ARCTIC OCEAN
ARCTIC OCEAN
SVALBARD (NORWAY)
Barents Sea
Laptev Sea
East Siberian Sea
Bering Strait
Bering Sea
RUSSIAN FEDERATION
SWEDEN
FINLAND
ÅLAND ISLANDS (FINLAND)
Helsinki
Stockholm
Tallinn
ESTONIA
Baltic Sea
Riga
LATVIA
LITHUANIA
Vilnius
Minsk
Moscow
BELARUS
Warsaw
POLAND
Prague
Kyiv
UKRAINE
SLOVAKIA
Vienna
Bratislava
Budapest
HUNGARY
Zagreb
CROATIA
MOLDOVA
Chişinău
ROMANIA
Bucharest
BOSNIA AND HERZEGOVINA
SERBIA
BULGARIA
Sofia
Skopje
Tirana
ALBANIA
GREECE
Athens
MALTA
Black Sea
GEORGIA
Tbilisi
ARMENIA
Yerevan
AZERBAIJAN
Baku
Ankara
TURKEY
Astana
KAZAKHSTAN
UZBEKISTAN
Tashkent
TURKMENISTAN
Aşgabat
Almaty
Bishkek
KYRGYZSTAN
Dushanbe
TAJIKISTAN
Ulan Bator
MONGOLIA
DEMOCRATIC PEOPLE'S REPUBLIC OF KOREA
Beijing
Pyongyang
Seoul
REPUBLIC OF KOREA
Sea of Japan
JAPAN
Tokyo
PEOPLE'S REPUBLIC OF CHINA
East China Sea
Nicosia
CYPRUS
SYRIA
Beirut
LEBANON
Damascus
ISRAEL
Amman
JORDAN
Baghdad
IRAQ
Tehran
IRAN
AFGHANISTAN
Kabul
Islamabad
PAKISTAN
Mediterranean Sea
Tripoli
Sirte
LIBYA
Cairo
EGYPT
PALESTINIAN AUTONOMOUS AREAS
Kuwait City
KUWAIT
BAHRAIN
Manama
QATAR
Doha
Riyadh
UAE
Abu Dhabi
Muscat
SAUDI ARABIA
OMAN
Red Sea
New Delhi
NEPAL
Kathmandu
Thimphu
BHUTAN
BANGLADESH
Dhaka
INDIA
Taipei
TAIWAN
MACAO (CHINA)
HONG KONG (CHINA)
Tropic of Cancer
MYANMAR
Nay Pyi Taw
Yangon
Hanoi
Vientiane
LAOS
THAILAND
VIET NAM
Bangkok
CAMBODIA
Phnom-Penh
South China Sea
Manila
PHILIPPINES
Philippine Sea
CHAD
Khartoum
SUDAN
ERITREA
Asmara
San'a
YEMEN
N'Djamena
DJIBOUTI
Addis Ababa
ETHIOPIA
SOMALIA
CENTRAL AFRICAN REPUBLIC
Bangui
DEMOCRATIC REPUBLIC OF THE CONGO
CONGO, REP.
UGANDA
Kampala
KENYA
Mogadishu
Nairobi
RWANDA
Kigali
BURUNDI
Bujumbura
Kinshasa
Dodoma
Dar es Salaam
TANZANIA
Victoria
SEYCHELLES
ANGOLA
Lubumbashi
ZAMBIA
Lusaka
MALAWI
Lilongwe
Harare
ZIMBABWE
MOZAMBIQUE
Moroni
COMOROS
MAYOTTE (FRANCE)
Mozambique Channel
MADAGASCAR
Antananarivo
MAURITIUS
Port Louis
RÉUNION (FRANCE)
NAMIBIA
BOTSWANA
Gaborone
Pretoria
Maputo
Mbabane
SWAZILAND
LESOTHO
Maseru
SOUTH AFRICA
Bay of Bengal
SRI LANKA
Colombo
Sri Jayawardenepura
MALDIVES
BRITISH INDIAN OCEAN TERRITORY (UNITED KINGDOM)
INDIAN OCEAN
COCOS ISLANDS (AUSTRALIA)
CHRISTMAS ISLAND (AUSTRALIA)
BRUNEI
Bandar Seri Begawan
Kuala Lumpur
Putrajaya
MALAYSIA
SINGAPORE
Jakarta
INDONESIA
Dili
TIMOR-LESTE
PAPUA NEW GUINEA
Port Moresby
NORTHERN MARIANA ISLANDS (USA)
GUAM (USA)
PALAU
PACIFIC OCEAN
MARSHALL ISLANDS
FEDERATED STATES OF MICRONESIA
NAURU
KIRIBATI
SOLOMON ISLANDS
Honiara
Coral Sea
VANUATU
Port Vila
TUVALU
TOKELAU (NEW ZEALAND)
WALLIS AND FUTUNA ISLANDS (FRANCE)
SAMOA
AMERICAN SAMOA (USA)
FIJI
Suva
NIUE (NZ)
TONGA
NEW CALEDONIA (FRANCE)
NORFOLK ISLAND (AUSTRALIA)
AUSTRALIA
Canberra
Tasman Sea
NEW ZEALAND
Wellington
ANTARCTICA
40°
80°
120°
160°
80°
40°
0°
40°

South America
Central America
and the
Caribbean
2011

South America Central America and the Caribbean 2011

19th Edition

LONDON AND NEW YORK

First published 1985
Ninteenth Edition 2011

Albert House, 1–4 Singer Street, London EC2A 4BQ, United Kingdom
(Routledge is an imprint of the Taylor & Francis Group, an Informa business)

ISBN: 978-1-85743-562-7
ISSN 0258-0661

Editor: Jackie West

Associate Editor: Katie Dawson

Regional Organizations Editors: Catriona Appeatu Holman, Helen Canton

Statistics Editor: Philip McIntyre

Statistics Researchers: Abhinav Srivastava (Lead Researcher), Mohd Khalid Ansari, Prerna Kumra, Jasmeet Singh

Directory Researchers: Arijit Khasnobis (Lead Researcher), Rima Kar, Surmeet Kaur, Thoithoi Pukhrambam

Contributing Editor: Katharine Murison

Contributing Editors (Commodities): Gareth Wyn Jones, Simon Chapman

Associate Editor, Directory Research: James Middleton

Publisher and Series Editor: Joanne Maher

Typeset in New Century Schoolbook

Typeset by Data Standards Limited, Frome, Somerset

Printed and bound in Great Britain by Polestar Wheatons, Exeter

FOREWORD

The 19th edition of SOUTH AMERICA, CENTRAL AMERICA AND THE CARIBBEAN provides a survey of the political and economic life both of the region and of the more than 50 countries and territories within it. The volume contains three distinct, though complementary, areas. Part One consists of seven introductory articles, covering a variety of subjects of regional significance, including the shifting political landscape in Latin America; the politics of energy; the moves towards autonomy in the Caribbean Overseas Territories; the war on drugs in Mexico; gender and development in the region; Latin America in the global financial crisis; and trade preferences in the Caribbean. In Part Two the main political and economic events in each of the 50 countries and territories in the region are examined in detail. In addition, all statistical and directory material has been extensively updated. Comprehensive coverage of international organizations and research institutes active in Latin America and the Caribbean is included, as are books and periodicals relevant to the region. Extensive background information on the region's major primary commodities is also provided.

There was a vote for continuity at elections held in many countries in the region during the year under review: in Bolivia, left-wing President Evo Morales was returned for a second term in office in December 2009, while in March 2010 José Mujica succeeded his Frente Amplio compadre Tabaré Vázquez as Uruguayan head of state. In Costa Rica and Colombia, too, power was kept within party lines, with Laura Chinchilla taking over from fellow Partido Liberación Nacional member Oscar Arias in the former in May, and Juan Manuel Santos succeeding his ally Alvaro Uribe in the latter in August. By contrast, in Trinidad and Tobago the People's Partnership coalition achieved an unexpected victory at the polls in May, and in the same month former dictator Desi Bouterse regained power in Suriname. In Chile a right-wing grouping led by Sebastiá Piñera unseated the ruling Concertación alliance in early 2010. Piñera took office weeks after a powerful earthquake had devastated part of the country, and the reconstruction effort was likely to dominate the agenda of the new Government.

Although the Chilean tremor was stronger in magnitude, the earthquake that struck Haiti on 12 January 2010 was more devastating: more than 200,000 people were estimated to have been killed, with a further 250,000 injured, and 1.2m. people made homeless or displaced. Much of the capital, Port-au-Prince, and surrounding areas were destroyed. The international community was quick to offer emergency aid and funding for the relief effort, and at a UN donor conference in March some US $5,300m. was pledged for the reconstruction project, although by mid-year only a small percentage of the promised total had materialized.

The Editors are grateful to all the contributors for their articles and advice, and to the numerous governments and organizations that provided statistical and other information.

August 2010

HEALTH AND WELFARE STATISTICS: SOURCES AND DEFINITIONS

Total fertility rate Source: WHO Statistical Information System. The number of children that would be born per woman, assuming no female mortality at child-bearing ages and the age-specific fertility rates of a specified country and reference period.

Under-5 mortality rate Source: WHO Statistical Information System. Defined by WHO as the probability of a child born in a specific year or period dying before reaching the age of five, if subject to the age-specific mortality rates of that year or period.

HIV/AIDS Source: UNAIDS. Estimated percentage of adults aged 15 to 49 years living with HIV/AIDS. < indicates 'fewer than'.

Health expenditure Source: WHO Statistical Information System.

US $ per head (PPP)

International dollar estimates, derived by dividing local currency units by an estimate of their purchasing-power parity (PPP) compared with the US dollar. PPPs are the rates of currency conversion that equalize the purchasing power of different currencies by eliminating the differences in price levels between countries.

% of GDP

GDP levels for OECD countries follow the most recent UN System of National Accounts. For non-OECD countries a value was estimated by utilizing existing UN, IMF and World Bank data.

Public expenditure

Government health-related outlays plus expenditure by social schemes compulsorily affiliated with a sizeable share of the population, and extrabudgetary funds allocated to health services. Figures include grants or loans provided by international agencies, other national authorities, and sometimes commercial banks.

Access to water and sanitation Source: WHO/UNICEF Joint Monitoring Programme on Water Supply and Sanitation (JMP) (Progress on Drinking Water and Sanitation, 2010 Update). Defined in terms of the percentage of the population using improved facilities in terms of the type of technology and levels of service afforded. For water, this includes house connections, public standpipes, boreholes with handpumps, protected dug wells, protected spring and rainwater collection; allowance is also made for other locally defined technologies. Sanitation is defined to include connection to a sewer or septic tank system, pour-flush latrine, simple pit or ventilated improved pit latrine, again with allowance for acceptable local technologies. Access to water and sanitation does not imply that the level of service or quality of water is 'adequate' or 'safe'.

Carbon dioxide emissions Source: World Bank, World Development Indicators database, citing the Carbon Dioxide Information Analysis Center (sponsored by the US Department of Energy). Emissions comprise those resulting from the burning of fossil fuels (including those produced during consumption of solid, liquid and gas fuels and from gas flaring) and from the manufacture of cement.

Human Development Index (HDI) Source: UNDP, *Human Development Report* (2009). A summary of human development measured by three basic dimensions: prospects for a long and healthy life, measured by life expectancy at birth; knowledge, measured by adult literacy rate (two-thirds' weight) and the combined gross enrolment ratio in primary, secondary and tertiary education (one-third weight); and standard of living, measured by GDP per head (PPP US $). The index value obtained lies between zero and one. A value above 0.8 indicates high human development, between 0.5 and 0.8 medium human development, and below 0.5 low human development. A centralized data source for all three dimensions was not available for all countries. In some cases other data sources were used to calculate a substitute value; however, this was excluded from the ranking. Other countries, including non-UNDP members, were excluded from the HDI altogether. In total, 182 countries were ranked for 2007.

ACKNOWLEDGEMENTS

The editors gratefully acknowledge the co-operation, interest and enthusiasm of all the authors who have contributed to the volume. We are also indebted to the many organizations connected with the region, particularly the national statistical offices. We owe special thanks to a number of embassies and ministries. We are also grateful to the University of Southampton Cartographic Unit for supplying the maps included in the Geography sections.

The editors gratefully acknowledge particular indebtedness for permission to reproduce material from the following sources: the United Nations' statistical databases and *Demographic Yearbook*, *Statistical Yearbook*, *Monthly Bulletin of Statistics*, *Industrial Commodity Statistics Yearbook* and *International Trade Statistics Yearbook*; the United Nations Educational, Scientific and Cultural Organization's *Statistical Yearbook* and Institute for Statistics database; the *Human Development Report* of the United Nations Development Programme; the Food and Agriculture Organization of the United Nations' statistical database; the statistical databases of the UNCTAD/WTO International Trade Centre; the statistical databases of the World Health Organization; the International Labour Office's statistical database and *Yearbook of Labour Statistics*; the World Bank's *World Bank Atlas*, *Global Development Finance*, *World Development Report* and *World Development Indicators*; the International Monetary Fund's statistical database, *International Financial Statistics* and *Government Finance Statistics Yearbook*; the World Tourism Organization's *Compendium* and *Yearbook of Tourism Statistics*; the UN Economic Commission for Latin America and the Caribbean's Statistical Yearbook; the US Geological Survey; and the International Telecommunication Union. We are also grateful to the International Institute for Strategic Studies, Arundel House, 13–15 Arundel Street, London WC2R 3DX, for the use of defence statistics from *The Military Balance 2010*.

EXPLANATORY NOTE ON THE DIRECTORY SECTION

The Directory section of each chapter covering a major country is arranged under the following, or similar, headings, where they apply:

THE CONSTITUTION

THE GOVERNMENT
- HEAD OF STATE
- CABINET/COUNCIL OF MINISTERS
- MINISTRIES

LEGISLATURE

ELECTION COMMISSION

POLITICAL ORGANIZATIONS

DIPLOMATIC REPRESENTATION

JUDICIAL SYSTEM

RELIGION

THE PRESS

PUBLISHERS

BROADCASTING AND COMMUNICATIONS
- TELECOMMUNICATIONS
- RADIO
- TELEVISION

FINANCE
- CENTRAL BANK
- STATE BANKS
- DEVELOPMENT BANKS
- COMMERCIAL BANKS
- BANKING ASSOCIATIONS
- STOCK EXCHANGE
- INSURANCE

TRADE AND INDUSTRY
- GOVERNMENT AGENCIES
- DEVELOPMENT ORGANIZATIONS
- CHAMBERS OF COMMERCE
- INDUSTRIAL AND TRADE ASSOCIATIONS
- EMPLOYERS' ASSOCIATIONS
- MAJOR COMPANIES
- UTILITIES
- TRADE UNIONS

TRANSPORT
- RAILWAYS
- ROADS
- SHIPPING
- CIVIL AVIATION

TOURISM

DEFENCE

EDUCATION

THE CONTRIBUTORS

Charles Arthur. Freelance journalist specializing in Caribbean politics and economics.

Dr Ame Bergés. Lecturer in the Economics of Latin America at the Institute for the Study of the Americas, University of London, United Kingdom.

Andrew Bounds. Former Central America correspondent of the *Financial Times*.

Dr Ed Brown. Lecturer in Human Geography at the University of Loughborough, United Kingdom.

Dr Julia Buxton. Senior Research Fellow at the Centre for Co-operation and Security, Department of Peace Studies at the University of Bradford, United Kingdom.

Prof. Peter A. R. Calvert. Emeritus Professor of Comparative and International Politics at the University of Southampton, United Kingdom.

Dr Peter Clegg. Lecturer at the Arthur Lewis Institute of Social and Economic Studies of the University of the West Indies, Kingston, Jamaica.

John Crabtree. Research Associate at the Latin American Centre at the University of Oxford, United Kingdom.

Prof. David Fleischer. Professor of Political Science at the Instituto Sociedade, População e Natureza at the University of Brasília, Brazil.

Lila Haines. Economic historian specializing in the Cuban economy, currently working for a major international development organization.

Annette Hester. Senior Associate (non-resident) of the William E. Simon Chair in Political Economy at the Center for Strategic and International Studies, Washington, DC, USA.

Prof. Antoni Kapcia. Professor of Latin American History and Director of the Centre for Research on Cuba at the University of Nottingham, United Kingdom.

Prof. Colin M. Lewis. Senior Lecturer in Latin American Economic History at the London School of Economics and Political Science, United Kingdom.

James McDonough. Editor and Publisher at EPIN Publishing, USA.

Dr Cathy McIlwaine. Reader in Geography in the Department of Geography at Queen Mary, University of London, United Kingdom.

Dr Fiona Macaulay. Lecturer in Development Studies at the Department of Peace Studies at the University of Bradford, United Kingdom.

Sandy Markwick. Writer and researcher specializing in Latin American affairs.

Sir Keith Morris. Former British Ambassador to Colombia.

Katharine Murison. Freelance writer and researcher specializing in Latin American and African affairs.

Pablo Navarrete. Freelance writer and researcher on Latin America.

Thomas Andrew O'Keefe. President, Mercosur Consulting Group Ltd, Washington, DC, USA.

Dr Francisco Panizza. Senior Lecturer in Latin American Politics at the London School of Economics and Political Science, United Kingdom.

Prof. Jenny Pearce. Professor of Latin American Politics at the University of Bradford, United Kingdom.

Rod Prince. Journalist specializing in Caribbean affairs.

Dr Pia Riggirozzi. Lecturer in the Department of Politics at the University of Sheffield, United Kingdom.

Dennis Rodgers. Senior Research Fellow at the Brooks World Poverty Institute at the University of Manchester, United Kingdom.

Diego Sánchez-Ancochea. Lecturer in the Political Economy of Latin America at the University of Oxford, United Kingdom.

Helen Schooley. Writer specializing in Latin American affairs.

Jeremy Thorp. Former British Ambassador to Colombia.

Phillip Wearne. Writer and researcher specializing in Latin American affairs.

Prof. Sidney Weintraub. Holder of the William E. Simon Chair in Political Economy at the Center for Strategic and International Studies, Washington, DC, USA.

Mark Wilson. Writer and researcher specializing in Caribbean affairs.

CONTENTS

PART THREE

Regional Information

ABBREVIATIONS

Abog.	Abogado
AC	Acre
Acad.	Academician; Academy
Adm.	Admiral
admin.	administration
AG	Aktiengesellschaft (Joint Stock Company)
Ags	Aguascalientes
a.i.	ad interim
AID	(US) Agency for International Development
AIDS	acquired immunodeficiency syndrome
AK	Alaska
AL	Alabama, Alagoas
ALADI	Asociación Latino-Americana de Integración
Alt.	Alternate
AM	Amazonas; Amplitude Modulation
amalg.	amalgamated
AP	Amapá
Apdo	Apartado (Post Box)
approx.	approximately
Apt	Apartment
Apto	Apartamento
AR	Arkansas
asscn	association
assoc.	associate
asst	assistant
Aug.	August
auth.	authorized
Ave	Avenue
Av., Avda	Avenida (Avenue)
AZ	Arizona
BA	Bahia
BCN	Baja California Norte
BCS	Baja California Sur
Bd	Board
Blvd, Blvr	Boulevard
b/d	barrels per day
Bldg	Building
BP	Boîte Postale (Post Box)
br.(s)	branch(es)
Brig.	Brigadier
BSE	bovine spongiform encephalopathy
BTN	Brussels Tariff Nomenclature
C	Centigrade
c.	circa; cuadra(s) (block(s))
CA	California; Compañía Anónima
CACM	Central American Common Market
Camp.	Campeche
cap.	capital
Capt.	Captain
CARICOM	Caribbean Community and Common Market
CCL	Caribbean Congress of Labour
Cdre	Commodore
CE	Ceará
Cen.	Central
CEO	Chief Executive Officer
CET	Common External Tariff
cf.	confer (compare)
Chair.	Chairman
Chih.	Chihuahua
Chis	Chiapas
Cia, Cía	Companhia, Compañía
Cie	Compagnie
c.i.f.	cost, insurance and freight
C-in-C	Commander-in-Chief
circ.	circulation
CIS	Commonwealth of Independent States
cm	centimetre(s)
CMEA	Council for Mutual Economic Assistance
Cnr	Corner
CO	Colorado
Co	Company
Coah.	Coahuila
Col	Colonel
Col.	Colima, Colonia
Comm.	Commission
Commdr	Commander
Commdt	Commandant
Commr	Commissioner
Confed.	Confederation
Cont.	Contador
Corpn	Corporation
CP	Case Postale; Caixa Postal (Post Box)
C por A	Compañía por Acciones (Joint Stock Company)
Cres.	Crescent
CSTAL	Confederación Sindical de los Trabajadores de América Latina
CT	Connecticut
CTCA	Confederación de Trabajadores Centroamericanos
Cttee	Committee
cu	cubic
cwt	hundredweight
DC	District of Columbia, Distrito Central
DE	Delaware, Departamento Estatal
Dec.	December
Del.	Delegación
Dem.	Democratic; Democrat
Dep.	Deputy
dep.	deposits
Dept	Department
devt	development
DF	Distrito Federal
Dgo	Durango
Diag.	Diagonal
Dir	Director
Div.	Division
DN	Distrito Nacional
dpto	departamento
Dr(a)	Doctor(a)
Dr.	Drive
DR-CAFTA	Dominican Republic-Central American Free Trade Agreement
dwt	dead weight tons
E	East, Eastern
EC	Eastern Caribbean; European Community
ECCB	Eastern Caribbean Central Bank
ECLAC	(United Nations) Economic Commission for Latin America and the Caribbean
Econ.	Economist
ECOSOC	(United Nations) Economic and Social Council
ECU	European Currency Unit
Ed.(s)	Editor(s)
Edif.	Edificio (building)
edn	edition
EEC	European Economic Community
EFTA	European Free Trade Association
e.g.	exempli gratia (for example)
eKv	electron kilovolt
eMv	electron megavolt
Eng.	Engineer; Engineering
Ens.	Ensanche (suburb)
ES	Espírito Santo
Esc.	Escuela; Escudos; Escritorio
esq.	esquina (corner)
est.	established; estimate, estimated
etc.	et cetera
eV	eingetragener Verein
EU	European Union
excl.	excluding
exec.	executive
Ext.	Extension
F	Fahrenheit
f.	founded
FAO	Food and Agriculture Organization
FDI	foreign direct investment
Feb.	February
Fed.	Federation; Federal
FL	Florida
FM	frequency modulation
Fri.	Friday
fmrly	formerly
f.o.b.	free on board
Fr	Father
Fr.	Franc
ft	foot (feet)
FTA	free trade agreement

g gram(s)
GA Georgia
GATT General Agreement on Tariffs and Trade
GDP gross domestic product
Gen. General
GM genetically modified
GmbH Gesellschaft mit beschränkter Haftung (Limited Liability Company)
GMT Greenwich Mean Time
GNP gross national product
GO Goiás
Gov. Governor
Govt Government
Gro Guerrero
grt gross registered tons
GSP Global Social Product
Gto Guanajuato
GWh gigawatt hours

ha hectares
HE His (or Her) Eminence; His (or Her) Excellency
hg hectogram(s)
Hgo Hidalgo
HGV Heavy goods vehicle
HI Hawaii
HIPC heavily indebted poor country
HIV human immunodeficiency virus
hl hectolitre(s)
HLTF High Level Task Force
HM His (or Her) Majesty
Hon. Honorary (or Honourable)
HQ Headquarters
HRH His (or Her) Royal Highness
HS Harmonized System

IA Iowa
ibid. ibidem (in the same place)
IBRD International Bank for Reconstruction and Development (World Bank)
ICC International Chamber of Commerce
ID Idaho
IDA International Development Association
IDB Inter-American Development Bank
i.e. id est (that is to say)
IGAD Intergovernmental Authority on Development
IL Illinois
ILO International Labour Organization
IMF International Monetary Fund
IN Indiana
in (ins) inch (inches)
Inc Incorporated
incl. including
Ind. Independent
Ing. Engineer
Insp. Inspector
Inst. Institute, Instituto
Int. International
IRF International Road Federation
irreg. irregular
Is Islands
ISIC International Standard Industrial Classification
ITUC International Trade Union Confederation
IUU illegal, unreported and unregulated

Jal. Jalisco
Jan. January
Jr Junior
Jt Joint

kg kilogram(s)
kHz Kilohertz
km kilometre(s)
KS Kansas
kW kilowatt(s)
kWh kilowatt hours
KY Kentucky

LA Louisiana
lb pound(s)
LIBOR London Inter-Bank Offered Rate
Lic. Licenciado
Licda Licenciada
LNG liquefied natural gas
LPG liquefied petroleum gas
Lt, Lieut Lieutenant
Ltd, Ltda Limited, Limitada

m metre(s)
m. million
MA Maranhão; Massachusetts
Maj. Major
Man. Manager; managing
MD Maryland
MDG Millennium Development Goal
ME Maine
mem. member
MEV mega electron volt
Méx. México
mfrs manufacturers
MG Minas Gerais
Mgr Monseigneur; Monsignor
MHz megahertz
MI Michigan
Mich. Michoacán
Mlle Mademoiselle
mm millimetre(s)
Mme Madame
MN Minnesota
MO Missouri
Mon. Monday
Mor. Morelos
movt movement
MP Member of Parliament
MS Mato Grosso do Sul; Mississippi
MSS Manuscripts
MT Montana
MW megawatt(s); medium wave
MWh megawatt hour(s)

N North, Northern
n.a. not available
NAFTA North American Free Trade Agreement
Nat. National
NATO North Atlantic Treaty Organization
Nay. Nayarit
NC North Carolina
NCO Non-Commissioned Officer
ND North Dakota
NE Nebraska
NGO Non-governmental organization
NH New Hampshire
NJ New Jersey
NL Nuevo León
NM New Mexico
NMP net material product
No(.) number, número
Nov. November
nr near
nrt net registered tons
NV Naamloze Vennootschap (Limited Company); Nevada
NY New York

OAS Organization of American States
Oax. Oaxaca
Oct. October
OECD Organisation for Economic Co-operation and Development
OECS Organisation of Eastern Caribbean States
Of. Oficina
OH Ohio
OK Oklahoma
OPEC Organization of the Petroleum Exporting Countries
op. cit. opere citato (in the work quoted)
opp. opposite
OR Oregon
Org. Organization
ORIT Organización Regional Interamericana de Trabajadores
oz troy ounces

p. page
PA Pará, Pennsylvania
p.a. per annum
Parl. Parliament(ary)
PB Paraíbo
PC Privy Counsellor
PE Pernambuco
Perm. Rep. Permanent Representative
PI Pianí
pl. place
PLC Public Limited Company
PMB Private Mail Bag
POB Post Office Box
pp. pages

PR	Paraná
PRGF	Poverty Reduction and Growth Facility
Pres.	President
Prin.	Principal
Prof.	Professor
Propr	Proprietor
Prov.	Province; Provincial
Pte	Private
Pty	Proprietary
p.u.	paid up
publ.	publication; published
Publr(s)	Publisher(s)
Pue.	Puebla
Pvt.	Private
Q. Roo	Quintana Roo
QC	Queen's Counsel, Québec
q.v.	quod vide (to which refer)
Qro	Querétaro
Rd	Road
reg., regd	register; registered
reorg.	reorganized
Rep.	Republic; Republican; Representative
Repub.	Republic
res	reserve(s)
retd	retired
Rev.	Reverend
RI	Rhode Island
RJ	Rio de Janeiro
Rm	Room
RN	Rio Grande do Norte
RO	Rondônia
Rpto	Reparto
RR	Roraima
RS	Rio Grande do Sul
Rt	Right
S	South; Southern; San
SA	Société Anonyme, Sociedad Anónima (Limited Company)
SA de CV	Sociedad Anónima de Capital Variable (Variable Capital Company)
SACN	South American Community of Nations
SARL	Sociedade Anônima de Responsabilidade Limitada (Joint Stock Company of Limited Liability)
Sat.	Saturday
SC	Santa Catarina, South Carolina
SD	South Dakota
SDR(s)	Special Drawing Right(s)
Sec.	Secretary
Sen.	Senior; Senator
Sept.	September
Sgt	Sergeant
Sin.	Sinaloa
SITC	Standard International Trade Classification
SJ	Society of Jesus
SLP	San Luis Potosí
s/n	sin número (no number)
Soc.	Society
Son.	Sonora
SP	São Paulo
Sq.	Square
sq	square (in measurements)
Sr	Senior; Señor
Sra	Señora
St(s)	Saint(s); Street(s)
Sta	Santa
Ste	Sainte
subs.	subscriptions; subscribed
Suc.	Sucursal
Sun.	Sunday
Supt	Superintendent
Tab.	Tabasco
Tamps	Tamaulipas
Tce	Terrace
tech., techn.	technical
tel.	telephone
TEU	20-ft equivalent unit
Thurs.	Thursday
TJ	tetrajoule
Tlax.	Tlaxcala
TN	Tennessee
TO	Tocatins
Treas.	Treasurer
Tue.	Tuesday
TV	television
TX	Texas
u/a	unit of account
UEE	Unidade Ecónomica Estatal
UK	United Kingdom
UN	United Nations
UNCED	United Nations Conference on Environment and Development
UNCTAD	United Nations Conference on Trade and Development
UNDP	United Nations Development Programme
UNESCO	United Nations Educational, Scientific and Cultural Organization
UNHCHR	United Nations High Commissioner for Human Rights
UNHCR	United Nations High Commissioner for Refugees
Univ.	University
UNWTO	World Tourism Organization
USA (US)	United States of America (United States)
USAID	United States Agency for International Development
USSR	Union of Soviet Socialist Republics
Urb.	Urbanización (urban district)
UT	Utah
VA	Virginia
VAT	Value-Added Tax
v-CJD	new variant Creutzfeldt-Jakob disease
Ver.	Veracruz
VHF	Very High Frequency
VI	(US) Virgin Islands
viz.	videlicet (namely)
vol.(s)	volume(s)
W	West; Western
WA	Washington
Wed.	Wednesday
WFTU	World Federation of Trade Unions
WHO	World Health Organization
WI	Wisconsin
WTO	World Trade Organization
WV	West Virginia
WY	Wyoming
yr	year
Yuc.	Yucatán

INTERNATIONAL TELEPHONE CODES

To make international calls to telephone and fax numbers listed in *South America, Central America and the Caribbean*, dial the international code of the country from which you are calling, followed by the appropriate country code for the organization you wish to call (listed below), followed by the area code (if applicable) and telephone or fax number listed in the entry.

	Country code	+ GMT*
Anguilla	1264	–4
Antigua and Barbuda	1268	–4
Argentina	54	–3
Aruba	297	–4
Bahamas	1242	–5
Barbados	1246	–4
Belize	501	–6
Bermuda	1441	–4
Bolivia	591	–4
Brazil	55	–3 to –4
British Virgin Islands	1284	–4
Cayman Islands	1345	–4
Chile	56	–4
Colombia	57	–4
Costa Rica	506	–6
Cuba	53	–4
Dominica	1767	–4
Dominican Republic	1809	–4
Ecuador	593	–4
El Salvador	503	–6
Falkland Islands	500	–4
French Guiana	594	–3
Grenada	1473	–4
Guadeloupe	590	–4
Guatemala	502	–6
Guyana	592	–4
Haiti	509	–4
Honduras	504	–6
Jamaica	1876	–4
Martinique	596	–4
Mexico	52	–6 to –7
Montserrat	1664	–4
Netherlands Antilles	599	–4
Nicaragua	505	–6
Panama	507	–4
Paraguay	595	–4
Peru	51	–4
Puerto Rico	1787	–4
Saint-Barthélemy	590	–4
Saint Christopher and Nevis	1869	–4
Saint Lucia	1758	–4
Saint-Martin	590	–4
Saint Vincent and the Grenadines	1784	–4
Suriname	597	–3
Trinidad and Tobago	1868	–4
Turks and Caicos Islands	1649	–4
US Virgin Islands	1340	–4
Uruguay	598	–3
Venezuela	58	–4½

* Time difference in hours – Greenwhich Mean Time (GMT). The times listed compare the standard (winter) times. Some countries adopt Summer (Daylight Saving) Times—i.e. + 1 hour for part of the year.

Note: Telephone and fax numbers using the Inmarsat ocean region code 870 are listed in full. No country or area code is required, but it is necessary to precede the number with the international access code of the country from which the call is made.

South America

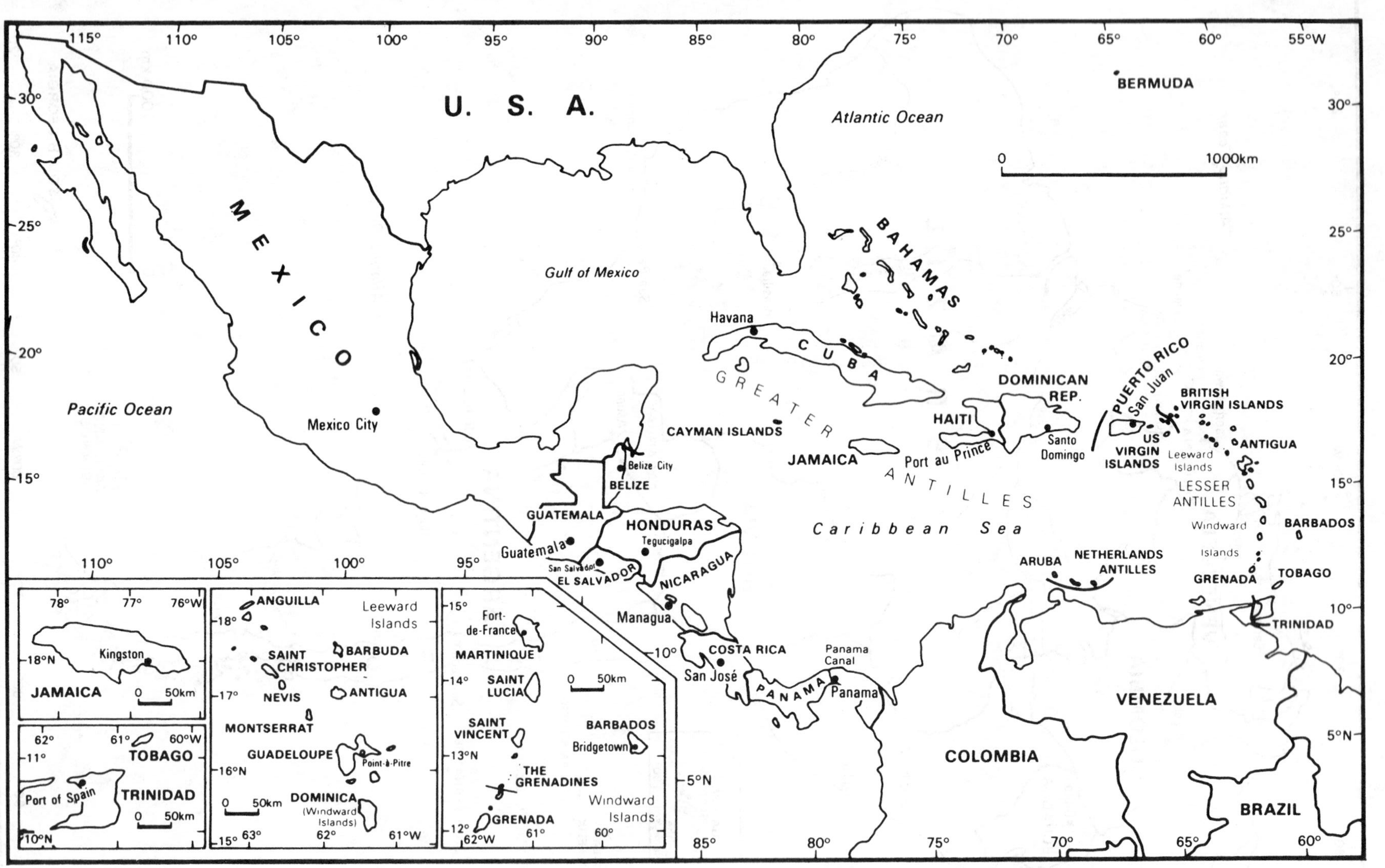

Central America and the Caribbean

PART ONE

General Survey

LATIN AMERICA'S NEW ELECTORAL AND ECONOMIC CYCLES: THE END OF THE PINK TIDE?

Dr FRANCISCO PANIZZA

In 2010 Latin America was in the middle of the second wave of elections of the 21st century: between 2009 and 2012 all countries of the region, with the exception of Paraguay, were set to hold presidential and legislative elections. Elections give citizens the chance to pass judgment on incumbents and choose between different political and ideological alternatives. An earlier wave of elections that took place during 2005–06 produced major political changes in the region that were commonly perceived as signalling a region-wide shift to the political left and a vote against incumbent administrations and personnel. In 2009, at the beginning of the current electoral wave, 13 out of 18 major Latin American countries had left-of-centre Presidents and nearly two-thirds of Latin Americans lived under some form of left-leaning government. No general trend can be identified in the ongoing electoral wave but the polls so far have pointed towards an increasingly fragmented political landscape. In some of the countries that have recently held elections—most notably Bolivia, Costa Rica, Ecuador, El Salvador and Uruguay—left or left-of-centre Presidents have been elected or re-elected. However, while it is too early to claim that the leftward regional trend has now come to a halt or that the region is tilting back to the right, the left suffered a considerable setback in Chile when local businessman Sebastián Piñera Echeñique, the candidate of the centre-right coalition Coalición por el Cambio (Coalition for Change), was elected to the presidency in January 2010, thereby bringing an end to two decades of government by the left-of-centre Concertación de Partidos por la Democracia (CPD). In Colombia, an anticipated upset by Antanas Mockus Sivickas, the presidential candidate of Partido Verde (PV—Green Party), did not materialize and the right-wing candidate, Juan Manuel Santos, of Partido Social de la Unidad Nacional (Partido de la U—Social Party of National Unity) was elected to succeed President Alvaro Uribe Vélez in a run-off election held on 20 June. In Panama another right-of-centre businessman, Ricardo Martinelli Berrocal, triumphed over the candidate of the ruling left-of-centre Partido Revolucionario Democrático (PRD—Party of the Democratic Revolution) in a poll held in May 2009. In the following month, in what was a major setback for the left in Central America, the Honduran left-of-centre President, José Manuel Zelaya Rosales, was deposed by the military, and in elections subsequently held in November the conservative Partido Nacional (PN—National Party) candidate, Porfirio Lobo Sosa, emerged victorious, under highly controversial circumstances (see the chapter on Honduras).

Just as no clear trend has so far emerged with regard to the political leanings of the winners of electoral contests, so too has there been no clear trend from the standpoint of continuity versus change. In presidential contests in 2009 and early 2010, opposition candidates won in Chile, El Salvador, Honduras and Panama. Conversely, Presidents Juan Evo Morales Aima and Rafael Correa Delgado were re-elected in Bolivia and Ecuador, respectively, and in Colombia, Costa Rica and Uruguay, countries in which re-election of the incumbent was not allowed, the respective candidates of the ruling parties—Juan Manuel Santos, Laura Chinchilla and José Mújica—were elected in their stead.

The political landscape of the region was expected to become clearer after forthcoming elections in the larger countries of the region, Brazil, Mexico and Argentina, as well as in Venezuela and Peru. In Brazil, the highly popular President Luiz Inácio Lula da Silva was constitutionally barred from running again; elections due to take place in October 2010 appeared to be finely balanced between the candidate of the incumbent left-of-centre party, Partido dos Trabalhadores (PT—Workers' Party), Dilma Rousseff, and the centre-right candidate, José Serra. In Venezuela the September 2010 legislative elections could see an upsurge in support for the opposition, even if the ruling Partido Socialista Unido de Venezuela (PSUV—United Socialist Party of Venezuela) was likely to remain the largest party in the Assembly; presidential elections were due to take place in 2012. There were as yet no clear favourites for the presidential elections scheduled to be held in Argentina and Mexico in 2011 and 2012, respectively, although in the former the Government of President Cristina Fernández de Kirchner was highly unpopular at mid-2010, and, in opinion polls conducted in the latter, the centrist Partido Revolucionario Institutional (PRI—Institutional Revolutionary Party) was leading both the ruling right-wing Partido Acción Nacional (PAN—National Action Party) and the left-wing Partido de la Revolución Democrática (PRD—Party of the Democratic Revolution).

How can we interpret the current shifts in the region's political landscape? Moreover, what do electoral results tell us about citizens' level of satisfaction with democratic governance and, more specifically, with the condition of their countries and the performance of their rulers? Answering these questions requires us to look beyond the headlines about the leftward trend that have dominated political narratives on Latin America over the past half decade, and to acknowledge that, while the region's political landscape did indeed change considerably in the first decade of the 21st century, the nature and scope of this change was far less straightforward than simply being a generalized turn to the left. It also requires us to take into account the very different economic contexts of the 2005–06 and the 2009–12 electoral rounds.

It is useful to underscore the fact that not all countries in the region chose left or left-of-centre Presidents during the past electoral wave. Colombia, Mexico and Peru constituted important exceptions to the regional trend by electing Presidents on the centre-right of the political spectrum. Moreover, in a region that was dominated by parties of the centre-right for most of the 1990s, arguably the vote for left-of-centre candidates in the closing years of the 20th century and the early years of the current century represented as much a vote against the status quo as an ideological shift towards the left. Surveys conducted by the polling organization Corporación Latinobarómetro between 1996 and 2007 showed little variation in the citizens' self-identification in the political spectrum, with the average voter located just slightly to the right of centre; only in Uruguay, Guatemala and Chile did citizens position themselves to the left of centre. According to the same survey, in Bolivia and Venezuela, the countries with arguably the most radical left-wing administrations in South America, electors placed themselves almost exactly at the centre of the scale.

While relations between politics and economics are far from straightforward, votes for opposition parties often reflect citizens' discontent with economic conditions. In the case of Latin America, votes for left and left-of-centre opposition candidates reflected a generalized disappointment with the neoliberal reforms of the 1990s. It is surely not a coincidence that the rise of the left coincided with 'the lost half-decade' of 1998–2002, in which per caput gross domestic product (GDP) contracted and the number of people living in poverty increased. When elections take place in the context of poor economic performances, incumbents tend to be punished, regardless of their political orientation. As most incumbents were from the right and centre-right, dissatisfaction with the status quo opened a window of opportunity for left-wing as well as anti-establishment candidates. In that sense, the victories of left and left-of-centre political candidates had as much to do with popular demands for change as with the specific content of the change package on offer. The gap between the promises and delivery of neo-liberalism provided left and left-of-centre candidates with a compelling narrative about the failures of free market reforms. In the electoral campaigns these candidates rallied against neo-liberalism and its domestic and international political patrons, the traditional parties of the centre-right, the US Administration and the IMF and other multilateral financial institutions that marshalled the reforms. However, a note of caution is necessary with regard to the dangers of sweeping generalizations. Free market reforms surely over-promised and under-delivered but they performed better in some countries (most notably in Chile) than in others, and, while many citizens were disappointed with the overall outcome of the reforms, they also valued the gains made in terms of low inflation, access to credit, economic opening and new job opportunities for the educated middle classes. There was also a considerable gap between the anti-neo-liberal rhetoric of left-of-centre presidential candidates and their policies once in office. In some countries, particularly Venezuela and Bolivia, and to a lesser extent Argentina and Ecuador, there has been a considerable departure from the principles of free market economics that dominated economic policy-making in the 1990s. In others, such as Brazil, Chile and Uruguay, left-of-centre administrations have maintained the market-friendly economic policies of the 1990s and combined these with a comparatively more activist state and more aggressive social policies.

Economic conditions changed quite radically in the second half of the 1990s and these changes further influenced electoral performances. While the 'lost half-decade' of 1998–2002 provided the background to the rise of the left, the economic boom during 2003–08 provided the economic context of their political success. Between 2003 and 2008 regional GDP growth averaged nearly 5% annually, with per caput GDP increasing by over 3% per annum. With annual economic growth for Latin America and the Caribbean at 4.6%, 2008 marked both the sixth consecutive year of growth and the end of a period that has very few precedents in the economic history of the region. Open unemployment, poverty and inequality went on a downward trend, while real average wages and consumption rose. Higher tax revenue resulting from economic growth allowed left-of-centre governments to increase public spending while simultaneously eliminating or narrowing the fiscal deficit and repaying external debt obligations. Inflation remained low by the region's historical standards, although the commodities boom that boosted economic growth during the period also brought back inflationary pressures, particularly in Venezuela and Argentina. Paradoxically, the economic upturn was at least partly the result of the macroeconomic discipline preached by free market advocates and of the commodities boom that was the offshoot of the process of capitalist globalization denounced by the left. Given the economic bonanza, it is not surprising that in 2006 polls saw the re-election of left-wing administrations such as those headed by Presidents Lula da Silva in Brazil and Hugo Chávez Friás in Venezuela, and the election of Michelle Bachelet in Chile, as well as of right-wing ones, such as that of President Uribe in Colombia, and the election of Felipe Calderón of the incumbent centre-right PAN, in Mexico.

By contrast, the downturn in global economic conditions from late 2008 constitutes the background to the current wave of elections. After six years of uninterrupted growth, the GDP of Latin America and the Caribbean declined by an estimated 1.8% and per caput GDP decreased by nearly 2.9% in 2009, according to figures from the Economic Commission for Latin America and the Caribbean (ECLAC). The effects of the crisis were channelled through the real sectors of the economies. Exports plunged, income from remittances and tourism fell, and foreign direct investment decreased by 37%. Domestic activity also declined in most countries as a result of the tighter credit conditions in the private banking sector, which increased public sector lending failed to ameliorate. Comparatively, however, the region has, thus far, been less badly affected by the global crisis than the developed world, and the recession has been shallower and more short-lived than past regional ones, such as the 'lost decade' of the 1980s or the recession of 1997–02. Already in the second half of 2009 positive signs began to emerge in the economies of the region. These have continued into 2010, in which year GDP growth is projected by ECLAC at 4.1%. Within the overall regional context of negative growth in 2009, some countries performed better than others, with Bolivia, Peru and Uruguay among the countries that were able to avoid recession, and Paraguay, Mexico and Venezuela among the worst affected.

While past recessions provoked mass protests and political turmoil, this was not the case in the 2008–09 downturn. In the early 2000s dissatisfaction with the economic conditions manifested itself in mass popular protests in Argentina, Bolivia and Ecuador, leading to the resignation of constitutionally elected Presidents in all three countries. By contrast, there have been no mass protests of similar magnitude since the start of the current economic cycle. As noted above, there has also not been as uniform a swing from left to right or from incumbency to opposition. In some countries, such as in Brazil, the Government was able to apportion the blame for the crisis to the developed world (according to President Lula, it was caused by 'white blue-eyed people' and not by 'blacks, poor or indigenous peoples'), while taking credit for the economic stimulus that has allowed growth to resume at a relatively high rate. In Chile, the then President Bachelet's popularity rose as a result of her Government's management of the crisis, and in Uruguay President Tabaré Vázquez Rosas ended his mandate in March 2010 with an approval rating of over 60% after the country avoided falling into recession. Conversely, in Venezuela, which has been hit particularly hard by a combination of falling oil prices and output, together with a prolonged drought, opinion polls show a significant decline in support for President Chávez. Incumbents are also unpopular in Argentina and Mexico, although the strong economic recovery currently under way in the two countries may help ruling parties to regain popularity prior to presidential elections in 2011 and 2012, respectively.

Despite the recession, the most recent available figures available at mid-2010 indicated a slow but steady rise in support for democracy in the region, while significant differences between countries confirm a picture of considerable political fragmentation. According to Latinobarómetro's 2009 poll, support for democracy had increased by 11 percentage points from its trough in 2001. There were, however, significant country variations: popular support for democracy ranged from 90% in Venezuela and Uruguay to 62% in Mexico. Support for democracy has risen the most in Venezuela and El Salvador (16 percentage points in 13 years) followed by Bolivia and Brazil (12 points), while the level of support has actually dwindled in other countries, including Mexico (by 9 points), Ecuador (6 points) and Argentina (4 points). While there has been a steady but unspectacular general rise in support for democracy, satisfaction with democracy, which measures democratic performance, has risen steeply from 29% in 2003, at the end of the 'lost half-decade' of economic growth, to 44% in 2009, the highest level since polls began in 1995. Unexpectedly, the biggest rise in democratic satisfaction occurred during the economic downturn of 2008–09, during which satisfaction climbed from 37% to 44%. This was in contrast to the 2001–02 recession (during which support for democracy had fallen concomitantly with economic decline) and may be linked to the legacy of the years of economic boom, to the impact of social policies and to specific political factors such as rotations in office, as observed, for instance, in Bolivia, Ecuador and Paraguay, and the fact that democracy has brought political change, allowing the left to come to power in many countries.

POPULISTS, SOCIAL DEMOCRATS AND THE RETURN OF THE RIGHT

While evidence from opinion polls suggests a growing democratic culture, the new electoral cycle attests to the resilience of democracy in the region. However, democracy is not defined by culture and elections alone, and, while elections are overwhelmingly the route to power in the region, in 2009 Latin America experienced its first military coup since the current wave of democratization began over 30 years ago: the military coup in Honduras in June was a reminder of the weakness of political institutions in many countries of the region.

Historically, and with some notable exceptions, democracy in Latin America has not fitted into the traditional liberal democratic pattern of strong institutions, rule of law, 'checks and balances' and market-oriented economies. Rather, it has been weakly institutionalized, populist, personalist, majoritarian and economically statist rather than market-oriented. To overcome these weaknesses, the model of democratic politics that dominated the political landscape of the mid-1990s placed a strong emphasis on the institutional and procedural elements of liberal democracy. Still haunted by the memories of the polarized politics that contributed to the democratic breakdowns of the 1970s, political stability was to be underpinned by a predominantly centrist consensus. Technocratic élites, which had gained considerable political leverage in the wake of the 1980s debt crisis and subsequent free market reformation, emphasized the importance of good governance as a condition for economic development. Civil society was no longer perceived as an arena for the mobilization of subordinate social sectors against elitist political orders or as a locus of resistance to tyrannical governments, but was redefined as the realm of voluntary associations engaged in bolstering citizens' mutual relations of trust, a realm that was being 'empowered' to perform the social development role that states were no longer fit to undertake. However, governability, centrist politics, technocratic good governance and a de-politicized civil society were no recipes for stasis. Rather, as has been well documented, the 1990s was a decade of radical social, political and economic change in Latin America, dominated by the expansion of market relations at both the domestic and international levels.

It is not the purpose of this essay to map the nature and scope of the changes of the 1990s, still less so their social costs and benefits, an undertaking that has been carried out extensively elsewhere. Suffice to say that the economic and social changes produced deep political dislocations from which new forms of politicization have taken shape throughout the region. As part of this process, political systems have been renewed, government élites have been replaced and the predominance of politics over institutions and of politicians over technocrats has been reasserted. While political change has been a common trend throughout the region, there are significant variations in the ways in which the new politics have been shaped by national processes. Communalities and variations can be accounted for by the weight of national histories in a region that shares many common legacies, by the common impact of the free market reformation on societies with very different socioeconomic structures and levels of economic development, and by the regional and domestic institutional contexts in which political change has taken place in different forms and at varying paces.

Democratic institution-buildin, is not a one-dimensional process, and the rise to office of left-of-centre administrations in the early years of the 21st century is had contrasting impacts upon the countries' respective political institutions. In some cases, most notably in Chile and Uruguay, institutional strength has an intrinsic historical legacy and, if anything, has become stronger under left-of-centre administrations. In other cases, such as in Brazil, it has been a relatively more recent and incomplete process, to which the PT has also made a significant contribution. By contrast, Bolivia, Ecuador and Venezuela can be characterized as Schumpeterian electoral democracies that combine electoral contests with processes of de-institutionalization followed by attempts to establish new political institutions on bases different to those of liberal democracy.

Weak democratic institutions allow elections to coexist in these countries with para-institutional forms of political activity (such as civil disobedience and mass protests) that run alongside electoral politics in different combinations. In some cases, as in Honduras in 2009, attempts to change the country's institutional order without regard for institutional procedures, or attempts to reach a consensus, can increase polarization and lead to democratic breakdowns. In other cases, the de-institutionalization of politics has led to conflicts of power and to the fall of Presidents. Since 1993 some 14 freely elected Presidents have been unable to complete their constitutional terms in office, some as a result of impeachment, while others were thrown out of office by popular opposition. At the start of the second decade of the 21st century, the differences between countries with strong and weak institutions remain as apparent as ever and have served as the basis for distinguishing between two types of left-of-centre Governments in the region, namely populists and social democrats.

A contentious and normatively highly charged concept, for which there is no agreed definition, populism by its very nature denotes an opposition to the status quo. As such, it appeals to the disenfranchised and the never enfranchised, who do not feel represented by existing institutions. Populism is the politics of anti-politics, with populist leaders presenting themselves as outsiders against vested economic interests and the political class. The anti-status quo element of populism makes it a common movement within societies deeply polarized on socio-economic, religious, ethnic and/or regional grounds, in which important sections of the population regard themselves as oppressed or discriminated against by the dominant élite, and in which the state is unable to secure social cohesion. Politically, populism has been characterized by a strong, personalist leadership, a direct appeal to the people unmediated by political institutions, and a preference for majoritarian rather than pluralist forms of democracy. Populism mistrusts political parties and representative institutions, which it argues are divisive of the people. Instead, it favours corporatist-style participative institutions that are intended to give direct voice to the people, organized in trade unions, neighbourhood associations and other 'grass-roots' organizations. Populism often includes a nationalist appeal, as the 'people' and the 'nation' become one and the same in their common cause against their internal (corrupt politicians, the economic élite, a dominant ethnic group) and external (imperialist nations, international organizations, multinational corporations, etc.) enemies. Populism has a foundational dimension: it promises to do away with the existing unjust and corrupt social order and to instigate a more inclusive one in its place.

While populism is not necessarily left-wing, the latest wave of Latin American populism is linked to popular backlashes against the inequalities and economic dislocations of neo-liberalism in the context of weakly institutionalized and exclusionary democracies. Populist-oriented governments have emerged in countries in which traditional parties are historically weak or have fallen into disrepute because of their inability to address popular grievances. Populism has also taken root where significant ethnic and regional groups have been systematically discriminated against or excluded from full participation in political life and where there is a history of anti-systemic movements. This has particularly been the case in Bolivia and Ecuador. In a region dominated by the USA, the populist stance has a strong element of anti-Americanism, a trend that was exacerbated in the past decade by the deep unpopularity across the region of US President George W. Bush. Economically, radical populism has been associated with opposition to the neo-liberal policies of the 1990s, particularly the privatization of state-owned enterprises. Populism has been significantly strong in oil- and gas-rich countries, in which the privatization of state-owned oil companies was perceived as relinquishing to foreign companies the country's most valuable assets, and in which oil revenues have not trickled down to the poor.

Representatives of radical left populism in the region are the Governments of Presidents Chávez of Venezuela, Morales of Bolivia and Correa of Ecuador. The Government of President Cristina Fernández of Argentina, like that of her predecessor and husband, Néstor Kirchner, demonstrates some elements of radical populism but operates in a politically more institutionalized, economically more developed and socially less polarized society that limits the appeal of populism. Radical left populist governments have been characterized by a partial return to the nationalist and interventionist economic policies of the 1960s. These governments have distanced themselves from the so-called Washington Consensus and placed a renewed emphasis on economic redistribution and the regaining of state control over oil and other national assets. In the past, economic populism was also characterized by irresponsible fiscal policies that used public spending to promote short-term economic growth at the expense of long-term economic stability. In their latter-day incarnation, radical left populist governments have become more aware of the importance of sound macroeconomic policies. However, without falling into the massive public deficits and hyperinflationary excesses of the past, some of these governments, particularly the Venezuela Government, have experienced renewed inflationary pressures that threaten to undermine their political bases of support.

The rise to office of Chávez in Venezuela provides an example of the politics of radical populism. As the imprisoned leader of a junior officers' rebellion in 1992 against the Government of President Carlos Andrés Pérez Rodríguez, which sought to impose a series of neo-liberal reforms, Chávez became a hero of the Venezuelan poor. Prior to the 1988 presidential election, Chávez capitalized on his image as a political outsider by campaigning against the *partidocracia*—the corrupt patronage-based party system that had dominated Venezuelan politics for the previous four decades. Upon his election as President, Chávez maintained the radical rhetoric that characterized his electoral campaigns, variously describing his critics as 'squalid', 'oligarchs', 'conspirators' and 'fascists'. He frequently invokes 'popular sovereignty' and calls on the people to defend the 'Bolivarian Revolution' when his Government's agenda has encountered resistance. In instances where the judiciary, Congress or the electoral administration have raised objections to government policy, Chávez has threatened reprisal and dismissal. A central target of his antagonism has been the USA, particularly former President Bush, whom he accused of being a 'murderer' and a 'war criminal'.

The politics and policies of President Chávez have deeply divided Venezuelan society. They have also antagonized the US Administration and received a mixed reception elsewhere in Latin America. In the view of his supporters, the President has deepened Venezuelan democracy, opened channels for popular participation and incorporated the excluded majority into the political system; supporters also argue that, while previous administrations favoured the middle classes, Chávez's Government has used oil revenue to benefit the poor. To his critics, however, Chávez is an authoritarian ruler who has destroyed the country's liberal democracy, centralized power, harassed his critics and squandered oil revenue in order to consolidate his political base at home and pursue his megalomaniac dreams of Latin American leadership abroad.

Since being elected to the presidency, Chávez has used the economic windfall of high oil prices to finance social programmes and consolidate his political base. To this purpose he has implemented a series of special programmes, the so-called *misiones* (missions), to promote health care, housing, remedial education and food subsidies among the poor. These programmes are designed not only to bring the benefits of the welfare state to the poor, especially those in the informal sector, but also to alter the governance of the economy from one emphasizing atomistic participation in the market to one relying on co-operatives and state co-ordination. There are conflicting figures regarding the impact of Chávez's social policies on the Venezuelan poor, and more research is needed to reveal the true picture of its achievements and shortcomings; however, according to figures from ECLAC, the percentage of Venezuelans living below the poverty line fell from 49.9% in 1999 to 27.6% in 2008. Even Chávez's critics acknowledge that the *misiones* have helped sections of the population that previously had no access to social programmes. However, questions remain with regard to the sustainability of the Government's social policy, and, indeed, of its overall economic programme in light of falling oil prices and mounting fiscal and economic problems. According to the IMF, Venezuelan GDP declined by 3.3% in 2009, and, while the rest of the region resumed economic growth during the first half of 2010, the Venezuelan economy was expected to shrink by a further 2.6% during 2010 as a whole. In March 2009 Chávez unveiled a series of measures intended to offset lower oil revenues, which account for about 50% of the national budget, and in January 2010 he unexpectedly ordered a devaluation of the national currency, the bolívar fuerte, with the aim of easing fiscal problems (oil royalties are denominated in US dollars) but this was expected to increase inflation, which was already in excess of 30%.

In 2005 Chávez redefined his beliefs as '21st century socialism with a Venezuelan inflexion'. Although it is still not entirely clear what socialism in this context means, after his re-election in December 2006, with almost 63% of the vote, Chávez intensified his campaign to turn Venezuela into a socialist state. An enabling law passed in February 2007 by the Asamblea Nacional (National Assembly)—which at mid-2010 was wholly controlled by Chávez's supporters as a result of a boycott by the opposition of the 2005 legislative elections—allowed the President to rule by decree for a period of 18 months in order to effect a transformation of Venezuelan society. As a means of attaining this goal, Chávez has started to implement a far-reaching nationalization programme aimed at recovering state ownership of strategic sectors. He has already re-nationalized the country's largest electricity and telecommunications companies, which were privatized during the 1990s, and in May 2007 he took control of the last remaining private oil companies in the country; in 2009 the National Assembly passed a law that would allow the Government to take over oil service contractors, including several US and British firms that were owed up to a year in back fees. He has also nationalized the entire cement industry and the country's largest steel maker, as well as a number of private banks, while the remaining private banks have been threatened with nationalization if they fail to give priority to financing the country's industrial sector at low cost.

Political changes have mirrored economic ones. Following his electoral victory at the end of 2006, Chávez appealed for the disbandment of the multi-party coalition that backed his so-called Bolivarian Revolution and for the merging of the parties into a single new entity, the PSUV, which was formally founded in 2007. A proposal to remove the limit on the number of presidential terms that an incumbent could serve was included within a package of 69 constitutional changes narrowly rejected in a referendum in late 2007. However, in February 2009 the result of the 2007 referendum was reversed when Chávez won a new plebiscite that lifted limits on terms in office for elected officials, allowing him to stand for a second re-election. Chávez contended that he needed to remain in office beyond the end of his current term in 2012 in order to secure what he referred to as Venezuela's socialist revolution, but his opponents claim that the constitutional change will further concentrate power in the hands of the President and that the result of the 2009 plebiscite was manipulated by the Government by means of massive state funding and blanket national television coverage.

While President Chávez remains popular, especially among the poor, the deteriorating economic situation and high rates of crime appear to have eroded his appeal. According to some opinion polls, at mid-2010, for the first time since 2003, more people claimed to identify with the opposition than with Chávez. As a result of this apparent decline in the popularity of Chávez, the forthcoming legislative elections, due to be held in September 2010, were expected to be the most competitive since Chávez came to power in 1999. While the superior political organization of the forces that support Chávez, combined with the executive's use of state resources to favour the ruling party and the President's campaigning skills, meant that the Government would likely retain control of the Asamblea Nacional, a strong parliamentary representation from the opposition parties would go some way towards making the country's political institutions more pluralist and could give the opposition a platform from which to build up political support in the run-up to the presidential election due to be held in 2012.

President Morales of Bolivia is another regional representative of the national popular brand of left-wing politics. Bolivia is a country characterized by a weak state and a long history of popular mobilization. Popular protests over the exploitation of gas and oil resources by foreign companies forced the resignation of President Gonzalo Sánchez de Lozada in October 2003, and further protests brought down his successor, Carlos Mesa Gisbert, in March 2005. The country's indigenous majorities, the *quechuas* and the *aymaras*, have been historically discriminated against, both politically and economically, but they have become increasingly politically active and played an important role in the wave of popular mobilizations that contributed to bringing Morales to office. His victory in the presidential election of December 2005 was a significant milestone in Bolivia's troubled history of democracy, as it was the first time that a member of the country's indigenous majority was elected head of state. Morales' main electoral pledges were to hold elections for a constituent assembly to reform the country's discredited political institutions, devolve power to the indigenous communities, and reassert state control over oil and gas deposits. He also defended the right of Bolivian peasants to grow coca plants, which, he argued, were part of the country's cultural and economic heritage.

Morales won the 2005 presidential election with 53.7% of the valid votes cast, the highest share for any candidate since the country returned to democracy more than 20 years previously. He took office in early 2006 with a mandate for radical change and with high expectations among his popular base of support. The new President fulfilled one of his main electoral promises in striking fashion in May when he issued a decree nationalizing the country's oil and gas fields, and ordered the army to occupy the foreign companies' installations to secure them against sabotage. Foreign companies were to leave Bolivia unless they signed new contracts within six months recognizing state control. In October some 10 oil companies agreed new energy deals with the Government, which allowed the companies to continue operating in the country in partnership with the state-owned oil firm, Yacimientos Petrolíferos Fiscales Bolivianos (YPFB). The companies have also agreed to pay the state higher royalties for their oil and gas sales. Telecommunications and mines were also nationalized and price controls were imposed on gas and foodstuffs, while the state distributed subsidized food to the poor. Morales' Government used the extra revenue accrued from higher gas royalties and prices to expand welfare provision, including the introduction of a non-contributory old age pension and targeted cash handouts to poor households conditional upon their children's school attendance. Some estimates suggest that the payments reached one-quarter of Bolivia's 10m. citizens in 2009. In June 2006 the President launched a programme of agrarian reform by giving more than 30,000 sq miles of land to indigenous peasant communities. The land handed over was state-owned, but Morales declared that his Government would also seize private holdings that were deemed not to be in productive use, in order to meet his target of redistributing around one-fifth of Bolivia's total land area over a five-year period.

The principal danger facing the Morales administration has its origin in the country's deep regional and ethnic cleavages, fissures that threatened to lead to civil unrest and even secessionist attempts if not properly managed. In February 2008 the opposition-controlled eastern departments that manage most of the country's oil, gas and agricultural wealth staged referendums to back their calls for further autonomy from the central Government. The Government dismissed the referendums as illegal and separatist. In an attempt to resolve the political stalemate, a recall referendum was held in August 2008 on the mandates of the President, the Vice-President and nine regional governors, which Morales won with an enhanced majority. After a long and politically fractious process of constitutional reform that brought the country to the brink of armed confrontation between the Government and the opposition, a compromise agreement was reached and the new Constitution was approved, by a large majority of the popular vote, in a plebiscite held in January 2009. However, the constitutional proposal was defeated in four of Bolivia's nine regions, showing the ongoing polarization of Bolivian society. The new Constitution established state control over key economic sectors and granted new social, political and economic rights to Bolivia's indigenous groups, but failed to resolve some fundamental issues that could potentially lead to further political unrest.

President Morales further consolidated his hold on power by winning a second term in office in December 2009 with 64.2% of the popular vote and a wider margin of victory than in 2005. His share of the vote was significantly improved in the opposition strongholds of Santa Cruz, Tarija, Beni and Pando, which made the prospects of secession appear more remote. It was the first time since 1964 that an incumbent Bolivian President had secured re-election to a second term. The ruling party, Movimiento al Socialismo (MAS—Movement for Socialism), also won a decisive two-thirds' majority in the Senado Nacional (National Senate), previously controlled by the opposition. Morales' main priority in his second mandate was fully to implement the new Constitution and advance his programme of economic nationalism. In May 2010 the Government nationalized four electricity generation companies. Critics of Morales' economic policy claim that nationalizations are discouraging much-needed foreign investment and depriving the country of technical and managerial expertise. They note that gas production has fallen since the outset of the programme of nationalization, owing to poor management by YPFB and declining private investment. Government sources counterclaim that they are not against foreign investment but 'want partners not patrons', and stress that their main priority is to promote the industrialization of the country's raw materials.

Together with Chávez and Morales, President Correa of Ecuador completes the trio of South American leaders that have been regarded as populist. The context of Correa's electoral triumph in November 2006 bears strong similarities to the circumstances of Chávez's and Morales' victories. Over the previous decade Ecuador had been blighted by political instability and social tensions, during which time the country had had eight different Presidents, three of whom had been thrown out of office by street protests. It had a highly fragmented and weakly institutionalized party system that bred political volatility. Traditional parties were in decline, discredited because of allegations of corruption and economic mismanagement. Similar to Bolivia, Ecuador is traversed by regional and ethnic fault lines, the main one being between the coastal areas, dominated by an entrepreneurial creole élite, and the Andean highlands, characterized by the strong influence of increasingly politically active indigenous communities. About one-half of Ecuador's 13m. population live on or below the poverty line and an estimated 1m. Ecuadoreans have migrated abroad in search of a better life. Correa campaigned for the presidency as much as a political outsider as a left-wing candidate, attacking the country's political institutions and traditional political parties, and denouncing political corruption within the existing order. His political movement, Alianza País (Patria Altiva i Soberana), did not field any congressional candidates. Correa strongly denounced the Washington Consensus and what he perceived to be the evils of neo-liberalism. He advocated renegotiating oil contracts with multinational oil companies to increase royalties and use the revenue for the redistribution of wealth. One of the first measures that Correa implemented upon assuming office was to expel the World Bank's representative in the country. The Ecuadorean Minister of Finance stated that the Government would not submit its economic programme for the inspection of the IMF.

In the early days of his presidency, Correa embarked on a high-risk political strategy that entailed a series of rapid-fire plebiscites and elections giving him the electoral legitimacy to redraw the country's political institutions without too much consideration for the letter of the law. During a four-year period he entered five major political campaigns: to win the presidency; to win the right to call for a constitutional assembly; to elect his candidates for the assembly; to secure approval of a new constitution; and to win presidential re-election. Throughout his campaigns Correa has used extreme confrontational tactics to target the *partidocracia* and what he called 'the long and dark neo-liberal night', and combined the politics of antagonism with policies of economic redistribution. In the 2006 electoral campaign Correa launched a programme to register voters as potential beneficiaries of his prospective welfare policies. In his first months in office he doubled poverty assistance payments and credits available for housing loans, and reduced electricity rates for low-income consumers. He combined his redistributionist policies with high-profile confrontations with multinational companies, including a Brazilian construction company, and in 2008 defaulted on what his Government considered the 'illegitimate external debt'. Correa channelled the windfall from higher oil prices into targeted social programmes and higher public sector salaries; he also raised the minimum wage. However, Correa has stressed that he does not intend to copy Chávez's political and economic models. Moreover, Correa's grip on power is less strong than that of the Venezuelan President. Alianza País is a heterogeneous political force composed of radical and moderate Left-wingers. He does not have full control of the armed forces, which are the country's historic arbiters of power, and Ecuador's regional and ethnic divisions make it difficult to centralize power.

Correa was re-elected to a second term in April 2009, securing 52% of the vote, comfortably defeating his closest rival, Lucio Gutiérrez, who won only 28%. It was the first time in thirty years that the country had re-elected a President. Alianza País won the largest number of seats in the Asamblea Nacional, although it did not secure an absolute majority. In his inaugural speech, Correa promised to continue his so-called 'socialist revolution', the aim of which was to end poverty, and the so-called 'citizens' revolution', which strove for equality among all citizens. However, Correa's twin revolutions have encountered opposition from both the left and the right. In 2009 indigenous organizations mobilized against a water management bill that they claimed amounted to privatization and would negatively impact on farmers. At least one protester died in clashes between indigenous peasants and the police. The President is also distrusted by businesses, which are critical of his nationalist economic policy and weary of what they regard as excessive public spending. Conflicts with foreign companies have negatively affected investment in oil production and electricity generation, leading to declining oil output and frequent power cuts. To finance the budget deficit the Government is likely to have to borrow more than US $4,000m. in 2010, which could be costly following Ecuador defaulting on one-third of its foreign debt in December 2008.

While displaying significant differences from the radical left-wing populist politics of Chávez, Morales and Correa, the administrations of Néstor Kirchner (2003–07) and Cristina Fernández de Kirchner (2007–11) in Argentina do demonstrate some similar elements. However, Néstor Kirchner was not a political outsider in the mould of Chávez or Morales and he operated in a more institutionalized political system. He came to office in 2003 in a country in which the previous year's economic crisis had produced a popular backlash against the political establishment, crystallized in the slogan *'Que se vayan todos'* ('all politicians out'). Elected to the presidency with just 24.3% of the total votes, Néstor Kirchner sought to increase his popular support by denouncing neo-liberalism and appealing to the national popular tradition of his Peronist party, Partido Justicialista (PJ—Justicialist Party). He also sought to build an image as a defender of the Argentine people against powerful domestic and foreign interests. He clashed with the IMF, with the owners of privatized public utilities, with the country's external debt holders and even with the Roman Catholic Church. He forged a close political and economic alliance with Chávez, whose Government bought around US $5,000m. of Argentine debt between 2005 and early 2010. He concentrated power in the executive, ruling by decree and broadening his political base of support by co-opting opposition state governors through the allocation of financial resources to the provinces on a discretionary basis and by forging alliances with social movements sympathetic to his policies, such as the *piquetero* movement.

The economic policy of the administration of Néstor Kirchner can be characterized as 'neo-developmentalist', after developmentalism, the interventionist economic doctrine that dominated economic policy-making in Latin America in the 1960s and the 1970s. In its current version, neo-developmentalism combines fiscal orthodoxy and heterodox state interventionism in a policy mix aimed at promoting exports and substituting imports. To this purpose, the Kirchner administration maintained high budgetary primary surpluses and supported a high US dollar export strategy. Export taxes, predominantly on highly priced primary exports such as beef, wheat and soya beans, were used to fund state spending and subsidize the public utilities, the tariffs of which have been frozen since the devaluation of the peso in 2002. Government funds were also used to support domestic industry. To offset the threat of rising inflation, Kirchner resorted to price controls, 'voluntary' agreements with producers and, allegedly, to the manipulation of the retail price index. Among the measures introduced to lower the price of foodstuffs by increasing domestic supply was the banning of exports of certain cuts of beef. Kirchner's economic policies resulted in high rates of economic growth that brought down unemployment into single figures and boosted his popularity, contributing to the electoral triumph of his wife, Cristina Fernández, in October 2007.

President Cristina Fernández de Kirchner has largely followed the politics and policies of her husband. However, she has hardly enjoyed a 'honeymoon' period. In the month following her inauguration in December 2007 she faced street protests in the capital, Buenos Aires, after power cuts left districts without energy for three days. More damagingly, in March 2008 a farmers' strike in protest at high export taxes for agricultural commodities precipitated a political crisis in which angry farmers erected road blocks and disgruntled middle-class inhabitants staged political protests in major cities. Protests also reflected growing discontent among sectors of the population regarding crime, energy shortages and rising inflation. As a result of her perceived mismanagement of the confrontation with the farmers, her popularity has waned and, contending with an increasingly difficult economic situation, her Government has come to rely increasingly on the core support of the PJ in the industrial belt of Buenos Aires province. Allegations of impropriety have also damaged the popularity of the Kirchners. The Government's loss of support was reflected in the June 2009 mid-term election, in which the ruling party, Frente para la Victoria (FPV), lost control of both houses of the Congreso (Congress). The party lost in the four main electoral districts, including the key province of Buenos Aires, home to more than 60% of the population. Increasing political polarization had led to legislative gridlock and to tensions between the executive and the legislature. In an attempt to boost its popularity, the Government abandoned its initial fiscal prudence and increased spending on pensions, social security and infrastructure. Political tensions were likely to increase still further in the run-up to the presidential poll due to be held in October 2011, in which Néstor Kirchner, widely expected to be fielded as the candidate of the ruling party, was likely to face opposition from the right wing of the PJ and from a coalition of opposition forces.

The administrations of Lula in Brazil and of Tabaré Vázquez and José Mújica of Uruguay are examples of the new social-democratic left in Latin America. In contrast with radical populism, the social-democratic left has gained office in countries in which representative institutions—legislatures and political parties—have a higher degree of legitimacy than in those countries in which populist policies are dominant, and the checks and balances of a liberal democracy prevent an excessive concentration of power in the executive. Often with their roots in traditional parties of the left, the social-democratic left has shifted from its radical roots towards the centre, as a result of the combination of political experience, electoral calculations and economic constraints. In power, the social-democratic left has adopted and adapted many of the market-friendly policies of the Washington Consensus, while attempting to redress its negative social impact by means of targeted social programmes and increasing investment in human capital. Social-democratic governments have sought to attract foreign investment to create the jobs that will both lift people out of poverty and provide tax revenue for investment in health and education. While seeking a more autonomous foreign policy with regard to the USA than their centre-right predecessors, centre-left governments have generally maintained good relations with the US Administration and with the multilateral financial agencies, such as the IMF and the World Bank.

In Brazil, three consecutive electoral defeats convinced Lula, leader of the PT, to broaden the party's electoral appeal prior to the 2002 election by promulgating an image of political moderation and economic responsibility. After winning the election, the new Government maintained a significant degree of continuity with the market-friendly economic policies of the previous administration of former President Fernando Henrique Cardoso, while expanding already existing social programmes and introducing new ones. After a difficult first year in office, economic growth picked up in the remaining three years of Lula's mandate. While the Government's moderate economic policies disappointed traditional PT supporters, the combination of low inflation, economic growth and targeted social programmes resulted in a reduction of economic inequality and in income gains for the poorest sectors of the population.

Satisfied with their welfare gains, in October 2006 voters rewarded Lula with a new four-year mandate. In his second term in office the administration of Lula has moved towards a more varied model of economic development that combines orthodox macroeconomic policies based on continuous fiscal discipline and inflation-targeting with increasing public and private investment in infrastructure and a more interventionist industrial policy. Brazil was not immune to the 2008–09 global recession, but compared with the situation in other countries the recession in Brazil was short and shallow (GDP contracted only modestly in 2009, by 0.2%). In an attempt to lessen the impact of the global downturn, the Government followed an activist policy of granting public investment and loans to ailing companies from the state-owned banks. Boosted by internal demand, and external demand from China and other emerging markets, the economy rebounded strongly in late 2009 and was expected to grow by over 6% in 2010. As a result of Lula's extremely high levels of popularity, together with the robust condition of the economy, the candidate of the ruling PT party, Dilma Rousseff, was expected to win the presidential contest due to be held in October 2010, although it was likely to be a close contest with the more experienced opposition candidate, José Serra.

In Uruguay, the left-of-centre Government of President Tabaré Vázquez, which took office in March 2005, followed a market-friendly economic policy that had as its main goal the attraction of foreign investment. The Government's economic programme, which was inspired by the Chilean model, combined macroeconomic orthodoxy, fiscal prudence, corporatist agreements on wage demands between trade unions and businesses, and an emergency social programme similar to Brazil's family grant scheme. The Vázquez administration's management of the economy was remarkably successful. In its first four years in office, GDP grew by an average of 7%, while inflation was kept under control. Unemployment declined from a peak of almost 20% in 2002 to single figures in 2008 and there was a concomitant 13.7% reduction in the number of persons living below the poverty line. As part of a strategy of opening up new markets for exports, in January 2007, in a move that surprised its traditional left-wing supporters, the Government signed a Trade and Investment Framework Agreement (TIFA) with the USA, which could lead to a future free trade agreement. Like other countries of the region, Uruguay suffered from the impact of the 2008–09 worldwide recession, but, while the economy slowed, it still registered positive growth of almost 3% in 2009. In November of that year the citizens rewarded the ruling Frente Amplio (FA) administration's social and economic policies by electing the party's candidate, José Mújica Cordano, as the new President (Vázquez was constitutionally barred from seeking re-election). In its first months in office, the new Mújica administration has shown considerable continuity with the policies of its predecessor, reaffirming the Vázquez administration's priorities of promoting domestic and international private investment, maintaining macroeconomic stability and investing in social policies.

The victory of the conservative candidate Sebastián Piñera in a run-off presidential contest in Chile in January 2010 brought an end to two decades of rule by the centre-left CPD. It was the first time in half a century that a right-wing candidate had won a presidential election in that country. Piñera's victory, however, was more a reflection of a desire for political change than of a rightwards shift. The outgoing President, Michelle Bachelet, ended her mandate with high approval ratings and would have had a good chance of winning a second mandate had she not been constitutionally proscribed from seeking re-election. During its 20 years in office the CPD had won four presidential elections and transformed Chile economically, socially and politically. Successive CPD administrations largely followed the free market economic model of the military Government headed by Gen. Augusto Pinochet, but implemented important measures to ensure that the benefits of economic growth reached those most in need. Since 1990 Chile has been the most successful economy in Latin America. The share of Chileans living below the poverty line fell from 38% in 1990 to less than 14% in 2006. There was also considerable investment in education, health and infrastructure. In line with the CPD's free market policies, Bachelet signed a landmark free trade agreement with the People's Republic of China. Her Government saved much of the windfall revenue from high copper exports in an US $11,000m. offshore sovereign fund, part of which was used to boost economic growth during the recession. However, the slowdown in the country's high rates of economic growth, internal divisions within the CPD and a general weariness with a political coalition that had been in office for almost two decades contributed to a mood of disillusionment with the Government that was capitalized on by Piñera. A multimillionaire businessman, Piñera campaigned as a social liberal and promised to maintain many of the CPD's social and economic policies while fighting crime and boosting economic growth and employment. However, just days before Piñera took office Chile was devastated by an earthquake that killed around 500 people and inflicted heavy damage to infrastructure, business and homes estimated at around $30,000m. President Piñera has since promised to afford absolute priority to the task of helping the victims of the earthquake and reconstructing the country's infrastructure.

FOREIGN POLICY

One of the effects of Piñera's victory in Chile was to tilt the regional balance of forces to the right. While former President Bachelet was part of the group of left-of-centre South American leaders that dominated the region, President Piñera is closer to the newly elected right-wing Colombian President, Juan Manuel Santos. However, relations with the centre-right Peruvian Government of President Alan García were expected to remain strained by disputes over territorial waters and other historical grievances. Divisions among the right are mirrored by differences between left and left-of-centre leaders, crystallized in an unacknowledged low-level competition for regional primacy between Presidents Lula and Chávez, a contest in which the Brazilian President is increasingly enjoying the upper hand.

In an attempt to foster regional integration, 12 South American countries signed a treaty on 23 May 2008 in Brasília agreeing to the establishment of a Union of South American Nations (UNASUR). This new entity, modelled on the European Union (EU), was to seek to unite South America's two existing customs unions, the Southern Common Market (Mercosur/Mercosul) and the Andean Community, and to foster closer political ties between the countries of the region. As part of the initiative, member states agreed in principle to create a Brazil-sponsored South American Defence Council (CSD) as a forum to co-ordinate defence and security affairs. UNASUR and the CSD can be seen as part of Brazil's strategy to assert itself as a regional superpower and to increase South America's autonomy from the USA. However, at mid-2010 it was too early to know whether UNASUR would boast any real substance or prove merely to be another 'talking shop' for South America's leaders.

Meanwhile, Chávez has aggressively used his country's oil wealth to pursue a foreign policy aimed at promoting his 'Bolivarian' idea of Latin American integration and to consolidate his regional leadership. In joining Mercosur in 2007, Venezuela sponsored the establishment of the so-called Alternative Bolivariana para las Americas (ALBA—the Bolivarian Alternative for the Americas—renamed the Bolivarian Alliance for the Peoples of our America, Alianza Bolivariana para los Pueblos de Nuestra América, in 2009), which at mid-2010 included Bolivia, Cuba, Dominica, Nicaragua, Saint Vincent and the Grenadines, and Venezuela, as an alternative project for political and economic integration under Chávez's leadership. Chávez has openly supported political allies such as Morales in Bolivia, Daniel Ortega Saavedra, the leader of Frente Sandinista de Liberación Nacional (FSLN—Sandinista National Liberation Front), in Nicaragua and the defeated presidential candidate Ollanta Humala in Peru. He has financed grassroots and cultural organizations throughout the region and sought to court public opinion in other countries, thereby undermining the leaders therein, with initiatives such as the sale of cheap heating oil to poor urban dwellers in the

USA. He has sold petroleum to Cuba and a number of small Caribbean countries at sub-market prices and has signed a co-operation agreement with Ecuador that includes the refining of up to 100,000 barrels per day of Ecuador's crude petroleum. However, the decline in oil prices as a result of the 2008–09 global economic crisis, together with mounting domestic problems, have limited Chávez's political and economic resources to pursue his regional diplomacy.

While the victory of Barack Obama in the US presidential elections in November 2008 was widely welcomed in Latin America, the new US Administration has yet to draw up a coherent policy framework for the region. The Obama Administration must also confront the issue of declining US political and economic influence in Latin America. During his first months in office, President Obama sought to ease tensions between the USA and some of Latin America's more radical left-wing Governments, including those of Cuba and Venezuela, and has established close political relations with the Brazilian Government of Lula, whom he regards as a natural regional leader. However, dialogue with Cuba has stalled and the US Administration was criticized by some Latin American countries for not being sufficiently forceful in demanding the restoration of the deposed Honduran President Zelaya following the military coup of June 2009. While remaining healthy, US relations with the Brazilian Government have been strained by Lula's amicable relationship with the Iranian President, Mahmoud Ahmadinejad, and by Lula's reluctance publicly to denounce what the USA regards as the authoritarian measures of Chávez. In June 2009, shortly after Lula announced that he had successfully mediated a deal on the issue of Iran's nuclear facilities, Obama cancelled a scheduled trip to Brazil, on the explicit grounds that it was inappropriate while an electoral campaign was taking place in the country, but the cancellation was widely interpreted as a signal of the displeasure of the US Administration at the nuclear deal.

CONCLUSIONS

As it entered the second decade of the 21st century, Latin America was an increasingly politically diverse region. With the notable exception of Cuba, the region remained ruled by democratic governments, although in June 2009 it experienced, in Honduras, the first successful military removal of a democratically elected President in over three decades. Elections were mostly free and fair but there was great variety in the shape and strength of political institutions, with some countries appearing as increasingly consolidated liberal democracies while in others fragile political institutions remained strained by deep social and political divisions. The new electoral cycle still under way was likely to augment the picture of regional diversity. While left and left-of-centre governments remain in office in many countries, there has not been a uniform swing to either side of the political spectrum. Rather, as can be expected in a democratic election, citizens have chosen to reward incumbents that have performed well or voted for change when the incumbents have been less successful.

In general, the countries of the region have dealt with the economic and political fallout from the 2008–09 global economic recession with a surprising degree of success—a sign, perhaps, of increasing political and economic stability. If sustained, the economic recovery under way at mid-2010 would give the Latin American countries the chance to build on the economic and social gains of the past decade. However, not all countries were likely to progress at the same rate, and, while considerable progress has been made in recent years with regard to the reduction of poverty, much remained to be done to breach the gap between the region's 'haves' and 'have nots'. Whether conservative, radical populists or moderate social democrats, the governments of the region were in a race against time to construct fairer and more prosperous societies as the foundation for a consolidated democratic order.

Internationally, Latin America continued to reassert its autonomy from the USA. The creation of new regional associations, such as UNASUR, mark a new era for the integration of the countries of South America. The relative decline of US influence within the region, and the political and economic problems experienced by President Chávez in Venezuela, have allowed Brazil further to advance its status as a regional superpower with increasing aspirations to become a major global player. However, political divisions within the countries of the region, together with a reluctance to share sovereignty in supranational institutions, remained a major obstacle to the achievement of deeper integration.

MEXICO AND THE WAR ON DRUGS

GARETH A. JONES

Media headlines suggest that Mexico has descended into a spiral of drugs-related violence that has prompted assessments of a failed state, with possibly regional implications. As President Felipe Calderón put it in 2009, 'organized crime is in search of territorial control, there will be a war with no quarter given because there is no possibility of living with the drugs cartel (*el narco*). There is no turning back; it is them or us.' The escalation of violence prompted the US Department of Defense's 2008 *Joint Operating Environment* assessment to observe that:

> In particular, the growing assault by the drug cartels and their thugs on the Mexican government over the past several years reminds one that an unstable Mexico could represent a homeland security problem of immense proportions to the United States.

The report continued:

> In terms of worst-case scenarios for the Joint Force and indeed the world, two large and important states bear consideration for a rapid and sudden collapse: Pakistan and Mexico.... Any descent by Mexico into chaos would demand an American response based on the serious implications for homeland security alone.

By some accounts, intervention might not come soon enough. A nightmare scenario (envisaged by Sullivan and Elkus, 2008) predicts, 'A lawless Mexico will be a perfect staging ground for terrorists seeking to operate in North America. American policy-makers must act to protect our southern flank.' It is a view shared by a range of private security consultancies and blogs, which endorse the thesis that 'third-phase cartels', no longer limited to regional power bases, may associate with 'third-generation gangs' that have shifted from turf-based affiliations to transnational networks, with the potential to conduct 'fourth generation warfare'. Noting, for example, US Southern Command estimates that Central America has around 70,000 gang members, and that both transnational gangs and drugs-trafficking organizations (DTOs) share cell-like structures, it is argued that such organizations may be attractive to the militant Islamist al-Qa'ida (Base) organization, the Lebanese militant group Hezbollah, or anti-capitalist groups looking for 'plug and go' networks to extend their cause.

'Failed state' discussion has mostly been met with disdain in Mexico. Nevertheless, a recent survey revealed that one in seven residents of Ciudad Juárez would be willing to invite the US Federal Bureau of Investigation (FBI) or the UN to provide security and nearly six out of 10 would accept their presence nation-wide. For the US Administration, Mexico has risen up the agenda. As recently as 2007, Mexico ranked 12th on the recipient list for funding through US foreign operations programmes. Mexico was deemed capable of financing its own anti-DTO initiatives and to require only occasional technical assistance and training in counter-insurgency measures. That view has changed. In 2010 rumours persisted that US Joint Special Operations Command had already approved a decision for Special Forces to operate covertly in Mexico to capture or eliminate DTO 'kingpins'. Publicly, the Mérida Initiative, begun in 2008, commits the USA to funding a series of regional security measures covering Mexico and Central America. To date, Mexico has been the largest recipient of the US $1,400m. package: the 2010 budgetary request for anti-drugs and security assistance to Mexico was $485.6m.

This essay departs from the temptation to interpret the 'war on drugs' from a US and military perspective, to predict the future and to offer only pessimistic readings of the present situation. Instead, it considers how the 'war' has been shaped by the structure of the drugs industry and the Mexican state's response. The essay notes how the political legitimacy of past regimes motivated but also undermined present-day control efforts. It considers how the Manichean 'them or us' approach reduces multiple conflicts to an idea of the state as the counterpoint to DTOs, implicitly calling upon society to enjoin an endeavour to save the nation. Yet, contrary to the rhetoric, the state is not 'under siege' from DTOs bent on its destruction. The DTOs need the state. Rather, the 'war' is about resisting the attempts of DTOs to regain a presence within the state that they held during the 1980s and 1990s, under circumstances today in which a different political class is competing for power and the state itself is increasingly decentralized and democratic.

THE SPIRAL OF VIOLENCE

Media reports present us continuously with images of dead bodies and blood-stained streets, with claims that the northern Mexican cities of Tijuana and Ciudad Juárez are today's equivalent of Colombia's Cali or Medellín, and with accounts of personal tragedies and fear. In fact, if considered against levels of violence during the period from 1910 through the 1930s, or with Colombia or parts of Central America at any point over the preceding 30 years, Mexico in 2010 was not more violent, nor was it the 'most violent' country in the region. It was the case that Mexico was more violent than the USA, but many US cities, for example New Orleans and Detroit, had higher murder rates than those recorded both in Mexico generally and in major Mexican cities in particular. It is important therefore to understand levels and trends for data on violence and to appreciate their unevenness.

A frequently cited headline figure in early 2010 was the death of more than 23,000 people since the announcement of a 'war on drugs' in Mexico in late 2006. This figure, for the new category of 'drugs-related violence', was initially estimated by national newspapers but was subsequently confirmed by the Mexican Government. Since 2006, there appeared to have been a dramatic increase from 2,200 drugs-related murders to 2,725 in 2007, to possibly over 6,500 in 2008 and to as many as 7,600 in 2009. Put another way, the 'war on drugs' claimed almost twice as many lives during 2009 as, officially, there were civilians killed in Iraq. An increase in the number of deaths in cities such as Nuevo Laredo, Tijuana, Culiacán and, especially, Ciudad Juárez (also known simply as Juárez) gave credence to the rhetoric of 'war'. In 2008 about 1,600 people were killed in Juárez, a figure that rose to 2,575 in 2009, pushing the homicide rate for the state of Chihuahua, in which the city is located, to 143 per 100,000 people. Drugs violence has been significant enough to affect the national homicide rate. According to the office of the Attorney General, 28,887 people were murdered in 2007, suggesting a rate of around 28 per 100,000, with drugs-related deaths accounting for almost 10% of homicides. The almost trebling of drugs-related violence between 2007 and 2009 indicates a further significant impact on the homicide rate attributed to the 'war'.

Data on homicide are conventionally considered to be reasonably accurate—murder rarely goes unreported—if an unreliable indicator of people's sense of fear. Yet the data for Mexico are open to interpretation for a variety of reasons, especially in relation to the popularization of the term 'drugs-related'. Homicide data in Mexico exclude deaths where the cause is not established or a body is not produced. However, describing a death as being 'drugs-related' immediately suggests the cause before forensic evidence can be assessed, or even a body is found. Of course, defining an execution in plain sight as a '*narcoejecución*' might be straightforward, but claims for 'disappearances', sometimes based on confessions of DTO members, are difficult to confirm, given the proficiency of DTOs at disposing of bodies using acid baths and mass graves. Suspicion abounds that it suits the Government to categorize as many deaths as possible as 'drugs-related' to bolster legitimacy for the 'war'. Inconsistencies between government departments in the data on homicide are cited to support this theory: the national statistics institute, for example, puts the 2008 homicide rate at 10.6 per 100,000 people. Critics might also wish to consider how a newly popularized term is deployed to capture an empirical trend. 'Drugs-related' was rarely used until about 2000, yet DTOs were responsible for murders during the 1990s and before—victims were mostly shippers (*transportistas*) who had lost consignments or distributors unable to pay for advances—with a figure of 1,000 per year suggested by one source. As the same source commented, before 2000 Mexico did not have a 'narrative' around which to discuss drugs-related killings: the 'war on drugs' has provided that narrative.

THE RISE OF THE *NARCO*

To understand the rise of the DTO, we must appreciate changes to the commodity chains for drugs and to the relative importance of Mexico. Although the focus of attention has been the trade in cocaine, the earliest significant DTOs, dating from the 1960s and 1970s, were involved in the production and/or shipment of marijuana and black tar heroin, with Mexican DTOs supplying about one-third of all heroin and marijuana entering the USA by 1991. The shift to cocaine, from the late 1970s, was an extension of these operations and was already significant by the 1980s. In 1991 about 350 metric tons of cocaine was already passing through Mexico. Since then, cocaine has grown in relative importance to DTO operations, with current shipments through Mexico estimated at over 1,000 tons and worth perhaps as much as US $38,000m. However, it is the impact of cocaine on DTO business practices and relations with the state that we must understand if we want to appreciate the path to 'war'.

The precursor to these changes was the development of relations between Colombian traffickers and the early Mexican DTOs during the 1970s, when it is alleged that Juan Ramón Matta Ballesteros, a Honduran national, linked Alberto Sicilia Falcón, a Cuban émigré and head of drugs-smuggling through Tijuana, to the Cali-based DTO of Benjamín Herrera Zuleta. Sicilia Falcón's operation was soon challenged by the emerging DTO of Miguel Angel Félix Gallardo, Rafael Caro Quintero and Ernesto Fonseca Carrillo, which began to link the Mexican states of Sinaloa, Sonora, Durango and Jalisco, becoming known as the Guadalajara DTO, and by the Gulf DTO of Juan García Abrego, which became involved with the Cali DTO from around the mid-1980s. Before their involvement with cocaine, these DTOs shipped marijuana and black tar heroin in one direction and took advantage of high tariffs to 'import' a variety of consumer goods in the other. The DTO structures were based on strong family links and ties to regions, restricted by relations with farms and intermediary suppliers, and dependent on specific border crossing points where bribery could be arranged. Cocaine, however, would transform these thin networks into complex structures with transnational reach, more diversified business interests and, most important of all, closer links with the state.

The Mexican DTOs offered their Colombian counterparts a number of advantages over the service provided by *transportistas* operating air or maritime routes from Peru or through Venezuela and the Caribbean. In addition to air and maritime routes, both via the west coast and the Gulf of Mexico, Mexican DTOs could provide access to tested mechanisms for crossing the land border. Critically, Mexican DTOs could switch transit routes and means quickly according to the anti-drugs operations of either the Mexican or US state, and reduce risks by having products in transit for shorter periods. Above all, however, Mexico offered opportunities for net bulk access to US markets. The high value to weight ratio of cocaine made it worthwhile to maximize the number of shipments, but Mexican DTOs began to use larger shipments; although a single interdiction might lose millions of dollars, the value of the larger loads would more than compensate. Stockpiling drugs ready for large shipments became a key component of the Mexican model. Offering reliability, frequency and bulk access, the main DTOs could charge higher fees—as much as one-half of a shipment's value—as well as operate as 'price makers', using their capacity to either flood or restrict the market in the short run and increase profit margins.

The arrangements between Mexican and Colombian DTOs have not remained stable over time. Mexican DTOs have tended to operate with a variety of Colombian DTOs. The Juárez DTO of Amado Carrillo Fuentes, for example, had strong links with Rodríguez Orejuela of Cali, as well as with the Ochoa brothers in Medellín, while Osiel Cárdenas, who took over the Gulf DTO from García Abrego, also built connections with Cali traffickers, despite being in competition with the Juárez DTO. More recently, it was revealed that, although in conflict with each other, both the Sinaloa and Beltrán Leyva DTOs (an off-shoot of the Sinaloa DTO and named after the five brothers who founded it) had developed and maintained ties with the Norte del Valle DTO of Colombia. Despite the perceived shift of power away from Colombian DTOs to their Mexican counterparts, the latter do not appear to have become involved with the refinement and shipping of cocaine out of Colombia, Peru and Bolivia. They have, however, increased their presence in Central America since the late 1990s. This is logical for a number of reasons. First, the shift to cocaine allowed Mexican DTOs to extend their geographical reach from a local area to the region in order to secure imports. Expanding into Guatemala and Honduras provided more opportunities to diversify drugs routes, particularly given the relative power of Mexican DTOs compared with those in both countries. Second, it seems likely that the Mexican DTOs identified Guatemalan and Honduran political structures as being susceptible to infiltration and corruption, especially in areas such as Petén and San Marcos in Guatemala. As DTOs have extended their operations over larger areas and become more complex, they have adopted cell-like structures in order to avoid infiltration bringing down the whole network. By 2000 it was claimed that the Juárez DTO involved 3,300 people in 300 cells spread over 17 Mexican states.

Perhaps the most significant impact of DTOs' involvement in cocaine was the change it made to their relationships with the Mexican state. Alberto Sicilia Falcón later claimed that his DTO was protected by the Dirección Federal de Seguridad (DFS), the agency tasked from 1947 with ensuring the internal security of Mexico, which, in practice, meant the suppression of left-wing movements. Sicilia identified as his principal contact Miguel Nazar Haro, allegedly the head of a secret group called the White Brigade during the 'dirty war', DFS deputy director from 1978–82 and subsequently director. Nazar Haro was an important player in a close group of politicians headed by two key figures, Fernando Gutiérrez Barrios and Manuel Bartlett. Gutiérrez Barrios joined the DFS in 1952, becoming its director during 1964–70, before entering politics formally, serving in a variety of elected posts, including as Governor of Veracruz (1986–88). Bartlett rose through the ranks of the Partido Revolucionario Institucional (PRI, Institutional Revolutionary Party), becoming Secretary of the Interior between 1982 and 1988. Crucially, despite shifts in ideology and personality during the final decades of its 70-year rule, which lasted until 2000, this *camarilla* (cabal) has always remained near the centre of power. Under the so-called 'new broom' of President Carlos Salinas (1988–94), Gutiérrez Barrios was appointed Secretary of the Interior and Bartlett Secretary of Public Education, before the latter became Governor of the state of Puebla. Nor has the *camarilla* disappeared with the death of Gutiérrez Barrios in 2000 and the decline of Bartlett, now a senator: rather, it has recreated itself around another generation, headed by Manlio Fabio Beltrones, who has served as Under-Secretary of the Interior (1988–91), as Governor of Sonora (1991–97) and as a senator.

The key point is that under the tutelage of Gutiérrez Barrios the DFS became a 'state within a state', negotiating with DTOs and protecting the political system. For the most part, the arrangement established with DTOs was the same as that applied to groups involved in other forms of organized crime or to leading trade union officials: keep certain activities away from public scrutiny, do not become involved in politics and provide funds or favours when requested. DTOs were encouraged to divide Mexico into *plazas* (territories), within which organizations would avoid each other or co-operate. In return, the state offered the 'guarantee' of protection and sometimes more. In the mid-1980s, for example, the US Drug Enforcement Administration (DEA) discovered interior ministry and army personnel working at a 220-acre ranch in Chihuahua used for growing marijuana and owned by Rafael Caro Quintero. Some DTO heads were even issued with DFS identification cards by José Antonio Zorilla Pérez, Nazar Haro's successor, making them all but 'untouchable' within the criminal justice system. The line between the state and the DTOs was even more blurred by kinship arrangements. When Rodolfo Sánchez Duarte, the son of the Sinaloa Governor Leopoldo Sánchez Celis, was killed in 1990, allegedly on the orders of DTO head Héctor 'El Güero' Palma Salazar in retaliation for the killing of his wife and children at the behest of Miguel Angel Félix Gallardo, it was noted that Félix Gallardo was godfather to Rodolfo Sánchez. With these connections in place, the DTOs were akin to textbook cartels.

Control of the press was vital to the protection of DTOs and the maintenance of the PRI's rule. The scandal that forced the dissolution of the DFS in 1985 illustrates this symbiosis. In 1984 the respected journalist Manuel Buendía was shot outside his office in Mexico City. The director of the DFS, Zorrilla Pérez, was initially instructed to head the investigation to find Buendía's killers but was himself arrested in 1989, along with the suspect, a DFS agent called Juan Rafael Moro Ávila, and was sentenced to prison, eventually serving 19 years. Most accept, however, that Moro Ávila and Zorilla Pérez were scapegoats. One theory is that the decision to kill Buendía was taken at the behest of another *camarilla* member, the Secretary of Defence, Juan Arévalo Gardoqui (1982–88). Arévalo Gardoqui may have been keen for Buendía not to file his latest story—the offer by leading DTOs to provide the Government with funds in order to avert the need to seek IMF assistance after Mexico announced its inability to pay debt interest in November 1982. Moro Ávila's accomplice in the murder was alleged to have been an agent of military intelligence, although he was never formally identified. Mexico's Secretary of Planning and the Budget at the time of the debt crisis was Carlos Salinas, who did indeed manage to avoid IMF intervention. As President, Salinas announced the arrest of Moro Ávila on national Freedom of the Press Day.

The truth about the killing of Buendía and the link with the DFS notwithstanding, the period from 1985 to about 1990 marked a critical juncture in state-DTO relations. At the moment when Mexican DTO involvement in the trafficking of cocaine was growing, the mechanism to negotiate protection with the state shifted to rely less on the mediation of the security apparatus. This link would remain. According to the DEA, four of the five Attorney-Generals that served during the administration of Carlos Salinas had links with DTOs, and the Procuraduría de Justicia Federal (PFJ, Judicial Police) and the successor to the DFS, the Centro de Investigación y Seguridad Nacional, were widely regarded as being compromised. However, DTOs now felt able to make deals direct with secretaries of state, including, according to the DEA, those responsible for key portfolios such as transport and agriculture. The quid pro quo in these arrangements would not be loyalty-protection but funding-enrichment. Cash-rich DTOs used 'shell' companies and financed the acquisition of equity in privatized enterprises, as well as the enormous number of state concessions and infrastructure programmes. Seminal to this argument is the allegation that the President's brother, Raúl Salinas, developed business relations with García Abrego of the Gulf DTO, as well as with individuals accused of money-laundering for the DTO, notably the fugitive President of the Banco Unión, Carlos Cabal Peniche. Despite only receiving a government salary, Raúl Salinas had bank accounts and real estate worth hundreds of millions of US dollars. The change in DTO-state relations may have extended to the PRI's presidential candidate for the 1994 election, Luis Donaldo Colosio, who was murdered during the electoral campaign. Some years after the assassination, a senior source in the PRI claimed that the Tijuana DTO might have found out about an agreement made by Colosio's team to favour the Sinaloa DTO once in office.

Carlos Salinas's successor as President, Ernesto Zedillo (1994–2000), distanced his administration from Gutiérrez Barrios and Bartlett. Lacking a personal power base, his strategy was to rely on a balance of technocrats, mostly former secretaries of state and directors of agencies in the Salinas administration, and politicians linked with the Atlacomulco group. Headed by the patriarch Carlos Hank González, this group had been engrained in the political structure of Mexico since the 1960s. Hank had served as Governor of the state of Mexico, Regent of Mexico City, Secretary of Tourism and Secretary of Agriculture. His power, however, extended to business interests in real estate, petrol stations, construction, an airline, shipping, sport and gambling, and banking in Mexico and the USA. These interests have been the subject of investigations in the USA by the DEA, the FBI, the National Drug Intelligence Center and the Federal Reserve Board, which have also examined the role of Hank's children, most notoriously his eldest son, who also served one term as Mayor of Tijuana. Uniquely, Hank probably had links with more than one DTO. Members of the Atlacomulco group rose to prominence during Zedillo's presidency: notably, Emilio Chuayffet, a former Governor of the state of Mexico, was appointed Secretary of the Interior, while Arturo Montiel served as a senior official at the Secretariat of State for the Interior and later as Governor of the state of Mexico. Roberto Madrazo, former Governor of Tabasco and a 'rising star' of the PRI, is a member of the Hank group and also a close ally of Manlio Fabio Beltrones, a protégé of Gutiérrez Barrios. Many doubt if the President, commanding a fragile legitimacy, was able to keep in check powerful interest groups.

The PRI's loss of the presidency in 2000 to the candidate of the Partido Acción Nacional (PAN, National Action Party), Vicente Fox, was widely celebrated, but the aftermath of his election had serious implications for the DTOs. In one version of events, popular in Washington, 'drugs-related' violence is an unintended consequence of democracy, although, as often stated, this idea lacks analytical traction. There are, perhaps, four dimensions to the way in which democratization has changed DTO-state relations and been partly responsible for violence. First, the loss of electoral power for the PRI, and with it access to business opportunities and corruption channels, put pressure on lower level party officials who now lacked the means to maintain the loyalty of *matones* (thugs), in some cases integrated into police forces, which therefore threatened the careful management of crime. In the second half of the 1990s, at the same time as the PRI began to recognize its loss of power, people began to notice an increase in street crime, car theft and abduction. Crime, moreover, became less predictable and possibly more violent. Small-scale criminals would see opportunities for working for shippers, dealers and, more formally, the DTOs: some smaller DTOs used organized crime to raise sufficient capital for involvement in the drugs trade.

Second, democracy increased the number of actors with whom DTOs had to deal, and who were, in turn, freer of central control. Previously, a mayor or governor would be closely monitored from the centre, reports from *madrinas* (informants) going back to the Secretariat of State for the Interior, the PRI and, if required, the President. If deemed necessary, action could be taken. The decline of the PRI meant that the monitoring system collapsed, although one interviewee suggested that Vicente Fox would still receive reports from the provinces but gave them little attention. Third, democracy raised the price for political co-operation. Politicians were now in a position to make deals with one DTO over another. Accusations were made in this regard against former Governors such as Francisco Labastida (Sinaloa) and Manlio Fabio Beltrones, while in May 2010 Mario Villanueva, Governor of Quintana Roo in 1993–99, became the first former governor to be extradited to the USA on charges of illicit gain from the drugs trade. Villanueva had been Mayor of Cancún, a city synonymous with money-laundering and where five of the last seven mayors have been arrested for connections with DTOs.

The case of Cancún's recent Mayor, Gregorio Sánchez, illustrates the fourth dimension, known as *narco-democracia* ('narco-democracy'). Sánchez was arrested in May 2010, shortly before elections to the governorship of Quintana Roo, for which he was the candidate of the Partido de la Revolución Democrática (PRD, Party of the Democratic Revolution) and ahead in the polls. The judge who issued the arrest warrant had been involved in the arrests in 2009 of 10 mayors in the state of Michoacán, all from the PRD and PRI, on the eve of elections. Charges were subsequently withdrawn, fuelling the suspicion that an association with drugs was being used as 'mud' to 'dirty' opposition candidates and justify the presence of the army during elections. One interesting response from the PRI during the lead-up to the July 2009 mid-term congressional elections and the July 2010 gubernatorial polls was its representation of itself as the party of 'stability', a barely veiled suggestion that it could broker deals with the main DTOs.

THE PAN AND THE 'WAR ON DRUGS'

The DTOs therefore emerged from a radical restructuring of politics and the state; they did not suddenly expand to take on a stable state. As the PAN replaced the PRI in government, reaccommodating the DTOs in a new political bargain was impossible. President Vicente Fox and his successor from December 2006, Felipe Calderón (also of the PAN), headed administrations that lacked the means and motivation to broker deals with the DTOs. However, Fox and Calderón had to control the DTOs without the guaranteed loyalty of agencies within the state, notably those involved with intelligence-gathering, policing and criminal prosecution. Both were, thus, confronted with the problem of having to conduct a profound reform of the state as part of the 'war on drugs', rather than in preparation for such a conflict.

Particular concerns were municipal and state police forces, widely criticized for their lack of professional training and co-ordination. Reforming the municipal police in all 2,438 municipalities, many of which were controlled by mayors from opposition parties, was a daunting task. Instead, the National Programme for the Control of Drugs 2000–06 envisaged the use of federal police agents and the army in conventional policing roles. In 2005 Operation Secure Mexico began in the states of Tamaulipas, Sinaloa and Baja California, with army units and federal agents replacing municipal police. The move received a hostile reaction in Nuevo Laredo, Tamaulipas, when federal agents were shot at by municipal police before the 700-strong force was made to stand down. This approach continued under Calderón, who disarmed 2,300 police officers in Tijuana, Baja California, and deployed federal police and the army to the city. More subtly, Calderón has also extended an approach adopted by President Zedillo by installing military officers in police roles, allocating senior posts to those with experience of anti-drugs operations. The appointment in 2008 of Gen. Javier del Real Magallanes, a former chief of the intelligence section of the armed forces and head of anti-drugs operations for north-east Mexico, as Under-Secretary of Police Strategy and Intelligence in the Secretariat of State for Public Security was regarded as particularly significant.

While relying on federal agencies, both Fox and Calderón had to cope with the knowledge that these same forces are compromised by links with DTOs. In a move that was more than a little suggestive of political expediency, six months after taking office President Calderón removed 284 federal police commanders, including the commanders of federal police agencies in all 31 states and the Federal District of Mexico, on grounds of corruption. Unlike at the local level, nationally neither Fox nor Calderón have had much option but to undertake reform. Fox created the Secretariat of State for Public Security to improve co-ordination between the security and justice systems, and a new federal agency for criminal investigation, the Agencia Federal de Investigación (AFI), to replace the much discredited PJF. Under Calderón, the powers of the federal agencies have been expanded, with provision made for the use of wire-taps, searches without a warrant and the confiscation of property from people convicted of serious crime. Calderón also sought to co-ordinate efforts by placing the public security police (Policía Federal Preventiva, PFP) and the AFI under a single command. In 2005, however, a report by the office of the Attorney-General had indicated that 1,500 of 7,000 AFI agents were under investigation for criminal activity and that 457 were facing charges, including for the illegal detention and disappearance of DTO members. In 2009 Calderón was forced to replace the AFI with a 'new' federal police agency, the Policía Federal Ministerial, although it subsequently recruited former AFI personnel, and the PFP became the Policía Federal. New officers are screened for drugs use and are subject to background financial checks.

In the circumstances, it is not surprising that President Calderón has made extensive use of the military. What marks the Calderón approach as different from those of his predecessors, however, is the scale of deployment and the almost constant mobilization of units in parts of the country. Less than two weeks after taking office, Calderón launched Operation Michoacán, involving agents from the AFI, 5,300 troops and special forces. By 2009 48,750 army personnel were assigned to more than 20 anti-drugs operations. Approximately one-third of the army was on drugs-related duty at any time, with a 2008 study by the Secretary of National Defence predicting that mobilization might need to be long-term. This is not a scenario that pleases all senior officers. Concerns have been expressed at the use of the military for internal security, at problems of desertion and at the rising number of human rights cases levelled at the army.

WINNING THE WAR?

If the 'war on drugs' is about 'them or us', which side is winning? Most assessments are ambivalent. First, considering the number of people detained on drugs-related charges, this figure has amounted to about 12,000 per year since 2000, with a small increase since 2006. The Government argues that these arrests are significant in number and disrupt DTO operations. Critics suggest that most of those apprehended are small-scale dealers or shippers rather than high-level bosses or those involved in money-laundering. Not for nothing are DTO leaders known colloquially as *cucarachas* (cockroaches), able to scuttle away from trouble. However, even the impact of high-profile arrests may be short-term. A recent DEA poster proclaimed successes against the Tijuana DTO, with 'arrested' stamped over photographs of seven of the nine leading members, including Javier and Eduardo Arellano Félix. Shortly afterwards a new poster was issued with photographs of a different 10 'most wanted' members of the organization.

One significant achievement concerns extradition. In the past an arrested DTO head could be assured of remaining in Mexico and in communication with the organization. Major bosses such as Miguel Angel Félix Gallardo, Rafael Caro Quintero and Osiel Cárdenas have all managed their organizations from Mexican prisons. In late 2005, however, the Mexican Supreme Court overturned a prohibition on extraditing fugitives who could face the death penalty. Extraditions quickly followed, 41 in 2005 and 63 in 2006. DTO leaders dislike prison life in the USA, unable to see family, to communicate with lieutenants or to arrange the protection of fellow DTO inmates. Retribution has been dramatic. Although denied as being sabotage, an aeroplane crash in Mexico City in November 2008, in which the Secretary of the Interior, Juan Camilo Mouriño, and all others on board were killed, is claimed privately to have been the work of DTOs. Also in the aircraft was José Luis Santiago Vasconcelos, formerly Assistant Attorney-General for International Affairs and Assistant Attorney-General at the federal agency charged with investigating organized crime, who was responsible for arranging the extradition of 15 major traffickers in January 2006.

A second gauge relates to interdiction of drugs or their means of production in Mexico. The Calderón Government claimed that in the first years of the 'war' 33,019 farms for the cultivation of opium poppy were seized and 777 laboratories for processing cocaine and/or methamphetamine were destroyed. The numbers represent an increase on previous years, but critics have noted the definitional difficulties with the description 'farms' and that laboratories can be reassembled at other locations within days. Between 2006 and 2010 the Mexican military claimed to have seized 22 metric tons of cocaine, which would represent about 3% of the total quantity of cocaine being transported through Mexico to the USA, as well as 337 kg of opium paste and 233 kg of heroin. Although DEA and police reports in the USA have indicated an increase in street prices for cocaine, suggesting difficulties of supply, this may be due to production difficulties in Colombia. Indeed, the interdiction of cocaine has declined on the US side by almost one-half since 2006, whereas that of heroin has trebled since 2005. This might support the US Department of Justice's claim, in its report *National Drug Threat Assessment 2010*, that Mexican DTOs may be switching back to heroin as the export of choice. Whether this assessment is accurate, or justifies being considered a success, is difficult to judge.

A third indicator relates to claims that increased levels of 'drugs-related' violence are the result of DTO infighting (as arrests and interdiction mount) or inter-DTO conflicts during which the DTOs might fight each other to a standstill. Both theories have some merit. Although a process that began during the 1990s, when pacts with the state broke down, it seems as if the DTOs have become more violent both against the state and against other DTOs as a means to preserve territorial control and to extend into zones controlled by others. To these ends, the 'war' has accelerated and diversified the emergence of new violent actors. First, several paramilitary groups, either linked with one DTO or acting as mercenaries, have been established. The best known of these are the Zetas, formed by Arturo Guzmán Decena from a group of around 30 members of the air unit of the special forces, supported with recruitment from Guatemalan special forces (*Kaibiles*). Initially under the command of the Gulf DTO, the Zetas used their military training to mount sophisticated attacks, often using high-powered weaponry and combined with a ruthless exhibitionism of violence. In counterpart, the Negros and Pelones have operated on behalf of the Sinaloa DTO, most famously in the attempted takeover of Nuevo Laredo in 2005, although the Negros may have since shifted allegiance to the Beltrán Leyva DTO or become independent under the direction of Edgar Valdez Villareal (also known as La Barbie).

A second dimension to drugs-related violence is the use of gangs, including groups from the USA and Central America. The most substantive example is the Juárez DTO's use of La Línea, a paramilitary group reported to draw upon the 7,000 members of the Aztecas gang based in both Juárez and El Paso. Reports also suggest that the Sinaloa DTO has employed members of the Mexicles (Partido Revolucionario Mexicano) and Artistas Asesinos (AA). The Mexicles were formed in the US prison system, first in Texas with affiliation across the south-west, with membership estimates ranging from 1,200–14,000, while the AA is believed to have around 600 members. The Tijuana DTO has used individuals from La Eme gang in the US state of California to conduct attacks in Mexico and the USA. There have been some reports of members of Mara Salvatrucha, a gang that originated in the US city of Los Angeles but subsequently spread to other parts of North and Central America, being used as enforcers to attack rival gangs, but DTOs have been wary of any more permanent associations with mostly untrained, drug-using young men with untested loyalties. Transnational gangs have so far come from the north and have not been integrated into the DTO structure.

The argument that increasing levels of violence indicate the break-up of the DTOs requires some caution. A brief history of DTOs reveals a propensity to fragment and realign. In the 1990s the Guadalajara DTO divided into the Tijuana and Sinaloa DTOs, after which the Sinaloa DTO headed by Joaquín 'El Chapo' Guzmán split, with the Beltrán Leyva brothers forming their own DTO. The Beltrán Leyva DTO subsequently associated with the Juárez and Tijuana DTOs, although these were in conflict, and grew rapidly in just two years until elder brother Arturo was killed in December 2009. The Juárez DTO survived the death of Amado Carrillo Fuentes in 1997, in part through maintaining a family line, as well as through Juan José Esparragoza Moreno's use of his Guadalajara DTO connections to broker a pact with the Sinaloa DTO and to draw upon support from the Caro Quintero Sonora DTO, which reformed around brothers Miguel and Jorge after lead figure Rafael was extradited to the USA. The arrangement between the Juárez, Sinaloa and Sonora DTOs is sometimes referred to as The Federation. A more fragile arrangement may have been negotiated by Esparragoza between the Juárez DTO and the Zetas, the latter having gained some control over the Gulf DTO, with reports suggesting that in 2008–09 the Zetas might have supplanted Osiel Cárdenas or become joint heads. However, subsequent reports signalled the dissolution of the Zetas, as original members were killed or captured, only for indications in 2010 to suggest a split in the organization, with a new group, the New Zetas Organization, emerging, acting as both a paramilitary group and a DTO, and with links to a revived Beltrán Leyva DTO.

Finally, the Tijuana DTO declined after the arrests of Benjamín and Eduardo Arellano Félix and the 2002 death of Ramón Arellano Félix, but subsequently reappeared, despite having fewer links with other organizations. After a power battle between Eduardo, Javier, Francisco and Enedina Arellano Félix, Eduardo and Enedina emerged as the new heads of the DTO, and when Javier and Eduardo were arrested, Enedina took control, passing responsibilities to her son Luis Fernando Sánchez Arellano. A 2008 split with former lieutenant Teodoro García Simenthal did not so much weaken the Tijuana DTO as necessitate the promotion of cell leaders. García Simenthal's arrest in January 2010 removed a rival who had formed links with another new and important DTO, Familia Michoacana, which has attempted to consolidate control of Michoacán and Guerrero, supported initially by the Gulf DTO and Zetas, although currently a rival of the latter, amid rumours of links to the Sinaloa DTO.

CONCLUSION

The 'war on drugs' declared by President Calderón in 2006 added a narrative thread to a conflict that had been under way for more than a decade and which has its origins in the 1980s. Then, a shift by DTOs into cocaine necessitated changes to their organization and practice, which coincided with political changes that resulted in a more complicated state structure. As the PRI lost its apparently hegemonic grip on politics, as a group of politicians tied to the state security apparatus competed with politicians with business interests, as the state apparatus itself decentralized and the media became less controlled, so a space opened for DTOs to become more autonomous. More and larger DTOs emerged, although not to challenge the state, as interests remained largely coterminous. Beholden to groups in the PRI for stability, President Zedillo had limited scope to act against the DTOs. His successors had little room for manoeuvre, as the organs of the state were unreliable allies in tackling the DTOs, prompting recourse to the military, Mexico's most trusted public institution.

Rather than risk Mexico becoming a failed state, one can conclude that the 'war on drugs' is an attempt to reassert the role of the state. On assuming the presidency in December 2006, Calderón inherited a country in which the reach of government, even in the arenas of 'public security', did not stretch nation-wide. In October 2006 the Secretariat of State for Public Security recognized that no part of Mexico was immune from the drugs trade, and two years later Calderón claimed that there were perhaps as many as 2,204 'zones of impunity' where, aside from an army presence, DTOs operated under limited constraint. A year later the President announced that the Government was regaining control, leaving no more than 233 areas in which DTO influence exceeded that of the state, although a 2009 report by the Secretariat of State for Public Security identified 353 such municipalities. Like most wars, the fight is as much about the integrity of the nation and the quality of government as the status of the enemy.

BIBLIOGRAPHIC REFERENCES

Astorga, L., and Shirk, D. A. 'Drug Trafficking Organizations and Counter-Drug Strategies in the U.S.-Mexican Context'. Working Paper Series on U.S.-Mexico Security Cooperation, Mexico Institute, Woodrow Wilson International Center for Scholars, and Trans-Border Institute, University of San Diego, April 2010.

Dudley, S. S. 'Drug Trafficking Organizations in Central America: *Transportistas*, Mexican Cartels and *Maras*'. Working Paper Series on U.S.-Mexico Security Cooperation, Mexico Institute, Woodrow Wilson International Center for Scholars, and Trans-Border Institute, University of San Diego, May 2010.

Fernández Menéndez, J., and Ronquillo, V. *De los Maras a los Zetas: los Secretos del Narcotráfico, de Colombia a Chicago*. Mexico City, Editorial Grijalbo, 2006

Sullivan, J. P., and Elkus, A. 'State of Siege: Mexico's Criminal Insurgency'; internet smallwarsjournal.com (accessed 21 May 2010). Bethesda, MD, Small Wars Foundation, 2008.

AUTONOMY IN THE CARIBBEAN OVERSEAS TERRITORIES: THIS FAR AND NO FURTHER!

Dr PETER CLEGG

INTRODUCTION

Various islands in the Caribbean region have not yet gained independent status. They still have constitutional relationships with former colonial mother countries, be it the Caribbean Overseas Territories with the United Kingdom, the Netherlands Antilles and Aruba with the Netherlands, Puerto Rico and the US Virgin Islands with the USA, and Guadeloupe, Martinique and French Guiana with France. The status of the non-independent Caribbean remains problematic. None of the islands wishes to stand on its own as a sovereign state. However, many governments and political parties of the islands are not satisfied with the status quo, and thus there has been considerable debate with regard to the extent to which greater autonomy might be provided to them. While the metropolitan powers have been generally willing to grant more autonomy, a situation is now developing whereby further change is highly unlikely, and in some cases there has in fact been a moderate repatriation of powers. This essay considers the nature of the political relationships in place, the important reforms that are being undertaken in an attempt to re-energize and reorganize links between the Caribbean overseas territories and their metropolitan centres, and the likelihood that an end point is being neared with regard to the awarding of further autonomy.

THE UNITED KINGDOM OVERSEAS TERRITORIES

The collapse of the Federation of the West Indies precipitated a period of decolonization in the English-speaking Caribbean, which began with Jamaica and Trinidad and Tobago gaining their independence in 1962. Despite the trend towards self-rule across the region a number of smaller British territories were reluctant to follow suit. As a consequence, the British authorities had to establish a new governing framework for them, and the West Indies Act of 1962 was approved for this purpose. The Act remains today the foremost provision for the British Virgin Islands, the Cayman Islands, Montserrat and the Turks and Caicos Islands. The fifth territory, Anguilla, was dealt with separately owing to its long association with Saint Christopher and Nevis, and the Anguilla Act 1980 became the principal source of authority.

Each Constitution allocates government responsibilities to the Crown (i.e. the British Government and the Governor) and the Overseas Territory, according to the nature of the responsibility. Those powers generally reserved for the Crown include defence and external affairs, as well as responsibility for internal security and the police, international and 'offshore' financial relations, and the public service. The Crown also has responsibility for the maintenance of good governance. Meanwhile, individual territory governments have control over all aspects of policy that are not overseen by the Crown, including the economy, education, health, social security and immigration. However, ultimate control lies with the United Kingdom as the territories are constitutionally subordinate. Nevertheless, the arrangements were not intended to be permanent; rather, they were originally proposed as stepping stones on the route to independence, and so the relationship is rather uncertain.

For example, the British Government, via its Governors, is reluctant to use its full powers, even in areas where the Governor has responsibility—rather, consensus and persuasion are preferred. The United Kingdom is aware of the importance of maintaining relations with democratically elected governments, and this is particularly true of those Overseas Territories—the majority—that are no longer in receipt of British state funding. A further constraint is the limited power wielded by the Governor in certain circumstances. There remains a problem with issues that are in the mid-spectrum. Of course, the Governor can use his or her constitutional powers, including recourse to Commissions of Inquiry, and the British Government can introduce Orders in Council, but there is a reluctance to do so owing to the controversy caused by such actions. Thus, Governors have few intermediate levers between influence on the one hand and the constitutional power on the other, despite the responsibilities that they must discharge. Problems can be exacerbated by the dependence of key British responsibilities on local government funding, which is not always sufficient. The Constitutions also provide continuous opportunities for 'turf wars' between the Governor and local ministers. In order to manage most effectively this sometimes difficult relationship, the United Kingdom strives to achieve a balance between allowing territories the fullest autonomy that they desire and ensuring that it can discharge its responsibilities and minimize its exposure to potential liabilities. The United Kingdom can face moral, political and legal obligations to give support when a territory's resources are insufficient to meet its commitments, and thus the former must retain certain levers of control.

Despite such constraints the territories' constitutional link with the United Kingdom retains its popularity, in particular, because it helps to preserve their stability. Many of the citizens within the territories regard continuing dependence as a safeguard against weak or corrupt government. The political ties are also important for the economies of the territories, as they provide a measure of sovereign protection, which helps to reassure potential investors. The influence of English law and language and the United Kingdom's responsibility for defence and external affairs have been valuable. Furthermore, the quasi-independent status that exists for the territories provides room for manoeuvre in political and economic matters and creates an ambiguity that attracts international capital. British support has facilitated the transition into successful economies of many of the territories. For example, the Cayman Islands had a GDP per head of US $50,717 in 2007 (according to UN estimates), and is the world's leading centre for 'hedge funds', while the British Virgin Islands had a GDP per head of US $53,302 in 2008 (UN estimate), and is the leading domicile for international business companies. In short, these territories recognize the advantages of retaining their present status, particularly if a comparison is made with the perilous economic position of many independent countries of the Caribbean.

From the 1960s British Governments, both Labour and Conservative, followed a policy of 'benign neglect', which allowed problems to fester. From 1997, however, the Labour Government attempted to heighten its observance of obligations toward the territories. The first step was the launch of a review of the United Kingdom's relationship with its territories in August 1997. Its purpose was 'to ensure that the relationship reflected the needs of the territories and Britain alike, and to give the territories confidence in our [the United Kingdom's] commitment to their future'. It was based on the principle that 'Britain's links to the territories should be based on a partnership, with obligations and responsibilities for both sides'. In March 1999 the review was published as the 'Partnership for Progress and Prosperity', which set out recommendations on a range of issues, such as the constitutional link, financial standards, good governance and human rights. The latter issues highlighted the United Kingdom's desire that the territories should meet certain standards set by the Government and the wider international community, and a number of changes were made in accordance with this approach. One very controversial change was the decriminalization of consensual private homosexual acts between adults made in 2001 via an Order in Council.

In terms of the constitutional link, the British Government maintained that reform should be evolutionary, and set in motion during 2001 a constitutional review process for the Overseas Territories. For the first time the process was supposedly 'locally owned and driven rather than directed from London'. Despite this, the United Kingdom had clear lines beyond which reform was not possible unless independence was the end objective. In a memorandum submitted to the House of Commons' Foreign Affairs Committee in October 2003 by the Parliamentary Under-Secretary, Foreign and Commonwealth Office (FCO), Bill Rammell, strict limits were placed on territories' constitutional room for manoeuvre. The concluding sentence of the memorandum stated: 'OT governments should not expect that in the Constitutional Reviews ... the UK will agree to changes in the UK Government's reserved powers, or which would have implications for the independence of the judiciary and the impartiality of the civil service'. So, in the new Constitutions agreed upon recently for the British Virgin Islands, the Cayman Islands, and the Turks and Caicos Islands, only limited new responsibilities were devolved to the territories. For example, the changes in the British Virgin Islands' Constitution Order 2007 included the introduction of a human rights chapter, provision for the devolution of new powers to the British Virgin Islands' Government in the field of international affairs, and the creation of a National Security Council to afford ministers greater influence in police matters.

However, it could be argued that such changes have further exacerbated, rather than resolved, the structural and operational problems in the United Kingdom's relationship with its Overseas Territories. Indeed, the new Constitution introduced in the Turks and Caicos Islands in 2006 actually contributed to the breakdown in good governance in that territory. As a Commission of Inquiry stated, 'The 2006 Constitution, to a far greater extent than its 1988 predecessor, leaves individual Cabinet Ministers with a wealth of discretions, by way of grants, exemptions, concessions, discounts etc. to override or side-step matters of principle or orderly and fair administration'.

Serious allegations of corruption in the Turks and Caicos Islands that led to the resignation, in March 2009, of the territory's Premier, Michael Misick, are certainly not representative of the Overseas Territories as a whole, but the deep-seated problems in the territory highlight grave failures in the United Kingdom's approach to the Overseas Territories in general. A detailed picture of the situation in the Turks and Caicos Islands was revealed by a Commission of Inquiry led by Sir Robin Auld, a former British High Court judge. The Commission was appointed in July 2008, an interim report was completed in February 2009, and the full report was released in July of the same year. Auld's criticisms were numerous, but his fundamental argument was that there was 'a high probability of systemic corruption in government and the legislature and among public officers in the TCI'. Particular areas of concern included the 'bribery by overseas developers and other investors of Ministers and/or public officers, so as to secure Crown (public) land on favourable terms, coupled with government approval for its commercial development'; the 'serious deterioration in the Territory's systems of governance and public financial management and control'; the 'concealment of conflicts of interest at all levels of public life, and consequent venality'; and the manipulation and abuse of Belongerships (a status that confers rights normally associated with citizenship, including the right to vote and to whom Crown land may be disposed). Stemming from these and many other points of contention, Auld recommended the instigation of criminal investigations into the conduct of former Premier Misick, whose resignation had been prompted by the publication of the Commission's interim report, and of three of his former cabinet ministers.

The criticisms and recommendations against senior members of the Government were, of course, highly damaging, but perhaps even more significant was the Commission's emphasis on the systemic nature of the corruption. Throughout the Commission's report, fundamental weaknesses in the system of governance in the Turks and Caicos Islands were highlighted. The outcome of such weaknesses was that the Turks and Caicos Islands' 'democratic traditions and structures [were] tested almost to beyond breaking point'. Owing to these broader concerns, Auld appealed for 'urgent and wide-ranging systemic change', and in particular the partial suspension of the Turks and Caicos Islands' 2006 Constitution, the implementation of interim direct rule by the British Government, and reforms to the Constitution and other aspects of the system of governance in the territory to help prevent future abuses of power. Subject to such wide-ranging criticisms, the British Government had little choice but to act, and key parts of the Constitution were suspended in August 2009 for a period of up to two years, including those relating to ministerial government and the House of Assembly. The Governor, Gordon Wetherell, was given the power to take charge of government matters, subject to instruction from the FCO. Soon after an anti-corruption team was dispatched to the Turks and Caicos Islands to investigate and prosecute criminal cases as a result of the Commission's report.

While recognizing that it can be difficult to assess whether an issue is serious enough to merit intervention, a report by the House of Commons' Foreign Affairs Committee in 2008, which had first requested a Commission of Inquiry, stated clearly that in the case of the Turks and Caicos Islands '[the British Government's] approach has been too hands off'. As a consequence, the Committee argued, 'The Government must take its oversight responsibility for the Overseas Territories more seriously—consulting across all Overseas Territories more on the one hand while demonstrating a greater willingness to step in and use reserve powers when necessary on the other'. Despite the United Kingdom's decision finally to establish a Commission of Inquiry, the collapse in governance in the Turks and Caicos Islands suggested that London had been excessively lax in its dealings with at least some of the Overseas Territories. Indeed, in February 2010 the Director of the Overseas Territories Division within the FCO stated that a review of the existing constitutional, political and electoral arrangements would take place over the ensuing six months to ensure 'that the principles of good governance will be upheld [and] that the sorts of things which happened in the previous administration do not happen again. This will mean that there will be greater British presence in TCI after the elections in 2011 than existed before August 2009'.

A similar tightening of British control is also being seen in the economic sphere. During the global economic downturn, the Overseas Territories have suffered from reduced activity in their financial services sector and declines in tourist arrivals and construction. The negative impact on public finances has thus been significant, particularly for Anguilla, the Cayman Islands and the Turks and Caicos Islands (the latter's situation being exacerbated by the previous administration's corruption and mismanagement). In response, the United Kingdom has shown a new determination to help correct the structural imbalances in the Overseas Territories' economies, and this is, of course, both welcome and necessary. While it is unfortunate that the United Kingdom waited so long to act, its action nevertheless serves as another indication that the British Government has realized that a stronger hand is required to oversee its territories. Thus, with this shift in policy, the situation in the Turks and Caicos Islands and the conclusion of recent constitutional reviews, it is clear that the territories should not expect further increases in autonomy for the foreseeable future, unless, of course, they commit to independence.

THE NETHERLANDS ANTILLES AND ARUBA

The Charter for the Kingdom of the Netherlands, which underpins the present relationship, was agreed in 1954, and laid out the arrangements for a federal state, comprising three autonomous countries of supposedly equal standing: the Netherlands, Suriname and the Netherlands Antilles (comprising Aruba, Curaçao, Bonaire, Saba, St Eustatius and St Maarten). In 1975 Suriname left the Kingdom and became an independent country, and in 1986 Aruba after obtaining *status aparte* seceded from the Netherlands Antilles, but remained part of the Kingdom as a separate country. Despite the changes in the membership of the Kingdom, the original provisions of the Charter remained largely in place, in part because any changes required the consent of all parties. In principle, although not always in practice, the countries of the Kingdom are autonomous in relation to internal matters, such as government finance, social and economic development, cultural affairs, housing and education, while the Kingdom oversees defence, foreign affairs, Dutch nationality, and extradition. Beyond the country-level autonomy, the Charter stipulates areas of communal responsibility, which by statute require the partners to co-operate. In the areas of human rights and freedoms, the rule of law and good governance, responsibility is shared between each country and the Kingdom, although ultimate responsibility for safeguarding standards in public life rests with the Kingdom. In the charter, Articles 48 to 52 allow for higher supervision—in essence a tool of last resort—which allows the Dutch Crown to impose its authority. However, as with the United Kingdom, and for the same reasons, the Dutch authorities have been reluctant to use this power.

When the Charter was signed it was expected that the Caribbean countries would seek their independence at some time in the future, and as a consequence the Netherlands agreed to give them a significant measure of autonomy. Although Suriname gained its independence in 1975, in the early 1990s a broad political consensus emerged that the Netherlands Antilles and Aruba would be better off remaining part of the Kingdom, primarily owing to their relatively good economic performance, as well as the ready support of the Netherlands. Therefore the temporary nature of the provisions of the Kingdom became permanent, and the Dutch Government in turn felt that a stronger role for the Kingdom was needed to more effectively oversee good governance in the territories. However, there was very strong opposition to this from the islands, and no reform was possible. So the Dutch Government employed its financial assistance to the region to effect changes at the local level in areas such as the organization of the Antillean Government, prison conditions, police operations and criminal investigations. However, this rather piecemeal approach was not a substitute for proper reform.

As well as problems in Kingdom relations, the operation of the Netherlands Antilles was questioned. The government structure consisted of two tiers: the national level and the island level, with elections held every four years. However, as the island elections took place during the mid-point of the national government there was little time for stable government and effective policy-making. Further, after Aruba left the Netherlands Antilles the territory was out of balance and dominated by Curaçao, the largest island by far. Curaçao felt that its interests were not being met because of the demands of the smaller islands, while those islands felt that Curaçao dominated the Antillean Government. As a result of these structural problems within the Kingdom and Antillean relationships, a number of serious difficulties manifested themselves in the Netherlands Antilles, including corruption involving prominent political figures, a substantial public debt, a high murder rate, significant levels of drugs-trafficking, inadequate environmental safeguards, and widespread social dislocation. There was also increasing public concern in the Netherlands about the situation in the Antilles, in part owing to associated alarm about the poor level of integration of young Antillean migrants in the Netherlands, caused to an extent by their native language being Papiamento rather than Dutch.

With such problems the Dutch Government made several attempts to negotiate with the islands to improve standards of governance, but until recently all efforts had failed. However, in 2004 attitudes changed owing to the worsening levels of violence and drugs-trafficking in the Netherlands Antilles that created a growing image of a failed state, and all parties agreed that the Antillean construct should be disbanded and a new set of relationships established. During 2004 and 2005 referendums were held in the islands and all but St Eustatius voted for the dissolution of the Netherlands Antilles, and that was sufficient to bring the Antilles to an end. After a period of initial negotiations it was agreed in October 2006 that Bonaire, St Eustatius and Saba would become part of the Netherlands as public authorities. This meant that the islands would be overseen by the Netherlands while retaining local government functions. Then, in November, the two larger territories, Curaçao and St Maarten, signed an agreement with the Dutch Government to become autonomous islands within the Kingdom, a similar status to that of Aruba. However, there was a pact that the Kingdom would oversee the public finances and the rule of law of the two islands. It was also agreed that the public debt of the Netherlands Antilles and of the island governments would be largely forgiven.

Despite expectations, the deadline of 15 December 2008 for the dissolution of the Netherlands Antilles was not met, following a series of disputes between the Kingdom partners. For example, the decision to place Curaçao's finances under Dutch control was not welcomed by some on the island. Riots broke out in June 2008 after the local council agreed to the proposals, with protestors targeting Dutch nationals. On the Dutch side, meanwhile, several legislators from across the political divide argued that St Maarten was not ready to attain country status owing to what they saw as its poor record in dealing with organized crime and drugs-trafficking. Nevertheless, in December an outline agreement was signed between the island authorities of the Netherlands Antilles and the Government of the Netherlands that would allow for the break-up of the island group on 10 October 2010. One component of the deal was a Dutch pledge to take on 70% of the Netherlands Antilles' combined debt—some €1,700m.—in return for legal and financial controls. Curaçao and St Maarten, which would each attain a new, independent country status, agreed to strict Dutch supervision of their budgets and the creation of a Public Prosecutor's Office.

Despite strong expectations that the 10 October 2010 deadline would be met, the final phase of the dissolution process proved to be difficult. For example, in mid-May 2009 Curaçao voted, in a non-binding referendum, to support the island becoming an autonomous territory, but around 48% of voters rejected the plan. The opposition denounced the planned increase in administrative powers for the Dutch as 'neocolonialism'. In October Bonaire's new Government dismissed the idea of becoming a public authority of the Netherlands, and instead argued for 'free association' status. Unsurprisingly, the Dutch were dismayed by the volte-face, arguing that everything had been agreed, and if public authority status was not acceptable the only other option would be independence for Bonaire. In the end, Bonaire agreed to adhere to the original agreement. Then, in April 2010, the Dutch Acting State Secretary for the Interior and Kingdom Relations announced that St Maarten would in theory attain statehood, but it would not in practice fully function as such in the initial stage. Rather, there was to be a number of built-in guarantees, including assurances that there would be a functioning system of law and order and good governance. There was criticism in some quarters that such caveats to full country status broke the terms of the 2006 agreement, but the Dutch Government was determined finally to complete the process of dissolution. Similarly, strong opposition in Bonaire, St Eustatius and Saba islands to the introduction of gay marriage, abortion and euthanasia were overcome. These changes were necessary to allow Bonaire, St Eustatius and Saba to accede to the Dutch Constitution. Thus, the process of reform in the Dutch Caribbean was nearing completion. However, it had been a protracted and divisive process, and the degree of autonomy had been quite strictly limited. Notwithstanding some probable fine-tuning of the new arrangements, further reform was unlikely for the foreseeable future.

PUERTO RICO AND THE US VIRGIN ISLANDS

The current status of the Commonwealth of Puerto Rico was established in 1952, under Law 600. After the USA took control of Puerto Rico following the Spanish-Cuban-American War of 1898 and until 1952, the territory was an unincorporated territory that was 'foreign to the United States in a domestic sense' as it was neither a state of the USA nor a sovereign republic. Despite this, Puerto Ricans were granted US citizenship in 1917. Hence, they are US citizens by statute, and can move freely to the USA. When Law 600 was passed this set out a new structure for relations that remains today, providing a greater degree of autonomy. Puerto Rico's current status provides for local gubernatorial, legislative and mayoral elections, but not the right to vote in US federal elections. Instead, there is a Puerto Rican Resident Commissioner in Washington, DC, who is able to participate in congressional debates but cannot vote on bills or any other pieces of legislation. Puerto Ricans living in the USA, however, are able to vote for the US

President. Puerto Rico has limited self-government in areas such as taxation, economic development, education, health, housing, culture and language, while the US Government retains control over citizenship, defence, diplomacy, currency, immigration, transportation, customs and foreign trade. Further, the US Government has the authority to undertake unilateral action on a range of issues, including the right to revoke any law inconsistent with the Constitution of the USA, and to award or rescind regulatory privileges or advantages, such as US citizenship. The US Congress may even repeal Law 600 or annul Puerto Rico's Constitution. Thus, it is clear that Puerto Rico is subordinate to the federal Government.

As the Cold War came to an end the question of Puerto Rico's status re-emerged as a key issue, and several attempts were made to resolve the issue in the early 1990s. In 1993 a referendum was held which offered three options: statehood (complete annexation to the US federal system as a state), independence, or remaining a commonwealth but with increased federal funding and autonomy. Neither statehood nor the commonwealth option enjoyed a clear majority, with the support of 46.2% and 48.4% of voters, respectively, while independence scored a mere 4%. A second referendum was held in 1998, but again the result was not decisive. There were five options on the ballot paper (statehood, independence, two definitions of commonwealth status, and 'none of the above'), and 'none of the above' was the most popular, obtaining 50.2% of the vote, compared with 46.5% for statehood. This was a consequence of serious dissatisfaction regarding the design of the referendum by the administration of Pedro Rosselló without the agreement of the other political parties. In the decade that followed the question of Puerto Rico's status declined in prominence as a political issue.

There were several reasons for the downgrading of the status issue. First, there was no consensus on the best way forward, with most Puerto Ricans supporting either statehood or a new form of commonwealth. Second, Puerto Rico accrues substantial economic benefits from its relationship with the USA and many in the territory were concerned that political change would undermine these benefits. Puerto Rico is an upper-middle income economy with a sizeable manufacturing sector, particularly in pharmaceuticals and electronics. Moreover, 30% of Puerto Rico's budget is accounted for by US federal grants, much of which is distributed as social welfare programmes to a large proportion of families. Third, national identity among the Spanish-speaking Puerto Ricans is strong, with a majority seeing themselves as a distinct nation and sharing a Puerto Rican, and not an American or Latino identity. However, Puerto Ricans do not wish to relinquish their US citizenship. Thus, the paradoxical nature of national identity helped to muddy the political waters.

However, the status issue has now once again taken centre stage. One reason is that the territory is in the midst of its worst economic contraction in modern history. It suffered economic recessions in 2005/06 and 2006/07, the first to have affected the country while the US economy was expanding. In 2009 the territory was close to bankruptcy because of the recession in the USA, and the situation remained parlous at mid-2010. The result has been worsening social conditions with rising unemployment, significant poverty, drugs-trafficking and a high murder rate, prompting uneasy speculation in Puerto Rico that the lack of consensus on the status issue has caused a dangerous degree of stagnation to set in. A second and related reason is that funding caps have been placed on federal programmes, such as health care and housing schemes, owing to Puerto Rico's commonwealth status, which puts it at a disadvantage *vis-à-vis* other parts of the USA.

Concerns with regard to Puerto Rico's economic vulnerability coincided with increasing political support for a comprehensive addressing of the status issue. For example, prior to his election in November 2008, US President Barack Obama pledged to resolve the issue of the territory's status during his first term in office. Puerto Rico's Resident Commissioner, Pedro Pierluisi (a Democrat), and Governor, Luis Fortuno (a Republican), lobbied members of the US Congress to support a bill that would allow Puerto Ricans to vote again on the status issue. The bill would establish a two-step process. First, there would be a vote to decide whether Puerto Rico should remain a commonwealth. If most voters voted for a different status, a second ballot would offer a choice of independence, statehood, sovereignty associated with the USA, or continued commonwealth status after all. In late April 2010 the efforts of Pierluisi and Fortuno began to pay dividends when the US House of Representatives passed the Puerto Rico Democracy Act, with both Democratic and Republican support, and reinforcing the increasingly prevalent view that the status issue could soon be resolved, with statehood being a distinct possibility. Independence was not expected to be chosen.

In contrast to Puerto Rico, political status is not an issue in the US Virgin Islands, including St Thomas, St Croix and St John. The lack of a strong distinct national identity, the domination of English, its small size, the limited population (112,000—compared with 4m. for Puerto Rico) and its narrow productive base (mainly tourism) make it difficult and perhaps impossible for the islands to move to either statehood or full independence. At present the islands are an organized non-incorporated territory, governed by a US Congressional Organic Act, and overseen by the US Office for Insular Affairs. This legal and administrative structure means that the US Virgin Islands has less political and economic autonomy than Puerto Rico. In March 2010 a new draft Constitution was presented to the US Congress for consideration, but, if enacted, it would not fundamentally change the balance of power between the US Virgin Islands and the USA.

THE FRENCH OVERSEAS DEPARTMENTS

Unlike the British, Dutch and US territories, the French Overseas Departments in the Caribbean are actually part of France. However, the political, economic and social challenges facing the Départements d'Outre-Mer (DOM) are similar to those in the other non-sovereign countries in the region. The law of assimilation of 19 March 1946 granted Martinique, Guadeloupe and French Guiana (together with Réunion in the Indian Ocean) the administrative status of Department so that all territorial institutions operate like their metropolitan equivalents in France. In addition, laws and regulations enacted in Paris apply automatically to the DOM. A Préfet nominated by Paris represents the state and has responsibility for foreign relations, defence, law and order and the provision of the national service. A Conseil Général manages the Department. Directly elected by the inhabitants of the Department, the Conseil controls a local budget and oversees social issues, economic initiatives and day-to-day administration. Also, locally elected deputies and senators represent each DOM in the French parliament. Then in 1982 French President François Mitterand introduced greater decentralization into the system that established a new level of government—the Region—with a directly elected body, the Conseil Régional, whose main role was to promote social, economic, cultural and scientific development of the Region. In principle, each region was to cover a few Departments. For geographical and political reasons it was impossible to incorporate the four DOM within a single region. Thus four overseas regions were established; one for each DOM. Martinique, Guadeloupe, French Guiana and Réunion each then became a Department and a Region. The Region operates on the same geographical territory, same population and same electorate as the Department. This reform has caused significant problems for the DOM in terms of overlapping activities, increased administrative costs and local political rivalry.

Aware of the bureaucratic tensions in the DOM Prime Minister Lionel Jospin and his socialist government established a new programme for the territories in 2000, entitled Loi d'Orientation pour l'Outre-Mer or LOOM. This gave members of the Conseil Général and Conseil Régional in each DOM an opportunity to discuss and submit to the Prime Minister any proposal regarding an evolution of their status, including a move towards independence. However, the changes suggested were rather moderate, and focused on administrative reform. Notwithstanding, with the defeat of the Socialists in the 2002 French parliamentary elections, the LOOM process was halted and the Conservatives introduced a new decentralization reform. In response, the elected representatives of Martinique and Guadeloupe submitted a request for local referendums to take place on the evolution of their status. They asked for the reunification of the Conseil Général and the Conseil Régional within a single elected assembly. In December 2003 the votes were held, but the results were unexpected as the change was rejected in both territories. The outcomes highlighted the concern of voters that if any alteration was made, their social and economic advantages emanating from the French state might be threatened, and that many voters feared that gathering local power in the hands of one person could lead to a decline in democratic standards and to a risk of autocracy. They seemed to have thought that keeping two local bodies with two presidents would guarantee a certain degree of competition considered to be positive for the management of their Department.

Although the administrative structures of Guadeloupe and Martinique remained unchanged, Saint-Barthélemy and Saint-Martin, two islands administratively attached to Guadeloupe, used their right under the decentralization reform to revise their status. Both islands expressed a wish to escape Guadeloupe's management and become two distinct territories. During the local referendums that took place both electorates voted overwhelmingly in favour of this new status that would allow them legislative speciality, more local power and a more direct link with Paris. On 7 February 2007 the French Parliament approved legislation granting Saint-Barthélemy and Saint-Martin their new status. They are now known as French overseas collectivities (Collectivités d'Outre-Mer or COM).

The political and legal assimilation of the DOM has taken place along with enormous injections of money from mainland France and increasingly from the European Union (EU), which has produced high levels of development. For example, assistance from EU Structural Funds during 2000–06 accounted for €809m. out of a total public budget of €1,980m. in Guadeloupe, and €674m. out of a total of €1,700m. in Martinique. Financial transfers are spent on social security, health care, education, tax breaks, and public employment. However, there are concerns about a model that does not allow the DOM to achieve self-sustained development despite good rates of growth. Indeed, growth is paradoxically derived from a considerable decline in the productive capacities of the territories. Thus, the significant monetary transfers provided have actually impeded economic development. In particular, the implementation of social legislation conceived for a developed country (i.e. mainland France) has distorted the economic performance of the small and formerly underdeveloped DOM. So they have been transformed from producer economies to heavily assisted welfare-based ones. The result is that 80% of required foods are imported and exports amount to only one-seventh of imports, high unemployment is endemic, and crime levels are increasing.

Some of these structural problems, exacerbated by the effects of the global financial crisis, were the cause of widespread protests in the DOM during the early part of 2009. Guadeloupe, in particular, was badly affected by a six-week general strike. Workers demanded action over low wages (in comparison with mainland France rather than with the rest of the Caribbean) and the high cost of living, which is, in part, caused by the high level of imports from France. Particular ire was directed at the 'Beke' class, white descendants of colonial plantation owners, who allegedly exploited their monopoly power in retail and construction in order to maintain high prices and their privileged lifestyles. Eventually, an agreement was reached on a number of issues, including paying workers on the minimum wage an extra €200 per month and lowering the cost of basic staples and commodities.

In July 2010 French President Nicolas Sarkozy visited Guadeloupe and Martinique, where he held discussions with local politicians and members of civil society. Sarkozy's visit, which was intended to facilitate the French Government's efforts to rebuild relations with the territories, coincided with a consultation process, initiated in April by the French Government with the aim of addressing the underlying concerns within the Departments. Key issues that were considered included the development of local production, the pricing mechanisms for goods and services, and the ways in which social dialogue could be improved. Another outcome was the decision to organize referenda in Martinique and French Guiana on the issue of whether the local governments should be granted more autonomy. However, in January 2010 the voters in both Departments rejected the proposals by a convincing margin. As before, voters were not prepared to countenance any weakening of the political and economic ties with the French Government. Thus, the opportunity for further autonomy was not seized, and the issue was not expected to be revisited in the medium term.

CONCLUSION

In many respects the overseas territories in the Caribbean, regardless of the metropolitan power with which they are associated and the specific nature of that relationship, have a privileged position within the international system. The territories' citizens have a final guarantee against autocracy and economic collapse; many territories receive sizeable monetary assistance that has helped them in creating relatively high levels of development; and nationals possess the citizenship of their metropolitan powers, and in the case of the British, Dutch and French territories have freedom of movement across the EU. Consequently, there are no serious demands for independence in any of the territories. Furthermore, after a period of constitutional reflection and, in some cases, change, the likelihood of the territories gaining further autonomy is very remote. In the British Overseas Territories and the Dutch Caribbean, further autonomy will now only be given with independence, and in select areas there has been a modest repatriation of powers to the respective central Governments in the United Kingdom and the Netherlands. In the French DOM there is no desire for further autonomy, as clearly evidenced in a series of local referenda. Finally, while the situation in Puerto Rico is more difficult to predict because the status issue is still to be fully considered, it is evident that independence is not a feasible option and many Puerto Ricans hope that statehood can be achieved, thereby locking the territory into the federal structure of the USA. For all territories, irrespective of their specific circumstances, it is a case of this far and no further with regard to the question of additional autonomy, and this will almost certainly remain the case for some time to come.

RESILIENCE AND TRANSFORMATION: LATIN AMERICA IN THE GLOBAL FINANCIAL CRISIS

Dr PIA RIGGIROZZI

The global financial crisis that emerged in 2007–08, and particularly affected the developed world, is evidence of a new economic trend that has given new space for alternative responses to the neo-liberal paradigm in Latin America. New models of political and economic governance seem to be taking shape, both at domestic and regional levels of governance, driven by new trade and financial relations as well as new political dynamics and institutional frameworks. Of course, Latin American countries are not immune to the adversities of the international political economy, as the recent global financial downturn and the current crisis in the Euro-zone have showed. Yet, unlike during past episodes, Latin America was somewhat cushioned from the effects of these crises and the consequent recession. In fact, there is something of an irony in how the region faced the recent problems. The capacity to buffer the swinging trends of the global economy, specifically the latest global financial crisis, must be understood in light of the severe and comprehensive crisis of neo-liberal governance experienced across the region in the late 1990s and early 2000s. This proved to be a turning point from which an alternative model of political and economic governance has developed across the region. Economic recovery in this context has been engineered through a combination of export-led growth, devaluation and stimulation of industry. Social stability, meanwhile, seems to have been achieved through populist welfare measures, political inclusion and job creation. These elements, which coincided with China's accession to the World Trade Organization (WTO) in 2001, resulting in a bonanza of high commodity prices, helped the region to weather the financial crisis. Paradoxically, a severely weakened financial sector meant that the region was able to escape the consequences of the sub-prime crisis that erupted in the economies of the industrialized world in 2007–08. As a consequence there has been a new accommodation of actors and alliances that suggests a fresh opportunity for alternative projects to emerge in a landscape of seemingly unchallenged neo-liberal rule.

This article analyses these trends with particular focus on two main developments: the effects of the global financial crisis on Latin American countries; and the effects of the crisis of neo-liberalism on inter-American relations. The chapter is divided into four parts. The first part considers the effects of the global financial crisis on Latin American economies as they advance post-neo-liberal models of political and economic governance. The second part brings a note of caution to optimistic narratives about Latin American capacity to weather the global storm. The third part speculates on the re-accommodation of actors and alliances in the 'historical backyard' of the USA, suggesting that an unprecedented shifting of sub-regional leadership is affecting inter-American relations. This analysis places particular attention on the increasing diffusion of financial and ideological power, epitomized in the region by Venezuela's oil diplomacy, Brazil's regional leadership and China's role in the global political economy. The last part of this chapter closes with some concluding remarks.

FACING THE GLOBAL CRISIS: HOW THE CURRENT DOWNTURN DIFFERS FROM PREVIOUS EXPERIENCES

Contrary to historical trends, Latin American countries' openness to international competition during the last decade has not left them more vulnerable to the current global economic downturn. This remarkable achievement contrasts sharply with the experience of these countries in previous international crises. In the past Latin America oscillated with the movements of international trade and financial markets and thus the region was often vulnerable to international economic turmoil.

On this occasion Latin America was better positioned to face the crisis. This time some fundamentals were different: in general, growth across the region had been sustained since the mid-2000s, export-led growth had secured a significant amount of foreign reserves, and above all a more diversified portfolio of trade and finance had been achieved, driven by the participation of China, India and Venezuela in the region. These factors are being embraced by a new political economy, manifested in alternative models of growth and democracy that differ from those that governed the region in the heyday of US neo-liberalism during the 1980s and 1990s.

The legacies of neo-liberalism hit a point of no return in the early 2000s, amidst a downturn in growth following currency difficulties and rising indebtedness (especially pronounced in Argentina, Bolivia, Venezuela and to a lesser extent Brazil and Chile). Looking back, the privatization of state public services, the casualization of labour and rising unemployment in many countries that dutifully implemented neo-liberal reforms in the previous decades left many without the resources to cope with the failure of economic and financial deregulation in the region. By the mid-1990s disillusionment with the charms of open markets and of neo-liberalism began to creep in. Popular demonstrations, spontaneous organizations of civil society demanding more responsive political economies, and a gradual articulation of alternative views to neo-liberalism, echoing emerging forms of identity politics, meant that in Latin America neo-liberalism as a political economic project was ill-fated (see Grugel and Riggirozzi 2009).

Progressively, in much of Latin America, most profoundly in Argentina and Venezuela, followed by Bolivia, Brazil, Ecuador, Uruguay and Paraguay, new Left-leaning candidates were elected to office. The election of Lula in Brazil in 2002 (re-elected in 2006) was followed by that of Néstor Kirchner in Argentina in 2003 (and of Cristina Fernández Kirchner in 2008), Tabaré Vásquez in Uruguay in 2004 (followed by José Mújica who took office on 1 March 2010), Evo Morales in Bolivia in 2005, Rafael Correa in Ecuador in 2006 and Fernando Lugo in Paraguay in 2008. Only Chile is facing the prospect of swinging to the 'right' for the first time in two decades after Sebastián Piñera won 51.6% of the vote in the presidential election of January 2010.

In marked contrast to the intractable radicalism of the leftist projects of half a century ago, the new projects across the region share a mission to re-found the nation-state, in the promise of achieving a new compromise of social transformation and economic viability. Yet, despite strong criticism of neo-liberalism and a denunciation of the exclusionary policies and practices of capitalism, government policies do not represent a revolutionary attack on capitalism as such (except in Venezuela) but rather a search for alternative strategies of development and a new approach to inter and intra-hemispheric relations. Latin America's leftists are not, in any serious way, 'anti-capitalist' in marked contrast to historical leftist projects in the region. Current governance projects in Latin America acknowledge the importance of the market and, indeed, have made clear that they welcome both private and foreign investment. This marks a crucial turning point across the region that since the mid-2000s allowed reformist candidates to win presidential elections.

Of course, the current search for post-neo-liberal governance across the region is strongly informed by each country's unique historical experience. However, beyond these differences between countries, and tensions between continuity and change, there is an emergence of a fresh outlook characterized by the search for an alternative paradigm which reconciles a pragmatic belief in a role for state management and a search for a new social contract anchored in prudent macro-economics. We can thus argue that while the current financial crisis posed a significant challenge to the political economy in the region, this has not meant an alteration to the emerging alternative models.

An important element of stabilization in the light of the global crisis has been the rapid growth of the export market over the past five years, which brought with it a renewed trust of national and international business. The crisis of neo-liberalism across the region coincided with an increasing diffusion of financial and ideological power, epitomized by the emergence of Venezuela's participation in the region and China's role in the global political economy, and in particular as a trading partner in South America. In contrast to the pressures on developing countries' policy choices during the 1980s and 1990s, the current shifts in power, authority and resources at the global level are far from diminishing the autonomy of national states but rather fostering new spaces for policy contestation in developing countries. The consolidation of China, India and other emerging markets has reshaped trade relationships. Latin America has faced a strong and sustained demand for raw materials from these countries, steering not only national growth and accumulation of reserves but also a new role in the world economy. This at the same time has helped to redress the traditional unfair terms of exchange that marked a historical dependency of Latin American countries in the global political economy. In sum, political developments and trade-related growth mean that in Latin America post-neo-liberal governance is taking shape based on vigorous expansion in domestic demand and commodity abundance, allowing for an increased level of reserves and in some cases counter-cyclical policies that helped to mitigate the effects of the global financial crisis.

Unlike past global recessions, the recent financial recession found Latin America in a stronger position to defend itself against the worst effects of the crisis. In the past, Latin America was trapped in high debt levels, dependence on foreign aid, and exchange rate rigidity that reduced monetary and fiscal policy space. This time, crisis management comprised three elements: first, accommodative policies that helped underpin domestic demand; second, good fundamentals (sound financial systems, solid balance sheets) that helped the region recover and attract capital flows; and third, higher commodity prices and external demand that supported growth in many economies, given their dependence on commodity-related earnings (IMF 2010: 58).

From 2003 to 2008, the regional economy grew by an annual average of nealy 5%. Latin America finished 2008 with a growth rate of more than 4% (ECLAC 2008: 18). This made it the sixth consecutive year of growth for the region, a record in the last 40 years. The year 2009 started with very grim prospects as world demand suffered a significant downturn but quickly experienced a rebound, taming the negative prospects of Latin American growth for 2009 and 2010. GDP in Latin America is projected to grow at 4% in 2010 and 2011, although prospects vary considerably across the region (IMF 2010: 59). The key element this time is that trade and financial openness have been accompanied by the building of resilient mechanisms that bolstered the ability to withstand negative shocks.

Positive predictions expect the recovery to be especially strong in many commodity-exporting, financially integrated economies, which account for about two-thirds of the region's GDP. In Brazil, growth in 2010 is expected to rebound to over 5%, led by strong private consumption and investment. Despite a devastating earthquake, Chile's GDP is projected to grow at about 4% in 2010 and 6% in 2011, supported by highly accommodative policies, a recovery in commodity prices, and reconstruction efforts. For some, export-led models of growth were not only the driver of crisis management but even led in some cases, such as Argentina, Venezuela and Ecuador, to a policy of 'desendeudamiento' (de-borrowing) (Riggirozzi 2007: 137; also Cooper and Momani 2005) augmenting the margin of manoeuvre for negotiation and a reduction of external debt to international financial institutions. In Mexico, on the contrary, growth is expected to rebound to 4% in 2010, helped in part by the US recovery. In Peru, the top growth performer of the region, GDP is projected to expand by 6% in 2010. Likewise, foreign direct investment (FDI) flows to Latin America and the Caribbean also represent an element for positive predictions. FDI is expected to rebound in 2010, rising by 40–50%, after dropping in 2009 as a result of the global crisis. This expected increase would allow the region to resume the levels of FDI of 2007 (see ECLAC 2009a). Of course, growth and investment prospects are not uniform across the region, with more subdued results expected in Central American economies.

What all this means is that Latin America comes out of this crisis with much less economic contraction than anticipated. Despite recession in 2009 the economies weathered the global storm. In terms of political economy, there is now an opportunity to argue that the policies of 'open market nationalism', particularly significant in South America, demonstrate how over recent years Latin America has learned some of the hard lessons of the limits of protectionist policies of the 1940s–50s and of the debt crisis of the 1980s. The emergence of a new political economy in the aftermath of the crisis of neo-liberalism seems to indicate that the historical divorce between openness and left-leaning policies is reaching a new compromise, while exposure to a more globalized world becomes a force for a more positive engagement.

CAUSE FOR CAUTIOUS OPTIMISM?

The spectacular recovery of the economy after 2003 allowed for the introduction of a range of anti-poverty policies at the domestic level, mostly in the form of cash transfer and targeted social spending. These programmes, largely adopted in Mexico, Brazil, Argentina, Chile, Nicaragua and Honduras, provide money to poor families, conditional on certain behaviour, such as sending children to school or bringing them to health centres on a regular basis, alongside job creation and investments in education (Cortés 2009). Latin America, then, faces the global recession with milder social problems and only a partial reversal of the robust poverty reduction gains that the region achieved in the five years prior to the crisis. According to the World Bank, while 60m. Latin Americans are estimated to have left the poverty ranks during 2002–08, more than 9m. people joined the poor in 2009 (see table below), and that number would have been greater had it not been for the fact that Latin American governments were able to maintain existing and implement new social assistance programmes, including conditional cash transfer schemes (World Bank 2010; Riggirozzi 2010). In its *Social Panorama of Latin America 2009*, ECLAC announced a cautious increase of the region's poverty rate by 1.1%, where extreme poverty climbed by 0.8% compared with 2008. In other words, the number of people below the poverty line will rise from 180m. to 189m., or 34.1% of the region's population, while the ranks of the destitute were to increase to 76m. Some countries may experience a greater increase in poverty than the regional average, such as Mexico, owing to lower GDP and deteriorating employment and salaries (see ECLAC 2009b).

The current crisis will nevertheless have less impact on regional poverty than prior crises, such as the 'Mexican crisis' in 1995, the 'Asian crisis' in 1998–2000 and that of Argentina in 2001–02. For now, the region has been able to maintain the purchasing power of salaries, low inflation, and social spending. But control over social expenditure as a whole remains tight and most of the funding for post-2002 social programmes is politically contentious as they are mainly financed from taxes on the export sector. In this scenario, it is plausible to speculate that despite export-led growth, this approach to development is still vulnerable to a fall in export prices in the international market, as explained in the following section, or to political opposition from the exporting élites. Domestically, the heavy reliance on targeted social spending and cash transfers at the cost of other redistributive measures, such as changing taxation structure, have also created potential flaws. All such programmes in Latin America will only ever have partial coverage and satisfy basic needs, excluding important segments of the poor (Cortés 2009: 63). From this perspective, the current context of international economic crisis is opening a 'technical' dilemma about how to finance social development and at the same time a 'political' debate about how to institutionalize a coherent model of governance across the region. Whether the current international financial crisis poses a significant challenge to the emergent alternative models across the region is debatable. While some countries, especially Brazil, Chile and Peru, may be better prepared to weather the global economic downturn, no country in the region is immune to the social consequences and the worsening levels of poverty, inequality and job informality as a result of the crisis. The important question is thus whether, in the present circumstances, a new political economic project across the region will permit a redistribution of income, or, at the very least, the adoption of effective anti-poverty policies and measures to promote social inclusion.

Poverty and Extreme Poverty in Latin America, 1980–2009 (millions of people)

Year	Poverty	Extreme Poverty
1980	135.9	62.4
1990	200.2	93.4
1997	203.8	88.8
1999	211.4	89.4
2002	221.4	97.4
2004	217.4	87.6
2006	194.4	71.3
2007	184.4	68.4
2008	180	71
2009	189	76

Source: Economic Commission for Latin America and the Caribbean (ECLAC).

While ECLAC's figures indicate a reversal of the recent trend toward poverty reduction in the region, unemployment, and the quality of employment, is also presenting decreased to low records supported by sustained economic growth and a strengthening of the services sector in many countries. Notable reductions are observed in Argentina, Chile, Peru, Venezuela and several of the Central American and Caribbean countries. Altogether, the region shed about 3.5m. jobs during last year's recession—albeit at a slower pace than in the recessions of the late 1990s. Colombia, Chile and Mexico were hardest hit, with workers in the manufacturing and construction sectors most affected. Vulnerabilities in the job market are inherently linked to the nature of export-led growth models, which are particularly affected in a global recession. According to ECLAC, about 95% of the region's GDP and 90% of Latin America's population reside in countries that are net commodity exporters (ibid).

Although the region was better prepared than before to handle external shocks, the global crisis has been driving down export volumes and prices, remittances, FDI and the demand for tourism services. By mid-2008 it became evident that commodity prices were moving adversely for Latin America. In this context, while the crisis of neo-liberalism in Latin America in the early 2000s opened a new political space, the current international turmoil exposes the limits of export-led growth. In Chile, for example, the rise in copper prices hides the fact that the country's export profile remains limited to mineral and agricultural goods, with copper accounting for 45% of all exports. A similar situation is faced in Argentina, where fluctuating export prices precipitated a nationalization of the pension system as a way of maintaining fiscal balance. The decline in commodity prices has also affected Brazil's manufactured goods exports as well as exporters of petroleum, such as Venezuela, Mexico, Peru and Ecuador. The lower demand from US consumers particularly affects Mexico and Central America, in light of their close ties to the US economy, as does the decline in remittances. The countries that are likely to suffer most are those that entered into 'free trade' agreements with the USA, such as the North American Free Trade Agreement (NAFTA) and the Central America-Dominican Republic Free Trade Agreement (CAFTA-DR) (see Weisbrot, Schmitt and Sandoval 2008).

Urban and rural employment has been particularly affected, both in terms of quantity and quality, by the drop in overseas demand for agricultural, mining and industrial products. According to a recent International Labour Organization (ILO) report, as a consequence of the recent global crisis there has been a clear, negative impact on labour markets in the region, as the unemployment rate is estimated to have risen to 8.2% in 2009. The Mexican economy suffered most in the region from the economic crisis as it contracted by 7.3%, in part due to the country's high trade integration and dependence on the USA. The outlook for 2010 is a resumption of economic growth at a modest rate of 2.9%. The recovery, however, is expected to be led by strong growth in Brazil, projected at 3.5%, after registering a contraction in 2009 of 0.7% (ILO 2010: 30-31). What all this points to is that real weaknesses in the model are not dissimilar to the period of export-led growth in the first part of the 20th century. How far this export-led growth is sustainable in the current scenario is now highly debatable, as is Latin America's 'immunity' to the crisis.

Politically and economically the current context means that Latin America is now facing a call for more conservatism in policy-making and therefore concerns and unwillingness to embrace radical economic change. In the current context, therefore, the models of more nationalist economic management that emerged over the last half-decade have yet to prove themselves. The current economic crisis will certainly test the capacity of new nationalistic projects to deal with global pressures and domestic demands for social inclusion and democracy while at the same time sustaining open markets. This is particularly pressing considering that between 2010 and 2012 there will be 11 presidential elections in the region, including critical contests in some of the region's biggest countries, namely Brazil, Mexico, Colombia, Argentina and Peru.

The capacity to react to the crisis and to protect the economy varies from country to country and depends on several factors, principally on their ability to change fiscal policies and to expand expenditure using fiscal income; access to foreign resources and foreign credit; the robustness of the national financial sector; and the balance on the capital and current accounts. In addition, any possible deterioration in social conditions will challenge domestic support for populist policies and the (finely) balanced relationship between mobilization and resistance, realigning actors domestically and across the borders.

The most likely scenario is, then, a more moderately nationalist pattern in which states attempt to extract some revenues from exports to channel into the development of domestic businesses and look towards greater intra-regional trade, where co-operation may be accelerated in view of the need to counter the impending effects of the global crisis. These dynamics are not only affecting the political economic spectrum in Latin American governance but also reshaping inter-American relations.

RESILIENCE AND TRANSFORMATION IN INTER-AMERICAN RELATIONS

Hemispheric relations have historically been dictated by the financial and ideological power of the USA, occasionally forcing out Governments it found adverse to its interests. Financial liberalization and the imposition of free markets across the developing world via the 'Washington Consensus' were crucial elements in the architecture of US power in the 1980s and 1990s. Credit rationing at the time meant that most developing countries ultimately had little choice but to accept the dictates of the rules on development that were undoubtedly sponsored by Washington. But two decades later, the failure of the Washington Consensus to deliver economic and political stability opened a new cycle of ideological contestation of political and economic projects in the region.

Latin American countries are in fact part and parcel of a changing international political economy, contributing to a process of political and ideological decentralization that is changing the nature of hemispheric power relations. As Latin American countries are diversifying their international economic and political relations, they become less reliant on the USA. Paradoxically, the emergence of a development approach rejecting US policy advice does not seem to have seriously disrupted inter-American relations. Certainly there have been tensions, focused mainly on Venezuela and, to a lesser extent, Bolivia. But the USA, especially under the Administration of George W. Bush, has been much less concerned with events in Latin America than usual. With the US Government caught in the quandary of the Middle East, its Latin American policy was basically reduced to a series of bilateral deals concerning trade and periodic initiatives on migration and drugs.

What is certain, however, is that a new map of regional co-operation is emerging out of new forms of overlapping regional governance projects that are independent of US rule. The eruption of Chávez and, to a large extent the emergence of China as a trade and financial actor, have transformed Latin American foreign policies while fracturing consensus around a model of integration based on the US economy.

Latin America is currently reshaping its patterns of regional integration. This development is fundamental in that it challenges the traditional transit to regional integration based on the US economy and US-led rule. This is manifested in two main projects: one, mainly Brazilian-led, which builds on the already established Mercado Común del Sur (MERCOSUR) yet expanded to include new members such as Chile, Bolivia, and Venezuela. While the incorporation of Venezuela in MERCOSUR injected a more nationalist tone into its discourse, the expanded MERCOSUR seeks to balance the risk-adverse mentality of business élites with new social demands.

The second, more radical, project emerged as 'counter-hegemonic' models of regional integration, led by Venezuela's Bolivarian Alliance for the Peoples of our America (ALBA), grouping Cuba, Bolivia, Ecuador, Nicaragua, Dominica, and Honduras. In contrast to MERCOSUR, ALBA has taken a particularly confrontational line in trying to challenge the USA with regard to almost all issues on the inter-American agenda. ALBA represents an unprecedented attempt to foster an agenda that is not based primarily on trade liberalization but actually on welfare co-operation and solidarity, placing a distinctive emphasis on civil society participatory practices in planning and administration. The promises of ALBA have been accompanied by a region-wide set of initiatives by Venezuela, including the purchase of Bolivia's leading micro-credit institution and a large share of the bonds issued by Argentina. Since 2004 Venezuela has been exchanging oil for the services of 30,000 Cuban doctors and teachers, and has developed social programmes providing housing and education in Nicaragua, Cuba and Honduras.

Venezuela and Argentina have also become strategic partners in the start-up of the Banco del Sur in early 2008. The inauguration of the first Latin American Banco del Sur is not only a reflection of the search for autonomy in policy formulation and implementation but also in the introduction of an alternative financial architecture in response to the new regional political and economic trend. If it succeeds in terms of goals and achievements, such an institution could play a significant role in regional monetary policy and provide resources to secure sound balance of payments finance. A major distinction from established international financial institutions, such as the Inter-American Development Bank and the World Bank, is that the Banco del Sur will not operate on the basis of conditional loans but intends to advance a more democratic decision-making process for its operations. The extent to which these initiatives can consolidate coherent and resilient projects is still to be seen. Nevertheless, they need to be taken as part of valid transformative arrangements shaping a new space for thinking about and negotiating alternative models for co-operation.

Likewise, Brazil and Venezuela, although emerging as silent competitors for regional leadership and political style, are ushering in consensus mechanisms with new players capable of making that balance viable. Such policy direction is evident in the efforts of the newly created Union of South American Nations (UNASUR), signed under the auspices of Brazil in March 2008. UNASUR brings together countries of resilient institutions such as the Andean Community of Nations with those of MERCOSUR, with the promise of political and economic co-operation and development. UNASUR is fundamentally a political project, conciliatory in its discourse and comprehensive in its objectives, which rank from free trade areas to social and security alliance. UNASUR does not position itself as anti-US, as opposed to the more confrontational, counter-hegemonic and activist rhetoric of ALBA. It rather addresses concrete problems of underdevelopment and dependency, elaborating a more conciliatory discourse and programme, articulating ideas within a framework of open economies. Its moderate ideological position means it also aims at strengthening the representation and leverage of the South in international forums of negotiation. One significant mechanism under the umbrella of UNASUR is the Initiative for the Integration of Regional Infrastructure in South America (IIRSA) which has already formulated an ambitious project list to boost infrastructural integration throughout the continent. Acknowledging the current demand for energy, various South American Presidents have also designed an energy integration strategy for the region. For example, Venezuela and Brazil launched a joint petrochemical plant, which is a clear step towards energy co-operation and integration. Central to their integration plans, the leaders discussed the construction of the gas pipeline, set to be built by Petrosur, a new venture between Petróleos de Venezuela, Petrobras, and Enarsa, respectively the Venezuelan, Brazilian, and Argentinian state-owned oil companies. Another important initiative is the South American Defense Council aimed at resolving conflicts and promoting military co-operation. This initiative potentially resists US interference in the South, balancing the authority of the existing Organization of American States (OAS) as a US-led defence mechanism (Riggirozzi 2010).

What these regional projects show is that long-standing projects of integration and co-operation cohabit with more radical alternatives that for some may reflect the difference between social democratic responses to neo-liberalism and populist appeals to radical change. This regional arena, however, does not represent a smooth, harmonious development. Compromising and amalgamating sub-regional projects beyond rhetoric and goodwill politics will certainly account for coherent and cohesive post-neo-liberal regional governance. Key actors such as Chile, Peru, Colombia and Mexico still remain firmly focused on the US market (partly as a result of trade dependence on US markets). This, for instance, created friction within the old scheme of the Andean Community leading Venezuela to announce its plans to leave the scheme, after Colombia and Peru reached free trade agreements with the USA. Brazil for its part has a political and diplomatic style of its own. Pragmatism and moderation in this case means an opportunity to play a role beyond the regional stage, using new regional projects as a platform for enhancing its negotiation capacity and leverage in other international forums such as the WTO or G20. MERCOSUR, meanwhile, struggles to come to terms with Venezuela's more radical alternative proposals, while keeping the dynamism of oil-funded trade and infrastructure projects. Current tensions among some South American nations pose the main challenge for UNASUR, while ideological differences, even amongst the left, exist. Geopolitically, there are also long-existing border issues, reheated confrontation between Venezuela and Colombia, and even a new advent of militarism in Central America—including a military coup in Honduras—that expose the limits of an alternative regional response.

The politicized regional arena echoes a nebulous yet important spirit of change in the region. Although there are important differences, what unites most of these countries is a real need to re-found the nation state, to re-embed socially responsive models of development and social justice, and to distance themselves from the USA over a number of key issues. In this context, Obama's Administration has still to reduce divisions and mistrust in inter-American relations by renewing the focus of Washington's policy towards Latin America as well as a new and more political sense of the region.

RECONSTRUCTING INTER-AMERICAN RELATIONS. THE CHALLENGES AHEAD

A new spirit of trust and improved policies are critical to rebuilding a constructive partnership between the USA and the region. President Barack Obama began his Administration with an exceptional opportunity to strike a new tone with Latin America's leaders in the Fifth Summit of the Americas in Port of Spain, Trinidad, in April 2009. There are five key areas pending in the hemispheric agenda: energy and climate change, migration, trade, organized crime and drugs-trafficking, and US–Cuban relations. A significant aspect of the summit was the emergent common interest on matters that can potentially serve as bases for new initiatives and agreements. These interests revolved around issues of poverty, migration, drugs, energy, and climate change. Cuba has been the other measure by which to test Obama's pledge to improve relations in the region. While Obama was not prepared to lift the embargo, he did make a concession before arriving at the Summit of the Americas, lifting restrictions on Cuban Americans who wish to visit family or send remittances to Cuba; and more recently he welcomed a decision by the Organization of American States (OAS) to lift a 47-year-old suspension and allow Cuba to be readmitted to the organization. Although the summit did not produce a final common agreement, it smoothed things over, given the tensions that emerged in the previous summit held in Mar del Plata (Buenos Aires, Argentina) in 2005, creating a renewed space for the treatment of substantive topics beyond classic trade talks. More encouragingly, the Obama Administration announced a Micro-finance Growth Fund for the Western Hemisphere, a timely policy as the global economic crisis begins to hurt the countries of Latin America and the Caribbean. The Obama Administration called for US $100m. in initial capital and an ultimate goal of US $250m. for the Fund. It also recognized the need to recapitalize the IADB to ensure steady flows of capital to the region, crucial to bringing about an economic recovery in the hemisphere.

The overwhelming receptiveness of the hemisphere's leaders to President Obama is encouraging. In a symbolic move, Obama's visit to Brazil before the summit denotes a *de facto* recognition of Brazil as 'spokesman' for the most moderate Latin American left-leaning Governments as well as a leader on a wide range of international issues, including global trade negotiations, nuclear non-proliferation, environmental protection, reform of international institutions, food and energy production. These trends might potentially herald a new geopolitical understanding of the region, which in turn may start a new chapter in inter-American relations.

But this opening needs to be consolidated to form a new platform for relations. There are three main problems that challenge trust-building in inter-American relations: the position towards the recent coup in Honduras which overthrew a civilian democratic Government. The differences in position towards the political-institutional crisis in Honduras. The countries of MERCOSUR and ALBA do not recognize the current Honduran military Government, while the USA has been lenient in the conflict. A second issue of tension relates to the presence of the USA in Colombia. Colombia allowed the USA to establish a military base in the country and this has triggered political tensions between Colombia and Venezuela. Colombia is allied with the USA not only in economic terms but also in its fight against the guerrilla force, FARC. This inflamed a territorial conflict between neighbours Colombia and Venezuela, with symbolic politics and antagonistic declarations. The third issue relates to the presence of Iran in the region. The political alliance between ALBA countries and Iran is vehemently questioned by the US Administration as is the position of Brazil which hosted an official visit by the Iranian President in 2009. These tensions are in addition to the ongoing 'narco-terrorism' in Mexico.

While the complete nature of Obama's Latin American platform remains to be seen, there is no doubt that Obama's stance on hemispheric affairs will differ from that of the Bush White House. This, in a context of an undeniable search for alternative models of socio-economic governance across the region, is critical for restoring the leverage of the US on regional projects.

CONCLUSION

Latin America is at a crucial point in its history. Old models of political and economic development are being dismantled and a new range of governments in the region are redefining the goals of policy making. At the same time, there is a new appeal to the region in terms of development models that differ markedly from the model of the 1990s.

Significantly, the current crisis of neo-liberalism across the region coincided with an increasing diffusion of financial and ideological power, epitomized by the emergence of Venezuela's participation in the region and China's role in the global political economy. The impact of Chávez and, to a large extent the emergence of China as a trade and financial actor, has transformed Latin American foreign policies while fracturing consensus around a model of integration based on the US economy. The search for a more autonomous developmental space currently experienced in Latin America has been engineered through conscious attempts to diversify through co-operation and networking. These factors are governing two unprecedented developments in the region: a new platform for regional relations beyond the 'Washington Consensus'; and the high level of reserves accumulated as a consequence of new dynamics of trade and finance that strengthened the regional position, weathering the stormy global financial crisis. The Asian appetite for the region's commodities has indeed turned into a great source of revenue for Latin America. At the same time, the presence of Chávez has transformed Latin American foreign policies. Venezuela has been a key player engaging in a region-wide set of initiatives and spreading its oil wealth throughout the continent. There is, in this context, an unprecedented new game of sub-regional leadership which, whatever direction it takes, will certainly affect US participation in the region.

Any assessment of the processes of political, social and economic transformation taking place in Latin America can only be tentative. Far from forming coherent institutionalized, long-term programmes of development, this analysis postulates that the emergence of alternative models of governance involving broader aspects of the political and economic life of Latin American countries is still in the making. A longer-term perspective indicates that there are difficulties ahead. For instance, growth has been secured in many economies largely via the effect of soaring commodity prices. Yet these trends are highly contingent on those of global markets. Furthermore, the easing of international conditions left more room for government interventionism, but this can create mistrust among foreign investors and some domestic businesses. Likewise, the problems ofpoverty, extreme poverty and unemployment are still far from resolution and tackling these issues is a delicate task, balancing the 'distribution game' between business and labour. At the same time, the economic recovery, as well as the political space in many parts of the region, is being challenged by the current context of international financial crisis, which is particularly hitting the social arena. The current context of the international financial crisis that is now joining an emerging crisis in the Euro-zone, poses particular concerns for South American economies, especially as these economies rely on Europe for nearly 40% of their foreign investments, and for almost 20% of their exports (see ECLAC 2009a).

The extent to which a post-neo-liberal project can be successful is thus currently a matter of debate. The fact that the Latin American region has realigned its strategy towards an alternative course for development and governance is a significant change. Its resilience, however, will largely depend on the sustainability of growth through primary exports in the long term.

REFERENCES

Cooper, A. and Momani, B. 'Negotiating out of Argentina's Financial Crisis: Segmenting the International Creditors', in *New Political Economy*, Vol. 10, No. 3. London, Routledge, 2005.

Cortés, R. 'Social Policy in Latin America in the Post-Neoliberal Era', in *Governance after Neoliberalism in Latin America*. New York, NY, Palgrave Macmillan, 2009.

Economic Commission for Latin America and the Caribbean (ECLAC). *Economic Survey of Latin America and the Caribbean 2007–08*. internet http://www.eclac.org/cgi-bin/getProd.asp?xml=/publicaciones/xml/3/33873/P33873.xml=/de/tpl-i/p9f.xsl=/ tpl-i/top-bottom.xsl. Santiago, 2008.

Economic Commission for Latin America and the Caribbean (ECLAC-2009a). *Foreign Direct Investment in Latin America and the Caribbean*. internet http://www.eclac.org/publicaciones/xml/2/39422/inversion2009i.pdf. 2009.

Economic Commission for Latin America and the Caribbean (ECLAC-2009b). *Preliminary Overview of the Economies of Latin America and the Caribbean*. internet http://www.cepal.org/ cgibin/getProd.asp?xml=/ publicaciones/ xml/ 3/ 38063/ P38063.xml=/ de/ tpl-i/ p9f.xsl=/ de/ tpl/ top-bottom.xsl. 2009.

Grugel, J. and Riggirozzi, P. 'Governance after Neo-Liberalism in Latin America.' Basingstoke, Palgrave Macmillan, 2009.

International Labour Organization (ILO). *Global Economic Trends*. internet http://www.ilo.org/wcmsp5/groups/public/—ed_emp/—emp_elm/—trends/documents/publication/ wcms_120471.pdf. Geneva, 2010.

International Monetary Fund (IMF). *World Economic Outlook*. internet http://www.imf.org/external/pubs/ft/weo/2010/01/ pdf/text.pdf. Washington, DC, 2010

Riggirozzi, P. 'Argentina: State Capacity and Leverage in External Negotiations', in *Power and Politics after Financial Crises*. Basingstoke, Palgrave Macmillan, 2007.

Riggirozzi, P. 'Crisis, resilience and transformation: the Changing Architecture of Regionalism in Latin America'. Paper presented at International Studies Association Convention, New Orleans, LA, February 2010.

Weisbrot, M., Schmitt, J., and Sandoval, L. 'The Economic Impact of a US Slowdown on the Americas'. CEPR, Issue Brief, March. internet http://www.cepr.net/documents/publications/ recession_americas_2008_02.pdf. Accessed 8 May 2009.

THE POLITICS OF ENERGY IN LATIN AMERICA

ANNETTE HESTER and Prof. SIDNEY WEINTRAUB

Revised and updated by THOMAS ANDREW O'KEEFE

INTRODUCTION

The Western hemisphere as a whole was a net importer of 6.2m. barrels per day (b/d) of petroleum in 2008. The oil import and export figures in 2008 were: USA, net imports of 10.9m. b/d; Canada, net exports of 1.5m. b/d; Mexico, net exports of 1.1m. b/d; and South and Central America, net exports of 2.1m. b/d (BP, 2009). Most trade in natural gas in the hemisphere moves by pipeline, hence to nearby countries, but Trinidad and Tobago exported 7,470m. cubic metres (cu m) of liquefied natural gas (LNG) to the USA in 2008, or about 75% of net total LNG imports (BP, 2009 and US Energy Information Administration, November 2009, Caribbean). Hemispheric trade in LNG is becoming important in South America as countries can no longer rely on supplies from their neighbours. By 2010 LNG had replaced the natural gas Chile once imported from Argentina through pipelines. Two facilities for LNG imports have come on line in Brazil since 2008 to reduce dependence on Bolivia. Argentina inaugurated a floating LNG import terminal at Bahía Blanca in 2008 for similar reasons. The focus here on oil and natural gas is based on the fact that they are the energy sources most heavily traded across national boundaries—more so than coal, electricity (which is, however, often traded between neighbouring countries), biofuels and other alternatives to fossil fuels—and that the political tension concerning energy in the hemisphere emerges most intensely in international trade.

The following tables provide additional contextual information on production, consumption, and trade of oil and gas in Latin America and the Caribbean, showing net exporters and importers separately.

Petroleum and Natural Gas (2007)

Petroleum (million barrels)	Production	Exports
Argentina	237.0	21.0
Brazil	639.3	153.8
Colombia	193.6	82.7
Ecuador	186.5	123.9
Mexico	1,126.3	617.1
Peru	28.2	10.0
Trinidad and Tobago	43.8	29.2
Venezuela	1,116.8	759.0

Petroleum (million barrels)	Consumption	Imports
Argentina	217.6	0.3
Brazil	641.6	147.9
Chile	71.9	74.3
Colombia	117.3	2.8
Ecuador	60.3	—
Mexico	502.1	—
Peru	58.6	40.2
Venezuela	357.8	—

Natural gas ('000 million cu m)	Production	Exports
Argentina	51.0	3.1
Bolivia	13.6	11.0
Brazil	17.3	—
Colombia	8.8	—
Mexico	79.0	1.2
Peru	6.7	—
Trinidad and Tobago	42.3	21.5
Venezuela	33.9	—

Natural gas ('000 million cu m)	Consumption	Imports
Argentina	49.1	2.0
Brazil	23.7	10.6
Chile	4.5	2.8
Colombia	8.5	—
Ecuador	0.9	—
Mexico	66.9	9.4
Peru	3.9	—
Trinidad and Tobago	19.2	—
Venezuela	30.4	—

Source: Organización Latinoamericana de Energía (OLADE), Sistema de Información Económica Energética.

Although North America is not included in this study, it is an important sub-region in any analysis of the politics of energy in the rest of the hemisphere because the USA is the continent's most important oil market. Oil exports (including crude and products) to the USA from non-North American hemispheric countries were 2.4m. b/d in 2008, out of total world exports from these countries of 3.6m. b/d (BP, 2009). In other words, nearly 70% of the exports are destined for the US market. Because the USA is so dependent on oil imports, it has a natural interest in the region's energy politics, particularly when circumstances lead to lower oil production.

THE INFLUENCE OF POLITICS ON ENERGY POLICIES

The most serious impediments to energy co-operation in the region lie primarily above ground. This does not mean that there is no co-operation in regard to energy among countries in the region: there is considerable investment across national boundaries; joint refining facilities exist between countries; pipelines are jointly financed to facilitate trade; subsidized exports of oil products are sent to poorer countries of the region; much energy information is shared; periodic meetings of energy officials take place; long-term contracts are negotiated; and much more. Problems arise when politics take precedence over actions that would be economically beneficial. Political impediments include intense nationalism, the playing out of historical grievances, and resentments stemming from perceived or actual exploitation by more powerful neighbours.

There are many examples of these situations. For instance, Bolivia will not sell natural gas to Chile, or even allow a pipeline to be built to take natural gas to the optimal port for transformation into LNG for export if that port is in Chile. This is based on resentment dating from Bolivia's loss of access to the sea after its defeat by Chile in the War of the Pacific (1879–84). Peru is reluctant to ship natural gas to Chile because it also lost territory after its defeat in the same war. Bolivia nationalized foreign-owned gas production facilities in 2006 owing to fears that foreign resource companies have exploited and continue to exploit the country; and the Bolivian authorities even sent in troops to occupy Brazilian-owned refineries, partly because of Brazil's large economic role in Bolivia. Ecuador took over an oil facility of the US-owned Occidental Petroleum Country on the grounds that it failed to abide fully by Ecuadorean laws. Other examples abound.

Energy has also played a decisive role in internal politics. Two successive presidents were forcefully ousted in Bolivia because they were seen as compromising the country's control of its gas resources. Ecuador has had more than 10 presidents during the last 15 years, something in large part related to oil policy. Argentine President Néstor Kirchner (2003–07) prevented producers from charging prices that would permit them to make a profit from their natural gas sales to residential consumers in order to increase his popularity, thereby leading to a cessation of new investments. Venezuela charges artificially low domestic prices for gasoline (petrol) so that President

Hugo Chávez Frías might further his influence. Until recently, guerrilla groups frequently attacked oil pipelines in Colombia.

The great majority of countries in the region have established national oil companies (NOCs) to manage their oil and gas operations; this is a modest manifestation of nationalist oil policies ('modest' because NOCs are not all alike). There is less purely political interference in the operations of Brazilian Petrobras (Petróleo Brasileiro, SA) and Colombian Ecopetrol (Empresa Colombiana de Petróleos) than in most other NOCs, which are commonly used to provide patronage or overtaxed to augment governmental revenue; the outstanding example of the latter is Mexican Petróleos Mexicanos (PEMEX). The only two countries in the hemisphere with significant oil and gas production that do not have NOCs are the USA and Canada. Petrobras has been more successful during the past 15 to 20 years in finding and operating new oil and gas deposits than has PEMEX. There are many reasons for this outcome, chief among them the fact that Brazilian governments have consistently addressed energy security with pragmatism. Starting in the 1970s, in response to the two oil crises, the military dictators chose to invest substantial amounts in technology research to make viable the only hydrocarbon reserves Brazil had, which were found offshore from the Brazilian coast. The military rulers also created the 'pro-alcohol' programme, which was the precursor for the ethanol boom Brazil was experiencing in the late 2000s. Successor governments continued to treat Petrobras largely as a commercial operation, while Mexico, having significant hydrocarbon deposits, used PEMEX as a 'cash cow' for the state and as a means of promoting nationalist emotions.

OIL AND GAS POLITICS IN KEY SUPPLIER COUNTRIES IN THE REGION

Venezuela

Venezuela has the largest proven reserves of conventional oil in the region, indeed in the hemisphere, with 99,400m. barrels at the end of 2008. (The second largest proven conventional reserves in the hemisphere are in the USA, of about 30,500m. barrels, while the largest reserves, taking into account conventional and unconventional sources, are Canada's, of 179,300m. barrels). Confining the discussion to the region under discussion, Brazil is placed second, because of recent discoveries, with 12,600m. barrels of proven reserves at the end of 2008 (BP, 2009). Brazil, given its large population (191.5m.) and sizeable economy (with gross national income—GNI—per head of US $10,700, measured on an international purchasing power-parity—PPP—basis), still has only a limited capacity to export oil. The comparable figures for Venezuela are a population of 28.4m. and per head GNI in PPP terms of $12,830 (Population Reference Bureau, 2010). Venezuela's recoverable unconventional oil reserves in the Orinoco tar belt are enormous—estimated to be 270,000m. barrels—but they are not yet considered economical, consequently are not included in proven reserves, and are not being fully exploited. Venezuela's natural gas reserves are also the largest in the region, but are only marginally exploited at present, in part, because of limited pipelines.

The emphasis on Venezuela's substantial oil and natural gas reserves should be examined in conjunction with the political role that President Chávez is playing on the hemispheric and global scenes. Chávez has made frequent comments on what he considers the malign influence of the USA in the region. Nevertheless, by absorbing 42.3% of Venezuelan crude and refined oil exports in 2008, the USA remains by far the country's largest export market (OPEC, 2009). Chávez has stated that he hopes over time to send the bulk of Venezuela's oil exports to the People's Republic of China, but he is constrained by significantly higher transportation costs and because most of the refining capacity for the heavy oil Venezuela produces is currently in the USA. Even so, in 2008 China imported almost 120,000 b/d of crude oil from Venezuela, up from only 39,000 b/d in 2005 (US Energy Information Administration, February 2010, Venezuela).

When the price of oil has been high, President Chávez has engaged in costly political activities. For example, Venezuela has supplied oil on concessional terms to countries in Central America and the Caribbean, including Cuba; it has bought Argentine and Ecuadorean debt to help the finances of these countries; it reached agreement with Brazil in 2005 to build a 200,000 b/d refinery in north-eastern Brazil at an initial estimated cost of US $5,000m. (a sum that has subsequently risen to $13,000m.); and Chávez has worked closely with like-minded heads of state of the region, including Evo Morales of Bolivia, Rafael Correa of Ecuador, Daniel Ortega of Nicaragua, and former Argentine President Kirchner as well as his wife, Cristina Fernández de Kirchner, the current Argentine head of state. Chávez's economic goal is to bring what he calls '21st century socialism' to Venezuela. He has diverted revenue received from oil exports to other *misiones*, as he calls them, which include costly heavy industry and expensive social welfare programmes; in the process he has neglected maintenance of Venezuela's energy infrastructure.

Chávez's ideological leaning, coupled with the financial resources he had until late 2008 to expand his influence, unsettled the political atmosphere in the hemisphere. Past and current presidents of Brazil, Chile (exempting rightist Sebastian Piñera who took office in March 2010) and Uruguay, ran for election as leftists but practised largely mainstream economic policies once in office. President Alan García of Peru is the head of the main left-wing party of the country, but his policies have nothing in common with those of Chávez. Relations between President Alvaro Uribe of Colombia and Chávez have usually been tense. None the less, Colombia supplies natural gas to Venezuela. In short, there are manifest political divisions among the countries of South America and these are reflected in their energy policies.

In recent years, the Chávez administration has mandated that international oil companies (IOCs) operating in Venezuela must enter into joint ventures with state-owned PDVSA (Petróleos de Venezuela, SA), which enjoys majority ownership of any oil projects. Taxes and royalty payments on new and existing projects have been increased. The Venezuelan Government has also exhibited a marked preference for working with NOCs. In 2009 Venezuela nationalized the assets of many service contractors that supported oil production in the Lake Maracaibo region (e.g. barges, maintenance, and natural gas processing units) when they failed to negotiate reductions on unpaid fees owed by PDVSA. By contrast, Chávez has taken a more laissez-faire approach towards natural gas exploration, production, transportation, and distribution. Operators are allowed 100% ownership and pay internationally competitive royalty rates and other taxes to the Venezuelan Government.

Mexico

In 1938 the then President, Lázaro Cardenas, expropriated the holdings of IOCs operating in Mexico. PEMEX was given an exclusive monopoly to explore, produce, refine, and market oil and natural gas. The country's highly restrictive oil and gas policy, enshrined in its Constitution, prohibits private sector equity investment in the hydrocarbons sector. That factor, combined with PEMEX's role as a 'cash cow' for the federal budget, has led to years of underinvestment in the exploration and development of new reserves and the expansion of refining capacity. Oil production in Mexico peaked in 2004 at 3,400m. b/d and has since dropped by about one-quarter. Shrinking reserves are exacerbated by rising domestic demand and generous subsidies that undermine conservation efforts or the development of alternative energy resources. PEMEX also lacks the expertise and technology required to explore for oil in the deep waters of the Gulf of Mexico. Although currently one of the world's top 10 crude oil-exporting nations, the failure to adopt major reforms means that Mexico may cease to be a net exporter of oil within a few years and risks finding itself importing oil some time around 2025 (Fuentes Berain and Rico, 2009).

Amending Mexico's Constitution to permit private sector investment in the petroleum industry requires a two-thirds' majority vote in the federal Senate and Chamber of Deputies as well as a two-thirds vote in each of the state legislatures. Given this huge hurdle, recent Mexican governments have preferred to chip away at the monopoly powers of PEMEX rather than boldly make constitutional changes. The Partido Revolucionario Institucional (PRI) Government of Ernesto Zedillo Ponce de León (1994–2000) introduced the concept of a multi-service contract through which PEMEX engages outside firms to perform specific exploration or extraction services for a set fee. The subsequent Government of Vicente Fox Quesada (2000–06) expanded the use of such contracts in an attempt to increase oil and natural gas production. The multi-service contracts, however, have been of limited appeal to major oil and gas companies, which prefer the greater revenue streams generated by full or joint risk concession contracts.

In April 2008 President Felipe Calderón Hinojosa of the centre-right Partido Acción Nacional, himself a former energy minister, presented legislation to the opposition-controlled Congress that included modest proposals to reverse the sharp decline in oil production. A diluted version was finally approved in October 2008 that included bonus payments if a project is finished ahead of schedule, results in greater output than originally anticipated, or involves the transfer of new technology that reduces costs. Furthermore, PEMEX was given more financial and decision-making autonomy in procurement decisions, and four independent members were added to PEMEX's existing 11-member board of directors that was dominated by government and union representatives. A new National Petroleum Commission under the jurisdiction of the Secretariat of State for Energy was authorized to oversee hydrocarbon exploration and production operations and to design a new regulatory framework. The bonus provisions with respect to multi-service contracts were subsequently abrogated when challenged by the PRI as unconstitutional (despite voting in favour of the original legislation) after the PRI and its Partido Verde Ecologista de México allies gained an absolute majority of seats in the lower house in the mid-term elections of July 2009.

Mexico's tax collections currently represent a paltry 11% of gross domestic product (GDP), which is low even by Latin American standards. The inability or unwillingness to create effective tax laws with meaningful penalties for non-payment is the reason that PEMEX provides about 40% of the federal Government's total annual income and has little funds available for reinvestment purposes. In March 2010 the Calderón Government presented a third tax reform bill in as many years in an attempt to reduce the country's heavy dependence on PEMEX for revenue (Thompson, 19 March 2010).

As recently as 1999, Mexico both imported and exported natural gas, but gas exports have fallen significantly and imports keep rising to meet increasing demand from the state-controlled electricity generation sector. To handle these growing imports, Mexico has increased its pipeline interconnection points at the border with the USA. Interestingly, Mexico opened the transport, storage, and distribution of natural gas to domestic private sector participation as well as to companies from Canada and the USA as a result of the North American Free Trade Agreement.

Brazil

Given Brazil's size and relatively successful economic growth since the late 1990s, the country is a natural leader in South America, although Venezuela has sought to challenge this role. Despite this, Brazil has maintained cordial relations with Venezuela, escaping the animosity that prevailed between Venezuela and the USA during the Administration of George W. Bush (2001–09), all the while avoiding the close support to Venezuela given by Chávez's allies in South America, notably Bolivia and Ecuador. One example of this is the approval by Brazil of Venezuela's entry as a full member of the Southern Common Market (MERCOSUR/MERCOSUL), whose four full members are Argentina, Brazil, Paraguay, and Uruguay.

When the organization of Petrobras was altered in the 1990s, the new structure proved to be beneficial. Petrobras remains an NOC in which the Government retains the controlling voting share (55.7% of the common shares), giving it control on policy issues (Petrobras, May 2008). The remainder of the common shares and 85% of the preferred shares trade publicly on a number of stock exchanges. The value of this public/private combination is that Petrobras simultaneously demonstrates to its private shareholders that it is seeking to maximize profits even as it operates in a way that the Government believes is in the national interest. Petrobras enters into joint ventures with other companies, both IOCs and other NOCs. Petrobras runs its own technical training programmes, but its joint ventures, especially with IOCs, have enabled it to upgrade its technical capacities. Two of the recent discoveries from these joint ventures, the Tupi oil- and gasfield in the Santos Basin and the Jupiter gasfield offshore from Rio de Janeiro are in deep water, in the Tupi case about 4 km–5 km below the ocean floor. Tupi apparently contains 5,800m.–8,000m. barrels of recoverable reserves (including both oil and natural gas). Preliminary estimates of the total extent of recoverable oil and natural gas reserves in the entire subsalt reserve (including Tupi and subsequent discoveries such as Carioca, Iara, and Guara) has exceeded 50m. barrels of oil equivalent (US Energy Information Administration, September 2009, Brazil). The Jupiter gasfield, when and if its reserves are exploited, will help Brazil become self-sufficient in natural gas, whereas today about one-half of the country's gas consumption is imported from Bolivia. It is expected to take more than five years to resolve the technical problems of bringing the deepwater gas and oil to the surface and building the infrastructure to make them marketable.

A political question that should be asked is whether Brazil, were it to become self-sufficient in natural gas, would nevertheless continue to purchase gas from Bolivia. Brazil does have an important interest in preventing the economic collapse of its neighbour and, unless Bolivia is able to earn enough from gas exports to Argentina or is able to reach an agreement to use a Chilean port for liquefaction of natural gas or sell natural gas directly to Chile, Brazil may have a compelling geostrategic interest to continue gas imports from Bolivia.

A change in the entire energy sector regulatory framework in 1995 also charged the national petroleum agency (Agência Nacional de Petróleo, Gás Natural e Biocombustíveis—ANP) with monitoring the oil sector and issuing exploration and production licences. In 1997 the Government deregulated oil prices, freeing them from state control, and opened the oil sector to competition by eliminating the monopoly enjoyed by Petrobras (US Energy Information Administration, September 2009, Brazil). These regulatory changes at the government level, and organizational changes at the company level, reduced the extent of political influence over Brazil's energy sector, while also providing improved technical and market influence. This diminished nationalist orientation could shift, however, if a new regulatory framework, presented by the administration of President Lula da Silva in August 2009, for exploiting the pre-salt reserves becomes law. As proposed, new production sharing agreements would replace the concession arrangements normally utilized elsewhere, and Petrobras would hold a minimum 30% operating stake in each pre-salt project. A new regulatory agency (Petrosal) would be created to oversee pre-salt projects. Furthermore, a development fund would be established to manage government revenues obtained from the pre-salt operations to invest in education, health, the environment, and other socio-economic projects. Finally, Petrobras would be capitalized by granting it offshore reserves not otherwise licensed to anyone (thereby also increasing the Government's percentage in Petrobras common stock with voting rights).

Brazil's energy policy turned out to be quite prescient when some 40 years ago the country began research, stimulated by heavy subsidies, into the conversion of sugar cane to ethanol as a substitute for gasoline in vehicle transportation, and also into the use of the bagasse from the cane to generate electricity. Today Brazil is the second largest producer (after the USA) and the world's largest exporter of ethanol. The direct subsidies have long since expired and production is highly efficient and internationally competitive, but Brazil is hindered from exporting ethanol to the USA in significant quantities by that country's 2.5% ad valorem tariff and high surcharge of 54 US cents per gallon, plus massive subsidies provided to corn-based ethanol producers that artificially lower their prices to end users. Brazil exports some ethanol indirectly in diluted form via Caribbean and Central American countries that have preferential trade access to the US market. In May 2008 sugar cane became the second largest contributor to Brazil's energy matrix, surpassing hydroelectricity. Moreover, in April and May 2008 ethanol consumption exceeded that of gasoline. Undoubtedly, this is owing to the fact that about one-half of Brazil's automobile fleet (and 90% of new vehicles sold) comprises 'flex-fuel' cars that can work with any combination of gasoline and ethanol; ethanol accounts for more than 50% of the country's current light vehicular fuel (US Energy Information Administration, September 2009, Brazil).

Bolivia

In 2008 Bolivia exported 10,900m. cu m of natural gas to Brazil, equivalent to about 90% of Bolivia's exports of this product (BP, 2009). The gas is transported under a 20-year bilateral take-or-pay contract signed in 1999 (and subsequently amended), primarily through the 3,400-km GASBOL pipeline from Río Grande (south of Santa Cruz) in Bolivia, to Porto Alegre, Brazil, via São Paulo. These imports from Bolivia constitute about one-half of Brazil's natural gas needs and are vital for the economy of São Paulo state. In March 2010 Bolivia and Argentina amended their 2006 agreement by which Argentina purchases natural gas under a similar take-or-pay arrangement as the contract with Brazil but for a higher price. The amendment calls for substantially increasing shipments above the current 4.5m.–5m. cu m per day (Business Monitor International, 1 March 2010). Increased exports have necessitated construction of a 50-km interconnector pipeline to Argentina to supplement the existing YABOG pipeline built in the 1970s.

The politics of these natural gas shipments are complex. The nationalization of hydrocarbon resources in 2006 was accompanied by Bolivian insistence on the renegotiation of natural gas contracts with Argentina and Brazil. Based on its long-term contract with Bolivia, Petrobras was reluctant to accept higher prices for the imported natural gas, but eventually agreed because of the importance of gas to the Brazilian economy and Brasília's geopolitical interest in stabilizing an impoverished neighbour. In light of the nationalization and price renegotiations, foreign investors held back on new investment to augment Bolivia's gas exploration. Bolivia does not produce enough natural gas to meet all its obligations for domestic use and the contracted levels of exports to both Brazil and Argentina. The gas may be in the ground, but the funds for new investment to extract it have only recently begun to materialize. One reason for the willingness by some IOCs to start increasing investment in Bolivia is the more pragmatic approach adopted by President Morales from 2009, including ending YPFB's (Yacimientos Petrolíferos Fiscales Bolivianos) monopoly on the provision of oil and gas services in October of that year.

President Morales has, to a large extent, emulated Venezuelan President Chávez. Chávez established a constituent assembly to change the Constitution, as did Morales; Chávez demanded a controlling majority stake by the domestic NOC in foreign-owned oil projects and higher royalty payments and taxes, as Morales has done with regard to Bolivia's natural gas. Venezuela altered contracts and Bolivia has done the same. To a great extent, both have succeeded, albeit with some costs, but there are differences in the two situations. Venezuelan oil has a global market, while Bolivia's pipeline gas sales rely on the markets of neighbouring countries. The Venezuelan Government was, at least until mid-2008, flush with money, but Bolivia, despite higher receipts for gas exports, was not. PDVSA is an established NOC, albeit weakened since the strike and subsequent dismissal in 2002 of many of its technicians when the industrial action failed to remove Chávez from power, whereas YPFB lacks the capacity to operate the country's nationalized gas fields. Moreover, opposition within Bolivia is much more vociferous than in Venezuela, and in 2008 several provinces conducted referendums to obtain popular support for their pleas for more autonomy from the central Government. The autonomy movement has abated, however, since the January 2009 plebiscite when 61% of Bolivians approved a new constitution (that included provisions for enhanced local autonomy), as well as the December 2009 election in which Morales was re-elected with 64% of the vote (including a majority in the autonomy-seeking department of Tarija), while his supporters also obtained a two-thirds' majority in both congressional chambers.

Argentina

Argentina is currently South America's largest natural gas producer and gas provides the primary energy source for generating electricity. Yet Argentina has serious, self-inflicted problems with regard to its natural gas. Following the country's economic crisis in 2001, Argentina converted end-user charges for natural gas and electricity from US dollars into sharply devalued Argentine pesos at an artificial one-to-one rate of exchange and froze them. Following his election in 2003, President Kirchner waited years to gradually increase energy prices for large commercial end-users while keeping those for residential users frozen. One motive was to contain inflation, but another was to enhance his political popularity after he won the presidency with a minority vote.

The energy-related consequences of this policy were to stimulate the use of natural gas by consumers and to stifle new exploration investment. There have been shortages of natural gas and electricity, such as occurred in June 2007, when Argentina experienced an unusually cold winter. Since 2004 Argentina has also imposed restrictions on the export of natural gas to Brazil, Chile, and Uruguay (see the section on Chile, below). Argentina also finds it necessary to import natural gas from Bolivia and electricity from Brazil at a price higher than paid for by residential consumers. The country has also utilized PDVSA as an intermediary to import overpriced substitute fuel oil to power Argentine dual combination thermal plants. Since her election in 2007, President Fernández de Kirchner has slowly begun restoring the market mechanism for setting electricity and natural gas prices for residential end-users.

Argentina's former NOC, YPF (Yacimientos Petrolíferos Fiscales) was privatized in 1993 and in 1999 merged with the Spanish oil company Repsol (now Repsol YPF) which dominates oil and gas exploration and production in the country. A new NOC, Energía Argentina, SA (ENARSA), was created in 2004, and has responsibility for promoting oil and gas exploration in the country, albeit with limited funds, and for managing natural gas imports from Bolivia, as well as LNG imports.

Argentina's political problems in relation to energy are both internal (such as the heavy subsidy provided to residential electricity and natural gas usage and the discouragement of investment that would increase supplies) and external (being an unreliable contractual partner). The need to import natural gas from Bolivia has also strained relations with Brazil as the two countries negotiate how to apportion Bolivian gas between them.

Chile

Chile is paying a high price for energy politics in South America. It has limited energy resources and until 2005 relied heavily on imports of Argentine natural gas for electricity generation since these began in the late 1990s. Chile's other neighbours have been unwilling (Bolivia) or reluctant (Peru) to export natural gas to Chile. There is the added problem that none of these three countries has enough current production to divert natural gas exports to Chile, but this constraint could be eliminated were incentives for additional investment to be put in place in Argentina and Bolivia. Chile has chosen to act cautiously, and built two LNG import terminals in central and northern Chile. The terminal in central Chile, near Quintero, became fully operational in June 2009, while the one in Mejillones in northern Chile commenced operations in May 2010. Both terminals import LNG primarily from Trinidad and Tobago.

Peru

Despite a long history of oil production and active fields, Peru is a net oil importer. Peru could potentially become an important natural gas producer and exporter as it further develops its Camisea project. The country is not caught up in the sub-regional energy politics that affect some other South American energy producers. It has even held talks about shipping natural gas to Chile (to which it lost territory in the 19th century War of the Pacific) if there are sufficient supplies. On the other hand, the internal energy politics in Peru are similar to those that exist elsewhere, namely, the interplay between environmental and cultural degradation, as well as demands that national needs be prioritized over exports, versus what are seen as the positive economics of hydrocarbons production. In May 2009 violence erupted in the Amazon region of north-eastern Peru when the army broke up a river blockade by indigenous groups furious at a decree issued by President García that permitted oil drilling in two special reserves created to protect tribes that have had little or no contact with the outside world. A state of emergency was also declared in the jungle regions of Loreto, Amazonas, Ucayali, and Cusco. In the following month at least 30 people were killed in clashes between the police and indigenous people in Bagua in northern Peru, over the implementation of land use regulations affecting the petroleum industry that allowed the central Government to disregard local community input.

The Camisea field is located in Peru's south-eastern Amazon Basin. The location is an environmentally sensitive area that is populated by impoverished indigenous tribes and that could be devastated by insensitive operations. For these reasons, moving ahead with the project was opposed by many organizations including Oxfam America and Friends of the Earth, which are concerned by both the likely degradation of the environment and the adverse impact on indigenous communities associated with the project. In any event, the project began in 2004 and has moved ahead, supported by consecutive Peruvian Presidents, as well as by multinational financial institutions such as the International Finance Corporation, which is part of the World Bank group, and the Inter-American Development Bank (IDB). These institutions, particularly the IDB, have imposed environmental conditions on their financing of the project and have encouraged royalty payments to the municipalities containing the indigenous groups. There have been problems, such as leaks in the pipeline system, but there is general support for the project in Peru because of the anticipated economic benefits.

An LNG consortium, led by Hunt Oil of the USA, broke ground in January 2006 on a liquefaction terminal at Pampa Melchorita, around 170 km south of Lima. The terminal, set to begin operations before the end of 2010, was expected to receive natural gas piped in from Camisea to be exported in liquefied form, primarily to the northern Pacific coast of Mexico for sale in Mexico and the USA. Since 2009, however, strong nationalist factions within the country have forced President García to renegotiate contracts with IOCs and limit the amount of natural gas from Camisea that can be exported until domestic needs are satisfied.

Ecuador

Ecuador has experienced considerable domestic political turmoil in addition to energy conflict externally. The constant changes of presidents since the mid-1990s sent a message of instability to the world. Rafael Correa was first elected President in November 2006. Following approval of a new Constitution in 2008, he was re-elected with 52% of the popular vote in 2009. In 2007 the Correa administration began converting production sharing contracts with IOCs into service contracts for which they earn a fixed fee for extracting oil for Petroecuador (Empresa Estatal Petróleos del Ecuador), the country's NOC. The move is intended to increase the Government's share of oil revenues to fund ambitious public spending programmes. Correa has also increased the windfall tax on surplus oil profits from 50% to 99% (subsequently reduced to 70% for those companies maintaining their investment plans in the country and withdrawing international arbitration claims against Ecuador) (Business Monitor International, 1 December 2008).

Ecuador's oil reserves are the third largest in South America and the oil sector accounts for almost one-half of export earnings and one-third of tax revenues (US Energy Information Administration, April 2009, Ecuador). Having peaked in 2006, oil production has been declining ever since. Petroecuador now controls about one-half of the oil production in the country. Despite its large crude oil exports, Ecuador is a net importer of refined petroleum products, owing to a lack of sufficient domestic refining capacity. In 2007 Ecuador rejoined the Organization of the Petroleum Exporting Countries (OPEC) after having pulled out in 1992, unable to pay its membership dues. Ecuador is also a member of the Bolivarian Alliance for the Peoples of our America (Alianza Bolivariana para los Pueblos de Nuestra América—ALBA), led by Venezuelan President Chávez.

Colombia

Colombia, despite the turmoil stemming from the violent actions of the country's guerrilla movements (the Fuerzas Armadas Revolucionarias de Colombia—Ejército del Pueblo, FARC—EP; and the Ejército de Liberación Nacional, ELN), has an energy policy that is largely non-political beyond the measures taken to minimize the damage done by these two guerrilla groups to energy operations (DeShazo and McLean, 2007). In any event, the security situation in the country has improved in recent years, with few attacks against oil and natural gas infrastructure (US Energy Information Administration, March 2010, Colombia).

Colombia is currently a modest net exporter of oil. At the start of the 21st century declining production of mature fields raised fears that the country might become an importer of oil by the end of the decade, despite the fact that only 15% of Colombia's sedimentary basins had been explored. This led to fiscal and regulatory reforms during the presidency of Alvaro Uribe Vélez (2002–10) designed to make the country more attractive to investors. These measures include a sliding scale royalty rate and forcing the NOC, Ecopetrol, to compete more with private operators. In addition, some 20% of Ecopetrol is now in the hands of private owners. Colombia also has a well regarded regulatory agency, Agencia Nacional de Hídrocarburos (ANH). ANH has been offering many offshore blocks for exploration. In September 2008 ANH awarded 10 companies licences to conduct oil exploration in an area near the Venezuelan border known as the Llanos Basin. As a result of the increased new investment, Colombian oil production reached a record 725,000 b/d in November 2009, compared with an average of 625,000 b/d in 2008. (Business Monitor International, 1 December 2009). Colombia has large deposits of low-sulphur, high quality bituminous coal that is relatively clean-burning. Most of the coal that is extracted is exported to Europe, North America, and Latin America, as the country relies primarily on hydropower to generate electricity.

Trinidad and Tobago

Trinidad and Tobago is noteworthy because it is the largest exporter of LNG to the USA and one of the largest LNG exporters in the world. Its proven natural gas reserves of 48,000,000m. cu m (at the end of 2008) constitutes 0.3% of known global reserves (BP, 2009). LNG exports are the most significant contributor to Trinidad and Tobago's economy (energy provides some 50% of government revenue) and successive governments, despite their often disparate ideologies, have been careful not to allow politics to get in the way of this profitable trade. This does not prevent lively debate in the country over how the revenue from these exports should be used and whether more attention should be paid to the environmental damage from gas and oil production.

An audit conducted by Texas-based Ryder Scott found that the country's onshore and shallow water natural gas reserves would run out by 2019. The Government's failure to offer more generous fiscal incentives for high risk, high cost drilling, coupled with increased use of domestically produced shale gas in the USA, has dampened multinational interest in exploring for new, deep sea natural gas reserves off Trinidad.

The advent of PetroCaribe, a Venezuelan initiative to sell oil to Caribbean island nations under highly favourable repayment terms, raised concerns in 2005 and 2006 that the agreement would compromise Trinidadian oil product sales within the Caribbean Community and Common Market (CARICOM). Trinidad and Tobago, together with Barbados, refused to sign the PetroCaribe agreement. The anger in Trinidad and Tobago over PetroCaribe subsided when the Chávez Government promised (as yet unfulfilled) to utilize Trinidadian facilities to convert Venezuelan natural gas into LNG for export and to refine Venezuelan crude destined for Caribbean nations that lack such capability. Trinidad and Tobago thereafter acquiesced to CARICOM's waiving of the common external tariff on imported Venezuelan oil. Further ameliorating the tension was the fact that Trinidad and Tobago was able to find other markets for its displaced oil exports. A binational Trinidadian and Venezuelan commission in 2007 resolved competing claims over underwater natural gas reserves at the Loran field, but other similar disputes have yet to be settled.

CONCLUSIONS

The region examined in this essay is quite disparate. The countries that produce and export oil and gas in this region are all in South America, except for the Caribbean state of Trinidad and Tobago. All the South American countries that produce sufficient oil or gas to be able to export meaningful amounts of one or both of these products have been mentioned above. Many of these, including Brazil, Argentina, and Venezuela, are both exporters and importers of one or both of these products. Other South American countries, including Chile, Paraguay and Uruguay, are dependent on imports.

The remaining countries of the region in Central America and the Caribbean (other than Trinidad and Tobago) are oil- and gas-deficient and the cost of importing these products is high. Venezuela provides oil to these countries under preferential lending arrangements and Mexico, to an extent, does so at subsidized prices.

All producing countries in the region have NOCs. These vary in terms of effectiveness. Petrobras (Brazil) and Ecopetrol (Colombia) are at the high end of technical capacity and YPFB (Bolivia) and Petroecuador are at the weaker end. Two of the most respected regulatory bodies are in Brazil and Colombia; it appears that an NOC can be effective if it can concentrate on technical issues, leaving the regulatory aspects to another competent agency. The least effective NOCs and regulatory bodies are subject to a high degree of political influence over their countries' energy operations. The most effective NOCs and regulatory bodies are not devoid of political involvement, but technical expertise forms the basis of their operations. The different emphases stem from the nature of the particular governments and the differing relative influence of governments and market factors.

Despite the sharp fall in the price of hydrocarbons following the global financial implosion in 2008, the relatively quick recovery from recession by emerging markets has led to a rebound in prices as world demand has shifted decidedly in favour of Asia. This ensures that the oil and gas industries will continue to play a crucial role in the economies of the Latin American fossil fuel producers. Indeed, GDP growth rates in both exporting and importing countries depend heavily on the prices of these necessary products. The benefits to the energy sector from technical efficiencies in operating and in regulatory agencies can be significant, but the costs of politically motivated inefficiencies may be more considerable still.

BIBLIOGRAPHY

BP. *Statistical Review of World Energy 2009*. London, BP plc, 2009.

Business Monitor International. 'Petrobras Investment Plan Under Growing Threat', in *Americas Oil and Gas Insights*. May 1, 2010.

'Correa Threatens to Take Over Oil Fields: Risk Analysis', in *Americas Oil and Gas Insights*. 1 April 2010.

'BPTT Needs Investment to Sustain Output', in *Americas Oil and Gas Insights*. 1 March 2010.

'Brazil's Oil Reform Takes a Step Forward', in *Americas Oil and Gas Insights*. 1 March 2010.

'Bolivia-Argentina Gas Deal: The Buenos Aires Perspective', in *Americas Oil and Gas Insights*. 1 March 2010.

'Mejillones LNG Facility to Become Operational in May', in *Americas Oil and Gas Insights*. 1 March 2010.

'Mexico to Revisit Oil Contract Rules', in *Americas Oil and Gas Insights*. 1 March 2010.

'BPTT Says T&T Needs US$8-10bn. Of Investment', in *Americas Oil and Gas Insights*. 1 February 2010.

'Total Announces Investment at Incahuasi Complex', in *Americas Oil and Gas Insights*. 1 February 2010.

'Ecopetrol Boosts 2010 Capex 11%', in *Americas Oil and Gas Insights*. 1 December 2009.

'Most of Camisea's Gas Reserved for Domestic Market', in *Americas Oil and Gas Insights*. 1 September 2009.

'Lima Scraps Amazon Land Laws', in *Americas Oil and Gas Insights*. 1 June 2009.

'Chávez Secures Law to Seize Service Players', in *Americas Oil and Gas Insights*. 1 May 2009.

'Second LNG Terminal Comes on Line', in *Americas Oil and Gas Insights*. 1 May 2009.

'Petroecuador to Delay Energy Projects as Government Cuts Spending', in *Americas Oil and Gas Insights*. 1 April 2009.

'Correa Threatens IOCs With Expulsion', in *Americas Oil and Gas Insights*. 1 December 2008.

'Senate Approves Watered-Down Energy Reform Bills', in *Americas Oil and Gas Insights*. 1 October 2008.

'Venezuela and T&T Agree to Gas Field Division', in *Americas Oil and Gas Insights*. 1 April 2007.

DeShazo, P., and McLean, P. *Back From The Brink: Evaluating Progress in Colombia, 1999–2007*. Washington, DC, CSIS Press, 2007.

Fuentes Berain, R., and Rico, D. *Oil in Mexico: Pozo de Pasiones*. Washington, DC, Woodrow Wilson International Center for Scholars (Mexico Institute), 2009.

Organization of the Petroleum Exporting Countries. *OPEC Annual Statistical Bulletin 2008*. Vienna, OPEC, 2009.

Thompson, A. 'Mexico Plans Tax Changes to Boost Growth', in *Financial Times*. 19 March 2010.

US Energy Information Administration. *Country Analysis Brief: Colombia*. www.eia.doe.gov/cabs/Colombia/Full.html (accessed 1 May 2010). Washington, DC, Energy Information Administration, March 2010.

Country Analysis Briefs: Venezuela. www.eia.doe.gov/emeu/cabs/Venezuela/Full.html (accessed 1 May 2010). Washington, DC, Energy Information Administration, February 2010.

Country Analysis Briefs: Caribbean. www.eia.doe.gov/emeu/cabs/Caribbean/LNG.html (accessed 1 May 2010). Washington, DC, Energy Information Administration, November 2009.

Country Analysis Briefs: Brazil. www.eia.doe.gov/emeu/cabs/Brazil/Full.html (accessed 1 May 2010). Washington, DC, Energy Information Administration, September 2009.

Country Analysis Briefs: Ecuador. www.eia.doe.gov/emeu/cabs/Ecuador/Full.html (accessed 1 May 2010). Washington, DC, Energy Information Administration, April 2009.

Country Analysis Briefs: Mexico. www.eia.doe.gov/emeu/cabs/Mexico/Full.html (accessed 1 May 2010). Washington, DC, Energy Information Administration, March 2009.

Weintraub, S., Hester, A., and Prado, V. R. (Eds). *Energy Cooperation in the Western Hemisphere: Benefits and Impediments*. Washington, DC, CSIS Press, 2007.

Other internet resources

Petrobras; internet www2.petrobras.com.br (accessed 14 May 2008).

Population Reference Bureau; internet www.prb.org/datafinder.aspx (accessed 1 May 2010).

GENDER AND DEVELOPMENT IN 21ST CENTURY LATIN AMERICA

Dr FIONA MACAULAY

INTRODUCTION

Gender relations have undergone significant changes in Latin America in the last few decades. The representation of women in political decision-making posts has been steadily rising, and equality between men and women is now enshrined in legislation throughout the region, even if many forms of lived discrimination still exist. Family structures in the region have also been undergoing change owing to the forces of economic and cultural globalization. On the other hand, democratization has also been accompanied by a rise in insecurity, crime and violence, which affect women and men in quite distinct ways, while economic restructuring has reshaped the labour market for both men and women. This essay examines the different challenges that rapidly changing social roles are posing to men and boys, and women and girls, across Latin America by addressing some key development issues: political representation, legislation and public policy processes, employment and the labour market, health and reproduction, the family, and violence.

POLITICAL REPRESENTATION AND PARTICIPATION

Political life in Latin America was heavily male-dominated until the 1970s, with the exception of Argentina under the Peronists and Cuba under communism. In Argentina the Partido Justicialista (PJ), the ruling Peronist party, courted the female vote and introduced a party quota that resulted in female deputies constituting 22% of the legislature in the 1950s. Cuba followed its socialist peers by introducing a quota for the national congress that led to a similar level of female representation by 1980. However, in the immediate aftermath of the 1980s transitions to democracy in the region, female representation dropped sharply as male political leaders of the historic parties returned from exile. Feminist movements in the region were dismayed by this remasculinization of a public sphere in which women had played a key role through civil society organizations during the years of military rule. Turning their attention to institutional arrangements, they pressed for space within the parties. By 2010 Latin American countries had an average of nearly 20% female representation in the lower (or single) house of their national legislatures, just above the world average of 18.7%. However, this aggregate figure has been slow to rise since a significant increase in the 1990s, during which decade most of the quota laws were introduced. It also masks significant variations. Cuba, Costa Rica and Argentina rank in the top 11 internationally, with 43.2%, 38.6% and 36.5%, respectively, while, by contrast, Brazil and Panama remain unable to muster 10%.

This rise in female parliamentary representation has little to do with the features normally associated with modernization, such as income levels, urbanization, secularization or family structure. It is largely the result of institutional engineering—i.e. the quota laws introduced by the majority of Latin American countries, spearheaded by Argentina in 1991. This is generally statutory legislation requiring all parties to reserve a minimum percentage of places (normally between 20% and 40%, for women or, in some cases, both sexes) on candidate lists. Some leftist parties followed their European counterparts by voluntarily imposing unilateral quotas for their lists in the absence of statutory legislation. Reserved seats on party governing bodies gave women more status and increased the likelihood both that they would be selected as parliamentary candidates and, moreover, that they would be elected. Parties such as Mexico's Partido de la Revolución Democrática and Brazil's Partido dos Trabalhadores have elected proportionately more women to congress than their rivals. The rise of radical indigenous politics in the Andes has also given a boost to affirmative action: in 2009 Ecuador and Bolivia both introduced quota provisions in their revised Constitutions.

In Central America, female representation rose faster in El Salvador and Nicaragua than in neighbouring Honduras or Guatemala, owing largely to the unilateral party quotas adopted by the two former revolutionary parties, the Frente Farabundo Martí de Liberación Nacional (35%) and the Frente Sandinista de Liberación Nacional (30%). However, party quotas render overall levels of female representation hostage to the relative electoral strength of that party, and the percentage of women legislators in El Salvador and Nicaragua has remained at around 20%. Gender quotas were absent from the Central American peace accords of the 1990s, in contrast to other countries that have more recently emerged from armed conflict, where female representation has overtaken the levels seen in Latin America.

However, the numerical impact of quotas has been constrained by the electoral systems in the region. They work best in closed list proportional representation systems (where voters select a party, not an individual), with reasonable party and district magnitude (number of seats available to win in each district), a placement mandate in law (male and female candidates proportionately interspersed throughout the list), and mechanisms of enforcement. Quotas do not work easily in 'first-past-the-post' systems: a revived bill seeking to apply a statutory quota of 40% to Chile's system of two seats per district did not prosper, despite the support of former President Michelle Bachelet. Open list systems, such as that in force in Brazil, where the electorate selects an individual candidate for office, are also problematic, although Peru, with 27.5% female representation in the lower house, bucked this trend, demonstrating that the opportunities or obstacles often lie in the detail of individual electoral system design. Despite its complex sub-list system, in 2009 Uruguay introduced a statutory quota that was to apply from the 2014 elections. As the percentage of female legislative candidates in the region was still only 24% in 2009, in some countries (among them Panama and Costa Rica) parties are required to spend a percentage of their public funding on encouraging female political participation. Women are also increasingly holding the levers of power within government: in 2009 women constituted 20.5% of heads of parliamentary commissions in Latin America, and frequently led the lower or upper legislative chambers.

The perception of women in the political sphere has also shifted significantly. Parties have increasingly come to regard female candidates as an asset rather than a liability. In 2009 Michelle Bachelet left the Chilean presidency with an approval rating of 83%, while Laura Chinchilla was elected President of Costa Rica, joining Peronist Cristina Fernández de Kirchner, who has governed Argentina since December 2007. In the early 21st century voters exhibited higher levels of trust in women politicians, whom they rated as more honest, competent and responsible than men. In a poll conducted in 2007 by the Gallup Organization, an international statistical research organization, 61% of women and 47% of men in nine countries agreed that 'women in politics have done a better job than men'; interestingly, the highest rate of concurrence with this view was recorded in Brazil, which has one of the lowest percentages of women in the national legislature. Nevertheless, female representation still lagged far behind that of men in majoritarian positions such as senator or provincial governor. Furthermore, while female representation remained highest in municipal government, this was only the case in those offices with least power. By 2009 women held an average of 22.3% of city councillor posts in 16 countries, partly owing to decentralization legislation containing quota provisions (as in Ecuador) or quota laws covering municipal elections (as in Bolivia, Brazil, the Dominican Republic and Costa Rica—which leads the region with 47.6% female councillors); however, in the same year women held only 8.2% of mayoral offices, although the extension of the Venezuelan gender quota to local elections has suddenly rendered that country untypical, with 18% female mayors).

The electoral quotas have also influenced appointments of women to executive posts. Across the region, 23% of cabinet posts were held by women, with some countries governed by the centre-left or by female Presidents, such as Costa Rica, Chile, Ecuador, Nicaragua, Bolivia, Peru and Uruguay, appointing equal numbers of men and women or adhering to an informal 'quota' of one-third, although this sometimes drops in the course of the administration. Women were also breaking into non-traditional policy areas beyond the traditional portfolios of health, education, social welfare and women's rights. The last decade has seen the appointment of several female Ministers of Defence, perhaps a symbolic underscoring of civilian control over masculine military establishments.

The challenge for gender equality in the region is to break through the 'ceilings' of representation that the quotas inadvertently enforce, and extend the quotas to all types of elected and appointed public office. Existing equality legislation needs to be enforced by the courts, and democracy in the region will be strengthened by increasing the opportunities available to both men and women for participation in decision-making through, for example, genuinely decentralized government and consultation processes over public spending. The local democracy processes underway in Venezuela are suggestive: some 60% of the 10,000 local community councils (each composed of 200 families) are headed by women and engage with the state on practical service delivery issues such as water, health, energy and communications.

LEGISLATION AND STATE POLICY

The changes in political representation and voice have affected public policy in the region in a myriad of ways, particularly with regard to gender equality. The last quarter century has seen the removal of anachronistic and discriminatory provisions from national and sub-national constitutions and legal codes, improving women's political, sexual, reproductive, labour, family and human rights. Labour codes no longer prohibit women from working in particular situations, and now define and outlaw sexual harassment, give pregnant women and lactating mothers enhanced labour rights, and prevent gender discrimination through unequal pay and intrusive investigation into women's reproductive history. Civil codes accord full legal powers and rights to married women, both over their property and their children, and protect women and their dependants in the case of divorce, widowhood or denial of paternity.

Women's movements mobilized to elect a notable number of representatives to the special assemblies convened in a number of countries to revise or draft constitutions following democratization or major political regime shifts. As a result, the region's constitutions explicitly outlaw sexual discrimination, extend women's rights, and incorporate international human rights treaties such as the 1979 UN Convention on the Elimination of all Forms of Discrimination Against Women. In Ecuador the constitutional assembly that had been elected under a 50% quota law discussed issues such as women's right to sexual pleasure, and the Constitution that was approved in 2008 maintained and extended rights that had been won a decade earlier.The new Constitution approved by Bolivians in 2009 contained 90 articles on women's rights and gender equality, such as equal pay for equal work, sexual and reproductive rights for men and women, the right of women to land regardless of marital status, and a recognition of the economic value of work within the home. In a concurrent process, many constitutions now also give indigenous groups greater recognition and autonomy, creating a new set of gender dynamics and negotiations in local communities that now have the power to elect their own representatives and run their own affairs using customary law as well as the civil legal system. Increased awareness of racial inequality, as evidenced by new race quota provisions and anti-discrimination laws, will benefit black and indigenous women the most, as they tend to receive the most prejudiced treatment in the labour market.

Despite these advances in the legal principle of gender equality, there is still a need for secondary, enabling legislation and public policies in the form of gender mainstreaming—i.e. a cross-sectoral approach that integrates into all areas of public policy a recognition of the differences between men's and women's life paths, interests and needs, based on reproduction and the current sexual division of labour. Every Latin American country has established some national unit to achieve this, through the constitution, law or decree. However, these units, and their effectiveness, vary enormously in relation to the extent of political support and institutional resources that they receive, and whether or not they were institutionally protected from co-option by parties and political leaders. Some such units, as in Brazil, Chile, Costa Rica, the Dominican Republic, Guatemala, Haiti, Honduras and Paraguay, have ministerial status, and are answerable directly to the President. Elsewhere, in Colombia, Mexico and Peru, for example, they are located within the President's office and thus are more closely tied to his or her person and fortunes. Although many of these units have, on occasion, been vulnerable to budget cuts and political manipulation, the majority have gradually risen in institutional status since their establishment in the 1980s and early 1990s. They have also tended to broaden their mandates, from an early focus on traditional welfare and social policy functions, addressing women's practical gender needs within the existing sexual division of labour and gender relations, to an emphasis on gender equality and human rights. In order to have an impact across the spectrum of public policy and governance, most such units collaborate with secondary mechanisms in government, such as national councils and commissions on specific issues; gender units located within line ministries; intra-agency task forces, for instance on domestic violence; and 'observatories', a new accountability mechanism that provides citizens with gender-disaggregated data on social policy and spending. The units also co-operate with gender equality mechanisms at provincial/state and municipal level. As numbers of women elected to public office have increased over the last two decades, their support for gender units, legislation and public policy has proven to be crucial.

FAMILY, REPRODUCTIVE RIGHTS, SEXUALITY AND HEALTH

One of the key areas affected by new gender legislation is the family, a social structure that has been undergoing rapid changes in recent years owing to demographic shifts, economic cycles, altered labour market conditions, migration, and cultural and policy-related factors affecting fertility and reproductive choice. Some countries such as Mexico, Costa Rica and Puerto Rico retain a more patriarchal family structure, in which men continue to exercise authority over daughters and wives—especially in poorer and more rural communities—and divorce, informal unions, single person households and unwed child-bearing are relatively uncommon. The opposite can be said of the more matrifocal societies in the Caribbean, for example in the Dominican Republic. The region has seen urban households decline in size with an increase in single person households, often men, in Argentina and Uruguay, in which there is also a notably higher proportion of older people. Although the proportion of female-headed households has risen across the region, at varying rates, it would be wrong to assume that these are necessarily single parent households, as women increasingly head households containing other adults. Similarly, there has been an increase in male-headed single parent households, especially among the middle and upper classes, as norms of masculinity change and men take on more child-rearing responsibilities. The evolving role of fathers is evidenced by the introduction of paternity leave in the continent. Cuba's 1970 Family Code was a forerunner, allowing either the father or the mother to take a year off work for childcare. More recently, Uruguay, Venezuela and Brazil gave new fathers two weeks of paid leave, Colombia increased its provision to eight days, while Chile offered a compulsory five days. Meanwhile, paid maternity leave provision stands at an average of three months in the region.

Likewise, attitudes regarding reproductive rights and sexuality have become steadily more liberal, despite the continuing influence of the Roman Catholic Church and the increasing popularity of Evangelicalism. Generally, a number of forms of contraception, including the so-called 'morning after pill', were available in the region, which has a high incidence (71%) of contraceptive use, with access limited primarily by inadequate health care services and social attitudes. Along with Asia, Latin America is the region with the highest prevalence of female sterilization being carried out as a means of contraception, with the rate reaching as much as 40% in Brazil, Puerto Rico and the Dominican Republic. In some cases, very high levels of sterilization, particularly of poor, rural or ethnic minority women, often allegedly without their full consent or free choice, have been linked to state population control policies. However, there is increasing evidence of more highly educated women now freely choosing sterilization as a method of birth control. The use of condoms, which also protect against HIV/AIDS infection, has gradually been rising, especially among unmarried women. However, very few married women use this contraceptive method; social norms and gender roles render many women unable to negotiate with their male partners on the subject of condoms, and thus leave them vulnerable to sexually transmitted diseases.

HIV/AIDS is a major health concern for both sexes in the region, where up to 2m. people are estimated to be infected. Over the last decade HIV/AIDS has become 'feminized', with the infection rate among women increasing faster than that among men, and in 2006 women constituted one-half of the adults with the HIV virus. Where previously infection was associated with intravenous drugs use or homosexual activity, transmission is now linked to men in heterosexual relationships using the commercial sex trade, or having sex with other men. Targeting safe sex education at men is therefore crucial, but has been problematic owing to a combination of machismo and homophobia. In some countries, homosexual males account for as much as 40% of HIV infection, and Peru, Brazil and Mexico have all targeted this group and its associated social prejudice, the last appointing an HIV-positive homosexual man as the public figurehead of its prevention campaign. However, despite still-conservative social attitudes, gay rights movements have achieved notable successes: all countries in the region have now decriminalized sodomy and homosexualtiy, and many have enshrined the principle of non-discrimination against homosexuals in various areas of legislation, although the armed forces and police continue to discriminate through existing military codes. Mexico, Brazil, Argentina, Colombia and Uruguay have all introduced civil partnership and co-habitation ordinances, and most major cities in the region now host an annual 'Gay Pride' march. It appears that there is a strong relationship between tolerance to homosexuality and levels of education and development.

Restrictive legislation and social and religious attitudes also produce an estimated 4m. abortions in Latin America annually, most performed under clandestine and often dangerous conditions, accounting for 12%–30% of maternal deaths. An estimated 800,000 terminations result in complications requiring medical treatment each year. Since the mid-20th century, most countries in Latin America have permitted so-called 'therapeutic abortion' in cases where there is a danger to the mother's life or the pregnancy resulted from sexual assault; however, access to terminations under these very limited conditions was extremely poor. Abortion was completely illegal under all circumstances in two countries—El Salvador and Chile; abortion is legal in only three nations in South America and the Caribbean—Cuba, Guyana and Puerto Rico (which follows US federal law). In recent years the pendulum has swung in both directions on the abortion issue. Conservative legislators in countries such as Argentina and El Salvador attempted to nullify existing provision for abortion by changing the text of the Constitution, adding the words 'from the moment of conception' to the article guaranteeing the right to life. On the other hand, elsewhere, in Colombia, Mexico and Brazil, for example, abortion laws have been liberalized in response to changing social attitudes, pressure from the women's movement, and the advice of health professionals who regarded the level of illegal abortions as a major public health crisis. In Chile the 'morning after pill' has been sold since 2002 and was made freely available during the presidency of Bachelet, despite challenges through the courts by the Catholic Church and the conservative opposition. It would seem that, throughout most of the region, professional and political concern about preventive public health measures is beginning to trump the more traditional religious influences. That said, women's own preferences and health needs have yet to be prioritized: at around one-third of all deliveries, Latin America has one of the highest caesarean rates in the world, with all the associated health risks and the clear inequalities of the maternity services available in the private and public sectors.

VIOLENCE

Increasing violence in the region constituted another major health risk affecting men and women differently. Women were most directly victimized by domestic violence, while men tended to be the primary perpetrators of domestic and criminal violence, as well as the chief victims of social and drugs- and gun-related violence. Numerous surveys have shown domestic violence to be a major problem in the region. Between 30% and 75% of adult women with partners are reported to suffer psychological abuse and between 10% and 30% are victims of physical violence. The region's penal codes have been revised to define rape and sexual crimes as offences against personal physical freedom and integrity rather than against public morals, and to eradicate all judgments on the victim's sexual history or honour. Some codes even protect men as potential victims. In 1994 Latin America became the first region to appoint a Special Rapporteur on Women's Rights and to draft and approve its own domestic violence norms, in the form of the Organization of American States' Convention on the Prevention, Punishment and Eradication of Violence against Women, known as the Belém do Pará Convention. This, together with the Platform for Action resulting from the UN Fourth World Conference on Women, which was held in Beijing, People's Republic of China, in September 1995, prompted a flurry of legislation, with new national laws approved in virtually every country in the hemisphere. Such new provisions began to reveal the extent of the problem. Following the enactment of the Chilean law, the number of domestic violence cases before the courts rose from 1,419 in 1994 to 73,559 in 1999, an exponential increase that was repeated around the region.

The region's laws were quite progressive, generally specifying protection measures that the courts could apply, such as exclusion orders and injunctions, and temporary child support orders. They detailed the powers and responsibilities of the authorities (police, courts and social services) with respect to protecting and assisting victims. The definitions of domestic violence were extensive, encompassing not only physical assault, but also psychological, emotional, financial and sexual abuse, even rape within marriage. However, few of these laws characterized this abuse as a specific offence within the penal code. Most defined 'low level' domestic violence as a primarily civil offence and designated non-criminal courts or authorities—generally family magistrates or local civil courts—as the first ports of call. In some countries, particularly those in which the Roman Catholic Church was politically influential, such as Chile, Peru, and Argentina, these laws initially stipulated that the couple had to pass through a compulsory conciliation procedure that placed family unity above the victim's right to protection; however, such legislation was later modified, upon the realization that the process did little to protect women from future cycles of violence. The civil and criminal sanctions applicable to offenders ranged from fines to imprisonment. However, in many cases men could be ordered to attend group therapy, and women's groups in the region were increasingly working in conjunction with men in order to reduce the social acceptability and prevalence of domestic violence. Brazil was one of the last countries to pass a dedicated law, the Maria da Penha law, which was approved in 2006; the legislation is innovative in establishing special courts for domestic violence cases, as well as offering protection to domestic workers from abuse in the workplace. Brazil pioneered dedicated women's police stations in the mid-1980s and Ecuador, Nicaragua, Peru and others have followed suit. The percentage of women police officers in the region is also rising—it has reached 27% in

Nicaragua—owing to quotas in some locations, and as part of efforts elsewhere to curb police violence and corruption: the bulk of Mexico City's traffic police are now female. It remains to be seen whether this will encourage more gender-sensitive policing.

Despite the changes in the law, the attitudes of society and of the criminal justice system have been slower to change, particularly with regard to sexual violence, which is prevalent in the region, but still woefully under-reported. Another more sinister phenomenon that emerged in the last decade of the 20th century was that of a series of multiple murders of women. The murders began in Ciudad Juárez in Mexico in 1993 and spread to Guatemala, where 2,200 women were killed in 2000–05. In the latter year alone 624 women were murdered. Only 9% of the homicides have reportedly been investigated by the police and only one murderer has been convicted. In 2009 the Inter-American Court of Human Rights held the Mexican state responsible for failure to protect its female citizens and properly to investigate the killings.

Such high levels of 'femicidal' and social violence are linked in Central America to the drugs trade, to the guns and violent masculinity left over from the civil wars of the 1980s and to the boom in gang culture and (semi-)organized crime. In the case of El Salvador, the gangs were a US import, as the US authorities decided to deport the children of Salvador refugees and migrants who had been involved with Hispanic gangs in Los Angeles, California. In Nicaragua, gangs were formed in the social crisis that followed the end of Sandinista rule in 1990. In 2006 it was estimated that there were around 70,000–100,000 gang members in the isthmus, young men with few prospects in search of an identity, an assertion of their masculinity, or income from drugs and criminal activity. However, gang membership came at a high price: Latin America had a homicide rate twice the world average and violence was the leading cause of death for young men from poor neighbourhoods aged between 15 and 24 years. In 2000 men were 13 times more likely than women to be murdered in Colombia, 13 times in El Salvador and 16 times in Venezuela. Some countries have attempted to address the problem through gun amnesties and control, and diversion strategies, but many gang members still enter the juvenile justice system or prison, if they survive. In El Salvador the incarceration rate has soared to 176 per 100,000 population owing to the criminalization of the *maras* (gangs). For their families and communities, the rise in social, criminal and gang violence has shattered the social fabric and greatly increased collective insecurity. In Mexico competition between rival cartels seeking to control cocaine transshipments through the cities bordering the USA has resulted in extreme levels of violence: nine out of 10 drug-related killings are of young men aged between 18 and 32 years, often carried out with grisly brutality. Such is the vulnerability of boys in the Brazilian city of Rio de Janeiro, for example, to forced recruitment by local drugs-traffickers that they have been classified as 'child soldiers', and thus as victims, rather than as perpetrators.

One intriguing 'exit strategy' for both men and women in low-income neighbourhoods rife with violence has been to join the new evangelical churches in the region. These offered not only the possibility of conversion and 'rebirth', but also an alternative version of 'respectable' masculinity that allowed young men to reject more destructive types of masculinity prevalent in their peer group. It appeared that women convert first to Pentecostalism and then recruit their menfolk. In exchange for accepting the man as the head of household, women gain a reduction in conflict in the home and greater disposable income, as less money is spent on male status activity such as drinking. Men have also increasingly been recruited into anti-violence activities, often 'self-help' and therapeutic groups that examine their own vulnerability to male-on-male violence as well as their complicity with violence against women and children. A number of projects seek explicitly to divert young men from violence and crime through sport, occupational training and education.

EDUCATION, EMPLOYMENT AND INCOME STRATEGIES

Changes in household composition, demographics and labour market opportunities owing to the impacts of globalization have affected men and women differently. Whereas the male economically active population (EAP) has remained static at around 72% over the last three decades, the female EAP has increased to over 40%, rising to well in excess of 60% among those aged 25–59 years. However, women's participation rate in paid employment varies, with the lowest rates in Chile, Mexico and Central America. Some 33m. women joined the labour market between 1990 and 2004, with much of the growth occurring in the service sector, in which women were already strongly represented. Over 15% of women worked in domestic service during this period and this was increasing as more middle-class women entered the labour market. Female employment has been increased by improved education, urban growth, declining fertility rates and changing social attitudes, although Chile, where all these factors of modernization are present, but where female employment, particularly in the poorer sectors, remains low, provides an exception to this rule. The level of female-headed households has continued to rise, varying between 19% and 31%, and many women are the sole wage earner. This shift was largely precipitated by the economic pressures of the 1980s and 1990s, as structural adjustment policies affected traditional areas of male employment, and reduced per caput income. Privatization of public services and new patterns of consumption also increased the dependence of households on multiple incomes. However, the female unemployment rate was higher than the equivalent rate for men in the region. Women also tended to be employed in the most poorly paid jobs in the informal sector, and the income disparity between men and women stood at 70%, the highest rate world-wide. This gender gap is apparently resistant to women's educational qualifications. In Latin America as a whole, women outnumber men in secondary and tertiary education, although this is qualified by both social class and ethnic origins.

Globalization has produced a number of changes in male and female employment patterns. Structural adjustment and market opening caused an increase in urban, male, manufacturing-related unemployment as both men and women were pushed into the informal sector. Women managed to find jobs in new areas, such as the export-processing zones that opened up in Central America, Mexico and the Caribbean. Although this was initially because employers offered them lower wages, and expected them to have lower levels of unionization, in some cases women successfully campaigned for better working conditions. Some economies, such as the Chilean fruit-exporting sector, preferred to employ women for seasonal agricultural work for similar reasons. However, despite women's increased access to informal sector, seasonal, service and certain manufacturing jobs, they remained vulnerable, owing to their lack of social protection. A number of countries have been extending their social security systems to cover the most vulnerable in society, typically rural workers, the urban informal sector, and women who have worked as domestics or within their own homes. More recent land reform processes, for example in Brazil, have also been more gender-sensitive, awarding joint land titles to couples, whether married or not, and giving women access to agricultural loans.

Women were also increasingly migrating through the region, to the USA and to Europe, in search of better jobs. Latin America was the first region to have equal numbers of men and women emigrating. Many migrant women ended up in domestic service, such as the Salvadoreans who moved to the USA during the civil war in the 1980s and many of the Peruvian migrants in Chile. By the early 21st century, migration constituted a household survival strategy, as many who leave are heads of household. Remittances earned by women can therefore form a substantial part of national economies. However, migration also has its darker side, and migration to work in the sex industry overseas and the trafficking of women from Latin America was also increasing. An estimated 50,000 women from the Dominican Republic and 75,000 from Brazil were working as prostitutes in Europe. Brazil was a major country of origin for trafficked women and children.

In recognition of the vulnerability of poor families to falling wages and unemployment, several countries, notably Brazil, Mexico, Honduras, Nicaragua, Colombia, Ecuador, El Salvador and Chile, have introduced 'conditional cash transfers', essentially monthly grants made to low-income families as long as they take responsibility for human capital formation in their family, such as ensuring that their children attend school and are vaccinated, or attending re-training or literacy classes themselves. By 2009 the Brazilian scheme, the *bolsa família*, was assisting 11m. families. In virtually all cases, the grants are paid direct to the mother, regardless of whether or not she is head of the household, thus constituting an unprecedented transfer of economic resources to impoverished women, resulting in an increase in family income, child welfare and women's empowerment. Women in receipt of the Mexican Progresa/ Oportunidades grants, which reaches 4m. families, were far more likely to use contraceptives than women outside the scheme. Similarly, micro-credit projects such as Banco de Desarrollo de la Mujer (BANMUJER—Women's Development Bank), set up in Venezuela in 2001, also offer women more economic autonomy. However, some argue that this makes women responsible for 'administering poverty' and neglects low-income un- or under-employed men, which brings its own longer-term social consequences.

CONCLUSION: THE MYTH OF MACHISMO?

Social attitudes and gender relations have changed a great deal in Latin America during the last two decades, with improved representation and participation of women in decision-making, legal protection of equality between the sexes, equal access to education and labour force participation, and ongoing debates concerning issues such as sexuality and reproduction. The monolithic conception of Latin American machismo has been challenged, with men's social roles, differential levels of power and vulnerabilities now more subtly understood. Patriarchal attitudes and ideas of hegemonic masculinity have been challenged more notably in the southern cone, whereas conservative attitudes and high levels of gender-based violence are still more entrenched in Mexico and Central America, owing both to the characteristics of the respective social structures therein, and to more recent pressures such as civil wars and the deluge of drugs-related violence. These pressures have had the effect of relegitimizing certain forms of violent masculinity and have rendered women more vulnerable to sexual and domestic assault, as well as leaving young men prey to gang and drug culture. One of the greatest pending challenges is to reform the criminal justice system in order to increase human security for both men and women, together with their families.

TRADE PREFERENCES IN THE CARIBBEAN

MARK WILSON

After 44 months of negotiations and 10 months of further delay, an Economic Partnership Agreement (EPA) between the European Union (EU) and the Caribbean Forum (CARIFORUM) grouping of Caribbean states[1] was signed on 15 October 2008 in Barbados. This was seen as a breakthrough by the EU, as it was the only one of six proposed regional agreements with groups of former African, Caribbean and Pacific colonies (the ACP countries) to be negotiated and initialled (on 16 December 2007) by the target date of 31 December 2007. The initialling and signature followed a long series of negotiations. After preparatory work running from 2002, the first round of talks began in Jamaica in April 2004, with the aim of reaching agreement on priorities for support of Caribbean integration and negotiating targets by September 2005, and a draft partnership agreement in 2006. Other proposed EPAs, with four regional groups of African countries and with the Pacific island states, were at varying but less advanced stages of negotiation in mid-2010, with most non-Caribbean ACP countries covered by interim agreements.

Some of the delays between initialling and signature were unavoidable. On the EU side, it took several months for the agreement to be adopted by the EU General Council, and for all the necessary legal checks to be completed. Time was also required to translate the agreement into the 23 EU official languages. The 404-page text of the agreement with its additional annexes was made public only on 21 March 2008. Signing of the document was originally scheduled for April and was subsequently cancelled and rescheduled at least four times.

Also contributing to the delays were concerns over the proposed agreement, voiced in particular by Guyanese President Bharrat Jagdeo at a meeting of Caribbean Community and Common Market (CARICOM) Heads of Government on 1–4 July 2008 in Antigua. His views reflected a body of opinion both within the Caribbean and beyond, which raised concerns during the EPA negotiations and argued that after the initialling of the agreement it should be renegotiated. Meanwhile, EU sources and other Caribbean Governments pressed for the agreement to be signed in its existing form.

On the face of it, the Caribbean would appear to have gained much from the agreement, while its direct benefits for the EU were modest. The EU's December 2007 target date for completion of EPA negotiations was not an arbitrary one. A new agreement was needed to replace the trade component of the Cotonou Agreement, negotiated in 2000 between the EU and 78 former colonies in Africa, the Caribbean and the Pacific. This gave most African, Caribbean and Pacific exports duty-free access to the EU, and made special provision for traditional agricultural exports such as sugar, bananas, rice and rum.

Under World Trade Organization (WTO) rules, trade agreements must either be reciprocal, or must be extended to all developing countries, including large and rapidly growing economies such as China and India. The trade elements of the Cotonou Agreement were non-reciprocal, and in addition extended only to the 78 members of the ACP group. They were allowed by the WTO only under a special waiver negotiated with some difficulty in 2001, which expired at the end of 2007. Without a WTO waiver or a new agreement, the EU would have been obliged to deal with Caribbean imports under the much less generous Generalised System of Preferences, ending special arrangements for traditional agricultural exports and imposing tariffs on many goods. Importers of Jamaican goods, for example, would have had to pay tariffs to the annual value of US $70m. on exports of sugar, rum, bananas and alumina. The 'Everything but Arms' initiative, announced in February 2001, gives duty-free and quota-free access to 49 of the world's poorest countries, but in the Caribbean extends only to Haiti, as other CARIFORUM members have middle-income economies.

The EPA has been structured to fall just within the agreed international criteria for reciprocal trade agreements, but makes significant concessions to the view that continuing protection is needed for the small and vulnerable economies of the Caribbean. Caribbean exports to Europe (other than sugar and rice, for which there are special arrangements during transition periods which are outlined below) were duty-free from the start of 2008, while duties on most goods exported from Europe to the Caribbean are to be phased out over an extended 25-year period—a much longer time frame than in other comparable agreements. The CARIFORUM countries are to reduce tariffs on 52.8% of imports from the EU from the start of 2011; most of these goods were already zero-rated or subject only to nuisance tariffs. The proportion is expected to rise to 56% in 2013, and then in stages to 86.9% by 2033. However, even within these limits, tariffs may be reinstated to protect 'infant industries'. The Caribbean is also to retain protective trade barriers on a permanent basis for sensitive products currently making up 13.1% of imports from Europe, including some agricultural commodities and processed foods. Tariffs such as those on wines and spirits whose main purpose was to raise revenue will also remain permanently in place. The Caribbean retains the right to maintain other taxes on imports such as customs user fees, excise taxes, stamp duties and environmental levies for up to 10 years. For those agricultural imports on which duty is to be removed, the EU is to phase out subsidies for its own domestic producers.

The 2008 EPA also provided for liberalization of trade in services for most CARICOM members, with Haiti and the Bahamas negotiating separate services agreements in 2009 and 2010. The EU has agreed to open 94% of listed service sectors to Caribbean competition. The larger CARICOM economies have agreed to allow European operators access to 75% of their service sectors, while the smaller economies are committed to 65%. Many of the service sectors opened for competition by Caribbean states were already open in practice to outside participation, or are areas in which Caribbean companies are not active, and are not likely to operate in the future. There is no provision for opening Caribbean health, education, water supply and other public services to international competition, although naturally governments may decide to open up these sectors if they choose, for example by inviting outside contractors to manage water services. Neither side has opened up audio-visual services, internal transport, air transport and related services, the arms trade, or mining and the processing of nuclear materials.

All EU member states will now allow free access for 29 categories of professional and supply services for up to six months, subject to visa requirements. Entertainment services received significant attention during the negotiations. Of the 27 EU member states, 25 agreed to free access for providers of entertainment services from the Caribbean (the exceptions were Austria and Germany, which will allow only authors and dance instructors). Coproduced audio-visual products and services involving European and Caribbean creative teams will qualify as European works.

For tourism, financial services, computing, telecommunications and courier services, the EU will provide assistance to develop capacity and training, sectoral standards, regulatory regimes, and mutual skills recognition for professions such as accountancy or engineering. There will be continuing dialogue on the regulation of e-commerce.

The EPA text draws a link to the fundamental principles of the Cotonou Agreement. Its stated aims include poverty reduction through trade partnership, regional integration, economic co-operation, good governance, and greater integration of the Caribbean within the world economy.

The areas of concern, known within the WTO since 1996 as the 'Singapore Issues', covering investment, competition policy, transparency in government procurement and trade facilitation, have been covered in the EPA, but in a generalized fashion with very few specific commitments. There were also provisions intended to deal with anti-competitive business practices, and an agreement in principle to pass legislation to prevent abuse of market power and dominance. If this proposal were followed through by CARIFORUM states, among the companies affected would be European-owned companies such as Cable & Wireless, whose affiliates still retain a dominant position in some Caribbean telecommunications markets.

The EU and the large Caribbean states would implement intellectual property commitments, for example under the WTO Trade-related Aspects of Intellectual Property Rights agreement; however, the smaller Caribbean countries would not have to apply the EPA's intellectual property provisions. There is no provision for market access in public procurement contracts, although there are some provisions to encourage transparency where access is allowed. The EPA does not rule out measures by the EU or Caribbean partners to prevent tax evasion, or to protect public morals, public security or human, plant and animal health. However, there are specific measures to assist Caribbean exporters in meeting health requirements for agricultural exports.

When the EPA was signed in 2008, the negotiation process for trade in services was still not complete. The Bahamas and Haiti were initially expected to finalize an agreement on trade in services during the six months following signature of the EPA, a period which ran to April 2009, and expired without an agreement. The Bahamas was seen as a special case because of its economic dependence on tourism, international finance and other services, as was Haiti because of the weak overall state of its economy. Haiti signed the EPA on 10 December 2009, with some adjustments to its initial tariff commitments, but had not ratified by mid-2010, in part because of the disruption caused by the January 2010 earthquake. An initial offer on trade in services made in April 2009 by the Bahamas, where protectionist sentiment runs strong, was very limited, preserving major sectors such as retailing, construction of buildings with fewer than 250 rooms, legal and real estate services. However, a services and investment agreement was initialled on 27 January 2010, and covered telecommunications, transport, financial services and tourism.

In addition to the agreements on trade in goods and services, the EU will provide development support for regional integration and for increased competitiveness, to be channelled through the proposed Regional Development Fund of the Caribbean Community. There will also be development assistance for infrastructural development, export marketing, quality standards, and other areas of activity. However, most EU aid programmes remain as structured by the Cotonou Agreement, which runs to 2020; the 10th European Development Fund package, which falls under Cotonou, provides for €23,000m. in development assistance to the ACP countries over seven years from 2007. This includes €165m. of regional assistance to the Caribbean, of which €33m. is specifically linked to the EPA.

The EPA also promotes free trade within the CARIFORUM group, between CARICOM and the Dominican Republic. Duty-free provision for imports from Europe will apply immediately within CARIFORUM, while other market access arrangements for Europe will be extended to CARIFORUM within one year for the larger CARICOM members, and two years for the smaller members, but not for at least five years for Haiti, by far the poorest country in the region and an immediate neighbour of the Dominican Republic. The agreement also provides for any preferential treatment extended by the EU or by CARIFORUM countries to other states and groupings outside Europe and the Caribbean to be extended also to the EPA signatories. The Dominican Republic resubmitted an earlier application for membership of CARICOM in May 2009.

The institutional framework established to oversee the operation of the EPA is similar to the structure covering the Cotonou Agreement. A ministerial CARIFORUM-EU Council will meet at least every two years; between its meetings there is a Trade and Development Committee. There is also a Parliamentary Committee, and a Consultative Committee to engage civil society in the implementation process. The joint ministerial council held its first meeting on 17 May 2010, and took procedural steps to further the full implementation of the EPA. Problems to be addressed include disagreements and continuing trade barriers between the CARICOM members and the Dominican Republic.

ARGUMENTS FOR AND AGAINST THE EPA

In January 2008 the CARICOM Council for Trade and Economic Development (COTED) initiated an independent review of the agreement. A 'Reflections Group' of national, CARICOM and Organisation of Eastern Caribbean States (OECS) officials, with representatives of the Regional Negotiating Machinery and other stakeholders, reported to COTED in February.

In a wide range of trade negotiations over the past decades, Caribbean countries have emphasized the need for special and differential treatment for small states, with continuing one-way trade privileges and protection for domestic industries over an extended period. The security afforded by tariffs and barriers to entry for small and medium-scale manufacturers and service providers of varying efficiency is emphasized by the exclusion of the benefits to consumers and businesses of access to more competitive markets with a wider choice of prices, product type and quality.

Opposition to the EPA has been voiced by several Caribbean academics and trade unionists, drawn in some cases from the post-independence generation, which saw development in terms of a free-standing economy with a growing manufacturing sector and only limited use of goods and services from overseas. There were concerns that the very limited provisions in the agreement for investment, competition policy, government procurement and intellectual property rights went beyond existing WTO commitments. The more alarmist commentators, such as the Trinidadian trade unionist David Abdullah, suggested that the EPA would wipe out Caribbean food production and lead to the total collapse of several Caribbean economies. In the Bahamas, there has been widespread opposition from lobby groups to the principle of free trade in goods and services, although in an unusual display of bipartisanship both main parties supported the signature of the agreement in October 2008. There have also been forceful criticisms from non-governmental organizations and charities, such as Oxfam International.

The most significant opposition to the agreement came from Guyanese President Jagdeo, who said in June 2008 that signature could be delayed for some years without adverse consequences, complaining of the potential loss of customs revenue and of price guarantees for sugar exports. He argued that the EU had acted in bad faith, had conducted unfair negotiations, in which it held all the trump cards, and had imposed an unreasonable deadline; he also argued that the agreement would lead to a loss of economic sovereignty, and as late as September proposed scrapping the EPA in favour of an agreement covering only the trade in goods. There was also opposition to the agreement from influential regional figures of Guyanese origin, such as the former Commonwealth Secretary-General, Sir Shridath Ramphal, and Sir Ronald Sanders, who is now an Antiguan citizen and served as a diplomat for that country. The Guyanese stance was supported by Saint Lucia, which stated on 19 August that it would not sign, and by opposition parties in several islands. In the event, Saint Lucia signed along with its CARIFORUM partners on 15 October, and Guyana separately in Brussels on 20 October. Guyanese brinkmanship secured only a commitment from the EU for a five-yearly review of the EPA and for implementation to pay regard to CARICOM integration processes. A call by Guyana for a delay in implementation of the EPA received a favourable vote from the EU-ACP Joint Parliamentary Assembly on 26 February 2009, but appeared unlikely to produce material changes to the schedule. However, in keeping with Guyana's wishes, CARICOM agreed in April to disband its Caribbean Regional Negotiating Machinery, which had co-ordinated regional positions in talks leading to the EPA, and to adopt other mechanisms for future trade negotiations, including those currently under way with Canada.

One area of concern for Guyana was proposals (outlined below) to reduce the EU's general duty on rice imports from €65 per metric ton. At a time of sharply increasing international rice prices, this promised significant benefit to European consumers. It would reduce the value to Guyana of the increased rice quota and duty-free exports granted by the EPA, although it should be noted that under the 'Everything but Arms' initiative, rice from countries such as Viet Nam and Bangladesh already enjoyed duty-free access to the EU. Guyana and Suriname are the only rice exporters in the Caribbean. In contrast to Suriname, Guyana is not a banana exporter, and would therefore not be threatened by a Latin American challenge to the EU's banana regime.

Although opposition to the agreement has been widely expressed, the view that the EPA does not go far enough in liberalizing trade and economic relations has been less frequently argued. Tariffs on most imported goods do not protect local industries in the Caribbean, because there are no significant local producers to protect; this would apply to motor vehicles, consumer electronics, textiles and a wide range of foods, drinks, consumer and capital goods.

Tariffs are an important source of revenue for regional governments, particularly those that have no significant income or corporate taxation. In the Bahamas, for example, one-half of government revenue is raised from taxes on imports. But arguably, even in the absence of income tax, a sales tax or value-added tax could efficiently and equitably replace customs duties. Tariffs also raise domestic consumer prices. Indeed, in the early months of 2008 most Caribbean Governments removed duties on many foods and agricultural products to slow the rate of inflation. These included some items for which permanent protection had been carefully negotiated under the EPA. Among the goods for which tariffs will be permanently retained are inputs which form an important cost component for the hotel, restaurant and tourism industries, including furniture, structural steel, linen, wines and spirits. It can also be argued that tighter rules on transparency, public procurement and competition policy would assist in the economic, social and political development of the region, and should not be rejected as a foreign imposition.

TRADITIONAL AGRICULTURAL EXPORTS

The signature of the EPA followed an extended period during which the special arrangements made for former Caribbean colonies as exporters of traditional agricultural products—principally bananas, sugar, rice and rum—had been eroded. The remaining market privileges are scheduled, in most cases, to disappear altogether within a few years. At the same time, the small states of the Caribbean have been concerned about more general trade liberalization initiatives—principally the WTO agreements.

The new EPA has replaced the trade chapters of the 20-year Cotonou Agreement, signed in Benin in June 2000 by heads of state and government from ACP countries and EU members. The Cotonou Agreement, in turn, followed a succession of five-year Lomé Conventions, the first of which came into force on 1 April 1976. These linked Europe's former ACP colonies with the European Community and its successor, the EU. Each convention combined an aid package, export earnings stabilization schemes, special market access arrangements for most traditional exports, and one-way duty-free status for most ACP manufactured exports to Europe. In contrast to earlier agreements, however, the new EPAs will not cover the full ACP grouping, but will be separately negotiated for regions such as the Caribbean or West Africa.

In some respects, the former trading arrangements were a success. Traditional agricultural producers lived in a fairly secure world. Small farmers could grow bananas, rice and, in some cases, sugar cane, sure of a steady export market, and usually a predictable price. The same was true for private and state-owned companies producing sugar and rum. However, the cost of production remained high, while there was much less success in stimulating non-traditional exports. Indeed, the proportion of EU imports originating in the wider ACP group crept steadily down, from 6.7% in 1976 to only 3.0% in 2000; the EU imported goods to the value of €40,000m. from the ACP grouping in 2006, but €70,000m. from Switzerland. Four commodities—oil, diamonds, cocoa and timber—made up more than 50% of ACP exports to the EU. Producers of traditional commodities in the Caribbean are a diverse group. Most attention has been given internationally to small farmers, a vulnerable group whose problems have direct implications not only for the economy but for social and political stability. These farmers were the traditional mainstay of the banana industry in the Windward Islands (Dominica, Grenada, Saint Lucia and Saint Vincent and the Grenadines), and they also produced a significant proportion of rice in Guyana and Suriname, and of sugar cane grown in certain countries, such as Belize. A second broad group are the larger private sector players; these assumed a major role, for example, in Jamaica's sugar and banana industries, as well as in rice-growing and -processing. These are rural employers of great local importance. Rum distillers such as Demerara Distillers in Guyana, Angostura Ltd in Trinidad and Tobago or J. Wray and Nephew in Jamaica are more closely integrated in their countries' corporate sector, where in some cases they play a leading role (the last two linked to a regional conglomerate, CL Financial, which was in severe financial difficulty in 2009). A third group of commodity producers are the large state-owned companies, which in some cases originated with the nationalization of foreign-owned sugar estates following independence. These include the Guyana Sugar Corporation (Guysuco), and, with rather different origins, the Surinamese former banana producer Surland, now restructured and marked for privatization as the Stichting Behoud Bananensector Suriname (SBBS).

Although Caribbean governments are rightly keen to defend the interests of their traditional agricultural producers, the role of this sector in most regional economies declined steadily in importance during the second half of the 20th century. By the early 21st century the main source of foreign exchange on most Caribbean islands was tourism. There are exceptions: in Trinidad and Tobago the energy sector is the driving force of the economy; in Jamaica and Suriname, and to a lesser extent in Guyana, bauxite plays a major role. Of €8,400m. in Caribbean exports to the EU in 2008, oil, natural gas and steel from Trinidad and Tobago accounted for 47% and refractory grade bauxite from Guyana for 10%. However, traditional agriculture remains of great importance in many countries as a source of employment, and has until now underpinned the social and economic stability of large parts of the rural Caribbean.

Bananas

Of the traditional agricultural sectors, banana cultivation has, until recently, played the most important social and economic role, and its problems have therefore attracted the most international attention. In the Windward Islands the colonial authorities fostered banana growing in the 1950s as a response to the demise of the sugar industry on some islands and owing to the difficulties faced by some other commercial crops. Small farmers, many with holdings of less than half a hectare, sold fruit to island-wide growers' associations, which in turn supplied Geest Bananas Ltd, a British company that shipped the produce to the United Kingdom. In contrast to most tropical crops, bananas provide a year-round cash income, as harvesting is continuous. In contrast to tree crops, the time-lag from planting to harvest is measured in months, not years. Additionally, production is possible in a wide variety of conditions, allowing even farmers with marginal land to participate in the industry, albeit at low yields. This pattern of very small farms was not universal, however. Most banana farms in Belize measure 40–200 ha, while in Jamaica the role of small farmers was supplemented by a few large commercial estates. In Suriname a state-owned company, the former Surland (and now SBBS), has been the only banana exporter.

Dependence on the banana industry was greatest in the small economies of the Windward Islands, and in particular in Dominica, an island with only 71,612 people in 2008 and a per-head income among the lowest in the English-speaking Caribbean. In 1992 bananas comprised some 55% of merchandise exports, and in 1990 some 30% of all foreign exchange earnings, exceeding tourism. More importantly, most rural households were in some way directly involved with the banana industry. Together, the 10,000 small producers in the Windward Islands in 1992 supplied 45% of the British banana market. In Jamaica, with a similar total production, the economic importance of the crop was much smaller, at 3.8% of merchandise exports in 1992 and 1.7% of foreign exchange earnings in the same year.

Until 1993 the British market was preserved for the Caribbean banana exporters,[2] with a small quantity of so-called 'dollar bananas'[3] from Latin America permitted only when supplies fell short. With the single European market in operation from 1992, this system could no longer operate. To protect the interests of the traditional producers, a complex system of licences, tariffs and quotas was developed. The USA, as well as several Latin American banana producers, used the machinery of the WTO to challenge this new EU banana import regime; in 1997 they obtained a ruling broadly in their favour, which held that there should be changes in the quota and licence system. The EU moved to a tariff for non-ACP bananas, with a duty-free quota for ACP producers; this in turn was challenged and was, in April 1999, found to violate WTO rules. After a brief 'trade war', in which the USA imposed punitive tariffs on selected European imports, a new licensing system was agreed. This was to run from 2001, with a transition to a tariff-only system from 2006, which until 2008 would incorporate residual privileges for ACP producers. This new regime necessitated a WTO waiver, which was forthcoming in November 2001.

In a free market situation, the price of South and Central American bananas in the United Kingdom is around 30% below that of Windward Islands fruit. This is in part because of greater economies of scale on the very large estates that operate there, and in part because agricultural wages are much lower; in Ecuador, the country holding the largest share of the EU market, salaries are around one-quarter of the levels prevailing in the Eastern Caribbean. There is also a quality issue, although it should be made clear that importers and supermarkets use this word in a rather specialized sense, to denote a bright colour, uniform size and unblemished skin, rather than taste.

The various EU import regimes in force since 1992 were designed to protect the interests of Caribbean and other traditional producers, but succeeded only to a limited extent. At times, for example in 1998–2000, illegally imported fruit, in excess of quotas, flooded the European market (so-called 'banana-laundering'). Partly because of the limited success of these import regimes, and partly because of the underlying imbalance between demand and supply, prices have moved unevenly downwards, creating uncertainty for the growers and leading to many abandoning the industry. Exports have declined across the region. In Dominica, for example, the value of banana exports in 2006 was US $6.0m., compared with $30.1m. in 1992, falling further to $3.6m. in 2007 as a result of Hurricane Dean. In Jamaica, banana exports fell from $39.5m. in 1992 to just $12.8m. in 2004, reaching an exceptional low of $4.7m. in 2005, following crop damage from Hurricane Ivan in the previous year. Although exports recovered to $13.4m. in 2006, they were down to $9.2m. in 2007 following Hurricane Dean, and came to a halt in 2008 after further damage resulting from Tropical Storm Gustav.

There has been substantial EU assistance to Caribbean banana producers. Part has been from payments under the former Stabilization of Export Earnings (Stabex) scheme, triggered by decreasing banana earnings and totalling €200.9m. for the Windward Islands alone for the crop years 1995–99, with an additional €189.0m. from a Special Programme of Assistance for the banana industry.

Banana growers in the Windward Islands increased their share of the final supermarket price by moving into international transport, ripening and distribution. The West Indies Banana Development Company (Wibdeco)—owned jointly by four island governments and banana growers' associations—in 1996 entered into a joint venture with an Irish company, Fyffes Group, to buy the shipper and distributor Geest Bananas Ltd; the purchase was financed with loans totalling £20m. from the Allied Irish Bank. Direct sales contracts were negotiated with British supermarkets.

In late 2004 and in 2005 interest focused on the tariff structure to be adopted when quotas were finally phased out at the beginning of 2006. The EU proposed a tariff of €230 per metric ton for Latin American and other non-traditional producers. CARICOM continued to lobby for a tariff of €275 per ton. Latin American producers argued for a much lower tariff of €70 per ton, claiming that a higher rate would cost them some of their existing market share, which was 63% in the former 15-member EU and close to 100% in the 10 new member states. On 30 March Honduras, Colombia, Costa Rica, Panama and Guatemala referred the issue to the WTO for arbitration, and obtained a ruling in their favour on 1 August. On 12 September the EU made a revised proposal of €187 per ton, and a further round of arbitration was initiated on 26 September, with the new EU proposal also rejected, this time on 27 October.

The 2006 deadline was therefore reached with no clarity on the future nature of the EU import regime. At the same time, Suriname and Belize suffered from the operation of the quota system. Quotas were issued to companies, rather than to nations. This benefited the Windward Islands and Jamaican producers, which owned their own export and marketing companies. However, the two other Caribbean producers were forced to buy unused quotas from other suppliers. Quotas were in short supply in 2005: for Suriname, the cost of buying quotas tripled to €9m., and at the end of the year they were not available at any price, forcing SBBS to dump quantities of unsaleable fruit. From 1 March 2006 the EU initiated a new regime without formal international agreement. The tariff was €176 per metric ton, a figure to which Latin American producers remain opposed, and was challenged within the WTO by Ecuador in November 2006 and by Colombia in March 2007. Against earlier expectations, a duty-free quota of 775,000 tons was retained for ACP producers, but with modifications that would benefit Suriname and Belize: 60% of quotas were allocated on a 'first come first served' basis, with only 40% on the former historic supplier system. This system was retained with modifications for 2007.

There have been efforts to increase earnings by exploiting niche markets. There is a premium price for smaller fruit, which is now packaged and sold separately. Most Windwards fruit meets employment and environmental 'Fair Trade' standards, and is sold with a 'social premium', which is paid to community groups for infrastructural or social development projects.

More emphasis has been placed also on the substantial regional market, where CARICOM has a punitive tariff on Latin American bananas. Windwards bananas are exported to Trinidad and Tobago and Barbados. Jamaicans consume an estimated 120,000 metric tons per year. Falling prices and the cost of spraying against Black Sigatoka disease, which arrived in the island only in the 1990s, have driven smaller domestic producers out of business. After suffering heavy damage from 'Hurricane Dean' in 2007 and 'Tropical Storm Gustav' in 2008, the main commercial producer Jamaica Producers' Association abandoned the export market altogether, with some capacity switched to production of snack foods for local and regional markets, and the closure of its large banana estate in St Thomas, in eastern Jamaica, with the loss of 400 jobs.

Restructuring has been most far-reaching in the case of the state-owned Surinamese producer Surland, which closed in April 2002 after sustaining heavy losses and accumulating substantial debts, laying off 2,000 staff. With an €18m. EU assistance programme and US $7.3m. in working capital from the Inter-American Development Bank, the company was then restructured as the SBBS, and a full replanting exercise using tissue culture, new irrigation systems, and cableways for transport of fruit was undertaken. Exports were resumed in March 2004, and privatization of the company was expected, as soon as a finalized EU import regime gives some degree of market certainty. An exercise of this sort is not possible, however, with the large number of relatively small, private sector growers that remain active in the Windward Islands, or even with the somewhat larger farmers active in Belize and Jamaica.

With the EPA initialled in December 2007, Caribbean bananas enjoyed full duty-free and quota-free access to the EU from January 2008. This was of particular benefit to Suriname and Belize, which suffered from the former quota system, but of less use to the OECS producers, which had difficulty in maintaining production volumes and in the past received funds from the sale of unused quotas. There were continuing EU assistance programmes for regional banana industries; J $630m. to assist with recovery from 'Hurricane Dean' and for rural economic diversification in banana growing areas was agreed for Jamaica in January.

In February 2008 the WTO ruled in favour of a US challenge to the pre-EPA banana import regime. This followed a ruling in December 2007 in favour of a challenge by Ecuador. The EU held however, that with a WTO-compatible partnership agreement at that time initialled if not signed, the ruling was only of historic importance.

The EPA commits the EU in principle to maintaining preferential access for Caribbean bananas within the multilateral trading system for as long as possible and to ensure that any unavoidable preference erosion is phased over a long period. However, with continuing challenges to the EU banana regime expected, WTO Director-General Pascal Lamy proposed in July 2008 that Latin American countries and the EU agree to a settlement under which the EU would reduce its tariff on Latin American and other non-traditional banana suppliers from €176 to €114 per metric ton by 2016. The European Commission said immediately that it was ready to accept these proposals. In the event, this proposal lapsed with the failure of broader 'Doha round' WTO negotiations. A further EU proposal in February 2009 to cut tariffs to €136 per ton by 2011 and €114 by 2016 also received an initially negative reception from the CARICOM Council for Trade and Development. An initial offer of further financial assistance for the transition period was seen as inadequate by ACP banana producers. An agreement with Latin American banana producers negotiated in December 2009 and formally signed on 31 May 2010 follows the Lamy proposals, and provides for an immediate tariff cut from €176 per ton to €148 per ton, with further cuts to €114 per ton by 2016. The EU announced a further €190m. in compensatory assistance to ACP banana producers, who had, however, asked for €250m.

Sugar

Sugar was the economic mainstay of most of the Caribbean from the 18th century until the 1950s. In contrast to bananas, the industry was dominated by large estates, with heavy capital investment in factories producing raw sugar from cane. After independence, large estates and sugar factories were in most cases nationalized, as in Guyana, Trinidad and Tobago and Saint Christopher and Nevis,[4] such that the fortunes of the industry became an important component of the public sector financial balance. Loss of trade preferences does not therefore carry quite the same emotional charge as for bananas, but does, nevertheless, have major social and economic implications.

Physical conditions in most of the Caribbean are not ideal for cane production: problems include low rainfall and uneven terrain in Barbados, field layouts unsuited to mechanization in Guyana, and the small scale to which the former industry was constrained in Saint Christopher and Nevis. Productivity is generally low, while wage levels are much higher than in producers such as Brazil, although, of course, lower than in others such as Australia. Factory equipment is, in many cases, antiquated, while Barbados in particular was plagued by a many-layered and costly management structure for what, by international standards, have been small production units. For these and other reasons, costs are extremely high by international standards.

The Caribbean sugar industry, which dominated the world market until the early 19th century, is no longer of great international significance. The CARICOM producers account for close to 1.0% of world sugar exports (or 0.3% of world production). Within most Caribbean economies, sugar is now overshadowed. In Barbados, for example, sugar made up 5% of GDP in 1980, but only 0.8% in 2006, in which year it accounted for only 1.0% of foreign exchange earnings and less than 2% of employment. In Guyana, however, sugar in 2003 still employed 7% of the labour force, and in 2008 produced 16.7% of total exports, and comprised 7.0% of GDP. Even in the economies where sugar has least overall importance, it remains significant as an employer of unskilled rural labour, which would be difficult for other industries to absorb. In Barbados, a tourism-based economy where sugar still dominates the rural landscape, closure of the industry would have far-reaching environmental and visual implications.

The sugar protocol of the Lomé Conventions until 2006 allocated Caribbean producers' export quotas to the EU, at a guaranteed price, which, from 1993 to 2006, remained fixed at €523.70 per metric ton. From the late 1990s until 2004 this was around three times the fluctuating free market price for raw sugar. World sugar prices doubled in 2004–06, to reach an average of 14.8 US cents per pound, and averaged 13.1 US cents per pound in 2008, at which level they were close to €212 per metric ton. This was approximately 47% of the EU's 2009 sugar price. This market has absorbed almost all of CARICOM's sugar exports, and indeed some producers, such as Barbados, have imported lower-cost sugar so as to use their own crop to supply the EU quota.

In June 2005 the EU announced a 39% cumulative cut in sugar prices to €319.50 per metric ton by July 2009; in November 2005 this was modified to 36%, with the first reduction from July 2006, and a final price of €335.17 per ton. The annual cost to the 18 ACP sugar producers was estimated at €300m. from 2010, of which €60m. would be borne by the Caribbean, including €39m. to be lost by Guyana alone. To assist with restructuring, the EU agreed a total of €667.3m. for 2007–10, with a further amount to be agreed for 2010–13. Of the total amount, €295.4m., or 44%, was allocated to the six Caribbean producers, with €84.2m. going to Guyana, €77.5m. for Jamaica, €45.1m. for Belize, €42.3m. for Saint Christopher and Nevis, €41.6m. for Trinidad and Tobago, and €34.7m. for Barbados, subject in all cases to agreement on spending proposals.

With a major reduction in the EU sugar price expected, the highest-cost producers have been forced to reconsider the future of their sugar industries. In 2003 Trinidad and Tobago closed its state-owned sugar company Caroni Ltd. For the 9,200 staff, this closure was cushioned by redundancy payments totalling TT $724m., with an additional TT $300m. pension fund enhancement; with Trinidad's energy sector expanding, most employees have found other work and overall unemployment has continued its downward trend. A successor, the Sugar Manufacturing Company, continued for four years to buy cane from independent farmers, but, with output well below target, it was closed in 2007. The Saint Christopher and Nevis Government announced in December 2004 (two months after a general election) that the sugar industry would be closed on completion of the next annual crop, in mid-2005. With the island's tourism prospering, any negative economic impact has been absorbed. Much of the land is to be used for proposed resorts or golf courses, and the railway formerly used to take cane to the factory has been transformed into a 'scenic ride'.

In June 2008 Jamaica agreed the sale of its five state-owned sugar factories to a Brazilian sugar and ethanol company, Infinity Bio Energy. However, this proposed sale fell through under the impact of the global financial crisis. In June 2009 the Government announced the proposed sale of two of the five factories to local private sector interests with a 50-year lease of the adjacent estates. At this point, the debts of the state-owned sugar company of Jamaica were reported as US $180m. and were growing at $22.5m. a year. Talks were in progress in mid-2010 for the divestment of the remaining three estates, with a commission of enquiry into sugar industry policy appointed in June.

In the two mainland producers, Guyana and Belize, there is a realistic prospect of continuing profitability. Guyana, which was responsible for 52% of CARICOM sugar production in 2008, completed a US $181m. sugar factory in 2009, with a co-generation plant to produce electricity for the public power supply, and planned to add a refinery for further processing of raw sugar, subject to a successful feasibility study and the availability of appropriate financing. Work is in progress to bring an additional 130 sq km of land into cane production. Finance was provided by the People's Republic of China, the World Bank and the Caribbean Development Bank, as well as from retained earnings. This initiative is expected to reduce costs to around US $265 per ton. Proposals are also in place for the modernization of other existing sugar factories in Guyana. Guyana and Belize will enjoy a continuing advantage in the Caribbean market, which charges a Common External Tariff of

40% on sugar and some other agricultural products, and where there is a significant saving in freight costs over extra-regional producers. Local earnings from sugar exports have also been increased through sales of packaged and branded sugar; in 2003 Guysuco launched its Demerara Gold product in selected markets, and in June 2009 signed a $12m. agreement to increase packaged production from 8,000 to 40,000 metric tons. There has also been a pilot project to produce organic sugar.

In the year ending July 2008 CARICOM produced 510,500 metric tons of sugar. Exports totalled 470,000 tons, of which 91% went to the EU. Under the EPA, the guaranteed price for sugar will be rapidly phased out. The EU renounced its sugar protocol in September 2007, in advance of the final EPA. This effectively ends the protocol with effect from October 2009. Sugar exports to the EU were priced at €497 per ton until October 2008, and then at €434 for the remaining year of the protocol. During the transition period, there was some benefit from an increase in sugar quotas of 60,000 tons, of which 30,000 tons was allocated to the Dominican Republic, and the remainder to CARICOM producers. From October 2009 until 2012, importers will pay a reference price, which will be at least 90% of the price used for domestic EU producers; Caribbean producers complained that in 2009, with world prices at a 28-year high, this made the EU less lucrative than other potential export markets, while EU prices were affected in 2010 by the fall in the value of the euro against the US dollar, to which Caribbean currencies are linked. There will be no quotas or duties, but until September 2015 there will be a safeguard clause allowing the EU to reimpose duties if sugar imports from the ACP countries exceed 3.5m. tons. There will be free access to the EU from October 2015.

Rice

Suriname and Guyana are the only ACP countries that export rice to Europe. They are small producers by international standards, with exports in 2009 totalling 261,000 tons from Guyana and approximately 40,000 tons from Suriname. However, rice has been a mainstay of both countries' agricultural sectors, and has provided a livelihood for several thousand small farmers, as well as for a smaller number of large agriculturalists, millers and processors.

Following a deep decline in the national economy in the 1980s, the Guyanese rice industry in particular prospered in the 1990s, with improved plant varieties and technology, better irrigation, duty-free concessions for inputs, a more favourable pricing system, and privatization of state-owned rice mills. Production peaked in 1999; since then, however, a changing economic environment has brought problems.

Until 1997 Caribbean and other ACP rice could be exported duty- and quota-free to Europe if it was processed in one of the EU's overseas countries and territories. In the Caribbean there were rice mills in Curaçao (part of the Netherlands Antilles), Saint Vincent and Montserrat, none of which grow rice. From 1997 this route into the EU market was limited to 35,000 tons. An additional quota of 145,000 tons for direct exports to the EU was subject to a tariff, and to regulations on timing and security deposits, which made it difficult for local exports to exploit the quota's full potential benefit. To compound these problems, local weather patterns were disrupted by a drought brought about by El Niño (a periodic warming of the tropical Pacific Ocean) and then by flooding caused by the reverse phenomenon, La Niña. There was also a decline in world prices. The export price of Surinamese rice fell by 40% from 1997 to 2001. According to local industry sources, prices were by the end of this period one-third below production costs.

During the rice boom Guyanese millers and farmers had borrowed extensively from local banks, while Surinamese farmers were forced to borrow owing to their country's severe macroeconomic difficulties. Lower prices after the late 1990s left many producers in both Suriname and Guyana unable to service their debts. This was a problem not only for the rice industry, but also for those countries' financial sectors. In Guyana total rice industry debt had, by 2001, reached $ G12,000m. in principal with $ G4,600m. in accumulated interest, owed by 1,380 farmers, and necessitating $ G6,000m. in loan loss provision by commercial banks.

By 2005 world rice prices had recovered, rising by 75% in 2001–06. In February 2002 the Guyanese Government brokered a debt-forgiveness scheme, writing off accumulated interest and 25% of principal owed for debts of less than $ G10m., with repayment of the remaining amount rescheduled over 10 years. There has also been some assistance from the EU, in the shape of a €24m. aid package for Caribbean rice, agreed in 2003. Of this aid, €11.7m. was allocated to Guyana and €9.3m. to Suriname for appropriate credit facilities, market and product research, institution and capacity-building, research and development, as well as drainage and irrigation support for the low-lying coastal farmlands of both countries. These funds, while useful, fell far short of meeting the full restructuring needs of the rice industry. In Guyana a debt relief programme for small farmers was agreed in principle in February 2002, although implementation was not immediate. However, a long-term strategy was needed to resolve the long-term problems of the industry.

An alternative to the EU market is that of CARICOM, with imports of over 170,000 tons per year. Guyana supplies almost one-half of this market, and also exports rice to Suriname. However, the tariff on extra-regional imports, at 25%, is lower than for sugar, while islands such as Jamaica have in some years imported substantial quantities of subsidized US rice.

International rice prices doubled in 2008 (falling back to some extent in 2009), to the benefit of Guyana and Suriname. Rice exporters also benefited from the EPA, as the 2007 quota of 145,000 tons for rice exports was be increased to 187,000 tons for 2008 and 250,000 tons for 2009, with duty- and quota-free access to the EU from January 2010. However, rice producers were concerned at prospects within the WTO trade negotiations of reducing the tariff on rice from €65 per ton. After lobbying by Guyana, the ACP Council of Ministers recommended in June 2008 that rice should be treated as a 'preference related product', rather than a 'tropical product', conferring special treatment for an extended period. This proposal remained the subject of intense negotiations in mid-2010. Difficulties included the importance of rice as a commodity to several major developing countries. However, the WTO talks failed to reach an overall conclusion, and the former rice tariff remained in place for a transition period still to be determined.

Rum

Rum is, of course, not directly an agricultural product, but is intimately linked in its history and development to the sugar industry. Most Caribbean countries make rum, including several that no longer have a sugar industry and use imported molasses. Caribbean brands have for many years had strong local visibility, but until recently the mainstay of the Caribbean rum industry was production of bulk rum for blending overseas. Trinidad and Tobago's rum company, Angostura Holdings Ltd, for example, produced spirit for Bacardi, whose Bahamian blending and bottling plant exported to Europe under the Lomé Conventions. A quota system for Caribbean rum was in force until 2000, giving producers little incentive to invest in larger-scale production facilities, but assuring duty-free access for a steady quantity of product. Rum producers are not in the same social need category as small banana growers, but do impact significantly on Caribbean economies.

Under a 'zero-for-zero' agreement on white spirits, the EU and the USA phased out most tariffs on imported rum and certain other spirits from most sources from July 1997 to January 2003. While Caribbean rums retained a very slight tariff advantage, this agreement opened the EU market to lower cost, third-country producers with much greater economies of scale. The best-adapted regional rum producers have moved from bulk exports to developing their own brands in export markets. This requires considerable capital investment; it can take US $30m. over five to 10 years to gain recognition in a major market. Some companies, such as Demerara Distillers of Guyana, have successfully promoted brands in selected international niche markets, gaining a small share of a business carrying much higher margins than bulk rum. Others are affiliated with international majors. Mount Gay Distilleries in Barbados is majority-owned by Rémy-Cointreau, which in turn is part of the Maxxium alliance. As with traditional agricultural products, the EU has a €70m. assistance programme running originally from 2002 to 2007, but later extended to June 2010 for institutional capacity-building, plant modernization, pollution control and, crucially, overseas distribution and marketing. In some countries, rum exports have increased as sugar has declined. In Barbados, for example, rum comprised 12.5% of domestic exports in 2009, up from 3.6% in 1991, growing from Bds $8.8m. to Bds $57.2m. in absolute terms, and some 40% more than the value of sugar exports. Under the EPA, rum can be exported duty- and quota-free to the EU.

PROSPECTS

Each of the Caribbean's traditional export commodities seems likely to survive in some form. However, survival is unlikely for some groups of producers, such as the smaller banana growers, and some national industries, such as sugar production on those islands where the industry is most heavily in loss. Where traditional industries do survive, they will employ less labour, and smaller independent businesses will play a sharply reduced role. This implies job losses, mainly among unskilled and semi-skilled staff in rural areas, who are not well placed for retraining or redeployment. Financing of social 'safety nets' is important, but will prove only a temporary palliative. More important is the growth of alternative export industries and securely based domestic production to absorb labour released by the traditional sectors, and replace them as a source of foreign exchange. Nevertheless, the most promising exchange earner on a region-wide basis remains tourism.

FOOTNOTES

[1] The Caribbean Forum (CARIFORUM) includes the 12 independent English-speaking Caribbean countries—Antigua and Barbuda, the Bahamas, Barbados, Belize, Dominica, Grenada, Guyana, Jamaica, Saint Christopher and Nevis, Saint Lucia, Saint Vincent and the Grenadines and Trinidad and Tobago—and the British Overseas Territory of Montserrat. It also includes Haiti and Suriname, which, along with their English-speaking regional neighbours, are members of the Caribbean Community and Common Market (CARICOM); and the Dominican Republic, which is not a CARICOM member. The scope of this article extends to the English-speaking CARICOM members and Suriname, but not to Haiti nor to the Dominican Republic, where issues relating to the export of agricultural commodities are different in nature.

[2] At the same time, the French market was preserved for its former colonies and Overseas Departments, with similar historic arrangements in place for some other European importers, and a low-cost free market system in operation in Germany.

[3] This term originated in the 1950s, when the United Kingdom gave preference to trade with the 'sterling area', comprising mainly Commonwealth countries keeping a proportion of their currency reserves in British pounds, as against the 'dollar area', which included the USA and Latin America.

[4] Trinidad and Tobago and Saint Christopher and Nevis are used when referring to the Governments of that country. Trinidad and Saint Kitts are used when referring to the individual islands on which sugar was grown. No sugar has been grown in recent times on the islands of Tobago or Nevis.

PART TWO

Country Surveys

ANGUILLA

Geography

PHYSICAL FEATURES

The United Kingdom Overseas Territory of Anguilla is in the north-eastern Caribbean and is the most northerly part of the Leeward Islands in the Lesser Antilles. The territory includes the islet of Sombrero, the pivot of the Lesser Antilles, between the main arc of the archipelago running south-eastwards and the Virgin Islands running westwards. The British Virgin Islands lie some 40 km (25 miles) to the west of the territory, but the nearest neighbour is only 8 km to the south—the French (northern) part of the island of Saint Martin (Sint Maarten), which is under the jurisdiction of Guadeloupe (and, therefore, part of France). Anguilla itself was previously part of the federation of Saint Christopher (Kitts)-Nevis-Anguilla, but seceded and reverted to British colonial status (Saint Kitts is over 110 km to the south-east). Anguilla comprises over 96 sq km (37 sq miles) of territory, the main island itself consisting of 91 sq km. This makes the colony the smallest territory in the Caribbean.

The main island, aligned roughly south-west to north-east, is long and narrow, which is why the French named it after an eel (Anguilla), echoing the Carib name, which meant a sea serpent (Malliouhana). It is a low, coral-and-limestone island, about 26 km in length and never wider than 5 km. The highest point on Anguilla is at Crocus Hill (65 m or 213 ft). Most of the more rugged terrain is at the north-eastern end of the island, where it faces into the Atlantic weather, sheltering some denser vegetation than the usual scrub of the arid interior behind 30-m cliffs. There are some areas of wetland along the 60 km or so of coastline, favoured by the island's varied bird life, but it tends to be the clear seas favoured by coral and the many wide, sandy beaches that draw more lucrative visitors.

Apart from the detached islets of Scrub Island, at the north-eastern tip of the main island, and the even smaller Anguillita, at the south-western tip, the territory also comprises a number of other islands and cays. To the north-west of the mainland is Dog Island and, just to the east of that, the Prickley Pear Cays and Seal Island. Further to the north-west, almost 50 km from Anguilla itself, is the sea-washed rock of Sombrero, uninhabited since its lighthouse was automated. The light, 51 m (166 ft) above the sea, serves shipping using the Anegada Passage from the Atlantic Ocean into the Caribbean Sea. The island, just over 1.5 km long, not even 0.5 km wide and around 10 m above sea level, is particularly rich in bird life.

CLIMATE

The climate is a subtropical one, tempered by the north-eastern trade winds off the Atlantic. The lack of altitude means Anguilla often misses the rains, but also that it is prone to flooding, particularly during the June–September hurricane

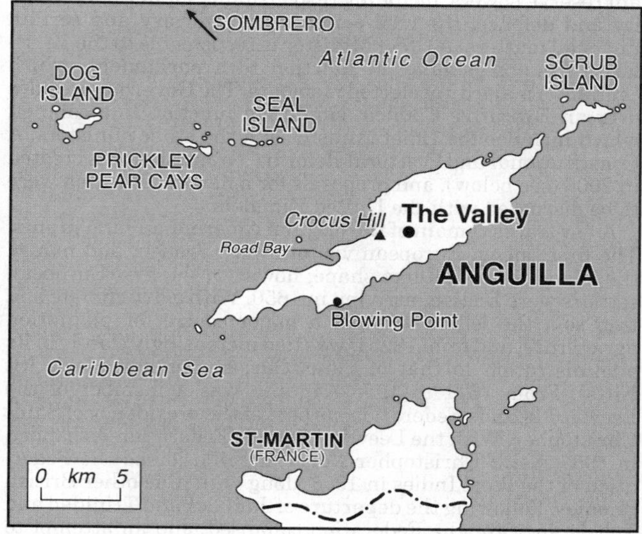

season. Annual rainfall is 36 ins (914 mm) per year and falls mainly between September and December. The mean temperature is 80°F (27°C), varying little over the course of the year.

POPULATION

There are some white and some mulatto (mixed-race) people native to Anguilla, but most of the population is black. Everyone speaks English, the official language, and most are adherents of one or other of numerous Christian denominations. According to figures from the 1990s, 40% of the population was nominally Anglican and 33% Methodist, with the Seventh-day Adventists, Baptists and Roman Catholics the next largest groups.

Official estimates put the total population at 15,736 at mid-2009, with about 1,600 living in and around the capital, The Valley, which is located in the centre of the island, near the northern coast. Across the island, to the south-west, is the ferry terminal of Blowing Point, although the main anchorage is at Road Bay, directly north of that port. The ferry gives easy access to the French and Dutch island of Saint Martin/Sint Maarten, encouraging tourism, but also helpful for emigration, which was a major demographic problem until the end of the 20th century.

History

MARK WILSON

Anguilla is a United Kingdom Overseas Territory. A Governor, who is the representative of the British monarch, has important reserve powers, including responsibility for national security and defence, the civil service, the judiciary and certain financial matters. A Chief Minister is responsible to the Legislative Council, similar in function to a parliament, which contains a majority of elected members. The Governor presides over an Executive Council, similar in function to a cabinet, which includes the Chief Minister and the other ministers. A Constitutional and Electoral Reform Commission was created in 2006 (see below), and proposals for a new constitution were to be discussed with the United Kingdom.

A few traces remain of the original Amerindian inhabitants. The first known European visitors were French, and named the island for its eel-like shape; however, the first European settlers were British, arriving in 1650. With a dry climate and thin soil, the island was not a major centre for plantation agriculture, and from 1825 it was tied increasingly closely in its administration to that of Saint Christopher and Nevis (St Kitts). From 1871 to 1956 Anguilla was a member of the Leeward Islands Federation, as part of the presidency of Saint Christopher. With the Leeward Islands Federation disbanded in 1957, Saint Christopher-Nevis-Anguilla joined the Federation of the West Indies in 1958 along with nine other British colonies. Following the departure of Jamaica and Trinidad and Tobago in 1962, the Federation collapsed, and an attempt to unite the remaining colonies as the 'little eight' was unsuccessful. Along with its neighbours, Saint Christopher-Nevis-Anguilla became a British Associated State in 1967, responsible for its own internal affairs, with the United Kingdom retaining control of external affairs and defence.

However, this arrangement was fiercely resisted by Anguilla, which feared domination by its larger neighbour, and in particular by Robert Llewellyn Bradshaw, leader of the St Kitts-Nevis-Anguilla Labour Party, which, in spite of its name, never had a substantial following outside the larger island.

Ronald Webster, leader of the People's Progressive Party (PPP), led a movement to break away from the three-island grouping. On 8 March 1967 Government House was burnt down, and on 30 May the island's small police detachment was expelled to the island of Saint Christopher. An armed attack on Saint Christopher on 10 June was unsuccessful, but a plebiscite held on 11 July recorded 1,813 votes in favour of separation from the three-island grouping (there were five votes against). A further plebiscite in February 1969 resulted in 1,739 votes to four in favour of an independent republic. However, this move was rejected by the United Kingdom, which at this time faced a more menacing rebellion in Rhodesia (now Zimbabwe). William Whitlock, a British junior minister, was despatched to Anguilla as an envoy in early March, but was ejected from the island. On 19 March 300 British paratroops and marines invaded, followed by a detachment from the Metropolitan Police Force; thereafter the island was administered under a resident Commissioner. The British police left in 1972, when Anguilla established its own force.

From 1980, following Bradshaw's death and the inauguration of a new administration in Saint Christopher and Nevis, Anguilla formally became a British Dependent Territory under a Governor, and from 1998, a United Kingdom Overseas Territory. In local politics, office alternated between the PPP and the Anguilla National Alliance (ANA) of Emile (later Sir Emile) Gumbs, who held office in 1977–80 and from 1984 until his retirement in 1994. Thereafter, the two-party system became less clear. A general election in March 1994 gave two seats each to the ANA, the Anguilla United Party (AUP), and the Anguilla Democratic Party (ADP). A former ANA Minister of Finance, Osbourne Fleming, took the seventh legislative seat. Hubert Hughes, also a former ANA minister, but now leader of the AUP, formed a coalition with Victor Banks of the ADP, and became Chief Minister. In May controversy arose over the proposed appointment by the Governor of a nominated member to the Legislative Council, David Carty, who had failed to win a legislative seat in the March election. Hughes objected to Carty's nomination, and alleged that he had not been consulted over the appointment, a charge denied by the Governor. Despite a ruling in Carty's favour by the Constitutional Court, the Speaker refused to swear him in as a member of the House of Assembly in December 1995.

Anguilla was severely damaged by Hurricane Luis in October 1995. Hughes was critical of what he saw as insufficient support from the United Kingdom. The announcement by the British Government in January 1997 that it was considering the extension of its powers in the Dependent Territories of the Caribbean attracted further criticism from Hughes, as did the proposed reactivation of the Governor's reserve powers, whereby the Governor (with the consent of the British Government) can amend, veto or introduce legislation without the consent of the local legislature.

In a legislative election held on 4 March 1999, the AUP held its two seats, as did the ADP. Hughes therefore continued in office as leader of a coalition Government. The ANA, with Fleming now a member, also retained its three seats. However, in June the ADP leader and Minister of Finance, Victor Banks, left the governing coalition following a dispute about the ADP's role in government. Hughes therefore no longer enjoyed the support of a majority of the elected members; however, with several appointed members also sitting in the Legislative Council, the constitutional position was unclear. To force an eventual resolution, Banks and the three ANA members withdrew from the House of Assembly, thus denying it a quorum. This left the Government unable, in December 1999, to introduce a budget for 2000 or implement any policy. A fresh elections was called for 3 March 2000.

The election of March 2000 left the ANA still with three parliamentary seats, the AUP still with two seats, while Banks (representing the ADP) and Edison Baird (an Independent) each held one. Fleming was appointed Chief Minister (and Minister of Home Affairs, Tourism, Agriculture, Fisheries and Environment) with support from four of the seven elected members. Banks became Minister of Finance, Economic Development, Investment and Commerce.

In February 2000 the island's Governor, Robert Harris, who had not enjoyed good relations with the Hughes Government, and who had reportedly felt frustrated by the political crisis, departed Anguilla. He was succeeded by Peter Johnstone, who, in turn, was replaced by Alan Huckle in May 2004. In the same month Edison Baird replaced Hubert Hughes as Leader of the Opposition after Albert Hughes resigned from the AUP and transferred his support to Baird.

Following Anguilla's inclusion on an Organisation for Economic Co-operation and Development (OECD) blacklist of tax havens in 2000, the Government introduced a number of articles of legislation to combat money-laundering on the island, including the establishment of a 'Money Laundering Reporting Authority'. OECD removed Anguilla from the list in March 2002, declaring that the Government had made sufficient commitments to improve transparency and effective exchange of information on tax matters by the end of 2005. The establishment of a new financial regulatory body, the Anguilla Financial Services Commission, in 2004 represented a further commitment to transparency within the sector. However, in April 2009 Anguilla was included in OECD's so-called 'grey list' of territories that had committed to improving transparency in the financial sector but had not yet substantially implemented such change.

In June 2001 the Government officially approved the draft of its National Telecommunications Policy, which would liberalize the telecommunications sector. Cable & Wireless, the territory's sole telecommunications provider, in April 2003 signed an agreement with the Government to open the market for competition. In August the Government commenced the sale of 6m. shares at US $1 each in the Anguilla Electricity Company, a profit-making public utility, in order to raise funds for the EC $49.2m. expansion and reconstruction of Wallblake

Airport (renamed Clayton J. Lloyd International Airport in 2010). The proceeds of the sale were primarily to go towards lengthening the airport's runway in order to accommodate larger aircraft.

At the general election held on 21 February 2005 there were some variations in party names or affiliations, but the same members were returned to government as in the previous ballot. The Anguilla United Front, an alliance comprising the ADP and the ANA, led by Osbourne Fleming, won four seats, while the Anguilla National Strategic Alliance secured two seats and the Anguilla United Movement (as the AUP had been renamed) attained one. However, it was anticipated that some of the existing representatives would retire from active politics prior to the holding of the next election. With the economy prospering, the Government was anxious to avoid the dangers of economic 'overheating' and social dislocation; to this effect, in October it announced that it would consider no additional investment proposals until May 2008; this moratorium was afterwards extended, although it was of less relevance in 2009 with most major projects at a halt from mid-2009. The Government expressed concern over the erosion of traditional values in Anguilla, and over short-term labour unrest on camps for migrant construction workers in 2007, stressing a desire to avoid the pattern of development that had evolved on neighbouring islands such as Saint Martin. In July 2006 Andrew George took office as Governor, in succession to Alan Huckle; Stanley Everton Reid, a lawyer and the country's first indigenous Deputy Governor, was sworn in later the same month. A report of the British parliamentary select committee on foreign affairs, completed in mid-2008, disclosed allegations that a single developer had been given permission for three large projects as a result of bribes paid to Anguillan government ministers, and recommended an independent inquiry; the Chief Minister denied the reports.

In January 2006 the Governor established a Constitutional and Electoral Reform Commission, to advance the work done by the previous electoral commission in 2001–04. A report detailing its recommendations was submitted to the Governor in August of that year. A series of public consultations commenced in March 2007. However, subsequent discussions with the United Kingdom were postponed, to allow the formation of a smaller committee comprising elected Assembly members from the Government and opposition parties assisted by local jurists; this body conducted public consultations throughout the island, and the resulting proposals were expected to be discussed with the United Kingdom in 2009, after which consultations between representatives of the Governments of Anguilla and the United Kingdom were to begin. The change of government in early 2010, however, meant discussions were delayed. Areas identified as in need of urgent amendment included the administration of justice, transparency in judicial proceedings, enforcement of constitutional rights, and the appointment of the island Governor and deputies. Furthermore, it recommended the expansion and restructuring of the Executive Council and House of Assembly to enable more efficient delivery of government functions, while increased responsibilities were to be conferred upon the Chief Minister and certain limitations imposed upon the Governor's powers, in order to improve the democratic process. Extensive electoral and judicial reform was also advocated. Broadly interpreted, the Commission's recommendations sought to advance Anguilla's ambitions towards greater responsibility for locally elected institutions, with the Governor's powers mainly limited to defence and security. The United Kingdom would, however, retain ultimate authority over constitutional questions and continue to possess significant reserve powers.

A general election was held on 15 February 2010. The AUM, led by former Chief Minister Hubert Hughes, won four of the seven elected seats in the House of Assembly. The AUF's parliamentary representation was reduced to two seats while the remaining seat was secured by the APP. The AUF leader, Victor Banks, lost his seat in the Valley South constituency. Hughes' new administration included Edison Baird as Deputy Chief Minister and Minister of Social Development and Walcott Richardson in the key post of Minister of Home Affairs, including Labour, Lands and Immigration. Lowering the unemployment rate was one of the stated priorities of the new Council. Hughes also took on the finance portfolio. In the following month the Chief Minister and the Governor announced the formation of a government task force further to improve financial transparency in Anguilla. The territory had recently been removed from OECD's 'grey list' of jurisdictions that failed to meet international tax standards (see above). One of the AUM's electoral pledges had been to strengthen the economically important financial sector.

Economy

MARK WILSON

Anguilla is a United Kingdom Overseas Territory in the eastern Caribbean, with an area of 96 sq km and a population, according to the Eastern Caribbean Central Bank (ECCB), of some 15,700 at mid-2009. Immigration resulting from economic prosperity resulted in average annual population growth peaking at 8.8% in 2005, and averaging 3.9% in 2006–08. Anguilla is an associate member of the Caribbean Community and Common Market, or CARICOM, whose larger members formed a single market at the start of 2006, with Anguilla and the smaller islands joining from July that year. It is also a member of the Organisation of Eastern Caribbean States, which links nine of the smaller Caribbean territories, while the ECCB, based in Saint Christopher and Nevis, supervises its financial affairs.

The island has a prosperous middle-income economy, with an estimated per-head gross domestic product (GDP) of US $19,087 in 2008. A downturn in international demand for Caribbean tourism in 2001–02 resulted in GDP contracting by 3.1% following Hurricane Lenny. However, these troubles were followed by a period of growth, which averaged 16.6% a year in 2004–07, before declining sharply in 2008, to 2.1%, as international tourism investment again slowed significantly. Unemployment has been low by regional standards—the rate was 7.8% in 2002, and was much lower by 2007–08, when labour shortages were a major concern and significant hotel construction projects employed workers from India, Mexico and elsewhere. According to the ECCB, there was a budgetary deficit of EC $29.5m. in 2008, equivalent to some 3.8% of GDP. The deficit was estimated to have increased significantly in the following year, when recurrent expenditure was estimated at EC $241m. and capital spending at EC $98m. Public debt totalled EC $152.7m. (equivalent to some 65% of GDP) in late 2008. The new Government announced it would have to borrow from the United Kingdom to cover capital outlays in 2010 in an attempt to stimulate the economy.

Tourism is the mainstay of the economy, with hotels and restaurants accounting for 16.5% of GDP in 2008; the main attractions are the island's tranquillity, the clear surrounding waters, low rainfall, and white, sandy beaches. According to the Caribbean Tourism Organization, there were 68,284 stopover visitors in 2008, a 13.7% decrease compared with the previous year, with total spending of EC $274m. (compared with EC $309m. in the previous year). Numbers were expected to decrease further in 2009, with a 21% decline in the first two months of the year. The USA accounted for 58.9% of visitor arrivals in 2008. The ratio of tourists to local population is higher than on such islands as Antigua and Barbuda, Barbados or Jamaica. Most tourists stay in high-cost, luxury accommodation, and their high spending power per head is of considerable economic benefit. The island is not a port of call for cruise ships, which helps preserve its pleasant atmosphere. An EC $49.2m. improvement programme at Wallblake Airport (renamed Clayton J. Lloyd International Airport in July 2010) was completed in December 2004, after several delays, to accommodate mid-range jets operated by American Airlines, the main international carrier.

Residential, commercial, public sector and tourism-related investment has resulted in a high level of construction activity, which contributed 27.7% of GDP in 2008. A wave of luxury tourism proposals from 2000 gave rise to widespread concerns over economic overheating and rapid social change. Tourism-related investments proposed or in progress in 2005, and scheduled for completion by 2021, totalled US $1,800m., close to more than nine times the annual level of GDP. To guard against the economic and social consequences of too fast a pace of growth, in October 2005 the Government announced a 20-month moratorium on new development proposals, until May 2008. The moratorium was later extended, with a tourism master plan prepared in 2009, building on an economic and social impact analysis completed in 2008. However, the pace of tourism-related construction slowed sharply from the second half of 2008, with several hotel projects delayed or cancelled. The construction sector was estimated to have contracted by some 55% in 2009. There is no significant agricultural sector, but a few small-scale farmers keep livestock and grow food crops. There has also been some recent development of commercial fishing. There is no manufacturing industry.

There is a small 'offshore' financial sector, which has been reasonably well regulated. Following pressure from the Organisation for Economic Co-operation and Development (OECD), which, in June 2000, included Anguilla on a list of tax havens, efforts were made to improve the transparency of the sector. Legislation to control money-laundering was strengthened, and the Government made a commitment to move towards the international exchange of information in criminal and civil tax investigations. As a result of these efforts, in 2002 OECD removed Anguilla from its 'blacklist'. However, in 2009 Anguilla was included in OECD's so-called 'grey list' of jurisdictions that had committed to improving transparency in the financial sector, but had not yet substantially implemented such change. Online company registration through an approved agent is quick and cost-effective: a total of 1,097 International Business Companies and 123 other financial service companies were added to the register in 2006. The outgoing Government of Osbourne Fleming made efforts to raise financial standards and in March 2010 Anguilla was removed from the list. The incoming administration of Hubert Hughes pledged to promote the financial services sector while ensuring that Anguilla remained on OECD's 'white list'. The Government has made efforts to develop e-commerce, while one source of income has been from the sale of internet addresses ending in the island's registered suffix, 'ai' (although there were concerns in some quarters that websites using this suffix might be carrying material deemed inappropriate to Anguilla's image, as 'ai' means 'love' in Chinese).

The island is in the heart of the hurricane belt, and has been damaged by several storms in recent years—including Luis in 1995, Georges in 1998, and Lenny in 1999.

Statistical Survey

Source (unless otherwise stated): Government of Anguilla, The Secretariat, The Valley; tel. 497-2451; fax 497-3389; e-mail stats@gov.ai; internet gov.ai/statistics.

AREA AND POPULATION

Area (sq km): 96 (Anguilla 91, Sombrero 5).

Population: 11,430 (males 5,628, females 5,802) at census of 9 May 2001. *Mid-2009* (projected estimate): 15,736 (Source: Eastern Caribbean Central Bank).

Density (at mid-2009): 163.9 per sq km.

Population by Age and Sex (at 2001 census): *0–14:* 3,202 (males 1,590, females 1,612); *15–64:* 7,356 (males 3,632, females 3,724); *65 and over:* 872 (males 406, females 466); *Total* 11,430 (males 5,628, females 5,802).

Principal Towns (population at 2001 census): South Hill 1,495; North Side 1,195; The Valley (capital) 1,169; Stoney Ground 1,133. *Mid-2009* (UN estimate, incl. suburbs): The Valley 1,635 (Source: UN, *World Urbanization Prospects: The 2009 Revision*).

Births, Marriages and Deaths (2008): Registered live births 154 (birth rate 9.9 per 1,000); Registered marriages 54 (marriage rate 3.5 per 1,000); Registered deaths 57 (death rate 3.7 per 1,000). *2009:* Registered live births 181; Registered marriages 58; Registered deaths 46.

Life Expectancy (years at birth): 80.7 (males 78.1; females 83.3) in 2009 (Source: Pan American Health Organization).

Economically Active Population (persons aged 15 years and over, census of 9 May 2001): Agriculture, fishing and mining 183; Manufacturing 135; Electricity, gas and water 81; Construction 830; Trade 556; Restaurants and hotels 1,587; Transport, storage and communications 379; Finance, insurance, real estate and business services 433; Public administration, social security 662; Education, health and social work 383; Other community, social and personal services 164; Private households with employed persons 164; Activities not stated 871; *Total employed* 5,644 (males 3,014, females 2,630); Unemployed 406 (males 208, females 198); *Total labour force* 6,050 (males 3,222, females 2,828). *July 2002:* Total employed 5,496 (males 3,009, females 2,487); Unemployed 465 (males 204, females 261); Total labour force 5,961 (Source: ILO).

HEALTH AND WELFARE

Total Fertility Rate (children per woman, 2009): 1.8.

Under-5 Mortality Rate (per 1,000 live births, 1997): 34.0.

Physicians (per 1,000 head, 2003): 1.2.

Hospital Beds (per 1,000 head, 2008): 2.2.

Health Expenditure (% of GDP, 2004): 4.2.

Access to Water (% of persons, 2004): 60.

Access to Sanitation (% of persons, 2004): 99.

Sources: Caribbean Development Bank, *Social and Economic Indicators 2004* and Pan American Health Organization.

For definitions, see explanatory note on p. vi.

AGRICULTURE, ETC.

Fishing (metric tons, live weight, 2008): Marine fishes 460; Caribbean spiny lobster 232; Stromboid conchs 9; Total catch 701. Source: FAO.

INDUSTRY

Electric Energy ('000 kWh): 80,110 in 2006; 88,999 in 2007; 89,728 in 2008. Source: Eastern Caribbean Central Bank.

FINANCE

Currency and Exchange Rates: 100 cents = 1 Eastern Caribbean dollar (EC $). *Sterling, US Dollar and Euro Equivalents* (31 May 2010): £1 sterling = EC $3.937; US $1 = EC $2.700; €1 = EC $3.344; EC $100 = £25.40 = US $37.04 = €29.91. *Exchange Rate:* Fixed at US $1 = EC $2.70 since July 1976.

Budget (EC $ million, 2009): *Revenue:* Tax revenue 111.6 (Taxes on domestic goods and services 44.7, Taxes on international trade and transactions 65.4, Taxes on property 1.5); Non-tax revenue 36.7; Total 148.3. *Expenditure:* Current expenditure 202.4 (Personal emoluments 90.7, Other goods and services 48.4, Transfers and subsidies 55.0, Interest payments 8.3); Capital expenditure 10.6; Total 213.0. Source: Eastern Caribbean Central Bank, *Annual Economic and Financial Review 2009*.

Cost of Living (Consumer Price Index; base: 2005 = 100): All items 113.9 in 2007: 121.7 in 2008; 120.8 in 2009. Source: IMF, *International Financial Statistics*.

Gross Domestic Product (EC $ million at constant 1990 prices): 397.90 in 2006; 470.82 in 2007; 477.07 in 2008. Source: Eastern Caribbean Central Bank.

Expenditure on the Gross Domestic Product (EC $ million at current prices, 2008): Government final consumption expenditure 114.75; Private final consumption expenditure 690.48; Gross fixed capital formation 491.98; *Total domestic expenditure* 1,297.21; Exports of goods and services 366.85; *Less* Imports of goods and services 879.84; *GDP in purchasers' values* 784.22. Source: Eastern Caribbean Central Bank.

Gross Domestic Product by Economic Activity (EC $ million at current prices, 2008): Agriculture (including crops, livestock and fishing) 9.35; Mining and quarrying 13.42; Manufacturing 12.60; Electricity and water 23.84; Construction 179.70; Wholesale and retail trade 31.58; Hotels and restaurants 111.90; Transport and Communications 89.18; Banks and insurance 82.01; Real estate and housing 10.28; Government services 104.44; Other services 9.35; *Sub-total* 677.65; *Less* Financial intermediation services indirectly measured 48.08; *Gross value added in basic prices* 629.57; Taxes, *less* subsidies, on products 154.65; *GDP in purchasers' values* 784.22. Source: Eastern Caribbean Central Bank.

Balance of Payments (EC $ million, 2009): Goods (net) –453.47; Services (net) 99.18; *Balance on goods and services* –354.28; Income (net) –20.99; *Balance on goods, services and income* –375.27; Current transfers (net) –8.46; *Current balance* –383.73; Capital account (net) 38.11; Direct investment (net) 166.06; Portfolio investment (net) 14.15; Other investments (net) 94.52; Net errors and omissions 40.90; *Overall balance* –29.99. Source: Eastern Caribbean Central Bank.

EXTERNAL TRADE

Principal Commodities (EC $ million, 2005): *Imports:* Food and live animals 57.4; Beverages and tobacco 25.1; Mineral fuels, lubricants, etc. 34.6; Chemicals and related products 22.7; Basic manufactures 61.9; Machinery and transport equipment 101.6; Miscellaneous manufactured articles 36.4; Total (incl. others) 350.6. *Exports* (incl. re-exports): Food and live animals 13.9; Beverages and tobacco 7.5; Basic manufactures 1.5; Machinery and transport equipment 14.8; Miscellaneous manufactured articles 1.9; Total (incl. others) 39.8.

Principal Trading Partners (EC $ million, 2005): *Imports:* Barbados 3.7; Guadeloupe 7.3; Guyana 6.6; Netherlands Antilles 22.3; Puerto Rico 27.4; Trinidad and Tobago 29.8; United Kingdom 16.1; USA 177.6; US Virgin Islands 5.6; Total (incl. others) 350.6. *Exports* (incl. re-exports): British Virgin Islands 1.7; Guadeloupe 0.8; Guyana 4.8; Netherlands Antilles 9.3; Saint Lucia 2.1; United Kingdom 10.7; USA 3.7; Total (incl. others) 39.8.

TRANSPORT

Road Traffic (motor vehicles in use at 31 December 2006): Passenger cars 4,155; Vans and lorries 92; Motorcycles and mopeds 22; Total 4,269 (Source: IRF, *World Road Statistics*).

Shipping: *Merchant Fleet* (registered at 31 December 2008): 4; Total displacement 805 grt. Source: Lloyd's Register-Fairplay, *World Fleet Statistics*.

TOURISM

Visitor Arrivals: 164,067 (stop-overs 77,652, excursionists 86,415) in 2007; 127,862 (stop-overs 68,284, excursionists 59,578) in 2008; 109,159 (stop-overs 55,848, excursionists 53,311) in 2009.

Visitor Arrivals by Place of Residence (2008): Canada 4,970; Caribbean 11,215; Germany 1,001; Italy 2,552; United Kingdom 5,730; USA 65,728; Total (incl. others) 127,861.

Tourism Receipts (EC $ million): 309.2 in 2007; 275.6 in 2008; 229.1 in 2009. Source: Eastern Caribbean Central Bank, *Annual Economic and Financial Review 2008*.

COMMUNICATIONS MEDIA

Radio Receivers (1997): 3,000 in use.

Television Receivers (1999): 1,000 in use.

Telephones (2009): 6,300 main lines in use.

Mobile Cellular Telephones (2009): 27,000 subscribers.

Internet Users (2009): 3,700.

Broadband Subscribers (2009): 3,700.

Sources: partly UN, *Statistical Yearbook*; International Telecommunication Union.

EDUCATION

Pre-primary (2007/08, unless otherwise indicated): 11 schools (2003); 43 teachers; 450 pupils (males 221, females 229).

Primary (2007/08, unless otherwise indicated): 8 schools (2003); 114 teachers; 1,610 pupils (males 817, females 793).

Secondary (2007/08, unless otherwise indicated): 1 school (2002/03); 96 teachers (2006/07); 1,008 pupils (males 505, females 503).

Tertiary (2007/08): 14 teachers; 54 students (9 males, 45 females).

Pupil-teacher Ratio (primary education, UNESCO estimate): 14.1 in 2007/08 (Source: UNESCO Institute for Statistics).

Adult Literacy Rate (UNESCO estimates): 95.4% (males 95.1%; females 95.7%) in 1995. Source: UNESCO, *Statistical Yearbook*.

Source (unless otherwise indicated): UNESCO Institute for Statistics.

Directory

The Constitution

The Constitution, established in 1976, accorded Anguilla the status of a British Dependent Territory. It formally became a separate dependency on 19 December 1980, and is administered under the Anguilla Constitution Orders of 1982 and 1990. British Dependent Territories were referred to as United Kingdom Overseas Territories from February 1998 and draft legislation confirming this change and granting citizens rights to full British citizenship and residence in the United Kingdom was published in March 1999. The British Overseas Territories Act entered into effect in May 2002. The British Government proposals also included the requirement that the Constitutions of Overseas Territories should be revised in order to conform to British and international standards. The process of revision of the Anguillan Constitution began in September 1999.

The British monarch is represented locally by a Governor, who presides over the Executive Council and the House of Assembly. The Governor is responsible for defence, external affairs (including international financial affairs), internal security (including the police), the public service, the judiciary and the audit. The Governor appoints a Deputy Governor. On matters relating to internal security, the public service and the appointment of an acting Governor or Deputy Governor, the Governor is required to consult the Chief Minister. The Executive Council consists of the Chief Minister and not more than three other ministers (appointed by the Governor from the elected members of the legislative House of Assembly) and two ex officio members (the Deputy Governor and the Attorney-General). The House of Assembly is elected for a maximum term of five years by universal adult suffrage and consists of seven elected members, two ex officio members (the Deputy Governor and the Attorney-General) and two nominated members who are appointed by the Governor, one upon the advice of the Chief Minister, and one after consultations with the Chief Minister and the Leader of the Opposition. The House elects a Speaker and a Deputy Speaker.

The Governor may order the dissolution of the House of Assembly if a resolution of no confidence is passed in the Government, and elections must be held within two months of the dissolution.

The Constitution provides for an Anguilla Belonger Commission, which determines cases of whether a person can be 'regarded as belonging to Anguilla' (i.e. having 'belonger' status). A belonger is someone of Anguillan birth or parentage, someone who has married a belonger, or someone who is a citizen of the United Kingdom Overseas Territories from Anguilla (by birth, parentage, adoption or naturalization). The Commission may grant belonger status to those who have been domiciled and ordinarily resident in Anguilla for not less than 15 years.

The Government

HEAD OF STATE

Queen: HM Queen ELIZABETH II.

Governor: WILLIAM ALISTAIR HARRISON (took office 21 April 2009).

EXECUTIVE COUNCIL

(July 2010)

The Government is formed by the Anguilla United Movement.

Chief Minister and Minister of Finance, Economic Development, Investments and Tourism: HUBERT B. HUGHES.

Deputy Chief Minister and Minister of Social Development: EDISON BAIRD.

Minister of Home Affairs, including Labour, Natural Resources, Lands, Physical Planning and Immigration: WALCOTT RICHARDSON.

Minister of Infrastructure, Communications, Utilities, Housing, Agriculture and Fisheries: EVAN GUMBS.

Parliamentary Secretary with responsibility for Tourism: HAYDN HUGHES.

Deputy Governor: STANLEY EVERTON REID.

Attorney-General: WILHELM C. BOURNE.

MINISTRIES

Office of the Governor: Government House, POB 60, The Valley; tel. 497-2622; fax 497-3314; e-mail governorsoffice@gov.ai.

Office of the Chief Minister: The Secretariat, POB 60, The Valley; tel. 497-2518; fax 497-3389; e-mail chief-minister@gov.ai.

All ministries are based in The Valley, mostly at the Secretariat (tel. 497-2451; internet www.gov.ai).

Legislature

HOUSE OF ASSEMBLY

Speaker: BARBARA WEBSTER-BOURNE.

Clerk to House of Assembly: ADELLA RICHARDSON.

Election, 15 February 2010

Party	% of votes	Seats
Anguilla United Movement (AUM)	32.67	4
Anguilla United Front (AUF)	39.39	2
Anguilla Progressive Party (APP)	14.71	1
Independent candidates	13.24	—
Total	100.00	7

In addition, there were 39 spoiled ballots. There are also two ex officio members and two nominated members.

Political Organizations

Anguilla Progressive Party (APP): The Valley; Leader BRENT DAVIS.

Anguilla United Front (AUF): The Valley; internet www.unitedfront.ai; f. 2000 by the alliance of the Anguilla Democratic Party and the Anguilla National Alliance; Leader VICTOR F. BANKS.

Anguilla United Movement (AUM): The Valley; f. 1979; revived 1984; previously known as the Anguilla United Party—AUP; conservative; Leader HUBERT B. HUGHES.

Judicial System

Justice is administered by the High Court, Court of Appeal and Magistrates' Courts. One of the 16 Puisne Judges of the Eastern Caribbean Supreme Court's High Court division, concurrently accredited to Montserrat, arbitrates in sittings of the High Court.

Puisne Judge: JANICE MESADIS GEORGE-CREQUE.

Religion

CHRISTIANITY

The Anglican Communion

Anglicans in Anguilla are adherents of the Church in the Province of the West Indies, comprising nine dioceses. Anguilla forms part of the diocese of the North Eastern Caribbean and Aruba. According to figures from the last census (2001), 29% of the population are Anglican.

Bishop of the North Eastern Caribbean and Aruba: Rt Rev. LEROY ERROL BROOKS, St Mary's Rectory, POB 180, The Valley; tel. 497-2235; fax 497-8555; e-mail brookx@anguilla.net.com.

The Roman Catholic Church

The diocese of St John's-Basseterre, suffragan to the archdiocese of Castries (Saint Lucia), includes Anguilla, Antigua and Barbuda, the British Virgin Islands, Montserrat and Saint Christopher and Nevis. The Bishop resides in St John's, Antigua. Some 5.7% of the population are Roman Catholic, according to census figures.

Roman Catholic Church: St Gerard's, POB 47, The Valley; tel. 497-2405; e-mail stgerards@caribcable.com; internet www.stgerards-anguilla.org.

Other Christian Churches

According to the last census, 24% of the population are Methodist.

Methodist Church: POB 5, The Valley; tel. 497-2612; fax 497-8460; e-mail methodism@anguillanet.com; Supt Minister Rev. Dr H. CLIFTON NILES.

The Seventh-day Adventist, Baptist, Church of God, Pentecostal, Apostolic Faith and Jehovah's Witnesses Churches and sects are also represented.

The Press

Anguilla Life Magazine: POB 1622, The Valley; tel. 497-3080; fax 497-4196; e-mail anguillalife@anguillanet.com; 3 a year; Publr and Editor CLAIRE DEVENER; circ. 10,000.

Anguilla Official Gazette: House of Assembly, POB 60, The Valley; tel. 497-5081; fax 498-2210; internet gazette.gov.ai; monthly; govt news-sheet.

The Anguillian Newspaper: POB 98, The Valley; tel. 497-3823; fax 497-8706; e-mail theanguillian@anguillanet.com; internet www.anguillian.com; weekly; Editor A. NAT HODGE.

The Light: Sandy Hill, POB 1373, The Valley; tel. 497-5058; fax 497-5641; e-mail thelight@anguillanet.com; internet www.thelightanguilla.com; f. 1993; owned by Hodgeco Publishing Inc; weekly; newspaper; Editor GEORGE C. HODGE.

What We Do in Anguilla: Sandy Hill, POB 1373, The Valley; tel. 497-5641; fax 497-5795; e-mail thelight@anguillanet.com; f. 1987; monthly; tourism; Editor GEORGE C. HODGE; circ. 50,000.

Broadcasting and Communications

TELECOMMUNICATIONS

LIME: POB 77, The Valley; tel. 804-2994; e-mail customerservice@time4lime.com; internet www.time4lime.com; fmrly Cable & Wireless (Anguilla) Ltd; name changed as above 2008; contact centres in Jamaica and Saint Lucia; CEO DAVID SHAW; Exec. Vice-Pres. (Leeward Islands) DAVIDSON CHARLES.

Wireless Ventures (Anguilla) Ltd: Babrow Bldg, The Valley; tel. 498-7500; fax 498-7510; e-mail customercareanguilla@digicelgroup.com; internet www.digicelanguilla.com; owned by Digicel Ltd (Bermuda); fmrly AT&T Wireless; Country Man. STEPHENIE BROOKS.

BROADCASTING

Radio

The Caribbean Beacon: Long Rd, POB 690, The Valley; Head Office: POB 7008, Columbus, GA 31908, USA; tel. 497-4340; fax 497-4311; f. 1981; privately owned and operated; religious and commercial; broadcasts 24 hours daily; Pres. MELLISA SCOTT; CEO B. MONSELL HAZELL.

Klass 92.9 FM: POB 339, The Valley; tel. 497-3791; e-mail request@klass929.com; internet www.klass929.com; f. 2006; commercial; Owner ABNER BROOKS, Jr.

Kool FM: North Side, The Valley; tel. 497-0103; fax 497-0104; e-mail kool@koolfm103.com; internet www.koolfm103.com; commercial; Man. ASHLEY BROOKS.

Radio Anguilla: Dept of Information and Broadcasting, Secretariat, POB 60, The Valley; tel. 497-2218; fax 497-5432; e-mail radioaxa@anguillanet.com; internet www.radioaxa.com; f. 1969; owned and operated by the Govt of Anguilla since 1976; 250,000 listeners throughout the north-eastern Caribbean; broadcasts 17 hours daily; Dir FARRAH BANKS; Programme Man. KEITH STONE GREAVES.

UP Beat Radio 97.7 FM: Cedar Ave, Rey Hill, POB 5045, The Valley, AI 2640; tel. 498-3354; fax 497-5995; e-mail info@hbr1075.com; internet hbr1075.com; f. 2001; commercial; music and news programmes.

ZJF FM: POB 333, The Valley; tel. 497-3919; fax 497-3909; f. 1989; commercial; Man. SELWYN BROOKS.

Television

Anguilla TV: tel. 662-7365; e-mail donna@islandeyetv.com; internet www.islandeyetv.com; operated by Eye TV; terrestrial channels 3 and 9; 24-hour local and international English language programming; Exec. Producer DONNA DAVIS.

Caribbean Cable Communications (Anguilla): Edwin Wallace Rey Dr., POB 336, The Valley; tel. 497-3600; fax 497-3602; e-mail customersupport@caribcable.com; internet www.caribcable.com; also broadcasts to Nevis; Pres. LEE BERTMAN.

Finance

(cap. = capital; res = reserves; dep. = deposits; m. = million; amounts in EC dollars)

CENTRAL BANK

Eastern Caribbean Central Bank: Fairplay Commercial Complex, POB 1385, The Valley; tel. 497-5050; fax 497-5150; e-mail eccbaxa@anguillanet.com; internet www.eccb-centralbank.org; HQ in Basseterre, Saint Christopher and Nevis; bank of issue and central monetary authority for Anguilla, Antigua and Barbuda, Dominica, Grenada, Montserrat, Saint Christopher and Nevis, Saint Lucia and Saint Vincent and the Grenadines; Gov. Sir K. DWIGHT VENNER; Country Man. MARILYN BARTLETT-RICHARDSON.

COMMERCIAL BANKS

Caribbean Commercial Bank (Anguilla) Ltd: POB 23, The Valley; tel. 497-3917; fax 497-3570; e-mail service@ccb.ai; internet www.ccb.ai; f. 1976; Chair. OSBOURNE B. FLEMING; Man. Dir STARRY WEBSTER-BENJAMIN.

FirstCaribbean International Bank Ltd: POB 140, The Valley; tel. 497-2301; fax 497-2980; e-mail care@firstcaribbeanbank.com; internet www.firstcaribbeanbank.com; f. 2002 following merger of Caribbean operations of Barclays Bank PLC and CIBC; Exec. Chair. MICHAEL MANSOOR; CEO JOHN D. ORR.

National Bank of Anguilla Ltd (NBA): POB 44, The Valley; tel. 497-2101; fax 497-3310; e-mail nbabankl@anguillanet.com; internet www.nba.ai; f. 1985; 5% owned by Govt of Anguilla; cap. 30.7m., res 69.2m., dep. 928.1m. (March 2008); CEO E. VALENTINE BANKS.

Scotiabank Anguilla Ltd: Fairplay Commercial Centre, POB 250, The Valley; tel. 497-3333; fax 497-3344; e-mail bns.anguilla@scotiabank.com; internet www.scotiabank.com; Man. Dir KERWIN BAPTISTE.

There are 'offshore' foreign banks based on the island, but most are not authorized to operate in Anguilla. There is a financial complex known as the Caribbean Commercial Centre in The Valley.

TRUST COMPANIES

Barwys Trust Anguilla Ltd: Caribbean Suite, The Valley; tel. 497-2189; fax 497-5007; e-mail info@barwys.com; internet www.barwys.com; Man. JOSEPH BRICE.

Codan Trust Co (Anguilla) Ltd: Mitchell House, POB 147, The Valley; tel. 498-6789; fax 498-8423; e-mail anguilla@conyersdill.com; internet www.conyersdill.com; subsidiary of Conyers, Dill and Pearman, Bermuda; Man. GARETH THOMAS.

First Anguilla Trust Co Ltd: Mitchell House, POB 174, The Valley, AI 2640; tel. and fax 498-8800; e-mail information@firstanguilla.com; internet www.firstanguilla.com; owned by Webster Dyrud Mitchell; f. 1995; Dir PAM WEBSTER.

GenevaTrust: National Bank Corporate Bldg, Caribbean Suite, Airport Rd, The Valley; tel. 870-3178; fax 870-3949; e-mail geneva@genevatrust.com; internet www.genevatrust.com; f. 2005; as the GenevaTrust Corpn; subsidiary of Geneva Assurance Ltd; CEO NADINE DE KOKER.

Global Trustees (Anguilla) Ltd: 201 The Rogers Office Bldg, Edwin Wallace Rey Dr., George Hill; tel. 498-5858; fax 497-5504; e-mail anguilla@gcsl.info; internet www.gcsl.info; fmrly Hansa Bank and Trust Co; Man. Dir CARLYLE K. ROGERS.

Intertrust (Anguilla) Ltd: National Bank Corporate Bldg, Airport Rd, POB 1388, The Valley; tel. 497-2189; fax 497-5007; e-mail toni.niekoop@intertrustgroup.com; internet www.intertrustgroup.com; fmrly Fortis Intertrust (Anguilla) Ltd; Dir TONI NIEKOOP.

Lutea (Anguilla) Ltd: S1 South, Auckland House, POB 1533, The Quarter; tel. 498-0340; fax 498-0341; e-mail acharles@lutea.com; internet www.lutea.com; owned by the Lutea Group of Cos, administered in Jersey (United Kingdom); Man. AINE CHARLES.

Mossack Fonseca & Co (British Anguilla) Ltd: Quantum Bldg, Suite 29, Caribbean Commercial Centre, The Valley; tel. 498-7777; fax 497-3727; e-mail britishanguilla@mossfon.com; internet www.mossfon.com; Administrator CUTELYN CARTY.

Sinel Trust (Anguilla) Ltd: POB 821, The Valley; fax 497-8289; e-mail arichardson@sineltrust.com; CEO ALEX RICHARDSON.

REGULATORY AUTHORITIES

Anguilla Financial Services Commission: The Secretariat, POB 1575, The Valley; tel. 497-5881; fax 497-5872; e-mail info@fsc.org.ai; internet www.fsc.org.ai; f. 2004 to replace the Financial Services Dept of the Ministry of Finance, Economic Development, Investment, Tourism and Commerce; Chair. HELEN HATTON.

Financial Services Regulatory Commission: The Valley; internet www.fsrc.gov.ag; f. 2002; responsible for the regulation and supervision of all institutions licensed under the International Business Corpns Act of 2002; CEO JOHN BENJAMIN.

STOCK EXCHANGE

Eastern Caribbean Securities Exchange: based in Basseterre, Saint Christopher and Nevis; tel. (869) 466-7192; fax (869) 465-3798; e-mail info@ecseonline.com; internet www.ecseonline.com; f. 2001; regional securities market designed to facilitate the buying and selling of financial products for the eight member territories—Anguilla, Antigua and Barbuda, Dominica, Grenada, Montserrat, Saint Christopher and Nevis, Saint Lucia, and Saint Vincent and the Grenadines; Chair. Sir K. DWIGHT VENNER; Gen. Man. and CEO TREVOR E. BLAKE.

INSURANCE

A-Affordable Insurance Services Inc: Old Factory Plaza, POB 6, The Valley; tel. 497-5757; fax 497-2122.

British American Insurance Co Ltd: Herbert's Commercial Centre, POB 148, The Valley; tel. 497-2653; fax 497-5933; e-mail britam@anguillenet.com.

Caribbean Alliance Insurance Co Ltd: POB 1377, The Valley; tel. 497-3525; fax 497-3526; e-mail info@d3ent.com.

D-3 Enterprises Ltd: Caribbean Commercial Complex, POB 1377, The Valley; tel. 497-3525; fax 497-3526; e-mail d-3ent@anguillanet.com; internet www.d-3enterprises.com; Man. Dir CLEMENT RUAN.

Gulf Insurance Ltd: c/o Ferry Boat Inn, POB 189, Blowing Point; tel. 497-6613; fax 497-6713; e-mail ferryb@anguillanet.com; internet www.gulfinsuranceltd.com; Contact MARJORIE MCCLEAN.

Malliouhana-Anico Insurance Co Ltd (MAICO): Herbert's Commercial Centre, POB 492, The Valley; tel. 497-3712; fax 497-3710; e-mail maico@anguillanet.com; Man. MONICA HODGE.

National Caribbean Insurance Co Ltd: Caribbean Commercial Complex, POB 323, The Valley; tel. 497-2865; fax 497-3783.

National General Insurance Co N.V. (NAGICO): c/o Fairplay Management Services, POB 79, The Valley; tel. 497-2976; fax 497-3303; e-mail fairplay@anguillanet.com; internet www.nagico.com.

Trade and Industry

DEVELOPMENT ORGANIZATION

Anguilla Development Board: Cannon Ball Office Complex, Wallblake Rd, POB 285, The Valley; tel. 497-2595; fax 497-2959; f. 1979; provides financial and technical assistance to fishing, agriculture, tourism and industry; Gen. Man. ALTHEA HODGE.

CHAMBER OF COMMERCE

Anguilla Chamber of Commerce and Industry: POB 321, The Valley; tel. and fax 497-3880; e-mail acoci@caribcable.com; internet www.anguillachamber.com; Pres. JOHN BENJAMIN; Exec. Dir CALVIN BARTLETT.

INDUSTRIAL AND TRADE ASSOCIATION

Anguilla Financial Services Association (AFSA): POB 1071, The Valley; tel. 498-4224; fax 498-4220; e-mail support@anguillafsd.com; internet www.anguillafsc.com; Pres. JOHN D. K. LAWRENCE.

UTILITIES

Electricity

Anguilla Electricity Co Ltd: POB 400, The Valley; tel. 497-5200; fax 497-5440; e-mail info@anglec.com; internet www.anglec.com; f. 1991; operates a power station and 12 generators; Chair. RODNEY REY; Gen. Man. THOMAS HODGE.

Transport

ROADS

Anguilla has 140 km (87 miles) of roads, of which 100 km are tarred.

SHIPPING

The principal port of entry is Sandy Ground on Road Bay. There is a daily ferry service between Blowing Point and Marigot (St Martin). The first phase of the Anguilla Ports Development Project commenced in July 2006 with the development of Road Bay; upon completion in October, extensive work began at Blowing Point to create three new piers, two of which were to be devoted to ferry and passenger services. Construction of the new facilities was completed in 2007.

Link Ferries: Little Harbour; tel. 497-2231; fax 497-3290; e-mail fbconnor@anguillanet.com; internet www.link.ai; f. 1992; daily services to Julianna International Airport (St Martin) and charter services to neighbouring islands and offshore quays; Capt. and Owner FRANKLYN CONNOR.

CIVIL AVIATION

Clayton J. Lloyd International Airport (known as Wallblake Airport until July 2010), 3.2 km (2 miles) from The Valley, has an asphalt-surfaced runway with a length of 1,665 m (5,462 ft). Reconstruction and expansion of the airport was completed in 2004. Most of the cost of the EC $49.2m. project was allocated to the extension of the runway to accommodate mid-range aircraft. LIAT and Winair regional airlines also operate from Clayton J. Lloyd International Airport.

American Eagle: POB 659, Clayton J. Lloyd International Airport; tel. 497-3131; fax 497-3502; regional partner co of American Airlines; operates scheduled flights from Puerto Rico 3 times a day (December to April) and once daily (May to November); Regional Man. EVETTE NEGRON.

Anguilla Air Services: POB 559, Clayton J. Lloyd International Airport; tel. 498-5922; fax 498-5921; e-mail info@anguillaairservices.com; internet www.anguillaairservices.com; f. Dec. 2006; operates passenger and cargo charter flights from Anguilla to neighbouring islands; official carrier for Winair (Winward Islands Airways) in Anguilla; Man. Dir CARL THOMAS.

Trans Anguilla Airways (2000) Ltd (TAA): POB 1329, Clayton J. Lloyd International Airport; tel. 497-8690; fax 497-8689; e-mail transang@anguillanet.com; internet www.transanguilla.com; f. 1996; air charter service in the Eastern Caribbean; Chair. JOSHUA GUMBS.

Tourism

Anguilla's sandy beaches and unspoilt natural beauty attract tourists and also day visitors from neighbouring St Martin/St Maarten. Tourism receipts totalled an estimated EC $229.1m. in 2009, and there were 746 hotel rooms on the island in 2005. Visitor arrivals totalled 109,159 in 2009.

Anguilla Hotel and Tourism Association: Coronation Ave, POB 1020, The Valley; tel. 497-2944; fax 497-3091; e-mail ahta@anguillanet.com; internet www.ahta.ai; f. 1981; Exec. Dir TRUDY NIXON.

Anguilla Tourist Board: Coronation Ave, POB 1388, The Valley, AI 2640; tel. 497-2759; fax 497-2710; e-mail atbtour@anguillanet.com; internet www.anguilla-vacation.com; Dir CANDIS NILES.

Defence

The United Kingdom is responsible for the defence of Anguilla. According to the 2008 budget address, proposed recurrent expenditure on the Royal Anguilla Police Force was EC $10.9m. (equivalent to 5.5% of total recurrent expenditure), representing a 26% increase on the allocation for 2007.

Education

Education is free and compulsory between the ages of five and 16 years. Primary education begins at five years of age and lasts for six years. Secondary education, beginning at 11 years of age, lasts for a further six years. There are six government primary schools and one government secondary school. According to UNESCO estimates, in 2007/08 enrolment at primary schools included 93% of children in the relevant age-group, while in 2004/05 enrolment at secondary schools included 91% of pupils in the relevant age-group. A 'comprehensive' secondary school education system was introduced in 1986. Post-secondary education is undertaken abroad. A new five-year strategic Education Development Plan was being discussed by the Government in 2010. According to the 2008 budget address, government expenditure on education was to total EC $22m. in that year, equivalent to 11% of proposed recurrent expenditure and an increase of 21% on the allocation for 2007.

ANTIGUA AND BARBUDA

Geography

PHYSICAL FEATURES

Antigua and Barbuda is in the Leeward Islands, in the north-eastern Caribbean, the Atlantic Ocean spreading to the east. The country's nearest neighbour is the British dependency of Montserrat, 43 km (27 miles) to the south-west of Antigua island, but only 24 km south-east of Redonda, the uninhabited western outpost of Antigua and Barbuda. Guadeloupe, a part of France, lies to the south and Saint Christopher (Kitts) and Nevis to the west. The islands that continue the chain of the Lesser Antilles to the north-west are variously parts of the Dutch and French Antilles. Antigua and Barbuda has a total surface area of 442 sq km (171 sq miles), Antigua (280 sq km) being larger than Barbuda (161 sq km). Redonda covers only 1.6 sq km.

Most of the country consists of a flat, coral or limestone terrain, but there are higher areas anciently formed by volcanic activity (southern Antigua and Redonda). This contributes to an irregular shoreline of many beaches and harbours on the main island (in total, the country has 153 km of coastline). Antigua was the largest of the British Leeward Islands and, historically, the site of an important port (English Harbour) for the Royal Navy in the West Indies. The arid island is about 23 km long (east–west) and 18 km wide, and its complex coast is girdled by reefs and islets. In the south-west the largely treeless highlands culminate in Boggy Peak (402 m—1,319 ft). Boggy Peak was renamed Mount Obama in 2009.

By contrast, Barbuda, 42 km north of Antigua, is an entirely low-lying island (the highest point above sea level, in the north-eastern, ambitiously named Highlands, reaches only 38 m), with smoother shores and only one harbour, the large Codrington Lagoon on the west. The Lagoon is formed by the south-westward jutting Palmetto Point on the central western coast and a long, narrow spit of land heading northwards from there and culminating in Cedar Tree Point, which runs in a north-easterly direction to form the narrow sea entrance. The other side of this northern entrance to the lagoon is formed by Goat Island (which is actually connected to the mainland by a narrow isthmus). South of the Lagoon is the world's largest colony of frigate birds, and the island is home to many other birds and to turtles.

The rocky, scrubby cone of Redonda, 55 km west-south-west of Antigua, lies in the western or inner of the two chains of islands that the Lesser Antilles split into here, between Montserrat and Nevis. It is just over 1.5 km long (north–south) and barely 0.5 km wide. Redonda has achieved some notoriety as a putative kingdom, established by the Irish Shiell family from Montserrat seven years before the United Kingdom formally annexed the island in 1872 (placing it under the jurisdiction of the Antiguan authorities). Those authorities never bothered to dispute the royal title, which became particularly noted in British literary circles after the Second World War, when the poet John Gawsworth ('King Juan') promoted its court with the creation of an 'intellectual aristocracy'. The title is now disputed, but sovereignty of Redonda is firmly vested in the Crown of Antigua and Barbuda, while actual possession by goats and birds is seldom challenged.

CLIMATE

Antigua and Barbuda is prone to hurricanes and droughts, the low altitudes drawing little of the moisture carried by the constant Atlantic trade winds. Antigua receives more rainfall than Barbuda, at some 45 ins (1,143 mm) annually. Most rainfall is in September–November, at the end of the hurricane season. Average monthly temperatures range between 73°F and 85°F (23°C–29°C).

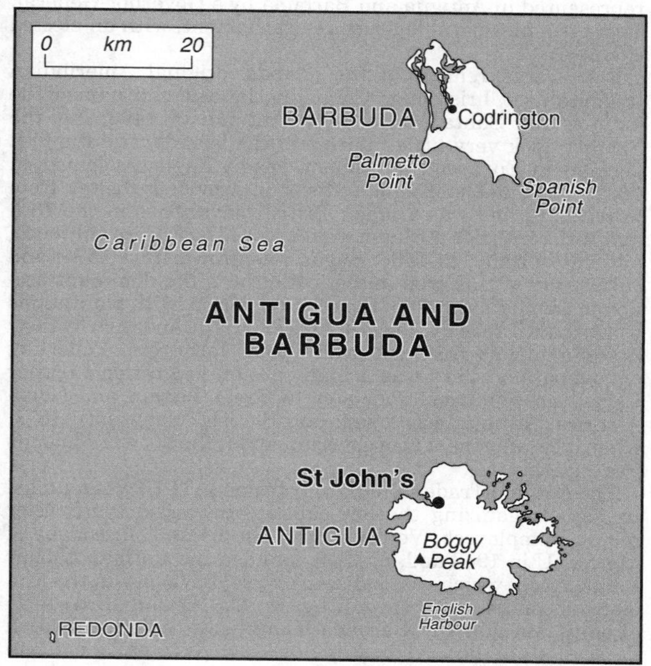

POPULATION

Most people are black, but there are some native whites (traditionally of British or Portuguese descent), as well as more recent communities from Syria and Lebanon. Moreover, as much as 10% of the population is reckoned to have emigrated from the Dominican Republic. Such groups often retain use of their own languages, but English is the official tongue. An English patois is also widely spoken. Most people are Christian, the main denomination being the Anglican Communion, as represented by the Church in the Province of the West Indies, although there are also Roman Catholic, Moravian and Protestant communities.

There were 77,426 people in the country at the time of the May 2001 census (over 98% of them on Antigua), and, according to official projections, this figure had increased to 89,138 by mid-2009. There is a large immigrant population, notably from the Dominican Republic and, since 1995, from Montserrat—some 3,000 are reckoned to have fled the volcano to Antigua. Saint John's, in the north, is the national capital, the largest city and the main port. It had an estimated population of 26,580 people in mid-2009, according to UN estimates, while the chief town of Barbuda, Codrington, is home to most of the island's population of some 1,500. For administrative purposes, Barbuda is separate from Antigua (Redonda is also a separate unit), and the main island is divided into six parishes.

History

MARK WILSON

Antigua and Barbuda is a constitutional monarchy within the Commonwealth. Queen Elizabeth II is Head of State, and is represented in Antigua and Barbuda by a Governor-General. There is a bicameral legislature, Parliament, with an elected chamber.

Few traces remain of the islands' original Amerindian inhabitants. Christopher Columbus landed and named the main island Santa María de la Antigua in 1493, but the Spanish took very little interest in the islands, and the first permanent European settlement was by English colonists in 1632. The inlet of English Harbour provided shelter from hurricanes, and was a major British naval base in the 18th and 19th centuries. Antigua was captured by France only once, and very briefly, in 1666. Sugar was grown from 1674, and cultivation of this crop and of cotton was the dominant economic activity for most of the colonial period, with plantations worked until 1834 by slaves of African origin, and then by their descendants as free, but badly paid, labourers. Following emancipation, there was a high rate of emigration to other Caribbean countries, and later to Great Britain and North America. Antigua was a separate British colony until 1871, when it became the seat of government for the Leeward Islands Federation.

The Antigua Trades and Labour Union (ATLU) was founded in 1939, organizing the low-paid sugar workers and other manual employees. Vere C. Bird, Sr, became President of the ATLU in 1943 and, in 1946, founded the Antigua Labour Party (ALP), which won a decisive election victory in the first elections under universal suffrage in 1951. During Bird's term of office Antigua and Barbuda, along with the other British possessions in the Caribbean, enjoyed steady improvements in living standards, education and social services. As a result, he won the fierce loyalty of most lower-income Antiguans.

Following the dissolution of the Leeward Islands Federation in 1957, Antigua and Barbuda joined the Federation of the West Indies in 1958, along with nine other British colonies. Following the departure of Jamaica and Trinidad and Tobago in 1962, the Federation collapsed and an attempt to unite the remaining colonies as the 'little eight' was unsuccessful. Along with its neighbours, Antigua and Barbuda became a British Associated State in 1967, responsible for its internal affairs, with the United Kingdom retaining control of external affairs and defence.

Vere Bird's ALP remained in government until February 1971, when George Walter's Progressive Labour Movement (PLM) began a troubled period in office. Regaining power in 1976, the ALP presided over the transition to independence on 1 November 1981.

After 1976 the ALP won six successive election victories. The Bird family retained control of the party machinery, and continued to enjoy loyal popular support. Almost 29% of the labour force was employed directly by the state, and many public employees felt a close and personal bond with the ALP's leadership. Several small and large private sector businesses had close links with ALP government ministers. Until November 2000 no radio or television station deemed to be critical of the Government was licensed to operate.

However, the Government's political credibility was damaged over an extended period by a series of scandals. Of these, the most widely documented concerned a Colombian diplomatic note, dated 3 April 1990 and delivered to the Antiguan permanent representative at the Organization of American States (OAS), stating that Israeli-manufactured weapons found on the property of a known Colombian drugs-trafficker had been traced to a delivery made to the Antigua Defence Force. The Prime Minister's eldest son, Vere Bird, Jr, was Minister of National Security at the time. The Governor-General appointed a British Queen's Counsel, Sir Louis Blom Cooper, to undertake a Commission of Inquiry. His conclusions included a recommendation that Vere Bird, Jr, 'should not hold any public office again'. Bird, Jr, was consequently dismissed from his post and banned for life from holding government office. The head of the Defence Force was also removed from office.

The Inquiry's conclusions helped to settle a succession struggle within the Bird family. Vere Bird, Sr, retired as leader of the ALP in September 1993, at the age of 84, and was succeeded by another son, Lester Bryant Bird, who led the party into an election on 8 March 1994. The campaign was hard fought. Three small opposition parties had merged in 1992 to form the United Progressive Party (UPP), led by Baldwin Spencer, a senior official of the Antigua Workers' Union. At the election, the UPP increased its parliamentary representation from one seat to five. The ALP's share of the popular vote declined to 54%, from 64% in 1989, but the party retained 11 seats, and Lester Bird became Prime Minister. In May 1996 Vere Bird, Jr, was controversially appointed to the post of Special Adviser to the Prime Minister.

At the next election, held on 9 March 1999, the ALP's share of the popular vote was reduced slightly further, to 53%, but the party gained an additional seat from the UPP by a margin of eight votes. A Commonwealth observer team criticized the electoral process, while independent observers noted that large numbers of voters had been given generous gifts of food, or had been allowed to import vehicles duty free in what the Prime Minister referred to as an exercise in 'poverty alleviation'. Vere Bird, Jr, was appointed Minister of Agriculture, Lands and Fisheries, on the basis that he had been elected to Parliament by voters who were aware of the findings of the Blom Cooper Commission of Inquiry.

In 2001 a further serious controversy developed over the management of the Government's Medical Benefits Scheme, which prompted the dismissal, in May, of the Attorney-General, Errol Cort, and the Leader of Government Business in the Senate, George 'Bacchanal' Walker. The Government reluctantly agreed to appoint a Commission of Inquiry into the management of the Scheme. In April 2002, following fraud allegations arising from the Inquiry, a minister resigned. The report of the Inquiry, published in July, detailed serious and systematic mismanagement, and recommended that the Director of Public Prosecutions should consider prosecuting 14 public officials, including two former health ministers. Some of these were subsequently charged.

In advance of the 2004 general election, a completely new electoral register was, with the assistance of the Electoral Office of Jamaica, prepared for the first time since 1975. Elimination of the names of the deceased and non-residents reduced the list by more than one-fifth, while voters were issued with identity cards including a photograph and fingerprint, decreasing the risk that illegitimate votes would be cast. At the election, held on 23 March, the UPP increased its share of the vote to 55%, securing 12 of the 17 seats, with an additional seat for the UPP's ally, the Barbuda People's Movement. The ALP took only 42% of the vote and four seats; both Lester Bird and Vere Bird, Jr, were defeated. Voter turn-out, at 91%, was extremely high, and the election was widely seen as a watershed in national politics. Baldwin Spencer became Prime Minister, and committed his Government to a pragmatic reformist programme and the control of corruption and mismanagement. None the less, the ALP retained a strong core of support, particularly in the civil service and police. Immediately before the election, a large number of files at the Prime Minister's office were destroyed, making it difficult for the incoming Government to establish the true state of public finances, debt or contracts with the private sector. Errol Cort, who had switched parties before the election, took Lester Bird's seat for the UPP and became finance minister in the new Cabinet.

The increasing prevalence of crime in the Caribbean region in recent years was also an important issue in Antigua, where the number of violent crimes had escalated rapidly: reported murders had risen from three, in both 2004 and 2005, to 12 in 2006 and 19 in 2007. The number of reported murders declined slightly to 14 in 2008 and 13 in 2009, but among those killed in

2008 were a British honeymoon couple shot in their hotel cottage, whose deaths brought unwelcome international attention. The increase in violent crime was attributed to an escalation in drugs-related gang disputes, and in part to an increase in the number of criminal deportees repatriated from the USA. Drugs transshipment is a continuing problem; the Government in 2009 estimated that 60% of the cocaine passing through the islands was destined for the United Kingdom, with 25% for the USA and 10% for the neighbouring island of Saint-Martin.

The IMF observed that the new Government had achieved progress in its attempt to restabilize the economy; however, the political atmosphere remained strongly polarized in 2008. Investigations into allegations against members of the former ALP administration led to criminal charges against Lester Bird, several former cabinet ministers, and their financial associates, but procedural issues were raised to delay their progress through the judicial system. The office of the Special Task Force against Corruption and Organised Crime was damaged in an arson attack in January 2008. After a series of faction fights, the ALP seemed better able to display unity as a new election approached. Divisions also opened within the UPP from 2005, weakening its public image: one focus of contention was the Antigua Public Utilities Authority, which operates electricity, water and domestic telecommunications services, and the governing board of which was dismissed in November 2005 following indications of financial malpractice. However, in a by-election on 26 March 2008 the UPP convincingly held the seat of the late Minister of Agriculture, Lands, Marine Resources and Agro Industries, Charlesworth Samuel, who had died in January, with 94% of votes cast. The ALP did not feel able to contest the poll, leaving the field open to two small opposition groups.

A further problem was continuing partisan support for the ALP from former political appointees in the police force and public service. There was widespread concern over the shooting in October 2006 of Denfield 'Tody' Thomas, the driver of the Minister of Culture Eleston Adams; following an official inquiry, a police officer was found guilty of his murder in October 2009. A report on the Royal Police Force of Antigua and Barbuda by Alphonse Breau, a retired Assistant Commissioner of the Royal Canadian Mounted Police, was completed in August 2007, and concluded that the force was debilitated by political polarization, and suffered from weak operational standards, poor leadership, as well as problems with corruption, management, training and communications, and insufficient material resources. A former member of the Ottawa Police Service, Gary Nelson, was appointed Commissioner of Police in Antigua from the start of March 2008, supported by three other Canadian officers on two-year contracts. Lester Bird stated that he viewed the appointments with 'utter abhorrence'. For reasons that were not clear, one Canadian officer resigned in July, and one in August, while Gary Nelson's contract was not renewed at the end of his six-month probationary period on 31 August. However, a new Canadian Commissioner and other senior staff were appointed, of whom three remained in place in mid-2010 with extensions to their initial two-year contracts. Nevertheless, a significant element within the police force remained hostile to the new leadership and to the Government in mid-2010.

Allen Stanford, an investor of Texan origin (USA) who now has Antiguan citizenship, played an important role in the island's affairs from the early 1990s, when he moved his 'offshore' banking activities from Montserrat, following their closure by the British authorities. He enjoyed a close relationship with the ALP Government that was then in office, acquiring Antiguan citizenship and developing 'onshore' (Bank of Antigua) and 'offshore' (Stanford International Bank) banks, property, construction and leisure companies, a daily newspaper (Antigua Sun), and a regional airline, Caribbean Star. The Stanford group was Antigua's second largest employer after the Government. However, Stanford distanced himself from the Bird regime ahead of the March 2004 election. Disagreements over a resort project developed by Stanford (see Economy) appear to have contributed to his rupture with the UPP Government in 2007, and Stanford's move to a new accommodation with the ALP, on the nomination of which he had been conferred with a knighthood in 2006 (the title was revoked in 2009). Closure of his airlines by early 2007 indicated growing financial difficulties, although Stanford was heavily involved in costly international and regional cricket sponsorship. The US authorities in February 2009 charged Stanford and several of his companies with organizing a fraudulent investment scheme; the case remained before the courts in mid-2010. Indicating the weakness of local financial regulation, the Antiguan Financial Services Regulatory Commission had in late 2008 given a clean bill of health to the Stanford International Bank. Its chief executive officer, Leroy King, was indicted by a grand jury in Houston, Texas, in June 2009 for alleged corruption, and a court in Antigua ordered his extradition in April 2010; he remained in Antigua under house arrest in early July.

At a general election on 12 March 2009, the UPP Government lost ground to the ALP opposition, still led by Lester Bird. The UPP's share of the popular vote declined to 51.1%, compared with 55% in 2004, and from 12 to nine seats, while the ALP moved to 47.0% and seven seats. Lester Bird, now 71 years of age and still ALP leader, regained his seat from Errol Cort. The Barbuda result was again narrow, with Trevor Walker of the Barbuda People's Movement defeating the ALP candidate by a single vote. The voter turn-out was 81%, a high figure, but down from 91% in 2004. The polling process did not run smoothly, with polling stations opening up to six hours late, and voters' lists, identity cards and ballot papers not ready for the scheduled start of the poll. However, election observers from the OAS, the Commonwealth and the Caribbean Community saw no evidence that either rival party was disproportionately affected.

Following the election, there was some remaining political uncertainty. Six defeated ALP candidates initiated a legal challenge to the result, and an unsuccessful UPP candidate challenged the electoral list. There were widespread reports that Walker and several UPP members of Parliament, including Cort (now Minister of National Security), were offered substantial inducements to change sides. The Deputy Prime Minister Wilmoth Daniel resigned that post in early May 2009, but remained in the Cabinet with responsibility for health. Meanwhile, the High Court ruled in March that polling day irregularities were such that the election of three members of Parliament, including Spencer, was invalid, and that by-elections should be held for those seats. Following appeals from the three members concerned, an order was obtained allowing them to retain their seats (and the Government its majority) pending a final ruling. The Court of Appeal received final written submissions from each side in July.

A dispute with the USA over restrictions on the use by US residents of internet gambling sites based in Antigua remained unresolved in mid-2008: an April 2005 ruling by a World Trade Organization (WTO) appellate body stated that while the USA was entitled to regulate gambling, some existing legislation discriminated against 'offshore' jurisdictions. However, Antigua maintained that the USA made no attempt to modify its legislation to ensure compliance with the ruling before the expiry of an April 2006 deadline. In October 2006 the US Congress approved legislation (the Unlawful Internet Gambling Enforcement Act) outlawing credit card payments to internet gambling websites, a move that the WTO in turn ruled illegal in March 2007. The USA announced in May that it would withdraw from any commitments relating to gambling under the General Agreement on Trade in Services (GATS), while Antigua attempted to gain wider international support for its position. As licenser and regulator for 32 internet gambling concerns within its jurisdiction, Antigua alleged that the prohibitive new legislation implemented by the USA had resulted in lost earnings, amounting to an estimated US $90m., and caused the loss of some 2,800 jobs, an estimate that most sources believed to be greatly exaggerated. Since the introduction of earlier US online gambling restrictions in 2000 it was claimed that revenue from the industry had declined from US $1,000m. a year to US $130m. in 2006. Licence fees and charges totalled almost US $2.8m. The Government in June 2007 claimed the right to impose sanctions to the value of US $3,400m. (three times the national gross domestic product) in compensation against the USA, through the withdrawal of intellectual property protection in Antigua for US trademarks, patents and industrial designs. Australia, Canada, India, Japan and the European Union also filed compensation claims. A WTO panel in December awarded Antigua the right to impose sanctions, but to the much lower value of US $21m. a year; the USA offered US $500,000. The World Intellectual Property Organization held that, notwithstanding the WTO ruling, Antigua remained bound by its obligations under the Berne Convention. The USA contended that the terms it had originally negotiated under the Agreement did not explicitly refer to internet gambling, thus rendering it exempt from the payment of the compensation. Nevertheless, the USA maintained its restrictions on internet gambling, and in November 2009 the founder of online gambling company BetOnSports was sentenced to 51 months in prison for violating racketeering and other laws.

In June 2006, at the annual meeting of the International Whaling Commission, Antigua voted, along with other members of the Organisation of Eastern Caribbean States (OECS), in favour of an end to a 20-year commercial whaling ban, despite lacking a recent whaling tradition and scientific expertise in the relevant issues. The Government's pro-whaling stance brought allegations that Japanese financial assistance had amounted to bribery (Japan led the campaign to end the ban), and that the vote had jeopardized relations with environmental groups and other foreign investors. Furthermore, at the Commission's 59th annual meeting in May 2007, Antigua was among several OECS countries to confirm their concurrence with a request, issued by Saint Vincent and the Grenadines, for an increase to those islands' commercial whaling quotas. An appeal for the protection of the indigenous and coastal population's rights to preserve their supposed traditional fishing practices—and for acknowledgement of earlier recommendations, by Saint Christopher and Nevis, that a policy of appropriate management of marine resources be adopted as opposed to a complete ban—was presented to the Commission. Opposition to the proposed establishment of a marine mammal sanctuary in the French West Indies was also reiterated, particularly as marine territorial boundaries between the French dependencies and several Eastern Caribbean nations remained in dispute.

The island of Barbuda has maintained an independent political tradition, in spite of its small population, and there have been several complex disputes between the islanders and the central Government over land development and other matters. An elected Council manages some aspects of the island's affairs. In the 2004 general election, the UPP-aligned Barbuda People's Movement (BPM) and the ALP-aligned Barbuda People's Movement for Change (BPMC) each won 400 votes. A re-run election on 20 April resulted in a narrow win for the BPM, with 408 votes to 394 for the BPMC. The new Member of Parliament, Trevor Walker, was appointed Minister of State with Responsibility for Barbuda Affairs, thus integrating the smaller island into the national decision-making process. After winning the seat in 2009 by a single vote, he took cabinet responsibility for works and transport. In March 2005 the BPM also won the island council election, which ended a deadlock arising from the BPM and the BPMC each having won four seats at the 2003 election.

Economy

MARK WILSON

Antigua and Barbuda is the third smallest country in the Western hemisphere, in terms of population, with some 89,139 inhabitants living on its 442 sq km in 2009. However, the islands have developed a relatively prosperous middle-income economy, with a per-head gross domestic product (GDP) at market prices of US $10,500 in 2009. The pace of economic growth picked up in the mid-2000s, increasing from a rise of 2.0% in 2001 to an average of 7.7% in 2003–07. However, the important tourism sector has been broadly stagnant since the mid-1990s, with a further downturn in 2008 and 2009 as international demand declined sharply; remittances from overseas migrants and investment inflows also decreased. GDP grew by only 0.2% in 2008, and contracted by 8.5% in 2009. Arrivals of stop-over tourists grew by only 1.5% in 2008, before contracting by 11.8% in 2009 as the international recession resulted in fewer tourist arrivals and reduced investment; the construction sector moved from 5% growth in 2008 to a contraction of 25% in 2009, as private and public sector activity slowed sharply, while the balance of payments deficit widened to 2.7% of GDP. The staging of the Cricket World Cup in Antigua and Barbuda (and other Caribbean islands) in 2007 contributed to construction sector growth of 19.5% in 2005 and an estimated 35% in 2006, but was disappointing in terms of tourism revenues. Unemployment is fairly low (estimated at 8.1% in 2001, and believed to have declined further from then to 2007, before increasing in 2008–10), and wages are high enough to attract immigrants from less prosperous Caribbean countries such as Dominica, the Dominican Republic and Guyana. There is concern about the extent of government debt: according to IMF estimates, total foreign and domestic government debt peaked in 2003 at EC $2,989m. (or 147% of GDP), much of it private borrowing at commercial rates. Debt had been reduced to an estimated 90% of GDP by December 2008, partly because of negotiated partial debt forgiveness and restructuring. However, the economic contraction of 2009 increased the debt-to-GDP ratio to 115% (according to IMF estimates) by the end of that year, with arrears at 53% of GDP. In 2005 as much as 29% of the labour force was employed directly by the Government, while wages and salaries accounted for some 64% of recurrent revenue, a rate that was reduced to 45% by 2009 (and was expected to be reduced further); public sector salaries were frozen in 2009. The previous (Antigua Labour Party—ALP) regime found increasing and obvious difficulty in paying salaries on time and in meeting regular financial commitments. The 2005 budget, the first presented for a full year by the new United Progressive Party (UPP) Government, aimed to narrow the gap with new taxes, including an income tax for the highest paid 25% of the population, while the efficiency of tax collections improved sharply and a value-added tax was introduced in 2007. The overall fiscal deficit moved from 12.4% of GDP in 2001 to 6.4% in 2007. Around 1,000 public service jobs (equivalent to 8% of total employment in the sector) were shed from 2006 through voluntary redundancy and early retirement programmes, contributing to a planned 20% reduction in public sector salary costs, which were projected at EC $350m. for 2008, down from EC $406m. in 2007. However, the economic difficulties of 2009 sharply decreased revenue and raised expenditure, with the fiscal deficit widening again to 14.8% of GDP. The IMF in June 2010 approved a US $117.8m. loan, while the Government agreed to a three-year plan involving spending reductions, revenue-raising measures, public sector reform, a debt-management strategy and policy reforms to mitigate financial sector risks.

Antigua and Barbuda is a member of the Caribbean Community and Common Market (CARICOM), the larger members of which formed the Caribbean Single Market at the start of 2006, with Antigua and Barbuda and the smaller islands joining on 3 July, following the resolution of economic and regional development concerns. It is also a member of the Organisation of Eastern Caribbean States, which links nine of the smaller Caribbean territories (Antigua and Barbuda, Dominica, Grenada, Montserrat, Saint Christopher (St Kitts) and Nevis, Saint Lucia, and Saint Vincent and the Grenadines, with Anguilla and the British Virgin Islands as associate members), while the Eastern Caribbean Central Bank, based in neighbouring Saint Christopher and Nevis, supervises its financial affairs. Antigua is of much greater economic significance than Barbuda, which is two-thirds the area of the main island, but which has a population of only some 1,500. A third island, Redonda, is much smaller and is uninhabited.

The main source of foreign exchange revenue is the service sector, principally tourism. Net earnings from services were 25.1% of GDP in 2009, with gross tourism earnings at US $303.7m., or 27.6% of GDP, which was not, however, enough to cover the deficit on merchandise trade, which was estimated at 49.9% of GDP. The islands' main attractions are their white sandy beaches, of which there are reputed to be 365. There are also fine historic naval sites at English Harbour, Nelson's Dockyard and Shirley Heights in the south-east of the island. There were 234,410 stop-over tourist arrivals in 2009, of whom 35% came from the USA, 40% from Europe (mostly the United Kingdom) and 6% from Canada. Cruise ship passengers outnumber stop-over tourists, and totalled 712,792 in 2009, although, with much lower per-head spending, they made a smaller contribution to the economy with only 4% of total tourist spending in 2005. Yachting and pleasure-boating is also an important and growing activity, centred on English Harbour, with 3,761 yachts bringing 21,226 visitors in 2009; Antigua's annual sailing week in April attracts several hundred yachts from across the Caribbean and world-wide. Barbuda has a small tourism industry, with three luxury hotels. In addition to tourism, an 'offshore' medical school, Indian-owned since 2008 (Manipal Education), generated significant year-round spending by its 1,000 students, as well as staff.

The tourism industry has been somewhat stagnant in recent years. In 2009 hotels and restaurants accounted for an estimated 7.5% of GDP, down from a peak value of 15.6% in 1994. High labour costs have been a particular problem for the sector. Relations of the former ALP Government with established investors were not always good, and some of the more intractable disputes remained unsettled in 2010. The industry suffered in 2001–03 from a downturn in the international economy. A slight recovery was witnessed in 2004, but the international economic recession brought serious difficulties from 2008, with stop-over arrivals declining by 11.8% in 2009.

Antigua serves as a hub for airline services to the smaller neighbouring islands, and is the headquarters of the major Eastern Caribbean airline, LIAT, which in October 2007 acquired some assets of Caribbean Star Airlines, established in 2000 by Stanford. The controlling shareholders of the airline are the Governments of Antigua, Barbados and St Vincent. However, the financial stability of the airline has been uneven, and it was affected by labour disputes in 2009–10.

There is an 'offshore' financial services sector, which has at times been a source of international concern. In 1999 the USA, the United Kingdom and other countries instructed their financial institutions to apply 'enhanced scrutiny' to transactions with Antigua and Barbuda; however, legislation to control money-laundering and financial fraud has since been more strictly enforced, and most restrictions had been lifted by 2001. The USA signed a Tax Information Exchange Treaty with Antigua and Barbuda in December of that year, although it is still listed by the US State Department as a jurisdiction of 'primary concern' for money-laundering, with attention focusing on investment fraud and advance fee fraud as much as on funds derived from narcotics. Even though the country was never included on the Financial Action Task Force's list of 'non-co-operative' jurisdictions, Antigua and Barbuda was placed on a list of so-called tax havens by the Organisation for Economic Co-operation and Development (OECD, based in Paris, France) in June 2000; it was removed from this list in 2002 after the Government signed a commitment to move towards the exchange of information with civil and criminal tax investigators by 2005. However, Antigua and Barbuda withdrew from this agreement in 2004, citing the failure of some OECD members to make similar commitments, and in April 2008 OECD included the islands in a 'grey list' of countries that did not yet have a significant number of Tax Information Exchange Agreements in place. In 2009 there were 18 licensed 'offshore' banks; more than 30 other banks had been closed for regulatory reasons since 1999. There were also 2,967 International Business Corporations in 2009, down from 15,000 in 1997, as well as 20 internet gambling companies, supervised in principle by the Directorate of Overseas Gaming, to which the owners of these sites paid annual licence fees of almost US $2.8m. In 2003 Antigua challenged US restrictions on internet gambling through the structures of the World Trade Organization (WTO), and in April 2005 received a ruling that was interpreted as partly in its favour. However, by mid-2008 the USA had failed to modify its regulatory regime to achieve compliance (having outlawed credit card payments to internet gambling sites in 2006) and stated in May 2007 that it would withdraw from any commitments on gambling made under the General Agreement on Trade in Services (GATS). The WTO in March 2007 made a further ruling in favour of Antigua, which attempted vigorously to gather international support for its stance. Nevertheless, the USA maintained its restrictions on internet gambling, and in November 2009 the founder of online gambling company BetOnSports was sentenced to 51 months in prison for violating racketeering and other laws. Indicating international recognition, Antigua in November 2008 received 'white list' status from the United Kingdom, allowing internet casinos to advertise for British customers. Plans were announced in the 2009 budget for a US $20m. horse-racing complex.

Allen Stanford, a US entrepreneur of Texan origin, moved to Antigua in the early 1990s after the closure of his Montserrat 'offshore' bank by the British authorities. He enjoyed a close relationship with the ALP Government that was then in office, acquiring Antiguan citizenship and developing many businesses. The Stanford group was Antigua's second largest employer after the government, to which it provided loans totalling US $85m., then more than 10% of GDP. However, Stanford distanced himself from the Lester Bird regime ahead of the March 2004 election. An agreement, announced in November 2004, with the incoming UPP administration provided for further funding, as well as a US $18.5m. debt cancellation. Stanford also announced plans for a EC $3,000m. resort development, to employ 1,000 people on completion, on a site previously earmarked under the ALP Government in 1997 for a Malaysian initiative that failed to materialize; however, a dispute over land ownership delayed progress on the scheme. Disagreements over this project appear to have contributed to Stanford's rupture with the Government in 2007, and his move to a new accommodation with the ALP, on the nomination of which he had been conferred with a knighthood in 2006 (the title was revoked in 2009). Closure of his airlines by early 2007 indicated growing financial difficulties, while a US $2,000m. Stanford Caribbean Investment Fund promised in 2002 came to nothing, although group companies claimed US $50,000m. in funds under management, with 30,000 clients, and Stanford was heavily involved in international and regional cricket sponsorship. The US authorities in February 2009 charged Stanford and several of his companies with organizing a fraudulent investment scheme, charges that remained before the courts in mid-2010. His local bank was taken over by an Eastern Caribbean consortium, while the assets of his 'offshore' operation fell far short of the amount needed to pay depositors. Indicating the weakness of local financial regulation, the Antiguan Financial Services Regulatory Commission had in late 2008 given a clean bill of health to the Stanford International Bank. Its chief executive officer, Leroy King, was indicted by a grand jury in Houston, Texas, in June 2009 for alleged corruption, and a court in Antigua ordered his extradition in April 2010; he remained in Antigua under house arrest in early July.

The Government has emphasized the importance of new technology, and telemarketing is seen as a promising area of activity. However, the islands have lagged behind their neighbours in liberalizing the telecommunications industry. Domestic landline services are provided by the state-owned Antigua Public Utilities Authority. However, Southern Caribbean Fibre landed a cable in March 2007, and an end is expected to the international voice call monopoly currently held by the local LIME (Cable & Wireless). There is also competition in cellular telephony. The state of infrastructures is uneven, however, with inadequate electricity supply and frequent power cuts.

Since the closure of the sugar industry, most of the land has been uncultivated. Agriculture accounted for only 1.7% of GDP in 2009, with a further 1.9% from fishing. The state owns most rural land. This has given it close control over residential, commercial and tourism-orientated development projects. There is a very small manufacturing sector, which contributed an estimated 1.8% of GDP in 2009, compared with 3.4% in 1990. It includes a brewery and a paints company, which cater mainly for the domestic market.

Statistical Survey

Source (unless otherwise stated): Ministry of Information, Broadcasting, Telecommunications, Science & Technology, Coolidge Business Complex, Sir George Walter Highway, Antigua; tel. 468-4600; e-mail minfinance@antigua.gov.ag; internet www.ab.gov.ag.

AREA AND POPULATION

Area: 441.6 sq km (170.5 sq miles).

Population: 62,922 at census of 28 May 1991; 76,886 (males 36,107, females 40,779) at census of 28 May 2001. *Mid-2009* (projected estimate): 89,138 (Source: Eastern Caribbean Central Bank).

Density (mid-2009): 201.9 per sq km.

Population by Age and Sex (2007): *0–14:* 24,276 (males 12,098, females 12,178); *15–64:* 55,721 (males 25,668, females 30,053); *65 and over:* 5,906 (males 2,576, females 3,330); *Total* 85,903 (males 40,342, females 45,561).

Principal Town: St John's (capital), population 24,451 at 2001 census. *Mid-2009* (UN estimate, incl. suburbs): St John's 26,580 (Source: UN, *World Urbanization Prospects: The 2009 Revision*).

Births, Marriages and Deaths (2007 unless otherwise indicated): Live births 1,240 (birth rate 14.44 per 1,000); Marriages 1,863; Deaths 504 (death rate 5.87 per 1,000). *2008:* Birth rate 16.8 per 1,000; Death rate 6.1 per 1,000. *2009:* Birth rate 16.6 per 1,000; Death rate 5.9 per 1,000 (Source: Pan American Health Organization).

Life Expectancy (years at birth, WHO estimates): 74 (males 73; females 75) in 2008. Source: WHO, *World Health Statistics*.

Employment (persons aged 15 years and over, official estimates, 2008): Agriculture, hunting and forestry 789; Fishing 290; Mining and Quarrying 121; Manufacturing 1,754; Electricity, gas and water supply 585; Construction 3,557; Wholesale and retail trade 5,516; Hotels and restaurants 5,783; Transport, storage and communications 3,203; Financial intermediation 1,195; Real estate, renting and business activities 1,665; Public administration and defence 4,986; Education 1,956; Health and social work 1,955; Other community, social and personal service activities 3,057; Households with employed persons 1,485; Extra-territorial organizations and bodies 572; Total employed 38,470 (males 19,321, females 19,149). Source: ILO.

HEALTH AND WELFARE

Key Indicators

Total Fertility Rate (children per woman, 2008): 2.1.

Under-5 Mortality Rate (per 1,000 live births, 2008): 12.

Physicians (per 1,000 head, 1999): 0.2.

Hospital Beds (per 1,000 head, 2006): 2.4.

Health Expenditure (2007): US $ per head (PPP): 946.

Health Expenditure (2007): % of GDP: 4.7.

Health Expenditure (2007): public (% of total): 69.4.

Access to Water (% of persons, 2004): 96.

Access to Sanitation (% of persons, 2004): 91.

Total Carbon Dioxide Emissions ('000 metric tons, 2006): 425.0.

Total Carbon Dioxide Emissions Per Head (metric tons, 2006): 5.0.

Human Development Index (2007): ranking: 47.

Human Development Index (2007): value: 0.868.

For sources and definitions, see explanatory note on p. vi.

AGRICULTURE, ETC.

Principal Crops ('000 metric tons, 2008, FAO estimates): Cantaloupes and other melons 0.9; Vegetables (incl. melons) 3.3; Guavas, mangoes and mangosteens 1.5; Fruits (excl. melons) 8.2.

Livestock ('000 head, 2008, FAO estimates): Asses 1.7; Cattle 14.6; Pigs 3.0; Sheep 20.0; Goats 37.0; Poultry 110.0.

Livestock Products ('000 metric tons, 2008, FAO estimates): Cattle meat 0.6; Cows' milk 5.4; Hen eggs 0.3.

Fishing (metric tons, live weight, 2008): Groupers and seabasses 258; Snappers and jobfishes 525; Grunts and sweetlips 216; Parrotfishes 259; Surgeonfishes 236; Triggerfishes and durgons 72; Caribbean spiny lobster 165; Stromboid conchs 1,357; Total catch (incl. others) 3,521.

Source: FAO.

INDUSTRY

Production (1988 estimates unless otherwise indicated): Rum 4,000 hectolitres; Wines and vodka 2,000 hectolitres; Electric energy (2007) 118m. kWh. Source: partly UN Industrial Commodity Statistics Database and Yearbook.

FINANCE

Currency and Exchange Rates: 100 cents = 1 Eastern Caribbean dollar (EC $). *Sterling, US Dollar and Euro Equivalents* (31 May 2010): £1 sterling = EC $3.937; US $1 = EC $2.700; €1 = EC $3.344; EC $100 = £25.41 = US $37.04 = €29.91. *Exchange rate:* Fixed at US $1 = EC $2.700 since July 1976.

Budget (EC $ million, 2008): *Revenue:* Tax revenue 692.4; Other current revenue 43.6; Capital revenue 5.2; Total 741.2, excl. grants received 30.0. *Expenditure:* Current expenditure 766.3 (Wages and salaries 300.4, Goods and services 185.0, Interest payments 102.6, Pensions 58.0, Transfers and subsidies 120.3); Capital expenditure 225.0; Total 991.3. Source: Eastern Caribbean Central Bank.

International Reserves (US $ million at 31 December 2009): IMF special drawing rights 19.61; Foreign exchange 108.24; Total 127.85. Source: IMF, *International Financial Statistics*.

Money Supply (EC $ million at 31 December 2009): Currency outside depository corporations 146.13; Transferable deposits 1,012.48; Other deposits 2,044.21; Broad money 3,202.82. Source: IMF, *International Financial Statistics*.

Cost of Living (Consumer Price Index; base: January 2001 = 100): 116.7 in 2007; 117.5 in 2008; 120.4 in 2009. Source: Eastern Caribbean Central Bank.

Expenditure on the Gross Domestic Product (EC $ million at current prices, 2008): Government final consumption expenditure 610.28; Private final consumption expenditure 989.67; Gross capital formation 2,571.85; *Total domestic expenditure* 4,171.80; Exports of goods and services 1,595.06; *Less* Imports of goods and services 2,517.91; *GDP at market prices* 3,248.95. Source: Eastern Caribbean Central Bank.

Gross Domestic Product by Economic Activity (EC $ million at current prices, 2008): Agriculture, hunting, forestry and fishing 84.88; Mining and quarrying 69.66; Manufacturing 49.72; Electricity and water 80.08; Construction 594.11; Trade 276.22; Restaurants and hotels 233.45; Transport and communications 529.66; Finance, insurance, real estate and business services 442.34; Government services 415.99; Other community, social and personal service activities 170.50; *Sub-total* 2,946.61; *Less* Financial intermediation services indirectly measured 238.09; *Gross value added in basic prices* 2,708.52; Taxes, less subsidies, on products 540.43; *GDP in market prices* 3,248.95. Source: Eastern Caribbean Central Bank.

Balance of Payments (EC $ million, 2009): Goods (net) –1,397.26; Services (net) 712.75; *Balance on goods and services* –684.51; Income (net) –122.00; *Balance on goods, services and income* –806.51; Current transfers (net) 40.31; *Current balance* –766.20; Capital account (net) 9.41; Direct investment (net) 375.92; Portfolio investment (net) –35.60; Other investments (net) 306.06; Net errors and omissions 74.30; *Overall balance* –36.12. Source: Eastern Caribbean Central Bank.

EXTERNAL TRADE

Total Trade (EC $ million): *Imports f.o.b.:* 1,727.4 in 2006; 1,761.9 in 2007; 1,544.3 in 2008. *Exports f.o.b.:* 68.1 in 2006; 72.9 in 2007; 66.7 in 2008. Source: Eastern Caribbean Central Bank.

Principal Commodities (US $ million, 2007): *Imports:* Food and live animals 85.7 (Meat and meat preparations 18.7; Vegetables and fruit 18.4); Beverages and tobacco 27.7 (Beverages 25.6); Crude materials (inedible) except fuels 15.3; Mineral fuels, lubricants, etc. 36.3 (Refined petroleum products 35.5); Chemicals and related products 43.3; Basic manufactures 93.5; Machinery and transport equipment 163.5 (Telecommunications and sound equipment 29.6; Road vehicles 46.7); Miscellaneous manufactured articles 106.4; Total (incl. others) 573.1. *Exports:* Beverages and tobacco 2.1 (Beverages 2.0); Crude materials (inedible) except fuels 0.6; Chemicals and related products 1.2 (Pigments, paints, varnishes, etc. 0.8); Basic manufactures 9.4 (Textiles, yarn, fabrics, made-up articles, etc. 3.2; Iron and steel 1.3); Machinery and transport equipment 19.7 (General industrial machinery and equipment 1.0; Telecommunications and sound equipment 8.1; Road vehicles 1.7); Miscellaneous manufactured articles 8.5; Total (incl. others) 98.6. Source: UN, *International Trade Statistics Yearbook*.

Principal Trading Partners (US $ million, 2007): *Imports:* Barbados 7.5; Brazil 5.2; Canada 13.4; China, People's Republic 7.6; Dominica 5.1; Dominican Republic 7.0; France (incl. Monaco) 5.3; Italy 15.9; Jamaica 5.0; Japan 24.6; Netherlands Antilles 23.8; Switzerland (incl. Liechtenstein) 7.9; Trinidad and Tobago 22.3; United Kingdom 36.8; USA 333.3; Total (incl. others) 573.1. *Exports:* Anguilla 2.8; Barbados 8.1; Dominica 6.0; France (incl. Monaco) 3.1; Germany 1.2; Jamaica 1.4; Netherlands Antilles 30.5; Nicaragua 3.9; Saint Christopher and Nevis 3.9; Saint Lucia 1.6; Saudi Arabia 1.6; United Kingdom 4.1; USA 23.2; Total (incl. others) 98.6. Source: UN, *International Trade Statistics Yearbook*.

TRANSPORT

Road Traffic (registered vehicles, 1998): Passenger motor cars and commercial vehicles 24,000. Source: UN, *Statistical Yearbook*.

Shipping (international freight traffic, '000 metric tons, 1990): Goods loaded 28; Goods unloaded 113 (Source: UN, *Monthly Bulletin of Statistics*). *Merchant Fleet* (registered at 31 December): 1,195 vessels (total displacement 9,536,889 grt) in 2008 (Source: Lloyd's Register-Fairplay, *World Fleet Statistics*).

Civil Aviation (traffic on scheduled services, 2005): Kilometres flown (million) 5; Passengers carried ('000) 778; Passenger-km (million) 123; Total ton-km (million) 11. Source: UN, *Statistical Yearbook*.

TOURISM

Visitor Arrivals: 959,260 (261,786 stop-over visitors, 24,686 yacht passengers, 672,788 cruise ship passengers) in 2007; 888,881 (265,844 stop-over visitors, 25,913 yacht passengers, 597,124 cruise ship passengers) in 2008; 965,431 (234,410 stop-over visitors, 21,226 yacht passengers, 709,795 cruise ship passengers) in 2009.

Tourism Receipts (EC $ million): 912.2 in 2007; 901.7 in 2008; 823.8 in 2009.

Source: Eastern Caribbean Central Bank.

COMMUNICATIONS MEDIA

Radio Receivers (1997): 36,000 in use*.

Television Receivers (1999): 33,000 in use*.

Telephones (2009): 37,400 main lines in use†.

Mobile Cellular Telephones (2009): 134,900 subscribers†.

Internet Users (2009): 65,000†.

Broadband (2009): 14,900 subscribers†.

Personal Computers: 17,500 (206.9 per 1,000 persons) in 2006†.

Daily Newspapers (2004): 2.

Non-daily Newspapers (1996): 4*.

* Source: UNESCO, *Statistical Yearbook*.

† Source: International Telecommunication Union.

‡ Source: UN, *Statistical Yearbook*.

EDUCATION

Pre-primary (2006/07 unless otherwise indicated): 21 schools (1983); 180 teachers (all females); 2,318 pupils (males 1,179, females 1,139). Source: UNESCO Institute for Statistics.

Primary (2006/07 unless otherwise indicated): 55 schools (2000/01); 538 teachers (males 41, females 497); 11,569 students (males 5,911, females 5,658). Source: UNESCO Institute for Statistics.

Secondary (2006/07 unless otherwise indicated): 14 schools (2000/01); 394 teachers (males 116, females 278); 7,838 students (males 3,830, females 4,008). Source: UNESCO Institute for Statistics.

Special (2000/01): 2 schools; 15 teachers; 61 students.

Tertiary (1986): 2 colleges; 631 students.

Pupil-teacher ratio (primary education, UNESCO estimate): 21.5 in 2006/07. Source: UNESCO Institute for Statistics.

Adult Literacy Rate: 99.0% in 2008 (males 98.4, females 99.4). Source: UNESCO Institute for Statistics.

Directory

The Constitution

The Constitution, which came into force at the independence of Antigua and Barbuda on 1 November 1981, states that Antigua and Barbuda is a 'unitary sovereign democratic state'. The main provisions of the Constitution are summarized below.

FUNDAMENTAL RIGHTS AND FREEDOMS

Regardless of race, place of origin, political opinion, colour, creed or sex, but subject to respect for the rights and freedoms of others and for the public interest, every person in Antigua and Barbuda is entitled to the rights of life, liberty, security of the person, the enjoyment of property and the protection of the law. Freedom of movement, of conscience, of expression (including freedom of the press), of peaceful assembly and of association is guaranteed, and the inviolability of family life, personal privacy, home and other property is maintained. Protection is afforded from discrimination on the grounds of race, sex, etc., and from slavery, forced labour, torture and inhuman treatment.

THE GOVERNOR-GENERAL

The British sovereign, as monarch of Antigua and Barbuda, is the Head of State and is represented by a Governor-General of local citizenship.

PARLIAMENT

Parliament consists of the monarch, a 17-member Senate and the House of Representatives, which is composed of 17 elected members. Senators are appointed by the Governor-General: 11 on the advice of the Prime Minister (one of whom must be an inhabitant of Barbuda), four on the advice of the Leader of the Opposition, one at his own discretion and one on the advice of the Barbuda Council. The Barbuda Council is the principal organ of local government in that island, whose membership and functions are determined by Parliament. The life of Parliament is five years.

Each constituency returns one Representative to the House who is directly elected in accordance with the Constitution.

The Attorney-General, if not otherwise a member of the House, is an ex officio member but does not have the right to vote.

Every citizen over the age of 18 is eligible to vote.

Parliament may alter any of the provisions of the Constitution.

THE EXECUTIVE

Executive authority is vested in the Monarch and exercisable by the Governor-General. The Governor-General appoints as Prime Minister that member of the House who, in the Governor-General's view, is best able to command the support of the majority of the members of the House, and other ministers on the advice of the Prime Minister. The Governor-General may remove the Prime Minister from office if a resolution of no confidence is approved by the House and the Prime Minister does not either resign or advise the Governor-General to dissolve Parliament within seven days.

The Cabinet consists of the Prime Minister and other ministers and the Attorney-General.

The Leader of the Opposition is appointed by the Governor-General as that member of the House who, in the Governor-General's view, is best able to command the support of a majority of members of the House who do not support the Government.

CITIZENSHIP

All persons born in Antigua and Barbuda before independence who, immediately prior to independence, were citizens of the United Kingdom and Colonies automatically become citizens of Antigua and Barbuda. All persons born outside the country with a parent or grandparent possessing citizenship of Antigua and Barbuda automatically acquire citizenship, as do those born in the country after independence. Provision is made for the acquisition of citizenship by those to whom it would not automatically be granted.

The Government

HEAD OF STATE

Queen: HM Queen ELIZABETH II.

Governor-General: LOUISE LAKE-TACK (took office on 17 July 2007).

CABINET
(July 2010)

The Cabinet comprised members of the United Progressive Party.

Prime Minister and Minister of Foreign Affairs: BALDWIN SPENCER.

Minister of Health, Social Transformation and Consumer Affairs: WILMOTH STAFFORD DANIEL.

Minister of National Security: Sen. Dr ERROL CORT.

Minister of Agriculture, Lands, Housing and the Environment: HILSON BAPTISTE.

Minister of Tourism, Civil Aviation and Culture: HERBERT JOHN MAGINLEY.

Minister of Finance, Economy and Public Administration: HAROLD E. E. LOVELL.

Minister of Works and Transport: TREVOR MYKE WALKER.

Minister of Education, Sports, Youth and Gender Affairs: Dr JACQUI QUINN-LEANDRO.

Attorney-General and Minister of Legal Affairs: JUSTIN L. SIMON.

Minister of State in the Ministry of Legal Affairs: Sen. JOANNE MAUREEN MASSIAH.

Minister of State in the Ministry of Education, Sports, Youth and Gender Affairs: WINSTON VINCENT WILLIAMS.

Minister of State in the Ministry of Tourism, Civil Aviation and Culture: ELESTON MONTGOMERY ADAMS.

Minister of State in the Office of the Prime Minister: Sen. Dr EDMOND MANSOOR.

Minister of State in the Ministry of Agriculture, Lands, Housing and the Environment: CHANLAH CODRINGTON.

Minister of State in the Ministry of Works and Transport: ELMORE CHARLES.

Minister of State in the Ministry of National Security: COLIN V. A. DERRICK.

MINISTRIES

Office of the Prime Minister: Queen Elizabeth Hwy, St John's; tel. 462-4956; fax 462-3225; internet www.antigua.gov.ag.

Ministry of Agriculture, Lands, Housing and the Environment: Queen Elizabeth Hwy, St John's; tel. 462-1543; fax 462-6104.

Ministry of Education, Sports, Youth and Gender Affairs: Govt Office Complex, Queen Elizabeth Hwy, St John's; tel. 462-4959; fax 462-4970; e-mail doristeen.etinoff@ab.gov.ag.

Ministry of Finance, Economy and Public Administration: Govt Office Complex, Parliament Dr., St John's; tel. 462-5015; fax 462-4860; e-mail minfinance@antigua.gov.ag.

Ministry of Foreign Affairs: Queen Elizabeth Hwy, St John's; tel. 462-1052; fax 462-2482; e-mail foreignaffairs@ab.gov.ag; internet www.foreignaffairs.gov.ag.

Ministry of Health, Social Transformation and Consumer Affairs: St John's.

Ministry of Legal Affairs: Government Complex, Queen Elizabeth Hwy, St John's; tel. 462-0017; fax 462-2465; e-mail legalaffairs@ab.gov.ag.

Ministry of National Security: Govt Office Complex, Parliament Dr., St John's.

Ministry of Tourism, Civil Aviation and Culture: Government Office Complex, Bldg 1, Queen Elizabeth Hwy, St John's; tel. 462-0480; fax 462-2483; e-mail mblackman@tourism.gov.ag.

Ministry of Works and Transport: St John's.

Legislature

PARLIAMENT

Senate

President: HAZELYN FRANCIS.

There are 17 nominated members.

House of Representatives

Speaker: D. GISELLE ISAAC-ARRINDELL.

Ex Officio Member: The Attorney-General.

Clerk: SYLVIA WALKER.

General Election, 12 March 2009

Party	Votes cast	%	Seats
United Progressive Party	21,205	51.1	9
Antigua Labour Party	19,460	47.0	7
Barbuda People's Movement	474	1.1	1
Independents	194	0.5	—
Organisation for National Development	119	0.3	—
Total	41,452	100.0	17

Election Commission

Antigua and Barbuda Electoral Commission (ABEC): Queen Elizabeth Hwy, POB 664, St. John's; tel. 562-4191; fax 562-4331; e-mail eleccom@candw.ag; internet www.abec.gov.ag; f. 2003; Chief Elections Officer LORNA SIMON.

Political Organizations

Antigua Labour Party (ALP): Upper Nevis St, St John's; tel. 562-7405; e-mail alpelection@hotmail.com; internet www.votealp.com; f. 1946; Leader LESTER BRYANT BIRD; Chair. and Dep. Leader GASTON BROWNE.

Barbuda People's Movement (BPM): Codrington; campaigns for separate status for Barbuda; allied to United Progressive Party; Parliamentary Leader THOMAS HILBOURNE FRANK; Chair. FABIAN JONES.

Barbuda People's Movement for Change (BPMC): Codrington; f. 2004; effectively replaced Organisation for National Reconstruction, which was f. 1983 and re-f. 1988 as Barbuda Independence Movt; advocates self-govt for Barbuda; supports the Antigua Labour Party; Pres. ARTHUR SHABAZZ-NIBBS.

Barbudans for a Better Barbuda: Codrington; f. 2004 by fmr Gen. Sec. of Barbuda People's Movement for Change; Leader ORDRICK SAMUEL.

First Christian Democratic Movement (FCDM): St John's; f. 2003; Leader EGBERT JOSEPH.

National Movement for Change (NMC): St John's; f. 2003; Leader ALISTAIR THOMAS.

Organisation for National Development: Upper St Mary's St, St John's; f. 2003 by breakaway faction of the United Progressive Party; Chair. GLENTIS GOODWIN; Sec.-Gen. VALERIE SAMUEL.

United Progressive Party (UPP): UPP Headquarters Bldg, Upper Nevis St, POB 2379, St John's; tel. 481-3888; fax 481-3877; e-mail info@uppantigua.com; internet www.uppantigua.com; f. 1992 by merger of the Antigua Caribbean Liberation Movt (f. 1979), the Progressive Labour Movt (f. 1970) and the United National Democratic Party (f. 1986); Leader BALDWIN SPENCER; Chair. LEON (CHAKU) SYMISTER.

Diplomatic Representation

EMBASSIES IN ANTIGUA AND BARBUDA

China, People's Republic: Cedar Valley, POB 1446, St John's; tel. 462-1125; fax 462-6425; e-mail chinaemb_ag@mfa.gov.cn; internet ag.chineseembassy.org/eng; Ambassador (vacant).

Cuba: Friars Hill, St John's; tel. 562-5864; fax 562-5867; e-mail cubanembassy@candw.ag; Ambassador JOSÉ MANUEL INCLÁN EMBADE.

Venezuela: Jasmine Court, Friar's Hill Rd, POB 1201, St John's; tel. 462-1574; fax 462-1570; e-mail embaveneantigua@yahoo.es; Ambassador JAVIER FLORENCIO LÓPEZ MORILLO.

Judicial System

Justice is administered by the Eastern Caribbean Supreme Court (ECSC), based in Saint Lucia, which consists of a High Court of Justice and a Court of Appeal. Two of the Court's 16 High Court Puisne Judges are resident in and responsible for Antigua and Barbuda, and preside over the Court of Summary Jurisdiction on the islands. One of two ECSC Masters, chiefly responsible for procedural and interlocutory matters, is also resident in Antigua. Magistrates' Courts in the territory administer lesser cases.

Acting Chief Justice: HUGH ANTHONY RAWLINS (resident in Saint Lucia).

Puisne Judges: ERROL THOMAS, LOUISE BLENMAN.

Master: CHERYL MATHURIN.

Solicitor-General: LEBRECHT HESSE.

Religion

The majority of the inhabitants profess Christianity, and the largest denomination is the Church in the Province of the West Indies (Anglican Communion).

CHRISTIANITY

Antigua Christian Council: POB 863, St Mary's St, St John's; tel. 461-1135; fax 462-2383; f. 1964; five mem. churches; Pres. Rt Rev. DONALD J. REECE (Roman Catholic Bishop of St John's-Basseterre); Treas. MARY-ROSE KNIGHT.

The Anglican Communion

Anglicans in Antigua and Barbuda are adherents of the Church in the Province of the West Indies. The diocese of the North Eastern Caribbean and Aruba comprises 12 islands: Antigua, St Kitts, Nevis, Anguilla, Barbuda, Montserrat, Dominica, Saba, St Martin/St Maarten, Aruba, St Bartholomew and St Eustatius. The See City is St John's, Antigua. According to the latest census (2001), some 26% of the population are Anglicans.

Bishop of the North Eastern Caribbean and Aruba: Rt Rev. LEROY ERROL BROOKS, Bishop's Lodge, POB 23, St John's; tel. 462-0151; fax 462-2090; e-mail dioceseneca@candw.ag.

The Roman Catholic Church

The diocese of St John's-Basseterre, suffragan to the archdiocese of Castries (Saint Lucia), includes Anguilla, Antigua and Barbuda, the British Virgin Islands, Montserrat and Saint Christopher and Nevis. The Bishop participates in the Antilles Episcopal Conference (whose Secretariat is based in Trinidad and Tobago). Some 10% of the population are Roman Catholics, according to the 2001 census.

Bishop of St John's-Basseterre: (vacant), Chancery Offices, POB 863, St John's; tel. 461-1135; fax 462-2383; e-mail djr@candw.ag.

Other Christian Churches

According to the 2001 census, some 12% of the population are Seventh-day Adventists, 11% are Pentecostalists, 10% are Moravians, 8% are Methodists and 5% are Baptists.

East Caribbean Baptist Mission: POB 2678, St John's; tel. 462-2894; fax 462-6029; e-mail admin@baptistantigua.org; internet www.baptistantigua.org; f. 1991; mem. congregation of the Baptist Circuit of Churches in the East Caribbean Baptist Mission; Presiding Elder Dr HENSWORTH W. C. JONAS.

Methodist Church: c/o POB 863, St John's; Supt Rev. ELOY CHRISTOPHER.

St John's Church of Christ: Golden Grove, Main Rd, St John's; tel. and fax 461-6732; e-mail stjcoc@candw.ag; Contact Evangelist CORNELIUS GEORGE.

St John's Evangelical Lutheran Church: Woods Centre, POB W77, St John's; tel. and fax 462-2896; e-mail sjlutheran@candw.ag; Principal E. JOHN FREDRICH; Pastors Rev. ANDREW JOHNSTON, Rev. JOSHUA STERNHAGEN, Rev. JASON RICHARDS, Rev. PAUL WORKENTINE.

The Press

Antigua Sun: 15 Pavilion Dr., Coolidge, POB W263, St John's; tel. 480-5960; fax 480-5968; e-mail editor@antiguasun.com; internet www.antiguasunonline.com; f. 1997; circ. 3,000; daily, Mon. to Fri.; weekend publication *SUN Weekend* publ. Saturday; publ. by Sun Printing and Publishing Ltd; Man. Editor TIMOTHY PAYNE; Dir of Operations PATRICK HENRY.

Daily Observer: LIAT Rd, Coolidge, POB 1318, St John's; tel. 480-1750; fax 480-1757; e-mail dailyobserver@candw.ag; internet www.antiguaobserver.com; ind.; Publr WINSTON A. DERRICK; Editor MICKEL BRANN; circ. 5,000.

The Worker's Voice: Emancipation Hall, 46 North St, POB 3, St John's; tel. 462-0090; f. 1943; 2 a week; official organ of the Antigua Labour Party and the Antigua Trades and Labour Union; Editor NOEL THOMAS; circ. 6,000.

Publishers

Antigua Printing and Publishing Ltd: Factory Rd, POB 670, St John's; tel. 462-1265; fax 462-6200.

Caribbean Publishing Co Ltd: Ryan's Place, Suite 1B, High St, POB 1451, St John's; tel. 462-2215; fax 462-0962.

Treasure Island Publishing Ltd: POB W283, Wood Centre, St John's; tel. and fax 463-7414; e-mail colettif@candw.ag.

West Indies Publishing Ltd: 3 Jasmine Court, Friars Hill Road, POB W883, St John's; tel. 461-0565; fax 461-9750; e-mail wip@candw.ag; internet www.westindiespublishing.com; f. 1992.

Broadcasting and Communications

TELECOMMUNICATIONS

Antigua Public Utilities Authority Personal Communications Services (APUA PCS): Cassada Gdns, POB 416, St John's; tel. 480-7000; fax 480-7476; internet www.apua.ag; f. 2000; digital mobile cellular telephone network; sale of 67% to Irish-owned consortium Digicel agreed in Nov. 2005; Gen. Man. ALLAN WILLIAMS.

Digicel Antigua and Barbuda: Antigua Wireless Ventures Ltd, POB W32, St John's; tel. 480-2050; fax 480-2060; e-mail customercareantiguaandbarbuda@digicelgroup.com; internet www.digicelantiguaandbarbuda.com; acquired Cingular Wireless' Caribbean operations and licences in 2005; owned by an Irish consortium; Chair. DENIS O'BRIEN; Eastern Caribbean CEO KEVIN WHITE.

LIME: 42–44 St Mary's St, POB 65, St John's; internet www.time4lime.com; fmrly Cable & Wireless (Antigua and Barbuda) Ltd; name changed as above 2008; contact centres in Jamaica and Saint Lucia; CEO RICHARD DODD.

BROADCASTING

Radio

ABS Radio: POB 590, St John's; tel. 462-3602; e-mail alex@hotmail.com; internet www.cmatt.com/abs.htm; f. 1956; subsidiary of Antigua and Barbuda Broadcasting Service (see Television); Programme Man. KENNY NIBBS.

Abundant Life Radio: Codrington Village, Barbuda; tel. 562-4821; e-mail afternoonpraise@gmail.com; internet www.abundantliferadio.com; f. 2001; began broadcasting in Antigua in 2003; Christian station; daily, 24-hour broadcasts; Man. Dir EVANGELIST CLIFTON FRANCOIS.

Caribbean Radio Lighthouse: POB 1057, St John's; tel. 462-1454; fax 462-7420; e-mail info@radiolighthouse.org; internet www.radiolighthouse.org; f. 1975; religious broadcasts in Spanish and English; operated by Baptist Int. Mission Inc (USA); Gen. Man. JERRY BAKER.

Caribbean Relay Co Ltd: POB 1203, St John's; tel. 462-0994; fax 462-0487; e-mail cm-crc@candw.ag; jtly operated by British Broadcasting Corpn and Deutsche Welle.

Crusader Radio: Redcliffe St, POB 2379, St John's; tel. 562-4610; fax 481-3892; e-mail crusaderradio@candw.ag; internet www.crusaderradio.com; f. 2003; Crusader Publishing & Broadcasting Ltd; official station of the UPP; Station Man. DAVID GEORGE.

Gem Radio Network: Tristan's Crescent Cedar Valley, POB W939, St John's; tel. 744-7768; fax 720-7017; e-mail gemfmstereo@gmail.com.

Observer Radio: internet www.antiguaobserver.com; f. 2001; independently owned station; Gen. Man. WINSTON A. DERRICK.

ZDK Liberty Radio International (Radio ZDK): Grenville Radio Ltd, Bryant Pasture, Bird Rd, Ottos, POB 1100, St John's; tel. 462-1100; fax 462-1116; e-mail mail@radiozdk.com; internet www.radiozdk.com; f. 1970; commercial; also operates SUN Radio; Programme Dir IVOR BIRD; CEO E. PHILIP.

Television

Antigua and Barbuda Broadcasting Service (ABS): Directorate of Broadcasting and Public Information, POB 590, St John's; tel. 462-0010; fax 462-4442; scheduled for privatization; Dir-Gen. HOLLIS HENRY; CEO DENIS LEANDRO.

ABS Television: POB 1280, St John's; tel. 462-0010; fax 462-1622; f. 1964; Programme Man. JAMES TANNY ROSE.

CTV Entertainment Systems: 25 Long St, St John's; tel. 462-0346; fax 462-4211; cable television co; transmits 33 channels of US television 24 hours per day to subscribers; Programme Dir K. BIRD.

Finance

(cap. = capital; res = reserves; dep. = deposits; m. = millions; brs = branches)

BANKING

The Eastern Caribbean Central Bank, based in Saint Christopher, is the central issuing and monetary authority for Antigua and Barbuda.

ABI Bank Ltd (ABIB): ABI Financial Center, 156 Redcliffe St, POB 1679, St John's; tel. 480-2700; fax 480-2750; e-mail abib@abifinancial.com; internet www.abifinancial.com/ABIB; f. 1990 as Antigua Barbuda Investment Bank Ltd; part of the ABI Financial Group; cap. EC $21.2m., res EC $38.1m., dep. EC $997.8m. (Sept. 2008); Chair. SYLVIA O'MARD; Country Man. EVERETT CHRISTIAN; 3 brs.

Antigua and Barbuda Development Bank: 27 St Mary's St, POB 1279, St John's; tel. 462-0838; fax 462-0839; f. 1974; Gen. Man. DON CHARLES.

Antigua Commercial Bank: St Mary's and Thames Sts, POB 95, Loans, St John's; tel. 481-4200; fax 481-4229; e-mail acb@acbonline.com; internet www.acbonline.com; f. 1955; auth. cap. EC $5m.; Chair. DAVIDSON CHARLES; Man. GLADSTON JOSEPH; 2 brs.

Bank of Antigua: 1000 Airport Blvd, Pavilion Dr., POB 315, Coolidge; tel. 462-4282; fax 480-5433; e-mail JCharles@ecabank.com; internet www.bankofantigua.com; f. 1981; total assets EC $560m. (Dec. 2007); Pres. HENRICUS E. J. M. VAN BERGEN; Gen. Man. JOANNA CHARLES (acting); 3 brs.

Bank of Nova Scotia: High and Market Sts, POB 342, St John's; tel. 480-1500; fax 480-1554; e-mail bns.antigua@soctiabank.com; internet www.antigua.scotiabank.com; f. 1961; subsidiary of Bank of Nova Scotia, Canada; Country Man. MARLON RAWLINS; 2 brs.

Caribbean Union Bank Ltd: Friars Hill Rd, POB W2010, St John's; tel. 481-8278; fax 481-8290; e-mail customerservice@caribbeanunionbank.com; internet www.caribbeanunionbank.com; f. 2005; total assets US $42.4m. (Sept. 2007); Chair. LUDOLPH BROWN; Man. Dir VERE I. HILL; 2 brs.

FirstCaribbean International Bank (Barbados) Ltd: High and Market Sts, POB 225, St John's; tel. 480-5000; fax 462-4910; internet www.firstcaribbeanbank.com; adopted present name in 2002 following merger of Caribbean operations of CIBC and Barclays Bank PLC; Barclays relinquished its stake in 2006; Exec. Chair. MICHAEL MANSOOR; CEO JOHN D. ORR; 2 brs.

Global Bank of Commerce Ltd (GBC): Global Commerce Centre, Old Parham Rd, POB W1803, St John's; tel. 480-2240; fax 462-1831; e-mail customer.service@gbc.ag; internet www.globalbank.ag; f. 1983; int. financial services operator; total assets US $74.4m.; shareholder equity US $8.1m.; Chair. and CEO BRIAN STUART-YOUNG; Gen. Man. WINSTON ST AGATHE; 1 br.

RBTT Bank Caribbean Ltd: 45 High St, POB 1324, St John's; tel. 462-4217; fax 462-5040; e-mail info@ag.rbtt.com; internet www.rbtt.com; total assets TTD $53.5m.; shareholder equity TTD $5m. (March 2008); Chair. PETER J. JULY; Br. Man. BERNARD LEONCE.

In 2005 there were 15 registered 'offshore' banks in Antigua and Barbuda.

Regulatory Body

Financial Services Regulatory Commission (FSRC): FCIB Bldg, Old Parham Rd, POB 2674, St John's; tel. 481-1170; fax 463-0422; e-mail anuifsa@candw.ag; internet www.fsrc.gov.ag; fmrly known as International Financial Sector Regulatory Authority, adopted current name in 2002; Chair. ALTHEA CRICK; Administrator and CEO JOHN BENJAMIN.

STOCK EXCHANGE

Eastern Caribbean Securities Exchange: tel. (869) 466-7192; fax (869) 465-3798; e-mail info@ecseonline.com; internet www.ecseonline.com; based in Basseterre, Saint Christopher and Nevis; f. 2001; regional securities market designed to facilitate the buying and selling of financial products for the eight mem. territories—Anguilla, Antigua and Barbuda, Dominica, Grenada, Montserrat, St Kitts and Nevis, St Lucia and St Vincent and the Grenadines; Chair. and Man. Dir Sir K. DWIGHT VENNER; Gen. Man. and CEO TREVOR E. BLAKE.

INSURANCE

Several foreign companies have offices in Antigua. Local insurance companies include the following:

ABI Insurance Co Ltd (ABII): ABI Financial Center, 156 Redcliffe St, POB 2386, St John's; tel. 480-2825; fax 480-2834; e-mail abii@abifinancial.com; internet www.abifinancial.com/ABII; f. 2000; subsidiary of the ABI Financial Group; Internal Auditor AVONELLE WATSON.

Antigua Insurance Co Ltd (ANICOL): Long St, POB 511, St John's; tel. 480-9000; fax 480-9035; e-mail anicol@candw.ag; internet www.anicolinsurance.com.

General Insurance Co Ltd: Upper Redcliffe St, POB 340, St John's; tel. 462-2346; fax 462-4482; Man. Dir PETER BLANCHARD.

Selkridge Insurance Agency Ltd: 7 Woods Centre, Friars Hill Rd, POB W306, St John's; tel. 462-2042; fax 462-2466; e-mail selkins@candw.ag; internet www.selkridgeinsuranceantigua.com; f. 1961; agents for American Life Insurance Company (ALICO) and Caribbean Alliance Insurance; Man. CHARLENE SELKRIDGE.

State Insurance Corpn: Redcliffe St, POB 290, St John's; tel. 481-7804; fax 481-7860; e-mail stateins@candw.ag; f. 1977; govt-owned; plans for privatization announced in Feb. 2010; Chair. Dr VINCENT RICHARDS; Gen. Man. LYNDELL BUTLER.

Trade and Industry

DEVELOPMENT ORGANIZATIONS

Antigua and Barbuda Investment Authority: Sagicor Financial Centre, POB 80, St John's; tel. 481-1000; fax 481-1020; e-mail abia@antigua.gov.ag; internet www.investantiguabarbuda.org; f. 2007; Exec. Dir LESTROY SAMUEL.

Barbuda Development Agency: St John's; economic devt projects for Barbuda.

Development Control Authority: Cecil Charles Bldg, 1st Floor, Cross St, POB 895, St John's; tel. 462-6427; fax 462-1919; developing lands, regulating construction; Chair. CHANLAH CODRINGTON.

St John's Development Corpn: Thames St, POB 1473, St John's; tel. 462-3925; fax 462-3931; e-mail info@stjohnsdevelopment.com; internet www.stjohnsdevelopment.com; f. 1986; manages the Heritage Quay Duty Free Shopping Complex, Vendors' Mall, Public Market and Cultural and Exhibition Complex; Exec. Dir Sen. ANTHONY STUART.

CHAMBER OF COMMERCE

Antigua and Barbuda Chamber of Commerce and Industry Ltd: Cnr of North and Popeshead Sts, POB 774, St John's; tel. 462-0743; fax 462-4575; e-mail chamcom@candw.ag; f. 1944 as Antigua Chamber of Commerce Ltd; name changed as above in 1991; Pres. EVERETT CHRISTIAN; Exec. Dir HOLLY PETERS.

INDUSTRIAL AND TRADE ASSOCIATIONS

Antigua Cotton Growers' Association: Central Cotton Station, Friars Hill Rd, St John's; tel. 462-3871; fax 462-4962; f. 1945.

Antigua Fisheries Limited: Market St, POB 781, St John's; tel. 462-0512; e-mail fisheries@candw.ag; partly funded by the Antigua and Barbuda Development Bank; executing agency for the Antigua Fisheries Development Project (2004); aims to help local fishermen; Dir MICHAEL JAMES.

Antigua and Barbuda Manufacturers' Association (ABMA): POB 115, St John's; tel. 462-1536; fax 462-1912.

Antigua and Barbuda Marine Association (ABMA): English Harbour, St John's; tel. 562-5085; e-mail info@abma.ag; internet www.abma.ag; protection and improvement of marine industry; Pres. JOHN DUFFY.

EMPLOYERS' ORGANIZATIONS

Antigua and Barbuda Employers' Federation: Upper High St, POB 298, St John's; tel. and fax 462-0449; e-mail aempfed@candw.ag; internet abef-anu.org; f. 1950; affiliated to the International Organization of Employers and the Caribbean Employers' Confederation; 135 mems; Chair. ACRES STOWE; Exec. Sec. HENDERSON BASS.

Antigua and Barbuda Small Business Association Ltd (ABSBA): Cross and Tanner Sts, POB 1401, St John's; tel. and fax 461-5741; Pres. LAWRENCE KING.

UTILITIES

Antigua Public Utilities Authority (APUA): Cassada Gardens, POB 416, St John's; tel. 480-7505; fax 462-4131; e-mail support@apua.ag; internet www.apua.ag; f. 1973; generation, transmission and distribution of electricity; internal telecommunications; colln, treatment, storage and distribution of water; transferred to the authority of the Office of the Prime Minister Dec. 2006; Gen. Man. ESWORTH MARTIN.

Antigua Power Co Limited: Old Parham Rd, POB 10, St John's; tel. 460-9461; fax 460-9462; e-mail cmills@candw.ag; electricity provider; Gen. Man. CALID HASSAD.

TRADE UNIONS

Antigua and Barbuda Meteorological Officers' Association: c/o V. C. Bird Int. Airport, Gabatco, POB 1051, St John's; tel. and fax 462-4606; Pres. CICELY CHARLES.

Antigua and Barbuda Nurses Association (ABNA): Nurses HQ, Queen Elizabeth Hwy, St John's; tel. 462-0251; fax 462-5003; Pres. CLARISSA CHRISTOPHER; Sec. ELAINE EDWARDS.

Antigua and Barbuda Public Service Association (ABPSA): Popeshead St, POB 1285, St John's; tel. 461-5821; fax 562-4571; e-mail abpsa_tradeunion@yahoo.com; Pres. JAMES SPENCER; Gen. Sec. EMILE FLOYD; 365 mems.

Antigua and Barbuda Trades Union Congress (ABTUC): c/o Antigua and Barbuda Workers' Union, Freedom Hall, Newgate St, POB 940, St John's; tel. 462-0442; fax 462-5220; e-mail awu@candw.ag; Pres. MAURICE CHRISTIAN; Gen. Sec. NATASHA MUSSINGTON.

Antigua and Barbuda Union of Teachers: c/o Ministry of Education, Govt Office Complex, Queen Elizabeth Hwy, POB 853, St John's; tel. and fax 462-3750; e-mail teachersunion@candw.ag; internet www.abut.edu.ag; f. 1926; Pres. VERNEST MACK; Gen. Sec. ASHWORTH AZILLE.

Antigua and Barbuda Workers' Union (ABWU): Freedom Hall, Newgate St, POB 940, St John's; tel. 462-2005; fax 462-5220; e-mail awu@candw.ag; f. 1967 following split with ATLU; not affiliated to any party; Pres. Sen. CHESTER HUGHES; Gen. Sec. Sen. DAVID MASSIAH; 10,000 mems.

Antigua Trades and Labour Union (ATLU): 46 North St, POB 3, St John's; tel. 462-0090; fax 462-4056; e-mail atandlu@hotmail.com; f. 1939; affiliated to the Antigua Labour Party; Pres. WIGLEY GEORGE; Gen. Sec. STAFFORD JOSEPH; about 10,000 mems.

Transport

ROADS

There are 384 km (239 miles) of main roads and 781 km (485 miles) of secondary dry-weather roads. Of the total 1,165 km (724 miles) of roads, only 33% are paved.

SHIPPING

The main harbour is the St John's Deep Water Harbour. It is used by cruise ships and a number of foreign shipping lines. There are regular cargo and passenger services internationally and regionally. At Falmouth, on the south side of Antigua, is a former Royal Navy dockyard in English Harbour. The harbour is now used by yachts and private pleasure craft.

Antigua and Barbuda Port Authority: Terminal Bldg, Deep Water Harbour, POB 1052, St John's; tel. 484-3400; fax 462-4243; e-mail abpa@port.gov.ag; internet www.port.gov.ag; f. 1968; responsible to Ministry of Works, Transportation and the Environment; Chair. WALTER ARMSTRONG; Port Man. AGATHA C. DUBLIN.

Caribbean Forwarders Ltd: Friars Hill Rd, POB 530, St John's; tel. 480-1100; fax 480-1120.

Tropical Shipping: Antigua Maritime Agencies Ltd, Milburn House, Old Parham Rd, POB W1310, St John's; tel. 562-2934; fax 937-3976; internet www.tropical.com; f. 1992; operates between Canada, USA and the Caribbean; Pres. RICK MURRELL.

Vernon Edwards Shipping Co: Thames St, POB 82, St John's; tel. 462-2034; fax 462-2035; e-mail vedwards@candw.ag; cargo service to and from San Juan, Puerto Rico; Man. Dir VERNON G. EDWARDS, Jr.

The West Indies Oil Co Ltd: Friars Hill Rd, POB 230, St John's; tel. 462-1207; fax 462-7968; e-mail marinedept@westindiesoil.com; f. 1970; petroleum refiner and supplier of petroleum products; facilities in Antigua and Dominica; operates storage site for fuel shipments under the Venezuelan PetroCaribe initiative for distribution locally and to other OECS countries; Contact NIXON D'SOUZA.

CIVIL AVIATION

Antigua's V. C. Bird (formerly Coolidge) International Airport, 9 km (5.6 miles) north-east of St John's, is modern and accommodates jet-engined aircraft. There is a small airstrip at Codrington on Barbuda. Antigua and Barbuda Airlines, a nominal company, controls international routes, but services to Europe and North America are operated by foreign airlines. Antigua and Barbuda is a shareholder in, and the headquarters of, the regional airline LIAT, which acquired Caribbean Star Airlines (another regional airline also based in Antigua) in 2007. Other regional services are operated by Caribbean Airlines (Trinidad and Tobago) and Air BVI (British Virgin Islands).

LIAT (1974) Ltd: POB 819, V. C. Bird Int. Airport, St John's; tel. 480-5713; fax 480-5717; e-mail customerrelations@liatairline.com; internet www.liatairline.com; f. 1956 as Leeward Islands Air Transport Services; privatized in 1995; shares are held by 11 regional govts (30.8%), Caribbean Airlines (29.2%), LIAT employees (13.3%) and private investors (26.7%); buyout arrangement reached in July 2007 in which LIAT would acquire all remaining shares in Caribbean Star; scheduled passenger and cargo services to 19 destinations in the Caribbean; charter flights are also undertaken; Chair. JEAN STEWART HOLDER; CEO BRIAN CHALLENGER (acting).

Tourism

Tourism is the country's main industry. Antigua offers a reputed 365 beaches, an annual international sailing regatta and Carnival week, and the historic Nelson's Dockyard in English Harbour (a national park since 1985). Barbuda is less developed, but is noted for its beauty, wildlife and beaches of pink sand. In 2009 there were some 234,410 stop-over visitors and 709,795 cruise ship passengers. Expenditure by all visitors was estimated at EC $823.8m. in that year.

Antigua & Barbuda Cruise Tourism Association (ABCTA): POB 2208, St John's; tel. 480-1244; fax 462-0170; e-mail abcta@candw.ag; f. 1995; Pres. NATHAN DUNDAS; 42 mems.

Antigua and Barbuda Department of Tourism: c/o Ministry of Tourism, Civil Aviation and Culture, Queen Elizabeth Hwy, POB 363, St John's; tel. 462-0480; fax 462-2483; e-mail deptourism@antigua.gov.ag; internet www.antigua-barbuda.org; Dir-Gen. CORTHWRIGHT MARSHALL.

Antigua Hotels and Tourist Association (AHTA): Island House, Newgate St, POB 454, St John's; tel. 462-0374; fax 462-3702; e-mail ahta@candw.ag; internet www.antiguahotels.org; Chair. TED ISAAC; Exec. Dir NEIL FORRESTER.

Defence

There is a small defence force of 170 men (army 125, navy 45). The US Government leases two military bases on Antigua. Antigua and Barbuda participates in the US-sponsored Regional Security System. The defence budget in 2008 was estimated at EC $21m.

Education

Education is compulsory for 11 years between five and 16 years of age. Primary education begins at the age of five and normally lasts for seven years. Secondary education, beginning at 12 years of age, lasts for five years, comprising a first cycle of three years and a second cycle of two years. In 2000/01 there were 55 primary and 14 secondary schools; the majority of schools are administered by the Government. In 2006/07 some 11,569 primary school pupils and 7,838 secondary school pupils were enrolled. An estimated 88% of children in the appropriate age-group were enrolled in primary education in 2008. Teacher training and technical training are available at the Antigua State College in St John's. An extra-mural department of the University of the West Indies offers several foundation courses leading to higher study at branches elsewhere. Government expenditure on education in 2008 was projected at EC $76.9m., equivalent to 9.7% of total budgetary expenditure.

Bibliography

For works on the Caribbean generally, see Select Bibliography (Books)

Antigua and Barbuda Foreign Policy and Government Guide, 5th edn. USA International Business Publications, 2004.

Coram, R. *Caribbean Time Bomb: The United States' Complicity in the Corruption of Antigua*. New York, NY, William Morrow & Co, 1993.

Dyde, B. *The Unsuspected Isle: A History of Antigua*. Oxford, Macmillan Caribbean, 2003.

Henry, P. *Shouldering Antigua and Barbuda: The Life of V. C. Bird*. London, Hansib Publishing (Caribbean) Ltd, 2010.

Lazarus-Black, M. *Legitimate Acts and Illegal Encounters: Law and Society in Antigua and Barbuda*. Washington, DC, Smithsonian Institution Press, 1994.

Lowes, S., *et al*. *Antigua and Barbuda (World Bibliographical Series)*. Santa Barbara, CA, ABC-CLIO, 1995.

Nicholson, D. V. *The Story of the Arawaks in Antigua and Barbuda*. Antigua Archaeological Society, Fort Collins, CO, Linden Press.

ARGENTINA

Geography

PHYSICAL FEATURES

The Argentine Republic is the second largest country in Latin America, after Brazil, and occupies the broad territories east of the Andes in the tapering southern half of South America. Along the Andes, from north to south, Argentina and Chile share the second longest land border in the Americas, at 5,150 km (3,198 miles), and it continues from north to south across the Isla Grande de Tierra del Fuego (the south-western city of Ushuaia is the most southerly city in the world). To the north is Bolivia (beyond an 832 km border) and to the north-east Paraguay (1,880 km). Also in the north-east, between south-eastern Paraguay and southern Brazil, Argentina extends an arm between the Paraná and Uruguay rivers; Brazil lies to the north, east and south-east of this region (the border is 1,224 km in length). The border with Uruguay (579 km) continues along the River Uruguay to the sea—Uruguay lies east across the river, but also to the north-east where the Argentinian capital, Buenos Aires, faces it across the great Río de la Plata (River Plate) estuary. In all, Argentina covers 2,780,403 sq km (1,073,519 sq miles), although it also claims a further 28,202 sq km of territory in the South Atlantic (the two British dependencies of the Falkland Islands and of South Georgia and the South Sandwich Islands) and in Antarctica (where its claims partly overlap those of Chile and, again, of the United Kingdom).

Argentina lies between the converging lines drawn by the Continental Divide and the eastern coast of South America, but also includes the eastern part of the main island of Tierra del Fuego, the tip of the eastward-curling tail of the continent, which ends in a broken mass of islands (mainly held by Chile). Argentina includes the Islas de los Estados just to the east (further east, and a little north, are the Falklands, which Argentina claims as the Islas Malvinas). The country's coastline, bulging in the north-east, then bitten by broad gulfs or bays southwards, is 4,989 km in length. Northern Argentina does not have a coast, but thrusts into the centre of the continent, extending the country's maximum length to some 3,330 km (it is 1,384 km at its widest), making north and south very different prospects, depending on latitude. Moreover, the terrain not only varies between the tropical rainforest of the north through fertile plains to the bleak landscape of Patagonia, but in the essential contrast between the plains and the high Andes. Indeed, Argentina contains both the highest and the lowest places in South America: Cerro Aconcagua (6,962 m or 22,841 ft), the highest mountain in the world outside the great ranges in the middle of Asia, is west of Mendoza; and the Laguna del Carbón (–105 m) is near Puerto San Julián in southern Patagonia. The country can be divided into the Andean highlands, the northern lowlands, the central plains of the Pampas (*pampa*) and the windswept Patagonian steppe.

The lower Patagonian Andes in the south (seldom exceeding 3,600 m) mount northwards into the main Andean cordillera, where some peaks rise above 6,400 m. Parallel ranges and spurs extend the mountainous terrain, which is generally inhospitable, except in some of the broader valleys, deep into north-western Argentina. Just south of here, in central Argentina, is the only other highland of significance, the Sierra de Córdoba (less than 3,000 m). The plains beneath these heights consist of the southern, Argentine, part of the Gran Chaco in the north, the Pampas stretching south for about 1,600 km and Patagonia in the narrower south. From the far north to the Colorado many rivers disappear into sinks or empty into marshes, and the northern and central plains are dotted with lakes and swampy wetlands. In the north and north-east subtropical and tropical conditions vary the landscape with rainforest, notably the tannin-rich quebracho trees (which thrive on the peculiarly saline soil of the Chaco), but generally grasslands dominate the vast, sometimes gently undulating, but largely treeless, plains. Forests cover only

19% of Argentina, while pasturelands cover 52%. Vegetation also includes the pine forests of the Andes and of Tierra del Fuego, the hardy shrubs and brambles of Patagonia and the cacti and thorny bushes of the arid, mountainous north-west—but grasslands dominate. The Pampas proper, the main region of fertile farmland and rich grazing for livestock, falls gently from about 600 m at the base of the Andean system in the west to sea level. Patagonia, semi-arid and with a more tortured terrain, has sharp contrasts between heights of over 1,500 m and depressions deeper than 30 m below sea level. Its desolate plains end in a lake district of waters fed by glaciers and icecaps (Argentina has 30,200 sq km of inland waters in total). The main rivers of the south, the Negro and the Colorado, are further north, while the most important rivers in the north are those that drain into the Plate—the Paraguay, the Paraná and the Uruguay. The fauna native to this varied land ranges from, for instance, the parrots, jaguars, tapirs and monkeys of the north, through the rheas (American ostriches), armadillos, martens and deer of the Pampas, to the Andean condors, llamas, alpacas and guanacos.

CLIMATE

Apart from a small tropical area in the north-east and the subtropical Chaco (the Tropic of Capricorn passes through northernmost Argentina), most of the country has a temperate climate, although it is arid in the north-west, and the dry south gradually tends to the subarctic. Most of the country is shadowed by the Andes and most rainfall is in the east. Altitude also affects the temperature. The lower Patagonian Andes leave the south exposed to the prevailing westerlies, which descend less humid from the mountains. The semi-arid Pampas ranges from cool to humid subtropical. The Pampas and the north-east can be subjected to violent windstorms, known as pamperos, while flooding and earthquakes can add to the natural hazards of the country. Average annual rainfall is at its height in the north (over 1,500 mm or some 60 ins), becoming drier to the west and south—Buenos Aires, on the north-east coast, but at a central latitude, receives 950 mm (37 ins). The average minimum and maximum temperatures in Buenos Aires range from winter's 8°C and 15°C (46°F–50°F) in July to mid-summer's 20°C–30°C (67°F–86°F) in January. To the west, in the foothills of the Andes, the extremes can be more pronounced, while in the far north there have been summer temperatures of 45°C (113°F) recorded, and the average winter temperature in western (inland) Patagonia is 0°C (32°F).

POPULATION

Most Argentines are of European origin (85%), especially of Spanish and Italian extraction (but also British, French, German and Russian, for instance). Although most of the rest of the population are Mestizos, of mixed descent, these are relatively few compared to other Latin American countries and mainly originate from elsewhere in South America. Only about 1% of the population is Amerindian. Other ethnic groups are also well represented, such as the 1m. or so of Arab descent, and the Jews that form one of the largest Jewish communities in the world outside Israel. This rich racial diversity does not compromise the predominance of the Roman Catholic Church (nominally some 90% of the population—but with less than 20% practising), but it means that other Christian denominations (2%) and faiths (Jews 2%, others 4%—including Muslims or native traditions) are represented. The official language is Spanish, although some minorities also retain use of their own tongues for domestic purposes, and English, Italian, German and French are not uncommon. The three remaining Amerindian languages are Tehuelche, Guaraní and Quechua, most speakers of native tongues living in the north and west of the country.

According to official mid-year estimates, in 2010 the total population of Argentina was 40.5m., which was relatively small compared with the vast territory that it inhabited. Moreover, about one-third of the total lived in the greater metropolitan area of Buenos Aires, the capital. In all, some 86% of the population is classed as urban. After Buenos Aires (the city proper had an estimated population of almost 3.1m. in mid-2010), the chief cities of Argentina are Córdoba (1.3m. at the 2001 census—north-west of Buenos Aires, its old rival, and midway to the Chilean border) and Rosario (0.9m.—upriver from Buenos Aires, on the Paraná). Argentina is a federal republic constituted of 23 provinces and one autonomous city (the Federal Capital, Buenos Aires).

History

Prof. COLIN M. LEWIS

INTRODUCTION

On 25 May 2010 Argentina celebrated the bicentenary of its independence, an occasion marked with patriotic pride and fervour, popular sentiments that did not extend to the incumbent administration of President Cristina Fernández de Kirchner. Since the revolutionary struggle for liberation from Spain at the beginning of the 19th century, key political questions confronting the Argentine people have included the nature of the state and the place of the Republic within the international community. The counterpoints of internationalism and isolationism, democracy and authoritarianism have dominated the political discourse and process of institution-building. These tensions have become particularly acute since the Second World War. Indeed, with the return of democratic government in 1983, the struggle to construct a fully functioning democracy within the context of a globalizing world has intensified and shows little prospect of achieving definitive resolution. While official statements vaunted 200 years of liberty and progress, democracy and freedom, and social rights and the rule of law, critics of the regime observed increasing political uncertainty and a deepening economic crisis that would test the institutions of the state and the resilience of society.

CONSTRUCTING THE NATION AND DEMOCRACY

Modern institutions began to take shape after 1853, following the overthrow of the dictator Gen. Manuel de Rosas in the previous year. The liberal 1853 Constitution, which established a federal, republican system of government, was probably unique in that it accorded the vote to all native-born males without subjecting electors to property or literacy tests. The substance of federalism was secured in 1880 with the 'nationalization' of the city of Buenos Aires, which was separated from the province and became the national capital. Subsequent political developments of critical importance include: electoral reform in 1912, which made the ballot secret, established the principle of compulsory voting, and provided semi-proportional representation for runner-up parties; the 1930 military coup, which overturned a democratically elected Government, inaugurating a cycle of 'restricted politics'; the 1946 electoral 'rupture' of Peronism; the approval of the short-lived 1949 Constitution (which extended the vote to women); the overthrow of Gen. Juan Domingo Perón in 1955; the 1976 military coup, which resulted in the installation of the so-called *Proceso de Reorganización Nacional*, a bloody regime characterized by mass torture, murder and the 'disappearance' of thousands during the 'dirty war'; the return of democracy in 1983; and the 2001 economic crisis that witnessed street protest and appeared to threaten complete institutional collapse.

Conventionally presented as a model for national consolidation, arrangements encapsulated in the 1853 Constitution and 1880 federalization of Buenos Aires could also be depicted as the project of a confederation of regional oligarchies increasingly dominated by the propertied classes of the littoral provinces. Irrespective of the rights accorded by the 1853 Constitution, before the early 20th century access to political life remained restricted. This resulted in an explosion of demands for political participation by the middle classes around 1900, and by the working classes in the 1940s. Accordingly, in the 1910s, the Radicals (Unión Cívica Radical—UCR) 'captured' the state and in the 1940s the Peronists did likewise. This widening of the political system occurred in a much shorter space of time than in many countries. However, the process of political inclusion was neither linear nor without problems. There were setbacks, such as the 1930–43 'infamous decade' of oligarchic reaction when elections were rigged and the UCR banned, the proscription of Peronism from the 1950s to the early 1970s under unstable military and civilian governments, and the horrors of the *Proceso*. It is worth recording that since 1983, notwithstanding several profound economic crises that in earlier periods would undoubtedly have triggered military intervention, democratic politics have prevailed. The basic provisions of the 1853 Constitution (modified in 1994) continue.

STATE-BUILDING: OLIGARCHIC AND EARLY DEMOCRATIC POLITICS

By the 1880s mass immigration from Western Europe had made Argentina the third most populous country in Latin America after Brazil and Mexico. It was also the most urban: approximately one-half of the population lived in cities by 1914. Argentina was on course to becoming one of the wealthiest societies of the early 20th century. During this period Argentine statesmen conceived of their country as a second USA and, indeed, as a potential rival to the 'Colossus of the North'.

The result was the emergence of a civil society, enmeshed with the building of a state. The relationship between institutional consolidation and the emergence of political order was direct and causal. However, it was unclear to what extent nation-building occurred within a state open to all, or in a less permeable, more restricted structure. The 1880s saw the development of the Partido Autonomista Nacional (PAN), a coalition of regional oligarchies that came to monopolize national politics and eclipsed other organizations. Because the PAN did not have a well-defined internal organization, factional confrontations proliferated and came to replace open electoral contests. In effect, internal manoeuvring and intrigue within the PAN emerged as a substitute for competitive party politics. Real politics was conducted inside the PAN, rather than the institutions of the state, an arrangement that facilitated order rather than democratic consolidation and which survived virtually unchallenged until 1916. Why did this arrangement survive for so long? The answer is fairly simple: resource growth that underwrote an expansion in the supply of public goods. The stalemate of Argentine sectional and regional political rivalry before the 1880s can be largely explained by a scarcity of state resources. This changed with the liberal, economically internationalist project of the late 19th century. Thus the PAN functioned as a mechanism for conflict resolution through a 'negotiated' distribution of assets, an easily managed process when the fiscal asset base was growing, as was the case until the 1920s. The loose nature of the oligarchic alliance required a strong executive, thereby establishing another enduring feature of the Argentine political system, in order to ensure an effective distribution of assets.

Mass immigration, population growth and urbanization transformed society and politics. That the PAN became more centralized, and possibly isolated, was suggested by popular protest triggered by the commercial and financial panic of 1889–90 (the Baring Crisis), which provoked a series of events prefiguring those of 2001–02. Street protests in 1889 ultimately resulted in 'reform from within', a reconstruction of oligarchic politics that reflected the growing influence of the coastal provinces, particularly that of the province of Buenos Aires, and the changing nature of society. The regime was concerned that the managed elections would need to be given a more patriotic and, possibly, more democratic patina. Electoral reform, sponsored by President Roque Sáenz Peña (1910–13) in 1912, led to the first free and fair elections in Argentine political history in 1916 and the defeat of the PAN, which did not survive the ensuing Radical ascendancy of 1916–30. The rules of the political game had changed.

Mass and class politics did not necessarily imply ideology-based politics. Nevertheless, it was generally accepted that mass politics erupted into Argentine political life in the 1910s, and that the UCR was its initial beneficiary. The UCR successfully courted three distinct groups: dissident interior oligarchies; the growing urban, professional middle classes; and sections of the enfranchised working class (in 1914 around 70% of the Buenos Aires working class had been born abroad and was therefore effectively disenfranchised; rates of naturalization were very low). Two of these social classes were epitomized by UCR Presidents of the period: Hipólito Yrigoyen (1916–22 and 1928–30), a teacher and minor public official, and Marcelo T. de Alvear (1922–28), scion of an aristocratic family and prominent lawyer. These three groups remained the bases of party support during the years of proscription in the 1930s, and the time of unequal contest with the Peronists in the 1940s and 1950s. The heterogeneous character of party membership probably accounted for the broadly conservative yet reformist stance of the UCR in the 1910s and 1920s. After the 1950s the party became more closely identified with the urban and rural middle class, though it undoubtedly attracted substantial support from the working class in the 1980s and the 1990s.

The 1929 world-wide economic depression brought an end to the democratic experiment and the return of 'oligarchic authoritarianism'. Institutional and conjunctural explanations are offered for the collapse of Argentine democracy in the 1930s. Arguably, fully functioning democratic organization had insufficient time to become firmly embedded before the shock struck. Critics have pointed to the authoritarian personality of Yrigoyen, and have accused him of an abuse of power. Indeed, for some he was a proto-populist who fostered an exclusionary approach to politics and to government. If the PAN deployed electoral fraud, Yrigoyen did not hesitate to use UCR majorities in the Congreso to overturn inconvenient results in provincial contests, nor to appoint federal administrators (*interventores*) to secure the desired electoral outcome. Like the PAN, the UCR also emerged as a 'distributional coalition', channelling state resources to friends of the regime and denying them to its enemies. This exclusionary approach to politics, and parties that functioned as distributional electoral alliances, appeared to have become key features of Argentine political life.

For some, the UCR was too progressive, provoking an inevitable conservative backlash; for others, it was insufficiently radical and failed to restructure Argentine society and polity so as to secure democracy. Opponents certainly accused UCR administrations of corruption and protested against the 'tyranny of democracy'—that is, the party's ability, and methods used, to win elections. The inertia of the administration in 1929–30, as the country slipped into economic crisis, fostered disillusion, providing an opportunity for democratic opponents of the regime, as well as enemies of fledgling democracy per se. This probably explains why the 1930 military coup attracted a fair measure of support: there was general antipathy towards an elected administration seen as failing the Republic. During the 1930s economic internationalism and liberal democracy were under threat not only in Argentina; regimes abroad, especially Benito Mussolini's Italy and Francisco Franco's Spain (primary sources of immigration to Argentina in the early 20th century), served as an inspiration to anti-democratic elements in Argentina.

THE RISE, CONTAINMENT AND SURVIVAL OF PERONISM

Although originating in a military putsch, and dependent on the armed forces and police to contain opposition, the 'Concordancia' administrations of the 1930s presented a largely civilian façade. The regime might be described as technocratic-authoritarian, possibly prefiguring more overtly militaristic administrations of the third quarter of the 20th century. The opportunist army clique responsible for the ouster of Yrigoyen exhibited distinctly fascist tendencies and was rapidly marginalized, displaced by traditionalist elements that manifested an unfashionable commitment to internationalism and 'guided' democracy. Politically, the Concordancia was a disparate grouping of liberals, conservatives and reformist socialists, precisely those groups that had been unable to dent the UCR stranglehold on the presidency in the 1920s. Initially, the regime sought legitimacy in efficient macroeconomic management and, with the stabilization of the economy in the mid-1930s, in a measured return to democracy. Accident, in the form of the death of several consummate political operators, and the approach of the Second World War derailed the projected phased return to open politics. The regime lurched to the right, destroying the fragile party political balance that had delivered stability in the executive and legislature. Concurrently, elements within the military, mainly 'crypto-fascists', railed against the subordinate role assigned to the armed forces and the pro-Allied stance of the administration, notwithstanding its formal declaration of neutrality.

In 1943 a group of officers, of whom Col Juan Domingo Perón was one, acted. The technocrats and oligarchs were turned out and a full military administration was installed. However, the armed forces were divided and ill-prepared for administration. Elections were called in 1946. To the surprise of many, not least the US ambassador, who had campaigned actively in favour of the Alianza Democrática (the umbrella grouping established by existing political parties, some of whom had formed part of the Concordancia), Perón won fairly decisively. Between 1943 and 1945 Perón had assiduously cultivated the support of organized labour. As a result, he became the presidential candidate of the Partido Laborista, the hastily constructed political wing of the Confederación General de Trabajadores (CGT—General Confederation of Labour). Soon, independent labour leaders were sidelined and the Partido Laborista became the Partido Justicialista (PJ). In association with his charismatic wife, Eva Duarte de Perón ('Evita'), Perón established a regime that would become increasingly centralist, statist and anti-liberal. Its main sources of support were organized labour, developmentalist military officers, nationalists and, at least in the early years, elements of the Roman Catholic hierarchy attracted by the authoritarian, traditionalist, anti-secularist, moralistic stance of the administration.

Like the UCR in the 1910s and 1920s, the PJ of the 1940s defied easy definition. In electoral terms, the overwhelming strength of the party lay with the working class, largely the urban working class. The PJ also enjoyed solid support in the north-west of the country, where rural workers were effectively organized and marshalled by trade union leaders. State sector workers, too, were a major electoral bulwark. Nevertheless, the Peronists have not always enjoyed the unquestioning electoral support of labour, nor been exclusively dependent on it. As victories at elections in 1973, 1989, 1992 and 1995 indicated, the party often captured substantial support from the middle class; conversely, it failed to mobilize important elements of the working class in 1982 and 1999. More a movement than a party, the PJ has proven to be the least institutionalized political organization in Argentina. Rather, Peronism is a contending alliance of factions headed by regional leaders. These features derived from, and conferred power on, a highly personalistic leadership. This tradition, established by Perón, perfected by Carlos Saúl Menem (1989–99), and extended by later Presidents, precluded a democratic internal organization of the party. The legacy of Menem, reinforced under the administrations of Néstor Carlos Kirchner (2003–07) and his wife, Cristina Fernandéz (2007–), meant that the PJ continues as a constellation of competing sectional and regional interests.

The 1946–55 Peronist administration, the *peronato*, can be divided into several distinct sub-periods. The first, which lasted until around 1949, was characterized by high levels of popular support, rapid social progress, economic nationalism verging on autarky and increasing centralization. This was the 'golden age' of Peronism, largely financed from windfall export earnings. The second phase ran from 1949 to about 1952 (when 'Evita' died). During this period high levels of mass support continued, but social tensions increased and the regime became much more authoritarian as the economy faltered. The final period witnessed the fracturing of the 'Peronist family': workers and nationalists were antagonized by a return to liberal orthodoxy reflected in wage cuts and the opening of the economy to foreign investment. The armed forces became alarmed at the threat of internal disorder. Intellectuals pointed to the isolation of the regime. The Roman Catholic Church was antagonized by proposed government interventions in education, family life and orchestrated demands for the canonization of 'Evita'.

Military governments of 1955 proposed to excise Peronism from Argentine politics and the Argentine psyche, to restore the market economy, and to prepare the country for an ordered return to civilian rule. However, the outcome was quite different. The political history of the following two decades indicated that it was as difficult to live without Perón as to live with him. The nation was riven: for every committed Peronist, there was an equally vehement anti-Peronist. Equally, from the 1950s until the 1980s there would be only conditional support for democracy, and little consensus about the international position of the country.

Reconstructing society and polity, and re-establishing the international position of the country, exercised successive regimes in the 1950s and 1960s, but possibilities and outcomes remained confused. These were neatly illustrated by the coups of 1955. The first, headed by Gen. Eduardo Lonardi, persecuted Peronists and set about dismantling some of the agencies of economic intervention. However, the Lonardi regime appeared disinclined to eradicate other aspects of statism and nationalism, revoking contracts granted to foreign oil companies awarded during the last years of the *peronato*. The second coup of 1955 led to the installation of a more internationalist regime, headed by Gen. Pedro Aramburu (1955–58). Deregulation and export promotion were applied with vigour and Argentina submitted membership applications to the World Bank and IMF. Having tamed (or terrorized) Peronists, in 1958 Aramburu's regime gave way to the elected presidency of Radical Arturo Frondizi (1958–62), which encapsulated the inconsistencies in domestic politics and the difficulties of devising a sustainable external strategy. Although he had enjoyed a reputation as a radical nationalist, on assuming office Frondizi announced the award of risk concessions to foreign oil corporations. This was part of the so-called 'battle for oil'. The second campaign, the 'battle for healthy money', was based on an IMF adjustment package, a measure which also implied a pro-internationalist position.

Partly for electoral purposes, Frondizi sought to balance a liberal, internationalist stance in economic and trade policy with a radical diplomatic programme, courting communist Cuba and the Non-aligned Movement, a stance that echoed Peronist rhetoric about a 'Third Position' that was neither capitalist nor communist. Frondizi made the mistake of receiving communist guerrilla commander Ernesto 'Che' Guevara on a secret visit to Buenos Aires. This was too much for the military, though whether Frondizi's removal from office was owing to liberal international economics, adventurous diplomacy, or an ambiguous relationship with the Peronists remained unclear. Successive civilian administrations of the 1960s, always closely scrutinized by the military, were no more successful in restabilizing domestic politics or redefining the international position of the country.

With the failure of the sterile regime of Gen. Juan Carlos Onganía (1966–70), and a rise in political protest characterized by urban uprisings, factory occupations, a spate of kidnappings directed against the heads of national and foreign corporations, and mounting guerrilla violence, an exhausted public and anxious military looked to the exiled Perón for salvation. After Gen. Onganía's regime there followed the short-lived military presidencies of Gen. Roberto Levingston (1970–71) and Gen. Alejandro Agustín Lanusse (1971–73), under whose Government Perón was permitted to return from exile in Madrid, Spain, where he had been sheltered by Franco. In July 1973 the elected, acting President, Héctor José Cámpora of the PJ, resigned. Perón arrived in a country that appeared to be falling apart. Standing for the presidency and vice-presidency, respectively, Perón and his new wife, Maria Estela ('Isabelita') Martínez de Perón, easily won the ballot. However, at 78 years of age, Perón was losing his touch, and was demonstrably unable to contain conflict within the movement, as shown by gun battles at party gatherings and on the streets. Assuming the presidency on the death of her husband, 'Isabelita' proved particularly ineffective. A believer in the occult, she soon became dependent on corrupt and criminal associates. The last days of her regime were ignominious, with the open operation of official 'death squads', near anarchy and spiralling inflation. In this context, the military regime that took over in 1976 was almost welcomed.

Declaring a policy of alignment with the 'western, Christian, free world', despite murdering its own citizens and strengthening commercial links with Eastern Europe, the military regimes of the 1976–82 period subscribed to the doctrine of 'national security' initially popularized in US–Latin American policy-making circles. According to this doctrine, the principal threat to the nation was from internal subversion sponsored by an international Marxist conspiracy that took advantage of domestic social tensions. Following a dose of military discipline (more accurately, the use of state terror) and liberal economics, Argentine society would be purged of subversive elements.

Estimates of the number who 'disappeared' during the 'dirty war' range between 10,000 and 30,000. For every individual murdered, there were probably two or three fortunate enough to escape into exile. Nevertheless, for the regime and for the Argentine people, the defining moment occurred in 1982, when the domestic and international actions of the dictatorship descended into a tragicomedy of errors, culminating in the invasion of the Falkland Islands (Islas Malvinas) in April. These British-ruled islands in the South Atlantic had been claimed by Argentina since 1833. The events leading up to the invasion illustrated the arrogance and ignorance of the regime, which had completely misread both its influence abroad and the place of Argentina in the Americas and the wider world. Following the collapse of the liberal, debt-led economic programme, as the stock market went into meltdown with a series of spectacular bank failures, the currency collapsed and the country approached default, and fearful of a resurgence of street protest, the regime felt compelled to act. Deluded by his own rhetoric, misled by civilian foreign policy advisers and convinced of the capacity of the armed forces, it was a supremely confident Gen. Leopoldo Fortunato Galtieri who announced from the balcony of the presidential palace, the Casa Rosada, to an enthusiastic crowd on 2 April that Argentine forces had taken Port Stanley in the Falklands. However, following Argentine defeat by the British on 14 June, when crowds next appeared outside the Casa Rosada it was not to cheer. A military that had few qualms about waging war on Argentines had neither the organizational capacity nor the ability to resist the British task force dispatched to recover the islands. So ended the only foreign campaign undertaken by the Argentine military in the 20th century.

THE RETURN OF DEMOCRACY

Political optimism and economic crisis were the inheritance of the incoming UCR Government of President Raúl Alfonsín in December 1983. A human rights lawyer who had consistently opposed the military and the war, Alfonsín was a committed democrat and constitutionalist. He represented the new face of Argentine politics, in contrast to the 'wheeler-dealers' who had dominated both the UCR and the PJ since the 1940s. Perhaps this, as well as the murky association of some Peronists with the outgoing military regime, explained the electoral triumph of the UCR in the elections of 30 October. Alfonsín's victory was a watershed in Argentine political history: it was the first time that the PJ had been defeated in free, fully democratic elections.

The new administration was confronted by an expectant electorate demanding that those responsible for human rights abuses during the 'dirty war' be brought to justice. It also faced a cowed but dangerous armed forces, a recalcitrant and divided opposition, an empty treasury, and an international banking community determined that the democratic Government honour the foreign debt that had been accumulated and squandered by the military (approximately one-quarter of the US $42,000m. debt accumulated by the generals and admirals remains accounted for). For Alfonsín, the restoration of democracy was a moral and practical imperative, as was principled internationalism. Indeed, the best means of securing civilian government at home would be to improve relations with neighbouring countries through the formation of the Southern Common Market (Mercado Común del Sur—Mercosur), the resolution of border disputes with Chile, the renunciation of the use of force in the settlement of international disputes, engagement in international forums and a commitment to the rule of international law. The need to resolve the debt crisis made internationalism even more of a priority. Effective participation in multilateral agencies such as the World Bank and the IMF and constructive dialogue in world bodies were, Alfonsín believed, the only options.

Anticipating rewards for democratization from international institutions and foreign governments (and assuming that these would put pressure on the international banks), the administration initially prioritized social spending and negotiations with the military over debt resolution. This was all the more pressing, as the Government had to confront a number of barrack protests. Although these hardly threatened a coup (being concerned with affronts to 'military dignity' and spending cuts), they still represented a challenge to the Government and to the construction of democratic institutions. The armed forces had to be made democratically accountable and incorporated into society. The question of Argentina's outstanding foreign debt, meanwhile, would have to wait. Drift, rather than strategy, typified the early economic stance of the Alfonsín presidency, though neither the debt nor the economy could be ignored indefinitely. A stand-by loan was obtained from the IMF in 1984, and when this failed to stabilize the economy, the heterodox 'Austral Plan' was launched in 1985. Initially popular, the Plan could have succeeded, but it was sabotaged by debt overhang, some technical flaws and, principally, by an electoral timetable that gave opponents ample opportunity to mobilize against it. The Plan ended in hyperinflation that cost the UCR dear in the 1989 elections, and resulted in the transfer of power to the incoming President, Carlos Saúl Menem of the PJ, five months earlier than required by the Constitution.

To its critics, the legacy of democracy in 1989 was fiscal indiscipline and social disorder, manifest in the looting of supermarkets. These problems were real, but they should not be allowed to deflect attention from the lasting achievements of Alfonsín. For the first time in Argentine political history, an administration of one political hue, which had gained office as the result of free, unrestricted elections, handed over the government of the country to another freely elected administration of a different political party. Moreover, although the transfer of power occurred earlier than that provided for by the Constitution, at a moment of institutional crisis, there was no military intervention. Previously, lesser economic crises had resulted in coups. Even if the Peronist victory in 1989 owed more to a protest against the UCR than a vote of confidence in Menem, the PJ victory was resounding. This, coupled with his skills as a coalition builder, gave Menem considerable freedom of manoeuvre. He employed these advantages to construct a broad alliance within and outside the traditional ranks of Peronism and, indeed, the party. Thus was formed the so-called popular-business alliance, which was to be responsible for the neo-liberal economic project designed to secure the new President's position in power, if not to institutionalize democracy. Differences between elected Governments of the 1980s and 1990s were substantial, but all subscribed to an internationalist agenda. For Menem and Alfonsín, internationalism, economic stability and civilian rule were interconnected.

Menem (1989–95 and 1995–99) espoused 'realism' in politics and international economic relations. Following currency stabilization in 1991, the so-called 'Convertibility Plan', foreign investment increased—as did the foreign debt. Internationalism also assumed a distinctly pro-US stance, reflected in positions taken in international forums and conflicts. The aspirations of the regime were signalled by the pledging of Argentine frigates to the international coalition involved in the Gulf War of 1991, the proposal to join the North Atlantic Treaty Organization (NATO), renewed commitment to Mercosur, which was gradually transformed from a free trade zone into something approaching a common market, and efforts to foster close collaboration between Mercosur and the European Union.

Ever the consummate populist politician, Menem reconfigured the PJ in his image and divided the opposition. He also secured constitutional reform in order to be able to stand for a second consecutive presidential term. Constitutional change was prepared by the Olivos Pact, an agreement between Menem and former President Alfonsín. The principal modifications introduced by the 1994 Constitution included an increase in provincial representation in the Senate from two to three seats, the granting of province-style autonomy to the federal capital, a reduction of the length of the presidential term from six to four years, and a provision allowing a sitting President to seek immediate re-election (hitherto a consecutive presidential term had been proscribed, incumbents being required to stand down for at least one term). The 1994 settlement facilitated the re-election of Menem and secured the 'Convertibility Plan'. The lessons of the PJ's mid-term electoral victories during Menem's first term, and Menem's second triumph in the 1995 presidential election, were that the electorate demanded economic stability and would not support political groupings deemed unlikely to continue strategies that had delivered monetary order. Nevertheless, before and after 1995 Menem's political project represented a threat to democracy: he undermined democracy within the PJ, repeatedly changed the rules of the political game and institutionalized corruption. None the less, voters had few qualms about returning the PJ to office in 1995. Economic instability had driven traditional politics off the agenda. However, with an opposition alliance of the UCR and the Frente País Solidario (Frepaso) painstakingly constructed after 1997, and with both major political groupings committed to macroeconomic stability, the electorate was finally presented with a real choice in 1999.

The opposition victory in the 1999 presidential and congressional elections can be viewed as a demand for economic stability and political accountability. Society demanded a correspondence between economic and political transparency. The elections were another benchmark in the consolidation of Argentine democracy. The third consecutive constitutionally prescribed change of government since 1983, the 1999 elections appeared to confirm institutional stability and offer a distinct opportunity for democratic consolidation. The UCR's Fernando de la Rúa was elected President for the opposition Alianza para el Trabajo, la Justicia y la Educación, suggesting that the UCR had been forgiven by the electorate for the chaos of 1989. Carlos 'Chacho' Alvarez of Frepaso was elected Vice-President. Even if the economy was already moving into recession, there was confidence that corruption was on the wane and that democracy and stability could be saved. However, disappointment soon set in.

In retrospect, perhaps the Peronists were not as corrupt as popularly perceived, nor the Radicals as honest. In both parties there were those who struggled for greater internal democracy and accountability, while there were also those who were prepared repeatedly to bend the rules. For the Alianza, this became clear in 2000 when it was revealed that President de la Rúa had systematically bribed opposition senators in order to secure legislative majorities. Budget slippage (often a mask for illegal transfers of funds) and nepotism seemed to be as much a feature of the Alianza administration as that of Menem and the PJ. Álvarez resigned in disgust. Drift, and an apparent inability to resolve the spiralling political and economic crises, became almost as much a feature of the de la Rúa administration in 2001 as of the Yrigoyen Government in 1929–30. While other sectors bore the brunt of unemployment and falling wages, the political class continued to spend more on itself. Public anger was demonstrated in the October 2001 mid-term elections: the tallies of blank protest votes cast in such key areas as the gubernatorial contest in the province of Buenos Aires, and the senate contest in the city of Buenos Aires, were larger than the number of votes secured by the winning candidates. Less than two months later, with the imminent collapse of the 'Convertibility Plan', came street demonstrations and government paralysis. De la Rúa was forced to flee the Casa Rosada by helicopter as the streets around the palace were filled with tear gas and protestors.

DEMOCRACY WITHOUT DEMOCRATIC INSTITUTIONS?

In December 2001 Ramón Puerta, the President of the Senado, was sworn in as acting President of the Republic, in the absence of a Vice-President (the position had not been filled following the resignation of Álvarez). Within the space of two weeks, from 20 December 2001 to 1 January 2002, the presidency changed hands on five occasions as public protests continued. Ultimately, a joint session of both houses of the Congreso elected Eduardo Duhalde as President. A former Governor of the province of Buenos Aires, Duhalde was the PJ candidate who had lost to de la Rúa in 1999.

Duhalde managed to hold both the administration and the country together, although he was less successful in keeping the PJ united. Although he had been nominated to serve out only the remainder of de la Rúa's term, it soon became clear that Duhalde aspired to stand for a further full four years—in effect, engineering his own election. He was prevented from doing so by an anti-Buenos Aires alliance of PJ Governors from interior provinces, fearful of the power amassed by the Buenos Aires faction of the party. Although there was no effective opposition, Peronist factions were unable to agree on a candidate for the 2003 election. Several Peronists indicated their willingness to stand, foremost among them being former President Menem and Néstor Carlos Kirchner, erstwhile Governor of the sparsely populated Patagonian province of Santa Cruz. Kirchner was favoured by Duhalde, who viewed his Santa Cruz colleague as malleable and able to defeat Menem, from whom Duhalde intended to wrest control of the PJ. In the event, Menem won the first round of the presidential election that was held on 27 April 2003, obtaining 24.34% of the votes cast, ahead of Kirchner's 21.99%. A former UCR minister, Ricardo López Murphy, came third with 16.35% of the ballot.

In mid-May 2003, four days before the second-round run-off was scheduled, and with opinion polls showing that Kirchner was likely to win twice as many votes, Menem withdrew from the contest. He did so partly to be able to claim that he had never been defeated in an election and, it was asserted, to deny Kirchner the legitimacy of a landslide victory. Was this also a ploy to precipitate chaos and yet another presidential contest? In the event, Kirchner managed to marginalize both Menem and Duhalde. Following his inauguration, the new President immediately began to build a 'transverse alliance', based on groupings within and outside the PJ. By favouring particular candidates in a succession of elections, such as the mayoral contest in Buenos Aires and interior governorships, and by supporting different factions in the October 2005 mid-term congressional elections, Kirchner created a loose confederation of individuals and sectional interests in key provinces who were beholden to him. Personality-driven leadership and the granting (or withholding) of favours, rather than institutional organization and internal accountability, remained the mechanisms of government and the instruments of power.

The strategy paid off. Economic recovery, under way by 2003, and the successful renegotiation of the outstanding foreign debt in February 2005 generated massive federal fiscal surpluses. A judicious disposal of these funds secured for Kirchner the acquiescence of many provincial administrators and the isolation of troublesome groups, including antagonistic segments of the PJ and the labour movement. The allocation of federal funds was also deployed to divide a weak formal opposition: Kirchner bought the adhesion of some sections of the UCR and marginalized others. Although Kirchner and his then Minister of the Economy, Roberto Lavagna, were not responsible for the economic recovery, their delivery of exchange stability and relatively low levels of inflation, as well as new social assistance programmes, were notable achievements. Furthermore, their resolute stance in negotiations with the IMF and private foreign creditors generated confidence and domestic political capital: nationalist rhetoric, and debt write-down, yielded a considerable electoral dividend.

Nationalist posturing was not without cost, however. Bombastic language in international forums, and unilateral action against neighbouring countries, such as restricting imports from Brazil and suspending energy supplies to Chile, gained Argentina few allies. More worrying still, Argentina's continued uncompromising opposition to the establishment of a modern European-financed cellulose plant in Uruguay occasioned a sharp deterioration in diplomatic relations between the two countries, creating an impasse that the regime in Buenos Aires seemed unable, or unwilling, to resolve. As a result, the country's closest allies in Latin America appeared to be Venezuela and Bolivia, a 'left-wing' association that raised eyebrows in the US Government, irked other members of Mercosur and made few friends for Argentina overseas. Despite membership of the Group of 20 (G20) organization, and participation in such forums as the left-of-centre Summit of Progressive Leaders, Argentina witnessed a decline in its international standing, in contrast to countries such as Brazil and Chile. The close association cultivated during the two Kirchner presidencies with Venezuelan President Lt-Col (retd) Hugo Chávez Frías undoubtedly complicated relations within Mercosur, not least because the increasingly nationalist and statist language of the regime in Buenos Aires was seen elsewhere in the bloc as undermining the ethos of Mercosur and its relationship with overseas partners.

By 2006, with rising world commodity prices further fuelling economic growth and a dramatic increase in fiscal resources at the disposal of the federal Government, the rhetoric and action of the administration became even more populist and nationalist. Both at home and abroad the Government seemed consciously to be resurrecting the language and imagery of the first Peronist administration of the 1940s, a rhetoric that became even more pronounced after 2008. Néstor Carlos Kirchner showed himself to be unafraid to promote members of his family to high office. Cristina Fernández, obtained a seat in the Senado in October 2005, which proved to be the launch-pad for a successful presidential campaign two years later. Despite some setbacks in the final year of his presidency, notably the election of anti-Kirchner or opposition candidates to provincial governorships and the mayoralty of Buenos Aires, crude political arm-twisting and massive discretionary expenditure meant that Kirchner was able to deliver the presidency to his wife, as he stepped down as head of state to assume the leadership of the PJ.

In the polls on 28 October 2007, the electorate was offered a choice of three Peronist factions and a plethora of opposition groupings. Although Fernández failed to take the three major cities (Buenos Aires, Córdoba and Rosario), she nevertheless obtained 44.9% of the vote. Her margin of victory over her nearest rival, Elisa Carrió of the centre-left Coalición Cívica, who obtained 23.0%, was well ahead of the 10 percentage points necessary to avoid a run-off election. The other principal candidate, Kirchner's former Minister of Economy and Production, Lavagna, of the centre-right Una Nación Avanzada, won 16.9% of votes cast. In effect, the three candidates who topped the presidential poll represented new electoral alliances, ephemeral groupings quite distinct from the former political parties, the PJ and the UCR. This points to a state of flux and lack of institutionality in Argentine politics and political life, where traditional allegiances and national structures are breaking down. Although initially muted by continuing economic prosperity, these developments subsequently became more pronounced, as demonstrated by the mid-term congressional elections held in June 2009.

Despite a calculated attempt on the part of the Government to minimize anticipated losses by bringing forward the elections from 25 October 2009 to 28 June, on the pretext that early elections would enable legislators to focus their efforts on resolving the negative effects of global economic crisis, the results of the polls were a clear snub to the Government, which lost its majority in both legislative chambers. In the Cámara de Diputados, the administration lost 19 seats, securing just 110 out of 257 seats. A further four seats were lost in the Senado, reducing the Government's representation in the upper chamber to just 34 out of 75 seats. These losses were attributed to mismanagement of the economy, chaotic handling of farmer protests, a simmering dispute over taxation and gross manipulation of prices that had united diverse rural and urban groups and caused an irreparable rupture between President Fernández and her Vice-President, escalating anxiety about crime and security issues, and fears about inflation triggered by government manipulation of the official agency responsible for collating macroeconomic data. Furthermore, considerable unease had been prompted by the way in which the Kirchners had undermined democratic accountability and manipulated the media—most notably in mid-2009 when tax inspectors raided the offices of a well-regarded newspaper that had become critical of the Fernández administration.

Several constructions can be placed on the election results. First, the fungibility of political institutions and self-regard of the political class should be noted—bringing forward the date of the elections required agreement among diverse party interests and was not simply a project of the regime. Second, the Government lost the elections; the opposition did not win. However, the magnitude of its loss cannot be exaggerated. Néstor Kirchner was defeated by the candidate of the Unión PRO centre-right opposition alliance in the contest for a congressional seat in the province of Buenos Aires, an electoral district in which the former President had previously been considered to be unassailable, and resigned as head of the PJ. Kirchner still secured a seat in the lower house as a result of the proportional representation voting system but his electoral loss provides a telling example of the fading fortunes of the Government. Third, the opposition remained divided. Although Coalición Cívica Afirmación para una República Igualitaria (CC ARI—a centre-left coalition nominally led by party President Elisa Carrío) came a close second to the official party list (gaining 29% of the popular vote compared with the latter's 31%), CC ARI was extremely loose and rather different from the constellation that Carrío had headed in 2007. Fourth, the most spectacular gains were registered by the fairly recently formed Unión PRO, headed by businessman Francisco de Naváez. Whether some of these changes could be presented as democratic and generational renewal or as instability in the party political system remained a matter of conjecture. However, what could not be doubted was the existence of major discontent with existing institutions and political arrangements at a time when the country was being exposed to a problematic conjuncture of the global economic crisis and domestic political fragility.

When Néstor Kirchner stepped down as President in 2007, conspiracy theorists argued that he had handed power to his wife in order to enable a far-stretching Kirchner dynasty. Had he been elected in 2007, having served two consecutive terms he would have been constitutionally debarred from contesting the presidency again at any point in the future. By allowing Cristina Fernández to assume power in 2007, he ensured his eligibility to stand for re-election in 2011, which would in turn ensure her own in 2015—an interminable tango of the Kirchners. Despite growing antagonism towards the administration, at mid-2010 that possibility continued to be discussed, even as the 'lame duck' presidency of Fernández limped to its probable demise in presidential and congressional elections due to be held in October 2011. That said, with opposition forces continuing to show little ability to settle their differences, the key political contest will be that conducted among distinct wings of the bitterly fractious PJ, of which Néstor Kirchner remains the titular head. In that contest, Kirchner's immediate predecessor as President, and former mentor, Eduardo Duhalde, is the man to watch. Caretaker President in 2001–02, former Governor of the province of Buenos Aires, sometime Vice-President to Menem, and late king-maker of the PJ, Duhalde is a political surviver. His reappearance on the political stage will be regarded as ominous by many who recall the slogan of the early 1990s: 'Menem roba; Duhalde mata' ('Menem steals; Duhalde kills').

ARGENTINA BEYOND THE BICENTENARY

Profound institutional problems remain. State institutions—the authority of the Congreso, the independence of the judiciary, the accountability and technical proficiency of key government agencies—weakened by Menem, de la Rúa and the Kirchners, remain fragile. Such representative organizations as political parties, labour unions and professional associations that traditionally form the bulwark of civil society in a mature democracy are weak. The style and practice of politics remain authoritarian and much of the language of the current political discourse seems to be trapped in the 1946–55 period. Little has been done since the 2001 crisis to strengthen democratic structures: on the contrary, an increased emphasis on personalities rather than institutions has remained the hallmark of recent administrations. The executive appears isolated from the reality of the day-to-day existence of the vast majority of citizens, and is subject to little congressional or judicial scrutiny. Press freedom has been seriously undermined. Corruption and a lack of transparency continue. Legislative inertia and the incidence of extra-legal official action have increased. While, in a formal sense, democracy and electoral politics survive, and the Constitution presents the image of a liberal, market economy, it remains unclear to whom the Argentine state 'belongs', where the country is positioned internationally, and whether or not the political system has the capacity to manage the crisis that will in all likelihood mature in 2010–11.

Economy

Prof. COLIN M. LEWIS

Optimists predicted that 2010 would see the Argentine economy 'bottom out', with recovery setting in towards the end of the year. However, these forecasts are now being revised, which is bad news for the administration, with legislative and presidential elections due in October 2011. Between 2003 and 2007 growth averaged approximately 9% per annum. With the the onset of the recession in late 2008, the rate declined to about 5%. In 2009 growth was negative, with estimates ranging from 2% to 5%. Aggregate growth rates between 2003 and 2008 set a new historical record, and ensured that while the 2003–05 period was one of recovery from the economic downturn that started in 1998, after 2005 the economy grew. Gross domestic product (GDP) per head in mid-2008 was around 7% higher than at the height of the previous boom, which ended in 1998. Current estimates suggest that GDP per caput is now significantly lower than at its 2007/08 peak, and is likely to fall. The lessons of the recent economic history of the Republic are that each successive crisis has been deeper than its predecessor, and that recovery has taken longer. Current domestic trends and the international conjuncture—reactions to the global financial panic of 2008–09 and the European debt crisis of 2010—indicate that this pattern will be repeated.

Argentina continues to present a paradox. Around 1900 the country featured among the 10 wealthiest economies in the world, ranked in terms of GDP per caput, and in 1950 it was the 12th wealthiest. Yet, according to one estimate, by 2010 Argentina ranked 82nd in the world economic league table. How could a country so favourably endowed with natural resources, and which was so well placed in international economic rankings until the mid-20th century, have fallen so precipitately from grace, on the way occasioning the largest recorded default on international debt in 2001–02? Why did a country that was the bread basket of the world in 1900 become an economic 'basket case' by the early 21st century? This paradox can only be understood by recognizing that the economic problems confronting the country are deep-seated and, thus far, continue to elude lasting resolution.

RESOURCES AND EXPORT-LED GROWTH

The second largest country in South America, after Brazil, Argentina comprises a little over 2.78m. sq km. It is about one-third of the size of the continental USA, or similar in area to Western Europe. Almost the whole of the Republic is situated in the temperate zone of the southern hemisphere, though, owing to the sheer size of the country, there are considerable variations in climate and topography, a variety matched only by the range and wealth of natural resources. Over the last decade or so the north-west and Patagonia have developed rapidly as centres of mining and energy production, with known deposits of oil and natural gas in the region being the third largest in Latin America. Along the Andes, in addition to traditional activities such as sheep-raising and wine production, new agricultural commodities were being developed and the region was beginning to realize fully its potential as a source of hydroelectric generation. The Pampas, representing the agricultural heartland of the country, had the potential to produce high yields of commodities without the use of chemicals or artificial fertilizers, according Argentina a competitive advantage in the lucrative and expanding 'organic' foods market, as well as an apparently limitless capacity to respond to surging global demand for more traditional temperate-region staples. Similarly dependent on the natural environment, new activities such as 'eco-tourism' and 'extreme sports' were emerging in the far north and south. Critically, the ability to harness Argentina's abundant natural wealth and utilize its topographical and climatic diversity has depended on a number of interrelated factors, such as an efficient infrastructure, a stable political environment and an appropriate international trade regime.

Factor endowments underpinned the liberal growth model of the so-called *Belle Époque* (1870s–1910s), an arrangement that facilitated the production of a broadening mix of commodities for global markets. A few statistics confirm the wealth and capacity of the Pampas. The outward movement of the frontier ensured that the area under cultivation doubled in the 1880s, had doubled again by 1900, and thereafter doubled at five-year intervals, by 1905, 1910, and 1915. During this period the country became, successively, a major world supplier of wool, cereals (principally wheat and maize), and, with the development of refrigerated shipping, quality frozen and chilled meat, especially high-premium chilled beef. No other economy experienced such an exponential increase in the area under cultivation in such a short space of time, or exhibited such a dynamic primary commodity export profile.

As reflected in the first Baring Crisis of 1889–90, export-led growth was volatile. In a series of events that foreshadowed those of 2001–02, by the end of the 1880s overseas investors doubted the capacity or willingness of the state to extract sufficient income to honour its obligations. The supply of new credits dried up, gold flowed abroad, and the Government broke its bond with domestic and foreign creditors. There were riots and armed confrontations on the streets. Asset values fell and the recession deepened. The 1889–90 shock was a crisis of development and a crisis of corruption. There were also overtones of a fiscal crisis, a crisis of state capacity. However, buoyant world demand for commodities and the broad scope of pre-1889 infrastructural modernization—embracing, principally, railways, ports and utilities—in conjunction with a new wave of immigration, soon facilitated the recovery of production and trade, and yet another investment boom. Despite the instability of the arrangement, such growth cycles validated the liberal model of economic openness and global engagement based on comparative natural advantage.

The First World War, however, weakened the export model. Structural change in the international economy provoked, and was intensified by, domestic policy responses that had a profound impact upon economic and political institutionalism. During the 1920s world growth slowed and there was greater instability, not least in commodity prices. Hence, earlier economic stimulants such as trade expansion, foreign capital inflows and immigration, were less pronounced. The terms of trade were beginning to move against Argentine exports, and the scope for commodity diversification became increasingly limited as the frontier closed.

Broad changes in commodity production and export between the 1880s and 1920s would not have been possible without institutional flexibility and macroeconomic efficiency, notwithstanding the massive growth in the resource base, notably through the incorporation of new land and the flow of foreign investment and immigrants. Commodity production and diversification was, hence, accompanied by aggregate output growth. In the early 1930s there was a sharp contraction in the area of land under cultivation, which pointed to structural rigidity and a looming crisis of production. Between the 1930s and the 1980s an increase in the production of one commodity tended to be accompanied by a contraction in the supply of another. Moreover, after the 1940s the economy seemed incapable of increasing exports without constraining domestic consumption, or vice versa. Growth in one sector often occurred in parallel to retrenchment in other parts of the economy as factor inputs relocated: increased industrial production implied a contraction in resources available for agriculture, while generating inputs for agriculture meant curtailing resources available for manufacturing. Consequently, for much of the period encompassing the 1940s–80s there was only modest growth in productivity and aggregate production. Consumption and accumulation similarly appeared as alternatives rather than complementary adjuncts to growth: consumption constrained the supply of resources available for investment, while enhancing savings capacity implied curbing consumption. This was the anatomy of an economy experiencing 'stop-go' growth and structural sclerosis.

SUSTAINABLE INDUSTRIALIZATION: ILLUSION OR REALITY?

Pessimism about the robustness of world trade and finance in the post-Second World War period fostered in Argentina a policy shift towards state-sponsored national development, founded on positive assumptions about the capacity of domestic institutions. As in other countries, government intervened in the productive sectors and assumed a substantial role in the social sphere. The critical difference between Argentina and many other countries was that the issue of how to fund state growth was not addressed systematically. Initially, intervention was financed by wartime windfall gains in export prices and fiscal reforms introduced during the early depression years. Thereafter, inflation taxation became the easy expedient. From the early 1940s to the early 1950s, as the economy closed, Argentine rates of inflation were noticeably higher than those of comparable economies. There was a second, more pronounced phase of divergence from international rates of price change in the mid-1950s and late 1960s, and a third cycle of divergence, from the early 1970s to the late 1980s, when inflation rates were vastly higher than those of other countries, and which culminated in bouts of hyperinflation in 1989–90.

It would be easy to blame these problems on populist strategies implemented by Peronist administrations between 1946 and 1955. Arguably, it was not these strategies *per se* that provoked a break in the national growth trajectory and divergence from other economies. Rather the cause lay in the way in which these strategies were implemented. Pro-industry ideas promulgated by the UN's Economic Commission for Latin America (as the Economic Commission for Latin America and the Caribbean was then known) and associated with the analysis of international commodity trade by Raúl Prebisch, former Director-General of the central bank, had a broad appeal. Developmentalist (*desarrollista*) ideology was widely embraced during the presidency of Arturo Frondizi (1958–62). There was a concerted effort to address the problem of arbitrary policy change and to resolve structural deficiencies in a systematic fashion. Targeting such sectors as steel and energy was designed to correct the bias towards 'horizontal' industrial expansion, manifest during the rule of Col Juan Domingo Perón (1946–55) when policy distortions had favoured light industries, geared towards the manufacture of basic wage goods, and the proliferation of small firms. The Frondizi project targeted 'downstream' basic industries and larger firms. In its own terms, the project was successful. Growth rates were high, if unpredictable. However, public sector deficits grew and, despite an improvement in the terms of trade, soaring imports and erratic export expansion soon caused deficits in the balance of payments.

By the mid-1960s manufacturing accounted for around one-third of total economic activity, the composition of industrial output was more diverse than hitherto, and firms were larger. These two phenomena were related and largely driven by the 'transnationalization' of business. The participation of foreign firms became particularly pronounced in sectors such as petrochemicals, machinery and equipment, motor vehicles, chemicals and non-ferrous metals. Increases in the scale of production were consistent with modest real reductions in the price of manufactures and efficiency gains. However, while foreign-owned corporations tended to invest in technology upgrading, national firms invested less and kept productions costs low by recruiting cheap, unskilled labour that was flooding into the cities from the countryside. The presence of the state (mainly military-owned firms) in manufacturing also grew. Across the manufacturing sector, a productivity gap was opening: all-round efficiency gains in sectors such as petrochemicals, chemicals and cellulose, and (some) metallurgical sectors were offset by slow productivity growth in other branches. This constrained expansion in overall productivity limited structural improvements in macroeconomic efficiency. Moreover, all businesses, however technically advanced, were dependent on the policy regime. Protection, access to cheap credit and subsidized inputs, an exchange rate tailored to the needs of manufacturing, and official interventions in the labour market, were critical to firm profitability. Regulation and intervention, though, fostered rent-seeking and corruption. As the productivity gap widened, distributional conflict (among economic sectors and between social groups) became a pronounced feature of the development model.

The 'bureaucratic-authoritarian' military regime installed in 1966, and presided over by Gen. Juan Carlos Onganía (1966–70), promised to resolve the efficiency gap and restore economic discipline. Onganía proposed the presentation of a 'business-friendly' face to the outside world. Foreign investment increased, precipitating another cycle of transnational corporate expansion which, associated with structural developments sustained from the Frondizi presidency, facilitated a surge in the manufacture of consumer durables, notably motor vehicles and electrical goods. The pro-business policy stance of the regime did not bring much relief to the agricultural sector, which continued to suffer pressure to generate resources (notably foreign exchange) essential for industrial development. The international oil crisis of 1973 prompted another policy shift, associated with the return from exile of Perón, who believed rising world commodity prices would end sluggish growth. As in the late 1940s, windfall taxes on agricultural exports supported an expansion in public expenditure, which increased by more than 50% in real terms from 1972 to 1975. However, the boom could not last. After 1975 commodity prices and foreign reserves fell sharply. Despite fiscal innovation, taxes failed to keep pace with expenditure and the public sector deficit was monetized. Inflation escalated and there was another crisis in the balance of payments: the twin structural constraints of the post-Second World War period had returned with devastating effect. Conditions were thus aligned for the 1976 coup, and renewed efforts to restore the productivity deficit and stabilize the economy.

A REVOLUTION IN PRODUCTIVITY: RESTRUCTURING IN AUTHORITARIAN AND DEMOCRATIC CONTEXTS

Many sectors of society initially greeted with relief the so-called Proceso de Reorganización Nacional initiated by the armed forces in March 1976. There was a sense that things could not get worse. The incoming military Government signalled a profound rupture with the pro-manufacturing consensus articulated by both civilian and military administrations since the 1940s. The collapse of the corporatist industrial alliance in the chaos of the last months of the administration of 'Isabelita' Martínez de Perón (1974–76), and the utter exhaustion of civil society, contributed to the new regime's autonomous power. 'Efficiency', 'accumulation' and 'shock therapy' became the catchphrases of the moment. The economy was opened and wages cut: foreign capital flowed in, investment levels recovered and export volumes soared; there was a near 40% contraction in real wages. Inflation was brought under control, falling from an average monthly rate above 30% in the period immediately preceding the coup to almost zero by June 1976. Subsidies were reduced and by 1977 the primary deficit had fallen to a quarter of its 1975 level, remaining low for the remainder of the decade. With the 'depoliticization' of decision-making, the junta's economic team enjoyed considerable protection from sectoral lobbying, an advantage that would not be lost on later Ministers of the Economy. None the less, there were limits to 'reform'. Public expenditure was not brought fully under control and the military refused to relinquish businesses acquired since the 1940s, despite a supposed commitment to market economics. Further, the armed forces exempted themselves from the discipline of the market and, in so doing, imposed greater fiscal pressure on other branches of official expenditure. As a share of the budget, military expenditure doubled in real terms during the second half of the decade.

There were other flaws with the model. Access to foreign funds, and an opportunity to import technology, should have enabled businesses to become more efficient. Tariff reduction, which accompanied the general liberalization of imports, should also have induced greater competitiveness among domestic firms pursuing business in both the home market and the international trade arena. Rooted in market logic, the economic model combined incentives and penalties. Unfortunately, not all economic agents behaved as expected. Rising government and household demand for credit meant that the financial sector was the main beneficiary of the boom: those with liquid assets found it more profitable to lend to the banks than to invest in production. Although companies raised funds to finance modernization, lending pressures limited the stock of resources available to business and drove up the real cost of domestic borrowing, even before the global spike in interest rates made further borrowing impracticable. Moreover, by 1980 public expenditure was higher than in 1976, and the budget deficit even larger. External indebtedness was becoming uncontrollable just as international interest rates were on the increase. Yet another boom was proving unsustainable: the era of 'easy money' (*plata dulce*) was about to end for companies, for consumers and for a Government that had based its legitimacy on growth, exchange rate stability and low inflation. All the signs of a structural crisis were in place: as in 1889, 1953–55, 1968, 1976, 1989, 1998 and 2001 there was evidence of financial sector distress, bankruptcies were on the increase, default on the domestic and external debt was in prospect, international reserves were contracting and the rate of exchange was unsustainable.

When the debt crisis and Falklands debacle (see History) resulted in the collapse of the Proceso regime in the 1982, the scene was set for a heterodox solution to the 'productivity crisis'. Launched in June 1985, the 'Austral Plan' was conceived as a 'war on inflation' by Juan Vital Sourrouille, Minister of the Economy. The project was a controversial blend of Keynesianism and monetarism. Acknowledging the need for macroeconomic stability, it broke the policy mould by seeking to stabilize through growth, rather than via a 'corrective' recession. Implemented in a democratic framework, unlike earlier 'corrections' of 1968 and 1976, the Austral Plan was another policy shock intended to change attitudes. A new currency, the austral, was phased in according to a sliding conversion table designed to prevent windfall gains and losses that often accompany sharp devaluations. A freeze on wages and prices was similarly adjusted for residual inflation, with fairly generous corrections being allowed for basic wages, and presented as a social pact involving the state, labour and business. Indexation was outlawed: the courts were banned from enforcing index clauses in contracts that linked prices to the rate of inflation. The Government committed itself to fiscal and monetary responsibility and privatization was on the agenda. Together, these measures and promises were intended to promote co-operation between all major interest groups—labour, business, taxpayers and the state—thereby ending the cycles of distributional conflict that had plagued the Argentine economy and society since the 1940s.

Unfortunately, economic agents did not always co-operate, and the state appeared reluctant or unable to honour its side of the bargain. Although inflation remained controlled at historically low monthly rates from July 1985 until the beginning of 1986, and public confidence remained high, investment did not increase as hoped. Crucially, the freezing of wages and prices was extended beyond its intended time span, a step largely motivated by the imminence of elections. A wages and prices shock, such as that applied in July 1985, could work only once: the imposition of a second round of shock treatment reduced the credibility of the policy model and the administration, indicating that the strategy was unravelling. By February 1989 central bank reserves were exhausted, the currency was in free fall and hyperinflation had become inevitable. When presidential and congressional elections were held in May 1989, the monthly rate of price increases touched 150%, representing an annual inflation rate of 5,000%. The scene was set for another dose of liberal correction.

Having initially toyed with populist economic solutions to the crisis, in January 1991 President Carlos Saúl Menem (1989–95, 1995–99) appointed Domingo Cavallo as Minister of the Economy. Cavallo implemented the 'Convertibility Plan' based on a new monetary system and the 'reform of the state': privatization, the liberalization of capital markets and a renewed opening of the economy. Following a substantial devaluation, the domestic currency was to be completely underwritten by US dollars and foreign reserves held by the central bank, which was to be freed from political control and prohibited from printing money (that is, monetizing the fiscal deficit). Apart from a small fiduciary limit, domestic currency would only be issued against US dollar reserves, and the bank would exchange dollars and local currency on demand at the official rate. The new parity was supported by an act of the Congreso, rather than a central bank directive. The Convertibility Plan introduced a dual (or 'competitive') monetary system: pesos and US dollars circulated in parallel and were virtually interchangeable. Private debts could be settled in pesos or dollars (or any other foreign currency chosen by contracting parties). The US dollar enjoyed the status of quasi-legal tender, with the exception that the government would only accept payment of taxes in pesos. The central bank became, in effect, a currency board. Opening the economy, along with the removal of controls on exchange and capital transactions and the abolition of price controls, was intended to discipline the private sector. A hard currency would deliver hard prices and compel businesses to take hard, rational decisions. Reform of the state meant removing the principal fiscal pressure points, specifically deficits generated by state-owned enterprises, provincial administrations and social security funds. The balance of the federal budget was to be restored by, on the revenue side, tax reform—entailing modernization of the fiscal structure and increasing the efficiency of tax collection—and, on the expenditure side, by the disposal of state enterprises, pension privatization and imposing discipline on the provinces.

Despite some technical flaws, the Convertibility Plan was successful, chiefly because there was a large measure of popular support and a reasonable (though not equitable) distribution of hardship. During the early years of the arrangement there was economic growth with low inflation. From 1991 to the end of 1994 output grew at an average annual rate of just under 8%, while the annual rate of inflation fell sharply from 84% to less than 4%. Unemployment rose, but remained below 10% until 1994, despite the accelerating pace of privatization, and investment increased. In addition, the project survived major shocks, namely the Mexican currency crisis of December 1994 (known as the 'tequila crisis') and the resignation of Cavallo in August 1996. However, despite the re-stabilization of the economy, and the beginning of profound structural reform, the success of the Convertibility Plan was undermined by corruption.

By the late 1990s the Menem administration had become a distributionist confederacy that preyed on the remnants of the failing state, conditions that contributed to opposition victories in the 1999 presidential and congressional elections. Institutionalized corruption exacted an economic and political price. Given the unforgiving nature of the Convertibility Plan, the economic price of fiscal delinquency was even greater. Failure to close the fiscal gap resulted in renewed state borrowing. Unfortunately, credit was not cheap. One of the recurring surprises, for proponents of the Plan, was that interest rates remained stubbornly high, despite the removal of the risk to the exchange rate associated with the new currency regime. There were several reasons for this. First, the markets harboured doubts about the technicalities of sustaining the project, doubts that intensified after 1999, as debt-service and the fiscal gap necessitated additional borrowing. Second, as during the mid-1980s, a rising government demand for credit kept rates high. Third, corruption drove the deficit. If Menem had little intention of curbing corruption, the Government of President Fernando de la Rúa that took office in December 1999 seemed equally unable, or unwilling, to curb expenditure. From 1991 to 2001 the fiscal deficit averaged 2% of GDP. Given the currency arrangement, a fiscal deficit of this order might have been sustainable for a year or two, but not for a whole decade.

The immediate causes of the ensuing crisis dated from early 2001 and unfolded in two phases. The first phase occurred in early April when recently reappointed Minister of the Economy, Domingo Cavallo, made a decision to adjust the Convertibility Law and modify the Central Bank Charter. This followed the largest ever monthly withdrawal of deposits from the banking system: in March some US $5,500m. flowed out of the banks, compared with the previous record of $4,600m. at the height of the tequila crisis in 1994. Between April and mid-July another run on the banks resulted in the withdrawal of a further $10,000m., precipitating a corresponding shrinkage of the domestic money supply and capital stock. This provoked a further credit slump—at a time when the economy was already more than three years into recession and bankruptcies were running at record levels—and precipitated the second phase: 'Plan Cero' (a monthly balancing of the budget) represented a desperate last attempt to reassure the public and the IMF, which was beginning to display a marked reluctance to advance further credit. This was followed in December, however, by the freezing of bank accounts, public outrage and the collapse of the de la Rúa presidency. By this time more than $20,000m. had been removed from the domestic banking system. The country was without credit and without money—or money of any value.

THE RETURN OF POPULIST ECONOMICS

The intensity and extent of the 2001–02 crisis was reflected in a series of protests aimed at the political class and the banks, and the succession of five Presidents in two weeks. Symbolically, on 1 January 2002 the Congreso offered the presidency to Eduardo Duhalde, a Peronist and former Governor of the province of Buenos Aires, who had been defeated by de la Rúa in the 1999 presidential election. Remaining in office until May 2003, the Duhalde administration was forced to take difficult decisions in order to secure a positive legacy for its successor. Though seemingly inevitable in retrospect, these decisions were hugely problematic at the time. The dual peso/US dollar monetary arrangement was abandoned, debt default was officially announced, the freeze on bank accounts was extended (with some minor exceptions), and an interim arrangement was sought with the IMF. Measures were taken to support the banking system and state finances, and a series of price agreements was negotiated with utility companies to prevent total social collapse. The principal anxieties were of a return of hyperinflation, precipitous devaluation of the peso, and violent public disorder. In the event, these fears were not realized, largely owing to the prudence of the regime (it had little alternative) and disciplined action by the new Minister of the Economy, Roberto Lavagna, appointed in April 2002. Lavagna was the sixth appointee to that post in 12 months, but he remained in office until November 2005, having been reappointed by Duhalde's successor, Néstor Carlos Kirchner (2003–07). President Kirchner was in turn succeeded by his wife, Cristina Fernández de Kirchner, in December 2007. This husband-to-wife succession ensured the strengthening and deepening of neo-populist economics that have characterized the post-2005 period.

An immediate benefit of debt default was the non-payment of interest and amortization charges. This reduced pressure on the budget—already contracting owing to the recession and near paralysis of the economy caused by the crisis—and allowed scarce fiscal resources to be devoted to emergency projects. A new revenue-sharing agreement was implemented in mid-2002 between the federal Government and the provinces, securing political support for the administration and preventing the failure of the state, while considerable sums were applied to social relief. Primary budget surpluses were soon being generated, and emergency taxes on exports gave the Government access to foreign exchange. This facilitated non-inflationary funding of government expenditure, notably the innovative Heads of Households Programme (Programa Jefes y Jefas de Hogar), targeted at the poorest members of society (at the height of the 2001–02 crisis over 55% households were categorized as living below the poverty line), and gave the central bank access to foreign exchange with which to manage the exchange rate. The rate of exchange remained remarkably stable from April 2003 until mid-2007, settling at around three pesos to the US dollar. From June 2007, however, the peso fell steadily against the dollar; in view of the increasingly parlous condition of the dollar, this decline was suggestive of domestic and international anxiety about both the peso and the quality of economic management in Argentina.

Until 2006 the economic team was generally well regarded, and was credited with securing social order and facilitating economic recovery and growth—or, at least, with not doing anything that jeopardized this recovery and growth. The principal features of the policy regime (described as 'neo-Keynesian') were: the accumulation of substantial fiscal surpluses and international reserves; price controls; targeted expenditure, initially focused mainly on emergency social projects and later the economic and social infrastructure; and, until very recently, exchange rate stability and low inflation. Most accounts acknowledged that the economic team had regained control of the economy by 2003, enabling the slow and arduous process of reconstructing the economic structures to begin. Luck, which now appears to be running out, also played a part, namely, the 'China effect' boom in commodity prices.

The extent of recovery and growth was demonstrated by several indicators. In most recent years the primary fiscal surpluses have stabilized at around 3%. The rate of open unemployment, which reached more than 22% in early 2002 and was approximately 10% in mid-2006, returned to 'historic' (pre-Convertibility Plan) levels of around 6% in 2008. The proportion of households living below the poverty line is now 15%, down from 55% in 2002. In 2007 industrial output grew by 9.9%—the highest ever recorded annual increase—improving upon 8.3% growth in 2006. Investment remained strong, and consumer and business surveys revealed high levels of confidence until 2008. Other achievements of the pre-2008 period included revenue-sharing agreements with the provinces, the renegotiation of the foreign and domestic debt with major institutional investors (the exception being individuals who refused to accept the deal—the so-called 'hold-outs'—who accounted for only a small proportion of total liabilities) and the repayment of international agency loans.

These achievements, however, should be considered in context. First, the level of external indebtedness remained high (being higher in real terms than it was before the 2001 crisis), while current debt service charges (expressed as a proportion of GDP) also remain above 2001 levels, despite the 2005 agreement. Second, until the surge in direct foreign investment associated with the commodity boom and Chinese-style growth rates, capital flows from overseas were among the lowest in Latin America (at around 2% of GDP), reflecting a lack of confidence in the country and the Government. Critically, until the Government turned its attention to this issue in 2008, there was acute under-investment in several sectors, including transport, energy generation and supply, and key branches of manufacturing. Stalled tariff-adjustment negotiations with utility companies inhibited recapitalization and motivated a distrust of foreign business: since 2008, as the rhetoric and substance of economic policy became increasingly nationalistic, some international consortia have gradually, sometimes vociferously, withdrawn from Argentina. Official suspension of energy supplies to Chile and Brazil at around the same time further undermined the predictability of contracts. As a result, and notwithstanding belated action being taken by the authorities, power blackouts occurred, prompting memories of the energy shortages experienced between the 1950s and the 1970s. Recession has partly resolved the problem, but the investment deficit remains. Third, the current tax regime is unsustainable: government finances have become dependent on export taxes. Initially justified as an emergency measure, when reapplied during the 2001–02 crisis, and subsequently presented as an 'equity' levy on an agro-export sector benefiting from the surge in commodity prices, these taxes have become counter-productive. Accompanied by export bans, successive increases in export tax rates between 2007 and 2009 have resulted in massive rural decapitalization (reversing a trend towards capital upgrading initiated in the 1990s), a switch to less heavily taxed commodities, and producer strikes. Farmer protests, accompanied by highway blockades and empty shelves in supermarkets, became a pronounced feature of 2008–09, and succeeded in uniting various farming groups and urban consumers against the Government. The emergency legislation providing for export taxes was to expire in mid-2010. Since the Government had lost its majority in the lower house of the Congreso in the mid-term congressional election of June 2009, there was doubt as to whether or not the legal basis of the current fiscal regime would be renewed, adding further to the economic uncertainty.

2010–11: DENOUEMENT OR MODEL CHANGE?

Admiration for Argentinian economic management waned considerably after mid-2006, partly owing to the increasing use of populist language and an apparent unwillingness to address underlying economic problems, notwithstanding the prevailing strength of the fiscal and external accounts at that time. The country's reputation has been further undermined during recent economic crises.

Government responses to post-2008 crises have been to: 'intervene' in the official agency responsible for compiling macroeconomic statistics; redirect supplies from overseas to the domestic market; exert pressure on producers; increase subsidies to key economic actors (notably transport and energy firms); nationalize and loot private pension funds (the overseas investment of which was liquidated to retire tranches of the foreign debt); and redeploy currency reserves to service foreign debt—a move that provoked the resignation of the head of the central bank and an expansion of nationalist-statist rhetoric. Oligopolistic and anti-national 'forces' have been blamed for the crises and, in 2010, overtly protectionist measures were applied. This has fooled nobody, as indicated by scepticism over official inflation data and anxiety about the weakening exchange rate. While the administration refused to accept that inflation was above 10%, most independent sources pointed to rates of around 30%, even as the economy entered recession, and few accepted that the recovery in industrial output and fall in unemployment recorded at the beginning of 2010 could be sustained.

A series of events in the first half of 2010 highlighted the difficulties confronting the country. The fragility of recovery in the real economy and fiscal accounts was emphasized by a dependence on volatile upward trends in prices rather than on output expansion, as well as on efforts to curb imports. A projected return to the markets to raise new finance—for the first time since before the collapse of the Convertibility Plan—which included a settlement with the 'hold-outs' who refused to accept the 2005 debt settlement, stalled as prospective investors were unsettled by the terms of a domestic debt swap, the federal Government attempted to shore up bankrupt provinces and creditors assessed Argentina's macroeconomic fundamentals.

Basic flaws in macroeconomic strategy are now becoming manifest on an obtrusively large scale. Social spending in 2002 and 2003 undoubtedly prevented a social catastrophe and helped to contain a political crisis. 'Neo-Keynesianism' also contributed to economic reactivation after 2003. With production approaching full capacity around 2007/08 in several sectors, infrastructural bottlenecks appeared, and, with growth running at about 9%, the economy no longer required further stimulation, but the Government did not readjust strategy in the run-up to the 2007 presidential election. Unsurprisingly, with the economy contracting, neither did it do so in advance of the 2009 mid-term congressional election. Rather, with historically large primary surpluses, an increasing proportion of government expenditure has been absorbed by subsidies: compensation to oil companies to keep domestic fuel prices below international levels, subsidies to transport companies to cover rising costs and compensate for the failure to adjust charges, and diverse subsidies to producers and consumers. The list is endless, driven by official efforts to check price increases and contain inflationary pressure. No economy can run on subsidies for ever. Although the arrangement seemed sustainable when the fiscal and external accounts remained in substantial surplus, the shortcomings of the Government's macroeconomic management are now becoming clear at precisely the moment when greater flexibility and efficiency is required to manage responses to global financial and currency crises that have compounded domestic structural weaknesses.

The current crisis facing Argentina is multi-dimensional and largely of domestic making. Tax policy has compromised agricultural production. This has resulted in a sharp contraction in exports, compounded by adverse weather conditions that have further undermined output and overseas trade. Once the bread basket of the world and energy self-sufficient, in 2011 Argentina faces the prospect of importing commodities it once exported. The fall in export production is also reducing government tax receipts, which are likely to decline further as the economy enters recession, given the pro-cyclical nature of the tax system. Substantial surpluses that were accumulated during good years were largely used to finance current consumption—well beyond the requirements of Keynesian economic reactivation—thus compromising investments that might have increased general efficiency. Investment was also discouraged by policy rhetoric that inhibited inflows of capital from overseas while fostering capital flight. Official expenditure patterns have also, recently, been responsible for increasing social inequality. Between 2003 and 2006 economic recovery produced a marked decline in absolute poverty and some improvement in inequality. Since then, rates of inequality have been on the increase and absolute poverty rose as the recession began to bite.

In international surveys of economic competitiveness and transparency, Argentina has a very low score compared with countries at a similar level of development; these scores have deteriorated over the last few years. There has been a similar deterioration in social indices and evaluations of economic management and policy consistency. This is the problem confronting the country as anxiety about the global economy and international volatility continues. How, and in what direction, will the policy model change? The present assumption is that there are two options: to overhaul the fiscal and financial structures, and to foster investment in productive efficiency; or to effect a further closure and statization of the economy in order to monetize the deficit. Neither option is costless, though the latter fits more with the short-sightedness of the current administration.

Statistical Survey

Sources (unless otherwise stated): Instituto Nacional de Estadística y Censos, Avda Julio A. Roca 609, C1067AAB Buenos Aires; tel. (11) 4349-9200; fax (11) 4349-9601; e-mail ces@indec.mecon.gov.ar; internet www.indec.mecon.gov.ar; Banco Central de la República Argentina, Reconquista 266, C1003ABF Buenos Aires; tel. (11) 4348-3500; fax (11) 4348-3955; e-mail sistema@bcra.gov.ar; internet www.bcra.gov.ar.

Area and Population

AREA, POPULATION AND DENSITY

Area (sq km)	2,780,403*
Population (census results)†	
15 May 1991	32,615,528
17–18 November 2001	
Males	17,659,072
Females	18,601,058
Total	36,260,130
Population (official projected estimates at mid-year)	
2008	39,745,613
2009	40,134,425
2010	40,518,951
Density (per sq km) at mid-2010	14.6

* 1,073,519 sq miles. The figure excludes the Falkland Islands (Islas Malvinas) and Antarctic territory claimed by Argentina.

† Figures exclude adjustment for underenumeration, estimated to have been 0.9% at the 1991 census.

POPULATION BY AGE AND SEX

(official estimates at mid-2010)

	Males	Females	Total
0–14	5,165,193	4,991,118	10,156,311
15–64	12,980,712	13,187,635	26,168,347
65 and over	1,700,766	2,493,527	4,194,293
Total	19,846,671	20,672,280	40,518,951

ADMINISTRATIVE DIVISIONS

(official projected estimates at mid-2010)

	Area (sq km)	Population	Density (per sq km)	Capital
Buenos Aires—City	203	3,058,309	15,065.6	—
Buenos Aires—Province	307,571	15,315,842	49.8	La Plata
Catamarca	102,602	404,240	3.9	San Fernando del Valle de Catamarca
Chaco	99,633	1,071,141	10.8	Resistencia
Chubut	224,686	470,733	2.1	Rawson
Córdoba	165,321	3,396,685	20.5	Córdoba
Corrientes	88,199	1,035,712	11.7	Corrientes
Entre Ríos	78,781	1,282,014	16.3	Paraná
Formosa	72,066	555,694	7.7	Formosa
Jujuy	53,219	698,474	13.1	San Salvador de Jujuy
La Pampa	143,440	341,456	2.4	Santa Rosa
La Rioja	89,680	355,350	4.0	La Rioja
Mendoza	148,827	1,765,685	11.9	Mendoza
Misiones	29,801	1,111,443	37.3	Posadas
Neuquén	94,078	565,242	6.0	Neuquén
Río Negro	203,013	603,761	3.0	Viedma
Salta	155,488	1,267,311	8.2	Salta
San Juan	89,651	715,052	8.0	San Juan
San Luis	76,748	456,767	6.0	San Luis
Santa Cruz	243,943	234,087	1.0	Río Gallegos
Santa Fe	133,007	3,285,170	24.7	Santa Fe
Santiago del Estero	136,351	883,573	6.5	Santiago del Estero
Tierra del Fuego	21,571	133,694	6.2	Ushuaia
Tucumán	22,524	1,511,516	67.1	San Miguel de Tucumán
Total	2,780,403	40,518,951	14.6	—

PRINCIPAL TOWNS

(population at 2001 census)*

Buenos Aires (capital)	2,776,138	Malvinas Argentinas†	290,691
Córdoba	1,267,521	Berazategui†	287,913
La Matanza†	1,255,288	Bahía Blanca†	284,776
Rosario	908,163	Resistencia	274,490
Lomas de Zamora†	591,345	Vicente López†	274,082
La Plata†	574,369	San Miguel†	253,086
General Pueyrredón†	564,056	Posadas	252,981
San Miguel de Tucumán	527,150	Esteban Echeverría†	243,974
Quilmes†	518,788	Paraná	235,967
Almirante Brown†	515,556	Pilar†	232,463
Merlo†	469,985	San Salvador de Jujuy	231,229
Salta	462,051	Santiago del Estero	230,614
Lanús†	453,082	José C. Paz†	230,208
General San Martín†	403,107	Guaymallén	223,365
Moreno†	380,503	Neuquén	201,868
Santa Fe	368,668	Formosa	198,074
Florencio Varela†	348,970	Godoy Cruz	182,563
Tres de Febrero†	336,467	Escobar†	178,155
Avellaneda†	328,980	Hurlingham†	172,245
Corrientes	314,546	Las Heras	169,248
Morón†	309,380	Ituzaingó	158,121
Tigre†	301,223	San Luis	153,322
San Isidro†	291,505	San Fernando†	151,131

* In each case, the figure refers to the city proper. At the 2001 census the population of the Buenos Aires agglomeration was 12,045,921.

† Settlement within the Province of Buenos Aires.

Mid-2010 ('000, incl. suburbs, UN estimates): Buenos Aires 13,074; Córdoba 1,493; Rosario 1,231; Mendoza 917; San Miguel de Tucumán 831 (Source: UN, *World Urbanization Prospects: The 2009 Revision*).

BIRTHS, MARRIAGES AND DEATHS

	Registered live births		Marriages		Registered deaths	
	Number	Rate (per 1,000)	Number	Rate (per 1,000)	Number	Rate (per 1,000)
2001	683,495	18.2	130,533	3.5	285,941	7.6
2002	694,684	18.3	122,343	3.3	291,190	7.7
2003	697,952	18.4	129,049	3.4	302,064	8.0
2004	736,261	19.3	128,212	3.4	294,051	7.7
2005	712,220	18.5	132,720	3.4	293,529	7.6
2006	696,451	17.9	134,496	3.5	292,313	7.5
2007	700,792	17.8	136,437	3.5	315,852	8.0
2008	746,460	18.8	133,060	3.3	302,133	7.6

Sources: Dirección de Estadísticas e Información en Salud (DEIS) and UN, *Demographic Yearbook* and *Population and Vital Statistics Report*.

Life expectancy (years at birth, WHO estimates): 76 (males 72; females 79) in 2008 (Source: WHO, *World Health Statistics*).

ECONOMICALLY ACTIVE POPULATION
(labour force survey of 31 urban agglomerations, persons aged 10 years and over, 2006)

	Males	Females	Total
Agriculture, hunting and forestry	59,242	13,640	72,882
Fishing	8,215	821	9,036
Mining and quarrying	34,127	5,687	39,814
Manufacturing	988,343	422,321	1,410,664
Electricity, gas and water	38,066	5,991	44,057
Construction	854,764	29,917	884,681
Wholesale and retail trade; repair of motor vehicles, motorcycles and personal and household goods	1,263,477	755,160	2,018,637
Hotels and restaurants	213,854	166,975	380,829
Transport, storage and communications	557,431	86,613	644,044
Financial intermediation	95,938	93,497	189,435
Real estate, renting and business activities	528,349	281,460	809,809
Public administration and defence; compulsory social security	444,379	324,337	768,716
Education	185,900	620,900	806,800
Health and social work	163,470	426,735	590,205
Other community, social and personal services	317,127	229,607	546,734
Private households with employed persons	18,151	778,801	796,952
Extra-territorial organizations and bodies	2,031	164	2,195
Sub-total	5,772,864	4,242,626	10,015,490
Activities not adequately described	13,854	11,161	25,015
Total employed	5,786,718	4,253,787	10,040,505
Unemployed	488,935	560,263	1,049,198
Total labour force	6,275,653	4,814,050	11,089,703

2007 (labour force survey of 31 urban agglomerations at January–March, '000 persons aged 10 years and over): Total employed 10,052; Unemployed 1,095; Total labour force 11,147.

2008 (labour force survey of 31 agglomerations at January–March, '000 persons aged 10 years and over): Total employed 10,216; Unemployed 938; Total labour force 11,154.

2009 (labour force survey of 31 agglomerations at January–March, '000 persons aged 10 years and over): Total employed 10,370; Unemployed 948; Total labour force 11,318.

Health and Welfare

KEY INDICATORS

Total fertility rate (children per woman, 2008)	2.2
Under-5 mortality rate (per 1,000 live births, 2008)	15
HIV (% of persons aged 15–49, 2007)	0.5
Physicians (per 1,000 head, 1998)	3.01
Hospital beds (per 1,000 head, 2000)	4.1
Health expenditure (2007): US $ per head (PPP)	1,322
Health expenditure (2007): % of GDP	10.0
Health expenditure (2007): public (% of total)	50.8
Access to water (% of persons, 2008)	97
Access to sanitation (% of persons, 2008)	90
Total carbon dioxide emissions ('000 metric tons, 2006)	173,409.8
Carbon dioxide emissions per head (metric tons, 2006)	4.4
Human Development Index (2007): ranking	49
Human Development Index (2007): value	0.866

For sources and definitions, see explanatory note on p. vi.

Agriculture

PRINCIPAL CROPS
('000 metric tons)

	2006	2007	2008
Wheat	14,663	16,487	8,428
Rice, paddy	1,193	1,080	1,246
Barley	1,268	1,482	1,690
Maize	14,446	21,755	22,017
Rye	17	77	34
Oats	243	472	291
Sorghum	2,328	2,795	2,937
Potatoes	1,944	1,950*	1,950*
Sweet potatoes*	330	340	340
Cassava (Manioc)*	172	175	175
Sugar cane*	26,450	29,950	29,950
Beans, dry	323	328	337
Soybeans (Soya beans)	40,537	47,483	46,232
Groundnuts, with shell	347	600	625
Olives*	170	160	160
Sunflower seed	3,760	3,498	4,646
Artichokes*	88	90	90
Tomatoes*	670	680	680
Pumpkins, squash and gourds*	290	300	300
Chillies and peppers, green*	126	127	127
Onions, dry	698	700*	700*
Garlic	136	140*	140*
Carrots and turnips*	230	231	231
Watermelons*	126	126	126
Cantaloupes and other melons*	80	85	85
Bananas*	181	182	182
Oranges*	765	766	766
Tangerines, mandarins, clementines and satsumas*	500	520	520
Lemons and limes*	1,250	1,260	1,260
Grapefruit and pomelos*	175	176	176
Apples*	1,280	1,300	1,300
Pears	510	520	520*
Peaches and nectarines*	260	270	270
Plums and sloes*	155	128	128
Grapes	2,881†	2,900*	2,900*
Tea	72	76*	76*
Mate*	280	290	300
Tobacco, unmanufactured*	165	170	170

* FAO estimate(s).

† Unofficial figure.

Aggregate production ('000 metric tons, may include official, semi-official or estimated data): Total cereals 34,204 in 2006, 44,187 in 2007, 36,681 in 2008; Total roots and tubers 2,446 in 2006, 2,465 in 2007–08; Total vegetables (incl. melons) 3,175 in 2006, 3,222 in 2007–08; Total fruits (excl. melons) 8,035 in 2006, 8,102 in 2007–08.

Source: FAO.

LIVESTOCK
('000 head, year ending September, FAO estimates)

	2005	2006	2007
Horses	3,655	3,650	3,680
Asses	98	98	98
Mules	185	185	185
Cattle	50,167	50,700	50,750
Pigs	1,830	2,260	2,270
Sheep	12,450	12,400	12,450
Goats	4,200	4,200	4,250
Chickens	95,000	95,000	96,000
Ducks	2,355	2,400	2,450
Geese	140	140	150
Turkeys	2,900	2,900	2,950

2008: Figures assumed to be unchanged from 2007 (FAO estimates).

Source: FAO.

LIVESTOCK PRODUCTS
('000 metric tons)

	2005	2006	2007
Cattle meat	2,980	2,800*	2,830*
Sheep meat*	52	52	52
Pig meat*	185	225	230
Horse meat*	56	56	57
Chicken meat	1,010	1,159	1,160*
Cows' milk	9,909	10,494	10,500*
Butter and ghee*	55	55	55
Cheese*	360	360	360
Hen eggs	310*	484†	480*
Honey*	110	105	81
Wool, greasy*	60	60	60

* FAO estimate(s).
† Unofficial figure.

2008: Production assumed to be unchanged from 2007 (FAO estimates).

Source: FAO.

Forestry

ROUNDWOOD REMOVALS
('000 cubic metres, excl. bark)

	2005	2006	2007
Sawlogs, veneer logs and logs for sleepers	3,455	3,486	2,920
Pulpwood	5,970	5,514	5,744
Other industrial wood	421	499	590
Fuel wood	4,372	4,372*	4,297*
Total	14,218	13,871*	13,551*

* FAO estimate.

2008: Production assumed to be unchanged from 2007 (FAO estimates).

Source: FAO.

SAWNWOOD PRODUCTION
('000 cubic metres, incl. railway sleepers)

	2005	2006	2007
Coniferous (softwood)	1,079	1,078	822
Broadleaved (hardwood)	660	1,025	694
Total	1,739	2,103	1,516

2008: Production assumed to be unchanged from 2007 (FAO estimates).
Source: FAO.

Fishing

('000 metric tons, live weight)

	2006	2007	2008
Capture	1,172.0	985.4	995.1
Southern blue whiting	31.3	19.0	19.8
Argentine hake	353.1	301.7	263.3
Patagonian grenadier	124.6	98.8	110.3
Argentine red shrimp	44.4	47.6	47.4
Patagonian scallop	80.0	53.7	58.7
Argentine shortfin squid	292.1	233.1	255.5
Aquaculture	2.5	3.0	2.7*
Total catch	1,174.5	988.4	997.8*

* FAO estimate.

Note: The data exclude aquatic animals, recorded by number rather than by weight. The number of minke whales caught was 1 in 2008. The number of dolphins and toothed whales caught was 101 in 2006; 1 in 2007; 27 in 2008. The number of broad-nosed and spectacled caimans caught was 4,535 in 2006; 7,208 in 2007; 4,261 in 2008.

Source: FAO.

Mining

('000 metric tons, unless otherwise indicated)

	2005	2006	2007
Crude petroleum ('000 cu metres)	38,323	38,249	37,175
Natural gas (million cu metres)	48,738	51,665	50,891
Lead ore*	10.7	12.1†	17.0†
Zinc ore*	30.2	29.8†	27.0†
Lithium‡	5.9	6.3	6.7
Silver ore (kg)*	263,766	245,124†	255,567†
Copper ore*	187.3	180.1†	180.2†
Gold ore (kg)*§	27,904	44,131	42,021
Boron	632.8	533.5†	669.6†
Gypsum (crude)	1,073.3	1,202.8†	1,226.5†
Clay (common)	6,373.7	6,832.2†	8,429.9†
Salt	1,845.6	1,917.7†	2,357.7†
Sand:			
for construction§	20,194.1	21,143.5	28,381.3
Silica (glass) sand	461.2	446.2†	456.2†
Limestone	12,267.0	12,993.4†	16,152.3†
Stone (various crushed)§	11,533.5	12,692.4	22,586.5
Rhodochrosite (kg)	118,200	78,832†	50,593†
Gemstones (kg)	80,579	53,355†	12,745†

* Figures refer to the metal content of ores and concentrates.
† Provisional.
‡ Lithium oxide (Li_2O) content.
§ Estimates.

2008: Crude petroleum 36,523,000 cu metres.

Industry

SELECTED PRODUCTS
('000 metric tons, unless otherwise indicated)

	2007	2008	2009
Wheat flour	4,398	4,781	4,668
Beer (sales, '000 hectolitres)*	15,850	18,190	18,640
Wine (sales, '000 hectolitres)	11,166	10,677	10,292†
Cigarettes (sales, million packets)	2,057	2,173	2,120
Paper (excl. newspaper)	1,594	1,543	1,544†
Aluminium	286	394	413
Iron (primary)	4,393	4,282	2,849
Crude steel	5,387	5,541	4,013
Rubber tyres for motor vehicles ('000, excl. tractors)	12,079	10,977	n.a.
Portland cement	9,602	9,703	9,385
Refined petroleum ('000 cu metres)	37,185	35,226†	33,572†
Ethylene	696	682	738
Urea	1,019	882	1,116
Ammonia	669	572	690
Washing machines ('000 units)	969	765	903†
Home refrigerators ('000 units)	646	451	643†
Air conditioning units (domestic, '000)	1,006	1,374	570†
Motor vehicles ('000)	351	399	380
Electric energy (million kWh)	111,503†	n.a.	n.a.

* Estimates.
† Provisional figure.

Finance

CURRENCY AND EXCHANGE RATES

Monetary Units

100 centavos = 1 nuevo peso argentino (new Argentine peso).

Sterling, Dollar and Euro Equivalents (31 May 2010)

£1 sterling = 5.699 new pesos;
US $1 = 3.909 new pesos;
€1 = 4.841 new pesos;
100 new pesos = £17.55 = $25.58 = €20.66.

Average Exchange Rate (new pesos per US $)

2007 3.096
2008 3.144
2009 3.710

Note: From April 1996 to December 2001 the official exchange rate was fixed at US $1 = 99.95 centavos. In January 2002 the Government abandoned this exchange rate and devalued the peso: initially there was a fixed official exchange rate of US $1 = 1.40 new pesos for trade and financial transactions, while a free market rate was applicable to other transactions. In February, however, a unified 'floating' exchange rate system, with the rate to be determined by market conditions, was introduced.

CENTRAL GOVERNMENT BUDGET

(million new pesos)

Revenue	2007	2008	2009*
Current revenue	149,462.8	212,740.9	241,644.4
Tax revenue	102,352.0	153,297.4	173,768.5
Social security contributions	40,305.1	46,379.1	58,257.1
Sale of public goods and services	860.8	1,024.0	1,067.6
Property income	2,333.6	6,587.9	2,584.7
Other non-tax revenue	3,089.2	3,925.2	4,130.5
Current transfers	522.1	1,527.2	1,565.9
Capital revenue	1,148.1	1,382.2	1,304.5
Total	1150,611.0	214,123.1	242,948.9

Expenditure	2007	2008	2009*
Current expenditure	128,884.6	179,091.4	200,938.7
Consumption expenditure	21,851.5	29,046.6	34,034.7
Remuneration	15,189.2	20,127.3	22,958.6
Goods and services	6,661.0	8,917.5	11,072.3
Other	1.3	1.7	3.8
Property income	17,598.7	22,686.8	24,484.9
Interest	17,596.1	22,684.1	24,479.4
Other income	2.6	2.7	5.4
Social security benefits	50,961.4	65,053.7	81,541.9
Other current expenditure	20.5	8.8	8.8
Current transfers	38,452.5	62,295.6	60,868.4
Private sector	21,968.3	38,899.1	36,530.7
Public sector	16,065.3	22,958.4	23,887.5
External sector	418.8	438.1	450.2
Capital expenditure	19,414.2	26,644.0	32,901.0
Real direct investment	7,632.9	10,092.7	11,657.4
Capital transfers	9,489.0	15,262.5	19,952.0
Financial investment	2,292.3	1,288.8	1,291.7
Total	148,298.8	205,735.4	233,839.7

* Preliminary figures.

Note: Budget figures refer to the consolidated accounts of the central Government only.

Source: Oficina Nacional de Presupuesto, Secretaría de Hacienda, Ministerio de Economía, Buenos Aires.

INTERNATIONAL RESERVES

(US $ million at 31 December)

	2007	2008	2009
Gold (national valuation)	1,434	1,514	1,932
IMF special drawing rights	507	494	3,170
Foreign exchange	44,175	44,360	42,922
Total	46,116	46,368	48,024

Source: IMF, *International Financial Statistics*.

MONEY SUPPLY

(million new pesos at 31 December)

	2007	2008	2009
Currency outside banks	67,067	74,099	86,054
Demand deposits at commercial banks	39,148	37,604	45,059
Total money	106,215	111,703	131,113

Source: IMF, *International Financial Statistics*.

COST OF LIVING

(Consumer Price Index for Buenos Aires metropolitan area; annual averages; base: April 2008 = 100)

	2007	2008	2009
Food and beverages	93.7	100.1	102.9
Housing and basic services	91.7	101.0	104.8
Clothing	102.1	103.2	116.2
Transport and communications	91.3	101.0	112.1
All items (incl. others)	93.1	101.1	107.5

NATIONAL ACCOUNTS

(million new pesos at current prices, preliminary)

Expenditure on the Gross Domestic Product

	2007	2008	2009
Government final consumption expenditure	105,013	138,827	174,002
Private final consumption expenditure	475,876	595,012	667,375
Increase in stocks*	94	18,931	3,176
Gross fixed capital formation	196,622	240,486	239,637
Total domestic expenditure	777,605	993,256	1,084,190
Exports of goods and services	200,080	252,772	244,569
Less Imports of goods and services	165,230	213,269	183,300
Gross domestic product (GDP) in market prices	812,456	1,032,758	1,145,458
GDP at constant 1993 prices	359,170	383,444	386,704

* Including statistical discrepancy.

Gross Domestic Product by Economic Activity

	2007	2008	2009
Agriculture, forestry and hunting	68,253	90,780	77,208
Fishing	1,849	2,399	2,155
Mining and quarrying	35,557	35,688	38,512
Manufacturing	158,821	201,175	224,188
Electricity, gas and water supply	10,991	12,321	13,459
Construction	46,359	56,554	60,158
Wholesale and retail trade	86,318	112,481	128,767
Hotels and restaurants	19,969	25,083	27,349
Transport, storage and communications	64,106	80,279	86,695
Financial intermediation	36,366	48,648	59,845
Real estate, renting and business activities	81,907	104,244	121,024
Public administration and defence*	43,698	58,186	73,170
Education, health and social work	61,344	81,027	97,229
Other community, social and personal service activities†	30,630	38,343	47,884
Sub-total	746,168	947,208	1,057,643
Value-added tax	65,124	84,265	90,843
Import duties	7,015	8,988	7,700
Less Financial intermediation services indirectly measured	5,851	7,702	10,728
GDP in market prices	812,456	1,032,758	1,145,458

* Including extra-territorial organizations and bodies.
† Including private households with employed persons.

BALANCE OF PAYMENTS
(US $ million)

	2007	2008	2009
Exports of goods f.o.b.	55,980	70,021	55,750
Imports of goods f.o.b.	–42,525	–54,557	–37,130
Trade balance	13,456	15,464	18,621
Exports of services	10,363	12,070	10,954
Imports of services	–10,876	–13,096	–11,711
Balance on goods and services	12,943	14,438	17,864
Other income received (net)	–5,941	–7,552	–9,272
Balance on goods, services and income	7,002	6,886	8,592
Current transfers (net)	353	150	2,701
Current balance	7,355	7,037	11,292
Capital account (net)	121	181	70
Net investment in banking sector	1,583	1,733	–985
Net investment in public sector	2,401	–537	–756
Net investment in private sector	1,572	–9,458	–7,457
Net errors and omissions	66	1,054	–817
Overall balance	13,098	9	1,346

External Trade

PRINCIPAL COMMODITIES
(US $ million)

Imports c.i.f.	2007	2008*	2009†
Mineral fuels, lubricants and related products	2,692	4,133	2,436
Paper and cardboard	835	975	742
Rubber and manufactures of rubber	889	1,078	705
Organic chemicals and related products	2,258	3,114	2,030
Pharmaceutical products	939	1,141	1,208
Plastic and manufactures of laminate	2,051	2,226	1,750
Metalliferous ore	1,146	1,146	n.a.
Electrical machinery	5,831	6,526	4,972
Vehicles	6,956	9,367	5,778
Nuclear reactors, boilers, machines and mechanical appliances	7,508	9,066	6,086
Optical instruments and apparatus, etc.	919	1,090	989
Total (incl. others)	44,707	57,423	38,781

Exports f.o.b.	2007	2008*	2009†
Meat and meat products	1,619	1,926	2,065
Milk and milk products	786	1,015	n.a.
Skins and leathers	970	897	663
Fish	1,072	1,256	1,085
Fats and oils	5,493	7,059	4,479
Cereals	4,661	6,772	3,214
Oil seeds and oleaginous fruits	3,696	4,887	1,980
Mineral fuels, lubricants and related materials	6,111	6,717	5,656
Mineral by-products	1,551	1,117	n.a.
Metalliferous ore	1,497	1,856	n.a.
Plastic and manufactures of laminate	1,203	1,478	1,225
Vehicles	5,306	6,491	5,373
Nuclear reactors, boilers and mechanical appliances	1,442	1,823	1,538
Total (incl. others)	55,980	70,021	55,669

* Provisional figures.
† Preliminary figures.

PRINCIPAL TRADING PARTNERS
(US $ million)*

Imports c.i.f.	2007	2008†	2009‡
Brazil§	14,523	17,687	11,819
Chile§	708	952	665
China, People's Republic‖	5,127	7,143	4,823
France (incl. Monaco)	1,061	1,451	810
Germany	2,131	2,534	1,994
Italy	1,072	1,205	850
Japan	1,200	1,378	909
Mexico	1,337	1,595	1,164
Paraguay	1,056	1,783	699
Spain	813	1,054	788
United Kingdom	445	545	376
USA	5,352	7,023	5,106
Uruguay§	458	527	348
Total (incl. others)	44,707	57,423	38,781

Exports f.o.b.	2007	2008†	2009‡
Belgium	409	543	457
Bolivia	463	606	580
Brazil§	10,498	13,259	11,373
Canada	350	470	466
Chile§	4,180	4,716	4,389
China, People's Republic‖	5,363	6,598	3,668
Colombia	576	808	874
France (incl. Monaco)	605	914	446
Germany	1,265	1,475	1,412
Italy	1,387	1,688	1,501
Japan	686	505	494
Mexico	1,439	1,347	932
Netherlands	1,797	2,959	2,392
Paraguay	779	1,086	843
Peru	958	1,313	793
South Africa	1,000	1,013	664
Spain	2,065	2,744	1,854
United Kingdom	694	814	762
USA	4,347	5,514	3,465
Uruguay§	1,173	1,762	1,606
Venezuela	1,178	1,418	1,042
Total (incl. others)	55,980	70,021	55,669

* Imports by country of origin; exports by country of destination.
† Provisional figures.
‡ Preliminary figures.
§ Including free trade zones.
‖ Including Hong Kong and Macao.

Transport

RAILWAYS
(traffic)

	2006	2007	2008
Passengers carried ('000)	437,522	425,760	450,914
Freight carried ('000 tons)	23,917	24,927	23,619
Passenger-km (million)	8,796	8,248	9,053
Freight ton-km (million)	12,628	12,871	12,024

ROAD TRAFFIC
('000 motor vehicles in use)

	2003	2004	2005
Passenger cars	4,668	4,926	5,230
Commercial vehicles	1,198	1,684	1,775

Source: UN, *Statistical Yearbook*.

2007 ('000 motor vehicles in use at 31 December): Total vehicles 12,399.9 (Source: IRF, *World Road Statistics*).

SHIPPING

Merchant Fleet
(registered at 31 December)

	2006	2007	2008
Number of vessels	565	569	576
Total displacement ('000 grt)	837.8	838.0	785.3

Source: Lloyd's Register-Fairplay, *World Fleet Statistics*.

International Sea-borne Freight Traffic
('000 metric tons)

	1996	1997	1998
Goods loaded	52,068	58,512	69,372
Goods unloaded	16,728	19,116	19,536

Goods unloaded: 16,320 in 2004; 22,92222,992 in 2007; 25,836 in 2008; 16,044 in 2009.

Source: UN, *Monthly Bulletin of Statistics*.

Total maritime freight handled ('000 metric tons): 130,775 in 2003; 135,001 in 2004; 152,921 in 2005; 152,074 in 2006; 168,260 in 2007 (Source: Dirección Nacional de Puertos).

CIVIL AVIATION

	2006	2007	2008
Kilometres flown (million)	172	178	186
Passengers carried ('000)	12,736	14,735	15,105
Passenger-km (million)	16,714	19,145	20,038
Total freight carried ('000 metric tons)	215	389	306

Tourism

TOURIST ARRIVALS BY REGION
('000 arrivals at Ezeiza International Airport)

	2007	2008	2009
Europe	563.3	614.5	550.0
North America	340.0	346.5	300.4
South America	1,247.1	1,232.7	1,015.8
Brazil	497.7	600.6	456.2
Chile	270.6	190.0	160.6
Total (incl. others)	2,298.1	2,327.2	1,999.5

Tourism receipts (US $ million): 2,472 in 2006; 3,048 in 2007; 3,370 in 2008.

Communications Media

	2007	2008	2009
Telephones ('000 main lines in use)	9,500.0	9,742.8	9,764.1
Mobile cellular telephones ('000 handsets in use)	40,401.8	46,508.8	51,891.0
Internet users ('000)	10,246.4	11,212.2	12,244.0
Broadband subscribers ('000)	2,600.0	3,185.3	3,542.6

Personal computers: 3,500,000 (90.4 per 1,000 persons) in 2005.

Television receivers ('000 in use): 11,800 in 2001.

Radio receivers ('000 in use): 24,300 in 1997.

Book production: 13,148 titles in 2001.

Daily newspapers: 184 in 2004 (average circulation 1,363,000).

Sources: mainly UNESCO Institute for Statistics and *Statistical Yearbook*, and International Telecommunication Union.

Education

(2007 unless otherwise indicated)

	Institutions	Teachers	Students
Pre-primary	16,499	86,663	1,364,909
Primary	22,164	307,830	4,645,843
Secondary	21,281	141,389	3,464,698
Basic	14,155	44,210	2,112,511
Specialized	7,126	97,179	1,352,187
Higher			
University*	37	n.a.	1,273,156
Non-university	1,901	16,516	540,771

* 2004.

Source: partly Red Federal de Información Educativa, *Relevamiento 2004* and *Relevamiento 2007*.

Pupil-teacher ratio (primary education, UNESCO estimate): 16.3 in 2005/06 (Source: UNESCO Institute for Statistics).

Adult literacy rate (UNESCO estimates): 97.7% (males 97.6%; females 97.7%) in 2008 (Source: UNESCO Institute for Statistics).

Directory

The Constitution

The return to civilian rule in 1983 represented a return to the principles of the 1853 Constitution, with some changes in electoral details. In August 1994 a new Constitution was approved, which contained 19 new articles, 40 amendments to existing articles and the addition of a chapter on New Rights and Guarantees. The Constitution is summarized below:

DECLARATIONS, RIGHTS AND GUARANTEES

Each province has the right to exercise its own administration of justice, municipal system and primary education. The Roman Catholic religion shall enjoy state protection; freedom of religious belief is guaranteed to all other denominations. The prior ethnical existence of indigenous peoples and their rights, as well as the common ownership of lands they traditionally occupy, are recognized. All inhabitants of the country have the right to work and exercise any legal trade; to petition the authorities; to leave or enter the Argentine territory; to use or dispose of their properties; to associate for a peaceable or useful purpose; to teach and acquire education; and to express freely their opinion in the press without censorship. The State does not admit any prerogative of blood, birth, privilege or titles of nobility. Equality is the basis of all duties and public offices. No citizens may be detained, except for reasons and in the manner prescribed by the law; or sentenced other than by virtue of a law existing prior to the offence and by decision of the competent tribunal after the hearing and defence of the person concerned. Private residence, property and correspondence are inviolable. No one may enter the home of a citizen or carry out any search in it without their consent, unless by a warrant from the competent authority; no one may suffer expropriation, except in case of public necessity and provided that the appropriate compensation has been paid in accordance with the provisions of the laws. In no case may the penalty of confiscation of property be imposed.

LEGISLATIVE POWER

Legislative power is vested in the bicameral Congreso (Congress), comprising the Cámara de Diputados (Chamber of Deputies) and the Senado (Senate). The composition of the Chamber of Deputies is determined according to the population of each province. Deputies are directly elected for a four-year term and are eligible for re-election; approximately one-half of the membership of the Chamber shall be renewed every two years. The Senate comprises 72 members (three from each province), directly elected for a six-year term, with one-third of the seats renewable every two years. The Vice-President of the Nation sits as President of the Senate.

The powers of Congress include regulating foreign trade; fixing import and export duties; levying taxes for a specified time whenever the defence, common safety or general welfare of the State so requires; contracting loans on the nation's credit; regulating the internal and external debt and the currency system of the country; fixing the budget; and facilitating the prosperity and welfare of the nation. Congress must approve required and urgent decrees and delegated legislation. Congress also approves or rejects treaties, authorizes the Executive to declare war or make peace, and establishes the strength of the Armed Forces in peace and war.

EXECUTIVE POWER

Executive power is vested in the President, who is the supreme head of the nation and controls the general administration of the country. The President issues the instructions and rulings necessary for the execution of the laws of the country, and takes part in drawing up and promulgating those laws. The President appoints, with the approval of the Senate, the judges of the Supreme Court and all other competent tribunals, ambassadors, civil servants, members of the judiciary, senior officers of the Armed Forces and bishops. The President may also appoint and remove, without reference to another body, the cabinet ministers. The President is Commander-in-Chief of all the Armed Forces. The President and Vice-President are elected directly for a four-year term, renewable only once.

JUDICIAL POWER

Judicial power is exercised by the Supreme Court and all other competent tribunals. The Supreme Court is responsible for the internal administration of all tribunals.

PROVINCIAL GOVERNMENT

The 23 provinces retain all the power not delegated to the federal Government. They are governed by their own institutions and elect their own governors, legislators and officials. The City of Buenos Aires has its own autonomous Government.

The Government

HEAD OF STATE

President of the Nation: CRISTINA ELISABET FERNÁNDEZ DE KIRCHNER (took office 10 December 2007).

Vice-President: JULIO CÉSAR CLETO COBOS.

CABINET
(July 2010)

The Cabinet is composed of members of the Frente para la Victoria-Partido Justicialista alliance.

Cabinet Chief: ANÍBAL DOMINGO FERNÁNDEZ.

Minister of the Interior: ANÍBAL FLORENCIO RANDAZZO.

Minister of Foreign Affairs, International Trade and Worship: HÉCTOR MARCOS TIMERMAN.

Minister of Defence: NILDA GARRÉ.

Minister of Economy and Public Finance: AMADO BOUDOU.

Minister of Industry and Tourism: DÉBORA ADRIANA GIORGI.

Minister of Education: ALBERTO ESTANISLAO SILEONI.

Minister of Science, Technology and Productive Innovation: LINO BARAÑAO.

Minister of Labour, Employment and Social Security: CARLOS TOMADA.

Minister of Federal Planning, Public Investment and Services: JULIO MIGUEL DE VIDO.

Minister of Health: JUAN LUIS MANZUR.

Minister of Justice, Security and Human Rights: JULIO ALAK.

Minister of Social Development: ALICIA KIRCHNER.

Minister of Agriculture, Livestock and Fisheries: JULIÁN ANDRÉS DOMÍNGUEZ.

MINISTRIES

General Secretariat to the Presidency: Balcarce 50, C1064AAB Buenos Aires; tel. and fax (11) 4344-3600; e-mail dgi@presidencia.gov.ar; internet www.secretariageneral.gov.ar.

Office of the Cabinet Chief: Avda Julio Argentino Roca 782, C1067ABP Buenos Aires; tel. (11) 4331-1951; e-mail prensa@jgm.gov.ar; internet www.jgm.gov.ar.

Ministry of Agriculture, Livestock and Fisheries: Avda Paseo Colón 982, C1063 Buenos Aires; tel. (11) 4349-2000; fax (11) 4349-2589; internet www.minagri.gob.ar.

Ministry of Defence: Azopardo 250, C1107ADB Buenos Aires; tel. (11) 4346-8800; e-mail prensa@mindef.gov.ar; internet www.mindef.gov.ar.

Ministry of Economy and Public Finance: Hipólito Yrigoyen 250, C1086AAB Buenos Aires; tel. (11) 4349-5000; e-mail infoprensa@mecon.gov.ar; internet www.mecon.gov.ar.

Ministry of Education: Pizzurno 935, C1020ACA Buenos Aires; tel. (11) 4129-1000; e-mail info@me.gov.ar; internet www.me.gov.ar.

Ministry of Federal Planning, Public Investment and Services: Hipólito Yrigoyen 250, 11°, Of. 1112, C1086AAB Buenos Aires; tel. (11) 4349-5000; internet www.minplan.gov.ar.

Ministry of Foreign Affairs, International Trade and Worship: Esmeralda 1212, C1007ABR Buenos Aires; tel. (11) 4819-7000; e-mail webmaster@mrecic.gov.ar; internet www.cancilleria.gov.ar.

Ministry of Health: 9 de Julio 1925, C1073ABA Buenos Aires; tel. (11) 4379-9000; fax (11) 4381-2182; e-mail consultas@msal.gov.ar; internet www.msal.gov.ar.

Ministry of Industry and Tourism: Hipólito Yrigoyen 250, C1086AAB Buenos Aires; internet www.minprod.gob.ar.

Ministry of the Interior: 25 de Mayo 101/145, C1002ABC Buenos Aires; tel. (11) 4339-0800; fax (11) 4331-6376; internet www.mininterior.gov.ar.

Ministry of Justice, Security and Human Rights: Sarmiento 329, C1041AAG Buenos Aires; tel. (11) 5300-4000; e-mail prensa@jus.gov.ar; internet www.jus.gov.ar.

Ministry of Labour, Employment and Social Security: Leandro N. Alem 650, C1001AAO Buenos Aires; tel. (11) 4311-2913; fax (11) 4312-7860; e-mail consultas@trabajo.gov.ar; internet www.trabajo.gov.ar.

Ministry of Science, Technology and Productive Innovation: Avda Córdoba 831, C1054AAH Buenos Aires; tel. (11) 4891-8300; fax (11) 4312-8364; e-mail contacto@mincyt.gov.ar; internet www.mincyt.gov.ar.

Ministry of Social Development: 9 de Julio 1925, 14°, C1073ABA Buenos Aires; tel. (11) 4379-3648; e-mail privadaministro@desarrollosocial.gov.ar; internet www.desarrollosocial.gov.ar.

President and Legislature

PRESIDENT

Election, 28 October 2007

Candidates	Votes	% of valid votes cast
Cristina E. Fernández de Kirchner (Frente para la Victoria)	8,652,293	45.28
Elisa M. A. Carrió (Coalición Cívica)	4,403,642	23.05
Roberto Lavagna (Concertación Una Nación Avanzada*)	3,230,236	16.91
Alberto J. Rodríguez Saá (Frente Justicia, Unión y Libertad)	1,459,174	7.64
Others	1,361,795	7.13
Total†	19,107,140	100.00

* Electoral alliance founded by the Movimiento de Integración y Desarrollo.

† In addition, there were 1,331,010 blank and 241,176 spoiled ballots.

CONGRESO

Cámara de Diputados
(Chamber of Deputies)

President: EDUARDO ALFREDO FELLNER.

The Cámara has 257 members, who hold office for a four-year term, with approximately one-half of the seats renewable every two years. The last election was held on 28 June 2009.

Distribution of Seats by Legislative Bloc, January 2010

	Seats
Frente para la Victoria—Partido Justicialista	87
Unión Cívica Radical (UCR)	43
Peronismo Federal*	29
Coalición Cívica†	19
Propuesta Republicana (PRO)	11
Frente Cívico por Santiago‡	7
Partido Socialista	6
Unión Peronista§	6
Nuevo Encuentro Popular y Solidario	5
Generación para un Encuentro Nacional	5
Movimiento Proyecto Sur	5
Frente Cívico—Córdoba‖	3
Movimiento Popular Neuquino	3
Si por la Unidad Popular	3
De la Concertación‡	2
Corriente de Pensamiento Federal	2
Partido Justicialista La Pampa	2
Libres del Sur	2
Córdoba Federal¶	2
Others	15
Total	257

* A faction of the Partido Justicialista, led by, *inter alia*, Alberto Rodríguez Saá.
† Supported by the Coalición Cívica Afirmación para una República Igualitaria.
‡ Comprising mainly members of the Frente para la Victoria and the UCR.
§ Dissident members of the Partido Justicialista who split from the Frente para la Victoria.
‖ Comprising members of the Partido Nuevo Contra la Corrupción, por la Honestidad y la Transparencia.
¶ Comprising members of the Unión por Córdoba.

Following the 2009 elections the following blocs were also represented in the Cámara de Diputados: Diálogo por Buenos Aires, Partido de la Concertación—FORJA, Proyecto Progresista, Consenso Federal, Frente Cívico y Social de Catamarca, Demócrata de Mendoza, Valores para mi País, Frente de Todos, Renovador de Salta, Partido Liberal de Corrientes, Peronismo Jujeño, Frente Peronista Federal, Partido Federal Fueguino, Salta Somos Todos and Demócrata Progresista.

Senado
(Senate)

President: JULIO CÉSAR CLETO COBOS.

The Senate has 72 directly elected members, three from each province. One-third of these seats are renewable every two years. The last election was held on 28 June 2009.

Distribution of Seats by Legislative Bloc, January 2010

	Seats
Frente para la Victoria—Partido Justicialista	30
Unión Cívica Radical (UCR)	14
Frente Cívico y Social de Catamarca	2
Justicialista San Luís	2
Justicialista 8 de Octubre	2
Partido Justicialista La Pampa	2
Por Tierra del Fuego	2
Others	18
Total	72

Provincial Administrators

(July 2010)

Head of Government of the Autonomous City of Buenos Aires: MAURICIO MACRI (PRO).

Governor of the Province of Buenos Aires: DANIEL OSVALDO SCIOLI (PJ).

Governor of the Province of Catamarca: Dr EDUARDO BRIZUELA DEL MORAL (UCR).

Governor of the Province of Chaco: JORGE MILTON CAPITANICH (PJ).

Governor of the Province of Chubut: Dr MARIO DAS NEVES (PJ).

Governor of the Province of Córdoba: JUAN SCHIARETTI (PJ).

Governor of the Province of Corrientes: RICARDO COLOMBI (UCR).

Governor of the Province of Entre Ríos: SERGIO DANIEL URRIBARRI (PJ).

Governor of the Province of Formosa: Dr GILDO INSFRÁN (PJ).

Governor of the Province of Jujuy: WALTER BASILO BARRIONUEVO (PJ).

Governor of the Province of La Pampa: OSCAR MARIO JORGE (PJ).

Governor of the Province of La Rioja: LUIS BEDER HERRERA-TERESITA LUNA (PJ).

Governor of the Province of Mendoza: CELSO ALEJANDRO JAQUE (PJ).

Governor of the Province of Misiones: MAURICE FABIÁN CLOSS (FR).

Governor of the Province of Neuquén: JORGE SAPAG (MPN).

Governor of the Province of Río Negro: Dr MIGUEL ANGEL SAIZ (UCR).

Governor of the Province of Salta: JUAN MANUEL URTUBEY (PJ).

Governor of the Province of San Juan: Dr JOSÉ LUIS GIOJA (PJ).

Governor of the Province of San Luis: Dr ALBERTO RODRÍGUEZ SAÁ (PJ).

Governor of the Province of Santa Cruz: DANIEL ROMAN PERALTA (PJ).

Governor of the Province of Santa Fe: HERMES BINNER (PS).

Governor of the Province of Santiago del Estero: Dr GERARDO ZAMORA (UCR).

Governor of the Province of Tierra del Fuego: MARÍA FABIANA RÍOS (ARI).

Governor of the Province of Tucumán: JOSÉ JORGE ALPEROVICH (PJ).

Election Commissions

Cámara Nacional Electoral (CNE): Avda 25 de Mayo 245, C1002ABE Buenos Aires; tel. (11) 4331-8421; internet www.pjn.gov.ar/cne/index.php; f. 1971; Pres. Dr SANTIAGO HERNÁN CORCUERA.

Dirección Nacional Electoral: 25 de Mayo 101, 3°, Of. 346, C1002ABC Buenos Aires; tel. (11) 4346-1683; fax (11) 4346-1634; e-mail dineprivada@mininterior.gov.ar; internet www.mininterior.gov.ar/elecciones/dine.asp; part of the Ministry of the Interior.

Political Organizations

Coalición Cívica Afirmación para una República Igualitaria (CC ARI): Callao 143, C1022AAB Buenos Aires; tel. (11) 4384-1268; e-mail arinacional@ari.org.ar; internet www.ccari.org.ar; f. 2001 as Alternativa por una República de Iguales; progressive party; contested the 2009 elections as part of the Acuerdo Cívico y Social alliance; Pres. ELISA M. A. CARRIÓ; Sec.-Gen. CARLOS LÓPEZ IGLESIAS; 48,000 mems.

Frente para la Victoria (FPV): e-mail webmaster@diarioelsol.com.ar; internet www.frenteparalavictoria.org; f. 2003 as faction of the PJ supporting presidential campaign of Néstor Carlos Kirchner; supported presidential candidacy of Cristina Fernández de Kirchner; centre-left electoral alliance, contested 2009 congressional elections with, *inter alia*, the PJ.

Generación para un Encuentro Nacional (GEN): Riobamba 67, 1°, C1025ABA Buenos Aires; tel. (11) 4951-9503; e-mail gen@partidogen.com.ar; internet www.partidogen.com.ar; f. 2007; contested the 2009 elections as part of the Acuerdo Cívica y Social alliance; Leader MARGARITA ROSA STOLBIZER.

Libres del Sur: Humberto I 542, San Telmo, C1103ACL Buenos Aires; tel. (11) 4307-3724; e-mail contacto@libresdelsur.org.ar; internet www.libresdelsur.org.ar; Leader CECILIA MERCHÁN.

Movimiento por la Dignidad y la Independencia (Modin): Yrigoyen 820, 2°G, C1086AAN Buenos Aires; e-mail modin@funescoop.com.ar; internet www.modin.org.ar; f. 1991; nationalist; Pres. JOSÉ ALEJANDRO BONACCI; 7,000 mems.

Movimiento de Integración y Desarrollo (MID): Ayacucho 49, C1025AAA Buenos Aires; tel. (11) 4954-0817; e-mail midinterior@mid.org.ar; internet www.mid.org.ar; f. 1963; Leader CARLOS ZAFFORE; Gen. Sec. EFRAÍN GUSTAVO PUYÓ PEÑA; 51,000 mems.

Movimiento Popular Neuquino (MPN): Neuquén; internet www.mpn.org.ar; f. 1961; provincial party; 112,000 mems.

Movimiento Proyecto Sur: Sarandí 56, C1088AAI Buenos Aires; tel. (11) 4952-3103; e-mail sur@proyecto-sur.com.ar; internet www.proyecto-sur.com.ar; f. 2001 as an alliance comprising Partido Socialista Auténtico, Partido Proyecto Sur and Buenos Aires para Todos; Pres. FERNANDO 'PINO' SOLANAS.

Nuevo Encuentro: Buenos Aires; f. 2009; centre-left; forms the Nuevo Encuentro Popular y Solidario bloc in the Congreso; Leader MARTÍN SABBATELLA.

Partido Comunista de Argentina: Entre Ríos 1039, C1080ABQ Buenos Aires; tel. and fax (11) 4304-0066; e-mail info@pca.org.ar; internet www.pca.org.ar; f. 1918; Leader PATRICIO ECHEGARAY.

Partido Demócrata Cristiano (PDC): Combate de los Pozos 1055, C1222AAK Buenos Aires; tel. (11) 4305-1229; fax (11) 4306-8242; e-mail pdcblog@fibertel.com.ar; internet democracia-cristiana .blogspot.com; f. 1954; Pres. Dr CARLOS LIONEL TRABOULSI; Sec.-Gen. CARLOS PÉREZ; 51,000 mems.

Partido Demócrata Progresista (PDP): Chile 1934, C1227AAD Buenos Aires; tel. (11) 4942-9930; e-mail info@demoprogresista.org .ar; internet www.demoprogresista.org.ar; f. 1914; contested the 2009 elections as part of the PRO alliance; Pres. JOSÉ EDUARDO DE CARA; Gen. Sec. OSCAR MOSCARIELLO; 36,000 mems.

Partido Intransigente: Riobamba 482, C1025ABJ Buenos Aires; tel. (11) 4954-2283; e-mail nacional@pi.org.ar; internet www.pi.org .ar; f. 1957; left-wing; contested the 2009 elections as part of the Frente para la Victoria alliance; Pres. Dr ENRIQUE GUSTAVO CARDESA; Sec. CARMELO S. PRUDENTE; 57,000 mems.

Partido Justicialista (PJ): Domingo Matheu 128/130, C1082ABD Buenos Aires; tel. (11) 4954-2450; fax (11) 4954-2421; e-mail contacto@pj.org.ar; internet www.pj.org.ar; f. 1945; Peronist party; contested the 2009 elections as part of the Frente para la Victoria alliance; Pres. NESTÓR CARLOS KIRCHNER; Vice-Pres. DANIEL OSVALDO SCIOLI; 3.6m. mems.

Partido Nacional Contra la Corrupción, por la Honestidad y la Transparencia: Córdoba; internet www.partidonuevocordoba .com.ar; Pres. LUIS ALFREDO JUEZ.

Partido Obrero: Ayacucho 444/8, C1026AAB Buenos Aires; tel. (11) 4953-3824; fax (11) 4954-5829; e-mail secprensa@po.org.ar; internet www.po.org.ar; f. 1982; Trotskyist; Pres. NÉSTOR PITROLA; Vice-Pres. GABRIELA ARROYO; 26,000 mems.

Partido Recrear para el Crecimiento (RECREAR): Avda de Mayo 605, 9°, Buenos Aires; tel. (11) 4342-2400; e-mail juntanacional@recrear.org.ar; internet recrear.org.ar; f. 2002; forms part of the PRO bloc in the Congreso; Pres. ESTEBAN BULLRICH; Sec. JAVIER PRIDA; 59,000 mems.

Partido Socialista (PS): Entre Ríos 488, 2°, Buenos Aires; tel. (11) 4383-2395; e-mail pscen@ar.inter.net; internet www .partidosocialista.org.ar; f. 2002 following merger of the Partido Socialista Democrático and the Partido Socialista Popular; contested the 2009 elections as part of the Acuerdo Cívica y Social alliance; Pres. RUBÉN HÉCTOR GIUSTINIANI; Sec.-Gen. ROBERTO CARLOS; 115,000 mems.

Partido Socialista Auténtico: Sarandí 56, C1081ACB Buenos Aires; tel. and fax (11) 4952-3103; e-mail consultas@psa.org.ar; internet www.psa.org.ar; contested the 2009 elections as part of the Movimiento Proyecto Sur alliance; Pres. FERNANDO 'PINO' SOLANAS; Sec.-Gen. MARIO MAZZITELLI; 13,000 mems.

Propuesta Republicana (PRO): Alsina 1325, C1088AAI Buenos Aires; e-mail info@pro.com.ar; internet www.pro.com.ar; f. 2005; part of the Unión PRO alliance; Leader MAURICIO MACRI.

Solidaridad e Igualdad (SI): Buenos Aires; internet www .espaciosi.org; f. 2008 as breakaway grouping from ARI; centre-left; forms the Sí por la Unidad Popular bloc in the Congreso; Leader EDUARDO MACALUSE.

Unión del Centro Democrático (UCeDé): Hipólito Yrigoyen 636, 6° B Buenos Aires; tel. (11) 4381-3763; internet ucedenacional .blogspot.com; f. 1980; Pres. JORGE PEREYRA DE OLAZÁBAL; Sec. Gen. HUGO EDUARDO BONTEMPO; 77,000 mems.

Unión Cívica Radical (UCR): Alsina 1786, C1088AAR Buenos Aires; tel. and fax (11) 5199-0600; e-mail webmaster@ucr.org.ar; internet www.ucr.org.ar; f. 1890; moderate; contested the 2009 elections as part of the Acuerdo Cívica y Social alliance; Pres. ERNESTO SANZ; Gen. Sec. JESÚS RODRÍGUEZ; 2.5m. mems.

Unión por Córdoba: Córdoba; internet www.unionporcordoba .com; forms the Córdoba Federal bloc in the Congreso; Leader FRANCISCO J. FORTUNA.

Unión Popular: Calcena 518, 4°, Buenos Aires; Pres. OLGA OVANESOFF; Vice-Pres. JOSÉ FERNANDO HERRERA; 16,000 mems.

OTHER ORGANIZATIONS

Asociación Madres de Plaza de Mayo: Hipólito Yrigoyen 1584, C1089AAD Buenos Aires; tel. (11) 4383-0377; fax (11) 4954-0381; e-mail madres@madres.org; internet www.madres.org; f. 1979; formed by mothers of those who 'disappeared' during the years of military rule, it has since become a broad-based grouping with revolutionary socialist aims; Pres. ESTELA DE CARLOTTO; Founder and Leader HEBE MARÍA PASTOR DE BONAFINI.

Corriente Clasista y Combativa (CCC): e-mail info@cccargentina.org.ar; internet www.cccargentina.org.ar; radical grouping; Leader CARLOS 'PERRO' SANTILLÁN.

Movimiento Barrios de Pie: e-mail correos@barriosdepie.org.ar; internet www.barriosdepie.org.ar; f. 2001; moderate grouping; Leader JORGE CEBALLOS.

Movimiento Libres del Sur: Humberto I° 542, Buenos Aires; tel. (11) 4307-3724; e-mail contacto@libresdelsur.org.ar; internet libresdelsur.org.ar; f. 2006; alliance of pro-President Kirchner *piquetero* groups; Leader HUMBERTO TUMINI.

Numerous other *piquetero* groupings also exist.

Diplomatic Representation

EMBASSIES IN ARGENTINA

Albania: Juez Tedín 3036, 4°, C1425CWH Buenos Aires; tel. (11) 48093574; fax (11) 48152512; e-mail embassy.buenosaires@mfa.gov .al; Ambassador REZAR BREGU.

Algeria: Montevideo 1889, C1021AAE Buenos Aires; tel. (11) 4815-1271; fax (11) 4815-8837; e-mail argeliae@interserver.com.ar; Ambassador AHCÈNE BOUKHELFA.

Angola: La Pampa 3452–56, C1430BXD Buenos Aires; tel. (11) 4554-8383; fax (11) 4554-8998; Ambassador MANUEL ARAGÃO.

Armenia: José Andrés Pacheco de Melo 1922, C1126AAD Buenos Aires; tel. (11) 4816-8710; fax (11) 4812-2803; e-mail armenia@fibertel.com.ar; Ambassador VLADIMIR KARMIRSHALYAN.

Australia: Villanueva 1400, C1426BMJ Buenos Aires; tel. (11) 4779-3500; fax (11) 4779-3581; e-mail info.ba.general@dfat.gov.au; internet www.argentina.embassy.gov.au; Ambassador JOHN RICHARDSON.

Austria: French 3671, C1425AXC Buenos Aires; tel. (11) 4807-9185; fax (11) 4805-4016; e-mail buenos-aires-ob@bmeia.gv.at; internet www.austria.org.ar; Ambassador Dr ROBERT ZISCHG.

Belarus: Cazadores 2166, C1428 Capital Federal, Buenos Aires; tel. (11) 4788-9394; fax (11) 4788-2322; e-mail argentina@belembassy .org; internet www.argentina.belembassy.org; Chargé d'affaires a.i. GEORGY KISLYAK.

Belgium: Defensa 113, 8°, C1065AAA Buenos Aires; tel. (11) 4331-0066; fax (11) 4331-0814; e-mail BuenosAires@diplobel.fed.be; internet www.diplomatie.be/buenosaires; Ambassador CRISTINA FUNES-NOPPEN.

Bolivia: Corrientes 545, 2°, C1043AAF Buenos Aires; tel. (11) 4394-1463; fax (11) 43940460; e-mail embolivia-baires@ree.gov.bo; internet www.embajadadebolivia.com.ar; Ambassador MARÍA LEONOR ARAUCO LEMAITRE.

Brazil: Cerrito 1350, C1010ABB Buenos Aires; tel. (11) 4515-2400; fax (11) 4515-2401; e-mail info@embrasil.org.ar; internet www.brasil .org.ar; Ambassador ENIO CORDEIRO.

Bulgaria: Mariscal A. J. de Sucre 1568, C1428DUT Buenos Aires; tel. (11) 4781-8644; fax (11) 4781-1214; e-mail embular@uolsinectis .com.ar; internet www.mfa.bg/buenos-aires; Ambassador STEFAN APOSTOLOV.

Canada: Tagle 2828, C1425EEH Buenos Aires; tel. (11) 4808-1000; fax (11) 4808-1111; e-mail bairs-webmail@international.gc.ca; internet www.canadainternational.gc.ca/argentina-argentine; Ambassador TIMOTHY JOSEPH MARTIN.

Chile: Tagle 2762, C1425EEF Buenos Aires; tel. (11) 4808-8600; fax (11) 4804-5927; e-mail data@embajadadechile.com.ar; internet www .embajadadechile.com.ar/home.asp; Ambassador ADOLFO ZALDÍVAR LARRAÍN (designate).

China, People's Republic: Crisólogo Larralde 5349, C1431APM Buenos Aires; tel. (11) 4547-8100; fax (11) 4545-1141; e-mail chinaemb_ar@mfa.gov.cn; internet ar.chineseembassy.org/esp; Ambassador GANG ZENG.

Colombia: Carlos Pellegrini 1363, 3°, C1011AAA Buenos Aires; tel. (11) 4325-0258; fax (11) 4322-9370; e-mail emargent@embajadacolombia.int.ar; internet www.embajadacolombia.int.ar; Ambassador ALVARO EDUARDO GARCÍA JIMÉNEZ.

Congo, Democratic Republic: Forest 1570, C1430EON Buenos Aires; tel. (11) 4552-3942; e-mail rdcbuenos@hotmail.com; Chargé d'affaires a.i. YEMBA LOHAKA.

Costa Rica: Pacheco de Melo 1833, 5°, C1126AAD Buenos Aires; tel. (11) 4802-6297; fax (11) 4801-3222; e-mail embarica@fibertel.com.ar; Ambassador RICARDO JAIME TOLEDO CARRANZA.

Croatia: Gorostiaga 2104, C1426CTN Buenos Aires; tel. (11) 4777-6409; fax (11) 4777-9159; e-mail croemb.ar@mvpei.hr; Ambassador MIRA MARTINEC.

Cuba: Virrey del Pino 1810, Belgrano, C1426EGF Buenos Aires; tel. (11) 4782-9049; fax (11) 4786-7713; e-mail info@ar.embacuba.cu;

internet www.embacuba.com.ar; Ambassador ARAMÍS FUENTE HERNÁNDEZ.

Czech Republic: Junín 1461, C1113AAM Buenos Aires; tel. (11) 4807-3107; fax (11) 4800-1088; e-mail buenosaires@embassy.mzv.cz; internet www.mzv.cz/buenosaires; Ambassador ŠTĚPÁN ZAJAC.

Denmark: Avda Leandro N. Alem 1074, 9°, C1001AAS Buenos Aires; tel. (11) 4312-6901; fax (11) 4312-7857; e-mail bueamb@um.dk; internet www.buenosaires.um.dk; Ambassador HENRIK BRAMSEN HAHN.

Dominican Republic: Santa Fe 830, 7°, C1059ABP Buenos Aires; tel. (11) 4312-9378; fax (11) 4894-2078; e-mail consuldo@hotmail.com; Ambassador GUILLERMO EDUARDO PIÑA-CONTRERAS.

Ecuador: Quintana 585, 9°, C1129ABB Buenos Aires; tel. (11) 4804-0073; fax (11) 4804-0074; e-mail embecuador@embecuador.com.ar; Ambassador GONZALO EDUARDO WELLINGTON SANDOVAL CÓRDOVA.

Egypt: Virrey del Pino 3140, C1426EHF Buenos Aires; tel. (11) 4553-3311; fax (11) 4553-0067; e-mail embegypt@fibertel.com.ar; Ambassador SOHA ELFAR.

El Salvador: Suipacha 1380, 2°, C1011ACD Buenos Aires; tel. (11) 4325-0849; fax (11) 4328-7428; e-mail elsalvador@fibertel.com.ar; internet www.embajadaelsalvador.com.ar; Ambassador GUILLERMO RUBIO FUNES.

Finland: Santa Fe 846, 5°, C1059ABP Buenos Aires; tel. (11) 4312-0600; fax (11) 4312-0670; e-mail sanomat.bue@formin.fi; internet www.finlandia.org.ar; Ambassador JUKKA PIETIKÄINEN.

France: Cerrito 1399, C1010ABA Buenos Aires; tel. (11) 4515-2930; fax (11) 4515-0120; e-mail ambafr@abaconet.com.ar; internet www.embafrancia-argentina.org; Ambassador JEAN-PIERRE ASVAZADOURIAN.

Germany: Villanueva 1055, C1426BMC Buenos Aires; tel. (11) 4778-2500; fax (11) 4778-2550; e-mail info@buenos-aires.diplo.de; internet www.buenos-aires.diplo.de; Ambassador GÜNTER KNIESS.

Greece: Arenales 1658, C1061AAT Buenos Aires; tel. (11) 4811-4811; fax (11) 4816-2600; e-mail gremb.bay@mfa.gr; Ambassador MICHAEL CHRISTIDIS.

Guatemala: Juncal 802, 3° H, C1062ABF Buenos Aires; tel. (11) 4313-9160; fax (11) 4313-9181; e-mail embagua@ciudad.com.ar; Ambassador LUIS FERNANDO GONZÁLEZ DAVISON.

Haiti: Avda Figueroa Alcorta 3297, C1425CKL Buenos Aires; tel. (11) 4802-0211; fax (11) 4802-3984; e-mail embajadahaiti@fibertel.com.ar; Ambassador JEAN MARIE MICHEL RAYMOND MATHIEU.

Holy See: Marcelo T. de Alvear 1605, C1014AAD Buenos Aires; tel. (11) 4813-9697; fax (11) 4815-4097; e-mail nunciaturaapostolica@speedy.com.ar; Apostolic Nuncio Most Rev. ADRIANO BERNARDINI (Titular Archbishop of Faleri).

Honduras: Avda Callao 1564, 2A, C1024AAO Buenos Aires; tel. (11) 4806-9914; fax (11) 4806-9880; e-mail embajadadehonduras@fibertel.com.ar; Ambassador CARMEN ELEONORA ORTEZ WILLIAMS.

Hungary: Plaza 1726, C1430DGF Buenos Aires; tel. (11) 4553-4646; fax (11) 4555-6859; e-mail mission.bue@kum.hu; internet www.mfa.gov.hu/emb/buenosaires; Ambassador PÁL VARGA KORITÁR.

India: Torre Madero, 19°, Avda Eduardo Madero 942, C1106ACW Buenos Aires; tel. (11) 4393-4001; fax (11) 4393-4063; e-mail indemb@indembarg.org.ar; internet www.indembarg.org.ar; Ambassador RENGARAJ VISWANATHAN.

Indonesia: Mariscal Ramón Castilla 2901, C1425DZE Buenos Aires; tel. (11) 4807-2211; fax (11) 4802-4448; e-mail emindo@tournet.com.ar; internet www.indonesianembassy.org.ar; Ambassador SUNTEN ZEPHYRIMUS MANURUNG.

Iran: Avda Figueroa Alcorta 3229, C1425CKL Buenos Aires; tel. (11) 4802-1470; fax (11) 4805-4409; e-mail embajadairan@fibertel.com.ar; Chargé d'affaires a.i. SEYED ALI PAKDAMAN.

Ireland: Avda del Libertador 1068, Edif. Bluesky, 6°, Recoleta, C1112ABN Buenos Aires; tel. (11) 5787-0801; fax (11) 5787-0802; e-mail info@irlanda.org.ar; internet www.embassyofireland.org.ar; Ambassador JAMES MCINTYRE.

Israel: Avda de Mayo 701, 10°, C1084AAC Buenos Aires; tel. (11) 4338-2500; fax (11) 4338-2624; e-mail info@buenosaires.mfa.gov.il; internet buenosaires.mfa.gov.il; Ambassador DANIEL GAZIT.

Italy: Billinghurst 2577, C1425DTY Buenos Aires; tel. (11) 4011-2100; fax (11) 4011-2159; e-mail segreteria.buenosaires@esteri.it; internet www.ambbuenosaires.esteri.it; Ambassador GUIDO WALTER LA TELLA.

Japan: Bouchard 547, 17°, C1106ABG Buenos Aires; tel. (11) 4318-8200; fax (11) 4318-8210; e-mail taishikan@japan.org.ar; internet www.ar.emb-japan.go.jp; Ambassador HITOHIRO ISHIDA.

Korea, Republic: Avda del Libertador 2395, C1425AAJ Buenos Aires; tel. (11) 4802-9665; fax (11) 4803-6993; e-mail argentina@mofat.go.kr; internet www.embcorea.org.ar; Ambassador KIM BYUNG KWON.

Kuwait: Uruguay 739, C1015ABO Buenos Aires; tel. (11) 4374-7202; fax (11) 4374-8718; e-mail info@embajadadekuwait.com.ar; internet www.embajadadekuwait.com.ar; Ambassador SAUD ABD AL-AZIZ AL-ROOMI.

Lebanon: Avda del Libertador 2354, C1425AAW Buenos Aires; tel. (11) 4802-0466; fax (11) 4802-0929; e-mail embajada@ellibano.com.ar; internet www.ellibano.com.ar; Ambassador Dr HICHAM SALIM HAMDAN.

Libya: Virrey del Pino 3432, C1426EHL Buenos Aires; tel. (11) 4553-4669; fax (11) 4551-6187; e-mail oficinapopularlibia@hotmail.com; Ambassador ABDULGADER O. EL-KHAIR.

Lithuania: Mendoza 1018, C1428DJN, Buenos Aires; tel. (11) 4788-2153; fax (11) 4785-7915; e-mail embajada@lituania.org.ar; internet ar.mfa.lt; Ambassador VACLOVAS ŠALKAUSKAS.

Malaysia: Villanueva 1040, C1426BMD Buenos Aires; tel. (11) 4776-2553; fax (11) 4776-0604; e-mail mwbaires@fibertel.com.ar; Ambassador Dato' ZULKIFLI BIN YAACOB.

Mexico: Arcos 1650, C1426BGL Buenos Aires; tel. (11) 4118-8800; fax (11) 4118-8837; e-mail embamexarg@interlink.com.ar; internet www.embamex.int.ar; Ambassador FRANCISCO EDUARDO DEL RÍO LÓPEZ.

Morocco: Castex 3461, C1425CDG Buenos Aires; tel. (11) 4801-8154; fax (11) 4802-0136; e-mail sifamarruecos@fibertel.com.ar; Ambassador LARBI REFFOUH.

Netherlands: Edif. Porteño II, Olga Cossenttini 831, 3°, C1107BVA Buenos Aires; tel. (11) 4338-0050; fax (11) 4338-0060; e-mail bue@minbuza.nl; internet www.embajadaholanda.int.ar; Ambassador HENDRIK JACOB WILLEM SOETERS.

New Zealand: Carlos Pellegrini 1427, 5°, C1011AAC Buenos Aires; tel. (11) 4328-0747; fax (11) 4328-0757; e-mail kiwiarg@speedy.com.ar; internet www.nzembassy.com/buenosaires; Ambassador DARRYL DUNN.

Nicaragua: Santa Fe 1845, 7°, Of. B, C1123AAA Buenos Aires; tel. (11) 4811-0973; fax (11) 4816-6315; e-mail zmasis@cancilleria.gob.ni; Ambassador ZORAYA FAVIOLA MASIS MAYORGA.

Nigeria: Juez Estrada 2746, Palermo, C1425CPD Buenos Aires; tel. (11) 4808-9245; fax (11) 4807-1782; e-mail info@nigerianembassy.org; internet www.nigerianembassy.org.ar; Ambassador EMPIRE NDUKA KANU.

Norway: Carlos Pelegrini 1427, 2°, C1011AAC Buenos Aires; tel. (11) 4328-8717; fax (11) 4328-9048; e-mail emb.buenosaires@mfa.no; internet www.noruega.org.ar; Ambassador NILS HAUGSTVEIT.

Pakistan: Gorostiaga 2176, C1426CTN Buenos Aires; tel. (11) 4775-1294; fax (11) 4776-1186; e-mail parepbaires@fibertel.com.ar; internet www.embassypakistan.com.ar; Ambassador NAELA CHOHAN.

Panama: Santa Fe 1461, 1°, C1060ABA Buenos Aires; tel. (11) 4811-1254; fax (11) 4814-0450; e-mail epar@fibertel.com.ar; internet www.embajadadepanama.com.ar; Ambassador MARIO BOYD GALINDO.

Paraguay: Las Heras 2545, C1425ASC Buenos Aires; tel. (11) 4802-3826; fax (11) 4807-7600; e-mail embaparba@fibertel.com.ar; Chargé d'affaires a.i. MARCELO ELISEO SCAPINNI RICCIARDI.

Peru: Avda del Libertador 1720, C1425AAQ Buenos Aires; tel. (11) 4802-2000; fax (11) 4802-5887; e-mail contacto@embajadadelperu.com.ar; internet www.embajadadelperu.com.ar; Ambassador JUDITH DE LA MATTA FERNÁNDEZ DE PUENTE.

Philippines: Blvd Lidoro Quinteros 1386, C1428BXR Buenos Aires; tel. (11) 4782-4752; fax (11) 4788-9692; e-mail pheba@fibertel.com.ar; internet www.buenosairespe.com.ar; Ambassador REY A. CARANDANG.

Poland: Alejandro María de Aguado 2870, C1425CEB Buenos Aires; tel. (11) 48081700; fax (11) 48081701; e-mail emb@buenosaires.polemb.net; internet www.buenosaires.polemb.net; Ambassador JACEK BAZAŃSKI.

Portugal: Maipú 942, 17°, C1006ACN Buenos Aires; tel. (11) 4312-3524; fax (11) 4311-2586; e-mail embpor@buenosaires.dgaccp.pt; internet www.embaixadaportugal.com.ar; Ambassador JOAQUIM JOSÉ LEMOS FERREIRA MARQUES.

Romania: Arroyo 962–970, C1007AAD Buenos Aires; tel. (11) 4326-5888; fax (11) 4322-2630; e-mail embarombue@rumania.org.ar; internet www.rumania.org.ar; Ambassador ION VÎLCU.

Russia: Rodríguez Peña 1741, C1021ABK Buenos Aires; tel. (11) 4813-1552; fax (11) 4815-6293; e-mail embrusia@fibertel.com.ar; internet www.argentina.mid.ru; Ambassador ALEKSANDR K. DOGADIN.

San Marino: Avda Presidente Manuel Quintana 175, 1°A, CP 1011, Buenos Aires; tel. (11) 4815-9070; fax (11) 4815-3787; e-mail embajada@consulatosanmarino.org.ar; Ambassador STEFANO PISA MONTEROSA.

Saudi Arabia: Alejandro María de Aguado 2881, C1425CEA Buenos Aires; tel. (11) 4802-0760; fax (11) 4806-1581; e-mail aremb@mofa.gov.sa; Ambassador ISAM ABED AL-THAGAFI.

Serbia: Marcelo T. de Alvear 1705, C1060AAG Buenos Aires; tel. (11) 4812-9133; fax (11) 4812-1070; e-mail serbembaires@ciudad.com.ar; Ambassador GORDANA VIDOVIĆ.

Slovakia: Figueroa Alcorta 3240, C1425CKY Buenos Aires; tel. (11) 4801-3917; fax (11) 4801-4654; e-mail emb.buenosaires@mzv.sk; Ambassador PAVEL ŠÍPKA.

Slovenia: Santa Fe 846, 6°, C1059ABP Buenos Aires; tel. (11) 4894-0621; fax (11) 4312-8410; e-mail vba@gov.si; internet www.buenosaires.veleposlanistvo.si; Ambassador AVGUŠTIN VIVOD.

South Africa: Marcelo T. de Alvear 590, 8°, C1058AAF Buenos Aires; tel. (11) 4317-2900; fax (11) 4317-2963; e-mail embajador.argentina@foreign.gov.za; internet www.sudafrica.org.ar; Ambassador ANTHONY LEON.

Spain: Mariscal Ramón Castilla 2720, C1425DZA Buenos Aires; tel. (11) 4802-6031; fax (11) 4802-0719; e-mail emb.buenosaires@maec.es; internet www.embajadaenargentina.es; Ambassador RAFAEL ESTRELLA PEDROLA.

Sweden: Tacuari 147, 6°, C1071AAC Buenos Aires; tel. (11) 4329-0800; fax (11) 4342-1697; e-mail ambassaden.buenos-aires@foreign.ministery.se; internet www.swedenabroad.com/buenosaires; Ambassador ARNE LENNART RODIN.

Switzerland: Santa Fe 846, 12°, C1059ABP Buenos Aires; tel. (11) 4311-6491; fax (11) 4313-2998; e-mail bue.vertretung@eda.admin.ch; internet www.eda.admin.ch/buenosaires; Ambassador CARLA DEL PONTE.

Syria: Callao 956, C1023AAP Buenos Aires; tel. (11) 4813-2113; fax (11) 4814-3211; Ambassador RIYAD AS-SINEH.

Thailand: Vuelta de Obligado 1947, 12°, C1428ADC Buenos Aires; tel. (11) 4780-0555; fax (11) 4782-1616; e-mail thaiembargen@fibertel.com.ar; internet www.thaiembargen.org; Ambassador ANUCHA OSATHANOND.

Tunisia: Ciudad de la Paz 3086, C1429ACD Buenos Aires; tel. (11) 4544-2618; fax (11) 4545-6369; e-mail atbuenosaires@infovia.com.ar; Chargé d'affaires a.i. SLIM BEN JAFFAR.

Turkey: 11 de Septiembre 1382, C1426BKN Buenos Aires; tel. (11) 4788-3239; fax (11) 4784-9179; e-mail turquia@fibertel.com.ar; internet buenosaires.be.mfa.gov.tr; Ambassador HAYRI HAYRET YALAV.

Ukraine: Conde 1763, C1426AZI Buenos Aires; tel. (11) 4552-0657; fax (11) 4552-6771; e-mail embucra@embucra.com.ar; internet www.mfa.gov.ua/argentina; Ambassador OLEKSANDR TARANENKO.

United Arab Emirates: Olleros 2021, C1426BRK Buenos Aires; tel. 4771-9716; fax 4772-5169; Ambassador MOHAMMED ISA AL-QATTAM AL-ZA'ABI.

United Kingdom: Dr Luis Agote 2412, C1425EOF Buenos Aires; tel. (11) 4808-2200; fax (11) 4808-2274; e-mail askinformation.baires@fco.gov.uk; internet ukinargentina.fco.gov.uk; Ambassador SHAN MORGAN.

USA: Avda Colombia 4300, C1425GMN Buenos Aires; tel. (11) 5777-4533; fax (11) 5777-4240; internet argentina.usembassy.gov; Ambassador VILMA S. MARTINEZ.

Uruguay: Las Heras 1907, C1127AAB Buenos Aires; tel. (11) 4807-3040; fax (11) 4807-3050; e-mail urubaires@embajadadeluruguay.com.ar; internet www.embajadadeluruguay.com.ar; Ambassador GUILLERMO JOSÉ POMI BARRIOLA.

Venezuela: Virrey Loreto 2035, C1426DXK Buenos Aires; tel. (11) 4788-4944; fax (11) 4784-4311; e-mail embaven@arnet.com.ar; Ambassador Gen. (retd) ARÉVALO ENRIQUE MÉNDEZ ROMERO.

Viet Nam: 11 de Septiembre 1442, C1426BKP Buenos Aires; tel. (11) 4783-1802; fax (11) 4782-0078; e-mail sqvnartn@fibertel.com.ar; Ambassador VAN LUNG THAI.

Judicial System

SUPREME COURT

Corte Suprema

Talcahuano 550, 4°, C1013AAL Buenos Aires; tel. (11) 4370-4600; fax (11) 4340-2270; e-mail jurisprudencia@cjsn.gov.ar; internet www.csjn.gov.ar.

The members of the Supreme Court are appointed by the President, with the agreement of at least two-thirds of the Senate. Members can be dismissed by impeachment. In December 2006 the Congreso approved legislation reducing the number of judges from nine to five.

President: RICARDO LUIS LORENZETTI.

Vice-President: ELENA I. HIGHTON DE NOLASCO.

Justices: EUGENIO RAÚL ZAFFARONI, ENRIQUE SANTIAGO PETRACCHI, JUAN CARLOS MAQUEDA, CARLOS S. FAYT, CARMEN MARÍA ARGIBAY.

OTHER COURTS

Judges of the lower, national or further lower courts are appointed by the President, with the agreement of the Senate, and can be dismissed by impeachment. From 1999, however, judges were to retire on reaching 75 years of age.

The Federal Court of Appeal in Buenos Aires has three courts: civil and commercial, criminal, and administrative. There are six other courts of appeal in Buenos Aires: civil, commercial, criminal, peace, labour, and penal-economic. There are also federal appeal courts in La Plata, Bahía Blanca, Paraná, Rosario, Córdoba, Mendoza, Tucumán and Resistencia. In 1994, following constitutional amendments, the Office of the Attorney-General was established as an independent entity and a Council of Magistrates was envisaged. In 1997 the Senate adopted legislation to create the Council.

The provincial courts each have their own Supreme Court and a system of subsidiary courts. They deal with cases originating within and confined to the provinces.

Attorney-General: Dr ESTEBAN RIGHI.

Religion

CHRISTIANITY

The Roman Catholic Church

Some 90% of the population are Roman Catholics.

Argentina comprises 14 archdioceses, 51 dioceses (including one each for Uniate Catholics of the Ukrainian rite, of the Maronite rite and of the Armenian rite), four territorial prelatures and an apostolic exarchate for Catholics of the Melkite rite. The Bishop of San Gregorio de Narek en Buenos Aires is also the Apostolic Exarch of Latin America and Mexico for Catholics of the Armenian rite, and the Archbishop of Buenos Aires is also the Ordinary for Catholics of other Oriental rites.

Bishops' Conference: Suipacha 1034, C1008AAV Buenos Aires; tel. (11) 4328-0993; fax (11) 4328-9570; e-mail seccea@cea.org.ar; internet www.cea.org.ar; f. 1959; Pres. Cardinal JORGE MARIO BERGOGLIO (Archbishop of Buenos Aires).

Armenian Rite

Bishop of San Gregorio de Narek en Buenos Aires: VARTÁN WALDIR BOGHOSSIAN, Charcas 3529, C1425BMU Buenos Aires; tel. (11) 4824-1613; fax (11) 4827-1975; e-mail exarmal@pcn.net.

Latin Rite

Archbishop of Bahía Blanca: GUILLERMO JOSÉ GARLATTI, Avda Colón 164, B8000FTO Bahía Blanca; tel. (291) 455-0707; fax (291) 452-2070; e-mail arzobis@arzobispadobahia.org.ar.

Archbishop of Buenos Aires: Cardinal JORGE MARIO BERGOGLIO, Rivadavia 415, C1002AAC Buenos Aires; tel. (11) 4343-0812; fax (11) 4334-8373; e-mail arzobispado@arzbaires.org.ar; internet www.arzbaires.org.ar.

Archbishop of Córdoba: CARLOS JOSÉ ÑAÑEZ, Hipólito Irigoyen 98, X5000JHN Córdoba; tel. and fax (351) 422-1015; e-mail info@arzobispado.org.ar; internet www.arzobispadocba.org.ar.

Archbishop of Corrientes: ANDRÉS STANOVNIK, 9 de Julio 1543, W3400AZA Corrientes; tel. and fax (3783) 422436; e-mail info@corrientes.arzobispado.net; internet corrientes.arzobispado.net.

Archbishop of La Plata: HÉCTOR RUBÉN AGUER, Calle 14 Centro 1009, B1900DVQ La Plata; tel. (221) 425-1656; e-mail arzobispadodelaplata@speedy.com.ar; internet www.arzolap.org.ar.

Archbishop of Mendoza: JOSÉ MARÍA ARANCIBIA, Catamarca 98, M5500CKB Mendoza; tel. (261) 423-3862; fax (261) 429-5415; e-mail arzobispadomza@supernet.com.ar.

Archbishop of Mercedes-Luján: AGUSTÍN ROBERTO RADRIZZANI, Calle 22 745, B6600HDU Mercedes; tel. (2324) 432-412; fax (2324) 432-104; e-mail arzomerce@yahoo.com.ar; internet www.basilicadelujan.org.

Archbishop of Paraná: MARIO LUIS BAUTISTA MAULIÓN, Monte Caseros 77, E3100ACA Paraná; tel. (343) 431-1440; fax (343) 423-0372; e-mail arzparan@arzparan.org.ar.

Archbishop of Resistencia: FABRICIANO SIGAMPA, Bartolomé Mitre 363, Casilla 35, H3500BLG Resistencia; tel. and fax (3722) 441908; e-mail arzobrcia@arnet.com.ar.

Archbishop of Rosario: JOSÉ LUIS MOLLAGHAN, Córdoba 1677, S2000AWY Rosario; tel. (341) 425-1298; fax (341) 425-1207; e-mail arzobros@uolsinectis.com.ar; internet www.delrosario.org.ar.

Archbishop of Salta: MARIO ANTONIO CARGNELLO, España 596, A4400ANL Salta; tel. (387) 421-4306; fax (387) 421-3101; e-mail arzobispadosalta@arnet.com.ar; internet www.arquidiocesissalta .org.ar.

Archbishop of San Juan de Cuyo: ALFONSO ROGELIO DELGADO EVERS, Bartolomé Mitre 250 Oeste, J5402CXF San Juan; tel. (264) 422-2578; fax (264) 427-3530; e-mail arzobispadosanjuan@infovia .com.ar.

Archbishop of Santa Fe de la Vera Cruz: JOSÉ MARÍA ARANCEDO, Avda Brig.-Gen. E. López 2720, S3000DCJ Santa Fe; tel. (342) 459-1780; fax (342) 459-4491; e-mail curia@arquisantafe.org.ar; internet www.arquisantafe.org.ar.

Archbishop of Tucumán: LUIS HÉCTOR VILLALBA, Avda Sarmiento 895, T4000GTI San Miguel de Tucumán; tel. (381) 431-0617; e-mail arztuc@arnet.com.ar; internet www.arztucuman.org.ar.

Maronite Rite

Bishop of San Charbel en Buenos Aires: CHARBEL GEORGES MERHI, Eparquía Maronita, Paraguay 834, C1057AAL Buenos Aires; tel. (11) 4311-7299; fax (11) 4312-8348; e-mail mcharbel@hotmail .com.

Melkite Rite

Apostolic Exarch: ABDO ARBACH, Exarcado Apostólico Greco-Melquita, Corrientes 276, X5000ANF Córdoba; tel. (351) 421-0625.

Ukrainian Rite

Bishop of Santa María del Patrocinio en Buenos Aires: Rt Rev. MIGUEL MYKYCEJ, Ramón L. Falcón 3950, Casilla 28, C1407GSN Buenos Aires; tel. (11) 4671-4192; fax (11) 4671-7265; e-mail pokrov@ ciudad.com.ar.

The Anglican Communion

The Iglesia Anglicana del Cono Sur de América (Anglican Church of the Southern Cone of America) was formally inaugurated in Buenos Aires in April 1983. The Church comprises seven dioceses: Argentina, Northern Argentina, Chile, Paraguay, Peru, Bolivia and Uruguay. The Primate is the Bishop of Argentina.

Bishop of Argentina: Rt Rev. GREGORY J. VENABLES, 25 de Mayo 282, C1002ABF Buenos Aires; tel. (11) 4342-4618; fax (11) 4331-0234; e-mail diocesisanglibue@fibertel.com.ar; internet www .anglicanaargentina.org.ar.

Bishop of Northern Argentina: (vacant), Casilla 187, A4400ANL Salta; tel. (387) 431-1718; fax (387) 431-2622; e-mail sinclair@salnet .com.ar; jurisdiction extends to Jujuy, Salta, Tucumán, Catamarca, Santiago del Estero, Formosa and Chaco.

Other Christian Churches

Federación Argentina de Iglesias Evangélicas (Argentine Federation of Evangelical Churches): José María Moreno 873, C1424AAI Buenos Aires; tel. and fax (11) 4922-5356; e-mail presidencia@faie .org.ar; internet www.faie.org.ar; f. 1938; 23 mem. churches; Pres. NICOLÁS ROSENTHAL; Sec. Rev. ADOLFO PEDROZA.

Convención Evangélica Bautista Argentina (Baptist Evangelical Convention): Virrey Liniers 42, C1174ACB Buenos Aires; tel. and fax (11) 4864-2711; e-mail ceba@sion.com; internet www.ceba .sion.com; f. 1908; Pres. NÉSTOR GOLLUSCIO.

Iglesia Evangélica Congregacional (Evangelical Congregational Church): Perón 525, E3100BBK Paraná; tel. (43) 21-6172; e-mail iecsecretaria@yahoo.com.ar; f. 1924; 100 congregations, 8,000 mems, 24,000 adherents; Pres. Rev. CLAUDIO DIETZ.

Iglesia Evangélica Luterana Argentina (Evangelical Lutheran Church of Argentina): Ing. Silveyra 1639-41, B1607BQM Villa Adelina, Buenos Aires; tel. (11) 4735-4155; fax (11) 4766-7948; e-mail ielapresidente@arnet.com.ar; internet www.iela.org.ar; f. 1905; 28,000 mems; Pres. EDGARDO ELSESER.

Iglesia Evangélica Luterana Unida (United Evangelical Lutheran Church): Marcos Sastre 2891, C1417FYE Buenos Aires; tel. (11) 4501-3925; fax 4504-7358; e-mail ielu@ielu.org; internet www.ielu.org; 11,000 mems; Pres. Rev. ALAN ELDRID.

Iglesia Evangélica Metodista Argentina (Methodist Church of Argentina): Rivadavia 4044, 3°, C1205AAN Buenos Aires; tel. (11) 4982-3712; fax (11) 4981-0885; e-mail secretariaadministracion@ iglesiametodista.org.ar; internet www.iglesiametodista.org.ar; f. 1836; Bishop NELLIE RITCHIE.

Iglesia Evangélica del Río de la Plata (Evangelical Church of the Plate River): Mariscal Sucre 2855, C1428DVY Buenos Aires; tel. (11) 4787-0436; fax (11) 4787-0335; e-mail secretario@ierp.org.ar; internet www.iglesiaevangelica.org; f. 1899; 25,200 mems; Pres. FEDERICO HUGO SCHÄFER; Gen. Sec. JUAN ABELARDO SCHVINDT.

JUDAISM

There are about 230,000 Jews in Argentina, mostly in Buenos Aires.

Delegación de Asociaciones Israelitas Argentinas (DAIA) (Delegation of Argentine Jewish Associations): Pasteur 633, 7°, C1028AAM Buenos Aires; tel. and fax (11) 4378-3200; e-mail daia@daia.org.ar; internet www.daia.org.ar; f. 1935; Pres. ALDO DONZIS; Exec. Dir JORGE ELBAUM.

The Press

PRINCIPAL DAILIES

Buenos Aires

Ambito Financiero: Paseo Colón 1196, C1063ACY Buenos Aires; tel. (11) 4349-1500; fax (11) 4349-1505; e-mail mensajesaleditor@ ambito.com.ar; internet www.ambito.com.ar; f. 1976; morning (Mon.–Fri.); business; Pres. ORLANDO MARIO VIGNATTI; Dir GUSTAVO ISAACK; circ. 115,000.

Boletín Oficial de la República Argentina: Suipacha 767, C1008AAO Buenos Aires; tel. and fax (11) 4322-4055; e-mail dnro@boletinoficial.gov.ar; internet www.boletinoficial.gov.ar; f. 1893; morning (Mon.–Fri.); official records publ; Dir Dr JORGE EDUARDO FEIJOÓ; circ. 15,000.

Buenos Aires Herald: Avda San Juan 141, C1064AEB Buenos Aires; tel. and fax (11) 4349-1524; e-mail info@buenosairesherald .com; internet www.buenosairesherald.com; f. 1876; English; morning; independent; Dir ORLANDO VIGNETTI; circ. 20,000.

Clarín: Piedras 1743, C1140ABK Buenos Aires; tel. (11) 4309-7500; fax (11) 4309-7559; e-mail cartas@claringlobal.com.ar; internet www .clarin.com; f. 1945; morning; independent; Dir ERNESTINA HERRERA DE NOBLE; circ. 342,749 (daily), 686,287 (Sunday).

Crónica: Juan de Garay 40, C1063ABN Buenos Aires; tel. (11) 5550-8608; fax (11) 4361-4237; e-mail gerenciacomercial@cronica.com.ar; internet www.cronica.com.ar; f. 1963; morning and evening; Dirs MARIO ALBERTO FERNÁNDEZ (morning), RICARDO GANGEME (evening); circ. 330,000 (morning), 190,000 (evening), 450,000 (Sunday).

El Cronista Comercial: Paseo Colón 740/6, 1°, C1063ACU Buenos Aires; tel. (11) 4121-9300; fax (11) 4121-9301; e-mail info@cronista .com; internet www.cronista.com; f. 1908; morning; Dir FERNANDO GONZÁLEZ; circ. 65,000.

La Nación: Bouchard 551, C1106ABG Buenos Aires; tel. (11) 4319-1600; fax (11) 4319-1969; e-mail cescribano@lanacion.com.ar; internet www.lanacion.com.ar; f. 1870; morning; independent; Pres. JULIO SAGUIER; circ. 150,000.

Página 12: Solís 1525, C1134ADG Buenos Aires; tel. (11) 6772-4444; fax (11) 6772-4428; e-mail publicidad@pagina12.com.ar; internet www.pagina12.com.ar; f. 1987; morning; independent; Dir ERNESTO TIFFENBERG; Pres. FERNANDO SOKOLOWICZ; circ. 280,000.

La Prensa: Azopardo 715, C1107ADK Buenos Aires; tel. (11) 4349-1000; e-mail informaciongeneral@laprensa.com.ar; internet www .laprensa.com.ar; f. 1869; morning; independent; Dir FLORENCIO ALDREY IGLESIAS; circ. 100,000.

La Razón: Río Cuarto 1242, C1168AFF Buenos Aires; tel. and fax (11) 4309-6000; e-mail lectores@larazon.com.ar; internet www .larazon.com.ar; f. 1992; evening; Dir OSCAR MAGDALENA; circ. 62,000.

PRINCIPAL PROVINCIAL DAILIES

Catamarca

El Ancasti: Sarmiento 526, 1°, K4700EML Catamarca; tel. (3833) 431385; fax (3833) 453995; e-mail lector@elancasti.net.ar; internet www.elancasti.com.ar; f. 1988; morning; Dir MARCELO SOSA; circ. 9,000.

Chaco

Norte: Carlos Pellegrini 744, H3500CDP Resistencia; tel. (3722) 428204; fax (3722) 426047; internet www.diarionorte.com; f. 1968; Dir MIGUEL ANGEL FERNÁNDEZ; circ. 16,500.

Chubut

Crónica: Namuncurá 122, U9000BVD Comodoro Rivadavia; tel. (297) 447-1200; fax (297) 447-1780; internet www.diariocronica.com .ar; f. 1962; morning; Dir DANIEL CÉSAR ZAMIT; circ. 15,000.

Córdoba

Comercio y Justicia: Félix Paz 310, Alto Alberdi, X5002IGQ Córdoba; tel. and fax (351) 488-0088; e-mail redaccion@ comercioyjusticia.info; internet www.comercioyjusticia.com.ar; f. 1939; morning; economic and legal news with periodic supplements on architecture and administration; Pres. EDUARDO POGROBINKI; Dir JAVIER ALBERTO DE PASCUALE; circ. 5,800.

La Voz del Interior: Monseñor P. Cabrera 6080, X5008HKJ Córdoba; tel. (351) 475-7000; fax (351) 475-7282; e-mail lavoz@

lavozdelinterior.com.ar; internet www.lavozdelinterior.com.ar; f. 1904; morning; independent; Dir Dr CARLOS HUGO JORNET; circ. 57,000.

Corrientes

El Litoral: Hipólito Yrigoyen 990, W3400AST Corrientes; tel. and fax (3783) 411524; e-mail redaccion@el-litoral.com.ar; internet www.el-litoral.com.ar; f. 1960; morning; Dir CARLOS A. ROMERO FERIS; circ. 25,000.

Entre Ríos

El Diario: Buenos Aires y Urquiza, E2823XBC Paraná; tel. (343) 423-1000; fax (343) 431-9104; e-mail info@eldiarioentrerios.com.ar; internet www.eldiario.com.ar; f. 1914; morning; Dir Dr LUIS F. ETCHEVEHERE; circ. 7,100.

El Heraldo: Quintana 42, E3200XAE Concordia; tel. (345) 421-5304; fax (345) 421-1397; e-mail admin@elheraldo.com.ar; internet www.elheraldo.com.ar; f. 1915; evening; Editor Dr CARLOS LIEBERMANN; circ. 10,000.

Mendoza

Los Andes: San Martín 1049, M5500AAK Mendoza; tel. (261) 449-1200; fax (261) 420-2011; e-mail aguardiola@losandes.com.ar; internet www.losandes.com.ar; f. 1982; morning; Chair. RAÚL FLAMARIQUE; Pres. ARTURO GUARDIOLA; circ. 30,400.

Misiones

El Territorio: Quaranta No. 4307, N3301GAC Posadas; tel. and fax (3752) 451844; internet www.territoriodigital.com.ar; f. 1925; Dir GONZALO PELTZER; circ. 4,800.

Provincia de Buenos Aires

El Atlántico: Bolívar 2975, B7600GDO Mar del Plata; tel. (223) 435462; e-mail info@diarioelatlantico.com; internet www.diarioelatlantico.com.ar; f. 1938; morning; Dir OSCAR ALBERTO GASTIARENA; circ. 20,000.

La Capital: Champagnat 2551, B7604GXA Mar del Plata; tel. (223) 478-8490; fax (223) 478-1038; e-mail diario@lacapitalnet.com.ar; internet www.lacapitalnet.com.ar; f. 1905; Dir FLORENCIO ALDREY IGLESIAS; circ. 32,000.

El Día: Avda A, Diagonal 80 815, B1900CCI La Plata; tel. (221) 425-0101; fax (221) 423-2996; e-mail lectores@eldia.com; internet www.eldia.com; f. 1884; morning; independent; Dir RAÚL E. KRAISELBURD; circ. 54,868.

Ecos Diarios: Calle 62, No. 2486, B7630XAF Necochea; tel. and fax (2262) 430754; e-mail ecosdiar@satlink.com; internet www.ecosdiarios.com; f. 1921; morning; independent; Dir GUILLERMO A. IGNACIO; circ. 2,300.

La Nueva Provincia: Rodríguez 55, B8000HSA Bahía Blanca; tel. (291) 459-0000; fax (291) 459-0001; e-mail redaccionweb@lanueva.com.ar; internet www.lanueva.com.ar; f. 1898; morning; independent; Dir DIANA JULIO DE MASSOT; circ. 14,000.

El Nuevo Cronista: 5 Calle 619, B8000XAV Mercedes; tel. (11) 2324-4001; internet www.nuevocronista.com.ar; Dir JAVIER GUEVARA.

El Popular: Vicente López 2626, B7400CRH Olavarría; tel. and fax (22) 8442-0502; e-mail redaccion@elpopular.com.ar; internet www.diarioelpopular.com.ar; f. 1899; morning; Dir JORGE GABRIEL BOTTA; circ. 6,100.

El Sol: Hipólito Yrigoyen 122, B1878FND Quilmes; tel. and fax (11) 4257-6325; e-mail elsol@elsolquilmes.com.ar; internet www.elsolquilmes.com.ar; f. 1927; Dir RODRIGO GHISANI; circ. 25,000.

La Voz del Pueblo: San Martín 991, B7500IKJ Tres Arroyos; tel. (2983) 430680; fax (2938) 430682; e-mail vecinos@lavozdelpueblo.com.ar; internet www.lavozdelpueblo.com.ar; f. 1902; morning; independent; Dir ALBERTO JORGE MACIEL; circ. 3,400.

Río Negro

Río Negro: 9 de Julio 733, R8332AAO General Roca; tel. (2941) 439300; fax (2941) 439638; e-mail publicidadonline@rionegro.com.ar; internet www.rionegro.com.ar; f. 1912; morning; Dir JULIO RAJNERI; Co-Dir NÉLIDA RAJNERI DE GAMBA; circ. 30,000.

Salta

El Tribuno: Avda Ex Combatientes de Malvinas 3890, A4412BYA Salta; tel. (387) 424-6200; fax (387) 424-6240; e-mail redaccion@eltribuno.com.ar; internet www.eltribuno.com.ar; f. 1949; morning; Dir ROBERTO E. ROMERO; circ. 20,000.

San Juan

Diario de Cuyo: Mendoza 380 Sur, J5402GUH San Juan; tel. (264) 429-0038; fax (264) 429-0063; e-mail comercialdc@diariodecuyo.com.ar; internet www.diariodecuyo.com.ar; f. 1947; morning; independent; Dir FRANCISCO B. MONTES; circ. 14,450.

San Luis

El Diario de La República: Lafinur 924, D5700ASO San Luis; tel. and fax (2623) 422037; e-mail redaccion@eldiariodelarepublica.com; internet www.eldiariodelarepublica.com; f. 1966; Dir FELICIANA RODRIGUEZ SAÁ; circ. 7,650.

Santa Fe

La Capital: Sarmiento 763, S2000CMK Rosario; tel. (341) 420-1100; fax (341) 420-1114; internet www.lacapital.com.ar; f. 1867; morning; independent; Dirs ORLANDO MARIO VIGNATTI, DANIEL EDUARDO VILA; circ. 40,000.

El Litoral: 25 de Mayo 3536, S3002DPJ Santa Fe; tel. (342) 450-2500; fax (342) 450-2530; e-mail litoral@litoral.com.ar; internet www.litoral.com.ar; f. 1918; morning; independent; Dir GUSTAVO VÍTTORI; circ. 16,500.

Santiago del Estero

El Liberal: Libertad 263, G4200CZC Santiago del Estero; tel. (385) 422-4400; fax (385) 422-4538; e-mail redaccion@elliberal.com.ar; internet www.elliberal.com.ar; f. 1898; morning; Dir ANTONIO ENRIQUE CASTIGLIONE; circ. 30,000.

Tucumán

La Gaceta: Mendoza 654, T4000DAN San Miguel de Tucumán; tel. (381) 484-2200; fax (381) 431-1597; e-mail redaccion@lagaceta.com.ar; internet www.lagaceta.com.ar; f. 1912; morning; independent; Dir DANIEL DESSEIN; circ. 54,000.

WEEKLY NEWSPAPER

Diario Perfil: Chacabuco 271,8°, C1069AAE Buenos Aires; tel. (11) 4341-9000; fax (11) 4341-8988; e-mail perfilcom@perfil.com.ar; internet www.diarioperfil.com.ar; f. 2005; Saturday and Sunday; Dir JORGE FONTEVECCHIA; circ. 38,600.

PERIODICALS

Aeroespacio: Dorrego 4019, C1425GBE Buenos Aires; tel. and fax (11) 4514-1561; e-mail info@aerospacio.com.ar; internet www.aeroespacio.com.ar; f. 1940; every 2 months; aeronautics; Dir DANIEL M. RUSSO; circ. 24,000.

Billiken: Azopardo 565, C1307ADG Buenos Aires; tel. (11) 4346-0107; fax (11) 4343-7040; e-mail billiken@atlantida.com.ar; internet www.billiken.com.ar; f. 1919; weekly; children's magazine; Dir JUAN CARLOS PORRAS; circ. 54,000.

Caras: Chacabuco 271, C1069AAE Buenos Aires; tel. (11) 4341-9000; fax (11) 4341-8988; e-mail correocaras@perfil.com.ar; internet www.revista-caras.com.ar; f. 1992; weekly; celebrities; Dir LILIANA CASTAÑO; circ. 41,000.

Chacra: The New Farm Company, SA, Paseo Colón 728, 7°B, C1063ACU Buenos Aires; tel. (11) 4342-4390; e-mail agritotal@agritotal.com; internet www.agritotal.com; f. 1930; monthly; farm and country magazine; Dir RUBÉN BARTOLOMÉ; circ. 12,000.

El Economista: Córdoba 632, 2°, C1054AAS Buenos Aires; tel. (11) 4322-7360; fax (11) 4322-8157; e-mail redaccion@eleconomista.com.ar; internet www.eleconomista.com.ar; f. 1951; weekly; financial; Dir Dr D. RADONJIC; circ. 37,800.

El Federal: Tucumán 1, 19° y 20°, C1049AAA Buenos Aires; tel. (11) 4318-7700; e-mail comercial@infomedia.com.ar; weekly; farming and countryside; Dir FABIÁN CASAS; circ. 18,900.

Fortuna: Chacabuco 271, C1069AAE Buenos Aires; tel. (11) 4341-9000; fax (11) 4341-8988; e-mail correofortuna@perfil.com.ar; internet www.revista-fortuna.com.ar; f. 2003; weekly; economics and business; Editor JUAN PABLO DE SANTIS; circ. 4,700.

Gente: Azopardo 565, C1307ADG Buenos Aires; tel. (11) 4346-0240; e-mail genteonline@atlantida.com.ar; internet www.gente.com.ar; f. 1965; weekly; general; Dir JORGE DE LUJÁN GUTIÉRREZ; circ. 45,000.

El Gráfico: Balcarce 510, 1064 Buenos Aires; tel. (11) 5235-5100; e-mail elgrafico@elgrafico.com.ar; internet www.elgrafico.com.ar; f. 1919; monthly; sport; Editor MARTIN MAZUR; circ. 24,150.

Mercado: Peru 263, 2°, CP, C1067AAE Buenos Aires; tel. (11) 5166-9400; fax (11) 4343-7880; e-mail info@mercado.com.ar; internet www.mercado.com.ar; f. 1969; monthly; business; Dir MIGUEL ANGEL DIEZ; circ. 28,000.

Mundo Israelita, SA: Corrientes 4006, 4°, Of. 35, C1032ABS Buenos Aires; tel. (11) 4861-2224; fax (11) 4861-8434; e-mail mundoeditor@hotmail.com; internet www.mundoisraelita.com.ar; f. 1923; owned by Mundo Editor, SA; fortnightly; Jewish interest; Editor-Dir Dr Corina Schvartzapel; circ. 1,500.

Noticias de la Semana: Chacabuco 271, C1069AAE Buenos Aires; tel. (11) 4341-9000; fax (11) 4341-8988; e-mail correonoticias@perfil.com.ar; internet www.revista-noticias.com.ar; f. 1977; weekly; news and current affairs; Editor Gustavo González; circ. 63,000.

Para Ti: Azopardo 565, C1107ADG Buenos Aires; tel. (11) 4331-4591; fax (11) 4331-3272; e-mail parati@atlantida.com.ar; internet www.parati.com.ar; f. 1922; weekly; women's interest; Dir Juan Carlos Porras; circ. 35,000.

La Prensa Médica Argentina: Junín 917, 2°D, C1113AAA Buenos Aires; tel. and fax (11) 4961-9213; e-mail presmedarg@hotmail.com; internet www.prensamedica.com.ar; f. 1914; monthly; medical; Editor Dr Pablo A. López; circ. 8,000.

Prensa Obrera: Ayacucho 444, C1026AAB Buenos Aires; tel. (11) 4953-3824; fax (11) 4953-7164; e-mail prensaobrera@po.org.ar; internet www.po.org.ar; f. 1982; weekly; publ. of Partido Obrero; circ. 16,000.

Saber Vivir: Magallanes 1315, C1288ABA Buenos Aires; tel. (11) 4303-2305; e-mail sabervivir@gentille.biz; f. 1999; fortnightly; health; Dir Ricardo Gentille; circ. 81,000.

Veintitrés: Serrano 1139, C1414DEW Buenos Aires; tel. (11) 4775-0300; e-mail lectores@veintitres.com; internet www.elargentino.com/medios-120-Veintitres.html; f. 1998; weekly; political and cultural; Dir Roberto Caballero; circ. 35,000.

NEWS AGENCIES

Diarios y Noticias (DYN): Julio A. Roca 636, 8°, C1067ABO Buenos Aires; tel. (11) 4342-3040; fax (11) 4342-3043; e-mail editor@dyn.com.ar; internet www.dyn.com.ar; f. 1982; Chair. José Pochat; Dir Hugo E. Grimaldi.

Noticias Argentinas, SA (NA): Dr Mariano Moreno 769, 3°, C1091AAO Buenos Aires; tel. and fax (11) 4331-3850; e-mail infogral@noticiasargentinas.com; internet www.noticiasargentinas.com; f. 1973; Pres. Fernando Cuello; Dir Guillermo Vucetich.

Télam, SE: Bolívar 531, C1066AAK Buenos Aires; tel. (11) 4339-0330; fax (11) 4339-0353; e-mail telam@telam.com.ar; internet www.telam.com.ar; f. 1945; state-owned; Pres. (vacant).

PRESS ASSOCIATION

Asociación de Entidades Periodísticas Argentinas (ADEPA): Chacabuco 314, 3°, C1069AAH Buenos Aires; tel. and fax (11) 4331-1500; e-mail adepa@adepa.org.ar; internet www.adepa.org.ar; f. 1962; Pres. Gustavo Vittori; Sec.-Gen. Carlos Rago.

Publishers

Aguilar, Altea, Taurus, Alfaguara, SA de Ediciones: Leandro N. Alem 720, C1001AAP Buenos Aires; tel. (11) 4119-5000; fax (11) 4119-5021; e-mail info@alfaguara.com.ar; internet www.alfaguara.com.ar; f. 1946; part of Grupo Santillana Argentina; general, literature, children's books; Dir-Gen. David Delgado de Robles.

Aique Grupo Editor, SA: Francisco Acuña de Figueroa 352, C1180AAF Buenos Aires; tel. and fax (11) 4865-5152; e-mail editorial@aique.com.ar; internet www.aique.com.ar; f. 1976; educational; Dir-Gen. María Pía Gagliardi.

Amorrortu Editores, SA: Paraguay 1225, 7°, C1057AAS Buenos Aires; tel. (11) 4816-5812; fax (11) 4816-3321; e-mail info@amorrortueditores.com; internet www.amorrortueditores.com; f. 1967; academic, social sciences and humanities; Man. Dir Horacio de Amorrortu.

a–Z Editora, SA: Paraguay 2351, C1121ABK Buenos Aires; tel. (11) 4961-4036; fax (11) 4961-0089; e-mail contacto@az.com.ar; internet www.az.com.ar; f. 1976; educational, children's, literature, social sciences, medicine, law; Pres. Dante Omar Villalba.

Biblioteca Nacional de Maestros: c/o Ministerio de Educación, Pizzurno 935, planta baja, C1020ACA Buenos Aires; tel. (11) 4129-1272; fax (11) 4129-1268; e-mail gperrone@me.gov.ar; internet www.bnm.me.gov.ar; f. 1884; Dir Graciela Perrone.

Cosmopolita, SRL: Piedras 744, C1070AAP Buenos Aires; tel. (11) 4361-8925; fax (11) 4361-8049; e-mail editorialcosmopolita@fullzero.com.ar; internet www.ed-cosmopolita.com.ar; f. 1940; science and technology; Man. Dir Ruth F. de Rapp.

Crecer Creando Editorial: Callao 1225, 14°B, C1023AAF Buenos Aires; tel. and fax (11) 4812-4586; e-mail info@crecercreando.com.ar; internet www.crecercreando.com.ar; educational.

De Los Cuatro Vientos Editorial: Balcarce 1053, Local 2, C1064AAU Buenos Aires; tel. and fax (11) 4300-0924; e-mail info@deloscuatrovientos.com.ar; internet www.deloscuatrovientos.com.ar; Dir Pablo Albornoz.

Distribuidora Lumen, SRL: Viamonte 1674, C1055ABF, Buenos Aires; tel. (11) 4373-1414; fax (11) 4375-0453; e-mail ventas@lumen.com.ar; internet www.lumen.com.ar; f. 1958; imprints include Lumen (religion, spirituality etc.), Magisterio (educational), Lumen-Hvmanitas (social sciences) and Lohlé-Lumen (politics, philosophy, literature).

Ediciones Atril: Hortiguera 1411, C1406CKI Buenos Aires; tel. (11) 4924-3003; e-mail atril@interlink.com.ar.

Ediciones de la Flor SRL: Gorriti 3695, C1172ACE Buenos Aires; fax (11) 4963-5616; e-mail edic-flor@datamarkets.com.ar; internet www.edicionesdelaflor.com.ar; f. 1966; fiction, poetry, theatre, juvenile, humour and scholarly; Co-Dirs Ana María T. Miler, Daniel Divinsky.

Ediciones Gránica: Lavalle 1634, 3° G, C1048AAN Buenos Aires; tel. (11) 4374-1456; fax (11) 4373-0669; e-mail granica.ar@granicaeditor.com; internet www.granicaeditor.com; management, reference.

Ediciones Macchi, SA: Alsina 1535/37, C1088AAM Buenos Aires; tel. (11) 446-2506; fax (11) 446-0594; e-mail info@macchi.com; internet www.macchi.com; f. 1947; economic sciences; Pres. Raúl Luis Macchi.

Ediciones Manantial, SRL: Avda de Mayo 1365, 6°, Of. 28, C1085ABD Buenos Aires; tel. (11) 4383-6059; fax (11) 4383-7350; e-mail info@emanantial.com.ar; internet www.emanantial.com.ar; f. 1984; social science, education and psychoanalysis; Gen. Man. Carlos A. de Santos.

Ediciones Nueva Visión, SAIC: Tucumán 3748, C1189AAV Buenos Aires; tel. (11) 4864-5050; fax (11) 4863-5980; e-mail ednuevavision@ciudad.com.ar; f. 1954; psychology, education, social sciences, linguistics; Man. Dir Haydée P. de Giacone.

Ediciones del Signo: Julián Alvarez 2844, 1° A, C1425DHT Buenos Aires; tel. (11) 4804-4147; fax (11) 4782-1836; e-mail edicionesdelsigno@arnet.com.ar; internet www.edicionesdelsigno.com.ar; f. 1995; philosophy, psychoanalysis, politics and scholarly.

Editorial Albatros, SACI: Torres Las Plazas, J. Salguero 2745, 5°, C1425DEL Buenos Aires; tel. (11) 4807-2030; fax (11) 4807-2010; e-mail info@albatros.com.ar; internet www.albatros.com.ar; f. 1945; technical, non-fiction, social sciences, sport, children's books, medicine and agriculture; Pres. Andrea Inés Canevaro.

Editorial Argenta Sarlep, SA: Corrientes 1250, 3°, Of. F, C1043AAZ Buenos Aires; tel. and fax (11) 4382-9085; e-mail argenta@millic.com.ar; internet www.editorialargenta.com; f. 1970; literature, poetry, theatre and reference.

Editorial Bonum: Corrientes 6687, C1427BPE Buenos Aires; tel. and fax (11) 4554-1414; e-mail ventas@editorialbonum.com.ar; internet www.editorialbonum.com.ar; f. 1960; religious, educational and self-help.

Editorial Catálogos, SRL: Independencia 1860, C1225AAN Buenos Aires; tel. and fax (11) 4381-5708; e-mail catalogos@ciudad.com.ar; internet www.catalogossrl.com.ar; religion, literature, academic, general interest and self-help.

Editorial Claretiana: Lima 1360, C1138ACD Buenos Aires; tel. (11) 427-9250; fax (11) 427-4015; e-mail editorial@editorialclaretiana.com.ar; internet www.editorialclaretiana.com.ar; f. 1956; Catholicism; Man. Dir Domingo Angel Grillia.

Editorial Claridad, SA: Juncal 3451, C1425AYT Buenos Aires; tel. and fax (11) 4804-0472; e-mail editorial@heliasta.com.ar; internet www.heliasta.com.ar; f. 1922; literature, biographies, social science, politics, reference, dictionaries; Pres. Dra Ana María Cabanellas.

Editorial Don Bosco (EDB): Don Bosco 4069, C1206ABM Buenos Aires; tel. (11) 4883-0111; fax (11) 4883-0115; e-mail mperezs@edb.com.ar; internet www.edb.com.ar; f. 1993; religious and educational; Pres. P. Roque Sella; Editorial Dir Juan L. Rodríguez.

Editorial Errepar: Paraná 725, C1017AAO Buenos Aires; tel. (11) 4370-8025; fax (11) 4383-2202; e-mail clientes@errepar.com; internet www.errepar.com; legal texts.

Editorial Grupo Cero: Mansilla 2686, planta baja 2, C1425BPD Buenos Aires; tel. 4966-1710; e-mail baires@grupocero.org; internet www.grupocerobuenosaires.com; fiction, poetry and psychoanalysis; Dir Miguel Oscar Menassa.

Editorial Guadalupe: Mansilla 3865, C1425BQA Buenos Aires; tel. (11) 4826-8587; fax (11) 4823-6672; e-mail ventas@editorialguadalupe.com.ar; internet www.editorialguadalupe.com.ar; f. 1895; social sciences, religion, anthropology, children's books and pedagogy; Man. Dir Lorenzo Goyeneche.

Editorial Heliasta, SRL: Juncal 3451, C1425AYT Buenos Aires; tel. and fax (11) 4804-0472; e-mail editorial@heliasta.com.ar; internet www.heliasta.com.ar; f. 1944; literature, biography, dictionaries, legal; Pres. Dra Ana María Cabanellas.

Editorial Hispano-Americana, SA (HASA): Alsina 731, C1087AAK Buenos Aires; tel. (11) 4331-5051; internet www.hasa.com.ar; f. 1934; science and technology; Pres. Prof. HÉCTOR OSCAR ALGARRA.

Editorial Inter-Médica, SAICI: Junín 917, 1°, C1113AAC Buenos Aires; tel. (11) 4961-9234; fax (11) 4961-5572; e-mail info@inter-medica.com.ar; internet www.inter-medica.com.ar; f. 1959; medicine and veterinary; Pres. SONIA MODYEIEVSKY.

Editorial Juris: Moreno 1580, S2000DLF Rosario, Santa Fe; tel. (341) 426-7301; e-mail editorial@editorialjuris.com; internet www.editorialjuris.com; f. 1952; legal texts; Dir LUIS MAESANO.

Editorial Kier, SACIFI: Santa Fe 1260, C1059ABT Buenos Aires; tel. (11) 4811-0507; fax (11) 4811-3395; e-mail ediciones@kier.com.ar; internet www.kier.com.ar; f. 1907; Eastern doctrines and religions, astrology, parapsychology, tarot, I Ching, occultism, cabbala, freemasonry and natural medicine; Pres. HÉCTOR S. PIBERNUS; Dir CRISTINA GRIGNA; Mans SERGIO PIBERNUS, OSVALDO PIBERNUS.

Editorial Losada, SA: Corrientes 1551, C1042AAB Buenos Aires; tel. (11) 4375-5001; fax (11) 4373-4006; e-mail losada@editoriallosada.com; internet www.editoriallosada.com; f. 1938; general; Pres. JOSÉ JUAN FERNÁNDEZ REGUERA.

Editorial Médica Panamericana, SA: Marcelo T. de Alvear 2145, C1122AAG Buenos Aires; tel. (11) 4821-5520; fax (11) 4825-5006; e-mail info@medicapanamericana.com.ar; internet www.medicapanamericana.com.ar; f. 1962; medicine and health sciences; Pres. HUGO BRIK.

Editorial Mercosur: Dean Funes 923/25, C1231ABI Buenos Aires; tel. (11) 4822-4615; e-mail info@editorialmercosur.com; internet www.editorialmercosur.com; self-help and general interest.

Editorial del Nuevo Extremo: Juncal 4651, C1425BAE Buenos Aires; tel. (11) 4773-3228; fax (11) 473-8445; e-mail editorial@delnuevoextremo.com; internet www.delnuevoextremo.com; general interest.

Editorial Sigmar, SACI: Belgrano 1580, 7°, C1093AAQ Buenos Aires; tel. (11) 4383-3045; fax (11) 4383-5633; e-mail editorial@sigmar.com.ar; internet www.sigmar.com.ar; f. 1941; children's books; Man. Dir ROBERTO CHWAT.

Editorial Stella: Viamonte 1984, C1056ABD Buenos Aires; tel. (11) 4374-0346; fax (11) 4374-8719; e-mail admin@editorialstella.com.ar; internet www.editorialstella.com.ar; general non-fiction and textbooks; owned by Asociación Educacionista Argentina.

Editorial Sudamericana, SA: Humberto 545, 1°, C1103ACK Buenos Aires; tel. (11) 4300-5400; fax (11) 4362-7364; e-mail info@edsudamericana.com.ar; internet www.edsudamericana.com.ar; f. 1939; general fiction and non-fiction; Gen. Man. OLAF HANTEL.

Editorial Troquel, SA: Olleros 1818, 4° I, C1426CRH Buenos Aires; tel. and fax (11) 4779-9444; e-mail editorial@troguel.com.ar; internet www.troquel.com.ar; f. 1954; general literature, religion, philosophy and education; Pres. GUSTAVO A. RESSIA.

Editorial Zeus, SRL: Balcarce 730, S2000DNP Rosario, Santa Fe; tel. (341) 449-5585; fax (341) 425-4259; e-mail editorialzeus@citynet.net.ar; internet www.editorial-zeus.com.ar; legal texts; Editor and Dir GUSTAVO L. CAVIGLIA.

Emecé Editores, SA: Avda Independencia 1668, C1100ABQ Buenos Aires; tel. (11) 4124-9100; fax (11) 4124-9190; f. 1939; fiction, non-fiction, biographies, history, art, essays; Pres. ALFREDO DEL CARRIL; Editorial Dir ALBERTO DÍAZ.

EUDEBA (Editorial Universitaria de Buenos Aires): Rivadavia 1573, C1033AAF Buenos Aires; tel. (11) 4383-8025; fax (11) 4383-2202; e-mail eudeba@eudeba.com.ar; internet www.eudeba.com.ar; f. 1958; university textbooks and general interest publs; Pres. MÓNICA PINTO; Gen. Man. LUIS QUEVEDO.

Galerna: Lambaré 893, C1185ABA Buenos Aires; tel. (11) 4867-1661; fax (11) 4862-5031; e-mail contacto@galerna.net; internet www.galernalibros.com; fiction, theatre, poetry and scholarly; Man. HUGO LEVÍN.

Gram Editora: Cochabamba 1652, C1148ABF Buenos Aires; tel. (11) 4304-4833; fax (11) 4304-5692; e-mail grameditora@infovia.com.ar; internet www.grameditora.com.ar; education; Man. MANUEL HERRERO MONTES.

Grupo Santillana Argentina: Avda Leandro N. Alem 720, C1001AAP Buenos Aires; tel. (11) 4119-5000; e-mail info@santillana.com.ar; internet www.santillana.com.ar; f. 1963; part of Grupo Editorial Santillana (Spain); education; Dir-Gen. DAVID DELGADO DE ROBLES.

Kapelusz Editora, SA: San José 831, C1076AAQ Buenos Aires; tel. (11) 5236-5000; fax (11) 5236-5005; e-mail jvergara@kapelusz.com.ar; internet www.kapelusz.com.ar; f. 1905; textbooks, psychology, pedagogy, children's books; Vice-Pres. RAFAEL PASCUAL ROBLES.

LexisNexis Argentina: Carlos Pellegrini 887, 1°, Buenos Aires; tel. (11) 5236-8888; e-mail info@ed-depalma.com; internet www.lexisnexis.com.ar; f. 1999 upon acquisition of Depalma and Abeledo-Perrot; periodicals and books covering law, politics, sociology, philosophy, history and economics.

Plaza y Janés, SA: Buenos Aires; tel. (11) 4486-6769; popular fiction and non-fiction; Man. Dir JORGE PÉREZ.

Siglo Veintiuno Editores: Tucumán 1621, 7° N, C1050AAG Buenos Aires; tel. and fax (11) 4373-8516; e-mail info@sigloxxieditores.com.ar; internet www.sigloxxieditores.com.ar; social science, history, economics, art; Dir-Gen. JAIME LABASTIDA; Editorial Dir CARLOS E. DIEZ.

PUBLISHERS' ASSOCIATIONS

Cámara Argentina del Libro: Avda Belgrano 1580, 4°, C1093AAQ Buenos Aires; tel. (11) 4381-8383; fax (11) 4381-9253; e-mail cal@editores.org.ar; internet www.editores.org.ar; f. 1938; Pres. CARLOS DE SANTOS.

Cámara Argentina de Publicaciones: Lavalle 437, 6°, Of. D, C1047AAI Buenos Aires; tel. (11) 5218-9707; e-mail info@publicaciones.org.ar; internet www.publicaciones.org.ar; f. 1970; Pres. MARÍA PÍA GAGLIARDI; Sec. ROBERTO LIGHTOWLER.

Broadcasting and Communications

Secretaría de Comunicaciones: Sarmiento 151, 4°, C1041AAC Buenos Aires; tel. (11) 4318-9410; fax (11) 4318-9432; internet www.secom.gov.ar; co-ordinates 30 stations and the international service; Sec. CARLOS LISANDRO SALAS.

Comité Federal de Radiodifusión (COMFER): Suipacha 765, 9°, C1008AAO Buenos Aires; tel. (11) 4320-4900; fax (11) 4394-6866; e-mail comfer@comfer.gov.ar; internet www.comfer.gov.ar; f. 1972; controls various technical aspects of broadcasting and transmission of programmes; Insp. JUAN GABRIEL MARIOTTO.

TELECOMMUNICATIONS

Regulatory Bodies

Cámara de Informática y Comunicaciones de la República Argentina (CICOMRA): Córdoba 744, 2°, C1054AAT Buenos Aires; tel. (11) 4325-8839; fax (11) 4325-9604; e-mail cicomra@cicomra.org.ar; internet www.cicomra.org.ar; f. 1985; Pres. NORBERTO CAPELLÁN.

Comisión Nacional de Comunicaciones (CNC): Perú 103, 9°, C1067AAC Buenos Aires; tel. (11) 4347-9242; fax (11) 4347-9244; internet www.cnc.gov.ar; f. 1996; Insp. CEFERINO NAMUNCURÁ.

Major Operators

AT&T Argentina: Alicia Moreau de Justo 400, C1107AAH Buenos Aires; internet www.att.com; Pres. of Global Operations PAULINO DO REGO BARROS, Jr.

Cía Ericsson, SACI: Güemes 676, 1°, Vicente López PCIA, B1638CJF Buenos Aires; tel. (11) 4319-5500; fax (11) 4315-0629; e-mail infocom@cea.ericsson.se; internet www.ericsson.com.

Claro Argentina: Avda de Mayo 878, C1084AAQ Buenos Aires; internet www.cti.com.ar; f. 1994 as CTI Móvil; bought by América Móvil, SA de CV (Mexico) in 2003; mobile cellular telephone services; Dir-Gen. CARLOS ZENTENO.

Movistar: Corrientes 655, C1043AAG Buenos Aires; tel. (11) 4130-4000; internet www.movistar.com.ar; 98% owned by Telefónicas Móviles, SA (Spain); operates mobile telephone network.

Telcosur, SA: Don Bosco 3672, 5°, C1206ABF Buenos Aires; tel. (11) 4865-9060; e-mail telcosur@tgs.com.ar; internet www.telcosur.com.ar; f. 1998; 99% owned by Transportador de Gas del Sur (TGS); Operations Man. EDUARDO VIGILANTE; Commercial Man. EDUARDO MARTÍN.

Telecom Argentina: Alicia Moreau de Justo 50, C1107AAB Buenos Aires; tel. (11) 4968-4000; fax (11) 4968-1420; e-mail inversores@intersrv.telecom.com.ar; internet www.telecom.com.ar; provision of telecommunication services in the north of Argentina; Pres. ENRIQUE GARRIDO.

RADIO

Radio Nacional Argentina (RNA): Maipú 555, C1006ACE Buenos Aires; tel. (11) 4325-4590; fax (11) 4325-4313; e-mail direccionrna@radionacional.gov.ar; internet www.radionacional.gov.ar; five national radio stations: Nacional; Nacional Folklórica; Nacional Clásica; RPN 93.7; and RAE (q.v.); 39 provincial stations; Exec. Dir EDUARDO GARCÍA CAFFI.

Radiodifusión Argentina al Exterior (RAE): Maipú 555, C1006ACE Buenos Aires; tel. (11) 4325-6368; fax (11) 4325-9433; e-mail rae@radionacional.gov.ar; f. 1958; broadcasts in seven languages to all areas of the world; Dir LUIS MARÍA BARASSI (acting).

Asociación de Radiodifusoras Privadas Argentinas (ARPA): Juan D. Perón 1561, 8°, C1037ACC Buenos Aires; tel. (11) 4371-5999; fax 4382-4483; e-mail arpaorg@arpa.org.ar; internet www.arpa.org.ar; f. 1958; assn of privately owned commercial stations; Pres. ALBERTO VEIGA; Exec. Dir HECTOR J. PARREIRA.

TELEVISION

The national television network is regulated by the Comité Federal de Radiodifusión (see above). The following are some of the more important television stations in Argentina: Argentina Televisora Color LS82 Canal 7, LS83 (Canal 9 Libertad), LV80 Telenueva, LU81 Teledifusora Bahiense SA, LV81 Canal 12 Telecor SACI, Dicor Difusión Córdoba, LV80 TV Canal 10 Universidad Nacional Córdoba, and LU82 TV Mar del Plata SA.

The Argentine Government holds a 20% stake in the regional television channel Telesur, which began operations in May 2005 and is based in Caracas, Venezuela.

Asociación de Teleradiodifusoras Argentinas (ATA): Córdoba 323, 6°, C1054AAP Buenos Aires; tel. (11) 4312-4208; fax (11) 4315-4681; e-mail info@ata.org.ar; internet www.ata.org.ar; f. 1959; assn of 23 private television channels; Pres. CARLOS FONTÁN BALESTRA; Exec. Dir CARLOS MOLINERO.

América: Fitzroy 1650, Buenos Aires; internet www.america2.com.ar; Programme Man. LILIANA PARODI.

Canal 9: Dorrego 1708, C1414CKZ Buenos Aires; tel. (11) 777-2321; fax (11) 777-9620; e-mail webmaster@canal9.com.ar; internet www.canal9.com.ar; f. 1960; private channel; Pres. CARLOS GAUSTEIN; Dir-Gen. ENRIQUE TABOADA.

Canal 13: Lima 1261, C1138ACA Buenos Aires; tel. (11) 4305-0013; fax (11) 4307-0315; e-mail prensa@artear.com; internet www.canal13.com.ar; f. 1989; leased to a private concession in 1992; Programme Man. ADRIÁN SUAR.

LS82 TV Canal 7: Figueroa Alcorta 2977, C1425CKI Buenos Aires; tel. (11) 4802-6001; fax (11) 4802-9878; e-mail info@canal7argentina.com.ar; internet www.canal7argentina.com.ar; state-controlled channel; Controller RICARDO PALACIO; Dir of News ANA DE SKALON; Dir of Drama LEONARDO BECHINI.

Telefé (Canal 11): Pavón 2444, C1248AAT Buenos Aires; tel. (11) 4941-9549; fax (11) 4942-6773; e-mail prensa@telefe.com; internet www.telefe.com.ar; private channel; Programme Man. CLAUDIO VILLARRUEL.

Finance

(cap. = capital; res = reserves; dep. = deposits; m. = million; brs = branches; amounts in nuevos pesos argentinos, unless otherwise stated)

BANKING

Central Bank

Banco Central de la República Argentina: Reconquista 266, C1003ABF Buenos Aires; tel. (11) 4348-3500; fax (11) 4348-3955; e-mail sistema@bcra.gov.ar; internet www.bcra.gov.ar; f. 1935 as a central reserve bank; bank of issue; all capital is held by the state; cap. 12,263m., res 18,031m., dep. 95,873m. (Dec. 2007); Pres. MERCEDES MARCO DEL PONT.

Government-owned Commercial Banks

Banco del Chubut: Rivadavia 615, Rawson, U9103ANG Chubut; tel. (2965) 482505; fax (2965) 484196; internet www.bancochubut.com.ar; Pres. Dr CARLOS ALBERTO GARCÍA LOREA.

Banco de la Ciudad de Buenos Aires: Sarmiento 630, C1005AAH Buenos Aires; tel. (11) 4329-8600; fax (11) 4329-8729; e-mail bcdad39@sminter.com.ar; internet www.bancociudad.com.ar; municipal bank; f. 1878; cap. 871m., res 570m., dep. 9,102m. (Dec. 2008); Chair. and Pres. FEDERICO STURZENEGGER; 51 brs.

Banco de Inversión y Comercio Exterior, SA (BICE): 25 de Mayo 526/32, C1002ABL Buenos Aires; tel. (11) 4317-6900; fax (11) 4311-5596; e-mail informatica@bice.com.ar; internet www.bice.com.ar; f. 1991; cap. and res 1,130.4m. (Dec. 20047); Pres. MAURO ALEM; Gen. Man. JORGE GIACOMOTTI.

Banco de la Nación Argentina: Bartolomé Mitre 326, Capital Federal Of. 235, C1036AAF Buenos Aires; tel. (11) 4347-6000; fax (11) 4347-6316; e-mail mbravo@bna.com.ar; internet www.bna.com.ar; f. 1891; national bank; cap. 2,510.1m., res 5,311.4m., dep. 50,613m. (Dec. 2007); Pres. JUAN CARLOS FÁBREGA; Gen. Man. RUBÉN DARIO NOCERA; 645 brs.

Banco de la Pampa SEM: Carlos Pellegrini 255, L6300DRE Santa Rosa; tel. (2954) 451-0000; e-mail cexterior@blp.com.ar; internet www.blp.com.ar; f. 1958; cap. 128.5m., res 43.3m., dep. 1,725.5m. (June 2008); Chair. LAURA AZUCENA GALLUCCIO; Gen. Man. CARLOS DESINANO; 51 brs.

Banco de la Provincia de Buenos Aires: Calle 7, 726, B1900TFS La Plata, Buenos Aires; tel. (11) 4347-0238; fax (11) 4348-9496; e-mail delriom@bpba.com.ar; internet www.bapro.com.ar; f. 1822; provincial govt-owned bank; cap. 1,250m., res 1,760m., dep. 22,876m. (Dec. 2008); Pres. GUILLERMO FRANCOS; Gen. Man. EDUARDO ORDÓÑEZ; 385 brs.

Banco de la Provincia de Córdoba: San Jerónimo 231/235, X5000AGD Córdoba; tel. (351) 420-7507; fax (351) 420-7492; internet www.bancor.com.ar; f. 1873; provincial bank; cap. 210.2m., res 10.4m., dep. 4,491.3m. (Dec. 2008); Pres. MARIO CUNEO; Gen. Man. PABLO VIERA; 150 brs.

Banco Provincia del Neuquén: Avda Argentina 41, 1°, Q8300AYA Neuquén; tel. (299) 449-6618; fax (299) 449-6622; internet www.bpn.com.ar; f. 1960; cap. 42.3m., res 56.2m., dep. 1,199.7m. (Dec. 2007); Pres. OMAR GUTIÉRREZ; Gen. Man. ADRIANA VELASCO; 22 brs.

Banco de Tierra del Fuego: Maipú 897, V9410BJQ Ushuaia; tel. (2901) 441600; fax (2901) 441601; e-mail info@bancotdf.com.ar; internet www.bancotdf.com.ar; national bank; Pres. RICARDO IGLESIAS; Gen. Man. JORGE CERROTA; 8 brs.

Nuevo Banco de la Rioja, SA: Rivadavia 702, F5300ACU La Rioja; tel. (3822) 430575; fax (3822) 430618; e-mail nblrsa@nblr.com.ar; internet www.nblr.com.ar; f. 1994; provincial bank; cap. 44.5m., dep. 134.0m., total assets 180.7m. (Dec. 2003); Pres. ELIAS SAHAD; Gen. Man. CLAUDIA L. DE BRIGIDO; 13 brs.

Nuevo Banco de Santa Fe, SA: 25 de Mayo 2499, S3000FTS Santa Fe; tel. (342) 450-4700; fax (342) 440150; e-mail contactobc@bancobsf.com.ar; internet www.bancobsf.com.ar; f. 1847 as Banco Provincial de Santa Fe, adopted current name in 1998; provincial bank; cap. 90.8m., res 176.5m., dep. 3,637.6m. (Dec. 2005); Chair. ENRIQUE ESKINAZI; Exec. Dir MARCELO BUIL; 108 brs.

Private Commercial Banks

Banco BI Creditanstalt, SA: Bouchard 547, 24° y 25°, C1106ABG Buenos Aires; tel. (11) 4319-8400; fax (11) 4319-8230; e-mail info@bicreditanstalt.com.ar; internet www.bicreditanstalt.com.ar; f. 1971 as Banco Interfinanzas; adopted current name 1997; cap. 41.1m., res 403.7m., dep. 14m. (Dec. 2008); Pres. Dr MIGUEL ANGEL ANGELINO; Gen. Man. RICARDO RIVERO HAEDO.

Banco CMF, SA: Macacha Güemes 150, Puerto Madero, C1106BKD Buenos Aires; tel. (11) 4318-6800; fax (11) 4318-6859; e-mail info@bancocmf.com.ar; internet www.bancocmf.com.ar; f. 1978 as Corporación Metropolitana de Finanzas, SA; adopted current name in 1999; cap. 145.9m., res 38.7m., dep. 613.1m. (Dec. 2008); Pres. and Chair. JOSÉ ALBERTO BENEGAS LYNCH; Gen. Man. MARCOS PRIETO.

Banco COMAFI: Roque S. Peña 660, C1035AAO Buenos Aires; tel. (11) 4347-0400; fax (11) 4347-0404; e-mail contactenos@comafi.com.ar; internet www.comafi.com.ar; f. 1984; assumed control of 65% of Scotiabank Quilmes in April 2002; total assets US $410.1m. (June 2001); Pres. GUILLERMO CERVIÑO; Vice-Pres. EDUARDO MASCHWITZ; 56 brs.

Banco de Corrientes: 9 de Julio 1002, esq. San Juan, W3400AYQ Corrientes; tel. (3783) 479300; fax (3783) 479372; e-mail bcteservicios@bcoctes.com.ar; internet www.bancodecorrientes.com.ar; f. 1951; est. as Banco de la República de Corrientes; adopted current name in 1993, after transfer to private ownership; cap. and res 117.8m., dep. 737.5m. (Dec. 2008); Pres. Dr ALEJANDRO ABRAHAN; Gen. Man. CARLOS GUSTAVO MACORATTI; 33 brs.

Banco Finansur, SA: Sarmiento 700, esq. Maipú, Buenos Aires; tel. (11) 4324-3400; fax (11) 4322-4687; e-mail bafin@bancofinansur.com.ar; internet www.bancofinansur.com.ar; f. 1973; est. as Finansur Compañía Financiera, SA; adopted current name in 1993; cap. 25.7m., res 10.8m., dep. 321.3m. (Dec. 2008); Pres. JORGE SÁNCHEZ CÓRDOVA; 4 brs.

Banco de Galicia y Buenos Aires, SA: Juan D. Perón 407, Casilla 86, C1038AAI Buenos Aires; tel. (11) 6329-0000; fax (11) 6329-6100; e-mail bancogalicia@bancogalicia.com.ar; internet www.bancogalicia.com.ar; f. 1905; cap. 562.3m., res 1,193.3m., dep. 14,008.8m. (Dec. 2008); Chair. ANTONIO R. GARCÉS; 232 brs.

Banco Industrial: San Martin 549, Azul 7300, Buenos Aires; tel. (2281) 431779; e-mail sucazul@bancoindustrial.com.ar; internet www.bancoindustrial.com.ar; f. 1971; cap. 25.7m., res 96.8m., dep. 1,004.9m. (Dec. 2007); Pres. CARLOTA EVELINA DURST; Gen. Man. CLAUDIO MITEFF; 30 brs.

Banco Itaú Buen Ayre, SA: 25 de Mayo 476, 2°, C1002ABJ Buenos Aires; tel. (11) 4378-8400; fax (11) 4394-1057; e-mail contactenos@itau.com.ar; internet www.itau.com.ar; fmrly Banco Itaú Argentina, SA; renamed as above following purchase of Banco del Buen Ayre, SA, in 1998; subsidiary of Banco Itaú, SA (Brazil); 117 brs.

Banco Macro, SA: Sarmiento 447, 4°, C1041AAI Buenos Aires; tel. (11) 5222-6500; fax (11) 5222-6624; e-mail investorelations@macro.com.ar; internet www.macro.com.ar; f. 1995 as Banco Bansud by merger; merged with Banco Macro in 2002; adopted current name

2006; cap. 683.9m., res 881.0m., dep. 12,673.4m. (Dec. 2008); Pres. JORGE HORACIO BRITO; 400 brs.

Banco Mariva, SA: Sarmiento 500, C1041AAJ Buenos Aires; tel. (11) 4321-2200; fax (11) 4321-2292; e-mail info@mariva.com.ar; internet www.mariva.com.ar; f. 1980; cap. 7.1m., res 22.5m., dep. 282.3m. (Dec. 2006); Pres. RICARDO MAY.

Banco Patagonia, SA: Juan D. Perón 500, C1038AAJ Buenos Aires; tel. (11) 4132-6300; fax (11) 4132-6059; e-mail international@bancopatagonia.com.ar; internet www.bancopatagonia.com.ar; f. 1912; fmrly Banco Sudameris; adopted current name in 2004 following merger with Banco Patagonia; cap. 748.2m., res 404.1m., dep. 6,991.1m. (Dec. 2008); Chair. JORGE GUILLERMO STUART MILNE.

Banco Regional de Cuyo, SA: San Martín 841, M5500AAI Mendoza; tel. (261) 449-8800; fax (261) 449-8801; internet www.bancoregional.com.ar; f. 1961; Pres. and Gen. Man. JOSÉ FEDERICO LÓPEZ; 20 brs.

Banco de San Juan: Ignacio de la Roza 85, J5402DCA San Juan; tel. (264) 429-1000; fax (264) 421-4126; internet www.bancosanjuan.com; f. 1943; 20% owned by provincial govt of San Juan; 80% privately owned; Pres. ENRIQUE ESKENAZI; Gen. Man. MARIA SILVINA BELLANTIG TARDIO; 9 brs.

Banco Santander Río, SA: Bartolomé Mitre 480, C1036AAH Buenos Aires; tel. (11) 4341-1000; fax (11) 4341-1020; internet www.santanderrio.com.ar; f. 1908 as Banco Río de la Plata; adopted current name 2007; owned by Banco Santander (Spain); cap. 1,078.9m., res 215.8m., dep. 17,311.1m. (Dec. 2007); Pres. JOSÉ LUIS ENRIQUE CRISTOFANI; 276 brs.

Banco Santiago del Estero: Belgrano 529/37 Sur, G4200AAF Santiago del Estero; tel. (385) 450-2300; fax (385) 450-2316; e-mail info@bse.com.ar; internet www.bse.com.ar; Pres. NÉSTOR CARLOS ICK; Gen. Man. ALDO RENÉ MAZZOLENI.

Banco Supervielle, SA: Reconquista 330, C1003ABH Buenos Aires; tel. (11) 4324-8000; fax (11) 4324-8090; internet www.supervielle.com.ar; f. 1887; cap. 238.6m., res 15.8m., dep. 2,470.4m. (Dec. 2007); Pres. JUAN CARLOS NOUGUES; Gen. Man. JOSE LUIS PANERO; 79 brs.

Banco de Valores, SA: Sarmiento 310, C1041AAH Buenos Aires; tel. (11) 4323-6900; fax (11) 4323-6942; e-mail info@banval.sba.com.ar; internet www.bancodevalores.com; f. 1978; cap. 10.0m., res 58.6m., dep. 546.0m. (Dec. 2008); Pres. HÉCTOR JORGE BACQUÉ; 1 br.

BBVA Banco Francés, SA: Reconquista 199, C1003ABC Buenos Aires; tel. (11) 4346-4000; fax (11) 4346-4320; internet www.bancofrances.com; f. 1886 as Banco Francés del Río de la Plata, SA; changed name to Banco Francés, SA, in 1998 following merger with Banco de Crédito Argentino; adopted current name in 2000; cap. 471.4m., res 901.3m., dep. 17,281.6m. (Dec. 2008); Pres. JORGE C. BLEDEL; Dir RICARDO MORENO; 308 brs.

HSBC Bank Argentina, SA: Florida 229, C1005AAE Buenos Aires; tel. (11) 4320-2800; fax (11) 4132-2409; internet www.hsbc.com.ar; f. 1978 as Banco Roberts, SA; name changed to HSBC Banco Roberts, SA, in 1998; adopted current name in 1999; cap. 1,792.0m., res –193.6m., dep. 10,088.0m. (June 2008); Pres. ANTONIO M. LOSADA; 68 brs.

Nuevo Banco de Entre Ríos, SA: Monte Caseros 128, E3100ACD Paraná; tel. (343) 423-1200; fax (343) 421-1221; e-mail info@nuevobersa.com.ar; internet www.nuevobersa.com.ar; f. 1935; provincial bank; transferred to private ownership in 1995; cap. 20.4m., dep. 624.5m. (Dec. 2002); Pres. ENRIQUE ESKENAZI; Gen. Man. LUIS NÚÑEZ; 73 brs.

Standard Bank Argentina: Della Paolera 265, 13°, C1001ABA Buenos Aires; tel. (11) 4820-9200; fax (11) 4820-2050; e-mail standardbank.argentina@standardbank.com; internet www.standardbank.com.ar; f. 2005; cap. 847.0m., dep. 6,246.4m. (Dec. 2007), res –697,000 (Dec. 2006)); CEO EDUARDO SPANGENBERG; 96 brs.

Co-operative Bank

Banco Credicoop Cooperativo Ltdo: Reconquista 484, C1003ABJ Buenos Aires; tel. (11) 4320-5000; fax (11) 4324-5891; e-mail credicoop@bancocredicoop.coop; internet www.bancocredicoop.coop; f. 1979; cap. 848,000, res 730m., dep. 8,581.5m. (June 2008); Chair., Pres. and CEO CARLOS HELLER; Gen. Man. GERARDO GALMÉS; 244 brs.

Bankers' Associations

Asociación de Bancos Argentinos (ADEBA): Juan D. Perón 564, 6°, C1038AAL Buenos Aires; tel. and fax (11) 5238-7790; e-mail info@adebaargentina.com.ar; internet www.adebaargentina.com.ar; f. 1972; Pres. JORGE HORACIO BRITO; 28 mems.

Asociación de Bancos de la Argentina (ABA): San Martín 229, 10°, 1004 Buenos Aires; tel. (11) 4394-1836; fax (11) 4394-6340; e-mail webmaster@aba-argentina.com; internet www.aba-argentina.com; f. 1999 by merger of Asociación de Bancos de la República Argentina (f. 1919) and Asociación de Bancos Argentinos (f. 1972); Pres. Lic. MARIO LUIS VICENS; 27 mems.

Asociación de Bancos Públicos y Privados de la República Argentina (ABAPPRA): Florida 470, 1°, C1005AAJ Buenos Aires; tel. and fax (11) 4322-5342; e-mail info@abappra.com.ar; internet www.abappra.com; f. 1959; Pres. JUAN CARLOS FABREGA; Exec. Dir DEMETRIO BRAVO AGUILAR; 31 mems.

STOCK EXCHANGES

Mercado de Valores de Buenos Aires, SA: 25 de Mayo 367, 8°–10°, C1002ABG Buenos Aires; tel. and fax (11) 4316-6000; e-mail merval@merval.sba.com.ar; internet www.merval.sba.com.ar; f. 1929; Pres. PABLO ALDAZABAL.

There are also stock exchanges at Córdoba, Rosario, Mendoza and La Plata.

Supervisory Authority

Comisión Nacional de Valores (CNV): 25 de Mayo 175, C1002ABC Buenos Aires; tel. (11) 4329-4600; fax (11) 4331-0639; e-mail webadm@cnv.gov.ar; internet www.cnv.gob.ar; monitors capital markets; Pres. ALEJANDRO VANOLI.

INSURANCE

In June 2008 there were 179 insurance companies operating in Argentina, of which 100 were general insurance companies. The following is a list of those offering all classes or a specialized service.

Supervisory Authority

Superintendencia de Seguros de la Nación: Julio A. Roca 721, 5°, C1067ABC Buenos Aires; tel. (11) 4338-4000; fax (11) 4331-9821; e-mail consultasydenuncias@ssn.gov.ar; internet www.ssn.gov.ar; f. 1938; Supt Dr GUSTAVO MARCELO MEDONE.

Major Companies

Argos Cía Argentina de Seguros Generales, SA: Esmeralda 288, 7°, C1035ABF Buenos Aires; tel. (11) 4323-1200; fax (11) 4323-1299; internet www.argos-seguros.com; Pres. LUIS KSAIRI.

Aseguradora de Créditos y Garantías, SA (ACG): Maipú 71, 4°, C1084ABA Buenos Aires; tel. (11) 4320-7200; fax (11) 4320-7277; e-mail infoacg@bristolgroup.com.ar; internet www.bristolgroup.com.ar; f. 1961; part of the Bristol Group; Pres. HORACIO G. SCAPPARONE.

Aseguradores de Cauciones, SA: Paraguay 580, C1057AAF Buenos Aires; tel. (11) 5235-3700; fax (11) 5235-3784; e-mail consultas@caucion.com.ar; internet www.caucion.com.ar; f. 1968; all classes; Pres. JOSÉ DE VEDIA.

Caja de Seguros, SA: Fitz Roy 957, C1414CHI Buenos Aires; tel. (11) 4857-8118; fax (11) 4857-8001; internet www.lacaja.com.ar; f. 1992; Pres. GERARDO WERTHEIN.

Chiltington Internacional, SA: Reconquista 559, 8°, C1003ABK Buenos Aires; tel. (11) 4312-8600; fax (11) 4312-8884; e-mail msmith@chiltington.com.ar; internet chiltington.com; f. 1982; Pres. MARTIN SMITH.

Chubb Argentina de Seguros, SA: Ing. Butty 240, 16°, C1001AFB Buenos Aires; tel. (11) 4510-1500; fax (11) 4510-1545; e-mail argentinainfo@chubb.com; internet www.chubb.com/international/argentina; f. 2003; Pres. JOHN D. FINNEGAN.

Cía Argentina de Seguros de Créditos a la Exportación, SA: Corrientes 345, 7°, C1043AAD Buenos Aires; tel. (11) 4313-4303; fax (11) 4313-2919; e-mail info@casce.com.ar; internet www.casce.com.ar; f. 1967; covers credit and extraordinary and political risks for Argentine exports; Pres. EDUARDO ANGEL FORNS.

El Comercio, Cía de Seguros a Prima Fija, SA: Maipú 71, baja, C1084ABA Buenos Aires; tel. (11) 4324-1300; fax (11) 4393-1311; internet www.bristolgroup.com.ar; f. 1889; all classes; part of the Bristol Group; Pres. HORACIO G. SCAPPARONE; Vice-Pres. ANTONIO ALTIERI.

General & Cologne Re (Sur), Cía de Reaseguros, SA: Manuela Saenz 323–343, 7°, C1107BPA Buenos Aires; tel. (11) 4114-7000; fax (11) 4114-7001; e-mail jcomerio@genre.com; internet www.genre.com; Gen. Man. JUAN J. COMERIO.

Mapfre Argentina: Juana Manso 205, C1107CBE Buenos Aires; tel. (11) 4320-9439; fax (11) 4320-9444; internet www.mapfre.com.ar; all classes; Exec. Pres. DIEGO SERGIO SOBRINI.

La Meridional, Cía Argentina de Seguros, SA: Juan D. Perón 646, C1038AAN Buenos Aires; tel. (11) 4909-7000; fax (11) 4909-7455; e-mail lameridional@chartisinsurance.com; internet www.lameridional.com; f. 1949; part of America Int. Group, Inc (USA); life and general; Pres. JAIME DE JESÚS CALVO DEL ROSARIO.

Metropol Cía Argentina de Seguros, SA: Sarmiento 1182–1190, 3º, Buenos Aires; tel. (11) 4443-3830; Pres. CARLOS ALBERTO PINO.

Prudential Seguros, SA: Leandro N. Alem 855, 5°, C1001AAD Buenos Aires; tel. (11) 4891-5000; internet www.prudentialseguros .com.ar; Pres. MARTÍN EDUARDO GAUTO.

Royal & Sun Alliance Seguros (Argentina), SA (RSA): Lima 653, Buenos Aires; tel. (11) 4339-0000; fax (11) 4331-1453; internet www.rsagroup.com.ar; life and general; Pres. FERRARO ROBERTO PASCUAL.

Victoria Seguros, SA: Florida 556, C1005AAL Buenos Aires; tel. (11) 4322-1100; fax (11) 4325-9016; e-mail seguros@victoria.com.ar; internet www.victoria.com.ar; f. 1921; Pres. SEBASTIÁN BAGÓ; Vice-Pres. and Exec. Dir DANIEL RICARDO SALAZAR.

Zurich Argentina Cía de Seguros, SA: Cerrito 1010, C1010AAV Buenos Aires; tel. (11) 4819-1010; internet www.zurich.com.ar; f. 1947; all classes; Pres. CARLOS RAMÓN LODEIRO.

Insurance Association

Asociación Argentina de Cías de Seguros (AACS): 25 de Mayo 565, 2°, C1002ABK Buenos Aires; tel. (11) 4312-7790; fax (11) 4312-6300; e-mail info@aacs.org.ar; internet www.aacs.org.ar; f. 1894; 31 mems; Pres. FRANCISCO ASTELARRA.

Trade and Industry

GOVERNMENT AGENCIES

Agencia Nacional de Desarrollo de Inversiones (ProsperAr): Florida 375, 8°B, C1005AAG Buenos Aires; tel. (11) 4328-9510; e-mail info@prosperar.gov.ar; internet www.prosperar.gov.ar; promotion of investment in Argentina; Dir Dra BEATRIZ NOFAL.

Consejo Federal de Inversiones: San Martín 871, C1004AAQ Buenos Aires; tel. (11) 4317-0700; fax (11) 4315-1238; e-mail info@cfired.org.ar; internet www.cfired.org.ar; f. 1959; federal board to co-ordinate domestic and foreign investment and provide technological aid for the provinces; Sec.-Gen. JUAN JOSÉ CIÁCERA.

Dirección de Forestación (DF): Paseo Colón 982, Anexo Jardín, C1063ACW Buenos Aires; tel. (11) 4349-2124; fax (11) 4349-2102; e-mail bfores@minagri.gob.ar; internet www.forestacion.gov.ar; assumed the responsibilities of the national forestry commission (Instituto Forestal Nacional—IFONA) in 1991, following its dissolution; supervised by the Secretaría de Agricultura, Ganadería, Pesca y Alimentos; maintains the Centro de Documentación e Información Forestal; Dir GUSTAVO CORTÉS.

Instituto de Desarrollo Económico y Social (IDES): Aráoz 2838, C1425DGT Buenos Aires; tel. (11) 4804-4949; fax (11) 4804-5856; e-mail ides@ides.org.ar; internet www.ides.org.ar; f. 1960; investigation into social sciences and promotion of social and economic devt; 1,100 mems; Pres. MARIANO PLOTKIN.

Ministry of Agriculture, Livestock and Fisheries: see The Government (Ministries).

Oficina Nacional de Control Comercial Agropecuario (ONCCA): Paseo Colón 922, C1063ACW Buenos Aires; tel. (11) 4349-2492; fax (11) 4349-2005; e-mail infooncca@mecon.gov.ar; internet www.oncca.gov.ar; oversees the agricultural sector; supervised by the Secretaría de Agricultura, Ganadería, Pesca y Alimentos; Pres. JUAN MANUEL CAMPILLO.

Organismo Nacional de Administración de Bienes (ONABE): José Ramos Mejía 1302, 3°, Of. 300, C1104AJN Buenos Aires; tel. (11) 4318-3658; e-mail sistemas@onabe.gov.ar; internet www.onabe.gov .ar; f. 2000; responsible for administration of state property; supervised by the Ministry of Federal Planning, Public Investment and Services; Dir JOSÉ FRANCISCO LÓPEZ; Exec. Dir FERNANDO MIGUEL SUÁREZ.

DEVELOPMENT ORGANIZATIONS

Instituto Argentino del Petróleo y Gas: Maipú 639, C1006ACG Buenos Aires; tel. (11) 4325-8008; fax (11) 4393-5494; e-mail informa@iapg.org.ar; internet www.iapg.org.ar; f. 1957; promotes the devt of petroleum exploration and research; Pres. ERNESTO LÓPEZ ANADÓN.

Instituto para el Desarrollo Social Argentino (IDESA): Montevideo 451, 3°, Of. 33, C1019ABI Buenos Aires; tel. (11) 4371-1177; internet www.idesa.org; centre for research in public policies related to social devt; Pres. OSVALDO GIORDANO; Exec. Dir ALEJANDRA TORRES.

Sociedad Rural Argentina: Florida 460, C1005AAJ Buenos Aires; tel. (11) 4324-4700; e-mail prensa@sra.org.ar; internet www.sra.org .ar; f. 1866; private org. to promote the devt of agriculture; Pres. Dr HUGO LUIS BIOLCATI; 9,400 mems.

CHAMBERS OF COMMERCE

Cámara Argentina de Comercio: Leandro N. Alem 36, C1003AAN Buenos Aires; tel. (11) 5300-9000; fax (11) 5300-9058; e-mail difusion2@cac.com.ar; internet www.cac.com.ar; f. 1927; Pres. CARLOS RAÚL DE LA VEGA.

Cámara de Comercio de los Estados Unidos en la República Argentina (AMCHAM): Viamonte 1133, 8°, C1053ABW Buenos Aires; tel. (11) 4371-4500; fax (11) 4371-8400; e-mail amcham@amchamar.com.ar; internet www.amchamar.com.ar; f. 1918; US Chamber of Commerce; CEO ALEJANDRO DÍAZ.

Cámara de Comercio Exterior de Rosario: Córdoba 1868, Rosario, S2000AXD Santa Fe; tel. and fax (341) 425-7147; e-mail consultas@commerce.com.ar; internet www.commerce.com.ar; f. 1958; deals with imports and exports; Pres. JUAN CARLOS RETAMERO; Vice-Pres. GUILLERMO BECCANI; 150 mems.

Cámara de Comercio, Industria y Producción de la República Argentina: Florida 1, 4°, C1005AAA Buenos Aires; tel. (11) 4331-0813; fax (11) 4331-9116; e-mail cacipra@fibertel.com.ar; internet www.cacipra.org.ar; f. 1913; Pres. Dr CAYETANO NINO ROTA; 1,500 mems.

Cámara de Comercio Italiana de Rosario: Córdoba 1868, 1°, S2000AXD, Rosario; tel. and fax (341) 426–68789; e-mail ngonzalez@italrosario.com; internet www.ccir.com.ar; f. 1985; promotes Argentine–Italian trade; Dir GUSTAVO MICATROTTA.

Cámara de Exportadores de la República Argentina: Roque Sáenz Peña 740, 1°, C1035AAP Buenos Aires; tel. and fax (11) 4394-4482; e-mail contacto@cera.org.ar; internet www.cera.org.ar; f. 1943; export promotion; 700 mems; Pres. Dr ENRIQUE S. MANTILLA.

Similar chambers are located in most of the larger centres, and there are many other foreign chambers of commerce.

INDUSTRIAL AND TRADE ASSOCIATIONS

Asociación Argentina de Productores Porcinos: Florida 520, C1005AAL Buenos Aires; internet www.porcinos.org.ar; f. 1922; promotion of pork products; Pres. JUAN LUIS UCCELLI.

Asociación Argentina de Químicos y Coloristas Textiles: Simbrón 5756, C1408BHJ Buenos Aires; tel. (11) 4644-3996; fax (11) 4644-7520; e-mail aaqct@aaqct.org.ar; internet www.aaqct.org .ar; f. 1954; textile industry; Pres. GUILLERMO CEVASCO.

Asociación de Importadores y Exportadores de la República Argentina: Manuel Belgrano 124, 1°, C1092AAO Buenos Aires; tel. (11) 4342-0010; fax (11) 4342-1312; e-mail aiera@aiera.org.ar; internet www.aiera.org; f. 1966; Pres. HORACIO CONSOLO; Man. ADRIANO A. DE FINA.

Consorcio de Exportadores de Carnes Argentinas (ABC): San Martín 575, 5°B, C1004AAK Buenos Aires; tel. (11) 4394-9734; fax (11) 4394-9658; e-mail gerencia@abc-consorcio.com.ar; internet www.abc-consorcio.com.ar; f. 2002 following the merger between the Asociación de Industrias Argentinas de Carnes and several meat exporters; meat industry; refrigerated and canned beef and mutton; Pres. MARIO DARÍO RAVETTINO.

Bodegas de Argentina: Thames 2334, 16A, C1425FIH Buenos Aires; tel. (11) 5786-1220; fax (11) 5786-1266; e-mail info@bodegasdeargentinaac.com; internet www.bodegasdeargentina.org; f. 2001 following merger between Centro de Bodegueros de Mendoza and Asociación Vitivinícola Argentina; wine industry; Pres. ÁNGEL VESPA.

Cámara de la Industria Aceitera de la República Argentina—Centro de Exportadores de Cereales: Bouchard 454, 7°, C1106ABS Buenos Aires; tel. (11) 4311-4477; fax (11) 4311-3899; internet www.ciaracec.com.ar; f. 1980; vegetable oil producers and grain exporters; Pres. RAÚL PADILLA.

Cámara de Sociedades Anónimas: Libertad 1340, C1016ABB Buenos Aires; tel. and fax (11) 4000-7399; fax (11) 4000-7703; e-mail camsocanon@camsocanon.com; internet www.camsocanon.com; Pres. HORACIO DE LAS CARRERAS; Man. EDUARDO BACQUÉ.

Confederación Argentina de la Mediana Empresa (CAME): Florida 15, 3°, C1005AAA Buenos Aires; tel. (11) 5556-5556; fax (11) 5556-5502; e-mail info@came.org.ar; internet www.came.org.ar; f. 1956; fmrly Coordinadora de Actividades Mercantiles Empresariales; adopted current name 2006; small and medium enterprises; Pres. OSVALDO CORNIDE.

Confederaciones Rurales Argentinas: México 628, 2°, C1097AAN Buenos Aires; tel. (11) 4300-4451; internet www.cra .org.ar; f. 1943; promotion and devt of agricultural activities; 13 federations comprising over 300 mem. orgs, representing 109,000 farmers; Pres. MARIO LLAMBÍAS.

Federación Agraria Argentina (FAA): Alfonsina Storni 745, S2000DYA Rosario, Santa Fe; tel. (341) 512-2000; fax (341) 512-2001; e-mail comunicacion@faa.com.ar; internet www.faa.com.ar; f. 1912; oversees the interests of small and medium-sized grain producers; Pres. EDUARDO BUZZI.

Federación Lanera Argentina: 25 de Mayo 516, 4°, C1002ABL Buenos Aires; tel. (11) 4878-8800; fax (11) 4878-8804; e-mail info@

flasite.com; internet www.flasite.com; f. 1929; wool industry; Pres. Raúl Ernesto Zamboni; Sec. Juan Pablo Lefebvre; 40 mems.

EMPLOYERS' ORGANIZATION

Unión Industrial Argentina (UIA): Avda de Mayo 1147/57, C1085ABB Buenos Aires; tel. (11) 4124-2300; fax (11) 4124-2301; e-mail uia@uia.org.ar; internet www.uia.org.ar; f. 1887; re-established in 1974 with the fusion of the Confederación Industrial Argentina (CINA) and the Confederación General de la Industria; following the dissolution of the CINA in 1977, the UIA was formed in 1979; asscn of manufacturers, representing industrial corpns; Pres. Héctor Méndez; Sec. Dr José Ignacio de Mendiguren.

MAJOR COMPANIES

AcerBrag, SA (Aceros Bragado): Panamericana Km 49.5, Edif. Boreau Pilar, 1°, 1629 Pilar, CD1629 Buenos Aires; tel. (11) 4006-7100; internet www.acerbrag.com; f. 1969; foundry, mill rolls, bearing trucks, laminating; 53% owned by Votorantim Metais, Brazil; Pres. Luisa Vara; 495 employees.

Acindar, SA: Estanislao Zeballos 2739, B1643AGY Beccar, Buenos Aires; tel. (11) 4719-8500; fax (11) 4719-8501; e-mail sac@acindar.com.ar; internet www.acindar.com.ar; f. 1942; production of iron and steel; part of ArcelorMittal group (Luxembourg); Pres. and CEO Arturo Acevedo; 3,922 employees.

Agrometal, SA: Misiones 1974, X2659BIN Monte Maiz, Córdoba; tel. (34) 6847-1311; fax (34) 6847-1804; internet www.agrometal.com; manufacture of agricultural machinery; Chair. Rosana María Negrini.

Alpargatas, SAIC: Regimiento de Los Patricios 1142, C1265AER Buenos Aires; tel. (11) 4303-0041; fax (11) 4303-2401; internet www.alpargatas.com.ar; f. 1885; textile and footwear manufacturers; Pres. Márcio Luiz Simoes Utsch; 4,000 employees.

ALUAR (Aluminio Argentino, SAIC): Pasteur 4600, B1644AMV Victoria, Buenos Aires; tel. (11) 4725-8060; fax (11) 4725-8091; internet www.aluar.com.ar; f. 1970; aluminium production; Pres. Javier Madanes Quintanilla; 2,216 employees.

Atanor, SCA: Albarellos 4914, B1605AFR Munro, Buenos Aires; tel. (11) 4721-3400; internet www.atanor.com.ar; f. 1943; producers of chemicals, petrochemicals, agrochemicals and sugar; Pres. Miguel Angel González; 768 employees.

Bayer Argentina, SA: Ricardo Gutiérrez 3652, B1605EHD Munro, Buenos Aires; tel. (11) 4762-7000; fax (11) 4762-7100; internet www.bayer.com.ar; f. 1911; production of chemicals, agrochemicals and pharmaceuticals; parent co Bayer AG, Germany; Pres. Werner Wenning.

BGH, SA: Brasil 731, C1154AAK Buenos Aires; tel. (11) 4309-2001; fax (11) 6310-4033; e-mail info@bgh.com.ar; internet www.bgh.com.ar; electronic appliances manufacturers; f. 1913 as Boris Garfunkel e Hijos; Pres. Alberto Hojman; Gen. Man. Eduardo Scarpello.

Boldt, SA: Aristóbulo del Valle 1257, C1295ADA Buenos Aires; tel. (11) 4309-5400; fax (11) 4361-3435; e-mail contact@boldt.com.ar; internet www.boldt.com.ar; information technology, telecommunications, land and leisure management; Chair. Antonio Angel Tabanelli; 932 employees.

Borax Argentina, SA: Huaytiquina 227, Campo Quijano, A4407AVE Salta; tel. (38) 7490-4030; fax (38) 4920-4031; e-mail boraxargentina@borax.com; internet www.borax.com/borax4h.html; owned by Rio Tinto; mining of borates; Pres. Alberto Trunzo.

CANALE, SA: Martín García 320, C1165ABP Buenos Aires; tel. (11) 4307-4000; fax (11) 4307-3003; f. 1975; manufacturers of biscuits; Gen. Man. Carlos Mollineri; 1,688 employees.

Celulosa Argentina, SA: Dardo Rocha 3278, Martínez, 1640 Buenos Aires; tel. (11) 4717-6077; e-mail contacto.comercial@celulosaargentina.com.ar; internet www.celulosaargentina.com.ar; f. 1929; manufacturers of paper and paper products; Pres. Douglas Albrecht; 1,900 employees.

Cementos Minetti (Juan Minetti, SA): A. Moreau de Justo 140, 1°, C1107AAD Buenos Aires; tel. (11) 4510-4800; fax (11) 4510-4859; e-mail conexion@grupominetti.com.ar; internet www.cementosminetti.com.ar; f. 1932; manufacturers of hydraulic cement; Pres. Dr Juan Javier Negri; Gen. Man. Otmar Hübscher; 830 employees.

Cervecería y Maltería Quilmes, SAICA: 12 de Octubre y Gran Canaria s/n, B1878AAB Quilmes, Buenos Aires; tel. (11) 4394-1700; fax (11) 4326-0026; e-mail contacto@cerveceriaymalteriaquilmes.com; internet www.cerveceriaymalteriaquilmes.com; f. 1888; beer and malt producers; Exec. Dir Felipe Rodríguez Laguens; 4,700 employees.

Chevron Argentina: Peron 925, 4°, C1038AAS Buenos Aires; tel. (11) 4320-7400; internet www.chevron.com/countries/argentina; wholly owned subsidiary of Chevron Corpn, USA; Pres. Ian Partridge.

Compañía Azucarera Concepción, SA: San Martín 662, 5°, C1004AAN Buenos Aires; tel. (11) 4311-3444; fax (11) 4312-0418; owned by Atanor, SCA; manufacturers of sugar cane and alcohol; Pres. Horacio García González; 3,289 employees.

Disco, SA: Larrea 847, 1°, 1117 Buenos Aires; tel. (11) 4964-8000; fax (11) 4964-8039; e-mail feedback@disco.com.ar; internet www.disco.com.ar; f. 1961; owned by Cencosud, SA (Chile); supermarket chain; CEO Alfredo García Pye.

Dow Química Argentina, SA: Eduardo Madero 900, 7°, C1106ACV Buenos Aires; tel. (11) 4319-0100; fax (11) 4319-0381; e-mail fbepoli@dow.com; internet www.dow.com; fmrly PBBPolisur, SA; wholly owned by Dow Chemical since 2005; petrochemicals; Chair. and CEO Andrew N. Liveris.

Dycasa, SA: Avda Leandro N. Alem 986, 4°, C1001AAR Buenos Aires; tel. (11) 4318-0200; fax (11) 4318-0230; e-mail info@dycasa.com.ar; internet www.dycasa.com; construction; Pres. Pablo Ruiz Parrilla.

Eco de los Andes, SA: 12 de Octubre y Gran Canaria, C1878AAB Quilmes; internet www.ecodelosandes.com.ar; f. 1994; 51% owned by Nestlé Waters (Switzerland) and 49% owned by Quilmes Industrial, Luxembourg; bottled water producer.

Esso SA Petrolera Argentina: Carlos María Della Paolera 297, 12°, C1001ADA Buenos Aires; tel. (11) 4319-1400; fax (11) 4319-1163; f. 1911; active in all spheres of the petroleum industry; subsidiary of Exxon Corpn, USA; Man. Jens Dreyer; Public Relations Man. Tomás D. Hess; 2,000 employees.

Ferrum, SA de Cerámica y Metalurgia: España 496, B1870BWJ Avellaneda, Buenos Aires; tel. (11) 4222-1500; fax (11) 4229-6244; e-mail info@ferrum.com; internet www.ferrum.com; f. 1911; manufacturers of sanitary products and building materials; Pres. Ing. Guillermo Viegener; Man. Dir Daniel H. Calabró.

Ford Argentina, SA: Henry Ford/Ruta Panamericana s/n, Ricardo Rojas, 1617 Buenos Aires; tel. (11) 4756-9000; fax (11) 4756-9001; internet www.ford.com.ar; f. 1913; manufacture of motor vehicles; owned by Ford Motor Co, USA; Pres. Enrique Alemañy; 5,200 employees.

General Electric Technical Services Co, Inc: Leandro N. Alem 619, 9°, 1001 Buenos Aires; tel. (11) 4313-2880; fax (11) 4313-2880; internet www.ge.com/ar; f. 1920; sales of industrial equipment; engineering services; subsidiary of International General Electric Co, USA; Pres. Alejandro Bottan; 900 employees.

Grimoldi, SA: Zapiola 1863, B1712ISQ Castelar, Buenos Aires; e-mail sugerencias@mail.grimoldi.com.ar; internet www.grimoldi.com.ar; footwear retailers; Pres. Alberto Luis Grimoldi.

Grupo Estrella, SA: Constituyentes 2995, C1427BLA Buenos Aires; tel. (11) 4254-8100; fax (11) 4522-3022; e-mail info@quimicaestrella.com.ar; f. 1906; fmrly Química Estrella, SACII; pharmaceutical manufacturers; Pres. Guillermo Nelson García Abal; 600 employees.

IBM Argentina, SA: Hipólito Yrigoyen 2149, Martínez, C1089AAO Buenos Aires; tel. (11) 4898-4898; fax (11) 4313-2360; e-mail ibm_directo@ar.ibm.com; internet www.ibm.com.ar; f. 1923; computer hardware and software; owned by IBM Corpn, USA; Gen. Man., Spanish South America and Pres., IBM Argentina Miguel Becerra; Gen. Man. Guillermo Cascio; 7,200 employees.

Inversiones y Representaciones, SA (IRSA): Edif. Intercontinental Plaza, 22°, Moreno 877, C1091AAQ Buenos Aires; tel. (11) 4323-7400; fax (11) 4323-7480; e-mail finanzas@irsa.com.ar; internet www.irsa.com.ar; f. 1943; land and property development; Chair. Eduardo Sergio Elsztain.

Kraft Foods, SA Argentina: Henry Ford 3200, B1610BKW Ricardo Rojas, Tigre, Buenos Aires; tel. (33) 2741-2600; e-mail consultas.ar@kraftla.com; internet www.kraftfoods.com.ar; f. 1933; chocolate, sweets and frozen confectionery; owned by Kraft Foods, Inc (USA); Pres., Latin America Gustavo Abelenda.

Ledesma, SAAIC: Corrientes 415, 8°, C1043AAE Buenos Aires; tel. (11) 4378-1555; fax (11) 4325-7666; e-mail adiciancio@ledesma.com.ar; internet www.ledesma.com.ar; f. 1908; sugar producers; Pres. Dr Carlos Pedro Blaquier; 3,970 employees.

Loma Negra, CIASA: Bouchard 680, C1106ABJ Buenos Aires; tel. (11) 4319-3000; fax (11) 4319-3003; e-mail info@lomanegra.com.ar; internet www.lomanegra.com.ar; f. 1926; subsidiary of Camargo Corrêa, SA (Brazil); cement and building materials manufacturing; Dir-Gen. Ricardo Lima.

Massalin Particulares, SA: Leandro N. Alem 466, 9°, C1003AAR Buenos Aires; tel. and fax (11) 4319-4100; f. 1980; owned by Philip Morris Int; cigarette and tobacco producers; Pres., Latin America and Canada James R. Mortensen; 2,600 employees.

Mercedes Benz Argentina, SACIFIM: Blvd Azucena Villaflor 435, Puerto Madero, C1107CII Buenos Aires; tel. (11) 4808-8700; fax (11) 4808-8701; e-mail soledad.carranza@daimler.com; internet www.mercedes-benz.com.ar; f. 1951; manufacturers of trucks, buses and engines; subsidiary of Daimler Benz AG, Germany; Pres. MATTHIAS BARTH; 1,600 employees.

Molinos Río de la Plata, SA: Uruguay 4075, B1644HKG Victoria, Buenos Aires; tel. (11) 4340-1100; fax (11) 4340-1200; e-mail atconsum@molinos.com.ar; internet www.molinos.com.ar; f. 1902; manufacturers of flour and grain products; part of the Pérez Companc group; COO GUILLERMO GARCÍA; 5,000 employees.

Morixe Hermanos, SA: Santa Fe 846, 8°, C1059ABP Buenos Aires; tel. (11) 4312-8500; fax (11) 4431-4079; e-mail info@morixehnos.com.ar; internet www.morixe.com.ar; f. 1923; flour and grain processing; Pres. JORGE JERÓNIMO DE ACHÁVAL.

Nestlé Argentina: Libertador 1855, Vicente López, C1425AAE Buenos Aires; tel. (11) 4329-8100; fax (11) 4329-8200; e-mail servicios.alconsumidor@ar.nestle.com; internet www.nestle.com.ar; manufacturers of condensed milk, instant coffee, milk powder and confectionery; subsidiary of Nestlé, SA, Switzerland; f. 1930; Pres. and Dir-Gen. PABLO DEVOTO; 3,400 employees.

Nobleza-Piccardo, SAICF: San Martín 645,CP 899, B1650HVE Buenos Aires; tel. (11) 4724-8444; fax (11) 4313-2499; internet www.noblezapiccardo.com; f. 1898; cigarette and tobacco manufacturers; owned by British American Tobacco; Pres. and Gen. Man. MARK M. COBBEN; 1,200 employees.

Peugeot Citroën Argentina, SA: Juan Domingo Perón 1001, Villa Bosch, 1682 Provincia de Buenos Aires; tel. (11) 4734-3005; fax (11) 4734-3007; internet www.peugeot.com.ar; f. 1965 as Sevel Argentina, SA; subsidiary of PSA Peugeot Citroën, France; automobile manufacturers; Pres. and Dir-Gen. JAVIER VARELA SOBRADO; 3,600 employees.

Philips Argentina, SA: Vedía 3892, C1430DAL Buenos Aires; tel. (11) 4546-7777; fax (11) 4546-7600; internet www.philips.com.ar; f. 1935; manufacturers of electrical equipment; subsidiary of Koninklijke Philips Electronics NV, Netherlands; CEO GUSTAVO VERNA.

Pirelli Neumaticos, SAIC: Cervantes 1901, Merlo, 1722 Buenos Aires; tel. (11) 4489-6000; fax (11) 4489-6603; internet www.pirelli.com.ar; Dir, Admin. FRANCISCO GORI; f. 1948; 1,900 employees.

Pluspetrol Exploración y Producción, SA: Edif. Pluspetrol, Lima 339, C1073AAG Buenos Aires; tel. (11) 4340-2222; fax (11) 4340-2215; e-mail rrhh-cv@pluspetrol.net; internet www.pluspetrol.net; f. 1977; oil and gas exploration and production; Chair. and Pres. LUIS ALBERTO REY; Country Man. ALFREDO POLI; 497 employees.

Renault Argentina, SA: Fray Justo María de Oro 1744, 1414 Buenos Aires; tel. (11) 4778-2000; fax (11) 4778-2023; e-mail src-renault.argentina@renault.com; internet www.renault.com.ar; f. 1955 as Ciadea, SA; subsidiary of Renault, SA, France; motor vehicle manufacturers; Pres. DOMINIQUE MACIET; 2,211 employees.

Repsol YPF, SA: Macacha Güemes 515, CP 1364, C1106BKK Buenos Aires; tel. (11) 4329-2000; fax (11) 4329-5717; e-mail federico.etiennot@ypf.com; internet www.ypf.com; f. 1922 as Yacimientos Petrolíferos Fiscales, a state-owned company; bought by Repsol (Spain) and adopted current name 1992; petroleum and gas exploration and production; Exec. Pres. ANTONI BRUFAU NIUBÓ; Dir-Gen., YPF ANTONIO GOMIS SÁEZ; 9,750 employees.

Rigolleau, SA: Lisandro de la Torre 1651, Berazategui, B1884MFK Buenos Aires; tel. (11) 4256-2010; fax (11) 4256-2544; e-mail info@rigolleau.com.ar; internet www.rigolleau.com.ar; f. 1882; makers of glass and glass products; Pres. ENRIQUE FRANCISCO CATTORINI; 1,485 employees.

Roggio, SA: La Voz del Interior 8500, X5000FMR Córdoba; tel. (351) 638-0000; fax (351) 638-0001; e-mail contacto@roggio.com.ar; internet www.roggio.com.ar; f. 1908; group of construction companies; Pres. VITO REMO ROGGIO; 2,156 employees.

Shell Compañía Argentina de Petróleo, SA: Roque Saenz Peña 788, C1035AAP Buenos Aires; tel. (11) 4130-2000; e-mail shelldirecto.arg@shell.com; internet www.shell.com.ar; f. 1922; active in all spheres of the petroleum industry; owned by Royal Dutch Shell; Pres. in Argentina JUAN JOSÉ ARANGUREN.

Tabacal Agroindustria: Leandro N. Alem 986, 9°, C1001AAR Buenos Aires; tel. (11) 5167-2100; fax (11) 4576-7720; e-mail ingenio@tabacal.com.ar; internet www.tabacal.com.ar; f. 1920; sugar and alcohol production; owned by Seaboard Corpn of the USA; Pres. HUGO ROSSI.

Techint Compañía Técnica Internacional, SACI: Torre Bouchard Plaza, Hipólito Bouchard 557, C1106ABG Buenos Aires; tel. (11) 4018-4100; fax (11) 4018-1000; e-mail info@techint.com; internet engineering.techint.com; f. 1945; steel and petroleum extraction and refining; part of the Techint Group; Exec. Pres. and CEO CARLOS BACHER.

Ternium, SA: Edif. Carlos Pellegrini, 20°, Leandro N. Alem 1067, C1001AAF Buenos Aires; tel. (11) 4018-2100; fax (11) 4018-1026; e-mail aparej@siderar.com; internet www.ternium.com; f. 1962; part of the Techint Group; manufacturers of steel; also operates in Mexico and Venezuela; Pres. PAOLO ROCCA; CEO DANIEL NOVEGIL; 5,695 employees.

UTILITIES

Regulatory Authorities

Compañía Administradora del Mercado Mayorista Eléctrico, SA (CAMMESA): Avda Madero 942, 1°, C1106ACW Buenos Aires; tel. (11) 4319-3700; e-mail agentes@cammesa.com.ar; internet portalweb.cammesa.com; f. 1992; responsible for administering the wholesale electricity market; 20% state-owned, 80% by electricity companies; Pres. JULIO MIGUEL DE VIDO (Minister of Federal Planning, Public Investment and Services).

Ente Nacional Regulador de la Electricidad (ENRE): Avda Eduardo Madero 1020, 10°, C1106ACX Buenos Aires; tel. (11) 4510-4600; fax (11) 4510-4210; internet www.enre.gov.ar; f. 1993; agency for regulation and control of electricity generation, transmission and distribution; Pres. MARIO DE CASAS.

Ente Nacional Regulador del Gas (ENARGAS): Suipacha 636, 10°, C1008AAN Buenos Aires; tel. (11) 4325-2500; fax (11) 4348-0550; internet www.enargas.gov.ar; regulates and monitors gas utilities; Insp. ANTONIO LUIS PRONSATO.

Electricity

Central Puerto, SA (CEPU): Tomás Edison 2701, C1104BAB Buenos Aires; tel. (11) 4317-5000; fax (11) 4317-5099; e-mail info@centralpuerto.com; internet www.centralpuerto.com; electricity generating co; Pres. BERNARDO VELAR DE IRIGOYEN.

Comisión Nacional de Energía Atómica (CNEA): Avda del Libertador 8250, C1429BNP Buenos Aires; tel. (11) 4704-1000; fax (11) 4704-1154; e-mail comunicacion@cnea.gov.ar; internet www.cnea.gov.ar; f. 1950; nuclear energy science and technology; operates three nuclear power stations for research purposes; Pres. NORMA LUISA BOERO.

Comisión Técnica Mixta de Salto Grande (CTMSG): Leandro N. Alem 449, C1003AAE Buenos Aires; tel. (11) 5554-3400; fax (11) 5554-3402; e-mail ctmsgda@sion.com; internet www.saltogrande.org; operates Salto Grande hydroelectric station, which has an installed capacity of 650 MW; joint Argentine-Uruguayan project; Pres., Argentine delegation ENRIQUE TOPOLANSKY; Gen. Mans CARLOS MASCINO (Argentina), HUGO MAQUEIRA (Uruguay).

Dirección Provincial de Energía: Calle 55, 629,e/7 y 8, La Plata, B1900BGY Buenos Aires; tel. and fax (221) 427-1185; e-mail dpe@dpe.mosp.gba.gov.ar; internet www.dpe.mosp.gba.gov.ar; f. 1957 as Dirección de Energía de la Provincia de Buenos Aires; name changed as above in 2000; electricity co for province of Buenos Aires; Dir NÉSTOR CALLEGARI.

Empresa Distribuidora y Comercializadora Norte, SA (EDENOR): Azopardo 1025,16° y 17°, C1107ADQ Buenos Aires; tel. (11) 4348-2121; fax (11) 4334-0805; e-mail ofitel@edenor.com.ar; internet www.edenor.com.ar; f. 1992; distribution of electricity; Pres. ALEJANDRO MACFARLANE.

Empresa Distribuidora Sur, SA (EDESUR): San José 140, C1076AAD Buenos Aires; tel. (11) 4381-8981; fax (11) 4383-3699; e-mail prensa@edesur.com.ar; internet www.edesur.com.ar; f. 1992; distribution of electricity; Gen. Man. JOSÉ MARÍA HIDALGO.

Endesa Costanera, SA (CECCO): España 3301, C1107ANA Buenos Aires; tel. (11) 4307-3040; fax (11) 4300-4168; e-mail comercialweb@ccostanera.com.ar; internet www.endesacostanera.com; subsidiary of Endesa (Spain); generation, transmission, distribution and sale of thermal electric energy; Pres. JOSEPH M. HIDALGO MARTÍN-MATEOS; Gen. Man. JOSÉ MIGUEL GRANGED BRUÑEN.

Energía Argentina, SA (ENARSA): Avda Libertador 1068, 2°, C1112ABN Buenos Aires; tel. and fax (11) 4801-9325; e-mail contacto@enarsa.com.ar; internet www.enarsa.com.ar; f. 2004; state-owned; generation and distribution of electricity, especially from renewable sources; exploration, extraction and distribution of natural gas and petroleum; Pres. EXEQUIEL OMAR ESPINOSA.

Entidad Binacional Yacyretá: Eduardo Madero 942, 21°, C1106ACW Buenos Aires; tel. (11) 4510-7500; e-mail rrpp@eby.org.ar; internet www.eby.org.ar; operates the hydroelectric dam at Yacyretá on the Paraná river; owned jointly by Argentina and Paraguay; completed in 1998, it is one of the world's largest hydroelectric complexes, consisting of 20 generators with a total generating capacity of 3,200 MW; 14,673 GWh of electricity produced in 2007; Exec. Dir OSCAR ALFREDO THOMAS.

Hidronor Ingeniería y Servicios, SA (HISSA): Hipólito Yrigoyen 1530, 6°B, C1089AAD Buenos Aires; tel. and fax (11) 4382-6316; fax (11) 4382-5111; e-mail hidronor@ciudad.com.ar; internet www.hidronor.com; f. 1967; fmrly HIDRONOR, SA, the largest producer of electricity in Argentina; responsible for developing the hydroelectric potential of the Limay and neighbouring rivers; Pres. CARLOS

Alberto Rocca; transferred to private ownership in 1992 and divided into the following companies.

Central Hidroeléctrica Alicurá, SA: Leandro N. Alem 712, 7°, C1001AAP Buenos Aires.

Central Hidroeléctrica Cerros Colorados, SA: Leandro N. Alem 690, 12°, C1001AAO Buenos Aires.

Central Hidroeléctrica El Chocón, SA: Suipacha 268, 9°, Of. A, C1008AAF Buenos Aires.

Hidroeléctrica Piedra del Aguila, SA: Tomás Edison 1251, C1104AYL Buenos Aires; tel. and fax (11) 4311-3296; Pres. Dr Jérôme Ferrier; Gen. Man. Horacio Turri.

Transener, SA: Paseo Colón 728, 6°, C1063ACU Buenos Aires; tel. (11) 4342-6925; fax (11) 4342-7147; e-mail info-trans@transx.com.ar; internet www.transener.com.ar; energy transmission co; Gen. Man. Carlos A. González.

Petrobrás Energía, SA: Maipú 1, 22°, C1084ABA Buenos Aires; tel. (11) 4344-6000; fax (11) 4344-6315; internet www.petrobras.com.ar; f. 1946 as Pérez Companc, SA; petroleum interests acquired by Petrobrás of Brazil in 2003; operates the hydroelectric dam at Pichi Picún Leufu; Exec. Dir Décio Fabricio Oddone da Costa.

Gas

Asociación de Distribuidores de Gas (ADIGAS): Diagonal Norte 740, 5° b, C1035AAP Buenos Aires; tel. (11) 4393-8294; e-mail consultas@adigas.com.ar; internet www.adigas.com.ar; f. 1993 to represent newly privatized gas companies; Gen. Man. Carlos Alberto Alfaro.

Distribuidora de Gas del Centro, SA: Ituzaingó 774, Córdoba; tel. (351) 468-8108; fax (351) 468-1568; e-mail clientescentro@ecogas.com.ar; internet www.ecogas.com.ar/appweb/leo/centro/centro.php; state-owned co; distributes natural gas in Córdoba, Catamarca and La Rioja; Pres. Eduardo A. Hurtado.

Distribuidora de Gas Cuyana, SA: Ituzaingó 774, Córdoba; tel. (351) 468-8108; fax (351) 468-1568; e-mail clientescuyo@ecogas.com.ar; internet www.ecogas.com.ar/appweb/leo/cuyo/cuyo.php; state-owned co; distributes natural gas in Mendoza, San Juan, San Luis; Pres. Eduardo A. Hurtado.

Energía Argentina, SA (ENARSA): see Electricity.

Gas Natural Ban, SA: Isabel la Católica 939, C1268ACS Buenos Aires; tel. (11) 4754-1137; e-mail comercial@gasnaturalban.com.ar; internet www.gasnaturalban.com.ar; f. 1992; distribution of natural gas; Gen. Man. Horacio Cristiani.

Metrogás, SA: Gregorio Aráoz de Lamadrid 1360, C1267AAB Buenos Aires; tel. (11) 4309-1000; fax (11) 4309-1025; e-mail atencionclientes@metrogas.com.ar; internet www.metrogas.com.ar; f. 1992; gas distribution; Dir. Gen. Andrés Cordero.

Transportadora de Gas del Norte, SA: Don Bosco 3672, 3°, C1206ABF Buenos Aires; tel. (11) 4008-2000; fax (11) 4008-2242; internet www.tgn.com.ar; f. 1992; distributes natural gas; Gen. Man. Freddy Cameo.

Transportadora de Gas del Sur, SA (TGS): Don Bosco 3672, 6°, C1206ABF Buenos Aires; tel. (11) 4865-9050; fax (11) 4865-9059; e-mail totgs@tgs.com.ar; internet www.tgs.com.ar; f. 1992; processing and transport of natural gas; Gen. Dir Carlos Seijo.

Water

Agua y Saneamientos Argentinos, SA (AySA): Tucumán 752, C1049APP Buenos Aires; tel. (11) 6319-0000; fax (11) 6139-2460; e-mail prensa@aysa.com.ar; internet www.aysa.com.ar; f. 2006; 90% state-owned; distribution of water in the Buenos Aires metropolitan area; Pres. Dr Carlos Humberto Ben.

TRADE UNIONS

Central de Trabajadores de la Argentinos (CTA): Piedras1065, C1070AAU Buenos Aires; tel. (11) 4307-3829; fax (11) 4300-1015; e-mail organizacion@cta.org.ar; internet www.cta.org.ar; f. 1992; dissident trade union confederation; Gen. Sec. Hugo Yasky.

Confederación General del Trabajo (CGT) (General Confederation of Labour): Azopardo 802, C1107ADN Buenos Aires; tel. (11) 4334-0596; fax (11) 4334-0599; e-mail secgral@cgtra.org.ar; internet www.cgtra.org.ar; f. 1930; Peronist; represents approx. 90% of Argentina's 1,100 trade unions; Sec.-Gen. Hugo Moyano.

CGT Azul y Blanca: Avda Belgrano 1280, C1093AAN Buenos Aires; f. 2008 by dissident faction of CGT comprising c. 60 unions; Sec.-Gen. Luis Barrionuevo.

Transport

Comisión Nacional de Regulación del Transporte (CNRT): Maipú 88, Apdo 129, C1000WAB Buenos Aires; tel. (11) 4819-3000; e-mail msenet@mecon.gov.ar; internet www.cnrt.gov.ar; regulates domestic and international transport services.

Secretaría de Transporte de la Nación: Hipólito Yrigoyen 250, 12°, C1086AAB Buenos Aires; tel. (11) 4349-7254; fax (11) 4349-7201; e-mail transporte@minplan.gov.ar; internet www.transporte.gov.ar.

RAILWAYS

There are direct rail links with the Bolivian Railways network to Santa Cruz de la Sierra and La Paz; with Chile, through the Las Cuevas–Caracoles tunnel (across the Andes) and between Salta and Antofagasta; with Brazil, across the Paso de los Libres and Uruguayana bridge; with Paraguay (between Posadas and Encarnación by ferry-boat); and with Uruguay (between Concordia and Salto). In 2005 there were 32,170 km of tracks.

Plans for the privatization of the state-run Ferrocarriles Argentinos (FA) were first initiated in 1991. In 1993 central government funding for the FA was suspended and responsibility for existing intercity passenger routes was devolved to respective provincial governments. However, owing to lack of resources, few provinces successfully assumed the operation of services, and many trains were suspended. At the same time, long-distance freight services were sold as six separate 30-year concessions (including lines and rolling stock) to private operators. In the mid-1990s the FA was replaced by Ente Nacional de Administración de Bienes Ferroviarios (ENABIEF), which assumed responsibility for railway infrastructure and the rolling stock not already sold off. The Buenos Aires commuter system was divided into eight concerns (one of which incorporates the underground railway system) and was offered for sale to private operators as 10- or 20-year (subsidized) concessions. The railway network is regulated by the Comisión Nacional de Regulación del Transporte (CNRT—see above). Plans for a 710-km high-speed railway linking Buenos Aires, Rosario and Córdoba were announced by the Government in 2006, and the contract for construction of the line was awarded in 2008.

Cámara de Industriales Ferroviarios: Alsina 1609, 1°, C1088AAO Buenos Aires; tel. (11) 4371-5571; e-mail cifra@24horas.com; private org. to promote the devt of Argentine railway industries; Pres. Ana María Guibaudi.

Ferrovías: Ramos Mejía 1430, C1104AJO Buenos Aires; tel. (11) 4314-1444; fax (11) 3311-1181; internet www.ferrovias.com.ar; f. 1994; operates northern commuter line (Belgrano Norte) in Buenos Aires; Pres. Gabriel Romero.

Metrovías (MV): Bartolomé Mitre 3342, C1201AAL Buenos Aires; tel. (11) 4959-6800; fax (11) 4866-3037; e-mail info@metrovias.com.ar; internet www.metrovias.com.ar; f. 1994; operates subway (Subterráneos de Buenos Aires—Subte, q.v.), a light rail line (Premetro) and Urquiza commuter line; Pres. Aldo Roggio.

Trenes de Buenos Aires, SA (TBA): Avda Ramos Mejía 1358, C1104AJN Buenos Aires; tel. (11) 4317-4400; fax (11) 4317-4409; e-mail prensa@tbanet.com.ar; internet www.tbanet.com.ar; took over operations of the Mitre and Sarmiento commuter lines from state in 1995; 400 km of track; Pres. Marcelo Calderón; Vice-Pres. Jorge Alvarez.

Unidad de Gestión Operativa Ferroviaria de Emergencia, SA (UGOFE): internet www.ugofe.com.ar; f. 2005; consortium of Ferrovías, Metrovías and TBA formed to assume control of three lines (Belgrano Sur, Roca and San Martín) following termination of concession held by Metropolitano (f. 1995); 304-km network.

The following consortia were awarded 30-year concessions to operate rail services in the 1990s:

ALL Mesopotámica: Santa Fe 4636, 3°, C1425BHV Buenos Aires; tel. (11) 4778-2425; fax (11) 4778-2493; internet www.rrdc.com/op_argentina_all_meso.html; f. 1993 as Ferrocarril Mesopotámico; bought by Brazil's América Latina Logística, SA, in 1999; operates freight services on the Urquiza lines; Exec. Dir Roberto Monteiro; 2,240 km of track.

Ferrobaires: Gen. Hornos 11, 4°, C1154ACA Buenos Aires; tel. (11) 4305-5174; fax (11) 4305-5933; e-mail calidadservicio@ferrobaires.gba.gov.ar; internet www.ferrobaires.gba.gov.ar; f. 1993; owned by the govt of the Province of Buenos Aires; local services; Pres. G. Crespo.

Ferroexpreso Pampeano, SA (FEPSA): Conesa 1073, C1426AQU Buenos Aires; tel. (11) 4014-7900; operates services on the Rosario–Bahía Blanca grain lines; 5,094 km of track.

Ferrosur Roca (FR): Bouchard 680, 8°, C1106ABJ Buenos Aires; tel. (11) 4319-3900; fax (11) 4319-3901; e-mail ferrosur@elsitio.net; internet www.ferrosur.com.ar; f. 1993; operator of freight services on the Roca lines; 3,000 km of track.

Nuevo Central Argentino, SA (NCA): Avda Eduardo Madero 1020, 16°, C1106ACX Buenos Aires; f. 1993; operates freight services on the Bartolomé Mitre lines; 5,011 km of track.

Buenos Aires also has an underground railway system:

Subterráneos de Buenos Aires (Subte): Bartolomé Mitre 3342, C1201AAL Buenos Aires; tel. (11) 4862-6844; fax (11) 4864-0633; internet www.sbase.com.ar; f. 1913; completely state-owned in 1951–93, responsibility for operations was transferred in 1993 to a private consortium, Metrovías (q.v.), with a 20-year concession; fmrly controlled by the Municipalidad de la Ciudad de Buenos Aires; six underground lines totalling 42.9 km, 74 stations, and a 7.4 km light rail line (Premetro) with 17 stations; three additional lines planned; Pres. JORGE ALBERTO IRIGOIN.

ROADS

In 2003 there were 231,374 km of roads, of which 30.0% were paved. Four branches of the Pan-American highway run from Buenos Aires to the borders of Chile, Bolivia, Paraguay and Brazil. In 1996 9,932 km of main roads were under private management.

Asociación Argentina de Empresarios Transporte Automotor (AAETA): Bernardo de Irigoyen 330, 6°, C1072AAH Buenos Aires; tel. (11) 4334-3254; fax (11) 4334-6513; e-mail info@aaeta.org.ar; internet www.aaeta.org.ar; f. 1941; Pres. Dr JUAN ZUNINO.

Dirección Nacional de Vialidad: Julio A. Roca 783, C1067ABC Buenos Aires; tel. (11) 4343-8520; internet www.vialidad.gov.ar; controlled by the Secretaría de Transportes; Gen. Man. NELSON GUILLERMO PERIOTTI.

Federación Argentina de Entidades Empresarias de Autotransporte de Cargas (FADEEAC): Sánchez de Bustamante 54, C1173AAB Buenos Aires; tel. (11) 4860-7700; fax (11) 4383-7870; e-mail fadeeac@fadeeac.org.ar; internet www.fadeeac.org.ar; Pres. LUIS A. MORALES.

There are several international passenger and freight services, including:

Autobuses Sudamericanos, SA: Tres Arroyos 287, C1414EAC Buenos Aires; tel. (11) 4857-3065; fax (11) 4307-1956; f. 1928; international bus services; car and bus rentals; charter bus services; Pres. ARMANDO SCHLECKER HIRSCH; Gen. Man. MIGUEL ANGEL RUGGIERO.

INLAND WATERWAYS

There is considerable traffic in coastal and river shipping, mainly carrying petroleum and its derivatives.

Dirección Nacional de Vías Navegables: España 221, 4°, Buenos Aires; tel. (11) 4361-5964; internet www.sspyvn.gov.ar; part of the Ministry of Federal Planning, Public Investment and Services, Transport Secretariat; responsible for the maintenance and improvement of waterways and dredging operations; Dir Dr JOSÉ BENI.

SHIPPING

There are more than 100 ports, of which the most important are Buenos Aires, Quequén and Bahía Blanca. There are specialized terminals at Ensenada, Comodoro Rivadavia, San Lorenzo and Campana (petroleum); Bahía Blanca, Rosario, Santa Fe, Villa Concepción, Mar del Plata and Quequén (cereals); and San Nicolás and San Fernando (raw and construction materials). In 2008 Argentina's merchant fleet totalled 576 vessels, with a combined aggregate displacement of approximately 785,300 grt.

Administración General de Puertos: Avda Ing. Huergo 431, 1°, C1107AOE Buenos Aires; tel. (11) 4343-2425; fax (11) 4331-0298; e-mail institucionales@puertobuenosaires.gov.ar; internet www.puertobuenosaires.gov.ar; f. 1956 as a state enterprise for administration of all national sea- and river-ports; following privatization of much of its activity in mid-1990s, operates the port of Buenos Aires; Gen. Man. Dr JORGE FRANCISCO CHOLVIS.

Capitanía General del Puerto: Julio A. Roca 734, 2°, C1067ABP Buenos Aires; tel. (11) 434-9784; f. 1967; co-ordination of port operations; Port Capt. Capt. PEDRO TARAMASCO.

Administración General de Puertos (Santa Fe): Duque 1 Cabacera, Santa Fe; tel. (42) 41732.

Consorcio de Gestión del Puerto de Bahía Blanca: Dr Mario M. Guido s/n, 8103 Provincia de Buenos Aires; tel. (91) 57-3213; Pres. JOSÉ E. CONTE; Sec.-Gen. CLAUDIO MARCELO CONTE.

Terminales Portuarias Argentinas: Buenos Aires; operates one of five cargo and container terminals in the port of Buenos Aires.

Terminales Río de la Plata: Buenos Aires; operates one of five cargo and container terminals in the port of Buenos Aires.

Other private shipping companies operating on coastal and overseas routes include:

Antártida Pesquera Industrial: Calle Dr M. Moreno 1270, 5°, C1091AAZ Buenos Aires; tel. (11) 4381-0167; fax (11) 4381-0519; Pres. J. M. S. MIRANDA; Man. Dir J. R. S. MIRANDA.

Astramar Cía Argentina de Navegación, SAC: Buenos Aires; tel. (11) 4311-3678; fax (11) 4311-7534; Pres. ENRIQUE W. REDDIG.

Bottacchi SA de Navegación: Buenos Aires; tel. (11) 4392-7411; fax (11) 411-1280; Pres. ANGEL L. M. BOTTACCHI.

Maruba S. en C. por Argentina: Maipú 535, 7°, C1006ACE Buenos Aires; tel. (11) 4322-7173; fax (11) 4322-3353; Chartering Man. R. J. DICKIN.

CIVIL AVIATION

Argentina has 10 international airports (Aeroparque Jorge Newbery, Córdoba, Corrientes, El Plumerillo, Ezeiza, Jujuy, Resistencia, Río Gallegos, Salta and San Carlos de Bariloche). Ezeiza, 35 km from Buenos Aires, is one of the most important air terminals in Latin America.

Aerolíneas Argentinas: Bouchard 547, 9°, C1106ABG Buenos Aires; tel. (11) 4317-3000; fax (11) 4320-2116; internet www.aerolineas.com.ar; f. 1950; bought by Grupo Marsans (Spain) in 2001; renationalization pending in 2008; services to North and Central America, Europe, the Far East, New Zealand, South Africa and destinations throughout South America; the internal network covers the whole country; passengers, mail and freight are carried; Gen. Man. MARIANO RECALDE.

Austral Líneas Aéreas (ALA): Corrientes 485, 9°, C1043AAE Buenos Aires; tel. (11) 4317-3600; fax (11) 4317-3777; internet www.austral.com.ar; f. 1971; domestic flights.

LAN Argentina: Avda Cerrito 866, Buenos Aires; tel. (11) 4378-2200; fax (11) 4378-2298; internet www.lan.com; subsidiary of LAN Airlines, SA (Chile); services between airports in Argentina, Chile and the USA.

Líneas Aéreas del Estado (LADE): Perú 710, C1068AAF Buenos Aires; tel. (11) 4361-7071; fax (11) 4362-4899; e-mail director@lade.com.ar; internet www.lade.com.ar; f. 1940.

Sol Líneas Aéreas: Aeropuerto Internacional Rosario, Avda Jorge Newbery s/n, 2000 Rosario; tel. (11) 6091-0032; e-mail contacto@sol.com.ar; internet www.sol.com.ar; f. 2005; services between destinations in Argentina and Uruguay.

Tourism

Argentina's superb tourist attractions include the Andes mountains, the lake district centred on Bariloche (where there is a National Park), Patagonia, the Atlantic beaches and Mar del Plata, the Iguazú falls, the Pampas and Tierra del Fuego. Arrivals at Ezeiza International Airport in 2009 totalled some 2.0m. In 2008 tourism receipts amounted to US $3,370m.

Asociación Argentina de Agencias de Viajes y Turismo (AAAVYT): Viamonte 640, 10°, B6015XAA Buenos Aires; tel. (11) 4325-4691; fax (11) 4322-9641; e-mail secretaria@aaavyt.org.ar; internet www.aaavyt.org.ar; f. 1951; Pres. TOMÁS RICARDO ROZA; Sec. VERÓNICA REINHOLD.

Instituto Nacional de Promoción Turística: Suipacha 1111, 20°, C1088AAW Buenos Aires; tel. (11) 4316-1600; fax (11) 4313-6834; e-mail inprotur@turismo.gov.ar; internet www.argentina.travel.

Defence

As assessed at November 2009, Argentina's Armed Forces numbered an estimated 73,100: Army 38,500, Navy 20,000 (including Naval Air Force), Air Force 14,600. There were also paramilitary forces numbering 31,240. In April 1995 conscription was ended and a professional (voluntary) military service was created in its place.

Defence Budget: An estimated 8,520m. new pesos in 2009.

Chair. of the Joint Chiefs of Staff: Brig.-Gen. JORGE CHEVALIER.

Chief of Staff (Army): Lt-Gen. LUIS ALBERTO POZZI.

Chief of Staff (Navy): Adm. JORGE OMAR GODOY.

Chief of Staff (Air Force): Brig.-Gen. NORMANDO CONSTANTINO.

Education

Education from pre-school to university level is available free of charge. Education is officially compulsory for all children at primary level, between the ages of six and 14 years. Secondary education lasts for between five and six years, depending on the type of course: the normal certificate of education (bachillerato) takes five years, a course leading to a commercial bachillerato lasts five years, and one leading to a technical or agricultural bachillerato takes six years. Technical education is supervised by the Consejo Nacional de Educación Técnica. Non-university higher education, usually leading to a teaching qualification, is for three or four years, while university courses last for four years or more. There were 37 state universities and some 48 private universities in 2004. Enrolment at primary schools in 2005 included 99% of the relevant age-group, while enrolment at secondary schools in 2007 included 79% of pupils in the relevant age-group. Government expenditure on education and culture for 2009 was forecast at 13,723.5m. new pesos (representing 5.9% of total budgeted public expenditure).

Bibliography

For works on South America generally, see Select Bibliography (Books)

Alexander, R. *A History of Organized Labor in Argentina*. Westport, CT, Praeger Publrs, 2003.

Alonso, P. *Between Revolution and the Ballot Box: The Origins of the Argentine Radical Party*. Cambridge, Cambridge University Press, 2000.

Arceneaux, C. L. *Bounded Missions: Military Regimes and Democratization in the Southern Cone and Brazil*. University Park, PA, Penn State University Press, 2001.

Auyero, J. *Poor People's Politics: Peronist Survival Networks and the Legacy of Evita*. Durham, NC, Duke University Press, 2001.

Barton, R., and Tedesco, L. *The State of Democracy in Latin America: Post-Transitional Conflicts in Argentina and Chile*. London, Routledge, 2004.

Blustein P. *And the Money Kept Rolling in (and Out): Wall Street, the IMF, and the Bankrupting of Argentina*. London, Public Affairs, 2005.

Brennan, J. P., and Rougier, M. *The Politics of National Capitalism: Peronism and the Argentine Bourgeoisie, 1946-1976*. University Park, PA, Pennsylvania State University Press, 2009.

Chudnovsky, D., and López, A. *The Elusive Quest for Growth in Argentina*. Basingstoke, Palgrave Macmillan, 2007.

Corrales, J. *Presidents Without Parties: The Politics of Economic Reform in Argentina and Venezuela in the 1990s*. University Park, PA, Penn State University Press, 2002.

Dominguez, J. I., and Shifter, M. (Eds). *Constructing Democratic Governance in Latin America (An Inter-American Dialogue Book)*. Baltimore, MD, Johns Hopkins University Press, 2003.

Epstein, E. (Ed.). *Broken Promises? The Argentine Crisis and Argentine Democracy*. Lanham, MD, Lexington Books, 2006.

Fuentes, C. *Contesting the Iron Fist: Advocacy Networks and Police Violence in Democratic Argentina and Chile*. London, Routledge, 2004.

Goñi, U. *The Real Odessa: How Perón Brought the Nazi War Criminals to Argentina*. London, Granta, 2000.

Grimson, A., and Kessler, G. *On Argentina and the Southern Cone: Neoliberalism and National Imaginations*. London, Routledge, 2005.

Guy, D. J. *Women Build the Welfare State: Performing Charity and Creating Rights in Argentina, 1880-1955*. Durham, NC, Duke University Press, 2009.

Helmke, G. *Courts Under Constraints: Judges, Generals, and Presidents in Argentina (Cambridge Studies in Comparative Politics)*. Cambridge, Cambridge University Press, 2005.

Karush, M. B. *Workers or Citizens: Democracy and Identity in Rosario Argentina, 1912–1930*. Alberquerque, NM, University of New Mexico Press, 2002.

Karush, M. B., and Chamosa, O. (Eds). *The New Cultural History of Peronism: Power and Identity in Mid-Twentieth-Century Argentina*. Durham, NC, Duke University Press, 2010.

Levine, L. W. W., Levine, L. W., and Ortiz, F. *Inside Argentina from Peron to Menem: 1950–2000 from an American Point of View*. Ojai, CA, Edwin House Publishing, 2001.

Levitsky, S. *Transforming Labour-Based Parties in Latin America: Argentine Peronism in Comparative Perspective*. Cambridge, Cambridge University Press, 2003.

(Ed.). *Argentine Democracy: The Politics of Institutional Weakness*. Philadelphia, PA, University of Pennsylvania Press, 2006.

Lewis, D. K. *The History of Argentina*. Westport, CT, Greenwood Publishing Group, 2001.

Lewis, P. H. *Guerrillas and Generals: The 'Dirty War' in Argentina*. Westport, CT, Greenwood Publishing Group, 2001.

Llanos, M. *Privatization and Democracy in Argentina: An Analysis of President-Congress Relations*. Boston, MA, St Martin's Press, 2002.

Marchak, P. *God's Assassins: State Terrorism in Argentina in the 1970s*. Montréal, QC, McGill-Queens University Press, 2002.

Middlebrook, M. *The Fight for the Malvinas*. London, Pen & Sword Books, 2003.

Mussa, M. *Argentina and the IMF: From Triumph to Tragedy*. Washington, DC, Institute for International Economics, 2002.

Norden, D., and Russell, R. *The United States and Argentina: Changing Relations in a Changing World*. London, Routledge, 2002.

Osiel, M. J. *Mass Atrocity, Ordinary Evil and Hannah Arendt: Criminal Consciousness in Argentina's Dirty War*. New Haven, CT, Yale University Press, 2002.

Podalsky, L. *Specular City: The Transformation of Culture, Consumption and Space after Peron*. Philadelphia, PA, Temple University Press, 2002.

Powers, N. *Grassroots Expectations of Democracy and Economy: Argentina in Comparative Perspective*. Pittsburgh, PA, University of Pittsburgh Press, 2001.

Robben, A. C. G. M. *Political Violence and Trauma in Argentina*. Philadelphia, PA, University of Pennsylvania Press, 2005.

Rock, D. *State Building and Political Movements in Argentina, 1860–1916*. Palo Alto, CA, Stanford University Press, 2002.

Politics in Argentina, 1890–1930: The Rise and Fall of Radicalism. Cambridge, Cambridge University Press, 2009.

Romero, J. L. *Las Ideas Políticas en Argentina*. Buenos Aires, Fondo de Cultura Económica Argentina, 2002.

Romero, L. A. *A History of Argentina in the Twentieth Century*. University Park, PA, Penn State University Press, 2002.

Sabato, H. *The Many and the Few: Political Participation in Republican Buenos Aires*. Palo Alto, CA, Stanford University Press, 2001.

Sheinin, D. M. K. *Argentina and the United States: An Alliance Contained*. Athens, GA, University of Georgia Press, 2006.

Spektorowski, A. *The Origins of Argentina's Revolution of the Right*. Notre Dame, IN, University of Notre Dame Press, 2001.

Teichman, J. A. *The Politics of Freeing Markets in Latin America: Chile, Argentina, and Mexico*. Chapel Hill, NC, University of North Carolina Press, 2001.

Wright, T. C. *State Terrorism in Latin America: Chile, Argentina, and International Human Rights*. Lanham, MD, Rowman & Littlefield Publrs, 2007.

ARUBA

Geography

PHYSICAL FEATURES

Aruba is a constituent of the tripartite Kingdom of the Netherlands, together with the metropolitan country in Europe and the other Dutch Caribbean islands grouped in the Netherlands Antilles (including Aruba, until it gained *status aparte* in 1986). The island of Aruba is one of the Lesser Antilles, lying in the southern Caribbean, the most westerly of that part of the chain paralleling the South American coast. Indeed, the island lies but some 25 km (16 miles) north of mainland Venezuela (the Paraguná peninsula). It is 68 km west of Curaçao, the chief island of the Netherlands Antilles. With Curaçao and Bonaire, Aruba constitutes what the Dutch confusingly call the 'Leeward Islands' (*Benedenwindse Eilands*). They are more familiarly called the 'ABC islands'. Aruba covers an area of 193 sq km (74.5 sq miles).

Aruba is the smallest of the three Dutch islands in the southern Caribbean. It is about 32 km at its longest (running from the south-east to the north-west) and almost 10 km at its widest. The island tapers fairly evenly towards the south-east, but the northerly facing weather coast extends further than the other, gentler shore, as, to the north-west of the capital, Oranjestad, the coast turns abruptly towards the north-east, curving into a western coastline that arcs up to the pointing north-western tip of Aruba. Most of the main towns and tourist resorts are on the leeward, reef-fringed western and southern shores. There are over 68 km of seashore. The interior (*cunucu*) of the dry island is naturally covered by scrub, cacti and wind-bent divi divi (*watapana*) trees, and little land is farmed. The lack of trees results from human exploitation of the scarce wood resources, although the more endangered native species are now protected, and there are replanting programmes and initiatives designed to keep goats out of vulnerable areas. Bird life is rich, particularly during November–January, when migratory species swell the local avian population. The terrain is generally flat, although there are some hills, the highest being Jamanota (189 m or 620 ft). There are no rivers.

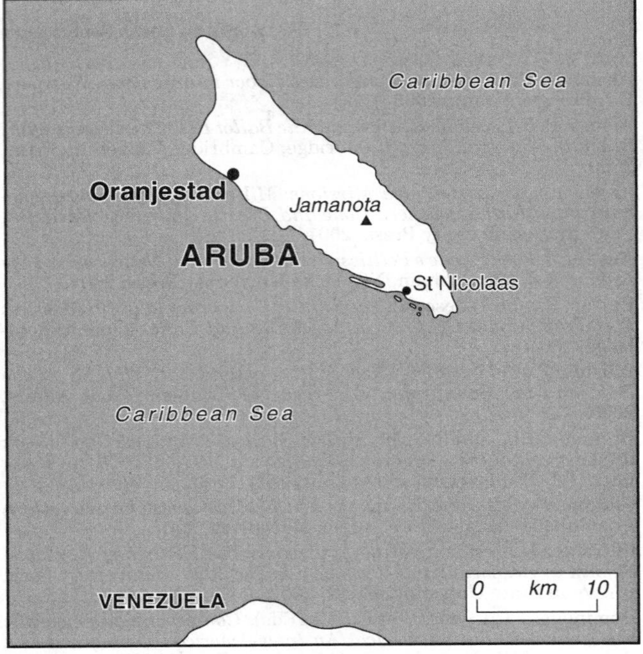

CLIMATE

Aruba has an even, tropical marine climate, with minimal seasonal temperature variation—the average is fairly constant at 27°C (81°F), seldom registering below 26°C or above 32°C. August, September and October are the hottest months, while December–February is slightly cooler than the rest of the year. The island is outside the Caribbean hurricane belt (although it is constantly cooled by the trade winds) and is very dry. There are only an average of 510 mm (20 ins) of rainfall per year, mostly falling in October–December.

POPULATION

The main ethnic group (80%) is of mixed white and Amerindian (Arawak) race (there have been no full-blooded Amerindians since the late 19th century), but, as a long-established and cosmopolitan trading centre, Aruba has attracted a rich diversity of communities and racial groups. As in the other southern Dutch Antilles, this varied background has given rise to a widely spoken Creole language, Papiamento, of mixed Portuguese, Spanish, Dutch and English descent. The official language is Dutch, although English and Spanish are also widely spoken. The historic influence of Latin America on this part of the Dutch Caribbean is revealed by estimates of religious affiliation—the principal faith of Aruba is the Roman Catholic denomination of Christianity, to which more than 80% of the population adhere. A further 8% are Protestant Christians, while other groups represented include Hindus, Muslims, Jews and Confucians.

The total population in mid-2010 was an estimated 108,888, although during the course of a typical year well over 600,000 more visit as stopping tourists and almost that number again as passing cruise ship passengers. Oranjestad (with a population of some 33,112 at mid-2009) is at the more northerly end of the south-western coast, with the 'oil town' of Sint Nicolaas at the southern end. Inland, near the western shore, is Noord, and in the centre of the island lies Santa Cruz.

History

CHARLES ARTHUR

Aruba's history has been closely linked to those of five other Caribbean islands that were colonized by the Dutch in the 17th century and administered as one entity by the Netherlands from 1845 until 1986. In that year Aruba left the federation of the Netherlands Antilles, having been granted *status aparte* by the Dutch Government, to become a self-governing part of the Kingdom of the Netherlands.

Aruba, which had been inhabited for some centuries by Arawak people, was discovered by the Spanish in 1499. The Spanish colony was limited in scope, and in contrast to most other Caribbean islands, Aruba did not develop a plantation society. Instead, the Spanish sent many of the indigenous people to Hispaniola (today the island shared by Haiti and the Dominican Republic), where they were enslaved in the mines. In the 1630s the Dutch West India Company developed an increasingly strong presence on Aruba, and in 1648 the Dutch took formal possession of the island. Apart from a brief spell under British control in 1805–16, Aruba remained a Dutch colony until after the Second World War. Periods of economic prosperity occurred during the 18th century when the island thrived first as a source of sea salt and then as a trading centre, and were further evidenced during the 19th century when gold was discovered and vigorously mined until the early years of the 20th century, when the supply dwindled and mining ceased to be prosperous. The basis of the island's modern day economy was established in 1929 when, following the discovery of extensive oil reserves in the neighbouring territory of Venezuela, the Lago Oil and Transport Company (a subsidiary of the Standard Oil Company of the USA, now the Exxon Mobil Corporation) established an oil refinery at the eastern end of the island, at Sint Nicolaas. At around the same time, Royal Dutch Shell built another refinery on the opposite end of the island. The refining of oil transformed the island's economy and ensured another period of economic prosperity.

In the years following the end of the Second World War, Aruba's economy received a further boost when the capital city of Oranjestad became a regular port of call for Caribbean cruise ships. A tourism industry soon developed, at first limited to cruise ship visits, and in 1959 the first luxury hotel opened in Aruba. The increasing wealth and prosperity encouraged islanders to agitate for a separation from the other Dutch colonies in the Caribbean. Although its status as a Dutch colony came to an end in 1951, when it formed its own government within the political structure of the Netherlands Antilles, in 1954 it was made part of the federation of the Netherlands Antilles along with Bonaire and Curaçao, and the three islands further to the north, St Eustatius, St Maarten and Saba. Aruba's citizens increasingly came to resent the unequal relationship with these, for the most part, poorer islands. The island's main political party, the Movimentu Electoral di Pueblo (MEP—People's Electoral Movement), campaigned for independence for Aruba, and in a referendum in March 1977 some 82% of those taking part voted in favour of withdrawal from the Antillean federation. Following drawn-out negotiations with the Dutch, in 1983 agreement was reached providing for Aruba's secession from the federation in 1986 and full independence 10 years later. In the interim it was agreed that Aruba would maintain a co-operative union in monetary and economic affairs with the other five members of the federation, and that the Netherlands would maintain its authority over matters of foreign affairs and defence.

Although the MEP fell from power in November 1985, a four-party coalition led by the Arubaanse Volkspartij (AVP—Aruba People's Party) led the island into its new *status aparte* on 1 January 1986. However, by this time an economic downturn, precipitated by the closure of the Sint Nicolaas refinery in 1985, had made many islanders less enthusiastic about the prospects of full independence. Then, as the economy experienced a rapid recovery based on extensive public works in support of a booming tourism industry, opinion shifted further away from a movement towards full independence and towards the achievement of greater autonomy within an association with the five islands of the Netherlands Antilles. In March 1994 the Governments of Aruba, the Netherlands and the Netherlands Antilles decided to abandon plans for full independence for Aruba unless it was approved by a referendum and by a majority of two-thirds in the Staten (parliament).

Aruba's electoral system is based on proportional representation, and, as no one party is usually able to win a majority of seats in the 21-seat Staten, the result of the elections held once every four years has traditionally been the creation of unstable coalition governments. Throughout the 1990s and early years of the 21st century, the primary issue for the two main parties, the MEP and the AVP, has been the negotiations concerning Aruba's relations with the Netherlands and the Netherlands Antilles. Following a split between the AVP and its main coalition partner, the Organisacion Liberal Arubano (OLA—Aruban Liberal Organization), there was a general election in December 1997. The contest failed to produce a clear result, with votes evenly divided between the MEP, the AVP, and the OLA. After negotiations between the MEP and the AVP to form a coalition failed, a new alliance between the AVP and OLA was formed, consigning the MEP to opposition. This coalition then collapsed in June 2001, following the withdrawal of the OLA's support for the AVP's plan to privatize the Aruban Tourism Authority, and in further legislative elections the MEP won an absolute majority, securing 12 seats. It formed Aruba's first ever one-party government. In the general election held on 23 September 2005 the MEP won another outright victory, winning 11 seats to the AVP's eight.

Part of the MEP's continuing appeal was linked to economic expansion and, in particular, the Government's creation of around 1,500 new public sector jobs. However, in late 2008 the economy began to struggle as a result of much-reduced global demand owing to the international financial crisis. Aruba's economic woes deepened during 2009 with a decline in the number of tourist visitors and the closure, in September, of the Valero Aruba Refinery (the largest oil refinery on the island—see Economy).

Popular disillusion with the deteriorating economic conditions was a key determinant in the legislative election held on 25 September 2009, from which the opposition AVP emerged victorious, with 48% of the vote and 12 of the 21 seats in the Staten. The AVP had held power twice previously as part of coalitions, but, having now garnered a legislative majority, the party would be able to govern unhindered by political pact-making and compromise. The MEP secured only eight seats, with its share of the vote declining to 36% (from 43% in 2005); the remaining seat was won by the Democracia Real (DR—Real Democracy) party. MEP leader and outgoing Prime Minister Nelson Oduber, who had presided over a fractious and deteriorating relationship with the Netherlands Government, blamed the party's poor performance on interference by the Dutch authorities—an investigation into corruption on the island had been launched by the Netherlands shortly prior to the election. AVP leader Michiel Eman was inaugurated as Prime Minister on 30 October.

The majority of the Government's early initiatives focused on the economy. Moves to halve an unpopular business tax and enhance social security payments proved popular. Longer-term initiatives aimed to revive a flagging tourism industry and improve relations with the Netherlands. Speaking on the occasion of the new Government's 100th day in power at the beginning of February 2010, Eman contended that his Government had shifted the political focus away from a small élite by introducing policies to benefit underprivileged Arubans.

As Aruba's prosperous economy is heavily dependent on tourism, the disappearance of a US teenager in Aruba in May 2005 had serious repercussions. With the disappearance remaining unsolved and the investigation generating considerable controversy, the incident has damaged relations between Aruba and the USA, and deterred US tourists from visiting the island. The Governor of Alabama—the home state of the missing person, Natalee Holloway—and the Alabama

Senate criticized the Aruban authorities for failing to solve the case and called, unsuccessfully, for the US Government to impose a travel and tourism boycott of Aruba. Following widespread media coverage in the USA that focused on the police's lack of progress in solving the disappearance, there was a downturn in US tourist arrivals. In early 2008 the case returned to the headlines after a journalist recorded an apparent confession, but no arrests were made, owing to a lack of sufficient evidence. The issue again inflamed the frequently strained relations between Aruba and the Netherlands in December when the Dutch police commissioner criticized the Aruban police's handling of the case. Hero Brinkman, a Dutch member of parliament representing the anti-immigration Freedom Party, used the renewed media interest in the Holloway case to repeat his charge of endemic corruption in Aruba. This in turn provoked a threat to boycott the twice-yearly meeting of members of parliament from Aruba, the Netherlands Antilles and the Netherlands (the Parliamentary Consultation of the Kingdom—POK) by Prime Minister Oduber, Minister of Justice Rudy Croes and two other Aruban ministers. The consultation went ahead in January 2009, but only after Brinkman had been expelled from the Netherlands delegation by his colleagues for continuing to insult the Aruban delegates.

Aruba's relations with the Netherlands deteriorated still further in March–April 2009 when the MEP denounced what it regarded as an overbearing attitude and unnecessary interference by the Netherlands in the island's affairs. The diplomatic row followed the leaking in February of a controversial report by a Dutch delegation to Aruba, which contained serious allegations about Oduber, and the brother of Minister of Justice Croes. Following the leaking of the report, Croes accused the Netherlands of spying, while Oduber, in a letter to the Dutch authorities, declared that the report had undermined confidence between the island's authorities and the Netherlands. Further discord erupted in April when the Dutch media reported that Dutch members of parliament had decided to boycott the next POK meeting. Aruban government officials argued that the postponement was a further example of Dutch disrespect towards Aruba's authorities. The new AVP Government acted quickly to distance itself from what it perceived to be the outgoing administration's obstructive policy, with Eman vowing to mend the relationship with the Netherlands. The Netherlands' State Secretary for the Interior and Kingdom Relations, Ank Bijleveld-Schouten, attended the new Government's inauguration ceremony. In subsequent bilateral talks, the two sides reached an agreement under the terms of which the Netherlands would carry out a review of public administration, with the aim of recommending reforms to bolster the integrity and quality of Aruba's Government and to improve law and order on the island. In a further sign of improving relations with the Dutch Government, Bijleveld-Schouten revisited Aruba in February 2010 to discuss further support for the Government's planned reforms in education and tourism-related construction projects.

In the first half of 2010 the new AVP Government moved to improve relations with powerful neighbours in the region. In early May, while in the Costa Rican capital, San José, for the inauguration of the new President of that country, Eman held discussions with Colombian President Alvaro Uribe Vélez. The talks were reported to have covered the issue of the possible reopening of the Valero Aruba Refinery; a Colombian oil company was believed to be discussing plans for the refinery with the owners, Valero Energy Corporation. During his stay in Costa Rica, Eman also initiated diplomatic moves to heal fractured relations with another Latin American neighbour, Venezuela. The Aruban leader visited the Venezuelan embassy in San José for talks with the Vice Minister of Foreign Affairs for Latin America and the Caribbean, Francisco Arias Cárdena. While the official report on the talks referred merely to discussion of 'matters of common interest', one of the key issues to be discussed was believed to have been the strained relations between the Dutch Government and the socialist Government of the Venezuelan President, Lt-Col (rtd) Hugo Chávez Frías. At the end of 2009 and again at the beginning of 2010, the Venezuelan Government had claimed that the USA and the Netherlands were using Aruba (and the Netherlands Antilles) as a staging post for a planned military intervention to overthrow President Chávez.

An issue of international concern has been the growing use of Aruba for the transshipment of illegal drugs from producing countries in South America to users in North America and Europe. According to the US authorities, Aruba attracts drugs-traffickers because of its good infrastructure, excellent flight connections, and relatively light sentences for drugs-related crimes that are served in prisons with comparatively good living conditions. In 1996 the USA included Aruba on its list of major drugs transit countries but since then the Aruban authorities have initiated concerted action to address the problem to the satisfaction of the USA, which currently praises Aruban co-operation in the fight against drugs-trafficking. In 1999 the USA began naval patrols from a base on Aruba as part of efforts to intercept deliveries of drugs from the South American mainland.

There have been similar developments in relation to concerns about money-laundering in Aruba's financial services sector, in particular that drugs-traffickers were taking advantage of lax regulation. Although Aruba has a small 'offshore' financial sector compared to more established 'offshore' jurisdictions, the sector has grown in recent years, which, combined with the presence of casinos and free zones, has made it vulnerable to exploitation. However, since concerns were initially expressed, the Aruban authorities have improved regulation and oversight, and in 1999 the international anti-money-laundering body, the Financial Action Task Force (FATF), concluded that an 'active approach' taken by the authorities had led to Aruba 'being in substantial compliance with most of the FATF recommendations'. Although Aruba no longer appears on the blacklist of international tax havens published by the Organisation for Economic Co-operation and Development (OECD), it was included on a 'grey list' of around 40 countries that, while co-operating with efforts to improve transparency, do not yet meet international standards. The list was published at the Group of 20 (G20) summit in London, United Kingdom, in April 2009. In response, Aruba was taking action to sign tax treaties with other countries in order to meet the criteria required for upgrade to the 'white' section of the OECD list.

OUTLOOK

Although the AVP Government enjoyed widespread popular support at mid-2010, longevity of success would depend heavily on its ability to boost economic growth and lower the unemployment rate. The economy suffered a sharp contraction in 2009 and any recovery during 2010 was likely to be slow. High unemployment was expected to be exacerbated by necessary cutbacks in the context of a deteriorating fiscal balance. In the short term, the Government was to focus its efforts on reopening the Valero refinery, promoting tourism and negotiating additional financial aid from the new Government in the Netherlands.

Economy

CHARLES ARTHUR

For much of the 20th century Aruba's economy revolved around oil-processing, but in the mid-1980s, following the closure of the Lago refinery, there was an enforced move to concentrate instead on the development of the tourism sector. Tourism showed especially strong growth in the 1990s and, as a consequence, tourism-related industries—particularly construction—boomed, contributing to strong economic growth and to a low unemployment rate. Today Aruba's main industries are tourism, 'offshore' financial services, transport (mainly shipping) and oil-refining. The island possesses few natural resources, and is heavily dependent on imports, including food and manufactures.

Between 1987 and 1993 the economy grew at an average annual rate of 10% and throughout the 1990s growth remained steady, largely owing to a vibrant tourism industry and investment in oil-refining, averaging 5.1% per year in 1991–2000. After such a prolonged period of economic success, the trend abated in the early years of the 21st century when gross domestic product (GDP) decreased, in real terms, by 0.7% in 2001 and by 2.6% in 2002 as a result of the terrorist attacks in the USA in September 2001, the effects of which badly affected the tourism and construction sectors. A modest revival in tourism and a sharp increase in investment in 2003 prompted a recovery, and in 2004 the continued revival of the tourism sector and related growth in construction contributed to strong GDP growth of 7.4%. Aruba became one of the most prosperous economies in the region, and in 2006 its GDP per head, at US $23,299, was among the highest in the Caribbean. However, as the performance of the tourism sector weakened again, economic growth slowed to 1.0% in 2005, to 0.6% in 2006 and 2.1% in 2007. In 2008 Aruba recorded barely positive real GDP growth of just 0.8%, and in 2009 the economy fell into a deep recession, contracting by 7.6%, according to the central bank, owing to a marked decline in US tourism demand and a fall in investment.

Aruba has enjoyed relatively low unemployment rates since the early 1990s. Its tourism and refining industries have attracted migrant labour to cover the shortfalls in its labour market, resulting in an increase in the population from 67,423 in 1991 to an estimated 105,676 in December 2008. This has made Aruba the second most densely populated island in the Caribbean after Barbados. For most of the 1990s the average unemployment rate was 6.0%—some 7.5%–8.0% of women and 4.5%–5.5% of men. Unemployment declined slightly between 2000 and 2008, but rose again in 2009 owing to the deterioration in the wider economy and exacerbated in particular by the closure in September of the Valero Aruba Refinery (see below). Most of the island's employment is in the wholesale, retail and repair trades, with hotels, restaurants and oil refineries the other principal employers.

Tourism remained the mainstay of the Aruban economy, accounting for some 40% of Aruba's GDP in the early 2000s—the hotels and restaurants sector alone was estimated to provide 10.5% of Aruba's GDP in 2002—and generating, directly or indirectly, some 35% of the island's jobs. The sandy white beaches, particularly along the southern coast, are a major attraction, along with reefs offering good diving and liberal casino laws. The construction of new hotels and an aggressive marketing campaign have succeeded in effecting and maintaining a continuous boom in the sector during the early years of the 21st century. The number of stop-over visitors and total tourism receipts increased every year between 2002 and 2005. However, dependence on tourism leaves the economy vulnerable to outside shocks. This was highlighted in mid-2005 when a US teenager went missing on the island, generating large amounts of negative publicity in the USA, which is by far the most important source of visitors. As a result, the number of stop-over tourists visiting Aruba declined in 2006 to 694,400 (from 732,500 in 2005). By 2008, however, stop-over arrivals had recovered to 826,774, while the number of cruise ship visitors amounted to 556,090; total tourist arrivals in that year stood at 1,382,864. The tourism sector performed poorly in early 2009 but recovered in the second half of the year. The number of cruise ship arrivals in 2009 totalled just over 600,000, representing a year-on-year increase of 8%. In the first months of 2010 the sector entered a slump as economic problems in North America and Europe negatively impacted on the amounts that cruise passengers spent ashore.

The USA accounted for 65% of tourists in 2008. Some 9% of stop-over visitors came from Europe and 14% from Venezuela in that year. By far the largest share of tourist visitors from Europe comes from the Netherlands. In 2006 a new daily direct flight from New York to Aruba was inaugurated, and in late 2008 Delta Airlines (USA) announced a second daily flight from Atlanta, and Copa Airlines (Panama) inaugurated a four-times-per-week service from Panama City. In March 2009 the Dutch national carrier, KLM, discontinued its Amsterdam–Aruba route, citing the declining profitability and popularity of the service. However, subsequent lobbying later in the year by the incoming Arubaanse Volkspartij (AVP—Aruba People's Party) Government, elected in September, persuaded KLM to resume its twice-weekly service between the two destinations; flights recommenced in February 2010. There was further good news for the tourism sector in May when a United Kingdom-based tour operator, Thomson, announced a new weekly direct flight to Aruba from the British city of Manchester. The new flight may be the first result of a major advertising campaign launched by the Aruba Tourism Authority's marketing agency in early 2010 with a view to raising the profile of the island among British consumers.

Oil-refining is the other dominant industry in Aruba. In 1929 the Lago Oil and Transport Company, a subsidiary of US energy company ExxonMobil, built a refinery at the eastern end of the island. At the time it was the largest refinery in the world, employing more than 8,000 people, and for most of the 20th century it was the main driver of Aruba's economy. In 1985 Exxon closed the refinery owing to a reduced worldwide demand for oil, causing a profound shock to the Aruban economy. In 1989 the Coastal Oil Company, attracted by fiscal concessions, bought the Lago oil refinery facility and reopened it on a smaller scale. Coastal increased its production capacity from 150,000 barrels per day (b/d) in 1989 to 280,000 b/d in 2000. Another US-based company, El Paso, took over Coastal in 2001. However, the quantity of oil refined declined, from a high of 83.4m. barrels in 2000 to 52.4m. barrels in 2002, and in March 2004 Coastal sold the refinery. The new owner, the US Valero Energy Corpn, renamed the facility the Valero Aruba Refinery, and in 2006 it had a total throughput capacity of 315,000 b/d. However, by 2007 this had declined to 275,000 b/d. In March 2008 Valero announced plans to sell the refinery because high oil prices had narrowed processing margins, and the global economic downturn had made financing more difficult. Valero subsequently announced that the refinery was to be closed in June 2009, owing to a reduced demand for oil stemming from the global economic crisis; in the event, the closure was postponed until September, resulting in the loss of over 700 jobs. The refinery's importance to the economy was reflected by the substantial contribution to GDP of the industrial sector, which was an estimated 10.2% in 2006. In January 2010 negotiations between the Government and Valero resulted in the resolution of a long-running dispute regarding unpaid taxes, reviving hopes for an eventual sale of the refinery. Valero was reported to be holding talks regarding the potential acquisition of the refinery with a Colombian oil company. A lengthy closure would inevitably undermine growth, employment, tax revenue and the trade balance.

A financial services sector developed in the late 1980s, and grew strongly in the 1990s, helped by the deregulation of the financial services industry and better legislation. The 'offshore' financial sector is important to Aruba, although it is small compared with other Caribbean 'offshore' centres. In April 2008 Aruba was taken off a blacklist of international tax havens published by the Organisation for Economic Co-operation and Development (OECD). However, it remained on a so-called 'grey list' of countries that, although co-operating with efforts to improve transparency, did not yet meet international standards. The Aruban authorities signalled their intention to take further action to sign tax treaties with other countries in order to meet the criteria required to gain upgrade to the 'white' section of OECD's list.

Owing to the scarcity of arable land, the poor quality of the soil and the shortage of water for irrigation, Aruba's agricultural sector is small. The main commercial crop is aloes, which are used in the manufacture of cosmetics and pharmaceuticals. All other local crops are consumed domestically, and Aruba depends heavily on imports of food. There is a small fishing industry. The manufacturing sector is also small with the main sub-sectors being oil-refining and free zone re-exports. Since the 1990s the tourism boom and a housing shortage has boosted construction activity, and made this sector one of the main drivers of economic growth in Aruba. Storms in 1995 destroyed many of these projects, and a buoyant period of construction of hotels, shops and housing followed. The construction sector has experienced steady growth since 2002, in particular in relation to the building of condominiums, the expansion of the number of hotel rooms, and other real estate developments. Condominium construction had been expected to boom in the period 2008–12, with more than 2,000 new units planned for resort areas and other parts of the island, such as Weststraat (Oranjestad), Palm Beach, Malmok and Tierra del Sol. However, the global economic crisis has led to the suspension of many of these projects.

The Queen Beatrix International Airport outside Oranjestad is served by numerous airlines linking the island with the Caribbean, North, Central and South America, and Europe. After substantial renovation and expansion, the airport was expected to be able to handle 2.6m. passengers a year by 2010. The national airline, Air Aruba, was declared bankrupt in 2000, and investors associated with the Dutch Air Holland Group established a new company, Royal Aruban Airlines (RAA), to take over Air Aruba's routes. The company was finally granted a flying licence in 2003, but although RAA has plans to fly to Europe, Africa and various destinations in the Americas, it currently only operates flights to Curaçao and to Fort Lauderdale, FL, in the USA. The regional Exel Group, owned by KLM, began regional services under the ArubaExel banner in 2004. Aruba has no railway system, but the road network is in good condition. The main port is at Oranjestad where the harbour can accommodate large ocean-going vessels.

In 2002 the Staten passed a law allowing the liberalization of the telecommunications market. The state telecommunications company Servicio di Telecomunicacion di Aruba NV (SETAR) was privatized in January 2003. Competition in mobile telephony rapidly increased with three other companies acquiring mobile licences. The explosion in mobile phone use was reflected in the relative percentages of adults with subscriptions to fixed line (38%) and mobile telephone services (144%) in 2007.

Exports through the island's free zone showed buoyant growth in the mid-1990s, peaking at US $295m. in 1997, but have since fallen as demand has dropped away. Refined oil is now Aruba's most important merchandise export, bringing earnings of $4,500m. in 2006, from $3,700m. of imported crude. In the absence of any significant local manufacturing, most consumer items, foodstuffs and machinery items are imported. In 2005, for the first time in many years, Aruba did not register a merchandise trade deficit, but in subsequent years the deficit has been resumed. In 2006 it was $120m., increasing to $159m. in 2007 and $497m. in 2008. Aruba's main trading partners were the USA, the Netherlands, the Netherlands Antilles, and Venezuela.

With the exception of 2000 and 2003, the Government has run a fiscal deficit in every year since achieving *status aparte* in 1986. Successive Governments have attempted to reduce the deficit, apart from in 2001–02, when a counter-cyclical spending policy was adopted. After a good economic and fiscal performance in 2003, when the fiscal accounts moved into surplus, the Government loosened policy in 2004, resulting in a deficit of 9.3% of GDP. Continued deficits have led to an accumulation of public debt. At mid-2010 the fiscal outlook remained poor, with revenue set to decline from already reduced levels in 2009. Unless measures to adjust the fiscal mismatch were taken, the cost of public health, social security and pensions looked likely to grow beyond fiscally sustainable levels.

In early 2008 the IMF praised the Aruban authorities for their promotion of an open, market-oriented economy and for the progress made in tightening fiscal policy in recent years. However, the IMF also sounded words of caution on Aruba's economic development, stemming from the island's vulnerability to external shocks because of its heavy dependence on tourism and the high level of public debt. By early 2009 tourism statistics indicated that the slump predicted following the onset of the global economic crisis in late 2008 had begun. Although the tourism industry showed signs of a recovery in the second half of 2009, with the number of both cruise ship arrivals and stop-over visitors increasing, mixed data for the first two months of 2010 cast doubt on the strength of that upturn. The number of cruise ship arrivals declined by 7.4% year-on-year in January–February, while the number of stop-over visitors increased by just 2.0%. The central bank noted with concern that preliminary tourism receipts data, adjusted for inflation, showed an 18.5% year-on-year contraction in January (the second consecutive monthly double-digit decline). The discrepancy between the small increase in stop-over visitors and the declining value of tourism receipts indicated that tourists were spending less.

In late 2009 the new AVP Government announced several measures designed to boost credit growth and consumer spending in an effort to initiate an economic recovery. The stimulus measures included halving the Belasting op Bedrijfsomzette (a business turnover tax introduced in 2007) from 3.0% to 1.5%; the tax was to be completely repealed by January 2011. According to government estimates, the reduction and subsequent removal of this tax would translate into a 10% reduction in the cost of producing local goods and services, resulting in lower prices for consumers and the possibility of improved margins for local businesses.

Statistical Survey

Sources (unless otherwise stated): Central Bureau of Statistics, Ministry of Finance and Economic Affairs, Sun Plaza Bldg, 3rd Floor, L. G. Smith Blvd 160, Oranjestad; tel. 5837433; fax 5838057; internet www.cbs.aw; Centrale Bank van Aruba, J. E. Irausquin Blvd 8, POB 18, Oranjestad; tel. 5252100; fax 5252101; e-mail cbaua@setarnet.aw; internet www.cbaruba.org.

AREA AND POPULATION

Area: 180 sq km (69.5 sq miles).

Population: 90,506 (males 43,434, females 47,072) at census of 14 October 2000; 106,050 (males 50,748, females 55,302) at 31 December 2008 (official estimate). *Mid-2010* (UN estimate): 108,888 (Source: UN, *World Population Prospects: The 2008 Revision*.

Density (at mid-2010): 604.9 per sq km.

Population by Age and Sex (UN estimates at mid-2010): *0–14:* 20,374 (males 10,301, females 10,073); *15–64:* 76,594 (males 36,662, females 39,932); *65 and over:* 11,920 (males 5,104, females 6,816); *Total* 108,888 (males 52,067, females 56,821). Source: UN, *World Population Prospects: The 2008 Revision*.

Principal Town (UN estimate, mid-2009): Oranjestad (capital) 33,112. Source: UN, *World Urbanization Prospects: The 2009 Revision*.

Births, Marriages and Deaths (2008, unless otherwise indicated): Live births 1,218 (birth rate 11.6 per 1,000); Marriage rate 5.1 per 1,000 (2007); Deaths 523 (death rate 5.0 per 1,000).

Life Expectancy (years at birth, 2009): 74.9 (males 72.3; females 77.5). Source: Pan American Health Organization.

Immigration and Emigration (2008): Immigration 2,885; Emigration 2,053.

Economically Active Population (persons aged 15 years and over, October 2007): Agriculture, hunting and forestry 352; Mining and quarrying 17; Manufacturing, electricity, gas and water 3,945; Construction 6,500; Wholesale and retail trade, repairs 7,283; Hotels and restaurants 8,712; Transport, storage and communications 2,832; Financial intermediation 1,905; Real estate, renting and business activities 6,811; Public administration, defence and social security 3,983; Education 1,589; Health and social work 3,177; Other community, social and personal services 3,218; Private households with employed persons 1,163; Extra-territorial organizations and bodies 33; *Sub-total* 51,520; Activities not adequately defined 87; *Total employed* 51,607; Unemployed 3,124; *Total labour force* 54,731 (males 28,629, females 26,102). Source: ILO.

HEALTH AND WELFARE

Total Fertility Rate (children per woman, 2009): 1.7.

Under-5 Mortality Rate (per 1,000 live births, 2009): 17.2.

Physicians (per 1,000 head, 1999): 1.28.

Hospital Beds (per 1,000 head, 2003): 3.2.

Health Expenditure (% of GDP, 2005): 8.5.

Total Carbon Dioxide Emissions ('000 metric tons, 2006): 2,308.3.

Carbon Dioxide Emissions Per Head (metric tons, 2006): 22.5.

Source: partly Pan American Health Organization.

For definitions, see explanatory note on p. vi.

FISHING

Total catch (metric tons, live weight, 2008): 151 (Groupers 16, Snappers and jobfishes 40, Wahoo 50, Other marine fishes 45). Source: FAO.

INDUSTRY

Electric Energy (million kWh, 2008): 913.6.

FINANCE

Currency and Exchange Rates: 100 cents = 1 Aruban gulden (guilder) or florin (A Fl.). *Sterling, Dollar and Euro Equivalents* (31 May 2010): £1 sterling = A Fl. 2.610; US$1 = A Fl. 1.790; €1 = A Fl. 2.217; A Fl. 100 = £3.83 = $55.87 = €45.11. Note: The Aruban florin was introduced in January 1986, replacing (at par) the Netherlands Antilles guilder or florin (NA Fl.). Since its introduction, the currency has had a fixed exchange rate of US$1 = A Fl. 1.79.

Budget (A Fl. million, 2009, provisional): *Revenue:* Tax revenue 928.9; Non-tax revenue 180.0 (incl. grants 23); Total 1,108.9. *Expenditure:* Wages 315.0; Wage subsidies 153.8; Goods and services 205.2; Interest payments 116.4; Investments 41.2; Transfer to the General Health Insurance (AZV) 127.6; Total (incl. others) 1,229.2.

International Reserves (US $ million at 31 December 2009): Gold 122.9; Foreign exchange 578.2; *Total* 701.1. Source: IMF, *International Financial Statistics*.

Money Supply (A Fl. million at 31 December 2009): Currency outside banks 174.6; Demand deposits at commercial banks 1,373.1; Total money (incl. others) 1,547.7. Source: IMF, *International Financial Statistics*.

Cost of Living (Consumer Price Index; base: 2006 = 100): All items 109.9 in 2007; 107.9 in 2008; 115.2 in 2009.

Gross Domestic Product (A Fl. million at constant 2000 prices): 2,014.8 in 2007; 2,029.1 in 2008; 1,875.0 in 2009.

Expenditure on the Gross Domestic Product (A Fl. million at current prices, 2009, estimates): Final consumption expenditure 3,616; Gross capital formation 1,361; *Total domestic expenditure* 4,976; Exports of goods and services 3,051; *Less* Imports of goods and services 3,332; *GDP in purchasers' values* 4,695.

Gross Domestic Product by Economic Activity (A Fl. million at current prices, 2008): Agriculture, hunting, forestry and fishing 19; Mining and utilities 432; Manufacturing 182; Construction 331; Wholesale, retail trade, restaurants and hotels 977; Transport, storage and communications 396; Other activities 2,366; *Total gross value added* 4,703; Net taxes on products 173 (figure obtained as a residual); *GDP in purchasers' values* 4,876. Source: UN National Accounts Main Aggregates Database.

Balance of Payments (US $ million, 2008): Exports of goods f.o.b. 3,700.6; Imports of goods f.o.b. –4,197.9; *Trade balance* –497.3; Exports of services 1,687.5; Imports of services –1,127.3; *Balance on goods and services* 62.9; Other income received 74.6; Other income paid –180.0; *Balance on goods, services and income* –42.5; Current transfers received 66.4; Current transfers paid –180.2; *Current balance* –156.3; Capital account (net) 160.4; Direct investment abroad –3.4; Direct investment from abroad 187.0; Portfolio investment assets –3.0; Portfolio investment liabilities 66.4; Financial derivatives liabilities –10.0; Other investment assets 80.4; Other investment liabilities –86.1; Net errors and omissions –10.0; *Overall balance* 225.3. Source: IMF, *International Financial Statistics*.

EXTERNAL TRADE

Principal Commodities (A Fl. million, 2009): *Imports c.i.f.:* Live animals and animal products 121.1; Food products 213.5; Chemical products 200.5; Base metals and articles thereof 103.2; Machinery and electrical equipment 409.7; Transport equipment 103.3; Total (incl. others) 1,783.1. *Exports f.o.b.:* Live animals and animal products 0.8; Machinery and electrical equipment 9.0; Transport equipment 7.5; Art objects and collectors' items 10.1; Total (incl. others) 55.1. Note: Figures exclude transactions involving mineral fuels and those of the Free Trade Zone of Aruba.

Principal Trading Partners (A Fl. million, 2009): *Imports c.i.f.:*Brazil 28.8; Colombia 33.7; Japan 31.3; Netherlands 306.6; Netherlands Antilles 43.7; Panama 58.9; USA 964.8; Venezuela 27.5; Total (incl. others) 1,783.1. *Exports f.o.b.:* Colombia 0.9; Netherlands 11.0; Netherlands Antilles 14.9; USA 14.5; Venezuela 2.1; Total (incl. others) 55.1. Note: Figures exclude transactions of the petroleum sector and those of the Free Trade Zone of Aruba.

TRANSPORT

Road Traffic (motor vehicles registered, December 2008): Passenger cars 49,372; Lorries 1,013; Buses 279; Taxis 367; Rental cars 3,603; Government cars 518; Motorcycles 1,604; Total (incl. others) 56,900.

Shipping: *Arrivals* (2008): 1,433 vessels. *Merchant Fleet* (vessels registered at 31 December 2008): Number of vessels 1; Total displacement 221 grt (Source: Lloyd's Register-Fairplay, *World Fleet Statistics*).

Civil Aviation: *Aircraft Landings:* 16,842 in 2006; 17,177 in 2007; 18,563 in 2008. *Passenger Arrivals:* 810,322 in 2006; 896,605 in 2007; 967,710 in 2008.

TOURISM

Tourist Arrivals: 1,253,848 (772,073 stop-over visitors, 481,775 cruise ship passengers) in 2007; 1,382,864 (826,774 stop-over visitors, 556,090 cruise ship passengers) in 2008; 1,419,391 (812,623 stop-over visitors, 606,768 cruise ship passengers) in 2009.

Tourism Receipts (A Fl. million): 2,242.3 in 2007; 2,522.4 in 2008; 2,314.1 in 2009.

COMMUNICATIONS MEDIA

Radio Receivers (1997): 50,000 in use.

Television Receivers (1997): 20,000 in use.

Telephones (2009): 38,300 main lines in use.

Mobile Cellular Telephones (2009): 128,000 subscribers.

Internet Users (2009): 24,000.

Broadband Subscribers (2009): 22,000.

Personal Computers: 10,000 (97.4 per 1,000 persons) in 2006.

Daily Newspapers (1996): 13 titles (estimated circulation 73,000 copies per issue).

Sources: mainly UNESCO, *Statistical Yearbook*; International Telecommunication Union; UN, *Statistical Yearbook*.

EDUCATION

Pre-primary (September 2007, unless otherwise indicated): 28 schools; 2,740 pupils (2007/08); 148 teachers.

Primary (September 2007, unless otherwise indicated): 43 schools; 9,977pupils (2007/08); 579 teachers.

General Secondary (September 2007, unless otherwise indicated): 14 schools; 7,549 pupils (2007/08); 562 teachers.

Technical-Vocational (September 2007, unless otherwise indicated): 2 schools (2000/01); 1,632 pupils; 124 teachers.

Community College (1999/2000): 1 school; 1,187 pupils; 106 teachers.

University (September 2007): 1 university; 128 students; 18 tutors.

Teacher Training (September 2007): 1 institution; 236 students; 55 teachers.

Special Education (September 2007): 4 schools; 466 pupils; 75 teachers.

Private, Non-aided (September 2007): 5 schools; 413 pupils; 40 teachers.

International School (2000/01): 1 school; 154 pupils; 25 teachers.

Pupil-teacher Ratio (primary education, UNESCO estimate): 17.3 in 2007/08 (Source: UNESCO Institute for Statistics).

Adult Literacy Rate (UNESCO estimates, 2008): 98.1% (males 98.2%; females 98.0%) (Source: UNESCO Institute for Statistics).

Directory

The Constitution

On 1 January 1986 Aruba acquired separate status (*status aparte*) within the Kingdom of the Netherlands. The form of government is similar to that for the Netherlands Antilles, and is embodied in the Charter of the Kingdom of the Netherlands (operational from 20 December 1954). The Netherlands, the Netherlands Antilles (Antilles of the Five) and Aruba each enjoy full autonomy in domestic and internal affairs, and are united on a basis of equality for the protection of their common interests and the granting of mutual assistance. In economic and monetary affairs there is a co-operative union between Aruba and the Antilles of the Five, known as the 'Union of the Netherlands Antilles and Aruba'.

The Governor, who is appointed by the Dutch Crown for a term of six years, represents the monarch of the Netherlands in Aruba. The Government of Aruba appoints a minister plenipotentiary to represent it in the Government of the Kingdom. Whenever the Netherlands Council of Ministers is dealing with matters coming under the heading of joint affairs of the realm (in practice mainly foreign affairs and defence), the Council assumes the status of Council of Ministers of the Kingdom. In that event, Aruba's Minister Plenipotentiary takes part, with full voting powers, in the deliberations.

A legislative proposal regarding affairs of the realm and applying to Aruba as well as to the metropolitan Netherlands is sent, simultaneously with its submission, to the Staten Generaal (the Netherlands parliament) and to the Staten (parliament) of Aruba. The latter body can report in writing to the Staten Generaal on the draft Kingdom Statute and designate one or more special delegates to attend the debates and furnish information in the meetings of the Chambers of the Staten Generaal. Before the final vote on a draft the Minister Plenipotentiary has the right to express an opinion on it. If he disapproves of the draft, and if in the Second Chamber a three-fifths' majority of the votes cast is not obtained, the discussions on the draft are suspended and further deliberations take place in the Council of Ministers of the Kingdom. When special delegates attend the meetings of the Chambers, this right devolves upon the delegates of the parliamentary body designated for this purpose.

The Governor has executive power in external affairs, which he exercises in co-operation with the Council of Ministers. He is assisted by an advisory council, which consists of at least five members appointed by him.

Executive power in internal affairs is vested in a nominated Council of Ministers, responsible to the Staten. The Aruban Staten consists of 21 members, who are elected by universal adult suffrage for four years (subject to dissolution), on the basis of proportional representation. Inhabitants have the right to vote if they have Dutch nationality and have reached 18 years of age.

The Government

HEAD OF STATE

Queen of the Netherlands: HM Queen BEATRIX.

Governor: FREDIS J. REFUNJOL (took office 7 May 2004).

COUNCIL OF MINISTERS

(July 2010)

The Government is formed by the Arubaanse Volkspartij.

Prime Minister and Minister of General Affairs: MICHIEL GODFRIED EMAN.

Minister of Integration, Infrastructure and the Environment: OSLIN BENITO SEVINGER.

Minister of Finance, Communications, Utilities and Energy: MIKE ERIC DE MEZA.

Minister of Tourism, Transport and Labour: OTMAR ENRIQUE ODUBER.

Minister of Justice and Education: ARTHUR LAWRENCE DOWERS.

Minister of the Economy, Social Affairs and Culture: MICHELLE JANICE HOOYBOER-WINKLAAR.

Minister of Public Health and Sports: RICHARD WAYNE MILTON VISSER.

Minister Plenipotentiary and Member of the Council of Ministers of the Realm for Aruba in the Netherlands: EDWIN BIBIANO ABATH.

Minister Plenipotentiary of the Realm for Aruba in Washington, DC (USA): JOCELYNE CROES.

MINISTRIES

Office of the Governor: Plaza Henny Eman 3, POB 53, Oranjestad; tel. 5834445; fax 5820730; e-mail info@kabga.aw; internet www.kabga.aw.

Office of the Prime Minister: Government Offices, L. G. Smith Blvd 76, Oranjestad; tel. 5880300; fax 5880024.

Ministry of the Economy, Social Affairs and Culture: L. G. Smith Blvd 76, Oranjestad; tel. 5885455; fax 5827526.

Ministry of Finance, Communications, Utilities and Energy: L. G. Smith Blvd 76, Oranjestad; tel. 5835455; fax 5827538.

Ministry of General Affairs: L. G. Smith Blvd 76, Oranjestad; tel. 5830001; fax 5827513; e-mail rekenkamer@aruba.gov.aw.

Ministry of Integration, Infrastructure and the Environment: L. G. Smith Blvd 76, Oranjestad; tel. 5828368; fax 5827564.

Ministry of Justice and Education: L. G. Smith Blvd 76, Oranjestad; tel. 5830004; fax 5827518.

Ministry of Public Health and Sports: L. G. Smith Blvd 76, Oranjestad; tel. 5825751; fax 5827569.

Ministry of Tourism, Transport and Labour: L. G. Smith Blvd 76, Oranjestad; tel. 5827718; fax 5827556.

Office of the Minister Plenipotentiary for Aruba in the Netherlands: R. J. Schimmelpennincklaan 1, 2517 JN The Hague, Netherlands; tel. (70) 3566200; fax (70) 3451446; e-mail info@arubahuis.nl; internet www.arubahuis.nl.

Office of the Minister Plenipotentiary for Aruba in Washington, DC: 4200 Linnean Ave, NW, Washington, DC 20008, USA; tel. (202) 274-2601; fax (202) 237-8303; e-mail was-plvcdp@minbuza.nl.

Legislature

STATEN

President: RENDOLF A. LEE.

General Election, 25 September 2009

Party	Seats
Arubaanse Volkspartij	12
Movimentu Electoral di Pueblo	8
Democracia Real	1
Total	21

Political Organizations

Arubaanse Volkspartij (AVP) (Aruba People's Party): Avda Alo Tromp 56, Oranjestad; tel. 5830911; fax 5837963; e-mail info@avparuba.net; internet www.avparuba.net; f. 1942; advocates Aruba's separate status; Leader MICHIEL GODFRIED EMAN.

Democracia Real (Real Democracy): Oranjestad; f. 2004; Leader AINDIN BIKKER.

Movimentu Electoral di Pueblo (MEP) (People's Electoral Movement): Santa Cruz 74D, Oranjestad; tel. 5854495; fax 5850768; e-mail mep@setarnet.aw; internet www.mep.aw; f. 1971; socialist; 1,200 mems; Pres. and Leader NELSON ORLANDO ODUBER.

Movimento Patriotico Arubano (MPA) (Aruban Patriotic Movement): Oranjestad; Leader MONICA KOCK ARENDS.

Organisacion Liberal Arubano (OLA) (Aruban Liberal Organization): Oranjestad; f. 1991; Leader GLENBERT FRANCOIS CROES.

Partido Patriotico di Arubà (PPA) (Patriotic Party of Aruba): Clavelstraat 5, Sint Nicolaas; tel. 5844609; e-mail nisbet@ppa-aruba.org; internet www.ppa-aruba.org; f. 1949; social democratic; opposed to complete independence for Aruba; Leader BENEDICT (BENNY) JOCELYN MONTGOMERY NISBET.

RED Democratico (RED Democratic Network): Belgiestraat 14, Oranjestad; tel. 5820213; e-mail info@red.aw; internet www.red.aw; f. 2003; Leader ARMANDO LAMPE.

Judicial System

Legal authority is exercised by the Court of First Instance. Appeals are heard by the Joint High Court of Justice of the Netherlands Antilles and Aruba.

Attorney-General of Aruba: ROBERT PIETERSZ.

Solicitor-General of Aruba: NICO JÖRG.

Courts of Justice: J. G. Emanstraat 51, Oranjestad; tel. 5822294; fax 5821241; e-mail griffiekopie@setarnet.aw.

Religion

CHRISTIANITY

The Roman Catholic Church

Roman Catholics form the largest religious community, numbering more than 80% of the population. Aruba forms part of the diocese of Willemstad, comprising the Netherlands Antilles and Aruba. The Bishop resides in Willemstad (Curaçao, Netherlands Antilles).

Roman Catholic Church: J. Yrausquin Plein 3, POB 702, Oranjestad; tel. 5821434; fax 5821409.

The Anglican Communion

Within the Church in the Province of the West Indies, Aruba forms part of the diocese of the North Eastern Caribbean and Aruba. The Bishop is resident in The Valley, Anguilla.

Anglican Church: Holy Cross, Weg Seroe Pretoe 31, Sint Nicolaas; tel. 5845142; fax 5843394; e-mail holycross@setarnet.aw.

Protestant Churches

Baptist Church: Aruba Baptist Mission, SBC, Paradera 98-C; tel. 5883893.

Church of Christ: Pastoor Hendrikstraat 107, Sint Nicolaas; tel. 5848172.

Church of Jesus Christ of Latter Day Saints: Dadelstraat 16, Oranjestad; tel. 5823507.

Dutch Protestant Church: Wilhelminastraat 1, Oranjestad; tel. 5821435.

Evangelical Church of San Nicolas: Jasmijnstraat 7, Sint Nicolaas; tel. 5848973; e-mail ecsnaua@gmail.com; f. 1970.

Faith Revival Center: Rooi Afo 10, Paradera; tel. 5831010; fax 5833070.

Iglesia Evangelica Pentecostal: Asamblea di Dios, Reamurstraat 2, Oranjestad; tel. 5831940.

Jehovah's Witnesses: Guyabastraat 3, Oranjestad; tel. 5828963.

Methodist Church: Longfellowstraat, Oranjestad; tel. 5845243.

New Apostolic Church: Goletstraat 5A, Oranjestad; tel. 5833762.

Pentacostal Apostolic Assembly: Bernhardstraat 185; tel. 5848710; fax 5845699.

Seventh-day Adventist: Weststraat, Oranjestad; tel. 5845896.

JUDAISM

There are approximately 130 Jews in Aruba.

Beth Israel Synagogue: Adriaan Laclé Blvd, Oranjestad; tel. 5823272; fax 5823534; e-mail jcommaruba@gmail.com; internet bethisrael-aruba.blogspot.com; Rabbi MARIO GUREVICH.

BAHÁ'Í FAITH

Spiritual Assembly: Bucutiweg 19, Oranjestad; tel. 5823104; Contact M. CHRISTIAN.

The Press

DAILIES

Amigoe di Aruba: Bilderdijkstraat 16-2, POB 323, Oranjestad; tel. 5824333; fax 5822368; e-mail amigoearuba@setarnet.aw; internet www.amigoe.com; f. 1884; Dutch; Dir WILLEM DA COSTA GOMEZ; Editor JEAN MENTENS; circ. 12,000 (in Aruba and Netherlands Antilles).

Aruba Today: Weststraat 22, Oranjestad; tel. 5827800; fax 5827093; e-mail info@arubatoday.com; internet www.arubatoday.com; English; Editor-in-Chief JULIA C. RENFRO.

Bon Dia Aruba: Weststraat 22, Oranjestad; tel. 5827800; fax 5827044; e-mail infor@bondia.com; internet www.bondia.com; Papiamento; Dirs JOHN CHEMALY, JOHN CHEMALY, Jr.

Diario: Engelandstraat 29, POB 577, Oranjestad; tel. 5826747; fax 5828551; e-mail noticia@diarioaruba.com; internet www.diarioaruba.com; f. 1980; Papiamento; morning; Editor and Man. JOSSY M. MANSUR; circ. 15,000.

The News: Italiestraat 5, POB 300, Oranjestad; tel. 5824725; fax 5889430; e-mail thenewsaruba@setarnet.aw; f. 1951; English; Dir SONIA WEVER-SCHOUTEN; Editor-in-Chief MARGARET BONARRIVA-WEVER; circ. 6,900.

La Prensa: Bachstraat 6, POB 566, Oranjestad; tel. 5821199; fax 5828634; e-mail laprensa@laprensacur.com; internet www.laprensacur.com; f. 1929; Papiamento; Editor THOMAS C. PIETERSZ.

NEWS AGENCIES

Algemeen Nederlands Persbureau (ANP) (The Netherlands): Caya G. F. (Betico) Croes 110, POB 323, Oranjestad; tel. 5824333; fax 5822368; internet www.anp.nl.

Aruba News Agencies: Bachstraat 6, Oranjestad; tel. 5821243.

Publishers

Aruba Experience Publications NV: Verbindingsweg 2, POB 634, Oranjestad; tel. 5834467; fax 5384520; e-mail info@arubaexperience.com; internet www.arubaexperience.com; f. 1985; Gen. Man. FRANCO SNEEK.

Caribbean Publishing Co Ltd (CPC): L. G. Smith Blvd 116, Oranjestad; tel. 5820485; fax 5820484.

De Wit Stores NV: L. G. Smith Blvd 110, POB 386, Oranjestad; tel. 5823500; fax 5821575; e-mail info@dewitvandorp.com; f. 1948; Gen. Man. LYANNE BEAUJON.

Editorial Charuba: Lagoenweg 31, Oranjestad; tel. 7301512; fax 5884574; e-mail alivaro@hotmail.com; f. 1982; Pres. ALICE VAN ROMONDT.

Gold Book Publishing: L. G. Smith Blvd 116, Oranjestad; tel. 5820485; fax 5820484; internet www.caribbeanhotelassociation.com; a division of the Caribbean Hotel and Tourism Asscn, based in Miami, FL, USA; Chair. WARREN BINDER.

Oranjestad Printing NV: Italiestraat 5, POB 300, Oranjestad; Man. Dir GERARDUS J. SCHOUTEN.

ProGraphics Inc: Italiestraat 5, POB 201, Oranjestad; tel. 5824550; fax 5833072; e-mail prographics@setarnet.aw; f. 2001; fmrly VAD Printers Inc; Publr H. VAN DER PUTTEN.

Van Dorp Aruba NV: Caya G. F. (Betico) Croes 77, POB 596, Oranjestad; tel. 5823076; fax 5823573.

Broadcasting and Communications

TELECOMMUNICATIONS

Digicel Aruba: Marisol Bldg, L. G. Smith Blvd 60, POB 662, Oranjestad; tel. 5222222; fax 5222223; e-mail customercarearuba@digicelgroup.com; internet www.digicelaruba.com; f. 2003; owned by an Irish consortium; established a mobile cellular telephone network connecting Aruba with Bonaire and Curaçao in July 2006; Chair. DENIS O'BRIEN; CEO (Dutch Caribbean) HANS LUTE; Gen. Man. (Aruba) BERT SCHREUDERS.

Servicio di Telecomunicacion di Aruba (SETAR): Seroe Blanco z/n, POB 13, Oranjestad; tel. 5251000; fax 5251515; e-mail sysop@setarnet.aw; internet www.setar.aw; f. 1986; Man. Dir ROLAND CROES.

BROADCASTING

Radio

Canal 90 FM Stereo: Van Leeuwenhoekstraat 26, Oranjestad; tel. 5828952; fax 837340; e-mail info@canal90fm.aw; internet www.canal90fm.aw/index2.htm; Producer M. GRAVENHORST.

Cristal Sound 101.7 FM: J. G. Emanstraat 124A, Oranjestad; tel. 5820017; fax 5820144.

Hit 94 FM: Caya Ernesto Petronia 68, Oranjestad; tel. 5820694; fax 5820494; e-mail hit94@setarnet.aw; internet www.hit94fm.com; f. 1993; Dir JOHNNY HABIBE.

Magic 96.5 FM: Caya G.F. Betico Croes 164, Oranjestad; tel. 5865353; fax 5835354; internet www.magic965.com; Owner and Dir ERIN J. CROES; Producer RUBEN GARCIA.

Radio 1270 AM: Bernardstraat 138, POB 28, Sint Nicolaas; tel. 5845602; fax 5827753; commercial station; programmes in Dutch, English, Spanish and Papiamento; Dir F. A. LEAUER; Station Man. J. A. C. ALDERS.

Radio Carina FM: Datustraat 10A, Oranjestad; tel. 5821450; fax 5831955; commercial station; programmes in Dutch, English, Spanish and Papiamento; Dir-Gen. ALBERT R. DIEFFENTHALER.

Radio Caruso Booy FM: G. M. de Bruynewijk 49, Savaneta; tel. 5847752; fax 5843351; e-mail sira@setarnet.aw; commercial station; broadcasts for 24 hrs a day; programmes in Dutch, English, Spanish and Papiamento; Pres. HUBERT ERQUILLES ANTONIO BOOY; Gen. Man. SIRA BOOY.

Radio Kelkboom: Bloemond 14, POB 146, Oranjestad; tel. 5821899; fax 5834825; e-mail radiokelkboom@setarnet.aw; internet www.watapana-aruba.com; f. 1954; commercial radio station; affiliated with Radio Nederland Wereldomroep (Netherlands) and Voice of America (USA); programmes in Papiamento, Dutch, English and Spanish; Man. Dir EMILE A. M. KELKBOOM.

Radio Victoria: Washington 23A, POB 5291, Oranjestad; tel. and fax 5873444; e-mail radiovictoria@setarnet.aw; internet www.radiovictoriaaruba.org; f. 1958; religious and cultural FM radio station owned by the Radio Victoria Foundation; programmes in Dutch, English, Spanish, Papiamento, Dutch, Tagalog, Creole and Mandarin; Pres. N. J. F. ARTS.

Voz di Aruba (Voice of Aruba): Van Leeuwenhoekstraat 26, POB 219, Oranjestad; tel. 5823355; fax 5837340; commercial radio station; programmes in Dutch, English, Spanish and Papiamento; also operates Canal 90 on FM; Dir A. M. ARENDS, Jr.

Television

ABC Aruba Broadcasting Co NV (ATV): Royal Plaza Suite 223, POB 5040, Oranjestad; tel. 5838150; fax 5838110; e-mail 15atv@setarnet.aw.

Telearuba NV: Pos Chiquito 1A, POB 392, Oranjestad; tel. 5851000; fax 5851111; e-mail info@telearuba.aw; internet www.telearuba.aw; f. 1963; fmrly operated by Netherlands Antilles Television Co; commercial; acquired by SETAR in March 2005; Gen. Man. M. MARCHENA.

Finance

(cap. = capital; res = reserves; dep. = deposits; m. = million; brs = branches; amounts in Aruban florin, unless otherwise stated)

BANKING

Central Bank

Centrale Bank van Aruba: J. E. Irausquin Blvd 8, POB 18, Oranjestad; tel. 5252100; fax 5252101; e-mail cbaua@setarnet.aw; internet www.cbaruba.org; f. 1986; cap. 10.0m., res 224.9m., dep. 814.2m. (Dec. 2008); Chair. A. J. SWAEN; Pres. JANE R. FIGAROA-SEMELEER.

Commercial Banks

Aruba Bank NV: Camacuri 12, POB 192, Oranjestad; tel. 5277777; fax 5277715; e-mail info@arubabank.com; internet www.arubabank.com; f. 1925; acquired Interbank Aruba NV in Dec. 2003; total assets US $260m. (Dec. 2004); Chair. B. W. H. GUIS; Man. Dir and CEO EDWIN TROMP; 5 brs.

Banco di Caribe NV: Vondellaan 31, POB 493, Oranjestad; tel. 5232000; fax 5832422; e-mail bdcaua@setarnet.aw; internet www.bancodicaribe.com; f. 1987; Gen. Man. and CEO IDEFONS D. SIMON; Man. (Aruba) EDUARDO DE KORT; 1 br.

Caribbean Mercantile Bank Aruba: Caya G. F. (Betico) Croes 53, POB 28, Oranjestad; tel. 5823118; fax 5830919; e-mail executive_office@cmbnv.com; internet www.cmbnv.com; f. 1963; cap. 4.0m., res 109.6m., dep. 1,110.8m. (Dec. 2008); Chair. LIONEL CAPRILES, II; Gen. Man. Dir J. E. WOLTER; 6 brs.

RBTT Bank Aruba NV: Italiestraat 36, Sasakiweg, Oranjestad; tel. 5233100; fax 58821576; e-mail info@tt.rbtt.com; internet www.rbtt.com; f. 2001; fmrly First National Bank of Aruba NV (f. 1985 and acquired by Royal Bank of Trinidad and Tobago Ltd in 1998); total assets US $111.5m. (Dec. 2003); Chair. PETER J. JULY; 6 brs.

Investment Bank

AIB NV: Wilhelminastraat 34–36, POB 1011, Oranjestad; tel. 5827327; fax 5827461; e-mail info@aib-bank.com; internet www.aib-bank.com; f. 1987 as Aruban Investment Bank; name changed as above in April 2004; total assets 149.0m. (Dec. 2005); Man. Dir FRENDSEL W. GIEL; Asst Man. Dir HERRY M. KOOLMAN.

Mortgage Bank

Fundacion Cas pa Comunidad Arubano (FCCA): Sabana Blanco 66, Oranjestad; tel. 5238800; fax 5836272; e-mail info@fcca.com; internet www.fcca.com; f. 1979; Man. Dir PETER VAN POPPEL.

INSURANCE

There were eight life insurance companies and 13 non-life insurance companies active in Aruba in December 2007.

Association

Insurance Association of Aruba (IAA): Sun Plaza 202, Oranjestad; tel. 5825500; fax 5822126; e-mail prakash.gupta@aig.com; Pres. PRAKASH GUPTA; 10 mems.

Trade and Industry

DEVELOPMENT ORGANIZATIONS

Department of Agriculture, Husbandry and Fisheries: Piedra Plat 114A, Oranjestad; tel. 5858102; fax 5855639; e-mail dlvv@aruba.gov.aw; internet www.overheid.aw; f. 1976; Dir T. G. DAMIAN.

Department of Economic Affairs, Commerce and Industry (Directie Economische Zaken, Handel en Industrie): Sun Plaza Bldg, L. G. Smith Blvd 160, Oranjestad; tel. 5821181; fax 5834494; e-mail deaci@setarnet.aw; internet www.arubaeconomicaffairs.aw; f. 1986; Dir MARIA DIJKHOFF-PITA.

CHAMBER OF COMMERCE AND INDUSTRY

Chamber of Commerce and Industry Aruba: J. E. Irausquin Blvd 10, POB 140, Oranjestad; tel. 5821120; fax 5883200; e-mail secretariat@arubachamber.com; internet www.arubachamber.com; f. 1930; Pres. EDWIN A. ROOS; Exec. Dir LORRAINE C. DE SOUZA.

TRADE ASSOCIATION

Aruba Trade and Industry Association (ATIA): ATIA Bldg, Pedro Gallegostraat 6, Dakota, POB 562, Oranjestad; tel. 5827593; fax 5833068; e-mail atiaruba@setarnet.aw; internet www.atiaruba.org; f. 1945; Pres. STEPHEN DAAL; Chair. and Sec. FRANK SNIJDERS; 250 mems.

MAJOR COMPANIES

Albo Aruba NV: Barcadera 122, Oranjestad; tel. 5285808; fax 5853766; e-mail info@alboaruba.com; internet www.alboaruba.com; f. 1980, combining Albo Bonaire NV and Bonbocemi NV; civil construction; wholly owned subsidiary of Albo Holding Co NV since 1986; Man. Dir FOLKERT G. VAN DER WOUDE.

Arena Contractors: L. G. Smith Blvd 116, Oranjestad; tel. 5881310; fax 5838514; internet www.arenacontractorsnv.com; f. 2006; clay products; Man. Dir EDITH MARIA PEREZ.

Aruba Aloe Balm NV: Pitastraat 115, Hato, Oranjestad; tel. 5883222; fax 5826081; e-mail customerservice@arubaaloe.com; internet www.arubaaloe.com; f. 1890; aloe-based skin-care products; Man. Dir LOUIS POSNER.

Arubaanse Verffabriek NV (Arvefa): L. G. Smith Blvd 144, POB 297, Oranjestad; tel. 5822519; fax 5827225; e-mail farts@arvefaaruba.com; internet www.arvefaaruba.com; f. 1969; manufactures paints and fillers; Man. FRED ARTS.

Arubaanse Wegenbouw Maatschappij NV (Aruba Road Construction Co): Barcadera 122, Oranjestad; tel. 5853007; fax 5853766; e-mail info@alboaruba.com; internet www.awmaruba.com; f. 1960; wholly owned subsidiary of Albo Holding Co NV; Man. Dir MICHIEL J. L. DAEMS; 100 employees.

Aruba Candle Co NV: Franlinstraat z/n, POB 240, Oranjestad; tel. and fax 5821958; candles, disinfectants; Dir MICHAEL SALADIN.

Aruba Marriott Resort and Stellaris Casino: L. G. Smith Blvd 101, Palm Beach, Oranjestad; tel. 5869000; fax 5206227; e-mail marriott@setarnet.aw; internet www.marriottaruba.com; Gen. Man. RICK ZEOLLA; 670 employees.

Aruba Trading Company: Weststraat 15–17, POB 156, Oranjestad; tel. 5823950; fax 5832165; e-mail info@arubatrading.com; internet www.arubatrading.com; f. 1928; distribution of general goods, incl. food and drink, clothing and household items; Man. Dir ANDREW L. BARBOUR; 80 employees.

ATCO (Associated Transport Company): Sabana Blanco 2, POB 189, Oranjestad; tel. 5821523; fax 5886761; e-mail info@atco.aw; internet www.atcoaruba.com; f. 1949; part of MetaCorp conglomerate; provides heavy lift and transport equipment services to construction and petrochemical industries; manufacturer of concrete and paving materials; operates waste management and recycling services.

Barcadera Cement Aruba: c/o J. G. Emanstraat 118A, POB 614, Oranjestad; tel. 5837286; fax 5831545; e-mail info@thielcorp.aw; internet www.thielcorp.aw; subsidiary of Thiel Materials NV; cement producers; Dir ANTHONY THIEL.

Brouwerij Nacional Balashi NV: POB 5317, Balashi; tel. 5922544; fax 5236544; internet www.balashi.com; f. 1997; brewery; owned by MetaCorp NV conglomerate; Man. Dir EDUARD L. J. DE VEER.

Carex Paper Products NV: Belgiëstraat 5, Oranjestad; tel. 5821404; fax 5831114; e-mail carexpaper@setarnet.aw; internet www.carexpaper.com; manufactures toilet paper, kitchen towels; Gen. Man. PATRICK MELCHIORS.

Caribbean Paint Factory Aruba NV: Sabana Blanco 16A, POB 273, Oranjestad; tel. 5825339; fax 5837063; e-mail akamermans@setarnet.aw; internet www.cpfaruba.com; f. 1986; paint manufacturer; Dir ANTONY KAMERMANS.

Heineken Aruba NV: Frankinstraat 6, Oranjestad; tel. 5833390; e-mail patrick.melchiors@heineken.com; internet www.heinekeninternational.com; Gen. Man. PATRICK MELCHIORS.

Hoori NV: Balashi 70, POB 1176, Oranjestad; tel. 5856400; fax 5851466; manufactures disposable plastic materials; Dir MOON CHIU CHAN.

Hyatt Regency Aruba Resort & Casino: J. A. Irausquin Blvd 85, Palm Beach, Oranjestad; tel. 5861234; fax 5861682; e-mail adventure.concierge@hyatt.com; internet www.aruba.hyatt.com; f. 1990; Hyatt Hotels Corpn; Gen. Man. SUSAN SANTIAGO; 670 employees.

Ling & Sons: Schotlandstraat 41, Oranjestad; tel. 5832370; fax 5887718; e-mail info@lingandsons.com; internet www.lingandsons.com; f. 1965; groceries retailer and wholesaler; mem. of the Independent Grocers Asscn; Gen. Man. CLIFTON LING.

R. J. van der Sar NV: Barcadera 9, POB 299, Oranjestad; tel. 5850631; fax 5850645; internet volsar@setarnet.aw; internet www.vandersarnv.com; f. 1975; manufactures disinfectants, soaps, detergents; Dir ROBERT NIEUW.

Valero Energy Corporation: 5 Lago Weg, Sint Nicolaas; internet www.valero.com; owns island's oil refinery, Valero Aruba Refining Co NV; refinery closed in Sept. 2009; negotiations to sell refinery ongoing in mid-2010; CEO WILLIAM R. KLESSE.

UTILITIES

Electricity and Water

Utilities Aruba NV: Arulex Center, Punta Brabo z/n; tel. 5828277; fax 5828682; e-mail utilities.aruba.hhenriquez@gmail.com; govt-owned holding co; Man. Dir HAROLD HENRIQUEZ.

Electriciteit-Maatschappij Aruba (ELMAR) NV: Wilhelminastraat 110, POB 202, Oranjestad; tel. 5237100; fax 5828991; e-mail info@elmar.aw; internet www.elmar.aw; independently managed co, residing under Utilities Aruba NV; electricity distribution; Man. Dir A. O. RAFINÉ; 160 employees.**Water en Energiebedrijf Aruba (WEB) NV:** Balashi 76, POB 575, Oranjestad; tel. 5254600; fax 5857681; e-mail info@webaruba.com; internet www.webaruba.com; f. 1991; independently managed co, residing under Utilities Aruba NV; production and distribution of industrial and potable water, and electricity generation; Man. Dir JOSSY M. LACLÉ.

Gas

Aruba Gas Supply Company Ltd (ARUGAS): Barcadera z/n, POB 190, Oranjestad; tel. 5851198; fax 5852187; e-mail webmaster@arugas.com; internet www.arugas.com; f. 1940.

BOC Gases Aruba NV: Balashi z/n, POB 387, Oranjestad; tel. 5852624; fax 5852823; e-mail bocaruba@setarnet.aw; internet www.boc-gases.com; acquired by the Linde Group global industrial gases and engineering org. in 2006; Man. Dir J. KENT MASTERS (responsible for Americas, South Pacific and Africa).

TRADE UNIONS

Federacion di Trahadornan di Aruba (FTA) (Aruban Workers' Federation): Bernhardstraat 23, Sint Nicolaas; tel. 5845448; fax 5845504; e-mail fetraua@setarnet.aw; f. 1964; independent; affiliated with the International Trade Union Confederation; Pres. JOSÉ RUDOLF (RUDY) GEERMAN; Vice-Pres. JANE ANASTACIA BRAAFHART.

There are also several unions for government and semi-government workers and employees.

Transport

There are no railways, but Aruba has a network of all-weather roads.

Arubus NV: Sabana Blanco 67, Oranjestad; tel. 5882300; fax 5828633; e-mail info@arubus.com; internet www.arubus.com; f. 1979; state-owned company providing public transport services; runs a fleet of 48 buses; Dir FRANKLIN KUIPERI.

SHIPPING

The island's principal seaport is Oranjestad, whose harbour can accommodate ocean-going vessels. There are also ports at Barcadera and Sint Nicolaas.

Aruba Ports Authority NV: Port Administration Bldg, L. G. Smith Blvd 23, Oranjestad; tel. 5826633; fax 5832896; e-mail info@arubaports.com; internet www.arubaports.com; f. 1981; responsible for the administration of the ports of Oranjestad and Barcadera; Man. Dir JUAN ALFONSO BOEKHOUDT.

Valero Aruba Refining Co NV: Lagoweg 5, POB 2150, Sint Nicolaas; tel. 5894904; fax 5849087; internet www.valero.com; f. 1989; acquired by Valero in 2004; petroleum refinery, responsible for the administration of the port of Sint Nicolaas; closed in Sept. 2009; negotiations to sell refinery ongoing in mid-2010; Gen. Man. RAYMOND A. BUCKLEY.

Principal Shipping Companies

Aruba Stevedoring Co (ASTEC), NV: Port Administration Bldg, L. G. Smith Blvd 23, Oranjestad; tel. 5822558; fax 5834570; e-mail astec_admin@setarnet.aw.

SEL Maduro & Sons (Aruba) Inc: Rockefellerstraat 1, Oranjestad; tel. 5282343; fax 5826003; internet www.selmaduro.com; ship husbandry and port agent; also provides container services, cargo services, moving services, real estate and travel services; Man. Dir HANS VAN ESVELD; Man. GRACEO DUNLOCK (Shipping and Container Services).

Valero Aruba Marine Services: Lagoweg, POB 2150, Sint Nicolaas; tel. 5894742; fax 5894554.

VR Shipping NV: Executive Bldg, Frankrijkstraat 1, POB 633, Oranjestad; tel. 5821953; fax 5825988; e-mail info@vrshipping.com; internet www.vrshipping.com; f. 1975 as Anthony Veder & Co; name changed as above 2000.

CIVIL AVIATION

The Queen Beatrix International Airport (Aeropuerto Internacional Reina Beatrix), about 2.5 km from Oranjestad, is served by numerous airlines (including Dutch Antilles Express, based in Curaçao, Netherlands Antilles), linking the island with destinations in the Caribbean, Europe, the USA, and Central and South America. After renovation and expansion, the airport was expected to be able to handle 2.6m. passengers per year by 2010. In November 2000 the national carrier, Air Aruba, was declared bankrupt.

Aruba Airport Authority NV: Queen Beatrix International Airport, Wayaca z/n, Oranjestad; tel. 5242424; fax 5834229; e-mail p.steinmetz@airportaruba.com; internet www.airportaruba.com; Man. Dir PETER STEINMETZ.

Tourism

Aruba's white sandy beaches, particularly along the southern coast, are an attraction for foreign visitors, and tourism is a major industry. The number of hotel rooms totalled 7,441 in early 2009. In 2009 some 1,419,391 tourists visited Aruba, of which 812,623 were stop-over visitors and 606,768 were cruise ship passengers. Most stop-over visitors came from the USA (65.3% in 2008), Venezuela (13.6%) and the Netherlands (5.0%). Receipts from tourism totalled A Fl. 2,314.1m. in 2009.

Aruba Cruise Tourism: Suite 230, Royal Plaza Mall, L. G. Smith Blvd 94, POB 5254, Oranjestad; tel. 5833648; fax 5835088; e-mail info@arubabycruise.com; internet www.arubabycruise.com; f. 1995 as the Cruise Tourism Authority—Aruba; name changed as above in 2005; non-profit government organization; Exec. Dir KATHLEEN ROJER.

Aruba Hotel and Tourism Association (AHATA): L. G. Smith Blvd 174, POB 542, Oranjestad; tel. 5822607; fax 5824202; e-mail info@ahata.com; internet www.ahata.com; f. 1965; 101 mems; Pres. and CEO ROB SMITH; Chair. EWALD BIEMANS.

Aruba Tourism Authority (ATA): L. G. Smith Blvd 172, Eagle, Oranjestad; tel. 5823777; fax 5834702; e-mail ata.aruba@aruba.com; internet www.aruba.com; f. 1953; Man. Dir MYRNA JANSEN-FELICIANO.

Defence

The Netherlands is responsible for Aruba's defence, and military service is compulsory. The Dutch-appointed Governor is Commander-in-Chief of the armed forces on the island. A Dutch naval contingent is stationed in the Netherlands Antilles and Aruba. In May 1999 the USA began air force and navy patrols from a base on Aruba as part of efforts to prevent the transport of illegal drugs.

Education

A Compulsory Education Act was introduced in 1999 for those aged between four and 16. Kindergarten begins at four years of age. Primary education begins at six years of age and lasts for six years. Secondary education, beginning at the age of 12, lasts for up to six years. In 2007/08 enrolment at primary schools included 99% of pupils in the relevant age-group, while the comparable ratio at secondary schools was 75%. The main language of instruction is Dutch, but Papiamento (using a different spelling system from that of the Netherlands Antilles) is used in kindergarten and primary education and in the lower levels of technical and vocational education. Papiamento is also being introduced into the curriculum in all schools. Aruba has two institutes of higher education: the University of Aruba, comprising the School of Law and the School of Business Administration, and the Teachers' College. There is also a community college. However, the majority of students continue their studies abroad, generally in the Netherlands. General government expenditure on education in 2008 amounted to A Fl. 308.3m., equivalent to 17.5% of total expenditure.

Bibliography

Croes, R. R. *Anatomy of Demand in International Tourism: The Case of Aruba*. Saarbrücken, LAP LAMBERT Academic Publishing, 2010.

Haanappel, P., *et al* (Eds). *The Civil Code of the Netherlands Antilles and Aruba*. Kluwer Law International, 2002.

International Monetary Fund, *The Kingdom of the Netherlands—Aruba: 2007 Article IV Consultation—Staff Report; Public Information Notice on the Executive Board Discussion; and Statement by the Executive Director for the Kingdom of the Netherlands—Aruba*. Washington, DC, IMF Staff Country Report, 2008.

Oostindie, G. *Paradise Overseas: The Dutch Caribbean: Colonialism and its Transatlantic Legacies*. Oxford, Macmillan Caribbean, 2004.

Schoenhals, K. *Netherlands Antilles and Aruba*. Oxford, Clio Press, 1993.

THE BAHAMAS

Geography

PHYSICAL FEATURES

The Commonwealth of the Bahamas forms part of the West Indies, but, as it is located to the north of the Greater Antilles and east of Florida (USA), the archipelago lies in the Atlantic Ocean, not the Caribbean Sea. The island chain begins some 80 km (50 miles) off the coast of south-eastern Florida, arcing south and east to tail off in the Turks and Caicos Islands, a British dependency that lies just over 60 km south-east of Mayaguana and to the west of Great Inagua, the southernmost of the Bahamas. The country ends here, just to the north of the Windward Passage between the Antillean islands of Cuba and Hispaniola, giving the Bahamas two more international neighbours less than 100 km from its shores—Haiti to the south-east and Cuba to the south. The Tropic of Cancer bisects the country, crossing Long Island. The myriad islands of the Bahamas cover 13,939 sq km (5,382 sq miles), of which 3,870 sq km are enclosed or inland waters.

There are almost 700 islands and some 2,000 cays (keys) and rocky islets in the Bahamas, giving the country coastlines that total 3,542 km in length. Most of the islands are coralline, usually flat, many of the larger ones being long and thin. Low hills relieve the landscape in places, the highest point in the country being Mt Alvernia (63 m or 207 ft) on Cat Island (once believed to be the San Salvador where the Italian navigator Christopher Columbus first set foot in the Americas). This terrain, as well as the dry climate, does not support much arable land. In the north of the archipelago is Grand Bahama, the main island nearest to Florida, while to its east, marking the other edge of the Little Bahama Bank, are Little Abaco and Great Abaco. To the south of Grand Bahama is the Great Bahama Bank, marked above sea level by the landmass of Andros, the largest island in the country, as well as Bimini and Berry and Williams Islands. East of Andros, beyond the continuation of the Northeast Providence Channel known as the Tongue of the Ocean (which plunges some 6,000 m beneath the surface), rises the relatively small, but densely populated, island of New Providence, the location of Nassau, the national capital. East of New Providence, Eleuthera continues the chain of long, thin islands heading south from Great Abaco, with Cat Island and Long Island following. East of Cat Island and Long Island is, among others, the island now called San Salvador (formerly Watling Island), while to the west is Great Exuma, another long, thin stretch of territory. By now heading more east than south, the remaining large islands of the Bahamas include Crooked and Acklins Islands and, beyond the Mayaguana Passage, Mayaguana itself and, to its south, Little Inagua (where Bahamian territory comes closest to the Turks and Caicos Islands—West Caicos) and Great Inagua, the latter dominated by Lake Rosa at its heart. Particularly to the west of the main chain of islands and islets, numerous reefs and cays dot the ocean, extending the country's territorial waters to cover well over 0.25m. sq km. The Andros Barrier Reef is the third largest such reef in the world and the largest after that of Belize in the Americas.

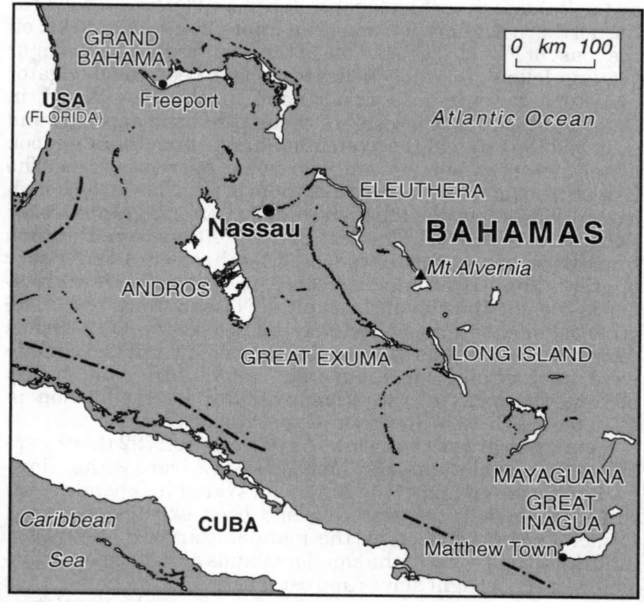

CLIMATE

The climate is tropical marine, moderated by the Gulf Stream and the Atlantic trade winds. The islands are prone to hurricanes, which can be particularly devastating given the low-lying terrain. Precipitation is not profuse, and the annual average is 1,360 mm (53 ins), falling mostly in June and then the four months thereafter. Seasonal variations in temperature are slight, with the weather always being warm—the month with the highest average daily maximum temperature is August (89.3°F or 31.8°C), while the lowest daily minimum is in January (62.1°F or 16.7°C).

POPULATION

The population is predominantly black (about 85% of African descent, according to the 1990 census), but there is a substantial white population (12%), which, statistically, does not include those of Hispanic descent (3%). The people of the Bahamas are generally Christian, the largest denomination being the Baptists (35%), but there are also numerous other Protestant denominations, as well as sizeable Anglican (15%) and Roman Catholic (14%) communities. Apart from the Creole spoken by some Haitian immigrants, the main language in use, as well as the official one, is English.

At mid-2010 the total population of the Bahamas was 346,900. Just over two-thirds of the population lived in the capital, Nassau, on New Providence. In mid-2009 the city and its suburbs housed an estimated 247,659. The other islands, of which about 29 are inhabited, are known as the Out Islands or Family Islands. The more populous ones are Grand Bahama, where the second largest city, Freeport, is located, Eleuthera, the original site of settlement by the British, and Andros. The country is divided into 21 administrative districts.

History

MARK WILSON

INTRODUCTION

The nearly 700 islands and 2,000 uninhabited cays that make up the Bahamian archipelago stretch in a 1,220 km arc towards the northern edge of the Caribbean from a point some 80 km off the coast of Florida (USA). One of the islands, San Salvador or Watling Island, is widely believed to have been the navigator Christopher Columbus's first landfall in the New World, in October 1492. The Spanish are thought to have deported and enslaved the original Lucayan inhabitants, but otherwise took little interest in the dry and somewhat barren islands. The British also found little to attract them to the islands, although a royal charter permitting their exploitation was granted to Sir Robert Heath in 1629. The first British settlers were Puritans from Bermuda, who arrived on Eleuthera in 1647. Other migrants from Bermuda also came, to seek salt. New Providence became the site of the capital, Nassau, from 1666. The other islands became collectively known as the Out Islands and, more recently, as the Family Islands. The soil and climate were not suitable for commercial agriculture, and piracy became the basis of the economy, until its eradication in 1719 by the British Governor, Capt. Woodes Rogers.

Population growth was slow. As recently as 1782 there were only 4,000 inhabitants, of whom some 43% were white. However, with the ending of the American War of Independence at this time, loyalist settlers who had been expelled from the former British colonies on the mainland arrived. New Englanders settled some of the smaller islands as fishermen, while southerners brought slaves and established cotton plantations on some of the larger islands. Within four years, the population had grown to 8,950, of whom 67% were black. However, the cotton plantations were soon abandoned, owing to insect pests and soil exhaustion. In total, fewer than 10,000 slaves were landed in the colony, and many were freed from bondage long before emancipation in 1834, when the population was an estimated 21,000. Then, as now, whites formed a significant minority. A further minority group originated directly from Africa, without any experience of New World slavery: several Bahamian villages were constructed on land granted to Africans freed by the British navy from captured Spanish vessels, which were intercepted *en route* to Cuba, following the abolition of the slave trade. Poor soil and a dry climate continued to prevent the development of plantation agriculture. The economy was based successively on plundering wrecks, gun--running during the American Civil War (1861–65), the cultivation of citrus and pineapples, sponge-fishing and the smuggling of rum and whisky during the US 'Prohibition' of alcoholic liquors in 1919–33.

Although there was some miscegenation, a rigid colour bar prevented black advancement. Accordingly, when a representative House of Assembly was established in 1729, it was an exclusive preserve of the white settlers and merchants. Despite being briefly suspended in 1776, when the colony was captured by the rebel American colonists, and again in 1782 when it surrendered to the Spanish, the House of Assembly remained a permanent feature of Bahamian politics.

Although free black property owners were able to vote from 1807, and the Assembly had four non-white members by as early as 1834, political and economic life was controlled, to all intents and purposes, by a white merchant élite, the so-called 'Bay Street Boys' (named after Nassau's main commercial street). This oligarchy practised blatant electoral bribery in small Out Island constituencies, where the secret ballot was not introduced until 1949. The élite's electoral power was challenged by just a small number of black and mixed-race members and by Sir Etienne Dupuch's *Nassau Tribune*.

POLITICAL AWAKENING

Black political awakening can be traced to the so-called Burma Road riots in 1942. By this time, after centuries of extreme variations in the island's fortunes, the economy was beginning to expand, with tourism growing steadily from the 1920s and the construction of US military bases required by the Second World War. The riots erupted over the issue of differential wages paid during the construction of a US Air Force base, to foreign and white workers on the one hand and to black Bahamians on the other. Two people were killed and 25 injured in the riots, which were followed by significant pay increases for black workers. The colony's first political party, the Progressive Liberal Party (PLP), was founded by a group of mixed-race professionals in 1953. In 1956 Sir Etienne Dupuch successfully advocated legislation to outlaw racial discrimination in public places. The 'Bay Street Boys' responded to the formation of the PLP by creating the United Bahamian Party (UBP). Lynden (later Sir Lynden) Pindling, a newly qualified black lawyer, later took over the leadership of the PLP, breaking with an older generation of mainly mixed-race PLP politicians. A tourism industry strike in 1958 was followed by universal male suffrage and the creation of four seats in New Providence, to reduce under-representation of the most densely populated island. The UBP benefited from the continuing over-representation of the less populous islands and won a majority of seats in the 1962 election, with only 36% of the popular vote, less than the 45% polled by the PLP. However, reports of the privately owned Grand Bahama Port Authority, which had recently been granted a casino licence, paying large consultancy fees to cabinet ministers severely damaged the reputation of the oligarchy.

INDEPENDENCE

In the historic January 1967 general election vigorous PLP campaigning resulted in each party winning 18 seats in the 38-seat House of Assembly. The sole representative of the Labour Party held the balance of power, and pledged his support for the PLP, which was therefore able to form a Government; Pindling, hailed as the 'Black Moses', became premier. The racial strife and economic collapse confidently predicted by the UBP never materialized, and a series of constitutional reforms was soon introduced. Because of the insistence by the PLP on black advancement, local control over immigration was regarded as especially important, and the import of mainly white, expatriate labour became progressively restricted.

The PLP won the 1968 election, securing 29 legislative seats; after further endorsement at a general election in 1972, the PLP led the country to independence in 1973. There was, however, growing middle-class resentment at Pindling's dictatorial style of leadership, while allegations of corruption became widespread. Dissident members resigned from the PLP, and in 1972 merged with the remnants of the UBP to form a new opposition party, the Free National Movement (FNM).

By the mid-1970s drugs-trafficking and money-laundering had become significant activities in the Bahamas. In 1984 the total value of the illegal drugs trade passing through the islands was conservatively estimated at some US $800m. Worse still was a virtual epidemic in the local use of drugs. Violent crime increased dramatically as addiction began to affect members of all social classes across the Bahamas. Initially, Pindling resisted pressure from the US Administration, notably the Drug Enforcement Agency (DEA). However, in 1983 he was publicly accused by a US television network of personal involvement and was forced to establish a Royal Commission to investigate the issue.

The Commission reported in December 1984. Although no evidence was published implicating Pindling, the same could not be said of several other ministers. However, a minority report noted a prominent Bahamian businessman, Everette Bannister, had made substantial payments to Pindling, enabling the Prime Minister to spend more than eight times his official salary (in early 1989 Bannister was indicted in the USA, on charges of conspiring with the Colombian Medellín cartel to transport drugs through the Bahamas). However, few dismissals followed and Pindling was re-endorsed as party leader at the 1985 PLP convention. Two cabinet ministers, Hubert Ingraham and Perry Christie, who also shared a legal practice, resigned in protest. These two later both served as Prime Minister, with Ingraham leading an FNM Government for 10 years from 1992, and Christie succeeding him in 2002, as leader of a PLP Government.

The damage caused to Bahamian-US relations was serious. The US Administration's concern went beyond trafficking: the strict banking secrecy laws, under which US and other 'offshore' banks in the islands operated, were also criticized because of their misuse by criminals. Moreover, US companies and individuals who used Bahamian banks deprived the US Internal Revenue Service (IRS) of tax income. Consequently, the Bahamas was excluded from the US Caribbean Basin Initiative, and tax concessions were not granted to US insurance companies wishing to exploit Bahamian 'offshore' facilities, nor to US corporations holding conventions in the islands. The Bahamas Government denounced US demands that the DEA and IRS be allowed access to bank records and be permitted to search for drugs as an 'imperialist' infringement of sovereignty.

Aware of increasing public concern and international pressure, Pindling realized that co-operation with the USA was essential. A compromise was reached: drugs searches in the Bahamas could be made by the US Coastguard and the DEA, but only with the Bahamian police involved. The first such joint operation took place as early as April 1985, in Bimini, when the authorities seized 34,000 metric tons of marijuana, 2,500 kg of processed cocaine and US $1.4m. worth of aircraft and ships. Expenditure on coastguard and defence forces was increased, and several notable Colombian smugglers were arrested, including Carlos Lehder Rivas. Other measures followed: free passage and diplomatic immunity were granted to DEA agents; a joint drugs-interdiction force was formed; and in 1989 both countries signed a Mutual Legal Assistance Treaty (M-LAT), providing for collaboration in the investigation of criminal allegations within the 'offshore' industry. A similar agreement was also signed with Canada. However, drugs-trafficking continued to pose a problem, despite the limited success of anti-smuggling measures.

At the end of the 1980s Pindling's confidence was such that he was dismissive of accusations (made by Lehder at his trial in Miami, Florida, USA) that Lehder had given him US $400,000. In 1991 elected representatives were required to state their assets for the first time; 10 of the 13 cabinet ministers and 25 members of the Assembly declared more than $1m. Local opinion was, if anything, surprised at the modesty of the amounts reported.

DOMESTIC POLITICS AND THE RISE OF THE FNM

The PLP remained the dominant political force in the 1980s, accusing the FNM of subservience to the USA and to local white Bahamian interests. However, the party lost some ground in the 1987 election, winning 31 seats to the FNM's 16 in an enlarged 49-seat House of Assembly. Christie and Ingraham were elected as independents, but in 1990 Ingraham joined the FMN, becoming party leader one month later after the death of Cecil Wallace-Whitfield. Perry Christie rejoined the PLP shortly afterwards.

Prospects for the FNM improved as the economy worsened. Measures taken under US pressure against cocaine-smuggling and money-laundering reduced the free flow of funds into the economy from the mid-1980s. A consequent fall in consumer demand induced a recession in the formal sector of the economy, followed by an 11% decline in tourist arrivals in 1989–92. As a result, Pindling was forced to introduce three successive austerity budgets and restraints on credit. In addition, the Government was damaged by new scandals, this time over widespread corruption in state-owned businesses. A vigorous campaign by the FNM resulted in the defeat of the PLP in the general election of August 1992. Ingraham became Prime Minister, and the extent of economic mismanagement and of corrupt practices in several public corporations under the PLP regime only then began to become apparent.

The FNM's confident campaign prior to the March 1997 general election culminated in a clear victory, with the party winning 34 of the 40 seats in a reduced House of Assembly. Sir Lynden Pindling, diminished by a series of scandals and suffering the adverse effects of treatment for cancer, resigned as PLP leader in April, and later announced his retirement from Parliament, after 41 years. Perry Christie succeeded him as party leader. In September the PLP's parliamentary strength was reduced to only five seats when the Government won a by-election in Pindling's old seat, South Andros. The PLP was further damaged in 2000 by the resignation of its deputy leader, Bernard Nottage, who subsequently formed a rival party, the Coalition for Democratic Reform.

In spite of the FNM's 10-year record of economic success, and a dramatic improvement in the standard of government, the party was increasingly perceived as élitist, autocratic and subservient to the interests of foreign investors. From the late 1990s expansion of large hotels such as Sun International's Atlantis resort on Paradise Island gave rise to concerns over beach access. There was vigorous trade union opposition in 2000 to the proposed privatization of the Bahamas Telecommunications Corporation (BaTelCo). From late 2000 sections of the financial community and the legal profession were disturbed by the Government's willingness to co-operate with international moves by the Financial Action Task Force on Money Laundering (FATF, based in Paris, France), and by the Organisation for Economic Co-operation and Development's (OECD, also based in Paris) initiative against tax evasion (see below).

These considerations laid the ground for a sharp turnaround in the fortunes of the two main parties, which gathered force from mid-2001. In line with Ingraham's long-standing commitment to step down as premier after two terms in office, the FNM held a convention to elect a leader in August, from which Orville Alton Thompson (Tommy) Turnquest, emerged as the victor. Turnquest was widely accused of having used improper methods to influence delegates, and was seen as a significantly less substantial figure than Ingraham. His father, Sir Orville Alton Thompson Turnquest, was Governor-General, but, in order to prevent a possible conflict of interest, he was replaced in this office by Dame Ivy Dumont, a respected former Minister of Education.

An FNM proposal to amend the Constitution, originally put forward before the 1997 election, suddenly gathered pace at the beginning of 2002. Five proposed amendments were put to a referendum on 27 February. These included: the appointment of an independent Director of Public Prosecutions; the establishment of an independent body to oversee teachers' employment; the appointment of an independent Parliamentary Electoral Commissioner; and the creation of a Boundaries Commission. The PLP voted for the amendments in Parliament, but campaigned for a 'no' vote in the referendum, on the grounds that the reforms had been rushed and ill-prepared. To the consternation of the Government, the population rejected all five proposals by large margins.

THE 2002 ELECTIONS

A general election was held on 2 May 2002, close to the constitutional deadline. The PLP increased its share of the popular vote to 52%, taking 29 of the 40 seats. The FNM's legislative representation was reduced to seven seats, with the four remaining seats and the remaining votes taken by independent candidates. Only one FNM cabinet minister was re-elected to Parliament; Turnquest lost his seat, but was nominated by his party to the Senate and remained party leader. However, the position of Leader of the Opposition, which, according to the Constitution, must be taken by a member of the lower house, was given to Alvin Smith, a former junior education minister. Perry Christie was appointed Prime Minister.

The new Government pledged the establishment of a national health insurance system, as well as constitutional reform; commissions were subsequently established to develop detailed proposals with regard to these commitments. The commission on health insurance reported in May 2004, with annual costs later estimated at US $235m., but implementation was not expected until after an anticipated 2007 general election. A constitutional reform commission reported in

March 2006: it recommended the replacement of Queen Elizabeth II as head of state with a President, who would have some limited real powers, including the appointment of independent senators, of the Chief Justice, and of other judges. Other proposals included the creation of an independent electoral and boundaries commission. None of these proposals was fulfilled during the Christie Government's single term in office.

Christie suffered a stroke in May 2005, but made a good recovery and was able to lead his party into a general election two years hence. His team was strengthened in November 2005, when Bernard Nottage rejoined the PLP, and was made Minister of Health and National Insurance, with responsibility for the development of the health insurance scheme, in a February 2006 cabinet reorganization.

The Bahamas' judicial system underwent significant disruption in November 2006 when the Cabinet's failure to appoint a commission to review judicial salaries was declared illegal by a supreme court ruling, and therefore to have compromised the independence of the judiciary. Closure of the country's magistrates' courts was anticipated pending the outcome of an appeal. Despite the judicial pay controversy, in December a contingent of Law Lords from the Privy Council sat in the Court of Appeal in Nassau, the first instance of the country's final appellate court operating outside London, United Kingdom. The Bahamas retained the Privy Council as its final appellate court, in contrast to several other Caribbean countries that had instituted the Caribbean Court of Justice following its inauguration in April 2005.

RETURN OF THE FNM

A general election was held on 2 May 2007, exactly five years after the previous poll. After a closely fought campaign, the FNM took 23 of the 41 seats in the enlarged House of Assembly, with the remaining 18 going to PLP members and allied independents. The FNM took 49.8% of the popular vote, with 47.0% going to the PLP and its allies, and the remainder to non-aligned independents and a minor party. Voter turn-out was high, at 91.3%. The FNM won six seats with majorities of fewer than 75 votes (equivalent to less than 2% of votes cast), while the PLP won four with equally narrow majorities. The PLP contested the results in three constituencies. The courts rejected one challenge in January 2008, with a second dropped in April, and a third dismissed in December. The PLP's parliamentary strength was weakened in January 2008, when a member of parliament, Kenyatta Gibson, left the party to sit as an independent; he formally joined the FNM a year later.

Hubert Ingraham returned as Prime Minister after the poll, also assuming the portfolio for finance; Turnquest, once more in the House of Assembly, became Minister of National Security, while Zhivargo Laing emerged as another influential figure, being appointed Minister of State in the Ministry of Finance. The PLP has remained weak and divided since the election, with a question over Christie's long-term future as party leader; however, he was re-elected by a party conference in October 2009, with 1,158 votes to 204 for his nearest rival, Bernard Nottage. To the embarrassment of the party, a PLP senator and former member of parliament, Pleasant Bridgewater, was charged with conspiracy in January 2009 after an alleged attempt to extort US $25m. from the US actor John Travolta after the sudden death of his son on Grand Bahama. A court process ended in October with a mistrial, when a FNM member of parliament Picewell Forbes mistakenly told a party convention that Bridgewater had been found innocent; the jury was still deliberating at the time, and the judge aborted the process fearing jury contamination. A PLP member of parliament, Malcolm Adderly, resigned his seat at the start of 2010 following his appointment as a judge. A by-election was held in his Elizabeth seat on 16 February. The PLP had won by 47 votes in 2007; on this occasion a recount initially gave 1,501 votes to the FNM candidate and 1,499 to the PLP. However, a court ruling on March 24 awarded five disputed votes to the PLP, giving them victory by a margin of three votes.

REGIONAL ISSUES

In the late 1990s there was a resurgence in drugs-trafficking in the Bahamas, as the Mexican route for Colombian cocaine became more difficult and Haiti, just south of the Bahamas, increased its importance as a transshipment point, as did Jamaica. A report published in March 2005 by the US Department of State suggested that around 20 metric tons of cocaine were transshipped each year through the Jamaica–Cuba–Bahamas corridor. Moreover, an earlier analysis of balance-of-payments statistics by the US embassy in Nassau suggested that cocaine- and marijuana-smuggling resulted in foreign exchange inflows of US $200m.–$300m. annually, a sum which would have been equivalent to 11%–17% of formal-sector merchandise imports, or 4%–7% of gross domestic product. On this basis, the report suggested drugs transshipment might rival, or even surpass, the Bahamian banking industry in economic impact. In 2008 25 suspicious speedboats were detected in or over Bahamian waters but could not be intercepted. There are an estimated 12 to 15 major drugs-trafficking organizations operating in the country.

The USA included the Bahamas on a list of 20 major drugs source or transshipment countries and a list of 60 major money-laundering countries, with close to 5% of US cocaine imports passing through the islands in 2009. Co-operation between the US and Bahamian authorities is generally fairly close. However, strong differences over counter-narcotics policy surfaced under the PLP Government in December 2002 when Bahamian representatives walked out of a meeting of a joint task-force in a protest against opening remarks by the erstwhile US ambassador to the Bahamas, J. Richard Blankenship. Blankenship had demanded an inquiry into the 1992 'Lorequin' incident, in which cocaine from a US-controlled drugs shipment reportedly went astray, and the reform of the defence force, which was blamed for the incident. An inquiry into the Lorequin incident was completed in September 2004; it criticized defence force officers but did not recommend prosecutions, while a US $3m. national counter-narcotics plan was made public in June, and a new maritime agreement with the USA was signed in the same month. A Canadian consultancy, Emergo International, completed a full review of the defence force in January 2006. Preliminary findings indicated a 'desperate' need for reorganization; the final report, however, was not made public. The then serving Commissioner of Police, Reginald Ferguson, said in March 2009 that police corruption was a major concern. The USA has donated six fast interceptor boats to the coastguard, and was planning to build a hanger on the southern island of Inagua, allowing it to station helicopters there for work in the southern Bahamas and Turks and Caicos. The coastguard also had two 60-metre vessels and a number of smaller craft, based in Nassau, Inagua and Grand Bahama, as well as fixed-wing surveillance aircraft.

Drugs-trafficking and violent crime continued to be a problem in the 2000s. The murder rate rose from 14 per 100,000 in 2004 to 27 per 100,000 in 2009. The reach of the drugs trade was illustrated in the 2006 trial of two men accused of murdering the son of the Minister of Trade in 2002; both defence and prosecution alleged that the killing stemmed from the theft of a commercial consignment of cocaine. Although the authorities succeeded in dismantling several drugs-trafficking organizations in 2002–04, others remained in operation. Extradition from the Bahamas to the USA was also difficult. One high-profile alleged trafficker, Samuel 'Ninety' Knowles, resisted extradition from 2001 until August 2006, when he was sent for trial in Florida; he was found guilty in March 2008 of trafficking several tons of cocaine and sentenced to 35 years in prison with the forfeiture of US $14m. in alleged drug proceeds. Two other alleged traffickers, Dwight and Keva Major, were extradited in 2008 after a five-year legal battle. Raising further doubt over the judicial system, the Judicial and Legal Services Commission in April appointed a supreme court judge, Rubie Nottage, who was considered by the USA to have been a fugitive from arrest since 1989 on racketeering charges connected to alleged laundering of drugs proceeds, and could face arrest if she travelled to that country; however, she left office in October, having reached retirement age.

In January 2007 the PLP Government was accused by the FNM, then in opposition, of colluding with US authorities to induce five Bahamian employees of the Lynden Pindling International Airport to travel to the USA for the purposes of arrest and trial on charges of drugs-trafficking by scheduling training sessions in Florida; all five either pleaded guilty or were found guilty on trial. Aggregate cocaine seizures in 2003 totalled 4.0 metric tons, but, more typically, 1.8 tons in January–October 2009 (when approximately 11 tons of marijuana were also recovered). The police Drug Enforcement Unit also seized US $3.9m. cash in suspected drugs proceeds in 2008, as well as five vessels and an aircraft in 2007.

In June 2000 the Bahamas was included by the FATF on a 'blacklist' of jurisdictions considered to be failing in attempts to combat money-laundering. As a result, the Government devoted considerable political attention to reform of the 'off-shore' financial sector. New legislation established a Financial Intelligence Unit in October, improved the mechanism for international co-operation in criminal proceedings, and required international business companies to keep records showing their beneficial ownership. A further law was passed increasing the regulatory capacity of the Central Bank. As a result of the measures, in June 2001 the FATF removed the Bahamas from its list of non-co-operative countries. An agreement to exchange information on tax with the USA was signed in January 2002 and came into effect a year later. Illustrating the continuing use of the Bahamas by controversial figures, Viktor Kožený, a Czech-born financier with Grenadian, Venezuelan and Irish nationality, was, in 2010, resisting extradition to both the USA and the Czech Republic on corruption charges linked, *inter alia*, to privatizations in Azerbaijan. His attorney, Philip Davis, was a PLP member of parliament, a former legal partner of Perry Christie, and was elected deputy leader of the PLP in October 2009. Arrested in 2005, Kožený was released on bail in April 2007. The high court initially ruled in his favour in October 2007 on the basis that corruption of foreign officials was not an offence in the Bahamas; the state lost a local appeal in April 2010, but said that it would lodge a further appeal to the Privy Council on behalf of the US authorities.

Another ongoing security concern was illegal migration from Haiti. The census of 2000 reported that mainly legal migrants from Haiti made up 7% of the resident population, with illegal migrants a further 10% on some estimates; however, in 2000–08 approximately 51,000 Haitian illegal migrants and refugees were deported from the Bahamas, with a peak figure of 7,589 in 2001, while a further 15,500 were intercepted at sea in 2000–08 by the coastguard. There was a substantial resident population of Haitian origin; 11% of all births nationally were to Haitian mothers, rising to more than 50% in major public clinics on the island of Abaco. There was also a substantial volume of illegal migration from Jamaica and Cuba, while illegal migrants from the People's Republic of China also used the Bahamas as a transit point for entry to the USA.

Economy

MARK WILSON

The economy of the Bahamas is one of the most prosperous of the Caribbean and Latin American nations, with a per-head gross domestic product (GDP) of some US $21,307 in 2008, a higher figure than any independent country in Latin America and the Caribbean (the Bahamian dollar is at par with the US dollar). However, the economy experienced difficulties in 2008–10 as a result of the international recession, with its Standard & Poor's credit rating reduced from A– to BBB+, although its Moody's rating remained at A3. The country was rated 52nd of 177 countries in the UN Development Programme's Human Development Index for 2009—sixth in the Latin America and Caribbean region after Barbados, which was placed 37th, Chile (44th), Antigua-Barbuda (47th) Argentina (49th), Uruguay (50th) and Cuba (51st).

Following a recession in 1988–93, from 1993 there was continuous economic growth, which peaked in 1998 at 6.9%. During 2001–04 the economy was virtually stagnant, and was indeed negative for three of these four years, with tourism performing weakly. Economic expansion recovered to 5.0% in 2005, but growth slipped back to 1.9% in 2007. As the international recession hit US consumer demand in 2008–09, financial services, tourist arrivals and hotel construction slowed, and GDP contracted, by 1.7% in 2008 and then more steeply, by 4.3%, in 2009. Foreign direct investment has been very high since the late 1990s and rose from 4.2% of GDP in 2002 to 13.8% in 2008, although it fell back to 10.1% in 2009, with major hotel projects on hold. Growth since the mid-1990s was prompted largely by new hotel investment, initially stimulated by the sale to new investors and subsequent renovation of the dilapidated properties of the Government's Hotel Corporation, then by further development, and by the increased hotel occupancy of stop-over visitors. As the economy expanded, unemployment came down from a 1992 peak of 14.8% to 7.6% in 2006, but then rose again to 14.2% in 2009 as the recession hit.

There is no personal or corporate income tax in the Bahamas. Duties on imports made up 48.7% of the Government's recurrent revenue in 2007/08 (or 54.8% of tax revenue); this declined sharply in 2008/09 to 37.9% (52.6% of tax revenue) as imports fell in line with the slowing economy. With high taxes on consumption of goods, retail prices were high, although the inflation rate was relatively low. Retail prices increased at an average annual rate of 1.9% in 1998–2007, spiking briefly at 4.5% in 2008, as international energy and food commodity costs rose sharply, but falling back to 2.1% in 2009. Taxes directly related to tourism (hotel occupancy tax, departure tax and gaming tax) made up a further 10.2% of Government revenue in 2008/09. However, the small tax base posed problems. In spite of successive tax increases, government revenue was equivalent to only an estimated 17.5% of GDP in 2009/10, down from 19.7% in 2007/08 as the economy slowed, and much lower than the proportion prevailing in other Caribbean islands, such as Barbados, where government revenue was equivalent to 31.1% of GDP in 2005. The Bahamas was given observer status at the World Trade Organization (WTO) in 2000 and applied for membership in 2001, with accession negotiations expected to conclude in 2013 or later. WTO membership would require a restructuring of the revenue system, with a move away from import duties and towards excise duties, sales tax or a value added tax to protect the tax base while avoiding the need for an income tax. Membership of the Caribbean Community and Common Market (CARICOM) single market and economy was not likely as public opinion remained strongly opposed to free trade. The Government signed an Economic Partnership Agreement (EPA) with the European Union (EU) in October 2008: this makes a commitment to free trade for most imports from the EU after a 25-year transition period running from 2011. However, the Bahamas did not commit to the EPA's stipulations on trade in services, and on 27 January 2010 reached a separate agreement, which was more restrictive than those adopted by other Caribbean countries, reserving activities such as retailing, real estate, advertising and restaurants for Bahamian businesses.

The fiscal deficit generally remained low from the mid-1990s until 2001/02: the overall deficit fell to 0.3% in 2000/01, with the recurrent fiscal account in surplus. However, both recurrent and overall fiscal accounts moved sharply into deficit from the last quarter of 2001, with revenue adversely affected by the downturn in tourism and in domestic consumer demand. The deficit averaged 2.7% of GDP from 2001/02 to 2006/07, dipping to 1.8% for 2007/08, but rose sharply to 4.9% in 2008/09 and an estimated 5.7% in 2009/10 as the international recession affected revenues and led to additional spending commitments, setting back the Government's earlier proposals for achieving a balanced budget by 2012/13. Total public and government-guaranteed debt increased from 34% of GDP in 2000 to 44% in 2008 and to 53% in 2009. This was considered to be a fairly manageable figure by Caribbean standards, but the rate of increase in the ratio became a source of serious concern. Central government debt was 45% of GDP in 2009; this was significantly above the Government's target range of 30%–35%. Interest payments on debt were US $154.2m. in 2008/09, up from $116.9m. in 2005/06, and equivalent to 11.6% of the revenue of $1,324.2m. With substantial domestic borrowing, the foreign debt-service ratio net of refinancing was modest, at an estimated 2.7% of the estimated value of exports of goods and services in 2009. Salaries and related expenses accounted for 51.4% of total recurrent expenditure in 1993/94, and 40.3% in 2008/09, marking a decrease in public sector employment and an increase in public salary restraint.

Most government-owned hotels were sold in the mid-1990s. However, plans first mooted in 1997 to privatize the Bahamas Telecommunications Corporation (BaTelCo) failed to bear fruit by mid-2010, although the Government did intend to complete the sale of a 51% stake to reduce the borrowing requirement. Also by mid-2010, no progress had been made on long-standing suggestions for the privatization of the Bahamas Electricity Corporation (BEC) or the national airline, Bahamasair Holdings Ltd, which had a history of heavy financial losses. However, an agreement was finalized with a Canadian company in 2006 for the management of Lynden Pindling International Airport (formerly Nassau International Airport) under a 30-year contract, with a $410m. redevelopment plan in progress in 2010 and billed by the Prime Minister as the largest public sector project ever undertaken in the Bahamas.

In 1955 an area of 603 sq km (233 sq miles), approximately one-third of the island of Grand Bahama, was granted to the privately owned Grand Bahama Port Authority (GBPA), with important tax concessions under the Hawksbill Creek Agreement. Freeport, which owed its existence entirely to that Agreement, developed considerably. The GBPA aimed originally to construct a manufacturing centre. The focus then shifted to tourism and residential development. Within Freeport, the operation of the port and airport, land development and the management of the water and electricity supply were private sector activities. Under successive Progressive Liberal Party (PLP) Governments, Grand Bahama was regarded as an opposition stronghold, and was consequently neglected by the central administration. The petroleum refinery and cement plant were closed, and tourism stagnated. In 1993, with the Free National Movement in office, the Hawksbill Creek Agreement was extended to 2054, with tax exemptions running to 2015. This contributed to renewed economic development, with a Hong Kong-owned company, Hutchison Whampoa, the principal investor. A complex legal dispute developed from 2004 between the British shareholders in the GBPA, Sir Jack Hayward and the heirs of his associate Edward St George. This interrupted the smooth development of the company, but appeared to have been resolved in mid-2010, and both parties were expected to search for buyers through the US investment bank JP Morgan. In 2009 the Government of the Bahamas decided not to renew the work permit of the GBPA Chairman Hannes Babak, and the Government retained ultimate control over new investors. The Government was believed to favour a major role for Hutchison Whampoa in any corporate restructuring. A public-private sector partnership in 2010 also agreed a US $60m. container port development on Arawak Cay, relieving pressure on the city centre waterfront.

The Out Islands, or Family Islands, varied enormously in the degree of economic development achieved. In the northern Bahamas, activities such as tourism and fishing brought prosperity to a number of islands, including Abaco, Spanish Wells, Eleuthera and Bimini. In contrast, some islands in the southern Bahamas, such as Mayaguana, Acklins and Crooked Island, had small populations and a very limited range of economic activity. Stimulating growth on these islands with airport development and an 'anchor' tourism project formed a central element of the Government's economic agenda in the 2000s, but progress on this agenda slowed from 2007 as a difficult borrowing environment halted most resort construction.

TOURISM

Tourism was the basis of prosperity in the Bahamas, and remained by far the most important sector of the economy. The islands are closer to the USA than are most other destinations in the Caribbean region. For this reason, commercial tourism developed comparatively early, with the construction of the Royal Victoria Hotel in Nassau commencing just before the American Civil War of the 1860s. Luxury winter tourism developed further between 1920 and 1940, and from the 1950s jet travel opened the islands as a mass-market destination. The number of stop-over tourists increased from 32,000 in 1949 to 1.5m. in 2006 (dipping to 1.3m. in 2009). Such a marked long-term increase led to rapid growth in commercial activity and a significant increase in living standards.

Following a fall in tourist arrivals in the early 1990s, a vast increase in tourism-related investment prompted a recovery in the sector. This investment totalled US $1,500m.–$2,000m. over five years and involved hotel construction and refurbishment, an extension to Nassau International Airport and new air links. As a result, room occupancy in Nassau increased from 52.0% in 1992 to 76.0% in 1999, in spite of a greatly increased room stock (from 13,541 to 14,153). Occupancy in the capital was 77.1% in 2006, but fell to 61.2% in 2008 owing to lower tourism demand. Compounding the difficulties, average room rates fell by 8.3% in 2009, and room occupancy was down by 4.7 percentage points across the Bahamas. Meanwhile, tourism receipts rose to $2,153m. in 2008, falling back to $1,938m. in 2009 under the impact of the international recession. The opening of 'private island' facilities by cruise lines and a refurbished cruise port facility in Nassau contributed to an increase in cruise ship passenger arrivals, which totalled 3.4m. in 2009. The Bahamas received more than twice as many cruise ship passengers as any other Caribbean destination, although with much lower per-head spending ($167 in 2007) than stop-over tourists ($2,021).

The increase in tourism investment in the late 1990s involved the reconstruction of most of the existing hotels in Nassau, followed, in 1999–2001, by the major properties on Grand Bahama. This activity involved the extensive development, at a cost of US $450m., of the Sun International (later Kerzner International) Atlantis resort on Paradise Island. After completion of its Phase II, the project included 2,395 rooms, as well as a marina, a casino and a conference facility, and had 5,600 staff, equivalent to about 4% of national employment. Following the Government's decision to invest substantially in airport, road, water and electricity improvements, and its commitment to a further 11 years of tax concessions and up to $4m. per year in marketing assistance over five years, in May 2003 Kerzner International announced a further $600m. Phase III expansion, increased in scope to $1,000m. one year later. This included 1,500 additional hotel rooms for completion by the end of 2007, and increased staff numbers to 9,000. In 2004 Kerzner purchased the neighbouring Club Méditerranée property on Paradise Island for $40m., and in 2005 the company bought the island's Hurricane Hole marina.

Another very large tourism investment was proposed in 2005. The Baha Mar Development Company, owned by a locally resident investor, agreed in March to buy the Wyndham Nassau Resort, Crystal Palace Casino and Nassau Beach Hotel, and in May finalized the purchase of the Radisson Cable Beach Resort, the last remaining major property of the state-owned Hotel Corporation, along with a substantial area of government-owned land. For a renovation and construction investment estimated at US $2,600m. on a site of 4 sq km, the project aimed to develop hotels with 3,450 rooms, a 0.7-ha casino, a golf course, 1 ha of convention space, residential units and a marina, and to employ a staff of 6,500 on completion. This development scheme was delayed following the withdrawal of the proposed casino partner in March 2008, while the existing properties were racking up large losses. An agreement was reached in July 2010 for a joint venture with the Export-Import Bank of China and China State Construction Engineering Corporation. However, there was some local disquiet over the proposed employment of up to 7,000 Chinese workers in the construction phase, and government approval was required for work permits.

Most of Nassau's hotel properties were large, and many belonged to international chains, a great asset for US marketing, which relied heavily on branding. On Grand Bahama, much of the available accommodation was previously owned by the Hotel Corporation and had, by the 1990s, become rather dilapidated. In 1997 the largest properties were sold to Hutchison Whampoa, which undertook a US $400m. redevelopment and reopened the Our Lucaya complex, with 1,350 rooms in late 2000. The island remained a relatively weak area for Bahamian tourism. The Princess Resort and Casino was sold in 2000 and reopened after a $42m. renovation as the 965-room Resort at Bahamia; renamed the Royal Oasis, it was closed after Hurricane Frances in 2004, with substantial debts owed to the Government, staff and local businesses, and remained closed in mid-2010. In spite of their excellent beaches and wildlife resources, the Family Islands remained relatively undeveloped until the 2000s. There were few direct air links to the north-eastern USA, and travel via Nassau could be inconvenient. Airport improvements in Nassau and the Family Islands formed an important component of the Government's economic strategy, and large-scale developments were by 2010 built or planned on several islands, including Eleuthera, Abaco and San Salvador. In 2006 proposals were published for large-scale resorts (with airports to serve them) on smaller and more remote islands, such as Rum Cay, which had only 70 inhabitants, or Mayaguana, with 262; the Government's aim was for each island to have at least one 'anchor' property to underpin its development. However, weakness in the US tourism, real estate and financial markets from mid-2007 delayed projects that were still in the planning stage and were not in some cases expected to move forward. A $140m. resort on Exuma completed in 2003, ran into financial difficulties and was purchased and renovated by the Sandals group, re-opening successfully in 2010.

Agriculture and manufacturing were poorly developed, and tourism operators purchased little locally. Food, furnishings and even souvenirs were generally shipped in from Miami, Florida, USA; some construction projects imported pre-assembled and pre-fitted hotel rooms, thus minimizing the need for local labour. For this reason, retained earnings were poor. In addition, many major hotel projects were given important tax concessions, reportedly equivalent in value to 20% of the development cost for the Atlantis Phase III projects.

Stop-over arrivals in 2005 were at an all-time high of 1.6m., an increase of 5.3% since 1998; however, numbers dipped in 2009 following the introduction in 2007 of a passport requirement by the USA for returning residents and a sharp downturn in consumer demand. Stop-over tourist numbers were 9.3% lower than in 2008. Hotel occupancy fell across the Bahamas to 49.4% in 2009 from 54.1% in 2008, with the average daily room rate in dollars down by 8.3%. With some hotels closed for all or part of the year, the average number of available rooms was 11,436, down from 12,061 in 2008, and total room revenue for Bahamian hotels fell by 20.6% to US $407.7m. from $513.5m. in 2008. Cruise ship passenger numbers in 2009 showed a 97% increase since 1998, and a 14% increase over 2008, with short cruises from Florida to the Bahamas providing a low-cost form of Caribbean travel. In 2007 the hotels and restaurants sector directly contributed an estimated 11.4% of GDP, while in 2009 travel receipts comprised 66.0% of earnings from goods and services, and covered 76.3% of the value of all goods imported to the Bahamas. Owing to the proximity of the USA, the European market was less important to the Bahamian tourism industry than it was to that of the rest of the Caribbean. In 2009 some 80.5% of stop-over arrivals were estimated to have travelled from the USA. In the same year 8.1% of visitors came from Canada and 5.9% came from Europe.

'OFFSHORE' FINANCE AND REGISTRATION

Nassau is a major international financial centre, with domestic and international banking and insurance accounting for 8.6% of GDP in 2007. In 2005 international banks in the Bahamas managed US $316,500m. in assets. In 2006 a further $205,000m. was managed by 725 mutual funds. Despite this, by the 1990s the Bahamas had lost its former dominant position as an 'offshore' financial centre. From being one of the world's best known 'offshore' centres, dating from the 1920s, the financial services industry in the Bahamas declined almost every year from the early 1980s until 1991. Whereas in 1976 some 49% of Organisation for Economic Co-operation and Development (OECD) 'offshore' assets in developing countries were administered from Nassau, by 1998 its market share was only 10%. In the world-wide ranking of the financial centres of metropolitan and developing countries, Nassau declined from third place in 1976 to 15th by 1998. Nassau lost market share partly because there was no longer a tax advantage in booking large international loans 'offshore', which had in any event accounted for relatively little value added. However, in the more economically significant business of private banking and trust management, the reputation of the Bahamas was severely damaged by extensive money-laundering activity. Suffering from the country's image of corruption and disreputability, and with many financial institutions having to defend themselves against the persistent enquiries of overseas law-enforcement and tax authorities (mainly from the USA), a number of institutions reduced their operations or chose alternative centres, notably the Cayman Islands. Aggressive marketing of company registration and other services by newer financial centres, such as the British Virgin Islands, also allowed them to capture a share of the market that they did not thereafter relinquish.

Resolute action was taken to cleanse the industry of illegal funds and to remove the minority damaging the industry's reputation. The reforms began in 1989, with more rapid progress being made after the 1992 elections and the change of government. By 1991 the industry was once more expanding. Legislation was updated on international business companies and mutual funds in 1995, on money-laundering in 1996 and on trusts in 1998. From 1998 the Financial Services Promotion Board handled overseas marketing of financial services. However, the captive insurance sector was less developed than in Bermuda, Barbados and other jurisdictions that, unlike the Bahamas, enjoyed tax concessions granted by the US or Canadian authorities.

In June 2000 the intergovernmental body charged with combating money-laundering, the Financial Action Task Force on Money Laundering (FATF, based in Paris, France) included the Bahamas in a list of 15 'non-co-operative' jurisdictions. The FATF criticized: the practice of issuing bearer shares, which made beneficial ownership of financial assets impossible to trace; long delays and restricted responses to requests for judicial assistance; and rules that allowed intermediaries to avoid revealing the names of their clients. Along with the other jurisdictions cited, the Bahamas was the subject of an advisory statement from the US Treasury, which asked US financial institutions to apply 'enhanced scrutiny' to transactions with the country. In response, the Bahamian authorities accelerated their efforts to bring the jurisdiction into line with international requirements, and 11 new financial reform measures were passed by Parliament by the end of the year. As a result, the Bahamas was removed from the FATF 'black list' in June 2001. In January 2002 the Bahamas concluded a tax information-exchange agreement with the USA. However, in 2010 the US Department of State continued to classify it as a jurisdiction of 'primary concern' for money-laundering, largely because of the size of the 'offshore' sector; it also appealed for reforms such as a public registry of beneficial owners of 'offshore' entities, and provision of adequate resources to investigate and prosecute apparent breaches of regulations and to comply with international information requests. The Bahamas International Securities Exchange (BISX) opened in 2000, and at the end of March 2010 was trading the shares of 24 local companies with total market capitalization of US $3,079m. However, with market turnover sluggish, at $25.4m. for 2009, commission income was low. (In 2002 and 2004 the Exchange had been in severe financial difficulty and had required government financial support.)

Local expenditure by 'offshore' companies was US $233.8m. in 2008, an increase from $106.0m. in 2003, and equivalent to 10.7% of the visible trade deficit; however, this fell to $179.6m. in 2009 as the international recession hit financial services. Total employment in banking was 4,662 in 2006, close to 3% of the employed labour force. Although expatriates continued to play an important role, by the start of the 21st century Bahamian nationals held a high proportion of professional positions.

During the 1990s company registration, in particular, witnessed spectacular growth, following the International Business Company Act of 1990. Financial sector professionals in the Bahamas have always insisted that most 'offshore' business is legitimate. As a result of new requirements that beneficial owners should be identifiable, the number of new International Business Companies (IBCs) registered in 2003 was less than one-fifth of the new registrations recorded in 2000, while many existing IBCs failed to renew their registration. In 2009 there were 160,000 registered IBCs, of which 44,000 were active. The licences of 183 'shell' banks (banks registered in the jurisdiction but with no staff or offices there) were revoked in 1999–2003 as the result of a new requirement that 'offshore' banks must maintain a physical presence in the Bahamas. With other licences lapsing later, 105 'offshore' banks and trust companies remained in operation in June 2008 with public licences, with a further 145 on restricted licences. However, the requirement to maintain an office and employ staff meant that the remaining banks each had a more significant economic impact.

Legal challenges were made against various aspects of the new financial legislation, but no major challenge succeeded. The 2002–07 PLP Government had pledged to review the financial legislation introduced in 2000–01, but had not, in practice, relaxed controls significantly. A number of criminal investigations and troubling incidents in 2002–10 underlined the need for continuing regulatory vigilance; the PLP treasurer Sidney Cambridge was in 2009 charged with money-laundering in Florida. The FATF in 2004 expressed concern that the Government was lax in responding to regulatory requests, and in April 2009 placed the Bahamas on a 'grey list' of countries that had not yet taken sufficient steps to negotiate tax information exchange agreements with international partners; the Bahamas at that point had only one, with the USA. However, 21 agreements had been concluded by April 2010, allowing the Bahamas to be placed on the 'white list'. Meanwhile, legislation approved in 2003 provided a legal basis for e-commerce, while legislation approved in 2004 extended the civil law concept of investment foundations to the Bahamas, established Purpose Trusts, and allowed IBCs to establish segregated accounts to protect assets against creditors.

The other area of 'offshore' activity that continued to perform well into the 2000s was that of ship registration. The Bahamas ship registry, relaunched after the adoption of the Bahamas Maritime Authority Act in 1995, was the world's third largest in terms of gross registered tonnage, behind Panama and Liberia. It was managed by the Bahamas Maritime Authority, which had offices in London, United Kingdom, Nassau and New York, USA, and by December 2008 had registered 1,446 vessels with total displacement of 47m. grt. The international container-transshipment terminal at Freeport, Grand Bahama, was capable of handling 950,000 container units per year and acted as an intercontinental hub port serving North America, the Caribbean and South America. A US $75m. expansion from 2003 increased the capacity to 1.5m. container units, and an additional expansion to 3.5m.-unit capacity was planned. A $30m. airport improvement programme was completed in 2004, and a 320-ha industrial park has also been developed. Ross University School of Medicine planned to open a 126-acre campus on Grand Bahama for overseas medical students in 2010, and began initial teaching activities in 2009.

INDUSTRY

Industrial development was a relatively late arrival in the Bahamas, dating from 1960 and the formation of the Grand Bahama Development Company, based in the free trade zone in Freeport, itself only established by the 1955 Hawksbill Creek Agreement. Freeport was at first dominated by ship-bunkering and petroleum-refining. However, proposals to develop Grand Bahama as a major industrial centre did not come to fruition; refining operations at the Bahamas Oil Refining Company (BORCO) ceased in 1985, and a cement plant built to serve the US market also closed. In the 1990s high labour and utilities costs, and the small size of the local market, combined to limit severely the development of industrial activity, although a number of manufacturers produced for the local market, among them a brewery, soft-drinks companies, paper converters and printers. Bacardi operated a rum distillery in Nassau, which made use of imported molasses and bulk rum to produce blended rums for export to Europe under the Cotonou Agreement. Rum exports totalled US $20.3m. in 2007 or 5.5% of domestic exports. However, the Bacardi plant closed in 2009: with production concentrated in a larger plant in Puerto Rico, duties on all rum entering the European market had been cut, greatly reducing the comparative advantage of Bahamian production.

Of greater significance were a number of enclave industries located on Grand Bahama that benefited from the island's tax concessions and port facilities. A Freeport company had facilities for the repair of containers, fabrication of steel structures and instrumentation system maintenance. There is also a plant producing expandable polystyrene. The US $75m. Grand Bahama Shipyard cruise ship repair facility was established in 2000. A 320-m dry dock, the largest in the Americas, was in operation from early 2002, and by 2009 there were two additional dry docks on the site. Although engineering skills shortages held the number of local staff to 320 by this date, a training centre was attempting to increase the number of Bahamian staff. A separate operation included the world's largest covered yacht repair facility. Also on Grand Bahama, Gold Rock Creek studios opened in 2005 as an international centre for filming, with two very large water tanks for marine scenes; however, there had been very little use of this facility, and its future was uncertain in mid-2010 because of the consequent lack of financial success. The former oil refinery on Grand Bahama was operated as an oil storage facility, and in May 2008 was sold by the Venezuelan state oil company, Petróleos de Venezuela (PDVSA), to a private equity firm, First Reserve Corporation (80%), and a Dutch tank terminal operator, Royal Vopak (20%), under the name Vopak Terminal Bahamas; the purchasers planned to expand storage capacity to 27.5m. barrels at a cost of $350m, making it the largest storage facility serving the eastern USA. Three separate proposals were made in 2001 to establish a liquefied natural gas regasification terminal and handling facilities in either Grand Bahama or the small island of Ocean Cay. The proposed facilities would serve Florida via an underwater pipeline. With local environmental concerns strong, the two proposals for Grand Bahama were abandoned by mid-2006; however, there appeared in 2010 to be a possibility that the Ocean Cay scheme would eventually proceed, in spite of repeated delays. On the remote island of Inagua in the southern Bahamas, the main employer was the US-owned Morton Salt Company (owned since 2008 by a German company, K+S Aktiengesellschaft), which produced salt through the evaporation of sea water. Production is reduced in periods of high rainfall. Exports of salt in 2007 were worth $6.6m. or 1.7% of domestic exports. Salt production was set back by Hurricane Ike in 2008, with structures damaged and stockpiles dissolved by heavy rainfall.

Industry (including construction and utilities) employed 16% of the working population in 2009 (construction accounted for 12%). Manufacturing contributed some 4.5% of GDP in 2007, with construction contributing a further 15.2%, electricity and water 4.9% and mining and quarrying 0.4%. However, high wages and costs continued to be serious disadvantages. Installed electricity capacity in Nassau and the Family Islands (excluding Grand Bahama) in 2010 was 438 MW. BEC invested US $290m. in capital projects in 1995–2010,

There has been some interest in petroleum and natural gas exploration. Negotiations were in progress in 2010 for an agreed maritime boundary with Cuba, which would allow exploration of promising areas to the south of the small island of Cay Sal; maritime boundary talks have also been held with the USA, and with the United Kingdom in relation to the Turks and Caicos islands. Past oil exploration initiatives have not met with success, however. There was drilling by a US company on Grand Bahama Bank from 1986, but with no positive results; Kerr McGee and Talisman of Canada abandoned a licence for an area north of Grand Bahama in 2006 after completing a seismic survey in 2004; Bahamas Offshore Petroleum, owned by Hardman Resources of Australia, also completed a seismic survey of a separate offshore concession awarded in 2005. Exploration licences were proposed in 2010 for the Norwegian firm Statoil in partnership with a British (Isle of Man) company BPC in waters close to Cay Sal, and for Atlantic Petroleum and Bahamas Petroleum in waters offshore from Grand Bahama.

AGRICULTURE AND FISHING

Agriculture (excluding fishing) never played a leading role in the Bahamian economy, and in 2007 it was estimated to account for only 0.4% of GDP. More than 80% of food was imported. Agricultural resources are severely limited since rainfall is low, few areas have groundwater for irrigation and much of the land consists of bare limestone rock with only scattered patches of soil.

In 2008 agricultural production accounted for only 1% of total land area. There were small-scale farmers on many of the Family Islands, who produced livestock, fruit and vegetables in limited quantities for local markets. Larger commercial farms on New Providence, the most populous island, produced eggs and poultry, constituting one-half of agricultural production in 2001; however, the largest of these was forced to close in 2002 as a result of reduced protection from imports. Feed and other supplies were imported. Ornamental plants and flowers accounted for another 10%–15% of agricultural production. Following government efforts in the early 1990s to make land available to local and foreign investors for fruit and vegetable farming, by 1995 over 8,000 ha were devoted to citrus fruit cultivation. To protect local producers, imports of some crops, such as bananas, were restricted. A number of sizeable agro-businesses in the larger islands of the northern Bahamas operated as enclave industries, growing citrus and other fruit and vegetable crops for export. Some farms used crushed limestone rock as a growing medium, and nutrients were sometimes added to groundwater used for irrigation. Total exports of fruit and vegetables amounted to US $10.3m. in 1999. However, commercial citrus production experienced a serious setback in 2004–05, when all trees on two major farms, covering a total of 2,500 ha, were uprooted after an outbreak of citrus canker disease, so that fruit and vegetable exports were down to $1.2m. in 2007.

Commercial fishing remained an important economic activity on some of the smaller islands, such as Spanish Wells, making up about 0.9% of national GDP in 2007, and supplying 22.0% of domestic exports. Exports of crawfish (spiny lobster) amounted to US $81.4m. in 2007, with another $1.9m. from other fisheries exports; fears of overfishing led to tighter limits on the catch per vessel from mid-2006. Such primary economic activities, however, remained peripheral in their contribution to the national wealth of the Bahamas.

Statistical Survey

Source (unless otherwise stated): Department of Statistics, Clarence A. Bain Building, Thompson Boulevard, P. O. Box N-3904, Nassau; tel. 302-2400; fax 325-5149; e-mail dpsdp@bahamas.gov.bs; internet statistics.bahamas.gov.bs/index.php; The Central Bank of the Bahamas, Frederick St, POB N-4868, Nassau; tel. 322-2193; fax 322-4321; e-mail cbob@centralbankbahamas.com; internet www.centralbankbahamas.com.

AREA AND POPULATION

Area: 13,939 sq km (5,382 sq miles).

Population: 255,095 at census of 2 May 1990; 303,611 (males 147,715, females 155,896) at census of 1 May 2000. *By Island* (2000): New Providence 210,832; Grand Bahama 46,994; Eleuthera 7,999; Andros 7,686. *Mid-2010* (official estimate): 346,900.

Density (mid-2010): 24.9 per sq km.

Population by Age and Sex ('000, official estimates at mid-2010): *0–14:* 87.0 (males 44.4, females 42.6); *15–64:* 238.7 (males 116.0, females 122.7); *65 and over:* 21.2 (males 8.8, females 12.4); *Total* 346.9 (males 169.2, females 177.7).

Principal Town (incl. suburbs, UN estimate): Nassau (capital) 247,659 in mid-2009. Source: UN, *World Urbanization Prospects: The 2009 Revision*.

Births, Marriages and Deaths (2006): Registered live births 4,594 (birth rate 13.9 per 1,000); Registered deaths 1,751 (death rate 5.3 per 1,000); Registered marriages 5,375 (marriage rate 16.3 per 1,000). *2008:* Registered live births 5,124; Registered deaths 1,863 (death rate 5.5 per 1,000) (Source: UN, *Population and Vital Statistics Report*).

Life Expectancy (years at birth, WHO estimates): 75 (males 72; females 78) in 2008. Source: WHO, *World Health Statistics*.

Economically Active Population (persons aged 15 years and over, excl. armed forces, 2009): Agriculture, hunting, forestry and fishing 4,530; Mining, quarrying, electricity, gas and water 2,595; Manufacturing 5,315; Construction 17,345; Wholesale and retail trade 22,185; Hotels and restaurants 24,315; Transport, storage and communications 10,985; Finance, insurance, real estate and other business services 19,405; Community, social and personal services 50,550; *Sub-total* 157,225; Activities not adequately defined 580; *Total employed* 157,805 (males 80,335, females 77,470); Unemployed 26,215 (males 13,565, females 12,650); *Total labour force* 184,020 (males 93,900, females 90,120).

HEALTH AND WELFARE

Key Indicators

Total Fertility Rate (children per woman, 2008): 2.0.

Under-5 Mortality Rate (per 1,000 live births, 2008): 13.

HIV/AIDS (estimated % of persons aged 15–49, 2007): 3.0.

Physicians (per 1,000 head, 1998): 1.1.

Hospital Beds (per 1,000 head, 2006): 3.2.

Health Expenditure (2007): US $ per head (PPP): 1,987.

Health Expenditure (2007): % of GDP: 7.3.

Health Expenditure (2007): public (% of total): 51.0.

Access to Water (% of persons, 2004): 97.

Total Carbon Dioxide Emissions ('000 metric tons, 2006): 2,136.1.

Total Carbon Dioxide Emissions Per Head (metric tons, 2006): 6.5.

Human Development Index (2007): ranking: 52.

Human Development Index (2007): value: 0.856.

For sources and definitions, see explanatory note on p. vi.

AGRICULTURE, ETC.

Principal Crops ('000 metric tons, 2008, FAO estimates): Sweet potatoes 0.9; Sugar cane 5.8; Bananas 3.8; Lemons and limes 9.4; Grapefruit and pomelos 13.0; Vegetables (incl. melons) 25.6; Fruits (excl. melons) 30.0.

Livestock ('000 head, year ending September 2008, FAO estimates): Cattle 0.8; Pigs 5.0; Sheep 6.5; Goats 14.5; Poultry 3,000.

Livestock Products ('000 metric tons, 2008, FAO estimates): Chicken meat 8.1; Cows' milk 0.7; Goat's milk 1.1; Hen eggs 0.9.

Forestry ('000 cubic metres, 2008, FAO estimates): *Roundwood Removals (excl. bark):* Sawlogs and veneer logs 17 (output assumed to be unchanged since 1992); *Sawnwood Production (incl. railway sleepers):* Coniferous (softwood) 1.4 (output assumed to be unchanged since 1970).

Fishing (metric tons, live weight, 2008): Capture 9,117 (Nassau grouper 171; Snappers 936; Caribbean spiny lobster 6,896; Stromboid conchs 858); *Total catch* 9,117. Note: Data for aquaculture were not available.

Source: FAO.

MINING

Production ('000 metric tons, 2007, estimates): Unrefined salt 882.3; Aragonite 1.1. *2008:* Unrefined salt 1,024.4. Source: US Geological Survey.

INDUSTRY

Production (million kWh, 2008): Electric energy 2,206.5.

FINANCE

Currency and Exchange Rates: 100 cents = 1 Bahamian dollar (B $). *Sterling, US Dollar and Euro Equivalents* (31 May 2010): £1 sterling = B $1.458; US $1 = B $1.000; €1 = B $1.238; B $100 = £68.59 = US $100.00 = €80.75. *Exchange Rate:* Since February 1970 the official exchange rate, applicable to most transactions, has been US $1 = B $1, i.e. the Bahamian dollar has been at par with the US dollar. There is also an investment currency rate, applicable to certain capital transactions between residents and non-residents and to direct investments outside the Bahamas. Since 1987 this exchange rate has been fixed at US $1 = B $1.225.

General Budget (B $ million, 2008/09, budget, preliminary): *Revenue:* Taxation 1,129.9 (Taxes on international trade and transactions 594.8; Taxes on property 84.6; Taxes on companies 97.2); Other current revenue 194.2; Capital revenue 0.1; Total 1,324.2. *Expenditure:* Current expenditure 1,422.7 (Wages and salaries 573.1; Goods and services 322.2; Interest payments 154.2; Subsidies and transfers 373.1); Capital expenditure and net lending 262.9; Total 1,685.5.

International Reserves (B $ million at 31 December 2009): IMF special drawing rights 179.0; Reserve position in IMF 9.8; Foreign exchange 821.0; Total 1,009.8. Source: IMF, *International Financial Statistics*.

Money Supply (B $ million at 31 December 2009): Currency outside banks 208; Demand deposits at deposit money banks 1,038; Total money (incl. others) 1,252. Source: IMF, *International Financial Statistics*.

Cost of Living (Consumer Price Index; base: 2005 = 100): All items 104.9 in 2007; 109.7 in 2008; 111.9 in 2009. Source: IMF, *International Financial Statistics*.

Gross Domestic Product (B $ million at current prices): 6,508.8 in 2005; 6,875.6 in 2006 (provisional); 7,234.0 in 2007 (preliminary).

Expenditure on the Gross Domestic Product (B $ million at current prices, 2007, preliminary): Government final consumption expenditure 976.1; Private final consumption expenditure 5,108.6; Change in stocks 65.8; Gross fixed capital formation 2,733.2; *Total domestic expenditure* 8,883.7; Exports of goods and services 3,278.4; *Less* Imports of goods and services 4,928.1; *GDP in purchasers' values* 7,234.0.

Gross Domestic Product by Economic Activity (B $ million at current prices, 2006, provisional): Agriculture, hunting, forestry and fishing 106.8; Mining and quarrying 51.2; Manufacturing 301.2; Electricity and water 234.8; Construction 738.2; Wholesale and retail trade 795.9; Restaurants and hotels 701.2; Transport, storage and communications 596.2; Finance, insurance, real estate and business services 1,893.9; Government services 397.1; Education 301.4; Health 207.3; Other community, social and personal services 388.4; *Sub-total* 6,713.5; *Less* Financial intermediation services indirectly measured 442.0; *Gross value added in basic prices* 6,271.4; Net indirect taxes 604.1; *GDP in purchasers' values* 6,875.6.

Balance of Payments (B $ million, 2009, preliminary): Exports of goods f.o.b. 665.8; Imports of goods f.o.b. –2,540.1; *Trade balance* –1,874.3; Services (net) 1,074.4; *Balance on goods and services* –799.9; Other income (net) –209.5; *Balance on goods, services and income* –1,009.4; Current transfers (net) 82.3; *Current balance* –927.1; Capital account (net) –31.7; Financial account (net) 1,104.6; Net errors and omissions 107.1; *Overall balance* 253.0.

EXTERNAL TRADE

Principal Commodities (B $ million, 2009, distribution according to HS): *Imports c.i.f.:* Food and live animals 417.8; Beverages and tobacco 69.0; Crude materials, inedible, excl. fuels 65.8; Mineral products 557.1; Products of chemical or allied industries 272.1; Manufactured goods classified chiefly by material 394.3; Machinery and transport equipment 529.0; Miscellaneous manufactured articles 280.0; Total (incl. others) 2,699.0. *Exports (incl. re-exports) f.o.b.:* Food and live animals 67.0; Mineral products 112.1; Products of chemical or allied industries 251.3; Machinery and transport equipment 74.4; Total (incl. others) 584.9.

Principal Trading Partners (non-petroleum transactions, B $ million, 2009): *Imports c.i.f.:* United Kingdom 7.0; USA 2,023.8; Total (incl. others) 2,141.8. *Exports f.o.b.:* United Kingdom 19.0; USA 307.8; Total (incl. others) 472.8.

TRANSPORT

Road Traffic (vehicles in use, '000): Passenger cars 90 (2002); Commercial vehicles 25 (2001); Total 27,058 (2007). Sources: IRF, *World Road Statistics*; Auto and Truck International (Illinois), *World Automotive Market Report*.

Shipping: *Merchant Fleet* (vessels registered at 31 December 2008): Number 1,446; Displacement ('000 grt) 46,543 (Source: Lloyd's Register-Fairplay, *World Fleet Statistics*). *International Sea-borne Freight Traffic* (estimates, '000 metric tons, 1990): Goods loaded 5,920; Goods unloaded 5,705 (Source: UN, *Monthly Bulletin of Statistics*).

Civil Aviation (2005): Kilometres flown (million) 8; Passengers carried ('000) 1,020; Passenger-km (million) 277; Total ton-km of freight (million) 26. Source: UN, *Statistical Yearbook*.

TOURISM

Visitor Arrivals ('000): 4,601 (1,487 by air, 3,114 by sea) in 2007; 4,394 (1,393 by air, 3,001 by sea) in 2008; 4,645 (1,252 by air, 3,393 by sea) in 2009.

Tourism Receipts (B $ million): 2,057 in 2006; 2,192 in 2007; 2,153 in 2008 (Source: partly World Tourism Organization).

COMMUNICATIONS MEDIA

Radio Receivers: 215,000 in use in 1997.

Television Receivers: 73,000 in use in 1999.

Personal Computers: 40,000 (122.9 per 1,000 persons) in 2005.

Telephones: 129,000 main lines in use in 2009.

Mobile Cellular Telephones: 358,800 subscribers in 2009.

Internet Users: 115,800 in 2009.

Broadband Subscribers: 31,600 in 2009.

Daily Newspapers (1996, unless otherwise indicated): 3 titles (total circulation 28,000 copies); 4 titles in 2004.

Sources: UN, *Statistical Yearbook*; UNESCO, *Statistical Yearbook*; International Telecommunication Union.

EDUCATION

Pre-primary (2002/03, unless otherwise indicated): 20 schools (1996/97); 338 teachers (all females); 3,771 pupils (males 1,931, females 1,840).

Primary (2006/07, unless otherwise indicated): 113 schools (1996/97); 2,420 teachers (males 458, females 1,962); 37,122 pupils (males 18,913, females 18,209).

Secondary (2006/07, unless otherwise indicated): 37 junior/senior high schools (1990); 2,788 teachers (males 848, females 1,940); 34,217 students (males 16,974, females 17,243).

Tertiary (1987): 249 teachers; 5,305 students. In 2002 there were 3,463 students registered at the College of the Bahamas.

Pupil-teacher Ratio (primary education, UNESCO estimate): 15.8 in 2007/08.

Sources: UNESCO, *Statistical Yearbook*; UN, Economic Commission for Latin America and the Caribbean, *Statistical Yearbook*; Caribbean Development Bank, *Social and Economic Indicators 2001*.

Adult Literacy Rate (UNESCO estimates): 95.0% (males 95.0%; females 95.0%) in 2003. Source: UN Development Programme, *Human Development Report*.

Directory

The Constitution

A representative House of Assembly was first established in 1729, although universal adult suffrage was not introduced until 1962. A new Constitution for the Commonwealth of the Bahamas came into force at independence, on 10 July 1973. The main provisions of the Constitution are summarized below.

Parliament consists of a Governor-General (representing the British monarch, who is Head of State), a nominated Senate and an elected House of Assembly. The Governor-General appoints the Prime Minister and, on the latter's recommendation, the remainder of the Cabinet. Apart from the Prime Minister, the Cabinet has no fewer than eight other ministers, of whom one is the Attorney-General. The Governor-General also appoints a Leader of the Opposition.

The Senate (upper house) consists of 16 members, of whom nine are appointed by the Governor-General on the advice of the Prime Minister, four on the advice of the Leader of the Opposition and three on the Prime Minister's advice after consultation with the Leader of the Opposition. The House of Assembly (lower house) has 41 members. A Constituencies Commission reviews numbers and boundaries at intervals of not more than five years and can recommend alterations for the approval of the House. The life of Parliament is limited to a maximum of five years.

The Constitution provides for a Supreme Court and a Court of Appeal.

The Government

HEAD OF STATE

Queen: HM Queen ELIZABETH II.

Governor-General: Sir ARTHUR FOULKES (took office 14 April 2010).

THE CABINET
(July 2010)

The Cabinet is formed by the Free National Movement.

Prime Minister and Minister of Finance: HUBERT ALEXANDER INGRAHAM.

Deputy Prime Minister and Minister of Foreign Affairs: THEODORE BRENT SYMONETTE.

Minister of National Security: ORVILLE (TOMMY) TURNQUEST.

Minister of Tourism and Aviation: VINCENT VANDERPOOL-WALLACE.

Minister of Agriculture and Marine Resources: LAWRENCE (LARRY) CARTWRIGHT.

Minister of Education: T. DESMOND BANNISTER.

Minister of Health: Dr HUBERT MINNIS.

Minister of Public Works and Transport: NEKO C. GRANT.

Minister of the Environment: Dr EARL D. DEVEAUX.

Attorney-General and Minister of Legal Affairs: JOHN K. F. DELANEY.

Minister of Labour and Social Development: DION FOULKES.

Minister of Housing: KENNETH RUSSELL.

Minister of Youth, Sports and Culture: CHARLES T. MAYNARD.

Minister of State for Lands and Local Government: BYRAN WOODSIDE.

Minister of State for Immigration: W. A. BRANVILLE MCCARTNEY.

Minister of State in the Ministry of the Environment: PHENTON NEYMOUR.

Minister of State for Finance and Public Service: ZHIVARGO LAING.

Minister of State for Social Development: LORETTA BUTLER-TURNER.

MINISTRIES

Attorney-General's Office and Ministry of Legal Affairs: 7th Floor, Post Office Bldg, East Hill St, POB N-3007, Nassau; tel. 502-0400; fax 322-2255.

Office of the Prime Minister: Sir Cecil Wallace Whitfield Centre, West Bay St, POB CB-10980, Nassau; tel. 327-5826; fax 327-5806; e-mail info@opm.gov.bs.

Office of the Deputy Prime Minister: Goodman's Corporate Bay Centre, POB N-3746, Nassau; tel. 322-7624; fax 328-8212; e-mail brentsymonette@bahamas.gov.bs.

Ministry of Agriculture and Marine Resources: Levy Bldg, East Bay St, POB N-3028, Nassau; tel. 325-7502; fax 322-1767; e-mail nathanieladderley@bahamas.gov.bs.

Ministry of Education: Thompson Blvd, POB N-3913, Nassau; tel. 502-2700; fax 322-8491; e-mail info@bahamaseducation.com; internet www.bahamaseducation.com.

Ministry of the Environment: 3rd Floor, Dockendale House, West Bay St, POB N-3040, Nassau; tel. 328-2701; e-mail earldeveaux@bahamas.gov.bs.

Ministry of Finance: Cecil Wallace-Whitfield Centre, West Bay St, POB N-3017, Nassau; tel. 327-1530; fax 327-1618; e-mail mofgeneral@bahamas.gov.bs; internet www.bahamas.gov.bs/finance.

Ministry of Foreign Affairs and Immigration: Goodman's Bay Corporate Centre, West Bay St, POB N-3746, Nassau; tel. 322-7624; fax 328-8212; e-mail mofa@bahamas.gov.bs; internet www.mfabahamas.org.

Ministry of Health: Meeting St, POB N-3730, Nassau; tel. 502-4700; fax 325-5421; internet www.bahamas.gov.bs/health.

Ministry of Housing: Claughton House, Frederick St, POB N-4849, Nassau; tel. 322-6027; fax 322-6064.

Ministry of Labour and Social Development: Post Office Bldg, 2nd Floor, East Hill St, POB N-3008, Nassau; tel. 323-7814; fax 325-1920.

Ministry of National Security: East Hill St, POB N-3746, Nassau; tel. 322-7624; fax 328-8212.

Ministry of Public Works and Transport: John F. Kennedy Dr., POB N-8156, Nassau; tel. 322-4830; fax 326-6629; e-mail admin@mowt.bs; internet www.bahamas.gov.bs/publicworks.

Ministry of Tourism and Aviation: Bolam House, George St, POB N-3701, Nassau; tel. 302-2000; fax 302-2098.

Ministry of Youth, Sports and Culture: POB 3913, Nassau; tel. 502-0600; internet myscems.bahamas.gov.bs.

Legislature

PARLIAMENT

Senate

President: LYNN HOLOWESKO.

There are 16 nominated members.

House of Assembly

Speaker: ALVIN SMITH.

The House has 41 members.

General Election, 2 May 2007

Party	Seats
Free National Movement (FNM)	23
Progressive Liberal Party (PLP)	18
Total	41

Election Commission

Office of the Parliamentary Commissioner: c/o Ministry of National Security, Farrington Road, POB N-1653, Nassau; tel. 325-2888; fax 322-1637; e-mail errolbethel@hotmail.com; internet www.bahamas.gov.bs/parliamentary; Chair. ERROL W. BETHEL.

Political Organizations

Bahamas Democratic Movement (BDM): 71 Marathon Rd, POB SS 5685, Nassau; tel. 341-3991; fax 393-9777; e-mail info@bdmparty.com; internet www.bdmparty.com; f. 2000; Leader CASSIUS V. STUART; Chair. TOLONUS SANDS.

Free National Movement (FNM): 144 Mackey St, POB N-10713, Nassau; tel. 393-7853; fax 393-7914; e-mail info@freenationalmovement.org; internet www.freenationalmovement.org; f. 1972; Leader HUBERT ALEXANDER INGRAHAM; Deputy Leader BRENT T. SYMONETTE.

Progressive Liberal Party (PLP): Sir Lynden Pindling Centre, PLP House, Farrington Rd, POB N-547, Nassau; tel. 326-9688; fax 328-0808; internet www.myplp.com; f. 1953; centrist party; Leader PERRY G. CHRISTIE; Deputy Leader PHILIP (BRAVE) DAVIS.

Diplomatic Representation

EMBASSIES IN THE BAHAMAS

China, People's Republic: 3 Orchard Terrace, Village Rd, POB SS-6389, Nassau; tel. 393-1415; fax 393-0733; e-mail chinaemb_bs@mfa.gov.cn; internet bs.china-embassy.org; Ambassador HU DINGXIAN.

Cuba: 61 Miller House, Collins Ave, POB EE-15679, Nassau; tel. 356-3473; fax 356-3472; e-mail cubanembassy@coralwave.com; internet embacu.cubaminrex.cu/bahamas; Ambassador JOSÉ LUIS PONCE CARABALLO.

Haiti: Sears House, Shirley St and Sears Rd, POB N-3036, Nassau; tel. 326-0325; fax 322-7712; Ambassador LOUIS HAROLD JOSEPH.

USA: Mosmar Bldg, Queen St, POB N-8197, Nassau; tel. 322-1181; fax 328-7838; e-mail embnas@state.gov; internet nassau.usembassy.gov; Ambassador NICOLE A. AVANT.

Judicial System

The Judicial Committee of the Privy Council (based in the United Kingdom), the Bahamas Court of Appeal, the Supreme Court and the Magistrates' Courts are the main courts of the Bahamian judicial system.

All courts have both a criminal and civil jurisdiction. The Magistrates' Courts are presided over by professionally qualified Stipendiary and Circuit Magistrates in New Providence and Grand Bahama, and by Island Administrators sitting as Magistrates in the Family Islands.

Whereas all magistrates are empowered to try offences that may be tried summarily, a Stipendiary and Circuit Magistrate may, with the consent of the accused, also try certain less serious indictable offences. In September 2006 the Bahamas' sole coroner's court was disbanded and magistrates endowed with the power to hear inquests. The jurisdiction of magistrates is, however, limited by law.

The Supreme Court consists of the Chief Justice, two Senior Justices and six Justices. The Supreme Court also sits in Freeport, with two Justices.

Appeals in almost all matters lie from the Supreme Court to the Court of Appeal, with further appeal in certain instances to the Judicial Committee of the Privy Council.

Supreme Court of the Bahamas

Bank Lane, POB N-167, Nassau; tel. 322-3315; fax 323-6463; internet www.bahamassupremecourt.gov.bs; Chief Justice Sir BURTON HALL.

Registrar of the Supreme Court: DONNA NEWTON (acting), The Registry, Ansbacher House, East and Shirley Sts, POB N-167, Nassau; tel. 322-4348; fax 325-6895; e-mail registrar@courts.gov.bs.

Court of Appeal: Claughton House, 3rd Floor, POB N-3209, Nassau; tel. 328-5400; fax 323-4659; e-mail info@courtofappeal.org.bs; internet www.courtofappeal.org.bs; Pres. Dame JOAN SAWYER.

Magistrates' Courts: POB N-421, Nassau; tel. 325-4573; fax 323-1446; 15 magistrates and a circuit magistrate.

Office of the Attorney-General: Post Office Bldg, 3rd Floor, East Hill St, POB N-3007, Nassau; tel. 322-1141; fax 322-2255; Dir of Legal Affairs DEBORAH FRASER; Dir of Public Prosecutions BERNARD TURNER.

Registrar-General: JACINDA BUTLER (acting), Rodney Bain Bldg, 50 Shirley St, POB N-532, Nassau; tel. 322-3316; fax 322-5553; e-mail registrargeneral@bahamas.gov.bs; internet www.bahamas.gov.bs/rgd.

Religion

Most of the population profess Christianity, but there are also small communities of Jews and Muslims.

CHRISTIANITY

Bahamas Christian Council: POB N-3103, Nassau; tel. 326-7114; f. 1948; 27 mem. churches; Pres. Rev. PATRICK PAUL.

The Baptist Church

According to the latest available census figures (2000), some 35% of the population are Baptists.

Bahamas National Baptist Mission and Education Convention: Nassau; mem. of the Baptist World Alliance; 270 churches and c. 75,000 mems; Pres. WILLIAM THOMPSON.

The Roman Catholic Church

The Bahamas comprises the single archdiocese of Nassau. According to the latest available census figures (2000), some 14% of the population are Roman Catholics. The Archbishop participates in the Antilles Episcopal Conference (whose Secretariat is based in Port of Spain, Trinidad). The Turks and Caicos Islands are also under the jurisdiction of the Archbishop of Nassau.

Archbishop of Nassau: Most Rev. PATRICK PINDER, The Hermitage, West St, POB N-8187, Nassau; tel. 322-8919; fax 322-2599; e-mail rcchancery@batelnet.bs.

The Anglican Communion

Anglicans in the Bahamas, who account for some 15% of the population, according to the 2000 census, are adherents of the Church in the Province of the West Indies. The diocese also includes the Turks and Caicos Islands.

Archbishop of the West Indies, and Bishop of Nassau and the Bahamas: Most Rev. DREXEL WELLINGTON GOMEZ, Bishop's Lodge, Sands Rd, POB N-656, Nassau; tel. 322-3015; fax 322-7943; internet www.bahamas.anglican.org.

Other Christian Churches

According to the latest available census figures (2000), 8% of the population are Pentecostalists, 5% belong to the Church of God, 4% are Methodists and 4% are Seventh-day Adventists.

Bahamas Conference of the Methodist Church: POB SS-5103, Nassau; tel. 393-3726; fax 393-8135; e-mail bcmc@bahamasmethodist.org; internet bahamasmethodist.org; 34 mem. churches; Pres. WILLIAM HIGGS.

Bahamas Conference of Seventh-day Adventists: Tonique Williams-Darling Hwy, POB N-356, Nassau; tel. 341-4021; fax 341-4088; e-mail info@bahamasconference.org; internet www.bahamasconference.org; Pres. Dr LEONARD JOHNSON.

Greek Orthodox Church: Church of the Annunciation, West St, POB N-823, Nassau; tel. 326-0850; fax 326-0851; e-mail frtedbita@annunciation.bs.goarch.org; internet www.annunciation.bs.goarch.org; f. 1928; part of the Archdiocese of North and South America, based in New York (USA); Priest Rev. TEODOR BITA.

Other denominations include African Methodist Episcopal, the Assemblies of Brethren, Christian Science, the Jehovah's Witnesses, the Salvation Army, Presbyterian and Lutheran churches.

OTHER RELIGIONS

Bahá'í Faith

Bahá'í National Spiritual Assembly: POB N-7105, Nassau; tel. 326-0607; e-mail nsabaha@mail.com; internet www.bs.bahai.org.

Islam

There is a small community of Muslims, numbering 292 at the 2000 census.

Islamic Centre: Carmichael Rd, POB N-10711, Nassau; tel. 341-6612; fax 364-6233; e-mail jamaa.ahlussunnah@gmail.com; internet www.geocities.com/nassaumasjid.

Judaism

Most of the Bahamian Jewish community, numbering 228 at the 2000 census, are based on Grand Bahama.

Bahamas Jewish Congregation Synagogue: Luis de Torres Synagogue, POB F-42515, Freeport; tel. 373-2008; fax 373-2130; e-mail hurst100@yahoo.com; Pres. GEOFF HURST.

The Press

NEWSPAPERS

The Abaconian: Marsh Harbour, POB AB-20551, Abaco; tel. 367-2677; fax 367-3677; e-mail davralph@batelnet.bs; internet abaconian.com; f. 1993; local news; Editor DAVE RALPH.

The Bahama Journal: Media House, East St North, POB N-8610, Nassau; tel. 325-3082; fax 325-3996; internet www.jonesbahamas.com; f. 1987; daily; circ. 5,000.

The Freeport News: Cedar St, POB F-40007, Freeport; tel. 352-8321; fax 351-3449; e-mail oswald@nasguard.com; internet freeport

.nassauguardian.net; f. 1961; owned by *The Nassau Guardian*; daily; Gen. Man. DORLAN COLLIE; Editor OSWALD T. BROWN; circ. 5,000.

The Nassau Guardian: 4 Carter St, Oakes Field, POB N-3011, Nassau; tel. 302-2300; fax 328-8943; e-mail editor@nasguard.com; internet www.thenassauguardian.com; f. 1844; daily; Pres. ANTHONY FERGUSON; Man. Editor ERICA WELLS; circ. 15,000.

The Punch: Farrington Rd, POB N-4081, Nassau; tel. 322-7112; fax 323-5268; e-mail thepunch@coralwave.com; f. 1990; 2 a week; Publr and Editor IVAN JOHNSON; circ. 25,000.

The Tribune: Shirley St, POB N-3207, Nassau; tel. 322-1986; fax 328-2398; e-mail tips@tribunemedia.net; internet www.tribune242.com; f. 1903; daily; Publr EILEEN CARRON; Man. Editor JOHN FLEET; circ. 15,000.

PERIODICALS

The Bahamas Financial Digest: Miramar House, 2nd Floor, Bay and Christie Sts, POB N-4824, Nassau; tel. 322-5030; fax 326-2849; e-mail bfd@bahamas.net.bs; internet bfd-financial.com/Digest/digest.html; f. 1973; 4 a year; business and investment; Publr and Editor MICHAEL A. SYMONETTE; circ. 15,890.

Bahamas Tourist News: Fred Ramsay Bldg, Shirley Park St, Nassau; tel. 322-3724; fax 322-4527; e-mail starpub@batelnet.bs; f. 1962; monthly; Editor BOBBY BOWER; circ. 371,000 (annually).

Nassau City Magazine: Miramar House, Bay and Christie Sts, POB N-4824, Nassau; tel. 356-2981; fax 326-2849.

Official Gazette: Government Publications, c/o Cabinet Office, POB N-7147, Nassau; tel. 322-2805; weekly; publ. by the Cabinet Office.

What's On Bahamas: Woodes Rogers Wharf, POB CB-11713, Nassau; tel. 323-2323; fax 322-3428; e-mail info@whatsonbahamas.com; internet www.whatsonbahamas.com; monthly; Publr NEIL ABERLE.

Publishers

Dupuch Publications Ltd: Oakes Field, POB N-7513, Nassau; tel. 323-5665; fax 323-5728; e-mail info@dupuch.com; internet www.dupuch.com; f. 1959; publishes *Bahamas Handbook*, *Trailblazer* maps, *What To Do* magazines, *Welcome Bahamas* and *Dining and Entertainment Guide*; Publr ETIENNE DUPUCH, Jr.

Guanima Press Ltd: East Bay St, POB CB-13151, Nassau; e-mail guanimapressltd@yahoo.com; internet www.guanimapress.com; tel. and fax 393-3221; Owner P. MEICHOLAS.

Media Enterprises Ltd: 31 Shirley Park Ave, POB N-9240, Nassau; tel. 325-8210; fax 325-8065; e-mail info@bahamasmedia.com; internet www.bahamasmedia.com; f. 1986; educational and other non-fiction books; Pres. and Gen. Man. LARRY A. SMITH; Publishing Dir NEIL E. SEALEY.

Printing Tours and Publishing: Miramar House, Bay and Christie Sts, POB N-4846, Nassau; tel. 356-2981; fax 356-7118.

Star Publishers Ltd: Fred Ramsay Bldg, Shirley Park St, Nassau; tel. 322-3724; fax 322-4527; e-mail starpub@bahamas.net.bs; CEO BOB BOWER.

Broadcasting and Communications

TELECOMMUNICATIONS

Bahamas Telecommunications Co (BTC): John F. Kennedy Dr., POB N-3048, Nassau; tel. 302-7008; fax 326-8423; internet www.btcbahamas.com; f. 1966, fmrly known as BaTelCo; state-owned; 51% scheduled for privatization in mid-2010; Exec. Chair. JULIAN FRANCIS; Acting Pres. and CEO KIRK GRIFFIN.

Cable Bahamas Ltd: Robinson Rd at Marathon, POB CB-13050, Nassau; tel. 356-8940; fax 356-8997; e-mail info@cablebahamas.com; internet www.cablebahamas.com; f. 1995; provides cable television and internet services; Chair. and CEO BRENDAN PADDICK; Dir and Pres. ANTHONY BUTLER.

BROADCASTING

Radio

Broadcasting Corporation of the Bahamas: 3rd Terrace, Centreville, POB N-1347, Nassau; tel. 502-3800; fax 322-6598; e-mail yourcomments@znsbahamas.com; internet www.znsbahamas.com; f. 1936; govt-owned; operates the ZNS radio and television network; Chair. CALSEY JOHNSON; Gen. Man. EDWIN LIGHTBOURNE.

Radio ZNS Bahamas: internet www.znsbahamas.com; f. 1936; broadcasts 24 hours per day on 4 stations: the main Radio Bahamas ZNS1, Radio New Providence ZNS2, which are both based in Nassau, Radio Power 104.5 FM, and the Northern Service (ZNS3—Freeport); Station Man. ANTHONY FORSTER; Programme Man. TANYA PINDER.

Cool 96 FM: Yellow Pine St, POB F-40773, Freeport, Grand Bahama; tel. 351-2665; fax 352-8709; e-mail cool96@coralwave.com; internet cool96fm.com; f. 1995; opened office in Nassau in Jan. 2005; Pres. and Gen. Man. ANDREA GOTTLIEB.

Love 97 FM: Bahamas Media House, East St North, POB N-3909, Nassau; tel. 356-2555; fax 356-7256; e-mail twilliams@jonescommunications.com; internet www.jonesbahamas.com; operated by Jones Communications Ltd.

More 94 FM: Carmichael Rd, POB CR-54245, Nassau; tel. 361-2447; fax 361-2448; e-mail media@more94fm.com; internet www.more94fm.com.

One Hundred JAMZ: Shirley and Deveaux St, POB N-3207, Nassau; tel. 677-0950; fax 356-5343; e-mail michelle@100jamz.com; internet www.100jamz.com; operated by *The Tribune* newspaper; Gen. Man. STEPHEN HAUGHEY; Programme Dir ERIC WARD.

Television

Broadcasting Corporation of the Bahamas: see Radio.

Bahamas Television: f. 1977; broadcasts for Nassau, New Providence and the Central Bahamas; transmitting power of 50,000 watts; full colour; Programme Man. CARL BETHEL.

US television programmes and some satellite programmes can be received. Most islands have a cable television service.

Finance

The Bahamas developed into one of the world's foremost financial centres (there are no corporation, income, capital gains or withholding taxes or estate duty), and finance has become a significant feature of the economy. In June 2008 there were 105 'offshore' banks and trust companies in operation in the islands, with a further 145 on restricted licences.

BANKING

(cap. = capital; res = reserves; dep. = deposits; m. = million; brs = branches)

Central Bank

The Central Bank of the Bahamas: Frederick St, POB N-4868, Nassau; tel. 302-2600; fax 322-4321; e-mail cbob@centralbankbahamas.com; internet www.centralbankbahamas.com; f. 1974; bank of issue; cap. B $3.0m., res B $116.7m., dep. B $336.2m. (Dec. 2008); Gov. and Chair. WENDY M. CRAIGG.

Development Bank

The Bahamas Development Bank: Cable Beach, West Bay St, POB N-3034, Nassau; tel. 702-5700; fax 327-5047; internet bahamasdevelopmentbank.com; f. 1978 to fund approved projects and channel funds into appropriate investments; total assets B $58.3m. (Dec. 2004); Chair. DARRON CASH; Man. Dir ANTHONY WOODSIDE; 1 br.

Principal Banks

Bank of the Bahamas Ltd (Bank of the Bahamas International): Claughton House, Shirley and Charlotte Sts, POB N-7118, Nassau; tel. 326-2560; fax 325-2762; e-mail info.bob@bankbahamas.com; internet www.bankbahamasonline.com; f. 1970; est. as Bank of Montreal (Bahamas and Caribbean); name changed as above in 2002; 50% owned by Govt, 50% owned by c. 4,000 Bahamian shareholders; cap. B $30.4m., res B $28.5m., dep. B $617.1m. (June 2008); Chair. MACGREGOR ROBERTSON; Man. Dir PAUL MCWEENEY; 11 brs.

Banque Privée Edmond de Rothschild Ltd (Switzerland): Lyford Financial Centre, Lyford Cay #2, West Bay St, POB SP-63948, Nassau; tel. 702-8000; fax 702-8008; e-mail dswaby@bper.ch; internet www.edmond-de-rothschild.bs; f. 1997; owned by Banque Privée Edmond de Rothschild SA (Switzerland); cap. 15.0m. Swiss francs, res 18.0m. Swiss francs, dep. 87.0m. Swiss francs (Dec. 2008); Chair. BENJAMIN DE ROTHSCHILD; CEO CLAUDE MESSULAM.

BSI Overseas (Bahamas) Ltd (Italy): Goodman's Bay Corporate Centre, West Bay St, Sea View Dr., POB N-7130, Nassau; tel. 502-2200; fax 502-2230; e-mail info@bsibank.com; internet www.bs.bsibank.com; f. 1969 as Banca della Svizzera Italiana (Overseas) Ltd; name changed as above 1990; wholly owned subsidiary of BSI SA Lugano; cap. US $10.0m., res US $17.4m., dep. US $4,919.3m. (Dec. 2008); Chair. GIORGIO GHIRINGHELLI; CEO ALFREDO GYSI.

Canadian Imperial Bank of Commerce (CIBC) (Canada): Goodman's Bay Corporate Centre, West Bay St, POB 3933, Nassau; tel. 356-1800; fax 322-3692; e-mail privatebanking@cibc.com; internet www.cibc.com; Pres. GERALD T. MCCAUGHEY; Area Man. TERRY HILTS; 9 brs.

Citibank NA (USA): Citibank Bldg, 4th Floor, Thompson Blvd, Oakes Field, POB N-8158, Nassau; tel. 302-8500; fax 323-3088; internet www.citibank.com; CEO RAUL ANAYA; 2 brs.

Commonwealth Bank Ltd: The Plaza, Mackey St, POB SS 5541, Nassau; tel. 502-6200; fax 394-5807; e-mail cbinquiry@combankltd.com; internet www.combankltd.com; f. 1960; total assets B $1,179.2m. (Dec. 2007); Pres., CEO and Dir WILLIAM BATEMAN SANDS, Jr; Chair. T. BASWELL DONALDSON; 11 brs.

Crédit Agricole Suisse Bank & Trust (Bahamas) Ltd: Goodman's Bay Corporate Centre, Ground Floor, POB N-3015, Nassau; tel. 502-8100; fax 502-8166; internet www.ca-suisse.bs; f. 1978; 100% owned by Crédit Agricole (Suisse) SA, Geneva; fmrly National Bank of Canada (International) Ltd; name changed as above 2008; cap. US $20.0m., dep. US $175.6m., total assets US $498.9m. (Oct. 2006); Pres. JEAN-MARIE SANDER; Dir-Gen. JEAN-PAUL CHIFFLET.

Crédit Suisse (Bahamas) Ltd (Switzerland): Bahamas Financial Centre, 4th Floor, Shirley and Charlotte Sts, POB N-4928, Nassau; tel. 356-8100; fax 326-6589; internet www.credit-suisse.com/bs; f. 1968; subsidiary of Crédit Suisse Zurichportfolio and asset management, 'offshore' company management, trustee services, foreign exchange; cap. US $12.0m., res US $20.0m., dep. US $579.2m. (Dec. 2004); CEO BRADY W. DOUGAN.

FirstCaribbean International Bank Ltd: Bahamas International Banking Centre, Shirley St, POB N-8350, Nassau; tel. 322-8455; fax 326-6552; internet www.firstcaribbeanbank.com; f. 2002; est. following merger of Caribbean operations of Barclays Bank PLC and CIBC; Barclays Bank relinquished its stake to CIBC in June 2006; total assets B $4,668.5m.; Exec. Chair. MICHAEL MANSOOR; CEO JOHN ORR; 16 brs.

Guaranty Trust Bank Ltd: Lyford Manor Ltd, Lyford Cay, POB N-4918, Nassau; tel. 362-7200; fax 362-7210; e-mail info@guarantybahamas.com; internet www.guarantybahamas.com; f. 1962; cap. US $18.0m., res US $0.4m., dep. US $99.6m. (Jan. 2007); Chair. Sir WILLIAM C. ALLEN; Man. Dir JAMES P. COYLE.

HSBC Private Banking (Bahamas) Ltd (Switzerland): Centre of Commerce, 3rd Floor, Suite 306, 1 Bay St, POB N-4917, Nassau; tel. 502-2555; fax 502-2566; internet www.hsbcprivatebank.com/offices/bahamas.html; e-mail hfccfint@bahamas.net.bs; f. 1971 as Handelsfina Int.; name changed as above in 2002; cap. US $5.0m., res US $15.5m., dep. US $581.3m. (Dec. 1999); Chair. STUART T. GULLIVER; CEO CHRISTOPHER MEARES.

Overseas Union Bank and Trust (Bahamas) Ltd (Switzerland): Kings Court, 250 Bay St, POB N-8184, Nassau; tel. 322-2476; fax 323-8771; f. 1980; cap. US $5.0m., res US $6.2m., dep. US $97.9m. (Dec. 1997); Chair. Dr CARLO SGANZINI; Gen. Man. URS FREI.

Pictet Bank and Trust Ltd (Switzerland): Bldg No. 1, Bayside Executive Park, West Bay St and Blake Rd, POB N-4837, Nassau; tel. 302-2222; fax 327-6610; e-mail pbtbah@bahamas.net.bs; internet www.pictet.com; f. 1978; cap. US $1.0m., res US $10.0m., dep. US $126.2m. (Dec. 1995); Chair. FRANCIS HODGSON; Pres. and Man. YVES LOURDIN.

Private Investment Bank Ltd: Devonshire House, Queen St, POB N-3918, Nassau; tel. 302-5950; fax 302-5970; e-mail pibbank@pib.bs; f. 1984; est. as Bank Worms and Co International Ltd; renamed in 1990, 1996 and 1998; in 2000 merged with Geneva Private Bank and Trust (Bahamas) Ltd; wholly owned by Banque de Patrimoines Privés Genève BPG SA (Switzerland); cap. US $3.0m., res US $12.0m., dep. US $165.4m. (Dec. 2008); Chair. and Dir JEAN-FRANÇOIS FURRER.

Royal Bank of Canada Ltd (Canada): 323 Bay St, POB N-7549, Nassau; tel. 322-8700; fax 328-7145; e-mail banks@rbc.com; internet www.rbc.com; f. 1869; Chair. DAVID P. O'BRIEN; Pres. and CEO GORDON M. NIXON; 25 brs.

Scotiabank (Bahamas) Ltd (Canada): Scotiabank Bldg, Rawson Sq., POB N-7518, Nassau; tel. 356-1697; fax 356-1689; e-mail scotiabank.bs@scotiabank.com; internet www.bahamas.scotiabank.com; Man. Dir BARRY MALCOM; Chair. ANTHONY C. ALLEN; 20 brs.

SG Hambros Bank and Trust (Bahamas) Ltd (United Kingdom): SG Hambros Bldg, West Bay St, POB N-7788, Nassau; tel. 302-5000; fax 326-6709; e-mail renaud.vielfaure@socgen.com; internet www.privatebanking.societegenerale.com; f. 1936; above name adopted in 1998; cap. B $2.0m., res –B $3.2m., dep. B $435.2m. (Dec. 2008); Chair. WARWICK NEWBURY; Head RENAUD VIELFAURE.

UBS (Bahamas) Ltd (Switzerland): UBS House, East Bay St, POB N-7757, Nassau; tel. 394-9300; fax 394-9333; internet www.ubs.com/bahamas; f. 1968; est. as Swiss Bank Corpn (Overseas) Ltd, name changed as above 1998; wholly owned by UBS AG (Switzerland); cap. US $4.0m., dep. US $420.2m. (Dec. 1997); Chair. KASPAR VILLIGER; CEO OSWALD J. GRÜBEL.

Principal Bahamian Trust Companies

Ansbacher (Bahamas) Ltd: Ansbacher House, 308 East Bay St, POB N-7768, Nassau; tel. 322-1161; fax 326-5020; e-mail info@ansbacher.bs; internet www.ansbacher.bs; incorporated 1957 as Bahamas International Trust Co Ltd; name changed 1994; acquired by AF Holdings Ltd 2009; cap. B $1.0m., res B $9.7m., dep. B $190.3m. (Sept. 1998); Man. Dir MICHAEL MAYHEW-ARNOLD.

Bank of Nova Scotia Trust Co (Bahamas) Ltd: Scotia House, 404 East Bay St, POB N-3016, Nassau; tel. 502-5700; fax 393-0582; e-mail scotiatrust@coralwave.com; internet www.bahamas.scotiabank.com; wholly owned by the Bank of Nova Scotia; Vice-Pres. and Head JAMES STOOKE.

Winterbotham Trust Co Ltd: Winterbotham Pl., Marlborough and Queen Sts, POB N-3026, Nassau; tel. 356-5454; fax 356-9432; e-mail adavidson@winterbotham.com; internet www.winterbotham.com; total assets US $14.1m. (Dec. 2007); Pres. and Man. Dir GEOFFREY HOOPER; CEO ALAN MCLEOD DAVIDSON; 2 brs.

Bankers' Organizations

Association of International Banks and Trust Companies in the Bahamas: Goodman's Bay Corporate Centre, West Bay St, POB N-7880, Nassau; tel. 356-3898; fax 328-4663; e-mail info@aibt-bahamas.com; internet www.aibt-bahamas.com; f. 1976; Chair. JAN F. C. MEZULANIK.

Bahamas Financial Services Board (BFSB): Goodman's Bay Corporate Centre, 1st Floor, West Bay St, POB N-1764, Nassau; tel. 326-7001; fax 326-7007; e-mail info@bsfb-bahamas.com; internet www.bfsb-bahamas.com; f. 1998; jt govt/private initiative responsible for overseas marketing of financial services; CEO and Exec. Dir WENDY C. WARREN; Chair. CRAIG (TONY) GOMEZ.

Bahamas Institute of Financial Services (BIFS): Verandah House, Market St and Trinity Pl., POB N-3202, Nassau; tel. 325-4921; fax 325-5674; e-mail info@bifs-bahamas.com; internet www.bifs-bahamas.com; f. 1974; est as Bahamas Institute of Bankers; name changed as above March 2003; Pres. TANYA MCCARTNEY; Exec. Dir KIM W. BODIE.

STOCK EXCHANGE

Bahamas International Securities Exchange (BISX): 50 Exchange Place, Bay St, POB EE-15672, Nassau; tel. and fax 323-2330; e-mail info@bisxbahamas.com; internet www.bisxbahamas.com; f. 2000; 21 local companies listed at May 2010; Chair. IAN FAIR; CEO KEITH DAVIES.

INSURANCE

The leading British and a number of US, Canadian and Caribbean companies have agents in Nassau and Freeport. Local insurance companies include the following:

Allied Bahamas Insurance Co Ltd: 93 Collins Ave, POB N-1216, Nassau; tel. 326-5439; fax 356-5472; general, aviation and marine.

BAF Financial: Independence Dr., POB N-4815, Nassau; tel. 461-1000; fax 361-2524; e-mail info@mybafsolutions.com; internet bahamas.mybafsolutions.com; f. 1920; est. as British American Insurance Co; name changed to British American Financial in 2007 when comprehensive range of financial services added; rebranded as above in 2010; wholly owned by local consortium, BAB Holdings Ltd, since Feb. 2007; Chair. BASIL L. SANDS; Pres. and CEO CHESTER COOPER.

Bahamas First General Insurance Co Ltd: 32 Collins Ave, POB SS-6238, Nassau; tel. 302-3900; fax 302-3901; e-mail info@bahamasfirst.com; internet www.bahamasfirst.com; f. 1983; Pres. and CEO PATRICK G. W. WARD.

ColinaImperial Insurance Ltd: 308 Bay St, POB N-4728, Nassau; tel. 396-2100; fax 396-2188; e-mail info@colinaimperial.com; internet www.colinaimperial.com; Colina Insurance Co merged with Global Life Assurance Bahamas in July 2002; operates under above name; fully owned subsidiary of Colina Holdings Bahamas Ltd; Chair. TERENCE HILTS; Exec. Vice-Chair. EMANUEL M. ALEXIOU.

Commonwealth General Insurance Co Ltd: POB N-4200, Nassau; tel. 322-8210; fax 322-5277; Man. Dir ALBERT ARCHER.

Family Guardian Insurance Co Ltd (FamGuard): East Bay St, POB SS-6232, Nassau; tel. 396-4000; fax 393-1100; e-mail info@familyguardian.com; internet www.familyguardian.com; f. 1965; life and health; fully owned subsidiary of FamGuard Corpn Ltd; Pres. and CEO PATRICIA A. HERMANNS.

Summit Insurance Co Ltd: Island Traders Bldg, East Bay St, POB SS-19028, Nassau; tel. 394-2351; fax 394-2353; e-mail info@summitbah.com; internet www.summitbahamas.com; f. 1994; Chair. CEDRIC A. SAUNDERS; Gen. Man. and Dir TIMOTHY N. INGRAHAM.

Association

Bahamas General Insurance Association: Royal Palm Mall, Unit 8, Mackey St, POB N-860, Nassau; tel. 394-6625; fax 394-6626; e-mail bgia@coralwave.com; internet www.bahamasinsurance.org; Chair. TIMOTHY INGRAHAM; Co-ordinator ROBIN B. HARDY; 18 mems.

Trade and Industry

DEVELOPMENT ORGANIZATIONS

Bahamas Agricultural and Industrial Corpn (BAIC): Levy Bldg, East Bay St, POB N-4940, Nassau; tel. 322-3740; fax 322-2123; e-mail nasoffice@baic.gov.bs; internet www.bahamas.gov.bs/baic; f. 1981; an amalgamation of Bahamas Development Corpn and Bahamas Agricultural Corpn for the promotion of greater co-operation between tourism and other sectors of the economy through the development of small and medium-sized enterprises; Chair. EDISON KEY; Gen. Man. BENJAMIN RAHMING.

Bahamas Financial Services Board (BFSB): see Finance—Bankers' Organizations.

Bahamas Investment Authority: Cecil V. Wallace-Whitfield Centre, West Bay St, POB CB-10980, Nassau; tel. 327-5970; fax 327-5907; e-mail bia@bahamas.gov.bs; operates from the Office of the Prime Minister.

Nassau Paradise Island Promotion Board: Hotel Center, S. G. Hambros Bldg, West Bay St, Nassau; tel. 322-8381; fax 326-5346; e-mail rknowles@bahamashotels.org; internet www.nassauparadiseisland.com; f. 1970; Chair. GEORGE R. MYERS; Sec. MICHAEL C. RECKLEY; 30 mems.

CHAMBERS OF COMMERCE

Bahamas Chamber of Commerce: Shirley St and Collins Ave, POB N-665, Nassau; tel. 322-2145; fax 322-4649; e-mail info@thebahamaschamber.com; internet www.thebahamaschamber.com; f. 1935 to promote, foster and protect trade, industry and commerce; Pres. KHAALIS ROLLE; over 700 mems.

Grand Bahama Chamber of Commerce: 5 Mall Dr., POB F-40808, Freeport, Grand Bahama; tel. 352-8329; fax 352-3280; e-mail gbchamber@batelnet.bs; internet www.gbchamber.com; Pres. GREGORY MOSS; Exec. Dir MERCYNTH FERGUSON; 264 mems.

EMPLOYERS' ASSOCIATIONS

Bahamian Contractors' Association: POB N-9286, Nassau; tel. 322-2145; fax 322-4649; e-mail info@bahamiancontractors.org; internet bahamascontractors.com; f. 1959; Pres. STEPHEN WRINKLE; Sec. ROBIN OGILVIE.

Bahamas Employers' Confederation (BECon): Bahamas Chamber of Commerce Bldg, Collins Ave and Shirley St, POB N-166, Nassau; tel. 328-5719; fax 322-4649; e-mail becon@bahamasemployers.org; internet www.bahamasemployers.org; f. 1966; Pres. and Dir BRIAN NUTT.

Bahamas Hotel Employers' Association: SG Hambros Bldg, West Bay, POB N-7799, Nassau; tel. 322-2262; fax 502-4221; e-mail bhea4mcr@hotmail.com; f. 1958; Pres. J. BARRIE FARRINGTON; Exec. Vice-Pres. MICHAEL C. RECKLEY; 16 mems.

Bahamas Institute of Chartered Accountants: Maritima House, 2nd Floor, Frederick St, POB N-7037, Nassau; tel. 326-6619; fax 326-6618; e-mail secbica@batelnet.bs; internet www.bica.bs; f. 1971; Pres. REECE CHIPMAN.

Bahamas Motor Dealers' Association (BMDA): POB SS-6213, Nassau; tel. 302-1030; internet www.bmda.bs; 17 mem. cos.

Bahamas Real Estate Association: Dowdeswell St, POB N-8860, Nassau; tel. 356-4578; fax 356-4501; e-mail info@bahamasrealestateassociation.com; internet www.bahamasrealestateassociation.com; f. 1959; Pres. PATRICIA BIRCH; Sec. JAMES NEWBOLD; more than 600 mems.

Bahamas Society of Engineers: POB SS-6533, Nassau; tel. 394-5544; fax 394-6885; e-mail crreiss@reisseng.com; internet www.bahamasengineers.org; f. 1998; Pres. C. ROBERT REISS; Sec. MARIO BASTIAN.

Professional Engineers Board (PEB): 3 21st Century Rd, POB N-3817, Nassau; tel. 328-3574; e-mail info@pebahamas.org; internet www.pebahamas.org; f. 2004; Chair. MICHAEL MOSS.

MAJOR COMPANIES

Aquapure Water Ltd: Bernard Rd, POB SS-6244, Nassau; tel. 394-1904; fax 393-1936; e-mail aquapure@bahamas.net.bs; f. 1975; produces purified and deionized bottled water; Dir JOHN MCSWEENEY.

Baha Mar Development Co Ltd: Baha Mar Resorts Ltd, West Bay St, POB N-8306, Nassau; tel. 677-9000; fax 677-9001; e-mail info@bahamar.com; internet www.bahamar.com; subsidiary of Baha Mar Resorts, Ltd; purchased Wyndham Nassau Resort, Crystal Palace Casino, Nassau Beach Hotel and Radisson Cable Beach Resort in 2005; developer of a 1,000 acre resort at Nassau; jt venture with Export-Import Bank of China and China State Construction Engineering Corpn; Chair. and CEO SARKIS IZMIRLIAN; Pres. DON ROBINSON.

Bahama Palm Groves Ltd: Don Mackely Blvd, POB 20096, Marsh Harbour, Abaco; tel. 367-3086; fax 367-2223; f. 1986; fruit sellers; Man. Dir RANDY KEY; 287 employees.

Bahamas Marine Construction Co Ltd: House of Mosko, Bay St and Victoria Ave, POB N-7512, Nassau; tel. 325-1654; fax 326-5127; e-mail crogers@mosko.com; internet www.mosko.com/building/marine.html; f. 1980; owned by the Mosko Group of Companies, Bahamas; focuses on the construction of ports, docks and marinas; Chair. JAMES GEORGE MOSKO; Contact CHRIS ROGERS; 111 employees.

Bahamas Realty Ltd: POB N-1132, Nassau; tel. 396-0000; fax 396-0010; e-mail brealty@bahamasrealty.bs; internet www.bahamasrealty.bs; f. 1978 as Caribbean Management and Sales Ltd; real estate; Pres. ROBIN B. BROWNRIGG; CEO LARRY ROBERTS.

Bahamas Supermarkets Ltd: East West Hwy, POB N-3738, Nassau; tel. 393-2830; fax 393-1232; e-mail feedback@bahamassupermarkets.com; internet www.citymarketbahamas.com; f. 1968; 8% stake fmrly held by Winn-Dixie Holdings (Florida, USA); acquired by local group of cos, BSL Holdings Ltd, in 2006; Pres. (Store Operations) STEPHEN SMOLLETT; 800 employees; 11 stores.

Butler and Sands Co Ltd: John F. Kennedy Dr., POB N-51, Nassau; tel. 322-8104; fax 326-6655; f. 1949; distribution of alcoholic beverages; Pres. MARK A. G. FINLAYSON; CEO GARRET O. FINLAYSON; 150 employees.

Freeport Concrete Co Ltd (FCC): First Commercial Centre, 3rd Floor, POB F-42647, Freeport; tel. 352-7511; fax 351-3669; internet www.fccbahamas.com; f. 1995; ready-mix concrete manufacturers and building supplies retailers; Pres., Dir and CEO RAY SIMPSON; Chair. HANNES BABAK.

Grand Bahama Development Co Ltd: G. B. Port Authority Bldg, Pioneers Way and East Mall, POB F-42666, Freeport; tel. 352-3601; fax 352-3602; e-mail infosupport@gbdevco.com; internet www.gbdevco.com; f. 1961; holding co; Pres. and CEO GRAHAM TORODE; 300 employees.

Grand Bahama Snack Food Wholesale: Queen's Hwy, POB F-40797, Freeport; tel. 352-8868; fax 352-4173; e-mail gn@batelnet; f. 1960; snack food and drinks wholesalers and retailers; Pres. GWENDOLYN NEWBOLD.

H. G. Christie Ltd: Millar's Court, POB N-8164, Nassau; tel. 322-1041; fax 326-5642; e-mail sales@hgchristie.com; internet www.hgchristie.com; f. 1922; real estate service; Pres. PETER CHRISTIE; Vice-Pres. JOHN CHRISTIE.

Hutchison Port Holdings (HPH): Headquarters Bldg, Container Port Rd, Queen's Hwy, POB F-42465, Freeport; tel. 350-8000; fax 350-8044; internet www.freeportcontainerport.com; port holding co; owned by Hutchison Whampoa of Hong Kong; subsidiaries include Grand Bahama Airport Co, Freeport Container Port and Freeport Harbour Co; Man. Dir JOHN E. MEREDITH; CEO GARY GILBERT.

J. S. R. Real Estate Ltd: Pioneers Professional Plaza, POB F-40093, Freeport; tel. 352-7201; fax 352-7203; e-mail vanlew@coralwave.com; internet jsrbahamasrealestate.com; f. 1957; real estate, developments, condominiums, residency and investing; Pres. LEE VAN LEW.

Morton Salt Co (Bahamas): Gregory St, Matthew Town, Inagua; tel. 339-1300; internet www.mortonsalt.com; f. 1954 when West Chemical Co was amalgamated into Morton Salt Co; bought by K+S Aktiengesellschaft (Germany) in 2008; Man. Dir GLEN BANNISTER.

Mosko's United Construction Ltd: House of Mosko, Bay St and Victoria Ave, POB N-641, Nassau; tel. 322-2571; fax 325-2571; e-mail tmcdermott@mosko.com; internet www.mosko.com/building/united; f. 1958; owned by the Mosko Group of Cos, Bahamas; Pres. GEORGE MOSKO; Contact TOM MCDERMOTT; 567 employees.

PharmaChem Technologies Grand Bahama Ltd (Novasep—Freeport): West Sunrise Hwy, POB F-42430, Freeport; tel. 352-8171; fax 352-7078; e-mail info@pharmachemtech.com; f. 1967 by Syntex; manufacturer of pharmaceutical products; acquired by Novasep (France) in 2007; Pres. PIETRO STEFANUTTI; Gen. Man. RANDY S. THOMPSON.

Polymers International Ltd: Queen's Hwy, POB F-42684, Freeport; tel. 352-3506; fax 352-2779; e-mail gebelhar@polymersintl.com; f. 1997; manufacturer of polystyrene products; subsidiary of Dart Container (USA); COO JOSEPH GREGORY EBELHAR, III; 50 employees.

Super Value/Portion Control: Golden Gates Shopping Centre, Blue Hill and Carmichael Rds, POB N-3039, Nassau; tel. 361-5220; fax 361-5583; e-mail svssltd@batelnet.bs; f. 1965; groceries wholesale and retail co; Pres. RUPERT WINER ROBERTS, Jr; Vice-Pres M. A. ROBERTS, CANDY KELLY; 567 employees.

Taylor Industries Ltd: 111 Shirley St, POB N-4806, Nassau; tel. 322-8941; fax 328-0453; e-mail generalinfo@taylor-industries.com; internet www.taylor-industries.com; f. 1945; electrical appliances and supplies; Pres. and Gen. Man. DEREK TAYLOR; 87 employees.

Templeton Global Advisors Ltd: Lyford Cay, POB N-7759, Nassau; tel. 362-4600; fax 362-4308; e-mail csweeti@templeton.com; f. 1986; investment consultants and security brokers; Pres. CINDY SWEETING; 400 employees.

Vopak Terminal Bahamas: West Sunrise Highway, POB F-42435, Freeport; tel. 352-9811; fax 352-4029; e-mail jim.miller@vopak.com; internet www.vopak.com; f. 1964; petroleum distribution; fmrly BORCO Bahamas Oil Refining Co International Ltd; 80% owned by First Reserve Corpn (United Kingdom), 20% owned by Royal Vopak (Netherlands); Pres. RAYMOND JONES; Commercial Dir JIM MILLER; 108 employees.

UTILITIES

Electricity

Bahamas Electricity Corpn (BEC): Big Pond and Tucker Rds, POB N-7509, Nassau; tel. 302-1000; fax 323-6852; e-mail customercare@bahamaselectricity.com; internet www.bahamaselectricity.com; f. 1956; state-owned; provides electricity to approx. 96,000 customers; Exec. Chair. MICHAEL MOSS; Gen. Man. KEVIN A. BASDEN.

Grand Bahama Power Co (GBPC): POB F-40888, Freeport; tel. 350-9000; fax 352-8449; e-mail evismissick@gb-power.com; internet www.gb-power.com; f. 1962 as Freeport Power Co Ltd; 55% owned by Marubeni Caribbean Power Holdings Inc; Pres. and CEO ALAN KELLEY.

Gas

Tropigas: Gladstone Rd, POB SS-5833, Nassau; tel. 361-2695; fax 341-4875.

Water

Bahamas Water and Sewerage Corpn (WSC): 87 Thompson Blvd, POB N-3905, Nassau; tel. 302-5500; fax 302-5080; e-mail wcinfo@wsc.com.bs; internet www.wsc.com.bs; f. 1976; operates under the auspices of the Ministry of Public Works and Transport; Chair. and acting Gen. Man. ANTON A. SAUNDERS.

TRADE UNIONS

All Bahamian unions are members of one of the following:

Commonwealth of the Bahamas Trade Union Congress: 3 Warwick St, POB N-3399, Nassau; tel. 394-6301; fax 394-7401; e-mail tuc@bahamas.net.bs; Pres. OBIE FERGUSON, Jr; Vice-Pres. CLEOLA HAMILTON; 12,500 mems.

National Congress of Trade Unions (NCTUB): Horseshoe Dr., POB GT-2887, Nassau; tel. 356-7459; fax 356-7457; e-mail office@nctu-bahamas.org; internet nctu-bahamas.org; Pres. JOHN PINDER; Gen. Sec. ROBERT FARQUHARSON; 20,000 mems.

The main unions are as follows:

Airport, Airline and Allied Workers' Union: Workers' House, Harold Rd, POB N-3364, Nassau; tel. 323-5030; fax 326-8763; e-mail aaawu@batelnet.com; f. 1958; Pres. NELLERENE HARDING; Gen. Sec. GLADSTONE ADDERLEY; 550 mems.

Bahamas Communications and Public Officers' Union: Farrington Rd, POB N-3190, Nassau; tel. 322-1537; fax 323-8719; e-mail union@bcpou.com; internet bcpou.org; f. 1973; Pres. BERNARD EVANS; Gen. Sec. DENISE WILSON; 2,100 mems.

Bahamas Doctors' Union: School Lane, Nassau; tel. 326-4166; Pres. FRANCIS WILLIAMS; Gen. Sec. GEORGE SHERMAN.

Bahamas Electrical Workers' Union: 52 Poinciana Dr., POB GT-2535, Nassau; tel. 322-4289; fax 322-4711; e-mail bewupresident2002@hotmail.com; Pres. DENNISE WILLIAMS; Gen. Sec. STEPHANO GREENE.

Bahamas Gaming and Allied Workers' Union: Taxi Union Bldg, Old Airport Rd, POB F-43070, Freeport; tel. 375-9804; fax 352-8837; e-mail bgawu@hotmail.com; Pres. DENNIS BRITTON; Gen. Sec. TIFFANY MARTIN.

Bahamas Hotel, Catering and Allied Workers' Union: Harold Rd, POB GT-2514, Nassau; tel. 325-0807; fax 325-6546; e-mail bhcawu@batelnet.com; f. 1958; Pres. NICOLE MARTIN; Gen. Sec. DARRIN WOODS; 6,500 mems.

Bahamas Maritime Port and Allied Workers' Union: Prince George Docks, Wulff Rd, POB FF-6501, Nassau; tel. 322-2049; fax 322-5545; e-mail fnrodgers@hotmail.com; Pres. FREDERICK N. RODGERS; Gen. Sec. MUNSINE DAVIS.

Bahamas Musicians' and Entertainers' Union: Horseshoe Dr., POB N-880, Nassau; tel. 322-3734; fax 323-3537; f. 1958; Pres. PERCIVAL SWEETING; Gen. Sec. PORTIA NOTTAGE; 410 mems.

Bahamas Nurses' Union: Centreville, Eighth Terrace, POB N-11530, Nassau; tel. and fax 325-3008; e-mail bnu_17199@hotmail.com; Pres. CLEOLA HAMILTON; Gen. Sec. ANEKA JOHNSON.

Bahamas Public Services Union: Wulff Rd, POB N-4692, Nassau; tel. 325-0038; fax 323-5287; e-mail bpsu@batelnet.bs; f. 1959; Pres. JOHN PINDER; Sec.-Gen. STEVEN J. MILLER; 4,247 mems.

Bahamas Taxi-Cab Union: Nassau St, POB N-1077, Nassau; tel. 323-5818; fax 323-6919; e-mail btcunion@coralwave.com; internet www.bahamastaxicabunion.com; Pres. LEON GRIFFIN; Gen. Sec. ROSCOE WEECH.

Bahamas Union of Teachers: Teachers' National Secretariat, 104 Bethel Ave, Stapledon Gardens, POB N-3482, Nassau; tel. 323-4491; fax 323-7086; e-mail idatp@hotmail.com; internet www.bahamasunionofteachers.com; f. 1945; Pres. BELINDA WILSON; Sec.-Gen. STEPHEN MCPHEE; over 3,800 mems.

Eastside Stevedores' Union: Wulff Rd, POB GT-2813, Nassau; tel. 322-4069; fax 323-7566; f. 1972; Pres. DAVID BETHEL; Gen. Sec. HAROLDINE STUBBS, Jr.

Transport

ROADS

There are about 1,600 km (994 miles) of roads in New Providence and 1,368 km (850 miles) in the Family Islands, mainly on Grand Bahama, Cat Island, Eleuthera, Exuma and Long Island. In 1999 57.4% of roads were paved.

SHIPPING

The principal seaport is at Nassau (New Providence), which can accommodate the very largest cruise ships. Passenger arrivals exceed 2m. annually. The other main ports are at Freeport (Grand Bahama), where a container terminal opened in 1997, and Matthew Town (Inagua). There are also modern berthing facilities for cruise ships at Potters Cay (New Providence), Governor's Harbour (Eleuthera), Morgan's Bluff (North Andros) and George Town (Exuma).

The Bahamas converted to free-flag status in 1976. The fleet's aggregate displacement was 46,542,634 grt in December 2008 (the third largest national fleet in the world).

There is a weekly cargo and passenger service to all the Family Islands.

Bahamas Maritime Authority: POB N-4679, Nassau; tel. 356-5772; fax 356-5889; e-mail nassau@bahamasmaritime.com; internet www.bahamasmaritime.com; f. 1995; promotes ship registration and co-ordinates maritime administration; state-owned; Deputy Dir ERMA MACKEY.

Freeport Harbour Co Ltd: POB F-42465, Freeport; tel. 350-8000; fax 350-8044; internet www.freeportcontainerport.com; owned by Hutchison Port Holdings (HPH), Hong Kong; CEO GARY GILBERT; Dir ORLANDO FORBES.

Grand Bahama Port Authority (GBPA): Pioneer's Way and East Mall, POB F-42666, Freeport; tel. 350-9002; fax 352-6184; e-mail fstubbs@gbpa.com; internet www.gbpa.com; f. 1955; receivers were appointed to operate co in Nov. 2006 pending outcome of contested ownership trial, which was resolved in 2010; Chair. HANNES BABAK; Pres. IAN ROLLE.

Nassau Port Authority: Prince George Wharf, POB N-8175, Nassau; tel. 322-8832; fax 322-5545; e-mail portaja@batelnet.bs; regulates principal port of the Bahamas; Port Dir ANTHONY J. ALLENS.

Principal Shipping Companies

Bahamas Ferries: Potters Cay West, Nassau; tel. 323-2166; fax 393-7451; e-mail hr@bahamasferries.com; internet www.bahamasferries.com; f. 1999; services Spanish Wells, Harbour Island, Current Island and Governors Harbour in Eleuthera, Morgan's Bluff and Fresh Creek in Andros, Sandy Point in Abaco and George Town in Exuma; Gen. Man. ALAN BAX.

Cavalier Shipping: Arawak Cay, POB N-8170, New Providence; tel. 328-3103; fax 323-8866.

Dockendale Shipping Co Ltd: Dockendale House, 3rd Floor, West Bay St, POB N-3033, Nassau; tel. 325-0448; fax 328-1542; e-mail dscopr@dockendale.com; internet www.dockendale.com; f. 1973; ship management; Man. Dirs LESLIE J. FERNANDES, KAMMANA VALLURI.

Freeport Ship Services: 8 Logwood Rd, POB F-40423, Freeport; tel. 351-4343; fax 351-4332; e-mail info@freeportshipservices.com;

internet www.freeportshipservices.com; f. 2003; privately owned co; affiliated to United Shipping Co Ltd; agents, customs brokers, logistics providers, chandlers; Pres. JEREMY CAFFERATA; Gen. Man. TROY CARTWRIGHT.

Grenville Ventures Ltd: 43 Elizabeth Ave, POB CB-13022, Nassau.

HJH Trading Co Ltd: POB N-4402, Nassau; tel. 392-3939; fax 392-1828.

Teekay Shipping Corporation: TK House, Bayside Executive Park, West Bay St & Blake Rd, POB AP-59212, Nassau; tel. 502-8820; fax 502-8840; internet www.teekay.com; petroleum transportation; Chair. C. SEAN DAY; Pres. and CEO BJORN MOLLER.

Tropical Shipping Co Ltd: Container Terminals Ltd, John Alfred Dock, Bay St, POB N-8183, Nassau; tel. 322-1012; fax 323-7566; internet www.tropical.com.

United Shipping Co (Nassau) Ltd: Centreville House, 5th Floor, Terrace 2, West Centreville, POB N-4005, Nassau; tel. 322-1341; fax 323-8779; e-mail operations@unitedshippingnassau.com; internet www.uscbahamas.com; sister co of Freeport Ship Services; Chair. TERRY MUNDAY; Pres. FRED HALL.

CIVIL AVIATION

Lynden Pindling International Airport (formerly Nassau International Airport) (15 km—9 miles—outside the capital), Freeport International Airport (5 km—3 miles—outside the city, on Grand Bahama) and Marsh Harbour International Airport (on Abaco Island) are the main terminals for international and internal services. There are also important airports at West End (Grand Bahama) and Rock Sound (Eleuthera) and some 50 smaller airports and landing strips throughout the islands. A B $30m. airport-improvement programme was completed in 2004, and an estimated US $200m. development of Lynden Pindling International Airport was planned, with the first new terminal expected to open in 2010. Construction of a further international airport terminal on the island of Mayaguana (563 km—350 miles—south-east of Nassau) commenced in 2007.

Bahamasair Holdings Ltd: Windsor Field, POB N-4881, Nassau; tel. 702-4100; fax 702-4180; e-mail astuart@bahamasair.com; internet up.bahamasair.com; f. 1973; state-owned, proposed privatization plans shelved indefinitely by 2009; scheduled services between Nassau, Freeport, Cuba, Jamaica, Dominican Republic, Turks and Caicos Islands, destinations within the USA and 20 locations within the Family Islands; Chair. J. BARRIE FARRINGTON; Man. Dir HENRY WOODS.

Western Air Limited: San Andros International Airport, POB AP 532900, Nassau; tel. 329-4000; fax 329-4013; e-mail info@westernairbahamas.com; internet www.westernairbahamas.com; f. 2001; private, wholly Bahamian-owned company; scheduled services between Nassau, Freeport, San Andros and Bimini, and on-demand charter flights throughout the Bahamas, the Caribbean and Central and South America; Pres. and CEO REX ROLLE.

Tourism

The mild climate and beautiful beaches attract many tourists. In 2009 tourist arrivals totalled some 4,645,000, including 3,393,000 visitors by sea. The majority of stop-over arrivals (82.7% in 2007) were from the USA. Receipts from the tourism industry stood at B $2,153m. in 2008.

Bahamas Hotel Association: SG Hambros Bldg, Goodman's Bay, POB N-7799, Nassau; tel. 322-8381; fax 502-4220; e-mail bha@bahamashotels.org; internet www.bhahotels.com; Pres. RUSSELL MILLER; Exec. Vice-Pres. FRANK COMITO.

Hotel Corporation of the Bahamas: Marlborough St & Navy Lion Rd, POB N-9520, Nassau; tel. 356-4571; fax 356-4846; operates from Office of the Prime Minister; Chair. MICHAEL SCOTT; Chief Exec. DEEPAK BHATNAGER (acting).

Nassau Tourism and Development Board: POB N-4740, Nassau; tel. 326-0992; fax 323-2998; e-mail linkages@batelnet.bs; f. 1995; Chair. CHARLES KLONARIS.

Defence

The Royal Bahamanian Defence Force, a paramilitary coastguard, is the only security force in the Bahamas, and numbered 860, as assessed at November 2009. Increasing concerns over rising crime levels in the Caribbean region prompted the recruitment of an additional 100 personnel to the Royal Bahamas Defence Force and 200 officers to the Royal Bahamas Police Force in 2007.

Defence Budget: an estimated B $46m. in 2008.

Commodore: CLIFFORD WELLINGTON SCAVELLA.

Education

Education is compulsory between the ages of five and 16 years, and is provided free of charge in government schools. There are several private and denominational schools. Primary education begins at five years of age and lasts for six years. Secondary education, beginning at the age of 11, also lasts for six years and is divided into two equal cycles. In 2007/08 91% of children in the relevant age-group were enrolled at primary level, while 85% of children in the relevant age-group were enrolled at secondary level. The University of the West Indies has an extra-mural department in Nassau, offering degree courses in hotel management and tourism. Ross University School of Medicine began initial teaching activities in 2009 and planned to open a 126-acre campus on Grand Bahama for overseas medical students in 2010. Technical, teacher-training and professional qualifications can be obtained at the two campuses of the College of the Bahamas.

Government expenditure on education in 2008/09 was budgeted at B $278m. (or 17.7% of total spending from the General Budget).

Bibliography

For works on the Caribbean generally, see Select Bibliography (Books)

Block, A. A. *Masters of Paradise: Organized Crime and the Internal Revenue Service in the Bahamas*. Piscataway, NJ, Transaction Publrs, 1997.

Craton, M., and Saunders, G. *Islanders in the Stream: A History of the Bahamian People: From the Ending of Slavery to the Twenty-First Century*, Vol. I. Athens, GA, University of Georgia Press, 1998.

Islanders in the Stream: A History of the Bahamian People: From the Ending of Slavery to the Twenty-First Century, Vol II. Athens, GA, University of Georgia Press, 2000.

Culmer Jenkins, O., and Saunders, G. *Bahamian Memories*. Gainesville, FL, University Press of Florida, 2000.

Eneas, G. *Agriculture in the Bahamas: Historical Development 1492–1992*. Nassau, Media Publishing Ltd, 1998.

Howard, R. *Black Seminoles in the Bahamas*. Gainesville, FL, University Press of Florida, 2002.

Johnson, H. *Bahamas—Slavery to Servitude*. Gainesville, FL, University Press of Florida, 1997.

Johnson, W. B. *Race Relations in the Bahamas 1784–1834: The Nonviolent Transformation from a Slave to a Free Society*. Fayetteville, AK, University of Arkansas Press, 1999.

Keegan, W. F. *The People Who Discovered Columbus*. Gainesville, FL, University Press of Florida, 1992.

Kelly, R. C., Ewing, D., Doyle, S., and Youngblood, D. *Country Review, Bahamas, 1998/1999*. Commercial Data International, 1998.

McCartney, D. M. *Bahamian Culture and Factors Which Impact Upon It*. Pittsburgh, PA, Dorrance Publishing Co Inc., 2004.

McCulla, P. E. *Bahamas*. Broomall, PA, Chelsea House Publrs, 1998.

Storr, V. H. *Enterprising Slaves and Master Pirates: Understanding Economic Life in the Bahamas*. Bern, Switzerland, Peter Lang Publishing, 2004.

Strachan, I. *Paradise and Plantation: Tourism and Culture in the Anglophone Caribbean*. Charlottesville, VA, University of Virginia Press, 2002.

Toogood, M. *The Bahamas: Portrait of an Archipelago*. Oxford, Macmillan Caribbean, 2004.

BARBADOS

Geography

PHYSICAL FEATURES

Barbados lies in the Lesser Antilles, between the Atlantic Ocean and the Caribbean Sea. It is the most easterly of the West Indian islands, and its nearest neighbour is Saint Vincent and the Grenadines, about 160 km (100 miles) to the west. The island nation has an area of 430 sq km (166 sq miles).

The wider southern part of the island of Barbados continues in the north-west, tapering northwards. The terrain is generally flat limestone scored by deep, vegetation-filled gullies, gently rising into a central highland area, especially in the north-east, where Mt Hillaby reaches 336 m (1,103 ft). The 97 km (156 miles) of coast are more rugged in the east and north, protecting the island from the worst of the oceanic weather and sheltering the gentler waters and beaches of the west. Reefs surround much of Barbados. There are rivers in the north-eastern Scotland District, where the ancient limestone cap has been eroded to expose even older rocks. The well-watered island is fertile, and two types of flora warrant particular mention: the typical local fig trees, with their aerial roots, which are believed to be the origin of the island's name (Los Barbados, 'the bearded ones', of Pedro a Campos of Portugal in 1536); and the grapefruit, which originates on Barbados. Wildlife includes the Barbados green monkey (vervet monkeys originally transported from West Africa), the red-footed tortoise, and *Leptotyphlops carlae*, the world's smallest snake, which was discovered in 2006.

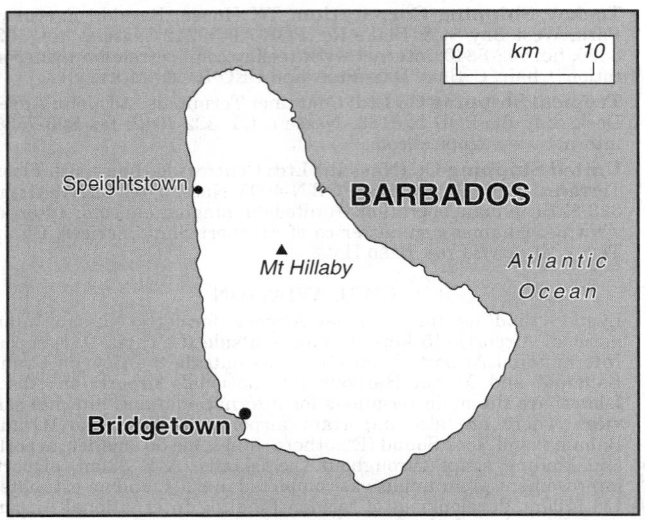

CLIMATE

The climate is tropical, but exposure to the Atlantic alleviates the extremes. Indeed, when the wind is strong off the ocean, certainly in the highlands it can become chilly. Generally, the average temperature is 27°C (81°F). The rainy season is between June and October, when there are likely to be hurricanes, although Barbados is on the edge of the region prone to them.

POPULATION

The people of the island, Barbadians (Bajans), are now predominantly black (89% at the 1990 census), but there is still a white community (3%), with the balance comprising mixed-race and Asian groups. Most of the people are Christians, the largest denomination being the Anglican Church, claiming the adherence of 28% of the population, followed by Pentecostalists with 19%, Adventists 5% and Methodists 5%. Roman Catholics account for 4% of the islanders. More than 100 religions and sects are represented on the island. There are small Muslim and Jewish communities—the synagogue is built on the site of one of the first two built in the Americas. English is the universal and official language.

The total population was a provisional 257,000 in mid-2010, making Barbados one of the most densely populated countries in the Caribbean. The capital and main port, Bridgetown, is on the south-western coast. On the coast in the north-west, Speightstown is the chief commercial centre for the north of the island. There are 11 parishes.

History

MARK WILSON

The Amerindians who settled Barbados from around AD 350 left the island during the 16th century, so that the first British settlers, who arrived in 1627, found no indigenous inhabitants. Barbados remained under British sovereignty until political independence in 1966, thereby earning itself the sobriquet 'Little England', and Barbadians played an important role in the settlement and administration of Britain's other Caribbean possessions. The first British settlers were smallholders growing tobacco and other crops, using the labour of indentured servants. However, fundamental change came with the introduction in the 1640s of sugar cane, by Dutch merchants, who brought plants from the Dutch settlements in Brazil. Sugar production required considerable labour and capital for the manufacturing process, a large work-force and extensive acreage, so large estate-owners supplanted the smallholders and, increasingly, slaves (of African origin) replaced the European servants. Although the first slaves arrived in 1627, they were few in number until the 1640s. By 1655 slaves formed 47% of a population of 43,000 and by 1712 they formed 77% of a total population of some 54,500. Many whites moved on to other British settlements in the Caribbean or on to the American mainland. Those who stayed, unless they were landowners, became craftsmen, overseers or merchants, or in some cases led a marginal and socially isolated existence as 'poor whites'. The black slave population was harshly treated and there were attempted slave revolts in 1675, 1692, 1702 and 1816. Slavery was eventually abolished in 1834, but its legacy was a highly stratified class-based society, still based, to some extent, on gradations of colour.

The British settlers established a House of Assembly in 1639 to represent their interests. Based on the 'representational system', the franchise was strictly limited by a property qualification. *De facto* power was exercised by the House of Assembly through its control of the public purse; hence it was able to hinder any attempt at reform by successive Governors. In 1876 the British Governor, John Pope Hennessey, proposed the establishment of a confederation to link Barbados and the Windward Islands. This suggestion was resisted by the Assembly, but was seen by many blacks as a partial solution to their difficulties. Eight people were killed in the ensuing Confederation Riots, and Pope Hennessey was subsequently transferred to Hong Kong. The first mixed-race member of the Assembly, Samuel Jackman Prescod, was elected in 1843, and the franchise was significantly widened in 1884. However, even the reformed property qualification continued to exclude the majority of blacks from the franchise. In 1856 the Assembly introduced district medical officers, and a Board of Education was formed in 1878, under the influence of the Anglican bishop, John Mitchinson. A non-white professional middle class emerged during the 19th century; Sir Conrad Reeves, a mixed-race politician and lawyer, was Chief Justice from 1886 to 1902. However, further political and social advance was to wait until the rise of the labour movement in the 1930s.

Charles Duncan O'Neal founded the Democratic League, influenced by Fabian principles, in 1924. Its first member, Chrissie Brathwaite, was elected to the Assembly in the same year, and the Working Men's Association was founded in 1926. The poor economic climate and the impoverished condition of most Barbadians led, as was also the case in most of the other British West Indian territories, to labour disturbances. In July 1937 14 people were killed and 47 injured in island-wide riots. A later commission of inquiry expressed no surprise at the disturbances, once the inequalities in Barbadian society at the time were revealed. The Barbados Progressive League was founded in 1938, its leaders including Grantley (later Sir Grantley) Adams. It secured five seats in the House of Assembly in 1940 and was strengthened considerably by an alliance with the Barbados Workers' Union (BWU), founded by Adams and Hugh Springer. In 1943 the League successfully campaigned for an extension of the franchise. In the 1944 general election the League won seven seats, while eight were attained by Wynter Crawford's more radical West Indian National Congress Party and eight by the traditionalist Electors' Association, established by the landowning and merchant élite. Adams and other elected members subsequently joined the Executive Committee, the principal policy-making instrument. The League was renamed the Barbados Labour Party (BLP) in 1946, and achieved growth at the expense of both other parties in the elections held in 1946 and 1948.

Universal adult suffrage was introduced in 1950 and in the general election held in 1951 the BLP won 16 of the 24 seats. Ministerial government was introduced in 1954 and Adams was appointed Premier. He subsequently became Prime Minister of the West Indies Federation, from January 1958 until its dissolution in 1962, and was succeeded as Premier of Barbados by Dr Hugh Cummins.

Following the 1951 election victory, those who favoured a more socialist approach, such as Errol Barrow, became disenchanted with those, like Adams, who favoured gradualist policies. In 1955 a small group, later named the Democratic Labour Party (DLP), led by Barrow, split from the BLP and joined forces with former members of the Congress Party. The BLP won 15 seats in the subsequent 1956 election, with the DLP and the Progressive Conservative Party each obtaining four. In October 1961 full internal self-government was granted and, in the ensuing general election, the DLP won 16 seats to the BLP's five, with one Independent seat and four for the traditionalist Barbados National Party. Britain tried to promote an association of Barbados with the neighbouring Leeward and Windward Islands, following the collapse of the West Indies Federation in 1962. However, this attempt was unsuccessful, and Barrow led Barbados to separate independence in November 1966 and became its first Prime Minister. Thereafter, a two-party system, based on the two Labour parties, prevailed.

The DLP was ousted from power in 1976 and the BLP leader, J. M. G. M. (Tom) Adams, son of Sir Grantley Adams, became Prime Minister. The BLP also won the 1981 election, securing 17 of the 27 seats in the newly enlarged House of Assembly. Adams played a leading role in support of the US military intervention in Grenada in 1983. He died suddenly in 1985 and was succeeded by Bernard St John, under whose leadership the BLP was heavily defeated by the DLP in the May 1986 election, when the BLP won only three seats. St John lost his seat and a former Minister of Foreign Affairs, Henry (later Sir Henry) Forde, assumed the BLP leadership. Errol Barrow once again became Prime Minister. The underlying reason for the Government's defeat lay in the country's past history. The issue of racism and 'white power' was never far from the surface; the BLP had become too closely identified, in many people's view, with the light-coloured business élite, from which it received substantial funds. Barrow, on the other hand, appealed to the black population and promised tax reforms to aid the black middle class. There was also dissatisfaction with the BLP's strong identification with US policy in the region, which offended nationalist sensibilities. Barrow's stand on this and other regional issues made him an imposing political force. His sudden death in June 1987 was, however, not entirely unexpected, given his refusal of medical advice pertaining to his strenuous work schedule. He was succeeded by his one-time deputy, Erskine Sandiford.

Sandiford's first political test was the resignation, in September 1987, of the Minister of Finance, Dr Richard (Richie) Haynes, who regarded himself as a possible future Prime Minister. At the same time, the economic situation began to deteriorate, partly as a result of Haynes' tax measures and partly owing to the closure in 1986 of the island's main manufacturing operation, a semi-conductor plant. In 1989 Haynes formed the National Democratic Party (NDP), with three other DLP parliamentarians, thus displacing Forde as the official Leader of the Opposition. In the general election of January 1991 the BLP won 10 seats to the DLP's 18. The fortunes of the BLP were restored with those of the two-party system; all four NDP members lost their seats. Support for the Sandiford regime declined rapidly thereafter, as austerity measures were introduced as a condition of IMF assistance to the economy, made necessary by a serious economic crisis. This situation was exploited to great effect by a rejuvenated BLP, led by a dynamic new leader, Owen Arthur. The BLP won a majority of seats at the general election of September 1994. Arthur became Prime Minister.

Arthur, a former professional economist, promoted economic recovery and international competitiveness in order to reduce the high levels of unemployment in the country. He proved himself capable of populist gestures, passing a constitutional amendment forbidding future reductions in pay for public employees. He also significantly broadened the BLP's support base, retaining its links with the business community while at the same time attracting a considerable number of nationalist intellectuals and trade unionists. In 1997 a public holiday to mark Emancipation Day was declared, and a National Heroes' Day was introduced on the anniversary of the birth of Sir Grantley Adams. The anniversary of the 1937 Confederation Riots was declared a 'day of national significance', and a pilot project was commenced towards the teaching of black studies in primary and secondary schools.

Support from across the political spectrum and a rapidly growing economy helped the BLP to achieve an unprecedented victory in the general election of 20 January 1999, winning 26 of the 28 seats in the House of Assembly. The opposition DLP emerged from the election severely weakened, gaining only two seats; a dispute from September 2001 between its two members of parliament over the party leadership further undermined its strength.

In August 2000 Arthur announced that a referendum would be held on the replacement of the monarch with a republic, a proposal that had the support of all political parties. However, a series of fierce political controversies in Trinidad and Tobago over the constitutional powers of the President in 2000–02 led to an enhanced appreciation of the need for careful consideration of the relationship between an elected government and a ceremonial President. In 2002 the Deputy Prime Minister and Minister of Foreign Affairs and Foreign Trade, Billie Miller, announced that new constitutional legislation would be drafted by the end of the year; however, the only change made was an amendment approved in September to override human rights judgments by the Privy Council, making it easier to make use of the death penalty.

A general election was held in May 2003, one year ahead of the constitutional deadline. With a strong economic record, in spite of a recent downturn in tourism, Owen Arthur led the BLP to a third successive electoral victory. However, the DLP increased its share of the popular vote to 44% and its parliamentary strength to seven seats; moreover, the Government held a further four seats by only narrow margins. Some voters were concerned over allegations of serious mismanagement in tourism, waste disposal and other public sector projects, and were at the same time concerned to temper the perceived arrogance of the BLP Government, while expecting it to remain in office. Clyde Mascoll was appointed opposition leader, quieting the DLP's leadership dispute. However, David Thompson was elected in November 2005 to the newly created post of party leader, and in January 2006 was chosen by a majority of elected opposition parliamentarians as constitutional Leader of the Opposition. Mascoll then defected from the DLP to the BLP, bringing the parliamentary strength of the ruling party to 24.

In February 2005 Arthur resurrected the proposal for Barbados' transformation to a republic with the announcement that a referendum to decide the issue—first disclosed as an objective of the BLP's third term in office by the Governor-General in June 2003—would be held by the end of the year. However, it was later announced that the referendum would be further postponed. It had been hoped that the 40th anniversary of Barbados' independence from British colonial rule, celebrated in November 2006, would induce the promised referendum. However, such a consultation remained unrealized in mid-2010 after Deputy Prime Minister Mia Mottley revoked a statement made in 2007 in which she had announced that the referendum would be held concurrently with the next legislative elections.

A general election was held on 15 January 2008, with the BLP again suffering from allegations of arrogance and mid-scale corruption, as well as from concerns over rising food and energy prices and the management of public sector infrastructure projects. The DLP returned to office after winning 20 of the 30 legislative seats and 52.7% of the popular vote, forming a new Government led by David Thompson, who took direct responsibility for finance, economic affairs and development, labour, the civil service, and energy, which portfolio includes responsibility for offshore oil and gas exploration. Arthur resigned as BLP leader immediately after the election, and was succeeded by Mottley. A BLP member of Parliament, Hamilton Lashley, left the party in September 2008 to sit as an independent; he had originally been elected as a DLP member in 1994, but joined the BLP in 1998, serving as social transformation minister until losing the cabinet post in 2006. He joined the DLP in May 2010, increasing its strength to 21 seats. There were minor cabinet reshuffles in November 2008 and March 2010. More significantly, the Prime Minister announced on 30 June that he would take a two month leave of absence overseas for health reasons; he said that major surgery was a possibility. The Deputy Prime Minister, Minister of Home Affairs and Attorney-General, Freundel Stuart, was appointed Acting Prime Minister, and in turn appointed a new Attorney-General and Minister of Home Affairs, Adriel Brathwaite.

Legislation enacted in May 2005 made Barbados one of only two countries to make the new Caribbean Court of Justice (CCJ—inaugurated in the previous month in Trinidad and Tobago) its final court of appeal, replacing the Privy Council in London, United Kingdom. The CCJ issued its first significant ruling in November 2006, endorsing a decision of the Court of Appeal of Barbados to commute to life imprisonment the death penalties requested against two convicted murderers, and so demonstrating the CCJ's ambivalence on the reinstatement of capital punishment (the last execution in Barbados occurred in 1984).

Barbados played a leading role in the 2000s in moves by 'offshore' financial centres to block initiatives by the Organisation for Economic Co-operation and Development (OECD, based in Paris, France) against tax havens, and by the intergovernmental Financial Action Task Force on Money Laundering (FATF, also based in Paris—see Economy). However, the country has an active anti-money-laundering policy although it remains vulnerable to laundering of both locally derived drugs proceeds and of overseas funds derived mainly from fraud operations. The 'offshore' financial sector is relatively clean, with a strong international reputation, and benefits from a network of 22 double taxation treaties, of which the latest, with the People's Republic of China and Panama, were signed in 2010—a single Caribbean Community and Common Market (CARICOM) treaty with 14 regional partners brings the number of countries covered to 35.

A dispute with Trinidad and Tobago over the delimitation of the Exclusive Economic Zone and fishing rights for Barbadian vessels within Tobago waters escalated in 2004, after almost 10 years of intermittent negotiations. Although fisheries issues attracted most attention, considerable importance was also attached to geological structures close to the median line between the countries that may contain significant quantities of petroleum and natural gas. In February Barbados imposed a temporary licensing requirement on some Trinidad and Tobago exports, and referred the maritime dispute for arbitration under the UN Convention on the Law of the Sea. A tribunal ruled in 2006, establishing a boundary following the line of equidistance between the two states for most of its length and reaching to the limits of the 200 nautical mile Exclusive Economic Zone. This gave Barbados a large area to the south-east, which had been claimed by Trinidad and Tobago, and was thought to have potential for deep-water petroleum and gas exploration. The tribunal rejected the Barbadian claim to a large area to the north of Tobago, but instructed the two countries to negotiate a fishing agreement for this area 'in good faith'; however, no significant progress on this front had been made by mid-2010. The Permanent Court of Arbitration's ruling conferred security on these new demarcations of jurisdiction, enabling Barbados in mid-2007 to open the auctioning of oil exploration rights for offshore blocks to leading hydrocarbon companies. A bid round for 24 offshore blocks was opened in June 2008. With oil prices low and capital markets weak at that point, results were disappointing. BHP Billiton was awarded two blocks, with a three-year seismic survey and data analysis programme. Barbados was in 2008 the first small island state to claim a further 150 nautical miles of Extended Continental Shelf beyond the Exclusive Economic Zone under Article 76 of the UN Convention on the Law of the Sea, acting a full year ahead of the deadline for such submissions. Maritime boundaries have also been agreed with Guyana, and in October 2009 with France (covering the French Overseas Department of Martinique).

Although Barbados is better ordered than most Caribbean islands, violent crime and drugs-trafficking are of serious concern. The US Department of State reported an increase in cocaine transshipment through Barbados since 2004, while marijuana is imported from Saint Vincent and Jamaica. Barbados police estimated around 5% of total drug consignment volumes remained on the island for local consumption in 2009, with 60% moving on to the United Kingdom, 15% to Canada, 10% to the USA and 10% to other Caribbean markets. Marijuana is imported by between eight and 12 local traffickers, and cocaine mainly by Trinidadians, Guyanese, Venezuelans and Colombians, who use pleasure boats, 'mules', and air cargo. The US Department of State noted concerns over corruption within the coastguard, as go-fast boats appear able to penetrate local defences. The murder rate of seven per 100,000 population in 2009 was the lowest for 10 years, down from a peak of 13 per 100,000 in 2006, and among the lowest in the Caribbean; suspects were identified for 63% of murders in 2009, in contrast to a detection rate of 5% for Jamaica. The US Department of the Treasury froze the assets of a Barbados-registered 'offshore' company, Kattus Corporation, in 2006 after it was implicated in the operations of a Colombian drugs cartel, foregrounding concerns about the susceptibility of the 'offshore' financial sector to corruption and criminal exploitation. In an effort to improve marine security, Barbados extended the capabilities of its coastguard from 2006, the completion in the previous year of a new coastguard headquarters and base paving the way for the delivery in 2007–09 of three 42-m offshore patrol vessels. Barbados in June 2010 agreed to borrow US $65m. from ING Bank to finance the purchase of eight smaller boats, a coastal radar system, and two helicopters.

Economy

MARK WILSON

Barbados is more economically and socially developed than most of the English-speaking Caribbean, with a per-head gross domestic product (GDP) at market prices of US $14,126 in 2010, among the highest in the region. The island functions as an air transport hub for the eastern Caribbean and is the site of the headquarters of several regional organizations. With high standards of education, infrastructure and health care, in 2009 the island was ranked higher than any other economy in Latin America and the Caribbean by the Human Development Index, produced by the UN Development Programme, although, at 37th world-wide, it had slipped from 31st place in 2007 and remained behind most members of the Organisation for Economic Co-operation and Development (OECD). The relative success was all the more remarkable because the country had one of the highest population densities in the world (some 639.7 per sq km in December 2010, with a population of 275,719 living on an area of 431 sq km).

GDP grew by an average of 2.9% per year in 1996–2007, interrupted by a 2.6% contraction in 2001—caused by a downturn in the tourism sector—which was barely noticed by most Barbadian consumers owing to the economy's underlying strength and the Government's counter-cyclical spending programme. Although some consumer prices are high by international standards, the underlying rate of inflation has generally been modest. Inflation averaged 2.1% per year in 1994–2004. The rate then rose sharply, reaching 8.2% in 2008, in part because of higher international oil prices, but declined again in 2009, to 4.4%.

However, the Barbadian economy experienced severe difficulties in 2008–10 as a result of the global economic recession and a decline in tourism demand. The economy moved from 3.8% growth in 2007 to a contraction of 0.2% in 2008; it then contracted sharply, by 5.7% in 2009. Unemployment rose to 10.6% in March 2010, from 7.4% in 2007, and would have risen further but for government commitments aimed at protecting key sectors such as construction.

In the 1990s successive governments took a reasonably cautious approach to budgeting and overall fiscal deficits remained under control, with the current account largely in surplus. The introduction of value-added tax (VAT) in 1997 contributed to the deficit reaching a low point of 0.1% of GDP in 1999. The fiscal deficit rose sharply, to 6.4% of GDP, with counter-cyclical spending in 2002, but averaged a manageable 2.7% in 2003–07, albeit with some substantial extra-budgetary spending, for example on improvements to the airport. However, the deficit increased again significantly as a result of the economic downturn, reaching 6.4% of GDP in 2008 and 8.4% in 2009, as revenue from VAT, import duties and corporate income tax fell sharply, while spending on goods, services and tourism promotion increased, as did transfers and subsidies to the public hospital, the University of the West Indies. The deficit was financed mainly by a bond issue led by the Bank of Nova Scotia in Trinidad and Tobago, and by borrowing from local institutions. In February 2010 the IMF proposed: reducing government spending; introducing a more efficient system of tax collection; and broadening the tax base to support the fixed exchange rate regime, improve debt dynamics and reduce the pressure on external reserves—this would in turn stimulate private sector investment in Barbados (five months earlier the Fund had expressed concerns that debt could reach unsustainable levels). The Barbadian authorities, however, maintained that too tight a fiscal policy would deepen the recession and weaken business confidence.

The ratio of public debt (including government guaranteed debt) to GDP rose to an estimated 110% at the end of 2009, up from 91% in 2008. Over the longer term, debt had risen from 74% in 2000; the increase would have been greater but for the 2004 sale of the state's majority holding in the Barbados National Bank, to Republic Bank (of Trinidad and Tobago) and the sale of a 51% stake in the Insurance Corporation of Barbados to BF&M Ltd of Bermuda in November 2005. The Government noted that one-quarter of its borrowing was from the National Insurance Scheme. Debt interest was projected at 5% of foreign exchange earnings for 2010, and at 18% of government revenue.

The current account of the balance of payments was in surplus from 1992 to 1996, with high and rising earnings from tourism and other services compensating for a permanent negative balance on merchandise trade. Continuing economic growth from 1997, however, brought about a rapid increase in imports of consumer and capital goods, resulting in a current account deficit, which rose incrementally from US $49.3m. in 1997 to US $367m. in 2005, a level equivalent to more than 12% of GDP and admitted by the Government to be unsustainable. The deficit fell back to US $178m. in 2007, but was recorded at US $422m. in 2008 as imports reached an all-time high of US $1,698m. and tourism earnings stagnated. In 2009, however, a sharp fall in imports outpaced the decline in tourism, and the current account deficit was down to US $229m. Balancing the current account payments deficit, there have been strong capital inflows, averaging US $308m. in 2004–09. The nature of these flows varied, with long-term private sector investments peaking at US $775m. in 2007, but falling to US $48m. in 2009 as tourism investments slowed.

From the 1990s net international reserves increased strongly. From a low point of Bds $38.9m. in 1991, reserves reached a high of Bds $1,510.2m. in May 2002. Reserves generally follow a strong seasonal pattern, with tourism inflows during the early part of the year, a peak in the second quarter and net ouflows thereafter. In addition, there are periodic capital inflows from precautionary borrowing, tourism-related investments and other sources. The recent high point was Bds $1,702.8m. in May 2008. In 2009 foreign exchange reserves increased as a result of public sector inflows from the Bank of Nova Scotia bond issue and an allocation of Special Drawing Rights; the usual first quarter net increase was absent, and reserves from March to June were below the January level. The first half of 2010 was also unusually weak, with low tourism receipts, although reserves remained comfortable, at 19 weeks' import cover in June 2010.

Economic growth in the 1990s had been preceded by economic stagnation from the mid-1980s, which had forced the Government to seek the assistance of the IMF. This downturn had followed two decades of political stability and economic prosperity. In 1991 the Government was forced to introduce a severe austerity programme, as a precondition of an IMF agreement. This coincided with a period of severe difficulties for the sugar industry (until the 1970s the principal foreign exchange earner), which recorded low production. A downturn in tourism (which from the 1970s had replaced the sugar industry as the principal economic sector) was also experienced, associated with a recession in North America. With stricter macroeconomic policies, there were sharp increases in interest rates and in unemployment. While the stabilization programme provided immediate relief to the economy, recovery began only in 1993, when economic conditions improved in Barbados' main tourism and export markets. In 1993 the Government, the private sector and the trade unions agreed a tripartite two-year protocol covering wages, prices and conditions of employment, which reflected a high degree of consensus regarding social and economic goals. New protocols agreed in subsequent years had considerable symbolic importance in cementing the national traditions of consensus and compromise.

TOURISM

Barbados has a well-established tourism industry, directly employing 10.1% of the working population in 2010. Following a decline in the sector in the early 1990s, brought about by weak market conditions, a fall in charter plane services and an increasingly poor reputation for value for money, the industry entered a period of strong growth; stop-over tourist arrivals increased by 34.3% between 1992 and 2000, to reach 545,027 in the latter year, then the highest number recorded. As a result of uncertain market conditions in the USA and a decrease in the local purchasing power of sterling for tourists from the United Kingdom, the number of stop-over arrivals decreased to 497,899 in 2002, but, by 2007, had recovered to a new high of 574,533. However, stop-over arrivals were slightly down in 2008, and in 2009 fell to 518,564, 9.7% below the figure for 2007.

Tourism accounted for an estimated 18% of GDP in 2009 and contributed 64% of foreign exchange earnings from goods and non-factor services. Barbados is a home port for some cruises in the eastern Caribbean, and consequently cruise traffic brings more benefits to the local economy than to some other islands. The number of cruise ship passengers rose from 99,168 in 1984 to 721,270 in 2004, then fluctuated as cruise lines switched routes, and totalled 635,746 in 2009.

Labour costs in Barbados were much higher than in some competing destinations and the landscape less immediately striking. However, the island enjoyed a high percentage of repeat visitors. All-inclusive holiday packages accounted for a relatively small market share, thus encouraging spending outside hotel premises. The closure of the Barbados Hilton for reconstruction in 1999 meant that no major international chains were represented on the island for some years, and there were no properties with more than 300 rooms; however, a new Bds $117m. 350-room Hilton was opened in June 2005. There were 152 registered properties in 2009, with a total of 6,606 rooms. New construction slowed under the impact of the economic recession in 2009–10, while several properties had been converted to self-catering condominiums and apartments. Industry concerns included high operating costs and a low room-occupancy rate, which was 72% in the first quarter of 2009, traditionally the peak season, and below 50% for much of the year. Barbados' tourism has been particularly successful in the United Kingdom, which in 2008 accounted for some 39.6% of tourist arrivals, slipping to 37.5% in 2009 as the British market weakened. The lack of large brand name hotels was partly responsible for Barbados' poor performance in North America, which also impeded the development of conference and incentive tourism. However, there was some reversal in this trend from 2005 following the opening of the new Hilton hotel, as well as special discounting promotions in the US market. As a result, US tourists comprised 23.6% of the total in 2009 (compared with 20.6% in 2000).

Tourist accommodation was, from the 1950s, concentrated on the sheltered south and west coasts, which were highly urbanized. By the 1990s further expansion depended largely on the development of inland or east-coast sites, with the use of sports facilities to compensate for the distance from the sea, or on the redevelopment of sites that were already used for tourism or other urban purposes—such as the reconstruction of the Barbados Hilton on the south coast, along with the planned redevelopment of the adjacent former Mobil petroleum refinery site for tourism. Attempts were made to attract a major international chain for this project. Several major proposals were under development or discussion in mid-2010, but others which had been expected to move forward were on hold. The Government intended to acquire the historic, but derelict, Sam Lord's property on the south-east coast from CL Financial, a Trinidadian insurance conglomerate which was experiencing severe financial difficulties. Construction of a Four Seasons resort on the former Cunard Paradise Beach property on the west coast, a site which had been unused since the early 1990s, was halted in February 2009 with the developers also in financial difficulties, and efforts by the Barbadian Government to assist the resumption of work by offering a 20% equity sake in return for a US $60m. loan guarantee had not borne fruit by mid-2010.

FINANCIAL AND INFORMATION SERVICES

Barbados has a well-developed local banking and insurance industry. The largest regional commercial bank, FirstCaribbean International, is headquartered in Barbados. With assets of US $10,200m. in April 2010, it was formed in 2002 through a merger of the Caribbean interests of the Canadian Imperial Bank of Commerce (CIBC) and Barclays Bank (which sold its interest to CIBC in 2006). Sagicor, a major insurance company with interests throughout the region and assets in 2009 of US $4,460m., was also formed in 2002 through the merger of the two largest Barbados-based insurers, followed by a demutualization exercise; in June 2005 it expanded into North America, buying an unlisted US company, American Founders' Life, for US $58m., and is listed on the London Stock Exchange as well as on Caribbean exchanges. There was a small local stock exchange, on which 18 locally based companies had a market capitalization of Bds $8,407m. in July 2010, with one additional company listed on the so-called 'small cap' market. In addition, four Trinidadian and Jamaican companies had cross-listings on the Barbados exchange, bringing total capitalization in July 2010 to Bds $10,594m. Several major Barbados-based companies passed into Trinidadian control after 2000. The majority of Sagicor's shares are now held by Trinidad residents, while in 2008 Trinidadian group Neal & Massy completed the purchase of the major local conglomerate, Barbados Shipping and Trading.

The 'offshore' financial sector, mainly specializing in insurance, was encouraged by the negotiation of 22 double taxation agreements with a total of 35 other countries by mid-2010, the full network creating niche opportunities not open to larger 'offshore' sectors such as those of the Bahamas, Bermuda or the Cayman Islands. The sector was a significant employer and foreign exchange earner; under Barbados regulations a high proportion of 'offshore' entities maintained an office and employed local staff, rather than existing simply on paper. Barbados has a fairly high standard of financial regulation. Since Barbados is a 'low tax' rather than 'no tax' regime, 'offshore' companies contributed more than 50% of corporate income tax revenue in 2009 and more than 10% of total government revenue. The number of new 'offshore' entities registered grew steadily up to 2008; however, only 270 were registered in January–September 2009, down from 463 during the first nine months of 2008. There is an active anti-money-laundering regime, which was further strengthened by new legislation in 1998 and 2001, while bank supervision was reinforced in 2002. Active regulation discouraged more dubious clients, but attracted businesses such as captive insurance companies. A total of 3,334 International Business Companies were registered in December 2008 under legislation passed in 1991; additionally, there were 228 exempt and qualified exempt insurance companies, six mutual fund companies and 57 'offshore' banks, with total assets of an estimated US $32,000m.

International developments in the first decade of the 21st century placed all 'offshore' financial services sectors under increasing pressure. Following a World Trade Organization ruling, US foreign sales corporations, a niche market for Barbados, were phased out from 2000. The island's inclusion on the OECD list of 'unco-operative tax havens' in that year received a hostile reaction from the Barbadian Government, which played a leading role in international lobbying by 'offshore' centres against OECD's initiative and that of the Financial Action Task Force on Money Laundering (based in Paris, France). Barbados was removed from the OECD list in 2002, after the organization modified its criteria for the definition of a tax haven. Although, unlike many other jurisdictions included on OECD's blacklist, Barbados did not pledge to reform its financial sector, the Government did introduce legislative changes intended to improve financial transparency, as well as demonstrating a willingness to enter into tax information exchange agreements with other countries. For this reason Barbados was the only Caribbean country to be placed on a 'white' list of financial jurisdictions by the OECD in April 2009.

Telecommunications-based and informatics industries originated in the early 1980s with data-entry operations, moving on to software and call centre activities. Employment in the sector reached 2,972 in December 1997, but fell subsequently, to 1,128 by December 2001, recovering unevenly to 1,770 by the end of 2006. By the mid-1990s routine data-entry work was handled by scanning systems, and work that was still done manually could be sourced more cheaply from countries with lower labour and telecommunications costs. Labour costs in Barbados were cheaper than in the USA, and the island had a higher standard of education and a more adaptable English-speaking labour force than many of its competitors and was also in the same time zone as the eastern USA. With new cellular-service providers in operation, and competitive fixed-wireless, broadband, international fibre-optic cable and local landline services already licensed, liberalization of the telecommunications sector was well advanced in 2010.

MANUFACTURING

The manufacturing sector was in a depressed state from the mid-1980s, and the restraints on credit and consumer spending, imposed progressively from 1991, resulted in bankruptcies and factory closures. Economic recovery in the late 1990s failed to benefit most manufacturing industries because of the gradual erosion of protective barriers against imports. The principal manufacturing industries employed over 15,000 people in 1986, but only 10,000, representing about 7.8% of the total active work-force, in 2010; manufacturing accounted for 7.7% of GDP in 2009. However, Barbados had a surprisingly wide range of manufacturing industries, producing consumer products for the local and regional market, although labour costs were higher than in most Caribbean islands and power costs much higher than in Trinidad and Tobago. A strong point has been the rum industry, with products such as Malibu produced locally for export as well as traditional Barbadian brands. Rum exports increased from Bds $8.5m. in 1994 to Bds $57.2m. in 2009, at which point they exceeded the value of sugar exports by 41%. The closure of the small petroleum refinery in 1998 was a gain for the economy, as refinery products could be imported more cheaply from Trinidad and Tobago, and a valuable site was released for eventual tourism development.

Following the removal of most trade barriers in the 1990s, the clothing and wooden furniture industries virtually disappeared. However, the more efficient producers in other branches of manufacturing managed to survive and, in some cases, to expand their export sales. The remaining heavy industrial plant was the Arawak cement plant in the north of the island, owned by a Trinidadian company, which used local limestone and low-cost pet coke fuel. After having been closed for some years, the kiln reopened in 1997. Capacity was 360,000 metric tons; however, with the economy in recession in 2009, production was only 251,000 tons, 20.7% lower than in 2007, with 45% of the plant's output being exported. The construction industry contributed 5.3% of GDP in 2009.

Petroleum production was another industrial activity. Crude petroleum production began in 1973, and rose to 679,000 barrels in 1985, before declining to 328,000 barrels in 1997 as wells were depleted. An onshore drilling programme begun in that year increased production from 1998, and total extraction reached 708,500 barrels in 1999, equivalent to one-third of local consumption. However, continued drilling programmes have had disappointing results, and output fell to 289,700 barrels in 2008, close to 10% of local consumption. With the closure of the local refinery, crude petroleum is exported to Trinidad and Tobago for refining; partly to protect this arrangement, in 2008 Barbados remained outside Venezuela's PetroCaribe preferential oil supply agreement. Natural gas production stood at 20.6m. cu m in 2008. There is a piped supply to most urban and suburban areas, while some electric generation capacity transferred to natural gas from 1999. With local gas resources limited in extent, there are outline proposals to import gas from Trinidad and Tobago, by pipeline or possibly by barge as compressed natural gas. A US-based company, Conoco Inc, operated an offshore petroleum and gas exploration programme in partnership with the French concern Elf Aquitaine (now part of Total); initial seismic surveys showed promising deep-water geological prospects. The first exploratory well, drilled in December 2001, produced disappointing results. The southern boundaries of the Exclusive Economic Zone were fixed by arbitration under the UN Convention on the Law of the Sea in April 2006; international oil companies, including Shell and ExxonMobil, subsequently expressed interest, with a bidding round for exploration and production contracts completed in September 2008. However, the response was disappointing, with the financial environment inauspicious for high-risk deep water exploration, and only two blocks were awarded, in January 2009 to BHP Billiton, which planned a three-year programme of seismic survey and data analysis.

SUGAR AND AGRICULTURE

Sugar was the mainstay of the economy until the rise of the tourism industry in the mid-20th century. In 1946 the sugar industry accounted for 37.8% of GDP and 55% of foreign exchange earnings, employing some 25,100 people. By 2009, however, the industry accounted for only 0.3% of GDP, 1.0% of foreign exchange earnings from goods and services, and less than 1.0% of total employment.

In spite of a guaranteed price for exports to Europe, under the Lomé Convention and, from June 2000, the Cotonou Agreement, the sugar industry suffered from severe economic problems from the 1980s. These related in part to high production costs and inefficiencies associated with the traditional management system. Farmers also left many sugar farms uncultivated, in order to capitalize upon the high prices that could sometimes be obtained for land set aside for urban development. By 1992 a high proportion of estates had borrowed heavily from the state-owned Barbados National Bank and had accumulated debts greater than the value of their assets. Barbados Sugar Industries Ltd, which owned and operated the factories, was forced into receivership. The factories and the most heavily indebted estates were placed under the management of the Barbados Agricultural Management Company, which from 1994 was run on a management contract by a British company, Booker-Tate. The initial contract expired in June 1998 and, after several temporary extensions, Booker-Tate's direct involvement was phased out.

As a result of declining production, in 2003 Barbados surrendered part of its valuable European Union (EU) quota of 54,000 metric tons of sugar (worth some US $24m. in foreign exchange), which was not fulfilled from 1991 to 1995, nor after 2001; production of raw cane sugar in 2010 was only 25,490 tons. No use was made in the 2000s of the US quota, which was reduced from 14,239 tons to 8,000 tons in 1995. From 1990 the rum industry was forced to import most of its rising annual requirement of molasses. Production costs for Barbados sugar were estimated at close to Bds $2,000 per ton in the years after 2000. With the euro relatively strong in mid-2008, the EU sugar price was equivalent to around Bds $1,575 per ton, and was close to three times the world market price. Additional, locally funded subsidies were already required to keep the industry afloat. After extended discussions, in November 2005 the EU finalized proposals for a cumulative 36% cut in the sugar price, to €319.50, by 2010. It was concluded that to maintain the industry in its current form would be increasingly costly, while closure would carry a heavy political and environmental price. The Government in January 2006 outlined proposals for a US $156m. sugar factory to be completed by 2008, producing brown sugar, molasses for the rum industry, 30 MW of electric power, and ethanol. However, with a change of government in 2008, this proposal was dropped, with no announcement of an alternative strategy. In 2007, meanwhile, the EU proposed grant aid of €34.6m. for sugar industry restructuring or other measures. The soil holds nutrients well, but is thin. Rainfall is generally adequate, but there are occasional severe droughts. Groundwater supplies are not sufficient for large-scale irrigation. These problems impede the development of other agricultural activities. There is some commercial production of vegetables and root crops. The island is virtually self-sufficient in poultry products and in fresh milk, activities that depend to a significant extent on imported inputs. There is some pig farming and lamb is produced from the local Black Belly short-haired sheep. However, despite some self-sufficiency, agricultural production (including fishing, but excluding sugar) contributed only an estimated 2.2% of GDP in 2009 and (including sugar) employed 3.3% of the working population in 2010.

Statistical Survey

Sources (unless otherwise stated): Barbados Statistical Service, National Insurance Bldg, 3rd Floor, Fairchild St, Bridgetown; tel. 427-7841; fax 435-2198; e-mail barstats@caribsurf.com; internet www.barstats.gov.bb; Central Bank of Barbados, Tom Adams Financial Centre, Spry St, POB 1016, Bridgetown; tel. 436-6870; fax 427-9559; e-mail cbb.libr@caribsurf.com; internet www.centralbank.org.bb.

AREA AND POPULATION

Area: 430 sq km (166 sq miles).

Population: 257,082 (provisional) at census of 2 May 1990; 250,010 (males 119,926, females 130,084) (provisional) at census of 1 May 2000; 257,000 at mid-2010 (Source: UN, *World Population Prospects: The 2008 Revision*).

Population by Age and Sex (population in '000, UN estimates at mid-2010): *0–14:* 44 (males 22, females 22); *15–64:* 186 (males 92, females 94); *65 and over:* 27 (males 10, females 17); *Total* 257 (males 125, females 132) (Source: UN, *World Population Prospects: The 2008 Revision*).

Density (at mid-2010): 597.7 per sq km.

Ethnic Groups (*de jure* population, excl. persons resident in institutions, 1990 census): Black 228,683; White 8,022; Mixed race 5,886; Total (incl. others) 247,288.

Parishes (population at 2000 census, preliminary): Christ Church 49,498; St Andrew 5,254; St George 17,868; St James 22,741; St John 8,873; St Joseph 6,805; St Lucy 9,328; St Michael 83,684; St Peter 10,699; St Philip 22,864; St Thomas 12,397; *Total* 250,010.

Principal Towns (population at 2000 census, preliminary): Bridgetown (capital) 5,996; Speightstown 2,604; Holetown 1,087; Oistins 1,203. *Mid-2009* (population in '000, incl. suburbs): Bridgetown 112 (Source: UN, *World Urbanization Prospects: The 2009 Revision)*.

Births, Marriages and Deaths (2007, unless otherwise indicated): Live births 3,537 (birth rate 12.9 per 1,000); Marriages (2000) 3,518 (marriage rate 13.1 per 1,000); Deaths 2,213 (death rate 8.1 per 1,000). Source: partly UN, *Population and Vital Statistics Report*.

Life Expectancy (years at birth, WHO estimates): 74 (males 71; females 77) in 2008. Source: WHO, *World Health Statistics*.

Economically Active Population (labour force sample survey, '000 persons aged 15 years and over, excl. armed forces, January–March 2010): Agriculture, forestry and fishing 4.2; Manufacturing 10.0; Electricity, gas and water 3.5; Construction and quarrying 12.9; Wholesale and retail trade 19.0; Tourism 12.9; Transport, storage and communications 7.0; Finance and insurance 8.2; Professional, scientific and technical services 3.8; Administrative and support services 8.2; Public administration and defence 6.5; Education 8.7; Health and social welfare 7.5; Household employees 6.1; Other services 9.5; *Sub-total* 128.0; Not classified 0.2; *Total employed* 128.2 (males 66.5, females 61.7); Unemployed 15.2 (males 7.8, females 7.4); *Total labour force* 143.3 (males 74.3, females 69.0).

HEALTH AND WELFARE

Key Indicators

Total Fertility Rate (children per woman, 2008): 1.5.

Under-5 Mortality Rate (per 1,000 live births, 2008): 11.

HIV/AIDS (% of persons aged 15–49, 2007, estimate): 1.2.

Physicians (per 1,000 head, 1999): 1.2.

Hospital Beds (per 1,000 head, 2005): 6.7.

Health Expenditure (2007): US $ per head (PPP): 1,263.

Health Expenditure (2007): % of GDP: 7.0.

Health Expenditure (2007): public (% of total): 64.0.

Total Carbon Dioxide Emissions ('000 metric tons, 2006): 1,337.4.

Total Carbon Dioxide Emissions Per Head (metric tons, 2006): 5.3.

Human Development Index (2007): ranking: 37.

Human Development Index (2007): value: 0.903.

For sources and definitions, see explanatory note on p. vi.

AGRICULTURE, ETC.

Principal Crops ('000 metric tons, 2008, FAO estimates): Sweet potatoes 2.2; Yams 0.9; Avocados 0.6; Pulses 1.0; Coconuts 2.3; Tomatoes 1.1; Cucumbers 1.5; Chillies and peppers, green 0.8; Onions, dry 0.5; String beans 1.1; Carrots and turnips 0.5; Okra 0.7; Maize, green 0.3; Bananas 0.7.

Livestock ('000 head, year ending September 2007, FAO estimates): Horses 1.3; Asses 2.3; Mules 2.0; Cattle 11.0; Pigs 20.0; Sheep 11.5; Goats 5.2; Poultry 3,658.

Livestock Products ('000 metric tons, 2008, FAO estimates): Cattle meat 0.2; Pig meat 2.6; Chicken meat 14.0; Cows' milk 7.2; Hen eggs 2.1.

Forestry ('000 cubic metres, 2008, FAO estimates): Roundwood removals 11.1.

Fishing (metric tons, live weight, 2008): Total catch 3,551 (Yellowfin tuna 156; Flying fishes 2,354; Common dolphinfish 693).

Source: FAO.

MINING

Production (2008, provisional, unless otherwise indicated): Natural gas 20.9m. cu m (2007); Crude petroleum 289,692 barrels; Cement 301,427,000 metric tons.

INDUSTRY

Selected Products (2007, unless otherwise indicated): Raw sugar 30,300 metric tons (2008, provisional); Rum 11,000,000 litres (2003); Beer 8,500,000 litres; Cigarettes 65m. (1995); Batteries 17,165 (official estimate, 1998); Electric energy 950.3m. kWh (2008, provisional). Sources: partly UN Industrial Commodity Statistics Database, and IMF, *Barbados: Statistical Appendix* (May 2004).

FINANCE

Currency and Exchange Rates: 100 cents = 1 Barbados dollar (Bds $). *Sterling, US Dollar and Euro Equivalents* (31 May 2010): £1 sterling = Bds $2.916; US $1 = Bds $2.000; €1 = Bds $2.477; Bds $100 = £34.29 = US $50.00 = €40.37. *Exchange Rate*: Fixed at US $1 = Bds $2.000 since 1986.

Budget (Bds $ million, year ending 31 March 2009): *Revenue:* Tax revenue 2,351.2 (Direct taxes 1,018.0, Indirect taxes 1,333.2); Non-tax revenue and grants 175.8; Total (incl. others) 2,540.8. *Expenditure:* Current 2,691.6 (Wages and salaries 800.4, Other goods and services 376.0, Interest payments 395.8, Transfers and subsidies 1,119.5); Capital (incl. net lending 38.2) 286.8; Total 2,978.4.

International Reserves (US $ million at 31 December 2009): IMF special drawing rights 88.33; Reserve position in IMF 9.00; Foreign exchange 777.18; Total 874.51. Source: IMF, *International Financial Statistics*.

Money Supply (Bds $ million at 31 December 2009): Currency outside depository corporations 494.0; Transferable deposits 3,092.9; Other deposits 5,539.4; *Broad money* 9,126.4. Source: IMF, *International Financial Statistics*.

Cost of Living (Consumer Price Index; base: 2005 = 100): All items 111.6 in 2007; 120.7 in 2008; 125.1 in 2009. Source: IMF, *International Financial Statistics*.

Gross Domestic Product (Bds $ million at constant 1974 prices): 1,023.6 in 2004; 1,065.3 in 2005; 1,106.4 in 2006 (preliminary).

Expenditure on the Gross Domestic Product (Bds $ million at current prices, 2006, preliminary): Government final consumption expenditure 1,360.3; Private final consumption expenditure 3,706.7; Increase in stocks 876.3; Gross fixed capital formation 839.7; *Total domestic expenditure* 6,783.0; Exports of goods and services 4,142.6; *Less* Imports of goods and services 4,442.6; Statistical discrepancy 18.1; *GDP in purchasers' values* 6,501.1.

Gross Domestic Product by Economic Activity (estimates, Bds $ million at current prices, 2006, preliminary): Agriculture, hunting, forestry and fishing 175.1; Mining and quarrying 53.0; Manufacturing 357.1; Electricity, gas and water 197.3; Construction 361.1; Wholesale and retail trade 893.8; Hotels and restaurants 612.9; Transport, storage and communications 330.2; Finance, insurance, real estate and business services 1,165.5; Government services 854.2; Other community, social and personal services 383.5; *GDP at factor cost* 5,383.7; Indirect taxes, *less* subsidies 1,117.4; *GDP in purchasers' values* 6,501.1.

Balance of Payments (Bds $ million, 2008): Exports of goods f.o.b. 979.1; Imports of goods f.o.b. –3,463.8; *Trade balance* –2,484.6; Exports of services 3,201.6; Imports of services –1,410.7; *Balance on goods and services* –693.7; Other income received 357.0; Other income paid –599.6; *Balance on goods, services and income* –936.3;

Current transfers received 281.1; Current transfers paid –187.5; *Current balance* –842.8; Capital and financial accounts (net) 330.2; Net errors and omissions 14.2; *Overall balance* –498.3.

EXTERNAL TRADE

Principal Commodities (excluding petroleum, Bds $ million, 2008, provisional): *Imports c.i.f.:* Food and live animals 489.3; Beverages and tobacco 107.3; Crude materials (inedible) except fuels 102.4; Mineral fuels, lubricants, etc. 622.5; Animal and vegetable oils and fats 32.0; Chemicals 374.5; Manufactured goods classified chiefly by material 494.8; Machinery and transport equipment 785.9; Miscellaneous manufactured articles 462.3; Miscellaneous transactions and commodities 22.0; Total 3,493.0. *Exports f.o.b.:* Food and live animals 114.5; Beverages and tobacco 94.3; Crude materials (inedible) except fuels 15.3; Mineral fuels, lubricants, etc. 49.3; Animal and vegetable oils and fats 11.8; Chemicals 119.7; Manufactured goods classified chiefly by material 86.9; Machinery and transport equipment 53.8; Miscellaneous manufactured articles 179.0; Miscellaneous transactions and commodities 5.4; Total 730.1 (incl. re-exports 203.8).

Principal Trading Partners (excluding petroleum, Bds $ million, 2008, provisional): *Imports c.i.f.:* Canada 121.4; CARICOM 885.5; Germany 56.3; Japan 126.4; United Kingdom 185.0; USA 1,274.4; Total (incl. others) 3,493.0. *Exports f.o.b.:* Canada 20.7; CARICOM 315.1; United Kingdom 82.3; USA 187.4; Total (incl. others) 730.1 (incl. re-exports 203.8).

TRANSPORT

Road Traffic (motor vehicles in use, 2007): Passenger cars 103,535; Buses and coaches 631; Lorries and vans 15,151; Motorcycles and mopeds 2,525. Source: International Road Federation, *World Road Statistics*.

Shipping (estimated freight traffic, '000 metric tons, 1990): Goods loaded 206; Goods unloaded 538 (Source: UN, *Monthly Bulletin of Statistics*). *Total Goods Handled* ('000 metric tons, 2009): 1,064 (Source: Barbados Port Authority). *Merchant Fleet* (vessels registered at 31 December 2008): Number of vessels 126; Total displacement 725,242 grt (Source: Lloyd's Register-Fairplay, *World Fleet Statistics*).

Civil Aviation (1994): Aircraft movements 36,100; Freight loaded 5,052.3 metric tons; Freight unloaded 8,548.3 metric tons.

TOURISM

Tourist Arrivals ('000 persons): *Stop-overs:* 573.9 in 2007; 567.6 in 2008; 518.6 in 2009 (provisional). *Cruise-ship passengers:* 616.4 in 2007; 597.5 in 2008; 635.7 in 2009 (provisional).

Tourist Arrivals by Country ('000 persons, 2009, provisional): Canada 63.8; Germany 7.0; Trinidad and Tobago 26.3; Other CARICOM 62.5; United Kingdom 190.6; USA 122.3; Total (incl. others) 518.6.

Tourism Receipts (US $ million, excl. passenger transport): 1,057 in 2006; 1,199 in 2007; 1,192 in 2008 (provisional) (Source: World Tourism Organization).

COMMUNICATIONS MEDIA

Radio Receivers (1999): 175,000 in use.

Television Receivers (2000): 83,000 in use.

Telephones (2009): 135,700 main lines in use.

Mobile Cellular Telephones (2009): 337,100 subscribers.

Personal Computers: 40,000 (157.9 per 1,000 persons) in 2005.

Internet Users (2009): 142,000.

Broadband Subscribers (2009): 57,300.

Newspapers: *Daily* (1996): 2 (circulation 53,000); (2004): 2 titles. *Non-daily* (1990): 4 (estimated circulation 95,000).

Sources: partly UNESCO, *Statistical Yearbook*, UN, *Statistical Yearbook*, and International Telecommunication Union.

EDUCATION

Pre-primary (2007/08, unless otherwise indicated): 84 schools (1995/96); 363 teachers (males 9, females 354); 5,931 pupils (males 2,955, females 2,976).

Primary (2007/08, unless otherwise indicated): 109 schools (2005/06); 1,698 teachers (males 351, females 1,347); 22,849 pupils (males 11,648, females 11,201).

Secondary (2005/06, unless otherwise indicated): 32 schools; 1,430 teachers (males 589, females 841); 20,337 pupils (males 10,117, females 10,220) (2007/08).

Tertiary (2006/07, unless otherwise indicated): 4 schools (2002); 786 teachers (males 403, females 383); 11,405 students (males 3,648, females 7,757).

Sources: Ministry of Education, Youth Affairs and Sport and UNESCO Institute for Statistics.

Pupil-teacher Ratio (primary education, UNESCO estimate): 13.5 in 2007/08 (Source: UNESCO Institute for Statistics).

Adult Literacy Rate (UN estimates): 99.7% (males 99.7%; females 99.7%) in 2003. Source: UN Development Programme, *Human Development Report*.

Directory

The Constitution

The parliamentary system has been established since the 17th century, when the first Assembly sat, in 1639, and the Charter of Barbados was granted, in 1652. A new Constitution came into force on 30 November 1966, when Barbados became independent. Under its terms, protection is afforded to individuals from slavery and forced labour, inhuman treatment, deprivation of property, arbitrary search and entry, and racial discrimination; freedom of conscience, expression, assembly, and movement are guaranteed.

Executive power is nominally vested in the British monarch, as Head of State, represented in Barbados by a Governor-General, who appoints the Prime Minister and, on the advice of the Prime Minister, appoints other ministers and some senators.

The Cabinet consists of the Prime Minister, appointed by the Governor-General as being the person best able to command a majority in the House of Assembly, and not fewer than five other ministers. Provision is also made for a Privy Council, presided over by the Governor-General.

Parliament consists of the Governor-General and a bicameral legislature, comprising the Senate and the House of Assembly. The Senate has 21 members: 12 appointed by the Governor-General on the advice of the Prime Minister, two on the advice of the Leader of the Opposition and seven as representatives of such interests as the Governor-General considers appropriate. The House of Assembly has (since 2003) 30 members, elected by universal adult suffrage for a term of five years (subject to dissolution). The minimum voting age is 18 years.

The Constitution also provides for the establishment of Service Commissions for the Judicial and Legal Service, the Public Service, the Police Service and the Statutory Boards Service. These Commissions are exempt from legal investigation; they have executive powers relating to appointments, dismissals and disciplinary control of the services for which they are responsible.

The Government

HEAD OF STATE

Queen: HM Queen ELIZABETH II.

Governor-General: Sir CLIFFORD HUSBANDS (appointed 1 June 1996).

THE CABINET
(July 2010)

The Cabinet is formed by the Democratic Labour Party.

Acting Prime Minister and Acting Minister of Finance and Investment, Telecommunications and Energy: FREUNDEL STUART.

Attorney-General and Minister of Home Affairs: ADRIEL BRATHWAITE (acting).

Minister of International Business and International Transport: GEORGE HUTSON.

Minister of Economic Empowerment, Innovation, Trade, Industry and Commerce: Dr DAVID ESTWICK.

Minister of the Environment, Water Resources and Drainage: Dr DENIS LOWE.

Minister of Foreign Affairs and Foreign Trade: MAXINE MCCLEAN.

Minister of Health: DONVILLE INNISS.

Minister of Housing and Lands: MICHAEL LASHLEY.

Minister of Community Development and Culture: STEVEN BLACKETT.

Minister of Youth, Family and Sports: STEPHEN LASHLEY.

Minister of Social Care, Constituency Empowerment, Urban and Rural Development: CHRISTOPHER SINCKLER.

Minister of Tourism: RICHARD SEALY.

Minister of Transport and Works: JOHN BOYCE.

Minister of Agriculture: HAYNESLEY BENN.

Minister of Education and Human Resource Development: RONALD JONES.

Minister of Labour: Dr ESTHER BYER SUCKOO.

Minister of State for Economic Empowerment, Trade, Industry and Commerce: PATRICK TODD.

Minister of State, Finance, Investment, Telecommunications and Energy: DARCY BOYCE.

MINISTRIES

Office of the Prime Minister: Government HQ, Bay St, St Michael; tel. 436-6435; fax 436-9280; e-mail info@primeminister.gov.bb; internet www.primeminister.gov.bb.

Ministry of Agriculture: Graeme Hall, POB 505, Christ Church; tel. 428-4150; fax 420-8444; e-mail info@agriculture.gov.bb; internet www.agriculture.gov.bb.

Ministry of Community Development and Culture: The Warrens Office Complex, 4th Floor, Warrens, St Michael; tel. 310-1700; fax 421-2171; e-mail info@comdev.gov.bb; internet www.comdev.gov.bb.

Ministry of Economic Empowerment, Innovation, Trade, Industry and Commerce: Pelican Industrial Estate, Fontabelle, St Michael; tel. 426-4452; fax 431-0056.

Ministry of Education and Human Resource Development: Elsie Payne Complex, Constitution Rd, St Michael; tel. 430-2705; fax 436-2411; e-mail mined1@caribsurf.com; internet www.mes.gov.bb.

Ministry of Environment, Water Resources and Drainage: S.P. Musson Bldg, Hinks St, St Michael; tel. 467-5700; fax 437-8859; e-mail envirobdos@gov.bb.

Ministry of Finance, Investment, Telecommunications and Energy: Government HQ, Bay St, St Michael; tel. 426-3179; fax 436-9280.

Ministry of Foreign Affairs and Foreign Trade: 1 Culloden Rd, St Michael; tel. 431-2200; fax 429-6652; e-mail barbados@foreign.gov.bb; internet www.foreign.gov.bb.

Ministry of Health: Jemmott's Lane, St Michael; tel. 426-5570; fax 426-4669.

Ministry of Home Affairs: General Post Office Bldg, Level 5, Cheapside, St Michael; tel. 228-8950; fax 437-3794; e-mail mha@caribsurf.com.

Ministry of Housing and Lands: National Housing Corpn Bldg, 'The Garden', Country Rd, St Michael; tel. 467-7801; fax 435-0174.

Ministry of International Business and International Transport: The Warrens Office Complex, 3rd Floor, Warrens, St Michael; tel. 310-2200; fax 424-2533.

Ministry of Labour: The Warrens Office Complex, 3rd Floor West, Warrens, St Michael; tel. 310-1400; fax 425-0266; e-mail mol@labour.gov.bb; internet labour.caribyte.com/index.

Ministry of Social Care, Constituency Empowerment, Urban and Rural Development: The Warrens Office Complex, 4th Floor, Warrens, St Michael; tel. 310-1604; fax 424-2908; e-mail info@socialtransformation.gov.bb; internet www.socialcare.gov.bb.

Ministry of Tourism: Sherbourne Conference Centre, Two Mile Hill, St Michael; tel. 430-7504; fax 436-4828; e-mail barmot@sunbeach.net; internet www.barmot.gov.bb.

Ministry of Transport and Works: The Pine, St Michael; tel. 429-2863; fax 437-8133; e-mail mpttech@caribsurf.com.

Ministry of Youth, Family and Sports: Constitution Rd, St Michael; tel. 430-2704; fax 436-8909.

Office of the Attorney-General: Cedar Court, Wildey Business Park, Wildey Rd, St Michael; tel. 431-7700; fax 228-5433; e-mail attygen@caribsurf.com.bb.

Legislature

PARLIAMENT

Senate

President: BRANFORD M. TAITT.

There are 21 members.

House of Assembly

Speaker: ISHMAEL ROETT.

General Election, 15 January 2008

Party	% of total	Seats
Democratic Labour Party (DLP)	52.66	20
Barbados Labour Party (BLP)	47.14	10
Total (incl. others)	100.00	30

Election Commission

Electoral and Boundaries Commission: National Insurance Bldg, Ground Floor, Fairchild St, Bridgetown 11122; tel. 426-5909; fax 437-8229; e-mail electoral@barbados.gov.bb; Chief Electoral Officer ANGELA TAYLOR.

Political Organizations

Barbados Labour Party (BLP): Grantley Adams House, 111 Roebuck St, Bridgetown; tel. 429-1990; fax 427-8792; e-mail will99@caribsurf.com; internet labourparty.wordpress.com; f. 1938 as Barbados Progressive League, name changed as above 1946; moderate social democrat; Leader MIA MOTTLEY; Gen. Sec. WILLIAM DUGUID.

Clement Payne Movement (CPM): Crumpton St, Bridgetown; tel. 435-2334; fax 437-8216; e-mail cpmbarbados2@yahoo.com; f. 1988 in honour of national hero; non-electoral founding assoc. of the PEP; links to the Pan-Caribbean Congress and promotes international Pan-Africanism; Pres. DAVID A. COMISSIONG; Gen. Sec. BOBBY CLARKE.

People's Empowerment Party (PEP): Crumpton St, Bridgetown; tel. 429-9902; fax 437-8216; e-mail pepbarbados@yahoo.com; f. 2006 by the Clement Payne Movt; left-of-centre; Leader DAVID COMISSIONG.

Democratic Labour Party (DLP): 'Kennington', George St, Belleville, St Michael; tel. 429-3104; fax 427-0548; internet www.dlpbarbados.org; f. 1955; Pres. and Leader DAVID J. H. THOMPSON; Gen. Sec. CHRISTOPHER SINCKLER.

Diplomatic Representation

EMBASSIES AND HIGH COMMISSIONS IN BARBADOS

Brazil: The Courtyard, Hastings, POB BB15156, Christ Church; tel. 427-1735; fax 427-1744; e-mail brasemb@caribsurf.com; internet www.brazilbb.org; Ambassador APPIO CLAUDIO ACQUARONE.

Canada: Bishops Court Hill, Pine Rd, POB 404, Bridgetown; tel. 429-3550; fax 429-3780; e-mail bdgtn@international.gc.ca; internet www.canadainternational.gc.ca/barbados-barbade; High Commissioner RUTH ARCHIBALD.

China, People's Republic: 17 Golf View Terrace, Golf Club Rd, POB 428, Rockley, Christ Church; tel. 435-6890; fax 435-8300; e-mail chineseembbds@caribsurf.com; internet bb.chineseembassy.org; Ambassador WEI QIANG.

Cuba: Palm View, Erdiston Dr., Pine Rd, St Michael; tel. 435-2769; fax 435-2534; e-mail embajadadecuba@sunbeach.net; Ambassador PEDRO ANDRÉS GARCÍA ROQUE.

United Kingdom: Lower Collymore Rock, POB 676, Bridgetown; tel. 430-7800; fax 430-7860; e-mail britishhcb@sunbeach.net; internet www.britishhighcommission.gov.uk/barbados; High Commissioner PAUL BRUMMELL.

USA: Wildey Business Park, Wildey, POB 302, Bridgetown BB 14006; tel. 436-4000; fax 227-4088; e-mail bridgetownclo@state.gov; internet bridgetown.usembassy.gov; Chargé d'affaires a.i. D. BRENT HARDT.

Venezuela: Hastings, Main Rd, Christ Church; tel. 435-7619; fax 435-7830; e-mail embaven@sunbeach.net; Ambassador JUAN CARLOS VALDEZ GONZALES.

Judicial System

Justice is administered by the Supreme Court of Judicature, which consists of a High Court and a Court of Appeal. Final appeal lies with the Caribbean Court of Justice (CCJ), which was inaugurated in Port of Spain, Trinidad and Tobago, on 16 April 2005; previously, final appeals were administered by the Judicial Committee of the Privy Council in the United Kingdom. There are Magistrates' Courts for lesser offences, with appeal to the Court of Appeal.

Supreme Court: Judiciary Office, Coleridge St, Bridgetown; tel. 426-3461; fax 246-2405.

Chief Justice: Sir DAVID SIMMONS.

Justices of Appeal: FREDERICK WATERMAN; PETER A. WILLIAMS; JOHN CONNELL; SHERMAN MOORE.

Judges of the High Court: ELNETH KENTISH; CHRISTOPHER BLACKMAN; WILLIAM CHANDLER; MARGARET REIFER; KAYE GOODRIDGE; RANDALL WORRELL; JACQUELINE CORNELIUS; SONIA RICHARDS.

Registrar of the Supreme Court: S. MAUREEN CRANE-SCOTT.

Office of the Attorney-General: Cedar Court, Wildey Business Park, Wildey, St Michael; tel. 431-7700; fax 228-5433; e-mail attygen@caribsurf.com.

Attorney-General: FREUNDEL J. STUART.

Solicitor-General: JENNIFER C. EDWARDS.

Religion

More than 100 religious denominations and sects are represented in Barbados, but the vast majority of the population profess Christianity.

CHRISTIANITY

Barbados Christian Council

Caribbean Conference of Churches Bldg, George St and Collymore Rock, St Michael; tel. 426-6014; Chair. Rt Rev. JOHN WALDER DUNLOP HOLDER

The Anglican Communion

According to the latest available census figures (2000), some 28% of the population are Anglicans. Anglicans in Barbados are adherents of the Church in the Province of the West Indies, comprising eight dioceses. The Archbishop of the Province is the Bishop of Nassau and the Bahamas, resident in Nassau, the Bahamas. In Barbados there is a Provincial Office (St George's Church, St George) and an Anglican Theological College (Codrington College, St John).

Bishop of Barbados: Rt Rev. JOHN WALDER DUNLOP HOLDER, Anglican Diocese of Barbados, Mandeville House, Henry's Lane, Collymore Rock, St Michael; tel. 426-2761; fax 426-0871; e-mail mandeville@sunbeach.com; internet www.anglican.bb.

The Roman Catholic Church

According to the 2000 census, some 4% of the population are Roman Catholics. Barbados comprises a single diocese (formed in January 1990, when the diocese of Bridgetown-Kingstown was divided), which is suffragan to the archdiocese of Port of Spain (Trinidad and Tobago). The Bishop participates in the Antilles Episcopal Conference (currently based in Port of Spain, Trinidad and Tobago).

Bishop of Bridgetown: (vacant), Bishop's House, Ladymeade Gardens, St Michael, POB 1223, Bridgetown; tel. 426-3510; fax 429-6198; e-mail rcbishopbgl@caribsurf.com.

Other Churches

According to the 2000 census, other significant denominations in terms of number of adherents include Pentecostal (19% of the population), Adventist (5%), Methodist (5%), Church of God (2%) Jehovah's Witnesses (2%) and Baptist (2%).

Baptist Churches of Barbados: Emmanuel Baptist Church, President Kennedy Dr., Bridgetown; tel. 426-2697; e-mail emmbaptc@caribsurf.com.

Church of God (Caribbean Atlantic Assembly): St Michael's Plaza, St Michael's Row, POB 1021, Bridgetown; tel. 427-5770; Pres. Rev. VICTOR BABB.

Church of Jesus Christ of Latter-Day Saints (Mormons)—West Indies Mission: 14 Walkers Terrace, St George; tel. 429-1385; fax 435-6486.

Church of the Nazarene: District Office, Eagle Hall, St Michael; tel. 425-1067; fax 435-6486.

Methodist Church: Bethel Church Office, Bay St, Bridgetown; tel. and fax 426-2223; e-mail methodist@caribsurf.com.

Moravian Church: Calvary Office, Roebuck St, St Michael; tel. 426-2337; fax 228-4381; e-mail calvarymoravian@sunbeach.net; Supt Rev. ERROL CONNOR.

Seventh-day Adventists (East Caribbean Conference): Brydens Ave, Brittons Hill, POB 22, St Michael; tel. 429-7234; fax 429-8055; e-mail info@eastcarib.org; internet eastcarib.org; Pres. DAVID BECKLES.

Wesleyan Holiness Church: General Headquarters, Whitepark Rd, Bank Hall; tel. 429-4888; internet www.carringtonwesleyan.org; District Supt Rev. C. WILLIAMS.

Other denominations include the Abundant Life Assembly, the African Orthodox Church, the Apostolic Church, the Assemblies of Brethren, the Berean Bible Brethren, the Bethel Evangelical Church, Christ is the Answer Family Church, the Church of God the Prophecy, the Ethiopian Orthodox Church, the Full Gospel Assembly, Love Gospel Assembly, the New Testament Church of God, the Pentecostal Assemblies of the West Indies, the People's Cathedral, the Salvation Army, Presbyterian congregations, the African Methodist Episcopal Church and the Mt Olive United Holy Church of America.

ISLAM

According to the 2000 census, around 1% of the population are Muslims.

Islamic Teaching Centre: Harts Gap, Hastings, Bridgetown; tel. 427-0120.

JUDAISM

According to the 2000 census, there are 96 Jews on the island (less than 1% of the population).

Jewish Community: Shaare Tzedek Synagogue, Rockley New Rd, Christ Church; Nidhe Israel Synagogue, Synagogue Lane, POB 651, Bridgetown; tel. 437-0907; fax 437-0829; Pres. JACOB HASSID; Sec. SHARON ORAN.

HINDUISM

According to the census of 2000, there are 840 Hindus on the island (less than 1% of the population).

Hindu Community: Hindu Temple, Roberts Complex, Government Hill, St Michael, BB 11066; tel. 434-4638.

The Press

Barbados Advocate: POB 230, St Michael; tel. 467-2000; fax 434-1000; e-mail news@barbadosadvocate.com; internet www.barbadosadvocate.com; f. 1895; daily; Exec. Editor GILLIAN MARSHALL; circ. 11,413.

The Broad Street Journal: Boarded Hall House, Boarded Hall, St. George; tel. 230-5687; e-mail bsj@caribsurf.com; internet www.broadstreetjournalbarbados.com; f. 1993; weekly; business; Editor PATRICK R. HOYOS.

The Nation: Nation House, Fontabelle, POB 1203, St Michael BB11000; tel. 430-5400; fax 427-6968; e-mail roxannegibbs@nationnews.com; internet www.nationnews.com; f. 1973; daily; also publishes *The Midweek Nation*, *The Weekend Nation*, *The Sun on Saturday*, *The Sunday Sun* (q.v.) and *The Visitor* (a free publ. for tourists); owned by One Caribbean Media Ltd; Publr VIVIAN-ANNE GITTENS; Exec. Editor ROXANNE GIBBS; circ. 31,533 (Daily), 51,440 (Sun.).

Sunday Advocate: POB 230, St Michael; tel. 467-2000; fax 434-1000; e-mail news@sunbeach.net; internet www.barbadosadvocate.com; f. 1895; Editor REUDON EVERSLEY; Exec. Editor GILLIAN MARSHALL; circ. 17,490.

The Sunday Sun: Nation House, Fontabelle, POB 1203, St Michael BB11000; tel. 430-5400; fax 427-6968; e-mail roxannegibbs@nationnews.com; internet www.nationnews.com; f. 1977; owned by One Caribbean Media Ltd; Publr VIVIAN-ANNE GITTENS; Exec. Editor ROXANNE GIBBS; circ. 48,824.

NEWS AGENCY

Caribbean Media Corporation (CMC): Harbour Industrial Estate, Unit 1B, Bldg 6A, St Michael, BB 11145; tel. 467-1037; fax 429-4355; e-mail admin@cmccaribbean.com; internet www.cananews.net; f. 2000; formed by merger of Caribbean News Agency (CANA) and Caribbean Broadcasting Union; Dir PATRICK COZIER.

Publishers

Advocate Publishers (2000) Inc: POB 230, Fontabelle, St Michael; tel. 467-2000; fax 434-2020; e-mail news@barbadosadvocate.com.

Business Tutors: 124 Chancery Lane, Christ Church; tel. 428-5664; fax 429-4854; e-mail pchad@caribsurf.com; business, management, computers.

Miller Publishing Co: Edgehill, St Thomas; tel. 421-6700; fax 421-6707; e-mail info@barbadosbooks.com; internet www.barbadosbooks.com; f. 1983; publishes general interest books, tourism and business guides; Jt Man. Dirs KEITH MILLER, SALLY MILLER.

Nation Publishing Co Ltd: Nation House, POB 1203, Fontabelle, St Michael; tel. 430-5400; fax 427-6968; internet www.onecaribbeanmedia.net; owned by One Caribbean Media Ltd; Pres. and Editor-in-Chief VIVIAN-ANNE GITTENS.

National Cultural Foundation of Barbados: West Terrace, St James; tel. 424-0909; fax 424-0916; internet www.ncf.bb; Chair. KENNETH D. KNIGHT; CEO DEVERE BROWNE.

Broadcasting and Communications

TELECOMMUNICATIONS

Digicel Barbados Ltd: The Courtyard, Hastings, Christ Church; tel. 434-3444; fax 426-3444; e-mail BDS_CustomerCare_External@digicelgroup.com; internet www.digicelbarbados.com; f. 2001; awarded licence to operate cellular telephone services in March 2003; approval granted in Jan. 2006 for the acquisition of Cingular Wireless' operation in Barbados; owned by an Irish consortium; CEO BARRY O'BRIEN.

LIME: Carlisle House, Hincks St, Bridgetown, St Michael; tel. 292-5050; e-mail CallCenterSupport@time4lime.com; internet www.time4lime.com; f. 1984; fmrly Cable & Wireless (Barbados) Ltd; Barbados External Telecommunications Ltd became Cable & Wireless BET Ltd; name changed as above in 2008; provides international telecommunications services; contact centres in Jamaica and Saint Lucia; owned by Cable & Wireless PLC (United Kingdom); CEO DAVID SHAW.

Sunbeach Communications: 'San Remo', Belmont Rd, St Michael; tel. 430-1569; fax 228-6330; e-mail customerservice@sunbeach.net; internet www.sunbeach.net; f. 1995 as an internet service provider; licence to operate cellular telephone services obtained in March 2003; launch of cellular operations postponed indefinitely in 2007; Vtel (Saint Lucia) acquired controlling 52.9% share in Dec. 2006; CEO MARWAN ZAWAYDEH.

TeleBarbados Inc: CGI Tower, 6th Floor, Warrens, St Michael; tel. 620-1000; fax 620-1010; e-mail info@telebarbados.com; internet www.telebarbados.com; f. 2005; internet and private telecommunications network provider; awarded licence to operate fixed-line service in 2005; Pres. BRIAN HARVEY; Vice-Pres. PATRICK HINKSON.

BROADCASTING

Radio

Barbados Broadcasting Service Ltd: Astoria, St George, Bridgetown; tel. 437-9550; fax 437-9203; e-mail action@sunbeach.net; f. 1981; operates BBS FM and Faith 102.1 FM (religious broadcasting).

Caribbean Broadcasting Corporation (CBC): The Pine, POB 900, Wildey, St Michael; tel. 467-5400; fax 429-4795; e-mail customerservices@cbc.bb; internet www.cbcbarbados.bb; f. 1963; operates 3 radio stations; Gen. Man. LARS SÖDERSTRÖM.

CBC Radio 900 AM: Caribbean Broadcasting Corpn, The Pine, St Michael; tel. 434-1900; fax 429-4795; f. 1963; spoken word and news.

Quality 100.7 FM: Caribbean Broadcasting Corpn, The Pine, St Michael; tel. 434-1007; fax 429-4795; e-mail dsthill@cbc.bb; internet www.cbc.bb/index.pl/radio3; international and regional music, incl. folk, classical, etc.

The One 98.1 FM: Caribbean Broadcasting Corpn, The Pine, St Michael; tel. 434-1981; fax 429-4795; internet www.981fm.net; f. 1984; popular music.

Starcom Network Inc: River Rd, POB 1267, Bridgetown; tel. 430-7300; fax 426-5377; internet www.starcomnetwork.net; f. 1935 as Radio Distribution; owned by One Caribbean Media Ltd; operates 4 radio stations; Man. Dir VICTOR FERNANDES.

Gospel 790 AM: Bridgetown; tel. 467-7355; e-mail gospel@starcomnetwork.net; internet www.gospel975.com; f. 2000; gospel music; Supervisor RONALD CLARKE.

Hott 95.3 FM: Bridgetown; tel. 434-4688; e-mail hott@starcomnetwork.net; internet www.hott953.com; f. 1997; popular music.

Love FM 104: Bridgetown; tel. 434-5683; e-mail love@starcomnetwork.net; f. 1988 as Yess Ten-Four FM; popular music; Supervisor GAYNELLE MARSHALL; Programme Dir DENNIS JOHNSON.

VOB 92.9 FM: Bridgetown; tel. 430-1790; e-mail tellit@vob929.com; internet www.vob929.com; f. 1981; current affairs, sport, music; Programme Dir DENNIS JOHNSON.

Television

CBC TV: The Pine, POB 900, Wildey, St Michael; tel. 467-5400; fax 429-4795; e-mail news@cbcbarbados.bb; internet www.cbcbarbados.bb; f. 1964; part of the Caribbean Broadcasting Corpn (q.v.); Channel Eight is the main national service, broadcasting 24 hours daily; a maximum of 115 digital subscription channels will be available through Multi-Choice Television; Programme Man. CECILY CLARKE-RICHMOND.

DIRECTV: Nation House, Roebuck St, Bridgetown, St Michael; tel. 435-7362; fax 228-5553; e-mail directv@starcomnetwork.net; digital satellite television service; owned by the Starcom Network; Administrator M. OWANA SKEETE.

Finance

In December 2008 there were approximately 3,334 International Business Companies and 57 'offshore' banks registered in Barbados.

BANKING

(cap. = capital; res = reserves; dep. = deposits; brs = branches; m. = million; amounts in Barbados dollars unless otherwise indicated)

Central Bank

Central Bank of Barbados: Tom Adams Financial Centre, Spry St, POB 1016, Bridgetown BB11126; tel. 436-6870; fax 427-9559; e-mail info@centralbank.org.bb; internet www.centralbank.org.bb; f. 1972; bank of issue; cap. 2.0m., res 16.0m., dep. 739.7m. (Dec. 2008); Gov. R. DELISLE WORRELL.

Commercial Banks

Barbados National Bank Inc. (BNB): Independence Sq., POB 1002, Bridgetown; tel. 431-5700; fax 228-3287; e-mail info@bnbbarbados.com; internet www.bnbbarbados.com; f. 1978 by merger; privatized in 2003; 65% of shares owned by Republic Bank Ltd (Trinidad and Tobago); cap. 48.0m., res 94.6m., dep. 2,283.5m. (Sept. 2008); Chair. RONALD F. D. HARFORD; Man. Dir and CEO ROBERT LE HUNTE; 9 brs.

FirstCaribbean International Bank Ltd: Warrens, POB 503, St Michael; tel. 367-2300; fax 424-8977; e-mail firstcaribbeanbank@firstcaribbeanbank.com; internet www.firstcaribbeanbank.com; f. 2002; previously known as CIBC West Indies Holdings, adopted present name following merger of CIBC West Indies and Caribbean operations of Barclays Bank PLC; Barclays relinquished its stake to CIBC in June 2006; cap. US $1,116.8m., res US $–372m., dep. US $9,251.6m. (Oct. 2008); Chair. MICHAEL K. MANSOOR; CEO JOHN ORR; 9 brs.

RBTT Bank Barbados Ltd: Lower Broad St, POB 1007C, Bridgetown; tel. 431-2500; fax 431-2530; internet www.rbtt.com/bb/personal; f. 1984; est. as Caribbean Commercial Bank Ltd; purchased by RBTT Financial Holdings, Trinidad and Tobago in 2004 when current name adopted; acquired by Royal Bank of Canada in 2008; cap. 25.0m., res 6.0m., dep. 258.5m. (Dec. 2002); Chair. GORDON M. NIXON; CEO SURESH SOOKOO; 4 brs.

Regional Development Bank

Caribbean Development Bank: Wildey, POB 408, St Michael BB11000; tel. 431-1600; fax 426-7269; e-mail info@caribank.org; internet www.caribank.org; f. 1970; cap. US $157.4m., res US $338m., total assets US $1,177.1m. (Dec. 2008); Pres. Dr COMPTON BOURNE.

Trust Companies

Barbados International Bank and Trust Co: Bissex House, Bissex, St Joseph; tel. 422-4629; fax 422-7994; e-mail bdosintlbank&trustco@caribsurf.com; f. 1981; 'offshore' banking; Chair. DOUGLAS LEESE.

Bayshore Bank and Trust (Barbados) Corpn: Lauriston House, Lower Collymore Rock, POB 1132, Bridgetown, St Michael BB11000; tel. 430-8650; fax 430-5335; e-mail info@bayshorecapital.com; internet www.bayshorebank.com; chartered bank with affiliates in the Cayman Islands and Toronto, Canada; acquired by J&T Bank and Trust Inc in 2008; Chair. and CEO JOHN BUJOUVES.

Clico Mortgage & Finance Corporation: Clico Corporate Centre, Walrond St, Bridgetown; tel. 431-4716; fax 426-6168; e-mail info@

clicomortgage.com; internet www.clicomortgage.com; f. 1984; incorporated as the Caribbean Commercial Trust Co Ltd; name changed as above in 1998; subsidiary of the C. L. Financial Group, based in Trinidad and Tobago; sale to Barbados Public Workers' Cooperative Credit Union approved in Oct. 2009; Chair. LEROY C. PARRIS; Pres. and CEO ANDREW N. ST JOHN.

Concorde Bank Ltd: The Corporate Centre, Bush Hill, Bay St, POB 1161, St Michael; tel. 430-5320; fax 429-7996; e-mail concorde@concordebb.com; f. 1987; cap. US $2.0m., res US $2.0m., dep. US $7.6m. (June 2008); Pres. and Chair. GERARD LUSSAN; Man. MARINA CORBIN.

FirstCaribbean International Trust and Merchant Bank (Barbados) Ltd: Warrens, POB 503, St Michael; tel. 367-2300; fax 424-8977; internet www.firstcaribbeanbank.com; known as CIBC Trust and Merchant Bank until 2002; Exec. Chair. MICHAEL MANSOOR; CEO JOHN D. ORR.

Globe Finance Inc: Rendezvous Court, Suite 6, Rendezvous Main Rd, Christ Church BB15112; tel. 426-4755; fax 426-4772; e-mail info@globefinanceinc.com; internet www.globefinanceinc.com; f. 1998; offers loans and hire-purchasing financial services; Gen. Man. RONALD DAVIS.

Royal Bank of Canada Financial Corporation: Bldg 2, 2nd Floor, Chelston Park, Collymore Rock, POB 986, St Michael; tel. 467-4300; fax 429-3800; internet www.rbcroyalbank.com; Pres. and CEO GORDON M. NIXON; Man. N. L. (ROY) SMITH.

St Michael Trust Corpn: Braemar Court, Deighton Rd, St Michael BB14017; tel. 467-6677; fax 467-6678; e-mail info@stmichael.bb; internet www.stmichaeltrust.com; f. 1987; Pres. IAN HUTCHISON.

STOCK EXCHANGE

Barbados Stock Exchange (BSE): Carlisle House, 1st Floor, Hincks St, Bridgetown; tel. 436-9871; fax 429-8942; e-mail marlon.yarde@bse.com.bb; internet www.bse.com.bb; f. 1987 as the Securities Exchange of Barbados; in 1989 the Govts of Barbados, Trinidad and Tobago and Jamaica agreed to link exchanges; cross-trading began in April 1991; reincorporated in 2001; Gen. Man. MARLON YARDE.

INSURANCE

The leading British and a number of US and Canadian companies have agents in Barbados. In December 2008 there were 228 exempt and qualified exempt insurance companies registered in the country. Local insurance companies include the following:

Insurance Corporation of Barbados Ltd (ICBL): Roebuck St, Bridgetown; tel. 434-6000; fax 426-3393; e-mail icb@icb.com.bb; internet www.icb.com.bb; f. 1978; 51% owned by BF&M Ltd of Bermuda; cap. Bds $39m.; Chair. R. JOHN WIGHT; Man. Dir WISMAR A. GREAVES; Gen. Man. DENIS A. BRADSHAW.

Sagicor: Sagicor Financial Centre, Lower Collymore Rock, St Michael; tel. 467-7500; fax 436-8829; e-mail info@sagicor.com; internet www.sagicor.com; f. 1840; est. as Barbados Mutual Life Assurance Society (BMLAS); changed name as above in 2002 after acquiring majority ownership of Life of Barbados (LOB) Ltd; listed on the London international stock exchange in May 2007; Chair. STEPHEN MCNAMARA; Pres. and CEO DODRIDGE D. MILLER.

United Insurance Co Ltd: United Insurance Centre, Lower Broad St, POB 1215, Bridgetown; tel. 430-1900; fax 436-7573; e-mail mail@unitedinsure.com; internet unitedinsure.com; f. 1976; Man. Dir H. A. TOPPIN; Gen. Man. DAVID ALLEYNE.

Association

Insurance Association of the Caribbean Inc: The Thomas Pierce Bldg, Lower Collymore Rock, St Michael BB11115; tel. 427-5608; fax 427-7277; e-mail info@iac-caribbean.com; internet www.iac-caribbean.com; regional asscn; Pres. DOUGLAS CAMACHO; Country Dir DAVIS BROWNE.

Trade and Industry

GOVERNMENT AGENCY

Barbados Agricultural Management Co Ltd (BAMC): Warrens, POB 719C, St Michael; tel. 425-0010; fax 425-0007; internet agriculture.gov.bb; f. 1993; Gen. Man. CARL SIMPSON.

DEVELOPMENT ORGANIZATIONS

Barbados Agriculture Development and Marketing Corpn (BADMC): Fairy Valley, Christ Church; tel. 428-0250; fax 428-0152; e-mail andrew.skeete@badmc.org; internet agriculture.gov.bb; f. 1993 by merger; programme of diversification and land reforms; CEO ANDREW SKEETE.

Barbados Investment and Development Corpn (BIDC): Pelican House, Princess Alice Hwy, POB 1250, Bridgetown, BB 11000; tel. 427-5350; fax 426-7802; e-mail bidc@bidc.org; internet www.bidc.com; f. 1992 by merger; facilitates the devt of the industrial sector, especially in the areas of manufacturing, information technology and financial services; offers free consultancy to investors; provides factory space for lease or rent; administers the Fiscal Incentives Legislation; Chair. DON MARSHALL; CEO WILBUR T. 'BASIL' LAVINE (acting).

Barbados Small Business Association: 1 Pelican Industrial Park, Bridgetown; tel. 228-0162; fax 228-0163; e-mail theoffice@sba.org.bb; internet www.sba.org.bb; f. 1974; non-profit org. representing interests of small businesses; Pres. CELESTE FOSTER.

CHAMBER OF COMMERCE

Barbados Chamber of Commerce and Industry: Braemar Court, Deighton Rd, St Michael; tel. 620-4750; fax 620-2907; e-mail bcci@bdscham.com; internet www.bdscham.com; f. 1825; 220 mem. firms; some 345 reps; Pres. GLENDA MEDFORD; Exec. Dir LISA GALE.

INDUSTRIAL AND TRADE ASSOCIATIONS

Barbados Agricultural Society: The Grotto, Beckles Rd, St Michael; tel. 436-6683; fax 435-0651; e-mail bdosagriculturalsociety@caribsurf.com; Pres. TYRONE POWER; CEO JAMES PAUL.

Barbados Association of Medical Practitioners (BAMP): BAMP Complex, Spring Garden, St Michael; tel. 429-7569; fax 435-2328; e-mail bamp@sunbeach.net; internet www.bamp.org.bb; Pres. Dr CARLOS CHASE.

Barbados Association of Professional Engineers: Christie Bldg, Garrison Hill, St Michael BB14038; tel. 429-6105; fax 434-6673; e-mail engineers@caribsurf.com; internet www.bape.org; f. 1964; Pres. ANTONIO ELCOCK; Hon. Sec. D. ANDRE ALLEYNE; 213 mems.

Barbados Hotel and Tourism Association (BHTA): 4th Ave, Belleville, St Michael; tel. 426-5041; fax 429-2845; e-mail info@bhta.org; internet www.bhta.org; f. 1952 as the Barbados Hotel Asscn; adopted present name in 1994; non-profit trade asscn; Pres. WAYNE CAPALDI.

Barbados Manufacturers' Association: Suite 201, Bldg 8, Harbour Industrial Park, St Michael; tel. 426-4474; fax 436-5182; e-mail info@bma.bb; internet www.bma.org.bb; f. 1964; Pres. IAN PICKUP; Exec. Dir BOBBI MCKAY; 110 mem. firms.

EMPLOYERS' ORGANIZATION

Barbados Employers' Confederation (BEC): Braemar Court, Deighton Rd, POB 33B, Brittons Hill, St Michael; tel. 435-4753; fax 435-2907; e-mail becon@barbadosemployers.com; internet barbadosemployers.com; f. 1956; Pres. IAN GOODING-EDGHILL; Exec. Dir ANTHONY WALCOTT; 235 mems (incl. assoc. mems).

MAJOR COMPANIES

ADM Barbados Mills Ltd: Flour Mill Complex, Spring Garden Hwy, POB 260, Bridgetown, St Michael; tel. 427-8880; fax 427-8886; e-mail cecil_hypolite@admworld.com; internet www.admworld.com; f. 1977; manufacturer of flour and other grain-derived products; Gen. Man. CECIL HYPOLITE; more than 40 employees.

Arawak Cement Co Ltd: Checker Hall, St Lucy; tel. 439-9880; fax 439-7976; e-mail arawak@arawakcement.com.bb; internet www.arawakcement.com.bb; f. 1981; manufacture and marketing of cement and lime (quicklime and hydrated lime); 100% owned by Trinidad Cement Ltd; sales US $30m. (2003); Chair. JEFFREY MCFARLANE; Gen. Man. RUPERT GREENE; more than 250 employees.

Banks Holdings Ltd (BHL): POB 507C, Wildey, St Michael, BB11000; tel. 227-6700; fax 427-0772; e-mail bhl@banksholdings.com.bb; internet www.thebhlgroup.com; f. 1991, after Banks (Barbados) Breweries acquired Barbados Bottling Co Ltd; beverage conglomerate; Chair. Sir ALLAN FIELDS; CEO and Man. Dir RICHARD COZIER.

Banks (Barbados) Breweries Ltd: Wildey, St Michael; tel. 227-6750; fax 227-6790; e-mail info@banksbeer.com; internet www.banksbeer.com; f. 1961; brewing and bottling of alcoholic and non-alcoholic beverages; Gen. Man. AKASH RAGBIR.

B & B Distribution Ltd: Newton, Christ Church; tel. 418-2900; fax 418-2970; e-mail bandb@banksholdings.com.bb; f. 1994; distribution of finished BHL products; Gen. Man. HARRY ROBERTS.

Barbados Bottling Co Ltd: Newton, Christ Church; tel. 418-3300; fax 418-3350; e-mail bbc@banksholdings.com.bb; manufacturer of soft drinks; f. 1944; acquired by BHL in 1992; Gen. Man. WILLIAM HASLETT.

Barbados Dairy Industries Ltd: The Pine, St Michael; tel. 430-4100; fax 227-6660; e-mail phd@banksholdings.com.bb; f. 1966; acquired by BHL in 1997; manufacturer of dairy and related products; sales US $29m. (2003); Man. Dir CLYDE GIBSON.

Duraplast Inc: Newton Industrial Park, Christ Church; tel. 418-9761; fax 418-9765; e-mail duraplast@banksholdings.com.bb; f. 2001; manufacture of roofing tiles; Plant Man. HALDENE GREEN.

Plastic Containers Ltd: Thornbury Hill, Christ Church; tel. 428-7780; fax 428-7112; e-mail pcl@banksholdings.com.bb; acquired by BHL in 1991; manufacturers of plastic bottles; Gen. Man. RICHARD HINKSON.

Barbados Shipping and Trading Co Ltd: see section on Shipping.

BICO Ltd: Harbour Industrial Park, Bridgetown, BB11145; tel. 430-2100; fax 426-2198; e-mail admin@bicoicecream.com; internet www.bicoicecream.com; f. 1901; manufacturer and distributor of ice cream; distributor of frozen dough and pastries; operators of public cold-storage facilities; sales Bds $16.6m. (2006); Chair. F. EDWIN THIRLWELL; 120 employees.

BRC West Indies Ltd: Cane Garden, St Thomas; tel. 425-0371; fax 425-2941; e-mail brc@caribsurf.com; internet www.brcwestindies.com; f. 1979; manufacturer of wire mesh and steel products; sales Bds $24m. (1998); Chair. R. S. WILLIAMS; Gen. Man. PETER COLLETT; 42 employees.

Bryden's Distribution (Barbados) Ltd: Barbarees Hill, POB 403, Bridgetown, St Michael; tel. 431-2600; fax 426-0755; e-mail barbados@brydens.com; internet www.brydens.com/barbados; f. 1898; wholly owned subsidiary of ANSA McAL (Barbados); member of the Trinidad-based ANSA McAL Group; manufacturers' representative and distributor for food and beverages, pharmaceuticals, photographic supplies, personal care and household cleaners; sales US $70m.; CEO ANDREW LEWIS; 1,200 employees.

Collins Ltd: 4A Warrens Industrial Park, POB 203C, Bridgetown, St Michael; tel. 426-4246; fax 436-7876; e-mail colcar@caribsurf.com; distributor of pharmaceuticals, hospital supplies, toiletries, confectionery, canned and snack foods throughout the Caribbean; Sales Man. KIM TOPPIN; 185 employees.

DaCosta Mannings: POB 103, Bridgetown; tel. 431-8700; fax 429-5905; e-mail info@dmi.bb; internet www.dacostamannings.com; f. 1995 after merger of DaCosta Ltd and Mannings, Wilkinson & Challenor; trade in building materials, furniture and hardware products; subsidiary of Barbados Shipping & Trading Company (see under Shipping); Chair. G. A. A. KING; Man. Dir T. A. MAHON; 276 employees.

Edghill Associates Ltd: Websters Industrial Park, Wildey, St Michael; tel. 427-2941; fax 426-5958; e-mail edghill@caribsurf.com; heavy construction; Dir RICHARD EDGHILL; 300 employees.

Goddard Enterprises Ltd (GEL): Mutual Bldg, 2nd Floor, Lower Broad St, POB 502, Bridgetown; tel. 430-5700; fax 436-8934; e-mail gelinfo@thegelgroup.com; internet www.goddardenterprisesltd.com; f. 1921; rum production, meat processing, bakery production, in-flight and airport-terminal catering, duty-free sales, lumber and building supplies, air conditioning and electrical contracting, insurance and financial services, shipping agent, automotive agency; sales Bds $889m. (2008/09); Chair. JOSEPH N. GODDARD; Man. Dir MARTIN PRITCHARD; 4,412 employees in the Caribbean, Central and Latin America (2008/09).

Hanschell Inniss Ltd: Goddard's Complex, Kensington, Fontabelle, St Michael; tel. 426-3544; fax 427-6938; e-mail camilla_greaves@goddent.com; internet www.hanschellinnissltd.com; manufacture and distribution of food and soft drinks; f. 1884; owned by Goddard Enterprises Ltd since 1973; Gen. Man. CAMILLA GREAVES; 190 employees.

Kitco International Ltd: Sefton Lodge, Brittons Cross Rd, St Michael; Canadian co, opened Barbados br. in Jan. 2010; precious metals dealers.

Mico Garment Factory Ltd: Harbour Industrial Park, Harbour Rd, POB 621, Bridgetown; tel. 426-1883; fax 429-7267; e-mail misons@trinidad.net; f. 1964; manufacture of clothing; Chair. MOHAMMED IBRAHIM JUMAN; Man. Dir ANSAR JUMAN; 143 employees.

Mount Gay Distilleries Ltd: POB 208, Brandon's Gap, Deaco's Rd, POB 208, Bridgetown; tel. 425-8757; fax 425-8770; e-mail cjordan@caribsurf.com; internet www.mountgay.com; f. 1955; owned by Rémy-Cointreau, part of the Maxxium alliance; rum distilling; Man. Dir DAVID MEYERS; 55 employees.

Roberts Manufacturing Co Ltd: POB 1275, Lower Estate, Bridgetown, St Michael; tel. 429-2131; fax 426-5604; e-mail roberts@rmco.com; internet www.rmco.com; f. 1944; subsidiary of Barbados Shipping and Trading Co Ltd (see under Shipping); manufacturers of shortening, margarine, edible oils and animal feeds; sales Bds $64m. (2006); Chair. A. C. FIELDS; Gen. Man. MICHAEL A. CLARKE; 160 employees.

R. L. Seale and Co Ltd: Clarence House, Tudor Bridge, POB 864, St Michael; tel. 426-0334; fax 436-6003; e-mail rseale@caribsurf.com; f. 1926; manufacture and distribution of rum, sale of food; sales US $55m. (2003); Chair. and Man. Dir Sir DAVID SEALE; 275 employees.

The West Indies Rum Distillery Ltd: Brighton, Black Rock, St Michael; tel. 425-9301; fax 425-7236; e-mail info@westindiesrum.com; internet www.westindiesrum.com; f. 1893; 88% shares owned by Goddard Enterprises Ltd; main brands are Cockspur, Malibu, Gilbeys and Popov; Man. Dir ANDREW HASSELL; 62 employees.

C. O. Williams Construction Ltd: POB 871E, Lears, St Michael; tel. 436-3910; fax 427-5336; e-mail info@cow.bb; internet www.cow.bb; f. 1960; Chair. Sir CHARLES OTHNEIL WILLIAMS.

UTILITIES

Electricity

Barbados Light and Power Co (BL & P): POB 142, Garrison Hill, St Michael; tel. 430-4300; fax 228-1396; internet www.blpc.com.bb; f. 1911; electricity generator and distributor; operates 3 stations with a combined capacity of 209,500 kW; Chair. IAN CUMMING; Man. Dir PETER WILLIAMS.

Gas

Barbados National Oil Co Ltd (BNOCL): POB 175, Woodbourne, St Philip; tel. 420-1800; fax 420-1818; e-mail ronhewitt@bnocl.com; internet www.bnocl.com; f. 1982; exploration and extraction of petroleum and natural gas; state-owned; Gen. Man. RONALD HEWITT; 88 employees.

National Petroleum Corporation (NPC): Wildey, POB 175, St Michael; tel. 430-4020; fax 426-4326; e-mail customerserv@npc.com.bb; internet npc.com.bb; gas production and distribution; Chair. HARCOURT LEWIS; Gen. Man. JAMES BROWNE.

Water

Barbados Water Authority: Pine East-West Blvd, The Pine, St Michael; tel. 427-3990; fax 426-4507; e-mail bwa@caribsurf.com; internet www.bwa.bb; f. 1980; Exec. Chair. ARNI WALTERS; Gen. Man. DENIS YEARWOOD.

TRADE UNIONS

Principal unions include:

Barbados Secondary Teachers' Union: The Patrick Frost Centre, Eighth Ave, Belleville, St Michael; tel. and fax 429-7676; e-mail bstu_org@yahoo.com; internet www.bstu.org; f. 1949; Pres. MARY-ANN REDMAN; Gen. Sec. ERSKINE PADMORE; 375 mems.

Barbados Union of Teachers: Merry Hill, Welches, POB 58, St Michael; tel. 436-6139; fax 426-9890; e-mail but@hotmail.com; internet butbarbados.org; f. 1974; Pres. KAREN BEST; Gen. Sec. HERBERT GITTENS; 1,800 mems.

Barbados Workers' Union (BWU): 'Solidarity' House, Harmony Hall, POB 172, St Michael; tel. 426-3492; fax 436-6496; e-mail bwu@caribsurf.com; internet www.bwu-bb.org; f. 1941; operates a Labour College; Pres.-Gen. LINDA BROOKS; Gen. Sec. Sir ROY TROTMAN; 25,000 mems.

National Union of Public Workers: Dalkeith Rd, POB 174, St Michael; tel. 426-7774; fax 436-1795; e-mail nupwbarbados@sunbeach.net; f. 1944 as the Barbados Civil Service Assn; present name adopted in 1971; Pres. WALTER MALONEY; Gen. Sec. JOSEPH GODDARD; c. 8,000 mems.

Transport

ROADS

Ministry of Transport and Works: The Pine, St Michael; tel. 429-2863; fax 437-8133; internet www.publicworks.gov.bb; maintains a network of 1,600 km (994 miles) of paved roads; Permanent Sec. DAVID DAISLEY (acting).

SHIPPING

Bridgetown harbour has berths for eight ships and simultaneous bunkering facilities for five. In October 2003 the Government announced a 10-year plan to expand the harbour, at an estimated cost of US $101m. The plan was to include the construction of a new sugar terminal and a new cruise ship pier. Construction commenced in 2004.

Barbados Port Inc: University Row, Princess Alice Hwy, Bridgetown; tel. 430-4700; fax 429-5348; e-mail administrator@barbadosport.com; internet www.barbadosport.com; f. 1979 as the Barbados Port Authority and was incorporated in 2003; Chair. DAVID HARDING; Man. Dir and CEO EVERTON WALTERS.

The Shipping Association of Barbados: Trident House, 2nd Floor, Broad St, Bridgetown; tel. 427-9860; fax 426-8392; e-mail info@shippingbarbados.com; internet www.shippingbarbados.com; f. 1981; Pres. GLYNE ST HILL; Vice-Pres. MARC SAMPSON.

Principal Shipping Companies

Barbados Shipping and Trading Co Ltd (B. S. & T.): The Auto Dome, 1st Floor, Warrens, St Michael; tel. 417-5110; fax 417-5116; e-mail info@bsandtco.com; internet www.bsandtco.com; f. 1920; acquired by energy and industrial asscn Neal & Massy (Trinidad and Tobago) in March 2008; Chair. GERVASE WARNER; CEO G. ANTHONY KING.

Bernuth Agencies: T. Geddes Grant White Park Rd, Bridgetown; tel. 431-3343; e-mail info@bernuth.com; internet www.bernuth.com; Pres. Capt. JORDAN MONOCANDILOS; Port Co-ordinator MARIA KIRKLAND.

Carlisle Shipping Ltd: Musson Bldg, Ground Floor, Hincks St, Bridgetown; tel. 430-4803; fax 431-0051; e-mail shipping@tggbarbados.com.

DaCosta Mannings Inc (DMI): DMI Corporate Office, The Autodome, Warrens, POB 103, St Michael; tel. 431-8700; fax 228-8590; e-mail support@dacostamannings.com; internet dacostamannings.com; f. 1995 following merger of DaCosta Ltd and Manning, Wilkinson & Challenor Ltd; shipping and retail company; acquired the shipping lines of T. Geddes Grant Bros in 2002; Chair. G. A. A. KING; Man. Dir T. A. MAHON.

Hassell, Eric and Son Ltd: Carlisle House, Hincks St, Bridgetown; tel. 436-6102; fax 429-3416; e-mail info@erichassell.com.bb; internet www.erichassell.com.bb; shipping agent, stevedoring contractor and cargo fowarder; Man. Dir ERICA LUKE; Operations Man. NOEL WALCOTT.

Tropical Shipping: Goddards Complex, Fontabelle Rd, St Michael; tel. 426-9990; fax 426-7750; e-mail president@tropical.com; internet www.tropical.com; Pres. RICK MURRELL.

CIVIL AVIATION

The principal airport is Grantley Adams International Airport, at Seawell, 18 km (11 miles) from Bridgetown. A US $100m. contract to build a new arrivals terminal was awarded in late 2001. The first phase of the project was under construction in 2006. Barbados is served by a number of regional and international airlines, including Air Jamaica, LIAT (1974) Ltd (Antigua), Air Canada and British Airways. An inter-island service, operating flights between Saint Lucia and Barbados (three days a week), was launched by the US-based American Eagle carrier in September 2007.

Barbados Civil Aviation Department: Grantley Adams Industrial Park, Bldg 4, Christ Church; tel. 428-0952; fax 428-7333; e-mail aisbarbados@sunbeach.net; internet www.bcad.gov.bb; Ministry of International Business and International Transport departments operating as internal regulator of air transport; Dir E. ANTHONY ARCHER.

Tourism

The natural attractions of the island consist chiefly of the warm climate and varied scenery. In addition, there are many facilities for outdoor sports of all kinds. Tourism receipts (including passenger transport) totalled US $1,192m. in 2008. In 2009 the number of stop-over tourist arrivals was an estimated 518,600, while the number of visiting cruise ship passengers was an estimated 635,700. There were some 7,000 hotel rooms on the island in 2003.

Barbados Hotel and Tourism Association (BHTA): see Trade and Industry.

Barbados Tourism Authority: Harbour Rd, POB 242, Bridgetown; tel. 427-2623; fax 426-4080; e-mail btainfo@barbados.org; internet www.barbados.org; f. 1993 to replace Barbados Board of Tourism; offices in Europe, South America and the USA; Chair. RALPH TAYLOR; Pres. and CEO STUART LAYNE.

Defence

The Barbados Defence Force is divided into regular defence units and a coastguard service with armed patrol boats. The total strength of the armed forces, as assessed at November 2009, was an estimated 610, comprising an army of 500 members and a navy (coastguard) of 110. There was also a reserve force of 430 members.

Defence Budget: an estimated Bds $65.0m. (US $32.5m.) in 2009.

Chief of Staff: Col ALVIN QUINTYNE.

Education

Education is compulsory for 12 years, between five and 16 years of age. Primary education begins at the age of five and lasts for seven years. Secondary education, beginning at 12 years of age, lasts for six years. In 2007/08 22,849 pupils were enrolled at primary schools, while there were 20,337 pupils at secondary schools. Tuition at all government schools is free. There were 11,405 students in higher education in 2006/07. Degree courses in arts, law, education, natural sciences and social sciences are offered at the Cave Hill campus of the University of the West Indies; three higher education training establishments, although remaining administratively discrete, were to be consolidated to form the University College of Barbados. A two-year clinical-training programme for medical students is conducted by the School of Clinic Medicine and Research of the University, while an in-service training programme for teachers is provided by the School of Education. Government expenditure on education for 2005/06 was Bbs $425.7m. (equivalent to 21.8% of total current expenditure).

Bibliography

For works on the Caribbean generally, see Select Bibliography (Books)

Beckles, H. *A History of Barbados: From Amerindian Settlement to Caribbean Single market*, 2nd Edn. Cambridge, Cambridge University Press, 2007.

Broberg, M. *Barbados*. New York, NY, Chelsea House Publications, 1998.

Carmichael, T. A. *Barbados: Thirty Years of Independence*. Kingston, Ian Randle Publrs, 1996.

Drummond, I., and Marsden, T. *The Condition of Sustainability*. London, Routledge, 1999.

Girvan, N. (Ed.). *Poverty, Empowerment and Social Development in the Caribbean*. Bridgetown, Canoe Press, 1997.

Gragg, L. *Englishmen Transplanted: The English Colonization of Barbados 1627-1660*. Oxford, Oxford University Press, 2003.

Jones, C. *Engendering Whiteness: White Women and Colonialism in Barbados and North Carolina, 1627-1865*. Manchester, Manchester University Press, 2007.

Ligon, R. *A True and Exact History of the Island of Barbados*. London, Frank Cass Publrs, 1998.

Menard, R. R. *Sweet Negotiations: Sugar, Slavery, and Plantation Agriculture in Early Barbados*. Charlottesville, University of Virginia Press, 2006.

Schomburg, R. *History of Barbados*. London, Frank Cass Publrs, 1998.

BELIZE

Geography

PHYSICAL FEATURES

Belize is on the north-eastern shores of Central America. Mexico lies to the north, beyond a 250-km (155-mile) border, and Guatemala to the west and south, beyond a 266-km border, with Honduras in the south-east, across the Gulf of Honduras. Belize is a Central American, Commonwealth country, which was known as British Honduras until 1973, when it was a dependent territory of the United Kingdom. It became independent only in 1981, the last country on the American mainland to do so, but its history and culture have made it more usually associated with the anglophone West Indian states than with its Spanish-speaking neighbours (it is the only Central American country not to have a Pacific coast). These neighbours also have territorial claims on Belize, with Guatemala going so far as only to recognize the country's independence in September 1991. The Organization of American States (OAS) is currently mediating the disputes over Guatemala's territorial claims and its rights of maritime access to the Caribbean. There are also problems associated with the 2000 agreement on managing disagreements within the 'Lines of Adjacency' (1 km either side of the Belize–Guatemala border), which attempt to limit illegal immigration (by 'squatters') coming into Belize. Honduras claims the Sapodilla Cays. The current total area of Belize covers 22,965 sq km (8,867 sq miles), making it about the size of Wales (United Kingdom) but with a population less than that of Cardiff, the Welsh capital.

The territory of Belize, which includes 160 sq km of inland waters and a maritime littoral of 386 km, is a flat, swampy coastal plain, with low mountains in the south. A resurvey of the Maya Mountains recently superseded Victoria Peak, in the south-east, with the nearby peak of Doyle's Delight (1,174 m or 3,853 ft) as the highest point in the country. The low-lying north of the country was once the bed of the sea, and supports scrubby vegetation or dense tropical hardwood forest. Particularly in this area, the landscape is typified by jungles laced with a seasonally navigable river network. Central Belize has sandy soil, supporting savannah grasslands, while to the south the land rises into the lofty Mountain Pine Ridge area and, thence, the Maya Mountains, which continue west into Guatemala. Here rainfall fuels the many streams, such as the Macal (which, with the Mopan, becomes the River Belize). South of the watershed is a more precipitous landscape, with short, fast streams carrying fertile soils and detritus to the coast, which permits not only a flourishing agriculture but also the longer-established tropical rainforest. Belize's shores are guarded by a coral barrier-reef system that is second in size only to the Great Barrier Reef of Australia. This extends the territory of the country to include a number of islands and cays (mangrove cays and island cays) off shore, in the Caribbean Sea. At almost 300 km in length, it is certainly the longest reef in the Americas. Two-fifths of the country, including the marine environment, is protected by parks and reserves.

CLIMATE

The climate is tropical and very hot and humid, despite the prevailing winds off the Caribbean. The country has an annual mean temperature of 79°F (26°C), with maximums seldom above 96°F (36°C) or below 60°F (16°C), even at night. The rainy season is in May–November, with hurricanes likely from June. The coast is prone to flooding, particularly in the south. The dry season is in February–May. Average annual rainfall ranges from 50 ins (1,270 mm) in the north to 170 ins (4,320 mm) in the south. Complications in this pattern have been observed in recent years (noticeably owing to the El Niño phenomenon and global warming).

POPULATION

The original racial balance in Belize has changed since independence, and particularly during the 1980s, mainly owing to immigration. The growing mixed Maya-Spanish, or Mestizo, population accounts for 46% of the total, while the previously dominant, black Creole population accounts for 28%. The autochthonous Amerindians consist mainly of the Maya (10%), although there are also immigrant, mixed-race Garifuna ('Black Carib'—6%) peoples. Other groups include those of European descent (including German Mennonites), 'East' Indians and Chinese. This changing balance of population has not had a discernible effect on the pattern of religious adherence, with Roman Catholics accounting for about one-half of the population. Other Christian denominations command the faith of the majority of the remainder of the population (mainly Pentecostalists, Anglicans, Seventh-day Adventists, Methodists and Mennonites). English is the official language, but immigration (often, originally, illegal) from the neighbouring Hispanic countries means that Spanish is now widely spoken. There is also a Creole dialect in use and native speakers of Amerindian tongues such as Maya, Garifuna and Ketchi.

The total population was 333,200, according to estimates for mid-2009, making Belize the smallest country of Central America in terms of population (El Salvador is slightly smaller in extent). The capital since 1972 has been Belmopan, in the centre of the country, although, according to official estimates, it still had a population of only 20,000 at mid-2009. The old capital on the coast, Belize City, remains the largest urban centre (66,700), and San Ignacio near the central western border also has a larger population than the capital. The chief town of the south is Punta Gorda. The country is the least urbanized in Central America, with only about 10% of the population living in urban areas. Belize is divided into six districts.

History

CHARLES ARTHUR

Revised for this edition by MARK WILSON

INTRODUCTION

The lands on the eastern side of the Central American isthmus that are today known as Belize were once part of the Mayan system of city states, but when the Spanish arrived in the 16th century these had long since collapsed. Spain never achieved uncontested control over the territory or the indigenous Maya, and the first Europeans to establish a permanent presence were British buccaneers and woodcutters who settled in coastal areas near present-day Belize City. The first recorded British settlement was established in 1638. Disease and destructive Spanish colonial policies had decimated the Mayan population, and those who survived lived inland, away from the coast. The country has remained sparsely populated ever since. In 1763 the Treaty of Paris granted British subjects the privilege of wood-cutting along the coast of the Gulf of Honduras, but retained Spanish sovereignty over the territory, and Spanish forces throughout the 18th century attempted to expel the British settlers. In 1798 defeat in a series of battles fought around the islands and reefs off the coast, known as the battle at St George's Caye, was Spain's last attempt to gain control, and Spain in 1802 recognized British sovereignty under the Treaty of Amiens. In 1859 the neighbouring country to the west, Guatemala, signed a treaty recognizing its border with British Honduras, on the understanding that a road would be constructed linking Guatemala with the Caribbean coast (the road was not built and, as a result, Guatemala later declared the treaty invalid). 'Bayman' settlers had elected their own magistrates as early as 1738, although these were recognized neither by Spain nor the United Kingdom. A formal Constitution with a legislative assembly was introduced in 1854 to replace the earlier public meeting of settlers, and in 1862 Belize became the colony of British Honduras, although it remained a dependency of Jamaica until 1884.

During the 18th century several thousand African slaves were brought into the territory, many of them via islands in the Caribbean but some direct from Africa, and were put to work felling logwood and later mahogany. By the time slavery was abolished in British colonies in 1833 the population comprised Africans, Mestizos (of mixed Mayan and European descent), indigenous Mayas, and a number of Garifuna (mixed African and Amerindian people originally deported from St Vincent to the Honduran island of Roatán in 1797), as well as a mainly British colonial élite. In the mid-19th century the still small population was significantly augmented when thousands of Mayan and Mestizo refugees from the Caste War of Yucatán (1847–1901) fled south into British Honduras. Many of them settled in the north of the colony where they established small farms. The appointed Legislative Council, which replaced the Assembly from 1871, included some Creole members from 1892.

Well into the 20th century the social and economic life of the colony revolved around the felling and export of timber, although the industry was depressed for extended periods from the mid-19th century. Extraction of chicle, a naturally occurring by-product of the sapodilla tree, for use in chewing gum was an important activity from the 1880s. Logging companies continually moved further into the interior in search of mahogany, and permanent settlements were established. Unlike the other Central American countries, a plantation economy was not developed, and with logging requiring relatively few workers, the population remained quite small. The timber industry came to be dominated by a handful of companies, one of which, the British Honduras Company (renamed the Belize Estate and Produce Company—BEC—in 1875), eventually owned one-half of the private land in the colony, representing one-fifth of the entire territory. The timber exporters initially also controlled the lucrative import trade, supplying nearly all the materials and produce required by the small middle class.

The Great Depression of the early 1930s had serious repercussions in British Honduras. Export prices were reduced, imports dropped sharply, and unemployment increased. In 1931 a major hurricane destroyed most of the capital, Belize City, adding to the mounting social and economic problems. During the 1930s workers began to organize to demand better pay, as well as an end to exploitative conditions of employment, and the unemployed to demand jobs. After a wave of strikes and demonstrations in 1934, reforms introduced in 1936 included elections for six of the 13 seats on the Legislative Council, albeit with a very restrictive property limit on the franchise. Further reforms in 1941 and 1943 permitted trade unions, and reduced some of the restrictions on workers' rights. The Second World War revived the timber industry and stimulated work opportunities abroad, but from 1945 widespread unemployment and poverty among the working class, especially in Belize City, galvanized a movement that questioned both the colonial set-up and the dominance of the small number of wealthy landowners and merchants. The devaluation of the currency on the last day of 1949 (in line with Sterling devaluation three months earlier) resulted in price increases and the immediate worsening of the workers' situation. Protests against devaluation evolved into a campaign against the entire colonial system, and in September 1950 the People's United Party (PUP) formed with the objective of gaining political and economic independence for the people of the colony. The PUP was closely aligned with the General Workers' Union (GWU), and in October 1952 the two called a national strike to protest against worsening economic conditions. After 10 days the Government and the main companies, but not including the BEC, agreed to negotiate with the union for better wages and working conditions. The BEC held out and succeeded in breaking the strike without making any concessions, but the strike was considered a victory and the prestige of the PUP and the GWU were considerably enhanced. The PUP then focused on a campaign to win universal suffrage. Several years of campaigning, during which a number of leading figures were jailed for sedition, culminated in 1954 with a new Constitution allowing all literate citizens over the age of 21 to vote, and in a general election held in the same year the PUP, under the leadership of George Price, won eight of the nine seats in the new Legislative Assembly with 66% of the popular vote.

THE RISE OF THE PUP

There followed a long period of PUP domination of the political scene. In 1961, after a constitutional reform introducing the ministerial system, the party won all 18 seats in an enlarged legislature, and Price was appointed First Minister by the British Governor. Further reforms led to a new Constitution in 1964 that significantly reduced the powers of the British Governor, and set up a Cabinet of Ministers headed by a Premier who would be the leader of the majority party in a bicameral National Assembly, composed of a House of Representatives and a Senate. The reforms effectively granted the colony internal self-government, and in an election in 1965 another PUP landslide victory over the opposition National Independence Party saw Price become Premier. Under Price the decision was taken to move the capital away from Belize City, which was prone to hurricane damage, and over several years a new capital, Belmopan, was built at the exact geographical centre of the country; Hurricane Hattie in October 1961 flooded much of Belize City with a three-metre storm surge, destroyed 40% of its buildings and killed 265 people. In January 1972 Belmopan was declared the new capital, although Belize City remains the nation's largest city and port. In June 1973 the colony was officially renamed Belize. There was a significant change, too, at the level of party politics when in September 1973 the three main opposition parties—liberals and social democrats concerned about the PUP's apparent progression to one-party rule—merged to form the United Democratic Party (UDP). In the general election of 1974 the UDP won six of the 18 seats in the House of Representatives, and in the following year confirmed its arrival as a major political force by winning control of six of the nine seats on the Belize City Council.

During the 1960s and 1970s the PUP followed a centre-left orientation with a focus on leading the colony to full independence. For over two decades this aim was thwarted because of concerns over the territorial claims of neighbouring Guatemala. In 1945 Guatemala had cited the failure of the British to build a road through the colony to the Caribbean coast as reason to renege on the 1859 treaty, and a new Guatemalan Constitution declared British Honduras to be part of Guatemala. After the colony was granted self-government in 1964 Guatemala renewed its land claim, and threatened to use force if the colony became independent without first settling the claim. Protracted negotiations continued throughout the 1960s but collapsed in 1972, at which point the United Kingdom established a permanent military garrison in the colony to deter any prospect of a Guatemalan invasion. In 1975, after more than a decade of fruitless negotiations, the Government of Guatemala demanded that Belize give up all the land south of the Monkey River—approximately one-quarter of the colony's territory—as a way of settling the dispute. Faced with this escalation the PUP Government embarked on a new strategy designed to win international support for its independence and for its territorial integrity. A concerted campaign succeeded in winning the advocacy of the Caribbean Community and Common Market (CARICOM) and the Non-aligned Movement. The Central American republics were also gradually won over, and the fall of the Somoza dictatorship in Nicaragua in 1979 deprived Guatemala of its most committed supporter in the region. A series of UN resolutions concerning the issue were considered, but each time the USA abstained. Finally, in 1980, the USA changed its policy of neutrality and voted in favour of a UN resolution calling for the independence of Belize, with all its territory, before the next UN session in 1981.

INDEPENDENCE

At home, the move towards independence convulsed party politics. In the general election of November 1979 the PUP ran on a platform endorsing independence. The UDP, by contrast, favoured delaying independence until the territorial dispute with Guatemala had been resolved, and pinned its hopes on winning the youth vote, as the suffrage had been extended to those of 18 years of age and over. The election became a referendum on independence, and although the PUP won only 52% of the vote, it carried 13 of the 18 seats in the House of Representatives and thus received a mandate for the preparation of an independence constitution. Following the UN resolution in favour of Belize's independence, the Price administration made a last attempt to reach an agreement with Guatemala. In March 1981 the United Kingdom, Guatemala and Belize signed the Heads of Agreement document outlining proposals for Guatemala to recognize an independent Belize within its existing borders. This depended upon reaching agreement on allowing Guatemala to use certain coastal cays, enjoy free port facilities and the freedom of transit on two roads, as well as a number of other border and national security issues. The proposals were interpreted by some sections of the Belizean population as unacceptable concessions, and trade unionists and students led a strike and a number of violent protests against the agreement, prompting the Government to declare a state of emergency. The UDP was unable to offer any new approach to the issue and failed to capitalize on the public disenchantment with the Government. When Guatemala again withdrew from the negotiations under domestic right-wing pressure, the United Kingdom confirmed it would protect an independent Belize. Independence was declared on 21 September 1981 without any agreement with Guatemala, and with the UDP boycotting the independence ceremony.

During the 1960s and 1970s the colony's economy had grown rapidly, mainly as a consequence of the expeditious emergence of a thriving sugar sector. By the 1970s sugar accounted for almost 70% of all export revenues. This dependency on one commodity left the newly independent country highly vulnerable to external shocks, and in the early 1980s the collapse of the international sugar price seriously damaged the economy. In the general election of 1984 the UDP focused on economic issues, and played on a general feeling that the PUP and its leader George Price had been in power for too long. The UDP also stressed its positive record in local government and capitalized on the popularity of its leader, Manuel Esquivel, the former mayor of Belize City. The party proceeded to win 21 of the 28 seats in the newly enlarged House of Representatives, ending 30 years of PUP domination. The UDP confirmed its strength when it prevailed in the municipal elections in March 1985, winning control of five of the eight municipal councils. The new Government carried out an economic adjustment programme in conjunction with the IMF, including cuts in public expenditure and the provision of incentives to diversify the economy. The reforms, together with favourable changes in the international economy—particularly the revival of the sugar market—contributed to a profound economic recovery during the late 1980s. Buoyed by the country's strong economic growth, in late 1989 Esquivel called an election several months sooner than necessary. However, the PUP campaigned strongly on a nationalist platform, criticizing the UDP Government's policy of selling Belizean citizenship to Hong Kong, Taiwanese and other overseas citizens (although similar 'economic citizenship' programmes were operated by PUP governments in 1979–84 and after 1998) and accusing it of excessive reliance on foreign investment to the detriment of Belizeans. The combination of the PUP's effective 'Belizeans First' campaign and the existence of internal divisions within the UDP contributed to a narrow victory for Price's PUP.

Party politics in Belize has continued to be dominated by the PUP and the UDP, with third parties failing to make any lasting impact. There are few ideological differences between the two parties, and neither holds any exclusive appeal for either of Belize's two main ethnic groups—the English-speaking Creoles of black African descent, and the Spanish-speaking Mestizos, although the UDP has stronger support among the Creoles, while the PUP is more popular among Hispanic voters in the north of the country. The electorate has often been more or less evenly divided in its support for the two, and in several elections the difference in the numbers voting for each party has been a matter of just one or two per cent. The close-fought nature of Belize's electoral contests was highlighted in 1993 when the UDP polled 49% of the vote against the PUP's 51%, but returned to power as it had won 16 seats against the PUP's 13 in the 29-seat House of Representatives.

THE DOMESTIC RAMIFICATIONS OF INTERNATIONAL POLITICS

The UDP's second term in office was notable for the continuing repercussions of Guatemala's territorial claim. In 1991 Guatemala had recognized Belize's right to exist, and as a result in 1993 the United Kingdom decided there was no longer any need to maintain a permanent military presence in Belize. The progressive reduction in the size of the British military force, from a high of 1,350, had pronounced negative effects on the Belizean economy, and added to economic woes that turned the electorate against the UDP Government. The public was also disenchanted by the renewal of the Guatemalan threat following the UDP's suspension of a non-aggression pact agreed between the two countries under the previous PUP administration. In March 1994 Guatemala renewed its territorial claim. Prime Minister Esquivel added fuel to the fire in mid-1994 when he claimed that Guatemala was encouraging peasant farmers to cross the border and settle in Belize.

By 1998 the incumbent UDP was widely perceived as incompetent, especially in terms of managing the economy. In 1996 a government survey had revealed that one-third of the population lived below the poverty line. Accusations of ministerial corruption exacerbated the discontent. Meanwhile, in opposition, the PUP had regrouped under a new leader, Said Musa, who had replaced the veteran George Price in 1996. In the August 1998 election the PUP won a substantial 60% of the vote, taking 26 of the 29 seats. Esquivel lost his seat and immediately resigned as UDP leader, being replaced by Dean Barrow.

The new PUP Government inherited an economy in a precarious state, with unemployment at 14% and a constrictive dependence on exports of sugar, citrus fruits and bananas. Earlier attempts to diversify had seen the development of a financial services sector and a shipping registry system, and the PUP relied on these to attract foreign investment. However, from 1999 the USA and the United Kingdom began to raise serious concerns about the country's 'offshore' banking system.

A particular focus was put on the financial empire established in Belize by the billionaire businessman Michael (from 2000 Lord) Ashcroft in the early 1990s. Ashcroft—who spent much of his childhood in Belize, holds dual Belizean-British nationality, was treasurer of the British Conservative Party in 1998–2001, and has since 2005 been its deputy chairman—was alleged to have made large donations to the PUP when it was in opposition. He benefited also from several pieces of legislation introduced by the new PUP Government; these included a law giving tax-exempt status to companies including Ashcroft's 'offshore' holding company Belize Holdings, and the granting of the exclusive right to the Ashcroft-owned Belize Bank to set up 'offshore' companies in Belize for US and British citizens.

THE 2003 GENERAL ELECTION

In March 2003 the PUP called an election, and focused its campaign on several years of steady economic growth and its record of increased spending on health, education and housing. The UDP strongly criticized the Government for alleged corruption, but although it succeeded in increasing its share of the vote, it was not enough to stop the PUP from emerging victorious. The PUP won 53% of the vote to the UDP's 46%, giving the PUP 22 seats and the UDP seven. The election result was notable for being the first time that either party had won two consecutive elections since independence.

In terms of domestic politics, the PUP's second term proved disastrous, and there were frequent charges of corruption and poor macro-economic management from the opposition UDP, as well as business organizations and international observers, as the expansionary fiscal policies, rapidly rising debt and widespread mismanagement of the PUP's first term had destroyed public trust while necessitating unpopular austerity measures. In January 2005 civil unrest broke out in Belmopan, provoked by the release of a new national budget that instituted significant tax increases. On 21 January a large demonstration at the National Assembly called by the National Trade Union Congress of Belize (NTUCB) and the Belize Chamber of Commerce ended in violent clashes between protesters and riot police. The following day the Belize National Teachers' Union added to the pressure on the Government by launching a strike that left the majority of schools closed. A planned general strike was averted when the Government negotiated a deal with the NTUCB that included salary increases for its members and a suspension of the budget's tax increases pending a review. The Government then reneged on the deal, and in mid-March, as Government machinations regarding the ownership of the privatized telecommunications monopoly Belize Telecommunications Ltd continued, the Belize Communication Workers' Union began protests to demand renationalization, including a work-stoppage that cut off phone lines across the country and international connections. Anti-Government protests culminated in a riot in Belize City on 20 April, as a result of which one person was killed, 27 people injured, and 98 arrested. After the Government turned to the IMF to negotiate adjustments in debt payments, and agreed to renationalize the water service, the protest movement faded away for a time. In local elections in March 2006 the full strength of the opposition was demonstrated when the UDP swept to power in all nine city and municipal councils, taking 64 of the 67 seats and 60% of the popular vote. The Government continued to be dogged by financial problems, and it was forced to default on debt payments in December 2006, and to renegotiate the country's external debt in early 2007 with international creditors. The opposition repeatedly aired accusations of corruption, and in 2006 Musa was forced to appoint commissions to investigate the Social Security Board (SSB) and the Development Finance Corporation (DFC). The SSB investigation resulted in resignations and dismissals of key personnel, while the report into the DFC found that it had authorized the use of millions of dollars in public, domestic, and international loan funds inappropriately to assist the business interests of certain citizens. Further problems arose over the Government's handling of the health sector, and in particular the decision to guarantee the debts of a private health company, Universal Health Services. In May 2007 the issue of the loan guarantee split the Government, and Prime Minister Musa dismissed three ministers who objected to it, in a further twist to the faction fights that had led to 10 cabinet reorganizations since October 2001. There were also further anti-Government protests that only subsided once Musa announced that the company's debt of US $16m. had been renegotiated and could be serviced without the need for 'tax-payer involvement'. (The issue was to return to haunt the PUP when, following the February 2008 election, it was revealed that some US $10m. donated to the Government by Venezuela for public housing had been used to pay the debt guarantee and ended up with Ashcroft's Belize Bank.)

THE 2008 GENERAL ELECTION AND THE BARROW GOVERNMENT

The 2008 election produced a clear victory for the UDP. In recent years the UDP had repeatedly accused the Musa administration of corruption and mismanagement, and it made these charges the focus of its campaign, while the PUP used US $10m. in Venezuelan funds to make cash payments to voters. Both parties promised to implement measures to lessen the impact of the increasing cost of living: the PUP by abolishing income tax for the lower paid, and the UDP by lowering or eliminating the general sales tax on a number of basic consumer items, but these issues were swamped by concern over mismanagement and corruption. Discontent with the PUP's role in a series of financial scandals and UDP leader Barrow's appeal to young first-time voters contributed to a 7 February election result in which the UDP won 57% of the vote to the PUP's 41%, giving the UDP 25 seats and the PUP six. Barrow became the first black Prime Minister of Belize. As has been the trend throughout the country's history, third parties failed to make any impact, garnering just 2% of the total vote. Musa stood down as PUP leader following the defeat, and a party convention on 30 March selected Johnny Briceño as his successor, one of three members of parliament from the party's reformist wing; however, deep splits persisted within the party. Immediately after the declaration of the election results, Barrow sought to allay fears that tenured public servants appointed under his predecessor would be dismissed, and vowed to investigate missing public funds and other aspects of alleged government corruption. One of his first actions was to appoint a team to investigate what had happened to the US $10m. that the country had received from Venezuela for public housing under the previous administration.

Hampered by severe financial difficulties, the new Government was also enmeshed in a series of complex court cases with locally prominent companies, some of them linked to Lord Ashcroft, described by the Premier in his March 2009 budget presentation as 'close to acquiring the status of an enemy of the people'. Belize Bank was in August 2008 forced under protest to pay the disputed Venezuelan US $10m. to the Government, although the rights of the case remained subject to legal dispute, both locally and before the London Court of Arbitration, as did the Bank's tax liabilities and those of its parent company, BB Holdings. However, an attempt to charge Musa and former Minister of Housing and Urban Development Ralph Fonseca with theft was defeated after initial court hearings. There was also a complex dispute with the telecommunications company, restructured as Belize Telemedia Ltd (BTL). With the dispute still unresolved, the BTL was nationalized by act of parliament in August 2009. By mid-2010 the amount of compensation due to its former owners had yet to be settled, and legal wrangling over the rights and status of the former shareholders was still ongoing. Meanwhile, there were repeated disputes over allowable rates and charges between

Canadian-owned Belize Electricity Ltd and the Public Utilities Commission. An affiliate of Lufthansa Consulting, Newco, won a US $4.3m. arbitration settlement in June 2008, in compensation for the Musa Government's cancellation of an airport management contract. There were also bitter feuds between farmers and processors in the citrus and sugar industries; these disputes threatened to take on a political dimension, but as of mid-2010 had not directly involved the Government.

The Government in April 2008 proposed constitutional reforms under which Prime Ministers would be limited to three parliamentary terms in office; public contracts would be open to scrutiny; the state's right to mineral deposits would be strengthened; there would be no requirement to hold a referendum on legislation affecting human rights, although voters could in some circumstances force one to be held; and an additional independent senator would deprive the Government of its upper-house majority. While most of these proposals were approved by the National Assembly in August, they remained subject to legal challenges; although some questions were resolved in favour of the Government, these constitutional reforms were not yet in force at mid-2010. Meanwhile, the Government's continuing electoral strength was apparent in local elections in March 2009, where it again won 64 of the 67 seats; the PUP took only three in the Orange Walk district, Briceño's home base. However, the Government was embarrassed by charges of corruption and mismanagement levelled both before and after the elections against the high-profile mayor of Belize City, Zenaide Moya-Flowers. She was re-elected, but the charges remained before the courts in mid-2010. She had by that time lost the support of the majority of councillors, all UDP members; an attempt by the party to expel her remained stalled at mid-2010 pending the consideration of her appeal.

In June 2009 the Barrow Government announced its intentions to replace the Privy Council (based in the United Kingdom) with the Caribbean Court of Justice as Belize's final court of appeals. Following an amendment to the Constitution, this change came into effect at the beginning of June 2010.

Successive Belizean administrations have grappled with the seemingly intractable dispute with Guatemala, but without much success. In 1998 a joint commission to address immigration and cross-border traffic was established, and in May 2000 bilateral talks under the aegis of the Organization of American States (OAS) began in Washington, DC, USA. However, continuing tensions on the border undermined the talks. In November 2001 three Guatemalans were killed during an altercation with Belizean security forces in Toledo, the country's southernmost district. Proposals presented in September 2002 provided for a US $200m. international assistance package; an international border ecological park shared with Honduras; and concessions by Belize and Honduras to allow Guatemala a corridor of territorial sea and a narrow Exclusive Economic Zone in the Caribbean. However, Guatemala rejected the proposals in August 2003 for domestic political reasons.

Although intermittent border incidents have continued, an international 'Group of Friends' continued to press for a resolution, and a bilateral co-operation agreement signed in February 2003 provided for a transition process and confidence-building measures. An Agreement on a Framework for Negotiations was signed, again with guidance from the OAS, in September 2005, providing for a joint Belizean-Guatemalan commission to encourage initiatives in bilateral trade, tourism and resource conservation. This was followed by a partial scope trade agreement, which was concluded, in principle, in June 2006, but remained unratified by Guatemala's legislature until October 2009; as a result, the agreement was not implemented until April 2010. Meanwhile, with no agreed settlement to the bilateral border dispute in sight, the OAS in November 2007 proposed referral of the dispute to the International Court of Justice for binding arbitration. Both sides agreed to the proposal in December 2008, subject, however, to simultaneous referendums in each country. This process was approved by the Belizean legislature; however, with Guatemalan public opinion in particular susceptible to nationalist rhetoric, there had been no progress on the Guatemalan side by mid-2010. Sporadic minor border skirmishes continued to be reported.

Relations with Mexico and other Central Amercian neighbours remain good, and Belize is the only country to be a member of both the CARICOM group and the Central American Integration System. Although English remains the sole official language, Belize is in practice bilingual and multicultural, with the 2001 census reporting Mestizos as 46% of the population, followed by Creoles (28%), Amerindians (10%) and Garifuna (6%). The remaining 10% were more recent migrants, including Taiwanese and Chinese, Syrians and Lebanese, and Mennonites from North America.

Another international relations issue has been the use of Belizean territory for the transshipment of illicit drugs. Although Belize had been removed from the US President's list of major drug transit countries in 1999, during the early years of the 21st century there was strong evidence that the country—and its territorial waters—was being used for the transshipment of cocaine from Colombia to Mexico, and ultimately to the USA. US authorities reported that underdeveloped infrastructure and a small population limited local efforts to suppress the cocaine-trafficking, with problems compounded by corruption, ineffective money-laundering legislation and weak enforcement of laws regulating 'offshore' financial interests. In Belize the problem was regarded as serious, not only because of local drugs consumption, but also because of the involvement of drugs-traffickers in money-laundering and with the increasingly murderous criminal street gangs, particularly in Belize City; there were 94 murders in 2009, a rate of 29 per 100,000, approximately five times that of the USA. In 2008 port authorities intercepted several large shipments of pseudo-epehedrine, a chemical used in the manufacture of crystal methedrine, thought to be intended for use in Mexico. Strong US support for anti-trafficking drives focused on assistance to police counter-narcotics units, the Defence Force, the recently formed Belize National Coast Guard, investigative, forensic and prosecutor units, and the Financial Intelligence Unit. Significant concerns exist regarding the effectiveness of the police force, not least because a significant number of officers have been charged with corruption, murder and other serious offences.

Economy

CHARLES ARTHUR

Revised for this edition by MARK WILSON

During the colonial period the economy was based on the export of a series of commodities: logwood in the 17th and 18th centuries, mahogany in the 19th century, and then sugar from the middle of the 20th century. In the second half of the 20th century there was some diversification of the economy. Non-traditional exports—principally citrus products, bananas and papaya—flourished, a single export garment factory was established, and tourism began to develop. In the 1990s the country's 'offshore' financial services and fishing sectors were also successful. By the end of the 20th century the economy was expanding rapidly, although it remained vulnerable to the impact of hurricanes and changes in the terms of trade for its main exports and to macro-economic difficulties resulting from a rapid increase in government debt and serious mismanagement of state institutions. Expansionary fiscal policies produced a spurt in gross domestic product (GDP), peaking at 13.0% in 2000, with growth averaging 5.3% in 2001–06, but slowing sharply to 1.3% in 2007. After a partial recovery in growth to 3.6% in 2008, the economy stagnated in 2009, with zero growth.

The population was estimated at 333,200 in mid-2009. The labour force grew in the course of the late 20th century as migrant workers from Central America (some of them fleeing political violence) eased periodic labour shortages. In addition, the influx of a great many immigrants each year, many of whom stay and settle in Belize, has changed the ethnic composition of the population and created a source of social tension, with Belizeans of Hispanic mestizo origin now the largest ethnic group. There were approximately 30,000 economically active individuals in 1970, with the number rising to 46,000 in 1980 and to more than 60,000 by 1990. By 2009 the number of employed workers had increased to 120,500. Nevertheless, the labour force in Belize remains small in relation to those of the neighbouring Central American republics. Unemployment increased to 13.1% in 2009, reflecting the impact of the slowing economy, but also indicating a lack of opportunities and the disincentive effect on the unemployed of receiving remittances from family members living abroad. In 2008 remittances from approximately 59,000 emigrants—most living in the USA—totalled US $113m., or 8% of GDP, although in the following year the comparable figures declined to $76m. and 5.6% of GDP, as the effects of the global economic downturn took hold. The alleviation of poverty continued to be a major challenge. An official survey conducted in 2009 classed some 43% of the population as poor, up from 33% at the time of the previous survey in 2002.

AGRICULTURE, FISHING AND FORESTRY

Agriculture is a mainstay of the economy, accounting for 10.7% of GDP in 2009, 18.0% of employment in 2006 and 52% of exports in 2009.

Sugar cane is grown mainly by small farmers in northern Belize, with a single sugar factory at Tower Hill operated by Belize Sugar Industries Ltd (BSI), which produced 93,277 metric tons in 2009. Sugar accounted for 13% of domestic exports in 2008, with most sold to the European Union (EU). However, the guaranteed EU sugar price has been cut in recent years, and the outlook for the industry was uncertain in view of high costs and the end of the EU sugar protocol from 2009, although there would be some continuing price protection until 2012. The EU agreed 'accompanying measures', including grant aid of €45.2m. for Belize for 2007–10, and a further amount for the period to 2013. The Belize Sugar Cane Farmers' Association (BSCFA) obtained Fairtrade certification in 2008, resulting in additional revenue of US $60 per metric ton, which was to be spent on development of the industry and social development in the sugar cane belt; however, these benefits were removed for a period during 2009–10 owing to the BSCFA's failure to adhere to Fairtrade guidelines. The industry has also been damaged by industrial disputes; in January and February 2009 violent protests by sugar farmers prevented the use of a 'core sampler' to gauge the quality of cane deliveries and resulted in 12 people being injured and one fatality in a confrontation with police. At mid-2010 there was also an ongoing dispute between the BSCFA and a breakaway group, the United Cane Farmers' Association, which received official recognition in December 2009. The Belcogen co-generation plant, construction of which was completed in 2009, was intended to generate 13.5 MW of electricity from sugar cane waste, of which 9 MW was to be sold to Belize Electricity Ltd (BEL—see Energy and Infrastructure, below); however, the plant severely underperformed in its first season of operation, producing only 1 MW of power, and significantly increasing ash pollution.

Citrus fruit production—mainly oranges and grapefruit—expanded in the 1980s when foreign demand for citrus concentrate for use in the production of fruit juice soared, and in the 1990s the sector was developed further when new areas were planted with citrus trees. Citrus concentrates accounted for 15.1% of total exports in 2009; nearly all the citrus fruit grown is processed for export. In the late 2000s the Belize Citrus Growers' Association (BCGA) had 1,000 members, mostly in the Stann Creek valley and in central and southern Belize, of whom the 65 largest with more than 40 ha accounted for three-quarters of total production. A Barbados beverage company, Banks Holdings Ltd, acquired a 47% stake in the processing company Citrus Products of Belize Ltd in 2007, following which a major investment programme has upgraded processing, packaging and by-product technology. New borrowing resulted in a financial loss for the year to September 2009, with no dividend paid to the BCGA, which led to a bitter dispute between the BCGA and Citrus Products of Belize over board membership and company policy, a dispute that remained unresolved at mid-2010.

Bananas are grown mainly by small and medium farms of 40 ha–200 ha in southern Belize, with sales and marketing co-ordinated by the Banana Growers' Association. Bananas accounted for 13.7% of exports in 2009, with most sold to the EU under preferential marketing arrangements. However, the degree of protection has been substantially reduced since the 1990s and the remaining tariff advantage was to be reduced further by 2016. Costs were higher than those of Latin American producers, but lower than those of the Caribbean islands, and the future of the industry was uncertain. The industry has suffered hurricane damage, and from an outbreak of Sigatoka disease in 2006, but production rose by 26% in 2008 as the industry recovered, and remained relatively stable in 2009; in the latter year banana exports totalled 80,424 metric tons.

The other significant export crop is papaya, which is grown mainly by large farms in northern Belize for the US market, and accounted for 4.5% of exports in 2009. The industry suffered badly from Hurricane Dean in 2007, which destroyed a large part of the crop; production declined further in 2008 and 2009. Traditionally the crops grown for the local market include corn, sorghum, rice and beans.

The fishing sector expanded rapidly in the 1990s when shrimp-farming began in earnest, supplementing more traditional activities such as offshore fishing for lobster and conch, but after peaking at 5% of GDP in 2005, fisheries output represented only 2.8% of GDP in 2009. Low prices, disease outbreaks and the high cost of intensifying production techniques contributed to a decline in farmed shrimp, while the capture of wild marine shrimp also declined, reflecting the over-exploitation of shrimp fishing grounds in southern Belize and repeated hurricane damage to marine habitats. Fishing and fish-processing employed just over 2,000 people in 2006 (2% of the labour force), with most marine commercial fishers organized in marketing and processing co-operatives. After contracting sharply in 2005–07, shrimp output stabilized at a lower level, and the negative effect on this sector was partly offset by an expansion in the production of cobia and tilapia fish for the export market. Marine products accounted for 9.3% of total exports in 2009.

Forestry lost its role as the leading sector of the Belizean economy decades ago, and by 2006 its demise was reflected in the fact that the industry employed just 733 people. The sector's contribution to GDP in 2007 was a mere 0.5%.

MANUFACTURING AND CONSTRUCTION

The manufacturing sector is small, and accounted for an estimated 12.5% of GDP in 2008 (excluding petroleum extraction, which is grouped statistically with manufacturing). The major activities are the processing of primary products, principally sugar, citrus fruit and shrimp, and food-processing for the domestic market, as well as production of consumer products such as beer (Belikin) and soft drinks. There was until January 2008 a single US-owned company, Williamson Industries, producing work-wear for export. This benefited from trade concessions under the Caribbean Basin Initiative, but could not survive increased competition from the People's Republic of China with the end of the Multi-Fibre Arrangement in 2005.

Construction accounted for 5.4% of GDP in 2009. Major projects in progress in that year included the hydroelectric dams and associated power plant at Vaca Falls on the Macal river, and the Belcogen co-generation plant at the Tower Hill sugar factory. Both involved Chinese construction companies, in spite of the close political and diplomatic relationship between Belize and Taiwan. Both private and public sector construction have suffered in recent years from depressed demand, although some aid-financed public sector construction and infrastructure projects have moved forward.

PETROLEUM EXTRACTION

A small firm, Belize Natural Energy Ltd (BNE), struck petroleum in the Spanish Lookout field, some 55 km north-west of the capital, Belmopan, in 2005. This followed 50 years of intermittent exploration by small local and overseas companies. In 2006—the first year of production—the volume of petroleum extracted reached 811,000 barrels, and the boost from oil production added almost 4% to GDP in 2006–07, accounting for most of the overall cumulative GDP growth of 5.9% over the two years. Production rose to 1.61m. barrels in 2009, but output from the field was expected to decline gradually to 284,000 barrels in 2019, as reserves were depleted. However, BNE discovered a smaller field at Never Delay in the Cayo District, and this was declared commercial in 2009. At mid-2010 BNE and other companies had been granted further exploration and production licences, onshore and offshore, and enjoyed some promising prospects. However, there was opposition to offshore drilling from influential non-governmental organizations, and from the People's United Party (PUP), which issued most of the offshore licences prior to being ousted from government by the United Democratic Party (UDP) in the 2008 legislative election (see History). All of Belize's oil is exported, as there is no local refinery; oil accounted for 25% of exports in 2009, down from 39% in 2008 as a result of lower international oil prices. The petroleum industry has been an important source of revenue for a cash-strapped administration since 2006, but tax mechanisms have been a continuing source of dispute with BNE. A windfall tax on oil profits was enacted in 2009, but would come into effect only with prices over US $90 per barrel, while proposals for an oil revenue investment fund have not been followed through.

ENERGY AND INFRASTRUCTURE

Despite the recent petroleum discovery, the lack of any refining capacity means that all fossil fuels are imported; fuels accounted for 15% of imports in 2008. Easing the burden to some extent, Belize signed up in June 2006 to Venezuela's Petrocaribe initiative, a deal under which Venezuela supplies oil to Belize (and other Caribbean countries) on preferential terms, with a proportion of purchases financed by low-interest loans.

BEL, the privatized electricity supplier, is 70% owned by a Canadian company, Fortis, and regulated by the Public Utilities Commission, with which it has had frequent disputes over rates and charges, which are, however, the second lowest among the members of the Caribbean Community and Common Market (CARICOM), after Trinidad and Tobago's. With peak demand of 74 MW in 2009, BEL had three generation plants, but bought much of its supply from Mexico's national power company, the Comisión Federal de Electricidad; electricity purchases accounted for 2.9% of Belize's total imports in 2009. Reducing dependence on fossil fuels and on imports, another Fortis company, the Belize Electric Company Ltd (BECOL), has since 2000 built two hydroelectric plants at Mollejón and Chalillo on the Macal river, despite vigorous environmental objections. These provided about 25% of the nation's electricity supply—depending on water levels—and a third plant at Vaca Falls was under construction in 2010. BEL also had a 15-year contract with an independent power producer, Hydro Maya, which supplied 3 MW, purchased 10 MW from Belize Aquaculture in the south of the country, and intended to buy 9 MW at peak season from BSI when performance at its Belcogen plant had improved. Completion of the Vaca and Belcogen projects would provide an additional 30 MW, ending the need for imports from Mexico in normal circumstances. In 2009 electricity and water supply accounted for 5.4% of GDP.

Belize has four major roads, connecting the former capital, Belize City, with the two official crossings on the Belize–Mexico border, and the one with Guatemala, and another linking with southern Belize. Regular bus services operate to and from all main towns. The main airport, the Philip S. W. Goldson International Airport, is situated 16 km from Belize City. During 2006 work began on the expansion of the international airport by extending the runway and building a new four-lane airport road. Upon completion, the 7,300 ft runway will be able to accommodate European Airbus and Boeing 767 transatlantic aircraft with a capacity of 200–300 passengers. Domestic air services provide connections to all the main towns and to four of the offshore islands. A modern weather radar system, part of the World Meteorological Network, gives early warning of approaching hurricanes. The main port, which is capable of handling containerized shipping, is in Belize City. The second largest port, Commerce Bight, just south of Dangriga, has recently been improved to accommodate the medium-sized vessels required to handle increased exports of bananas and citrus products. Both are operated by Port of Belize Ltd, which was privatized in 2002.

Belize was among the first Central American countries to privatize its national telecoms company in 1998–92, and the monopoly held by Belize Telecommunications Ltd (BTL) ended formally in 2002. The current successor company, Belize Telemedia Ltd, had competition from a mobile start-up company, SpeedNet Ltd, which began operations in 2004, but the two companies appeared to have been in allied ownership, with both companies reportedly possessing indirect links to the billionaire businessman Lord Michael Ashcroft. BTL's ownership history since privatization has been complex, and subject to a convoluted series of legal disputes, involving at times the Public Utilities Commission, Lord Ashcroft, the Government, and Robert Prosser, an entrepreneur based in the US Virgin Islands. Matters were complicated by large government-guaranteed debts incurred by a failed internet start-up company, Intelco. In 2008–09 BTL was in dispute with the Government over a 2005 'accommodation agreement' negotiated in secret by the former Musa administration, under which BTL claims tax privileges and a 14% guaranteed return on investment; the Government, meanwhile, increased the rate of business taxation on telephone companies from 19% to 24.5% of gross sales revenue in December 2008. With legal proceedings over these and other issues in progress, BTL was nationalized in August 2009, leading to further complex disputes regarding compensation and other issues. Meanwhile, Telemedia had in 2008 extended its interests to television, acquiring a controlling stake in one of the two national networks, Channel 5 Belize, which was excluded from the 2009 nationalization. According to the World Bank, in 2006 51% of the population subscribed to fixed-line or mobile services, while 12% used the internet. In 2008 there were 31,100 fixed lines in use, and 160,000 mobile phone subscribers, according to the International Telecommunication Union.

TOURISM AND ENVIRONMENT

The tourism industry began to expand substantially in the 1980s, and it has since overtaken agricultural production as the most important source of foreign exchange for the Belizean economy. In 2009 tourism earnings of BZ $431m. were equivalent in value to 88% of domestic exports, and to 16% GDP. The number of hotel rooms increased from 3,708 in 1995 to 5,789 in 2006. This success is based on the appeal of a combination of factors: the climate, the second longest barrier reef in the world, numerous islands, excellent fishing and safe waters, extensive undeveloped rainforest areas, and important Mayan ruins. The authorities have encouraged controlled development, aware of the danger of damaging the country's ecological balance, and Belize has developed a reputation for eco-tourism. The number of stop-over visitors rose steadily to a peak of 251,422 in 2007, but declined thereafter, falling back to 232,373 in 2009, owing to weak international demand; of these, 60% were from the USA, 7% from Canada, and 13% from Europe. With the opening of a cruise ship facility in Belize City, cruise passenger numbers increased from 48,116 in 2001 to a peak of 851,436 in 2004. However, cruise traffic has since fluctuated, to 705,219 in 2009, as cruise lines again shifted their itineraries. Proposals for new cruise port facilities have been under consideration since 2004, but were in abeyance in 2010. In 2009 hotels and restaurants accounted for 4.0% of GDP, and in 2006 they provided just under 14,000 jobs, meaning that tourism retained its position as the country's fourth largest employer.

Belize is one of the world's most biologically diverse nations, with the integrity of its natural resources still very much intact. With only 333,200 people inhabiting 22,965 sq km (8,867 sq miles), the population density, at 14.5 per sq km, is the lowest in Central America and one of the lowest in the world. In recent decades, as tourism has emerged as one of the main motors of the economy, the authorities have led efforts to balance development with conservation of the country's natural resources: 46% of the land is under some form of legally protected status, and there is an extensive network of marine conservation areas. The Protected Areas Conservation Trust Act was adopted in 1996, introducing a small conservation fee to be paid by each tourist on departure from the country, and a 20% commission from cruise ship passenger fees. The Trust issues grants for the conservation, preservation, enhancement and management of Belize's natural resources and protected areas. Protecting the country's natural and historical environment will be critical to the sustainability of Belize's tourism industry, and there is concern about both the number of tourists, who may damage some of the country's main attractions, and the recent discovery of petroleum in the Cayo District, which has triggered interest in Belize on the part of other petroleum companies engaged in exploration activities within protected marine and forest areas. There are also concerns that the low-lying coastal zone, offshore islands and barrier reef are vulnerable to rising sea levels and any increase in hurricane activity.

TRADE AND BALANCE OF PAYMENTS

While tourism and other services, as well as remittances, are increasingly important, the economy continues to be characterized by a small productive base, and like any other small country relies heavily on foreign trade. In recent years the rising cost of imports—particularly fuel—has meant that the merchandise trade deficit has widened. At the same time, there were increased imports of capital goods for electricity generation, telecommunications and the oil industry, while domestic exports increased more slowly in spite of growing oil sales. In 2008 the merchandise trade deficit was more than 23% of GDP. Major domestic exports were agricultural products (sugar, bananas, citrus and papayas) at 47%, fisheries products (8%) and oil (37%). Sales of imported goods from free zones, principally at Corozal on the Mexican border, brought net earnings equivalent to 8% of domestic exports. The merchandise trade deficit was covered in part by net earnings from tourism and other services, and by remittances from overseas Belizeans, with a current account deficit in 2008 of 11% of GDP. This was covered by a capital account surplus, with substantial foreign direct investment in oil, real estate, tourism and other sectors, as well as official assistance inflows.

In 2008 the USA was the market for 42% of exports, principally shrimp and marine products, papaya, and oil. The United Kingdom took 20% of exports, mainly sugar and bananas, with a further 7% to other European countries. Exports to Central America, mainly oil, accounted for 21%, with 5% to CARICOM members, including citrus products. The USA was also the main source of imports, at 34%, with 19% from Central America and a further 9% from Mexico. Only 1.5% of imports were sourced from the United Kingdom, and 4% from mainland Europe.

PUBLIC FINANCES

During the first years of the 21st century Belize had extremely high levels of external debt, low reserves, and a high current account deficit, making it vulnerable to external shocks. This resulted from budget deficits running as high as 11.3% of GDP in 2001, and averaging 7.5% in 2002–06, with a high level of public borrowing, some of it on onerous commercial terms, and major unannounced tax concessions and loan guarantees granted to favoured private sector companies. The impact of years of expansionary policies, driven by increased government spending and borrowing, was confirmed when in July 2006 the Government announced it would not be able to meet its repayment obligations to external creditors. Efforts to restructure the country's external debt of almost US $1,000m. were completed in February 2007. Holders of eligible debt exchanged their claims for a new 22-year 'superbond', with interest initially reduced to 4.25%. However, this would increase to 6.0% from 2010, and to 8.5% from 2012, with twice yearly principal repayments running for 10 years from 2019 to 2029.

Despite the successful debt-restructuring, the debt burden remains high and was equivalent to 87% of GDP in 2009, although this was down from more than 100% in 2004. External reserves remain low, although they had risen to 4.2 months of import cover in 2009, from only 0.6 months in 2005.

From 2007 revenues were enhanced by income from the newly discovered Spanish Lookout oilfield, and under international and domestic pressure the deficit was reined back to 1.9% of GDP in 2006 and 1.2% in 2007. Following the election of the UDP Government in 2008, the overall fiscal balance moved to a surplus of 1.5% of GDP, the first positive fiscal balance for 20 years, in spite of an increase in capital spending on externally funded projects. This resulted in part from strong oil revenues in the first three quarters. In both 2007 and 2008 the fiscal balance benefited from substantial grants from Venezuela, the Republic of China (Taiwan) and other sources, which in 2008 were equivalent to 2.0% of GDP, while external interest payments declined as a result of the 2007 debt-restructuring. The fiscal balance also benefited in 2008 from the strong stance taken by the UDP Government in relation to disputed tax payments by major private sector companies, which was upheld at this time by the courts but would be subject to reverse in the event of an adverse ruling at final appeal. Despite the improved fiscal balance, the economy suffered in 2008 from a sharp downturn in international tourism, high international commodity prices, severe flood damage in June and October, and weak performance by most major export sectors, while grant inflows fell from 3.3% of GDP in 2007 to 1.3% of GDP in 2009. As a result, the fiscal balance deteriorated sharply to a 2.8% deficit in 2009, and the budget for 2010/11 increased value-added tax from 10.0% to 12.5%, and also raised the tax rates on oil and electricity production. In spite of these measures, the IMF in 2010 expected the fiscal deficit to increase further in 2010/11, and argued for spending restraint and pension reform. The Fund also expressed concern regarding an increase in non-performing loans within the banking system, stressing the need for vigilant offshore and domestic bank supervision.

OUTLOOK

Belize has potential for further development in commercial agriculture and tourism, while petroleum exploration is in progress and has fair prospects of success. Prices declined by 1.1% in 2009 as a result of lower fuel costs. The continuing move towards transparency and improved public finances is expected to bring positive results, while hydroelectric and co-generation plants will reduce dependence on fossil fuels. However, there are concerns over the erosion and removal of EU trade preferences for sugar and bananas, while more broadly the economy remains vulnerable to fluctuations in the price of its major export commodities, to weakness in international demand for tourism, and to hurricanes. More immediately, the Government remains in conflict with major local and foreign-owned companies over taxation, compensation for nationalization and other matters, and an adverse court ruling on final appeal would seriously affect public finances. With interest payments on the 'superbond' increasing from 2010 and due to increase again from 2012, the IMF in 2009 proposed a significant but attainable fiscal adjustment to produce a 4% primary surplus by 2011 in order to bring down the high debt level inherited from the former PUP Government; however, at mid-2010 this appeared to be an overly ambitious target.

Statistical Survey

Sources (unless otherwise stated): Statistical Institute of Belize, 1902 Constitution Drive, Belmopan; tel. 822-2207; internet www.statisticsbelize.org.bz; Central Bank of Belize, Gabourel Lane, POB 852, Belize City; tel. 223-6194; fax 223-6226; e-mail cenbank@btl.net; internet www.centralbank.org.bz.

AREA AND POPULATION

Area: 22,965 sq km (8,867 sq miles).

Population: 189,774 at census of 12 May 1991; 240,204 (males 121,278, females 118,926) at census of 12 May 2000; 333,200 (males 166,500, females 166,700) at mid-2009 (official estimate).

Density (mid-2009): 14.5 per sq km.

Population by Age and Sex (official estimates at mid-2009): *0–14:* 122,700 (males 62,600, females 60,100); *15–64:* 193,500 (males 95,100, females 98,400); *65 and over:* 17,000 (males 8,800, females 8,200); *Total* 333,200 (males 166,500, females 166,700).

Districts (official estimates at mid-2009): Belize 100,100; Cayo 80,800; Orange Walk 49,500; Corozal 37,300; Stann Creek 34,500; Toledo 31,000.

Principal Towns (official estimates at mid-2009): Belize City (former capital) 66,700; San Ignacio/Santa Elena 19,900; Belmopan (capital) 20,000; Orange Walk 16,700; Dangriga (fmrly Stann Creek) 12,500; San Pedro 12,900; Corozal 9,400; Benque Viejo 9,300; Punta Gorda 5,500.

Births, Marriages and Deaths (provisional figures, 2003): Registered live births 7,440 (birth rate 27.3 per 1,000); Registered marriages 1,713 (marriage rate 6.3 per 1,000); Registered deaths 1,277 (death rate 4.7 per 1,000). *2005* (provisional): Registered live births 8,396; Registered deaths 1,369 (Source: UN, *Population and Vital Statistics Report*).

Life Expectancy (years at birth, WHO estimates): 72 (males 69; females 76) in 2008. Source: WHO, *World Health Statistics*.

Economically Active Population (April 2006): Agriculture 18,406; Forestry 733; Fishing 2,070; Mining and quarrying 434; Manufacturing 7,363; Electricity, gas and water 879; Construction 7,390; Wholesale and retail trade and repairs 16,722; Tourism (incl. restaurants and hotels) 13,981; Transport, storage and communications 4,352; Financial intermediation 1,800; Real estate, renting and business activities 2,431; General government services 9,345; Community, social and personal services 16,041; Other 285; *Total employed* 102,233. *Total labour force* (persons aged 14 years and over, September 2009): 144,363 (employed 126,188, unemployed 18,176).

HEALTH AND WELFARE

Key Indicators

Total Fertility Rate (children per woman, 2008): 2.9.

Under-5 Mortality Rate (per 1,000 live births, 2008): 19.

HIV/AIDS (% of persons aged 15–49, 2007): 2.1.

Physicians (per 1,000 head, 2000): 1.1.

Hospital Beds (per 1,000 head, 2006): 1.3.

Health Expenditure (2007): US $ per head (PPP): 279.

Health Expenditure (2007): % of GDP: 4.0.

Health Expenditure (2007): public (% of total): 65.1.

Access to Water (% of persons, 2008): 99.

Access to Sanitation (% of persons, 2008): 90.

Total Carbon Dioxide Emissions ('000 metric tons, 2006): 817.1.

Carbon Dioxide Emissions Per Head (metric tons, 2006): 2.7.

Human Development Index (2007): ranking: 93.

Human Development Index (2007): value: 0.772.

For sources and definitions, see explanatory note on p. vi.

AGRICULTURE, ETC.

Principal Crops ('000 metric tons, 2008): Rice, paddy 11.8; Maize 37.1; Sorghum 10.7; Sugar cane 980.1; Beans, dry 3.7; Fresh vegetables 3.6 (FAO estimate); Bananas 68.1; Plantains 3.0; Oranges 239.5; Grapefruit and pomelos 61.0; Papayas 27.0. *Aggregate Production* ('000 metric tons, may include official, semi-official or estimated data): Vegetables (incl. melons) 9.4; Fruits (excl. melons) 403.3.

Livestock ('000 head, year ending September 2008): Horses 5 (FAO estimate); Cattle 81; Pigs 13; Sheep 10; Chickens 1,670 (FAO estimate).

Livestock Products ('000 metric tons, 2008): Cattle meat 1.7; Chicken meat 12.6; Pig meat 1.1; Cows' milk 2.9; Hen eggs 2.1.

Forestry (2008): *Roundwood Removals* ('000 cubic metres, excl. bark): Sawlogs, veneer logs and logs for sleepers 41; Fuel wood 674 (FAO estimate); Total 715. *Sawnwood Production* ('000 cubic metres, incl. railway sleepers, FAO estimates): Coniferous (softwood) 5; Broadleaved (hardwood) 30; Total 35.

Fishing ('000 metric tons, live weight, 2008): Capture 4.6 (Albacore 0.4; Caribbean spiny lobster 0.6; Stromboid conchs 1.9; Yellowfin tuna 1.3); Aquaculture 9.5 (White leg shrimp 7.3—FAO estimate); Total catch 14.2 (FAO estimate).

Source: FAO.

INDUSTRY

Production (2005, unless otherwise indicated): Raw sugar 100,435 long tons; Molasses 37,074 long tons; Cigarettes 78 million; Beer 1,891,000 gallons; Batteries 6,000; Flour 26,959,000 lb; Fertilizers 26,874,000 short tons; Garments 611,900 items; Soft drinks 4,929,000 gallons; Citrus concentrates 2,973,000 gallons (2004); Single strength juices 2,102,000 gallons (2004). Source: IMF, *Belize: Selected Issues and Statistical Appendix* (October 2006).

FINANCE

Currency and Exchange Rates: 100 cents = 1 Belizean dollar (BZ $). *Sterling, US Dollar and Euro Equivalents* (31 May 2010): £1 sterling = BZ $2.916; US $1 = BZ $2.000; €1 = BZ $2.477; BZ $100 = £34.29 = US $50.00 = €40.37. *Exchange rate*: Fixed at US $1 = BZ $2.000 since May 1976.

Budget (BZ $ million, year ending 31 March 2009, draft budget): *Revenue*: Taxation 628.8 (Taxes on income and profits 225.8; Taxes on property 7.1; Taxes on goods and services 244.4; International trade and transactions 151.6); Other current revenue 92.2; Capital revenue 8.5; Total 729.5, excl. grants (87.4). *Expenditure*: Current expenditure 649.6 (Personal emoluments 262.9; Pensions 39.9; Goods and services 237.9; Debt service 108.9); Capital expenditure 175.2; Total 824.8.

International Reserves (US $ million at 31 December 2009): IMF special drawing rights 31.62; Reserve position in the IMF 6.64; Foreign exchange 175.42; Total 213.68. Source: IMF, *International Financial Statistics*.

Money Supply (BZ $ million at 31 December 2009): Currency outside depository corporations 154.52; Transferable deposits 558.77; Other deposits 1,379.89; *Broad money* 2,093.17. Source: IMF, *International Financial Statistics*.

Cost of Living (Consumer Price Index; base: 2005 = 100): All items 106.6 in 2007; 113.5 in 2008; 112.2 in 2009. Source: IMF, *International Financial Statistics*.

Expenditure on the Gross Domestic Product (BZ $ million at current prices, 2008): Government final consumption expenditure 430.4; Private final consumption expenditure 1,758.8; Increase in stocks 48.2; Gross fixed capital formation 691.8; *Gross domestic expenditure* 2,929.2; Exports of goods and services 1,687.1; *Less* Imports of goods and services 1,903.4; Statistical discrepancy 4.6; *GDP at market prices* 2,717.4.

Gross Domestic Product by Economic Activity (BZ $ million at current prices, 2008): Agriculture and forestry 228.8; Fishing 59.1; Mining and quarrying 13.5; Manufacturing 339.2; Electricity and water 61.0; Construction 124.1; Wholesale and retail trade, repairs 400.7; Restaurants and hotels 117.4; Transport, storage and communications 283.4; Financial intermediation 205.3; Real estate, renting and business services 196.9; Community, social and personal services 177.0; General government services 277.6; *Sub-total* 2,484.0; Taxes, less subsidies, on products 353.6; *Less* Financial intermediation services indirectly measured 120.2; *GDP at market prices* 2,717.4.

Balance of Payments (US $ million, 2008): Exports of goods f.o.b. 471.9; Imports of goods f.o.b. –788.1; *Trade balance* –316.2; Exports of services 386.5; Imports of services –169.6; *Balance on goods and services* –99.3; Other income received 5.9; Other income paid –162.5; *Balance on goods, services and income* –255.9; Current transfers (net)111.6; *Current balance* –144.4; Capital account (net) 9.0; Financial account (net) 225.9; Net errors and omissions –32.4; *Overall balance* 58.2 (Source: IMF, *International Financial Statistics*).

EXTERNAL TRADE

Principal Commodities (BZ $ million, 2009): *Imports c.i.f.:* Food and live animals 156.5; Mineral fuels and lubricants 209.5; Chemicals and related products 125.2; Manufactured goods 178.1; Miscellaneous manufactured articles 94.8; Machinery and transport equipment 266.9; Commercial free zone 156.5; Export processing zone 104.9; Total (incl. others) 1,336.4. *Exports f.o.b.:* Orange concentrate 84.9; Marine products (excl. aquarium fish) 49.4; Sugar 89.1; Bananas 66.7; Papaya 21.8; Grapefruit concentrate 13.9; Total (incl. others) 501.2.

Principal Trading Partners (BZ $ million, 2009): *Imports c.i.f.:* USA 464.2; Mexico 136.9; United Kingdom 18.9; Canada 12.2; Total (incl. others) 1,336.4. *Exports f.o.b.* (excl. re-exports): USA 162.5; United Kingdom 158.9; Mexico 11.1; Total (incl. others) 501.2.

TRANSPORT

Road Traffic (vehicles in use, 1998): Passenger cars 9,929; Buses and coaches 416; Lorries and vans 11,339; Motorcycles and mopeds 270. *2007* (vehicles in use): Total vehicles 54,225. Source: IRF, *World Road Statistics*.

Shipping (sea-borne freight traffic, '000 metric tons, 1996): Goods loaded 255.4; Goods unloaded 277.1. *Merchant Fleet* (vessels registered at 31 December 2008): Number of vessels 418; Total displacement 1,214,594 grt (Source: Lloyd's Register-Fairplay, *World Fleet Statistics*).

Civil Aviation (2002): Passenger arrivals 174,038. Source: IMF, *Belize: Statistical Appendix* (April 2004).

TOURISM

Tourist Arrivals: 903,240 (cruise ship passengers 655,931, stop-over visitors 247,309) in 2006 (preliminary); 875,550 (cruise ship passengers 624,128, stop-over visitors 251,422) in 2007; 842,396 (cruise ship passengers 597,370, stop-over visitors 245,026) in 2008 (preliminary).

Tourism Receipts (US $ million): 174.7 in 2005; 252.9 in 2006; 292.7 in 2007 (preliminary).

Source: Belize Tourism Board.

COMMUNICATIONS MEDIA

Radio Receivers (1997): 133,000 in use*.

Television Receivers (2000): 44,000 in use†.

Telephones (2009): 31,200 main lines in use†.

Mobile Cellular Telephones (2009): 161,800 subscribers†.

Personal Computers (2007): 45,000 (144.5 per 1,000 persons) in use†.

Internet Users (2009): 36,000†.

Broadband Subscribers (2009): 8,000†.

Book Production (1996): 107 titles*.

Non-daily Newspapers (1996): 10 (circulation 80,000)*.

* Source: UNESCO, *Statistical Yearbook*.

† Source: International Telecommunication Union.

EDUCATION

Pre-primary (2007/08, unless otherwise indicated): 142 schools (2005/06), 348 teachers, 5,801 students.

Primary (2007/08, unless otherwise indicated): 288 schools (2005/06), 2,299 teachers, 51,994 students.

Secondary (2005/06, unless otherwise indicated): 50 schools (2005/06), 1,835 teachers, 31,120 students.

Higher (1997/98, unless otherwise indicated): 12 institutions, 228 teachers, 3,581 students (2008/09).

Pupil-teacher Ratio (primary education, UNESCO estimate): 22.6 in 2007/08.

Source: fmr Ministry of Education, Youth and Sports; UNESCO Institute for Statistics.

Adult Literacy Rate (UNESCO estimates): 76.9% (males 77.1%; females 76.7%) in 2003. Source: UN Development Programme, *Human Development Report*.

Directory

The Constitution

The Constitution came into effect at the independence of Belize on 21 September 1981. Its main provisions are summarized below:

FUNDAMENTAL RIGHTS AND FREEDOMS

Regardless of race, place of origin, political opinions, colour, creed or sex, but subject to respect for the rights and freedoms of others and for the public interest, every person in Belize is entitled to the rights of life, liberty, security of the person, and the protection of the law. Freedom of movement, of conscience, of expression, of assembly and of association, and the right to work are guaranteed, and the inviolability of family life, personal privacy, home and other property, and human dignity is upheld. Protection is afforded from discrimination on the grounds of race, sex, etc., and from slavery, forced labour and inhuman treatment.

CITIZENSHIP

All persons born in Belize before independence who, immediately prior to independence, were citizens of the United Kingdom and Colonies automatically become citizens of Belize. All persons born outside the country having a husband, parent or grandparent in possession of Belizean citizenship automatically acquire citizenship, as do those born in the country after independence. Provision is made such that persons who do not automatically become citizens of Belize may be registered as such. (Belizean citizenship was also offered, under the Belize Loans Act 1986, in exchange for interest-free loans of US $25,000 with a 10-year maturity. The scheme was officially ended in June 1994, following sustained criticism of alleged corruption on the part of officials. A revised economic citizenship programme, offering citizenship in return for a minimum investment of US $75,000, received government approval in early 1995, but was ended in 2002.)

THE GOVERNOR-GENERAL

The British monarch, as Head of State, is represented in Belize by a Governor-General, a Belizean national.

Belize Advisory Council

The Council consists of not less than six people 'of integrity and high national standing', appointed by the Governor-General for up to 10 years upon the advice of the Prime Minister. The Leader of the Opposition must concur with the appointment of two members and be consulted about the remainder. The Council exists to advise the Governor-General, particularly in the exercise of the prerogative of mercy, and to convene as a tribunal to consider the removal from office of certain senior public servants and judges.

THE EXECUTIVE

Executive authority is vested in the British monarch and exercised by the Governor-General. The Governor-General appoints as Prime Minister that member of the House of Representatives who, in the Governor-General's view, is best able to command the support of the majority of the members of the House, and appoints a Deputy Prime Minister and other Ministers on the advice of the Prime Minister. The Governor-General may remove the Prime Minister from office if a resolution of no confidence is approved by the House and the Prime Minister does not, within seven days, either resign or advise the Governor-General to dissolve the National Assembly. The Cabinet consists of the Prime Minister and other Ministers.

The Leader of the Opposition is appointed by the Governor-General as that member of the House who, in the Governor-General's view, is best able to command the support of a majority of the members of the House who do not support the Government.

THE LEGISLATURE

The Legislature consists of a National Assembly comprising two chambers: the Senate, with 12 nominated members; and the House of Representatives, with 31 elected members. The Assembly's normal term is five years. An amendment to the Constitution in January 2002 expanded the appointed Senate to 12 persons from eight. Senators are appointed by the Governor-General: six on the advice of the Prime Minister; three on the advice of the Leader of the Opposition or on the advice of persons selected by the Governor-General; and one each on the advice of the Belize Council of Churches together with the Evangelical Association of Churches, the Belize Chamber of Commerce and Industry and the Belize Better Business Bureau, and the National Trade Union Congress in agreement with the Civil Society Steering Committee. If any person who is not a Senator is elected to be President of the Senate, he or she shall be an ex-officio Senator in addition to the 12 nominees.

Each constituency returns one Representative to the House, who is directly elected in accordance with the Constitution.

If a person who is not a member of the House is elected to be Speaker of the House, he or she shall be an ex-officio member in addition to the 31 members directly elected. Every citizen older than 18 years is eligible to vote. The National Assembly may alter any of the provisions of the Constitution.

The Government

HEAD OF STATE

Queen: HM Queen ELIZABETH II.

Governor-General: Sir COLVILLE YOUNG (appointed 17 November 1993).

THE CABINET
(July 2010)

The Government is formed by the United Democratic Party.

Prime Minister and Minister of Finance: DEAN O. BARROW.

Deputy Prime Minister and Minister of Natural Resources and the Environment: GASPAR VEGA.

Minister of Foreign Affairs and Foreign Trade: WILFRED ELRINGTON.

Minister of Economic Development, Commerce, Industry and Consumer Protection: ERWIN CONTRERAS.

Minister of Education and Youth: PATRICK FABER.

Minister of Defence: CARLOS PERDOMO.

Minister of Housing and Urban Development: MICHAEL FINNEGAN.

Minister of Works: ANTHONY (BOOTS) MARTINEZ.

Minister of Tourism, Civil Aviation and Culture: MANUEL HEREDIA, Jr.

Minister of Health: PABLO MARIN.

Minister of Labour, Local Government and Rural Development: GABRIEL MARTINEZ.

Minister of the Public Service, Governance Improvement, Elections and Boundaries and Sports: JOHN SALDIVAR.

Minister of Agriculture and Fisheries: RENE MONTERO.

Minister of Transport, Communications and National Emergency Management: MELVIN HULSE.

Minister of Human Development and Social Transformation: PETER EDEN MARTINEZ.

Minister of Public Utilities, Information and Broadcasting: ELVIN PENNER.

Ministry of Police and Public Security: DOUGLAS SINGH.

Attorney-General: BERNARD PITTS.

MINISTRIES

Office of the Prime Minister and Ministry of Finance: New Administration Bldg, Belmopan; tel. 822-2345; fax 822-0898; e-mail cabinet@btl.net; internet www.mof.gov.bz (finance).

Ministry of Agriculture and Fisheries: West Block Bldg, 2nd Floor, Belmopan; tel. 822-2241; fax 822-2409; e-mail minaf@btl.net; internet www.agriculture.gov.bz.

Ministry of the Attorney-General: General Office, Belmopan; tel. 822-2504; fax 822-3390; internet www.belizelaw.org.

Ministry of Defence: Belmopan.

Ministry of Economic Development, Commerce, Industry and Consumer Protection: Belmopan; tel. 822-2526; fax 822-3673; e-mail econdev@btl.net.

Ministry of Education and Youth: West Block Bldg, Belmopan; tel. 822-2380; fax 822-3389; e-mail moeducation.moes@gmail.com; internet www.moes.gov.bz.

Ministry of Foreign Affairs and Foreign Trade: NEMO Bldg, POB 174, Belmopan; tel. 822-2167; fax 822-2854; e-mail belizemfa@btl.net; internet www.mfa.gov.bz (foreign affairs); www.foreigntrade.gov.bz (foreign trade).

Ministry of Health: East Block Bldg, Independence Plaza, Belmopan; tel. 822-2068; fax 822-2942; e-mail seniorsecretary@health.gov.bz; internet health.gov.bz/moh.

Ministry of Housing and Urban Development: Curl Thompson Bldg, Belmopan; tel. 822-1039; fax 822-3337; e-mail info@housing.gov.bz.

Ministry of Human Development and Social Transformation: West Block, Independence Plaza, Belmopan; tel. 822-2161; fax 822-3175; e-mail mhd@btl.net.

Ministry of Labour, Local Government and Rural Development: Belmopan; tel. 822-2297; fax 822-0156; e-mail secretary@labour.gov.bz.

Ministry of Natural Resources and the Environment: Market Sq., Belmopan; tel. 822-2226; fax 822-2333; e-mail info@mnrei.gov.bz; internet www.mnrei.gov.bz.

Ministry of Police and Public Security: Curl Thompson Bldg, Belmopan; tel. 822-2817; fax 822-2195; e-mail minofnatsec@mns.gov.bz.

Ministry of the Public Service, Governance Improvement, Elections and Boundaries and Sports: Belmopan; tel. 822-3765; fax 822-2206; e-mail ceo@mps.gov.bz.

Ministry of Public Utilities, Information and Broadcasting: General Office, Belmopan; tel. 822-3336; fax 822-0433.

Ministry of Tourism, Civil Aviation and Culture: General Office, Belmopan; tel. 227-2801; fax 227-2810; e-mail dcabelize@btl.net; internet www.belizetourism.org (tourism); www.nichbelize.org (culture).

Ministry of Transport, Communications and National Emergency Management: Belmopan; tel. 822-2692; fax 822-3317; e-mail belizetransport@yahoo.com; internet www.nemo.bz (emergency management).

Ministry of Works: New 2 Power Lane, Belmopan; tel. 822-2136; fax 822-3282; e-mail works@btl.net.

Legislature

NATIONAL ASSEMBLY

The Senate

President: ANDREA GILL.

There are 12 nominated members in addition to the current ex officio President.

House of Representatives

Speaker: EMIL ARGUELLES.

Clerk: HERBERT PANTON.

General Election, 7 February 2008

	Votes cast	% of total	Seats
United Democratic Party (UDP)	66,203	57.0	25
People's United Party (PUP) .	47,624	41.0	6
Others	2,367	2.0	—
Total	116,194	100.0	31

Election Commissions

Elections and Boundaries Commission: Belize City; e-mail electbound@btl.net; internet www.elections.gov.bz; f. 1978; appointed by Governor-Gen; Chair. ALBERTO AUGUST.

Elections and Boundaries Department: Charles Bartlett Hyde Bldg, Mahogany St Extension, POB 913, Belize City; tel. 222-4042; fax 222-4991; e-mail electbound@btl.net; internet www.elections.gov.bz; f. 1989; dept of the Office of the Prime Minister; Chief Elections Officer RUTH MEIGHAN.

Political Organizations

People's National Party (PNP): Belize City; e-mail info@pnpbelize.org; internet www.pnpbelize.org; f. 2007; Leader WIL MAHEIA.

People's United Party (PUP): 3 Queen St, Belize City; tel. 223-2428; fax 223-3476; internet www.pup.org.bz; f. 1950; based on organized labour; publs *The Belize Times*; Leader JOHN BRICEÑO; Chair. FRANCIS FONSECA; Sec.-Gen. HENRY USHER; Deputy Leaders GODFREY SMITH, VILDO MARIN.

United Democratic Party (UDP): South End Bel-China Bridge, POB 1898, Belize City; tel. 227-2576; fax 227-6441; e-mail unitedd@btl.net; internet www.udp.org.bz; f. 1974 by merger of People's Development Movement, Liberal Party and National Independence Party; conservative; Leader DEAN BARROW; Chair. DOUGLAS SINGH.

Diplomatic Representation

EMBASSIES AND HIGH COMMISSION IN BELIZE

Brazil: 12 Floral Park Ave, POB 548, Belmopan; tel. 822-0460; fax 822-0461; e-mail embbrazil@btl.net; internet www.embaixadadobrasilembelize.org; Ambassador ROBERTO PIRES COUTINHO.

China (Taiwan): 20 North Park St, POB 1020, Belize City; tel. 227-8744; fax 223-3082; e-mail embroc@btl.net; internet www.taiwanembassy.org/bz; Ambassador DAVID WU.

Costa Rica: 1 Marigold St, Orchid Garden Area, POB 288, Belmopan; tel. 822-1582; fax 822-1583; e-mail embaticabz@gmail.com; Ambassador EDGAR GARCÍA MIRANDA.

Cuba: 6087 Manatee Dr., Buttonwood Bay, POB 1775, Belize City; tel. 223-5345; fax 223-1105; e-mail embacuba@btl.net; internet embacu.cubaminrex.cu/beliceing; Ambassador MANUEL JAVIER RUBIDO DÍAZ.

El Salvador: 49 Nanche St, POB 215, Belmopan; tel. 823-3404; fax 823-3569; e-mail embasalva@btl.net; Ambassador JULIO MILTON PARADA DOMINGUEZ.

Guatemala: 8 A St, King's Park, POB 1771, Belize City; tel. 223-3150; fax 223-5140; e-mail embbelice@minex.gob.gt; Ambassador MANUEL ARTURO TÉLLEZ MIRALDA.

Honduras: 114 Bella Vista, POB 285, Belize City; tel. 224-5889; fax 223-0562; e-mail embahonbe@yahoo.com; Ambassador SANDRA ROSALES ABELLA.

Mexico: 3 North Ring Rd, Embassy Sq., Belmopan; tel. 822-2480; fax 822-2487; e-mail embamexbze@btl.net; internet www.sre.gob.mx/belice; Ambassador LUÍS MANUEL LÓPEZ MORENO.

Nicaragua: 124 Barrack Rd, Belize City; tel. 223-3868; fax 223-2666; e-mail embanicbelize@btl.net; Ambassador GILDA MARIA BOLT GONZALEZ (resident in El Salvador).

United Kingdom: Embassy Sq., POB 91, Belmopan; tel. 822-2146; fax 822-2761; e-mail brithicom@btl.net; internet ukinbelize.fco.gov.uk; High Commissioner PATRICK ASHWORTH.

USA: Floral Park Rd, POB 286, Belmopan; tel. 822-4011; fax 822-4012; e-mail embbelize@state.gov; internet belize.usembassy.gov; Ambassador VINAI K. THUMMALAPALLY.

Venezuela: 17 Orchid Garden St, POB 49, Belmopan; tel. 822-2384; fax 822-2022; e-mail embaven@btl.net; Chargé d'affaires ALEXANDER YAÑEZ DELEUZE.

Judicial System

Summary Jurisdiction Courts (criminal jurisdiction) and District Courts (civil jurisdiction), presided over by magistrates, are established in each of the six judicial districts. Summary Jurisdiction Courts have a wide jurisdiction in summary offences and a limited jurisdiction in indictable matters. Appeals lie to the Supreme Court, which has jurisdiction corresponding to the English High Court of Justice and where a jury system is in operation. From the Supreme Court further appeals lie to a Court of Appeal, established in 1967, which holds an average of four sessions per year. Since 1 June 2010 final appeals are made to the Caribbean Court of Justice, based in Trinidad and Tobago, rather than to the Privy Council in the United Kingdom.

Court of Appeal: Belize City; tel. 227-2907; internet www.belizelaw.org; Pres. ELLIOTT MOTTLEY; Justices of Appeal MANUEL SOSA, DENYS BARROW, DENNIS MORRISON.

Magistrates' Court: Paslow Bldg, Belize City; tel. 227-7164; Chief Magistrate MARGARET GABB-MACKENZIE.

Supreme Court: Supreme Court Bldg, Belize City; tel. 227-7256; fax 227-0181; e-mail chiefjustice@btl.net; internet www.belizelaw.org/supreme_court/chief_justice.html; Registrar ALDO SALAZAR; Chief Justice Dr ABDULAI OSMAN CONTEH.

Religion

CHRISTIANITY

Most of the population are Christian, the largest denomination being the Roman Catholic Church.

Belize Council of Churches: 149 Allenby St, POB 508, Belize City; tel. 227-7077; f. 1957 as Church World Service Cttee; present name adopted 1984; 9 mem. churches, 4 assoc. bodies; Pres. Rev. LEROY FLOWERS.

The Roman Catholic Church

According to the latest available census figures (2000), some 50% of the population are Roman Catholics. Belize comprises the single diocese of Belize City-Belmopan, suffragan to the archdiocese of Kingston in Jamaica. The Bishop participates in the Antilles Episcopal Conference (whose secretariat is based in Port of Spain, Trinidad and Tobago).

Bishop of Belize City-Belmopan: DORICK MCGOWAN WRIGHT, Bishop's House, 144 North Front St, POB 616, Belize City; tel. 223-2122; fax 223-1922; e-mail episkopos@btl.net.

The Anglican Communion

Anglicans in Belize, accounting for some 5% of the population at the 2000 census, belong to the Church in the Province of the West Indies, comprising eight dioceses. The Archbishop of the Province is the Bishop of the North Eastern Caribbean and Aruba, resident in St John's, Antigua and Barbuda.

Bishop of Belize: Rt Rev. PHILIP S. WRIGHT, Rectory Lane, POB 535, Belize City; tel. 227-3029; fax 227-6898; e-mail bzediocese@btl.net; internet www.belize.anglican.org.

Protestant Churches

According to the 2000 census, some 7% of the population are Pentecostalists, 5% Seventh-day Adventists, 4% Mennonites, 3% Baptists and 3% Methodists.

Mennonite Congregations in Belize: POB 427, Belize City; tel. 823-0137; fax 823-0101; f. 1958; in 2003 there were an estimated 3,575 mems living in 8 Mennonite settlements, the largest of which was Altkolonier Mennonitengemeinde with 1,728 mems; Bishop AARON HARDER.

Methodist Church in the Caribbean and the Americas (Belize/Honduras District) (MCCA): 75 Albert St, POB 212, Belize City; tel. 227-7173; fax 227-5870; f. 1824; c. 1,827 mems; District Pres. Rev. DAVID GOFF.

Other denominations active in the country include the Presbyterians, Moravians, Jehovah's Witnesses, the Church of God, the Nazarene Church, the Assemblies of Brethren and the Salvation Army.

OTHER RELIGIONS

There are also small communities of Hindus (367, according to the census of 2000), Muslims (243 in 2000) and Bahá'ís (205 in 2000), together accounting for less than 1% of the population.

The Press

Amandala: Amandala Press, 3304 Partridge St, POB 15, Belize City; tel. 202-4476; fax 222-4702; e-mail info@amandala.com.bz; internet www.amandala.com.bz; f. 1969; 2 a week; independent; Publr EVAN X. HYDE; Editor RUSSELL VELLOS; circ. 45,000.

Ambergris Today: Pescador Dr., POB 23, San Pedro Town, Ambergris Caye; tel. 226-3462; fax 226-3483; e-mail ambertoday@btl.net; internet www.ambergristoday.com; weekly; independent; Editor DORIAN NUÑEZ.

The Belize Times: 3 Queen St, POB 506, Belize City; tel. 224-5757; fax 223-1940; e-mail belizetime@btl.net; internet www.belizetimes.bz; f. 1956; weekly; party political paper of PUP; Editor-in-Chief MIKE RUDON, Jr; circ. 6,000.

Belize Today: Belize Information Service, East Block, POB 60, Belmopan; tel. 822-2159; fax 822-3242; monthly; official; circ. 17,000.

Government Gazette: Print Belize Ltd, 1 Power Lane, Belmopan; tel. 822-0194; fax 822-3367; e-mail admin@printbze.com; internet www.printbelize.com/content; f. 1871; official; weekly; CEO LAWRENCE J. NICHOLAS.

The Guardian: Ebony St and Bel-China Bridge, POB 1898, Belize City; tel. 207-5346; fax 227-5343; e-mail guardian@btl.net; internet www.guardian.bz; weekly; party political paper of UDP; Editor ALFONSO NOBLE; circ. 5,000.

The Reporter: 147 Allenby St, POB 707, Belize City; tel. 227-2503; fax 227-8278; e-mail editor@belizereporter.bz; internet www.reporter.bz; f. 1967; weekly; Editor ANN MARIE WILLIAMS; circ. 6,500.

The San Pedro Sun: POB 35, San Pedro Town, Ambergris Caye; tel. 226-2070; fax 226-2905; e-mail spsun@sanpedrosun.net; internet www.sanpedrosun.net; f. 1993; weekly; Editors RON SNIFFIN, TAMARA SNIFFIN.

Publishers

Angelus Press Ltd: 10 Queen St, POB 1757, Belize City; tel. 223-5777; fax 227-8825; e-mail angel@btl.net; internet www.angeluspress.com; Gen. Man. AMPARO M. NOBLE.

Cubola Productions: Montserrat Casademunt, 35 Elizabeth St, Benque Viejo del Carmen; tel. 823-2083; fax 823-2240; e-mail cubolabz@btl.net; internet www.cubola.com; Dir MONTSERRAT CASADEMUNT.

Print Belize Ltd: 1 Power Lane, Belmopan; tel. 822-2293; fax 882-3367; e-mail admin@printbelize.com; internet www.printbelize.com; f. 1871; responsible for printing, binding and engraving requirements of all govt depts and ministries; publications include annual govt estimates, govt magazines and the official *Government Gazette*; CEO LAWRENCE J. NICHOLAS.

Broadcasting and Communications

TELECOMMUNICATIONS

In September 2001 the Government announced that the telecommunications sector was to be liberalized.

Public Utilities Commission (PUC): regulatory body for the telecommunications sector; see Utilities—Regulatory Body.

Belize Telemedia Ltd: Esquivel Telecom Centre, St Thomas St, POB 603, Belize City; tel. 223-2868; fax 223-1800; e-mail prdept@btl.net; internet www.belizetelemedia.net; f. May 2007; fmrly Belize Telecommunications Ltd (subsidiary of Innovative Communication Corpn (ICC) until taken over by the Govt in Feb. 2005); nationalized Aug. 2009; Exec. Chair. NESTOR VASQUEZ.

SpeedNet Communications Ltd: 2 Bishop St, Belize City; tel. 280-1000; fax 223-1919; e-mail Smartbelizecity@speednet-wireless.com; internet www.smart-bz.com; f. 2003, commenced services in 2005; mobile cellular telecommunications provider under the brand name Smart; Man. (IT) SEAN DUNCAN.

BROADCASTING

Regulatory Authority

Belize Broadcasting Authority (BBA): Belize City; tel. and fax 223-3953; e-mail broadcasting_bze@hotmail.com; regulatory authority; part of the Ministry of Public Utilities, Transport, Communications and National Emergency Management; Chair. LOUIS LESLIE.

Radio

Love FM: 7145 Slaughterhouse Rd, POB 1865, Belize City; tel. 203-2098; fax 203-0529; e-mail lovefm@btl.net; internet www.lovefm.com; f. 1992; purchased Friends FM in 1998; CEO RENE VILLANUEVA, Sr.

Radio Krem Ltd: 3304 Partridge St, POB 15, Belize City; tel. 222-4299; fax 202-4469; e-mail kremwub@hotmail.com; internet www.krembz.com; commercial; purchased Radio Belize in 1998.

Other private radio stations broadcasting in Belize include: Estereo Amor, More FM, My Refuge Christian Radio, Radio 2000 and Voice of America.

Television

Centaur Cable Network (CTV): 31 Clarke St, Orange Walk Town, Orange Walk; tel. 670-2216; fax 322-2216; internet www.ctv3belizenews.com; f. 1989; commercial.

Channel 5 Belize: Great Belize Productions Ltd, 2882 Coney Dr., POB 1314, Belize City; tel. 223-7781; fax 223-4936; e-mail gbtv@btl.com; internet www.channel5belize.com; f. 1991; CEO AMALIA MAI.

Tropical Vision (Channel 7): 73 Albert St, Belize City; tel. 223-5589; fax 227-5602; e-mail tvseven@btl.net; internet 7newsbelize.com; commercial; Man. Dir NESTOR VASQUEZ.

Finance

(cap. = capital; res = reserves; dep. = deposits; brs = branches; amounts in BZ $, unless otherwise indicated)

BANKING

Central Bank

Central Bank of Belize: Gabourel Lane, POB 852, Belize City; tel. 223-6194; fax 223-6226; e-mail cenbank@btl.net; internet www.centralbank.org.bz; f. 1982; cap. 10m., res 21.4m., dep. 324.7m. (2008); Gov. GLENFORD YSAGUIRRE; Chair. ALAN SLUSHER.

Development Bank

Development Finance Corporation: Bliss Parade, Belmopan; tel. 822-2360; fax 822-3096; e-mail info@dfcbelize.org; internet www.dfcbelize.org; f. 1972; ceased to finance loans following a govt review in Dec. 2004; issued cap. 10m.; 5 brs.

Other Banks

Atlantic Bank Ltd: Cnr Freetown Rd and Cleghorn St, POB 481, Belize City; tel. 223-4123; fax 223-3907; e-mail atlantic@atlabank.com; internet www.atlabank.com; f. 1971; 52% owned by Honduran co Sociedad Nacional de Inversiones, SA (SONISA); dep. 161.0m., total assets 191.9m. (2001); Gen. Man. SANDRA BEDRAN; 8 brs.

Atlantic International Bank Ltd: Cnr Freetown Rd and Cleghorn St, POB 481, Belize City; tel. 223-3152; fax 223-3528; e-mail banking@atlabank.com; internet www.atlanticibl.com; affiliated to Atlantic Bank Ltd; Gen. Man. RICARDO PELAYO.

Belize Bank Ltd: 60 Market Sq., POB 364, Belize City; tel. 227-7132; fax 227-2712; e-mail bblbz@belizebank.com; internet www.belizebank.com; subsidiary of BCB Holdings; cap. US $102.2m., res US $5.2m., dep. US $660.9m. (March 2008); Chair. LYNDON GUISEPPI; Marketing Man. MISTY MICHAEL; 10 brs.

British Caribbean Bank International: 60 Market Sq., Belize City; tel. 227-0697; fax 227-0983; e-mail services@bcbankinternational.com; internet bcbankinternational.com; fmrly Belize Bank, Turks & Caicos.

Caye International Bank Ltd (CIBL): Coconut Dr., San Pedro, POB 11, Ambergris Caye; tel. 226-2388; fax 226-2892; e-mail cibl@btl.net; internet www.cayebank.bz; Pres. PETER A. ZIPPER; Exec. Vice-Pres. JOY A. FLOWERS.

FirstCaribbean International Bank Ltd (Barbados): 21 Albert St, POB 363, Belize City; tel. 227-7211; fax 227-8572; e-mail care@firstcaribbeanbank.com; internet www.firstcaribbeanbank.com; f. 2002 by merger of CIBC West Indies Holdings and Barclays Bank PLC Caribbean operations; Barclays relinquished its stake to CIBC in June 2006; Exec. Chair. MICHAEL MANSOOR; Exec. Dir JOHN ORR.

Heritage Bank Ltd: 106 Princess Margaret Dr., POB 1988, Belize City; tel. 223-6783; fax 223-6785; e-mail services@banking.bz; internet www.alliancebankbelize.bz; f. 2001 as Alliance Bank of Belize Ltd; name changed as above in 2010; dep. 6,876m., total assets 113.7m.; 3 brs.

Heritage International Bank and Trust Ltd: 35 Barrack Rd, POB 1867, Belize City; tel. 223-5698; fax 223-0368; e-mail services@banking.bz; internet heritageibt.com; f. 1998 as Provident Bank and Trust of Belize; name changed as above in 2010; cap. US $6.0m., res US $1.5m., dep. US $105.9m. (2004); Chair. JOY VERNON GODFREY; Pres. JOSÉ MARIN.

There is also a government savings bank. In late 2001 the Government amended the exchange-control regulations to allow foreign-currency exchange bureaux.

INSURANCE

The insurance sector is regulated by the Office of the Supervisor of Insurance, part of the Ministry of Finance.

Atlantic Insurance Company Ltd: Atlantic Bank Bldg, 3rd Floor, Cnr Cleghorn St and Freetown Rd, POB 1447, Belize City; tel. 223-2657; fax 223-2658; e-mail info@atlanticinsurancebz.com; internet www.atlanticinsurancebz.com; f. 1990; part of the Atlantic Group of Companies; holding company, Sociedad Nacional de Inversiones, SA, (SONISA); Gen. Man. MARTHA GUERRA.

Belize Insurance Centre: 212 North Front St, Belize City; tel. 227-7310; fax 227-4803; e-mail info@belizeinsurance.com; internet www.belizeinsurance.com; f. 1972; insurance broker; subsidiary of Fraser Fontaine & Kong Ltd (Jamaica); Chair. G. RICHARD FONTAINE; Gen. Man. CYNTHIA AWE.

RF & G Insurance Co Ltd: Gordon House, 1 Coney Dr., POB 661, Belize City; tel. 223-5734; fax 223-6734; e-mail info@rfginsurancebelize.com; internet www.rfginsurancebelize.com; f. 2005 by merger of F&G Insurance and Regent Insurance; underwriters of all major classes of insurance; mem. of the Roe Group of Companies; Chair. CHRISTOPHER ROE; Man. Dir GUY HOWISON.

RF & G Life Insurance Company Ltd: Gordon House, 4th Floor, 1 Coney Dr., POB 661, Belize City; tel. 223-5734; fax 223-6734; e-mail info@rfglife.com; internet www.rfglife.com; f. 2005 through merger of the Life and Medical portfolios of F&G Insurance Company into Regent Life; mem. of the Roe Group of Companies; Chair. BRIAN D. ROE; Gen. Man. RHONDA LECKY.

Trade and Industry

STATUTORY BODIES

Banana Control Board: c/o Ministry of Agriculture and Fisheries, West Block Bldg, 2nd Floor, Belmopan; management of banana industry; in 1989 it was decided to make it responsible to growers, not an independent executive.

Belize Agricultural Health Authority: Cnr Forest Dr. and Hummingbird Hwy, POB 169, Belmopan; tel. 822-0818; fax 822-0271; e-mail baha@btl.net; internet www.baha.bz; CEO GABINO CANTO; Man. Dir EDWIN MARTINEZ.

Belize Marketing and Development Corporation (BMDC): 117 North Front St, POB 633, Belize City; tel. 227-7402; fax 227-7656; f. 1948 as Belize Marketing Board to encourage the growing of staple food crops; renamed as above in 2003; promotes domestic produce; Man. Dir ROQUE MAI.

Coastal Zone Management Authority (CZMAI): POB 1884, Belize City; tel. 223-0719; fax 223-5738; e-mail czmbze@btl.net; internet www.coastalzonebelize.org; Man. Dir VIRGINIA VASQUEZ (acting).

Pesticides Control Board (PCB): Central Farm, Cayo District; tel. 824-2640; fax 824-3486; e-mail pcbinfo@btl.net; internet www.pcbbelize.com; Chair. EUGENE WAIGHT.

DEVELOPMENT ORGANIZATION

Belize Trade and Investment Development Service (BELTRAIDE): 14 Orchid Garden St, Belmopan; tel. 822-3737; fax 822-0595; e-mail beltraide@belizeinvest.org.bz; internet www.belizeinvest.org.bz; f. 1986 as a joint govt and private sector institution to encourage export and investment; Exec. Chair. LOURDES SMITH.

CHAMBERS OF COMMERCE

American Chamber of Commerce of Belize: 5½ Miles Western Hwy, Cucumber Beach, Marina, POB 75, Belize City; tel. 222-4344; fax 222-4265; e-mail office@amchambelize.org; internet www.amchambelize.org; Pres. BILL MACKENZIE; Sec. BOB STEVENS.

Belize Chamber of Commerce and Industry (BCCI): 4792 Coney Dr., Withfield Tower, 1st Floor, POB 291, Belize City; tel. 223-5330; fax 223-5333; e-mail bcci@belize.org; internet www.belize.org; f. 1920; Pres. AMPARO MASSON; Sec. BRYON BOWMAN; 300 mems.

EMPLOYERS' ASSOCIATIONS

Banana Growers' Association: Big Creek, Independence Village, Stann Creek District; tel. 523-2000; fax 523-2112; e-mail banana@btl.net; Chair. EUGENE ZABANEH.

Belize Citrus Growers Association (BCGA): Mile 9, Stann Creek Valley Rd, POB 7, Dangriga, Stann Creek District; tel. 522-3585; fax 522-2686; e-mail info@belizecitrus.org; internet www.belizecitrus.org; f. 1967; CEO BRIDGET CULLERTON; Exec. Sec. JUDITH WILLIAMS.

Belize Livestock Producers' Association (BLPA): 47½ miles Western Hwy, POB 183, Belmopan; tel. 822-3883; e-mail blpa@btl.net; internet www.blpabz.org; f. 1972; Chair. Dr ERROL VANZIE.

Belize Sugar Cane Farmers' Association (BSCFA): 34 San Antonio Rd, Orange Walk; tel. 322-2005; fax 322-3171; f. 1959 to assist cane farmers and negotiate with the Sugar Cane Board and manufacturers on their behalf; Dir ALFREDO ORTEGA; CEO CARLOS MAGANA; 16 district brs.

United Cane Farmers' Association: Orange Walk; f. 2009; breakaway faction of the BSCFA; Rep. WILFREDO MAGAÑA.

MAJOR COMPANIES

BCB Holdings Ltd: 60 Market Sq., POB 1764, Belize City; tel. 227-2660; fax 227-5854; e-mail info@bbholdingslimited.com; internet www.bcbholdings.com; fmrly Carlisle Holdings Ltd, changed name to BB Holdings in 2005; current name adopted 2009; holding co with banking and financial services operations in Belize; investments in infrastructure development and agro-processing and distribution in Central America and the Caribbean region; Chair. Lord MICHAEL ASHCROFT; CEO LYNDON GUISEPPI; 437 employees.

Belize Brewing Co Ltd: 1 King St, POB 1068, Belize City; tel. 227-2602; fax 225-3195; e-mail belikin@bowenbz.com; internet www.thebeerofbelize.com; f. 1968; subsidiary of Bowen & Bowen Ltd; producers of malt liquors; Gen. Man HILLY MARTINEZ; 120 employees.

Belize Estate Co Ltd: Slaughterhouse Rd, POB 151, Belize City; tel. 227-7031; fax 227-7062; e-mail bec@btl.net; f. 1875; subsidiary of Bowen & Bowen Ltd; importers, shipping agents, main agents for Kia and Ford, Lloyd's agent for Belize, operation of tourist enterprises; Man. Dir WILLIAM F. BOWMAN; 94 employees.

Belize Natural Energy Ltd (BNE): Spanish Lookout Rd, Mile 3, POB 279, Iguana Creek, Cayo, Belmopan; tel. 823-0354; fax 823-0415; e-mail info@belizeenergy.bz; internet www.belizenaturalenergy.bz; f. 2002; owned by US and Irish interests; oil and gas exploration and production; Pres. and CEO Dr GILBERT CANTON; Dir SUSAN MORRICE.

Belize Sugar Industries Ltd: Tower Hill, POB 29, Orange Walk Town; tel. 322-2150; fax 322-3247; e-mail ceobelizesugar@btl.net; f. 1935; public co; raw sugar manufacturers; Man. Dir JOSÉ MONTALVO; Financial Controller ALVARO ALPUCHE; 650 employees.

Castillo Sanchez & Burrell, LLP (CSB): 40A Central American Blvd, POB 1235, Belize City; tel. 227-3020; fax 227-5792; e-mail info@csb-llp.com; internet www.csb-llp.com; accountancy, management consultancy, 'offshore' services; Sr Partner GIACOMO SANCHEZ.

Citrus Products of Belize Ltd: 12 Miles, Stann Creek Valley Rd, Pomona Village, Stann Creek District; tel. 522-0036; fax 522-2136; e-mail info@citrusproductsbelize.com; internet www.citrusproductsbelize.com; f. 1948 as Citrus Co of Belize Ltd; present name adopted in 2002; citrus fruit growers and processors; 46.58% owned by Bank Holdings Ltd of Barbados; Chair. MICHAEL DUNCKER; CEO Dr HENRY CANTON.

Esso Standard Oil SA Ltd: Caesar Ridge Rd, POB 328, Belize City; tel. 227-7323; fax 227-7726; e-mail ecgss@btl.net; petroleum exploration and distribution; Man. JOSÉ ESPAT.

Femagra Industries Ltd: ½ Mile, Hummingbird Hwy, POB 65, Belmopan City; tel. 822-3909; fax 882-3910; e-mail fernando@femagra.com; internet www.femagra.com; f. 1984; chemical- and food-processing, water-purifying; Gen. Man. FERNANDO MOLINA.

Hofius Ltd: 19 Albert St, POB 226, Belize City; tel. 227-7231; fax 227-4751; e-mail hofiusace@btl.net; f. 1892; hardware and home products, real estate sales, boats and marine fittings, food distribution; CEO JOHN CRUMP; 50 employees.

Madisco: 42 Cleghorn St, POB 34, Belize City; tel. 224-4153; fax 223-1797; e-mail sales@madisco.bz; internet www.madisco.bz; mem. of the Roe Group (q.v.); marketing and distribution; Contact Person JOHN NICHOLSON.

Marine Farms Belize: Mile 5½ Western Highway, POB 1778, Belize City; tel. 222-5038; fax 222-4102; e-mail info@marinefarmsbelize.com; internet www.marinefarmsbelize.com; f. 2006; owned by Marine Farms ASA (Norway); fish farming and processing; CEO BJØRN MYRSETH; 30 employees (2007).

Netkom Internet Solutions: 18 Leslie St, Kings Park, POB 855, Belize City; tel. 223-3274; e-mail support@netkombelize.com; internet www.mybelizeadventure.com/netkombelize; internet consultancy and provider of digital media production services.

Northern Fishermen Cooperative Society: 49 North Front St, POB 647, Belize City; tel. 224-4448; fax 223-0978; e-mail norficoop@btl.net; producers, processors and exporters of seafood products; Gen. Man. ROBERT USHER.

Prosser Fertilizer and Agrotec Co: Mile 8 Western Hwy, POB 566, Belize City; tel. 223-5410; fax 222-5548; e-mail prosserfertilizer@gmail.com; manufacture of industrial chemicals and fertilizers; Pres. HERBERT MASSON; CEO SALVADOR ESPAT.

The Roe Group: Gordon House, 1 Coney Dr., Belize City; tel. 223-6124; fax 227-1357; e-mail info@roegroupbelize.com; internet www.roegroupbelize.com; f. 1961; 16 cos; agriculture, distribution and sales, financial services, manufacturing, real estate and tourism; Chair. BRIAN D. ROE; CEO CHRISTOPHER ROE.

Sol Belize Ltd: 2.5 miles Northern Hwy, POB 608, Belize City; tel. 223-0406; fax 223-0704; e-mail info@solpetroleum.com; internet www.solpetroleum.com; f. 1938; subsidiary of Interamericana Trading Ltd (Barbados); marketing and distribution of petroleum, petroleum products and chemical products; Chair. KYFFIN D. SIMPSON; Gen. Man. JOE HABET; 14 employees.

Texaco Belize Ltd: 4½ miles Western Hwy, POB 627, Belize City; tel. 224-340; fax 224-355; subsidiary of Texaco Inc, USA; exploration and production of petroleum and gas, refining and distribution of petroleum and gas products; Man. HECTOR LÓPEZ.

UTILITIES

Regulatory Body

Public Utilities Commission (PUC): 41 Gabourel Lane, POB 300, Belize City; tel. 223-4938; fax 223-6818; e-mail info@puc.bz; internet www.puc.bz; regulatory body, headed by 7 commissioners; replaced the Offices of Electricity Supply and of Telecommunications following enaction of the Public Utilities Commission Act in 1999; Chair. JOHN AVERY.

Electricity

Belize Electricity Co Ltd (BECOL): 115 Barrack Rd, POB 327, Belize City; tel. 227-0954; fax 223-0891; e-mail bel@btl.net; internet www.fortisinc.com; wholly owned subsidiary of Fortis Inc (Canada); operates Mollejón 25.2–MW hydroelectric plant and Chalillo 7.3–MW hydroelectric facility, which supply electricity to Belize Electricity Ltd (BEL—see below); Pres. and CEO H. STANLEY MARSHALL.

Belize Electricity Ltd (BEL): 2½ miles Northern Hwy, POB 327, Belize City; tel. 227-0954; fax 223-0891; e-mail pr@bel.com.bz; internet www.bel.com.bz; fmrly Belize Electricity Board, changed name upon privatization in 1992; Govt held 51% of shares until 1999; 70% owned by Fortis Inc (Canada), 27% owned by Social Security Board; Pres. and CEO LYNN R. YOUNG; Chair. RODWELL WILLIAMS; 242 employees.

Water

Belize Water Services Ltd: Central American Blvd, POB 150, Belize City; tel. 222-4757; fax 222-4759; e-mail bws_ceosec@btl.net; internet www.bws.bz; f. 1971 as Water and Sewerage Authority (WASA); changed name upon privatization in March 2001; renationalized in Oct. 2005 prior to partial reprivatization in early 2006; Chair. HERMAN LONGSWORTH; Company Sec. ALVAN HAYNES.

TRADE UNIONS

National Trade Union Congress of Belize (NTUCB): POB 2359, Belize City; tel. 822-0677; fax 822-0283; e-mail ntucb@btl.net; Pres. DYLAN RENEAU; Gen. Sec. JAVIER ROBERTS.

Principal Unions

Belize Communications Workers' Union (BCWU): POB 1291, Belize City; tel. 223-4809; fax 224-4300; e-mail bcwu@btl.net; f. 1989; Pres. MARK GLADDEN; Gen. Sec. BERNARD PITTS.

Belize Energy Workers' Union: c/o Belize Electricity Ltd, 2½ miles Northern Hwy, POB 1066, Belize City; tel. 227-0954; Pres. MARVIN MORA; Gen. Sec. DORLA STAINE.

Belize National Teachers' Union: NGO Crescent, POB 382, Belize City; tel. 223-4811; fax 223-5233; e-mail admin@bntubelize.org; internet www.bntubelize.org; f. 1970 following merger between the British Honduras Union of Teachers' (BHUT) and the Catholic Education Association (CEA); adopted present name in 1976; Pres. JAIME PANTI; Exec. Sec. GEORGE FRAZER; 1,000 mems.

Belize Workers' Union: Tate St, Orange Walk Town; tel. 822-2327; Pres. HORRIS PATTEN.

Christian Workers' Union: 107B Cemetery Rd, POB 533, Belize City; tel. 227-2150; fax 227-8470; e-mail cwu@btl.net; f. 1962; general; Pres. ANTONIO GONZÁLEZ; Gen. Sec. JAMES MCFOY; 1,000 mems.

Public Service Union of Belize: Hilltop Complex, POB 458, Belmopan; tel. 802-3885; fax 822-0283; e-mail belizepsu@btl.net; f. 1922; public workers; Pres. JACQUELINE WILLOUGHBY-SANCHEZ; Gen. Sec. MARIO CALIZ; 1,600 mems.

Transport

Department of Transport: 1 Power Lane, Belmopan; tel. 822-2038; fax 822-2291; e-mail departmentoftransport@yahoo.com; Chief Officer JOHN S. BRIGGS.

RAILWAYS

There are no railways in Belize.

ROADS

There are 2,872 km of roads, of which some 2,210 km (1,600 km of gravel roads, 300 km of improved earth roads and 310 km of unimproved earth roads) are unpaved. In 2004 construction of a double-lane bridge over the Sibun River was completed, funded by a BZ $3.6m. European Union (EU) grant and some BZ $1m. from the Government. In 2006 construction of another two-lane bridge, this time over Silver Creek, was completed. The bridge was intended to expedite the transport of produce and other products from the southern agricultural area to markets in Belize City along the Hummingbird Highway and also provide access for emergency aid to the southern communities of Belize during the hurricane season. A north–south highway, funded by the Government and international donors, was also under construction.

SHIPPING

There is a deep-water port at Belize City and a second port at Commerce Bight, near Dangriga (formerly Stann Creek), to the south of Belize City. There is a port for the export of bananas at Big Creek and additional ports at Corozal and Punta Gorda. Nine major shipping lines operate vessels calling at Belize City, including the Carol Line (consisting of Harrison, Hapag-Lloyd, Nedlloyd and CGM). A proposal to develop a cruise ship port at Port Loyola at a cost of BZ $963.5m. was submitted to parliament in October 2004. Work had commenced on the project by September 2007; however, a dispute between the operating companies and the Government of that time severely compromised future development.

Belize Ports Authority: 120 North Front St, POB 633, Belize City; tel. 223-0716; fax 223-0710; e-mail info@portauthority.bz; internet www.portauthority.bz; f. 1980; Commr of Ports Maj. (retd) LLOYD JONES.

Marine & Services Ltd: 95 Albert St, POB 611, Belize City; tel. 227-2112; fax 227-5404; e-mail businessmanager@marineservices.bz; internet www.marineservices.bz; f. 1975; shipping and cargo services, cruise line agent; Dir SHAUN FINNETTY; Man. JOSE GALLEGO.

Port of Belize Ltd: Caesar Ridge Rd, POB 2674, Belize City; tel. 227-3571; fax 227-3571; e-mail info@portofbelize.com; internet www.portofbelize.com; operates the main port facility; Chair. LUKE ESPAT; CEO RAINELDO GUERRERO.

CIVIL AVIATION

Philip S. W. Goldson International Airport, 16 km (10 miles) from Belize City, can accommodate medium-sized jet-engined aircraft. There are 37 airstrips for light aircraft on internal flights near the major towns and offshore islands.

Belize Airports Authority (BAA): POB 1564, Belize City; tel. 225-2045; fax 225-2439; e-mail bzeaa@btl.net; CEO PABLO ESPAT.

Maya Island Air: Municipal Airstrip, Bldg 1, 2nd Floor, POB 458, Belize City; tel. 223-1140; fax 223-0576; e-mail regional@mayaislandair.com; internet www.mayaregional.com; f. 1961 as merger between Maya Airways Ltd and Island Air; operated by Belize Air Group; internal services, centred on Belize City, and charter flights to neighbouring countries; CEO LOUIS ZABANEH; Gen. Man. FERNANDO TREJOS.

Tropic Air: San Pedro, POB 20, Ambergris Caye; tel. 226-2012; fax 226-2338; e-mail reservations@tropicair.com; internet www.tropicair.com; f. 1979; operates internal services and services to Guatemala; Chair. CELI MCCORKLE; Man. Dir JOHN GREIF, III.

Tourism

The main tourist attractions are the beaches and the barrier reef, diving, fishing and the Mayan archaeological sites. There are nine major wildlife reserves (including the world's only reserves for the jaguar and for the red-footed booby), and government policy is to develop 'eco-tourism', based on the attractions of an unspoiled environment and Belize's natural history. The country's wildlife also includes howler monkeys and 500 species of birds, and its barrier reef is the second largest in the world. There were 5,789 hotel rooms in Belize in 2006. In 2008 there were 842,396 tourist arrivals, of which some 597,370 were cruise ship passengers. Tourism receipts totalled US $292.7m. in 2007, according to preliminary figures.

Belize Tourism Board: 64 Regent St, POB 325, Belize City; tel. 227-2420; fax 227-2423; e-mail info@travelbelize.org; internet www.travelbelize.org; f. 1964; fmrly Belize Tourist Bureau; 8 mems; Chair. GASPAR GUERRERO; Dir TRACY TAEGAR-PANTON.

Belize Tourism Industry Association (BTIA): 10 North Park St, POB 62, Belize City; tel. 227-1144; fax 227-8710; e-mail info@btia.org; internet www.btia.org; f. 1985; promotes sustainable tourism; Pres. ROSELLA ZABANEH; Exec. Dir ANDREW GODOY; 500 mems.

Defence

The Belize Defence Force was formed in 1978 and was based on a combination of the existing Police Special Force and the Belize Volunteer Guard. Military service is voluntary, but provision has been made for the establishment of National Service, if necessary, to supplement normal recruitment. As assessed at November 2009, the regular armed forces totalled approximately 1,050 and there were some 700 militia reserves. In 1994 all British forces were withdrawn from Belize, and in 2008 some 30 troops remained to organize training for jungle warfare. On 28 November 2005 the Belize National Coast Guard Service was inaugurated to combat drugs-trafficking, illegal immigration and illegal fishing in Belize's territorial waters. The Coast Guard comprised 58 volunteer officers from the Belize Defence Force, the Belize Police Department, the Customs and Excise Department, the National Fire Service, the Department of Immigration and Nationality Services, the Port Authority and the Fisheries Department.

Defence Budget: an estimated BZ $38m. in 2008.

Belize Defence Force Commandant: Brig.-Gen. DARIO TAPIA.

Education

Education is compulsory for all children for a period of 10 years between the ages of five and 14 years. Primary education, beginning at five years of age and lasting for eight years, is provided free of charge, principally through subsidized denominational schools under government control. In 2007/08 enrolment at primary institutions included 98% of children in the relevant age-group. Secondary education, beginning at the age of 13, lasts for four years. Enrolment at secondary schools in 2006/07 included 63% of students in the relevant age-group (males 61%; females 66%).

In 1997/98 there were 2,853 students enrolled in 12 other educational institutions, which included technical, vocational and teacher-training colleges. There is an extra-mural branch of the University of the West Indies in Belize. In 2000 the University of Belize was formed through the amalgamation of five higher education institutions, including the University College of Belize and Belize Technical College. Budgetary expenditure on education in the financial year 2004/05 was projected at BZ $152.6m., representing 26.7% of total spending by the central Government.

Bibliography

For works on the Caribbean generally, see Select Bibliography (Books)

Barry, T., and Vernon, D. *Inside Belize*. London, Latin America Bureau, 1995.

Cutlack, M. *Belize, Ecotourism in Action*. London, Macmillan, 1993.

Grant, C. H. *The Making of Modern Belize: Politics, Society and British Colonialism in Central America*. Cambridge, Cambridge University Press, 2008.

Guderjan, Thomas H. *The Nature of an Ancient Maya City: Resources, Interaction, and Power at Blue Creek, Belize*. Tuscaloosa, AL, University of Alabama Press, 2007.

Kroshus Medina, L. *Negotiating Economic Development: Identity Formation and Collective Action in Belize*. Tucson, AZ, University of Arizona Press, 2004.

MacPherson, A. S. *From Colony to Nation: Women Activists and the Gendering of Politics in Belize, 1912–1982*. Lincoln, NE, University of Nebraska Press, 2007.

Moberg, M. *Myths of Ethnicity and Nation: Immigration, Work and Identity in the Belize Banana Industry*. Knoxville, TN, University of Tennessee Press, 1997.

Musa, S., and Smith, G. P. (Eds). *Belize: A Caribbean Nation in Central America—Selected Speeches of Said Musa*. Kingston, Ian Randle Publrs, 2006.

Norton, N. *Belize*. London, Cadogan Press, 1997.

Phillips, M. D. *Belize*. Lanham, MD, University Press of America, 1996.

Roessingh, C. *The Belizean Garifuna: Organization of Identity in an Ethnic Community in Central America*. Amsterdam, Rozenberg, 2002.

Simmons, D. C. *Confederate Settlements in British Honduras*. Jefferson, NC, McFarland & Co, 2001.

Sutherland, A. *The Making of Belize*. Westport, CT, Bergin & Garvey, 1998.

Thomson, P. *History of Belize*. Oxford, Macmillan Caribbean, 2005.

Turner, B. L., and Harrison, P. D. (Eds). *Pulltrouser Swamp: Ancient Maya Habitat, Agriculture and Settlement in Northern Belize*. Salt Lake City, UT, University of Utah Press, 2000.

Twigg, A. *Understanding Belize: A Historical Guide*. Madeira Park, BC, Harbour Publishing, 2006.

BERMUDA

Geography

PHYSICAL FEATURES

Bermuda lies in the North Atlantic, about 900 km (560 miles) east of Cape Hatteras in North Carolina (USA), and is an Overseas Territory of the United Kingdom (indeed, it is the oldest British colony). Although geographically part of North America, Bermuda shares many of the features of the West Indian islands, and is generally included in that region—it is north-west of the Bahamian archipelago and north of the Virgin Islands. Bermuda, located on what were called the Somers Islands, has an area of only 53.3 sq km, making it the smallest territory in the Western hemisphere.

Bermuda is built of coral perching on the southern rim of the summit of an underwater volcanic mountain. The 103 km (64 miles) of coastline define some 138 islands and islets, which are strung out across 35 km, running south-westwards from St George's Island to hook around the Great Sound in the south and taper off in a more northerly direction. There are many surrounding reefs, banks and islets. About 20 of the islands are inhabited and seven are linked by bridges and causeways. South of St George's is St David's Island, then Great Bermuda or Main Island (23 km in length). The landscape is richly vegetated, although there is now little land used for farming (over two-fifths of the territory is kept rural and undeveloped), with low hills separated by fertile depressions. The highest point is in the far south, at Gibbs Hill (78 m or 256 ft), itself surmounted by a 36-m, cast-iron lighthouse.

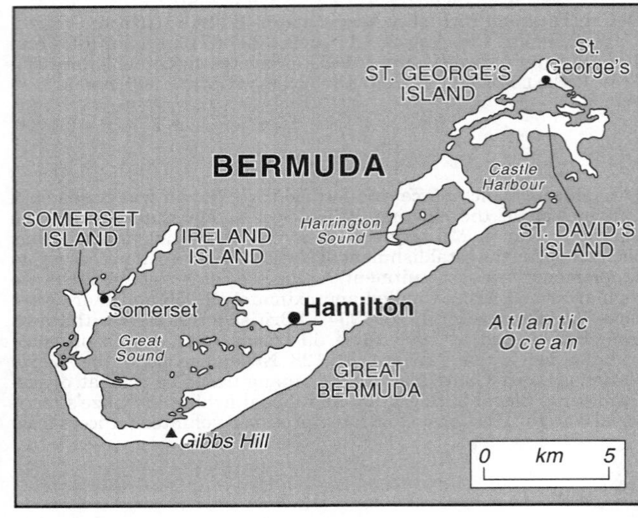

CLIMATE

The subtropical climate is influenced by the Gulf Stream, which enables Bermuda to consist of the most northerly coral islands in the world. The weather is mild, but humid, with strong winds common in winter. Hurricanes can occur between June and November. The good, year-round rainfall (averaging some 1,500 mm—59 ins—annually) makes up for the scarcity of natural freshwater resources. The annual average temperature is 76°F (24°C), ranging between an average minimum of 59°F (15°C) in February and a maximum of 85°F (29°C) in August.

POPULATION

Bermuda, named for the Spanish sailor who visited it in the early years of the 16th century, was only inhabited in the 17th century, by the British. The black population forms the majority (61% of the total in 2000), but whites still comprise 39%. Most people are Christian, with the main (of many) denominations being the Anglican Church (23%), the Roman Catholic Church and the African Methodist Episcopalian Church. English is the official language. There is a reasonably significant Portuguese-speaking community.

The total population at the time of the 2000 census was 62,059, giving a population density of some 1,164 per sq km; this had increased to an officially projected 64,566 (1,211.4 per sq km) by mid-2010. Bermuda is the most densely populated territory of the Americas. The capital is at Hamilton, near the centre of Main Island and on the north-eastern shores of the Great Sound, which had an estimated population of 11,535 in 2009. It is one of two municipalities in the territory, the other being that of St George's, the original settlement and old capital in the north. There are also three villages on the islands, while for administrative purposes there are nine parishes.

History

Bermuda is a Crown Colony of the United Kingdom. The British monarch is represented in the islands by a Governor.

The 1968 Constitution gave Bermuda (the oldest British colony, established in 1684) internal self-government. The 1968 elections were won by the moderate, multiracial United Bermuda Party (UBP). However, Bermudian society was riven by racial tensions and in the early 1970s there was a considerable level of violence. Shooting incidents in 1973 notably resulted in the assassination of the Governor of the Colony. At the 1976 election the UBP remained in power, although it lost seats to the mainly black, pro-independence, left-wing Progressive Labour Party (PLP). The PLP won 46% of the vote, but only 14 of the 40 seats in the House of Assembly. In 1980 the UBP only narrowly retained power, but regained the seats it had lost in the following election, in 1983. Meanwhile, in 1982, John (later Sir John) W. Swan became party leader and Premier. The UBP won a decisive victory in the 1985 elections; in 1989 it lost seats, although it maintained its majority. The UBP remained in government after the general election of October 1993 (the first to be held since the voting age was lowered from 21 to 18 years), having won 22 seats (the remaining 18 seats were secured by the PLP).

On 16 August 1995 a referendum was held on independence from the United Kingdom, despite the strenuous opposition of the PLP, which stated that the issue should be decided in a general election, and urged its supporters to boycott the poll. In the referendum, which had a relatively low turn-out (for Bermuda) of 59%, some 74% of participants registered their opposition to independence. The debate polarized opinion within the ruling party, and Swan subsequently resigned as Premier and as leader of the UBP. The erstwhile finance minister, Dr David Saul, succeeded him in both posts. Saul remained neutral on the independence issue, and the divisions within the UBP deepened under his leadership. A motion of censure against him, prompted by Saul's decision to authorize the establishment of a foreign-owned franchise restaurant in Bermuda (in contravention of a ruling by the Bermuda Monetary Authority), was approved, with the support of five UBP members, in the House of Assembly in June 1996. Having failed to restore party unity, Saul resigned as Premier and UBP leader in March 1997. Pamela Gordon replaced him.

In August 1996 the Leader of the Opposition, Frederick Wade, died. In November the party's Deputy Leader, Jennifer Smith, was elected to the leadership of the organization.

Deep divisions within the UBP were exposed once again and overshadowed the party's campaign for the parliamentary elections in November 1998. At these elections, the PLP received 54% of the votes cast, winning 26 seats and its first ever majority in the House of Assembly. With 44% of the ballot, the UBP secured the remaining seats. On becoming the first PLP Premier, Jennifer Smith declared that no immediate moves towards independence were planned, although it remained a stated aim of the party. She also reassured the international business community that her Government would seek to enhance Bermuda's attraction as an international business centre, and that she would resist any attempts to alter the island's tax status. In February 1999, nevertheless, the Premier reassured members of the Organisation for Economic Co-operation and Development (OECD) that Bermuda would strive to improve regulation of the 'offshore' financial services sector.

In March 1999 the British Government published draft legislation confirming that its Dependencies were to be referred to as United Kingdom Overseas Territories; the document stated that all such territories would be required to comply with European standards on human rights and financial regulation. In October it was announced that in accordance with these reforms, corporal and capital punishment were to be abolished in Bermuda.

Following OECD's investigation into tax havens, in June 2000 Bermuda pledged to conform to international standards on financial transparency before the end of 2005. This was likely to include the abolition of the 60/40 rule, by which all businesses aimed at the local market had to be 60%-owned by a Bermudian individual or entity. The Government had, however, pledged to maintain its existing tax system, which included no income tax.

Aside from the worrying decline in the tourism industry and the increase in the value of drugs seizures by Bermudian customs, the most important issue the Government faced during the first six months of 2001 was that of constitutional change. The Government and the opposition UBP fundamentally disagreed about proposed changes to the voting system and electoral boundaries. Racial issues were at the heart of the conflict, with the PLP claiming the present system favoured the traditionally 'white' UBP. In December 2000 the House of Assembly approved a motion requesting the British Government to approve the establishment of a boundaries commission, which would recommend the size of the island's constituencies. In January 2001 the UBP submitted an 8,500-signature petition to the British Government, demanding a constitutional conference or referendum before any changes were made. Gordon also claimed that some Bermudians had refused to sign the petition, fearing recriminations. The British Foreign and Commonwealth Office (FCO), however, stated that a constitutional conference was unnecessary, and in April it began consultations over the proposed changes. The commission recommended reducing the number of seats in the House of Assembly by four, to 36. In addition, whereas deputies had previously been elected from 20 two-member constituencies, under the proposed scheme each member of parliament would be elected by a separate constituency. The FCO approved the changes before the July 2003 general election.

In November 2001 Sir John Vereker succeeded Sir Thorold Masefield as Governor of Bermuda.

In May 2002 the British Overseas Territories Act, having received royal assent in the United Kingdom in February, came into force and granted British citizenship to the people of its Overseas Territories, including Bermuda. Under the new law Bermudians would be able to hold British passports and work in the United Kingdom and anywhere else in the European Union.

In mid-2002 the issue of financial transparency and corporate governance in Bermuda re-emerged following the collapse of the US energy concern Enron and several other multinational firms in late 2001 and early 2002. The indictment on tax-evasion charges of Dennis Kozlowski, the former CEO of Tyco International Ltd, a manufacturer of electronic security systems with a nominal headquarters on the island, fuelled a growing campaign in the US media and the US Congress against the perceived lack of financial regulation and scrutiny in Bermuda. Since 1997, it was reported, nine major US companies had reincorporated in Bermuda and the Cayman Islands.

Elections to the smaller 36-seat House of Assembly were held on 24 July 2003 and were dominated by resentment towards wealthy foreign workers and criticism of the personal style of Smith, regarded by many as uncommunicative and aloof. The PLP retained its majority in parliament, securing 22 seats, but its share of the popular vote was reduced to 52% (compared with 48% for the UBP). Smith resigned as Premier after it emerged that she had retained her seat, in what was regarded as a 'safe' PLP constituency, by just eight votes. She was replaced by the erstwhile Minister of Works and Engineering, W. Alexander Scott. Scott's first Cabinet consisted of 12 members (including C. Eugene Cox, who retained the finance portfolio), despite the PLP's pre-election pledge to reduce its size to eight in order to reduce costs.

Following the death of Cox in January 2004, his daughter, Paula Ann Cox, the erstwhile Minister of Education and Justice and Attorney-General, was appointed as Minister of Finance. The reorganization also included the appointment of Larry Mussenden as Minister of Justice and Attorney-General, while Terry Lister moved to the education ministry. In February the Premier announced that his Government would initiate a 'relaxed public discussion' on the subject of achieving independence from the United Kingdom. In July Scott effected a minor cabinet reorganization after Maurine Webb resigned as Minister of Tourism, Telecommunications and E-Commerce. Responsibility for tourism was transferred to Ewart Brown; Michael Scott, the erstwhile Minister of Legislative Affairs, was allocated Webb's other portfolios.

In February 2005 a Supreme Court judge ruled as discriminatory and unlawful the Government's policy of deferring the right to apply for parole for prisoners convicted of drugs-smuggling until they had served one-half of their sentence. Prisoners convicted of non-drugs, non-sexual or non-violent offences were allowed to apply for parole after serving one-third of their sentence. In July the Misuse of Drugs Amendment Act introduced legislation allowing courts to fine those convicted of drugs offences up to US $1m. and to impose prison sentences of between 10 years and life. Despite the designation of a dedicated cabinet minister and employment of an eminent British police officer as Assistant Commissioner specializing in drugs crime prevention, drugs-related violent crime escalated during 2006. Police authorities had valued Bermuda's drugs trade at an estimated US $200m. by August of that year.

On 27 October 2006 Scott's premiership ended after he was defeated in a PLP leadership contest; party delegates voted in former Minister of Transport and Tourism and Deputy Premier Brown as his successor. Brown had resigned from his ministerial responsibilities earlier that month, demonstrating his intention to contest the party leadership; he was formally inaugurated as party leader on 30 October, resuming the transport and tourism portfolio and announcing limited changes to the Government's composition: a ministerial post was created for matters of social rehabilitation, to be occupied by erstwhile Minister of Community Affairs and Sports Dale Butler, whose newly vacated portfolio was assumed by Wayne Perinchief; Paula Ann Cox, the Minister of Finance, assumed the additional role of Deputy Premier.

The new Government's stated intention to address disruptive racial tensions among the island's communities was a matter of particular pertinence to the opposition UBP, embroiled as it was in an internal racial discrimination controversy which, in January 2007, precipitated the resignations of House of Assembly member Jamahl Simmons and party Chair Gwyneth Rawlins. Both alleged serious charges of racial discrimination against factions within the party. Demands for the resignation of leader Wayne Furbert ensued, with senior members asserting that intra-party schisms and dissension arising from the racism dispute threatened to undermine the UBP's political power. Such public wrangling further provoked speculation of an early general election—ahead of the 2008 deadline dictated constitutionally—whereby Premier Brown might take advantage of an opposition in disarray. Following a vote of no confidence by a majority within the UBP, Furbert yielded to party pressure and resigned on 29 March; deputy leader, Michael Dunkley, was elected unopposed as his successor on 2 April.

In December 2004 the Senate approved the Ombudsman Act, which created the post of Ombudsman to investigate complaints against the Government, although ministers would be exempt from the Ombudsman's remit; Arlene Brock was appointed to this post in May 2005. In January of that year the Bermuda Independence Commission was established, in co-operation with the UN Committee on Decolonization, in order to investigate and report on the implications of transition to self-rule. In November the Commission submitted its report; however, its findings were criticized for being biased, as they failed to include contributions from the UBP, using only the ruling PLP's submission. In an attempt to quell the criticism, Scott declared that discussions would take place in 2006 regarding the future status of Bermuda. However, public opinion remained strongly in favour of maintaining links with the United Kingdom: according to opinion polls in June 2006, only 20% of the public supported independence, while an overwhelming 65% opposed complete secession from the United Kingdom. In March both the UN and the British Government indicated their support for a referendum on the issue; however, Scott maintained that the question of independence should be decided at the next general election. The issue of independence created political tension between the population's black majority, from which the PLP drew much of its support, and the white minority.

The issue of future independence for Bermuda arose again in March 2007 when Premier Brown declared such an eventuality 'inevitable', but unlikely to feature prominently in preparations for the impending election. Pursuing such a contentious objective was deemed likely to jeopardize the PLP's chances of success. Brown indicated that constitutional revisions must be effected and the entrenchment of economic dependence upon the United Kingdom in the national ideology be reversed before advances towards such an historical development could be achieved. However, relations with the United Kingdom had become increasingly strained following the unauthorized disclosure, by a source within the Bermudian police force, of documents relating to a scandal in which the Premier, among other high-profile government officials, was implicated. Brown maintained that the previous inquiry into the alleged corrupt arrangement between government personnel (including himself) and the state-owned Bermuda Housing Corporation (BHC)—whereby substantial sums of public money were appropriated for private benefit—had exonerated him of any wrongdoing. Moreover, he blamed Governor Sir John Vereker for failing to ensure the documents' security, thereby allowing the information into the public realm.

Despite speculation that the events had gravely damaged Premier Brown's reputation and the PLP's popularity, in a general election held on 18 December 2007 the PLP secured a third consecutive term in office with 52.5% of the votes cast, while the UBP won 47.3% of the ballot. The parties' representation in the legislature remained as at the 2003 election: 22 seats for the PLP and 14 seats for the UBP. Brown was duly sworn in as Premier two days later. Allegations of corruption and issues of race featured prominently in the election campaign, with PLP candidates employing inflammatory rhetoric to suggest that the UBP, if elected, would install a regime oppressive to the black population. After failing to win the constituency seat he contested, Michael Dunkley was replaced as leader of the UBP by Kim Swan, who had been the party's leader in the Senate for six years. Meanwhile, on 12 December Richard Gozney was inaugurated as Governor of Bermuda.

There was continued tension in 2008 between the Government and local media sources after David Burch, the Minister of Labour, Home Affairs and Housing, announced in March that his ministry was to cease advertising in and subscribing to *The Royal Gazette*, the country's most widely read daily newspaper. This was followed by a government-wide ban on the same activities, justified as an attempt to reduce the amount of money spent by the Government on print media advertising and subscriptions. However, the editor of the newspaper, William (Bill) Zuill, claimed that the action was politically motivated in response to his publication's support for public access to information and due to the Government's perception that *The Royal Gazette* supported the opposition UBP, which the editor denied. Furthermore, the newspaper had been the vessel of publication of the leaked report relating to the BHC.

The allegations of corruption at the BHC featured in a report issued by the FCO regarding the British Overseas Territories in July 2008, which recommended that the Government make clear the measures it had taken to investigate the allegations and also advised it to improve transparency on a wider scale, to include the establishment of an independent electoral commission. The document further recommended the extension of voting rights to 'non-Belongers' and an end to the practice of conscription.

A political dispute developed in mid-June 2009 after it was revealed that the PLP Government had agreed with US authorities to allow four Chinese Uygur (Uighur) Muslim separatists to settle in Bermuda following their release from the US detention centre at Guantánamo Bay, Cuba. The UBP claimed that Premier Brown had acted 'autocratically' by accepting the former detainees without consultation with either the Cabinet, the Governor or the British Government. On 20 June the opposition brought a motion of no confidence in the House of Assembly, which the Government survived by 22 to 11 votes. Following the vote, the Minister of Culture and Social Rehabilitation, Dale Butler, resigned in protest at the Premier's handling of the affair. Neletha Butterfield was appointed to succeed him. The FCO also remonstrated with the Government for its lack of consultation, claiming that the matter fell outside the Bermudian authorities' remit. None the less, following a security assessment of the Uygurs, the FCO concluded that they did not pose a 'significant risk', and in November the British monarch, Queen Elizabeth II, undertook a three-day visit to Bermuda to mark the 400th anniversary of its settlement by the British.

Continued divisions within the UBP prompted the defection from the party of five members of the House of Assembly in September and October 2009, reducing its representation in the chamber to nine seats. While two, including former UBP leader Wayne Fubert, subsequently chose to sit as independents in the House of Assembly, three joined other erstwhile members of the UBP in forming a new political organization, the Bermuda Democratic Alliance (BDA), in November. Craig Cannonier, a businessman, and Michael Fahy, a former UBP senator, were elected as leader and Chairman of the BDA, respectively, at the party's inaugural conference in February 2010. Meanwhile, there was speculation regarding a successor to Premier Brown, who had declared his intention to stand down on completion of his four-year term as leader of the PLP in October, with the Deputy Premier Cox widely reported to be the main contender.

Scrutiny of Bermuda's burgeoning financial services industry intensified in 2006, with an increased incidence of money-laundering and embezzlement. The arrest in Bermuda of Dutch businessman and oil magnate John Deuss in October attracted considerable local and international media interest; Deuss was compelled to resign as Chairman and CEO of Bermuda Commercial Bank following allegations of money-laundering, among other illegal practices, and extradited to the Netherlands. Despite this, and reports of other such offences, the House of Assembly ratified the Investment Funds Act 2006 in December; the legislation was designed to facilitate the registration and licensing of investment funds in the territory, by eliminating 'unnecessary' administrative protocols, and to encourage further expansion in a sector already attractive to international fund operators. Bermuda's financial sector was criticized in February 2007 for its resistance to regulatory mechanisms and reluctance to engage in transparency exercises accepted, albeit hesitantly, by its Cayman Islands counterparts. In May 2008 the House of Commons Select Committee on Public Accounts reported that in 2005 the rate of non-compliance with anti-money-laundering measures was relatively high, at 22%, as were the number of suspicious activity reports in 2006, at 380. Scrutiny of the financial sector was compounded in July when the FCO report (see above) recommended that the country make further progress in improving financial regulation, particularly with regards to combating money-laundering. In April 2009 Bermuda was included in OECD's so-called 'grey list' of territories that had committed to but not yet implemented an internationally agreed standard of transparency measures. However, Bermuda was the first jurisdiction to be removed from the list two months later after it signed its 12th tax information-sharing agreement. By May 2010 the Government had signed a further seven accords.

In July 2003 Bermuda became an associate member of the Caribbean Community and Common Market (CARICOM).

Economy

Despite the growth of financial services, it was estimated that tourism still accounted for almost one-half of foreign exchange earnings and, directly and indirectly, for 65% of employment in 1996. The service industries as a whole engaged 86.0% of the employed labour force in 2009, according to preliminary figures. In that year 11.8% of the employed labour force worked in restaurants and hotels. Visitor expenditure in 2004 accounted for an estimated 8.6% of gross domestic product (GDP). The majority of visitors come from the USA (some 73.2% of total arrivals by air in 2009), Canada and the United Kingdom. Although the number of cruise-ship passengers increased in 1998, 1999 and 2000, there was a large decrease (of 14.4%) in 2001, partly owing to the repercussions of the terrorist attacks on the USA on 11 September. The number of air arrivals fell consistently in 1998–2001. In late 2002, in an effort to halt the consequent decline in tourism receipts, the Bermuda Alliance for Tourism launched a rebranding of Bermuda as a luxury destination, in order to attract higher-spending visitors. The number of cruise-ship passengers and air arrivals increased in that year (by 11.5% and 3.1%, respectively); however, the sector suffered a further decline in 2003 when the number of arrivals by air fell by 9.5%. In terms of tourism receipts, which decreased by 9.6%, this decline was not significantly offset by a 13% rise in the number of cruise-ship passengers, who generally spend far less per head than tourists arriving by air. In 2004 a total of 477,754 tourists visited Bermuda; the relatively low level of expenditure in that year was attributed to the closure of a major hotel following damage caused by Hurricane Fabian in late 2003. Despite another severe and prolonged hurricane season in 2005, visitor arrivals increased in that year, to 516,827, although again only owing to a rise in low-spending cruise-ship tourists, the high cost of flights from the USA having discouraged a recovery in the number of visitors arriving by air. However, in 2006 the number of tourists visiting by air increased to the highest level in six years, contributing to an overall rise of 22.9% in visitor arrivals to 635,027. A continued emphasis on tourism to diversify the economy away from the reliance on the insurance sector remained evident, with tourist numbers increasing further in 2007, to 659,572. Arrivals by air and on cruise ships rose by 2.2% and 5.4% respectively. However, the number of tourist arrivals declined by 16.6% in 2008, to 550,021, as a result of the international financial crisis. In 2009 visitor arrivals increased slightly, by 0.8%, to 554,388, but an 11.2% rise in cruise ship arrivals, resulting partly from the opening of a mega-cruise port early that year, masked a 10.5% decline in arrivals by air. Moreover, visitor expenditure declined by 16.0% in the first three quarters of 2009 compared with the same period of 2008, amounting to B $276m. Employment in hotels also contracted in 2009, by 7.6%, while hotel occupancy rates fell by 13.4%, although promotional offers by larger hotels mitigated this decline.

According to preliminary data, 30.3% of the employed workforce were engaged directly in the financial, insurance, real estate and business sectors in 2009. 'Offshore' commercial and financial services were a significant foreign exchange earner. International business accounted for 24.0% of GDP in 2008, while the number of companies registered in Bermuda at the end of 2009 totalled 15,392 (compared with 13,841 in 2001 and 15,631 in 2008). The GDP of the international business sector rose at an average annual rate of 9.2% in 2003–08; it increased by 16.6% in 2007, but declined by 4.4% in 2008. The Bermudian insurance industry was estimated to have doubled during the last decade of the 20th century and by 2000 was the world's third largest. In March 2002 the US Department of the Treasury began an investigation into the reasons many formerly US-based firms had relocated to Bermuda. In late 2001 the industry came under huge pressure from claims made in connection with the September terrorist attacks in the USA, although increased demand for insurance and reinsurance services led to a number of new companies being formed at the same time. In 2008 the insurance industry was adversely affected not only by the global economic downturn but also by high claims following the passing of Hurricanes Ike and Gustav in September. There were indications towards the end of 2009 of an improvement in the performance of the international business sector, particularly the insurance industry, with many companies reporting positive results.

Bermuda is almost entirely dependent on imports, mainly from the USA, and has few export commodities. Therefore, it consistently records a large visible trade deficit (B $1,067m. in 2009). Receipts from the service industries normally ensure a surplus on the current account of the balance of payments ($615m. in 2009). The USA is the principal source of imports (providing 71.1% of total imports in 2008) and the principal market for exports. Other important trading partners include Canada, the United Kingdom and France. The main exports are rum, flowers, medicinal and pharmaceutical products, and re-exported petroleum products. Machinery and transport equipment, basic manufactures, and food, beverages and tobacco are the primary imports.

Industry (including manufacturing, construction, quarrying and public utilities) contributed 8.7% of GDP and employed 12.2% of the work-force in 2009, according to preliminary figures. The principal industrial sector is construction, which (including quarrying) contributed 5.8% of GDP and engaged 8.9% of the employed labour force in that year. Smaller industries include ship repair, small boat building and manufacture of paint, perfume, pharmaceuticals, mineral-water extracts and handicrafts. Energy requirements are met primarily by the import of mineral fuels (accounting for 9.2% of total imports in 2007). Industrial GDP increased by 2.5% in 2008.

Bermuda's overall GDP increased, in real terms, at an average annual rate of 3.9% in 2003–08. GDP growth of 0.7% was recorded in 2008; in 2007 GDP per head was estimated to be the highest in the world at US $91,477. However, GDP was estimated to have contracted by 2.5% in 2009, as a result of the impact of global recession on the tourism and international business sectors. According to official projections, a return to positive growth, of around 0.5%–1.0%, was forecast for 2010, although this was conditional on a sustained recovery in the US economy. In 2008/09 Bermuda recorded a budgetary deficit of $241.4m. (including capital expenditure, interest on debt and sinking fund contributions); the deficit was anticipated to narrow to $193.9m. (revised from $147.7m.) in 2009/10, and to $143.5m. in 2010/11. The average annual rate of inflation was 3.2% in 2000–09. Consumer prices increased by 4.8% in 2008 and by 1.8% in 2009. The official unemployment rate was recorded at 4.5% in May 2009.

Statistical Survey

Source: Dept of Statistics, Cabinet Office, POB HM 3015, Hamilton HM MX; tel. 297-7761; fax 295-8390; e-mail statistics@gov.bm; internet www.statistics.gov.bm.

AREA AND POPULATION

Area: 53.3 sq km (20.59 sq miles).

Population (civilian, non-institutional): 58,460 at census of 20 May 1991; 62,059 (males 29,802, females 32,257) at census of 20 May 2000. *Mid-2010* (official projection): 64,566.

Density (mid-2010): 1,211.4 per sq km.

Population by Age and Sex (official projections at mid-2010): *0–14:* 11,184 (males 5,683, females 5,501); *15–64:* 45,069 (males 21,696, females 23,373); *65 and over:* 8,313 (males 3,376, females 4,937); *Total* 64,566 (males 30,755, females 33,811).

Principal Town (2009, UN estimate): Hamilton (capital) 11,535. Source: UN, *World Urbanization Prospects: The 2009 Revision*.

Births, Marriages and Deaths (2006): Live births 798 (birth rate 12.5 per 1,000); Marriages 876 (marriage rate 13.7 per 1,000); Deaths 461 (death rate 7.2 per 1,000). Note: Figures for births and deaths exclude non-residents and foreign service personnel and their dependants (Sources: UN, *Population and Vital Statistics Report*; UN, *Demographic Yearbook*). *2009:* Birth rate 11.6; Death rate 7.3 (Source: Pan American Health Organization).

Life Expectancy (years at birth, 2009): 80.0 (males 77.2; females 83.7). Source: Pan American Health Organization.

Employment (excluding unpaid family workers, 2008): Agriculture, forestry, fishing, mining and quarrying 717; Manufacturing 915; Electricity, gas and water 412; Construction 3,649; Wholesale and retail trade 4,766; Hotels and restaurants 4,869; Transport and communications 2,602; Financial intermediation 2,907; Real estate 625; Business activities 4,326; Public administration 4,223; Education, health and social services 3,279; Other community, social and personal services 2,162; International business activity 4,761; *Total employed* 40,213. *2009:* Total employed 36,549.

HEALTH AND WELFARE

Total Fertility Rate (children per woman, 2009): 2.0.

Physicians (per 1,000 head, 2005): 2.1.

Hospital Beds (per 1,000 head, 2008): 3.2.

Health Expenditure (% of GDP, 2004): 4.3.

Health Expenditure (public, % of total, 1995): 53.2.

Total Carbon Dioxide Emissions ('000 metric tons, 2006): 564.3.

Carbon Dioxide Emissions Per Head (metric tons, 2006): 8.8.

Source: partly Pan American Health Organization.

For other sources and definitions, see explanatory note on p. vi.

AGRICULTURE, ETC.

Principal Crops (metric tons, 2008, FAO estimates): Potatoes 1,000; Carrots and turnips 380; Vegetables and melons 3,010; Bananas 363.

Livestock (2008, FAO estimates): Cattle 650; Horses 1,000; Pigs 650.

Livestock Products (metric tons, 2008, FAO estimates): Cows' milk 1,550; Hen eggs 300.

Fishing (metric tons, live weight, 2008): Groupers 54; Snappers and jobfishes 37; Wahoo 117; Yellowfin tuna 15; Carangids 49; Caribbean spiny lobster 34; Total catch (incl. others) 400.

Source: FAO.

INDUSTRY

Electric Energy (production, million kWh): 617 in 2005; 631 in 2006; 643 in 2007. Source: UN Industrial Commodity Statistics Database.

FINANCE

Currency and Exchange Rates: 100 cents = 1 Bermuda dollar (B $). *Sterling, US Dollar and Euro Equivalents* (31 May 2010): £1 sterling = B $1.458; US $1 = B $1.000; €1 = B $1.238; B $100 = £68.59 = US $100.00 = €80.75. *Exchange Rate:* The Bermuda dollar is at par with the US dollar. Note: US and Canadian currencies are also accepted.

Budget (B $ million, 2010/11): Total current account revenue 1,058.8; Total current account expenditure 991.3; Total capital expenditure 143.9.

Cost of Living (Consumer Price Index; base: 2000 = 100): All items 124.1 in 2007; 130.0 in 2008; 132.4 in 2009. Source: ILO.

Gross Domestic Product (US $ million at constant 1996 prices): 3,981.8 in 2006; 4,150.4 in 2007; 4,177.9 in 2008.

Expenditure on the Gross Domestic Product (B $ million at current prices, 2008, UN estimates): Government final consumption expenditure 1,284.3; Private final consumption expenditure 4,811.6; Gross fixed capital formation 1,219.4; Change in inventories 63.3; *Total domestic expenditure* 7,378.6; Exports of goods and services 2,626.6; *Less* Imports of goods and services 3,573.1; *GDP in purchasers' values* 6,432.1. Source: UN Statistics Division, National Accounts Main Aggregates Database.

Gross Domestic Product by Economic Activity (B $ million at current prices, 2008): Agriculture, forestry and fishing 48.2; Manufacturing 90.0; Electricity, gas and water 97.8; Construction and quarrying 370.1; Wholesale and retail trade and repair services 435.4; Restaurants and hotels 308.0; Transport and communications 297.1; Financial intermediation 922.4; Real estate and renting activities 876.1; Business activities 596.7; Public administration 326.4; Education, health and social work 397.4; Other community, social and personal services 120.7; International business activity 1,543.9; *Sub-total* 6,430.2; *Less* Imputed bank service charges 583.0; Taxes and duties on imports 245.9; *GDP in purchasers' values* 6,093.1.

Balance of Payments (B $ million, 2009): Exports of goods f.o.b. 21; Imports of goods f.o.b. –1,067; *Trade Balance* –1,046; Receipts from services and income 3,028; Payments on services and income –1,355; *Balance on goods, services and income* 627; Current transfers (net) –13; *Current balance* 615; Direct investment (net) –88; Portfolio investment (net) –1,691; Other investments (net) 2,203; Reserve assets (net) –18; *Overall balance* 1,021.

EXTERNAL TRADE

Principal Commodities (US $ million): *Imports* (2008): Food and live animals 134.5; Beverages and tobacco 58.7; Mineral fuels and lubricants 102.6 (Petroleum and petroleum products 99.0); Chemicals and related products 76.1 (Medicinal and pharmaceutical products 33.4); Basic manufactures 149.4; Machinery and transport equipment 248.7; Total (incl. others) 1,146.8. *Exports* (2003): Total 57.0.

Principal Trading Partners (US $ million, 2008): *Imports:* Canada 76.5; Caribbean countries 12.3; United Kingdom 39.8; USA 815.4; Total (incl. others) 1,146.8. *Exports* (1995): France 7.5; United Kingdom 3.9; USA 31.3; Total (incl. others) 62.9. *2003:* Total exports 57.

Source: partly UN, *International Trade Statistics Yearbook*.

TRANSPORT

Road Traffic (vehicles in use, 2007): Private cars 22,617; Motorcycles 19,232; Buses, taxis and limousines 765; Trucks and tank wagons 4,142; Other 1,196; *Total* 47,952.

Shipping: *Ship Arrivals* (2004): Cruise ships 161; Cargo ships 186; Oil and gas tankers 21. *Merchant Fleet* (registered at 31 December 2008): 153; Total displacement 9,592,499 grt (Source: Lloyd's Register-Fairplay, *World Fleet Statistics*). *International Freight Traffic* ('000 metric tons, 1990): Goods loaded 130; Goods unloaded 470 (Source: UN, *Monthly Bulletin of Statistics*).

Civil Aviation (1999): Aircraft arrivals 6,024; Passengers 354,026; Air cargo 4,761,444 kg; Air mail 422,897 kg.

TOURISM

Visitor Arrivals: 659,572 (arrivals by air 305,548, cruise ship passengers 354,024) in 2007; 550,021 (arrivals by air 263,613, cruise ship passengers 286,408) in 2008; 554,388 (arrivals by air 235,860, cruise ship passengers 318,528) in 2009.

Tourism Receipts (US $ million, incl. passenger transport): 513.2 in 2007; 401.8 in 2008; 331.3 in 2009.

COMMUNICATIONS MEDIA

Radio Receivers (1997): 82,000 in use.

Television Receivers (1999): 70,000 in use.

Telephones (2009): 57,700 main lines in use.

Mobile Cellular Telephones (2009): 85,000 subscribers.

Personal Computers: 14,250 (225 per 1,000 persons) in 2004.

Internet Users (2009): 55,000.

Broadband Subscribers (2009): 40,000.

Daily Newspapers (2004): 1 (estimated circulation 16,708).

Non-daily Newspapers (2004): 2 (estimated circulation 22,650).

Sources: mainly UNESCO, *Statistical Yearbook*; UN, *Statistical Yearbook*; International Telecommunication Union.

EDUCATION

Pre-primary (1999, unless otherwise indicated): 12 schools (2006); 191 teachers; 429 pupils.

Primary: 17 (and 5 middle) schools (2006); 567 teachers (2005/06); 4,678 pupils (2005/06) (Source: partly UNESCO Institute for Statistics).

Senior: 18 schools (1999); 747 teachers (2005/06); 4,518 pupils (2005/06)*.

Higher: 1 institution (2002); 88 teachers (2006/07); 886 students (2006/07).

* Including 7 private schools.

2004: Local student enrolment 10,594 (government schools including pre-school 6,370, private schools excluding pre-school 3,512, Bermuda College 712); Teachers 1,310.

Pupil-teacher Ratio (primary education, UNESCO estimate): 8.3 in 2005/06. Source: UNESCO Institute for Statistics.

Adult Literacy Rate (UNESCO estimates): 99% (males 98%; females 99%) in 1998 (Source: UNESCO, *Statistical Yearbook*).

Directory

The Constitution

The Constitution, introduced on 8 June 1968 and amended in 1973 and 1979, contains provisions relating to the protection of fundamental rights and freedoms of the individual; the powers and duties of the Governor; the composition, powers and procedure of the Legislature; the Cabinet; the judiciary; the public service and finance.

The British monarch is represented by an appointed Governor, who retains responsibility for external affairs, defence, internal security and the police.

The Legislature consists of the monarch, the Senate and the House of Assembly. Three members of the Senate are appointed at the Governor's discretion, five on the advice of the Government leader and three on the advice of the Opposition leader. The Senate elects a President and Vice-President. The House of Assembly, consisting of 36 members elected under universal adult franchise, elects a Speaker and a Deputy Speaker, and sits for a five-year term.

The Cabinet consists of the Premier and at least six other members of the Legislature. The Governor appoints the majority leader in the House of Assembly as Premier, who in turn nominates the other members of the Cabinet. They are assigned responsibilities for government departments and other business and, in some cases, are assisted by Permanent Cabinet Secretaries.

The Cabinet is presided over by the Premier. The Governor's Council enables the Governor to consult with the Premier and two other members of the Cabinet nominated by the Premier on matters for which the Governor has responsibility. The Secretary to the Cabinet, who heads the public service, acts as secretary to the Governor's Council.

Voters must be British subjects aged 18 years or over (lowered from 21 years in 1990), and, if not possessing Bermudian status, must have been registered as electors on 1 May 1976. Candidates for election must qualify as electors, and must possess Bermudian status.

Under the British Overseas Territories Act, which entered into effect in May 2002, Bermudian citizens have the right to United Kingdom citizenship and the right of abode in the United Kingdom. British citizens do not enjoy reciprocal rights.

The Government

HEAD OF STATE

Queen: HM Queen ELIZABETH II.

Governor and Commander-in-Chief: Sir RICHARD HUGH GOZNEY (took office 12 December 2007).

Deputy Governor: DAVID ARKLEY.

CABINET
(July 2010)

The Government is formed by the Progressive Labour Party.

Premier and Minister of Tourism and Transport: Dr EWART FREDERICK BROWN.

Deputy Premier, Minister of Finance and Economic Development: PAULA A. COX.

Minister of Health: WALTER H. ROBAN.

Minister of the Environment and Sports: GLENN A. BLAKENEY.

Minister of Education: ELVIN JAMES.

Minister of Labour, Home Affairs and Housing: DAVID BURCH.

Minister of Energy, Telecommunications and E-Commerce: MICHAEL SCOTT.

Minister of Works and Engineering: DERRICK V. BURGESS.

Minister of Culture and Social Rehabilitation: D. NELETHA I. BUTTERFIELD.

Attorney-General and Minister of Justice: Sen. KIM N. WILSON.

Minister without Portfolio: ZANE DE SILVA.

MINISTRIES

Office of the Governor: Government House, 11 Langton Hill, Pembroke HM 13; tel. 292-3600; fax 292-6831; e-mail depgov@ibl.bm; internet www.gov.bm.

Office of the Premier: Cabinet Office, Cabinet Bldg, 105 Front St, Hamilton HM 12; tel. 292-5501; fax 292-0304; e-mail premier@gov.bm; internet www.gov.bm.

Ministry of Culture and Social Rehabilitation: Melbourne House, Suite 304, 11 Parliament St, POB HM 788, Hamilton HM CX; tel. 296-1574; fax 295-2066.

Ministry of Education: Dundonald Pl., 14 Dundonald St, POB HM 1185, Hamilton HM EX; tel. 278-3300; fax 278-3348; e-mail reve@gov.bm; internet www.moed.bm.

Ministry of Energy, Telecommunications and E-Commerce: F. B. Perry Bldg, 2nd Floor, 40 Church St, POB HM 101, Hamilton HM 12; tel. 292-4595; fax 295-1462; e-mail gtelecom@gov.bm; internet www.mtec.bm.

Ministry of the Environment and Sports: Government Administration Bldg, 3rd Floor, 30 Parliament St, Hamilton HM 12; tel. 297-7590; fax 292-2349.

Ministry of Finance and Economic Development: Government Administration Bldg, 30 Parliament St, Hamilton HM 12; tel. 295-5151; fax 295-5727.

Ministry of Health: Continental Bldg, 25 Church St, Hamilton HM 12; tel. 278-4900; fax 292-2622; e-mail wjones@gov.bm; internet www.health.gov.bm.

Ministry of Justice and Attorney-General's Chambers: Penthouse Floor, Global House, 43 Church St, Hamilton HM 12; tel. 292-2463; fax 292-3608; e-mail agc@gov.bm.

Ministry of Labour, Home Affairs and Housing: Government Administration Bldg, 1st Floor, 30 Parliament St, Hamilton HM 12; tel. 297-7819.

Ministry of Tourism and Transport: Global House, 43 Church St, Hamilton HM 12; tel. 295-3130; fax 295-1013; e-mail clwhitter@gov.bm; internet www.bermudatourism.com.

Ministry of Works and Engineering: General Post Office Bldg, 3rd Floor, 56 Church St, POB HM 525, Hamilton HM 12; tel. 297-7699; fax 295-0170; e-mail nfox@bdagov.bm; internet www.wae.gov.bm.

Legislature

SENATE

President: CAROL ANN MARIE BASSETT.

Vice-President: Dr IDWAL WYN (WALWYN) HUGHES.

There are 11 nominated members.

HOUSE OF ASSEMBLY

Speaker: STANLEY W. LOWE.

Deputy Speaker: Dr JENNIFER M. SMITH.

Clerk to the Legislature: SHERNETTE WOLFE; tel. 292-7408; fax 292-2006; e-mail smwolffe@gov.bm.

General Election, 18 December 2007

Party	% of votes	Seats
Progressive Labour Party	52.5	22
United Bermuda Party	47.3	14
Total (incl. others)	100.0	36

Political Organizations

Bermuda Democratic Alliance (BDA): Hamilton; e-mail info@thealliance.bm; internet www.thealliance.bm; f. 2009 by fmr mems of the United Bermuda Party; Leader CRAIG CANNONIER; Chair. MICHAEL FAHY; Sec. TONI DANIELS.

Progressive Labour Party (PLP): Alaska Hall, 16 Court St, POB 1367, Hamilton HM 17; tel. 292-2264; fax 295-7890; e-mail info@plp.bm; internet www.plp.bm; f. 1963; advocates the 'Bermudianization' of the economy, more equitable taxation, a more developed system of welfare and preparation for independence; Leader Dr EWART FREDERICK BROWN; Chair. ANTHONY SANTUCCI.

United Bermuda Party (UBP): Central Office, 3rd Floor, Bermudiana Arcade, 27 Queen St, Hamilton HM 11; tel. 295-0729; fax 292-7195; e-mail info@ubp.bm; internet www.ubp.bm; f. 1964; policy of participatory democracy, supporting system of free enterprise; Leader KIM SWAN; Chair. JEFF SOUSA; Sec. JANET BRIDGEWATER.

Judicial System

Chief Justice: RICHARD GROUND.

President of the Court of Appeal: EDWARD ZACCA.

Registrar of Supreme Court and Court of Appeal: MICHAEL J. MELLO.

Director of Public Prosecutions: RORY FIELD.

The Court of Appeal was established in 1964, with powers and jurisdiction of equivalent courts in other parts of the Commonwealth. The Supreme Court has jurisdiction over all serious criminal matters and has unlimited civil jurisdiction. The Court also hears civil and criminal appeals from the Magistrates' Courts. The three Magistrates' Courts have jurisdiction over all petty offences, and have a limited civil jurisdiction.

Religion

CHRISTIANITY

The Anglican Communion

According to the latest available census figures (2000), some 23% of the population are Anglicans. The Anglican Church of Bermuda consists of a single, extra-provincial diocese, directly under the metropolitan jurisdiction of the Archbishop of Canterbury, the Primate of All England.

Bishop of Bermuda: Rt Rev. PATRICK WHITE, Bishop's Lodge, 18 Ferrar's Lane, Pembroke HM 08, POB HM 769, Hamilton HM CX; tel. 292-6987; fax 292-5421; internet www.anglican.bm.

The Roman Catholic Church

According to the latest available census figures (2000), some 15% of the population are Roman Catholics. Bermuda forms a single diocese, suffragan to the archdiocese of Kingston in Jamaica. The Bishop participates in the Antilles Episcopal Conference (currently based in Port of Spain, Trinidad and Tobago).

Bishop of Hamilton in Bermuda: ROBERT JOSEPH KURTZ, 2 Astwood Rd, POB HM 1191, Hamilton HM EX; tel. 232-4414; fax 232-4447; e-mail rjkurtz@northrock.bm.

Protestant Churches

According to the 2000 census, 11% of the population are African Methodist Episcopalians, 7% are Seventh-day Adventists, 4% are Pentecostalists and 4% are Wesleyan Methodists. The Presbyterian Church, the Church of God, the Salvation Army, the Brethren Church and the Baptist Church are also active in Bermuda.

Baptist Church: Emmanuel Baptist Church, 35 Dundonald St, Hamilton HM 10; tel. 295-6555; fax 296-4491; Pastor RONALD K. SMITH.

Wesley Methodist Church: 41 Church St, Hamilton HM 12; tel. 292-0418; fax 295-9460; e-mail info@wesley.bm; internet www.wesley.bm; Rev. CALVIN STONE.

The Press

Bermuda Magazine: POB HM 283, Hamilton HM HX; tel. 295-0695; fax 295-8616; e-mail cbarclay@ibl.bm; f. 1990; quarterly; Editor-in-Chief CHARLES BARCLAY.

The Bermuda Sun: 19 Elliott St, POB HM 1241, Hamilton HM FX; tel. 295-3902; fax 292-5597; e-mail feedback@bermudasun.bm; internet www.bermudasun.bm; f. 1964; 2 a week; official govt gazette; Publr RANDY FRENCH; Editor TONY MCWILLIAM; circ. 12,500.

The Bermudian: POB HM 283, Hamilton HM AX; tel. 232-7041; fax 232-7042; e-mail info@thebermudian.com; internet www.thebermudian.com; f. 1930; monthly; pictorial and lifestyle magazine; Editor TINA STEVENSON; circ. 7,500.

Bermudian Business Online: POB HM 283, Hamilton HM AX; tel. 232-7041; fax 232-7042; e-mail info@thebermudian.com; internet www.bermudianbusiness.com; f. 1996; publ. by The Bermudian Publishing Co Ltd; Publr TINA STEVENSON; circ. 2,500.

Preview Bermuda: 19 Elliott St, POB HM 3273, Hamilton HM PX; tel. 292-4155; fax 292-4156; e-mail info@previewbermuda.com; internet www.previewbermuda.com; monthly magazine; caters to tourists and visitors to Bermuda; Publr JACKIE STEVENSON; circ. 15,000 per month.

The Royal Gazette: 2 Par-la-Ville Rd, POB HM 1025, Hamilton HM DX; tel. 295-5881; fax 292-2498; e-mail letters@royalgazette.bm; internet www.theroyalgazette.com; f. 1828; morning daily; incorporates The Colonist and Daily News (f. 1866); Editor WILLIAM J. ZUILL; Man. Dir KEITH JENSEN; circ. 17,500.

TV Week: 2 Par-la-Ville Rd, Hamilton HM 08; tel. 295-5881.

The Worker's Voice: 49 Union Sq., Hamilton HM 12; tel. 292-0044; fax 295-7992; e-mail biu@ibl.bm; fortnightly; organ of the Bermuda Industrial Union; Editor-in-Chief LAVERNE FURBERT.

Publisher

Bermudian Publishing Co Ltd: POB HM 283, Hamilton HM AX; tel. 232-7041; fax 232-7042; e-mail info@thebermudian.com; internet www.thebermudian.com; social sciences, sociology, sports; Editor TINA STEVENSON.

Broadcasting and Communications

TELECOMMUNICATIONS

Bermuda Digital Communications/CellularOne: 22 Reid St, Hamilton HM 11; tel. 296-4010; fax 296-4020; e-mail info@cellularone.bm; internet www.cellularone.bm; f. 1998; mobile cellular telephone operator; CEO KURT EVE.

Bermuda Telephone Co (BTC): 30 Victoria St, POB 1021, Hamilton HM DX; tel. 295-1001; fax 295-1192; e-mail customersupport@btc.bm; internet www.btc.bm; f. 1987; Pres. and CEO FRANCIS R. MUSSENDEN.

Cable & Wireless (Bermuda) Ltd: 1 Middle Rd, Smith's FL 03, POB HM 151, Hamilton HM AX; tel. 497-7000; fax 297-7159; e-mail helpdesk@bda.cwplc.com; internet www.cw.com/bermuda; new fibre-optic submarine cable, 'Gemini Bermuda', replaced satellite dish in October 2007 as facilitator of Cable & Wireless' global communications services; CEO EDDIE SAINTS.

Digicel Bermuda: Washington Mall, 22 Church St, Phase II, POB 896, Hamilton HM 11; tel. 500-5000; fax 295-3235; e-mail info.bermuda@digicelgroup.com; internet www.digicelbermuda.com; f. 2005; CEO (Bermuda) WAYNE MICHAEL CAINES.

TeleBermuda International Ltd (TBI): Victoria Pl., 1st Floor, 31 Victoria St, POB HM 3043, Hamilton HM 10; POB HM 3043, Hamilton HM NX; tel. 296-9000; fax 296-9010; e-mail business@telebermuda.com; internet www.telebermuda.com; f. 1997; a division of GlobeNet Communications, provides an international service; owns a fibre-optic network connecting Bermuda and the USA; Pres. and CEO GREGORY SWAN.

BROADCASTING

Radio

Bermuda Broadcasting Co: POB HM 452, Hamilton HM BX; tel. 295-2828; fax 295-4282; e-mail zbmzfb@bermudabroadcasting.com; f. 1982 as merger of ZBM (f. 1943) and ZFB (f. 1962); operates 4 radio stations; Man. Dir ULRIC P. (RICK) RICHARDSON; Comptroller MALCOLM R. FLETCHER.

DeFontes Broadcasting Co Ltd (VSB): 94 Reid St, POB HM 1450, Hamilton HM FX; tel. 292-0050; fax 295-1658; e-mail news@vsbbermuda.com; internet www.vsbbermuda.com; f. 1981 as St George's Broadcasting Co; commercial; 4 radio stations; Pres. KENNETH DEFONTES; Station Man. MIKE BISHOP.

Television

Bermuda Broadcasting Co: see Radio; operates 2 TV stations (Channels 7 and 9).

Bermuda Cablevision Ltd: 19 Laffan St, POB 1642, Hamilton HM GX; tel. 292-5544; fax 295-3023; e-mail info@cablevision.bm; internet www.cablevision.bm; f. 1988; 180 channels; Pres. DAVID LINES; Gen. Man. TERRY ROBERSON.

DeFontes Broadcasting Co Ltd (VSB): see Radio; operates 1 TV station.

Finance

(cap. = capital; res = reserves; dep. = deposits; m. = million; brs = branches; amounts in Bermuda dollars)

BANKING

Central Bank

Bermuda Monetary Authority: BMA House, 43 Victoria St, Hamilton HM 12; tel. 295-5278; fax 292-7471; e-mail info@bma.bm; internet www.bma.bm; f. 1969; central issuing and monetary authority; cap. 20.0m., res 22.5m., total assets 188.1m. (Dec. 2008); Chair. ALAN COSSAR; CEO JEREMY COX.

Commercial Banks

Bank of N. T. Butterfield & Son Ltd: 65 Front St, POB HM 195, Hamilton HM 12; tel. 298-4691; fax 292-4365; e-mail contact@bntb.bm; internet www.bm.butterfieldgroup.com; f. 1858; inc 1904; cap. 98.4m., res 455.0m., dep. 9,801.2m. (Dec. 2008); Chair. ROBERT MULDERIG; Pres. and CEO BRADFORD KOPP; 4 brs.

Bermuda Commercial Bank Ltd: Bermuda Commercial Bank Bldg, 19 Par-la-Ville Rd, POB 1748, Hamilton HM GX; tel. 295-5678; fax 295-8091; e-mail enquiries@bcb.bm; internet www.bermuda-bcb.com; f. 1969; cap. 13.8m., res 18.2m., dep. 407.6m. (Sept. 2008); COO HORST E. FINKBEINER, II; Chief Financial Officer GREG REID.

HSBC Bank Bermuda Ltd: 6 Front St, POB HM 1020, Hamilton HM 11; tel. 295-4000; fax 295-7093; e-mail customer.care@hsbc.bm; internet www.hsbc.bm; f. 1889; fmrly Bank of Bermuda Ltd; 100% acquired by HSBC Asia Holdings BV (Netherlands) in Feb. 2004; name changed as above in May 2010; cap. 30.0m., res 309.0m., dep. 8,134.7m. (Dec. 2008); Chair. JOHN D. CAMPBELL; CEO PHILIP BUTTERFIELD; 6 brs.

STOCK EXCHANGE

Bermuda Stock Exchange: 3rd Floor, Washington Mall, Church St, POB 1369, Hamilton HM FX; tel. 292-7212; fax 292-7619; e-mail info@bsx.com; internet www.bsx.com; f. 1971; 707 listed equities, funds, debt issues and depositary programmes; Chair. DAVID BROWN; Pres. and CEO GREG WOJCIECHOWSKI.

INSURANCE

Bermuda had a total of some 1,600 registered insurance companies in 2002, the majority of which are subsidiaries of foreign insurance companies, or owned by foreign industrial or financial concerns. Many of them have offices on the island.

Bermuda Insurance Market Information Office: Cedarpark Centre, 48 Cedar Ave, POB HM 2911, Hamilton HM LX; tel. 292-9829; fax 295-3532; e-mail biminfo@bii.bm; internet www.bermuda-insurance.org; division of the Bermuda Insurance Development Council; Dir DAVID FOX.

Major Companies

ACE Bermuda: ACE Global HQ, 17 Woodbourne Ave, POB HM 1015, Hamilton HM DX; tel. 295-5200; fax 298-9620; e-mail info@acebermuda.com; internet www.acebermuda.com; total revenue $14,154m. (Dec. 2007); Pres. and CEO G. REES FLETCHER; Chair. EVAN G. GREENBERG; Regional Exec. ALLISON TOWLSON.

Argus Insurance Co Ltd: Argus Insurance Bldg, 14 Wesley St, POB HM 1064, Hamilton HM EX; tel. 295-2021; fax 292-6763; e-mail insurance@argus.bm; internet www.argus.bm; Pres. and CEO GERALD D. E. SIMONS; Chair. SHEILA E. NICOLL.

Bermuda Insurance Development Council (IDC): c/o Bermuda Insurance Institute, The Cedar Parkade Bldg, 48 Cedar Ave, POB HM 2911, Hamilton HM LX; tel. 292-9829; fax 296-3840; e-mail fox@bii.bm; internet www.bermuda-insurance.org; sub-cttee of the Insurance Advisory Council; Chair. ROGER GILLETT.

Bermuda Insurance Management Association (BIMA): POB HM 2993, Hamilton HM HX; tel. 279-7925; fax 2962-8846; e-mail peter.willitts@libertybermuda.com; f. 1978; manages over 1,200 insurance and reinsurance cos; liaises with govt and other financial orgs with regard to insurance industry issues; Pres. PETER WILLITTS.

Paumanock Insurance Co Ltd: Windsor Place, 3rd Floor, 18 Queen St, Hamilton; tel. 292-2404; fax 292-2648.

XL Insurance Co Ltd: XL House, 1 Bermudiana Rd, Hamilton HM 08; tel. 292-8515; fax 292-5280; e-mail contact.xli@xlgroup.com; internet www.xlinsurance.com; CEO DAVID B. DUCLOS.

Trade and Industry

GOVERNMENT AGENCY

Bermuda Registrar of Companies: Government Administration Bldg, 30 Parliament St, Hamilton HM HX; tel. 294-9244; fax 292-6640; e-mail jfsmith@gov.bm; internet www.roc.gov.bm; Registrar of Companies STEPHEN LOWE.

DEVELOPMENT ORGANIZATION

Bermuda Small Business Development Corpn (BSBDC): Sofia House, 48 Church St, POB HM 637, Hamilton HM CX; tel. 292-5570; fax 295-1600; e-mail bdasmallbusiness@gov.bm; internet www.bsbdc.bm; f. 1980; funded jtly by the Govt and private banks; guarantees loans to small businesses; responsible for establishing economic empowerment zones; Gen. Man. MICHELLE KHALDUN.

CHAMBER OF COMMERCE

Bermuda Chamber of Commerce: 1 Point Pleasant Rd, POB HM 655, Hamilton HM CX; tel. 295-4201; fax 292-5779; e-mail info@bermudacommerce.com; internet www.bermudacommerce.com; f. 1907; Pres. STEPHEN W. G. TODD; Exec. Dir DIANE GORDON; 750 mems.

INDUSTRIAL AND TRADE ASSOCIATION

Bermuda International Business Association (BIBA): The Windsor Place, 1st Floor, 22 Queen St, Hamilton HM 12; tel. 292-0632; fax 292-1797; e-mail info@biba.org; internet www.biba.org; Chair. VICKI COELHO; CEO CHERYL PACKWOOD.

EMPLOYERS' ASSOCIATIONS

Bermuda Employers' Council: 4 Park Rd, Hamilton HM 11; tel. 295-5070; fax 295-1966; e-mail mlaw@bec.bm; internet www.bec.bm; f. 1960; advisory body on employment and labour relations; Pres. WILLIAM DESILVA; Exec. Dir MARTIN LAW; 420 mems.

Construction Association of Bermuda: POB HM 238, Hamilton HM AX; tel. 292-0633; fax 292-0564; e-mail caob@logic.bm; internet www.constructionbermuda.com; f. 1968; Pres. J. ANDREW PEREIRA; 90 mems.

Hotel Employers of Bermuda: c/o Bermuda Hotel Asscn, 'Carmel', 61 King St, Hamilton HM 19; tel. 295-2127; fax 292-6671; e-mail jharvey@bdahotels.bm; f. 1968; Pres. JONATHAN CRELLIN; CEO JOHN HARVEY; 8 mems.

UTILITY

BELCO Holdings Ltd: 27 Serpentine Rd, POB HM 1026, Hamilton HM DX; tel. 295-5111; fax 292-8975; e-mail info@belco.bhl.bm; internet www.belcoholdings.bm; f. 1906; holding co for Bermuda Electric Light Co Ltd, and Bermuda Gas and Utility Co Ltd; Chair. J. MICHAEL COLLIER; Pres. and CEO A. L. VINCENT INGHAM.

TRADE UNIONS

In 2007 trade union membership was estimated at approximately 9,140. There are nine registered trade unions, eight of which profess membership of the Bermuda Trades Union Congress.

Bermuda Industrial Union: 49 Union Sq., Hamilton HM 12; tel. 292-0044; fax 295-7992; e-mail biu@biu.bm; f. 1946; Pres. CHRIS FURBERT; Gen. Sec. HELENA BURGESS; 5,202 mems.

Bermuda Trades Union Congress (BTUC): POB 2080, Hamilton HM HX; tel. 292-6515; fax 292-0697; e-mail mcharles@ibl.bm; Pres.

ANTHONY WOLFFE; Gen. Sec. MICHAEL CHARLES; principal mems of the BTUC include:

Bermuda Federation of Musicians and Variety Artists: Reid St, POB HM 6, Hamilton HM AX; tel. 291-0138; Sec.-Gen. LLOYD H. L. SIMMONS; 318 mems.

Bermuda Public Services Union: POB HM 763, Hamilton HM CX; tel. 292-6985; fax 292-1149; e-mail osimmons@bpsu.bm; internet www.bpsu.bm; re-formed 1961; Pres. ARMELL L. THOMAS; Gen. Sec. EDWARD G. BALL, Jr; c. 3,500 mems.

Bermuda Union of Teachers: 72 Church St, POB HM 726, Hamilton HM CX; tel. 292-6515; fax 292-0697; e-mail butunion@ibl.bm; internet www.bermudaunionofteachers.org; f. 1919; Pres. KEISHA DOUGLAS; Gen. Sec. MICHAEL A. CHARLES; 700 mems.

Transport

ROADS

There are some 225 km (140 miles) of public highways and 222 km of private roads, with almost 6 km reserved for cyclists and pedestrians. Each household is permitted only one passenger vehicle, and visitors may only hire mopeds, to limit traffic congestion.

SHIPPING

The chief port of Bermuda is Hamilton, with a secondary port at St George's. Both are used by freight and cruise ships. There is also a 'free' port, Freeport, on Ireland Island. In 2000 it was proposed to enlarge Hamilton docks in order to accommodate larger cruise ships. There remained, however, fears that such an enlargement would place excessive strain on the island's environment and infrastructure. Bermuda is a 'free-flag' nation, and at December 2008 the shipping register comprised 153 vessels, totalling 9,592,499 grt.

Department of Marine and Ports Services: POB HM 180, Hamilton HM AX; tel. 295-6575; fax 295-5523; e-mail marineports@bolagov.bm; Dir of Marine and Ports Services FRANCIS RICHARDSON; Deputy Dir and Harbour Master DAVID SIMMONS.

Department of Maritime Administration: Magnolia Pl., 2nd Floor, 45 Victoria St, POB HM 1628, Hamilton HM GX; tel. 295-7251; fax 295-3718; e-mail maradros@gov.bm; Chief Surveyor (vacant); Registrar of Shipping ANGELIQUE BURGESS.

Principal Shipping Companies

B & H Ocean Carriers Ltd: Par-la-Ville Pl., 3rd Floor, 14 Par-la-Ville Rd, POB HM 2257, Hamilton HM JX; tel. 295-6875; fax 295-6796; e-mail info@bhcousa.com; internet www.bhocean.com; f. 1988; Chair. MICHAEL S. HUDNER.

Benor Tankers Ltd: Cedar House, 41 Cedar Ave, Hamilton HM 12; Pres. CARL-ERIK HAAVALDSEN; Chair. HARRY RUTTEN.

Bermuda Forwarders Ltd: 2 Mill Creek Park, POB HM 511, Hamilton HM CX; tel. 292-4600; fax 292-1859; e-mail info@bermudaforwarders.com; internet www.bermudaforwarders.com; international import and export handlers; Pres. TOBY KEMPE.

Bernhard Schulte Shipmanagement (Bermuda) Ltd Partnership: Richmond House, 12 Par-la-Ville Rd, POB HM 2089, Hamilton HM HX; tel. 295-0614; fax 292-1549; e-mail management@amlp.bm; internet www.bs-shipmanagement.com; f. 2008 by the merger of Hanseatic Shipping, Dorchester Atlantic Marine, Eurasia Group and Vorsetzen Bereederungs-und Schiffahrtskontor; owned by the Schulte Group; CEO ANDREAS DROUSSIOTIS; Man. Dir JENS ALERS.

BEST Shipping: 6 Addendum Lane South, POB HM 335, Hamilton HM BX; tel. 292-8080; fax 295-1713; e-mail dsousa@best.bm; internet www.best.bm; f. 1987 as Bermuda Export Sea Transfer Ltd; sea and air freight services; Pres. and Man. Dir DAVID SOUSA.

Container Ship Management Ltd: 14 Par-la-Ville Rd, POB HM 2266, Hamilton HM JX; tel. 295-1624; fax 295-3781; e-mail csm@csm.bm; internet www.bcl.bm/csm; Pres. and CEO GEOFFREY FRITH.

Gearbulk Holding Ltd: Par-la-Ville Pl., 14 Par-la-Ville Rd, POB HM 2257, Hamilton HM JX; tel. 295-2184; fax 295-2234; internet www.gearbulk.com; f. 1968; Pres. ARTHUR E. M. JONES.

Golden Ocean Group Ltd: Par-la-Ville Pl., 14 Par-la-Ville Rd, POB HM 1593, Hamilton HM 08; tel. 295-6935; fax 295-3494; e-mail tor@frontmgt.no; internet www.goldenocean.no; Chair. and Pres. JOHN FREDRIKSON.

Meyer Shipping: Waverley Bldg, 35 Church St, Hamilton HM 12; tel. 296-9798; fax 295-4556; e-mail shipping@meyer.bm; internet www.meyer.bm; f. 1867; subsidiary of the Meyer Group of Companies; CEO J. HENRY HAYWARD.

Norwegian Cruise Line: 3rd Floor, Reid House, Church St, POB 1564, Hamilton; internet www.ncl.com; Chair. EINAR KLOSTER.

Shell Bermuda (Overseas) Ltd: Shell House, Ferry Reach, POB 2, St George's 1.

Unicool Ltd: POB HM 1179, Hamilton HM EX; tel. 295-2244; fax 292-8666; Pres. MATS JANSSON.

Worldwide Shipping Ltd: 22 Church St, Suite 412, POB HM 1862, Hamilton HM 11; tel. 295-3770; fax 295-3801.

CIVIL AVIATION

The former US Naval Air Station (the only airfield) was returned to the Government of Bermuda in September 1995, following the closure of the base and the withdrawal of US forces from the islands. Bermuda does not have its own airline. From May 2006 the island was served by the low-cost US airline JetBlue, in addition to other British, Canadian and US airlines.

Department of Civil Aviation: Channel House, Suite 2, 12 Longfield Rd, Southside, St. David's DD 03, POB GE 218, St George's GE BX; tel. 293-1640; fax 293-2417; e-mail info@dca.gov.bm; internet www.dca.gov.bm; responsible for all civil aviation matters; Dir of Civil Aviation THOMAS DUNSTAN.

L.F. Wade International Airport: 3 Cahow Way, St George's GE CX; tel. 293-2470; e-mail dao@gov.bm; internet www.bermudaairport.aero; fmrly Bermuda International Airport, adopted present name 2007; Gen. Man. AARON ADDERLEY.

Tourism

Tourism is the principal industry of Bermuda and is government-sponsored. The great attractions of the islands are the climate, scenery, and facilities for outdoor entertainment of all types. In 2009 a total of 554,388 tourists (including 318,528 cruise ship passengers) visited Bermuda. In 2007 the industry earned an estimated US $569m. In 2006 there were 56 licensed hotels, 2,824 rooms and 5,698 beds.

Bermuda Department of Tourism: Global House, 43 Church St, Hamilton; tel. 292-0023; fax 292-7537; e-mail webmaster@bermudatourism.com; internet www.bermudatourism.com; Dir of Tourism BILLY GRIFFITH.

Bermuda Hotel Association: 'Carmel', 61 King St, Hamilton HM 19; tel. 295-2127; fax 292-6671; e-mail jharvey@bdahotels.bm; internet www.experiencebermuda.com; Pres. FRANK STOCEK; Exec. Dir JOHN HARVEY; 37 mem. hotels.

Defence

The local defence force is the Bermuda Regiment, with a strength of some 630 men and women in 1999. The Regiment employs selective conscription. According to the 2008/09 budget statement, the Government of Bermuda allocated B $8.5m. of its current account expenditure to defence and $57.1m. to the police force for the fiscal year 2007/08 (which, combined, was equivalent to 7.3% of total current expenditure). It was expected to provide $9.0m. and $62.8m. to those departments, respectively, in 2008/09.

Education

There is free compulsory education in government schools between the ages of five and 16 years, and a number of scholarships are awarded for higher education and teacher training. There are also seven private secondary schools, which charge fees. In 2005/06 enrolment at primary and secondary level institutions was equivalent to an estimated 92% of children in the relevant age-groups. The Bermuda College accepts students over the age of 16, and is the only post-secondary educational institution. Extramural degree courses are available through Queen's University, Canada, and Indiana and Maryland Universities, USA. A major public education reform programme was scheduled to be implemented in 2010–15.

BOLIVIA

Geography

PHYSICAL FEATURES

The Republic of Bolivia lies at the heart of the South American continent, in the centre-west, set on the high Andes, but reaching down into the Amazon basin. The country is landlocked, and has been since 1884, when it lost the Atacama Desert region to Chile (with which it still maintains demands for a sovereign corridor to the Pacific). The border with Chile, 861 km (535 miles) in extent, is in the south-west, while the rest of the western border, further north, is with Peru (900 km in extent). Brazil (with which Bolivia has a long, 3,400-km border) is to the north and north-east, the other landlocked country of the continent, Paraguay (750 km), to the south-east, and Argentina (832 km) to the south. The country is the fifth largest in South America, the size of France and Spain together, and covers 1,098,581 sq km (424,164 sq miles).

Bolivia's maximum length, from north to south, is about 1,530 km and its maximum breadth 1,450 km. Known as a 'rooftop of the world' from the setting of its lofty plateau amid the high Andes (which account for about one-third of the territory), the country also reaches down the eastern slopes of the mountains into vast grassy plains threaded by rivers with densely forested banks (Oriente). The high plateau is known as the *altiplano* and the lower slopes and valleys as the Yungas, while in the south-east the plains of the Amazonian–Chaco lowlands are known as the Llanos. The Andes form two main ranges in western Bolivia, the lower Cordillera Occidental along the border with Chile and, further inland, the great peaks of the broader Cordillera Oriental (Cordillera Real), also crossing from north to south, but in the centre-west of the country. Between the ranges is the main plateau, about 800 km long and 130 km wide, arid in the south, but in the north the country shares Lake Titicaca, the highest navigable lake in the world (at 3,805 m or 12,488 ft), with Peru. The region consists of snowy peaks and broad, windy plateaux over 4,000 m above sea level, often barren but for ichu (a coarse grass). The highest peak is Illimani (6,462 m). The Yungas consists of the lower, eastern slopes of the Cordillera Oriental, the fertile, forested and well watered, but steep, valleys, separating the plateau region and the plains. Then, east and north-east of the mountains are the great Amazonian plains. South of them, beyond the low Chiquitos hills, is the Bolivian portion of the dry plains of the fought-over Chaco, the Llanos. Vast swathes of the plains become swampland during the rainy season, but the drier parts provide rich grazing for livestock. The plains are covered by great grasslands, although along the rivers, particularly in the north-east, there are stretches of dense tropical rainforest (forests cover about one-half of the country). Rivers drain either into the Amazon basin or into the system of the Río de la Plata (River Plate)—the lowest point in Bolivia, at 90 m above sea level, is the Paraguay river, part of the latter system, as it leaves the country. This vast, sparsely populated and rough countryside also enables Bolivia to have become the world's third largest cultivator of coca (after Colombia and Peru).

CLIMATE

The country is situated entirely in the tropics, but its varied elevation gives it a wide range of climates. It is cold and dry in the mountainous south-west, but it is much warmer and wetter lower down. Being south of the Equator, winter is in the middle of the calendar year. The mean annual temperature in the *altiplano*, where most people live, is 8°C (46°F) and in the Llanos 26°C (79°F). The Yungas is more subtropical than the higher slopes. The main rain-bearing winds are those that cross the Amazon basin, and the north-east, particularly, is prone to flooding during the wet season (December–January),

although droughts here are equally possible. The Llanos gets drier towards the south.

POPULATION

Most people are Amerindian, native American, and have only been involved in the activities of the state and the benefits of its economy since the 1950s, when greater social mobility was encouraged, to the detriment of the white ruling élite. About 56% of the population are reckoned to be Amerindian, or predominantly Amerindian, and 30% *mestizo* (predominantly of Spanish descent), with the rest white, apart from a small number of those of African descent. Bolivia was, anciently, home to a flourishing Aymará civilization based around Titicaca, but was later conquered by the Quechua-speaking Incas from the north. The Quechua peoples alone are put at about one-quarter of the population, while the Aymará now fall short of one-fifth. Given that only 36% of Bolivians use Spanish as their principal language, it is no surprise to find that Quechua and Aymará have joined it as official languages. Guaraní is the main one of the other indigenous languages in use. Although other aspects of native tradition are powerful in Bolivian culture, some homogeneity was provided by the prevalence of at least nominal, if adapted, Roman Catholic Christianity (still over 80% of the population). There are also increasing numbers of Protestant denominations, particularly the more evangelical ones, while the Bahá'ís claim almost 3%.

The total population at mid-2010 was put at an estimated 10.4m., with most people living in the mountains (although the eastern lowlands have become more populated since the second half of the 20th century, owing to the exploitation of the hydrocarbons resources here), but less than two-fifths in rural areas. Bolivia is one of the least-densely populated Latin American countries. The administrative capital and largest city (with its suburbs) is La Paz, in the west, at the northern end of the *altiplano*, and, at 3,640 m, the highest capital in the world. The judicial and constitutional capital is Sucre, in the centre-south. Between them, also in the highlands, are Cochabamba, at the centre of a fertile farming area, and the mining town of Oruro, more to the west. To the east, on the edge of the plains, is Santa Cruz de la Sierra, which is the only metropolis in Bolivia to have over 1m. people in the city proper. The country is divided into nine departments for administrative purposes.

History

JOHN CRABTREE

INTRODUCTION

Indigenous civilizations flourished in what is now Bolivia long before the Spanish Conquest in the 16th century. In the mid-15th century the Inca empire extended its control over highland Bolivia, integrating the region around Lake Titicaca, and by the late 15th century Inca rule stretched from southern Colombia to northern Argentina. The Spanish invasion in 1533 quickly led to the creation of a new empire, with the establishment of the cities of Chuquisaca (today's Sucre) and La Paz during the 1540s. The discovery of enormous silver deposits at the Cerro Rico in Potosí in 1545 conferred on these territories huge economic importance, and by the end of the 16th century Potosí had become the largest city in the Americas. The development of mining in Potosí and elsewhere provided the stimulus for agricultural development in the inter-Andean valleys which became the territory's main 'bread basket'.

COLONIAL AND REPUBLICAN BOLIVIA

Spanish rule was exercised from Lima in Peru and lasted until the independent republic of Bolivia was established in 1825. As elsewhere in the Spanish colonies, the indigenous population was reduced to subservient status. However, indigenous culture proved more durable in the central Andes, and there were many rebellions against Spanish rule. The most important were the rebellions of Tupac Amaru and Tupaj Katari in southern Peru and western Bolivia, respectively. Both were put down with great violence. The decline in the power of Lima in the late 18th century encouraged the atomization of empire and the development of local power centres. In Bolivia, the most important was Chuquisaca, where independence was proclaimed following Simón Bolívar's victories over the Spanish armies in Peru. Bolivia's first President was José Antonio de Sucre.

At the outset, Bolivia was composed of a number of quasi-independent 'departments' that loosely reflected the system of *intendencias* (mayoralties) established by the colonial administration. However, Bolívar, after whom the new country was named, rejected federalism as a system of government. The struggle for hegemony between power centres, particularly between Sucre and La Paz, was one of the main factors behind Bolivia's chronic instability during much of the 19th century. The supremacy of La Paz was finally clinched after a civil war in 1899. Meanwhile, the country was dealt a rude shock during the War of the Pacific (1879–83), when it lost its Pacific department, based on Antofagasta, to Chile. Bolivia has repeatedly sought to regain its access to the sea, but so far without success.

The Chaco War and its Legacy

Bolivia's territorial integrity continued to suffer at the hands of its neighbours. In 1903 it lost Acre to Brazil, and then in 1935—following the Chaco War (1932–35)—it lost a large swathe of this semi-desert region to Paraguay. The experience of this bloody war, involving the mobilization of indigenous peasants, became one of the main catalysts of the development of Bolivian nationalism and causes of the 1952 'national' revolution. Meanwhile, domestic politics stabilized in the 1880s with the emergence of an élite-run two-party system, a system that was already showing signs of weakness and which was dealt a body blow by the disastrous defeat in the Chaco.

The emergence of new forces in Bolivian politics, particularly on the left, became evident in the 1930s. Nationalist military governments, opposed to the élite (known in Bolivia as the *rosca*), sought to engineer important reforms. In 1937 (two years before the Mexican petroleum nationalization), the Government of David Toro Ruilova took the Bolivian assets of Standard Oil into state control, establishing Yacimientos Petrolíferos Fiscales Bolivianos (YPFB). In 1938 the Government of Germán Busch created a Ministry of Labour. That year also saw a constitutional reform that, among other things, rejected economic liberalism in favour of greater state intervention. In 1941 the Movimiento Nacionalista Revolucionario (MNR) was established; the new party eschewed class-based politics and followed a nationalist ideology, influenced by the development of populist movements elsewhere in Latin America. Reflecting the increased salience of organized labour, the mineworkers in 1943 set up the Federación Sindical de Trabajadores Mineros de Bolivia (FSTMB). A coup that year brought to power Gualberto Villaroel, backed by the increasingly influential MNR. However, Villaroel and the MNR were overturned by an élite-backed coup in 1946.

THE 1952 REVOLUTION AND ITS LEGACY

The revolution of 1952 represented an important watershed in Bolivian history in the 20th century, finally breaking the power of the mining élites—the so-called 'tin barons' (the Patiño, Aramayo and Hochschild families)—and ushering in a period of state-led development. The 1952 revolution occurred in the wake of the MNR's election victory in the previous year. This had been met with a military coup that prevented the MNR's presidential candidate, Víctor Paz Estenssoro, from taking power. The revolution involved three days of fighting in which armed workers and deserting conscripts overwhelmed the army. Some 600 people died in the battles. Paz Estenssoro became the new President, with the other main MNR leader, Hernán Siles Zuazo, his Vice-President.

Reformist Impulse

The new Government introduced some far-reaching changes. The first of these was universal suffrage, giving the vote to the country's previously marginalized indigenous peasant population. It then announced the nationalization of the country's largest mines, belonging to Patiño, Aramayo and Hochschild, which, in turn, led to the formation of the Corporación Minera de Bolivia (COMIBOL). Finally, in 1953, the Government announced its agrarian reform programme. This involved the formal ending of peonage and the division of large landed estates among the *campesinos* (peasantry), as they became known after 1952. In fact, the reform programme was more a ratification of the land seizures that had taken place the year before. In terms of territory, the land reform had most impact in the *altiplano* and the inter-Andean valleys; it did not affect the eastern half of the country where there was little pressure on available land and no organized *campesino* presence.

The revolution greatly added to the power of organized labour in Bolivia. Led by the FSTMB, which had played an important role in the insurrection, the new Government swiftly organized existing unions into a powerful confederation, the Central Obrera Boliviana (COB). The COB was effectively dominated by the mineworkers. The key figure linking the Government and the new union structure was Juan Lechín Oquendo. At the same time as pushing through the agrarian reform, the MNR Government sought to organize its peasant base into peasant unions.

Conservative Shift

Concerned by this leftwards lurch in Bolivian politics, coming as it did at the height of the Cold War, the US Administration sought to coax the new Government into a more moderate position. In particular, the USA sought to wean Paz Estenssoro away from Lechín and the COB. The economic crisis of 1956–57, which ended in rampant inflation, provided the opportunity to win over key sectors of the MNR leadership. The USA was able to provide much-needed finance in return for a stabilization plan that ran counter to the MNR's more left-wing policies. This was institutionalized in 1961 by the Plan Triangular (backed by the USA, the Federal Republic of Germany and the Inter-American Development Bank), which sought to rehabilitate the country's mines on the condition that COMIBOL was reorganized and its number of employees reduced.

The post-revolutionary Governments—that of Paz Estenssoro (1952–56 and 1960–64) and Siles Zuazo (1956–60)—also strove to develop the eastern part of the country, developing agriculture so as to reduce Bolivia's dependence on mining exports. This diversification strategy had been suggested in the 1940s by the US Bohan Commission. Economic integration was facilitated by the completion in 1954 of a highway linking Santa Cruz with Cochabamba and La Paz. In the 1950s and early 1960s large-scale funding was made available to develop cash crop agriculture, and the MNR Governments devised official programmes to encourage migration of labour from the west of the country to the eastern lowlands. Spurred on economically by the development of petroleum resources in Santa Cruz department, growth rates far outpaced those of other parts of Bolivia. This encouraged, in turn, the emergence of a powerful, conservative élite, concerned to promote its departments' interests irrespective of the rest of the country. Its mouthpiece was the Comité Pro-Santa Cruz.

Military Predominance, 1964–78

The period of MNR rule was brought to an abrupt end in November 1964, when the armed forces took power. Paz Estenssoro was overthrown by his Vice-President, Gen. René Barrientos Ortuño. In 1966 Barrientos, who enjoyed a good deal of popularity, won a presidential election. However, he died in a plane crash in 1969. He was succeeded by his Vice-President, Luis Adolfo Siles Salinas, who in turn was overthrown in a coup in the same year by Gen. Alfredo Ovando Candía. In October 1970 Ovando was himself thrown out of office by a leftist army general, Juan José Torres González. Pursuing an agenda of radical reforms, Torres was ejected in 1971 in a coup organized by Col (later Gen.) Hugo Bánzer Suárez and the right wing of the army. Bánzer went on to rule Bolivia for a comparatively long period, until 1978.

The new Bánzer administration enjoyed the decided support of the USA and the new élite of Santa Cruz. Effectively destroyed in 1952, the army had emerged as a key factor of political power in the years that followed. The USA provided important support in terms of money and training. However, as the ideological gyrations that took place after the death of Barrientos suggested, the army was not a cohesive force in political terms. Under Bánzer, however, the army adopted a more right-wing posture. It sought further to secure Santa Cruz's privileged position and to curb the power of the COB and the FSTMB.

Contested Interlude, 1978–82

The fall of Bánzer in 1978 led to a period of short-lived Governments, both military and civilian. Under US pressure to return the country to democracy, three presidential elections in so many years (1978, 1979 and 1980) failed to resolve the log-jam in Bolivian politics. Then, in 1980, in a coup designed to put an end to this short-lived 'democratic opening', a group of military officers closely connected to Bolivia's drugs production interests seized power. Three military Presidents ensued: Gen. Luis García Meza (1980–81), Gen. Celso Torrelio Villa (1981–82) and Gen. Guido Vildoso Calderón (1982). None of these Governments managed to generate domestic legitimacy and, externally, they faced US hostility because of two new departures in that country's foreign policy: the salience of illegal narcotics production and the support for democratization in Latin America. Economic crisis led to the military finally handing over power in 1982 to Siles Zuazo, the victor of the presidential election in 1980.

RETURN TO CONSTITUTIONAL RULE

The presidency of Siles Zuazo marked the beginning of the democratic period in Bolivian politics which has lasted to the present day. However, the Siles Government found itself wracked by internal dissension between the parties of which it was composed: Siles's Movimiento Nacionalista Revolucionario de Izquierda (MNRI—Siles had left the MNR proper and formed his own party in 1971), the Movimiento de la Izquierda Revolucionaria (MIR) and the Partido Comunista de Bolivia (PCB). It also had to contend with the effects of the debt crisis and simultaneously confront serious labour unrest. The Government was unable to control prices in a process of escalating hyperinflation. Responding finally to a general strike called by the COB, Siles was obliged to hold a presidential election one year early. This was duly held in July 1985, and was won by Siles's old partner in the 1952 revolution, Víctor Paz Estenssoro.

The Return of Paz Estenssoro, 1985–89

The return of Paz Estenssoro to the presidency, after 21 years, opened a new chapter in the life of this wily and experienced politician. The man who had led Bolivia as it entered its most interventionist period was the same man who presided over a period of economic liberalization. The so-called New Economic Policy, warmly supported by the international financial community, was a determined effort to achieve stabilization via trade and currency liberalization and fiscal and monetary orthodoxy. It had major social costs, however, which the Government did little to mitigate. In particular, the New Economic Policy involved a massive reorganization of the public sector, particularly the state mining industry. Responding also to a sharp collapse in tin prices on international metals markets, the Government effectively closed down this sector, with the loss of some 25,000 jobs.

Although elected with the support of the MIR, Paz Estenssoro quickly moved into a working relationship with Bánzer's right-wing Acción Democrática Nacionalista (ADN). His policies were premised on close collaboration with the business sector, and all ties with the unions—relations with which had never recovered from the wide-ranging dismissals of FSTMB members—were severed. One of the main architects of stabilization was one of Bolivia's wealthiest private sector mine owners, Gonzalo Sánchez de Lozada. The Government also won the enthusiastic support of the World Bank, which provided Bolivia with a much-needed financial infusion. The positive effects of stabilization on domestic prices were quickly felt, helping to provide political support for the Paz Estenssoro administration. The President also found himself the beneficiary of the declining political clout of both the trade union movement and the army. The former mounted several attempts to protest against the Government's policies, but these had little effect. The reputation of the latter had been badly damaged by its former involvement in drugs-trafficking.

Jaime Paz Zamora, 1989–93

The 1989 elections brought to office Jaime Paz Zamora, leader of the MIR and Paz Estenssoro's nephew. Although Paz Zamora was actually third-placed in the elections, he managed to engineer a pact with Bánzer (who came second) to deprive the front-running MNR candidate, Sánchez de Lozada, of the presidency. Under Bolivia's electoral rules at the time, a run-off vote in the newly elected Congreso Nacional (Congress) was held if no candidate achieved an overall majority (50% plus one) of votes. Although Bánzer failed this time in his ambition to return to the presidency by constitutional means, the ADN was given a great deal of influence in the new Government, which continued the broad pro-business thrust of the previous administration. A timid privatization programme was launched. However, in spite of this conversion, Paz Zamora never enjoyed the trust of the USA owing to his alleged connections with drug interests.

The late 1980s and early 1990s saw the emergence of parties that drew their support primarily from popular sectors and which had a populist message. These were Conciencia de Patria (Condepa), set up in 1988, and Unión Cívica Solidaridad (UCS), established in 1989. These parties represented an important departure from the more traditional parties, and offered a conduit for dissent. They tended to prosper at the expense of the older parties of the left. Another growing force was the emergence of indigenist politics, particularly among Aymará-speaking peoples of the *altiplano*. This was associated with the so-called Kataristas, who sought to create an independent force among the peasantry, shaking off the links with the state cultivated first by the MNR and then by the military after the 1964 coup. Katarismo involved various strands that veered from class-based politics through to a more overt form of race politics. However, indigenist politics was not just confined to the *altiplano*: in 1990 ethnic groups from the east of the country marched from Trinidad in Beni to La Paz to demand rights for lowland indigenous tribes as well.

Sánchez de Lozada, 1993–97

Deprived of the presidency in 1989, Sánchez de Lozada narrowly managed to achieve his ambition in 1993 with the help of UCS, the Movimiento Bolivia Libre, a splinter group from the MIR, and a small faction of the Kataristas. Sánchez de Lozada was primarily concerned to pursue the liberalizing agenda he had begun as Paz Estenssoro's Minister of Planning, as well as to consolidate the model politically by speading the benefits of reform more widely. His 'Plan de Todos' (Plan for All) gave pride of place to privatization, which he argued was the key to sustainable growth and thus higher living standards. He called his model 'capitalization', since it was a hybrid scheme of privatization that involved foreign partners 'capitalizing' state companies by investing the estimated value of the company and taking management control. The existing stock value of the company would then be invested and provide income for a pension benefit called the Bonosol. By far the most important public company to be capitalized was YPFB.

Another key reform designed to build political support was Popular Participation, which involved the expansion of municipal government. Not only did it create a large number of municipalities in rural areas where the state had hardly existed previously, it also greatly increased the amount of spending channelled through them. It provided a mechanism through which to tackle extreme poverty, harnessing local civil society in exercising oversight into the way government money was applied. Its critics, however, charged that it sought to strengthen the hand of the President at the local level and to sap the strength of departmental-level institutions. Other innovative reforms pursued by the Sánchez de Lozada administration included plurilingual educational reforms and an attempt to revamp agrarian reform and apply it to eastern Bolivia.

Consensus Breakdown: the Bánzer Government, 1997–2002

The hope that such reforms would help keep the MNR in power, however, proved misplaced, and in the 1997 elections Bánzer emerged victorious at the head of what he called his 'mega-coalition'—an amalgam of the ADN, the MIR, UCS and Condepa. This proved an unwieldy mixture of elements, and the Government soon gained an unfortunate reputation for crony politics, corruption and graft. Though Bánzer was elected for a five-year term, his ailing health meant that he had to resign a year early, in 2001, and confer power on his youthful Vice-President, Jorge 'Tuto' Quiroga Ramírez, who served out Bánzer's last year in office.

Virulent opposition emerged to Bánzer and his policies in a number of areas. First, and most significant, was the reaction of the country's coca farmers, led by Juan Evo Morales Aima, to Bánzer's 'zero tolerance' policy on drugs-cultivation. Use of the army to eradicate coca in the Chapare district of Cochabamba brought an energetic response from the *cocaleros*, many of them displaced mineworkers who had lost their jobs in 1985. Second, there were growing signs of unrest on the *altiplano*, where indigenist leader Felipe Quispe emerged as the *mallku*, or the self-styled leader of the 'Aymará nation'. Quispe became adept at the use of road-blocks and other forms of direct action to make demands on the Government. Finally, the attempt to privatize water supplies in Cochabamba precipitated the so-called 'Water War', a massive local protest in 1999 and 2000, which ended with the Government ignominiously backing down and cancelling a contract with the US multinational Bechtel.

Breakdown in the System of Pacts

The return of Sánchez de Lozada to office in 2002, having only narrowly beaten Evo Morales in the presidential election, compounded this sense of growing tension. Sánchez de Lozada failed to bring 'new ideas' to the fore in the way he had in his first administration. However, it was his handling of plans to sell Bolivian gas to the USA via a pipeline passing through northern Chile that proved the catalyst for the premature collapse of his Government. Riots in El Alto, dubbed the 'Gas War', resulted in a violent stand-off, in which many were killed. Deserted by his allies and with doubts as to the loyalty of the army, Sánchez de Lozada agreed to step down from office in October 2003, less than 15 months after assuming the presidency. He was replaced by his Vice-President, Carlos Mesa Gisbert, who switched sides at the last moment and agreed to meet a list of opposition demands known as the 'October agenda'.

President Mesa moved ahead with demands to put a series of questions about gas exploitation to a referendum. This authorized the Government to push ahead with a new hydrocarbons law that was much more nationalist in flavour than the scheme devised in 1996 by Sánchez de Lozada to attract foreign investors. However, ultimately, Mesa was reluctant to put his name to new legislation approved by the Congreso. With the tide of public unrest rapidly rising once again, he resigned in June 2005, giving way to a short interim administration headed by the President of the Supreme Court, Eduardo Rodríguez Veltzé, whose main achievement was to hold fresh presidential and legislative elections in December. Elections were also held for departmental prefects for the first time.

EVO MORALES, 2006–

The landslide victory of Evo Morales in the presidential election of 18 December 2005, with a massive 53.7% of the votes cast (avoiding the need for a vote in the Congreso), represented a landmark in recent Bolivian history. His party, the Movimiento al Socialismo (MAS), also won a majority of seats, 72, in the 130-seat Cámara de Diputados, and only narrowly missed winning a majority in the Senado, securing 12 of the 27 upper house seats. The election therefore brought to an end the discredited system of party pacts. Morales was the first 'indigenous' head of state in a country where a *mestizo* minority had traditionally predominated. His rise to power from the humblest of backgrounds added to this symbolism, augmenting his legitimacy.

New Policy Direction

Morales abandoned the neo-liberal policies that had prevailed since 1985. The first major sign of this was his 'renationalizing' of Bolivia's oil and gas industry in May 2006, forcing foreign investors to sign new contracts that enhanced the role of YPFB and greatly increased the taxes payable to the state. All investors in the oil and gas industries ended up signing the new contracts, thereby avoiding international arbitration proceedings. Morales's Government also sought to extend power to those who had traditionally been excluded from Bolivian politics, especially the country's indigenous majority. Morales's first Cabinet included many from the social movements that had opposed successive previous Governments. Indeed, the MAS was less a political party as such, more a coalition of disparate social movements, united mainly by their support for Morales.

The new President made more of an impression outside Bolivia than any of his recent predecessors. His election was widely perceived as part of a changing 'tide' in Latin America towards support for the left. He immediately forged close ties with the left-wing administrations of Venezuela and Cuba, but at the same time developed a close rapport with Presidents Luiz Inácio Lula da Silva in Brazil and Néstor Carlos Kirchner in Argentina. The election of Morales brought a marked improvement in relations with Chile, where a left-leaning head of state, Michelle Bachelet Jeria, also took office in early 2006. The US Administration of George W. Bush avoided outright confrontation with Bolivia, in spite of marked differences between the two countries over coca cultivation.

Opposition to Morales

However, domestic opposition to Morales quickly made itself felt over his plans to rewrite the country's Constitution. Elected in July 2006, a Constituent Assembly was given one year to produce a draft constitution, which would then be submitted to a referendum. The conservative minority in the Constituent Assembly, backed by strong support from Santa Cruz and other anti-Morales strongholds, adroitly used its influence to stymie the MAS's agenda. The opposition was particularly insistent that the Government honour commitments towards greater regional and departmental autonomy. Due to the extent of opposition, the deadline for completing the constitution was extended to December 2007. In the end, with that deadline fast approaching and the opposition blocking final agreement, the MAS majority and its allies approved their own constitutional text, with the main opposition party, Poder Democrático y Social (PODEMOS), boycotting the final sessions.

Negotiating the New Constitution

In defiance of the new constitutional text, the opposition—led by the civic authorities in Santa Cruz—published a 'statute of autonomy' for the department at the end of 2007, a document proclaiming a wide measure of independence from central Government. Similar pronouncements were made subsequently in Tarija, Beni and Pando. Negotiations between the Government and opposition prefects proved fruitless. Refusing any compromise, the authorities in Santa Cruz held a referendum on the autonomy proposal. Overwhelming local support for the autonomy statute in Santa Cruz led to similar outcomes in Beni, Pando and Tarija.

However, in the second half of 2008 the Morales Government managed to regain the initiative. In a recall referendum held in August, Morales was ratified as President by two-thirds of the electorate. Although the prefects of the four eastern departments were also ratified, two opposition prefects—those of La Paz and Cochabamba—were voted out of office. A bout of political violence in September in the eastern *media luna* ended in international mediation and the signing of an agreement that paved the way to a referendum on a somewhat amended version of the new constitution in January 2009. The Constitution, duly ratified, was promulgated by Morales at the beginning of February.

Morales's Re-election

Fresh presidential and legislative elections under the terms of the new Constitution were held on 6 December 2009. In the presidential election, Morales and his Vice-President, Alvaro Marcelo García Linera, were re-elected for a further five-year term, with Morales securing a massive 64.2% of the vote compared with only 26.5% for Manfred Reyes Villa, candidate of the recently formed right-wing Plan Progreso para Bolivia–Convergencia Nacional. In the legislative poll, the MAS won 88 seats in the 130-seat Cámara de Diputados and 26 seats in the newly enlarged 36-seat Senado Nacional. Altogether the MAS won more than two-thirds of the seats in the renamed Asamblea Legislative Plurinacional, sufficient (should it wish to do so) to amend the Constitution. Morales announced a reorganization of cabinet portfolios in late January 2010. Further polls were held in April to elect departmental governors (as prefects became known), departmental assemblies, local mayors and local councils. These too produced positive results for the MAS, though not on the same scale as the presidential election. At the departmental level, the party won six out of nine governorships, with opposition incumbents winning in Santa Cruz, Beni and Tarija, but not in Pando. At the municipal level, the MAS won in only three out of 10 major cities (the nine departmental capitals plus El Alto), although it won the great majority of mayoral contests in rural areas.

CONCLUSION AND PROSPECTS

Having been re-elected in 2009, President Morales seemed to be in a strong position to push ahead with his Government's agenda of implementing the terms of the new Constitution. He enjoyed electoral legitimacy, a strong popular following, and was in charge of a Government with the fiscal resources to implement its plans. The opposition appeared demoralized and leaderless at the national level. Yet renewed political conflict seemed likely. The élites of eastern Bolivia remained largely unreconciled to accepting the MAS agenda, and their acquiescence would be required to set up the complex system of autonomies anticipated in the 2009 Constitution. There were also signs of unrest among some social movements, whose radicalized leadership sought to challenge Morales on the left. Morales' standing seemed sufficient to prevent challenges emerging from within the MAS. However, the promise he made in 2008 to opposition leaders not to stand for subsequent re-election in 2014 (in order to win their acceptance of a constitutional referendum) seemed likely to raise the issue of eventual succession. By mid-2010 it was by no means clear who such an eventual successor might be, or, indeed, whether Morales would in the end honour his promise not to seek further re-election.

Economy

JOHN CRABTREE

MACROECONOMY

Overall Policy Direction

Macroeconomic policy has undergone an important shift in recent years in Bolivia. From the mid-1980s to the late 1990s Bolivia adopted policies of economic liberalization and privatization, consistent with the recommendations of the so-called 'Washington Consensus'. However, popular discontent about the meagre social returns from these policies forced governments to revise such policies and then finally to abandon them. The election of Evo Morales to the presidency in December 2005 marked a particularly sharp turning-point in policy, ushering in a period of resumed interventionism and the rejection of the US-backed trade liberalization agenda. On taking office, the new Government immediately rejected the notion of Bolivia's joining the US-backed, and now stalled, Free Trade Area of the Americas (FTAA) initiative, in favour of a deal with Venezuela and Cuba. The forcible renegotiation of oil and gas contracts, announced in May 2006, also had overtones of resurgent economic nationalism.

The strategic objectives of the new Morales administration were set out in its five-year development plan, published in June 2006. This set out a blueprint for policy until 2011, and sought to make Bolivia a fairer and more democratic society, less dependent on the international economy as the source of growth. The plan was based on the assumption that investment would increase substantially, therefore helping to expand productive capacity. It was less clear, however, where this investment would come from, and whether it would be made in those sectors best placed to maximize social benefits. In the past, the majority of investment has been absorbed by the hydrocarbons industry. However, the linkages between this and the rest of the economy have been notoriously weak, and there were concerns that the new Government's hydrocarbons 'nationalization' policy (see below) would act as a disincentive to foreign investment. Given the growth of gas and mining revenues, the economy was more dependent on primary exports than ever.

Economic Growth

In 2009 Bolivia emerged relatively unscathed from the global downturn. Its gross domestic product (GDP) increased by 3.4%, one of the highest rates in Latin America. This followed growth of 6.1% in 2008, 4.6% in 2007 and 4.8% in 2006. The recent dynamic in the economy is largely derived from both buoyant international prices for and increased output of the country's main commodity exports, notably minerals and natural gas. The increased rhythm of growth pushed GDP per head (at current prices) up to US $1,460 in 2008, according to World Bank figures. However, the decline in commodity prices in the second half of 2008, combined with falls in both investment income and remittances, reduced the rhythm of growth in 2009. A modest recovery seemed likely in 2010.

Following many years of stagnation, Bolivia's rate of growth recovered in the mid-1990s, in part because of the investment stimulated by the privatization programme of President Gonzalo Sánchez de Lozada (1993–97), especially in hydrocarbons. The building of new infrastructure—particularly the gas pipeline to Brazil—provided a fillip to the economy. However, Bolivia found itself highly exposed to economic crises within its larger neighbours—first Brazil in the late 1990s and then Argentina in the early 2000s. The slowing of growth rates from 1998 coincided with the collapse in the popularity of successive governments and the onset of a wave of protests that was to lead to the assumption of office by the new Morales administration. The Morales Government has taken advantage of higher growth to increase social spending.

Inflation

Inflation reached a high point of nearly 14% on an annualized basis at the beginning of 2008, largely as a result of the increase in food and fuel import prices. However, since then it has been on a declining trajectory and at the end of 2009 it was below 1%, although prices increased slightly in the first quarter of 2010. Government policy has been to use cautious monetary and exchange rate policies to prevent the emergence of inflationary pressures. In the early 1980s Bolivia was considered a byword for reckless monetary and fiscal policies that resulted in hyperinflation. Stabilization was one of the main achievements of the Víctor Paz Estenssoro Government (1985–89) and its successors. Although Bolivia ran large fiscal deficits through the 1990s, it was able to finance these by drawing down generous credits from the international financial and aid communities. Since 2006 Bolivia has run a fiscal surplus, with higher revenues derived mainly from the hike in hydrocarbon production tax rates.

Foreign Trade

In 2009 Bolivia saw its trade surplus fall to US $470m.,largely owing to a fall in export revenues. By contrast, the trade surplus reached a record $1,467m. in 2008, up from $1,003m. in 2007. Exports in 2009 totalled $4,847m., down from $6,448m. in 2008, reflecting a sharp decline in the value of gas exports to Brazil. Brazil reduced substantially the volume of gas purchased in 2009, since its own energy needs were met by plentiful hydroelectricity supplies. Total imports for 2009 were $4,377m., compared with a record $4,980m. in 2008. Bolivia benefited from the boom in world mineral prices up until mid-2008, in what had previously been a depressed sector. This was particularly the case for zinc, silver and gold, but tin prices were also up on previous years. Mineral prices have rebounded since their sharp fall in 2008. Bolivia's export performance has also profited from the San Cristóbal zinc and silver mine coming on stream in 2007. Silver now vies with zinc as the country's single most important mineral export. Buoyant world prices have encouraged higher production from mines that were previously abandoned in the 1980s.

Export performance in 2009 was also affected by the withdrawal of US trade preferences with the curtailment of the Andean Trade Preferences and Drug Eradication Act (ATPDEA). Most hit were exporters of manufactured items, particularly textiles and clothing. Bolivia is a founder member of the Comunidad Andina de Naciones (CAN—Andean Community of Nations) and an associate member of the Southern Common Market (Mercado Común del Sur—Mercosur), set up by Brazil, Argentina, Paraguay and Uruguay. It is also a member of the Alternativa Bolivariana para nuestra America (ALBA—Bolivarian Alternative for the Americas,), alongside Venezuela, Ecuador and Cuba. Moreover, Bolivia enjoys access to the European Union (EU)'s Generalized System of Preferences, although it did not join with Colombia and Peru in negotiating a free trade agreement with the EU; these two countries agreed bilateral accords with the EU in early 2010.

Balance of Payments

Improved terms of trade have helped to improve the balance of payments situation in recent years. However, these tailed off in 2009, reflecting a deterioration on both the capital and current account. According to preliminary central bank figures, in 2009 Bolivia recorded an overall surplus of US $352m., compared with a surplus in 2008 of $2,374m. The current account surplus was down to $800m. in 2009, compared with $2,015m. the year before and $1,591m. in 2006. By the first quarter of 2010 net foreign reserves stood at $9,726m., up from $5,989m. at the end of 2007. The balance of payments in 2009 also benefited from a modest positive net inflow of foreign investment (slower than in previous years) and the continued remittances from Bolivians living abroad, as well as the effects of debt relief from multilateral lenders, principally the World Bank. Remittances fell slightly in 2009, with an increase from Argentina partly offsetting the falls from Spain and the USA.

Fiscal Situation

Preliminary central bank figures suggested that the public sector fiscal surplus in the first half of 2009 was considerably lower than in 2008, with increased spending outmatching a small increase in fiscal revenues. The surplus in 2008 was slightly higher than in 2007, but lower than in 2006. The greatly improved fiscal performance of recent years reflects the hike in taxes on gas output since the 'nationalization' of gas in 2006, though reduced sales to Brazil in 2009 reduced government revenues. The size of the fiscal surplus also reflects an inability to spend the money at the Ministry of Finance's disposal. As recently as 2003 Bolivia's fiscal deficit stood at 9.0% of GDP. Part of the reason for this shortfall was the privatization of pensions, which reduced levels of revenue from pension contributions while existing spending commitments continued.

ECONOMIC SECTORS

Hydrocarbons

Petroleum was first discovered in Bolivia in 1927. Until the sector was nationalized in 1937, the main company involved was Standard Oil of New Jersey. Under the state company that emerged, Yacimientos Petrolíferos Fiscales Bolivianos (YPFB), no major new discoveries were made, and it was only in 1953 that Bolivia became self-sufficient in oil. In 1954 state policy changed, and private investment was sought, the main company being Bolivian Gulf Oil. New discoveries of petroleum and gas were made by Bolivian Gulf Oil, and pipelines were constructed linking Bolivia to the Pacific and to Argentina. In 1969 the assets of Bolivian Gulf Oil were taken over by YPFB. From the 1970s to the 1990s a stable system was created in which the private and public sectors coexisted, with YPFB awarding operating contracts to private sector companies. Then, in 1996, the Sánchez de Lozada Government 'capitalized' YPFB and turned over production to the private sector through shared risk contracts. Attracted by the generous terms on offer, several major international oil and gas companies invested in Bolivia, principal among them Petrobras of Brazil, Repsol of Spain, Total of France and British Gas (known as BG from 1997). The new regime quickly led to important discoveries in the gas sector, these mainly concentrated in the department of Tarija. Proven reserves of gas increased from 4,200,000m. cu ft in 1998 to 28,700,000m. cu ft in 2003; proven plus probable reserves increased from 6,600,000m. cu ft to 54,900,000m. cu ft over the same period. Bolivia had the second largest gas reserves in South America, after Venezuela. To exploit this gas potential, a pipeline was constructed, at a cost of US $450m., linking Río Grande in Bolivia with São Paulo in Brazil. Production increased from an average of just under 500m. cu ft per day in 1999 to 1,224m. cu ft per day in 2004, greatly increasing Bolivia's export earnings.

At the beginning of the 21st century attention was devoted to developing new markets for Bolivian gas, and a project was designed to export gas to Mexico and the USA by piping it across the Andes, liquefying it and then shipping it northwards. The project sparked a furious polemic within Bolivia. This partly focused on the transshipment of gas through Chile, Bolivia's traditional enemy, but it also raised wider questions about the terms on which foreign companies were operating in Bolivia and the modest returns to the Bolivian economy. The resultant 'Gas War' of October 2003 led to the ousting of Sánchez de Lozada, who had narrowly regained the presidency in 2002. His successor, Carlos Mesa Gisbert, found himself obliged to hold a referendum in July 2004 on the country's approach to the gas question, and, in particular, on the proposal to build a Chilean pipeline. The referendum compelled the Government to reformulate its hydrocarbons legislation, and a new law was finally approved in May 2005. This raised the taxes payable by foreign investors and changed the contractual relationship between them and YPFB.

Following the victory of Evo Morales and the Movimiento al Socialismo in the 2005 elections, the new administration announced its intentions to 'nationalize' (for the third time) the hydrocarbons industry. In a show of force, troops were sent into two of the largest gasfields on 1 May 2006 to make nationalization effective. Foreign companies were given 180 days in which to switch to new contracts or else leave the country. In the event, all the companies accepted the new terms offered to them within the deadline prescribed. As well as switching the contracts to service contracts, the new regulations established substantially higher new tax rates payable to the state: the highest rate established was 81% of the value of production. The new legislation afforded a greatly enhanced role to YPFB in the production process. In May 2008 the Government extended its ownership of the industry by acquiring a majority shareholding in several pipeline companies.

The second main strand in the Morales administration's gas policy was to renegotiate the terms whereby Argentina and Brazil bought gas from Bolivia. In the case of Argentina, in October 2006 the Government of Néstor Carlos Kirchner agreed to increase both the volume purchased and price paid for Bolivian gas. Plans were also announced to build a new pipeline to Santa Fe. Argentina committed to buying up to 27.7m. cu m per day by 2010, up from 7m. cu m per day. It has so far failed to meet these targets. Brazil proved more resistant than Argentina, but eventually—in March 2007—agreed to increase the price payable for some of the gas bought from Bolivia; nevertheless, the price paid fell in 2009, mirroring the world-wide decline in the prices of hydrocarbons. There is a reasonable probability that Bolivia's declining gas reserves will increase again once more systematic prospecting gets under way. However, foreign oil and gas companies (most of which have recovered their initial investment in Bolivia) have shown themselves reluctant to devote more resources to exploration while the contractual conditions are relatively unfavourable and prices remain depressed. The main exception has been Petrobras, which is under pressure to meet the short- to medium-term energy shortfall in Brazil. In 2009 hydrocarbons accounted for 41% of total exports.

Mining

From the earliest colonial times, what was to become Bolivia found itself integrated into the world economy as a supplier of minerals. The discovery of the enormous silver reserves of the Cerro Rico in Potosí gave the country huge economic significance. The importance of silver mining declined by the 19th century, and in the 20th century tin mining became the economic mainstay. During the course of the 20th century, however, the ore grades of Bolivian tin declined progressively. Tin mining was dominated in the first half of the 20th century by the Patiño, Hochschild and Aramayo families, but by the time the mines were nationalized in 1952, ore grades were falling fast. With its underground mines, Bolivia found it increasingly difficult to compete with open-cast tin mining in Indonesia, Malaysia and Brazil. In 1985 the world tin market collapsed, and Bolivia was obliged to close its main mining centres and dismiss some 25,000 mineworkers. The only major mining centre to continue in production was at Huanuni, which was sold to the private sector in the 1990s. Other private sector mining companies, however, were better placed than the former state mining company, Corporación Minera de Bolivia (COMIBOL), to stay in business.

The recovery of prices in the early 2000s led to a revival of interest in the mining sector. A steady rise in mineral prices, stimulated mainly by demand from the People's Republic of China and India for raw materials, pushed up the value of exports. In the main this was because of higher prices, but these in turn prompted miners to expand production to meet the demand. Central Bank figures indicate that the official value of exports of (non-hydrocarbons) minerals stood at US $369.3m. in 2003; by 2009, this had reached $1,847m. The decline in world mineral prices towards the end of 2008 did affect Bolivia, but export values fell only by a fairly modest 4.8%. The composition of exports has changed greatly, meanwhile, particularly since the 1990s. Tin is no longer the main source of foreign exchange in the mining industry, having been overtaken by zinc and silver. Zinc accounted for just over one-third of export revenue from minerals in 2009, according to provisional figures ($688m.), followed by silver ($610m.) and then tin ($235m.).

After the virtual closure of COMIBOL in 1985, the structure of the industry changed radically. The so-called 'minería mediana' (privately owned mines) took over from the public sector. The most important company here until recently was Sinchi Wayra, the firm owned by former President Sánchez de Lozada. In 2005 Sánchez de Lozada sold Sinchi Wayra, which owned several of Bolivia's most profitable mines, as well as the smelter at Vinto (near Oruro), to the Swiss-based company Glencore International AG. In February 2007, however, the Morales Government announced that it was taking Vinto, built and formerly owned by the state, back into public ownership. It considered that Vinto had been improperly acquired by the private sector at a reduced price. The Government also had plans to relaunch COMIBOL and to give it a much more prominent role in the industry.

Although officially closed in 1985 and their labour force disbanded, many of the former state-owned mines continued to be operated by self-employed workers who sold the ores they extracted to private intermediaries. The rise in mineral prices in the years after 2003 attracted workers back into the industry. At Siglo XX, for instance, formerly Bolivia's most important tin mine, there were more workers in 2007 than in 1985, mostly operating in extremely dangerous conditions.

As well as seeking to revive COMIBOL, the Morales Government took steps to increase the taxes payable by the sector to the state. These declined to very low levels after 1985. According to official figures, mining contributed only US $58m. to the state in 2006 on exports earnings of over $1,000m. The Government sought to make the new Complementary Mining Tax (Complementario a la Minería) incremental, so that its yield reflected the upward shift in international prices. However, the implementation of such reforms encountered significant resistance from miners and mining companies, not least from the self-employed sector of 'cooperativistas'.

As in the case of hydrocarbons, a major problem is the lack of investment. Mining investment has been at a very low level for more than 50 years, and relatively little of the country has been properly prospected. Investors have been deterred by political instability and by the existence of more attractive operating conditions in neighbouring countries, notably in Chile and Peru. None the less, the San Cristóbal mine and the San Bartolomé scheme, both in Potosí, have substantially increased Bolivia's productive capacity in silver. The San Cristóbal project, which will be Bolivia's largest silver mine, entered into production in 2007. San Bartolomé is a project to apply new technology to reworking the tailings of the historic Cerro Rico mine, just outside the city of Potosí. Furthermore, in 2007 the Government signed a contract with Jindal Power and Steel Ltd of India, together with its local subsidiary, Jindal Steel Bolivia, to develop the giant El Mutún iron ore deposit in eastern Santa Cruz, close to the Brazilian frontier. However, the contract has been dogged by disagreements between Jindal and the Government, and there is a possibility that Jindal may withdraw altogether from Bolivia. Another scheme is to develop lithium from the Salar de Uyuni in Potosí. Bolivia has the world's largest reserves of this commodity, a key element in the development of batteries for use in electric cars. The Morales Government is seeking foreign investment to develop lithium, but on the basis of industrializing its use.

Agriculture

Although Bolivia's main contribution to international commerce is through the extraction of hydrocarbons and minerals (which accounted for 6.6% and 6.3% of GDP, respectively, in 2008), agriculture contributed more than 13% of GDP in that year and is an important source of employment. While rapid urbanization has reduced the proportion of people living on the land, Bolivia remains a much more rural country than most in Latin America. Agriculture is highly segmented, reflecting the geographical diversity of the country. There are three main types of agriculture: small-scale peasant agriculture in the highlands, where the quality of the soil is mainly poor, and where there is a mixture of livestock rearing (mainly alpacas and llamas) and basic crops such as potatoes and some grains; small-scale agriculture (mainly crops) in the inter-Andean valleys (principally around Cochabamba, Sucre and Tarija) where the quality of the land is considerably better and the climate less extreme; and extensive export-orientated agriculture and cattle-rearing in the eastern lowland departments of Santa Cruz and Beni.

From a commercial point of view, the most dynamic sector in recent years has been soya. Produced mainly in Santa Cruz, soya took over in the 1980s from more traditional crops (such as sugar and cotton) as Bolivia's prime agricultural export commodity. Soya products (including oil) accounted for exports of US $465m. in 2009, up from $329m. in 2008. The scale of soya production depends both on climatic and market conditions. Bolivia has enjoyed a niche within the CAN as a privileged supplier of soya to Peru and Colombia. However, its comparative advantages over much larger and lower-cost producers threatened to be eroded if the CAN and Mercosur eventually were to merge and South America become a free trade area. Moreover, the growth in soya cultivation has taken place with scant regard for ecological considerations, and there are growing problems of desertification emerging in parts of the Bolivian lowlands.

Other forms of export agriculture also come predominantly from the lowlands. In 2009 these included sugar (US $68m.) timber ($64m.) and Brazil nuts ($64m.). In all probability timber exports are worth more than the official figure suggests, since the scale of illegal logging in Bolivia is large. Brazil nuts provide an important livelihood for small-scale producers in Beni and Pando departments, the main market being the EU. Other agricultural exports include coffee and cotton.

Coca

One of Bolivia's most lucrative forms of agriculture is coca, the raw material for cocaine. Coca has been grown in Bolivia since earliest times, and it is still widely used as a palliative to stave off hunger and fatigue. It also has religious uses. However, its economic importance in recent decades lies in its illegal use for the manufacture of cocaine. Since the 1980s successive governments have come under strong pressure from the USA to eradicate coca. These attempts have led to strenuous resistance from those whose livelihoods depend on coca production. The *cocaleros* have emerged in recent years as one of Bolivia's best organized and most militant social movements, and the political rise of President Evo Morales, former leader of the Chapare *cocaleros*, owes much to attempts to eradicate coca.

Coca eradication reached its peak under the Government of Hugo Bánzer Suárez (1997–2001), whose strict stance on coca cultivation was strongly supported by the US Administration. The fall in coca acreages at that time has since been reversed, reflecting the increased political power at the national level of the *cocaleros*. At its maximum, coca production in Bolivia involved cultivation of 48,000 ha in 1996, according to figures published by the UN Office on Drugs and Crime. In 2008 the area under cultivation was 30,500 ha, an increase of 6% on the previous year and the third consecutive annual increase. The main production areas are in the Yungas valleys of La Paz department and the lowland Chapare district of Cochabamba: the area cultivated increased in both regions in 2008. The policy of the Morales Government has been more permissive towards coca production than some of its predecessors. However, the Government asserted that it was doing more to stem illegal shipments of cocaine and cocaine paste. In 2008 there was a 12.5% decrease in the area eradicated over the previous year, but cocaine seizures were up, therefore perhaps vindicating Morales's stated policy of targeting drugs-traffickers rather than the peasant producers of coca. However, the Morales Government has been strongly criticized by Washington for not doing enough to counter drugs trafficking, particularly since Morales expelled officials from the US Drug Enforcement Administration at the end of 2008.

Manufacturing

Manufacturing accounted for 16.9% of GDP in 2008. However, Bolivia is one of South America's least industrialized countries. Much of what is classed as manufacturing is simply light processing of agricultural or mineral production. None the less, rapid urbanization has led to a growing demand for manufactured goods, and a proportion of these is produced locally. Bolivia has also increased its exports of manufactured goods in recent years, especially in areas such as clothing, textiles and jewellery. Major Bolivian cities, including La Paz, Cochabamba and Santa Cruz, all have industrial areas, and manufacturing is of ever greater importance in providing urban employment.

The most important market for manufactured goods is the USA, where ATPDEA acted as an important spur to export activity in this area. However, since Bolivia's access to ATPDEA benefits was ended in 2009, Bolivian exporters—mainly in El Alto—have suffered market loss.

Transport

Given its geographic location at the centre of South America, Bolivia has major potential as a transport hub for the region. In particular, it offers a route by which output from Brazil can reach the Pacific for transshipment to Asia. However, the country's rugged terrain and the poor quality of its infrastructure have hindered the development of this potential. Its railway network, privatized in the 1990s, is in a poor state of repair, especially the eastern section in Santa Cruz, and the eastern and western networks do not interconnect. Major efforts have been made to upgrade road connections to facilitate international transport. However, the maintenance of road networks is poor, and climatic conditions are such that land transport links are frequently interrupted.

Tourism

Bolivia has experienced a large increase in international tourist arrivals over the last 20 years. Its dramatic geography and its cultural wealth mean that it has a great appeal to tourists. However, beyond the main cities, tourism infrastructure—such as hotels and restaurants—is often not of a high standard. Poor transport is also a deterrent, particularly the paucity and relative expense of international air links. Moreover, as elsewhere in Latin America, increasing crime rates can present a disincentive to visitors to the country.

CONCLUSIONS AND PROSPECTS

Growth was expected to increase moderately in 2010, following a slowdown in 2009 that reflected a downturn in the export economy. Higher growth rates would probably have positive multiplier effects both in terms of employment and government finance. The country's external accounts are cushioned by relatively high international reserves. Bolivia continues to experience difficulties in diversifying its economy, and the discovery of large reserves of natural gas has done little to resolve this problem. It has, however, substantially alleviated the country's fiscal and balance of payments problems. The Bolivian Government in the last few years has no longer been in a position in which policy is effectively determined by conditions set down by the IMF and the World Bank, and this has given the Morales administration greater room for manoeuvre. However, new investment has been scant and more is needed if Bolivia's productive potential is to be expanded, particularly in the hydrocarbons sector. Investors have been deterred by the Morales Government's nationalist economic policies and by perceptions of high political risk. Ultimately, however, Bolivia is a country with large untapped natural resources, and some investors might be prepared to risk funds if they are convinced that the rules of the game (albeit less favourable than in the past) are now likely to prove more stable.

Statistical Survey

Sources (unless otherwise indicated): Instituto Nacional de Estadística, José Carrasco 1391, Casilla 6129, La Paz; tel. (2) 222-2333; fax (2) 222-693; internet www.ine.gov.bo; Banco Central de Bolivia, Ayacucho esq. Mercado, Casilla 3118, La Paz; tel. (2) 240-9090; fax (2) 240-6614; e-mail bancocentraldebolivia@bcb.gov.bo; internet www.bcb.gov.bo.

Area and Population

AREA, POPULATION AND DENSITY

Area (sq km)	
Land	1,084,391
Inland water	14,190
Total	1,098,581*
Population (census results)†	
3 June 1992	6,420,792
5 September 2001	
Males	4,123,850
Females	4,150,475
Total	8,274,325
Population (official projections)	
2008	10,027,644
2009	10,227,299
2010	10,426,154
Density (per sq km) at 2010	9.5

* 424,164 sq miles.

† Figures exclude adjustment for underenumeration. This was estimated at 6.92% in 1992.

POPULATION BY AGE AND SEX

(official projections, 2010)

	Males	Females	Total
0–14	1,903,360	1,830,821	3,734,181
15–64	3,086,854	3,128,450	6,215,304
65 and over	211,760	264,909	476,669
Total	5,201,974	5,224,180	10,426,154

DEPARTMENTS

(official projections, 2010)

	Area (sq km)*	Population	Density (per sq km)	Capital ('000)
Beni	213,564	445,234	2.1	Trinidad (92,587)
Chuquisaca	51,524	650,570	12.6	Sucre (284,032)
Cochabamba	55,631	1,861,924	33.5	Cochabamba (618,376)
La Paz	133,985	2,839,946	21.2	La Paz (835,361)
Oruro	53,588	450,814	8.4	Oruro (216,724)
Pando	63,827	81,160	1.3	Cobija (41,948)
Potosí	118,218	788,406	6.7	Potosí (154,693)
Santa Cruz	370,621	2,785,762	7.5	Santa Cruz de la Sierra (1,616,063)
Tarija	37,623	522,339	13.9	Tarija (194,313)
Total	1,098,581	10,426,154	9.5	

* As at 2001 census.

PRINCIPAL TOWNS

(official projections, 2010)

Santa Cruz de la Sierra	1,616,063	Sacaba	155,668
El Alto	953,253	Potosí	154,693
La Paz (administrative capital)	835,361	Yacuiba	112,096
Cochabamba	618,376	Quillacollo	99,050
Sucre (legal capital)	284,032	Montero	96,106
Oruro	216,724	Trinidad	92,587
Tarija	194,313	Riberalta	87,501

BIRTHS AND DEATHS

(annual averages, UN estimates)

	1995–2000	2000–05	2005–10
Birth rate (per 1,000)	32.6	30.2	27.3
Death rate (per 1,000)	9.0	8.2	7.6

Source: UN, *World Population Prospects: The 2008 Revision*.

Life expectancy (years at birth, WHO estimates): 67 (males 65; females 68) in 2008 (Source: WHO, *World Health Statistics*).

ECONOMICALLY ACTIVE POPULATION

(labour force survey, '000 persons aged 10 years and over)

	2005	2006	2007
Agriculture, hunting, forestry and fishing	1,643.6	1,797.4	1,686.7
Mining and quarrying	71.0	55.5	72.4
Manufacturing	465.5	477.8	514.9
Electricity, gas and water supply	13.9	13.0	15.4
Construction	275.3	248.1	316.3
Wholesale and retail trade; repair of motor vehicles, motorcycles and personal and household goods	629.3	647.3	673.8
Hotels and restaurants	171.4	186.7	159.3
Transport, storage and communications	256.3	251.5	272.4
Financial intermediation	13.1	23.3	28.0
Real estate, renting and business activities	104.6	152.0	136.9
Public administration and defence; compulsory social security	91.1	115.2	152.3
Education	192.7	217.9	222.9
Health and social work	64.0	96.9	109.3
Other community, social and personal service activities	153.0	147.5	149.0
Private households with employed persons	108.3	119.6	160.7
Extra-territorial organizations and bodies	4.0	0.6	1.9
Total employed	4,257.2	4,550.3	4,672.4
Unemployed	245.2	243.5	255.0
Total labour force	4,502.4	4,793.8	4,927.4
Males	2,468.2	2,624.6	2,699.4
Females	2,034.2	2,169.2	2,228.0

Source: ILO.

Health and Welfare

KEY INDICATORS

Total fertility rate (children per woman, 2008)	3.5
Under-5 mortality rate (per 1,000 live births, 2008)	54
HIV/AIDS (% of persons aged 15–49, 2007)	0.2
Physicians (per 1,000 head, 2001)	1.2
Hospital beds (per 1,000 head, 2006)	1.1
Health expenditure (2007): US $ per head (PPP)	200
Health expenditure (2007): % of GDP	5.0
Health expenditure (2007): public (% of total)	69.2
Access to water (% of persons, 2008)	86
Access to sanitation (% of persons, 2008)	25
Total carbon dioxide emissions ('000 metric tons, 2006)	11,395.0
Carbon dioxide emissions per head (metric tons, 2006)	1.2
Human Development Index (2007): ranking	113
Human Development Index (2007): value	0.729

For sources and definitions, see explanatory note on p. vi.

Agriculture

PRINCIPAL CROPS
('000 metric tons)

	2005	2006	2007
Wheat	131.2	143.7	165.2
Rice, paddy	479.3	446.5	369.1
Barley	74.0	75.2	72.6
Maize	738.4	894.4	770.4
Sorghum	203.7	271.0	336.3
Potatoes	761.9	754.9	735.3
Cassava (Manioc)	370.5	371.3	360.6
Sugar cane	5,112.2	6,201.1	6,419.3
Brazil nuts*	40.0	41.0	42.0
Chestnuts	57.1	55.0*	55.0*
Soybeans (Soya beans)	1,693.1	1,619.0	1,595.9
Sunflower seeds	80.9	101.0	191.3
Tomatoes	127.7	126.2	124.3
Pumpkins, squash and gourds	117.0*	19.7	20.0
Onions, dry	32.3	33.3	33.3
Peas, green	25.1	25.0	25.0
Broad beans, horse beans, dry*	13.5	13.6	13.6
Carrots and turnips	28.7	29.3	29.3
Maize, green	32.2	34.3	34.8
Watermelons*	22.9	23.0	24.0
Bananas	180.9	181.7	182.5
Plantains	443.4	443.8	445.9
Oranges	87.7	89.7	91.6
Tangerines, mandarins, clementines and satsumas	35.4	36.5	37.8
Lemons and limes	26.9†	27.7	28.0
Grapefruit and pomelos	7.6	7.9	8.0
Peaches and nectarines	16.6	17.0*	17.0*
Grapes	33.3	33.6	32.9
Pineapples	13.4	14.0	14.5
Papayas*	23.4	23.0	23.0
Coffee, green	25.0	25.3	25.4

* FAO estimate(s).
† Unofficial figure.

Aggregate production ('000 metric tons, may include official, semi-official or estimated data): Total cereals 1,660 in 2005, 1,866 in 2006, 1,749 in 2007; Total roots and tubers 1,190 in 2005, 1,176 in 2006, 1,146 in 2007; Total vegetables (incl. melons) 491 in 2005, 396 in 2006, 397 in 2007; Total fruits (excl. melons) 901 in 2005, 908 in 2006, 915 in 2007.

2008: Production assumed to be unchanged from 2007 (FAO estimates).

Source: FAO.

LIVESTOCK
('000 head, year ending September)

	2006	2007	2008
Horses	456	465	465*
Asses*	635	635	635
Mules*	82	82	82
Cattle	7,718	7,894	7,894*
Pigs	2,488	2,592	2,592*
Sheep	8987	9,177	9,177*
Goats	1,926	1,960	1,960*
Chickens	80,598	73,388	80,424
Ducks*	295	295	295
Turkeys*	155	155	155

* FAO estimate(s).

Source: FAO.

LIVESTOCK PRODUCTS
('000 metric tons)

	2005	2006	2007
Cattle meat*	175.0	170.0	170.0
Sheep meat*	18.0	18.0	18.0
Goat meat*	5.8	5.8	5.8
Pig meat*	107.5	107.5	107.5
Chicken meat†	153.8	140.0	140.0
Cows' milk	315.0*	253.9	260.8
Sheep's milk*	29.3	29.2	29.3
Goats' milk*	11.4	11.7	11.7
Hen eggs	53.9†	59.3*	62.6*
Wool, greasy*	8.8	8.6	8.6

* FAO estimate(s).
† Unofficial figure(s).

2008: Figures assumed to be unchanged from 2007 (FAO estimates).

Source: FAO.

Forestry

ROUNDWOOD REMOVALS
('000 cubic metres, excl. bark)

	2006	2007	2008
Sawlogs, veneer logs and logs for sleepers*	910	910	910
Fuel wood†	2,270	2,289	2,309
Total†	3,180	3,199	3,219

* Unofficial figures.
† FAO estimates.

Source: FAO.

SAWNWOOD PRODUCTION
('000 cubic metres, incl. railway sleepers)

	2004	2005	2006
Coniferous (softwood)*	1	1	2
Broadleaved (hardwood)	402	408	459
Total*	403	409	461

* Unofficial figures.

2007–08: Figures assumed to be unchanged from 2006 (FAO estimates).

Source: FAO.

Fishing

(metric tons, live weight)

	2006*	2007	2008
Capture	6,350	6,000*	6,797*
Freshwater fishes	5,200	4,851	5,787
Rainbow trout	300	299*	160
Silversides (sand smelts)*	850	850	850
Aquaculture	455	585	631*
Rainbow trout	230	130	194
Total catch	6,805	6,585*	7,428*

* FAO estimate(s).

Note: Figures exclude crocodiles and alligators, recorded by number rather than by weight. The number of spectacled caimans caught was: 44,443 in 2006; 49,115 in 2007; 51,618 in 2008.

Source: FAO.

Mining

(metric tons, unless otherwise indicated; figures for metallic minerals refer to the metal content of ores)

	2006	2007	2008
Crude petroleum ('000 barrels)	14,882	15,027*	14,233*
Natural gas (million cu m)	14,689	15,230	15,374*
Copper	218	606	731
Tin	17,669	15,972	17,319
Lead	11,955	22,798	81,602
Zinc	172,747	214,053	383,618
Tungsten (Wolfram)	868	1,107	1,148
Antimony	5,460	3,881	3,905
Silver (kg)	472,208	524,989	1,114,000
Gold (kg)	9,628	8,818	8,405

* Preliminary figure.

Source: US Geological Survey.

Industry

SELECTED PRODUCTS

('000 42-gallon barrels, unless otherwise indicated)

	2006	2007	2008
Cement ('000 metric tons)	1,636	1,739	1,985
Liquefied petroleum gas	855	895	850*
Distillate fuel oil	4,615	4,880	4,600*
Kerosene	153	131	130*
Motor spirit (petrol)	3,877	4,558	4,300*

* Preliminary figure.

Electric energy (million kWh): 4,778 in 2005.

2001 (provisional): Flour ('000 metric tons) 788; Carbonated drinks ('000 hl) 1,996; Beer ('000 hl) 1,586; Cigarettes (packets) 75,373; Alcohol ('000 litres) 29,099.

Source: partly US Geological Survey.

Finance

CURRENCY AND EXCHANGE RATES

Monetary Units

100 centavos = 1 boliviano (B).

Sterling, Dollar and Euro Equivalents (30 April 2010)

£1 sterling = 10.760 bolivianos;
US$1 = 7.020 bolivianos;
€1 = 9.347 bolivianos;
100 bolivianos = £9.29 = $14.25 = €10.70.

Average Exchange Rate (bolivianos per US$)

2007	7.85
2008	7.24
2009	7.02

GENERAL BUDGET

(national treasury budget, million bolivianos, preliminary)

Revenue (all current)	2007	2008	2009
Tax revenue	12,679.5	14,379.2	15,271.7
Internal	11,691.1	13,357.4	14,108.5
Customs	746.8	780.6	922.4
Duties on hydrocarbons	1,152.6	1,085.8	2,636.5
Other current revenue	384.2	354.6	1,166.2
Repayment of loans	23.3	n.a.	n.a.
Current transfers	252.8	672.6	n.a.
Grants	402.0	236.1	328.4
Total	14,894.4	16,728.3	19,402.8

Expenditure	2007	2008	2009
Current expenditure	15,617.6	18,851.9	23,443.7
Personal services	8,310.7	9,187.7	10,731.1
Goods and services	727.4	890.2	1,088.0
Interest on debt	2,243.3	2,781.9	2,396.0
External	1,059.8	1,063.1	834.2
Internal	1,183.5	1,718.8	1,561.8
Current transfers	4,336.2	5,992.2	8,619.9
Payments	3,472.6	3,877.2	4,440.8
Capital expenditure	287.0	417.7	883.8
Total	15,904.6	19,269.6	24,327.5

INTERNATIONAL RESERVES

(US$ million at 31 December)

	2007	2008	2009
Gold (national valuation)	764.3	794.5	997.6
IMF special drawing rights	42.3	42.3	258.5
Reserve position in IMF	14.0	13.7	13.9
Foreign exchange	4,497.7	6,871.4	7,311.3
Total	5,318.3	7,721.9	8,581.3

Source: IMF, *International Financial Statistics*.

MONEY SUPPLY

(million bolivianos at 31 December)

	2007	2008	2009
Currency outside depository corporations	13,117	15,807	17,080
Transferable deposits	14,528	19,279	18,723
Other deposits	31,497	37,483	45,334
Broad money	59,142	72,569	81,137

Source: IMF, *International Financial Statistics*.

COST OF LIVING

(Consumer Price Index for urban areas; base: 2000 = 100)

	2006	2007	2008
Food and beverages	122.2	138.9	174.5
Fuel and light	124.1	125.5	n.a.
Clothing and footwear	119.1	125.1	134.1
Rent	112.7	113.1	n.a.
All items (incl. others)	121.6	132.2	150.7

2009: Food and beverages 176.8; All items (incl. others) 155.8.

Source: ILO.

NATIONAL ACCOUNTS

(million bolivianos at current prices, preliminary)

Expenditure on the Gross Domestic Product

	2007	2008	2009
Government final consumption expenditure	14,481.7	16,025.0	17,904.5
Private final consumption expenditure	65,127.9	75,100.3	79,733.2
Increase in stocks	−981.6	366.9	598.9
Gross fixed capital formation	16,625.3	20,818.1	20,059.7
Total domestic expenditure	95,253.3	112,310.3	118,296.3
Exports of goods and services	43,053.4	54,199.4	43,484.0
Less Imports of goods and services	35,297.4	45,815.9	40,053.5
GDP at market prices	103,009.2	120,693.8	121,726.7
GDP at constant 1990 prices	28,524.0	30,277.8	31,294.3

Gross Domestic Product by Economic Activity

	2007	2008	2009
Agriculture, hunting, forestry and fishing	10,312.4	12,603.3	13,575.5
Mining and quarrying	12,656.7	17,181.5	15,779.3
Manufacturing	11,758.4	13,479.7	14,140.7
Electricity, gas and water	2,255.8	2,436.6	2,631.4
Construction	2,470.1	2,792.6	3,027.8
Trade	6,990.3	8,468.5	8,779.1
Transport, storage and communications	9,657.8	10,147.0	10,723.5
Finance, insurance, real estate and business services	8,890.2	10,062.3	10,642.8
Government services	11,354.9	12,600.9	14,507.8
Other services	6,895.6	7,597.5	8,308.4
Sub-total	83,242.3	97,369.7	102,116.1
Value-added tax Import duties }	22,927.7	27,123.7	23,562.6
Less Imputed bank charge	3,160.8	3,799.7	3,951.9
GDP in purchasers' values	103,009.2	120,693.8	121,726.7

BALANCE OF PAYMENTS
(US $ million)

	2006	2007	2008
Exports of goods f.o.b.	3,874.5	4,458.3	6,447.8
Imports of goods f.o.b.	–2,632.1	–3,243.5	–4,641.0
Trade balance	1,242.4	1,214.8	1,806.9
Exports of services	476.6	499.4	499.7
Imports of services	–826.6	–899.7	–1,039.3
Balance on goods and services	892.5	814.5	1,267.2
Other income received (net)	–397.3	–489.5	–536.4
Balance on goods, services and income	495.2	325.1	730.9
Current transfers received (net)	822.2	1,266.2	1,284.2
Current balance	1,317.5	1,591.2	2,015.0
Capital account (net)	1,813.2	1,180.2	9.7
Direct investment (net)	277.8	363.3	509.3
Portfolio investment assets	25.1	–29.9	–208.1
Other investment assets (net)	–1,891.5	–1,128.0	–24.5
Net errors and omissions	–103.3	–111.7	–102.9
Overall balance	1,438.8	1,865.1	2,198.5

Source: IMF, *International Financial Statistics*.

External Trade

PRINCIPAL COMMODITIES
(distribution by SITC, US $ million)

Imports c.i.f.	2007	2008	2009
Food and live animals	279.5	402.2	351.7
Crude materials (inedible) except fuels	112.1	84.2	56.3
Mineral fuels, lubricants, etc.	293.4	579.1	498.7
Chemicals and related products	603.0	868.4	776.6
Basic manufactures	704.7	988.5	868.5
Machinery and transport equipment	1,296.8	1,771.7	1,523.9
Miscellaneous manufactured articles	252.3	323.6	295.5
Total (incl. others)	3,588.0	5,100.2	4,466.9

Exports f.o.b.	2007	2008	2009
Food and live animals	470.5	577.8	673.9
Crude materials (inedible) except fuels	1,206.7	1,712.6	1,686.0
Mineral fuels, lubricants, etc.	2,290.8	3,548.7	2,114.2
Animal and vegetable oils, fats and waxes	203.2	290.3	245.3
Basic manufactures	310.3	421.9	290.5
Machinery and transport equipment	2.0	1.6	1.5
Miscellaneous manufactured articles	150.9	145.1	146.0
Total (incl. others)	4,821.8	6,932.9	5,365.5

PRINCIPAL TRADING PARTNERS
(US $ million)

Imports c.i.f.	2007	2008	2009
Argentina	589.9	729.8	622.4
Brazil	719.1	925.3	787.1
Chile	227.8	350.6	238.2
China, People's Republic	312.1	445.1	375.1
Colombia	70.6	111.7	98.8
France (incl. Monaco)	29.6	57.1	42.7
Germany	85.4	92.0	97.0
Italy	31.1	45.1	43.9
Japan	359.4	501.7	311.0
Korea, Republic	20.5	31.3	24.9
Mexico	62.1	109.9	96.3
Paraguay	41.5	46.8	27.9
Peru	227.1	354.4	321.9
Spain	53.7	55.4	47.5
Sweden	69.9	98.4	83.3
USA	408.3	522.4	603.1
Venezuela	47.7	253.2	310.5
Total (incl. others)	3,588.0	5,100.2	4,466.9

Exports	2007	2008	2009
Argentina	422.2	493.3	432.8
Belgium-Luxembourg	131.9	157.4	189.6
Brazil	1,748.2	3,023.1	166.7
Canada	104.7	87.3	69.9
Chile	56.4	78.1	74.3
China, People's Republic	57.5	129.4	130.6
Colombia	158.5	216.2	292.4
Japan	407.1	214.3	303.5
Korea, Republic	198.6	812.5	494.9
Panama	66.1	24.7	57.6
Peru	226.1	275.9	287.4
Switzerland (incl. Liechtenstein)	159.9	162.1	167.3
United Kingdom	105.8	90.0	74.3
USA	413.8	486.9	450.0
Venezuela	241.4	250.0	299.3
Total (incl. others)	4,821.8	6,932.9	5,365.5

Transport

RAILWAYS
(traffic)

	2002	2003	2004
Passenger-kilometres (million)	280	283	286
Net ton-kilometres (million)	873	901	1,058

Source: UN, *Statistical Yearbook*.

ROAD TRAFFIC
(motor vehicles in use at 31 December)

	2002	2003	2004
Passenger cars	26,229	127,222	138,729
Buses	27,226	43,588	49,133
Lorries and vans	30,539	225,028	251,801
Motorcycles	1,125	15,467	19,426

2007: Passenger cars 174,912; Buses 6,996; Lorries and vans 468,763; Motorcycles 34,982.

Source: IRF, *World Road Statistics*.

SHIPPING

Merchant Fleet
(registered at 31 December)

	2006	2007	2008
Number of vessels	68	75	56
Total displacement ('000 grt)	107.5	102.9	74.7

Source: Lloyd's Register-Fairplay, *World Fleet Statistics*.

CIVIL AVIATION
(traffic on scheduled services)

	2005	2006	2007
Kilometres flown (million)	22	13	4
Passenger-km (million)	1,903	1,413	287
Freight ton-km (million)	25	11	1

Source: UN Commission for Latin America and the Caribbean, *Statistical Yearbook*.

Tourism

ARRIVALS AT HOTELS
(regional capitals only)

Country of origin	2004	2005	2006
Argentina	36,320	41,610	54,622
Brazil	29,745	32,400	35,077
Canada	8,120	8,297	10,745
Chile	14,948	19,234	26,515
France	24,416	25,167	27,304
Germany	19,804	20,308	23,707
Israel	12,149	9,405	12,171
Italy	8,480	8,101	9,744
Japan	7,469	7,226	7,505
Netherlands	9,764	8,625	9,651
Peru	68,739	77,380	84,867
Spain	12,140	11,974	15,531
Switzerland	8,531	8,519	9,964
United Kingdom	20,616	20,801	22,650
USA	38,066	37,758	41,378
Total (incl. others)	390,888	413,267	496,489

Tourism receipts (US $ million, excl. passenger transport): 244 in 2006; 292 in 2007; 275 in 2008 (provisional).

Source: World Tourism Organization.

Communications Media

	2007	2008	2009
Telephones ('000 main lines in use)	678.2	690.0	810.2
Mobile cellular telephones ('000 subscribers)	3,254.4	4,830.0	7,148.4
Internet users ('000)	1,000.0	1,050.0	1,102.5
Broadband subscribers ('000)	34.0	65.6	282.4

Source: International Telecommunication Union.

Personal computers: 220,000 (24.0 per 1,000 persons) in 2005 (Source: International Telecommunication Union).

Television receivers ('000): 990 in use in 2000 (Source: International Telecommunication Union).

Radio receivers ('000): 5,250 in use in 1997 (Source: UNESCO, *Statistical Yearbook*).

Daily newspapers: 18 in 1996 (average circulation 420,000 copies) (Source: UNESCO, *Statistical Yearbook*).

Education

(2006/07, unless otherwise indicated, estimates)

	Institutions	Teachers	Students ('000) Males	Females	Total
Pre-primary	2,294*	6,126	121.1	116.9	238.0
Primary	12,639†	62,430	771.5	740.5	1,512.0
Secondary:					
general	n.a.	57,912	543.2	508.8	1,052.0
technical/ vocational	n.a.	2,148‡	17.3§	32.3§	49.6§
Tertiary	n.a.	15,685	193.8	158.8	352.6

* 1988.
† 1987.
‡ 2003/04.
§ 2002/03.

Pupil-teacher ratio (primary education, UNESCO estimate): 24.2 in 2006/07.

Adult literacy rate (UNESCO estimates): 90.7% (males 96.0%; females 86.0%) in 2007.

Source: UNESCO Institute for Statistics.

Directory

The Constitution

Bolivia became an independent republic in 1825 and received its first Constitution in November 1826. Since that date a number of new Constitutions have been promulgated. Following the *coup d'état* of November 1964, the Constitution of 1947 was revived. Executive power is vested in the President, who chairs the Cabinet. A revised Constitution was signed into law in February 2009, according to which, the President, who is elected by direct suffrage for a five-year term, can seek re-election for a second consecutive term. (According to an electoral law passed in 2009, in the wake of the new Constitution, presidential and legislative elections were to be held in December 2009, one year before they were constitutionally due.) In the event of the President's death or failure to assume office, the Vice-President or, failing the Vice-President, the President of the Senado Nacional (Senate), of the Congreso Nacional (Congress) or of the Supreme Court, in that order, becomes interim Head of State.

The President has power to appoint members of the Cabinet and diplomatic representatives from a panel proposed by the Senate. The President is responsible for the conduct of foreign affairs and is also empowered to issue decrees and to initiate legislation by special messages to Congress.

The Congreso consists of a 36-member Senado and a 130-member Cámara de Diputados (Chamber of Deputies). The Congreso meets annually and its ordinary sessions last only 90 working days, which may be extended to 120. Each of the nine departments (La Paz, Chuquisaca, Oruro, Beni, Santa Cruz, Potosí, Tarija, Cochabamba and Pando), into which the country is divided for administrative purposes, elects four senators. Members of both houses are elected for five years (although elections were held one year early in 2009, according to the terms of legislation approved in April 2009).

The supreme administrative, political and military authority in each department is vested in a prefect appointed by the President (in 2005, however, the first direct elections for departmental prefects were held). The sub-divisions of each department, known as provinces, are administered by sub-prefects. The provinces are further divided into cantons. There are 94 provinces and some 1,000 cantons. The capital of each department has its autonomous municipal council and controls its own revenue and expenditure.

Public order, education and roads are under national control.

A decree issued in July 1952 conferred the franchise on all persons who had reached the age of 21 years, whether literate or illiterate. Previously the franchise had been restricted to literate persons. (The voting age for married persons was lowered to 18 years at the 1989 elections.)

A revised Constitution was approved by some 61% of voters in a referendum in January 2009 and came into effect in the following month. The new Constitution provided for greater autonomy for indigenous communities, enshrined state control over key economic sectors (most notably natural resources), imposed restrictions on the size of land holdings, removed Roman Catholicism as the state religion and aimed to make the judiciary more transparent and accountable. Congress was expected to draft regulations for the new articles of the Constitution during 2009.

The Government

HEAD OF STATE

President: JUAN EVO MORALES AIMA (took office 22 January 2006, re-elected 6 December 2009).

Vice-President: ALVARO MARCELO GARCÍA LINERA.

THE CABINET
(July 2010)

The Cabinet is composed of members of the Movimiento al Socialismo.

Minister of Foreign Affairs and Worship: DAVID CHOQUEHUANCA CÉSPEDES.

Minister of the Interior: SACHA SERGIO LLORENTI SOLIZ.

Minister of National Defence: RUBÉN SAAVEDRA SOTO.

Minister of Justice: NILDA COPA CONDORI.

Minister of Finance: LUIS ALBERTO ARCE CATACORA.

Minister of Development Planning: ELBA VIVIANA CARO HINOJOSA.

Minister of the Presidency: OSCAR COCA ANTEZANA.

Minister of Autonomy: CARLOS ROMERO.

Minister of Institutional Transparency and the Fight against Corruption: NARDI SUXO ITURRY.

Minister of Health and Sport: SONIA POLO ANDRADE.

Minister of Labour, Employment and Social Security: CARMEN TRUJILLO CÁRDENAS.

Minister of Education: ROBERTO AGUILAR.

Minister of Rural Development and Lands: NEMESIA ACHACOLLO TOLA.

Minister of Hydrocarbons and Energy: FERNANDO VICENTI VARGAS.

Minister of Mines and Metallurgy: JOSÉ ANTONIO PIMENTEL CASTILLO.

Minister of Public Works, Services and Housing: WALTER JUVENAL DELGADILLO TERCEROS.

Minister of Water and the Environment: MARÍA ESTHER UDAETA VELÁZQUEZ.

Minister of the Legal Defence of State: ELIZABETH ARISMENDI CHUMACERO.

Minister of Culture: ZULMA YUGAR PÁRRAGA.

Minister of Productive Development and Plural Economy: ANTONIA RODRÍGUEZ MEDRANO.

MINISTRIES

Office of the President: Palacio de Gobierno, Calle Ayacucho, esq. Comercio s/n, La Paz; tel. and fax (2)220-2321; e-mail correo@presidencia.gob.bo; internet www.presidencia.gob.bo.

Office of the Vice-President: Edif. de la Vicepresidencia del Estado, Calle Ayacucho, esq. Mercado 308, Casilla 7056, La Paz; tel. (2) 214-2000; fax (2) 220-1211; internet www.vicepresidencia.gob.bo.

Ministry of Autonomy: Edif. Cámara Nacional de Comercio, 11°, Avda Mariscal Santa Cruz 1392, Casilla 1397, La Paz; tel. (2) 211-0930; fax (2) 211-3613; e-mail prensa@autonomia.gob.bo; internet www.autonomia.gob.bo.

Ministry of Culture: Palacio Chico, Calle Ayacucho, esq. Potosí, Casilla 7846, La Paz; tel. (2) 220-0910; fax (2) 220-2628; e-mail despacho@minculturas.gob.bo; internet www.minculturas.gob.bo.

Ministry of Development Planning: Avda Mariscal Santa Cruz, esq. Oruro 1092, Casilla 12814, La Paz; tel. (2) 211-6000; fax (2) 231-7320; e-mail comunicacion@planificacion.gov.bo; internet www.planificacion.gov.bo.

Ministry of Education: Avenida Arce 2147, Casilla 3116, La Paz; tel. and fax (2) 244-2414; e-mail webmaster@minedu.gob.bo; internet www.minedu.gob.bo.

Ministry of Finance: Edif. Palacio de Comunicaciones, 19°, CP 3744, La Paz; tel. (2) 220-3434; fax (2) 235-9955; e-mail ministro_web@economiayfinanzas.gob.bo; internet www.economiayfinanzas.gob.bo.

Ministry of Foreign Affairs and Worship: Plaza Murillo, Calle Ingavi, esq. Calle Junín, La Paz; tel. (2) 240-8900; fax (2) 240-8905; e-mail mreuno@rree.gob.bo; internet www.rree.gob.bo.

Ministry of Health and Sport: Plaza del Estudiante, esq. Cañada Strongest s/n, La Paz; tel. (2) 249-0554; fax (2) 248-6654; e-mail info@sns.gov.bo; internet www.sns.gov.bo.

Ministry of Hydrocarbons and Energy: Edif. Palacio de Comunicaciones, 12°, Avda Mariscal Santa Cruz, esq. Calle Oruro, La Paz; tel. (2) 237-4050; fax (2) 214-1307; e-mail minehidro@hidrocarburos.gob.bo; internet www.hidrocarburos.gob.bo.

Ministry of Institutional Transparency and the Fight against Corruption: Edif. Capitán Ravelo, 3-9°, Calle Capitán Ravelo 2101, esq. Montevideo, La Paz; tel. 211-5773; fax 215-3084; internet www.transparencia.gob.bo.

Ministry of the Interior: Avda Arce 2409, esq. Belisario Salinas 2409, Casilla 7110, La Paz; tel. (2) 244-0466; fax (2) 237-1334; e-mail mail@mingobierno.gob.bo; internet www.mingobierno.gob.bo.

Ministry of Justice: Avda 16 de Julio (El Prado) 1769, La Paz; tel. (2) 212-4725; fax (2) 231-5468; e-mail ministerio@justicia.go.bo; internet www.justicia.gob.bo.

Ministry of Labour, Employment and Social Security: Calle Yanacocha, esq. Mercado, Zona Central, La Paz; tel. (2) 240-8606; fax (2) 237-1387; e-mail info@mintrabajo.gob.bo; internet www.mintrabajo.gob.bo.

Ministry of the Legal Defence of State: Edif. Hansa, 4°, Avda Mariscal Santa Cruz, La Paz; tel. and fax (2) 211-8454; e-mail mdle@defensalegal.gob.bo; internet www.defensalegal.gob.bo.

Ministry of Mines and Metallurgy: Edif. Palacio de Comunicaciones, 14°, Avda Mariscal Santa Cruz, Casilla 8686, La Paz; tel. (2) 231-0846; fax (2) 239-1241; e-mail mineria@mineria.gob.bo; internet www.mineria.gob.bo.

Ministry of National Defence: Calle 20 de Octubre 2502, esq. Pedro Salazar, La Paz; tel. (2) 243-2525; fax (2) 243-3153; e-mail utransparencia@mindef.gob.bo; internet www.mindef.gob.bo.

Ministry of the Presidency: Palacio de Gobierno, Calle Ayacucho, esq. Comercio s/n, La Paz; tel. (2) 215-3913; fax (2) 237-1388; e-mail correo@presidencia.gob.bo; internet www.presidencia.gob.bo.

Ministry of Productive Development and Plural Economy: Edif. Centro de Comunicaciones, 20°, Avda Mariscal Santa Cruz, esq. Calle Oruro, La Paz; tel. (2) 212-4235; fax (2) 212-4240; e-mail contacto@produccion.gob.bo; internet www.produccion.gob.bo.

Ministry of Public Works, Services and Housing: Edif. Centro de Comunicaciones, 5°, Avda Mariscal Santa Cruz, esq. Calle Oruro, La Paz; tel. (2) 211-9999; internet www.oopp.gob.bo.

Ministry of Rural Development and Lands: Avda Camacho 1471, entre Calle Bueno y Loaysa, La Paz; tel. (2) 211-1103; fax (2) 211-1067; e-mail despacho@agrobolivia.gov.bo; internet www.agrobolivia.gov.bo.

Ministry of Water and the Environment: Capitán Castrillo 434, entre Calles 20 de Octubre y Héroes del Acre, Zona San Pedro, La Paz; tel. 211-5571; fax 211-8582; e-mail gary.suarez@minagua.gov.bo; internet www.mmaya.gob.bo.

President and Legislature

PRESIDENT

Election, 6 December 2009

Candidate	Valid votes	% of valid votes cast
Juan Evo Morales Aima (MAS)	2,943,209	64.22
Manfred Reyes Villa Leopoldo Fernández (PPB–CN)	1,212,795	26.46
Samuel Doria Medina (UN)	258,971	5.65
René Joaquino Suárez González (AS)	106,027	2.31
Others	61,784	1.35
Total (incl. others)*	4,582,786	100.00

* In addition, there were 156,290 blank votes and 120,364 spoiled votes.

ASAMBLEA LEGISLATIVA PLURINACIONAL

President of the Senado Nacional: ANA MARÍA ROMERO DE CAMPO (MAS).

President of the Cámara de Diputados: HÉCTOR ARCE (MAS).

General Election, 6 December 2009

Party	Seats	
	Cámara de Diputados	Senado Nacional
Movimiento al Socialismo (MAS)	88	26
Plan Progreso para Bolivia—Convergencia National (PPB–CN)	37	10
Frente de Unidad Nacional (UN)	3	—
Alianza Social (AS)	2	—
Total	130	36

Election Commission

Corte Nacional Electoral (CNE): Avda Sánchez Lima, esq. Pedro Salazar, Sopocachi, CP 8748, La Paz; tel. (2) 242-4221; fax (2) 241-6710; e-mail cne@cne.org.bo; internet www.cne.org.bo; Pres. ANTONIO JOSÉ I. COSTAS SITIC.

Political Organizations

Acción Democrática Nacionalista (ADN): Edif. Illimani II, No 2512, Of. 12, Avda 6 de agosto y Pedro Salazar, La Paz; f. 1979; right-wing; Leader GUILLERMO FORTÚN SUÁREZ.

Alianza Social (AS): Calle Fortunato Gumiel s/n, Potosí; tel. (2) 622-6150; internet alianzasociallapaz.blogspot.com; f. 2006; Leader RENÉ JOAQUINO CABRERA.

Bolivia Social Demócrata (BSD): Edif. Arco Iris, planta baja, Of. 01, Calle Yanacocha 441, La Paz; tel. 247-0768; e-mail rimech@hotmail.com; internet www.boliviasocialdemocrata.org; f. 2003; Pres. Dr RIME CHOQUEHUANCA AGUILAR.

Comité Cívico pro Santa Cruz (CCSC): Avda Cañada Strongest 70, CP 1801, Santa Cruz; tel. (3) 334-2777; fax (3) 334-1812; internet www.comiteprosantacruz.org.bo; f. 1950; right-wing autonomist grouping; Pres. LUIS NÚÑEZ.

Comité Cívico de Tarija (CCT): Tarija; right-wing autonomist grouping; Pres. WALDEMAR PERALTA.

Consenso Popular (CP): alle Solíz de Olguín 447, esq. Avda Velarde, Santa Cruz; e-mail oscarortizantelo@gmail.com; internet www.consenso-popular.bo; f. 2009; fmr dissident grouping of PODEMOS; Leader OSCAR ORTIZ ANTELO.

Federación de Juntas Vecinales (FEJUVE): El Alto; left-wing grouping campaigning for civil rights and the nationalization of industries and utilities; Pres. GILMAR DURÁN; Sec.-Gen. JORGE CHURA.

Frente Revolucionario de Izquierda (FRI): Avda Busch 1191 y Pasaje Jamaica, Miraflores, La Paz; tel. (2) 222-5488; e-mail waltervr2002@yahoo.es; left-wing; f. 1978; Leader OSCAR ZAMORA MEDINACELI.

Frente de Unidad Nacional (UN): Calle Fernando Guachalla, esq. Jacinto Benavente 2190, La Paz; tel. and fax (2) 211-5110; e-mail info@unidad-nacional.com; internet www.unidad-nacional.com; f. 2003; left-wing; Leader SAMUEL DORIA MEDINA.

Frente para la Victoria (FPV): Edif. Ugarte de Ingeniería, Penthouse 1, Calle Loayza, La Paz; tel. (2); e-mail fpvbolivia@hotmail.com; f. 2006; Leader ELISEO RODRÍGUEZ PARI.

Movimiento Indígena Pachakuti (MIP): indigenous movement; f. 2002; Leader FELIPE QUISPE HUANCA.

Movimiento de la Izquierda Revolucionaria-Nueva Mayoría (MIR-NM): Avda América 119, 2°, La Paz; f. 1971 as Movimiento de la Izquierda Revolucionaria; split into several factions in 1985; adopted present name in 2005; left-wing; Leader JAIME PAZ ZAMORA.

Movimiento Nacionalista Revolucionario (MNR): Avda Hernando Siles 21, Curva Sur del Estado Hernando Siles, La Paz; tel. (2) 212-8475; fax (2) 212-8479; e-mail mnr@bolivian.com; internet www.bolivian.com/mnr; f. 1942; centre-right; Leader DANIEL ARANA VACA; Sec.-Gen. FRANKLIN ANAYA VÁZQUEZ; 165,000 mems.

Movimiento Revolucionario Túpac Katarí de Liberación (MRTKL): Avda Baptista 939, Casilla 9133, La Paz; tel. (2) 235-4784; f. 1978; peasant party; Leader VÍCTOR HUGO CÁRDENAS CONDE; Sec.-Gen. NORBERTO PÉREZ HIDALGO; 80,000 mems.

Movimiento al Socialismo (MAS): Calle Benedicto Vincenti 960, Sopocachi, La Paz; tel. 72970205 (mobile); e-mail info@masbolivia.com; internet www.masbolivia.com; f. 1987; also known as the Movimiento al Socialismo—Instrumento Político por la Soberanía de los Pueblos (MAS—IPSP); left-wing; promotes equality for indigenous people, peasants and workers; Leader JUAN EVO MORALES AIMA.

Movimiento Sin Miedo (MSM): Calle 20 de Octubre y Conchitas, frente al colegio Bolívar, La Paz; tel. 70514444 (mobile); e-mail landaeta93@hotmail.com; internet www.bolivian.com/msm/index.html; f. 1999; left-wing; Leader JUAN DEL GRANADO COSÍO.

Movimiento de Unidad Social Patriótica (MUSPA): Edif. Bejarano, Planta Baja, Of. 7, Avda Montes 630 (Frente cine México), La Paz; tel. (2) 245-2648; e-mail juangabriel757@hotmail.com; f. 2005; Leader JUAN GABRIEL BAUTISTA.

Partido Demócrata Cristiano (PDC): Calle Colón 812, 2°, esq. Sucre, Casilla 4345, La Paz; tel. 70655693 (mobile); e-mail josuva2002@hotmail.com; f. 1954; contested the 2009 election in alliance with PODEMOS; Pres. JORGE SUÁREZ VARGAS.

Partido Obrero Revolucionario (POR): Correo Central, La Paz; internet www.por-bolivia.org; f. 1935; Trotskyist; Leader GUILLERMO LORA.

Plan Progreso para Bolivia—Convergencia Nacional (PPB—CN): Plaza del Estudiante 1907, Of. Radio Ciudad, Zona Central, La Paz; tel. 71520200 (mobile); e-mail jlparedesm@hotmail.com; internet www.planprogreso.org; f. 2007; Leader JOSÉ LUIS PAREDES MUÑOZ.

Poder Democrático y Social (PODEMOS): La Paz; right-wing; split into two factions in March 2009; contested the 2009 elections in alliance with the PDC; Leader JORGE QUIROGA RAMÍREZ.

Pueblos por la Libertad y la Soberanía (PULSO): La Paz; f. 2007; Leader ALEJANDRO VÉLIZ LAZO.

Unión Cívica Solidaridad (UCS): Edif. La Primera Bloque B, 17°, Of. 7 y 8, Avda Mariscal Santa Cruz 1364, La Paz; tel. (2) 236-0297; fax (2) 237-2200; e-mail unidadcivicasolidaridad@hotmail.com; f. 1989; populist; Leader JOHNNY FERNÁNDEZ SAUCEDO; 102,000 mems.

Diplomatic Representation

EMBASSIES IN BOLIVIA

Argentina: Calle Aspiazú 497, esq. Sánchez Lima, Casilla 64, La Paz; tel. (2) 241-7737; fax (2) 242-2727; e-mail ebolv@mrecic.gov.ar; Ambassador HORACIO ANTONIO MACEDO.

Brazil: Edif. Multicentro, Torre B, Avda Arce s/n, esq. Rosendo Gutiérrez, Sopocachi, Casilla 429, La Paz; tel. (2) 216-6400; fax (2) 244-0043; e-mail embajadabrasil@brasil.org.bo; internet www.brasil.org.bo; Ambassador FREDERICO CEZAR DE ARAUJO.

China, People's Republic: Calle 1 8532, Los Pinos, Calacoto, Casilla 10005, La Paz; tel. (2) 279-3851; fax (2) 279-7121; e-mail emb-china@kolla.net; Ambassador QU SHENGWU.

Colombia: Calle 9, No 7835, Casilla 1418, Calacoto, La Paz; tel. (2) 278-4491; fax (2) 279-6011; e-mail elapaz@cancilleria.gov.co; internet www.embajadaenbolivia.gov.co; Ambassador JESÚS EDGAR PAPAMIJA DIAGO.

Cuba: Calle Gobles 6246, entre calles 11 y 12, Bajo Irpavi, Zona Sur, La Paz; tel. (2) 272-1646; fax (2) 272-3419; e-mail embacuba@acelerate.com; internet embacu.cubaminrex.cu/bolivia; Ambassador RAFAEL DAUSÁ CÉSPEDES.

Denmark: Edif. Fortaleza, 9°, Avda Arce 2799, esq. Cordero, Casilla 9860, La Paz; tel. (2) 243-2070; fax (2) 243-3150; e-mail lpbamb@um.dk; internet www.amblapaz.um.dk; Ambassador MORTEN ELKJÆR.

Ecuador: Calle 10, No 8054, Calacoto, Casilla 406, La Paz; tel. (2) 278-4422; fax (2) 277-1043; e-mail eecuabolivia@mmrree.gov.ec; Ambassador SUSANA ALVEAR CRUZ.

Egypt: Avda Ballivián 599, esq. Calle 12, Casilla 2956, La Paz; tel. (2) 278-6511; fax (2) 278-4325; e-mail embajadaegipto@acelerate.com; Ambassador HANI MUHAMMAD BASYONI MAHMOUD.

France: Avda Hernando Silés 5390, esq. Calle 8 de Obrajes, Casilla 717, La Paz; tel. (2) 214-9900; fax (2) 214-9901; e-mail information@ambafrance-bo.org; internet www.ambafrance-bo.org; Ambassador ANTOINE GRASSIN.

Germany: Avda Arce 2395, esq. Belisario Salinas, Casilla 5265, La Paz; tel. (2) 200-1500; fax (2) 244-1441; e-mail info@la-paz.diplo.de; internet www.la-paz.diplo.de; Ambassador Dr PHILIPP SCHAUER.

Holy See: Avda Arce 2990, San Jorge, Casilla 136, La Paz; tel. (2) 243-1007; fax (2) 243-2120; e-mail nunapobol@entelnet.bo; Apostolic Nuncio Most Rev. GIAMBATTISTA DIQUATTRO (Titular Archbishop of Giru Mons).

Italy: Calle 5 (Jordán Cuellar) 458, Obrajes, Casilla 626, La Paz; tel. (2) 278-8506; fax (2) 278-8178; e-mail segreteria.lapaz@esteri.it; internet www.amblapaz.esteri.it; Ambassador SILVIO MIGNANO.

Japan: Calle Rosendo Gutiérrez 497, esq. Sánchez Lima, Casiila 2725, La Paz; tel. (2) 241-9110; fax (2) 241-1919; e-mail coop japon@acelerate.com; Ambassador KAZUO TANAKA.

Korea, Republic: Edif. Torre Lucía, 6°, Calle 13, Calacoto, La Paz; tel. (2) 211-0361; fax (2) 211-0365; e-mail coreabolivia@gmail.com; internet www.bol.mofat.go.kr; Ambassador KIM HONG-RAK.

Mexico: Avda Ballivián 1174, entre Calles 17 y 18, Calacoto, Casilla 430, La Paz; tel. (2) 277-1871; fax (2) 277-1855; e-mail embamex@embamexbolivia.org; internet www.sre.gob.mx/bolivia; Ambassador JOSÉ RAFAEL CERVANTES VILLARREAL.

Netherlands: Edif. Hilda, 7°, Avda 6 de Agosto 2455, Casilla 10509, La Paz; tel. (2) 244-4040; fax (2) 244-3804; e-mail lap@minbuza.nl; internet www.mfa.nl/lap-es; Ambassador MARTIN DE LA BEY.

Panama: Calle 10, No 7853, Calacoto, Casilla 678, La Paz; tel. (2) 278-7334; fax (2) 279-7290; e-mail empanbol@ceibo.entelnet.bo; Ambassador AUGUSTO LUIS VILLARREAL AMARANTO.

Paraguay: Edif. Illimani II, 1°, Of. 101, Avda 6 de Agosto, esq. Pedro Salazar, Sopocachi, Casilla 882, La Paz; tel. (2) 243-3176; fax (2) 243-2201; e-mail embaparbolivia@mre.gov.py; Chargé d'affaires a.i. MARÍA GRACIELA CABALLERO BÁEZ.

Peru: Calle Fernando Guachalla 300, Sopocachi, Casilla 668, La Paz; tel. (2) 244-1250; fax (2) 244-1240; e-mail embbol@caoba.entelnet.bo; Ambassador MANUEL RODRÍGUEZ CUADROS.

Russia: Avda Walter Guevara Arce 8129, Calacoto, Casilla 5494, La Paz; tel. (2) 278-6419; fax (2) 278-6531; e-mail embrusia@acelerate.com; Ambassador LEONID E. GOLUBEV.

Spain: Avda 6 de Agosto 2827, Casilla 282, La Paz; tel. (2) 243-3518; fax (2) 243-2752; e-mail emb.lapaz@maec.es; internet www.maec.es/embajadas/lapaz; Ambassador RAMÓN SANTOS MARTÍNEZ.

Switzerland: Calle 13, esq. Avda 14 de Setiembre, Obrajes, Casilla 9356, La Paz; tel. (2) 275-1225; fax (2) 214-0885; e-mail paz.vertretung@eda.admin.ch; internet www.eda.admin.ch/lapaz; Ambassador PASCAL AEBISCHER.

United Kingdom: Avda Arce 2732, Casilla 694, La Paz; tel. (2) 243-3424; fax (2) 243-1073; e-mail ukinbolivia@gmail.com; internet www.ukinbolivia.fco.gov.uk; Ambassador NIGEL BAKER.

USA: Avda Arce 2780, Casilla 425, La Paz; tel. (2) 216-8000; fax (2) 216-8111; e-mail consularlapaz@state.com; internet bolivia.usembassy.gov; Chargé d'affaires a.i. JOHN S. CREAMER.

Uruguay: Edif. Monroy Velez, 7°, Calle 21, San Miguel 8350, Calacoto, La Paz; tel. (2) 279-1482; fax (2) 279-3976; e-mail urulivia@acelerate.com; Ambassador DIEGO ZORRILLA DE SAN MARTÍN LLAMAS.

Venezuela: Calle 12 esq. Costanerita 1000, Obrajes, Casilla 441, La Paz; tel. (2) 278-8501; fax (2) 278-8254; e-mail embvzla@acelerate.com; Ambassador CRISBERLEE GONZÁLES FERRER.

Judicial System

CONSTITUTIONAL COURT

Tribunal Constitucional de Bolivia: Nicolás Ortiz 149, Sucre; tel. (4) 644-0455; fax (4) 642-1871; e-mail tribunal@tc.gov.bo; internet tribunalconstitucional.gob.bo; f. 1994; Pres. F. JUAN LANCHIPA.

SUPREME COURT

Corte Suprema

Parque Bolívar, Casilla 211, Sucre; tel. (4) 645-3200; fax (4) 646-2696; e-mail cortesuprema@poderjudicial.gov.bo; internet suprema.poderjudicial.gov.bo.

Judicial power is vested in the Supreme Court. There are 12 members, appointed by Congress for a term of 10 years. The court is divided into four chambers of three justices each. Two chambers deal with civil cases, the third deals with criminal cases and the fourth deals with administrative, social and mining cases. The President of the Supreme Court presides over joint sessions of the courts and attends the joint sessions for cassation cases.

President of the Supreme Court: BEATRIZ SANDÓVAL (acting).

DISTRICT COURTS

There is a District Court sitting in each Department, and additional provincial and local courts to try minor cases.

ATTORNEY-GENERAL

In addition to the Attorney-General at Sucre (appointed by the President on the proposal of the Senate), there is a District Attorney in each Department as well as circuit judges.

Attorney-General: MARIO URIBE MELENDRES.

Religion

The majority of the population are Roman Catholics. Religious freedom is guaranteed. There are a number of Bahá'ís and a small Jewish community, as well as various Protestant denominations, in Bolivia.

CHRISTIANITY

The Roman Catholic Church

Some 83% of the poulation are Roman Catholics. Bolivia comprises four archdioceses, six dioceses, two Territorial Prelatures and five Apostolic Vicariates.

Bishops' Conference

Conferencia Episcopal Boliviana, Calle Potosí 814, Casilla 2309, La Paz; tel. (2) 240-6855; fax (2) 240-6941; e-mail asc@scbbs-bo.com.

f. 1972; Pres. Cardinal JULIO TERRAZAS SANDOVAL (Archbishop of Santa Cruz de la Sierra).

Archbishop of Cochabamba: Most Rev. TITO SOLARI CAPELLARI, Avda Heroínas 152, esq. Zenteno Anaya, Casilla 129, Cochabamba; tel. (4) 425-6562; fax (4) 425-0522; e-mail arzobispado@iglesia.org; internet www.iglesiacbba.org.

Archbishop of La Paz: Most Rev. EDMUNDO LUIS FLAVIO ABASTOFLOR MONTERO, Calle Ballivián 1277, Casilla 259, La Paz; tel. (2) 220-3690; fax (2) 220-3840; e-mail arzonslp@ceibo.entelnet.bo; internet www.arzobispadolapaz.org.

Archbishop of Santa Cruz de la Sierra: Cardinal JULIO TERRAZAS SANDOVAL, Calle Ingavi 49, Casilla 25, Santa Cruz; tel. (3) 332-4416; fax (3) 333-0181; e-mail asc@scbbs-bo.com.

Archbishop of Sucre: Most Rev. JESÚS GERVASIO PÉREZ RODRÍGUEZ, Calle Bolívar 702, Casilla 205, Sucre; tel. (4) 645-1587; fax (4) 646-0336; e-mail arzsucre@mara.scr.entelnet.bo.

The Anglican Communion

Within the Iglesia Anglicana del Cono Sur de América (Anglican Church of the Southern Cone of America), Bolivia forms part of the diocese of Peru. The Bishop is resident in Lima, Peru.

Protestant Churches

Baptist Union of Bolivia: Casilla 2199, La Paz; tel. (2) 222-9538; Pres. Rev. AUGUSTO CHUJO.

Convención Bautista Boliviana (Baptist Convention of Bolivia): Casilla 3147, Santa Cruz; tel. and fax (3) 334-0717; f. 1947; Pres. EIRA SORUCO DE FLORES.

Iglesia Evangélica Metodista en Bolivia (Evangelical Methodist Church in Bolivia): Casillas 356 y 8347, La Paz; tel. (2) 249-1628; fax (2) 249-1624; autonomous since 1969; 10,000 mems; Bishop Rev. CARLOS INTIPAMPA.

BAHÁ'Í FAITH

National Spiritual Assembly of the Bahá'ís of Bolivia: Casilla 1613, La Paz; tel. (2) 278-5058; fax (2) 278-2387; e-mail noticias@bahai.org.bo; internet bahai.org.bo; mems resident in 5,161 localities; Gen. Sec. BADÍ HERNÁNDEZ.

The Press

DAILY NEWSPAPERS

Cochabamba

Opinión: Calle General Acha 252, Casilla 287, Cochabamba; tel. (4) 425-4400; fax (4) 441-5121; e-mail opinion@opinion.com.bo; internet www.opinion.com.bo; f. 1985; Dir EDWIN TAPIA FRONTANILLA; Chief Editor ANTONIO RIVERA M.

Los Tiempos: Edif. Los Tiempos, Plaza Quintanilla, Casilla 525, Cochabamba; tel. (4) 425-4562; fax (4) 425-4577; e-mail contactos@lostiempos.com; internet www.lostiempos.com; f. 1943; morning; independent; Dir FERNANDO CANELAS TÁRDIO; Man. Editor ALCIDES FLORES MONCADA; circ. 19,000.

La Paz

El Diario: Calle Loayza 118, Casilla 5, La Paz; tel. (2) 215-0900; fax (2) 215-0902; e-mail redinfo@diario.net; internet www.eldiario.net; f. 1904; morning; conservative; Dir ANTONIO CARRASCO GUZMÁN; Man. Editor RODRIGO TICONA ESPINOZA; circ. 55,000.

Jornada: Edif. Almirante Grau 672, Zona San Pedro, Casilla 1628, La Paz; tel. (2) 248-8163; fax (2) 248-7487; e-mail cartas@jornadanet.com; internet www.jornadanet.com; f. 1964; evening; independent; Dir DAVID RÍOS ARANDA; circ. 11,500.

La Prensa: Mayor Lopera 230, Villa Fátima, Casilla 5614, La Paz; tel. (2) 221-8821; fax (2) 221-8851; e-mail laprensa@laprensa.com.bo; internet www.laprensa.com.bo; Pres. JUAN CARLOS RIVERO J.; Chief Editor CARLOS MORALES PEÑA.

La Razón: Colinas de Santa Rita, Alto Auquisamaña (Zona Sur), Casilla 13100, La Paz; tel. (2) 277-1415; fax (2) 277-0908; e-mail jcrocha@la-razon.com; internet www.la-razon.com; f. 1990; Dir EDWIN HERRERA S.; Man. Editor PATRICIA CUSICANQUI H.; circ. 35,000.

Oruro

La Patria: Avda Camacho 1892, Casilla 48, Oruro; tel. (2) 525-0781; fax (2) 525-0782; e-mail info@lapatria.com.bo; internet www.lapatriaenlinea.com; f. 1919; morning; independent; Dir ENRIQUE MIRALLES BONNECARRERE; circ. 6,000.

Potosí

El Potosí: Calle Cochabamba 35 (Junto a Unidad Sanitaria), Potosí; tel. (2) 622-2601; fax (2) 622-7835; e-mail elpotosi@entelnet.bo; internet www.elpotosi.net; f. 2001; Pres. GONZALO CANELAS TARDÍO; Man. Editor GUILLERMO BULLAÍN IÑIGUEZ.

Santa Cruz

El Deber: Avda El Trompillo 1144, 2º, Casilla 2144, Santa Cruz; tel. (3) 353-8000; fax (3) 353-9053; e-mail web@eldeber.com.bo; internet www.eldeberdigital.com; f. 1953; morning; independent; Dir Dr PEDRO RIVERO MERCADO; Man. Editor TUFFÍ ARÉ VÁZQUEZ; circ. 35,000.

El Día: Avda Cristo Redentor 3355, Casilla 5344, Santa Cruz; tel. (3) 343-4040; fax (3) 342-4041; e-mail eldia@eldia.com.bo; internet www.eldia.com.bo; f. 1987; Dir EDUARDO BOWLES; Man. Editor RÓGER CUÉLLAR.

La Estrella del Oriente: Calle Republiquetas 353, Santa Cruz; tel. (3) 332-9011; fax (3) 332-9012; e-mail central@laestrelladeloriente.com; internet www.laestrelladeloriente.com; f. 1864; Pres. CARLOS SUBIRANA SUÁREZ; Dir (vacant).

El Mundo: Parque Industrial MZ-7, Casilla 1984, Santa Cruz; tel. (3) 346-4646; fax (3) 346-3322; e-mail redaccion@mail.elmundo.com.bo; internet www.elmundo.com.bo; f. 1979; morning; owned by Santa Cruz Industrialists' Asscn; Dir GERMÁN CASASSA ZAPATA; Chief Editor BENITO JESÚS ESPÍNDOLA; circ. 15,000.

Sucre

Correo del Sur: Calle Kilómetro 7, No 202, Casilla 242, Sucre; tel. (4) 646-3202; fax (4) 646-0152; e-mail publicidad_impresa@correodelsur.com; internet www.correodelsur.com; f. 1987; Dir MARCO ANTONIO DIPP MUKLED; Man. Editor RAYKHA FLORES COSSIO.

PERIODICALS

Actualidad Boliviana Confidencial (ABC): Fernando Guachalla 969, Casilla 648, La Paz; f. 1966; weekly; Dir HUGO GONZÁLEZ RIOJA; circ. 6,000.

Aquí: Casilla 10937, La Paz; tel. (2) 234-3524; fax (2) 235-2455; f. 1979; weekly; circ. 10,000.

Bolivia Libre: Edif. Esperanza, 5°, Avda Mariscal Santa Cruz 2150, Casilla 6500, La Paz; fortnightly; govt organ.

Carta Cruceña de Integración: Casilla 3531, Santa Cruz de la Sierra; weekly; Dirs HERNÁN LLANOVARCED A., JOHNNY LAZARTE J.

Comentarios Económicos de Actualidad (CEA): Casilla 312097, La Paz; tel. (2) 242-4766; fax (2) 242-4772; e-mail veceba@caoba.entelnet.bo; f. 1983; fortnightly; articles and economic analyses; Editor GUIDO CÉSPEDES.

Información Política y Económica (IPE): Calle Comercio, Casilla 2484, La Paz; weekly; Dir GONZALO LÓPEZ MUÑOZ.

Informe R: La Paz; weekly; Editor SARA MONROY.

Notas: Edif. Mariscal de Ayacucho, 5°, Of. 501, Calle Loayza 233, Casilla 5782, La Paz; tel. (2) 233-5577; fax (2) 233-7607; internet www.noticiasfides.com; f. 1963; publ. by ANF; weekly; political analysis; Editor JOSÉ GRAMUNT DE MORAGAS.

El Noticiero: Sucre; weekly; Dir DAVID CABEZAS; circ. 1,500.

Prensa Libre: Sucre; tel. (4) 646-2447; fax (4) 646-2768; e-mail prelibre@mara.scr.entelnet.bo; f. 1989; weekly; Dir JULIO PEMINTEL A.

Servicio de Información Confidencial (SIC): Elías Sagárnaga 274, Casilla 5035, La Paz; weekly; publ. by Asociación Nacional de Prensa; Dir JOSÉ CARRANZA.

Siglo XXI: La Paz; weekly.

Unión: Sucre; weekly; Dir JAIME MERILES.

Visión Boliviana: Calle Loayza 420, Casilla 2870, La Paz; 6 a year.

PRESS ASSOCIATIONS

Asociación Nacional de la Prensa: Claudio Aliaga 1290, 2°, San Miguel, La Paz; tel. (2) 279-4208; internet www.anpbolivia.com; f. 1976; private; Pres. MARCO ANTONIO DIPP MUKLED; Exec. Dir JUAN JAVIER ZEBALLOS GUTIÉRREZ.

Asociación de Periodistas de La Paz: Avda 6 de Agosto 2170, Edif. Las Dos Torres, Casilla 477, La Paz; tel. (2) 243-0345; fax (2) 243-6006; internet www.aplp.org.bo; f. 1929; Pres. RONALDO GREBE LÓPEZ; Vice-Pres. MARIÁN DELINA OTAZÚ.

NEWS AGENCIES

Agencia Boliviana de Información: Avda Camacho 1485, Casilla 6500, La Paz; tel. (2) 211-3782; fax (2) 220-4370; e-mail abi@comunica.gov.bo; internet www.abi.bo; govt-owned; Dir JORGE REY CUBA AKIYAMA; Man. Editor RUBÉN DAVID SANDI LORA.

Agencia de Noticias Fides (ANF): Edif. Mariscal de Ayacucho, 5°, Of. 501, Calle Loayza, Casilla 5782, La Paz; tel. (2) 236-5152; fax (2) 236-5153; internet www.noticiasfides.bo; f. 1963; owned by the Roman Catholic Church; Dir JOSÉ GRAMUNT DE MORAGAS; Editors JAIME LOAYZA ZEGARRA (morning), DAVID NIÑO DE GUZMÁN (evening).

Publishers

Ediciones Runa: Calle Ladislao Cabrera 611, Cochabamba; tel. (4) 451-1551; e-mail edicionesruna@yahoo.com; internet www.geocities.com/edicionesruna; f. 1968; juvenile, educational and scholarly.

Editora Khana Cruz, SRL: Avda Camacho 1372, Casilla 5920, La Paz; tel. (2) 237-0263; Dir GLADIS ANDRADE.

Editora Lux: Edif. Esperanza, Avda Mariscal Santa Cruz, Casilla 1566, La Paz; tel. (2) 232-9102; fax (2) 234-3968; f. 1952; Dir FELICISIMO TARILONTE PÉREZ.

Editorial los Amigos del Libro: Avda Ayacucho 0–156, Casilla 450, Cochabamba; tel. (4) 450-4150; fax (4) 411-5128; e-mail gutten@amigol.bo.net; internet www.librosbolivia.com; f. 1945; general; Man. Dir WERNER GUTTENTAG; Gen. Man. INGRID GUTTENTAG.

Editorial Bruño: Loayza 167, Casilla 4809, La Paz; tel. (2) 233-1254; fax (2) 233-5043; f. 1964; Dir IGNACIO LOMAS.

Editorial Don Bosco: Avda 16 de Julio 1899, Casilla 4458, La Paz; tel. (2) 237-1449; fax (2) 236-2822; f. 1896; social sciences and literature; Dir GRAMAGLIA MAGLIANO.

Editorial Icthus: La Paz; tel. (2) 235-4007; f. 1967; general and textbooks; Man. Dir DANIEL AQUIZE.

Editorial Popular: Plaza Pérez Velasco 787, Casilla 4171, La Paz; tel. (2) 235-0701; f. 1935; textbooks, postcards, tourist guides, etc.; Man. Dir GERMÁN VILLAMOR.

Editorial Puerta del Sol: Edif. Litoral Sub Suelo, Avda Mariscal Santa Cruz, La Paz; tel. (2) 236-0746; f. 1965; Man. Dir OSCAR CRESPO.

Empresa Editora Proinsa: Avda Saavedra 2055, Casilla 7181, La Paz; tel. (2) 222-7781; fax (2) 222-6671; f. 1974; school books; Dirs FLOREN SANABRIA G., CARLOS SANABRIA C.

Gisbert y Cía, SA: Calle Comercio 1270, Casilla 195, La Paz; tel. (2) 220-2626; fax (2) 220-2911; f. 1907; textbooks, history, law and general; Pres. JAVIER GISBERT; Promotions Man. MARÍA DEL CARMEN SCHULCZEWSKI; Admin. Man. ANTONIO SCHULCZEWSKI.

Ivar American: Calle Potosí 1375, Casilla 6016, La Paz; tel. (2) 236-1519; Man. Dir HÉCTOR IBÁÑEZ.

Librería Dismo Ltda: Calle Comercio 806, Casilla 988, La Paz; tel. (2) 240-6411; fax (2) 231-6545; e-mail dismo@caoba.entelnet.bo; Dir TERESA GONZÁLEZ DE ALVAREZ.

Librería Editorial Juventud: Plaza Murillo 519, Casilla 1489, La Paz; tel. (2) 240-6248; f. 1946; textbooks and general; Dir GUSTAVO URQUIZO MENDOZA.

Librería El Ateneo, SRL: Calle Ballivián 1275, Casilla 7917, La Paz; tel. (2) 236-9925; fax (2) 239-1513; Dirs JUAN CHIRVECHES D., MIRIAN C. DE CHIRVECHES.

Librería La Paz: Edif. Artemis, Calle Campos y Villegas, Casilla 539, La Paz; tel. (2) 243-4927; fax (2) 243-5004; f. 1900; Dirs EDUARDO BURGOS R., CARLOS BURGOS M.

Librería La Universal, SRL: Calle Ingavi 780, Casilla 2869, La Paz; tel. (2) 228-6634; f. 1958; Man. Dir ROLANDO CONDORI SALINAS.

Librería San Pablo: Calle Colón 627, Casilla 3152, La Paz; tel. (2) 232-6084; f. 1967; Man. Dir MARÍA DE JESÚS VALERIANO.

Santillana de Ediciones, SA: Avda Arce 2333, La Paz; tel. (2) 441-122; fax (2) 442-208; e-mail info@santillanabo.com; internet www.santillanabo.com; Gen. Man. ANDRÉS CARDÓ.

PUBLISHERS' ASSOCIATION

Cámara Boliviana del Libro: Calle Capitán Ravelo 2116, Casilla 682, La Paz; tel. and fax (2) 211-3264; e-mail cabolib@entelnet.bo; f. 1947; Pres. ERNESTO MARTÍNEZ ACCHINI; Vice-Pres. CAROLA OSSIO B.; Gen. Man. ANA PATRICIA NAVARRO.

Broadcasting and Communications

TELECOMMUNICATIONS

Cámara Nacional de Medios de Comunicación: Casilla 2431, La Paz.

Empresa Nacional de Telecomunicaciones (ENTEL): Calle Federico Zuazo 1771, Casilla 4450, La Paz; tel. (2) 231-3030; fax (2) 239-1789; e-mail contacto@entelsa.entelnet.bo; internet www.entel.bo; f. 1965; privatized under the Govt's capitalization programme in 1995; reverted to state ownership in 2008; Pres. LEONARDO BASCOPÉ TAMAYO.

Superintendencia de Telecomunicaciones: Calle 13, No 8260, Calacoto, La Paz; tel. (2) 277-2266; fax (2) 277-2299; e-mail supertel@ceibo.entelnet.bo; internet www.sittel.gov.bo; f. 1995; govt-controlled broadcasting authority; Supt JORGE NAVA AMADOR.

BROADCASTING

Regulatory Authority

Asociación Boliviana de Radiodifusoras (ASBORA): Edif. Jazmín, 10°, Avda 20 de Octubre 2019, Casilla 5324, La Paz; tel. (2) 236-5154; fax (2) 236-3069; broadcasting authority; Pres. RAÚL NOVILLO ALARCÓN.

Radio

The majority of radio stations are commercial. Broadcasts are in Spanish, Aymará and Quechua.

Educación Radiofónica de Bolivia (ERBOL): Calle Ballivian 1323, 4°, Casilla 5946, La Paz; tel. (2) 204-0111; fax (2) 203-888; e-mail erbol@erbol.com.bo; internet www.erbol.com.bo; asscn of 28 educational radio stations in Bolivia; Dir ANDRÉS GÓMEZ VELA.

Radio Fides: La Paz; e-mail sistemas@radiofides.com; internet www.radiofides.com; f. 1939; network of 28 radio stations; Roman Catholic; Pres. EDUARDO PÉREZ IRIBARNE.

Red Patria Nueva: Avda Camacho 1485, 6°, La Paz; tel. (2) 220-0473; fax (2) 200-390; e-mail illimani@comunica.gov.bo; internet www.patrianueva.bo; f. 1932 as Compañía Radio Boliviana; govt-owned network; broadcasts across the country, often as Radio Illimani; Dir IVÁN MALDONADO CORTÉZ.

Television

ATB Red Nacional (Canal 9): Avda Argentina 2057, Casilla 9285, La Paz; tel. and fax (2) 222-9922; internet www.atb.com.bo; f. 1985; privately owned television network.

Bolivisión (Canal 4): Santa Cruz; tel. (2) 240-8585; e-mail jimmystrauch@redbolivision.tv; internet www.redbolivision.tv; f. 1997; privately owned television network; Exec. Pres. ERNESTO ASBÚN GAZAUI; Gen. Man. JEANNETTE ARRÁZOLA RIVERO.

Red Uno: Calle Romecín Campos 592, Sopocachi, La Paz; tel. (2) 242-1111; e-mail notivision@reduno.com.bo; internet www.reduno.com.bo; f. 1985; commercial television station; offices in La Paz, Santa Cruz and Cochabamba; Dir MARIO ROJAS.

Televisión Boliviana (TVB—Canal 7): Edif. La Urbana, 6° y 7°, Avda Camacho 1485, Casilla 900, La Paz; tel. (2) 202-900; fax (2) 203-015; internet www.televisionboliviana.tv.bo; f. 1969; govt network operating stations in La Paz, Oruro, Cochabamba, Potosí, Chuquisaca, Pando, Beni, Tarija and Santa Cruz; Gen. Man. MIGUEL N. MONTERO VACA.

Televisión Universitaria (Canal 13): Edif. 'Hoy', 12°–13°, Avda 6 de Agosto 2170, Casilla 13383, La Paz; tel. (2) 244-1313; internet tvu.umsa.bo; f. 1980; educational programmes; stations in Oruro, Cochabamba, Potosí, Sucre, Tarija, Beni and Santa Cruz; Dir ROBERTO CUEVAS RAMÍREZ.

Unitel (Canal 9): Km 5, Carretera antigua a Cochabamba, Santa Cruz; tel. (3) 352-7686; fax (3) 352-7688; e-mail comercialpz@unitel.com.bo; internet www.unitel.tv; f. 1997; privately owned television network; Gen. Man. YAMILE IBAÑEZ CORREA.

Finance

(cap. = capital; res = reserves; dep. = deposits; m. = million; br(s) = branch(es); amounts are in bolivianos, unless otherwise stated)

BANKING

Supervisory Authority

Autoridad de Supervisión del Sistema Financiero: Plaza Isabel la Católica 2507, Casilla 447, La Paz; tel. (2) 243-1919; fax (2) 243-0028; e-mail asfi@asfi.gov.bo; internet www.asfi.gov.bo; f. 1928; fmrly Superintendencia de Bancos y Entidados Financieras; name changed as above in 2009; Exec. Dir Lic. REYNALDO YUJRA SEGALES.

Central Bank

Banco Central de Bolivia: Avda Ayacucho, esq. Mercado, Casilla 3118, La Paz; tel. (2) 240-9090; fax (2) 240-6614; e-mail bancocentraldebolivia@bcb.gob.bo; internet www.bcb.gob.bo; f. 1911 as Banco de la Nación Boliviana; name changed as above in 1928; bank of issue; cap. 515.8m., res 6,265.2m., dep. 42,497.1m. (Dec. 2008); Pres. GABRIEL LOZA TELLERÍA; Gen. Man. EDUARDO PARDO.

Commercial Banks

Banco Bisa, SA: Avda 16 de Julio 1628, Casilla 1290, La Paz; tel. (2) 231-7272; fax (2) 239-0033; e-mail bancobisa@grupobisa.com; internet www.bisa.com; f. 1963; cap. 542.0m., res 157.2m., dep. 5,735.0m. (Dec. 2008); Pres., CEO and Chair. Ing. JULIO LEÓN PRADO.

Banco de Crédito de Bolivia, SA: Calle Colón, esq. Mercado 1308, Casilla 907, La Paz; tel. (2) 233-0444; fax (2) 231-9163; e-mail cnavarro@bancred.com.bo; internet www.bancodecredito.com.bo; f. 1993 as Banco Popular del Perú, SA; name changed as above 1994; owned by Banco de Crédito del Perú; cap. 315.5m., res 189.6m., dep. 5,518.1m. (Dec. 2008); Chair. DIONISIO ROMERO; Gen. Man. DIEGO A. CAVERO BELAUNDE; 8 brs.

Banco Económico, SA-SCZ: Calle Ayacucho 166, Casilla 5603, Santa Cruz; tel. (3) 315-5500; fax (3) 336-1184; e-mail baneco@baneco.com.bo; internet www.baneco.com.bo; f. 1990; dep. US $244.9m., cap. US $24.4m., total assets US $269.3m. (Dec. 2006); Pres. IVO MATEO KULJIS FÜCHTNER; 25 brs.

Banco Ganadero, SA-Santa Cruz: Calle Bolivar 99, esq. Beni, Santa Cruz; tel. (3) 336-1616; fax (3) 336-1617; internet www.bg.com.bo; f. 1994; cap. 137.4m., res 1.4m., total assets 2,057.6m. (Dec. 2006); Pres. FERNANDO MONASTERIO NIEME; Gen. Man. RONALD GUTIÉRREZ LÓPEZ.

Banco Mercantil Santa Cruz, SA: Calle Ayacucho, esq. Mercado 295, Casilla 423, La Paz; tel. (2) 240-9040; fax (2) 240-9158; e-mail asalinas@bancomercantil.com.bo; internet www.bmsc.com.bo; f. 1905 as Banco Mercantil, SA; acquired Banco Santa Cruz in 2006 and changed name as above; cap. 413.3m., res 149.5m., dep. 9,842.7m. (Dec. 2008); Exec. Vice-Pres. ALBERTO VALDES ANDREATTA; Pres. EMILIO UNZUETA ZEGARRA; 46 brs.

Banco Nacional de Bolivia: Avda Camacho, esq. Colón 1296, Casilla 360, La Paz; tel. (2) 233-2323; fax (2) 231-0695; e-mail info@bnb.com.bo; internet www.bnb.com.bo; f. 1871; 67.27% owned by Grupo Bedoya; cap. 565.8m., res 86.5m., dep. 7,518.5m. (Dec. 2008); Pres. ARTURO BEDOYA SÁENZ; Gen. Man. PABLO BEDOYA SÁENZ; 9 brs.

Banco Solidario, SA (BancoSol): Calle Nicolás Acosta 289, Casilla 13176, La Paz; tel. (2) 248-4242; fax (2) 248-6533; e-mail info@bancosol.com.bo; internet www.bancosol.com.bo; f. 1992; cap. 147.7m., res 35.2m., dep. 2,415.1m. (Dec. 2008); Gen. Man. KURT KÖNIGSFEST.

Banco Unión, SA: Calle Loayza 255, Edif. de Ugarte Ingeniería, 10°, Of. 1001, La Paz; e-mail info@bancounion.com.bo; internet www.bancounion.com.bo; f. 1982; cap. 132.9m., res 78.4m., dep. 2,911.5m.

(Dec. 2008); Pres. José Rolando Claros Bustillo; Gen. Man. Marcia Villarroel Gonzáles; 7 brs.

Credit Institution

PRODEM: Avda Camacho 1277, esq. Colón, La Paz; tel. (2) 211-3227; fax (2) 214-7632; e-mail info@prodemffp.com.bo; internet www.prodemffp.com; f. 2000; microcredit institution; Gen. Man. Bladimir Reverón Madrid; 250 brs.

Banking Association

Asociación de Bancos Privados de Bolivia (ASOBAN): Edif. Cámara Nacional de Comercio, 15°, Avda Mariscal Santa Cruz, esq. Colombia 1392, Casilla 5822, La Paz; tel. (2) 237-6164; fax (2) 239-1093; e-mail info@asoban.bo; internet www.asoban.bo; f. 1957; Pres. Juan Carlos Salaues; Vice-Pres Kurt Koenigfest Sanabria, Ronald Gutierrez Lopez; 18 mems.

STOCK EXCHANGE

Supervisory Authorities

Autoridad de Fiscalización y Control Social de Pensiones: Calle Reyes Ortiz, esq. Federico Zuazo, Edif. Torres Gundlach Este, 5°, Casilla 10794, La Paz; tel. (2) 233-1212; fax (2) 231-2223; e-mail ap@ap.gob.bo; internet www.ap.gob.bo; Exec. Dir Javier Lijerón Loayza.

Bolsa Boliviana de Valores, SA: Calle Montevideo 142, Casilla 12521, La Paz; tel. (2) 244-3232; fax (2) 244-2308; e-mail info@bolsa-valores-bolivia.com; internet www.spvs.gov.bo; f. 1989; Gen. Man. Federico Knaudt.

INSURANCE

Supervisory Authority

Autoridad de Fiscalización y Control Social de Pensiones: see Stock Exchange—Supervisory Authorities.

Major Companies

Adriatica Seguros y Reaseguros, SA: Calle Libertad, esq. Cañoto 879, Casilla 1515, Santa Cruz; tel. (3) 336-6667; fax (3) 336-0600; f. 1995; Pres. Antonio Olea Baudoin.

Alianza, Cía de Seguros y Reaseguros, SA: Avda 20 de Octubre 2680, esq. Campos, Zona San Jorge, Casilla 1043, La Paz; tel. (2) 243-2121; fax (2) 243-2713; e-mail info@alianzaseguros.com; internet www.alianza.com.bo; f. 1991; Pres. Juan Manuel Peña Roca.

Alianza Vida Seguros y Reaseguros, SA: Avda Viedma 19, Casilla 7181, Santa Cruz; tel. (3) 337-5656; fax (3) 337-5666; e-mail alejandroy@alianzaseguros.com; internet www.alianza.com.bo; f. 1999; Pres. Raúl Adler K.; Gen. Man. Alejandro Ybarra Carrasco.

Bisa Seguros y Reaseguros, SA: Edif. San Pablo, 13°, Avda 16 de Julio 1479, Casilla 3669, La Paz; tel. (2) 235-2123; fax (2) 239-2500; internet www.bisaseguros.com; f. 1991; part of Grupo Bisa; Pres. Julio León Prado; Exec. Vice-Pres. Alejandro MacLean Céspedes.

La Boliviana Ciacruz de Seguros y Reaseguros, SA: Calle Colón, esq. Mercado 288, Casilla 628, La Paz; tel. (2) 220-3131; fax (2) 220-4087; e-mail rodrigo.bedoya@zurich.com; internet www.boliviana-ciacruz.com; f. 1946; owned by Zurich Bolivia group; all classes; Pres. Gonzalo Bedoya Herrera; Gen. Man. Rodrigo Bedoya Diez de Medina.

Bupa Insurance (Bolivia), SA: Edif. Tacuaral Equipetrol, Of. 203, Avda San Martín 1800, Santa Cruz; tel. (3) 341-2842; fax (3) 341-2832; e-mail bolivia@bupa.com.bo; internet bolivia.ihi.com; health insurance; Pres. Per Bay Jørgensen.

Credinform International, SA de Seguros: Edif. Credinform, Calle Potosí, esq. Ayacucho 1220, Casilla 1724, La Paz; tel. (2) 231-5566; fax (2) 220-3917; e-mail credinform@credinformsa.com; internet www.credinformsa.com; f. 1954; all classes; Pres. Dr Robín Barragán Peláez; Gen. Man. Miguel Angel Barragán Ibargüen.

Grupo Fortaleza, SA: Avda Arce 2799, esq. Cordero, La Paz; tel. and fax (2) 243-4142; e-mail nhinojosa@grupofortaleza.com.bo; internet www.grupofortaleza.com.bo; Pres. Guido Hinojosa; Gen. Man. Martha O. Lucca Suárez.

Nacional Vida Seguros de Personas, SA: Avda Monseñor Rivero 223, esq. Asunción, Santa Cruz; tel. (3) 371-6262; fax (3) 333-7969; e-mail nacionalvida@nacionalvida.com.bo; internet www.nacionalvida.com.bo; f. 1999; Pres. Juan Carlos Antelo Salmón; Gen. Man. José Luis Camacho Miserendino.

Seguros Illimani, SA: Edif. Mariscal de Ayacucho, 10°, Calle Loayza 233, Casilla 133, La Paz; tel. (2) 220-3040; fax (2) 239-1149; e-mail sisalp@entelnet.bo; internet www.segurosillimani.com.bo; f. 1979; all classes; Gen. Man. Josefina Soliz de Foronda.

Seguros y Reaseguros Generales 24 de Septiembre, SA: Avda Ejército Nacional 487, Santa Cruz; tel. and fax (3) 354-8484; e-mail seguros@caoba.entelnet.com.bo; f. 2001; Pres. Col Roberto Foronda; Gen. Man. Josefina Soliz de Foronda.

La Vitalicia: Edif. Hoy, Avda 6 de Agosto 2860, Casilla 8424, La Paz; tel. (2) 212-5355; fax (2) 211-3480; e-mail aibanez@grupobisa.com; internet www.lavitaliciaseguros.com; f. 1988; part of Grupo Bisa; Pres. Julio León Prado; Gen. Man. Luis Alfonso Ibañez Montes.

Insurance Association

Asociación Boliviana de Aseguradores: Edif. Castilla, 5°, Of. 510, Calle Loayza, esq. Mercado 250, Casilla 4804, La Paz; tel. (2) 220-1014; fax (2) 220-1088; e-mail aba@ababolivia.org; internet www.ababolivia.org; f. 1962; Pres. Hugo de Grandchant Salazar; Gen. Man. Carlos Baudoin Dávalos.

Trade and Industry

GOVERNMENT AGENCIES

Centro de Promoción Bolivia (CEPROBOL): Calle Mercado 1328, Edif. Mariscal Ballivián, 18°, Casilla 10871, La Paz; tel. (2) 233-6886; fax (2) 233-6996; e-mail ceprobol@ceprobol.gov.bo; internet www.ceprobol.gov.bo; f. 1998; under the Ministerio de Relaciones Exteriores y Culto; promotes exports and foreign investment; Exec. Dir Martín López.

Sistema de Regulación Sectorial (SIRESE): Edif. Capitán Ravelo, 4°, Calle Capitán Ravelo 2101, Casilla 9647, La Paz; tel. (2) 244-4545; fax (2) 244-4017; e-mail sg@sirese.gov.bo; internet www.sirese.gov.bo; f. 1994; regulatory body for the formerly state-owned companies and utilities; oversees the general co-ordination and growth of the regulatory system and the work of its Superintendencies of Electricity, Hydrocarbons, Telecommunications, Transport and Water; Supt-Gen. Reynaldo Irigoyen Castro.

DEVELOPMENT ORGANIZATIONS

Centro de Estudios para el Desarrollo Laboral y Agrario (CEDLA): Avda Jaimes Freyre 2940, esq. Muñoz Cornejo, Casilla 8630, La Paz; tel. (2) 241-2429; fax (2) 241-4625; e-mail jgomez@cedla.org; internet www.cedla.org; f. 1985; agrarian and labour development; Exec. Dir Javier Gómez Aguilar.

Corporación de las Fuerzas Armadas para el Desarrollo Nacional (COFADENA): Avda 6 de Agosto 2649, Casilla 1015, La Paz; tel. (2) 237-7305; fax (2) 236-0900; e-mail info@fbmcofadena.com; f. 1972; industrial, agricultural and mining holding co and devt org. owned by the Bolivian armed forces; Gen. Man. Col José Edgar Blacutt Barrón.

Fondo Nacional de Desarrollo Regional (FNDR): La Paz; tel. (2) 417-575; e-mail evalda@fndr.gov.bo; internet www.fndr.gov.bo; f. 1987; promotes local and regional devt, offering financing and support; assumed temporary responsibility for water supply in La Paz in Jan. 2007 following annulment of contracts with private water cos; Exec. Dir Edson Valda Gómez.

CHAMBERS OF COMMERCE

Cámara de Comercio e Industria de Pando: Avda Teniente Coronel Cornejo 80, Casilla 277, Cobija; tel. (3) 842-3139; fax (3) 842-2291; e-mail cicpando@entelnet.bo; Pres. Nemesio Ramírez.

Cámara de Comercio de Oruro: Edif. Cámara de Comercio, Pasaje Guachalla, La Plata, Casilla 148, Oruro; tel. (2) 525-2615; fax (2) 525-0606; e-mail camacor@coteor.net.bo; f. 1895; Pres. Fernando Dehne Franco; Gen. Man. Víctor Hugo Rodríguez García; 165 mems.

Cámara de Comercio y Servicios de Cochabamba: Calle Sucre E-0336, Casilla 493, Cochabamba; tel. (4) 425-7715; fax (4) 425-7717; e-mail gerencia@cadeco.org; internet www.cadeco.org; f. 1922; Pres. Javier Guzmán Aguirre.

Cámara Departamental de Comercio de Beni: Casilla 96, Trinidad; tel. (3) 462-2399; fax (3) 462-0910; Pres. Eduardo Avila Alverdi; Sec.-Gen. José Mamerto Durán.

Cámara Departamental de Industria y Comercio de Tarija (CAINCOTAR): Avda Bolívar, Suite 3000, 1°, Zona Central, Casilla 74, Tarija; tel. (6) 664-2737; fax (6) 611-3636; e-mail info@cictja.com; internet www.cictja.org; Pres. Julio Kohlberg Campero.

Cámara de Exportadores de La Paz (CAMEX): Avda Arce 2021 esq. Goitia, Sopocachi, Casilla 789, La Paz; tel. (2) 244-4310; fax (2) 244-2842; e-mail info@camexbolivia.com; internet www.camexbolivia.com; f. 1993; Pres. Guillermo Pou Munt.

Cámara de Exportadores de Santa Cruz (CADEX): Avda Velarde 131, Santa Cruz; tel. (3) 332-1509; e-mail cadex@cadex

.org; internet www.cadex.org; f. 1986; Gen. Man. OSWALDO BARRIGA KARLBAUM.

Cámara de Industria y Comercio de Chuquisaca: Calle España 64, 2°, Casilla 33, Sucre; tel. (4) 645-1194; fax (4) 645-1850; f. 1923; Pres. MARCELO CUELLAR.

Cámara de Industria, Comercio y Servicios y Turismo de Santa Cruz (CAINCO): Torre Cainco, Avda Las Américas, 7°, Casilla 180, Santa Cruz; tel. (3) 333-4555; fax (3) 334-2353; e-mail cainco@cainco.org.bo; internet www.cainco.org.bo; f. 1915; Pres. ELAR EDUARDO PAZ VARGAS.

Cámara Nacional de Comercio: Edif. Cámara Nacional de Comercio, Avda Mariscal Santa Cruz 1392, 1° y 2°, Casilla 7, La Paz; tel. (2) 237-8606; fax (2) 239-1004; e-mail cnc@boliviacomercio.org.bo; internet www.boliviacomercio.org.bo; f. 1929; 30 brs and special brs; Pres. OSCAR ALBERTO CALLE ROJAS.

Cámara Nacional de Exportadores (CANEB): Avda Arce 2017, esq. c. Goitia, Casilla 12145, La Paz; tel. (2) 244-3529; fax (2) 244-1491; e-mail secretaria@caneb.org.bo; internet www.caneb.org.bo; f. 1969; fmrly Asociación Nacional de Exportadores de Bolivia; adopted current name in 1993; Pres. EDUARDO BRACAMONTE VELASCO.

Cámara Nacional de Industrias de Bolivia: Edif. Cámara Nacional de Comercio, 14°, Avda Mariscal Santa Cruz 1392, Casilla 611, La Paz; tel. (2) 237-4477; fax (2) 236-2766; e-mail ragreda@bolivia-industry.com; internet www.bolivia-industry.com; f. 1937; eight depts throughout Bolivia; Pres. DANIEL SÁNCHEZ SOLIZ.

INDUSTRIAL AND TRADE ASSOCIATIONS

Asociación Nacional de Exportadores de Café (ANDEC): Calle Nicaragua 1638, Casilla 9770, La Paz; tel. (2) 224-4290; fax (2) 224-4561; e-mail andec@caoba.entelnet.bo; controls the export, quality and marketing of coffee producers; Exec. Pres. CARMEN DONOSO DE ARAMAYO.

Cámara Agropecuaria del Oriente: Avda Roca y Coronado s/n, (Predios de Fexpocruz), Casilla 116, Santa Cruz; tel. (3) 352-2200; fax (3) 352-2621; e-mail cao@cotas.com.bo; internet www.cao.org.bo; f. 1964; agriculture and livestock assn for eastern Bolivia; Gen. Man. EDILBERTO OSINAGA ROSADO.

Cámara Boliviana de Hidrocarburos: Radial 17 1/2 y Sexto Anillo, Casilla 3920, Santa Cruz; tel. (3) 353-8799; fax (3) 357-7868; e-mail cbh@cbh.org.bo; internet www.cbh.org.bo; f. 1986; Pres. JOSÉ MAGELA BERNARDES.

Cámara Forestal de Bolivia: Prolongación Manuel Ignacio Salvatierra 1055, Casilla 346, Santa Cruz; tel. (3) 333-2699; fax (3) 333-1456; e-mail camaraforestal@cfb.org.bo; internet www.cfb.org.bo; f. 1969; represents the interests of the Bolivian timber industry; Pres. PEDRO COLANZI SERRATE.

Comité Boliviano de Productores de Antimonio: Edif. El Condor, Batallón Colorados 1404, 14°, Casilla 14451, La Paz; tel. (2) 244-2140; fax (2) 244-1653; f. 1978; controls the marketing, pricing and promotion policies of the antimony industry; Pres. MARIO MARISCAL MORALES; Sec.-Gen. Dr ALCIDES RODRÍGUEZ J.

EMPLOYERS' ASSOCIATIONS

Asociación Nacional de Mineros Medianos: Calle Pedro Salazar 600, esq. Presbítero Medina, Casilla 6190, La Paz; tel. (2) 241-7522; fax (2) 241-4123; e-mail anmm@caoba.entelnet.bo; f. 1939; asscn of 14 private medium-sized mining cos; Pres. HUMBERTO RADA; Sec.-Gen. Dr EDUARDO CAPRILLES.

Confederación de Empresarios Privados de Bolivia (CEPB): Calle Méndez Arcos 117, Plaza España, Zona Sopacachi, Casilla 4239, La Paz; tel. (2) 242-0999; fax (2) 242-1272; e-mail cepb@cepb.org.bo; internet www.cepb.org.bo; largest national employers' org.; Pres. RODRIGO AGREDA; Exec. Sec. ANDRÉS TÓRREZ VILLA-GÓMEZ.

There are also employers' federations in Santa Cruz, Cochabamba, Oruro, Potosí, Beni and Tarija.

STATE HYDROCARBON COMPANY

Corporación Minera de Bolivia (COMIBOL): Avda Camacho 1396, esq. Loayza, La Paz; tel. (2) 268-2100; fax (2) 235-7979; e-mail comibol@comibol.gov.bo; internet www.comibol.gov.bo; f. 1952; state mining corpn; owns both mines and processing plants; Pres. HUGO MIRANDA RENDÓN; 26,000 employees.

Empresa Metalúrgica Vinto (EMV): Carretera Potosí Km 7, Casilla 612, Oruro; tel. (2) 527-8094; fax (2) 527-8024; e-mail info@vinto.gob.bo; internet www.vinto.gob.bo; f. 1966; smelting of non-ferrous minerals and special alloys; majority of shares previously owned by Glencore (Switzerland); renationalized in 2007; took control of Glencore-owned Vinto-Antimony plant in 2010 following renationalization; Gen. Man. RAMIRO VILLAVICENCIO NIÑO DE GUZMÁN; 950 employees.

MAJOR COMPANIES

ADM-SAO, SA: Parque Industrial Pl-M9, Casilla 1295, Santa Cruz; tel. (3) 346-0888; fax (3) 346-3941; e-mail admsao@admworld.com; internet www.admsao.com; f. 1976; edible vegetable oils and soyabean products; Pres. ANDRÉS PETRICEVIC; Gen. Man. VALMOR SCHAFFER; 560 employees.

Ametex, SA (América Textil): Calle Yanacachi 1489, Villa Fatima, La Paz; textile exporter to the USA; Pres. MARCOS IBERKLEID; 3,500 employees.

Cervecería Boliviana Nacional, SA: Avda Montes 400, Casilla 421, La Paz; tel. (2) 245-5455; fax (2) 245-5375; e-mail cbn@pacena.com; f. 1920; brewing; Pres. JOHNNY FERNÁNDEZ SAUCEDO; Gen. Man. JUAN MEDINACELLI VALENCIA; 275 employees.

Cervecería Santa Cruz, SA: Avda Busch, 3er Anillo Interno, Santa Cruz; tel. (3) 353-5000; fax (3) 353-7070; f. 1952; owned by Quilmes Industrial, SA (Argentina); brewing; Pres. HERMANN WILLE; Gen. Man. RICARDO LÓPEZ ECHEVERRÍA; 220 employees.

Cervecería Taquiña, SA: Avda Centenario Final, Casilla 494, Cochabamba; f. 1895; owned by Quilmes Industrial, SA (Argentina); brewing; Pres. ERNESTO ASBÚN GIZAUI; Gen. Man. FAUSTINO ARIAS REY; 345 employees.

Compañía Industrial Azucarera San Aurelio, SA: Avda San Aurelio, esq. 4 Anillo, Zona Sud, Casilla 94, Santa Cruz; tel. (3) 353-4343; fax (3) 352-1182; e-mail ciasacomercial@ciasa.com.bo; internet www.sanaurelio.com; sugar refining and alcohol distillery; Pres. RAMÓN AURELIO GUTIÉRREZ SOSA; Gen. Man. MARIO E. TEJADA; 800 employees.

Compañía Industrial Maderera Ltda (CIMAL): Parque Industrial Pesado 10, Santa Cruz; tel. (3) 342-2595; fax (3) 342-3995; f. 1974; sawmill operations; Pres. CRISTÓBAL RODA DAZA; Gen. Man. LARRY HANSLER; 265 employees.

Compañía Industrial de Tabacos, SA: Avda Chacaltaya 2141, Zona Achachicala, Casilla 210, La Paz; tel. (2) 230-5353; fax (2) 230-7272; e-mail citsa@citbolivia.com; internet www.citbolivia.com; f. 1934; cigarette manufacturers; Pres. RAÚL ADLER KAVLIN; Gen. Man. JORGE H. PAREJA; 200 employees.

Cooperativa Boliviana de Cemento Industrias y Servicios (COBOCE): Avda San Martín 558, Cochabamba; tel. (2) 426-2547; fax (2) 422-2485; e-mail cem@coboce.com; internet www.coboce.com; f. 1966; manufacture and distribution of cement; Gen. Man. EDWIN TAPIA FRONTANILLA; 455 employees.

Drogueria Inti, SA: Calle Lucas Jaimes 1959, Casilla 1421, La Paz; tel. (2) 222-0200; fax (2) 221-1981; e-mail drogueria@inti.com.bo; internet www.inti.com.bo; f. 1947; manufacture and distribution of pharmaceuticals; Pres. FRIEDRICH OHNES TANZER; Man. DALGAS CHRISTIAN SCHILLING; 365 employees.

Empresa Minera Unificada, SA (EMUSA): Edif. EMUSA, 6°, Avda 20 de Octubre 1963, Sopocachi, Casilla 291, La Paz; tel. (2) 242-3275; fax (2) 242-2755; e-mail emusapre@entelnet.bo; f. 1946; mining and processing of metal ores; Pres. LUIS MERCADO; 416 employees.

Empresa Petrolera Chaco, SA: Edif. Centro Empresarial Equipetrol, 6°, Avda San Martín 1700, Equipetrol Norte, Casilla 6428, Santa Cruz; tel. (3) 345-3700; fax (3) 345-3710; internet www.chaco.com.bo; f. 1999; wholly owned subsidiary of BP (United Kingdom); oil and gas exploration and production; Exec. Pres. PEDRO TORQUEMADA LÉON.

Fábrica Nacional de Cemento, SA (FANCESA): Pasaje Armando Alba No 80, Sucre; tel. (4) 645-3882; fax (4) 644-1221; e-mail info@fancesa.com; internet www.fancesa.com; f. 1959; manufacturers of cement; Pres. IVÁN ARCIÉNEGA; Gen. Man. WILMER ASTETE; 300 employees.

Ferrari Ghezzi Ltda: Avda 6 de Octubre 5049, Aroma y Rodriguez, Casilla 371, Oruro; tel. (2) 527-9361; fax (2) 527-5130; e-mail sfida_sa@hotmail.com; internet www.sfida.com.bo; f. 1935; subsidiary of SFIDA Inversiones, SA; food production and processing; Gen. Man. PEDRO PEREZ BLACUTT; 500 employees.

Gravetal Bolivia, SA: Edif. Banco Nacional de Bolivia, 6° y 7°, René Moreno 258, Casilla 5503, Santa Cruz; tel. (3) 336-3601; fax (3) 332-4723; e-mail gerencia@gravetal.com.bo; internet www.gravetal.com.bo; f. 1992; production of soyabean oil and soyabean meal; Pres. JUAN VALDIVIA ALMANZA; Vice-Pres. ROBERTO MANZANILLA; Gen. Man. JUAN JOSÉ RIC RIVERA.

Industrias de Aceite, SA (FINO): Carretera al Norte Km 6.5; Casilla 1759, Santa Cruz; tel. (3) 344-3000; fax (3) 344-3020; e-mail fino@fino.com.bo; internet www.fino.com.bo; f. 1944; owned by Grupo Romero of Peru; manufacture of edible vegetable oils; Pres. JUAN JAVIER LLOSA ISENRICH; Gen. Man. RENZO VALAREZO CINO; 1,080 employees.

Ingenio Azucarero Guabirá, SA: Carretera al Norte Km 56, Casilla 2069, Guabirá, Montero, Santa Cruz; tel. (3) 345-2021; fax (3) 345-2024; e-mail regional_scz@entelnet.bo; internet guabira.com; f. 1956; processing and refining of sugar cane and alcohol distillation; Pres. CRISTÓBAL RODA VACA; Gen. Man. RUDIGER TREPP DEL C.

Jindal Steel Bolivia, SA (JSB): Edif. Tacuaral, 4º, Of. 402–403, Avda San Martín 1800, Equipetrol Norte, Santa Cruz; tel. (3) 341-6000; e-mail marketing@jindalsteel.com; internet www.jindalsteelpower.com; subsidiary of Jindal Steel & Power Ltd, India; operates in a joint venture with Empresa Siderurgica Del Mutun (ESM); mining and steel manufacture; Man. Dir NAVEEN JINDAL.

Manufactura Boliviana, SA (MANACO): Avda Tomas Bata, esq. Blanco Galindo, Quillacollo, Casilla 513, Cochabamba; tel. (4) 426-3012; fax (4) 426-3013; e-mail manaco@manaco-bo.com; internet www.bata.com; f. 1940; manufacturers of footwear; part of the Bata group; Pres. PABLO DERMIZAKY PEREDO; Gen. Man. CARLOS BUSTAMENTE MORALES; 771 employees.

La Papelera, SA: Avda Clemente Inofuentes 836, entre 14 y 15, Calacoto, La Paz; tel. (2) 279-3947; fax (2) 279-3952; e-mail lapapelera@papelera.com; internet www.lapapelera.com; f. 1941; paper and plastics manufacturers; Pres. EMILIO VON BERGEN; Gen. Man. JUAN CARLOS ARNEZ; 150 employees.

Petrobras Bolivia, SA: Avda Grigotá, esq. Calle los Troncos 5, Casilla 6866, Santa Cruz; tel. (3) 358-6030; fax (3) 358-6031; e-mail petrobrasbolivia@petrobras.com.bo; internet www.petrobras.com.bo; subsidiary of Petrobras (Brazil); oil and gas exploration and production; f. 1995; Gen. Man. CLAUDIO CASTEJON; 1,500 employees.

Petroquim, SRL: 4to Anillo s/n, P.I. Mz. 25, CP 3445, Santa Cruz; tel. (3) 348-8000; fax (3) 348-8200; e-mail info@petroquim.net; internet www.petroquim.net; petrochemicals; Gen. Man. ANDRÉS RODRÍGUEZ.

Pluspetrol Bolivia Corporation, SA: Avda Grigota, esq. Calle Las Palmas, Santa Cruz; tel. (3) 352-0606; fax (3) 354-8080; e-mail ocosta@pluspetrol.net; internet www.pluspetrolbolivia.com.bo; f. 1997; oil and gas exploration and production; Chair. and Pres. LUIS ALBERTO REY.

Sinchi Wayra, SA: Edif. Multicentro, Torre B, 1° y 2°, Avda Arce, esq. Rosendo Gutiérrez 2299, Casilla 4326, La Paz; tel. (2) 244-4849; fax (2) 244-4126; e-mail fhartmann@sinchiwayra.com.bo; f. 1965; mining and processing of lead and zinc ores and precious metals; wholly owned by a subsidiary of Glencore (Switzerland); Pres. EDUARDO CAPRILES; 1,456 employees.

Sociedad Boliviana de Cemento, SA (SOBOCE): Calle Mercado 1075, 1°, Casilla 557, La Paz; tel. (2) 240-6040; fax (2) 240-7440; e-mail info@soboce.com; internet www.soboce.com; f. 1925; manufacturers of cement; Pres. JUAN CARLOS REQUENA; Gen. Man. ARMANDO GUMUCIO; 710 employees.

Sociedad Comercial e Industrial Hansa Ltda (HANSA): Edif. Hansa, Calle Yanacocha, esq. Mercado 1004, Casilla 10800, La Paz; tel. (2) 214-9800; fax (2) 240-7788; e-mail gpetit@hansa.com.bo; internet www.hansa.com.bo; f. 1954; import and trading of telecommunications equipment, hardware, industrial machinery, motor vehicles and mining equipment; Pres. GEORGES PETIT; 370 employees.

UTILITIES

Electricity

Superintendencia de Electricidad: Avda 16 de Julio 1571, La Paz; tel. (2) 231-2401; fax (2) 231-2393; e-mail webmaster@superele.gov.bo; internet www.superele.gov.bo; f. 1994; regulates the electricity sector; Supt JERGES MERCADO SUÁREZ.

Alternative Energy Systems Ltd (Talleres AES): Los Cafetales 2753, Alto Queru Queru, Casilla 4082, Cochabamba; tel. and fax (4) 445-3973; e-mail aesbol@freeyellow.com; internet aesbol.freeyellow.com; f. 1986; specialist manufacturers of alternative energy products including small water turbines, equipment for small hydro plants and pumping stations; Gen. Man. MIGUEL ALANDIA.

Compañía Boliviana de Energía Eléctrica, SA (COBEE): Avda Hernando Siles 5635, Casilla 353, La Paz; tel. (2) 278-2474; fax (2) 278-5920; e-mail cobee@cobee.com; internet www.cobee.com; f. 1925; largest private power producer and distributor, serving the areas of La Paz and Oruro; generated 27.2% of Bolivia's total electricity output in 2002; mainly hydroelectric; Pres. and Gen. Man. JOSÉ ANTONIO RAMÍREZ MURILLO.

Compañía Eléctrica Central Bulo Bulo, SA (CECBB): Avda San Martín 1700, Centro Empresarial Equipetrol Norte, 6°, Casilla 6428, Santa Cruz; tel. (3) 366-3606; fax (3) 366-3601; e-mail ramon.bascope@chaco.com.bo; f. 1999; generator co; owned by Empresa Petrolera Chaco, SA; 101.2 MW capacity in 2002; Gen. Man. RAMÓN BASCOPE PARADA.

Compañía Eléctrica Sucre, SA (CESSA): Calle Ayacucho 254, Sucre; tel. (4) 645-3126; fax (4) 646-0292; e-mail cessa@mara.scr.entelnet.bo; internet www.cessasucre.com; f. 1924; electricity distributor; Gen. Man. JOSÉ ANAVE LEÓN.

Cooperativa Rural de Electrificación Ltda (CRE): Avda Busch, esq. Honduras, Santa Cruz; tel. (3) 336-6666; fax (3) 332-4936; e-mail webmaster@cre.com.bo; internet www.cre.com.bo; f. 1965; electricity distributor; Gen. Man. CARMELO PAZ DURÁN; Sec.-Gen. JOSÉ ERNESTO ZAMBRANA.

Electropaz: Avda Illimani 1973, Miraflores, Casilla 10511, La Paz; tel. (2) 222-2200; fax (2) 222-3756; e-mail cpacheco@electropaz.com.bo; internet www.electropaz.com.bo; f. 1995; distributor serving La Paz area; Gen. Man. Ing. MAURICIO VALDEZ CÁRDENAS.

Empresa Nacional de Electricidad, SA (ENDE): Avda Ballivián 503, Edif. Colón, 8°, Casilla 565, Cochabamba; tel. (4) 452-0317; fax (4) 452-0318; e-mail ende@ende.bo; internet www.ende.bo; f. 1962; former state electricity co; privatized under the Govt's capitalization programme in 1995 and divided into three arms concerned with generation, transmission and distribution, respectively; Gen. Man. RAFAEL ALARCÓN ORIHUELA.

The following companies were renationalized in May 2010 and placed under the control of ENDE:Empresa Corani, SA: Avda Oquendo 654, Edif. Las Torres Sofer I, 9°, Casilla 5165, Cochabamba; tel. (4) 423-5700; fax (4) 425-9148; e-mail corani@corani.com; internet www.corani.com; f. 1995; generator co; 802.60 GWh generation in 2006 in conjunction with Santa Isabel; Pres. FREDERICK P. RENNER.

Empresa Eléctrica Valle Hermoso, SA (EVH): Calle Tarija 1425, esq. Adela Zamudio, Cala Cala, Cochabamba; tel. (4) 424-0544; fax (4) 428-6838; e-mail central@evh.com.bo; internet www.evh.com.bo; f. 1995; generator co.; 347.41 MW capacity in 2002; Pres. ENRIQUE HERRERA SORIA.

Empresa de Generación Guaracachi, SA (EGSA): Avda Brasil y Tercer Anillo Interno, Casilla 336, Santa Cruz; tel. (3) 346-4632; fax (3) 346-5888; e-mail central@egsa.com.bo; internet www.guaracachi.com.bo; f. 1995; generator co; 445 MW capacity in 2008; Pres. PETER EARL.

Empresa de Luz y Fuerza Eléctrica Cochabamba, SA (ELFEC): Avda Heroínas 0-686, Casilla 89, Cochabamba; tel. (4) 420-0125; fax (4) 425-9427; e-mail sugerencias@elfec.com; internet www.elfec.com; f. 1908; electricty distributor; Gen. Man. JAVIER DE UDAETA.

Hidroeléctrica Boliviana, SA: Avda Fuerza Naval 22, Zona Calcoto, La Paz; tel. (2) 277-0765; fax (2) 277-0933; e-mail hb@hidrobol.com; internet www.hidrobol.com; 317 GWh generation in 2008; Gen. Man. Ing. ANGEL ZANNIER CLAROS.

Gas

Numerous distributors of natural gas exist throughout the country, many of which are owned by the petroleum distributor, Yacimientos Petrolíferos Fiscales Bolivianos (YPFB).

Yacimientos Petrolíferos Fiscales Bolivianos (YPFB): Calle Bueno 185, 6°, Casilla 401, La Paz; tel. and fax (2) 237-0210; e-mail webmaster@ypfb.gov.bo; internet www.ypfb.gov.bo; f. 1936; exploration, drilling, production, refining, transportation and distribution of petroleum; partially privatized in 1996; Pres. CARLOS VILLEGAS QUIROGA; 4,900 employees.

Water

Superintendencia de Saneamiento Básico (SISAB): Edif. Cámara de Comercio, Avda Mariscal Santa Cruz 1392, 4° y 16°, Casilla 4245, La Paz; tel. (2) 231-0801; fax (2) 231-0554; e-mail contactos@sisab.gov.bo; f. 1999; regulates urban water supplies and grants service concessions and licences; Govt announced plans to replace SISAB with a decentralized regulatory authority in 2008/09; Supt ALVARO CAMACHO GARNICA.

Empresa Pública Social de Agua y Saneamiento (EPSAS): Avda de las Américas 705, Villa Fátima, Casilla 9359, La Paz; tel. (2) 221-0295; fax (2) 221-2454; e-mail info@epsas.com.bo; f. 2007; state-owned water and sewerage provider in La Paz and El Alto; Gen. Man. VÍCTOR RICO.

CO-OPERATIVE

Instituto Nacional de Co-operativas (INALCO): Edif. Lotería Nacional, 4°, Avda Mariscal Santa Cruz y Cochabamba, La Paz; tel. (2) 237-4366; fax (2) 237-2104; e-mail inalcolp@ceibo.entelnet.bo; f. 1974; Pres. DAVID AYAVIRI.

TRADE UNIONS

Central Obrera Boliviana (COB): Edif. COB, Calle Pisagua 618, Casilla 6552, La Paz; tel. (2) 352-426; fax (2) 281-201; e-mail postmast@cob-bolivia.org; f. 1952; main union confederation; 800,000 mems; Exec. Sec. PEDRO MONTES.

Affiliated unions:

Central Obrera Departamental de La Paz: Estación Central 284, La Paz; tel. (2) 235-2898; Exec. Sec. GENARO TORRICO.

Confederación Sindical Unica de los Trabajadores Campesinos de Bolivia (CSUTCB): Avda Saavedra 2045, Miraflores, Casilla 11589, La Paz; tel. (2) 224-6232; fax (2) 224-6300; e-mail csutcb_tk@hotmail.com; internet www.csutcb.org; f. 1979; peasant farmers' union; Exec. ISAAC AVALOS CUCHALLO.

Federación de Empleados de Industria Fabril: Edif. Fabril, 5°, Plaza de San Francisco, La Paz; tel. (2) 240-6799; fax (2) 240-7044; Exec. Sec. ALEX GÁLVEZ.

Federación Sindical de Trabajadores Mineros de Bolivia (FSTMB): Plaza Venezuela 147, Casilla 14565, La Paz; tel. (2) 235-9656; fax (2) 231-7764; e-mail fstmb1944@hotmail.com; internet http://sites.google.com/site/fstmb2003/; f. 1944; mineworkers' union; Leader MIGUEL ZUBIETA; Exec. Sec. GUIDO MISMA CRISPIN; 27,000 mems.

Federación Sindical de Trabajadores Petroleros de Bolivia: Calle México 1504, La Paz; tel. (2) 235-1748; Exec. Sec. NEFTALÍ MENDOZA DURÁN.

Central Obrera Regional (COR): El Alto; Exec. Sec. EDGAR PATANA.

Confederación General de Trabajadores Fabriles de Bolivia (CGTFB): Avda Armentia 452, Casilla 21590, La Paz; tel. (2) 237-1603; fax (2) 232-4302; e-mail dirabc@bo.net; f. 1951; manufacturing workers' union; Exec. Sec. ANGEL ASTURIZAGA.

Transport

RAILWAYS

Empresa Nacional de Ferrocarriles (ENFE): Estación Central de Ferrocarriles, Plaza Zalles, Casilla 428, La Paz; tel. (2) 232-7401; fax (2) 239-2677; f. 1964; privatized in 1995; re-nationalized in 2007; administers most of the railways in Bolivia; holding co for unauctioned former state assets; total networks: 3,608 km (1999); Andina network: 2,274 km; Oriental (Eastern) network: 1,424 km; Pres. J. L. LANDÍVAR.

Empresa Ferroviaria Andino, SA: Casilla 4350, La Paz; tel. and fax (2) 239-145; e-mail efasa@fca.com.bo; internet www.fca.com.bo; f. 1996; Pres. MIGUEL SEPÚLVEDA CAMPOS.

Empresa Ferroviaria Oriental, SA (FCOSA): Avda Montes Final s/n, Casilla 108, Santa Cruz; tel. (3) 338-7000; e-mail ferroviaria@ferroviariaoriental.com; internet www.ferroviariaoriental.com; f. 1996; 50.0% owned by Genesee & Wyoming Inc (USA); Gen. Man. MARÍA MUÑOZ.

There are plans to construct a railway line with Brazilian assistance, to link Cochabamba and Santa Cruz. Plans were also mooted for the construction of a rail link between Santa Cruz and Mutún on the border with Brazil.

ROADS

In 2004 Bolivia had some 60,282 km of roads, of which an estimated 3,979 km (6.6%) were paved. Almost the entire road network is concentrated in the *altiplano* region and the Andes valleys. A 560-km highway runs from Santa Cruz to Cochabamba, serving a colonization scheme on virgin lands around Santa Cruz. The Pan-American Highway, linking Argentina and Peru, crosses Bolivia from south to north-west. In 1997 the Government announced the construction of 1,844 km of new roads in the hope of improving Bolivia's connections with neighbouring countries.

INLAND WATERWAYS AND SHIPPING

By agreement with Paraguay in 1938 (confirmed in 1939), Bolivia has an outlet on the River Paraguay. This arrangement, together with navigation rights on the Paraná, gives Bolivia access to the River Plate and the sea. The River Paraguay is navigable for vessels of 12-ft draught for 288 km beyond Asunción, in Paraguay, and for smaller boats another 960 km to Corumbá in Brazil. In late 1994 plans were finalized to widen and deepen the River Paraguay, providing a waterway from Bolivia to the Atlantic coast in Uruguay. However, work on the project was delayed, owing largely to environmental concerns.

In 1974 Bolivia was granted duty-free access to the Brazilian coastal ports of Belém and Santos and the inland ports of Corumbá and Port Velho. In 1976 Argentina granted Bolivia free port facilities at Rosario on the River Paraná. In 1992 an agreement was signed with Peru, granting Bolivia access to (and the use, without customs formalities, of) the Pacific port of Ilo. Most of Bolivia's foreign trade is handled through the ports of Matarani (Peru), Antofagasta and Arica (Chile), Rosario and Buenos Aires (Argentina) and Santos (Brazil). An agreement between Bolivia and Chile to reform Bolivia's access arrangements to the port of Arica came into effect in January 1996.

Bolivia has over 14,000 km of navigable rivers, which connect most of Bolivia with the Amazon basin.

CIVIL AVIATION

Bolivia has 30 airports, including the two international airports at La Paz (El Alto) and Santa Cruz (Viru-Viru).

Dirección General de Aeronaútica Civil: Edif. Palacio de Comunicaciones, 4°, Avda Mariscal Santa Cruz 1278, Casilla 9360, La Paz; tel. (2) 237-4142; internet www.dgac.gov.bo; f. 1947; Exec. Dir Gen. LUIS TRIGO ANTELO.

AeroSur: Calle Colón y Avda Irala 616, Casilla 3104, Santa Cruz; tel. (3) 336-4446; fax (3) 363-1384; e-mail ventas@aerosur.com; internet www.aerosur.com; f. 1992 by merger of existing charter cos following deregulation; privately owned; Pres. HUMBERTO ROCA; Gen. Man. CARLOS MEYER.

Boliviana de Aviación: Calle Jordán 202, esq. Nataniel Aguirre, Cochabamba; tel. (4) 414-0873; fax (4) 411-4643; e-mail ventasweb@boa.bo; internet www.boa.gov.bo; f. 2007; state-owned; Gen. Man. RONALD CASSO CASSO.

Lloyd Aéreo Boliviano, SA (LAB): Casilla 132, Aeropuerto 'Jorge Wilstermann', Cochabamba; tel. (4) 425-1270; fax (4) 425-0766; e-mail presidencia@labairlines.com.bo; internet www.labairlines.com.bo; f. 1925; privatized under the Govt's capitalization programme in 1995; jtly owned by Bolivian Govt (48%), and private interests (52%); operates a network of scheduled services to 12 cities within Bolivia and to 21 international destinations in South America, Central America and the USA; Pres. Ing. ERNESTO ASBÚN; Gen. Man. MARIA VICTORIA CALDERÓN GONZALES.

Transportes Aéreos Bolivianos (TAB): El Alto, Internacional Aeropuerto, Casilla 12237, La Paz; tel. (2) 264-0556; e-mail tabair@tab.aero; internet www.tab.aero; f. 1977; regional scheduled and charter cargo services; Gen. Man. LUIS GUERECA PADILLA; Chair. PETER MARLIN GURD.

Transportes Aéreos Militares: Avda Montes 738, esq. Jose Maria Serrano, La Paz; tel. (2) 268-1101; fax (2) 268-1102; internet www.tam.bo; internal passenger and cargo services; Dir-Gen. REMBERTO DURÁN.

Tourism

Bolivia's tourist attractions include Lake Titicaca, at 3,810 m (12,500 ft) above sea level, pre-Incan ruins at Tiwanaku, Chacaltaya in the Andes mountains, which has the highest ski-run in the world, and the UNESCO World Cultural Heritage Sites of Potosí and Sucre. In 2006 some 496,489 foreign visitors arrived at hotels in Bolivian regional capitals. In 2008 receipts from tourism totalled a provisional US $275m. Tourists come mainly from South American countries, the USA and Europe.

Asociación Boliviana de Agencias de Viajes y Turismo (ABAVYT): Calle Boliviar 27, 2°, Zonca Central, Santa Cruz; tel. (3) 332-7110; fax (3) 332-1634; e-mail abavyt@caoba.entelnet.bo; internet www.abavyt.org; f. 1984; Pres. LESLIE CRONENBOLD SALVATIERRA.

Defence

As assessed at November 2009, Bolivia's armed forces numbered 46,100: army 34,800 (including 25,000 conscripts), navy 4,800, air force 6,500. There was also a paramilitary force numbering 37,100. Military service, lasting one year, is selective.

Defence Expenditure: budgeted at 1,700m. bolivianos in 2009.

Commander-in-Chief of the Armed Forces: Gen. RAMIRO DE LA FUENTE.

General Commander of the Army: Maj.-Gen. RAMIRO DE LA FUENTE.

General Commander of the Air Force: Maj.-Gen. DANIEL SALAZAR OSORIO.

General Commander of the Naval Forces: Vice-Adm. ARMANDO PACHECO GUTIÉRREZ.

Education

Primary education, beginning at six years of age and lasting for eight years, is officially compulsory and is available free of charge. Secondary education, which is not compulsory, begins at 14 years of age and lasts for up to four years. In 2006/07 enrolment at primary schools included 94% of pupils in the relevant age-group. In that year enrolment at secondary schools included 70% of students in the relevant age-group. There are eight state universities and two private universities. The Government of Evo Morales, which took office in 2006, launched an education programme, 'Yo sí puedo', to alleviate levels of illiteracy. Expenditure on education by the central Government in 2006 was 6,328.5m. bolivianos, according to preliminary figures, representing 19.5% of total spending.

Bibliography

For works on South America generally, see Select Bibliography (Books)

Crabtree, J. *Patterns of Protest: Politics and Social Movements in Bolivia*. London, Latin America Bureau, 2005.

Dunkerley, J. *Bolivia: Revolution and the Power of History in the Present. Essays*. London, Institute for the Study of the Americas, 2007.

Fifer, J. V. *Bolivia: Land, Location and Politics Since 1825*. Cambridge, Cambridge University Press, 2008.

Gamarra, E. A. *Bolivia on the Brink*. New York, Council on Foreign Relations, 2007.

Gotkowitz, L. *A Revolution for Our Rights: Indigenous Struggles for Land and Justice in Bolivia*. Durham, NC, Duke University Press, 2008.

Grey Postero, N. *Now We Are Citizens: Indigenous Politics in Post-Multicultural Bolivia*. Palo Alto, CA, Stanford University Press, 2006.

Grindle, M., and Domingo, P. (Eds). *Proclaiming Revolution: Bolivia in Comparative Perspective*. London, Harvard University David Rockefeller Center for Latin American Studies and the Institute for Latin American Studies, 2003.

Gustafson, B. D. *New Languages of the State: Indigenous Resurgence and the Politics of Knowledge in Bolivia*. Durham, NC, Duke University Press, 2009.

Healy, K. *Llamas, Weavings and Organic Chocolate: Multilateral Grassroots Development in the Andes and Amazon of Bolivia*. Notre Dame, IN, University of Notre Dame Press, 2000.

Hylton, F., and Thomson, S. *Revolutionary Horizons: Popular Struggle in Bolivia*. London and New York, Verso, 2007.

James, D. (Ed.). *The Complete Bolivian Diaries of Che Guevara*. New York, Cooper Square Press, 2000.

Jemio, L. C. *Debt, Crisis and Reform in Bolivia: Biting the Bullet*. The Hague, Institute of Social Studies, 2001.

Klein, H. S. *Bolivia: The Evolution of a Multi-Ethnic Society*. New York, Oxford University Press, 1982.

A Concise History of Bolivia. Cambridge, Cambridge University Press, 2003.

Kohl, B., and Farthing, L. *Impasse in Bolivia: Neoliberal Hegemony and Popular Resistance*. London, Zed Books, 2006.

Lehman, K. D. *Bolivia and the United States: A Limited Partnership*. Athens, GA, University of Georgia Press, 1999.

López Levy, M. *Bolivia*. Oxford, Oxfam Publishing, 2001.

Muñoz-Pogossian, B. *Electoral Rules and the Transformation of Bolivian Politics: The Rise of Evo Morales*. Basingstoke, Palgrave Macmillan, 2010.

Olivera, O. *¡Cochabamba! Water War in Bolivia*. Cambridge, MA, Southend Books, 2004.

Powers, W. *Whispering in the Giant's Ear: A Frontline Chronicle from Bolivia's War on Globalization*. New York, Bloomsbury USA, 2006.

Rhyne, E. *Mainstreaming Microfinance: How Lending to the Poor Began, Grew and Came of Age in Bolivia*. Bloomfield, CT, Kumarian Press, 2001.

Saldana, R. *Fertile Ground: Che Guevara and Bolivia*. New York, Pathfinder Press, 2001.

Sándor John, S. *Bolivia's Radical Tradition: Permanent Revolution in the Andes*. Tucson, AZ, University of Arizona Press, 2009.

BRAZIL

Geography

PHYSICAL FEATURES

The Federative Republic of Brazil is the largest country in Latin America, occupying much of the east of South America. Nearly one-half of the continent is in Brazil. Its longest border is with Bolivia (3,400 km or 2,111 miles), which lies to the south-west, then Paraguay (1,290 km of border). Brazil then thrusts southwards, between the Atlantic coast and an extension of Argentina (1,224 km) to the west, ending in a 985-km border with Uruguay to the south. In the north is the Guianan coast (from east to west, French Guiana—673 km, Suriname—597 km and Guyana—1,119 km) and then Venezuela (2,200 km). Colombia pushes south to form the northern part of the western border (1,643 km), in north-west Brazil, with Peru also lying to the west, beyond a 1,560-km frontier. Of all the South American territories, only Ecuador and Chile do not have borders with Brazil. Brazil has an uncontested territorial dispute with Uruguay over small river islands in the Quarai (Cuareim) and the Arroio Invernada (Arroyo de la Invernada). Somewhat smaller than the USA, Brazil covers an area of 8,514,877 sq km (3,287,611 sq miles), making it the fifth largest country in the world.

Brazil, which also includes a number of offshore islands and islets, has 7,491 km of coastline, formed where South America bulges eastwards and then begins to taper south. The Amazon enters the Atlantic on the north-eastern coast of South America, and the mouth of the river is complicated by many channels and islands (the largest is Marajó), as well as swamps, mangroves and flooding, features common until higher land begins in eastern Brazil. Here the north-eastern highlands make the coast more defined, smoother and drier, with stretches of dunes, although there are still occasional mangroves and lagoons beyond São Roque cape, where the eastern bulge of the continent turns south. To the south-west, beneath the south-eastern highlands, the shore is varied by sandy spits and beaches, as well as lagoons and marshes, but for 1,000 km beyond Rio de Janeiro, the coastal plains are reduced to occasional patches, as the highlands often come sheer to the sea. Most of the country's territory, however, is defined by political rather than natural borders, although in the north the Guianan highlands help establish the line. These forested heights cover only 2% of the country and are generally considered to be part of the Amazon basin, but they also include Brazil's highest mountain, Pico da Neblina (3,014 m or 9,892 ft), which lies in the north-west, on the border with southern Venezuela. The Amazon basin itself, which accounts for about one-third of the country, spreads across the north of Brazil, pushing it west, deeply into the heart of the continent. Brazil also shares the basin of the much smaller River Plate (Río de la Plata) system, in the south, while coastal plains constitute the only other area of lowland in the country. In the midst of these other features, and in marked contrast to the dense jungles of the Amazonian lowlands, are the open Brazilian highlands, an eroded plateau of jumbled mountain ranges and river valleys, running from the easternmost end of the country towards the south-west, generally just inland from the coast. However, once human and economic geography is taken into account, Brazil is usually described as consisting of five regions: the north (most of the Amazon basin and the Guianan highlands—45% of the territory, but only 7% of the population); the north-east (essentially the eastern bulge, the north-eastern end of the Brazilian highlands—the area first settled by Europeans and their African slaves); the south-east (the other, higher end of the highlands—11% of the territory, but 43% of the population); the south (the smallest region, temperate in climate); and, finally, the landlocked centre-west, sparsely populated, but including the capital city, Brasília (this region is a transitional region, including the edges of the Amazonian plains to the north, the Brazilian highlands to the south and east, and the upper lowlands of the River Plate basin in the west). All

these vast territories include surprisingly little fertile land and, although the range of crops produced is wide, relatively small amounts of land are cultivated. Grasslands are used extensively for pasture.

The main lowland area of Brazil is the Amazon basin, which is flat, or gently rolling, seldom exceeding 150 m above sea level and covered in the largest rainforest in the world. The Amazon and its tributaries are prone to seasonal flooding, inundating the level, swampy areas known as varzeas. Similarly, the headwaters of the Paraná and Paraguay can flood the important wetlands of the Pantanal, where the hills of the Brazilian highlands yield to the plains of the River Plate basin (the Chaco spreads through Paraguay to the south). The Pantanal forms the western end of the centre-west region, dividing the Amazonian north from the south-eastern highlands. Finally, there are the coastal plains, extending for thousands of kilometres from the north-east to the border with Uruguay. Up to 60 km in width in the north-east, the coastal plains are negligible south of Rio de Janeiro, where the Serra do Mar form a sharp edge along the shore. The plains only broaden again in the far south, as they widen towards the Pampas and, inland, the Chaco.

The Brazilian highlands are a huge block of geologically ancient rocks, falling away to the north-east and north. In the south-eastern region of the country the highlands consist of a complex mass of ridges and ranges, some dropping steeply into the sea, and generally with elevations of around 1,200 m, although the highest summits reach about 2,800 m. The main ranges include the Serra do Mar and the Serra da Mantiqueira. Inland from the coastal ranges is a broad plateau, hills lowering themselves into the centre-west and towards the Amazonian lowlands. Likewise, the highlands fall away to the north-east, as they parallel the coast and form the solid core of the eastern bulge of South America. Here are low, rolling hills, with the semi-arid interior known as the Sertão. As mentioned above, the north side of the Amazon basin is defined by the highlands separating Brazil from the Guiana coast and from the drainage area of the Orinoco. Out of these highlands, but mainly from the Andes to the west, flow the main rivers of Brazil, which can be grouped in eight systems, together carrying about one-fifth of the world's running water. The Amazon itself is the second longest river in the world, after the Nile in

Africa, at 6,516 km (most of it flowing through Brazil, but still navigable into Peru). However, some of its tributaries are mighty rivers in themselves, notably the Tocantins, which joins the Amazon from the south, near its mouth. The second river system is that of the south-draining Paraná, which empties into the Plate (between Uruguay and Argentina), draining much of the south, south-east and centre-west of Brazil. The principal river of the eastern plateau region is the São Francisco, which flows north through the highlands until it turns east into the Atlantic.

The vegetation of this varied landscape is diverse, ranging from tropical and temperate woodland, through savannah and often swampy grasslands, to semi-arid scrub. Many of the species sheltering in these environments are still unknown, although already threatened, particularly by deforestation, and also by mining and industrial pollution. Wooded areas account for 58% of Brazil's total, but it is the great jungle of the Amazon, the largest rainforest (despite massive and continuing encroachments) in the world, covering two-fifths of Brazil's territory, which dominates. The luxuriant vegetation hosts a massively varied array of ecosystems and a good proportion of the many species found in Brazil. There are almost 400 species of mammal found in Brazil—such as endangered jaguars, rare bush dogs, anteaters, deer (for instance, the endangered Pantanal deer), monkeys, and tapirs—but, more impressively perhaps, the country has among the most diverse populations of birds (1,635 species) and amphibians (502 species), as well as 1,500 species of freshwater fish, of which more than two-thirds are found in the Amazon basin. There are over 100,000 invertebrate species, of which 70,000 are insects, although it should be noted that, given the scale, all these figures are estimates. Much of this wealth is threatened, the Amazon increasingly affected by deforestation since the 1970s (much of the eastern and southern uplands have already been denuded of their widest variety since 1500), although some 3.3m. sq km of rainforest remain. One tree species should be mentioned, as it gave the country its name—the pau brasil or brazilwood tree provided dyewood, the first commodity to be exported by Europeans from Brazil. Grasslands have also been economically exploited (pasture covers 22% of the country), with both savannah and rich wetlands used for ranching—in areas such as the Pantanal, the Sertão, the Cerrado (in the centre-west, where the rainforest yields to a more open and varied landscape of trees and bushes, as well as grassland) and the Campos of the far south.

CLIMATE

Over such a large area, the climate is obviously extremely varied. All but the extreme north (the Equator passes across the mouth of the Amazon) and the far south lies within the Tropic of Capricorn (which passes through São Paulo). Most of the country has annual average temperatures of over 22°C (72°F), but in the far south and in the high country it occasionally falls lower than this, with seasonal variations also more pronounced. Northern Brazil largely has a tropical wet climate, with much rainfall and virtually no dry season. Temperatures average 25°C (77°F), varying more between night and day than by time of year, and average rainfall is about 2,200 mm per year. It is oppressively humid in the Amazon. In central Brazil rainfall (1,600 mm annually) is more seasonal, typical for a savannah area (80% falls in summer, October–March). The interior north-east, or Sertão, is even more pronouncedly seasonal in its little rainfall (only 800 mm per year—almost all falling within only two or three months), although precipitation is very liable to fail completely, causing drought (temperatures are extremely hot, able to exceed 40°C—104°F). In the south-east the tropical climate is moderated by altitude, with winter temperatures averaging below 18°C (64°F) and annual rainfall at 1,400 mm (falling mainly in the summer). The south has a subtropical climate, verging on the temperate, with cool winters that can produce a few frosts and even some snow at higher elevations. Annual rainfall is 1,500 mm, fairly evenly spread throughout the year.

POPULATION

Brazil is the only lusophone country in the Western hemisphere, owing to the 1494 Treaty of Tordesillas, which modified a papal arbitration between Portugal and Spain of the previous year. Most of the 'New World' was accorded to Spain, but moving the original Line of Demarcation further west ensured that Portugal gained territory here too. By the 1777 Treaty of Ildefonso (confirming principles established in 1750), Portugal also gained vast territories west again of the 1494 Line. As a result, modern Brazil is a unique blending of Portuguese settlers and their forcibly imported African labour with native Amerindians and later waves of immigration (usually from Europe). There is also a noticeably more relaxed attitude to race in Brazil than in many countries, with the Portuguese joined by many other European settlers and the African slaves taken not only from West Africa (as in much of the Caribbean), but also from Congo, Angola and Mozambique. About 55% of the population are classed as white (principally, 15% of mainly Portuguese descent, 11% Italian, 10% Spanish and 3% German), 22% of mixed white and black descent (mulatto), 12% Mestizo (mixed white and Amerindian) and 6% black. Amerindians now account for only about 1% of the population, with some other minority immigrant communities (such as those of Arab or Japanese descent) also enjoying a similar size. There is considerable regional variation in the distribution of the ethnic groups, with over 70% black or mulatto in the north-east, the old slave-worked region, while the urban south-east is 66% white and only 33% black, and the south is 82% white, being settled after the slave era by a variety of groups from Europe. There is some element of standing in racial definition, with the élite generally white, but those of mixed race particularly enjoy considerable social mobility. Portuguese, with some regional variation, is the most widely used as well as the official language, although German and Italian, for instance, are still used in parts of the south (English and French tend to be the main second languages of the educated). Local dialects have incorporated Amerindian and African words. There are still over 100 indigenous Amerindian languages, of which the main ones belong to the Tupí, Gê, Arawak, Carib (Garib) and Nambicuara groups. Caribs and Arawaks are the main peoples of the north, the Tupí-Guaraní of the east coast and the Amazon river valley, the Gê of eastern and southern Brazil, and the Pano in the west. Most Amerindians survive in the north and west. Virtually all groups, excluding the more remote tribes of the Amazon and more recent immigrants from non-Christian backgrounds, tend to be at least nominally Roman Catholic (76%), making Brazil the largest Roman Catholic country in the world. Christian adherence is sometimes supplemented by parallel belief systems. Perhaps 6% of the population are classified as Protestant Christian. Some of the urban middle classes are also followers of Spiritualism (involving reincarnation, communication with the dead, etc.), while Afro-Brazilian blendings have produced religions such as Candomblé, Macumba and Umbanda (the identity of Christian saints with African deities, the distinctive use of music and a belief in spirit possession, etc.), relatively widespread in areas such as the north-east. There are also some Buddhists and Jews, as well as a number of continuing, if with few adherents, aboriginal belief systems.

The total population was estimated at almost 193.3m. in mid-2010, making Brazil the second most populous country in the Americas after the USA. The social legacy of a plantation society means there is still much inequality and poverty, especially in the countryside, although after massive urban migration the rural population accounts for only about one-fifth of the total. One-fifth of Brazilians live in cities of over 1m., the largest being São Paulo, the biggest city in South America and the country's main industrial centre (an estimated 11.0m. at mid-2009). The second most populous city is the old capital (1763–1960), Rio de Janeiro, which remains an important port and the commercial centre of the country (6.2m.). Both cities were founded on the scant coastal plains of the south-east region, Rio de Janeiro further east up the coast. The cities, with the Federal District, are the most densely populated parts of the country. Brasília (2.6m. in mid-2009), the federal capital since 1960, was purposely located away from the coast (four-fifths of Brazilians live within 350 km of the sea) and from the crowded south-east, nearer the centre of the country. Salvador (3.0m.) and Fortaleza (formerly Ceará—2.5m.), both in the north-east, and Belo Horizonte (2.5m.), in Minas Gerais, to the north of Rio de Janeiro, all have populations of a similar size to that of the capital. The other cities of over 1m. are Curitiba and Porto Alegre in the south, Recife (formerly Pernambuco) on the north-east coast, the great inland Amazonian city of Manaus, Belém, at the mouth of the river, Goiânia, to the south-west of the Federal District of Brasília, and Campinhas, to the north-west of São Paulo (Guarulhos, a suburb of São Paulo, is also classed as a separate city, and had 1.3m. people in mid-2009). Brazil is a federal country, consisting of 26 states and one Federal District (Distrito Federal).

History

Prof. DAVID FLEISCHER

Revised for this edition Dr FRANCISCO PANIZZA

Brazil was Portugal's only American colony, and survived as a single unit after independence to become Latin America's only Portuguese-speaking nation. During the period of Portuguese colonial rule, millions of Africans were forcibly transported to Brazil to work as slaves. As a result of the flight of the Portuguese royal family to the colony in 1808, Brazil attained independence in 1822 under Prince Pedro, who became Emperor Pedro I of Brazil. The country remained a monarchy until 1889, when a republic was declared, one year after the abolition of slavery. A federalist Constitution was adopted in 1891. This First Republic became a decentralized, federal regime and endured until it was overthrown in 1930, in a revolution that brought Dr Getúlio Vargas to power. Vargas oversaw the introduction of a new and more centralized Constitution in 1934, but established a military-backed dictatorship in 1937 rather than retire from the presidency following elections due to be held in 1938. During this 15-year period, Vargas recentralized the political system, initiated state reforms, encouraged import substitution and developed the steel industry. The new regime (the 'Estado Novo') lasted until 1945, when the military withdrew its support and forced Vargas from power.

THE RESTORATION OF DEMOCRACY

The restoration of democracy with the new Constitution of 1946 gave most Brazilians their first experience of political involvement and inaugurated nearly two decades of continuous but unstable party competition. The period was dominated by Vargas, now presenting himself, with some success, as a champion of the masses, and his heirs. They were grouped in the broadly conservative, rural-based Partido Social Democrático and the leftist and increasingly influential, urban-based Partido Trabalhista Brasileiro (PTB), and opposed by the liberal União Democrática Nacional (UDN) and at times by the Partido Social Progressista. Vargas was elected to the presidency in 1950, but committed suicide in 1954, when the military demanded his resignation.

Over the next 10 years Brazil gradually declined into a state of acute political crisis. Industrialization proceeded rapidly under the presidency of Juscelino Kubitschek (1956–61), but the economic strains that were created, and the political tensions arising out of urbanization and swift social change, proved too great for the fragile political system. As pressure mounted for social and structural reform, the UDN secured the presidency for the first time, through an independent, Jânio Quadros, at elections in October 1960. Within seven months of taking power in January 1961, Quadros resigned, alleging lack of support from the Congresso Nacional (National Congress), and the country was plunged into crisis. He was succeeded by the Vice-President, PTB leader João Goulart, after the military had forced the Congresso to change from a presidential to a parliamentary system, with Tancredo de Almeida Neves as Prime Minister.

Under pressure from the left to adopt a radical programme, Goulart at first hesitated but, after regaining presidential powers in a referendum held in January 1963, and lacking a majority in the Congresso Nacional, he moved to respond to such demands by decree. Before the ensuing radicalization was far advanced, the military intervened, seizing power on 1 April 1964. The military coup brought an end to two decades of fragile democracy, marked by a refusal on the part of the privileged élites to countenance any degree of social reform, and a general failure on the part of political parties to establish themselves as independent actors, rather than as clientelistic groupings reliant upon the patronage powers of the state.

MILITARY RULE AFTER 1964

The 21-year military regime was a curious hybrid, quite distinct from the military governments in Argentina, Chile, Peru and Uruguay. The armed forces concentrated power in their own hands, but kept the Congresso Nacional in session (except for an extended period in 1968–69 and briefly in 1977) while denying it autonomy, and held regular elections for the Congresso, state legislatures, and local mayors and city councils. Successive purges removed all but the most moderate opponents of the regime. The five military Presidents were vested with power to govern by decree, and the parties existing in 1964 were replaced by a two-party system in 1966, with pro-Government forces congregating in the majority Aliança Renovadora Nacional (ARENA) and the remaining opposition members grouped in the Movimento Democrático Brasileiro (MDB).

The dictatorship was at its most harsh between 1968 and 1974, particularly under Gen. Emílio Garrastazu Médici. The already highly authoritarian Constitution approved in 1967 was heavily amended in 1969 to strengthen further the power of the military executive, and the elections of 1970, held in conditions that made meaningful competition impossible, gave emphatic majorities to the government party. Throughout this period, the retention of a system of political parties, combined with a concentration of powers of decision in the military executive, pushed to extremes the tendency for the governing party to act as a clientelistic machine. In 1974 Gen. Ernesto Geisel (1974–79), relying on the appeal of limited liberalization and Brazil's burst of economic growth after a period of recession had ended in 1967, allowed more open elections. The electoral system protected the government majority, but the unexpected gains that were made by the MDB, particularly in the elections for one-third of the Senado Federal (Federal Senate), may be seen in retrospect as marking the beginning of the long retreat of the military from power. Following the 1973 petroleum crisis, Brazil's economy stagnated, but the less restricted elections in November 1974 provided political legitimacy to, and bolstered support for, Geisel's regime.

From 1974 onwards the military lacked a natural majority in the country, but persisted in holding elections on schedule, seeking to maintain their hold on power by a series of expedient measures such as the indirect election (to all intents and purposes, the appointment) of one-third of the Senado Federal in 1978. This failed to conceal either their unpopularity or their waning self-confidence. Geisel's successor, Gen. João Baptista de Figueiredo (1979–85), was the beneficiary of a decision to prolong the presidential mandate by one year, but it fell to him to oversee the departure of the military from power.

An attempt to regain the initiative by dissolving the two-party system in 1979 in a bid to divide the opposition and to halt the advance of the reorganized and increasingly effective MDB, failed in its objective. ARENA was shorn of some of its moderate elements and reconstituted as the Partido Democrático Social (PDS), while a number of new opposition parties appeared, led by the renamed Partido do Movimento Democrático Brasileiro (PMDB), which was reduced to half the strength of its predecessor, the MDB. Most prominent among the new parties were the Partido dos Trabalhadores (PT), led by Luiz Inácio Lula da Silva, a labour union organizer, and the Partido Democrático Trabalhista (PDT), led by Goulart's brother-in-law, Leonel de Moura Brizola.

THE WANING OF MILITARY AUTHORITY

By 1982 five years of social mobilization and protest, focused primarily on the factories and working-class communities of São Paulo, and co-ordinated as much by the Roman Catholic Church as by the parties and labour unions, had put the military on the defensive. The 1982 elections gave the governorships of the 10 leading states to the opposition (with direct gubernatorial elections for the first time since 1965) and would have given the combined opposition forces a majority in the Câmara dos Deputados (Chamber of Deputies) had the PTB not formed a coalition with the PDS. In April 1984 a substantial vote by the Câmara in favour of an amendment to the Constitution, introducing direct elections, failed to gain the required two-thirds' majority. However, the military executive lost control of its own party, and the official nomination for its presidential candidate went to the civilian industrialist and financier, Paulo Salim Maluf, former Governor of São Paulo. His aggressive style provoked a division of the government party and led, eventually, to the formation of the Partido da Frente Liberal (PFL). This grouping gave its support to the PMDB candidate, Tancredo Neves, and secured the vice-presidential candidacy for José Sarney, erstwhile leader of the pro-Government PDS. As a result, the electoral college that was to elect the President became opposition-controlled. Lacking other options, the military accepted Neves' victory, achieved by a massive 300-vote majority in the 686-member college when voting took place on 15 January 1985. The transfer of power took place as scheduled on 15 March, but Neves, then 74 years old, required surgical treatment on the eve of his accession. As a result, José Sarney was sworn in as acting President. He assumed full presidential powers after Neves' death in April.

THE RETURN TO DEMOCRACY, 1985

Brazil returned to competitive liberal democracy in challenging circumstances. Economic growth was faltering as inflation spiralled far beyond the levels it had reached when the military intervened in 1964, but was somewhat alleviated by monthly monetary correction of contracts and salaries. Socially, the strains of rapid industrialization and urbanization over previous decades had been exacerbated by the sharp worsening of income distribution over the period of military rule, leading to growing malnutrition and absolute poverty in urban and rural areas alike. Amid a general recognition of the need for political and social reform and substantial economic redistribution, civilian politicians were under pressure to address a range of issues that had been neglected during the military period. Initial suspicion arising from Sarney's recent links with the armed forces limited his popular appeal, and his relations with the dominant PMDB proved to be difficult. However, he pledged to implement the programme that Neves had proposed, including the convocation of a National Constituent Assembly and the introduction of direct elections to the presidency, and he reached a peak of popularity in 1986, as a consequence of the temporary success of the Cruzado Plan, an anti-inflation, price and wage freeze programme announced in February. The election, in November, of the Congresso Nacional marked the first stage in the transition to the adoption of a new constitution and a full return to democracy; the election was also a zenith for the PMDB, which won 22 of the 23 state governorships and absolute majorities in both houses of the Congresso.

However, the apparent economic and political success of the transition to democracy proved short-lived. The key measures of the Cruzado Plan were abandoned immediately after the November 1986 elections, and it collapsed altogether in early 1987. Debates over the new constitution were dominated by rivalry between the President and the unicameral National Constituent Assembly, and conflict over the extent to which commitments to social reform should be written into the document. Part of the problem lay in the changed character of the once reformist PMDB. Since its establishment as the leading opposition force in the 1970s, it had attracted the support of conservatives who abandoned the PDS as its prospects faded. Thus, by 1986 the PMDB was no longer a party committed to genuine reform. A new Constitution was finally promulgated in October 1988. It provided for a five-year presidential term and adopted a conservative stance with regard to land reform in particular. The PMDB split in June 1988, with many of its founders moving into a new social democratic party, the Partido da Social Democracia Brasileira (PSDB), including the political exile and São Paulo senator, Fernando Henrique Cardoso, and federal deputy José Serra. Signs of a serious challenge from the left emerged in the municipal elections of November 1988, at which da Silva's hitherto small PT gained control of the city of São Paulo, as well as 37 other major towns and cities across the country.

THE RISE AND FALL OF COLLOR DE MELLO

The first direct presidential election since 1960 was held on 15 November 1989. In the first round of voting Fernando Collor de Mello, leader of the tiny Partido de Reconstrução Nacional (PRN) took 30.5% of the valid votes cast, compared with da Silva's 17.2%, while Brizola came third with 16.5%. As the Constitution required an absolute majority, a second round of voting was held, just over one month later, at which Collor de Mello defeated da Silva, obtaining 53% of the votes cast compared with 47% for da Silva.

President Collor de Mello introduced a radical reform programme aimed at reducing public employment, lowering government expenditure and liberalizing the economy. At the same time, in 1991, Brazil, in conjunction with Argentina, Paraguay and Uruguay, began to establish the free trade zone known as Mercosul (Mercado Comum do Sul, or, in Spanish, Mercado Común del Sur—Mercosur). However, the initial results of these reforms were disappointing, with a sharp recession in 1990 followed by a resumption of inflation in 1991. Collor de Mello found his popularity and congressional support dwindling, even after the poor performance of the left at legislative elections held in October 1990, where the PRN also achieved disappointing results.

President Collor de Mello's position deteriorated further in 1992 as he failed to persuade the PSDB and other congressional parties to support a new reform programme, and he resorted to governing by decree. The Câmara dos Deputados subsequently voted to bring forward a referendum on changing to a parliamentary system of government. However, Collor de Mello intervened and in December 1991 the Senado defeated the measure. After a series of corruption scandals emerged in early 1992, causing further ministerial resignations, in May Collor de Mello's brother, Pedro, began a national campaign against the President's campaign manager, treasurer and confidant, Paulo César Farias. The ensuing succession of corruption scandals soon involved the President himself and ultimately led to his downfall. After a joint congressional investigating committee reported in favour of impeachment, the Câmara voted to commence impeachment proceedings and Collor de Mello was suspended from office on 28 September. The Senado later convicted Collor de Mello of 'political crimes' and he was impeached on 30 December. The Vice-President, former senator Itamar Franco, who had been appointed acting President in September, was confirmed as President on the same day.

THE TRANSITION TO DEMOCRACY IN CRISIS, 1993–94

With the coming to power of Franco, the crisis surrounding the attempted transition to democracy deepened further. A number of serious problems, some with deep historical roots, made decisive action imperative, but Franco lacked both the necessary political experience and the organized political support that would have made effective government possible. Inflation continued to worsen and threatened to spiral entirely out of control. Economic growth also continued to falter, while levels of foreign investment dwindled as international confidence in the Brazilian economy declined further. On the political side, pressure was already mounting for reform of the 1988 Constitution, while public discontent with politicians in general brought the future of the transition into question. Most seriously, Brazil's political party system, chronically weak and prone to fragmentation throughout the republican period, appeared once again to be in terminal decline. No party was able to elect a President, to provide majority support in the Congresso Nacional for the resulting administration, nor to exert sufficient authority over powerful élites to achieve either economic stability or social reform. These difficulties combined to make the situation of the Franco Government, and the political system as a whole, extremely precarious by the beginning of 1994.

Economic affairs were dominated by the effort to introduce a credible programme of economic adjustment backed by fiscal reforms. There was an urgent need to reduce inflation dramatically, restore growth, balance the budget and address the pressing problem of the steadily worsening distribution of income. The new Minister of Finance, Fernando Henrique Cardoso, therefore sought repeatedly, but largely unsuccessfully, to introduce a series of wide-ranging structural reforms to the fiscal system. By early 1994 he had succeeded in introducing a limited fiscal reform package incorporating selected expenditure reductions and the establishment of a Social Emergency Fund. The compulsory transfer of large resources from the federal to the state and local governments was also reduced, but remained a serious obstacle to the achievement of a balanced budget.

THE PRESIDENTIAL ELECTION AND THE REAL PLAN, 1994

With the Government weak and the Congresso Nacional discredited, the immediate beneficiaries were the PT and da Silva, who emerged as the left wing's leading contender in the presidential election that was scheduled for October 1994. A consensus eventually emerged in the Government, with business and army circles favouring the candidacy of centrist Minister of Finance Cardoso. The final stages of the Franco presidency were dominated by the long-awaited and much-postponed programme of economic reform, the centrepiece of which was the introduction, on 1 July 1994, of a new currency, the real, pegged to the US dollar. The initial impact of the measures, known as the Real Plan, appeared broadly positive as inflation was dramatically reduced and the real incomes of poorer groups increased. This was a very powerful election instrument, and at the election, on 3 October, Cardoso secured the presidency without the need to proceed to a second ballot. PSDB governors were also elected in the important central states of São Paulo, Minas Gerais and Rio de Janeiro. The election of Cardoso and his allies appeared to demonstrate that Brazilian voters had opted for a path of continuity with moderate reform rather than radical change or conservative reaction.

CARDOSO'S FIRST TERM, 1995–98

When President Cardoso assumed office on 1 January 1995 he had committed himself to a series of key constitutional reforms, aimed at accelerating the modernization of the economic and social fabric and overcoming the federal Government's fiscal crisis. The principal reforms envisaged were: a liberalization of the petroleum, electricity and telecommunications sectors; the permitting of foreign investment in mining and hydroelectric projects; a reform of the civil service; a major overhaul of the social security system; fundamental alterations to the federal Government's taxation and budgetary regimes; and an increased emphasis on achieving a more even pattern of landholding in rural areas. Cardoso achieved some initial success with his proposed reforms with the approval, in early 1995, of constitutional changes terminating state monopolies and permitting foreign investment in the sectors mentioned above. In addition, the programme of economic liberalization was given impetus by the full implementation of the Mercosul free trade area on 1 January 1995. Furthermore, in December Brazil signed an agreement to establish a Free Trade Area of the Americas (FTAA). However, the reform programme encountered a number of obstacles during 1996 and 1997. In particular, as had long been the case, the Government found it very difficult to exercise control over the budget deficit. The constitutionally mandated transfers of funds between the federal Government and the state and municipal governments led to a weakening of the federal Government's fiscal position as expenditures expanded. Slow progress in the reform of the civil service and the social security system meant that other major items of expenditure could not be reduced in compensation. The lack of progress in the reform of the landholding system resulted in a growing number of confrontations between landless peasants, represented by the Movimento dos Trabalhadores Rurais Sem Terra (MST), and landowners. The impasse in the reform programme was exacerbated by divisions between the two main parties of the coalition: President Cardoso's social democratic PSDB and the conservative PFL.

Although fiscal, social security and administrative reforms remained delayed by the Congresso Nacional throughout 1996 and most of 1997, considerably more progress was made with the privatization and economic liberalization programmes. In 1996 steps were taken towards the sale of the Brazilian electricity network, Centrais Elétricas Brasileiras, SA (Eletrobras). The privatization of the federal rail network, Rede Ferroviária Federal, SA, was completed in the following year. The huge mining group, Companhia Vale do Rio Doce, SA, was privatized in May 1997. From 1997 onwards a series of other major privatizations occurred, many in the energy sector. By far the most significant privatization to date, however, was implemented in the telecommunications sector with the sale of the subsidiaries of Telecomunicações Brasileiras, SA in July 1998. The Government also accelerated its attempts to privatize the state banking sector in the late 1990s. In August 1997 legislation enabling the liberalization of the petroleum sector became law. In a radical departure, the new regulatory framework for the sector allowed the participation of foreign enterprises in the exploration for petroleum within Brazil. This clearly eroded the monopoly status that the state-owned Petróleo Brasileiro, SA (Petrobras) had enjoyed since its foundation in 1953. With the new legislation in place, a series of exploration concessions were auctioned off to both domestic and foreign bidders between 1998 and 2001.

Despite the achievements in economic policy described above, lack of progress on constitutional reform left unaddressed a series of lingering macroeconomic problems. In particular, the Brazilian economy remained unable to escape from its tendency to accumulate heavy internal and external deficits. The persistence of these deficits became an increasing source of concern to international investors in 1997, and serious doubts were expressed in international financial markets as to the ability of the Brazilian Government to avoid a rapid, unplanned devaluation of the real. In order to maintain the valuation of the currency and avoid a resurgence of inflation, President Cardoso introduced a series of emergency measures intended to lower the budget deficit in November. The atmosphere of urgency surrounding the implementation of the measures did, however, have some favourable political effects. In underlining the need for further progress on structural reform, the crisis induced notable advances in the passage of important legislation through the Câmara dos Deputados. After an extraordinary session of the Congresso Nacional in January 1998, crucial social security reforms were successfully enacted, while the Government's civil service reforms were finally approved in March, although amendments were enforced by the Congresso. By the beginning of August a second term in office for Cardoso's Government appeared inevitable. However, international financial events during that month caused the Government considerable unease, demonstrated once again the vulnerability of Brazil's economy, and prompted renewed concern among investors over the scale of Brazil's external and fiscal deficits. As financial disruption increased world-wide, investors began to withdraw resources from Brazil in ever-increasing quantities, causing a sharp decline in international reserves and testing the Government's ability to defend the value of the real.

By September 1998 Brazil was experiencing a period of economic crisis in which the sustainability of the Real Plan seemed increasingly in doubt. The political effects of this crisis, however, ultimately proved far from unfavourable for the Government. Emphasizing the technical competence of his economic policy team, President Cardoso undertook an effective last-minute election campaign. At the presidential election held on 4 October Cardoso became the first President to be re-elected for a consecutive term in office, securing 53% of the valid votes cast, compared with 32% for his closest rival, da Silva. The results of the legislative and gubernatorial elections, however, were not as favourable for Cardoso's PSDB. Although the governing coalition in the Câmara dos Deputados secured 377 of the 513 seats, the PSDB's 99 seats did not constitute a significant increase in the party's overall legislative representation, although it was considerably more than the 60 seats won by Cardoso's party in 1994. The election of populist, anti-Cardoso state governors in Minas Gerais, Rio de Janeiro and Rio Grande do Sul provided focal points for increasingly vocal regional opposition to the federal Government.

CARDOSO'S SECOND TERM, 1998–2002

Despite the generally favourable domestic and international reaction to Cardoso's re-election, Brazil's economic situation continued to deteriorate in late 1998. In November a US $41,000m. agreement was concluded with the IMF, imposing stronger fiscal austerity on Brazil. In December the Câmara dos Deputados voted to reject a significant government fiscal reform measure affecting public-employee pension contributions. The failure of this legislation increased concerns over the Government's ability to meet IMF targets and led to further outflows of foreign capital. By January 1999 it became apparent that the fixed exchange-rate policy pursued by the Government was becoming untenable. Moreover, in the same month, former President Itamar Franco, the newly elected Governor of Minas Gerais, declared that the state was defaulting on its debt to the federal Government and on a loan to a French bank consortium, thus indirectly precipitating the devaluation of the real. By the second week of January the drain of foreign exchange reserves had become significant. Faced with the imminent prospect of a complete depletion of reserves, on 13 January the Central Bank announced that the real was to float freely against the US dollar. Following the flotation, the real swiftly depreciated. With the Real Plan apparently in ruins, one of its key architects, the President of the Central Bank, Gustavo Franco, resigned.

While the devaluation of the real did not affect the economy as severely as had been predicted, it did have the effect of galvanizing congressional opinion in favour of accelerating the fiscal and structural reform programme. In an important measure designed to reduce the recurrent deficits of the social security system, the Congresso Nacional finally approved the Fator Previdenciário in November 1999, which created a greater correspondence between social security contributions and pension payments in the private sector. Furthermore, in April 2000 legislation on fiscal responsibility was approved by the Senado, establishing stricter regulations for the setting of state and municipal budgets with harsh penalties for deficit spending. Moreover, the Congresso approved both the budgets for 2000 and 2001 with minimal amendments. However, the Cardoso Government remained frustrated in its attempts to introduce comprehensive taxation reform.

Accelerated progress in the area of fiscal reform coincided with a number of political developments in early 2000. In mid-February Cardoso's PSDB announced a new congressional alliance with the centrist PTB. This alliance further increased the divisions between the PSDB and its leading coalition partner in the Congresso Nacional, the centre-right PFL. In August the PTB announced that it was to dissolve its alliance with the PSDB, thus re-establishing the PFL as the largest party in the Câmara dos Deputados.

Left-wing opposition parties performed well in the municipal elections of October 2000, in advance of the presidential election of 2002. Furthermore, throughout 2000 and 2001 the Government and Congresso Nacional were embroiled in an extensive scandal involving allegations of embezzlement and corruption at senior levels. Moreover, further evidence of high-level corruption had emerged in November 2000 following the publication of a report by another congressional investigating committee on organized drugs-trafficking and crime in Brazil, implicating a number of state deputies and mayors, as well as members of the Congresso Nacional, prosecutors, police, the judiciary and the armed forces.

The controversy surrounding allegations of high-level corruption, and the departure in May 2001 of the President of the Senado, Antônio Carlos Magalhães (who, before resigning amid allegations of impropriety, had led a campaign against government corruption), both acted to stall the Government's ambitious legislative programme and to taint the Government's hard-won reputation for competent economic management. By mid-2001 the weakening of the real prompted the authorities to increase interest rates and lower growth forecasts. To add to the Government's difficulties, unusually low levels of rainfall had led to water in hydroelectric reservoirs falling to critically low levels. The authorities were forced to implement an emergency programme of energy conservation that further reduced economic growth and adversely affected the Government's popularity, and demonstrated that the privatization programme for the electricity sector had been a failure.

In the months preceding the October 2002 presidential election President Cardoso's coalition found itself in severe difficulties. Its most cohesive party, the PFL, had withdrawn from the governing coalition in March, the support of the PMDB was doubtful, and the PTB had declared its support for the candidacy of Ciro Gomes of the Partido Progressista Socialista (PPS). Nevertheless, Cardoso attempted to mobilize support for the PSDB candidate, José Serra, and succeeded in persuading the PMDB to enter into a formal alliance with the PSDB. By April Serra had emerged as second favourite in the presidential contest, behind the PT's da Silva, who was running in alliance with the Partido Liberal (PL) candidate, José Alencar. However, following press revelations in May regarding a number of scandals dating back to the mid- and late 1990s, the PSDB candidate's popularity decreased significantly. In the same month it also became apparent to international financial markets that Brazil's macroeconomic situation was deteriorating, and analysts questioned Brazil's capacity to honour its large debt. Amid insinuations that Brazil was in danger of suffering the economic crisis recently experienced by Argentina were an 'incompetent' President and economic team to be elected, da Silva's popularity rating also fell. The concerns by the international financial community regarding an imminent da Silva victory had a considerable negative impact on Brazil in mid-2002. Banks sharply reduced short-term trade credits, Brazil's risk evaluation soared, the real devalued strongly against the US dollar, and international reserves dwindled. As in 1998, the Cardoso Government again sought IMF assistance and quickly concluded a new 15-month agreement, worth US $30,000m., in August 2002. In order to allay fears, the PT's campaign platform took a sharp turn to the centre and attracted the support of several prominent business leaders.

The elections of October 2002 produced a decisive victory for the left. In the presidential contest da Silva nearly achieved an absolute majority (46.4%) in the first round, held on 6 October. Gomes, and Antônio Garotinho of the Partido Socialista Brasileiro (PSB), supported da Silva in the 27 October run-off, in which the PT candidate defeated Serra by an unprecedented margin, attracting 61.3% of the valid votes cast. In elections to the Congresso Nacional, the pro-da Silva parties elected 218 deputies and 31 senators, a considerable increase over 1998, but still fewer than the respective 257- and 41-member absolute majorities. The PT returned the largest delegation in the Câmara dos Deputados, with 91 federal deputies.

THE PT IN POWER

Lula da Silva was sworn in as President on 2 January 2003, and the new Congresso Nacional took office on 1 February. Da Silva's cabinet was recruited from his electoral coalition, with a heavy concentration of PT militants, along with representatives from other allied parties. However, two prominent business leaders were also appointed, to the Ministries of Development, Industry and Trade and of Agriculture, Fisheries and Food Supply. The choice of former BankBoston President Henrique Meirelles to head the Central Bank particularly irritated the more radical PT deputies and senators. Many had feared that the new da Silva Government's policy initiatives would be impeded in the Congresso by a lack of majorities. However, the new President's team (led by Cabinet Chief José Dirceu) adroitly used the same power mechanisms (federal appointments and disbursements) as Cardoso to consolidate absolute majorities.

The new Minister of Finance, Antônio Palocci, and his economic team unequivocally pursued a fiscal austerity programme even more rigorous than that of the previous Government. Such a policy won enthusiastic approval from the IMF, which endorsed loan disbursements scheduled for March and June 2003. In the first five months of 2003 the trade surplus, tax collections and foreign direct investment all increased significantly, while the current account deficit decreased. Brazil's risk evaluation improved significantly. Inflation declined in April, May and June, but the Central Bank maintained a high basic interest rate. As a result, gross domestic product declined by 0.1% in the first quarter of 2003 and unemployment increased to over 20%. The Government claimed that this was part of the negative economic situation inherited from the Cardoso period.

On assuming office, the PT Government faced the problem of high deficits in a stagnating economy with low inflation. Thus, the da Silva Government's two key priorities were social security and tax reforms. Da Silva's proposals to reform the deficit-ridden social security system were deemed 'heresy' by PT radicals, who had previously shown strong opposition in the Congresso to the more modest reform proposals of the Cardoso Government. A first round vote on social security reform in August 2003 was only narrowly approved by the lower house, while a separate vote on the introduction of an 11% levy on public servants' pensions was even more of a trial for the Government, being approved only with votes from opposition deputies. None the less, in late September a more cohesive government coalition was able to approve the tax reform in the lower house without help from the opposition. Following a record five months of deliberations, in December the Senado finally approved the two reforms, but only after senators had demanded that changes be made to the legislation.

In January 2004 President da Silva effected a cabinet reorganization, in which representatives of the PMDB were appointed to the Government in an attempt to shore up support for his administration in the Congresso Nacional. Nevertheless, in early 2004 the President encountered several political reverses and defeats. In February a videotape exposed allegedly corrupt campaign finance dealings in May 2002 by his congressional relations chief, Waldomiro Diniz. In April the PL's three senators declared themselves no longer aligned with the ruling coalition, thus reducing the Government's majority in the Senado to just three seats. In June the Government encountered great difficulties in sustaining its decree increasing the minimum wage by only R $20 in successive votes in the Congresso; the Senado subsequently rejected the Government's plan and voted to increase the minimum wage by R $35, to R $275 per month. Finally, the Supreme Court threatened to declare a major part of the 2003 social security reform unconstitutional.

A four-month recess of the Congresso Nacional due to municipal elections delayed the Government's reform agenda in the second half of 2004. However, in early 2005 the Congresso approved protracted judicial reforms that established external control councils for the judiciary and public prosecutors. A long-awaited new bankruptcy law was also approved, and took effect in early June. The legislation enabled struggling businesses to negotiate debts and therefore to remain operational. The Government was weakened in February after the PT lost the presidency of the Câmara dos Deputados. Severino Cavalcanti of the Partido Progressista (PP) was elected to head the lower house, defeating both the 'official' PT candidate, Eduardo Greenhalgh, and the 'dissident' PT candidate, Virgílio Guimarães. Although the PP was part of the pro-Government bloc in the Câmara, Cavalcanti pursued an independent strategy as President of the chamber and, as a result, the Government's legislative agenda encountered obstacles.

In May 2005 several cases of government corruption were revealed by federal police investigations, and a major scandal erupted in early June. A videotape emerged that allegedly showed proof that a bribes-for-contracts scheme was in operation at the state postal service, the Empresa Brasileira de Correios e Telégrafos. The recipient of the bribes, Maurício Marinho, a senior postal service employee, claimed on the tape that the scheme was operated by PTB appointees, organized by Roberto Jefferson Monteiro, the party's national president. A similar scheme was subsequently revealed to be in operation at the state-owned reinsurance institution, the IRB-Brasil Resseguros. Jefferson denied the allegation and, in turn, publicly accused the PT of operating a bribery scheme in 2003 and 2004, whereby PL and PP deputies received a monthly allowance ('*mensalão*') of R $30,000 for voting for government-sponsored legislation. Jefferson also alleged that in 2004 the PT had promised the PTB some R $20m. in financial support for the municipal election campaign, but that only R $4m. had actually been transferred to party funds. Testifying before the Câmara dos Deputados's ethics council (Conselho de Ética e Decoro Parlamentar) in mid-June, Jefferson repeated his earlier accusation that President da Silva's Cabinet Chief, José Dirceu, had organized the bribery scheme. As a result, Dirceu resigned his influential position in the Government; he was replaced by Dilma Vana Rousseff, hitherto Minister of Mines and Energy. The PT's Secretary-General, President and Treasurer also resigned their posts in July after being implicated in the scandal. In late May the Congresso Nacional instituted an investigating committee to examine the accusations relating to the postal service and, following Jefferson's testimony, into the *mensalão* allegations. In mid-June 2005 Jefferson took a leave of absence from the PTB presidency while the investigations continued.

The *mensalão* scandal produced three congressional investigating committees (known as CPIs—Comissões Parlamentares de Inquéritos), which in September 2005 proposed that 19 deputies be expelled from the Congresso Nacional. (By June 2006 four deputies had resigned, three had been expelled—including Jefferson and Dirceu—11 absolved and one still awaited a decision.) Following the discovery that PT officers had signed dubious loan contracts with two banks to disguise the *mensalão* operations, they too were forced to resign, and in September new officers were elected, including Ricardo Berzoini of the pro-da Silva Campo Majoritário faction as party President. Nevertheless, the PT refused to reform its institutions, and thus the party's image suffered considerable damage.

THE 2006 PRESIDENTIAL ELECTION

The CPIs had a negative impact on President da Silva's poll ratings in late 2005, and the leaders of the opposition PSDB and PFL appeared confident that da Silva would be easy to defeat in the elections. As a result, these parties refrained from advocating the President's impeachment. However, by early 2006 da Silva's approval ratings had improved considerably. The da Silva Government achieved this reversal of fortune through circumstance and a series of popular measures: rates of inflation, unemployment and interest had all decreased, special consigned credit loans were introduced, as was a substantial increase in the minimum wage. Furthermore, the Bolsa Família allowance programme met with considerable success, benefiting some 11m. poor families. In September, however, the Government was again implicated in a scandal after the federal police arrested a group of PT militants at a São Paulo hotel. The party members had suitcases filled with R $1.7m. in cash and were allegedly negotiating the purchase of a damaging dossier from the perpetrators of a scandal in which federal health officials in 2003 had accepted bribes in return for buying ambulances and other emergency equipment at inflated prices. Eight PT militants were involved, some with close ties to the President and others holding federal government posts.

At the first round presidential ballot, held on 1 October 2006, President da Silva received 48.6% of the valid votes cast, just short of an absolute majority. Da Silva's failure to secure a second term without need for a second ballot was attributed to the so-called 'dossier scandal' in the previous month. The PSDB's candidate, São Paulo Governor Geraldo Alckmin, came a close second, receiving 41.6% of the valid votes cast. Heloísa Helena, representing the Partido Socialismo e Liberdade, garnered 6.9% of the ballot while Cristovam Buarque of the PDT won 2.6%. At the run-off ballot, held on 29 October, the PSDB candidate Alckmin was unable to close the gap, and received 2,425,191 fewer votes than in the first round, equivalent to 39.2% of the valid votes, compared to the 60.8% of the vote attracted by the incumbent President. Da Silva's performance in both rounds was similar to that of the 2002 election.

In concurrent elections to the Senado, in which 27 seats (one per state) were contested, the PFL elected six senators, the PSDB five, the PMDB four and the PT only two. As a result, the PFL counted 18 senators in total and thus was expected to choose the new Senado President. The PMDB had 15 senators but, through several senators switching party allegiance, its representation advanced to 20 senators by February 2007, when the Câmara and Senado were scheduled to elect their new presiding officers. As a result, the PMDB re-elected Senator Renan Calheiros (a staunch ally of the President) to lead the upper house.

Following the scandals that plagued the PT in 2005 and 2006, many observers predicted that the President's party might return only 60 or 70 federal deputies in the lower house elections and fall to third or fourth rank in the Câmara. However, the PT returned 83 deputies (fewer than the 91 elected in 2002) and became the second largest party, behind the PMDB with 89 deputies. By tradition, the largest party in the legislature selected the new Câmara President; however, the PMDB agreed to support the PT candidate, Arlindo Chinaglia, in return for the PT's support of the PMDB candidate in the Senado. It was also agreed that in 2009 the reverse would occur: the PT would elect the speaker of the upper house and the PMDB the Câmara President. Following considerable political manoeuvring similar to that seen after the 2002 election, the pro-da Silva coalition in the Câmara constructed an 11-party alliance that was equivalent to 70% of the chamber. A total of 21 parties elected at least one deputy.

DA SILVA'S SECOND TERM

President da Silva's new Government was not fully constituted until late March 2007, as the President had to take into consideration the demands of the 11 parties that comprised his coalition when it came to allocating government appointments. The close PT-PMDB alliance ensured that two cabinet positions were allocated to the PMDB's senate grouping and two for its lower house representatives; the appointment of PMDB party member José Gomes Temporão as Minister of Health completed the PMDB's ministerial quota. To accommodate the PSB, a new Special Secretariat for Ports was dismembered from the Ministry of Transport. The PDT's decision to join the coalition was recognized in the party's national President, Carlos Lupi, being appointed Minister of Labour. In contrast, the cabinet quota of the PT was reduced to accommodate the PMDB and other coalition partners, much to the displeasure of party members. Cabinet Chief Dilma Rousseff and Secretary-General of the Presidency Luiz Dulci remained in their posts, while Minister of Institutional Relations Tarso Genro was appointed Minister of Justice in March and was succeeded by Walfrido do Mares Guia of the PTB, who had been Minister of Tourism in da Silva's first term.

Early in his second term, President da Silva changed the armed forces commandants. The new Chief of Staff of the Air Force, Brig.-Gen. Juniti Saito, faced an almost immediate institutional crisis: a national air travel 'blackout' provoked by flight controllers who were dissatisfied with their working conditions and who demanded 'demilitarization' of this sector, in which 80% of air traffic controllers were non-commissioned officers in the air force. In May 2007 the Senado and Câmara installed CPIs to investigate the issues surrounding the crash, in late September 2006, of an aeroplane in northern Mato Grosso, which killed all 154 on board. Flight controllers were accused of causing the disaster. A further aeroplane crash, at São Paulo's Congonhas airport in July 2007, killed almost 200 people and increased pressure on the Government to reform the aviation sector. Following the disaster, in late July Minister of Defence Waldir Pires was dismissed from his post. Pires was succeeded by Nelson Jobim, a former Minister of Justice, who moved quickly to force the replacement of the directorate of the Agência Nacional de Aviação Civil.

In February 2007 the Higher Electoral Court (Tribunal Superior Eleitoral—TSE) rendered an important interpretation of election and party legislation: that the mandate of those elected under proportional representation belonged to the party and not to the individual deputy. Thus, when a deputy changed parties, he or she would lose the seat and be replaced by the next alternate on that party's list. By late March 37 deputies had changed parties since their election in October 2006. Three opposition parties (the PFL, PSDB and PPS) had lost 22 deputies to the pro-Government coalition parties and immediately sought redress in the Supremo Tribunal Federal (Supreme Federal Court) to restore their lost seats. In October the Supreme Court confirmed the TSE resolution, and the TSE began receiving cases from the state election courts requesting the replacement of elected officials who had changed parties after the February TSE resolution.

In April 2007 the federal police began a sequence of operations against alleged corruption within the judiciary and executive. In May a major operation led to the arrests of 46 people suspected of involvement in a scandal whereby a construction firm, Guatama Construtora, was alleged to have bribed federal and state government officials in order to secure procurement contracts. Several governors and former governors were implicated, and in late May the Minister of Mines and Energy, Silas Rondeau, was forced to resign. In June the federal police launched an operation against illegal organized gambling operations in nine states. As in the *mensalão* affair in 2005 and the 'dossier scandal' in September 2006, several people from the PT and close to the President were implicated. However, the scandals were not confined to the PT: in May 2007 the powerful PMDB Senado President, Renan Calheiros, was accused of allowing a lobbyist for a construction company, Mendes Júnior, to make child support payments for his illegitimate child. Although Calheiros insisted the money was his and he had done nothing wrong, the case threatened to weaken the PT-PMDB alliance. Federal police and auditors subsequently identified a scheme of false sales receipts and other discrepancies relating to Calheiros's attempts to justify this expenditure. The Senado's ethics council investigated Calheiros on five counts and recommended his expulsion from the Senado. However, he refused to take a leave of absence from the Senado presidency and used his office to favour his defence. In September the Senado voted not to expel Calheiros, although in the following month he took a 45-day leave of absence. Finally, in December Calheiros resigned the presidency of the Senado, and later on the same day the upper house again voted not to expel him. This episode consumed nearly six months and prevented the Congresso Nacional from approving any major legislation during that time. Meanwhile, in August the Supreme Court indicted 40 people, including a number of deputies, implicated in the *mensalão* scandal of 2005. The law on parliamentary immunity stipulated that deputies could only be tried on criminal charges at the Supreme Court, and this was the first time the court had accepted any such indictments.

During da Silva's first term many development projects, especially new hydroelectric installations, were delayed or thwarted owing to the refusal of the Brazilian Institute of Environment and Renewable Natural Resources (Instituto Brasileiro do Meio Ambiente e dos Recursos Naturais Renováveis—IBAMA) to grant the projects environmental impact licences. The President became frustrated by these impediments to economic growth, and in April 2007 dismissed most of the leadership in the Ministry of the Environment and transferred the conservation responsibilities of IBAMA to a new body. In response to the division of their organization, IBAMA employees called a national protest strike in May. Da Silva subsequently recruited expert technicians from the World Bank and the Inter-American Development Bank to elaborate the impact licences for two new hydroelectric plants on the Madeira River. The concessions to construct the plants were subsequently awarded in December 2007 and May 2008, respectively. Also in May 2008 the Minister of the Environment, Marina Silva, resigned and returned to her seat in the Senado. Silva had opposed a number of President da Silva's policies, including the hydroelectric schemes and other plans for development of the Amazon region, on environmental grounds. Carlos Minc, hitherto Secretary of the Environment in the state government of Rio de Janeiro, was appointed to replace her. Silva's resignation was criticized by a number of international environmental organizations, which held her in high esteem for her stance on ecological issues in Brazil.

Meanwhile, in December 2007 the opposition in the Senado was able to defeat a constitutional amendment to renew the Contribuição Provisória Sobre Movimentação Financeira (CPMF), a tax of 0.38% on financial transactions that had been introduced in 1993 under President Franco. In addition to raising some R $40,000m. a year in federal revenues, the levy was a useful tool for identifying tax evasion. In June 2008, however, the Câmara dos Deputados approved the creation of the Contribução Social para a Saude, a 0.1% tax on financial transactions for the sole purpose of funding health care. In spite of the loss of the CPMF, federal revenues increased in 2008.

Municipal elections held on 5 and 26 October 2008 resulted in gains for both the PMDB (which won the greatest number of votes and of mayoralties) and the PT, and a decline in the share of the vote for the PSDB and the Democratas (DEM—as the PFL had been renamed in 2007). However, the PT suffered a defeat in the high-profile contest for Mayor of São Paulo, where its candidate, Marta Suplicy (who had resigned as Minister of Tourism in June in order to stand for election), failed to unseat the incumbent Gilberto Kassab of the DEM. Kassab's victory was considered to have strengthened the position of the Governor of São Paulo state, José Serra of the PSDB (the defeated candidate in the 2002 presidential election), who had endorsed Kassab's candidacy and was regarded as a probable nominee for the presidential election due in October 2010.

In 2009 some of President da Silva's supporters began a movement to amend the Constitution in order to allow the President to serve for a third consecutive term. Da Silva rejected the move and started instead to promote his Cabinet Chief, Dilma Rousseff, as his chosen successor. In spite of her cabinet position, Rousseff was little known in the country. Moreover, she had only recently joined the PT and her candidacy was resisted by some senior party members. Although constitutionally barred from engaging in electoral politics, President da Silva toured the country with Rousseff, inaugurating public works financed by the Government's successful Growth Acceleration Programme (Programa de Aceleração do Crecimento—PAC). During these events, the President introduced Rousseff as 'the mother of the PAC'. In April of that year Rousseff announced that she had undergone treatment for cancer, raising speculation that she would not be able to stand for the presidency, but she has since apparently made a full recovery, and in June 2010 was confirmed as the PT's nominee for head of state.

THE 2010 ELECTIONS

Presidential, congressional and state elections were scheduled to take place on 3 October 2010. If no presidential candidate received more than one-half of the vote, a run-off ballot would take place on 31 October. As in the past four elections, the main rival to the PT's candidate would come from the centre-right PSDB. Two state governors emerged as contenders for that party's presidential nomination, the Governor of Minas Gerais, Aécio Neves, and the Governor of São Paulo, José Serra. In April the PSDB again confirmed Serra as its presidential candidate. Early opinion polls gave Serra a considerable lead over Rousseff, but as she gained more public recognition, Rousseff began to cut Serra's advantage and opinion polls in May put the two candidates level. A third candidate, Marina Silva, from the Partido Verde (PV), trailed well behind, with around 10% of voting intentions. The outcome of the election was set to be close and almost certainly would go to a second round, but political and economic circumstances gave Rousseff the edge over her main rival. The economy was rebounding strongly from the short and shallow recession of 2009, with record numbers of jobs being created. Rousseff was seeking to capitalize on da Silva's extraordinary high popularity and while the President was constitutionally barred from campaigning on her behalf, he would do everything within his power to secure her victory. Serra avoided directly criticizing Lula. Instead he sought to project an image of experience and competence (he was Minister of Health and of Planning under President Cardoso, as well as a senator and Mayor of São Paulo), in contrast with Rousseff's relative inexperience: despite having occupied several positions in the Government, she had never run for office. Rousseff campaigned on the record of President da Silva's administrations, comparing it with that of the last PSDB administration under Cardoso. She also warned that a victory for Serra would put the Government's popular social programmes, such as the PAC, under threat.

Whoever wins the election will need to form a broad multiparty coalition to achieve a congressional majority, which made it difficult for any Government to shift too much from the political centre. There was relatively very little that separated the two leading candidates in terms of economic policy. Neither candidate was expected to deviate from current economic policies. They were both committed to maintaining macroeconomic stability and a broadly orthodox, market friendly, economic model mixed with redistributive social policies and varied levels of state intervention. Rousseff favoured a more activist state and a bigger role for state enterprises, particularly in sectors such as banking and petroleum and gas production. Serra was likely to favour a bigger role for the private sector and to promote lower public spending to make possible cuts in interest rates and a more competitive exchange rate without the risk of overheating the economy. However, he was also in favour of using the financial muscle of the state development bank, the Banco Nacional de Desenvolvimento Econômico e Social (BNDES) to promote domestic investment.

FOREIGN POLICY UNDER THE PT

During his first term in office, President da Silva was active in foreign affairs and undertook a large number of visits overseas. This policy continued into his second term. Brazil continued to pursue its ambition to gain access to one of the proposed additional permanent seats on the UN Security Council, a goal opposed by Argentina and Mexico. To this end, in 2004 Brazil accepted the command of the UN Stabilization Mission in Haiti and contributed 1,200 troops. Furthermore, in 2005 the Group of Four (G4), comprising Brazil, India, Japan and Germany, was organized for the purpose of supporting one another's bid for a permanent seat. Brazil led demands from a group of emerging nations towards the Group of Eight industrialized countries (G8) for a reduction of subsidies and protectionist policies, particularly subsidies on agricultural products. The strong stance adopted by Brazil on this issue at the fifth Ministerial Conference of the World Trade Organization (WTO) in Cancún, Mexico, in September 2003 effectively deadlocked negotiations towards the proposed Free Trade Area of the Americas (FTAA) promoted by the USA. Negotiations resumed in February 2005, but no advances were made. In June 2004 a complaint against US cotton subsidies brought by Brazil was upheld by the WTO, and in August a similar complaint against European Union (EU) sugar subsidies was sustained.

Da Silva held several meetings in 2006 with Presidents Néstor Kirchner of Argentina and Hugo Chávez of Venezuela to discuss the effective nationalization, in May, of petroleum and gas reserves by Bolivia, Venezuela's possible membership of Mercosul, and the possible construction of a US $23,000m. gas pipeline from Venezuela through Brazil to Argentina. Many commentators in Brazil suspected that the Venezuelan head of state had influenced Bolivian President Evo Morales' announcement that all gas and oil contracts with foreign companies, including the Brazilian energy company Petrobras, be renegotiated. In 2006 Brazil received about 50% of its natural gas supply from Bolivia after completion of the Bolivia–Brazil pipeline project. Petrobras also operated two refineries in Bolivia and accounted for about 20% of that nation's foreign exchange. Bolivia demanded renegotiation of Petrobras' contracts as a service provider for the Bolivian state petroleum company, Yacimientos Petrolíferos Fiscales Bolivianos, and an increase in the price of exported gas. Petrobras affirmed that it had invested some US $400m. in its two installations, but Bolivia offered only $60m. in compensation; in May 2007 a final price of $112m. was agreed upon.

During a visit to Brazil by US President George W. Bush in March 2007, the main topic under discussion was ethanol: Brazil proposed promotion of an organization of ethanol-exporting countries and enhancement of Brazilian-US biofuel co-operation. At a meeting in Washington, DC, in the following month the two leaders agreed to try to reactivate the WTO's stalled 'Doha round' of trade negotiations and to establish a joint private sector biofuels study group. Despite US concerns, President da Silva asserted that Brazil would continue its programmes with Iran within the criteria set by the UN Security Council.

In December 2004 Brazil was one of 12 countries that were signatories to the agreement, signed in Cusco, Peru, creating the South American Community of Nations (Comunidade Sul-Americana de Nações), intended to promote greater regional economic integration. The organization was renamed the Union of South American Nations (União das Nações Sul-Americanas—UNASUL/Unión de Naciones Suramericanas—UNASUR) at the South American Energy Summit held in Venezuela in April 2007. UNASUL was formally constituted in May 2008 at a summit in Brasília attended by the Presidents of all 12 member nations. Following Colombia's military incursion into Ecuador in March 2008 and the resulting diplomatic confrontation, President da Silva was active in promoting the establishment of a South American Defence Council, under the auspices of UNASUL, to guarantee peace and security in the region. The Council was duly inaugurated at a summit in Santiago, Chile, in March 2009.

In 2005 Brazil and Argentina pressured the other members of Mercosul for the admission of Venezuela as a full member of the grouping. In late May 2007 the Brazilian Senado approved a resolution requesting, unsuccessfully, that President Chávez not close down the Venezuelan television network Radio Caracas Television (RCTV). In response, Chávez called the Senado 'George Bush's parrot'. An opposition-led senate group threatened to veto Venezuela's membership of Mercosul as a result. By mid-2010 the Senado had yet to ratify Venezuela's admission to the bloc.

In 2007 President da Silva began a world-wide campaign promoting the production of biofuels. During an FAO conference in Rome, Italy, in June 2008, da Silva emphatically rejected accusations that Brazil's increasing biofuel production had contributed to sharp increases in food prices on international markets. He defended the production by tropical nations of ethanol from sugar cane, saying that it did not take agricultural land out of production, while criticizing the USA's use of maize for the same purpose.

Relations with Paraguay appeared likely to be affected by the election of Fernando Lugo as President in April 2008. During his election campaign Lugo had pledged to renegotiate the 1973 bilateral treaty for the construction and utilization of the Itaipú hydroelectric scheme, on the border between the two countries. Under the terms of the treaty, each side was obliged to sell any portion of its electricity allocation that it did not use to the other country at below the market rate, a situation that Lugo considered unfavourable towards Paraguay. In December the Brazilian Minister of Foreign Affairs, Celso Amorim, rejected Paraguay's demands for the right to sell its surplus energy on the open market and for a pardon of some US $19,000m. of debt resulting from the scheme, declaring that they were 'unrealistic'.

In 2010 da Silva continued with his high profile campaign to project Brazil as a global player with the ultimate goal of securing a permanent seat in a reformed UN Security Council. As part of this strategy, the President continued to develop political and economic links with the developing world (south–south relations) and with other emerging powers, particularly with the other so-called BRIC countries: Russia, India and the People's Republic of China. President da Silva has been a strong voice in the G-20 group of nations, joining the other BRIC countries in demanding reform of international financial and political institutions better to reflect a changing world order. In this context, Brazil has sought to assert a growing autonomy from the USA while projecting the country as a consensus builder and an honest broker in international affairs. While relations with the USA are generally good and the Administration of Barack Obama sees Brazil as a regional leader and a stabilizing force in Latin America, there have been frictions between the two countries, particularly concerning Lula's claim to have brokered a deal with Iran regarding the processing of nuclear fuel that the USA considered merely a delaying tactic by Iran to prevent the imposition of sanctions. The US Government has also been uneasy over President da Silva's reluctance to voice concerns about the erosion of democracy in Venezuela and his failure to condemn human rights abuses in Cuba. If elected, Rousseff was expected to continue da Silva's autonomous foreign policy as a regional power with global interests. A Serra administration would seek closer ties with the USA and take a more critical stance towards other left-leaning Latin American governments, particularly Venezuela. Serra was also expected to give a higher priority to Brazil's global role at the expense of its regional political and economic engagement with organizations such as Mercosul and UNASUL.

Economy

Dr AME BERGÉS

INTRODUCTION

Brazil is among the largest economies and most populous countries in the world, with a gross domestic product (GDP) of US $2,025,000m. (on an international purchasing-power parity basis) and some 193.7m. inhabitants in 2009. Despite being the world's largest coffee exporter in the 19th century, Brazil became one of the region's earliest industrial powers, as coffee profits were invested in nascient industrial and commercial enterprises. These enterprises benefited further when the First and Second World Wars interrupted trade, effectively providing protection from losses. By 1947 manufacturing had replaced agriculture as the principal sector; however, this structural change would not become evident in export composition until the last quarter of the 20th century, when export composition not only shifted toward manufactures, but towards increasingly sophisticated, high-technology and heavy manufactures, including telecommunications equipment, aircraft, and automobiles. With a strong currency, rapidly increasing exports, and a comparatively low ratio of foreign debt to GDP of 14%, Brazil is poised to become a world power.

After a slow start in the first years of the 21st century, Brazil experienced strong and sustained economic growth from 2004, until succumbing (albeit briefly) to the global financial crisis towards the end of 2008. Market conditions for Brazil this decade have generally been very good: not only has global demand for hydrocarbons and biofuels been on the rise, but

Brazil has also made progress in global high technology, information technology, software and services markets. Non-income measures of living standards, such as life expectancy at birth and literacy rates, also improved dramatically over the course of the 20th century, rising from 29.4 to 71.7 years and from 34.7% to 88.6%, respectively, between 1900 and 2008. These gains were made possible in large part by health and education initiatives during the period of inward-looking growth in the middle decades of the 20th century and by public spending priorities in the 1990s and 2000s, which were designed to reduce poverty through innovative programmes, including conditional cash transfers and broadening social protection coverage.

Twenty years ago, Brazil's economic growth record was very different. Growth had been particularly slow and volatile from the mid-1980s onwards as a result of the debt crisis and the hyperinflationary episodes of that decade, followed by the currency crisis of 1998–99, the 2001 energy crisis and Argentina's economic crisis of the same year, which drastically cut demand for Brazilian imports.

The hyperinflationary episodes would prove instrumental in generating the political capital needed to push through the market-oriented economic reforms that were initiated under President Fernando Collor de Mello (1990–92) and strengthened under President Fernando Henrique Cardoso (1995–2002). However, growing dissatisfaction with fiscal austerity, worsening income and social inequality, heightened popular support for the Partido dos Trabalhadores (PT) and resulted in the victory of Luiz Inácio Lula da Silva in the 2002 presidential election—to the chagrin of many foreign investors who feared a reversal of market-friendly policies. These concerns would prove to be unfounded, since the da Silva Government not only retained Cardoso's fiscal and monetary policies but also gave the Banco Central do Brasil operational independence, whilst expanding social programmes.

With favourable commodity prices during 2004–07, the Brazilian economy grew by an annual average of 4.5%, the fastest rate for 20 years. In the last quarter of 2007 the economy grew by 5.4%, inflation was reduced to below 4.5% and international reserves exceeded US $190,000m. Record growth was sustained until the end of 2008, when the global downturn and the collapse in petroleum and other commodity prices resulted in a contraction in GDP of 0.8% and caused Brazil to enter into recession in the first quarter of 2009. Although it was widely speculated that economic recovery would be protracted due to weak world export demand, the Brazilian economy had recovered by September 2009, owing, in part, to a healthy international reserves position, counter-cyclical fiscal policies, and strong domestic demand.

PRODUCTION

The service sector remains the largest component of Brazilian GDP, comprising 66.0% in 2008, followed by the industrial sector at 28.5% and agriculture at 5.5%. Since 2004 agriculture and mining have been the fastest-growing sectors of the Brazilian economy, owing, in part, to high global commodity prices and to policy initiatives designed to create a more favourable business climate and encourage investment.

Agriculture

Brazil is the world leader in the production of sugar, coffee, orange juice, and tropical fruits for export, the world's second largest soybean producer, and among the top producers of cotton, beef, and poultry for export. Genetically-modified and non-biotech crops enjoy an uneasy co-existence in Brazil. Between 2006 and 2010 Brazil moved from third to second largest cultivator of genetically modified crops after the USA, whilst also being a major source of non-biotech soybeans and soybean meal. The agribusiness sector (which includes processing and distribution) accounted for 36% of total exports and 25% of the labour force in 2008. Brazil's main agricultural products are beef (accounting for 21% of the value of agricultural production in 2009), followed by soybeans (16%), sugar cane (10%), maize (7%) and milk (7%).

The state of São Paulo is the agricultural centre of Brazil, contributing 20.3% of total production and 58.8% of sugar cane production. Surging commodity prices prompted record levels of sugar cane, soybean and maize production in 2008, and the grain harvest is expected to meet these levels in 2010, owing to productivity gains and favourable rainfall. Agricultural output is projected to grow by more than 40% in the next decade—significantly more than projections for the world's other two main agricultural producers, India (21%) and China (26%).

Better farm management practices, along with investment in modern equipment and soil improvements made possible through programmes such as the Land-Based Poverty Alleviation Project (Crédito Fundiário—Combate à Pobreza Rural), have contributed to a rise in productivity gains. Based on the earlier community-centred pilot programme, 'Cédula da Terra', these efforts have seen land distributed to some 372,500 families between 1995 and 2008. Rural poverty and concerns about domestic food prices have resulted in the implementation of a number of programmes charged with the multiple aims of productivity improvements, environmental conservation and tackling rural poverty and unemployment. These include the National Programme for the Strengthening of Family Agriculture (Programa Nacional de Fortalecimento da Agricultura Familiar—PRONAF), which extends financial support at preferential interest rates for equipment purchases, land recovery and development, and the Agriculture and Stockbreeding Integration Programme (Programa de Integração Lavoura-Pecuária—PROLAPEC), which provides grants for the recovery of deforested lands and the implementation of more environmentally friendly agricultural practices.

Industry

Brazil has a sophisticated and diverse industrial sector. Production includes automobiles, rail cars and locomotives, aircraft and satellites, iron ore, steel, petrochemicals, and consumer products such as footwear, toys and electronics. Industrial output grew by 8% in 2004, but declined to 2.9% in 2006, before recovering to 5.9% in 2007. Industrial output growth slowed down in 2008 to 4.4%, but recovered rapidly in 2009, owing, in part, to the fiscal stimulus package. Foremost in industrial output are capital goods (with 19.5% growth in 2007) and durable goods (9.2%), stimulated by strong consumer demand, favourable credit conditions, and expansion in the construction sector, as preparations to host the football World Cup in 2014 and the 2016 Olympic Games proceed.

Among the most dynamic industrial sectors in Brazil are petroleum and ethanol. With more than 12,620m. barrels of proven petroleum reserves in January 2009, Brazil has the second largest reserves in South America, after Venezuela. In 2009 petroleum production was estimated at 2.1m. barrels per day (b/d), compared with 2.32m. b/d in 2007 and 2.64m. b/d in 2008. The state-owned oil company, Petróleo Brasileiro, SA (Petrobras), controls over 95% of crude petroleum production, and has expanded output in recent years, with plans to spend at least US $39,000m. on exploration and production projects in Brazil up to 2011. In 2007 Petrobras announced the discovery of an offshore oilfield reportedly containing reserves equivalent to some 8,000m. barrels of oil, the world's biggest oil discovery since 2000. Petrobras is also the largest producer and wholesale supplier of natural gas in Brazil, with control of 90% of the country's natural gas reserves (amounting to proven natural gas reserves of 365,000m. cu m in January 2009).

Brazil is also one of the world's largest producers of ethanol derived from sugar cane. The Government of Lula da Silva has sought to capitalize on the global search for less environmentally damaging energy alternatives by promoting investment in ethanol and biodiesel production, and by pioneering research into cellulosic ethanol (derived from non-food plants). However, international and non-governmental organizations have warned that the displacement of staple food crops in favour of sugar cane, and the diversion of food plants away from food uses, could provoke a global food price crisis and contribute to deforestation.

Domestic ethanol production, combined with higher domestic prices for petrol and government regulations supporting the use of biofuels (which accounted for 22.3% of fuel use in 2009, compared with 8.3% in 2008), have contributed to a massive increase in the use of flexible-fuel vehicles. More than one-half of the cars manufactured in Brazil are flexible-fuel vehicles, and 80% of new cars sold can run on ethanol. Brazil's automobile manufacturing industry is sizeable. Brazil is among the ten largest automobile-manufacturing countries in the world by volume, and flexible-fuel vehicle sales were projected to rise annually by 15.7% in 2007–10. General Motor and Toyota have recently announced plans to establish and/or increase car production in Brazil, with the aim of expanding sales in Brazil and South America.

Brazil also has some of the largest domestic consumer markets in the world, with the third largest soft drinks market, the fourth largest car market, and the fifth largest beer market and telecommunications market in the world. The food and beverages market accounted for 9.5% of GDP in 2005, and Brazil also has one of the largest confectionery markets in the world. The sheer size and potential of Brazil's consumer markets have made it an attractive destination for foreign investment, and indeed both domestic consumption and foreign direct investment are credited with Brazil's rapid economic recovery from the 2008 global financial crisis.

Hydroelectric power accounts for 83% of Brazil's total electricity supply. This heavy reliance on hydroelectricity has been problematic during years of below-average rainfall. Despite large natural gas reserves, electricity derived from natural gas comprises only a small share of total supply. Brazil currently has two nuclear power plants. In 2007 the Government approved plans for the state-owned Eletrobrás Termonuclear, SA (Eletronuclear) to resume construction of a third plant (Angra-3), and began the process of applying for permission from the Instituto Brasileiro do Meio Ambiente e dos Recursos Naturais Renováveis (IBAMA—the environmental regulatory agency) to begin operations at the plant.

Services

The Brazilian banking system—the largest in Latin America—remains highly concentrated, with the ten largest banks accounting for 80% of total banking sector assets in 2005. Although some of the largest banks are foreign owned, foreign participation in the banking system has been quite limited, especially relative to the rest of Latin America, accounting for about 27% of total deposits. The four largest banks are all Brazilian: Banco do Brasil (18% of total assets) and Caixa Econômica Federal (13%), both of which are owned by the federal Government, followed by Banco Bradesco, SA (12%) and Banco Itaú, SA (10%), which are private banks.

TRADE

Brazil's export performance in the early 2000s resulted in a current account deficit of 4.6% of GDP in 2001 being transformed into a current account surplus over five consecutive years, reaching the equivalent of 1.8% of GDP in 2004. However, in 2008 the trade surplus became a trade deficit, as imports exceeded exports due to falling world demand during the international economic crisis.

Brazil's main export trading partners in 2008 were the European Union (EU, which accounted for 23.5% of the total), the USA (14.7%), the People's Republic of China (11.6%) and Argentina (8.7%). In 2008 exports to the other BRIC countries (Russia, India and China) grew by 14.4%, those to the North American Free Trade Agreement (NAFTA) countries (Canada, Mexico and the USA) by 18.3% and those to Latin American countries by 22.8%. In 2009 China became Brazil's main trade partner. A notable trend is the expansion of exports to non-traditional markets, notably Africa and the Middle East (which increased by 14.6% and 10.9%, respectively, in 2007).

Export composition has changed radically since the 1960s, when manufactures contributed just 3% of total exports and food and agricultural raw materials accounted for some 88% of exports. The share of manufactures declined from 52.2% in 2007 to 46% in 2009, while the share of primary products rose to 40% of total exports, stimulated by record prices and favourable production conditions. Among Brazil's most important exports are soybeans and soymeal, iron ore and concentrates, beef and poultry, and crude petroleum and fuels. In 2007 high commodity prices raised growth in exports of fuels (of 28.8%) and ores and metals (12.6%), as well as in exports of maize grains (317.2%), chicken meat (43.7%), tobacco leaves (28.9%), soy chaff and grains (21.9% and 18.0%, respectively), pork (17.0%) and coffee grains (14.9%). The fastest growing manufacture and semi-manufactured exports in 2007 were iron alloys (74.4%), oil (52.7%), aircraft (45.0%), engines and generators (28.0%), pulp (21.0%), iron ore (17.5%), and pumps and compressors (14.5%).

Manufactures have also become increasingly sophisticated. During the 1990s there was greater export market penetration of high- and medium-technology products, notably aircraft (accounting for 12.1% of total exports in 1990–99), transport equipment parts (4.2%), telecommunications equipment (5.7%), and automobiles (5.0%). Between 2000 and 2006, however, the share of high-technology exports fell steadily from 18.6% to 12.1%.

High world prices for fuels and commodities, combined with more favourable domestic tax and export policies, saw Brazilian exports more than double from US $73,000m. in 2003 to $161,000m. in 2007 and $197,000m. in 2008. In 2009 exports fell to 158,900m. due to weak world demand, while imports—driven by higher domestic food and energy prices and a swelling of consumer credit before the onset of the crisis, and by expansionary fiscal and monetary policy after the crisis—have continued to grow. The largest source of import growth has been consumer goods, followed by capital goods, fuels and lubricants, and intermediary goods and raw materials.

Brazil's main import trading partners in 2008 were the EU (21.4%), the USA (15.2%), China (11.8%) and Argentina (8.1%). Among the fastest growing markets were the EU (demonstrating a 92.1% increase in imports in 2006–07), Africa (39.1%) and Asia (33.3%). Manufactures account for the greatest share of imports (of about 73% since 2000), including machinery, electrical and transport equipment, chemical products, petroleum, automotive parts and electronics.

Appreciation of the national currency, together with an expansion in domestic consumer credit (from 75.8% of GDP in 2004 to 92.8% in 2006) and falling interest rates, fuelled stronger growth of imports. By 2007 the current account surplus had fallen to 0.3% of GDP, with deficits of US $28,300 and $24,300 recorded in 2008 and 2009, respectively, although these figures also reflected weak export performance due to falling world demand.

FOREIGN DIRECT INVESTMENT

Foreign direct investment (FDI), which reached US $34,600m. in 2007 and a record $45,100m. in 2008, has been instrumental in compensating for the deficit in the current account. FDI net inflows fell dramatically in 2009, to $25,900m. In 2008 the main sources of FDI were the USA, Luxembourg, the Netherlands and Japan. In 2007 FDI was orientated towards financial services (15.4% of the total), basic metallurgy and steel (10.3%), and vehicles (7.2%). In 2008 mineral extraction received 24.3% of the total, followed by metals (11.4%), financial services (8.7%) and foodstuffs (5.1%).

Many of the multinational companies currently operating in Brazil acquired local operations through debt-equity swaps in the late 1980s and early 1990s under President Collor de Mello's National Privatization Programme (Programa Nacional de Desestatização—PND), which saw 33 state-owned enterprises sold between 1990 and 1994, including Empresa Brasileira de Aeronáutica, SA (Embraer), an aircraft and aerospace services company. The big push toward privatization at both federal and state levels came in the late 1990s under President Cardoso. Between 1995 and 1998 some 80 state-owned enterprises were privatized, including the Companhia Vale do Rio Doce mining company (formerly CVRD, now Vale), as well as railways, telecommunications, ports, electricity distribution and generation, and water and sanitation services.

Brazil is a particularly attractive market for FDI, owing to the growth potential implied by an increasingly affluent middle class and an expanding domestic consumer market. The presence of multinational companies is particularly salient in the consumer products segment, especially food, beverages and confectionery.

Despite the opening up of the petroleum sector in 1997, foreign operations in that sector are few and far between. The first foreign crude petroleum production operation in Brazil was Royal Dutch Shell's Bijupira-Salema project in the Campos Basin. The first and only upstream oil project without any participation from Petrobras is Devon Energy Corporation's Polvo field, which began production in August 2007. Other important foreign companies in the Brazilian petroleum sector are Chevron and Norsk Hydro.

An interesting trend is the emergence of Brazil as an important source of FDI abroad. In 2006 outward FDI flows exceeded inflows by US $9,400m. Outward foreign direct investment from Brazil had reached almost $21,000 in 2008, and nearly $104,000m. by August 2009, making Brazil the second most important source of FDI among developing countries after China. The greatest contributor to Brazil's outward FDI is Companhia Vale do Rio Doce, which has mining operations and investments in Finland, Canada, Australia, Mongolia, China, India, Angola, South Africa, Chile and Peru, followed by Petroleo Brasiliero, SA (Petrobras) and Metalúrgica Gerdau, SA. Other major Brazilian multinationals include heavy construction companies and high-technology groups, such as Votorantim (one of the ten largest cement companies in the world), Camargo Corrêa, Embraer, Itautec and Odebrecht. The rapid increase in outward investment is also, in good measure, the result of the rapid internationalization of a small number of established enterprises in the food and beverages sector (including Sadia, Perdigão Agroindustrial and AmBev) and the personal care and cosmetics products sector.

MACROECONOMIC POLICY

Higher commodity prices and investment inflows underpinned a rapid increase in Brazil's international reserves since 2003. These nearly doubled from US $49,000m. in 2003 to $85,000m. in 2006. International reserves have continued to swell, reaching $173,000m. in 2007 and $197,400m. in December 2008, making Brazil a net creditor with the rest of the world for the first time. By May 2009 Brazil's international reserves reached $202,000m. and these have continued to grow, despite the global financial crisis—a testament to investor perceptions about the stability and attractiveness of the Brazilian economy. Indeed, Brazil was able to achieve economic recovery within a relatively short period, with a record 9% growth rate for the first quarter of 2010, prompting the Government to revise its forecast for 2010 upwards, from 5.5% to 6.5%.

Monetary Policy

The accumulation of foreign reserves was, until recently, accompanied by the steady appreciation of the Brazilian currency, the real. The Cardoso Government's Plano Real of 1994—under which the cruzeiro real was replaced by the real, which was devalued and pegged to the US dollar—restrained inflation rates, bringing them down from around 2,500% in 1993 to 22.4% in 1995 and to 1.6% in 1997. In the wake of the Russian financial crisis of 1997 and the Asian crisis of 1998, however, inflation once again began to rise. This, coupled with dwindling foreign reserves, raised doubts about the Banco Central do Brasil's ability to defend the currency peg. In 1999 the central bank abandoned the exchange rate peg in favour of a flexible exchange rate regime with an inflation target, raising the benchmark interest rate (Sistema Especial de Liquidação e Custódia—SELIC) from 25% to 45% to tighten the money supply. The real lost 68.5% of its value between 2000 and 2005, with inflation falling from 8.9% in 1999 (and a peak of 12.5% in 2002 at the height of Argentina's economic crisis) to an average of around 3.8% in 2006–08. This controlled inflation led the central bank to reduce the SELIC rate from 19.75% in September 2005 to 13.25% in December 2006 and 11.25% in September 2007. The central bank introduced minimum reserve requirements on inter-bank deposits in January 2008, and raised the benchmark rate to 11.75% in April 2008 in response to rising food and energy prices, but subsequently lowered bank reserve requirements and reduced interest rates to record lows of 10.25% in May 2009 and 8.75% in October 2009, in an effort to stimulate the economy. In April 2010 the Banco Central do Brasil raised the SELIC to 9.5% and again in June to 10.25%, in an attempt to restrain consumption and to help meet the Government's 4.5% inflation target. Amid the global financial crisis, the currency depreciated against the US dollar from 1.56 reais to the dollar in August 2008 to 2.51 in December 2008, but the trend was reversed in 2009, when the value of the currency reached pre-crisis levels, as a result of strong foreign investment inflows.

Fiscal Policy

Higher commodity prices and swelling international reserves made it possible for Brazil to retire its debt to the IMF in December 2005, two years ahead of schedule. By the end of 2007 the country's gross external debt had fallen to US $193,200m., from $236,600m. in 2003. These favourable external account indicators, in part, led the Standard & Poor's and Fitch Ratings credit rating agencies to raise Brazil's sovereign credit rating to 'investment' grade in 2008. Despite a rise in debt of $211,300m. in September 2008, by mid-2009 Brazil's management of the downturn in the global economy (which was marked by a continued increase in international reserves of 23.4% in 2009) strengthened hopes for a relatively rapid economic recovery.

A commitment to fiscal austerity, enshrined in legislation on fiscal responsibility enacted in 2000, was instrumental in the decrease in the ratio of external debt to GDP, enabling the da Silva administration consistently to surpass the budget surplus targets without sacrificing public sector investment. Municipal and state governments also saw dramatic improvement in their balances, the latter converting a budget deficit of 0.58% in 2002 into a budget surplus of 0.70% of GDP in 2006. As a consequence of the recession and falling tax revenues, in 2009 the budget surplus declined to the lowest level in eight years, of about 2.1% of GDP, compared with 3.5% of GDP in 2008.

Brazil's public internal debt, however, remained high at 50.6% of GDP in 2007 and 51.1% of GDP in the first quarter of 2008, well above the emerging market average of 30%. One of the largest components of fiscal outlays are personnel costs and pensions. Brazil's social security deficit widened to R $42,070m. in 2006—equivalent to 9% of current expenditure—as a result of increases in the overall number of payments and in the amount paid to beneficiaries, as payments are themselves linked to the inflation-adjusted minimum wage. The deficit widened further to R $43,600m. in 2009, owing to minimum wage increases, as well as a slowing of job creation, which adversely affected revenue from social security contributions. The growth in social security revenues has been further undermined by an extensive informal labour market.

Given the difficulties associated with retrenchment of public expenditure, which in many cases would require amendment to the Constitution, the burden of fiscal adjustment has fallen upon public investment on the one hand, and on greater tax collection on the other.

From 3.4% of GDP in 1986, public investment has fallen sharply to 2.1% of GDP in 2004 and 0.3% of GDP in 2007. Falling public investment, coupled with the downward pressure that high interest rates and business taxes have exerted on private investment, has, in turn, seen fixed investment as a share of GDP fall from an average of 21.5% in the 1980s to 19.6% in the 1990s, 19.1% in 2000–05 and 16.8% in 2006 and an estimated 17% in 2009. In an effort to reverse the downward trend in productive investment, the da Silva Government introduced the Growth Acceleration Plan (Plano de Aceleração do Crescimento—PAC) in 2007. The PAC promotes investment through public-private partnerships in infrastructure development, as well as projects in petroleum and gas, transportation, sanitation, and housing. In May 2008 the Government announced a productive development policy package that would reduce taxes and extend government loans to favoured industries, including agribusiness, nanotechnology, biotechnology, perfume, biodiesel and oil and gas. These policies were expected to raise productive investment from 17.6% of GDP in 2007 to 21% of GDP by 2010. With the second phase of the Growth Acceleration Programme beginning in March 2010, combined investments were expected to reach R $1,590,000,000m.

Record levels of tax collection helped ensure that the Government met its primary surplus targets. Brazil's tax-to-GDP ratio rose from an average of 22.9% in the 1980s to 27.1% in 1994 and reaching almost 35% of GDP in 2007—more than double the average for Latin America—and 38.8% in 2008. However, the expiration of the 0.83% tax on monetary and financial transactions (Contribuição Provisória sobre Movimentação Financeira—CPMF) in December 2007, which had generated revenues equivalent to 1.5% of GDP, was expected to increase the pressure for structural fiscal reform and for reducing and eliminating tax evasion. However, the economic stimulus package caused a sharp decline in the primary budget surplus to 2% of GDP in 2009 (the lowest level in eight years).

LABOUR MARKETS AND SOCIAL POLICY

The services sector provides employment for 66% of the economically active population, while agriculture contributes 20% and industry 14%. Labour market indicators have improved significantly since the 1980s and 1990s. The Brazilian labour force expanded from 62.4m. in 1990 to 83.4m. in 2000 and 99.5m. in 2007. Unemployment fell to an historic low of 9.4% in 2007, and unemployment in the six largest metropolitan areas fell from 12.3% in 2003 to 11.5% in 2004. The decline in unemployment continued despite the crisis, falling to 7.4% in 2009, while minimum wage increases have exceeded the rate of inflation. Notwithstanding the sustained growth in formal job creation and real wages, employment in the non-agricultural informal sector grew from 37% of non-agricultural employment in 1990–2004 to 45% in 2007.

At the same time as employment figures have improved, poverty and inequality rates have also fallen to historically low figures, partly due to the rise in earnings and to targeted income support programmes, which reach around 20% of the population. The percentage of the population living in poverty declined from 40.8% in 1992 to 32.9% in 2002 and from 31% in 2005. Income distribution has also improved, evident in the decline in the Gini coefficient (a measure of income inequality) from 0.640 in 1999 to 0.566 in 2005. These social programmes have helped to mitigate the impact of the global financial crisis, with poverty rates falling to 26% in 2008 and a marginal increase in the Gini coefficient to 0.567 in 2009.

Targeted income support and land-based poverty alleviation programmes have been instrumental in reducing extreme poverty in rural and urban areas. The percentage of the population living in extreme poverty decreased by some 31% to 13.4% in 2002, from 19.3% a decade earlier. Rural income inequality also declined. Under the land-based Crédito Fundiário programme, beneficiaries saw their income increase by an average of 181% in 1998–2003 and by 145% in 2003–05. In addition, the Gini coefficient in rural areas fell from 0.577 in 1999 to 0.538 in 2006, and from 0.625 to 0.593 in urban areas. The much praised Bolsa Família programme expanded coverage from 8.5m. families by the end of 2005 to 12.5m. households in 2009. Bolsa Família ties cash transfers to children's school attendance and participation in various government vaccination and nutrition programmes.

Brazil has also seen dramatic improvements in health and education indicators. Infant mortality decreased from 45.2 per thousand births in 1992 to 27.8 in 2002 and to 22.6 in 2009. Under-nourishment fell from 12% of the population in 1990–92 to 7% in 2002–04. Literacy rates improved from 86.9% in 2000 to 88.6% in 2005, rising to 90% in 2007, while the number of children in the relevant age-group attending school rose from 85% in 1990 to 97% in 2005. Moreover, 93% of school-age children in the poorest 20% of the population were enrolled in school in 2001, compared to 70% in 1990.

OUTLOOK

The Brazilian economy has become more resilient and stable since 2002, as attested by its rapid recovery from the global financial crisis, reduction in foreign debt, restraint of inflation to more manageable levels, and lowering of interest rates. Brazil has also become less export dependent; indeed, the economy withstood the global crisis as a result of buoyant domestic demand. The Government has intensified efforts to promote innovation and investment in research and development, with the promulgation of the 'innovation law' of 2004 (which encourages co-operation between the public and private sectors in scientific research projects), the PAC, and a new industrial policy framework. At the same time, the labour force is becoming more skilled, with a 28% increase in the number of people aged 25 and older who have attained tertiary education between 2000 and 2005.

Although poised to becoming a world power, Brazil continues to face a number of short- and long-term economic challenges, including management of the inflation rate and the appreciation of the real, and raising investment levels. At a level of 17% in 2009, Brazil's low investment share of GDP remains a concern, especially compared with that of Russia (20%), India (32.1%), and China (42.6%). On the social side, questions remain about the extent to which extended coverage of the Bolsa Família programme can be sustainably financed, since it lost 87% of its funding when the CPMF expired in December 2007. Brazil also faces the difficult challenge of environmental protection and presenting itself as a global leader in efforts to combat climate change, on the one hand—Brazil reportedly accounts for nearly all of Latin America's investment in renewable energy—while at the same time negotiating the interests of agro-business, transport, and non-renewable energy.

Statistical Survey

Sources (unless otherwise stated): Economic Research Department, Banco Central do Brasil, SBS, Quadra 03, Bloco B, 70074-900 Brasília, DF; tel. (61) 3414-1074; fax (61) 3414-2036; e-mail coace.depec.@bcb.gov.br; internet www.bcb.gov.br; Instituto Brasileiro de Geografia e Estatística (IBGE), Centro de Documentação e Disseminação de Informações (CDDI), Rua Gen. Canabarro 706, 2° andar, Maracanã, 20271-201 Rio de Janeiro, RJ; tel. (21) 2142-4781; fax (21) 2142-4933; e-mail ibge@ibge.bov.br; internet www.ibge.gov.br.

Area and Population

AREA, POPULATION AND DENSITY

Area (sq km)	8,514,877*
Population (census results)†	
1 August 1996	157,070,163
1 August 2000	
Males	83,576,015
Females	86,223,155
Total	169,799,170
Population (official projected estimates at mid-year)‡	
2008	189,612,814
2009	191,480,630
2010	193,252,604
Density (per sq km) at mid-2010	22.7

* 3,287,611 sq miles.

† Excluding Indian jungle population (numbering 45,429 in 1950).

‡ Projections adjusted to reflect data obtained from a partial population count carried out on 1 April 2007, when the total population was estimated at 183,987,291.

POPULATION BY AGE AND SEX

(official projected estimates at mid-2010)

	Males	Females	Total
0–14	25,080,983	24,358,469	49,439,452
15–64	63,970,759	66,648,690	130,619,449
65 and over	5,741,210	7,452,493	13,193,703
Total	94,792,952	98,459,652	193,252,604

ADMINISTRATIVE DIVISIONS

(official population projections at mid-2009)

State	Area (sq km)	Population	Density (per sq km)	Capital
Acre (AC)	152,581	691,132	4.5	Rio Branco
Alagoas (AL)	27,768	3,156,108	113.7	Maceió
Amapá (AP)	142,815	626,609	4.4	Macapá
Amazonas (AM)	1,570,746	3,393,369	2.2	Manaus
Bahia (BA)	564,693	14,637,364	25.9	Salvador
Ceará (CE)	148,826	8,547,809	57.4	Fortaleza
Espírito Santo (ES)	46,078	3,487,199	75.7	Vitória
Goiás (GO)	340,087	5,926,300	17.4	Goiânia
Maranhão (MA)	331,983	6,367,138	19.2	São Luís
Mato Grosso (MT)	903,358	3,001,692	3.3	Cuiabá
Mato Grosso do Sul (MS)	357,125	2,360,498	6.6	Campo Grande
Minas Gerais (MG)	586,528	20,033,665	34.2	Belo Horizonte
Pará (PA)	1,247,690	7,431,020	6.0	Belém
Paraíba (PB)	56,440	3,769,977	66.8	João Pessoa
Paraná (PR)	199,315	10,686,247	53.6	Curitiba
Pernambuco (PE)	98,312	8,810,256	89.6	Recife
Piauí (PI)	251,529	3,145,325	12.5	Teresina
Rio de Janeiro (RJ)	43,696	16,010,429	366.4	Rio de Janeiro
Rio Grande do Norte (RN)	52,797	3,137,541	59.4	Natal
Rio Grande do Sul (RS)	281,749	10,914,128	38.7	Porto Alegre
Rondônia (RO)	237,576	1,503,928	6.3	Porto Velho
Roraima (RR)	224,299	421,499	1.9	Boa Vista
Santa Catarina (SC)	95,346	6,118,743	64.2	Florianópolis
São Paulo (SP)	248,209	41,384,039	166.7	São Paulo
Sergipe (SE)	21,910	2,019,679	92.2	Aracaju
Tocantins (TO)	277,621	1,292,051	4.7	Palmas
Distrito Federal (DF)	5,802	2,606,885	449.3	Brasília
Total	8,514,877	191,480,630	22.5	—

PRINCIPAL TOWNS

(official projections at mid-2009)*

São Paulo	11,037,593	Santo André	673,396
Rio de Janeiro	6,186,710	Uberlândia	634,345
Salvador	2,998,056	Contagem	625,393
Brasília (capital)	2,606,885	São José dos Campos	615,871
Fortaleza	2,505,552	Feira de Santana	591,707
Belo Horizonte	2,452,617	Sorocaba	584,313
Curitiba	1,851,215	Ribeirão Preto	563,107
Manaus	1,738,641	Cuiabá	550,562
Recife	1,561,659	Aracaju	544,039
Belém	1,437,600	Juíz de Fora	526,706
Porto Alegre	1,436,123	Aparecida de Goiânia	510,770
Guarulhos	1,299,283	Londrina	510,707
Goiânia	1,281,975	Ananindeua	505,512
Campinas	1,064,669	Belford Roxo	501,544
São Luís	997,098	Joinville	497,331
São Gonçalo	991,382	Niterói	479,384
Maceió	936,314	São João de Meriti	469,827
Duque de Caxias	872,762	Betim	441,748
Nova Iguaçu	865,089	Campos dos Goytacazes	434,008
São Bernardo do Campo	810,979	São José do Rio Preto	419,632
Natal	806,203	Mauá	417,458
Teresina	802,537	Santos	417,098
Campo Grande	755,107	Vila Velha	413,548
Osasco	718,646	Caxias do Sul	410,166
João Pessoa	702,235	Florianópolis	408,161
Jaboatão dos Guararapes	687,688		

* Figures refer to *municípios*, which may contain rural districts.

BIRTHS, MARRIAGES AND DEATHS
(official estimates based on annual registrations)

	Live births		Marriages	Deaths	
	Number*	Rate (per 1,000)	Number	Number	Rate (per 1,000)
2003	3,426,727	19.2	748,981	993,685	5.6
2004	3,329,120	18.4	806,968	1,013,657	5.6
2005	3,329,431	18.2	835,846	996,931	5.4
2006	3,172,000	17.1	889,828	1,023,814	5.5
2007	3,080,266	16.4	916,006	1,036,405	5.5
2008	3,107,927	16.4	959,901	1,060,365	5.6

* Including births registered but not occurring during that year: 604,265 in 2003; 510,202 in 2004; 448,243 in 2005; 368,062 in 2006; 324,895 in 2007; 309,885 in 2008.

Life expectancy (official estimates, years at birth): 72.9 (males 69.1; females 76.7) in 2008.

ECONOMICALLY ACTIVE POPULATION
('000 persons aged 10 years and over, labour force sample survey at September)*

	2006	2007	2008
Agriculture, hunting, forestry and fishing	17,264	16,579	16,100
Industry (excl. construction)	13,236	13,846	13,995
Manufacturing industries	12,497	13,105	13,266
Construction	5,837	6,107	6,905
Commerce and repair of motor vehicles and household goods	15,748	16,309	16,093
Hotels and restaurants	3,395	3,351	3,592
Transport, storage and communication	4,064	4,374	4,596
Public administration	4,452	4,504	4,531
Education, health and social services	8,018	8,379	8,539
Domestic services	6,782	6,732	6,626
Other community, social and personal services	3,800	3,711	4,083
Other activities	6,505	6,684	7,134
Sub-total	89,100	90,577	92,194
Activities not adequately defined	218	209	201
Total employed	89,318	90,786	92,395
Unemployed	8,210	8,060	7,106
Total labour force	97,528	98,846	99,500

* Data coverage excludes rural areas of Acre, Amapá, Amazonas, Pará, Rondônia and Roraima.

Health and Welfare

KEY INDICATORS

Total fertility rate (children per woman, 2008)	1.9
Under-5 mortality rate (per 1,000 live births, 2008)	22
HIV/AIDS (% of persons aged 15–49, 2007)	0.6
Physicians (per 1,000 head, 2000)	1.2
Hospital beds (per 1,000 head, 2002)	2.6
Health expenditure (2007): US $ per head (PPP)	762
Health expenditure (2007): % of GDP	5.7
Health expenditure (2007): public (% of total)	74.6
Access to water (% of persons, 2008)	97
Access to sanitation (% of persons, 2008)	80
Total carbon dioxide emissions ('000 metric tons, 2006)	352,268.0
Carbon dioxide emissions per head (metric tons, 2006)	1.9
Human Development Index (2007): ranking	75
Human Development Index (2007): value	0.813

For sources and definitions, see explanatory note on p. vi.

Agriculture

PRINCIPAL CROPS
('000 metric tons)

	2006	2007	2008
Wheat	2,485	4,114	5,886
Rice, paddy	11,527	11,061	12,100
Barley	203	236	237
Maize	42,662	52,112	59,018
Oats	406	238	232
Sorghum	1,605	1,441	1,966
Buckwheat*	51	52	52
Potatoes	3,152	3,551	3,676
Sweet potatoes	519	530	519*
Cassava (Manioc)	26,639	26,541	25,878
Yams*	240	250	250
Sugar cane	477,411	549,707	648,921
Beans, dry	3,458	3,169	3,461
Brazil nuts, with shell	29	30	30*
Cashew nuts, with shell	244	141	240
Soybeans (Soya beans)	52,465	57,857	59,917
Groundnuts, with shell	250	263	297
Coconuts	2,978	2,831	2,759
Oil palm fruit*	590	660	660
Castor oil seed	95	113	120
Sunflower seed	87	105	146
Tomatoes	3,363	3,431	3,934
Onions, dry	1,346	1,360	1,300
Garlic	88	99	92
Watermelons	1,947	2,093	1,950*
Cantaloupes and other melons	500	495	510*
Bananas	6,956	7,098	7,117
Oranges	18,032	18,685	18,390
Tangerines, mandarins, clementines and satsumas	1,270	1,206	1,273*
Lemons and limes	1,031	1,019	1,040*
Grapefruit and pomelos*	71	72	72
Apples	863	1,115	1,121
Peaches and nectarines	200	186	200*
Grapes	1,257	1,372	1,403
Guavas, mangoes, mangosteens	1,217	1,272	1,272*
Avocados	164	154	166*
Pineapples	2,561	2,676	2,492
Persimmons	168	160	169*
Cashew-apple*	1,660	1,660	1,660
Papayas	1,898	1,812	1,900*
Coffee, green	2,573	2,249	2,791
Cocoa beans	212	202	208
Mate	434	438	436*
Sisal	248	245	246
Tobacco, unmanufactured	900	909	850
Natural rubber	105	113	114*

* FAO estimate(s).

Aggregate production ('000 metric tons, may include official, semi-official or estimated data): Total cereals 59,149 in 2006, 69,442 in 2007, 79,682 in 2008; Total roots and tubers 30,549 in 2006, 30,871 in 2007, 30,323 in 2008; Total vegetables (incl. melons) 9,643 in 2006, 9,888 in 2007, 10,196 in 2008; Total fruits (excl. melons) 38,012 in 2006, 39,195 in 2007, 38,988 in 2008.

Source: FAO.

LIVESTOCK
('000 head, year ending September)

	2006	2007	2008
Cattle	205,886	199,752	175,437*
Buffaloes	1,157	1,132	1,132†
Horses	5,749	5,602	5,650†
Asses	1,187	1,163	1,163†
Mules	1,386	1,343	1,343†
Pigs	35,174	35,945	40,000†
Sheep	16,019	16,239	16,500†
Goats	10,401	9,450	9,500†
Chickens	1,011,516	1,127,658	1,200,000†
Ducks†	3,600	3,600	3,600
Turkeys†	16,800	22,000	23,000

* Unofficial figure.
† FAO estimate(s).

Source: FAO.

LIVESTOCK PRODUCTS
('000 metric tons)

	2006	2007	2008
Cattle meat*	9,020	9,303	9,024
Sheep meat†	77	78	79
Goat meat†	29	29	29
Pig meat*	2,830	2,990	3,015
Horse meat†	21	22	22
Chicken meat	8,164	8,988	10,216
Cows' milk	26,186	26,944	27,752*
Goats' milk†	135	137	137
Hen eggs	1,760	1,779	1,825†
Other poultry eggs	74	79	79†
Natural honey	36	35	35†
Wool, greasy	11	11	11†

* Unofficial figure(s).
† FAO estimate(s).

Source: FAO.

Forestry

ROUNDWOOD REMOVALS
('000 cubic metres, excl. bark, FAO estimates)

	2006	2007	2008
Sawlogs, veneer logs and logs for sleepers	54,903	52,243	49,355
Pulpwood	55,115	60,964	58,182
Other industrial wood	8,736	8,313	7,853
Fuel wood	138,783	139,831	140,916
Total	257,537	261,351	256,306

Source: FAO.

SAWNWOOD PRODUCTION
('000 cubic metres, incl. railway sleepers)

	2006	2007	2008*
Coniferous (softwood)	9,078	9,577	9,532
Broadleaved (hardwood)	14,719	14,837	15,455
Total	23,797	24,414	24,987

* Unofficial figures.

Source: FAO.

Fishing

('000 metric tons, live weight)

	2006	2007	2008*
Capture	779.1	783.2	775.0
Characins	100.2	95.4	95.4
Freshwater siluroids	44.8	40.3	40.3
Weakfishes	42.3	46.5	46.5
Whitemouth croaker	45.6	44.4	44.4
Brazilian sardinella	54.2	55.9	55.9
Aquaculture	271.7	289.1	290.2
Common carp	45.8	36.6	36.6
Tilapias	71.3	95.1	96.0
Whiteleg shrimp	65.0	65.0	65.0
Total catch	1,050.8	1,072.2	1,065.2

* FAO estimates.

Note: Figures exclude aquatic mammals, recorded by number rather than by weight. The number of whales and dolphins caught was: 256 in 2006; 1,799 in 2007; 27 in 2008. Also excluded are crocodiles: the number of broad-nosed, black and spectacled caimans caught was: 723 in 2006; 10,254 in 2007; 8 in 2008.

Source: FAO.

Mining

('000 metric tons, unless otherwise indicated)

	2006	2007	2008[1]
Hard coal[2]	6,220	6,697	6,732
Crude petroleum ('000 barrels)	628,797	638,018	876,000
Natural gas (million cu m)	17,706	18,152	18,941
Iron ore:			
gross weight	317,800	354,674	351,677
metal content	211,020	235,504	233,514
Copper (metric tons)	219,700	218,367	220,000
Nickel ore (metric tons)[3]	82,492	58,317	54,060
Bauxite	23,236	25,461	28,098
Lead concentrates (metric tons)[3]	25,764	24,574	24,600
Zinc (metric tons)	272,311	265,126	248,874
Tin concentrates (metric tons)[3]	9,030	9,634	10,558
Chromium ore (metric tons)[4]	228,721	253,254	256,300
Tungsten concentrates (metric tons)[3]	525	537	550
Ilmenite (metric tons)	127,200	130,000	130,000
Rutile (metric tons)	2,100	3,000	3,000
Zirconium concentrates (metric tons)[5]	25,120	26,739	26,739
Silver (kg)[6]	30,000	36,000	36,500
Gold (kg)[7]	43,082	50,000	54,000
Bentonite (beneficiated)	235	239	239
Kaolin (beneficiated)	2,455	2,480	2,674
Magnesite (beneficiated)	383	399	399
Phosphate rock[8]	5,932	6,185	6,343
Potash salts[9]	403	424	383
Fluorspar (Fluorite) (metric tons)[10]	63,604	65,924	63,573
Barite (Barytes) (beneficiated) (metric tons)	19,151	13,311	7,321
Quartz (natural crystals) (metric tons)	14,195	22,561	22,600
Salt (unrefined):			
marine	5,122	5,365	5,370
rock	1,622	1,621	1,650
Gypsum and anhydrite (crude)	1,712	1,923	1,923
Graphite (natural) (metric tons)	76,194	76,194	76,200
Asbestos (fibre) (metric tons)	227,304	254,204	287,673
Mica (metric tons)[11]	4,000	4,000	4,000
Vermiculite concentrates (metric tons)	19,279	18,952	20,089
Talc (crude)	389	401	401
Pyrophyllite (crude)[11]	200	200	200
Diamonds, gem and industrial ('000 carats)[11,12]	181	182	182

[1] Preliminary figures.
[2] Figures refer to marketable products.
[3] Figures refer to the metal content of ores and concentrates.
[4] Figures refer to the chromic oxide (Cr_2O_3) content.
[5] Including production of baddeleyite-caldasite.
[6] Figures refer to primary production only. The production of secondary silver (in kilograms, estimated production) was: 39,000 in 2006; 32,000 in 2007; 32,500 in 2008 (preliminary figure).
[7] Including official production by independent miners (*garimpeiros*): 5,175 kg in 2006; 5,210 kg in 2007; 5,627 in 2008 (preliminary figure).
[8] Figures refer to the gross weight of concentrates. The phosphoric acid (P_2O_5) content (in '000 metric tons) was: 2,111 in 2006; 2,185 in 2007; 2,242 in 2008 (preliminary figure).
[9] Figures refer to the potassium oxide (K_2O) content.
[10] Acid-grade and metallurgical-grade concentrates.
[11] Estimated production.
[12] Figures refer to officially reported diamond output plus official Brazilian estimates of diamond output by independent miners (*garimpeiros*).

Source: US Geological Survey.

Industry

SELECTED PRODUCTS

('000 metric tons, unless otherwise indicated)

	2005	2006	2007
Beef—fresh or chilled	3,179	3,277	3,425
Frozen poultry meats and giblets	4,332	4,294	5,464
Sugar (granulated)	20,356	20,479	18,230
Beer ('000 hl)	92,148	100,176	100,203
Soft drinks ('000 hl)	103,474	115,860	126,422
Gas-diesel oil (distillate fuel oil, '000 cu m)	39,244	43,005	40,658
Residual fuel oils ('000 cu m)	18,354	16,197	26,817
Naphthas for petrochemicals ('000 cu m)	9,905	10,605	11,915
Liquefied petroleum gas	11,467	11,595	12,171
Ethylene—unsaturated	3,019	3,103	2,830
Fertilizers with nitrogen, phosphorus and potassium	17,084	16,923	18,377
Chemical wood pulp, cellulose	7,099	7,147	7,894
Iron	10,326	10,110	10,504
Iron ore*	297,365	429,958	456,453
Hot rolled coils of carbon steel—uncoated	4,983	5,222	6,345
Motor vehicles (units)	2,122,117	2,178,148	2,473,586
Trucks (units)†	105,579	87,543	106,235
Motorcycles (units)	1,170,459	1,373,932	1,759,425
Mobile cellular telephones (units)	64,284,671	61,720,056	68,432,559

* Prepared forms, including concentrates, ball bearings, etc.

† Vehicles with diesel engines and maximum load capacity in excess of five metric tons.

Electric energy (million kWh): 402,938 in 2005; 419,336 in 2006; 444,583 in 2007 (Source: UN Industrial Commodity Statistics Database).

Finance

CURRENCY AND EXCHANGE RATES

Monetary Units

100 centavos = 1 real (plural: reais).

Sterling, Dollar and Euro Equivalents (31 May 2010)

£1 sterling = 2.648 reais;
US \$1 = 1.816 reais;
€1 = 2.249 reais;
100 reais = £37.77 = \$55.07 = €44.47.

Average Exchange Rates (reais per US \$)

2007	1.9471
2008	1.8338
2009	1.9994

Note: In March 1986 the cruzeiro (CR \$) was replaced by a new currency unit, the cruzado (CZ \$), equivalent to 1,000 cruzeiros. In January 1989 the cruzado was, in turn, replaced by the new cruzado (NCZ \$), equivalent to CZ \$1,000 and initially at par with the US dollar (US \$). In March 1990 the new cruzado was replaced by the cruzeiro (CR \$), at an exchange rate of one new cruzado for one cruzeiro. In August 1993 the cruzeiro was replaced by the cruzeiro real, equivalent to CR \$1,000. On 1 March 1994, in preparation for the introduction of a new currency, a transitional accounting unit, the Unidade Real de Valor (at par with the US \$), came into operation, alongside the cruzeiro real. On 1 July 1994 the cruzeiro real was replaced by the real (R \$), also at par with the US \$ and thus equivalent to 2,750 cruzeiros reais.

BUDGET

(R \$ million)

Revenue	2007	2008	2009
National treasury revenues	477,142	551,344	555,054
Gross revenues*	490,924	564,723	569,846
Taxes and welfare contributions	432,556	484,702	n.a.
Restitutions	−13,772	−13,388	−14,737
Fiscal incentives	−10	−1	−55
Social security revenues	140,412	163,355	182,008
Urban	136,166	158,383	177,444
Rural	4,245	4,973	4,564
Central bank revenues	1,319	1,959	2,242
Total	618,873	716,658	739,305

Expenditure	2007	2008	2009
Transfers to state and local governments	105,605	133,076	127,684
Treasury expenditures	268,186	295,907	344,657
Payroll*	116,372	130,829	151,653
Worker support fund (FAT)	18,472	21,026	27,433
Economic subsidies and grants†	10,021	5,980	5,411
Assistance benefits (LOAS/RMV)	14,192	16,036	18,946
Other current and capital expenditures	108,608	120,993	140,035
Transfer to central bank	521	1,043	1,180
Social security benefits	185,293	199,562	224,876
Central bank expenditures	1,964	2,431	2,872
Sovereign Fund of Brazil‡	—	14,244	—
Total	561,048	645,220	700,089

* Excludes the employer share of federal civil service payments from revenues originating in contributions to the Social Security Plan (CPSS) and personnel outlays.

† Includes outlays on grants to regional funds and spending on the restructuring of liabilities.

‡ Expenses related to paid-in capital for the Fiscal Investment and Stabilization Fund (FFIE) from the Sovereign Fund of Brazil.

Source: Ministério da Fazenda, Brasília, DF.

CENTRAL BANK RESERVES

(US \$ million at 31 December)

	2007	2008	2009
Gold (national valuation)	901	940	1,175
IMF special drawing rights	2	1	1
Foreign exchange	179,431	192,843	231,888
Total	180,334	193,784	233,064

Source: IMF, *International Financial Statistics*.

MONEY SUPPLY

(R \$ million at 31 December)

	2007	2008	2009
Currency outside depository corporations	82,166	92,360	105,816
Transferable deposits	149,820	130,017	143,091
Other deposits	1,403,181	1,695,406	1,971,284
Securities other than shares	10,898	24,621	29,481
Broad money	1,646,064	1,942,404	2,249,672

Source: IMF, *International Financial Statistics*.

COST OF LIVING
(Consumer Price Index; base: 2000 = 100)

	2004	2005	2006
Food	146.5	151.0	151.0
Clothing and footwear	135.2	147.3	156.1
Rent	148.6	158.3	165.7
All items (incl. others)	141.7	151.4	157.8

2007: Food 161.2; All items (incl. others) 163.5.

2008: Food 182.3; All items (incl. others) 172.8.

2009: All items 181.2.

Source: ILO.

NATIONAL ACCOUNTS
(R$ million at current prices)

National Income and Product

	2007	2008	2009
Gross domestic product (GDP) in market prices	2,661,344	3,004,881	3,143,015
Wages and salaries	875	1,041	1,218
Primary incomes received from abroad (net)	–55,684	–72,815	–65,296
Gross national income (GNI)	2,606,534	2,933,107	3,078,937
Current transfers received from abroad (net)	7,829	7,916	6,684
Net national disposable income	2,614,363	2,941,023	3,085,621

Expenditure on the Gross Domestic Product

	2007	2008	2009
Final consumption expenditure	2,133,196	2,400,746	2,626,525
Households; Non-profit institutions serving households	1,594,134	1,812,467	1,972,431
General government	539,062	588,279	654,094
Gross capital formation	487,761	598,382	518,951
Gross fixed capital formation	464,137	560,892	525,838
Changes in inventories; Acquisitions, less disposals, of valuables	23,624	37,490	–6,887
Total domestic expenditure	2,620,957	2,999,128	3,145,476
Exports of goods and services	355,671	414,257	354,235
Less Imports of goods and services	315,283	408,505	356,696
GDP in market prices	2,661,344	3,004,881	3,143,015
GDP at constant 2000 prices*	1,492,381	1,569,089	1,566,108

* Source: IMF, *International Financial Statistics*.

Gross Domestic Product by Economic Activity

	2007	2008	2009
Agriculture, hunting, forestry and fishing	127,267	151,268	163,953
Mining and quarrying	53,669	82,652	35,913
Manufacturing	389,620	399,749	418,789
Electricity, gas and water	81,791	88,332	94,365
Construction	111,201	128,206	137,378
Trade, restaurants and hotels	277,371	317,675	321,064
Transport, storage and communications	109,783	129,929	138,014
Information services	87,731	92,484	98,465
Financial intermediation, insurance, and related services	175,608	193,149	195,978
Real estate and renting	194,457	208,359	227,389
Government, health and education services	353,724	401,557	450,296
Other services	325,640	362,946	420,496
Gross value added in basic prices	2,287,858	2,556,304	2,702,100
Taxes, less subsidies, on products	373,486	448,577	440,913
GDP in market prices	2,661,344	3,004,881	3,143,015

Note: Totals may not be equal to the sum of components, owing to rounding.

BALANCE OF PAYMENTS
(US$ million)

	2007	2008	2009
Exports of goods f.o.b.	160,649	197,942	152,995
Imports of goods f.o.b.	–120,617	–173,107	–127,647
Trade balance	40,032	24,836	25,347
Exports of services	23,954	30,451	27,750
Imports of services	–37,173	–47,140	–47,011
Balance on goods and services	26,813	8,146	6,087
Other income received	11,493	12,511	8,826
Other income paid	–40,784	–53,073	–42,510
Balance on goods, services and income	–2,478	–32,416	–27,597
Current transfers received	4,972	5,317	4,661
Current transfers paid	–943	–1,093	–1,398
Current balance	1,551	–28,192	–24,334
Capital account (net)	756	1,055	1,129
Direct investment abroad	–7,067	–20,457	10,084
Direct investment from abroad	34,585	45,058	25,949
Portfolio investment assets	286	1,900	2,975
Portfolio investment liabilities	48,104	–767	46,159
Financial derivatives assets	88	298	322
Financial derivatives liabilities	–799	–610	–166
Other investment assets	–18,552	–5,269	–33,141
Other investment liabilities	31,683	8,143	17,229
Net errors and omissions	–3,152	1,810	1,373
Overall balance	87,484	2,969	47,578

Source: IMF, *International Financial Statistics*.

External Trade

PRINCIPAL COMMODITIES
(US$ million)

Imports f.o.b.	2006	2007	2008
Capital goods	18,924	25,125	35,932
Industrial machinery	5,310	7,356	10,992
Parts of capital goods for industry	2,109	4,186	5,420
Moveable transport equipment	1,405	1,882	3,487
Parts and accessories of industrial machinery	1,352	1,825	2,418
Consumer goods	11,955	16,027	22,526
Non-durable goods	5,879	7,776	9,816
Foodstuffs	1,728	2,082	2,812
Pharmaceuticals	2,171	2,908	3,493
Durable goods	6,076	8,251	12,710
Passenger vehicles	1,914	3,121	5,343
Mineral fuels and lubricants	15,197	20,085	31,464
Raw materials and intermediate goods	45,274	59,381	83,056
Chemicals and pharmaceutical goods	12,240	15,672	21,185
Intermediate goods and parts thereof	7,818	8,839	11,132
Minerals	9,205	11,631	15,447
Transport equipment, parts and spares	553	768	990
Agricultural products (excl. foodstuffs)	3,036	5,529	10,955
Total (incl. others)	91,351	120,617	172,978

Exports f.o.b.	2006	2007	2008
Basic goods	40,285	51,596	73,028
Iron ore and concentrates	8,949	10,558	16,539
Crude petroleum and fuels	6,894	8,905	13,556
Soybeans and products thereof	5,663	6,709	10,952
Coffee (not roasted)	2,928	3,378	4,131
Beef and poultry	7,082	8,935	n.a.
Semi-manufactured goods	19,523	21,800	27,073
Sugar (raw)	3,936	3,130	3,650
Iron and steel in primary forms	2,277	2,340	4,002
Wood pulp	2,479	3,012	3,901
Manufactured goods	75,018	83,943	92,683
Passenger cars	4,597	4,653	4,916
Aeroplanes	3,241	4,719	5,495
Parts and accessories for motor vehicles and tractors	2,972	3,186	3,510
Flat-rolled products of iron or non-alloy steel	2,718	2,532	1,921
Devices, transmitters, receivers and components	3,068	2,353	2,550
Total (incl. others)	137,807	160,649	197,942

PRINCIPAL TRADING PARTNERS
(US $ million)*

Imports f.o.b.	2006	2007	2008
Argentina	8,053	10,404	13,258
Belgium-Luxembourg	997	1,191	1,689
Canada	1,194	1,708	3,210
Chile	2,866	3,462	3,952
China, People's Republic	7,990	12,621	20,044
France	2,838	3,525	4,678
Germany	6,503	8,669	12,027
Italy	2,570	3,348	4,613
Japan	3,840	4,609	6,807
Korea, Republic	3,106	3,391	5,413
Mexico	1,310	1,979	3,125
Netherlands	786	1,116	1,477
Paraguay	296	434	657
Spain	1,431	1,843	2,472
United Kingdom	1,417	1,956	2,551
USA	14,817	18,888	25,810
Uruguay	618	786	1,018
Total (incl. others)	91,351	120,617	172,978

Exports f.o.b.	2006	2007	2008
Argentina	11,740	14,417	17,606
Belgium-Luxembourg	3,015	3,912	4,494
Canada	2,281	2,362	1,866
Chile	3,914	4,264	4,792
China, People's Republic	8,402	10,749	16,403
France	2,669	3,472	4,126
Germany	5,691	7,211	8,851
Italy	3,836	4,464	4,765
Japan	3,895	4,321	6,115
Korea, Republic	1,963	2,047	3,119
Mexico	4,458	4,260	4,281
Netherlands	5,749	8,841	10,483
Paraguay	1,234	1,648	2,488
Spain	2,330	3,476	4,074
United Kingdom	2,829	3,301	3,792
USA	24,773	25,314	27,648
Uruguay	1,013	1,288	1,644
Total (incl. others)	137,807	160,649	197,942

* Imports by country of purchase; exports by country of last consignment.

Transport

RAILWAYS
(figures are rounded)

	2003	2004	2005
Passengers ('000)			
Long distance	1,553	1,557	1,451
Metropolitan	133,900	141,900	144,300
Passenger-km ('000, long distance only)	469,330	475,186	451,943
Freight ('000 metric tons)	345,111	377,776	388,592
Freight ton-km (million)	182,644	205,711	221,633

Source: Agência Nacional de Transportes Terrestres (ANTT), Ministério dos Transportes, Brasília.

ROAD TRAFFIC
(motor vehicles in use at 31 December)

	2004	2005	2006
Passenger cars	24,936,541	26,309,256	27,868,564
Lorries	1,636,535	1,703,715	1,768,221
Vans	1,218,922	1,674,532	2,036,030
Coaches	2,661,614	2,441,858	2,328,596
Motorcycles and mopeds	7,039,675	8,070,148	9,360,696
Total (incl. others)	39,240,875	42,071,961	45,372,640

2007 (motor vehicles in use at 31 December): Passenger cars 30,282,855; Vans and lorries 5,709,063; Buses and coaches 1,985,761; Motorcycles and mopeds 10,921,686; Total 48,899,365 (Source: IRF, *World Road Statistics*).

SHIPPING

Merchant Fleet
(registered at 31 December)

	2006	2007	2008
Number of vessels	525	538	569
Total displacement ('000 grt)	2,281	2,290	2,359

Source: Lloyd's Register-Fairplay, *World Fleet Statistics*.

International Sea-borne Freight Traffic
('000 metric tons)

	2003	2004	2005
Goods loaded	376,188	417,723	452,742
Goods unloaded	194,602	202,997	196,677

CIVIL AVIATION
(embarked passengers, mail and cargo)

	2006	2007	2008
Number of passengers ('000)	47,702	51,029	56,205
Passenger-km (million)*	49,218	52,045	n.a.
Freight ton-km ('000)†	7,728,482	7,832,290	8,403,749

* Source: UN Economic Commission for Latin America and the Caribbean, *Statistical Yearbook*.

† Including mail.

Source: mostly Departamento de Aviação Civil (DAC), Comando da Aeronáutica, Ministério da Defesa, Brasília.

Tourism

FOREIGN TOURIST ARRIVALS

Country of origin	2007	2008	2009
Argentina	921,679	1,017,675	1,211,159
Bolivia	61,990	84,072	83,454
Canada	63,983	62,681	63,296
Chile	260,439	240,087	170,491
France	254,367	214,440	205,860
Germany	257,740	254,264	215,595
Italy	268,685	265,724	253,545
Japan	63,381	81,270	66,655
Mexico	58,804	77,193	68,028
Netherlands	83,566	81,936	75,518
Paraguay	212,022	217,709	180,373
Portugal	280,438	222,558	183,697
Spain	216,891	202,624	174,526
Switzerland	72,763	61,169	72,736
United Kingdom	176,970	181,179	172,643
USA	695,749	625,506	603,674
Uruguay	226,111	199,403	189,412
Total (incl. others)	5,025,834	5,050,099	4,802,217

Source: Instituto Brasileiro de Turismo—EMBRATUR, Brasília.

Receipts from tourism (US $ million, excluding passenger transport): 4,316 in 2006; 4,953 in 2007; 5,785 in 2008 (provisional) (Source: World Tourism Organization).

Communications Media

	2007	2008	2009
Telephones in use ('000 main lines)	39,399.6	41,235.2	41,497.0
Mobile cellular telephones ('000 subscribers)	120,980.1	150,641.4	173,959.4
Internet users ('000)*	58,717.0	72,027.7	75,943.6
Broadband subscribers ('000)	7,609.5	10,098.0	14,540.9

* Estimates.

Personal computers: 30,000,000 (161.2 per 1,000 persons) in 2005.

Source: International Telecommunication Union.

Radio receivers ('000 in use): 71,000 in 1997 (Source: UNESCO, *Statistical Yearbook*).

Television receivers ('000 in use): 58,283 in 2000 (Source: International Telecommunication Union (ITU)).

Book production ('000 titles): 21,689 in 1998 (Source: UNESCO Institute for Statistics).

Daily newspapers: 532 (average circulation, '000 copies): 6,552 in 2004 (Source: UNESCO Institute for Statistics).

Non-daily newspapers: 2,472 in 2004 (Source: UNESCO Institute for Statistics).

Education

(2009, unless otherwise indicated)

	Institutions	Teachers	Students
Pre-primary	106,563	309,881*	6,699,109
Literacy classes (Classe de Alfabetização)†	27,670	37,508	598,589
Primary	152,251	1,665,341*	31,512,884
Secondary	25,923	519,935*	8,288,520
Higher‡	2,252	338,890	5,080,056

* 2006 figure.
† 2003 figures.
‡ Preliminary figures for 2008.

Source: Ministério da Educação, Brasília.

Pupil-teacher ratio (primary education, UN estimate): 23 in 2007/08 (Source: UNESCO Institute for Statistics).

Adult literacy rate (UNESCO estimates): 90.0% (males 89.8%; females 90.2%) in 2007 (Source: UNESCO Institute for Statistics).

Directory

The Constitution

A new Constitution was promulgated on 5 October 1988. The following is a summary of the main provisions:

The Federative Republic of Brazil, formed by the indissoluble union of the States, the Municipalities and the Federal District, is constituted as a democratic state. All power emanates from the people. The Federative Republic of Brazil seeks the economic, political, social and cultural integration of the peoples of Latin America.

All are equal before the law. The inviolability of the right to life, freedom, equality, security and property is guaranteed. No one shall be subjected to torture. Freedom of thought, conscience, religious belief and expression are guaranteed, as is privacy. The principles of habeas corpus and 'habeas data' (the latter giving citizens access to personal information held in government data banks) are granted. There is freedom of association, and the right to strike is guaranteed.

There is universal suffrage by direct secret ballot. Voting is compulsory for literate persons between 18 and 69 years of age, and optional for those who are illiterate, those over 70 years of age and those aged 16 and 17.

Brasília is the federal capital. The Union's competence includes maintaining relations with foreign states, and taking part in international organizations; declaring war and making peace; guaranteeing national defence; decreeing a state of siege; issuing currency; supervising credits, etc.; formulating and implementing plans for economic and social development; maintaining national services, including communications, energy, the judiciary and the police; legislating on civil, commercial, penal, procedural, electoral, agrarian, maritime, aeronautical, spatial and labour law, etc. The Union, States, Federal District and Municipalities must protect the Constitution, laws and democratic institutions, and preserve national heritage.

The States are responsible for electing their Governors by universal suffrage and direct secret ballot for a four-year term. The organization of the Municipalities, the Federal District and the Territories is regulated by law.

The Union may intervene in the States and in the Federal District only in certain circumstances, such as a threat to national security or public order, and then only after reference to the Congresso Nacional (National Congress).

LEGISLATIVE POWER

Legislative power is exercised by the Congresso Nacional (National Congress), which is composed of the Câmara dos Deputados (Chamber of Deputies) and the Senado Federal (Federal Senate). Elections for deputies and senators take place simultaneously throughout the country; candidates for the Congresso must be Brazilian by birth and have full exercise of their political rights. They must be at least 21 years of age in the case of deputies and at least 35 years of age in the case of senators. The Congresso meets twice a year in ordinary sessions, and extraordinary sessions may be convened by the President of the Republic, the Presidents of the Câmara and the Senado, or at the request of the majority of the members of either house.

The Câmara is made up of representatives of the people, elected by a system of proportional representation in each State, Territory and the Federal District for a period of four years. The total number of deputies representing the States and the Federal District will be established in proportion to the population; each Territory will elect four deputies.

The Senado is composed of representatives of the States and the Federal District, elected according to the principle of majority. Each State and the Federal District will elect three senators with a mandate of eight years, with elections after four years for one-third of the members and after another four years for the remaining two-thirds. Each Senator is elected with two substitutes. The Senado approves, by secret ballot, the choice of Magistrates (when required by the Constitution), of the Attorney-General of the Republic, of the Ministers of the Accounts Tribunal, of the Territorial Governors, of the president and directors of the central bank and of the permanent heads of diplomatic missions.

The Congresso is responsible for deciding on all matters within the competence of the Union, especially fiscal and budgetary arrangements, national, regional and local plans and programmes, the strength of the armed forces, and territorial limits. It is also responsible for making definitive resolutions on international treaties, and for authorizing the President to declare war.

The powers of the Câmara include authorizing the instigation of legal proceedings against the President and Vice-President of the Republic and Ministers of State. The Senado may indict and impose sentence on the President and Vice-President of the Republic and Ministers of State.

Constitutional amendments may be proposed by at least one-third of the members of either house, by the President or by more than one-half of the legislative assemblies of the units of the Federation. Amendments must be ratified by three-fifths of the members of each house. The Constitution may not be amended during times of national emergency, such as a state of siege.

EXECUTIVE POWER

Executive power is exercised by the President of the Republic, aided by the Ministers of State. Candidates for the Presidency and Vice-Presidency must be Brazilian-born, be in full exercise of their political rights and be over 35 years of age. The candidate who obtains an absolute majority of votes will be elected President. If no candidate attains an absolute majority, the two candidates who have received the most votes proceed to a second round of voting, at which the candidate obtaining the majority of valid votes will be elected President. The President holds office for a term of four years and (under an amendment adopted in 1997) is eligible for re-election.

The Ministers of State are chosen by the President, and their duties include countersigning acts and decrees signed by the President, expediting instructions for the enactment of laws, decrees and regulations, and presentation to the President of an annual report of their activities.

The Council of the Republic is the higher consultative organ of the President of the Republic. It comprises the Vice-President of the Republic, the Presidents of the Câmara and Senado, the leaders of the majority and of the minority in each house, the Minister of Justice, two members appointed by the President of the Republic, two elected by the Senado and two elected by the Câmara, the latter six having a mandate of three years.

The National Defence Council advises the President on matters relating to national sovereignty and defence. It comprises the Vice-President of the Republic, the Presidents of the Câmara and Senado, the Minister of Justice, military Ministers and the Ministers of Foreign Affairs and of Planning.

JUDICIAL POWER

Judicial power in the Union is exercised by the Supreme Federal Court; the Higher Court of Justice; the Regional Federal Courts and federal judges; Labour Courts and judges; Electoral Courts and judges; Military Courts and judges; and the States' Courts and judges. Judges are appointed for life; they may not undertake any other employment. The Courts elect their own controlling organs and organize their own internal structure.

The Supreme Federal Court, situated in the Union capital, has jurisdiction over the whole national territory and is composed of 11 ministers. The ministers are nominated by the President after approval by the Senado, from Brazilian-born citizens, between the ages of 35 and 65 years, of proved judicial knowledge and experience.

The Government

HEAD OF STATE

President: LUIZ INÁCIO LULA DA SILVA (PT) (took office 2 January 2003, re-elected 29 October 2006).

Vice-President: JOSÉ ALENCAR GOMES DA SILVA (PRB).

THE CABINET
(July 2010)

The Cabinet is composed of members of the Partido dos Trabalhadores (PT), the Partido Socialista Brasileiro (PSB), the Partido do Movimento Democrático Brasileiro (PMDB), the Partido Progressista (PP), the Partido Verde (PV), the Partido Democrático Trabalhista (PDT) and Independents.

Cabinet Chief: DILMA VANA ROUSSEFF (PT).

Minister of Foreign Affairs: CELSO LUIZ NUNES AMORIM (Ind.).

Minister of Justice: LUIZ PAULO BARRETO (Ind.).

Minister of Finance: GUIDO MANTEGA (PT).

Minister of Defence: NELSON AZEVEDO JOBIM (PMDB).

Minister of Agriculture and Food Supply: WAGNER GONÇALVES ROSSI (PMDB).

Minister of Agrarian Development: GUILHERME CASSEL (PT).

Minister of Labour and Employment: CARLOS ROBERTO LUPI (PDT).

Minister of Transport: PAULO SÉRGIO PASSOS (Ind.).

Minister of Cities: MÁRCIO FORTES DE ALMEIDA (PP).

Minister of Planning, Budget and Administration: PAULO BERNARDO SILVA (PT).

Minister of Mines and Energy: MÁRCIO PEREIRA ZIMMERMANN (PMDB).

Minister of Culture: JOÃO LUIZ (JUCA) SILVA FERREIRA (PV).

Minister of the Environment: ISABELLA MÔNICA VIEIRA TEIXEIRA (Ind.).

Minister of Development, Industry and Foreign Trade: MIGUEL JOÃO JORGE FILHO (Ind.).

Minister of Education: FERNANDO HADDAD (PT).

Minister of Health: JOSÉ GOMES TEMPORÃO (PMDB).

Minister of Institutional Relations: ALEXANDRE ROCHA SANTOS PADILHA (PT).

Minister of National Integration: GEDDEL QUADROS VIEIRA LIMA (PMDB).

Minister of Social Security: CARLOS EDUARDO GABAS (PT).

Minister of Social Development and the Fight against Hunger: MÁRCIA HELENA CARVALHO LOPES (PT).

Minister of Communications: JOSÉ ARTUR FILARDI LEITE (PMDB).

Minister of Science and Technology: SÉRGIO MACHADO REZENDE (PSB).

Minister of Sport: ORLANDO SILVA DE JESUS JÚNIOR (PT).

Minister of Tourism: LUIZ EDUARDO PEREIRA BARRETO FILHO (PT).

Comptroller-General: JORGE HAGE SOBRINHO.

There are also five Special Secretaries.

MINISTRIES

Office of the President: Palácio do Planalto, 3° andar, Praça dos Três Poderes, 70150-900 Brasília, DF; tel. (61) 3411-1200; fax 3411-2222; e-mail protocolo@planalto.gov.br; internet www.presidencia.gov.br.

Office of the Civilian Cabinet: Palácio do Planalto, 4° andar, Praça dos Três Poderes, 70150-900 Brasília, DF; tel. (61) 3411-1221; fax 3411-2222; e-mail casacivil@planalto.gov.br; internet www.casacivil.planalto.gov.br.

Ministry of Agrarian Development: Esplanada dos Ministérios, Bloco A, 8º andar, Ala Norte, 70050-902 Brasília, DF; tel. (61) 2020-0002; fax (61) 2020-0061; e-mail miguel.rossetto@mda.gov.br; internet www.mda.gov.br.

Ministry of Agriculture and Food Supply: Esplanada dos Ministérios, Bloco D, Anexo B, 70043-900 Brasília, DF; tel. (61) 3218-2828; fax (61) 3218-2401; e-mail gm@agricultura.gov.br; internet www.agricultura.gov.br.

Ministry of Cities: Edif. Telemundi II, 14º andar, Setor de Autarquias Sul, Quadra 01, Lote 01/06, Bloco H, 700700-10 Brasília, DF; tel. (61) 2108-1000; fax (61) 2108-1415; e-mail cidades@cidades.gov.br; internet www.cidades.gov.br.

Ministry of Communications: Esplanada dos Ministérios, Bloco R, 8° andar, 70044-900 Brasília, DF; tel. (61) 3311-6000; fax (61) 3311-6731; e-mail imprensa@mc.gov.br; internet www.mc.gov.br.

Ministry of Culture: Esplanada dos Ministérios, Bloco B, 4° andar, 70068-900 Brasília, DF; tel. (61) 2024-2000; fax (61) 3225-9162; e-mail gm@cultura.gov.br; internet www.cultura.gov.br.

Ministry of Defence: Esplanada dos Ministérios, Bloco Q, 70049-900 Brasília, DF; tel. (61) 3312-4000; fax (61) 3225-4151; e-mail faleconosco@defesa.gov.br; internet www.defesa.gov.br.

Ministry of Development, Industry and Foreign Trade: Esplanada dos Ministérios, Bloco J, 70053-900 Brasília, DF; tel. (61) 2027-7000; fax (61) 2027-7230; e-mail asint@desenvolvimento.gov.br; internet www.desenvolvimento.gov.br.

Ministry of Education: Esplanada dos Ministérios, Bloco L, 8° andar, Sala 805, 70047-900 Brasília, DF; tel. (61) 2022-7842; fax (61) 2022-7858; e-mail acsgabinete@mec.gov.br; internet www.mec.gov.br.

Ministry of the Environment: Esplanada dos Ministérios, Bloco B, 5°–9° andares, 70068-900 Brasília, DF; tel. (61) 2028-1057; fax (61) 2028-1756; e-mail webmaster@mma.gov.br; internet www.mma.gov.br.

Ministry of Finance: Esplanada dos Ministérios, Bloco P, 5° andar, 70048-900 Brasília, DF; tel. (61) 3412-2000; fax (61) 3412-1721; e-mail gabinete.df.gmf@fazenda.gov.br; internet www.fazenda.gov.br.

Ministry of Foreign Affairs: Palácio do Itamaraty, Térreo, Esplanada dos Ministérios, Bloco H, 70170-900 Brasília, DF; tel. (61) 3411-8006; fax (61) 3225-8002; e-mail imprensa@itamaraty.gov.br; internet www.itamaraty.gov.br.

Ministry of Health: Esplanada dos Ministérios, Bloco G, 70058-900 Brasília, DF; tel. (61) 3315-3200; fax (61) 3224-2563; internet www.saude.gov.br.

Ministry of Justice: Esplanada dos Ministérios, Bloco T, 70064-900 Brasília, DF; tel. (61) 3429-3000; fax 3224-0954; e-mail acs@mj.gov.br; internet www.mj.gov.br.

Ministry of Labour and Employment: Esplanada dos Ministérios, Bloco F, 5° andar, 70059-900 Brasília, DF; tel. (61) 3317-6000; fax (61) 3317-8245; e-mail ouvidoria@mte.gov.br; internet www.mte.gov.br.

Ministry of Mines and Energy: Esplanada dos Ministérios, Bloco U, 70065-900 Brasília, DF; tel. (61) 3319-5555; fax (61) 3319-5074; e-mail gabinete@mme.gov.br; internet www.mme.gov.br.

Ministry of National Integration: Esplanada dos Ministérios, Bloco E, 8° andar, 70067-901 Brasília, DF; tel. (61) 3414-5814; fax 3321-5914; e-mail impresa@integracao.gov.br; internet www.integracao.gov.br.

Ministry of Planning, Budget and Administration: Esplanada dos Ministérios, Bloco K, 7° andar, 70040-906 Brasília, DF; tel. (61) 2020-4102; fax (61) 3321-77452020-5009; e-mail ministro@planejamento.gov.br; internet www.planejamento.gov.br.

Ministry of Science and Technology: Esplanada dos Ministérios, Bloco E, 4° andar, 70067-900 Brasília, DF; tel. (61) 3317-7500; fax (61) 3317-7764; e-mail webgab@mct.gov.br; internet www.mct.gov.br.

Ministry of Social Development and the Fight against Hunger: Esplanada dos Ministérios, Bloco C, 5° andar, 70046-900 Brasília, DF; tel. (61) 3433-1029; e-mail ministro.mds@mds.gov.br; internet www.mds.gov.br.

Ministry of Social Security: Esplanada dos Ministérios, Bloco F, 8° andar, 70059-900 Brasília, DF; tel. (61) 2021-5000; fax (61) 2021-5407; e-mail gm.mps@previdencia.gov.br; internet www.mps.gov.br.

Ministry of Sport: Esplanada dos Ministérios, Bloco A, 70054-906 Brasília, DF; tel. (61) 3217-1800; fax (61) 3217-1707; e-mail gabmin@esporte.gov.br; internet www.esporte.gov.br.

Ministry of Tourism: Esplanada dos Ministérios, Bloco U, 2° e 3° andar, 70065-900 Brasília, DF; tel. (61) 2023-7024; fax (61) 2023-7096; e-mail ouvidoria@turismo.gov.br; internet www.turismo.gov.br.

Ministry of Transport: Esplanada dos Ministérios, Bloco R, 6° andar, 70044-900 Brasília, DF; tel. (61) 2029-7000; fax (61) 2029-7876; e-mail paulo.passos@transportes.gov.br; internet www.transportes.gov.br.

Secretariat of Institutional Relations of the Presidency of the Republic: Palácio do Planalto, 4° andar, Sala 13, Praça dos Três Poderes, 70150-900 Brasília, DF; tel. (61) 3411-1042; fax (61) 3411-1470; e-mail sripr@planalto.gov.br; internet www.relacoesinstitucionais.gov.br.

President and Legislature

PRESIDENT

Election, First Round, 1 October 2006

Candidate	Votes	% of valid votes
Luiz Inácio Lula da Silva (PT)	46,662,365	48.61
Geraldo Alckmin (PSDB)	39,968,369	41.64
Heloísa Helena (P-SOL)	6,575,393	6.85
Cristovam Buarque (PDT)	2,538,844	2.64
Ana Maria Rangel (PRP)	126,404	0.13
José Maria Eymael (PSDC)	63,294	0.07
Luciano Bivar (PSL)	62,064	0.06
Total*	95,996,733	100.00

* In addition, there were 8,823,412 invalid votes.

Election, Second Round, 29 October 2006

Candidate	Votes	% of valid votes
Luiz Inácio Lula da Silva (PT)	58,295,042	60.83
Geraldo Alckmin (PSDB)	37,543,178	39.17
Total*	95,838,220	100.00

* In addition, there were 1,351,448 blank ballots and 4,808,553 spoiled ballots.

CONGRESSO NACIONAL

Câmara dos Deputados

Chamber of Deputies: Palácio do Congresso Nacional, Edif. Principal, Praça dos Três Poderes, 70160-900 Brasília, DF; tel. (61) 3216-0000; internet www.camara.gov.br.

President: MICHEL TEMER (PMDB).

The Chamber has 513 members who hold office for a four-year term.

General Election, 1 October 2006

Party	Votes	% of valid votes	Seats
Partido do Movimento Democrático Brasileiro (PMDB)	13,580,517	14.57	89
Partido dos Trabalhadores (PT)	13,989,859	15.01	83
Partido da Social Democracia Brasileira (PSDB)	12,691,043	13.62	65
Partido da Frente Liberal (PFL)*	10,182,308	10.93	65
Partido Progressista (PP)	6,662,309	7.15	42
Partido Socialista Brasileiro (PSB)	5,732,464	6.15	27
Partido Democrático Trabalhista (PDT)	4,854,017	5.21	24
Partido Liberal (PL)†	4,074,618	4.37	23
Partido Trabalhista Brasileiro (PTB)	4,397,743	4.72	22
Partido Popular Socialista (PPS)	3,630,462	3.90	21
Partido Verde (PV)	3,368,561	3.61	13
Partido Comunista do Brasil (PC do B)	1,982,323	2.13	13
Partido Social Cristão (PSC)	1,747,863	1.88	9
Partido Trabalhista Cristão (PTC)	806,662	0.87	4
Partido Socialismo e Liberdade (P-SOL)	1,149,619	1.23	3
Partido da Mobilização Nacional (PMN)	875,686	0.94	3
Partido de Reedificação da Ordem Nacional (PRONA)†	907,494	0.97	2
Partido Humanista da Solidariedade (PHS)	435,328	0.47	2
Partido Trabalhista do Brasil (PT do B)	311,833	0.33	1
Partido dos Aposentados da Nação (PAN)	264,682	0.28	1
Partido Republicano Brasileiro (PRB)	244,059	0.26	1
Total (incl. others)‡	93,184,830	100.00	513

* Refounded in 2007 as Democratas (DEM).

† In late 2006 the PL and the PRONA merged to form the Partido da República (PR).

‡ In addition, there were 11,593,921 blank or invalid votes. The rate of participation was 83.27% of the total of 125,827,119 registered voters.

Senado Federal

Federal Senate: Palácio do Congresso Nacional, Praça dos Três Poderes, 70165-900 Brasília, DF; tel. (61) 3311-4141; fax (61) 3311-3190; e-mail webmaster.secs@senado.gov.br; internet www.senado.gov.br.

President: JOSÉ SARNEY (PMDB).

The 81 members of the Senate are elected by the 26 states and the Federal District (three senators for each) according to the principle of majority. The Senate's term of office is eight years, with elections after four years for one-third of the members and after another four years for the remaining two-thirds.

In the elections of 1 October 2006 27 seats were contested. In that month the PMDB was represented by 20 senators, the PFL and the PSDB by 16 each, the PT by 12, the PTB and the PDT by four each, the PL by three, the PSB and the PRB by two each, and the P-SOL and the PC do B by one each.

Governors

STATES

Acre: BINHO MARQUES (PT).

Alagoas: TEOTÔNIO BRANDÃO VILELA FILHO (PSDB).

Amapá: PEDRO PAULO DIAS DE CARVALHO (PP).

Amazonas: OMAR JOSÉ ABDEL AZIZ (PMN).

Bahia: JACQUES WAGNER (PT).

Ceará: CID GOMES (PSB).

Espírito Santo: PAULO HARTUNG (PMDB).

Goiás: ALCIDES RODRIGUES FILHO (PP).

Maranhão: ROSEANA SARNEY (PMDB).

Mato Grosso: SILVAL CUNHA BARBOSA (PMDB).

Mato Grosso do Sul: ANDRÉ PUCCINELLI (PMDB).

Minas Gerais: ANTÔNIO ANASTASIA (PSDB).

Pará: ANA JÚLIA CAREPA (PT).

Paraíba: JOSÉ MARANHÃO (PMDB).

Paraná: ORLANDO PESSUTI (PMDB).

Pernambuco: EDUARDO HENRIQUE ACCIOLI CAMPOS (PSB).

Piauí: WILSON NUNES MARTINS (PSB).

Rio de Janeiro: SÉRGIO CABRAL FILHO (PMDB).

Rio Grande do Norte: IBERÊ PAIVA FERREIRA DE SOUZA (PSB).

Rio Grande do Sul: YEDA CRUSIUS (PSDB).

Rondônia: JOÃO APARECIDO CAHULLA (PPS).

Roraima: JOSÉ DE ANCHIETA JÚNIOR (PSDB).

Santa Catarina: LEONEL ARCÂNGELO PAVAN (PSDB).

São Paulo: ALBERTO GOLDMAN (PSDB).

Sergipe: MARCELO DÉDA (PT).

Tocantins: CARLOS HENRIQUE GAGUIM (PMDB).

FEDERAL DISTRICT

Brasília: ROGÉRIO ROSSO (PMDB).

Election Commission

Tribunal Superior Eleitoral (TSE): Praça dos Tribunais Superiores, Bloco C, 70096-900 Brasília, DF; tel. (61) 3316-3000; fax (61) 3316-3002; e-mail webmaster@tse.gov.br; internet www.tse.gov.br; f. 1945; Pres. ENRIQUE RICARDO LEWANDOWSKI; Inspector Gen. Elections FELIX FISCHER.

Political Organizations

In 2009 a total of 27 political parties were registered with the Tribunal Superior Eleitoral.

Democratas (DEM): Senado Federal, Anexo 1, 26° andar, 70165-900 Brasília, DF; tel. (61) 3311-4305; fax (61) 3224-1912; e-mail democratas25@democratas.org.br; internet www.dem.org.br; f. 1985 as the Partido da Frente Liberal; refounded in 2007 under present name; Pres. RODRIGO MAIA; Sec.-Gen. JAYME CAMPOS.

Partido Comunista do Brasil (PC do B): Rua Rego Freitas 192, 01220-907, São Paulo, SP; tel. and fax (11) 3054-1800; e-mail comitecentral@pcdob.org.br; internet www.pcdob.org.br; f. 1922; Pres. JOSÉ RENATO RABELO; Sec.-Gen. WALTER SORRENTINO; 185,000 mems.

Partido Democrático Trabalhista (PDT): Rua do Teatro 39, Praça Tiradentes, 20010-190 Rio de Janeiro, RJ; tel. (21) 2232-1016; fax (21) 2232-0121; e-mail fio@pdt.org.br; internet www.pdt.org.br; f. 1980; fmrly the Partido Trabalhista Brasileiro, renamed 1980 when that name was awarded to a dissident group following controversial judicial proceedings; mem. of Socialist International; Pres. CARLOS LUPI; Sec.-Gen. MANOEL DIAS.

Partido da Mobilização Nacional (PMN): Rua Martins Fontes, 197, 3º andar, Conj. 32, 01050-906 São Paulo, SP; tel. 3214-4261; fax 3120-2669; e-mail pmn33@pmn.org.br; internet www.pmn.org.br; f. 1984; Pres. OSCAR NORONHA FILHO; Sec.-Gen. TELMA RIBEIRO DOS SANTOS.

Partido do Movimento Democrático Brasileiro (PMDB): Câmara dos Deputados, Edif. Principal, Ala B, Sala 6, Praça dos Três Poderes, 70160-900 Brasília, DF; tel. (61) 3215-9206; fax (61) 3215-9220; e-mail pmdb@pmdb.org.br; internet www.pmdb.org.br; f. 1980 by moderate elements of fmr Movimento Democrático Brasileiro; merged with Partido Popular in 1982; Pres. MICHEL TEMER; Sec.-Gen. MAURO LOPES; factions include the Históricos and the Movimento da Unidade Progressiva (MUP).

Partido Popular Socialista (PPS): SCS, Quadra 7, Bloco A, Edif. Executive Tower, Sala 826/828, Pátio Brasil Shopping, Setor Comercial Sul, 70307-901 Brasília, DF; tel. (61) 3218-4123; fax (61) 3218-4112; e-mail pps23@pps.org.br; internet www.pps.org.br; f. 1922; Pres. ROBERTO FREIRE; Sec.-Gen. RUBENS BUENO.

Partido Progressista (PP): Senado Federal, Anexo 1, 17° andar, Sala 1704, 70165-900 Brasília, DF; tel. (61) 3311-3041; fax (61) 3322-6938; e-mail pp@pp.org.br; internet www.pp.org.br; f. 1995 as Partido Progressista Brasileiro by merger of Partido Progressista Reformador, Partido Progressista and Partido Republicano Progressista; adopted present name 2003; right-wing; Pres. FRANCISCO DORNELLES; Sec.-Gen. BENEDITO DOMINGOS.

Partido da República (PR): SCN, Edif. Liberty Mall, Quadra 02, Bloco D, Torre A, Salas 601/606, Asa Norte, 70712-903 Brasília, DF; tel. and fax (61) 3202-9922; e-mail pr22@partidodarepublica.org.br; internet www.partidodarepublica.org.br; f. 2006 by merger of Partido Liberal and Partido de Reedificação da Ordem Nacional; Pres. SÉRGIO VICTOR TAMER.

Partido Republicano Brasileiro (PRB): SDS, Bloco L 30, Edif. Miguel Badya, 3° andar, Sala 320, 70394-901 Brasília, DF; tel. and fax (61) 3223-9069; e-mail faleconosco@prb10.org.br; internet www.prb10.org.br; f. 2005 as Partido Municipalista Renovador; name changed as above in 2006; political wing of Igreja Universal do Reino de Deus; Pres. VITOR PAULO ARAÚJO DOS SANTOS.

Partido Social Cristão (PSC): Rua Pouso Alegre, 1388, Santa Teresa, 31015-030 Belo Horizonte, MG; tel. (31) 3467-1390; fax (31) 3467-6522; e-mail psc@psc.org.br; internet www.psc.org.br; f. 1970 as Partido Democrático Republicano; Pres. VITOR JORGE ADBALA NÓSSEIS; Sec.-Gen. ANTONIO OLIBONI.

Partido da Social Democracia Brasileira (PSDB): SGAS, Quadra 607, Edif. Metrópolis, Asa Sul, Cobertura 2, 70200-670 Brasília, DF; tel. (61) 3424-0500; fax (61) 3424-0515; e-mail tucano@psdb.org.br; internet www.psdb.org.br; f. 1988; centre-left; formed by dissident mems of parties incl. the PMDB, PFL, PDT, PSB and PTB; Pres. SÉRGIO GUERRA; Sec.-Gen. RODRIGO DE CASTRO.

Partido Social Liberal (PSL): SCS, Quadra 01, Bloco E, Edif. Ceará, Sala 1004, 70303-900 Brasília, DF; tel. (61) 3322-1721; fax (61) 3032-6832; e-mail contato@pslnacional.org.br; internet www.pslnacional.org.br; f. 1994; Pres. LUCIANO CALDAS BIVAR; Sec.-Gen. ROBERTO SIQUEIRA.

Partido Socialismo e Liberdade (P-SOL): SCS, Quadra 1, Bloco E, Edif. Ceará, Salas 1203–04, 70303-900 Brasília, DF; tel. (61) 3963-1750; fax (61) 3039-6356; e-mail secreteria@psol.org.br; internet www.psol.org.br; f. 2004 by fmr PT mems; Pres. HELOÍSA HELENA; Sec.-Gen. AFRÂNIO TADEU BOPPRÉ.

Partido Socialista Brasileiro (PSB): SCLN 304, Bloco A, Sobreloja 1, Entrada 63, 70736-510 Brasília, DF; tel. and fax (61) 3327-6405; e-mail psb@psbnacional.org.br; internet www.psbnacional.org.br; f. 1945 as the Esquerda Democrática, renamed 1947; Pres. EDUARDO CAMPOS; Sec.-Gen. RENATO CASAGRANDE.

Partido dos Trabalhadores (PT): SCS, Quadra 2, Bloco C, Edif. Toufic, Sala 256, 70302-000 São Paulo, SP; tel. (11) 3213-1313; fax (11) 3213-1360; e-mail presidencia@pt.org.br; internet www.pt.org.br; f. 1980; first independent labour party; associated with the *autêntico* br. of the trade union movt; 500,000 mems; Pres. JOSÉ EDUARDO DUTRA; Sec.-Gen. JOSÉ EDUARDO CARDOZO.

Partido Trabalhista Brasileiro (PTB): SEPN, Quadra 504, Bloco A, Edif. Ana Carolina, Sala 100, Cobertura, 70730-521 Brasília DF; tel. (61) 2101-1414; fax (61) 2101-1400; e-mail ptb@ptb.org.br; internet www.ptb.org.br; f. 1980; Pres. ROBERTO JEFFERSON MONTEIRO FRANCISCO; Sec.-Gen. ANTÔNIO CARLOS DE CAMPOS MACHADO.

Partido Trabalhista Cristão (PTC): SCS, Quadra 8, Edif. Venâncio 2000, Bloco B-50, Salas 133–35, 70333-900 Brasília, DF; tel. (61)

3039-6791; fax (61) 3039-6382; e-mail ptcnacional@uol.com.br; internet www.ptcnacional.com.br; f. 1989 as the Partido da Reconstrução Nacional, renamed 1997; Christian party; Pres. DANIEL S. TOURINHO; Sec.-Gen. RIVAILTON PINTO VELOSO DA SILVA.

Partido Verde (PV): Edif. Miguel Badya, Bloco L, Sala 218, Asa Sul, 70394-901 Brasília, DF; tel. (61) 3366-1569; e-mail nacional@pv.org.br; internet www.pv.org.br; Pres. JOSÉ LUIZ DE FRANÇA PENNA; Organizing Sec. CARLA PIRANDA.

Other political parties include the Partido da Causa Operária (PCO; internet www.pco.org.br), the Partido Republicano Progressista (PRP; internet www.prp.org.br), Democrata Cristão (PSDC; internet www.psdc.org.br), the Partido Trabalhista do Brasil (PT do B; internet www.ptdob.org.br) and the Partido Humanista da Solidariedade (PHS; internet www.phs.org.br).

OTHER ORGANIZATIONS

Movimento dos Trabalhadores Rurais Sem Terra (MST): Alameda Barão de Limeira, 1232 Campos Elíseos, 01202-002 São Paulo, SP; tel. (11) 3361-3866; e-mail semterra@mst.org.br; internet www.mst.org.br; landless peasant movt; Pres. JOÃO PEDRO STÉDILE; Nat. Co-ordinator GILMAR MAURO.

Other rural movements include the Organização da Luto no Campo (OLC) and the Movimento de Liberação dos Sem Terra (MLST), a dissident faction of the MST.

Diplomatic Representation

EMBASSIES IN BRAZIL

Algeria: SHIS, QI 09, Conj. 13, Casa 01, Lago Sul, 70472-900 Brasília, DF; tel. (61) 3248-4039; fax (61) 3248-4691; e-mail sanag277@terra.com.br; Ambassador MUHAMMAD ACHACHE.

Angola: SHIS, QL 06, Conj. 5, Casa 01, 71620-055 Brasília, DF; tel. (61) 3248-4489; fax (61) 3248-1567; e-mail embangola@embaixadadeangola.com.br; internet www.embaixadadeangola.com.br; Ambassador LEOVIGILDO DA COSTA E SILVA.

Argentina: SHIS, QL 02, Conj. 01, Casa 19, Lago Sul, 70442-900 Brasília, DF; tel. (61) 3364-7600; fax (61) 3364-7666; e-mail ebras@mrecic.gov.br; internet www.brasil.embajada-argentina.gov.ar; Ambassador JUAN PABLO LOHLÉ.

Australia: SES, Av. Das Nações, Quadra 801, Conj. K, Lote 7, 70200-010 Brasília, DF; tel. (61) 3226-3111; fax (61) 3226-1112; e-mail embaustr@dfat.gov.au; internet www.brazil.embassy.gov.au; Ambassador NEIL ALLAN MULES.

Austria: SES, Av. das Nações, Quadra 811, Lote 40, 70426-900 Brasília, DF; tel. (61) 3443-3111; fax (61) 3443-5233; e-mail brasilia-ob@bmeia.gv.at; internet www.embaixadadaaustria.com.br; Ambassador HANS-PETER GLANZER.

Barbados: Brasília, DF; Ambassador YVETTE GODDARD.

Belgium: SES, Av. das Nações, Quadra 809, Lote 32, 70422-900 Brasília, DF; tel. (61) 3443-1133; fax (61) 3443-1219; e-mail brasilia@diplobel.org; internet www.diplomatie.be/brasilia; Ambassador CLAUDE MISSON.

Benin: SHIS, QI 9, Conj. 11, Casa 24, Lago Sul, 71625-110 Brasília, DF; tel. (61) 3248-2192; fax (61) 3263-0739; e-mail ambabeninbrasilia@yahoo.fr; Ambassador ISIDORE BENJAMIN AMÉDÉE MONSI.

Bolivia: SHIS, QI 19, Conj. 13, Casa 19, Lago Sul, 71655-130 Brasília, DF; tel. (61) 3366-3432; fax (61) 3366-3136; e-mail embolivia@embolivia.org.br; internet www.embolivia.org.br; Ambassador JOSÉ ALBERTO GONZÁLES SAMANIEGO.

Botswana: SHIS, QI 09, Conj. 17, Casa 16, Lago Sul, 70316-000 Brasília, DF; tel. (61) 3366-5563; fax (61) 3248-6713; Ambassador DIABI JACOB MMUALEFE.

Bulgaria: SEN, Av. das Nações, Quadra 801, Lote 08, 70432-900 Brasília, DF; tel. (61) 3223-6193; fax (61) 3323-3285; e-mail bulgaria@linkexpress.com.br; internet www.mfa.bg/brazil; Ambassador NIKOLAY TZATCHEV.

Cameroon: SHIS, QI 09, Conj. 07, Casa 01, 71625-070 Brasília, DF; tel. (61) 3248-5403; fax (61) 3248-0443; e-mail embcameroun@embcameroun.org.br; internet www.embcameroun.org.br; Ambassador MARTIN AGBOR MBENG.

Canada: SES, Av. das Nações, Quadra 803, Lote 16, 70410-900 Brasília, DF; tel. (61) 3424-5400; fax (61) 3424-5490; e-mail brsla@international.gc.ca; internet www.canada.org.br; Ambassador PAUL HUNT.

Cape Verde: SHIS, QL 14, Conj. 03, Casa 08, Lago Sul, 71640-035 Brasília, DF; tel. (61) 3248-0543; fax (61) 3364-4059; e-mail embcvbrasil@embcv.org.br; internet www.embcv.org.br; Ambassador DANIEL ANTÓNIO PEREIRA.

Chile: SES, Av. das Nações, Quadra 803, Lote 11, Asa Sul, 70407-900 Brasília, DF; tel. (61) 2103-5151; fax (61) 3322-0714; e-mail embchile@embchile.org.br; internet chileabroad.gov.cl/brasil; Ambassador JORGE MONTERO FIGUEROA.

China, People's Republic: SES, Av. das Nações, Quadra 813, Lote 51, Asa Sul, 70443-900 Brasília, DF; tel. (61) 2198-8200; fax (61) 3346-3299; e-mail chinaemb_br@mfa.gov.cn; internet br.china-embassy.org/por; Ambassador QIU XIAOQI.

Colombia: SES, Av. das Nações, Quadra 803, Lote 10, 70444-900 Brasília, DF; tel. (61) 3226-8997; fax (61) 3224-4732; e-mail ebrasili@cancilleria.gov.co; internet www.embajadaenbrasil.gov.co; Ambassador MARÍA ELVIRA POMBO HOLGUÍN.

Congo, Democratic Republic: SHIS, QL 13, Conj. 08, Casa 21, Lago Sul, CP 71635-080 Brasília, DF; tel. (61) 3365-4822; fax (61) 3365-4823; e-mail ambaredeco@ig.com.br; Chargé d'affaires a.i. BAUDOUIN MAYOLA MA LULENDO.

Congo, Republic: SHIS, QL 8, Conj. 05, Casa 06, Lago Sul, 71620-255 Brasília, DF; tel. and fax (61) 3532-0440; e-mail ambacobrazza@gmail.com; Ambassador (vacant).

Costa Rica: SRTV/N 701, Conj. C, Ala A, Salas 308/310, Edif. Centro Empresarial Norte, 70719-903 Brasília, DF; tel. (61) 3032-8450; fax (61) 3032-8452; e-mail embcr.brasil@gmail.com; Ambassador JORGE ALFREDO ROBLES ARIAS.

Côte d'Ivoire: SEN, Av. das Nações, Lote 09, 70473-900 Brasília, DF; tel. (61) 3321-7320; fax (61) 3321-1306; e-mail cotedivoire@cotedivoire.org.br; internet www.cotedivoire.org.br; Ambassador DAOUDA DIABATE.

Croatia: SHIS, QI 09, Conj. 11, Casa 03, 71625-110 Brasília, DF; tel. (61) 3248-0610; fax (61) 3248-1708; e-mail croemb.brasilia@mvpei.hr; Ambassador RADE MARELIĆ.

Cuba: SHIS, QI 05, Conj. 18, Casa 01, Lago Sul, 71615-180 Brasília, DF; tel. (61) 3248-4710; fax (61) 3248-6778; e-mail embacuba@uol.com.br; internet embacu.cubaminrex.cu/brasil; Ambassador CARLOS RAFAEL ZAMORA RODRIGUEZ.

Cyprus: Naoum Plaza Hotel, Quarto 1611, Brasília, DF; tel. (61) 3322-4545; fax (61) 3322-4949; Ambassador MARTHA A. MAVROMMATIS.

Czech Republic: SHIS, QI 9, Conj. 16, Casa 3, Lago Sul, 71625-160 Brasília, DF; tel. (61) 3242-7785; fax (61) 3242-7833; e-mail brasilia@embassy.mzv.cz; internet www.mzv.cz/brasilia; Ambassador IVAN JANČÁREK.

Denmark: SES, Av. das Nações, Quadra 807, Lote 26, 70200-900 Brasília, DF; tel. (61) 3878-4500; fax (61) 3878-4509; e-mail bsbamb@um.dk; internet www.ambbrasilia.um.dk; Ambassador SVEND ROED NIELSEN.

Dominican Republic: SHIS, QL 06, Conj. 07, Casa 02, 71626-075 Brasília, DF; tel. (61) 3248-1405; fax (61) 3364-3214; e-mail embaixada@republicadominicana.org.br; internet www.republicadominicana.org.br; Ambassador HÉCTOR DIONISIO PÉREZ FERNÁNDEZ.

Ecuador: SHIS, QL 10, Conj. 08, Casa 01, 71630-085 Brasília, DF; tel. (61) 3248-5560; fax (61) 3248-1290; e-mail embeq@solar.com.br; internet www.embequador.org.br; Ambassador EDUARDO RODRIGO ALFONSO MORA-ANDA.

Egypt: SEN, Av. das Nações, Lote 12, 70435-900 Brasília, DF; tel. (61) 3323-8800; fax (61) 3323-1039; e-mail embegito@opengate.com.br; internet www.opengate.com.br/embegito; Ambassador AHMED HASSAN IBRAHIM DARWISH.

El Salvador: SHIS, QL 10, Conj. 01, Casa 15, Lago Sul, 71630-015 Brasília, DF; tel. (61) 3364-4141; fax (61) 3364-2459; e-mail elsalvador@embelsalvador.brte.com.br; Ambassador RINA DEL SOCORRO ANGULO.

Equatorial Guinea: SHIS, QL 10, Conj. 09, Casa 01, Lago Sul, 70630-095 Brasília, DF; tel. (61) 3364-4185; fax (61) 3364-1641; e-mail embaixada@embrge.brtdata.com.br; Ambassador TEODORO BIYOGO NSUÉ OKOMO.

Finland: SES, Av. das Nações, Quadra 807, Lote 27, 70417-900 Brasília, DF; tel. (61) 3443-7151; fax (61) 3443-3315; e-mail sanomat.bra@formin.fi; internet www.finlandia.org.br; Ambassador ILPO ILMARI MANNINEN.

France: SES, Av. das Nações, Quadra 801, Lote 04, 70404-900 Brasília, DF; tel. (61) 3222-3999; fax (61) 3222-3917; e-mail france@ambafrance.org.br; internet ambafrance-br.org/france_bresil; Ambassador YVES EDOUARD SAINT-GEOURS.

Gabon: SHIS, QL 08, Conj. 03, Casa 01, Lago Sul, 71620-235 Brasília, DF; tel. (61) 3248-3536; fax (61) 3248-2241; e-mail embgabao@terra.com.br; Ambassador BENJAMIN LEGNONGO-NDUMBA.

Germany: SES, Av. das Nações, Quadra 807, Lote 25, 70415-900 Brasília, DF; tel. (61) 3442-7089; fax (61) 3443-7508; e-mail info@alemanja.org; internet www.brasilia.diplo.de; Ambassador WILFRIED GROLIG.

Ghana: SHIS, QL 10, Conj. 08, Casa 02, 71630-085 Brasília, DF; tel. (61) 3248-6047; fax (61) 3248-7913; e-mail ghaembra@zaz.com.br; Ambassador SAMUEL KOFI DADEY.

Greece: SES, Av. das Nações, Quadra 805, Lote 22, 70480-900 Brasília, DF; tel. (61) 3443-6573; fax (61) 3443-6902; e-mail gremb.bra@mfa.gr; internet www.emb-grecia.org.br; Ambassador DIMITRI ALEXANDRAKIS.

Guatemala: SHIS, QI 07, Conj. 13, Casa 09, Lago Sul, 71615-330 Brasília, DF; tel. (61) 3248-4175; fax (61) 3248-6678; e-mail embaguate.brasil@gmail.com; Ambassador CARLOS JIMÉNEZ LICONA.

Guinea: SHIS, QL 02, Conj. 07, Casa 09, Lago Sul, 71610-075 Brasília, DF; tel. (61) 3365-1301; fax (61) 3365-4921; e-mail ambaguibrasil@terra.com.br; Ambassador FODÉ TOURÉ.

Guyana: SHIS, QI 05, Conj. 19, Casa 24, 71615-190 Brasília, DF; tel. (61) 3248-0874; fax (61) 3248-0886; e-mail embguyana@embguyana.org.br; internet www.embguyana.org.br; Ambassador HARRY NARINE NAWBATT.

Haiti: SHIS, QI 11, Conj. 06, Casa 13, Lago Sul, 71625-260 Brasília, DF; tel. (61) 3248-6860; fax (61) 3248-7472; e-mail embhaiti@terra.com.br; Ambassador IDALBERT PIERRE-JEAN.

Holy See: SES, Av. das Nações, Quadra 801, Lote 01, 70401-900 Brasília, DF; tel. (61) 3223-0794; fax (61) 3224-9365; e-mail nunapost@solar.com.br; Apostolic Nuncio Most Rev. LORENZO BALDISSERI (Titular Archbishop of Diocletiana).

Honduras: SHIS, QI 19, Conj. 07, Casa 34, Lago Sul, 71655-070 Brasília, DF; tel. (61) 3366-4082; fax (61) 3366-4618; e-mail embhonduras@ig.com.br; Ambassador VICTOR MANUEL LOZANO URBINA.

Hungary: SES, Av. das Nações, Quadra 805, Lote 19, 70413-900 Brasília, DF; tel. (61) 3443-0836; fax (61) 3443-3434; e-mail mission.brz@kum.hu; internet www.mfa.gov.hu/emb/brasilia; Ambassador Dr CSABA PÓLYI.

India: SHIS, QL 08, Conj. 08, Casa 01, 71620-285 Brasília, DF; tel. (61) 3248-4006; fax (61) 3248-7849; e-mail indemb@indianembassy.org.br; internet www.indianembassy.org.br; Ambassador BELLUR SHAMARAO PRAKASH.

Indonesia: SES, Av. das Nações, Quadra 805, Lote 20, 70479-900 Brasília, DF; tel. (61) 3443-8800; fax (61) 3443-6732; e-mail contato@embaixadadaindonesia.org; internet www.embaixadadaindonesia.org; Ambassador BALI MONIAGA.

Iran: SES, Av. das Nações, Quadra 809, Lote 31, 70421-900 Brasília, DF; tel. (61) 3242-5733; fax (61) 3224-9640; e-mail iransefa@mail.comsats.net.pk; internet brasilia.mfa.gov.ir; Ambassador Dr MOHSEN SHATERZADEH YAZDI.

Iraq: SES, Av. das Nações, Quadra 815, Lote 64, 70430-900 Brasília, DF; tel. (61) 3346-2822; fax (61) 3346-7034; e-mail brzemb@iraqmfamail.com; Ambassador BAKER FATTAH HUSSEIN.

Ireland: SHIS, QL 12, Conj. 05, Casa 09, Lago Sul, 71630-255 Brasília, DF; tel. (61) 3248-8800; fax (61) 3248-8816; e-mail brasiliaembassy@dfa.ie; internet www.embaixada-irlanda.org.br; Ambassador FRANK SHERIDAN.

Israel: SES, Av. das Nações, Quadra 809, Lote 38, 70424-900 Brasília, DF; tel. (61) 2105-0500; fax (61) 2105-0555; e-mail info@brasilia.mfa.gov.il; internet brasilia.mfa.gov.il; Ambassador GIORA BECHER.

Italy: SES, Av. das Nações, Quadra 807, Lote 30, 70420-900 Brasília, DF; tel. (61) 3442-9900; fax (61) 3443-1231; e-mail ambasciata.brasilia@esteri.it; internet www.ambbrasilia.esteri.it; Ambassador GHERARDO LA FRANCESCA.

Japan: SES, Av. das Nações, Quadra 811, Lote 39, 70425-900 Brasília, DF; tel. (61) 3442-4200; fax (61) 3442-2499; e-mail consularjapao@yawl.com.br; internet www.br.emb-japan.go.jp; Ambassador AKIRA MIWA.

Jordan: SHIS, QI 09, Conj. 18, Casa 14, Lago Sul, 71625-180 Brasília, DF; tel. (61) 3248-5414; fax (61) 3248-1698; e-mail emb.jordania@apis.com.br; Ambassador RAMEZ ZAKI ODEH GOUSSOUS.

Kenya: SHIS, QL 10, Conj. 08, Casa 08, Lago Sul, 71630-085 Brasília, DF; tel. (61) 3364-0691; fax (61) 3364-0978; e-mail brazil@mfa.go.ke; internet www.kenyaembassy.com.br; Ambassador (vacant).

Korea, Democratic People's Republic: SHIS, QI 25, Conj. 10, Casa 11, Lago Sul, 71660-300 Brasília, DF; tel. (61) 3367-1940; fax (61) 3367-3177; e-mail embrpdcoreia@hotmail.com; Ambassador RI HWA GUN.

Korea, Republic: SEN, Av. das Nações, Lote 14, 70436-900 Brasília, DF; tel. (61) 3321-2500; fax (61) 3321-2508; e-mail emb-br@mofat.go.kr; internet bra-brasilia.mofat.go.kr; Ambassador KYONG-LIM CHOI.

Kuwait: SHIS, QI 05, Chácara 30, Lago Sul, 71600-550 Brasília, DF; tel. (61) 3213-2333; fax (61) 3248-0969; e-mail kuwait@opendf.com.br; Ambassador WALEED AHMAD M. AL-KANDARI.

Lebanon: SES, Av. das Nações, Quadra 805, Lote 17, 70411-900 Brasília, DF; tel. (61) 3443-5552; fax (61) 3443-8574; e-mail embaixada@libano.org.br; internet www.libano.org.br; Ambassador FOUAD EL-KHOURY GHANEM.

Libya: SHIS, QI 15, Chácara 26, Lago Sul, 71600-750 Brasília, DF; tel. (61) 3248-6710; fax (61) 3248-0598; e-mail emblibia@terra.com.br; Ambassador SALEM OMAR ABDULLAH AZ-ZUBAIDI.

Malaysia: SHIS, QI 05, Chácara 62, Lago Sul, 70477-900 Brasília, DF; tel. (61) 3248-5008; fax (61) 3248-6307; e-mail mwbrasilia@terra.com.br; internet www.kln.gov.my/perwakilan/brasilia; Ambassador SUDHA DEVI.

Mauritania: SHIS, QI 9, conj. 14, casa 3, Lago Sul, 71925-140 Brasília, DF; tel. (61) 3797-3995; fax (61) 3263-6944; e-mail ambarimbrasilia@mauritania.org.br; internet www.mauritania.org.br; Ambassador N'DIAYE KANE.

Mexico: SES, Av. das Nações, Quadra 805, Lote 18, 70412-900 Brasília, DF; tel. (61) 3204-5200; fax (61) 3204-5201; e-mail embamexbra@cabonet.com.br; internet portal.sre.gob.mx/brasil; Ambassador ALEJANDRO DE LA PEÑA NAVARRETE.

Morocco: SEN, Av. das Nacões, Quadra 801, Lote 02, Asa Norte, 70432-900 Brasília, DF; tel. (61) 3321-3994; fax (61) 3321-0745; e-mail sifamabr@onix.com.br; internet www.embmarrocos.org.br; Ambassador MUHAMMAD LOUAFA.

Mozambique: SHIS, QL 12, Conj. 07, Casa 09, Lago Sul, 71630-275 Brasília, DF; tel. (61) 3248-4222; fax (61) 3248-3917; e-mail embamoc-bsb@uol.com; internet www.mozambique.org.br; Ambassador MURADE ISAAC MIGUIGY MURARGY.

Myanmar: SHIS, QI 13, Conj. 08, Casa 09, Lago Sul, 71635-080 Brasília, DF; tel. (61) 3248-3747; fax (61) 3364-2747; e-mail mebrsl@brnet.com.br; Ambassador HTEIN WIN.

Namibia: SHIS QI 09, Conj. 08, Casa 11, Lago Sul, 71625-080 Brasília, DF; tel. (61) 3248-6274; fax (61) 3248-7135; e-mail info@embassyofnamibia.org.br; internet www.embassyofnamibia.org.br; Ambassador HOPELONG UUSHONA IPINGE.

Nepal: SHIS QI 11, Conj.03, Casa 20, Lago Sul, 71630-085 Brasília, DF; tel. (61) 3541-1320; fax (61) 3541-1229; Ambassador PRADHUMNA BIKRAM SHAH.

Netherlands: SES, Av. das Nações, Quadra 801, Lote 05, 70405-900 Brasília, DF; tel. (61) 3961-3200; fax (61) 3961-3234; e-mail bra@minbuza.nl; internet www.mfa.nl/brasil; Ambassador KEES PIETER RADE.

New Zealand: SHIS, QI 09, Conj. 16, Casa 01, 71625-160 Brasília, DF; tel. (61) 3248-9900; fax (61) 3248-9916; e-mail zelandia@nwi.com.br; internet www.nzembassy.com/brazil; Ambassador MARK JULIAN TRAINOR.

Nicaragua: SHIS, QL 22, Conj. 10, Casa 13, Lago Sul, 71650-305 Brasília, DF; tel. (61) 3366-3297; fax (61) 3366-5213; e-mail mromerom@cancilleria.gob.ni; Ambassador SARA MARÍA TÓRREZ RUIZ.

Nigeria: SEN, Av. das Nações, Lote 05, 70800-400 Brasília, DF; tel. (61) 3208-1700; fax (61) 3226-5192; e-mail admin@nigerianembassy-brazil.org; internet www.nigerianembassy-brazil.org; Ambassador KAYODE GARRICK.

Norway: SES, Av. das Nações, Quadra 807, Lote 28, 70418-900 Brasília, DF; tel. (61) 3443-8720; fax (61) 3443-2942; e-mail emb.brasilia@mfa.no; internet www.noruega.org.br; Ambassador TURID B. RODRIGUES EUSÉBIO.

Pakistan: SHIS, QL 12, Conj. 02, Casa 19, Lago Sul, 71630-225 Brasília, DF; tel. (61) 3364-1632; fax (61) 3248-0246; e-mail parepbrasilia@yahoo.com; internet www.pakistan.org.br; Ambassador ALAMGIR BASHAR KHAN BABAR.

Panama: SES, Av. das Nações, Quadra 803, Lote 9, 70200-030 Brasília, DF; tel. (61) 3323-2885; fax (61) 3248-2834; e-mail empanamabr@embaixada.brte.com.br; Ambassador GABRIELA GARCÍA CARRANZA.

Paraguay: SES, Av. das Nações, Quadra 811, Lote 42, 70427-900 Brasília, DF; tel. (61) 3242-3732; fax (61) 3242-4605; e-mail secretaria@embaparaguai.org.br; internet www.embaparaguai.org.br; Ambassador (vacant).

Peru: SES, Av. das Nações, Quadra 811, Lote 43, 70428-900 Brasília, DF; tel. (61) 3242-9933; fax (61) 3225-9136; e-mail embperu@embperu.org.br; internet www.embperu.org.br; Ambassador RICARDO JORGE GHIBELLINI HARTEN.

Philippines: SEN, Av. das Nações, Lote 01, 70431-900 Brasília, DF; tel. (61) 3223-5143; fax (61) 3226-7411; e-mail brasiliape@turbo.com.br; Ambassador EVA G. BETITA.

Poland: SES, Av. das Nações, Quadra 809, Lote 33, 70423-900 Brasília, DF; tel. (61) 3212-8000; fax (61) 3242-8543; e-mail embaixada@polonia.org.br; internet www.polonia.org.br; Ambassador JACEK JUNOSZA KISIELEWSKI.

Portugal: SES Sul, Av. das Nações, Quadra 801, Lote 02, 70402-900 Brasília, DF; tel. (61) 3032-9600; fax (61) 3032-9642; e-mail embaixadadeportugal@embaixadadeportugal.org.br; internet www.embaixadadeportugal.org.br; Ambassador JOÃO MANUEL GUERRA SALGUEIRO.

Qatar: SHIS, QL 20, Conj. 01, Casa 19, Lago Sul, 71650-115 Brasília, DF; tel. (61) 3366-1005; fax (61) 3366-1115; e-mail qatarbsb@embcatar.org.br; Ambassador JAMAL NASSER SULTAN AL-BADR.

Romania: SEN, Av. das Nações, Lote 06, 70456-900 Brasília, DF; tel. (61) 3226-0746; fax (61) 3226-6629; e-mail romenia@solar.com.br; Ambassador MIHAI ZAMFIR.

Russia: SES, Av. das Nações, Quadra 801, Lote A, 70476-900 Brasília, DF; tel. (61) 3223-3094; fax (61) 3226-7319; e-mail emb@embrus.brte.com.br; internet www.brazil.mid.ru; Ambassador SERGUEY POGÓSSOVITCH AKOPOV.

Saudi Arabia: SHIS, QL 10, Conj. 09, Casa 20, 70471-900 Brasília, DF; tel. (61) 3248-3523; fax (61) 3284-1142; e-mail bremb@mofa.gov.sa; internet www.saudiembassy.org.br; Ambassador MUHAMMAD AMIN BIN ALI BIN MUHAMMAD KURDI.

Senegal: SEN, Av. das Nações, Lote 18, 70800-400 Brasília, DF; tel. (61) 3223-6110; fax (61) 3322-7822; e-mail senebrasilia@senebrasilia.com.br; internet www.senebrasilia.org.br; Ambassador FODÉ SECK.

Serbia: SES, Av. das Nações, Quadra 803, Lote 15, 70409-900 Brasília, DF; tel. (61) 3223-7272; fax (61) 3223-8462; e-mail embaixadaservia@terra.com.br; Ambassador LJUBOMIR MILIC.

Slovakia: SES Av. das Nações, Quadra 805, Lote 21B, 70200-902 Brasília, DF; tel. (61) 3443-1263; fax (61) 3443-1267; e-mail eslovaca@brasil.mfa.sk; Ambassador BRANISLAV HITKA.

South Africa: SES, Av. das Nações, Quadra 801, Lote 06, 70406-900 Brasília, DF; tel. (61) 3312-9500; fax (61) 3322-8491; e-mail brasilia.general@foreign.gov.za; internet www.africadosul.org.br; Ambassador BANGUMZI SIFINGO.

Spain: SES, Av. das Nações, Quadra 811, Lote 44, 70429-900 Brasília, DF; tel. (61) 3701-1600; fax (61) 3242-1781; e-mail emb.brasilia@maec.es; Ambassador CARLOS ALONSO ZALDÍVAR.

Sri Lanka: SHIS, QI 09, Conj. 09, Casa 07, Lago Sul, 71625-090 Brasília, DF; tel. (61) 3248-2701; fax (61) 3364-5430; e-mail lankaemb@yawl.com.br; Ambassador ADAM MAZNAVEE JAUFER SADIQ.

Sudan: SHIS, QI 11, Conj. 5, Casa 13, Lago Sul, 71625-250 Brasília, DF; tel. (61) 3248-4835; fax (61) 3248-4833; e-mail sudanbrasilia@yahoo.com; Ambassador ABD ELGHANI ELNAIM AWAD ELKARIM.

Suriname: SHIS, QI 09, Conj. 08, Casa 24, 71625-080 Brasília, DF; tel. (61) 3248-6706; fax (61) 3248-3791; e-mail surinameemb@terra.com.br; Ambassador GEORGINE MAVIS DEMON-BELGRAEF.

Sweden: SES, Av. das Nações, Quadra 807, Lote 29, 70419-900 Brasília, DF; tel. (61) 3442-5200; fax (61) 3443-1187; e-mail ambassaden.brasilia@foreign.ministry.se; internet www.suecia.org.br; Ambassador ANNIKA MARKOVIC.

Switzerland: SES, Av. das Nações, Quadra 811, Lote 41, 70448-900 Brasília, DF; tel. (61) 3443-5500; fax (61) 3443-5711; e-mail bra.vertretung@eda.admin.ch; internet www.dfae.admin.ch/brasilia; Ambassador WILHELM MEIER.

Syria: SEN, Av. das Nações, Lote 11, 70434-900 Brasília, DF; tel. (61) 3226-0970; fax (61) 3223-2595; e-mail embsiria@uol.com.br; Chargé d'affaires a.i. GHASSAN OBEID.

Tanzania: SHIS, QI 09, Conj. 16, Casa 20, Lago Sul, 71615-190 Brasília, DF; tel. (61) 3364-2629; fax (61) 3248-3361; e-mail tanrepbrasilia@yahoo.com.br; Ambassador JORAM MUKAMA BISWARO.

Thailand: SEN, Av. das Nações, Lote 10, 70433-900 Brasília, DF; tel. (61) 3224-6943; fax (61) 3223-7502; e-mail thaiemb@linkexpress.com.br; internet www.thaiembassy.org/brasilia; Ambassador CHAKARIN CHAYABONGSE.

Timor-Leste: SHIS, QI 11, Conj. 10, Casa 19, Lago Sul, 71625-300 Brasília, DF; tel. and fax (61) 3366-2755; e-mail embaixada@embaixadatimorleste.com.br; Ambassador DOMINGOS FRANCISCO DE JESUS DE SOUSA.

Trinidad and Tobago: SHIS, QL 02, Conj. 02, Casa 01, 71665-028 Brasília, DF; tel. (61) 3365-1132; fax (61) 3365-1733; e-mail trinbagoemb@gmail.com; Ambassador MONICA JUNE CLEMENT.

Tunisia: SHIS, QI 11, Conj. 06, Casa 06, Lago Sul, 71625-260 Brasília, DF; tel. (61) 3248-7366; fax (61) 3248-7355; e-mail at.brasilia@terra.com.br; Ambassador SEIFEDDINE CHERIF.

Turkey: SES, Av. das Nações, Quadra 805, Lote 23, 70452-900 Brasília, DF; tel. (61) 3242-1850; fax (61) 3242-1448; e-mail turquia@conectanet.com.br; internet www.turquia.org.br; Ambassador DURMUŞ ERSIN ERÇIN.

Ukraine: SHIS, QI 05, Conj. 04, Casa 02, Lago Sul, 71615-040 Brasília, DF; tel. (61) 3365-1457; fax (61) 3365-2127; e-mail emb_br@mfa.gov.ua; internet www.mfa.gov.ua/brazil; Ambassador VOLODYMYR LAKOMOV.

United Arab Emirates: SHIS, QI 05, Chácara 54, 70800-400 Brasília, DF; tel. (61) 3248-0717; fax (61) 3248-7543; e-mail uae@uae.org.br; internet www.uae.org.br; Ambassador YOUSEF ALI AL-USAIMI.

United Kingdom: SES, Av. das Nações, Quadra 801, Conj. K, Lote 08, 70408-900 Brasília, DF; tel. (61) 3329-2300; fax (61) 3329-2369; e-mail press.brasilia@fco.gov.uk; internet ukinbrazil.fco.gov.uk; Ambassador ALAN CHARLTON.

USA: SES, Av. das Nações, Quadra 801, Lote 03, 70403-900 Brasília, DF; tel. (61) 3312-7000; fax (61) 3312-7676; e-mail ircbsb@state.gov; internet brasilia.usembassy.gov; Ambassador THOMAS A. SHANNON, Jr.

Uruguay: SES, Av. das Nações, Quadra 803, Lote 14, 70450-900 Brasília, DF; tel. (61) 3322-1200; fax (61) 3322-6534; e-mail urubras@emburuguai.org.br; internet www.emburuguai.org.br; Ambassador CARLOS DANIEL AMORÍN TENCONI.

Venezuela: SES, Av. das Nações, Quadra 803, Lote 13, 70451-900 Brasília, DF; tel. (61) 2101-1011; fax (61) 3321-0871; e-mail emb@embvenezuela.org.br; internet www.embvenezuela.org.br; Ambassador MAXIMILIAN SANCHEZ ARVELAIZ.

Viet Nam: SHIS, QI 09, Conj. 10, Casa 01, Lago Sul, 71625-100 Brasília, DF; tel. (61) 3364-5876; fax (61) 3364-5836; e-mail embavina@yahoo.com; internet www.vietnamembassy-brazil.org/vi; Ambassador NGUYÊN DUONG TUONG.

Zambia: SHIS, QL 10, Conj. 6, Casa 10, Lago Sul, 71630-065 Brasília, DF; tel. and fax (61) 3248-3277; e-mail zambiansbrasil@embaixadazambia.org.br; Ambassador JOEL NGO.

Zimbabwe: SHIS, QI 03, Conj. 10, Casa 13, 71605-300 Brasília, DF; tel. (61) 3365-4801; fax (61) 3365-4803; e-mail zimbrasilia@uol.com.br; internet www.zimbabue-brasilia.org.br; Ambassador THOMAS SUKUTAI BVUMA.

Judicial System

The judicial powers of the State are held by the following: the Supreme Federal Court, the Higher Court of Justice, the five Regional Federal Courts and Federal Judges, the Higher Labour Court, the 24 Regional Labour Courts, the Conciliation and Judgment Councils and Labour Judges, the Higher Electoral Court, the 27 Regional Electoral Courts, the Electoral Judges and Electoral Councils, the Higher Military Court, the Military Courts and Military Judges, the Courts of the States and Judges of the States, the Court of the Federal District and of the Territories and Judges of the Federal District and of the Territories.

The Supreme Federal Court comprises 11 ministers, nominated by the President and approved by the Senado. Its most important role is to rule on the final interpretation of the Constitution. The Supreme Federal Court has the power to declare an act of Congress void if it is unconstitutional. It judges offences committed by persons such as the President, the Vice-President, members of the Congresso Nacional, Ministers of State, its own members, the Attorney-General, judges of other higher courts, and heads of permanent diplomatic missions. It also judges cases of litigation between the Union and the States, between the States, or between foreign nations and the Union or the States, disputes as to jurisdiction between higher Courts, or between the latter and any other court, in cases involving the extradition of criminals, and others related to the writs of habeas corpus and habeas data, and in other cases.

The Higher Court of Justice comprises 33 members, appointed by the President and approved by the Senado. Its jurisdiction includes the judgment of offences committed by State Governors. The Regional Federal Courts comprise at least seven judges, recruited when possible in the respective region and appointed by the President of the Republic. The Higher Labour Court comprises 17 members, appointed by the President and approved by the Senado. The judges of the Regional Labour Courts are also appointed by the President. The Regional Electoral Courts are composed of seven members. The Higher Military Court comprises 15 life members, appointed by the President and approved by the Senate: three from the navy, four from the army, three from the air force and five civilian members. The States are responsible for the administration of their own justice, according to the principles established by the Constitution.

SUPREME FEDERAL COURT

Supremo Tribunal Federal: Praça dos Três Poderes, 70175-900 Brasília, DF; tel. (61) 3217-3000; fax (61) 3217-4412; internet www.stf.jus.br.

President: GILMAR FERREIRA MENDES.

Vice-President: ANTÓNIO CEZAR PELUZO.

Justices: JOSÉ CELSO DE MELLO FILHO, MARCO AURELIO MENDES DE FARIAS MELLO, ELLEN GRACIE NORTHFLEET, CARLOS AYRES BRITTO, JOAQUIM BENEDITO BARBOSA GOMES, EROS ROBERTO GRAU, ENRIQUE RICARDO LEWANDOWSKI, CÁRMEN LÚCIA ANTUNES ROCHA, JOSÉ ANTÔNIO DIAS TOFFOLI.

Procurator-General: ROBERTO MONTEIRO GURGEL SANTOS.

Religion

CHRISTIANITY

Conselho Nacional de Igrejas Cristãs do Brasil (CONIC) (National Council of Christian Churches in Brazil): Edif. Ceará, Sala 713, SCS, Quadra 01, Bloco E, 70303-900 Brasília, DF; tel. and fax (61) 3321-8341; e-mail conic.brasil@terra.com.br; internet www.conic.org.br; f. 1982; eight mem. churches; Pres. Pastor CARLOS AUGUSTO MÖLLER; Exec. Sec. Rev. LUIZ ALBERTO BARBOSA.

The Roman Catholic Church

Brazil comprises 41 archdioceses, 214 dioceses (including one each for Catholics of the Maronite, Melkite and Ukrainian Rites), 13 territorial prelatures and one personal apostolic administration. The Archbishop of São Sebastião do Rio de Janeiro is also the Ordinary for Catholics of other Oriental Rites in Brazil (estimated at 10,000 in 1994). According to the latest available census figures (2000), some 74% of the population are Roman Catholics.

Bishops' Conference: Conferência Nacional dos Bispos do Brasil, SES, Quadra 801, Conj. B, 70401-900 Brasília, DF; tel. (61) 2103-8300; fax (61) 2103-8303; e-mail cnbb@cnbb.org.br; internet www.cnbb.org.br; f. 1952; statutes approved 2002; Pres. GERALDO LYRIO ROCHA (Archbishop of Mariana, MG); Sec.-Gen. DIMAS LARA BARBOSA.

Latin Rite

Archbishop of São Salvador da Bahia, BA, and Primate of Brazil: Cardinal GERALDO MAJELLA AGNELO, Cúria Metropolitana, Rua Martin Afonso de Souza 270, 40100-050 Salvador, BA; tel. (71) 328-6699; fax (71) 328-0068; e-mail gma@atarde.com.br.

Archbishop of Aparecida, SP: RAYMUNDO DAMASCENO ASSIS.

Archbishop of Aracaju, SE: JOSÉ PALMEIRA LESSA.

Archbishop of Belém do Pará, PA: ALBERTO TAVEIRO CORRÊA.

Archbishop of Belo Horizonte, MG: WALMOR OLIVEIRA DE AZEVEDO.

Archbishop of Botucatu, SP: MAURÍCIO GROTTO DE CAMARGO.

Archbishop of Brasília, DF: JOÃO BRAZ DE AVIZ.

Archbishop of Campinas, SP: BRUNO GAMBERINI.

Archbishop of Campo Grande, MS: VITÓRIO PAVANELLO.

Archbishop of Cascavel, PR: MAURO APARECIDO DOS SANTOS.

Archbishop of Cuiabá, MT: MILTON ANTÔNIO DOS SANTOS.

Archbishop of Curitiba, PR: MOACYR JOSÉ VITTI.

Archbishop of Diamantina, MG: JOÃO BOSCO OLIVER DE FARIA.

Archbishop of Feira de Santana, BA: ITAMAR NAVILDO VIAN.

Archbishop of Florianópolis, SC: MURILO SEBASTIÃO RAMOS KRIEGER.

Archbishop of Fortaleza, CE: JOSÉ ANTÔNIO APARECIDO TOSI MARQUES.

Archbishop of Goiânia, GO: WASHINGTON CRUZ.

Archbishop of Juiz de Fora, MG: GIL ANTÔNIO MOREIRA.

Archbishop of Londrina, PR: ORLANDO BRANDES.

Archbishop of Maceió, AL: ANTÔNIO MUNIZ FERNANDES.

Archbishop of Manaus, AM: LUIZ SOARES VIEIRA.

Archbishop of Mariana, MG: GERALDO LYRIO ROCHA.

Archbishop of Maringá, PR: ANUAR BATTISTI.

Archbishop of Montes Claros, MG: JOSÉ ALBERTO MOURA.

Archbishop of Natal, RN: MATIAS PATRÍCIO DE MACÊDO.

Archbishop of Niterói, RJ: ALANO MARIA PENA.

Archbishop of Olinda e Recife, PE: ANTONIO FERNANDO SABURIDO.

Archbishop of Palmas, PR: (vacant).

Archbishop of Paraíba, PB: ALDO DE CILLO PAGOTTO.

Archbishop of Porto Alegre, RS: DADEUS GRINGS.

Archbishop of Porto Velho, RO: MOACYR GRECHI.

Archbishop of Pouso Alegre, MG: RICARDO PEDRO CHAVES PINTO FILHO.

Archbishop of Ribeirão Preto, SP: JOVIANO DE LIMA JÚNIOR.

Archbishop of São Luís do Maranhão, MA: JOSÉ BELISÁRIO DA SILVA.

Archbishop of São Paulo, SP: Cardinal ODILO PEDRO SCHERER.

Archbishop of São Sebastião do Rio de Janeiro, RJ: ORANI JOÃO TEMPESTA.

Archbishop of Sorocaba, SP: EDUARDO BENES DE SALES RODRIGUES.

Archbishop of Teresina, PI: SÉRGIO DA ROCHA.

Archbishop of Uberaba, MG: ALOÍSIO ROQUE OPPERMANN.

Archbishop of Vitória, ES: LUIZ MANCILHA VILELA.

Archbishop of Vitória da Conquista, BA: LUIS GONZAGA SILVA PEPEU.

Maronite Rite

Bishop of Nossa Senhora do Líbano em São Paulo, SP: EDGAR MADI.

Melkite Rite

Bishop of Nossa Senhora do Paraíso em São Paulo, SP: FARES MAAKAROUN.

Ukrainian Rite

Bishop of São João Batista em Curitiba, PR: VALDOMIRO KOUBETCH.

The Anglican Communion

Anglicans form the Episcopal Anglican Church of Brazil (Igreja Episcopal Anglicana do Brasil), comprising eight dioceses.

Igreja Episcopal Anglicana do Brasil: Av. Ludolfo Boehl 256, Teresópolis, 91720-150 Porto Alegre, RS; tel. and fax (51) 3318-6200; internet www.ieab.org.br; f. 1890; 103,021 mems (1997); Primate Rt Rev. MAURÍCIO JOSÉ ARAÚJO DE ANDRADE; Sec.-Gen. Rev. FRANCISCO DE ASSIS DA SILVA.

Protestant Churches

According to the 2000 census, 15% of the population are Evangelical Christians.

Igreja Cristã Reformada do Brasil (Christian Reformed Church of Brazil): Rua Domingos Rodrigues, 306/Lapa, 05075-000 São Paulo, SP; tel. (11) 3260-7514; f. 1932; Pres. Rev. ANTÔNIO BONZOI; 500 mems.

Igreja Evangélica de Confissão Luterana no Brasil (IECLB): Rua Senhor dos Passos 202, 4° andar, 90020-180 Porto Alegre, RS; tel. (51) 3284-5400; fax (51) 3284-5479; e-mail secretariageral@ieclb.org.br; internet www.luteranos.org.br; f. 1949; 715,000 mems; Pres. Pastor Dr WALTER ALTMANN; Vice-Pres. Pastor HOMERO SEVERO PINTO.

Igreja Evangélica Congregacional do Brasil: Rua Dom Pedro 1616, 85960-000 Marechal Cândido Rondon, PR; tel. (45) 254-2448; e-mail web@iecb.org.br; internet www.iecb.org.br; f. 1942; 148,836 mems (2000); Pres. Rev. H. DORIVAL L. SEIDEL.

Igreja Evangélica Luterana do Brasil: Av. Cel. Lucas de Oliveira 894, Bairro Mont'Serrat, 90440-010 Porto Alegre, RS; tel. (51) 3332-2111; fax (51) 3332-8145; e-mail ielb@ielb.org.br; internet www.ielb.org.br; f. 1904; 236,345 mems; Pres. Rev. PAULO MOISÉS NERBAS; Sec. Rev. Dr RONY RICARDO MARQUARDT.

Igreja Maná do Brasil: Travesa da Imprensa 26, Centro 12900-460 Bragança Paulista, SP; tel. (11) 4032-8104; e-mail adm_brasil@igrejamana.com; internet www.igrejamana.com.

Igreja Metodista do Brasil: Av. Piassanguaba 3031, Planalto Paulista, 04060-004 São Paulo, SP; tel. (11) 2813-8600; fax (11) 2813-8632; e-mail sede.nacional@metodista.org.br; internet www.metodista.org.br; 136,470 mems (2002); Exec. Sec. Bishop JOÃO CARLOS LOPES.

Igreja Presbiteriana Unida do Brasil (IPU): Av. Jeronimo Monteiro 400, Edif. Vitória Center, 1210/1, 29010-360 Vitória, ES; tel. and fax (27) 3256-6598; e-mail ipu@ipu.org.br; internet www.ipu.org.br; f. 1978; Moderator Rev. ENOC TEIXEIRA WENCESLAU.

BAHÁ'Í FAITH

Comunidade Bahá'í do Brasil (Bahá'í Community of Brazil): SHIS, QL 08, Conj. 02, CP 7035, 71620-970 Brasília, DF; tel. (61) 3364-3594; fax (61) 3364-3470; e-mail info@bahai.org.br; internet www.bahai.org.br; f. 1965; Sec. CARLOS ALBERTO SILVA.

BUDDHISM

Sociedade Budista do Brasil (Buddhist Society—Rio Buddhist Vihara): Dom Joaquim Mamede 45, Lagoinha, Santa Tereza, 20241-390 Rio de Janeiro, RJ; tel. (21) 2526-1411; e-mail sbbrj@yahoo.com; internet www.geocities.com/sbbrj; f. 1972; Pres. JORGE ALOICE GOMES.

OTHER RELIGIONS

Sociedade Taoísta do Brasil (Daoist Society): Rua Cosme Velho 355, Cosme Velho, 22241-090 Rio de Janeiro, RJ; tel. (21) 2225-2887; e-mail info@taoismo.org.br; internet www.taoismo.org.br; f. 1991.

The Press

The most striking feature of the Brazilian press is the relatively small circulation of newspapers in comparison with the size of the population. The newspapers with the largest circulations are *O Dia* (250,000), *O Globo* (350,000), *Folha de São Paulo* (287,627), and *O Estado de São Paulo* (242,000). The low circulation is mainly owing to high costs resulting from distribution difficulties. In consequence, there are no national newspapers. In 2004 a total of 532 daily newspaper titles, with an average circulation of 6,552,000, and 2,472 non-daily newspapers were published in Brazil.

DAILY NEWSPAPERS

Belém, PA

O Liberal: Av. 25 de Setembro 2473, Marco, 66093-000 Belém, PA; tel. (91) 3216-1138; e-mail redacao@orm.com.br; internet www.orm.com.br/oliberal; f. 1946; Pres. Lucidea Maiorana; circ. 20,000.

Belo Horizonte, MG

Diário da Tarde: Av. Getúlio Vargas 291, 30112-020 Belo Horizonte, MG; tel. (31) 3263-5229; internet www.estaminas.com.br/dt; f. 1931; evening; Editor Fábio Proença Doyle; total circ. 150,000.

Diário do Comércio: Av. Américo Vespúcio 1660, Nova Esperança, 31230-250 Belo Horizonte, MG; tel. (31) 3469-2049; fax (31) 3469-2043; e-mail redacaodc@diariodocomercio.com.br; internet www.diariodocomercio.com.br; f. 1932; Editor Osires Fecci.

Estado de Minas: Av. Getúlio Vargas 291, 8° andar, 30112-020 Belo Horizonte, MG; tel. (31) 3263-5800; fax (31) 3263-5424; e-mail gerais.em@uai.com.br; internet www.uai.com.br/em; f. 1928; morning; independent; Chief Editor Josemar Gimenez Resende; circ. 65,000.

Hoje em Dia: Rua Padre Rolim 652, Santa Efigênia, 30130-916 Belo Horizonte, MG; tel. (31) 3236-8000; fax (31) 3236-8010; e-mail comercial@hojeemdia.com.br; internet www.hojeemdia.com.br; Editorial Dir Carlos Lindenburg.

Blumenau, SC

Jornal de Santa Catarina: Rua Bahia 2291, 89031-002 Blumenau, SC; tel. (48) 3221-1400; fax (48) 3221-1405; e-mail redacao@santa.com.br; internet www.santa.com.br; f. 1971; Dir (vacant); circ. 25,000.

Brasília, DF

Correio Brasiliense: SIG, Quadra 02, Lote 340, 70610-901 Brasília, DF; tel. (61) 3214-1100; fax (61) 3214-1157; e-mail geral@correioweb.com.br; internet www.correiobraziliense.com.br; f. 1960; Pres. and Dir Álvaro Teixeira da Costa; circ. 30,000.

Jornal de Brasília: SIG, Trecho 1, Lotes 585/645, 70610-400 Brasília, DF; tel. (61) 3343-8000; fax (61) 3226-6735; e-mail redacao@jornaldebrasilia.com.br; internet www.jornaldebrasilia.com.br; f. 1972; Editor-in-Chief Jorge Eduardo Antunes; circ. 25,000.

Campinas, SP

Correio Popular: Rua 7 de Setembro 189, Vila Industrial, 13035-350 Campinas, SP; tel. (19) 3736-3050; fax (19) 3234-8984; e-mail webmaster@rac.com.br; internet www.cpopular.com.br; f. 1927; Editorial Dir Nelson Homem de Mello; circ. 40,000.

Curitiba, PR

O Estado do Paraná: Rua João Tschannerl 800, Jardim Mercês, Vista Alegre, 80820-010 Curitiba, PR; tel. (41) 3331-5000; fax (41) 3335-2838; e-mail oestado@parana-online.com.br; internet www.parana-online.com.br; f. 1951; Pres. Paulo Cruz Pimentel; Dir Supt Yvonne Lunardelli Pimentel; circ. 15,000.

Gazeta do Povo: Rua Pedro Ivo 459, Centro, 80010-020 Curitiba, PR; tel. (41) 3321-5000; fax (41) 3321-5300; e-mail atendimento@tudoparana.com; internet www.gazetadopovo.com.br; f. 1919; Pres. Edmundo Lemanski; circ. 40,000.

Tribuna do Paraná: Rua João Tschannerl 800, Jardim Mercês, Vista Alegre, 80820-010 Curitiba, PR; tel. (41) 3331-5000; fax (41) 3335-2838; e-mail tribuna@parana-online.com.br; internet www.parana-online.com.br; f. 1956; Man. Editor Rafael Tavares; circ. 15,000.

Florianópolis, SC

O Estado: Rodovia SC-401, Km 3, 88030-900 Florianópolis, SC; tel. and fax (48) 3239-8888; internet www.oestado.com.br; f. 1915; Pres. José Matusalém de Carvalho Comelli; Gen. Editor Sandra Annuseck; circ. 20,000.

Fortaleza, CE

Diário do Nordeste: Editora Verdes Mares Ltda, Praça da Impresa, C.G.C. 07209-299 Fortaleza, CE; tel. (85) 3266-9773; fax (85) 3266-9797; e-mail aloredacao@diariodonordeste.com.br; internet diariodonordeste.globo.com; Editorial Dir Ildefonso Rodrigues.

Jornal O Povo: Av. Aguanambi 282, 60055 Fortaleza, CE; tel. (85) 3255-6250; fax (85) 3231-5792; e-mail centraldeatendimento@opovo.com.br; internet opovo.uol.com.br; f. 1928; evening; Exec. Editor Fátima Sudário; Editor-in-Chief Erick Guimarães; circ. 20,000.

Goiânia, GO

Diário da Manhã: Av. Anhanguera 2833, Setor Leste Universitário, 74610-010 Goiânia, GO; tel. (62) 3267-1000; internet www.dm.com.br; f. 1980; Editor Batista Custódio; circ. 16,000.

O Popular: Rua Thómas Edson, Quadra 07, Setor Serrinha, 74835-130 Goiânia, GO; tel. (62) 3250-1220; fax (62) 3250-1270; e-mail dca@opopular.com.br; internet www.opopular.com.br; f. 1938; Editor Elisângela Nascimento; circ. 65,000.

João Pessoa, PB

Correio da Paraíba: Av. Pedro II, Centro, João Pessoa, PB; tel. (83) 3216-5000; fax (83) 3216-5009; e-mail assinante@portalcorreio.com.br; internet www.correiodaparaiba.com.br; Exec. Dir Beatriz Ribeiro.

Londrina, PR

Folha de Londrina: Rua Piauí 241, 86010-420 Londrina, PR; tel. (43) 3374-2020; fax (43) 3339-1412; e-mail editorial@folhadelondrina.com.br; internet www.bonde.com.br/folha; f. 1948; Editor-in-Chief Oswald Petrin; circ. 40,000.

Manaus, AM

A Crítica: Av. André Araújo 1924a, Aleixo-Cidade das Comunicações, 69060-001 Manaus, AM; tel. (92) 3643-1200; fax (92) 3643-1234; internet www.acritica.com.br; f. 1949; Dir Rita Araújo Calderaro; circ. 19,000.

Natal, RN

Diario de Natal: Av. Deodoro da Fonseca 245, Petrópolis, 59012-600 Natal, RN; tel. (84) 4009-0166; e-mail redacao.rn@diariosassociados.com.br; internet www.diariodenatal.com.br; Exec. Editor Juliska Azevedo.

Niterói, RJ

O Fluminense: Rua da Conceição 188, Loja 118, Niterói Shopping, Niterói, RJ; tel. (21) 2620-6168; fax (21) 2620-8636; e-mail redacao@ofluminense.com.br; internet www.ofluminense.com.br; f. 1878; Man. Editor Sandra Duarte; circ. 80,000.

A Tribuna: Rua Barão do Amazonas 31, Ponta D'areia, 2403-0111 Niterói, RJ; tel. (21) 2719-1886; e-mail icarai@urbi.com.br; internet www.atribunarj.com.br; f. 1936; daily; Dir-Supt Gustavo Santano Amóro; circ. 10,000.

Palmas, TO

O Girassol: Av. Teotônio Segurado 101 Sul, Conj. 01, Edif. Office Center, Lote 06, Sala 408, 77015-002 Palmas, TO; tel. and fax (63) 3225-5456; e-mail ogirassol@uol.com.br; internet www.ogirassol.com.br; Editor-in-Chief Wilbergson Estrela Gomes; Exec. Editor Sonielson Luciano de Sousa.

Porto Alegre, RS

Zero Hora: Av. Ipiranga 1075, Azenha, 90169-900 Porto Alegre, RS; tel. (51) 3218-4300; fax (51) 3218-4700; e-mail geral@zerohora.com.br; internet www.zerohora.com.br; f. 1964; Editorial Dir Ricardo Stefanelli; circ. 165,000 (Mon.), 170,000 (weekdays), 240,000 (Sun.).

Recife, PE

Diário de Pernambuco: Rua do Veiga 600, Santo Amaro, 50040-110 Recife, PE; tel. (81) 2122-7555; fax (81) 2122-7544; e-mail faleconosco@diariodepernambuco.com.br; internet www.diariodepernambuco.com.br; f. 1825; morning; independent; Editorial Dir Vera Ogando; circ. 47,000.

Ribeirão Preto, SP

Jornal Tribuna da Ribeirão Preto: Rua São Sebastião 1380, Centro, 14015-040 Ribeirão Preto, SP; tel. and fax (16) 3632-2200; e-mail tribuna@tribunariberao.com.br; internet www.tribunaribeirao.com.br; Editor HILTON HARTMANN; circ. 16,000.

Rio de Janeiro, RJ

O Dia: Rua Riachuelo 359, Centro, 20235-900 Rio de Janeiro, RJ; fax (21) 2507-1228; internet odia.terra.com.br; f. 1951; morning; centrist labour; Editor-in-Chief ALEXANDRE FREELAND; circ. 250,000 (weekdays), 500,000 (Sun.).

O Globo: Rua Irineu Marinho 35, CP 1090, 20233-900 Rio de Janeiro, RJ; tel. (21) 2534-5000; fax (21) 2534-5510; internet oglobo.globo.com; f. 1925; morning; Editor-in-Chief RODOLFO FERNANDES; circ. 350,000 (weekdays), 600,000 (Sun.).

Jornal do Brasil: Av. Paulo de Frontin 568, Fundos, Rio Comprido, 20261-243 Rio de Janeiro, RJ; tel. (21) 2323-1000; e-mail jb@jbonline.com.br; internet www.jbonline.terra.com.br; f. 1891; print edn suspended July 2010, online only; Catholic, liberal; NELSON TANURE; Vice-Pres. RICARDO CARVALHO.

Jornal do Commercio: Rua do Livramento 189, 20221-191 Rio de Janeiro, RJ; tel. and fax (21) 2223-8500; e-mail jornaldocommercio@jcom.com.br; internet www.jornaldocommercio.com.br; f. 1827; morning; Pres. MAURICIO DINEPI; circ. 31,000 (weekdays).

Jornal dos Sports: Rua Pereira de Almeida 88, Praça de Bandeira, 20260-100 Rio de Janeiro, RJ; tel. (21) 2563-0363; e-mail redacao@jsports.com.br; internet jsports.uol.com.br; f. 1931; morning; sporting daily; Editor THIAGO VIANA; circ. 39,000.

Salvador, BA

Correio da Bahia: Rua Professor Aristides Novis 123, Federação, 40210-630 Salvador, BA; tel. (71) 3533-3030; fax (71) 3203-1045; e-mail comercial@correiodabahia.com.br; internet www.correiodabahia.com.br; f. 1978; Editor-in-Chief SERGIO COSTA.

A Tarde: Rua Prof. Milton Cayres de Brito 204, Caminho das Árvores, 41820-570 Salvador, BA; tel. (71) 3340-8500; fax (71) 3231-8800; e-mail suporte@atarde.com.br; internet www.atarde.com.br; f. 1912; evening; Editor-in-Chief FLORISVALDO MATTOS; circ. 54,000.

Santarém, PA

O Impacto—O Jornal da Amazônia: Av. Presidente Vargas 3728, Caranazal, 68040-060 Santarém, PA; tel. (93) 3523-3330; fax (93) 3523-9131; e-mail oimpacto@oimpacto.com.br; internet www.oimpacto.com.br; Editor-in-Chief JERFFESON ROCHA.

Santo André, SP

Diário do Grande ABC: Rua Catequese 562, Bairro Jardim, 09090-900 Santo André, SP; tel. (11) 4435-8100; fax (11) 4434-8250; e-mail online@dgabc.com.br; internet www.dgabc.com.br; f. 1958; Exec. Editor MARCELO RUIZ; circ. 78,500.

Santos, SP

A Tribuna: Rua João Pessoa 129, 2º e 3º andares, Centro, 11013-900 Santos, SP; tel. (13) 2102-7000; fax (13) 3219-7329; e-mail atribuna@atribuna.com.br; internet www.atribuna.com.br; f. 1984; Exec. Editor ARMINDA AUGUSTO; Editor-in-Chief CARLOS CONDE; circ. 40,000.

São Luís, MA

O Imparcial: Empresa Pacotilha Ltda, Rua Assis Chateaubriand s/n, Renascença 2, 65075-670 São Luís, MA; tel. (98) 3212-2000; e-mail redacao@oimparcial.com.br; internet www.oimparcial.com.br; f. 1926; Editor-in-Chief PEDRO HENRIQUE FREIRE; circ. 8,000.

São Paulo, SP

DCI (Diário Comércio, Indústria e Serviços): Rua Bacaetava 191, 1° andar, 04705-010 São Paulo, SP; tel. (11) 5094-5200; fax (11) 5095-5308; e-mail redacao@dci.com.br; internet www.dci.com.br; f. 1933; morning; Editorial Dir MÁRCIA RAPOSO; circ. 50,000.

Diário do Comércio: Associação Comercial de São Paulo, Rua Boa Vista 51, 6° andar, Centro, 01014-911 São Paulo, SP; tel. (11) 3244-3322; fax (11) 3244-3046; e-mail faleconosco@dcomercio.com.br; internet www.dcomercio.com.br; Pres. GUILHERME AFIF DOMINGOS.

Diário de São Paulo: Rua Major Quedinho 90, Centro, São Paulo, SP; tel. (11) 3235-7800; internet www.diariosp.com.br; f. 1884; fmrly *Diário Popular*; evening; owned by O Globo; Editor-in-Chief NELSON NUNES; circ. 90,000.

O Estado de São Paulo: Av. Celestino Bourroul 68, 1° andar, 02710-000 São Paulo, SP; tel. (11) 3856-5400; fax (11) 3856-2940; e-mail falecom.estado@grupoestado.com.br; internet www.estado.com.br; f. 1875; morning; independent; Editor JULIO DE MESQUITA NETO; circ. 242,000 (weekdays), 460,000 (Sun.).

Folha de São Paulo: Alameda Barão de Limeira 425, 6° andar, Campos Elíseos, 01202-900 São Paulo, SP; tel. (11) 3224-4759; fax (11) 3224-7550; e-mail falecomagente@folha.com.br; internet www.folha.uol.com.br; f. 1921; morning; Editor CAMILA MARQUES; circ. 287,627 (weekdays), 342,614 (Sun.).

Gazeta Mercantil: Vila Olimpia, Rua Ramos Batista 444, 11° andar, CP 04552-020 São Paulo, SP; tel. (11) 2126-5000; e-mail relacionamento@gazetamercantil.com.br; internet www.gazeta.com.br; f. 1920; business paper; Pres. LUIZ FERREIRA LEVY; circ. 80,000.

Jornal da Tarde: Av. Eng. Caetano Álvares 55, Bairro do Limão, 02598-000 São Paulo, SP; tel. (11) 3856-2234; fax (11) 3856-2940; e-mail pergunta.jt@grupoestado.com.br; internet www.jt.com.br; f. 1966; evening; independent; Dir FERNÃO LARA MESQUITA; circ. 120,000, 180,000 (Mon.).

Vitória, ES

A Gazeta: Rua Charic Murad 902, 29050 Vitória, ES; tel. (27) 3321-8333; fax (27) 3321-8720; e-mail ahees@redegazeta.com.br; internet gazetaonline.globo.com; f. 1928; Exec. Editor ANDRÉ HEES; circ. 19,000.

PERIODICALS

Rio de Janeiro, RJ

Antenna-Eletrônica Popular: Av. Marechal Floriano 151, Centro, 20080-005 Rio de Janeiro, RJ; tel. (21) 2223-2442; fax (21) 2263-8840; e-mail antenna@anep.com.br; internet www.anep.com.br; f. 1926; monthly; telecommunications and electronics, radio, TV, hi-fi, amateur and CB radio; Dir MARIA BEATRIZ AFFONSO PENNA; circ. 15,000.

Conjuntura Econômica: Rua Barão de Itambi 60, 7º andar, Botafogo, 22231-000 Rio de Janeiro, RJ; tel. (21) 2559-6040; fax (21) 2559-6039; e-mail conjunturaeconomica@fgv.br; internet www.fgv.br/ibre/cecon; f. 1947; monthly; economics and finance; published by Fundação Getúlio Vargas; Editor-in-Chief CLAUDIO CONCEIÇÃO; circ. 15,000.

ECO21: Av. Copacabana 2, Gr. 301, 22010-122 Rio de Janeiro, RJ; tel. (21) 2275-1490; e-mail eco21@eco21.com.br; internet www.eco21.com.br; f. 1990; monthly; ecological issues; Editor RENÉ CAPRILES.

São Paulo, SP

Ana Maria: Editora Abril, Av. das Nações Unidas 7221, 05425-902 São Paulo, SP; tel. (11) 3037-2000; fax (11) 3037-4734; e-mail anamaria.abril@atleitor.com.br; internet mdemulher.abril.com.br/revistas/anamaria; weekly; women's interest; Editor-in-Chief LIDICE-BAH; circ. 222,171.

Caros Amigos: Rua Paris 856, Sumaré, 01257-040 São Paulo, SP; tel. (11) 2594-0355; fax (11) 2594-0351; e-mail atendimento.carosamigos@tmktbrasil.com.br; internet www.carosamigos.com.br; f. 1997; monthly; political; Editor HAMILTON OCTAVIO DE SOUZA; circ. 50,000.

Caras: Editora Abril, Av. das Nações Unidas 7221, 05425-902 São Paulo, SP; tel. (11) 3037-2000; fax (11) 3037-4734; e-mail redacaoonline@caras.com.br; internet www.caras.com.br; f. 1993; weekly; celebrities; Dir EDGARDO MARTOLIO; circ.308,465.

CartaCapital: Alameda Santos 1800, 7º B, 01418-200 São Paulo, SP; tel. (11) 3474-0161; e-mail redacao@cartacapital.com.br; internet www.cartacapital.com.br; f. 1994; weekly; politics and economics; Editor-in-Chief MINO CARTA; circ. 32,570.

Casa e Jardim: Av. Jaguaré 1485, 05346-902 São Paulo, SP; tel. (11) 3767-7000; fax (11) 3767-7936; e-mail casaejardim@edglobo.com.br; internet revistacasaejardim.globo.com; f. 1953; monthly; homes and gardens, illustrated; Editor-in-Chief ARTUR DE ANDRADE; circ. 100,811.

Claudia: Editora Abril, Av. das Nações Unidas 7221, Pinheiros, 05425-902 São Paulo, SP; tel. (11) 3037-2000; fax (11) 5087-2100; e-mail claudia.abril@atleitor.com.br; internet claudia.abril.com.br; f. 1962; monthly; women's interest; Editor-in-Chief LÚCIA BARROS; circ. 402,940.

Contigo!: Editora Abril, Av. das Nações Unidas 7221, 5° andar, 05425-902 São Paulo, SP; tel. (11) 3037-2000; fax (11) 3037-4734; e-mail contigo.abril@atleitor.com.br; internet contigo.abril.com.br; f. 1963; weekly; entertainment and celebrity news; Dir FELIX FASSONE; circ. 148,569.

Criativa: Av. Jaguaré 1485, 05346-902 São Paulo, SP; tel. (11) 3767-7812; fax (11) 3767-7771; e-mail criativa@edglobo.com.br; internet revistacriativa.globo.com; monthly; women's interest; Editor-in-Chief MARIANA WEBER; circ. 100,314.

Digesto Econômico: Associação Comercial de São Paulo, Rua Boa Vista 51, Centro, 01014-911 São Paulo, SP; tel. (11) 3244-3092; fax

(11) 3244-3355; e-mail admdiario@acsp.com.br; internet www.acsp.com.br; fortnightly; Pres. ELVIO ALIPRANDI; Chief Editor JOÃO DE SCANTIMBURGO.

Elle: Editora Abril, Av. das Nações Unidas 7221, 16° andar, Pinheiros, 05425-902 São Paulo, SP; tel. (11) 3037-3545; fax (11) 3037-5451; e-mail elle.abril@atleitor.com.br; internet www.elle.com.br; f. 1988; monthly; women's interest; Editor-in-Chief ELIANA SANCHEZ; circ. 100,000.

Época: Av. Jaguaré 1485, 05346-902 São Paulo, SP; tel. (11) 3767-7000; e-mail epocadir@edglobo.com.br; internet revistaepoca.globo.com; f. 1998; news weekly; Editor HELIO GUROVITZ; circ. 416,744.

Exame: Editora Abril, Av. das Nações Unidas 7221, Pinheiros, 05425-902 São Paulo, SP; tel. (11) 3037-2000; fax (11) 3037-2027; e-mail redacao.exame@abril.com.br; internet www.exame.com.br; f. 1967; 2 a week; business; Editorial Dir CLÁUDIA VASSALLO; circ. 168,300.

ISTOÉ: Rua William Speers 1088, 05067-900 São Paulo, SP; tel. (11) 3618-4200; fax (11) 3618-4324; e-mail leitor@istoe.com.br; internet www.istoe.com.br; politics and current affairs; Editorial Dir CARLOS JOSÉ MARQUES; circ. 340,764.

Máquinas e Metais: Alameda Olga 315, 01155-900 São Paulo, SP; tel. (11) 3824-5300; fax (11) 3666-9585; e-mail infomm@arandanet.com.br; internet www.arandanet.com.br; f. 1964; monthly; machine and metal industries; Editor JOSÉ ROBERTO GONÇALVES; circ. 15,000.

Marie Claire: Av. Jaguaré 1485, 05346-902 São Paulo, SP; tel. (11) 3767-7000; fax (11) 3767-7833; e-mail mclaire@edglobo.com.br; internet revistamarieclaire.globo.com; monthly; women's interest; Editorial Dir MÔNICA DE ALBUQUERQUE LINS SERINO; circ. 199,831.

Micromundo-Computerworld do Brasil: Rua Caçapava 79, 01408 São Paulo, SP; tel. (11) 3289-1767; e-mail editor@computerworld.com.br; internet www.computerworld.com.br; f. 1976; bimonthly; computers; Editor FABIANA MONTE; circ. 38,000.

Nova Escola: Editora Abril, Av. das Nações Unidas 7221, 6° andar, 05425-902 São Paulo, SP; tel. (11) 3037-2000; fax (11) 3037-4322; e-mail novaescola@atleitor.com.br; internet revistaescola.abril.com.br; f. 1986; monthly; education; Dir GABRIEL GROSSI; circ. 451,125.

Placar: Editora Abril, Av. das Nações Unidas 7221, 14° andar, Pinheiros, 05425-902 São Paulo, SP; tel. (11) 3037-2000; fax (11) 5087-2100; e-mail placar.abril@atleitor.com.br; internet placar.abril.com.br; f. 1970; monthly; soccer; Editor SÉRGIO XAVIER; circ. 127,000.

Quatro Rodas: Av. das Nações Unidas 7221, 14° andar, 05425-902 São Paulo, SP; fax (11) 3037-5039; internet quatrorodas.abril.com.br; f. 1960; monthly; motoring; Editor SÉRGIO BEREZOVSKY; circ. 190,139.

Revista O Carreteiro: Rua Palacete das Aguias 395, Vila Alexandria, 04635-021 São Paulo, SP; tel. (11) 5035-0000; fax (11) 5031-8647; e-mail revista@ocarreteiro.com.br; internet www.revistaocarreteiro.com.br; f. 1970; monthly; transport; Editor JOÃO GERALDO; circ. 100,000.

Saúde: Editora Abril, Av. das Nações Unidas 7221, 16° andar, Pinheiros, 05425-902 São Paulo, SP; tel. (11) 3037-4885; fax (11) 3037-4867; e-mail saude.abril@atleitor.com.br; internet saude.abril.com.br; monthly; health; Editor LÚCIA HELENA DE OLIVEIRA; circ. 183,250.

Superinteressante: Editora Abril, Avenida das Nações Unidas 7221, 8º andar, 05425-902 São Paulo, SP; tel. (11) 3037-2000; fax (11) 3037-5891; e-mail superleitor.abril@atleitor.com.br; internet super.abril.com.br; f. 1987; monthly; popular science; Dir SÉRGIO GWERCMAN; circ. 354,947.

Veja: Editora Abril, Av. das Nações Unidas 7221, Pinheiros, 05425-902 São Paulo, SP; tel. (11) 3347-2121; fax (11) 3037-5638; e-mail veja@abril.com.br; internet vejaonline.abril.com.br; f. 1968; news weekly; Editor EURÍPEDES ALCÂNTARA; circ. 1,099,078.

Viva Mais: Editora Abril, Av. das Nações Unidas 7221, 05425-902 São Paulo, SP; tel. (11) 3037-2000; fax (11) 3037-4734; e-mail vivamais.abril@atleitor.com.br; internet mdemulher.abril.com.br; weekly; women's interest; Editor MÔNICA KATO; circ. 219,940.

NEWS AGENCIES

Agência o Estado de São Paulo: Av. Eng. Caetano Alvares 55, Bairro do Limão, 02588-900 São Paulo, SP; tel. (11) 3856-3500; fax (11) 3856-2940; internet www.estadao.com.br; Rep. SAMUEL DIRCEU F. BUENO.

Agência O Globo: Rua Irineu Marinho 70, 4° andar, Cidade Nova, 20230-901 Rio de Janeiro, RJ; tel. (21) 2534-5656; e-mail agenciaoglobo@oglobo.com.br; internet www.agenciaoglobo.com.br; f. 1974; Man. RICARDO MELLO.

Agência JB (Agência Jornal do Brasil): Av. Paulo de Frontin 568, Fundos, Rio Comprido, 20261-243 Rio de Janeiro, RJ; tel. (21) 2101-4148; fax (21) 2101-4428; e-mail ajb@jb.com.br; internet www.agenciajb.com.br; f. 1966; Exec. Dir EDGAR LISBOA.

Folhapress: Alameda Barão de Limeira 401, 4° andar, Campos Elíseos, 01202-900 São Paulo, SP; tel. (11) 3224-3123; fax (11) 3224-4778; e-mail folhapress@folhapress.com.br; internet www.folhapress.com.br; Gen. Man. RAIMUNDO CUNHA.

PRESS ASSOCIATIONS

Associação Brasileira de Imprensa (ABI): Rua Araújo Porto Alegre 71, Centro, 20030-012 Rio de Janeiro, RJ; tel. (21) 2282-1292; e-mail abi@abi.org.br; internet www.abi.org.br; f. 1908; asscn for journalistic rights and assistance; 4,000 mems; Pres. MAURÍCIO AZÊDO.

Associação Nacional de Editores de Revistas (ANER): Rua Deputado Lacerda Franco 300, 15°, Conj. 155, 05418-000 São Paulo, SP; tel. (11) 3030-9390; fax (11) 3030-9393; e-mail info@aner.org.br; internet www.aner.org.br; f. 1986; Pres. ROBERTO MUYLAERT; Exec. Dir MARIA CÉLIA FURTADO.

Federação Nacional dos Jornalistas (FENAJ): SCLRN 704, Bloco F, Loja 20, 70730-536 Brasília, DF; tel. (61) 3244-0650; fax (61) 3242-6616; e-mail fenaj@fenaj.org.br; internet www.fenaj.org.br; f. 1946; represents 31 regional unions; Pres. SÉRGIO MURILLO DE ANDRADE.

Publishers

Ao Livro Técnico Indústria e Comércio, Ltda: Rua Sá Freire 36/40, São Cristóvão, 20930-430 Rio de Janeiro, RJ; tel. (21) 2580-6230; fax (21) 2580-9955; internet www.editoraaolivrotécnico.com.br; f. 1933; textbooks, children's and teenagers' fiction and non-fiction, art books, dictionaries; Man. Dir REYNALDO MAX PAUL BLUHM.

Atual Editora, Ltda: São Paulo, SP; tel. (11) 5071-2288; fax (11) 5071-3099; e-mail atendprof@atualeditora.com.br; internet www.atualeditora.com.br; f. 1973; school and children's books, literature; Dirs GELSON IEZZI, OSVALDO DOLCE.

Barsa Planeta Internacional: Av. Francisco Matarazzo 1500, 4º andar, Edif. New York, Centro Empresarial Agua Branca, 05001-100 São Paulo, SP; tel. (11) 3225-1990; fax (11) 3225-1960; e-mail atendimento@barsaplaneta.com.br; internet brasil.planetasaber.com; f. 1949; reference books.

Cengage Learning: Condomínio E-Business Park, Rua Werner Siemens 111, Prédio 20, Espaço 03, Lapa de Baixo, 05069-900 São Paulo, SP; tel. (11) 3665-9900; fax (11) 3665-9901; e-mail milagros.valderrama@cengage.com; internet www.cengage.com.br; f. 1960 as Editora Pioneira; architecture, computers, political and social sciences, business studies, languages, children's books; Dir MILAGROS VALDERRAMA.

Ebid-Editora Páginas Amarelas, Ltda: Rua São José 90, 4° andar, 20010-020 Rio de Janeiro, RJ; tel. (21) 3824-8287; fax (21) 3824-8300; f. 1947; commercial directories.

Ediouro Publicações, SA: Rua Nova Jerusalém 345, CP 1880, Bonsucesso, 21042-235 Rio de Janeiro, RJ; tel. (21) 3882-8416; e-mail editoriallivros@ediouro.com.br; internet www.ediouro.com.br; f. 1939; general; Pres. JORGE CARNEIRO.

Editora Abril, SA: Av. das Nações Unidas 7221, Pinheiros, 05425-902 São Paulo, SP; tel. (11) 3037-2000; fax (11) 5087-2100; e-mail abril@abril.com.br; internet www.abril.com.br; f. 1950; magazines; Pres. ROBERTO CIVITA.

Editora Atica, SA: Rua Barão de Iguape 110, 01507-900 São Paulo, SP; tel. (11) 3346-3000; fax (11) 3277-4146; e-mail editora@atica.com.br; internet www.atica.com.br; f. 1965; textbooks, Brazilian and African literature; Pres. VICENTE PAZ FERNANDEZ.

Editora Atlas, SA: Rua Conselheiro Nébias 1384, 01203-904 São Paulo, SP; tel. (11) 3357-9144; fax (11) 3221-5859; e-mail diretoria@editora-atlas.com.br; internet www.editoraatlas.com.br; f. 1944; business administration, economics, accounting, law, education, social sciences; Pres. LUIZ HERRMANN, Jr.

Editora do Brasil, SA: Rua Conselheiro Nébias 887, Campos Elíseos, CP 4986, 01203-001 São Paulo, SP; tel. (11) 3226-0211; fax (11) 3222-5583; e-mail editora@editoradobrasil.com.br; internet www.editoradobrasil.com.br; f. 1943; education; Pres. Dr CARLOS COSTA.

Editora Brasiliense, SA: Rua Airi 22, Tatuapé, 03310-010 São Paulo, SP; tel. and fax (11) 6198-1488; e-mail brasilienseedit@uol.com.br; internet www.editorabrasiliense.com.br; f. 1943; education, racism, gender studies, human rights, ecology, history, literature, social sciences; Man. YOLANDA C. DA SILVA PRADO; Vice-Pres. MARIA TERESA B. DE LIMA.

Editora Campus: Rua Sete de Setembro 111, 16° andar, 20050-002 Rio de Janeiro, RJ; tel. (21) 3970-9300; fax (21) 2507-1991; e-mail c.rothmuller@campus.com.br; internet www.campus.com.br; f. 1976; business, computing, non-fiction; imprint of Elsevier since 2002; Man. Dir CLAUDIO ROTHMULLER.

Editora Delta, SA: Av. Nilo Peçanha 50, 2817, 20020-100 Rio de Janeiro, RJ; tel. (21) 2262-5243; internet www.delta.com.br; f. 1930; reference books; Pres. ANDRÉ KOOGAN BREITMAN.

Editora Educacional Brasileira, SA: Rua XV de Novembro 178, Salas 101/04, CP 7498, 80000 Curitiba, PR; tel. (41) 2223-5012; f. 1963; biology, textbooks and reference books.

Editora Expressão e Cultura—Exped, Ltda: Estrada dos Bandeirantes 1700, Bloco H, 22710-113 Rio de Janeiro, RJ; tel. (21) 2444-0649; fax (21) 2444-0651; e-mail exped@ggh.com.br; internet www.exped.com.br; f. 1966; textbooks, literature, reference; Gen. Man. RICARDO AUGUSTO PAMPLONA VAZ.

Editora FTD, SA: Rua Rui Barbosa 156, Bairro Bela Vista, 01326-010 São Paulo, SP; tel. (11) 3253-5011; fax (11) 3288-0132; internet www.ftd.com.br; f. 1902; textbooks; Pres. JOÃO TISSI.

Editora Globo, SA: Av. Jaguaré 1485/1487, 05346-902 São Paulo, SP; tel. (11) 3767-7400; fax (11) 3767-7870; e-mail globolivros@edglobo.com.br; internet globolivros.globo.com; f. 1957; fiction, engineering, agriculture, cookery, environmental studies; Gen. Man. JUAN OCERIN.

Editora e Gráfica Miguel Couto, SA: Rua da Passagem 78, Loja A, Botafogo, 22290-030 Rio de Janeiro, RJ; tel. (21) 2541-5145; f. 1969; engineering; Dir PAULO KOBLER PINTO LOPES SAMPAIO.

Editora Lê, SA: Rua Januária 437, Floresta, Belo Horizonte, MG; tel. (31) 3423-3200; e-mail editora@le.com.br; internet www.le.com.br; f. 1967; textbooks.

Editora Lemi, SA: Av. Nossa Senhora de Fátima 1945, CP 1890, 30000 Belo Horizonte, MG; tel. (31) 3201-8044; f. 1967; administration, accounting, law, ecology, economics, textbooks, children's books and reference books.

Editora Melhoramentos, Ltda: Rua Tito 479, 05051-000 São Paulo, SP; tel. (11) 3874-0854; fax (11) 3874-0855; e-mail blerner@melhoramentos.com.br; internet www.melhoramentos.com.br; f. 1890; general non-fiction, children's books, dictionaries; Dir BRENO LERNER.

Editora Michalany, Ltda: Rua Laura dos Anjos Ramos 420, Jardim Santa Cruz—Interlagos, 04455-350 São Paulo, SP; tel. (11) 5611-3414; fax (11) 5614-1592; e-mail editora@editoramichalany.com.br; internet www.editoramichalany.com.br; f. 1965; biographies, economics, textbooks, geography, history, religion, maps; Dir DOUGLAS MICHALANY.

Editora Moderna, Ltda: Rua Padre Adelino 758, Belenzinho, 03303-904 São Paulo, SP; tel. (11) 6090-1316; fax (11) 6090-1369; e-mail moderna@moderna.com.br; internet www.moderna.com.br; Pres. RICARDO ARISSA FELTRE.

Editora Nova Fronteira, SA: Rua Bambina 25, Botafogo, 22251-050 Rio de Janeiro, RJ; tel. (21) 2131-1111; fax (21) 2537-2659; e-mail sac@novafronteira.com.br; internet www.novafronteira.com.br; f. 1965; fiction, psychology, history, politics, science fiction, poetry, leisure, reference; Pres. CARLOS AUGUSTO LACERDA.

Editora Record, SA: Rua Argentina 171, São Cristóvão, CP 884, 20001-970 Rio de Janeiro, RJ; tel. (21) 2585-2000; fax (21) 2585-2085; e-mail record@record.com.br; internet www.record.com.br; f. 1941; general fiction and non-fiction, education, textbooks, fine arts; Pres. SÉRGIO MACHADO.

Editora Revista dos Tribunais, Ltda: Rua do Bosque 820, 01136-000 São Paulo, SP; tel. (11) 3613-8400; fax (11) 3613-8474; e-mail gerencia.mkt@rt.com.br; internet www.rt.com.br; f. 1912; law and jurisprudence books and periodicals; Dir CARLOS HENRIQUE DE CARVALHO FILHO.

Editora Rideel, Ltda: Av. Casa Verde 455, Casa Verde, 02519-000 São Paulo, SP; tel. and fax (11) 6238-5100; e-mail sac@rideel.com.br; internet www.rideel.com.br; f. 1971; general; Dir ITALO AMADIO.

Editora Saraiva: Av. Marquês de São Vicente 1697, CP 2362, 01139-904 São Paulo, SP; tel. (11) 3933-3366; fax (11) 861-3308; e-mail diretoria.editora@editorasaraiva.com.br; internet www.editorasaraiva.com.br; f. 1914; education, textbooks, law, economics; Pres. JORGE EDUARDO SARAIVA.

Editora Scipione, Ltda: Praça Carlos Gomes 46, 01501-040 São Paulo, SP; tel. (11) 3241-2255; e-mail scipione@scipione.com.br; internet www.scipione.com.br; f. 1983; owned by Editora Abril, SA; school books, literature, reference; Dir LUIZ ESTEVES SALLUM.

Editora Vozes, Ltda: Rua Frei Luís 100, CP 90023, 25689-900 Petrópolis, RJ; tel. (24) 2233-9000; fax (24) 2231-4676; e-mail editorial@vozes.com.br; internet www.vozes.com.br; f. 1901; Catholic publrs; theology, philosophy, history, linguistics, science, psychology, fiction, education, etc.; Dir ANTÔNIO MOSER.

Instituto Brasileiro de Edições Pedagógicas, Ltda (Editoras IBEP Nacional): Av. Alexandre Mackenzie 619, Jaguaré, 05322-000 São Paulo, SP; tel. (11) 6099-7799; fax (11) 6694-5338; e-mail editoras@ibep-nacional.com.br; internet www.ibep-nacional.com.br; f. 1965; textbooks, foreign languages and reference books; Dirs JORGE YUNES, PAULO C. MARTI.

Lex Editora, SA: Rua da Consolação 77, 01301-000 São Paulo, SP; tel. (11) 2126-6000; fax (11) 2126-6001; e-mail wsoares@aduaneiras.com.br; internet www.lex.com.br; f. 1937; legislation and jurisprudence; Dir CARLOS SERGIO SERRA.

Livraria Francisco Alves Editora, SA: Rua Uruguaiana 94, 13° andar, centro, 20050-091 Rio de Janeiro, RJ; tel. (21) 2221-3198; fax (21) 2242-3438; f. 1854; textbooks, fiction, non-fiction; Pres. CARLOS LEAL.

Livraria José Olympio Editora, SA: Rua da Glória 344, 4° andar, Glória, 20241-180 Rio de Janeiro, RJ; tel. (21) 2509-6939; fax (21) 2242-0802; f. 1931; juvenile, science, history, philosophy, psychology, sociology, fiction; Dir MANOEL ROBERTO DOMINGUES.

Pallas Editora: Rua Frederico de Albuquerque 56, Higienópolis, 21050-840 Rio de Janeiro, RJ; tel. and fax (21) 2270-0186; e-mail pallas@alternex.com.br; internet www.pallaseditora.com.br; f. 1980; Afro-Brazilian culture.

PUBLISHERS' ASSOCIATIONS

Associação Brasileira de Editores de Livros (Abrelivros): Rua Turiassu 143, Conj. 101/102, 05005-001 São Paulo, SP; tel. and fax (11) 3826-9071; e-mail contato@abrelivros.org.br; internet www.abrelivros.org.br; f. 1991; 27 mems; Pres. JOÃO ARINOS RIBEIRO DOS SANTOS.

Associação Brasileira do Livro (ABL): Av. 13 de Maio 23, 16° andar, Sala 1619/1620, 20031-000 Rio de Janeiro, RJ; tel. and fax (21) 2240-9115; e-mail abralivro@uol.com.br; Pres. ADENILSON JARBAS CABRAL.

Câmara Brasileira do Livro: Cristiano Viana 91, 05411-000 São Paulo, SP; tel. and fax (11) 3069-1300; e-mail marketing@cbl.org.br; internet www.cbl.org.br; f. 1946; Pres. ROSELY BOSCHINI.

Sindicato Nacional dos Editores de Livros (SNEL): Rua da Ajuda 35, 18° andar, Centro, 20040-000 Rio de Janeiro, RJ; tel. (21) 2533-0399; fax (21) 2533-0422; e-mail snel@snel.org.br; internet www.snel.org.br; 200 mems; Pres. SONIA MACHADO JARDIM.

There are also regional publishers' associations.

Broadcasting and Communications

TELECOMMUNICATIONS

Regulatory Authority

Agência Nacional de Telecomunicações (ANATEL): SAUS Quadra 06, Blocos C, E, F e H, 70070-940 Brasília, DF; tel. (61) 2312-2000; fax (61) 2312-2264; e-mail biblioteca@anatel.gov.br; internet www.anatel.gov.br; f. 1998; regional office in each state; Pres. RONALDO MOTA SARDENBERG.

Major Operators

Amazônia Celular: Av. Solferina Ricci Pace 470, Vale do Jatobá, 30664-000 Belo Horizonte, MG; internet www.amazoniacelular.com.br; mobile cellular provider in the Amazon region; 1.3m. customers; Pres. JOSÉ MAURO METTRAU CARNEIRO DA CUNHA; CEO LUIZ EDUARDO FALCO PIRES CORREA.

AT&T Brazil: Torre Sul, 7°, Rua James Joule 65, São Paulo, SP; internet www.att.com.

Brasil Telecom: SIA Sul, Área dos Servicos Públicos, Lote D, Bloco B, 71215-000 Brasília, DF; tel. (61) 3415-1128; fax (61) 3415-1133; internet www.brasiltelecom.com.br; fixed line services in nine states and Federal District; fixed line and mobile cellular networks; Chair. SÉRGIO SPINELLI SILVA JÚNIOR; Pres. LUIZ EDUARDO FALCO PIRES CORRÊA.

Claro: Rua Mena Barreto 42, Botafogo, 22271-100 Rio de Janeiro, RJ; internet www.claro.com.br; f. 2003 by mergers; owned by América Móvil, SA de CV (Mexico); mobile cellular provider; 30.2m. subscribers (2007).

CTBC (Companhia de Telecomunicações do Brasil Central): Av. Afonso Pena 3928, Bairro Brasil, 38400-668 Uberlândia, MG; internet www4.ctbctelecom.com.br; f. 1954; owned by Grupo Algar; mobile and fixed line provider in central Brazil.

Empresa Brasileira de Telecomunicações, SA (Embratel): Av. Presidente Vargas 1012, CP 2586, 20179-900 Rio de Janeiro, RJ; tel. (21) 2519-8182; e-mail cmsocial@embratel.net.br; internet www.embratel.com.br; f. 1965; operates national and international telecommunications system; owned by Telmex (Teléfonos de Mexico, SA).

Oi (Tele Norte Leste Participações, SA): Rua Lauro Müller 116, 22° andar, Botafogo, Rio de Janeiro, RJ; tel. (21) 2815-2921; fax (21) 2571-3050; internet www.novaoi.com.br; f. 1998 as Tele Norte Leste; fixed line and mobile operator; Pres. JOSÉ MAURO METTRAU CARNEIRO DA CUNHA; CEO LUIZ EDUARDO FALCO.

Sercomtel Celular, SA: Rua João Cândido 555, 86010-000 Londrina, PR; tel. 0800 400 4343; e-mail casc@sercomtel.com.br; internet www.sercomtelcelular.com.br; f. 1998; mobile cellular network provider; Pres. JOÃO BATISTA DE REZENDE.

Telefônica SP: Rua Martiniano de Carvalho 851, Bela Vista, 01321-000 São Paulo, SP; tel. (11) 3549-7200; fax (11) 3549-7202; e-mail webmaster@telesp.com.br; internet www.telesp.com.br; fmrly Telecomunicações de São Paulo (Telesp), privatized in 1998; subsidiary of Telefónica, SA (Spain); 41m. customers.

Telemig Celular: internet www.telemigcelular.com.br; mobile cellular provider in Minas Gerais; 2.6m. customers.

TIM (Telecom Italia Mobile): Av. das Américas 3434, 5° andar, Barra da Tijuca, 22640-102 Rio de Janeiro, RJ; internet www.tim.com.br; f. 1998 in Brazil; owned by Telecom Italia (Italy); mobile cellular provider; 24.1m. customers (2006); Pres. GIORGIO DELLA SETA FERRARI CORBELLI GRECO; CEO MARIO CESAR PEREIRA DE ARAUJO.

Vivo: Av. Chucri Zaidan 2460, 5°, 04583-110 São Paulo, SP; tel. (11) 5105-1001; internet www.vivo.com.br; owned by Telefónica Móviles, SA of Spain; Telefónica bought Portugal Telecom's share in 2010; mobile telephones; Pres. ROBERTO OLIVEIRA DE LIMA; 24.6m. customers.

BROADCASTING

RADIOBRÁS (Empresa Brasileira de Radiodifusão): SCRN 502, Bloco B 80, Edif. Marilda Figueiredo, Sala 308, CP 070747, 70720-502 Brasília, DF; tel. (61) 3327-4348; fax (61) 3327-4378; e-mail faleconosco@radiobras.gov.br; internet www.radiobras.gov.br; f. 1975; state-run radio and television network; Pres. JOSÉ ROBERTO GARCEZ.

Radio

The main broadcasting stations in Rio de Janeiro are: Rádio Nacional, Rádio Globo, Rádio Eldorado, Rádio Jornal do Brasil, Rádio Tupi and Rádio Mundial. In São Paulo the main stations are Rádio Bandeirantes, Rádio Mulher, Rádio Eldorado, Rádio Gazeta and Rádio Excelsior; and in Brasília: Rádio Nacional, Rádio Alvorada, Rádio Planalto and Rádio Capital.

The state-run corporation RADIOBRÁS (q.v.) owns the following radio stations:

Rádio Nacional AM de Brasília: CP 259, 7017-750 Brasília, DF; f. 1958; Man. CRISTINA GUIMARÃES.

Rádio Nacional da Amazônia: CP 258, 70359-970 Brasília, DF; internet www.radiobras.gov.br; f. 1977; Man. SOFÍA HAMMOE.

Rádio Nacional FM de Brasília: CP 070747, 70720-502 Brasília, DF; f. 1977; broadcasts to the Federal District and surrounding areas; Man. CARLOS SENNA.

Rádio Nacional do Rio de Janeiro: f. 2004.

Television

The main television networks are:

RBS TV: Rua do Acampamento 2250B, Passo do Príncipe, 96425-250 Bagé, RS; tel. (53) 240-5300; internet www.rbs.com.br; f. 1957; major regional network; operates Canal Rural and TVCOM; Group Pres. JAYME SIROTSKY.

TV Bandeirantes: Rádio e Televisão Bandeirantes Ltda, Rua Radiantes 13, Morumbi, 05699-900 São Paulo, SP; tel. (11) 3742-3011; fax (11) 3745-7622; e-mail cat@band.com.br; internet www.band.com.br; 65 TV stations and repeaters throughout Brazil; Pres. JOÃO CARLOS SAAD.

TV Brasil Internacional: CP 08840, 70312-920 Brasília, DF; tel. (61) 3799-5889; fax (61) 3799-5888; e-mail tvbrasilinternacional@ebc.com.br; internet www.ebc.com.br; f. 2005; owned by Empresa Brasil de Comunicação (EBC); broadcasts internationally via satellite in Portuguese; Gen. Co-ordinator MARILENA CHIARELLI.

TV da Gente: internet www.tvdagente.com.br; f. 2005; part of Grupo Bandeirantes de Comunicação; Afro-Brazilian channel; Founder JOSÉ DE PAULA NETO.

TV Nacional (Canal 2): Brasília, DF; tel. (21) 3327-4523; public tv station; broadcasts to the Federal District and surrounding areas; owned by RADIOBRÁS; Head ANDREÁ FASSINA.

TV Record—Rede Record de Televisão—Radio Record, SA: Rua de Várzea 240, Barra Funda, 01140-080 São Paulo, SP; tel. (11) 3660-4761; fax (11) 3660-4756; e-mail tvrecord@rederecord.com.br; internet www.tvrecord.com.br; Pres. JOÃO BATISTA R. SILVA; Exec. Vice-Pres. H. GONÇALVES.

TV Rede Globo: Rua Lopes Quintas 303, Jardim Botânico, 22460-010 Rio de Janeiro, RJ; tel. (21) 2540-2000; fax (21) 2294-2092; e-mail webm@redeglobo.com.br; internet www.redeglobo.com.br; f. 1965; 8 stations; national network; Dir ADILSON PONTES MALTA.

TV SBT—Sistema Brasileira de Televisão—Canal 4 de São Paulo, SA: Av. Das Comunicações 4, Vila Jaraguá, 06278-905 São Paulo, SP; tel. (11) 7087-3000; fax (11) 7087-3509; internet www.sbt.com.br; Vice-Pres. GUILHERME STOLIAR.

Broadcasting Associations

Associação Brasileira de Emissoras de Rádio e Televisão (ABERT): SCN Quadra 04, Bloco B, No 100, 5° andar, Sala 501, Centro Empresarial Varig, 70710-500 Brasília, DF; tel. and fax (61) 2104-4600; e-mail abert@abert.org.br; internet www.abert.org.br; f. 1962; Pres. DANIEL PIMENTEL SLAVIERO; Exec. Dir FLÁVIO CAVALCANTI JÚNIOR.

There are regional associations for Bahia, Ceará, Goiás, Minas Gerais, Rio Grande do Sul, Santa Catarina, São Paulo, Amazonas, Distrito Federal, Mato Grosso and Mato Grosso do Sul (combined), and Sergipe.

Finance

(cap. = capital; res = reserves; dep. = deposits; m. = million; brs = branches; amounts in reais, unless otherwise stated)

BANKING

Conselho Monetário Nacional (CMN): Setor Bancário Sul, Quadra 03, Bloco B, Edif. Sede do Banco do Brasil, 21° andar, 70074-900 Brasília, DF; tel. (61) 3414-1945; fax (61) 3414-2528; e-mail cmn@bcb.gov.br; f. 1964; est. to formulate monetary policy and to supervise the banking system; Pres. GUIDO MANTEGA (Minister of Finance).

Central Bank

Banco Central do Brasil: SBS, Quadra 03, Mezanino 01, Bloco B, 70074-900 Brasília, DF; tel. (61) 3414-1414; fax (61) 3223-1033; e-mail secre.surel@bcb.gov.br; internet www.bcb.gov.br; f. 1965; est. to execute the decisions of the Conselho Monetário Nacional; bank of issue; total assets 1,047,092.4m. (Dec. 2008); Gov. HENRIQUE DE CAMPOS MEIRELLES; 10 brs.

State Commercial Banks

Banco do Brasil, SA: SBS, Quadra 01, Bloco C, Lote 32, Edif. Sede III, 70073-901 Brasília, DF; tel. (61) 3310-3406; fax (61) 3310-2561; e-mail ri@bb.com.br; internet www.bb.com.br; f. 1808; cap. 13,780.0m., res 16,157.3m., dep. 369,366.5m. (Dec. 2008); Pres. and Vice-Chair. ALDEMIR BENDINE; 15,133 brs.

Banco do Estado do Pará: Edif. Banpará, 4° andar, Av. Presidente Vargas 251, Campina, 66010-000 Belém, PA; tel. (91) 3210-3233; fax (91) 3241-7163; internet www.banparanet.com.br; f. 1961; cap. 105.8m., res 16.4m., dep. 1,255.1m. (Dec. 2008); Pres. AFFONSO RODRIGUES VIANNA NETO; 42 brs.

Banco do Estado do Rio Grande do Sul, SA (Banrisul): Rua Caldas Junior 108, 7° andar, 90018-900 Porto Alegre, RS; tel. (51) 3215-2501; fax (51) 3215-1715; e-mail cambio_dg@banrisul.com.br; internet www.banrisul.com.br; f. 1928; cap. 2,300.0m., res 779.1m., dep. 16,763.6m. (Dec. 2008); Pres. FERNANDO GUERREIRO DE LEMOS; 352 brs.

Banco do Nordeste do Brasil, SA: Av. Pedro Ramalho 5700, Passaré, 60740-000 Fortaleza, CE; tel. (85) 3299-3000; fax (85) 3299-3674; e-mail info@banconordeste.gov.br; internet www.banconordeste.gov.br; f. 1952; cap. 1,299.0m., res 498.5m., dep. 4,455.2m. (Dec. 2008); Pres. ROBERTO SMITH; 186 brs.

BANESTES, SA—Banco do Estado do Espirito Santo: Edif. Palas Center, Bloco B, 9° andar, Av. Princesa Isabel 574, Centro, 29010-931 Espirito Santo, ES; tel. (27) 3383-1545; fax (27) 3383-1398; e-mail ri@banestes.com.br; internet www.banestes.com.br; f. 1937; cap. 436.3m., res 131.0m., dep. 7030.5m. (Dec. 2008); Pres. BRUNO PESSANHA NEGRIS; CEO ROBERTO DA CUNHA PENEDO; 140 brs.

Private Banks

Banco ABC Brasil, SA: Av. Juscelino Kubitschek 1400, 3°–5° andares, 04543-000 São Paulo, SP; tel. (11) 3170-2000; fax (11) 3170-2001; e-mail sac.abcbrasil@abcbrasil.com.br; internet www.abcbrasil.com.br; f. 1989 as Banco ABC—Roma SA; 84% owned by Arab Banking Corpn BSC (Bahrain); cap. 1,004.4m., res 157.3m., dep. 3,077.0m. (Dec. 2008); Pres. and Gen. Man. TITO ENRIQUE DA SILVA NETO; 2 brs.

Banco Alfa de Investimento, SA: Alameda Santos 466, Cerqueira César, 01418-000 Paraíso, SP; tel. (11) 3175-5074; fax (11) 3171-2438; e-mail alfanet@alfanet.com.br; internet www.alfanet.com.br; f. 1998; cap. 382.0m., res 544.0m., dep. 7,935.2m. (Dec. 2008); Pres. PAULO GUIHERME MONTEIRO LOBATO RIBEIRO; 12 brs.

Banco da Amazônia, SA: Av. Presidente Vargas 800, 3° andar, 66017-000 Belém, PA; tel. (91) 4008-3421; fax (91) 4008-3243; e-mail cambio@bancoamazionia.com.br; internet www.bancoamazonia

.com.br; f. 1942; state-owned; cap. 1,205.2m., res 680.3m., dep. 2,185.2m. (Dec. 2008); Pres. ABIDIAS JOSÉ DE SOUZA JÚNIOR; 104 brs.

Banco BBM, SA: Av. Tancredo Neves 1632, Caminho das Arvores, 41820-020 Salvador, BA; tel. (71) 4009-6000; fax (71) 4009-6001; internet www.bancobbm.com.br; f. 1858; est. as Banco de Bahia; present name adopted 1998; cap. 413.1m., res 324.1m., dep. 5,139.1m. (Dec. 2008); Pres. PEDRO HENRIQUE MARIANI BITTENCOURT; 7 brs.

Banco BMG, SA: Av. Alvares Cabral 1707, Santo Agostinho, 30170-001 Belo Horizonte, MG; tel. (31) 3290-3000; fax (31) 3290-3100; e-mail bancobmg@bancobmg.com.br; internet www.bancobmg.com .br; f. 1930; cap. 1,399.7m., res 617.5m., dep. 4,076.2m. (Dec. 2008); Pres. FLÁVIO PENTAGNA GUIMARÃES; 10 brs.

Banco Bradesco, SA: Cidade de Deus, Vila Yara, 06029-900 Osasco, SP; tel. (11) 3684-4011; fax (11) 3684-4630; internet www .bradesco.com.br; f. 1943; est. as Banco Brasileiro de Descontos; present name adopted 1989; cap. 23,000.0m., res 11,256.5m., dep. 255,537.0m. (Dec. 2008); Chair. LÁZARO DE MELLO BRANDÃO; CEO LUIZ CARLOS TRABUCO CAPPI; 3,092 brs.

Banco Brascan, SA: Av. Almirante Barroso 52, 30° andar, Centro, 20031-000 Rio de Janeiro, RJ; tel. (21) 3231-3000; fax (21) 3231-3231; internet www.bancobrascan.com.br; f. 1968; cap. 169.0m., res 7.0m., dep. 428.7m. (Dec. 2008); Pres. ANTÔNIO PAULO DE AZEVEDO SODRE.

Banco BTG Pactual, SA: Torre Corcovado, 6°, Praia de Botafago 501, 22250-040 Rio de Janeiro, RJ; tel. (21) 3262-9600; fax (21) 2514-8600; internet www.btgpactual.com; f. 1983; fmrly Banco UBS Pactual; present name adopted 2008 following acquisition by BTG Pactual; cap. 555.0m., res 884.3m., dep. 6,320.8m. (Dec. 2008); Pres. ANDRÉ ESTEVES; 5 brs.

Banco Dibens, SA: Rua Boa Vista 162, 6° andar, Centro, 01014-000 São Paulo, SP; tel. (11) 5019-8101; fax (11) 5019-8103; internet www .dibens.com.br; f. 1989; jtly owned by UNIBANCO and Grupo Verdi; cap. 179.2m., res 23.6m., dep. 1,420.3m. (Dec. 2005); Pres. CARLOS HENRIQUE ZANVETTOR; 23 brs.

Banco Fibra: Av. Presidente Juscelino Kubitschek 360, 4° ao 9° andar, 04543-000 São Paulo, SP; tel. (11) 3847-6700; fax (11) 3847-6962; e-mail bancofibra@bancofibra.com.br; internet www .bancofibra.com.br; f. 1989; cap. 706.4m., res 2.4m., dep. 6,311.7m. (Dec. 2008); CEO ANTONIO DE LIMA NETO.

Banco Finasa BMC, SA: Av. das Nações Unidas 12995, 25° andar, 04578-000 São Paulo, SP; tel. (11) 5503-7711; fax (11) 3523-0037; internet www.bradescopromotora.com.br; f. 1939; est. as Banco Mercantil de Crédito, SA; renamed Banco BMC SA in 1990; adopted current name in 2008 after merger with Bank Finasa; owned by Banco Bradesco; cap. 22,010.0m., res 536.1m., dep. 37,976.0m. (Dec. 2008); Pres. LÁZARO DE MELLO BRANDÃO.

Banco Industrial do Brasil: Av. Juscelino Kubitschek 1703, 2°–4° andares, Itaim Bibi, 04543-000 São Paulo, SP; tel. (11) 3049-9671; fax (11) 3049-9810; internet www.bancoindustrial.com.br; f. 1994; cap. 360.3m., res 20.3m., dep. 956.3m. (Dec. 2008); Pres. CARLOS ALBERTO MANSUR.

Banco Industrial e Comercial, SA (Bicbanco): Av. Paulista 1048, Bela Vista, 01310-100 São Paulo, SP; tel. (11) 2173-9000; fax (11) 2173-9101; internet www.bicbanco.com.br; f. 1938; cap. 1,434.2m., res 255.0m., dep. 5,600.3m. (Dec. 2008); Pres. JOSÉ BEZERRA DE MENEZES; 38 brs.

Banco Indusval, SA (Banco Indusval Multistock): Rua Boa Vista, 7°–12° andares, Centro, 01014-000 São Paulo, SP; tel. (11) 3315-6777; fax (11) 3315-0130; e-mail banco@indusval.com.br; internet www.indusval.com.br; f. 1980; cap. 371.0m., res 77.5m., dep. 852.0m. (Dec. 2008); Pres. MANOEL FELIX CINTRA NETO.

Banco Itaú, SA: Praça Alfredo Egydio de Souza Aranha 100, Torre Itaúsa, 04344-902 São Paulo, SP; tel. (11) 5019-8101; fax (11) 5019-8103; e-mail investor.relations@itau.com.br; internet www.itau.com .br; f. 1944; est. as Banco Central de Crédito; present name adopted 1973; merger with Unibanco announced in Nov. 2008; cap. 40,175.0m., res 406.0m., dep. 366,234.3m. (Dec. 2008); Pres. and CEO SERGIO RIBEIRO DA COSTA WERLANG; 3,044 brs.

Banco Itaú BBA, SA: Av. Brig. Faria Lima 3400, 3° ao 8° andar, 04538-132 São Paulo, SP; tel. (11) 3708-8000; fax (11) 3708-8172; e-mail bancoitaubba@itaubba.com.br; internet www.itaubba.com .br; f. 1967; est. as Banco do Estado de Minas Gerais, SA; acquired by Banco Itaú in 2002; present name adopted 2004; cap. 4,223.1m., res 1,437.6m., dep. 94,118.3m. (Dec. 2008); Pres. and CEO CANDIDO BOTELHO BRACHER; 6 brs.

Banco Mercantil do Brasil, SA: Rua Rio de Janerio 680, Centro, 30160-912 Belo Horizonte, MG; tel. (31) 3057-4450; fax (31) 3079-8422; e-mail sac@mercantil.com.br; internet www.mercantil.com.br; f. 1943; est. as Banco Mercantil de Minas Gerais, SA; cap. 214.4m., res 306.6m., dep. 4,988.2m. (Dec. 2008); Pres. MILTON DE ARAÚJO; 171 brs.

Banco Paulista, SA: Av. Brigadeiro Faria Lima, 1355 Jardim Paulistano, 2° andar, 01452-002 São Paulo, SP; tel. (11) 3299-2000; fax (11) 3299-2362; e-mail cambiobp@bancopaulista.com.br; internet www.bancopaulista.com.br; f. 1989; cap. 107.0m., res 15.7m., dep. 818.0m. (Dec. 2008); Pres. ALVARO AUGUSTO VIDIGAL.

Banco de Pernambuco, SA (Bandepe): Edif. Bandepe, 5° andar, Cais do Apolo 222, Bairro do Recife, 50030-230 Recife, PE; tel. (11) 3174-9957; fax (11) 3174-7101; internet www.bandepe.com.br; f. 1938; est. as Banco do Estado de Pernambuco; present name adopted 2000; owned by Grupo Santander Brasil; cap. 2,768.4m., res 150.3m., dep. 1,095.8m. (Dec. 2005); Pres. JOSE DE MENEZES BERENGUER NETO; 66 brs.

Banco Pine, SA: Eldorado Business Tower, Av. das Nações Unidas 8501, 30° andar, 05425-070 São Paulo, SP; tel. (11) 3372-5200; fax (11) 3372-5404; e-mail bancopine@uol.com.br; internet www .bancopine.com.br; f. 1997; cap. 422.6m., res 35.0m., dep. 404.5m. (Dec. 2008); Man. Dirs Dr NELSON NOGUEIRA PINHEIRO, NORBERTO NOGUEIRA PINHEIRO.

Banco Real, SA: Av. Brigadeiro Luís Antônio 1824, 9° andar, 01317-002 Bela Vista, SP; tel. (11) 3174-9615; fax (11) 3174-7052; internet www.bancoreal.com.br; f. 1925; acquired by Grupo Santander (Spain) in 2008; cap. 7,593.7m., res 2,092.0m., dep. 73,754.7m. (Dec. 2006); 847 brs.

Banco Rural, SA: Rua Rio de Janeiro 927, 14º andar, 30160-041 Belo Horizonte, MG; tel. (31) 2126-5000; fax (31) 2126-5096; e-mail rural002@rural.com.br; internet www.bancorural.com.br; f. 1964; est. as Banco Rural de Minas Gerais; present name adopted 1980; cap. 277.7m., res 34.9m., dep. 1,387.0m. (Dec. 2008); Pres. KÁTIA RABELLO; 26 brs.

Banco Safra, SA: Av. Paulista 2100, 9° andar, 01310-930 São Paulo, SP; tel. (11) 3175-7309; fax (11) 3175-8466; internet www.safra.com .br; f. 1940; cap. 2,008.0m., res 700.5m., dep. 41,211.5m. (Dec. 2008); Pres. CARLOS ALBERTO VIEIRA; 99 brs.

Banco Santander, SA: Av. Presidente Juscelino Kubitschek, 2041 Vila Olimpia, 04543-011 São Paulo, SP; tel. (11) 3553-5447; fax (11) 3553-7778; internet www.santander.com.br; f. 2006; est. as Banco Santander Banespa, SA by merger; present name adopted 2007; owned by Banco Santander, SA (Spain); cap. 47,152.2m., res 1,641.6m., dep. 90,461.8m. (Dec. 2008); Pres. FABIO COLLETTI BARBOSA.

Banco Société Générale Brasil, SA: Av. Paulista 2300, 9° andar, Cerqueira Cesar, 01310-300 São Paulo, SP; tel. (11) 3217-8000; fax (11) 3217-8090; e-mail faleconosco@sgcib.com; internet www .sgbrasil.com.br; f. 1981; est. as Banco Sogeral; present name adopted 2001; cap. 1,388.0m., res –201.5m., dep. 721.2m. (Dec. 2008); Pres. FRANÇOIS DOSSA.

Banco Votorantim, SA: Av. das Nações Unidas 14171, Torre A, 18° andar, Vila Gertrudes, 04794-000 São Paulo, SP; tel. (11) 5171-1000; fax (11) 5171-1900; e-mail sac@bancovotorantim.com.br; internet www.bancovotorantim.com.br; f. 1991; cap. 3,380.0m., res 2,982.2m., dep. 62,420.4m. (Dec. 2008); Pres. WILSON MASAO KUZUHARA.

Banif—Banco Internacional do Funchal (Brasil), SA: Rua Minas de Prata 30, 16°–17° andares, 04552-080 São Paulo, SP; tel. (11) 3165-2000; fax (11) 3167-3960; e-mail bc_matriz@bancobanif .com.br; internet www.bancobanif.com.br; f. 1999 as Banco Banif Primus, SA; present name adopted 2005; owned by Banif Comercial SGPS, SA (Portugal); cap. 128.2m., res 17.0m., dep. 1.5m. (Dec. 2008); Pres. ANTONIO JÚLIO MACHADO RODRIGUES.

Development Banks

Banco de Desenvolvimento de Minas Gerais, SA (BDMG): Rua da Bahia 1600, 30160-907 Belo Horizonte, MG; tel. (31) 3219-8000; fax (31) 3226-3292; internet www.bdmg.mg.gov.br; f. 1962; owned by the state of Minas Gerais; long-term credit operations; cap. 909.3m., res 26.6m., total assets 1,994.5m. (Dec. 2008); Pres. PAULO DE TARSO ALMEIDA PAIVA.

Banco Nacional do Desenvolvimento Econômico e Social (BNDES): Av. República do Chile 100, Centro, 20031-917 Rio de Janeiro, RJ; tel. (21) 2172-7447; fax (21) 2172-6266; e-mail gerai@ bndes.gov.br; internet www.bndes.gov.br; f. 1952 to act as main instrument for financing of devt schemes sponsored by the Govt and to support programmes for the devt of the national economy; charged with supervision of privatization programme of the 1990s; cap. 12,500.1m., res 576.4m., dep. 8,617.0m. (June 2002); Chair. LUCIANO COUTINHO.

Investment Bank

Banco Fininvest, SA: Rua da Passagem 170, 7° andar, 20030-021 Rio de Janeiro, RJ; tel. (21) 3097-4725; fax (21) 3820-5323; internet www.fininvest.com.br; f. 1961 as Fininvest SA Crédito Financiamento e Investimento; present name adopted 1989; owned by Unibanco; cap. 3,165.8m., res 674.7m., dep. 937.7m. (Dec. 2008); Pres. ALVARO OSÓRIO LONGO MUSA DOS SANTOS.

State-owned Savings Bank

Caixa Econômica Federal: SBS, Quadra 04, Lotes 3–4, 16° andar, 70092-900 Brasília, DF; tel. (61) 3206-3171; fax (61) 3206-9732; e-mail genit@caixa.gov.br; internet www.caixa.gov.br; f. 1861; cap. 9,292.0m., res 3,412.6m., dep. 218,347.0m. (Dec. 2008); Pres. MARIA FERNANDA RAMOS COELHO; 2,088 brs.

Foreign Banks

Banco Sumitomo Mitsui Brasileiro, SA: Av. Paulista 37, 11° andar, Paraiso, 01311-902 São Paulo, SP; tel. (11) 3178-8000; fax (11) 3178-8194; internet www.smbcgroup.com.br; f. 1958; present name adopted 2001; cap. 409.4m., res 10.6m., dep. 431.0m. (Dec. 2008); Pres. TOSHIRO KUBOTA; 1 br.

Banco de Tokyo-Mitsubishi UFJ Brasil, SA: Av. Paulista 1274, Bela Vista, 01310-925 São Paulo, SP; tel. (11) 3268-0211; fax (11) 3268-0453; internet www.br.bk.mufg.jp; f. 1972 as Banco de Tokyo; cap. 186.9m., res 118.7m., dep. 380.0m. (Dec. 2008); Pres. TOSHIFUMI MURATA; 2 brs.

Deutsche Bank SA—Banco Alemão: Av. Brigadeiro Faria Lima 3900, 13–15° andares, Itaim Bibi, 04598-132 São Paulo, SP; tel. (11) 2113-5000; fax (11) 2113-5100; internet www.deutsche-bank.com.br; f. 1911; cap. 415.2m., res 572.8m., dep. 7,709.3m. (Dec. 2008); Pres. BERNANDO PARNES.

HSBC Bank Brasil SA-Banco Multiplo: Edif. Palácio Avenida, 4° andar, Travessa Oliveira Belo 34, Centro, 80020-030 Curitiba, PR; tel. (41) 3321-6161; fax (41) 3321-6075; internet www.hsbc.com.br; f. 1997; cap. 2,289.2m., res 1,154.6m., dep. 72,136.3m. (Dec. 2008); Pres. BERNANDO PARNES; 939 brs.

Banking Associations

Associação Nacional dos Bancos de Investimentos (ANBID): Edif. Eldorado Business Tower, Av. das Nações Unidas 8501, 21° andar, 05425-070 São Paulo, SP; tel. (11) 3471-4200; fax (11) 3471-4230; e-mail anbid@anbid.com.br; internet www.anbid.com.br; investment banks; Pres. MARCELO FIDÊNCIO GIUFRIDA; Supt LUIZ KAUFMAN.

Federação Brasileira dos Bancos: Avda Brigadeiro Faria Lima 1485, 14° andar, Torre Norte, Pinheiros, 01452-921 São Paulo, SP; tel. (11) 3244-9800; fax (11) 3031-4106; e-mail imprensa@febraban.org.br; internet www.febraban.org.br; f. 1966; Pres. FABIO COLLETTI BARBOSA; Dir-Gen. WILSON ROBERTO LEVORATO; 120 mems.

Sindicato dos Bancos dos Estados do Rio de Janeiro e Espírito Santo: Av. Rio Branco 81, 19° andar, 20040-004 Rio de Janeiro, RJ; tel. (21) 2253-1538; fax (21) 2253-6032; e-mail aberj@aberj.com.br; internet www.aberj.com.br; f. 1935; Pres. CARLOS ALBERTO VIEIRA.

Sindicato dos Bancos dos Estados de São Paulo, Paraná, Mato Grosso e Mato Grosso do Sul: Rua Líbero Badaró 293, 13° andar, 01905 São Paulo, SP; f. 1924; Pres. PAULO DE QUEIROZ.

There are other banking associations in Maceió, Salvador, Fortaleza, Belo Horizonte, João Pessoa, Recife and Porto Alegre.

STOCK EXCHANGES

Comissão de Valores Mobiliários (CVM): Rua 7 de Setembro 111, Centro, 20050-901 Rio de Janeiro, RJ; tel. (21) 3554-8686; fax (21) 3554-8211; e-mail ouvidor@cvm.gov.br; internet www.cvm.gov.br; f. 1977 to supervise the operations of the stock exchanges and develop the Brazilian securities market; regional offices in Brasília and São Paulo; Chair. MARIA HELENA DOS SANTOS FERNANDES DE SANTANA.

BM&F BOVESPA, SA: Praça Antônio Prado 48, Rua XV e Novembro, 275 Centro, 01010-901 São Paulo, SP; tel. (11) 2565-4000; e-mail ri@bmfbovespa.com.br; internet www.bmfbovespa.com.br; f. 2008 by merger of Bolsa de Mercadorias e Futuros (BM&F—Mercantile and Futures Exchange) and Bolsa de Valores de São Paulo (BOVESPA—São Paulo Stock Exchange); offices in Brasília, Rio de Janeiro, Porto Alegre, Campo Grande, Santos, New York (USA) and Shanghai (People's Republic of China); Pres. ARMENIO FRAGA NETO; CEO EDEMIR PINTO.

Bolsa de Valores do Rio de Janeiro (BVRJ): Praça XV de Novembro 20, 20010-010 Rio de Janeiro, RJ; tel. (21) 2514-1069; fax (21) 2514-11107; e-mail info@bvrj.com.br; internet www.bvrj.com.br; f. 1845; focuses on the trading of fixed income govt bonds and foreign exchange; Chair. EDSON FIGUEIREDO MENEZES; Supt-Gen. SÉRGIO PÓVOA.

There are commodity exchanges at Paraná, Porto Alegre, Vitória, Recife, Santos and São Paulo.

INSURANCE

Supervisory Authorities

Conselho de Recursos do Sistema Nacional de Seguros Privados, de Previdência Abierta e de Capitalização (CRSNSP): Rua Buenos Aires 256, 20061-000 Rio de Janeiro, RJ; tel. (21) 3806-9815; f. 1966 as Conselho Nacional de Seguros Privados (CNSP); changed name in 1998; part of the Ministry of Finance; Pres. FRANCISCO TEIXEIRA DE ALMEIDA; Sec. THERESA CHRISTINA CUNHA MARTINS.

Superintendência de Seguros Privados (SUSEP): Av. Presidente Vargas, 730 Centro, 20071-900 Rio de Janeiro, RJ; tel. (21) 3233-4000; e-mail gabin@susep.gov.br; internet www.susep.gov.br; f. 1966; part of the Ministry of Finance; offices in Brasília, São Paulo and Porto Alegre; Pres. GUIDO MANTEGA (Minister of Finance); Supt PAULO DOS SANTOS.

Principal Companies

The following is a list of the principal national insurance companies, selected on the basis of assets. The total assets of insurance companies operating in Brazil were R $226,707m. in November 2008.

Bradesco Seguros e Previdência, SA: Rua Barão de Itapagipe 225, 20269-900 Rio de Janeiro, RJ; tel. (21) 2503-1101; fax (21) 2293-9489; internet www.bradescoseguros.com.br; f. 1934; general; Pres. LUIZ CARLOS TRABUCO CAPPI.

Bradesco Vida e Previdência, SA: Cidade de Deus s/n, Vila Yara, São Paulo, SP; tel. (11) 3684-2122; fax (11) 3684-5068; internet www.bradescoprevidencia.com.br; f. 2001; life insurance; Pres. MARCO ANTÔNIO ROSSI.

Brasilprev Seguros e Prevedência, SA: Rua Verbo Divino 1711, Chácara Santo Antônio, 04719-002 São Paulo, SP; tel. (11) 5185-4240; e-mail atendimento@brasilprev.com.br; internet www.brasilprev.com.br; f. 1993; all classes; 50% owned by Banco do Brasil; Pres. TARCÍSIO GODOY.

Caixa Seguros: SCN Quadra 01, Bloco A, Edif. 1, 15–17° andares, Asa Norte, 70711-900 Brasília, DF; tel. (61) 2192-2400; fax (61) 3328-0600; internet www.caixaseguros.com.br; f. 1967; fmrly Sasse, Cia Nacional de Seguros; adopted current name 2000; general; Pres. THIERRY MARC CLAUDE CLAUDON.

Caixa Vida e Previdência, SA: SCN Quadra 1, Bloco A, Edif. 1, 15° andar, 70711-900 Brasília, DF; tel. (61) 2192-2400; fax (61) 3328-0600; internet www.caixavidaeprevidencia.com.br; part of Caixa Seguros group.

Cia de Seguros Aliança do Brasil, SA (BB Seguros): Rua Manuel da Nóbrega 1280, 9° andar, 04001-004 São Paulo, SP; tel. (11) 4689-5638; internet www.aliancadobrasil.com.br; f. 1996; Pres. JAIME LUIZ KALSING.

HSBC Vida e Previdência (Brasil), SA: Rua Teniente Francisco Ferreira de Souza 805, Bloco 1, Ala 4, Vila Hauer, 81570-340 Curitaba, PR; tel. (41) 3217-4555; fax (41) 3321-8800; e-mail spariz@hsbc.com.vr; internet www.hsbc.com.br; f. 1938; all classes; Supt Dir VILSON ANDRADE; Pension Funds Dir SIDNEY PARIZ.

Icatu Hartford Seguros, SA: Praça 22 de Abril 36, 20021-370 Rio de Janeiro, RJ; tel. (21) 3824-3900; e-mail atendimento_internet@icatuhartford.com.br; internet www.icatu-hartford.com.br; Pres. MARIA SILVIA BASTOS MARQUES.

IRB-Brasil Resseguros: Av. Marechal Câmara 171, Castelo, 20020-901 Rio de Janeiro, RJ; tel. (21) 2272-0200; fax (21) 2240-8775; e-mail info@irb-brasilre.com.br; internet www.irb-brasilre.com.br; f. 1939; state-owned reinsurance co; fmrly Instituto de Resseguros do Brasil; Pres. EDUARDO HITIRO NAKAO.

Itaú Seguros, SA: Praça Alfredo Egydio de Souza Aranha 100, Bloco A, 04344-920 São Paulo, SP; tel. (11) 5019-3322; fax (11) 5019-3530; e-mail itauseguros@itauseguros.com.br; internet www.itauseguros.com.br; f. 1921; all classes; Pres. LUIZ DE CAMPOS SALLES.

Liberty Seguros, SA: Rua Dr Geraldo Campos Moreira 110, 04571-020 São Paulo, SP; tel. (11) 5503-4000; fax (11) 5505-2122; internet www.libertyseguros.com.br; f. 1906; general; Pres. LUIS EMILIO MAURETTE.

Marítima Seguros, SA: Rua Col Xavier de Toledo 114, 10° andar, São Paulo, SP; tel. (11) 3156-1000; fax (11) 3156-1712; internet www.maritima.com.br; f. 1943; Pres. FRANCISCO CAIUBY VIDIGAL; Dir-Gen. MILTON BELLIZIA FILHO.

Porto Seguro Cia de Seguros Gerais: Rua Guaianazes 1238, 12° andar, 01204-001 São Paulo, SP; tel. (11) 3366-5199; fax (11) 3366-5140; internet www.portoseguro.com.br; f. 1945; life, automotive and risk; Pres. JAYME BRASIL GARFINKEL.

Santander Seguros, SA: internet www.santander.com.br; part of Banco Santander.

Sul América, SA: Rua da Quitanda 86, 20091-000 Rio de Janeiro, RJ; tel. (21) 2506-8585; fax (21) 2506-8807; internet www.sulamerica.com.br; f. 1895; life and risk; Pres. PATRICK ANTONIO CLAUDE DE LARRAGOITI LUCAS.

Tokio Marine Seguradora, SA: Rua Samapiao Viana 44, 04004-902 Paraíso, SP; tel. (11) 3054-7000; internet www.tokiomarine.com.br; f. 1969 as Real Seguros, SA; adopted current name 2008; owned by Tokio Marine Holdings (Japan); general.

Unibanco Seguros e Previdência: Av. Eusébio Matoso 1375, 05423-180 São Paulo, SP; tel. (11) 3039-4082; fax (11) 3039-4074; internet www.unibancoseguros.com.br; subsidiary of União de Bancos Brasileiros, SA (Unibanco); life; Pres. JOSÉ CASTRO ARAÚJO RUDGE.

Insurance Associations

Federação Nacional dos Corretores de Seguros Privados e de Resseguros, de Capitalização, de Previdência Privada e das Empresas Corretoras de Seguros e de Resseguros (FENACOR): Rua Senador Dantas 74, 10° andar, 20031-205 Rio de Janeiro, RJ; tel. (21) 3077-4777; fax (21) 3077-4798; e-mail presidencia@fenacor.com.br; internet www.fenacor.com.br; f. 1975; Pres. ARMANDO VERGÍLIO DOS SANTOS, Jr.

Federação Nacional das Empresas de Seguros Privados e de Capitalização (FENASEG): Rua Senador Dantas 74, 12° andar, Centro, 20031-200 Rio de Janeiro, RJ; tel. (21) 2510-7777; e-mail fenaseg@fenaseg.org.br; internet www.fenaseg.org.br; f. 1951; Pres. JOÃO ELISIO FERRAZ DE CAMPOS.

Trade and Industry

GOVERNMENT AGENCIES

Agência Nacional de Petróleo, Gás Natural e Biocombustíveis (ANP): Av. Rio Branco 65, 12° andar, 20090-004 Rio de Janeiro, RJ; tel. (21) 2112-8100; fax (21) 2112-8129; internet www.anp.gov.br; f. 1998; regulatory body of the petroleum, natural gas and biofuels industries; Dir-Gen. HAROLDO BORGES RODRIGUES LIMA.

Agência de Promoção de Exportações do Brasil (APEX Brasil): Edif. Apex-Brasil, SBN, Quadra 02, Lote 11, 70040-020 Brasília, DF; tel. (61) 3426-0202; fax (61) 3426-0263; e-mail apex@apexbrasil.com.br; internet www.apexbrasil.com.br; f. 2003; promotes Brazilian exports; CEO ALESSANDRO GOLOMBIEWSKI TEIXEIRA.

Câmara de Comércio Exterior (CAMEX): Ministério do Desenvolvimento, Indústria e Comércio Exterior, Bloco J, 70053-900 Brasília, DF; tel. (61) 2109-7483; e-mail camex@desenvolvimento.gov.br; internet www.desenvolvimento.gov.br; f. 2003; part of Ministry of Development, Industry and Foreign Trade; formulates and co-ordinates export policies; Exec. Sec. MÁRIO MUGNAINI JÚNIOR.

Companhia de Pesquisa de Recursos Minerais (CPRM): Av. SGAN, Quadra 603, Conj. J, Parte A, 1° andar, 70830-030 Brasília, DF; tel. (61) 2192-8252; fax (61) 3224-1616; e-mail cprmsede@df.cprm.gov.br; internet www.cprm.gov.br; mining research, attached to the Ministry of Mines and Energy; regional offices in Belém, Belo Horizonte, Goiânia, Manaus, Porto Alegre, Recife, Salvador and São Paulo; Pres. AGAMENON SÉRGIO LUCAS DANTAS.

Conselho Nacional de Desenvolvimento Científico e Tecnológico (CNPq): Edif. Sede CNPq, 3° andar, Sala 300, SEPN 507, Bloco B, 70740-901 Brasília, DF; tel. (61) 2108-9000; fax (61) 2108-9394; e-mail presidencia@cnpq.br; internet www.cnpq.br; f. 1951; scientific and technological development council; Pres. CARLOS ALBERTO ARAGÃO DE CARVALHO FILHO.

Conselho Nacional de Desenvolvimento Rural Sustentável (CONDRAF): Edif. Palácio do Desenvolvimento, 8° andar, SBN, Quadra 01, Bloco D, 70057-900 Brasília, DF; tel. (61) 2191-9880; e-mail condraf@mda.gov.br; internet sistemas.mda.gov.br/condraf; f. 2000 to promote sustainable rural development; Pres. GUILHERME CASSEL (Minister of Agrarian Development).

Departamento Nacional da Produção Mineral (DNPM): SAN, Quadra 1, Bloco B, 3° andar, 70041-903 Brasília, DF; tel. (61) 3312-6666; fax (61) 3225-8274; e-mail dire@dnpm.gov.br; internet www.dnpm.gov.br; f. 1934; responsible for geological studies and control of exploration of mineral resources; part of Ministry of Mines and Energy; Dir-Gen. MIGUEL ANTONIO CEDRAZ NERY.

Empresa Brasileira de Pesquisa Agropecuária (EMBRAPA): Edif. Sede, Parque Estação Biológica (PqEB) s/n, Av. W3 Norte (final), CP 40315, 70770-901 Brasília, DF; tel. (61) 3448-4433; fax (61) 3448-4890; e-mail presid@sede.embrapa.br; internet www.embrapa.br; f. 1973; attached to the Ministry of Agriculture and Food Supply; agricultural research; Pres. PEDRO ANTONIO ARRAES PEREIRA.

Instituto Brasileiro de Geografia e Estatística (IBGE): Av. Franklin Roosevelt 166, 10° andar, Castelo, 20271-201 Rio de Janeiro, RJ; tel. (21) 2142-4503; fax (21) 2142-4933; e-mail ibge@ibge.gov.br; internet www.ibge.gov.br; f. 1936; produces and analyses statistical, geographical, cartographic, geodetic, demographic and socio-economic information; Pres. (IBGE) EDUARDO PEREIRA NUNES; Supt (CDDI) DAVID WU TAI.

Instituto Brasileiro do Meio Ambiente e Recursos Naturais Renováveis (IBAMA): Edif. Sede IBAMA, SCEN Trecho 2, 70818-900 Brasília, DF; tel. (61) 3316-1001; fax (61) 3226-1025; e-mail presid.sede@ibama.gov.br; internet www.ibama.gov.br; f. 1989; responsible for the annual formulation of national environmental plans; authorizes environmentally sensitive devt projects; Pres. ABELARDO BAYMA AZEVEDO.

Instituto Nacional de Colonização e Reforma Agraria (INCRA): Edif. Palácio do Desenvolvimento, SBN, Quadra 01, Bloco D, 70057-900 Brasília, DF; tel. (61) 3411-7474; fax (61) 3411-7404; e-mail publico@incra.gov.br; internet www.incra.gov.br; f. 1970; land reform agency; Pres. ROLF HACKBART.

Instituto Nacional de Metrologia, Normalização e Qualidade Industrial (INMETRO): Rua Santa Alexandrina 416, 10° andar, Rio Comprido, 20261-232 Rio de Janeiro, RJ; tel. (21) 2563-2800; fax (21) 2563-2970; e-mail caint@inmetro.gov.br; internet www.inmetro.gov.br; f. 1973; part of Ministry of Development, Industry and Foreign Trade; Pres. JOÃO ALZIRO HERZ DA JORNADA.

Instituto Nacional da Propriedade Industrial (INPI): Praça Mauá 7, 18° andar, Centro, 20081-240 Rio de Janeiro, RJ; tel. (21) 2139-3000; fax (21) 2263-2539; e-mail inpipres@inpi.gov.br; internet www.inpi.gov.br; f. 1970; part of Ministry of Development, Industry and Foreign Trade; intellectual property, etc.; Pres. JORGE DE PAULA COSTA ÁVILA.

Instituto de Pesquisa Econômica Aplicada (IPEA): Av. Presidente Antônio Carlos 51, 15° andar, 20020-010 Rio de Janeiro, RJ; tel. (21) 3804-8000; fax (21) 2240-1920; e-mail faleconosco@ipea.gov.br; internet www.ipea.gov.br; also has an office in Brasília; f. 1970; economics and planning institute; Pres. LUIZ HENRIQUE PROENÇA SOARES.

REGIONAL DEVELOPMENT ORGANIZATIONS

Companhia de Desenvolvimento dos Vales do São Francisco e do Parnaíba (CODEVASF): Edif. Manoel Novaes, SGAN, Quadra 601, Conj. 1, 70830-901 Brasília, DF; tel. (61) 3312-4611; fax (61) 3312-4680; e-mail orlandoc@codevasf.gov.br; internet www.codevasf.gov.br; f. 1974; promotes integrated development of resources of São Francisco and Parnaíba Valley; part of Ministry of National Integration; Pres. ORLANDO CESAR DA COSTA CASTRO.

Superintendência do Desenvolvimento da Amazônia (SUDAM): Av. Almirante Barroso 426, Marco, 66090-900 Belém, PA; tel. (91) 4008-5442; fax (91) 4008-5456; e-mail gabinete@ada.gov.br; internet www.ada.gov.br; f. 2001 to co-ordinate the devt of resources in Amazon region; Dir-Gen. DJALMA BEZERRA MELLO.

Superintendência de Desenvolvimento do Nordeste (SUDENE): Praça Ministro João Gonçalves de Souza s/n, Engenho do Meio, 50670-900 Recife, PE; tel. (81) 2102-2114; fax (81) 2102-2575; e-mail gabinete@sudene.gov.br; internet www.sudene.gov.br; f. 2007 to replace Agência de Desenvolvimento do Nordeste (f. 2001); Supt PAULO SÉRGIO DE NORONHA FONTANA.

Superintendência da Zona Franca de Manaus (SUFRAMA): Av. Ministro João Gonçalves de Souza s/n, Distrito Industrial, 69075-830 Manaus, AM; tel. (92) 3321-7000; fax (92) 3237-6549; e-mail cas@suframa.gov.br; internet www.suframa.gov.br; assists in the development of the Manaus Free Zone; Supt FLÁVIA SKROBOT BARBOSA GROSSO.

AGRICULTURAL, INDUSTRIAL AND TRADE ORGANIZATIONS

Associação Brasileira do Alumínio (ABAL): Rua Humberto I 220, 4° andar, Vila Mariana, 04018-030 São Paulo, SP; tel. (11) 5904-6450; fax (11) 5904-6459; e-mail aluminio@abal.org.br; internet www.abal.org.br; f. 1970; represents aluminium producing and processing cos; 66 mem. cos; Pres. ADJARMA AZEVEDO.

Associação Brasileira de Celulose e Papel—Bracelpa: Rua Olimpíadas, 66, 9° and Bairro Vl. Olímpia São Paulo, São Paulo, SP; tel. (11) 3018-7800; fax (11) 3018-7813; e-mail faleconosco@bracelpa.org.br; internet www.bracelpa.org.br; f. 1932; pulp and paper asscn; Exec. Dir ELIZABETH CARVALHAES.

Associação Brasileira das Indústrias de Óleos Vegetais (Abiove) (Brazilian Association of Vegetable Oil Industries): Av. Vereador José Diniz 3707, 7° andar, Conj. 73, 04603-004 São Paulo, SP; tel. (11) 5536-0733; fax (11) 5536-9816; e-mail abiove@abiove.com.br; internet www.abiove.com.br; f. 1981; 10 mem. cos; Pres. CARLO LOVATELLI.

Associação Brasileira dos Produtores de Algodão (ABRAPA): Edif. Antônio Ernesto de Salvo, Térreo, SGAN, Quadra 601, Lote K, 70830-903 Brasília, DF; tel. (61) 2109-1606; fax (61) 2109-1607; e-mail faleconosco@abrapa.com.br; internet www.abrapa.com.br; f. 1999; cotton producers' asscn; Pres. HAROLDO RODRIGUES DA CUNHA.

Associação Comercial do Rio de Janeiro (ACRJ): Rua da Calendária 9, 11°–12° andares, Centro, 20091-020 Rio de Janeiro, RJ; tel. and fax (21) 2514-1229; e-mail acrj@acrj.org.br; internet www.acrj.org.br; f. 1820; Pres. JOSÉ LUIZ ALQUÉRES.

Associação Comercial de São Paulo (ACSP): Rua Boa Vista 51, Centro, 01014-911 São Paulo, SP; tel. (11) 3244-3322; fax (11) 3244-3355; e-mail infocem@acsp.com.br; internet www.acsp.com.br; f. 1894; Pres. ALENCAR BURTI.

Associação de Comércio Exterior do Brasil (AEB) (Brazilian Foreign Trade Association): Av. General Justo 335, 4° andar, 20021-130 Rio de Janeiro, RJ; tel. (21) 2544-0048; fax (21) 2544-0577; e-mail aebbras@aeb.org.br; internet www.aeb.org.br; exporters' asscn; Pres. BENEDICTO FONSECA MOREIRA.

Associação Nacional dos Fabricantes de Veículos Automotores (ANFAVEA): Av. Indianópolis 496, 04062-900 São Paulo, SP; tel. (11) 2193-7800; fax (11) 2193-7825; internet www.anfavea.com.br; f. 1956; motor vehicle manufacturers' asscn; Pres. CLEDORVINO BELINI.

Centro das Indústrias do Estado de São Paulo (CIESP): Av. Paulista 1313, 01311-923 São Paulo, SP; tel. (11) 3549-3232; e-mail atendimento@ciesp.com.br; internet www.ciesp.org.br; f. 1928; asscn of small and medium-sized businesses; Pres. PAULO ANTONIO SKEF.

Confederação da Agricultura e Pecuária do Brasil (CNA): SGAN, Quadra 601, Modulo K, 70830-903 Brasília, DF; tel. (61) 2109-1400; fax (61) 2109-1490; e-mail cna@cna.org.br; internet www.canaldoprodutor.com.br; f. 1964; national agricultural confederation; Pres. KÁTIA REGINA DE ABREU.

Confederação Nacional do Comércio (CNC): Av. General Justo 307, 20021-130 Rio de Janeiro, RJ; tel. (21) 3804-9200; e-mail cncrj@cnc.com.br; internet www.portaldocomercio.org.br; national confederation comprising 35 affiliated federations of commerce; Pres. ANTÔNIO JOSÉ DOMINGUES DE OLIVEIRA SANTOS.

Confederação Nacional da Indústria (CNI) (National Confederation of Industry): Edif. Roberto Simonsen, SBN, Quadra 01, Bloco C, 70040-903 Brasília, DF; tel. (61) 3317-9993; fax (61) 3317-9994; e-mail sac@cni.org.br; internet www.cni.org.br; f. 1938; national confederation of industry comprising 27 state industrial federations; membership of some 1,016 employers' unions; Pres. ARMANDO DE QUEIROZ MONTEIRO NETO; Exec. Dir JOSÉ AUGUSTO COELHO FERNANDES.

Conselho dos Exportadores de Café Verde do Brasil (CECAFE): Av. Nove de Julho 4865, Torre A, Conj. 61, Chácara Itaim, 01407-200 São Paulo, SP; tel. (11) 3079-3755; fax (11) 3167-4060; e-mail cecafe@cecafe.com.br; internet www.cecafe.com.br; f. 1999 through merger of Federação Brasileira dos Exportadores de Café and Associação Brasileira dos Exportadores de Café; council of green coffee exporters; Pres. JOÃO ANTÔNIO LIAN; Dir-Gen. GUILHERME BRAGA ABREU PIRES FILHO.

Federação das Indústrias do Estado do Rio de Janeiro (FIRJAN): Centro Empresarial FIRJAN, Av. Graça Aranha 1, Rio de Janeiro, RJ; tel. (21) 2563-4389; e-mail centrodeatendimento@firjan.org.br; internet www.firjan.org.br; regional manufacturers' asscn; 103 affiliated syndicates representing almost 16,000 cos.

Federação das Indústrias do Estado de São Paulo (FIESP): Av. Paulista 1313, 01311-923 São Paulo, SP; tel. (11) 3549-4499; e-mail relacionamento@fiesp.org.br; internet www.fiesp.org.br; regional manufacturers' asscn; Pres. PAULO ANTONIO SKAF.

Instituto Aço Brasil: Av. Rio Branco 181, 28° andar, 20040-007 Rio de Janeiro, RJ; tel. (21) 3445-6300; fax (21) 2262-2234; e-mail acobrasil@acobrasil.org.br; internet www.acobrasil.org.br; f. 1963; fmrly Instituto Brasileiro de Siderurgia (IBS); steel cos' org.; Pres. ANDRÉ BIER GERDAU JOHANNPETER; Exec. Chair MARCO POLO DE MELLO LOPES.

Instituto Brasileiro do Mineração (IBRAM) (The Brazilian National Mining Association): SHIS, Quadra 12, Conj. 0, Casa 4, 71630-205 Brasília, DF; tel. (61) 3364-7200; fax (61) 3364-7272; e-mail ibram@ibram.org.br; internet www.ibram.org.br; f. 1976 to foster the development of the mining industry; Pres. and Dir PAULO CAMILLO VARGAS PENNA.

Instituto Nacional de Tecnologia (INT): Av. Venezuela 82, 8° andar, 20081-312 Rio de Janeiro, RJ; tel. (21) 2123-1100; fax (21) 2123-1284; e-mail dcom@int.gov.br; internet www.int.gov.br; f. 1921; co-operates in national industrial development; Dir DOMINGOS MANFREDI NAVEIRO.

Serviço de Apoio às Micro e Pequenas Empresas (Sebrae): SEPN, Quadra 515, Lote 03, Bloco C, Asa Norte, 70770-530 Brasília, DF; tel. (61) 3348-7100; fax (61) 3347-3581; internet www.sebrae.com.br; f. 1972; supports small and medium-sized enterprises; Pres. PAULO TARCISO OKAMOTTO.

União Democrática Ruralista (UDR): Av. Col Marcondes 983, 6° andar, Sala 62, Centro, 19010-080 Presidente Prudente, SP; tel. (11) 3221-1082; fax (11) 3232-4622; e-mail udr.org@uol.com.br; internet www.udr.org.br; landowners' org.; Pres. LUIZ ANTÔNIO NABHAN GARCIA.

União da Industria de Cana-de-Açúcar (UNICA): Av. Brigadeiro Faria Lima 2179, 9° andar, Jardim Paulistano, 01452-000 São Paulo, SP; tel. (11) 3093-4949; fax (11) 3812-1416; e-mail unica@unica.com.br; internet www.unica.com.br; f. 1997; sugar and bioethanol asscn; offices in Washington, DC, USA, and Brussels, Belgium; Pres. MARCOS SAWAYA JANK; Exec. Dir EDUARDO LEÃO DE SOUSA.

STATE HYDROCARBONS COMPANIES

Petróleo Brasileiro, SA (Petrobras): Av. República do Chile 65, Centro, 20031-912 Rio de Janeiro, RJ; tel. (21) 3224-1510; fax (21) 3224-6055; e-mail sac@petrobras.com.br; internet www.petrobras.com.br; f. 1953; production of petroleum and petroleum products; owns 16 oil refineries; net profit US $16,645m. (2009); Pres. JOSÉ SÉRGIO GABRIELLI DE AZEVEDO; Sec.-Gen. HÉLIO SHIGUENOBU FUJIKAWA; 53,933 employees; subsidiary cos are Petrobras Transporte, SA (Transpetro), Petrobras Comercializadora de Energia, Ltda, Petrobras Negócios Eletrônicos, SA, Petrobras International Finance Company (PIFCO) and Downstream Participações, SA, and cos listed below:

Petrobras Biocombustível, SA (Petrobras Biofuel): Av. República do Chile 65, Centro, 200.031-912 Rio de Janeiro, RJ; tel. (21) 3224-1510; fax (21) 3224-6055; e-mail biocombustivel@petrobras.com.br; internet www.petrobrasbiocombustivel.com.br; f. 2008; three biodiesel plants in Candeias, Quixadá and Montes Claros; Pres. JOSÉ SÉRGIO GABRIELLI DE AZEVEDO.

Petrobras Distribuidora, SA: Rua General Canabarro 500, Maracanã, 20271-900 Rio de Janeiro, RJ; tel. (21) 3876-4477; fax (21) 3876-4977; internet www.br.com.br; f. 1971; distribution of all petroleum by-products; Pres. JOSÉ LIMA DE ANDRADE NETO; 3,758 employees.

Petrobras Gás, SA (Gaspetro): Av. República do Chile 65, Centro, 20031-912 Rio de Janeiro, RJ; tel. (21) 3534-0439; fax (21) 3534-1080; e-mail sac@petrobras.com.br; internet www.gaspetro.com.br; f. 1998; Pres. JOSÉ SÉRGIO GABRIELLI DE AZEVEDO; Dir (Gas and Energy) MARIA DAS GRAÇAS SILVA FOSTER.

Petrobras Química, SA (Petroquisa): Av. República do Chile 65, 9° andar, Centro, 20031-912 Rio de Janeiro, RJ; tel. (21) 3224-1455; fax (21) 2262-1521; e-mail contato.petroquisa@petrobras.com.br; internet www.petroquisa.com.br; f. 1968; petrochemicals industry; controls 27 affiliated companies and four subsidiaries; Pres. JOSÉ SÉRGIO GABRIELLI DE AZEVEDO.

Pré-Sal Petróleo, SA: f. 2010; state-owned; manages exploration of petroleum and natural gas beneath the salt layer along the Brazilian coast; Pres. MÁRCIO PEREIRA ZIMMERMANN (Minister of Mines and Energy).

MAJOR COMPANIES

Chemicals, Petrochemicals and Petroleum

Braskem, SA: Edif. Eldorado Business Tower, 23° e 24° andares, Av. das Nações Unidas 8501, Pinheiros, 05425-070 São Paulo, SP; tel. (11) 3443-9999; fax (11) 3443-9017; internet www.braskem.com.br; f. 2002; part of Odebrecht group; 18 chemical plants; Chair. MARCELO BAHIA ODEBRECHT; CEO BERNARDO AFONSO DE ALMEIDA GRADIN; 4,800 employees.

Empresas Petróleo Ipiranga, SA (IPQ): Rua Francisco Eugênio 329, 20948-900 Rio de Janeiro, RJ; tel. (21) 2574-5858; fax (21) 2569-8796; internet www.ipiranga.com.br; f. 1959; petroleum, petroleum products and natural gas; Pres. JOÃO PEDRO GOUVÊA VIEIRA; Vice-Pres. SÉRGIO SILVEIRA SARAIVA; 3,653 employees.

Distribuidora de Productos de Petróleo Ipiranga, SA: Av. Dolores Alcaraz Caldas 90, Praia das Belas, 90110-180 Porto Alegre, RS; tel. (51) 3216-4353; fax (51) 3216-4066; internet www.ipiranga.com.br; f. 1957; distribution of petroleum derivatives; cap. US $1,482.4m., sales $9,772.5m. (2005); Pres. SÉRGIO SILVEIRA SARAIVA; Vice-Pres. CARLOS ALBERTO MARTINS BASTOS; 1,500 employees.

Metals and Mining

Aços Villares, SA: Av. Nações Unidas 8501, Bloco A, 5° andar, Pinheiros, 05425-070 São Paulo, SP; tel. (11) 3094-6600; fax (11) 094-6524; internet www.villares.com.br; f. 1944; part of Sidenor group; steel producers; Pres. PAULO FERNANDO BINS DE VASCONCELLOS; CEO ANDRÉ BIER GERDAU JOHANNPETER; 4,307 employees.

Alcoa Alumínio, SA: Av. Nações Unidas 12901, Torre Oeste 16° andar, Brooklin Novo, 04578-000 São Paulo, SP; tel. (11) 3741-5988; fax (11) 3741-8300; internet www.alcoa.com.br; f. 1965; subsidiary of Alcoa Inc, USA; extraction and processing of bauxite; Pres. (Latin America and Caribbean) FRANKLIN FEDER; 4,447 employees.

ArcelorMittal Brasil: Av. Carandaí 1115, 30130-915 Belo Horizonte, MG; tel. (31) 3219-1122; fax (31) 3235-4294; internet www.arcelor.com.br; f. 1921; formed by merger of Companhia Siderúrgica Belgo-Mineira, Companhia Siderúrgica de Tubarão, and Vega do Sul; owned by ArcelorMittal, Luxembourg; steel mill; bought

ACESITA in 2010; Pres. JOSÉ ARMANDO CAMPOS; CEO BENJAMIN MÁRIO BAPTISTA FILHO; 15,000 employees.

Companhia Brasileira de Metalurgia e Mineração (CBMM): Córrego da Mata s/n, CP 8, 38183-970 Araxá, MG; tel. (34) 3669-3000; fax (34) 3669-3100; e-mail cbmm@cbmm.com.br; internet www.cbmm.com.br; f. 1955; extraction and processing of niobium, manufacturing of niobium products; CEO FERNANDO ROBERTO MOREIRA SALLES.

Companhia Siderúrgica Nacional (CSN): Rua San José 20, Grupo 1602, Centro, 20010-020 Rio de Janeiro, RJ; tel. (21) 2141-1800; fax (21) 2586-1400; internet www.csn.com.br; f. 1941; privatized 1993; steel; Chair. and CEO BENJAMIN STEINBRUCH; 8,000 employees.

Companhia Vale do Rio Doce, SA (Vale): Av. Graça Aranha 26, 6° andar, Bairro Castelo, 20030-900 Rio de Janeiro, RJ; tel. (21) 3814-4477; fax (21) 3814-4040; internet www.vale.com; f. 1942; fmr state-owned mining co, privatized in 1997; owns and operates two systems: in the north, the Carajás iron ore mine and railway, and port of Ponta da Madeira; in the south, the Itabira iron ore mine, the Vitória–Minas railway and the port of Tubarão; largest gold producer in Latin America; also involved in forestry and pulp production, aluminium and other minerals; Pres. and CEO ROGER AGNELLI; 15,500 employees.

Grupo Gerdau: Av. Farrapos 1811, 90220-005 Porto Alegre, RS; tel. (51) 3323-2000; fax (51) 3323-2222; internet www.gerdau.com.br; f. 1901; long steel group; Pres. JORGE GERDAU JOHANNPETER; CEO ANDRÉ BIER GERDAU JOHANNPETER; cos in the group include Gerdau Ameristeel Corpn, Metalúrgica Gerdau, SA and co listed below.

Mineraçaõ Corumbaense Reunida, SA (MCR): Rua do Cabral 1555, 79332-030 Corumbá, MS; tel. (67) 3234-2333; fax (67) 3234-2236; owned by Vale SA; iron ore production.

Rio Tinto Brasil: Rua Lauro Müller 116, 35° andar, Botafogo, 22290-160 Rio de Janeiro, RJ; tel. (21) 2197-4200; fax (21) 2197-4214; e-mail externo.rtb@riotinto.com.br; internet www.riotinto.com.br; f. 1971; mining and transport of minerals; subsidiary cos include Rio Tinto Desenvolvimentos Minerais, Ltda and Transbarge Navegación, SA.

SMS Siemag Serviços Industriais, Ltda: Rua Timbiras 1754, 13° andar, Lourdes, 30140-061 Belo Horizonte, MG; tel. (31)2125-1100; fax (31)2125-1408; e-mail consulta@sms-siemag.com.br; internet www.sms-siemag.com.br; f. 1977; subsidiary of SMS Siemag, Germany; steel mills and hot metal production; Pres. and CEO KAY MAYLAND.

Usinas Siderúrgicas de Minas Gerais, SA (USIMINAS): Rua Prof. José Vieira de Mendonça 3011, Engenho Nogueira, CP 806, 31310-260 Belo Horizonte, MG; tel. (31) 3499-8000; fax (31) 3499-8899; e-mail imprensa@usiminas.com.br; internet www.usiminas.com.br; f. 1956; steel mill; privatized in 1991; Chair. ISRAEL VAINBOIM; CEO WILSON NÉLIO BRUMER.

Votorantim Metais: Praça Ramos de Azevedo 254, 5º e 6° andar, 01037-912 São Paulo, SP; tel. (11) 2159-3100; fax (11) 3361-3628; internet www.vmetais.com.br; part of Votorantim Group; aluminium and zinc extraction and processing, long steel; subsidiary cos include Companhia Mineira do Metais, Companhia Niquel Tocatins and Companhia Paraibuna de Metais; Man. Dir JOÃO BOSCO SILVA; 3,500 employees.

White Martins Gases Industriais, Ltda: Rua Mayrink Veiga 9, Centro, 20090-050 Rio de Janeiro, RJ; tel. (21) 2588-6622; fax (21) 2588-6683; e-mail atendimento@sac.whitemartins.com.br; internet www.whitemartins.com.br; f. 1912; almost 100% owned by Praxair; manufacturers and distributors of industrial gases, welding equipment and seamless cylinders; CEO RICARDO S. MALFITANO; 10,000 employees.

Motor Vehicles and Aircraft

Companhia Fabricadora de Peças (COFAP): Av. Alexandre de Gusmão 1395, Capuava, 09110-901 Santo André, SP; tel. (11) 4474-1357; fax (11) 4474-1357; e-mail erv.saopaulo@marellicofap.com.br; internet www.mmcofap.com.br; f. 1951; manufacturers of motor-vehicle components; Pres. EDISON DUARTE LINO; 7,100 employees.

Empresa Brasileira de Aeronáutica, SA (Embraer): Av. Brig. Faria Lima 2170, Putim, 12227-901 São José dos Campos, SP; tel. (12) 3927-4404; fax (12) 3922-6070; e-mail investor.relations@embraer.com.br; internet www.embraer.com; f. 1969 as a state-owned enterprise; privatized in 1994; aeronautics industry; Chair. MAURÍCIO NOVIS BOTELHO; Pres. and CEO FREDERICO FLEURY CURADO; 17,375 employees.

Fiat do Brasil, SA: Rodovia Fernão Dias s/n, BR 381, km 429, 32560-460 Betim, MG; tel. (31) 3529-2855; e-mail bogutchi@fiat.com; internet www.fiat.com.br; produces 730,000 vehicles per year; Pres. and Dir CLEDORVINO BELINI; 9,400 employees.

Ford Brasil, Ltda: Av. Taboão 899, Prédio 6, CP 9308, 09655-900 São Bernardo do Campo, SP; tel. (11) 4174-8235; fax (11) 848-9057; internet www.ford.com.br; f. 1987; subsidiary of Ford Motor Co of the USA; motor vehicles; Pres. MANOEL DE OLIVEIRA; 6,500 employees.

General Motors do Brasil: Rodovia BR 290, Km 67, Gravataí, RS; tel. (51) 3430-1718; internet chevrolet.com.br; f. 1925; subsidiary of General Motors Co of the USA; Pres. JAIME ARDILA; 21,180 employees.

Iochpe-Maxion, SA: Rua Luigi Galvani 146, 13° andar, 04575-020 São Paulo, SP; tel. (11) 5508-3800; fax (11) 5506-7353; e-mail ri@iochpe.com.br; internet www.iochpe-maxion.com.br; f. 1918; motor-vehicle manufacturers; Chair. IVONCY BROCHMANN IOSCHPE; Pres. and CEO DANIEL IOSCHPE; 6,500 employees.

Mercedes-Benz do Brasil, SA: Av. Mercedes Benz 679, Distrito Industrial, 13054-750 Campinas, SP; tel. (19) 3725-3333; fax (19) 3725-3635; internet www.mercedes-benz.com.br; f. 1953 as Mercedes Benz do Brasil, SA; subsidiary of DaimlerChrysler AG of Germany; motor-car, truck and bus-chassis production; Pres. JÜRGEN ZIEGLER; 13,209 employees.

Volkswagen do Brasil, SA: Via Anchieta km 23, 5, CP 1048, 09823-990 São Bernardo do Campo, SP; tel. (11) 4347-2355; fax (11) 578-0947; e-mail info@vm.com.br; internet www.volkswagen.com.br; f. 1953; subsidiary of Volkswagen AG of Germany; manufacture of trucks and passenger commercial vehicles; Pres. THOMAS SCHMALL; 22,000 employees.

Rubber, Textiles and Paper

Celulose Nipo-Brasileira (CENIBRA): Rua Bernardo Guimarães 245, 8° andar, Bairro Funcionários, 30140-080 Belo Horizonte, MG; tel. (31) 3235-4041; fax (31) 3235-4002; e-mail comercial@cenibra.com.br; internet www.cenibra.com.br; f. 1973; owned by Japan Brazil Paper and Pulp Resources Development Co Ltd (JBP); eucalyptus pulp paper; Pres. PAULO EDUARDO DE ROCHA BRANT; 1,600 employees.

Fibria Celulose, SA: Alameda Santos 1357, 6º andar, 01419-908 São Paulo, SP; tel. (11) 2138-4000; e-mail ir@fibria.com.br; internet www.fibria.com.br; f. 2009; following merger between Aracruz Celulose and Votorantim Celulose e Papel (VCP); CEO CARLOS AUGUSTO LIRA AGUIAR; 15,000 employees.

Indústrias Klabin de Papel e Celulose, SA (Klabin): Av. Brig. Faria Lima 3600, Itaim Bibi, 04538-132 São Paulo, SP; tel. (11) 3225-4000; fax (11) 3225-4067; e-mail invest@klabin.com.br; internet www.klabin.com.br; f. 1934; manufacturers of paper and paper products; Chair. ARMANDO KLABIN; Gen. Man. REINOLDO POERNBACHER; 13,432 employees.

LANXESS Elastomers of Brazil, SA: Rua Marumbi 600, Campos Elíseos, 25221-000 Duque de Caxias, RJ; tel. (21) 2667-1241; fax (21) 2776-1510; internet www.lanxess.com.br; f. 1977 as a subsidiary of Petroquisa; 70% shares bought by LANXESS Holdings in 2008; synthetic rubber; CEO JÖRG SCHNEIDER; 900 employees.

Pirelli Pneus, SA: Av. Capuava 603, Vila Homero Thon, 09111-310 Santo André, SP; fax (11) 4998-5512; e-mail webpneus@pirelli.com.br; internet www.pirelli.com.br; f. 1988; owned by Pirelli of Italy; makers of rubber inner tubes and tyres; CEO CARLOS REDONDO; 6,798 employees.

Stora Enso Arapoti, Ltda: Alameda Itú 852, 6° e 8° andar, Cerqueira César, 01421-001 São Paulo, SP; tel. (11) 3065-5200; fax (11) 3065-5214; internet www.storaenso.com; f. 1998; fmrly Vinson Indústria de Papel Arapoti Ltda and Vinson Empreendimentos Agricolas Ltda; bought by Stora Enso (Finland) in 2006; paper manufacturers; Pres. NILS GRAFSTRÖM.

Suzano Papel e Celulose, SA: Av. Tancredo Neves 274, Bloco B, Sala 121, 122 e 123, Caminho das Árvores, 41820-020 Salvador, BA; tel. (71) 3037-9062; fax (71) 3037-9313; e-mail suzano@suzano.com.br; internet www.suzano.com.br; f. 1923; makes and distributes eucalyptus pulp and paper products; Pres. DAVID FEFFER; CEO ANTONIO MACIEL NETO; 3,425 employees.

Tecelagem Kuehnrich, SA (TEKA): Rua Paulo Kuehnrich 68, Bairro Itoupava Norte, 89052-900 Blumenau, SC; tel. (47) 3321-5000; fax (47) 3321-5050; e-mail sac@teka.com.br; internet www.teka.com.br; f. 1935; textile manufacturers; Pres. FREDERICO KUEHNRICH NETO; CEO LUIZ FERNANDO BRANDT; 4,500 employees.

Construction

Camargo Corrêa, SA: Rua Funchal 160, Vila Olímpia, 04551-903 São Paulo, SP; tel. (11) 3841-5511; fax (11) 3841-5849; e-mail camargo@camargocorrea.com.br; internet www.camargocorrea.com.br; f. 1946; heavy construction, engineering, cement; part of the Camargo Corrêa Group; 25 subsidiary cos; Chair. VITOR HALLACK; Man. Dir JOSÉ ALBERTO DINIZ; 56,800 employees.

Construtora Andrade Gutierrez, SA: Av. do Contorno 8123, Cidade Jardim, 30110-910 Belo Horizonte, MG; tel. (31) 3290-6699; internet www.agsa.com.br; f. 1948; subsidiary of Andrade Gutierrez, SA; heavy construction and civil engineering; CEO ROGÉRIO NORA DE SÁ; 34,161 employees.

Construtora Norberto Odebrecht, SA: Praia de Botafogo 300, 10° andar, Botafogo, 22250-040 Rio de Janeiro, RJ; tel. (21) 2559-3000; fax (21) 2552-4448; e-mail info@odebrecht.com.br; internet www.odebrecht-ec.com; f. 1944; part of Odebrecht group; subsidiaries include CBPO Engenharia Ltda, Odebrecht Empreendimentos Imobiliários Ltda, Lumina Engenharia Ambiental Ltda; CEO MARCELO BAHIA ODEBRECHT; 27,159 employees.

Construtora Queiroz Galvão, SA: Av. Rio Branco 156, 30° andar, Centro, 20040-901 Rio de Janeiro, RJ; tel. (21) 2131-7100; fax (21) 2131-9367; internet www.queirozgalvao.com; f. 1953; civil-engineering and construction projects; Pres. ANTÔNIO DE QUEIROZ GALVÃO; Man. Dir JOÃO ANTÔNIO DE QUEIROZ GALVÃO; 7,450 employees.

Food and Drink

AmBev (Companhia de Bebidas das Américas): Corporate Park, Renato Paes de Barros 1017, 4° andar, 04530-001 São Paulo, SP; tel. (11) 2122-1370; e-mail ci@ambev.com.br; internet www.ambev.com.br; f. 1999 following merger of Brahma and Antarctica beer producers; bought by InBev (Belgium) in 2004; beer and soft drinks maker, produces Brahma beer; CEO JOÃO MAURICIO GIFFONI DE CASTRO NEVES; Pres. (Latin America) LUIZ FERNANDO EDMOND; 13,000 employees.

Brasil Foods, SA (BRF): Av. Escola Politécnica 760, Jaguaré, 05350-901 São Paulo, SP; tel. (11) 3718-5301; fax (11) 3718-5287; e-mail sac@brasilfoods.com; internet www.brasilfoods.com; f. 1934 as Perdigão; adopted present name in 2009 after merger with Sadia, SA; food-processing and packaging; Pres. and Dir NILDEMAR SECCHES; 27,000 employees.

Bunge Alimentos, SA: Rodovia Jorge Lacerda, Km 20, Poço Grande, 89110-000 Gaspar, SC; tel. (47) 3331-2222; fax (47) 3331-2005; internet www.bungealimentos.com.br; f. 2000 by merger of Santista Alimentos and Ceval Alimentos; agricultural processing; CEO PEDRO PARENTE; 9,793 employees.

Carrefour Brasil: Rua George Eastman 213, São Paulo, SP; internet www.grupocarrefour.com.br; f. 1975 in Brazil; grocery sales, etc.; CEO JEAN-MARC PUEYO; 500 stores (2010); 48,000 employees.

Companhia Brasileira de Distribuição/Grupo Pão de Açúcar: Av. Brig. Luís Antonio 3126, Jardim Paulista, 01402-901 São Paulo, SP; tel. (11) 3886-0533; fax (11) 3884-2677; e-mail cbd.ri@paodeacucar.com.br; internet www.grupopaodeacucar.com.br; f. 1948; supermarkets, hypermarkets and electrical stores; Chair. ABILIO DOS SANTOS DINIZ; CEO ENÉAS CÉSAR PESTANA NETO; 70,656 employees.

Sadia, SA: Rua Senador Attílio Fontana 86, Centro, 89700-000 Concórdia, SC; tel. (49) 3444-3000; fax (49) 3444-3001; e-mail ri@sadia.com.br; internet www.sadia.com.br; f. 1944; refrigeration, meat-packing, animal feeds; merged with Perdigão in May 2009 to form Brasil Foods, SA (BRF); complete merger of stocks and operations pending; CEO JOSÉ JULIO CARDOSO DE LUCENA; 40,000 employees.

Walmart: Av. Tucunaré 125, Alphaville, 06460-020 Barueri, SP; tel. (11) 2103-5800; fax (11) 2103-5776; e-mail imprensa@wal-mart.com; internet www.walmartbrasil.com.br; f. 1995; subsidiary cos incl. Bompreço, SA and Sonae Distribuição Brasil, SA; grocery sales, etc.; Pres. HÉCTOR NÚÑEZ; 21,000 employees.

Pharmaceuticals

Aché Laboratórios Farmacêuticos, SA: Rodovia Presidente Dutra, Km 222,2, Porto da Igreja, 07034-904 Guarulhos, SP; tel. (11) 2608-6000; fax (11) 2608-6178; e-mail cac@ache.com.br; internet www.ache.com.br; f. 1966 as Prodoctor Produtos Farmacêuticos; Dir-Gen. JOSÉ RICARDO MENDES DA SILVA; 2,600 employees.

Biosintética: Av. das Nações Unidas 22428, Jurubatuba, 04795-916 São Paulo, SP; tel. (11) 5546-6822; fax (11) 5546-6800; internet www.ache.com.br; acquired by Aché in 2005; cardiovascular medication and other products; Nat. Man. MIRIAM FERREIRA OLIVEIRA.

EMS Indústria Farmacêutica, Ltda: Rodovia Jornalista Francisco Aguirre Proença, Km 08, Bairro Chacara Assay, 13186-481 Hortolândia, SP; tel. (19) 3887-9800; fax (19) 3887-9515; e-mail sac@ems.com.br; internet www.ems.com.br; f. 1964.

Eurofarma: Av. das Nações Unidas 22215, Jurubatuba, 04795-100 São Paulo, SP; tel. and fax (11) 5521-0232; e-mail euroatende@eurofarma.com.br; internet www.eurofarma.com.br; f. 1972 as Billi Farmacêutica; products include prescription and oncological medications; Pres. MAURIZIO BILLI.

JP Indústria Farmacêutica, SA: Av. Presidente Castelo Branco 999, Lagoinha, 14095-000 Ribeirão Preto, SP; tel. (16) 3512-3500; fax (16) 3512-3510; e-mail sac@jpfarma.com.br; internet www.jpfarma.com.br; f. 1966; hospital supplies and medications; Exec. Pres. ANDRÉ ALI MERE.

Libbs: Rua Josef Kryss 250, Barra Funda, 01140-050 São Paulo, SP; tel. (11) 3879-2500; fax (11) 3879-0957; e-mail heloisio.rodrigues@libbs.com.br; internet www.libbs.com.br; f. 1958; general pharmaceutical products; 1,050 employees.

Medley, SA, Indústria Farmacêutica: Rua Macedo Costa 55, Jardim Santa Genebra, 13080-180 Campinas, SP; tel. (19) 3708-8222; fax (19) 3708-8227; internet www.medley.com.br; brand and generic products; Pres. JAIRO YAMAMOTO.

Miscellaneous

Duratex, SA: Av. Paulista 1938, 5° andar, Bela Vista, 01310-942 São Paulo, SP; tel. (11) 3179-7733; fax (11) 3179-7355; internet www.duratex.com.br; f. 1951; mfrs of hardboard and plywood, ceramic products and bathroom fixtures; part of Itaúsa Group; CEO HENRI PENCHAS; 6,785 employees.

Electrolux do Brasil, SA: Rua Verbo Divino 1488, 7° andar, Conj. 72B, 04719-904 São Paulo, SP; tel. (11) 5188-1155; fax (11) 5188-1281; e-mail eluxfct@electrolux.com.br; internet www.electrolux.com.br; f. 1926; makers of refrigerators, freezers and vacuum cleaners; CEO RUY HIRSCHHEIMER; 431 employees.

Elevadores Atlas Schindler, SA: Av. do Estado 6116, Cambuci, 01516-900 São Paulo, SP; tel. (11) 6120-5161; fax (11) 2020-5478; e-mail sac.brasil@br.schindler.com; internet www.atlas.schindler.com; f. 1918; produces and maintains lifts and escalators; Pres. LUIS DEL BARRIO; 4,500 employees.

Empresa Brasileira de Correios e Telégrafos (Correios): Edif. Sede dos Correios, SBN, Quadra 1, Bloco A, 15° andar, 70002-900 Brasília, DF; tel. (61) 3426-2450; fax (61) 3327-5455; e-mail presidencia@correios.com.br; internet www.correios.com.br; f. 1969; state-owned; posts and telegraph; Pres. CARLOS HENRIQUE CUSTÓDIO; 108,000 employees.

Globex Utilidades, SA: Av. Tenente Rebelo 675, 21241-460 Irajá, RJ; tel. (21) 2472-8509; fax (21) 3372-7019; internet www.pontofrio.com.br; f. 1946; retail of household goods; Chair. and CEO ROBERTO BRITTO; 8,300 employees.

Itaú Tecnologia, SA (Itautec): Av. Paulista 2028, 15° andar, Bela Vista, 01310-200 São Paulo, SP; tel. (11) 3543-3000; e-mail ri@itautec.com; internet www.itautec.com.br; f. 1979; part of Itaúsa Group; mfrs of computer hardware; Chair. RICARDO EGYDIO SETUBAL; CEO MÁRIO ANSELONI; 5,347 employees.

Lojas Americanas, SA: Rua Sacadura Cabral 102, Saúde, 20081-260 Rio de Janeiro, RJ; tel. (21) 2206-6300; internet ri.lasa.com.br; f. 1929; retail chain; part of the Carrefour Group; Pres. CARLOS ALBERTO DA VEIGA SICUPIRA; 8,490 employees.

Saint-Gobain Vidros, SA: Av. Santa Marina 482, Agua Blanca, 05036-903 São Paulo, SP; tel. (11) 2246-7600; fax (11) 3611-0299; internet www.saint-gobain-vidros.com.br; f. 1896 as Companhia Vidraria Santa Marina; subsidiary of Groupe Saint-Gobain, France; glass manufacturers; Chair. JEAN JACQUES FAUST; 3,120 employees.

Souza Cruz, SA: Rua Candelária 66, Centro, 20091-900 Rio de Janeiro, RJ; tel. (21) 3849-9000; fax (21) 3849-9643; e-mail sac@scruz.com.br; internet www.souzacruz.com.br; f. 1903; manufacturers of cigarettes and tobacco; subsidiary of British American Tobacco; Pres. MARK MARTIJN COBBEN; 5,955 employees.

Votorantim Participações: Rua Amauri 255, 01448-000 São Paulo, SP; tel. (11) 3704-3300; fax (11) 3167-1550; internet www.votorantim.com.br; f. 1918; part of Votorantim Group; holding co with interests in cement, paper, metals, chemicals and financial services; Pres. CARLOS ERMÍRIO DE MORAES; 28,000 employees.

Whirlpool, SA: Edif. Plaza Centenário, Av. das Nações Unidas 12995, 32° andar, 04578-000 São Paulo, SP; tel. (11) 6940-1000; e-mail ana.paiva@cdn.com.br; internet www.whirlpool.com.br; f. 2006; with the re-organization of Multibrás, SA Eletrodomésticos and Empresa Brasileira de Compressores, SA-Embraco; retail of household appliances; Pres. (Latin America) JOSÉ DRUMMOND JÚNIOR; 8,000 employees.

Xerox Brasil: Av. Rodriques Alves 261, 20220-360 Rio de Janeiro, RJ; tel. (21) 4009-1212; fax (21) 4009-2749; e-mail webmaster@xerox.com.br; internet www.xerox.com.br; office equipment, technology; Pres. YORAM LEVANON.

UTILITIES

Regulatory Agencies

Agência Nacional de Energia Elétrica (ANEEL): SGAN 603, Módulo J, 70830-030 Brasília, DF; tel. (61) 2192-8600; e-mail aneel@aneel.gov.br; internet www.aneel.gov.br; f. 1939 as Conselho Nacional de Águas e Energia Elétrica, present name adopted 1996; Dir-Gen. NELSON JOSÉ HÜBNER MOREIRA.

Comissão Nacional de Energia Nuclear (CNEN): Rua General Severiano 90, Botafogo, 22290-901 Rio de Janeiro, RJ; tel. (21) 2173-2000; fax (21) 2173-2003; e-mail corin@cnen.gov.br; internet www

.cnen.gov.br; f. 1956; state org. responsible for management of nuclear power programme; Pres. Odair Dias Gonçalves.

Electricity

In December 2005 seven out of a total of 17 hydroelectric power-stations were successfully auctioned by ANEEL. Following a drought in 2002, the Government attempted to diversify the electricity-production sector, by encouraging the development of wind power and biofuels.

Centrais Elétricas Brasileiras, SA (Eletrobrás): Av. Presidente Vargas 409, 13° andar, Centro, 20071-003 Rio de Janeiro, RJ; tel. (21) 2514-5151; fax (21) 2514-6479; e-mail pr@eletrobras.gov.br; internet www.eletrobras.com; f. 1962; holding company responsible for planning, financing and managing Brazil's electrical energy programme; 54% govt-owned; Pres. José Antonio Muniz Lopes.

Centrais Elétricas do Norte do Brasil, SA (Eletronorte): SCN, Quadra 6, Conj. A, Blocos B e C, Entrada Norte 2, Asa Norte, 70716-901 Brasília, DF; tel. (61) 3429-5151; fax (61) 3328-1463; e-mail ouvidoria@eln.gov.br; internet www.eln.gov.br; f. 1973; serves Amapá, Acre, Amazonas, Maranhão, Mato Grosso, Pará, Rondônia, Roraima and Tocantins; Pres. Jorge Nassar Palmeira.

Boa Vista Energia, SA: Av. Capitão Ene Garcêz 691, Centro, 69310-160 Boa Vista, RR; tel. (95) 2621-1400; e-mail ouvidoria@boavistaenergia.gov.br; internet www.boavistaenergia.gov.br; f. 1997; subsidiary of Eletronorte; electricity distribution; Pres. Carlos Augusto Andrade Silva.

Manaus Energia, SA (ME): Manaus, AM; tel. (92) 3621-1110; internet www.manausenergia.gov.br; f. 1895; became subsidiary of Eletronorte in 1997; electricity distributor; Pres. Flávio Decat de Moura.

Companhia de Geração Térmica de Energia Elétrica (CGTEE): Rua Sete de Setembro 539, 90010-190 Porto Alegre, RS; tel. (51) 3287-1500; fax (51) 3287-1566; internet www.cgtee.gov.br; f. 1997; became part of Eletrobrás in 2000; Dir-Pres. Sereno Chaise.

Companhia Hidro Elétrica do São Francisco (Chesf): 333 Edif. André Falcão, Bloco A, Sala 313 Bongi, Rua Delmiro Golveia, 50761-901 Recife, PE; tel. (81) 229-2000; fax (81) 229-2390; e-mail chesf@chesf.com.br; internet www.chesf.gov.br; f. 1948; Exec. Dir Dilton da Conti Oliveira.

Eletrobras-Distribuição Rondônia, SA (CERON): Av. Imigrantes 4137, Industrial, 76821-063 Porto Velho, RO; tel. (69) 3216-4000; internet www.ceron.com.br; f. 1968; Dir-Pres. Pedro Carlos Hosken Vieira.

Eletrobrás Termonuclear, SA (Eletronuclear): Rua da Candelária 65, Centro, 20091-906 Rio de Janeiro, RJ; tel. (21) 2588-7000; fax (21) 2588-7200; internet www.eletronuclear.gov.br; f. 1997 by fusion of the nuclear branch of Furnas with Nuclebrás Engenharia (NUCLEN); operates two nuclear facilities, Angra I and II; Angra III under construction; Pres. Miguel Colasuonno; CEO Othon Luiz Pinheiro da Silva.

Eletrosul Centrais Elétricas, SA (Eletrosul): Rua Deputado Antônio Edu Vieira 999, Pantanal, 88040-901 Florianópolis, SC; tel. (48) 3231-7000; fax (48) 3234-4040; internet www.eletrosul.gov.br; f. 1968; Pres. Eurides Luiz Mescolotto.

Furnas Centrais Elétricas, SA: Rua Real Grandeza 219, Bloco A, 16° andar, Botafogo, 22281-031 Rio de Janeiro, RJ; tel. (21) 2528-3970; fax (21) 2528-4480; e-mail presiden@furnas.com.br; internet www.furnas.com.br; f. 1957; Pres. Carlos Nadalutti Filho.

Companhia de Eletricidade do Acre (ELETROACRE): Rua Valério Magalhães 226, Bairro do Bosque, 69909-710 Rio Branco, AC; tel. (68) 3212-5700; fax (68) 3223-1142; internet www.eletroacre.com.br; f. 1965; Pres. Pedro Carlos Hosken Vieira.

Companhia de Eletricidade do Estado da Bahia (COELBA): Av. Edgard Santos 300, Cabula IV, 41186-900 Salvador, BA; tel. (71) 370-5130; fax (71) 370-5132; internet www.coelba.com.br; f. 1960; Pres. Moisés Afonso Sales Filho.

Companhia de Eletricidade do Estado do Rio de Janeiro (CERJ): Rua Visconde do Rio Branco 429, Centro, 24020-003 Niterói, RJ; tel. (21) 2613-7120; fax (21) 2613-7196; e-mail cerj@cerj.com.br; internet www.cerj.com.br; f. 1907; privatized in 1996; Pres. Cristián Eduardo Fierro Montes.

Companhia Energética de Alagoas (CEAL): Av. Fernandes Lima 3349, Gruta de Lourdes, 57057-900 Maceió, AL; tel. (82) 2126-9247; internet www.ceal.com.br; f. 1961; Commercial Dir Ronaldo Ferreira.

Companhia Energética do Amazonas (CEAM): Manaus, AM; internet www.ceam-am.com.br; f. 1964; owned by Eletrobrás; electricity generating and distribution co; Pres. Dr Willamy Moreira Frota.

Companhia Energética de Brasília (CEB): SIA/SAPS, Trecho 01, Lotes 1745/1755, Ala 01-A, Brasília, DF; tel. 0800 610196; e-mail info@ceb.com.br; internet www.ceb.com.br; services in Distrito Federal; also operates gas distribution co CEBGAS.

Companhia Energética do Ceará (COELCE): Av. Barão de Studart 2917, Dionísio Torres, 60120-002 Fortaleza, CE; tel. (85) 3247-1444; fax (85) 3216-4088; e-mail ouvidoria@coelce.com.br; internet www.coelce.com.br; f. 1971; Pres. and Dir Cristián Eduardo Fierro Montes.

Companhia Energética do Maranhão (CEMAR): Av. Colares Moreira 477, Renascença II, São Luis, MA; internet www.cemar-ma.com.br; f. 1958 as Centrais Elétricas do Maranhão; changed name as above in 1984; owned by PPL Global, Inc, USA; Tech. Dir Marcelino Machadoda Cunha Neto.

Companhia Energética de Minas Gerais (CEMIG): Av. Barbacena 1200, 30190-131 Belo Horizonte, MG; tel. (31) 3299-4900; fax (31) 3299-3700; e-mail atendimento@cemig.com.br; internet www.cemig.com.br; f. 1952; 51% state-owned, 33% owned by Southern Electric Brasil Partipações Ltda; Pres. Djalma Bastos de Morais.

Companhia Energética de Pernambuco (CELPE): Av. João de Barros 111, Sala 301, 50050-902 Recife, PE; tel. (81) 3217-5168; e-mail celpe@celpe.com.br; internet www.celpe.com.br; state distributor of electricity; CEO José Humberto Castro.

Companhia Energética do Piauí (CEPISA): Av. Maranhão 759, Sul, 64001-010 Teresina, PI; tel. (86) 3228-8000; internet www.cepisa.com.br; f. 1962; 99% of shares bought by Eletrobrás in 1997; distributor of electricity in state of Piauí; Pres. Flávio Decat de Moura.

Companhia Energética de São Paulo (CESP): Av. Nossa Senhora do Sabará 5312, Bairro Pedreira, 04447-011 São Paulo, SP; tel. (11) 5613-2100; fax (11) 3262-5545; e-mail inform@cesp.com.br; internet www.cesp.com.br; f. 1966; Pres. Mauro Guilherme Jardim Arce.

Companhia Paranaense de Energia (COPEL): Rua Coronel Dulcídio 800, 80420-170 Curitiba, PR; tel. (41) 3331-4209; fax (41) 3331-4376; e-mail copel@copel.com; internet www.copel.com; f. 1954; state distributor of electricity and gas; Pres. João Bonifácio Cabral Júnior; Exec. Dir Rubens Ghilardi.

Companhia Paulista de Força e Luz (CPFL): Rodovia Campinas Mogi-Mirim Km 2.5, 10388-900 Campinas, SP; tel. (19) 3253-8704; fax (19) 3252-7644; internet www.cpfl.com.br; provides electricity through govt concessions; Pres. Wilson Pinto Ferreira Júnior.

Eletricidade de São Paulo, SA (ELETROPAULO): Av. Alfredo Egidio de Souza Aranha 100, 04791-900 São Paulo, SP; tel. (11) 5546-1467; fax (11) 3241-1387; e-mail administracao@eletropaulo.com.br; internet www.eletropaulo.com.br; f. 1899; acquired by AES in 2001; Pres. Marc André Perreira.

Espírito Santo Centrais Elétricas, SA (ESCELSA): Rua José Alexandre Buaiz 160, 8° andar, Ed. London Office Tower, Enseada do Suá, 29050-955 Vitória, ES; tel. (27) 3321-9000; fax (27) 3322-0378; e-mail ri@energiasdobrasil.com.br; internet www.escelsa.com.br; f. 1968; Dir-Pres. Agostinho Gonçalves Barreira.

Grupo Energisa Cataguazes-Leopoldina: Praça Rui Barbosa 80, 36770-901 Cataguases, MG; tel. (32) 3429-6000; fax (32) 3429-6317; internet www.cataguazes.com.br; f. 1905 as Companhia Força e Luz Cataguazes-Leopoldina, adopted current name in 2008; subsidiary of Energisa, SA; concerned with generation and distribution of electrical energy; Dir-Pres. Ricardo Perez Botelho.

Indústrias Nucleares do Brasil, SA (INB): Rua Mena Barreto 161, Botafogo, 22271-100 Rio de Janeiro, RJ; tel. (21) 2536-1600; fax (21) 2537-9391; e-mail inbrio@inb.gov.br; internet www.inb.gov.br; f. 1988; Pres. Alfredo Tranjan Filho.

Itaipú Binacional: Av. Tancredo Neves 6731, 85866-900 Foz de Iguaçu, PR; tel. (45) 3520-5252; fax (45) 3520-3015; e-mail itaipu@itaipu.gov.br; internet www.itaipu.gov.br; f. 1974; jtly owned by Brazil and Paraguay; hydroelectric power station on Brazilian–Paraguayan border; 94,684,781 MWh produced in 2008; Dir-Gen. (Brazil) Jorge Miguel Samek.

LIGHT—Serviços de Eletricidade, SA: Av. Marechal Floriano 168, CP 0571, 20080-002 Rio de Janeiro, RJ; tel. (21) 2211-7171; fax (21) 2233-1249; e-mail light@lightrio.com.br; internet www.lightrio.com.br; f. 1905; electricity generation and distribution in Rio de Janeiro; fmrly state-owned, sold to a Brazilian-French-US consortium in 1996; controlled by EdF (France) from 2002; in 2006 79.4% holding sold to Brazilian group Rio Minas Energia Participaçoes, SA (RME) with EdF retaining 10% share; generating capacity of 850 MW; Pres. José Luiz Alquéres.

Gas

Companhia Distribuidora de Gás do Rio de Janeiro (CEG): Av. Pedro II 68, São Cristóvão, 20941-070 Rio de Janeiro, RJ; tel. (21) 2585-7575; fax (21) 2585-7070; internet www.ceg.com.br; f. 1969; gas distribution in the Rio de Janeiro region; privatized in July 1997; Pres. BRUNO ARMBRUST.

Companhia de Gás de Alagoas, SA (ALGÁS): Rua Artur Vital da Silva, 04, Gruta de Lourdes, 57052-790 Maceió, AL; tel. (82) 3218-7767; fax (82) 3218-7742; e-mail algas@algas.com.br; internet www.algas.com.br; 51% state-owned; Dir and Pres. Dr GERSON FONSECA.

Companhia de Gás de Bahia (BAHIAGÁS): Av. Tancredo Neves 450, Sala 1801, Edif. Suarez Trade, Caminho das Arvores, 41820-901 Salvador, BA; tel. (71) 3206-6000; fax (71) 3206-6001; e-mail bahiagas@bahiagas.com.br; internet www.bahiagas.com.br; f. 1991; 51% state-owned; Pres. DAVIDSON DE MAGALHÃES SANTOS.

Companhia de Gás do Ceará (CEGÁS): Av. Santos Dumont 7700, 5°–11° andares, 60190–800 Fortaleza, CE; tel. (85) 3266–6900; fax (85) 3265-2026; e-mail cegas@secrel.com.br; internet www.cegas.com.br; 51% owned by the state of Amazonas; Pres. Dr JOSÉ REGO FILHO.

Companhia de Gás de Minas Gerais (GASMIG): Av. do Contorno 6594, 10º andar, Belo Horizonte, MG; tel. (31) 3265-1000; fax (31) 3265-1103; e-mail gasmig@gasmig.com.br; internet www.gasmig.com.br; Pres. JOSÉ CARLOS DE MATTOS.

Companhia de Gás de Pernambuco (COPERGÁS): Av. Eng. Domingo Ferreira 4060, 15° andar, 51021-040 Recife, PE; tel. (81) 3463-2000; e-mail copergas@copergas.com.br; internet www.copergas.com.br; 51% state-owned; Pres. Dr ALDO GUEDES.

Companhia de Gás do Rio Grande do Sul (SULGÁS): Rua 7 de Setembro 1069, Edif. Santa Cruz, 5° andar, 90010-190 Porto Alegre, RS; tel. and fax (51) 3287-2200; internet www.sulgas.rs.gov.br; f. 1993; 51% state-owned; 49% owned by Petrobras; Pres. DANIEL ANDRADE.

Companhia de Gás de Santa Catarina (SCGÁS): Rua Antônia Luz 255, Centro Empresarial Hoepcke, 88010-410 Florianópolis, SC; tel. (48) 3229-1200; fax (48) 3229-1230; internet www.scgas.com.br; f. 1994; 51% state-owned; Pres. IVAN CÉSAR RANZOLIN.

Companhia de Gás de São Paulo (COMGÁS): Rua Olimpíadas 205, 10° andar, Vila Olímpia, 04551-000 São Paulo, SP; tel. (11) 4504-5000; e-mail investidores@comgas.com.br; internet www.comgas.com.br; f. 1978; distribution in São Paulo of gas; sold in April 1999 to consortium including British Gas PLC and Royal Dutch/Shell Group; Pres. LUIS DOMENECH.

Companhia Paraibana de Gás (PBGÁS): Av. Epitácio Pessoa 4840, Sala 210, 1° andar, Tambaú, 58030-001 João Pessoa, PB; tel. (83) 3247-7609; fax (83) 3247-2244; e-mail cicero@pbgas.com.br; internet www.pbgas.pb.gov.br; f. 1995; 51% state-owned; Pres. and Dir FRANCISCO DE ASSIS QUINTANS.

Companhia Paranaense de Gás (COMPAGÁS): Rua Pasteur 463, Edif. Jatobá, 7° andar, Batel, 80250-080 Curitaba, PR; tel. (41) 3312-1900; fax (41) 3222-6633; e-mail compagas@mail.copel.br; internet www.compagas.com.br; f. 1998; 51.0% owned by Copel Participaçoes, SA, 24.5% by Gaspetro and 24.5% by Mitsui Gás e Energia do Brasil; Pres. Dr ANTÔNIO FERNANDO KREMPEL.

Companhia Potiguar de Gás (POTIGÁS): Av. Brancas Dunas 485, Lojas 1 e 2, Salas de 101 a 106, Candelária, 59064-720 Natal, RN; tel. (84) 3204-8500; e-mail ismael@potigas.com.br; internet www.potigas.com.br; 17% state-owned; Pres. MARCELO ROSADO CAETANO MAIA BATISTA.

Companhia Rondoniense de Gás, SA (RONGÁS): Av. Carlos Gomes 1223, Sala 403, Centro, 78903-000 Porto Velho, RO; tel. and fax (69) 3229-0333; e-mail rongas@rongas.com.br; internet www.rongas.com.br; f. 1998; 17% state-owned; Pres. JOSÉ SANGUANINI.

Empresa Sergipana de Gás, SA (EMSERGÁS): Av. Heráclito Rollemberg, 1712, Farolândia, SE; tel. (79) 3243-8500; e-mail emsergas@infonet.com.br; internet www.sergipegas.com.br; Pres. FERNANDO AKIRA OTA.

Water

Águas e Esgotos do Piauí (AGESPISA): Av. Mal Castelo Branco 101, Cabral, 64000 Teresina, PI; tel. (86) 3223-9300; internet www.agespisa.com.br; f. 1962; state-owned; water and waste management; Pres. MERLONG SOLANO NOGUEIRA.

Companhia de Agua e Esgosto de Ceará (CAGECE): Rua Lauro Vieira Chaves 1030, Fortaleza, CE; tel. (85) 3101-1735; fax (85) 3101-1742; internet www.cagece.com.br; state-owned; water and sewerage services; Gen. Man. JOSÉ DE RIBAMAR DA SILVA.

Companhia Algoas Industrial (CINAL): Rodovia Divaldo Suruagy, Km 12, 57160-000 Marechal Deodoro, AL; tel. (82) 3218-2500; fax (82) 3269-1199; internet www.cinal.com.br; f. 1982; management of steam and treated water; Dir Pres. FRANCISCO CARLOS RUGA.

Companhia Espírito Santense de Saneamento (CESAN): Av. Governador Bley 186, Edif. BEMGE, 29010-150 Vitória, ES; tel. (27) 3132-8200; fax (27) 2127–5000; e-mail comunica@cesan.com.br; internet www.cesan.com.br; f. 1968; state-owned; construction, maintenance and operation of water supply and sewerage systems; Pres. RICARDO MAXIMILIANO GOLDSCHMIDT.

Companhia Estadual de Aguas e Esgotos (CEDAE): Rua Sacadura Cabral 103, 9° andar, 20081-260 Rio de Janeiro, RJ; tel. (21) 2296-0025; fax (21) 2296-0416; internet www.cedae.rj.gov.br; f. 1975; state-owned; water supply and sewerage treatment; Pres. ALBERTO JOSÉ MENDES GOMES.

Companhia Pernambucana de Saneamento (COMPESA): Av. Cruz Cabugá 1387, Bairro Santo Amaro, 50040-905 Recife, PE; tel. (81) 3412-9180; fax (81) 3412-9181; internet www.compesa.com.br; state-owned; management and operation of regional water supply in the state of Pernambuco; Pres. JOÃO BOSCO DE ALMEIDA.

Companhia Riograndense de Saneamento (CORSAN): Rua Caldas Júnior 120, 18° andar, 90010-260 Porto Alegre, RS; tel. (51) 3215-5600; e-mail ascom@corsan.com.br; internet www.corsan.com.br; f. 1965; state-owned; management and operation of regional water supply and sanitation programmes; Dir MÁRIO RACHE FREITAS.

Companhia de Saneamento Básico do Estado de São Paulo (SABESP): Rua Costa Carvalho 300, 05429-900 São Paulo, SP; tel. (11) 3388-8000; internet www.sabesp.com.br; f. 1973; state-owned; supplies basic sanitation services for the state of São Paulo, including water treatment and supply; Pres. GESNER JOSÉ DE OLIVEIRA FILHO.

TRADE UNIONS

Central Unica dos Trabalhadores (CUT): Rua Caetano Pinto 575, Brás, 03041-000 São Paulo, SP; tel. (11) 2108-9200; fax (11) 2108-9310; e-mail duvaier@cut.org.br; internet www.cut.org.br; f. 1983; central union confederation; left-wing; 3.5m. mems; Pres. ARTHUR ENRIQUE DA SILVA SANTOS; Gen. Sec. SEVERE QUINTINO MARQUES.

Confederação Nacional dos Metalúrgicos (Metal Workers): Alameda dos Tupinás 248, Planalto Paulista, 04069-000 São Paulo, SP; tel. (11) 5584-8440; e-mail imprensa@cnmcut.org.br; internet www.cnmcut.org.br; f. 1992; Pres. CARLOS ALBERTO GRANA; Gen. Sec. VALTER SANCHES.

Confederação Nacional das Profissões Liberais (CNPL) (Liberal Professions): SAU/SUL, Quadra 06, Bloco K, Edif. Belvedere, 70070-915 Brasília, DF; tel. (61) 2103-1683; e-mail cnpldf@cnpl.org.br; internet www.cnpl.org.br; f. 1953; 260,000 mems (2007); Pres. FRANSCISCO ANTONIO FEIJÓ; Sec.-Gen. LUIZ SERGIO DA ROSA LOPES.

Confederação Nacional dos Trabalhadores na Indústria (CNTI) (Industrial Workers): SEP/NORTE, Quadra 505, Conj. A, 70730-540 Brasília, DF; tel. (61) 3448-9900; fax (61) 3448-9956; e-mail cnti@cnti.org.br; internet www.cnti.org.br; f. 1946; Pres. JOSÉ CALIXTO RAMOS; Sec.-Gen. JOSÉ SEBASTIÃO DOS SANTOS.

Confederação Nacional dos Trabalhadores no Comércio (CNTC) (Commercial Workers): Av. W/5 Sul, SGAS Quadra 902, Bloco C, 70390-020 Brasília, DF; tel. (61) 3217-7100; fax (61) 3217-7122; e-mail cntc@cntc.com.br; internet www.cntc.com.br; f. 1946; Pres. ANTÔNIO ALVES DE ALMEIDA.

Confederação Nacional dos Trabalhadores em Transportes Marítimos, Fluviais e Aéreos (CONTTMAF) (Maritime, River and Air Transport Workers): SDS, Edif. Venâncio V, Grupos 501503, 70393-900 Brasília, DF; tel. (61) 3225-0789; fax (61) 3322-6383; e-mail conttmaf@conttmaf.org.br; internet www.conttmaf.org.br; f. 1957; Pres. SEVERINO ALMEIDA FILHO.

Confederação Nacional dos Trabalhadores em Comunicações e Publicidade (CONTCOP) (Communications and Advertising Workers): SCS, Quadra 02, Edif. Serra Dourada, 7° andar, 70300-902 Brasília, DF; tel. (61) 3224-7926; fax (61) 3224-5686; e-mail contcop@contcop.org.br; internet www.contcop.org.br; f. 1964; 350,000 mems; Pres. ANTÔNIO MARIA THAUMATURGO CORTIZO.

Confederação Nacional dos Trabalhadores nas Empresas de Crédito (CONTEC) (Workers in Credit Institutions): SEP-SUL, Av. W/4, EQ 707/907, Conj. A/B, 70390-078 Brasília, DF; tel. (61) 3244-5833; fax (61) 3224-2743; e-mail contec@yawl.com.br; internet www.contec.org.br; f. 1958; Pres. LOURENÇO FERREIRA DO PRADO.

Confederação Nacional dos Trabalhadores em Estabelecimentos de Educação e Cultura (CNTEEC) (Workers in Education and Culture): SAS, Quadra 4, Bloco B, 70070-908 Brasília, DF; tel. (61) 3321-4140; fax (61) 3321-2704; internet www.cnteec.org.br; f. 1966; Pres. MIGUEL ABRÃO NETO.

Confederação Nacional dos Trabalhadores na Agricultura (CONTAG) (Agricultural Workers): SMPW, Quadra 01, Conj. 02, Lote 02, Núcleo Bandeirante, 71735-102 Brasília, DF; tel. (61) 2102-2288; fax (61) 2102-2299; e-mail contag@contag.org.br; internet www.contag.org.br; f. 1964; represents 25 state federations and 3,630 syndicates, 15m. mems; Pres. MANOEL JOSÉ DOS SANTOS; Sec.-Gen. DAVID WYLKERSON RODRIGUES DE SOUZA.

Força Sindical (FS): Rua Galvão Bueno 782, Liberdade, São Paulo, SP; tel. and fax (11) 3348-9000; e-mail secgeral@fsindical.org.br; internet www.fsindical.org.br; f. 1991; 2.1m. mems (2007); Pres. PAULO PEREIRA DA SILVA; Sec.-Gen. JOÃO CARLOS GONÇALVES.

União Geral dos Trabalhadores (UGT): Rua Formosa 367, 4° andar, 01049-000 São Paulo, SP; tel. (11) 2111-7300; fax (11) 2111-7301; e-mail ugt@ugt.org.br; internet www.ugt.org.br; f. 2007 by merger of Confederação Geral dos Trabalhadores with two other unions; Pres. RICARDO PATAH; Sec.-Gen. FRANCISCO CANINDÉ PEGADO DO NASCIMENTO.

Transport

Ministério dos Transportes: see section on the Government (Ministries).

Agência Nacional de Transportes Terrestres (ANTT): SBN, Quadra 2, Bloco C, 70040-020 Brasília, DF; tel. (61) 3410-1990; e-mail ouvidoria@antt.gov.br; internet www.antt.gov.br; f. 2002; govt agency; oversees road and rail infrastructure; Dir-Gen. JOSÉ ALEXANDRE NOGUEIRA RESENDE.

RAILWAYS

In 2006 there were 29,013 km of railway lines. There are also railways owned by state governments and several privately owned railways. In 2001 railways accounted for 20.7% of all freight traffic, and in 2002 for 1.0% of passenger transport.

América Latina Logistica do Brasil, SA (ALL): Rua Emilio Bertolini 100, Cajuru, Curitiba, PR; tel. (41) 2141-7555; e-mail caall@all-logistica.com; internet www.all-logistica.com; f. 1997; 6,586 km in 2003; Pres. BERNARDO HEES.

Associação Nacional dos Transportadores Ferroviários (ANTF): Quadra 01, Bloco J, Ed. CNT, Torre A 6°, Sala 605, 70070-010 Brasília, DF; tel. (61) 3226-5434; fax (61) 3221-0135; internet www.antf.org.br; promotes railway devt; 11 mem. cos; Pres. JULIO FONTANA NETO; Exec. Dir RODRIGO VILAÇA.

Companhia Brasileira de Trens Urbanos (CBTU): Estrada Velha da Tijuca 77, Usina, 20531-080 Rio de Janeiro, RJ; tel. (21) 2575-3399; fax (21) 2571-6149; e-mail imprensa@cbtu.gov.br; internet www.cbtu.gov.br; f. 1984; fmrly responsible for suburban networks and metro systems throughout Brazil; 252 km in 1998; the transfer of each city network to its respective local government was under way; Pres. ELIONALDO MAURÍCIO MAGALHÃES MORAES.

Gerência de Trens Urbanos de João Pessoa (GTU/JP): Praça Napoleão Laureano 1, 58010-040 João Pessoa, PB; tel. (83) 3241-4240; fax (83) 3241-6388; e-mail gecomjp@cbtu.gov.br; 30 km.

Gerência de Trens Urbanos de Maceió (GTU/MAC): Rua Barão de Anadiva 121, 57020-630 Maceió, AL; tel. (82) 2123-1701; fax (82) 223-4024; e-mail gecommac@cbtu.gov.br; 32 km.

Superintendência de Trens Urbanos de Belo Horizonte (STU/BH-Demetrô): Rua Janúaria 181m, 31110-060 Belo Horizonte, MG; tel. (31) 3250-3900; fax (31) 3250-4053; e-mail decombh@cbtu.gov.br; f. 1986; 21.3 km open in 2002; Gen. Man. M. L. L. SIQUEIRA.

Superintendência de Trens Urbanos de Natal: Praça Augusto Severo 302, 59012-380 Natal, RN; tel. (84) 3221-3355; fax (84) 3211-4122; e-mail esegundo@cbtu.gov.br; internet natal.cbtu.gov.br; f. 1984; 56 km; Supt ERLY SEGUNDO.

Superintendência de Trens Urbanos de Recife (STU/REC): Rua José Natário 478, Areias, 50900-000 Recife, PE; tel. (81) 3252-6100; fax (81) 3455-4422; f. 1985; 53 km open in 2002; Supt FERNANDO ANTÔNIO C. DUEIRE.

Superintendência de Trens Urbanos de Salvador (STU/SAL): Praça Onze de Decembro s/n, Bairro Calçada, 40410-360 Salvador, BA; tel. (71) 313-9512; fax (71) 313-8760; 14 km.

Companhia Cearense de Transportes Metropolitanos, SA (Metrofor): Rua 24 de Maio 60, 60020-001 Fortaleza, CE; tel. (85) 3101-7100; fax (85) 3101-4744; e-mail metrofor@metrofor.ce.gov.br; internet www.metrofor.ce.gov.br; f. 1997; 46 km; Dir RÔMULO DOS SANTOS FORTES.

Companhia Ferroviária do Nordeste: Av. Francisco de Sá 4829, Bairro Carlito Pamplona, 60310-002 Fortaleza, CE; tel. (85) 4008-2525; e-mail kerley@cfn.com.br; internet www.cfn.com.br; 4,534 km in 2003; Dir MARTINIANO DIAS.

Companhia do Metropolitano de São Paulo: Rua Augusta 1626, 01304-902 São Paulo, SP; tel. (11) 3371-7274; fax (11) 3371-7329; e-mail ouvidoria@metrosp.com.br; internet www.metro.sp.gov.br; f. 1974; 4-line metro system, 61.3 km open in 2007; Pres. JOSÉ JORGE FAGALI.

Companhia Paulista de Trens Metropolitanos (CPTM): Av. Paulista 402, 5° andar, 01310-000 São Paulo, SP; tel. (11) 3371-1530; fax (11) 3285-0323; e-mail usuario@cptm.sp.gov.br; internet www.cptm.sp.gov.br; f. 1992 to incorporate suburban lines fmrly operated by the CBTU and FEPASA; 286 km; Dir and Pres. SÉRGIO HENRIQUE PASSOS AVELLADA.

Empresa de Trens Urbanos de Porto Alegre, SA: Av. Ernesto Neugebauer 1985, 90250-140 Porto Alegre, RS; tel. (51) 3363-8000; e-mail secos@trensurb.com.br; internet www.trensurb.gov.br; f. 1985; 33.8 km open in 2004; Pres. MARIO FORTES DE ALMEIDA.

Estrada de Ferro do Amapá (EFA): Av. Santana 429, Porto de Santana, 68925-000 Santana, AP; tel. (96) 231-1719; fax (96) 281-1175; f. 1957; operated by Indústria e Comércio de Minérios, SA; 194 km open in 2003; Dir Supt JOSÉ LUIZ ORTIZ VERGULINO.

Estrada de Ferro Campos do Jordão: Rua Martin Cabral 87, CP 11, 12400-000 Pindamonhangaba, SP; tel. (12) 3644-7408; fax (12) 3643-2951; f. 1924; operated by the Tourism Secretariat of the State of São Paulo; Dir ARTHUR FERREIRA DOS SANTOS.

Estrada de Ferro Carajás: Av. Graça Aranha 26, 20030-000 RJ; tel. (21) 3814-4477; fax (21) 3814-4040; f. 1985 for movement of minerals from the Serra do Carajás to the port at Ponta da Madeira; operated by Companhia Vale do Rio Doce; 892 km open in 2002; Supt JUARES SALIBRA.

Estrada de Ferro do Jari: Vila Munguba s/n, Monte Dourado, 68230-000 Pará, PA; tel. (91) 3736-6526; fax (91) 3736-6490; e-mail ascarvalho@jari.com.br; transportation of timber; 70 km open; Operations Man. PABLO ASSIS GUZZO.

Estrada de Ferro Mineração Rio do Norte, SA: Praia do Flamengo 200, 5° e 6° andares, 22210-030 Rio de Janeiro, RJ; tel. (21) 2205-9112; fax (21) 2545-5717; 35 km open in 2003; Pres. ANTÔNIO JOÃO TORRES.

Estrada de Ferro Paraná-Oeste, SA (FERROESTE): Av. Iguaçú 420, 7° andar, 80230-902 Curitiba, PR; tel. (41) 3901-7400; fax (41) 3233-2147; e-mail ferroest@pr.gov.br; internet www.pr.gov.br/ferroeste; f. 1988; serves the grain-producing regions in Paraná and Mato Grosso do Sul; privatized in 1996; 248 km in 2005; Pres. SAMUEL GOMES.

Estrada de Ferro Vitória-Minas: Av. Carandaí 1115, 13° andar, Funcionários, 30130-915 Belo Horizonte, MG; tel. (31) 3279-4545; fax (31) 3279-4676; f. 1942; operated by Companhia Vale de Rio Doce; transport of iron ore, general cargo and passengers; 905 km open in 2003; Dir JOSÉ FRANCISCO MARTINS VIVEIROS.

Ferrovia Bandeirante, SA (Ferroban): Rua Dr Sales de Oliveira 1380, Vila Industral, 13035-270 Campinas, SP; tel. (19) 3735-3100; fax (19) 3735-3196; f. 1971 by merger of five railways operated by São Paulo State; transferred to private ownership in Nov. 1998; fmrly Ferrovia Paulista; 4,236 km open in 2003; Dir JOÃO GOUVEIA FERRÃO NETO.

Ferrovia Centro Atlântica, SA: Rua Sapucaí 383, Floresta 30150-904, Belo Horizonte, MG; tel. (31) 3279-5520; fax (31) 3279-5709; e-mail thiers@centro-atlantica.com.br; internet www.fcasa.com.br; f. 1996 following the privatization of Rede Ferroviária Federal, SA; owned by Companhia Vale do Rio Doce since 2003; industrial freight; 8,000 km.

Ferrovia Norte-Sul: Av. Marechal Floriano 45, Centro, 20080-003 Rio de Janeiro, RJ; tel. (21) 2291-2185; fax (21) 2263-9119; e-mail valecascom@ferrovianortesul.com.br; internet www.ferrovianortesul.com.br; 2,066 km from Belém to Goiânia; Dir JOSÉ FRANCISCO DAS NEVES.

Ferrovia Novoeste, SA: Rua do Rócio 351, 3° andar, 04552-905 São Paulo, SP; tel. (11) 3845-4966; fax (11) 3841-9252; e-mail silviam@uol.com.br; 1,622 km in 2003; Man. Dir NÉLSON DE SAMPAIO BASTOS.

Ferrovia Tereza Cristina, SA (FTC): Rua dos Ferroviários 100, Bairro Oficinas, 88702-230 Tubarão, SC; tel. (48) 3621-7724; fax (48) 3621-7747; e-mail comunicacao@ftc.com.br; internet www.ftc.com.br; 164 km in 2007; Man. Dir BENONY SCHMITZ FILHO.

Ferrovias Norte do Brasil, SA (FERRONORTE): Rua do Rócio 351, 3° andar, Vila Olímpia, 04552-905 São Paulo, SP; tel. (11) 3845-4966; fax (11) 3841-9252; f. 1988; 403 km in 2003; affiliated with Ferrovia Novoeste and Ferroban; Man. Dir NELSON DE SAMPAIO BASTOS.

Metrô Rio: Av. Presidente Vargas 2000, Col. Centro, 20210-031 Rio de Janeiro, RJ; tel. (21) 3211-6300; e-mail sac@metrorio.com.br; internet www.metrorio.com.br; 2-line metro system, 42 km open in 1997; operated by Opportans Concessão Metroviária, SA; Pres. ALVARO J. M. SANTOS.

MRS Logística, SA: Praia de Botafogo 228, Sala 1201E, Ala B, Botafogo, 22359-900 Rio de Janeiro, RJ; tel. (21) 2559-4610; internet www.mrs.com.br; f. 1996; 1,974 km in 2003; CEO JULIO FONTANA NETO.

Transporte Urbano do Distrito Federal (DFTRANS): SGON, Quadra 6, Lote Único, Garagem da TCB, 70610-600; tel. (61) 3324-0376; e-mail ouvidoriadftrans@yahoo.com.br; internet www.dftrans.df.gov.br; the first section of the Brasília metro, linking the capital with the western suburb of Samambaia, was inaugurated in 1994; Dir PAULO HENRIQUE B. MUNHOZ DA ROCHA.

ROADS

In 2003 there were 1,751,862 km of roads in Brazil, of which 196,094 km were paved. Brasília has been a focal point for inter-regional development, and paved roads link the capital with every region of Brazil. The building of completely new roads has taken place predominantly in the north. Roads are the principal mode of transport, accounting for 61.1% of freight traffic in 2001, and 95% of passenger traffic, including long-distance bus services, in 2002. Major projects include the 5,000-km Trans-Amazonian Highway, running from Recife and Cabedelo to the Peruvian border, the 4,138-km Cuiabá–Santarém highway, which will run in a north–south direction, and the 3,555-km Trans-Brasiliana project, which will link Marabá, on the Trans-Amazonian Highway, with Aceguá, on the Uruguayan frontier. A 3.5–km bridge linking Manaus with Iranduba over the Rio Negro, a tributary of the Amazon, was scheduled to open in November 2010. In 2004 an agreement was reached to construct a highway linking the Brazilian state of Acre with the coast of Peru.

Departamento Nacional de Infra-Estrutura de Transportes (DNIT) (National Roads Development): SAN, Quadra 3, Lote A, Edif. Núcleo dos Transportes, 70040-902 Brasília, DF; tel. (61) 3315-4000; fax (61) 3315-4050; e-mail diretoria.geral@dner.gov.br; internet www.dner.gov.br; f. 1945 to plan and execute federal road policy and to supervise state and municipal roads in order to integrate them into the national network; Pres. PAULO SÉRGIO OLIVEIRA PASSOS; Exec. Dir JOSÉ HENRIQUE SADOK DE SÁ.

INLAND WATERWAYS

River transport plays only a minor part in the movement of goods. There are three major river systems, the Amazon, the Paraná and the São Francisco. The Amazon is navigable for 3,680 km, as far as Iquitos in Peru, and ocean-going ships can reach Manaus, 1,600 km upstream. Plans have been drawn up to improve the inland waterway system, and one plan is to link the Amazon and Upper Paraná to provide a navigable waterway across the centre of the country.

Agência Nacional de Transportes Aquaviários (ANTAQ): SEPN, Quadra 514, Conj. E, Edif. ANTAQ, 70760-545 Brasília, DF; tel. (61) 3447-1035; fax (61) 3447-1040; e-mail asc@antaq.gov.br; internet www.antaq.gov.br; Dir-Gen. FERNANDO ANTÔNIO BRITO FIALHO.

Administração das Hidrovias do Nordeste (AHINOR): Rua da Paz 561, 65020-450 São Luiz, MA; tel. and fax (98) 3231-5122; e-mail ahinor@elo.com.br; internet www.ahinor.gov.br; Pres. JOSÉ OSCAR FRAZÃO FROTA.

Administração da Hidrovia do Paraguai (AHIPAR): Rua Treze de Junho 960, Corumbá, 79300-040 MS; tel. (67) 3231-2841; fax (67) 3231-2661; internet www.ahipar.gov.br; Supt FERMIANO YARZON.

Administração da Hidrovia do Paraná (AHRANA): Av. Brig. Faria Lima 1884, 6° andar, 01451-000 São Paulo, SP; tel. (11) 2106-1600; fax (11) 3815-5435; e-mail ahrana@ahrana.gov.br; internet www.ahrana.gov.br; Supt LUIZ EDUARDO GARCIA.

Administração da Hidrovia do São Francisco (AHSFRA): Praça do Porto 70, Distrito Industrial, 39270-000 Pirapora, MG; tel. (38) 3741-2555; fax (38) 3741-2510; e-mail superint@ahsfra.gov.br; internet www.ahsfra.gov.br; Supt SEBASTIÃO MARQUES DE OLIVEIRA.

Administração das Hidrovias da Amazônia Oriental (AHIMOR): Rua Joaquim Nabuco 8, Nazaré, 66055-300 Belém, PA; tel. (91) 3039-7700; fax (91) 3039-7721; e-mail ahimor@ahimor.gov.br; internet www.ahimor.gov.br; Supt ALBERTINO DE OLIVEIRA E SILVA.

Administração das Hidrovias do Sul (AHSUL): Praça Oswaldo Cruz 15, 3° andar, 90030-160 Porto Alegre, RS; tel. (51) 3228-3677; fax (51) 3226-9068; e-mail ahsul@uol.com.br; Supt JOSÉ LUIZ F. DE AZAMBUJA.

Administração das Hidrovias do Tocantins e Araguaia (AHITAR): ACSE Conj. 02, Lote 33 1º andar, Sala 02, 77020-024 Palmas, TO; tel. (62) 3215-3171; fax (62) 3213-1904; e-mail tarlis@ahitar.gov.br; internet www.ahitar.gov.br; Supt TARLIS JUNQUEIRA CALEMAN.

Empresa de Navegação da Amazônia, SA (ENASA): Rodovia Arthur Bernardes 1000, Val-de-Cães, 66115-000 Belém, PA; tel. (91) 3257-6868; fax (91) 3257-4308; f. 1967; cargo and passenger services on the Amazon River and its principal tributaries, connecting the port of Belém with all major river ports; Pres. LORIWAL DE MAGALHÃES; 48 vessels.

SHIPPING

There are more than 40 deep-water ports in Brazil, all but one of which (Imbituba) are directly or indirectly administered by the Government. The majority of ports are operated by state-owned concerns (Cia Docas do Pará, Estado de Ceará, Estado do Rio Grande do Norte, Bahia, Paraíba, Espírito Santo, Rio de Janeiro and Estado de São Paulo), while a smaller number (including Suape, Cabedelo, São Sebastião, Paranaguá, Antonina, São Francisco do Sul, Porto Alegre, Itajaí, Pelotas and Rio Grande) are administered by state governments.

The ports of Santos, Rio de Janeiro and Rio Grande have specialized container terminals handling more than 1,200,000 TEUs (20-ft equivalent units of containerized cargo) per year. Santos is the major container port in Brazil, accounting for 800,000 TEUs annually. The ports of Paranaguá, Itajaí, São Francisco do Sul, Salvador, Vitória and Imbituba cater for containerized cargo to a lesser extent.

Total cargo handled by Brazilian ports in 2002 amounted to 529m. metric tons.

Brazil's merchant fleet comprised 569 vessels, with a combined aggregate displacement of some 2,359,371 grt, in December 2008.

Departamento de Marinha Mercante: Coordenação Geral de Transporte Maritimo, Av. Rio Branco 103, 6° e 8° andar, 20040-004 Rio de Janeiro, RJ; tel. (21) 2221-4014; fax (21) 2221-5929; Dir PAULO OCTÁVIO DE PAIVA ALMEIDA.

Port Authorities

Administração do Porto de Manaus (SNPH): Rua Marquês de Santa Cruz 25, Centro, 69005-050 Manaus, AM; tel. and fax (92) 3621-4300; e-mail falecom@portodemanaus.com.br; internet www.portodemanaus.com.br; private; operates the port of Manaus.

Administração do Porto de São Francisco do Sul (APSFS): Av. Eng. Leite Ribeiro 782, CP 71, 89240-000 São Francisco do Sul, SC; tel. (47) 3471-1200; fax (47) 3471-1211; e-mail chiodini@apsfs.sc.gov.br; internet www.apsfs.sc.gov.br; Pres. PAULO CÉSAR CORTES CORSI.

Administração dos Portos de Paranaguá e Antonina (APPA): Rua Antonio Pereira 161, 83221-030 Paranaguá, PR; tel. (41) 3420-1100; fax (41) 3423-4252; e-mail appasupe@pr.gov.br; internet www.portosdoparana.pr.gov.br; Supt. EDUARDO REQUIÃO DE MELLO E SILVA.

Companhia Docas do Espírito Santo (CODESA): Av. Getúlio Vargas 556, Centro, 29010-945 Vitória, ES; tel. (27) 3132-7360; fax (27) 3132-7311; internet www.portodevitoria.com.br; f. 1983; Dir HENRIQUE GERMANO ZIMMER.

Companhia das Docas do Estado de Bahia: Av. da França 1551, 40010-000 Salvador, BA; tel. (71) 3320-1100; fax (71) 3320-1375; e-mail codeba@codega.com.br; internet www.codeba.com.br; administers the ports of Salvador, Aratu and Ilhéus; Pres. MARCO ANTÔNIO ROCHA MEDEIROS.

Companhia Docas do Estado de Ceará (CDC): Praça Amigos da Marinha s/n, Mucuripe, 60182-640 Fortaleza, CE; tel. (85) 3266-8800; fax (85) 3266-88943-2433; internet www.docasdoceara.com.br; administers the port of Fortaleza.

Companhia Docas do Estado de São Paulo (CODESP): Av. Conselheiro Rodrigues Alves s/n, Macuco, 11015-900 Santos, SP; tel. (13) 3202-6565; fax (13) 3202-6411; internet www.portodesantos.com; administers the ports of Santos, Charqueadas, Estrela, Cáceres and Corumbá/Ladário, and the waterways of Paraná (AHRANA), Paraguai (AHIPAR) and the South (AHSUL); Dir-Pres. JOSÉ ROBERTO CORREIA SERRA.

Companhia Docas de Imbituba (CDI): Porto de Imbituba, Av. Presidente Vargas 100, 88780-000 Imbituba, SC; tel. (48) 3255-0080; fax (48) 3255-0701; e-mail docas@cdiport.com.br; internet www.cdiport.com.br; private sector concession to administer the port of Imbituba; Pres. NILTON GARCIA DE ARAUJO.

Companhia Docas do Pará (CDP): Av. Presidente Vargas 41, 2° andar, 66010-000 Belém, PA; tel. (91) 3182-9029; fax (91) 3241-1741; e-mail deusa@cdp.com.br; internet www.cdp.com.br; f. 1967; administers the ports of Belém, Miramar, Santarém Obidos, Altamira, São Francisco, Marabá and Vila do Conde; Dir-Pres. CLYTHIO RAYMOND SPERANZA BACKZ VAN.

Companhia Docas da Paraíba (DOCAS-PB): Porto de Cabedelo, Rua Presidente João Pessoa s/n, 58310-000 Cabedelo, PB; tel. (83) 3250-3006; fax (83) 3250-3005; e-mail gvp@docaspb.com.br; internet www.docas.pb.gov.br; administers the port of Cabedelo; Dir-Pres. EURÍPEDES BALSANUFO DE SOUSA MELO.

Companhia Docas do Rio de Janeiro (CDRJ): Rua do Acre 21, 20081-000 Rio de Janeiro, RJ; tel. (21) 2219-8617; fax (21) 2253-0528; e-mail cdrj@portosrio.gov.br; internet www.portosrio.gov.br; administers the ports of Rio de Janeiro, Niterói, Itaguaí and Angra dos Reis; Pres. JOSÉ LUZ DE MELLO.

Companhia Docas do Rio Grande do Norte (CODERN): Av. Hildebrando de Góis 220, Ribeira, 59010-700 Natal, RN; tel. (84) 4005-5311; e-mail administrativo@codern.com.br; internet www.codern.com.br; administers the ports of Areia Branca, Natal and Maceió; Dir-Pres. EMERSON FERNANDES DANIEL JÚNIOR.

Empresa Maranhense de Administração Portuária (EMAP): Av. dos Portugueses n/n, Itaquí, 65085-370 São Luís, MA; tel. (98) 3216-6000; fax (98) 3216-6060; internet www.portodoitaqui.ma.gov.br; f. 2001 to administer port of Itaquí as concession from the state of Maranhão; Pres. ANGELO JOSÉ DE CARVALHO BAPTISTA.

Sociedade de Portos e Hidrovias do Estado de Rondônia (SOPH): Terminal dos Milagres 400, Balsa, 78900-750 Porto Velho, RO; tel. (69) 3229-2134; fax (69) 3229-3943; e-mail soph@soph.ro.gov.br; internet portodeportovelho.ro.gov.br; operates the port of Porto Velho; Dir OBEDES OLIVEIRA DE QUEIROZ.

SUAPE—Complexo Industrial Portuário Governador Eraldo Gueiros: Rodovia PE-060, Km 10, Engenho Massangana, 55590-972 Ipojuca, PE; tel. (81) 3527-5000; fax (81) 3527-5066; e-mail suape@suape.pe.gov.br; internet www.suape.pe.gov.br; administers the port of Suape.

Superintendência do Porto de Itajaí: Rua Blumenau 5, Centro, 88305-101 Itajaí, SC; tel. (47) 3341-8023; fax (47) 3341-8075; e-mail atendimento@portoitajai.com.br; internet www.portoitajai.com.br; Supt ANTÐNIO AYRES DOS SANTOS, Jr.

Superintendência do Porto de Rio Grande (SUPRG): Av. Honório Bicalho s/n, CP 198, 96201-020 Rio Grande do Sul, RS; tel. (53) 3231-1366; fax (53) 3231-1857; internet www.portoriogrande.com.br; f. 1996.

Superintendência do Porto de Tubarão: Porto de Tubarão, 29072-970 Vitória, ES; tel. (27) 3228-1053; fax (27) 3228-1682; operated by the Companhia Vale do Rio Doce mining co; Port Dir CANDIDO COTTA PACHECO.

Superintendência de Portos e Hidrovias do Estado do Rio Grande do Sul (SPH): Av. Mauá 1050, 4° andar, 90010-110 Porto Alegre, RS; tel. and fax (51) 3288-9200; e-mail executiva@sph.rs.gov.br; internet www.sph.rs.gov.br; administers the ports of Porto Alegre, Pelotas and Cachoeira do Sul, the São Gonçalo canal, and other waterways; Dir-Supt GILBERTO CUNHA.

State-owned Company

Companhia de Navegação do Estado de Rio de Janeiro: Praça 15 de Novembro 21, 20010-010 Rio de Janeiro, RJ; tel. (21) 2533-6661; fax (21) 2252-0524; Pres. MARCOS TEIXEIRA.

Private Companies

Aliança Navegação e Logística, Ltda: Rua Verbo Divino 1547, Bairro Chácara Santo Antônio, 04719-002 São Paulo, SP; tel. (11) 5185-5600; fax (11) 5185-5624; e-mail alianca@sao.alianca.com.br; internet www.alianca.com.br; f. 1950; cargo services to Argentina, Uruguay, Europe, Baltic, Atlantic and North Sea ports; Pres. ARSÊNIO CARLOS NÓBREGA.

Companhia de Navegação do Norte (CONAN): Av. Rio Branco 23, 25° andar, 20090-003 Rio de Janeiro, RJ; tel. (21) 2223-4155; fax (21) 2253-7128; f. 1965; services to Brazil, Argentina, Uruguay and inland waterways; Chair. J. R. RIBEIRO SALOMÃO.

Companhia de Navegação do São Francisco (FRANAVE): Av. São Francisco 1517, 39270-000 Pirapora, MG; tel. (38) 3741-1444; fax (38) 3741-1164; Pres. JOSÉ HUMBERTO BARATA JABUR.

Companhia Libra de Navegação: Av. Rio Branco, 4, 6° e 7° andares, 20090-000 Rio de Janeiro; tel. and fax (21) 2213-9700; e-mail atendimento.brasil@csavgroup.com; internet www.libra.com.br.

Frota Oceânica e Amazonica, SA (FOASA): Av. Venezuela 110, CP 21-020, 20081-310 Rio de Janeiro, RJ; tel. (21) 2203-3838; fax (21) 2253-6363; e-mail foasa@pamar.com.br; f. 1947; Pres. JOSÉ CARLOS FRAGOSO PIRES; Vice-Pres. LUIZ J. C. ALHANATI.

Petrobras Transporte, SA (TRANSPETRO): Edif. Visconde de Itaboraí, Av. Presidente Vargas 328, 20091-060 Rio de Janeiro, RJ; tel. (21) 3211-7848; e-mail ouvidoria@transpetro.com.br; internet www.transpetro.com.br; f. 1998; absorbed the Frota Nacional de Petroleiros (FRONAPE) in 1999; transport of petroleum and related products; 53 vessels; Pres. SERGIO DE OLIVEIRA MACHADO.

Vale do Rio Doce Navegação, SA (DOCENAVE): Av. Graça Aranha 26, 8°–9° andar, 20005-900 Rio de Janerio, RJ; fax (21) 3814-4971; internet www.docenave.com.br; bulk carrier to Japan, Arabian Gulf, Europe, North America and Argentina; Pres. ALVARO DE OLIVEIRA FILHO.

Wilson Sons Agência Marítima: Rua Jardim Botânico 518, 3° andar, 22461-000 Rio de Janeiro, RJ; tel. (21) 2126-4222; fax (21) 2126-4190; e-mail box@wilsonsons.com.br; internet www.wilsonsons.com.br; f. 1837; shipping agency, port operations, towage, small shipyard.

CIVIL AVIATION

In 2006 there were 2,498 airports and airstrips and 857 helipads. Of the 67 principal airports, 22 are international, although most international traffic is handled by the two airports at Rio de Janeiro and two at São Paulo. There were 18,024 aircraft registered in Brazil in 2008.

Agência Nacional de Aviação Civil: Aeroporto International de Brasília, Setor de Concessionárias, Lote 5, 71608-900 Brasília, DF; tel. (61) 3366-9200; internet www.anac.gov.br; f. 2006; Dir-Pres. SOLANGE PAIVA VIEIRA.

Empresa Brasileira de Infra-Estrutura Aeroportuária (Infraero): SCS, Quadra 04, Bloco A, 58, Edif. Infraero, 6° andar, 70304-902 Brasília, DF; tel. (61) 3312-3222; fax (61) 3321-0512; e-mail webmaster@infraero.gov.br; internet www.infraero.gov.br; Pres. Brig. CLEONILSON NICÁCIO SILVA.

Principal Airlines

GOL Transportes Aéreos, SA: Rua Tamios 246, Jardim Aeropuerto, 04630-000 São Paulo, SP; tel. (11) 5033-4200; internet www.voegol.com.br; f. 2001; low-cost airline, acquired VARIG, SA in 2007; Man. Dir CONSTANTINO OLIVEIRA JÚNIOR.

Líder Táxi Aéreo, SA: Av. Santa Rosa 123, 31270-750 Belo Horizonte, MG; tel. (31) 3490-4500; fax (31) 3490-4600; internet www.lideraviacao.com.br; helicopters and small jets; f. 1958; Pres. JOSÉ AFONSO ASSUMPÇÃO.

Oceanair Linhas Aéreas, Ltda: Av. Marechal Câmara 160, Sala 1532, Centro, 20020-080 Rio de Janeiro, RJ; tel. (21) 2544-2181; fax (21) 2215-7181; internet www.oceanair.com.br; f. 1998; domestic services; Pres. GERMAN EFROMOVICH.

Pantanal Linhas Aéreas, SA: Av. das Nações Unidas 10989, 8° andar, Conj. 81, 04578-000 São Paulo, SP; tel. (11) 3040-3900; fax (11) 3846-3424; e-mail sac@voepantanal.com.br; internet www.voepantanal.com.br; f. 1993; regional services.

TAM Linhas Aéreas, SA (Transportes Aéreos Regionais—TAM): Av. Jurandir 856, Lote 4, 1° andar, Jardim Ceci, 04072-000 São Paulo, SP; tel. (11) 5582-8811; fax (11) 5578-5946; e-mail tamimprensa@tam.com.br; internet www.tam.com.br; f. 1976; scheduled passenger and cargo services from São Paulo to destinations throughout Brazil and in Argentina, Paraguay, Europe and the USA; Pres. DAVID BARIONI NETO.

VARIG LOG (VARIG Lógistica, SA): Rua Fidencio Ramos 223, 04551-010 São Paulo, SP; tel. (11) 3119-7003; e-mail atendimento.variglog@variglog.com; internet www.variglog.com; f. 2000; owned by Volo do Brasil; cargo airline.

Tourism

In 2009 some 4.8m. tourists visited Brazil. In 2008 receipts from tourism totalled an estimated US $5,785m. Rio de Janeiro, with its famous beaches, is the centre of the tourist trade. Like Salvador, Recife and other towns, it has excellent examples of Portuguese colonial and modern architecture. The modern capital, Brasília, incorporates a new concept of city planning and is the nation's showpiece. Other attractions are the Iguaçu Falls, the seventh largest (by volume) in the world, the tropical forests of the Amazon basin and the wildlife of the Pantanal.

Associação Brasileira da Indústria de Hotéis (ABIH): SCN, Quadra 01, Bloco F, Lojas 121 e 125, Térreo, 70711-905 Brasília, DF; tel. and fax (61) 3326-1177; e-mail abihnacional@abih.com.br; internet www.abih.com.br; f. 1936; hoteliers' asscn; Pres. ERALDO ALVES DA CRUZ.

Instituto Brasileiro de Turismo (EMBRATUR): SCN, Quadra 02, Bloco G, 3° andar, 70710-500 Brasília, DF; tel. (61) 3429-7777; fax (61) 3429-7710; e-mail presidencia@embratur.gov.br; internet www.braziltour.com; f. 1966; Pres. JEANINE PIRES.

Defence

As assessed at November 2009, Brazil's armed forces numbered 327,710: army 190,000 (including 70,000 conscripts); navy 67,000 (including at least 3,200 conscripts; also including 1,387 in the naval air force and 15,520 marines); and air force 70,710. Reserves numbered 1,340,000 and there were some 395,000 in the paramilitary Public Security Forces, state militias under army control. Military service lasts for 12 months and is compulsory for men between 18 and 45 years of age.

Defence Budget: R $51,400m. in 2008.

Chief of Staff of the Air Forces: Gen. JUNITI SAITO.

Chief of Staff of the Army: Lt-Gen. ENZO MARTINS PERI.

Chief of Staff of the Navy: Adm. JÚLIO SOARES DE MOURA NETO.

Education

Education is free in official schools at primary and secondary level. Primary education is compulsory between the ages of seven and 14 years and lasts for eight years. Secondary education begins at 15 years of age and lasts for three years. In 2008 enrolment in primary schools included 94% of children in the relevant age-group, while enrolment in secondary schools included 82% of those in the relevant age-group. The federal Government is responsible for higher education, and in 2008 there were 183 universities, of which 97 were state-administered. Numerous private institutions exist at all levels of education. Federal government expenditure on education was R $18,905m. in 2006.

Bibliography

For works on South America generally, see Select Bibliography (Books)

Amann, E., Baer, W., and Coes, D. (eds). *Energy, Bio Fuels and Development: Comparing Brazil and the United States*. Abingdon, Routledge, 2010.

Ames, B. *The Deadlock of Democracy in Brazil*. Ann Arbor, MI, University of Michigan Press, 2001.

Andersen, L., Granger, C. W. J., Reis, J. E., Weinhold, D., and Wunder, S. *The Dynamic of Deforestation and Economic Growth in the Brazilian Amazon*. Cambridge, Cambridge University Press, 2002.

Arestis, P., and Saad-Filho, A. (eds). *Political Economy of Brazil: Recent Economic Performance*. Basingstoke, Palgrave Macmillan, 2007.

Arias, E. D. *Drugs and Democracy in Rio de Janeiro: Trafficking, Social Networks, and Public Security*. Chapel Hill, NC, University of North Carolina Press, 2006.

Arruda, M. *External Debt (Brazil and the International Financial Crisis)*. London, Pluto Press Ltd, 2000.

Baer, W. *The Brazilian Economy (Growth and Development)*. New York, NY, Praeger Publrs, 2001.

Bailey, S. R. *Legacies of Race: Identities, Attitudes, and Politics in Brazil*. Palo Alto, CA, Stanford University Press, 2009.

Baiocchi, G. *Militants and Citizens: The Politics of Participatory Democracy in Porto Alegre*. Palo Alto, CA, Stanford University Press, 2005.

Baumann, R. *Brazil in the 1990s*. Basingstoke, Palgrave Macmillan, 2001.

Bourne, R. *Lula of Brazil: The Story So Far*. London, Zed Books, 2008.

Branford, S., and Kucinski, B. *Brazil: Carnival of the Oppressed*. London, Latin America Bureau, 1995.

Lula and the Workers' Party in Brazil. New York, NY, The New Press, 2005.

Branford, S., and Rocha, J. *Cutting the Wire: The Story of the Landless Movement in Brazil*. London, Latin America Bureau, 2002.

Bruhn, K. *Urban Protest in Mexico and Brazil*. Cambridge, Cambridge University Press, 2008.

Cardoso, F. E., and Font, M. (Ed.). *Charting a New Course*. Lanham, MD, Rowman & Littlefield Publrs, 2001.

Cardoso, F. H. *The Accidental President of Brazil: A Memoir*. New York, PublicAffairs, 2006.

Castro, P. F. *Fronteras Abiertas: Expansionismo y Geopolítica en el Brasil Contemporáneo*. Madrid, Editores Siglo XXI, 2002.

de Paula, L. E. *Financial Liberalization and Economic Performance: Brazil at the Crossroads*. Abingdon, Routledge, 2010.

Dillon Soares, G. A. *A Democracia Interrompida*. Rio de Janeiro, RJ, Editora FGV, 2001.

Font, M. A., Spanakos, A., and Bordin, C. *Reforming Brazil (Western Hemisphere Studies)*. Lanham, MD, Lexington Books, 2004.

Foweraker, J. *The Struggle for Land: A Political Economy of the Pioneer Frontier in Brazil from 1930 to the Present Day*. Cambridge, Cambridge University Press, 2002.

Freyre, G. *The Masters and the Slaves: A Study in the Development of Brazilian Civilization*. New York, NY, Alfred A. Knopf, 1946.

Gordon, L. *Brazil's Second Chance: En Route toward the First World*. Washington, DC, The Brookings Institution, 2001.

Guilhoto, J. M. J., and Hewings, G. J. D. (Eds). *Structure and Structural Change in the Brazilian Economy*. Aldershot, Ashgate Publishing Ltd, 2001.

Hirst, M. *The United States and Brazil: A Long Road of Unmet Expectations*. London, Routledge, 2005.

Johnson, O. A., III. *Brazilian Party Politics and the Coup of 1964*. Gainesville, FL, University Press of Florida, 2001.

Le Breton, B. *Trapped: Modern-Day Slavery in the Brazilian Amazon*. Bloomfield, CT, Kumarian Press, 2003.

Matos, C. *Journalism and Political Democracy in Brazil*. Lanham, MD, Lexington Books, 2008.

Mendes, C. *Fight for the Forest: Chico Mendes in his own Words*. London, Latin America Bureau, 1989.

Montero, A. *Brazilian Politics: Reforming a Democratic State in a Changing World*. Cambridge, Polity Press, 2006.

Newitt, M. (Ed.). *The First Portuguese Colonial Empire*. Exeter, University of Exeter Press, 2002.

Platt, D., and Neate, P. *Bolado: Life, Death and Survival Strategies in the Favelas*. London, Latin America Bureau, 2006.

Reiter, B. *Negotiating Democracy in Brazil: The Politics of Exclusion*. Boulder, CO, FirstForum Press, 2008.

Reiter, B., and Mitchell, G. L. (Eds). *Brazil's New Racial Politics*. Boulder, CO, Lynne Rienner Publishers, 2009.

Revkin, A. *The Burning Season: The Murder of Chico Mendes and the Fight for the Amazon Rain Forest*. Washington, DC, Shearwater Books, 2004.

Ribeiro, D. *The Brazilian People (The Formation and Meaning of Brazil)*. Gainesville, FL, University Press of Florida, 2000.

Rocha, S. *Pobreza no Brasil: Afinal de que se trata?* Rio de Janeiro, RJ, Editora, FGV, 2003.

Rohter, L. *Brazil on the Rise: The Story of a Country Reformed*. Basingstoke, Palgrave Macmillan, 2010.

Smith, J. *A History of Brazil*. Harlow, Longman, 2002.

Telles, E. E. *Race in Another America: The Significance of Skin Color in Brazil*. Princeton, NJ, Princeton University Press, 2006.

Trebat, T. J., and Knight, A. (Ed.). *Brazil's State-Owned Enterprises: A Case Study of the State as Entrepreneur*. Cambridge, Cambridge University Press, 2007.

Wolfe, J. *Autos and Progress: The Brazilian Search for Modernity*. New York, NY, OUP USA, 2010.

Wolford, W. *The Land is Ours Now: Social Mobilization and the Meanings of Land in Brazil*. Durham, NC, Duke University Press, 2010.

Woodard, J. P. *A Place in Politics@ Sao Paulo, Brazil, from Seigneurial Republicanism to Regionalist Revolt*. Durham, NC, Duke University Press, 2009.

THE BRITISH VIRGIN ISLANDS

Geography

PHYSICAL FEATURES

The British Virgin Islands is an Overseas Territory of the United Kingdom in the West Indies. The Virgin Islands lie at the north-western end of the Lesser Antilles, the chain that defines the edge of the Caribbean Sea, north and east of which is the Atlantic Ocean. To the east of the British Virgin Islands, beyond the shipping lane known as the Anegada Passage, Anguilla (another British dependency) and the other Leeward Islands continue the arc of the Lesser Antilles south--eastwards, while to the west of the US Virgin Islands (formerly the Danish West Indies) is Puerto Rico and the other Greater Antilles. The Virgin Islands themselves are divided between two sovereignties, the smaller, eastern group being British, the rest constituting a Territory of the USA. South-west from Tortola, the main island of the British Virgin Islands, across a narrow sea channel, is the US Virgin Island of St John. The main island of Puerto Rico (another US Territory) is almost 100 km (60 miles) to the west. The British Virgin Islands has a total area of 153 sq km (59 sq miles).

The British Virgin Islands consists of between 40 and 60 islands, islets and cays (with only about 80 km of coastline between them) strewn over almost 3,450 sq km of sea. Of the main islands, 16 are inhabited and 20 uninhabited. The largest island is Tortola (54 sq km), where the capital is located. The next in size are Anegada (39 sq km), Virgin Gorda (21 sq km) and Jost Van Dyke (9 sq km). The last is west of Tortola, while Virgin Gorda is to the east (beyond the small clump of the Dog Islands), and the more isolated Anegada is north of Virgin Gorda. At the centre of the archipelago, like an 'inland sea', is the 30-km Sir Francis Drake Channel, which runs north-eastwards from St John to Virgin Gorda, flanked by Tortola (on the northern side) and by a string of islands including Norman, Peter, Salt, Cooper and Ginger (to the south). Most of the main islands are hilly and steep (the highest point is Mt Sage on Tortola, at 521 m or 1,710 ft), the result of long-past volcanic activity, which has made the islands fertile and lush with tropical greenery. However, there are also extensive coral reefs, themselves adding to the land area, most notably in the northern island of Anegada, which is flat and coralline. South of Anegada is the 18-km Horseshoe Reef, one of the largest reefs in the world—some 300 ships are believed to have been wrecked on and around the island. Only on Tortola are there open streams, and these are seasonal. The complicated island geography has, historically, attracted pirates, but it is now tourists, particularly yachters, who are drawn to the scattered islands, sometimes perilous reefs, hidden coves and sandy beaches. Some tree species can only be found on the Virgin Islands, as can the smallest lizard in the world, the cotton ginner or dwarf gecko, while Anegada, by contrast, shelters the last survivors of the indigenous variety of rock iguana, which can grow to over 1.5 m.

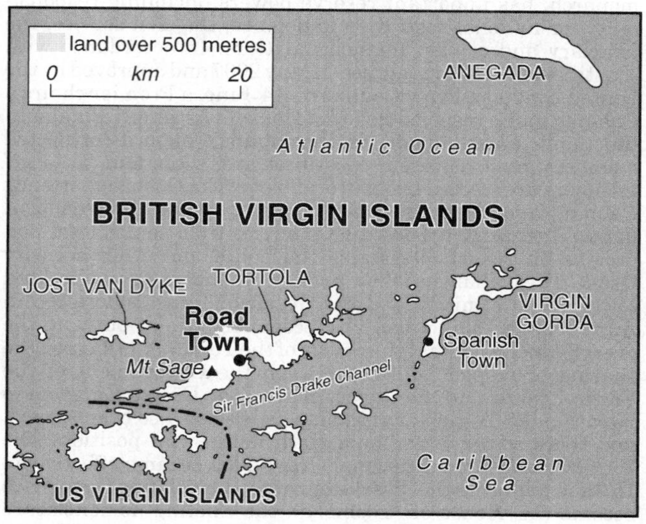

CLIMATE

The climate is subtropical and humid, moderated by the trade winds off the Atlantic. The hilly terrain helps capture some of the 1,350 mm (53 ins) of rainfall received in an average year. However, the British Virgin Islands are in the hurricane belt, which can strike to devastating effect. Temperature variations are relatively mild, ranging between 22°C–28°C (72°F–82°F) in winter (December–March) and 26°C–32°C (79°F–90°F) in summer.

POPULATION

Most of the population is black (83%) and Christian (33% Methodist, 21% from other Protestant denominations, 17% Anglican—Episcopal—and 11% Roman Catholic). English is the official and most widely spoken language. Links with the neighbouring US Virgin Islands are strong.

The total population was projected at 29,537 in mid-2010. It is reckoned to have almost doubled in the last 20 years of the 20th century, with only about one-half of the present population judged to be of British Virgin Islands origin, the rest being drawn by opportunities in tourism and construction. The capital is Road Town, on the south coast of Tortola, the most populous (82% of the total) as well as the largest island. Fifteen other islands are also inhabited, although most of the rest of the population is on Virgin Gorda (itself once the centre of population), the chief settlement of which is Spanish Town.

History

MARK WILSON

The British Virgin Islands is a United Kingdom Overseas Territory. A Governor, who is the representative of the British monarch, has important reserve powers, including responsibility for national security and defence, the civil service, the judiciary and certain financial matters. In accordance with constitutional reforms agreed in May 2007 and approved by the United Kingdom Privy Council on 14 June, a Premier chairs a Cabinet, and is responsible to the House of Assembly, similar in function to a parliament, which contains a majority of elected members; nine represent constituencies, while four 'at large' members are elected by an overall vote. The Governor attends Cabinet, and shares responsibility for setting its agenda. A national security council allows advice from senior local politicians on issues relating to the police and other security issues. These changes follow a constitutional review submitted to the Chief Minister and the Governor for consideration in April 2005, with a total of 116 recommendations, but with the overall conclusion that the people of the Territory preferred the sharing of responsibilities between the Government of the Virgin Islands and the Government of the United Kingdom to be continued. A charter of human rights has also been agreed, and there is provision for a sixth ministerial position. The Virgin Islands Constitutional Order 2007 became effective on 15 June following the dissolution of the Legislative Council (to become the 'House of Assembly'); the existing nomenclature describing the Premier ('Chief Minister') and Cabinet ('Executive Council') was retained, however, until immediately after the general election on 20 August. With a headquarters building completed in 2009, the British Virgin Islands was host to a commercial court which served the islands participating in the Eastern Caribbean court system.

Few traces remain of the original Amerindian inhabitants. The Virgin Islands were named by Christopher Columbus in 1493. The first European settlers were from the Netherlands, but the islands were British from 1666. There was an elected Assembly from 1773. From 1871 to 1956 the British Virgin Islands formed part of the Leeward Islands Federation. From 1951 the local Legislative Council was given four elected representatives, equal in number to the nominated members, with the franchise extended to adults passing a literacy test. The islands did not join the Federation of the West Indies in 1958, possibly because islanders saw their future as more closely linked to the neighbouring US Virgin Islands. Instead they were, from 1960, a separate British Dependent Territory, first under an Administrator, then under a Governor. From February 1998 they were, along with the United Kingdom's other remaining dependencies, designated a United Kingdom Overseas Territory.

In 1967 a new Constitution established the office of Chief Minister. For most of the succeeding period, the Virgin Islands Party (VIP) has held office, led by H. Lavity Stoutt until his death in May 1995, and then by Ralph T. O'Neal. The United Party (UP) formed a coalition during 1983–86, with an independent member, Cyril Romney, as Chief Minister.

In 1986 the VIP then returned to office, winning five out of the nine elected seats in that year, and six seats in 1989, but losing its absolute majority in a general election on 20 February 1995. Four 'at large' members had been added to the nine constituency representatives, against the wishes of the VIP; with the composition of the Legislative Council altered in this way, the VIP took six seats, with two for the UP, two for the Concerned Citizens' Movement (CCM), and three independents. However, one of the independents joined the VIP, which was thus able to form an administration with a majority of a single seat. At the general election of 17 May 1999 the VIP retained its single-seat majority, winning seven seats, in spite of a strong challenge from the National Democratic Party (NDP), which had been formed only in 1998 and which took five seats. The remaining seat was held by the CCM.

A brief political crisis began on 20 July 2000, when the appointment of Eileene L. Parsons as Minister for Health, Education, Culture and Welfare was revoked. Parsons then joined the NDP, a move that would have deprived the VIP of its majority, had not the single CCM member, Ethlyn E. Smith, defected to join the Government as Minister for Health and Welfare. O'Neal's support was increased from seven to eight seats in February 2001 when another opposition member, Mark Vanterpool, joined the VIP.

Reported corruption on an airport-improvement project precipitated a serious political crisis in 2001–02. Following a report presented to the Governor on 9 November 2001, several people were arrested, including the Government's financial secretary Allen Wheatley, the budget co-ordinator and the former head of the telephone services management unit. In March 2002 they were charged in court with conspiracy to defraud the Government and related offences; they received sentences of between six and nine months in January 2004. The Attorney-General appealed in March 2004 against the leniency of the sentences. A report by the Government's chief auditor in September 2003 also expressed concern over the neglect of established procedures for the award of government contracts. An opposition-proposed motion of no confidence in the Legislative Council was defeated in May, with O'Neal expressing a lack of concern about the issue. The standing of the Government was severely weakened and, with a constitutional review in progress, strong pressure for stricter financial management was expected from the British authorities. However, the Chief Minister argued for greater local autonomy and a reduction in the Governor's reserve powers, while a report by the United Kingdom's Centre for Management and Policy Studies commented on the 'almost total breakdown' in the relationship between elected ministers and senior civil servants. In addition to corruption, drugs-related crime is also a serious problem. The police commissioner was shot by a discontented constable in 2004. Several murders in 2003–06 appeared to be drugs-related. A police Drug and Violent Crime Task Force was formed in 2005 and a new visa regime implemented by the Government in April 2007; the latter required that, in order to enter the Territory, Jamaican nationals without residency or 'belonger' status obtain a visa, in an effort to enhance immigration monitoring and curb the numbers of non-British Virgin Islanders residing in the country illegally.

In May 2002 the British Overseas Territories Act, having received royal assent in the United Kingdom in February, came into force and granted British citizenship to the people of its Overseas Territories, including the British Virgin Islands. Under the new law, British Virgin Islanders would be able to hold British passports and work in the United Kingdom and anywhere else in the European Union.

After 17 years in office, the VIP relinquished control of the legislature after a general election, which was held on 16 June 2003. The NDP secured eight seats compared with the VIP's five after a campaign that was dominated by the issues of alleged corruption, management of public sector capital projects and relations with the United Kingdom. The VIP, which claimed returning officers failed to account for all ballots issued and votes cast, demanded a recount in two constituencies; however, the complaint was rejected by the High Court. The new Chief Minister, Orlando Smith, appointed Ronnie Skelton as Minister of Finance, Health and Welfare, Paul Wattley as Minister of Communications and Works, Lloyd Black as Minister of Education and Culture, and J. Alvin Christopher as Minister of Natural Resources and Labour. In an effort to improve strategic planning for public sector capital spending, the new Government decided to reappraise a controversial US $77m. hospital project, and ended a dispute with the Caribbean Development Bank over the appointment of contractors to complete an airport-improvement project; as a result, work on the runway started in October 2003, after a delay of 15 months, and was completed in May 2004. A contract was signed for a modified US $64m. hospital project in December 2006. Anti-corruption legislation targeted at politicians and public figures was debated by the Legislative Council in December 2003. The Minister of Communications and Works,

Paul Wattley, died in July of that year. The NDP won the ensuing by-election with 54% of the votes cast, increasing its legislative representation to nine seats; J. Alvin Christopher became Wattley's successor in September, while Eileene Parsons replaced Christopher as Minister for Natural Resources and Labour. Christopher was removed from his tenure at the Ministry of Communications and Works in May 2006, after disagreeing with his colleagues over proposals for the liberalization of the telecommunications sector, in place of the monopoly still held by Cable & Wireless. However, he remained a member of the NDP, having broken with the former VIP Government in 2002. He was replaced in the ministerial portfolio by Elmore Stoutt.

A new Constitution negotiated with the United Kingdom after broad public consultations was agreed by the Legislative Council in May 2007. A Cabinet chaired by a Premier replaced the Executive Council chaired by the Governor. Police and security remained the Governor's responsibility, but with advice from a new National Security Council in which elected politicians were to participate.

At a general election on 20 August 2007, the VIP returned to office, taking 10 of the 13 seats, with Ralph O'Neal as Premier. A former Deputy Governor, Dancia Penn Sallah, was appointed Deputy Premier and Minister of Health and Social Development. The NDP held only two seats, and Christopher, running as an independent, took one. The VIP took 52.5% of the popular vote in the single-member constituencies (leaving aside the 'at large' seats), with 35.2% going to the NDP and 12.2% to independent candidates. The NDP had presided over a period of strong economic growth, with completion of several infrastructural projects, and its period in office had been largely free of accusations of corruption. However, there was widespread public concern over the rapid pace of economic development, led mainly by investors from outside the British Virgin Islands. As during his previous administration, O'Neal developed a difficult relationship with the British-appointed Governor, whom he accused in February 2008 of favouring the NDP opposition. O'Neal also objected to the appointment in August 2008 of Inez Archibald, who was Speaker of the Legislative Council before the 2007 general election, as Deputy Governor.

In the British Virgin Islands, as in most of the Caribbean, there is concern over violent crime. There were six murders in the territory in 2007 and eight in 2008, resulting in a murder rate of 31 per 100,000 inhabitants, more than five times that of the USA. However, there was only one murder in 2009, a significant improvement. Most killings appear to be directly or indirectly drugs-related. The Government in 2008 announced the recruitment of seven additional police officers from the United Kingdom. The islands are a short distance from the US Virgin Islands, which are within the US customs and immigration area, and are therefore an attractive staging post for drugs- and human-trafficking. There have also been several instances of serious fraud, some of which have involved the 'offshore' financial sector. Assets to the value of US $45m. held in the British Virgin Islands by three International Business Company subsidiaries of a Bermuda-registered entity, the IPOC International Growth Fund, were confiscated in May 2007 following a guilty plea on charges of perverting the course of justice during a money-laundering investigation linked to the Russian telecommunications industry. Indicating a history of weak public sector management, the Governor, David Pearey, in March 2009 appointed a commission of inquiry into alleged evasion of stamp duty in 2000–06, headed by a former Eastern Caribbean Chief Justice, Brian Alleyne. A report was submitted to the Governor in March 2010, and was handed to the Cabinet in July. The opposition in June 2010 called for an inquiry into the Government's relations with a British company, Biwater Holdings Ltd, after agreements to purchase a generator and to operate a Build-Own-Operate-Transfer desalination, water supply and sewerage contract were both reportedly negotiated without tender.

A new Governor, William Boyd McCleary, was appointed in December 2009 to succeed Pearey on his retirement at the beginning of August 2010.

Economy

MARK WILSON

The British Virgin Islands is situated in the Eastern Caribbean and had an estimated population of 28,213 in mid-2008, occupying 153 sq km of territory. Immigration resulting from economic prosperity led to an average annual population growth of 3.5% in 1995–2005. Of the total population, 83% lived on the island of Tortola. Virgin Gorda, with 14%, is developing rapidly, and there is 1% each on Anegada and Jost Van Dyke.

The British Virgin Islands is an associate member of the Caribbean Community and Common Market, or CARICOM, whose larger members formed a single market and economy at the start of 2006. It is also a member of the Organisation of Eastern Caribbean States, which links nine of the smaller Caribbean territories. However, the islands do not participate in the Eastern Caribbean Central Bank and have no separate central banking arrangements, using US currency for all purposes.

The islands have an extremely prosperous economy, with a per-head gross domestic product (GDP) of US $38,818 in 2009, and an unemployment rate of an estimated 3.1% in 2008. Average annual growth was close to 4% in 1995–99.

The economy slowed in 2000–03, largely reflecting an international downturn in tourism. Revenue in 2002 was almost 10% below the original budget projection, forcing the Government to draw heavily on fiscal reserves. However, the brisk pace of growth was resumed from 2004; growth averaged 4.3% in 2004–07, although GDP contracted by 0.6% in 2008 as investment and tourism demand fell. In 2006 there was a current account surplus of US $31.6m., equivalent to 3.1% of GDP. The current account surplus increased to $31.9m. in 2007. Debt-servicing has increased, but takes up only 4.6% of current revenues. However, the economy of the British Virgin Islands suffered in 2008 and 2009, as the international economic downturn adversely affected international financial services, tourism and hotel construction. The recurrent surplus for 2008 was $9.0m., in place of an original budget projection of $37.6m., while for 2009 revenue fell by 3.6% and spending by 1.6%, with a resulting overall deficit of $6.9m. Additional cost-cutting measures were announced in June 2010. Public debt increased to $151.7m. at the end of 2009.

Financial and business services made up 33.7% of GDP in 2008. The very large 'offshore' financial sector, administered by an independent Financial Services Commission, specializes in the registration of International Business Companies (IBCs), with a cumulative total of 445,865 active companies by June 2008, up from 56,025 in 1991. However, the number of new incorporations was adversely affected by the international recession and competition from other jurisdictions, falling from 77,022 in 2007 to 61,716 in 2008. British Virgin Island companies may be listed on the New York, Nasdaq, Toronto, Singapore or Hong Kong stock exchanges, or on the London stock exchange's AIM international market for smaller and growing companies. There were 392 captive 'offshore' insurance companies. There were 2,849 active licensed mutual funds, but 'offshore' banking is not well developed, a deliberate choice by the authorities who are hesitant to take on the regulatory problems involved. Legislation on trusts introduced in 2003 was designed to broaden the basis of the 'offshore' sector, and to control possible abuse of existing regulations. Fees from the 'offshore' sector were estimated at US $170m. in

2009, or just over 58% of total government revenue. Following international pressure, in particular from the Organisation for Economic Co-operation and Development (OECD), which, in June 2000, had included the British Virgin Islands on its list of tax 'havens', legislation to improve transparency in the financial sector was introduced. In early 2002 the Government committed itself to improving the islands' financial sector to meet OECD guidelines by 2005. A Tax Information Exchange Treaty with the USA was signed in April 2002, followed, in October 2008, by tax information exchange agreements with the United Kingdom and Australia. In 2004 further legislation was introduced, eliminating the distinction between 'onshore' and 'offshore' taxation regimes, specifically in order to correspond to OECD and European Union standards; a transitional period ended in January 2007. The US Department of State continued until 2009 to list the British Virgin Islands as of 'primary concern' for money-laundering, demanding tougher penalties, stricter reporting requirements and additional regulatory staff; however, in 2010 it was upgraded to country of 'concern', an intermediate category. OECD in an April 2009 review placed the British Virgin Islands on a so-called 'grey' list of countries that had not yet done enough to implement tax transparency in spite of making a general commitment to earlier guidelines; however, sufficient tax information exchange agreements had been signed by August 2009 for the British Virgin Islands to be removed from the list. The 'offshore' sector also suffered from the sharp downturn in international economic activity from 2008, with new IBC registrations around 20% lower in 2008 than in 2007, and major professional practices laying off staff. Work permit applications were down sharply in 2009.

Tourism is the other mainstay of the economy, with hotels and restaurants accounting for 15.9% of GDP in 2008. On the smaller islands in the group, there is the added benefit of near-complete privacy. The number of stop-over tourists reached 295,625 in 2001, before decreasing slightly to some 281,696 in 2002. However, stop-over numbers rebounded to a record figure of 317,758 in 2003, increasing even further, to some 358,056 in 2007, but falling sharply to 304,283 in 2009 as international demand weakened. Creating further concerns, the main international carrier, American Airlines, reduced flights to the British Virgin Islands from September 2008. However, a new carrier BVI Airways began services to nearby islands from February 2010. Yachting is an important segment of the tourism industry; against the trend, yacht tourism increased in 2009. Most tourists stay in luxury accommodation; their high spending power per head is of further economic benefit. However, there were complaints that cruise ship traffic was diluting the islands' 'exclusive' image (there were some 530,327 cruise ship passengers in 2009). Visitor expenditure totalled some US $437m. in 2005.

Residential, commercial, public sector and tourism-related investment has resulted in a high level of construction activity, making up 6.5% of GDP in 2008. Mismanagement and alleged corruption in public sector capital projects was a major concern until 2003, when the incoming National Democratic Party (NDP) Government attempted to address this issue, reappraising a US $77m. hospital project, and reaching an agreement with the Caribbean Development Bank that allowed a long-delayed airport runway improvement to be completed. The NDP was defeated in the general election of August 2007, but there was no indication of renewed corrupt activities following the return to office of the Virgin Islands Party. Transport and communications contributed 12.4% of GDP in 2008.

Agriculture comprised only 0.4% of GDP in 2008, with a few small farmers keeping livestock and growing food crops. There is also a small-scale fishing industry, which contributed 0.5% of GDP in 2008. Manufacturing (2.5% of GDP in 2008) is limited to small-scale activities such as printing and the blending and bottling of rum. Electric power supply has been a problem, in spite of the addition of new generating capacity. The BVI Electricity Corporation was, in July 2005, given permission to borrow US $32m. for its capital programme and repayment of existing debt. In 2006 the Chief Minister stressed the importance of economic diversification; in conjunction with this policy, the Government established a guarantee facility to enable small businesses lacking collateral to secure financial loans.

The territory is in the heart of the hurricane belt, and has been damaged by several storms in recent years. There is, however, no volcanic risk, although earthquakes have been known to occur.

Statistical Survey

Source: Development Planning Unit, Central Administrative Complex, Road Town, Tortola VG1110; tel. 494-3701; fax 494-3947; e-mail dpu@dpu.org; internet dpu.gov.vg.

AREA AND POPULATION

Area: 153 sq km (59 sq miles). *Principal Islands* (sq km): Tortola 54.4; Anegada 38.8; Virgin Gorda 21.4; Jost Van Dyke 9.1.

Population: 16,115 at census of 12 May 1991; 23,161 (males 11,436, females 11,725) at census of 21 May 2001; 29,537 (official projection) in 2010; *By Island* (2001 census): Tortola 19,282; Virgin Gorda 3,203; Anegada 250; Jost Van Dyke 244; Other 182 (Other islands 86, Boats 96); Total 23,161.

Density (2010): 193.1 per sq km.

Population by Age (official projections, 2010): *0–14:* 7,404; *15–64:* 20,368; *65 and over:* 1,765; *Total* 29,537.

Principal Town: Road Town (capital), population 9,384 (UN estimate, incl. suburbs, mid-2009). Source: UN, *World Urbanization Prospects: The 2009 Revision*.

Births, Marriages and Deaths (2007 unless otherwise indicated): 279 live births (birth rate 10.1 per 1,000); 419 marriages (marriage rate 15.2 per 1,000); 109 deaths (2008—death rate 3.9 per 1,000). *2009:* Crude birth rate 14.6 per 1,000; Crude death rate 4.4 per 1,000 (Source: Pan American Health Organization).

Life Expectancy (years at birth, estimates): 77.3 (males 76.0; females 78.6) in 2009. Source: Pan American Health Organization.

Employment (2005): Agriculture, hunting and forestry 78; Fishing 14; Mining and quarrying 37; Manufacturing 404; Electricity, gas and water supply 145; Construction 1,260; Wholesale and retail trade 1,624; Hotels and restaurants 2,573; Transport, storage and communications 454; Financial intermediation 797; Real estate, renting and business activities 1,307; Public administration and social security 5,142; Education 1,119; Health and social work 141; Other community, social and personal service activities 724; Private households with employed persons 404; *Sub-total* 16,223; Not classifiable by economic activity 9; *Total* 16,232. *2010:* Total employed 18,796.

HEALTH AND WELFARE

Total Fertility Rate (children per woman, 2009): 1.7.

Physicians (per 1,000 head, 1999): 1.15.

Hospital Beds (per 1,000 head, 2006): 1.8.

Health Expenditure (% of GDP, 1995): 3.9. *2004* (public expenditure only): 2.3.

Health Expenditure (public, % of total, 1995): 36.5.

Source: Pan American Health Organization.

For definitions, see explanatory note on p. vi.

AGRICULTURE, ETC.

Livestock ('000 head, 2008, FAO estimates): Cattle 2.4; Sheep 6.1; Goats 10.0; Pigs 1.5.

Fishing (metric tons, live weight, 2008, FAO estimates): Snappers 320; Boxfishes 30; Jacks and crevalles 25; Caribbean spiny lobster 40; Marine fishes 770; Total catch (incl. others) 1,200.

Source: FAO.

INDUSTRY

Electric Energy (production, million kWh): 45 in 2005; 48 in 2006–07. Source: UN Industrial Commodity Statistics Database.

FINANCE

Currency and Exchange Rate: United States currency is used: 100 cents = 1 US dollar ($). *Sterling and Euro Equivalents* (31 May 2010): £1 sterling = US $1.458; €1 = US $1.238; US $100 = £68.59 = €80.75.

Budget (US $ million, 2006): *Revenue:* Total recurrent revenue 247.9. *Expenditure:* Recurrent expenditure 222.6; Capital expenditure 38.6; Total expenditure 261.2. *2007* (US $ million, projections): Total recurrent revenue 265.0; Total expenditure 267.9 (Recurrent expenditure 221.5, Capital expenditure 46.4).

Cost of Living (Consumer Price Index; base: 1995 = 100): All items 139.4 in 2006; 142.9 in 2007; 153.1 in 2008.

Gross Domestic Product (US $ million at constant 1990 prices): 900 in 2006; 915 in 2007; 939 in 2008. Source: UN Statistics Division, National Accounts Main Aggregates Database.

Expenditure on the Gross Domestic Product (US $ million at current prices, 2008): Government final consumption expenditure 110; Private final consumption expenditure 445; Gross fixed capital formation 292; Changes in inventories –20; *Total domestic expenditure* 827; Exports of goods and services 1,330; *Less* Imports of goods and services 942; *GDP in purchasers' values* 1,215. Source: UN Statistics Division, National Accounts Main Aggregates Database.

Gross Domestic Product by Economic Activity (US $ million at current prices, 2008): Agriculture, hunting, forestry and fishing 12; Mining, manufacturing and utilities 63 (Manufacturing 36); Construction 73; Wholesale, retail trade, restaurants and hotels 362; Transport, storage and communication 149; Other activities 572; *Total gross value added* 1,231; Net taxes on products –16 (figure obtained as a residual); *GDP in purchasers' values* 1,215 (Source: UN Statistics Division, National Accounts Main Aggregates Database).

EXTERNAL TRADE

Principal Commodities (US $ '000): *Imports c.i.f.* (1997): Food and live animals 31,515; Beverages and tobacco 8,797; Crude materials (inedible) except fuels 1,168; Mineral fuels, lubricants, etc. 9,847; Chemicals 8,816; Basic manufactures 31,715; Machinery and transport equipment 47,019; Total (incl. others) 116,379. *Exports f.o.b.* (1996): Food and live animals 368; Beverages and tobacco 3,967; Crude materials (inedible) except fuels 1,334; Total (incl. others) 5,862. *2001* (exports, US $ million): Animals 0.1; Fresh fish 0.7; Gravel and sand 1.4; Rum 3.6; Total 28.13.

Principal Trading Partners (US $ '000): *Imports c.i.f.* (1997): Antigua and Barbuda 1,807; Trinidad and Tobago 2,555; United Kingdom 406; USA 94,651; Total (incl. others) 166,379. *Exports f.o.b.* (1996): USA and Puerto Rico 1,077; US Virgin Islands 2,001; Total (incl. others) 5,862. *1999:* Imports 208,419; Exports 2,081.

Source: mainly UN, *International Trade Statistics Yearbook*.

TRANSPORT

Road Traffic (motor vehicles registered and licensed, 2005): 13,392 (Private vehicles 9,201, Commercial vehicles 2,102, Rental vehicles 1,196, Taxis 483, Government 275, Motorcycles 135).

Shipping: *International Freight Traffic* ('000 metric tons, 2002): Goods unloaded 145.6. *Cargo Ship Arrivals* (2002): 2,027. *Merchant Fleet* (vessels registered, at 31 December 2008): 13; Total displacement 16,293 grt (Sources: British Virgin Islands Ports Authority; Lloyd's Register-Fairplay, *World Fleet Statistics*).

Civil Aviation (passenger arrivals): 153,391 in 2003; 220,239 in 2004 (estimate); 220,116 in 2005 (estimate).

TOURISM

Visitor Arrivals ('000): 356.2 stop-over visitors, 444.0 cruise ship passengers in 2006; 358.1 stop-over visitors, 575.2 cruise ship passengers in 2007; 345.9 stop-over visitors, 571.7 cruise ship passengers in 2008.

Tourism Revenue (US $ million, incl. passenger transport): 342 in 2003; 393 in 2004; 437 in 2005. Source: World Tourism Organization.

COMMUNICATIONS MEDIA

Radio Receivers (1997): 9,000 in use.

Television Receivers (1999): 4,000 in use.

Telephones (2009): 20,100 main lines in use.

Mobile Cellular Telephones (2009): 24,000 subscribers.

Daily Newspapers (2004): 1.

Non-daily Newspapers (2004, unless otherwise indicated): 8 (estimated circulation 4,000 in 1996).

Sources: UNESCO, *Statistical Yearbook*; UN, *Statistical Yearbook*; International Telecommunication Union.

EDUCATION

Pre-primary: 5 schools (1994/95); 45 teachers (2005/06); 653 pupils (2005/06).

Primary: 21 schools (2006); 215 teachers (2006/07); 3,044 pupils (2006/07).

Secondary: 7 schools (2006); 223 teachers (2006/07); 1,921 pupils (2006/07).

Tertiary (2004/05): 110 teachers; 1,200 pupils.

Pupil-teacher Ratio (primary education, UNESCO estimate): 14.2 in 2006/07.

Sources: UNESCO Institute for Statistics; Caribbean Development Bank, *Social and Economic Indicators*.

Directory

The Constitution

The British Virgin Islands have had a representative assembly since 1774. Following a United Kingdom Government invitation in 2001 for its Overseas Territories to institute programmes of constitutional reform, a new Constitution for the British Virgin Islands was finalized in May 2007 and formally ratified by the Privy Council of the United Kingdom in June. The Virgin Islands Constitutional Order 2007 became effective (largely—see below) from 15 June and represented the first comprehensive revision of the territory's Constitution since the revision that had precipitated the 1977 Constitution, which it replaced. Under the terms of the 2007 Constitution, the Governor is responsible for defence and internal security (including the police force), external affairs, terms and conditions of service of public officers, and the administration of the Courts. The Governor also possesses reserved legislative powers in respect of legislation necessary in the interests of his special responsibilities and fulfils the role of Presiding Officer at meetings of the Cabinet (formerly the 'Executive Council'). The Cabinet comprises the Premier (formerly 'Chief Minister'), one ex officio member (the Attorney-General), and four other ministers (appointed by the Governor on the advice of the Premier); a Cabinet Secretary sets the Cabinet's agenda under consultation with the Premier. The House of Assembly (formerly 'Legislative Council') consists of a Speaker, chosen from among the elected members of—or those eligible for election to—the Assembly, one ex officio member (the Attorney-General) and 13 elected members (nine members from one-member electoral districts and four members representing the territory 'at large').

The new Constitution also makes provision for the formation of a sixth government ministry, while a National Security Council, comprised of the Governor, Premier, Attorney-General, Commissioner of Police and a named government minister, advises the Governor upon matters of internal security and policing of the territory. A Fundamental Rights Chapter, ensuring the protection of citizens' human rights and freedoms, is also in effect. By mid-2009 a Public Service Commission and Judicial and Legal Services Commission had been instituted, while preparations for a Human Rights Commission were ongoing.

The division of the islands into nine electoral districts, instead of seven, came into effect at the November 1979 general election. The four 'at large' seats were introduced at the February 1995 general election. The minimum voting age was lowered from 21 years to 18 years.

Under the British Overseas Territories Act, which entered into effect in May 2002, British Virgin Islanders have the right to United Kingdom citizenship and the right of abode in the United Kingdom. British citizens do not enjoy reciprocal rights.

The Government

HEAD OF STATE

Queen: HM Queen ELIZABETH II.

Governor: WILLIAM BOYD MCCLEARY (assumed office 20 Aug. 2010).

Deputy Governor: INEZ ARCHIBALD.

CABINET
(July 2010)

The Government is formed by the Virgin Islands Party.

Premier and Minister of Finance and Tourism: RALPH TELFORD O'NEAL.

Deputy Premier and Minister of Health and Social Development: DANCIA PENN-SALLAH.

Minister of Natural Resources and Labour: OMAR HODGE.

Minister of Education and Culture: ANDREW FAHIE.

Minister of Communications and Works: JULIAN FRASER.

Attorney-General: KATHLEEN QUARTEY AYENSU.

MINISTRIES

Office of the Governor: 20 Waterfront Dr., POB 702, Road Town, Tortola VG1110; tel. 494-2345; fax 494-5582; e-mail bvigovernor@gov.vg; internet www.bvi.gov.vg.

Office of the Deputy Governor: Central Administration Bldg, West Wing, 33 Admin Dr., Road Town, Tortola VG1110; tel. 494-3701; fax 494-6481; e-mail webmaster@dgo.gov.vg; internet www.dgo.gov.vg.

Office of the Premier: 33 Admin Dr., Wickham's Cay 1, Road Town, Tortola VG1110; tel. 468-0026; fax 468-6413; e-mail premieroffice@gov.vg.

Ministry of Communications and Works: 33 Admin Dr., Wickham's Cay 1, Road Town, Tortola VG1110; tel. 468-2183; fax 494-3873; e-mail mcw@gov.vg.

Ministry of Education and Culture: 33 Admin Dr., Wickham's Cay 1, Road Town, Tortola VG1110; tel. 468-2036; fax 468-0021; e-mail bvimecgov@hotmail.com.

Ministry of Finance and Tourism: 33 Admin Dr., Wickham's Cay 1, Road Town, Tortola VG1110; tel. 494-3701; fax 494-6180; e-mail finance@gov.vg; internet www.finance.gov.vg.

Ministry of Health and Social Development: 33 Admin Dr., Wickham's Cay 1, Road Town, Tortola VG1110; tel. 468-3701; fax 494-5018.

Ministry of Natural Resources and Labour: 33 Admin Dr., Wickham's Cay 1, Road Town, Tortola VG1110; tel. 468-2147; fax 494-4283; e-mail nrl@gov.vg.

HOUSE OF ASSEMBLY

Speaker: ROY HARRIGAN.

Clerk: (vacant), Richard C. Stoutt Bldg, Wickham's Cay I, POB 2390, Road Town, Tortola VG1110; tel. 494-4757; fax 494-4544; e-mail JHodge@gov.vg; internet www.legco.gov.vg.

General Election, 20 August 2007

Party	% of vote	Seats
Virgin Islands Party	45.2	10
National Democratic Party	39.6	2
Independent	15.2	1
Total	100.0	13

Political Organizations

Concerned Citizens' Movement (CCM): Road Town, Tortola VG1110; f. 1994 as successor to Independent People's Movt; Leader ETHLYN SMITH.

National Democratic Party (NDP): Road Town, Tortola VG1110; f. 1998; Chair. RUSSELL HARRIGAN; Leader ORLANDO SMITH.

Virgin Islands Party (VIP): Road Town, Tortola VG1110; e-mail info@viparty.com; internet www.viparty.com; Chair. RALPH T. O'NEAL.

Judicial System

Justice is administered by the Eastern Caribbean Supreme Court (ECSC), based in Saint Lucia, which consists of two divisions: the High Court of Justice and the Court of Appeal. There are two resident High Court Judges. A visiting Court of Appeal, comprised of the Chief Justice and two Judges of Appeal, sits twice a year in the British Virgin Islands. There is also a Magistrates' Court, which hears prescribed civil and criminal cases. The final Court of Appeal is the Privy Council in the United Kingdom. Under the terms of the 2007 Constitution, a Judicial and Legal Services Commission, chaired by the Chief Justice, was established to counsel the Governor in matters relating to judicial appointments and regulation of the territory's legal system. In April 2009 the ECSC announced the establishment of a new division of the court, based on Tortola, to preside over all stages of litigation concerning major domestic, international or cross-border commercial claims. Justice Edward Alexander Banner was to preside over the new Commercial Court, which became operational in June 2009.

Resident Judges: INDRA HARIPRASHAD-CHARLES, RITA JOSEPH-OLIVETTI.

Magistrate: VALERIE STEPHENS.

Registrar: PAULA AJARIE.

Magistrate's Office: Magistrates Court, POB 140, Road Town, Tortola VG1110; tel. 494-3460; fax 494-2499; e-mail magistrate@vigilate.org.

Religion

CHRISTIANITY

The Roman Catholic Church

The diocese of St John's-Basseterre, suffragan to the archdiocese of Castries (Saint Lucia), includes Anguilla, Antigua and Barbuda, the British Virgin Islands, Montserrat and Saint Christopher and Nevis. The Bishop is resident in St John's, Antigua. According to official estimates from 2005, 10% of the population are Roman Catholics.

The Anglican Communion

The British and US Virgin Islands form a single, missionary diocese of the Episcopal Church of the United States of America. The Bishop of the Virgin Islands is resident on St Thomas in the US Virgin Islands. According to official estimates from 2005, 17% of the population are Anglicans.

Protestant Churches

Various Protestant denominations are represented, principally the Methodist Church (an estimated 33% of the population in 2005). Others include the Church of God (9%), Seventh-day Adventist (6%), and Baptist Churches (5%).

The Press

The BVI Beacon: 10 Russell Hill Rd, POB 3030, Road Town, Tortola VG1110; tel. 494-3434; fax 494-6267; e-mail bvibeacn@surfbvi.com; internet www.bvibeacon.com; f. 1984; Thurs; covers local and international news; also operates from the US Virgin Islands; Editor LINNELL M. ABBOTT; circ. 3,400.

The BVI StandPoint: Wickham's Cay, POB 4311, Road Town, Tortola VG1110; tel. 494-8106; fax 494-8647; e-mail editorial@vistandpoint.com; internet www.vistandpoint.com; fmrly BVI PennySaver, adopted current name in 2001; Tues. and Fri.; covers local and international news; Publr ELTON CALLWOOD; Editor CARMILITA JAMIESON; circ. 18,000.

The Island Sun: 112 Main St, POB 21, Road Town, Tortola VG1110; tel. 494-2476; fax 494-5854; e-mail issun@candwbvi.net; internet islandsun.com; f. 1962; Fri.; publ. by Sun Enterprises (BVI) Ltd; Editor VERNON W. PICKERING; circ. 3,000.

The Welcome (The British Virgin Islands Welcome Tourist Guide): POB 133, Road Town, Tortola; tel. 494-2413; fax 494-4413; e-mail jim@bviwelcome.com; internet www.bviwelcome.com; f. 1971; every 2 months; general, tourist information; Publr and Editor CLAUDIA COLLI; annual circ. 176,000.

Publishers

Caribbean Publishing Co (BVI) Ltd: POB 3403, Road Town, Tortola VG1110; tel. 494-2060; fax 494-3060; e-mail bvi-sales@caribpub.com; Gen. Man. MICHAEL ARNOLD.

Island Publishing Services Ltd: POB 133, Road Town, Tortola VG1110; tel. 494-2413; fax 494-4413; e-mail info@bviwelcome.com; publishes *The British Virgin Islands Welcome Tourist Guide* (q.v.), *BVI Restaurant and Food Guide* (annual), *The Limin' Times* (weekly entertainment guide), and *The British Virgin Islands Cruise Ship Visitors' Guide* (annual).

Broadcasting and Communications

TELECOMMUNICATIONS

A Telecommunications Regulatory Commission was established under the Telecommunications Act 2006 in October to facilitate the liberalization of the telecommunications sector, which had commenced earlier that year. In April 2007 a Telecommunications Liberalization Act was ratified by the Government; the legislation prepared the market for the addition of further operators after a period of three years, until which time the market would be restricted to the existing three service providers. However, the market was subsequently opened to applications from alternative operators after Digicel pursued a successful lawsuit against the restriction: the first unitary licences were issued in June 2007, and Digicel was granted a mobile licence in December.

Regulatory Bodies

Telecommunications Regulatory Commission: LM Business Centre, 3rd Floor, 27 Fish Lock Rd, Road Town, POB 4401, Tortola; tel. 468-4165; fax 494-6786; e-mail contact@trc.vg; internet www.trc.vg; f. Oct. 2006; regulatory body; Chair. COLLIN SCATLIFFE; CEO TOMAS LAMANAUSKAS.

Telephone Services Management Unit: Deputy Governor's Office, Central Administration Bldg, 2nd Floor, West Atrium, Road Town, Tortola VG1110; tel. 494-4728; fax 494-6551; e-mail tsmu@bvigovernment.org; govt agency; Man. REYNELL FRASER.

Principal Companies

Caribbean Cellular Telephone (CCT Global Communications): Geneva Pl., 333 Waterfront Dr., POB 267, Road Town, Tortola VG1110; tel. 494-3825; fax 494-4933; internet www.cctwireless.com; f. 1986 as CCT Boatphone; mobile cellular telephone operator; Gen. Man. JOSE LUIS FERNANDEZ.

Digicel: POB 4168, Road Town, Tortola VG1110; tel. 494-2048; fax 494-0111; e-mail bvicustomercare@digicelgroup.com; internet www.digicelbvi.com; granted licence to operate mobile cellular telephone network in British Virgin Islands in Dec. 2007; CEO ALAN BATES (British Virgin Islands).

LIME: Cutlass Bldg, Wickham's Cay 1, POB 440, Road Town, Tortola VG1110; tel. 494-4444; fax 494-2506; e-mail support@candwbvi.net; internet www.time4lime.com; f. 1967 as Cable & Wireless (WI) Ltd; name changed as above 2008; Exec. Vice-Pres. (British Virgin Islands) JOEL ABDINOOR; Country Man. VANCE LEWIS.

BROADCASTING

Radio

Virgin Islands Broadcasting Ltd—Radio ZBVI: Baughers Bay, POB 78, Road Town, Tortola VG1110; tel. 494-2250; fax 494-1139; e-mail zbvi@caribsurf.com; internet www.zbvi.vi; f. 1965; commercial; Gen. Man. HARVEY HERBERT; Operations Man. SANDRA POTTER WARRICAN.

Television

BVI Cable TV: Fishlock Rd, POB 644, Road Town, Tortola VG1110; tel. 494-3831; fax 494-3205; operated by Innovative Communication Corporation, based in the US Virgin Islands; programmes from US Virgin Islands and Puerto Rico; secured a licence to compete in the newly liberalized telecommunications market in June 2007; 53 channels; Gen. Man. LUANNE HODGE.

Finance

BANKING

Regulatory Authority

Financial Services Commission: Pasea Estate, POB 418, Road Town, Tortola VG1110; tel. 494-1324; fax 494-5016; e-mail enquiries@bvifsc.vg; internet www.bvifsc.vg; f. 2002; independent financial services regulator; Chair. ROBIN GAUL; Man. Dir and CEO ROBERT MATHAVIOUS.

Commercial Banks

Ansbacher (BVI) Ltd: International Trust Bldg, POB 659, Road Town, Tortola VG1110; tel. 494-3215; fax 494-3216.

Banco Popular de Puerto Rico: POB 67, Road Town, Tortola VG1110; tel. 494-2117; fax 494-5294; e-mail internet@bppr.com; internet www.bancopopular.com; Pres. and CEO RICHARD L. CARRIÓN; Man. SANDRA SCATLIFFE.

Bank of Nova Scotia (Canada): Wickham's Cay 1, POB 434, Road Town, Tortola VG1110; tel. 494-2526; fax 494-4657; e-mail joycelyn.murraine@scotiabank.com; internet www.bvi.scotiabank.com; f. 1967; Man. Dir JOYCELYN MURRAINE.

DISA Bank (BVI) Ltd: POB 985, Road Town, Tortola VG1110; tel. 494-4977; fax 494-4980; Man. ROSA RESTREPO.

First Bank Virgin Islands: Road Town Business Centre, Wickham's Cay 1, Road Town, POB 435, Tortola VG1110; tel. 494-2662; fax 494-3863; e-mail e-firstbank@firstbankpr.com; internet www.firstbankvi.com; f. 1994; est. as a commercial bank in Puerto Rico; CEO AURELIO ALEMÁN-BERMUDEZ.

FirstCaribbean International Bank Ltd: Wickham's Cay 1, POB 70, Road Town, Tortola VG1110; tel. 852-9900; fax 494-4315; e-mail barcbvi@surfbvi.com; internet www.firstcaribbeanbank.com; f. 2003 following merger of Caribbean operations of Barclays Bank PLC and CIBC; Barclays relinquished its stake in 2006; CEO JOHN D. ORR; Man. MICHAEL SPENCER; 2 brs.

Rathbone Bank (BVI) Ltd: POB 986, Road Town, Tortola VG1110; tel. 494-6544; fax 494-6532; e-mail rathbone@surfbvi.com; Man. Dir CORNEL BAPTISTE.

VP Bank (BVI) Ltd: 3076 Sir Francis Drake's Highway, POB 3463, Road Town, Tortola VG1110; tel. 494-1100; fax 494-1199; e-mail info.bvi@vpbank.com; internet www.vpbank.vg; Man. Dir Dr PETER REICHENSTEIN.

Development Bank

National Bank of the Virgin Islands Ltd: New Social Security Bldg, Wickham's Cay 1, POB 275, Road Town, Tortola VG1110; tel. 494-3737; fax 494-3119; e-mail admin@natbankvi.com; internet www.natbankvi.com; f. 1976; fmrly Development Bank of the British Virgin Islands; state-owned; Chair. KENNETH HODGE.

TRUST COMPANIES

Abacus Trust and Management Services Ltd: 333 Waterfront Dr., Road Town, Tortola VG1110; tel. 494-4388; fax 494-3088; e-mail info@mwmabacus.com; internet www.mwmabacus.com; f. 1994; Man. MEADE MALONE.

Aleman, Cordero, Galindo and Lee Trust (BVI) Ltd: POB 3175, Road Town, Tortola VG1110; tel. 494-4666; fax 494-4679; e-mail alcogalbvi@alcogal.com; Man. GABRIELLA CONTE.

AMS Trustees Ltd: Sea Meadow House, POB 116, Road Town, Tortola VG1110; tel. 494-3399; fax 494-3041; e-mail enquiries@amsbvi.com; internet www.amsbvi.com; subsidiary of the AMS Group (British Virgin Islands); Man. Dir NICHOLAS CLARK.

Belmont Trust Ltd: Belmont Chambers, Tropic Isle Bldg, Nibbs St, POB 3443, Road Town, Tortola VG1110; tel. 494-5800; fax 494-2545; e-mail info@belmontbvi.net; internet www.belmontbvi.com; Man. Dir ANDREA DOUGLAS.

CCP Financial Consultants Ltd: Ellen Skelton Bldg, Fishers Lane, POB 681, Road Town, Tortola VG1110; tel. 494-6777; fax 494-6787; e-mail ccp@surfbvi.com; internet www.ccpbvi.com; Man. JOSEPH ROBERTS.

Citco BVI Ltd: Wickham's Cay, POB 662, Road Town, Tortola VG1110; tel. 494-2217; fax 494-3917; e-mail bvi-trust@citco.com; internet www.citco.com; Man. NICOLA GILLESPIE.

HSBC International Trustee (BVI) Ltd: Woodbourne Hall, POB 916, Road Town, Tortola VG1110; tel. 494-5414; fax 494-2417; e-mail kenneth.morgan@htvg.vg; Dir KENNETH MORGAN.

Hunte & Co Services Ltd: Omar Hodge Bldg, 3rd Floor, Wickham's Cay I, POB 3504, Road Town, Tortola; tel. 495-0232; fax 495-0229; internet www.hunteandco.com; Office Man. DEBORAH BLANFORD.

Maples and Calder BVI: Sea Meadow House, POB 173, Road Town, Tortola VG1110; tel. 852-3000; fax 852-3097; e-mail bviinfo@maplesandcalder.com; internet www.maplesandcalder.com; Managing Partners CLINTON HEMPEL, ARABELLA DI LORIO.

Midocean Management and Trust Services (BVI) Ltd: 9 Columbus Centre, Pelican Dr., POB 805, Road Town, Tortola VG1110; tel. 494-4567; fax 494-4568; e-mail midocean@maitlandbvi.com; owned by Maitland Group; Man. ELIZABETH WILKINSON.

Moore Stephens International Services (BVI) Ltd: Palm Grove House, Wickham's Cay I, POB 3186, Road Town, Tortola VG1110; tel. 494-3503; fax 494-3592; e-mail moorestephens@moorestephensbvi.com; internet www.moorestephens.com; Man. NICHOLAS LANE.

TMF (BVI) Ltd: POB 964, Road Town, Tortola VG11900; tel. 494-4997; fax 494-4999; e-mail bvi@tmf-group.com; internet www.tmf-group.com; Man. GRAHAM COOK.

Totalserve Trust Company Ltd: 197 Main St, POB 3540, Road Town, Tortola VG1110; tel. 494-6900; fax 494-6990; e-mail bvi@totalserve.eu; internet www.totalservecy.com; Man. DENESHAR MEADE.

Tricor Services (BVI) Ltd: POB 3340, Road Town, Tortola VG1110; tel. 494-6004; fax 494-6404; e-mail info@bvi.tricorglobal.com; internet www.bvi.tricorglobal.com; Man. PATRICK A. NICHOLAS.

Trident Trust Company (BVI) Ltd: Trident Chambers, Wickham's Cay, POB 146, Road Town, Tortola VG1110; tel. 494-2434; fax 494-3754; e-mail bvi@tridenttrust.com; internet www.tridenttrust.com; Man. BARRY R. GOODMAN.

At the beginning of 2007 there were some 2,600 active mutual and hedge funds registered with the British Virgin Islands International Finance Centre.

INSURANCE

ALTA Insurance Management (BVI) Ltd: POB 4623, Road Town, Tortola VG1110; tel. 494-9670; fax 494-9690; e-mail gtaylor@altaholdings.com; internet www.altaholdings.com; Man. GREGORY TAYLOR.

AMS Insurance Management Services Ltd: Sea Meadow House, POB 116, Road Town, Tortola VG1110; tel. 494-4078; fax 494-8589; e-mail dlloyd@amsbvi.com; internet www.amsbvi.com; Man. DEREK LLOYD.

Belmont Insurance Management Ltd: Belmont Chambers, Tropic Isle Bldg, Nibbs St, POB 3443, Road Town, Tortola VG1110; tel. 494-5800; fax 494-2545; e-mail info@belmontbvi.com; internet www.belmontbvi.com; Man. Dir ANDREA DOUGLAS.

Caledonian Insurance Services (BVI) Ltd: 4th Floor, Rodus Bldg, Road Town, Tortola VG1110; tel. 949-0050; fax 814-4875; e-mail insurance@caledonian.com; internet www.caledonian.com; f. 2005; Dir HARRY THOMPSON.

Captiva Global Ltd: POB 4428, Road Town, Tortola VG1110; tel. 494-4111; fax 494-4222; e-mail info@captiva.vg; internet www.captiva.vg; Man. Dir HARRY J. THOMPSON.

Caribbean Insurers Ltd (CIL): Mirage Bldg, POB 129, Road Town, Tortola VG1110; tel. 494-2728; fax 494-4393; e-mail info@caribbins.com; internet www.caribbeaninsurers.com; f. 1973; part of the Caribbean Insurers Group; Chair. and CEO JOHN WILLIAMS.

HWR Insurance Management Services Ltd (Harneys Insurance): Craigmuir Chambers, POB 71, Road Town, Tortola VG1110; tel. 494-2233; fax 494-3547; e-mail bvi@harneys.com; internet www.harneys.com; Man. Dir DAVID SPYER.

Marine Insurance Office (BVI) Ltd (MIO): Mill Mall, Wickham's Cay 1, POB 874, Road Town, Tortola VG1110; tel. 494-3795; fax 494-4540; e-mail info@mioinsurance.com; internet mioinsurance.com; f. 1985; Man. WESLEY WOOLHOUSE.

Osiris Insurance Management Ltd: Coastal Bldg, Wickham's Cay 11, POB 2221, Road Town, Tortola VG1110; tel. 494-9820; fax 494-6934; e-mail info@osiristrust.com; internet osiristrust.com; Man. Dir MILES WALTON.

Trident Insurance Management (BVI) Ltd: POB 146, Road Town, Tortola VG1110; tel. 494-4078; fax 494-2519; e-mail trident@surfbvi.com; Man. DEREK LLOYD.

TSA Insurance Management Ltd: POB 3443, Road Town, Tortola VG1110; tel. 494-5800; fax 494-6563; e-mail jwilliams@surfbvi.com; Man. JOHN WILLIAMS.

USA Risk Group (BVI) Inc: 30 Main St, Suite 450, Burlington, VT05401; tel. 371-2225; fax 371-2220; e-mail info@usarisk.com; internet www.usarisk.com; Pres. STUART H. GRAYSTON.

Several US and other foreign companies have agents in the British Virgin Islands. In 2006 57 new 'captive' insurers were registered by the British Virgin Islands International Financial Centre, increasing the total such registered to more than 400.

Trade and Industry

GOVERNMENT AGENCY

Trade and Investment Promotion Department: Chief Minister's Office, Central Administration Bldg, 33 Administration Dr., Road Town, Tortola VG1110; tel. 494-5007; fax 494-5657; e-mail trade@bvigovernment.org.

CHAMBER OF COMMERCE

British Virgin Islands Chamber of Commerce and Hotel Association: Tropic Aisle Bldg, Wickham's Cay 1, POB 376, Road Town, Tortola VG1110; tel. 494-3514; fax 494-6179; e-mail info@bviccha.org; internet www.bviccha.org; f. 1986; Chair. BIRNEY M. HARRIGAN; Pres. (Business and Commerce) DEBORAH O'NEAL; Pres. (Hotels and Tourism) ROMNEY PENN; 250 mems.

UTILITIES

Electricity

British Virgin Islands Electricity Corpn (BVIEC): Long Bush, POB 268, Road Town, Tortola VG1110; tel. 494-3911; fax 494-4291; e-mail bviecgm@bvielectricity.com; internet www.bvielectricity.com; f. 1979; privatization pending; Chair. MARGARET PENN; Gen. Man. LEROY ABRAHAM.

Water

Water and Sewerage Dept: Water & Sewerage Compound, Baughers Bay, Road Town, POB 130, Tortola VG1110; tel. 468-3416; fax 494-6746; e-mail wsd@gov.vg; f. 1980; publs quarterly newsletter *The Vapour* ; Dir. JULIAN WILLOCK.

Transport

ROADS

In 2002 there were 132 km (82 miles) of access roads, 77 km of primary roads, 37 km of secondary roads and 90 km of tertiary roads. In 2005 13,392 vehicles were licensed, 9,201 of which were private vehicles.

Public Works Department: Baughers Bay, POB 284, Tortola VG1110; tel. 494-2722; fax 494-4740; e-mail pwd@bvigovernment.org; responsible for road maintenance; Dir DREXEL GLASGOW (acting).

SHIPPING

There are two direct steamship services, one from the United Kingdom and one from the USA. Motor launches maintain daily mail and passenger services with St Thomas and St John, US Virgin Islands. A new cruise ship pier, built at a cost of US $6.9m. with assistance from the Caribbean Development Bank, was opened in Road Town in 1994 and was later expanded. Further expansion work was completed in December 2008.

British Virgin Islands Ports Authority: Port Purcell, POB 4, Road Town, Tortola VG1110; tel. 494-3435; fax 494-2642; e-mail bviports@bviports.org; internet www.bviports.org; f. 1991; Chair. CARL DAWSON; Man. Dir VINCENT VICTOR O'NEAL.

Tropical Shipping: Port Purcell Seaport, Island Shipping and Trading, POB 250, Road Town, Tortola VG1110; tel. 494-2674; fax 494-3505; e-mail lmoses@tropical.com; internet www.tropical.com; Man. LEROY MOSES.

CIVIL AVIATION

Terrance B. Lettsome (formerly Beef Island) Airport, about 16 km (10 miles) from Road Town, has a runway with a length of 1,500 m (4,921 ft). A new US $65m. airport terminal was opened at the airport in March 2002. Captain Auguste George Airport on Anegada has been designated an international point of entry and was resurfaced in the late 1990s. In June 2008 the Government signed an agreement with Halcrow Group Ltd of the United Kingdom to develop the airport on Virgin Gorda, including an extension to the runway to allow larger aircraft to land.

British Virgin Islands Airports Authority: POB 4416, Road Town, Tortola VG1110; tel. 852-9000; fax 852-9045; internet www.bviaa.com; f. 2005; Man. Dir DENNISTON FRASER.

Tourism

The main attraction of the islands is their tranquillity and clear waters, which provide excellent facilities for sailing, fishing, diving and other water sports. In 2004 there were an estimated 1,370 hotel rooms. There are also many charter yachts offering overnight accommodation. There were some 345,934 stop-over visitors and 571,700 cruise ship passengers in 2008. The majority of tourists are from the USA. Receipts from tourism totalled some US $437m. in 2005.

British Virgin Islands Chamber of Commerce and Hotel Association: see Chamber of Commerce.

British Virgin Islands Tourist Board: 2nd Floor, AKARA Bldg, DeCastro St, Road Town, Tortola VG1110; tel. 494-3134; fax 494-3866; e-mail info@bvitourism.com; internet www.bvitourism.com; Chair. TERRY WALWYN.

Defence

The United Kingdom is responsible for the defence of the islands.

Education

Primary education is free, universal and compulsory between the ages of five and 11. Secondary education is also free and lasts from 12 to 16 years of age. In 2005/06 some 653 pupils were attending pre-primary schools; in 2006/07, according to UNESCO estimates, enrolment at primary schools included 93% of children in the relevant age-group, while enrolment at secondary schools included 84% of pupils in the relevant age category. Higher education is available at the University of the Virgin Islands (St Thomas, US Virgin Islands) and elsewhere in the Caribbean, in North America and in the United Kingdom. Central government expenditure on education in 2008 was estimated at US $40.4m. (equivalent to 14.2% of total expenditure).

THE CAYMAN ISLANDS

Geography

PHYSICAL FEATURES

The Cayman Islands is a United Kingdom Overseas Territory in the Caribbean Sea, mid-way between Cuba and Honduras. The islands are located about 240 km (150 miles) south of Cuba and some 290 km north-west of Jamaica, upon which the Territory was once dependent (before Jamaican independence). The Caymans are separated from Jamaica by the Cayman Trench, the deepest part of the Caribbean. The territory covers an area of only 262 sq km (102 sq miles).

The three islands are low, limestone-and-coral formations, largely surrounded by coral reef, and with shorelines ill-defined by mangrove swamps. The largest island is Grand Cayman (about 35 km—22 miles—long, with an average width of some 6 km), which constitutes three-quarters of the territory's land area, although about one-half of it is wetland. The island is aligned along an east–west axis, tapering in the south-west before a northward-extending spit defines the western shore of the 110-sq-km shallow lagoon, the North Sound, as well as the sheltered west coast of the whole island (notably the West Bay and its Seven Mile Beach). The other two islands are long and narrow, aligned more to the north-east, end to end and separated by an 8-km channel. They lie 128 km to the east of Grand Cayman, and a little north, slightly closer to both Cuba and Jamaica than the largest island. Low-lying and swampy Little Cayman (26 sq km) is about 16 km long and seldom more than 1.5 km wide. Cayman Brac (39 sq km) is the most easterly of the islands. It is about 19 km long and about 2 km wide, but reaches the highest point in the territory, where a huge limestone outcrop, called The Bluff (43 m—a Gaelic word for a bluff is brac), rises along the centre of the island. The islands' land and marine environments are extensively protected, in an effort to preserve the bird and animal life, some of it unique (a species of orchid on Grand Cayman, for instance, trees on Cayman Brac and Cayman parrots). The islands were originally named, and, indeed, settled for the large turtle population, although they have long been named with the Carib word for the marine crocodile that also lived here.

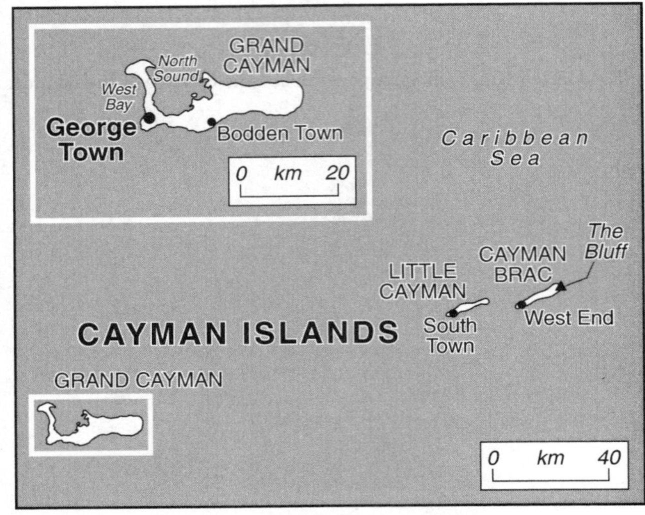

CLIMATE

The climate is subtropical marine, with warm, wet summers between May and October (in the latter part of this season hurricanes occasionally occur) and milder, dryer winters. Rain is essential to the freshwater supply. Average annual rainfall is about 1,290 mm (50 ins), and the average annual temperature is 28.5°C (83.3°F).

POPULATION

A mixed-race population (40%) is balanced by roughly equal black and white communities (each about 20%), as well as expatriates of various ethnic groups. About one-third of the population are foreign workers. The islanders are predominantly Christian and all are English-speaking.

The population in December 2008 was officially estimated at 57,009. At the census of October 1999 95.1% of the population lived on Grand Cayman, 4.6% on Cayman Brac and only 0.3% on Little Cayman. The capital is George Town in the south-west of Grand Cayman, which had an estimated population of 32,000 at mid-2009. West Bay (to the north of the capital) and Bodden Town (on the central southern coast) are the other main centres on Grand Cayman. The main settlements on the other two islands are West End on Cayman Brac and South Town on Little Cayman. The territory is divided into eight administrative districts.

History

The Cayman Islands constitute a United Kingdom Overseas Territory, with a Cabinet (known as the Executive Council until 2003) headed by the Governor, who is the representative of the British monarch.

Grand Cayman became a British colony in 1670, with the two smaller islands settled only in 1833. Until 1959 all three islands were a dependency of Jamaica. In 1962 a separate Administrator for the islands was appointed (redesignated Governor in 1971). The Constitution was revised in 1972, 1992 and 1994. The Governor is Chairman of the Cabinet (comprising four other official members and five members elected by the Legislative Assembly from among their own number). The Legislative Assembly comprises three members appointed by the Governor and 15 elected members.

In the absence of formal political parties, elections to the Assembly were contested every four years by independents and by individuals standing as 'teams'. In August 1991, however, the territory's first formal political organization since the 1960s was formed, the Progressive Democratic Party. It opposed various provisions of the proposed constitutional reforms. It developed into a broad coalition and was renamed the National Team, and then won 12 of the 15 elective seats at the general election of November 1992. The new Government did not seek the introduction of a post of chief minister. At a general election on 20 November 1996 the National Team remained in power, winning nine seats in the Legislative Assembly.

A serious problem for the Cayman Islands in recent years has been drugs-related crime. In the 1990s an estimated 75% of all thefts and burglaries in the islands were attributed, directly or indirectly, to the drugs trade. The Mutual Legal Assistance Treaty (signed in 1986, and ratified by the US Senate in 1990) between the Cayman Islands and the USA provides for the mutual exchange of information for use in combating crime (particularly drugs-trafficking and money-laundering). Further legislation relating to the abuse of the financial sector by criminal organizations was approved in November 1996.

In March 1999 the British Government published draft legislation confirming that its Dependencies were to be referred to as United Kingdom Overseas Territories; the document stated that all such territories would be required to comply with European standards on human rights and financial regulation. In May 2002 the British Overseas Territories Act, having received royal assent in the United Kingdom in February, came into force and granted British citizenship to the people of its Overseas Territories, including the Cayman Islands. Under the new law, Caymanians would be able to hold British passports and work in the United Kingdom and elsewhere in the European Union.

On 8 November 2000 the governing National Team suffered a heavy defeat in the general election. It lost six of its nine seats, including that held by Truman Bodden, the Leader of Government Business. The newly elected Legislative Assembly voted for Kurt Tibbetts of the Democratic Alliance to be Leader of Government Business.

In November 2001 several members of the Legislative Assembly formed the United Democratic Party (UDP). McKeeva Bush, the leader of the new party and Deputy Leader of Government Business and Minister of Tourism, Environment and Transport, claimed that at least 10 members of the 15-member Assembly were UDP supporters. Subsequently, the approval of a motion of no confidence (by nine votes to five, with one abstention) against the Leader of Government Business resulted in Tibbetts and Edna Moyle, the Minister of Community Development, Women's Affairs, Youth and Sport, leaving the Executive Council. Bush became the new Leader of Government Business, while two other UDP legislators joined the Cabinet. In May 2002, at the UDP's inaugural convention, Bush was formally elected leader of the party. In the same month it was announced that the five opposition members of the Legislative Assembly had formed a new political party, the People's Progressive Movement (PPM), led by Tibbetts.

In March 2002 a three-member Constitutional Review Commission, appointed by the Governor in May 2001, submitted a new draft constitution. The proposed document had to be debated by the Legislative Assembly and then approved by the British Parliament before being formally adopted. The draft constitution, made public in April, included the creation of the office of Chief Minister, proposed a full ministerial government, and incorporated a bill of rights. The opposition demanded a referendum on the recommendations, on the grounds that the UDP had rejected several of the proposals, despite strong public support for the changes, but Bush forwarded the proposals to the British Foreign and Commonwealth Office (FCO), via the Governor's office. In December Bush and the leader of the opposition, Tibbetts, travelled to the United Kingdom in order to review the proposed constitution with FCO officials. Consensus, however, proved impossible to achieve. Furthermore, the UDP announced in February 2004 that it would not participate in the constitutional review process before the next elections, due by November of that year. For its part, the PPM called for a public referendum on the issue.

In May 2002 it was announced that the Cayman Islands had become an associate member of the Caribbean Community and Common Market (CARICOM). In the same month Bruce Dinwiddy succeeded Peter Smith as Governor.

In January 2003 Bush accused the United Kingdom of undermining the course of Cayman Islands' justice, after a routine money-laundering case was dismissed amid allegations of espionage and obstruction of justice by British intelligence agents. The trial collapsed after it was alleged that the Director of the Cayman Islands Financial Reporting Unit and a key witness in the trial had passed information about the case to an unnamed agency of the British Government, understood to be the Secret Intelligence Service (MI6). It was claimed that MI6 wished to protect the names of its sources within the Caribbean 'offshore' banking community. Bush demanded that the British Government pay for the failed trial, estimated to have cost some US $5m., and for any negative repercussions the affair might have for the reputation of the territory's banking sector. The United Kingdom, however, refused to compensate the Cayman Islands and maintained that although its intelligence agencies might have helped in the investigation, they had never interfered in the case. In March the Attorney-General, David Ballantyne, resigned amid accusations that he was aware that British intelligence agents were working covertly in the Cayman Islands; in July Samuel Bulgin, the Solicitor-General, was appointed as Ballantyne's permanent successor.

The legislative election scheduled to take place in November 2004 was postponed by six months following the devastation caused by Hurricane Ivan in September of that year. In response to the hurricane Governor Dinwiddy enacted the Emergency Powers Act, allowing him to extend the remit of his authority and impose a curfew until the restoration of full electricity supplies, as a deterrent to looting. In early 2005 Linford Pierson left the UDP and established the People's Democratic Alliance, in advance of the rescheduled election. The opposition PPM secured nine of the 15 seats available in the ballot that was held on 11 May; the UDP won only five mandates and the remaining seat was occupied by an independent candidate. The outgoing UDP Government had been criticized for its management of the aftermath of the hurricane and also for the decision to grant Caymanian 'belonger' status to 3,000 residents in 2003, which was interpreted by many as an attempt to increase in the party's favour the number of those eligible to vote, prior to the election. The leader of the PPM, Kurt Tibbetts, once again became the Leader of Government Business and committed the administration to holding a referendum on increased autonomy in the territory. On 18 May the Legislative Assembly elected Anthony Eden, Alden McLaughlin, Arden McLean and Charles Clifford to the Cabinet. Stuart Jack succeeded Bruce Dinwiddy as Governor from November 2005.

Informal talks on constitutional modernization were held between the Government and representatives of the FCO in March 2006, with the aim of recommencing the constitutional review process, which had been dormant since 2004. The establishment of a Constitutional Review Secretariat, to initiate renewed efforts towards constitutional reform in the territory, was announced by the Government in February 2007. In January 2008 the Government launched a series of public consultations ahead of a referendum scheduled to be held in May. The FCO affirmed in April that the new constitution must include a bill of rights and, in response, the Government postponed the referendum to allow a longer period of public deliberation. The UDP voiced strong objections to the revised date for the ballot of 30 July, contending that this did not allow for a sufficient period of preparation and discussion, and in June the Government postponed the referendum once more until May 2009 in order for it to be held concurrently with a general election. This was to allow for the finalization of a draft constitution following the conclusion of discussions with the United Kingdom.

In an effort to enhance constitutional democracy, Tibbetts announced in November 2006 that a Freedom of Information Bill—intended to promote government transparency and accountability—was to be debated in the Legislative Assembly, prior to a public consultation exercise. A National Archives and Public Records Bill, governing the preservation of government records was approved in March 2007, as a preparatory step towards examination of the Freedom of Information Bill, which had been subject to delays. The legislation was finally approved in August, and in the following month the Freedom of Information Unit was officially opened. The law eventually became effective on 5 January 2009.

The general election was held on 20 May 2009, at which the opposition UDP defeated the incumbent PPM, securing nine of the 15 available seats. The PPM secured five seats and the remaining one was taken by an independent candidate. The rate of voter participation was 80.56% of the electorate. McKeeva Bush was sworn in as Leader of Government Business on 27 May.

In the concurrent referendum on the draft constitution some 62% of voters supported the changes (the votes of 50% plus one were required for the result to be binding). As a result, on 10 June 2009 the Privy Council approved the new charter, which came into force on 6 November. The new Constitution gave greater autonomy to the Cabinet, replacing the Governor-appointed Financial Secretary with an elected Minister of Finance—a portfolio assumed by Bush, whose post of Leader of Government Business was also redesignated Premier. Under the Constitution, the Premier was limited to serving a maximum of two consecutive four-year terms in office. Juliana O'Connor-Connolly, the Minister of District Administration, Works and Gender Affairs, was additionally appointed to the newly created post of Deputy Premier. Although the Governor retained overall control of foreign affairs, certain aspects of external dealings were delegated to the Cabinet. A Bill of Rights, Freedom and Responsibilities was also scheduled to come into effect in November 2012. Duncan Taylor succeeded Stuart Jack as Governor in January 2010.

Following criticism, by the Organisation for Economic Co-operation and Development (OECD) and the IMF, of the regulatory mechanisms governing operations in the Cayman Islands financial services sector, together with the suggestion by the US newspaper *The Washington Post* that alleged abstruse financial legislation was permitting its exploitation as a tax haven, the territory renewed efforts to bolster its international reputation as a legitimate and prestigious financial centre. In November 2006 the Cayman Islands Monetary Authority (CIMA) announced amendments to the Mutual Funds Law, last revised in 2003, including new, more stringent requirements for the administration of funds and raising the minimum subscription for registered funds from US $50,000 to $100,000. However, in June 2007 the US Senate Finance Committee reported that it had identified some 18,000 registered companies purportedly maintaining headquarters at a single address in the Caribbean island nation, and subsequently commissioned an inquiry into the anomaly by the Government Accountability Office, which concluded that US companies were using the haven to hide illegal activity or evade income tax payment. It was estimated that evasion of US tax obligations by such entities—achieved by establishing 'offshore' subsidiaries on the islands—had resulted in a $100,000m. shortfall in tax-based revenue and precipitated a growing sentiment of hostility between the two nations' respective regulatory authorities. However, in May 2008 the United Kingdom's Select Committee on Public Accounts reported that there had been a considerable expansion of the capacity of financial regulators on the islands since 2000, allowing more successful investigative activities in relation to suspicious activity reports, of which there were 244 in 2005. Nevertheless, the collapse in 2008 of several Cayman Island-based hedge funds, exacerbating the global financial crisis, caused increased attention to be focused on the territory's financial institutions. US President Barack Obama announced in May 2009 that he intended to implement stringent new laws governing tax havens, and called for more transparency from the 'offshore' sector.

In April 2009, meanwhile, OECD included the territory on its 'grey list' of 'unco-operative tax havens', namely those that had committed to an internationally agreed standard of transparency but had yet to implement it. However, in August the territory was removed from the list after signing its 12th bilateral tax information sharing agreement. By May 2010 the Cayman Islands had signed a further three such accords.

Amendments to the Cayman Islands' immigration regime in November 2005 required that persons originating from Costa Rica, El Salvador, Guatemala and Jamaica hold a visa in order to enter the territory. The maximum fine for living illegally in the Cayman Islands was CI $20,000. Amendments to the 2004 Term Limit Policy, or 'rollover law', which limited the term for which work permits may be granted to seven years, were promulgated in October 2006.

Economy

Following the introduction of secrecy laws in respect of bank accounts and other professional information in the late 1960s, and the easing of foreign exchange regulations in the 1970s (finally abandoned entirely in 1980), the islands developed as one of the world's major 'offshore' financial markets. In 1999 the sector contributed some 36% of gross domestic product (GDP), while financial services employed 10.2% of the labour force in a sample survey dated October–November 2008. There were 333 licensed banks and trust companies and 8,819 registered mutual funds on the islands at the end of March 2010. The absence of any form of direct taxation has also made the islands notorious as a tax haven.

In 1986 a treaty of mutual assistance was signed with the USA, providing access for US law-enforcement agencies to the financial records of Cayman Islands banks, in cases where serious criminal activity is suspected. In November 1996 the powers of the authorities to investigate such cases were augmented. The Cayman Islands Monetary Authority (CIMA), responsible for managing the islands' currency and reserves and for regulating the financial sector, began operations in 1997.

In June 2000 the Cayman Islands were included on a list, compiled by the Financial Action Task Force on Money Laundering (FATF, based in Paris, France), of those jurisdictions considered to be 'non-co-operative' in international efforts to combat money-laundering. The Government's prompt response in addressing the FATF's concerns resulted in the Cayman Islands' removal from the list in 2001. The CIMA was given increased powers, and efforts were made to eliminate so-called 'shell banks' on the islands (those banks registered in the jurisdiction but with no staff or offices).

In anticipation of the publication by the Organisation for Economic Co-operation and Development (OECD) of a blacklist of 'unco-operative tax havens', in early 2000 the Government of the Cayman Islands made a commitment to the elimination of harmful tax practices. In November 2001, in a further move to increase international confidence in its financial regulation, the Government signed a tax information exchange agreement with the USA, designed to reduce the potential for abuse of the tax system. (The agreement took effect with regard to criminal tax evasion in January 2004 and would do so for further aspects of the tax regime from 2006.) The Government also agreed to respond to any US requests for assistance in investigations into the collapse of the major US energy company Enron, which was suspected of financial malpractice. (Reports presented to the US Securities and Exchange Commission in 2002 claimed that Enron used 692 companies in the Cayman Islands to avoid paying taxes in the USA. Furthermore, in 2006 the territory was once again associated with financial malpractice, albeit not within its borders, through a legal case regarding the sale of a company registered in the Cayman Islands by British bankers to Enron.) However, fears remained that reforms to the financial services sector would reduce the islands' ability to attract international business.

From late 2002 the financial sector faced further disruption when the United Kingdom, under pressure from a European Union (EU) investigation into tax evasion, demanded that the Cayman Islands disclose the identities and account details of Europeans holding private savings accounts on the islands. The Cayman Islands, along with some other United Kingdom Overseas Territories facing similar demands, claimed it was being treated unfairly compared with more powerful European countries, such as Switzerland and Luxembourg, and refused to make any concessions. The British Paymaster-General demanded that the Cayman Islands enact the necessary legislation to implement the EU's Savings Tax Directive by 30 June 2004. The Legislative Assembly, after the British Government pledged to safeguard the territory's interests, voted to accept British/EU demands by 1 January 2005. (As a result of the agreement, recognition was granted to the Cayman Islands Stock Exchange by the United Kingdom's Inland Revenue body.) However, the implementation of the regulations was delayed until July 2005 and the Cayman Islands authorities were able to negotiate some exemptions. Meanwhile, the investigation into the collapse of Parmalat, an Italian food company, which had 10 subsidiary companies in the Cayman Islands, focused further attention on the regulatory apparatus of the territory's financial sector in 2003–04. Nevertheless, in a March 2005 assessment of the financial sector, the IMF commended the system of financial regulation and compliance culture in the territory, particularly in relation to anti-money-laundering measures. The islands continued to be a leading 'offshore' insurance domicile, ranked as the second largest (after Bermuda) in the international insurance market. However, by early 2007 many US companies with 'offshore' subsidiaries had come under the scrutiny of the US Congress. Some prominent US politicians claimed that 'offshore' operations lose the US Treasury millions of dollars in tax revenue every year. The companies register in order to avoid the 35% tax burden imposed by the US Internal Revenue Service on 'onshore' company profits. A Stop Tax Haven Abuse Act was delivered to the US Senate in February 2007; it was not considered before the end of that session of Congress, but was reintroduced under the same title in March 2009. In 2008 an address in George Town was found to be the registered office of some 18,000 companies, a situation which prompted the General Accountability Office to conclude that the islands were being used by US citizens to avoid taxes and to conceal illegal activity. In April 2009 OECD included the Cayman Islands on its so-called 'grey list' of territories that had committed to but not yet implemented an internationally agreed standard of transparency measures, but the conclusion of a 12th bilateral tax information sharing agreement in August enabled its removal from the list. In early 2010, amid reports that several companies had decided to relocate their businesses out of the Cayman Islands, the Government announced plans to offer permanent residency to workers in the financial sector in exchange for US $1m.

In addition to 'offshore' financial services, the tourism sector contributes strongly to the economy. Both of these sectors benefit from the Cayman Islands' political stability, good infrastructure and extensive development. Tourism was estimated to account for almost one-quarter of GDP and, directly or indirectly, 50% of employment. Visitor expenditure earned an estimated US $519m. in 2004, and although this figure decreased significantly to $353m. the following year, the figure subsequently recovered in 2006, when receipts totalled $509m. Most tourists are from the USA (79.1% of stop-over arrivals in 2009). Visitor arrivals totalled 1.8m. in 2009. The industry is marketed towards the wealthier visitor. Since 1987 the Government has limited the number of cruise ship passengers. The Cayman Islands also maintains the largest registry of luxury yachts of over 100 ft in length in the world. The tourism sector was adversely affected by the destruction wreaked by Hurricane Ivan in September 2004. The CIMA estimated that 90% of properties on the islands had been damaged in some way by the hurricane, while the Economic Commission for Latin America and the Caribbean estimated economic damage of $3,400m. Since the late 1990s the Government has attempted to limit tourist numbers in order to minimize damage to the environment. The number of tourists arriving by cruise ship increased in 2005 (partly owing to the destruction of other ports in the region by the hurricane), but those actually staying on the islands decreased by some 35%. Travel by air had been negatively affected by the steep increase in fuel prices in 2005, with arrivals declining by some 35.4%. In 2006 there was a recovery in air arrival numbers, which increased by 59.3%, while numbers of cruise ship passengers continued to grow. By 2007, however, the number of tourists arriving by cruise ship had declined by 11%, in contrast with air arrival numbers, which increased by a further 8.3%. With North America and Europe accounting for 92% of total air arrivals in 2009, the recession in those regions was detrimental to tourism in the Cayman Islands in 2008–09. Although the number of visitors arriving by air actually rose in 2008, by 3.9%, partly owing to increased airline services to the islands, a decline of 10.2% in air arrival numbers was recorded in 2009. Cruise ship passenger numbers declined by 9.5% in 2008 and by 2.1% in 2009. Both air and cruise ship arrival numbers increased in the first quarter of 2010 on a year-on-year basis, raising tentative hopes of a recovery in the sector.

There is also an active construction sector (contributing 9.7% of GDP in 2008), owing to post-hurricane reconstruction activities and the expansion of the tourism and commercial sectors. This high rate of activity also benefited the real estate and utilities sectors and the wholesale, retail trade, restaurant and hotel sector (which contributed 23.6% of GDP in 2008). Another consequence of Hurricane Ivan was the need for an enlarged labour force; this demand caused the population to increase by some 9.5% in 2005. Employment increased by 22.5% in 2005, bringing the official unemployment rate to 3.5% (the lowest since 1994). By 2008, however, the unemployment rate had risen to 4.0%.

The agricultural and light industrial sectors are small, and more than 90% of the islands' food needs are imported. In particular, agriculture is limited by infertile soil, low rainfall and high labour costs. Traditional fishing activities, chiefly of turtles, declined from 1970, particularly after the USA imposed an import ban on turtle products in 1979 (the islands possess the world's only commercial turtle farm). Agriculture contributed 0.4% of GDP in 2008.

The economic growth rate was 1.0% in 2000, 0.6% in 2001 and 1.7% in 2002. Growth remained stable, at 2.0%, in 2003, but slowed to 0.9% in 2004 as a result of the impact of Hurricane Ivan. In 2005 the territory achieved its highest rate of economic growth since 1994, at 6.6%, primarily owing to the activity generated by its recovery programme, from within the private sector. However, the economy also experienced its highest rate of inflation since that year, at 7.3%, largely as a result of rising housing costs following the destruction of buildings by Hurricane Ivan. In 2006 economic growth was recorded at 4.6%, with the rate of inflation slowing to just 0.8%. GDP growth declined to 2.2% in 2007 and to 1.1% in 2008, while rising food costs led to increases in the inflation rate of 2.9% and 4.1%, respectively. The economy contracted by 3.6% in the first three quarters of 2009 owing to the adverse effect of the global downturn on its principal sectors (tourism, financial services and construction), and consumer prices declined by an annual average of 1.3% in the year overall, as domestic demand weakened. None the less, the Caymanian Government resisted pressure from the British Government to introduce direct taxes in the 2009/10 budget. Instead, it announced rises in work permit, transaction and banking licence fees, as well as cuts in public sector salaries and the divestment of several assets, in an attempt to reduce the fiscal deficit, which was forecast to expand to CI $156m. in 2009/10. The British Government subsequently agreed to permit the Islands to borrow an additional CI $225m. during that year. Concerns regarding the widening budget deficit increased in early 2010, although an independent report on potential new sources of revenue, which had been commissioned at the request of the British Government, concluded that the introduction of direct taxes would place the Cayman Islands at a competitive disadvantage compared with other international financial centres and recommended, rather, that public expenditure be reduced.

Statistical Survey

Sources: Government Information Services, Cricket Sq., Elgin Ave, George Town, Grand Cayman; tel. 949-8092; fax 949-5936; The Information Centre, Economic and Statistics Office, Government Administration Bldg, Grand Cayman; tel. 949-0940; fax 949-8782; e-mail infostats@gov.ky; internet www.eso.ky.

AREA AND POPULATION

Area: 262 sq km (102 sq miles). The main island of Grand Cayman is about 197 sq km (76 sq miles), about one-half of which is swamp. Cayman Brac is 39 sq km (15 sq miles); Little Cayman is 26 sq km (11 sq miles).

Population: 39,410 (males 19,311, females 20,099) at census of 10 October 1999 (Grand Cayman 37,473, Cayman Brac 1,822, Little Cayman 115). *2008* (estimated population at 31 December): 57,009.

Density (31 December 2008): 217.6 per sq km.

Population by Age and Sex (official estimates at 31 December 2008): *0–14:* 10,633 (males 5,247, females 5,386); *15–64:* 43,502 (males 21,741; females 21,761); *65 and over:* 2,874 (males 1,275, females 1,599); *Total* 57,009 (males 28,263, females 28,746).

Principal Towns (labour force survey, 2008): George Town (capital) 29,764; West Bay 12,119; Bodden Town 9,119. *Mid-2009* (UN estimate, incl. suburbs): George Town 31,723 (Source: UN, *World Urbanization Prospects: The 2009 Revision*).

Births, Marriages and Deaths (2008): Live births 793 (birth rate 14.2 per 1,000); Marriages 487 (marriage rate 8.7 per 1,000); Deaths 166 (death rate 3.0 per 1,000).

Life Expectancy (years at birth, 2009): 80.4 (males 77.8; females 83.1). Source: Pan American Health Organization.

Economically Active Population (sample survey, persons aged 15 years and over, October–November 2008): Agriculture and fishing 697; Manufacturing, mining, printing and publishing 790; Construction 5,796; Electricity, gas and water supply 553; Wholesale and retail trade 4,732; Restaurants and hotels 4,300; Transport, post and telecommunication 1,684; Financial services 3,773; Public administration 2,095; Education, health and social work 2,971; Other community, social and personal service activities 1,912; Private households with employed persons 2,752; Real estate, renting and business services 5,020; Extra-territorial organizations and bodies (calculated as residual) 5; *Sub-total* 37,080; Not classifiable by economic activity 370; *Total employed* 37,450; Unemployed 1,549; *Total labour force* 38,999 (Caymanian 17,686, non-Caymanian 21,313).

HEALTH AND WELFARE

Total Fertility Rate (children per woman, 2009): 1.9.

Physicians (per 1,000 head, 2005): 1.4.

Health Expenditure: % of GDP (1997): 4.2.

Health Expenditure: public (% of total, 1997): 53.2.

Total Carbon Dioxide Emissions ('000 metric tons, 2006): 516.6.

Total Carbon Dioxide Emissions Per Head (metric tons, 2006): 9.8.

Source: mainly Pan American Health Organization.

For definitions, see explanatory note on p. vi.

AGRICULTURE, ETC.

Livestock ('000 head, 2008, FAO estimates): Cattle 1.3; Goats 0.3; Pigs 0.4; Chickens 6.

Fishing (metric tons, live weight, 2008): Total catch 125 (all marine fishes).

Source: FAO.

INDUSTRY

Electric Energy (production, million kWh): 535.7 in 2006; 584.4 in 2007; 596.8 in 2008.

FINANCE

Currency and Exchange Rates: 100 cents = 1 Cayman Islands dollar (CI $). *Sterling, US Dollar and Euro Equivalents* (31 May 2010): £1 sterling = CI $1.215; US $1 = 83.333 CI cents; €1 = CI $1.032; CI $100 = £82.30 = US $120.00 = €96.90. *Exchange rate:* Fixed at CI $1 = US $1.20.

Budget (CI $ million, 2008): *Revenue:* Taxes on international trade and transactions 176.9; Taxes on other domestic goods and services 238.0; Taxes on property 41.1; Other tax revenue 1.9; Non-coercive revenue 64.3 (Sales of goods and services 59.7); Total 522.2. *Expenditure:* Current expenditure 488.7 (Personnel costs 245.2, Supplies and consumable goods 97.8, Subsidies 105.5, Transfer payments 28.4, Interest payments 11.7); Extraordinary expenses 1.7; Other executive expenses 12.3; Capital expenditure and net lending 150.6; Total 653.3.

Cost of Living (Consumer Price Index; base: June 2008 = 100): All items 96.2 in 2007; 100.1 in 2008; 98.8 in 2009.

Gross Domestic Product (CI $ million at constant 2007 prices): 2,461.4 in 2006; 2,569.5 in 2007; 2,598.8 in 2008.

Gross Domestic Product by Economic Activity (CI $ million in current prices, 2007): Agriculture 8.2; Fishing 2.2; Mining and quarrying 29.6; Manufacturing 29.5; Electricity and water supply 82.4; Construction 139.3; Wholesale and retail trade 236.4; Hotels and restaurants 96.3; Transport, storage and communication 175.5; Finance and insurance 1,374.9; Real estate, renting and business services 532.3; Public administration and defense 169.4; Education 62.7; Health and social work 69.8; Other services 93.5; *Sub-total* 3,102.0; *Less* Financial intermediation services indirectly measured 532.5; *GDP in purchasers' values* 2,569.5. *2008:* GDP in purchasers' values 2,704.4.

EXTERNAL TRADE

Principal Commodities (CI $ million, 2008): *Imports c.i.f.:* Food and live animals 95.6; Beverages and tobacco 35.5; Petroleum products and gas 135.6; Chemicals and related products 30.3; Basic manufactures 77.5; Machinery and transport equipment 94.8; Miscellaneous manufactured articles 342.2; Total (incl. others) 876.5. *Exports f.o.b.:* Total 13.8.

Principal Trading Partners (CI $ million, 2008): *Imports c.i.f.:* Jamaica 5.7; Japan 4.0; Netherlands Antilles 138.8; United Kingdom 3.0; USA 652.8; Total (incl. others) 876.5. *Exports f.o.b.:* USA 11.8; Total (incl. others) 13.8.

TRANSPORT

Road Traffic ('000 motor vehicles in use, 2002): Passenger cars 23.8; Commercial vehicles 6.4.

Shipping: *International Freight Traffic* ('000 metric tons): Goods loaded 735 (1990); Goods unloaded 239,138 (2000). *Cargo Vessels* (2007): Vessels 10, Calls at port 551. *Merchant Fleet* (vessels registered at 31 December 2008): 153; Total displacement 2,977,609 grt. (Source: Lloyd's Register-Fairplay, *World Fleet Statistics*).

TOURISM

Visitor Arrivals ('000): 2,197.4 (arrivals by air 267.3, cruise ship passengers 1,930.1) in 2006; 2,007.2 (arrivals by air 291.5, cruise ship passengers 1,715.7) in 2007; 1,855.9 (arrivals by air 302.9, cruise ship passengers 1,553.1) in 2008.

Stay-over Arrivals by Place of Origin ('000, 2008): Canada 18.5; Europe 21.2; USA 240.5; Total (incl. others) 302.8. Source: Cayman Islands Tourism Department, George Town.

Tourism Receipts (US $ million, incl. passenger transport): 356 in 2005; 513 in 2006; 479 in 2007. Source: World Tourism Organization.

COMMUNICATIONS MEDIA

Radio Receivers: 36,000 in use in 1997.

Television Receivers: 23,239 in use in 1999.

Telephones: 38,000 main lines in use in 2009.

Mobile Cellular Telephones (subscribers): 33,800 in 2008.

Fixed and Mobile Telecommunication Lines (number in service): 110,656 in 2005.

Internet Users: 24,000 in 2009.

Daily Newspapers: 2 (circulation 15,400) in 2004.

Source: mainly International Telecommunication Union.

EDUCATION

(30 September 2008)

Institutions (excl. Lighthouse School): Government 16; Private 10; Total 26.

Enrolment: *Government:* Pre-primary 34; Primary 2,283; Middle 1,136; Secondary 1,126; Total 4,579. *Private:* Pre-primary 347; Primary 1,455; Middle 458; Secondary 673; Total 2,933.

Pupil-teacher Ratio (primary education, UNESCO estimate): 12.1 in 2007/08. Source: UNESCO Institute for Statistics.

Adult Literacy Rate: 98.9% in 2008 (males 98.7%, females 99.0%). Source: UNESCO Institute for Statistics.

Directory

The Constitution

A new Constitution was enacted in 2009. Although it afforded Cayman Islanders more autonomy, the new Constitution extended many of the terms of the previous 1959 charter: the Governor, who is appointed for four years, is responsible for defence and internal security, external affairs, and the public service. The Governor appoints the Premier. As well as the Chairman (the Governor) and the Premier, the Cabinet comprises the Deputy Premier, the Attorney-General and the Cabinet Secretary (all of whom are appointed by the Governor in consultation with the Premier) and five other Ministers elected by the Legislative Assembly from their own number. The Governor assigns ministerial portfolios to the elected members of the Cabinet, in consultation with the Premier. There are 15 elected members of the Legislative Assembly (elected by direct, universal adult suffrage for a term of four years) and three official members appointed by the Governor. The Legislative Assembly was to be expanded to 18 members by 2013. The Speaker presides over the Assembly. The new Constitution establishes a National Security Council, to advise the Governor on internal security policy. The United Kingdom retains full control over foreign affairs. A Bill of Rights, Freedom and Responsibilities was scheduled to come into effect in November 2012.

The Government

HEAD OF STATE

Queen: HM Queen ELIZABETH II.

Governor: DUNCAN TAYLOR (assumed office 15 January 2010).

CABINET
(July 2010)

The Government is formed by the United Democratic Party.

Chairman: DUNCAN TAYLOR (The Governor).

Premier and Minister of Finance, Tourism and Development: W. MCKEEVA BUSH.

Deputy Governor and Minister of Internal and External Affairs*: DONOVAN EBANKS.

Attorney-General and Minister of Legal Affairs*: SAMUEL BULGIN.

Cabinet Secretary*: ORRETT CONNOR.

Minister of Health, Environment, Youth, Sports and Culture: MARK SCOTLAND.

Minister of Education, Training and Employment: ROLSTON ANGLIN.

Deputy Premier and Minister of District Administration, Works and Gender Affairs: JULIANA O'CONNOR-CONNOLLY.

Minister of Community Affairs and Housing: MIKE ADAM.

A District Commissioner, Ernie Scott, represents the Governor on Cayman Brac and Little Cayman.

* Appointed by the Governor.

GOVERNMENT OFFICES

Office of the Governor: The Professional Centre, Suite 202, 2nd Floor, Smith Rd, POB 10261, George Town, Grand Cayman KY1-1003; tel. 244-2401; fax 945-4131; e-mail staffoff@candw.ky; internet www.ukincayman.fco.gov.uk.

All official government offices and ministries are located in the Government Administration Bldg, Elgin Ave, George Town, Grand Cayman.

Ministry of Community Affairs and Housing: tel. 244-2424; fax 949-3896; e-mail dorine.whittaker@gov.ky.

Ministry of District Administration, Works and Gender Affairs: tel. 244-2412; fax 945-2922; e-mail foi.mpc@gov.ky; internet www.dapah.gov.ky.

Ministry of Education, Training and Employment: tel. 244-2417; fax 949-9343; e-mail brighterfutures@gov.ky; internet www.education.gov.ky.

Ministry of Finance, Tourism and Development: tel. 244-2458; fax 945-1746; e-mail tedc@gov.ky; internet www.caymanislands.ky (Dept of Tourism).

Ministry of Health, Environment, Youth, Sports and Culture: tel. 244-2318; fax 949-1790; e-mail h&hs@gov.ky; internet www.hsa.ky (Health Services Authority).

Ministry of Internal and External Affairs: tel. 244-3179; fax 946-5453; e-mail foi.pie@gov.ky; internet www.pie.gov.ky.

Ministry of Legal Affairs: tel. 244-2405; fax 949-6079; e-mail agc@gov.ky; internet www.caymanjudicial-legalinfo.ky.

LEGISLATIVE ASSEMBLY

Legislative Assembly: 33 Fort St, POB 890, George Town, Grand Cayman KY1-1103; tel. 949-4236; fax 949-9514; internet www.legislativeassembly.ky; Clerk ZENA MERREN-CHIN.

Members: The Deputy Governor, the Attorney-General, and 15 elected members. According to the terms of the 2009 Constitution, the number of elected members was to be increased to 18 at the next dissolution of the Legislative Assembly, when the Deputy Governor was to give up his seat. An Electoral Boundaries Commission also was to be established to review constituency boundaries. The most recent election to the Assembly was on 20 May 2009.

Speaker: MARY LAWRENCE.

Election Commission

Elections Office: Smith Road Professional Centre, 2nd Floor, 150 Smith Rd, George Town, Grand Cayman; tel. 949-8047; fax 949-2977; e-mail electionsoffice@candw.ky; internet www.electionsoffice.ky; Supervisor of Elections KEARNEY SIDNEY GOMEZ.

Political Organizations

People's Progressive Movement (PPM): POB 10526 APO, Grand Cayman; tel. 945-1776; f. 2002; Leader D. KURT TIBBETTS; Chair. ANTONY DUCKWORTH.

United Democratic Party (UDP): Godfrey Nixon Rd, George Town, Grand Cayman; tel. 943-3338; e-mail info@udp.ky; internet www.udp.ky; tel. 943-3338; fax 943-3339; f. 2001; Leader W. MCKEEVA BUSH; Gen. Sec. ROLSTON ANGLIN.

Judicial System

There is a Grand Court of the Islands (with Supreme Court status), a Summary Court, a Youth Court and a Coroner's Court. The Grand Court has jurisdiction in all civil matters, admiralty matters, and in trials on indictment. Appeals lie to the Court of Appeal of the Cayman Islands and beyond that to the Privy Council in the United Kingdom. The Summary Courts deal with criminal and civil matters (up to a certain limit defined by law) and appeals lie to the Grand Court.

Chief Justice: ANTHONY SMELLIE.

President of the Court of Appeal: EDWARD ZACCA.

Clerk of the Courts of the Islands: VALDIS FOLDATS, Court's Office, Edward St, George Town, Grand Cayman KY1-1106; tel. 949-4296; fax 949-9856; e-mail valdis.foldats@gov.ky.

Religion

CHRISTIANITY

The oldest established denominations are (on Grand Cayman) the United Church of Jamaica and Grand Cayman (Presbyterian), and (on Cayman Brac) the Baptist Church. Anglicans are adherents of the Church in the Province of the West Indies (Grand Cayman forms part of the diocese of Jamaica). Within the Roman Catholic Church, the Cayman Islands forms part of the archdiocese of Kingston in

Jamaica. According to the latest available census figures (1999), some 26% of the population are adherents of the Church of God, 12% belong to the United Church, 11% are Roman Catholics, 9% are Baptists, 8% are Seventh-day Adventists, 6% are Anglicans and 5% are Pentecostalists.

The Press

The Cayman Islands Journal: The Compass Centre, Shedden Rd, POB 1365, George Town, Grand Cayman; tel. 949-5111; fax 949-7675; internet www.compasscayman.com/journal; publ. by Cayman Free Press; monthly; broadsheet business newspaper; Publr BRIAN UZZELL.

Cayman Net News: 85 North Sound Rd, Alissta Towers, POB 10707, Grand Cayman; tel. 946-6060; fax 949-0679; e-mail news@caymannetnews.com; internet www.caymannetnews.com; internet news service; publishes weekly newspaper (f. 2006); Publr and Editor-in-Chief DESMOND SEALES.

Caymanian Compass: The Compass Centre, Shedden Rd, POB 1365, George Town, Grand Cayman; tel. 949-5111; fax 949-7675; internet www.compasscayman.com; f. 1965; publ. by the Cayman Free Press; 5 a week; Publr BRIAN UZZELL; circ. 10,000.

The Chamber: POB 1000, George Town, Grand Cayman; tel. 949-8090; fax 949-0220; e-mail info@caymanchamber.ky; internet www.caymanchamber.ky; f. 1965; monthly; newsletter of the Cayman Islands Chamber of Commerce; Editor WIL PINEAU; circ. 5,000.

Christian Lifestyle: GKF Bldg, Godfrey Nixon Way, POB 1217, Grand Cayman KY1 1108; tel. 926-2507; fax 947-2228; e-mail editor@cstylemagazine.com; internet www.christianlifestylemagazine.com; f. 2008; publ. every 2 months; Editor KAREN CHIN.

Gazette: Gazette Office, Government Information Service, Cayman Islands Government, Aqua World Mall, Merrendale Dr., Grand Cayman; tel. 949-8092; fax 949-5936; e-mail caymangazette@gov.ky; internet www.gazettes.gov.ky; official govt newspaper; publ. fortnightly on Monday; Editor-in-Chief PATRICIA EBANKS.

Key to Cayman: The Compass Centre, Shedden Rd, POB 1365 George Town, Grand Cayman KY1 1108; tel. 949-5111; fax 949-7675; e-mail cfp@candw.ky; internet keytocayman.com; 2 a year; free tourist magazine; publ. by the Cayman Free Press; Cayman Free Press also publs *Caymanian Compass* newspaper and accompanying supplements, *Cayman Islands Journal*, *Cayman Islands Yearbook & Business Directory*, *Cayman Islands Map*, and *Inside Out*, a home and living magazine; Publr BRIAN UZZELL.

Publishers

Caribbean Publishing Co (Cayman) Ltd: 1 Paddington Pl., Suite 306, North Sound Way, POB 688, George Town, Grand Cayman; tel. 949-7027; fax 949-8366; internet www.caribbeanwhitepages.com; f. 1978.

Cayman Free Press Ltd: The Compass Centre, Shedden Rd, POB 1365, George Town, Grand Cayman; tel. 949-5111; fax 949-7675; e-mail info@cfp.ky; internet www.caymanfreepress.com; f. 1965.

Government Information Service: Gazette Office, Cayman Islands Govt, Cricket Sq., Elgin Ave, Grand Cayman; tel. 949-8092; fax 949-5936; e-mail caymangazette@gov.ky; internet www.gazettes.gov.ky; publr of official govt releases, *Gazette*.

Progressive Publications Ltd: Economy Printers Bldg, POB 764, George Town, Grand Cayman; tel. 949-5780; fax 949-7674.

Tower Marketing: Grand Cayman; tel. 623-6700; fax 769-6700; e-mail lynne@tower.com.ky; internet www.tower.com.ky; f. 1999; Man. Dir LYNNE BYLES.

Broadcasting and Communications

REGULATORY AUTHORITY

Information and Communications Technology Authority (ICTA): Alissta Towers, 3rd Floor, 85 North Sound Rd, POB 2502, Grand Cayman KY1-1104; tel. 946-4282; fax 945-8284; e-mail info@icta.ky; internet www.icta.ky; f. 2002; responsible for the regulation and licensing of telecommunications, broadcasting, and all forms of radio which includes ship, aircraft, mobile and amateur radio and the management of the Cayman Islands internet domain; Chair. SAMUEL JACKSON; Man. Dir DAVID ARCHBOLD.

TELECOMMUNICATIONS

Digicel Cayman: Cayman Financial Centre, 36A Roys Dr., POB 700, George Town, Grand Cayman; tel. 623-3444; fax 623-3329; e-mail Care-cayman.customercare@digicelgroup.com; internet www.digicelcayman.com; f. 2003; owned by an Irish consortium; acquired the operations of Cingular Wireless (fmrly those of AT&T Wireless) in the country in 2005 (www.cingular.ky); CEO DENIS O'BRIEN.

LIME: Anderson Sq. Bldg, Anderson Sq., Sheddon Rd, POB 293, George Town, Grand Cayman; tel. 949-7800; fax 949-7962; e-mail cs@candw.ky; internet www.time4lime.com; f. 1966 as Cable & Wireless (Cayman Islands) Ltd; name changed as above 2008; Cable & Wireless' monopoly over the telecommunications market ended in 2004; Exec. Vice-Pres.(Cayman Islands) JOEL ABDINOOR; Country Man. ANTHONY RITCH.

TeleCayman: Cayman Corporate Centre, 4th Floor, POB 704 GT, Grand Cayman; tel. 769-1000; fax 769-0999; e-mail customer@telecayman.com; internet www.telecayman.com; f. 2003; provides telephone and internet services; Senior Vice-Pres. GILBERT CHALIFOUX.

WestTel Ltd: Governors Sq., West Bay Rd, POB 31117, Grand Cayman; tel. 745-5555; fax 743-5554; e-mail support@westtel.ky; internet www.westtel.ky; f. 2003; provides telephone and internet services; independent affiliate of WestStar TV Ltd cable television co; Chief Technical Officer MICHAEL EDENHOLM.

BROADCASTING

Radio

Radio Cayman: Elgin Ave, POB 1110 GT, George Town, Grand Cayman KY1-1102; tel. 949-7799; fax 949-6536; e-mail rcnews@gov.ky; internet www.radiocayman.gov.ky; started full-time broadcasting 1976; govt-owned commercial radio station; service in English; operates Radio Cayman One and Breeze FM; Dir NORMA MCFIELD.

Radio Heaven 97 FM: GKF Industrial Park, Godfrey Nixon Way, POB 31481 SMB, George Town, Grand Cayman; tel. 949-2797; fax 949-2707; e-mail contact@heaven97.com; internet www.heaven97.com; f. 1997; owned by Christian Communications Association; Christian broadcasting, music and news; commercial station.

Radio ICCI-FM: International College of the Cayman Islands, POB 136, Grand Cayman KY1-1501; tel. 947-1100; fax 947-1210; e-mail icci@icci.edu.ky; internet www.icci.edu.ky; f. 1973; radio station of the International College of the Cayman Islands; educational and cultural; Pres. Dr ELSA M. CUMMINGS.

Radio Vibe: Rankin's Plaza, 21 Eclipse Dr., POB 10734, Grand Cayman KY1-1007; tel. 949-8243; fax 946-9867; e-mail info@vibefm.ky; internet www.vibefm-cayman.com; operated by Paramount Media Services, in addition to Spin FM; Man. KENNY RANKINE.

Radio Z99.9 FM: 256 Crewe Rd, Suite 201, Crighton Bldg, POB 30110, Grand Cayman KY1-1201; tel. 945-1166; fax 945-1006; e-mail info@z99.ky; internet www.z99.ky; owned by Hurley's Entertainment Corpn Ltd; Man. Dir RANDY MERREN.

Television

Cayman Adventist Television Network (CATN/TV): POB 515, Grand Cayman KY1-1106; tel. 949-2739; e-mail mission@candw.ky; internet www.tagnet.org/cayman/tv.html; f. 1996; local and international programmes, mainly religious; Pres. JEFFREY THOMPSON.

Cayman Christian TV Ltd: POB 964, Grand Cayman KY1-1102; relays Christian broadcasting from the Trinity Broadcasting Network (USA); Vice-Pres. FRED RUTTY.

CITN Cayman 27: 45 Eclipse Way, POB 30563, Grand Cayman KY1-1203; tel. 745-0207; fax 749-1002; e-mail hlofters@weststartv.com; internet www.cayman27.com.ky; f. 1992 as Cayman International Television Network; 24 hrs daily; local and international news and US entertainment; 10-channel cable service of international programmes by subscription; Station Man. RICK ALPERT.

WestStar TV Ltd: 45 Eclipse Way, POB 31117, Grand Cayman KY1-1205; tel. 745-5555; e-mail info@weststartv.com; internet www.weststartv.com; f. 1993; operates wireless cable television service; affiliated to WestTel Ltd; Operations Man. RICHARD CORBIN.

Finance

(cap. = capital; res = reserves; dep. = deposits; m. = million; brs = branches)

Banking facilities are provided by commercial banks. The islands have become an important centre for 'offshore' companies and trusts. In 2008 there were 93,693 companies registered in the Cayman Islands. At the end of June 2010 there were 324 licensed banks and trusts and a total of 8,929 registered mutual funds. The islands are well-known as a tax haven because of the absence of any form of direct taxation. In September 2009 assets held by banks registered in the Cayman Islands totalled US $1,800,000m.

Cayman Islands Monetary Authority (CIMA): 80E Shedden Rd, Elizabethan Sq., POB 10052 APO, George Town, Grand Cayman

KY1-1001; tel. 949-7089; fax 945-2532; e-mail contactpublicrelations@cimoney.com.ky; internet www.cimoney.com.ky; f. 1997; responsible for managing the territory's currency and reserves and for regulating the financial services sector; cap. CI $9.9m., res CI $20.1m., dep. CI $78.9m. (Jun. 2008); Chair. GEORGE MCCARTHY; Man. Dir CINDY SCOTLAND.

PRINCIPAL BANKS AND TRUST COMPANIES

AALL Trust and Banking Corpn Ltd: AALL Bldg, POB 1166, George Town, Grand Cayman; tel. 949-5588; fax 945-5772; internet www.aall.com; Chair. ERIK MONSEN; Man. Dir KEVIN DOYLE.

Appleby Trust (Cayman) Ltd: Clifton House, 75 Fort St, POB 190, Grand Cayman KY1-1104; tel. 949-4900; fax 949-4901; e-mail cayman@applebyglobal.com; internet www.applebyglobal.com; f. 2006 following acquisition of business interests of Ansbacher (Cayman) Ltd; offices in Bermuda; Man. Dir HUW ST J. MOSES.

Atlantic Security Bank: POB 10340, George Town 1097, Grand Cayman; internet www.asbnet.com; f. 1981 as Banco de Crédito del Peru International, name changed as above 1986; Chair. DIONISIO ROMERO; Pres. CARLOS MUÑOZ.

Julius Baer Bank and Trust Co Ltd: Windward Bldg 3, Suite 310, Regatta Office Park, West Bay Rd, POB 1100, George Town, Grand Cayman; tel. 943-2237; fax 949-6096; e-mail charles.farrington@juliusbaer.com; internet www.juliusbaer.ch; f. 1974; 100% owned by Julius Baer Holding Ltd (Switzerland); Man. Dir CHARLES FARRINGTON.

Banco Português do Atlântico: POB 30124, Grand Cayman; tel. 949-8322; fax 949-7743; e-mail bcpjvic@candw.ky; Gen. Man. HELENA SOARES CARNEIRO.

Banco Safra (Cayman Islands) Ltd: c/o Bank of Nova Scotia, POB 501, George Town, Grand Cayman; tel. 949-2001; fax 949-7097; f. 1993; res US $124.5m., dep. US $268.8m. (Dec. 2007).

BANIF-Banco Internaçional do Funchal (Cayman) Ltd: Genesis Bldg, 3rd Floor, POB 32338 SMB, George Town, Grand Cayman; tel. 945-8060; fax 945-8069; e-mail banifcay@candw.ky; internet www.banif.pt; Chair., Exec. Bd Dr JOAQUIM FILIPE MARQUES DOS SANTOS; Chair., Admin. Bd HORÁCIO DA SILVA ROQUE.

Bank of Bermuda (Cayman) Ltd: British American Tower, 3rd Floor, POB 513, George Town, Grand Cayman; tel. 949-9898; fax 949-7959; internet www.bankofbermuda.bm; f. 1968 as a trust; converted to a bank in 1988; total assets US $1,041m. (July 2001); Chair. HENRY B. SMITH; Man. Dir ALLEN BERNARDO.

Bermuda Trust (Cayman) Ltd: 5th Floor, Bermuda House, POB 513, George Town, Grand Cayman; tel. 949-9898; fax 949-7959; internet www.bankofbermuda.bm; f. 1968 as Arawak Trust Co; became subsidiary of Bank of Bermuda in 1988; bank and trust services; Chair. JOHN CAMPBELL; Man. Dir KENNETH GIBBS.

BFC Bank (Cayman) Ltd: Trafalgar Pl., POB 1765, George Town, Grand Cayman; tel. 949-8748; fax 949-8749; e-mail bfc@candw.ky; f. 1985; FC Financière de la Cité, Geneva, 99.9%; cap. US $0.8m., res US $3.7m., dep. US $33.5m. (March 2001); Chair. SIMON C. TAY; Resident Man. CHERRYLEE BUSH.

Butterfield Bank (Cayman) Ltd: Butterfield House, 68 Fort St, POB 705, George Town, Grand Cayman KY1-1107; tel. 949-7055; fax 949-7004; e-mail info@ky.butterfieldbank.com; internet www.ky.butterfieldgroup.com; f. 1967; name changed as above in 2004, fmrly Bank of Butterfield International (Cayman) Ltd; subsidiary of Bank of N. T. Butterfield & Son Ltd, Bermuda; cap. US $16.5m., dep. US $3,116.8m. (Dec. 2008); Exec. Vice-Pres. (Int.) GRAHAM BROOKS; Man. Dir CONOR J. O'DEA; 3 brs.

Caledonian Bank and Trust Ltd: Caledonian House, 69 Dr Roy's Dr., POB 1043, George Town, Grand Cayman KY1-1102; tel. 949-0050; fax 949-8062; e-mail info@caledonian.com; internet www.caledonian.com; f. 1970; Chair. WILLIAM S. WALKER; Man. Dir DAVID WALKER.

Cayman National Bank Ltd: Cayman National Bank Bldg, 4th Floor, 200 Elgin Ave, POB 1097, George Town, Grand Cayman; tel. 949-4655; fax 949-7506; e-mail cnb@caymannational.com; internet www.caymannational.com; f. 1974; subsidiary of Cayman National Corpn; cap. CI $2.4m., res CI $42.7m., dep. CI $776.6m. (Sept. 2008); Chair. BENSON O. EBANKS; Pres. STUART DACK; 6 brs.

CITCO Bank and Trust Co Ltd: 89 Nexus Way, 2nd Floor, Camana Bay, POB 31105, Grand Cayman KY1-1205; tel. 945-3838; fax 945-3888; e-mail cayman-bank@citco.com; internet www.citco.com; Man. Dir ROBERT THOMAS.

Deutsche Bank (Cayman) Ltd: Boundary Hall, Cricket Sq., 171 Elgin Ave, POB 1984, George Town, Grand Cayman KY1-1104; tel. 949-8244; fax 949-8178; e-mail dmg-cay@candw.ky; internet www.dboffshore.com; f. 1983 as Morgan Grenfell (Cayman) Ltd; name changed to Deutsche Morgan Grenfell (Cayman) Ltd in 1996; name changed as above in 1998; cap. US $5.0m., res US $20.3m., dep. US $129.3m. (Dec. 1998); Chair. MARK HIRST; Regional Head JANET HISLOP.

Deutsche Bank International Trust Co (Cayman) Ltd: POB 1984, George Town, Grand Cayman; tel. 949-8244; fax 949-7866; f. 1999; Regional Man. TIM GODBER.

Deutsche Girozentrale Overseas Ltd: POB 694, George Town, Grand Cayman; tel. 914-9483; fax 949-0626; Man. Dir RAINER MACH.

Fidelity Bank (Cayman) Ltd: POB 914, George Town, Grand Cayman KY1-1103; tel. 949-7822; fax 949-6064; e-mail bank@fidelitycayman.com; internet www.fidelitycayman.com; f. 1979; Pres. and CEO BRETT HILL.

FirstCaribbean International Bank Ltd: POB 68, 25 Main St, George Town, Grand Cayman KY1-1102; tel. 949-7300; fax 949-7179; internet www.firstcaribbeanbank.com; f. 2002 following merger of Caribbean operations of Barclays Bank PLC and CIBC; Barclays relinquished its stake to CIBC in June 2006; Exec. Chair. MICHAEL MANSOOR; CEO JOHN D. ORR; Cayman Islands Contact MARK MCINTYRE.

Fortis Bank (Cayman) Ltd: Grand Pavilion Commercial Centre, 802 West Bay Rd, POB 2003, George Town, Grand Cayman; tel. 949-7942; fax 949-8340; e-mail phil.brown@ky.fortisbank.com; internet www.fortis.com; f. 1984 as Pierson, Heldring & Pierson (Cayman) Ltd; name changed to Mees Pierson (Cayman) Ltd in 1993; present name adopted in June 2000; Man. Dir ROGER HANSON.

HSBC Financial Services (Cayman) Ltd: HSBC House, 68 West Bay Rd, POB 1109, George Town, Grand Cayman KY1-1102; tel. 949-7755; fax 949-7634; e-mail hbky.information@ky.hsbc.com; internet www.hsbc.ky; f. 1982; CEO GONZALO JALLES.

LGT Bank in Liechtenstein (Cayman) Ltd: UBS House, 227 Elgin Ave, POB 852, George Town, Grand Cayman; tel. 949-7676; fax 949-8512; e-mail lgt.cayman@lgt.com; internet www.lgt-bank-in-liechtenstein.com.

Merrill Lynch Bank and Trust Co (Cayman) Ltd: Harbour Centre, 4th Floor, North Church St, George Town, Grand Cayman; tel. 814-6405; fax 949-8895; internet www.ml.com.

RBS Coutts (Cayman) Ltd: Coutts House, 1446 West Bay Rd, POB 707, George Town, Grand Cayman KY1-1107; tel. 945-4777; fax 945-4799; e-mail info@rbscoutts.com; internet www.rbscoutts.com; f. 1967; fmrly NatWest International Trust Corpn (Cayman) Ltd; 100% owned by Royal Bank of Scotland International (Holdings) Ltd (Jersey); CEO GERHARD H. MÜLLER.

Royal Bank of Canada: 24 Shedden Rd, POB 245, Grand Cayman KY1-1104; tel. 949-4600; fax 949-7396; internet www.royalbank.com; Man. HARRY C. CHISHOLM.

Royal Bank of Canada Trust Co (Cayman) Ltd: 24 Shedden Rd, POB 1586 GT, Grand Cayman KY1-1110; tel. 949-9107; fax 949-5777; internet www.rbcprivatebanking.com/cayman-islands.html; Man. Dir DEANNA BIDWELL.

Scotiabank and Trust (Cayman) Ltd: Scotia Centre, 6 Cardinal Ave, POB 689, George Town, Grand Cayman KY1-1107; tel. 949-2001; fax 949-7097; e-mail scotiaci@candw.ky; internet www.cayman.scotiabank.com; f. 1968; fmrly Bank of Nova Scotia Trust Company (Cayman) Ltd; present name adopted Dec. 2003; Man. Dir FARRIED SULLIMAN.

UBS Fund Services (Cayman Islands) Ltd: UBS House, 227 Elgin Ave, POB 852, George Town, Grand Cayman KY1-1103; tel. 914-1060; fax 914-4060; internet www.ubs.com/cayman-funds; Man. Dir DARREN STAINROD.

Development Bank

Cayman Islands Development Bank: Cayman Financial Centre, 36B Dr Roy's Dr., POB 1271 GT, George Town, Grand Cayman; tel. 949-7511; fax 949-6168; e-mail angela.miller@gov.ky; f. 2002; replaced the Housing Devt Corpn and the Agricultural and Industrial Devt Bd; under the jurisdiction of the Ministry of Finance, Tourism and Development; Devt Finance Institution Gen. Man. RALPH LEWIS.

Banking Association

Cayman Islands Bankers' Association: Macdonald Sq., Fort St, POB 676, George Town, Grand Cayman; tel. 949-0330; fax 945-1448; e-mail ciba@candw.ky; internet www.cibankers.org; Pres. DAVID WALKER; Sec. GARY DARWENT; 86 full mems, 250 assoc. mems.

STOCK EXCHANGE

Cayman Islands Stock Exchange (CSX): 4th Floor, Elizabethan Sq., POB 2408, George Town, Grand Cayman KY1-1105; tel. 945-6060; fax 945-6061; e-mail csx@csx.com.ky; internet www.csx.com.ky; f. 1996; more than 3,000 cos listed (July 2009); Chair. ANTHONY B. TRAVERS; CEO VALIA THEODORAKI.

INSURANCE

Several foreign companies have agents in the islands. A total of 760 insurance companies were registered as of June 2010. In particular, the islands are a leading international market for health insurance. Local companies include the following:

AON Cayman National Insurance Brokers Ltd: Buckingham Sq., 720 West Bay Rd, POB 69, George Town, Grand Cayman KY1-1102; tel. 949-0111; fax 949-8163; e-mail cnib@caymannational.com; internet www.caymannational.com; part of the Cayman National Corpn; Gen. Man. MARY MELLIN.

British Caymanian Insurance Agency Ltd: Elizabethan Sq., POB 74 GT, Grand Cayman KY1-1002; tel. 949-8699; fax 949-8411; e-mail gderry@candw.ky; Man. DERRY GRAHAM.

Cayman Insurance Centre: POB 10056, Cayman Business Park; tel. 814-7222; e-mail linda.key@cic.com.ky; internet www.cic.com.ky; Pres. LINDA CHAPMAN-KEY.

Cayman Islands National Insurance Co (CINICO): Cayman Centre, 1st Floor, Dorcy Dr, Airport Rd, George Town, POB 10112, Grand Cayman KY1-1001; tel. 949-8101; fax 949-8226; e-mail debanks@cinico.ky; internet www.cinico.ky; govt-owned; Chair. DALE CROWLEY; Gen. Man. CAROLE APPLEYARD.

Insurance Company of the West Indies (Cayman) Ltd (ICWI): 93 Hospital Rd, POB 461, Grand Cayman KY1-1106; tel. 949-6970; fax 949-6929; e-mail icwi@candw.ky; internet www.icwi.com/cayman; subsidiary of Insurance Company of the West Indies, Jamaica; Pres. PAUL LABOR; Man. HEATHER LANIGAN.

Island Heritage Insurance Co Ltd: Atlantic Star House, 128 Lawrence Blvd, POB 2501, Grand Cayman KY1-1104; tel. 949-7280; fax 945-6765; e-mail info@islandheritage.com.ky; internet www.islandheritageinsurance.com; general insurance; Chair. and CEO GARTH MACDONALD.

Sagicor Life of the Cayman Islands Ltd: 198 North Church St, POB 1087, George Town, Grand Cayman KY1-1102; tel. 949-8211; fax 949-8262; e-mail customerservice@sagicor.com; internet www.sagicor.com; f. 2004 by merger between Global Life and Capital Life; Country Man. CLAUDETTE SAINT-REID.

Sagicor General Insurance (Cayman) Ltd: 3rd Floor, Harbour Pl., 103 South Church St, POB 2171, Grand Cayman KY1-1105; tel. 949-7028; fax 949-7457; e-mail askus@sagicor.ky; internet www.sagicor.ky; fmrly Cayman General Insurance Co Ltd; renamed as above in 2006 following acquisition of 51% interest by Sagicor Life of the Cayman Islands Ltd (q.v.).

Trade and Industry

GOVERNMENT AGENCY

National Investment Council: Cayman Corporate Centre, 1st Floor, Hospital Rd, POB 10087 APO, Grand Cayman KY1-1001; tel. 945-0943; fax 945-0941; e-mail info@investcayman.gov.ky; internet www.investcayman.ky; f. 2003 as Cayman Islands Investment Bureau; renamed 2010 and merged into Dept of Commerce and Investment.

CHAMBER OF COMMERCE

Cayman Islands Chamber of Commerce: Macdonald Sq., 2nd Floor, Fort St, POB 1000, George Town, Grand Cayman KY1-1102; tel. 949-8090; fax 949-0220; e-mail info@caymanchamber.ky; internet www.caymanchamber.ky; f. 1965; Pres. STEWART BOSTOCK; CEO WIL PINEAU; 594 corporate mems and 78 associates.

TRADE ASSOCIATION

Cayman Finance: POB 11048, Grand Cayman; tel. 946-6000; fax 946-6001; e-mail info@caymanfinances.com; internet www.caymanfinances.com; f. 2003 as Cayman Islands Financial Services Association; name changed as above in Oct. 2009; aims to promote the integrity and transparency of the financial services sector; Chair ANTHONY TRAVERS.

EMPLOYERS' ORGANIZATION

Human Resources Department: 4th Floor, Tower Bldg, Grand Cayman; tel. 949-0941; fax 945-6057; Dir DALE M. BANKS.

UTILITIES

Electricity

Electricity Regulatory Authority: Grand Pavilion, Suite 2, West Bay Rd, POB 10189, Grand Cayman KY1-1002; tel. 949-8372; fax 947-9598; e-mail general@caymanera.com; internet caymanera.com; f. 2005; Chair. SHERRI BODDEN-COWAN; Man. Dir PHILIP THOMAS.

Caribbean Utilities Co Ltd (CUC): Corporate HQ & Plant, 457 North Sound Rd, POB 38, George Town, Grand Cayman; tel. 949-5200; fax 949-5203; e-mail service@cuc.ky; internet www.cuc-cayman.com; Pres. and CEO J. F. RICHARD HEW; Chair. DAVID RITCH.

Cayman Brac Power and Light Co Ltd (CBP&L): Stake Bay Point, POB 95, Stake Bay, Cayman Brac; tel. 948-2224; fax 948-2204; e-mail braclite@candw.ky; Gen. Man. JONATHAN TIBBETTS.

Water

Cayman Islands Water Authority: 13G Red Gate Rd, POB 1104 GT, George Town, Grand Cayman KY1-1102; tel. 949-2837; fax 949-0094; e-mail info@waterauthority.ky; internet www.waterauthority.ky; Dir Dr GELIA FREDERICK-VAN GENDEREN; Chair. JONATHAN PIERCY.

Consolidated Water Co Ltd (CWCO): Windward 3, 4th Floor, Regatta Office Park, POB 1114, George Town, Grand Cayman KY1-1102; tel. 945-4277; fax 949-2957; e-mail info@cwco.com; internet ir.cwco.com; f. 1973; Pres. and CEO FREDERICK W. MCTAGGART; Dir and Chair. WILMER F. PERGANDE.

Transport

ROADS

There are some 406 km (252 miles) of motorable roads, of which 304 km are surfaced with tarmac. The road network connects all districts on Grand Cayman and Cayman Brac (which has 76 km of motorable road), and there are 43 km of motorable road on Little Cayman (of which about 18 km are paved). According to the 2009 budget address, US $5.3m. was to be allocated for ongoing improvements to the islands' road network.

SHIPPING

George Town is the principal port and a new port facility was opened in July 1977. Cruise liners, container ships and smaller cargo vessels ply between the Cayman Islands, Florida, Jamaica and Costa Rica. There is no cruise ship dock in the Cayman Islands. Ships anchor off George Town and ferry passengers ashore to the North or South Dock Terminals in George Town. The number of cruise ship passengers is limited to 6,000 per day. The port of Cayman Brac is Creek; there are limited facilities on Little Cayman. In December 2008 the shipping register comprised 153 vessels, with combined displacement totalling 2,977,609 grt.

Maritime Authority of Cayman Islands (MACI): Strathvale House, 2nd Floor, 90 North Church St, POB 2256, Grand Cayman KY1-1107; tel. 949-8831; fax 949-8849; e-mail maci.consulting@cishipping.com; internet www.cishipping.com; f. 2005; wholly govt-owned; legal entity responsible for: enforcement of international maritime laws and conventions; implementation of maritime safety and security, Cayman Islands marine environment laws; formation of national maritime policy; representation and protection of national maritime interests at international forums; also undertakes vessel and mortgage registration, advisory and marine survey and audit services fmrly administered by CISR; Chair. SHARON E. ROULSTONE; CEO A. JOEL WALTON.

Port Authority of the Cayman Islands: Harbour Dr., POB 1358 GT, George Town, Grand Cayman KY1-1108; tel. 949-2055; fax 949-5820; e-mail support@caymanport.com; internet www.caymanport.com; Chair. STEFAN BARAUD.

Principal Shipping Companies

Cayman Islands Shipping Registry: Strathvale House, 2nd Floor, 90 North Church St, POB 2256, Grand Cayman KY1-110; tel. 949-8831; fax 949-8849; e-mail cisrky@cishipping.com; internet www.cishipping.com; f. 1993; division of Maritime Authority of Cayman Islands (MACI); Dir A. JOEL WALTON.

Seaboard Marine (Cayman): Mirco Commerce Centre, 2nd Floor, Industrial Park, POB 1372, George Town, Grand Cayman KY1-1108; tel. 949-4977; fax 949-8402; e-mail info@seaboardcayman.com; internet www.seaboardcayman.com; Man. Dir ROBERT FOSTER.

Thompson Shipping Co Ltd: Cayman Shipping Centre, 2nd Floor, 432 Eastern Ave, POB 188, George Town, Grand Cayman KY1-1004; tel. 949-8044; fax 949-8349; e-mail info@thompsonshipping.com; internet www.thompsonshipping.com; f. 1977; agent for Thompson Line, a div. of Tropical Shipping; Contact Person SUSAN GABRUCH.

CIVIL AVIATION

There are two international airports in the Territory: Owen Roberts International Airport, 3.5 km (2 miles) from George Town, and Gerrard Smith International Airport on Cayman Brac. Both are capable of handling jet-engined aircraft. Edward Bodden Airport on Little Cayman can cater for light aircraft. Several scheduled carriers serve the islands.

Civil Aviation Authority of the Cayman Islands (CAACI): Unit 2, Cayman Grand Harbour Complex, Shamrock Rd, POB 10277, George Town, Grand Cayman KY1-1003; tel. 949-7811; fax 949-0761; e-mail civil.aviation@caacayman.com; internet www.caacayman

.com; f. 1987; Dir-Gen. RICHARD SMITH; Chair. SHERIDAN BROOKS-HURST.

Cayman Airways Ltd: 91 Owen Roberts Dr., POB 10092, Grand Cayman KY1-1001; tel. 949-8200; fax 949-7607; e-mail customerrelations@caymanairways.net; internet www.caymanairways.com; f. 1968; wholly govt-owned since 1977; operates local services and scheduled flights to Jamaica, Honduras and the USA; Pres. and CEO FABIAN WHORMS.

Island Air: Airport Rd, POB 2433, George Town, Grand Cayman KY1-1105; tel. 949-5252; fax 949-1073; e-mail res@islandair.ky; internet islandair.ky; f. 1987; operates daily scheduled services between Grand Cayman, Cayman Brac and Little Cayman; Man. Dir MARCUS CUMBER.

Tourism

The Cayman Islands are a major tourist destination, the majority of visitors coming from North America. The tourism industry was badly affected by the damage caused by Hurricane Ivan in September 2004, severely reducing available accommodation and a major reconstruction effort was undertaken in 2005. The beaches and opportunities for diving in the offshore reefs form the main attraction for most tourists. In 2007 there were an estimated 4,484 hotel rooms. In 2008 there were 302,879 arrivals by air (compared with 291,503 in 2007) and some 1,553,053 cruise visitors (compared with 1,715,666 in 2007). The USA remained the core market for stay-over visitors to the islands (79.4% in 2008). In 2007 the tourism industry earned an estimated US $479m.

Cayman Islands Department of Tourism: Cricket Sq., POB 67, George Town, Grand Cayman KY1-1102; tel. 949-0623; fax 949-4053; internet www.caymanislands.ky; f. 1965; Dir SHOMARI SCOTT (acting).

Cayman Islands Tourism Association (CITA): Largatos Bldg, 73 Lawrence Blvd, POB 31086 SMB, Grand Cayman; tel. and fax 949-8522; e-mail info@cita.ky; internet www.cita.ky; f. 2001 as a result of the amalgamation of the Cayman Tourism Alliance and the Cayman Islands Hotel and Condominium Asscn; Pres. KARIE BERGSTROM; Exec. Dir KEN THOMPSON.

Sister Islands Tourism Association (SITA): POB 187, Cayman Brac KY2-2101; tel. and fax 948-1345; e-mail sita@candw.ky; internet www.sisterislands.com; Pres. PETER HILLENBRAND (acting).

Defence

The United Kingdom is responsible for the defence of the Cayman Islands.

Education

Schooling is compulsory for children between the ages of five and 15 years. It is provided free in 16 government-run schools, and there are also 10 private schools. Primary education, from five years of age, lasts for six years; in 2007/08 enrolment at primary schools included an estimated 85% of pupils in the relevant age-group. Secondary education is for seven years; enrolment at secondary-level institutions in 2007/08 included an estimated 81% of students in the relevant age-group. There were also 381 children enrolled at pre-primary schools in 2008. The Cayman Islands Law School, Community College of the Cayman Islands, University College of the Cayman Islands and the International College of the Cayman Islands number among providers of tertiary level education in the territory. Budgetary spending on education in 2009/10 was approved at US $176.3m.

CHILE

Geography

PHYSICAL FEATURES

The Republic of Chile occupies the narrow strip of territory between the Andes and the Pacific in the southern part of South America. The country is 4,329 km (2,688 miles) in length, but never more than 180 km in width, and its border along the mountainous Continental Divide is primarily with Argentina (5,150 km in extent). The north of the country (Atacama was gained from Bolivia in the 1880s, although that country still pursues a claim for a sovereign corridor to the Pacific through Chile) has a western frontier with land-locked Bolivia (861 km of border) and a short northern one with Peru (160 km). Chile has an issue with Peru over maritime economic boundaries, otherwise its only other territorial dispute concerns its claim in Antarctica (which conflicts with Argentine and British claims). Chile has a total area of 756,096 sq km (291,930 sq miles—excluding the 1.25m. sq km of the Antarctic claim).

Chile includes many of the clustered islands into which the continent disintegrates in the south-west and in the eastward flick of its tail, as well as an often deeply indented shore, so that it has a total coastline of 6,435 km. The country also includes a number of islands in the Pacific proper—notably Isla de Pascua (Easter Island or Rapa Nui—the most distant, at 3,790 km west of the north-central mainland), but also Sala y Gómez, Islas de los Desventurados and Archipiélago Juan Fernández. The first is famous for the isolated Polynesian civilization that flourished here long before the arrival of Europeans and erected the great stone statues (moai), and the last includes one island named for a shipwrecked sailor (Alexander Selkirk) and another for the fictional character he inspired (Robinson Crusoe).

Chile itself consists of the narrow lands west of the Andes, from the Atacama Desert in the north to the Patagonian icefields. It is a geologically unstable area, with earthquakes common and volcanoes active in the mountains, and the coasts are sometimes struck by tsunamis. The arid north is dominated by some of Chile's highest mountains, where the main Andean cordillera is at its widest and includes broad plateaux and soaring peaks (including the country's highest, Ojos del Salado—6,893 m or 22,615 ft—on the border with Argentina). Here the country forms the Atacama Desert, reputedly the driest in the world, but also rich in minerals and, especially, nitrates. Central Chile, with its more Mediterranean-type climate, sees a clear definition between the main line of the Andes and the lower coastal range, with an intervening Central Valley. The Andes are lower and narrower here, pierced by the best passes to the east, and the coast has many good harbours. Between is the Central Valley, some 40–80 km in width, with fertile, deep alluvial soils, particularly between the Aconcagua and Bío-Bío rivers (from just north of Santiago, the capital, south to Concepción). South of Puerto Montt the interior valley or plateau between the Andean and coastal ranges disappears beneath the sea, the coastal mountains continuing as a mass of islands off shore, itself untidy with fjords and inlets. Archipelagic Chile extends from Chiloé all the way down to Tierra del Fuego (of which Argentina has the eastern part) and the Isla Hornos, with its famous Cabo de Hornos (Cape Horn). On the mainland, the Andes are lower than in the north (seldom more than 1,800 m), the lowlands forming the desolate, undulating plains of Patagonia that sweep down to the tip of the continent and over into Argentina. Apart from areas of permanent ice (the Patagonian ice cap is reckoned to be the largest after those of Antarctica and Greenland), this is a steppe country of coarse grasses and shrubs, while the north of Chile is a true desert, with very little vegetation at all. The vegetation of the central regions ranges, however, from cacti and scrub in the north to some dense rainforest south of Valdivia. Flora and fauna is not as rich in Chile as it is beyond the high Andes, although the coastal waters are teeming with life. The rivers, all short and steep (vital to irrigation and electricity generation), have few fish (mainly the introduced trout) and few of the larger birds common on the continent are found here. However, there is a Chilean pine (with edible nuts), and animal species include the llama, the alpaca, the chinchilla, the Andean wolf, the puma, the huemal (a large deer) and the pudu (a small deer).

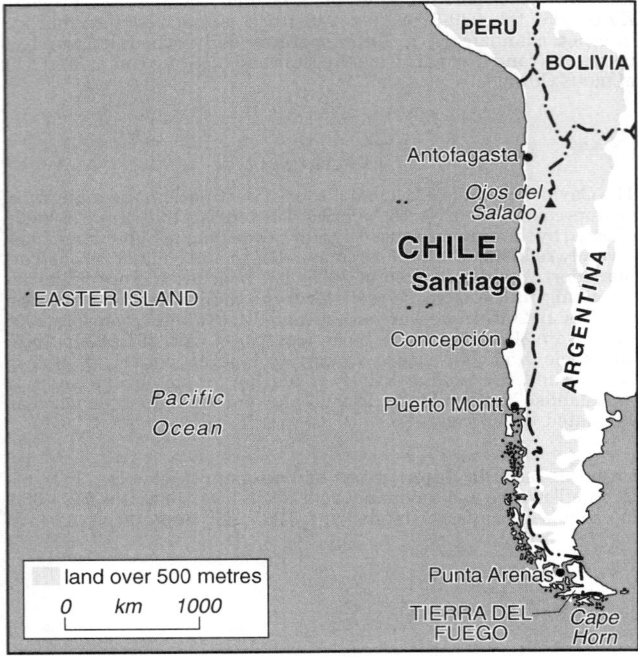

CLIMATE

The climate is very varied across such a long country, but is generally moderated by oceanic influences. The northern region is one of the driest areas of the world, although temperatures are moderated by the cold offshore Humboldt or Peru Current. Average temperatures at Antofagasta range from 12°–16°C (54°–61°F) in July up to 18°–23°C (64°–73°F) in January, but rainfall is only 2 mm (barely 0.1 ins) per year. Rainfall increases southwards, reaching 360 mm (14 ins) at Santiago in the Central Valley, where it falls mainly in the winter months of May–August. The winters, apart from being fairly wet, are mild, and the summers are cool. The average temperatures range from 3°–15°C (37°–59°F) in July to 12°–29°C (54°–84°F) in January. In the south it is a temperate marine climate, cooler and still wetter, with rain falling fairly evenly throughout the year and reaching levels of, at most, about 5,000 mm (much falling as snow) near the Straits of Magellan. Strong winds and cyclonic storms are common. The annual average temperature at Punta Arenas is 7°C (45°F).

POPULATION

The early, mainly Spanish, settlers from Europe intermarried with the local Amerindians (predominantly the Araucanian Mapuche tribes, who boast of never having succumbed to the Quechua-speaking Incas), and mixed-race Mestizos now comprise well over 90% of the population. Subsequent European immigration was not as important to Chile as to many other South American countries, although immigration by Germans to the Valdivia–Puerto Montt area was influential, and other groups to make a significant contribution were from the United Kingdom, France, Italy, Switzerland, Austria and the former

Yugoslavia. Only about 2% of the population is now unmixed European. According to the 2002 census, 4.6% of the total population claimed to be unmixed Amerindians. The latter are principally Mapuche (87% of the ethnic minority total), who survive mainly in the south, with some Aymará in the north (7%) and the Polynesian-descended Rapa Nui (1%) on Easter Island. There are a few other groups, including the aboriginal peoples of Patagonia and Tierra del Fuego. The official language, however, and that in almost total use is Spanish. Some of the other European-descended groups retain some use of their ancestral languages, but the aboriginal languages, including the seven Araucanian dialects, are struggling to survive. Most of the population is Roman Catholic, with about 70% acknowledging adherence, but Protestants (in Chile defined as all non-Roman Catholic Christians except for the Orthodox, Mormons, Seventh-day Adventists and Jehovah's Witnesses) claimed 15%. There is a relatively high figure of 8% given for those expressing no religious affiliation.

According to official estimates, the total population was 17.1m. in mid-2010. Some 90% of the population lived in the central region. About one-third of the total population lived in and around the capital city alone. Greater Santiago had a population of 4.7m. at the 2002 census, with the next largest city being just to the south-west of the capital proper—Puente Alto (492,915). Other major population centres are Antofagasta, in the north, the neighbouring cities of Viña del Mar and Valparaíso, on the coast to the north-west of Santiago, and Talcahuano and Concepción, also close to each other, mid-way down the central region. The country is divided into 15 regions.

History

SANDY MARKWICK

In 1536, when Diego de Almagro arrived to pave the way for the Spanish colony of Santiago, an indigenous population of around 500,000 inhabited the land that was to become Chile. The Inca empire had extended its reach as far south from Cusco (Cuzco) as the Maule river in the centre of modern Chile, but could not overcome fiercely resistant Mapuche Indian communities. The Mapuche resisted European colonialism too, but as occurred elsewhere in the Americas, indigenous Indians (Amerindians) were subjugated by disease and superior military force. Intermittent armed conflict with central government in post-colonial Chile persisted into the late 19th century. Colonial Chile, a distant and geographically isolated territory of the Spanish crown, had a minor economic role, principally focused on producing fruit and grains for export by sea to Lima.

INDEPENDENCE

War in Europe unleashed the forces of independence in Chile. Napoleon Bonaparte's invasion of Spain led landowning oligarchs in Chile to forge self-government while ostensibly remaining loyal to the imprisoned Spanish King, Ferdinand VII. Modern Chileans commemorate independence on 18 September, although the events of that day in 1810 were less decisive: a junta of Criollo (Creole) leaders issued a declaration of self-government and simultaneously declared loyalty to the ousted Spanish King.

Self-rule escalated into demands for permanent, full-scale independence. Internecine conflict among local élites stemmed from regional tensions, personal rivalries and arguments between conservatives and liberals over the role of the Roman Catholic Church. Conflict descended into civil war between the forces of José Miguel Carrera and Bernardo O'Higgins Riquelme, whose fragile truce could not resist Spanish royalist forces from the Viceroyalty of Peru resuming control following the Battle of Rancagua in 1814.

Independence forces exiled in Argentina came under the command of José de San Martín, who led an expedition over the Andes in early 1817 and dealt a decisive blow for independence at Maipú in April 1818. San Martín's ambitions extended beyond independence for Chile to liberation of all of the Americas and he prepared his forces to fight against the Viceroyalty in Lima.

O'Higgins assumed dictatorial powers in Chile and focused on restoring order in remaining royalist strongholds and eradicating support for rivals. O'Higgins was a controversial leader whose authoritarian tendencies alienated liberals within the oligarchy, while his attempts to restrict the powers of the Church and to reform the system of land tenure aroused the opposition of conservative and landowning interests. In 1823, with the state virtually bankrupt, troops loyal to rival oligarchic interests both north and south forced his resignation. Instability and intermittent civil war continued after the exile of O'Higgins as rival élite factions dominated by anti-clerical liberals competed for control with conservatives and regional military leaders (*caudillos*).

AUTOCRATIC REPUBLIC, 1831–91

Conservative Domination, 1831–61

Following a military defeat of forces loyal to the Liberal President Ramón Freire Serrano at Lircay in 1830, an era of domination by conservative factions commenced, which lasted until 1861. A merchant from Valparaíso, Diego Portales, although never assuming the presidency, was the power behind the scenes until his assassination in 1837.

Portales brokered a new Constitution in 1833, which centralized government by granting sweeping powers to the President over elections, the legislature, judiciary and public appointments throughout the country. The military was brought under civilian control and its successes in a war against the Peruvian-Bolivian Confederation in 1836–39 instilled in the young country a sense of national identity. Meanwhile, Portales repealed liberal reforms that had targeted Church privileges, thereby reinforcing its loyalty and underpinning the Church's role as an institution of social control.

Divisions within Chile's ruling classes centred on the degree of power centralized in the office of the President in Santiago and the privileged role of the Church. Despite abortive attempts by liberals to remove conservatives from power in 1835, 1851 and 1859, the Constitution of 1833 gave Chile a period of relative stability in 19th century South America. The Constitution survived until 1925, albeit with amendments reducing presidential powers in 1891. Fundamental to Chile's relative stability was the small and homogeneous ruling class interconnected by ties of family and commerce. Regional, church-state and, to a lesser extent, ethnic tensions were less acute in Chile than elsewhere in South America. Stability during this period proved to be a springboard for territorial expansion and economic development. The construction of ports and railways, increased immigration and advances in education accelerated trade, modernization and growth.

Liberal Domination, 1861–91

A realignment of political forces saw a succession of Liberal Presidents from the middle of the century to 1891. Reforms were introduced gradually. Church control was reduced in education and with the introduction of civil registrations of births, marriages and deaths. Power transferred peacefully between successive Liberal Presidents serving a single term: Federico Errázuriz Zañartu (1871–76); Aníbal Pinto Garmendia (1876–81); and Domingo Santa María González (1881–86).

During the 19th century mining, not agriculture, was the leading force in the economy. Agricultural exports suffered from the long distances to key markets and from competition from Argentina. Silver and copper production grew rapidly from the 1840s and by 1870 Chile controlled approximately 25% of the world copper market.

Tensions with Chile's northern neighbours over the activities of Chilean nitrate mining operations in disputed territory led to the War of the Pacific (1879–83). Chile was victorious and gained territory in the north from Peru and Bolivia. Chile also acquired valuable deposits of nitrates, which became the country's leading export, used for fertilizer and explosives, and the main driver of the economy until the First World War. Foreign investors, mostly European, owned two-thirds of nitrate fields by 1884.

The pattern of peaceful transitions of power ended dramatically with civil war during the term of President José Manuel Balmaceda. The Congreso (Congress), which had gradually claimed increased authority over the budgets and ministerial appointments, led a rebellion against the President's attempts to bypass congressional influence. Balmaceda had proposed that a public works programme be paid for using taxes raised from the nitrate industry. His plans were met with opposition in the Congreso from northern mining interests allied to the Catholic hierarchy and landowning and merchant élites controlling parliament.

Opposition in the Congreso received support from the bulk of the navy, under Capt. Jorge Montt Alvarez, while the army was predominantly loyal to Balmaceda. Northern rebel forces supported by foreign-dominated mining interests mobilized to sail south to depose the President and defeated the army near Valparaíso before taking Santiago. Balmaceda sought refuge in the Argentine embassy, where he committed suicide.

PARLIAMENTARY REPUBLIC, 1891–1925

The new President, Jorge Montt, took office with the Congreso now strengthened in its powers over the executive, particularly in relation to its authority over cabinet appointees. This period in Chilean history was characterized by the expansion of suffrage and the growing importance of new parties representing a more urbanized electorate of middle-class and skilled workers and provincial élites. Despite this, the Congreso remained largely dominated by landowning élites, who controlled local elections through patronage, corruption and intimidation of rural voters.

After 1900 workers became more militant as they made demands for wages to protect them from inflation. Labour unrest peaked in 1917–20. The system of government was increasingly under strain as Chile transformed into an urbanized society whose population was suffering under the strains of spiralling inflation and the country's dependence on volatile nitrate exports, which had declined markedly with the outbreak of the First World War (international trade was interrupted and Germany was forced to develop artificial alternatives).

In this context President Arturo Alessandri Palma took office in 1920, representing an alliance of reformist liberals, radicals and democrats. Once in power a Conservative Congreso blocked his legislative agenda, which featured a proposed labour code and social welfare reform. The deadlock led to agitation by military officers and demands for improvements in military salaries. Alessandri left the country and thus a long period of civilian government was interrupted by the military junta that took charge. The junta was divided, and in January 1925 a faction favouring the restoration of Alessandri to the presidency took control. Alessandri's return to office in March was short-lived (he was deposed again by the military), but during his tenure the Constitution of 1925 was ratified, which made official the separation of church and state and gave workers the legal right to organize. The President was to be directly elected and the power to select cabinet appointees shifted from the legislature, now bi-cameral, to the executive.

Labour reform governed industrial relations up until the early 1970s. Union activity was permitted but restricted and subject to government controls. Unions relied on political party allies to lobby on their behalf, as the state became the mediator in industrial disputes.

Col Carlos Ibáñez del Campo, the most powerful political figure during this time, formally assumed the presidency in 1927. He expanded the role of the state, promoting industry and the modernization of infrastructure, and the economy initially expanded as a result, until it was affected by the Great Depression of 1929–31. Rapid economic decline led to mass unemployment, falling government revenues and growing deficits. Ibáñez's orthodox economic response to the crisis and his use of repression led to widespread unrest and his eventual exile in Argentina in 1931.

CIVILIAN DEMOCRACY, 1925–73

A period of short-lived Governments, including a 12-day 'Socialist Republic' led by Marmaduke Grove, eventually led to a third period in power for Arturo Alessandri after his victory in the 1932 elections. Economic recovery followed increased public spending, expansion of the money supply, a shift to import tariffs to nurture domestic industry and a revival of copper exports.

Alessandri's presidency marked the beginning of one of the longest periods of stable civilian government in South America. The fragmentation of the party system led to highly competitive elections and effective government required participation in coalitions. Electoral participation was high and results respected. Initially it was a restricted democracy, with only middle- and upper-class males enfranchised. Voting was extended to women in 1949, and to landless rural labourers and the urban poor with the introduction of universal suffrage in 1970.

Once the reforming alternative to the forces of conservatism, Alessandri turned the powers of the state to control the threat posed by organized labour and leftist parties. The Frente Popular, a coalition of communists, radicals, socialists and unions, united in opposition to the Government and in 1938 its candidate, Pedro Aguirre Cerda, won a narrow victory in the presidential election, with 50.3% of the vote.

In power, the Frente Popular Government pursued the development of a mixed economy and a goal of national industrial expansion using high tariffs for imports to make domestic manufacturing viable and provide government credit to new enterprises. Modernization rather than radical redistribution was the priority.

The Frente Popular was a heterogeneous coalition, which proved difficult to maintain. After it disbanded its followers supported two Radical Party presidencies, namely those of Juan Antonio Ríos Morales (1942–46) and Gabriel González Videla (1946–52). These Governments were pragmatic in balancing demands for radical social reform from left-wing groups with a need to appease landowning interests in the Congreso. They maintained a prohibition on unionization of rural labour, mindful of preventing a pretext for military intervention.

A broad consensus behind populist development strategies of the 1930s and 1940s could be forged in a context of economic growth and development. However, divisions widened with economic stagnation and high inflation, and as demands for social reform threatened landowning interests in rural areas represented by conservatives and liberals.

Jorge Alessandri Rodríguez, the son of former President Alessandri, was elected to the presidency in 1958, representing a conservative-liberal alliance. Salvador Allende Gossens, the candidate of the Frente de Acción Popular (FRAP—Popular Action Front), a coalition of socialists and communists, came second, polling 29% of the votes. Eduardo Frei Montalva of the Partido Demócrata Cristiano (PDC—Christian Democratic Party), came third, with 21%. The PDC promoted economic and social reform, but stood against liberalism's emphasis on the individual and the collectivism and atheism of Marxism. The PDC displaced the radicals as the party of the centre. A more ideological organization, it was less inclined to seek coalition and reflected a hardening of positions across the political spectrum.

A three-way split of the electorate in the 1958 elections between left-wing, right-wing and centre parties dictated electoral politics in Chile into the early 1970s. With increased voter registration the FRAP and the PDC both had high expectations that they could increase their vote from the urban poor and landless labourers, with promises of land reform, in the 1964 elections.

The PDC won the election of 1964, with Frei once again as its presidential candidate, by persuading the conservative-liberal alliance to support it in order to prevent a Marxist victory. Frei received 55.7% of the votes to Allende's 38.6%, promising a 'revolution in liberty', a reformist programme, to distinguish his programme from that advocated by the FRAP.

The electoral coalition with the conservative-liberal alliance did not survive into government and Frei encountered an opposition-dominated legislature. Frei's programme involved popular expansionary measures to increase consumption and production. However, he was forced into a retreat when confronted with inflation and increasing militancy on the part of unions.

Frei was the first Chilean President to implement an agrarian reform bill. Despite its agricultural potential Chile imported substantial volumes of food produce. Land distribution was uneven and land use inefficient, and the difficulties of sustaining an existence in the countryside led many rural poor to move to the cities during the 1950s. The law came into effect in 1967 after obstacles from both conservatives, representing landowners, and left-wing groups that felt it was not sufficiently radical.

Under the new law large estates were divided, and expropriated lands given to rural workers, but by 1970 only 21,000 landless peasant families had benefited from the reform, far short of the 100,000 target. This was the result of a combination of bureaucracy, technical problems and obstructionism by landowners. The disappointments assisted Allende in attracting the votes of the rural poor in 1970, while alienating conservative élites.

Another major plank of the Frei Government was the 'Chileanization' of the mining sector, a centrist option falling short of nationalizing mines, which were owned and operated predominantly by foreign companies. The law introduced by Frei authorized the Government to buy 51% of the shares of the largest mine owned by the Braden Copper Co. Frei was taking care not to scare away foreign investors and was criticized heavily by left-wing interests for being too moderate.

The Presidency of Salvador Allende

The PDC nominated Radomiro Tomic, a founding father of the party on its left wing, as its presidential candidate in 1970. The conservatives and liberals had formed a single party, the Partido Nacional (PN—National Party), in 1966, and nominated Jorge Alessandri as its candidate. Allende again represented the left, whose Unidad Popular (UP—Popular Unity) coalition had supplanted the FRAP. With the PN and the PDC fighting separately, Allende secured the presidency, winning 36.6% of the votes cast.

Allende's objectives centred on creating a mixed economy, placing major enterprises under state control while leaving untouched small retail operations and companies upon which the state depended for the supply of technology. Allende's intention was to build an alliance of the middle and working classes by expanding the state sector and increasing mass consumption while targeting the privileges of the élite.

The UP Government nationalized certain foreign-owned operations, sometimes without compensation. Nationalist sentiment had grown and Frei's Chileanization policy was perceived as a failure. Some foreign companies were bought at book value, while others were allowed to continue to operate unaffected where the goods and services they provided were considered essential.

Chile became a highly politicized society. Workers mobilized independently of the Government to occupy firms, demanding nationalization and thereby accelerating the process. Nationalizations alienated the PDC as well as the USA under President Richard Nixon, who used his considerable influence to isolate Chile from the international economy. The USA halted new credit to Chile in a bid to force Allende to request moratoriums on debt repayments (which he did in 1971) and to undermine the country's credit rating. A severe shortage of financing ensued as loans from multilateral institutions stopped and direct investment from overseas receded.

Allende accelerated and deepened the agrarian reform that Frei had initiated, partly prompted by a wave of land seizures. In 1965 some 55% of agricultural land was part of farms exceeding 200 acres; by 1973 only 2.9% of land was on private estates of this size. Land expropriations went ahead faster than the Government's ability to provide credit, access to services and equipment needed by co-operatives or small landowners.

An initial series of populist measures, including price freezes and wage increases, led to a consumer boom and a short-term redistribution of wealth. Real income for Chilean workers increased by an average 40% in 1971. Gross domestic product (GDP) grew rapidly and there was full employment, while inflation fell to 20%. During this early phase the UP attained its greatest popularity, winning 49.7% of the votes cast in the 1971 local elections.

However, problems began to appear from 1972. GDP declined by 5% as private firms responded negatively to price controls and the threat of expropriation, while the state did not have resources to invest. In response to a widening fiscal deficit, Allende increased the money supply. Meanwhile, an overvalued currency, a rise in imports to meet consumer demand, capital flight and a 30% drop in copper prices contributed to a US $315m. trade deficit in 1971, following a $91m. surplus in 1970. Agricultural production fell, the effect of low prices, a lack of investment and administrative bottlenecks. Price controls contained inflationary pressures in 1971, but prices rose rapidly in 1972 and increased by 190% in the first nine months of 1973.

There was a huge voter turn-out in the March 1973 congressional elections. The PN and the PDC sought to win two-thirds of the seats to allow them to impeach Allende. In fact, the UP increased its share of the national vote to 43%, the first time in Chile that a governing party had increased its vote mid-term, but its gains were not sufficient to win majority control in the Cámara de Diputados or in the Senado.

The Nixon Administration, implacably opposed to Allende's regime, generously aided the Chilean military and provided covert assistance to opposition groups in a bid to destabilize the Government. Opposition groups mobilized protests, strikes and workplace lock-outs from 1972, paralysing the Chilean economy, which was concentrated on copper and trucking industries.

The Allende Government provides an illustration of the difficulties of introducing radical socialist reform in a pluralist democracy, as it requires the government to attract support beyond organized urban labour and landless peasants, necessitating groups within the middle classes and independent traders to oppose traditional élite agricultural and industrial interests. As Chile became increasingly polarized and tensions rose, so too did the threat of military intervention, particularly as it became clear that attempts by Allende to negotiate with the Congreso had failed.

THE PINOCHET DICTATORSHIP

On 11 September 1973, in a well-planned military overthrow, the air force attacked La Moneda (the presidential palace), where Allende was making a last stand, having refused offers of exile. Allende died inside the palace, where he is widely believed to have committed suicide. The coup was organized by a military junta, featuring the army, navy, national police and the air force. The Commander-in-Chief of the Army, Gen. Augusto Pinochet Ugarte, soon emerged as the dominant figure.

On assuming control, the military began purging government and civilian institutions of UP sympathizers at local and national level. The military junta closed the Congreso, censored the media, ousted suspected opponents from positions in schools and universities and banned union and political party activities. Institutions were dismantled and replaced, thenceforth under the direct authority of the military. The goal was stabilization through brutal repression and the imposition of a bureaucratic-authoritarian regime intent on remaining in power for an indefinite period. The most egregious human rights abuses took place in the first four years of the dictatorship, when thousands were murdered, jailed, tortured and exiled.

Pinochet consolidated his position by assuming dictatorial powers. He declared himself head of state and commander-in-chief of the armed forces, and improved pay and conditions in the military to secure its loyalty. His control of appointments ensured that by 1980 all active-service generals owed him their positions.

The economic goals of the Pinochet regime represented a radical shift from the past. From 1975 neo-liberal policies were accelerated and deepened under the control of a cadre of civilian radical advocates of free market reform. They were known as the 'Chicago Boys' because many had been trained at the University of Chicago (USA), where they had come under the influence of neo-liberal thinkers Milton Friedman and Friedrich von Hayek. The regime determined to reduce the role of the state in the economy through privatizations, tariff reductions and reduced public spending. Until 1981 this resulted in notable economic success. The fiscal deficit was virtually eliminated, the economy grew strongly and inflation fell from around 500% at the time of the coup to 10% in 1982. Nevertheless, economic success came at the cost of high unemployment and regressive redistribution of wealth, while foreign debt increased massively, to US $17,000m., the highest in the world per caput, as the Government sought capital from international organizations and bilateral aid.

By 1982 the initial success of growth and falling inflation was over and in its place came recession and bankruptcies. The problems were compounded by a decline in international copper prices and by the international debt crisis. Recovery during the late 1980s was based on an export boom encouraged by a highly competitive real exchange rate and low tariffs. In contrast to the *laissez-faire* policies of the 'Chicago Boys', which had led to currency appreciation, economic policy was more pragmatic from the mid-1980s, involving active macroeconomic management to achieve exchange-rate stability. Chile diversified exports and markets, which contributed to the country achieving one of the highest GDP growth rates in Latin America.

A new constitution drafted under Pinochet in 1980 (and implemented in 1981) was designed to re-establish a semblance of civilian government while simultaneously entrenching the military's position by giving it a supervisory role in government and creating a weak legislature. Notably, the Constitution limited the power of the Congreso by preventing it from initiating legislation that required budgetary approval, and ensured that further constitutional reform was virtually impossible by creating nine seats in the Senado (one-third of the total) for nominees of the regime. The Constitution planned for a distant restoration of civilian rule. It provided for a referendum in 1988 on whether Pinochet would remain in charge for a further eight years, and also stipulated that Pinochet would remain Commander-in-Chief of the Army for a period of eight years after relinquishing the presidency.

The regime took steps to control any future transition to civilian government and attempted to ensure that the military would retain significant power and influence to protect its members from prosecution. Among these were the amnesty law of 1978, preventing prosecution for human rights crimes between 1973 and 1978, Pinochet's own continued position as head of the army, the lack of civilian control over military appointments and the existence of non-elected senators appointed by the military who could block constitutional reform. A protracted return to civilian rule ensued for much of the 1980s. Civil society and political activity slowly became more openly active as support for authoritarianism diminished with the economic crisis and international pressure for a return to democracy.

RESTORATION OF CIVILIAN GOVERNMENT

In the referendum held in October 1988, in accordance with the 1981 Constitution, 55% of the electorate voted for a return to civilian democracy, obliging the regime to hold elections within one year. In 1989 consensus was reached between the right-wing Partido Renovación Nacional (RN–National Renewal) and the Concertación de Partidos por la Democracia (CPD–Coalition of Parties for Democracy), a centre-left coalition of 17 anti-Pinochet groups, regarding further constitutional reform. These reforms would reduce the presidential term to four years, increase the number of senators from 26 to 38 (thereby diminishing the influence of the nine non-elected senators) and require a two-thirds majority in the Congreso for amendments to the Constitution. The reforms were endorsed in a referendum later that year.

The Government of President Aylwin, 1990–94

In the presidential election of December 1989 Patricio Aylwin Azócar, representing the CPD, was the victor. Aylwin was a member of the PDC, which, along with the Partido Socialista de Chile (PS—Chilean Socialist Party), was the dominant party within the coalition. He took office on 11 March 1990.

In economic policy Aylwin showed that times had changed since the 1932–70 period of civilian government. Where his predecessors in the PDC had advocated price controls, high tariff barriers and economic nationalism, Aylwin's presidency was to mark the start of a new consensus in civilian politics towards a social democratic model of moderately redistributive policies allied to macroeconomic prudence and trade liberalism. Aylwin placed emphasis on the market, not the state, as the key driver of the economy. To this end, he maintained the broad thrust of the economic policies of the military regime's later years, although increases in public spending were funded through tax rises rather than financed by deficits.

How best to remove the vestiges of military rule was an issue for Aylwin and his successors, as was the best way to tackle unsolved human rights crimes. Aylwin created the Truth and Reconciliation Commission (Comisión Nacional de Verdad y Reconciliación) to investigate human rights abuses by the military. The exercise was a compromise designed to establish the facts and to identify victims entitled to compensation, but which was not intended to lead to prosecutions. The Commission documented nearly 3,000 deaths at the hands of the regime. Pinochet resisted attempts to force his resignation and the armed forces remained loyal to him. The Commission was limited in its scope from the outset, its main success being that it ended the legal limbo that families of the 'disappeared' found themselves in, and that it undermined the military's interpretation of this period of Chilean history, forcing it to defend its actions. Aylwin declared the period of reconciliation over in 1991, although the scars in Chilean society remained visible for many years.

The Government of President Frei, 1994–2000

The presidential election of December 1993 resulted in a convincing victory, with 58% of the votes cast, for another CPD candidate, Eduardo Frei Ruiz-Tagle, a PDC Senator and son of former President Frei. In concurrent elections to the Congreso, the CPD failed to win the two-thirds majority required to amend Pinochet's 1981 Constitution.

While progress towards full civilian democracy was secure, tensions with the military persisted over its autonomy and budgets, its influence in government institutions and investigations into human rights crimes. Pinochet retired from the army at 83 years of age in March 1998 and assumed his seat as Senator-for-life, which thus granted him immunity from prosecution. This was to be tested in October when, on a private visit to the United Kingdom, Pinochet was arrested following an extradition request from a Spanish judge investigating human rights abuses against Spanish citizens during his regime. The Chilean Government protested at the arrest on the grounds that he was protected by diplomatic immunity. Following protracted legal and diplomatic deliberations, the British judicial authorities released Pinochet in March 2000, citing ill health as preventing the former dictator from understanding trial proceedings.

The Pinochet affair in the United Kingdom was hugely controversial in Chile and illustrated lingering divisions within Chilean society over the military dictatorship. The episode forced Chile to re-examine the period of dictatorship and the extent to which it had achieved reconciliation under restored civilian rule.

The Government of President Lagos, 2000–06

CPD candidate Ricardo Lagos Escobar narrowly defeated Joaquín Lavín Infante of the right-wing Alianza por Chile (APC—Alliance for Chile), formed in 1999 as a successor to the Unión por Chile, in a second-round ballot for the presidency in January 2000. It was illustrative of the strength of civilian government in Chile that victory for Lagos, a member of the PS, did not raise fears of military intervention. It was also a sign of the pragmatism and consensual politics that had replaced the ideological divisions that characterized civilian politics before Pinochet. Like Frei before him, Lagos pursued pragmatic liberal economic management and consensus. He maintained a policy of fiscal prudence, signed numerous bilateral free trade agreements (FTAs) and sought private investment to upgrade basic infrastructure via build-operate-transfer concessions. He also secured significant health reform.

The contentious issue of military privileges was settled during the Lagos presidency. A Supreme Court ruling revoked Pinochet's parliamentary immunity in August 2000, shortly after his return from detention in the United Kingdom. Pinochet faced charges of tax evasion, kidnapping and murder, although claims and counterclaims about whether he was fit to stand trial were protracted. Pinochet resigned as Senator-for-life in 2002. Residual institutionalized military authority over civilian government was brought to an end when, in 2004, the Supreme Court overturned the amnesty law of 1978, which had protected members of the armed forces, a move which opened the way for investigations into multiple human rights abuses. Finally, Chile's transition to full democracy was completed with the constitutional reform of 2005, which eliminated seats for non-elected senators and senators-for-life.

The Government of President Bachelet, 2006–10

Strong economic growth boosted the popularity of the Lagos Government and helped ensure the CPD was victorious in the presidential election in December 2005, the fourth consecutive victory for the coalition. The CPD candidate, Michelle Bachelet Jeria, won 46.0% of the votes cast, while the right-wing vote was split between Sebastián Piñera Echeñique of the RN, who secured 25.4% of the vote, and Joaquín Lavín of the Unión Demócrata Independiente (UDI—Independent Democratic Union), with 23.2%. Bachelet won a second-round contest in January 2006, winning 53.5% of the votes to Piñera's 46.5%. Bachelet, the first female President of Chile, was inaugurated in March for a newly reduced four-year term of office. Despite her affiliation to Nueva Izquierda (New Left, a faction within the PS), Bachelet was a modern social democrat intent on promoting social reforms while maintaining fiscal orthodoxy and price and exchange-rate stability.

Congressional elections held simultaneously with the first ballot for the presidency secured majorities for the CPD in both the Cámara de Diputados, with 65 out of 120 seats, and the Senado, where it won 11 seats, bringing its total to 20 out of 38 seats. Bachelet was the first of the post-Pinochet civilian Presidents to benefit from a majority in the Congreso, partly a consequence of the abolition of seats for non-elected senators. However, she had to deal with a more fractious alliance than her predecessors. The consensus politics that had characterized four successive CPD presidential terms since the end of military rule had, in part, reflected the political will to consolidate civilian democracy; with the vestiges of the military regime dismantled, tensions over the management of the economy and the routine concerns of mature civilian politics increasingly came to the surface.

Following a strike and the occupation of schools by secondary school students in May 2006, the Government announced a series of immediate measures to enhance education infrastructure and promised further reform, made public in April 2007, to improve funding and the quality of teaching. The protest was the largest popular mobilization since the return of civilian democracy.

Further pressure on the Bachelet Government stemmed from a series of corruption scandals involving CPD politicians under the Lagos administration, which only came to light at the end of 2006. President Bachelet responded by swiftly announcing measures to improve transparency in public administration.

In September 2006 a new fiscal responsibility law was passed, designed to increase transparency in the rules for managing the fiscal surplus. In 2006, aided by burgeoning copper exports as a result of high global prices, the surplus was equivalent to 7.7% of GDP, affording the Government room for manoeuvre in social investment, including covering its minimum pensions liabilities. The budget for 2007, approved by the Congreso in November 2006, was the most expansionary since the restoration of civilian democracy, with spending set to rise by 8.9% in real terms; however, it remained in line with the fiscal rule of achieving a surplus equivalent to 1% of GDP. The right-wing Alianza por Chile abstained in the congressional vote to approve the budget, the first time since 1990 that the Congreso had failed to reach consensus in support of the budget. In December 2006 the Government published a significant pension reform bill, increasing benefits to the poor and less affluent by providing a universal minimum pension and subsidies for workers' pension contributions.

Bachelet continued the free trade outlook of her predecessors, making Chile one of the most open trading nations in the world. In 2006 Bachelet signed bilateral FTAs with Colombia, Japan, Peru and Panama, and announced that negotiations for additional FTAs had commenced with Australia and Viet Nam. Numerous FTAs were already operational, including those with the People's Republic of China, Canada, the USA and Mexico, confirming Chile's dependence on trade.

Gen. Pinochet died in December 2006. President Bachelet, whose own family had been victims of repression under Pinochet's regime, precluded a state funeral normally given to former Presidents. He was, however, buried with full military honours as a former Commander-in-Chief, at which event the Government was represented by the Minister of Defence. The funeral arrangements were a microcosm of the post-dictatorship compromise in Chile. Pinochet's death was expected to improve the electoral prospects of the opposition Alianza por Chile, which had suffered from close relations between Pinochet and the UDI, one of the Alianza's two constituent parties.

Following the mismanaged introduction of a new integrated transport network in Santiago in February 2007, in March Bachelet issued a public apology and effected her second major cabinet reshuffle. The President was careful to balance the composition of her new Cabinet to spread positions across CPD parties sensitive to internal tensions within the coalition.

The budget approved for 2008 maintained public spending growth of 8.9% in real terms, consistent with spending growth in 2007, and followed a relaxation of the fiscal surplus rule from 1% to 0.5% of GDP from 2008. A more expansionary policy was expected to exert further inflationary pressures already straining from high international food and fuel prices.

In January 2008 the ruling coalition was left with a minority in both legislative chambers, following the PDC decision in December 2007 to expel a senator who had sided with the opposition on an important vote and the subsequent defection of five other PDC deputies who announced plans to form a new centrist political grouping. The Alianza por Chile took control of committees in the Cámara de Diputados for the first time since 1990, chairing 13 of a total of 29.

The Government's declining popularity, in part owing to high prices, energy shortages and crime, and in the face of a resurgent opposition, was evidenced in municipal elections in October 2008, in which the Alianza por Chile made strong gains, receiving the largest share of votes (40.6%—compared with 38.5% for the CPD) and taking control of 142 municipalities (up from 104), including mayoralties previously considered CPD strongholds.

The Government's response to the global economic downturn from early 2009 helped to boost President Bachelet's approval ratings in the middle of that year to their highest level since the start of her administration, according to opinion polls. Popular discontent over the Government's conservative approach to spending windfall earnings from copper exports up to 2008 gave way to appreciation of the fact that strong public finances in 2009 allowed the Government to increase spending significantly, and thus offset the effects of the fall in demand. The budget approved for 2009 increased public spending by 5.7% in real terms, which, although down from 8.9% in 2008, was expansionary when pessimistic GDP growth forecasts were taken into account. In January 2009 the Government announced a US $4,000m. stimulus package comprising spending increases and tax cuts.

In May 2009 the Alianza por Chile formally joined forces with a number of independent politicians, regional groupings and splinter groups formerly aligned with the ruling CPD to form the Coalición por el Cambio (Coalition for Change). Among the new members of the broader opposition coalition was the social-democratic ChilePrimero, which split from the Partido por la Democracia (PPD) in 2007. In an apparent realignment of the Chilean political landscape, the conservative opposition increasingly occupied the centre ground, assisted by the high approval ratings of Piñera, formerly President of the RN and now the candidate of the Coalición por el Cambio.

The Government of President Sebastian Piñera, 2010–

Presidential election were held on 13 December 2009. Piñera secured the highest number of votes in the presidential poll, garnering 44.1% of the ballot, ahead of the candidate of the CPD, former President Eduardo Frei Ruiz-Tagle, who won 29.6% of the vote, and the independent Marco Enríquez-Ominami (formerly of the PS), who gained 20.1%. A fourth candidate, Jorge Arrate MacNiven, representing the communist-led Juntos Podemos Más alliance, attained 6.2% of the ballot. In a run-off election, held on 17 January 2010, Piñera defeated Frei, attracting 51.6% of the total votes.

The result brought to an end 20 years of centre-left dominance of government since the return of democracy. The prospect of a Piñera presidency raised expectations of reforms in the health and education sectors and pro-business reform of labour legislation. However, the new Government's freedom of manoeuvre was constrained by a Congreso finely balanced between Piñera's Coalición por el Cambio and the CPD. In congressional elections held simultaneously with the first ballot for the presidency in December 2009, the Coalición became the largest party in the Cámara de Diputados, securing 58 seats—three short of a majority and one more than the CPD. An agreement with the centrist Partido Regionalista de los Independientes (PRI—Independent Regionalist Party), which had three deputies, gave Piñera's Government a narrow majority in the lower house. In the Senado, the CPD secured 19 of the 38 seats; of the remainder, 16 were won by the Coalición.

The new Government was further constrained by an urgent requirement to lead a reconstruction programme in the aftermath of a devastating earthquake that struck Chile's central region in February 2010. Homes and infrastructure in the Maule and Biobío regions, and particularly in Chile's second largest city, Concepción, were destroyed with damages to homes and infrastructure estimated at US $20,900m. The disaster prompted a large-scale humanitarian response. Outgoing President Bachelet declared a state of emergency and deployed 10,000 soldiers to assist in the relief effort and to maintain order. The disaster forced the new Government's original spending programme to be sidelined even before Piñera had taken office and ensured that reconstruction efforts would dominate spending plans for the duration of his four-year term.

Economy

SANDY MARKWICK

Chile's landmass of 756,096 sq km occupies a distinctive geographic position, extending 4,329 km from the Atacama desert, bordering Peru in the north, to the icecaps of southern Patagonia. The breadth of the country does not exceed 180 km between the Pacific Ocean to the west and the Andes to the east. The fertile Central Valley extends north–south between the Andes and the lower coastal range. Additionally, the Pacific islands of Rapa Nui (Easter Island) and Juan Fernández form part of Chile. The extension of Chile over close to 40° of latitudinal spread and its variation in topography partly account for its mineral wealth and climate diversity, with heavy rainfall in the south distinct from the temperate Central Valley and the extremely arid north.

Chile is located on a fault line dividing the Nazca and South American tectonic plates, rendering it prone to earthquakes. In February 2010 an earthquake measuring 8.8 on the moment magnitude scale (MMS) struck off the coast of the central Maule region, causing serious damage throughout central Chile (home to 80% of the population), including the capital, Santiago, in the north of the affected zone. The worst-hit area was Chile's second largest city, Concepción. Hundreds of people were killed, with many more injured and/or made homeless. In addition to the direct human casualties, the earthquake had a devastating impact on the Chilean economy. The cost of the damages was estimated at US $20,900m., with estimated losses in Chilean gross domestic product (GDP) of $7,600m.

The population in mid-2010 was estimated at 17.1m., with growth rates of 1.0% per year, down from 2.1% in the 1960s. Chile's population is ageing as a result of a slowing population growth rate and increases in life expectancy. Chileans over 40 years of age accounted for an estimated 38.0% of the total population in mid-2010, compared with 27.7% in 1992. Life expectancy at birth was 78.5 years in 2008, up from 63.4 years in 1975. Meanwhile, the rate of infant mortality per 1,000 live births had declined to 9 by 2008, from 78 in 1970. There was significant emigration in the 1970s and 1980s for both political and economic reasons. However, the re-establishment of civilian democracy and a robust economy slowed emigration rates from the 1990s, and in 2007 the net migration balance was close to zero.

Economic activity is concentrated in a central region between the Aconcagua and Bío-Bío rivers, where around two-thirds of the population live and which includes the capital, Santiago, and Chile's other main cities. In 2010 an estimated 50.8% of the population lived in the greater Santiago area and in the neighbouring Valparaíso region. The country has become increasingly urbanized, with 87.1% of the population estimated to be living in towns, compared with 60% in 1960. In recent decades a centralizing tendency has been slowed by strong growth in mining, concentrated in the north, and tourism and non-traditional exports, such as salmon farming and methanol production, in the south.

Standards of living are high in Chile in comparison with the rest of Latin America. GDP per head, estimated at just over US $9,525 in 2009, ranked second after Venezuela. The proportion of Chileans considered poor fell from 38.6% in 1990 to 13.7% in 2006. The large-scale humanitarian impact of the earthquake in February 2010 was expected to interrupt temporarily a trend toward higher living standards. According to official figures, unemployment rose to an average of 7.8% in 2008, up from 7.1% in 2007, reflecting slowing economic activity. The trend continued in 2009, with unemployment rising to an annual average of 9.7%, the highest rate since 2005. Unemployment declined to 8.5% in February 2010, reflecting Chile's emergence from recession in mid-2009.

The improvement in health indicators reflects increased access to drinking water and investment in sewage infrastructure and education as well as a focus on preventative care such as free vaccination. Public spending on health was low under the military dictatorship of Gen. Augusto Pinochet Ugarte (1973–90), but increased markedly after 1990. About two-thirds of health services are provided by the public sector, supported by statutory national health service deductions from employees' gross earnings. A compulsory health insurance policy with a flat-rate premium was approved by the Congreso (Congress) in 2004.

Despite large-scale protests in 2006 by secondary school students demanding increased investment in education, educational standards are high in comparison with the rest of South America. Compulsory school education for a period of eight years reaches 98.5% of the population (up from 80% in 1960) and helped to reduce the adult illiteracy rate to 4.0% in

2008. Data released by the Ministry of Education for 2007 indicated improving overall levels of education: in that year 18% of Chileans aged between 25 and 34 years had completed further education, compared with 11% of the population aged between 45 and 54. Enrolment rates in further education in Chile compare favourably with the South American regional average.

ECONOMIC STRUCTURE, SIZE AND PERFORMANCE

For most of its history, primary exports have been the key component fuelling Chile's economy. With the fertile Central Valley, a long Pacific Ocean coastline and abundant mineral wealth, exports traditionally focused on wheat and leather, fish and mining products. Chile was the world's largest copper producer and a significant producer of gold, silver, molybdenum and nitrates.

Following severe recession in the 1980s, a result of a global debt crisis, low copper prices and large current account deficits, a period of sustained recovery ensued that continued into the 21st century. Increasingly open markets gave a boost to traditional exports and encouraged the development of newer commodities such as fruit, wine and wood products as well as transport and other export services.

An increasingly diversified export sector has been the principal driver of economic growth since the 1980s. A pattern of sustained growth was interrupted in 1999, when the economy contracted by 1.0% as a result of a global economic slowdown and drought in Chile. However, by 2000 growth had been restored, measuring 4.4%. Modest growth averaging 3.2% in 2001–03 reflected a downturn in the global economy. Higher growth rates after 2004 were primarily a result of dramatic increases in international copper prices. The economy grew at an average annual rate of 5.1% in 2004–07, led initially by transport and communications, electricity, gas and water, machinery, basic metals and fishing, with a trend towards slower growth in 2006 as a result of lower investment, faster import growth, high energy costs and a month-long strike at the Escondida copper mine, the world's largest. Growth slowed to 3.2% in 2008, a result of reduced domestic demand stemming from declining consumer confidence amid a downturn in the global economy, higher credit costs and depreciation of the peso. Growth in the fourth quarter of 2008 slowed to 0.2%, with contractions in year-on-year economic activity in November and December. The decline continued into 2009 as Chile followed most economies into recession, registering a contraction of 11.1% during the year to April. Recovery, in which positive growth was recorded, in subsequent quarters resulted in a decline of 1.5% for 2009 as a whole. Total GDP amounted to an estimated US $163,322.5m. in 2009. In that year services contributed 61.8% of GDP, industry 32.9% and agriculture (including fishing) 5.4% (expressed at constant 2003 prices). Damage caused by the earthquake in February 2010 negatively impacted on GDP, contributing to a decline of 1.5% in that month; however, output throughout the year increased by 1.0%, and growth increased further, to 3.8%, in April.

Successive governments since the 1970s have targeted inflation control as a principal pillar of economic policy. The Banco Central de Chile (central bank) set a target range of 2%–4%. Consumer prices increased by an average annual rate of 3.9% in 2006–07. Annual inflation increased to 7.8% in December 2007 as a result of rising international food and energy prices, as well as a harsh winter that affected domestic harvests. Annual average inflation during 2008 rose to 8.7%, but declined after peaking at 9.9% in October. At the end of 2008 the annual inflation rate was 7.1%. The trend in declining prices continued into 2009, in which year the first annual deflation rate was recorded since the 1930s. Weak domestic demand and cheaper imports resulting from an appreciation of the peso, combined with low electricity and food prices and a fall in interest rates, resulted in a decline in prices of 1.4% at the end of the year. Prices began rising again at the start of 2010 owing to restored economic growth and higher fuel prices. In April 2010 the rate of inflation stood at 0.9%.

Total external debt increased steadily, from US $25,700m. in 1995 to $74,807m. in early 2010. Nevertheless, successive governments since the 1980s have prudently managed debt repayments, incurring no penalties on principal arrears. Of the total debt, 81.4% was private sector debt and 76.4% was due for maturity in the long term.

MANUFACTURING AND CONSTRUCTION

Adjustment to a new competitive environment after protective tariff barriers were dismantled in the 1970s proved difficult for some domestic industries, notably textiles, and with low levels of investment the contribution of industry to GDP declined from the mid-1970s until the early 1990s. Recovery from the mid-1990s saw the contribution of industry to GDP increase by an average 4% per year. The best performing sub-sectors during this recovery period were petrochemicals and plastics, basic metals, paper and transport equipment. Manufacturing output grew by an average annual rate of 3.6% in the period 2001–05. Output was static in 2006 across all sub-sectors, but growth, of 3.1%, was restored in 2007, led by capital goods manufacturing, which grew by 18.5%. In 2007 the print and paper sub-sector was the most dynamic, growing by 18.4% during that year as a result of the entry into operation of two large cellulose plants. In 2008 the manufacturing sector overall was again static. The best performing sub-sectors were metal products, machinery and equipment, which grew by 3.4% during the year, and print and paper, which grew by 3.1%. The global downturn reduced demand in manufacturing, output of which declined by 6.7% in 2009, with consumer goods the worst-performing category. Machinery manufacturing, textiles and metals ranked among the worst-performing sub-sectors.

Construction output grew by an average annual rate of 4.7% during 2001–06, by 5.4% in 2007 and by 9.7% in 2008, led by investments in the mining and energy sectors. Sectoral output declined by 5.2% in 2009, a consequence of reduced investment, itself stemming from overall recession in the economy. Construction's share of the employed labour force was 8.8% in 2008, while the sector's contribution to total GDP in 2009 was 7.5%. Manufacturing accounted for 13.0% of jobs in 2008 and contributed an estimated 12.0% of GDP in 2009, compared with 15.0% in 2008 and 16.3% in 2007.

MINING

Northern Chile is rich in minerals. Chile has approximately 30% of the world's proven reserves of copper as well as significant reserves of nitrates, molybdenum, selenium, iodine and gold. Deposits are of high quality and close to the surface, making exploitation easier, while the short distances to the coastal ports facilitate exports of mining products. Since the early 1980s Chile has been the largest copper producer in the world. In 2006 the country produced 5.4m. metric tons of refined copper, equivalent to 36% of global output.

A three-fold increase in output since 1990 was the result of large-scale investment, dominated by the private sector, although the Corporación Nacional del Cobre de Chile (Codelco), the state copper concern, also expanded its operations. The largest mine, La Escondida, located in the northern Atacama desert, was owned mostly by British and Australian interests (Rio Tinto and BHP Billiton, respectively). It was opened in 1990, and, following expansion in 2001–02, became the world's largest copper mine, with an annual capacity of 1.2m. metric tons of fine copper. Further investment in copper installations, including US $11,500m. from Codelco, was set to increase capacity by 2012. The mining sector contributed an estimated 6.7% to total GDP in 2009, unchanged from 2008 but down from 7.3% in 2007, and engaged just 1.5% of the employed labour force in 2008.

A copper boom since 2003, on top of the growth of the 1990s, was fuelled by demand from the USA and the People's Republic of China. In that year the average price of copper rose by 14.1%; it increased further, reaching record highs, by rates of 61.2% in 2004, 28.4% in 2005 and 82.7% in 2006. Prices peaked at close to US $4 per pound in April 2008, but declined rapidly after August, reaching less than $1.50 per pound in December.

The spectacular increase in international copper prices was largely responsible for an increase in copper export earnings that averaged 63.2% during 2004–06; export earnings increased by a further 15.5% in 2007, to reach a record US $37,583m. In response to the high copper prices and export earnings, the Government introduced a reform of the tax regime in March 2006, in order to tax operating profits and reduce the ability of companies to use technical 'loopholes' to shelter earnings.

Offsetting the positive benefits of the boom was an appreciation of the peso, which undermined the competitiveness of other exports. The value of the peso rose in real terms by 11.7% in 2004, 8.5% in 2005 and 5.8% in 2006, and reached a 10-year high of 431 pesos to the US dollar in March 2008. This, together with declining copper prices as a result of the global economic downturn from the second half of 2008, contributed to a decrease in the value of copper exports in 2008 and 2009, by 12.9% and 16.5%, respectively. In the latter year copper exports totalled US $27,454m., representing 52.4% of total merchandise export revenue and 90.1% of total mining sector exports in that year. Meanwhile, molybdenum exports fell by 15.2% in 2008, and by a further 59.2% in 2009 to reach $1,330m. in the latter year, down from a record high of $3,845m. in 2007. Mining exports declined by 11.9% in 2008, and by a further 20.2% in 2009, to reach US $30,461m. in the latter year.

As well as reducing tax revenues accruing to the Government from mining companies, falling copper prices also reversed the trend in peso appreciation, and in the second half of 2008 the exchange rate fell to 680 pesos to the dollar. The peso recovered modestly to 564 to the dollar in May 2009, bolstered by confidence in the Government's expansionary response to the downturn. The appreciation continued into 2010, with the peso trading at 520.62 to the dollar in April 2010, having fallen back slightly from 500.66 in January. The decline in copper prices also allayed concerns that aluminium and plastic alternatives to copper would be developed more quickly, fears that had recalled the decline of Chile's nitrate industry in the early 20th century.

ENERGY SUPPLY

Chile is a significant net energy importer, a consequence of having modest hydrocarbon reserves estimated at 155m. metric tons of low-quality coal, 45,000m. cu m of natural gas and less than 30m. barrels of petroleum, located off shore in the extreme south. Thermoelectricity, largely using imported fuel, accounted for an estimated 61.6% of the country's installed energy capacity and 57.2% of electricity generation in 2009, with hydroelectricity making up the remainder. Alternative energy generation, including wind power, was statistically insignificant. Thermoelectricity generation relied mostly on natural gas, and to a lesser extent coal and diesel fuel. Heavy rainfall and mountainous topography in the south provides huge potential to generate energy from hydroelectricity. However, installed power-generating capacity from hydroelectric installations, at 5,014 MW in 2007, was just 21% of its 24,000 MW potential as estimated by the National Energy Commission (Comisión Nacional de Energía—CNE). There were plans to build four hydroelectric dams in the southern Aisén region, which would provide a total capacity of 2,430 MW. The project, located in an area of exceptional natural wilderness, provoked opposition from environmental groups.

Chile needs an estimated 7,000 MW of new generating capacity to keep pace with demand up to 2015. Reliance on hydroelectricity and imported fuel makes power supplies vulnerable to periods of low rainfall and external forces. In response to Chile's energy insecurity, President Michelle Bachelet Jeria created a ministerial position to head the CNE in 2007 to focus on combating the problem. The Minister of the CNE, Marcelo Tokman Ramos, intended to make progress in expanding electricity generation and transmission capacity. Plans were made to diversify the sector in order to reduce dependence on a narrow range of sources and to meet the shortfall in energy supplies. The CNE announced a schedule of investment in new generation and transmission capacity up to 2015. The plan included increasing generating capacity by 2,000 MW through new coal-based installations and by 1,905 MW through plants fuelled by liquefied natural gas (LNG). Construction of an LNG port terminal, which was to have a daily capacity to convert LNG back into gas of 10m. cu m, at Quintero, near Santiago, was initiated, and the terminal began operations in 2009. Meanwhile, as a temporary solution, the Government encouraged the installation of small-scale diesel generators. The GDP of the electricity, gas and water sector rose by 15.7% in 2009, following a fall in output during 2007–08 that had been attributable to a reduced supply of imported gas from Argentina and drought.

SERVICES

In 2008 some 64.6% of the employed labour force was engaged in the service sector, principally in tourism, retail and financial services. The retail sector is modern, highly competitive and dominated by domestic chains that have expanded into operations in other Latin American countries. Retail operations engaged an estimated 19.9% of the employed labour force in 2008. Chile's diverse range of scenery, particularly the unspoilt lakes and fjords in the south, along with opportunities for skiing, beach and mountaineering holidays, attract large numbers of visitors and support a robust tourism sector. There were 2.7m. visits from abroad in 2008, representing an average annual increase of 12.5% since 2003. The contribution of the tourism sector, manifested in demand for transport, travel services, hotels and restaurants, was estimated to be 3.1% of GDP in 2006. Chile earned an estimated US $2,030m. from overseas visitors in 2008. A total of 55.9% of visitors came from neighbouring countries (Argentina, Bolivia and Peru), while 9.4% came from North America and 14.9% from Europe. Visitors from further afield typically spent more than visitors from neighbouring countries, reflecting the greater average length of stay. European visitors accounted for 28.4% of tourism revenues, compared with 19.1% contributed by North American visitors and 21.6% by visitors from neighbouring countries.

The country's sophisticated financial services sub-sector outperformed other areas of the economy in 2004–06, and increased by an average of 5.9% in 2001–07 and by a further 1.2% and 4.6% in 2008 and 2009, respectively. Around 608,000 people, or 9.6% of the labour force, were employed in financial services in 2008. Chile introduced a private pension scheme in 1980, based on individual accounts and private pension fund administration, which was a model for pension reform for other governments in South and Central America as well as in Eastern Europe; however, critics highlighted the number of Chileans who were unable to make sufficient contributions and remained outside the system.

Banks in Chile are prudently capitalized under the supervision of the Superintendencia de Bancos e Instituciones Financieras. Many foreign and national banks operate in the country, holding total deposits of 67,530,090m. pesos in March 2010, up 1.4% during the previous 12 months. Total stock market capitalization in 2008 amounted to US $231,106m., representing an increase of 42% compared with the previous year; by April 2010 this figure had increased to $242,157m. Share transactions totalling $41,577m. took place in 2009, an annual increase of 7.3%.

Financial deregulation has helped nurture dynamic capital markets, with a wide range of financial services available. Deregulation of capital markets was implemented in December 2001 to increase liquidity and encourage savings and investment. A second reform ('MK2'), approved by the Congreso in March 2007, included measures to promote the development of a risk capital industry through tax incentives and greater flexibility in investment regulations. The reform also targeted deregulation to help develop mutual funds and markets in derivatives and bonds.

TRANSPORT AND COMMUNICATIONS

Transport infrastructure and internal transport services are well developed. Private investment through build-operate-transfer (BOT) concessions has led to a modern motorway network serving the central region where most of the population lives, as well as urban toll roads. There were 17,269 km of paved roads in 2007.

The state railway company, Empresa de los Ferrocarriles del Estado (EFE), formerly managed a rail network extending from Iquique in the far north to Puerto Montt in the south. Shorter lines extended west–east connecting main towns. New investment was limited. Freight services were privatized in 1995, as was Ferronor, the northern railway division, in 1996, but plans to sell other parts of the network were abandoned under President Ricardo Lagos Escobar, who increased funds for EFE to modernize central and southern services.

A large network of airports, including 17 that host scheduled commercial routes, complements the road and rail infrastructure and is particularly useful to shorten travel times, given Chile's considerable distances and mountainous terrain. Foreign investment increased the capacity of Santiago's international airport terminal threefold following a BOT concession awarded in 1997. A second runway was added in 2005. BOT concessions were also awarded to expand the most important regional airports, thus releasing government funds for investment in smaller airports.

In 1999 the Government awarded BOT concessions to modernize the ports at Valparaíso, Iquique, San Vicente and San Antonio, the largest in the country, and to build a fifth at Mejillones in the north. Investment was expected to increase annual handling capacity from 28m. metric tons in 2002 to 77m. tons in 2015. Chile has an important merchant marine dominated by Compañía Sud Americana de Vapores (CSAV), which became the principal shipping company in South America with acquisitions of smaller, competitor companies in Brazil and Uruguay.

Telecommunications are the most advanced in the region. Chile had the highest penetration of mobile cellular telephone users, with 88.1 users for every 100 inhabitants in 2007. Fixed-line penetration peaked at 22.3% in 2001 and stood at 21.0% in 2008. The incumbent operator, Telefónica CTC Chile, operating under the Movistar brand, encountered increased competition from new cable television entrants to the market providing 'triple play' services that featured fixed-line telephony and broadband internet access as well as television services. At 8.5 subscriptions per 100 inhabitants in 2008, Chile had the highest broadband internet access rates in Latin America. The transport and communications sub-sector accounted for 8.5% of the employed labour force in 2008.

AGRICULTURE

Diversity in climate and soil type ensures that there is considerable agricultural potential. Furthermore, natural barriers in the form of desert to the north, the Andes to the east and the ocean to the west protect crops and livestock from disease and pests.

Since the 1990s free trade agreements (FTAs) have boosted agriculture and encouraged modern and efficient production processes. Output from cultivation of crops grew faster than the economy as a whole during 2004–07. The sector grew by 8.3% in 2004, by 9.3% in 2005 and by 6.6% in 2006. The performance of the fishing industry was volatile, depending on the annual catch. Fishing output grew by 19.1% in 2004, followed by growth of just 0.9% in 2005 and a contraction of 3.5% in 2006. Slow growth followed in 2007–08, output having been undermined by the Infectious Salmon Anaemia (ISA) virus imported in contaminated salmon eggs. Nevertheless, fishing production growth outpaced that of crops in 2007 and 2008, underpinning overall sector growth of 0.9% and 4.1%, respectively. In 2009 a contraction in fishing output offset moderate growth in crop cultivation, leading to sluggish overall growth in the sector of just 0.5%. Agricultural performance was expected to be hit hard by the earthquake of February 2010, which caused extensive damage to irrigation infrastructure and fishing and forestry production plants. In 2008 11.5% of the employed labour force was engaged in agriculture, hunting, forestry and fishing.

The valleys of central Chile provide excellent conditions for vineyards. Planting and wine-making capacity increased rapidly from the 1980s as Chilean wine secured a growing share of the world wine market. There were 13,947 vineyards producing grapes for wine in 2006, covering 116,792 ha, compared with 11,252 vineyards covering 63,550 ha in 1997. Chile became the world's fifth largest exporter of wine in 2004, having been ranked seventh in 1996. Wine producers in Chile focus on good-quality wine for export principally to the United Kingdom, Canada and the USA. Chile produced 868.8m. litres of wine in 2008, following production of 827.8m. litres of wine in 2007. Chile exported 591m. litres in 2008, a 3.6% decline in terms of volume following a 17.9% increase the year before. Despite the lower volumes, higher prices saw export earnings increase by 9.7% to US $1,378m., following a 30.8% increase in 2007. Wine exports were static during 2009, amounting to $1,381m. Damage caused to wine storage facilities by the February 2010 earthquake resulted in the loss of an estimated 13% of production stock from 2009.

Fruit and vegetable production was boosted by free trade. Chile is one of the most important suppliers of fruit to world markets. Total fruit exports were valued at US $3,011m. in 2009, down 11.1% year-on-year, following growth in the previous two years of 20.7% and 17.0%. The main fruit export was grapes, which earned $1,155m. in export earnings in 2009, down 9.2% during the year, ending a trend of consistent growth since 2000. After grapes, apples, kiwis and blueberries were the most important fruit exports. Olive oil production has risen significantly since 2003, when the domestic market was supplied by imports and there was only a marginal export business. Other important products in the fruit and vegetable sub-sector included peaches, almonds and avocados (some 75% of the 200,000 metric tons produced in 2006 were exported). Access to new markets via FTAs was expected to boost the fruit industry, supported by investment in new plantations.

Although exports of meat are modest, this sub-sector is growing in importance, fuelled by new FTAs. Chile produced 1.5m. metric tons in 2008, up from 1.1m. in 2004. Meat exports earned US $567.7m. in 2005, up 34.3% during the year following an increase of some 61% in 2004. Exports increased slightly in 2006, stemming from the appreciation of the peso as well as bans on beef imported from Argentina and Brazil, where there had been outbreaks of foot-and-mouth disease. Faster growth, of 9.3%, was restored in 2007. Investment is under way to increase meat production capacity. Pork remains the most important product, although its relative share of meat exports has diminished owing to the introduction in 2006 of quotas for the export of beef and poultry to the USA under a bilateral FTA in 2004.

Chile is one of the world's largest suppliers of fish and fish products, although it ranked behind its northern neighbour, Peru. Fishing exports represented an average of 10.7% of total exports during 1995–2005. Regulations introduced in 2002 were designed to limit industrial fishing operations to combat over-fishing. Southern Chile's extensive network of lakes and fjords are rich in salmon. Since the mid-1980s a salmon-farming industry has emerged and, at over 35% of world market share, now rivals Norway's. The most important markets for Chilean salmon were the USA and Japan. Strong production growth during the 1990s led to a fall in international prices and export earnings declined to US $1,538m. in 2001. In response, the industry cut production to restore prices. Export earnings increased to $1,775m. in 2003. An emphasis on higher-value salmon products resulted in a rapid rise in export earnings in 2005, when they increased by 16.7% to $2,518m., compared with an 8% rise in export volumes to 383,700 metric tons. This pattern continued in 2006 when Chile exported 387,141 tons, less than 1% more than the quantity exported in 2005, while earnings rose by 20.4%, to $3,032m. The ISA virus affected the industry from 2007. In 2009 Chile exported 250,000 tons of salmon, according to preliminary estimates, down 52% compared with the previous year. Notwithstanding this massive decline, export revenue decreased by just 17% during the year, assisted by higher international prices. The number of salmon cultivation centres in which the ISA virus was present declined from the end of 2009. However, hopes for a swift recovery in the sub-sector were dealt a devastating blow by the February 2010 earthquake, which caused large-scale damage to tinning and freezing plants. Reconstruction of the sector's infrastructure was expected to take a minimum of one year.

There is an abundance of temperate rainforests, with over 10.5m. ha of protected natural forest and 2.7m. ha planted and managed for wood and wood products. Forestry increased in importance during the late 20th century and by 1993 had become the second largest foreign exchange earner, accounting for 13.1% of total export revenue. Increased investment, supported by government subsidies and a benign tax regime, led to a further expansion of the sector and a shift in emphasis away from the primary resource towards higher value processed products, including cellulose. Processing capacity increased with the construction of new cellulose plants beginning in 2004 in Valdivia, Nueva Aldea and Santa Fe. Cellulose exports rose by 14.3% in 2006, by 73.8% in 2007 and by a further 8.2% in 2008 to reach US $2,366m. in the latter year. Exports declined by 23.2% in 2009 to $1,978m. Earthquake damage in February 2010 caused widespread disruption to production in the forestry industry; however, all plants were expected to resume normal operations by October. Meanwhile, investment in forestry brought the industry into conflict with environmental groups opposed to the displacement of natural forest by faster-growing non-native trees, and with Mapuche Indians over land rights.

FOREIGN TRADE

From its colonial origins until the 1930s, Chile was a trading nation whose economy relied on exports. Primary resources or products with minimal processing dominated exports. Fish, wheat and leather products were significant, but the most important exports were minerals, particularly nitrates until the First World War, copper and gold.

From the 1930s governments introduced protective import tariffs to create a domestic market for Chilean manufacturing and to nurture a domestic industrial base. Chile reverted to an export-led growth model in the mid-1970s, resulting in merchandise trade surpluses, which continued into the 21st century. Since the 1990s governments have deepened free trade with a succession of bilateral FTAs, including with the European Union (implemented in 2003), the USA (2004), China (2006) and Japan (2007), making it among the most open in the world economy. Exports of goods and services grew in real terms by an average of 8.4% during the period 1990–2005, while import growth averaged 10.7% during the same period.

Traditional exports, notably copper, dominated and further outstripped other commodities following a boom in copper prices from 2003. Copper accounted for 55.7% of merchandise export earnings in 2006 and 55.5% in 2007. A sharp fall in international prices for copper saw its share of export earnings decline to 49.4% in 2008. Despite a fall in the value of copper exports in 2009, the proportion of copper exports as a proportion of total merchandise exports rose to 52.4% in that year, as global demand for Chilean exports fell during the global economic downturn, resulting in a 19.5% decline in total merchandise exports earnings. However, there was a long-term trend towards diversifying exports. Significant non-traditional exports included cellulose, wood and wood products, fruit, salmon, wine, methanol, meat, seeds and metal-processing equipment.

Imports increased during the 1990s, accompanying economic growth and a rise in foreign direct investment (FDI). In 2009 imports of intermediate goods, including petroleum, represented 55.3% of total imports, while 21.1% of total imports were consumer products and 16.7% were capital goods.

Around 90% of exports were split broadly evenly between markets in Europe, the Americas and Asia. China, which overtook the USA as the largest single market in 2007, took 23.1% of Chilean exports in 2009 (up from 8.8% in 2006), followed by the USA with 11.3% (down from 16.1% in 2006). The third most important export market was Japan, with a 9.0% share of Chilean exports in 2009. The Netherlands was the most important primary European destination for Chile's exports, taking 3.8% of the total in that year, although much of this was transported to other European markets. Imports were less diversified, with Latin America supplying 32.4% of all goods and services entering Chile in 2009. The USA was the single largest source of imports for Chile in 2009, accounting for 18.7% of the total, followed by China with 13.3%. Argentina (11.9%) and Brazil (7.4%) were the next most important suppliers.

A surplus in the country's merchandise trade balance, of US $13,981.5m. was reported in 2009, an improvement on the $8,847m. surplus recorded in 2008, but still significantly down from surpluses of $23,653m. in 2007 and $22,587m. in 2006, which had been underpinned by record copper prices. Nevertheless, a surplus equivalent to 8.6% of GDP was a significant increase from the 5.2% of GDP registered in 2008 (and also stood up well against the comparable figures of 8.8% and 7.7% in 2007 and 2006, respectively), and was the result of the decline in import value outpacing that of exports during the global economic downturn.

Current Account

Chile traditionally had current account deficits constituting a services account deficit and, more significantly, deficits on the income account associated with profit remittances sent overseas by foreign companies. Remittances tended to correlate positively with export performance. During 1999–2003 the average deficit was equivalent to 1% of GDP. During 2004–07 Chile reported current account surpluses stimulated by demand for Chilean exports, particularly copper, from fast-growing China, which resulted in high international prices. The merchandise trade surplus outpaced accompanying growth in remittances by foreign investors, and Chile reported current account surpluses equivalent to 1.1% of GDP in 2005, 3.6% in 2006 and 4.4% in 2007. In 2008 the decline in the trade surplus during the year was not sufficiently offset by improvements in the services and income balances to prevent the current account going into deficit, equivalent to 2.0% of GDP, for the first time since 2003. In 2009 a 31% decline in the value of imports ensured the restoration of a current account surplus, despite a concomitant decline in export earnings. The surplus amounted to US $4,217m., equivalent to 2.6% of GDP.

FOREIGN DIRECT INVESTMENT

Foreign investors were significant protagonists in the economic development of Chile in the 19th century, notably focusing on the nitrate industry. From the 1930s to 1973 a shifting popular consensus increasingly favoured restricting the terms of engagement governing foreign investors' participation in the economy. Antagonism towards foreign investors reached a head during the presidency of Salvador Allende (1970–73), whose socialist experiment included nationalizing several (mainly US) foreign companies, including some without compensation. The confiscation of US-owned assets contributed to the US Government of President Richard Nixon undertaking a campaign to destabilize the Allende regime, to which it was already implacably opposed.

The military dictatorship that took charge in 1973 ushered in an era of free market reform that persisted following the restoration of civilian democracy in 1990. In the 2000s foreign investment continued to be encouraged by a liberal and stable environment as well as dynamism in the economy. Chile's stock of foreign direct investment (FDI) amounted to US $60,600m. in 2005, the highest in Latin America relative to both population size and GDP.

Mining was traditionally the main focus of foreign investment in Chile and continued to be following liberalization from the mid-1970s. Around 33.0% of FDI went into mining operations during 1974–2006, followed by electricity, gas and water utilities (20.5%), manufacturing (12.5%), transport and telecommunications (11.6%) and financial services (10.0%). The USA was the main source of foreign investment, accounting for 25.5% in this period, followed by Spain (22.1%), Canada (15.7%), the United Kingdom (9.0%), Australia (4.9%) and Japan (2.9%).

A decline in FDI inflows followed a peak in the late 1990s, but inflows recovered strongly after 2003, mainly driven by investment in copper (encouraged by high international prices). Direct investment in Chile amounted to US $121,639m. in 2009, up from $99,476m. in 2008. Meanwhile, Chilean companies' investments outside the country amounted to some $41,200m. in 2009, up from $31,763m. in 2008.

OUTLOOK

The Chilean economy remains one of the most developed in Latin America, with living standards among the highest. Chile did not escape the global recession that afflicted most economies in 2008–09, as demand for Chilean exports registered a significant decline. However, the country's sound fiscal position and strong banking system ensured the downturn was relatively mild compared with other regional economies. The Government was well positioned to provide monetary and fiscal stimulus to combat recession and the deteriorating global economy. A conservative approach to windfall earnings from exceptionally high copper prices in 2006–08 meant that the Government had significant international reserves of more than US $21,000m., as well as savings in sovereign wealth funds amounting to $27,000m., to support stimulus initiatives. In January 2009 the Government announced a $4,000m. stimulus package comprising spending increases and tax cuts. Additionally, the central bank eased monetary policy by rapidly cutting base interest rates from 8.25% at the end of 2008 to a record low of 1.25% in May 2009. Positive economic growth returned in mid-2009. In April 2010 year-on-year GDP growth stood at 3.8%. However, the massive earthquake that struck central Chile in February of that year threatened the economic recovery. The incoming Government of President Sebastián Piñera Echeñique, elected in January, was forced to discard his economic plans in favour of a massive reconstruction programme that was likely to occupy his entire four-year term and to rule out hopes of reducing the fiscal deficit. Piñera announced a reallocation of funds from the 2010 budget to tackle immediate issues arising from the earthquake, including the provision of housing and temporary employment. To pay for long-term reconstruction, the Government was expected to access Chile's offshore sovereign fund as well as to introduce temporary corporate tax rises. The relatively minor extent of damage inflicted by the earthquake on major industrial infrastructure provided hope that the lasting economic impact would be minimized. Chile's major ports and airports were largely unscathed, as was the key mining sector, primarily located in the far north of the country.

Statistical Survey

Sources (unless otherwise stated): Instituto Nacional de Estadísticas (INE), Avda Bulnes 418, Casilla 498-3, Correo 3, Santiago; tel. (2) 366-7777; fax (2) 671-2169; e-mail inesdadm@reuna.cl; internet www.ine.cl; Banco Central de Chile, Agustinas 1180, Santiago; tel. (2) 696-2281; fax (2) 698-4847; e-mail bcch@bcentral.cl; internet www.bcentral.cl.

Area and Population

AREA, POPULATION AND DENSITY*

Area (sq km)	756,096†
Population (census results)‡	
22 April 1992	13,348,401
24 April 2002	
Males	7,447,695
Females	7,668,740
Total	15,116,435
Population (official estimates at mid-year)	
2008	16,763,470
2009	16,928,873
2010	17,094,270
Density (per sq km) at mid-2010	22.6

* Excluding Chilean Antarctic Territory (approximately 1,250,000 sq km).
† 291,930 sq miles.
‡ Excluding adjustment for underenumeration.

POPULATION BY AGE AND SEX
(official estimates at mid-2008)

	Males	Females	Total
0–14	1,990,619	1,919,869	3,910,488
15–64	5,692,767	5,719,088	11,411,855
65 and over	614,433	826,694	1,441,127
Total	8,297,819	8,465,651	16,763,470

REGIONS
(2002 census)

	Area (sq km)	Population	Density (per sq km)	Capital
Tarapacá	42,225.8	238,950	5.7	Iquique
Antofagasta	126,049.1	493,984	3.9	Antofagasta
Atacama	75,176.2	254,336	3.4	Copiapó
Coquimbo	40,579.9	603,210	14.9	La Serena
Valparaíso	16,396.1	1,539,852	93.9	Valparaíso
El Libertador Gen. Bernardo O'Higgins	16,387.0	780,627	47.6	Rancagua
Maule	30,296.1	908,097	30.0	Talca
Biobío	37,068.7	1,861,562	50.2	Concepción
La Araucanía	31,842.3	869,535	27.3	Temuco
Los Lagos	48,583.6	716,739	14.8	Puerto Montt
Aisén del Gen. Carlos Ibáñez del Campo	108,494.4	91,492	0.8	Coihaique
Magallanes y Antártica Chilena	1,382,291.1	150,826	0.1	Punta Arenas
Metropolitan Region (Santiago)	15,403.2	6,061,185	393.5	—
Los Ríos*	18,429.5	356,396	19.3	Valdivia
Arica y Parinacota*	16,873.3	189,644	11.2	Arica
Total†	2,006,096.3	15,116,435	7.5	—

* New regions created in 2007 from provinces previously contained within the Tarapacá and Los Lagos regions; census data for these regions has been reallocated, based on the data recorded for the relevant provinces, retrospectively.
† Including Chilean Antarctic Territory (approximately 1,250,000 sq km).

PRINCIPAL TOWNS

(2002 census)

Gran Santiago (capital)	4,668,473	Talca	201,797
Puente Alto	492,915	Arica	185,268
Antofagasta	296,905	Puerto Montt	175,938
Viña del Mar	286,931	Los Angeles	166,556
Valparaíso	275,982	Coquimbo	163,036
Talcahuano	250,348	Chillán	161,953
San Bernardo	246,762	La Serena	160,148
Temuco	245,347	Osorno	145,475
Iquique	216,419	Valdivia	140,559
Concepción	216,061	Calama	138,402
Rancagua	214,344		

Mid-2010 (incl. suburbs, UN estimates): Gran Santiago 5,951,554; Valparaíso 872,591 (Source: UN, *World Urbanization Prospects: The 2009 Revision*).

BIRTHS, MARRIAGES AND DEATHS

	Registered live births*		Registered marriages		Registered deaths	
	Number	Rate (per 1,000)	Number	Rate (per 1,000)	Number	Rate (per 1,000)
1998	270,637	18.3	73,456	5.0	80,257	5.4
1999	263,867	17.6	69,765	4.6	81,984	5.5
2000	261,993	17.2	66,607	4.4	78,814	5.2
2001	259,059	16.8	64,088	4.2	81,873	5.3
2002	251,559	16.1	60,971	3.9	81,079	5.2
2003	246,827	15.6	56,659	3.6	83,672	5.3
2004	242,276	15.1	53,403	3.3	86,138	5.4
2005	242,980	14.9	53,842	3.3	86,102	5.3

* Adjusted for underenumeration.

2006: Live births 231,383 (birth rate 14.1 per 1,000); Deaths 85,639 (death rate 5.2 per 1,000) (Source: UN, *Population and Vital Statistics Report*).

2007: Live births 240,569 (birth rate 14.5 per 1,000); Deaths 93,000 (death rate 5.6 per 1,000) (Source: UN, *Population and Vital Statistics Report*).

Marriages: 58,155 (3.5 per 1,000) in 2006 (Source: UN, *Demographic Yearbook*).

Life expectancy (years at birth, WHO estimates): 78 (males 75; females 82) in 2008 (Source: WHO, *World Health Statistics*).

ECONOMICALLY ACTIVE POPULATION*

('000 persons aged 15 years and over, February–April, preliminary)

	2008	2009
Agriculture, hunting, forestry and fishing	806.5	762.8
Mining and quarrying	93.3	99.1
Manufacturing	880.1	873.7
Electricity, gas and water	37.2	34.7
Construction	582.3	553.6
Trade, restaurants and hotels	1,317.4	1,303.0
Transport, storage and communications	586.4	578.0
Financing, insurance, real estate and business services	589.1	621.0
Community, social and personal services	1,739.5	1,774.1
Total employed	6,631.7	6,599.9
Unemployed	549.2	716.3
Total labour force	7,180.9	7,316.2

* Figures are based on sample surveys, covering 36,000 households, and exclude members of the armed forces. Estimates are made independently, therefore totals are not always the sum of the component parts.

Health and Welfare

KEY INDICATORS

Total fertility rate (children per woman, 2008)	1.9
Under-5 mortality rate (per 1,000 live births, 2008)	9
HIV/AIDS (% of persons aged 15–49, 2007)	0.3
Physicians (per 1,000 head, 2003)	1.1
Hospital beds (per 1,000 head, 2005)	2.3
Health expenditure (2007): US $ per head (PPP)	863
Health expenditure (2007): % of GDP	6.2
Health expenditure (2007): public (% of total)	58.7
Access to water (% of persons, 2008)	96
Access to sanitation (% of persons, 2008)	96
Total carbon dioxide emissions ('000 metric tons, 2006)	60,056.6
Carbon dioxide emissions per head (metric tons, 2006)	3.7
Human Development Index (2007): ranking	44
Human Development Index (2007): value	0.878

For sources and definitions, see explanatory note on p. vi.

Agriculture

PRINCIPAL CROPS

('000 metric tons)

	2006	2007	2008
Wheat	1,404	1,096	1,238
Rice, paddy	160	110	121
Barley	137	56	96
Maize	1,382	1,123	1,365
Oats	435	341	384
Potatoes	1,391	834	966
Sugar beet	2,200	1,518	1,208
Beans, dry	50	19	20
Rapeseed	47	41	67
Cabbages and other brassicas*	63	42	42
Lettuce and chicory*	93	95	95
Tomatoes*	1,250	1,270	1,270
Pumpkins, squash and gourds*	105	110	110
Chillies and peppers, green*	43	22	22
Onions, dry*	385	290	290
Carrots and turnips*	102	100	100
Maize, green*	200	165	165
Watermelons*	57	47	47
Cantaloupes and other melons*	48	46	46
Oranges*	145	155	155
Lemons and limes	168	180	180
Apples*	1,380	1,370	1,370
Pears*	180	160	160
Peaches and nectarines*	295	268	268
Plums and sloes*	260	300	300
Grapes*	2,300	2,350	2,350
Avocados*	220	250	250
Kiwi fruit*	160	170	170

* FAO estimates.

Aggregate production ('000 metric tons, may include official, semi-official or estimated data): Total cereals 3,566 in 2006, 2,823 in 2007, 3,302 in 2008; Total roots and tubers 1,401 in 2006, 844 in 2007, 975 in 2008; Total vegetables (incl. melons) 2,666 in 2006, 2,473 in 2007–08; Total fruits (excl. melons) 5,217 in 2006, 5,337 in 2007–08.

Source: FAO.

LIVESTOCK

('000 head, year ending September)

	2006	2007	2008*
Horses	350*	320	320
Cattle	3,900*	3,789	3,800
Pigs	2,855	2,957	2,960
Sheep	3,400*	3,938	3,950
Goats	735*	739	740
Chickens	97,000*	98,000*	99,000
Turkeys	27,000*	28,000*	28,500

* FAO estimate(s).

Source: FAO.

LIVESTOCK PRODUCTS
('000 metric tons)

	2006	2007	2008
Cattle meat	237.6	241.7	240.3
Sheep meat	11.1	10.3	11.0
Pig meat	467.9	498.7	522.4
Horse meat	9.4	8.6	8.6*
Chicken meat	523.2	485.8	507.0†
Cows' milk	2,400	2,450	2,550
Goats' milk*	9.9	10.0	10.0
Hen eggs	124.3†	137.2†	140.0*
Wool, greasy	10.3*	9.9	9.9*

* FAO estimate(s).
† Unofficial figure.

Source: FAO.

Forestry

ROUNDWOOD REMOVALS
('000 cubic metres, excluding bark)

	2006	2007	2008
Sawlogs, veneer logs and logs for sleepers	18,725	17,866	16,475
Pulpwood	14,283	20,359	23,232
Other industrial wood	209	192	171
Fuel wood	13,488	14,216	14,955
Total	46,705	52,633	54,833

Source: FAO.

SAWNWOOD PRODUCTION
('000 cubic metres, including railway sleepers)

	2006	2007	2008
Coniferous (softwood)	8,378	8,015	7,005
Broadleaved (hardwood)	340	325	301
Total	8,718	8,340	7,306

Source: FAO.

Fishing

('000 metric tons, live weight)

	2006	2007	2008
Capture	3,859.6	3,507.1	3,170.3
Patagonian grenadier	73.4	63.7	73.6
Araucanian herring	440.1	281.4	795.1
Anchoveta (Peruvian anchovy)	995.2	1,393.7	1,116.7
Chilean jack mackerel	1,379.9	1,302.8	896.2
Chub mackerel	368.8	297.2	133.0
Jumbo flying squid	251.0	124.4	145.7
Aquaculture*	759.1	756.1	821.4
Atlantic salmon*	376.5	331.0	388.8
Coho (silver) salmon	118.2	105.5	92.3
Rainbow trout	150.6	164.4	149.4
Total catch*	4,618.7	4,263.2	3,991.7

* FAO estimates.

Note: Figures exclude aquatic plants ('000 metric tons): 336.1 in 2006 (capture 301.1, aquaculture 35.0); 335.8 (capture 312.2, aquaculture 23.7) in 2007; 406.2 (capture 384.6, aquaculture 21.7) in 2008.

Source: FAO.

Mining

('000 metric tons, unless otherwise indicated)

	2006	2007	2008
Copper (metal content)	5,361	5,557	5,330
Coal	674	288	534
Iron ore*	8,629	8,818	9,316
Calcium carbonate	7,145	7,196	7,295
Zinc—metal content (metric tons)	36,238	36,453	40,519
Molybdenum—metal content (metric tons)	43,278	44,912	33,687
Manganese (metric tons)†	37,169	26,808	18,273
Gold (kilograms)	42,100	41,527	39,162
Silver (kilograms)	1,607	1,936	1,405
Petroleum (crude)	1,061	931	966

* Gross weight. The estimated iron content is 61%.
† Gross weight. The estimated metal content is 32%.

Source: US Geological Survey.

Industry

SELECTED PRODUCTS
('000 metric tons, unless otherwise indicated)

	2005	2006	2007
Beer ('000 hectolitres)	4,754	4,518	5,501
Wine*	789	802	792
Soft drinks ('000 hectolitres)	44	107	181
Cigarettes (million)	16,428	18,073	18,654
Non-rubber footwear ('000 pairs)	5,178	3,791	3,928
Particle board ('000 cu metres)	501	522	515
Mattresses ('000)	1,530	1,534	1,535
Jet fuel	574	660	537
Motor spirit (petrol)	2,257	2,482	2,349
Kerosene	89	58	93
Distillate fuel oils	3,534	3,717	3,623
Residual fuel oils	2,306	2,646	2,445
Cement	4,014.0	3,999.6	4,368.5
Tyres ('000)	6,536	4,830	5,254
Blister copper	4,408	2,024	1,936
Refined copper, unwrought	168	158	124
Electric energy (million kWh)	52,484	55,320	58,509

2002 ('000 metric tons, unless otherwise indicated): Refined sugar 532; Wine 562.3*; Cigarettes (million) 13,839; Non-rubber footwear ('000 pairs) 5,280; Particle board ('000 cu metres) 448; Mattresses ('000) 1,126; Sulphuric acid 2,720; Jet fuel 126; Kerosene 152; Residual fuel oils 1,368; Cement 3,522; Blister copper 1,439; Refined copper, unwrought 2,850; Electric energy 45,983m. kWh.

2003 ('000 metric tons, unless otherwise indicated): Wine 668.2*; Cigarettes (million) 13,776; Non-rubber footwear ('000 pairs) 6,257; Mattresses ('000) 1,144; Sulphuric acid 2,866; Cement 3,550; Blister copper 1,542; Refined copper, unwrought 2,900; Electric energy 45,239m. kWh.

* Source: FAO.

Source (unless otherwise indicated): UN Industrial Commodity Statistics Database.

Finance

CURRENCY AND EXCHANGE RATES

Monetary Units
100 centavos = 1 Chilean peso.

Sterling, Dollar and Euro Equivalents (31 May 2010)
£1 sterling = 775.671 pesos;
US $1 = 531.010 pesos;
€1 = 658.841 pesos;
10,000 Chilean pesos = £12.89 = $18.80 = €15.18.

Average Exchange Rate (pesos per US $)

2007	522.464
2008	522.461
2009	560.860

GOVERNMENT FINANCE
(general government transactions, non-cash basis, million pesos)

Summary of Balances

	2006	2007	2008
Revenue	20,060,506	23,533,726	23,442,851
Less Expense	12,254,914	13,788,342	16,043,295
Net operating balance	7,805,592	9,745,384	7,399,556
Less Net acquisition of non-financial assets	1,821,484	2,194,291	2,719,299
Net lending/borrowing	5,984,108	7,551,093	4,680,257

Revenue

	2006	2007	2008
Net tax revenue	13,221,062	16,166,375	16,498,254
Gross copper revenue	4,431,123	4,141,792	3,198,958
Social security contributions	1,050,396	1,148,647	1,289,225
Grants	92,689	44,700	64,662
Property income	363,202	1,002,931	1,197,113
Operating revenue	440,315	465,508	528,119
Other revenue	461,719	563,773	666,520
Total	20,060,506	23,533,726	23,442,851

Expense

Expense by economic type	2006	2007	2008
Compensation of employees	2,760,449	3,107,938	3,544,891
Use of goods and services	1,397,872	1,665,347	1,699,922
Consumption of fixed capital	509,280	566,332	647,842
Interest	539,103	521,302	439,691
Subsidies and grants	3,690,111	4,320,326	5,454,813
Social benefits	3,346,885	3,590,192	4,084,099
Other expense	11,214	16,905	172,037
Total	12,254,914	13,788,342	16,043,295

Source: Dirección de Presupuestos, Santiago.

INTERNATIONAL RESERVES
(US $ million at 31 December)

	2007	2008	2009
Gold (national valuation)	5.4	5.7	8.8
IMF special drawing rights	53.2	56.8	1,147.1
Reserve position in IMF	88.4	167.0	287.1
Foreign exchange	16,695.3	22,848.6	23,847.8
Total	16,842.3	23,078.1	25,290.8

Source: IMF, *International Financial Statistics*.

MONEY SUPPLY
('000 million pesos at 31 December)

	2007	2008	2009
Currency outside depository corporations	2,429.1	2,676.2	2,935.4
Transferable deposits	6,327.4	7,679.7	8,495.3
Other deposits	39,349.2	45,243.6	39,391.5
Securities other than shares	24,239.7	24,582.4	28,538.3
Broad money	72,345.4	80,181.8	79,360.5

Source: IMF, *International Financial Statistics*.

COST OF LIVING
(Consumer Price Index for Santiago; base: 2000 = 100)

	2007	2008	2009
Food (incl. beverages)	120.5	139.8	147.4
Rent, fuel and light	135.7	151.9	154.7
Clothing (incl. footwear)	81.2	81.4	70.8
All items (incl. others)	122.7	133.4	135.3

Source: ILO.

NATIONAL ACCOUNTS
('000 million pesos at current prices, preliminary)

Expenditure on the Gross Domestic Product

	2007	2008*	2009†
Government final consumption expenditure	9,371.7	10,603.2	12,235.6
Private final consumption expenditure	46,870.2	52,808.3	54,795.7
Increase in stocks	602.7	553.8	–2,191.5
Gross fixed capital formation	16,983.4	21,816.5	19,631.6
Total domestic expenditure	73,828.0	85,781.8	84,471.5
Exports of goods and services	40,561.3	39,976.0	34,929.2
Less Imports of goods and services	28,539.5	36,495.2	27,809.5
GDP in purchasers' values	85,849.8	89,262.6	91,591.3
GDP at constant 2003 prices	62,646.1	64,954.9	63,963.5

Gross Domestic Product by Economic Activity

	2007	2008*	2009†
Agriculture and forestry	2,374.2	2,404.9	2,206.3
Fishing	715.7	553.6	651.4
Mining and quarrying	19,567.8	15,665.9	14,157.0
Copper	18,136.0	13,847.0	12,436.0
Manufacturing	11,255.4	11,212.3	11,004.7
Electricity, gas and water	2,205.9	3,159.5	4,320.9
Construction	5,532.6	7,002.2	6,899.3
Trade, restaurants and hotels	6,979.6	7,980.2	8,108.8
Transport	4,440.3	4,672.3	5,018.8
Communications	1,646.5	1,747.4	1,972.2
Financial services‡	11,811.1	13,134.4	13,740.6
Sale of real estate	3,752.4	4,149.2	4,377.7
Personal services§	8,089.0	9,132.7	10,166.7
Public administration	3,200.6	3,640.8	3,868.4
Sub-total	81,571.0	84,455.5	86,492.8
Value-added tax	6,269.0	7,237.3	7,290.0
Import duties	685.8	600.7	555.0
Less Imputed bank service charge	2,676.0	3,030.9	2,746.6
GDP in purchasers' values	85,849.8	89,262.6	91,591.3

* Provisional figures.
† Preliminary figures.
‡ Including insurance, renting of property and business loans.
§ Including education.

BALANCE OF PAYMENTS
(US $ million)

	2007	2008	2009
Exports of goods f.o.b.	67,972	66,464	53,735
Imports of goods f.o.b.	–44,031	–57,617	–39,754
Trade balance	23,941	8,848	13,982
Exports of services	8,962	10,785	8,507
Imports of services	–9,950	–11,656	–9,581
Balance on goods and services	22,954	7,976	12,907
Other income received	6,325	6,296	5,352
Other income paid	–24,950	–19,719	–15,659
Balance on goods, services and income	4,329	–5,447	2,601
Current transfers received	3,857	3,879	2,531
Current transfers paid	–728	–945	–914
Current balance	7,458	–2,513	4,217
Capital account (net)	16	3	15
Direct investment abroad	–2,573	–7,988	–7,983
Direct investment from abroad	12,534	15,181	12,702
Portfolio investment assets	–15,953	–11,615	–13,893
Portfolio investment liabilities	–508	2,773	2,008
Financial derivatives assets	2,608	11,718	8,650
Financial derivatives liabilities	–2,154	–12, 670	–8,945
Other investment assets	–11,098	3,536	–1,772
Other investment liabilities	6,906	6,392	6,766
Net errors and omissions	–449	1,645	–116
Overall balance	–3,214	6,461	1,648

Source: IMF, *International Financial Statistics*.

External Trade

PRINCIPAL COMMODITIES
(distribution by SITC, US $ million, preliminary)

Imports c.i.f.	2006	2007	2008
Food and live animals	2,101.4	2,783.2	3,750.2
Mineral fuels, lubricants, etc.	8,447.8	11,378.7	16,189.1
Petroleum, petroleum products, etc.	7,154.5	9,738.2	13,956.1
Gas, natural and manufactured	888.8	1,126.0	1,281.0
Chemicals and related products	3,921.5	4,723.2	6,423.7
Basic manufactures	4,034.9	4,642.6	6,536.5
Iron and steel	1,023.9	1,119.2	2,234.7
Machinery and transport equipment	11,705.6	13,732.1	17,179.0
Machinery specialized for particular industries	1,482.1	1,863.7	2,285.8
General industrial machinery equipment and parts	1,750.5	2,047.3	2,662.4
Office machines and automatic data-processing equipment	964.6	1,259.3	1,391.4
Telecommunications and sound equipment	1,783.3	1,769.2	1,893.8
Other electrical machinery apparatus, etc.	1,302.2	1,411.9	1,762.3
Road vehicles and parts*	3,436.2	4,245.4	5,176.7
Miscellaneous manufactured articles	3,154.0	3,615.4	4,307.9
Total (incl. others)	38,409.1	46,966.3	61,903.0

* Data on parts exclude tyres, engines and electrical parts.

Exports f.o.b.	2006	2007	2008
Food and live animals	8,008.3	8,834.0	10,362.3
Fish, crustaceans and molluscs and preparations thereof	3,032.4	3,114.4	3,369.4
Vegetables and fruit	3,240.3	3,726.8	4,685.8
Feeding-stuff for animals (excl. unmilled cereals)	568.9	621.9	547.6
Beverages and tobacco	1,010.8	1,313.4	1,451.4
Beverages	980.5	1,279.9	1,403.8
Crude materials (inedible) except fuels	18,416.3	22,936.9	18,909.8
Cork and wood	1,287.1	1,281.8	1,297.3
Pulp and waste paper	1,362.8	2,352.8	2,618.5
Metalliferous ores and metal scrap	15,355.0	18,852.9	14,386.3
Mineral fuels, lubricants, etc.	1,059.7	835.7	949.6
Chemicals and related products	2,557.1	2,417.1	3,279.7
Basic manufactures	23,673.6	27,901.6	26,788.6
Non-ferrous metals	21,246.2	25,127.2	23,555.3
Machinery and transport equipment	806.3	1,039.0	1,155.3
Total (incl. others)	58,116.4	68,295.8	66,455.5

Total imports c.i.f. (revised): 35,899.8 in 2006; 44,030.7 in 2007; 57,609.6 in 2008; 39,707.9 in 2009.

Total exports f.o.b. (revised): 58,680.1 in 2006; 67,665.8 in 2007; 66,455.5 in 2008; 53,024.1 in 2009.

PRINCIPAL TRADING PARTNERS
(US $ million, revised)

Imports c.i.f.	2007	2008	2009
Angola	924.8	1,599.3	38.0
Argentina	3,976.8	4,645.1	4,291.3
Brazil	4,242.9	4,942.9	2,699.3
Canada	924.6	949.3	697.8
China, People's Republic	5,525.3	7,510.1	5,599.9
Colombia	799.2	1,927.6	1,284.5
Finland	234.3	266.0	226.4
France	762.5	892.8	625.6
Germany	1,498.6	1,856.7	1,492.7
Italy	695.1	783.4	720.0
Japan	1,824.8	2,917.8	1,467.4
Korea, Republic	3,022.0	3,020.5	2,087.0
Mexico	1,330.1	1,708.9	1,164.9
Peru	1,674.9	1,840.1	705.5
Spain	811.9	888.5	989.9
Sweden	391.6	485.3	375.2
United Kingdom	358.1	459.9	1,001.0
USA	7,117.0	10,750.1	7,228.1
Total (incl. others)	44,030.7	57,609.6	39,707.9

Exports f.o.b.	2007	2008	2009
Argentina	810.9	992.7	738.7
Belgium	759.9	784.9	843.5
Brazil	3,379.6	3,805.6	2,710.3
Canada	1,184.6	1,393.5	1,191.3
China, People's Republic	10,345.7	9,233.9	12,308.8
Colombia	611.2	713.3	547.4
France	2,378.5	2,192.8	1,232.2
Germany	1,694.0	1,659.1	1,111.5
India	2,194.0	1,343.0	1,025.5
Italy	3,487.9	3,320.2	1,412.4
Japan	7,349.5	6,423.0	4,829.5
Korea, Republic	3,825.1	3,594.9	3,084.5
Mexico	2,355.6	2,202.1	1,430.5
Netherlands	3,984.4	4,213.2	2,030.3
Peru	1,242.4	1,611.7	1,351.1
Spain	1,270.5	1,768.6	1,086.6
United Kingdom	723.6	700.4	610.2
USA	8,700.0	7,929.5	5,939.4
Venezuela	845.3	1,213.0	756.3
Total (incl. others)	67,665.8	66,455.5	53,024.1

Transport

PRINCIPAL RAILWAYS

	2006	2007	2008
Passenger journeys ('000)	18,563	21,239	22,210
Passenger-km ('000)	843,131	731,921	759,367
Freight ('000 metric tons)	25,747	26,616	27,185
Freight ton-km (million)	3,660	3,957	4,293

ROAD TRAFFIC
(motor vehicles in use)

	2007	2008	2009
Passenger cars and jeeps (excl. taxis)	1,701,036	1,825,562	1,905,353
Minibuses and vans	148,423	153,906	156,566
Light trucks	524,206	551,913	567,445
Motorcycles and mopeds	63,257	87,545	96,213

SHIPPING

Merchant Fleet
(registered at 31 December)

	2006	2007	2008
Number of vessels	549	553	551
Total displacement ('000 grt)	935.6	908.1	863

Source: Lloyd's Register-Fairplay, *World Fleet Statistics*.

International Sea-borne Shipping
(freight traffic, '000 metric tons)

	2006	2007	2008
Goods loaded	43,813	44,653	46,386
Goods unloaded	31,226	37,744	40,904

CIVIL AVIATION
(traffic on scheduled services)

	2006	2007	2008
Kilometres flown (million)	128	139	147
Passengers ('000)	7,610.6	9,011.0	9,709.0
Passenger-km (million)	19,681	21,422	23,140
Freight (million ton-km)	4,257	4,185	4,279

Tourism

ARRIVALS BY NATIONALITY

	2007	2008	2009
Argentina	760,708	868,999	1,003,126
Bolivia	271,934	307,902	309,445
Brazil	228,779	261,080	216,801
France	61,069	62,984	63,623
Germany	71,170	75,579	67,592
Peru	252,626	252,573	269,669
Spain	68,557	61,551	56,212
United Kingdom	64,029	63,354	52,702*
USA	204,538	216,280	208,566
Total (incl. others)	2,506,756	2,698,659	2,749,913

* Including only England, Wales and Scotland.

Source: Servicio Nacional de Turismo.

Tourism receipts (US $ million, excl. passenger transport): 1,213 in 2006; 1,478 in 2007; 1,757 in 2008 (provisional) (Source: World Tourism Organization).

Communications Media

	2007	2008	2009
Telephones ('000 main lines in use)	3,459.6	3,526.4	3,575.4
Mobile cellular telephones ('000 subscribers)	13,955.2	14,796.6	16,450.2
Internet users ('000)	5,162.2*	5,456.2*	5,767.1
Broadband subscribers ('000)	1,302.3	1,427.2	1,665.1

* Estimate.

Radio receivers ('000 in use): 5,180 in 1997.

Daily newspapers: 59 in 2004 (average circulation 816,000 copies).

Personal computers: 2,300,000 (141.1 per 1,000 persons) in 2005.

Sources: mainly UNESCO, *Statistical Yearbook*; UN, *Statistical Yearbook*; International Telecommunication Union.

Education

(2004, unless otherwise indicated)

	Institutions	Teachers	Students
Pre-primary		16,528	287,454
Special primary		7,673	92,536
Primary	n.a.*	75,854	2,269,388
Secondary		49,144	989,039
Adult		1,897†	131,237
Higher (incl. universities)†	226	n.a.	567,114

* Many schools offer more than one level of education; a detailed breakdown is given below.

† Figure(s) for 2003.

Schools (2004): Pre-primary: 640; Special 766; Primary 3,679; Secondary 517; Adult 292; Pre-primary and special 10; Pre-primary and primary 3,172; Pre-primary and secondary 1; Special and primary 22; Special and adult 3; Primary and secondary 380; Primary and adult 82; Secondary and adult 156; Pre-primary, special and primary 52; Pre-primary, primary and secondary 1,070; Pre-primary, primary and adult 261; Special, primary and secondary 2; Primary, secondary and adult 49; Pre-primary, special, primary and secondary 13; Pre-primary, special, primary and adult 7; Pre-primary, primary, secondary and adult 106; Pre-primary, special, primary, secondary and adult 5.

2006/07: *Teachers:* Pre-primary 21,858; Primary 66,862; Secondary 67,970; Tertiary 54,649. *Students:* Pre-primary 407,418; Primary 1,679,017; Secondary 1,611,631; Tertiary 753,398 (Source: UNESCO Institute for Statistics).

Pupil-teacher ratio (primary education, UNESCO estimate): 25.1 in 2006/07 (Source: UNESCO Institute for Statistics).

Adult literacy rate (UNESCO estimates): 98.6% (males 98.6%; females 98.7%) in 2008 (Source: UNESCO Institute for Statistics).

Directory

The Constitution

The 1981 Constitution, described as a 'transition to democracy', separated the presidency from the Junta and provided for presidential elections and for the re-establishment of the bicameral legislature, consisting of an upper chamber (Senado) of both elected and appointed senators, who are to serve an eight-year term, and a lower chamber (Cámara de Diputados) of 120 deputies elected for a four-year term. There is a National Security Council consisting of the President of the Republic, the heads of the Armed Forces and the police, and the Presidents of the Supreme Court and the Senado.

In July 1989 a national referendum approved 54 reforms to the Constitution, including 47 proposed by the Government and seven by the Military Junta. Among provisions made within the articles were an increase in the number of directly elected senators from 26 to 38, the abolition of the need for the approval of two successive Congresos for constitutional amendments (the support of two-thirds of the Cámara de Diputados and the Senado being sufficient), the reduction in term of office for the President to be elected in 1989 from eight to four years, with no immediate re-election possible, and the redrafting of the provision that outlawed Marxist groups so as to ensure 'true and responsible political pluralism'. The President's right to dismiss the Congreso and sentence its members to internal exile was eliminated.

In November 1991 the Congreso approved constitutional changes to local government. The amendments provided for the replacement of centrally appointed local officials with directly elected representatives.

In February 1994 an amendment to the Constitution was approved whereby the length of the presidential term was reduced from eight to six years.

In September 2005 constitutional reforms came into force reducing the presidential term from six to four years, abolishing the positions of senators-for-life and appointed senators and providing for a presidential prerogative to dismiss the Commanders-in-Chief of the Armed Forces.

The Government

HEAD OF STATE

President: SEBASTIÁN PIÑERA ECHEÑIQUE (took office 11 March 2010).

THE CABINET
(July 2010)

A coalition of the Renovación Nacional, the Unión Demócrata Independiente and Independents.

Minister of the Interior: RODRIGO HINZPETER KIRBERG (RN).

Minister of Foreign Affairs: ALFREDO MORENO CHARME (Ind.).

Minister of National Defence: JAIME RAVINET DE LA FUENTE (Ind.).

Minister of Finance: FELIPE LARRAÍN BASCUÑÁN (Ind.).

Minister, Secretary-General of the Presidency: CRISTIÁN LARROULET VIGNAU (Ind.).

Minister, Secretary-General of the Government: ENA VON BAER JAHN (UDI).

Minister of the Economy, Economic Promotion and Reconstruction: JUAN ANDRÉS FONTAINE TALAVERA (Ind.).

Minister of Planning: FELIPE KAST SOMMERHOFF (UDI).

Minister of Education: JOAQUÍN LAVÍN INFANTE (UDI).

Minister of Justice: FELIPE BULNES SERRANO (RN).

Minister of Labour and Social Security: CAMILA MERINO CATALÁN (Ind.).

Minister of Public Works: HERNÁN DE SOLMINIHAC TAMPIER (Ind.).

Minister of Health: JAIME MAÑALICH MUXI (Ind.).

Minister of Housing and Urban Development: MAGDALENA MATTE LECAROS (Ind.).

Minister of Agriculture: JOSÉ ANTONIO GALILEA VIDAURRE (RN).

Minister of Mining: LAURENCE GOLBORNE RIVEROS (Ind.).

Minister of Transport and Telecommunications: FELIPE MORANDÉ LAVÍN (Ind.).

Minister of National Property: CATALINA PAROT DONOSO (RN).

Minister of the National Energy Commission: RICARDO RAINERI BERNAIN (Ind.).

Minister of the National Women's Service (Sernam): CAROLINA SCHMIDT ZALDÍVAR (Ind.).

Minister of the National Commission for Culture and the Arts: LUCIANO CRUZ-COKE CARVALLO (Ind.).

Minister of the National Environment Commission: MARÍA IGNACIA BENÍTEZ PEREIRA (UDI).

MINISTRIES

Ministry of Agriculture: Teatinos 40, 1°, Santiago; tel. (2) 393-5000; fax (2) 393-5135; internet www.minagri.gob.cl.

Ministry of the Economy, Economic Promotion and Reconstruction: Avda Libertador Bernardo O'Higgins 1449, Santiago Downtown Torre II, POB 8340487, Santiago; tel. (2) 473-3400; fax (2) 473-3403; e-mail economia@economia.cl; internet www.economia.cl.

Ministry of Education: Alameda 1371, 7°, Santiago; tel. (2) 390-4000; fax (2) 380-0317; e-mail consultas@mineduc.cl; internet www.mineduc.cl.

Ministry of Finance: Teatinos 120, 12°, Santiago; tel. (2) 473-2000; internet www.minhda.cl.

Ministry of Foreign Affairs: Teatinos 180, Santiago; tel. (2) 827-4200; internet www.minrel.gov.cl.

Ministry of Health: Enrique MacIver 541, 3°, Santiago; tel. (2) 574-0100; e-mail consulta@minsal.cl; internet www.minsal.cl.

Ministry of Housing and Urban Development: Alameda 924, POB 6513482, Santiago; tel. (2) 351-3000; fax (2) 633-7830; e-mail contactenos@minvu.cl; internet www.minvu.cl.

Ministry of the Interior: Palacio de la Moneda, Santiago; tel. (2) 690-4000; fax (2) 699-2165; internet www.interior.cl.

Ministry of Justice: Morandé 107, Santiago; tel. (2) 674-3100; fax (2) 698-7098; internet www.minjusticia.cl.

Ministry of Labour and Social Security: Huérfanos 1273, 6°, Santiago; tel. (2) 753-0400; e-mail mintrab@mintrab.gob.cl; internet www.mintrab.gob.cl.

Ministry of Mining: Teatinos 120, 9°, Santiago; tel. (2) 473-3000; fax (2) 698-9262; internet www.minmineria.cl.

Ministry of National Defence: Edif. Diego Portales, 22°, Villavicencio 364, Santiago; tel. (2) 222-1202; fax (2) 633-0568; e-mail correo@defensa.cl; internet www.defensa.cl.

Ministry of National Property: Alameda 720, Santiago; tel. (2) 351-2100; fax (2) 351-2160; e-mail consultas@mbienes.cl; internet www.bienes.cl.

Ministry of Planning (MIDEPLAN): Ahumada 48, 7°, Santiago; tel. (2) 675-1400; fax (2) 672-1879; internet www.mideplan.gov.cl.

Ministry of Public Works: Morandé 59, Of. 545, Santiago; tel. (2) 449-4000; fax (2) 361-2700; internet www.mop.cl.

Ministry of Transport and Telecommunications: Amunátegui 139, 3°, Santiago; tel. (2) 421-3000; fax (2) 421-3552; internet www.mtt.cl.

National Commission for Culture and the Arts: Fray Camilo Henríquez 262, Santiago; tel. (2) 589-7824; internet www.consejodelacultura.cl.

National Energy Commission: Alameda 1449, 13° y 14°, Edif. Santiago Downtown Torre II, Santiago; tel. (2) 365-6800; fax (2) 365-6611; internet www.cne.cl.

National Environment Commission: Teatinos 254/258, Santiago; tel. (2) 241-1800; fax (2) 240-5758; internet www.conama.cl.

National Women's Service (Sernam): Agustinas 1389, Santiago Centro, Santiago; tel. (2) 549-6100; fax (2) 549-6247; e-mail sernam@sernam.gov.cl; internet www.sernam.gov.cl.

Office of the Minister, Secretary-General of the Government: Palacio de la Moneda, Santiago; tel. (2) 690-4160; fax (2) 697-1756; e-mail cmladini@segegob.cl; internet www.segegob.cl.

Office of the Minister, Secretary-General of the Presidency: Moneda 1160, Santiago; tel. (2) 694-5855; fax (2) 694-5888; internet www.minsegpres.gob.cl.

President and Legislature

PRESIDENT

Election, 13 December 2009 and 17 January 2010

	First round % of votes	Second round % of votes*
Sebastián Piñera Echeñique (Coalición por el Cambio)	44.05	51.61
Eduardo Frei Ruiz-Tagle (CPD)	29.60	48.39
Marco Enriquez-Ominami Gumucio (Ind.)	20.13	—
Jorge Arrete MacNiven (Juntos Podemos Más)	6.21	—
Total	100.00	100.00

* Provisional results.

CONGRESO NACIONAL

The Congreso Nacional is located in Valparaíso.

Senado
(Senate)

President: JORGE PIZARRO SOTO (PDC).

The Senado has 38 members, who hold office for an eight-year term, with approximately one-half of the seats renewable every four years. The last election, to renew 18 of the 38 seats, was held on 13 December 2009. The table below shows the composition of the Senado following that election.

Distribution of Seats by Legislative Bloc, December 2009

	Seats
Concertación de Partidos por la Democracia (CPD)/ Juntos Podemos Más*	19
Coalición por el Cambio	16
Independents	3
Total	38

* The CPD and Juntos Podemos Más contested the congressional elections in alliance; however, the Partido Humanista, part of the Juntos Podemos Más grouping, did not participate in the alliance.

Cámara de Diputados
(Chamber of Deputies)

President: ALEJANDRA SEPÚLVEDA ORBENES (PRI).

General Election, 13 December 2009

Legislative bloc	% of valid votes	Seats
Coalición por el Cambio	43.44	58
Unión Demócrata Independiente	—	36
Renovación Nacional	—	19
Independents	—	3
Concertación de Partidos por la Democracia (CPD)/Juntos Podemos Más*	44.36	57
Partido Demócrata Cristiano	—	19
Partido por la Democracia	—	18
Partido Socialista de Chile	—	11
Partido Radical Socialdemócrata	—	5
Partido Comunista de Chile	—	3
Independents	—	1
Chile Limpio Vote Feliz†	5.40	3
Independents	6.77	2
Total	100.00	120

* The CPD and Juntos Podemos Más contested the congressional elections in alliance; however, the Partido Humanista, part of the Juntos Podemos Más grouping, did not participate in the alliance.

† Deputies in this bloc are aligned to the Partido Regionalista de los Independientes.

Election Commissions

Servicio Electoral: Esmeralda 611, Santiago; tel. (02) 731-5500; fax (02) 639-7296; e-mail partes@servel.cl; internet www.servel.cl; f. 1986; Dir JUAN IGNACIO GARCÍA RODRÍGUEZ.

Tribunal Calificador de Elecciones (TCE): Teatinos 391, Santiago; tel. (2) 463-8500; fax (2) 699-4464; e-mail secretaria@tribunalcalificador.cl; internet www.tribunalcalificador.cl; f. 1980; Pres. SERGIO MUÑOZ GAJARDO.

Political Organizations

In late 2009 there were 15 political parties registered with the Servicio Electoral.

Coalición por el Cambio: f. 2009 to support presidential candidacy of Sebastián Piñera; right-wing alliance.

Chile Primero: Moneda 812, Of. 1104, Santiago; tel. (2) 830-3906; e-mail contacto@chileprimero.cl; internet www.chileprimero.cl; f. 2007 by fmr mems of the PPD (q.v.); independent; Pres. ALBERTO PRECHT; Sec.-Gen. EDUARDO BASTÍAS.

Movimiento Humanista Cristiano: Santiago; internet www.mhcchile.cl; Pres. ROBERTO MAYORGA L.; Sec.-Gen. CARLOS PÉREZ O.

Norte Grande: Of. 502, Washington 2562, Antofagasta; tel. and fax (55) 22-8732; internet www.cantero.cl; Leader CARLOS CANTERO OJEDA; Sec. NORMA PLAZA.

Renovación Nacional (RN): Antonio Varas 454, Providencia, Santiago; tel. (2) 799-4200; fax (2) 799-4212; e-mail clarrain@rn.cl; internet www.rn.cl; f. 1988; right-wing; part of the Alianca por Chile coalition (f. 1999) which in turn forms part of the Coalición por el Cambio; Pres. CARLOS LARRAÍN PEÑA; Sec.-Gen. BRUNO BARANDA FERRÁN.

Unión Demócrata Independiente (UDI): Avda Suecia 286, Providencia, Santiago; tel. (2) 241-4200; fax (2) 233-6189; e-mail contacto@udi.cl; internet www.udi.cl; f. 1989; right-wing; part of the Alianca por Chile coalition (f. 1999) which in turn forms part of the Coalición por el Cambio; Pres. JUAN ANTONIO COLOMA; Sec.-Gen. VÍCTOR PÉREZ.

Concertación de Partidos por la Democracia (CPD): Londres 57, Santiago; tel. and fax (2) 639-7170; internet www.primariasconcertacion.cl; f. 1988 as the Comando por el No, an opposition front to campaign against the military regime in the plebiscite of 5 October 1988; adopted present name following plebiscite; Nat. Co-ordinator DOMINGO NAMUNCURA.

Partido Demócrata Cristiano (PDC): Alameda 1460, 2°, Santiago; tel. and fax (2) 376-0136; e-mail info@pdc.cl; internet www.pdc.cl; f. 1957; Pres. JUAN CARLOS LATORRE CARMONA; Sec. MOISÉS VALENZUELA MARTÍNEZ.

Partido por la Democracia (PPD): Santo Domingo 1828, Santiago; tel. and fax (2) 671-2320; e-mail presidencia@ppd.cl; internet www.ppd.cl; f. 1989; Pres. ADRIANA MUÑOZ D'ALBORA; Sec.-Gen. ALEJANDRO BAHAMONDES SAAVEDRA.

Partido Radical Socialdemócrata (PRSD): Londres 57, Santiago; tel. and fax (2) 633-6928; fax (2) 638-3353; e-mail ernestov@123mail.cl; internet www.partidoradical.cl; centre-left; Pres. JOSÉ ANTONIO GÓMEZ URRUTIA; Sec.-Gen. ERNESTO VELASCO RODRÍGUEZ.

Partido Socialista de Chile (PS): París 873, Santiago; tel. (2) 956-6700; fax (2) 956-6719; e-mail pschile@pschile.cl; internet www.pschile.cl; f. 1933; left-wing; mem. of Socialist International; Pres. FULVIO ROSSI; Sec.-Gen. MANUEL MONSALVE.

Juntos Podemos Más: e-mail info@podemos.cl; internet www.juntospodemosmas.cl; electoral alliance comprising:

Izquierda Cristiana de Chile (IC): Compañía 2404, Santiago; tel. (2) 672-9897; internet www.izquierdacristiana.cl; f. 1971; Pres. MANUEL JACQUES PARRAGUEZ; Sec.-Gen. BERNARDA PÉREZ CARRILLO.

Partido Comunista de Chile (PC): Avda Vicuña Mackenna 31, Santiago; tel. and fax (2) 222-2750; e-mail www@pcchile.cl; internet www.pcchile.cl; f. 1912; achieved legal status in Oct. 1990; Pres. GUILLERMO TEILLIER; Sec.-Gen. LAUTARO CARMONA.

Partido Humanista (PH): Livingstone 72, Santiago; tel. (2) 634-2614; e-mail eosorio@humanismo.cl; internet www.partidohumanista.cl; f. 1984; Pres. EFRÉN OSORIO JARA; Sec.-Gen. CÉSAR MONTENEGRO AMPUERO.

Movimiento Amplio Social (MAS): Calle Padre Alonso de Ovalle 720, Santiago; internet www.movimientoampliosocial.cl; f. 2008; contested the 2009 legislative elections in alliance with Fuerza País (q.v.); Pres. FERNANDO ALFREDO ZAMORANO FERNÁNDEZ; Sec.-Gen. FELIPE IGNACIO HAZBÚN MARÍN.

Partido Ecologista: O'Higgins 1104, Concepción; e-mail admin@partidoecologista.cl; internet partidoecologista.cl; f. 2002; Pres. ALEJANDRO IVÁN SAN MARTÍN BRAVO; Sec.-Gen. ISABEL LINCOLAO GARCÉS.

Partido Regionalista de los Independientes (PRI): Avda Miraflores 133, Of. 33, Santiago; tel. (2) 664-8773; internet www.chilepri.cl; f. 2006 following merger of Alianza National de Independientes and Partido de Acción Regionalista de Chile; Pres. ADOLFO ZALDÍVAR LARRAÍN; Sec.-Gen. EDUARDO SALAS CERDA.

Wallmapuwen: e-mail wallmapuwen@gmail.com; internet www.wallmapuwen.cl; f. 2005; campaigns for Mapuche rights; not officially registered; Sec.-Gen. PEDRO GUSTAVO QUILAQUEO.

Diplomatic Representation

EMBASSIES IN CHILE

Algeria: Monseñor Nuncio Sotero Sanz 221, Providencia, Santiago; tel. (2) 820-2100; fax (2) 820-2121; e-mail argelia_embajada@yahoo.fr; Ambassador NOURREDINE YAZID.

Argentina: Miraflores 285, Santiago; tel. (2) 582-2500; fax (2) 639-3321; e-mail embajador@embargentina.cl; internet www.embargentina.cl; Ambassador GINÉS GONZÁLEZ GARCÍA.

Australia: Isidora Goyenechea 3621, El Golf Torre B, 12° y 13°, Casilla 33, Correo 10 Las Condes, Santiago; tel. (2) 550-3500; fax (2) 331-5960; e-mail dima-santiago@dfat.gov.au; internet www.chile.embassy.gov.au; Ambassador VIRGINIA GRAVILLE.

Austria: Barros Errazuriz 1968, 3°, Santiago; tel. (2) 223-4774; fax (2) 204-9382; e-mail santiago-de-chile-ob@bmaa.gv.at; internet www.chile-embajadadeaustria.at; Ambassador WOLFGANG ANGERHOLZER.

Belgium: Edif. Forum, Avda Providencia 2653, 11°, Of. 1103, Santiago; tel. (2) 232-1070; fax (2) 232-1073; e-mail santiago@diplobel.org; internet www.diplomatie.be/santiago; Ambassador DIRK VAN EECKHOUT.

Brazil: Padre Alonso Ovalle 1665, Casilla 1497, Santiago; tel. (2) 698-2486; fax (2) 671-5961; e-mail embrasil@brasembsantiago.cl; internet www.brasembsantiago.cl; Ambassador MÁRIO VILALVA.

Bulgaria: Lota 2284, Providencia, Santiago; tel. (2) 421-1244; fax (2) 421-1245; e-mail embulch@mail.bg; internet www.mfa.bg/santiago; Ambassador VALERI YOTOV.

Canada: Edif. World Trade Center, Torre Norte, 12°, Nueva Tajamar 481, Santiago; tel. (2) 652-3800; fax (2) 652-3912; e-mail stago@international.gc.ca; internet www.canadainternational.gc.ca/chile-chili; Ambassador SARAH FOUNTAIN SMITH.

China, People's Republic: Pedro de Valdivia 550, Santiago; tel. (2) 233-9880; fax (2) 335-2755; e-mail embajadachina@entelchile.net; internet cl.china-embassy.org; Ambassador LU FAN.

Colombia: Isidora Goyenechea 3162, Of. 302, Las Condes, Santiago; tel. (2) 335-9948; fax (2) 335-8469; e-mail esantiag@cancilleria.gov.co; internet www.embajadaenchile.gov.co; Chargé d'affaires a.i. CARLOS JALLER ALVAREZ.

Costa Rica: Zurich 255, Of. 85, Las Condes, Santiago; tel. (2) 334-9486; fax (2) 334-9490; e-mail embacostarica@adsl.tie.cl; Ambassador JAN RUGE MOYA.

Croatia: Ezequias Alliende 2370, Providencia, Santiago; tel. (2) 269-6141; fax (2) 269-6092; e-mail embajada@croacia.cl; Ambassador VESNA TERZIĆ.

Cuba: Avda Los Leones 1346, Providencia, Santiago; tel. (2) 367-9738; fax (2) 367-9745; e-mail emcuchil@embacuba.cl; internet www.embacuba.cl; Ambassador ILENEA DÍAZ-ARGÜELLES ALASA.

Czech Republic: Avda El Golf 254, Santiago; tel. (2) 232-1066; fax (2) 232-0707; e-mail santiago@embassy.mzv.cz; internet www.mfa.cz/santiago; Ambassador ZDENĚK KUBÁNEK.

Denmark: Jacques Cazotte 5531, Casilla 19002, Correo 19, Vitacura, Santiago; tel. (2) 941-5100; fax (2) 218-1736; e-mail sclamb@um.dk; internet www.ambsantiago.um.dk/la; Ambassador KIM HØJLUND CHRISTENSEN.

Dominican Republic: Candelaria Goyenechea 4153, Vitacura, Santiago; tel. (2) 953-5750; fax (2) 953-5758; e-mail embrepdom@erd.co.cl; Ambassador PABLO ARTURO MARIÑEZ ALVAREZ.

Ecuador: Avda Providencia 1979 y Pedro Valdivia, 5°, Casilla 16007, Correo 9, Santiago; tel. (2) 231-5073; fax (2) 232-5833; e-mail embajadaecuador@adsl.tie.cl; internet www.embajadaecuador.cl; Ambassador FRANCISCO BORJA CEVALLOS.

Egypt: Roberto del Río 1871, Providencia, Santiago; tel. (2) 274-8881; fax (2) 274-6334; e-mail embassy.santiago@mfa.gov.eg; Ambassador ASHRAF YOSSEF ZAAZAA.

El Salvador: Coronel 2330, 5°, Of. 51, Casilla 16863, Correo 9, Santiago; tel. (2) 233-8324; fax (2) 231-0960; e-mail embasalva@adsl.tie.cl; internet www.rree.gob.sv/embajadas/chile.nsf; Ambassador AIDA ELENA MINERO REYES.

Finland: Alcántara 200, Of. 201, Las Condes, Casilla 16657, Correo 9, Santiago; tel. (2) 263-4917; fax (2) 263-4701; e-mail sanomat.snt@formin.fi; internet www.finland.cl; Ambassador IIVO SALMI.

France: Avda Condell 65, Casilla 38D, Providencia, Santiago; tel. (2) 470-8000; fax (2) 470-8050; e-mail ambassade@ambafrance-cl.org; internet www.france.cl; Ambassador MARYSE BOSSIÈRE.

Germany: Las Hualtatas 5677, Vitacura, Santiago; tel. (2) 463-2500; fax (2) 463-2525; e-mail info@santigo-de-chile.diplo.de; internet www.santiago.diplo.de; Ambassador MICHAEL GLOTZBACH.

Greece: Jorge Sexto 306, Las Condes, Santiago; tel. (2) 212-7900; fax (2) 212-8048; e-mail embassygr@grecia.cl; internet www.grecia.cl; Ambassador CHRYSSOULA KARYKOPOULOU-VLAVIANOU.

Guatemala: Zurich 255, Of. 55, Las Condes, Santiago; tel. (2) 586-4430; fax (2) 586-4437; e-mail embajada@guatemala.cl; internet www.guatemala.cl; Ambassador LUIS ALBERTO PADILLA MENÉNDEZ.

Haiti: Zurich 255, Of. 21, Las Condes, Santiago; tel. (2) 231-3364; fax (2) 231-0967; Ambassador ROLAND AUGUSTIN.

Holy See: Nuncio Sótero Sanz 200, Casilla 16836, Correo 9, Santiago (Apostolic Nunciature); tel. (2) 231-2020; fax (2) 231-0868; e-mail nunciatu@tie.cl; Apostolic Nuncio Most Rev. GIUSEPPE PINTO (Titular Archbishop of Pandosia).

Honduras: Zurich 255, Of. 51, Las Condes, Santiago; tel. (2) 234-4069; fax (2) 334-7946; e-mail honduras@tie.cl; Chargé d'affaires a.i. CESAR RAÚL MARIN GRANADOS.

Hungary: Avda Los Leones 2279, Providencia, Santiago; tel. (2) 274-2210; fax (2) 234-1227; e-mail huembstg@entelchile.net; internet www.mfa.gov.hu/emb/santiagodechile; Ambassador JÓZSEF KOSÁRKA.

India: Triana 871, Casilla 10433, Santiago; tel. (2) 235-2005; fax (2) 235-9607; e-mail info@embajadaindia.cl; internet www.embajadaindia.cl; Ambassador PRADEEP KUMAR KAPUR.

Indonesia: Avda Nueva Costanera 3318, Vitacura, Santiago; tel. (2) 207-6266; fax (2) 207-9901; e-mail kbristgo@entelchile.net; Ambassador IBRAHIM AMBONG.

Iran: Estoril 755, Las Condes, Santiago; tel. (2) 215-7582; fax (2) 215-7631; e-mail embiranchile@mail.com; Ambassador KAMBIZ JALALI.

Iraq: Alsacia 150, Of. 122, Las Condes, Santiago; tel. 8-1918665 (mobile); e-mail sanemb@iraqmfamail.com; Ambassador TAHA SHOKER MAHMOOD AL-ABASSI.

Israel: San Sebastián 2812, 5°, Las Condes, Santiago; tel. (2) 750-0500; fax (2) 750-0555; e-mail amb.sec@santiago.mfa.gov.il; internet santiago.mfa.gov.il; Ambassador DAVID DADONN.

Italy: Clemente Fabres 1050, Providencia, Santiago; tel. (2) 470-8400; fax (2) 223-2467; e-mail info.santiago@esteri.it; internet www.ambsantiago.esteri.it; Ambassador VINCENZO PALLADINO.

Japan: Avda Ricardo Lyon 520, Santiago; tel. (2) 232-1807; fax (2) 232-1812; e-mail contactoembajadajapon@gmail.com; internet www.cl.emb-japan.go.jp; Ambassador WATARU HAYASHI.

Jordan: Avda Presidente Errazuriz 2999, Of. 202, Las Condes, Santiago; tel. (2) 245-6210; fax (2) 245-6212; e-mail embajadadejordania@manquehue.net; Ambassador IBRAHIM AWAWDEH.

Korea, Republic: Alcántara 74, Casilla 1301, Santiago; tel. (2) 228-4214; fax (2) 206-2355; e-mail coremb@tie.cl; internet chl.mofat.go.kr; Ambassador YIM CHANG-SOON.

Lebanon: Alianza 1728, Vitacura, Casilla 19150, Correo 19, Santiago; tel. (2) 218-2835; fax (2) 219-3502; e-mail libano@vtr.net; Chargé d'affaires a.i. ALEJANDRO BITAR.

Malaysia: Tajamar 183, 10°, Of. 1002, Correo 35, Las Condes, Santiago; tel. (2) 233-6698; fax (2) 234-3853; e-mail mwstg@embdemalasia.cl; internet www.kln.gov.my/perwakilan/santiago; Chargé d'affaires a.i. ANIL FAHRIZA ADENAN.

Mexico: Félix de Amesti 128, Las Condes, Santiago; tel. (2) 583-8400; fax (2) 583-8484; e-mail info@emexico.cl; internet www.emexico.cl; Ambassador MARIO LEAL CAMPOS.

Morocco: Avda Juan XXIII 6152, Vitacura, Santiago; tel. (2) 218-0311; fax (2) 218-0176; e-mail ambmarch@terra.cl; Ambassador ABDELKADER CHAUI LUDIE.

Netherlands: Apoquinado 3500, 13°, Las Condes, Santiago; tel. (2) 756-9200; fax (2) 756-9226; e-mail stg@minbuza.nl; internet www.embajadadeholanda.cl; Ambassador JOHAN VAN DER WERFF.

New Zealand: El Golf 99, Of. 703, Las Condes, Santiago; tel. (2) 290-9800; fax (2) 458-0940; e-mail embajada@nzembassy.cl; internet www.nzembassy.cl; Ambassador ROSEMARY ANNE PATERSON.

Nicaragua: Zurich 255, Of. 111, Las Condes, Santiago; tel. (2) 234-1808; fax (2) 234-5170; e-mail embanic@embajadadenicaragua.tie.cl; Ambassador MARÍA LUISA ROBLETO AGUILAR.

Norway: San Sebastián 2839, Of. 509, Casilla 2431, Santiago; tel. (2) 234-2888; fax (2) 234-2201; e-mail emb.santiago@mfa.no; internet www.noruega.cl; Ambassador MARTIN TORE BJØRNDAL.

Pakistan: Espoz 2336, Vitacura, Santiago; tel. (2) 953-8686; fax (2) 953-8691; e-mail parepsantiao@hotmail.com; Ambassador BURHANUL ISLAM.

Panama: La Reconquista 640, Las Condes, Santiago; tel. (2) 202-5439; fax (2) 202-6318; e-mail embajadapanamachile@vtr.net; Ambassador MERCEDES ALFARO DE LOPEZ.

Paraguay: Huérfanos 886, 5°, Ofs 514–515, Santiago; tel. (2) 639-4640; fax (2) 633-4426; e-mail epychemb@entelchile.net; Ambassador TERUMI MATSUO DE CLAVEROL.

Peru: Avda Andrés Bello 1751, Casilla 16277, Providencia, Santiago; tel. (2) 339-2600; fax (2) 235-2053; e-mail embstgo@entelchile.net; Ambassador CARLOS PAREJA RÍOS.

Philippines: Félix de Amesti 367, Las Condes, Santiago; tel. (2) 208-1313; fax (2) 208-1400; e-mail embassyphil@vtr.net; Ambassador MARÍA CONSUELO PUYAT-REYES.

Poland: Mar del Plata 2055, Santiago; tel. (2) 204-1213; fax (2) 204-9332; e-mail embajador.polonia@entelchile.net; internet www.polonia.cl; Ambassador RYSZARD PIASECKI.

Portugal: Nueva Tajamar 555, Torre Norte 16°, Las Condes, Santiago; tel. (2) 203-0542; fax (2) 203-4004; e-mail embajada@embportugal.tie.cl; Ambassador JOSÉ MANUEL SANTA-MARINHA BELEZA PAES MOREIRA.

Romania: Benjamín 2955, Las Condes, Santiago; tel. (2) 231-1893; fax (2) 232-2325; e-mail embajada@rumania.tie.cl; internet www.rumania.cl; Ambassador VALENTIN FLOREA.

Russia: Avda Américo Vespucio 2127, Vitacura, Santiago; tel. (2) 208-6254; fax (2) 206-8892; e-mail embajada@rusia.tie.cl; internet www.chile.mid.ru; Ambassador YURIY A. FILÁTOV.

South Africa: Avda 11 de Septiembre 2353, 17°, Torre San Ramón, Santiago; tel. (2) 231-2862; fax (2) 231-3185; e-mail info.chile@foreign.gov.za; internet www.embajada-sudafrica.cl; Ambassador DUDUZILE MOERANE-KHOZA.

Spain: Avda Andrés Bello 1895, Casilla 16456, Providencia, Santiago; tel. (2) 235-2755; fax (2) 235-1049; e-mail emb.santiagodechile@mae.es; internet www.mae.es/embajadas/santiagodechile; Ambassador JUAN MANUEL CABRERA.

Sweden: Avda 11 de Septiembre 2353, 4°, Providencia, Santiago; tel. (2) 940-1700; fax (2) 940-1730; e-mail ambassaden.santiago-de-chile@foreign.ministry.se; internet www.embajadasuecia.cl; Ambassador EVA ZETTERBERG.

Switzerland: Avda Américo Vespucio Sur 100, 14°, Las Condes, Santiago; tel. (2) 928-0800; fax (2) 928-0135; e-mail san.vertretung@eda.admin.ch; internet www.eda.admin.ch/santiago; Ambassador YVONNEE BAUMANN.

Syria: Carmencita 111, Casilla 12, Correo 10, Santiago; tel. (2) 232-7471; fax (2) 231-1825; e-mail embajadasiria@tie.cl; Chargé d'affaires a.i. SAMI SALAMEH.

Thailand: Avda Américo Vespucio 100, 15°, Las Condes, Santiago; tel. (2) 717-3959; fax (2) 717-3758; e-mail rte.santiago@vtr.net; internet www.thaiembassy.org/santiago; Ambassador VIPAWAN NIPATAKUSOL.

Turkey: Edif. Montolin, Of. 71, Monseñor Sotero Sanz 55, Providencia, Santiago; tel. (2) 231-8952; fax (2) 231-7762; e-mail embturquia@123.cl; Ambassador MELIN MEHMET AKAT.

United Kingdom: Avda el Bosque Norte 0125, Santiago; tel. (2) 370-4100; fax (2) 370-4180; e-mail embsan@britemb.cl; internet ukinchile.fco.gov.uk; Ambassador JON BENJAMIN.

USA: Avda Andrés Bello 2800, Las Condes, Santiago; tel. (2) 232-2600; fax (2) 330-3710; internet www.usembassy.cl; Ambassador ALEJANDRO DANIEL WOLFF.

Uruguay: Avda Pedro de Valdivia 711, Santiago; tel. (2) 204-7988; fax (2) 204-7772; e-mail urusgo@uruguay.cl; internet www.uruguay.cl; Ambassador JUAN CARLOS PITA ALVARIZA.

Venezuela: Bustos 2021, Providencia, Santiago; tel. (2) 365-8700; fax (2) 223-1170; e-mail embavenez@embajadavenezuela.cl; internet embajadadevenezuela.cl; Ambassador MARÍA LOURDES URBANEJA DURANT.

Viet Nam: Avda Américo Vespucio Sur 833, Las Condes, Santiago; tel. (2) 244-3633; fax (2) 244-3799; e-mail sqvnchile@yahoo.com; Ambassador NGUYEN VAN TICH.

Judicial System

The Supreme Court consists of 21 members.

There are Courts of Appeal (in the cities or departments of Arica, Iquique, Antofagasta, Copiapó, La Serena, Valparaíso, Santiago, San Miguel, Rancagua, Talca, Chillán, Concepción, Temuco, Valdivia, Puerto Montt, Coyhaique and Punta Arenas) whose members are appointed from a list submitted to the President of the Republic by the Supreme Court. The number of members of each court varies. Judges of the lower courts are appointed in a similar manner from lists submitted by the Court of Appeal of the district in which the vacancy arises. Judges and Ministers of the Supreme Court do not continue in office beyond the age of 75 years.

Corte Suprema

Compañía 1140, 2°, Santiago; tel. (2) 873-5000; fax (2) 873-5276; e-mail mgonzalezp@poderjudicial.cl; internet www.poderjudicial.cl.

President of the Supreme Court: URBANO MARÍN VALLEJO.

Ministers of the Supreme Court: ORLANDO ANTONIO ALVAREZ HERNÁNDEZ, MILTON IVAN JUICA ARANCIBIA, NIBALDO SEGURA PEÑA, ADALIS SALVADOR OYARZUN MIRANDA, JAIME DEL CARMEN RODRÍGUEZ ESPOZ, RUBEN ALBERTO BALLESTEROS CARCAMO, SERGIO MANUEL MUÑOZ GAJARDO, MARGARITA ELIANA HERREROS MARTÍNEZ, HUGO ENRIQUE DOLMESTCH URRA, JUAN ARAYA ELIZALDE, RAÚL PATRICIO VALDES ALDUNATE, HÉCTOR GUILLERMO CARREÑO SEAMAN, PEDRO PIERRY ARRAU, GABRIELA PÉREZ PAREDES, SONIA MIREYA ARANEDA BRIONES, CARLOS GUILLERMO KÜNSEMÜLLER LOEBENFELDER, HAROLDO OSVALDO BRITO CRUZ, GUILLERMO ENRIQUE SILVA GUNDELACH; two vacancies.

Public Prosecutor: MÓNICA EUGENIA MALDONADO CROQUEVIELLE.

Secretary of the Court: ROSA MARÍA DEL C. PINTO EGUSQUIZA.

Religion

CHRISTIANITY

The Roman Catholic Church

According to the latest available census figures (2002), some 70% of the population aged 15 years and above are Roman Catholics. Chile comprises five archdioceses, 18 dioceses, two territorial prelatures and one apostolic vicariate.

Bishops' Conference

Conferencia Episcopal de Chile, Echaurren 4, 6°, Casilla 517-V, Correo 21, Santiago; tel. (2) 671-7733; fax (2) 698-1416; e-mail secretariageneral@episcopado.cl; internet www.iglesia.cl.

f. 1955 (statutes approved 2000); Pres. Rt Rev. ALEJANDRO GOIĆ KARMELIĆ (Bishop of Rancagua).

Archbishop of Antofagasta: PABLO LIZAMA RIQUELME, San Martín 2628, Casilla E, Antofagasta; tel. and fax (55) 26-8856; e-mail antofagasta@episcopado.cl; internet www.iglesiadeantofagasta.cl.

Archbishop of Concepción: RICARDO EZZATI ANDRELLO, Calle Barros Arana 544, Casilla 65-C, Concepción; tel. (41) 222-8173; fax (41) 223-2844; e-mail amoreno@episcopado.cl; internet www.arzobispadodeconcepcion.cl.

Archbishop of La Serena: MANUEL GERARDO DONOSO DONOSO, Los Carrera 450, Casilla 613, La Serena; tel. (51) 21-2325; fax (51) 22-5886; e-mail laserena@episcopado.cl; internet www.iglesia.cl/laserena.

Archbishop of Puerto Montt: CRISTIÁN CARO CORDERO, Calle Benavente 385, Casilla 17, Puerto Montt; tel. (65) 25-2215; fax (65) 27-1861; e-mail puertomontt@episcopado.cl; internet www.arzobispadodepuertomontt.cl.

Archbishop of Santiago de Chile: Cardinal FRANCISCO JAVIER ERRÁZURIZ OSSA, Erasmo Escala 1884, Casilla 30-D, Santiago; tel. (2) 696-3275; fax (2) 671-2042; e-mail curiasantiago@arzobispado.tie.cl; internet www.iglesiadesantiago.cl.

The Anglican Communion

Anglicans in Chile come within the Diocese of Chile, which forms part of the Anglican Church of the Southern Cone of America, covering Argentina, Bolivia, Chile, Paraguay, Peru and Uruguay.

Bishop of Chile: Rt Rev. HECTOR F. ZAVALA, Corporación Anglicana de Chile, Victoria Subercaseaux 41, Of. 301., Casilla 50675, Correo Central, Santiago; tel. (2) 638-3009; fax (2) 639-4581; e-mail diocesis@iach.cl; internet www.iglesiaanglicana.cl.

Other Christian Churches

According to the 2002 census, 15% of the population are Evangelical Christians, 1% are Jehovah's Witnesses and 1% are Mormons.

Iglesia Católica Apostólica Ortodoxa de la Santísima Virgen María (Orthodox Church of the Patriarch of Antioch): Avda Pedro de Valdivia 92, Providencia, Santiago; tel. (2) 231-7284; fax 232-0860; e-mail iglesia@iglesiaortodoxa.cl; internet www.iglesiaortodoxa.cl; Archbishop Mgr SERGIO ABAD.

Iglesia Evangélica Luterana en Chile: Pedro de Valdivia 3420-H, Dpto 33, Ñuñoa, Casilla 167–11, Santiago; tel. (2) 223-3195; fax (2) 205-2193; e-mail secretaria@ielch.cl; internet www.ielch.cl; f. 1937; Pres. Dra GLORIA ROJAS VARGAS; 3,000 mems.

Iglesia Metodista de Chile: Sargento Aldea 1041, Casilla 67, Santiago; tel. (2) 556-6074; fax (2) 554-1763; e-mail imech.chile@metodista.cl; internet www.metodista.cl; autonomous since 1969; Bishop NEFTALÍ ARAVENA BRAVO; 9,882 mems.

Iglesia Pentecostal de Chile: Manuel Rodríguez 1155, Curicó; tel. (75) 318640; e-mail iglesia@pentecostaldechile.cl; internet www

.pentecostaldechile.cl; f. 1947; Pres. Rev. SERGIO VELOSO TOLOSA; Bishop Rev. LUIS ULISES MUÑOZ MORAGA; 125,000 mems.

Jehovah's Witnesses: Avda Concha y Toro 3456, Casilla 267, Puente Alto; tel. (2) 428-2600; fax (2) 428-2609; Dir PEDRO J. LOVATO GROSSO.

Unión de Iglesias Evangélicas Bautistas de Chile: Miguel Claro 755, Providencia, Santiago; tel. (2) 264-1208; fax (2) 431-8012; e-mail centrobautista@ubach.cl; internet www.ubach.cl; f. 1908; Pres. RAQUEL CONTRERAS EDDINGER; Vice-Pres. JORGE QUINTEROS.

JUDAISM

There is a small Jewish community in Chile, numbering 14,976 at the 2002 census (less than 1% of the population).

Círculo Israelita de Santiago: Comandante Malbec 13210, Lo Barnechea, Santiago; tel. (2) 240-5000; fax (2) 243-6244; e-mail info@cis.cl; internet www.cis.cl; f. 1982; Dir-Gen. SERGIO JODORKOVSKY P.; Exec. Dir MARIO KIBLISKY.

Comunidad Israelita Sefardi de Chile: Avda Ricardo Lyon 812, Providencia, Santiago; tel. (2) 209-8086; fax (2) 204-7382; e-mail contacto@sefardies.cl; internet www.sefaradies.cl; Pres. MERY NACHARI GALVANI; Sec.-Gen. LEÓN HASSÓN T.

ISLAM

There is a small Muslim community in Chile, numbering 2,894 at the 2002 census (less than 1% of the population).

Centro Islámico de Chile: Mezquita As-Salam, Campoamor 2975, esq. Chile-España, Ñuñoa, Santiago; tel. (2) 343-1376; fax (2) 343-1378; e-mail contacto@islamenchile.cl; internet www.islamenchile.cl; f. 1925 as the Sociedad Unión Musulmana; Sec. MOHAMED RUMIE.

BAHÁ'Í FAITH

National Spiritual Assembly: Manuel de Salas 356, Casilla 3731, Ñuñoa, Santiago; tel. (2) 752-3999; fax (2) 752-3999; e-mail secretaria@bahai.cl; internet www.bahai.cl.

The Press

Most newspapers of nation-wide circulation in Chile are published in Santiago.

DAILIES

Santiago

La Cuarta: Diagonal Vicuña Mackenna 1870, Casilla 2795, Santiago; tel. (2) 551-7067; fax (2) 555-7071; e-mail contacto@lacuarta.cl; internet www.lacuarta.cl; f. 1984; morning; popular; Dir DIOZEL PÉREZ; circ. 146,000.

Diario Financiero: San Crescente 81, 2°, Las Condes, Santiago; tel. (2) 339-1000; fax (2) 231-3340; e-mail suscripciones@df.cl; internet www.df.cl; f. 1988; morning; Dir GUILLERMO TURNER OLEA; Gen. Man. EDUARDO POOLEY PELIZZOLA; circ. 20,000.

Diario Oficial de la República de Chile: Casilla 81-D, Agustinas 1269, Santiago; tel. (2) 698-3969; fax (2) 698-1059; e-mail info@diariooficial.cl; internet www.diariooficial.cl; f. 1877; Dir FLORENCIO CEBALLOS BUSTOS; circ. 10,000.

Estrategia: Luis Carrera 1289, Vitacura, Santiago; tel. (2) 655-6100; fax (2) 655-6439; e-mail estrategia@edgestion.cl; internet www.estrategia.cl; f. 1978; morning; business news; Dir VÍCTOR MANUEL OJEDA; circ. 33,000.

La Hora: Avda Vicuña Mackenna 1870, Santiago; tel. (2) 550-7000; fax (2) 550-7770; e-mail contacto@lahora.cl; internet www.lahora.cl; f. 1997; Mon.–Fri; distributed free of charge; Dir JAVIER FUICA DEL CAMPO; circ. 106,000.

El Mercurio: Avda Santa María 5542, Casilla 13-D, Santiago; tel. (2) 330-1111; fax (2) 242-6965; e-mail elmercurio@mercurio.cl; internet www.elmercurio.cl; f. 1900; morning; conservative; Dir CRISTIÁN ZEGERS; circ. 154,000 (Mon.–Fri.), 232,000 (weekends).

La Nación: Agustinas 1269, Casilla 81-D, Santiago; tel. (2) 787-0100; fax (2) 698-1059; e-mail mpmoya@lanacion.cl; internet www.lanacion.cl; f. 1917 to replace govt-subsidized *El Cronista*; morning; Propr Soc. Periodística La Nación; Gen. Man. FRANCISCO FERES NAZARALA; Dir MARCELO CASTILLO; circ. 11,000.

Santiago Times: Avda Santa María 227, Of. 12, Santiago; tel. and fax (2) 777-5376; e-mail editor@santiagotimes.cl; internet www.santiagotimes.cl; daily; national news in English; Gen. Editor BILL STOTT; 10,000 subscribers.

La Segunda: Avda Santa María 5542, Casilla 13-D, Santiago; tel. (2) 330-1111; fax (2) 242-6965; e-mail cartas@lasegunda.cl; internet www.lasegunda.com; f. 1931; owned by proprs of *El Mercurio*; evening; Dir PILAR VERGARA; circ. 40,000.

La Tercera: Avda Vicuña Mackenna 1870, Ñuñoa, Santiago; tel. (2) 551-7067; fax (2) 555-7071; e-mail latercera@latercera.cl; internet www.latercera.cl; f. 1950; morning; Dir CRISTIÁN BOFILL RODRÍGUEZ; circ. 91,000 (Mon.–Fri.), 201,000 (weekends).

Las Ultimas Noticias: Bellavista 0112, Providencia, Santiago; tel. (2) 730-3000; fax (2) 730-3331; e-mail ultimas.noticias@lun.cl; internet www.lun.cl; f. 1902; owned by the proprs of El Mercurio; morning; Dir AGUSTÍN EDWARDS DEL RÍO; circ. 133,000 (Mon.–Fri.), 176,000 (weekends).

Antofagasta

La Estrella del Norte: Manuel Antonio Matta 2112, Antofagasta; tel. (55) 45-3672; fax (55) 45-3671; internet www.estrellanorte.cl; f. 1966; evening; Dir SERGIO MONTIVERO; circ. 5,000.

El Mercurio de Antofagasta: Manuel Antonio Matta 2112, Antofagasta; tel. (55) 425-3600; fax (55) 425-3612; e-mail info@mercurioantofagasta.cl; internet www.mercurioantofagasta.cl; f. 1906; morning; conservative ind; Proprs Soc. Chilena de Publicaciones; Dir CARLOS RODRÍGUEZ PÉREZ; circ. 9,000.

Arica

La Estrella de Arica: San Marcos 580, Arica; tel. (58) 22-5024; fax (58) 25-2890; internet www.estrellaarica.cl; f. 1976; Dir REINALDO NEIRA RUIZ; circ. 10,000.

Atacama

Chañarcillo: Los Carrera 801, Casilla 198, Copiapó, Atacama; tel. and fax (52) 21-9044; internet www.chanarcillo.cl; f. 1992; morning; Dir ALBERTO BICHARA.

Calama

El Mercurio de Calama: Abaroa 2051, Calama; tel. (55) 45-8571; fax (55) 45-8172; e-mail cronicacalama@mercurio.cl; internet www.mercuriocalama.cl; f. 1968; propr Soc. Chilena de Publicaciones; Dir JAVIER ORELLANA VERA; circ. 4,500 (weekdays), 7,000 (Sun.).

Chillán

La Discusión: 18 de Septiembre 721, Casilla 479, Chillán; tel. (42) 21-2650; fax (42) 21-3578; internet www.diarioladiscusion.cl; f. 1870; morning; ind.; Dir RUSSEL CABRERA PARADA; circ. 5,000.

Concepción

El Sur: Calle Freire 799, Casilla 8-C, Concepción; tel. (41) 279-4760; fax (41) 279-4761; e-mail buzon@diarioelsur.cl; internet www.elsur.cl; f. 1882; morning; ind.; Gen. Editor VICTOR TOLOZA JIMÉNEZ; Dir ERNESTO MONTALBA; circ. 28,000 (weekdays), 45,000 (Sun.).

Copiapó

El Diario de Atacama: Atacama 724A, Copiapó; tel. (52) 21-8509; fax (52) 23-2212; internet www.diarioatacama.cl; f. 1970; morning; ind.; Gen. Editor CRIATIAN ANGEL ARDILLES; Dir DAVID DOLL PINTO; circ. 6,500.

Coyhaique

El Diario de Aysén: 21 de Mayo 410, Coyhaique; tel. (67) 234-850; fax (67) 232-318; e-mail contacto@diarioaysen.cl; internet www.diarioaysen.cl; f. 1981; Dir GABRIELA VICENTINI.

Curicó

La Prensa: Merced 373, Curicó; tel. (75) 31-0453; fax (75) 31-1924; e-mail aprensa@diariolaprensa.cl; internet diariolaprensa.cl; f. 1898; morning; right-wing; Dir MANUEL MASSA MAUTINO; circ. 6,000.

Iquique

La Estrella de Iquique: Luis Uribe 452, Iquique; tel. (57) 39-9311; fax (57) 42-7975; internet www.estrellaiquique.cl; f. 1966; evening; Dir CAUPOLICÁN MÁRQUEZ VERGARA; circ. 10,000.

La Serena

El Día: Brasil 431, La Serena; tel. (51) 20-0400; fax (51) 21-9599; internet www.diarioeldia.cl; f. 1944; morning; Dir FRANCISCO PUGA VERGARA; circ. 10,800.

Los Angeles

La Tribuna: Colo Colo 464, Casilla 15-D, Los Angeles; tel. (43) 31-3315; fax (43) 31-4987; e-mail gerencia@diariolatribuna.cl; internet www.diariolatribuna.cl; f. 1958; ind; Dir CIRILO GUZMÁN DE LA FUENTE; circ. 4,200.

Osorno

El Diario Austral de Osorno: O'Higgins 870, Osorno; tel. (64) 22-2300; fax (64) 24-6244; e-mail gcanales@australosorno.cl; internet www.australosorno.cl; f. 1982; Dir RICARDO ALT; circ. 6,500 (weekdays), 7,300 (Sun.).

Ovalle

El Ovallino: Vicuña Mackena 473, Ovalle; tel. (53) 433-031; internet www.elovallino.cl; f. 1989; Dir FRANCISCO PUGA.

Puerto Montt

El Llanquíhue: Antonio Varas 167, Puerto Montt; tel. (65) 432-400; fax (65) 432-401; internet www.diariollanquihue.cl; f. 1885; Dir MAURICIO RIVAS ALVEAR; circ. 4,800 (weekdays), 5,700 (Sun.).

Punta Arenas

La Prensa Austral: Waldo Seguel 636, Casilla 9-D, Punta Arenas; tel. (61) 20-4000; fax (61) 24-7406; e-mail redaccion@laprensaaustral.cl; internet www.laprensaaustral.cl; f. 1941; morning; ind.; Gen. Editor POLY RAÍN HARO; Dir ALEJANDRO TORO; circ. 10,000, Sunday El Magallanes ; f. 1894 12,000.

Quillota

El Observador: La Concepción 277, Casilla 1-D, Quillota; tel. (33) 312-096; fax (33) 311-417; e-mail elobser@entelchile.net; internet www.diarioelobservador.cl; f. 1970; Man. Dir ROBERTO SILVA BIJIT.

Rancagua

El Rancagüino: O'Carroll 518, Casilla 50, Rancagua; tel. (72) 327-400; e-mail info@elrancaguino.cl; internet www.elrancaguino.cl; f. 1915; ind.; Dir ALEJANDRO GONZÁLEZ; Gen. Man. FERNANDO REYES; circ. 10,000.

Talca

El Centro: Casa Matriz, Avda Lircay 3030, Talca; tel. (71) 51-5300; fax (71) 51-0310; e-mail diario@diarioelcentro.cl; internet www.diarioelcentro.cl; f. 1989; Dir ANTONIO FAUNDES MERINO.

Temuco

El Diario Austral de la Araucanía: Antonio Varas 945, Casilla 1-D, Temuco; tel. (45) 29-2929; fax (45) 23-9189; internet www.australtemuco.cl; f. 1916; propr Soc. Periodística Araucanía, SA; morning; commercial, industrial and agricultural interests; Dir JOSÉ MANUEL ALVAREZ; circ. 15,100 (weekdays), 23,500 (Sun.).

Tocopilla

La Prensa de Tocopilla: Bolívar 1244, Tocopilla; tel. (83) 81-3036; e-mail prensa@prensatocopilla.cl; internet www.prensatocopilla.cl; f. 1924; morning; ind.; Editor MARTÍN GONZÁLEZ; circ. 3,000.

Valdivia

El Diario Austral de Valdivia: Yungay 499, Valdivia; tel. (63) 24-2200; fax (63) 24-2209; internet www.australvaldivia.cl; f. 1982; Dir VERÓNICA MORENO AGUILERA; circ. 5,600.

Valparaíso

La Estrella: Esmeralda 1002, Casilla 57-V, Valparaíso; tel. (32) 226-4264; fax (32) 226-4108; internet www.estrellavalpo.cl; f. 1921; evening; ind.; Dir PEDRO URZÚA; owned by the proprs of *El Mercurio*; circ. 28,000 (weekdays), 35,000 (Sat.).

El Mercurio de Valparaíso: Esmeralda 1002, Casilla 57-V, Valparaíso; tel. (32) 226-4264; fax (32) 226-4138; e-mail info@mercuriovalpo.cl; internet www.mercuriovalpo.cl; f. 1827; owned by the proprs of *El Mercurio* in Santiago; morning; Dir MARCO ANTONIO PINTO ZEPADA; circ. 65,000.

PERIODICALS

Santiago

América Economía: tel. (2) 290-9400; fax (2) 206-6005; e-mail rferro@aeconomia.cl; internet www.americaeconomia.com; f. 1986; monthly; business; CEO ELÍAS SELMAN; Publr NILS STRANDBERG; Editorial Dir FELIPE ADULANTE.

CA (Ciudad/Arquitectura) Revista Oficial del Colegio de Arquitectos de Chile AG: Avda Libertador Bernardo O'Higgins 115, Santiago; tel. (2) 353-2300; fax (2) 353-2355; internet www.revistaca.cl; f. 1968; 4 a year; architecture; Dir PAULINA VILLALOBOS; circ. 3,500.

Caras: Rosario Norte 555, 18°, Santiago; tel. (2) 595-5000; e-mail revista@caras.cl; internet www.caras.cl; f. 1988; women's interest; Dir PATRICIA GUZMÁN.

Chile Agrícola: Teresa Vial 1170, Casilla 2, Correo 13, Santiago; tel. and fax (2) 522-2627; e-mail chileagricola@hotmail.com; f. 1975; 6 a year; organic farming; Dir RAÚL GONZÁLEZ VALENZUELA; circ. 7,000.

Chile Forestal: Paseo Bulnes 285, Of. 601, Santiago; tel. (2) 390-0213; fax (2) 696-6724; e-mail mespejo@conaf.cl; internet www.conaf.cl; f. 1974; 10 a year; state-owned; technical information and features on forestry sector; Editor RICARDO SAN MARTÍN; Dir MARIELA ESPEJO SUAZO; circ. 4,000.

Cinegrama: Avda Holanda 279, Providencia, Santiago; tel. (2) 422-8500; fax (2) 422-8570; e-mail cinegrama@cinegrama.cl; internet www.cinegrama.cl; f. 1987; monthly; cinema; Dir JUAN IGNACIO OTO; Editor LEYLA LÓPEZ.

The Clinic: Merced 280, Of. 71, Santiago; tel. (2) 633-9584; fax (2) 639-6584; internet www.theclinic.cl; fortnightly; political and social satire; Editor PABLO VERGARA; Gen. Man. JUAN PABLO BAROS.

Conozca Más: Rosario Norte 555, 18°, Las Condes, Santiago; tel. (2) 366-7100; fax (2) 246-2810; e-mail viamail@conozcamas.cl; internet www.conozcamas.cl; monthly; science; Dir PAULA AVILES; circ. 90,000.

Cosas: Almirante Pastene 259, Providencia, Santiago; tel. (2) 364-5100; fax (2) 235-8331; e-mail info@cosas.com; internet www.cosas.com; f. 1976; fortnightly; entertainment and lifestyle; Editor OSCAR SEPÚLVEDA PACHECO; circ. 40,000.

Creces: Luis Uribe 2610, Ñuñoa, Santiago; tel. and fax (2) 341-5829; e-mail creceswebmaster@entelchile.net; internet www.creces.cl; monthly; science and technology; Dir FERNANDO MÖNCKEBERG BARROS; circ. 12,000.

Ercilla: Avda Holanda 279, Providencia, Santiago; tel. (2) 422-8500; fax (2) 422-8570; e-mail ercilla@holanda.cl; internet www.ercilla.cl; f. 1936; weekly; general interest; conservative; Dir JUAN IGNACIO OTO; circ. 28,000.

Mujer a Mujer: Vicuña Mackenna 1870, Ñuñoa, Santiago; tel. (2) 550-7000; fax (2) 550-7379; e-mail mujer@latercera.cl; internet www.mujeramujer.cl; weekly; women's interest; Dir JACKELINE OTEY.

Paula: Vicuña Mackena 1962, Ñuñoa, Santiago; tel. (2) 550-7108; fax (2) 550-7195; e-mail cartas@paula.cl; internet www.paula.cl; f. 1967; monthly; women's interest; Dir MILENA VODANOVIC; Editor CAROLINA DÍAZ; circ. 85,000.

Punto Final: San Diego 31, Of. 606, Casilla 13954, Correo 21, Santiago; tel. and fax (2) 697-0615; e-mail punto@interaccess.cl; internet www.puntofinal.cl; f. 1965; fortnightly; politics; left-wing; Dir MANUEL CABIESES DONOSO; circ. 15,000.

¿Qué Pasa?: Vicuña Mackenna 1870, Ñuñoa, Santiago; tel. (2) 550-7523; fax (2) 550-7529; e-mail quepasa@copesa.cl; internet www.quepasa.cl; f. 1971; weekly; general interest; Dir CRISTIAN BOFILL; circ. 30,000.

Revista Mensaje: Cienfuegos 21, Santiago; tel. (2) 698-0617; fax (2) 671-7030; e-mail rrpp@mensaje.cl; internet www.mensaje.cl; f. 1951; monthly; national, church and international affairs; Dir ANTONIO DELFAU; circ. 6,000.

Semanario Datos Sur: Avda Urmeneta 231, Puerto Montt; tel. (65) 26-6700; e-mail info@datossur.cl; internet www.datossur.cl; weekly; regional, national and business news; Dir ALEX BERKHOFF ALCARRAZ.

El Siglo: e-mail elsiglo@elsiglo.cl; internet www.elsiglo.cl; f. 1940; monthly; publ. by the Communist Party of Chile (PCCh); Dir CLAUDIO DE NEGRI QUINTANA; circ. 15,000.

Vea: Avda Holanda 279, Providencia, Santiago; tel. (2) 422-8500; fax (2) 422-8572; e-mail revistavea@holanda.cl; internet www.vea.cl; f. 1939; weekly; general interest, illustrated; Dir JAIME GODOY CARTES; circ. 150,000.

PRESS ASSOCIATION

Asociación Nacional de la Prensa: Carlos Antúnez 2048, Providencia, Santiago; tel. 232-1004; fax 232-1006; e-mail info@anp.cl; internet www.anp.cl; f. 1951; Pres. GUILLERMO TURNER OLEA; Sec.-Gen. FERNANDO SILVA VARGAS.

NEWS AGENCIES

Agencia Chile Noticias (ACN): Carlos Antúnez 1884, Of. 104, Providencia, Santiago; tel. and fax (2) 717-9121; e-mail prensa@chilenoticias.cl; internet www.chilenoticias.cl; f. 1993; Editor NORBERTO PARRA H.

Agencia Orbe: Avda Phillips 56, Of. 66, Santiago; tel. (2) 251-7800; fax (2) 251-7801; e-mail prensa@orbe.cl; internet www.orbe.cl; f. 1955; Bureau Chief PATRICIA ESCALONA CÁCERES.

Business News Americas: San Patricio 2944, Las Condes, Santiago; tel. (2) 941-0300; fax (2) 232-9376; e-mail info@bnamericas

.com; internet www.bnamericas.com; internet-based business information; CEO GREGORY BARTON.

Chile Information Project (CHIP): Avda Santa María 227, Of. 12, Recoleta, Santiago; tel. (2) 737-5649; fax (2) 735-9044; e-mail info@chipsites.com; internet www.chipsites.com; English language; Dir STEPHEN J. ANDERSON.

UPI Chile: Avda Nataniel Cox 47, 9°, Santiago; tel. (2) 657-0874; fax (2) 698-6605; e-mail chilean_news@upi.com; internet www.upi.cl; Dir THOMAS R. FIELD.

Publishers

Carlos Quiroga Editorial: La Concepción 56, Of. 206, Providencia, Santiago; tel. and fax (2) 202-9825; e-mail cquiroga@carlosquiroga.cl; internet www.carlosquiroga.cl; children's and educational; Gen. Man. MARIANELLA MEDINA.

Edebé—Editorial Don Bosco: Avda Libertador B. O'Higgins 2373, Santiago; tel. (2) 437-8050; e-mail contacto@edebe.cl; internet www.edebe.cl; f. 1904 as Editorial Salesiana; adopted present name in 1996; general, political, biography, religious, children's; Dir JORGE RIVERA SMITH.

Ediciones B Chile: Monseñor Sótero Sanz 55, Of. 600, Providencia, Santiago; tel. (2) 231-6200; fax (2) 231-6300; e-mail mansieta@edicionesbchile.cl; children's and fiction; Gen. Man. MARILÉN WOOD.

Ediciones Mil Hojas: Avda Antonio Varas 1480, Providencia, Santiago; tel. (2) 274-3172; fax (2) 223-7544; e-mail milhojas@terra.cl; internet www.milhojas.cl; educational and reference.

Ediciones Universitarias de Valparaíso: Universidad Católica de Valparaíso, 12 de Febrero 187, Casilla 1415, Valparaíso; tel. (32) 227-3087; fax (32) 227-3429; e-mail euvsa@ucv.cl; internet www.euv.cl; f. 1970; literature, social and general sciences, engineering, education, music, arts, textbooks; Gen. Man. ALEJANDRO DAMIÁN VILARREAL.

Ediciones Urano: Avda Francisco Bilbao 2809, Providencia, Santiago; tel. (2) 341-6731; fax (2) 225-3896; e-mail infoch@edicionesurano.cl; internet www.edicionesurano.cl; f. 1983 in Spain, f. 1996 in Chile; self-help, mystical and scholarly.

Editec (Ediciones Técnicas Ltda): El Condor 844, Of. 205, Ciudad Empresarial, Huechuraba, Santiago; tel. (2) 757-4200; fax (2) 757-4201; e-mail editec@editec.cl; internet www.editec.cl; Pres. RICARDO CORTES DONOSO; Gen. Man. ROLY SOLIS SEPÚLVEDA.

Editorial Antártica, SA: San Francisco 116, Santiago; tel. (2) 639-3476; fax (2) 633-3402; e-mail plaborde@antartica.cl; internet www.antartica.cl; f. 1978; Gen. Man. PAUL LABORDE U.

Editorial Borlando: Avda Victoria 151, Santiago; tel. (2) 555-9566; fax (2) 555-9564; internet www.editorialborlando.cl; f. 1984; scholarly, juvenile, educational and reference; Dir-Gen. SERGIO BORLANDO PORTALES.

Editorial Cuatro Vientos Ltda: Maturana 19, Metro República, entre Brasil y Cumming, Santiago; tel. (2) 672-9226; fax (2) 673-2153; e-mail editorial@cuatrovientos.cl; internet www.cuatrovientos.net; f. 1980; Man. Editor JUAN FRANCISCO HUNEEUS COX.

Editorial y Distribuidora Lenguaje y Pensamiento Ltda: Avda 11 de Septiembre 1881, Of. 324, Metro Pedro de Valdivia, Santiago; tel. (2) 335-2347; e-mail contacto@lenguajeypensamiento.cl; internet www.editoriallenguajeypensamiento.cl; children's, educational; Gen. Man. MARÍA LORENA TERÁN.

Editorial Evolución, SA: Avda Alameda 171, Of. 307, Santiago; tel. (2) 638-9717; fax (2) 236-4796; e-mail info@evolucion.cl; internet www.evolucion.cl; business and management; Dir JUAN BRAVO CARRASCO.

Editorial Fondo de Cultura Económica Chile, SA: Paseo Bulnes 152, Santiago; tel. (2) 697-2644; fax (2) 696-2329; e-mail obravo@fcechile.cl; internet www.fcechile.cl.

Editorial Jurídica de Chile: Ahumada 8, 4°, Santiago; tel. (2) 461-9500; fax (2) 461-9501; e-mail covalle@editorialjuridica.cl; internet www.editorialjuridica.cl; f. 1945; law; Dir RAÚL TAVOLARI OLIVEROS.

Editorial Patris: José Manuel Infante 132, Providencia, Santiago; tel. (2) 235-1343; fax (2) 235-8674; e-mail edit.patris@entelchile.net; internet www.patris.cl; f. 1982; Catholic.

Editorial Renacimiento: Huérfanos 623, Santiago; tel. (2) 632-7334; fax (2) 633-9374; e-mail pedidos@editorialrenacimiento.com; internet www.editorialrenacimiento.com; f. 1977; Gen. Man. MANUEL VILCHES.

Editorial San Pablo: Avda Libertador B. O'Higgins 1626, Santiago; tel. (2) 720-0300; fax (2) 672-8469; internet www.sanpablochile.cl; Catholic texts; Dir-Gen. BRUNO BRESSAN.

Editorial Texido: Manuel Antonio Tocornal 1487, Santiago; tel. (2) 555-5534; f. 1969; Gen. Man. ELSA ZLATER.

Editorial Tiempo Presente Ltda: Almirante Pastene 329, Providencia, Santiago; tel. (2) 364-5100; fax (2) 235-8331; e-mail info@cosas.com; internet www.cosas.com; Gen. Man. MATÍAS PFINGSTHORN.

Editorial Universitaria, SA: Avda Libertador Bernardo O'Higgins 1050, Santiago; tel. (2) 487-0700; fax (2) 487-0702; e-mail comunicaciones@universitaria.cl; internet www.universitaria.cl; f. 1947; general literature, social science, technical, textbooks; Man. Dir RODRIGO CASTRO.

Empresa Editora Zig-Zag SA: Los Conquistadores 1700, 10°, Providencia, Santiago; tel. (2) 810-7400; fax (2) 810-7452; e-mail zigzag@zigzag.cl; internet www.zigzag.cl; f. 1905; general publrs of literary works, reference books and magazines; Pres. GONZALO VIAL C.; Gen. Man. RAMÓN OLACIREGUI.

Grupo Planeta: Avda 11 de Septiembre 2353, 16°, Providencia, Santiago; tel. (2) 652-9000; fax (2) 652-2912; e-mail info@planeta.cl; internet www.planeta.cl; non-fiction, philosophy, psychology; Dir-Gen. OSCAR M. ENRIQUE CORNÚ.

Lexis-Nexis Chile: Miraflores 383, 11°, Santiago; tel. (2) 510-5000; fax (2) 510-5110; e-mail informacion@lexisnexis.cl; internet www.lexisnexis.cl; legal, business, government and academic; f. 1973.

McGraw-Hill/Interamericana de Chile Ltda: Carmencita 25, Of. 51, Las Condes, Santiago; tel. (2) 661-3000; fax (2) 661-3000; e-mail christian_mendez@mcgraw-hill.com; internet www.mcgraw-hill.cl; educational and technical.

Norma de Chile, SA: Avda Providencia 1760, Of. 502, Providencia, Santiago; tel. (2) 236-3355; fax (2) 236-3362; e-mail ventasnorma@carvajal.cl; internet www.norma.com; f. 1960; part of Editorial Norma of Colombia; Gen. Man. ELSY SALAZAR CAMPO.

Pearson Educación de Chile: José Ananias 505, Macul, Santiago; tel. (2) 237-2387; fax (2) 237-3297; e-mail infopear@pearsoned.cl; internet www.pearsoneducacion.cl; Gen. Man. JAIME VALENZUELA S.

Pehuen Editores Ltda: María Luisa Santander 537, Providencia, Santiago; tel. (2) 225-6264; fax (2) 204-9399; e-mail epehuen@entelchile.net; internet www.pehuen.cl; f. 1983; literature and sociology; Pres. JORGE BARROS TORREALBA; Gen. Man. SEBASTIÁN BARROS CERDA.

RIL Editores: Alférez Real 1464, Providencia, CP 750-0960, Santiago; tel. (2) 223-8100; fax (2) 225-4269; e-mail ril@rileditores.com; internet www.rileditores.com; literature, poetry, scholarly and political; f. 1991 as Red Internacional del Libro Ltda; Dir ELEONORA FINKELSTEIN; Dir of Publications DANIEL CALABRESE.

PUBLISHERS' ASSOCIATION

Cámara Chilena del Libro AG: Avda Libertador B. O'Higgins 1370, Of. 501, Casilla 13526, Santiago; tel. (2) 672-0348; fax (2) 698-9226; e-mail prolibro@tie.cl; internet www.camlibro.cl; Pres. EDUARDO CASTILLO GARCÍA.

Broadcasting and Communications

TELECOMMUNICATIONS

Regulatory Authority

Subsecretaría de Telecomunicaciones (Subtel): Amunátegui 139, 5°, Casilla 120, Correo 21, Santiago; tel. (2) 421-3000; fax (2) 421-3553; e-mail subtel@subtel.cl; internet www.subtel.cl; f. 1977; part of the Ministry of Transport and Telecommunications; Under-Sec. PABLO BELLO ARELLANO.

Major Operators

AT&T Chile: Málaga 89, 7°, Santiago; tel. (2) 582-5000; fax (2) 585-5079; e-mail info@firstcom.cl; internet www.attla.cl; Pres. ALEJANDRO ROJAS; Gen. Man. CARLOS C. FERNÁNDEZ.

Claro Chile, SA: Avda del Cóndor 820, Ciudad Empresarial, Comuna de Huechuraba, Santiago; tel. (2) 444-5000; fax (2) 444-5170; internet www.clarochile.cl; acquired in Aug. 2005 by América Móvil, SA de CV (Mexico); fmrly Smartcom; Gen. Man. GERARDO MUÑOZ.

CMET Telecomunicaciones: Avda Los Leones 1412, Providencia, Santiago; tel. (2) 251-3333; fax (2) 274-9573; internet www.cmet.cl; f. 1978.

Empresa Nacional de Telecomunicaciones, SA—ENTEL Chile, SA: Andrés Bello 2687, 14°, Casilla 4254, Las Condes, Santiago; tel. (2) 360-0123; fax (2) 360-3424; internet www.entel.cl; f. 1964; operates the Chilean land satellite stations of Longovilo, Punta Arenas and Coihaique, linked to INTELSAT system; 52% owned by Telecom Italia; Pres. JUAN JOSÉ HURTADO VICUÑA; Gen. Man. RICHARD BÜCHI BUC.

Grupo GTD: Moneda 920, 11°, Santiago; e-mail soporte@gtdinternet.com; internet www.grupogtd.com; f. 1979; internet and telephone service provider; Pres. JUAN MANUEL CASANUEVA.

Movistar: Miraflores 130, Santiago; tel. (2) 661-6000; internet www.movistar.cl; privatized in 1988; owned by Telefónica, SA (Spain); fmrly known as Telefónica Chile; in 2009 adopted Movistar for all brands and products; operates fixed line, mobile and internet services; Pres. EMILIO GILOLMO LÓPEZ; Gen. Man. OLIVER FLÖGEL.

Telmex Chile: Rinconada El Salto 202, Huechuraba, Casilla 12, Santiago; tel. (2) 582-5787; fax (2) 585-5185; internet www.telmex.cl; subsidiary of Teléfonos de México, SA de CV; Pres. ALEJANDRO ROJAS PINAUD; Vice-Pres. and Gen. Man. EDUARDO DÍAZ CORONA JIMÉNEZ.

VTR GlobalCom: Reyes Lavalle 3340, 9°, Las Condes, Santiago; tel. (2) 310-1000; fax (2) 310-1560; internet www.vtr.cl; f. 1928 as Vía Transradio Chilena; present name adopted in 1999; 80% owned by Liberty Global Inc (USA), 20% owned by Cristalerías Chile of the Claro group; Exec. Pres. MAURICIO RAMOS.

BROADCASTING

Regulatory Authority

Subsecretaría de Telecomunicaciones: see under Telecommunications.

Radio

Agricultura (AM y FM): Avda Manuel Rodríguez 15, Santiago; tel. (2) 392-3000; fax (2) 392-3072; internet www.radioagricultura.cl; owned by Sociedad Nacional de Agricultura; Pres. MANUEL VALDÉS VALDÉS; Gen. Man. GUIDO ERRÁZURIZ MORENO.

Beethoven FM: Avda. Santa María 2670, 2°, Providencia, Santiago; tel. (2) 571-7056; fax (2) 274-3323; e-mail director@redfm.cl; internet www.beethovenfm.cl; f. 1981; mainly classical music; affiliate stations in Viña del Mar and Temuco; Dir ADOLFO FLORES.

Bío Bío La Radio: Avda Libertador B. O'Higgins 680, Concepción; tel. (41) 222-5660; fax (41) 222-6742; e-mail pandrade@laradio.cl; internet www.radiobiobio.cl; affiliate stations in Concepción, Los Angeles, Temuco, Ancud, Castro, Osorno, Puerto Montt, Santiago and Valdivia; Man. PATRICIO ANDRADE.

Duna FM: Avda Santa María 2670, 2°, Providencia, Santiago; tel. (2) 225-5494; fax (2) 225-6013; e-mail aholuigue@duna.cl; internet www.duna.cl; affiliate stations in Viña del Mar and Concepción; Pres. FELIPE LAMARCA CLARO; Dir A. HOLUIGUE.

Estrella del Mar AM: Eleuterio Ramírez 207, Ancud, Isla de Chiloé; tel. and fax (65) 62-2722; e-mail direccionrem@gmail.com; internet www.radioestrelladelmar.cl; f. 1982; station of the Roman Catholic diocese of San Carlos de Ancud; affiliate stations in Castro, Quellón, Melinka, Achao, Futaleufú, Palena and Chaitén; Man. Dir FELIPE TOMÁS MARTÍNEZ CARRASCO.

Festival AM: Quinta 124A, Viña del Mar; tel. (32) 268-4251; fax (32) 268-0266; e-mail schiesa@festival.cl; internet www.festival.cl; f. 1976; Dir-Gen. SANTIAGO CHIESA HOWARD.

Horizonte: Avda Pocuro 2151, Providencia, Santiago; tel. (2) 410-5400; fax (2) 410-5460; internet www.horizonte.cl; f. 1985; affiliate stations in Arica, Antofagasta, Iquique, La Serena, Viña del Mar, Concepción, San Antonio, Temuco, Villarrica, Puerto Montt, Punta Arenas and Osorno; Dir JULIÁN GARCÍA-REYES.

IberoAmericana Radio Chile: Eliodoro Yáñez 1783, Providencia, Santiago; tel. (2) 390-2000; fax (2) 390-2047; e-mail aaguirre@iarc.cl; internet www.iarc.cl; belongs to Grupo Latino de Radio (GLR), a subsidiary of Union Radio; Exec. Dir MARCELO ZÚÑIGA VETTIGER; Communications Man. ALEJANDRA AGUIRRE C.; the media group operates 11 radio stations.

40 Principales 101.7 FM: e-mail radio@los40.cl; internet www.los40.cl.

ADN Radio Chile 91.7 FM: e-mail radio@adnradio.cl; internet www.adnradio.cl; general and sports news.

Concierto 88.5 FM: e-mail radio@concierto.cl; internet www.concierto.cl; f. 1999; 1980s music; Gen. Man. JAIME VEGA DE KUYPER.

Corazón 101.3 FM: e-mail radio@corazon.cl; internet www.corazon.cl; f. 1997.

FMDos 98.5 FM: e-mail radio@fmdos.cl; internet www.fm2.cl; popular music.

Futuro 88.9 FM: e-mail radio@futuro.cl; internet www.futuro.cl; rock music.

Imagina 88.1 FM: e-mail radio@radioimagina.cl; internet www.radioimagina.cl; women's radio.

Pudahuel 90.5 FM: e-mail radio@pudahuel.cl; internet www.pudahuel.cl; f. 1966; Pres. SUSANA MUTINELLI ANCHUBIDART; Gen. Man. JOAQUÍN BLAYA BARRIOS.

Radioactiva 92.5 FM: e-mail info@radioactiva.cl; internet www.radioactiva.cl; dance music from 1970s to 2000.

Rock & Pop 94.1 FM: e-mail contacto@rockandpop.cl; internet www.rockandpop.cl; retro classics and 1990s music.

Uno 97.1 FM: e-mail contacto@radiounochile.cl; internet www.radiounochile.cl; Chilean national music.

Infinita FM: Avda Los Leones 1285, Providencia, Santiago; tel. (2) 754-4400; fax (2) 341-6727; internet www.infinita.cl; f. 1977; affiliate stations in Santiago, Viña del Mar, Concepción and Valdivia; Gen. Man. CARLOS ALBERTO PEÑAFIEL GUARACHI.

Para Ti FM: Vial 775, Puerto Montt, Santiago; tel. (65) 317-003; internet www.radioparati.cl; 16 affiliate stations throughout Chile; Gen. Man. FELIPE MOLFINO BURKERT.

Play FM: Alcalde Dávalos 164, Providencia, Santiago; tel. (2) 630-2600; fax (2) 630-2264; e-mail asanchez@13.cl; internet www.playfm.cl; f. 2006; Dir GABRIEL POLGATI; Gen. Man. XIMENA CALLEJÓN.

Radio Carolina: Avda Santa Maria 2670, 2°, Providence, Santiago; tel. (2) 571-7000; fax (2) 571-7002; internet www.carolina.cl; f. 1975; owned by COPESA, SA Chile; Contact HÉCTOR CABRERA.

Radio El Conquistador FM: El Conquistador del Monte 4644, Huechuraba, Santiago; tel. (2) 580-2000; e-mail radio@elconquistadorfm.cl; internet www.cqfm.cl; f. 1962; affiliate stations in Santiago, Iquique, Antofagasta, La Serena, Viña del Mar, Rancagua, Talca, Chillán, Concepción, Talcahuano, Pucón, Temuco, Villarrica, Lago Llanquihue, Osorno, Puerto Montt, Puerto Varas, Valdivia and Punta Arenas; Pres. JOAQUÍN MOLFINO.

Radio Cooperativa (AM y FM): Antonio Bellet 353, Casilla 16367, Correo 9, Santiago; tel. (2) 364-8000; fax (2) 236-0535; e-mail info@cooperativa.cl; internet www.cooperativa.cl; f. 1936; affiliate stations in Copiapó, Arica, Coquimbo, La Serena, Valparaíso, Concepción, Calama, Temuco and Castro; Pres. LUIS AJENJO ISASI; Gen. Man. SERGIO PARRA GODOY.

Radio Nacional de Chile: Santiago; tel. (2) 551-6954; fax (2) 551-6967; e-mail radionacionaldechile@gmail.com; internet www.radionacionalchile.tk; f. 1974; Gen. Man. SANTIAGO AGLIATI.

Radio Nueva Belén FM: Benavente 385, Puerto Montt; tel. (65) 25-8042; fax (65) 25-8084; e-mail nuevabelen@gmail.com; internet www.radionuevabelen.cl; f. 2005; owned by Archbishopric of Puerto Montt; Dir HÉCTOR ASENJO REYES; Gen. Man. CARLOS WAGNER CATALÁN.

Radio Polar: Bories 871, 2° y 3°, Punta Arenas; tel. (61) 24-1909; fax (61) 24-9001; e-mail secretaria@radiopolar.com; internet www.radiopolar.com; f. 1940; Pres. RENÉ VENEGAS OLMEDO.

Superandina FM: Avda Chacabuco 281, Los Andes; tel. (34) 42-2515; fax (34) 90-4091; e-mail radio@superandina.cl; internet www.superandina.cl; f. 1987; Dir JOSÉ ANDRÉS GÁLVEZ.

Universo FM: Antonio Bellet 223, Providencia, Santiago; tel. (2) 364-8000; e-mail alfredo@universo.cl; internet www.universo.cl; affiliate stations in 18 cities, including Iquique, Copiapó, La Serena, Ovalle, Concepción, Temuco, Puerto Montt, Coihayque and Punta Arenas; Commercial. Man. ALFREDO URETA Q.

Television

Corporación de Televisión de la Universidad Católica de Chile—Canal 13: Inés Matte Urrejola 0848, Providencia, Santiago; tel. (2) 251-4000; fax (2) 630-2683; internet www.canal13.cl; f. 1959; non-commercial; Pres. PATRICIO DEL SOL; Exec. Dir MERCEDES DUCCI BUDGE.

Corporación de Televisión de la Universidad Católica de Valparaíso: Agua Santa Alta 2455, Viña del Mar; tel. (32) 276-8500; fax (32) 261-0505; e-mail direccion@ucvtv.cl; internet www.ucvtv.cl; f. 1957; Pres. BERNARDO DONOSO; Exec. Dir ENRIQUE AIMONE.

Megavisión, SA—Canal 9: Avda Vicuña Mackenna 1348, Ñuñoa, Santiago; tel. (2) 810-8000; fax (2) 551-8369; e-mail mega@mcl.cl; internet www.mega.cl; f. 1990; Pres. RICARDO CLARO VALDÉS; Gen. Man. CRISTÓBAL BULNES SERRANO.

Red de Televisión SA/Chilevisión—Canal 11: Inés Matte Urrejola 0825, Casilla 16547, Correo 9, Providencia, Santiago; tel. (2) 461-5100; fax (2) 461-5371; e-mail contactoweb@chilevision.cl; internet www.chilevision.cl; Exec. Dir JAIME DE AGUIRRE HOFFA; Gen. Man. MARIO CONCA ROSENDE.

La Red Televisión TV: Manquehue Sur 1201, Las Condes, Santiago; tel. (2) 385-4000; fax (2) 385-4020; internet www.redtv.cl; e-mail administracion@lared.cl; f. 1991; Dir-Gen. JOSÉ MANUEL LARRAÍN.

Televisión Nacional de Chile—Canal 7: Bellavista 0990, Casilla 16104, Providencia, Santiago; tel. (2) 707-7777; fax (2) 707-7766; e-mail relaciones.publicas@tvn.cl; internet www.tvn.cl; f. 1969; govt network of 140 stations and an international satellite signal; Chair. MARIO PAPI BEYER; Exec. Dir DANIEL FERNÁNDEZ KOPRICH.

Broadcasting Associations

Asociación Nacional de Televisión (ANATEL): Guardia Vieja 255, Of. 1106, Providencia, Santiago; tel. (2) 331-9650; fax (2) 331-9803; e-mail info@anatel.cl; internet www.anatel.cl; 7 mem. networks; Pres. BERNARDO DONOSO RIVEROS; Sec.-Gen. HERNÁN TRIVIÑO OYARZUN.

Asociación de Radiodifusores de Chile (ARCHI): Pasaje Matte 956, 8°, Of. 801, Casilla 10476, Santiago; tel. (2) 639-8755; fax (2) 639-4205; internet www.archi.cl; f. 1933; more than 1,000 affiliated stations; Pres. LUIS PARDO SAINZ; Sec.-Gen. FERNANDO OCARANZA YÑESTA.

Finance

(cap. = capital; res = reserves; dep. = deposits; m. = million; brs = branches; amounts in pesos, unless otherwise specified)

BANKING

Supervisory Authority

Superintendencia de Bancos e Instituciones Financieras: Moneda 1123, 6°, Casilla 15-D, Santiago; tel. (2) 442-6200; fax (2) 441-0914; e-mail superintendente@sbif.cl; internet www.sbif.cl; f. 1925; affiliated to Ministry of Finance; Supt CARLOS BUDNEVICH LE-FORT.

Central Bank

Banco Central de Chile: Agustinas 1180, Santiago; tel. (2) 670-2000; fax (2) 670-2099; e-mail bcch@bcentral.cl; internet www.bcentral.cl; f. 1926; under Ministry of Finance until Dec. 1989, when autonomy was granted; bank of issue; cap. and res –1,934,993m., dep. 13,100,469m. (Dec. 2008); Pres. JOSÉ DE GREGORIO REBECO; Gen. Man ALEJANDRO ZURBUCHEN SILVA.

State Bank

Banco del Estado de Chile (BancoEstado): Avda Libertador B. O'Higgins 1111, Casilla 240V, Santiago; tel. (2) 970-7000; fax (2) 970-5711; internet www.bancoestado.cl; f. 1953; state bank; cap. 4,000m., res 528,853m., dep. 12,538,167m. (Dec. 2007); Pres. JOSÉ LUIS MARDONES SANTANDER; CEO PABLO PIÑERA ECHENIQUE; 214 brs.

Commercial Banks

Banco BICE: Teatinos 220, Santiago; tel. (2) 692-2000; fax (2) 696-5324; e-mail webmaster@bice.cl; internet www.bice.cl; f. 1979 as Banco Industrial y de Comercio Exterior; adopted present name 1988; cap. 32,142m., res 139,022m., dep. 2,210,594m. (Dec. 2008); Pres. and Chair. BERNARDO MATTE LARRAÍN; Gen. Man. RENÉ LÉHUEDÉ FUENZALIDA; 16 brs.

Banco Bilbao Vizcaya Argentaria Chile: Pedro de Valdivia 100, 17°, Providencia, Santiago; tel. (2) 679-1000; fax (2) 698-5640; e-mail ascarito@bbva.cl; internet www.bbva.cl; f. 1883 as Banco Hipotecario de Fomento Nacional; controlling interest acquired by Banco Bilbao Vizcaya (Spain) in 1998; adopted current name 2003; cap. €1,837m., res €20,619m., dep. €495,873m. (Dec. 2008); Chair. JOSÉ SAID SAFFIE; Gen. Man. and CEO IGNACIO LACASTA CASADO; 92 brs.

Banco de Chile: Ahumada 251, Casilla 151-D, Santiago; tel. (2) 637-1111; fax (2) 637-3434; internet www.bancochile.cl; f. 1894; 35.6% owned by SAOS, SA; cap. 1,106,491m., res –81,181m., dep. 14,243,238m. (Dec. 2008); Pres. and Chair. PABLO GRANIFO LAVÍN; CEO FERNANDO CAÑAS BERKOWITZ; 248 brs.

Banco de Crédito e Inversiones (Bci): Huérfanos 1134, Casilla 136-D, Santiago; tel. (2) 692-7000; fax (2) 695-3775; e-mail webmaster@bci.cl; internet www.bci.cl; f. 1937; cap. 564,503m., res 119,307m., dep. 11,602,495m. (Dec. 2008); Pres. and Chair. LUIS ENRIQUE YARUR REY; 112 brs.

Banco Desarrollo de Scotiabank: Avda Libertador B. O'Higgins 949, 3°, Casilla 320-V, Casilla 1, Santiago; tel. (2) 674-5000; fax (2) 671-5547; e-mail bdd@bandes.cl; internet www.bdd.cl; f. 1983; fmrly Banco del Desarrollo; above name adopted after acquisition by Scotiabank Chile in 2007; cap. 198,456m., res 751m., dep. 2,367,498m. (Dec. 2008); Pres. PETER CARDINAL; Gen. Man. JAMES EDWARD CALLAHAN; 83 brs.

Banco Internacional: Moneda 818, Casilla 135-D, Santiago; tel. (2) 369-7000; fax (2) 369-7367; e-mail banco@binter.cl; internet www.bancointernacional.cl; f. 1944; cap. 17,911m., res 8,566m., dep. 410,614m. (Dec. 2008); Pres. JULIO JARAQUEMADA L.; Gen. Man. JUAN ENRIQUE VILAJUANA R.

Banco Santander Chile: Bandera 140, 13°, Casilla 57-D, Santiago; tel. (2) 320-2000; fax (2) 320-8877; e-mail webmaster@santander.cl; internet www.santandersantiago.cl; f. 1926; cap. 891,303m., res 358,596m., dep. 17,532,905m. (Dec. 2008); subsidiary of Banco Santander (Spain); Chair. MAURICIO LARRAÍN GARCES; 72 brs.

Banco Security: Apoquindo 3150, Las Condes, Santiago; tel. (2) 584-4000; fax (2) 584-4058; internet www.bancosecurity.cl; f. 1981; fmrly Banco Urquijo de Chile; cap. 138,196m., res 32,263m., dep. 2,639,918m. (Dec. 2008); Pres. and Chair. FRANCISCO SILVA S.; Gen. Man. RENATO PEÑAFIEL MUÑOZ; 16 brs.

Corpbanca: Rosario Norte 660, Las Condes, Casilla 80-D, Santiago; tel. (2) 687-8000; fax (2) 672-6729; e-mail corpbanca@corpbanca.cl; internet www.corpbanca.cl; f. 1871 as Banco de Concepción, current name adopted in 1997; cap. 324,039m., res 102,958m., dep. 5,154,465m. (Dec. 2008); Chair. and Pres. ALVARO SAIEH BENDECK; CEO MARIO CHAMORRO; 64 brs.

HSBC Bank (Chile): Edif. Titanium, Avda Vitacura 2872, Las Condes, Santiago; tel. (2) 332-1904; fax (2) 299-7391; e-mail ricardo.navarrete@cl.hsbc.com; internet www.hsbc.cl; f. 2003 as HSBC Bank Chile; present name adopted in 2004; cap. 92,032m., res –822m., dep. 1,157,016m. (Dec. 2008); Chair. S. K. GREEN; CEO and Gen. Man. ALBERTO SILVA M.

Scotiabank Sud Americano: Morandé 226, Casilla 90-D, Santiago; tel. (2) 692-6000; fax (2) 698-6008; e-mail scotiabank@scotiabank.cl; internet www.scotiabank.cl; f. 1944; cap. 670,469m., res 117,067m., dep. 3,094,449m. (Dec. 2008); Pres. and Chair. PETER C. CARDINAL; CEO and Gen. Man JAMES CALLAHAN; 60 brs.

Banking Association

Asociación de Bancos e Instituciones Financieras de Chile AG: Ahumada 179, 12°, Santiago; tel. (2) 636-7100; fax (2) 698-8945; e-mail general@abif.cl; internet www.abif.cl; f. 1945; Pres. HERNÁN SOMERVILLE SENN; Gen. Man. ALEJANDRO ALARCÓN PÉREZ.

Other Financial Supervisory Bodies

Superintendencia de Administradoras de Fondos de Pensiones (SAFP) (Superintendency of Pension Funds): Teatinos 317, Santiago; tel. (2) 753-0100; fax (2) 753-0122; internet www.safp.cl; f. 1981; Supt SOLANGE BERSTEIN JÁUREGUI.

Superintendencia de Seguridad Social (Superintendency of Social Security): Huérfanos 1376, 5°, Santiago; tel. (2) 620-4500; fax (2) 696-4672; e-mail contacto@suseso.cl; internet www.suseso.gov.cl; f. 1927; Supt JAVIER FUENZALIDA SANTANDER.

STOCK EXCHANGES

Bolsa de Comercio de Santiago: La Bolsa 64, Casilla 123-D, Santiago; tel. (2) 399-3000; fax (2) 318-1961; e-mail chathaway@bolsadesantiago.com; internet www.bolsadesantiago.com; f. 1893; 32 mems; Pres. PABLO YRARRÁZAVAL VALDÉS.

Bolsa de Corredores—Valores de Valparaíso: Prat 798, Casilla 218-V, Valparaíso; tel. (32) 225-0677; fax (32) 221-2764; e-mail bolsadec.orred001@chilnet.cl; internet www.bovalpo.com; f. 1905; Pres. CARLOS F. MARÍN ORREGO; Man. ARIE JOEL GELFENSTEIN FREUNDLICH.

Bolsa Electrónica de Chile: Huérfanos 770, 14°, Santiago; tel. (2) 484-0100; fax (2) 484-0101; e-mail contactoweb@bolchile.cl; internet www.bolchile.cl; f. 1989; Gen. Man. JUAN CARLOS SPENCER OSSA.

INSURANCE

In 2007 there were 49 general and life insurance companies operating in Chile.

Supervisory Authority

Superintendencia de Valores y Seguros: Avda Libertador B. O'Higgins 1449, Casilla 834-0518, Santiago; tel. (2) 473-4000; fax (2) 473-4102; internet www.svs.cl; f. 1931; under Ministry of Finance; Supt GUILLERMO LARRAÍN RÍOS.

Principal Companies

ABN Amro (Chile) Seguros Generales, SA: Avda Apoquindo 3039, Las Condes, Santiago; tel. (2) 396-6600; fax (2) 396-6666; e-mail ccm.clientservice.santiago@cl.abnamro.com; internet www.abnamro.cl; Pres. CECILIA STAGNARO FRÍAS.

Ace Seguros de Vida, SA: Miraflores 222, 17°, Santiago; tel. (2) 549-8300; fax (2) 632-6289; e-mail juan.ortega@ace-ina.com; internet www.acelimited.com; Gen. Man. JUAN LUIS ORTEGA GARTERAS.

Aseguradora Magallanes, SA: Avda Alonso de Córdova 5151, 18°, Of. 1801, Las Condes, Santiago; tel. (2) 715-4848; fax (2) 715-4860; e-mail fvarela@magallanes.cl; internet www.magallanes.cl; f. 1957; general; Pres. EDUARDO DOMINGUEZ COVARRUBIAS; Gen. Man. FERNANDO VARELA VILLAROEL.

Axa Asistencia Chile: Josué Smith Solar 390, 6650378 Providencia, Santiago; tel. (2) 941-8900; fax (2) 941-8951; e-mail asistencia@axa-assistance.cl; internet www.axa-assistance.cl; f. 1936; general; Gen. Man. MARYLÚ FORTTES VALDIVIA.

Cardif Chile: Vitacura 2670, 13°, Las Condes, Santiago; tel. (2) 370-4800; fax (2) 370-4877; internet www.cardif.cl; f. 1997; owned by BNP Paribas (France); Gen. Man. FRANCISCO VALENZUELA CORNEJO.

Chilena Consolidada, SA: Pedro de Valdivia 195, Casilla 16587, Correo 9, Providencia, Santiago; tel. (2) 200-7000; fax (2) 274-9933; internet www.chilena.cl; f. 1853; owned by Zurich group; general and life; Pres. GASTÓN AGUIRRE SILVA; Gen. Man. JOSÉ MANUEL CAMPOSANO LARRAECHEA.

Chubb de Chile Compañía de Seguros Generales, SA: Gertrudis Echeñique 30, 4°, Santiago; tel. (2) 398-7000; fax (2) 398-7090; e-mail jecheverria@chubb.com; internet www.chubb.com/international/chile; f. 1992; general; Gen. Man. CLAUDIO M. ROSSI.

Cía de Seguros de Crédito Continental, SA: Avda Isidora Goyenechea 3162, 6°, Edif. Parque 1 Golf, Santiago; tel. (2) 636-4000; fax (2) 636-4001; e-mail comer@continental.cl; internet www.continental.cl; f. 1990; general; Gen. Man. FRANCISCO ARTIGAS CELIS.

Cía de Seguros de Vida Cruz del Sur, SA: El Golf 150, Santiago; tel. (2) 461-8000; fax (2) 334-7250; internet www.cruzdelsur.cl; f. 1992; life; Pres. ROBERTO ANGELINI; Gen. Man. MIKEL URIARTE PLAZAOLA.

Consorcio, SA: Edif. Consorcio, Avda El Bosque Sur 180, Providencia, Santiago; tel. (2) 230-4000; fax (2) 230-4050; internet www.consorcio.cl; f. 1916; life and general insurance; Pres. JUAN BILBAO HORMAECHE; Gen. Man. NICOLÁS GELLONA AMUNATEGUI.

Euroamérica Seguros de Vida, SA: Agustinas 1127, 3°, Casilla 21-D, Santiago; tel. (2) 479-9000; fax (2) 479-9428; internet www.euroamerica.cl; f. 1962; life; Pres. BENJAMIN I. DAVIS CLARKE; Gen. Man. CLAUDIO ASECIO FULGERI.

HDI Seguros, SA: Encomenderos 113, Casilla 185-D, Centro 192, Las Condes, Santiago; tel. (2) 422-9000; fax (2) 232-8209; internet www.hdi.cl; f. 1989 in Chile; general; CEO PATRICIO ALDUNATE.

ING Seguros de Vida, SA: Avda Suecia 211, Providencia, Santiago; tel. (2) 252-1464; fax (2) 364-2060; internet www.ingvida.cl; f. 1989; life; Gen. Man. RODRIGO GUZMÁN LEYTON.

Mapfre Seguros: Isidora Goyenechea 3520, 14°, Casilla 7550071, Las Condes, Santiago; tel. (2) 700-4000; fax (2) 694-7565; internet www.mapfreseguros.cl; f. 1991; general; Gen. Man. JULIO DOMINGO SOUTO.

Renta Nacional Compañías de Seguros, SA: Amunátegui 178, 2°, Santiago; tel. (2) 670-0200; fax (2) 670-0039; e-mail fbeytia@rentanac.cl; internet www.rentanac.cl; f. 1982; life; Pres. FRANCISCO JAVIER ERRÁZURIZ OVALLE.

Royal & Sun Alliance Seguros (Chile), SA: Providencia 1760, 4°, Santiago; tel. (2) 661-1000; fax (2) 661-1413; e-mail lacwebmaster@lacrso.royalsun.com; internet www.royalsunalliance.cl; f. 2000; Pres. VÍCTOR MANUEL JARPA RIVEROS.

Santander Seguros: Bombero Ossa 1068, 4°, Santiago; tel. (2) 676-4100; fax (2) 676-4220; internet www.santandersantiago.cl/santander_seguros/index.asp; life.

Seguros Interamericana: Agustinas 640, 9°, Casilla 111, Correo Central, Santiago; tel. (2) 630-3000; fax (2) 633-2239; internet www.interamericana.cl; f. 1980; life; Exec. Pres. RICARDO GARCÍA; Gen. Man. EDUARDO BUSTAMENTE.

Vida Security, SA: Apoquindo 3150, 8°, Las Condes, Santiago; tel. (2) 584-2400; internet www.vidasecurity.cl; f. 2002 through merger of Seguros Security and Seguros Previsión Vida; Pres. FRANCISCO SILVA SILVA; Gen. Man. ALEJANDRO ALZÉRRECA LUNA.

Insurance Association

Asociación de Aseguradores de Chile, AG: La Concepción 322, Of. 501, Providencia, Santiago; tel. (2) 236-2596; fax (2) 235-1502; e-mail seguros@aach.cl; internet www.aach.cl; f. 1931; Pres. MIKEL URIARTE PLAZAOLA.

Trade and Industry

GOVERNMENT AGENCIES

National Energy Commission (Comisión Nacional de Energía—CNE): see The Government—Ministries.

National Environment Commission (Comisión Nacional del Medio Ambiente—CONAMA): Teatinos 258, Santiago; tel. (2) 240-5600; fax (2) 244-3437; e-mail conama@conama.cl; internet www.conama.cl; f. 1994; environmental regulatory body; Minister MARÍA IGNACIA BENÍTEZ PEREIRA; Exec. Dir VERÓNICA FLORES SÁNCHEZ.

Corporación de Fomento de la Producción (CORFO): Moneda 921, Casilla 3886, Santiago; tel. (2) 631-8200; e-mail info@corfo.cl; internet www.corfo.cl; f. 1939; holding group of principal state enterprises; grants loans and guarantees to private sector; responsible for sale of non-strategic state enterprises; promotes entrepreneurship; Pres. JUAN ANDRÉS FONTAINE TALAVERA (Minister of the Economy, Economic Promotion and Reconstruction); Exec. Vice-Pres. CARLOS ALVAREZ VOULLIÈME; 13 brs.

PROCHILE (Dirección General de Relaciones Económicas Internacionales): Alameda 1315, 2°, Casilla 14087, Correo 21, Santiago; tel. (2) 565-9000; fax (2) 696-0639; e-mail info@prochile.cl; internet www.prochile.cl; f. 1974; bureau of international economic affairs; Dir ALICIA FROHMANN.

Servicio Nacional de Capacitación y Empleo (SENCE) (National Training and Employment Service): Teatinos 333, 8°, Santiago; tel. (2) 870-6222; fax (2) 696-7103; internet www.sence.cl; attached to Ministry of Labour and Social Security; Dir FERNANDO ROULIEZ FLECK.

STATE CORPORATIONS

Corporación Nacional del Cobre de Chile (CODELCO-Chile): Huérfanos 1270, Casilla 150-D, Santiago; tel. (2) 690-3000; fax (2) 690-3059; e-mail comunica@codelco.cl; internet www.codelco.com; f. 1976 as a state-owned enterprise with copper-producing operational divisions at Chuquicamata, Radomiro Tomić, Salvador, Andina, Talleres Rancagua and El Teniente; attached to Ministry of Mining; Pres. LAURENCE GOLBORNE RIVEROS (Minister of Mining); Exec. Pres. JOSÉ PABLO ARELLANO MARÍN; 18,496 employees.

Empresa Nacional de Petróleo (ENAP): Vitacura 2736, 10°, Las Condes, Santiago; tel. (2) 280-3000; fax (2) 280-3199; e-mail webenap@enap.cl; internet www.enap.cl; f. 1950; state-owned petroleum and gas exploration and production corpn; Pres. LAURENCE GOLBORNE RIVEROS (Minister of Mining); Gen. Man. ENRIQUE DÁVILA ALVEAL; 3,286 employees.

DEVELOPMENT ORGANIZATIONS

Comisión Chilena de Energía Nuclear: Amunátegui 95, Santiago; tel. (2) 470-2500; fax (2) 470-2570; e-mail oirs@cchen.cl; internet www.cchen.cl; f. 1965; govt body to develop peaceful uses of atomic energy; concentrates, regulates and controls all matters related to nuclear energy; Pres. ROBERTO HOJMAN GUIÑERMAN; Exec. Dir FERNÁNDO LÓPEZ.

Corporación Nacional de Desarrollo Indígena (Conadi): Aldunate 620, 8°, Temuco, Chile; tel. (45) 641-500; fax (45) 641-520; e-mail ctranamil@conadi.gov.cl; internet www.conadi.cl; promotes the economic and social development of indigenous communities; Nat. Dir AROLDO CAYUN ANTICURA.

Corporación Nacional Forestal (CONAF): Región Metropolitana, Valenzuela Castillo 1868, Santiago; tel. (2) 225-0428; fax (2) 225-0641; e-mail consulta@conaf.cl; internet www.conaf.cl; f. 1970 to promote forestry activities, enforce forestry law, promote afforestation, administer subsidies for afforestation projects and to increase and preserve forest resources; manages 13.97m. ha designated as National Parks, Natural Monuments and National Reserves; under Ministry of Agriculture; Dir MARÍA CATALINA BAU.

Empresa Nacional de Minería (ENAMI): MacIver 459, 2°, Casilla 100-D, Santiago; tel. (2) 637-5278; fax (2) 637-5452; e-mail eiturra@enami.cl; internet www.enami.cl; promotes the devt of small and medium-sized mines; attached to Ministry of Mining; partially privatized; Exec. Vice-Pres. JAIME PÉREZ DE ARCE ARAYA.

CHAMBERS OF COMMERCE

Cámara de Comercio de Santiago: Edif. Del Comercio, Monjitas 392, Santiago; tel. (2) 360-7000; fax (2) 633-3595; e-mail cpn@ccs.cl; internet www.ccs.cl; f. 1919; 1,300 mems; Pres. PETER HILL D.

Cámara de Comercio, Servicios y Turismo de Antofagasta: Latorre 2580, Of. 21, Antofagasta; tel. (55) 225-175; fax (55) 222-053; e-mail info@camaracomercioantofagasta.cl; internet www.camaracomercioantofagasta.cl; f. 1924; Pres. GONZALO SANTOLAYA GOICOVIC.

Cámara de Comercio, Servicios y Turismo de Temuco, AG: Vicuña Mackenna 396, Temuco; tel. (45) 210-556; fax (45) 237-047; e-mail info@camaratemuco.cl; internet www.camaratemuco.cl; Pres. HERNÁN VIGUERA LÓPEZ; Sec. PEDRO GUTIÉRREZ AYALA.

Cámara Nacional de Comercio, Servicios y Turismo de Chile: Merced 230, Santiago; tel. (2) 365-4000; fax (2) 365-4001; internet www.cnc.cl; f. 1858; Pres. PEDRO CORONA BOZZO; Pres., Int. Cttee ALEX THIERMANN I.; 120 mems.

Cámara de la Producción y del Comercio de Concepción: Cauplicán 567, 2°, Concepción; tel. (41) 224-1121; fax (41) 222-7903; e-mail lmandiola@cpcc.cl; internet www.cpcc.cl; f. 1927; Pres. PEDRO SCHLACK HARNECKER; Gen. Man. LEONCIO TORO ARAYA.

INDUSTRIAL AND TRADE ASSOCIATIONS

Servicio Agrícola y Ganadero (SAG): Avda Bulnes 140, Santiago; tel. (2) 345-1100; fax (2) 345-1102; e-mail dirnac@sag.gob.cl; internet www.sag.cl; under Ministry of Agriculture; responsible for the protection and devt of safe practice in the sector; Nat. Dir FRANCISCO JAVIER BAHAMONDE MEDINA.

Servicio Nacional de Pesca (SERNAPESCA): Victoria 2832, Valparaíso; tel. (32) 281-9100; fax (32) 25-6311; e-mail informaciones@sernapesca.cl; internet www.sernapesca.cl; f. 1978; govt regulator of the fishing industry; Dir FÉLIX INOSTROZA.

Sociedad Agrícola y Servicios Isla de Pascua (SASIPA): Hotu Matu'a s/n, Hanga Roa, Isla de Pascua; tel. (32) 210-0212; e-mail atencion@sasipa.cl; internet www.sasipa.cl; f. 1966; administers agriculture and public services on Easter Island; Pres. LUIS MANUEL RODRÍGUEZ CUEVAS.

EMPLOYERS' ORGANIZATIONS

Confederación del Comercio Detallista y Turismo de Chile, AG (CONFEDECH): Merced 380, 8°, Of. 74, Santiago; tel. (2) 639-1264; fax (2) 638-0338; e-mail comerciodetallista@confedech.cl; internet www.comerciodetallista.cl; f. 1938; retail trade; Nat. Pres. RAFAEL CUMSILLE ZAPAPA; Sec.-Gen. ROBERTO ZUÑIGA BELAUZARÁN.

Confederación de la Producción y del Comercio: Monseñor Sótero Sanz 182, Providencia, Santiago; tel. (2) 231-9764; fax (2) 231-9808; e-mail procomer@entelchile.net; internet www.cpc.cl; f. 1936; Pres. RAFAEL GUILISASTI GANA.

Affiliated organizations:

Asociación de Bancos e Instituciones Financieras de Chile AG: see Finance (Banking Association).

Cámara Nacional de Comercio, Servicios y Turismo de Chile: see Chambers of Commerce.

Cámara Chilena de la Construcción: Marchant Pereira 10, 3°, Providencia, CP 6640721, Santiago; tel. (2) 376-3300; fax (2) 371-3430; internet www.camaraconstruccion.cl; f. 1951; Pres. LUIS NARIO MATUS; Sec.-Gen. ARTURO DEL RÍO LEYTON; 17,442 mems.

Sociedad de Fomento Fabril, FG (SOFOFA): Avda Andrés Bello 2777, 3°, Las Condes, Santiago; tel. (2) 391-3100; fax (2) 391-3200; internet www.sofofa.cl; f. 1883; largest employers' org.; Pres. BRUNO PHILIPPI IRARRÁZABAL; Sec.-Gen. ANDRÉS CONCHA RODRÍGUEZ; 2,500 mems.

Sociedad Nacional de Agricultura—Federación Gremial (SNA): Tenderini 187, 2°, CP 6500978, Santiago; tel. (2) 639-6710; fax (2) 633-7771; e-mail info@sna.cl; internet www.sna.cl; f. 1838; landowners' asscn; controls Radio Stations CB 57 and XQB8 (FM) in Santiago, CB-97 in Valparaíso, CD-120 in Los Angeles, CA-144 in La Serena, CD-127 in Temuco; Pres. LUIS SCHMIDT MONTES.

Sociedad Nacional de Minería (SONAMI): Avda Apoquindo 3000, 5°, Santiago; tel. (2) 335-9300; fax (2) 334-9700; e-mail monica.cavallini@sonami.cl; internet www.sonami.cl; f. 1883; Pres. ALFREDO OVALLE RODRÍGUEZ; Gen. Man. ALBERTO SALAS MUÑOZ; 48 mem. cos.

CONUPIA (Confederación Gremial Nacional Unida de la Mediana y Pequeña Industria, Servicios y Artesanado): Phillips 40, 6°, Of. 63, Providencia, Santiago; tel. (2) 633-1492; internet www.conupia.cl; e-mail secgeneral@conupia.cl; f. 1966; small and medium-sized industries and crafts; Pres. PEDRO DAVIS URZÚA; Sec.-Gen. JOSÉ LUIS RAMÍREZ ZAMORANO.

MAJOR COMPANIES

Petroleum and Mining

Antofagasta Minerals, SA: Avda Apoquindo 4001, 18°, Las Condes, Santiago; tel. (2) 798-7000; fax (2) 798-7402; e-mail info@antofagasta.co.uk; internet www.antofagasta.co.uk; subsidiary of Antofagasta PLC, United Kingdom; copper mining; CEO MARCELO AWAD; 1,736 employees.

Compañía de Petróleos de Chile, SA (COPEC): Agustinas 1382, 1°–7°, Casilla 9391, Santiago 6500586; tel. (2) 690-7000; fax (2) 672-5119; e-mail icontact@copec.cl; internet www.copec.cl; f. 1934; manufacturers of petroleum products; owned by Angelini group following privatization in 1986; Pres. ROBERTO ANGELINI ROSSI; Gen. Man. LORENZO GAZMURI SCHLEYER; 8,500 employees.

Minera Escondida Ltda: Avda Américo Vespucio Sur 100, 9°, Las Condes, Santiago; tel. (2) 330-5000; fax (2) 207-6520; internet www.escondida.cl; f. 1985; 57.5% owned by BHP Billiton (Australia), 30% owned by Rio Tinto PLC (United Kingdom); copper mining and cathodes production; Pres. EDGAR BASTO; 2,189 employees.

Sociedad Punta del Cobre, SA (PYCOBRE): Avda El Bosque Sur 130, 14°, Las Condes, Santiago; tel. (2) 379-4560; fax (2) 379-4570; e-mail info@pucobre.cl; internet www.pucobre.cl; f. 1989; copper processing; Chair. FERNANDO HARAMBILLET ALONSO; Gen. Man. SEBASTIAN RÍOS RIVAS; 360 employees.

Sociedad Química y Minera de Chile, SA (SQM, SA): El Trovador 4285, Las Condes, Santiago; tel. (2) 425-2000; fax (2) 425-2060; e-mail admin_web@sqm.cl; internet www.sqm.cl; f. 1968; mining co; nitrates etc.; Pres. JULIO PONCE LEROU; CEO PATRICIO CONTESSE GONZÁLEZ; 3,418 employees.

Soprocal, Calerías e Industrias, SA: Avda Pedro de Valdivia 0193, Of. 31, Providencia, Santiago; tel. (2) 231-8874; fax (2) 233-3396; e-mail info@soprocal.cl; internet www.soprocal.cl; f. 1940; producers of lime; Exec. Chair. ALFONSO ROZAS OSSA; CEO ISMAEL CUEVAS ZANARTE; 72 employees.

Food and Beverages

Agrícola Nacional, SACEI (ANASAC): 300 Almirante Pastene, Providencia, Santiago; tel. (2) 470-6800; e-mail info@anasac.cl; internet www.anasac.cl; f. 1948; food, agricultural chemicals and pest control; Chair. FERNANDO MARTÍNEZ PEREZ-CANTO; 553 employees; CEO EUGENIO DE MARCHENA GÚZMAN.

Coca-Cola Embonor, SA: Santa María 2652, Arica; tel. (5) 820-2400; internet www.embonor.cl; f. 1943; bottling company for Coca-Cola; Chair. ANDRÉS VICUÑA GARCÍA-HUIDOBRO; Gen. Man. RODRIGO WOOD ARMAS; 4,193 employees.

Compañía Cervecerías Unidas, SA (CCU): Vitacura 2670, Las Condes, Santiago; tel. (2) 427-3000; fax (2) 427-3333; e-mail ccuir@ccu-sa.com; internet www.ccu-sa.com; f. 1902; part of Quiñenco conglomerate; 20% owned by Anheuser Busch of the USA; beverages; Pres. GUILLERMO LUKSIC CRAIG; Gen. Man. PATRICIO JOTTAR NASRALLAH; 4,500 employees.

Concha y Toro, SA: Avda Nueva Tajamar 481, Torre Norte, 15°, Santiago; tel. (2) 476-5000; fax (2) 203-6740; e-mail conchaytoro@banfivintners.com; internet www.conchaytoro.com; f. 1883; vintners; Chair. ALFONSO LARRAÍN; CEO EDUARDO GUILISASTI GANA.

Copefrut, SA: Panamericana Sur, Km 185, Curico; tel. (2) 209-220; fax (2) 380-905; e-mail copefrut@copefrut.cl; internet www.copefrut.cl; f. 1955; fruit producers and exporters; Chair. JOSÉ LUIS SOLER RUIZ; Gen. Man. FERNANDO CISTERNAS LIRA; 309 employees.

CORPESCA, SA: Avda El Golf 150, 15°, Las Condes, Santiago; tel. (2) 476 4000; internet www.corpesca.cl; f. 1955; fish oil and flour producers; Chair. ROBERTO ANGELINI ROSSI; CEO FRANCISO MUJICA ORTÚZAR; 600 employees.

Dos en Uno, SA: Placer 1324, Santiago; tel. (2) 520-8700; e-mail arcor@dosenuno.cl; internet www.dosenuno.cl; f. 1989; part of Grupo Arcor (Argentina); makers of biscuits, cakes, etc.; CEO RAÚL QUEMADA LERIA; 1,700 employees.

Embotelladora Andina, SA: Avda El Golf 40, 4° Las Condes, Santiago; tel. (2) 338-0500; fax (2) 338-0530; e-mail inv.rel@koandina.com; internet www.koandina.com; f. 1946; bottling company for Coca-Cola; also operates in Brazil and Argentina; Chair. JUAN CLARO GONZÁLEZ; CEO JAIME GARCÍA RIOSECO; 4,284 employees.

Empresas Iansa, SA: Rosario Norte 615, 23°, Las Condes, Santiago; tel. (2) 571-5400; fax (2) 565-5525; e-mail iansa@iansa.cl; internet www.empresasiansa.cl; f. 1953; sugar production, frozen fruit and vegetables, fruit juices, animal feed; fmrly known as Industria Azucarera Nacional, SA; Chair. JOAQUÍN NOGUERA WILSON; CEO JOSÉ LUIS IRARRÁZAVAL OVALLE; 1,255 employees (Dec. 2004).

Iansagro, SA: Km 385 Panamericana Sur, San Carlos, Chillán; tel. (42) 454-300; fax (42) 454-338; internet www.iansagro.cl; agricultural produce and animal feed; owned by Empresas Iansa, SA; Gen. Man. ALVARO PRIETO; 2,173 employees.

Empresas Santa Carolina, SA: Rodrigo de Araya 1431, Macul, Santiago; tel. (2) 450-3000; fax (2) 238-0307; internet www.santacarolina.cl; f. 1874; wine producers; part of Grupo CB conglomerate; Gen. Man. FELIPE DE LA JARA; 1,117 employees.

Fruticola Viconto, SA: Avda Apoquindo 4775, 16°, Las Condes, Santiago; tel. (2) 707-4200; fax (2) 707-4250; e-mail viconto@viconto.cl; internet www.viconto.cl; f. 1986; wholesale fruit exporters; Pres. ANDRÉS LARRAÍN SANTA MARÍA; Gen. Man. JOSE MANUEL GUILISASTI GANA; 200 employees.

Industrias Alimentícias Carozzi, SA: Camino Longitudinal Sur 5201, Km 23, Casilla 70, San Bernardo, Santiago; tel. (2) 377-6400; fax (2) 857-2579; internet www.carozzi.cl; f. 1898; food-processing; Pres. GONZALO BOFILL VELARDE; Gen. Man. JOSÉ JUAN LLUGANY RIGO-RIGHY; 5,584 employees.

Pesquera Itata, SA: Avda Presidente Riesco 5711, Of. 1201, Las Condes, Santiago; tel. (2) 782-5400; fax (2) 231-0973; e-mail info@itata.com; internet www.itata.com; f. 1948; fish and fish products; Pres. SERGIO SARQUIS MENASSA; Gen. Man. GERARDO BALBONTÍN; 307 employees.

Sociedad Pesquera Coloso, SA: Avda El Bosque Norte 0440, 10°, Las Condes, Santiago; tel. (2) 371-2600; fax (2) 203-5301; e-mail caracena@coloso.cl; internet www.coloso.cl; processed fish exporters; owners of Pesquera San José, SA; Pres. SERGIO LECAROS MENÉNDEZ; Gen. Man. DOMINGO JIMÉNEZ OLMO; 731 employees.

Viña Errázuriz, SA: Avda Nueva Tajamar 481, Torre Sur, Of. 503, Torre Sur, Las Condes, Santiago; tel. (2) 339-9100; fax (2) 203-6690; e-mail wine.report@errazuriz.cl; internet www.errazuriz.com;

f. 1870; wine producers; Pres. EDUARDO CHADWICK; Man. Dir FELIPE DE LA JARA; 180 employees.

Viña San Pedro, SA: Avda Vitacura 4380, 6°, Vitacura, Santiago; tel. (2) 477-5300; fax (2) 477-5307; e-mail info@sanpedro.cl; internet www.sanpedro.cl; f. 1865; wine producers; part of Grupo San Pedro Tarapacá; Pres. GUILLERMO LUKSIC CRAIG; Gen. Man. JAVIER BITAR HIRMAS; 347 employees.

Viña Undurraga, SA: Edif.Millenium, 21°, Avda Vitacura 2939, Las Condes, Santiago; tel. (2) 372-2900; fax (2) 372-2901; e-mail info@undurraga.cl; internet www.undurraga.cl; f. 1885; wine producers; Chair. MAURICIO PICCIOTTO KASSIN; Gen. Man. JOSÉ YURASZECK TRONCOSO; 576 employees.

Viñedos Emiliana, SA: Edif. World Trade Center, Avda Nueva Tajamar 481, Las Condes, Santiago; tel. (2) 353-9130; fax (2) 203-6227; e-mail info@emiliana.cl; internet www.emiliana.cl; f. 1986; wines and spirits producers; Chair. SERGIO CALVO SALAS; Gen. Man RAFAEL GUILISASTI GANA; 508 employees.

Wood, Pulp and Paper

Celulosa Arauco y Constitución, SA (ARAUCO): El Golf 150, 14°, Las Condes, Santiago; tel. (2) 461-7200; fax (2) 698-5987; internet www.arauco.cl; f. 1967; wood pulp and timber group; operations in Argentina and Brazil; Chair. JOSÉ TOMÁS GUZMÁN; CEO MATÍAS DOMEYKO; 35,000 employees.

Empresas CMPC, SA: Agustinas 1343, Santiago; tel. (2) 441-2000; fax (2) 672-1115; e-mail pfriedl@gerencia.cmpc.cl; internet www.cmpc.cl; f. 1920; paper and packaging manufacturers, cellulose, wood products and pulp; Chair. ELIODORO MATTE; Gen. Man. ARTURO MACKENNA; 11,919 employees.

Industrias Forestales, SA: Agustinas 1357, 9°, Santiago; tel. (2) 441-2050; fax (2) 695-7809; internet www.inforsa.cl; f. 1956; paper producers; Pres. WASHINGTON WILLIAMSON BENAPRÉS; Gen. Man. ANDRÉS LARRAÍN MARCHANT; 372 employees.

Construction Materials

Besalco, SA: Ebro 2705, Las Condes, Santiago; tel. (3) 334-4000; fax (3) 334-4031; e-mail besalco@besalco.cl; internet www.besalco.cl; f. 1944; civil engineering and construction; Pres. VICTOR BEZANILLA SAAVEDRA; Gen. Man. PAULO BEZANILLA SAAVEDRA; 7,200 employees.

Cemento Polpaico, SA: Avda El Bosque Norte 0177, Las Condes, Santiago; tel. (2) 337-6456; fax (2) 337-6324; e-mail ventaspolpaico@polpaico.cl; internet www.polpaico.cl; f. 1948; jtly owned by GASCO and Holcim of Switzerland; Pres. JUAN ANTONIO GUZMÁN MOLINARI; Gen. Man. LOUIS BEAUCHEMIN; 890 employees.

Cementos Bío-Bío, SA: Barros Errazuriz 1968, 4°, Casilla 16603, Providencia, Santiago; tel. (2) 560-7000; fax (2) 560-7001; internet www.cbb.cl; f. 1957; cement, forestry and raw materials; Pres. HERNÁN BRIANES GOICH; CEO JORGE MATUS CAMPOS; 1,128 employees.

Cerámicas Cordillera, SA: Avda Americo Vespucio 1001, Quilicura, Santiago; tel. (2) 387-4200; fax (2) 387-4321; e-mail cemento@melon.lafarge.cl; internet www.cordillera.cl; f. 1984; tiles, building materials; owned by Empresas Pizarreño SA; Pres. JORGE BENNETT URRUTIA; Gen. Man. JOSE IGNACIO URCELAY F.; 243 employees.

Compañía Industrial El Volcán, SA: Agustinas 1357, 10°, Santiago; tel. (2) 483-0500; fax (2) 380-9710; internet www.volcan.cl; f. 1916; makers of insulation and gypsum products; Pres. BERNARDO MATTE LARRAÍN; Gen. Man. ANTONIO LARRAÍN IBÁÑEZ; 287 employees.

Edelpa, SA (Envases del Pacífico, SA): Camino a Melipilla 13320, Maipú, Santiago 45; tel. (2) 385-4500; fax (2) 385-4600; e-mail comercial@edelpa.cl; internet www.edelpa.cl; f. 1984; plastic packaging and bottling producers; owners of Italprint, SA; Chair. JOSÉ DOMINGO ELEUCHANS URENDA; Gen. Man. OSCAR JAIME LÓPEZ; 506 employees.

Empresas Pizarreño, SA: Camino a Melipilla 10803, Maipú, Santiago; tel. (2) 391-2401; fax (2) 391-2402; e-mail info@pizarreno.cl; internet www.pizarreno.cl; f. 1935; owned by Etex of Belgium; plastic building materials; controls Cerámica Cordillera, SA; Chair. CANIO CORBO LIOI; Gen. Man. JORGE BENNETT URRUTIA; 2,553 employees.

Melón SA: Vitacura 2939, Las Condes, Santiago; tel. (2) 280-0000; fax (2) 280-0412; internet www.lafarge.cl; f. 1908 as Empresas Melón, SA; renamed Lafarge Chile in 2007; acquired by Grupo Brescia (Perú) and adopted present name in 2009; manufacturers of cement; Pres. PEDRO BRESCIA CAFFERATA; Gen. Man. JORGE EUGENÍN ULLOA; 77,000 employees (group).

Metals and Chemicals

Aceros Chile, SA: Avda Diego Portales Oriente 3499-A, Casilla 808-0776, San Bernardo, Santiago; tel. (2) 483-8700; fax (2) 483-8701; e-mail info@aceroschile.cl; internet www.aceroschile.cl; f. 1980; steelmakers; Gen. Man. HUGO GAIDO GÓMEZ; 188 employees.

CAP, SA: Gertrudis Echeñique 220, Las Condes, Santiago; tel. (2) 818-6000; fax (2) 818-6116; e-mail webmaster@cap.cl; internet www.cap.cl; f. 1946; steel producer and exporter; Pres. ROBERTO DE ANDRACA; Gen. Man. JAIME CHARLES; 4,746 employees.

Compañía Electro Metalúrgica, SA (Elecmetal): Avda Vicuña Mackenna 1570, Ñuñoa, Santiago; tel. (2) 361-4020; fax (2) 361-4021; e-mail info@me-elecmetal.com; internet www.elecmetal.cl; f. 1917; metal foundry, manufactures parts for heavy machinery; part of Cristalchile group; Chair. JAIME CLARO VALDÉS; Gen. Man. ROLANDO MEDEIROS SOUX; 3,653 employees.

Enaex, SA: Renato Sánchez 3859, Las Condes, Santiago; tel. (2) 837-7600; fax (2) 206-6752; e-mail enaex@enaex.cl; internet www.enaex.cl; f. 1920; industrial chemicals, incl. explosives; Chair. JUAN EDUARDO ERRÁRUIZ OSSA; Gen. Man. JUAN ANDRÉS ERRÁZURIZ DOMÍNGUEZ; 863 employees.

Instituto Sanitas, SA: Avda Américo Vespucio Norte 01260, Quilicura, Santiago; tel. (2) 444-6600; fax (2) 444-6651; e-mail sanitas@sanitas.cl; internet www.sanitas.cl; f. 1920; medicines and vaccines; Chair. JOAQUÍN BARROS FONTAINE; 171 employees.

Laboratorio Chile, SA: Avda Maratón 1315, Ñuñoa, Santiago; tel. (2) 365-5000; fax (2) 365-5100; e-mail pilar.rodriguez@labchile.cl; internet www.labchile.cl; f. 1896; pharmaceutical co; mem. of the Teva Group (Israel); CEO HERNÁN PFEIFER; 1,000 employees.

Madeco, SA: Ureta Cox 930, San Francisco 4760, San Miguel, Santiago; tel. (2) 520-1000; fax (2) 520-1140; e-mail cgt@madeco.cl; internet www.madeco.cl; f. 1944; metallurgy and packaging; part of Quiñenco conglomerate; Chair. GUILLERMO LUKSIC CRAIG; Gen. Man. CRISTIÁN MONTES LAHAYE; 2,949 employees.

Molymet, SA (Molibdenos y Metales, SA): Huérfanos 812, 6°, Casilla 1974, Santiago; tel. (2) 368-3600; fax (2) 368-3653; e-mail info@molymet.cl; internet www.molymet.cl; f. 1975; producers of industrial chemicals and ferroalloy ores; Chair. CARLOS HURTADO RUIZ-TAGLE; CEO JOHN GRAELL MOORE; 602 employees.

Tricolor, SA: Avda Claudio Arrau 9440, Pudahuel, Santiago; tel. (2) 290-8700; fax (2) 601-0055; e-mail contactenos@tricolor.cl; internet www.tricolor.cl; part of Grupo CB conglomerate; paint; Gen. Man. ROBERTO LEHMANN COSOI; 606 employees.

Textiles

Bata Chile, SA: Camino a Melipilla 9460, Maipú, Santiago; tel. (02) 560-4200; fax (02) 533-2931; e-mail bsochile@bata.cl; internet www.bata.cl; f. 1939; manufacturers and distributors of sportswear and shoes; Chair. FERNANDO RIVERA JIMÉNEZ; Gen. Man. GONZALO LANDAETA PEREIRA; 2,132 employees.

Retail

Cencosud, SA: Avda Kennedy 9001, Las Condes, Santiago; tel. (2) 959-0000; fax (2) 212-1469; e-mail contactoscl@cencosud.cl; internet www.cencosud.cl; f. 1952; retail conglomerate; Chilean concerns incl. Jumbo (hypermarkets), Santa Isabel (supermarkets), Easy (home improvement stores) and Paris (dept stores); operations in Argentina, Brazil, Colombia and Peru; Chair. HORST PAULMANN KEMNA; CEO DANIEL RODRÍGUEZ COFRÉ (acting).

D y S, SA (Distribución y Servicio, SA): Avda Presidente Eduardo Frei Montalva 8301, Quilicura, Santiago 7490562; tel. (2) 200-5000; fax (2) 200-5100; e-mail info@dys.cl; internet www.dys.cl; f. 1893; supermarket group, owns Ekono and Líder chains; Chair. FELIPE IBÁÑEZ SCOTT; CEO ENRIQUE OSTALÉ CAMBIASO; 17,000 employees.

Falabella, SACI: Rosas 1665, Santiago; tel. (2) 620-2000; fax (2) 620-2000; internet www.falabella.cl; f. 1889; dept stores and textiles; Pres. REINALDO SOLARI MAGNASCO; CEO JUAN BENAVIDES FELIÚ; 13,935 employees.

Sodimac, SA: Avda Presidente Eduardo Frei 3092, Renca, Casilla 3110, Santiago; tel. (2) 738-1000; fax (2) 641-8271; internet www.sodimac.cl; f. 1982; home improvement products retailers; Chair. JUAN PABLO DEL RÍO GOUDIE; CEO SANDRO SOLARI; 20,000 employees.

Information Technology

Adexus, SA: Miraflores 383, 20°, Santiago; tel. (2) 686-1000; fax (2) 686-1201; e-mail adexus@adexus.cl; internet www.adexus.com; information technology systems contractors; f. 1990 as Tandem Chile, SA; name changed 1998; Chair. PATRICIO DEL SANTE SCROGGIE; CEO CARLOS BUSSO VYHMEISTER; 500 employees.

Sonda, SA: Teatinos 500, Santiago; tel. (2) 657-5000; fax (2) 657-5410; e-mail info@sonda.com; internet www.sonda.com; f. 1974; information technology services; Pres. ANDRÉS NAVARRO HAEUSSLER; Gen. Man RAÚL VÉJAR OLEA; 2,400 employees.

Miscellaneous

Compañía Chilena de Fósforos, SA: Los Conquistadores 1700, 15°, Providencia, Santiago; tel. (2) 707-6200; fax (2) 231-5072; e-mail ventas@fosforos.cl; internet www.fosforos.cl; f. 1913; makers of safety matches and producers of wine; Pres. José Luis Vender Bresciani; Gen. Man. Viviana Horta Pometto; 1,776 employees.

Compañía Chilena de Tabacos, SA (Chiletabacos): Avda Isidora Goyenechea 3000, Casilla 267-V, Las Condes, Santiago; tel. (2) 464-6000; fax (2) 464-6241; internet www.chiletabacos.cl; f. 1909; subsidiary of British American Tobacco Co Ltd, United Kingdom; tobacco co; Pres. Carlos Francisco Cáceres; Gen. Man. Benjamin Kemball; 752 employees.

Compañía Tecno Industrial, SA (CTI, SA): Alberto Llona 777, Maipú, Santiago; tel. (2) 837-6000; fax (2) 532-8773; e-mail wadm@cti.cl; internet www.cti.cl; f. 1905; manufacturers of domestic electrical appliances; Chair. Juan Eduardo Errázuriz Ossa; CEO Mario Rodrigo Oportus Morales; 1,254 employees.

Compañias CIC, SA: Avda Esquina Blanca 960, Maipú, Santiago; tel. (2) 530-4000; fax (2) 557-4396; e-mail servicio@cic.cl; internet www.cic.cl; f. 1912; exporters of wooden furniture, mattresses, etc.; Chair. Leonidas E. Vial Echeverría; Gen. Man. Miguel Valenzuela Lagos; 994 employees.

Cristalerías de Chile, SA (Cristalchile, SA): Apoquindo 3669, 16°, Las Condes, Santiago; tel. (2) 787-8888; fax (2) 787-8800; e-mail gerencia@cristalchile.cl; internet www.cristalchile.cl; f. 1904; bottle and packaging producers; the group also controls winemakers Santa Rita, the *Diario Financiero* newspaper and the Megavisión television network; Chair. Baltazar Sánchez Guzmán; CEO Cirilo Elton González; 700 employees.

Sociedad El Tattersall, SA: Isidora Goyenechea 3600, 5°, Las Condes, Santiago; tel. (2) 362-3005; fax (2) 362-3002; e-mail sociedad@tattersall.cl; internet www.tattersall.cl; f. 1913; distributors of agricultural machinery; also represent Budget car rentals in Chile; Chair. Tomás Böttiger Müller; Gen. Man. Jorge Rodriguez Cifuentes; 501 employees.

Somela, SA: Avda Escobar Williams 600, Cerillos, Santiago; tel. (2) 837-6600; fax (2) 557-5667; e-mail contacto@somela.cl; internet www.somela.cl; f. 1950; manufacturers of domestic appliances; Chair. Isidoro Palma Penco; Gen. Man. Pablo Arriagada; 183 employees.

UTILITIES

Comisión Nacional de Energía: Teatinos 120, 7°, Clasificador 14, Correo 21, Santiago; tel. (2) 460-6800; fax (2) 365-6800; e-mail energia@cne.cl; internet www.cne.cl; Pres. Ricardo Raineri Bernain (Minister of the CNE); Exec. Sec. Rodrigo Iglesias Acuña.

Superintendencia de Electricidad y Combustibles (SEC): Avda Libertador B. O'Higgins 1449, 13°, Torre 1, Santiago; tel. (2) 756-5149; fax (2) 756-5155; e-mail pchotzen@sec.cl; internet www.sec.cl; Supt Patricia Chotzen Gutiérrez.

Electricity

AES Gener, SA: Mariano Sánchez Fontecilla 310, 3°, Santiago; tel. (2) 686-8900; fax (2) 686-8991; e-mail gener@gener.cl; internet www.gener.cl; f. 1981 as Chilectra Generación, SA; privatized in 1988; current name adopted in 1998; owned by AES Corpn (USA); responsible for operation of power plants Renca, Ventanas, Laguna Verde, El Indio, Altalfal, Maitenes, Queltehues and Volcán; Pres. Andrés Gluski; Gen. Man. Luis Felipe Cerón Cerón; 1,121 employees (group).

Eléctrica Santiago: Jorge Hirmas 2964, Renca, Santiago; tel. (2) 680-4760; fax (2) 680-4743; operates the Renca and the Nueva Renca thermoelectric plants in Santiago; installed capacity of 379 MW.

Empresa Eléctrica Guacolda, SA: Miraflores 222, 16°, Santiago; tel. (2) 362-4000; fax (2) 360-1675; internet www.guacolda.cl; operates a thermoelectric power station in Huasco; installed capacity of 304 MW; Pres. José Florencio Guzmán.

Energía Verde: O'Higgins 940, Of. 90, Concepción; tel. (41) 240-1900; fax (41) 225-3227; internet www.energiaverde.cl; operates 2 co-generation power-stations at Constitución and Laja and a steam plant at Nacimiento; supplies the Cabrero industrial plant; CEO Jaime Zuazagoitía.

Norgener, SA: Jorge Hirmas 2964, Renca, Santiago; tel. (2) 680-4870; fax (2) 680-4895; northern subsidiary supplying the mining industry; Exec. Dir Juan Carlos Olmedo.

Arauco Generación: El Golf 150, 14°, Las Condes, Santiago; tel. (2) 461-7200; fax (2) 698-5987; e-mail gic@arauco.cl; internet www.arauco.cl; f. 1994 to commercialize surplus power from pulp processing facility; Pres. José Tomás Guzmán; Gen. Man. Matías Domeyko.

Chilquinta Energía, SA: General Cruz 222, Valparaíso; tel. (32) 250-2000; fax (32) 223-1171; e-mail contactoweb@chiquinta.cl; internet www.chilquinta.cl; f. 1997 as Energas, SA; present name adopted in 2001; owned by Inversiones Sempra and PSEG of the USA; Pres. George Liparidis; Gen. Man. Cristián Arnolds.

Compañía Eléctrica del Litoral, SA: Avda Peñablanca 540, Algarrobo, Santiago; tel. (2) 481-195; fax (2) 483-313; internet www.litoral.cl; e-mail fmartine@litoral.cl; f. 1949; Gen. Man. Luis Contreras Iglesias.

Compañía General de Electricidad, SA (CGE): Teatinos 280, Santiago; tel. (2) 624-3243; fax (2) 680-7104; e-mail cge@cge.cl; internet www.cge.cl; installed capacity of 662 MW; Pres. Jorge Eduardo Marín Correa; Gen. Man. Pablo Guarda Barros.

Compañía Nacional de Fuerza Eléctrica, SA (CONAFE): Norte 13, Of. 810, Viña del Mar; tel. (32) 220-6100; fax (32) 227-1593; e-mail servicioclientes@conafe.cl; internet www.conafe.cl; f. 1945; Pres. José Luis Hornauer Herrmann; Gen. Man. Raúl Riveras Banderas.

Empresa Eléctrica de Magallanes, SA (Edelmag, SA): Croacia 444, Punta Arenas; tel. (71) 40-00; fax (71) 40-77; e-mail edelmag@edelmag.cl; internet www.edelmag.cl; f. 1981; 55% owned by CGE; Pres. Jorge Jordan Franulic; Gen. Man. Carlos Yáñez Antonucci.

Empresa Eléctrica del Norte Grande, SA (EDELNOR): El Bosque Norte 500, 9°, Vitacura, Santiago; tel. (2) 353-3200; fax (2) 353-3210; e-mail contacto@edelnor.cl; internet www.edelnor.cl; f. 1981; acquired by Codelco and Tractebel SA of Belgium in Dec. 2002; Pres. Jan Flachet; Gen. Man. Juan Clavería A.

Empresas Emel, SA: Avda Libertador B. O'Higgins 886, Central Post Office, 5° y 6°, Santiago; tel. (2) 376-6500; fax (2) 633-3849; internet www.emel.cl; holding co for the Emel group of electricity cos, bought by CGE in Nov. 2007; output in 2000 totalled 18,6124 MWh; Gen. Man. Ricardo Cruzat Ochagavía; Emel group includes:

ELECDA (Empresa Eléctrica de Antofagasta, SA): José Miguel Carrera 1587, Antofagasta 1250; tel. (55) 649-100; Regional Man. Felindo Concha Henríquez.

ELIQSA (Empresa Eléctrica de Iquique, SA): Zegeres 469, Iquique; tel. (57) 40-5400; fax (57) 42-7181; e-mail eliqsa@eliqsa.cl; Regional Man. Marco Antonio Sanquea Ramos.

EMELARI (Empresa Eléctrica de Arica, SA): Baquedano 731, Arica; tel. (58) 201-100; fax (58) 23-1105; Regional Man. Marco Antonio Sanquea Ramos.

EMELAT (Empresa Eléctrica Atacama, SA): Circunvalación Ignacio Carrera Pinto 51, Copiapó; tel. (52) 205-100; fax (52) 205-103; f. 1981; distribution co; Pres. Michael Friedlander; Regional Man. Gabriel Barraza Alcayaga.

EMELECTRIC (Empresa Eléctrica de Melipilla, Colchagua y Maule): Regional Mans Marco Antonio Carvajal, Sergio Quiroz Arias.

ENERSIS, SA: Avda Kennedy 5454, Casilla 1557, Vitacura, Santiago; tel. (2) 353-4400; fax (2) 378-4768; e-mail comunicacion@e.enersis.cl; internet www.enersis.com; f. 1981; holding co for Spanish group generating and distributing electricity through its subsidiaries throughout South America; 60.62% owned by Endesa, SA; Pres. Pablo Yrarrázaval V.; Gen. Man. Ignacio Antoñanzas Alvear; 10,957 employees.

Chilectra, SA: Santo Domingo 789, Casilla 1557, Santiago; tel. (2) 632-2000; fax (2) 639-3280; e-mail rrpp@chilectra.cl; internet www.chilectra.cl; f. 1921; transmission and distribution arm of ENERSIS; supplies distribution cos, including the Empresa Eléctrica Municipal de Lo Barnechea, Empresa Municipal de Til-Til, and the Empresa Eléctrica de Colina, SA; holds overseas distribution concessions in Argentina, Peru and Brazil; acquired by ENERSIS of Spain in 1999; Pres. Jorge Rosenblut; Gen. Man. Rafael López R.

Endesa Chile: Santa Rosa 76, Casilla 1392, Santiago; tel. (2) 630-9000; fax (2) 635-4720; e-mail comunicacion@endesa.cl; internet www.endesa.cl; f. 1943; installed capacity 4,035 MW (Feb. 2002); ENERSIS obtained majority control of Endesa Chile in April 1999; operates subsidiaries Pehuenche, Pangue, San Isidro y Celta; Pres. Mario Valcarce Durán; Gen. Man. Rafael Matea Alcalá.

SAESA (Sociedad Austral de Electricidad, SA): Manuel Bulnes 441, Osorno; tel. (64) 20-6200; fax (64) 20-6209; e-mail saesa@saesa.cl; internet www.saesa.cl; owned by PSEG Corpn of the USA; Pres. Robert Dougherty, Jr; Gen. Man. Eduardo Novoa Castellón.

Gas

Abastible, SA (Abastecedora de Combustible): Avda Vicuña Mackenna 55, Providencia, Santiago; tel. (2) 693-0000; fax (2) 693-9304; internet www.abastible.cl; f. 1956; owned by COPEC; Pres. Felipe Lamarca Claro; Gen. Man. José Odone.

AGA Chile, SA: Paseo Presidente, Errázuriz Echaurren 2631, Providencia, Santiago; e-mail callcentre@cl.aga.com; internet www.aga.cl; f. 1920; natural and industrial gases utility; owned by Linde Gas Corpn of Germany.

Compañía de Consumidores de Gas de Santiago (GASCO, SA): 1061 Santo Domingo, Casilla 8-D, Santiago; tel. (2) 694-4444; fax (2) 694-4370; e-mail info@gasco.cl; internet www.gasco.cl; natural gas utility; supplies Santiago and Punta Arenas regions; owned by CGE; Pres. MATÍAS PÉREZ CRUZ; Vice-Pres. JORGE MARÍN CORREA.

Electrogas: Alonso de Cordova 5900, Of. 401, Las Condes, Santiago; tel. (2) 299-3400; fax (2) 299-3490; e-mail carlos.andreani@electrogas.cl; f. 1998; subsidiary of Endesa Chile; CEO CARLOS ANDREANI.

GasAndes: Avda Chena 11650, Parque Industrial Puerta Sur, Las Condes, Santiago; tel. (2) 366-5960; fax (2) 366-5942; internet www.gasandes.com; distributes natural gas transported from the Argentine province of Mendoza via a 463-km pipeline.

GasAtacama Generación: Costanera Oriente s/n, Km 2.5, Barrio Industrial, Mejillones; tel. (55) 357-200; fax (55) 623-170; natural gas producer and transporter; Man. LUIS CAHUE.

GasValpo, SA: Camino Internacional 1420, Viña del Mar; tel. (32) 227-7000; fax (32) 221-3092; e-mail info@gasvalpo.cl; internet www.gasvalpo.cl; f. 1853; owned by AGL of Australia.

Empresas Lipigas: Las Urbinas 53, 13°, Of. 131, Providencia, Santiago; tel. (2) 650-3582; e-mail info@empresaslipigas.cl; internet www.empresaslipigas.cl; f. 1950; liquid gas supplier; also operates Agrogas, Enagas and Industrias Codigas; Pres. ERNESTO NOGUERA G.; Gen. Man. ANGEL MAFUCCI.

Water

Aguas Andinas, SA: Avda Presidente Balmaceda 1398, Santiago; tel. (2) 688-1000; fax (2) 698-5871; e-mail info@aguasandinas.cl; internet www.aguasandinas.cl; water supply and sanitation services to Santiago and the surrounding area; sold to a French-Spanish consortium in June 1999; Pres. ALFREDO NOMAN.

Empresa de Obras Sanitarias de Valparaíso, SA (Esval): Cochrane 751, Valparaíso; tel. (32) 220-9000; fax (32) 220-9502; e-mail infoesval@entelchile.net; internet www.esval.cl; f. 1989; sanitation and irrigation co serving Valparaíso; Pres. JUAN HURTADO VICUÑA; Gen. Man. GUSTAVO GONZÁLEZ DOORMAN; 377 employees.

Sigsig Ltda (Tecnagent) (Servicios de Ingeniería Sigren y Sigren Ltda): Presidente Errázuriz 3262, Casilla 7550295, Las Condes, Santiago; tel. (2) 335-2001; fax (2) 334-8466; e-mail tecnagent@tecnagent.cl; internet www.tecnagent.cl; f. 1986; Pres. RAÚL SIGREN BINDHOFF; Gen. Man. RAÚL A. SIGREN ORFILA.

TRADE UNIONS

Central Unions

Central Autónoma de Trabajadores (CAT): Sazié 1761, Santiago; tel. and fax (2) 657-8533; e-mail catchile@catchile.cl; internet www.catchile.cl; 107,000 mems (2007); Pres. OSCAR OLIVOS MADARIAGA; Sec.-Gen. ALFONSO PASTENE URIBE.

Central Unitaria de Trabajadores de Chile (CUT): Avda Libertador B. O'Higgins 1346, Santiago; tel. (2) 671-9020; fax (2) 672-0112; e-mail cutorganizacion@gmail.com; internet www.cutchile.cl; f. 1988; affiliated orgs: 20 asscns, 28 confederations, 64 federations, 35 unions; 670,000 mems (2009); Pres. ARTURO MARTÍNEZ MOLINA; Gen. Sec. JAIME GAJARDO ORELLANA.

Union Confederations

Agrupación Nacional de Empleados Fiscales (ANEF): Edif. Tucapel Jiménez, Alameda 1603, Santiago; tel. (2) 696-2957; fax 697-9764; e-mail info@anef.cl; internet www.anef.cl; f. 1943; affiliated to CUT; public-service workers; Pres. RAÚL DE LA PUENTE PEÑA; Sec.-Gen. ANGELA RIFO CASTILLO.

Colegio de Profesores de Chile: Moneda 2394, Santiago; tel. (2) 470-4200; fax (2) 470-4290; e-mail cpch@colegiodeprofesores.cl; internet www.colegiodeprofesores.cl; 80,000 mems; Pres. JAIME GAJARDO ORELLANA; Sec.-Gen. PEDRO CHULAK PIZARRO.

Confederación Nacional Campesina: Eleuterio Ramírez 1471, Santiago; tel. and fax (2) 696-2673; affiliated to CUT; Pres. EUGENIO LEÓN GAJARDO; Sec.-Gen. RENÉ ASTUDILLO R.

Confederación Nacional de Federaciones y Sindicatos de Gente de Mar, Portuarios y Pesqueros de Chile (CONGEMAR): Tomás Ramos 158–172, Valparaíso; tel. (32) 225-5430; fax (32) 225-7580; affiliated to CUT; Pres. WALTER ASTORGA LOBOS; Sec.-Gen. JUAN GUZMÁN CARRASCO.

Confederación Nacional de Federaciones y Sindicatos de Trabajadores Textiles y Ramos Similares (CONTEXTIL): Serrano 14, Of. 203, 2°, Santiago; tel. and fax (2) 638-6379; e-mail contextil@yahoo.es; affiliated to CUT; Pres. PATRICIA COÑOMÁN CARRILLO; Sec.-Gen. MARÍA FELISA GARAY ASTUDILLO.

Confederación Nacional de Sindicatos Agrícolas—Unidad Obrero Campesina (UOC): Eleuterio Ramírez 1463, Santiago; tel. and fax (2) 696-6342; e-mail confe.uocchile@uocchile.cl; affiliated to CUT; Pres. OSCAR VALLADARES GONZÁLEZ.

Confederación Nacional de Sindicatos, Federaciones y Asociaciones de Trabajadores del Sector Privado de Chile (CEPCH): Valentín Letelier 18, Santiago; tel. (2) 695-2252; trade union for workers in private sector; affiliated to CUT; Pres. ANGÉLICA CARVALLO PRENAFETA; Sec.-Gen. ISABEL GONZÁLEZ C.

Confederación Nacional de Sindicatos de Trabajadores de la Construcción, Maderas, Materiales de Edificación y Actividades Conexas: Almirante Hurtado 2069, Santiago; tel. and fax (2) 696-4536; e-mail cntc@chile.com; affiliated to CUT; Pres. JULIO ARANCIBIA.

Confederación Nacional de Sindicatos de Trabajadores Textiles, de la Confección y Vestuario (CONTEVECH): Agustinas 2349, Dpto 0555, Santiago; tel. (2) 789-8241; e-mail josesanmartinp@chile.com; affiliated to CUT; Pres. JOSÉ GERMÁN SAN MARTÍN PÉREZ.

Confederación Nacional de Suplementeros de Chile (CONASUCH): Tucapel Jiménez 26, Santiago; tel. (2) 784-3444; fax (2) 784-3449; e-mail conasuch1942@gmail.com; internet www.conasuch.cl; f. 1942; trade union for newspaper vendors; Pres. OSCAR ALISTE CARREÑO.

Confederación Nacional de Trabajadores del Comercio, Oficinas, Industrias y Servicios (CONSFETRACOSI): Almirante Simpson 70, Providencia, Santiago; tel. (2) 655-0301; fax (2) 222-7804; e-mail consfetracosi@gmail.com; internet consfetracosi.blogspot.com; f. 1995; affiliated to CAT; Sec. OSVALDO HERBACH ALVAREZ.

Confederación Nacional de Trabajadores Electrometalúrgicos, Mineros y Automotrices de Chile (CONSFETEMA): Vicuña Mackenna 3101, San Joaquín, Santiago; tel. (2) 238-1732; fax (2) 553-6494; e-mail consfetema@123mail.cl; Pres. LUIS SEPÚLVEDA DEL RÍO.

Confederación Nacional de Trabajadores Forestales de Chile (CTF): Concepción; tel. and fax (41) 220-0407; Pres. JORGE GONZÁLEZ CASTILLO; Sec.-Gen. SERGIO GATICA ORTIZ.

Confederación Nacional de Trabajadores de la Industria del Pan (CONAPAN): Tucapel Jiménez 32, 2°, Santiago; tel. and fax (2) 672-1622; affiliated to CUT; Pres. GUILLERMO CORTES MUÑOZ.

Confederación Nacional de Trabajadores Metalúrgicos (CONSTRAMET): Santa Rosa 101, esq. Alonso Ovalle, Santiago; tel. (2) 664-8581; fax (2) 638-3694; e-mail contrame@ctcinternet.cl; affiliated to CUT and the International Metalworkers' Federation; Pres. MIGUEL SOTO ROA; Sec.-Gen. ROBERTO BUSTAMENTE.

Confederación Nacional de Trabajadores del Transporte Terrestre de Chile (CONATRACH): Santiago; Pres. PEDRO MONSALVE.

Confederación de Sindicatos Bancarios y Afines: Agustinas 814, Of. 606, Santiago; tel. (2) 481-6122; fax (2) 481-6123; e-mail confederacionbancaria@gmail.com; internet www.bancariachile.cl; affiliated to CUT; Pres. ANDREA RIQUELME BELTRÁN; Sec.-Gen. LUIS MESINA MARÍN.

Confederación de Trabajadores del Cobre (CTC): Santiago; e-mail secretariageneral@confederaciondelcobre.cl; internet www.confederaciondelcobre.cl; f. 2007; copper workers' union; Pres. CRISTIÁN CUEVAS ZAMBRANO; Sec.-Gen. JULIO ARAYA OLIVA.

Transport

RAILWAYS

State Railways

Empresa de los Ferrocarriles del Estado (EFE): Avda Libertador B. O'Higgins 3170, Santiago; tel. (2) 376-8500; fax (2) 776-2609; e-mail contacto@efe.cl; internet www.efe.cl; f. 1851; 2,072 km of track in use (2006); Pres. JORGE RODRÍGUEZ GROSSI; Gen. Man. FRANCO FACCILONGO FORNO.

Private Railways

Empresa de Transporte Ferroviario, SA (Ferronor): Huérfanos 587, Ofs 301 y 302, Santiago; tel. (2) 638-0464; e-mail ferronor@ferronor.cl; internet www.ferronor.cl; 2,412 km of track (2006); operates cargo services only; Pres. ROBERTO PIRAZZOLI; Gen. Man. RODRIGO VALDIVIESO.

Ferrocarril de Antofagasta a Bolivia (FCAB): Bolívar 255, Casillas ST, Antofagasta; tel. (55) 20-6700; fax (55) 20-6220; e-mail webmaster@fcab.cl; internet www.fcab.cl; f. 1888; subsidiary of Antofagasta PLC (United Kingdom); operates an international railway to Bolivia and Argentina; cargo forwarding services; total track length 947 km (2006); Chair. ANDRÓNICO LUKSIC ABAROA; Gen. Man. M. V. SEPÚLVEDA.

Ferrocarril del Pacífico, SA (FEPASA): Málaga 120, 5°, Las Condes, Santiago; tel. (2) 412-1000; fax (2) 412-1040; e-mail oguevara@fepasa.cl; internet www.fepasa.cl; f. 1993; privatized freight services on EFE track; 19.83% owned by EFE; Pres. RAMÓN ABOITIZ MUSATADI; Gen. Man. GAMALIEL VILLALOBOS ARANDA.

Ferrocarril Tocopilla–Toco: Calle Arturo Prat 1060, Casilla 2098, Tocopilla; tel. (55) 81-2139; fax (55) 81-2650; owned by Sociedad Química y Minera de Chile, SA; 139 km (2006); Gen. Man. SEGISFREDO HURTADO GUERRERO.

Association

Asociación Chilena de Conservación de Patrimonio Ferroviario (ACCPF): Concha y Toro 10, Barrio Brasil, Santiago; tel. (2) 699-4607; fax (2) 280-0252; e-mail info@accpf.cl; internet www.accpf.cl; railway preservation asscn; Pres. SERGIO CARMONA MALATESTA; Sec.-Gen. CLAUDIO CURELLI MANN.

METROPOLITAN TRANSPORT

Metro de Santiago: Avda Libertador B. O'Higgins 1414, Santiago; tel. (2) 250-3000; fax (2) 937-2000; e-mail comunicaciones@metro.cl; internet www.metrosantiago.cl; started operations 1975; 5 lines, 84.4 km (2008); extension to 104.5 km scheduled for completion in 2010; Pres. RAPHAEL BERGOEING VELA; Gen. Man. HERNÁN VEGA MOLINA.

Transantiago: Nueva York 9, 10°, Santiago; tel. (2) 428-7900; fax (2) 428-7926; internet www.transantiago.cl; f. 2005; govt scheme to co-ordinate public transport in Santiago; comprises 10 bus networks and the Metro de Santiago.

ROADS

The total length of roads in Chile in 2001 was an estimated 79,605 km (49,464 miles), of which some 6,279 km were highways and some 16,410 km were secondary roads. The road system includes the entirely paved Pan-American Highway, extending 3,455 km from north to south.

SHIPPING

As a consequence of Chile's difficult topography, maritime transport is of particular importance. The principal ports are Valparaíso, Talcahuano, Antofagasta, San Antonio, Arica, Iquique, Coquimbo, San Vicente, Puerto Montt and Punta Arenas. Chile's merchant fleet amounted to 863,000 grt (comprising 551 vessels) at December 2008.

Supervisory Authorities

Asociación Nacional de Armadores: Blanco 869, 3°, Valparaíso; tel. (32) 221-2057; fax (32) 221-2017; e-mail info@armadores-chile.cl; internet www.armadores-chile.cl; f. 1931; shipowners' asscn; Pres. EUGENIO VALENZUELA CARVALLO.

Cámara Marítima y Portuaria de Chile, AG: Blanco 869, 2°, Valparaíso; tel. (32) 225-3443; fax (32) 225-0231; e-mail info@camport.cl; internet www.camport.cl; Pres. VICTOR PINO TORCHE; Vice-Pres. EDUARDO HARTWIG ITURRIAGA.

Dirección General de Territorio Marítimo y Marina Mercante: Errázuriz 537, 4°, Valparaíso; tel. (32) 220-8000; fax (32) 225-2539; e-mail webmaster@directemar.cl; internet www.directemar.cl; maritime admin. of the coast and national waters, control of the merchant navy; ship registry; Dir-Gen. FRANCISCO MARTÍNEZ VILLARROEL.

Cargo-handling Companies

Empresa Portuaria Antofagasta: Grecia s/n, Antofagasta; tel. (55) 25-1737; fax (55) 22-3171; e-mail afernandez@puertoantofagasta.cl; internet www.puertoantofagasta.cl; Pres. BLAS ENRIQUE ESPINOZA SEPÚLVEDA; Gen. Man. ALVARO FERNÁNDEZ SLATER.

Empresa Portuaria Arica: Máximo Lira 389, Arica; tel. (58) 25-5078; fax (58) 23-2284; e-mail puertoarica@puertoarica.cl; internet www.puertoarica.cl; Pres. FRANCISCO JAVIER GONZÁLEZ; Gen. Man. ALDO SIGNORELLI BONOMO.

Empresa Portuaria Austral: Avda B. O'Higgins 1385, Punta Arenas; tel. and fax (61) 24-1111; e-mail portspuq@epa.co.cl; internet www.epa.co.cl; Pres. YANKO VILICIC RASMUSSEN; Gen. Man. EDUARDO MANZANARES CASTESC.

Empresa Portuaria Chacabuco: Avda B. O'Higgins s/n, Puerto Chacabuco; tel. (67) 35-1198; fax (67) 35-1174; e-mail gerencia@chacabucoport.cl; internet www.portchacabuco.cl; Pres. LUIS ALBERTO MUSALEM; Gen. Man. ENRIQUE RUNÍN ZUÑIGA.

Empresa Portuaria Coquimbo: Melgareja 676, Coquimbo; tel. (51) 31-3606; fax (51) 32-6146; e-mail ptoqq@entelchile.net; internet www.puertocoquimbo.cl; Pres. HUGO MIRANDA RAMÍREZ.

Empresa Portuaria Iquique: Jorge Barrera 62, Iquique; tel. (57) 40-0100; fax (57) 41-3176; e-mail epi@epi.cl; internet www.epi.cl; f. 1998; Pres. MARCO ANTONIO BLAVIA BEYA.

Empresa Portuaria Puerto Montt: Angelmó 1673, Puerto Montt; tel. (65) 25-2247; e-mail info@empormontt.cl; internet www.empormontt.cl; Gen. Man. PATRICIO CAMPAÑA CUELLO.

Empresa Portuaria San Antonio: Alan Macowan 0245, San Antonio; tel. (35) 58-6000; fax (35) 58-6015; e-mail correo@saiport.cl; internet www.saiport.cl; f. 1998; Pres. PATRICIO ARRAU PONS; Gen. Man. ALVARO ESPINOSA ALMARZA.

Empresa Portuaria Talcahuano-San Vicente: Blanco Encalada 547, Talcahuano; tel. (41) 279-7600; fax (41) 279-7626; e-mail eportuaria@puertotalcahuano.cl; internet www.ptotalsve.cl; Pres. ELIANA CARABALL MARTINEZ; Gen. Man. LUIS ALBERTO ROSENBERG NESBET.

Empresa Portuaria Valparaíso: Errázuriz 25, 4°, Of. 1, Valparaíso; tel. (2) 244-8800; fax (2) 223-4427; e-mail comercial@epv.cl; internet www.epv.cl; Pres. GERMÁN CORREA DIAZ; Gen. Man. HARALD JAEGER KARL.

Principal Shipping Companies

Santiago

Agencias Universales, SA (AGUNSA): Edif. del Pacífico, 15°, Avda Andrés Bello 2687, Casilla 2511, Las Condes, Santiago; tel. (2) 203-9000; fax (2) 203-9009; e-mail agunsascl@agunsa.cl; internet www.agunsa.cl; f. 1960; maritime transportation and shipping, port and docking services; owned by Empresas Navieras, SA; Chair. JOSÉ MANUEL URENDA SALAMANCA; Gen. Man. LUIS MANCILLA PÉREZ.

Empresa Marítima, SA (Empremar Chile): Encomenderos 260, Piso 7°, Las Condes, Santiago; tel. (2) 469-6100; fax (2) 469-6199; internet www.empremar.cl; f. 1953; international and coastal services; Chair. LORENZO CAGLEVIC; Gen. Man. E. ESPINOZA.

Naviera Magallanes, SA (NAVIMAG): Avda El Bosque, Norte 0440, 11°, Of. 1103/1104, Las Condes, Santiago; tel. (2) 442-3150; fax (2) 442-3156; internet www.navimag.com; f. 1979; Chair. PEDRO LECAROS MENÉNDEZ; Gen. Man. HÉCTOR HENRÍQUEZ NEGRÓN.

Nisa Navegación, SA: Avda El Bosque Norte 0440, 11°, Casilla 2829, Santiago; tel. (2) 442-3100; fax (2) 203-5190; internet www.nisa.cl; Chair. PEDRO LECAROS MENÉNDEZ; Fleet Man. GABRIEL LUCHINGER.

Ultragas Ltda: Avda El Bosque Norte 500, 20°, Las Condes, Santiago; tel. (2) 630-1009; fax (2) 232-8856; e-mail ultragas@ultragas.cl; f. 1960; tanker services; Chair. DAG VON APPEN; Gen. Man. MICHAEL SCHRÖDER.

Valparaíso

Broom Valparaíso: Almirante Señoret 70, 10°, Valparaíso; tel. (32) 226-8200; fax (32) 221-3308; e-mail info@ajbroom.cl; internet www.broomgroup.com; f. 1920; ship owners and brokers; Pres. JAMES C. WELLS M; CEO ANDRÉS NUÑEZ SORENSEN.

Cía Chilena de Navegación Interoceánica, SA (CCNI): Plaza de la Justicia 59, Valparaíso; tel. (32) 227-5500; fax (32) 225-5949; e-mail info@ccni.cl; internet www.ccni.cl; f. 1930; regular sailings to Japan, Republic of Korea, Taiwan, Hong Kong, USA, Mexico, South Pacific, South Africa and Europe; bulk and dry cargo services; owned by Empresas Navieras, SA; Chair. BELTRÁN FELIPE URENDA; CEO FELIPE IRARRÁZAVAL.

Cía Sud Americana de Vapores (CSAV): Plaza Sotomayor 50, Casilla 49-V, Valparaíso; tel. (32) 220-3000; fax (32) 320-3333; e-mail info@csav.com; internet www.csav.com; f. 1872; regular services world-wide; bulk and container carriers, tramp and reefer services; Chair. JAIME CLARO VALDÉS; Gen. Man. JOAQUÍN BARROS FONTAINE.

Naviera Chilena del Pacífico, SA (Nachipa): Almirante Señoret 70, 6°, Casilla 370, Valparaíso; tel. (32) 250-0300; e-mail valparaiso@nachipa.com; internet www.nachipa.cl; cargo; Pres. PABLO SIMIAN ZAMORANO; Gen. Man. FELIPE SIMIAN FERNÁNDEZ.

Sudamericana Agencias Aéreas y Marítimas, SA (SAAM): Blanco 895, Valparaíso; tel. (32) 220-1000; fax (32) 220-1481; e-mail gerenciavap@saamsa.com; internet www.saam.cl; f. 1961; cargo services; Pres. DEMETRIO INFANTE; Gen. Man. ALEJANDRO GARCÍA-HUIDOBRO.

Punta Arenas

Cía Marítima de Punta Arenas, SA: Avda Independencia 830, Casilla 337, Punta Arenas; tel. (61) 22-1871; fax (61) 22-7514; f. 1949; shipping agents and owners operating in the Magellan Straits; Pres. PEDRO LECAROS MENÉNDEZ; Gen. Man. ARTURO STORAKER MOLINA.

Puerto Montt

Transmarchilay, SA (Transporte Marítimo Chiloé-Aysén): Angelmo 2187, Puerto Montt; tel. (65) 27-0000; fax (65) 27-0730; e-mail transporte@tmc.cl; internet www.transmarchilay.cl; f. 1971; Pres. HARALD ROSENQVIST; Gen. Man. ALVARO CONTRERAS.

CIVIL AVIATION

There are 330 airfields in the country, of which eight have long runways. Arturo Merino Benítez, 20 km north-east of Santiago, and

Chacalluta, 14 km north-east of Arica, are the principal international airports.

REGULATORY AUTHORITY

Dirección General de Aeronática Civil (DGAC): Miguel Claro 1314, Providencia, Santiago; tel. (2) 439-2000; fax (2) 436-8143; internet www.dgac.cl; f. 1930; Dir-Gen. Brig-Gen. JOSÉ HUEPE PÉREZ.

PRINCIPAL AIRLINES

Aerocardal: Aeropuerto Internacional Arturo Merino Benítez, Avda Diego Barros Ortiz s/n, Pudahuel, Santiago; tel. (2) 377-7400; fax (2) 377-7402; e-mail aerocard@aerocardal.com; internet www.aerocardal.cl; f. 1991; executive, charter and tourist services.

Aerovías DAP: Avda B. O'Higgins 891, Casilla 406, Punta Arenas; tel. (61) 61-6100; fax (61) 22-1693; e-mail ventas@aeroviasdap.cl; internet www.aeroviasdap.cl; f. 1980; domestic services; CEO ALEX PISCEVIC.

Línea Aérea Nacional de Chile (LAN-Chile): Américo Vespucio 901, Renca, Santiago; tel. (2) 565-2525; fax (2) 565-1729; internet www.lanchile.com; f. 1929; operates scheduled domestic passenger and cargo services, also Santiago–Easter Island; international services to French Polynesia, Spain, and throughout North and South America; Pres. JORGE AWAD MEHECH; Gen. Man. IGNACIO CUETO PLAZA.

Tourism

Chile has a wide variety of attractions for the tourist, including fine beaches, ski resorts in the Andes, lakes, rivers and desert scenery. Isla de Pascua (Easter Island) may also be visited by tourists. In 2009 there were 2,749,913 tourist arrivals. In 2008 receipts from tourism totalled an estimated $1,757m.

Servicio Nacional de Turismo (SERNATUR): Avda Providencia 1550, 2°, Santiago; tel. (2) 731-8419; fax (2) 236-1417; e-mail pcasanova@sernatur.cl; internet www.sernatur.cl; f. 1975; Dir Dr OSCAR SANTELICES ALTAMIRANO.

Asociación Chilena de Empresas de Turismo (ACHET): Avda Providencia 2019, Of. 42B, Santiago; tel. (2) 439-9100; fax (2) 439-9118; e-mail achet@achet.cl; internet www.achet.cl; f. 1945; 155 mems; Pres. GUILLERMO CORREA SANFUENTES; Man. LORENA ARRIAGADA GÁLVEZ.

Defence

As assessed at November 2009, Chile's armed forces numbered 60,560: army 35,000, navy 17,800 and air force 7,760. There were also paramilitary forces of 41,500 *carabineros*. Reserve troops numbered 40,000. Compulsory military service was ended in 2005.

Defence Expenditure: Expenditure was budgeted at 1,580,000m. pesos in 2009.

Chief of Staff of National Defence: Maj.-Gen. ALFREDO EWING PINOCHET.

Commander-in-Chief of the Army: Gen. MIGUEL FUENTE ALBA POBLETE.

Commander-in-Chief of the Navy: Adm. EDMUNDO GONZÁLEZ ROBLES.

Commander-in-Chief of the Air Force: Gen. RICARDO ORTEGA PERRIER.

Education

Primary education in Chile is free and compulsory for eight years, beginning at six or seven years of age. It is divided into two cycles: the first lasts for four years and provides a general education; the second cycle offers a more specialized schooling. Secondary education is divided into the humanities-science programme (lasting four years), with the emphasis on general education and possible entrance to university, and the technical-professional programme (lasting for up to six years). In 2007 enrolment at primary schools included 94% of children in the relevant age-group, while the comparable ratio for secondary enrolment was 85%. There are three types of higher education institution: universities, professional institutes and centres of technical information. In 2007 there were 753,398 students in tertiary education. The provision for education in the 2009 central government budget was 4,024,351m. pesos.

Bibliography

For works on South America generally, see Select Bibliography (Books)

Adler Lomnitz, L., and Melnick, A. *Chile's Political Culture and Parties*. Notre Dame, IN, University of Notre Dame Press, 2000.

Aguilera, P., and Fredes, R. (Eds). *Chile—The Other September 11: Reflections and Commentaries on the 1973 Coup in Chile*. New York, Ocean Press, 2006.

Angell, A. *Democracy after Pinochet: Politics, Parties and Elections in Chile*. London, Institute for the Study of the Americas, 2007.

Arceneaux, C. L. *Bounded Missions: Military Regimes and Democratization in the Southern Cone and Brazil*. University Park, PA, Penn State University Press, 2001.

Aroca, P. A., and Hewings, G. J. D. (Eds). *Structure and Structural Change in the Chilean Economy*. Basingstoke, Palgrave Macmillan, 2006.

Barr-Melej, P. *Reforming Chile: Cultural Politics, Nationalism and the Rise of the Middle Class*. Chapel Hill, NC, University of North Carolina Press, 2001.

Beckett, A. *Pinochet in Piccadilly: Britain and Chile's Hidden History*. London, Faber and Faber, 2002.

Berg, J. *Miracle for Whom?: Chilean Workers Under Free Trade*. London, Routledge, 2005.

Borzutzky, S. *Vital Connections: Politics, Social Security, and Inequality in Chile*. Notre Dame, IN, University of Notre Dame Press, 2002.

Borzutzky, S., and Oppenheim, L. (Eds). *After Pinochet: The Chilean Road to Democracy and the Market*. Gainesville, FL, University Press of Florida, 2006.

Collier, S., and Sater, W. *A History of Chile, 1808–1994*. Cambridge University Press, Cambridge Latin American Studies, 1996.

A History of Chile, 1808–2002. Cambridge University Press, Cambridge Latin American Studies, 2004 (2nd edn, Ed. Knight, A.).

Faundez, J. *Democratization, Development and Legality: Chile, 1831–1973*. Basingstoke, Palgrave Macmillan, 2007.

French-Davis, R. *Economic Reforms in Chile: From Dictatorship to Democracy*. Michigan, MI, University of Michigan Press, 2001.

Haughney, D. *Neoliberal Economics, Democratic Transition and Mapuche Demands for Rights in Chile*. Gainesville, FL, University Press of Florida, 2006.

Hawkins, D. G. *International Human Rights and Authoritarian Rule in Chile*. Lincoln, NE, University of Nebraska Press, 2002.

Hilbink, L. *Judges beyond Politics in Democracy and Dictatorship: Lessons from Chile (Cambridge Studies in Law and Society)*. Cambridge, Cambridge University Press, 2007.

Hite, K. *When the Romance Ended: Leaders of the Chilean Left, 1968–1998*. New York, Columbia University Press, 2000.

Londregan, J. *Legislative Institutions and Ideology in Chile: Political Economy of Institutions and Decisions*. Cambridge, Cambridge University Press, 2000.

Loveman, B. *Chile: The Legacy of Hispanic Capitalism*. New York, Oxford University Press Inc, 2001.

Meller, P. *The Unidad Popular and the Pinochet Dictatorship: A Political Analysis*. New York, St Martins Press, 2000.

Mount, G. *Chile and the Nazis: From Hitler to Pinochet*. Montréal, QC, Black Rose Books, 2001.

Nuñéz, R. C. *The Politics of Social Policy Change in Chile and Uruguay: Retrenchment versus Maintenance, 1973–1998*. London, Routledge, 2005.

O'Brien, P., and Roddick, J. *Chile, the Pinochet Decade*. London, Macmillan, 1983.

O'Shaughnessy, H. *Pinochet: The Politics of Torture*. London, Latin America Bureau, 1999.

Paley, J. *Marketing Democracy: Power and Social Movements in Post-Dictatorship Chile*. Los Angeles, CA, University of California Press, 2001.

Pollack, M. *The New Right in Chile 1973–1977*. Basingstoke, Macmillan, 2000.

Power, M. *Right-Wing Women in Chile: Feminine Power and the Struggle Against Allende*. Pennsylvania, PA, Penn State University Press, 2002.

Report of the National Commission on Political Imprisonment and Torture. Santiago, 2004.

Roberts, K. M. *Deepening Democracy? The Modern Left and Social Movements in Chile and Peru*. Palo Alto, CA, Stanford University Press, 1999.

Roht-Arriaza, N. *The Pinochet Effect: Transnational Justice in the Age of Human Rights*. Philadelphia, PA, University of Pennsylvania Press, 2006.

Rosemblatt, K. A. *Gendered Compromises: Political Cultures and the State in Chile, 1920–1950*. Chapel Hill, NC, University of North Carolina Press, 2000.

Sehnbruch, K. *The Chilean Labour Market: A Key to Understanding Latin American Labour Markets*. Basingstoke, Palgrave Macmillan, 2007.

Siavelis, P. *The President and Congress in Post-Authoritarian Chile: Institutional Constraints to Democratic Consolidation*. University Park, PA, Penn State University Press, 1999.

Silva, P. *In the Name of Reason: Technocrats and Politics in Chile*. University Park, PA, Pennsylvania State University Press, 2009.

Spooner, M. H. *Soldiers in a Narrow Land: The Pinochet Regime in Chile*. Los Angeles, CA, University of California Press, 1999.

Stern, S. J. *Reckoning with Pinochet: The Memory Question in Democratic Chile, 1989-2006*. Durham, NC, Duke University Press, 2010.

Taylor, M. *From Pinochet to the Third Way: Neoliberalism and Social Transformation in Chile*. London, Pluto Press, 2006.

Tinsman, H. *Partners in Conflict: The Politics of Gender, Sexuality and Labor in the Chilean Agrarian Reform, 1950–1973*. Durham, NC, Duke University Press, 2002.

Verdugo, P. *Chile, Pinochet and the Caravan of Death*. Boulder, CO, Lynne Rienner Publrs, 2001.

Vergara, A. *Copper Workers, International Business and Domestic Politics in Cold War Chile*. University Park, PA, Pennsylvania State University Press, 2008.

Wright, T. C. *State Terrorism in Latin America: Chile, Argentina, and International Human Rights*. Lanham, MD, Rowman & Littlefield Publrs, 2007.

COLOMBIA

Geography

PHYSICAL FEATURES

The Republic of Colombia is in north-western South America, the only country on that continent to have coastlines on both the Pacific Ocean and the Caribbean Sea, separated mid-way by the westward-heading Isthmus of Panama. The country's shortest land border (225 km or 140 miles), therefore, is with Panama, to the west, across the start of the Central American land bridge (until 1903 Panama was a province of Colombia). To the south lie Ecuador and Peru, the former on the coast beyond a 590-km frontier and the latter inland, the border extending for 1,496 km onto the Amazonian plains. Here Colombia also meets Brazil, which lies east and south of a 1,643-km border in the south-east of the country. The longest border, however, is with Venezuela, which lies to the east. Central Colombia thrusts further east than the rest of the country, while in the north Venezuela encroaches into the west. However, Colombia still has 1,760 km of north-west-facing shores on the Caribbean (1,448 km on the Pacific), giving it the right to maintain its possession of a number of islands and islets off shore. These are grouped in a single administrative unit, the smallest department in the country (44 sq km or 17 sq miles), San Andrés and Providencia, which also has jurisdiction over Roncador Cay and the Quita Sueño, Serrana and Serranilla Banks. However, Colombian possession of this territory impelled Nicaragua in 2001 to pursue a claim with the International Court of Justice (based in The Hague, Netherlands) involving 50,000 sq km of territorial waters—San Andrés is only 180 km east of Nicaragua, whereas it is some 700 km north of the Colombian mainland. Providencia is a further 80 km north. The still more distant Serranilla Bank is claimed by the USA (which recognized Colombian possession of Roncador, Serrana and Quita Sueño in 1981, when a 1972 treaty took effect) and, on occasion, by Honduras. Colombia also has a dispute over maritime boundaries in the Gulf of Venezuela, with Venezuela. The Pacific coast involves fewer formal international problems—Isla de Malpelo is the only Pacific island to be included in Colombian territory, although it adds little area to the overall national territory of 1,141,748 sq km (making the country a little bigger than Bolivia).

The western two-fifths of Colombia are dominated by the Andes and the coastal lowlands, with the east and south dominated, respectively, by the Llanos (the grassland plains of the Orinoco basin) and by the Selvas (the flat rainforest region typical of the Amazon basin). These torrid lowlands of the east are sparsely inhabited and little explored, watered by rivers that drain into the Atlantic—the Llanos by the Meta and other tributaries of the Orinoco, and the Selvas by the Caquetá and other Amazon tributaries. The most important river of Colombia, however, is the Magdalena, which cuts north through the Andes for about 1,540 km, through the most settled parts of the country, to empty into the Caribbean. The great Andean chain enters the country in the south-west, then splits into three cordilleras, the western, the lowest, the central, the highest, and the eastern. Like the coast, the volcanic ranges run slightly north of a south-west to north-east course. The region consists of soaring ranges separated by high plateaux, broad upland basins and deep, fertile valleys carrying powerful rivers. The Cordillera Occidental is a sheer wall of barren peaks rising to some 3,700 m (over 12,000 ft). The Cordillera Central has peaks over 5,500 m, the Cordillera Oriental some that are not much less, and both are under permanent snow at their summits. This, and a timberline at about 3,000 m, contrasts dramatically with the swampy tropical jungle the mountains descend to some 240 km short of the Caribbean coast. The Cordillera Oriental is distinguished by its densely populated plateaux and basins, usually between 2,400 m and 2,700 m, in one of which is the capital city, although there are also large centres in the Cordillera Central. Between the two ranges clefts the mighty Magdalena, serving as a transport conduit to the Atlantic (Caribbean) coast. On the other side of the Cordillera Central, to the west, is the Cauca, a tributary of the Magdalena, joining it some 320 km before it reaches the sea. These rivers link the highlands and the Atlantic lowlands, which are often marshy, but long settled. These lowlands are separated from Venezuela by a northward extension of the Cordillera Oriental, the Sierra de Perijá, and, on the north-western coast, the flat, semi-arid Gujaira peninsula (which forms the western bluff of the Gulf of Venezuela) to the east and the isolated mountain mass of the Sierra Nevada de Santa Marta to the west. This range on the Caribbean includes the country's highest point, Pico Cristóbal Colón (5,776 m or 18,957 ft)—named, like the country, for Christopher Columbus, the Genoese (Italian) navigator who claimed much of the continent for Spain. The nearby Pico Simón Bolívar, named for the great liberator of South America, has a similar elevation. In the south the Atlantic plains narrow, and the densely forested region on the border with Panama leads onto the Pacific coast, first the Serranía del Baudó and then the jungles and swamps of the coastal plains, watered by relatively short Andean rivers, such as the Patía in the south. This varied terrain gives Colombia a biodiversity reckoned to be second only to Brazil, sheltering in forests that cover almost one-half of the country and on pastureland that covers about two-fifths (although some of this is on the bleak high moors, *páramo*, between the mountain basins). The forest is densest in the tropical east, but deforestation is probably a greater threat in the north and west. There is also a problem with illegal smuggling of animals, which can have a severe effect on endangered populations—particularly threatened species include the yellow-eared parrot, the condor, the giant armadillo, the cotton-top marmoset, the white-footed tamarin, tapir and some alligators. Other fauna that flourish in the natural conditions of Colombia include hummingbirds, toucans, storks, pumas, jaguars, red deer, sloths and monkeys. The country's flora ranges from coconut and mangrove, through mahogany, oak, pine, balsam, rubber, ginger, tonka beans, etc., to the extensive (illegal) cultivation of coca (Colombia is the world's leading producer), opium poppies and cannabis.

CLIMATE

The Equator passes through the far south-east of Colombia, so most of the country lies within the Tropic of Cancer, but elevation makes a dramatic difference to the climate. The coastal lowlands and the deep Magdalena and Patía valleys, for instance, are very hot, with average annual temperatures of 24°C–27°C (75°F–81°F). From about 500 m the climate becomes subtropical, and then from about 2,300 m temperate (many people live at this level). It is only cold above 3,000 m (average temperatures ranging from –18°C to 13°C, 0°F–55°F). Seasonal variation, however, is slight—the capital, Bogotá, has average high temperatures of 19°C (66°F) in July and of 20°C (68°F) in January. The main seasons are the wet and dry seasons, the two periods of rain being in March–May and September–November, except on the Atlantic coast, where there is one long wet season, in May–October. Rain is heaviest on the Pacific coast, and it is drier in the north and on the slopes of the Cordillera Oriental. At Bogotá the average annual rainfall is 1,050 mm (41 ins), but at Barranquilla, on the Caribbean, it is 800 mm.

POPULATION

Before the advent of Europeans, there was a large Amerindian population in what is now Colombia, notably of the Chibcha (Muisca) people. There remain about 60 tribes scattered throughout the country, but unmixed Amerindians account for only about 1% of the population. The Spanish settlement and long years of colonial rule, as an imperial centre moreover, engrained a socially rigid class stratification, which is still strong. Family lineage, inherited wealth and racial background remain extremely important. The extremes of poverty in the country have not helped with widespread problems of social and political violence. Despite the pre-eminence of the old élite, most of the population (58%) are actually Mestizo, of mixed Spanish and Amerindian ancestry. However, 20% are of unmixed European ancestry, with 14% mulatto (black-white), 4% black and 3% black-Amerindian. The official language is Spanish, with Colombian Spanish said to be the purest in Latin America, but some native languages are still spoken by remoter groups and now have recognition under the Constitution. The Roman Catholic Church (which claims the nominal adherence of 87% of the population) also enjoys some official sanction, although it is not, formally, the state religion. There are small Protestant and Jewish minorities, with some even smaller Arab communities (in which there are some Muslims).

According to official projections, the total population was 45.5m. in mid-2010. About three-quarters live in urban centres, most above the courses of the Magdalena and the Cauca and on the Atlantic coast. The national capital is Bogotá. It is located in the centre of the country, towards the southern end of the Cordillera Oriental, and is the largest city in Colombia (an estimated 8.5m. in mid-2010). The cities of Medellín (3.6m.), in the north of the Cordillera Central, and Cali (2.4m. in mid-2010), in the southern Cauca valley, are next in size, followed by the Caribbean cities of Barranquilla, at the mouth of the Magdalena, and Cartagena, south-west along the coast. Colombia is a unitary republic consisting of 32 departments and one capital district (distrito capital—Bogotá).

History

Sir KEITH MORRIS

Colombia shares many features with the other Latin American countries and particularly with its Andean neighbours. However, its geography, and pre-Columbian and colonial history gave the country distinctive characteristics that were accentuated following independence and became increasingly marked in the 20th century. The Andes mountain range divides into three cordilleras when it enters Colombia. The Pacific coast is largely jungle and mangrove swamps. The 60% of the country to the east of the Andes is divided between the Llanos (savannah, much of which is flooded for nine months of the year) and Amazonian jungle. Many places are only accessible by air. With its capital at Bogotá (500 miles from the Caribbean ports of entry and 8,600 ft high in the Cordillera Oriental), the country was inevitably inward-looking and regional.

The regionalism was reinforced by the country's Amerindian heritage. Although Colombia had many different civilizations before the Spanish conquest in the 16th century (they reached a high level of sophistication, producing the finest gold work in the Americas), they were never united in a large state like the Inca or Aztec empires. Few of them have survived as distinct groups, and most were hispanicized, unlike those in Ecuador, Peru and Bolivia to the south. By the end of the colonial period the majority of Colombians were Mestizos (of mixed European and Amerindian descent) with significant European and mulatto minorities—the latter descended from the African slaves imported to work in the gold mines. The resulting lack of communal identity added individualism to the regionalism and localism, which geography and pre-colonial history had encouraged.

INDEPENDENCE AND THE 19TH CENTURY

Nueva Granada became a Viceroyalty in 1739. Santa Fe de Bogotá, as it was called in colonial times, inevitably had a great concentration of the region's lawyers and administrators. Simón Bolívar made it the target of his great independence campaign of 1819 and there established the capital of Gran Colombia, comprising present-day Colombia, Venezuela, Ecuador and Panama. However, Gran Colombia broke up amid much bitterness in 1830, leaving the Colombians with a strong preference for civilian government after their experience with Bolívar and his largely Venezuelan generals.

Following independence, Colombia's politics in the 19th century bore a great resemblance to those of its neighbours. It was a turbulent period with nine civil wars. These were essentially struggles for power between the two main currents of national political life that had, by the middle of the century, emerged as the Partido Liberal Colombiano (PL—Liberal Party) and the Partido Conservador Colombiano (PCC—Conservative Party). The only issue that consistently divided them was the greater or lesser role of the Roman Catholic Church: the PL contained anti-clerical elements. There was little dispute over economic policy, and both parties were at times federalist, at times centralist, though the Liberals inclined more towards the former. However, party allegiance was often decided as much by family and locality as by doctrine.

The collapse of Gran Colombia had other lasting effects. It left Colombia with the largest share of the Gran Colombian debt. The Colombian state's finances were therefore poor from the beginning. The country remained poor for the rest of the century, first because of the lack of large commodity discoveries and, second, owing to a weak external sector (the only effective form of taxation in 19th century Latin America was customs duties, which depended on foreign trade). As a result, the state was chronically weak with an army of only 2,000–3,000 men, which was frequently incapable of maintaining public order. No Colombian President could exercise the sort of authority that later enabled the Venezuelan leader, Gen. Juan Vicente Gómez (1908–35), effectively to disarm the Venezuelan population in the early 1900s. The Colombian Constitution alternated between extreme federalism (1863) and excessive centralism (1886). The latter was confirmed by the War of the Thousand Days (1899–1902), but the centralism was more policy than practice. Governments had to pay due respect to regional and local feeling.

EARLY 20TH CENTURY

Colombia's story in the 20th century was to diverge greatly from that of its neighbours. It was to have much greater constitutional stability (only one four-year military regime) and steadier economic development, but, paradoxically, more violence.

A consequence of the difficult geography and the poverty of the state, which was to plague Colombia throughout the 20th century, was the development of a frontier tradition. Colombia became a land of many internal frontiers as *colonos* (colonists) cleared the river valleys and advanced ever higher into the sierras, as well as opening up the Llanos and the jungle. As the state was absent in most of these areas, traditions of private justice prevailed. The ability to defend oneself became much admired, which may explain some of the tolerance shown to guerrillas to this day. The rural conflicts that afflicted Colombia in the late 20th and early 21st centuries led to many *colonos* taking their weapons and their frontier customs to the cities.

From the end of the War of the Thousand Days until the mid-1940s, Colombia enjoyed relative tranquillity. The Conservatives remained in power until 1930. The coffee and textile industries developed greatly, mainly in Medellín. In 1930 the Conservatives divided into factions, which allowed a moderate Liberal, Enrique Olaya Herrera, to govern in coalition with Conservatives. An attack by Peru on Colombia's Amazonian territories in 1931 ensured wide support for the new Government. President Alfonso López Pumarejo, who succeeded Olaya in 1934, introduced 'New Deal' type reforms, consolidating the Liberals' popular support. His successor, Eduardo Santos Montejo (1938–42), slowed the pace of reform.

Divisions within the PL led to a Conservative victory in 1946. However, by 1948 the Liberals had reunited behind the popular figure of Jorge Eliécer Gaitán, the dissident Liberal candidate in the 1946 elections. The assassination of Gaitán in Bogotá on 9 April 1948 led to an outbreak of civil unrest, known as the Bogotazo, with days of rioting, leaving several thousand dead. Gaitán, whose fiery oratory had won him a strong personal following, had been expected not only to regain the presidency for the Liberals in the 1950 elections, but also to introduce significant social change. The Government managed to restore order in the cities, but the conflict spread to the rural areas. 'La Violencia', as the period became known, continued until 1958 and may have claimed the lives of as many as 200,000 people.

FRENTE NACIONAL, 1958–74

The military, led by Gen. Gustavo Rojas Pinilla, took power in 1953. The coup, the only one in the 20th century, initially enjoyed popular support; this, however, waned as it became clear that Rojas did not intend to restore constitutional government. A military junta removed Rojas in 1957 and, in the following year, power was transferred to a Frente Nacional (National Front). This power-sharing agreement between the two traditional political parties provided for them to alternate in the presidency for four terms and to have an equal number of seats in the Cabinet and the Congreso (Congress). This was less undemocratic than it might appear, as under the Colombian system anyone could claim to be a Liberal or Conservative and the seats on both sides were strongly contested, with Communists winning some Liberal seats and Rojas's movement, the Alianza Nacional Popular (ANAPO), well represented on both sides.

Violence declined under the Frente Nacional as most of the remaining armed groups relinquished violence or were suppressed. However, the success of the Cuban revolution in 1959 gave fresh impetus to guerrilla activity. One of the surviving groups of Liberal guerrillas relaunched itself in the mid-1960s as the Fuerzas Armadas Revolucionarias de Colombia (FARC), the military wing of the pro-Soviet Communist Party, with strong support in some rural areas. The Ejército de Liberación Nacional (ELN), a Cuban-orientated movement, whose members were originally middle-class students and included several Roman Catholic priests, was founded at the same time. The Ejército Popular de Liberación (EPL), a smaller, Maoist guerrilla movement, followed in 1969.

Generally, the Frente Nacional's period of rule, which formally ended in 1974, was one of good economic growth and social progress, especially under Carlos Lleras Restrepo (1966–70), who gave much impetus to agrarian and administrative reform. In the 1970 presidential election, the narrow victory of the official Conservative candidate, Misael Pastrana, was challenged by the second placed candidate, Gen. Rojas, representing ANAPO. When Pastrana's victory was confirmed there were mass protests, as the result reinforced the popularly held view that the system was unfair and could not produce change peacefully. One consequence was the founding by some ANAPO supporters in 1974 of the Movimiento 19 de Abril (M-19), a non-Marxist guerrilla group, which, unlike the others, was initially city-based.

RETURN TO LIBERAL GOVERNMENT, 1974–82

In the presidential election of 1974 the Liberal candidate, Alfonso López Michelsen, won a decisive victory over the Conservative Alvaro Gómez and the ANAPO contender, María Eugenia Rojas de Moreno Díaz. Curiously, the fathers of all three were former Presidents. The expectations aroused by López Michelsen's victory were great. He was the first Liberal to win a fully competitive election since his father, whose name still symbolized progressive liberalism. However, he was committed to continue to govern in coalition with the Conservatives, and any attempt at constitutional reform faced formidable opposition in the Congreso and the Supreme Court. The world economy was also in recession following the 1973 oil crisis. In fact, the López Michelsen administration's most lasting achievement was probably the introduction of association contracts for oil exploration, at a time when other Latin American countries were nationalizing their oil industries. This would lead to the great discoveries at Caño Limón in 1982 and at Cusiana in 1991.

President López Michelsen's successor was Julio César Turbay Ayala. Turbay took a firm and unpopular stand against the Argentine invasion of the Falkland Islands (Islas Malvinas) in 1982. He also sought to solve the problems of urban terrorism and drugs-trafficking. His efforts met with some success, although his counter-insurgency campaign against guerrillas in 1982 provoked many allegations of human rights abuses by the armed forces.

THE DRUGS TRADE

The illegal drugs trade became the key factor in Colombia from the late 20th century. It began quietly in the 1970s with the cultivation and export of marijuana. Then, some Colombians saw the opportunity to gain a dominant role in the cocaine business. The coca paste was produced largely in Peru and Bolivia and flown to Colombia, which was strategically placed to process it into cocaine and ship it to the USA. By the early 1980s two groups in Medellín and Cali controlled most of the trade. Their activities were already on a large scale before the Government or society realized the extent of the threat. When challenged by the Government they retaliated and unleashed a cycle of violence that has continued to the present. In the case of the Medellín cartel under Pablo Escobar, violence escalated into 'narco-terrorism' (a direct assault on the state to force it to abandon the policy of extradition to the USA). The traffickers also hired paramilitaries to defend their newly acquired ranches from attack by the guerrillas. These paramilitary groups, often originally formed by the army, went increasingly on the offensive and killed many civilians in their counter-guerrilla war. Ironically, the traffickers often financed the very guerrillas that their paramilitaries had been fighting. Many cocaine laboratories and much of the coca cultivation were situated in the jungle in south-east Colombia, a stronghold of the FARC. (In 1982 the FARC added Ejército del Pueblo to its title, becoming FARC—EP for official purposes, although it remained commonly known by its shorter acronym.) The drugs cartels paid the FARC 'protection' money, which rapidly made the FARC into the world's richest guerrilla group. The advent of opium poppy cultivation in the early 1990s and the increase in coca cultivation from 1995 made the FARC and their paramilitary enemies in the Autodefensas Unidas de Colombia (AUC) even richer. From 2001 'Plan Colombia' (see below) led to a significant reduction in coca production, but the trend was reversed in 2005 as cultivation was switched to more inaccessible areas and smaller plots, increasing total coca acreage by some 8% on the previous year, according to the UN Office on Drugs and Crime. In 2006 total Colombian coca acreage was estimated to be 52% lower than in 2000; however, in 2007 it went up by 27%, only to fall by an unconfirmed 18% in 2008. Cultivation fell again in 2009 to 68,000 ha, a 60% fall over 10 years. That progress was being made against the Colombian coca trade was confirmed by the increase in Peru, where cultivation reached 59,000 ha in 2009. As Peruvian yields were higher, Peru displaced Colombia as foremost coca producer. The earnings from coca and cocaine in Colombia were estimated to have fallen from US $623m. in 2008 to $494m. in 2009. It looked as if a significant reduction in the profits of the trade was finally being made.

The impact of the drugs trade on Colombia went much further than the direct effects described above. It diverted and weakened the judicial system and security forces, allowing common criminality greater impunity and creating a culture of violence and contempt for any legal or moral restraints.

REFORM, PEACE AND NARCO-TERRORISM, 1982–90

In May 1982 the Conservative candidate, Belisario Betancur Cuartas, was elected to the presidency, mainly owing to divisions within the PL. Betancur had moved from the right of the party to its far left. However, with a Liberal majority in the Congreso he had to continue the tradition of coalition government. Like his predecessors, he followed a prudent economic policy and encouraged foreign investment. His innovations focused on foreign policy and peace issues. Under his leadership, Colombia, traditionally a loyal US ally, became a member of the Non-Aligned Movement as well as the Contadora Group, which assisted efforts to find a peaceful solution to the conflicts in Central America.

Domestically, Betancur attempted to resolve Colombia's internal conflict by agreement. He granted an amnesty to guerrilla prisoners and concluded cease-fires with the FARC, M-19 and the EPL. The FARC founded a political party, the Unión Patriótica (UP), which contested the 1986 elections. However, the cease-fires with both M-19 and the EPL broke down and in November 1985 the M-19 seized the Palace of Justice. In the ensuing recapture of the building by the army about 100 people were killed, including 11 judges, leading to strong public criticism of both the Government and the army. Many observers concluded that the cease-fires had benefited the guerrillas, particularly the FARC, which had used the time to build up its forces. Betancur also faced the beginnings of narco-terrorism when, in 1984, drugs-traffickers from Medellín assassinated the justice minister, Rodrigo Lara Bonilla, who had taken the first serious measures to combat their activities. Betancur concluded that extradition to the USA was the only effective means of addressing the problem.

The drugs-trafficking problem dominated the presidency of the Liberal Virgilio Barco Vargas, elected in 1986 by a decisive majority. His offer to the Conservatives of a limited participation in government was refused, which resulted in the first single-party Government since 1953. Barco shared Betancur's belief in extradition, but the Supreme Court twice ruled that such a treaty with the USA was unconstitutional. Barco, however, used emergency decrees to proceed with extraditions. The Medellín drugs cartel began a campaign of terror to force the Government to abandon this policy. In August 1989 it assassinated Luis Carlos Galán, the favourite to win the PL's presidential nomination in 1990. The M-19 and UP presidential candidates were also assassinated in early 1990. An aeroplane belonging to the national airline AVIANCA was exploded, as were government offices, and in the first seven months of 1990 more than 200 police officers were killed in Medellín. Barco refused to be intimidated and called successfully for international support to counter the cartel's threat.

Barco also continued the peace process with the guerrillas. The cease-fire with the FARC broke down in 1987, but in 1989 a settlement was reached with the M-19. They regrouped as the Alianza Democrática—M-19 (AD—M-19) and participated in the 1990 elections. Their presidential candidate, Carlos Pizarro, was assassinated by paramilitaries. Successful negotiations with the EPL, the Partido Revolucionario de Trabajadores (PRT) and the Comando Quintín Lame were also concluded in 1990. Sadly, hopes that the FARC and the ELN might also enter into peaceful dialogue were reduced by the killing of over 2,000 members of the UP, largely by paramilitaries linked to the Medellín cartel, although the FARC and ELN's strong financial position, despite the loss of support from the communist states, was probably the decisive factor. Many of the paramilitary groups had been set up by the army, but as they fell increasingly under the control of drugs cartels, they were declared illegal in 1989.

CÉSAR GAVIRIA TRUJILLO: THE REFORM PROJECT

César Gaviria Trujillo, the Liberal candidate elected President in May 1990, was determined to accelerate political reform and the liberalization of the economy, a policy known as *apertura* (opening). After decades in which the Congreso and the Supreme Court had opposed almost all constitutional change, an informal referendum, held at the time of the presidential election in 1990, produced a huge majority in favour of the election of a Constituent Assembly. It was elected in December, and the AD—M-19 and the Liberals received the largest share of the vote. Seats were also allocated to the EPL, the PRT and the Comando Quintín Lame as part of those groupings' peace settlements.

The Constituent Assembly drafted a new Constitution in 1991. It guaranteed every conceivable human right and took decentralization further, through the election of governors and the transfer of functions and central funds to departments and municipalities. It weakened the presidency by limiting emergency powers and providing for censure of ministers. A Constitutional Court was created, as was a prosecution service. Citizens were given the right to challenge almost any measure through an injunction (*tutela*), and extradition was prohibited. The Medellín cartel had halted its mass terrorist attacks when Gaviria took office, but had kidnapped several prominent figures. Gaviria offered the cartel the possibility of avoiding extradition if they released their hostages and surrendered, an offer that several prominent cartel members, including its leader, Pablo Escobar, accepted.

In his first year in office Gaviria liberalized labour markets, removed price controls and improved terms for foreign investment. He abolished import licences, drastically reduced tariffs and promoted rapid integration within the Andean community, especially with Venezuela and Ecuador. However, the liberalization of the political system was not completed by a peace settlement with the FARC and the ELN. Negotiations with both groups failed in Caracas, Venezuela, in 1991 and in Tlaxcala, Mexico, in 1992. This was followed in April 1992 by a drought, which, in a country that was 80% dependent on hydroelectric power, resulted in 13 months of power cuts. In July the Government was humiliated when Pablo Escobar escaped from his luxurious prison outside Medellín and returned to narco-terrorism. However, his organization was gradually dismantled and he was killed by the police in Medellín in December 1993. Gaviria's determination to persist with his reforms, in spite of reverses, was admired, and when he left office in 1994 his popularity was higher than that of any previous retiring President.

ERNESTO SAMPER PIZANO: SOCIAL REFORM AND POLITICAL CRISIS

In June 1994 the PL's Ernesto Samper Pizano was elected by a narrow margin in Colombia's first two-round presidential election. Two days later his defeated Conservative opponent, Andrés Pastrana Arango, disclosed the existence of taped conversations suggesting that the Cali drugs cartel had partly financed Samper's campaign, an accusation that cast a shadow over his whole presidency. An initial investigation cleared Samper, but one year later the case was reopened when his treasurer, Santiago Medina, and then his campaign manager (at the time his Minister of Defence) accused him of personal involvement. The Cámara de Representantes (House of Representatives) finally voted to clear him of any wrongdoing in June 1996, but this was perceived by many as a political, rather than a legal, verdict. This long-running political crisis, which was exacerbated by US policy (see below), made it difficult for Samper to carry out the social reform programme on which he had been elected. Always on the social-democratic wing of the party, Samper had made clear his reservations about the rapid pace of *apertura* pursued by Gaviria (under whom he had served as Minister of Economic Development until late 1991). As President he aimed not to reverse this policy, but to moderate it. He also promised to increase social spending to alleviate poverty, a problem hitherto neglected.

Samper's domestic problems were exacerbated by the response of the USA. Initially, the US Government stated that Samper, despite the allegations, would be judged on the results of his anti-narcotics policy. This proved to be quite successful, with the leaders of the Cali cartel captured in 1995. However, when Medina made his accusations against Samper in mid-1995 US policy shifted, and the Administration of President Bill Clinton (1993–2001) openly expressed its lack of confidence in Samper and demanded that further anti-narcotics legislation be passed (seizure of assets, stricter penalties and even the reintroduction of extradition). Samper eventually succeeded in getting these measures approved by the Congreso. Colombia was, meanwhile, refused certification for its anti-narcotic efforts in both 1996 and 1997 and only received a conditional certification in 1998. The consequences of decertification were severe: Colombia received no US export credits and the USA voted against loans to Colombia from multilateral banks. The confidence of both domestic and foreign investors inevitably declined. The fiscal deficit and foreign debt rose and economic growth slowed. The FARC and the ELN were correspondingly encouraged and saw no reason to negotiate with a President whom the USA considered corrupt. Foreign pressure, although it damaged his Government and the country, undoubtedly helped Samper to maintain a considerable level of popular support, as many Colombians resented such blatant US interference.

ANDRÉS PASTRANA ARANGO: THE PEACE PROCESS AND THE 'PLAN COLOMBIA'

The 1998 presidential contest was one of the closest fought in Colombian history. In the first round the Liberal candidate, Horacio Serpa Uribe, was less than one percentage point ahead of Pastrana, the defeated 1994 Conservative candidate. In the second round, however, Pastrana won by 500,000 votes. Many leading Liberals had supported Pastrana, believing him better placed to end Colombia's isolation, restore confidence in the economy and restart the peace process.

Unfortunately, the means to achieving the last two goals were often in conflict. Restoring economic confidence meant reducing the fiscal deficit sharply by cutting public expenditure and raising taxes. In the short term this worsened the recession Pastrana had inherited from the previous administration. It made it very difficult to maintain popular support for the peace process, which ideally required greater military spending (to protect the population and put pressure on the guerrillas) and increased social spending to mitigate rising unemployment.

Pastrana launched the peace process by taking the dramatic step of meeting Manuel Marulanda Vélez, leader of the FARC, in his jungle hideout. The new President's cabinet appointments reassured the markets that Colombia was returning to its prudent tradition of orthodox financial management. Relations with the USA immediately improved. The USA granted Colombia full certification in March 1999 and in 2000 gave US $1,300m. over two years to help restore peace and stability and reduce the drugs trade. This funding formed the US portion of Plan Colombia (see below). To persuade the rebels to negotiate, Pastrana had to cede them, temporarily, 41,000 sq km in south-east Colombia, from which all government troops were withdrawn. The FARC, having received this territory, successfully insisted on the removal of any restrictions before they would agree an agenda for the talks. Public support soon decreased sharply when it became clear the FARC was using the demilitarized zone as a safe haven and was keeping military prisoners and kidnapped civilians there. Public discontent increased when both the FARC and the ELN began to kidnap more indiscriminately, taking many middle-class and child victims.

President Pastrana's support for firmer military action against the FARC, while negotiating, and his success in winning substantially increased US aid for the armed forces ensured that military discontent with the peace process was contained. From 1998 the armed forces, the combined operations and intelligence capacity of which greatly improved, won all major engagements against the FARC. This contrasted with the last two years of the Samper administration when the army suffered several humiliating defeats. However, the FARC's capacity to launch guerrilla attacks was not affected and the number of kidnappings close to large cities rose. This led to increased support for the paramilitary AUC, whose numbers rose faster than those of the FARC. The AUC put the ELN under great pressure. The latter, which from 2000 was engaged sporadically in talks about negotiations with the Government, in turn exerted pressure with periodic mass kidnappings.

Central to Pastrana's strategy from 2000 was Plan Colombia. Its aims included increasing the efficiency of the security forces and the judicial system, eliminating drugs production through both eradication and crop substitution, and reducing unemployment. The international community was to fund almost 50% of the US $7,500m. Plan. The initial US contribution of $1,300m. included a military component of $1,000m., but also significant sums for judicial reform and human rights education. In 2001 the USA committed itself to providing a further $882m. under the new Andean Region Initiative, introduced following criticism of the Plan by worried neighbouring countries. The member states of the European Union (EU) also agreed to provide $300m. This was all to be devoted to economic and social projects, and the EU made it clear that its aid was not linked to Plan Colombia, with the military emphasis of which the EU differed.

However, the slow progress of peace negotiations, halted several times by the FARC, which made no concessions of substance, frustrated the Colombian public. President Pastrana visited Marulanda several times to keep the process going, but each time the FARC stalled the talks and committed another terrorist act. Some degree of international involvement from February 2001 raised hopes that the peace process would succeed, but, following the hijacking of an aeroplane and the kidnapping of a prominent senator by the FARC, an utterly disillusioned Pastrana ended the peace process on 20 February 2002 and ordered the armed forces to regain control of the demilitarized zone. The FARC responded by resorting to urban terrorism in an attempt to intimidate the public into calling for peace again. The result was the election of Alvaro Uribe Vélez to the presidency on 26 May, with 54% of the votes cast. The other main contender was Liberal Horacio Serpa, who won 32% of the votes. The Conservatives did not even field an official presidential candidate, preferring to support Uribe. Uribe was a dissident Liberal candidate who had been a strong critic of Pastrana's peace process and he proposed a dramatic increase in the security forces. In legislative elections, held earlier, on 10 March, the most significant gains were made by independents and supporters of Uribe. The official PL remained the largest single party in the Senado (Senate) and the Cámara de Representantes, although its representation was substantially reduced, as was the representation of the official Conservatives.

The failure of the peace process to resolve or even reduce the internal conflict eroded public support for President Pastrana. The austere economic measures his administration had to implement to restore Colombia's finances, while increasing spending on security, lost him even more support. Pastrana approached the end of his term as a deeply unpopular President. History may be kinder. Without his extraordinarily generous peace process it was unlikely that the international community would have given Colombia so much financial support or that Colombian public opinion would have decided that much greater sacrifices would be required to restore the authority of the state in order to end the internal conflict.

ALVARO URIBE VÉLEZ: TOWARDS DEMOCRATIC SECURITY

First Term: 2002–06

Colombian voters entered new territory in electing Alvaro Uribe to the presidency in 2002. For the first time they elected someone who was not the official candidate of one of the two traditional parties. A dissident Liberal, Uribe ran as an independent, without even the support of a faction within the PL. He was also the first President committed to ensuring the state's control of Colombia's entire territory, and protecting the lives of all Colombians became the central tenet of his election manifesto. The considerable success he achieved in improving security was to be a decisive factor in both the rapid economic recovery and in a dramatic political shift: constitutional change to allow presidential re-election, and his own subsequent re-election.

Uribe's Democratic Security Policy faced an immense challenge. The illegal groups had grown to unprecedented levels, and the FARC saw him as a serious threat. Consequently, the FARC signalled an urban terrorist campaign by firing mortar bombs (unsuccessfully) at the presidential palace during his inauguration on 7 August 2002. In order to defeat the illegal groups or convince them to negotiate seriously, Uribe increased the security forces by one-third during his first term. However, the economic restraints on these proposals were considerable. The economy was recovering very slowly from the 1999 recession, and the public sector deficit had to be reduced as Colombia's foreign debt neared the limits of sustainability. The new administration found that its predecessor had left a larger deficit than had been officially declared.

Nevertheless, the new President had two factors in his favour. First, the security forces had been modernized under Pastrana and the military equipment and training provided by the USA under Plan Colombia were at last starting to show results by 2002. Second, the Uribe Government enjoyed exceptionally high levels of public support. The public had decided that the internal conflict was simply no longer tolerable and felt that under Uribe progress was being made in addressing it. The President's community meetings almost every Saturday in a different provincial town, sometimes lasting over 12 hours, exemplified his personal commitment to resolve the country's problems. On taking office, Uribe declared a state of emergency, under which he levied a wealth tax to finance increased security. The move sent a message to Colombia and to the international community. The expansion of the army and the police force was reinforced by the recruitment of 'peasant soldiers', who would serve in their own districts. A network of 'informers' was also established to help protect the roads. Within months the main roads were largely safe during daytime. Police began moving back to the 160 or so municipalities whence they had been withdrawn following guerrilla pressure. By the end of 2003 all had a police presence again.

The coca eradication programme was stepped up, and by 2004 coca cultivation was less than one-half of the 2000 acreage, the Plan Colombia base line. In 2005 cultivation increased marginally as traffickers encouraged cultivation in new areas and in smaller plots that were less easy to detect, but it fell again in 2006. The FARC responded to the Government's measures by escalating, for a time, its campaign of urban terrorism and attacks on the country's infrastructure; however, the group was increasingly on the defensive, and by 2004, under strong pressure from the security forces, it had withdrawn from the area around Bogotá towards its bases in the jungles of the south-east. The FARC rejected the President's terms for negotiations, which included discussions under UN auspices, on condition of a cease-fire, and demanded a much larger demilitarized zone than the one that had operated under Pastrana. The ELN seemed to be falling increasingly under FARC influence as that group for a time moved to protect it from the AUC. In mid-2004 the ELN expressed interest in entering negotiations with the Government, under Mexican mediation, but withdrew from talks in early 2005, supposedly in protest at Mexican criticism of Cuba. Talks were renewed in Havana, Cuba, in February 2006, at which the ELN was granted political status, and by mid-2007 a cease-fire had been provisionally agreed; however, by mid-2010 it had still not been concluded. Chances for an eventual peace agreement had been increased by heavy losses suffered by the ELN in Arauca department at the hands of the FARC.

Meanwhile, the majority of the AUC (whose leader, Carlos Castaño, disappeared in early 2004) in July 2003 committed itself to a cease-fire, to be followed by negotiations and a phased demobilization. After many breaches of the cease-fire, in June 2004 the long-postponed negotiations began, and the demobilization of over 30,000 paramilitaries was completed by March 2006. The process took place under the Justice and Peace Act (Ley de Justicia y Paz) of June 2005, although this law was not approved by the Constitutional Court until June 2006. The Court amended the law, strengthening its provisions for punishing crimes committed by the paramilitaries, as many critics of the law, both in Colombia and internationally, had demanded. The amendments alarmed the paramilitary leaders, who threatened to remobilize the AUC in response. When some of them planned to leave their 'holiday camp'-style detention in November 2006 to resume the armed struggle, President Uribe had them transferred to Itagüí prison, much to their fury. There, they took turns in confessing their crimes. Anger at their treatment probably led to some of their allegations against congressmen and officials. The process was bound to be a long one, with confessions to be heard, assets seized and victims (of whom 50,000 had come forward) to interview. The task of integrating the rank-and-file members back into society was stretching government resources. A significant minority had either become common criminals or, in some cases, joined new groups working for drugs-traffickers who saw no difficulty in doing business with the FARC.

In December 2002 Uribe had succeeded in gaining congressional approval for unpopular tax, pension and labour reforms. These did much to ensure that he could increase security expenditure while reducing the public sector deficit, in line with a new IMF agreement. However, more reforms were needed, particularly in the pensions sector, to secure the fiscal position in the second half of his term. Uribe decided to achieve these reforms, together with political measures such as a reduction in the size of the Congreso, in a referendum in October 2003. The measures were approved by a large majority of those who voted, but the referendum failed because the turnout was just below the necessary 25%. The election of left-wing mayors in Bogotá and Medellín and a left-wing governor in the Valle del Cauca (Cali) was seen as a second defeat for Uribe, although it could also be interpreted as a sign that Colombian democracy was much more authentic than critics had claimed.

President Uribe had to return to the Congreso to obtain approval for further tax increases to meet the shortfall in finances forecast for 2005 and 2006. Despite the electoral setbacks and the unpopularity of extra taxes, Uribe's approval rating averaged about 70% in his first term, owing to steadily improving security, with rates of murders, kidnappings, massacres and attacks on small towns all much lower than in previous years and the economy recovering faster than expected. Against this background, a proposal to amend the Constitution to allow the re-election of a President, which had failed to receive congressional approval in 2003, was revived in 2004 and approved by the Congreso at the end of the year. The constitutional amendment was approved by the Constitutional Court in October 2005. The measure enjoyed majority support in the country, but had been opposed strongly by the PL and by a recently formed left-wing party, the Polo Democrático Independiente (which in 2006 merged with another group to become the Polo Democrático Alternativo—PDA).

The congressional elections of 12 March 2006 gave 89 of the 163 seats in the Cámara and 63 of the 100 seats in the Senado to pro-Uribe parties: the newly formed Partido Social de la Unidad Nacional (Partido de la U) took 29 seats in the lower house and 20 in the upper chamber, while the PCC, which had continued to support President Uribe, was second placed in both chambers (29 lower house seats and 18 senate places). The PL, the dominant party in the country since 1930, came third in the elections to the Senado, with 18 seats, although it did secure the most number of Cámara seats by a single party (35).

Uribe's victory in the first round of the presidential election on 28 May 2006 was expected, but its scale was not: with 7,397,835 votes, equivalent to 63.6% of the valid ballot, it was more than any presidential candidate had received in Colombian history. Equally surprising was the impressive 22.5% of the vote secured by the PDA candidate, Carlos Gaviria Díaz, who came second. The 12.1% vote for the PL candidate, Horacio Serpa Uribe, contesting his third presidential election, was an extraordinary humiliation. Finally, it seemed, the established political dominance of the PL and PCC had ended.

Second Term: 2006–10

Uribe's decisive victory and the congressional majority supporting him did not bring the results expected of it. The economy prospered at first, with growth of 6.8% in 2006 and 7.5% in 2007, the highest for nearly 30 years. Security continued to improve, although inevitably less rapidly than before, and reducing the drugs trade continued to prove difficult. Manual eradication was used increasingly, since aerial spraying was unpopular, but it was costly in lives and slow. The political situation soon became highly complicated as security-related issues created severe domestic and international problems. The Uribista majority immediately started to quarrel over posts in the new administration, and the tax reform approved by the Congreso in December 2006 was not nearly as radical as the Government had hoped. More seriously, the investigation by the Supreme Court into links between congressmen and paramilitaries, which began in December 2006, had by mid-2010 led to the arrest of or the opening of investigations into about 80 congressmen, as well as a number of local politicians. The majority of those involved came from Uribista parties and generally represented departments on the Caribbean coast, where paramilitary influence had been strong. The 'parapolitical' scandal, as it was called, damaged the President's standing, but not his popularity, and soured relations with the Congreso and between the executive and the Supreme Court. The two main legislative measures—a constitutional amendment to break permanently the link between rises in central government expenditure and transfers to local government, and ratification of the free trade agreement (FTA) with the USA—were finally approved in mid-2007 only after much difficulty and expensive government concessions on the constitutional amendment.

The flow of public confessions by the main paramilitary leaders, held, much to their annoyance, in Itagüí prison from November 2006 (although in May 2008 14 of the most prominent were extradited to the USA—see below), continued to bring to light new allegations against congressmen, officials and officers. The President insisted on the need for all the truth to come out, noting that without the Justice and Peace legislation the paramilitary leaders would still be committing massacres instead of confessing past crimes from prison.

The Supreme Court's methods of investigation, especially in arresting the President's first cousin, Mario Uribe, led to bitter exchanges in September 2007. A more serious clash ensued in June 2008 when the Supreme Court convicted a former congresswoman for having changed her vote in a congressional commission in return for favours, thus allowing the re-election amendment to go forward. The Supreme Court sent its decision to the Constitutional Court for its opinion, implicitly questioning the President's legitimacy. He reacted by calling for a referendum to approve a re-run of the 2006 election. However, the Constitutional Court immediately ruled that its decision could not be reconsidered, and the President dropped his proposal.

The departmental and local elections of October 2007 were the least violent and least affected by the intimidation of armed groups for a generation. The main Uribista parties did marginally worse than in the congressional elections of 2006. The PCC and the PL, particularly the former, fared well in rural areas but made no comebacks in the cities. The PDA won Bogotá emphatically against former Mayor Enrique Peñalosa, who had Uribista backing, but the new Mayor, Samuel Moreno Rojas, was not a new figure like his predecessor, Luis Eduardo Garzón, but the grandson of General Rojas Pinilla, the military dictator of the 1950s and himself a Senator since 1991. The PDA made little progress elsewhere apart from Nariño, where Antonio Navarro Wolff won the governorship of his own department as expected. Independents did well, as in 2003.

The 'parapolitical' scandal was seized on by the Democratic majority in the US Congress as grounds, together with the killings of trade unionists, for postponing ratification of the FTA with Colombia. The US Congress successfully insisted on the inclusion of clauses on labour rights and environmental protection in the accord. President Uribe made several visits to Washington, DC, USA, in 2006–07 to try to win support for ratification, but without success. In mid-2010 it seemed probable that the Administration of President Barack Obama would ask Congress to ratify the FTA, although ratification would be unlikely to occur before 2011. The Uribe administration's standing on the issue had been strengthened in May 2008 when 14 of the top paramilitary leaders, who had failed to meet the terms of the Justice and Peace Law by neither confessing all their crimes nor disclosing all assets and by continuing to run their businesses from Itagüí gaol, were extradited to the USA.

Policy towards the FARC led to even greater international complications. Pressure built up during 2006 and 2007 for a humanitarian agreement under which about 50 prominent hostages of the FARC, including former presidential candidate Ingrid Betancourt and three US contractors, would be exchanged for the 500 or so FARC prisoners in Colombian gaols. The FARC insisted on a demilitarized zone to negotiate the terms. Uribe refused but came under intense pressure both domestically and internationally, especially from France, where Betancourt, who had French as well as Colombian nationality, had become a national heroine. In mid-2007 Uribe released unilaterally a key FARC spokesman, at the request of French President Nicolas Sarkozy, and over 100 rank-and-file FARC prisoners. The FARC did not respond. In September Uribe asked the Venezuelan President, Lt-Col (retd) Hugo Chávez Frías, to use his good offices. This he did with enthusiasm until Uribe decided that he was intervening in Colombian internal affairs and abruptly ended his mandate in November. Chávez persevered, and the FARC released two small groups of prisoners to him in early 2008 with the co-operation of the Colombian authorities. In turn, Chávez called for the FARC to be given belligerent status.

Colombians reacted with a demonstration in February 2008 by millions for the liberty of all the 700 or so hostages held by the FARC. In early March Colombian forces bombed and briefly occupied a FARC camp inside Ecuador. Raúl Reyes, the FARC second-in-command and chief negotiator, was killed, and three computers were seized. President Chávez broke off diplomatic relations with Colombia, said he would stop trade and ordered nine battalions of troops to the frontier. President Rafael Correa of Ecuador also severed relations. A summit of the Rio Group was held days later in Santo Domingo, Dominican Republic, at which Uribe apologized for having entered Ecuadorean territory and promised not to allow it to happen again. Venezuela subsequently restored relations with Colombia. The Colombian authorities' possession of more than 30,000 computer files, the authenticity of which was confirmed by Interpol, may have influenced Chávez's decision, as well as food shortages in Venezuela, which made Colombian food imports vital at that time. Chávez, who had called a minute's silence in Reyes's honour, in June 2009 advised the FARC to release all its hostages and make peace. Although Correa also had agreed to resume relations with Colombia at the Santo Domingo meeting, and there was a renewal of bilateral co-operation, by mid-2010 diplomatic representation had not yet been fully restored.

Inside Colombia the FARC suffered further blows. Iván Ríos, another member of its seven-man Secretariat, was killed by his own men in mid-March 2008, and Manuel Marulanda, its founder and undisputed leader, died at the end of that month, although his death was not admitted until May. Even worse was to come for the group. In July 2008 a FARC commander was tricked into boarding a helicopter with 15 prisoners, including Ingrid Betancourt and the three US contractors, supposedly for transfer to the headquarters of Alfonso Cano, the new FARC leader, for negotiations for release. The helicopter in fact belonged to the Colombian army, and the hostages were released without a shot being fired. There was general rejoicing in Colombia, and the incident, known as Operación Jaque, received highly favourable coverage around the world. Betancourt, whose family had been fiercely critical of Uribe, praised him and the Colombian military highly. Uribe's public approval rating, which had reached 84% after the Santo Domingo summit, registered 91% in one poll. The polls showed historically high levels of optimism and majority support for a second re-election. To make this possible, the largest Uribista party, Partido de la U, began to promote a referendum to change the Constitution.

The euphoria did not last long. The army's reputation was damaged by allegations in October 2008 that, in order to meet body count targets, a dozen unemployed youths from Soacha near Bogotá had been recruited to work in Cúcuta, where they had been shot while dressed as guerrillas. It became clear that it had been far from the sole case of 'false positives'. Uribe acted swiftly and dismissed three generals and 24 other commissioned and non-commissioned officers. Investigations were started against several of them, but strong criticism continued to be voiced by human rights organizations, both domestic and international.

Meanwhile, relations between the Government and the Supreme Court were exacerbated in early 2009 by allegations that officials of the intelligence service, the Departamento Administrativo de Seguridad, had intercepted the telephone calls of Supreme Court justices and opposition politicians. Allegations that officials of the presidency had ordered these intercepts persisted in mid-2010 as did the tension between President and Supreme Court, complicated further by deadlock over the appointment of a new Fiscal General. Financial scandals also made Uribe's final year difficult, especially one involving agricultural subsidies. Gross domestic product (GDP) growth of only 0.1% in 2009 meant that unemployment rose above 12%, and although the financial system remained strong and growth resumed in the first quarter of 2010 the administration found it hard to deal with the effective bankruptcy of the public health system.

In the Congreso the passage of a political reform bill to correct the faults exposed by the 'parapolitical' scandal, and of legislation to provide for a referendum on a constitutional amendment to allow the President to serve a third term (for which 5m. signatures had been collected), occupied the first nine months of 2009. Both measures were finally approved, although the opposition to them was increasingly bitter. Together they were seen by critics as entrenching the ruling Uribista majority and undermining the separation of powers. The delay in approving the referendum increased the uncertainty. Even if the Constitutional Court, which had four months to decide, gave its consent it was not certain whether there would be time to hold a referendum. Under the constitutional amendment allowing an incumbent president to run for a second term, he had to declare his candidature by 30 November 2009. Uribe could not comply and so risked a legal challenge if elected. The announcement on 26 February 2010 of the Constitutional Court's decision against the referendum, which surprised many observers, was a relief to many Colombians, not least in putting an end to uncertainty. A referendum might not have been possible before the election and there was real doubt about the minimum turnout being achieved. Uribe's gracious acceptance of the Court's decision contributed to optimism about the political change to come. The congressional elections on 13 March reassured him that his main policies would be continued. The Partido de la U came first in both houses with increased representation. The PCC also made gains and came second. Although they only lost one seat in the Cámara, the PL dropped from first to third place. The PDA lost seats in both houses, dropping from 10 to five in the Cámara.

The other main loser in the 2010 elections was Germán Vargas Lleras's Cambio Radical, which lost almost one-half of its 15 seats in the Senado, the price of his determination to run for the presidency whether or not Uribe did. The new entrants were a striking contrast: the Partido de Integración Nacional (PIN), which won eight seats in the Senado and 14 in the Cámara, was formed from the merger of several small Uribista parties and its candidates were usually relatives or close associates of congressmen condemned or under investigation for their participation in the parapolitical scandal. The Partido Verde (Green Party), from which five senators and three representatives were elected, had significantly gained in influence when three former mayors of Bogotá—Antanas Mockus Šivickas, Enrique Peñalosa Londoño and Luis Eduardo ('Lucho') Garzón, decided to compete for the leadership, which they intended to use to launch their presidential campaigns. The three candidates held a primary on the same day of the general election, which Mockus won.

The presidential campaign saw Juan Manuel Santos of the Partido de la U take an early lead. This was as expected because he was believed to be Uribe's favoured candidate, with Noemí Sanín (PCC) in second place. However, the situation changed when an independent candidate, Sergio Fajardo, the ex-mayor of Medellín, realized that his chances were poor and joined Mockus's ticket as vice-presidential candidate. Mockus's ratings greatly improved, support for Sanín collapsed and Mockus even overtook Santos in some opinion polls. On 30 May 2010, however, Santos won 47% of the votes cast. Mockus came second with 22%, followed by Vargas Lleras with 10%, Gustavo Petro (PDA) 9%, Sanín 6 % and Rafael Pardo (PL) 4%. In the second round, held on 20 June, Santos was elected with 69% (9.0m. votes) to Mockus's 27% (3.6m. votes). The result of the election showed popular support for continuity but also for the 'cleaner' government that Mockus advocated. The failure of the FARC or other armed groups to disrupt the election or intimidate voters to any significant degree marked the progress that Colombia had made. A successful operation conducted in the week before the second round, which resulted in the release of a police general and other officers who had been held by the FARC for 12 years, cannot have harmed Santos's chances either.

INTERNATIONAL POLICY

Given Colombia's association in the popular mind with violence, it is worth stressing that the country has an impeccable record in international matters. Colombia has never attacked another country, and lost Panama through US intervention in 1903. Colombia has been a consistent opponent of the use of force to settle disputes and condemned the Argentine invasion of the Falkland Islands in 1982, despite pressure from most other Latin American countries. The country has contributed to UN peace-keeping operations since their inception.

A founder of the Andean Pact in 1969, Colombia under President Gaviria played a leading role in the 1990s in making economic integration a reality, initially with Venezuela and Ecuador. This was followed by the formation of a free trade area with Venezuela and Mexico in 1994. Colombia has since concluded FTAs with Chile and, in 2004, with the Mercado Común del Sur (Mercosur). In June 2004 Colombia, together with Ecuador and Peru, began negotiations for an FTA with the USA, which Colombia concluded in February 2006 (the Peru-USA agreement was signed in April). The Congreso ratified the FTA in June 2007, but the US Congress postponed its consideration of the accord until the outcome of the investigations into the 'parapolitical' scandal was known. Venezuela denounced the bilateral agreements as submission to US 'imperialism' and reacted by withdrawing from the Andean Community of Nations and the Group of Three (G-3, comprising Colombia, Mexico and Venezuela) in April and May 2007, respectively. This probably reflected more the increasingly anti-US policy of Venezuela under the presidency of Chávez than a worsening of relations with Colombia. Despite repeated, unproven allegations of Chávez's support for the FARC, the Colombian Government attempted with some success to avoid confrontation or involvement in Venezuela's own internal disputes. The building of a gas pipeline between Venezuela and Colombia was the first of several collaborative projects under way or planned in 2009.

Relations with Venezuela deteriorated sharply when in November 2007 President Uribe ended President Chávez's mandate as a negotiator with the FARC for hostage release. They reached their lowest point when Chávez broke off relations after the Colombian attack on the FARC camp in Ecuador in March 2008 (see above). Relations were restored after the Rio Group summit, and, despite ideological differences, Uribe and Chávez resumed their periodic meetings, while collaborative projects continued. Ecuador also severed relations but by mid-2010 they had been partially restored. Colombia had apologized for its incursion into Ecuador and promised not to repeat it, but insisted it was a defensive action against the FARC and not directed against Ecuador. Relations with Venezuela worsened again when Colombia in mid-2009 reached an agreement with the USA to allow US forces to use seven Colombian military bases for counter-terrorist and counter-narcotics operations. Chávez denounced this move as part of a US plan to intervene in Venezuela and took severe trade sanctions against Colombia. Colombian exports to Venezuela fell by 33% in 2009. Whether Colombian relations with Venezuela and Ecuador, as well as with Nicaragua, which was pursuing a case at the International Court of Justice against Colombia about offshore limits, would improve once Juan Manuel Santos took office remained to be seen.

Traditionally, Colombia has been a loyal US ally, although its role in the Non-aligned Movement from the 1980s led to some more independent stands. Close collaboration with the USA on anti-narcotics policy was established under President Barco and continued thereafter, albeit with difficulties under President Samper (see above). Under the Uribe administration, the relationship became even closer, and Colombia supported the US-led coalition against the regime of Saddam Hussain in Iraq in 2003. The Administration of President George W. Bush continued strongly to support Colombia, but the Democratic majority in Congress from January 2007 was less staunch in its support. The Obama Administration maintained US support for Colombia but delayed action over the ratification of the FTA signed in 2006, which had aroused much opposition among the Democratic majority in Congress. It seemed likely that the issue would not be debated until after the 2010 congressional elections, although President Obama's announcement in mid-2010 that the USA should double its exports in the next five years was a positive sign.

Colombia had long ceased to be the introverted Andean republic that President López Michelsen referred to as an 'Andean Tibet'. It had become an active and respected player, but one which, at the beginning of the 21st century, still needed international support to help cope with its internal problems; nevertheless, it was increasingly prepared to act to defend its own interests in a region which had become much more turbulent.

OUTLOOK

The political future of Colombia looked more settled in mid-2010 than it had since the months after Uribe's re-election in 2006. Indeed, it could be argued that the measure of Uribe's success was that his departure, despite his continuing popularity, had led to increased optimism about the future. An exceptional leader, who would never have been elected in normal times, had been succeeded by a President whose whole life had seemed to have been spent in preparation for the post. Colombia was no longer in crisis. Juan Manuel Santos's landslide victory in the second round of the presidential elections was the final of a series of events which had put an end to the political uncertainty that had reigned for the previous two years; an uncertainty all the more damaging because it coincided with the world economic crisis and the dramatic deterioration in Colombia's relations with Venezuela and Ecuador. Would the Constitution be changed to allow Uribe to run again? If not, could he pass on his popularity to a successor?

The first question was resolved by the Constitutional Court's surprising decision against the holding of a referendum to approve a second re-election. The victory of Uribista parties in the congressional elections on 13 March 2010 seemed to answer the second. It made Santos, the candidate whom Uribe hoped would succeed him, the clear favourite to win the presidency, but it was not until he won 47% in the first round that the outcome was certain. There had been doubts about the strength of 'Uribismo' and about Santos as a candidate. He had never run for office, unlike his five leading opponents, and came from Colombia's most prominent political family, which also owned *El Tiempo*—Colombia's leading daily.

Santos was, however, exceptionally well qualified for the presidency. He had successfully held the foreign trade, finance and defence portfolios under various administrations. His acceptance of the post of Minister of Defence was a daring political gamble by a politician who had been considered cautious. It had paid off: Operación Jaque in 2008 (see above) had put him firmly centre stage. While not a natural campaigner he had other political skills. He was well respected and liked in the Congreso, where his family connections were an asset. In 1993, as a junior member of Gaviria's Cabinet he had been elected by the Congreso as Designado, Vice-President in all but name, a post replaced by that of Vice-President in the 1991 Constitution. Having supported Horacio Serpa against Uribe in 2002 he had decided to back Uribe in 2006 and had founded the Partido de la U, the most successful of the Uribista parties. Santos also had great international experience, not only through his ministerial posts. He had studied at the University of Kansas, Harvard University (USA) and London School of Economics (United Kingdom). He had then spent eight years as Colombian representative to the International Coffee Organization in London.

Santos was never likely to inspire the popular devotion Uribe had—for a start he had not had to rescue the country from near collapse as Uribe had in 2002—but his experience and his skills as a manager, a delegator, a diplomat and a negotiator seemed well suited to the problems Uribe would leave him as a legacy. These included: a highly polarized political scene; the continuing parapolitical scandal which had led to the confrontation between the executive and the Supreme Court, exacerbated by the allegations of illegal interceptions of calls of judges and politicians; an army fearing it would be held to account for the false positives scandal, FARC and other drugs-related armed groups weakened but still posing a threat; strained diplomatic relations with Venezuela and Ecuador; an economy emerging from recession with high unemployment; and a bankrupt health system.

In his favour Santos had a most convincing mandate, reinforced by a campaign with historically low levels of violence which was contested by half a dozen candidates all with good credentials for the presidency, something unprecedented in Colombia and probably elsewhere, who frequently participated in televised debates. The emergence of Antanas Mockus as Santos's opponent in the second round—a figure who supported the democratic security policy and shared the economic philosophy of the administration but attacked it for corruption and abuse of power—demonstrated that there were no fundamental ideological divisions. Santos tried to capitalize on this by calling in the second round for a National Agreement and offering to include Mockus, and even Petro of the PDA, in his administration. They did not accept, but it none the less marked a clear change of political atmosphere. Santos also had the advantage of a congressional majority so large that he would be unlikely to be forced into debilitating wrangles over patronage to get his legislation through, especially as he would not have to use valuable political capital on re-election, as Uribe did in both his terms. Nor would he need to rely on the votes of the PIN, the heirs of parapolitica. One of the new President's first acts was to meet the justices of Colombia's four higher courts, sending a clear signal that he wanted to end the dispute with the Supreme Court.

In foreign affairs, the manner of Santos's election and Uribe's acceptance of his departure made a striking contrast with the situation in some of Colombia's neighbouring countries and had given Santos an uncontested legitimacy that his predecessors had not been able to enjoy. He had taken a conciliatory line with his neighbours which had been initially welcomed. His role as defence minister at the time of the incursion into Ecuador in March 2008 (see above) meant that he had been viewed with suspicion in Ecuador, where an arrest warrant had been issued for him, but his diplomatic skills would be deployed to reduce tension. His ease on the international scene and his negotiating skills would assist him, in contrast to Uribe's dislike of foreign affairs and impatience with endless Latin American summits. But if Chávez's internal difficulties were to lead him to seek an external threat, no degree of moderation on Colombia's part would stop him. Santos's more patient approach was likely also to play well in the USA and make it easier for the Obama Administration to get ratification of the FTA through the US Congress in 2011. His choice of Angelino Garzón, a former trade union leader, as his Vice-President, should also reduce the opposition of US congressional Democrats to the FTA, as it contrasted with the Uribe Administration's alleged failure to stop the assassinations of trade unionists.

Human rights groups would be unlikely to let Santos forget the scandal of false positives in 2008 during his time as defence minister. He could stress his decisive role in tackling such abuses, but would have to balance this with reassuring the security forces that their exposure to civilian courts would be limited. The good relations Santos had with the generals—traditionally a fractious group—would make this task easier.

He would need the fullest co-operation of the security forces to deliver a decisive blow against the FARC and the new drugs-related criminal groups, many of whom were ex-paramilitaries but who often collaborated with the FARC. The level of violence in Colombia, while much reduced under Uribe, was still much too high and showing signs of rising again. The successful operation to release police officers held by the FARC in June 2010 (see above) demonstrated that the increased sophistication of the security forces shown in Operacion Jaque had not diminished and suggested that further major advances were possible. There were no signs on FARC's part of interest in negotiations. This was not surprising since the Ley de Justicia y Paz and the International Criminal Court made an amnesty for the FARC leaders impossible. They would almost certainly prefer to fight on in the jungle or take refuge across the border rather than serve prison sentences, even short ones. Reducing the funding that the illegal groups received from the drugs trade was critical to weakening them decisively. UN figures in mid-2010 suggested that progress was being made in this regard (see above).

Santos had inherited an economy that was starting to grow again. It had weathered the world crisis quite well. Growth was expected by the IMF to be 2.3% in 2010. He aimed to reform the tax and the health systems and to create 2.4m jobs, reducing unemployment to single figures and halving poverty. Santos was optimistic that this could be achieved by a Colombia now seen by some observers as a rising star, one of the CIVETS (Colombia, Indonesia, Vietnam, Egypt, Turkey and South Africa). The CIVETS were to be the BRICs of the next decade, countries with a very bright future, large, youthful and growing populations, diverse and dynamic economies, and relative political stability. That Colombia should be thought of in such terms was a measure of the turnaround that Uribe had achieved and the confidence that Santos's election had created. If he could secure ratification of the FTAs with the USA and with the EU that would boost confidence even further.

The strength of Uribismo post-Uribe was the main lesson of the presidential and congressional elections of 2010. In the first round the total votes gained by Santos (Partido de la U), Vargas Lleras (Cambio Radical) and Sanín (PCC) added up to the number that Uribe had polled in 2006. Furthermore, in the presidential election the performance of the PCC and PL candidates was lamentable, despite Sanín and Pardo both being highly experienced and respected figures. With Cambio Radical and the PCC rejoining the Uribista coalition for the second round and for government and the PL coming on board too, the race for 2014 was already starting. Santos had a clear lead but Vargas Lleras, despite Cambio Radical's loss of congressional seats following his break with Uribe, had come across in the televised debates as the best prepared and the clearest thinker. If Santos decided not to run for re-election in 2014 Vargas Lleras would be well placed. This might make possible the creation of a single Uribista party, perhaps drawing in the followers of Felipe Arias in the PCC. Alternatively, as Santos came from a great PL family, the presence of the PL in his coalition might open the way for the union of his party with the Liberals.

The totally unexpected element of the election was the success of Mockus and the Green Party, with Mockus winning the same number of votes in the first round as Carlos Gaviria (PDA) had in 2006. The decision of the three ex-mayors of Bogotá to use the party as their vehicle and hold a primary on congressional election day caught the public imagination and brought the Greens five senators and three representatives. When Mockus started to outpoll the previously much more fancied former mayor of Medellín, Sergio Fajardo, the latter had the good sense to agree to be Mockus's running mate. The duo, both intellectuals who had run cities successfully, appealed to those tired of the old politics. Many younger voters gave their support. Mockus's campaign, which for several weeks looked capable of winning the presidency, faltered when he was put under pressure on international and security issues. The majority decided to play safe but Mockus's strong case against corruption and abuse of power won much support, especially among the young. Whether it could provide the basis for a national party had to be in doubt. The Green Party would be a small voice in Congress. Much would depend on their showing in the regional and municipal elections in October 2011.

The Mockus phenomenon had been a serious set-back for the PDA. It had already been damaged by the unpopularity of Samuel Moreno as mayor of Bogotá, whose administration was accused of corruption and clientelism. The PDA's chances of retaining control of the city were poor. Its internal divisions had remained deep. Much of the leadership had been less than wholehearted in their support for Petro's candidature. The emergence of a strong democratic left in Colombia appeared still blocked by the presence of the FARC.

Economy

Sir KEITH MORRIS

Revised for this edition by JEREMY THORP

INTRODUCTION

Throughout most of its history as both a Spanish colony and an independent state, Colombia has been impoverished. Neither gold-mining, which generated most of the money in the colonial era, nor agriculture, which provided most of the employment, proved to be a basis for sustained economic development. Connections and trade with the rest of the world were hampered by geography, as Colombia's main centres of population are in the highlands, with difficult access to the outside world. The lack of a major export commodity during most of the 19th century meant that, in a time when customs dues were the only effective means of raising revenue, the Colombian state lacked the resources either to maintain law and order or to build infrastructure. These factors and the small size of the market deterred both foreign investors and also immigrants. As a result, most of the economy was in Colombian hands; coffee, the country's main export from the late 19th century, remained firmly a Colombian concern.

During the 19th century Medellín became the country's economic stronghold, dominating coffee, gold-mining and the nascent textile industry. By the 1920s Colombia had become the world's leading exporter of mild coffee, but a brief coffee-led period of prosperity was ended by the Great Depression in the 1930s. This led to a policy of import substitution, with the aim of both promoting local industry and insulating the country against the world economy. With this policy in place, Colombia grew steadily until the 1990s, becoming a rare model of economic and financial stability in Latin America, especially during the chaotic 1970s and 1980s. It was the Government of President César Gaviria Trujillo (1990–94) that changed the direction of Colombia's economy, opening it up to global competition by reducing tariffs, abolishing many import restrictions, inviting foreign investment, embarking on a privatization programme and allowing the Colombian peso to float relatively freely.

However, the economy weakened in the second half of the 1990s. Although the administration of Ernesto Samper Pizano (1994–98) largely maintained the free market policies implemented by Gaviria, the economic downturn was triggered by a steep increase in central government spending. It was further aggravated by a clause in the new Constitution of 1991 that stipulated that any increase in the amount of central government funds be equalled in regional authority expenditure. The increasing cost of the civil conflict during Samper's presidency also undermined economic performance. The civil conflict and related violence cost the equivalent of an estimated 4% of gross domestic product (GDP). These factors combined to produce a sharp increase in the fiscal deficit, generating inflationary pressure, which led to interest- and exchange-rate instability, but failed to generate significant economic growth. Colombia's overall GDP increased at an average annual rate of 2.7% in 1995–98.

The Government of Andrés Pastrana Arango (1998–2002) inherited an incipient recession. The downturn was exacerbated by a sharp decline in international commodity prices and prevailing instability in emerging markets. In 1999 the economy registered a 4.2% contraction, the country's worst economic performance since records began at the start of the 20th century. The economic decline was in sharp contrast to the average 4% annual growth witnessed throughout the 1970s, 1980s and most of the 1990s. The depth of the recession in 1999 reduced inflation to a 30-year low of 11.2%, compared with 20.4% in 1998, but unemployment increased to 19.4%.

The Pastrana Government's fiscally conservative, orthodox economic programme for recovery was based on a three-year, US $3,000m., extended fund facility agreement approved by the IMF in December 1999. Conditions of the agreement included a reduction in the fiscal deficit to 3.6% of GDP from the unusually high 5.4% in 1999, growth of 3% and an inflation target of 10%. To meet the targets the Government reduced sharply social spending, increased taxes and limited automatic transfers to local authorities. However, its pension reforms were only partly completed and its privatization programme was much smaller than intended, owing to market conditions. Colombia lost its investment-grade sovereign debt rating in 1999 and was downgraded further in 2000.

Despite these negative signals, the economy began to recover in 2000, when GDP growth of 2.9% was recorded. The public sector deficit of 3.4% of GDP and an inflation rate of 9.5% improved on the IMF targets. The current account of the balance of payments went into surplus, helped by an increase in exports of 13%. However, the Pastrana Government's hopes that growth would increase at a faster rate in 2001 were disappointed. The US recession, exacerbated by the terrorist attacks of 11 September 2001, made it more difficult to export Colombian goods. Falling coffee and petroleum prices and production did not help. The economy grew by 1.5% in 2001. However, annual inflation was reduced to 8.6% and interest rates remained historically low. In 2002 growth was still sluggish, at 1.9%, and owed much to a recovery in construction, which was boosted by an increase in government-subsidized social housing. However, despite further cuts in spending in early 2002, the fiscal deficit rose to 3.7% of GDP, against an IMF target of 2.6%.

The state of the public finances was an unpleasant surprise to the incoming administration of President Alvaro Uribe Vélez, which took office in August 2002 and found that it would have to raise an extra 1% of GDP in addition to the 2% it was already committed to spending on increased security. A wealth tax of 1% for this purpose was immediately introduced under a state of emergency decreed by President Uribe in August. By the end of 2002 the legislature had approved significant tax, pension and labour reforms, and in January 2003 the IMF agreed a new, US $2,100m., three-year financing programme. The new Government's economic measures, combined with its success in improving the security situation, did much to restore confidence, and investment recovered. Gross domestic investment increased rapidly during 2003–05, and reached almost 25% of GDP in 2006. Strong economic conditions helped provide President Uribe with high approval ratings, and secured him a second term in office following a landslide victory in the May 2006 general election. Thereafter, foreign direct investment (FDI) continued to rise sharply. Increased investment led to renewed growth. In 2003 annual GDP growth was 4.1% (with industrial GDP rising by 7.2%) and the fiscal deficit was reduced to 2.7%, against the IMF target of 2.8%. Growth in 2004 was 4.7% and the fiscal deficit was reduced to 1.3% of GDP. Growth rose to 5.7% in 2005 and surpassed all expectations by reaching 6.9% in 2006, the highest realized in 30 years. Real GDP increased by 7.5% in 2007, a result attributed to the strong growth in the manufacturing and petroleum sectors (both of which had benefited from substantial investment). Strong internal demand and high commodity prices further aided growth in that year. Domestic investment reached 24.3% of GDP in 2007 and 25.0% in 2008, while FDI rose to $9,049m. and $10,583m. in 2007 and 2008, respectively. The combined public sector balance was reduced to -0.7% of GDP in both 2006 and 2007, and to -0.1% in 2008, and total public sector debt was reduced from 46.0% of GDP in 2003 to 32.3% in 2008. Sound economic management enabled a reduction in the rate of consumer price inflation, which fell to 4.5% in 2006, but began to increase thereafter (to 5.7% in 2007 and to 7.7% in 2008), reflecting rising international prices for energy and food, as well as increasing domestic consumption. Unemployment fell from a high of 20% in 2000 to just under 10.5% at the end of 2008. Poverty was reduced from a high of 60% in 1999 to 45% in 2006. The international financial crisis impacted adversely on growth in 2008 (see below), but the average annual growth rate in 2004–08 was still around 5.5%. Colombia is currently the third largest country in Latin America in terms of population and the fourth largest economy.

AGRICULTURE

Until the 1990s Colombia relied heavily on agriculture, a sector of the economy that was immensely diverse, owing to the country's varied topography. In 1960 agriculture (including forestry, fishing and hunting) employed over one-half of Colombia's total work-force, and more recently it accounted for 26% of GDP in 1976. In 2009 agricultural employment had fallen to 18.4%. The contribution of the sector to GDP was 8.5% in 2009. The long-term decline in agricultural employment was sharply accelerated during the economic liberalization of the early 1990s, when an estimated 100,000 jobs were lost in agriculture, as reduced tariffs made imports affordable. After 1994 the sector became more stable, despite the continuing violence in much of Colombia's rural areas. Much of Colombia's fertile arable land has been used for the illicit cultivation of coca (for cocaine production), and reports suggested that the spraying of coca crops with herbicide had also reduced conventional crop yields. However, since 1999 production has been increasing steadily. Agricultural GDP increased by a provisional 1.1% in 2009; average annual growth in 2001–07 was 3.1%. Growing interest in biodiesel, produced in Colombia from sugar cane and palm oil, seemed likely to spur increased growth: palm oil production increased by almost 40% in 2002–08.

Coffee

In 2009 coffee was Colombia's leading legal cash and export crop, and Colombian coffee still enjoyed an excellent reputation around the world, even though Colombia had lost its position as the world's second largest producer after Brazil to Viet Nam and Indonesia. Coffee had been overtaken in the 1990s by petroleum and its derivatives as the single most important export commodity. In the early 1980s coffee accounted for roughly one-half of total export earnings, but this figure had fallen to 4.7% by 2009. Coffee still accounted for about one-half of employment in agriculture. Some 500,000 families in Colombia worked in coffee plantations at this time, of whom 95% owned less than 5 ha, creating a rural middle class unusual in Latin America.

The coffee sector was well regulated. Policy was set by the semi-official Federación Nacional de Cafeteros de Colombia (FNC—National Federation of Coffee Growers). The Fondo Nacional del Café (National Coffee Fund) was established to help producers overcome sharp fluctuations in world prices. However, not even the Fund could cope with the fall in the coffee price following the collapse of the International Coffee Agreement in 1989. Colombia's response was to increase production, relying on its reputation as a high-quality producer. Production reached a high of 1.1m. metric tons in 1992. However, prices, which fluctuated during much of the 1990s, fell to a 100-year low, in real terms, by the turn of the century. This was owing, in part, to the dramatic entry of Vietnamese coffee (predominantly of the relatively low-quality robusta varieties, rather than the high-quality arabicas more commonly grown in Colombia), which rapidly overtook Colombia's own production capacity. Colombia's small farmers could not compete on cost with the large-scale Brazilian producers or the Vietnamese with their extremely low labour costs. Coffee exports in 2008 were worth US $1,883m., despite falling production as a result of adverse weather and a plant replacement programme. This represented a healthy increase on the $1,714m. recorded in the previous year, but still much lower than the $2,895m. recorded in 1997. Exports in 2009 were $1,543m. In 2002 the sector launched a series of high-quality specialist brands under the still popular 'Café de Colombia' name. By the end of 2004 the Colombian Arabica coffee price had reached $1.05/lb, more than enough to cover costs. It averaged $1.77/lb in 2009 and had risen to $2.05/lb in March 2010, reflecting the production difficulties mentioned above. The coffee zone, once Colombia's most prosperous and peaceful, has suffered greatly in recent years with coca cultivation appearing and the inevitable subsequent arrival of guerrilla and paramilitary organizations.

Bananas

Bananas have been Colombia's most contentious legal export, the subject of long-standing trade disputes. Although the banana is a traditional Colombian crop, it became part of the country's drive towards agricultural diversification designed to protect the economy from the fluctuations of the coffee market. Banana exports totalled US $837m. in 2009, equivalent to about 2.6% of total export revenues. Most of the bananas exported were grown in Uraba, in the north-west of the country, and Santa Marta in the central north. About 69,000 people were directly employed in the industry. The long-running dispute between the USA and the European Union (EU) about the latter's banana quotas was finally resolved at the end of 2009, with agreement that the tariff for Colombian bananas would be reduced from €175 to €148 as soon as the agreement was implemented, and subsequently to €114 in 2017 and €75 in 2020. The agreement, which in mid-2010 had yet to be approved by the European Parliament, promised substantial benefit to Colombia; with exports of around 1.7m. metric tons the EU was Colombia's biggest export market for bananas at this time.

Flowers

The cut-flower industry was the biggest success story of Colombia's agricultural diversification. It was launched in the late 1960s, and by the 1990s Colombia had become the world's second largest exporter. The industry is largely concentrated on the plain surrounding Bogotá, a choice influenced both by the climate and the presence of the international airport, vital for rapid movement of the flowers, which are mostly bound for the USA. The industry successfully coped with the overvalued peso of the mid-1990s and with increasing international competition. In 2009 cut-flower exports earned Colombia US $1,047m., about 3% of Colombia's total exports and not far below the highest annual figure ever recorded ($1,099m. in 2007).

Palm Oil

In 2009 Colombia, with 802,000 metric tons, was the world's fifth largest producer of palm oil, although its market share (1.9%) was very small when compared with Malaysia and Indonesia. About 235,000 ha were under cultivation in 2009. Production had increased rapidly from 672,000 tons in 2005. High international prices allowed for a significant increase in export revenue from this commodity in 2007 and even more in 2008, but a fall in prices resulted in a steep decline in the value of exports in 2009, to around US $112m. The sector was encouraged by successive governments, with a flexible credit system introduced in the late 1990s. The industry had considerable potential because the yields per hectare were some of the highest in the world and only a small proportion of the suitable land has yet been utilized. High costs, particularly of transportation from the interior, deterred expansion in the past, but total acreage sown for all palm production increased by over 90% in 2002–08, much of it near the Caribbean coast. Unfortunately, some plantations have been established by paramilitary leaders. There is also considerable potential for the export of the exotic fruits native to Colombia, such as star fruit and guanabana, although volumes will inevitably remain modest.

Staples

The traditional elements of the Colombian diet—apart from meat—are potatoes, maize, beans, rice, plantains, cassava and citrus. Domestic production of these crops was inevitably affected by the import liberalization of the early 1990s. Production stabilized thereafter. Rice production, which reached a low of 1.2m. metric tons in 1997, had recovered to 2.5m. tons in 2004 and fell slightly to 2.4m. tons in 2008. Raw sugar production, at around 1.7m. tons from the early 1990s, reached about 2.6m. tons in 2009. Potato output reached 2.9m. tons in the early 1990s. Output fell subsequently to 1.8m. tons, but recovered to around 2.8m. tons in 2008.

Livestock

Government initiatives to promote the supply of meat and dairy products through the use of subsidies led to an expansion in the amount of arable land dedicated to livestock. Almost 80% of the cattle population was based in the north-eastern pasture land of the Llanos. Production of cattle meat rose from 3.7m. tons slaughtered in 1995 to 3.9m. in 2000, but then declined between 2001 and 2003, before recovering to 4.1m. tons in 2008 (according to the Federación Colombiana de Ganaderos). A problem facing many ranchers was endemic guerrilla violence in cattle-raising areas. Wealthy ranch owners, particularly those with connections to the drugs trade, could afford to defend their landholdings, but, for the increasingly impoverished peasant class, the general level of insecurity was indicated by a fall of 600,000 ha in the area sown with arable crops between 1990 and 1995. The threat of guerrilla and paramilitary violence, although reduced in many areas, continued to depress levels of rural investment and discourage foreign involvement in the sector.

Agrarian Reform

Successive governments attempted to improve economic and social infrastructure in rural areas. President Samper pledged to increase such expenditure, but was impeded by the economic slowdown during his period of office. Despite the introduction of the first agrarian reform law in 1961, Colombia's record in this field has been disappointing. Considerable progress was made under the administration of President Carlos Lleras Restrepo (1966–70), but redistribution of land slowed thereafter. However, in early 2006 the seizure of many ranches owned by drugs-traffickers, combined with the prospect of many being surrendered by demobilized paramilitary leaders, promised a new opportunity for agrarian reform. According to the Colombian Institute for Rural Development (INCODER) some 250,000 ha were to be subject to redistribution in 2006–10; by 2009 about one-third of this objective had been achieved. The pattern of landholding varies greatly from region to region. The highlands of the Cordillera Oriental are mainly cultivated by smallholders, the majority of whom are often subsistence farmers. The coffee zone in the Cordillera Central is farmed in family-size commercial farms. The country's large cattle ranches are situated on the Caribbean coast and the Llanos. A longstanding obstacle to reforming the agricultural sector has been the question of legal title, as many internal migrants, or colonos, occupied land on Colombia's many internal frontiers. The legal position of these holdings has often remained obscure.

Drugs

The illicit drugs trade has undoubtedly both contributed to Colombia's economic growth and hindered it. Marijuana and coca have long been grown in the country, but the drugs trade really took off with the processing of cocaine from the late 1970s. Until the mid-1990s most of the coca paste used came from Peru and Bolivia, but when the supply, largely by light aircraft, was disrupted, coca cultivation in Colombia increased five-fold to replace it. Increased aerial spraying under 'Plan Colombia' reduced the overall area under cultivation by over one-half between 2001 and 2004, despite considerable replanting, according to UN figures (US figures were much higher). Hectares under cultivation increased by about 5% in 2005 but fell by slightly more in 2006. In 2007, according to UN estimates, production of coca in Colombia increased sharply to 99,000 ha, but fell to 68,000 ha in 2009, owing to a combination of manual eradication and aerial spraying. According to the UN Office on Drugs and Crime (UNODC), total farm-gate production of coca leaf and derivatives fell from $623m. in 2008 to $494m. in 2009, equivalent to about 3% of agriculture sector output. While Colombia remained the world's largest producer in 2008 (accounting for some 50% of production), its share of global coca output was observed to be declining. In the early 1990s there was an expansion, mainly in the south-west of the country, in the cultivation of the opium poppy—used to make heroin—and Colombia became the main supplier to the US market. However, acreage declined from 4,100 ha in 2003 to 356 ha in 2009. In early 2007 the Government claimed that production was no longer significant.

The benefits or otherwise of this hidden input were disputed, as, by its nature, the trade resisted quantification, and many conflicting and extravagant estimates have been made. One reputable study estimated that Colombian traffickers' net profits averaged between US $1,500m. and $2,500m. from 1982 to 1998, and that two-thirds of this was brought back to Colombia. This would represent an average of 3.8% of GDP per year. Government estimates have put the figure at closer to US $1,000m. per year, representing an average of 1.5%–2.0% of GDP, which seemed more likely, given that, for obvious reasons, a high proportion of drugs money is kept outside the country. The takeover by Mexican cartels of important drug supply routes to the USA that were previously controlled by Colombians may have reduced net profits further in recent years. The Colombian Government also regularly argued that the cost in terms of extra security expenditure and lost foreign investment was much higher than any gains. Certainly, the extra drugs-related crime—the guerrilla group Fuerzas Armadas Revolucionarias de Colombia (FARC) are believed to derive significant income from drug related activities in Colombia—and violence in rural areas, along with associated environmental damage, had a major negative impact. Nevertheless, while some rural areas remained effectively isolated from markets for legal agricultural produce, the attraction of growing illegal drugs crops, which would be collected by traffickers and which commanded a higher price, would persist. However, it was worth noting that many of the growers went to such areas specifically to grow such crops, often sent by the traffickers.

MINING AND ENERGY

Despite a long history of oil production, the largest coal reserves in Latin America, the world's largest emerald deposits and much gold, as well as great hydraulic resources, mining and energy only accounted for 1% of GDP in 1980. Major developments saw this figure reach 8.8% by 1999; after a decline in the early 2000s, the sector's share of GDP recovered to some 7.3% in 2009.

Coal

Colombia had the largest coal reserves in Latin America, estimated by the US Energy Information Administration (EIA) at 6,182m. metric tons in 2007. In 2008 it was the world's 10th largest producer and fourth largest exporter, with over 90% of domestic production exported. Production has expanded rapidly and in 2009 was 72m. tons, a decline of around 2.6% from the previous year. The leading coal producer was the El Cerrejón open-cast mine in the Guajira, one of the largest mines in the world. It was jointly developed by the state company, Carbones de Colombia (CARBOCOL), and International Resources Corporation (Intercor), a subsidiary of Exxon. Both CARBOCOL and Intercor were sold to an international consortium of BHP Billiton PLC, Anglo-American PLC and Glencore International AG in 2000 and 2002, respectively. In March 2006 Xstrata acquired Glencore's one-third stake in the mine for some US $1,700m. El Cerrejón exported 30.3m. tons of coal in 2009. The second largest producer in Colombia was the US company Drummond Ltd at its mine at La Loma in the César department, with production of 21.7m. tons in 2009. Coal is Colombia's second largest export. Exports of coal rose from US $595m. in 1995 to $5,413m. in 2009, equivalent to about 16% of total exports.

Petroleum and Gas

Colombia was a modest oil producer, usually producing a small surplus for export, from early in the 20th century until the major discoveries in the 1980s and 1990s. These followed the introduction of association contracts for oil exploration in the mid-1970s, which kept Colombia open to foreign companies just when most other developing countries were nationalizing their oil industries. The first important discovery was the Caño Limón field of an estimated 1,000m. barrels in Arauca in the early 1980s by Occidental. In 1991 a consortium led by British Petroleum (BP) discovered the Cusiana field in Casanare. This and the neighbouring Cupiagua field were estimated to hold between 1,500m. and 2,000m. barrels. Production at this field has fallen from 434,000 barrels per day (b/d) in 1998 to 81,000 b/d at the end of 2009. Total Colombian petroleum production in 2009 was 685,000 b/d, over 12% higher than in 2008, and following a period of static or declining production in 2003–07. Analysts have projected that production will be maintained or increase at these levels in the medium term and then decline gradually, barring major new discoveries. Exports reached a record 617,000 b/d at the end of 1998, but had declined to 171,000 b/d by 2004. By 2009 exports had increased to an estimated 513,000 b/d, with a value of US $10,200m., equivalent to around 31% of total exports, and proven crude petroleum reserves stood at 1,400m. barrels, equivalent to just over five years' production.

A tightening of the terms of the association contracts in 1989 led to a sharp fall in new exploration in the 1990s, which threatened to make Colombia a net importer by the mid-2000s. Much improved terms introduced in 1999 prompted a renewal of interest. Two medium-sized fields were discovered in 2001, and in March 2003 the discovery of large reserves (initially estimated at over 200m. barrels) at the Gibraltar-1 field was announced (a subsequent survey in 2004, however, greatly reduced the estimate of potential reserves, to 15m. barrels). The creation in 2003 of the Agencia Nacional de Hidrocarburos (ANH) to take over the regulatory side of the activities of the state-run Empresa Colombiana de Petróleos (Ecopetrol) and the new, improved terms that the ANH introduced in June 2004, the most attractive in Latin America, were welcomed by the international oil industry. Furthermore, the exploration of blocs off the Caribbean coast had already attracted interest from leading companies. The ANH signed 54 new contracts in 2007, 59 in 2008 and 64 in 2009. A survey compiled by US-based multinational company Halliburton in 2008 indicated that significant recoverable petroleum reserves—which could potentially increase total reserves to 20,000m. barrels—remained, as yet, untapped. The oil sector has also benefited from recent improvements in security, which has improved access to remote areas previously dominated by the FARC—see History.

Colombia's gas potential has never received the same investment as oil, owing largely to low local demand. However, there were important stand-alone natural gas fields off the Caribbean coast and a great deal of associated gas in the main oilfields. In recent years production has increased rapidly; from an average of 265,000m. cu ft in 2007 to 420,000m. cu ft in 2009. Proven gas reserves were estimated at about 4,400,000m. cu ft at the end of 2009, equivalent to about 12 years' production. The Empresa Colombiana de Gas (Ecogás) was established in 1997 to develop the distribution network, in which it invested US $1,000m. Ecogás was sold to the Empresa de Energía de Bogotá, SA, for $1,410m. in 2006. BP'S gas treatment facilities supply about 200m. cu ft from the Casanare fields to the Colombian market, roughly one-third of the national gas demand.

Metals

Despite Colombia's position as a leading producer of gold, the country's mines were not only small scale and technologically unsophisticated, but also located in remote areas heavily affected by guerrilla activity in the late 1990s. As a result, gold exports, which reached US $205m. in 1996, fell to $68m. in 2001. With a rising gold price, exports recovered thereafter, reaching $1,537m. in 2009, about 5% of total exports. The nickel industry, concentrated at the Cerromatoso plant, expanded steadily in the 1990s. Exports rose from $154m. in 1999 to $1,680m. in 2007, but fell sharply to $726m. in 2009, reflecting a fall in the price of the metal.

Emeralds

It was estimated that Colombia produced about 60% of the world's emeralds; however, large-scale smuggling made measurement exceptionally difficult. Emeralds were Colombia's fourth most valuable export commodity in the mid-1990s, although exports generally declined thereafter. Emerald exports were valued at US $154m. in 2008 and $88m. in 2009.

Power

Colombia made a massive investment in large hydroelectric projects in the 1970s and 1980s, and in 2006 this sector represented 78% of generating capacity. The El Niño extreme weather pattern caused a severe drought in 1992–93 that exposed the economy's vulnerability to this over-reliance on hydroelectric power. A rapid expansion of the thermal power stations was then undertaken both to reduce this reliance and to meet increasing demand. In the event, demand slowed with the 1999 recession: between 1995 and 2001 production only rose from 41,573 gWh to 43,173 gWh. Production reached an estimated 51,100m. kWh in 2008, according to the EIA. Domestic consumption was 38,600M. kWh in 2007 and installed capacity was about 13,200m. kilowatts. The thermal sector's capacity had risen to about 14% by 2008. The mid-1990s saw a major privatization programme, with the sale of eight companies for more than US $5,000m., largely to Spanish electricity concerns. The Government began to sell its stake in smaller regional electricity companies during 2009; a further sale of its stake in a major electricity company—ISAGEN—was again delayed.

MANUFACTURING

Manufacturing, which accounted for 14.1% of GDP in 2009, grew steadily under import substitution policies from the 1930s to 1990. The drastic reduction in tariffs and removal of import controls in 1991 under President Gaviria's policy of economic liberalization, known as the *apertura* (opening), led to an average annual contraction in the sector of 0.8% in 1995–2004, compared with average growth of 5% per year in the 1980s. As well as facing increased international competition, manufacturing had to cope with an overvalued currency for most of the decade and large-scale smuggling, which drugs-traffickers often used for money-laundering. Production grew steadily in the mid-2000s and by an estimated 6.8% and 10.0% in 2006 and 2007, respectively, but fell by 1.8% and 6.3% in 2008 and 2009 as the global crisis began to impact on the economy. Food and beverages, the largest sector, was adversely affected by increased import penetration; nevertheless, this industry experienced robust growth in 2004–06 and accounted for about 3.6% of GDP in 2009. The chemicals industry, in contrast, prospered, owing to major investment by multinational companies. The value of chemical exports increased from US $235m. in 1990 to $1,259m. in 2009, about 3.8% of total export revenues and about 4.0% less than in the previous year. The automobile industry was also in the hands of foreign multinationals. Three car-assembly plants produced a then record 80,000 units in 1997, but following the recession of 1999 annual production fell to 32,000. By 2007 the sector recorded a new high of 178,000 units, but this fell to 106,000 units in 2008. The textiles sector, based largely in Medellín, drove Colombia's industrialization from the beginning of the 20th century. The industry contributes some 3% of GDP and about 5% of exports, although the latter suffered a 42% reduction in 2009 compared with the previous year.

CONSTRUCTION

From the mid-1990s the highly cyclical construction industry suffered seriously from the economic slowdown and then the recession. A reduction in the amount of drugs money directed at speculative high-cost housing was one element in this decline, as was the increasingly rapid emigration of middle-class professionals. The Government attempted to revive the sector and employment by increasing expenditure on low-cost housing, but was constrained in the short term by budgetary restrictions and an unhelpful Constitutional Court ruling on mortgage rates. However, a recovery began in late 2000, which strengthened in subsequent years until a fall occurred in 2008. None the less, there was an impressive increase, of some 13%, in 2009, when the sector contributed about 6% of GDP.

TELECOMMUNICATIONS

Telecommunications, formerly the exclusive monopoly of the state communications company, were deregulated in the 1990s. Mobile licences were opened to international competition in the mid-1990s, and competition to the state concern for long-distance calls, the Empresa Nacional de Telecomunicaciones (TELECOM), was introduced in the late 1990s. In 2003 TELECOM itself, which was heavily indebted, was dissolved by the Government and reconstituted as Colombia Telecomunicaciones, SA. A 50% stake in the firm was acquired by Telefónica of Spain in April 2006 for US $370m. The industry as a whole expanded rapidly, outpacing the rest of the official economy, and in 2006 the sector represented 2.5% of GDP. In terms of access to fixed-line telecommunications, Colombia had 92 mobile phone subscribers, and 110 mobile phone and fixed-line subscribers per 100 inhabitants in 2008.

FINANCIAL SERVICES

Colombia's financial services sector and its regulation is well developed by regional standards, particularly in banking. Banking supervision had been more rigorously enforced after a crisis in 1982, when the Government was forced to renationalize 70% of the banking sector. In the 1990s most of the sector returned to private ownership, with foreign investors, principally from Spain, a significant presence. The banking sector prospered in the early 1990s, in large part owing to the privatization and liberalization process. However, as elsewhere in Latin America, the product range of banks was very limited and the banks were, therefore, over-dependent on loan income. As a result, they were not always prudent in their lending and, when the economy entered recession in 1998, many of the institutions found themselves in grave difficulty with large, unrecoverable debts. The problem was aggravated when interest rates were increased to record levels in late 1998, in order to reduce the public sector deficit. In 1999 the Government was forced to carry out a major bank rescue, estimated to have cost 7% of GDP. Return on assets of entities subject to the Colombian financial regulator was negative in 2000 and 2001 but rose to a peak of around 4.0% in 2006 before a contraction to about 2.3% in 2008, and a subsequent slight rise. Return on capital followed a similar trajectory and was about 20% in 2009. The percentage of regulatory capital held by the banking system to risk-weighted assets increased from 14.4% at the end of 2004 to 15.2% at the end of 2009. Overall, Colombian banks weathered the global financial crisis by strengthened capitalization and profitability in 2007–09. In 2007 foreign interests presided over 21% of Colombian banking assets, compared to 80% in Mexico. Indeed, Colombia was unique in Latin America in that a majority of its banks were locally owned, and the sector is highly concentrated (about 50% of banking assets are controlled by two domestic financial entities). None the less, foreign ownership was projected to increase as the country's investment profile improved. The stock exchanges in Bogotá, Cali and Medellín grew rapidly in 2005–06, as a result of the privatization and deregulation measures undertaken. Market capitalization remained small by international standards. Turmoil on global financial markets tempered the volume of trade in 2007 and 2008, but there was a sharp increase in traded volumes in 2009 as the domestic financial markets revived after the crisis of the previous year.

PRIVATIZATION AND INFRASTRUCTURE

The Gaviria administration made a modest start to privatizing Colombia's inadequate infrastructure in the early 1990s by transferring ports, railways and some power stations to the private sector. Concessions were let for construction or modernization of airports, roads and water utilities, and several banks were also sold. The Samper administration privatized a major part of the power-generation industry, as well as several other banks. The Pastrana administration was forced to cancel its plans to sell the remainder of the power sector, however, owing to changed market conditions, but the state coal company, CARBOCOL, was sold in late 2000. In mid-2004 the Uribe administration announced plans to privatize US $10,000m. of state assets over a five-year period. Sold first were two banks, Bancafe ($937m.) and Megabanco ($342m.). Ecogás was sold in 2006 to the Empresa de Energía de Bogotá, SA, for $1,410m., and a 50% stake in the state telecommunications firm was sold to Telefónica for $370m., also in 2006 (see above). In March 2007 52% of steel company Acerías Paz del Río was bought by Votorantim Metais of Brazil for $850m. In that year an Initial Public Offering of 10.1% of the state oil company Ecopetrol raised $10,100m., and the Government also sold several regional power distributors. The privatization of ISAGEN was delayed in the run up to the presidential election in 2010; a sale of an additional 9.9% of Ecopetrol was planned for 2011–12.

FOREIGN TRADE AND BALANCE OF PAYMENTS

After a long period of strong growth that began around 2002, Colombia's exports and imports in 2009 were inevitably hit by the market convulsions that had begun in 2008. Colombia's export earnings were traditionally dependent first on coffee and then on petroleum, both of which are vulnerable to highly volatile international prices. Petroleum exports fell to US $3,383m. in 2003 (26% of total exports), before recovering to $5,559m. in 2005 (26%) and to a record $12,213m. in 2008, up 67% on 2007, a result attributable to increased production and the escalating international price of crude petroleum. However, petroleum exports fell to $10,268m. in 2009, despite a volume increase. The overall contribution of receipts from this commodity to export revenue rose sharply from 13% in 2007 to about 31% in 2009. Coal exports have risen steadily, from $2,558m. in 2005 to $5,416m., or 16% of total exports, in 2009. Nickel exports generated $1,680m. in 2007, but fell in value to $726m., or 2% of total exports, in 2009. Non-traditional exports, in particular manufactures, bananas ($836m, or 2.5%, in 2009) and cut flowers ($1,046m., or 3.1%), which benefited from privileged access to the EU and US markets, were increasingly important. Helped by favourable commodity prices and international economic activity, total exports grew rapidly in the mid-2000s from $20,800m. in 2005 to $38,500m. in 2008 but fell to $33,787m. in 2009, an overall fall of nearly 13%. Imports also increased strongly as a result of exceptionally strong GDP growth. The *apertura* of the early 1990s and a steadily growing economy saw Colombia's imports—which had traditionally been fairly modest—grow rapidly, reaching $37,556m. in 2008 before falling to $31,054m. (a decrease of about 17%) in 2009. Colombia was able to report positive trade balances in most years from 1999. The trade balance was a $596m. deficit in 2007 but a surplus of $976m. was recorded in 2008 and of $2,560m. in 2009. The current account was in surplus in 1999 and 2000, but there was a widening deficit from 2001, reaching $6,883m. in 2008, before falling to $4,232m. in 2009, equivalent to about 1.8% of GDP. Exports to Venezuela—Colombia's second largest export market after the USA—fell by 33.5% in 2009, owing to a deterioration in relations between the two countries, and continued disruption would act as a damper on GDP growth.

INVESTMENT AND INDEBTEDNESS

FDI increased greatly during the 1990s, after the Andean Pact's abolition of its rule limiting foreign holdings to 49% in 1990. Much European money went into the petroleum industry and then into banks and power generation when these were privatized. FDI reached US $5,639m. in 1997. Following the end of the privatization programme, inflows declined to $2,237m. in 2000. Inflows of FDI rose from an average annual rate of about $2,730m. in 1996–2003 to a provisional $7,907m. in 2004–08, equivalent to about 3.5% of GDP, about 48% of which was in the oil and mining sector. Other important recipients of FDI are manufacturing, financial services, telecommunications and the retail, restaurants and hotels sectors. In 2005 FDI levels leapt to $10,252m., which included the purchase of Bavaria by SABMiller for $4,715m. and the sale of Compañía Colombiana de Tabaco (COLTABACO) to Philip Morris for $310m., the only major privatization in that year. FDI remained strong in 2007–09 at $9,049m., $10,583m. and $8,185m., respectively. Europe and North America are the biggest investors in Colombia.

Colombia was the only Latin American country that avoided major debt rescheduling in the 1980s. External debt grew slowly; from US $17,000m. in 1986, it reached $20,832m. in 2005, although this represented a real reduction, from 46% to 27% of GDP. Total external borrowing increased thereafter, to $53,600m. at the end of 2009, of which public debt was $36.900m., $15,600m. higher than at the end of 2008. Despite this increase the Colombian authorities had little difficulty in financing the debt through a positive capital account of $6,700m., placement of international bonds and multilateral loans. Public debt had fallen gradually as a percentage of GDP from 38.8% in 2005 to 32.3% in 2008; the increase in 2009 took the ratio to GDP to 35.1%. Total external debt has likewise fallen as a percentage of GDP, from 23.4% in 2006 to 21.3% in 2009, as has public debt that is external debt, from 15.3% in 2006 as a proportion of GDP to 15.2% in 2009. The bulk of external debt is owed by the public sector; private sector external indebtedness, at $16,900m. at the end of 2009, has declined to about 7% of GDP. Colombia's combined public and private external debt service as a percentage of exports had fallen from 35.4% in 2006 to 21.8% in 2009. Colombia's international reserves were equivalent to 4.8 months of imports in 2006 and 6.7 months in 2009. At the end of 2009 they stood at $24,995m., over 5% higher than one year previously.

OUTLOOK

The Uribe administration had introduced a number of policy measures after 2002. It was hoped that the new congressional majority would pass radical reforms to ensure financial viability. There was a need for higher spending on security and much increased investment in infrastructure, housing, education and health, while the public debt needed to be reduced. Some observers argued that the considerable economic successes of President Uribe's first administration owed more to his democratic security policy (homicides down by almost 40%, kidnappings down by 75%, most main roads secure) and to the benign international economic environment than to the President's economic reforms, which, although brave, did not go far enough in the view of many experts. The administration's first year tax, labour and pension reforms, which helped to restore confidence, should have been followed by more radical measures, put to the country in a referendum in October 2003. However, these failed, owing to a low voter turnout. The tax and pension reforms eventually approved by the Congress in 2004 and 2005, respectively, were not as far-reaching as was originally envisaged. Much of the administration's success in reducing the fiscal deficit was owing to a combination of higher tax revenues resulting from above average growth, high oil prices and local government fiscal prudence. Keeping the budget deficit within target in 2007 and beyond required more radical tax reform. Also required was a constitutional amendment to end the automatic increase of local government spending in line with central government spending, a policy that was scheduled to come into force in 2009. Unfortunately, rivalry within the new congressional majority meant the tax reform passed in late 2006 disappointed many within the Government, as well as observers. While a reduction in the rate of income and corporate taxation did ensue, because of the number of exemptions and reductions incorporated into the reforms they fell short of expectations. The inclusion of nine different rates for value-added tax also proved unpopular. Fiscal reform was further impeded in 2007 by the so-called 'parapolitical' scandal, which reduced the willingness of the majority to support unpopular measures. The parapolitical scandal also affected the prospects of the US Congress approving the free trade agreement (FTA) with Colombia that was signed in 2006: senior members of the new Democratic majority in the US Congress and their allies in the trade unions seized on it as a reason for delaying discussion of a measure many disliked for protectionist reasons. The FTA—and a similar one with the EU which was signed in May 2010—still awaited ratification in mid-2010; but an FTA with Canada was approved by the Canadian legislature at that time. While Colombia's economic prospects would be enhanced by these agreements, strong internal demand was also likely to engender a substantial increase in imports in the short term, as the removal of tariffs on goods imported from the USA led to a decline in prices. By extending the US Andean Trade Promotion Act (ATPDEA) in June 2007, the US Congress guaranteed, though on a temporary basis, the continuation of favourable terms of trade between the two countries until the FTA was finalized.

Colombia was inevitably affected by the global economic and financial crisis of 2008, but not too severely. Volatility in financial markets and a slowdown in economic activity resulting from a reduced demand for exports and lower commodity prices, lower investment and reduced workers' remittances from outside Colombia, and a drop in consumer confidence, resulted a sharp fall in GDP growth from 7.5% in 2007 to 2.5% in 2008. Exports, none the less, grew strongly in real terms, by 8.1% in the year as a whole, helped by strong oil and coal shipments, and FDI was at record levels. In 2009 overall, GDP hardly grew (0.1%) and unemployment rose (11.5% in the third quarter), but growth began to pick up in the second half of the year (3.4% in the fourth quarter of 2009 compared with the same quarter one year earlier, and provisional 4.4% on the same basis in the first quarter of 2010). Imports fell sharply, but the reduction in exports was less drastic owing to increased production of oil and coal and continued high commodity prices; mainly as a result the current account deficit declined by the equivalent of about 2% of GDP. Fiscal policy in 2009 contributed about 1% of GDP; however the Congress extended a wealth tax linked to security expenditure for another four years. In response to rising inflation in 2006–08 the central bank had tightened monetary policy to contain overheating pressures, but as the economy cooled the central bank's policy interest rate was lowered, from 10.0% at the end of 2008 to 3.5% in late 2009 and 3.0% in April 2010. Consumer price inflation fell to 2.0% in 2009, and the central bank's inflation target for 2010 was revised down from 3.5%-4.5% to 2%-4%. The Government had previously announced a programme of public and private investment in infrastructure, equivalent to over 10% of GDP. A continued strong external trade position enabled the Government to borrow on international markets; as a result, total public sector indebtedness as a percentage of GDP rose from 32.3% in 2008 to 35.1% in 2009, and international reserves rose by over 5% to US $24,995m. On 31 December 2009 the peso stood at 2,044 to the dollar, compared with 2,244 a year earlier.

The economy benefited in 2009 from increased capital spending, as regional governments made up for underspending in the previous year, and continued high commodity prices, increased government borrowing and continuing private capital inflows, despite the dip from the level in 2008. Growth was expected to pick up but not at the rate of the boom years of 2004–07—in mid-2010 the IMF's latest published forecast for that year was 2.3%—but with a higher rate in 2011 and subsequently. The IMF's medium term forecast suggested growth rising to 5.0% per annum until 2013 before levelling off at around 4.5%. The large inward flows of FDI in recent years was likely to have a positive impact on output, especially of oil and coal.

The risks to prospects in 2010 and the medium term included: uncertainty about the strength of the global economic recovery, affecting commodity prices; a deterioration in Colombia's ability to raise external financing (although its anticipated financing requirement for 2010 had already been covered); and increased political tensions with Venezuela, which could reduce activity and perhaps impact on domestic financial markets. As a precautionary measure the Government negotiated in May 2010 a new US $3.500m. flexible credit line with the IMF, without policy conditions; the previous year's $10,500m. credit line was not drawn upon. The IMF at the time congratulated the Colombian authorities on their appropriate response to the global crisis, commitment to a flexible exchange rate and to an inflation target regime.

The new President, Juan Manuel Santos, was expected to continue current economic policies emphasizing macroeconomic stability and improving the business environment. Among the tasks facing him upon taking office in August 2010 would be: reform of tax, pension and health care systems; social and infrastructure investment; job creation to lower the double-digit rate of unemployment and underemployment—Santos had pledged to create 2.4m. jobs by 2014; a reduction of the debt/GDP ratio to pre-2008 levels; and encouragement of FDI, including improvements in an inefficient judicial system. Santos also emphasized poverty reduction, which if achieved would impact on Colombia's high degree of income inequality. These were all challenging objectives, but they were necessary if their combined impact would be to permit a ratcheting up of Colombia's growth rate. As President-elect, Santos reportedly believed that Colombia could lift its economic growth rate to 6% per year.

In mid-2010 Colombia had so far weathered the global crisis quite well, helped by a track record of, until 2009: a reduction in the external debt-to-GDP ratio; sound public finances and a sustainable public debt position; a well-regulated banking sector, which had so far not been affected by the crisis; a lesser dependence than other countries on exports, which represented about 17% of GDP; and access to international capital markets on relatively favourable terms (Colombia's rating was just below investment grade status). However, on current expectations growth in 2010 and 2011 would remain below its potential, which would continue to hamper progress towards resolution of its long-running political and social problems.

Statistical Survey

Sources (unless otherwise stated): Departamento Administrativo Nacional de Estadística (DANE), Transversal 45 No 26-70, Interior I-CAN, Bogotá, DC; tel. (1) 597-8300; fax (1) 597-8399; e-mail dane@dane.gov.co; internet www.dane.gov.co; Banco de la República, Carrera 7A, No 14-78, 5°, Apdo Aéreo 3531, Bogotá, DC; tel. (1) 343-1111; fax (1) 286-1686; e-mail wbanco@banrep.gov.co; internet www.banrep.gov.co.

Area and Population

AREA, POPULATION AND DENSITY

Area (sq km)	1,141,748*
Population (census results)	
24 October 1993†	37,635,094
30 June 2005‡	
Males	21,169,835
Females	21,718,757
Total	42,888,592
Population (official projections at mid-year)	
2008	44,450,260
2009	44,977,758
2010	45,508,205
Density (per sq km) at mid-2010	39.9

* 440,831 sq miles.

† Revised figure, including adjustment for underenumeration. The enumerated total was 33,109,840 (males 16,296,539, females 16,813,301) in 1993.

‡ A 'census year' was conducted between 22 May 2005 and 22 May 2006, and a 'conciliated' total for 30 June 2005 was finally published in May 2007 (the original enumerated total was 41,298,706) incorporating adjustments for underenumeration, geographical undercoverage and underlying natural growth trends.

POPULATION BY AGE AND SEX
(official projections at mid-2010)

	Males	Females	Total
0–14	6,646,484	6,364,441	13,010,925
15–64	14,436,186	14,999,418	29,435,604
65 and over	1,383,090	1,678,586	3,061,676
Total	22,465,760	23,042,445	45,508,205

DEPARTMENTS
(census of 30 June 2005)*

Department	Area (sq km)	Population	Capital (with population†)
Amazonas	109,665	67,726	Leticia (32,450)
Antioquia	63,612	5,682,276	Medellín (2,233,660)
Arauca	23,818	232,118	Arauca (74,385)
Atlántico	3,388	2,166,156	Barranquilla (1,113,016)
Bolívar	25,978	1,878,993	Cartagena (895,400)
Boyacá	23,189	1,255,311	Tunja (152,419)
Caldas	7,888	968,740	Manizales (368,433)
Caquetá	88,965	420,337	Florencia (142,123)
Casanare	44,640	295,353	Yopal (103,754)
Cauca	29,308	1,268,937	Popayán (258,653)
César	22,905	903,279	Valledupar (348,990)
Chocó	46,530	454,030	Quibdó (110,032)
Córdoba	25,020	1,467,929	Montería (381,525)
Cundinamarca	22,623	2,280,037	Bogotá‡
Guainía	72,238	35,230	Puerto Inírida (15,827)
La Guajira	20,848	681,575	Riohacha (169,311)
Guaviare	42,327	95,551	San José del Guaviare (45,573)
Huila	19,890	1,011,418	Neiva (315,332)
Magdalena	23,188	1,149,917	Santa Marta (414,387)
Meta	85,635	783,168	Villavicencio (384,131)
Nariño	33,268	1,541,956	Pasto (383,846)
Norte de Santander	21,658	1,243,975	Cúcuta (585,919)
Putumayo	24,885	310,132	Mocoa (36,185)
Quindío	1,845	534,552	Armenia (272,574)
Risaralda	4,140	897,509	Pereira (428,397)
San Andrés y Providencia Islands	44	70,554	San Andrés (55,426)
Santander del Sur	30,537	1,957,789	Bucaramanga (509,918)
Sucre	10,917	772,010	Sincelejo (236,780)
Tolima	23,562	1,365,342	Ibagué (495,246)
Valle del Cauca	22,140	4,161,425	Cali (2,075,380)
Vaupés	65,268	39,279	Mitú (17,641)
Vichada	100,242	55,872	Puerto Carreño (12,897)
Capital District			
Bogotá, DC	1,587	6,840,116	—
Total	1,141,748	42,888,592	—

* A 'census year' was conducted between 22 May 2005 and 22 May 2006, and a 'conciliated' total for 30 June 2005 was finally published in May 2007 (the original enumerated total was 41,298,706) incorporating adjustments for underenumeration, geographical undercoverage and underlying natural growth trends.

† These amended figures for 11 November 2005 include an adjustment for geographical undercoverage and were announced in November 2006, prior to the publication of the final conciliated figures for 30 June 2005.

‡ The capital city, Bogotá, exists as the capital of a department as well as the Capital District. The city's population is included only in Bogotá, DC.

PRINCIPAL TOWNS
(estimated population at mid-1999)

Bogotá, DC (capital)	6,260,862	Neiva	300,052
Cali	2,077,386	Soledad	295,058
Medellín	1,861,265	Armenia	281,422
Barranquilla	1,223,260	Villavicencio	273,140
Cartagena	805,757	Soacha	272,058
Cúcuta	606,932	Valledupar	263,247
Bucaramanga	515,555	Montería	248,245
Ibagué	393,664	Itagüí	228,985
Pereira	381,725	Palmira	226,509
Santa Marta	359,147	Buenaventura	224,336
Manizales	337,580	Floridablanca	221,913
Bello	333,470	Sincelejo	220,704
Pasto	332,396	Popayán	200,719

Mid-2010 (incl. suburbs, UN estimates): Bogotá, DC 8,499,820; Medellín 3,593,821; Cali 2,401,004; Barranquilla 1,866,711; Bucaramanga 1,091,819; Cartagena 962,321; Cúcuta 774,343; (Source: UN, *World Urbanization Prospects: The 2009 Revision*).

BIRTHS, MARRIAGES AND DEATHS*

	Registered live births	Registered deaths
2000	752,834	187,432
2001	724,319	191,513
2002	700,455	192,262
2003	710,702	192,121
2004	723,099	188,933
2005	719,968	189,022
2006	714,450	192,814
2007	709,253	193,936
2008	714,477	196,394

* Data are tabulated by year of registration rather than by year of occurrence, although registration is incomplete. According to UN estimates, the average annual rates in 1995–2000 were: births 24.0 per 1,000, deaths 5.8 per 1,000; in 2000–05: births 22.0 per 1,000, deaths 5.6 per 1,000; and in 2005–10: births 20.6 per 1,000, deaths 5.5 per 1,000 (Source: UN, *World Population Prospects: The 2008 Revision*).

Registered marriages: 102,448 in 1980; 95,845 in 1981; 70,350 in 1986.

Life expectancy (years at birth, WHO estimates): 75 (males 72; females 79) in 2008 (Source: WHO, *World Health Statistics*).

ECONOMICALLY ACTIVE POPULATION
('000 persons aged 10 years and over)

	2006	2007	2008
Agriculture, hunting, forestry and fishing	2,059.2	3,035.0	3,054.5
Mining and quarrying	102.0	103.2	149.1
Manufacturing	1,998.0	2,361.4	2,335.6
Electricity, gas and water	62.9	83.7	78.7
Construction	755.2	905.1	878.5
Trade, restaurants and hotels	3,646.5	4,344.4	4,605.3
Transport, storage and communications	1,097.9	1,450.1	1,467.4
Financial intermediation	204.8	222.2	219.6
Real estate, renting and business activities	811.2	995.7	1,146.8
Community, social and personal services	3,183.0	3,567.3	3,463.3
Sub-total	13,920.8	17,068.0	17,398.8
Activities not adequately described	2,760.1	8.5	26.9
Total employed	16,680.9	17,076.5	17,425.7
Unemployed	2,424.8	2,089.2	2,245.7
Total labour force	19,105.7	19,165.7	19,671.4
Males	11,283.8	11,396.4	11,644.0
Females	7,821.9	7,769.3	8,027.4

Source: ILO.

Health and Welfare

KEY INDICATORS

Total fertility rate (children per woman, 2008)	2.4
Under-5 mortality rate (per 1,000 live births, 2008)	20
HIV/AIDS (% of persons aged 15–49, 2007)	0.6
Physicians (per 1,000 head, 2002)	1.4
Hospital beds (per 1,000 head, 2004)	1.2
Health expenditure (2007): US $ per head (PPP)	516
Health expenditure (2007): % of GDP	6.1
Health expenditure (2007): public (% of total)	84.2
Access to water (% of persons, 2008)	92
Access to sanitation (% of persons, 2008)	74
Total carbon dioxide emissions ('000 metric tons, 2006)	63,376.2
Carbon dioxide emissions per head (metric tons, 2006)	1.5
Human Development Index (2007): ranking	77
Human Development Index (2007): value	0.807

For sources and definitions, see explanatory note on p. vi.

Agriculture

PRINCIPAL CROPS
('000 metric tons)

	2006	2007	2008
Rice, paddy	2,248	2,313	2,792
Maize	1,531	1,733	1,727
Sorghum	156	118	134
Potatoes	2,208	2,823	2,373
Cassava (Manioc)	1,703	1,794	1,804
Yams	261	261	266
Sugar cane*	38,450	38,500	38,500
Beans, dry	137	156	161
Soybeans (Soya beans)	55	53	56
Coconuts	116	110*	110*
Oil palm fruit*	3,200	3,200	3,200
Cabbages and other brassicas*	143	145	145
Tomatoes	444	474	491
Chillies and peppers, green*	50	50	50
Onions, dry	275	334	334*
Carrots and turnips	226	231	299
Watermelons	88	89	88
Bananas	1,864	1,820	1,820*
Plantains	3,157	3,219	3,380
Oranges	405	353	353*
Mangoes, mangosteens and guavas	184	193	175
Avocados	192	194	184
Pineapples	397	435	436
Papayas	164	224	208
Coffee, green	725	757	689

* FAO estimate(s).

Aggregate production ('000 metric tons, may include official, semi-official or estimated data): Total cereals 3,972 in 2006, 4,214 in 2007, 4,707 in 2008; Total roots and tubers 4,266 in 2006, 4,978 in 2007, 4,543 in 2008; Total vegetables (incl. melons) 1,507 in 2006, 1,643 in 2007, 1,768 in 2008; Total fruits (excl. melons) 8,049 in 2006, 8,141 in 2007, 8,214 in 2008.

Source: FAO.

LIVESTOCK
('000 head, year ending September)

	2006	2007	2008
Horses	2,317	2,394	2,421
Asses	304	277	224
Mules	435	471	430
Cattle	26,129	26,703	26,878
Pigs	1,745*	1,914	1,830*
Sheep*	3,300	3,400	3,400
Goats*	1,180	1,200	1,200
Chickens*	145,000	150,000	155,000

* FAO estimate(s).

Source: FAO.

LIVESTOCK PRODUCTS
('000 metric tons)

	2006	2007	2008
Cattle meat	827.2	856.3	917.4
Sheep meat*	6.7	7.0	7.0
Goat meat*	6.8	6.9	6.9
Pig meat	148.2	177.2	169.8
Horse meat*	6.0	6.3	6.3
Chicken meat	849.8	924.9	1,010.7
Cows' milk	6,817	6,725	7,431
Hen eggs	525	498	542

* FAO estimates.

Source: FAO.

Forestry

ROUNDWOOD REMOVALS
('000 cu metres, excl. bark)

	2006	2007	2008*
Sawlogs, veneer logs and logs for sleepers	674	658	658
Pulpwood	842	808	808
Other industrial wood	121	145	145
Fuel wood	8,833	8,829	10,547
Total	10,470	10,440	12,158

* FAO estimates.

Source: FAO.

SAWNWOOD PRODUCTION
('000 cu metres, incl. railway sleepers)

	2006	2007	2008
Coniferous (softwood)	93	92	92*
Broadleaved (hardwood)	296	290	549†
Total	389	382	641

* FAO estimate.
† Unofficial figure.

Source: FAO.

Fishing

('000 metric tons, live weight)

	2006	2007	2008
Capture	109.6*	129.8*	135.0
Bigeye tuna	5.3	3.2	4.0
Characins*	7.1	7.1	7.1
Freshwater siluroids*	7.5	7.5	7.5
Other freshwater fishes*	5.4	5.4	5.4
Pacific anchoveta*	13.0	18.0	18.0
Skipjack tuna	21.3	17.9	22.1
Yellowfin tuna	14.2	20.9	21.6
Aquaculture*	70.1	66.6	66.4
Tilapias*	15.5	18.3	18.3
Pirapatinga*	1.6	2.3	2.2
Rainbow trout	2.4	1.1	1.0*
Whiteleg shrimp	21.6	20.3	20.3
Total catch*	179.8	196.4	201.4

* FAO estimate(s).

Note: Figures exclude crocodiles, recorded by number rather than by weight. The number of spectacled caimans caught was: 974,721 in 2006; 673,072 in 2007; 535,394 in 2008. The number of American crocodiles caught was: 9 in 2006; 250 in 2007; 367 in 2008.

Source: FAO.

Mining

('000 metric tons, unless otherwise indicated)

	2006	2007	2008
Gold (kilograms)	15,682	15,482	13,411
Silver (kilograms)	8,399	9,765	9,160
Salt	638	514	221
Hard coal	66,192	69,902	73,500
Iron ore*	644	624	475
Crude petroleum ('000 barrels)	193,085	193,815	214,620

* Figures refer to the gross weight of ore. The estimated iron content is 46%.

Source: US Geological Survey.

2009 ('000 metric tons): Crude petroleum 34,127 (Source: BP, *Statistical Review of World Energy*).

Industry

SELECTED PRODUCTS
('000 metric tons, unless otherwise indicated)

	2005	2006	2007
Sugar	2,683	2,415	2,277
Cement	9,959	n.a.	n.a.
Crude steel ingots (incl. steel for casting)*	842	1,221	1,260
Semi-manufactures of iron and steel (hot-rolled)*†	694	700	700
Gas-diesel (distillate fuel) oils	3,660	4,457	4,395
Residual fuel oils	3,056	2,792	3,318
Motor spirit (petrol)	4,252	3,618	3,164

* Source: US Geological Survey.
† Estimates.

Source: mostly UN Industrial Commodity Statistics Database.

2008 ('000 metric tons): Crude steel ingots (incl. steel for casting) 1,125; Semi-manufactures of iron and steel (hot-rolled) 700 (estimate) (Source: US Geological Survey).

Finance

CURRENCY AND EXCHANGE RATES

Monetary Units
100 centavos = 1 Colombian peso.

Sterling, Dollar and Euro Equivalents (31 May 2010)
£1 sterling = 2,867.6 pesos;
US $1 = 1,966.8 pesos;
€1 = 2,435.7 pesos;
10,000 Colombian pesos = £3.49 = $5.08 = €4.11.

Average Exchange Rate (pesos per US $)
2007 2,078.29
2008 1,967.71
2009 2,166.79

GOVERNMENT FINANCE
(budgetary central government transactions, non-cash basis, '000 million pesos, provisional figures)

Summary of Balances

	2005	2006	2007
Revenue	63,286	83,585	103,986
Less Expense	90,930	92,238	110,014
Net operating balance	−27,645	−8,654	−6,028
Less Net acquisition of non-financial assets	−21,087	3,780	1,694
Net lending/borrowing	−6,558	−12,433	−7,722

Revenue

	2005	2006	2007
Taxes	43,584	45,423	58,644
Taxes on income, profits and capital gains	16,461	15,240	17,336
Individuals	16,461	15,240	17,336
Taxes on goods and services	22,038	19,412	27,181
Social contributions	3,054	3,366	4,273
Grants	239	93	170
Other revenue	16,409	34,702	40,899
Total	63,286	83,585	103,986

Expense/Outlays

Expense by economic type	2005	2006	2007
Compensation of employees	17,344	17,322	20,468
Use of goods and services	4,026	4,528	5,645
Consumption of fixed capital	293	511	914
Interest	19,067	29,644	27,562
Subsidies	178	289	273
Grants	29,439	34,296	41,689
Social benefits	2,981	3,077	6,221
Other expense	17,602	2,571	7,240
Total	90,930	92,238	110,014

Source: IMF, *Government Finance Statistics Yearbook*.

Public sector account ('000 million pesos): *Revenue:* 132,247.1 in 2007; 130,672.9 in 2008; 138,982.2 in 2009. *Expenditure (incl. interest payments):* 134,040.4 in 2007; 128,478.3 in 2008; 149,898.8 in 2009.

INTERNATIONAL RESERVES
(US $ million at 31 December)

	2007	2008	2009
Gold (national valuation)	185	191	243
IMF special drawing rights	220	229	1,184
Reserve position in IMF	452	440	406
Foreign exchange	20,096	22,810	23,158
Total	20,953	23,670	24,991

Source: IMF, *International Financial Statistics*.

MONEY SUPPLY
('000 million pesos at 31 December)

	2007	2008	2009
Currency outside banks	22,417.2	24,351.6	25,671.2
Transferable deposits	20,943.6	23,075.9	24,796.3
Other deposits	54,175.8	58,409.5	66,134.6
Securities other than shares	47,106.4	65,538.9	68,579.6
Broad money	144,643.0	171,375.9	185,181.8

Source: IMF, *International Financial Statistics*.

COST OF LIVING
(Consumer Price Index for low-income families; base: 2000 = 100)

	2006	2007	2008
Food and beverages	150.5	162.5	182.6
Clothing and footwear	109.7	111.4	112.0
Rent, fuel and light*	121.1	126.4	132.5
All items (incl. others)	145.2	153.4	166.0

* Including certain household equipment.

2009: Food and beverages 189.6; All items (incl. others) 173.2.

Source: ILO.

NATIONAL ACCOUNTS
('000 million pesos at current prices, provisional figures)

Expenditure on the Gross Domestic Product

	2007	2008	2009
Final consumption expenditure	344,795	375,864	395,160
Households*	273,321	297,840	309,721
General government	71,474	78,024	85,439
Gross capital formation	105,046	119,560	120,475
Total domestic expenditure	449,841	495,424	515,634
Exports of goods and services	72,869	87,240	81,675
Less Imports of goods and services	90,871	104,305	99,613
GDP in market prices	431,839	478,360	497,697
GDP at constant 2000 prices	273,710	280,369	281,367

* Including non-profit institutions serving households.

Gross Domestic Product by Economic Activity

	2007	2008	2009
Agriculture, hunting, forestry and fishing	35,276	39,378	42,433
Mining and quarrying	27,705	36,055	32,055
Manufacturing	69,757	71,675	70,432
Electricity, gas and water	13,181	14,750	17,174
Construction	29,683	36,946	44,017
Wholesale and retail trade; repair of motor vehicles, motorcycles, and personal and household goods; hotels and restaurants	52,873	57,916	58,951
Transport, storage and communications	29,246	29,634	32,301
Financial intermediation, insurance, real estate, renting and business activities	65,197	74,191	76,256
Other community, social and personal service activities	72,712	78,765	86,144
Gross value added in basic prices	395,629	439,310	459,763
Taxes on products	36,781	39,692	38,527
Less Subsidies on products	571	642	594
GDP in market prices	431,839	478,360	497,697

BALANCE OF PAYMENTS
(US $ million)

	2007	2008	2009
Exports of goods f.o.b.	30,577	38,531	34,026
Imports of goods f.o.b.	−31,173	−37,556	−31,466
Trade balance	−596	976	2,560
Exports of services	3,636	4,137	4,191
Imports of services	−6,243	−7,188	−6,871
Balance on goods and services	−3,203	−2,075	−121
Other income received	1,855	1,745	1,204
Other income paid	−9,857	−12,065	−10,848
Balance on goods, services and income	−11,205	−12,395	−9,764
Current transfers received	5,642	5,898	5,238

—continued	2007	2008	2009
Current transfers paid	−413	−386	−619
Current balance	−5,977	−6,883	−5,146
Direct investment abroad	−913	−2,254	−3,025
Direct investment from abroad	9,049	10,583	7,201
Portfolio investment assets	−993	188	−3,181
Portfolio investment liabilities	1,884	−1,195	4,668
Other investment assets	−2,237	−173	−884
Other investment liabilities	3,532	2,267	2,103
Net errors and omissions	344	38	−296
Overall balance	4,688	2,571	1,441

Source: IMF, *International Financial Statistics*.

External Trade

PRINCIPAL COMMODITIES
(US $ million)

Imports c.i.f.	2007	2008	2009
Agricultural, livestock, hunting and forestry products	1,678	2,217	1,733
Prepared foodstuffs, beverages and tobacco	1,565	2,057	1,859
Textiles, clothing and leather products	1,350	1,488	1,307
Chemical products	6,097	7,362	6,119
Rubber and plastic goods	1,066	1,277	1,157
Metals and metal manufactures	3,218	3,898	2,530
Mechanical, electrical, office, telecommunications and medical equipment	9,581	11,558	9,438
Vehicles and transport equipment	5,840	6,142	6,179
Total (incl. others)	32,897	39,669	32,898

Exports f.o.b.	2007	2008	2009
Coffee	1,714	1,883	1,543
Coal	3,495	5,043	5,416
Petroleum and its derivatives	7,318	12,213	10,268
Prepared foodstuffs, beverages and tobacco	1,988	2,627	2,330
Textiles, clothing and leather products	2,434	2,747	1,492
Paper and publishing	797	871	764
Chemicals	2,169	2,674	2,482
Metal manufactures	1,963	2,357	2,422
Mechanical, electrical and office equipment	906	1,101	987
Vehicles and transport equipment	1,725	1,224	698
Total (incl. others)	29,991	37,626	32,853

PRINCIPAL TRADING PARTNERS
(US $ million)

Imports c.i.f.	2007	2008	2009
Brazil	2,394	2,328	2,147
China, People's Republic	3,327	4,549	3,715
Ecuador	733	810	695
Germany	1,205	1,557	1,338
Japan	1,231	1,153	825
Mexico	3,073	3,126	2,298
Spain	456	568	442
USA	8,569	11,437	9,456
Venezuela	1,366	1,198	563
Total (incl. others)	32,897	39,669	32,898

Exports f.o.b.	2007	2008	2009
Belgium	389	460	409
Ecuador	1,276	1,500	1,257
Germany	553	638	365
Japan	395	372	336
Mexico	495	617	536
Peru	806	855	788
USA	10,373	14,053	12,879
Venezuela	5,210	6,092	4,050
Total (incl. others)	29,991	37,626	32,853

Transport

RAILWAYS
(traffic)

	1996	1997	1998
Freight ('000 metric tons)	321	348	281
Freight ton-km ('000)	746,544	736,427	657,585

Source: Sociedad de Transporte Ferroviario, SA.

ROAD TRAFFIC
(motor vehicles in use at 31 December)

	1997	1998	1999
Passenger cars	1,694,323	1,776,100	1,803,201
Buses	126,362	131,987	134,799
Goods vehicles	179,530	183,335	184,495
Motorcycles	385,378	450,283	479,073

2007: Passenger cars 1,674,441; Buses 148,537; Vans and lorries 1,064,513; Motorcycles and mopeds 1,930,978.

Source: IRF, *World Road Statistics*.

SHIPPING

Merchant Fleet
(registered at 31 December)

	2006	2007	2008
Number of vessels	144	147	149
Total displacement ('000 grt)	96.2	90.8	91.4

Source: Lloyd's Register-Fairplay, *World Fleet Statistics*.

Domestic Sea-borne Freight Traffic
('000 metric tons)

	1987	1988	1989
Goods loaded and unloaded	772.1	944.8	464.6

International Sea-borne Freight Traffic
('000 metric tons)

	1999	2000	2001
Goods loaded	4,111	3,543	3,832
Goods unloaded	1,274	1,114	1,399

CIVIL AVIATION
(traffic)

	2003	2004	2005
Kilometres flown (million)	110	118	127
Passengers carried ('000)	8,665	8,829	9,984
Passenger-km (million)	8,299	9,045	9,688
Total ton-km (million)	1,390	1,926	1,982

Source: UN, *Statistical Yearbook*.

Tourism

TOURIST ARRIVALS

Country of origin	2005	2006	2007
Argentina	34,025	40,260	50,632
Brazil	27,209	31,757	41,145
Canada	24,471	27,123	28,279
Chile	19,091	23,770	29,371
Costa Rica	25,002	25,138	21,326
Ecuador	95,816	100,226	110,508
France	23,060	24,883	27,611
Germany	18,130	19,050	21,668
Italy	19,955	22,495	24,620
Mexico	42,580	52,042	60,340
Netherlands	15,721	16,459	17,104
Panama	28,811	31,181	31,459
Peru	44,490	47,750	58,332
Spain	57,064	66,432	66,748
United Kingdom	16,089	17,707	14,071
USA	235,386	259,226	265,651
Venezuela	113,674	141,599	196,863
Total (incl. others)	933,243	1,053,348	1,195,443

Tourism receipts (US $ million, excl. passenger transport): 1,554 in 2006; 1,669 in 2007; 1,844 in 2008 (provisional).

Source: World Tourism Organization.

Communications Media

	2007	2008	2009
Telephones ('000 main lines in use)	7,935.7	8,053.8	7,500.4
Mobile cellular telephones ('000 subscribers)	33,941.1	41,364.7	42,159.6
Internet users ('000)	12,331.9	17,329.7	20,788.8
Broadband subscribers ('000)	1,207.1	1,902.8	2,117.9

Radio receivers ('000 in use): 21,000 in 1997.

Television receivers ('000 in use): 11,396 in 2000.

Personal computers: 5,062,885 (112.5 per 1,000 persons) in 2008.

Book production: 5,302 titles in 1997.

Daily newspapers: 23 titles in 2004 (total average circulation 1,004,000).

Non-daily newspapers: 5 titles in 2004 (total average circulation 289,000).

Sources: UN, *Statistical Yearbook*; UNESCO, *Statistical Yearbook*; International Telecommunication Union.

Education

(2007/08 unless otherwise indicated)

	Institutions*	Teachers	Students ('000)		
			Males	Females	Total
Pre-primary	32,432	49,538†	672.0	640.5	1,312.5
Primary	55,869	187,821†	2,704.3	2,581.2	5,285.5
Secondary					
general	12,921	151,813‡	2,317.5	2,454.7	4,772.2
technical/vocational		12,527‡	143.5	165.7	309.2
Higher (incl. universities)	321	87,397§	757.5	729.7	1,487.2

* 2001/02.

† 2006/07.

‡ 2003/04.

§ 2005/06.

Sources: Ministerio de Educación Nacional and UNESCO Institute for Statistics.

Pupil-teacher ratio (primary education, UNESCO estimate): 29.4 in 2007/08 (Source: UNESCO Institute for Statistics).

Adult literacy rate (UNESCO estimates): 93.4% (males 93.3%; females 93.4%) in 2008 (Source: UNESCO Institute for Statistics).

Directory

The Constitution

A new, 380-article Constitution, drafted by a 74-member National Constituent Assembly, took effect from 6 July 1991. The new Constitution retained the institutional framework of a directly elected President with a non-renewable four-year term of office, together with a bicameral legislature composed of an upper house or Senate (with 102 directly elected members) and a lower house or House of Representatives (to include at least two representatives of each national department). In December 2004 the legislature approved a constitutional amendment to allow re-election of the President for a second term in office. The reform was approved by the Constitutional Court in October 2005, taking force prior to the May 2006 presidential election. A Vice-President is elected at the same time as the President, and also holds office for a term of four years.

The new Constitution also contained comprehensive provisions for the recognition and protection of civil rights, and for the reform of the structures and procedures of political participation and of the judiciary.

The fundamental principles upon which the new Constitution is based are embodied in articles 1–10.

Article 1: Colombia is a lawful state, organized as a single Republic, decentralized, with autonomous territorial entities, democratic, participatory and pluralist, founded on respect for human dignity, on the labour and solidarity of its people and on the prevalence of the general interest.

Article 2: The essential aims of the State are: to serve the community, to promote general prosperity, to guarantee the effectiveness of the principles, rights and obligations embodied in the Constitution, to facilitate the participation of all in the decisions which affect them and in the economic, political, administrative and cultural life of the nation, to defend national independence, to maintain territorial integrity and to ensure peaceful coexistence and the validity of the law.

The authorities of the Republic are instituted to protect the residents of Colombia, in regard to their life, honour, goods, beliefs and other rights and liberties, and to ensure the fulfilment of the obligations of the State and of the individual.

Article 3: Sovereignty rests exclusively with the people, from whom public power emanates. The people exercise power directly or through their representatives in the manner established by the Constitution.

Article 4: The Constitution is the highest authority. In all cases of incompatability between the Constitution and the law or other juridical rules, constitutional dispositions will apply.

It is the duty of nationals and foreigners in Colombia to observe the Constitution and the law, and to respect and obey the authorities.

Article 5: The State recognizes, without discrimination, the primacy of the inalienable rights of the individual and protects the family as the basic institution of society.

Article 6: Individuals are solely responsible to the authorities for infringements of the Constitution and of the law. Public servants are equally accountable and are responsible to the authorities for failure to fulfil their function or abuse of their position.

Article 7: The State recognizes and protects the ethnic diversity of the Colombian nation.

Article 8: It is an obligation of the State and of the people to protect the cultural and natural riches of the nation.

Article 9: The foreign relations of the State are based on national sovereignty, with respect for self-determination of people and with recognition of the principles of international law accepted by Colombia.

Similarly, Colombia's external politics will be directed towards Caribbean and Latin American integration.

Article 10: Spanish (Castilian) is the official language of Colombia. The languages and dialects of ethnic groups are officially recognized within their territories. Education in communities with their own linguistic traditions will be bilingual.

The Government

HEAD OF STATE

President: JUAN MANUEL SANTOS CALDERÓN (took office on 7 August 2010).

Vice-President: ANGELINO GARZÓN.

CABINET
(August 2010)

The Government is formed by the Partido Social de Unidad Nacional.

Minister of the Interior and Justice: GERMÁN VARGAS LLERAS.

Minister of Foreign Affairs: MARÍA ANGÉLICA HOLGUÍN.

Minister of Finance and Public Credit: JUAN CARLOS ECHEVERRY.

Minister of National Defence: RODRIGO RIVERA.

Minister of Agriculture and Rural Development: JUAN CAMILO RESTREPO.

Minister of Social Protection: MAURICIO SANTAMARÍA SALAMANCA.

Minister of Mines and Energy: CARLOS RODADO NORIEGA.

Minister of Trade, Industry and Tourism: SERGIO DÍAZ GRANADOS.

Minister of National Education: MARÍA FERNANDA CAMPO.

Minister of the Environment: SANDRA BESSUDO LION.

Minister of Information Technology and Communications: DIEGO MOLANO.

Minister of Transport: GERMÁN CARDONA GUTIÉRREZ.

Minister of Culture: MARIANA GARCÉS CÓRDOBA.

Minister of Housing and Territorial Development: BEATRIZ URIBE.

MINISTRIES

Office of the President: Palacio de Nariño, Carrera 8, No 7-26, Bogotá, DC; tel. (1) 562-9300; fax (1) 286-8063; internet www.presidencia.gov.co.

Ministry of Agriculture and Rural Development: Avda Jiménez, No 7-65, Bogotá, DC; tel. (1) 334-1199; fax (1) 284-1775; e-mail contactenos@minagricultura.gov.co; internet www.minagricultura.gov.co.

Ministry of Culture: Carrera 8, No 8-43, Bogotá, DC; tel. (1) 342-4100; fax (1) 342-1721; e-mail servicioalcliente@mincultura.gov.co; internet www.mincultura.gov.co.

Ministry of the Environment: Calle 37, No 8-40, Bogotá, DC; tel. (1) 332-3434; e-mail correspondencia@minambiente.gov.co; internet www.minambiente.gov.co.

Ministry of Finance and Public Credit: Carrera 8, No 6-64, Of. 305, Bogotá, DC; tel. (1) 381-1700; fax (1) 350-9344; e-mail atencioncliente@minhacienda.gov.co; internet www.minhacienda.gov.co.

Ministry of Foreign Affairs: Palacio de San Carlos, Calle 10, No 5-51, Bogotá, DC; tel. (1) 381-4000; fax (1) 381-4747; e-mail cancilleria@cancilleria.gov.co; internet www.cancilleria.gov.co.

Ministry of Housing and Territorial Development: Bogotá, DC.

Ministry of Information Technology and Communications: Edif. Murillo Toro, Carrera 8A entre, Calle 12 y 13, Apdo Aéreo 14515, Bogotá, DC; tel. (1) 344-3460; fax (1) 344-3434; e-mail info@mintic.gov.co; internet www.mintic.gov.co.

Ministry of the Interior and Justice: Palacio Echeverry, Carrera 9, No 14-10, Bogotá, DC; tel. (1) 444-3100; fax (1) 341-9583; e-mail atencionalcliente@mij.gov.co; internet www.mij.gov.co.

Ministry of Mines and Energy: Calle 43, No 57-31, Centro Administrativo Nacional (CAN), Bogotá, DC; tel. (1) 220-0300; fax (1) 222-3651; e-mail menergia@minminas.gov.co; internet www.minminas.gov.co.

Ministry of National Defence: Carrera 54, No 26–25, Centro Administrativo Nacional (CAN), 2°, Bogotá, DC; tel. (1) 266-0296; fax (1) 315-0111; e-mail usuarios@mindefensa.gov.co; internet www.mindefensa.gov.co.

Ministry of National Education: Calle 43, No 57-14, Centro Administrativo Nacional (CAN), Bogotá, DC; tel. (1) 222-2800; fax (1) 222-4578; e-mail dci@mineducacion.gov.co; internet www.mineducacion.gov.co.

Ministry of Social Protection: Carrera 13, No 32-76, Bogotá, DC; tel. (1) 330-5000; fax (1) 330-5050; e-mail atencionalciudadano@minproteccionsocial.gov.co; internet www.minproteccionsocial.gov.co.

Ministry of Trade, Industry and Tourism: Edif. Centro de Comercio Internacional, Calle 28, No 13A-15, 18°, Bogotá, DC; tel. (1) 606-7676; fax (1) 606-7521; e-mail info@mincomercio.gov.co; internet www.mincomercio.gov.co.

Ministry of Transport: Centro Administrativo Nacional (CAN), Of. 409, Avda El Dorado, Bogotá, DC; tel. (1) 324-0800; e-mail mintrans@mintransporte.gov.co; internet www.mintransporte.gov.co.

President and Legislature

PRESIDENT

Presidential Election, First Round, 30 May 2010

	Valid votes	% of votes cast
Juan Manuel Santos Calderón (Partido de la U)	6,802,043	46.67
Antanas Mockus Šivickas (PV)	3,134,222	21.51
Germán Vargas Lleras (CR)	1,473,627	10.11
Gustavo Petro Urrego (PDA)	1,331,267	9.13
Noemí Sanín (PCC)	893,819	6.13
Rafael Pardo Rueda (PL)	638,302	4.38
Others	75,336	0.52
Votos en blanco*	223,977	1.53
Total†	14,573,593	100.00

* Blank, valid votes.
† In addition, there were 208,427 invalid votes.

Presidential Election, Second Round, 20 June 2010

	Valid votes	% of votes cast
Juan Manuel Santos Calderón (Partido de la U)	9,028,942	69.13
Antanas Mockus Šivickas (PV)	3,587,975	27.47
Votos en blanco*	444,274	3.40
Total valid votes†	13,061,192	100.00

* Blank, valid votes.
† In addition, there were 235,732 invalid votes.

CONGRESO

Senado
(Senate)

President: AMANDO BENEDETTI.

General Election, 14 March 2010

	Seats
Partido Social de la Unidad Nacional (Partido de la U)	28
Partido Conservador Colombiano (PCC)	22
Partido Liberal Colombiano (PL)	17
Partido de Integración Nacional (PIN)	9
Partido Cambio Radical	8
Polo Democrático Alternativo (PDA)	8
Partido Verde	5
Movimiento MIRA	2
Compromiso Ciudadano por Colombia	1
Indigenous groups*	2
Total	102

* Under the terms of the Constitution, at least two Senate seats are reserved for indigenous groups.

Cámara de Representantes
(House of Representatives)

President: EDGAR GÓMEZ.

General Election, 14 March 2010

	Seats
Partido Social de Unidad Nacional (Partido de la U)	47
Partido Conservador Colombiano (PCC)	38
Partido Liberal Colombiano (PL)	37
Partido Cambio Radical	15
Partido de Integración Nacional (PIN)	12
Polo Democrático Alternativo (PDA)	4
Partido Verde	3
Movimiento MIRA	3
Movimiento Apertura Liberal	2
Alianza Social Indígena	1
Alternativa Liberal	1
Movimiento de Integración Regional (IR)	1
Indigenous groups*	2
Total	166

* Under the terms of the Constitution, at least two lower house seats are reserved for indigenous groups.

Election Commission

Consejo Nacional Electoral (CNE): Avda El Dorado 46–20, Centro Administrativo Nacional (CAN), 6°, Bogotá, DC; tel. (1) 220-0800; internet www.cne.gov.co; f. 1888 as Gran Consejo Electoral; refounded under current name in 1985; Pres. MARCO EMILIO HINCAPIÉ RAMÍREZ.

Political Organizations

Alianza Social Indígena: Calle 17, No 5-43, 8°, Bogotá, DC; tel. (1) 282-7474; fax (1) 286-8422; e-mail contactos@asicolombia.com; internet www.asicolombia.com; f. 1991; Leader HERNANDO CHINDOY.

Cambio Radical (CR): Carrera 7, No 26-20, 26°, Bogotá, DC; tel. (1) 210-7373; fax (1) 210-6868; e-mail cambioradical@cable.net.co; internet www.partidocambioradical.org; f. 1998; Pres. GERMÁN VARGAS LLERAS; Sec.-Gen. ANTONIO ALVAREZ LLERAS.

Compromiso Ciudadano por Colombia: Carrera 36, 8A-46, Of. 201, Medellín; tel. (4) 448-6048; fax (4) 312-7014; e-mail info@sergiofajardo.com; internet www.sergiofajardo.com; f. 2008; contested the 2010 presidential campaign in alliance with the Partido Verde (q.v.); Leader SERGIO FAJARDO.

Movimiento Apertura Liberal: Avda 3B, 5-70B, Latino, Cúcuta, Norte de Santander; tel. (7) 571-3729; e-mail correo@aperturaliberal.com; internet www.aperturaliberal.com; f. 1993; Nat. Dir Dr MIGUEL ANGEL FLORES RIVERA.

Movimiento de Autoridades Indígenas de Colombia (AICO): Calle 23, No 7-61, Of. 302, Bogotá DC; tel. (1) 286-8233; fax (1) 341-8930; e-mail aico@aicocolombia.org; internet www.aicocolombia.org; f. 1990; Pres. LUIS HUMBERTO CUASPUD.

Movimiento de Integración Regional (IR): 4-140 Avda 20 de Julio, San Andrés, Isla; tel. (1) 512-2193; e-mail ir@latinmail.com; Leader DORKY JAY JULIO.

Movimiento MIRA (Movimiento Independiente de Renovación Absoluta): Transversal 29, No 36-40, Bogotá, DC; tel. (1) 369-3222; fax 369-3210; e-mail webmaster1@webmira.com; internet www.webmira.com; f. 2000; Pres. CARLOS ALBERTO BAENA LÓPEZ.

Partido Alas: Calle 34, No 29-18, Bogotá, DC; tel. (1) 244-1213; fax (1) 269-7034; e-mail contactenos@alasequipocolombia.org; internet www.alasequipocolombia.org; conservative; contested 2006 election as Alas Equipo Colombia, in alliance with Movimiento Equipo Colombia; reverted to former name in 2009; Pres. ALFONSO MATOS; Sec.-Gen. JAVIER PINILLA PALACIO.

Partido Alianza Democrática Nacional (ADN): Of. 215, Calle 13, No 8-23, Bogotá, DC; tel. and fax (1) 283-7099; internet www.adnpartido.com; f. 2005 as Colombia Viva; present name adopted 2009.

Partido Colombia Democrática: Calle 41, No 13A-07, 2°, Bogotá, DC; tel. (1) 338-3624; fax (1) 338-2310; e-mail contactenos@colombiademocratica.com; internet www.colombiademocratica.com; f. 2003; conservative; Nat. Dir MARIO URIBE ESCOBAR; Sec.-Gen. GABRIEL SIERRA.

Partido Comunista Colombiano (PC): Calle 18A, No 14-56, Apdo Aéreo 2523, Bogotá, DC; tel. (1) 334-1947; fax (1) 281-8259; e-mail notipaco@pacocol.org; internet www.pacocol.org; f. 1930; Marxist-Leninist; Sec.-Gen. JAIME CAYCEDO TURRIAGO.

Partido Conservador Colombiano (PCC): Avda Carrera 24, No 37-09, La Soledad, Bogotá, DC; tel. (1) 597-9630; fax (1) 369-0053; e-mail presidencia@partidoconservador.com; internet www.partidoconservador.com; f. 1849; 2.9m. mems; Pres. FERNANDO ARAUJO PERDOMO; Sec.-Gen. BENJAMÍN HIGUITA RIVERA.

Partido de Integración Nacional (PIN): Carrera. 27A, No 48-33, Bogotá DC; tel. (1) 647-6411; fax (1) 657-3784; e-mail convergencia@intercable.net.co; f. 2009; pro-govt party; Sec.-Gen. RICARDO FLORES; Leader ALVARO CAICEDO.

Partido Liberal Colombiano (PL): Avda Caracas, No 36-01, Bogotá, DC; tel. (1) 593-4500; fax (1) 323-1070; e-mail direcciondecomunicaciones@partidoliberal.org.co; internet www.partidoliberal.org.co; f. 1848; Pres. CÉSAR GAVIRIA TRUJILLO; Sec.-Gen. MAURICIO JARAMILLO MORALES (designate).

Partido Social de la Unidad Nacional (Partido de la U): Carrera 7, No 32-16, 21°, Bogotá, DC; tel. and fax (1) 350-0215; internet www.partidodelau.com; f. 2005; conservative; Pres. JUAN MANUEL SANTOS.

Partido Verde (PV): Calle 36, No 28A–24, Bogotá, DC; tel. (1) 344-0864; fax (1) 608-1312; e-mail movilizacion@partidoverde.org.co; internet www.partidoverde.org.co; Pres. ANTANAS MOCKUS ŠIVICKAS.

Polo Democrático Alternativo (PDA): Carrera 17A, No 37-27, Bogotá, DC; tel. (1) 288-6188; e-mail info@polodemocratico.net; internet www.polodemocratico.net; f. 2002 as electoral alliance, constituted as a political party in July 2003; founded by fmr mems of the Movimiento 19 de Abril; fmrly Polo Democrático Independiente; adopted current name 2006; left-wing; Pres. JAIME DUSSÁN CALDERÓN (acting); Sec.-Gen. CARLOS BULA CAMACHO.

The following are the principal guerrilla groups in operation in Colombia:

Ejército de Liberación Nacional (ELN): internet www.eln-voces.com; Castroite guerrilla movt; f. 1964; 3,500 mems; political status recognized by the Govt in 1998; mem. of the Coordinadora Nacional Guerrilla Simón Bolívar; Leader NICOLÁS RODRÍGUEZ BAUTISTA.

Fuerzas Armadas Revolucionarias de Colombia—Ejército del Pueblo (FARC—EP): f. 1964, although mems active from 1949; name changed from Fuerzas Armadas Revolucionarias de Colombia to the above in 1982; fmrly military wing of the Communist Party; composed of 39 armed fronts and about 6,000–8,000 mems; political status recognized by the Govt in 1998; mem. of the Coordinadora Nacional Guerrilla Simón Bolívar; C-in-C GUILLERMO LEÓN SÁENZ VARGAS (alias Alfonso Cano).

Diplomatic Representation

EMBASSIES IN COLOMBIA

Algeria: Carrera 11, No 93-53, Of. 302, Bogotá, DC; tel. (1) 635-0520; fax (1) 635-0531; e-mail ambalgbg@cable.net.co; internet www.embargelia-colombia.org; Chargé d'affaires a.i. DJAMAL HABTICHE.

Argentina: Avda 40A, No 13-09, 16°, Apdo Aéreo 53013, Bogotá, DC; tel. (1) 288-0900; fax (1) 288-8868; e-mail embargentina@etb.net.co; Ambassador MARTÍN ANTONIO BALZA.

Austria: Edif. Fiducafé, 4°, Carrera 9, No 73-44, Bogotá, DC; tel. (1) 326-3680; fax (1) 317-7639; e-mail bogota-ob@bmeia.gv.at; internet www.embajadadeaustria.org.co; Ambassador ANDREAS LIEBMANN-HOLZMANN.

Belgium: Calle 26, No 4A-45, 7°, Apdo Aéreo 3564, Bogotá, DC; tel. (1) 380-0370; fax (1) 380-0340; e-mail bogota@diplobel.fed.be; internet www.diplomatie.be/bogota; Ambassador JORIS COUVREUR.

Bolivia: Calle 108A, No 21-42, Chicó Navarra, Bogotá, DC; tel. (1) 619-5509; fax (1) 619-6050; e-mail embolivia-bogota@rree.gov.bo; internet www.embajadaboliviacolombia.org; Chargé d'affaires a.i. MARÍO ARTURO SUAREZ VARGAS.

Brazil: Calle 93, No 14-20, 8°, Bogotá, DC; tel. (1) 218-0800; fax (1) 218-8393; e-mail sembaix@brasil.org.co; internet www.brasil.org.co; Ambassador VALDEMAR CARNEIRO LEÃO.

Canada: Carretera 7, No 114-33, 14°, Apdo Aéreo 110067, Bogotá, DC; tel. (1) 657-9800; fax (1) 657-9912; e-mail bgota@international.gc.ca; internet www.canadainternational.gc.ca/colombia-colombie; Ambassador GENEVIÈVE DES RIVIÈRES.

Chile: Calle 100, No 11B-44, Apdo Aéreo 90061, Bogotá, DC; tel. (1) 620-6613; fax (1) 619-3863; e-mail embajadachile@cable.net.co; Ambassador GUSTAVO AYARES OSSANDÓN.

China, People's Republic: Carrera 16, No 98-30, Bogotá, DC; tel. (1) 622-3215; fax (1) 622-3114; e-mail chinaemb_co@mfa.gov.cn; internet co.china-embassy.org; Ambassador GAO ZHENGYUE.

Costa Rica: Casa Barrio, Calle 118A, No 14-62, Santa Barbara, Bogotá, DC; tel. (1) 629-5095; fax (1) 691-8558; e-mail embacosta@etb.net.co; internet www.embajadadecostarica.org; Ambassador CLARA MONTERO MEJÍA.

Cuba: Carrera 9, No 92-54, Bogotá, DC; tel. (1) 621-7054; fax (1) 611-4382; e-mail embacuba@cable.net.co; internet embacu.cubaminrex.cu/colombia; Ambassador JORGE IVÁN MORA GODOY.

Czech Republic: Avda 7, No 114-33, Edif. The Royal Bank of Scotland, Ofs 603 y 604, Bogotá, DC; tel. (1) 640-0600; fax (1) 640-0599; e-mail bogota@embassy.msv.cz; internet www.mzv.cz/bogota; Ambassador ZDENĚK KREJČÍ.

Dominican Republic: Carrera 18, No 123-43, Bogotá, DC; tel. (1) 601-1670; fax (1) 620-7597; e-mail embajado@cable.net.co; Ambassador ANGEL LOCKWARD.

Ecuador: Edif. Fernando Mazuera, 7°, Calle 72, No 6-30, Bogotá, DC; tel. (1) 212-6549; fax (1) 212-6536; e-mail eecucolombia@mmrree.gov.ec; relations suspended in March 2008; Chargé d'affaires a.i. ANDRÉS TERÁN.

Egypt: Transversal 19A 101-10, Bogotá, DC; tel. (1) 256-2940; fax (1) 256-9255; e-mail embajadadeegipto@cable.net.co; Ambassador MOHAMED AHDY KHAIRAT.

El Salvador: Edif. El Nogal, Of. 503, Carrera 9, No 80-15, Bogotá, DC; tel. (1) 349-6765; fax (1) 349-6670; e-mail elsalvador@supercable.net.co; Ambassador JOAQUÍN ALEXANDER MAZA MARTELLI.

France: Carrera 11, No 93-12, Bogotá, DC; tel. (1) 638-1400; fax (1) 638-1430; e-mail amfrabog@andinet.com; internet www.ambafrance-co.org; Ambassador JEAN-MICHEL MARLAUD.

Germany: Avda El Dorado, Edif. World Business Port, 7°, Carrera 69, No 25B-44, Apdo 98833, Bogotá, DC; tel. (1) 423-2600; fax (1) 429-3145; e-mail info@bogota.diplo.de; internet www.bogota.diplo.de; Ambassador JÜRGEN CHRISTIAN MERTENS.

Guatemala: Calle 87, No 20-27, Of. 302, Bogotá, DC; tel. (1) 636-1724; fax (1) 610-1449; e-mail embcolombia@minex.gob.gt; Ambassador MANLIO FERNANDO SESENNA OLIVERO.

Holy See: Carrera 15, No 36-33, Apdo Aéreo 3740, Bogotá, DC (Apostolic Nunciature); tel. (1) 705-4545; fax (1) 285-1817; e-mail nunciatura@cable.net.co; Apostolic Nuncio Most Rev. ALDO CAVALLI (Titular Archbishop of Vibo).

Honduras: Calle 65, No 8-26, Of. 201, Bogotá, DC; tel. (1) 248-2195; fax (1) 217-1457; e-mail info@embajadadehonduras.org.co; internet www.embajadadehonduras.org.co; Ambassador HERNÁN ANTONIO BERMÚDEZ AGUILAR.

India: Calle 116, No 301, Torre Cusezar, Bogotá, DC; tel. (1) 637-3259; fax (1) 637-3451; e-mail central@embajadaindia.org; internet www.embajadaindia.org; Ambassador DEEPAK BHOJWANI.

Indonesia: Carrera 11, No 75-27, Bogotá, DC; tel. (1) 217-2404; fax (1) 326-2165; e-mail eindones@colomsat.net.co; internet www.indonesiabogota.org.co; Ambassador MICHAEL MENUFANDU.

Iran: Calle 96, No 11A-20, Apdo 93854, Bogotá, DC; tel. (1) 256-2862; fax (1) 256-2842; e-mail embairancolombia@yahoo.com; Ambassador AHMAD PABARJA.

Israel: Calle 35, No 7-25, 14°, Bogotá, DC; tel. (1) 327-7500; fax (1) 327-7555; e-mail info@bogota.mfa.gov.il; internet bogota.mfa.gov.il; Ambassador MERON REUBEN.

Italy: Calle 93B, No 9-92, Apdo Aéreo 50901, Bogotá, DC; tel. (1) 218-7206; fax (1) 610-5886; e-mail ambbogo.mail@esteri.it; internet www.ambbogota.esteri.it; Ambassador GEROLAMO SCHIAVONI.

Jamaica: Avda 19, No 106A-83, Of. 304, Apdo Aéreo 102428, Bogotá, DC; tel. (1) 612-3389; fax (1) 612-3479; e-mail emjacol@cable.net.com; Chargé d'affaires ELAINE TOWNSEND DE SÁNCHEZ.

Japan: Carrera 7A, No 71-21, 11°, Torre B, Bogotá, DC; tel. (1) 317-5001; fax (1) 317-5007; e-mail info@embjp-colombia.com; internet www.colombia.emb-japan.go.jp; Ambassador TATSUMARO TERAZAWA.

Korea, Republic: Calle 94, No 9-39, Bogotá, DC; tel. (1) 616-7200; fax (1) 610-0338; e-mail embcorea@mofat.go.kr; internet col.mofat.go.kr/index.jsp; Ambassador HONG SEONG-HOA.

Lebanon: Calle 74, No 11-88, CP 51084, Bogotá, DC; tel. (1) 348-1781; fax (1) 347-9106; e-mail info@embajadadellibano.org.co; internet www.embajadadellibano.org.co; Ambassador HASSAN MUSLIMANI.

Mexico: Edif. Teleport Business Park, Calle 113, No 7-21, Of. 204, Torre A, Barrio Santa Ana, Bogotá, DC; tel. (1) 629-4989; fax (1) 629-5121; e-mail emcolmex@etb.net.co; internet www.sre.gob.mx/colombia; Ambassador FLORENCIO SALAZAR ADAME.

Morocco: Carrera 23, No 104A-34, Bogotá, DC; tel. (1) 619-3681; fax (1) 619-3685; e-mail embamarruecos@etb.net.co; internet www.embajadamarruecosbogota.com; Ambassador NOUREDDINE KHALIFA.

Netherlands: Carrera 13, No 93-40, 5°, Apdo Aéreo 43585, Bogotá, DC; tel. (1) 638-4200; fax (1) 623-3020; e-mail bog@minbuza.nl; internet www.mfa.nl/bog; Ambassador MARION S. KAPPEYNE VAN DE COPPELLO.

Nicaragua: Calle 108A, No 25-42, Bogotá, DC; tel. (1) 619-8911; fax (1) 612-6050; e-mail embnicaragua@007mundo.com; Chargé d'affaires a.i. JULIO JOSÉ CALERO REYES.

Norway: Edif. Fiducafé, 8°, Of. 801, Carrera 9, No 73-44, Bogotá, DC; tel. (1) 317-7851; fax (1) 317-7858; e-mail emb.bogota@mfa.no; internet www.noruega.org.co; Ambassador VIBEKE KNUDSEN.

Panama: Calle 92, No 7A-40, Bogotá, DC; tel. (1) 257-5067; fax (1) 257-5068; e-mail embpacol@cable.net.co; internet www.empacol.org; Ambassador RICARDO ANGUIZOLA.

Paraguay: Calle 72, No 10-51, 10º, Of. 1001, Bogotá, DC; tel. (1) 347-0322; e-mail emboy@etb-net-co; Ambassador WALTER DANIEL BIEDERMANN MONTANER.

Peru: Calle 80A, No 6-50, Bogotá, DC; tel. (1) 257-0505; fax (1) 249-8581; e-mail embajadaperu@supercabletv.net.co; internet www.embajadadelperu.org.co; Ambassador JORGE VOTO-BERNALES GATICA.

Poland: Carrera 21, Calle 104A, No 23-48, Apdó Aereo 101363, Bogotá, DC; tel. (1) 214-0400; fax (1) 214-0854; e-mail bogota.amb.sekretariat@msz.gov.pl; internet www.bogota.polemb.net; Ambassador JACEK PERLIN.

Portugal: Calle 98, No 9-03, Of. 906, Bogotá, DC; tel. (1) 622-1649; fax (1) 236-5269; e-mail embporbog@cable.net.co; Ambassador AUGUSTO JOSÉ PESTANA SARAIVA PEIXOTO.

Romania: Carrera 7A, No 92-58, Chico, Bogotá, DC; tel. (1) 256-6438; fax (1) 256-6158; e-mail ambrombogota@etb.net.co; internet bogota.mae.ro; Ambassador MARIA SIPOS.

Russia: Carrera 4, No 75-02, Apdo Aéreo 90600, Bogotá, DC; tel. (1) 212-1881; fax (1) 210-4694; e-mail embajadarusia@cable.net.co; internet www.colombia.mid.ru; Ambassador VLADIMIR V. TRUJANOVSKI.

Spain: Calle 92, No 12-68, Apdo 90355, Bogotá, DC; tel. (1) 622-0090; fax (1) 621-0809; e-mail bogota@maec.es; internet www.mae.es/embajadas/bogota; Ambassador ANDRÉS COLLADO GONZÁLEZ.

Sweden: Edif. Avenida Chile, 8°, Calle 72, No 5-83, Apdo Aéreo 52966, Bogotá, DC; tel. (1) 325-6180; fax (1) 325-6181; e-mail embsueca@cable.net.co; internet www.swedenabroad.com/bogota; Ambassador LENA NORDSTRÖM.

Switzerland: Carrera 9, No 74-08, Of. 1101, 11°, Apdo Aéreo 251957, Bogotá, DC; tel. (1) 349-7230; fax (1) 349-7195; e-mail bog.vertretung@eda.admin.ch; internet www.eda.admin.ch/bogota; Ambassador DIDIER DIETER ULRICH PFIRTER.

United Kingdom: Edif. ING Barings, Carrera 9, No 76-49, 9°, Bogotá, DC; tel. (1) 326-8300; fax (1) 326-8302; e-mail ppa.bogota@fco.gov.uk; internet ukincolombia.fco.gov.uk; Ambassador JOHN DEW.

USA: Calle 24-bis, No 48-50, Apdo Aéreo 3831, Bogotá, DC; tel. (1) 315-0811; fax (1) 315-2197; e-mail AmbassadorB@state.gov; internet bogota.usembassy.gov; Ambassador PETER MICHAEL MCKINLEY.

Uruguay: Edif. El Nogal, Carrera 9A, No 80-15, 11°, Apdo Aéreo 101466, Bogotá, DC; tel. (1) 235-2748; fax (1) 248-3734; e-mail urucolom@etb.net.co; Ambassador SILVIA LOURDES IZQUIERDO VILA.

Venezuela: Carrera 11, No 87-51, 5°, Bogotá, DC; tel. (1) 644-5555; fax (1) 640-1242; e-mail embajada@embaven.org.co; internet www.embaven.org.co; Ambassador GUSTAVO MÁRQUEZ MARÍN.

Judicial System

CONSTITUTIONAL COURT

The constitutional integrity of the State is ensured by the Constitutional Court. The Constitutional Court is composed of nine judges who are elected by the Senate for eight years. Judges of the Constitutional Court are not eligible for re-election.

Corte Constitucional

Edif. del Palacio de Justicia, Calle 12, No 7-65, Bogotá, DC; tel. (1) 350-6200; fax (1) 336-8759; internet www.corteconstitucional.gov.co.

President: HUMBERTO ANTONIO SIERRA PORTO.

Judges: NILSON PINILLA PINILLA (Vice-Pres.), MANUEL JOSÉ CEPEDA ESPIÑOSA, JAIME CÓRDOBA TRIVIÑO, RODRIGO ESCOBAR GIL, MARCO GERARDO MONROY CABRA, CLARA INÉS VARGAS HERNÁNDEZ, JAIME ARAUJO RENTERÍA, MAURICIO GONZÁLEZ CUERVO.

SUPREME COURT OF JUSTICE

The ordinary judicial integrity of the State is ensured by the Supreme Court of Justice. The Supreme Court of Justice is composed of the Courts of Civil and Agrarian, Penal, and Laboral Cassation. Judges of the Supreme Court of Justice, of which there are 23, are selected from the nominees of the Higher Council of Justice and serve an eight-year term of office, which is not renewable.

Corte Suprema de Justicia

Edif. de Palacio de Justicia, Calle 12, No 7-65, Bogotá, DC; tel. (1) 562-2000; internet www.ramajudicial.gov.co.

President: Dr AUGUSTO IBÁÑEZ GUZMÁN.

Director of Public Prosecutions: MARIO GERMÁN IGUARÁN ARANA.

Court of Civil and Agrarian Cassation (seven judges): Pres. Dr WILLIAM NAMÉN VARGAS.

Court of Penal Cassation (nine judges): Pres. Dr SIGIFREDO DE JESÚS ESPINOSA PEREZ.

Court of Laboral Cassation (seven judges): Pres. Dr FRANCISCO JAVIER RICAURTE.

COUNCIL OF STATE

The Council of State serves as the supreme consultative body to the Government in matters of legislation and administration. It also serves as the supreme tribunal for administrative litigation (*Contencioso Administrativo*). It is composed of 27 magistrates, including a President.

Council of State

Edif. del Palacio de Justicia, 7-65 Calle 12, Bogotá, DC; tel. (1) 350-6700; internet www.ramajudicial.gov.co.

President: Dr ENRIQUE GIL BOTERO.

Religion

CHRISTIANITY

The Roman Catholic Church

Colombia comprises 13 archdioceses, 52 dioceses and 10 apostolic vicariates. Some 87% of the population are Roman Catholics.

Bishops' Conference

Conferencia Episcopal de Colombia, Carrera 47, No 84-85, Apdo Aéreo 7448, Bogotá, DC; tel. (1) 311-4277; fax (1) 311-5575; e-mail colcec@cec.org.co; internet www.cec.org.co.

f. 1978; statutes approved 1996; Pres. Rt Rev. RUBÉN SALAZAR GÓMEZ (Archbishop of Barranquilla).

Archbishop of Barranquilla: RUBÉN SALAZAR GÓMEZ, Carrera 45, No 53-122, Apdo Aéreo 1160, Barranquilla 4, Atlántico; tel. (5) 349-1145; fax (5) 349-1530; e-mail arquidio@arquidiocesibaq.org.co.

Archbishop of Bogotá: Cardinal PEDRO RUBIANO SÁENZ, Carrera 7A, No 10-20, Bogotá, DC; tel. (1) 350-5511; fax (1) 350-7290; e-mail cancilleria@arquidiocesisbogota.org.co.

Archbishop of Bucaramanga: ISMAEL RUEDA SIERRA, Calle 33, No 21-18, Bucaramanga, Santander del Sur; tel. (7) 642-4387; fax (7) 642-1361; e-mail sarqdbu@col1.telecom.com.

Archbishop of Cali: JUAN FRANCISCO SARASTI JARAMILLO, Carrera 4, No 7-17, Apdo Aéreo 8924, Cali, Valle del Cauca; tel. (2) 889-0562; fax (2) 883-7980; e-mail jsarasti@andinet.com.

Archbishop of Cartagena: JOSÉ ENRIQUE JIMÉNEZ CARVAJAL, Apdo Aéreo 400, Cartagena; tel. (5) 664-5308; fax (5) 664-4974; e-mail arzoctg@telecartagena.com.

Archbishop of Ibagué: FLAVIO CALLE ZAPATA, Calle 10, No 2-58, Ibagué, Tolima; tel. (8) 261-1680; fax (8) 263-2681; e-mail arguibague@hotmail.com.

Archbishop of Manizales: FABIO BETANCUR TIRADO, Carrera 23, No 19-22, Manizales, Caldas; tel. (6) 884-0114; fax (6) 882-1853; e-mail arquiman@epm.net.co.

Archbishop of Medellín: ALBERTO GIRALDO JARAMILLO, Calle 57, No 49-44, 3°, Medellín; tel. (4) 251-7700; fax (4) 251-9395; e-mail arquidiomed@epm.net.co.

Archbishop of Nueva Pamplona: (vacant), Carrera 5, No 4-87, Nueva Pamplona; tel. (7) 568-1329; fax (7) 568-4540; e-mail gumafri@hotmail.com.

Archbishop of Popayán: IVÁN ANTONIO MARÍN LÓPEZ, Calle 5, No 6-71, Apdo Aéreo 593, Popayán; tel. (2) 824-1710; fax (2) 824-0101; e-mail ivanarzo@emtel.net.co.

Archbishop of Santa Fe de Antioquia: ORLANDO ANTONIO CORRALES GARCÍA, Plazuela Martínez Pardo, No 12-11, Santa Fe de Antioquia; tel. (4) 853-1155; fax (4) 853-1596; e-mail arquistafe@edatel.net.co.

Archbishop of Tunja: LUIS AUGUSTO CASTRO QUIROGA, Calle 17, No 9-85, Apdo Aéreo 1019, Tunja, Boyacá; tel. (8) 742-2093; fax (8) 743-3130; e-mail arquidio@telecom.com.co.

Archbishop of Villavicencio: OSCAR URBINA ORTEGA, Carrera 39, No 34-19, Apdo Aéreo 2401, Villavicencio, Meta; tel. (8) 663-0337; fax (8) 665-3200; e-mail diocesisvillavicencio@andinet.com.

The Anglican Communion

Anglicans in Colombia are members of the Episcopal Church in the USA.

Bishop of Colombia: Rt Rev. FRANCISCO JOSÉ DUQUE GÓMEZ, Carrera 6, No 49-85, Apdo Aéreo 52964, Bogotá, DC; tel. (1) 288-3167; fax (1) 288-3248; e-mail iec@iglesiaepiscopal.org.co; internet www.iglesiaepiscopal.org.co.

Protestant Church

Iglesia Evangélica Luterana de Colombia: Calle 75, No 20C-54, Apdo Aéreo 51538, Bogotá, DC; tel. (1) 212-5735; fax (1) 212-5714; e-mail ofcentral@ielco.org; internet www.ielco.org; 3,000 mems; Pres. Bishop SIGIFREDO DANIEL BUITRAGO PACHÓN.

BAHÁ'Í FAITH

National Spiritual Assembly of the Bahá'ís of Colombia: Apdo Aéreo 51387, Bogotá, DC; tel. and fax (1) 268-1658; e-mail bahaicol@colombianet.net; internet www.bahaicol.org; Gen. Sec. XIMENA OSORIO V.; adherents in 1,013 localities.

JUDAISM

There is a community of about 4,200 Jews.

The Press

DAILIES

Bogotá, DC

El Espacio: Carrera 61, No 45-35, Avda El Dorado, Apdo Aéreo 80111, Bogotá, DC; tel. (1) 425-1570; fax (1) 410-4595; internet www.elespacio.com.co; f. 1965; evening; Dir JAIME ARDILA CASAMITJANA; Editor ALBERTO URIBE GÓMEZ; circ. 159,000.

El Espectador: Avda El Dorado 69-76, Bogotá, DC; tel. and fax (1) 423-2300; e-mail editorweb@elespectador.com.co; internet www.elespectador.com; f. 1887; published weekly from 2001–08; Editor LEONARDO RODRÍGUEZ.

El Nuevo Siglo: Calle 45A, No 102-02, Apdo Aéreo 5452, Bogotá, DC; tel. (1) 413-9200; fax (1) 413-8547; e-mail contacto@elnuevosiglo.com.co; internet www.elnuevosiglo.com.co; f. 1936; conservative; Dir JUAN GABRIEL URIBE; Editor ALBERTO ABELLO; circ. 68,000.

Portafolio: Avda El Dorado, No 59-70, Apdo Aéreo 3633, Bogotá, DC; internet www.portafolio.com.co; f. 1993; economics and business; Dir RICARDO AVILA PINTO.

La República: Calle 25 Bis, 102A-63, Bogotá, DC; tel. (1) 413-5077; fax (1) 413-3725; e-mail diario@larepublica.com.co; internet www.larepublica.com.co; f. 1954; morning; finance and economics; Editor JORGE EMILIO SIERRA M.; circ. 55,000.

El Tiempo: Avda El Dorado, No 59-70, Apdo Aéreo 3633, Bogotá, DC; tel. (1) 294-0100; fax (1) 410-5088; e-mail julguz@eltiempo.com.co; internet www.eltiempo.com; f. 1911; morning; Liberal; Dir ENRIQUE SANTOS CALDERÓN; circ. 265,118 (weekdays), 536,377 (Sundays).

Barranquilla, Atlántico

El Heraldo: Calle 53B, No 46-25, Barranquilla, Atlántico; tel. (5) 371-5000; fax (5) 371-5091; internet www.elheraldo.com.co; f. 1933; morning; liberal; Dir GUSTAVO BELL LEMUS; circ. 70,000.

La Libertad: Carrera 53, No 55-166, Barranquilla, Atlántico; tel. (5) 349-1175; fax (5) 349-1298; e-mail libertad@lalibertad.com.co; internet www.lalibertad.com.co; f. 1979; liberal; Dir ROBERTO ESPER REBAJE; Editor LUZ MARINA ESPER FAYAD; circ. 25,000.

Bucaramanga, Santander del Sur

El Frente: Calle 35, No 12-22, Apdo Aéreo 665, Bucaramanga, Santander del Sur; tel. (7) 42-5319; fax (7) 33-4541; internet www.elfrente.com.co; f. 1942; morning; conservative; Dir RAFAEL SERRANO PRADA; circ. 10,000.

Vanguardia Liberal: Calle 34, No 13-42, Bucaramanga, Santander del Sur; tel. (7) 680-0700; fax (7) 630-2443; e-mail erodriguez@vanguardialiberal.com.co; internet www.vanguardia.com; f. 1919; morning; liberal; Sunday illustrated literary supplement and women's supplement; Dir SEBASTIÁN HILLER GALVIS; circ. 48,000.

Cali, Valle del Cauca

Diario Occidente: Centro Comercial Chipichape, Bodega 2, 2°, Of. 220, Cali, Valle del Cauca; tel. (2) 680-2002; e-mail direccion@diariooccidente.com.co; internet www.diariooccidente.com.co; f. 1961; morning; conservative; Editor ROSA MARÍA AGUDELO AYERBE; circ. 25,000.

El País: Carrera 2A, No 24-46, Apdo Aéreo 4766, Cali, Valle del Cauca; tel. (2) 898-7000; e-mail diario@elpais.com.co; internet www.elpais.com.co; f. 1950; conservative; Dir and Gen. Man. MARÍA ELVIRA DOMÍNGUEZ; circ. 60,000 (weekdays), 120,000 (Saturdays), 108,304 (Sundays).

Cartagena, Bolívar

El Universal: Pie del Cerro Calle 30, No 17-36, Cartagena, Bolívar; tel. (5) 650-1050; fax (5) 650-1057; e-mail director@eluniversal.com.co; internet www.eluniversal.com.co; f. 1948; daily; liberal; Editor-in-Chief LEDIS CALO; Dir PEDRO LUIS MOGOLLÓN VÉLEZ; circ. 167,000.

Cúcuta, Norte de Santander

La Opinión: Avda 4, No 16-12, Cúcuta, Norte de Santander; tel. (7) 582-9999; fax (7) 571-7869; e-mail gerencia@laopinion.com.co; internet www.laopinion.com.co; f. 1960; morning; liberal; Dir Dr JOSÉ EUSTORGIO COLMENARES OSSA; circ. 27,000.

Manizales, Caldas

La Patria: Carrera 20, No 46-35, Manizales, Caldas; tel. (6) 878-1700; e-mail lapatria@lapatria.com; internet www.lapatria.com; f. 1921; morning; independent; Dir NICOLÁS RESTREPO ESCOBAR; circ. 22,000.

Medellín, Antioquia

El Colombiano: Carrera 48, No 30 sur-119, Apdo Aéreo 80636, Medellín, Antioquia; tel. (4) 331-5252; fax (4) 331-4858; e-mail elcolombiano@elcolombiano.com.co; internet www.elcolombiano.com; f. 1912; morning; conservative; Dir ANA MERCEDES GÓMEZ MARTÍNEZ; circ. 90,000.

El Mundo: Calle 53, No 74-50, Apdo Aéreo 53874, Medellín, Antioquia; tel. (4) 264-2800; fax (4) 264-3729; e-mail direccion@elmundo.com; internet www.elmundo.com; f. 1979; Dir GUILLERMO GAVIRIA ECHEVERRI; Editor IRENE GAVIRIA CORREA; circ. 37,200 (Mon.–Sat.), 55,000 (Sun.).

Montería, Córdoba

El Meridiano de Córdoba: Avda Circunvalar, No 38-30, Montería, Córdoba; tel. (4) 782-6888; fax (4) 782-6996; e-mail publicidad@elmeridianodecordoba.com; internet www.elmeridianodecordoba.com.co; f. 1995; morning; Dir WILLIAM ENRIQUE SALLEG TABOADA; circ. 18,000.

Neiva, Huila

Diario del Huila: Calle 8A, No 6-30, Neiva, Huila; tel. (8) 871-2458; fax (8) 871-2543; e-mail prensa@diariodelhuila.com; internet www.diariodelhuila.com; f. 1966; Dir JAVIER CABRERA PADRÓN; circ. 12,000.

Pasto, Nariño

Diario del Sur: Calle 18, No 47-160, Torobajo, San Juan de Pasto, Nariño; tel. (2) 731-0048; e-mail diariodelsur@diariodelsur.com.co; internet www.diariodelsur.com.co; f. 1983; Dir HERNANDO SUÁREZ BURGOS.

Pereira, Risaralda

El Diario del Otún: Carrera 8A, No 22-75, Apdo Aéreo 2533, Pereira, Risaralda; tel. (6) 335-1313; fax (6) 325-4878; e-mail luiscramirez@eldiario.com.co; internet www.eldiario.com.co; f. 1982; Administrative Dir JAVIER IGNACIO RAMÍREZ MÚNERA; Editor-in-Chief MARTHA LUCÍA MONSALVE TRUJILLO; circ. 30,000.

La Tarde: Carrera 9A, No 20-54, Pereira, Risaralda; tel. (6) 313-7676; fax (6) 335-5187; internet www.latarde.com; f. 1975; evening; Dir SONIA DÍAZ MANTILLA; circ. 30,000.

Popayán, Cauca

El Liberal: Carrera 3, No 2-60, Apdo Aéreo 538, Popayán, Cauca; tel. (28) 24-2418; fax (28) 23-3888; e-mail gerencia@elliberal.com.co; internet www.elliberal.com.co; f. 1938; Man. ANA MARIA LONDOÑO R.; Dir ISMENIA ARDILA DÍAZ; circ. 6,500.

Santa Marta, Magdalena

El Informador: Avda Libertador 12A-37, Santa Marta, Magdalena; e-mail eldirector@el-informador.com; internet www.el-informador.com; f. 1921; liberal; Dir ALFONSO VIVES CAMPO; circ. 26,000.

PERIODICALS

ART NEXUS/Arte en Colombia: Carrera 5, No 67-19, Apdo Aéreo 90193, Bogotá, DC; tel. (1) 312-9435; fax (1) 312-9252; e-mail info@artnexus.com; internet www.artnexus.com; f. 1976; quarterly; Latin American art, photography, visual arts; editions in English and Spanish; Pres. and Chief Editor CELIA SREDNI DE BIRBRAGHER; CEO SUSANNE BIRBRAGHER; circ. 26,000.

Cambio: Avda El Dorado No 59-70, 2°, Bogotá, DC; tel. (1) 294-0100; fax (1) 416-5643; internet www.cambio.com.co; weekly; current affairs; Dir RODRIGO PARDO.

Coyuntura Económica: Calle 78, No 9-91, Apdo Aéreo 75074, Bogotá, DC; tel. (1) 312-5300; fax (1) 212-6073; e-mail administrator@fedesarrollo.org; internet www.fedesarrollo.org; f. 1970; twice yearly; economics; published by Fundación para Educación Superior y el Desarrollo; Editor CAROLINA MEJÍA; circ. 500.

Cromos Magazine: Avda El Dorado 69-76, Bogotá, DC; tel. (1) 423-2300; fax (1) 423-7641; e-mail internet@cromos.com.co; internet www.cromos.com.co; f. 1916; weekly; illustrated; general news; Dir ALBERTO ZALAMEA; circ. 102,000.

Dinero: Calle 93B, No 13-47, Bogotá, DC; tel. (1) 646-8400; fax (1) 621-9526; e-mail correo@dinero.com; internet www.dinero.com; f. 1993; fortnightly; economics and business; Dir ROSARIO CÓRDOBA GARCÉS.

Economía Colombiana: Contraloría General de la República, Carrera 10, No 17-18, 19°, Bogotá, DC; tel. and fax (1) 353-7700; internet www.contraloriagen.gov.co; f. 1984; published by Contraloría General de la República; 6 a year; economics.

Informe Financiero: Dirección Economía y Finanzas, San Agustín 6-45, Of. 126A, Bogotá, DC; tel. (1) 282-4597; fax (1) 282-3737; published by Contraloría General de la República; monthly; economics.

Insurrección: internet www.eln-voces.com; f. 1998; fortnightly; fmrly Correo de Magdalena; organ of the Ejército de Liberación Nacional.

El Malpensante: Calle 35, No 14-27, Bogotá, DC; tel. (1) 320-0120; fax (1) 340-2808; e-mail contacto@elmalpensante.com; internet www.elmalpensante.com; f. 1996; monthly; literature; Dir MARIO JURSICH DURÁN.

Resistencia: e-mail elbarcinocolombia@yahoo.com; internet www.resistencianacional.net; f. 1993; quarterly; organ of the Fuerzas Armadas Revolucionarias de Colombia—Ejército del Pueblo.

Revista Diners: Calle 85, No 18-32, 6°, Bogotá, DC; tel. (1) 636-0508; fax (1) 623-1762; e-mail diners@cable.net.co; internet www.revistadiners.com.co; f. 1963; monthly; Dir GERMÁN SANTAMARÍA; circ. 110,000.

Revista Escala: Calle 30, No 17-752, Bogotá, DC; tel. (1) 287-8200; fax (1) 285-9882; e-mail escala@col-online.com; internet www.revistaescala.com; f. 1962; fortnightly; architecture; Dir DAVID SERNA CÁRDENAS; circ. 18,000.

Revista Fucsia: Calle 93B, No 13-47, Bogotá, DC; tel. (1) 646-8400; fax (1) 621-9526; e-mail correo@fucsia.com; internet www.revistafucsia.com; fortnightly; women's interest; Dir LILA OCHOA.

Semana: Calle 93B, No 13-47, Bogotá, DC; tel. (1) 646-8400; fax (1) 621-9526; e-mail director@semana.com; internet www.semana.com; f. 1982; general; weekly; Dir ALEJANDRO SANTOS RUBINO.

Tribuna Médica: Calle 8B, No 68A-41, y Calle 123, No 8-20, Bogotá, DC; tel. (1) 262-6085; fax (1) 262-4459; internet www.tribunamedica.com; f. 1961; monthly; medical and scientific; Editor JACK ALBERTO GRIMBERG; circ. 50,000.

Tribuna Roja: Calle 39, No 21-30, Bogotá, DC; tel. (1) 245-9647; e-mail tribojar@moir.org.co; internet tribunaroja.moir.org.co; f. 1971; quarterly; organ of the MOIR (pro-Maoist Communist party); Dir CARLOS NARANJO; circ. 300,000.

NEWS AGENCY

Colprensa: Diagonal 34, No 5-63, Apdo Aéreo 20333, Bogotá, DC; tel. (1) 287-2200; fax (1) 285-5915; e-mail colpre@elsitio.net.co; internet www.colprensa.com; f. 1980; Dir ALFONSO OSPINA TORRES.

PRESS ASSOCIATIONS

Asociación Nacional de Diarios Colombianos (ANDIARIOS): Calle 61, No 5-20, Apdo Aéreo 13663, Bogotá, DC; tel. (1) 212-8694; fax (1) 212-7894; internet www.andiarios.com; f. 1962; 32 affiliated newspapers; Pres. LUIS MIGUEL DE BEDOUT; Exec. Dir NORA SANÍN DE SAFFON.

Asociación Nacional de Medios de Comunicación (ASOMEDIOS): see Broadcasting and Communications.

Círculo de Periodistas de Bogotá (CPB): Calle 26, No 13A-15, Bogotá, DC; tel. (1) 282-5573; e-mail escribanos@cpb.org.co; internet www.cpb.org.co; f. 1946; Pres. MAURA ACHURY RAMÍREZ.

Publishers

Ediciones Aula XXI: Calle 19, No 44-10, Bogotá, DC; tel. (1) 574-3990; fax (1) 244-6129; e-mail gerencia@edicionesaulaxxi.com; internet www.edicionesaulaxxi.com; general interest, reference, fiction and educational; Legal Rep. CARLOS MARIO ESCOBAR BRAVO.

Ediciones Gaviota: Transversal 43, No 99-13, Bogotá, DC; tel. (1) 613-6650; fax (1) 613-9117; e-mail gaviotalibros@edicionesgaviota.com.co.

Ediciones Modernas: Carrera 41A, No 22F, Bogotá, DC; tel. (1) 269-0072; fax (1) 244-0706; e-mail edimodernas@edimodernas.com.co; internet www.empresario.com.co/edimodernas; f. 1991; juvenile.

Editora Cinco, SA: Calle 61, No 13-23, 7°, Apdo Aéreo 15188, Bogotá, DC; tel. (1) 285-6200; e-mail presidencia@editoracinco.com; recreation, culture, textbooks, general; Man. PEDRO VARGAS G.

Editorial Cypres Ltda: Carrera 15, No 80-36, Of. 302, Bogotá, DC; tel. (1) 691-0578; fax (1) 636-3824; e-mail cypres@etb.net.co; general interest and educational.

Editorial El Globo, SA: Calle 16, No 4-96, Apdo Aéreo 6806, Bogotá, DC.

Editorial Hispanoamérica: Carrera 56B, No 45-27, Bogotá, DC; tel. (1) 221-3020; fax (1) 315-5587; e-mail info@hispanoamerica.com.co; internet www.hispanoamerica.com.co; f. 1984; materials for primary education; Man. GABY TERESA CORTÉS; Editor ALVARO PINZÓN.

Editorial Kinesis: Carrera 25, No 18-12, Armenia; tel. and fax (6) 740-1584; e-mail editorial@kinesis.com.co; internet www.kinesis.com.co; physical education, recreation and sport; Dir DIÓGENES VERGARA LARA.

Editorial Leyer Ltda: Carrera 4, No 16-51 Bogotá, DC; tel. (1) 282-1903; fax (1) 282-2373; e-mail contacto@edileyer.com; internet www.edileyer.com; f. 1991; law; Dir HILDEBRANDO LEAL PÉREZ.

Editorial Paulinas: Calle 161A, No 31-50, Bogotá, DC; tel. (1) 522-0828; fax (1) 671-0992; e-mail ventasp@paulinas.org.co; internet www.paulinas.org.co; Christian and self-help.

Editorial San Pablo: Carrera 46, No 22A-90, Quintaparedes, Apdo Aéreo 080152, Bogotá, DC; tel. (1) 368-2099; fax (1) 244-4383; e-mail editorial@sanpablo.com.co; internet www.sanpablo.com.co; f. 1914; religion (Catholic); Editorial Dir Fr P. VICENTE MIOTTO; Editor AMPARO MAHECHA P.

Editorial Temis, SA: Calle 17, No 68D, Apdo Aéreo 46, Bogotá, DC; tel. (1) 424-7855; fax (1) 292-5801; e-mail editorial@editorialtemis.com; internet www.editorialtemis.com; f. 1951; law, sociology, politics; Man. Dir JORGE GUERRERO.

Editorial Voluntad, SA: Carrera 7A, No 24-89, 24°, Bogotá, DC; tel. (1) 241-0444; fax (1) 241-0439; e-mail voluntad@voluntad.com.co; internet www.voluntad.com.co; f. 1930; school books; Pres. GASTÓN DE BEDOUT.

Fondo de Cultura Económica: Calle 16, No 80-18, Bogotá, DC; tel. (1) 531-2288; fax (1) 531-1322; internet www.fce.com.co; f. 1934; academic; Dir CONSUELO SÁIZAR GUERRERO.

Fundación Centro de Investigación y Educación Popular (CINEP): Carrera 5A, No 33A -08, Apdo Aéreo 25916, Bogotá, DC; tel. (1) 245-6181; fax (1) 287-9089; e-mail cinep@cinep.org.co; internet www.cinep.org.co; f. 1972; education and social sciences; Exec. Dir MAURICIO GARCÍA-DURÁN.

Instituto Caro y Cuervo: Calle 10, No 4-69, Bogotá, DC; tel. (1) 342-2121; e-mail direcciongeneral@caroycuervo.gov.co; internet www.caroycuervo.gov.co; f. 1942; philology, general linguistics and reference; Man. Dir HERNANDO CABARCAS ANTEQUERA; Gen. Sec. LILIANA RIVERA OREJUELA.

Inversiones Cromos, SA: Avda El Dorado, No 69-76, Bogotá, DC; tel. (1) 423-2300; fax (1) 423-7641; e-mail internet@cromos.com.co; internet www.cromos.com.co; f. 1916; Dir ALBERTO ZALAMEA; Gen. Man. JORGE EDUARDO CORREA ROBLEDO.

Legis, SA: Avda El Dorado, No 81-10, Apdo Aéreo 98888, Bogotá, DC; tel. (1) 425-5200; e-mail servicio@legis.com.co; internet www.legis.com.co; f. 1952; economics, law, general; Man. JUAN ALBERTO CASTRO.

McGraw Hill Interamericana, SA: Carrera 11, No 93-46, Oficina 301, Bogotá, DC; tel. (1) 600-3800; fax (1) 600-3822; internet www.mcgraw-hill.com.co; university textbooks; Dir-Gen. CARLOS G. MÁRQUEZ.

Publicar, SA: Avda 68, No 75A-50, 2° y 4°, Centro Comercial Metrópolis, Apdo Aéreo 8010, Bogotá, DC; tel. (1) 646-5555; fax (1) 646-5596; e-mail m-navia@publicar.com; internet www.publicar.com; f. 1959; owned by the Carvajal Group; directories; Pres. MARÍA SOL NAVIA VELASCO.

Siglo del Hombre Editores, SA: Carrera 31A, No 25B-50, Bogotá, DC; tel. (1) 337-7700; fax (1) 337-7665; e-mail info@siglodelhombre.com; f. 1992; arts, politics, anthropology, history, humanities; Gen. Man. EMILIA FRANCO DE ARCILA.

Tercer Mundo Editores, SA: Grupo TM, SA, Calle 25B, No 31A-34, Bogotá, DC; tel. (1) 368-8645; e-mail grupotmsa@etb.net.co; internet grupotmsa.blogspot.com; f. 1963; social sciences.

Thomson PLM: Calle 98, No 19A-21, Apdo Aéreo 52998, Bogotá, DC; tel. (1) 257-4400; fax (1) 616-7620; internet www.plmlatina.com; medical; Commerical Dir DANILO SÁNCHEZ.

Villegas Editores: Avda 82, No 11-50, Interior 3, Bogotá, DC; tel. (1) 616-1788; fax (1) 616-0020; internet www.villegaseditores.com; f. 1985; illustrated and scholarly.

ASSOCIATIONS

Cámara Colombiana del Libro: Calle 35, No 5 A-05, Bogotá, DC; tel. (1) 323-0111; fax (1) 285-1082; e-mail camlibro@camlibro.com.co; internet www.camlibro.com.co; f. 1951; Pres. ENRIQUE GONZÁLEZ VILLA; 95 mems.

Fundalectura: Avda 40A Bis, No 16-46, Bogotá, DC; tel. (1) 320-1511; fax (1) 287-7071; e-mail contactenos@fundalectura.org.co; internet www.fundalectura.org; Exec. Dir CARMEN BARVO.

Broadcasting and Communications

REGULATORY AUTHORITIES

Comisión de Regulación de Comunicaciones (CRC): 28-01, Carrera 13, 8°, Bogotá, DC; tel. (1) 327-7000; fax (1) 327-7001; e-mail atencioncliente@crt.gov.co; internet www.crcom.gov.co; f. 2000; regulatory body; Exec. Dir CRISTHIAN OMAR LIZCANO ORTIZ.

Comisión Nacional de Televisión: Calle 72, No 12–77, Bogotá, DC; tel. (1) 595-3000; e-mail info@cntv.org.co; internet www.cntv.org.co; Dir JUAN ANDRÉS CARREÑO.

TELECOMMUNICATIONS

COMCEL: Bogotá, DC; internet www.comcel.com.co; f. 1994 as Occidente y Caribe Celular, SA (Occel); present name adopted in 2000; merged with Celcaribe in 2003; owned by América Móvil, SA de CV (Mexico); cellular mobile telephone operator.

Empresa de Telecomunicaciones de Bogotá, SA (ETB): Carrera 8, No 20-56, 3°–9°, Bogotá, DC; tel. (1) 242-3483; fax (1) 242-2127; e-mail adrimara@etb.com.co; internet www.etb.com.co; Bogotá telephone co; partially privatized in May 2003; Pres. FERNANDO CARRIZOSA RASCH-ISLA; Sec.-Gen. ANDRÉS PÉREZ VELASCO.

Telefónica Móviles Colombia (Movistar): Calle 100, No 7-33, Edif. Capital Tower, Bogotá, DC; tel. (1) 650-0000; fax (1) 650-1852; internet www.movistar.com.co; f. 2004 following acquisition of BellSouth's operations by Telefónica Móviles, a subsidiary of Telefónica, SA of Spain.

Telefónica Telecom: Carrera 70, No 108-84, Bogotá, DC; tel. (1) 593-5399; fax (1) 593-1252; internet www.telefonica.com.co; f. June 2003 following dissolution of state-owned Empresa Nacional de Telecomunicaciones (TELECOM, f. 1947); 50% bought by Telefónica, SA (Spain) in April 2006; Pres. ALFONSO GÓMEZ PALACIO.

BROADCASTING

Radio

The principal radio networks are as follows:

Cadena Melodía de Colombia: Calle 45, No 13-70, Bogotá, DC; tel. (1) 323-1500; fax (1) 288-4020; internet www.cadenamelodia.com; Pres. EFRAÍN PÁEZ ESPITIA.

Cadena Radial Auténtica: Calle 31A, No 16–12, Bogotá, DC; tel. (1) 285-2505; fax (1) 566-5814; e-mail contacto@

cadenaradialautentica.com; internet www.cadenaradialautentica .com; f. 1983; stations include Radio Auténtica and Radio Mundial; Religious (Roman Catholic); Pres. JORGE ENRIQUE GÓMEZ MONTEALEGRE.

Cadena Radial La Libertad Ltda: Carrera 53, No 55-166, Apdo Aéreo 3143, Barranquilla; tel. (5) 31-1517; fax (5) 32-1279; news and music programmes for Barranquilla, Cartagena and Santa Marta; stations include Emisora Ondas del Caribe (youth programmes), Radio Libertad (classical music programmes) and Emisora Fuentes.

Cadena Super: Calle 39A, No 18–12, Bogotá, DC; tel. (1) 234-7777; e-mail soporte@cadenasuper.com; internet www.cadenasuper.com; f. 1971; stations include Radio Super and Super Stereo FM; Pres. JAIME PAVA NAVARRO.

CARACOL, SA (Primera Cadena Radial Colombiana, SA): Edif. Caracol Radio, Calle 67, No 7-37, Bogotá, DC; tel. (1) 348-7600; fax (1) 337-7126; internet www.caracol.com.co; f. 1948; 107 stations; Pres. JOSÉ MANUEL RESTREPO FERNÁNDEZ DE SOTO.

Circuito Todelar de Colombia: Avda 13, No 84-42, Apdo Aéreo 27344, Bogotá, DC; e-mail mercadeo@todelar.com; internet www .todelar.com; tel. (1) 616-1011; fax (1) 616-0056; f. 1953; 74 stations; Pres. BERNARDO TOBÓN DE LA ROCHE.

Colmundo Radio, SA ('La Cadena de la Paz'): Diagonal 58, 26A-29, Apdo Aéreo 36750, Bogotá, DC; tel. (1) 217-8911; fax (1) 348-2746; e-mail correo@colmundoradio.com.co; internet colmundoradio.com .co; f. 1989; Dir ELVIA PILAR RODRÍGUEZ.

Organización Radial Olímpica, SA (ORO, SA): Calle 72, No 48-37, 2°, Apdo Aéreo 51266, Barranquilla; tel. (5) 358-0500; fax (5) 345-9080; internet www.oro.com.co; programmes for the Antioquia and Atlantic coast regions.

Radio Cadena Nacional, SA (RCN Radio): Carrera 13A, No 37-32, Bogotá, DC; tel. (1) 314-7070; fax (1) 288-6130; e-mail rcn@impsat .net.co; internet www.rcn.com.co; 116 stations; official network; Pres. FERNANDO MOLINA SOTO.

Radio Nacional de Colombia: Carrera 45, No 26-33, Bogotá, DC; tel. (1) 597-8000; fax (1) 597-8145; e-mail radio@rtvc.gov.co; internet www.radionacionaldecolombia.gov.co; f. 1940; national public radio; Dir GABRIEL GÓMEZ MEJÍA.

Television

Canal Institutional: Avda El Dorado 45, No 26–33, Bogotá, DC; tel. (1) 597-8081; fax (1) 597-8062; govt-owned; Co-ordinator LENNART RODRÍGUEZ.

Canal RCN Televisión: Avda Américas No 65–82, Bogotá, DC; tel. (1) 426-9292; e-mail quienessomos@canalrcn.com; internet www .canalrcnmsn.com; f. 1998; Pres. GABRIEL REYES.

Canal Uno: Centro Administrativo Nacional (CAN), Avda El Dorado, Bogotá, DC; tel. (1) 342-3777; fax (1) 341-6198; e-mail administrativa@telecolombia.com; internet www.telecolombia.com; formerly Cadena Uno; f. 1992; Dir FERNANDO BARRERO CHÁVEZ.

Caracol Televisión, SA: Calle 76, No 11-35, Apdo Aéreo 26484, Bogotá, DC; tel. (1) 319-0860; fax (1) 321-1720; internet www .canalcaracol.com; f. 1969; Pres. RICARDO ALARCÓN GAVIRIA.

Señal Colombia: Avda El Dorado 45, No 26–33, Bogotá, DC; tel. (1) 597-8132; fax (1) 597-8062; internet www.senalcolombia.tv; govt-owned; Co-ordinator YOLANDA BAUTISTA.

Teleantioquia: Edif. Anexo a EDATEL, 3°, Calle 41, No 52-28, Apdo Aéreo 8183, Medellín, Antioquia; tel. (4) 356-9900; fax (4) 356-9909; e-mail comunicaciones@teleantioquia.com.co; internet www .teleantioquia.com.co; f. 1985; Gen. Man. JUAN FERNANDO CASTRILLÓN BENJUMEA.

Telecafé: Carrera 19A, Calle 43, Sacatín contiguo Universidad Autónoma, Manizales, Caldas; tel. (6) 872-7100; fax (6) 872-7610; e-mail comunicaciones@telecafe.tv; internet www.telecafe.tv; f. 1986; govt-owned; broadcasts to the 'Eje Cafetero' (departments of Caldas, Quindío and Risaralda); Gen. Man. JORGE EDUARDO URREA GIRALDO.

TeleCaribe: Carrera 54, No 72-142, 4°, Barranquilla, Atlántico; tel. (5) 368-0183; fax (5) 360-7300; e-mail info@telecaribe.com.co; internet www.telecaribe.com.co; f. 1986; Pres. ARTURO SARMIENTO; Gen. Man. EDGAR REY SINNING.

Telepacífico: Calle 5A, No 38A-14, 3°, esq. Centro Comercial Imbanaco, Cali, Valle del Cauca; tel. (2) 518-4000; fax (2) 588-281; e-mail infotv@telepacifico.com; internet www.telepacifico.com; Gen. Man. VICTOR MANUEL SALCEDO.

TV Cúcuta: tel. (7) 574-7874; fax (7) 575-2922; f. 1992; Pres. JOSÉ A. ARMELLA.

ASSOCIATION

Asociación Nacional de Medios de Comunicación (ASOMEDIOS): Carrera 19C, No 85-72, Bogotá, DC; tel. (1) 611-1300; fax (1) 621-6292; e-mail asomedio@cable.net.co; internet www .asomedios.com; f. 1978; merged with ANRADIO (Asociación Nacional de Radio, Televisión y Cine de Colombia) in 1980; Pres. SERGIO ARBOLEDA CASAS.

Finance

(cap. = capital; res = reserves; dep. = deposits; m. = million; brs = branches; amounts in pesos)

Contraloría General de la República: Carrera 10, No 17-18, Torre Colseguros, 27°, Bogotá, DC; tel. (1) 353-7700; fax (1) 353-7616; e-mail mesaportal@contraloriagen.gov.co; internet www .contraloriagen.gov.co; f. 1923; Comptroller-Gen. JULIO CÉSAR TURBAY QUINTERO.

BANKING

Supervisory Authority

Superintendencia Financiera de Colombia: Calle 7, No 4-49, 11°, Apdo Aéreo 3460, Bogotá, DC; tel. (1) 594-0200; fax (1) 350-7999; e-mail super@superfinanciera.gov.co; internet www.superfinanciera .gov.co; f. 2006 following merger of the Superintendencia Bancaria and the Superintendencia de Valores; Supt ROBERTO BORRÁS POLANÍA.

Central Bank

Banco de la República: Carrera 7A, No 14-78, 5°, Apdo Aéreo 3551, Bogotá, DC; tel. (1) 343-1111; fax (1) 286-1686; e-mail wbanco@ banrep.gov.co; internet www.banrep.gov.co; f. 1923; sole bank of issue; cap. 12,711m., res 11,219,429m., dep. 11,180,129m. (Dec. 2007); Gov. JOSÉ DARÍO URIBE ESCOBAR; 17 brs.

Commercial Banks

Bogotá, DC

Banco Agrario de Colombia (Banagrario): Carrera 8, No 15-43, Bogotá, DC; tel. (1) 382-1400; fax (1) 599-5509; e-mail presidencia@ bancoagrario.gov.co; internet www.bancoagrario.gov.co; f. 1999; state-owned; Pres. DAVID GUERRERO PÉREZ; 732 brs.

Banco de Bogotá: Calle 36, No 7-47, 15°, Apdo Aéreo 3436, Bogotá, DC; tel. (1) 332-0032; fax (1) 338-3302; internet www.bancodebogota .com.co; f. 1870; cap. 2,382m., res 2,428,360m., dep. 19,165,336m. (Dec. 2007); Pres. Dr ALEJANDRO FIGUEROA JARAMILLO; 286 brs.

Banco de Comercio Exterior de Colombia, SA (BANCOLDEX): Calle 28, No 13A-15, 40°, Apdo Aéreo 240092, Bogotá, DC; tel. (1) 382-1515; fax (1) 286-2451; internet www.bancoldex.com; f. 1992; provides financing alternatives for Colombian exporters; affiliate trust co FIDUCOLDEX, SA, manages PROEXPORT (Export Promotion Trust); cap. 855,670m., res 371,804m., dep. 3,251,087m. (Dec. 2008); Pres. GUSTAVO ARDILA.

Banco GNB Sudameris, SA: Carrera 7, No 71-52, 19°, Torre B, Bogotá, DC; tel. (1) 325-5000; fax (1) 313-3259; internet www .sudameris.com.co; f. 2005 following merger of Banco Sudameris Colombia, SA and Banco Tequendama; cap. 42,766m., res 288,567m., dep. 3,370,258m. (Dec. 2008); Pres. and Chair. JORGE RAMÍREZ OCAMPO; 6 brs.

Banco Popular, SA: Calle 17, No 7-43, 3°, Bogotá, DC; tel. (1) 339-5449; fax (1) 281-9448; e-mail vpinternacional@bancopopular.com .co; internet www.bancopopular.com.co; f. 1950; cap. 77,253m., res 757,301m., dep. 7,630,371m. (Dec. 2008); Pres. HERNÁN RINCÓN GÓMEZ; 156 brs.

Banco Santander: Carrera 7, No 99-53, Bogotá, DC; tel. (1) 284-3100; fax (1) 281-0311; e-mail comex@santander.com.co; internet www.santander.com.co; f. 1961; fmrly Banco Comercial Antioqueño, SA; subsidiary of Banco Santander (Spain); cap. 218,731m., res 295,307m., dep. 4,757,079m. (Dec. 2008); Pres. ROMÁN BLANCO REINOSA; 30 brs.

BBVA Colombia: Carrera 9, No 72-21, 11°, Bogotá, DC; tel. (1) 312-4666; fax (1) 347-1600; internet www.bbva.com.co; f. 1956 as Banco Ganadero; assumed current name 2004; 95.2% owned by Banco Bilbao Vizcaya Argentaria, SA (Spain); cap. 89,779m., res 1,097,202m., dep. 13,263,307m. (Dec. 2007); Exec. Pres. OSCAR CABRERA IZQUIERDO; 279 brs.

Citibank Colombia, SA: Carrera 9A, No 99-02, 3°, Bogotá, DC; tel. (1) 638-2420; fax (1) 618-2606; internet www.citibank.com.co; wholly owned subsidiary of Citibank (USA); cap. 144,123m., res 709,653m., dep. 4,886,894m. (Dec. 2008); Chair. and CEO MANUEL MEDINA-MORA; 23 brs.

Helm Bank SA: Carrera 7, No 27-18, 19°, Bogotá, DC; tel. (1) 581-8181; e-mail servicio.empresarial@grupohelm.com; internet www .grupohelm.com; f. 1963 as Banco de Crédito; renamed Banco de Credito—Helm Financial Services in 2000; present name adopted in

2009; cap. 195,720m., res 618,756m., dep. 5,577,078m. (Dec. 2008); Pres. CARMIÑA FERRO IRIARTE; 26 brs.

HSBC Colombia, SA: Carrera 7, No 71-21, Of. 1601, Torre B, 16°, Apdo Aéreo 3532, Bogotá, DC; tel. (1) 334-5088; fax (1) 341-9433; e-mail columbia.contactenos@hsbc.com.co; internet www.hsbc.com.co; f. 1976 as Banco Anglo Colombiano; present name adopted in 2007; bought by HSBC Bank PLC (United Kingdom) in 2006; cap. 154,227m., res –5,037m., dep. 1,459,564m. (Dec. 2007); Pres. ROBERTO BRIGARD; 52 brs.

Cali

Banco de Occidente: Carrera 4, No 7-61, 12°, Apdo Aéreo 7607, Cali, Valle del Cauca; tel. (2) 886-1111; fax (2) 886-1298; e-mail dinternacional@bancodeoccidente.com.co; internet www.bancodeoccidente.com.co; f. 1965; cap. US $2m., res US $566.3m., dep. US $4,697m. (Dec. 2007); 78.2% owned by Grupo Aval Acciones y Valores; Pres. EFRAÍN OTERO ÁLVAREZ; 175 brs.

Medellín

Bancolombia, SA: Carrera 52, No 50-20, Medellín, Antioquia; tel. (4) 576-6060; fax (4) 513-4827; e-mail comunica@bancolombia.com.co; internet www.grupobancolombia.com; f. 1998 by merger of Banco Industrial Colombiano and Banco de Colombia; cap. 393,914m., res 4,464,566m., dep. 26,377,046m. (Dec. 2008); Pres. JORGE LONDOÑO SALDARRIAGA; Chair. DAVID EMILIO BOJANINI GARCÍA; 385 brs.

Development Bank

BCSC: Carrera 7, No 77-65, 11°, Bogotá, DC; tel. (1) 313-8000; fax (1) 321-6912; e-mail csgarzon@fundacion-social.com.co; internet www.bcsc.com.co; f. 1911 as Banco Caja Social; adopted current name 2005; cap. 185,392m., dep. 4,420,000m. (Dec. 2006); Pres. CARLOS UPEGUI CUARTAS; 260 brs.

Banking Associations

Asociación Bancaria y de Entidades Financieras de Colombia (Asobancaria): Carrera 9A, No 74-08, 9°, Bogotá, DC; tel. (1) 326-6612; fax (1) 326-6604; e-mail info@asobancaria.com; internet www.asobancaria.com; f. 1936; 56 mem. banks; Pres. MARÍA MERCEDES CUÉLLAR LÓPEZ.

Asociación Nacional de Instituciones Financieras (ANIF): Calle 70A, No 7-86, Bogotá, DC; tel. (1) 310-1500; fax (1) 235-5947; internet www.anif.org; f. 1974; Pres. Dr SERGIO CLAVIJO.

STOCK EXCHANGE

Bolsa de Valores de Colombia: Carrera 7, No 71-21, Edif. Bancafé, Torre B, Of. 1201, Bogotá, DC; tel. (1) 313-9800; fax (1) 313-9766; internet www.bvc.com.co; f. 2001 following merger of stock exchanges of Bogotá, Medellín and Occidente; Pres. JUAN PABLO CÓRDOBA GARCÉS; Sec.-Gen. ANGEL ALBERTO VELANDIA RODRÍGUEZ.

INSURANCE

Principal Companies

ACE Seguros, SA: Calle 72, No 10-51, 7°, Apdo Aéreo 29782, Bogotá, DC; tel. (1) 319-0300; fax (1) 319-0304; internet www.acelatinamerica.com; fmrly Cigna Seguros de Colombia, SA; Pres. PILAR LOZANO.

Afianzamiento y Seguros: Avda 9N, 16N-18, 2°, Cali; tel. (2) 667-4456; fax (2) 668-2232; Man. ALDEMAR SARRIA.

AIG Colombia Seguros de Vida: Carrera 7, No 99-53, 17°, Bogotá, DC; tel. (14) 358-1258; fax (14) 638-1299; e-mail servicio.cliente@alico.com.co; internet co.alico.com; sold to MetLife in 2010; Pres. SANTIAGO OSORIO; Sec. Gen. CONSUELO GONZÁLEZ.

Aseguradora Colseguros, SA: Carrera 13A, No 29-24, Parque Central Bavaria, Apdo Aéreo 3537, Bogotá, DC; tel. (1) 560-0600; fax (1) 561-6695; internet www.colseguros.com; subsidiary of Allianz AG, Germany; f. 1874; Pres. IGNACIO BORJA.

Aseguradora Solidaria de Colombia: Calle 100, No 9A-45, 8° y 12°, Bogotá, DC; tel. (1) 646-4330; fax (1) 296-1527; e-mail eguzman@solidaria.com.co; internet www.aseguradorasolidaria.com.co; Pres. CARLOS GUZMÁN PÉREZ.

BBVA Seguros: Carrera 11, No 87-51, Bogotá, DC; tel. (1) 219-1100; fax (1) 640-7995; internet www.bbvaseguros.com.co; f. 1994; Pres. FRANCISCO GONZÁLEZ.

Chubb de Colombia Cía de Seguros, SA: Carrera 7A, No 71-52, Torre B, 10°, Bogotá, DC; tel. (1) 326-6200; fax (1) 326-6210; e-mail informaciongeneral@chubb.com; internet www.chubb.com.co; f. 1972; Pres. MANUEL OBREGÓN; 4 brs.

Cía Aseguradora de Fianzas, SA (Confianza): Calle 82, No 11-37, 7°, Apdo Aéreo 056965, Bogotá, DC; tel. (1) 617-0899; fax (1) 610-8866; e-mail correos@confianza.com.co; internet www.confianza.com.co; f. 1979; Pres. LUIS ALEJANDRO RUEDA.

Cía Mundial de Seguros, SA: Calle 33, No 6B-24, 2° y 3°, Bogotá, DC; tel. (1) 285-5600; fax (1) 285-1220; e-mail mundial@mundialseguros.com.co; internet www.mundialseguros.com.co; f. 1995; Pres. ROBERTO VERGARA ORTIZ.

Cía de Seguros Bolívar, SA: Avda El Dorado, No 68B-31, Bogotá, DC; tel. (1) 341-0077; fax (1) 283-0799; internet www.segurosbolivar.com.co; f. 1939; Dir RAMÓN MENESES.

Cía de Seguros Colmena, SA: Calle 26, No 69C-03, 5° y 6°, Apdo Aéreo 5050, Bogotá, DC; tel. (1) 324-1111; fax (1) 324-0866; internet www.colmena-arp.com.co; Dir-Gen. JUAN MANUEL DÍAZ-GRANADOS.

Cía de Seguros de Créditos Comerciales (CREDISEGURO): Calle 7 Sur, No 42-70, Edif. Forum II, 8°, Antioquia; tel. (4) 444-0145; fax (4) 314-1990; e-mail adritoac@crediseguro.com.co; internet www.crediseguro.com.co; f. 1999; subsidiary of Mapfre.

Cía de Seguros de Vida Aurora, SA: Carrera 7, No 74-21, 1°, 2° y 3°, Bogotá, DC; tel. 319-2930; fax 345-4980; e-mail juan.otalvaro@segurosaurora.com; internet www.segurosaurora.com; f. 1967; Pres. EUDORO CARVAJAL IBAÑEZ.

Cía Suramericana de Seguros, SA: Centro Suramericana, Carrera 64B, No 49A-30, Apdo Aéreo 780, Medellín, Antioquia; tel. (4) 260-2100; fax (4) 260-3194; e-mail contactenos@suramericana.com; internet www.suramericana.com; f. 1944; Pres. GONZALO ALBERTO PÉREZ ROJAS.

Condor, SA, Cía de Seguros Generales: Carrera 7, No 74-21, Bogotá, DC; tel. (1) 612-0666; fax (1) 215-6121; internet www.seguroscondor.com.co; Pres. EUDORO CARVAJAL IBÁÑEZ.

La Equidad Seguros, Organización Cooperativa: Torre La Equidad Seguros, 13° y 14°, Carrera 9A, 99-07, Bogotá, DC; tel. (1) 592-2929; fax (1) 520-0169; e-mail equidad@laequidadseguros.coop; internet www.laequidadseguros.coop; Dir Dr CLEMENTE AUGUSTO JAIMES.

Generali Colombia—Seguros Generales, SA: Carrera 7A, No 72-13, 8°, Apdo Aéreo 076478, Bogotá, DC; tel. (1) 346-8888; fax (1) 255-1164; e-mail presidencia@generali.com.co; internet www.generali.com.co; f. 1937; Pres. EDUARDO SARMIENTO.

Global Seguros, SA: Carrera 9, No 74-62, Bogotá, DC; tel. (1) 313-9200; fax (1) 317-5376; internet www.globalseguroscolombia.com; Pres. RODRIGO URIBE BERNAL.

Liberty Seguros, SA: Calle 72, No 10-07, 6°, 7° y 8°, Bogotá, DC; tel. (1) 376-5330; fax (1) 217-9917; e-mail lhernandez@impsat.net.co; internet www.libertycolombia.com.co; f. 1954; fmrly Latinoamericana de Seguros, SA; Pres. MAURICIO GARCÍA ORTIZ.

Mapfre Seguros Generales de Colombia, SA: Carrera 14, No 96-34, Bogotá, DC; tel. (1) 650-3300; fax (1) 650-3400; internet www.mapfre.com.co; f. 1995; Pres. JOSÉ MANUEL INCHAUSTI.

Pan American de Colombia Cía de Seguros de Vida, SA: Carrera 7A, No 75-09, Apdo Aéreo 76000, Bogotá, DC; tel. (1) 326-7400; fax (1) 326-7390; e-mail servicioalclienteco@panamericanlife.com; internet www.panamericanlife.com; Gen. Man. MANUEL LEMUS.

La Previsora, SA, Cía de Seguros: Calle 57, No 9-07, Apdo Aéreo 52946, Bogotá, DC; tel. (1) 348-5757; fax (1) 540-5294; e-mail contactenos@previsora.gov.co; internet www.previsora.gov.co; f. 1914; Pres. DIEGO BARRAGÁN CORREA.

Royal and Sun Alliance Seguros (Colombia), SA: Avda 19, No 104-37, Bogotá, DC; tel. (1) 488-1010; fax (1) 214-0470; e-mail servicioalcliente@co.rsagroup.com; internet www.rsagroup.com.co; fmrly Seguros Fénix, SA; Pres. JOSÉ LUIS PLANA VILLARROEL.

Segurexpo de Colombia, SA: Calle 72, No 6-44, 12°, Apdo Aéreo 75140, Bogotá, DC; tel. (1) 326-6969; fax (1) 211-0218; e-mail segurexpo@segurexpo.com; internet www.segurexpo.com; f. 1993; Pres. JUAN PABLO LUQUE LUQUE.

Seguros Alfa, SA: Carrera 13, No 27-47, 22° y 23°, Apdo Aéreo 27718, Bogotá, DC; tel. (1) 344-4720; fax (1) 344-6770; e-mail presidencia@segurosalfa.com.co; internet www.segurosalfa.com.co; Pres. LUIS FERNANDO MATHIEU VALDERRAMA.

Seguros Colpatria, SA: Carrera 7A, No 24-89, 9°, Apdo Aéreo 7762, Bogotá, DC; tel. (1) 606-6121; fax (1) 561-2747; e-mail incidentesinternet@colpatria.com; internet www.colpatria.com; Pres. LUIS SANTIAGO PERDOMO MALDONADO.

Seguros del Estado, SA: Carrera 13, No 96-66, Apdo Aéreo 6810, Bogotá, DC; tel. (1) 218-0903; fax (1) 218-0913; e-mail omaida.moreno@segurosdelestado.com; internet www.segurosdelestado.com; Pres. JORGE MORA SÁNCHEZ.

Seguros de Riesgos Profesionales Suramericana, SA (ARP Sura): Centro Suramericana, Edif. Torre Suratep, Calle 49A, No 63-55, Bogotá, DC; tel. (1) 430-7100; fax (1) 231-8080; e-mail suratepenlinea@suratep.com.co; internet www.suratep.com; f. 1996; fmrly SURATEP; name changed as above in 2009; subsidiary of Cía Suramericana de Seguros; Gen. Man. IVÁN IGNACIO ZULUAGA LATORRE.

Skandia Seguros de Vida, SA: Avda 19, No 109-30, Apdo Aéreo 100327, Bogotá, DC; tel. (1) 620-5566; fax (1) 214-0038; e-mail cliente@skandia.com.co; internet www.skandia.com.co; Pres. Camilo Wills Franco.

Insurance Association

Federación de Aseguradores Colombianos (FASECOLDA): Carrera 7A, No 26-20, 11° y 12°, Apdo Aéreo 5233, Bogotá, DC; tel. (1) 344-3080; fax (1) 210-7041; e-mail fasecolda@fasecolda.com; internet www.fasecolda.com; f. 1976; 30 mems; Exec. Pres. Roberto Junguito Bonnet.

Trade and Industry

GOVERNMENT AGENCIES

Agencia Nacional de Hidrocarburos (ANH): Calle 99, No 9A-54, 14°, Bogotá, DC; tel. (1) 593-1717; fax (1) 593-1718; e-mail info@anh.gov.co; internet www.anh.gov.co; f. 2003; govt agency responsible for regulation of the petroleum industry; Dir-Gen. José Armando Zamora Reyes.

Departamento Nacional de Planeación: Calle 26, No 13-19, 14°, Bogotá, DC; tel. (1) 336-1600; fax (1) 281-3348; e-mail vgonzalez@dnp.gov.co; internet www.dnp.gov.co; f. 1958; supervises and administers devt projects; approves foreign investments; Dir-Gen. Carolina Rentería Rodríguez.

Superintendencia de Industria y Comercio (SUPERINDUSTRIA): Carrera 13, No 27-00, 5°, Bogotá, DC; tel. (1) 382-0840; fax (1) 382-2696; e-mail info@sic.gov.co; internet www.sic.gov.co; supervises chambers of commerce; controls standards and prices; Supt Gustavo Valbuena Quiñones.

Superintendencia de Sociedades (SUPERSOCIEDADES): Avda El Dorado, No 51-80, Apdo Aéreo 4188, Bogotá, DC; tel. (1) 324-5777; fax (1) 324-5000; e-mail webmaster@supersociedades.gov.co; internet www.supersociedades.gov.co; f. 1931; oversees activities of local and foreign corpns; Supt Hernando Ruiz López.

DEVELOPMENT AGENCIES

Agencia Presidencial para la Acción Social y la Cooperación Internacional: Calle 7, No 6-54, Bogotá, DC; tel. (1) 352-6666; fax (1) 284-4120; internet www.accionsocial.gov.co; f. 2005 following merger of Red de Solidaridad Social (RSS) and Agencia Colombiana de Cooperación Internacional (ACCI); govt agency intended to channel domestic and international funds into social programmes.

Asociación Colombiana de Ingeniería Sanitaria y Ambiental (ACODAL): Calle 39, No 14-75, Bogotá, DC; tel. (1) 245-9539; fax (1) 323-1407; internet www.acodal.org.co; f. 1956 as Asociación Colombiana de Acueductos y Alcantarillados; asscn promoting sanitary and environmental engineering projects; Pres. Maryluz Mejía de Pumarejo; Man. José Fernando Cárdenas.

Asociación Colombiana de las Micro, Pequeñas y Medianas Empresas (ACOPI): Carrera 15, No 36-70, Bogotá, DC; tel. and fax (1) 320-4783; e-mail comunicaciones@acopi.org.co; internet www.acopi.org.co; f. 1951; promotes small and medium-sized industries; Pres. Dr Norman Correa Calderón.

Centro Internacional de Educación y Desarrollo Humano (CINDE): Edif. Las Tres Carabelas, El Laguito, Cartagena; tel. (5) 665-5100; fax (5) 665-0319; e-mail cinde@cinde.org.co; internet www.cinde.org.co; education and social devt; f. 1977; Pres. Jaime Olarte Restrepo.

Corporación para la Investigación Socioeconómica y Tecnológica de Colombia (CINSET): Carrera 48, No 91-94, La Castellana, Bogotá, DC; tel. (1) 256-0961; fax (1) 218-6416; e-mail cinset@cinset.org.co; internet www.cinset.org.co; f. 1987; social, economic and technical devt projects; Pres. Norman Correa Calderón; Exec. Dir Juan Carlos Gutiérrez Arias.

Corporación Región: Calle 55, No 41-10, Medellín; tel. (4) 216-6822; fax (4) 239-5544; e-mail coregion@region.org.co; internet www.region.org.co; f. 1989; environmental, political and social devt; Pres. Rubén Hernando Fernández Andrade.

Fondo Financiero de Proyectos de Desarrollo (FONADE): Calle 26, No 13-19, 19°-22°, Apdo Aéreo 24110, Bogotá, DC; tel. (1) 594-0407; fax (1) 282-6018; e-mail fonade@colomsat.net.co; internet www.fonade.gov.co; f. 1968; responsible for channelling loans towards economic devt projects; administered by a cttee under the head of the Departamento Nacional de Planeación; FONADE works in close asscn with other official planning orgs; Gen. Man. Dr Elvira Forero Hernández.

Instituto Colombiano de Desarrollo Rural: Centro Administrativo Nacional (CAN), Avda Eldorado, Calle 43, No 57–41, Bogotá, DC; e-mail incoder@incoder.gov.co; internet www.incoder.gov.co; rural devt agency.

CHAMBERS OF COMMERCE

Confederación Colombiana de Cámaras de Comercio (CONFECAMARAS): Of. 502, Carrera 13, No 27-47, Apdo Aéreo 29750, Bogotá, DC; tel. (1) 346-7055; fax (1) 346-7026; e-mail confecamaras@confecamaras.org.co; internet www.confecamaras.org.co; f. 1969; 56 mem. orgs; Exec. Pres. Eugenio Marulanda Gómez.

Cámara Colombo Japonesa de Comercio e Industria: Calle 72, No 7-82, 7°, Bogotá, DC; tel. (1) 210-0383; fax (1) 349-0736; internet www.camaracolombojaponesa.com.co; f. 1988; Colombian-Japanese trade asscn; Pres. Jaime Roa Drews.

Cámara Colombo Venezolana: Calle 72, No 8-24, Of. 503, Edif. Suramericana, Bogotá, DC; tel. (1) 211-6224; fax (1) 211-6089; e-mail info@comvenezuela.com; internet www.comvenezuela.com; f. 1977; Colombian-Venezuelan trade asscn; 19 mem. cos; Pres. María Luisa Chippe.

Cámara de Comercio de Bogotá: Avda Eldorado, 68D-35, Bogotá, DC; tel. (1) 383-0300; fax (1) 284-7735; e-mail webmaster@ccb.org.co; internet www.ccb.org.co; f. 1878; 3,650 mem. orgs; Pres. Sergio Mutis Caballero.

Cámara de Comercio Colombo Americano: Of. 1209, Calle 98, No 22-64, Bogotá, DC; tel. (1) 623-7088; fax (1) 621-6838; e-mail website@amchamcolombia.com.co; internet www.amchamcolombia.com.co; f. 1955; Colombian-US trade asscn.

Cámara de Comercio Colombo Británica: Of. 409, Calle 95, No 13-55, Bogotá, DC; tel. (1) 621-2401; fax (1) 621-2431; e-mail britcham@colombobritanica.com; internet www.colombobritanica.com; Colombian-British trade asscn.

There are also local Chambers of Commerce in the capital towns of all the Departments and in many of the other trading centres.

INDUSTRIAL AND TRADE ASSOCIATIONS

Corporación de la Industria Aeronáutica Colombiana, SA (CIAC SA): Avda Calle 26, No 103-08, Entrada 1, Bogotá, DC; tel. (1) 413-8312; e-mail info@ciac.gov.co; internet www.ciac.gov.co; Gen. Man. Luis Fernando Medrano.

Industria Militar (INDUMIL): Calle 44, No 51-11, Apdo Aéreo 7272, Bogotá, DC; tel. (1) 220-7800; fax (1) 222-4889; internet www.indumil.gov.co; attached to Ministry of National Defence; Man. Col (retd) Carlos Enrique Villarreal Quintero.

Instituto Colombiano Agropecuario (ICA): Calle 37, No 8-43, 4° y 5°, Bogotá, DC; tel. (1) 285-5520; fax (1) 232-4689; e-mail info@ica.gov.co; internet www.ica.gov.co; f. 1962; attached to the Ministry of Agriculture and Rural Devt; institute for promotion, co-ordination and implementation of research into and teaching and devt of agriculture and animal husbandry; Gen. Man. Jaime Cárdenas López (acting).

Instituto Colombiano de Geología y Minería (INGEOMINAS): Diagonal 53, No 34-53, Apdo Aéreo 4865, Bogotá, DC; tel. (1) 222-1811; fax (1) 220-0582; e-mail henciso@ingeominas.gov.co; internet www.ingeominas.gov.co; f. 1968; responsible for mineral research, geological mapping and research including hydrogeology, remote sensing, geochemistry, geophysics and geological hazards; attached to the Ministry of Mines and Energy; Dir Mario Ballesteros Mejía.

Instituto Colombiano de Geología y Minería (INGEOMINAS): Diagonal 53, No 34-53, Apdo Aéreo 4865, Bogotá, DC; tel. (1) 222-1811; fax (1) 220-0582; e-mail henciso@ingeominas.gov.co; internet www.ingeominas.gov.co; f. 1968; responsible for mineral research, geological mapping and research including hydrogeology, remote sensing, geochemistry, geophysics and geological hazards; attached to the Ministry of Mines and Energy; Dir Mario Ballesteros Mejía.

EMPLOYERS' AND PRODUCERS' ORGANIZATIONS

Asociación Colombiana de Cooperativos (ASCOOP): Transversal 29, No 35-29, Bogotá, DC; tel. (1) 368-3500; fax (1) 268-4230; e-mail comunicaciones@ascoop.coop; internet www.ascoop.coop; promotes co-operatives; Exec. Dir Carlos E. Acero.

Asociación de Cultivadores de Caña de Azúcar de Colombia (ASOCAÑA): Calle 58N, No 3N-15, Apdo Aéreo 4448, Cali, Valle del Cauca; tel. (2) 664-7902; fax (2) 664-5888; internet www.asocana.com.co; f. 1959; sugar planters' asscn; Pres. Luis Fernando Londoño Capurro.

Asociación Nacional de Comercio Exterior (ANALDEX): Carrera 10, No 27, Int. 137, Of. 902, Apdo Aéreo 29812, Bogotá, DC; tel. (1) 342-0788; fax (1) 284-6911; e-mail analdex@analdex.org; internet www.analdex.org; exporters' asscn; Pres. Javier Díaz Molina.

Asociación Nacional de Empresarios de Colombia (ANDI): Carrera 43A, No 1-50, San Fernando Plaza, Torre 2, 9°, Apdo Aéreo 997, Medellín, Antioquia; tel. (4) 326-5100; fax (4) 326-0068; e-mail comercial@andi.com.co; internet www.andi.com.co; f. 1944; Pres. Luis Carlos Villegas Echeverri; 9 brs; 756 mems.

Asociación Nacional de Exportadores de Café de Colombia: Calle 72, No 10-07, Of. 1101, Bogotá, DC; tel. (1) 347-8419; fax (1) 347-

9523; e-mail asoexport@asoexport.org; internet www.asoexport.org; f. 1933; private asscn of coffee exporters; Pres. JORGE E. LOZANO MANCERA.

Federación Colombiana de Ganaderos (FEDEGAN): Calle 37, No 14-31, Apdo Aéreo 9709, Bogotá, DC; tel. (1) 245-3041; fax (1) 578-2020; e-mail fedegan@fedegan.org.co; internet www.fedegan.org.co; f. 1963; cattle raisers' asscn; about 350,000 affiliates; Exec. Pres. JOSÉ FÉLIX LAFAURIE RIVERA; Sec.-Gen. JAIME RAFAEL DAZA ALMENDRALES.

Federación Nacional de Cacaoteros: Carrera 17, No 30-39, Apdo Aéreo 17736, Bogotá, DC; tel. (1) 327-3000; fax (1) 288-4424; e-mail presidencia@fedecacao.com.co; internet www.fedecacao.com.co; fed. of cocoa growers; Gen. Man. Dr JOSÉ OMAR PINZÓN USECHE.

Federación Nacional de Cafeteros de Colombia (FEDERACAFE) (National Federation of Coffee Growers): Calle 73, No 8-13, Apdo Aéreo 57534, Bogotá, DC; tel. (1) 217-0600; fax (1) 217-1021; internet www.cafedecolombia.com; f. 1927; totally responsible for fostering and regulating the coffee economy; Gen. Man. (vacant); 203,000 mems.

Federación Nacional de Comerciantes (FENALCO): Carrera 4, No 19-85, 7°, Bogotá, DC; tel. (1) 350-0600; fax (1) 350-9424; e-mail fenalco@fenalco.com.co; internet www.fenalco.com.co; business fed; Pres. GUILLERMO BOTERO NIETO.

Federación Nacional de Cultivadores de Cereales y Leguminosas (FENALCE): Carrera 14, No 97-62, Apdo Aéreo 8694, Bogotá, DC; tel. (1) 218-2114; fax (1) 218-9463; e-mail fenalce@cable.net.co; internet www.fenalce.org; f. 1960; fed. of grain growers; Pres. CARLOS ADEL KAFRUNI; 30,000 mems.

Sociedad de Agricultores de Colombia (SAC) (Colombian Farmers' Society): Carrera 7A, No 24-89, 44°, Apdo Aéreo 3638, Bogotá, DC; tel. (1) 281-0263; fax (1) 284-4572; e-mail socdeagr@impsat.net.co; internet www.sac.org.co; f. 1871; Pres. RAFAEL MEJÍA LÓPEZ.

There are several other organizations, including those for rice growers, engineers and financiers.

MAJOR COMPANIES

The following are some of the leading industrial and commercial companies operating in Colombia:

Acerías Paz del Río, SA: Calle 100, No 13-21, 6°, Bogotá, DC; tel. (1) 651-7300; fax (1) 341-6497; e-mail presidenciaapdr@hotmail.com; internet www.pazdelrio.com.co; f. 1948; 52% bought by Votorantim Metais (Brazil) in 2007; mining and processing of iron ores; Pres. LUIS GUILLERMO PARRA DUSSÁN.

Almacenes Exito, SA: Carrera 48, 32B Sur, Apdo Aéreo 139, Envigado, Antioquia; tel. (4) 339-6507; fax (4) 331-4792; e-mail prensa.exito@grupo-exito.com; internet www.almacenesexito.com.co; f. 1949; wholesaling and retailing; Pres. Dr GONZALO RESTREPO LÓPEZ; 37,000 employees.

Alpina Productos Alimenticios, SA: Carrera 63, No 15-61, Bogotá, DC; tel. (1) 571-8609; e-mail alpina@alpina.com; internet www.alpina.com.co; f. 1978; food and food-processing; Pres. JULIÁN JARAMILLO; 2,800 employees.

Alumina (Aluminio Nacional, SA): Carretera 32, No 11-101, Acopi Yumbo, Cali, Valle del Cauca; tel. (2) 651-0400; fax (2) 664-5691; internet www.alumina.com.co; f. 1960 as Alumina Alcan de Colombia, present name adopted 1985; aluminium production.

Aluminio Reynolds Santo Domingo, SA: Calle 79, No 40-362, Via 40, Barranquilla; tel. (5) 330-0222; fax (5) 330-0210; e-mail comercial@aluminioreynolds.com.co; internet www.aluminioreynolds.com.co; 94% bought by Industrias Arfel, SA, in 2010; aluminium and metal products; f. 1955; Pres. EDUARDO GAITAN PARRA; 525 employees.

Bavaria, SA: Calle 94, No 7A-47, Bogotá, DC; tel. (1) 638-9000; fax (1) 638-9344; e-mail bavaria@bavaria.com.co; internet www.bavaria.com.co; f. 1889; acquired by SABMiller (United Kingdom and South Africa) in 2005; holding co with principal interests in brewing and the manufacture of soft drinks; also transport, telecommunications, construction, forestry and fishing; Pres. and CEO KARL LIPPERT; Sec.-Gen. JUAN MANUEL ARBOLEDA PERDOMO; 18,895 employees.

Cerveza Aguila, SA: Calle 10, No 38-280, Barranquilla; tel. (5) 350-4000; fax (5) 344-8815; internet www.cervezaaguila.com; f. 1913; brewery; parent co is Bavaria, SA; 980 employees.

BHP Billiton: internet www.bhpbilliton.com; f. 2001 following merger of BHP of Australia and British-South African co Billiton; mining and natural resources; part of consortium that bought Carbones de Colombia (CARBOCOL) in 2000 and Intercor (q.v.) in 2002.

BP Exploration Company (Colombia) Ltd: Carrera 9A, No 99-02, 9°, Bogotá, DC; tel. (1) 628-4000; fax (1) 611-1127; internet www.bp.com/colombia; f. 1972; subsidiary of BP, United Kingdom; exploration for hydrocarbons reserves; Pres. ALBERTO GALVIS; 500 employees.

Carbones del Cerrejón: Guasare, La Guajira; internet www.cerrejoncoal.com; f. 1976 as jt venture between state-owned Carbocol, SA and Intercor (USA); govt sold its share in 2002 to int. consortium; owned by Anglo American, BHP Billiton and Glencore Int. AG; coal mining and export; Pres. LEÓN TEICHER.

Carvajal, SA: Calle 29 Norte, No 6A-40, Apdo Aéreo 46, Cali; tel. (2) 667-5011; fax (2) 668-7644; internet www.carvajal.com.co; f. 1941; holding co with principal interests in printing and publishing; also construction, electronic components, telecommunications, trade, personal credit and the manufacture of office furniture; Pres. RICARDO OBREGÓN; 10,000 employees.

Cerro Matoso, SA: Calle 114, No 9-01, Torre A, Edif. Teleport Park, Montelíbano, Córdoba; tel. (5) 629-1570; fax (5) 629-1593; internet www.bhpbilliton.com; f. 1979; mining of ferrous ores; owned by BHP Billiton; Pres. RICARDO ESCOBAR; 950 employees.

Cervecería Leona, SA: Carretera Central del Norte Km 30, Vía Tunja, Tocancipa; tel. (1) 857-4425; fax (1) 857-4355; f. 1992; subsidiary of SABMiller PLC; brewery; Legal Rep. RICARDO HUMBERTO RESTREPO; 400 employees.

Cervecería Unión, SA: Carrera 50A, No 38-39, Itagüí, Medellín; tel. (4) 372-2400; fax (4) 372-3488; internet www.cerveceriaunion.com.co; f. 1931; brewery; parent company is Bavaria, SA; Dir-Gen. JORGE BONNELLS GALINDO; 900 employees.

Compañía Colombiana Automotriz, SA (CCA): Calle 13, No 38-54, Bogotá, DC; tel. (1) 277-7911; fax (1) 201-1836; e-mail cca@mazda.com.co; internet www.mimazda.com; f. 1973; automobile manufacturers; majority of shares held by Mazda Ltd and Mitsubishi Corpn of Japan; Pres. FABIO SÁNCHEZ FORERO; 1,169 employees.

Compañía Colombiana de Tabaco (COLTABACO): Medellín, Antioquia; tel. 319-9500; f. 1919; bought by Philip Morris (USA) in 2005; cigarette manufacturer; Dir (Corporate Affairs) HUMBERTO MORA; 1,062 employees.

Compañía Colombiana de Tejidos, SA (COLTEJER): Carretera 42, No 54A-161, Itagüí, Antioquia; tel. (4) 375-7500; fax (4) 372-8585; e-mail coltejer@coltejer.com.co; internet www.coltejer.com.co; f. 1907; textile manufacturers; Pres. RAFAEL KALACH MIRZRAHI; 5,922 employees.

Compañía de Galletas Noel, SA: Avda Guayabal, Carrera 52, No 2-38, Apdo 897, Medellín; tel. (4) 365-5999; fax (4) 285-4167; e-mail webmaster@noel.com.co; internet www.noel.com.co; f. 1933; subsiadiary of Grupo Nacional de Chocolates, SA; food production and processing including meat products, confectionery, powdered soft drinks and vegetable protein; Pres. ALBERTO HOYERO LOPERA; 2,000 employees.

Comunicación Celular, SA (COMCEL): Calle 90, No 14-37, Bogotá, DC; tel. (1) 616-9797; fax (1) 623-1287; internet www.comcel.com.co; f. 1992; mobile telecommunications; Pres. JUAN CARLOS ARCHILA CABAL; 1,203 employees.

Cristalería Peldar, SA: Calle 39S, No 48-180, Apdo Aéreo 215, Envigado; tel. (4) 378-8000; fax (4) 270-4225; e-mail peldar@peldar.com; internet www.peldar.com; f. 1962; manufacture of glass products; Pres. FREDERICO JOSÉ LLANO MOLINA; 1,800 employees.

Ecopetrol, SA: Edif. Ecopetrol, Carrera 13, No 36-24, 8°, Apdo Aéreo 5938, Bogotá, DC; tel. (1) 234-4000; fax (1) 234-4099; e-mail webmaster@ecopetrol.com.co; internet www.ecopetrol.com.co; f. 1951; state-owned co for the exploration, production, refining and transportation of petroleum; 10.1% sold to private ownership in 2007; Pres. JAVIER GUTIÉRREZ PEMBERTHY; 6,720 employees.

Enka de Colombia, SA: Of. 901, Carrera 37A, No 8-43, Apdo Aereo 5233, Medellín; tel. (4) 319-5106; fax (4) 319-5155; e-mail ventasymercadeo@enka.com.co; internet www.enka.com.co; f. 1964; manufacture of synthetic fibres; Pres. ALVARO HINCAPIÉ VÉLEZ; 1,450 employees.

ExxonMobil de Colombia, SA: Bogotá, DC; internet www.mobil.com.co; f. 2001 following the merger of Esso Colombiana with ExxonMobil; petroleum and gas exploration and extraction; Pres. CAMILO DURÁN.

Fabricato Tejicondor: Carrera 50, No 38-320, Bello, Antioquia; tel. (4) 448-3500; fax (4) 454-3407; e-mail contactenos@fabricato.com.co; internet www.fabricato.com.co; f. 1923; manufacture and export of cotton, textiles and synthetic fibre goods; Pres. ÓSCAR IVÁN ZULUAGA SERNA; 4,325 employees.

GM Colmotores: Avda Boyacá, No 36A-03 Sur, Bogotá, DC; tel. (1) 710-1111; fax (1) 270-8382; internet www.chevrolet.com.co; f. 1957; subsidiary of General Motors Corpn, USA; producers of passenger and commercial vehicles, spare parts and accessories; Pres. SANTIAGO CHAMORRO; 1,254 employees.

Incauca, SA: Carrera 9, No 28-103, Cali, Valle del Cauca; tel. (2) 418-3000; fax (2) 438-4909; e-mail incauca@incauca.com; internet www.incauca.com; f. 1963; cultivation and processing of sugar cane; Pres. Bd of Dirs CARLOS ARDILLA LÜLLE; 5,109 employees.

Ingenio Providencia, SA: Carrera 28, No 28-103, Palmira; tel. (2) 318-4500; fax (2) 438-4929; e-mail ingprovidencia@ingprovidencia.com; internet www.ingprovidencia.com; f. 1926; cultivation and wholesale of sugar cane; Pres. Pedro José Cabal Duque; 2,700 employees.

Leonisa Internacional: Carrera 51, No 13-158, Medellín; tel. (4) 350-6100; fax (4) 265-0617; e-mail info@leonisa.com; internet www.leonisa.com; f. 1956; manufacturers of men's and women's clothing; Pres. Luis Gilberto Giraldo; 2,000 employees.

Occidental Petroleum Corporation: Calle 77A, No 11-32, Apdo 92171, Bogotá, DC; tel. (1) 346-0111; fax (1) 211-6820; internet www.oxy.com; f. 1977; principal shareholder Occidental Petroleum Corpn of the USA; petroleum and gas exploration and production; Chair. Ray Irani; 681 employees.

Petrobras Colombia: Carrera 7, No 71-21, Torre B, 17°, Bogotá, DC; tel. (1) 313-5000; fax (1) 313-5070; internet www.petrobras.com; f. 1972; subsidiary of Petróleo Brasileiro, SA (Petrobras), Brazil; oil exploration and production; Gen. Man. Abílio Ramos.

Productora de Papeles, SA (PROPAL): Antigua Carrera Cali–Yumbo Km 12, Yumbo, Valle; tel. (2) 651-2000; fax (2) 669-9244; e-mail em1874@propal.com.co; internet www.propal.com.co; f. 1957; owners of two paper mills manufacturing paper products; Pres. Alfonso Ocampo Gaviria; 1,100 employees.

Promigas: Calle 66, No 67-123, Barranquilla; tel. (95) 371-3444; fax (95) 368-0515; e-mail promigas@promigas.com; internet www.promigas.com; f. 1974; natural gas distributor, network covers 60% of the country; Pres. Antonio Celia Martínez-Aparicio.

Smurfit Kappa Cartón de Colombia, SA: Calle 15, No 18-109, Puerto Isaacs, Yumbo; tel. (2) 691-4000; fax (2) 691-4199; e-mail comunicaciones@smurfitkappa.com.co; internet www.smurfit.com.co; manufacturers of paper and packaging materials; subsidiary of Jefferson Smurfit Group of Ireland; Pres. Bernardo Guzmán; 1,500 employees.

Sociedad de Fabricación de Automotores, SA (Sofasa Renault): Carretera Central del Norte, Km 17, Chía, Cundinamarca; tel. (1) 676-0108; e-mail servicioalcliente@sofasa.com.co; internet www.renault.com.co; f. 1973; manufacture of motor vehicles and spare parts; Pres. Germán Camilo Calle Sánchez; 873 employees.

Sociedad Kedahda, SA: Bogotá, DC; internet www.angloamerican.co.uk; f. 1917; subsidiary of Anglo-American PLC; thermal coal mining at Cerrejón.

Supertiendas y Droguerías Olímpica, SA: Carrera 36, No 38-03, Barranquilla; tel. (5) 371-0100; fax (5) 371-0292; internet www.olimpica.com.co; f. 1953; retailing; Pres. Antonio Char Chaljub; 4,600 employees.

Tecnoquímicas, SA: Calle 23, No 4-66, Cali; tel. (2) 883-9392; fax (2) 883-8859; e-mail rpacifico@tecnoquimicas.com.co; internet www.tecnoquimicas.com.co; f. 1934; manufacture of pharmaceuticals; Pres. Francisco José Barberi Ospina; 1,670 employees.

UTILITIES

Electricity

Corporación Eléctrica de la Costa Atlántica, SA ESP (Corelca): Centro Ejecutivo II, 5°, Calle 55, No 72-109, 9°, Barranquilla, Atlántico; tel. (5) 330-3000; fax (5) 330-3011; e-mail presidencia@corelca.com.co; internet www.corelca.com.co; responsible for supplying electricity to the Atlantic departments; generates more than 2,000m. kWh annually from thermal power stations; Gen. Man. Daniel Alsina Galofre.

Empresa de Energía de Bogotá, SA ESP (EEB): Of. Principal, 6°, Carrera 9A, No 73-44, Bogotá, DC; tel. (1) 326-8000; fax (1) 226-8010; e-mail webmaster@eeb.com.co; internet www.eeb.com.co; provides electricity for Bogotá area by generating capacity of 680 MW, mainly hydroelectric; Pres. Mónica de Greiff; Man. Dir Astrid Martínez Ortiz.

Instituto de Planificación y Promoción de Soluciones Energéticas para las Zonas No Interconectadas (IPSE): Carrera 12, No 84-12, 8°, Bogotá, DC; tel. (1) 644-9300; fax (1) 622-3461; e-mail ipse@ipse.gov.co; internet www.ipse.gov.co; f. 1999; attached to the Ministry of Mines and Energy; co-ordinates and develops energy supply in rural areas; Dir-Gen. Edigson Pérez Bedoya.

Interconexión Eléctrica, SA (ISA): Calle 12 Sur, No 18-168, El Poblado, Apdo Aéreo 8915, Medellín, Antioquia; tel. (4) 325-2270; fax (4) 317-0848; e-mail isa@isa.com.co; internet www.isa.com.co; f. 1967; created by Colombia's principal electricity production and distribution cos to form a national network; operations in Brazil, Ecuador, Peru, Bolivia and Central America; 52.9% state-owned; CEO Luis Fernando Alarcón Mantilla.

Isagen: Avda El Poblado, Carrera 43A, No 11A-80, Apdo Aereo 8762, Medellín, Antioquia; tel. (4) 316-5000; fax (4) 268-4646; e-mail isagen@isagen.com.co; internet www.isagen.com.co; f. 1995 following division of ISA (q.v.); 57.7% state-owned; generates electricity from three hydraulic and two thermal power plants; Gen. Man. Luis Fernando Rico Pinzón.

Gas

Empresa Colombiana de Gas (Ecogás): Of. 209, Centro Internacional de Negocios La Triada, Calle 35, No 19-41, Bucaramanga, Santander del Sur; tel. (7) 642-1000; fax (7) 642-6446; e-mail correspondencia@ecogas.com.co; internet www.ecogas.com.co; f. 1997; operation and maintenance of gas-distribution network; sold in 2006 to Empresa de Energía de Bogotá, SA; Dir Geronimo Manuel Guerra Cárdenas.

Gas Natural, SA ESP: Calle 71A, No 5-38, Bogotá, DC; tel. (1) 338-1199; fax (1) 288-0807; internet portal.gasnatural.com; f. 1987; owned by Gas Natural of Spain; distributes natural gas in Bogotá and Soacha; Dir-Gen. (Latin America) Sergio Aranda Moreno; Pres. María Eugenia Coronado.

TRADE UNIONS

Central Unitaria de Trabajadores de Colombia (CUT): Calle 35, No 7-25, 9°, Apdo Aéreo 221, Bogotá, DC; tel. and fax (1) 323-7550; e-mail comunicaciones@cut.org.co; internet www.cut.org.co; f. 1986; comprises 50 feds and 80% of all trade union members; Pres. Tarcisio Hora Godoy; Sec.-Gen. Domingo Tovar Arrieta.

Federación Colombiana de Educadores (FECODE): Carrera 13A, No 34-54, Bogotá, DC; tel. (1) 338-1711; fax (1) 285-3245; internet fecode.edu.co; Pres. Senén Niño Avendaño; Sec.-Gen. Luis Eduardo Varela.

Federación Nacional de Loteros (FECOLOT): Cale 27, No 25-38, Bogotá, DC; tel. (1) 232-1041; fax (1) 232-1045; lottery ticket sellers' union; Pres. Alberto Tarriba.

Federación Nacional Sindical Unitaria Agropecuaria (FENSUAGRO): Calle 17, No 10-16, Of. 104, Bogotá, DC; tel. (1) 286-7794; fax (1) 282-8871; e-mail fensuagro@hotmail.com; internet www.fensuagro.org; f. 1976 as Federación Nacional Sindical Agropecuaria (FENSA); comprises 37 unions, 7 peasant asscns, with 80,000 mems; Pres. Everto Díaz Montes.

Federación Nacional Sindicatos Bancarios Colombianos (FENASIBANCOL): Calle 30A, No 6-22, Of. 1601, Bogotá, DC; tel. (1) 287-5728; fax (1) 288-0235; e-mail fenasibancol@telecom.com.co; Pres. Roberto Moreno; Sec.-Gen. Cesar Augusto Cardenas.

Federación Nacional de Sindicatos de Trabajadores de Empresas y Entidades de Servicios Públicos y Oficiales (FENASINTRAP): Carrera 19, No 1C-47, Bogotá, DC; tel. (1) 246-4327; Pres. Roberto Rubiano Borja.

Federación Nacional de Trabajadores de Alimentación, Bebidas, Afines y Similar (Fentralimentación): Calle 8 sur, 68B-60, Bogotá, DC; tel. (1) 414-6505; fax (1) 290-0390; represents the food and drink industry; Pres. Alfonso López Freyle.

Federación Nacional de Trabajadores al Servicio del Estado (FENALTRASE): Calle 17, No 5-21, Of. 502, Bogotá, DC; tel. (1) 334-4815; e-mail fenaltrese@hotmail.com; Pres. Roberto Chamucero.

FUNTRAENERGETICA: Calle 16, No 13-49, Of. 201, Bogotá, DC; tel. (1) 334-0447; fax (1) 286-5259; e-mail funtraenergetica@colombia.com; f. 2001 following merger of Funtrammetal and Fedepetrol; represents workers in the energy sector; Pres. Joaquín Romero.

Unión Sindical Obrera de la Indústria del Petróleo (USO): Calle 38, No 13-37, Of. 302, Bogotá, DC; tel. (1) 234-4074; fax (1) 234-4399; e-mail prensa@usofrenteobrero.org; internet www.usofrenteobrero.org; f. 1922; petroleum workers' union; affiliated to CUT; Pres. Germán Alfredo Osman Mantilla; Sec.-Gen. Isnardo Lozano Gómez; 3,200 mems.

Unión de Trabajadores de Colombia (UTRAMMICOL): tel. (1) 288-5728; fax (1) 285-0663; e-mail utrammicol@multiphone.net.co; Pres. Luis Carlos Velásquez.

Confederación General del Trabajo (CGT): Calle 39A, No 14-52, Bogotá, DC; tel. (1) 288-1504; fax (1) 573-4021; e-mail cgt@etb.net.co; internet www.cgtcolombia.org; Sec.-Gen. Julio Roberto Gómez Esguerra.

Confederación de Trabajadores de Colombia (CTC) (Colombian Confederation of Workers): Calle 39, No 26A-23, 5°, Apdo Aéreo 4780, Bogotá, DC; tel. (1) 269-7119; e-mail ctc1@etb.net.co; internet www.ctc-colombia.com.co; f. 1934; mainly liberal; 600 affiliates, including 6 national orgs and 20 regional feds; admitted to the International Trade Union Confederation; Pres. Apecides Alvis Fernández; 400,000 mems.

Transport

Land transport in Colombia is rendered difficult by high mountains, so the principal means of long-distance transport is by air.

Superintendencia de Puertos y Transporte: Ministerio de Transporte, Edif. Estación de la Sabana, 3°, Calle 13, No 18-24, Bogotá, DC; tel. (2) 352-6700; e-mail info@superpuertos.gov.co; internet www.supertransporte.gov.co; f. 1992 as Superintendencia General de Puertos, present name adopted in 1998; part of the Ministry of Transport; oversees transport sector; Supt ALVARO HERNANDO CARDONA GONZÁLEZ.

Instituto Nacional de Concesiones (INCO): Edif. Ministerio de Transporte, Centro Administrativo Nacional (CAN), 3°, Avda El Dorado, Bogotá, DC; tel. (1) 324-0800; e-mail contactenos@inco.gov.co; internet www.inco.gov.co; govt agency charged with contracting devt of transport infrastructure to private operators; part of the Ministry of Transport; Gen. Man. ALVARO JOSÉ SOTO GARCÍA.

Instituto Nacional de Vías (INVIAS): Edif. INVIAS, Centro Administrativo Nacional (CAN), Carrera 59, No 26-60, Bogotá, DC; internet www.invias.gov.co; govt agency responsible for non-contracted transport infrastructure; Dir-Gen. ENRIQUE MARTÍNEZ ARCINIEGAS.

RAILWAYS

In 2000 there were 3,304 km of track. The Instituto Nacional de Concesiones (q.v.) operates the Red Ferrea del Atlántico and the Red Ferrea del Pacífico.

El Cerrejón Mine Railway: International Colombia Resources Corpn, Carrera 54, No 72-80, Apdo Aéreo 52499, Barranquilla, Atlántico; tel. (5) 350-5389; fax (5) 350-2249; internet www.elcerrejoncoal.com; f. 1989 to link the mine and the port at Puerto Bolívar; 150 km.

Ferrocarriles del Norte de Colombia, SA (FENOCO, SA): Calle 94A, No 11A-27, Bogotá, DC; tel. (1) 622-0505; operates the Concesión de la Red Férrea del Atlántico.

Metro de Medellín: Calle 44, No 46-001, Apdo Aéreo 9128, Medellín, Antioquia; tel. (4) 452-6000; fax (4) 452-4450; internet www.metrodemedellin.org.co; f. 1995; five-line metro system; Gen. Man. Dr RAMIRO MÁRQUEZ RAMÍREZ.

Sociedad de Transporte Férreo de Occidente, SA: Avda Vásquez Cobo, Estación Ferrocarril, 2°, Cali; tel. (2) 660-3314; fax (2) 660-3320; runs freight services between Cali and the port of Buenaventura.

Tren de Occidente, SA: Carrera 14, No 94A-24, Of. 202, Bogotá, DC; tel. (1) 635-9208; operates the Concesión de la Red Férrea del Pacífico.

ROADS

In 2002 there were 110,000 km of roads, of which 26,000 km were paved. The country's main highways are the Caribbean Trunk Highway, the Eastern and Western Trunk Highways and the Central Trunk Highway; there are also roads into the interior. There are plans to construct a Jungle Edge highway to give access to the interior, a link road between Turbo, Bahía Solano and Medellín, a highway between Bogotá and Villavicencio, and to complete the short section of the Pan-American Highway between Panama and Colombia.

Transmilenio: Edif. Ministerio de Transporte, Centro Administrativo Nacional (CAN), 3°, Avda El Dorado, No 66-63, Bogotá, DC; tel. (1) 220-3000; fax (1) 324-9870; internet www.transmilenio.gov.co; f. 2000; bus-based mass transit system in Bogotá.

INLAND WATERWAYS

The Magdalena–Cauca river system is the centre of river traffic and is navigable for 1,500 km, while the Atrato is navigable for 687 km. The Orinoco system has more than five navigable rivers, which total more than 4,000 km of potential navigation (mainly through Venezuela); the Amazon system has four main rivers, which total 3,000 navigable km (mainly through Brazil). There are plans to connect the Arauca with the Meta, and the Putumayo with the Amazon, and also to construct an Atrato–Truandó inter-oceanic canal.

SHIPPING

The four most important ocean terminals are Buenaventura on the Pacific coast and Santa Marta, Barranquilla and Cartagena on the Atlantic coast. The port of Tumaco on the Pacific coast is gaining in importance and there are plans for construction of a deep-water port at Bahía Solano. In December 2008 Colombia's merchant fleet comprised of 149 vessels, with a total displacement of some 91,400 grt.

Port Authorities

Sociedad Portuaria Regional de Barranquilla: Carrera 38, Calle 1A, Barranquilla, Atlántico; tel. (5) 371-6200; fax (5) 371-6310; e-mail info@sprb.com.co; internet www.sprb.com.co; privatized in 1993; Port Man. ERNESTO DURÁN GONZÁLEZ.

Sociedad Portuaria Regional de Buenaventura: Edif. de Administración, Avda Portuaria, Apdo 478-10765, Buenaventura; tel. 241-0700; internet www.puertobuenaventura.com; Port Man. VÍCTOR GONZÁLEZ.

Sociedad Portuaria Regional de Cartagena: Manga, Terminal Marítimo, Cartagena, Bolívar; tel. (5) 660-7781; fax (5) 650-2239; e-mail comercial@sprc.com.co; internet www.puertocartagena.com; f. 1993; Port Man. ALFONSO SALAS TRUJILLO.

Sociedad Portuaria de Santa Marta: Carrera 1, 10A-12, Apdo 655, Santa Marta; tel. (5) 421-1311; fax (5) 421-2161; e-mail spsm@spsm.com.co; internet www.spsm.com.co; Dir ARMANDO DUARTE-PELÁEZ; Gen. Man. MAURICIO SUÁREZ.

Principal Shipping Companies

Colombiana Internacional de Vapores, Ltda (Colvapores): Avda Caracas, No 35-02, Apdo Aéreo 17227, Bogotá, DC; e-mail colvabao@metrotel.net.co; internet www.colvapores.com; cargo services mainly to the USA.

Flota Mercante Grancolombiana, SA: Edif. Grancolombiana, Carrera 13, No 27-75, Apdo Aéreo 4482, Bogotá, DC; tel. (1) 286-0200; fax (1) 286-9028; f. 1946; owned by the Colombian Coffee Growers' Federation (80%) and Ecuador Development Bank (20%); one of Latin America's leading cargo carriers serving 45 countries world-wide; Pres. LUIS FERNANDO ALARCÓN MANTILLA.

Líneas Agromar, Ltda: Calle 73, Vía 40-350, Apdo Aéreo 3259, Barranquilla, Atlántico; tel. (5) 345-1111; fax (5) 345-9634; Pres. MANUEL DEL DAGO FERNÁNDEZ.

Naviera Blancamar, SA: El Bosque, No 20-05, Cartagena; tel. (5) 669-0197; fax (5) 662-3531.

Petromar Ltda: Bosque, Diagonal 23, No 56-152, Apdo Aéreo 505, Cartagena, Bolívar; tel. (5) 662-7208; fax (5) 662-7592; internet www.petromar.com; Pres. Capt. ALEX KOUTSAKIS.

Transportadora Colombiana de Graneles, SA (NAVESCO, SA): Avda 19, No 118-95, Of. 214-301, Bogotá, DC; tel. (1) 620-9035; fax (1) 620-8801; e-mail navesco@colomsat.net.co; Gen. Man. GUILLERMO SOLANO VARELA.

Several foreign shipping lines call at Colombian ports.

CIVIL AVIATION

Colombia has more than 100 airports, including 11 international airports: Bogotá, DC (El Dorado International Airport), Medellín, Cali, Barranquilla, Bucaramanga, Cartagena, Cúcuta, Leticia, Pereira, San Andrés and Santa Marta.

Airports Authority

Aeronaútica Civil (Aerocivil): Aeropuerto El Dorado, 4°, Bogotá, DC; tel. (1) 425-1000; e-mail quejasyreclamos@aerocivil.gov.co; internet www.aerocivil.gov.co; f. 1967 as Departamento Administrativo de Aeronáutica Civil, reorganized in 1992; part of the Ministry of Transport; develops and regulates the civil aviation industry; Pres. ANDRÉS URIEL GALLEGO.

National Airlines

AIRES (Aerovías de Integración Regional): El Dorado International Airport, Bogotá, DC; internet www.aires.com.co; f. 1981; domestic and international passenger services, domestic cargo services; CEO FRANCISCO JOSÉ MENDEZ GARCÍA.

AVIANCA (Aerovías Nacionales de Colombia, SA): Avda El Dorado, No 93-30, 5°, Bogotá, DC; tel. (1) 413-9511; fax (1) 413-8716; internet www.avianca.com; f. 1919; operates domestic services to all cities in Colombia and international services to the USA, France, Spain and throughout Central and Southern America; in Oct. 2009 announced merger with TACA of El Salvador (q.v.); Chair. ANDRÉS OBREGÓN SANTO DOMINGO; Pres. FABIO VILLEGAS.

Satena (Servicio de Aeronavegación a Territorios Nacionales): Avda El Dorado, No 103-08, Apdo Aéreo 11163, Bogotá, DC; tel. (1) 423-8530; e-mail presidencia@satena.com; internet www.satena.com; f. 1962; commercial enterprise attached to the Ministry of National Defence; internal services; CEO and Gen. Man. Gen. HECTOR CAMPO.

Tampa Cargo, SA: Terminal Internacional de Carga, Bodega 1, Avda El Dorado, No 116-87, Bogotá, DC; tel. (1) 439-7900; fax (1) 439-7998; e-mail info@tampacargo.com.co; internet www.tampacargo.com.co; f. 1973; operates international cargo services to destinations throughout the Americas; Exec. Dir RODRIGO PLATA.

In addition, Aerosucre and Líneas Aéreas Suramericanas (LAS) operate international and domestic charter cargo services.

Tourism

The principal tourist attractions are the Caribbean coast (including the island of San Andrés), the 16th-century walled city of Cartagena, the Amazonian town of Leticia, the Andes mountains rising to 5,700m above sea-level, the extensive forests and jungles, pre-Columbian relics and monuments of colonial art. In 2007 there were 1,195,443 visitors (compared with 1,053,348 in 2006), most of whom came from the USA, Ecuador and Venezuela. In 2008 tourism receipts were US $1,844m.

Ministry of Trade, Industry and Tourism: Edif. Centro de Comercio Internacional, Calle 28, No 13A-15, 18°, Bogotá, DC; tel. (1) 606-7676; fax (1) 696-7521; internet www.mincomercio.gov.co; Deputy Minister responsible for Tourism OSCAR RUEDA GARCÍA.

Asociación Colombiana de Agencias de Viajes y Turismo (ANATO): Carrera 19B, No 83-63, Apdo Aereo 7088, Bogotá, DC; tel. (1) 610-7099; fax (1) 236-2424; e-mail direccionejecutiva@anato.org; internet www.anato.org; f. 1949; Pres. Dr SERGIO DÍAZ-GRANADOS GUIDA; Exec. Dir ZULLY OSPINA DE COZZI.

Defence

As assessed at November 2009, Colombia's armed forces numbered 285,220, of whom the army comprised 237,466, the navy 34,620 (including 14,000 marines and 7,200 conscripts) and the air force 13,134. In addition there were some 61,900 reservists, of whom 54,700 were in the army, 4,800 in the navy, 1,200 in the air force and 1,200 in the joint services. There was also a paramilitary National Police Force numbering 144,097. Military service is compulsory for men (except for students) and lasts for 12–24 months.

Defence Budget: an estimated 12,100,000m. pesos in 2009.

Chief of Staff of the Armed Forces: Gen. FREDDY PADILLA DE LEÓN.

Commander of the Army: Gen. OSCAR ENRIQUE GONZÁLEZ PEÑA.

Commander of the Navy: Adm. GUILLERMO ENRIQUE BARRERA HURTADO.

Commander of the Air Force: Gen. JORGE BALLESTEROS RODRÍGUEZ.

Education

Education in Colombia commences at nursery level for children under six years of age. Primary education is free and compulsory for five years. Admission to secondary school is conditional upon the successful completion of these five years. Secondary education is for four years. Following completion of this period, pupils may pursue a further two years of vocational study, leading to the Bachiller examination. In 2008 a total of 4,927,782 students were in primary education and 4,231,718 attended secondary schools. In 2007/08 enrolment at primary and secondary schools included 90% and 71% of the school-age population, respectively. In 2009 there were an estimated 55,501 primary schools and 13,280 secondary schools. In 2007 there were 32 public universities in Colombia.

Bibliography

For works on South America generally, see Select Bibliography (Books)

Alesina, A. *Institutional Reforms: The Case of Colombia*. Cambridge, MA, MIT Press, 2005.

Ardila Galvis, C. *The Heart of the War in Colombia*. London, Latin America Bureau, 2000.

Aviles, W. *Global Capitalism, Democracy, and Civil-Military Relations in Colombia*. Albany, NY, State University of New York Press, 2007.

Bergquist, C. W. *Violence in Colombia, 1990–2000: Waging War and Negotiating Peace*. Wilmington, DC, Scholarly Resources Inc, 2001.

Betancourt, I. *Until Death Do Us Part: My Struggle to Reclaim Colombia*. London, Ecco Press, 2001.

Brittain, J. J. *Revolutionary Social Change in Colombia: The Origin and Direction of the FARC–EP*. London, Pluto Press, 2009.

Crandall, R. *Driven by Drugs: US Policy Toward Colombia*. 2nd Edn, Boulder, CO, Lynne Rienner Publrs, 2008.

Croce, E. *Programación Financiera: Métodos y Aplicación al caso de Colombia*. Washington, DC, IMF Publications, 2002.

Dudley, S. *Walking Ghosts: Murder and Guerrilla Politics in Colombia*. London, Routledge, 2004.

Earle, R. A. *Spain and the Independence of Colombia, 1808–1825*. Exeter, University of Exeter Press, 2000.

Gow, D. G. *Countering Development: Indigenous Modernity and the Moral Imagination*. Durham, NC, Duke University Press, 2008.

Hartlyn, J. *The Politics of Coalition Rule in Colombia*. Cambridge, Cambridge University Press, 2008.

Henderson, J. *Modernization in Colombia: The Laureano Gómez Years, 1889–1965*. Gainesville, FL, University Press of Florida, 2001.

Hernández Gamarra, A. *A Monetary History of Colombia*. Bogotá, DC, Villegas Editores, 2002.

Hinojosa, V. J. *Domestic Politics and International Narcotics Control*. London, Taylor & Francis, 2007.

Jaramillo, F. *Liberalization and Crisis in Colombian Agriculture*. Boulder, CO, Westview Press, 1998.

Kirk, R. *More Terrible Than Death: Drugs, Violence, and America's War in Colombia*. Jackson, TN, Perseus Books, 2004.

Kline, H. F. *State Building and Conflict Resolution in Colombia, 1986–1994*. Tuscaloosa, AL, University of Alabama Press, 1999.

Chronicle of a Failure Foretold: The Peace Process of Colombian President Andrés Pastrana. Tuscaloosa, AL, University of Alabama Press, 2007.

Livingstone, G. *Inside Colombia: Drugs, Democracy and War*. London, Latin America Bureau, 2002.

Londoño-Vega, P. *Religion, Society and Culture in Colombia: Antioquia and Medellín, 1850–1930*. Oxford, Clarendon Press, 2002.

McFarlane, A. *Colombia Before Independence*. Cambridge, Cambridge University Press, 2002.

Rausch, J. *Colombia: Territorial Rule and the Llanos Frontier*. Gainesville, FL, University Press of Florida, 1999.

Richani, N. *Systems of Violence: The Political Economy of War and Peace in Colombia*. Albany, NY, State University of New York Press, 2002.

Ruiz, B. *The Colombian Civil War*. Jefferson, NC, McFarland & Co, 2001.

Safford, F., and Palacios, M. *Colombia: Fragmented Land, Divided Society*. Oxford, Oxford University Press, 2001.

Sanchez, G., and Meertens, D. *Bandits, Peasants and Politics: The Case of 'La Violencia' in Colombia*. Austin, TX, University of Texas Press, 2001.

Schott, J. J. (Ed.). *Trade Relations between Colombia and the United States*. Washington, DC, Peterson Institute for International Economics, 2006.

Simons, G. *Colombia: A Brutal History*. London, Saqi Books, 2004.

Velez, A. U. *Showing Teeth to the Dragons*. Tuscaloosa, AL, University of Alabama Press, 2009.

Welna, C., and Galón, G. (Eds). *Peace, Democracy, and Human Rights in Colombia*. Notre Dame, IN, University of Notre Dame Press, 2007.

COSTA RICA

Geography

PHYSICAL FEATURES

The Republic of Costa Rica is the southernmost of the Central American countries, with Panama beyond the southern frontier (330 km or 205 miles in length). Nicaragua lies to the north (309 km). Although the border with Panama is across a narrower part of the isthmus, it is more convoluted and, therefore, longer. The country has coasts on both the Pacific (1,015 km) and the Caribbean (usually referred to as the Atlantic coast—212 km). The territory of the country includes the rugged Isla del Coco (Cocos Island), some 480 km south-west of continental Costa Rica. The country has a dispute with Nicaragua over navigational rights on the San Juan river on the border, exacerbated by the presence of many illegal Nicaraguan immigrants in the country. Costa Rica has a total area of 51,100 sq km (19,730 sq miles).

The San Juan, the outflow of Lake Nicaragua, flows into the Pacific and forms much of the north-eastern border. In the north-west the border skirts the south-western edges of Lake Nicaragua, to the east of the Cordillera de Guanacaste, on the Pacific side of which is the Nicoya peninsula. These mountains head inland eventually to join the higher, central ranges, culminating in the Cordillera de Talamanca, which thrusts up the spine of the country from the south. The region is also volcanic, with four volcanoes near San José, the capital, two of them active: Irazu last erupted destructively in the mid-1960s. The highest point is south of here at Cerro Chirripo (3,810 m or 12,504 ft), in the rugged Talamanca range. The capital city is located in a fertile, upland basin, the Meseta Central Valley, at an altitude of about 1,170 m. On either side of the mountains are coastal plains, the Pacific coast being more irregular in outline and the Atlantic coast lower, swampier and heavily forested (almost one-third of the country is wooded). Costa Rica is about 460 km at its maximum length, its axis running from south-east to north-west, with the northern border the widest part of the country (260 km). The country is very fertile and rich in biodiversity, among the most intense in the world, with a massive range of flora and fauna, notably bird life, flourishing in a huge range of ecosystems. Thirty nature reserves cover some 11% of the territory, with about twice as much again also gaining some form of protection, sheltering more than 200 species of mammals (including six species of wild cat), over 850 species of birds (including endemic species, such as two types of hummingbird and a tanager), 1,000 butterfly types and almost 200 amphibians and 220 reptiles. The country is reckoned to contain up to 13,000 varieties of flowering plant and 10% of the world's birds and butterflies. The isolation of the Isla del Coco has created another unspoilt natural haven for both land and marine life (here alone are three endemic bird species: the Cocos finch, flycatcher and cuckoo).

CLIMATE

The climate is tropical and subtropical, varied by the highlands and the competing weather systems of the Pacific and the Caribbean. The dry season is December–April. The onset of the rainy (or green) season can bring flooding in the coastal lowlands and, later, landslides in the mountainous interior, in a topography complicated by earthquakes and active volcanoes.

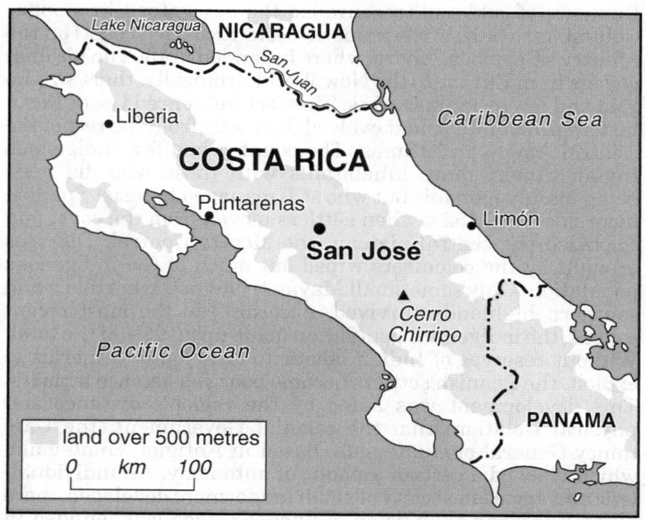

Hurricanes are likely along the Caribbean coast, where rainfall is greater than on the Pacific coast. Rainfall is also greater in the mountains. Annual precipitation varies enormously according to location, some places recording a remarkable 6,000 mm (234 ins), others as relatively little as 1,500 mm. The average for the whole country is 3,300 mm. Temperatures vary mainly with altitude, the coast experiencing thermometer readings between about 27°C and 32°C (81°–90°F), the Central Valley around 22°C (72°F) and the mountains being cooler still.

POPULATION

The white and Mestizo or mixed-race population, mainly of Spanish descent, accounts for 94% of the total, with blacks at 3%, and Amerindians and Chinese at 1% each. Traditionally a Roman Catholic country, the denomination still enjoys the adherence of about four-fifths of the population; however, evangelical Christian groups have gained many new followers, and non-Catholic Christians now represent more than one-sixth of the population. Spanish is the official language, but some English is spoken around Puerto Limón, which is the heart of black Creole culture, on the Caribbean. The Amerindian languages spoken in Costa Rica are all of the Chibcha group. Costa Ricans refer to themselves informally as 'Ticos'.

About one-half of the total population of 4.6m. (mid-2010 estimate) live in the central plateau (Meseta Central) around San José, the capital. There are several other large population centres in that region, but the principal cities of the Pacific coast are Puntarenas, on the Gulf of Nicoya, in the north-west, and further north, inland, Liberia. The main city of the Atlantic coast is Limón. Another important demographic statistic is the large number of foreign tourists who visit annually; these totalled 2.1m. in 2008. The country consists of seven provinces.

History

CATHY MCILWAINE

Based on earlier articles by Prof. JENNY PEARCE and DIEGO SÁNCHEZ-ANCOCHEA

Rumours of gold and treasure led the navigator Christopher Columbus to bestow the name of Costa Rica (rich coast) on the country's Caribbean shore, where he landed in 1502 on his final voyage from Europe to the New World. Ironically, there was no gold and few other resources. This fact influenced Costa Rican history profoundly and it evolved distinctly from the rest of the Central American isthmus. The country had few indigenous Indian (Amerindian) inhabitants with those who did exist being mainly nomadic but who still managed to resist Spanish incursion until 1522, when settlers moved from the coast and colonized the central plateau, the Meseta Central. Diseases brought by the colonizers wiped out much of the indigenous population. Only some small Mayan tribes in the northern and southern highlands survived. According to the most recent census, the indigenous population made up just 1% of the total. Without reserves of Indian labour to draw on or minerals to exploit, the Spanish settlers became poor subsistence farmers. This development was aided by the region's distance and physical isolation from the colonial Government, the Captaincy-General of Guatemala, based in Antigua, Guatemala, which allowed a certain amount of autonomy. An individualistic and agrarian society of small landowners developed, more along European than colonial lines. Cartago was founded in 1563, but there was no expansion of settlement until the beginning of the 18th century, when small groups left the Meseta Central to establish other cities. San José, now the capital of Costa Rica, was founded in 1737.

INDEPENDENCE

Costa Rica joined the other countries of the region in their declaration of independence from Spain in 1821 (following the Spanish Revolution of 1820). It became part of the newly formed Mexican Empire, which lasted for two years until 1823, when Costa Rica joined the United Provinces of Central America. When the federation collapsed in 1838 Costa Rica became an independent republic. Costa Rica's early governments were civilian, in contrast to the rest of the isthmus.

Coffee, introduced from Cuba in 1808, became the motor of Costa Rica's development. The Government offered free land and trees to coffee growers, encouraging the development of a large landowning peasantry, with a small aristocracy. The opening of the European market in 1845 and the establishment of a cart road to the port of Puntarenas on the Pacific the following year hastened development. In 1890 a railway opened between San José and Puerto Limón on the Caribbean, along the Reventazón valley. This facilitated the foundation of coffee plantations outside the Meseta Central towards the east. Bananas were introduced around Puerto Limón in 1878 by the United Fruit Company. Jamaican labourers were brought to Costa Rica to clear large areas of land along the Caribbean coast and to work on the plantations; when production reached its peak, in 1913, interest was then shown in the Pacific coast.

THE MOVE TOWARDS STABILITY

Between 1835 and 1899 Costa Rica was under military rule for one-half of the period as Conservative and Liberal élites contested power. However, in the early 20th century rising literacy rates increased political participation dramatically, laying the foundations for one of Latin America's most successful democratic systems. Progress was reversed briefly in 1917, when Federico Tinoco ousted the elected President, Alfredo González, who had introduced new taxes and reforms damaging to the coffee aristocracy. Two years later Tinoco's military dictatorship was ousted by a combination of popular revolt and guerrilla activity by Costa Rican exiles in Nicaragua. Julio Acosta's 1919 election victory restored democracy and constitutional order until 1948. The Communist party had grown powerful through the recession of the 1930s, taking especially strong hold in the union movement based in the banana plantations. However, it abandoned revolutionary policies in favour of social welfare, working with the Government of Dr Rafael Angel Calderón Guardia in the 1940s to introduce labour safeguards and a social security system. Calderón also formed an unlikely alliance with the Roman Catholic Church. The presidential election campaign of 1948 was characterized by violent protests, including a 15-day general strike. When the opposition candidate, Otilio Ulate Blanco, won, the government candidate, Calderón, contested the result and it was nullified. In March 1948 José Figueres Ferrer, a coffee farmer, led an uprising in support of Ulate. A month of fighting ensued until a truce was agreed, and Santos León Herrera was installed as the interim President. In May the Constitution was abrogated and Figueres and his junta took over government. A constitutional assembly convened in January 1949, formulating a new Constitution, which abolished the army, assigning its budget to education. During its months in office, the junta also nationalized the banking system and created a bureaucracy, which would become a strong political force during the second half of the 20th century. In November the junta resigned and Ulate, the President-elect, was inaugurated.

THE EMERGENCE OF THE PLN

Figueres, a social democrat, found Ulate too moderate, and withdrew his support for his presidency in 1952, forming the Partido de Liberación Nacional (PLN). He dominated Costa Rican politics for the next two decades, serving as President between 1953 and 1958 and, again, from 1970 to 1974. The PLN developed the so-called 'tico' model of heavy state intervention. The Figueres Governments and that of his PLN successor between 1974 and 1978, Daniel Oduber Quirós, nationalized large areas of the economy and extended the welfare state. Between 1958 and 1980 public social spending as a proportion of gross domestic product (GDP) increased from 8.7% to 23.6%. Intervening conservative administrations tended to favour private enterprise but were prevented from reducing state benefits by public opinion. Conservative government returned between 1978 and 1982 under Rodrigo Carazo Odio.

Elections in February 1982 gave a decisive victory to the PLN's presidential candidate, Luis Alberto Monge Alvarez, with 58% of the votes cast. The PLN also won a clear working majority in the Asamblea Legislativa (Legislative Assembly). The Monge administration was confronted by two big challenges: the domestic economic crisis and the external problem of conflict in the region, focusing on Costa Rica's northern neighbour, Nicaragua.

THE ARIAS PRESIDENCY

Although the Monge Government achieved only limited economic success, the PLN won a decisive, if surprising, victory at the presidential and legislative elections in February 1986. The PLN's victory was attributed to the dynamism and youth of its leader, Oscar Arias Sánchez, who, at the age of 44, was the youngest President in the country's history. It was also a reaction against the extremism of his main opponent, the right-wing Rafael Angel Calderón Fournier, the son of the former President. On taking office, President Arias announced his desire for the country to pursue a more independent policy, while at the same time recognizing the necessity of maintaining good relations with the USA to ensure continued foreign aid. The Government was keen to emphasize its commitment to the welfare state, promising the creation of 25,000 jobs and 20,000 dwellings each year.

However, its principal aim was reform of the economy through the promotion of a market-friendly model that concentrated on the promotion of exports. This set the political pattern for the following administrations, all of which promoted neo-liberal reforms in the face of protests from a citizenry nourished on 40 years of state-sponsored welfare. The Government renegotiated its huge public debt after its 1982 default. However, it had to agree to a number of structural adjustment policies with the IMF. Public sector strikes in 1988 were followed by protests by farmers, who were unhappy with the Government's policy of promoting the cultivation of cash crops to appease the IMF. Labour unrest increased in 1989 as trade unions, professional bodies and civic groups united to demonstrate against the Government. However, President Arias could claim substantial economic success. As well as the renegotiation of the country's foreign debt, during his term of office GDP grew by 4% each year, the annual inflation rate was reduced to less than 10% and unemployment declined to less than 4% of the total labour force.

In September 1989 a report by the Asamblea Legislativa's commission of inquiry into the extent of drugs-trafficking and related activities was published. The report was a blow to the PLN, as it implicated many political and business figures of involvement in illegal activities. This scandal, combined with a general desire for change, led to the victory of Calderón, of the Partido Unidad Social Cristiana (PUSC), in the presidential election of February 1990. The PUSC also secured a majority in the Asamblea Legislativa.

FROM CALDERÓN TO RODRÍGUEZ

The battle over the future of Costa Rica's welfare state and public sector utilities continued to dominate politics in the 1990s. It divided the country deeply and led to a gradual erosion of confidence in politicians and the political system. Costa Ricans were justifiably protective of the exceptional social harmony that the country enjoyed compared with others in the region. Nevertheless, economic adjustment measures adopted in order to qualify for further IMF credits and loans threatened the 'welfarism' that underpinned that harmony.

The presidency of Calderón (1990–94) was dominated by this issue. Overall economic performance during his administration was good, but the Government's privatization programme and reductions in expenditure on education and public health increased social and political tensions. The opposition PLN prevented the realization of the third phase of the structural-adjustment programme in 1993 by voting against its approval in the Asamblea Legislativa.

In 1994 José María Figueres Olsen, son of José Figueres Ferrer, the former President, stood as the PLN's presidential candidate, promising to improve housing, education, health and other social programmes, rather than implement the public sector reforms agreed by President Calderón with the World Bank. With this manifesto Figueres obtained a narrow victory in the elections of 6 February. As President, however, Figueres rapidly converted to free market economics: during 1995 he restored relations with the IMF and the World Bank by agreeing to a new structural adjustment programme, and signed a letter of intent with the IMF, which led to the release of loans from the Inter-American Development Bank (IDB) and the World Bank. Figueres sought to raise taxes to reduce the large and persistent fiscal deficit. In April the Government concluded an agreement with the opposition PUSC to ensure the implementation of tax increases and austerity measures agreed with the IMF. The PUSC was divided over this support for Figueres, while the President succeeded in consolidating his position within his own party, in spite of internal opposition to his shift to neo-liberal policies.

However, within the country as a whole social unrest increased. In 1996 protests and strikes led to the suspension of plans to privatize the energy and telecommunications monopoly, the Instituto Costarricense de Electricidad (ICE), in favour of a restructuring plan. Figueres's popularity decreased dramatically in 1995–96 as living standards fell, taxes increased, and the social spending that protected many Costa Ricans from poverty was drastically reduced. A presidential election in February 1998 resulted in victory for Miguel Angel Rodríguez Echeverría of the PUSC. The PUSC obtained 27 seats in the Asamblea Legislativa, compared with the PLN's 23 seats. There was a 28% abstention rate, compared with 19% in 1994, demonstrating the level of public disillusionment with the established parties.

THE RODRÍGUEZ ADMINISTRATION AND THE ACCELERATION OF SOCIAL CONFLICT

President Rodríguez, a neo-liberal economist, sought further to extend the process of liberalization and deregulation. He attracted foreign investment, signed free trade agreements and lowered tariff barriers. Annual GDP growth averaged more than 4% during his administration, but was confined to the new export-orientated sectors such as information technology, located in the free trade zones, and tourism. Traditional areas such as farming, food processing and manufacturing suffered, and most Costa Ricans did not feel the benefit of the economic expansion. Moreover, Rodríguez suffered a serious reverse in April 2000, when the largest popular protests in 30 years forced the Government to withdraw legislation that would have opened the energy and telecommunications industries to private investment. The protests reflected the popularity of the ICE among most Costa Ricans, but also the opposition of a majority of the population to the Government's neo-liberal policies. The privatization debate encapsulated the difficulties in implementing unpopular economic reforms aimed at reducing the level of state intervention in the economy.

In December 2000 Ottón Solís Fallas, a former PLN deputy and a former Minister of Planning, formed a breakaway party, the Partido de Acción Ciudadana (PAC). He sought to take advantage of social discontent with the economic reforms of the 1990s and the electorate's disillusionment with the two traditional parties. He attracted many members of the PLN and was able to use their experience to develop a national structure with surprising speed. He also attracted non-voters and some PUSC supporters.

The PAC campaigned for the February 2002 presidential and legislative elections on an anti-corruption platform and also pledged to halt privatization and free trade agreements. It won over many young, well-educated people, as well as rural voters. Rodolfo Araya Monge, who emerged as the PLN's presidential candidate, also promised assistance to farmers and other groups affected by economic liberalization. However, Abel Pacheco de la Espriella, the PUSC's nominee, surprisingly managed best to address the country's unease and won the election. Pacheco attracted 39% of the first round ballot, compared with Araya's 31%. Solís's strong performance in the first round of voting, when he was placed third with 26% of the vote, necessitated a second round of voting on 7 April. Pacheco won this, with 58% of the votes cast, against 42% polled by Araya. It was the first time that the PLN had lost successive elections and the result left it badly weakened. The success of the PAC in concurrently held legislative elections, together with a strong showing by the neo-liberal Movimiento Libertario (ML), signalled a transformation of the Costa Rican political system from a two-party to a multiparty system.

THE PACHECO ADMINISTRATION: SOCIAL STALEMATE AND CORRUPTION SCANDALS

President Pacheco's Government struggled to cope with a disaffected public and a divided legislature. At his inauguration in May 2002 Pacheco promised to be conciliatory while continuing to pursue moderate reform. His first challenge was to reduce the fiscal deficit to avoid further debt increases. The previous month a cross-party commission of former finance ministers had presented its long-delayed report, which concluded that higher taxes and reduced spending were needed to avoid severe financial and social instability by 2006. The main proposals were the replacement of sales tax with value-added tax and an extension of profits tax to the export zones. Along with a 3% reduction in spending, the moves would eliminate the fiscal deficit. However, the measures were unpopular. While the Government won legislative approval in December 2002 for a series of temporary tax rises and spending cuts, it was unable to implement a more permanent tax reform. The reform was approved by the Asamblea Legislativa, but was declared unconstitutional by the Constitutional Court in March 2006.

Tentative steps towards introducing the free market into traditionally publicly run areas proved politically costly and the Government faced continuous opposition. In October 2002 plans for a private US company to supervise the construction and staffing of a new maximum-security prison met with controversy. Following his objections to private sector involvement in the scheme, the Minister of Justice, José Miguel Villalobos, was dismissed. In early 2003 electrical workers failed to receive salary bonuses and further plans by the Government to reduce the ICE budget were criticized by unions and the institute's directors. ICE employees began strike action in May. At the same time, teachers also began industrial action in protest at their salary and pension arrangements. The disputes resulted in the resignation of the Ministers of Finance, Presidential Affairs and Education before the Government capitulated to the ICE's demands. In September 2004 protests by civil servants led to an increase in public sector wages. The Minister of Finance's opposition to this measure led to his resignation, which in turn provoked the departure of seven senior government officials. This brought to 14 the number of cabinet members who had resigned or been dismissed during Pacheco's administration.

Political uncertainty increased even further with the disclosure of two major corruption scandals in late 2004. The first involved the alleged payment of commissions to senior managers of the Costa Rican social security institute, the Caja Costarricense de Seguro Social (CCSS), a member of its board of directors and former President Calderón Fournier. Another finding of illegal commissions, this time in the ICE, followed this first scandal: the French telecommunication transnational corporation Alcatel allegedly made payments of several million US dollars to former President Rodríguez, as well as to senior ICE officials, in order to secure a lucrative contract. The corruption scandals resulted in the preventive imprisonment of both former Presidents (as well as Rodríguez's resignation as Secretary-General of the Organization of American States), and also affected the popular standing of the PUSC and of the PLN, the latter after it was alleged that a third former President, Figueres Olsen, also received payments from Alcatel, although no formal charges were made. Calderón's hearing did not begin until early 2008 and in November 2009 he was found guilty and sentenced to five years' imprisonment for misuse of public funds. Rodríguez's trial was ongoing in July 2010.

THE SECOND ARIAS ADMINISTRATION: A MIXED RECORD

On 5 February 2006 former President Arias, whose candidacy was permitted following a decision by the Constitutional Court in April 2003 to allow the re-election of former heads of state, won the presidential election by fewer than 20,000 votes. Arias, the PLN nominee, obtained 40.9% of the total votes cast, against 39.8% for Solís, the candidate of the PAC. The Asamblea Legislativa was also split: the PLN won 25 seats, while the PAC obtained 18, the right-wing ML secured six, and four small independent parties each took one seat. The PUSC was severely affected by the corruption scandal, securing only four legislative seats.

The elections and the first two years of the Arias administration were dominated by debates over the Dominican Republic-Central American Free Trade Agreement (DR-CAFTA) between five Spanish-speaking Central American countries (Costa Rica, El Salvador, Guatemala, Honduras and Nicaragua), the Dominican Republic and the USA. The free trade accord had been signed in May 2004 and by January 2005 had been approved by all seven signatories, but it still needed to be ratified by each country's legislature. The Agreement required Costa Rica to open three sectors of the telecommunications market—namely private network services, internet services and wireless services—and establish a regulatory framework, with the aim of promoting effective market access. Furthermore, the Agreement committed Costa Rica to a full liberalization of the insurance sector by 1 January 2011. DR-CAFTA had the support of Arias, Pacheco and a majority of the business sector, but was opposed by trade unions, universities and other groups in civil society. Opposition to DR-CAFTA galvanized the vote against Arias and helped Solís, who favoured its renegotiation, to obtain a large number of votes.

The schism over DR-CAFTA remained after the elections. In February 2007 thousands of Costa Ricans marched in the streets against the agreement, highlighting increasing social polarization. In April the Tribunal Supremo de Elecciones (TSE) granted the opposition's request to collect signatures (equivalent to 5% of the electorate) for a referendum on DR-CAFTA. The Arias administration responded by proposing a referendum of its own, which finally took place on 7 October 2007. After a spirited campaign in which the Government outspent the opposition, the Agreement was approved by a slim majority, with the 'yes' campaign garnering 51.6% of the total vote. In the subsequent months, the Asamblea Legislativa approved all the laws that were required as part of the Implementation Agenda, and on 1 January 2009 Costa Rica become the last signatory of DR-CAFTA to join the Agreement.

The approval of DR-CAFTA resulted in a short-term increase in the popularity of President Arias, but the Government was soon forced to respond to other challenges. An increase in the prices of food and petroleum during 2008 resulted in a rise in poverty levels. The global financial crisis also affected Costa Rica particularly severely. In February 2009 the Arias administration announced a stimulus package, called 'Plan Escudo', which expanded social programmes (including an increase in state pensions), created housing subsidies and promoted new infrastructure projects. The programme, financed with new loans from the World Bank and the IDB, was unable to avert a recession in the first half of the year. However, Plan Escudo did mitigate the economic downturn and also strengthened the popularity of the Arias administration in its last days in office, paving the way for the PLN candidate in the 2010 presidential election, Laura Chinchilla Miranda.

THE CHINCHILLA ADMINISTRATION: CONSENSUS-BUILDING

On 7 February 2010 Laura Chinchilla became Costa Rica's first woman President. Despite predictions that she would not win enough votes (40%) for a first round victory, Chinchilla won a comfortable 46.9% of the ballot against her main rivals, Ottón Solís Fallas of the PAC, who received 25.1% of votes and Otto Guevara Guth of the right-wing ML, with 20.9%. Analysts suggest that the PLN victory was the result of the failure of the opposition to unite into a single coalition owing to their ideological differences, which in turn reflected the wider fragmentation of the two-party system in Costa Rica. Despite this, on taking office in May, President Chinchilla did not have a simple majority in the Asamblea Legislativa; the PLN held only 24 of the 57 seats. The rest were held by seven other parties: the PAC (11 seats), the ML (nine seats), the PUSC (six seats), the Partido Accesibilidad sin Exclusión (four seats), and a further three minority parties with one seat each. This lack of a majority would make it difficult for Chinchilla to govern, making it essential for her to make alliances and build consensus across the parties. Indeed, her inaugural promise was to co-operate with all political parties and citizens and to craft agreements. Her Government followed closely in the footsteps of the previous Arias administration in which she served as Vice-President and Minister of Justice. Since taking office, the PLN has made an informal alliance with the ML on security reform and was expected to seek support from the PAC in order to approve higher rates of social spending.

As well as needing to build consensus, President Chinchilla's administration would provide continuity with the Arias administration in encouraging further foreign investment, free trade agreements and public–private partnerships in infrastructure development, as well as increased social welfare spending, especially on health and education. Arias's Plan Escudo was likely to continue at least throughout 2010. Chinchilla also fully supported the privatization processes established by entry into DR-CAFTA in 2009 (which were vehemently opposed by the PAC). The new President also planned to implement security measures to address problems of crime and drugs-trafficking. These policies, and especially social spending, would require tax reform which was widely resisted by the opposition. It was also anticipated that the fiscal deficit would grow to 3.7% of GDP in 2010 and that the inflation rate would remain at about 6%.

President Chinchilla's first month in office was difficult as she was forced to veto controversial legislation that entailed a 70% increase in legislators' salaries (on grounds that other public sector wages were much higher). Although the PLN initiated the bill and all parties supported it, popular opposition made it impossible for Chinchilla to vote in favour of it. This raised questions as to how far she would be able to forge alliances in order to make other necessary reforms. In addition, confusion was caused when three nominees for public positions had to resign because of problems with the nomination procedures (the Chief Executive officer of the national women's institute, Instituto Nacional de las Mujeres, a senior official at the Ministry of Culture, Youth and Sports, and the Ambassador to the UN). The main challenge for the Chinchilla administration in the next four years was to emphasize its ability to co-ordinate policies and to build alliances across the political spectrum.

FOREIGN POLICY: FROM REGIONAL CONFLICT TO TRADE CONFLICTS

Following the restoration of relative peace to the Central American region in the early 1990s,Costa Rican foreign policy was dominated by trade issues. Costa Rica, together with Chile and Mexico, has been one of the most active negotiators of free trade agreements in Latin America. The country sought to join the North American Free Trade Agreement (NAFTA), indicating the priority of trade relations with the USA and Mexico over those with its neighbours in the Central American Common Market. Costa Rica signed a free trade agreement with Mexico in 1994, giving some 86% of Costa Rican exports duty-free access to the Mexican market.

In December 2000 Costa Rica ratified a free trade agreement with Chile, and in November 2002 a similar accord with Canada came into effect. The return to power in 2006 of President Arias led again to a more critical view of the US Administration. Arias withdrew Costa Rican support for the ongoing conflict in Iraq and made critical statements about the expansionist approach of the USA under President George W. Bush. Nevertheless, the Arias Government sought to implement DR-CAFTA (see above) with the USA, which was expected to expand Costa Rican exports further. In December 2006 the Central American countries also began negotiating an association agreement with the European Union (EU). Costa Rica initially adopted a cautious position in the negotiations, but by the signing of the agreement in May 2010 had become a leading proponent of the accord.

The Arias administration effected other significant changes in foreign policy. In 2006 Costa Rica, together with El Salvador, moved its embassy in Israel from Jerusalem to Tel Aviv. In 2007 Costa Rica broke diplomatic relations with Taiwan and became the first Central American country to enter into diplomatic relations with the People's Republic of China. Both of these measures helped Costa Rica to secure a non-permanent seat on the UN Security Council in October 2007. In March 2009 Costa Rica re-established diplomatic relations with Cuba, which had been severed in 1961.

Relations with Nicaragua during the second Arias administration remained tense, despite several meetings between President Arias and the Nicaraguan President Daniel Ortega. Sporadic conflicts between both countries have occurred in the last 15 years. A long-running dispute over sovereignty of the San Juan river, which forms the border between the two countries, was finally settled in July 2009 following a final ruling by the International Court of Justice, to the satisfaction of both countries. However, tensions persisted over maritime rights and different positions in the negotiations of the association agreement with the EU and in the promotion of regional integration resulted in further discord between the two Governments in 2009.

Deepening regional integration would continue under the Chinchilla administration. The Central American free trade agreement with the EU was signed in May 2010 and was expected to be ratified in 2011. In February 2010 free trade agreement talks with Singapore and China paved the way for Costa Rica to seek to join the Asia-Pacific Economic Co-operation (APEC) group in 2011. China, in particular, was expected to increase its investment in Costa Rica, especially in the energy and manufacturing sectors. Relations with the USA continued to be strong, facilitated especially through DR-CAFTA.

OUTLOOK

The negotiations over DR-CAFTA brought into sharp focus the deep divisions within Costa Rican society and the mounting task ahead. Over the previous two decades the country had maintained intact its democratic institutions in the midst of military tensions in the region. Costa Rica also succeeded in attracting new foreign investment and generating high—though fluctuating—economic growth. However, Costa Ricans became increasingly disillusioned with the direction of the country, the growth of income inequality and the apparent corruption within its political class. Although DR-CAFTA had been implemented, the policy direction of the country was still uncertain. The negative impact of the global financial crisis, which increased the rate of poverty and inequality, contributed to further social and political tensions. The comfortable victory of Laura Chinchilla in the 2010 presidential election, despite the lack of a congressional majority, and the return to economic growth in 2010, however, provided some room for optimism in the short term.

Economy

CATHY MCILWAINE

Based on earlier articles by ANDREW BOUNDS and DIEGO SÁNCHEZ-ANCOCHEA

Costa Rica has one of the highest levels of human development in Latin America. In 2009 it was ranked 54th in the UN Human Development Index (a drop of one place from the previous year), below Argentina, Chile, Uruguay, Mexico and Cuba in the region. The literacy rate was 96% in 2008, with life expectancy at birth standing at 79.4 years and infant mortality at only 8.8 per 1,000 live births in 2009. Costa Rica was ranked 11th out of all non-OECD countries in the UN Human Poverty Index in 2009. This reflects a long-term commitment to social stability, political accountability and public spending in health and education. Costa Rica has one of the highest levels of social spending in Latin America and the Caribbean (17.7% of gross domestic product—GDP—in 2007). The economy has been historically stable. According to World Bank estimates, gross national income per head was US $6,060 in 2008, compared with the Latin American and Caribbean average of $6,780, although this is the highest in Central America.

STAGES OF ECONOMIC DEVELOPMENT

Belying its Spanish colonial name, Costa Rica, or rich coast, the country yielded few resources for its conquistadores to exploit. There were also few indigenous inhabitants to press into slave labour, and few that were there survived the European invasion. Thus, subsistence agriculture and smallholder farming was the norm until the introduction of large scale cultivation of first coffee and then bananas from the early 19th century. From then on, Costa Rica's development outpaced the rest of Central America. It was first to export coffee (in 1832), to establish a commercial bank (in 1864) and to build a railway (in 1890). After the 1948 civil war it departed even further from its Central American peers. Large sectors of the economy were nationalized and considerable state support given to smallholders, who made up the backbone of the agricultural economy and underpinned its commitment to democracy. A welfare state was established and public utilities expanded quickly under state ownership.

In the 1960s the Government sought to diversify the economy and promote new exports through import substitution within the Central American Common Market (CACM), attempting to build a domestic manufacturing industry through protectionist tariffs and export subsidies. Yet it was not until the 1990s, when the tourism sector expanded and vast foreign investment fostered first a textile, then a high-technology sector, that Costa Rica reduced its reliance on coffee and bananas. It sought to transform itself into a diversified exporter with world-class companies through a mixture of government incentives and a network of free trade agreements. However, success in the export sector was accompanied by problems in other spheres. By the 1980s high debt threatened to swamp the country, which also suffered the negative impact of the difficulties of the CACM, as well as the armed conflict in the region. The Government was forced to pursue a series of unpopular structural adjustment programmes with multilateral lending institutions. This proved difficult, owing to the strength and independence of Costa Rica's state-owned companies and the consensual nature of the political system. Successive governments also sought to develop non-traditional exports with incentive schemes, and reined in government spending. Nevertheless, large deficits had to be funded by heavy domestic and overseas borrowing, and in 1988 the country was forced to apply for IMF and World Bank help to reschedule its debts. While it gained temporary relief, progress over the subsequent 15 years was painstakingly slow because of public opposition to a diminution of the welfare state and an increase in taxes. The debt restructuring of 1988–89, better borrowing terms and more careful policy management reduced public external debt, from 43.7% of GDP in 1990 to an estimated 11.8% of GDP in 2008. Public internal debt grew rapidly in the 1990s, but has decreased in more recent times due to a small primary public surplus. Between 2002 and 2008 public internal debt as a percentage of GDP fell from 27.2% to just 16.8%.

From the 1990s Costa Rica followed an at times inconsistent path towards a neo-liberal policy model. Significant reforms were introduced, including changes to the pensions and tax systems and measures to promote foreign investment and to facilitate private sector participation in activities such as banking and power generation that had formerly been confined to the state sector. At the same time, however, other reforms such as the deregulation of the telecommunications industry failed, owing to the active opposition of a majority of the population. Costa Rica's economy expanded at an average annual rate of 5.5% between 2000 and 2008, one of the highest rates in Latin America. However, the economic model remained dependent on external forces and especially on ties with the USA, a problem that became evident after the advent of the global financial crisis in 2008. The USA was Costa Rica's main export partner in 2008, accounting for 23.9% of all exports, as well as the main source of imports, accounting for 42.7% of the total. This relationship and the global recession directly contributed to low economic growth of 2.8% in 2008 (less than any other country in Central America) and to an economic contraction of 1.1% in 2009. However, the recession in Costa Rica was mild, with forecasts for a recovery of 3.6% real GDP growth in 2010 and 3.5% in 2011. These broad patterns were also reflected in worsening unemployment rates. Unemployment in the early 2000s was relatively high by historical standards, with the combined rate of unemployment and underemployment at 15% in most years, with real minimum wages stagnating. Although the unemployment rate alone was reduced to 4.6% and 4.8% in 2007 and 2008, respectively, it increased to 7.8% in 2009, and was forecast to increase to 6.7% in 2010 and 2011, mainly owing to weak growth in the construction sector. This effectively brought the rate back to the levels that prevailed in the early 2000s.

Despite the projected recovery, indicating that Costa Rica could weather the global recession, the export-led model has created a dual economy and questioned the survival of the former institutional structure. While export sectors performed well, traditional producers faced the loss of government subsidies and protective measures. Poverty has been gradually decreasing in the last decade, from 20.3% of the population living in poverty in 2002, to 16.4% in 2008; extreme poverty, or indigence, has declined from 8.2% to 5.5% over the same period (although the 2008 figure was an increase from 5.3% in 2007). International poverty lines are favourable compared with the rest of Latin America, with 8.6% of the population living on less than US $2 per day and only 2.4% living on less than $1.25 in 2009. Income inequality continued its worsening trend that began in the early 1990s. The Gini Index, which measures income inequality was 47.2 in 2009 (where 0 equals absolute equality and 100 equals absolute inequality). This was an increase towards greater inequality from 46.5 in 2005. In 2009 the poorest 10% of the population had a 1.5% share of the national income compared with the richest 10%, which had 35.5%. Plan Escudo, a social and economic protection programme established by President Oscar Arias Sánchez in February 2009, has assisted in protecting Costa Rican businesses, the financial sector, workers and families from the worst effects of the global financial crisis.

AGRICULTURE

Agriculture, hunting, forestry and fishing contributed an estimated 6.4% of GDP and engaged 14% of the employed population in 2009. In 2008 the agricultural sector experienced a significant crisis, with negative growth of -2.3%. This continued in 2009 with a contraction of 2.5%, although there was a projected return to positive growth in 2010 and 2011 of 2.5% and 2.0%, respectively. The major agricultural commodities were coffee, bananas, pineapples, sugar and beef for export, and rice for domestic consumption. The Government's attempt to encourage non-traditional export crops meant that the country was no longer self-sufficient in staples and imported large quantities of maize, beans, rice and soybeans. The recuperation of coffee prices, together with the expansion of demand for pineapple and other non-traditional exports, contributed to a rise in the value of agricultural exports from 2002, reaching $2,112m. in 2008.

Bananas

Apart from a brief period in the mid-1980s, bananas have consistently been Costa Rica's main export commodity concentrated on the Pacific and Caribbean coasts. In 1985 the closure of the Pacific coast operations of Chiquita brought widespread economic depression to the region, since many of its towns were wholly dependent on the company's fortunes. Consequently, the Government purchased 1,700 ha of the abandoned plantations (which totalled 2,300 ha) and converted them to the cultivation of cocoa. Elsewhere, bananas were being replaced by more profitable crops such African palm, sugar cane and exotic fruits, especially pineapples.

The Costa Rican banana industry recovered gradually with incentives from the Government, but faced a new threat from the European Union (EU) quota system from 1993. The quota system, designed to protect banana production in the former European colonies, placed an annual limit of 2.0m. metric tons on banana imports from Latin American countries. This led to the flooding of non-EU markets and a significant decrease in banana prices in Costa Rica. Costa Rican producers were operating under severe pressure caused by falling prices, continuing market access problems and climatic adversity. There was also increasing competition from Ecuador, which rapidly became a bigger banana producer than Costa Rica. While Costa Rica had the world's highest productivity levels, it also had higher costs: the average worker earned US $18 per day, compared with $2 in Ecuador. In 2001 the EU and the USA settled the banana dispute. Under the terms of the deal, the EU was to introduce a transitional system, issuing licences according to historical trade patterns, in preparation for a tariff-only system from 2006. Nevertheless, a world banana surfeit continued, leading to the closure of four plantations, resulting in the loss of some 1,200 jobs, and the cancellation of contracts in Costa Rica by the three principal exporters, Chiquita Brands, the Banana Development Corporation and the Standard Fruit Company. This adversely affected independent farmers, who accounted for more than one-half of total production. From 2002 banana exports slowly recuperated but still constituted a small share of total exports. In 2008 banana exports totalled $690m. (just 7.3% of total export revenues), up from $221m. in 1988 and remaining the main agricultural export.

Coffee

Costa Rica grows only arabica highland coffee, which commands a premium on the world market, and uses technology to achieve some of the highest yields in the world. Sharp falls in the international price of coffee in 1992 caused bankruptcies and led many coffee growers to diversify into other crops. Although by 1998 output had regained its 1992 level, international prices reached a 30-year low in early 2001 and coffee production suffered, amounting to only 150,289 tons in that year. Central American producers, along with Mexico, Colombia and Brazil, agreed to retain up to 10% of their stocks in order to allow the price to rise. However, the arrangement proved difficult to enforce, especially in the face of increased production by Asian countries, particularly Viet Nam, which opposed the retention scheme. Prices fell by two-thirds between 1998 and 2002, but recovered in 2002–07, growing by a combined 140%. This contributed to the gradual recovery of coffee export receipts, which increased from $194m. in 2003 to $305m. in 2008. Nevertheless, production declined overall between 2004–09 from 150,730 tons to 124,055 tons in 2007 and from 1,887,000 bags in 2004 to 1,659,000 bags in 2009. Coffee is now Costa Rica's third most important agricultural export.

Sugar

Sugar production began to increase at the end of the 1990s, in spite of a reduction in the annual US sugar quota. Production continued to rise, and then output hovered around 340,000 metric tons in the early and mid-2000s. Owing to the international price increase, export earnings grew by 64% between 2005 and 2007; however, in 2008 they decreased from $49m. to $34m. The sector expected to receive a small boost after the Dominican Republic-Central America Free Trade Agreement (DR-CAFTA) came into force in January 2009, and especially since the USA granted Costa Rica a tariff-free import quota under the Agreement in June 2010. This would allow the import of nearly 14,000 tons of sugar from Costa Rica into the USA tariff free annually. Sugar is now Costa Rica's ninth most important agricultural export.

Other Crops

Crops for domestic consumption included maize, beans and rice, which were grown mainly on small farms with low yields, although advances were being made in rice cultivation, and the size of the units of production was also increasing. The Government gave priority for export incentives on traditional crops such as cocoa, African oil palm, cotton, vegetables, cut flowers, macadamia nuts, coconuts and tropical fruit. Although the EU imposed an 8.8% tariff on most of Costa Rica's fruit and vegetable exports in 2004 after ruling that it was too wealthy to continue to benefit from the General System of Preferences, non-traditional primary exports grew by a combined 55% between 2004 and 2008. The extraordinary success of pineapple exports was behind this strong performance: in 2003 exports of the fruit were worth US $207m., meaning it replaced coffee as the second biggest agricultural earner after bananas. Between 2003 and 2008 pineapple exports continued to increase, reaching $573m. in the latter year. In 2010 Costa Rica was the world's main exporter of pineapples.

Forestry and Fishing

Costa Rica has considerable forestry resources, but the Government imposed strict controls on their exploitation because of high historical rates of deforestation. A US $275m. programme to maintain and develop the forestry resource over the following 20 years was announced in 1990. A 1996 forestry law introduced incentives for reforestation and a law of biodiversity in 1998 ensured the protection of natural resources. Just over 26% of the country lies in 186 protected areas which include national parks, biological reserves, forest reserves and wildlife refuges. However, demand for sustainable wood continues to grow among rich, environmentally sensitive consumers. Some Costa Rican companies are exploiting this demand and others could follow, owing to the country's reputation for conservation. Costa Rica was a pioneer in the use of 'debt-for-nature' swaps (where a creditor nation forgives debt in return for environmental pledges) to protect its rainforest from the late 1980s. In 2007 the country agreed to a new swap with the US Government for US $12.6m., with an additional $1.26m. from environment protection organizations The Nature Conservancy and Conservation International, making it the largest swap ever made by the US Tropical Forest Conservation Act. Between 2005 and 2007 the proportion of forest area increased slightly, from 46.8% to 46.9%. Costa Rica has also been active in selling carbon credit offsets for the clean air its forests produce, a market that continued to grow despite US opposition to the Kyoto Protocol to reduce 'greenhouse' gases. Costa Rica is ranked third globally and first within the Americas in terms of the 2010 Environmental Performance Index, which measures the environmental performance of a country's policies.

During the 1990s the Government promoted the expansion of a fishing industry, mainly for shrimps, sardines, tuna and tilapia. Exports of fresh and frozen fish reached US $89.2m. in 2002 but decreased most years thereafter. In 2008 export revenues experienced a small recuperation, totalling $97.1m.

MINING AND POWER

Costa Rica has deposits of iron ore, bauxite, sulphur, manganese, mercury, gold and silver. However, by the beginning of the 21st century only the last two were mined. Canadian companies were most active, but mining remained a tiny industry because of strong environmental protection; in 2008 it accounted for just 0.2% of GDP. Policy towards mining exploitation has been inconsistent during the last few years. A mining code adopted in 2001 reduced taxes and improved the legal environment for mining operations. However, a law banning open-cast operations was enacted in 2002. In 2006 the Constitutional Court confirmed the ban in a ruling regarding the gold mining exploitation of Las Crucitas. In 2008 the Government of President Oscar Arias Sánchez reversed a moratorium on mining and gave permission for the Las Crucitas project to proceed, leading to protests from social groups and the Nicaraguan Government. In April 2010 the Constitutional Court ruled in favour of the continuation of the project and in the following month the new President, Laura Chinchilla Miranda, banned all gold mining in the country except in Las Crucitas.

The country also has substantial reserves of petroleum, but they have remained largely unexploited. In 1998 Costa Rica offered exploration concessions in the Caribbean to international companies. However, in 2002 the state environmental regulator refused foreign oil companies licences to prospect on environmental grounds. As a result of the state's refusal to allow the exploitation of petroleum reserves, Costa Rica has been compelled to import all its oil, mostly from Venezuela, under the Caracas Accord of 2000, which provided concessional financing for some of the cost. The petroleum refinery at Puerto Limón processes up to 25,000 barrels per day.

Costa Rica has virtually eliminated the need for petroleum products for electricity generation through its development of hydroelectric power resources and the use of fuel wood, bagasse (vegetable waste) and sugar cane alcohol. Geothermal energy from volcanoes was also developed, and investment in the national grid ensured that 95% of the population was covered by 2002. In 2007 an estimated 75% of all the annual electricity generated was hydroelectric, 14% geothermal, 6% gas and 3% wind power. By 2009 the proportion of electrical energy from clean sources increased to 99%, with the aim of becoming carbon neutral by 2021. Although the state electricity company, the Instituto Costarricense de Electricidad (ICE), generated the bulk of power, private producers have existed since 1990. In 2006 private plants generated 17.2% of the total.

Despite widespread opposition to privatization throughout the 1990s and 2000s, the entry into DR-CAFTA in 2009 led to the establishment of the principle to liberalize the energy, insurance and telecommunications sectors from 2010 onwards. In 2008 the Insurance Market Regulatory Law was passed, which broke up the Costa Rican insurance monopoly held for 84 years by the Instituto Nacional de Seguros. In January 2010 the Superintendencia General de Seguros was established in order to regulate the sector.

MANUFACTURING

With the manufacturing sector generating an estimated 18.4% of nominal GDP and industry as a whole representing 29% of GDP in 2008, Costa Rica was the most industrialized country in Central America. Rapid growth in this sector during the 1960s and 1970s owing to the creation of the CACM resulted in a high level of diversification. After a contraction in demand in the 1980s, growth returned from the early 1990s, with industrial GDP increasing in real terms by an average annual rate of 6% between 1990 and 2006. However, in 2006 growth in the industrial sector was 11.3%, although there was a contraction of 0.6% in 2008 and of 2.9% in 2009. Forecasts estimate a recovery in 2010 and 2011 of 3% and 2%, respectively.

Manufacturing is dominated by the free trade zones, representing 41% of the total value added in 2006 (second was food, beverages and tobacco, with a share of 19.5%). In 1998 Intel began production at an assembly plant in the free trade zone west of San José, with a second plant opening in June 2004. Although only 2,200 people were employed, Intel galvanized Costa Rica's export and growth figures. Between 2001 and 2007 exports from the free trade zones increased at an average annual rate of 13.5%, but in 2008 they entered into recession, decreasing by 3.1%. By 2010 the electronics industry was the focus of manufacturing, with textiles being unable to compete globally, especially relative to China. Overall though, in 2008, the 247 companies operating in free trade zones accounted for $4,980m. in exports (more than 54% of total exports). These companies exported more than 1,200 products to 106 different countries. At the end of 2009 the Government passed a law to encourage companies to establish in free trade zones outside the central valley and capital region.

TOURISM

Tourism became Costa Rica's largest single source of foreign exchange earnings in the 1990s following significant investment in the sector, with revenue increasing from US $679.2m. in 1994 to $2,250m. in 2008. In the latter year the total number of tourists was 2.09m (a combined increase of almost 15% over 2006). The country's reputation for political stability and relatively low crime attracts tourists to its fine beaches and extensive system of national parks and protected areas. The rainforest is accessible and bird-watching and trekking are popular. Costa Rica is home to an incredible variety of flora and fauna and is estimated to have 5% of the world's biodiversity, which has encouraged an important ecotourism sector.

The Government aimed to diversify from its dependence on North American visitors, and by 2007 less than 40% of all foreign tourists came from the USA (down from 51% in the previous year). The Government also encouraged a shift from small operators catering to independent tourists to large resorts, built around San José and the northern Pacific coast. It was envisaged that in the long term this might erode tourism's vital contribution to the Costa Rican economy, as more money would be repatriated by international owners of resorts. The tourism sector was adversely affected by the recession, with a decline in activity in the sector by 3.1% between 2009 and 2010, although there was an increase in visitor numbers. In 2009 Costa Rica ranked 42nd in the world (out of 133) and fourth in the Americas in the travel and tourism competitiveness index, which measures the attractiveness of a country as a place to establish a tourism business.

INFRASTRUCTURE

Costa Rica had an estimated 35,983 km of roads, of which about 25% were paved, increasing to 25.5% in 2007. The main road is the Pan-American Highway, which runs north–south and is fully paved. In 2003 public investment in roads increased by more than 37% in real terms, owing to the implementation of an extensive maintenance programme to improve the quality of some existing roads. However, since then public investment in transportation has been erratic due to fiscal constraints: in 2004 and 2005 it went down by a combined 43% in real terms, while in 2007 it increased by 88%.

There are five international ports in Costa Rica. Four are on the Pacific coast—Puntarenas, Calderas, Quepos, Golfito and Punta Morales—and one on the Atlantic Coast at Limón-Moín. The latter accounts for over 80% of cargo handled. The poor quality of port infrastructure was beginning to affect the competitiveness of exports by the end of the 1990s. The Pacific ports were leased to a private operator at the end of 2001. Trade unions prevented such a move on the Atlantic coast until an agreement in April 2010 to allow the ports of Limón and Moín to be opened for bidding from the private sector. There are firm plans to fund a new container terminal at Moín through a joint partnership between RECOPE (Refinadora Costarricense de Petróleo), the national oil refinery company, and the Chinese National Petroleum Corporation.

There were about 950 km of railway in 2006, of which a sizeable proportion were plantation lines. These were closed in 1995 when the state railway company, Instituto Costarricense de Ferrocarriles (INCOFER), suspended operations indefinitely, pending privatization, although the transport of cargo continued. In 2008 INCOFER bought trains and technical assistance from a Spanish company, FEVE, and by mid-2009 a wide range of rail lines had reopened.

Costa Rica has four international airports, two of which are located in San José: Juan Santamaría, which is one of the busiest in Central America, transporting an average of 1.5m. passengers per year, and the Tobías Bolaños International Airport in the Pavas area of San José. The other two are the Daniel Oduber Quirós International Airport in Liberia serving the Pacific coast and the Limón International Airport on the Caribbean coast. There are a further 38 small airports with paved runways located throughout the country.

The ICE is also responsible for telecommunications and by the 1990s had built an impressive land network. There were 32 telephone lines per 100 inhabitants in 2007, up from 24 in 2001. Despite initial delays in investing in advanced cellular and internet technology, the country was connected to the Maya fibre-optic cable and internet connections were established in schools and post offices in 2001. Further investments in 2005 and 2006 led to an increase in the number of cellular subscribers (from 25 per 100 inhabitants in 2005 to 34 in 2007). Secure internet servers per million people also increased considerably from 62 in 2005 to 98 in 2009. The approval of the General Telecommunications Law—triggered by the signing of DR-CAFTA—opened the door for gradual private participation in network services, internet services and wireless services from 2008. By 2010 a wide range of private internet provider firms had applied to the Superintendencia de Telecomunicaciones (SUTEL), which oversees the opening up of the telecommunications market to competition.

FINANCE AND INVESTMENT

Adverse economic conditions and a lack of fiscal reform precipitated a crisis in Costa Rica's public finances in the early 1980s, necessitating the implementation of a stabilization plan. By the early 1990s the Government was focused on reducing inflation through strict monetary control. Inflation has long been a problem for Costa Rica although it has been brought under control from 20.8% in 1988 to 12.7% in 2008. In 2009 it fell further, to 7.8% and consumer price reduction continued to be a priority for the Government; forecasts for 2010 and 2011 were estimated at 6.3% and 6.0%, respectively.

The fiscal deficit also continued to be a major preoccupation of successive governments given the general commitment to public spending. However, budget reductions and tax measures have been politically very difficult to pursue, especially owing to opposition from labour organizations. In the last decade there had been some progress with the deficit, which fell to only 2.1% in 2005 and transformed into a surplus under the Arias administration in 2007. However, the surplus was short-lived: in 2008 the public accounts again recorded a deficit, which was expected to increase significantly in 2009. The new Chinchilla Government (2010-) has committed to maintain the social and economic stimulus measures as part of the Plan Escudo, resulting in a continuation of an estimated fiscal deficit of 3.7% of GDP in 2010 (from 3.0% in 2009), declining to 3.5% in 2011. Linked with this, public expenditure is expected to rise to 18% of GDP in 2010 (an increase from 13.7% in 2009).

There was an increase in foreign direct investment (FDI) in the 1990s, as Costa Rica moved from being predominantly an exporter of coffee and bananas to an advanced technology and *maquila* ('offshore' assembly) exporter with a successful tourism industry. Total annual FDI increased from US $172m. in 1991 to a record $662m. in 2002. In the following four years FDI remained high, reaching a new record in 2008 in absolute terms ($2,016—equivalent to 6.7% of GDP). In 2008 US companies accounted for 60% of incoming investment; some 27% of investment was channelled into manufacturing, 24% into real estate, 21% into agriculture and 14% into tourism. In 2009 the Costa Rican Investment and Development Board (CINDE) noted that $304m. was invested by 29 foreign companies, which created 5,729 jobs. In particular, call centres expanded rapidly with 20 companies establishing such centres by the end of 2009, generating approximately 12,000 direct jobs.

BALANCE OF PAYMENTS AND THE EXTERNAL DEBT

Exports performed well in the 1990s, but strong economic growth and the reduction of import tariffs in 1993 contributed to a dramatic increase in the trade deficit. While the trade deficits were partially offset by increased tourism revenues and the operations of the free trade zones, they necessitated high levels of external borrowing. In 2000 the trade deficit totalled US $538.8m. increasing to $4,813m in 2008. This was partly compensated by the tourism sector, giving rise to a current account deficit of $2,669m.—more than double that of two years before. By 1995 Costa Rica's public external debt as a percentage of GDP had been reduced to 28%. Between 2000 and 2005 public external debt remained around 19% of GDP. In 2005 and 2006 the appreciation of the exchange rate and lower interest rates contributed to a further reduction in the public debt as a share of GDP. In 2008 the public external debt totalled $3,570m. (12.0% of GDP) and interest payments were equivalent to 0.8% of GDP.

OUTLOOK

Costa Rica illustrates as well as any other country in Latin America and the Caribbean both the opportunities and the threats that the current process of market-friendly globalization can bring. On the positive side, Costa Rica succeeded in increasing total exports and diversifying its export base. The arrival of multinational corporations in the high-technology and service sectors led to the creation of new, high-paying jobs, demonstrating the long-term importance of public investment in education. In 2006 and 2007 the country benefited from a new round of high foreign investment and expansion of non-traditional exports, partly driven by closer economic and political ties with China. At the same time, however, the country has also struggled to adapt to the new global conditions. Repeated efforts by different administrations to deepen the process of neo-liberal reforms were met with significant public opposition. Dissatisfaction with an economic model that has resulted in increasing inequality, and with the consolidation of a dual economy, was increasing, and social polarization was on the rise. The global financial crisis highlighted the contradictions of the Costa Rican model in 2008. Dependence on external markets, especially the USA, resulted in a recession. However, by 2010 the outlook was more optimistic as it was realized that Costa Rica had dealt with the effects of the global financial crisis better than anticipated, influenced partly by an effective social and economic stimulus and protection measures in the form of Plan Escudo. Costa Rica continued to face economic and social challenges but with a new Government in place in 2010, the economy looked set to return to growth, with the worst effects of the recession partly cushioned and privatization of the economy progressing steadily. Costa Rica also continued to be very well-placed on a range of indices of quality of life. In 2009 the Economist Intelligence Unit ranked Costa Rica 33rd out of 160 countries in its Quality of Life Index, ensuring it was ranked first in Latin America.

Statistical Survey

Sources (unless otherwise stated): Instituto Nacional de Estadística y Censos, Edif. Ana Lorena, Calle Los Negritos, de la Rotonda de la Bandera 450 m oeste, Mercedes de Montes de Oca, San José; tel. 2280-9280; fax 2224-2221; e-mail informacion@inec.go.cr; internet www.inec.go.cr; Banco Central de Costa Rica, Avdas Central y Primera, Calles 2 y 4, Apdo 10.058, 1000 San José; tel. 2233-4233; fax 2223-4658; internet www.bccr.fi.cr.

Area and Population

AREA, POPULATION AND DENSITY

Area (sq km)	
Land	51,060
Inland water	40
Total	51,100*
Population (census results)	
11 June 1984†	2,416,809
28 June 2000	
Males	1,902,614
Females	1,907,565
Total	3,810,179
Population (official estimates at mid year)	
2008	4,381,987
2009	4,438,995
2010	4,563,539
Density (per sq km) at mid-2010	89.3

* 19,730 sq miles.

† Excluding adjustment for underenumeration.

POPULATION BY AGE AND SEX

(official estimates at mid-2010)

	Males	Females	Total
0–14	577,415	548,647	1,126,062
15–64	1,597,219	1,539,921	3,137,140
65 and over	139,659	160,678	300,337
Total	2,314,293	2,249,246	4,563,539

PROVINCES
(official estimates at mid-2009)

	Area (sq km)	Population (estimates)	Density (per sq km)	Capital (with population)
Alajuela	9,757.5	838,508	85.9	Alajuela (258,967)
Cartago	3,124.7	497,940	159.4	Cartago (151,139)
Guanacaste	10,140.7	310,696	30.6	Liberia (57,063)
Heredia	2,657.0	411,271	154.8	Heredia (120,378)
Limón	9,188.5	408,738	44.5	Limón (107,981)
Puntarenas	11,265.7	424,082	37.6	Puntarenas (120,546)
San José	4,965.9	1,547,760	311.7	San José (356,174)
Total	51,100.0	4,438,995	86.9	—

PRINCIPAL TOWNS
(official estimates at mid-2009)

San José	356,174	Pérez Zeledón	142,774
Alajuela	258,967	Goicoechea	132,747
Desamparados	223,809	Pococí	123,699
San Carlos	154,250	Puntarenas	120,546
Cartago	151,139	Heredia	120,378

BIRTHS, MARRIAGES AND DEATHS

	Registered live births		Registered marriages		Registered deaths	
	Number	Rate (per 1,000)	Number	Rate (per 1,000)	Number	Rate (per 1,000)
2002	71,144	17.5	23,926	5.9	15,004	3.7
2003	72,938	17.6	24,448	5.9	15,800	3.8
2004	72,247	17.2	25,370	6.0	15,949	3.8
2005	71,548	16.8	25,631	6.0	16,139	3.8
2006	71,291	16.5	26,575	6.1	16,766	3.9
2007	73,144	16.7	26,010	5.9	17,071	3.9
2008	75,187	16.9	25,034	5.6	18,021	4.1
2009	75,000	16.6	23,920	5.3	18,560	4.1

Life expectancy (years at birth, WHO estimates): 78 (males 76; females 81) in 2008 (Source: WHO, *World Health Statistics*).

ECONOMICALLY ACTIVE POPULATION*
('000 persons aged 12 years and over, household survey, July)

	2007	2008	2009
Agriculture, hunting and forestry	244.75	235.06	224.32
Fishing	9.85	6.57	7.27
Mining and quarrying	2.61	2.17	1.59
Manufacturing	251.57	239.54	232.92
Electricity, gas and water supply	21.06	27.95	27.09
Construction	151.79	152.45	128.39
Wholesale and retail trade	366.51	377.61	390.13
Hotels and restaurants	108.27	100.31	105.74
Transport, storage and communications	125.72	143.05	148.73
Financial intermediation	49.47	53.34	49.04
Real estate, renting and business activities	121.62	137.58	130.28
Public administration activities	88.68	93.76	112.74
Education	110.74	112.55	114.63
Health and social work	64.01	64.67	73.07
Other community, social and personal service activities	72.70	81.13	75.78
Private households with employed persons	128.56	118.96	123.17
Extra-territorial organizations and bodies	1.12	2.70	5.39
Sub-total	1,919.04	1,949.39	1,950.29
Not classifiable by economic activity	6.61	8.32	5.22
Total employed	1,925.65	1,957.71	1,955.51
Unemployed	92.79	101.91	165.94
Total labour force	2,018.44	2,059.61	2,121.45

* Figures for activities are rounded to the nearest 10 persons, and totals may not be equivalent to the sum of component parts as a result.

Health and Welfare

KEY INDICATORS

Total fertility rate (children per woman, 2008)	2.0
Under-5 mortality rate (per 1,000 live births, 2008)	11
HIV/AIDS (% of persons aged 15–49, 2007)	0.4
Physicians (per 1,000 head, 2000)	1.3
Hospital beds (per 1,000 head, 2006)	1.3
Health expenditure (2007): US $ per head (PPP)	899
Health expenditure (2007): % of GDP	8.1
Health expenditure (2007): public (% of total)	72.9
Access to water (% of persons, 2008)	97
Access to sanitation (% of persons, 2008)	95
Total carbon dioxide emissions ('000 metric tons, 2006)	7,848.3
Carbon dioxide emissions per head (metric tons, 2006)	1.8
Human Development Index (2007): ranking	54
Human Development Index (2007): value	0.854

For sources and definitions, see explanatory note on p. vi.

Agriculture

PRINCIPAL CROPS
('000 metric tons)

	2006	2007	2008
Rice, paddy	175.8	179.6	248.0
Potatoes	55.8	66.1	66.1
Cassava (Manioc)	389.3*	397.9*	97.8
Sugar cane	4,600*	3,950*	3,504
Watermelons	46.6	46.9	49.3
Cantaloupes and other melons	291.3	251.8	197.3
Oil palm fruit	872.4	825.0	863.2
Bananas	2,268.0*	2,350.0*	1,881.8
Plantains	76.6	86.4	85.2
Oranges	448.8	424.0	278.0
Pineapples	1,805.0*	1,968.0	1,624.6
Coffee, green	101.0	124.1	107.3

* FAO estimate.

Aggregate production ('000 metric tons, may include official, semi-official or estimated data): Total cereals 188.8 in 2006, 199.1 in 2007, 260.5 in 2008; Total roots and tubers 521.1 in 2006, 535.6 in 2007, 211.0 in 2008; Total vegetables (incl. melons) 499.5 in 2006, 442.9 in 2007, 392.9 in 2008; Total fruits (excl. melons) 4,980.3 in 2006, 5,264.5 in 2007, 4,325.9 in 2008.

Source: FAO.

LIVESTOCK
('000 head, year ending September, FAO estimates)

	2006	2007	2008
Horses	115	120	120
Asses	8	8	8
Cattle	1,100	1,200	1,287
Pigs	573	676	729
Sheep	3	3	3
Goats	5	5	5
Chickens	25,900	28,100	19,500

Source: FAO.

LIVESTOCK PRODUCTS
('000 metric tons)

	2006	2007	2008
Cattle meat	75.3	80.8	87.5
Pig meat	40.7	48.0	51.9
Chicken meat	98.3	107.2	103.4
Cows' milk	823.8	890.0	881.6
Hen eggs	47.2	41.9	52.2
Honey*	1.3	1.3	1.3

* FAO estimates.

Source: FAO.

Forestry

ROUNDWOOD REMOVALS
('000 cubic metres, excl. bark, FAO estimates)

	2006	2007	2008
Sawlogs, veneer logs and logs for sleepers	952	952	952
Other industrial wood	246	246	246
Fuel wood	3,424	3,411	3,398
Total	4,622	4,609	4,596

Source: FAO.

SAWNWOOD PRODUCTION
('000 cubic metres, incl. railway sleepers)

	2004	2005	2006
Coniferous (softwood)*	12	12	23
Broadleaved (hardwood)	414	476	1,109*
Total*	426	488	1,132

* FAO estimate(s).

2007–08: Figures assumed to be unchanged from 2006 (FAO estimates).

Source: FAO.

Fishing

('000 metric tons, live weight)

	2006	2007	2008
Capture*	22.0	21.7	21.8
Clupeoids	2.2*	2.2	2.2*
Marlins, sailfishes, etc.	1.0*	0.9	0.9*
Tuna-like fishes	1.6*	1.4	1.4*
Common dolphinfish	2.9*	2.7	2.7*
Sharks, rays, skates, etc.	4.1	3.9	3.9
Other marine fishes	4.2	4.5	4.5
Aquaculture	20.0	25.8	27.0
Tilapias	13.5	19.8	21.2
Whiteleg shrimp	5.7	5.3	5.3
Total catch*	42.0	47.5	48.8

* FAO estimate(s).

Source: FAO.

Industry

SELECTED PRODUCTS
('000 metric tons, unless otherwise indicated)

	2005	2006	2007
Raw sugar	398	348	373
Kerosene	3	3	1
Distillate fuel oils	148	230	248
Residual fuel oils	235	295	328
Bitumen	13	26	22
Electric energy (million kWh)	8,252	8,697	9,050

Source: UN Industrial Commodity Statistics Database.

Cement ('000 metric tons): 1,900 in 2006 (estimate); 2,300 in 2007 (estimate); 2,500 in 2008 (Source: US Geological Survey).

Finance

CURRENCY AND EXCHANGE RATES

Monetary Units
100 céntimos = 1 Costa Rican colón.

Sterling, Dollar and Euro Equivalents (31 May 2010)
£1 sterling = 787.947 colones;
US $1 = 540.430 colones;
€1 = 669.268 colones;
10,000 Costa Rican colones = £12.69 = $18.50 = €14.94.

Average Exchange Rate (colones per US $)
2007 516.617
2008 526.236
2009 573.288

GENERAL BUDGET
(million colones)

Revenue	2005	2006	2007
Current revenue	2,218,904	2,754,039	3,370,533
Taxation	1,882,185	2,320,676	2,926,121
Income tax	324,224	394,095	531,552
Social security contributions	593,623	721,453	871,228
Taxes on property	48,751	62,860	83,478
Taxes on goods and services	797,608	1,006,111	1,269,413
Taxes on international trade	111,048	136,128	170,414
Other taxes	6,932	30	36
Other current revenue	105,802	193,845	166,625
Current transfers	–2,452	2,509	4,741
Operational surplus	233,369	237,010	273,046
Capital revenue	3,385	3,819	723
Total	2,222,288	2,757,859	3,371,257

Expenditure*	2005	2006	2007
Current expenditure	1,961,290	2,312,074	2,668,931
Wages and salaries	717,477	843,895	977,353
Social security contributions	4,399	4,958	5,807
Other purchases of goods and services	187,543	232,339	288,354
Interest payments	394,364	437,946	420,967
Internal	313,278	349,675	332,474
External	81,086	88,271	88,493
Current transfers	656,200	791,536	976,450
Operational deficit	1,307	1,401	—
Capital expenditure	342,705	361,115	495,165
Investment	230,897	227,311	312,749
Real sector	219,115	224,564	308,733
Financial sector	11,782	2,747	4,016
Capital transfers	111,808	133,803	182,417
Total	2,303,995	2,673,189	3,164,096

* Excluding lending minus repayments (million colones): 97 in 2005; –1,986.1 in 2006; –3,851.5 in 2007.

Note: Figures represent the consolidated accounts of central and local government activities.

Source: Ministerio de Haciendo, San José.

INTERNATIONAL RESERVES
(excl. gold, US $ million at 31 December)

	2007	2008	2009
IMF special drawing rights	0.11	0.30	208.30
Reserve position in IMF	31.61	30.83	31.38
Foreign exchange	4,081.90	3,767.53	3,826.49
Total	4,113.62	3,798.66	4,066.17

Source: IMF, *International Financial Statistics*.

MONEY SUPPLY

('000 million colones at 31 December)

	2007	2008	2009
Currency outside depository corporations	391.1	400.1	431.5
Transferable deposits	3,220.0	3,619.2	3,813.1
Other deposits	61.7	64.4	56.5
Securities other than shares	3,822.7	4,714.3	5,202.8
Broad money	7,495.5	8,798.0	9,504.0

Source: IMF, *International Financial Statistics*.

COST OF LIVING

(Consumer Price Index at July; base: July 2006 = 100)

	2007	2008	2009
Food and non-alcoholic beverages	116.2	143.8	152.7
Clothing and footwear	99.6	97.3	101.0
Housing	108.1	122.9	144.6
Medical care	110.5	122.3	136.7
Transport	105.1	123.5	117.9
Education	111.9	123.8	141.0
All items (incl. others)	108.8	124.2	132.7

NATIONAL ACCOUNTS

(million colones at current prices)

National Income and Product

	2007	2008*	2009*
GDP in purchasers' values	13,598,604.5	15,706,900.8	16,799,083.7
Net primary incomes from abroad	–386,258.0	–405,366.8	–558,120.1
Gross national income	13,212,346.5	15,301,534.1	16,240,963.6
Less consumption of fixed capital	793,219.3	910,272.1	973,568.1
Net national income	12,419,127.3	14,391,262.0	15,267,395.5
Net current transfers	242,561.2	233,097.8	188,694.3
Gross national disposable income	12,661,688.5	14,624,359.8	15,456,089.8

* Preliminary figures.

Expenditure on the Gross Domestic Product

	2007	2008*	2009*
Government final consumption expenditure	1,810,283.2	2,254,700.6	2,850,362.3
Private final consumption expenditure	9,087,357.9	10,649,261.2	11,619,043.9
Increase in stocks	390,263.8	665,652.0	–1,177,527.1
Gross fixed capital formation	2,964,052.8	3,656,673.6	3,490,313.3
Total domestic expenditure	14,251,957.7	17,226,287.4	16,782,192.4
Exports of goods and services	6,623,704.1	7,159,077.5	7,209,937.7
Less Imports of goods and services	7,277,057.2	8,678,464.0	7,193,046.4
GDP in purchasers' values	13,598,604.5	15,706,900.8	16,799,083.7
GDP at constant 1991 prices	2,042,033.1	2,099,560.4	2,077,106.8

* Preliminary figures.

Gross Domestic Product by Economic Activity

	2007	2008*	2009*
Agriculture, hunting, forestry and fishing	1,030,587.1	1,025,839.4	1,072,994.3
Mining and quarrying	31,696.7	35,625.7	29,729.3
Manufacturing	2,597,438.6	2,891,705.2	2,893,848.4
Electricity, gas and water	234,950.9	253,883.4	300,567.6
Construction	691,909.1	855,933.1	911,100.8
Trade, restaurants and hotels	2,408,320.6	2,815,067.6	2,850,508.3
Transport, storage and communications	1,219,654.3	1,410,793.4	1,522,866.2
Finance and insurance	780,319.7	946,601.9	1,048,182.6
Real estate	387,793.2	437,633.9	474,398.7
Other business services	646,910.9	803,271.3	964,351.7
Public administration	477,956.9	575,829.4	719,357.7
Other community, social and personal services	2,230,105.5	2,702,809.7	3,293,059.8
Sub-total	12,737,643.5	14,754,994.0	16,080,965.5
Less Imputed bank service charge	588,071	707,316.2	805,309.6
GDP at basic prices	12,149,572.6	14,047,677.8	15,275,655.9
Taxes on products	1,505,980.1	1,711,691.2	1,574,869.7
Less Subsidies	56,948.1	52,468.3	51,441.9
GDP in purchasers' values	13,598,604.5	15,706,900.8	16,799,083.7

* Preliminary figures.

BALANCE OF PAYMENTS

(US $ million)

	2006	2007	2008
Exports of goods f.o.b.	8,101.7	9,299.5	9,566.3
Imports of goods f.o.b.	–10,828.9	–12,284.9	–14,550.6
Trade balance	–2,727.1	–2,985.5	–4,984.3
Exports of services	2,971.7	3,552.2	4,084.9
Imports of services	–1,620.6	–1,818.1	–1,882.5
Balance on goods and services	–1,376.1	–1,251.4	–2,782.0
Other income received	1,135.1	707.7	689.0
Other income paid	–1,130.8	–1,572.4	–1,078.0
Balance on goods, services and income	–1,371.8	–2,116.1	–3,170.9
Current transfers received	586.1	734.6	706.6
Current transfers paid	–237.0	–264.8	–264.4
Current balance	–1,022.6	–1,646.4	–2,728.7
Capital account (net)	1.1	21.2	7.4
Direct investment abroad	–98.1	–262.4	–5.9
Direct investment from abroad	1,469.1	1,896.1	2,021.0
Portfolio investment assets	–509.3	–170.4	535.1
Portfolio investment liabilities	0—	0—	–93.5
Other investment assets	654.6	–155.8	–686.6
Other investment liabilities	370.4	1,124.4	642.8
Net errors and omissions	149.5	171.0	2.6
Overall balance	1,014.7	977.7	–305.9

Source: IMF, *International Financial Statistics*.

External Trade

PRINCIPAL COMMODITIES

(US $ million)

Imports c.i.f.	2006	2007	2008
Food and live animals	583.5	672.6	832.7
Mineral products	1,583.6	1,845.1	2,263.6
Basic manufactures	482.3	459.2	511.9
Chemicals and related products	1,321.3	1,388.6	1,673.3
Plastic materials and manufactures	933.2	989.7	1,014.1
Leather, hides and furs	61.4	66.7	52.3
Paper, paperboard and manufactures	48.5	59.7	70.3
Wood pulp and other fibrous materials	677.3	717.9	608.1
Silk, cotton and textile fibres	607.3	603.8	549.4
Footwear, hats, umbrellas, etc.	83.6	102.6	113.3
Stone manufactures, etc.	187.7	188.6	195.5
Natural and cultured pearls	56.4	44.2	44.0
Common metals and manufactures	1,114.4	1,198.4	1,450.2
Machinery and electrical equipment	3,905.5	4,298.6	4,395.4
Transport equipment	608.6	939.3	958.9
Optical and topographical apparatus and instruments, etc.	295.4	300.8	318.6
Total (incl. others)	12,740.2	14,095.2	15,289.4

Exports f.o.b.	2006	2007	2008
Food and live animals	2,026.6	2,302.6	2,518.3
Mineral products	57.6	64.9	95.3
Basic manufactures	726.3	881.3	876.4
Chemicals and related products	472.9	531.7	616.5
Plastic materials and manufactures	392.0	401.6	442.4
Leather, hides and furs	79.9	72.1	45.7
Paper, paperboard and manufactures	46.1	48.3	52.8
Wood pulp and other fibrous materials	172.9	198.6	227.7
Silk, cotton and textile fibres	514.5	430.9	321.2
Stone manufactures, etc.	87.4	93.8	106.5
Natural and cultured pearls	83.3	67.3	49.6
Common metals and manufactures	306.2	382.3	416.1
Machinery and electrical equipment	2,690.3	3,192.0	2,861.9
Transport equipment	31.6	41.4	40.7
Optical and topographical apparatus and instruments, etc.	685.4	779.7	990.0
Total (incl. others)	8,453.2	9,569.2	9,744.5

PRINCIPAL TRADING PARTNERS

(US $ million)

Imports c.i.f.	2006	2007	2008
Aruba	301.3	353.8	491.1
Brazil	490.0	500.9	420.1
China, People's Rep.	543.0	719.5	865.4
Colombia	332.6	357.9	401.3
Germany	190.9	226.1	272.0
Guatemala	289.5	246.6	296.8
Ireland	518.0	424.2	439.4
Japan	602.8	763.2	822.7
Korea, Republic	242.7	253.9	279.0
Mexico	664.4	778.4	941.2
USA	4,860.3	5,502.9	5,812.4
Venezuela	663.6	736.9	692.3
Total (incl. others)	12,740.2	14,095.2	15,289.4

Exports f.o.b.	2006	2007	2008
China, People's Rep.	557.7	844.8	613.0
El Salvador	235.0	258.5	270.1
Germany	198.4	236.8	219.0
Guatemala	319.1	350.4	359.1
Honduras	258.9	302.1	309.2
Hong Kong	523.1	560.1	390.8
Mexico	189.3	258.2	264.3
Netherlands	509.6	468.4	492.3
Nicaragua	298.9	367.8	399.5
Panama	245.0	300.4	387.5
USA	3,304.9	3,382.0	3,512.0
Total (incl. others)	8,453.2	9,569.2	9,744.5

Transport

ROAD TRAFFIC

(motor vehicles in use at 31 December)

	2002	2003	2004
Private cars	367,832	581,247	620,992
Buses and coaches	12,891	18,516	20,950
Goods vehicles	191,315	195,449	199,506
Road tractors	25,842	n.a.	n.a.
Motorcycles and mopeds	91,883	61,273	64,947

2007: Passenger cars 525,376; Buses and coaches 12,345; Lorries and vans 139,588; Motorcycles and mopeds 100,083.

Source: IRF, *World Road Statistics*.

SHIPPING

Merchant Fleet

(registered at 31 December)

	2006	2007	2008
Number of vessels	15	15	15
Total displacement ('000 grt)	3.6	3.6	3.6

Source: Lloyd's Register-Fairplay, *World Fleet Statistics*.

International Sea-borne Freight Traffic

('000 metric tons)

	1996	1997	1998
Goods loaded	3,017	3,421	3,721
Goods unloaded	3,972	4,522	5,188

Source: Ministry of Public Works and Transport.

CIVIL AVIATION

(scheduled services)

	2004	2005	2006
Kilometres flown (million)	24.4	26.9	13.3
Passenger-km (million)	2,173.0	2,305.8	2,216.0
Total ton-km (million)	10.2	10.4	10.0

Source: UN, mostly Economic Commission for Latin America and the Caribbean, *Statistical Yearbook*.

Tourism

FOREIGN TOURIST ARRIVALS BY COUNTRY OF ORIGIN

	2006	2007	2008
Canada	88,304	102,061	109,854
Colombia	27,706	31,299	33,644
El Salvador	46,414	48,976	46,837
France	24,392	25,939	34,622
Germany	37,847	40,285	44,705
Guatemala	41,057	43,864	40,840
Honduras	32,550	35,673	31,714
Italy	19,175	20,251	18,994
Mexico	56,419	61,436	59,545
Netherlands	24,303	28,014	30,615
Nicaragua	281,086	379,222	455,412
Panama	76,214	84,204	72,855
Spain	50,225	59,089	54,029
United Kingdom	27,890	37,580	40,250
USA	731,236	790,315	807,162
Total (incl. others)	1,725,261	1,979,789	2,089,174

Tourism receipts (US $ million, excl. passenger transport): 1,732 in 2006; 2,209 in 2007; 2,250 in 2008 (provisional) (Source: World Tourism Organization).

Communications Media

	2007	2008	2009
Telephones ('000 main lines in use)	1,436.7	1,437.7	1,492.6
Mobile cellular telephones ('000 subscribers)	1,508.2	1,886.6	1,950.3
Internet users	1,350.0	1,460.0	1,579.0
Broadband subscribers ('000)	107.4	107.4	275.0

Personal computers: 1,000,000 (231.0 per 1,000 persons) in 2005.

Radio receivers ('000 in use): 3,045 in 1999.

Television receivers ('000 in use): 930 in 2000.

Daily newspapers: 7 in 2004.

Non-daily newspapers: 42 in 2004.

Book production: 1,464 titles (excluding pamphlets) in 1998.

Sources: UNESCO, *Statistical Yearbook*, UN, *Statistical Yearbook*, International Telecommunication Union.

Education

(2007/08, unless otherwise indicated)

	Institutions*	Teachers	Students		
			Males	Females	Total
Pre-primary	2,705	7,421	55,499	52,442	107,941
Primary	4,007	28,186	275,839	258,977	534,816
Secondary	708	24,347	190,459	190,354	380,813
General	n.a.	21,033	161,453	160,508	321,961
Vocational	n.a.	3,314	29,006	29,846	58,852
Tertiary	52†	4,494‡	50,573§	60,144§	110,717§

* 2005.

† 1999.

‡ 2002/03.

§ 2004/05.

Source: mainly UNESCO Institute for Statistics.

Pupil-teacher ratio (primary education, UNESCO estimate): 19.0 in 2007/08 (Source: UNESCO Institute for Statistics).

Adult literacy rate (UNESCO estimates): 96.0% (males 95.7%; females 96.2%) in 2008 (Source: UNESCO Institute for Statistics).

Directory

The Constitution

The present Constitution of Costa Rica was promulgated in November 1949. Its main provisions are summarized below:

GOVERNMENT

The government is unitary: provincial and local bodies derive their authority from the national Government. The country is divided into seven provinces, each administered by a Governor who is appointed by the President. The provinces are divided into cantons, and each canton into districts. There is an elected Municipal Council in the chief city of each canton, the number of its members being related to the population of the canton. The Municipal Council supervises the affairs of the canton. Municipal government is closely regulated by national law, particularly in matters of finance.

LEGISLATURE

The government consists of three branches: legislative, executive and judicial. Legislative power is vested in a single chamber, the Legislative Assembly (Asamblea Legislativa), which meets in regular session twice a year—from 1 May to 31 July, and from 1 September to 30 November. Special sessions may be convoked by the President to consider specified business. The Assembly is composed of 57 deputies elected for four years. The chief powers of the Assembly are to enact laws, levy taxes, authorize declarations of war and, by a two-thirds' majority, suspend, in cases of civil disorder, certain civil liberties guaranteed in the Constitution.

Bills may be initiated by the Assembly or by the Executive and must have three readings, in at least two different legislative periods, before they become law. The Assembly may override the presidential vote by a two-thirds' majority.

EXECUTIVE

The executive branch is headed by the President, who is assisted by the Cabinet. If the President should resign or be incapacitated, the executive power is entrusted to the First Vice-President; next in line to succeed to executive power are the Second Vice-President and the President of the Legislative Assembly.

The President sees that the laws and the provisions of the Constitution are carried out, and maintains order; has power to appoint and remove cabinet ministers and diplomatic representatives, and to negotiate treaties with foreign nations (which are, however, subject to ratification by the Legislative Assembly). The President is assisted in these duties by a Cabinet, each member of which is head of an executive department.

ELECTORATE

Suffrage is universal, compulsory and secret for persons over the age of 18 years.

DEFENCE

The Costa Rican Constitution has a clause outlawing a national army. Only by a continental convention or for the purpose of national defence may a military force be organized.

The Government

HEAD OF STATE

President: LAURA CHINCHILLA MIRANDA (took office 8 May 2010).

First Vice-President: ALFIO PIVA MESÉN.

Second Vice-President: LUIS LIBERMAN GINSBURG.

THE CABINET
(July 2010)

The Government was formed by the Partido Liberación Nacional (PLN).

Minister of the Presidency: MARCO ANTONIO VARGAS DÍAZ.

Minister of Justice: HERNANDO PARÍS RODRÍGUEZ.

Minister of Planning and Economic Policy: LAURA ALFARO MAYKALL.

Minister of Finance: FERNANDO HERRERO ACOSTA.

Minister of Foreign Relations: RENÉ CASTRO.

Minister of Foreign Trade: ANABEL GONZÁLEZ CAMPABADAL.

Minister of Governance, Police and Public Security: JOSÉ MARÍA TIJERINO PACHECO.

Minister of Economy, Industry and Commerce: MAYI ANTILLÓN.

Minister of Decentralization and Local Government: JUAN MARÍN QUIRÓS.

Minister of Social Welfare: FERNANDO MARÍN ROJAS.

Minister of the Environment, Energy and Telecommunications: TEÓFILO DE LA TORRE ARGUELLO.

Minister of Labour and Social Security: SANDRA PISZK FEINZILBER.

Minister of Public Education: LEONARDO GARNIER RIMOLO.

Minister of Public Health: DR MARÍA LUISA AVILA AGÜERO.

Minister of Housing and Poverty: IRENE CAMPOS GÓMEZ.

Minister of Public Works and Transport: FRANCISCO JIMÉNEZ REYES.

Minister of Science and Technology: CLOTILDE FONSECA QUESADA.

Minister of Culture and Youth: MANUEL OBREGÓN LÓPEZ.

Minister of Tourism: CARLOS RICARDO BENAVIDES JIMÉNEZ.

Minister of Agriculture and Livestock: GLORIA ABRAHAM PERALTA.

Minister of Sport: GISELLE GOYENAGA CALVO.

MINISTRIES

Ministry of Agriculture and Livestock: Antigüo Colegio La Salle, Sabana Sur, Apdo 10094, 1000 San José; tel. 2231-2344; fax 2232-2103; e-mail sunii@mag.go.cr; internet www.mag.go.cr.

Ministry of Culture and Youth: Avdas 3 y 7, Calles 11 y 15, frente al parque España, San José; tel. 2255-3188; fax 2233-7066; e-mail mincjd@mcjd.go.cr; internet www.mcjdcr.go.cr.

Ministry of Decentralization and Local Government: San José.

Ministry of Economy, Industry and Commerce: Del Restaurante Princesa Marina 100 m sur, 100 m oeste y 50 m norte, Barrio La Guaria, Moravia, San José; tel. 2240-5222; fax 2297-1741; e-mail informacion@meic.go.cr; internet www.meic.go.cr.

Ministry of the Environment, Energy and Telecommunications: Avdas 8 y 10, Calle 25, Apdo 10104, 1000 San José; tel. 2233-4533; fax 2257-0697; e-mail prensa@minae.go.cr; internet www.minae.go.cr.

Ministry of Finance: Edif. Antigüo Banco Anglo, Avda 2a, Calle 3a, San José; tel. 2257-9333; fax 2255-4874; e-mail webmaster1@hacienda.go.cr; internet www.hacienda.go.cr.

Ministry of Foreign Relations: Avda 7 y 9, Calle 11 y 13, Apdo 10027, 1000 San José; tel. 2223-7555; fax 2257-6597; e-mail despacho.ministro@rree.go.cr; internet www.rree.go.cr.

Ministry of Foreign Trade: Apdo 2297, 1007 Centro Colón, San José; tel. 2299-4700; fax 2255-3281; e-mail pep@comex.go.cr; internet www.comex.go.cr.

Ministry of Governance, Police and Public Security: Apdo 55, 4874 San José; tel. 2227-4866; fax 2226-6581; internet www.msp.go.cr.

Ministry of Housing and Poverty: Of. Mall San Pedro, 7°, Costado Norte, Apdo 1753, 2050 San Pedro de Montes de Oca; tel. 2202-7900; fax 2202-7910; e-mail info@mivah.go.cr; internet www.mivah.go.cr.

Ministry of Justice: 50 m norte de la Clínica Bíblica, frente a la Escuela M. García Flamenco, 1000 San José; tel. 2256-6700; fax 2234-7959; e-mail justicia@gobnet.go.cr; internet www.mjp.go.cr.

Ministry of Labour and Social Security: Edif. Benjamín Núñez, 4°, Barrio Tournón, Apdo 10133, 1000 San José; tel. 2257-8211; internet www.ministrabajo.go.cr.

Ministry of Planning and Economic Policy: De Autos Subarú 200 m al Norte, Barrio Dent, San Pedro de Montes de Oca; tel. 2281-2700; fax 2253-6243; e-mail despacho@mideplan.go.cr; internet www.mideplan.go.cr.

Ministry of Public Education: Edif. Rofas, frente al Hospital San Juan de Dios, Apdo 10087, 1000 San José; tel. 2258-3745; fax 2248-1763; e-mail contraloriaservicios@mep.go.cr; internet www.mep.go.cr.

Ministry of Public Health: Calle 16, Avda 6 y 8, Apdo 10123, 1000 San José; tel. 2223-0333; fax 2255-2636; e-mail prensams@netsalud.sa.cr; internet www.ministeriodesalud.go.cr.

Ministry of Public Works and Transport: Plaza González Víquez, Calles 9 y 11, Avda 20 y 22, Apdo 10176, 1000 San José; tel. 2523-2000; fax 2255-0242; internet www.mopt.go.cr.

Ministry of Science and Technology: 50 m Este del Museo Nacional, Avda Segunda, Calles 19 y 17, Apdo 5589, 1000 San José; tel. 2248-1515; fax 2257-8895; e-mail micit@micit.go.cr; internet www.micit.go.cr.

Ministry of Social Welfare: San José; tel. 2202-4000; fax 2202-4069; e-mail informatica@imas.go.cr; internet www.imas.go.cr.

Ministry of Sport: San José.

Ministry of Tourism: Costado Este del Puente Juan Pablo II, sobre Autopista General Cañas, Apdo 777, 1000 San José; tel. 2299-5800; fax 2220-0243; internet www.ict.go.cr.

President and Legislature

PRESIDENT

Election, 7 February 2010

Candidate	Valid votes cast	% of valid votes
Laura Chinchilla Miranda (PLN)	896,516	46.91
Ottón Solís Fallas (PAC)	478,877	25.05
Otto Guevara Guth (ML)	399,788	20.92
Luis Fishman Zonzinski (PUSC)	74,114	3.88
Oscar López (PASE)	36,104	1.89
Mayra González (PRC)	13,945	0.73
Eugenio Trejo Benavides (Frente Amplio)	6,782	0.35
Rolando Araya (Alianza Patriótica)	3,158	0.16
Walter Muñoz (PIN)	2,049	0.11
Total (incl. others)	1,911,333	100.00

ASAMBLEA LEGISLATIVA

President: LUIS GERARDO VILLANUEVA MONGE.

General Election, 7 February 2010

Party	% of votes cast	Seats
Partido Liberación Nacional (PLN)	37.16	24
Partido Acción Ciudadana (PAC)	17.68	11
Movimiento Libertario (ML)	14.48	9
Partido Unidad Social Cristiana (PUSC)	8.05	6
Partido Accesibilidad sin Exclusión (PASE)	9.17	4
Partido Renovación Costarricense (PRC)	3.77	1
Frente Amplio	3.66	1
Partido Restauración Nacional	1.62	1
Total (incl. others)	100.00	57

Election Commission

Tribunal Supremo de Elecciones (TSE): Avda 1 y 3, Calle 15, Apdo 2163, 1000 San José; tel. 2287-5555; e-mail secretariatse@tse.go.cr; internet www.tse.go.cr; f. 1949; independent; Pres. Luis Antonio Sobrado González; Exec. Dir Fernando Víquez Jiménez.

Political Organizations

Alianza Democrática Nacionalista (ADN): Contiguo a casa 37, Barrio La Favorita, Pavas, San José; tel. 2232-8762; fax 2220-3041; e-mail info@adn.co.cr; internet www.adn.co.cr; f. 2004; Pres. José Miguel Villalobas Umaña; Sec.-Gen. Emilia María Rodríguez Arias.

Alianza Patriótica: Edif. Rojo, 2°, De la esquina sureste del Museo Nacional, 1 cuadra este a mano derecha, San José; tel. 2223-9595; fax 2223-9596; e-mail info@ap.cr; internet www.ap.cr; Pres. Mariano Figueres Olsen; Sec.-Gen. Arnoldo Mora Vaglio.

Frente Amplio: Apdo 16-1016, San José; tel. 8386-1835; fax 2243-2830; e-mail jmerino@asamblea.go.cr; Pres. José Merino Del Río.

Movimiento Libertario (ML): Of. de Cabinas San Isidro, Barrio Los Yoses Sur, Apdo 4674, 1000 San José; tel. 2283-8600; fax 2283-9600; e-mail otto@libertario.org; internet www.movimientolibertario.com; f. 1994; Pres. Otto Guevara Guth; Sec.-Gen. Mirna Patricia Pérez Hegg.

Partido Accesibilidad sin Exclusión (PASE): San José; tel. 2214-6110; internet www.oscarlopez.net; f. 2004; Leader Oscar López.

Partido Acción Ciudadana (PAC): 25 San Pedro, 425 m sur del Templo Parroquial, San José; tel. 2281-2727; fax 2280-6640; e-mail accionciudadana@pac.or.cr; internet www.pac.or.cr; f. 2000; centre party; Pres. Alberto Cañas Escalante; Sec.-Gen. Margarita Bolaños Arquín.

Partido Fuerza Democrática (FD): Edif. Colón, Apdo 1129, 1007 San José; tel. 2233-7850; fax 2273-3625; e-mail partidofuerzademocratica@hotmail.com; f. 1992 as coalition; later became national party; Pres. Marco Nuñez González; Sec.-Gen. Vladimir de la Cruz de Lemos.

Partido Integración Nacional (PIN): Edif. de Imágenes Médicas, 2°, Apdo 219, 2050 San Pedro de Montes de Oca, San José; tel. 2221-3300; fax 2500-0729; e-mail waltermunoz@costarricense.cr; internet www.pin.co.cr; f. 1996; Pres. Dr Walter Muñoz Céspedes; Sec.-Gen. Heiner Alberto Lemaitre Zamora.

Partido Liberación Nacional (PLN): Mata Redonda, 125 m oeste del Ministerio de Agricultura y Ganadería, Casa Liberacionista José Figueres Ferrer, Apdo 10051, 1000 San José; tel. 2232-5133; fax 2231-4097; e-mail secregeneralpln@ice.co.cr; internet www.pln.or.cr; f. 1952; social democratic party; affiliated to the Socialist International; 500,000 mems; Pres. Francisco Antonio Pacheco Fernández; Sec.-Gen. Antonio Calderón Castro.

Partido Patria Primero: 400 m norte de la Toyota Purdy Motor, Paseo Colón, San José; tel. 8368-9294; fax 2222-9667; f. 2004; Pres. Juan José Vargas Fallas; Sec. Wilberth Hernández Vargas.

Partido Renovación Costarricense (PRC): Centro Educativo Instituto de Desarrollo de Inteligencia, Hatillo 1, Avda Villanea, Apdo 31, 1300 San José; tel. 2254-3651; fax 2252-3270; e-mail jimmysos@costarricense.cr; f. 1995; Pres. Justo Orozco Alvarez; Vice-Pres. Rafael Matamoros Mesén.

Partido Rescate Nacional: Residencial Estefanía 14, Mata de Plátano, Goicoechea, San José; tel. 2234-9569; fax 2285-3282; e-mail delgadorojas@racsa.co.cr; f. 1996; Pres. Fabio Enrique Delgado Hernández; Sec.-Gen. Alejandro López Martínez.

Partido Restauración Nacional: Del Restaurante la Princesa Marina, 75 mnorte, portón amarillo, casa al fondo, contiguo al local de pinturas Protecto, Moravia, San Vicente; f. 2005; provincial party; Pres. Carlos Luis Avendaño Calvo.

Partido Unidad Social Cristiana (PUSC): 100 m al oeste del Hospital de Niños, Paseo Colón, Apdo 10095, 1000 San José; tel. 2280-2920; fax 2248-3678; e-mail info@partidounidadsocialcristiana.com; internet www.partidounidadsocialcristiana.com; f. 1983; Pres. Luis Fishman Zonzinski; Sec.-Gen. Juan Ignacio Mata Centeno.

Partido Vanguardia Popular: 400 m sur de la Iglesia Católica del distrito, Ciudad Desamparados, Apdo 690, 2400 San José; tel. 2225-8300; fax 2219-7976; e-mail upvargas@sol.racsa.co.cr; f. 1931 as Partido Pueblo Unido; renamed in 1995; Pres. Trino Barrantes Araya; Sec.-Gen. Humberto Elías Vargas Carbonell.

Unión Nacional: Frente a la Asociación China, Barrio Francisco Peralta, San José; tel. 2289-4670; fax 2234-3207; e-mail partidounionnacional@yahoo.com; f. 2004; Pres. Arturo Acosta Mora; Sec.-Gen. Hernán Ricardo Zamora Rojas.

Unión Para el Cambio (UPC): Ultima casa a la izquierda, 675 m sur del Banco Nacional, Barrio Roosevelt, Montes de Oca, San José; tel. 2280-0006; fax 2524-0534; e-mail info@upc.or.cr; internet www.upc.or.cr; f. 2004; Pres. Antonio Alvarez Desanti; Sec.-Gen. Rocío Alvarez Olaso.

Unión Patriótica (UP): 200 m norte del Centro Cultural Costarricense Norteamericano, Barrio Escalante, San José; tel. 2243-2050; fax 2551-0542; Pres. José Miguel Corrales Bolaños; Sec.-Gen. Rafael Angel Varela Granados.

Diplomatic Representation

EMBASSIES IN COSTA RICA

Argentina: McDonald's de Curridabat, 700 m sur y 25 m este, Apdo 1963, 1000 San José; tel. 2234-6520; fax 2283-9983; e-mail embarg@racsa.co.cr; Ambassador Juan José Arcuri.

Belgium: Los Yoses, 4a entrada, 25 m sur de la Subaru, Apdo 3725, 1000 San José; tel. 2225-6633; fax 2225-0351; e-mail sanjose@diplobel.fed.be; internet www.diplomatie.be/sanjose; Ambassador Grègoire Vardakis.

Bolivia: Barrio Francisco Peralta, de la Casa Italia 100 m Oeste, Apdo 84810, 1000 San José; tel. 2524-3491; fax 2280-0320; e-mail embocr@racsa.co.cr; Ambassador Martín Callisaya Coaquira.

Brazil: Edif. Torre Mercedes, 6°, Paseo Colón, Apdo 10132, 1000 San José; tel. 2295-6875; fax 2295-6874; e-mail embajada@embrasil.co.cr; Ambassador Hildebrando Tadeu Nascimento Valadares.

Canada: Oficentro Ejecutivo La Sabana, Edif. 5, 3°, detrás de la Contraloría, Centro Colón, Apdo 351, 1007 San José; tel. 2242-4400; fax 2242-4410; e-mail sjcra@international.gc.ca; internet www.sanjose.gc.ca; Ambassador Neil Reeder.

Chile: Casa 225, Los Yoses, del Automercado Los Yoses 225 m sur, Calle 39, Avdas 10 y 12, Apdo 10102, 1000 San José; tel. 2280-0037; fax 2253-7016; e-mail info@embachile.co.cr; internet www.embachile.co.cr; Ambassador Gonzalo Mendoza Negri.

China, People's Republic: De la casa de D. Oscar Arias, 100 m sur y 50 m este, Rohrmoser, Pavas, Apdo 1518, 1200 San José; tel. 2291-4811; fax 2291-4820; e-mail embchina_costarica@yahoo.com.cn; internet cr.chineseembassy.org/esp; Ambassador Li Changhua.

Colombia: Barrio Dent de Taco Bell, San Pedro, Apdo 3154, 1000 San José; tel. 2283-6871; fax 2283-6818; e-mail emcolcr@racsa.co.cr; Ambassador Luis Guillermo Fernández Correa.

Czech Republic: 75 m oeste de la entrada principal del Colegio Humboldt, Apdo 12041, 1000 San José; tel. 2296-5671; fax 2296-5595; e-mail sanjose@embassy.mzv.cz; internet www.mzv.cz/sanjose; Ambassador Pavel Prochazka.

Dominican Republic: McDonald's de Curridabat 400 sur, 100 m este, Apdo 4746, 1000 San José; tel. 2283-8103; fax 2280-7604; e-mail embdominicanacr@ice.co.cr; Ambassador Adonaida Medina Rodríguez.

Ecuador: De la casa de Oscar Arias 100 m norte, Rohrmoser, Apdo 1374, 1000 San José; tel. and fax 2232-1503; e-mail eecucostarica@mmrree.gov.ec; internet www.consuladoecuadorsj.com; Ambassador Daisy Tula Espinel de Alvarado.

El Salvador: Paseo Colón, Calle 30, Avda 1, No 53, Apdo 1378, 1000 San José; tel. 2257-7855; fax 2258-1234; e-mail embasacr@amnet.co.cr; Ambassador Sebastián Vaquerano López.

France: Carretera a Curridabat, de Mitsubishi 200 m sur y 25 m oeste, Apdo 10177, 1000 San José; tel. 2234-4167; fax 2234-4195; e-mail sjfrance@sol.racsa.co.cr; internet www.ambafrance-cr.org; Ambassador Fabrice Delloye.

Germany: Edif. Torre la Sabana, 8°, Sabana Norte, Apdo 4017, 1000 San José; tel. 2290-9091; fax 2231-6403; e-mail info@san-jose.diplo.de; internet www.san-jose.diplo.de; Ambassador Dr Wolf Daerr.

Guatemala: De Sabana Sur, del Gimnasio Fitsimons 100 sur y 50 m oeste, Apdo 328, 1000 San José; tel. 2291-6172; fax 2290-4111; e-mail embaguat@ice.co.cr; Ambassador Carlos Ramiro Santiago Morales.

Holy See: Barrio Rohrmoser, Centro Colón, Apdo 992, 1007 San José (Apostolic Nunciature); tel. 2232-2128; fax 2231-2557; e-mail nuapcr@racsa.co.cr; Apostolic Nuncio Right Rev. Pierre Nguyên Van Tot (Titular Archbishop of Rusticiana).

Honduras: Rohrmoser, Pavas, Apdo 2239, 1000 San José; tel. 2231-1642; fax 2291-5147; e-mail embhoncr@embajadahonduras.co.cr; internet www.embajadahonduras.co.cr; Ambassador Jaime Güell Bográn.

Israel: Edif. Centro Colón, 11°, Calle 38 Paseo Colón, Apdo 5147, 1000 San José; tel. 2221-6444; fax 2257-0867; e-mail info@sanjose.mfa.gov.il; internet sanjose.mfa.gov.il; Ambassador Ehud Moshe Eitam.

Italy: Los Yoses, 5a entrada, Apdo 1729, 1000 San José; tel. 2224-6574; fax 2225-8200; e-mail ambasciata.sanjose@esteri.it; internet www.ambsanjose.esteri.it; Ambassador DIEGO UNGARO.

Japan: Edif. Torre La Sabana, 10°, Sabana Norte, Apdo 501, 1000 San José; tel. 2232-1255; fax 2231-3140; e-mail embjapon@racsa.co.cr; internet www.cr.emb-japan.go.jp; Ambassador HIDEKAZU YAMAGUCHI.

Korea, Republic: 125 m norte del banco Cuscatlán, Rohrmoser, Paseo Colón, Apdo 838, 1007 San José; tel. 2220-3160; fax 2220-3168; e-mail koco@mofat.go.kr; internet cri.mofat.go.kr; Ambassador KWON TAE-MYUN.

Mexico: Avda 7A, No 1371, Apdo 10107, 1000 San José; tel. 2257-0633; fax 2258-2437; e-mail rmision@embamexico.or.cr; internet portal.sre.gob.mx/costarica; Ambassador ZADALINDA GONZALEZ Y REYNERO.

Netherlands: Oficentro Ejecutivo La Sabana (detrás de la Contraloría), Edif. 3, 3°, Sabana Sur, Apdo 10285, 1000 San José; tel. 2296-1490; fax 2296-2933; e-mail nethemb@racsa.co.cr; internet www.nethemb.or.cr; Ambassador JOHANNES VAN BONZEL.

Nicaragua: Avda Central 2540, Calle 25 bis, Barrio la California, Apdo 1382, 1000 San José; tel. 2221-2924; fax 2221-3036; e-mail embanic@racsa.co.cr; Ambassador HAROLD FERNANDO RIVAS REYES.

Panama: Del Antiguo Higuerón de San Pedro 200 m sur y 25 m este, Barrio La Granja, San Pedro de Montes de Oca, Apdo 103, 2050 San José; tel. 2280-1570; fax 2281-2161; e-mail panaembacr@racsa.co.cr; Ambassador JOSÉ JAVIER MULINO.

Paraguay: De la Kentucky de Plaza del Sol 600 m al sur y 50 m al este, 12 Curridabat, San Pedro de Montes de Oca, Apdo 2420, 2050 San José; tel. 2234–2932; fax 2234–0891; e-mail embapar@racsa.co.cr; Ambassador OSCAR BUENAVENTURA LLANES TORRES.

Peru: Del Colegio de Igenieros y Arquitectos, 350 m al norte, Urb. Freses, Curridabat, Apdo 4248, 1000 San José; tel. 2225-9145; fax 2253-0457; e-mail embaperu@amnet.co.cr; Ambassador MOISÉS TAMBINI DEL VALLE.

Russia: Barrio Escalante, 100 m norte y 150 m este de la Iglesia Santa Teresita, Apdo 6340, 1000 San José; tel. 2256-9181; fax 2221-2054; e-mail emrusa@sol.racsa.co.cr; Ambassador VLADIMIR TIKHONOVICH KURAEV.

Spain: Calle 32, entre Paseo Colón y Avda 2, Apdo 10150, 1000 San José; tel. 2222-1933; fax 2222-4180; e-mail embespcr@correo.mae.es; Ambassador ARTURO REIG TAPIA.

Switzerland: Edif. Centro Colón, 10°, Paseo Colón, Apdo 895, 1007 San José; tel. 2221-4829; fax 2255-2831; e-mail sjc.vertretung@eda.admin.ch; internet www.eda.admin.ch/sanjose; Ambassador HANS-RUDOLF HODEL.

United Kingdom: Edif. Centro Colón, 11°, Paseo Colón, Apdo 815, 1007 San José; tel. 2258-2025; fax 2233-9938; e-mail britemb@racsa.co.cr; internet www.ukincostarica.fco.gov.uk; Ambassador TOM KENNEDY.

Uruguay: Trejos Monte Alegre, Escazú, del Vivero Exótica. 900 m oeste y 100 m sur, Apdo 3448, 1000 San José; tel. 2288-3424; fax 2288-3070; e-mail embajrou@sol.racsa.co.cr; Ambassador OCTAVIO BRUGNINI GARCÍA LAGOS.

USA: Calle 120, Avda 0, Pavas, Apdo 920, 1200 San José; tel. 2519-2000; fax 2220-2305; e-mail info@usembassy.or.cr; internet sanjose.usembassy.gov; Ambassador ANNE SLAUGHTER ANDREW.

Venezuela: De la Casa de Don Óscar Arias, 100 m al sur, 400 m al oeste y 25 m al sur, Barrio Rohrmoser, Apdo 10230, 1000 San José; tel. 2220-3102; fax 2290-3806; e-mail embve.crsjo@mre.gob.ve; internet www.embajadadevenezuelaencostarica.org; Ambassador NELSON RAMÓN PINEDA PRADA.

Judicial System

Ultimate judicial power is vested in the Supreme Court, the justices of which are elected by the Legislative Assembly for a term of eight years, and are automatically re-elected for an equal period, unless the Assembly decides to the contrary by a two-thirds' vote. The Supreme Court justices sit in four courts: the First Court (civil, administrative, agrarian and commercial matters), the Second Court (employment and family), the Third Court (penal) and the Constitutional Court.

There are, in addition, appellate courts, criminal courts, civil courts and special courts. The jury system is not used. Judges of the lower courts are appointed by the Supreme Court's administrative body, the Supreme Council. The Supreme Council's members are elected by the Supreme Court.

The Supreme Court

Sala Constitucional de la Corte Suprema de Justicia, Apdo 5, 1003 San José; tel. 2295-3000; fax 2257-0801; e-mail sala4-informacion@poder-judicial.go.cr; internet www.poder-judicial.go.cr.

President of the Supreme Court: LUIS PAULINO MORA MORA.

Supreme Council

Members: MIRIAM ANCHÍA PANIAGUA, MARVIN MARTÍNEZ FERNÁNDEZ, MILENA CONEJO AGUILAR, ROCÍO CERVANTES BARRANTES.

Justices of the First Court: Dr ANABEL LEÓN FEOLI, Dr OSCAR GONZÁLEZ CAMACHO, Dr ROMÁN SOLÍS ZELAYA, Dr CARMENMARÍA ESCOTO FERNÁNDEZ, LUIS GUILLERMO RIVAS LOÁICIGA.

Justices of the Second Court: ORLANDO AGUIRRE GÓMEZ, ZARELA VILLANUEVA MONGE, Dr JULIA VARELA ARAYA, ROLANDO VEGA ROBERT.

Justices of the Third Court: JOSÉ MANUEL ARROYO GUTIÉRREZ, JESÚS RAMÍREZ QUIRÓS, Dr CARLOS CHINCHILLA SANDÍ, ALFONSO CHAVES RAMÍREZ, MAGDA PEREIRA VILLALOBOS.

Justices of the Constitutional Court: ANA VIRGINIA CALZADA MIRANDA, LUIS PAULINO MORA MORA, Dr FERNANDO CRUZ CASTRO, ADRIÁN VARGAS BENAVIDES, Dr ERNESTO JINESTA LOBO, Dr GILBERT ARMIJO SANCHO.

Religion

Under the Constitution, all forms of worship are tolerated. Roman Catholicism is the official religion of the country. Various Protestant churches are also represented.

CHRISTIANITY

The Roman Catholic Church

Costa Rica comprises one archdiocese and seven dioceses. Roman Catholics represent some 82% of the total population.

Bishops' Conference

Conferencia Episcopal de Costa Rica, Apdo 7288, 1000 San José; tel. 2221-3053; fax 2221-6662; e-mail seccecor@racsa.co.cr; internet www.iglesiacr.org.

f. 1977; Pres. Most Rev. HUGO BARRANTES UREÑA (Archbishop of San José de Costa Rica).

Archbishop of San José de Costa Rica: Most Rev. HUGO BARRANTES UREÑA, Arzobispado, Apdo 497, 1000 San José; tel. 2258-1015; fax 2221-2427; e-mail arzobispo@arquisanjose.org; internet www.arquisanjose.org.

The Anglican Communion

Costa Rica comprises one of the five dioceses of the Iglesia Anglicana de la Región Central de América.

Bishop of Costa Rica: Rt Rev. HÉCTOR MONTERROSO, Apdo 10520, 1000 San José; tel. 2225-0790; fax 2253-8331; e-mail iarca@amnet.co.cr.

Other Churches

Federación de Asociaciones Bautistas de Costa Rica: Apdo 1631, 2100 Guadalupe; tel. 2253-5820; fax 2253-4723; e-mail fabcr2@icc.co.cr; internet www.fabcr.org; f. 1946; represents Baptist churches; Pres. JOSÉ ARMANDO SOTO VILLEGAS.

Iglesia Evangélica Luterana de Costa Rica (Evangelical Lutheran Church of Costa Rica): Apdo 1512, Pavas, 1200 San José; tel. 2291-0986; fax 2291-0986; e-mail iglevlutcostarica@gmail.com; internet www.ielcor.org; f. 1955; German congregation; 600 mems; Pres. Rev. MATTHIAS VON WESTHERHOLT.

Iglesia Evangélica Metodista de Costa Rica (Evangelical Methodist Church of Costa Rica): Apdo 5481, 1000 San José; tel. 2236-2171; fax 2236-5921; e-mail iglesiametodistacr@yahoo.com; internet www.geocities.com/iglesiametodistacr; autonomous since 1973; affiliated to the United Methodist Church; 6,000 mems; Pres. Bishop LUIS F. PALOMO.

BAHÁ'Í FAITH

National Spiritual Assembly of the Bahá'ís of Costa Rica: Apdo 553, 1150 La Uruca; tel. 2520-2127; fax 2296-1033; e-mail info@bahaicr.org; internet www.bahaicr.org; f. 1942.

The Press

DAILIES

Al Día: Llorente de Tibás, Apdo 10138, 1000 San José; tel. 2247-4647; fax 2247-4665; e-mail mgomez@aldia.co.cr; internet www.aldia.co.cr; f. 1992; morning; independent; Dir EDGAR FONSECA; Editor MÓNICA GÓMEZ; circ. 60,000.

Boletín Judicial: La Uruca, Apdo 5024, San José; tel. 2296-9570; internet www.boletinjudicial.go.cr; f. 1878; journal of the judiciary; circ. 2,500.

Diario Extra: Edif. de La Prensa Libre, Calle 4, Avda 4, Apdo 177, 1009 San José; tel. 2223-6666; fax 2223-6101; e-mail redaccion@diarioextra.com; internet www.diarioextra.com; f. 1978; morning; independent; Dir WILLIAM GÓMEZ VARGAS; circ. 120,000.

La Gaceta: La Uruca, Apdo 5024, San José; tel. 2296-9570; e-mail direccion@imprenta.go.cr; internet www.lagaceta.go.cr; f. 1878; official gazette; Dir NELSON LOAIZA; circ. 5,300.

El Heraldo: 400 m al este de las oficinas centrales, Apdo 1500, San José; tel. 2222-6665; fax 2222-3039; e-mail info@elheraldo.net; internet www.elheraldo.net; f. 1994; morning; independent; Chief Editor VANESSA ESQUIVEL S.; Dir ERWIN KNOHR; circ. 30,000.

La Nación: Llorente de Tibás, Apdo 10138, 1000 San José; tel. 2247-4747; fax 2247-5022; e-mail agonzales@nacion.com; internet www.nacion.com; f. 1946; morning; independent; Dir YANANCY NOGUERA; circ. 90,000.

La Prensa Libre: Calle 4, Avda 4, Apdo 10121, 1000 San José; tel. 2223-6666; fax 2223-4671; e-mail plibre@prensalibre.co.cr; internet www.prensalibre.co.cr; f. 1889; evening; independent; Dir WILLIAM GÓMEZ VARGAS; Editor MARÍA ELENA JIMÉNEZ VEGA; circ. 56,000.

La República: Barrio Tournón, Guadalupe, Apdo 2130, 1000 San José; tel. 2522-3300; fax 2257-0401; e-mail redaccion@larepublica.net; internet www.larepublica.net; f. 1950; reorganized 1967; morning; independent; Dir LUIS ALBERTO MUÑOZ; circ. 61,000.

PERIODICALS

Abanico: Calle 4, Avda 4, Apdo 10121, 1000 San José; tel. 2223-6666; fax 2223-4671; e-mail abanico@diarioextra.com; internet www.prensalibre.co.cr; weekly supplement of La Prensa Libre; women's interests; circ. 50,000.

Actualidad Económica: San José; tel. 2226-6483; fax 2224-1528; e-mail wordmagic@live.com; internet www.actualidad.co.cr; Dir NORA RUIZ.

Buena Salud: Colegio de Médicos y Cirujanos de Costa Rica, Sabana Sur, Apdo 548, 1000 San José; tel. 2210-2200; fax 2232-2406; e-mail redaccion@medicos.cr; internet www.medicos.sa.cr; f. 1957; journal of the Colegio de Médicos; monthly; Dir DAISY CORRALES DÍAZ; circ. 5,000.

Contrapunto: La Uruca, Apdo 7, 1980 San José; tel. 2231-3333; f. 1978; fortnightly; publ. of Sistema Nacional de Radio y Televisión; Dir-Gen. BELISARI SOLANO; circ. 10,000.

Eco Católico: Calle 22, Avdas 3 y 5, Apdo 1064, San José; tel. 2222-8391; fax 2256-0407; e-mail info@elecocatolico.org; internet www.elecocatolico.org; f. 1931; Catholic weekly; Dir MARTÍN RODRÍGUEZ GONZÁLEZ; circ. 20,000.

El Financiero: Grupo Nación, Edif. Subsidiarias, Llorente de Tibás, 185-2120 Guadalupe; tel. 2247-5555; fax 2247-5177; e-mail redaccion@elfinancierocr.com; internet www.elfinancierocr.com; f. 1995; Dir JOSÉ DAVID GUEVARA MUÑOZ.

INCAE Business Review: Apdo 960-4050, Alajuela; tel. 2224-6598; fax 2433-9606; e-mail marlene.deestrella@incae.edu; internet conocimiento.incae.edu/ES/publicaciones; f. 1982; publ. by INCAE business school; Dir MARLENE DE ESTRELLA LÓPEZ.

Perfil: Llorente de Tibás, Apdo 1517, 1100 San José; tel. 2247-4345; fax 2247-5110; e-mail perfil@nacion.co.cr; internet www.perfilcr.com; f. 1984; fortnightly; women's interests; Dir ISABEL OVARES; Man. Editor THAIS AGUILAR ZÚÑIGA; circ. 16,000.

Revista Comunicación: Escuela de Ciencias del Lenguaje, Instituto Tecnológico de Costa Rica, Apdo 159-7050, Cartago; tel. 2550-9102; fax 2550-9144; e-mail recom@itcr.ac.cr; internet www.itcr.ac.cr/revistacomunicacion; f. 1977; 2 a year; publ. by Instituto Tecnológico de Costa Rica; Dir RONALD SOLANO JIMÉNEZ.

Semanario Universidad: San José; tel. 2207-5355; fax 2207-4774; e-mail semana@cariari.ucr.ac.cr; internet www.semanario.ucr.ac.cr; f. 1970; weekly; general; Dir LAURA MARTÍNEZ QUESADA; circ. 15,000.

The Tico Times: Calle 15, Avda 8, Apdo 4632, 1000 San José; tel. 2258-1558; fax 2223-6378; e-mail info@ticotimes.net; internet www.ticotimes.net; f. 1956; weekly; in English; Editor STEVE MACK; circ. 15,210.

Tiempos de Costa Rica: 100 m sur de Ferretería El Mar, San Pedro, San José; tel. 2280-2332; fax 2280-6840; e-mail admin@tdm.com; internet www.tdm.com; f. 1996; Costa Rican edition of the international Tiempos de Mundo; Dir and Publr FRANK I. GROW; Editor-in-Chief CARLOS VERDECIA.

PRESS ASSOCIATIONS

Colegio de Periodistas de Costa Rica: Sabana Este, Calle 42, Avda 4, Apdo 5416, San José; tel. 2233-5850; fax 2278-4345; e-mail director@comunicacionefectiva.com; internet www.colper.or.cr; f. 1969; 1,447 mems; Pres. RAÚL SILESKY JIMÉNEZ.

Sindicato Nacional de Periodistas: Colegio de Periodistas Sabana, 50 m sur de la Soda Tapia, San José; tel. 2222-7589; fax 2258-3229; e-mail sindicato@colper.or.cr; f. 1970; 200 mems; Sec.-Gen. LUIS CHAVEZ RODRÍGUEZ.

Publishers

Alef Editores: Apdo 146, 1017 San José; tel. 2255-0202; fax 2222-7878; e-mail alefreading@racsa.co.cr; Dir JOSÉ SUCCAR.

Caribe-Betania Editores: Apdo 1.307, San José; tel. 2222-7244; e-mail info@editorialcaribe.com; internet www.caribebetania.com; f. 1949 as Editorial Caribe; merged with Editorial Betania in 1992 and name changed as above; division of Thomas Nelson Publrs; religious textbooks; Exec. Vice-Pres. TAMARA L. HEIM; Dir JOHN STROWEL.

Editorial Costa Rica: Costado oeste del cementerio, Guadalupe de Goicoechea, Apdo 10010, San José; tel. 2255-5354; fax 2253-5091; e-mail difusion@editorialcostarica.com; internet www.editorialcostarica.com; f. 1959; govt-owned; cultural; Gen. Man. MARÍA ISABEL BRENES; Pres. Dr CLAUDIO MONGE PEREIRA.

Editorial Fernández Arce: 50 este de Sterling Products, la Paulina de Montes de Oca, Apdo 2410, 1000 San José; tel. 2224-5201; fax 2225-6109; internet www.fernandez-arce.com; f. 1967; textbooks for primary, secondary and university education; Dir Dr MARIO FERNÁNDEZ LOBO.

Editorial INBio: San José; tel. 2507-8183; e-mail editorial@inbio.ac.cr; internet www.inbio.ac.cr/editorial; part of Instituto Nacional de Biodiversidad; Man. FABIO ROJAS.

Editorial de la Universidad Autónoma de Centro América (UACA): Apdo 7637, 1000 San José; tel. 2234-0701; fax 2224-0391; e-mail info@uaca.ac.cr; internet www.uaca.ac.cr; f. 1981; Editor GUILLERMO MALAVASSI.

Editorial de la Universidad Estatal a Distancia (EUNED): Apdo 474, 2050 San Pedro; tel. 2253-2440; fax 2234-9138; e-mail editoria@uned.ac.cr; internet www.uned.ac.cr/editorial; f. 1979; Pres. Dr LUIS ALBERTO CAÑAS ESCALANTE; Dir RENÉ MUIÑOZ GUAL.

Editorial Universitaria Centroamericana (EDUCA): Ciudad Universitaria Rodrigo Facio, San Pedro, Montes de Oca, Apdo 64, 2060 San Pedro; tel. 2224-3727; fax 2253-9141; e-mail educa@sp.cusa.ac.cr; f. 1969; organ of the CSUCA; science, literature, philosophy; Dir ANITA DE FORMOSO.

Grupo Editorial Norma: Zona Franca Metropolitana Local 7B, Barreal de Heredia, Heredia; tel. 2293-1333; fax 2239-3947; e-mail gerencia@farben.co.cr; internet www.norma.com; Man. Editor ALEXANDER OBONAGA.

Grupo Santillana: La Uruca 78, 1150 San José; tel. 2220-4242; fax 2220-1320; e-mail santilla@santillana.co.cr; internet www.gruposantillana.co.cr; Dir ELSA MORALES CORDERO.

Imprenta Nacional: La Uruca, San José; tel. 2296-9570; e-mail callcenter@imprenal.go.cr; internet www.imprentanacional.go.cr; Dir-Gen. NELSON LOAIZA.

Librería Lehmann, Imprenta y Litografía, Ltda: Calles 1 y 3, Avda Central, Apdo 10011, San José; tel. 2522-4848; fax 2233-0713; e-mail servicio@librerialehmann.com; internet www.librerialehmann.com; f. 1896; general fiction, educational, textbooks; Man. Dir ANTONIO LEHMANN STRUVE.

Trejos Hermanos Sucesores, SA: Curridabat, Apdo 10096, San José; tel. 2224-2411; e-mail henry@trejoshnos.com; f. 1912; general and reference; Pres. ALVARO TREJOS; Man. HENRY CHAMBERLAIN.

PUBLISHING ASSOCIATION

Cámara Costarricense del Libro: Paseo de los Estudiantes, Apdo 1571, 1002 San José; tel. 2225-1363; fax 2252-4297; e-mail ccl@libroscr.com; internet www.libroscr.com; f. 1978; Pres. OSCAR CASTILLO.

Broadcasting and Communications

TELECOMMUNICATIONS

In June 2008 legislation was passed to end the monopoly over the telecommunications sector enjoyed by the Instituto Costarricense de Electricidad (ICE). Implementation of the reform was delayed until 2010, however.

Cámara Costarricense de Telecomunicaciones (CCTEL): Edif. Centro Colón, Apdo 591, 1007 San José; tel. and fax 2255-3422; e-mail cctel@cctel.org; internet cctel.org; Pres. MIGUEL LEÓN S.

Instituto Costarricense de Electricidad (ICE): govt agency for power and telecommunications (see Trade and Industry—Utilities)

Radiográfica Costarricense, SA (RACSA): Avda 5, Calle 1, Frente al Edif. Numar, Apdo 54, 1000 San José; tel. 2287-0087; fax 2287-0379; e-mail racsaenlinea@racsa.co.cr; internet www.racsa.co.cr; f. 1921; state telecommunications co, owned by ICE; Gen. Man. ROGER CARVAJAL BONILLA.

Superintendencia de Telecomunicaciones (SUTEL): San José; f. 2009; regulatory body for the telecommunications sector; forms part of the Autoridad Reguladora de los Servicios Públicos (ARESEP—see Trade and Industry).

RADIO

Asociación Costarricense de Información y Cultura (ACIC): Apdo 365, 1009 San José; f. 1983; independent body; controls private radio stations; Pres. JUAN FEDERICO MONTEALEGRE MARTÍN.

Cámara Nacional de Radio (CANARA): Paseo de los Estudiantes, Apdo 1583, 1002 San José; tel. 2256-2338; fax 2255-4483; e-mail info@canara.org; internet www.canara.org; f. 1947; Pres. LUIS ENRIQUE ORTIZ VAGLIO; Sec. GUSTAVO PIEDRA GUZMÁN.

Control Nacional de Radio (CNR): Edif. García Pinto, 2°, Calle 33, Avdas Central y Primera, Barrio Escalante, Apdo 1344, 1011 San José; tel. 2524-0455; fax 2524-0454; e-mail controlderadio@ice.co.cr; internet www.controlderadio.go.cr; f. 1954; governmental supervisory department; Dir MELVIN MURILLO ALVAREZ.

Non-commercial

Faro del Caribe: Apdo 2710, 1000 San José; tel. 2286-1755; fax 2227-1725; e-mail info@farodelcaribe.org; internet www.farodelcaribe.org; f. 1948; religious and cultural programmes in Spanish and English; Man. GEOVANNY CALDERÓN CASTRO.

Radio FCN Sonora (Family Christian Network): Apdo 60-2020, Zapote, San José; tel. 2209-8000; fax 2293-7993; e-mail info@fcnradio.com; internet www.fcnradio.com; Dir Dr DECAROL WILLIAMSON; Man. ALEXANDER PORRAS.

Radio Fides: Avda 4, Curia Metropolitana, Apdo 5079, 1000 San José; tel. 2258-1415; fax 2233-2387; e-mail emiliom@radiofides.co.cr; internet www.radiofides.co.cr; f. 1952; Roman Catholic station; Dir EMILIO OTÁROLA.

Radio Nacional: 1 km oeste del Parque Nacional de Diversiones, La Uruca, Apdo 7, 1980 San José; tel. 2231-3331; fax 2220-0070; e-mail rnacional@sinart.go.cr; internet www.sinart.go.cr; f. 1978; Exec. Pres. ALFONSO ESTEVANOVICH GONZALES; Dir SYLVIA CAAMAÑO RENCORET.

Radio Santa Clara: Santa Clara, San Carlos, Apdo 221, Ciudad Quesada, Alajuela; tel. and fax 2460-6666; e-mail radio@radiosantaclara.org; internet www.radiosantaclara.org; f. 1984; Roman Catholic station; Dir Rev. MARCO A. SOLÍS V.

Radio Universidad: Ciudad Universitaria Rodrigo Facio, San Pedro, Montes de Oca, Apdo 2060, 1000 San José; tel. 2234-3233; fax 2207-4832; e-mail radioucr@cariari.ucr.ac.cr; internet www.radiouniversidad.ucr.ac.cr; f. 1949; classical music; Dir GIZELLE BOZA SOLANO.

Commercial

There are about 80 commercial radio stations, including:

Grupo Centro: Apdo 6133, San José; tel. 2240-7591; fax 2236-3672; internet www.radiocentrocr.com; f. 1971; operates Radio Centro 96.3 FM, Radio 820 AM, Televisora Guanacasteca Channels 16 and 28; Dir ROBERTO HERNÁNDEZ RAMÍREZ.

Grupo Columbia: 200 m oeste de la Casa Presidencial, Zapote, Apdo 168-2020, San José; tel. 2224-7272; fax 2225-9275; e-mail columbia@columbia.co.cr; internet www.columbia.co.cr; operates Radio Columbia, Radio Dos, Radio 955 Jazz; Dir YASHÍN QUESADA ARAYA; Gen. Man. MIGUEL MONGE.

Radio Chorotega: Conferencia Episcopal de Costa Rica, Casa Cural de Santa Cruz, Apdo 92, 5175 Guanacaste; tel. and fax 2680-0447; e-mail ugiocr@hotmail.com; f. 1983; Roman Catholic station; Dir Rev. HUGO BRENES VILLALOBOS.

Radio Eco: Apdo 585, 1007 Centro Colón, San José; tel. 2220-1001; fax 2290-0970; e-mail info@radioeco.com; internet www.radioeco.com; Dir RICARDO ZAMORA; Gen. Man. LUIS ENRIQUE ORTIZ VAGLIO.

Radio Emaús: San Vito, Coto Brus; tel. and fax 2773-3101; e-mail radioemaus@racsa.co.cr; f. 1962; Roman Catholic station; religious programmes; Dir Rev. MIGUEL ANGEL BERGANZA.

Radio Monumental: Avda Central y 2, Calle 2, Apdo 800, 1000 San José; tel. 2296-6093; fax 2296-0413; e-mail ventas@monumental.co.cr; internet www.monumental.co.cr; f. 1929; operates 8 radio stations: Radio Monumental, Radio ZFM, Radio Reloj, Punto Cinco, EXA FM, Radio Fabulosa, Radio Favorita and 670 AM; Gen. Man. TERESA MARÍA CHÁVES ZAMORA.

Radio Musical: Apdo 854, 1000 San José; tel. 2518-2290; fax 2518-2270; e-mail info@radiomusical.com; internet www.radiomusical.com; f. 1951.

Radio Sendas de Vida: San José; tel. 2248-1148; fax 2233-1259; e-mail info@radiosendas.com; internet www.radiosendas.com; f. 1982; Christian station; Pres. CARLOS UMAÑA R.

TELEVISION

Government-owned

Sistema Nacional de Radio y Televisión Cultural (SINART): 1 km al oeste del Parque Nacional de Diversiones La Uruca, Apdo 7, 1980 San José; tel. 2231-6553; fax 2231-6604; e-mail sinart@racsa.co.cr; internet www.sinart.go.cr; f. 1977; cultural; Dir-Gen. DANNY HERNANDEZ.

Commercial

Alphavisión (Canal 19): Detrás de la Iglesia de Santa María y Griega, Carretera a Desamparados, Apdo 1490, San José; tel. 2226-9333; fax 2226-9095; f. 1987; Gen. Man. CECILIA RAMÍREZ.

Canal 54–Cable Mas: Detrás de la Iglesia Santa Marta, Carretera a Desamparados, San José; tel. 2286-3344; fax 2226-9092; e-mail canalcr@racsa.co.cr; internet www.teleplusdigital.com; f. 1996; Pres. ANTONIO ALEXANDRE GARCÍA.

Multivisión de Costa Rica, Ltda (Canal 9): 150 m oeste del Centro Comercial de Guadalupe, Apdo 4666, 1000 San José; tel. 2233-4444; fax 2221-1734; f. 1961; operates Radio Sistema Universal AM (f. 1956), Channel 9 (f. 1962), and FM (f. 1980); sold Channel 4 (f. 1964) to Repretel in 2000; Gen. Man. ARNOLD VARGAS.

Representaciones Televisivas Repretel (Canales 4, 6 y 11): Edif. Repretel, La Uruca del Hospital México, 300 m al oeste, Apdo 2860, 1000 San José; tel. 2299-7200; fax 2232-4203; e-mail info@repretel.com; internet www.repretel.com; f. 1993; Pres. FERNANDO CONTRERAS LÓPEZ; Gen. Man. JULIO MENA RIVERA; News Dir MARCELA ANGULO.

Televisora de Costa Rica (Canal 7), SA (Teletica): Costado oeste Estadio Nacional, Apdo 3876, San José; tel. 2290-6245; fax 2231-6258; e-mail escribanos@teletica.com; internet www.teletica.com; f. 1960; operates Channel 7; Pres. OLGA COZZA DE PICADO; Gen. Man. RENÉ PICADO COZZA.

Finance

(cap. = capital; res = reserves; dep. = deposits; m. = million; brs = branches; amounts in colones, unless otherwise indicated)

BANKING

Central Bank

Banco Central de Costa Rica: Avdas Central y Primera, Calles 2 y 4, Apdo 10058, 1000 San José; tel. 2243-3333; fax 2243-4566; internet www.bccr.fi.cr; f. 1950; total assets 2,516,806.3m. (Dec. 2008); state-owned; Pres. Dr RODRIGO BOLAÑOS ZAMORA; Gen. Man. ROY GONZÁLEZ ROJAS.

State-owned Banks

Banco de Costa Rica (BCR): Avdas Central y 2da, Calles 4 y 6, Apdo 10035,1000 San José; tel. 2287-9000; fax 2255-0911; e-mail ServiciosBancaElectronica@bancobcr.com; internet www.bancobcr.com; f. 1877; responsible for industry; cap. 80,942.5m., res 120,626.7m., dep. 1,615,338.3m. (Dec. 2008); Pres. LUIS CARLOS DELGADO MURILLO; Gen. Man. MARIO RIVERO TURCIOS; 260 brs.

Banco Nacional de Costa Rica: Avda 1–3, Calle 4, Apdo 10015, 1000 San José; tel. 2212-2000; fax 2255-0270; e-mail bncr@bncr.fi.cr; internet www.bncr.fi.cr; f. 1914; responsible for the agricultural sector; cap. 67,395.3m., res 174,733m., dep. 2,562,984m. (Dec. 2008); Pres. ALFREDO VOLIO PÉREZ; Gen. Man. FERNANDO NARANJO VILLALOBOS; 150 brs.

Banco Popular y de Desarrollo Comunal: Calle 1, Avda 2, Apdo 10190, 1000 San José; tel. 2211-7000; fax 2258-5259; e-mail popularenlinea@bp.fi.cr; internet www.bancopopular.fi.cr; f. 1969; cap. 24,991.2m. (2003); Pres. RODOLFO MADRIGAL SABORÍO; Gen. Man. GERARDOS PORRAS SANABRIA.

Private Banks

Banca Promérica, SA: El Cedral, Escazú Trejos Montealegre, Costado Oeste del Hipermás, Apdo 1289, 1200 San José; tel. 2505-7000; fax 2290-1991; e-mail solucion@promerica.fi.cr; internet www.promerica.fi.cr; 21 brs; Pres. EDGAR ZURCHER.

Banco BAC San José, SA: Calle Central, Avdas 3 y 5, Apdo 5445, 1000 San José; tel. 295-9797; fax 256-7200; e-mail info@bacsanjose.com; internet www.bacsanjose.com; f. 1986; fmrly Bank of America, SA; cap. 47,141.0m., res 20,257.2m., dep. 913,451.0m. (Dec. 2008); Pres. ERNESTO CASTEGNARO ODIO; Gen. Man. GERARDO CORRALES BRENES.

Banco BCT, SA: 150 m norte de la Catedral Metropolitana, San José; tel. 2212-8000; fax 2222-3706; e-mail info@corporacionbct.com; internet www.bancobct.com; f. 1984; total assets 13,794m. (1999); merged with Banco del Comercio, SA in 2000; Pres. LEONEL BARUCH.

Banco CMB (Costa Rica), SA: Oficentro Plaza Roble, Edif. El Patio, 4°, Guachipelín de Escazú; tel. 2201-0800; fax 2201-8311; e-mail citibab@sol.racsa.co.cr; internet www.latam.citibank.com/corporate/lacrco/spanish/index.htm; formerly Citibank (Costa Rica).

Banco Citibank de Costa Rica, SA: De La Rotonda Juan Pablo II, 150 m norte, Contiguo, La Uruca, Apdo 6531, 1000 San José; tel. 2299-0299; fax 2296-0026; e-mail cuscatlan@cuscatlancr.com; internet www.latinamerica.citibank.com/costarica/index.html; f. 1984 as Banco de Fomento Agrícola; changed name to Banco BFA in 1994; and became Cuscatlan in 2000; cap. 14,766.4m., dep. 244,747.3m. (Dec. 2007); current name adopted in 2008 after acquisition by Citi; Pres. RAÚL ARMANDO ANAYA E.; Gen. Man. JAIME ALBERTO MARTINEZ ALVAREZ.

Banco HSBC, SA: Barrio Tournón, Diagonal a Ulacit, Apdo 7983, 1000 San José; tel. 2257-1155; fax 2257-1167; e-mail interna@banex.com; internet www.hsbc.fi.cr; f. 1981 as Banco Agroindustrial y de Exportaciones, SA; became Banco Banex SA in 1987; incorporated Banco Metropolitano in 2001 and Banco Bancrecen in 2002; adopted present name in 2007; cap. 50,383.4m., res 14,291.5m., dep. 701,691.2m. (Dec. 2008); Pres. ALBERTO VALLARINO; Gen. Man. SERGIO RUIZ; 33 brs.

Banco Improsa, SA: Barrio Tournón, costado sur del Periódico La República, San José; tel. 2284-4000; fax 2284-4009; e-mail cramirez@improsa.com; internet www.improsa.com; Pres. MARIANELA ORTUÑO PINTO; Gen. Man. FRANCO NARANJO JIMÉNEZ.

Banco Lafise: Fuente de la Hispanidad 50m Este, San Pedro, Montes de Oca; tel. 2246-0800; fax 2280-5090; e-mail info@lafise.fi.cr; internet www.lafise.fi.cr; f. 1974; owned by Grupo Lafise; cap. 3,403.6m., res 258.0m., total assets 3,983.1m. (Dec. 2004); Pres. ROBERTO J. ZAMORA LLANES; Gen. Man. GILBERTO SERRANO.

Scotiabank Costa Rica: Frente a la esquina Noroeste de La Sabana, Edif. Scotiabank, Apdo 5395, 1000, San José; tel. 2210-4000; fax 2233-13766; e-mail scotiacr@scotiabank.com; internet www.scotiabankcr.com; f. 1995; Pres. CARLOS LOMELI ALONZO; Gen. Man. BRIAN W. BRADY; 13 brs.

Banking Association

Asociación Bancaria Costarricense: Apdo 7-0810, 1000 San José; tel. 2253-2898; fax 2225-0987; e-mail ejecutiva@abc.fi.cr; internet www.abc.fi.cr; Pres. FRANCO NARANJO.

STOCK EXCHANGE

Bolsa Nacional de Valores, SA: Parque Empresarial FORUM (Autopista Próspero Fernández), Apdo 03–6155, 1000 San José; tel. 2204-4848; fax 2204-4749; e-mail servicioalcliente@bolsacr.com; internet www.bolsacr.com; f. 1976; Pres. Dr ORLANDO SOTO ENRÍQUEZ; Vice-Pres. THOMAS FREDERICK ALVARADO ACOSTA.

INSURANCE

In 2008 the Legislative Assembly approved legislative reform effectively terminating the state monopoly of all insurance activities.

Caja Costarricense de Seguro Social: Avda 2da, entre calles 5 y 7, Apdo 10105, San José; tel. 2539-0000; fax 2222-1217; e-mail ibalmace@ccss.sa.cr; internet www.info.ccss.sa.cr; accident and health insurance; state-owned; Pres. Dr ILEANA BALMACEDA ARIAS.

Instituto Nacional de Seguros: Calles 9 y 11 bis, Avda 7, Apdo 10061, 1000 San José; tel. 2287-6000; fax 2255-3381; e-mail contactenos@ins-cr.com; internet portal.ins-cr.com; f. 1924; services of foreign insurance companies may be used only by authorization of the Ministry of Finance, and only after the Instituto has certified that it will not accept the risk; Exec. Pres. Dr GUILLERMO CONSTENLA UMAÑA; Vice-Pres. LUIS ALBERTO CASAFONT FLORES.

Superintendencia General de Seguros (SUGESE): San José; e-mail sugese@sugese.fi.cr; internet www.sugese.fi.cr; f. 2010; regulates the insurance sector; Supt JAVIER CASCANTE.

Trade and Industry

GOVERNMENT AGENCIES

Instituto Nacional de Vivienda y Urbanismo (INVU): Apdo 2534, San José; tel. 2221-5266; fax 2223-4006; internet www.invu.go.cr; housing and town planning institute; Exec. Pres. ELADIO PRADO CASTRO; Vice-Pres. JOSÉ MANUEL JIMÉNEZ GÓMEZ.

Promotora del Comercio Exterior de Costa Rica (PROCOMER): Calle 40, Avdas Central y 3, Centro Colón, Apdo 1278, 1007 San José; tel. 2299-4700; fax 2299-4881; e-mail info@procomer.com; internet www.procomer.com; f. 1997 to improve international competitiveness by providing services aimed at increasing, diversifying and expediting international trade; Pres. ANABEL GONZÁLEZ CAMPABADAL; Dir ROBERTO CALVO.

DEVELOPMENT ORGANIZATIONS

Cámara de Azucareros: Calle 3, Avda Fernández Güell, Apdo 1577, 1000 San José; tel. 2221-2103; fax 2222-1358; e-mail crazucar@racsa.co.cr; internet www.camaraazucarera.org.mx; f. 1949; sugar growers; 16 mems; Pres. FEDERICO CHAVARRÍA K.

Cámara Nacional de Bananeros: Edif. Urcha, 3°, Calle 11, Avda 6, Apdo 10273, 1000 San José; tel. 2222-7891; fax 2233-1268; e-mail canaba@racsa.co.cr; f. 1967; banana growers; Pres. EDUARDO ALVARADO S.; Exec. Dir MARÍA DE LOS ANGELES VINDAS.

Cámara Nacional de Cafetaleros: Condominio Oroki 4D, La Uruca, Apdo 1310, San José; tel. and fax 2296-8334; e-mail camcafe@ice.co.cr; f. 1948; 30 mems; coffee millers and growers; Pres. RODRIGO VARGAS RUÍZ; Exec. Dir GABRIELA LOBO H.

Central de Trabajadores de Costa Rica (CTCR): De Acueductos y Alcantarillados 175 m este, entre calles 11 y 13, Barrio Estudiante, San José; tel. 2221-5697; fax 2280-1187; f. 1984.

Corporación Bananera Nacional, SA (CORBANA): Zapote frente casa Presidencial, Apdo 6504-1000 San José; tel. 2202-4700; fax 2234-9421; e-mail corbana@racsa.co.cr; internet www.corbana.co.cr; f. 1971; public co; cultivation and wholesale of agricultural produce, incl. bananas; Pres. JORGE SAUMA; Man. ROMANO ORLICH.

Costa Rican Investment and Development Board (CINDE): Edif. Los Balcones, Plaza Roble, 4°, Guachipelin, Ezcazú; tel. 2201-2800; fax 2201-2867; e-mail invest@cinde.org; internet www.cinde.org; f. 1983; coalition for development of initiatives to attract foreign investment for production and export of new products; Chair. ALBERTO TREJOS; CEO EDNA CAMACHO.

Instituto del Café de Costa Rica: Calle 1, Avdas 18 y 20, Apdo 37, 1000 San José; tel. 2222-6411; fax 2222-2838; internet www.icafe.go.cr; e-mail promo@icafe.go.cr; f. 1933 to develop the coffee industry, to control production and to regulate marketing; Exec. Dir RONALD PETERS SEEVERS.

Sistema de Información del Sector Agropecuario: San José; tel. 2296-2579; fax 2296-1652; e-mail infoagro@mag.go.cr; internet www.infoagro.go.cr; dissemination of information to promote the agricultural sector.

CHAMBERS OF COMMERCE

Cámara de Comercio de Costa Rica: Urb. Tournón, 150 m noroeste del parqueo del Centro Comercial El Pueblo, Apdo 1.114, 1000 San José; tel. 2221-0005; fax 2223-157; e-mail camara@camara-comercio.com; internet www.camara-comercio.com; f. 1915; 900 mems; Exec. Dir ALONSO ELIZONDO BOLAÑOS.

Cámara de Industrias de Costa Rica: 350 m sur de la Fuente de la Hispanidad, San Pedro de Montes de Oca, Apdo 10003, San José; tel. 2202-5600; fax 2234-6163; e-mail cicr@cicr.com; internet www.cicr.com; Pres. JUAN MARÍA GONZÁLEZ VÁSQUEZ; Vice-Pres. ANGELA CRISTINA GARCÍA LEÓN.

Unión Costarricense de Cámaras y Asociaciones de la Empresa Privada (UCCAEP): De McDonald's en Sabana Sur, 400 m al sur, 100 m al este, 25 m al sur, San José; tel. 2290-5595; fax 2290-5596; e-mail uccaep@uccaep.or.cr; internet www.uccaep.or.cr; f. 1974; business fed.; Pres. MANUEL H. RODRÍGUEZ; Vice-Pres. JAIME MOLINA.

INDUSTRIAL AND TRADE ASSOCIATIONS

Asociación de Empresas de Zonas Francas (AZOFRAS): Plaza Mayor, 2°, Pavas, San José; tel. 2520-1635; fax 2520-1636; e-mail azofras@racsa.co.cr; internet www.azofras.com; f. 1990; Pres. JORGE BRENES; Exec. Dir TIMOTHY SCOTT HALL.

Cámara Nacional de Agricultura y Agroindustria: 300 metros sur y 50 metros este de McDonalds, Plaza del Sol, Curridabat, San José; tel. 2225-8245; fax 2280-0969; e-mail cnaacr@sol.racsa.co.cr; internet www.cnaacr.com; f. 1947; Pres. ALVARO SÁENZ SABORÍO; Exec. Dir EDGAR MATA RAMÍREZ.

Consejo Nacional de Producción: 125 m al sur de Yamuni La Sabana en Avda 10, Apdo 2205, San José; tel. 2257-9355; fax 2256-9625; e-mail sim@cnp.go.cr; internet www.mercanet.cnp.go.cr; f. 1948 to encourage agricultural and fish production and to regulate production and distribution of basic commodities; Pres. (vacant); Gen. Man. ZORAIDA FALLAS CORDERO.

Instituto de Desarrollo Agrario (IDA): Apdo 5054, 1000 San José; tel. 2224-6066; internet www.ida.go.cr; Exec. Pres. Dr CARLOS BOLAÑOS CÉSPEDES.

Instituto Mixto de Ayuda Social (IMAS): Calle 29, Avdas 2 y 4, Apdo 6213, San José; tel. 220-24247; fax 2224-6386; e-mail gerencia_general@imas.go.cr; internet www.imas.go.cr; Pres. JOSÉ ANTONIO LI PIÑAR.

Instituto Nacional de Fomento Cooperativo: Apdo 10103, 1000 San José; tel. 2256-2944; fax 2255-3835; e-mail info@infocoop.go.cr; internet www.infocoop.go.cr; f. 1973 to encourage the establishment of co-operatives and to provide technical assistance and credit facilities; Pres. FREDDY GONZÁLEZ ROJAS; Exec. Dir MARTÍN ROBLES ROBLES.

MAJOR COMPANIES

Agrosuperior, SA (SUPERIOR): Apdo 10116-1000, San José; tel. 2210-5300; fax 2231-5059; e-mail gherrera@abonossuperior.co.cr; internet www.abonossuperior.co.cr; holding co with interests in the fertilizer, utilities and industrial machinery sectors; Gen. Man. RICARDO FOURNIER VARGAS.

ArtinSoft: Torre La Sabana, 6°, 300 m oeste del Edif. del ICE, San José; tel. 2519-1000; fax 2519-1010; e-mail info@artinsoft.com; internet www.artinsoft.com; f. 1993; producer of computer software; partially owned by Intel (USA); CEO CARLOS ARAYA; Consulting Services Man. ALEXÁNDER GÓMEZ.

Atlas Eléctrica, SA: Carretera a Heredia, Km 12, Apdo 2166, 1000 San José; tel. 2277-2000; fax 2260-3930; e-mail atlaselectrica@atlas.co.cr; internet www.atlas.co.cr; f. 1961; manufacturers of domestic cooking and refrigeration appliances; Chair. LUIS GAMBOA ARGUEDAS; Man. DIEGO ARTIÑANO FERRIS; 750 employees.

BASF de Costa Rica, SA: Parque Industrial Zeta de Alajuela, Montecillos de Alajuela, Alajuela; tel. 2440-9110; fax 2201-8221; e-mail jose.chacon@basf.com; internet www.centroamerica.basf-cc.com; f. 1975; chemicals; owned by BASF, AG (Germany); Man. JOSÉ GUILLERMO CHACÓN RAMÍREZ.

Baxter Productos Medicos Ltd: Parque Industrial El Guarco, Cartago, San José; tel. 2573-7811; fax 2573-7433; e-mail zelayac@baxter.com; internet www.baxter.com; owned by Baxter International Inc (USA); medical products manufacturing and distribution; Pres. (Latin America) CARLOS ALSONSO; Technology Man. MIGUEL JIMÉNEZ.

Bayer Costa Rica, SA: Eurocenter II, Barreal de Heredia, San José; tel. 2223-6166; fax 2255-0693; e-mail bayer.costarica.bc@bayer-ca.com; internet www.bayer-ca.com; f. 1978; chemicals; Pres. MANFRED LOESEKEN; Country Head ANNETTE ROSENOW.

BDF Costa Rica, SA: Edif. El Pórtico, 1°, Centro Corporativo, Plaza Roble, Blvd Multiplaza, San José; tel. 2201-8020; fax 2201-8023; internet www.beiersdorf.co.cr; manufacturer of pharmaceuticals and toiletries; owned by Beiersdorf, AG (Germany); Dir-Gen. LUIS EMILIO WONG.

Bticino Costa Rica, SA: Frente al Cenada, Parque Industrial Heredia, Apdo 6563, 1000 San José; tel. 2298-5600; fax 2239-0472; e-mail bticino@racsa.co.cr; internet www.bticino.co.cr; f. 1975; manufacturer of electrical apparatus; Gen. Man. FEDERICO CALDERÓN.

CAMtronics, SA: Edif. 50, Parque Industrial Zona Franca Cartago, Cartago; tel. 2573-7366; fax 2573-7225; e-mail marketing@camtronicscr.com; internet www.camtronicscr.com; manufacturers of electronic equipment; Pres. and CEO ENRIQUE ORTIZ CARAZO.

Cemex Costa Rica: Edif. El Pórtico, 3°, Plaza Roble, Guachipelín de Escazú, Apdo 6558, 1000 San José; tel. and fax 2201-2000; fax 2201-8202; internet www.cemexcostarica.com; subsidiary of Cemex, SA de CV (Mexico); cement manufacturers; Country Dir CARLOS EMILIO GONZÁLEZ GALLEGOS.

Cibertec International, SA: 100 metros este de Fuente de Hispanidad, Calle privada, San Pedro de Montes de Oca, POB 149-2300, San José; tel. 2524-0002; fax 2280-5957; e-mail info@cibertec.com; internet www.cibertec.com; f. 1979; telecommunications equipment.

Colgate Palmolive (Costa Rica), SA: 400 m oeste, 400 m norte de la Plaza de Deportes, Barreal de Heredia, POB 10040-1000, San José; tel. 2298-4600; fax 2293-7171; e-mail juanita_espinoza@colpal.com; internet www.colgatecentralamerica.com; manufacturers of toiletries; Pres., Colgate Latin America JUSTIN SKALA; Vice-Pres. and Gen. Man. PEGGY GERICHTER.

Compañía Costarricense del Café, SA (CAFESA): La Uruca, Apdo 4588, 1000 San José; tel. 2232-2255; fax 2231-3640; e-mail cafesa@racsa.co.cr; f. 1956; manufacturer of agrochemicals, fertilizers; Pres. CARLOS ABREU MCDONOUGH; Gen. Man. DANIEL VALERIO BOLAÑOS.

Componentes Intel de Costa Rica, SA: Centro de Ciencia y Tecnologia Ultrapark, Ultra Park, Bldg 1B, La Aurora, Heredia; tel. 2298-6000; fax 2298-7206; e-mail intel.public.affairs@intel.com; internet www.intel.com/costarica; f. 1998; microprocessor manufacture and assembly; operates 2 factories; Group CEO PAUL S. OTELLINI; Gen. Man. MIKE FORREST.

Cooperativa Agrícola Industrial Victoria, RL (CoopeVictoria): Apdo 176–4100, San Isidro, Grecia, 41000 Alajuela; tel. 2494-1866; fax 2444-6346; e-mail victoria@coopevictoria.com; internet www.coopevictoria.com; f. 1949; co-operative of local coffee and sugar growers and processors; Dir JOSÉ EDUARDO HERNÁNDEZ CHAVERRI; Gen. Man. MARIO ANTONIO PINTO; 345 employees.

Cooperativa de Productores de Leche Dos Pinos, RL: Apdo 179-4060, Alajuela; tel. 2437-3000; fax 2437-3602; e-mail centrodecontactos@dospinos.com; internet www.dospinos.com; f. 1948; manufacturers of dairy products and fruit juices; Pres. CARLOS VARGAS ALFARO; 2,526 employees.

Corporación de Desarrollo Pinero de Costa Rica, SA (Pineapple Development Corporation—PINDECO): Apdo 4084-1000 San José; tel. 2222-9211; fax 2233-7808; f. 1971; subsidiary of Del Monte Fresh; cultivation and wholesale of pineapples; Dir-Gen. RODRIGO JIMÉNEZ; 4,800 employees.

Corporación Fischel: Edif. Club Unión, Calle 2, Avda 3, Frente al Correo, Apdo 410300, 1000 San José; tel. 2248-1692; fax 2248-1682; e-mail regente-s00@fischel.co.cr; internet www.fischel.co.cr; subsidiary of Instrumentarium Medko Medical Corpn; pharmaceutical manufacturers; Pres. EMILIO BRUCE JIMÉNEZ.

Corporación Pipasa, SA: 1.5 km al oeste de la Firestone, La Ribera de Belén, Apdo 22-4005, San Antonio Belén; tel. 2293-4801; fax 2293-0479; e-mail pipasa@sol.racsa.co.cr; internet www.crica.com/biz/pipcorp.html; f. 1969; owned by Rica Foods Inc, USA; production of meat products and animal feed; owns the As de Oro brand; Exec. Pres. DON VÍCTOR OCONITRILLO CONEJO; 1,670 employees.

Corrugados Belén, SA (CORBEL): Contiguo a Fábrica Firestone, Autopista General Cañas, Apdo 100-4005, Heredia; tel. 2239-0122; fax 2239-1023; e-mail rlizano@corbel.co.cr; internet www.corbel.co.cr; manufacturers of corrugated cardboard boxes; Gen. Man. RICARDO LIZANO.

DEMASA (Derivados de Maíz Alimenticios, SA): 2 Km al oeste de la Embajada Norteamericana, Pavas, Apdo 7299-1000 San José; tel. 2232-9110; fax 2290-1655; e-mail infopalmito@demasa.com; internet www.demasa.net; f. 1986; subsidiary of Gruma, Mexico; food processing; Pres. HANS J. BÜCHER CHÉVES; 2,500 employees.

Dole Fresh Fruit International Ltd: Centro Colon, POB 12, 1000 San José; tel. 2287-2170; fax 2287-2172; e-mail frans.wielemaker@dole.com; internet www.doleorganic.com; div. of Dole Food Co Inc; fmrly Standard Fruit Company; Dir, Organic Program FRANS WIELEMAKER; 3,250 employees.

Durman Esquivel, SA: 1 km al este del cruce de cinco esqs de Tibás, Calle Blancos, Apdo 6139-1000, San José; tel. 2436-4700; fax 2436-4800; e-mail costarica@durman.com; internet www.durman.com; f. 1959; subsidiary of Aliaxis, SA; manufacturer of plastic products; Pres. FRANCIS DURMAN; Overseas Man. RONALD CISNEROS.

Fertilizantes de Centroamérica, SA (FERTICA): De las Ofs de Pizza Hut, 50 m este, Oficentro Mediterráneo Of. 1, Pavas, 1000 San José; tel. 2231-2555; fax 2290-7571; e-mail ventas@fertica.com; internet www.fertica.com; f. 1961; manufacturers of chemical fertilizers; Pres. OSCAR ENRIQUEZ; 360 employees.

Florida Ice and Farm Company, SA: Apdo 2046-3000 Heredia; tel. 2437-6700; fax 2437-7000; e-mail info@florida.co.cr; internet www.florida.co.cr; f. 1966; 3 main subsidiaries: Florida Inmobiliaria, SA, Florida Capitales, SA, and Florida Bebidas, SA; Pres. RODOLFO JIMÉNEZ BORBÓN; 1,465 employees.

Holcim (Costa Rica), SA: Edif. Administrativo, Centro Industrial Holcim, 200 m este y 100 m sur de la Cruz Roja de San Rafael de Alajuela, Apdo 4301-1000, Alajuela; tel. 2205-2700; fax 2205-3000; e-mail contactenos-cri@holcim.com; internet www.holcim.com/cr; f. 1960; as Industria Nacional de Cemento (INCSA); owned by Holcim Ltd (Switzerland); manufacturers of cement; CEO SERGIO EGLOFF GERLI; 924 employees.

Hultec Terramix, SA: 150 m norte de La Cañada, Apdo 84140, 1000 San José; tel. 2205-1800; fax 2282-7559; e-mail hultec@hultec.com; internet www.hulteccr.com; f. 1976 as Hules Técnicos; manufacturers of rubber seals for PVC tubes; Pres. ALVARO GUTIÉRREZ; 673 employees.

Industrias Unidas Costa Rica, SA (IUSA): Zona Franca Metropolitana 2-C, Barreal de Heredia; tel. 2239-0011; fax 2239-0355; e-mail ticatex@sol.racsa.co.cr; internet www.iusa.com.sv; f. 1965; owned by Toyobo-Itochu y Marubeni (Japan); subsidiary of IUSA (El Salvador); manufacturers of textiles; Pres. NOBUYA ISHII; 400 employees.

Instituto Costarricense de Acueductos y Alcantarillados: Edif. La Llacuna, 9°, Costado de los Bomberos, Pavos, Apdo 5120-1000 San José; tel. 2242-5090; fax 2256-5642; e-mail administrador@aya.go.cr; internet www.aya.go.cr; f. 1961; construction and operation of water and sewerage services; Exec. Pres. OSCAR NÚÑEZ CALVO; Gen. Man. HEIBEL RODRÍGUEZ ARAYA; 2,975 employees.

Merck Sharp & Dohme: Apdo 10135, 1000 San José; tel. 2210-0210; fax 2232-2384; internet www.msd.co.cr; f. 1959; manufacturers of medical and pharmaceutical products; Contact Person NICOLE SCHMIDLIN; 335 employees.

Motorola Costa Rica, SA: Edif. El Portico, 1°, Plaza Roble, Escazu, San José; tel. 2201-1480; fax 2201-1496; internet www.motorola.com/cr; Pres. and CEO GREGORY Q. BROWN.

Nestlé Costa Rica, SA: 300 metros Oeste de Cenada en Barreal de Heredia, 1000 San José; tel. 2209-6600; fax 2239-2678; e-mail nestlecr@sol.racsa.co.cr; internet www.nestle.co.cr; chocolate producers; Exec. Vice-Pres. LUIS CANTARELL.

Refinadora Costarricense de Petróleo (Recope): Goicoechea, San Francisco de Guadalupe de la Iglesia 200 m oeste, Apdo 4351-1000 San José; tel. 2284-2700; fax 2255-4993; internet www.recope.go.cr; f. 1961; state petroleum co; Pres. JORGE ENRIQUE VILLALOBOS CLARE; 1,100 employees.

Roche Servicios, SA: Edif. 6A, 1 Km Noreste de Real Cariari, Zona Franca Ultrapark, Apdo 3438-1000, La Aurora, Heredia; tel. 2298-1500; fax 2298-1607; internet www.roche.com; medication and diagnostic instruments; Group CEO SEVERIN SCHWAN.

Siemens, SA: La Uruca, de la Plaza de Deptortes 200 m al este, Apdo 1002-1000 San José; tel. 2287-5050; fax 2221-5050; e-mail siemens@racsa.co.cr; internet www.siemens-centram.com/index_costarica.shtml; electronic systems, telecommunications equipment; Pres. and CEO PETER LÖSCHER; Gen. Man. ERWIN ELLER.

UTILITIES

Regulatory Body

Autoridad Reguladora de los Servicios Públicos (ARESEP): Sabana Sur, 400 m oeste de la Contraloría General de la República, Apdo 936, 1000 San José; tel. 2220-0102; fax 2290-0374; internet www.aresep.go.cr; f. 1996; oversees telecommunications, public utilities and transport sectors; Regulator FERNANDO HERRERO ACOSTA.

Electricity

Cía Nacional de Fuerza y Luz, SA (CNFL): Calle Central y 1, Avda 5, Apdo 10026, 1000 San José; tel. 2296-4608; fax 2296-3950; e-mail info@cnfl.go.cr; internet www.cnfl.go.cr; f. 1941; electricity co; mem. of ICE Group; Pres. TEÓFILO DE LA TORRE ARGUELLO.

Instituto Costarricense de Electricidad (ICE) (Costa Rican Electricity Institute): Apdo 10032, 1000 San José; tel. 2220-7720; fax 2220-1555; e-mail ice-si@ice.co.cr; internet www.ice.co.cr; f. 1949; govt agency for power and telecommunications; Exec. Pres. PEDRO PABLO QUIRÓS CORTÉZ; Dir EDUARDO DORYAN.

JASEC (Junta Administrativa del Servicio Eléctrico Municipal de Cartago): Apdo 179, 7050 Cartago; tel. 2550-6800; fax 2551-1683; e-mail agomez@jasec.co.cr; internet www.jasec.co.cr; f. 1964; Pres. LUIS GERARDO VILLANUEVA MONGE.

Water

Instituto Costarricense de Acueductos y Alcantarillados: Edif. Central, Pavas, 1000 San José; tel. 2242-5591; fax 2222-2259; e-mail centrodoc@aya.go.cr; internet www.aya.go.cr; water and sewerage; Pres. RICARDO SANCHO CHAVARRÍA.

TRADE UNIONS

Asociación Nacional de Empleados Públicos (ANEP): Apdo 5152, 1000 San José; tel. 2257-8233; fax 2257-8859; e-mail info@anep.or.cr; internet www.anep.or.cr; f. 1958; Sec.-Gen. ALBINO VARGAS BARRANTES.

Central del Movimiento de Trabajadores Costarricenses (CMTC) (Costa Rican Workers' Union): Calle 20, 75 m este de la Cinta Amarilla, Apdo 4137, 1000 San José; tel. 2222-5893; fax 2221-3353; e-mail cmtccr@racsa.co.cr; internet cmtcr.org; Pres. DENNIS CABEZAS BADILLA; Sec.-Gen. JOSÉ ANGEL OBANDO.

Central de Trabajadores de Costa Rica (CTCR): De Acueductos y Alcantarillados 175 m este, entre calles 11 y 13, Barrio Estudiante, San José; tel. 2221-5697; fax 2280-1187; f. 1984.

Confederación Costarricense de Trabajadores Democráticos (Costa Rican Confederation of Democratic Workers): Ofs Centrales del Banco Nacional, 13°, Apdo 2167, San José; tel. 2223-7903; fax 2212-2745; f. 1966; mem. of ITUC and ORIT; Sec.-Gen. OLGER CHAVES; 50,000 mems.

Confederación de Trabajadores Rerum Novarum (CTRN): Barrio Escalante, de la Rotonda el Farolito 250 m este, Apdo 31100, San José; tel. 2283-4244; fax 2234-2282; e-mail ctrn@ice.co.cr; internet www.rerumnovarum.or.cr; Pres. RODRIGO AGUILAR; Sec.-Gen. SERGIO SABORIO.

Confederación Unitaria de Trabajadores (CUT): Calles 1 y 3, Avda 12, Casa 142, Apdo 186, 1009 San José; tel. 2233-4188; fax 2221-4709; e-mail mcalde@racsa.co.cr; f. 1980 from a merger of the Federación Nacional de Trabajadores Públicos and the Confederación General de Trabajadores; 53 affiliated unions; Sec.-Gen. MIGUEL MARÍN CALDERÓN; c. 75,000 mems.

The Consejo Permanente de los Trabajadores, formed in 1986, comprises six union organizations and two teachers' unions.

Transport

Autoridad Reguladora de los Servicios Públicos (ARESEP): regulatory body for the telecommunications industry, public utilities and transport (see Trade and Industry—Utilities).

Cámara Nacional de Transportes: Del Banco Nacional de San Pedro, 600 m sur y 175 m oeste, Montes de Oca, San José; tel. 2283-1820; fax 2283-1712; e-mail canatram@racsa.co.cr; internet www.canatrans.com; national chamber of transport; Exec. Dir JAVIER REYNA.

RAILWAYS

AmericaTravel: Edif. INCOFER, Avda 20, Calle 2, Apdo 246, San José; tel. 2233-3300; fax 2223-3311; e-mail americatravel@ice.co.cr; internet www.americatravelcr.com; operates weekend tourist trains between San José and Caldera; Gen. Man. JUAN PANIAGUA ZELEDÓN.

Instituto Costarricense de Ferrocarriles (INCOFER): Calle Central, Avda 22 y 24, Apdo 1, 1009 San José; tel. 2222-8857; fax 2222-6998; e-mail incofer@sol.racsa.co.cr; internet www.mideplan.go.cr/pnd/actores/sector_publico/incofer; f. 1985; govt-owned; 471 km, of which 388 km are electrified; Pres. MIGUEL CARABAGUÍAZ.

INCOFER comprised:

División I: Atlantic sector running between Limón, Río Frío, Valle la Estrella and Siquirres. Main line of 109 km, with additional 120 km of branch lines, for tourists and the transport of bananas; services resumed in 1999.

División II: Pacific sector running from San José to Puntarenas and Caldera; 116 km of track, principally for transport of grain, iron and stone.

Note: In 1995 INCOFER suspended most operations, pending privatization, although some cargo transport continued. In 2008 INCOFER bought trains and technical assistance from a Spanish company, FEVE, and by mid-2009 a wide range of rail lines had reopened.

ROADS

In 2006 there were 35,983 km of roads, of which 25% were paved. In 2001 the construction of four major roads across the country began; the first road to be built was 74 km long, running from San José to San Ramón. In August 2008 the Inter-American Development Bank approved a loan of US $850m. for improvement works to the road infrastructure, as well as to railways and ports.

SHIPPING

Local services operate between the Costa Rican ports of Puntarenas and Limón and those of Colón and Cristóbal in Panama and other Central American ports. The multi-million dollar project at Caldera on the Gulf of Nicoya is now in operation as the main Pacific port; Puntarenas is being used as the second port. The Caribbean coast is served by the port complex of Limón/Moín. International services are operated by various foreign shipping lines. The Caldera and Puntarenas ports were opened up to private investment and operation from 2002.

Instituto Costarricense de Puertos del Pacífico (INCOP): Calle 36, Avda 3, Apdo 543, 1000 San José; tel. 2223-7111; fax 2223-4348; e-mail pnd@ns.mideplan.go.cr; internet www.mideplan.go.cr/pnd/actores/sector_publico/incop; f. 1972; state agency for the development of Pacific ports; Exec. Pres. ENRIQUE MONTEALEGRE MARTÍ.

Junta de Administración Portuaria y de Desarrollo Económico de la Vertiente Atlántica (JAPDEVA): Calle 17, Avda 7, Apdo 5.330, 1000 San José; tel. 2795-4747; fax 2795-0728; e-mail lrodriguez@japdeva.go.cr; internet www.japdeva.go.cr; state agency for the development of Atlantic ports; Exec. Pres. (vacant); Gen. Man. CARLOS THOMAS ARROYO.

CIVIL AVIATION

Costa Rica has four international airports: Juan Santamaría Airport, the largest, 16 km from San José at El Coco, Tobías Bolaños Airport in Pavas, Daniel Oduber Quirós Airport, at Liberia, and Limón International.

Fly Latin America: San José; tel. 2256-3222; e-mail info@flylatinamerica.net; internet www.flylatinamerica.com; operates services to 9 destinations in Central and South America; Pres. CHARLES STRATFORD; Man. RICHARD KRUG.

Nature Air: Tobías Bolaños Airport, San José; tel. 2299-6000; fax 2232–2516; e-mail ahuntley@natureair.com; internet www.natureair.com; flights from San José to 18 domestic destinations.

Servicios Aéreos Nacionales, SA (SANSA): Edif. TACA, La Uruca, San José; tel. 2290-3543; fax 2290-3538; e-mail info@flysansa.com; internet www.flysansa.com; subsidiary of TACA; international, regional and domestic scheduled passenger and cargo services; Man. Dir CARLOS MANUEL DELGADO AGUILAR.

Tourism

Costa Rica boasts a system of nature reserves and national parks unique in the world, covering one-third of the country. The main tourist features are the Irazú and Poás volcanoes, the Orosí valley and the ruins of the colonial church at Ujarras. Tourists also visit San José, the capital, the Pacific beaches of Guanacaste and Puntarenas, and the Caribbean beaches of Limón. Some 2,089,174 tourists visited Costa Rica in 2008, while tourism receipts totalled an estimated US $2,250m. Most visitors came from the USA (39%).

Cámara Nacional de Turismo de Costa Rica (CANATUR): San José; tel. 2234-6222; fax 2253-8102; e-mail info@tourism.co.cr; internet www.tourism.co.cr; Pres. GONZALO VARGAS.

Instituto Costarricense de Turismo (ICT): La Uruca, Costado Este del Puente Juan Pablo II, Apdo 777, 1000 San José; tel. 2299-5800; fax 2291-5675; e-mail info@visitcostarica.com; internet www.visitcostarica.com; f. 1955; Exec. Pres. CARLOS RICARDO BENAVIDES; Gen. Man. ALLAN RENÉ FLORES MOYA.

Defence

Costa Rica has had no armed forces since 1948. As assessed at November 2009, Rural and Civil Guards totalled 2,000 and 4,500 men and women, respectively. In addition, there were 2,500 Border Security Police. There was also a Coast Guard Unit numbering 400.

Security Budget: an estimated 105,000m. colones in 2009.

Minister of Governance, Police and Public Security: JOSÉ MARÍA TIJERINO PACHECO.

Education

Education in Costa Rica is free, and is compulsory between six and 15 years of age. Primary education begins at the age of six and lasts for six years. Official secondary education consists of a three-year basic course, followed by a more specialized course lasting two years. In 2007/08 secondary enrolment was equivalent to 89% of children in the relevant age-group. In 2005 there were 4,007 primary schools and 708 secondary schools. In 2004 government expenditure on the education system was 440,157.4m. colones, equivalent to 11.1% of total government spending.

Bibliography

For works on Central America generally, see Select Bibliography (Books)

Biesanz, M., *et al. The Ticos: Culture and Social Change in Costa Rica*. Boulder, CO, Lynne Rienner Publrs, 1998.

Booth, J. A. *Costa Rica: Quest for Democracy*. Boulder, CO, Westview Press, 1999.

Calderon, G. *The Life of Costa Rica*. Bogotá, DC, Villegas Editores, 2001.

Costa Rica Research Group. *Executive Report on Strategies in Costa Rica (Strategic Planning Series)*. San Diego, CA, Icon Group International, 2000.

Cruz, C. *Political Culture and Institutional Development in Costa Rica and Nicaragua: World-Making in the Tropics*. Cambridge, Cambridge University Press, 2005.

Edelman, M. *Peasants Against Globalisation: Rural Socialist Movements in Costa Rica*. Stanford, CA, Stanford University Press, 1999.

Evans, S. *The Green Republic: A Conservation History of Costa Rica*. Austin, TX, University of Texas Press, 1999.

Foreign Investment in Latin America and the Caribbean. Santiago, Economic Commission for Latin America and the Caribbean, 2004.

Harpelle, R. N. *The West Indians of Costa Rica*. Montréal, QC, McGill-Queen's University Press, 2001.

Helmuth, C. *Culture and Customs of Costa Rica*. Westport, CT, Greenwood Publishing Group, 2000.

Honey, M. *Hostile Acts: US Policy in Costa Rica in the 1980s*. Gainesville, FL, University Press of Florida, 1994.

Lehoucq, F. E., and Molina, I. *Stuffing the Ballot Box: Fraud, Electoral Reform, and Democratization in Costa Rica*. Cambridge, Cambridge University Press, 2006.

Longley, K. *The Sparrow and the Hawk: Costa Rica and the United States During the Rise of José Figueres*. Tuscaloosa, AL, University of Alabama Press, 1997.

Luetchford, P. *Fair Trade and a Global Commodity: Coffee in Costa Rica*. London, Pluto Press, 2007.

Palmer, S., and Molina, I. (Eds). *The Costa Rica Reader: History, Culture, Politics*. Durham, NC, Duke University Press, 2004.

Paus, E. *Foreign Investment, Development, And Globalization: Can Costa Rica Become Ireland?* Basingstoke, Palgrave Macmillan, 2005.

Reformas económicas, régimen cambiario y choques externos: efectos en el desarrollo económico, la desigualdad y la pobreza en Costa Rica, El Salvador y Honduras (Estudios y perspectivas). New York, NY, United Nations Educational, 2005.

Sandoval-García, C. *Threatening Others: Nicaraguans and the Formation of National Identities in Costa Rica (Latin America S.)*. Athens, OH, Ohio University Press, 2004.

Steigenga, T. J. *Politics of the Spirit: The Political Implications of Pentecostalized Religion in Costa Rica and Guatemala*. Moscow, ID, Lexington Books, 2001.

Wilson, B. M. *Costa Rica: Politics, Economics and Democracy*. Boulder, CO, Lynne Rienner Publrs, 1998.

Yashar, D. J. *Demanding Democracy: Reform and Reaction in Costa Rica and Guatemala, 1870s–1950s*. Stanford, CA, Stanford University Press, 1997.

CUBA

Geography

PHYSICAL FEATURES

The Republic of Cuba consists of the island of Cuba (the largest and westernmost of the Greater Antilles), the Isla de la Juventud (Isle of Youth, until 1978 the Isle of Pines—Isla de Pinos) and 1,600 small offshore islands. Cuba is the largest island in the West Indies, lying at the entrance to the Gulf of Mexico (to the north-west), and is washed by the Caribbean Sea to the south and west and by the Atlantic Ocean to the north-east. Cuba lies only 145 km (90 miles) north of Jamaica and, at the other, north-western end of the island, a similar distance south of Key West in Florida, USA. However, some of the more remote cays of the Bahamas lie much closer, and that country stretches across the north-eastern approaches to Cuba. Haiti is only 80 km to the east. The Yucatán peninsula of Mexico lies about 210 km to the west and the British dependency of the Cayman Islands some 240 km to the south. Cuba also has a 29-km land border in the south-west, where the USA has a lease on the area around its naval base on Guantánamo Bay, but Cuba retains sovereignty. Cuba, the largest country of the insular Caribbean, in terms of both extent and population, covers an area of 109,886 sq km (42,427 sq miles) or about 45% of the total surface area of the Antilles.

The island of Cuba, which is roughly the same size as the North Island of New Zealand or Newfoundland (Canada), is about 1,250 km long and between 32 km and 191 km wide. From a flattened, southern head of mountainous terrain, the island of Cuba extends back north-westwards into a narrowing tail that begins to turn towards the south-west when the island ends. This tail is attempting to encompass the 2,200-sq km Isla de la Juventud, which lies about 100 km to the south (north of a large, bisecting swamp, this island, famed for its citrus fruits, is generally dry and flat, although there are some hills). The Isla de la Juventud is by far the largest of the myriad offshore islands and cays that, together with extensive coral reefs, further complicate the heavily indented, 3,735-km coastline. In the north old coral and limestone has lifted into a steep shore of cliffs and bluffs, sheltering some fine harbours, while the south subsides into a low and often marshy littoral. Much of the terrain of this predominantly limestone island is flat or undulating plain, with wide and fertile valleys, and highlands of any significance only in the south-east. About one-quarter of Cuba's territory is mountainous, with three main ranges: the Cordillera de Guaniguanico (including the distinctive steep-sided, flat-topped mountains of the Sierra de los Organos and the more easterly Sierra del Rosario) at the north-western end of the island; the centre-west highlands, such as the Escambray; and the geologically more recent Sierra Maestra (largely volcanic in origin) in the far south-east, where Pico Turquino reaches 2,005 m (6,580 ft). Rivers tend to be short and fall steeply. The longest is the Cauto, in the east, at only 240 km, and the Toa (110 km long) is the widest river in Cuba.

Rivers and plentiful rainfall water an island still rich in biodiversity, although the almost entirely wooded island that the Spanish first settled on is now three-quarters savannah or plains (there are two main areas of savannah). About 4% of the island is swampy wetland, and a reforestation programme aims to increase the area under trees to 27% of the total. Meanwhile, Cuba is home to an extraordinary range of terrains and vegetation types, with the eastern end of the south-east being particularly rich in biodiversity (it claims to be the most diverse in the Caribbean, with almost one-third of the endemic species of the island). Over 7,000 species of flora have been identified on Cuba, of which about 3,000 are endemic. However, almost 1,000 have been made extinct, rare or endangered since the 17th century. Examples of native plants include the world's only carnivorous epiphyte (plants that live on other plants, but are not parasitic, like moss or orchids), about 100 types of palm (90 of which are endemic) and one of nature's largest flowers. Cuba might be more generally associated with claims of the world's smallest products of nature, however, particularly in the animal kingdom: the smallest frog, the Cuban pygmy frog, which is 12 mm (0.5 ins); the smallest mammal, the 55-mm butterfly bat (*mariposa*); the smallest scorpion, the 10-mm dwarf scorpion; and the smallest bird, the 63-mm bee hummingbird (*zunzuncito*). There is also a pygmy owl, tiny salamanders and the insect-eating rodent, the *almiquí*, which is a long-surviving species, a 'living fossil' (like the cork palm, the Cuban or rhombifer crocodile and the Cuban alligator). In all, there are almost 14,000 species of fauna, although about 1,500 are said to be near extinction. Many of the species have diversified into distinctly Cuban varieties—40% of mammal species (including some of the larger ones, such as manatees or sea cows and hutias), 85% of reptiles, 90% of amphibians and 96% of molluscs are said to be endemic. Protected areas cover 30% of Cuba, including its marine platform and four UNESCO biosphere reserves, although enforcement sometimes lacks infrastructure.

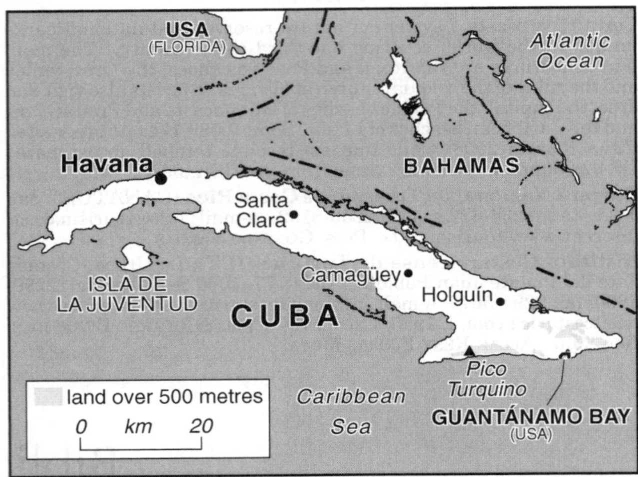

CLIMATE

The climate is subtropical, warm and humid, with the Atlantic trade winds alleviating extremes. A rainy season falls from May to October. During this time hurricanes occasionally trouble the eastern coasts. Drought is a more usual and general problem. Average annual rainfall in Havana (La Habana—the capital, in the north-west) is 1,730 mm (67 ins), but 860 mm in the east. The average annual temperature in Cuba is 25°C (77°F), but readings can rise to 33°C (91°F) in the shade even in Havana (the south-eastern city of Santiago de Cuba is hotter and drier) during the summer. The drier, winter months of December–April see temperatures nearer 20°C (68°F), but they can occasionally fall to as low as 8°C (46°F) in a north wind.

POPULATION

Just over one-half of the population (51%) is of mulatto or mixed-race ethnicity (mainly of Spanish and African descent), with a further 37% defined as white, 11% as black and 1% as Chinese. Numerous other influxes have influenced Cuba and its culture, notably in the south-east, where the French fled from revolution in Haiti in the early 19th century and, more recently, Jamaicans have settled. The oldest influences to modify Spanish colonial settlers, however, came from West Africa with the slaves brought to work the plantations. The most numerous group was of Yoruba speakers from south-western Nigeria, Benin (formerly Dahomey) and Togo. They are known in Cuba as *Lucumí*. The descendants of the Bantu-speaking peoples brought from the Congo basin are known as the *Congos*, while those from the Calabar region of southern Nigeria and Cameroon are known as the *Carabalí*. The Yoruba pantheon and legends were syncretized by the early *Lucumí* with the saints of the Christian religion they were formally required to adopt, forming the basis of the Regla de Ocha cult, or *Santería*. It is a religion without sects or missionaries and can co-exist without complication with both Christianity or the similarly syncretic cult of the *Congos*, the Regla Conga or Palo Monte. Some practise all three belief systems at once. The *Carabalí* originated not a cult, but a sort of masonic closed sect, the Abakuá Secret Society, which is open to men only and upholds values traditionally associated with masculinity (it is also known as *ñañiguismo*). Ostensibly, however, the predominant religion remains Roman Catholic Christianity and, prior to the advent of the current Communist regime and the official disapproval of religion (although this was eased from 1992), some 85% of the population were at least nominally Roman Catholic. In 2005 some 53% of the population were open adherents of Roman Catholicism (with another 10% belonging to other Christian denominations). There are also some Jews and a few that practise other faiths. Spanish is the official language.

About three-quarters of the total population of 11.2m. (as estimated in December 2009) are urbanized and some 2.1m. live in Havana, on the north coast. The capital is one of 15 provinces. The second city is Santiago de Cuba (with a population of over 426,840 at the end of 2009), in the south-east, followed by Camagüey, Holguín, Guantánamo and Santa Clara. There is a high level of illicit emigration from Cuba, particularly to the USA.

History

Prof. ANTONI KAPCIA

PRE-COLUMBIAN AND COLONIAL CUBA

When Christopher Columbus arrived in 1492, Cuba's indigenous population numbered about 60,000 Siboney in the west and more agriculturally advanced Arawaks (or Taínos) in the east. After Once Sebastián de Ocampo proved Cuba to be an island, in 1508, a period of exploration and rapid conquest followed. Between 1512 and 1515 the Spanish founded seven defined *villas* (settlements): Baracoa, Bayamo, Trinidad, Sancti Spíritus, Havana, Puerto Príncipe and Santiago de Cuba, the last serving as the capital city until it was replaced by Havana in the 1550s.

Thereafter, Cuba's colonial experience was unusual. First, the rapid decline of the indigenous population (to around 1,000 persons within 50 years), with few Spanish settlers, made Cuba initially one of Spain's 'whitest' colonies. Second, from 1561 Cuba's imperial significance came from its role as a port of call for Spanish-bound fleets transporting silver from the Americas, making Havana an economic hub, as well as a prime target for piracy, requiring a strong military presence.

In 1762–03 a brief but pivotal British occupation opened up trade with North America, changing the perspectives of locally born whites (*criollos*); about 5,000 slaves were imported during this period to develop sugar, establishing a historic nexus between sugar, slavery and colonialism. While *criollos* elsewhere saw decreasing incentives to remain Spanish, for those in Cuba there was every reason. Once the British Empire abolished, in 1807, the slave trade, only Spain could guarantee the *criollos* a significant slave supply, which was required for the development of Cuba's burgeoning sugar trade. Moreover, a violent slave rebellion in 1791 in the nearby French territory of Saint Domingue (now Haiti), coupled with the rising number of blacks owing to slave imports, increased fears among the whites of the possibility of revolt; as a result, the *criollos* welcomed Spain's military might.

However, as the Spanish excluded *criollos* politically and denied them access to capital, slave-based criollo planters were not able to modernize. Hence, while Spanish planters flourished, *criollo* production declined, pushing them towards separatism; however, fearful of the United Kingdom and the black majority, the *criollos* preferred annexation by the USA, which at that time imported about 40% of Cuba's sugar. This produced several revolts, supported by southern US interests, and three US Governments tried to purchase Cuba.

THE WARS OF INDEPENDENCE

When the US Civil War made annexation impossible, some *criollos* opted for independence; on 10 October 1868 Carlos Manuel de Céspedes launched a rebellion. The rebel ranks swelled with thousands of black guerrillas (*mambises*) equating political liberation with racial equality. However, with increased Spanish numbers, the war was confined to the east (Oriente), and, fearful of the implications of a largely black rebellion, the white rebels finally surrendered in 1878. The recalcitrant and popular *mulato* leader, Antonio Maceo, then led a second Oriente revolt, the 'Little War', in 1879–80.

By then, slavery was no longer a prominent issue; Spain had abolished slavery in 1817, although it was not effectively abolished until 1886. Henceforth, *criollo* planters were replaced by large modern US-owned sugar mills, and Spanish repression forced many to leave. One exile was the poet José Martí, who left Cuba in 1871, devoting his journalistic and political skills to campaigning for independence and founding the Cuban Revolutionary Party in 1892. In February 1895 Martí led an invasion of Oriente; although he was killed in May, the *mambises*' Liberation Army soon increased (to around 40,000) and reached the west.

Having been driven by a press campaign against alleged Spanish atrocities, by US companies' pleas, by an expansionist lobby, and by the unexplained explosion in Havana of the *USS Maine* in February 1889, the US Government declared war on Spain in April. Thus, the Cuban War of Independence became the Spanish–American War.

US INTERVENTION AND CONTROL

The war lasted until August 1898. The Treaty of Paris, signed by Spain and the USA in December of that year, established US control over Cuba, which lasted until Cuba was granted independence on 20 May 1902. During that period, social provision improved but US economic interests increased. Most controversially, the new Cuban Constitution included clauses from the so-called Platt Amendment, limiting the Cubans' right to sign treaties or contract loans, leasing territory on the island for US military bases and allowing unilateral US intervention in Cuba to quell unrest. Codified in a 1903 treaty, this legitimized neo-colonial control (and gave the USA Guantanamo Bay), provoking ongoing resentment. A 1903 Reciprocity Treaty, signed by Tomás Estrada Palma, the first President of the new Republic, confirmed economic dependence, while a second treaty signed by Estrada Palma incorporated the Platt Amendment. Under the terms of this second agreement, there was another period of US intervention in 1906–09, and again in 1912, when a protest staged by the Independent Party of Colour against the marginalization of black Cubans was forcefully repressed, resulting in the death of 3,000 people. A fourth period of US intervention occurred in 1917.

In 1920 collapsing sugar prices undermined political stability and faith in the neo-colonial system, producing a decade of union militancy (increasingly led by the Communist Party, founded in 1925), student radicalism and the election in 1924 of Gerardo Machado, whose presidency degenerated into corruption and authoritarianism.

The 1929 Wall Street Crash and ensuing Great Depression caused sugar prices to plummet still further, and resulted in more protests and a virtual labour insurrection, with student radicalism metamorphosing into armed conflict. US pressure led the army, in August 1933, to depose President Machado, whose interim replacement, Carlos Manuel de Céspedes (the younger), was overthrown in the following month by an alliance of students and mutinying non-commissioned officers under Sgt (later Gen.) Fulgencio Batista Zaldivar. Ramón Grau San Martín replaced Céspedes as President. However, Céspedes was denied recognition by the new non-interventionist US President, Franklin Roosevelt, and was unable to control the continuing unrest on all sides. Meanwhile, his Minister of the Interior, Antonio Guiteras, led calls for a deeper social revolution.

Sustained US pressure led Batista to seize power in January 1934, upon which he ruled dictatorially via 'puppet' Presidents until 1940, during which time he also enacted a populist programme giving farmers and entrepreneurs greater economic space, secured the end of the Platt Amendment and introduced various social reforms. In 1938 he legalized the Communist Party (subsequently renamed the People's Socialist Party—PSP—in 1944), allowing them to control the trade unions, in exchange for electoral support. That alliance ensured the approval of a progressive new Constitution in 1940, as well as facilitating his victory in the presidential election in the same year.

Batista retired in 1944, his presidency having overseen rampant corruption (through patronage, links with US crime and the degeneration of student radicalism into gangsterism). Grau, leader of the Authentic Cuban Revolutionary Party (Auténticos), was elected in his stead later that year, and was in turn replaced by Carlos Prío Socarrá, a fellow Auténtico, in 1948. Prío's rule was increasingly conservative and corrupt, and his term was brought to a premature end when Batista seized power on 10 March 1952, thereby preventing the electoral victory of the Cuban People's Party (Ortodoxos), led by the charismatic Eduardo Chibás. A strong candidate for the presidency, Chibás publicly committed suicide during a live radio broadcast in 1951, in a personal protest against the social injustice and political corruption that he deemed to be rife in Cuba.

The coup remained largely unchallenged, except for a protest movement among students, led by a former student activist, Fidel Castro Ruz. On 26 July 1953 a group of 132 rebels attacked two eastern military barracks, with the force of their assault concentrated on the Moncada garrison in Santiago de Cuba. Intended to spark a rebellion, the attack failed, resulting in the death of seven rebels (with a further 54 killed after arrest). Among those surviving were Castro and his younger brother, Raúl Castro Ruz, both of whom were captured, tried, and subsequently sentenced to 15 and 13 years' imprisonment, respectively, for their roles in the attack. Fidel Castro's defence speech at his trial was later published as 'History Will Absolve Me'.

In prison, the Castro brothers organized the 26 July Movement. Released as part of a general amnesty of political prisoners in 1955, they headed to Mexico, where they prepared for an invasion and guerrilla resistance against Batista, and met the Argentine radical Ernesto ('Che') Guevara. In November 1956 82 rebels sailed for eastern Cuba aboard the yacht *Granma*. However, they landed late, at the wrong place, missing by a couple of days a Santiago uprising that had been supposed to distract attention, and were dispersed under air attack. Two weeks later, around two dozen rebels regrouped in the nearby Sierra Maestra mountains.

Two years of guerrilla warfare followed, the rebels benefiting from mobility, growth, skilful publicity, peasant support and military prowess (especially the Castro brothers and Guevara). Meanwhile, the Batista regime faced economic stagnation, dissent, urban violence (provoking a repression that embarrassed the US Government into withholding arms in 1958), the guerrillas' superiority and the army's falling morale. By 1958 all alternatives to the 26 July Movement had disappeared or fallen into line, including the small Revolutionary Directorate (Directorio Revolucionario), the leader of which—José Antonio Echevarría—had been killed in an attack on Batista's palace in March 1957, and the PSP, which, having criticized Castro, joined the rebel alliance in 1958. The guerrilla movement's rapid westward advance from mid-1958 culminated in victory under Guevara in Santa Clara on 30 December 1958. The next day Batista fled, and Guevara entered Havana on 1 January 1959, a general strike ensuring control.

THE RADICALIZATION OF THE REVOLUTIONARY PROCESS

The first Government was a coalition combining representatives of the 26 July Movement, liberals and social democrats, under the presidency of a respected judge, Manuel Urrutia Lleó; Fidel Castro assumed the position of Prime Minister, with Raúl as his deputy. While they agreed on their main objectives (diversification of the economy, improved social welfare and better Cuban-US relations), they differed over their preferred means of attaining these ends, for the rebels had radicalized since 1953 through contact with the peasantry and the influence of radicals such as Guevara and the PSP.

The PSP's role led Urrutia to resign in July 1959, whereupon he was replaced by Osvaldo Dorticós Torrado, and prompted further protests. Fears of communism also prompted US concern, and caution soon turned to opposition, with the US Government and press criticizing the public trials of supporters of Batista (*batistianos*). After a goodwill visit to the USA by Castro in April 1959, US Vice-President Richard Nixon's concerns about the 'Communist threat' led him to approve plans by the US Central Intelligence Agency (CIA) to train Cuban exiles. In reality, although the PSP was involved in early planning of reforms, its presence was often resented by those critical of its former alliance with Batista.

The most significant of those reforms—land reform legislation passed in May 1959—outlawed large landholdings and guaranteed a minimum stake for farmers, prompting concern among US corporations, which feared expropriation, the implications of the establishment of a National Institute for Agrarian Reform and the trend towards co-operatives and 'people's farms'.

Other reforms abolished urban renting (later giving title to former tenants and re-housing the homeless and slum-dwellers in empty middle-class properties), expanded education and health, and banned racial discrimination. Meanwhile, from 1960–61 Cubans were mobilized in new 'mass organizations', the first of which were the citizens' militia, established in 1959, and the neighbourhood Committees for the Defence of the Revolution (CDR), set up in the following year; other organizations subsequently sprang up for women, private farmers, students and others. One existing organization, the trade union confederation (CTC), soon came under radical leadership, including PSP activists, fuelling fears of communism.

Looming fears of a US invasion were intensified, in February 1960, by a Cuban-Soviet agreement to exchange sugar (500,000 metric tons annually) for oil, sparking a rapid deterioration in US-Cuban relations: when US-owned refineries in Cuba refused to refine the oil, they were nationalized, beginning a process of steady elimination of the US quota for Cuban sugar, an increase in economic sanctions imposed by the USA against Cuba, steady nationalization of US enterprises within Cuba, and the increasing Soviet purchase of unsold Cuban sugar.

The USA severed diplomatic relations with Cuba in January 1961. In April, the CIA-trained Cuban exile forces launched an ill-fated attack on the southern Bay of Pigs (known locally as Playa Girón), with the support of the US Administration. The invasion was an unmitigated disaster for the USA: the 1,480 invaders were resisted by peasant militias; the Cuban army and air force lost 87 personnel, but took 1,180 prisoners; and the CDRs detained thousands of alleged collaborators.

The episode was a turning-point. It discredited the USA and drew a clear line between the Revolution and the old Cuba. It led to the expulsion of clergy and the nationalization of private schools; it established the CDRs as an ideal mechanism for the mobilization, involvement and politicization of Cubans; and it confirmed the shift towards socialism. In response to a shortage of private capital, upon Soviet advice, Cuba began to industrialize, centralize and nationalize; 70% of land was seized by the state in 1963. The middle classes now left in droves, fearing expropriation and rationing, and, in 1965, the US and Cuban Governments agreed to a regular airlifting of disgruntled Cubans off the island. By 1971 some 700,000 had left, removing valuable professional expertise but also a considerable source of potential unrest.

Meanwhile, two key processes were initiated in 1961. First, a high-profile literacy campaign enlisted 270,000 young volunteers to reduce illiteracy from around 23% to just 3% within a year. Besides its educational value, the campaign integrated and politicized both the 707,000 newly literate and their educators. Second, the 26 July Movement, PSP and DR were merged to form the Organizaciones Revolucionarias Integradas (ORI—Integrated Revolutionary Organizations); following widespread criticism, ORI was restyled in 1962 as the Partido Unido de la Revolución Socialista Cubana (PURSC—United Party of the Socialist Revolution of Cuba).

The growing mistrust between Cuba and the USA led to an incident in October 1962 commonly referred to as the Cuban Missile Crisis. Cuban fears and Soviet misjudgements led to the stationing of nuclear missiles in Cuba. A US ultimatum secured their withdrawal, following a tense 13 days, but, although the USA agreed (secretly) not to invade Cuba, the Soviet climb-down angered Castro.

That displeasure, coupled with other Cuban dissatisfactions, led to a growing distance between Cuba and the USSR, a distance that was exacerbated by a crisis in March 1962. Aníbal Escalante (ORI co-ordinator) was accused of using his position to enhance the PSP's power, leading to the demotion of many PSP activists within the newly formed PURSC. Thereafter, the ex-guerrillas pursued their own definition of socialist revolution, rejecting Soviet dictates. In 1965 the PURSC was replaced by the Partido Comunista de Cuba (PCC—Communist Party of Cuba).

Bitter theoretical differences finally led, in the mid-1960s, to a 'moral economy', maximizing sugar production (with a target of increasing output to 10m. metric tons by 1970) but, following Guevara's advice, emphasizing centralization and consciousness. This strategy reflected Cuba's isolation, which was formalized in 1962 by its suspension, in January, from the Organization of American States (OAS) and the imposition, in February, of a near-total trade embargo by the USA; the resulting 'siege mentality' and austerity led some to see Cuba's resources in its human capital and land, now the focus of all investment. In 1968 as part of the 'Revolutionary Offensive', all remaining non-agricultural private enterprises, numbering some 55,000, were nationalized in an attempt to combat declining production and increasing levels of absenteeism.

Independence was also true abroad. From 1962, Cuba actively supported guerrillas in the region and in Africa. Guevara left the country in 1965 and, after an abortive Congo campaign, began a struggle in Bolivia in 1966, until he was captured and killed in October 1967. By 1968 Cuba was fighting 'US imperialism' and challenging the Soviet policy of 'peaceful coexistence'.

POST-1970 INSTITUTIONALIZATION

A disastrous harvest in 1970 provoked a reassessment, as a result of which the 1960s strategy was replaced by an Eastern Bloc orthodoxy, which persuaded the Bloc's trading organization (the Council for Mutual Economic Assistance—CMEA) to admit Cuba as a full member in 1972, having previously refused. This gave Cuba economic stability, together with a reliable market (for diversified exports), manufactured imports, a more rational wage structure, rising standards and a move away from rationing.

The rethink also rehabilitated the former PSP members, now given economic and political responsibility in a strengthened PCC, which had its first party congress in 1975; party membership expanded from about 55,000 in 1975 to 500,000 in 1985. The first Constitution of the Revolution, implemented in 1976, created a Soviet-style 'people's power' system, with directly elected municipal assemblies subsequently electing the Government and other higher bodies. Cuba increasingly resembled the Socialist Bloc, with growing professional, military and educational links.

Relations with the USA also improved during the presidency of Jimmy Carter. In 1977 'interest sections' were opened in third-country embassies in Havana and Washington, DC, and Latin American countries could recognize and trade with Cuba. In 1979 Cuban-American emigrants returned on family visits, although protests (at Cubans' relative poverty) then led to an invasion of the Peruvian embassy by some 10,000 people wishing to emigrate. When the violence escalated, the Government allowed would-be emigrants to be collected by boat from Mariel, west of Havana; some 121,000 left the island.

Apparent 'Sovietization' was, however, misleading. Even Castro's 1968 endorsement of the Soviet invasion of Czechoslovakia was more complex than it seemed, and when, in 1975, Cuban troops arrived in Angola to defend the Movimento Popular de Libertação de Angola (MPLA—People's Movement for the Liberation of Angola) Government against South Africa, Cuba was simply continuing old links, and the Cuban action forced the USSR to supply and transport the operation. This popular involvement (halting the South Africans and then defeating them in 1988) opened a new overseas strategy: internationalism. This meant sending thousands of volunteer professionals to developing countries, supporting successful revolutions in Nicaragua and Grenada, and collaborating with sympathetic Latin American, Caribbean and African governments. This strategy, besides allowing young Cubans to travel, usually to poorer countries, gave Cuba international leverage and support against the US trade embargo.

In the 1980s, however, the influence of the CMEA began to decline, and the Cold War prompted the USSR President, Mikhail Gorbachev, to implement a series of reforms that directly affected Cuba: with trade and aid in crisis, urgent action was needed. This led to another strategic reassessment, at the 1986 PCC party congress, which led to a campaign of 'Rectification' (which was also in part a reaction to the bureaucratization and opportunism that had originated from the recent rapid expansion of the party); Rectification meant purging membership, economic streamlining and a return to some of the principles of the 1960s.

THE SPECIAL PERIOD

During 1989–91, the Eastern Bloc disintegrated, the CMEA was dissolved, and the USSR imploded, all in quick succession. Suddenly, Cuba had lost 80% of its trade and faced a hostile USA alone and militarily weakened, the armed forces having been cut by one-half. In August 1990 Fidel Castro declared a war footing, the start of a 'Special Period' (in peacetime). In 1992 the US Congress tightened the trade embargo against Cuba in the Cuban Democracy Act.

The scale of the crisis threatened the Revolution's existence. The economy shrank by 35% by 1994, with hitherto unthinkable levels of unemployment; oil supplies collapsed, affecting energy production and transport and worsening daily life and economic activity, and sugar output plummeted to less than 4m. metric tons annually.

The social effects were traumatic, total collapse being mitigated by rationing. Despite sustained spending, health and education standards fell, and people's expectations collapsed, with thousands leaving the PCC, and thousands more leaving Cuba illegally, as *balseros* (rafters). In August 1994 ferry hijackings produced clashes, deaths and unprecedented disturbances in Havana; when would-be emigrants were again allowed to leave by boat, some 35,000 left immediately, with a significant side-effect. Since 1966 illegal Cuban immigrants had uniquely been allowed permanent US residence and eventual citizenship; now Washington and Havana agreed to distinguish between those migrants caught at sea by the US Coastguard ('wet foot'), who were to be repatriated, and those migrants, who, if they reached US soil, could enjoy the 1966 rights ('dry foot').

Then, with the Revolution teetering on the brink of ruin, the economy began to recover, responding to a programme of unprecedented measures adopted at the PCC congress in 1991. Most significantly, the holding of US dollars was decriminalized in 1993; although this produced a new inequality between the dollar economy and the peso economy, dollar-denominated income from family remittances and tourism was crucial in facilitating the economic recovery. Tourism replaced sugar as Cuba's principal industry (one-half of Cuba's sugar mills were closed in 2003–04 alone), and annual tourist arrivals rose rapidly, reaching 2m. in 2000 and generating satellite economies, employment and revenue. Limited self-employment was tolerated in small-scale activities, allowing for the creation of private restaurants (*paladares*) and rented accommodation (*casas particulares*), both geared towards the tourist market. More fundamentally, in 1993 state lands became co-operatives, to incentivize farmers, who were now given titles and allowed to sell surplus produce commercially, as was the military.

These unprecedented reforms had no political parallel, but there were further, lesser changes. A political broadening included Cuba's churches, which, sharing leaders' concerns about social collapse, were now allowed greater autonomy to practise and publish, members being welcomed into the PCC. The National Assembly became directly elected in 1992, and workplace-based assemblies debated measures and reforms. Finally, one response to the collapse—the revitalization of barrio-level life, filling gaps left by the state—was formalized, through local regenerative 'workshops' and People's Councils.

However, for most Cubans, the daily preoccupation was on economic and social conditions, as the disintegration wrought by the combination of economic collapse and tourism undermined the old morality of collective solidarity and encouraged individualism, a vast 'black' market and a rise in petty criminality. Tourism, in particular, resurrected long-banished problems: hustling and female prostitution (*jineterismo*); racism, as black Cubans benefitted less from remittances than their white compatriots; illegal internal migration, worsening an already overcrowded Havana and creating shanties; and a 'brain drain' from sectors such as education and health.

Meanwhile, the USA loomed large. Although the trade embargo remained in place, the 'twin track' policy of the Administration of US President Bill Clinton advocated contacts with 'civil society' in Cuba. However, this partial opening angered émigrés, and, in February 1996, two aircraft from Brothers to the Rescue—a US-based activist organization formed by Cuban exiles—violated Cuban airspace to provoke a reaction; when the aircraft were shot down by the Cuban air force, resulting in the deaths of several US citizens, Clinton responded by signing the previously vetoed Cuban Liberty and Solidarity Act (commonly known as the Helms-Burton Act), allowing the embargo to be extended to include other countries that traded with, or invested in, Cuba, and giving it the force of a treaty, able to be repealed only by a two-thirds' congressional majority.

One window of Cuban opportunity opened in late 1999. Elián González, a six-year old boy whose mother died while attempting to take him illegally to Florida, USA, was rescued at sea, and thus was due to be deported. However, his US relatives refused to hand him over to the authorities. When, in April 2000, armed immigration officers seized him, flag-burning protests in Florida demonstrated public opinion. However, with the US presidential election approaching, the embargo could not be changed, and in November the Cuban-Americans in Florida were pivotal in electing George W. Bush who, determined to end the Cuban regime, revived the old hostility.

After the terrorist attacks against the USA on 11 September 2001, the Bush Administration implicitly included Cuba in its new 'axis of evil', campaigning to isolate Cuba and wean the European Union (EU) from its long-standing policy of engaging in dialogue and trade with the country. The US Interests Section began supporting dissidents materially, provoking the Cuban authorities who, in April 2003, arrested and imprisoned 75 activists. This persuaded the EU to impose diplomatic sanctions for a two-year period, pragmatism and Spanish pressure shifting them back to their 'common position'. In 2004 the Bush Administration restricted remittances and family visits to Cuba, in an attempt to starve the Cuban economy of US dollars, although the Cuban Government's response (banning the dollar as legal currency and replacing it with the convertible peso—thereby swelling the state coffers as Cubans exchanged their worthless dollars—and charging 10% for all dollar exchanges) led many Cuban-Americans to criticize the original measures.

One interruption to the general US–Cuban hostility came in November 2001, when, following a devastating hurricane, US enterprises were allowed to sell food and medicines to Cuba, if paid cash in advance, producing an increase in trade between Cuba and US agricultural states.

Elsewhere, foreign relations improved dramatically, especially in Latin America, where the election of leftist governments created more sympathy for Cuba, especially in Venezuela, whose President, Hugo Chávez, developed a close relationship with Fidel Castro. In 2002 the Cuban and Venezuelan Governments established the Alternativa Bolivariana para las Américas (ALBA—the Bolivarian Alternative for the Americas), intended as an alternative to the Free Trade Area of the Americas and renamed the Alianza Bolivariana para los Pueblos de Nuestra América (Bolivarian Alliance for the Peoples of our America in June 2009). The two Governments also agreed to an exchange of Cuban expertise for Venezuelan oil. Other governments also moved closer to Cuba, and the Caribbean Common Market (CARICOM), and even the OAS in 2009, voted to admit Cuba (although Cuba declined the latter invitation).

The Elián González affair also changed Cuban politics, leaders regarding it as an opportunity to revive political mobilization and target youth. Both were urgently needed. Mobilization had suffered from institutionalization and a crisis that left no time, means or inclination to engage in campaigning. Cuba's leaders reasoned that, having regained the ability to mobilize large numbers effectively owing to the incident, they should target the young; activists had long feared that young Cubans lacked ideological commitment and that, born during relative material security, they had developed unrealistic expectations and responded less to the discourse of an ageing leadership. However, from January 2000 it was Cuba's youth organizations that led six months of daily national campaigning and, once Elián returned to Cuba, in June, the campaign's mechanisms and enthusiasm were marshalled in a broader campaign.

The youth organization's campaigning began a new 'battle of ideas', which, recognizing that ideological commitment had suffered during the Special Period, urged Cubans to revive ideological fervour, resist capitalism and address the 'internet threat', rebuilding the ideological basis of a shattered nation. Internationally, this meant supporting both Latin America's struggle against globalization and the left-wing Government of Venezuela. Nationally, it reinvigorated debate (through television, public forums and academic centres) and revived the spirit of the literacy campaign (see above) by emphasizing the importance of reading, which had been a casualty of the Special Period. Above all, it trained young people through intensive schools to meet new social needs and shortages. In 2000 youth activists had realized the scale of poverty and the potential alienation of those unable to gain access to university. The first schools produced social workers who would work in the slums while studying at university, but similar schools addressed sectors depleted by the dual-currency 'brain drain' (primary teaching and nursing). Since this required an expansion of university provision, in 2002 a university branch was opened in each of Cuba's 169 municipalities, and a wider educational campaign developed televised university courses.

By 2005 the 'battle' was leading to absenteeism, exhaustion and inefficiency. This now coincided with a new development: namely, the increasing frailty of Fidel Castro, now almost 80 and losing his old vigour. On 1 August 2006 he announced that he was temporarily to cede power to his brother, Raúl, to allow him to undergo urgent surgery (for diverticulitis). The Cuban population seemed neither surprised nor disappointed, many seeing Raúl Castro as a legitimate historic leader, who, known for his efficiency and pragmatism, might bring economic change.

While uncertainty reigned, few major decisions were taken. However, in July 2007 Raúl Castro voiced public criticisms of Cuba's economic, political and social failings, and in September he launched a nation-wide consultation. However, whatever his intentions or the urgency of change (expectations being high), Raúl was limited in his scope. First, Fidel might either return or undermine reforms; second, Raúl recognized the need for balance. Then, in January 2008, on the eve of Assembly elections, Fidel resigned as head of state. Raúl was promptly elected to the presidency in February.

CUBA UNDER RAÚL CASTRO

Raúl Castro now began appointing his own people. Characteristically mixing efficiency with a trust of the military, most appointments were either junior politicians or guerrilla veterans. Two surprises were the appointment, in February 2008, of veteran José Ramón Machado Ventura, as Raúl's replacement as First Vice-President, and the dismissal, in March 2009, of two likely successors: the de facto prime minister, Secretary of the Council of Ministers Carlos Lage Dávila, and the Minister of Foreign Relations, Felipe Pérez Roque.

With Fidel Castro remaining General Secretary of the PCC, the new President still lacked total authority; however, the sixth party congress, due to have convened in 2002, had never met. Consequently, in 2008 Raúl Castro immediately convoked it for 2009, although it was again postponed (until late 2010 or 2011), with an unprecedented Special Conference due to make necessary personnel changes, although this too had yet to convene by mid-2010. The postponement was the result of a series of challenges during 2008: Cuba was hit by three successive hurricanes, which wreaked havoc on agricultural production, housing and infrastructure, while the global economic downturn from the latter half of 2008 raised imports prices and lowered export income. Therefore, despite small gestures (including greater access to computers and mobile phones), expectations of significant change were again put on hold.

Some improvements did materialize. In 2008–09 farmers were allowed access to unused public land, and Raúl sought to incentivize increased production and to improve efficiency and political consciousness by eliminating pilfering, absenteeism and ineffective work practices.

Barack Obama's election to the US presidency in November 2008 aroused unrealistic hopes among many Cubans for an amelioration in relations, unrealistic because of the trade embargo's legal status and because of Florida's continued electoral importance. Hence, Obama was limited to reversing the 2004 measures (in late 2009), softening hostility and resuming Clinton's 'twin track' policy. However, as Cuba's dissidents, inactive during the 2006–08 hiatus, revived activity in 2009–10, the authorities' firm response forced a return to traditional rhetoric from the US Administration, especially in March 2010, when one prisoner, Orlando Zapata Tamayo, died on hunger strike, and when the wives of the remaining 2003 prisoners (commonly known as the Ladies in White) were prevented from making their weekly protest.

In mid-2010, therefore, Raúl Castro's presidency faced more uncertainty than he had hoped or had many expected when he assumed the position on a permanent basis in 2008. With economic problems preventing faster change or improvement, with dissident activity once again making international headlines (although dissident groups remain as fragmented as ever and still lacked popular support), with official US attitudes seemingly fixed for the short to medium term at least, and with neither the PCC congress nor the Special Conference in sight, hopes of progress towards reform seemed far from assured.

Economy

LILA HAINES

ECONOMIC POLICY

For most of the period after the 1959 Revolution economic policy in Cuba was guided by a commitment to collective ownership of the means of production and, in particular following full membership (in 1972) of the Council for Mutual Economic Assistance (CMEA, or Comecon), to central planning. In the early 1990s the recession in Cuba's economy after the collapse of the Eastern European socialist (communist) bloc led to the introduction of austerity measures and a cautious reassessment of economic policy. The new approach focused on seeking inward investment and developing tourism to obtain convertible ('hard') currency in an attempt to alleviate the social effects of a precipitous decline in foreign trade, including the loss of vital food and fuel imports from the socialist bloc, while remaining faithful to the basic principles of socialism. The Government initially reduced domestic spending and non-essential imports and declared a 'special period in time of peace', an austerity programme that was marked by food shortages, less expenditure on power and public transport, and attempts to improve the efficiency of state enterprises. By 1993, however, the system was clearly in danger of collapse: the money supply was increasing rapidly; subsidies to loss-making industries were soaring; and the 'black market' (parallel, illegal economy) was expanding, with the state often unable to supply even basic rations. In July 1993 President Fidel Castro Ruz announced the legalization of the use of hard currency by Cubans, one of several cautious, although significant, economic reforms arising from policy decisions taken at the Fourth Congress of the Partido Comunista de Cuba (Communist Party of Cuba), held in 1991. Constitutional amendments passed in 1992 marginally liberalized the concept of property and the state's economic role, promised protection to foreign investors and granted limited recognition to private enterprise, thus preparing for new legislation and the use of new policy instruments from 1993.

Thereafter, a shift away from direct control of production was discernible and state enterprises were given greater operational freedom. However, the state retained ownership of the resource base and the Government continued to set economic priorities, to control the flow of essential commodities and to monitor carefully the use of hard currency finance. A law passed in 1998 aimed to raise managerial standards and to make enterprises self-financing, but also reaffirmed the state enterprise as the basic business unit in the national economy. This period also saw slow, but clear, changes in social attitudes and the business culture, resulting from overseas investment, a greater Western presence in foreign trade and the opening of new employment opportunities (mainly in tourism). Moves towards recentralizing economic management and tightening control over use of the US dollar in 2004–05 led to the emergence of concerns about the direction of policy. The concurrent increases in peso-denominated basic pay and social security rates, and the exchange rate revaluation suggested that the moves were expedients to deal with current problems, part of the pattern of pragmatic economic measures within a policy framework designed to protect the social system while attracting inward investment and expanding trade. Alternatively, these moves might have signalled a decision to return to a full command economy, if viewed as a new departure marked by Head of State Fidel Castro's announcement in March 2005 that the 'special period' of economic hardship, in force since the early 1990s, was over.

In 1994 the Government also began to use monetary and fiscal instruments of economic policy, which subsequently gained in importance. As part of this policy it introduced new taxes aimed at eradicating surplus liquidity, and reintroduced taxation on income from self-employment and hard currency earnings in 1995 and 1996, respectively. It also reduced subsidies to state enterprises and began to implement a system of profit taxation. Official data showed that these measures fulfilled the aims of increasing government revenues and curbing inflation. However, the effect on the money supply was difficult to measure owing to a number of factors, including the coexistence of several markets and currencies. For over three decades the state controlled the prices of all officially traded goods and provided a heavily subsidized 'basket' of essential products to all citizens. In 1994, when it became clear that it could no longer directly ensure minimum consumer supplies, the Government authorized the opening of non-regulated farm-produce markets and other retail outlets where prices responded to supply and demand. Together with the division of most state farms into smaller workers' co-operatives called Unidades Básicas de Producción Cooperativa (UBPC—Units of Basic Co-operative Production) from 1993, and the leasing of smallholdings to individuals, this measure helped to ease food shortages. However, agricultural output did not increase as much as had been hoped, owing, in large part, to the failure to address the inefficiencies in the sugar industry. In 2002 restructuring of the sugar industry began, thus finally recognizing the impracticality of trying to maintain agricultural and manufacturing practices left over from the era of secure socialist bloc markets. Much of the land used to cultivate sugar cane was to be turned over to other crops and forest, but the most recent official statistics suggest that much of that land is idle. The issue moved to centre stage during 2010, as President Raúl Castro Ruz (brother of the ailing former leader Fidel Castro who had succeeded him in 2008) urged the sector to focus on improving production in order to reduce food imports, and told a convention attended by 200,000 farmers that crops must be planted on idle land.

Cuba moved into the 21st century with its economy recovering from the collapse suffered a decade earlier, but still fragile and vulnerable to fluctuations in commodity prices on the world markets, particularly for sugar, oil and nickel, and to the repercussions of natural disasters such as hurricanes. Its biggest economic success, the development of the tourism sector, also brought with it an additional element of instability, as demonstrated by the decline in visitors to the region following the 11 September 2001 terrorist attacks on the USA and again during the recession sparked by the 2008 financial crisis. Growth of gross domestic product (GDP) slowed from 6.1% in 2000 to 1.5% in 2002, before increasing again, reaching 12.1% in 2006, then decreasing to just 1.4% in 2009, according to official government figures. In 1994 Cuba began to use GDP in place of the Soviet system of gross material product (GMP), which excluded the contribution of services (such as health and education). All data since then have been best estimates, using the 1981 GMP figures as the base year for the period 1994–2000. In 2001 the base year was adjusted to 1997, changing both the value and the sectoral composition of GDP in the years for which it is available; however, it remained unclear what difference this would make to analysis of earlier years.

The island economy continued to pursue a development strategy that took little account of the need to move away from carbon-heavy economic activities, even though Cuba signed the Kyoto Protocol on addressing climate change in 2002. Carbon emissions fell between 1994 and 2002, as a result of lower energy production and manufacturing. However, no official figures were available for greenhouse gas emissions after 2002. While total energy consumption fell, most power generation was oil-based and alternative energy remained a small and fluctuating part of overall output. Expansion of domestic and imported petroleum supplies was a policy priority.

THE FINANCIAL SECTOR

In 1994, in a radical departure from existing policy, foreign banks were authorized to open representative offices, but not branches, in Cuba. This move signalled the start of the reform of the domestic financial system. Banking had become a state monopoly in 1960 and, until the 1990s, the Banco Nacional de Cuba (BNC) and Banco Popular de Ahorro, the national savings bank, were the only domestic banking institutions. In 1995 a chain of exchange bureaux began to operate, trading in US dollars and both convertible and old pesos (see below). New banks were also established to provide commercial and private banking services and development financing. In 1997 the BNC's central banking functions passed to a new central bank, the Banco Central de Cuba (BCC); banking operations were also modernized. In addition, the insurance sector expanded and began to form joint ventures with overseas insurance companies. The aggregate value of the financial sector grew, in constant 2000 prices, from US $1,551.33m. in 1995 to $2,543.2m. in 2007. A number of overseas-based investment funds opened offices in Havana. In 1999 a monetary policy committee was established to set domestic interest rates.

In the immediate aftermath of hard currency liberalization in 1993, as the economy became more unbalanced and political tensions rose, the Cuban peso continued to fall rapidly in value against the US dollar in domestic transactions. The peso recovered, however, from its lowest rate of 120 pesos per dollar in mid-1994 to an average of 19–23 pesos per dollar from 1996 until late 2001, when it depreciated to approximately 26 pesos per dollar, largely owing to the negative effect on tourism of the terrorist attacks on the USA, before settling again at approximately 22 pesos per dollar. A 'convertible peso', at par with the US dollar, was introduced in December 1994 and by the late 1990s the US dollar circulated freely alongside the traditional and the convertible peso. Thus, there were in effect three currencies: the Cuban peso and the convertible peso, neither of which could be exchanged directly for foreign currency, and the US dollar. There were also three exchange rates. In April 2005 the convertible peso was devalued, apparently in response to the weakening of the US dollar in world markets; in policy terms it may also have reflected an intention to move towards an adjustable peg. A fourth official currency was introduced in 2002, when the euro became legal tender for hard currency transactions within the main tourist resorts. The move was motivated both by politics and by a wish to lower transaction costs caused by the dependence on the US dollar. Full currency convertibility remained unlikely while Cuba's foreign debt problem persisted. The budget deficit stood at 3.1% of GDP at current prices in 2006, down from 4.2% of GDP in the previous year.

US POLICY AND REFORM

Overall, US policy (notably the trade embargo) negatively affected the Cuban economy, mainly through higher import and other transaction costs, the loss of potential tourism and other services revenue, and a high-risk investment and trade climate. However, US trade sanctions, implemented with varying degrees of severity in response to political events and retained mainly as a result of pressure from a powerful Cuban exiles' lobby, failed to achieve their aim of bringing down the Castro Government. In October 2000, following an acrimonious passage through the US Congress, legislation was approved that allowed US food and medicine sales, but attached conditions (see below) that left most parties dissatisfied, including the then US President, Bill Clinton (1993–2001), who saw his power to ease or tighten travel restrictions removed. His successor, President George W. Bush (2001–09), retained and implemented trade sanctions (see below). When President Barack Obama (2009–) came into office he stated that his Administration's attitude to Cuba would be different to that of his predecessor. He initiated dialogue on the direction of future relations, while the new Cuban President, Raúl Castro, said that he was willing to discuss 'everything'. Obama eased restrictions on remittances and travel to Cuba by Cuban-Americans, widened the range and value of gifts that were permitted to be sent to the island, and allowed US companies to supply telecoms services to Cuba. However, he faced continuing opposition in the US legislature to deeper changes in economic relations, and on the Cuban side the rhetoric soon reverted to how it had been prior to Obama's election.

INFRASTRUCTURE

A central highway linking Pinar del Río in the west with Santiago de Cuba in the east forms the spine of a road system that totals over 60,000 km, of which approximately 29,000 km are paved roads. Causeways join the mainland to some of the offshore keys, which, since 1990, have been developed as tourism resorts. The functioning rail network fell to 8,193 km in length in 2007, largely as a result of the major rationalization of the sugar industry; just 5,076 km of the network transported passengers. Private car ownership remained low and the principal mode of transport in Cuba remained the bus, which had begun to offer improved services after 1998 following a period of severe curtailment post-1990 and which benefited from the import of buses from the People's Republic of China.

Havana handled more than one-half of the country's maritime cargo, making it by far the most important of 16 commercial seaports and 23 minor ports. The petroleum industry operated 11 sea terminals and 17 land storage facilities designed for domestic trade. New pipelines and tanker bases were constructed to support the growing nickel sector and, a little later, the expansion in the production and use of domestic crude petroleum.

Civil aviation enjoyed a dramatic, tourism-led expansion during the 1990s, and increasingly brought former military air bases into civilian use. The main carrier was the national airline, Empresa Consolidada Cubana de Aviación (Cubana). Cubana, the smaller local air companies and the national air services enterprise were brought under the umbrella of the newly formed Corporación de la Aviación Cubana in 1997. State and overseas investment modernized the island's airports and opened new facilities to handle international passengers.

Modernization of the telephone system began in 1994, when the Government approved the formation of a joint venture with overseas partners, Empresa de Telecomunicaciones de Cuba, SA (ETECSA). ETECSA continued to invest in modernization; there were 11 telephones per 100 of the population in 2007, compared with 5.9 in 2002, one of the lowest rates in Latin America. Internet services had been installed in post offices and this, together with a network of computer clubs and workplace use, gave almost 500,000 Cubans e-mail access. It was reported in 2007 that ETECSA also planned to extend the mobile cellular telephone network to remote areas, a move that would require arrangements for payments in local currency and would thus bring mobile cellular telephones officially into the peso economy for the first time. Soon after he became President in 2008, Raúl Castro confirmed that Cubans could legally acquire mobile telephones.

HUMAN RESOURCES AND EMPLOYMENT

The economically active population numbered some 5.03m. in 2008, or 74.7% of those of working age; the rate for women was 60.2% and that for men 87.7%. The estimated total population was 11,236,099 in 2008, rising to 11,239,566 in 2009. Estimated population growth was negative between 2005 and 2008, a trend which some commentators attributed to emigration.

The economic reforms of the 1990s initiated a shift away from the almost total state domination of employment that had resulted from the nationalization programmes of the 1960s. The state sector accounted for 77.5% of civilian employment at the end of 2000, compared with 95.4% in 1989; since then the percentage of the economically active population in private employment (including co-operatives) fluctuated from 16% to 20%, according to official statistics.

The unemployment rate fell from 5.4% in 2000 to 1.6% in 2008, according to official figures. However, it was probable that under-employment and low productivity were still serious problems. In the past, the UN's Economic Commission for Latin America and the Caribbean estimated that the real rate of unemployment was much higher than the official one. It was thought that the discrepancy could have resulted, at least in part, from the retention of former staff at government ministries and other agencies and state enterprises on the payroll until they found alternative employment. This approach was adopted in the process of restructuring the sugar industry, when 200,000 redundant workers were guaranteed redeployment or retraining.

In contrast to the moral stimulus approach that characterized the Ernesto ('Che') Guevara era of 'socialist economics', in the 1990s the granting of material incentives to employees became an important strand of policies aimed at stimulating greater labour productivity. Bonuses, in the form of scarce goods or hard currency, were introduced, first in the sectors considered to be of greatest importance for economic recovery, such as tourism and mining, and then gradually in other sectors. Salaries in joint ventures involving foreign capital were 15%–30% above sectoral averages, and both official and unofficial bonuses were often relatively generous. Salaries in the public services, in contrast, were largely frozen for a decade, until 1999 when employees in the education and public health sectors received an average 30% pay rise, followed by those in other sectors such as the police. The average mean monthly wage in state-owned and mixed ownership enterprises rose from 238 pesos in 2000 to 415 pesos in 2007, according to official statistics; the highest pay was in mining and the lowest was in the category 'commerce, hotels and restaurants', but it was likely that additional sources of income such as tips and bonuses were not included. Increases in social security and minimum wage rates were announced in 2005 in order to raise the income of the poorest sectors of society and thus reduce inequality, which had worsened during the 1990s.

In 2008 the services sector was by far the largest employer, engaging some 63.3% of the employed labour force, while agriculture (including hunting, forestry and fishing) employed around 18.6% of the labour force. However, the absolute numbers continued to fall in a growing work-force. Manufacturing industry employed approximately 11.0% and construction 5.0%. At 26,700 in 2008, the number employed in mining was statistically insignificant, but generated the highest share of export revenue. Investment in universal education after 1959 produced a well-educated work-force, which was perceived as an asset in attracting foreign investment; more recently there was increased investment in computer education to try to increase Cuba's ability to join the 'knowledge economy'.

FOREIGN TRADE

Prior to 1959 Cuba's main trading partner was the USA, which had consolidated its dominance after Cuban independence from Spain in 1898. In 1958, the year preceding the overthrow of Fulgencio Batista Zaldivar by the Castro-led revolutionaries, 68% of foreign trade was with the USA and Cuban sugar enjoyed preferential entry to the US market. This position changed radically in the early 1960s, when the new Government tried to implement a programme that it believed reflected its commitment to social justice.

After the Cuban Government had nationalized assets belonging to US companies, valued at over US $1,000m., the USA severed diplomatic relations in January 1961, supported the unsuccessful Bay of Pigs invasion by anti-Castro exiles in April and, in March 1962, extended to all goods the partial trade embargo that it had imposed on Cuba in 1960. The so-called Cuban Missile Crisis of October 1962, following the attempt by the Soviet Government to install nuclear weapons on the island, demonstrated Cuba's peripheral status in relation to the cold war 'superpowers' of the USA and the USSR. The country was left with little choice but to depend on the USSR for its trade revenue, as well as for aid to implement an ambitious social and economic development programme.

After 1962 foreign trade was conducted increasingly with the communist bloc, although China, Japan and some countries of Western Europe each took a small, but significant, share at various times. In 1989 over 80% of foreign trade was with Eastern Europe. As a result of the collapse of trade with the Soviet bloc from 1990, the value of merchandise trade plummeted from US $13,500m. in 1989 to less than $3,170m. in 1993. Recovery was slow and included a diversification of trading partners and greater integration with the world market. The direction of trade altered and services assumed an increasingly important share of export earnings. This was particularly notable in the bolstering of relations with Venezuela, with which the value of trade soared from 1,500m. pesos in 2004 to 4,900m. pesos in 2008, In the latter year Venezuela accounted for 11.3% of Cuba's total exports and 28.9% of its imports, primarily of Cuban medical services and of Venezuelan oil, respectively. The USA was the other significant new source of imports, surpassing 800m. pesos in value in 2008, according to official Cuban statistics. US food and medicine exports to Cuba were legalized on humanitarian grounds by an amendment to US regulations in October 2000, in the wake of major hurricane damage to the island. Trade with China also became increasingly important in the new millennium, with exports rising from 77.3m. pesos in 2003 to almost 1,000m. pesos in 2007, although they declined to 677m. pesos in 2008; meanwhile, imports from China quadrupled in value to over 2,000m. pesos in 2008.

The change in the composition of trade after 1990 was significant. Services comprised a growing share of overall foreign trade, mainly owing to increases in the tourism sector, but also as a result of the greatly diminished role of the sugar sector. Mining products (mainly nickel) accounted for almost 40% of goods exports, to the value of 1,400m. pesos, in 2008; tobacco exports were valued at 236.5m. pesos in the same year, with sugar and sugar by-products earning 235.8m. pesos and medical and pharmaceutical exports valued at 296.8m. pesos. Reuters news agency, quoting an unpublished report by the Ministry of Foreign Trade and Investment, suggested that Cuba was again exporting significant quantities of oil, and that this was likely to be due to a joint venture with Venezuela which supplied crude petroleum to a Cuban refinery. The export of services, in particular medical services to Venezuela, which enabled Cuba to increase its imports of oil from that country, made a strategic contribution to the recovery experienced up to 2008. In addition to the security provided by Venezuelan oil, Chinese and Western European machinery and equipment for energy and infrastructure expansion underpinned that short expansionist period, while food imports from the USA helped overcome the blow to agriculture caused by a series of hurricanes. However, it became increasingly clear in early 2009 that Cuba was facing another period of trade constraints as its two main sources of export revenues faced difficulties: income from tourism was decreasing, and nickel prices on the world market were falling, leading to consideration of a production cut.

THE US TRADE EMBARGO

The US trade embargo, implemented with varying degrees of severity since it was first imposed by President John F. Kennedy in 1960, was strengthened in 1992 when the Cuban Democracy Act (also known as the Torricelli Act) banned trade with Cuba by overseas subsidiaries of US companies. A further dimension was added in March 1996 when President Clinton signed into law the Cuban Liberty and Solidarity Act (commonly known as the Helms-Burton Act), which aimed to halt foreign investment in Cuba. It provoked exceptionally strong protests by other Western governments concerned by its attempted extraterritorial reach.

Contrary to international norms, this legislation potentially opened the US courts to claimants who had obtained US citizenship after their property in Cuba was nationalized. However, President Clinton repeatedly exercised his right to postpone the implementation of Title III, the section of the Act allowing US nationals to claim damages in US federal courts from overseas companies believed to be 'trafficking' in confiscated Cuban property. (Claims by former owners of such property resident in countries other than the USA had been settled.) Clinton's successor, George W. Bush, also suspended the implementation of Title III, despite his heightened anti-Cuban rhetoric. Title IV, which made executives of companies investing in Cuba (and their dependants) liable to exclusion from the USA, was implemented selectively.

After 1998 some restrictions were eased, allowing family visits and cash remittances by Cuban-Americans. In October 2000 legislation was passed that allowed US food and medicine sales to Cuba. However, the potential for such trade was restricted by the conditions attached, such as a ban on financing by US banks or official US credits, and a requirement for payment in cash. Other sanctions legislation, such as the Torricelli and Helms-Burton Acts and the 'Trading with the Enemy' Act, remained operational. These laws included a clause of the Torricelli Act that forbade ships to enter US ports within six months of entering a Cuban port for the purpose of trade. However, in February 2001 the USA granted the first licence to run a scheduled route to Cuba.

The US House of Representatives repeatedly approved a proposal to revoke restrictions on most travel to Cuba, but each time the Republican business managers removed the proposal from the budget bill to which it was attached at the committee stage. This was consistent with the more inflexible approach to Cuba adopted by the Bush Administration, which increased prosecutions against US residents for non-permitted travel and against third country nationals for infringing trade restrictions. In 2004 the Cuban authorities announced that they would waive the requirement that Cubans living in the USA apply for Cuban visas to visit the island. However, the US Government then introduced further travel restrictions, causing a decline in the number of US visitors to Cuba. Overall, US public and political opinion shifted against sanctions, as expressed in a range of campaigns by businesses and bills in Congress, but the Bush Administration remained committed to them. As noted above, Obama announced a change in approach to Cuba in 2009, beginning with a lifting of restrictions on remittances and travel to the island by Cuban-Americans. However, further loosening of the embargo faced the perennial problem of opposition within the US legislature. It did, however, appear that recognition of the need for a review of US policy to the island was growing.

FOREIGN INVESTMENT

Legal from 1982, foreign investment only became a priority for the Cuban Government following the collapse of the communist bloc at the end of the 1980s. In September 1995 foreign investment (up to 100%) was legalized in all sectors of the economy except defence, public health and education, and in 1996 a law was passed allowing the establishment of free trade zones and industrial parks with a view to attracting foreign investment in such areas. Foreign companies were expected to invest in the new type of nominally autonomous limited company (Sociedad Anónima), in which the state (or its nominee) was the major or only shareholder. US companies were prevented by their own laws from investing in Cuba, and the US Helms-Burton Act rendered negotiations with companies from third countries more difficult, although it did not halt the flow of overseas investment. At the end of 2001 cumulative investments and commitments totalled US $5,400m., according to official data, and almost 400 joint ventures and other forms of economic association with overseas companies were operating, with an estimated annual turnover of over $1,200m. However, rigorous administrative procedures required by the Cuban Government, combined with its decision to give preference to larger, more strategic investments, led to a decrease in the number of joint ventures in operation. Leaked official figures revealed that there were just 258 joint ventures and 115 joint-production contracts operating in Cuba in 2005. The decline was mainly owing to the closure of smaller companies, while the remaining ventures with foreign partners accounted for around one-half of total export earnings.

The United Nations Conference on Trade and Development reported inward flows of foreign direct investment (FDI) totalling US $26m. in 2006 and $17m. in 2007, with cumulative FDI stocks of $119m. in 2006 and $136m. in 2007. In 2000 the Government halted foreign involvement in real estate, one of the most sought-after investment opportunities, and the Cuban partners in property ventures bought back the units that had already been built. This was not surprising, as political opposition had prevented a planned real estate law from being enacted. As well as a growing preference on the part of the Cuban authorities for larger projects in strategic sectors, such as energy and infrastructure, there was also keen interest in partners who could offer loan finance. As tourism expansion slowed in recent years, the pace of hotel-building declined, which may have led to a fall in the amount of inward investment.

FOREIGN DEBT

The BCC estimated that the hard currency foreign debt amounted to US $12,000m. at the end of 2004. This appeared to be made up of two major elements, as reported by the Oficina Nacional de Estadísticas (ONE—Office for National Statistics): 'immobilized' debt, which had not been the object of restructuring since 1986, amounting to 7,591.7m. pesos; and 'active' debt, which totalled US $5,806m. in 2004, but had risen to $7,793.7m. in 2006. The latest BCC statistics available put the total debt in 2007 at 8,908.2m. pesos, of which 22.2% was short-term debt; however, it was noted that this referred solely to 'active' debt and that the 'immobilized' debt not subject to restructuring since 1986 amounted to 7,591.7m. pesos, of which 60.2% was the official debt due mainly to the 'Paris Club' of Western creditors. News reports estimated that the total external debt amounted to $52,799m. by the end of 2008.

As Cuba has no access to the World Bank or IMF, most of its official foreign debt is bilateral. Cuba suspended the servicing of bank and bilateral debt with Western governments in 1986, and in 1991 it was granted a moratorium on Soviet debt estimated at 15,000m. roubles. From the mid-1990s Cuba recommenced talks with its creditors and reached several debt-rescheduling agreements. Talks with 'Paris Club' creditors took place in 2000, but progress was prevented, in part, by indecision regarding the inclusion of the debt owed to Russia. In 2002 Cuba announced that it was unable to meet the terms of its 1998 agreement to service US $750m. of Japanese commercial debt. This was attributed to trade difficulties and seemed to be indicative of a change in the priorities of the BCC, forced upon it by the island's worsening trade balance. However, at the end of 2004 the BCC reported a stronger balance of payments, mainly as a result of strong growth in exports of both goods and services, and in April 2006 it made the unprecedented decision to obtain a listing for BCC debt on the London Stock Exchange to consolidate existing debts to the banks. This marked an important step towards achieving the BCC's aims of restructuring Cuba's finances and lowering the cost of financing, and was seen by some analysts as part of a series of adjustments designed to strengthen the Cuban peso and to prepare for eventual exchange rate unification. Nevertheless, it was reported in 2009 that Russia alone was asking for the equivalent of $20,000m. in compensation for pre-1990 debts, and that creditors were being asked to restructure the debt.

AGRICULTURE, FORESTRY AND FISHING

Agriculture has been one of the most unpredictable sectors of the Cuban economy, suffering from frequent droughts, low investment, poor productivity in many crops and, crucially, the central role of sugar long after it had become economically unviable for such reliance to continue. A study by Cuban experts reported that average rainfall had decreased by 10% over the previous 50 years, and had declined by 15% in eastern Cuba over the same period. Agriculture and fisheries accounted for 4.3% of GDP in 2009. Sugar output and its economic contribution diminished dramatically during the 1990s. The fall in the agricultural sector's contribution to national income reflected the effects of the post-Soviet economic crisis and endemic problems, some of which were broached, though not adequately addressed, in the mid-1990s. Foreign financing helped to overcome input shortages in sugar cane, tobacco and citrus fruits, although relief was short-lived in the case of sugar. The 1994 law legalizing free-market sales of agricultural produce (with some exclusions) helped to increase food availability, but production was still below national needs. Although legal, there was little foreign investment in agriculture—the sale of land was not allowed.

A 1993 law divided most state farms into over 4,000 co-operatives, or UBPCs. Small areas of land were leased to individuals for private cultivation, especially of coffee and tobacco, which helped stimulate output, although the number returning to the land was not significant. Official data showed that co-operatives and private farmers held 64% of agricultural land at the end of 2007, compared to under 20% in 1989; however, the state retained full ownership of some 55% of territory overall. In 2002 a new law reduced profit tax for small farmers by allowing them to retain 75% of their profits rather than the 50% previously permitted. A new government fund for agricultural credits was established in 2006, and farmers were promised faster payments and better access to bank credits after a legislative debate identified delayed payments to farmers by state distributors as a serious disincentive to production and delivery of produce, which also deprived farmers of resources to buy essential inputs. In 2008 the new Cuban leader, Raúl Castro, made more state land available to private farmers and co-operatives and devolved decisions regarding land use to the municipal level. Yet, despite these reforms, agriculture continued seriously to underperform, according to debates and ministerial speeches at the congress of the Asociación Nacional de Agricultores Pequeños (National Association of Small Farmers) in May 2010 (see Economic Policy, above).

The restructuring of the sugar industry, formerly Cuba's leading industry, which commenced in 2002, constituted the country's most significant economic policy reform since the early 1990s. The cumulative effect of shortages of inputs, spare parts and fuel had caused sugar production to fall significantly in the 1990s. The implementation by the USA of the Helms-Burton Act in 1996 led the few overseas banks and traders who had financed the industry to review their commitments. From 1997 the Government attempted to achieve greater efficiency and discipline, closing the least efficient sugar mills and ending the practice of cutting young cane. Meanwhile, export earnings were adversely affected by low sugar prices on the world market. Despite the concentration of production on better land, output did not improve. In recognition of the insurmountable problems and adverse market conditions, large tracts of land were taken out of sugar cane production and much of that land continued to lie idle despite the intention to turn it over to alternative uses.

The recovery of the tobacco industry, following a rapid decline during the early 1990s, was one of the clearest successes of economic reform. From an annual average of 43,000 metric tons in 1986–90, production fell rapidly, to 17,000 tons in 1993, before recovering in the late 1990s, owing to financing obtained from the main French and Spanish buyers and incentive schemes for producers. Output was expanded by allocating more land to private farmers, who produced over 80% of the tobacco. This allowed significant expansion in the production of cigars, to respond to growing demand on the world market. The sector opted for a high-quality image with premium prices on the international market. According to Cuban press reports, output in the 2008–09 season reached 55,000 metric tons, despite the damage caused by two major hurricanes in 2008.

Joint ventures provided inputs for a modern, foreign-financed citrus-juicing industry in the 1990s, which boosted production and export income. New directions included organic production, particularly of crops such as coffee, which could obtain premium export prices, and urban agriculture, which reportedly created thousands of new jobs while simultaneously improving domestic food supplies. Some Cuban orange juice exports received 'fair trade' accreditation.

The dairy industry was severely affected by the collapse of foreign trade relations with the Soviet bloc. Milk production plummeted because the national herd was bred to produce high yields from a feedlot system (according to which cattle were kept indoors and fed automatically) and adapted badly to grazing when cheap Soviet feed imports were curtailed. Overall, private farmers recorded the most notable output improvements, a phenomenon attributed largely to the incentive offered by the opening of largely deregulated farmers' markets. Irregularity characterized most food sectors, exacerbated since 1990 by the state of the economy but also by the susceptibility of Cuban agriculture to hurricane and other weather damage. A drought that lasted several years appeared to end in 2006, but new problems relating to humidity and heavy rainfall, as well as hurricane damage, looked likely to slow the recovery of the sector.

Fish farming was developed in the 1990s as the main source of fish for domestic consumers. Lobster-processing plants were modernized to respond to demand from exports and tourism. A scheme introduced in 1998, whereby fishing boats were leased as co-operatives to their crews, was reported to have raised the inshore catch. When not consumed in the tourism sector, lobster and other shellfish were exported, as was the catch from Cuba's deep-sea fishing fleet, but the island also imported seafoods.

Woodland covered 27.7% of Cuban territory by 2007, up from 18% in 1987, according to official data. However, like most of the economy, the sector suffered from resource shortages in the

1990s and by the end of the decade was seeking foreign investment.

The development of an urban farming sector attracted attention abroad among those interested in organic and environmentally safer cultivation and the preservation of scarce energy resources. There were no official statistics available to indicate what this form of cultivation contributed to national supplies, but it may have filled an important gap in localized food availability.

MINING AND ENERGY

Gold was the first economic resource developed by the Spaniards in Cuba, in 1515–38. Copper was mined from 1530 onwards. However, mining was thereafter of little economic importance in Cuba. One study valued total mining output between 1902 and 1950 at US $467m., approximately equivalent to a single post-Second World War sugar harvest.

The island developed production of industrial minerals such as zeolite, and in the 1990s copper, gold, silver and other metals received attention from foreign prospectors. However, deposits of such minerals were insignificant compared with Cuba's proven and estimated reserves of nickel and cobalt, which were among the world's largest. Output of unprocessed nickel plus cobalt increased from 26,900 metric tons in 1994 to a reported 70,000 tons in 2008. The increase was mainly the result of significant joint-venture agreements, particularly one with a Canadian corporation, which included a 50% Cuban share in a Canadian refinery, as well as more recent Chinese investment. A fourth ferro-nickel processing plant, in Las Camariocas, was planned involving Venezuelan investment; this was reported to be on schedule for completion in 2011. Nickel exports helped Cuba to offset recessionary factors.

Energy was one of the Cuban economy's weakest sectors, and the country depended on imported petroleum to generate over 80% of its electricity until the collapse of Soviet economic support forced Cuba to maximize its use of domestic sources. Some 13m. metric tons of petroleum were formerly imported annually from the USSR, on a barter basis, with around 2m. tons being re-exported. When Russian trade was established on a market-prices basis, Cuban petroleum imports decreased sharply. Cuba held international bidding rounds for petroleum exploration blocks beginning in 1993. Canadian and European companies began prospecting both onshore and offshore. While there were no major petroleum discoveries and some foreign companies withdrew from the project, small discoveries were made that allowed domestic petroleum extraction to supply about 45% of oil consumption by 2006. The Spanish petrochemicals company Repsol discovered petroleum in Cuba's deep-water territory in the Gulf of Mexico in 2004, in the only test drilling to date; in 2010 the Brazilian firm Petrobras was reported to be considering drilling an exploration well.

The Cuban reserves in the Gulf of Mexico aroused interest among US oil companies, representatives of which met with Cuban officials in Mexico City in early 2006. The US oil industry was reported to be calling for a review of the US sanctions legislation, which prevented them from investing in the development of Cuban economic assets, and in mid-2010 Washington licensed a US firm to advise Cuba on oil safety and environmental practices. Electricity-generating plants were converted to use domestic fuel and Canadian investment allowed natural gas to be harnessed for energy generation. Ensuring reliable and affordable sources for the remainder of Cuba's petroleum requirements proved problematic until Venezuela agreed in November 2001 to supply oil to Cuba in deals given high-profile support by left-wing Venezuelan President Lt-Col Hugo Chávez Frías and involving the supply of Cuban medical and educational services to Venezuela. Cuba became one of the signatories of the PetroCaribe accord, under the terms of which Caribbean nations were to be allowed to purchase Venezuelan oil at reduced prices. An agreement reached in 2006 with Petróleos de Venezuela (PDVSA), the Venezuelan state oil company, led to the modernization of a Soviet-built oil refinery in Cuba in order to process up to 65,000 barrels per day. In 2005 the Cuban authorities launched what they termed an 'energy revolution', intended to improve efficiency in household and commercial usage, as well as within the energy industry, and to reduce dependence on hydrocarbons. In 2007 the first major wind farm began to operate on the Isla de la Juventud and work was in progress on others. Solar power was also to be expanded.

INDUSTRY

From 1962 Cuba invested heavily in developing and diversifying an industrial base that had previously been dominated by sugar. In 1965–72 the main focus was on rehabilitating sugar mills (which had been nationalized with most existing industry in the early 1960s) and building up the production of spare parts, agricultural equipment, cement and fertilizers. Investment spending accelerated in 1976–90, so that by the end of the 1980s Cuba had developed a varied industrial base, ranging from food-processing and light industry to construction materials, chemicals, machine tools, paper and glass. However, there were several major weaknesses, which became clearer and more pronounced as industry came to a near standstill after Cuba's communist bloc markets disappeared. A steep fall in crucial petroleum imports led to the closure of most plants. This was exacerbated by the fuel inefficiency of many factories constructed with Soviet or Eastern European aid, which were often built for Comecon's rather than Cuba's needs, and the unsuitability of many products for Western markets. A heavy dependence on imported raw materials was most marked in the chemicals industry, which, according to one leading Cuban analyst, was at least 20 years behind its counterparts in most large and medium-sized Latin American countries.

In the 1990s the Government attempted to make industry more efficient through measures such as the division of large enterprises into smaller and more manageable entities, using only the most efficient lines and reducing staff. Such measures were believed to be essential for attracting inward investment to manufacturing and some sectors recorded higher output after 1994. Results were mixed, however, and growth was often linked to tourism, in cases such as construction materials and furniture, or to inward investment, as in nickel-processing and the beverages and tobacco sectors. It seemed, however, that many plants were still producing at a fraction of installed capacity, and, despite new investments, official figures showed that in 2008 the overall index of production was just 46.1% of the 1989 level. There was, however, one notable exception to the downward trend: manufacture of pharmaceutical and 'botanical' products in 2008 reached 822% of the 1989 level.

PHARMACEUTICALS AND HEALTH CARE

One area that continued to receive significant support from the Government throughout the 1990s crisis period was the indigenous pharmaceuticals and medical goods sector. The Government justified its decision to continue investing by reference to the need to protect the national health care service, and to recover the state's earlier spending on training and infrastructure. Laboratories and production lines were improved, the biotechnology sector's production capacity expanded and integrated research and production centres developed. A network of science parks organized the contribution of some 200 life science institutions to the national economy, and leading research and development centres began to form joint-venture agreements. Spending on science and technology totalled US $423.6m. in 2007, most of it from the state budget, and was mainly spent on research and development. The sector fulfilled the aim of providing the bulk of national medicines, but significant commercial results were slow to materialize until the 21st century, when exports of medicines and medical services rose in value and played a strategic role in enabling Cuba to import key requirements, particularly oil from Venezuela. In 2005 the Government established a new enterprise, Servicios Médicos Cubanos (Cuban Medical Services), to regulate the trade in medical services.

TOURISM

In the 1990s the international tourism sector in Cuba experienced rapid growth, having virtually disappeared after the USA banned travel to the island by its citizens in 1961.

Orientated primarily towards the domestic market for nearly 30 years, in the 1980s tourism was identified as a potentially rich source of convertible currency. Overseas investment was sought to help develop the industry, and the first agreement to build a joint-venture hotel was signed in 1989 with a leading Spanish hotel group. However, official sources claimed that foreign capital remained of less importance than that from national sources and, although the number and origin of foreign participants in the industry increased, most overseas companies managed, rather than owned, the hotels they operated. In 2006 there were over 300 hotels in international tourism centres, with nearly 52,000 rooms, employing 108,000 staff; there were, in addition, several thousand rooms in private homes.

Tourism became the principal source of foreign currency earnings by the end of the 1990s: gross hard currency revenue increased from US $243.4m. in 1990 to almost $2,359m. in 2008, according to amended official figures. Arrivals, mainly from Europe and Canada, rose from some 340,300 in 1990 to more than 2.4m. in 2009, according to the ONE. Canada was the principal country of origin, while the number of visitors from the USA looked set to rise following the Obama Administration's decision to lift restrictions on travel by Cuban-Americans; early reports indicated that there was a swift response, probably facilitated by an earlier decision on the part of the Cuban Government to allow visa-free entry to Cubans resident in the USA. Over the previous decade arrivals from the USA had fluctuated, from 34,956 legal visitors in 1997 to 84,529 in 2003, falling again to 36,808 in 2006, a trend that reflected the severity with which earlier US Administrations enforced travel restrictions on US citizens. There were 41,904 US arrivals to Cuba in 2008.

ECONOMIC OUTLOOK

Following another decline in GDP and tough external conditions, economic recovery was unlikely in the short term, and there was little indication that basic underlying factors would change in the medium term, with the national approach to the economy appearing to consist of cautious minor reforms, personnel changes at cabinet level and calls for greater effort by producers. There were hopes that the inauguration in 2008–09 of new Presidents in both Washington and Havana would usher in a new era in US-Cuban relations, and facilitate moves towards 'normal' economic conditions. Both Obama and Raúl Castro spoke of their readiness to discuss issues that have dominated relations between their countries for 50 years. Obama's initiative on travel restrictions looked likely to lead to a rise in visitors from the USA, thus providing a useful boost to Cuban tourism, which was expected to face a tougher trading climate in the current recession. However, Obama's ability to deliver a further easing of embargo restrictions was in question, as Congress remained divided on Cuban issues. Only minor concessions were made in other areas, but the potential for some further easing of economic restrictions in the course of the Obama presidency remained.

On taking office in 2008, the new Cuban President for his part decreed some small measures that were welcomed by the public, but they were fewer and more limited than some had hoped for. He replaced several key ministers, including the Minister of Economy and Planning, bringing older men of his own generation—mainly technocrats with a military background—into the Council of Ministers. Raúl Castro was not expected to implement any radical economic measures, and predictions that more sweeping changes would be sanctioned by the Cuban Communist Party Congress scheduled for late 2009 were dashed when that event was postponed. Information that leaked out about internal party consultations suggested that there were disagreements about future policy directions, and leadership proposals for relatively minor reforms such as relaxation of state control over small retail and service industries. A significant departure from strict fiscal control and central planning, or a retreat from the decentralization that had taken place since the early 1990s, was unlikely amid the current severe economic conditions.

GDP had recorded positive growth for over a decade, reflecting some recovery in important sectors, as well as greater security of key fuel imports. However, growth slowed sharply once again in 2009 and was unlikely to recover for several years. The economy was still operating considerably below capacity and remained highly vulnerable to external shocks. Oil supplies had been secure and affordable for some years while Venezuela was trading oil for medical services, but high indebtedness in the Venezuelan petroleum sector raised uncertainties about the future of that deal. Tourism, the largest source of foreign currency and fastest growth sector, appeared to be weathering the difficulties, although revenue failed to keep pace with visitor numbers; despite the contribution of visiting Cuban-Americans, the tourism sector too was expected to feel the effects of the recession for some time. Leaders, including President Raúl Castro, warned of economic hardship and urged greater productivity, but Cubans have heard such statements frequently over the years and might therefore not have taken them as seriously as their leaders hoped. Coupled with the external environment, as well as factors such as an ageing population and high emigration among the younger generation, the pace of recovery looked uncertain and slow.

Statistical Survey

Sources (unless otherwise stated): Cámara de Comercio de la República de Cuba, Calle 21, No 661/701, esq. Calle A, Apdo 4237, Vedado, Havana; tel. (7) 830-4436; fax (7) 833-3042; e-mail pdcia@camara.com.cu; internet www.camaracuba.cu; Oficina Nacional de Estadísticas, Calle Paseo 60, entre 3 y 5, Plaza de la Revolución, Vedado, Havana, CP 10400; tel. (7) 830-0053; fax (7) 833-3083; e-mail oneweb@one.gov.cu; internet www.one.cu.

Area and Population

AREA, POPULATION AND DENSITY

Area (sq km)	109,886*
Population (census results)	
11 September 1981	9,723,605
7–16 September 2002	
Males	5,597,233
Females	5,580,510
Total	11,177,743
Population (official estimates at 31 December)	
2007	11,236,790
2008	11,236,099
2009	11,242,628
Density (per sq km) at 31 December 2009	102.3

* 42,427 sq miles.

POPULATION BY AGE AND SEX
(official estimates at 31 December 2009)

	Males	Females	Total
0–14	1,012,951	951,390	1,964,341
15–64	3,958,672	3,915,241	7,873,913
65 and over	659,120	745,254	1,404,374
Total	5,630,743	5,611,885	11,242,628

PROVINCES
(official population estimates at 31 December 2009)

	Area (sq km)	Population	Density (per sq km)	Capital (population*)
Camagüey	15,615.0	782,582	50.1	Camagüey (306,393)
Ciego de Avila	6,783.1	422,643	62.3	Ciego de Avila (110,728)
Cienfuegos	4,180.0	405,545	97.0	Cienfuegos (143,356)
Ciudad de la Habana†	721.0	2,141,993	2,970.9	—
Granma	8,375.5	835,808	99.8	Bayamo (147,458)
Guantánamo	6,168.0	510,944	82.8	Guantánamo (208,055)
La Habana†	5,731.6	747,491	130.4	—
Holguín	9,292.8	1,037,326	111.6	Holguín (276,956)
Isla de la Juventud	2,419.3	86,256	35.7	Nueva Gerona (47,249)
Matanzas	11,802.7	690,223	58.5	Matanzas (132,046)
Pinar del Rio	10,904.0	729,292	66.9	Pinar del Rio (137,808)
Sancti Spíritus	6,736.5	465,542	69.1	Sancti Spíritus (98,682)
Santiago de Cuba	6,156.4	1,047,181	170.1	Santiago de Cuba (426,679)
Las Tunas	6,587.8	536,112	81.4	Las Tunas (152,799)
Villa Clara	8,412.4	803,690	95.5	Santa Clara (207,170)
Total	109,886.2	11,242,628	102.3	—

* Estimates at 31 December 2008.

† Ciudad de la Habana is the capital of La Habana province, but also a province in its own right.

PRINCIPAL TOWNS
(estimated population at 31 December 2009)

La Habana (Havana, the capital)	2,141,993	Las Tunas	153,128
Santiago de Cuba	426,840	Bayamo	147,638
Camagüey	305,701	Cienfuegos	143,894
Holguín	277,261	Pinar del Rio	137,320
Guantánamo	207,974	Matanzas	132,678
Santa Clara	206,379	Ciego de Avila	111,085

Note: Havana contained 12 municipalities with populations exceeding 100,000 at 31 December 2008; other highly populated municipalities included Cárdenas (109,097, Province of Matanzas), Manzanillo (131,425, Province of Granma), Palma Soriano and Contramaestre (123,064 and 104,575, respectively, Province of Santiago de Cuba) and Mayarí (103,884, Province of Holguín).

BIRTHS, MARRIAGES AND DEATHS*

	Registered live births†		Registered marriages‡		Registered deaths	
	Number	Rate (per 1,000)	Number	Rate (per 1,000)	Number	Rate (per 1,000)
2002	141,276	12.6	56,876	5.1	73,882	6.6
2003	136,795	12.2	54,739	4.9	78,434	7.0
2004	127,192	11.3	50,878	4.5	81,110	7.2
2005	120,716	10.7	51,831	4.6	84,824	7.5
2006	111,323	9.9	56,377	5.0	80,831	7.2
2007	112,472	10.0	56,781	5.1	81,927	7.3
2008	122,569	10.9	61,852	5.5	86,423	7.7
2009	130,036	11.6	54,969	4.9	86,943	7.7

* Data are tabulated by year of registration rather than by year of occurrence.

† Births registered in the National Consumers Register, established on 31 December 1964.

‡ Including consensual unions formalized in response to special legislation.

Life expectancy (years at birth, WHO estimates): 77 (males 76; females 79) in 2008 (Source: WHO, *World Health Statistics*).

ECONOMICALLY ACTIVE POPULATION
('000 persons aged 15 years and over, official estimates)

	2007	2008	2009
Agriculture, hunting, forestry and fishing	912.3	919.1	945.6
Mining and quarrying	25.7	26.7	27.0
Manufacturing	523.3	543.1	530.8
Electricity, gas and water	85.0	79.8	90.3
Construction	243.7	245.2	239.1
Trade, restaurants and hotels	613.6	610.2	628.2
Transport, storage and communications	289.3	301.4	297.1
Financing, insurance, real estate and business services	111.4	123.0	118.5
Community, social and personal services	2,063.4	2,099.7	2,195.8
Total employed	4,867.7	4,948.2	5,072.4
Unemployed	88.6	79.7	86.1
Total labour force	4,956.3	5,027.9	5,158.5

CIVILIAN EMPLOYMENT IN THE STATE SECTOR
('000 persons)

	1998	1999	2000
Agriculture, hunting, forestry and fishing	733.1	714.4	714.2
Mining and quarrying	47.3	20.8	20.8
Manufacturing	458.9	512.7	512.6
Electricity, gas and water	46.0	51.0	51.0
Construction	178.9	167.1	167.8
Trade, restaurants and hotels	355.2	375.2	375.2
Transport, storage and communications	175.2	157.4	157.4
Financing, insurance, real estate and business services	47.6	54.3	54.3
Community, social and personal services	964.5	952.1	951.8
Total	3,006.7	3,005.0	3,005.1

Health and Welfare

KEY INDICATORS

Total fertility rate (children per woman, 2008)	1.5
Under-5 mortality rate (per 1,000 live births, 2008)	6
HIV/AIDS (% of persons aged 15–49, 2007)	0.10
Physicians (per 1,000 head, 2002)	5.9
Hospital beds (per 1,000 head, 2006)	4.9
Health expenditure (2007): US $ per head (PPP)	917
Health expenditure (2007): % of GDP	10.4
Health expenditure (2007): public (% of total)	95.5
Access to water (% of persons, 2008)	94
Access to sanitation (% of persons, 2008)	91
Total carbon dioxide emissions ('000 metric tons, 2006)	29,605.1
Carbon dioxide emissions per head (metric tons, 2006)	2.6
Human Development Index (2007): ranking	51
Human Development Index (2007): value	0.863

For sources and definitions, see explanatory note on p. vi.

Agriculture

PRINCIPAL CROPS
('000 metric tons)

	2006	2007	2008
Rice, paddy	434.2	439.6	436.0
Maize	305.4	368.8	325.7
Potatoes	286.2	143.7	189.0
Sweet potatoes	303.0	414.0	375.0
Cassava (Manioc)	450.0	379.1	339.6
Yautia (Cocoyam)	175.0	207.8	240.0
Sugar cane	11,060.0	11,900.0	15,700.0
Beans, dry	70.6	97.2	97.2
Groundnuts, in shell*	10.0	10.0	10.0
Coconuts	103.9	124.6	105.6
Cabbages and other brassicas	172.8	182.3	186.7
Tomatoes	636.0	627.9	575.9
Pumpkins, squash and gourds	446.5	455.5	422.5
Cucumbers and gherkins	155.7	154.3	139.3
Chillies and peppers, green	62.1	55.8	63.7
Onions, dry	112.0	105.1	128.1
Garlic	33.6	34.8	34.8
Watermelons	71.9	64.6	60.4
Cantaloupes and other melons*	93.0	99.0	99.0
Bananas	339.5	385.9	280.8
Plantains	532.3	605.0	477.4
Oranges	178.4	302.8	200.4
Tangerines, mandarins, clementines and satsumas	19.0	20.2	19.9
Lemons and limes	6.1	6.0	5.4
Grapefruit and pomelos	169.6	140.0	166.1
Guavas, mangoes and mangosteens	308.2	311.5	355.2
Pineapples	45.4	51.6	55.4
Papayas	90.3	89.7	89.4
Coffee, green	13.5†	14.0*	14.0*
Tobacco, unmanufactured	29.7	25.6	21.5

* FAO estimate(s).
† Unofficial figure.

Aggregate production ('000 metric tons, may include official, semi-official or estimated data): Total cereals 744.1 in 2006, 809.5 in 2007, 762.2 in 2008; Total roots and tubers 1,330.2 in 2006, 1,378.6 in 2007, 1,392.5 in 2008; Total vegetables (incl. melons) 2,765.1 in 2006, 2,702.0 in 2007, 2,538.3 in 2008; Total fruits (excl. melons) 1,941.9 in 2006; 2,173.6 in 2007, 1,837.4 in 2008.

Source: FAO.

LIVESTOCK
('000 head, year ending September)

	2006	2007	2008
Cattle	3,737.2	3,787.4	3,821.3
Horses	482.8	506.1	534.0
Mules	21.0	20.7	20.5
Pigs	1,760.8	1,868.6	1,878.6
Sheep	2,761.3	2,653.1	2,675.0
Goats	1,170.9	1,126.1	1,134.0
Chickens	29,848	29,413	29,201

Source: FAO.

LIVESTOCK PRODUCTS
('000 metric tons)

	2006	2007	2008
Cattle meat	55.7	54.0	62.0
Pig meat	99.9	177.0	192.7
Chicken meat	31.2	33.5	33.1
Cows' milk	415.2	485.1	545.5
Hen eggs	103.0	103.5	102.4
Honey	6.9	6.2	5.1

Source: FAO.

Forestry

ROUNDWOOD REMOVALS
('000 cubic metres, excl. bark, FAO estimates)

	2006	2007	2008
Sawlogs, veneer logs and logs for sleepers	400	400	400
Other industrial wood	361	361	361
Fuel wood	1,584	1,413	1,273
Total	2,345	2,174	2,034

Source: FAO.

SAWNWOOD PRODUCTION
('000 cubic metres, incl. railway sleepers)

	2006*	2007	2008
Coniferous (softwood)	146	135	126
Broadleaved (hardwood)	97	60	56
Total	243	195	182

* FAO estimates.

Source: FAO.

Fishing

('000 metric tons, live weight)

	2006	2007	2008
Capture	27.6	28.8	27.9
Blue tilapia	1.4	3.1	2.8
Lane snapper	1.1	1.3	1.6
Caribbean spiny lobster	4.4	4.8	5.7
Aquaculture*	27.2	31.6	33.0
Silver carp	12.2	19.9	20.2
Total catch*	54.8	60.4	60.9

* FAO estimates.

Note: Figures exclude sponges (metric tons): 44 in 2006; 38 in 2007; 46 in 2008.

Source: FAO.

Mining

('000 metric tons unless otherwise indicated)

	2007	2008	2009
Crude petroleum	2,905.0	3,003.1	2,731.3
Natural gas (million cu metres)	1,217.9	1,161.0	1,155.3
Nickel (metal content)	3,332.5	3,289.5	3,949.0

Chromite: 27.9 in 2006.

Industry

SELECTED PRODUCTS

('000 metric tons unless otherwise indicated)

	2007	2008	2009
Crude steel	262.4	273.8	265.8
Grey cement	1,805.3	1,705.2	1,625.7
Corrugated asbestos-cement tiles	5,425.7	5,660.2	5,948.7
Colour television sets ('000)	118.3	94.2	79.4
Fuel oil	940.4	2,667.8	2,629.3
New tyres ('000)	68.9	66.4	42.8
Recapped tyres ('000)	71.3	67.6	56.9
Woven textile fabrics (million sq metres)	24.0	31.6	27.9
Cigarettes ('000 million)	13.8	14.2	13.4
Cigars (million)	411.9	386.7	373.2
Alcoholic beverages (excl. wines, '000 litres)	950.8	1,100.1	997.2
Beer ('000 hectolitres)	2,459.1	2,508.2	2,474.4
Soft drinks ('000 hectolitres)	3,505.8	3,713.3	3,747.8
Bicycles ('000)	37.6	53.3	36.4
Fishing vessels	421	927	263
Electric energy (million kWh)	17,622.5	17,661.8	17,801.8

Finance

CURRENCY AND EXCHANGE RATES

Monetary Units

100 centavos = 1 Cuban peso.

1 Cuban peso = 1 convertible peso (official rate).

Sterling, Dollar and Euro Equivalents (31 May 2010)

£1 sterling = 1.350 convertible pesos;

US $1 = 0.926 convertible pesos;

€1 = 1.147 convertible pesos;

100 convertible pesos = £74.08 = $108.00 = €87.21.

Note: The foregoing information relates to official exchange rates. For the purposes of foreign trade, the peso was at par with the US dollar during each of the 10 years 1987–96. In addition, a 'convertible peso' was introduced in December 1994. Although officially at par with the Cuban peso, in March 2005 the 'unofficial' exchange rate prevailing in domestic exchange houses was adjusted to 24 pesos per convertible peso.

STATE BUDGET

(million pesos)

Revenue	2008	2009	2010*
Tax revenue	25,847.0	25,447.7	24,835.0
Road and sales tax	13,219.9	12,791.0	11,342.4
Taxes on services	1,460.4	1,543.2	1,647.0
Taxes on utilities	2,950.0	2,660.7	2,811.5
Taxes on labour	3,956.2	4,267.7	4,593.0
Personal income tax	453.4	465.4	508.7
Other taxes	1,216.5	956.7	951.3
Social security contributions	2,590.6	2,763.0	2,981.1
Non-tax revenue	16,535.6	18,468.2	18,550.5
Transfers from state enterprises	3,240.0	3,100.4	3,256.9
Other non-tax revenue	13,295.6	15,367.8	15,293.6
Restitution payments	–327.0	–320.4	–320.4
Total	42,055.6	43,595.5	43,065.1

Expenditure	2008	2009	2010*
Current expenditure	41,755.5	41,800.0	41,770.8
Education	7,503.4	9,030.6	9,904.0
Public health	7,188.6	6,610.3	6,823.7
Defence and public order	2,036.8	2,126.2	2,206.1
Social security	4,400.0	4,704.0	4,900.0
Administration	1,456.5	1,525.9	1,522.3
Community services	1,688.8	1,717.2	1,664.6
Industry	2,108.5	2,157.3	801.7
Art and culture	1,314.9	1,327.2	1,321.5
Science and technology	570.3	603.6	663.6
Sport	547.2	617.9	717.8
Social assistance	940.2	934.0	885.8
Other activities	1,910.1	1,675.3	1,609.0
Subsidies, etc. to state enterprises	8,632.0	7,462.1	7,150.7
Subsidy for losses	1,053.0	n.a.	n.a.
Subsidy for price differentials	2,212.0	n.a.	n.a.
Others	5,367.0	n.a.	n.a.
Financial operations	1,300.0	1,308.4	1,400.0
Adjustment	158.0	—	200.0
Investment expenditure	4,500.0	4,811.2	3,237.0
Reserves	—	—	260.0
Total	46,255.6	46,611.2	45,267.8

* Approved budgetary proposal.

INTERNATIONAL RESERVES

(million pesos at 31 December)

	1987	1988
Gold and other precious metals	17.5	19.5
Cash and deposits in foreign banks (convertible currency)	36.5	78.0
Sub-total	54.0	97.5
Deposits in foreign banks (in transferable roubles)	142.5	137.0
Total	196.5	234.5

MONEY SUPPLY

(million pesos)

	2007	2008	2009
Currency in circulation	10,566.2	11,579.7	10,874.7
Savings	11,293.4	13,946.6	15,186.2
Total	21,859.6	25,526.3	26,060.9

NATIONAL ACCOUNTS

(million pesos at current prices)

Composition of Gross National Product

	2005	2006	2007
Compensation of employees	16,124.3	18,970.1	20,385.7
Operating surplus; Consumption of fixed capital	16,430.9	21,562.2	24,295.1
Gross domestic product (GDP) at factor cost	32,555.2	40,532.3	44,680.8
Indirect taxes, less subsidies	10,088.6	12,210.5	13,923.1
GDP in purchasers' values	42,643.8	52,742.8	58,603.9
Less Factor income paid abroad (net)	633.2	618.0	959.7
Gross national product	42,010.6	52,124.8	57,644.2

Expenditure on the Gross Domestic Product

	2005	2006	2007
Government final consumption expenditure	14,349.0	17,001.1	20,751.5
Private final consumption expenditure	22,559.5	29,429.9	30,299.4
Increase in stocks	773.2	700.0	290.0
Gross fixed capital formation	3,821.5	5,486.0	5,678.0
Total domestic expenditure	41,503.2	52,617.0	57,018.9
Exports of goods and services	8,962.9	9,869.7	11,917.9
Less Imports of goods and services	7,822.6	9,744.0	10,332.6
GDP in purchasers' values	42,643.8	52,742.8	58,603.9
GDP at constant 1997 prices	36,507.3	40,912.2	43,883.3

Gross Domestic Product by Economic Activity

	2005	2006	2007
Agriculture, hunting, forestry and fishing	1,860.8	1,795.9	2,291.8
Mining and quarrying	569.5	766.5	1,101.6
Manufacturing	5,393.5	6,333.4	7,415.7
Electricity, gas and water	559.4	985.0	1,137.3
Construction	2,398.2	3,320.9	3,217.2
Wholesale and retail trade, restaurants and hotels	10,103.8	14,449.8	15,043.2
Transport, storage and communications	3,640.2	4,001.9	4,423.1
Finance, insurance, real estate and business services	2,200.7	2,412.8	2,661.7
Community, social and personal services	15,423.6	18,086.7	20,651.8
Sub-total	42,149.7	52,152.9	57,943.4
Import duties	494.1	590.0	660.2
Total	42,643.8	52,742.9	58,603.6

2008 (million pesos at constant prices): Agriculture, hunting, forestry and fishing 1,897.9; Mining and quarrying 287.3; Manufacturing 6,358.9; Electricity, gas and water 657.2; Construction 2,848.0; Wholesale and retail trade, restaurants and hotels 10,530.5; Transport, storage and communications 4,019.0; Finance, insurance, real estate and business services 2,563.9; Education 3,675.8; Public administration and social security 1,772.2; Public health and social assistance 7,721.7; Other services 2,659.5; *Sub-total* 44,991.9; Import duties 698.0; *Total* 45,689.9.

2009 (million pesos at constant prices): Agriculture, hunting, forestry and fishing 1,981.2; Mining and quarrying 273.9; Manufacturing 6,230.9; Electricity, gas and water 664.7; Construction 2,883.7; Wholesale and retail trade, restaurants and hotels 10,540.6; Transport, storage and communications 4,186.2; Finance, insurance, real estate and business services 2,620.8; Education 3,797.1; Public administration and social security 1,805.6; Public health and social assistance 8,120.8; Other services 2,782.3; *Sub-total* 45,887.8; Import duties 419.5; *Total* 46,307.3.

BALANCE OF PAYMENTS
(million pesos)

	1999	2000	2001
Exports of goods	1,456.1	1,676.8	1,661.5
Imports of goods	–4,365.4	–4,876.7	–4,838.3
Trade balance	–2,909.3	–3,117.2	–3,076.2
Services (net)	2,162.7	2,223.0	2,212.8
Balance on goods and services	–746.6	–894.2	–863.4
Other income (net)	–514.1	–622.2	–502.2
Balance on goods, services and income	–1,260.7	–1,516.4	–1,365.6
Current transfers (net)	798.9	740.4	812.9
Current balance	–461.8	–776.0	–552.7
Direct investment (net)	178.2	448.1	38.9
Other long-term capital (net)	31.7	570.3	328.3
Other capital (net)	275.0	–213.0	227.3
Overall balance	23.1	29.4	41.8

2005 (million pesos): Exports of goods 2,159.4; Imports of goods –7,604.3; Goods acquired at seaports and airports 210.2; *Trade balance* –5,234.7; Services (net) 6,375.2; *Balance on goods and services* 1,140.5; Income (net) –633.2; Current transfers (net) –367.2; *Current balance* –140.1.

2006 (million pesos): Exports of goods 2,924.6; Imports of goods –9,497.9; Goods acquired at seaports and airports 243.0; *Trade balance* –6,330.3; Services (net) 6,456.0; *Balance on goods and services* 125.7; Income (net) –618.0; Current transfers (net) 277.7; *Current balance* –214.6.

2007 (million pesos): Exports of goods 3,701.4; Imports of goods –10,082.6; Goods acquired at seaports and airports 128.5; *Trade balance* –6,252.7; Services (net) 7,899.9; *Balance on goods and services* 1,647.2; Income (net) –959.7; Current transfers (net) –199.0; *Current balance* 488.5.

External Trade

PRINCIPAL COMMODITIES
('000 pesos)

Imports c.i.f.	2007	2008	2009
Food and live animals	1,548,923	2,205,342	1,494,102
Cereals and cereal preparations	671,795	1,128,738	647,682
Wheat and meslin (unmilled)	164,256	272,702	189,806
Rice	229,239	478,830	238,411
Mineral fuels, lubricants, etc.	2,382,884	4,561,798	2,648,703
Chemicals and related products	825,901	1,179,997	817,956
Basic manufactures	1,101,795	1,548,650	1,049,942
Iron and steel	223,017	318,408	264,254
Manufactures of metal	293,134	399,335	282,463
Machinery and transport equipment	3,005,681	3,154,618	1,784,808
Power-generating machinery and equipment	546,495	538,726	211,395
General industrial machinery and equipment and machine parts	487,243	686,096	423,087
Total (incl. others)	10,082,557	14,234,094	8,909,541

Exports f.o.b.	2007	2008	2009
Food and live animals	325,794	340,067	306,711
Fish, crustaceans and molluscs and preparations thereof	83,389	73,758	46,573
Fresh, chilled or frozen fish	82,363	73,620	46,471
Fruit and vegetables	32,011	26,271	27,881
Sugar, sugar preparations and honey	200,861	233,425	225,057
Beverages and tobacco	288,671	318,000	281,872
Crude materials (inedible) except fuels	2,143,823	1,483,700	880,434
Metalliferous ores and metal scrap	2,140,044	1,479,917	873,777
Chemicals and related products	332,286	347,929	567,775
Basic manufactures	117,162	137,887	100,518
Iron and steel	56,901	76,905	44,942
Machinery and transport equipment	171,714	164,454	169,362
Miscellaneous manufactured articles	139,433	58,417	61,312
Total (incl. others)	3,685,665	3,664,157	2,879,036

PRINCIPAL TRADING PARTNERS
('000 pesos)

Imports c.i.f.	2007	2008	2009
Algeria	225,469	243,698	169,163
Argentina	146,036	125,305	117,599
Brazil	382,087	600,141	508,913
Canada	436,723	655,778	291,834
Chile	74,522	73,990	52,999
China, People's Republic	1,518,084	1,480,791	1,171,485
Colombia	71,674	69,005	49,790
France	166,659	226,737	139,678
Germany	371,730	377,617	275,306
Italy	391,063	488,408	323,651
Japan	224,428	153,304	88,506
Mexico	204,703	369,144	303,485
Netherlands Antilles	882	698	249
Russia	291,788	268,745	195,406
Spain	982,305	1,232,473	752,536
Venezuela	2,243,242	4,473,223	2,604,988
Viet Nam	281,430	514,342	276,117
Total (incl. others)	10,079,210	14,234,094	8,909,541

Exports f.o.b.	2007	2008	2009
Belgium	17,253	10,849	8,218
Brazil	64,293	41,679	69,356
Canada	962,966	756,622	434,396
China, People's Republic	928,320	677,107	516,504
Dominican Republic	32,757	46,061	21,578
France	68,461	45,897	45,472
Germany	24,259	27,041	29,440
Japan	12,467	9,289	5,691
Mexico	14,975	14,160	14,502
Netherlands	435,514	288,599	236,853
Portugal	24,143	47,534	21,335
Russia	70,570	55,961	87,683
Spain	172,533	194,802	154,664
Switzerland	12,472	15,235	14,506
Venezuela	450,397	413,781	533,148
Total (incl. others)	3,685,665	3,664,157	2,879,036

Transport

RAILWAYS

	2007	2008	2009
Passenger-kilometres (million)	1,286	1,057	974
Freight ton-kilometres (million)	1,411	1,388	2,791

ROAD TRAFFIC
(motor vehicles in use at 31 December)

	1996	1997
Passenger cars	216,575	172,574
Buses and coaches	28,089	28,861
Lorries and vans	246,105	156,634

Source: International Road Federation, *World Road Statistics*.

SHIPPING

Merchant Fleet
(registered at 31 December)

	2006	2007	2008
Number of vessels	68	68	67
Total displacement ('000 grt)	65	61	60

Source: Lloyd's Register-Fairplay, *World Fleet Statistics*.

International Sea-borne Freight Traffic
('000 metric tons)

	1988	1989	1990
Goods loaded	8,600	8,517	8,092
Goods unloaded	15,500	15,595	15,440

Source: UN, *Monthly Bulletin of Statistics*.

CIVIL AVIATION
(traffic on scheduled services)

	2003	2004	2005
Kilometres flown (million)	19	21	22
Passengers carried ('000)	664	743	813
Passenger-kilometres (million)	2,036	2,241	2,422
Total ton-kilometres (million)	224	246	263

Source: UN, *Statistical Yearbook*.

Tourism

ARRIVALS BY COUNTRY OF RESIDENCE*

	2007	2008	2009
Canada	660,384	818,246	914,884
France	92,304	90,731	83,478
Germany	103,054	100,964	93,437
Italy	134,289	126,042	118,347
Mexico	92,120	84,052	61,487
Spain	133,149	121,166	129,224
United Kingdom	208,122	193,932	172,318
USA	40,521	41,904	52,455
Venezuela	33,593	31,931	28,657
Total (incl. others)	2,152,221	2,348,340	2,429,809

* Figures include same-day visitors (excursionists).

Tourism receipts (US $ million, incl. passenger transport): 2,399 in 2005; 2,414 in 2006; 2,415 in 2007 (Source: World Tourism Organization).

Communications Media

	2007	2008	2009
Telephones ('000 main lines in use)	1,043.1	1,103.6	1,167.5
Mobile cellular telephones ('000 subscribers)	198.3	331.7	443.0
Internet users ('000)	1,310.0	1,450.0	1,605.0
Broadband subscribers ('000)	1.9	2.0	2.0

Radio receivers ('000 in use): 3,900 in 1997.

Television receivers ('000 in use): 2,800 in 2000.

Book production: 1,004 titles published in 2001.

Daily newspapers: 2 in 2004 (average estimated circulation 727,600 copies).

Personal computers: 630,000 (56.2 per 1,000 persons) in 2008.

Sources: UNESCO, *Statistical Yearbook*; UN, *Statistical Yearbook*; International Telecommunication Union.

Education

(2009/10)

	Institutions	Teachers	Students
Pre-primary	1,110*	9,628	120,293
Primary	8,215	108,020	811,598
Secondary	1,946	95,904	871,473
Tertiary	65	62,509	606,863

* 2008/09 figure.

Pupil-teacher ratio (primary education, UNESCO estimate): 9.6 in 2007/08 (Source: UNESCO Institute for Statistics).

Adult literacy rate (UNESCO estimates): 99.8% (males 99.8%; females 99.8%) in 2008 (Source: UNESCO Institute for Statistics).

Directory

The Constitution

Following the assumption of power by the Castro regime, on 1 January 1959, the Constitution was suspended and a Fundamental Law of the Republic was instituted, with effect from 7 February 1959. In February 1976 Cuba's first socialist Constitution came into force after being submitted to the first Congress of the Communist Party of Cuba, in December 1975, and to popular referendum, in February 1976; it was amended in July 1992. The main provisions of the Constitution, as amended, are summarized below.

Note: On 27 July 2002 the Constitution was further amended to enshrine the socialist system as irrevocable and to ratify that economic, diplomatic and political relations with another state cannot be negotiated in the face of aggression, threat or pressure from a foreign power. A clause was also introduced making it impossible to remove these amendments from the Constitution.

POLITICAL, SOCIAL AND ECONOMIC PRINCIPLES

The Republic of Cuba is a socialist, independent and sovereign state, organized with all and for the sake of all as a unitary and democratic republic for the enjoyment of political freedom, social justice, collective and individual well-being and human solidarity. Sovereignty rests with the people, from whom originates the power of the State. The Communist Party of Cuba is the leading force of society and the State. The State recognizes, respects and guarantees freedom of religion. Religious institutions are separate from the State. The socialist State carries out the will of the working people and guarantees work, medical care, education, food, clothing and housing. The Republic of Cuba bases its relations with other socialist countries on socialist internationalism, friendship, co-operation and mutual assistance. It reaffirms its willingness to integrate with and co-operate with the countries of Latin America and the Caribbean.

The State organizes and directs the economic life of the nation in accordance with a central social and economic development plan. The State directs and controls foreign trade. The State recognizes the right of small farmers to own their lands and other means of production and to sell that land. The State guarantees the right of citizens to ownership of personal property in the form of earnings, savings, place of residence and other possessions and objects that serve to satisfy their material and cultural needs. The State also guarantees the right of inheritance.

Cuban citizenship is acquired by birth or through naturalization. The State protects the family, motherhood and matrimony, and directs and encourages all aspects of education, culture and science. All citizens have equal rights and are subject to equal duties.

The State guarantees the right to medical care, education, freedom of speech and press, assembly, demonstration, association and privacy. In the socialist society work is the right and duty, and a source of pride for every citizen.

GOVERNMENT

National Assembly of People's Power

The National Assembly of People's Power (Asamblea Nacional del Poder Popular) is the supreme organ of the State and is the only organ with constituent and legislative authority. It is composed of deputies, over the age of 18, elected by free, direct and secret ballot, for a period of five years. All Cuban citizens aged 16 years or more, except those who are mentally incapacitated or who have committed a crime, are eligible to vote. The National Assembly of People's Power holds two ordinary sessions a year and a special session when requested by one-third of the deputies or by the Council of State. More than one-half of the total number of deputies must be present for a session to be held.

All decisions made by the Assembly, except those relating to constitutional reforms, are adopted by a simple majority of votes. The deputies may be recalled by their electors at any time.

The National Assembly of People's Power has the following functions:

to reform the Constitution;

to approve, modify and annul laws;

to supervise all organs of the State and government;

to decide on the constitutionality of laws and decrees;

to revoke decree-laws issued by the Council of State and the Council of Ministers;

to discuss and approve economic and social development plans, and the state budget, monetary and credit systems;

to approve the general outlines of foreign and domestic policy, to ratify and annul international treaties, to declare war and approve peace treaties;

to approve the administrative division of the country;

to elect the President, First Vice-President, the Vice-Presidents and other members of the Council of State;

to elect the President, Vice-President and Secretary of the National Assembly;

to appoint the members of the Council of Ministers on the proposal of the President of the Council of State;

to elect the President, Vice-President and other judges of the People's Supreme Court;

to elect the Attorney-General and the Deputy Attorney-Generals;

to grant amnesty;

to call referendums.

The President of the National Assembly presides over sessions of the Assembly, calls ordinary sessions, proposes the draft agenda, signs the Official Gazette, organizes the work of the commissions appointed by the Assembly and attends the meetings of the Council of State.

Council of State

The Council of State is elected from the members of the National Assembly and represents that Assembly in the period between sessions. It comprises a President, one First Vice-President, five Vice-Presidents, one Secretary and 23 other members. Its mandate ends when a new Assembly meets. All decisions are adopted by a simple majority of votes. It is accountable for its actions to the National Assembly.

The Council of State has the following functions:

to call special sessions of the National Assembly;

to set the date for the election of a new Assembly;

to issue decree-laws in the period between the sessions of the National Assembly;

to decree mobilization in the event of war and to approve peace treaties when the Assembly is in recess;

to issue instructions to the courts and the Office of the Attorney-General of the Republic;

to appoint and remove ambassadors of Cuba abroad on the proposal of its President, to grant or refuse recognition to diplomatic representatives of other countries to Cuba;

to suspend those provisions of the Council of Ministers that are not in accordance with the Constitution;

to revoke the resolutions of the Executive Committee of the local organs of People's Power that are contrary to the Constitution or laws and decrees formulated by other higher organs.

For all purposes the Council of State is the highest representative of the Cuban state.

Head of State

The President of the Council of State is the Head of State and the Head of Government and has the following powers:

to represent the State and Government and conduct general policy;

to convene and preside over the sessions of the Council of State and the Council of Ministers;

to supervise the ministries and other administrative bodies;

to propose the members of the Council of Ministers to the National Assembly of People's Power;

to receive the credentials of the heads of foreign diplomatic missions;

to sign the decree-laws and other resolutions of the Council of State;

to exercise the Supreme Command of all armed institutions and determine their general organization;

to preside over the National Defence Council;

to declare a state of emergency in the cases outlined in the Constitution.

In the case of absence, illness or death of the President of the Council of State, the First Vice-President assumes the President's duties.

The Council of Ministers

The Council of Ministers is the highest-ranking executive and administrative organ. It is composed of the Head of State and Government, as its President, the First Vice-President, the Vice-Presidents, the Ministers, the Secretary and other members determined by law. Its Executive Committee is composed of the President, the First Vice-President, the Vice-Presidents and other members of the Council of Ministers determined by the President.

The Council of Ministers has the following powers:

to conduct political, economic, cultural, scientific, social and defence policy as outlined by the National Assembly;

to approve international treaties;

to propose projects for the general development plan and, if they are approved by the National Assembly, to supervise their implementation;

to conduct foreign policy and trade;

to draw up bills and submit them to the National Assembly;

to draw up the draft state budget;

to conduct general administration, implement laws, issue decrees and supervise defence and national security.

The Council of Ministers is accountable to the National Assembly of People's Power.

LOCAL GOVERNMENT

The country is divided into 14 provinces and 169 municipalities. The provinces are: Pinar del Río, Habana, Ciudad de la Habana, Matanzas, Villa Clara, Cienfuegos, Sancti Spíritus, Ciego de Avila, Camagüey, Las Tunas, Holguín, Granma, Santiago de Cuba and Guantánamo.

Voting for delegates to the municipal assemblies is direct, secret and voluntary. All citizens over 16 years of age are eligible to vote. The number of delegates to each assembly is proportionate to the number of people living in that area. A delegate must obtain more than one-half of the total number of votes cast in the constituency in order to be elected. The Municipal and Provincial Assemblies of People's Power are elected by free, direct and secret ballot. Nominations for Municipal and Provincial Executive Committees of People's Power are submitted to the relevant assembly by a commission presided over by a representative of the Communist Party's leading organ and consisting of representatives of youth, workers', farmers', revolutionary and women's organizations. The President and Secretary of each of the regional and the provincial assemblies are the only full-time members, the other delegates carrying out their functions in addition to their normal employment.

The regular and extraordinary sessions of the local Assemblies of People's Power are public. More than one-half of the total number of members must be present in order for agreements made to be valid. Agreements are adopted by simple majority.

JUDICIARY

Judicial power is exercised by the People's Supreme Court and all other competent tribunals and courts. The People's Supreme Court is the supreme judicial authority and is accountable only to the National Assembly of People's Power. It can propose laws and issue regulations through its Council of Government. Judges are independent, but the courts must inform the electorate of their activities at least once a year. Every accused person has the right to a defence and can be tried only by a tribunal.

The Office of the Attorney-General is subordinate only to the National Assembly and the Council of State, and is responsible for ensuring that the law is properly obeyed.

The Constitution may be totally or partially modified only by a two-thirds' majority vote in the National Assembly of People's Power. If the modification is total, or if it concerns the composition and powers of the National Assembly of People's Power or the Council of State, or the rights and duties contained in the Constitution, it also requires a positive vote by referendum.

The Government

Head of State: Gen. Raúl Castro Ruz (took office 24 February 2008).

COUNCIL OF STATE

President: Gen. Raúl Castro Ruz.

First Vice-President: José Ramón Machado Ventura.

Vice-Presidents: Juan Esteban Lazo Hernández, Lt-Gen. Abelardo Colomé Ibarra, Lt-Gen. Julio Casas Regueiro, Ramiro Valdes Menéndez, Gladys Bejerano Portela.

Secretary: Homero Acosta Alvarez.

Members: José Ramón Balaguer Cabrera, Roberto Fernández Retamar, Lt-Gen. Leopoldo Cintra Frías, Orlando Lugo Fonte, Tania León Silveira, Lt-Gen. Álvaro López Miera, Inés María Chapman Waugh, Iris Betancourt Téllez, Guillermo García Frías, Luis Saturnino Herrera Martínez, María Yolanda Ferrer Gómez, Regla Dayamí Armenteros Mesa, Dignora Montano Perdomo, Salvador Antonio Valdés Mesa, María del Carmen Concepción González, Juan José Rabilero Fonseca, Surina Acosta Brook, Liudmila Alamo Dueñas, Isis Angelina Diez Duardo, Kirenia Díaz Burke, Marino Alberto Murillo Jorge, Sergio Juan Rodrígiez Morales.

COUNCIL OF MINISTERS
(July 2010)

The Government is formed by the Partido Comunista de Cuba.

President: Gen. Raúl Castro Ruz.

Secretary: Brig.-Gen. José Amado Ricardo Guerra.

First Vice-President: José Ramón Machado Ventura.

Vice-Presidents: José Ramón Fernández Alvarez, Ricardo Cabrisas Ruiz, Ramiro Valdés Menéndez, Gen. Ulises Rosales del Toro, Marino Alberto Murillo Jorge, Gen. Antonio Enrique Lussón Batlle.

Minister of Agriculture: Gen. Ulises Rosales del Toro.

Minister of Auditing and Control: Gladys María Bejerano Portela.

Minister of Basic Industry: Yadira García Vera.

Minister of Construction: Fidel Fernando Figueroa de la Paz.

Minister of Culture: Abel Enrique Prieto Jiménez.

Minister of Domestic Trade: Jacinto Angulo Pardo.

Minister of Economy and Planning: Marino Alberto Murillo Jorge.

Minister of Education: Ena Elsa Velázquez Cobiella.

Minister of Finance and Prices: Lina Pedraza Rodríguez.

Minister of the Food Industry: María del Carmen Concepción González.

Minister of Foreign Relations: Bruno Rodríguez Parrilla.

Minister of Foreign Trade and Investment: Rodrigo Malmierca Díaz.

Minister of Higher Education: Miguel Díaz-Canel Bermúdez.

Minister of Information Technology and Communications: Ramiro Valdés Menéndez.

Minister of the Interior: Lt-Gen. Abelardo Colomé Ibarra.

Minister of the Iron, Steel and Engineering Industries: Brig.-Gen. Salvador Pardo Cruz.

Minister of Justice: María Esther Reus González.

Minister of Labour and Social Security: Margarita Marlene González Fernández.

Minister of Light Industry: Damar Maceo Cruz.

Minister of Public Health: Roberto Morales Ojeda.

Minister of the Revolutionary Armed Forces: Lt-Gen. Julio Casas Regueiro.

Minister of Science, Technology and the Environment: Dr José M. Miyar Barruecos.

Minister of Sugar: Orlando Celso García Ramírez.

Minister of Tourism: Manuel Marrero Cruz.

Minister of Transportation: César Ignacio Arocha Masid.

Minister, President of the Banco Central de Cuba: Ernesto Medina Villaveirán.

MINISTRIES

Ministry of Agriculture: Edif. MINAG, Avda Conill, esq. Carlos M. Céspedes, Nuevo Vedado, Plaza de la Revolución, 10600 Havana; tel. (7) 884-5370; fax (7) 881-2837; e-mail armando@minag.cu; internet www.minag.cu.

Ministry of Auditing and Control: Monserrate No 213, esq. Empedrado y Tejadillo, Habana Vieja, Havana; tel. (7) 868-2100; e-mail linacarm@minauditoria.cu; internet www.minauditoria.cu.

Ministry of Basic Industry: Avda Salvador Allende 666, entre Oquendo y Soledad, Havana; tel. (7) 878-7840; fax (7) 873-5345; e-mail ministerio.basica@oc.minbas.cu; internet www.minbas.cu.

Ministry of Construction: Avda Carlos Manuel de Céspedes, Calle 35, Plaza de la Revolución, 10600 Havana; tel. (7) 881-4745; fax (7) 855-5303; e-mail sitio@micons.cu; internet www.micons.cu.

Ministry of Culture: Calle 2, No 258, entre 11 y 13, Plaza de la Revolución, Vedado, CP 10400, Havana; tel. (7) 838-2223; e-mail atencion@min.cult.cu; internet www.min.cult.cu.

Ministry of Domestic Trade: Calle Habana 258, entre Empedrado y San Juan de Dios, Havana; tel. (7) 867-0133; fax (7) 867-0094; e-mail estadistica@cinet.cu.

Ministry of Economy and Planning: 20 de Mayo, entre Territorial y Ayestarán, Plaza de la Revolución, Havana; tel. (7) 881-9354; fax (7) 855-5371; e-mail mep@ceniai.inf.cu.

Ministry of Education: Calle 17, esq. O, Vedado, Havana; tel. (7) 838-2930; fax (7) 838-3105; e-mail despacho@mined.rimed.cu; internet www.rimed.cu.

Ministry of Finance and Prices: Calle Obispo 211, esq. Cuba, Habana Vieja, Havana; tel. (7) 867-1800; fax (7) 833-8050; e-mail bhcifip@mfp.gov.cu; internet www.mfp.cu.

Ministry of the Food Industry: Avda 41, No 4455, entre 48 y 50, Playa, Havana; tel. (7) 203-6801; fax (7) 204-0517; e-mail minal@minal.get.cma.net; internet www.minal.cubaindustria.cu.

Ministry of Foreign Relations: Calzada 360, esq. G, Vedado, Plaza de la Revolución, Havana; tel. (7) 836-4500; e-mail cubaminrex@minrex.gov.cu; internet www.cubaminrex.cu.

Ministry of Foreign Trade and Investment: Infanta y 23, Plaza de la Revolución, Miramar, Havana; tel. (7) 838-0436; fax (7) 204-3496; e-mail secretariataller@mincex.cu; internet www.mincex.cu.

Ministry of Higher Education: Calle 23, No 565, esq. F, Vedado, Plaza de la Revolución, Havana; tel. (7) 830-3674; e-mail sitio_mes@reduniv.edu.cu; internet www.mes.edu.cu.

Ministry of Information Technology and Communications: Avda Independencia No 2, entre 19 de Mayo y Aranguren, Plaza de la Revolución, Havana; tel. (7) 882-8000; fax (7) 885-4048; e-mail dircom@mic.cu; internet www.mic.gov.cu.

Ministry of the Interior: Sitio Minint, Plaza de la Revolución, Havana; tel. (7) 30-1566; fax (7) 855-6621; e-mail correominint@mn.mn.co.cu.

Ministry of the Iron, Steel and Engineering Industries: Avda Independencia y Calle 100, Havana; tel. (7) 265-3606; fax (7) 267-0501; e-mail yoli@sime.co.cu.

Ministry of Justice: Calle O, No 216, entre 23 y 25, Plaza de la Revolución, Apdo 10400, Havana 4; tel. (7) 838-3450; e-mail apoblacion@oc.minjus.cu; internet www.minjus.cu.

Ministry of Labour and Social Security: Calle 23, esq. Calles O y P, Vedado, Municipio Plaza de la Revolución, Havana; tel. (7) 838-0022; e-mail webmaster@mtss.cu; internet www.mtss.cu.

Ministry of Light Industry: Empedrado 302, esq. Aguiar, Havana; tel. (7) 867-0524; fax (7) 202-6187; e-mail comunicacion@minil.cu.

Ministry of Public Health: Calle 23, No 201, entre M y N, Vedado, Plaza de la Revolución, Havana; tel. (7) 835-2767; fax (7) 833-2195; e-mail apoblacion@infomed.sld.cu; internet www.sld.cu.

Ministry of the Revolutionary Armed Forces: Plaza de la Revolución, Havana; internet www.cubagob.cu/otras_info/minfar/far/minfar.htm.

Ministry of Science, Technology and the Environment: Industria y San José, Habana Vieja, Havana; tel. (7) 860-3411; fax (7) 866-8654; e-mail comunicacion@citma.cu.

Ministry of Sugar: Of. de Comunicación Institucional, Calle 23, No 171, entre N y O, Vedado, Havana; tel. (7) 832-9356; e-mail liobel@ocentral.minaz.cu.

Ministry of Tourism: Calle 3, No 6, entre F y G, Vedado, Plaza de la Revolución, Havana; tel. (7) 836-3245; fax (7) 836-4086; e-mail dircomunicacion@mintur.tur.cu; internet www.cubatravel.cu.

Ministry of Transportation: Avda Carlos Manuel de Céspedes, s/n, entre Tulipán y Lombillo, Plaza de la Revolución, 10600 Havana; tel. (7) 855-5030; fax (7) 884-1105; e-mail mitrans@mitrans.transnet.cu; internet www.transporte.cu.

Legislature

ASAMBLEA NACIONAL DEL PODER POPULAR

The National Assembly of People's Power was constituted on 2 December 1976. In July 1992 the National Assembly adopted a constitutional amendment providing for legislative elections by direct vote. Only candidates nominated by the Partido Comunista de Cuba (PCC) were permitted to contest the elections. At elections to the National Assembly conducted on 20 January 2008, all 614 candidates succeeded in obtaining the requisite 50% of valid votes cast. Of the 8.2m. registered voters, 96.89% participated in the elections. Only 4.76% of votes cast were blank or spoiled.

President: Ricardo Alarcón de Quesada.

Vice-President: Jaime Alberto Crombet Hernández-Baquero.

Secretary: Miriam Brito Sarroca.

Political Organizations

Partido Comunista de Cuba (PCC) (Communist Party of Cuba): Havana; e-mail root@epol.cipcc.inf.cu; internet www.pcc.cu; f. 1961 as the Organizaciones Revolucionarias Integradas (ORI) from a fusion of the Partido Socialista Popular (Communist), Fidel Castro's Movimiento 26 de Julio and the Directorio Revolucionario 13 de Marzo; became the Partido Unido de la Revolución Socialista Cubana (PURSC) in 1962; adopted current name in 1965; youth wing, the Unión de Jóvenes Comunistas (Young Communist League, First Sec. Liudmila Alamo Dueñas), comprises c. 500,000 mems; 150-member Central Committee, Political Bureau, 12-member Secretariat and five Commissions; 706,132 mems (1994).

Political Bureau

Dr Fidel Castro Ruz (First Sec.), Gen. Raúl Castro Ruz (Second Sec.), José Ramón Machado Ventura, Juan Esteban Lazo Hernández, Lt-Gen. Abelardo Colomé Ibarra, Pedro Ross Leal, Maj.-Gen. Ulises Rosales del Toro, Concepción Campa Huergo, Yadira García Vera, Abel Enrique Prieto Jiménez, Lt-Gen. Julio Casas Regueiro, Lt-Gen. Leopoldo Cintra Frías, Ricardo Alarcón de Quesada, José Ramón Balaguer Cabrera, Misael Enamorado Dáger, Lt-Gen. Ramón Espinosa Martín, Pedro Sáez Montejo, Jorge Luis Sierra Cruz, Miguel Mario Díaz Canel Bermúdez, Ramiro Valdés Menéndez, Salvador Valdés Mesa, Lt-Gen. Álvaro López Miera.

There are a number of dissident groups operating in Cuba. Among the most prominent of these are the following:

Arco Progresista: tel. 763-0912; e-mail arcoprogresista.gl@gmail.com; internet partidoarcoprogresista.org; f. 2003 as an alliance of three social-democratic groups in and outside Cuba: Corriente Socialista Democrática, Partido del Pueblo and Coordinadora Socialdemócrata en el Exilio; merged into a single party in 2008; Spokesperson Manuel Cuesta Morúa.

Asamblea para Promover la Sociedad Civil en Cuba: e-mail asambleacivil@bellsouth.net; internet www.asambleasociedadcivilcuba.info; f. 2002; alliance of 365 civil society asscns; Leader Martha Beatriz Roque Cabello.

Movimiento Cristiano Liberación (MCL): e-mail info@oswaldopaya.org; internet www.oswaldopaya.org; f. 1988; campaigns for peaceful democratic change and respect for human rights; associated with the Varela Project, established 1998 to petition the Govt for democratic freedoms; Leader Oswaldo Payá Sardiñas.

Partido Demócrata Cristiano de Cuba (PDC): 1236 SW 22 Ave, Miami, FL 33135, USA; tel. (305) 644-3395; fax (305) 644-3311; e-mail miyares@pdc-cuba.org; internet www.pdc-cuba.org; f. 1959 as Movimiento Demócrata Cristiano; adopted current name in 1991; Pres. Marcelino Miyares Sotolongo; Vice-Pres José Vázquez, René Hernández, Yaxys Cires.

Partido Liberal de Cuba: 20 de Mayo 531, Apto B-14, entre Marta Abreu y Línea del Ferrocarril, Cerro, 10600 Havana; tel. and fax (7) 878-4010; f. 1991 as Partido Liberal Democrático de Cuba; mem. of Liberal International; Pres. Héctor Maseda Gutiérrez (imprisoned in 2003), Reinaldo Hernández Cardona (acting).

Partido Liberal Nacional Cubano (PLNC): f. 2004 as Movimiento Liberal Cubano; adopted present name in 2009; part of Unidad Liberal de la República de Cuba; Pres. Fernando E. Palacio Mogar; Exec. Nat. Sec. Ronaldo Mendoza Mendez.

Partido Pro-Derechos Humanos de Cuba (PPDHC): f. 1988 to defend human rights in Cuba; Pres. Julián Enrique Martínez Báez (arrested in Dec. 2009); Nat. Sec. Ricardo Rubén Barreto Fuentes.

Partido Social Revolucionario Democrático de Cuba: 5900 Starlite Lane, Milton, FL 32570, USA; tel. and fax (305) 541-2334; e-mail psrdc@psrdc.org; internet www.psrdc.org; f. 1992; executive committee of 15 members; Pres. Jorge Valls; Exec. Sec. Roberto Simeon.

Partido Socialdemócrata de Cuba (PSC): Calle 36, No 105, Nuevo Vedado, 10600 Havana; tel. (7) 881-8203; e-mail vroca@pscuba.org; internet pscuba.org; f. 1996; Pres. Vladimiro Roca Antúnez; Exec. Sec. Carlos J. Menéndez Cervera; Sec.-Gen. Antonio Santiago Ruiz.

Partido Solidaridad Democrática (PSD): Calle Trocadero 414 bajos, entre Galiano y San Nicolás, Municipio Pio-Centro, 10200 Havana; tel. (7) 866-8306; e-mail gladyperez@aol.com; mem. of Liberal International; Pres. Fernando Sánchez López.

Unión Liberal Cubana: Paseo de la Retama 97, 29600 Marbella, Spain; tel. (91) 4340201; fax (91) 5011342; e-mail cubaliberal@mercuryin.es; internet www.cubaliberal.org; mem. of Liberal International; Founder and Chair. Carlos Alberto Montaner.

Diplomatic Representation

EMBASSIES IN CUBA

Algeria: Avda 5, No 2802, esq. 28, Miramar, Havana; tel. (7) 204-2835; fax (7) 204-2702; e-mail embhav@argelia.sytes.net; Ambassador ABDELLAH LAOUARI.

Angola: Avda 5, No 1012, entre 10 y 12, Miramar, Havana; tel. (7) 204-2474; fax (7) 204-0487; e-mail embangol@ceniai.inf.cu; Ambassador ANTONIO JOSÉ CONDESSE DE CARVAHLO.

Argentina: Calle 36, No 511, entre 5 y 7, Miramar, Havana; tel. (7) 204-2565; fax (7) 204-2140; e-mail embajador@ecuba.co.cu; Ambassador JULIANA ISABEL MARINO.

Austria: Avda 5A, No 6617, esq. 70, Miramar, Havana; tel. (7) 204-2825; fax (7) 204-1235; e-mail havanna-ob@bmeia.gv.at; Ambassador JOHANNES SKRIWAN.

Bahamas: Avda 5, No 3006, entre 30 y 32, Miramar, Playa, Havana; tel. (7) 206-9918; fax (7) 206-9921; e-mail embahamas@enet.cu; Ambassador VERNON E. L. BURROWS.

Belarus: Avda 5, No 6405, entre 64 y 66, Miramar, Havana; tel. (7) 204-7330; fax (7) 204-7332; e-mail cuba@belembassy.org; internet www.cuba.belembassy.org/es; Ambassador VLADIMIR A. ASTAPENKA.

Belgium: Calle 8, No 309, entre 3 y 5, Miramar, Havana; tel. (7) 204-4806; fax (7) 204-6516; e-mail havana@diplobel.fed.be; internet www.diplomatie.be/havana; Ambassador KONRAAD ADAM.

Belize: Edif. Barcelona, Of. 302, Centro de Negocios Miramar, Havana; tel. (7) 204-3504; fax (7) 204-3506; e-mail belizecuba@yahoo.es; Ambassador SAID BADHI GUERRA.

Benin: Calle 20, No 119, entre 1 y 3, Miramar, Havana; tel. (7) 204-2179; fax (7) 204-2334; e-mail ambencub@ceniai.inf.cu; Ambassador GRÉGOIRE LAITIAN HOUDÉ.

Bolivia: Calle 3A, entre 36A y 38, Miramar, Havana; tel. (7) 204-2426; fax (7) 204-2739; e-mail emboliviahaba@enet.cu; Chargé d'affaires a.i. RICHARD RIOJA.

Brazil: Lonja del Comercio, Calle Lamparilla, No 2, 4° K, Habana Vieja, 10100 Havana; tel. (7) 866-9052; fax (7) 866-2912; e-mail embhavana@brasilhavana.org; Ambassador BERNARDO PERICÁS.

Bulgaria: Calle B, No 252, entre 11 y 13, Vedado, Havana; tel. (7) 833-3125; fax (7) 833-3297; e-mail embulhav@ceniai.inf.cu; internet www.mfa.bg/havana; Ambassador TCHAVDAR MLADÉNOV NIKÓLOV.

Burkina Faso: Calle 40, No 516, entre 5A y 7ma, Miramar, Havana; tel. (7) 204-2895; fax (7) 204-1942; e-mail ambfaso@ceniai.inf.cu; Ambassador DANIEL OUÉDRAOGO.

Cambodia: Avda 5, No 7001, entre 70 y 72, Miramar, Havana; tel. (7) 204-1496; fax (7) 204-6400; e-mail cambohav@enet.cu; Ambassador PRES MANOLA.

Canada: Calle 30, No 518, esq. 7, Miramar, Havana; tel. (7) 204-2516; fax (7) 204-2044; e-mail havan@international.gc.ca; internet www.canadainternational.gc.ca/cuba; Ambassador JEAN-PIERRE JUNEAU.

Cape Verde: Calle 20, No 2001, esq. 7, Miramar, Havana; tel. (7) 204-2979; fax (7) 204-1072; e-mail embajadora@caboverde.co.cu; Ambassador CRISPINA ALMEIDA GOMES.

Chile: Avda 33, No 1423, entre 14 y 18, Miramar, Havana; tel. (7) 204-1222; fax (7) 204-1694; e-mail embachilecu@echile.cu; internet www.conchile-lahabana.cu; Ambassador ROLANDO DRAGO RODRÍGUEZ.

China, People's Republic: Calle C, entre 13 y 15, Vedado, Havana; tel. (7) 833-3005; fax (7) 833-3092; e-mail chinaemb_cu@mfa.gov.cn; Ambassador LIU YUQIN.

Colombia: Calle 14, No 515, entre 5 y 7, Miramar, Havana; tel. (7) 204-1248; fax (7) 204-0464; e-mail elhabana@cancilleria.gov.co; Ambassador JULIO LONDOÑO PAREDES.

Congo, Republic: Avda 5, No 1003, Miramar, Havana; tel. and fax (7) 204-9055; Ambassador PASCAL ONGEMBY.

Czech Republic: Avda Kohly, No 259, entre 41 y 43, Nuevo Vedado, CP 10600, Havana; tel. (7) 883-3201; fax (7) 883-3596; e-mail havana@embassy.mzv.cz; internet www.mzv.cz/havana; Chargé d'affaires a.i. VÍT KORSELT.

Dominica: Calle 36, No 507, entre 5 y 7, Miramar, Havana; Ambassador CLARKSON J. THOMAS.

Dominican Republic: Avda 5, No 9202, entre 92 y 94, Miramar, Havana; tel. (7) 204-8429; fax (7) 204-8431; e-mail edc@enet.cu; Ambassador JOSÉ MANUEL CASTILLO BETANCES.

Ecuador: Avda 5A, No 4407, entre 44 y 46, Miramar, Havana; tel. (7) 204-2034; fax (7) 204-2868; e-mail embecuador@yahoo.com; Ambassador EDGAR PONCE ITURRIAGA.

Egypt: Avda 5, No 1801, esq. 18, Miramar, Havana; tel. (7) 204-2441; fax (7) 204-0905; e-mail emegipto@enet.cu; Ambassador TAREK MOHEY ELDIN ELWASSIMY.

Equatorial Guinea: Calle 20, No 713, entre 7 y 9, Miramar, Havana; tel. (7) 204-1720; fax (7) 204-1724; Ambassador TERESA EFUA ASANGONO.

Ethiopia: Avda 5, No 6604, Apto 3, entre 66 y 68, Miramar, Havana; tel. (7) 206-9905; fax (7) 206-9907; e-mail info@embaethi.co.cu; Ambassador Dr BERHANU DIBABA KUMMA.

France: Calle 14, No 312, entre 3 y 5, Miramar, Havana; tel. (7) 201-3131; fax (7) 201-3107; e-mail internet.la-havane-amba@diplomatie.fr; internet www.ambafrance-cu.org; Ambassador FRÉDÉRIC DORÉ.

The Gambia: Calle 24, No 307, entre 3 y 5, Miramar, Havana; tel. and fax (7) 204-9242; e-mail mofacuba@ceniai.inf.cu; Ambassador PIERRE BIRAM TAMBA.

Germany: Calle 13, No 652, esq. B, Vedado, Havana; tel. (7) 833-2569; fax (7) 833-1586; e-mail info@havanna.diplo.de; internet www.havanna.diplo.de; Ambassador CLAUDE ROBERT ELLNER.

Ghana: Avda 5, No 1808, esq. 20, Miramar, Havana; tel. (7) 204-2153; fax (7) 204-2317; e-mail chancery@ghanaembassy.cu; internet www.ghanaembassy.cu; Ambassador DAVID SARPONG BOTENG.

Greece: Avda 5, No 7802, esq. 78, Miramar, Havana; tel. (7) 204-2995; fax (7) 204-9770; e-mail gremb@enet.cu; Ambassador PANTELIS CARCABASSIS.

Grenada: Avda 5, No 2006, entre 20 y 22, Miramar, Havana; tel. (7) 204-6764; fax (7) 204-6765; e-mail embgranada@enet.cu; Ambassador RAPHAEL JOSEPH.

Guatemala: Calle 20, No 301, entre 3 y 5, Miramar, Havana; tel. (7) 204-3417; fax (7) 204-8173; e-mail embagucu@ceniai.inf.cu; Ambassador HERBERT ESTUARDO MENECES CORONADO.

Guinea: Calle 20, No 504, entre 5 y 7, Miramar, Havana; tel. (7) 292-9212; fax (7) 204-1894; Ambassador HADIATOU SOW.

Guinea-Bissau: Avda 5, No 8203, entre 82 y 84, Miramar, Havana; tel. (7) 204-5742; fax (7) 204-2794; e-mail embaguib@enet.cu; Ambassador ABEL COELHO MENDONÇA.

Guyana: Calle 18, No 506, entre 5 y 7, Miramar, Havana; tel. (7) 204-2094; fax (7) 204-2867; e-mail embguyana@enet.cu; Ambassador Dr MITRADEVI ALI.

Haiti: Avda 7, No 4402, esq. 44, Miramar, Havana; tel. (7) 204-5421; fax (7) 204-5423; e-mail embhaiti@enet.cu; internet www.embhaiti.cu; Ambassador JEAN VICTOR GENEUS.

Holy See: Calle 12, No 514, entre 5 y 7, Miramar, Havana (Apostolic Nunciature); tel. (7) 204-2700; fax (7) 204-2257; e-mail csa@pcn.net; Apostolic Nuncio Most Rev. GIOVANNI ANGELO BECCIU (Titular Archbishop of Atella).

Honduras: Edif. Santa Clara, 1°, Of. 121 Centro de Negocios Miramar, Calle 3a No 123, entre 78 y 80 Calles, Miramar, Havana; tel. (7) 204-5496; fax (7) 204-5497; e-mail embhocu@enet.cu; Ambassador JUAN RAMÓN ELVIR SALGADO.

Hungary: Calle G, No 458, entre 19 y 21, Vedado, Havana; tel. (7) 833-3365; fax (7) 833-3286; e-mail mission.hav@kum.hu; internet www.mfa.gov.hu/kulkepviselet/cu/hu; Ambassador MIKLÓS DEÁK.

India: Calle 21, No 202, esq. K, Vedado, Havana; tel. (7) 833-3777; fax (7) 833-3287; e-mail hoc@indembassyhavana.cu; internet www.indembassyhavana.cu; Ambassador MITRA VASISHT.

Indonesia: Avda 5, No 1607, esq. 18, Miramar, Havana; tel. (7) 204-9618; fax (7) 204-9617; e-mail indonhav@ceniai.inf.cu; internet www.indohav.cu; Ambassador BANUA RADJA MANIK.

Iran: Avda 5, No 3002, esq. 30, Miramar, Havana; tel. (7) 204-2675; fax (7) 204-2770; e-mail embairan@enet.cu; Ambassador MOSTAFA ALAEI.

Italy: Avda 5, No 402, esq. 4, Miramar, Havana; tel. (7) 204-5615; fax (7) 204-5659; e-mail ambasciata.avana@esteri.it; internet www.amblavana.esteri.it; Ambassador MARCO BACCIN.

Jamaica: Calle 22, No 503, entre 5 y 7, Miramar, Havana; tel. (7) 204-2908; fax (7) 204-2531; e-mail embjmcub@enet.cu; Ambassador A'DALE GEORGE ROBINSON.

Japan: Centro de Negocios Miramar, Avda 3, Edif. 1, 5°, esq. 80, Miramar, Havana; tel. (7) 204-3355; fax (7) 204-8902; e-mail taisi@ceniai.inf.cu; internet www.cu.emb-japan.go.jp; Ambassador MASUO NISHIBAYASHI.

Korea, Democratic People's Republic: Calle 17 y Paseo, No 752, Vedado, Havana; tel. (7) 833-2313; fax (7) 833-3073; e-mail dprkorcuba@enet.cu; Ambassador KWON SUNG CHOL.

Laos: Avda 5, No 2808, esq. 30, Miramar, Havana; tel. (7) 204-1057; fax (7) 204-9622; e-mail embalao@enet.cu; Ambassador KHAMPO KYAKHAMPHITOUNE.

Lebanon: Calle 17A, No 16403, entre 164 y 174, Siboney, Havana; tel. (7) 208-6220; fax (7) 208-6432; e-mail lbcunet@ceniai.inf.cu; Ambassador JEAN MACARON.

Libya: Avda 7, No 1402, esq. 14, Miramar, Havana; tel. (7) 204-2192; fax (7) 204-2991; e-mail oficinalibia@ip.etecsa.cu; Ambassador SAAD DAHER ZAMUNA.

Malaysia: Avda 5, No 6612, entre 66 y 68, Miramar, Havana; tel. (7) 204-8883; fax (7) 204-6888; e-mail malhavana@kln.gov.my; internet www.kln.gov.my/perwakilan/havana; Ambassador YEAN YOKE HENG.

Mali: Calle 36A, No 704, entre 7 y 42, Miramar, Havana; tel. (7) 204-5321; fax (7) 204-5320; e-mail ambamali@ceniai.inf.cu; Ambassador FIDÈLE DIARRA.

Mexico: Calle 12, No 518, esq. Avda 7, Miramar, Playa, Havana; tel. (7) 204-2553; fax (7) 204-2717; e-mail embamex@embamexcuba.org; internet www.sre.gob.mx/cuba; Ambassador ENRIQUE GABRIEL JIMÉNEZ REMUS.

Mongolia: Calle 66, No 505, esq. 5A, Miramar, Havana; tel. (7) 204-2763; fax (7) 204-0639; e-mail embahavana@ceniai.inf.cu; Ambassador YADAMYN DELGERJAV.

Mozambique: Avda 7, No 2203, entre 22 y 24, Miramar, Havana; tel. (7) 204-2443; fax (7) 204-2232; e-mail embamoc@ceniai.inf.cu; Ambassador AMADEU PAULO SAMUEL DA CONCEICAO.

Namibia: Calle 36, No 504, entre 5 y 5A, Miramar, Havana; tel. (7) 204-1430; fax (7) 204-1431; e-mail embnamibia@embnam.co.cu; Ambassador CLAUDIA GRACE UUSHONA.

Netherlands: Calle 8, No 307, entre 3 y 5, Miramar, Havana; tel. (7) 204-2511; fax (7) 204-2059; e-mail hav@minbuza.nl; internet cuba.nlambassade.org; Ambassador RONALD MUYZERT.

Nicaragua: Calle 20, No 709, entre 7 y 9, Miramar, Havana; tel. (7) 204-1025; fax (7) 204-5387; e-mail nicaragua@embnicc.co.cu; Ambassador LUIS CABRERA GONZÁLEZ.

Nigeria: Avda 5, No 1401, entre 14 y 16, Miramar, Havana; tel. (7) 204-2898; fax (7) 204-2202; e-mail chancery@nigeria-havana.com; Ambassador SEGUN BAMIGBETAN BAJU.

Norway: Calle 30, No 315, entre 3 y 5, Miramar, Havana; tel. (7) 204-0696; fax (7) 204-0699; e-mail emb.havana@mfa.no; internet www.noruega-cuba.org; Ambassador JAN TORE HOLVIK.

Panama: Calle 26, No 109, entre 1 y 3, Miramar, Havana; tel. (7) 204-0858; fax (7) 204-1674; e-mail panaemba_cuba@panaemba.co.cu; Ambassador LUIS CARLOS CLEGHORN.

Paraguay: Calle 34, No 503, entre 5 y 7, Miramar, Havana; tel. (7) 204-0884; fax (7) 204-0883; e-mail cgphav@enet.cu; Ambassador LUIS DOMINGO LAINO GUANES.

Peru: Calle 30, No 107, entre 1 y 3, Miramar, Havana; tel. (7) 204-2632; fax (7) 204-2636; e-mail embaperu@embaperu.org; Ambassador GILMAR NÉSTOR CALDERÓN CUENCA.

Philippines: Avda 5, No 2207, esq. 24, Miramar, Havana; tel. (7) 204-1372; fax (7) 204-2915; e-mail philhavpe@enet.cu; Ambassador Dr MACARTHUR F. CORSINO.

Poland: Calle G, No 452, esq. 19, Vedado, Havana; tel. (7) 833-2439; fax (7) 833-2442; e-mail hawana.amb.sekretariat@msz.gov.pl; Ambassador MARZENNA ADAMCZYK.

Portugal: Avda 7, No 2207, esq. 24, Miramar, Havana; tel. (7) 204-0149; fax (7) 204-2593; e-mail embpthav@embporthavana.org; Ambassador LUIS JOSÉ MOREIRA DA SILVA BARREIROS.

Qatar: Avda 3, No 3407, entre 34 y 36, Miramar, Havana; tel. (7) 204-0587; fax (7) 204-0003; e-mail embajada@qatar.co.cu; Ambassador ALI BIN SAAD AL-KHARJI.

Romania: Calle 21, No 307, entre H y I, Vedado, Havana; tel. (7) 833-3325; fax (7) 833-3324; e-mail erumania@ceniai.inf.cu; Chargé d'affaires a.i. VASILE MACOVEI.

Russia: Avda 5, No 6402, entre 62 y 66, Miramar, Havana; tel. (7) 204-2686; fax (7) 204-1038; e-mail embrusia@newmail.cu; internet www.cuba.mid.ru; Ambassador MIKHAIL L. KAMYNIN.

Saint Lucia: Centro de Negocios Miramar, Edif. Jerusalen, Calle 3, No 403, entre 78 y 80, Miramar, Havana; tel. (7) 206-9609; fax (7) 206-9610; Ambassador Dr JOVITA ST. MARTHE.

Saint Vincent and the Grenadines: Centro de Negocios Miramar, Edif. Jerusalén, Of. 403, Avda 3 y Calle 80, Miramar, Havana; tel. (7) 206-9783; fax (7) 206-9782; e-mail embsvg@mtc.co.cu; Ambassador DEXTER E. M. ROSE.

Serbia: Avda 5, No 4406, entre 44 y 46, Miramar, Havana; tel. (7) 204-2488; fax (7) 204-2982; e-mail ambsrbhav@embajadaserbia.co.cu; Ambassador MILENA LUKOVIC-JOVANOVIC.

Slovakia: Calle 66, No 521, entre 5B y 7, Miramar, Havana; tel. (7) 204-1884; fax (7) 204-1883; e-mail embeslovaca@mzv.sk; Ambassador ZDENEK ROZHOLD.

South Africa: Avda 5, No 4201, esq. 42, Miramar, Havana; tel. (7) 204-9671; fax (7) 204-1101; e-mail mision@sudafrica.cu; Ambassador PHATSE JUSTICE PIITSO.

Spain: Cárcel No 51, esq. Zulueta, Havana; tel. (7) 866-8025; fax (7) 866-8006; e-mail emb.lahabana@mae.es; internet www.maec.es/embajadas/lahabana; Ambassador MANUEL CACHO QUESADA.

Sri Lanka: Calle 32, No 307, entre 3 y 5, Miramar, Havana; tel. (7) 204-2562; fax (7) 204-2183; e-mail sri.lanka@enet.cu; Ambassador TAMARA KUNANAYAKAM.

Suriname: Edif. Jerusalén, Of. 210, Centro de Negocios de Miramar, Calle 3, entre 78 y 80, Playa, Miramar Havana; tel. (7) 207-9559; fax (7) 207-9561; e-mail secembsur@mtc.co.cu; Ambassador IKE DESMOND ANTONIUS.

Sweden: Calle 34, No 510, entre 5 y 7, Miramar, Havana; tel. (7) 204-2831; fax (7) 204-1194; e-mail ambassaden.havanna@foreign.ministry.se; internet www.swedenabroad.com/havanna; Ambassador CAROLINE FLEETWOOD.

Switzerland: Avda 5, No 2005, entre 20 y 22, Miramar, Havana; tel. (7) 204-2611; fax (7) 204-1148; e-mail hav.vertretung@eda.admin.ch; internet www.eda.admin.ch/havana; Ambassador PETER BURKHARD.

Syria: Calle 20, No 514, entre 5 y 7, Miramar, Havana; tel. (7) 204-2266; fax (7) 204-9754; e-mail embsiria@ceniai.inf.cu; Ambassador MUHAMMAD CHAKER KHAYAT.

Timor-Leste: Calle 40A, No 301, esq. 3, Miramar, Havana; tel. (7) 206-9911; e-mail embtimor@enet.cu; Ambassador EGIDIO DE JESÚS.

Trinidad and Tobago: Avda 5, No 6603, entre 66 y 68, Miramar, Havana; tel. (7) 207-9603; fax (7) 207-9604; e-mail ttmissionscuba@enet.cu; Ambassador LESTER EFEBO WILKINSON.

Turkey: Avda 5, No 3805, entre 36 y 40, Miramar, Havana; tel. (7) 204-1204; fax (7) 204-2899; e-mail turkemb@gmail.com; Ambassador INCY TUMAY.

Ukraine: Avda 5, No 4405, entre 44 y 46, Miramar, Havana; tel. (7) 204-2586; fax (7) 204-2341; e-mail emb_cu@mfa.gov.ua; internet www.mfa.gov.ua/cuba; Ambassador TETIANA G. SAIENKO.

United Kingdom: Calle 34, No 702/4, esq. 7 y 17, Miramar, Havana; tel. (7) 214-2200; fax (7) 214-2218; e-mail embrit@ceniai.inf.cu; internet ukincuba.fco.gov.uk; Ambassador DIANNA MELROSE.

USA (Relations severed in 1961): Interests Section in the Embassy of Switzerland: Calzada, entre L y M, Vedado, Havana; tel. (7) 833-3551; fax (7) 833-1084; e-mail irchavana@state.org; internet havana.usinterestsection.gov; Principal Officer JONATHAN D. FARRAR.

Uruguay: Calle 36, No 716, entre 7 y 17, Miramar, Havana; tel. (7) 204-2311; fax (7) 206-9683; e-mail urucub@rou.co.cu; Ambassador ARIEL BERGAMINO.

Venezuela: Edif. Beijing, 2°, Centro de Negocios Miramar, Avda 3, entre 74 y 76, Miramar, Havana; tel. (7) 204-2612; fax (7) 204-9790; e-mail embajada@venezuela.co.cu; internet www.venezuelaencuba.co.cu; Ambassador RONALDO BLANCO LA CRUZ.

Viet Nam: Avda 5, No 1802, esq. 18, Miramar, Havana; tel. (7) 204-1525; fax (7) 204-5333; e-mail embavina@embavicu.org; internet www.vietnamembassy-cuba.org; Ambassador VU CHI CONG.

Yemen: Avda 5, No 8201, entre 82 y 84, Miramar, Havana; tel. (7) 204-1506; fax (7) 204-1131; e-mail gamdan-hav@enet.cu; Ambassador YAHYA AL-SYAGHI.

Zimbabwe: Avda 3, No 1001, entre 10 y 12, Miramar, Havana; tel. (7) 204-2857; fax (7) 204-2720; e-mail zimhavan@enet.cu; Ambassador JOHN SHUMBA MVUNDURA.

Judicial System

The judicial system comprises the People's Supreme Court, the People's Provincial Courts and the People's Municipal Courts. The People's Supreme Court exercises the highest judicial authority.

Public Prosecutor: JUAN ESCALONA REGUERA.

PEOPLE'S SUPREME COURT

The People's Supreme Court comprises the Plenum, the six Courts of Justice in joint session and the Council of Government. When the Courts of Justice are in joint session they comprise all the professional and lay judges, the Attorney-General and the Minister of Justice. The Council of Government comprises the President and Vice-Presidents of the People's Supreme Court, the Presidents of each Court of Justice and the Attorney-General of the Republic. The Minister of Justice may participate in its meetings.

President: Dr RUBÉN REMIGIO FERRO.

Vice-Presidents: OSVALDO SÁNCHEZ MARTÍN, EMILIA GONZÁLEZ PÉREZ, EDUARDO RODRÍGUEZ GONZÁLEZ.

Criminal Court

President: CARLOS ZARAGOZA PUPO.

Civil and Administrative Court

President: CARLOS M. DÍAZ TENREIRO.

Labour Court

President: Dr ANTONIO RAUDILLO MARTÍN SÁNCHEZ.

Court for State Security

President: PLÁCIDO BATISTA VERANES.

Economic Court

President: NARCISO COBO ROURA.

Military Court

President: Col JUAN MARINO FUENTES CALZADO.

Religion

There is no established Church, and all religions are permitted, though Roman Catholicism predominates. The Afro-Cuban religions of Regla de Ocha (Santería) and Regla Conga (Palo Monte) also have numerous adherents.

CHRISTIANITY

Consejo de Iglesias de Cuba (CIC) (Cuban Council of Churches): Calle 14, No 304, entre 3 y 5, Miramar, Playa, Havana; tel. (7) 204-2878; fax (7) 204-1755; e-mail iglesias@enet.cu; f. 1941; 25 mem. churches; Pres. Rev. MARCIAL MIGUEL HERNÁNDEZ SALAZAR.

The Roman Catholic Church

Cuba comprises three archdioceses and eight dioceses. Adherents represent some 53% of the total population.

Conferencia de Obispos Católicos de Cuba (COCC) (Bishops' Conference)

Calle 26, No 314, entre 3 y 5, Miramar, Apdo 635, 11300 Havana; tel. (7) 29-2298; fax (7) 24-2168; e-mail cocc@iglesiacatolica.cu; internet www.iglesiacubana.org.

f. 1983; Pres. DIONISIO GUILLERMO GARCÍA IBÁÑEZ (Archbishop of Santiago de Cuba).

Archbishop of Camagüey: JUAN GARCÍA RODRÍGUEZ, Calle Luaces, No 55, Apdo 105, 70100 Camagüey; tel. (32) 229-2268; fax (32) 228-7143; e-mail arzcam@cocc.co.cu.

Archbishop of San Cristóbal de la Habana: Cardinal JAIME LUCAS ORTEGA Y ALAMINO, Calle Habana No 152, esq. a Chacón, Apdo 594, 10100 Havana; tel. (7) 862-4000; fax (7) 866-8109; e-mail cocc@brigadoo.com.

Archbishop of Santiago de Cuba: DIONISIO GUILLERMO GARCÍA IBÁÑEZ, Sánchez Hechevarría No 607, Apdo 26, 90100 Santiago de Cuba; tel. (226) 25480; fax (226) 86186.

The Anglican Communion

Anglicans are adherents of the Iglesia Episcopal de Cuba (Episcopal Church of Cuba).

Bishop of Cuba: Rt Rev. MIGUEL TAMAYO ZALDÍVAR, Calle 6, No 273, Vedado, 10400 Havana; tel. (7) 832-1120; fax (7) 334-3293; e-mail episcopal@ip.etecsa.cu; internet www.cuba.anglican.org.

Protestant Churches

Convención Bautista de Cuba Oriental (Baptist Convention of Eastern Cuba): San Jerónimo, No 467, entre Calvario y Carnicería, Santiago de Cuba 90100; tel. (226) 62-3587; e-mail presidentecb@cbcor.co.cu; f. 1905; Pres. Rev. ENIO LEONCIO NAVARRO CASTELLANOS; Sec. Rev. ALEXI GARCÍA PUEBLA; more than 300 mem. churches.

Iglesia Metodista en Cuba (Methodist Church in Cuba): Calle K, No 502, 25 y 27, Vedado, 10400 Havana; tel. (7) 832-2991; fax (7) 832-0770; e-mail imecu@enet.cu; internet www.imecu.com; autonomous since 1968; 215 churches, 17,000 mems (2005); Bishop RICARDO PEREIRA DÍAZ.

Iglesia Presbiteriana Reformada en Cuba (Presbyterian-Reformed Church in Cuba): Salud 222, entre Lealtad y Campanario, 10200 Havana; tel. (7) 862-1219; fax (7) 866-8819; e-mail presbit@enet.cu; internet www.prccuba.org; f. 1890; 8,000 mems; Moderator Rev. Dr HÉCTOR MÉNDEZ.

Other denominations active in Cuba include the Apostolic Church of Jesus Christ, the Bethel Evangelical Church, the Christian Pentecostal Church, the Church of God, the Church of the Nazarene, the Free Baptist Convention, the Holy Pentecost Church, the Pentecostal Congregational Church and the Salvation Army.

The Press

DAILIES

Granma: Avda Gen. Suárez y Territorial, Plaza de la Revolución, Apdo 6187, CP 10699, Havana; tel. (7) 881-3333; fax (7) 881-9854; e-mail english@granma.cip.cu; internet www.granma.cubaweb.cu; f. 1965, to replace *Hoy* and *Revolución*; official Communist Party organ; Dir-Gen. LÁZARO BARREDO MEDINA; Editor-in-Chief OSCAR SÁNCHEZ SERRA; circ. 400,000.

Juventud Rebelde: Avda Territorial y Gen. Suárez, Plaza de la Revolución, Apdo 6344, CP 10600, Havana; tel. (7) 882-0155; fax (7) 883-8959; e-mail lectores@juventudrebelde.cu; internet www.juventudrebelde.cu; f. 1965; organ of the Young Communist League; Dir PELAYO TERRY CUERVO; circ. 250,000.

PERIODICALS

Adelante: Salvador Cisneros Betancourt 306, Camagüey; e-mail cip222@cip.enet.cu; internet www.adelante.cu; f. 1959; Dir Dr C. SANTIAGO LAJES CHOY; Editor JORGE LUIS PEIX AGÜERO; circ. 42,000.

Ahora: Salida a San Germán y Circunvalación, Holguín; e-mail director@ahora.cu; internet www.ahora.cu; f. 1962; Dir RODOBALDO MARTÍNEZ PÉREZ; Chief Editor JORGE L. CRUZ BERMÚDEZ; circ. 50,000.

Alma Mater: Prado 553, esq. Teniente Rey, Habana Vieja, Havana; e-mail almamater@editoraabril.co.cu; internet www.almamater.cu; f. 1922; aimed at a student readership; Chief Editor MIRIAM ANCÍZAR.

ANAP: Calle I, No 206, entre Línea y 13, Vedado, Havana; e-mail revista@anap.org.cu; internet www.campesinocubano.anap.cu; f. 1961; 6 a year; organ of the Asociación Nacional de Agricultores Pequeños; information for small farmers; Dir FÉLIX SIMÓN SANTA CRUZ; circ. 90,000.

Bohemia: Avda Independencia y San Pedro, Apdo 6000, Havana; tel. (7) 81-9213; fax (7) 33-5511; e-mail bohemia@bohemia.co.cu; internet www.bohemia.cu; f. 1908; fortnightly; politics; Dir JOSÉ FERNÁNDEZ VEGA; circ. 100,000.

El Caimán Barbudo: Casa Editora Abril, Prado 553, entre Dragones y Teniente Rey, Vedado, Havana; e-mail caimanbarbudo@editoraabril.co.cu; internet www.caimanbarbudo.cu; f. 1966; monthly; cultural; Dir FIDEL DÍAZ CASTRO; Editor RAFAEL GRILLO; circ. 47,000.

Cinco de Septiembre: Avda 54, No 3516, entre 35 y 37, CP 55100, Cienfuegos; tel. (43) 52-2144; e-mail admin@gmail.com; internet www.5septiembre.cu; f. 1980; Dir ALINA ROSELL CHONG; circ. 18,000.

Dedeté: Territorial y Gen. Suárez, Plaza de la Revolución, Apdo 6344, Havana; tel. (7) 82-0134; fax (7) 81-8621; e-mail contacto@dedete.cu; internet www.dedete.cu; f. 1969; monthly; humorous supplementary publ. of Juventud Rebelde; Dir ADÁN IGLESIAS TOLEDO; circ. 70,000.

La Demajagua: Amado Estévez, esq. Calle 10, Rpto R. Reyes, Bayamo; tel. (23) 42-4221; e-mail cip225@cip.enet.cu; internet www.lademajagua.co.cu; f. 1977; Dir LUIS CARLOS FRÓMETA AGÜERO; Editor GISLANIA TAMAYO CEDEÑO; circ. 21,000.

El Deporte, Derecho del Pueblo: Vía Blanca y Boyeros, Havana; tel. (7) 40-6838; f. 1968; monthly; sports supplement of Granma; Dir MANUEL VAILLANT CARPENTE; circ. 15,000.

El Economista de Cuba: Asociación Nacional de Economistas y Contadores de Cuba, Calle 22, No 901 esq. a 901, Miramar, Havana; tel. (7) 209-3303; fax (7) 202-3456; internet www.eleconomista.cubaweb.cu; monthly; business; Dir-Gen. ROBERTO VERRIER CASTRO; Editor ARLEEN RODRÍGUEZ DERIVET.

Escambray: Adolfo del Castillo 10, Sancti Spíritus; tel. (41) 32-3003; e-mail cip220@cip.enet.cu; internet www.escambray.cu; f. 1979 as daily; weekly from 1992; serves Sancti Spíritus province; Dir JUAN ANTONIO BORREGO DÍAZ; circ. 21,000.

Girón: Avda Camilo Cienfuegos No 10505, P. Nuero, Matanzas; e-mail cip217@cip.enet.cu; internet www.giron.co.cu; f. 1960; organ of the Communist Party in Matanzas province; Dir CLOVIS ORTEGA CASTAÑEDA; circ. 25,000.

Guerrillero: Colón 12 entre Juan Gualberto Gómez y Adela Azcuy, CP 20100, Pinar del Río; e-mail cip216@cip.enet.cu; internet www.guerrillero.co.cu; f. 1969; organ of Communist Party in Pinar del Río province; Dir ERNESTO OSORIO ROQUE; Editor MARLON RODRÍGUEZ ESTUPIÑÁN; circ. 33,000.

El Habanero: Gen. Suárez y Territorial, Plaza de la Revolución, Apdo 6187, Havana; e-mail internet@habanero.cip.cu; internet www.elhabanero.cubaweb.cu; f. 1987; Dir ANDRÉS HERNÁNDEZ RIVERO; circ. 21,000.

Invasor: Avda de los Deportes s/n, Ciego de Avila; e-mail cip221@cip.enet.cu; internet www.invasor.cu; f. 1979; provincial periodical; Dir MIGDALIA UTRERA PEÑA; Editor ROBERTO CARLOS DELGADO BURGOS; circ. 10,500.

Juventud Técnica: Prado 553, esq. Teniente Rey, Habana Vieja, Havana; tel. (7) 62-4330; e-mail jtecnica@editoraabril.co.cu; internet www.juventudtecnica.cu; f. 1965; every 2 months; scientific-technical; Dir Iramis Alonso Porro; Editor Dania Ramos; circ. 20,000.

Mar y Pesca: San Ignacio 303, entre Amargura y Teniente Rey, Habana Vieja, Havana; tel. (7) 861-5518; fax (7) 861-6280; e-mail mercado@mpesca.telemar.cu; internet www.cubamar.cu/marpesca; f. 1965; quarterly; fishing; Dir Mario Guillot Vega; circ. 20,000.

Muchacha: Galiano 264, entre Neptuno y Concordia, CP 10200, Havana; tel. (7) 861-5919; f. 1980; monthly; young women's magazine; published by the Cuban Women's Federation; Dir Ivette Vega; circ. 120,000.

Mujeres: Galiano 264, entre Neptuno y Concordia, CP 10200 Havana; tel. (7) 861-5919; e-mail mujeres@enet.cu; internet www.mujeres.cubaweb.cu; f. 1961; weekly; organ of the Cuban Women's Federation; Dir-Gen. Isabel Moya Richard; circ. 270,000.

El Nuevo Fenix: Independencia 52, esq. Honorato del Castillo, Sancti Spíritus; tel. (41) 327902; e-mail plss@ip.etecsa.cu; internet www.fenix.co.cu; f. 1999; published by Sancti Spíritus bureau of Prensa Latina (see News Agencies); Editor-in-Chief Raúl I. García Alvarez.

Opciones: Territorial esq. Gen. Suárez, Plaza de la Revolucíon, Havana; tel. (7) 881-8934; fax (7) 881-8621; e-mail opciones@jrebelde.cip.cu; internet www.opciones.cu; f. 1994; weekly; finance, commerce and tourism; Chief Editor Isabel Fernández Garrido.

Palante: Calle 21, No 954, entre 8 y 10, Vedado, Havana; e-mail cip319@cip.enet.cu; internet www.palante.co.cu; f. 1961; weekly; humorous; Dir Pedro Emigdio Viñas Alfonso; circ. 235,000.

Periódico 26: Avda Carlos J. Finlay s/n, Las Tunas CP 75100; e-mail cip224@cip.enet.cu; internet www.periodico26.cu; f. 2000; provincial periodical; Dir Ramiro Segura García; Chief Editor Oscar Góngora Jorge.

Pionero: Calle 17, No 354, Havana; tel. (7) 32-4571; e-mail pionero@editoraabril.co.cu; internet www.pionero.cu; f. 1961; monthly; children's magazine; Dir Lucía Sanz Araujo; circ. 210,000.

Prisma: Calle 21 y Avda G, No 406, Vedado, Havana; tel. (7) 832-3578; e-mail prisma@pubs.prensa-latina.cu; f. 1979; every two months; tourism; Man. Dir Luis Manuel Arce; circ. 15,000 (Spanish), 10,000 (English).

Revista Casa: 3 y G, Vedado, CP 10400, Havana; tel. (7) 838-2706; fax (7) 834-4554; e-mail revista@casa.cult.cu; internet www.casadelasamericas.com; f. 1959; 6 a year; Latin American theatre; Dir Roberto Fernández Retamar.

Sierra Maestra: Avda de Los Desfiles, Santiago de Cuba; e-mail cip226@cip.enet.cu; internet www.sierramaestra.cu; f. 1957; weekly; Dir Arnaldo Clavel Carmenaty; circ. 45,000.

Somos Jóvenes: Calle Prado, esq. a Teniente Rey, Havana; tel. (7) 862-5031; e-mail abadell@gmail.com; internet www.somosjovenes.cu; f. 1977; weekly; Dir Marietta Manso Martín; Editor Alicia Centelles; circ. 200,000.

Temas: Calle 23, No 1155, 5º entre 10 y 12, CP 10400, El Vedado, Havana; tel. and fax (7) 838-3010; e-mail temas@iciaic.cu; internet www.temas.cult.cu; f. 1995; quarterly; cultural, political; Dir Rafael Hernández; Chief Editor Alfredo Prieto.

Trabajadores: Territorial esq. Gen. Suárez, Plaza de la Revolución, CP 10698, Havana; tel. (7) 79-0819; fax (7) 55-5927; e-mail digital@trabaja.cip.cu; internet www.trabajadores.cu; f. 1970; organ of the trade union movt; Dir Jorge Luis Canela Ciurana; Chief Editor Omar Segura; circ. 150,000.

Tribuna de la Habana: Territorial esq. Gen. Suárez, Plaza de la Revolución, Havana; tel. (7) 881-8021; e-mail redac@tribuna.cip.cu; internet www.tribuna.co.cu; f. 1980; weekly; Dir Jesús Álvarez Ferrer; circ. 90,000.

Vanguardia: Calle Céspedes 5, esq. Plácido, Santa Clara, CP 50100, Matanzas; e-mail cip218@cip.enet.cu; internet www.vanguardia.co.cu; f. 1962; weekly; Dir F. A. Chang L.; circ. 45,000.

Venceremos: Avda Ernesto Che Guevara, Km 1½, CP 95400, Guantánamo; tel. (7) 32-7398; e-mail cip227@cip.enet.cu; internet www.venceremos.co.cu; f. 1962; economic, political and social publ. for Guantánamo province; Dir Yamilka Alvarez Ramos; Editor-in-Chief Jorge Cantalapiedra Luque; circ. 33,500.

Victoria: Carretera de la Fe, Km 1½, Plaza de la Revolución, Nueva Gerona, Isla de la Juventud; tel. (46) 32-4210; e-mail cip228@cip.enet.cu; internet www.victoria.co.cu; f. 1967; Dir Sergio Rivero Carrasco; Chief Editor Matilde Campos Joa; circ. 9,200.

Zunzún: Prado 553, CP 10500, Havana; e-mail zunzun@eabril.jovenclub.cu; internet www.zunzun.cu; f. 1980; children's magazine; Dir Adela Moro; Chief Editor Héctor Quintero.

PRESS ASSOCIATIONS

Unión Nacional de Escritores y Artistas de Cuba (UNEAC): Calle 17, No 354, entre G y H, Vedado, Havana; tel. (7) 838-3158; e-mail presidencia@uneac.co.cu; internet www.uneac.org.cu; f. 1961; Pres. Miguel Barnet Lanza.

Unión de Periodistas de Cuba (UPEC): Avda 23, No 452, esq. a I, Vedado, CP 10400, Havana; tel. (7) 832-4550; fax (7) 33-3079; e-mail vpetica@upec.co.cu; internet www.cubaperiodistas.cu; f. 1963; Pres. Tubal Páez Hernández.

NEWS AGENCIES

Agencia de Información Nacional (AIN): Calle 23, No 358, esq. J, Vedado, Havana; tel. (7) 881-6423; fax (7) 66-2049; e-mail igg@ain.cu; internet www.ain.cu; f. 1974; national news agency; Gen. Dir Esteban Ramírez Alonso.

Prensa Latina (Agencia Informativa Latinoamericana, SA): Calle 23, No 201, esq. N, Vedado, Havana; tel. (7) 838-3496; fax (7) 33-3068; e-mail difusion@prensa-latina.cu; internet www.prensa-latina.cu; f. 1959; Pres. Francisco González.

Publishers

Artecubano Ediciones: Calle 3, No 1205, entre 12 y 14, Playa, Havana; tel. (7) 203-8581; fax (7) 204-2744; e-mail cnap@cubarte.cult.cu; attached to the Ministry of Culture; Dir Rafael Acosta de Arriba.

Casa de las Américas: Calle 3 y Avda G, Plaza de la Revolución, Vedado, 10400 Havana; tel. (7) 552-7106; fax (7) 832-7272; e-mail admin@casa.cult.cu; internet www.casadelasamericas.com; f. 1959; Latin American literature and social sciences; Dir Roberto Fernández Retamar.

Casa Editora Abril: Prado 553, esq. Teniente Rey y Dragones, Habana Vieja, Havana; tel. (7) 862-7871; fax (7) 862-4330; e-mail eabril@jcce.org.cu; f. 1980; attached to the Union of Young Communists; cultural, children's literature; Dir Niurka Duménico García.

Ediciones Creart: Calle 4, No 205, entre Línea y 11, Plaza de la Revolución, Vedado, Havana; tel. (7) 832-9691; fax (7) 66-2582; e-mail creart@cubarte.cult.cu; f. 1994; Dir Tania Licea Jiménez.

Ediciones Unión: Calle 17, No 354, entre G y H, Plaza de la Revolución, Vedado, 10400 Havana; tel. (7) 55-3112; fax (7) 33-3158; e-mail editora@uneac.co.cu; f. 1962; publishing arm of the Unión de Escritores y Artistas de Cuba; Cuban literature, art; Dir Olga Marta Pérez Rodríguez.

Editora Política: Belascoaín No 864, esq. Desagüe y Peñalver, Havana; tel. (7) 879-8553; fax (7) 879-5688; e-mail editora@unap.cc.cu; f. 1963; publishing institution of the Communist Party of Cuba; Dir Santiago Dórquez Pérez.

Editorial Academia: Industria y Barcelona, Capitolio Nacional, 4°, Habana Vieja, 10200 Havana; tel. and fax (7) 863-0315; e-mail editorial@gecyt.cu; f. 1962; attached to the Ministry of Science, Technology and the Environment; scientific and technical; Dir Carlos J. Leyva Perdomo.

Editorial Arte y Literatura: Calle O'Reilly, No 4, esq. Tacón, Habana Vieja, Havana; tel. (7) 862-4326; fax (7) 833-8187; e-mail publicaciones@icl.cult.cu; f. 1967; traditional Cuban literature and arts; Dir Lourdes González.

Editorial Ciencias Médicas: Calle I esq. Línea, 11°, Plaza de la Revolución, Vedado, 10400 Havana; tel. (7) 832-5338; fax (7) 33-3063; e-mail ecimed@infomed.sld.cu; attached to the Ministry of Public Health; books and magazines specializing in the medical sciences; Dir Damiana Martín Laurencio.

Editorial Científico-Técnica: Calle 14, No 4104, entre 41 y 43, Playa, Havana; tel. (7) 203-6090; fax (7) 833-3441; e-mail nuevomil@cubarte.cult.cu; f. 1967; attached to the Ministry of Culture; technical and scientific literature; Dir Juan Rodríguez.

Editorial Félix Varela: San Miguel No 1011, entre Mazón y Basarrate, Plaza de la Revolución, Vedado, 10400 Havana; tel. (7) 877-5617; fax (7) 73-5419; e-mail elsa@enpses.co.cu; Dir Elsa Rodríguez.

Editorial Gente Nueva: Calle 2, No 58, entre 3 y 5, Plaza de la Revolución, Vedado, 10400 Havana; tel. (7) 833-9489; fax (7) 33-8187; e-mail gentenueva@icl.cult.cu; f. 1967; books for children; Dir Enrique Pérez Díaz.

Editorial José Martí: Calzada 259, entre I y J, Apdo 4208, Plaza de la Revolución, Vedado, 10400 Havana; tel. (7) 832-9838; fax (7) 33-3441; e-mail editjosemarti@ceniai.inf.cu; f. 1983; attached to the Ministry of Culture; foreign-language publishing; Dir Ana María Díaz.

Editorial Letras Cubanas: Calle O'Reilly, No 4, esq. Tacón, Habana Vieja, 10100 Havana; tel. (7) 862-4378; fax (7) 33-8187; e-mail elc@icl.cult.cu; f. 1977; attached to the Ministry of Culture; general, particularly classic and contemporary Cuban literature and arts; Dir DANIEL GARCÍA SANTOS.

Editorial de la Mujer: Calle Galiano, No 264, esq. Neptuno, Havana; tel. (7) 862-4905; e-mail mujeres@enet.cu; f. 1995; female literature; Dir ISABEL MOYA RICHARD.

Editorial Oriente: Santa Lucía 356, Santiago de Cuba; tel. (226) 22496; fax (226) 42387; e-mail edoriente@cultstgo.cult.cu; f. 1971; publishes works from the Eastern provinces; fiction, history, female literature and studies, art and culture, practical books and books for children; Dir AIDA BAHR.

Editorial Pablo de la Torriente Brau: Calle 11, No 160, entre K y L, Plaza de la Revolución, Vedado, 10400 Havana; tel. (7) 832-7581; e-mail centropablo@cubarte.cult.cu; f. 1985; publishing arm of the Unión de Periodistas de Cuba; Dir IRMA DE ARMAS FONSECA.

Editorial Pueblo y Educación: Avda 3A, No 4601, entre 46 y 60, Playa, Havana; tel. (7) 202-1490; fax (7) 204-0844; e-mail epe@ceniai.inf.cu; f. 1971; textbooks and educational publs; publishes Revista Educación (3 a year, circ. 2,200); Dir CATALINA LAJUD HERRERO.

Editorial Sanlope: Calle Gonzalo de Quesada, No 121, entre Lico Cruz y Lucas Ortiz, Las Tunas; tel. (31) 48191; fax (31) 47380; e-mail librolt@tunet.cult.cu; internet www.tunet.cult.cu/pagsec/institut/sanlope/index.html; f. 1991; attached to the Ministry of Culture; Dir VERENA GARCÍA MIRABAL.

GOVERNMENT PUBLISHING HOUSES

Instituto Cubano del Libro: Palacio del Segundo Cabo, Calle O'Reilly, No 4, esq. Tacón, Havana; tel. (7) 862-8091; fax (7) 33-8187; e-mail libro@cubarte.cult.cu; f. 1967; printing and publishing org. attached to the Ministry of Culture, which combines several publishing houses and has direct links with others; presides over the National Editorial Council (CEN); Pres. IROEL SÁNCHEZ.

Oficina Publicaciones del Consejo de Estado: Calle 17, No 552, esq. D, Plaza de la Revolución, Vedado, 10400 Havana; tel. (7) 832-9149; fax (7) 57-4578; e-mail palvarez@enet.cu; f. 1972; attached to the Council of State; books, pamphlets and other printed media on historical and political matters; Dir PEDRO ALVAREZ TABÍO.

PUBLISHING ASSOCIATION

Cámara Cubana del Libro: Calle 15, No 602, esq. C, Vedado, Havana; tel. (7) 833-6064; fax (7) 833-3441; e-mail maria@ccl.cult.cu; internet www.cubaliteraria.com/instituciones/camaradellibro; f. 1997; organizes the annual Havana International Book Fair; Pres. MARÍA MEDEROS MACHADO.

Broadcasting and Communications

TELECOMMUNICATIONS

Empresa de Telecomunicaciones de Cuba, SA (ETECSA): Calle 3, entre 76 y 78, Centro de Negocios Miramar, Havana; tel. (7) 266-6203; fax (7) 860-5144; e-mail atencion_usuarios@etecsa.cu; internet www.etecsa.cu; f. 1991; 27% owned by Telecom Italia International, SpA; merged with Empresa de Telecomunicaciones Celulares del Caribe, SA (C-Com) and Teléfonos Celulares de Cuba, SA (CUBACEL) in 2003; Exec. Pres. MAIMIR MESA RAMOS.

Empresa de Transporte de Señales de Telecomunicaciones (Transbit): Havana; state-owned; Pres. WALDO REBOREDO ARROYO.

Instituto de Investigación y Desarrollo de Comunicaciones (LACETEL): Avda Independencia, Km 14½, 1° de Mayo, Rancho Boyeros, CP 19210, Havana; tel. (7) 57-9265; fax (7) 649-5828; e-mail glauco@lacetel.cu; internet www.lacetel.cu; Dir-Gen. GLAUCO GUILLÉN NIETO.

Ministerio de la Informática y las Comunicaciones (Dirección de Regulaciones y Normas): Avda Independencia y 19 de Mayo, Plaza de la Revolución, Havana; tel. (7) 81-7654; e-mail infosoc@mic.cu; internet www.mic.gov.cu; regulatory authority.

Telecomunicaciones Móviles, SA (MOVITEL): Avda 47, No 3405, Reparto Kohly, Playa, Havana; tel. (7) 204-8400; fax (7) 204-4264; e-mail asela@movitel.co.cu; internet www.movitel.co.cu; mobile telecommunications; Dir-Gen. ASELA FERNÁNDEZ LORENZO.

BROADCASTING

Ministerio de la Informática y las Comunicaciones (Dirección de Frecuencias Radioeléctricas): see Ministries.

Empresa de Radiocomunicación y Difusión de Cuba (RADIOCUBA): Calle Habana 406, entre Obispo y Obrapía, Habana Vieja, Havana; tel. (7) 860-0796; fax (7) 860-3107; e-mail radiocuba@radiocuba.cu; f. 1995; controls the domestic and international broadcast transmission networks; Dir-Gen. JUSTO GERVACIO MORENO GARCÍA.

Instituto Cubano de Radio y Televisión (ICRT): Edif. Radiocentro, Avda 23, No 258, entre L y M, Vedado, Havana 4; tel. (7) 32-1568; fax (7) 33-3107; e-mail icrt@cecm.get.tur.cu; internet www.cubagob.cu/des_soc/icrt/index.htm; f. 1962; Pres. ERNESTO LÓPEZ DOMÍNGUEZ.

Radio

In 2009 there were seven national networks and one international network, 18 provincial radio stations and 25 municipal radio stations.

Habana Radio: Edif. Lonja del Comercio, Lamparilla 2, Plaza de San Francisco de Asís, Habana Vieja, Havana; tel. (7) 866-2706; e-mail sitioweb@habradio.ohc.cu; internet www.habanaradio.cu; f. 1999; run by the Oficina del Historiador de la Ciudad de La Habana; cultural and factual programmes; Dir Dr EUSEBIO LEAL SPENGLER.

Radio Cadena Agramonte: Calle Cisneros, No 310, entre Ignacio Agramonte y General Gómez, Camagüey; tel. (322) 29-5616; e-mail cip240@cip.enet.cu; internet www.cadenagramonte.cu; f. 1957; serves Camagüey; Dir ONELIO CASTILLO CORDERÍ.

Radio Enciclopedia: Calle N, No 266, entre 21 y 23, Vedado, 10400 Havana; tel. (7) 838-4586; e-mail epalacio@renciclopedia.icrt.cu; internet www.radioenciclopedia.cu; f. 1962; national network; instrumental music programmes; 24 hours daily; Dir-Gen. EDELSA PALACIO GORDO.

Radio Habana Cuba: Infanta 105, Apdo 6240, Havana; tel. (7) 877-6628; fax (7) 881-2927; e-mail radiohc@enet.cu; internet www.rhc.org; f. 1961; shortwave station; broadcasts in Spanish, English, French, Portuguese, Arabic, Esperanto, Quechua, Guaraní and Creole; Dir-Gen. ISIDRO BETANCOURT SILVA.

Radio Musical Nacional (CBMF): Calle N, No 266, entre 21 y 23, Vedado, Havana; tel. (7) 877-5527; e-mail rmusical@ceniai.inf.cu; internet www.cmbfradio.cu; f. 1948; national network; classical music programmes; 17 hours daily; Dir EDUARDO GRANADO CASTELLÓN.

Radio Progreso: Infanta 105, esq. a 25, 6°, Apdo 3042, Havana; tel. (7) 877-5519; e-mail progreso@ceniai.inf.cu; internet www.radioprogreso.cu; f. 1929; national network; mainly entertainment and music; 24 hours daily; Dir-Gen. LUIS FERNÁNDEZ PÉREZ.

Radio Rebelde: Avda 23, No 256, entre L y M, Vedado, Apdo 6277, Havana; tel. (7) 831-3514; fax (7) 33-4270; e-mail smabel@radiorebelde.icrt.cu; internet www.radiorebelde.com.cu; f. 1958; merged with Radio Liberación in 1984; national network; 24-hour news and cultural programmes, music and sports; Dir-Gen. SOFÍA MABEL MANSO DELGADO.

Radio Reloj: Edif. Radiocentro, Calle 23, No 258, entre L y M, Plaza de la Revolución, Vedado, Havana; tel. (7) 838-4185; fax (7) 838-4225; e-mail relojmailj@rreloj.icrt.cu; internet www.radioreloj.cu; f. 1947; national network; 24-hour news service; Dir OMAIDA ALONSO DIEZCABEZA.

Radio Taino: Edif. Radiocentro, Calle 23, No 258, entre L y M, Vedado, Havana; tel. (7) 55-4181; fax (7) 55-4490; e-mail pperez@rtaino.icrt.cu; internet www.radiotaino.cu; f. 1985; broadcasts in English and Spanish; Dir PEDRO MANUEL PÉREZ ROQUE.

Television

The Cuban Government holds a 19% stake in the regional television channel Telesur (q.v.), which began operations in May 2005 and is based in Caracas, Venezuela.

Instituto Cubano de Radio y Televisión—TV Cubana: Avda 23, No 258, Vedado, Havana; tel. (7) 55-4059; fax (7) 33-3107; internet www.tvcubana.icrt.cu; f. 1950; broadcasts through five channels: Canal Educativo, Canal Educativo 2, Cubavisión, Multivisión, Tele Rebelde; Pres. ERNESTO LÓPEZ DOMÍNGUEZ.

Canal Educativo: Avda 23, No 258, Vedado, Havana; tel. (7) 55-4059; fax (7) 33-3107; f. 2002; broadcasts on channel 13; educational; Dir IVÁN BARRETO.**Cubavisión:** Calle M, No 313, Vedado, Havana; e-mail info@cubavision.icrt.cu; internet www.cubavision.cubaweb.cu; broadcasts on channel 6.

Multivisión: f. 2008; broadcasts programmes from foreign networks.

Tele Rebelde: Mazón, No 52, Vedado, Havana; tel. (7) 32-3369; broadcasts on channel 2; Vice-Pres. GARY GONZÁLEZ.

Finance

(cap. = capital; res = reserves; dep. = deposits; m. = million; brs = branches)

BANKING

All banks were nationalized in 1960. Legislation establishing the national banking system was approved by the Council of State in 1984. A restructuring of the banking system, initiated in 1995, to accommodate Cuba's transformation to a more market-orientated economy, was proceeding in the mid-2000s. A new central bank, the Banco Central de Cuba (BCC), was created in 1997 to supersede the Banco Nacional de Cuba (BNC). The BCC was to be responsible for issuing currency, proposing and implementing monetary policy and the regulation of financial institutions. The BNC was to continue functioning as a commercial bank and servicing the country's foreign debt. The restructuring of the banking system also allowed for the creation of an investment bank, the Banco de Inversiones, to provide medium- and long-term financing for investment, and the Banco Financiero Internacional, SA, to offer short-term financing. A new agro-industrial and commercial bank was also to be created to provide services for farmers and co-operatives. The new banking system is under the control of Grupo Nueva Banca, which holds a majority share in each institution. In 2010 there were nine commercial banks, 12 non-banking financial institutions, nine representative offices of foreign banks and two representative offices of non-banking financial institutions operating in Cuba.

Central Bank

Banco Central de Cuba (BCC): Calle Cuba, No 402, Aguiar 411, Apdo 746, Habana Vieja, Havana; tel. (7) 860-4811; fax (7) 863-4061; e-mail webmaster@bc.gov.cu; internet www.bc.gov.cu; f. 1997; sole bank of issue; Pres. ERNESTO MEDINA VILLAVEIRÁN.

Commercial Banks

Banco de Crédito y Comercio (BANDEC): Amargura 158, entre Cuba y Aguiar, Habana Vieja, Havana; tel. (7) 861-4533; fax (7) 866-8968; e-mail ileana@oc.bandec.cu; f. 1997; Pres. ILEANA ESTÉVEZ.

Banco Exterior de Cuba: Calle 23, No 55, esq. P, Vedado, Municipio Plaza, Havana; tel. (7) 55-0795; fax (7) 55-0794; e-mail bec@bec.co.cu; f. 1999; cap. 431.1m. pesos and 18.9 convertible pesos, total assets 431.4m. pesos and 333.8m. convertible pesos (Dec. 2006); Pres. JACOBO PEISON WEINER.

Banco Financiero Internacional, SA: Avda 5, No 9009, esq. 92, Miramar, Municipio Playa, Havana; tel. (7) 267-5000; fax (7) 267-5002; e-mail bfi@bfi.com.cu; f. 1984; autonomous; finances Cuba's foreign trade; Pres. (vacant); Gen. Man. NIVALDO PULDÓN IBARZÁBAL (acting); 29 brs.

Banco Industrial de Venezuela-Cuba, SA (BIVC): Edif. Jerusalem, 2°, Of. 201, Centro de Negocios Miramar, Sector Miramar, Havana; tel. (7) 206-9650; f. 2005 as a subsidiary of state-owned Banco Industrial de Venezuela, SA.

Banco Internacional de Comercio, SA: 20 de Mayo y Ayestarán, Apdo 6113, 10600 Havana; tel. (7) 883-6038; fax (7) 883-6028; e-mail bicsa@bicsa.co.cu; f. 1993; cap. 198.7m. convertible pesos, res 24.2m. convertible pesos, dep. 1,877.1m. convertible pesos (Dec. 2006); Chair. and Pres. MARCOS DÍAZ.

Banco Metropolitano, SA: Avda 5 y Calle 112, Miramar, Municipio Habana Vieja, 11600 Havana; tel. (7) 204-3869; fax (7) 204-9193; e-mail bm@banco-metropolitano.com; internet www.banco-metropolitano.com; f. 1996; offers foreign currency and deposit account facilities; Pres. MANUEL VALE; Dir-Gen. PEDRO DE LA ROSA GONZÁLEZ.

Banco Nacional de Cuba (BNC): Aguiar 456, entre Amargura y Lamparilla, Habana Vieja, Havana; tel. (7) 862-8896; fax (7) 866-9390; e-mail bancuba@bnc.cu; f. 1950; reorganized 1997; Chair. IRMA MARTÍNEZ CASTRILLÓN.

Savings Bank

Banco Popular de Ahorro: Calle 16, No 306, entre 3ra y 5ta, Playa, Miramar, Havana; tel. (7) 204-2545; fax (7) 204-1180; e-mail presidencia@mail.bpa.cu; f. 1983; savings bank; Pres. JOSÉ LÁZARO ALARI MARTÍNEZ; 520 brs.

Investment Bank

Banco de Inversiones, SA: Avda 5, No 6802 esq. a 68, Miramar, Havana; tel. (7) 204-3374; fax (7) 204-3377; e-mail inversiones@bdi.cu; internet www.bdi.cu; f. 1996; Exec. Pres. RAÚL E. RANGEL.

INSURANCE

State Organizations

Empresa del Seguro Estatal Nacional (ESEN): Calle 5, No 306, entre C y D, Vedado, Havana; tel. (7) 832-2500; fax (7) 833-8717; e-mail rfo@esen.com.cu; internet www.ain.cu/publicidad/sitio esen/index.htm; f. 1978; motor and agricultural insurance; Dir-Gen. HUMBERTO BARRETO NARDO.

Seguros Internacionales de Cuba, SA (Esicuba): Cuba No 314, entre Obispo y Obrapía, Habana Vieja, Havana; tel. (7) 33-8400; fax (7) 33-8038; e-mail esicuba@esicuba.cu; f. 1963; reorganized 1986; all classes of insurance except life; Pres. RAMÓN MARTÍNEZ CARRERA.

Trade and Industry

GOVERNMENT AGENCIES

Ministry of Foreign Trade and Investment: see Ministries.

Centro para la Promoción del Comercio Exterior de Cuba (CEPEC): Infanta 16, esq. 23, 2°, Vedado, Municipio Plaza, Havana; tel. (7) 838-0428; fax (7) 833-2220; e-mail cepecdir@mincex.cu; internet www.cepec.cu; f. 1995; Dir-Gen. RAYSA COSTA BLANCO.

CHAMBER OF COMMERCE

Cámara de Comercio de la República de Cuba: Calle 21, No 661/701, esq. Calle A, Apdo 4237, Vedado, Havana; tel. (7) 830-4436; fax (7) 833-3042; e-mail camaracuba@camara.com.cu; internet www.camaracuba.cu; f. 1963; mems include all Cuban foreign trade enterprises and the most important agricultural and industrial enterprises; Pres. PEDRO ALVAREZ BORREGO; Sec.-Gen. IVÁN MARICHAL AGUILERA.

AGRICULTURAL ORGANIZATION

Asociación Nacional de Agricultores Pequeños (ANAP) (National Association of Small Farmers): Calle I, No 206, entre Linea y 13, Vedado, Havana; tel. (7) 32-4541; fax (7) 33-4244; internet www.campesinocubano.anap.cu; f. 1961; 331,874 mems; Pres. ORLANDO LUGO FONTE; Vice-Pres. EVELIO PAUSA BELLO.

STATE IMPORT-EXPORT BOARDS

Alimport (Empresa Cubana Importadora de Alimentos): Infanta 16, 3°, Apdo 7006, Havana; tel. (7) 54-2501; fax (7) 33-3151; e-mail precios@alimport.com.cu; f. 1962; controls import of foodstuffs and liquors; CEO PEDRO ALVAREZ BORREGO.

Autoimport (Empresa Central de Abastecimiento y Venta de Equipos de Transporte Ligero): Galiano 213, entre Concordia y Virtudes, Habana Vieja, Havana; tel. (7) 61-5322; fax (7) 66-6549; e-mail magda@autoimport.com.cu; imports cars, light vehicles, motor cycles and spare parts; Dir JOSÉ ARAÑABURU.

Aviaimport (Empresa Cubana Importadora y Exportadora de Aviación): Calle 182, No 126, entre 1 y 5, Rpto Flores, Playa, Havana; tel. (7) 273-0077; fax (7) 273-6365; e-mail dcom@aviaimport.avianet.cu; import and export of aircraft and components; Man. Dir MARCOS LAGO MARTÍNEZ.

Caribex (Empresa Comercial Caribe): Avda La Pesquera y Atarés, Puerto Pesquero de La Habana, 3°, Habana Vieja, Havana; tel. (7) 864-4135; fax (7) 864-4144; e-mail caribex@caribex.cu; internet www.caribex.cu; export of seafood and marine products; Dir D. RENÉ BESTEIRO.

Catec (Empresa Cubana Exportadora y Comercializadora de Productos y Servicios de la Ciencia y la Técnica Agraria): Calle 148, No 905, entre 9 y 9A, Rpto Cubanacán, Playa, Havana; tel. (7) 208-2164; fax (7) 204-6071; e-mail alina@catec.co.cu; internet www.catec.cu; exports, imports and markets scientific and technical products relating to the farming and forestry industries; Dir-Gen. OSVALDO CARVEJAL GABELA.

Construimport (Empresa Central de Abastecimiento y Venta de Equipos de Construcción y sus Piezas): Carretera de Varona, Km 1½, Capdevila, Havana; tel. (7) 645-2567; fax (7) 646-8943; e-mail equipo@construimport.co.cu; internet www.construimport.cubaindustria.cu; f. 1969; controls the import and export of construction machinery and equipment; Man. Dir DEYSI ROMAY SARDIÑAS.

Consumimport (Empresa Cubana Importadora de Artículos de Consumo General): Calle 23, No 55, 9°, Apdo 6427, Vedado, Plaza de Revolución, Havana; tel. (8) 36-7717; fax (8) 33-3847; e-mail comer@consumimport.infocex.cu; f. 1962; imports and exports general consumer goods; Dir MERCEDES REY HECHAVARRÍA.

Copextel (Corporación Productora y Exportadora de Tecnología Electrónica): Avda 11, entre 222B y 222C, Siboney, Playa, Havana; tel. (7) 273-0820; fax (7) 273-6540; e-mail copextel@copextel.com.cu; internet www.copextel.com.cu; f. 1985; exports LTEL personal computers and micro-computer software; Dir CIRO MURO.

Coprefil (Empresa Comercial y de Producciones Filatélicas): Avda 49, No 2831, esq. 49A, Rpto Kohly, Playa, Havana; tel. (7) 204-9668; fax (7) 204-5077; e-mail coprefil@coprefil.cu; imports and exports postage stamps, postcards, calendars, handicrafts, communications equipment, electronics, watches, etc.; Dir NELSON IGLESIAS FERNÁNDEZ.

Cubaelectrónica (Empresa Importadora y Exportadora de Productos de la Electrónica): Calle 22, No 510, entre 5 y 7, Miramar, Havana; tel. (7) 204-0178; fax (7) 204-1233; e-mail mariaisabel@columbus.cu; f. 1986; imports and exports electronic equipment and devices; Dir GERARDO LÓPEZ BRITO.

Cubaexport (Empresa Cubana Exportadora de Alimentos y Productos Varios): Calle 23, No 55, entre Infanta y P, 8°, Vedado, Apdo 6719, Havana; tel. (7) 838-0595; fax (7) 833-3587; e-mail cubaexport@cexport.mincex.cu; f. 1965; export of foodstuffs and industrial products; Man. Dir FRANCISCO SANTIAGO PICHARDO.

Cubahidráulica (Empresa Central de Equipos Hidráulicos): Carretera Vieja de Guanabacoa y Linea de Ferrocarril, Rpto Mañana, Guanabacoa, Havana; tel. (7) 797-0821; fax (7) 797-1627; e-mail cubahidraulica@enet.cu; internet www.cubahidraulica.com; f. 1995; imports and exports hydraulic and mechanical equipment, parts and accessories; Dir-Gen. OSMUNDO PAZ PAZ.

Cubalse (Empresa para Prestación de Servicios al Cuerpo Diplomático): Avda 3a y Final, Miramar, Havana; tel. (7) 201-2100; fax (7) 204-7994; e-mail relacion@cubalse.cu; internet www.cubalse.cu; f. 1974; imports consumer goods for the diplomatic corps and foreign technicians residing in Cuba; exports beverages, tobacco, leather goods and foodstuffs; other operations include real estate, retail trade, restaurants, clubs, automobile business, state-of-the-art equipment and household appliances, construction, investments, wholesale, road transport, freight transit, shipping, publicity, photography and video, financing, legal matters; Pres. HORACIO NAVAS.

Cubametales (Empresa Cubana Importadora de Metales, Combustibles y Lubricantes): Infanta 16, 4°, entre 23 y Humboldt, Apdo 6917, Vedado, Havana; tel. (7) 838-0531; fax (7) 838-0530; e-mail mcarmen@cubametal.mincex.cu; f. 1962; controls import of metals (ferrous and non-ferrous), crude petroleum and petroleum products; also engaged in the export of petroleum products and ferrous and non-ferrous scrap; Dir-Gen. MARY CARMEN ARENCIBIA VÁZQUEZ.

Cubaniquel (Empresa Cubana Exportadora de Minerales y Metales): Carretera Moa, Sagua Km 1½, Moa, CP 83330, Holguín; tel. (24) 60-8283; fax (24) 60-2156; e-mail cceac@cubaniquel.moa.minbas.cu; f. 1961; sole exporter of minerals and metals; Man. Dir ANGEL ROBERTO HERNÁNDEZ.

Cubatabaco (Empresa Cubana del Tabaco): Calle Nueva 75, entre Universidad y Pedroso, Cerro, Havana; tel. (7) 879-0253; fax (7) 33-8214; e-mail cubatabaco@cubatabaco.cu; internet www.cubatabaco.cu; f. 1962; controls export of leaf tobacco, cigars and cigarettes to France; Dir ALFREDO S. CALERO ACOSTA.

Cubazúcar (Empresa Cubana Exportadora de Azúcar y sus Derivados): Calle 23, No 55, 7°, Vedado, Apdo 6647, Havana; tel. (7) 54-2275; fax (7) 33-3482; e-mail producer@cubazucar.com; internet www.cubazucar.com; f. 1962; controls export of sugar, molasses and alcohol; Pres. JOSÉ LÓPEZ SILVERO.

Ecimetal (Empresa Importadora y Exportadora de Objetivos Industriales): Calle 23, No 55, 2°, esq. Plaza, Vedado, Havana; tel. (7) 55-0548; fax (7) 33-4737; e-mail ecimetal@infocex.cu; f. 1977; controls import and export of plant, equipment and raw materials for all major industrial sectors; Dir CONCEPCIÓN BUENO.

Ediciones Cubanas (Empresa de Comercio Exterior de Publicaciones): Obispo 527, esq. Bernaza, Apdo 47, Habana Vieja, Havana; tel. (7) 863-1989; fax (7) 33-8943; e-mail edicuba@cubarte.cult.cu; controls import and export of books and periodicals; Dir ROLANDO VERDÉS PINEDA.

Egrem (Estudios de Grabaciones y Ediciones Musicales): Calle 3, No 1008, entre 10 y 12, Miramar, Playa, Havana; tel. (7) 204-1925; fax (7) 204-2519; e-mail relaciones@egrem.co.cu; internet www.egrem.com.cu; f. 1964; controls the import and export of records, tapes, printed music and musical instruments; Dir-Gen. RACIEL RUIZ RODRÍGUEZ.

Emiat (Empresa Importadora y Exportadora de Suministros Técnicos): Avda 47, No 2828, entre 28 y 34, Rpto Kohly, Havana; tel. (7) 203-0345; fax (7) 204-9353; e-mail emiat@enet.cu; f. 1983; imports technical materials, equipment and special products; exports furniture, kitchen utensils and accessories; Man. FIDEL GARCÍA HERNÁNDEZ.

Emidict (Empresa Especializada Importadora, Exportadora y Distribuidora para la Ciencia y la Técnica): Calle 16, No 102, esq. Avda 1, Miramar, Playa, 13000 Havana; tel. (7) 203-5316; fax (7) 204-1768; e-mail emidict@ceniai.inf.cu; internet www.emidict.com.cu; f. 1982; controls import and export of scientific and technical products and equipment, live animals; scientific information; Dir-Gen. CARLOS CANALES ENRÍQUEZ.

Energoimport (Empresa Importadora de Objetivos Electro-energéticos): Amenidad No 124, entre Nueva y 20 de Mayo, Municipio Cerro, 10600 Havana; tel. (7) 70-2501; fax (7) 66-6079; e-mail andy@energonet.com.cu; internet www.energonet.com.cu; f. 1977; controls import of equipment for electricity generation; Dir-Gen. ANDRÉS MONTES PEREA.

Eprob (Empresa de Proyectos para las Industrias de la Básica): Avda 31A, No 1805, entre 18 y 20, Edif. Las Ursulinas, Miramar, Playa, Apdo 12100, Havana; tel. (7) 202-5562; fax (7) 204-2146; e-mail direccion@eprob.cu; f. 1967; exports consulting services, processing of engineering construction projects and supplies of complete industrial plants and turnkey projects; Man. Dir GLORIA EXPÓSITO DÍAZ.

Eproyiv (Empresa de Proyectos para Industrias Varias): Calle 31A, No 1815, entre 18 y 20, Playa, Havana; tel. (7) 202-7097; fax (7) 204-2149; e-mail dg-eproyiv@eproyiv.cu; internet www.eproyiv.cu; f. 1967; consulting services, feasibility studies, devt of basic and detailed engineering models, project management and turnkey projects; Dir MARTA ELENA HERNÁNDEZ DÍAZ.

Esi (Empresa de Suministros Industriales): Calle Aguiar, No 556, entre Teniente Rey y Muralla, Habana Vieja, Havana; tel. (7) 62-0696; fax (7) 33-8951; f. 1985; imports machinery, equipment and components for industrial plants; Dir-Gen. FRANCISCO DÍAZ CABRERA.

Fondo Cubano de Bienes Culturales: Calle 36, No 4702, esq. Avda 47, Rpto Kohly, Playa, Havana; tel. (7) 204-6428; fax (7) 204-0391; e-mail fcbc@fcbc.cult.cu; f. 1978; controls export of fine handicraft and works of art; Dir-Gen. GUILLERMO SOLENZAL MORALES.

Habanos, SA: Avda 3, No 2006, entre 20 y 22, Miramar, Havana; tel. (7) 204-0524; fax (7) 204-0491; e-mail habanos@habanos.cu; internet www.habanos.com; f. 1994; controls export of leaf and pipe tobacco, cigars and cigarettes to all markets; jt venture with Altadis, SA (Spain); Pres. OSCAR BASULTO TORRES; Dir-Gen. ADARGELIIO GARRIDO DE LA GRANA.

ICAIC (Instituto Cubano del Arte e Industria Cinematográficos): Calle 23, No 1155, Vedado, Havana 4; tel. (7) 55-3128; fax (7) 33-3032; e-mail webmaster@icaic.cu; internet www.cubacine.cu; f. 1959; production, import and export of films and newsreel; Dir CAMILO VIVES PALLÉS.

Maprinter (Empresa Cubana Importadora y Exportadora de Materias Primas y Productos Intermedios): Edif. MINCEX, Calle 23, No 55, entre P e Infanta, 8°, Plaza de la Revolución, Vedado, Havana; tel. (7) 878-0711; fax (7) 833-3535; e-mail direccion@maprinter.mincex.cu; internet www.maprinter.cu; f. 1962; controls import and export of raw materials and intermediate products; Dir-Gen. ODALYS ALDAMA VALDÉS.

Maquimport (Empresa Cubana Importadora de Maquinarias Equipos y Artículos de Ferretería): Calle 23, No 55, 6°, entre P e Infanta, Vedado, Apdo 6052, Havana; tel. (7) 838-0635; fax (7) 838-0632; e-mail direccion@maquimport.mincex.cu; imports industrial goods and equipment; Dir ARIEL HERNÁNDEZ GARCÍA.

Medicuba (Empresa Cubana Importadora y Exportadora de Productos Médicos): Máximo Gómez 1, esq. Egido, Habana Vieja, Havana; tel. (7) 862-4061; fax (7) 866-8516; e-mail dirgeneral@medicuba.sld.cu; f. 1962; enterprise for the export and import of medical and pharmaceutical products; Dir-Gen. JORGE LUIS MECÍAS CUBILLA.

Produimport (Empresa Central de Abastecimiento y Venta de Productos Químicos y de la Goma): Calle Consulado 262, entre Animas y Virtudes, Havana; tel. (7) 62-0581; fax (7) 62-9588; f. 1977; imports and exports spare parts for motor vehicles; Dir ARTURO J. CINTRA GÓNGORA.

Propes (Empresa Importadoro y Proveedora de Productos para la Pesca): Calle 22, No 2, esq. Calzada, Vedado, Havana; tel. (7) 830-3770; fax (7) 55-1729; e-mail pesmar@apropes.fishnavy.inf.cu; importer and distributor of a wide variety of equipment and accessories pertaining to the fishing industry; Dir-Gen. PEDRO BLAS ARTEAGA.

Quimimport (Empresa Cubana Importadora y Exportadora de Productos Químicos): Calle 23, No 55, entre Infanta y P, Apdo 6088, Vedado, Havana; tel. (7) 33-3394; fax (7) 33-3190; e-mail global@quimimport.infocex.cu; internet www.quimimport.cu; controls import and export of chemical products; Dir ARMANDO BARRERA MARTÍNEZ.

Suchel (Empresa de Jabonería y Perfumería): Calzada de Buenos Aires 353, esq. a Durege, Apdo 6359, Havana; tel. (7) 649-8008; fax (7) 649-5311; e-mail direccion@suchel.co.cu; f. 1977; imports materials for the detergent, perfumery and cosmetics industry, exports cosmetics, perfumes, hotel amenities and household products; Dir JOSÉ GARCÍA DÍAZ.

Tecnoazúcar (Empresa de Servicios Técnicos e Ingeniería para la Agro-industria Azucarera): Calle 12, No 310, entre 3 y 5, Miramar, Playa, Havana; tel. (7) 29-5441; fax (7) 33-1218; e-mail tecno@tecnoazucar.cu; internet www.tecnoazucar.cu; imports machinery and equipment for the sugar industry, provides technical and engineering assistance for the sugar industry; exports equipment and spare parts for sugar machinery; provides engineering and technical assistance services for sugar-cane by-product industry; Dir-Gen. HÉCTOR COMPANIONI ECHEMENDÍA.

Tecnoimport (Empresa Importadora y Exportadora de Productos Técnicos): Edif. La Marina, Avda del Puerto 102, entre Justiz y Obrapía, Habana Vieja, Havana; tel. (7) 861-5552; fax (7) 66-9777; e-mail celeste@ti.gae.com.cu; f. 1968; imports technical products; Dir ADEL IZQUIERDO RODRÍGUEZ.

Tecnotex (Empresa Cubana Exportadora e Importadora de Servicios, Artículos y Productos Técnicos Especializados): Avda 47, No 3419, Playa, Havana; tel. (7) 861-3536; fax (7) 66-6270; e-mail ailede@tecnotex.qae.com.cu; f. 1983; imports specialized technical and radiocommunications equipment, exports outdoor equipment and geodetic networks; Dir RENÉ ROJAS RODRÍGUEZ.

Tractoimport (Empresa Central de Abastecimiento y Venta de Maquinaria Agrícola y sus Piezas de Repuesto): Avda Rancho Boyeros y Calle 100, Apdo 7007, Havana; tel. (7) 45-2166; fax (7) 267-0786; e-mail direccion@tractoimport.co.cu; f. 1962; import of tractors and agricultural equipment; also exports pumps and agricultural implements; Dir-Gen. ABDEL GARCÍA GONZÁLEZ.

Transimport (Empresa Central de Abastecimiento y Venta de Equipos de Transporte Pesados y sus Piezas): Calle 102 y Avda 63, Marianao, Apdo 6665, 11500 Havana; tel. (7) 260-0329; fax (7) 267-9050; e-mail direccion@transimport.co.cu; internet www.transimport.co.cu; f. 1968; controls import and export of vehicles and transportation equipment; Dir-Gen. JUAN CARLOS TASSÉ BELLOT.

OTHER MAJOR COMPANIES

BrasCuba Cigarrillos, SA: Calle Princesa, No 202, entre Reyes y San José, Luyanó, Havana; tel. (7) 696-7510; fax (7) 866-9306; e-mail brascuba@ceniai.inf.cu; f. 1995; manufactures and markets cigarettes; jt venture between TabaCuba (Grupo Empresarial del Tobaco) and Souza Cruz, SA (Brazil); Pres. FLAVIO DE ANDRADE.

CariFin (Caribbean Finance Investments Ltd): Calle 22, No 313, entre 3 y 5, Miramar, Playa, Havana; tel. (7) 204-4147; fax (7) 204-4140; e-mail jcarracedo@carifin.cu; f. 1996 in the British Virgin Islands; started lending operations in Cuba in 1997; subsidiary of the Commonwealth Devt Corpn (United Kingdom) and Grupo Nueva Banca, SA (Cuba); financial services such as loans to businesses, international money transfers and leasing of equipment and machinery; Int. Man. JUAN J. CARRACEDO BOTIFOLL; 23 employees.

Corporación Cuba Ron, SA (CubaRon): Calle 200, No 1708, esq. 17, Rpto Atabey, Playa, Havana; tel. (7) 273-0102; fax (7) 273-6600; e-mail cubaron@cubaron.co.cu; internet www.cubaron.com; f. 1993; production, marketing and distribution of rum and other alcoholic beverages; Pres. LUIS PERDOMO HERNÁNDEZ.

Cubalub (Empresa Cubana de Lubricantes): Calle Oficios No 154, entre Amargura y Teniente Rey, 3°, Habana Vieja, 10100 Havana; tel. (7) 861-6512; fax (7) 867-9197; e-mail mabel@cubalub.cupet.cu; state-owned; manufactures and markets lubricants; Dir FAUSTINO LEÓN.

Cubapetróleo (Cupet): Oficios No 154, entre Amargura y Teniente Rey, Habana Vieja, 10100 Havana; tel. (7) 862-0551; fax (7) 862-7577; e-mail escobar@union.cupet.cu; state-owned; extraction and production of petroleum; Pres. FIDEL RIVERO PRIETO; Vice-Pres. JUAN FLEITES MELO.

Grupo Industrial Refrigeración y Calderas: Calle 31, No 19811, entre 198 y 208, La Coronela, La Lisa, Havana; tel. (7) 33-8090; fax (7) 33-8501; e-mail grupoc@rc.columbus.cu; f. 1985; manufacturer of refrigerators and air-conditioning appliances; Man. Dir EMILIO MARILL FREYRE DE ANDRADE; 2,200 employees.

Grupo Industrial Unecamoto: Calle 37, entre 208 y 212, La Coronela, La Lisa, Havana; tel. (7) 21-6665; fax (7) 33-6545; e-mail unecamoto@unecamoto.com.cu; produces automobile parts and accessories; Pres. CRISTÓBAL VÁZQUEZ EGAÑA.

TabaCuba (Grupo Empresarial del Tabaco): Calle 19, esq. M, No 102, Vedado, Havana; tel. (7) 53-5665; fax (7) 53-5732; f. 2000; state-owned; regulates tobacco cultivation and cigar production in Cuba; Pres. OSCAR BASULTO TORRES; Dir FÉLIX R. HERNÁNDEZ.

Unión de Empresas Constructoras Caribe, SA (UNECA, SA): Calle 7, esq. 41, No 701, entre 6 y 10, Miramar, Playa, CP 6020, Havana; tel. (7) 204-4582; fax (7) 209-6067; e-mail negocios@uneca.co.cu; internet www.uneca.com.cu; f. 1978; construction and engineering services; operates in South and Central America and the Caribbean and sub-Saharan Africa; est. turnover of US $12m. (2009); Chair. and CEO RICARDO DE JESÚS MENÉNDEZ CAMPOS.

UTILITIES

Electricity

Unión Nacional Eléctrica (UNE): Havana; public utility; Dir-Gen. VICENTE LEVY.

Water

Aguas de la Habana: Fomento y Recreo, Rpto Palatino, Cerro, Havana; tel. and fax (7) 642-4901; e-mail jmtura@ahabana.co.cu; water supplier; Dir-Gen. JOSEP OLLER HERNÁNDEZ.

Instituto Nacional de Recursos Hidráulicos (INRH) (National Water Resources Institute): Calle Humbolt, No 106, esq. a P, Plaza de la Revolución, Vedado, Havana; tel. (7) 836-5571; e-mail gisel@hidro.cu; internet www.hidro.cu; regulatory body; Pres. RENÉ MESA VILLAFAÑA.

TRADE UNIONS

All workers have the right to become members of a national trade union according to their industry and economic branch.

The following industries and labour branches have their own unions: Agriculture, Chemistry and Energetics, Civil Workers of the Revolutionary Armed Forces, Commerce and Gastronomy, Communications, Construction, Culture, Defence, Education and Science, Food, Forestry, Health, Light Industry, Merchant Marine, Mining and Metallurgy, Ports and Fishing, Public Administration, Sugar, Tobacco and Transport.

Central de Trabajadores de Cuba (CTC) (Confederation of Cuban Workers): Palacio de los Trabajadores, San Carlos y Peñalver, Havana; tel. (7) 78-4901; fax (7) 55-5927; e-mail digital@trabaja.cip.cu; f. 1939; affiliated to WFTU and CPUSTAL; 19 national trade unions affiliated; Gen. Sec. SALVADOR ANTONIO VALDÉS MESA.

Transport

The Ministry of Transportation controls all public transport.

RAILWAYS

The total length of railways in 1998 was 14,331 km, of which 9,638 km were used by the sugar industry. The remaining 4,520 km were public service railways operated by Ferrocarriles de Cuba. All railways were nationalized in 1960. In 2001 Cuba signed an agreement with Mexico for the maintenance and repair of rolling stock.

Ferrocarriles de Cuba: Edif. Estación Central, Egido y Arsenal, Havana; tel. (7) 70-1076; fax (7) 33-1489; f. 1960; operates public services; Dir-Gen. FERNANDO PÉREZ LÓPEZ; divided as follows:.**División Occidente:** serves Pinar del Río, Ciudad de la Habana, Havana province and Matanzas.

División Centro: serves Villa Clara, Cienfuegos and Sancti Spíritus.

División Centro-Este: serves Camagüey, Ciego de Avila and Tunas.

División Oriente: serves Santiago de Cuba, Granma, Guantánamo and Holguín.

División Camilo Cienfuegos: serves part of Havana province and Matanzas.

ROADS

In 1999 there were an estimated 60,858 km of roads, of which 4,353 km were highways or main roads. The Central Highway runs from Pinar del Río in the west to Santiago, for a length of 1,144 km. In addition to this paved highway, there are a number of secondary and 'farm-to-market' roads. A small proportion of these secondary roads is paved, but many can be used by motor vehicles only during the dry season.

SHIPPING

Cuba's principal ports are Havana (which handles 60% of all cargo), Santiago de Cuba, Cienfuegos, Nuevitas, Matanzas, Antilla, Guayabal and Mariel. Maritime transport has developed rapidly since 1959, and at 31 December 2008 Cuba had a merchant fleet of 67 ships (with a combined total displacement of some 60,000 grt). In late 2007 the Government announced expenditure of US $180m. on modernization of the country's ports in 2007–10.

Coral Container Lines, SA: Calle Oficios No 170, 1°, Habana Vieja, Havana; tel. (7) 67-0854; fax (7) 67-0850; e-mail caribe@coral.com.cu; f. 1994; liner services to Europe, Canada, Brazil and Mexico; 11 containers; Chair. and Man. Dir EVELIO GONZÁLEZ GONZÁLEZ.

Empresa Consignataria Mambisa: San José No 65, entre Prado y Zulueta, Habana Vieja, Havana; tel. (7) 862-2061; fax (7) 33-8111; e-mail mercedes@mambisa.transnet.cu; shipping agent, bunker suppliers; Man. Dir MERCEDES PÉREZ NEWHALL.

Empresa Cubana de Fletes (Cuflet): Calle Oficios No 170, entre Teniente Rey y Amargura, Apdo 6755, Havana; tel. (7) 61-2604; e-mail antares@antares.transnet.cu; freight agents for Cuban cargo; Man. Dir CARLOS SÁNCHEZ PERDOMO.

Empresa de Navegación Caribe (Navecaribe): Calle San Martín, No 65, 4°, entre Agramonte y Pasco de Martí, Habana Vieja,

Havana; tel. (7) 61-8611; fax (7) 33-8564; e-mail enccom@transnet.cu; f. 1966; operates Cuban coastal fleet; Dir RAMÓN DURÁN SUÁREZ.

Empresa de Navegación Mambisa: San Ignacio No 104, Apdo 543, Havana; tel. (7) 869-7901; fax (7) 61-0044; operates dry cargo, reefer and bulk carrier vessels; Gen. Man. GUMERSINDO GONZÁLEZ FELIÚ.

Naviera del Caribe (Carimar): Calle Oficios No 170, entre Amargura y Teniente Rey, 3°, Habana Vieja, Havana; tel. (7) 67-0925; fax (7) 204-8627; e-mail ftarrau@coral.com.cu.

Naviera Frigorífica Marítima (Friomar): 5a Avda y 240, Barlovento, Playa, Havana; tel. (7) 209-8171; fax (7) 204-5864; e-mail friocom@fishnavy.inf.cu; specializes in shipping of refrigerated cargo; Dir JORGE FERNÁNDEZ.

Naviera Mar América: 5a Avda y 246, Edif. No 3, 1°, Barlovento, Playa, Havana; tel. (7) 209-8076; fax (7) 204-8889; e-mail nubia@maramerica.fishnavy.inf.cu.

Naviera Petrocost: 5a Avda y 246, Barlovento, Playa, Havana; tel. (7) 209-8067; fax (7) 204-5113; e-mail aleida@petrocost.fishnavy.inf.cu; transports liquid cargo to domestic and international destinations.

Naviera Poseidon: 5a Avda y 246, Edif. No 3, 2°, Barlovento, Playa, Havana; tel. (7) 209-8073; fax (7) 204-8627; e-mail yepe@poseidon.fishnavy.inf.cu.

Nexus Reefer: 5a Avda y 246, Edif. No 7, 1°, Barlovento, Playa, Havana; tel. (7) 204-8205; fax (7) 204-8490; e-mail sandra@antares.fishnavy.inf.cu; merchant reefer ships; Gen. Dir QUIRINO L. GUTIÉRREZ LÓPEZ.

CIVIL AVIATION

There are a total of 21 civilian airports, with 11 international airports, including Havana, Santiago de Cuba, Camagüey, Varadero and Holguín. Abel Santamaría International Airport opened in Villa Clara in early 2001. In January 2003 the King's Gardens International Airport in Cayo Coco was opened. The airport formed part of a new tourist 'offshore' centre. The international airports were all upgraded and expanded during the 1990s and a third terminal was constructed at the José Martí International Airport in Havana. In 2001 three North American airlines were permitted to commence direct flights from Miami and New York to Havana. A programme of improvements to five of the country's international airports was announced by the Government in late 2007.

Aerocaribbean: Calle 23, No 64, esq. P, Vedado, Havana; tel. (7) 832-7584; fax (7) 336-5016; e-mail reserva@cacsa.avianet.cu; internet www.aero-caribbean.com; f. 1982; international and domestic scheduled and charter services; Chair. JULIÁN ALVAREZ INFIESTA.

Aerogaviota: Avda 47, No 2814, entre 28 y 34, Rpto Kolhy, Havana; tel. (7) 203-0668; fax (7) 204-2621; e-mail vpcom@aerogaviota.avianet.cu; f. 1994; operated by Cuban air force.

Empresa Consolidada Cubana de Aviación (Cubana): Aeropuerto Internacional José Martí, Terminal 1, Avda Rancho Boyeros, Havana; tel. (7) 266-4644; fax (7) 33-4056; e-mail pax@avianet.cu; internet www.cubana.co.cu; f. 1929; international services to North America, Central America, the Caribbean, South America and Europe; internal services from Havana to 14 other cities; Pres. RICARDO SANTILLÁN MIRANDA.

Instituto de Aeronáutica Civil de Cuba (IACC): Calle 23, No 64, Plaza de la Revolución, Vedado, Havana; tel. (7) 33-4949; fax (7) 33-4553; e-mail iacc@avianet.cu; internet www.cubagob.cu/des_eco/iacc/home.htm; f. 1985; Pres. ROGELIO ACEVEDO GONZÁLEZ.

Tourism

Tourism began to develop after 1977, with the easing of travel restrictions by the USA, and Cuba subsequently attracted European tourists. In 2008 the number of hotel rooms had reached 56,970. In 2007 receipts from tourism totalled an estimated US $2,415m. Tourist arrivals stood at an estimated 2,429,809 in 2009, compared with 2,348,340 in 2008.

Cubanacán: Calle 23, No 156, entre O y P, Vedado, 10400 Havana; tel. (7) 833-4090; fax (7) 22-8382; e-mail com_electronic@cubanacan.cyt.cu; internet www.cubanacan.cu; f. 1987; Pres. MANUEL VILA.

Empresa de Turismo Internacional (Cubatur): Calle F, No 157, entre Calzada y Novena, Vedado, Havana; tel. (7) 835-4155; fax (7) 836-3170; e-mail casamatriz@cubatur.cu; internet www.cubatur.cu; f. 1968.

Defence

As assessed at November 2009, according to Western estimates, Cuba's Revolutionary Armed Forces numbered 49,000 (including ready reserves, serving 45 days a year to complete active and reserve units): Army 38,000, Navy 3,000 and Air Force 8,000. There were an additional 39,000 army reserves. Cuba's paramilitary forces included 20,000 State Security troops, 6,500 border guards, a civil defence force of 50,000 and a Youth Labour Army of some 70,000. There was also a Territorial Militia, comprising an estimated 1m. men and women. Conscription for military service is for a two-year period from 17 years of age, and conscripts also work on the land. Despite Cuban hostility, the USA maintains a base at Guantánamo Bay, which comprised 482 naval, 127 marine and 293 army personnel as assessed at November 2009.

Defence Expenditure: The state budget for 2008 allocated 2,290m. pesos to defence and public order.

Minister of the Revolutionary Armed Forces: Lt-Gen. JULIO CASAS REGUEIRO.

Chief of Staff: Lt-Gen. ÁLVARO LÓPEZ MIERA.

Education

Education is universal and free at all levels. Education is based on Marxist-Leninist principles and combines study with manual work. Day nurseries are available for all children after their 45th day, and national schools at the pre-primary level are operated by the State for children of five years of age. Primary education, from six to 11 years of age, is compulsory, and secondary education lasts from 12 to 17 years of age, comprising two cycles of three years each. In 2008/09 primary enrolment included 99% of children in the relevant age-group, while secondary enrolment included 83% of the population in the appropriate age-group. In 2008/09 there were an estimated 710,978 students in higher education. Workers attending university courses receive a state subsidy to provide for their dependants. Courses at intermediate and higher levels lay an emphasis on technology, agriculture and teacher training. A Latin American School of Medicine opened in Havana in 1999. In 2009 budgetary expenditure on education was 9,030.6m. pesos (19.4% of total spending).

Bibliography

For works on the Caribbean generally, see Select Bibliography (Books)

Arboleya, J. *Havana–Miami: The US–Cuban Migration Conflict*. Melbourne, Ocean Press, 1996.

La Revolucion del Otro Mundo: Cuba y Estados Unidos en el horizonte del siglo XXI. Melbourne, Ocean Press, 2007.

Ayorinde, C. *Afro-Cuban Religiosity, Revolution, and National Identity*. Gainesville, FL, University Press of Florida, 2004.

Azicri, M., and Deal, E. (Eds). *Cuban Socialism in a New Century: Adversity, Survival and Renewal*. Gainesville, FL, University Press of Florida, 2005.

Azicri, M., and Kirk, J. M. *Cuba Today and Tomorrow*. Gainesville, FL, University Press of Florida, 2001.

Baez, A. C. *State Resistance to Globalisation in Cuba*. London, Pluto Press, 2004.

Basdeo, S., and Nicol, H. N. (Eds). *Canada, the United States, and Cuba: An Evolving Relationship*. Boulder, CO, Lynne Rienner Publrs, 2002.

Blight, J. A., and Welch, D. A. (Eds). *Intelligence and the Cuban Missile Crisis*. London, Frank Cass, 1998.

Brenner, P., *et al*. *The Cuba Reader: The Making of a Revolutionary Society*. New York, Grove Press, 1998.

Calvo, H., and Declercq, K. *The Cuban Exile Movement: Dissidents or Mercenaries?* Melbourne, Ocean Press, 2000.

Chaffee, W. A., and Prevost, G. (Eds). *Cuba: A Different America*. Lanham, MD, Rowman & Littlefield Publrs, 2002.

Chomsky, A., Carr, B., and Smorkaloff, P. M. (Eds). *The Cuba Reader*. Durham, NC, Duke University Press, 2004.

Chrisp, P. *The Cuban Missile Crisis*. London, Hodder Wayland, 2001.

Cirules, E. *The Mafia in Havana: A Caribbean Mob Story*. Melbourne, Ocean Press, 2004.

Cole, K. *Cuba: From Revolution to Development*. London, Pinter, 1998.

Coltman, L. *The Real Fidel Castro*. New Haven, CT, Yale University Press, 2003.

Eckstein, S. E. *Back from the Future: Cuba Under Castro*. London, Routledge, 2003.

The Immigrant Divide: How Cuban Americans Changed the US and Their Homeland. Abingdon, Routledge, 2009.

Erisman, H. M., and Kirk, J. M. *Redefining Cuban Foreign Policy: The Impact of the 'Special Period'*. Gainesville, FL, University Press of Florida, 2006.

Escalante, F. *The Cuba Project: CIA Covert Operations Against Cuba 1959–62*. St Paul, MN, Consortium, 2004.

Facio, E. (Ed.). *Cuba: Economic Challenges and the Globalization of Captialism*. Lanham, MD, Rowman & Littlefield Publrs, 2007.

Falcoff, M. *Cuba the Morning After: Normalization and its Discontents*. Washington, DC, AEI Press, 2003.

Farber, S. *The Origins of the Cuban Revolution Reconsidered*. Chapel Hill, NC, University of North Carolina Press, 2006.

Fernández, D. J. *Cuba Transitional*. Gainesville, FL, University Press of Florida, 2005.

Fernández, S. J. *Encumbered Cuba*. Gainesville, FL, University Press of Florida, 2002.

Ferrer, A. *Insurgent Cuba: Race, Nation, and Revolution, 1868–1898*. Chapel Hill, NC, University of North Carolina Press, 1999.

Franklin, J. *Cuba and the United States: A Chronological History*. Melbourne, Ocean Press, 1997.

Fuente, A. de la. *A Nation for All: Race, Inequality, and Politics in Twentieth-Century Cuba (Envisioning Cuba)*. Chapel Hill, NC, University of North Carolina Press, 2001.

García Luis, J. (Ed.). *Cuban Revolution Reader: A Documentary History of 40 Years of Revolution*. Melbourne, Ocean Press, 2000.

George, E. *The Cuban Intervention in Angola, 1965–1991: From Che Guevara to Cuito Cuanavale*. London, Routledge, 2005.

González, E., and McCarthy K. *Cuba After Castro: Legacies, Challenges and Impediments*. Santa Monica, CA, RAND Corpn, 2004.

González, M. *Che Guevara and the Cuban Revolution*. London, Bookmarks Publications, 2004.

Afro-Cuban Theology: Religion, Race, Culture, and Identity. Gainesville, FL, University Press of Florida, 2006.

Gott, R. *Cuba: A New History*. New Haven, CT, Yale University Press, 2004.

Gray, A. I., and Kapcia, A. (eds). *The Changing Dynamic of Cuban Civil Society*. Gainesville, FL, University Press of Florida, 2008.

Hirschfield, K. *Health, Politics and Revolution in Cuba since 1898*. Piscataway, NJ, Transaction Publrs, 2009.

Horowitz, I. L. (Ed.). *Cuban Communism, 1959–1995*, 10th edn. New Brunswick, NJ, Transaction Publrs, 2001.

Jenkins, G., and Haines, L. *Cuba: Prospects for Reform, Trade and Investment*. New York, Economist Intelligence Unit, 1995.

Kirk, J. M., and Padura Fuentes, L. *Culture and the Cuban Revolution*. Gainesville, FL, University Press of Florida, 2001.

Klepak, H. *Cuba's Military 1990–2005: Revolutionary Soldiers During Counter-Revolutionary Times*. London, Institute for the Study of the Americas, 2005.

Lambie, G. *Building Cuban Democracy*. Basingstoke, Palgrave Macmillan, 2005.

Leonard, T. M. *Encyclopedia of Cuban-United States Relations*. Jefferson, NC, McFarland & Co, 2003.

Levine, R. *Secret Missions to Cuba*. Basingstoke, Palgrave Macmillan, 2002.

Lievesley, G. *The Cuban Revolution: Past, Present and Future*. Basingstoke, Palgrave Macmillan, 2003.

López, J. J. *Democracy Delayed: The Case of Castro's Cuba*. Baltimore, MD, Johns Hopkins University Press, 2002.

MacDonald, T. H. *The Education Revolution: Cuba's Alternative to Neoliberalism*. London, Manifesto Press, 2009.

McCoy, T. *Cuba on the Verge: An Island in Transition*. New York, Little, Brown USA, 2003.

Meso-Lago, C., and Pérez-López, J. *Cuba's Aborted Reform: Socioeconomic Effects, International Comparisons, and Transition Policies*. Gainesville, FL, University Press of Florida, 2005.

Morales Domínguez, E., and Prevost, G. *United States–Cuban Relations: A Critical History*. Lanham, MD, Lexington Books, 2008.

Morley, M., and McGillion, C. *Cuba, the United States, and the Post-Cold War World: The International Dimensions of the Washington–Havana Relationship*. Gainesville, FL, University Press of Florida, 2005.

Moses, C. *Real Life in Castro's Cuba (Latin American Silhouettes)*. Wilmington, DE, Scholarly Resources, 1999.

Paris, M. L. *Embracing America*. Gainesville, FL, University Press of Florida, 2002.

Pedraza, S. *Political Disaffection in Cuba's Revolution and Exodus (Cambridge Studies in Contentious Politics)*. Cambridge, Cambridge University Press, 2007.

Pérez, Jr, L. A. *Cuba: Between Reform and Revolution*, 2nd edn. Oxford, Oxford University Press, 1995.

Cuba and the United States: Ties of Singular Intimacy, 2nd edn. Athens, GA, University of Georgia Press, 1997.

On Becoming Cuban: Identity, Nationality, and Culture. Chapel Hill, NC, University of North Carolina Press, 1999.

Winds of Change: Hurricanes and the Transformation of Nineteenth-Century Cuba. Chapel Hill, NC, University of North Carolina Press, 2001.

Pérez-López, J. F. *Cuba at a Crossroads (Politics and Economics After the Fourth Party Congress)*. Gainesville, FL, University Press of Florida, 1994.

Pérez-López, J. F., and Alvarez, J. *Reinventing the Cuban Sugar Agroindustry*. Lanham, MD, Rowman and Littlefield Pblrs, 2005.

Pérez-Stable, M. *The United States and Cuba: Intimate Enemies*. Abingdon, Routledge, 2010.

Piñeiro, M. *Che Guevara and the Latin American Revolution*. Melbourne, Ocean Press, 2006.

Purcell, S. K., and Rothkopf, D. (Eds). *Cuba: The Contours of Change*. Boulder, CO, Lynne Rienner Publrs, 2000.

Ritter, A. R. M. (Ed.). *The Cuban Economy (Pitt Latin American Series)*. Pittsburgh, PA, University of Pittsburgh Press, 2004.

Robins, N. A. *The Culture of Conflict in Modern Cuba*. Jefferson, NC, McFarland and Co, 2002.

Robinson, E. *Last Dance in Havana: The Final Days of Fidel and the Start of the New Cuban Revolution*. New York, Free Press, 2004.

Roman, P. *People's Power: Cuba's Experience with Representative Government*. Lanham, MD, Rowman & Littlefield Publrs, 2003.

Roy, J. *The Cuban Revolution (1959–2009): Relations with Spain, the European Union and the United States*. Basingstoke, Palgrave Macmillan, 2009.

Sánchez, G. *Cuba y Venezuela: Reflecciones y Debates*. Melbourne, Ocean Press, 2006.

Saney, I. *Cuba: A Revolution in Motion*. London, Zed Books, 2004.

Shaffer, K. R. *Anarchism and Countercultural Politics in Early Twentieth-Century Cuba*. Gainesville, FL, University Press of Florida, 2005.

Suchlicki, J. *Cuba: From Columbus to Castro and Beyond*. London, Brassey's, 2002.

Sweig, J. E. *Inside the Cuban Revolution: Fidel Castro and the Urban Underground*. Cambridge, MA, Harvard University Press, 2004.

Thomas, H. *Cuba or the Pursuit of Freedom*, revised edn. New York, First Da Capo Press, 1998.

White, M. J. *Missiles in Cuba: Kennedy, Khrushchev, Castro, and the 1962 Crisis*. Chicago, IL, Ivan R. Dee, 1997.

Whitney, R. *State and Revolution in Cuba*. Chapel Hill, NC, University of North Carolina Press, 2001.

Zebich-Knos, M., and Nicol, H. *Foreign Policy Toward Cuba: Isolation or Engagement?* Lanham, MD, Rowman and Littlefield Publrs, 2005.

DOMINICA

Geography

PHYSICAL FEATURES

The Commonwealth of Dominica is found in the central Lesser Antilles, the northernmost of the Windward Islands in the old British West Indies. Early colonization and rule by the French has left its mark on the island, reinforced by the continued French presence among Dominica's nearest neighbours. To the north are the main islands of Guadeloupe, an overseas department of the French Republic, and to the south the island of Martinique, another such department. Dominica is the largest of the anglophone islands in the Lesser Antilles (excluding Trinidad), covering an area of 751 sq km (290 sq miles).

Formed by volcanic activity, which is still prevalent on the island, Dominica is a mountainous land, lush and fertile, the most rugged of the Lesser Antilles. Its physical geography helped the long resistance of the native Carib Amerindians to European colonization. Dominica has the highest mountain in the eastern Caribbean, Morne Diablotins, at 1,447 m (4,749 feet). The high interior is covered by dense rainforest, which accounts for about 60% of the island and is protected by three national parks. The southernmost park, around Morne Trois Pitons (a UNESCO World Heritage Site), is considered to have the richest biodiversity in the Caribbean, but also contains five active volcanoes, fuelling about 50 fumaroles and hot springs, as well as Boiling Lake, one of the largest thermally active lakes in the world (its main rival is in New Zealand). Fertility has encouraged the wooded nature of the hills, and there is rich flora and fauna (including the sisserou or imperial parrot, which features on the country's flag, the red-necked or jacquot parrot, the forest thrush, the blue-headed hummingbird, turtles, a rare iguana and the crapaud—eaten as 'mountain chicken'—this last a large frog, which has found its main haven in Dominica since the devastating volcanic activity on Montserrat in the 1990s). The steep terrain and wet climate also give rise to numerous rivers, streams and waterfalls, many of which are seasonal. Little of the landscape is farmed. There are 148 km (92 miles) of coastline, with reefs offshore, and the island itself is about 47 km long (north–south, the northern end of the island leaning more towards the north-west) and 26 km wide.

CLIMATE

The climate is subtropical and the mountains attract rain, making the island relatively rich in water resources and often humid. The wettest month is August, and the driest months are in February–June. Average annual rainfall is high—in Roseau, the capital on the south-western coast, it is about 2,160 mm (85 ins), but in the mountains it is over some 8,640 mm (340 ins). The terrain makes the risk of flash flooding high, and the island also lies in the possible path of hurricanes, during June–October particularly. Daytime temperatures average between 70°F and 85°F (21°C–29°C), the hottest month being August, but it is much cooler in the highlands, especially at night.

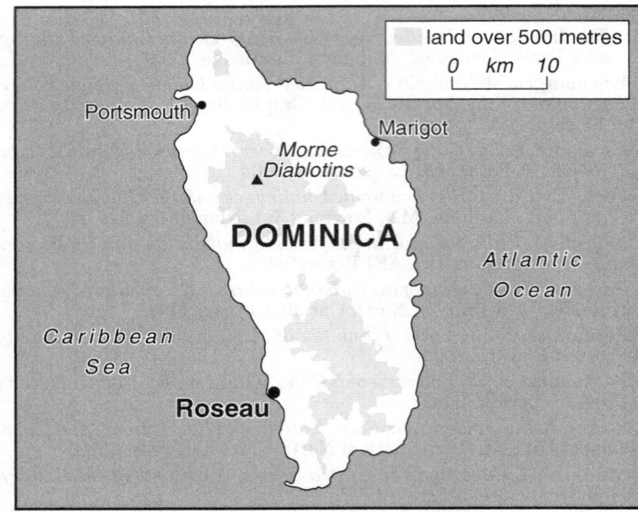

POPULATION

Ethnically, the island population is mainly black, but there are also whites and many of mixed race, as well as a more recent Syrian community. The legacy of previous rulers survives in the only extant Carib population of the West Indies (most living in the 15-sq-km Carib Territory, or Waitukubuli Karifuna area, on the rugged Atlantic coast) and in a thriving French Creole patois, the most widely spoken local dialect. Spoken Carib has not survived. In the north-west an English patois, Kokay, is spoken by the Methodist descendants of freed slaves from Antigua. The official language, however, is English, which is widely spoken, and the main Christian denomination is Roman Catholic (about 62% of the population), with a further 20% adhering to a number of other Christian churches.

The total population was estimated at 71,898 in mid-2009, with about two-fifths of the population living in and around the capital, Roseau, in the south-west, in one of the 10 parishes into which the country is divided. The second town, Portsmouth, is also on the western coast, but at the northern end. On the north-east Atlantic coast, Marigot, near to the airport, is the main town. As mentioned above, Dominica is the only island of the Caribbean to retain some of its pre-Columbian Amerindian population—about 3,000 Caribs, or those of mixed Carib descent, live on the north-eastern coast, just south of Marigot. The island is also noted for having the highest rate of centenarians in the world.

History

MARK WILSON

Dominica is a republic within the Commonwealth. It has a ceremonial President as head of state and a Prime Minister who leads the majority party in the unicameral House of Assembly, where elected representatives sit alongside appointed senators.

Dominica's original Carib Amerindian inhabitants, the Karifuna, knew the island as Waitukubuli—'tall is her body'—and survive in a small community at Salybia in the north-east. The island was given its present name by the explorer Christopher Columbus, who sighted it on Sunday 3 November 1493. Its mountainous topography discouraged early settlement, and it was declared neutral by England and France in 1600 and again in 1686. With the islands of Martinique and Guadeloupe in close proximity, French settlers gradually moved in during the 17th and early 18th centuries. The island was first claimed by the United Kingdom in 1759, and changed hands several times before finally becoming a British possession in 1805. However, the French creole language, aspects of French culture and the Roman Catholic religion remain firmly established today; Dominica is a member of La Francophonie as well as of the Commonwealth.

Despite the island's high rainfall and fertile soil, its broken terrain and poor communications made large-scale plantation agriculture less profitable than on some neighbouring islands. Commercial crops during the colonial period included coffee, cocoa, coconuts (for copra) and limes, as well as sugar. The island remained something of a backwater, although one administrator, Hesketh Bell, initiated significant infrastructural improvements between 1899 and 1905. Dominica formed part of the Leeward Islands Federation from 1833 until 1939.

The first elections with universal suffrage were held in 1951, with candidates supported by the Dominica Trade Union winning the majority of seats. In 1955 the Dominica Labour Party (DLP) was founded by Phyllis Shand Allfrey, a white Dominican and author of a well-known local novel, *The Orchid House*. However, an organized party system emerged more slowly than on most other islands. Dominica joined the Federation of the West Indies in 1958 along with nine other British colonies. When Jamaica and Trinidad and Tobago left in 1962, the Federation collapsed; an attempt to unite the remaining colonies as the 'little eight' was unsuccessful. Along with its neighbours, Dominica became a British Associated State in 1967. While it remained responsible for its internal affairs, the United Kingdom retained control of foreign relations and defence.

After winning an election held in 1971 the DLP was led from 1974 by Patrick John, who became the first Prime Minister upon the granting of independence on 3 November 1978. In February 1979 John announced that a 'Dominica Caribbean Free Port Authority' owned by Don Pierson, a developer from Texas, USA, would be given extensive rights over the northern third of the island. This proposal was abandoned owing to strong popular opposition. However, further disputes followed, including a strike by the civil service. On 29 May, in an attempt to disperse a large demonstration, the Defence Force shot and killed one person and left 10 injured. A general strike by the private sector then led to the resignation of several cabinet ministers, while the President, Frederick Degazon, suddenly left the island on 11 June. The former Governor, Sir Louis Cools-Lartigue, was installed as acting President, but resigned after only one day in office. Following arson attacks on the Court House and Registry shortly afterwards, the political opposition formed a Committee for National Salvation (CNS), together with private sector, business, labour and agricultural organizations. On 21 June, in an improvised procedure, Jenner Armour was sworn in as acting President; he then appointed one of John's former ministers, Oliver Seraphin, as Prime Minister.

These turbulent events were followed in August 1979 by 'Hurricane David', which devastated homes, roads, and the banana crop, leaving 37 people dead and 5,000 injured. In September the island was struck by a second powerful storm, 'Hurricane Frederick'.

The interim Government led by Seraphin was not an unqualified success, not least owing to disputes over the management of hurricane reconstruction efforts. At a general election held on 20 July 1980, Seraphin's followers were soundly defeated by the Dominica Freedom Party (DFP), and Eugenia Charles (later Dame Mary Eugenia Charles) became the Caribbean's first female Prime Minister. Premier Charles developed a strong reputation both within the island and internationally and was an articulate supporter of the invasion of Grenada in 1983.

In March 1981 the new Government stated that members of the small Defence Force were planning a coup to restore Patrick John to office, with the support of US and Canadian 'soldiers of fortune'—members of the extremist right-wing Ku Klux Klan, some of whom were intercepted in New Orleans, Louisiana, USA. The Defence Force was disbanded in April 1982, while John was tried and acquitted of attempting to overthrow the Government in the same year. However, following a retrial in 1985, John was sentenced to a 12-year prison term; he was released before the expiry of his sentence. Meanwhile, in 1985 the DLP, the Democratic Labour Party, the United Dominica Labour Party and the Dominica Liberation Movement united to form the Labour Party of Dominica; however, the merged organization remains known in practice as the DLP.

Although the DFP majority was reduced to a single seat in the general election of May 1990, Charles remained in office until 1995; she was replaced as leader of the DFP by Brian Alleyne, under whose leadership the party was defeated in a general election held on 12 June of that year. The Dominica United Workers' Party (UWP), led by Edison James, won 11 of the 21 seats in the House of Assembly; the DFP and the DLP secured five apiece.

Troubles in the banana industry undermined support for the UWP Government, and there was considerable controversy over its spending proposals, including one for the development of an airport. In a general election in January 2000, the UWP was reduced to nine seats. The DLP, led by Roosevelt (Rosie) Douglas, won 10 seats, securing 43% of the popular vote, and formed a coalition with the DFP, which won two seats. One UWP member subsequently defected from the party and joined the ruling coalition, strengthening the position of the new Government within the House of Assembly.

Douglas died unexpectedlyin October 2000. He was succeeded by his deputy, Pierre Charles.

In 2001 Canada announced that Dominicans travelling to Canada would require visas. This reflected growing international concern over Dominica's economic citizenship programme, under which passports were sold to non-citizens. Following the terrorist attacks in the USA in September, Dominica came under increased pressure to abandon the programme. Negotiations to allow Dominicans to travel without visas to the French Caribbean islands—Guadeloupe and Martinique—in March 2006 subsequently stalled, owing to the French departments' concerns regarding the conduct of illegal immigrants from Dominica, and Attorney-General Ian Douglas' criticism that such an arrangement would prove impractical in conjunction with existing travel restrictions.

In June 2002 the Government announced its intention to reduce the size of the Cabinet in an attempt to reduce expenditure. In July the Dominica Public Service Union organized a large-scale demonstration in the capital, Roseau, to protest against controversial tax increases introduced in a budget intended to bring about economic recovery. In November Frederick Baron, one of the two DFP members of parliament, announced that he would no longer support the Government, leaving it with backing from 11 of the 21 elected members.

With the economic situation remaining difficult, the Government was in a severely weakened condition in the first half of 2003, while the leadership of Charles was strongly questioned from within his own party. After suffering several bouts of ill health, Charles died in January 2004 and was succeeded by the 31-year-old Roosevelt Skerrit, hitherto Minister of Education, Youth and Sports.

In spite of the country's economic difficulties and a stringent austerity programme, Skerrit re-established the Government's popularity. At a general election in May 2005 the DLP took 52% of the popular vote, compared with 43% at the elections in 2000. The party won 12 of the 21 seats, and a further seat was taken by a close ally of the DLP, who ran as an independent; the UWP secured the remaining eight seats (and 44% of the votes cast). The DFP was defeated in each of two constituencies in which it fielded a candidate; however, its leader, Charles Savarin, was appointed as a senator and retained his place in Skerrit's new administration as Minister of Foreign Affairs, Trade, Labour and the Public Service.

The former UWP deputy leader, and spokesperson for finance and planning, Julius Timothy, changed party allegiance in September 2006 to join the DLP Cabinet as Minister of Planning and Economic Development, with additional responsibility for public housing, and for the development of 'offshore' financial services. Timothy also inherited governance of the Economic Citizenship programme, under the terms of which investors from Asia, Eastern Europe and elsewhere were able to purchase Dominican passports. This UWP defection increased the Government's strength to 13 of the 21 elected seats. However, there was some concern over Timothy's role in the previous UWP administration, which had borrowed heavily at commercial rates for an unrealistic airport project, and which seriously mismanaged the 'offshore' financial sector. Ambrose George was again dismissed from the Cabinet (he was at that point responsible for works and infrastructure) in November 2008, reportedly after asking to be paid for assistance in establishing an 'offshore' bank, the principal investor of which had previously been convicted of money-laundering.

The opposition team experienced its own troubles. Leader of the Opposition Edison James resigned from office in July 2007; Earl Williams, who had succeeded James as leader of the UWP the previous year, was inaugurated as his replacement. However, Williams resigned as party leader in August 2008 and subsequently left the island for New York, USA, after allegations that he had misappropriated the funds of legal clients.

At a general election on 18 December 2009 the DLP won a third parliamentary term with 18 of the 21 elected seats and 61.2% of the popular vote, compared with three seats and 34.9% for the UWP, and 2.4% for the DFP. The new UWP leader Ronald Green lost his seat, and the party alleged irregularities, such as special flights being provided for nationals resident overseas returning home to vote. The party also claimed that Skerrit was not qualified to sit in parliament as he had acquired French nationality as a child, in addition to his Dominican citizenship. In protest, the opposition staged a boycott of the House of Assembly, although one opposition member put in a single token appearance. The seats of the remaining two were declared vacant by the Speaker in May 2010. In two by-elections held on 9 July, the UWP retained both seats, declaring that having made its point about the 2009 poll, it would resume its active role as a parliamentary opposition.

Dominica is a comparatively peaceful island. However, murders increased from five in both 2006 and 2007 to eight in 2008 and to 13 in 2009, the latter figure equivalent to 19 per 100,000 population, around 3.5 times the US murder rate. The rising crime rate placed increased demands on the 434-strong police force. There are also reports of attacks on visiting yachts, The police estimate cocaine transshipment at 100 kg–200 kg weekly, while US sources report around 90 ha under marijuana cultivation. Two major traffickers were arrested in 2009, and one in 2008. Although the small 'offshore' financial sector had an uneven regulatory record, the island was not thought to be a major money-laundering risk.

In March 2004, following a visit to the Chinese capital, Beijing, Skerrit announced that Dominica would recognize the People's Republic of China in place of Taiwan. China had agreed to provide US $6m. in budgetary support, equivalent to around 8% of annual recurrent revenue, followed by EC $300m.–$330m. in grant aid for a road, the main hospital, a school and a sports stadium, equivalent in value to some 45% of one year's gross domestic product or 1.5 years' recurrent revenue. An embassy of the People's Republic of China was duly opened in Roseau in June. In 2005 Taiwan initiated legal action to recover US $12m. in debt contracted under assistance programmes in place before 2003.

Dominica's perceived attachment to so-called 'chequebook diplomacy' was criticized again in December 2004 when Japan provided funding of some EC $33m. for the construction of a fisheries complex on the island, allegedly in return for supporting the Japanese Government's pro-whaling stance. Dominica was among other member states of the Organisation of Eastern Caribbean States (OECS) criticized for voting in favour of the proposed lifting of a 20-year moratorium on commercial whaling—tendered by Japan—during the annual meeting of the International Whaling Commission (IWC) in June 2006. In April 2007 Prime Minister Skerrit made an official visit to Japan, following which he announced that Japanese funding for a further fisheries facility had been secured. Skerrit also stated his intention to renew Dominica's support for the Japanese Government's bid to resume commercial whaling. The President of the Caribbean Conservation Association and former Minister of the Environment in the Dominican Government, Atherton Martin, accused his country of behaving like 'an international prostitute' for agreeing to support Japan at the IWC while accepting financial assistance from the Japanese Government. Following Japan's success at the IWC meeting in Alaska, USA, in May, in securing permission to resume whaling activity, Edison James cautioned that the decision could adversely affect Dominica's tourism industry, a significant proportion of which came from whale-watching.

Dominica has developed friendly relations with Venezuela, although there was potential for a divisive dispute over maritime boundaries and the status of tiny Avez Island/Bird Rock 220 km to the west. Dominica benefits from Venezuela's PetroCaribe initiative, and in January 2008 ratified membership of the Alternativa Bolivariana para América Latina y el Caribe (ALBA—the Bolivarian Alternative for Latin America) group, along with Bolivia, Cuba and Nicaragua. Two other OECS members, Antigua and Barbuda and Saint Vincent and the Grenadines, also signed an initial statement supporting the ALBA initiative in February 2007. Venezuela has provided substantial grant aid, and proposed in January 2008 to build a small US $80m. petroleum refinery. At the same time Dominica maintained friendly relations with the USA, the United Kingdom, Canada and France, whose two overseas departments of Guadeloupe and Martinique are Dominica's nearest neighbours.

Economy

MARK WILSON

Dominica is the second smallest country in the Western hemisphere in terms of population, with 71,898 inhabitants living on its 751 sq km in mid-2009. The island has developed a modest middle-income economy, but the per-head gross domestic product (GDP) of US $3,932 in 2009 was marginally the lowest in the Eastern Caribbean. GDP contracted by 3.8% in 2001 and 4.0% in 2002, but then grew steadily at an average annual rate of 4.4% in 2003–08 as grant-funded assistance projects progressed. However, the economy contracted by 0.3% in 2009, according to IMF estimates, with construction declining by 20.9% after a 17.1% expansion in 2008, and investment, tourism and migrant remittances all suffering from the effects of the international recession. The rate of unemployment rose to 25% in 2003, according to World Bank estimates, but has since decreased.

The economic reversal in the early 2000s intensified the Government's financial difficulties; an overall deficit equivalent to around 8% of GDP in 2001 was financed partially through the accumulation of arrears. Debt rose sharply, reaching at least EC $779m. or 131% of GDP in late 2003, and included substantial amounts borrowed at commercial rates. Indeed, the Government has, since June 2002, refused to make payments on 1999 bond issues totalling US $47.5m. from two Trinidadian banks that it claims were illegally structured to Dominica's disadvantage. Total outstanding external debt reached US $231.5m. at the end of 2005. The budget for 2002/03 introduced a 4% stabilization levy (repealed in the 2004/05 budget) on gross annual incomes over EC $9,000 and other measures intended to raise revenue in an attempt to reduce the deficit to 5.2% of GDP. However, major savings on public sector staffing costs were rejected both by the Government and by trade unions.

Donor agencies, including the European Union (EU), the IMF and the World Bank, were closely involved in the discussion of possible measures to stabilize the economy. Concessional borrowing of EC $30m. in late 2002 included assistance from Barbados, Trinidad and Tobago, and Saint Vincent and the Grenadines, as well as from more obvious donor agencies. The IMF in August 2002 agreed a stand-by credit, with performance targets. However, a review of the IMF programme in March 2003 found that the island had failed to meet these targets. The 2003/04 budget included proposals for further reductions in expenditure, including a 5% pay cut for public servants. New policy targets were set in June 2003, and were followed by a US $11.4m. line of credit under the IMF's Poverty Reduction and Growth Facility. An IMF mission in February 2004 found that the new targets had been implemented. A further positive quarterly review followed in May 2004. The expectation of a further 10% reduction in salary costs over two years, to be achieved mainly through reduced staff numbers, was met with some hostility from the Dominica Public Service Union; nevertheless, public sector salary costs were reduced from 17% of GDP in 2002/03 to 13% by 2005/06. The fiscal outlook benefited significantly in March 2004 from an agreement by the People's Republic of China to provide substantial project grant aid in exchange for diplomatic recognition; however, this prompted Taiwan, a substantial existing creditor, to take legal action in November 2005 to recover US $12m. in debt incurred through earlier assistance programmes.

A third tranche of assistance was agreed with the IMF in August 2004, by which time 60% of eligible debt was covered by a restructuring programme. In the financial year ending in June 2005 there was a recurrent surplus of EC $31m., while a primary surplus of 3% of GDP was achieved two years ahead of the target date; further improvements in revenue collection followed the introduction of a value-added tax in 2006 in accordance with IMF recommendations. Creditors holding 70% of Dominica's debt had reached restructuring agreements by November 2005, with outstanding debt down by the end of the year to 108% of GDP—still a very high figure by international standards, but a great improvement on earlier levels. With an increase in capital spending finance, mainly by development grant assistance, GDP began to grow again from 2004, and the Government was able in mid-2005 to reverse the public sector pay reduction imposed in 2003, although a salary 'freeze' remained in effect until July 2006. Public debt was an estimated 95.5% of GDP in 2008, while the overall fiscal balance moved into a small surplus from 2005 (the surplus was equivalent to 0.8% of GDP in 2009). This represented a recovery in the Government's financial position, assisted by major grant inflows, which were equivalent to just over 11% of GDP from 2007 to 2009. A Growth and Social Protection Strategy for the period to 2010 was launched in January 2007, with completion of a three-year Poverty Reduction and Growth Facility at the end of 2006. The Government aimed to achieve a primary fiscal surplus of 1% of GDP in the budget for the financial year starting in July 2009 (based on IMF data released ahead of the July budget presentation). The public sector remains large, accounting for an average of 34.6% of GDP in 2000–04.

In February 2008 the IMF approved a US $3.3m. loan to Dominica to sustain the economy in the short term in light of ongoing reconstruction efforts as a result of 'Hurricane Dean': the loan was repayable from 2011 to 2013 at an interest rate of 0.5%. Damage from the hurricane was estimated at EC $162m., or 20% of GDP, with a loss of export earnings mainly from bananas at 4% of GDP.

Dominica is a member of the Caribbean Community and Common Market, or CARICOM, the larger members of which formed the Caribbean Single Market and Economy (CSME) at the start of 2006, followed by the addition of Dominica and the smaller islands in July. The regional development fund set aside US $250m. to bolster smaller market economies against the abolition of import taxes integral to the CSME, assuaging fears of unequal trading status and expediting the inauguration of the system. Dominica is also a member of the Organization of Eastern Caribbean States, which links nine of the smaller Caribbean territories, while its financial affairs are supervised by the Eastern Caribbean Central Bank, which has its headquarters in Saint Christopher and Nevis.

Agriculture accounted for 17.9% of GDP in 2008, reduced from 25.0% in 1990. The export of bananas to the United Kingdom had been the mainstay of the economy since the 1950s, and Dominica was more dependent on this activity than any other Caribbean country. In 1990 banana exports constituted 92.1% of total merchandise exports and generated 34.4% of foreign exchange earnings, while more than one-half of the country's work-force was involved to some extent with the industry. As a result of changes in the EU's import regime, banana exports decreased from 55,000 metric tons in 1993 to 10,599 tons in 2005, and, after a slight recovery to 11,407 tons in 2006, decreased further to 6,236 tons in 2009, representing an estimated 8.7% of merchandise exports by value. Significant EU grant aid was available for modernizing the banana industry and for enabling economic diversification, although the rate of disbursement was painfully slow. Small farmers produce a wide variety of fruits, vegetables and livestock products for the local market, with some produce exported to Barbados, Antigua and Barbuda, and the neighbouring French Overseas Departments of Martinique and Guadeloupe.

There is a small manufacturing sector, which in 2009 accounted for 4.2% of GDP, declining from 8.3% in 2004. The main exporter was Dominica Colgate Palmolive, which made soap from locally produced copra, as well as detergent and (until 2007) toothpaste, but the company downsized significantly in 2007–09.

The island has two small airports, but neither was capable of accommodating either night flights or long-haul aeroplanes. Connections to Europe and North America are made through larger regional airports such as those in Antigua or Barbados. The former Dominica United Workers' Party Government borrowed heavily at commercial rates to finance an ambitious airport project, which was later thought to have been neither technically nor commercially viable. The Labour Government that succeeded it in 2000 agreed EU funds in 2005 to upgrade the existing airports to allow night flights, and French funds to improve the road connection to the capital, Roseau; the drive currently takes up to two hours. There has also been Venezuelan and other assistance for airport improvements. Airport upgrading and associated road work was in progress in 2010, but running behind schedule, with night flight capability proposed by the end of the year.

There are few sandy beaches, and rainfall is much higher than on most Caribbean islands. These factors, as well as the lack of direct air access, have restricted the development of tourism. However, Dominica's wildlife and natural beauty have attracted visitors interested in the island's flora and fauna. Visitor expenditure rose from US $25m. in 1990 to US $71.6m. in 2008 (19.0% of GDP), declining to US $67.9m. in 2009. Stop-over arrivals totalled 85,271 in 2009, an 8.3% decrease compared with the peak year of 2006. In 2009 some 25.2% of arrivals were from North America and 7.8% from the United Kingdom; the largest groups were business and family visitors from other Caribbean islands. Stop-over tourists were easily outnumbered by the 485,768 cruise ship passengers in 2009; however, this group spends little money ashore, and accordingly brings fewer economic benefits than the numbers would indicate. Of some significance was the student and organizational spending of two US 'offshore' medical schools, the Ross University of Medicine in the north of the island and the smaller and more recently established All Saints University School of Medicine in the south.

There is a small 'offshore' financial sector, with 12,787 international business companies at the end of 2007, one international bank and three officially registered internet gambling operations. Unfortunately, the country has been accused of failing to meet internationally acceptable financial standards. In June 2000 Dominica was listed as a 'non-co-operative jurisdiction' on the issue of money-laundering by the Financial Action Task Force on Money Laundering (FATF, based in Paris, France) and as a harmful tax haven by the Organisation for Economic Co-operation and Development (OECD). Having made regulatory reforms, Dominica was conditionally de-listed by the FATF in October 2002, and is now listed by the US Department of State under 'other jurisdictions monitored' rather than as a country of concern. However, OECD in April 2008 included Dominica on a 'grey' list of countries that did not yet have a significant number of Tax Information Exchange Agreements in place. The 'economic citizenship' programme, under which Dominican nationality can be acquired in return for a cash investment, has been in place, under various guises, since independence. It is viewed with some suspicion internationally, as it is considered open to exploitation by criminals. The programme was relaunched in June 2002, with a fee of US $75,000 for individual applicants; 650 passports were sold in 1996–2002, and retaliatory measures included the imposition of a visa requirement by Canada in December 2001. Negotiations for visa-free travel for Dominicans to the neighbouring French Overseas Departments of Martinique and Guadeloupe collapsed in mid-2006; the existing prohibitive restrictions on immigration to those territories remained in place.

Dominica is at risk from hurricanes, of which the most recent was 'Hurricane Dean' in August 2007. Tropical storms, while less violent, can cause serious damage to the fragile banana plants. The island is also at risk from earthquakes. There are several volcanic centres, which are currently inactive; regional geologists suggest there is a 25% chance of a major eruption within the next 25 years. In the absence of recent eruptions, however, volcanic features such as the Boiling Lake and Valley of Desolation are attractions for the more energetic tourists. An investigation of geothermal power potential was completed in 2009, and proposed an initial 2-MW plant to open in 2011, followed by a further four plants with total capacity of 77 MW by 2017. With peak demand currently at 14.5 MW, this would, if successfully completed, leave a substantial potential for export to neighbouring islands, particularly Martinique and Guadeloupe.

Statistical Survey

Source (unless otherwise stated): Eastern Caribbean Central Bank; internet www.eccb-centralbank.org.

AREA AND POPULATION

Area: 751 sq km (290 sq miles).

Population: 71,727 (males 36,434, females 35,293) at census of 12 May 2001. *Mid-2009* (estimate): 71,898.

Density (mid-2009): 95.7 per sq km.

Population by Age and Sex (31 December 2006): *0–14:* 20,976 (males 10,759, females 10,217); *15–64:* 42,979 (males 22,280, females 20,699); *65 and over:* 7,226 (males 3,200, females 4,026); *Total* 71,180 (males 36,238, females 34,942) (Source: UN, *Demographic Yearbook*.

Population by Ethnic Group (*de jure* population, excl. those resident in institutions, 1981): Negro 67,272; Mixed race 4,433; Amerindian (Carib) 1,111; White 341; Total (incl. others) 73,795 (males 36,754, females 37,041). Source: UN, *Demographic Yearbook*.

Principal Town (population at 1991 census): Roseau (capital) 15,853. *Mid-2009* (UN estimate): Roseau 14,266 (Source: UN, *World Urbanization Prospects: The 2009 Revision*).

Births, Marriages and Deaths (registrations, 2002 unless otherwise indicated): Live births 1,081 (birth rate 15.4 per 1,000); Marriages (1998) 336 (marriage rate 4.4 per 1,000); Deaths 594 (death rate 8.4 per 1,000) (Source: UN, *Demographic Yearbook*). *2006:* Live births 1,058 (birth rate 14.9 per 1,000); Deaths 536 (death rate 7.5 per 1,000) (Source: UN, *Population and Vital Statistics Report*).

Life Expectancy (years at birth, WHO estimates): 74 (males 72; females 77) in 2008. Source: WHO, *World Health Statistics*.

Economically Active Population ('000 persons aged 15 years and over, 2001): Agriculture, hunting, forestry and fishing 5.22; Manufacturing (incl. mining and quarrying) 2.10; Utilities 0.41; Construction 2.42; Wholesale and retail trade, restaurants and hotels 5.12; Transport, storage and communications 1.56; Financing, insurance, real estate and business services 1.14; Community, social and personal services 6.77; *Sub-total* 24.73; Activities not adequately defined 0.08; *Total employed* 24.81; Unemployed 3.05; *Total labour force* 27.86 (males 17.03, females 10.83) (Source: ILO). *Mid-2010* (estimates): Agriculture, etc. 6,000; Total labour force 29,000 (males 17,000, females 12,000) (Source: FAO).

HEALTH AND WELFARE

Key Indicators

Total Fertility Rate (children per woman, 2008): 2.1.

Under-5 Mortality Rate (per 1,000 live births, 2008): 10.

Physicians (per 1,000 head, 1997): 0.5.

Hospital Beds (per 1,000 head, 2005): 3.9.

Health Expenditure (2007): US $ per head (PPP): 550.

Health Expenditure (2007): % of GDP: 6.2.

Health Expenditure (2007): public (% of total): 62.1.

Access to Water (% of persons, 2004): 97.

Access to Sanitation (% of persons, 2004): 84.

Total Carbon Dioxide Emissions ('000 metric tons, 2006): 117.2.

Total Carbon Dioxide Emissions Per Head (metric tons, 2006): 1.6.

Human Development Index (2007): ranking: 73.

Human Development Index (2007): value: 0.814.

For sources and definitions, see explanatory note on p. vi.

AGRICULTURE, ETC.

Principal Crops ('000 metric tons, 2008, FAO estimates): Sweet potatoes 1.9; Cassava 1.2; Yautia (Cocoyam) 4.6; Taro (Dasheen) 11.2; Yams 8.0; Sugar cane 4.8; Coconuts 12.0; Cabbages 0.8; Pumpkins 0.9; Cucumbers 1.8; Carrots 0.6; Bananas 30.0; Plantains 5.8; Oranges 7.2; Lemons and limes 1.1; Grapefruit 17.0; Guavas, mangoes and mangosteens 2.0; Avocados 0.7. *Aggregate Production* ('000 metric tons, may include official, semi-official or estimated data): Fruits (excl. melons) 64.7.

Livestock ('000 head, year ending September 2008, FAO estimates): Cattle 13.5; Pigs 5.0; Sheep 7.6; Goats 9.7; Chickens 190.

Livestock Products ('000 metric tons, 2008, FAO estimates): Cattle meat 0.6; Pig meat 0.4; Chicken meat 0.4; Cows' milk 6.1; Hen eggs 0.2.

Fishing (metric tons, live weight, 2008): Capture 694 (Skipjack tuna 45; Yellowfin tuna 124; Marlins, sailfishes, etc. 107; Common dolphinfish 125); Aquaculture 0; *Total catch* 694.

Source: FAO.

MINING

Pumice ('000 metric tons, incl. volcanic ash): Estimated production 100 per year in 1988–2004. Source: US Geological Survey.

INDUSTRY

Production (2006, metric tons, unless otherwise indicated, preliminary): Laundry soap 3,605; Toilet soap 4,296; Dental cream 1,376; Liquid disinfectant 1,861; Crude coconut oil 855 (2001); Coconut meal 331 (2001); Electricity 85.0 million kWh (2007). Sources: IMF, *Dominica: Statistical Appendix* (September 2007), and UN Industrial Commodity Statistics Database.

FINANCE

Currency and Exchange Rates: 100 cents = 1 Eastern Caribbean dollar (EC $). *Sterling, US Dollar and Euro Equivalents* (31 May 2010): £1 sterling = EC $3.937; US $1 = EC $2.700; €1 = EC $3.344; EC $100 = £25.40 = US $37.04 = €29.91. *Exchange Rate:* Fixed at US $1 = EC $2.70 since July 1976.

Budget (EC $ million, 2009): *Revenue:* Tax revenue 320.6 (Taxes on income and profits 55.9, Taxes on property 9.1, Taxes on domestic goods and services 185.9, Taxes on international trade and transactions 69.6); Other current revenue 29.5; Total 350.1, excl. grants received 61.7. *Expenditure:* Current expenditure 288.5 (Wages and salaries 125.7, Goods and services 84.4, Interest payments 14.1, Transfers and subsidies 64.3); Capital expenditure and net lending 155.1; Total 443.6.

International Reserves (US $ million at 31 December 2009): Reserve position in IMF 0.01; Foreign exchange 64.47; Total 64.48. Source: IMF, *International Financial Statistics*.

Money Supply (EC $ million at 31 December 2009): Currency outside depository corporations 50.68; Transferable deposits 180.69; Other deposits 844.57; *Broad money* 1,075.93. Source: IMF, *International Financial Statistics*.

Cost of Living (Retail Price Index, base: 2005 = 100): All items 105.9 in 2007; 112.6 in 2008; 112.7 in 2009 Source: IMF, *International Financial Statistics*.

Gross Domestic Product (EC $ million at constant 1990 prices): 621.1 in 2007; 643.2 in 2008; 638.0 in 2009. Source: IMF, *International Financial Statistics*.

Expenditure on the Gross Domestic Product (EC $ million at current prices, 2009): Government final consumption expenditure 187.5; Private final consumption expenditure 915.8; Gross fixed capital formation 263.1; *Total domestic expenditure* 1,366.4; Exports of goods and services 374.6; *Less* Imports of goods and services 726.4; Statistical discrepancy 5.2; *GDP in purchasers' values* 1,019.8. Source: IMF, *International Financial Statistics*.

Gross Domestic Product by Economic Activity (EC $ million at current prices, 2008): Agriculture, hunting, forestry and fishing 140.03; Mining and quarrying 9.44; Manufacturing 34.75; Electricity and water 45.41; Construction 94.42; Wholesale and retail trade 112.25; Restaurants and hotels 25.36; Transport 68.73; Communications 32.72; Finance and insurance 86.33; Real estate and housing 25.86; Government services 146.09; Other services 13.85; *Sub-total* 835.24; *Less* Financial intermediation services indirectly measured (FISIM) 64.41; *Gross value added in basic prices* 770.83; Taxes, less subsidies, on products 240.11; *GDP in market prices* 1,010.94.

Balance of Payments (US $ million, 2008): Exports of goods f.o.b. 36.3; Imports of goods f.o.b. –197.3; *Trade balance* –161.0; Services (net) 45.6; *Balance on goods and services* –115.5; Other income (net) –17.7; *Balance on goods, services and income* –133.2; Current transfers (net) 20.9; *Current balance* –112.3; Capital transfers 51.3; Direct investment from abroad 52.1; Portfolio investment (net) 1.2; Other investment (net) 6.5; Net errors and omissions –5.5; *Overall balance* –6.6. Source: IMF, *International Financial Statistics*.

EXTERNAL TRADE

Principal Commodities (US $ million, 2008): *Imports c.i.f.:* Food and live animals 37.1 (Meat and meat preparations 8.1; Cereals and cereal preparations 8.3); Mineral fuels and lubricants 36.3 (Petroleum and petroleum products 33.8); Animal and vegetable oils 7.3; Chemicals, etc. 20.3; Basic manufactures 39.0 (Paper products 6.8; Iron and steel 8.1); Machinery and transport equipment 56.3 (Telecommunications and sound equipment 4.4; Road vehicles 14.5); Miscellaneous manufactured articles 23.2; Total (incl. others) 232.4. *Exports f.o.b.:* Food and live animals 14.9 (Vegetables and roots and tubers 2.8; Bananas 8.0); Stone, sand and gravel 5.4; Chemicals, etc. 17.7 (Perfumes, cosmetics, toilet products, etc. 0.9; Soap 13.3; Disinfectants 0.1); Total (incl. others) 40.0. Source: UN, *International Trade Statistics Yearbook*.

Principal Trading Partners (US $ million, 2008): *Imports c.i.f.:* Barbados 4.2; Brazil 2.8; Canada 6.3; China, People's Republic 4.6; Colombia 2.5; Dominican Republic 5.0; France (incl. Monaco) 3.7; Grenada 3.5; Guyana 3.5; Jamaica 2.3; Japan 10.0; Netherlands 2.9; Saint Lucia 4.1; Saint Vincent and the Grenadines 2.6; Trinidad and Tobago 49.6; United Kingdom 10.7; USA 92.3; Venezuela 4.1; Total (incl. others) 232.4. *Exports f.o.b.:* Anguilla 1.0; Antigua and Barbuda 6.1; Barbados 1.1; France (incl. Monaco) 5.5; Guyana 2.1; Jamaica 6.5; Saint Christopher and Nevis 1.8; Saint Lucia 0.9; Saint Vincent and the Grenadines 1.0; Suriname 0.5; Trinidad and Tobago 3.5; United Kingdom 5.3; USA 1.2; Total (incl. others) 40.0. Source: UN, *International Trade Statistics Yearbook*.

TRANSPORT

Road Traffic (motor vehicles licensed in 1994): Private cars 6,491; Taxis 90; Buses 559; Motorcycles 94; Trucks 2,266; Jeeps 461; Tractors 24; Total 9,985. *2000* (motor vehicles in use): Passenger cars 8,700; Commercial vehicles 3,400. Source: partly UN, *Statistical Yearbook*.

Shipping: *Merchant Fleet* (registered at 31 December 2008): 111 vessels (total displacement 1,018,041 grt) (Source: Lloyd's Register-Fairplay, *World Fleet Statistics*); *International Freight Traffic* ('000 metric tons, estimates, 1993): Goods loaded 103.2; Goods unloaded 181.2.

Civil Aviation (1997): Aircraft arrivals and departures 18,672; Freight loaded 363 metric tons; Freight unloaded 575 metric tons.

TOURISM

Visitor Arrivals: 443,486 (88,035 stop-over visitors, 936 excursionists, 354,515 cruise ship passengers) in 2007; 470,332 (88,725 stop-over visitors, 936 excursionists, 380,671 cruise ship passengers) in 2008; 571,881 (85,271 stop-over visitors, 842 excursionists, 485,768 cruise ship passengers) in 2009.

Tourism Receipts (EC $ million): 201.1 in 2007; 193.2 in 2008; 183.3 in 2009.

COMMUNICATIONS MEDIA

Radio Receivers (1997): 46,000 in use.

Television Receivers (1999): 17,000 in use.

Telephones (2009): 17,500 main lines in use.

Mobile Cellular Telephones (2009): 106,000 subscribers.

Personal Computers: 13,000 (181.9 per 1,000 persons) in 2004.

Internet Users (2009): 28,000.

Broadband Subscribers (2009): 16,000.

Non-daily Newspapers (2004): 3.

Sources: mainly UNESCO, *Statistical Yearbook*, International Telecommunication Union and UN, *Statistical Yearbook*.

EDUCATION

Institutions (1994/95 unless otherwise indicated): Pre-primary 72 (1992/93); Primary 64; Secondary 14; Tertiary 2.

Teachers (2007/08 unless otherwise indicated): Pre-primary 135; Primary 500; General secondary 491; Secondary vocational 15; Tertiary 34 (1992/93).

Pupils (2007/08 unless otherwise indicated): Pre-primary 2,006 (males 1,020, females 986); Primary 8,369 (males 4,293, females 4,076); General secondary 7,162 (males 3,644, females 3,518); Secondary vocational 147; Tertiary 461 (1995/96).

Sources: UNESCO, *Statistical Yearbook*, Institute for Statistics; Caribbean Development Bank, *Social and Economic Indicators*; UN Economic Commission for Latin America and the Caribbean, *Statistical Yearbook*.

Pupil-teacher Ratio (primary education, UNESCO estimate): 16.7 in 2007/08 (Source: UNESCO Institute for Statistics).

Adult Literacy Rate (2004): 88.0%. Source: UN Development Programme, *Human Development Report*.

Directory

The Constitution

The Constitution came into effect at the independence of Dominica on 3 November 1978. Its main provisions are summarized below:

FUNDAMENTAL RIGHTS AND FREEDOMS

The Constitution guarantees the rights of life, liberty, security of the person, the protection of the law and respect for private property. The individual is entitled to freedom of conscience, of expression and assembly and has the right to an existence free from slavery, forced labour and torture. Protection against discrimination on the grounds of sex, race, place of origin, political opinion, colour or creed is assured.

THE PRESIDENT

The President is elected by the House of Assembly for a term of five years. A presidential candidate is nominated jointly by the Prime Minister and the Leader of the Opposition and on their concurrence is declared elected without any vote being taken; in the case of disagreement the choice will be made by secret ballot in the House of Assembly. Candidates must be citizens of Dominica aged at least 40 who have been resident in Dominica for five years prior to their nomination. A President may not hold office for more than two terms.

PARLIAMENT

Parliament consists of the President and the House of Assembly, composed of 21 elected Representatives and nine Senators. According to the wishes of Parliament, the latter may be appointed by the President—five on the advice of the Prime Minister and four on the advice of the Leader of the Opposition—or elected. The life of Parliament is five years.

Parliament has the power to amend the Constitution. Each constituency returns one Representative to the House who is directly elected in accordance with the Constitution. Every citizen over the age of 18 is eligible to vote.

THE EXECUTIVE

Executive authority is vested in the President. The President appoints as Prime Minister the elected member of the House who commands the support of a majority of its elected members, and other ministers on the advice of the Prime Minister. Not more than three ministers may be from among the appointed Senators. The President has the power to remove the Prime Minister from office if a resolution expressing no confidence in the Government is adopted by the House and the Prime Minister does not resign within three days or advise the President to dissolve Parliament.

The Cabinet consists of the Prime Minister, other ministers and the Attorney-General in an ex officio capacity.

The Leader of the Opposition is appointed by the President as that elected member of the House who, in the President's judgement, is best able to command the support of a majority of the elected members who do not support the Government.

The Government

HEAD OF STATE

President: Dr Nicholas Liverpool (assumed office 1 October 2003; began a second term 2 October 2008).

CABINET
(July 2010)

The Government is formed by the Dominica Labour Party.

Prime Minister and Minister of Finance, Foreign Affairs and Information Technology: Roosevelt Skerrit.

Attorney-General: Francine Baron Royer.

Minister of Housing, Lands, Settlement and Water Resources: Reginald Austrie.

Minister of Agriculture and Forestry: Matthew Walter.

Minister of Employment, Trade, Industry and Diaspora Affairs: Dr John Colin McIntyre.

Minister of the Environment, Natural Resources, Physical Planning and Fisheries: Dr Kenneth Darroux.

Minister of Education and Human Resource Development: Peter Saint Jean.

Minister of Social Services, Community Development and Gender Affairs: Gloria Shillingford.

Minister of Culture, Youth and Sports: Justina Charles.

Minister of Tourism and Legal Affairs: Ian Douglas.

Minister of Information, Telecommunication and Constituency Empowerment: Ambrose George.

Minister of Health: Julius Timothy.

Minister of Public Works, Energy and Ports: Rayburn Blackmore.

Minister of Carib Affairs: Ashton Graneau.

Minister of National Security, Labour and Immigration: Charles Savarin.

Parliamentary Secretary in the Office of the Prime Minister, responsible for Information Technology: Kelvar Darroux.

Parliamentary Secretary in the Ministry of Public Works: Johnson Drigo.

Parliamentary Secretary in the Ministry of Housing, Lands, Settlement and Water Resources: Ivor Stephenson.

MINISTRIES

Office of the President: Morne Bruce, Roseau; tel. 4482054; fax 4498366; e-mail presidentoffice@cwdom.dm; internet presidentoffice .gov.dm.

Office of the Prime Minister: 6th Floor, Financial Centre, Roseau; tel. 2663300; fax 4488960; e-mail pmoffice@cwdom.dm.

All other ministries are at Government Headquarters, Kennedy Ave, Roseau; tel. 4482401.

CARIB TERRITORY

This reserve of the remaining Amerindian population is located on the central east coast of the island. The Caribs enjoy a measure of local government and elect their chief.

Chief: Garnet Joseph.

Waitukubuli Karifuna Development Committee (WAIKADA): Salybia, Carib Territory; tel. 4457336; e-mail waikada@cwdom.dm.

Legislature

HOUSE OF ASSEMBLY

Speaker: Alix Boyd-Knight.

Clerk: Deirdre Jules.

Senators: 9.

Elected Members: 21.

General Election, 18 December 2009

Party	% of votes	Seats
Dominica Labour Party (DLP)	61.2	18
Dominica United Workers' Party (UWP)	34.9	3
Dominica Freedom Party (DFP)	2.4	—
Others	1.5	—
Total	100.0	21

Election Commission

Electoral Office: Cnr Turkey Lane and Independence St, Roseau; tel. 2663336; fax 4483399; e-mail elections@cwdom.dm; internet electoraloffice.gov.dm; Chief Elections Officer MERINA WILLIAMS.

Political Organizations

Dominica Freedom Party (DFP): 37 Great George St, Roseau; tel. 4482104; fax 4481795; e-mail freedompar2@yahoo.com; internet www.thedominicafreedomparty.com; f. 1968; Leader JUDITH PESTAINA.

Dominica Labour Party (DLP): 18 Hanover St, Roseau; tel. 4488511; e-mail dlp@cwdom.dm; internet www.togetherwemust.net; f. 1985 as a merger and reunification of left-wing groups, incl. the Dominica Labour Party (f. 1961); Leader ROOSEVELT SKERRIT; Deputy Leader AMBROSE GEORGE.

Dominica Progressive Party: Roseau; Leader ERNEST TAVERNIER.

Dominica United Workers' Party (UWP): 37 Cork St, POB 00152, Roseau; tel. 6134508; fax 4498448; e-mail secretariat@uwpdm.com; internet www.uwpdm.com; f. 1988; Leader RONALD GREEN.

People's Democratic Movement (PDM): 22 Upper Lane, POB 2248, Roseau; tel. 2354171; e-mail para@cwdom.dm; internet www.dapdm.org; f. 2006; Leader Dr WILLIAM E. 'PARA' RIVIERE.

Real Labour Party (RLP): Roseau; f. 2009 by mems of Labour Party of Dominica; Leader Dr SAM CHRISTIAN; Co-ordinator ADENAUER WARSHWOA DOUGLAS.

Diplomatic Representation

EMBASSIES IN DOMINICA

China, People's Republic: Ceckhall, Morne Daniel, POB 2247, Roseau; tel. 4490198; fax 4400088; e-mail chinaemb_dm@mfa.gov.cn; internet dm.chineseembassy.org; Ambassador DENG BOQING.

Cuba: Morne Daniel, POB 1170, Roseau; tel. 4490727; e-mail cubanembassy@cwdom.dm; internet embacu.cubaminrex.cu/dominica; Ambassador OSVALDO COBACHO MARTÍNEZ.

Venezuela: 20 Bath Rd, 3rd Floor, POB 770, Roseau; tel. 4483348; fax 4486198; e-mail embven@cwdom.dm; Ambassador CARMEN MARTÍNEZ DE GRIJALVA.

Judicial System

Justice is administered by the Eastern Caribbean Supreme Court (based in Saint Lucia), consisting of the Court of Appeal and the High Court. One of the 16 puisne judges of the High Court is resident in Dominica and presides over the Court of Summary Jurisdiction. The District Magistrate Courts deal with summary offences and civil offences involving limited sums of money (specified by law).

Puisne Judge: DAVIDSON BAPTISTE.

Registrar: REGINALD WINSTON.

Religion

Most of the population profess Christianity, but there are some Muslims, Bahá'ís and Jews. The largest denomination is the Roman Catholic Church.

CHRISTIANITY

The Roman Catholic Church

Dominica comprises the single diocese of Roseau, suffragan to the archdiocese of Castries (Saint Lucia). According to official figures from 2001, 62% of the population are Roman Catholics. The Bishop participates in the Antilles Episcopal Conference (currently based in Port of Spain, Trinidad and Tobago).

Bishop of Roseau: Rt Rev. GABRIEL MALZAIRE, Bishop Arnold Boghaert Catholic Centre, Turkey Lane, POB 790, Roseau; tel. 4482837; fax 4483404; e-mail bishop@cwdom.dm; internet www.dioceseofroseau.org.

The Anglican Communion

Anglicans in Dominica, representing less than 1% of the population in 2001, are adherents of the Church in the Province of the West Indies. The country forms part of the diocese of the North Eastern Caribbean and Aruba. The Bishop is resident in Antigua, and the Archbishop of the Province is the Bishop of the Bahamas and the Turks and Caicos Islands.

Other Christian Churches

According to official figures from 2001, 6% of the population are Seventh-day Adventists, 6% are Pentecostalists, 4% are Baptists and 4% are Methodists. In addition to the Christian Union Church, other denominations include Church of God, Presbyterian, the Assemblies of Brethren and Moravian groups, and the Jehovah's Witnesses.

Christian Union Church of the West Indies: Dominica Island District, 1 Rose St, Goodwill, POB 28, Roseau; tel. 4482725; e-mail marcusfrancis@hotmail.com; internet www.cccuhq.org; Island District Supt MARCUS FRANCIS.

BAHÁ'Í FAITH

National Spiritual Assembly: 79 Victoria St, POB 136, Roseau; tel. 4483881; fax 4488460.

The Press

The Chronicle: Wallhouse, Loubiere, POB 1764, Roseau; tel. 4487887; fax 4480047; e-mail thechronicle@cwdom.dm; f. 1909; Friday; progressive independent; Editor J. ANTHONY WHITE (acting); Gen. Man. J. ANTHONY WHITE; circ. 3,200.

Official Gazette: Office of the Prime Minister, 6th Floor, Financial Centre, Kennedy Ave, Roseau; tel. 2363300; fax 4488960; e-mail cabsec@cwdom.dm; weekly; circ. 550.

The Sun: Sun Inc, 50 Independence St, POB 2255, Roseau; tel. 4484744; fax 4484764; e-mail acsun@cwdom.dm; f. 1998; weekly; Editor CHARLES JAMES.

The Times: 15 Kennedy Ave, Roseau; tel. 4403949; fax 4404056; e-mail timesnews@cwdom.dm; f. 2004; Friday; Editor MATT PELTIER.

The Tropical Star: Canefield, Roseau; tel. 4484634; fax 4485984; e-mail tpl@cwdom.dm; weekly; Editor NIGEL LAWRENCE; circ. 3,000.

Broadcasting and Communications

TELECOMMUNICATIONS

Regulatory Authority

National Telecommunications Regulatory Commission of Dominica (NTRC Dominica): 42-2 Kennedy Ave, POB 649, Roseau; tel. 4400627; fax 4400835; e-mail secretariat@ntrcdm.org; internet www.ectel.int/ntrcdm; f. 2000 as the Dominican subsidiary of the Eastern Caribbean Telecommunications Authority (ECTEL)—established simultaneously in Castries, Saint Lucia, to regulate telecommunications in Dominica, Grenada, Saint Christopher and Nevis, Saint Lucia and Saint Vincent and the Grenadines; Chair. JULIAN JOHNSON.

Major Service Providers

Digicel Dominica: Wireless Ventures (Dominica) Ltd, POB 2236, Roseau; tel. 6161500; fax 4403189; e-mail customercare.dominica@digicelgroup.com; internet www.digiceldominica.com; acquired Cingular Wireless' Caribbean operations and licences in 2005; owned by an Irish consortium; acquired Orange Dominica in 2009; Chair. DENIS O'BRIEN; Country Man. RICHARD STANTON.

LIME: Hanover St, POB 6, Roseau; tel. 2551000; fax 2551111; e-mail pr@cwdom.dm; internet www.time4lime.com; fmrly Cable & Wireless Dominica; name changed as above 2008; Caribbean CEO RICHARD DODD.

BROADCASTING

Radio

Dominica Broadcasting Corporation: Victoria St, POB 148, Roseau; tel. 4483283; fax 4482918; e-mail dbsmanager@dbcradio.net; internet www.dbcradio.net; f. 1971; govt station; daily broadcasts in English; 2 hrs daily in French patois; 10 kW transmitter on the medium wave band; FM service; programmes received throughout Caribbean excluding Jamaica and Guyana; Chair. IAN MUNRO.

Kairi FM: 42 Independence St, POB 931, Roseau; tel. 4487331; fax 4487332; e-mail hello@kairifmonline.com; internet www.kairifm.com; f. 1994; CEO FRANKIE BELLOT; Gen. Man. STEVE VIDAL.

Voice of Life Radio (ZGBC): Gospel Broadcasting Corpn, Loubiere, POB 205, Roseau; tel. 4487017; fax 4400551; e-mail volradio@cwdom.dm; internet www.voiceoflife.com; f. 1975; 24 hrs daily FM; Gen. Man. CLEMENTINA MUNRO.

Television

There is no national television service, although there is a cable television network serving 95% of the island.

Marpin Telecom and Broadcasting Co Ltd: 5–7 Great Marlborough St, POB 2381, Roseau; tel. 5004107; fax 5002965; e-mail inettel@mtb.dm; internet www.marpin.dm; f. 1982, present name adopted in 1996; commercial; cable and internet services.

Finance

(cap. = capital; res = reserves; dep. = deposits; m. = million; brs = branches; amounts in East Caribbean dollars)

The Eastern Caribbean Central Bank, based in Saint Christopher, is the central issuing and monetary authority for Dominica.

Eastern Caribbean Central Bank—Dominica Office: Financial Centre, 3rd Floor, Kennedy Ave, POB 23, Roseau; tel. 4488001; fax 4488002; e-mail eccbdom@cwdom.dm; internet www.eccb-centralbank.org; Country Dir EDMUND ROBINSON.

BANKS

FirstCaribbean International Bank (Barbados) Ltd: Old Street, POB 4, Roseau; tel. 4482571; fax 4483471; internet www.firstcaribbeanbank.com; f. 2002 following merger of Caribbean operations of Barclays Bank PLC and CIBC; Barclays relinquished its stake to CIBC in June 2006; Exec. Chair. MICHAEL MANSOOR; CEO JOHN D. ORR; Country Dir PAUL FRAMPTON.

National Bank of Dominica: 64 Hillsborough St, POB 271, Roseau; tel. 2552300; fax 4483982; e-mail customersupport@nbd.dm; internet www.nbdominica.com; f. 1976 as the National Commercial Bank of Dominica; name changed as above after privatization in Dec. 2003; cap. 11.0m., res 18.6m., dep. 620.2m. (June 2008); 49% govt-owned; Chair. NORMAN ROLLE; Man. Dir GREGORY DE GANNES; 6 brs.

DEVELOPMENT BANK

Dominica Agricultural, Industrial and Development Bank (AID Bank): cnr Charles Ave and Rawles Lane, Goodwill, POB 215, Roseau; tel. 4482853; fax 4484903; e-mail aidbank@cwdom.dm; internet www.aidbank.com; f. 1971; responsible to Ministry of Finance, Foreign Affairs and Information Technology; provides finance for the agriculture, tourism, housing, education and manufacturing sectors; total assets 125.3m. (June 2006); Chair. AMBROSE SYLVESTER; Gen. Man. KINGSLEY THOMAS.

STOCK EXCHANGE

Eastern Caribbean Securities Exchange: based in Basseterre, Saint Christopher and Nevis; tel. (869) 466-7192; fax (869) 465-3798; e-mail info@ecseonline.com; internet www.ecseonline.com; f. 2001; regional securities market designed to facilitate the buying and selling of financial products for the eight member territories—Anguilla, Antigua and Barbuda, Dominica, Grenada, Montserrat, Saint Christopher and Nevis, Saint Lucia and Saint Vincent and the Grenadines; Chair. Sir K. DWIGHT VENNER; Gen. Man. and CEO TREVOR E. BLAKE.

INSURANCE

In 2006 there were 32 insurance companies operating in Dominica. Several British, regional and US companies have agents in Roseau. Local companies include the following:

First Domestic Insurance Co Ltd: 19–21 King George V St, POB 1931, Roseau; tel. 4498202; fax 4485778; e-mail insurance@cwdom.dm; internet www.firstdomestic.dm; f. 1993; Man. Dir and CEO CURTIS TONGE; Gen. Man. ROBERT TONGE.

Jeff's Services Ltd: 3 Goodwill Rd, Roseau; tel. 4483501; fax 4488856.

Windward Islands Crop Insurance Co (Wincrop): Vanoulst House, Goodwill, POB 469, Roseau; tel. 4483955; fax 4484197; f. 1987; regional; coverage for weather destruction of, mainly, banana crops; Man. KERWIN FERREIRA; brs in Grenada, Saint Lucia and Saint Vincent.

Trade and Industry

DEVELOPMENT ORGANIZATIONS

Invest Dominica Authority: Financial Centre, 1st Floor, Roseau; tel. 4482045; fax 4485840; e-mail investdominica@investdominica.dm; internet www.investdominica.dm; f. 1988 as National Development Corpn (NDC) by merger of Industrial Development Corpn (f. 1974) and Tourist Board; NDC disbanded in April 2007 by act of parliament and replaced by two separate entities, Invest Dominica and Discover Dominica (see Tourism) from 1 July 2007; promotes local and foreign investment to increase employment, production and exports; Chair. YVOR NASSIEF; Exec. Dir RHODA LETANG.

National Development Foundation of Dominica: POB 313, Roseau; tel. 4483240; fax 4480225; e-mail ndfd@cwdom.dom; f. 1981; promotes investment of funds and resources from local businesses and foreign agencies to facilitate economic and social devt projects in Dominica.

Organisation of the Eastern Caribbean States Export Development Unit (EDU): Financial Centre, 4th Floor, Kennedy Ave, POB 769, Roseau; tel. 4482240; fax 4485554; e-mail eduinfocenter@oecs.org; internet www.oecs.org/edu; f. 1997 as Eastern Caribbean States Export Devt and Agricultural Diversification Unit; reformed as above in 2000; OECS regional devt org.; Exec. Dir COLIN BULLY.

INDUSTRIAL AND TRADE ASSOCIATIONS

Dominica Association of Industry and Commerce (DAIC): 14 Church St, POB 85, Roseau; tel. and fax 4491962; e-mail daic@cwdom.dm; internet www.daic.dm; f. 1972 by a merger of the Manufacturers' Asscn and the Chamber of Commerce; represents the business sector, liaises with the Govt, and stimulates commerce and industry; 100 mems; Pres. GENEVIEVE ASTAPHAN; CEO ACHILLE CHRIS JOSEPH.

Dominica Banana Producers Ltd (DBPL): Vanoulst House, 2nd Floor, Charles Ave, POB 1620, Roseau; tel. 4482671; fax 4486445; e-mail dbpl@cwdom.dm; f. 1934 as Dominica Banana Growers' Asscn; restructured 1984 as the Dominica Banana Marketing Corpn; renamed as above in 2003; state-supported, scheduled for privatization; Chair. LUKE PREVOST; Gen. Man. RAYMOND AUSTRIE.

Dominica Export-Import Agency (DEXIA): Bay Front, POB 173, Roseau; tel. 4482780; fax 4486308; e-mail info@dexia.dm; internet www.dexia.dm; f. 1986; replaced the Dominica Agricultural Marketing Board and the External Trade Bureau; exporter of Dominican agricultural products, trade facilitator and importer of bulk rice and sugar; Chair. MARGARET GEORGE.

EMPLOYERS' ORGANIZATION

Dominica Employers' Federation: 14 Church St, POB 1783, Roseau; tel. 4482314; fax 4484474; e-mail def@cwdom.dm; f. 1966; Pres. ACKROYD BIRMINGHAM.

UTILITIES

Regulatory Body

Independent Regulatory Commission (IRC): 42-2 Kennedy Ave, 3rd Floor, Roseau; tel. 4406634; fax 4406635; e-mail admin@ircdominica.org; internet www.ircdominica.org; f. 2006 to oversee the electricity sector; Exec. Dir LANCELOT MCCARSKY.

Electricity

Dominica Electricity Services Ltd (Domlec): 18 Castle St, POB 1593, Roseau; tel. 2256000; fax 4485397; e-mail support@domleconline.com; internet www.domlec.dm; national electricity service; 72% owned by WRB Enterprises Ltd (USA) since takeover of the Commonwealth Devt Corpn's (United Kingdom) stake in 2004; Chair. ROBERT BLANCHARD, Jr; Gen. Man. COLLIN GROVER.

Water

Dominica Water and Sewerage Co Ltd (DOWASCO): 3 High St, POB 185, Roseau; tel. 4484811; fax 4485813; e-mail dowasco@cwdom.dm; internet www.dowasco.com; state-owned; Chair. LARRY BARDOUILLE; Gen. Man. BERNARD ETTINOFFE.

TRADE UNIONS

Dominica Amalgamated Workers' Union (DAWU): 43 Hillsborough St, POB 137, Roseau; tel. 4482343; fax 4480086; e-mail wawuunion@hotmail.com; f. 1960; Gen. Sec. ELIAS LEAH SHILLINGFORD (acting); 500 mems (1996).

Dominica Association of Teachers: 7 Boyd's Ave, POB 341, Roseau; tel. and fax 4488177; e-mail dat@cwdom.dm; internet www.dateachers.4t.com; Pres. CELIA NICHOLAS; Gen. Sec. ISABELLA PRENTICE; 630 mems (1996).

Dominica Public Service Union (DPSU): cnr Valley Rd and Windsor Lane, POB 182, Roseau; tel. 4482102; fax 4488060; e-mail dcs@cwdom.dm; f. 1940; registered as a trade union in 1960; representing all grades of civil servants, including firemen, prison officers, nurses, teachers and postal workers; Pres. MERVIN ANTHONY; Gen. Sec. THOMAS LETANG; 1,400 mems.

Dominica Trade Union: 70–71 Independence St, Roseau; tel. 4498139; fax 4499060; e-mail domtradun@hotmail.com; f. 1945; Pres. HAROLD SEALEY; Gen. Sec. LEO J. BERNARD NICHOLAS; 400 mems (1995).

National Workers' Union: 102 Independence St, POB 387, Roseau; tel. 4485209; fax 4481934; e-mail icss@cwdom.dm; f. 1977; Pres.-Gen. RAWLINGS F. A. JEMMOTT; Gen. Sec. FRANKLIN FABIEN; 450 mems (1996).

Waterfront and Allied Workers' Union: 43 Hillsborough St, POB 181, Roseau; tel. 4482343; fax 4480086; e-mail wawuunion@hotmail.com; f. 1965; Sec.-Treas. CURTIS AUGUSTUS; 1,500 mems.

Transport

ROADS

In 1999 there were an estimated 780 km (485 miles) of roads, of which about 50.4% was paved; there were also numerous tracks. A three-year Road Improvement Programme was announced in May 2007, under the Ninth European Development (EDF) National Indicative Programme, and was to include an allocation of EC $8m. towards financing the development and maintenance of the country's road network. Planned construction of an important road link between Petite Soufriere and Rosalie under the Ninth EDF, at an estimated cost of $12m., was yet to begin in 2009.

SHIPPING

A deep-water harbour at Woodbridge Bay serves Roseau, which is the principal port. Several foreign shipping lines call at Roseau, and there is a high-speed ferry service between Martinique and Guadeloupe, which calls at Roseau eight times a week. Ships of the Geest Line call at Prince Rupert's Bay, Portsmouth, to collect bananas, and there are also cruise ship facilities there. There are other specialized berthing facilities on the west coast.

Dominica Air and Seaport Authority (DASPA): Woodbridge Bay, Fond Cole, POB 243, Roseau; tel. 4484131; fax 4486131; e-mail daspa@cwdom.dm; f. 1972; air transit, pilotage and cargo handling; Gen. Man. BENOIT BARDOUILLE.

CIVIL AVIATION

Melville Hall Airport, 64 km (40 miles) from Roseau, and Canefield Airport, 5 km (3 miles) from Roseau, are the two airports on the island. A EC $15m. contract to upgrade Melville Hall Airport was signed with a French construction company in August 2004 and the Government redirected funds—which had been partly provided by the European Union—from the previous (Dominica United Workers' Party) administration's plan to build a brand new international airport for the development. The Government of Venezuela also contributed $9m. towards the expansion. Construction was expected to be completed by November 2009. A scheme to rebuild the road from Roseau to the airport at a cost of $54m., funded by the French Government, was expected to commence in the same year. The regional airline LIAT (based in Antigua and Barbuda, and in which Dominica is a shareholder) acquired its troubled rival, Caribbean Star Airline (also headquartered in Antigua and Barbuda), in late 2007. The two airlines had separately offered almost identical schedules, which, now consolidated, provide daily services and, together with Air Caraïbes, connect Dominica with all the islands of the Eastern Caribbean, including the international airports of Puerto Rico, Antigua, Guadeloupe and Martinique.

Tourism

The Government has designated areas of the island as nature reserves, to preserve the beautiful, lush scenery and the rich, natural heritage that constitute Dominica's main tourist attractions. Birdlife is particularly prolific, and includes several rare and endangered species, such as the Imperial parrot. There are also two marine reserves. Tourism is not as developed as it is among Dominica's neighbours, but the country is being promoted as an 'eco-tourism' and cruise destination. There were an estimated 571,881 visitors in 2009 (of whom 485,768 were cruise ship passengers). Receipts from tourism totalled an estimated EC $183.3m. in 2009.

Discover Dominica Authority: Financial Centre, 1st Floor, Roseau; tel. 4482045; fax 4485840; e-mail tourism@dominica.dm; internet www.discoverdominica.com; f. 1988 following merger of Tourist Board with Industrial Devt Corpn; CEO and Dir of Tourism COLIN PIPER.

Dominica Hotel and Tourism Association (DHTA): 17 Castle St, POB 384, Roseau; tel. 4403430; fax 4403433; e-mail dhta@cwdom.dm; internet www.dhta.org; Pres. SIMON WALSH; 98 mems.

Defence

The Dominican Defence Force was officially disbanded in 1981. There is a police force of about 325, which includes a coastguard service. The country participates in the US-sponsored Regional Security System.

Education

Education is free and is provided by both government and denominational schools. There are also a number of schools for the mentally and physically handicapped. Education is compulsory for 10 years between five and 15 years of age. Primary education begins at the age of five and lasts for seven years. Enrolment at primary schools during the academic year 2007/08 included an estimated 72% of children in the relevant age-group. Secondary education, beginning at 12 years of age, lasts for five years. In 2007/08, according to UNESCO estimates, enrolment at secondary schools included 68% of pupils in the relevant age-group. A teacher-training college and nursing school provide further education, and there is also a branch of the University of the West Indies on the island. In 2005 the Government announced that funding provided by Libya would pay for the construction of a primary school in Portsmouth and a high school in Goodwill, near Roseau. The 2008/09 budget allocated EC $13.6m. for educational assistance.

Bibliography

For works on the Caribbean generally, see Select Bibliography (Books)

Baker, P. L. *Centring the Periphery: Chaos, Order and the Ethnohistory of Dominica*. Kingston, University of the West Indies Press, 1996.

Barriteau, E. and Cobley, A. (Eds) *Enjoying Power: Eugenia Charles and Political Leadership in the Commonwealth Caribbean*. Kingston, University of the West Indies Press, 2006.

Honychurch, L. *The Dominica Story: A History of the Island*. Oxford, Macmillan Caribbean, 1995.

Paravisini-Gebert, L. *Phyllis Shand Allfrey: A Caribbean Life*. Piscataway, NJ, Rutgers University Press, 1996.

THE DOMINICAN REPUBLIC

Geography

PHYSICAL FEATURES

The Dominican Republic comprises almost two-thirds of the island of Hispaniola (Isla Española) in the Greater Antilles. It lies at the eastern end of the island, with Haiti to the west of the land border that runs for 360 km (224 miles), from north to south, across the widest part of Hispaniola. The next nearest neighbours are Puerto Rico, a US Commonwealth territory 120 km to the east (across the Mona Passage), and the Turks and Caicos Islands, a British territory 145 km to the north. The country has 1,288 km of coastline and a total area of 48,734 sq km (18,816 sq miles), including 597 sq km of inland waters. Although less than one-half the size of Cuba, the Dominican Republic is the second largest country of the insular Caribbean and about the same size as Costa Rica.

The Dominican Republic occupies that part of Hispaniola that tapers eastwards—in the south, this is from the Pedernales peninsula, which is just east of the border with Haiti and thrusts southwards to culminate in Cabo Beata. Like Haiti, the Dominican Republic is very rugged and mountainous (80%), but, unlike its neighbour, its hillsides have not been denuded of woodland. The highlands are cleft by fertile valleys, many of them broad, and there is one fairly extensive range of coastal plain, named for the capital, Santo Domingo, narrow to the west of the city, but broad and running to the end of the island in the east. The northern boundary of this plain is the range of hills called the Cordillera Oriental, which parallels the Atlantic coast, like the higher, north-western range, the Cordillera Septentrional. The highest mountains of the island and, indeed, of the West Indies are found in the Cordillera Central, where rise Pico Duarte (3,175 m or 10,420 ft) and its near twin, La Pelona. The Cordillera Central occupies the centre of the island, running eastwards out of the Massif du Nord in Haiti and eventually curving southwards to the Caribbean. A mere 85 km to the south-west of Pico Duarte is the lowest point in the Caribbean, where, 46 m below sea level, is the bitter lake, the 200-sq km Lago Enriquillo, in hot, arid surroundings between the rocky dryness of the remaining two mountain ranges, the Sierra de Neiba and, to the south of Enriquillo, the Sierra de Baharuco (a continuation of the Massif du Selle, in Haiti). The high, forested mountains of the Dominican Republic attract good rainfall, though the Cordillera Central tends to shadow the south-west of the country, but there are also some important rivers. The longest river of the Dominican Republic, watering the Ceiba Valley, is the north-westward-flowing Yaque del Norte, which exits into the sea near the border with Haiti. Other major rivers are the westward-flowing Yuna, the southward-flowing Yaque del Sur and, running into Haiti, the Artibonite. The main offshore islands, which are not significant in territorial extent, are Saona (south of the south-eastern end of the island) and the uninhabited Beata (off Cabo Beata). To the west of each is a smaller island, Catalina and Alto Velo, respectively. There are also three lacustrine islands in Enriquillo and some sandy cays off the northern coast. The range of the terrain and weather conditions makes for a wide variety of environments, ranging from the arid tropical forests of the west, for instance, to the pine woodland of the highlands. Native mammals are few and endangered, notably the hutia (*jutía*), a small rodent, the solenodon, an insectivore, and the manatee or sea cow. Birds are more numerous and include the endemic Hispaniolan woodpecker. There is a variety of parrots, parakeets and hummingbirds.

CLIMATE

The climate is subtropical maritime, experiencing little seasonal variation in temperature and with exposure to hurricanes for some months from the middle of the year, but particularly in September. The Dominican Republic suffers occasional flooding and more regular droughts, but generally

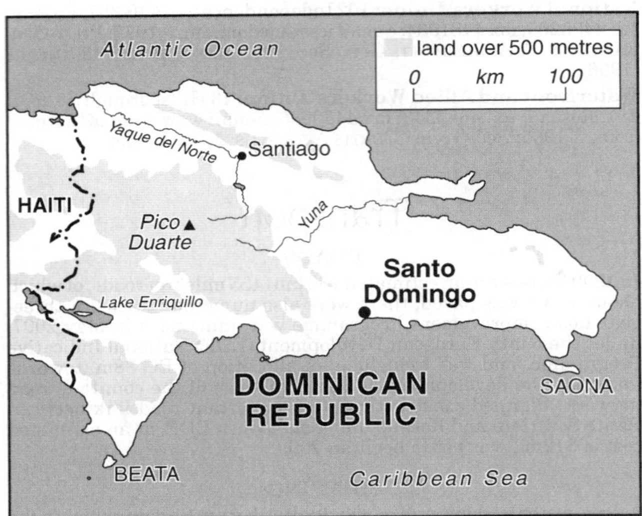

has good rainfall, although it is very affected by the geography of the island. Rainfall is greater with altitude and with exposure to the north-eastern trade winds off the Atlantic, so the Cordillera Septentrional can receive more than 2,500 mm (98 ins) per year, on average, but the valleys between ranges can be much dryer. The average annual temperature is about 25°C (77°F), with little seasonal variation, but, again, altitude has a major influence (below-freezing temperatures have been recorded atop Pico Duarte) and the north can be noticeably cooler under the influence of weather fronts coming out of the north.

POPULATION

Santo Domingo was the first Spanish capital in the Americas and the centre of early colonial expansion. African slaves began to arrive in the city in the 1520s, to replace the disappearing Amerindian population as labour. The proportion of black slaves in what is now called the Dominican Republic was never as high as in the French part of Hispaniola (Saint-Domingue, now Haiti); however, they still constituted an important part of the population and were later the object of 'liberating' incursions by their free western neighbours. Meanwhile, the mixing of Spanish and African stock produced the majority mixed-race population of today (65%), although social conditions have ensured that colour has remained an important issue into the present, with a complex vocabulary for skin colour and ethnic identity evolving. Whites and blacks each account for about 15% of the population now, because although many of the descendants of the original Spanish settlers fled at the time of independence amid fears of Haitian aggression, the ruling class considered it important to encourage new white immigration. Thus, groups of settlers from the Canary Islands (Spain) and Italy settled in the country, although there were also Syrians (known locally as Turcos), who came to establish businesses, and sugar-plantation workers from the anglophone Virgin and Leeward Islands (known as Cocolos). However, Spanish is the official language and the population remains overwhelmingly Roman Catholic, at least in nominal adherence. African traditions have also insinuated themselves into the religious scene, usually in parallel to more orthodox ecclesiastical practice. There is also an element of reconstructed *Taíno* (Amerindian) belief systems (the perceived legitimacy of which can also be observed in racial claims), all of which contribute to the local voodoo (*vodú dominicana*).

Connected to this is a widespread belief in and fear of witchcraft (*brujería*).

The total population of the Dominican Republic, according to official projections, was 9.9m. in 2010, making it the second most populous country of the Antilles. Social conditions are marked by income inequality and the fact that almost one-third of the population is under 14 years of age. There is a large immigrant Haitian population, most of whom have entered the country for work and often illegally. The capital and largest city, Santo Domingo (with a population of 2.2m. at mid-2010, according to a UN estimate), which is located midway along the southern coast, is constituted as a special National District (Distrito Nacional), in addition to the 31 provinces into which the country is divided. The second city of the republic is Santiago de los Caballeros (622,101 at the 2002 census), in the north-west, in the fertile and productive Ceiba Valley.

History

CHARLES ARTHUR

Revised for this edition by the editorial staff

The original inhabitants of the island on which Christopher Columbus landed in 1492 were the indigenous Tainos. They called their land Quisqueya, but, in honour of the Spanish monarchs who sponsored his voyage, Columbus named it La Isla Española (Hispanola). The Taino population, estimated to number 500,000 in 1492, was drastically reduced by disease and the brutal treatment administered by the Spanish. By the mid-16th century the genocide was complete and, in need of an alternative source of labour, the colonists began to import African slaves.

The first Spanish settlements were founded on the north coast, but as the colonists spread out in search of gold, they soon discovered the fertile plains in the centre of the country, an area known as the Cibao. A capital, Santo Domingo, was established on the south coast, and developed into the first European-style city in Latin America. With gold discoveries proving disappointingly small, Spanish colonial attentions turned instead to Mexico and Peru. Although the city of Santo Domingo remained an important staging post between Europe and the mainland of Central and South America, within a few decades of its establishment, the colony itself was receiving little attention.

During the 17th century European adventurers, many of French origin, began to settle and cultivate the coastal plains of the largely abandoned western part of the island. In 1697 Spain ceded these lands to France, and the French colony of Saint-Domingue quickly developed into a prosperous sugar-exporting slave economy, overshadowing its neighbour. The Spanish colony, Santo Domingo, as it was known, remained sparsely populated. The slave revolt that began in French Saint-Domingue in August 1791 initiated a chaotic and violent period, during which Spanish, French and British armies, and rebellious slaves, fought for control of the island. In 1795 Spain surrendered control of its colony to France, and then, between 1801 and 1803, Toussaint Louverture, leader of the slave insurrection, took control of the whole island. In 1803 the French regained control of Santo Domingo, but the same year suffered a final defeat in the west. Saint-Domingue became the independent black republic of Haiti in early 1804. Five years later the French abandoned their interest in the island, and Santo Domingo was handed back to Spain. In 1822 Haiti occupied its eastern neighbour, remaining until the declaration of Dominican independence in 1844. The new Dominican Republic was, however, plagued by political strife and violence, and in 1861 Spain granted a request to recolonize. This remarkable move proved a dismal failure, and after a 'War of Restoration' between Dominican nationalists and Spanish sympathizers, independence was regained in 1865.

The late 19th and early 20th centuries were periods of political and economic instability, broken only by the dictatorship of Ulises Heureaux (1882–99), and the 1916–24 occupation by the USA. During the late 1920s the head of the Dominican Army, Rafael Leonidas Trujillo Molina, established political control, and in May 1930 was elected President.

Trujillo's rule quickly developed into a dictatorship that was to last until 1961. Holding power direct as President or via 'puppet' leaders, Trujillo used coercion, bribery and blackmail to ensure the loyalty of his supporters, and torture and murder to repress his opponents. The regime was propped up by an ideology that endlessly stressed the nation's Hispanic, Catholic and white roots, and portrayed neighbouring Haiti and its people as a primitive, black, African threat. In 1937 a notorious episode in Trujillo's nation-building campaign saw the deployment of the Dominican armed forces into the previously barely governed regions near the border with Haiti, and the massacre of over 20,000 black people suspected of being Haitians.

Over time, the dictator and his family came to control 80% of the country's industrial production, including two-thirds of a booming sugar industry. Administrations in the USA viewed Trujillo with a mixture of admiration and distrust, but generally tolerated a regime that came to be regarded as an ally. However, following the 1959 Cuban revolution, US strategists decided that the dictator's excesses were making the country vulnerable to a Communist takeover. The traditional Dominican oligarchy had grown increasingly resentful of the Trujillo family's monopoly of economic and political power, and in May 1961 a group of middle-class Dominicans, acting with US intelligence support, had Trujillo assassinated.

Elections were held in December 1962, and Juan Bosch Gaviño, leader of the social democratic Partido Revolucionario Dominicano (PRD—Dominican Revolutionary Party), promising land reform and job creation, won an overwhelming victory and was inaugurated in February 1963. However, Bosch achieved little, and after only seven months was overthrown by a military coup. The military appointed a civilian junta, but it failed to establish any form of stability, and in 1965 armed conflict broke out between supporters and opponents of the exiled Bosch. In April, using the pretext of a looming Communist takeover, the USA deployed a large force of marines to side with the anti-Bosch faction. The Organization of American States (OAS) oversaw the establishment of a provisional Government, and new elections were held in June 1966. In the months preceding the deeply flawed elections, hundreds of PRD supporters were assassinated, and a strong military presence at polling stations ensured an easy victory for Joaquín Balaguer, the candidate favoured by the USA and the Dominican élite.

Balaguer established an authoritarian regime that carried out a brutal campaign of repression against PRD activists. As a result, the main opposition party boycotted elections in 1970 and 1974, handing Balaguer two further victories. The opposition's disarray deepened in 1973 when Bosch resigned from the PRD and formed his own new party, the Partido de la Liberación Dominicana (PLD—Party of Dominican Liberation). For three consecutive terms, Balaguer opened the country to foreign investment and enjoyed significant development assistance from the USA. A period of economic prosperity saw diversification into tourism and industrial free trade zones.

Pressure from the USA prompted a much more open electoral contest in May 1978, and the PRD's Silvestre Antonio Guzmán Fernández was elected President. Guzmán's Government had some success with its efforts to weaken the armed forces' influence on Dominican politics by dismantling the officer hierarchy that had supported Trujillo and Balaguer. However, it failed either to deliver the benefits expected by its supporters or efficiently to manage the economy. Despite its failings, the PRD won a second term in 1982, but the new Government led by President Salvador Jorge Blanco proved even more corrupt and incompetent than its predecessor. When an economic crisis prompted the application of austerity measures in 1984, popular protests against the Government degenerated into riots and military repression. With the left wing of the PRD fiercely criticizing the Government, elections held in May 1986 were won again by Balaguer and his Partido Reformista Social Cristiano (PRSC—Reformist Social Christian Party).

The second period of Balaguer government was one of instability and contestation. Economic problems fuelled increasing conflict between the authorities and a growing popular movement for social and political change. During 1988 a wave of strikes and anti-Government protests were met with fierce repression by the police and military. Balaguer was able to win yet another election in 1990 only because the opposition vote, although a majority, was divided between José Francisco Peña Gómez's PRD and Bosch's PLD.

The economy continued to falter, and in 1991 Balaguer was obliged to negotiate a new anti-inflationary austerity agreement with the IMF. Price controls and reductions in government expenditure led to more strikes and public protests. The 1994 elections saw Balaguer again facing the challenge of the PRD's Peña Gómez. The election campaign was dominated by racist slurs against Peña Gómez, with suggestions that his alleged Haitian ancestry made him unfit to govern. Amid allegations of widespread fraud, Balaguer was adjudged to have won a very narrow victory. In the face of deep popular discontent over what many felt was a stolen victory, Balaguer reached agreement with the PRD to limit his term of office to 18 months (later extended to two years) and to prohibit future Presidents from seeking consecutive terms in office.

The next presidential election was held in May 1996, and for the first time in three decades, Balaguer, by this time aged 89 and completely blind, was not a candidate. His influence on the outcome was, none the less, profound, as he refused to support the PRSC's candidate, who polled just 15% of the votes, and instead courted the PLD. None of the candidates achieved the 50% or more votes required for an outright victory according to a new voting system, and the two leading candidates, the PRD's Peña Gómez and the PLD's Leonel Fernández Reyna, entered a second round contest. A remarkable political alliance between lifetime foes, Balaguer and Bosch, resulted in PRSC and PLD supporters uniting in support of Fernández, ensuring his victory over Peña Gómez.

There were high expectations that the 43-year-old, US-educated Fernández would bring an end to the dominance of vested political and economic interests. However, his party, the PLD, was barely represented in the legislature, the Congreso Nacional (Congress), and the new President struggled to gain approval for intended reforms. Legislative elections in 1998 improved the PLD's position in the Congreso Nacional, but the party remained well short of a majority. The PRD's grip on the legislature allowed it to obstruct Fernández's initiatives. Stymied at home, Fernández focused on building up the country's links in the region, travelling extensively on diplomatic visits, and in 1998 negotiating free trade agreements with the Central American republics and the Caribbean Community (CARICOM).

By the 2000 presidential election there had been a rapprochement between Balaguer and his party, and the veteran politician stood as the PRSC candidate, while the PLD, unable to field the incumbent, Fernández, nominated Danilo Medina Sánchez as its nominee. The PRD's long-serving leader, Peña Gómez, had died in early 1998, and its candidate was Rafael Hipólito Mejía Domínguez. Mejía won 49.9% of the vote, against Medina's 24.9% and Balaguer's 24.6%. After Medina conceded defeat, the election commission, the Junta Central Electoral, awarded victory to Mejía, even though he had just failed to secure more than one-half of the votes cast.

The Mejía presidency proved immensely controversial. Public discontent grew rapidly as the country plunged into an economic crisis from 2002. Prices increased exponentially, salaries stagnated and jobs were lost. Persistent power cuts provoked public protests that frequently degenerated into violent clashes with the security services.

The Mejía administration responded by tightening monetary policy and implementing austerity measures, but only succeeded in pushing the economy into recession. The Government's standing fell further in April 2003 when it was forced to take over the country's second largest commercial bank, Banco Intercontinental (Baninter), after it collapsed because of widespread fraud. The Baninter rescue provoked public outrage when it was revealed that many leading politicians in previous administrations, including Mejía (a former Minister of Agriculture), had received illicit payments.

In foreign policy, Mejía was more successful, developing good relations with the US Administration of President George W. Bush by supporting US policy, in particular by contributing Dominican troops to the US-led international force that invaded Iraq in 2003. In 2004 the President also negotiated the inclusion of the Dominican Republic in a planned Central American Free Trade Agreement (which became known as DR-CAFTA) with the USA.

During the latter half of 2003 rising prices and the effects of further austerity measures led to a series of violent protests across the country. Clashes between protesters and police resulted in a number of deaths and hundreds of injuries. Anti-Government feeling increased when energy generators cut electricity supplies after the Government and distributors failed to pay their debts. Mejía moved to pre-empt a planned general strike by deploying the military and ordering the arrest of more than 100 activists and union leaders. Another nation-wide 48-hour general strike was held at the end of January 2004, and again the authorities deployed police and soldiers to patrol poor neighbourhoods of major cities.

In 2002 a constitutional amendment had been adopted allowing a President to serve two consecutive terms, and in early 2003 Mejía announced he would seek the PRD's candidacy for the 2004 presidential election. His re-election bid was not only unpopular with the public, but also met fierce opposition from within his own party. Senior figures, such as Vice-President Milagros Ortiz Bosch and party Chairman Hatuey Decamps, who were widely believed to harbour their own presidential ambitions, decried what they described as a betrayal of party principles. None the less, Mejía's candidacy was confirmed in January 2004.

In the months preceding the election Mejía attempted to recoup some of his lost support among the public by spending heavily on public works projects. Further street protests and anti-Government strikes indicated that this largesse failed to change public perceptions, and this was confirmed by the election result. The PLD's Fernández won an outright victory in the first round, held on 16 May 2004, polling 57.1% of the vote against Mejía's 33.7%. The PRSC's Rafael Eduardo Estrella Virella polled just 8.7%, a disastrous result for a party that had dominated Dominican politics for decades under Balaguer. Following the death of Balaguer in 2002, the PRSC had suffered from splits among party leaders, and these divisions only widened in the months preceding the election when three prominent leaders had supported the candidacy of the PLD's Fernández.

On taking office on 16 August 2004, Fernández immediately fulfilled a campaign promise to reduce the size of the armed forces. In a move designed to break the close ties that existed between his predecessor and the senior officer corps, 130 generals were given early retirement. Fernández was more hesitant about taking action on another pre-election pledge, combating government corruption, and caused controversy by selecting a number of officials for his new administration who had allegedly been involved in dubious dealings during his first presidency. Neither did he authorize judicial investigations into officials from the Mejía administration widely believed to have engaged in corruption. The reluctance to pursue PRD leaders was a tacit recognition of that party's strong position in the Congreso Nacional, and the need to avoid open conflict with it if his Government was to advance its planned legislation. In the Senado (Senate) the PRD held an overwhelming majority, with 29 of the 32 seats, while Fernández's PLD held only one. In the lower house, the Cámara de Diputados (Chamber of Deputies), the PLD was better placed, with 42 seats, but still lagged far behind the PRD, which held 72 of the 150 seats. A major priority for the new Government was securing congressional approval for DR-CAFTA. The Agreement had been brokered by the Mejía administration, but was strongly supported by the new administration. It was ratified by the Congreso in September 2005, but final implementation did not begin until March 2007.

The new Government struggled to resolve a number of issues that had undermined its predecessor. A crime wave, variously attributed to the economic crisis, the influence of drugs-traffickers and the impact of criminal deportees from the USA, continued to rage during the first year of Fernández's second presidency. Impeded by a weak and often corrupt police force, the authorities finally took decisive action in July 2005 when large numbers of police officers were deployed in marginalized neighbourhoods in Santo Domingo and the second largest city, Santiago. Criminal activity declined in these areas, but increased in previously relatively safe middle-class residential areas. Further measures were implemented in early 2006, including the provision of better communications and transport equipment for the police, and restrictions on the sale of alcohol.

Fernández also faced difficulties in trying to overcome the country's chronic electricity crisis. In mid-2006 a heat wave prompted increased demand for electricity for air-conditioning and refrigeration, and the country was once again beset by power cuts lasting between eight and 16 hours a day. With energy generation heavily dependent on oil imports, soaring prices in 2006 created further problems. The electricity sector remained one of the economy's key structural weaknesses. The new Government had more success with other aspects of the economy, making significant advances to counter the mismanagement and overspending of the Mejía presidency. An austerity budget was accepted by the Congreso Nacional, and at the beginning of 2005 negotiations with the IMF produced a crucial stand-by agreement, opening the way for additional multilateral disbursements.

The steps taken by the administration restored confidence in the economy and produced a strong recovery from the crisis of 2003–04. Public approval of this performance was reflected by the results of the legislative elections held in May 2006. Fernández's party, the PLD, won a major victory, securing comfortable working majorities in both chambers: the PLD secured 22 of the 32 seats in the Senado and 96 of the 178 seats in a newly enlarged Cámara de Diputados. In the months preceding the elections there had been speculation that a tentative electoral alliance between the main opposition parties, the PRD and the PRSC, would prevail. In response, the PLD had concluded a tactical alliance with a group of small parties, including the right-wing nationalist Fuerza Nacional Progresista (FNP), a move that showed how far the PLD had departed from its leftist origins.

Relations with Haiti became increasingly strained from 2006 as the neighbouring country's dire economic situation continued to prompt large numbers of Haitians to cross the border in search of a livelihood. Although Dominican employers were content to hire Haitian labour when necessary, the influx of Haitians was regarded by right-wing Dominicans as a threat that would fundamentally alter the country's ethnic composition. With the FNP stoking anti-Haitian prejudice, there were numerous incidents of violence against Haitians in the border regions, and the Dominican Army was repeatedly deployed to arrest and deport Haitian immigrants; nearly 20,000 Haitians were deported in 2006 and a further 17,000 in 2007. In early 2008 the Dominican military moved more troops to the border region following several incidents in which Haitians allegedly stole cattle and took them across the border into Haiti. Anti-Haitian sentiment grew when, following an outbreak of avian influenza in parts of the Dominican Republic, the Haitian authorities imposed a ban on the import of poultry and eggs from its neighbour. The Dominican Government was forced to buy large quantities of eggs and chickens from producers who would otherwise have gone out of business because of the ban. During 2008 poverty in Haiti was exacerbated by a series of natural disasters and continuing economic woes. At the same time, there was increased hardship in the Dominican Republic, prompting increased tensions around the perennially thorny issue of illegal Haitian immigrants. On the domestic front, with the PLD in firm control of both the executive and the legislature, public expectations were high. However, despite impressive economic growth, most Dominicans did not feel that their standard of living had increased as a result. A series of tax reforms in late 2006 created conflict with a previously supportive business sector, and there was growing disillusionment among the middle classes over the Government's general performance, particularly with regard to the rise of crime and criminal violence and the failure to reduce chronic electricity shortages.

In the months leading up to the May 2008 presidential election the Government faced a number of difficulties, including a series of corruption scandals and continuing labour unrest. Unions staged strikes, and for several weeks there were regular stoppages and demonstrations by teachers, taxi drivers and doctors. The protesters demanded higher public spending and salary increases, with transport drivers claiming that the rising cost of fuel required the authorities to increase fares. At the same time there was a constant stream of disclosures and allegations of misuse of public funds. However, despite these problems, Fernández's personal charisma and his success in restoring economic stability allowed him to retain his popularity. The main opposition candidate, the PRD's Miguel Vargas Maldonado, failed to dispel public perceptions that he had a strong connection to former President Mejía, for whom he served as Secretary of State for Public Works and Communications. Many Dominicans appeared to regard the Mejía Government as more corrupt than its successor, and remained distrustful of a party that had led the country into a financial crisis and profound economic instability in 2003–04. Heavy state spending, including increased subsidies and increases in the state payroll, and major public works such as the hastily completed Santo Domingo metro, shored up Fernández's election bid, and he secured an outright victory in the first round, held on 16 May, with 53.8% of valid votes cast. Vargas obtained 40.5% and the PRSC's Amable Aristy Castro just 4.6%, an even worse result than the party's disastrous showing in 2004. Four other candidates together polled a total of just 1.1%.

Fernández was inaugurated for his second consecutive term in August 2008 and enjoyed the traditional 'honeymoon' period afforded to every new administration. For example, serious problems surrounding the national electricity supply—there were frequent prolonged blackouts throughout the country—were initially tolerated by the public because of a general belief that the energy crisis was the result of high international oil prices. However, the Government's subsequent inability to guarantee the electricity supply, even after oil prices fell sharply, provoked violent public demonstrations towards the end of 2008. These prompted leading business organizations to propose sweeping reforms that included the privatization of the distribution companies. Critics claimed that political bureaucracy and incompetence had impaired the system, and that only professional private management could correct it.

By early 2009 public criticism of the Fernández Government had increased, with education, health and crime the prime areas of concern. A series of reports on the state of Dominican public education uniformly condemned its low quality and exposed a whole range of structural and curricular problems. The health sector also suffered from tighter fiscal conditions. The 2009 budget left many hospitals lacking funds to maintain adequate medical supplies or facilities. Crime became a major issue as the authorities struggled to cope with a rise in kidnapping, violent crime and drugs-trafficking.

Further public discontent with the PLD Government was incited when a large number of corruption cases came to light, suggesting an increasing lack of government accountability. One well-publicized case involved a clerk at the Dominican Consulate in the USA who was arrested in December 2008 for using his privileged visa status to smuggle Dominicans into the country. Another case concerned the PLD Senator for San Pedro de Macorís, who, while under investigation in the USA for Medicaid and tax fraud, was revealed to have been absent from most Senate sessions because he had been running a full-time dental clinic in New York, USA.

By mid-2009 the Government's inability to provide regular electricity, adequate water supply, and security against crime had sparked increasing public anger. These omissions, in tandem with a failure to execute needed infrastructural projects at the municipal level, provoked daily demonstrations in several cities. Many local public works projects, including bridges, roads, sewer lines and public buildings, remained paralysed for lack of funds. In another sign of increasing popular mobilization against the Government, demonstrations and strikes orchestrated by the Colegio Médico Dominicano (CMD—Dominican Medical Association) on the part of public health care employees gained momentum. A strike organized by the trade union federation for health workers, Coordinadora de los Gremios de la Salud, commenced in late July, with the police using tear gas to disperse protests by strikers. Meanwhile, a 48-hour general strike took place in support of demands for improvements in the provision of electricity and other public services, while protesters demonstrated outside the offices of the state electricity company, the Corporación Dominicana de Empresas Eléctricas Estatáles (CDEEE), to demand an end to power shortages. In August, amid allegations of nepotism and mismanagement, President Fernández replaced Rhadamés Segura as Executive Vice-President of the CDEEE. In September, following a decline in fiscal revenues resulting largely from the global economic downturn, the Government was forced to initiate formal negotiations with the IMF on a new stand-by arrangement; this was approved in November.

In October 2009 the Cámara de Diputados adopted amendments to more than 40 articles of the Constitution, despite public protests and criticism from civil society groups that opposed the more socially conservative provisions. The reforms stipulated a complete ban on abortion and defined marriage as being solely between a man and a woman. An unlimited number of non-consecutive presidential terms was to be permitted, thus allowing Fernández to contest the presidency again in 2016, following a term out of office. Among other provisions, administrative corruption of public officials was made a constitutional offence, while trade unionism, strikes, public education and swift justice with the presumption of innocence were established as constitutional rights. The revised Constitution came into force on 26 January 2010.

An earthquake with a magnitude of 7.0 devastated Haiti in January 2010, killing more than 100,000 people. In response, the Dominican Government waived visa restrictions for Haitians seeking emergency medical care, authorized nearly 300 flights carrying aid, donated US $11m. and despatched more than 100 soldiers to aid UN forces in stabilizing the country. This latter move was initially resisted by the Haitian Government, but it subsequently acquiesced.

The PLD achieved a decisive victory in legislative and municipal elections conducted on 16 May 2010, securing 31 of the Senado's 32 seats and 105 of the 183 seats in the enlarged Cámara de Diputados. The PRSC, which had formed an alliance with the PLD, took the remaining seat in the upper chamber and three seats in the lower chamber, where the PRD won 75 seats. The PLD also secured control of 92 of the 155 municipalities (20 more than in the 2006 elections). Voter turnout was low, at 56.4%, while polling was also marred by violence, in which five people were reportedly killed, and opposition accusations of voting irregularities and misuse of state funds by the PLD. The PLD's strong performance was attributed to signs of recovery in the economy and the popularity of social welfare programmes introduced by Fernández, as well as the failure of the divided PRD to present itself as a viable alternative. Under the amended Constitution, the newly elected legislators, mayors and councillors would exceptionally serve a term of six years (rather than four) to enable legislative, municipal and presidential elections to be held concurrently from 2016.

Economy

CHARLES ARTHUR

Revised for this edition by the editorial staff

As a Spanish colony until the mid-18th century, the economy of the Dominican Republic had languished, and cattle-rearing was the most important economic activity. Following independence, the growth of a sugar cane industry helped improve economic performance, but, despite a diversification into coffee and tobacco production, it contracted again in the early part of the 20th century. In the late 1960s and 1970s there was a period of economic expansion driven by international loans, high sugar prices on the world market, and President Joaquín Balaguer's extravagant public works programmes. During the 1980s loans ceased, and the economy struggled under the burdens of trade and budget deficits and heavy debts. Free trade zone manufacturing, tourism and services overtook agriculture as the dominant sectors of the economy. Economic growth in the second half of the 1980s and the early 1990s was erratic, reflecting bouts of government austerity policies, varying trends in the manufacturing-for-export free zone, construction and tourism sectors, as well as problems with the country's electricity supply. Then, after a decade of little to no growth, the economy grew in the late 1990s, expanding at an average rate of 7.7% per year from 1996 to 2000. This growth, based on increased activity in the tourism, construction, energy and manufacturing sectors, continued in 2001 and 2002; however, in 2003 there was negative growth, reflecting the Government of Rafael Hipólito Mejía Domínguez's mismanagement and corruption, and lower US demand for Dominican manufactured goods. There was modest growth again in 2004, and following the presidential election victory of Leonel Fernández Reyna in that year, the macroeconomic situation showed dramatic improvements. Inflation fell sharply in late 2004, and the Fernández administration successfully renegotiated debt repayments with the international community. Fiscal and financial targets of a stand-by agreement with the IMF were met, and in 2005 real gross domestic product (GDP) growth registered 9.3%. In 2006 GDP grew by 10.7%, one of the fastest rates in the world, as strong growth of US demand supported the recovery from the 2003–04 crisis. However, in 2007 real GDP growth slowed to 8.5%, partly as a consequence of the increase in international competition arising from trade liberalization under the Dominican Republic-Central American Free Trade Agreement (DR-CAFTA), which came into force in March 2007. The GDP growth rate slowed still further in 2008 and 2009, to 5.3% and to 3.5%, respectively, as the export-oriented sectors of the economy, notably mining and free trade zone manufacturing, suffered the effects of the global downturn. In November 2009 the IMF approved a 28-month stand-by arrangement, worth approximately US $1,700m., to support the Government's strategy to stabilize the economy. However, the deceleration in GDP experienced in 2009 was less severe than expected, mainly owing to significant expansion in the final quarter of the year, which continued into the first quarter of 2010, when year-on-year growth of 7.5% was recorded, as exports, imports and tax revenue all increased.

In the early years of the 21st century the population grew at around 1.5% per year. It numbered 9.9m. in 2010, according to official projections. The population density of 202.8 per sq km is one of the lowest in the Caribbean region. The composition of the Dominican labour force has undergone a profound shift over the last 50 years. In 1960 the agricultural sector employed 73% of the labour force; by the end of the 1980s it accounted for 35%, and by April 2010 the figure was just 15%. According to the central bank, the labour force totalled 4,368,912 in April

2010. Some 25% of employed workers were engaged in providing education, health, social and community services, while 22% of the employed labour force worked in wholesale and retail trades, 11% in manufacturing, and 8% in transport and communications. In April 2010 the official unemployment rate stood at 14.4%, having declined from 14.9% in October 2009.

An estimated 500,000 Haitians, nearly all of them undocumented, also live and work in the Dominican Republic. Haitian labour underpinned the sugar industry throughout the 20th century when workers were contracted for the duration of the cane harvest and then sent back. Over recent decades tens of thousands of Haitians have crossed the border illegally in search of a living, and they provide an important source of unskilled, casual labour in all forms of agriculture, as well as in the construction and tourism sectors.

Official and unofficial emigration throughout the 20th century has created a large expatriate population in the USA, predominantly in the New York City metropolitan area. These migrants provided an important contribution to the general economic health of their homeland by regularly sending remittances to family members in the Dominican Republic. At times of economic hardship, such as in 2003 and 2009, these remittances are crucial for families facing unemployment and poverty. The value of total remittances (both workers' and social) was estimated to have increased from US $1,877m. in 2000 to a preliminary $3,393m. in 2008, representing some 7% of GDP. The value of remittances to the Dominican Republic declined by 5.8% in 2009, to a preliminary $3,207.0m., as remittance flows to all of Latin America fell, in large part because of a slowdown in the US construction sector (82% of remittances entering the Dominican Republic come from the USA). Preliminary estimates indicated a year-on-year increase in the value of remittances to the Dominican Republic of 5.2% in the first quarter of 2010, reflecting an improvement in the US economy.

Since colonial times, the largest and most productive agricultural region has been the Cibao valley, situated in the north of the country. The main sugar-producing areas have been on the plains in the east and south-east. Traditional agriculture has been declining since the early 1980s under the weight of several adverse factors, including high interest rates, price controls, lack of investment, the subsidized sale by the Government of imported agricultural and livestock products, foreign competition, and tariffs on imported inputs. Despite a steady decline in importance over recent decades, agriculture (including livestock, forestry and fishing) continued to be one of the mainstays of the economy, providing employment for 546,299 people, according to a central bank survey conducted in April 2010. Agricultural exports have long ceased to be of critical importance to the economy. The traditional crops, sugar, coffee, cocoa and tobacco, accounted for approximately 40% of all exports in 1996, but in 2009 their value had fallen to 6% of the value of total exports (including exports from free trade zones). Since the late 1980s non-traditional crops, such as pineapples, oranges, bananas, vegetables and flowers, have increased in importance, and this diversification has boosted the ailing agricultural sector. None the less, the sector's contribution to GDP has declined in recent years, falling from 7.2% in 2005 to 6.0% in 2009. In 2009, however, agriculture was one of the strongest performing sectors in the economy, registering growth of 12.5%, after a poor performance in 2008, when agricultural GDP decreased by 3.4%.

The once dominant sugar industry has generally been in decline for many years. The state-owned Consejo Estatal del Azúcar (CEA) suffered from a lack of investment under successive governments, and its percentage of the total annual sugar output fell throughout the late 1990s. In 1999 the first Fernández Government sold off some CEA properties to a Mexican consortium. To compensate for the reduced yields produced by the state-owned enterprise, private companies, including the Central Romana Corporation and the Grupo Vicini, have increased their output to meet demand both for export and for domestic consumption. However, in 2004 output was so low that it was insufficient to meet domestic demand. The sugar sector has since made a partial recovery, but its share of total export earnings was just 2.2% in 2009. None the less, sugar remained the most important traditional agricultural export until that year, when it was overtaken by cocoa, exports of which increased by 55.3%, providing 3.0% of total export earnings. A possible lifeline for the sugar sector has been provided by the recent interest in bio-fuels as an alternative to increasingly expensive petroleum. Both foreign and local investors are exploring the possibilities of producing sugar cane in the Dominican Republic, with a view to transforming it into ethanol for local use and for export to the potentially vast US market.

Coffee was an important traditional agricultural crop from the mid-18th century, but towards the end of the 20th century the value of coffee exports decreased. In September 1998 Hurricane Georges damaged many of the country's coffee plantations, although in subsequent years there was a relative recovery. After a prosperous year in 2003, export earnings declined sharply in 2004. There was some recovery thereafter, but its contribution to the country's total exports was a mere 0.4% of the total value.

Manufacturing is the largest sector in the Dominican economy, accounting for 23.7% of GDP in 2009. This sector, which engaged 11% of the employed labour force in April 2010, is divided into two main sub-sectors: domestic manufacturing and free trade zone export manufacturing. Domestic manufacturing, which is the most significant in terms of profit margins, consists largely of food-processing operations, clothing and footwear, leather goods, and cement. Having registered negligible growth in 2003–04, the sector rebounded in 2005, increasing by 7.6% in that year. Growth was moderate in 2006–08, but slowed to 1.0% in 2009, when the sector contributed 20.5% of GDP. Manufacturing in free trade zones developed rapidly from the 1980s, mainly as a result of tax exemption incentives and a devaluation of the peso that made Dominican labour relatively cheap for foreign assembly companies. The most common product is garments, but footwear, electronic goods, jewellery, pharmaceuticals and cigars are also manufactured. Since 2000 the free trade zone sector has been struggling, losing its market share in the USA, its main market, particularly in the garments sector, which traditionally accounts for around 50% of merchandise exports. This trend accelerated following the phasing out of global quotas in January 2005, and Asian producers, particularly those in the People's Republic of China, gained further shares of the US market. In 2006 the GDP of the free trade zone sector fell by 8.0% compared with the previous year, and it contracted by a further 10.0% in 2007. In the aftermath of such a significant decline, in 2008 there was just a nominal contraction of 1.1%, but in 2009 a decrease of 14.6% was recorded, largely owing to weak demand resulting from the global downturn.

The construction industry experienced a boom in the latter half of the 1990s, but it was one of the sectors most affected by the 2003–04 crisis. A recovery began in 2005, when private, and to a lesser extent public, investment resumed. In 2006 the sector contributed 6.5% of GDP, growing by 24.6% compared with the previous year. Private financing increased significantly during this period, and there was an additional boost provided by the central Government's spending on the initial phase of the underground subway system in Santo Domingo. However, in 2007, despite increased public spending on construction during the year and a consistent growth in property services and prices, the level of construction activity increased by a modest 3.2%. By 2008 a slowdown in the property market had hit the construction industry hard and the sector declined (by 0.4%) for the first year since 2004. A further contraction, of 3.9%, was registered in 2009, when the sector contributed just 5.3% of GDP, but year-on-year growth of 19.4% in the first quarter of 2010 was encouraging.

The mining sector, dominated by ferro-nickel, is subject to wildly fluctuating international prices for metal. A fall in world prices forced the ferro-nickel mine at Bonao, in the centre of the country, to close in 1998, and again in 2001 and early 2002. In 2003, when nickel prices soared, it reopened once more. After rapid growth in 2004, mineral export growth fell slightly in 2005. Export earnings were US $380.8m. in 2005, compared with $390.0m. in 2004. In 2006 an increase in the volume of ferro-nickel exports and a rise in international nickel prices boosted nickel export earnings to $709.9m., and in 2007, as the international price rose yet further, export earnings increased by 54.8%, to $1,098.9m. However, in 2008 earnings declined to a preliminary $492.3m., after the international price crashed as slowing global economic activity dampened demand for the metal. In August the main ferro-nickel mining operator, the Swiss company Xstrata, suspended operations at the Falcondo mine. Prices and earnings fell further in 2009, the latter amounting to only a preliminary $4.1m. As a result, the GDP of the mining sector declined by 30.3% in 2008 and by 51.9% in 2009. There was significant foreign investment in the mining sector in 2009, however, and it was hoped that gold exports would commence in 2011.

The Dominican Republic was relatively late in developing its tourism potential, but quickly caught up during the 1970s and 1980s. The tourism trade is primarily focused on the country's beaches, which comprise about one-third of a 1,400-km coastline. The leading resort is Puerto Plata on the north coast, but Punta Cana and Romana-Bayahibe are also popular destinations. Tourism is the Dominican Republic's largest earner of foreign exchange, and a major source of employment, with 226,521 people employed in hotels, bars and restaurants in April 2010. The number of tourist arrivals increased steadily during 2002–07, but declined in 2008 as a result of the impact of the global economic downturn. A slight increase, to 4,414,756, was recorded in 2009, owing to a return to growth in the second half of the year following four consecutive quarters of decline, although receipts decreased in that year and the GDP of the hotels, bars and restaurants sub-sector contracted by 3.5%. Tourist arrivals from the USA accounted for 26% of tourists in 2009, with 28% coming from Europe. The generally rapid growth of the tourism sector in recent decades has given a strong boost to other sectors, notably the construction industry, but also to transport and commerce. Until now the focus has been on the budget end of the market, and all-inclusive package tours for holidaymakers from North America and Europe have become very popular. However, the structure of the Dominican tourism market is changing from the mass market model to a more high-end niche, and in 2007 the construction of several luxury, non-all inclusive, five-star hotels began. At the same time, according to the Asociación Dominicana de Compañías de Bienes Inmuebles de Turismo, the real estate market for holiday homes has also begun to evolve in this high-end direction, with estimated investment of US $1,500m. in 2007. The advantage of these developments for the country's economy is that high-end tourists tend to spend more in facilities outside the immediate hotel area, and therefore have a greater knock-on effect on the local economy.

In spite of recent years of growth and strong investment, the tourism sector is struggling to remain competitive as a result of challenges such as inadequate infrastructure, inefficient and costly electricity supply, and less frequent flights. There are international airports at Santo Domingo, Puerto Plata, Punta Cana, La Romana, Barahona, Samaná and Santiago. Punta Cana remained the principal arrival destination for tourists, receiving 43% of the country's total passenger arrivals in 2009. The main seaports are Santo Domingo, Haina, Boca Chica, and San Pedro de Macorís on the south coast, and Puerto Plata in the north. Facilities have been expanded at Haina, near Santo Domingo, which in 2005 handled 80% of imports. In late 2002 the Government announced plans for the construction of a mega-port at Manzanillo Bay in the north-west of the country, but progress with the project has been slow. A road-building programme during the late 1990s upgraded urban roads in Santo Domingo and the principal intercity routes. In 2005 there were a total of 17,000 km of roads. Traffic congestion increasingly brings gridlock to the capital, and in 2006 work began on a north–south underground railway system in city. The first line—14 km in length—entered into service in early 2009. Communications has been the fastest growing economic sector in recent years, and recorded a further 14% expansion during 2009. According to the Dominican Telecommunications Institute, 70% of people living in the Dominican Republic own a telephone. In 2009 there were 8.6m. mobile telephone subscribers, compared with just 705,431 in 2000. The spiralling growth in mobile use contrasted with a relatively stagnant growth in residential line connections. In 2009 there were 965,400 main lines in use, up from 894,200 in 2000. Some 39% of Dominicans have an internet connection. There were 2.7m. internet users in 2009, up from 327,100 in 2000.

The Dominican Republic has no oil resources and, aside from power supplied by a small hydroelectric sector, relies entirely on imported petroleum for its energy needs. This dependence has left the energy sector extremely vulnerable to movements in international oil prices. In 2006 82% of power output was produced by thermal (oil-fired) generators, nearly all of them running on imported fuel. Since the signing of the San José Agreement in 1980, most oil imports have been supplied by Mexico and Venezuela on preferential terms. Under the Caracas energy accord signed in October 2000, the Dominican Republic was given the option to purchase a further 20,000 barrels per day from Venezuela, but the supply was interrupted in 2002 and 2003, first by political instability in that country and then following a diplomatic row between the two Governments. In November 2005 President Fernández signed up to Venezuela's PetroCaribe agreement, under which Venezuela would meet all the Dominican Republic's oil needs on beneficial terms. More recently, the Dominican Government has responded enthusiastically to the prospects for developing bio-fuel production, and is currently exploring initiatives to produce bio-fuel from sugar cane and jatropha plants.

The electricity power sector has long been undermined by inadequate investment, high costs, theft and low collection rates, including recurrent payment arrears accumulated by the public sector. There have been frequent blackouts, obliging companies and households to turn to their own small-scale generators, and in 2004 the situation deteriorated still further when blackouts, sometimes lasting several days, prompted protests and civil unrest. The Fernández administration has struggled to overcome the sector's problems, despite making it one of its priorities on taking office. Debts in the sector, including government debt, amounted to more than US $500m. in 2007. In 2007 the authorities took the decision to criminalize electricity theft, a move intended to help reduce the need for budgetary support to the electricity sector, and following Fernández's re-election in May 2008, the authorities initiated a further attempt to reform the electricity supply sector. However, during 2008 the electricity industry continued to provide an unreliable service and customers experienced extended blackouts. Rolling blackouts reached unprecedented levels during the months of October and November 2008, with power shortages lasting up to 20 hours in some parts of the country. Further blackouts were expected in mid-2009, as a number of generators were due to be offline for maintenance and the barges contracted to provide additional substitute power had not arrived. As part of the stand-by arrangement agreed with the IMF in November, the Government committed itself to a reform of the electricity sector, developing a strategy in conjunction with the Inter-American Development Bank and the World Bank.

Since the early 2000s government finances have continued to fluctuate. A surplus of 2,984m. pesos in 2000 fell to 992m. pesos in 2001, and then, in 2002, a deficit of 299m. pesos was recorded. In 2003 the account returned to a surplus of 5,692m. pesos, but in the following year there was a deficit, of 6,917m. pesos, once more. A further deficit, of 4,012m. pesos, was recorded in 2005, and in 2006 the Government was obliged to prepare another tax reform. In 2007 there was a sharp improvement, largely as a result of a strong increase in revenue collection. However, loosening of fiscal policy in 2008, as a result of election spending and the international oil price shock, led to the largest deficit since 2004, of a preliminary 61,208.4m. pesos, equivalent to 3.9% of GDP. Although much lower oil prices removed one significant source of pressure in 2009, the Government still struggled to fund stimulus spending on infrastructure and local public works, as well as social programmes. A preliminary deficit of 57,210.2m. pesos (3.4% of GDP) was recorded in that year. Foreign investment has fluctuated in the 2000s, increasing by 25% in 2001, to a total of US $1,079m., and then falling again in 2002 and 2003. Foreign direct investment (FDI) inflows recovered to $1,123m. in 2005, reflecting a boost to business confidence brought about by the restoration of stability and economic recovery, and the resumption of tourism projects suspended owing to the earlier crisis. In early 2007 the Secretariat of State for the Economy,

Planning and Development announced that the Dominican Republic was the leading recipient of FDI in the Caribbean and Central America region, surpassing previous leading beneficiaries Trinidad and Tobago and Costa Rica. In 2007 FDI rose by 44%, to reach $1,563m., partly as a consequence of the entry into force of the DR-CAFTA agreement in March, and the recent Economic Partnership Agreement with the European Union. Inflows increased further in 2008, to a record $2,971m., before declining to a preliminary $2,158m. in 2009. The leading receiving sector in 2009 was mining, with $758m. (up by 83.2%), while the real estate sector attracted $401m. The telecommunications sector also brought a significant share of FDI in 2009, with $297m., an increase of 39.2%. Canada was the main source of FDI inflows ($770m.), followed by the USA ($589m.) and Mexico ($267m.).

The Dominican Republic's most important trading partner is the USA. Other important export markets include Haiti, Spain, the Netherlands and the People's Republic of China. During the early 21st century exports have continued to grow. Export earnings reached US $6,610m. in 2006 and rose by 8.3% the following year, almost entirely on account of the higher international price for nickel. Real export growth was sluggish, affected by a sharp decline in earnings from textile and shoe manufactures. At the same time, import spending surged. An 11.7% increase in import spending in 2007 was driven by strong demand for consumer goods imports (led by automobiles and electrical appliances) and rising oil costs. As a result, the current account deficit widened from $1,288m. in 2006 to $2,096m. in 2007. In 2008 the current account deficit reached a record $4,437m., driven by rising import costs and declining earnings from nickel and free zone exports. The deficit was halved in 2009, however, as the value of imports declined at a faster rate than remittances from abroad and the value of exports.

CONCLUSION

After returning to power in 2004, President Fernández had some success in restoring economic stability after the crisis of 2003–04. In 2005 inflation was at the lower end of the 5%–7% official target range. The currency remained relatively stable throughout the year, and official and commercial interest rates eased. Furthermore, international reserves continued to build after their virtual depletion in early 2004. However, while the impressive GDP growth rates in 2005 and 2006 reflected a strong recovery, growth slowed in 2007, 2008 and 2009, as a result of the collapse in global trade, a US recession and a sharp contraction in consumption, and the fiscal deficit increased substantially. The deterioration in the fiscal situation prompted the Government to seek assistance from the IMF, which approved a stand-by arrangement in November 2009 (see above). Stronger growth was recorded in the final quarter of 2009 and first quarter of 2010, reflecting a recovery in the US economy. Following a mission to the Dominican Republic in May 2010, the IMF welcomed the recent expansion in the economy, as well as government efforts to improve tax collection and bank supervision, but noted delays in the reform of the electricity sector. The Fund forecast GDP growth of 5.0%–5.5% for 2010.

Statistical Survey

Sources (unless otherwise stated): Oficina Nacional de Estadística, Edif. de Oficinas Gubernamentales, 9°, Avda México, esq. Leopoldo Navarro, Santo Domingo, DN; tel. 682-7777; fax 685-4424; e-mail info@one.gob.do; internet www.one.gob.do; Banco Central de la República Dominicana, Calle Pedro Henríquez Ureña, esq. Leopoldo Navarro, Apdo 1347, Santo Domingo, DN; tel. 221-9111; fax 686-7488; e-mail info@bancentral.gov.do; internet www.bancentral.gov.do.

Area and Population

AREA, POPULATION AND DENSITY

Area (sq km)	
Land	48,137
Inland water	597
Total	48,734*
Population (census results)	
24 September 1993	7,293,390
18–20 October 2002	
Males	4,297,326
Females	4,265,215
Total	8,562,541
Population (official projections)	
2008	9,625,207
2009	9,755,954
2010	9,884,371
Density (per sq km) at 2010	202.8

* 18,816 sq miles.

POPULATION BY AGE AND SEX

(official projections, 2010)

	Males	Females	Total
0–14	1,583,277	1,527,956	3,111,233
15–64	3,068,670	3,116,981	6,185,651
65 and over	283,335	304,152	587,487
Total	4,935,282	4,949,089	9,884,371

PROVINCES

(official population projections, 2010)

	Area (sq km)	Population	Density (per sq km)
Distrito Nacional Region			
Distrito Nacional	104.4	1,111,838	10,649.8
Santo Domingo	1,296.4	2,198,333	1,695.7
Valdesia Region			
Peravia	997.6	202,250	202.7
Monte Plata	2,632.1	210,365	79.9
San Cristóbal	1,265.8	660,009	521.4
San José de Ocoa	650.2	69,204	106.4
Norcentral Region			
Espaillat	839.0	237,101	282.6
Puerto Plata	1,856.9	327,510	176.4
Santiago	2,839.0	1,046,182	368.5
Nordeste Region			
Duarte	1,605.4	299,188	186.4
Hermanas Mirabal	440.4	103,259	234.5
María Trinidad Sánchez	1,271.7	141,678	111.4
Samaná	853.7	98,820	115.8
Enriquillo Region			
Baoruco	1,282.2	114,967	89.7
Barahona	1,739.4	200,602	115.3
Independencia	2,006.4	55,223	27.5
Pedernales	2,074.5	25,478	12.3
Este Region			
El Seibo	1,786.8	105,994	59.3
Hato Mayor	1,329.3	90,773	68.3
La Altagracia	2,474.3	229,428	92.7

—continued	Area (sq km)	Population	Density (per sq km)
La Romana	654.0	246,234	376.5
San Pedro de Macorís	1,255.5	337,108	268.5
El Valle Region			
Azua	2,531.8	242,109	95.6
Elías Piña	1,426.2	72,130	50.6
San Juan	3,569.4	245,377	68.7
Noroeste Region			
Dajabón	1,020.7	66,954	65.6
Monte Cristi	1,924.4	120,833	62.8
Santiago Rodríguez	1,111.1	54,865	49.4
Valverde	823.4	190,253	231.1
Cibao Central Region			
La Vega	2,287.0	429,563	187.8
Monseñor Nouel	992.4	194,505	196.0
Sánchez Ramírez	1,196.1	156,238	130.6
Total	48,137.0*	9,884,371	205.3*

* Land area only.

PRINCIPAL TOWNS
(population at census of October 2002)

Santo Domingo DN (capital)	2,302,759	San Felipe de Puerto Plata	146,882
Santiago de los Caballeros	622,101	Higuey	141,751
San Cristóbal	220,767	Moca	131,733
Concepción de la Vega	220,279	San Juan de la Maguana	129,224
San Pedro de Macorís	217,141	Monseñor Nouel	115,743
La Romana	202,488	Baní	107,926
San Francisco de Macorís	156,267	Bajos de Haina	80,835

Mid-2010 (incl. suburbs, UN estimate): Santo Domingo DN 2,180,150 (Source: UN, *World Urbanization Prospects: The 2009 Revision*).

BIRTHS, MARRIAGES AND DEATHS
(year of registration)

	Registered live births		Registered marriages		Registered deaths	
	Number	Rate (per 1,000)	Number	Rate (per 1,000)	Number	Rate (per 1,000)
2003	209,069	23.4	37,225	4.2	29,821	3.3
2004	198,304	21.8	38,642	4.3	34,325	3.8
2005	183,819	19.9	39,439	4.3	33,949	3.7
2006	174,393	18.3	42,375	4.5	33,060	3.5
2007	193,817	20.4	39,993	4.2	33,842	3.6

2008: Registered marriages 38,310 (4.0 per 1,000 persons).

Life expectancy (years at birth, WHO estimates): 73 (males 71; females 74) in 2008 (Source: WHO, *World Health Statistics*).

ECONOMICALLY ACTIVE POPULATION
('000 persons aged 10 years and over, official estimates at October 2009)

	Males	Females	Total
Agriculture, hunting, forestry and fishing	508.6	25.7	534.3
Mining and quarrying	10.7	0.5	11.2
Manufacturing	281.2	96.7	377.9
Electricity, gas and water supply	24.2	6.2	30.4
Construction	219.8	4.7	224.6
Wholesale and retail trade	545.8	246.2	792.0
Hotels and restaurants	98.8	115.9	214.6
Transport, storage and communications	257.6	18.0	275.6
Financial intermediation; Real estate, renting and business activities	45.8	39.1	84.9
Public administration and defence	105.2	63.6	168.9
Education; Health and social work; Other community, social and personal service activities	278.2	615.6	893.8
Total employed	2,375.9	1,232.3	3,608.2
Unemployed	257.0	374.1	631.1
Total labour force	2,632.9	1,606.4	4,239.3

Health and Welfare

KEY INDICATORS

Total fertility rate (children per woman, 2008)	2.6
Under-5 mortality rate (per 1,000 live births, 2008)	33
HIV/AIDS (% of persons aged 15–49, 2007)	1.1
Physicians (per 1,000 head, 2000)	1.88
Hospital beds (per 1,000 head, 2005)	2.0
Health expenditure (2007): US $ per head (PPP)	411
Health expenditure (2007): % of GDP	5.4
Health expenditure (2007): public (% of total)	35.9
Access to water (% of persons, 2008)	86
Access to sanitation (% of persons, 2008)	83
Total carbon dioxide emissions ('000 metric tons, 2006)	20,342.5
Carbon dioxide emissions per head (metric tons, 2006)	2.1
Human Development Index (2007): ranking	91
Human Development Index (2007): value	0.777

For sources and definitions, see explanatory note on p. vi.

Agriculture

PRINCIPAL CROPS
('000 metric tons)

	2006	2007	2008
Rice, paddy	626	656	644
Maize	31.0	29.4	26.8
Potatoes	42.3	41.8	33.0
Sweet potatoes	28.7	36.4	35.5
Cassava (Manioc)	128.4	128.3	100.2
Yautia (Cocoyam)	26.4	29.8	21.8
Sugar cane	4,713.1	4,823.9	4,823.9*
Beans, dry	29.0	28.5	21.0
Coconuts	92.6	94.9	94.9*
Oil palm fruit*	165.0	165.1	188.8
Tomatoes	254.3	211.6	243.0
Pumpkins, squash and gourds	36.2	36.5	39.5
Chillies and peppers, green	28.9	29.1	32.1
Onions, dry	43.0	48.0	49.4
Garlic	3.0	3.2	2.6
Carrots and turnips	21.2	19.9	19.7
Cantaloupes and other melons	30.4	18.9	18.9*

—continued	2006	2007	2008
Bananas	500.8	495.7	439.6
Plantains	542.8	504.6	340.4
Oranges	105.2	117.4	90.3
Guavas, mangoes and mangosteens*	170.0	170.0	170.0
Avocados	216.4	183.5	187.4
Pineapples	70.6	91.6	100.5
Papayas*	24.0	22.5	22.5
Coffee, green	41.4	41.2	41.2*
Cocoa beans	45.9	42.2	42.2*
Tobacco, unmanufactured*	12.0	12.0	12.0

* FAO estimate(s).

Aggregate production ('000 metric tons, may include official, semi-official or estimated data): Total cereals 657.9 in 2006, 686.7 in 2007, 671.7 in 2008; Total roots and tubers 250.9 in 2006, 263.8 in 2007, 216.2 in 2008; Total vegetables (incl. melons) 473.6 in 2006, 417.7 in 2007, 458.2 in 2008; Total fruits (excl. melons) 1,683.9 in 2006, 1,635.6 in 2007, 1,402.7 in 2008.

Source: FAO.

LIVESTOCK

('000 head, year ending September, FAO estimates)

	2005	2006	2007
Horses	345	348	350
Asses	151	151	151
Cattle	2,200.0	2,228.1	2,652.6
Pigs	580.0	580.0	580.0
Sheep	123.0	123.0	123.0
Goats	190.0	190.0	190.0
Chickens	86,000	91,000	100,500

2008: Production assumed to be unchanged from 2007 (FAO estimates).

Source: FAO.

LIVESTOCK PRODUCTS

('000 metric tons)

	2005	2006	2007
Cattle meat	73.2	84.2	101.1
Pig meat	78.0	72.2*	72.2*
Chicken meat	296.6	313.4	346.4
Cows' milk	461.4	512.4	548.3
Hen eggs	80.2	86.1*	86.0*
Honey*	4.9	4.3	4.6

* FAO estimate(s).

2008: Production assumed to be unchanged from 2007 (FAO estimates).

Source: FAO.

Forestry

ROUNDWOOD REMOVALS

('000 cubic metres, excl. bark)

	2006	2007	2008
Sawlogs, veneer logs and logs for sleepers	11	14	7
Other industrial wood*	3	3	3
Fuel wood*	878	887	895
Total*	892	904	905

* FAO estimates.

Source: FAO.

Fishing

('000 metric tons, live weight)

	2006	2007	2008
Capture	13.0	13.7	15.4
Tilapia	0.8	0.8	0.7
Groupers, seabasses	n.a.	0.6	0.7
Common carp	0.4	0.4	0.5
Snappers and jobfishes	1.5	1.3	1.2
King mackerel	0.2	0.1	0.3
Blackfin tuna	n.a.	n.a.	0.3
Caribbean spiny lobster	0.9	1.1	1.3
Stromboid conchs	1.0	1.3	1.6
Aquaculture*	1.0	1.0	1.0
Penaeus shrimps*	0.5	0.5	0.5
Total catch*	13.9	14.7	16.4

* FAO estimates.

Source: FAO.

Mining

('000 metric tons)

	2005	2006	2007
Ferro-nickel	61.1	76.7	84.0
Nickel (metal content of laterite ore)	53.1	4,096.2	4,062.5
Gypsum	370.1	355.6	350.0

2008: Production assumed to be unchanged from 2007 (estimates).

Source: US Geological Survey.

Industry

SELECTED PRODUCTS

('000 metric tons, unless otherwise indicated)

	2004	2005	2006*
Flour and derivatives ('000 quintales†)	2,516.4	2,543.2	1,581.5
Refined sugar	124.0	140.1	132.2
Cement	2,653.6	2,778.7	1,888.4
Beer ('000 hl)	3,546.1	4,540.9*	n.a.
Cigarettes (million)	3,445.9	3,300.3*	n.a.

* Preliminary figure(s).

† 1 quintale is equivalent to 46 kg.

2004 ('000 barrels, estimates): Motor spirit (petrol) 2,000; Jet fuel 1,900; Distillate fuel oil 2,900; Residual fuel oil 4,600 (Sources: US Geological Survey; UN, *Industrial Commodity Statistics Yearbook*).

Electric energy (million kWh): 12,899 in 2005, 14,150 in 2006; 14,839 in 2007 (Source: UN Industrial Commodity Statistics Database).

Finance

CURRENCY AND EXCHANGE RATES

Monetary Units
100 centavos = 1 Dominican Republic peso (RD $ or peso oro).

Sterling, Dollar and Euro Equivalents (31 May 2010)
£1 sterling = 53.805 pesos;
US $1 = 36.903 pesos;
€1 = 45.701 pesos;
1,000 Dominican Republic pesos = £18.59 = $27.10 = €21.88.

Average Exchange Rate (RD $ per US $)
2007 33.263
2008 34.624
2009 36.027

BUDGET
(RD $ million)

Revenue	2007	2008*	2009*
Tax revenue	217,965.0	236,166.1	220,373.6
Taxes on income and profits	55,232.0	58,534.7	54,127.7
Taxes on goods and services	128,207.6	139,766.7	132,411.8
Taxes on international trade and transactions	23,303.8	24,829.9	21,942.4
Other current revenue	18,046.5	10,744.2	5,837.4
Capital revenue	0.1	0.1	2.1
Total	236,011.5	246,910.4	226,213.2

Expenditure	2007	2008*	2009*
Current expenditure	177,291.2	227,269.4	223,391.4
Wages and salaries	48,485.0	58,787.3	68,495.1
Other services	15,364.7	31,560.1	29,592.2
Materials and supplies	18,363.8		
Current transfers	77,969.7	111,426.7	92,790.1
Interest payments	16,820.3	25,229.7	31,957.0
Internal debt	3,747.0	13,223.0	20,656.0
External debt	13,073.3	12,006.7	11,301.0
Capital expenditure	63,037.7	80,849.4	60,032.0
Machines and equipment	3,473.9	53,930.2	37,950.9
Construction of works and agricultural plantations	37,191.8		
Capital transfers	22,566.9	26,333.5	21,321.0
Total	240,328.9	308,118.8	283,423.4

* Preliminary figures.

INTERNATIONAL RESERVES
(US $ million at 31 December)

	2007	2008	2009
Gold*	15.3	15.9	19.9
IMF special drawing rights	98.6	36.0	275.6
Foreign exchange	2,447.8	2,235.6	2,609.5
Total	2,561.7	2,287.5	2,905.0

* Valued at market-related prices.

Source: IMF, *International Financial Statistics*.

MONEY SUPPLY
(RD $ million at 31 December)

	2007	2008	2009
Currency outside depository corporations	49,187	50,478	55,413
Transferable deposits	90,403	77,867	96,981
Other deposits	193,673	209,302	232,630
Securities other than shares	137,209	156,728	175,672
Broad money	470,472	494,376	560,695

Source: IMF, *International Financial Statistics*.

COST OF LIVING
(Consumer Price Index including direct taxes; base: 2000 = 100)

	2007	2008	2009
Food, beverages and tobacco	258.8	295.7	307.3
Clothing	205.2	219.1	232.5
Rent	262.9	277.1	299.3
All items (incl. others)	263.1	291.1	295.3

Source: ILO.

NATIONAL ACCOUNTS
(RD $ million at current prices)

Expenditure on the Gross Domestic Product

	2007	2008	2009
Final consumption expenditure	1,230,166.5	1,504,352.5	1,564,274.5
Households; Non-profit institutions serving households	1,128,669.0	1,383,957.8	1,432,777.4
General government	101,497.5	120,394.7	131,497.1
Gross capital formation	258,143.8	288,574.0	248,858.8
Gross fixed capital formation	256,331.0	286,457.4	246,585.6
Changes in inventories; Acquisitions, less disposals, of valuables	1,812.8	2,116.6	2,273.2
Total domestic expenditure	1,488,310.3	1,792,926.5	1,813,133.3
Exports of goods and services	392,577.4	401,703.0	373,490.8
Less Imports of goods and services	516,677.4	618,466.8	507,861.5
GDP in market prices	1,364,210.3	1,576,162.8	1,678,762.6
GDP at constant 1991 prices	314,592.9	331,126.8	342,564.1

Gross Domestic Product by Economic Activity

	2007	2008	2009
Agriculture, hunting, forestry and fishing	81,161.7	92,297.4	96,366.8
Mining and quarrying	9,284.2	5,415.1	2,184.3
Manufacturing	261,777.0	338,745.0	379,489.7
Local manufacturing	209,860.0	282,660.4	328,550.6
Free trade zones	51,917.0	56,084.6	50,939.1
Electricity and water	30,141.3	33,988.2	35,993.7
Construction	88,559.2	92,737.3	85,596.0
Wholesale and retail trade	127,753.1	148,069.5	142,390.8
Restaurants and hotels	145,732.7	159,793.5	158,984.5
Transport and storage	105,289.2	136,157.4	125,373.3
Communications	34,879.3	42,438.9	49,654.4
Finance, insurance and business activities	69,690.8	90,494.5	102,545.6
Real estate	113,795.7	125,698.3	139,676.2
General government services (incl. defence)	41,115.6	51,775.3	57,707.1
Education	42,080.1	50,135.9	61,309.1
Health	27,463.2	30,271.7	33,127.1
Other services	94,070.3	111,356.2	134,047.9
Sub-total	1,272,793.3	1,509,374.2	1,604,446.5
Less Financial intermediation services indirectly measured	37,706.1	46,440.4	53,727.1
Gross value added in basic prices	1,235,087.3	1,462,933.8	1,550,719.4
Taxes, *less* subsidies	129,123.1	113,229.0	128,043.2
GDP in market prices	1,364,210.3	1,576,162.8	1,678,762.6

BALANCE OF PAYMENTS
(US $ million)

	2006	2007	2008
Exports of goods f.o.b.	6,610.2	7,160.2	6,948.9
Imports of goods f.o.b.	–12,173.9	–13,597.0	–16,095.4
Trade balance	–5,563.7	–6,436.8	–9,146.5
Exports of services	4,567.2	4,794.1	4,938.6
Imports of services	–1,582.2	–1,773.2	–1,846.0
Balance on goods and services	–2,578.7	–3,415.9	–6,053.9
Other income received	699.7	811.5	681.9
Other income paid	–2,552.7	–2,892.5	–2,496.7
Balance on goods, services and income	–4,431.7	–5,496.9	–7,868.7
Current transfers received	3,365.6	3,654.8	3,699.4
Current transfers paid	–221.5	–253.6	–267.5
Current balance	–1,287.6	–2,095.7	–4,436.8
Capital account (net)	254.2	195.1	142.7
Direct investment from abroad	1,528.3	1,578.9	2,884.7
Portfolio investment assets	–328.6	177.4	102.8
Portfolio investment liabilities	1,101.8	776.1	–559.8
Other investment assets	–1,752.4	–692.5	425.2
Other investment liabilities	795.2	323.5	978.9
Net errors and omissions	–146.5	357.1	144.6
Overall balance	164.3	619.9	–317.7

Source: IMF, *International Financial Statistics*.

External Trade

PRINCIPAL COMMODITIES
(US $ million)*

Imports f.o.b.	2007	2008†	2009†
Consumer goods	5,810.9	6,857.0	5,341.1
Durable goods	1,020.1	946.6	641.9
Foodstuffs	506.7	619.4	625.6
Petroleum products	2,303.7	2,999.8	2,062.1
Raw materials	3,489.5	4,574.7	3,027.3
Artificial plastic materials	293.2	326.1	264.4
Petroleum and petroleum products	920.3	1,241.5	592.7
Cast iron and steel	489.6	751.3	360.4
Capital goods	1,796.9	2,132.2	1,589.5
For transport	294.8	329.9	148.3
For industry	377.7	409.1	336.7
Machinery	338.9	427.8	413.7
Total	11,097.3	13,564.0	9,957.9

* Figures exclude imports into free trade zones.

Exports f.o.b.	2007	2008†	2009†
Sugar and sugar cane derivatives	129.2	108.5	119.6
Raw cane sugar	98.0	77.3	91.7
Cocoa and cocoa manufactures	90.9	106.7	165.7
Cocoa beans	81.0	92.6	154.7
Tobacco and tobacco manufactures	16.5	13.5	11.8
Ferro-nickel	1,098.9	492.3	4.1
Other goods	871.7	1,113.3	1,024.6
Petroleum products	394.3	522.3	313.4
Total (incl. others)	2,635.0	2,394.0	1,678.3

* Figures exclude exports from free trade zones, which totalled: US $4,525.2m. in 2007; $4,354.1m. in 2008; $3,784.9m. in 2009.
† Preliminary figures.

PRINCIPAL TRADING PARTNERS
(US $ '000)

Imports c.i.f.	2006	2007	2008
Argentina	132,418.0	160,332.0	147,550.4
Brazil	223,388.1	346,067.4	393,484.8
Canada	72,943.4	139,358.5	151,567.9
China, People's Republic	513,886.5	829,928.4	1,203,144.5
Colombia	164,563.9	530,658.1	723,345.1
Costa Rica	95,170.2	136,629.4	186,127.0
Denmark	65,841.4	83,888.5	10,290.4
France	64,684.0	97,846.5	124,974.4
Germany	144,211.2	185,979.3	208,373.6
Guatemala	76,825.2	77,824.4	102,938.5
Italy	70,725.5	113,026.7	142,238.5
Japan	272,856.9	374,382.2	322,228.1
Mexico	157,559.3	717,462.1	836,918.6
Panama	213,570.0	271,592.9	233,234.1
Spain	225,552.6	324,500.2	404,841.7
Trinidad and Tobago	54,390.9	362,755.4	561,795.1
USA	2,523,852.2	3,768,887.2	4,235,600.0
Venezuela	57,714.2	720,269.1	1,397,450.1
Total (incl. others)	9,400,932.0	10,386,734.2	13,332,204.2

Exports f.o.b.	2006	2007	2008
Canada	84,336.1	24,494.1	29,379.9
China, People's Republic	59,543.1	232,157.1	72,829.4
Cuba	11,624.4	34,149.9	55,280.7
Germany	20,324.8	15,151.8	14,120.1
Haiti	137,411.7	154,451.4	240,007.2
Italy	10,585.1	24,029.0	25,506.1
Jamaica	20,243.0	27,851.3	54,322.1
Japan	28,849.1	72,137.2	28,858.3
Korea, Democratic People's Republic	181,250.2	134,984.2	18,785.5
Netherlands	85,603.5	354,979.0	106,539.4
Spain	36,240.0	82,403.2	156,567.9
United Kingdom	50,085.3	62,891.7	56,845.4
USA	568,688.7	704,416.6	534,826.5
Total (incl. others)	1,898,288.2	2,235,356.9	1,841,719.9

Transport

ROAD TRAFFIC
(motor vehicles in use)

	2003	2004	2005
Passenger cars ('000)	638.0	662.0	721.0
Commercial vehicles ('000)	320.0	329.0	351.0

Source: UN, *Statistical Yearbook*.

2007 (motor vehicles in use at 31 December): Passenger cars 602,671; Buses and coaches 64,236; Vans and Lorries 525,391; Motorcycles and mopeds 1,044,510 (Source: IRF, *World Road Statistics*).

SHIPPING

Merchant Fleet
(registered at 31 December)

	2006	2007	2008
Number of vessels	24	23	25
Total displacement ('000 grt)	10.0	9.7	10.1

Source: Lloyd's Register-Fairplay, *World Fleet Statistics*.

International Sea-borne Freight Traffic
('000 metric tons)

	1996	1997	1998
Goods loaded	112	152	139

Source: UN, *Monthly Bulletin of Statistics*.

CIVIL AVIATION
(traffic on scheduled services)

	1997	1998	1999
Kilometres flown (million)	1	1	0
Passengers carried ('000)	34	34	10
Passenger-km (million)	16	16	5
Total ton-km (million)	1	1	0

Source: UN, *Statistical Yearbook*.

Tourism

ARRIVALS BY NATIONALITY

	2007	2008	2009
Canada	591,871	639,796	650,111
France	287,147	279,408	247,038
Germany	214,942	206,940	178,533
Italy	140,423	127,383	115,775
Puerto Rico	104,227	97,592	107,610
Spain	267,365	239,638	231,275
United Kingdom*	217,490	206,372	176,180
USA	1,099,906	1,107,898	1,150,875
Total (incl. others)	4,428,005	4,398,743	4,414,756

* Includes arrivals from England and Scotland only.

Tourism receipts (US $ million, excl. passenger transport): 3,518 in 2005; 3,792 in 2006; 4,082 in 2007 (Source: World Tourism Organization).

Communications Media

	2007	2008	2009
Telephones ('000 main lines in use)	906.5	985.7	965.4
Mobile cellular telephones ('000 subscribers)	5,512.9	7,210.5	8,629.8
Internet users ('000)	1,733.1	2,072.1	2,701.3
Broadband users ('000)	193.1	267.9	396.3

Daily newspapers: 11 in 2004 (average circulation 365,000 copies).

Non-daily newspapers: 8 in 2000 (average circulation 215,000 copies).

Radio receivers ('000 in use): 1,440 in 1997.

Television receivers ('000 in use): 790 in 1998.

Personal computers: 200,000 (21.3 per 1,000 persons) in 2004.

Sources: UNESCO, *Statistical Yearbook*; UN, *Statistical Yearbook*; International Telecommunication Union.

Education

(2007/08, unless otherwise stated)

		Students		
	Teachers	Males	Females	Total
Pre-primary	9,183	113,156	109,085	222,241
Primary	66,539	686,476	619,185	1,305,661
Secondary	37,164	421,030	488,301	909,331
General	34,847	404,787	463,230	868,017
Vocational	2,317	16,243	25,071	41,314
Higher*	11,367	113,520	180,045	293,565

* Estimates for 2003/04.

Institutions: Primary 4,001 (1997/98); General secondary 1,737 (1996/97).

Source: UNESCO, mostly Institute for Statistics.

Pupil-teacher ratio (primary education, UNESCO estimate): 19.6 in 2007/08 (Source: UNESCO Institute for Statistics).

Adult literacy rate (UNESCO estimates): 88.2% (males 88.2%; females 88.3%) in 2007 (Source: UNESCO Institute for Statistics).

Directory

The Constitution

The Constitution of the Dominican Republic was promulgated on 28 November 1966, and amended in 1994, 2002 and 2010. The 2010 reforms amended the Constitution from 122 to 273 articles. Its main provisions are summarized below:

The Dominican Republic is a sovereign, free, independent state; no organizations set up by the State can bring about any act which might cause direct or indirect intervention in the internal or foreign affairs of the State or which might threaten the integrity of the State. The Dominican Republic recognizes and applies the norms of general and American international law and is in favour of and will support any initiative towards economic integration for the countries of America. The civil, republican, democratic, representative Government is divided into three independent powers: legislative, executive and judicial.

The territory of the Dominican Republic is as laid down in the Frontier Treaty of 1929 and its Protocol of Revision of 1936.

The life and property of the individual citizen are inviolable; there can be no sentence of death, torture nor any sentence which might cause physical harm to the individual. There is freedom of thought, of conscience, of religion, freedom to publish, freedom of unarmed association, provided that there is no subversion against public order, national security or decency. The right to life is inviolable from conception to death. There is freedom of labour and trade unions; freedom to strike, except in the case of public services, according to the dispositions of the law.

The State will undertake agrarian reform, dedicating the land to useful interests and gradually eliminating the latifundios (large estates). The State will do all in its power to support all aspects of family life. Marriage is defined as being between a man and a woman. Primary education is compulsory and all education is free. Social security services will be developed. Every Dominican has the duty to give what civil and military service the State may require. Every legally entitled citizen must exercise the right to vote, i.e. all persons over 18 years of age and all who are or have been married even if they are not yet 18. Children born in the Dominican Republic to foreign parents in transit or in the country illegally will not automatically be granted Dominican citizenship.

GOVERNMENT

Legislative power is exercised by Congress which is made up of the Senate and Chamber of Deputies, elected by direct vote. Senators, one for each of the 31 Provinces and one for the Distrito Nacional, are elected for four years; they must be Dominicans in full exercise of their citizen's rights, and at least 25 years of age. Their duties are to elect the President and other members of the Electoral and Accounts Councils, and to approve the nomination of diplomats. Deputies, one for every 50,000 inhabitants or fraction over 25,000 in each Province and the Distrito Nacional, are elected for four years and must fulfil the same conditions for election as Senators.

Decisions of Congress are taken by absolute majority of at least half the members of each house; urgent matters require a two-thirds' majority. Both houses normally meet on 27 February and 16 August each year for sessions of 90 days, which can be extended for a further 60 days. Any amendments to the Constitution must be approved by referendum.

Executive power is exercised by the President of the Republic, who is elected by direct vote for a four-year term. The President may not serve a consecutive term, although an unlimited number of non-consecutive terms are permitted. The successful presidential candidate must obtain an overall majority of the votes cast; if necessary, a second round of voting is held 45 days later, with the participation of the two parties that obtained the highest number of votes. The President must be a Dominican citizen by birth or origin, over 30 years of age and in full exercise of citizen's rights. The President must not have engaged in any active military or police service for at least a year prior to election. The President takes office on 16 August following the election. The President of the Republic is Head of the Public Administration and Supreme Chief of the armed forces and police forces. The President's duties include nominating Secretaries and Assistant Secretaries of State and other public officials, promulgating and publishing laws and resolutions of Congress and seeing to their faithful execution, watching over the collection and just investment of national income, nominating, with the approval of the Senate, members of the Diplomatic Corps, receiving foreign Heads of State, presiding at national functions, decreeing a State of Siege or Emergency or any other measures necessary during a public crisis. The President may not leave the country for more than 15 days without authorization from Congress. In the absence of the President, the Vice-President will assume power, or failing him or her, the President of the Supreme Court of Justice. From 2016 presidential elections are to be held at the same time as legislative and municipal elections, every four years.

LOCAL GOVERNMENT

Government in the Distrito Nacional and the Municipalities is in the hands of local councils, with members elected proportionally to the number of inhabitants, but numbering at least five. Each Province has a civil Governor, designated by the Executive.

JUDICIARY

Judicial power is exercised by the Supreme Court of Justice and the other Tribunals; no judicial official may hold another public office or employment, other than honorary or teaching. The Supreme Court is made up of at least 11 judges, who must be Dominican citizens by birth or origin, at least 35 years old, in full exercise of their citizen's rights, graduates in law and have practised professionally for at least 12 years. All Supreme Court judges must retire at the age of 75. The National Judiciary Council appoints the members of the Supreme Court, who in turn appoint judges at all other levels of the judicial system. There are nine Courts of Appeal, a Lands Tribunal and a Court of the First Instance in each judicial district; in each Municipality and in the Distrito Nacional there are also Justices of the Peace. Under the terms of the 2010 constitutional amendments, a Constitutional Court was to be established.

OTHER PROVISIONS

Elections are directed by the Central Electoral Board. The armed forces are essentially obedient and apolitical, created for the defence of national independence and the maintenance of public order and the Constitution and Laws.

The artistic and historical riches of the country, whoever owns them, are part of the cultural heritage of the country and are under the safe-keeping of the State. All beaches, rivers and water sources are part of the national heritage and belong to the people, respecting the rights of private property. Mineral deposits belong to the State. There is freedom to form political parties, provided they conform to the principles laid down in the Constitution. Justice is administered without charge throughout the Republic.

This Constitution can be reformed if the proposal for reform is supported in Congress by one-third of the members of either house or by the Executive. A special session of Congress must be called and any resolutions must have a two-thirds' majority. There can be no reform of the method of government, which must always be civil, republican, democratic and representative.

The Government

HEAD OF STATE

President: LEONEL FERNÁNDEZ REYNA (took office 16 August 2004; re-elected 16 May 2008).

Vice-President: DR RAFAEL FRANCISCO ALBURQUERQUE DE CASTRO.

CABINET
(July 2010)

The Government is formed by the Partido de la Liberación Dominicana.

Secretary of State for the Presidency: DR CÉSAR PINA TORIBIO.

Secretary of State for Foreign Affairs: CARLOS MORALES TRONCOSO.

Secretary of State for the Interior and Police: FRANKLIN ALMEYDA RANCIER.

Secretary of State for the Armed Forces: Lt-Gen. PEDRO RAFAEL PEÑA ANTONIO.

Secretary of State for Finance: VICENTE BENGOA ALBIZU.

Secretary of State for Education: MELANIO PAREDES.

Secretary of State for Agriculture: SALVADOR JIMÉNEZ.

Secretary of State for Public Works and Communications: VÍCTOR JOSÉ DÍAZ RÚA.

Secretary of State for Public Health and Social Welfare: DR BAUTISTA ROJAS GÓMEZ.

Secretary of State for Industry and Commerce: JOSÉ RAMÓN FADUL FADUL.

Secretary of State for Labour: MAXIMILIANO PUIG.

Secretary of State for Tourism: FRANCISCO JAVIER GARCÍA.

Secretary of State for Sport, Physical Education and Recreation: FELIPE (JAY) PAYANO.

Secretary of State for Culture: JOSÉ RAFAEL LANTIGUA.

Secretary of State for Higher Education, Science and Technology: LIGIA AMADA DE MELO.

Secretary of State for Women: ALEJANDRINA GERMÁN.

Secretary of State for Youth: FRANKLIN RODRÍGUEZ.

Secretary of State for the Environment and Natural Resources: DR JAIME DAVID FERNÁNDEZ MIRABAL.

Secretary of State for the Economy, Planning and Development: JUAN TEMÍSTOCLES MONTÁS.

Secretary of State for Public Administration: RAMÓN VENTURA CAMEJO.

Administrative Secretary to the Presidency: LUIS MANUEL BONETTI.

SECRETARIATS OF STATE

Office of the President: Palacio Nacional, Avda México, esq. Dr Delgado, Gazcue, Santo Domingo, DN; tel. 695-8000; fax 682-4558; internet www.presidencia.gob.do.

Secretariat of State for Agriculture: Autopista Duarte, Km 6.5, Los Jardines del Norte, Santo Domingo, DN; tel. 547-3888; fax 227-1268; e-mail agricultura@agricultura.gob.do; internet www.agricultura.gob.do.

Secretariat of State for the Armed Forces: Plaza de la Bandera, Avda 27 de Febrero, esq. Avda Luperón, Santo Domingo, DN; tel. 530-5149; fax 531-0461; e-mail directorrev@j2.mil.do; internet www.fuerzasarmadas.mil.do.

Secretariat of State for Culture: Centro de Eventos y Exposiciones, Avda George Washington, esq. Presidente Vicini Burgos, Santo Domingo, DN; tel. 221-4141; fax 688-2908; e-mail contacto@cultura.gob.do; internet www.cultura.gob.do.

Secretariat of State for the Economy, Planning and Development: Palacio Nacional, Avda México, esq. Dr Delgado, Bloque B, 2°, Santo Domingo, DN; tel. 221-5140; fax 221-8627; e-mail informacion@economia.gob.do; internet www.economia.gob.do.

Secretariat of State for Education: Avda Máximo Gómez, esq. Santiago 2, Gazcue, Santo Domingo, DN; tel. 688-9700; fax 689-8688; e-mail mlibreacceso@see.gob.do; internet www.see.gob.do.

Secretariat of State for the Environment and Natural Resources: Plaza Naco 28, Avda Tiradentes, esq. Fantico Falco, Ensanche Naco, Santo Domingo, DN; tel. 567-4300; fax 683-4774; e-mail contacto@medioambiente.gob.do; internet www.ambiente.gob.do.

Secretariat of State for Finance: Avda México 45, esq. Leopoldo Navarro, Apdo 1478, Santo Domingo, DN; tel. 687-5131; fax 682-0498; e-mail webmaster@finanzas.gob.do; internet www.hacienda.gob.do.

Secretariat of State for Foreign Affairs: Avda Independencia 752, Estancia San Gerónimo, Santo Domingo, DN; tel. 987-7001; fax 987-7002; e-mail relexteriores@serex.gob.do; internet www.serex.gov.do.

Secretariat of State for Higher Education, Science and Technology: Avda Máximo Gómez 31, esq. Pedro Henríquez Ureña, Santo Domingo, DN; tel. 731-1100; fax 535-4694; e-mail info@seescyt.gob.do; internet www.seescyt.gov.do.

Secretariat of State for Industry and Commerce: Edif. de Ofs Gubernamentales Juan Pablo Duarte, 7°, Avda México, esq. Leopoldo Navarro, Apdo 9876, Santo Domingo, DN; tel. 685-5171; fax 686-1973; e-mail info@seic.gob.do; internet www.seic.gov.do.

Secretariat of State for the Interior and Police: Edif. de Ofs Gubernamentales Juan Pablo Duarte, 13°, Avda México, esq. Leopoldo Navarro, Santo Domingo, DN; tel. 686-6251; fax 689-6599; e-mail info@seip.gob.do; internet www.seip.gob.do.

Secretariat of State for Labour: Centro de los Héroes, Avda Jiménez Moya 9,La Feria, Santo Domingo, DN; tel. 535-4404; fax 535-4833; e-mail oai@set.gob.do; internet www.set.gob.do.

Secretariat of State for Public Administration: Edif. de Ofs. Gubernamentales Juan Pablo Duarte, 12°, Avda México, esq. Leopoldo Navarro, Apdo 20031, Santo Domingo, DN; tel. 682-3298; fax 686-6652; e-mail seap@seap.gob.do; internet www.seap.gob.do.

Secretariat of State for Public Health and Social Welfare: Avda San Cristóbal, esq. Tiradentes, Ensanche La Fe, Santo Domingo, DN; tel. 541-3121; fax 540-6445; e-mail correo@sespas.gob.do; internet www.sespas.gov.do.

Secretariat of State for Public Works and Communications: Avda San Cristóbal, esq. Avda Tiradentes, Ensanche La Fe, Santo Domingo, DN; tel. 565-2811; fax 562-3382; e-mail info@seopc.gob.do; internet www.seopc.gov.do.

Secretariat of State for Sport, Physical Education and Recreation: Avda Correa y Cidrón, esq. John F. Kennedy, Estadio Olímpico, Centro Olímpico Juan Pablo Duarte, Santo Domingo, DN; tel. 565-3325; fax 563-6586; e-mail j.yapor@sedefir.gov.do; internet www.sedefir.gov.do.

Secretariat of State for Tourism: Edif. de Ofs Gubernamentales, Bloque D, Avda México, esq. 30 de Marzo, Apdo 497, Santo Domingo, DN; tel. 221-4660; fax 682-3806; e-mail info@sectur.gob.do; internet www.sectur.gob.do.

Secretariat of State for Women: Edif. de Ofs. Gubernamentales, Bloque D, 2°, Avda México, esq. 30 de Marzo, Santo Domingo, DN; tel. 685-3755; fax 686-0911; e-mail info@mujer.gob.do; internet www.mujer.gob.do.

Secretariat of State for Youth: Avda Jiménez de Moya 71, esq. Calle Desiderio Arias, Ensanche La Julia, Santo Domingo, DN; tel. 508-7227; fax 508-6686; e-mail info@juventud.gob.do; internet www.juventud.gob.do.

President and Legislature

PRESIDENT

Election, 16 May 2008

Candidate	Votes	% of valid votes cast
Leonel Fernández Reyna (PLD)	2,199,734	53.83
Miguel Vargas Maldonado (PRD)	1,624,066	40.48
Amable Aristy Castro (PRSC)	187,645	4.59
Others	45,096	1.10
Total	4,086,541	100.00

CONGRESO NACIONAL

The Congreso Nacional comprises a Senado and a Cámara de Diputados.

President of the Senado: Dr Reinaldo Pared Pérez (PLD).

President of the Cámara de Diputados: Julio César Valentín Jiminián (PLD).

General Election, 16 May 2010

	Seats	
	Senate	Chamber of Deputies
Partido de la Liberación Dominicana (PLD)	31	105
Partido Revolucionario Dominicano (PRD)	—	75
Partido Reformista Social Cristiano (PRSC)	1	3
Total	32	183

Election Commission

Junta Central Electoral (JCE): Avda 27 de Febrero, esq. Gregorio Luperón, Santo Domingo, DN; tel. 539-5419; e-mail webmaster@jce.do; internet www.jce.do; f. 1923; govt-appointed body; Pres. Dr Julio César Castaños Guzmán.

Political Organizations

In 2009 there were 23 political parties recognized by the Junta Central Electoral.

Alianza por la Democracia (APD): Benito Mención 10, Gazcue, Santo Domingo, DN; tel. 687-0337; fax 687-0360; f. 1992 by breakaway group of the PLD; Pres. Maximiliano Puig; Sec.-Gen. Carlos Luis Sánchez S.

Bloque Institucional Socialdemócrata (BIS): Avda Bolívar 24, esq. Uruguay, Ensanche Lugo, Apdo 5413, Santo Domingo, DN; tel. 682-3232; fax 682-3375; e-mail adm@bis.org.do; internet bis.org.do; f. 1989 by breakaway group of PRD under Dr José Francisco Peña Gómez; Sec.-Gen. Diómedes Remigio Pichardo.

Fuerza Nacional Progresista (FNP): Calle Emilio A. Morel 17, Ensanche La Fe, Santo Domingo, DN; tel. 732-0849; e-mail fuerza_nacional_progresista@hotmail.com; internet fuerzanacionalprogresista.blogspot.com; right-wing; Pres. Marino Vinicio Castillo; Sec.-Gen. José Ricardo Taveras B.

Partido Demócrata Popular: Carmen de Mendoza de Corniel 78, El Millón, Santo Domingo, DN; tel. 701-6035; Pres. Ramón Nelson Didiez Nadal; Sec.-Gen. Santa M. Ogando de Didiez.

Partido de la Liberación Dominicana (PLD): Avda Independencia 401, Santo Domingo, DN; tel. 685-3540; fax 687-5569; e-mail pldorg@pld.org.do; internet www.pld.org.do; f. 1973 by breakaway group of PRD; left-wing; Leader Leonel Fernández Reyna; Sec.-Gen. Reinaldo Pared Pérez.

Partido Quisqueyano Demócrata Cristiano (PQDC): Avda Bolívar 51, esq. Uruguay, Santo Domingo, DN; tel. 682-5873; fax 689-2881; e-mail pqd@verizon.net.do; f. 1968; right-wing; Pres. Elías Wessin Chávez; Sec.-Gen. Lorenzo Valdez Carrasco.

Partido Reformista Social Cristiano (PRSC): Avda Tiradentes, esq. San Cristóbal, Ensanche La Fe, Apdo 1332, Santo Domingo, DN; tel. 621-7772; e-mail s.seliman@codetel.net.do; f. 1964; centre-right party; Pres. Carlos Morales Troncoso; Sec.-Gen. Ramón Rogelio Genao.

Partido Revolucionario Dominicano (PRD): Avda Dr Comandante Enrique Jiménez Moya 14, Bella Vista, Santo Domingo, DN; tel. 687-2193; e-mail prensa_tribunalp.r.d@hotmail.com; internet prd.partidos.com; f. 1939; democratic socialist; mem. of Socialist International; Pres. Miguel Vargas Maldonado; Sec.-Gen. Orlando Jorge Mera.

Partido Revolucionario Independiente (PRI): Edif. Galerías Comerciales, Avda 57, Apdo 509, Santo Domingo, DN; tel. 221-8286; e-mail Trajano.S@codetel.net.do; f. 1985 after split by the PRD's right-wing faction; Pres. Dr Trajano Santana; Sec.-Gen. Dr Jorge Montes de Oca.

Partido de los Trabajadores Dominicanos (PTD): Avda Bolívar 101, esq. Dr Báez, Gazcue, Santo Domingo, DN; tel. 685-7705; fax 333-6443; e-mail contacto@ptd.org.do; internet www.ptd.org.do; f. 1979; Communist; Pres. José González Espinoza; Sec.-Gen. Antonio Florián.

Diplomatic Representation

EMBASSIES IN THE DOMINICAN REPUBLIC

Argentina: Avda Máximo Gómez 10, Apdo 1302, Santo Domingo, DN; tel. 682-2977; fax 221-2206; e-mail edomi@mreic.gov.ar; Chargé d'affaires a.i. Fernando Gustavo Edua Ricci.

Belize: Carretera La Isabela, Calle Proyecto 3, Arroyo Manzano 1, Santo Domingo, DN; tel. 567-7146; fax 567-7159; e-mail domrep@embelize.org; internet www.embelize.org; Ambassador R. Eduardo Lama S.

Brazil: Eduardo Vicioso 46a, esq. Avda Winston Churchill, Ensanche Bella Vista, Apdo 1655, Santo Domingo, DN; tel. 532-0868; fax 532-0917; e-mail contato@embajadadebrasil.org.do; internet www.embajadadebrasil.org.do; Ambassador João Solano Carneiro da Cunha.

Canada: Avda Winston Churchill 1099, Torre Citigroup en Acrópolis Center, 18°, Ensanche Piantini, Apdo 2054, Santo Domingo, DN; tel. 262-3100; fax 262-3108; e-mail sdmgo@international.gc.ca; internet www.canadainternational.gc.ca/dominican_republic-republique_dominicaine; Ambassador Todd Kuiack.

Chile: Avda Anacaona 11, Mirador del Sur, Santo Domingo, DN; tel. 532-7800; fax 530-8310; e-mail embaj.chile@verizon.net.do; Ambassador Manuel Enrique Hinojosa Muñoz.

China (Taiwan): Avda Rómulo Betancourt 1360, Secto Bella Vista, Santo Domingo, DN; tel. 508-6200; fax 508-6335; e-mail dom@mofa.gov.tw; internet www.roc-taiwan-do.com; Ambassador Isaac Tsai Meng-hung.

Colombia: Fernando Escobar 8, Ensanche Serralles, Santo Domingo, DN; tel. 562-5282; fax 562-3253; e-mail erdomini@cancilleria.gov.co; Ambassador MARIO MONTOYA URIBE.

Costa Rica: Calle Malaquías Gil 11 Altos, entre Abraham Lincoln y Lope de Vega, Ensanche Serralles, Santo Domingo, DN; tel. 683-7209; fax 565-6467; e-mail emb.costarica@codetel.net; Ambassador MARTA EUGENIA NÚÑEZ MADRIZ.

Cuba: Francisco Prats Ramírez 808, El Millón, Santo Domingo, DN; tel. 537-2113; fax 537-9820; e-mail embadom@verizon.net.do; internet embacu.cubaminrex.cu/dominicana; Ambassador JUAN DOMINGO ASTIASARÁN CEBALLO.

Ecuador: Edif. Optica Félix, Penthouse 601, Avda Abraham Lincoln 1007, Ensanche Piantini, Santo Domingo, DN; tel. 563-8363; fax 563-8153; e-mail mecuador@verizon.net.do; Ambassador CARLOS ALONSO MANRIQUE MUÑOZ.

El Salvador: Edif. Odontología Dominicana, 4°, Calle Haim López Penha 32, Ensanche Piantini, Santo Domingo, DN; tel. 565-4311; fax 541-7503; e-mail emb.salvador@codetel.net.do; Ambassador ERNESTO FERREIRO RUSCONI.

France: Calle Las Damas 42, esq. El Conde, Zona Colonial, Santo Domingo, DN; tel. 695-4300; fax 695-4311; e-mail ambafrance@ambafrance-do.org; internet www.ambafrance.org.do; Ambassador ROLAND DUBERTRAND.

Germany: Edif. Torre Piantini, 16° y 17°, Calle Gustavo Mejía Ricart 196, esq. Avda Abraham Lincoln, Ensanche Piantini, Santo Domingo, DN; tel. 542-8949; fax 542-8955; e-mail info@santo-domingo.diplo.de; internet www.santo-domingo.diplo.de; Ambassador CHRISTIAN GERMANN.

Guatemala: Edif. Corominas Pepín, 9°, Avda 27 de Febrero 233, Santo Domingo, DN; tel. 381-0249; fax 381-0278; e-mail embrepdominicana@minex.gob.gt; Ambassador GIOVANNI RENÉ CASTILLO POLANCO.

Haiti: Calle Juan Sánchez Ramírez 33, esq. Desiderio Valdez 33, Zona Universitaria, Santo Domingo, DN; tel. 686-8185; fax 686-6096; e-mail embajadahaiti@yahoo.com; Ambassador Dr FRITZ N. CINEAS.

Holy See: Avda Máximo Gómez 27, esq. César Nicolás Penson, Apdo 312, Santo Domingo, DN (Apostolic Nunciature); tel. 682-3773; fax 687-0287; Apostolic Nuncio Most Rev. JÓZEF WESOŁOWSKI (Titular Archbishop of Slebte).

Honduras: Calle Arístides García Mella, esq. Rodríguez Objío, Edif. El Buen Pastor VI, Apt 1B, 1°, Mirador del Sur, Santo Domingo, DN; tel. 482-7992; fax 482-7505; e-mail e.honduras@codetel.net.do; Chargé d'affaires a.i. ANTONIO JESÚS HANDAL.

Israel: Calle Pedro Henríquez Ureña 80, La Esperilla, Santo Domingo, DN; tel. 472-0774; fax 472-1785; e-mail info@santodomingo.mfa.gov.il; internet santodomingo.mfa.gov.il; Ambassador AMOS RADIAN.

Italy: Calle Rodríguez Objío 4, Gazcue, Santo Domingo, DN; tel. 682-0830; fax 682-8296; e-mail ambsdom.mail@esteri.it; internet www.ambsantodomingo.esteri.it; Ambassador ENRICO GUICCIARDI.

Jamaica: Avda Enriquillo 61A, Los Cacicazgos, Santo Domingo, DN; tel. 482-7770; fax 620-2497; e-mail emb.jamaica@codetel.net.do; Chargé d'affaires a.i. THOMAS F. ALLAN MARLEY.

Japan: Torre BHD, 8°, Avda Winston Churchill, esq. Luis F. Thomén, Ensanche Evaristo Morales, Apdo 9825, Santo Domingo, DN; tel. 567-3365; fax 566-8013; e-mail embjpn@codetel.net.do; internet www.do.emb-japan.go.jp; Ambassador vacant.

Korea, Republic: Calle Maniel 13, Los Cacicazgos, Santo Domingo, DN; tel. 482-3676; fax 482-6504; e-mail embcod@mofat.go.kr; internet dom.mofat.go.kr; Ambassador KANG SUNG-ZU.

Mexico: Arzobispo Meriño 265, esq. Las Mercedes, Zona Colonial, Santo Domingo, DN; tel. 687-7793; fax 687-7872; e-mail embamex@codetel.net.do; Ambassador ENRIQUE MANUEL LOAEZA TOVAR.

Morocco: Avda Abraham Lincoln 1009, Edif. Profesional EFA, 6°, Ensanche Piantini, Santo Domingo, DN; tel. 732-0409; fax 732-1703; e-mail sifamasdomingo@codetel.net.do; Ambassador BRAHIM HOUSSEIN MOUSSA.

Netherlands: Max Henríquez Ureña 50, entre Avda Winston Churchill y Abraham Lincoln, Ensanche Piantini, Apdo 855, Santo Domingo, DN; tel. 262-0320; fax 565-4685; e-mail std@minbuza.nl; internet www.holanda.org.do; Ambassador RITA D. RAHMAN.

Nicaragua: Avda Helios, Calle Corozal, No 6, Bella Vista, Santo Domingo, DN; tel. 535-1120; fax 535-1230; e-mail embanic-rd@codetel.net.do; Chargé d'affaires a.i. ROSA ADILIA VIZCAYA BRIONES.

Panama: Benito Monción 255, Gazcue, Santo Domingo, DN; tel. 688-3789; fax 685-3665; e-mail emb.panam@codetel.net.do; Ambassador ALBERTO MAGNO CASTILLERO.

Peru: Calle Mayreni 31, Urb. Los Cacicazgos, Santo Domingo, DN; tel. 482-3300; fax 482-3334; e-mail embaperu@codetel.net.do; Ambassador VICENTE ALEJANDRO AZULA DE LA GUERRA.

Qatar: Avda Sarasota 7, Santo Domingo, DN; tel. 533-7526; fax 532-8974; Ambassador SAUD ABD AL-AZIZ AL-SOWAIDI.

Spain: Avda Independencia 1205, Apdo 1468, Santo Domingo, DN; tel. 535-6500; fax 535-1595; e-mail embespdo@correo.mae.es; internet www.mae.es/embajadas/santodomingo; Ambassador DIEGO BERMEJO ROMERO DE TERREROS.

Switzerland: Edif. Aeromar, 2°, Avda Winston Churchill 71, esq. Desiderio Arias, Bella Vista, Apdo 3626, Santo Domingo, DN; tel. 533-3781; fax 532-3781; e-mail sdd.vertretung@eda.admin.ch; internet www.eda.admin.ch/santodomingo; Ambassador JACQUES GREMAUD.

United Kingdom: Edif. Corominas Pepin, 7°, Avda 27 de Febrero 233, Santo Domingo, DN; tel. 472-7111; fax 472-7574; e-mail brit.emb.sadom@codeltel.net.do; internet ukindominicanrepublic.fco.gov.uk; Ambassador STEVEN FISHER.

USA: Avda César Nicolás Pensón, esq. Leopoldo Navarro, Santo Domingo, DN; tel. 221-2171; fax 686-7437; e-mail irc@usemb.gov.do; internet santodomingo.usembassy.gov; Ambassador RAUL H. YZAGUIRRE (designate).

Uruguay: Edif. Gapo, Local 401, Avda Luis F. Thomen 110, Ensanche Evaristo Morales, Santo Domingo, DN; tel. 227-3475; fax 472-4231; e-mail embur@codetel.net.do; Ambassador LUIS ALBERTO CARRESE PRIETO.

Venezuela: Avda Anacoana 7, Mirador del Sur, Santo Domingo, DN; tel. 537-8882; fax 537-8780; e-mail embvenezuela@codetel.net.do; internet www.embavenezdominicana.org; Ambassador FRANCISCO AURA MAHUAMPI RODRÍGUEZ DE ORTIZ.

Judicial System

The Judicial Power resides in the Suprema Corte de Justicia (Supreme Court of Justice), the Cortes de Apelación (Courts of Appeal), the Juzgados de Primera Instancia (Tribunals of the First Instance), the municipal courts and the other judicial authorities provided by law. The Supreme Court is composed of 16 judges and the Attorney-General, and exercises disciplinary authority over all the members of the judiciary. The Attorney-General of the Republic is the Chief of Judicial Police and of the Public Ministry, which he or she represents before the Supreme Court of Justice. The Consejo Nacional de la Magistratura (National Judiciary Council) appoints the members of the Supreme Court, which in turn appoints judges at all other levels of the judicial system.

Corte Suprema de Justicia

Centro de los Héroes, Calle Juan de Dios Ventura Simó, esq. Enrique Jiménez Moya, Apdo 1485, Santo Domingo, DN; tel. 533-3191; fax 532-2906; e-mail suprema.corte@verizon.net.do; internet www.suprema.gov.do.

President: Dr JORGE A. SUBERO ISA.

Vice-President and President of First Court: Dr RAFAEL LUCIANO PICHARDO.

Second Vice-President: Dra EGLYS MARGARITA ESMURDOC.

President of Second Court: Dr HUGO ÁLVAREZ VALENCIA.

Justices: Dra MARGARITA A. TAVARES, VÍCTOR JOSÉ CASTELLANOS ESTRELLA, Dr JULIO IBARRA RÍOS, Dr EDGAR HERNÁNDEZ MEJÍA, Dra DULCE M. RODRÍGUEZ DE GORIS, Dra ANA ROSA BERGÉS DREYFOUS, Dr JUAN LUPERÓN VÁSQUEZ, Dr JULIO ANÍBAL SUÁREZ, Dra ENILDA REYES PÉREZ, Dr JOSÉ ENRIQUE HERNÁNDEZ MACHADO, Dr PEDRO ROMERO CONFESOR, Dr DARÍO OCTAVIO FERNÁNDEZ ESPINAL.

Attorney-General: Dr RADHAMÉS JIMÉNEZ PEÑA.

Religion

The majority of the inhabitants belong to the Roman Catholic Church, but freedom of worship exists for all denominations. The Baptist, Evangelist and Seventh-day Adventist churches and the Jewish faith are also represented.

CHRISTIANITY

The Roman Catholic Church

The Dominican Republic comprises two archdioceses and nine dioceses. Roman Catholics represent about 87% of the population.

Bishops' Conference

Conferencia del Episcopado Dominicano, Apdo 186, Calle Isabel la Católica 55, Santo Domingo, DN; tel. 685-3141; fax 685-0227; e-mail nicolas.clr@codetel.net.do; internet www.ced.org.do.

f. 1985; Pres. Cardinal NICOLÁS DE JESÚS LÓPEZ RODRÍGUEZ (Archbishop of Santo Domingo).

Archbishop of Santiago de los Caballeros: Most Rev. RAMÓN BENITO DE LA ROSA Y CARPIO, Arzobispado, Duvergé 14, Apdo 679,

Santiago de los Caballeros; tel. 582-2094; fax 581-3580; e-mail arzobisp.stgo@verizon.net.do.

Archbishop of Santo Domingo: Cardinal NICOLÁS DE JESÚS LÓPEZ RODRÍGUEZ, Arzobispado, Isabel la Católica 55, Apdo 186, Santo Domingo, DN; tel. 685-3141; fax 688-7270; e-mail nicolas.clr@codetel.net.do.

The Anglican Communion

Anglicans in the Dominican Republic are under the jurisdiction of the Episcopal Church in the USA. The country is classified as a missionary diocese, in Province IX.

Bishop of the Dominican Republic: Rt Rev. JULIO CÉSAR HOLGUÍN KHOURY, Santiago 114, Apdo 764, Santo Domingo, DN; tel. 688-6016; fax 686-6364; e-mail iglepidom@verizon.net.do; internet www.dominicanepiscopalchurch.org.

BAHÁ'Í FAITH

National Spiritual Assembly of the Bahá'ís of the Dominican Republic: Cambronal 152, esq. Beller, Santo Domingo, DN; tel. 687-1726; fax 687-7606; e-mail bahai.rd.aen@verizon.net.do; internet www.bahai.org.do; f. 1961; 402 localities.

The Press

Dirección General de Información, Publicidad y Prensa: Palacio Nacional, Santo Domingo, DN; f. 1983; govt supervisory body; Dir RAFAEL NÚÑEZ.

DAILIES

Santo Domingo

El Caribe: Calle Doctor Defilló 4, Los Prados, Apdo 416, Santo Domingo, DN; tel. 683-8100; fax 544-4003; e-mail editora@elcaribe.com.do; internet www.elcaribe.com.do; f. 1948; morning; circ. 32,000; Pres. FÉLIX M. GARCÍA; Dir MANUEL A. QUIROZ.

El Día: Avda San Martín 236, Santo Domingo, DN; tel. 565-5581; fax 540-1697; e-mail eldia@eldia.com.do; internet www.eldia.com.do; f. 2002; Dir RAFAEL MOLINA MORILLO; Editor FRANKLIN PUELLO.

Diario Libre: Avda Abraham Lincoln, esq. Max Henríquez Ureña, Santo Domingo, DN; tel. 476-7200; fax 616-1520; internet www.diariolibre.com; Dir ADRIANO MIGUEL TEJADA; Editor ELI HEILIGER.

Hoy: Avda San Martín 236, Santo Domingo, DN; tel. 565-5581; fax 567-2424; e-mail hoydigital@hoy.com.do; internet www.hoy.com.do; f. 1981; morning; Dir ALVAREZ VEGA; Man. Editors CLAUDIO ACOSTA, MARIEN CAPITÁN; circ. 40,000.

Listín Diario: Paseo de los Periodistas 52, Ensanche Miraflores, Santo Domingo, DN; tel. 686-6688; fax 686-6595; e-mail info@listindiario.com.do; internet www2.listindiario.com; f. 1889; morning; Dir-Gen. MIGUEL FRANJUL; Editor-in-Chief FABIO CABRAL; circ. 88,050.

La Nación: Calle San Antonio 2, Zona Industrial de Herrera, Santo Domingo, DN; tel. 537-2444; fax 537-4865; e-mail editor.nacion@codetel.net.do; afternoon.

El Nacional: Avda San Martín 236, Santo Domingo, DN; tel. 565-5581; fax 565-4190; e-mail elnacional@elnacional.com.do; internet www.elnacional.com.do; f. 1966; evening and Sunday; Dir RADHAMÉS GÓMEZ PEPÍN; circ. 45,000.

El Nuevo Diario: Avda Francia 41, Santo Domingo, DN; tel. 687-7450; fax 687-3205; e-mail redaccionnd@gmail.com; internet www.elnuevodiario.com.do; f. 1981; morning; Exec. Dir COSETTE BONNELLY; Editor LUIS BRITO.

El Siglo: Calle San Antón 2, Zona Industrial de Herrera, Apdo 20213, Santo Domingo, DN; tel. 518-4000; fax 518-4035; e-mail elsiglo@elsiglord.com; Editorial Dir OSVALDO SANTANA.

Santiago de los Caballeros

La Información: Carretera Licey, Km 3, Santiago de los Caballeros; tel. 581-1915; fax 581-7770; e-mail e.informacion@codetel.net.do; internet lainformacion.com.do; f. 1915; morning; Dir FERNANDO A. PÉREZ MEMÉN; circ. 15,000.

PERIODICALS AND REVIEWS

Agroconocimiento: Apdo 345-2, Santo Domingo, DN; monthly; agricultural news and technical information; Dir DOMINGO MARTE; circ. 10,000.

¡Ahora!: San Martín 236, Apdo 1402, Santo Domingo, DN; tel. 565-5581; e-mail revistaahora@internet.net.do; internet www.ahora.com.do; f. 1962; weekly; Editor RAFAEL MOLINA MORILLO.

La Campiña: San Martín 236, Apdo 1402, Santo Domingo, DN; f. 1967; Dir Ing. JUAN ULISES GARCÍA B.

Carta Dominicana: Avda Tiradentes 56, Santo Domingo, DN; tel. 566-0119; f. 1974; monthly; economics; Dir JUAN RAMÓN QUIÑONES M.

Deportes: San Martín 236, Apdo 1402, Santo Domingo, DN; f. 1967; sports; fortnightly; Dir L. R. CORDERO; circ. 5,000.

Eva: San Martín 236, Apdo 1402, Santo Domingo, DN; f. 1967; fortnightly; Dir MAGDA FLORENCIO.

Horizontes de América: Santo Domingo, DN; f. 1967; monthly; Dir ARMANDO LEMUS CASTILLO.

Letra Grande, Arte y Literatura: Leonardo da Vinci 13, Mirador del Sur, Avda 27 de Febrero, Santo Domingo, DN; tel. 531-2225; f. 1980; monthly; art and literature; Dir JUAN RAMÓN QUIÑONES M.

Renovación: José Reyes, esq. El Conde, Santo Domingo, DN; fortnightly; Dir OLGA QUISQUEYA VIUDA MARTÍNEZ.

Visión Agropecuaria: Autopista Duarte, Km 6.5, Los Jardines del Norte, Santo Domingo, DN; tel. 547-1193; e-mail visionagropecuaria27@gmail.com; newsletter of the Secretariat of State for Agriculture; 6 a year; Dir WILFREDO POLANCO; Editor ANTONIO CÁCERES.

NEWS AGENCY

La Noticia: Julio Verne 14, Santo Domingo, DN; tel. 535-0815; f. 1973; evening; Pres. JOSÉ A. BREA PEÑA; Dir BOLÍVAR BELLO.

Publishers

SANTO DOMINGO

Arte y Cine, C por A: San Martín 45, Santo Domingo, DN; tel. 682-0342; fax 686-8354.

Editora Alfa y Omega: José Contreras 69, Santo Domingo, DN; tel. 532-5577.

Editora de las Antillas: Santo Domingo, DN; tel. 685-2197.

Editora Dominicana, SA: 23 Oeste, No 3 Luperón, Santo Domingo, DN; tel. 688-0846.

Editora El Caribe, C por A: Calle Doctor Defilló 4, Los Prados, Apdo 416, Santo Domingo, DN; tel. 683-8100; fax 544-4003; e-mail editora@elcaribe.com.do; internet www.elcaribe.com.do; f. 1948; Dir MANUEL QUIROZ.

Editora Hoy, C por A: San Martín, 236, Santo Domingo, DN; tel. 566-1147.

Editora Listín Diario, C por A: Paseo de los Periodistas 52, Ensanche Miraflores, Apdo 1455, Santo Domingo, DN; tel. 686-6688; fax 686-6595; f. 1889; Pres. Dr ROGELIO A. PELLERANO.

Editorama, SA: Calle Eugenio Contreras, No 54, Los Trinitarios, Apdo 2074, Santo Domingo, DN; tel. 596-6669; fax 594-1421; e-mail editorama@editorama.com; internet www.editorama.com; f. 1970; Pres. JUAN ANTONIO QUIÑONES MARTE.

Editorial Padilla, C por A: Avda 27 de Febrero, Santo Domingo, DN; tel. 379-1550; fax 379-2631.

Editorial Santo Domingo: Santo Domingo, DN; tel. 532-9431.

Editorial Stella: Avda 19 de Marzo 304, Santo Domingo, DN; tel. 682-2281; fax 687-0835.

Julio D. Postigo e Hijos: Santo Domingo, DN; f. 1949; fiction; Man. J. D. POSTIGO.

Publicaciones Ahora, C por A: Avda San Martín 236, Apdo 1402, Santo Domingo, DN; tel. 565-5580; fax 565-4190; Pres. JULIO CASTAÑO.

Publicaciones América: Santo Domingo, DN; Dir PEDRO BISONÓ.

SANTIAGO DE LOS CABALLEROS

Editora el País, SA: Carrera Sánchez, Km 6½, Santiago de los Caballeros; tel. 532-9511.

Broadcasting and Communications

Instituto Dominicano de las Telecomunicaciones (INDOTEL): Avda Abraham Lincoln, No 962, Edif. Osiris, Santo Domingo, DN; tel. 732-5555; fax 732-3904; e-mail centrodeasistencia@indotel.org.do; internet www.indotel.org.do; f. 1998; Pres. Dr JOSÉ RAFAEL VARGAS.

TELECOMMUNICATIONS

Compañía Dominicana de Teléfonos, C por A (Claro—Codetel): Avda John F. Kennedy 54, Apdo 1377, Santo Domingo, DN; tel. 220-1111; fax 543-1301; e-mail servicioalcliente@codetel.net.do; internet www.codetel.net.do; f. 1930; owned by América Móvil, SA de CV (Mexico); operates mobile services as Claro and fixed-line services as Codetel; Pres. OSCAR PEÑA CHACÓN.

Ericsson República Dominicana: Edif. Empresarial Hylsa, 2°, Avda Winston Churchill, esq. Víctor Garrido Puello, Santo Domingo, DN; tel. 683-7701; fax 616-0962; f. 2000; mobile cellular telephone network provider; subsidiary of Telefon AB LM Ericsson (Sweden); Country Man. PETER FÄLLMAN.

Orange Dominicana, SA: Calle Víctor Garrido Puello 23, Edif. Orange, Ensanche Piantini, Santo Domingo, DN; tel. 859-6555; e-mail servicio.cliente@orange.com.do; internet www.orange.com .do; f. 2000; mobile cellular telephone operator, providing GSM network coverage to 89% of the Dominican Republic population; subsidiary of Orange, SA (France); Pres. FREDERICK DEBORD.

Tricom Telecomunicaciones de Voz, Data y Video: Avda Lope de Vega 95, Ensanche Naco, Santo Domingo, DN; tel. 476-6000; fax 567-4412; e-mail sc@tricom.com.do; internet www.tricom.net; f. 1992; Pres. and CEO CARL CARLSON; Chair. RICARDO VALDEZ ALBIZU.

BROADCASTING

Radio

There were some 130 commercial stations in the Dominican Republic. The government-owned broadcasting network, Radio Televisión Dominicana (see Television), operates nine radio stations.

Asociación Dominicana de Radiodifusoras Inc. (ADORA): Paul Harris 3, Centro de los Héroes, Santo Domingo, DN; tel. 535-4057; fax 535-4058; e-mail adora.org.do@gmail.com; internet adora-do.blogspot.com; f. 1964; Pres. SANDRA PONS.

Cadena de Noticias (CDN) Radio: Calle Doctor Defilló 4, Los Prados, Apdo 416, Santo Domingo, DN; tel. 683-8100; fax 544-4003; e-mail inforadio@cdn.com.do; internet www.cdn.com.do.

Television

Antena Latina, Canal 7: Calle Gustavo Mejía Ricart 45, Ensanche Naco, Santo Domingo, DN; tel. 412-0707; fax 333-0707; e-mail contacto@antenalatina7.com; internet www.antenalatina7.com; f. 1999; Pres. JOSÉ MIGUEL BONETTI.

Cadena de Noticias (CDN) Televisión: Calle Doctor Defilló 4, Los Prados, Apdo 416, Santo Domingo, DN; tel. 262-2100; fax 567-2671; e-mail direccion@cdn.com.do; internet www.cdn.com.do; broadcasts news on Channel 37.

Color Visión, Canal 9: Emilio A. Morel, esq. Luis Pérez, Ensanche La Fe, Santo Domingo, DN; tel. 566-5875; fax 732-9347; e-mail colorvision@codetel.net.do; internet www.colorvision.com.do; f. 1969; majority-owned by Corporación Dominicana de Radio y Televisión; commercial station; Dir-Gen. MANUEL QUIROZ MIRANDA.

Radio Televisión Dominicana, Canal 4: Dr Tejada Florentino 8, Apdo 869, Santo Domingo, DN; tel. 689-2120; e-mail rm.colombo@codetel.net.do; internet www.rtvd.com; govt station; Channel 4; Dir-Gen. RAMÓN EMILIO COLOMBO; Gen. Man. AGUSTÍN MERCADO.

Teleantillas, Canal 2: Autopista Duarte, Km 7½, Los Prados, Apdo 30404, Santo Domingo, DN; tel. 567-7751; fax 540-4912; e-mail webmaster@tele-antillas.tv; internet www.tele-antillas.tv; f. 1979; Gen. Man. HÉCTOR VALENTÍN BÁEZ.

Telecentro, Canal 13: Avda Pasteur 204, Santo Domingo, DN; tel. 687-9161; fax 542-7582; e-mail webmaster@telecentro.com.do; internet www.telecentro.com.do; Santo Domingo and east region; Pres. JOSÉ MIGUEL BÁEZ FIGUEROA.

Telemedios Dominicanos, Canal 25: 16 de Agosto, Santo Domingo, DN; tel. 583-2525; internet www.canal25net.tv; f. 1999; Dir CÉSAR HERNÁNDEZ.

Telemicro, Canal 5: Calle Mariano Cestero, esq. Enrrique, Santo Domingo, DN; tel. 689-0555; fax 686-6528; e-mail programacion@telemicro.com.do; internet www.telemicro.com.do; f. 1982.

Telesistema, Canal 11: Avda 27 de Febrero 52, esq. Máximo Gómez, Sector Bergel, Santo Domingo, DN; tel. 563-6661; fax 472-1754; e-mail info@telesistema11.tv; internet www.telesistema11.tv; Pres. JOSÉ L. CORREPIO.

Finance

(cap. = capital; res = reserves; dep. = deposits; m. = million; brs = branches; amounts in pesos)

BANKING

Supervisory Body

Superintendencia de Bancos: 52 Avda México, esq. Leopoldo Navarro, Apdo 1326, Santo Domingo, DN; tel. 685-8141; fax 685-0859; e-mail nmolina@supbanco.gov.do; internet www.supbanco.gov .do; f. 1947; Supt HAIVANJOE NG CORTIÑAS.

Central Bank

Banco Central de la República Dominicana: Calle Pedro Henríquez Ureña, esq. Leopoldo Navarro, Apdo 1347, Santo Domingo, DN; tel. 221-9111; fax 687-7488; e-mail info@bancentral.gov.do; internet www.bancentral.gov.do; f. 1947; cap. and res 2,371.4m., dep. 237,732.7m. (Dec. 2007); Gov. HÉCTOR VALDEZ ALBIZU; Man. PEDRO SILVERIO ALVAREZ.

Commercial Banks

Banco BHD, SA: Avda 27 de Febrero, esq. Avda Winston Churchill, Santo Domingo, DN; tel. 243-3232; fax 541-4949; e-mail servicio@bhd .com.do; internet www.bhd.com.do; f. 1972; cap. 3,608.0m., res 1,027.0m., dep. 55,422.0m. (Dec. 2008); Pres. LUIS EUGENIO MOLINA ACHÉCAR; 80 brs.

Banco Dominicano del Progreso, SA (Progreso): Avda John F. Kennedy 3, Apdo 1329, Santo Domingo, DN; tel. 378-3201; fax 227-3137; e-mail informacion@progreso.com.do; internet www.progreso .com.do; f. 1974; merged with Banco Metropolitano, SA, and Banco de Desarrollo Dominicano, SA, in 2000; cap. 3,500m., res –2,056m., dep. 20,380m. (Dec. 2007); Pres. JUAN B. VICINI LLUBERES; 20 brs.

Banco Múltiple Leon, SA: Avda John F. Kennedy 135, esq. Tiradentes, Apdo 1502, Santo Domingo, DN; tel. 476-2000; fax 473-2050; e-mail info@leon.com.do; internet www.leon.com.do; f. 1981; fmrly Banco Nacional de Crédito, SA; became Bancrédito, SA, in 2002; adopted current name Dec. 2003; cap. 1,951.1m., res 159.0m., dep. 26,672.6m. (Dec. 2008); Pres. and CEO MANUEL PEÑA-MORROS; 56 brs.

Banco Popular Dominicano: Avda John F. Kennedy 20, Torre Popular, Apdo 1441, Santo Domingo, DN; tel. 544-5555; fax 544-5899; e-mail contactenos@bpd.com.do; internet www.bpd.com.do; f. 1963; cap. 8,549.8m., res 1,630.2m., dep. 127,177.3m. (Dec. 2008); Pres., Chair. and Gen. Man. MANUEL ALEJANDRO GRULLÓN; 184 brs.

Banco de Reservas de la República Dominicana (Banreservas): Isabel la Católica 201, Apdo 1353, Santo Domingo, DN; tel. 960-2000; fax 685-0602; e-mail mensajeadministrador@banreservas .com; internet www.banreservas.com.do; f. 1941; state-owned; cap. 3,500.0m., res 6,488.1m., dep. 115,274.4m. (Dec. 2007); Pres. VICENTE BENGOA ALBIZU (Secretary of State for Finance); Administrator DANIEL TORIBIO; 112 brs.

Development Banks

Banco Agrícola de la República Dominicana: Avda G. Washington 601, Apdo 1057, Santo Domingo, DN; tel. 535-8088; fax 535-8022; e-mail bagricola@bagricola.gov.do; internet www.bagricola.gov.do; f. 1945; govt agricultural devt bank; Gen. Man. and Chair. PAÍNO ABREU COLLADO.

Banco BDI, SA: Avda Sarasota 27, esq. La Julia, Santo Domingo, DN; tel. 535-8586; fax 508-4384; internet www.bdi.com.do; Contact ROCÍO VALDEZ SALDIVAR.

Banco de Desarrollo Ademi, SA: Asociación ADEMI Madame Curie, C/21, La Esperilla, Santo Domingo, DN; tel. 732-4411; fax 732-4401; e-mail cnanita@ademi.org.do; internet www.ademi.org.do; Pres. MARGARITA DE FERRARI LLUBERES.

Banco de Desarrollo Agropecuario Norcentral, SA: Avda Independencia 801, esq. Avda Máximo Gómez, Santo Domingo, DN; tel. 686-0984; fax 687-0825.

Banco de Desarrollo de Exportación, SA: Fatino Falco, entre Avda Lope de Vega y Tiradentes 201, Santo Domingo, DN; tel. 566-5841; fax 565-1769.

Banco de Desarrollo Intercontinental, SA: Edif. Lilian, 5°, Avda Lope de Vega, esq. Gustavo Mejía Ricart, Santo Domingo, DN; tel. 544-0559; fax 563-6884.

Banco Nacional de la Construcción: Avda Alma Mater, esq. Pedro Henríquez Ureña, Santo Domingo, DN; tel. 685-9776; f. 1977; Gen. Man. LUIS MANUEL PELLERANO.

Banco de la Pequeña Empresa, SA: Avda Bolívar 233, entre Avda Abraham Lincoln y Avda Winston Churchill, Santo Domingo, DN; tel. 534-8383; fax 534-8385.

STOCK EXCHANGE

Bolsa de Valores de la República Dominicana, SA: Edif. Empresarial, 1°, Avda John F. Kennedy 16, Apdo 25144, Santo Domingo, DN; tel. 567-6694; fax 567-6697; e-mail info@bolsard .com; internet www.bolsard.com; Pres. MARÍA ANTONIA ESTEVA DE BISONO.

INSURANCE

Supervisory Body

Superintendencia de Seguros: Secretaría de Estado de Finanzas, Avda México 54, esq. Leopoldo Navarro, Santo Domingo, DN; tel.

221-2606; fax 685-5096; e-mail info@superseguros.gob.do; internet www.superseguros.gob.do; f. 1969; Supt EUCLIDES GUTIÉRREZ FÉLIX.

Insurance Companies

American Life and General Insurance Co, C por A: Edif. ALICO, 5°, Avda Abraham Lincoln, Apdo 131, Santo Domingo, DN; tel. 533-7131; fax 535-0362; e-mail caribalico@codetel.net.do; general; Gen. Man. FRANCISCO CABREJA.

Angloamericana de Seguros, SA: Avda Gustavo Mejía Ricard 8, esq. Hermanos Roque Martínez, Ensanche El Millón, Santo Domingo, DN; tel. 227-1002; fax 227-6005; e-mail angloseguros@angloamericana.com.do; internet www.angloamericana.com.do; f. 1996; Pres. NELSON HEDI HERNÁNDEZ P.; Vice-Pres. ESTEBAN BETANCES FABRÉ.

Atlántica Insurance, SA: Avda 27 de Febrero 365A, 2°, Apdo 826, Santo Domingo, DN; tel. 565-5591; fax 565-4343; e-mail atlanticains@codetel.net.do; Gen. Man. Lic. GERARDO PERALTA; Pres. GAMALIER PERALTA.

Bankers Security Life Insurance Society: Calle Gustavo Mejía Ricart 61, Apdo 1123, Santo Domingo, DN; tel. 544-2626; fax 567-9389; e-mail eizquierdo@bpd.com.do; Pres. Lic. ESTELA MA. FIALLO T.

BBVA Seguros: Santo Domingo, DN; f. 2006; bought by Scotiabank in 2007; Pres. MIGUEL JARSUN.

BMI Compañía de Seguros, SA: Avda Tiradentes 14, Edif. Alfonso Comercial, Apdo 916, Ensanche Naco, Santo Domingo, DN; tel. 562-6660; fax 562-6849; e-mail bmi@bmi.com.do; internet www.bmi.com.do; Exec. Vice-Pres. PEDRO DA CUNHA.

Bonanza Compañía de Seguros, SA: Avda John F. Kennedy, Edif. Bonanza, Santo Domingo, DN; tel. 565-5531; fax 566-1087; e-mail bonanza.dom@codetel.net.do; Pres. Lic. DARIO LAMA.

Centro de Seguros La Popular, C por A: Gustavo Mejía Ricart 61, Apdo 1123, Santo Domingo, DN; tel. 566-1988; fax 567-9389; f. 1965; general except life; Pres. Lic. ROSA FIALLO.

La Colonial, SA: Avda Sarasota 75, Bella Vista, Santo Domingo, DN; tel. 508-8000; fax 508-0608; e-mail info@lacolonial.com.do; internet www.lacolonial.com.do; f. 1971; general; Pres. Dr MIGUEL FERIS IGLESIAS; Exec. Vice-Pres. LUIS EDUARDO GUERRERO ROMÁN.

Compañía de Seguros Palic, SA: Avda Abraham Lincoln, esq. José Amado Soler, Apdo 1132, Santo Domingo, DN; tel. 562-1271; fax 562-1825; e-mail cia.seg.palic2@codetel.net.do; Pres. JOSÉ ANTONIO CARO GINEBRA; Exec. Vice-Pres. MILAGROS DE LOS SANTOS.

Confederación del Canadá Dominicana: Calle Salvador Sturla 17, Ensanche Naco, Santo Domingo, DN; tel. 544-4144; fax 540-4740; e-mail confedom@codetel.net.do; internet www.confedom.com; f. 1988; Pres. Lic. MOISES A. FRANCO.

Federal Insurance Company: Edif. La Cumbre, 4°, Avda Tiradentes, esq. Presidente González, Santo Domingo, DN; tel. 567-0181; fax 567-8909; e-mail eizquierdo@bpd.com.do; Pres. LUIS AUGUSTO GINEBRA H.

General de Seguros, SA: Avda Sarasota 55, esq. Pedro A. Bobea, Apdo 2183, Santo Domingo, DN; tel. 535-8888; fax 532-4451; e-mail info@gs.com.do; internet www.gs.com.do; f. 1981; general; Pres. Dr FERNANDO A. BALLISTA DÍAZ.

La Mundial de Seguros, SA: Avda Máximo Gómez, No 31, Santo Domingo, DN; tel. 685-2121; fax 682-3269; general except life and financial; Pres. PEDRO D'ACUNHA.

Progreso Compañía de Seguros, SA (PROSEGUROS): Avda John F. Kennedy 1, Ensanche Miraflores, Santo Domingo, DN; tel. 985-5000; fax 985-5187; e-mail juanga@progreso.com.do; internet www.proseguros.com.do; Pres. VICENZO MASTROLILLI; CEO CARLOS ROMARO.

Reaseguradora Hispaniola, SA: Avda Gustavo Mejía Ricart, Edif. 8, 2°, esq. Hermanos Roque Martínez, Ensanche El Millón, Santo Domingo, DN; tel. 548-7171; fax 548-6007; e-mail rehsa@verizon.net.do; Pres. NELSON HEDI HERNÁNDEZ P.

REHSA Compañía de Seguros y Reaseguros: Avda Gustavo Mejía Ricart, esq. Hermanas Roques Martínez, Ensanche El Millón, Santo Domingo, DN; tel. 548-7171; fax 584-7222; e-mail info@rehsa.com.do; internet www.rehsa.com.do; Gen. Man. NELSON HEIDI HERNÁNDEZ.

Seguros BanReservas: Avda Jiménez Moya, esq. Calle 4, Centro Technológico Banreservas, Ensanche La Paz, Santo Domingo, DN; tel. 960-7200; fax 960-5148; e-mail serviseguros@segbanreservas.com; internet www.segurosbanreservas.com; Pres. Lic. DANIEL TORIBIO MARMOLEJOS; Exec. Vice-Pres. RAFAEL MEDINA.

Seguros Constitución: Calle Seminario 55, Ensanche Piantini, Santo Domingo, DN; tel. 620-0765; fax 412-2358; e-mail info@solseguros.com.do; internet www.segconstitucion.com.do; fmrly El Sol de Seguros; above name adopted in 2008; Exec. Vice-Pres. SIMÓN MAHFOUD MIGUEL.

Seguros La Isleña, C por A: Edif. Centro Coordinador Empresarial, Avda Núñez de Cáceres, esq. Guarocuya, Santo Domingo, DN; tel. 567-7211; fax 565-1448; Pres. HUÁSCAR RODRÍGUEZ; Exec. Vice-Pres. MARÍA DEL PILAR RODRÍGUEZ.

Seguros Pepín, SA: Edif. Corp. Corominas Pepín, Avda 27 de Febrero 233, Santo Domingo, DN; tel. 472-1006; fax 565-9176; internet www.segurospepin.com; general; Pres. Dr BIENVENIDO COROMINAS PEPÍN.

Seguros San Rafael, C por A: Leopoldo Navarro 61, esq. San Francisco de Macorís, Edif. San Rafael, Apdo 1018, Santo Domingo, DN; tel. 688-2231; fax 686-2628; e-mail sanrafael@codetel.net.do; general; Administrator-Gen. RAMÓN PERALTA.

Seguros Universal: Avda Winston Churchill 1100, Evaristo Morales, Apdo 1242, Santo Domingo, DN; tel. 544-7200; fax 544-7999; e-mail escribenos@segurospopular.com.do; internet www.universal.com.do; f. 1964 as La Universal de Seguros; merged with Grupo Asegurador América in 2000; name changed as above in 2006; general; Pres. ERNESTO IZQUIERDO.

Insurance Association

Cámara Dominicana de Aseguradores y Reaseguradores, Inc: Edif. Torre BHD, 5°, Luis F. Thomen, esq. Winston Churchill, Apdo 601, Santo Domingo, DN; tel. 566-0014; fax 566-2600; e-mail cadoar@codetel.net.do; internet www.cadoar.org.do; f. 1972; Pres. Dr LUIS EDUARDO GUERRERO.

Trade and Industry

GOVERNMENT AGENCIES

Comisión Nacional de Energía (CNE): Calle Gustavo Mejía Ricart 73, esq. Agustín Lara, 3°, Ensanche Serralles, Santo Domingo, DN; tel. 732-2000; fax 547-2073; e-mail info@cne.gov.do; internet www.cne.gov.do; f. 2001; responsible for regulation and devt of energy sector; Pres. ENRIQUE RAMIREZ.

Comisión para la Reforma de la Empresa Pública: Edif. Gubernamental Dr Rafael Kasse Acta, 6°, Gustavo Mejía Ricart 73, esq. Agustín Lara, Ensanche Serrallés, Santo Domingo, DN; tel. 683-3591; fax 683-3114; e-mail Info@fonper.gov.do; internet www.fonper.gov.do; commission charged with divestment and restructuring of state enterprises; Pres. FERNANDO ROSA.

Consejo Estatal del Azúcar (CEA) (State Sugar Council): Calle Fray Cipriano de Utrera, Centro de los Héroes, Apdo 1256/1258, Santo Domingo, DN; tel. 533-1161; fax 533-1305; internet www.cea.gov.do; f. 1966; management of operations contracted to private consortiums in 1999 and 2000; Dir-Gen. JUAN FRANCISCO MATOS CASTAÑO.

Corporación Dominicana de Empresas Estatales (CORDE) (Dominican State Corporation): Avda General Antonio Duvergé, Apdo 1378, Santo Domingo, DN; tel. 533-5171; f. 1966 to administer, direct and develop state enterprises; Dir-Gen. LEONCIO ALMÁNZAR.

Instituto de Estabilización de Precios (INESPRE): Plaza de la Bandera, Apdo 86-2, Santo Domingo, DN; tel. 621-0020; fax 620-2588; e-mail informacion@inespre.gov.do; internet www.inespre.gov.do; f. 1969; price commission; Exec. Dir RICARDO JACOBO CABRERA.

Instituto Nacional de la Vivienda: Avda Pedro Henríquez Ureña, esq. Avda Alma Mater, Santo Domingo, DN; tel. 732-0600; fax 227-5803; e-mail invi@verizon.net.do; internet www.invi.gob.do; f. 1962; low-cost housing institute; Dir-Gen. ALMA FERNÁNADEZ DURÁN.

DEVELOPMENT ORGANIZATIONS

Centro para el Desarrollo Agropecuario y Forestal, Inc (CEDAF): Calle José Amado Soler 50, Ensanche Paraíso, CP 567-2, Santo Domingo, DN; tel. 565-5603; fax 544-4727; e-mail cedaf@cedaf.org.do; internet www.cedaf.org.do; f. 1987 to encourage the devt of agriculture, livestock and forestry; fmrly Fundación de Desarrollo Agropecuario, Inc; Pres. MARCIAL NAJRI; Exec. Dir JUAN JOSÉ ESPINAL.

Centro de Desarrollo y Competitividad Industrial (PROINDUSTRIA): Avda 27 de Febrero, esq. Avda Luperón, Plaza de las Banderas, Apdo 1462, Santo Domingo, DN; tel. 530-0010; fax 530-1303; e-mail info@proindustria.gov.do; internet www.cfi.gov.do; f. 1962 as Corporación de Fomento Industrial; restructured and name changed as above in 2007; industrial sector regulator; Dir-Gen. JOSÉ AUGUSTO IZQUIERDO.

Fundación Dominicana de Desarrollo (Dominican Development Foundation): Mercedes No 4, Apdo 857, Santo Domingo, DN; tel. 688-8101; fax 686-0430; e-mail info@fdd.org.do; internet www.fdd.org.do; f. 1962 to mobilize private resources for collaboration in financing small-scale devt programmes; 384 mems; Pres. ALEJANDRO FERNÁNDEZ; Exec. Dir FRANCISCO J. ABATE.

Instituto de Desarrollo y Crédito Cooperativo (IDECOOP): Avda Héroes de Luperón 1, Centro de los Héroes, Apdo 1371, Santo Domingo, DN; tel. 533-8131; fax 533-5149; e-mail idecoop@codetel.net.do; internet idecoop.gov.do; f. 1963 to encourage the devt of co-operatives; Pres. Pedro Corporán Cabrera; Dir Carlos Junior Espinal.

CHAMBERS OF COMMERCE

Cámara Americana de Comercio de la República Dominicana: Torre Empresarial, 6°, Avda Sarasota 20, Apdo 99999, Santo Domingo, DN; tel. 381-0777; fax 381-0286; e-mail amcham@codetel.net.do; internet www.amcham.org.do; Pres. Alejandro Peña Prieto; Exec. Vice-Pres. William M. Malamud.

Cámara de Comercio y Producción de Santo Domingo: Arzobispo Nouel 206, Zona Colonial, Apdo 815, Santo Domingo, DN; tel. 682-2688; fax 685-2228; e-mail ccpsd@camarasantodomingo.org.do; internet www.camarasantodomingo.org.do; f. 1910; 1,500 active mems; Pres. María Isabel Gassó; Sec. Fabiola Medina Garnes.

There are official Chambers of Commerce in the larger towns.

INDUSTRIAL AND TRADE ASSOCIATIONS

Asociación Dominicana de Hacendados y Agricultores (ADHA): 265 Avda 27 de Febrero, al lado de Plaza Central, Santo Domingo, DN; tel. 565-0542; fax 565-8696; farming and agricultural org.; Pres. Ricardo Barceló.

Asociación Dominicana de la Industria Eléctrica (ADIE): Santo Domingo, DN; f. 2009; electrical industry asscn; Pres. Marco de la Rosa.

Asociación Dominicana de Zonas Francas Inc (ADOZONA): Avda Sarasota 20, 4°, Torre Empresarial AIRD, Apdo 3184, Santo Domingo, DN; tel. 472-0251; fax 472-0256; e-mail info@adozona.org; internet www.adozona.org; f. 1988; Pres. Fernando Capellán.

Asociación de Industrias de la República Dominicana, Inc: Avda Sarasota 20, Torre Empresarial AIRD, 12°, Santo Domingo, DN; tel. 472-0000; fax 472-0303; e-mail aird@verizon.net.do; internet www.aird.org.do; f. 1962; industrial org.; Pres. Manuel Diez Cabral.

Centro Dominicano de Promoción de Exportaciones (CEDOPEX): Avda 27 de Febrero, esq. Avda Gregorio Luperón, Los Restauradores, Apdo 199-2, Santo Domingo, DN; tel. 530-5505; fax 530-8208; e-mail emartinez@cel-rd.gov.do; internet www.cei-rd.gov.do; promotion of exports and investments; Exec. Dir Eddy M. Martínez Manzueta.

Consejo Nacional de la Empresa Privada (CONEP): Avda Sarasota 20, Torre Empresarial, 12°, Ensanche La Julia, Santo Domingo, DN; tel. 472-7101; fax 472-7850; e-mail conep@conep.org.do; internet www.conep.org.do; Pres. Lisandro Macarrulla.

Consejo Nacional de Zonas Francas de Exportación (CNZFE): Edif. San Rafael, 5°, Avda Leopoldo Navarro 61, Apdo 21430, Santo Domingo, DN; tel. 686-8077; fax 686-8079; e-mail e.castillo@cnzfe.gob.do; internet www.cnzfe.gov.do; co-ordinating body for the free trade zones; Exec. Dir Luisa Fernández Durán.

Consejo Promotor de Inversiones (Investment Promotion Council): Avda Abraham Lincoln, Edif. Alico, 2°, Santo Domingo, DN; tel. 532-3281; fax 533-7029; Exec. Dir and CEO Frederic Emam Zadé.

Dirección General de Minería: Edif. de Ofs Gubernamentales, 10°, Avda México, esq. Leopoldo Navarro, Santo Domingo, DN; tel. 685-8191; fax 686-8327; e-mail direc.mineria@verizon.net.do; internet www.dgm.gov.do; f. 1947; govt mining and hydrocarbon org.; Dir-Gen. Octavio López.

Instituto Agrario Dominicano (IAD): Avda 27 de Febrero, Plaza la Bandera, Santo Domingo, DN; tel. 620-6585; fax 620-1537; e-mail info@iad.gob.do; internet www.iad.gob.do; Exec. Dir Héctor Rodríguez Pimentel.

Instituto de Innovación en Biotecnología e Industria (INDOTEC): Calle Oloff Palme, esq. Núñez de Cáceres, San Gerónimo, Apdo 392-2, Santo Domingo, DN; tel. 566-8121; fax 227-8808; e-mail sugerencias@iibi.gov.do; internet www.iibi.gov.do; fmrly Instituto Dominicano de Tecnología Industrial (INDOTEC); name changed as above in 2005; Pres. Francisco Javier García; Exec. Dir Dra Bernarda A. Castillo.

Instituto Nacional del Azúcar (INAZUCAR): Avda Jiménez Moya, Apdo 667, Santo Domingo, DN; tel. 532-5571; fax 533-2402; e-mail inst.azucar2@verizon.net.do; internet www.inazucar.gov.do; f. 1965; sugar institute; Exec. Dir Faustino Jiménez.

EMPLOYERS' ORGANIZATIONS

Confederación Patronal de la República Dominicana (COPARDOM): Torre Empresarial AIRD, Suite 207, Avda Sarasota 20, Santo Domingo, DN; tel. 381-4233; fax 381-4266; f. 1946; Pres. Radhamés Martínez.

Consejo Nacional de Hombres de Empresa, Inc: Edif. Motorámbar, 7°, Avda Abraham Lincoln 1056, Santo Domingo, DN; tel. 562-1666; Pres. José Manuel Paliza.

Federación Dominicana de Comerciantes: Carretera Sánchez Km 10, Santo Domingo, DN; tel. 533-2666; Pres. Ivan García.

MAJOR COMPANIES

Abbott Laboratories International: Apdo 846, CP 10117, Santo Domingo, DN; tel. 542-7181; fax 922-8029; internet www.abbott.com; manufacturers of nutritional and pharmaceutical products; Chair. and CEO Miles D. White.

Americana Departamentos, C por A: Avda John F. Kennedy, Km 5.5, Santo Domingo, DN; tel. 549-7777; fax 567-7063; e-mail info@americanadepartamentos.com; internet www.americana.com.do; f. 1944; distributors of hardware, houseware, animal food and construction materials; Pres. Luis García San Miguel; 400 employees.

Bermúdez: Calle J, esq. K, Zona Industrial de Herrera, Santo Domingo, DN; tel. 620-1852; fax 947-4200; e-mail export@bermudez.com.do; internet www.ronbermudez.com; f. 1852; rum production.

Bratex Dominicana, C por A: Zona Franca, Villa Mella, Santo Domingo, DN; tel. 568-1304; fax 568-5718; e-mail helpdesk@bratex.com.do; f. 1989; mfrs of knitted undergarments; Pres. Peter Weinerth; 5,000 employees.

Brugal & Co, C por A: Avda John F. Kennedy 57, Santo Domingo, DN; tel. 566-5651; e-mail contacto@edrington.co.uk; internet www.brugal.com.do; owned by Edrington Group (United Kingdom); rum production; Chair. George Arzeno Brugal; Exec. Pres. Franklin Baez Brugal; c. 1,000 employees.

Cartonajes Hernández, SA: Anibal Espinosa 366, Apdo 1162, Santo Domingo, DN; tel. 695-4008; fax 695-4058; e-mail geren.hdez@codetel.net.do; f. 1946; mfrs of cardboard and packaging materials; Pres. Ricardo Hernández Elmudesi; 285 employees.

Cementos Cibao, C por A: Carretera Baitoa Km 8.5, Palo Amarillo, Apdo 571, Santiago de los Caballeros; tel. 242-7111; fax 242-7135; e-mail cementoscibao@codetel.net.do; internet www.cementoscibao.com; f. 1964; mfrs of concrete and cement blocks; Pres. Huáscar Rodríguez; 516 employees.

Cemex Dominicana, C por A: Torre Acrópolis, 20°, Avda Winston Churchill 67, Ensanche Piantini, Santo Domingo, DN; tel. 683-4901; fax 683-4949; e-mail contactanos@cemexdominicana.com; internet www.cemexdominicana.com; f. 1976 as Cementos Nacionales, SA; name changed as above in 2000, following acquisition by Cemex, SA de CV, Mexico, in 1995; mfrs of cement and cement products; Dir-Gen. Carlos Jacks.

Central Romana Corporación: Apdo 891, La Romana, DN; tel. 523-3333; e-mail alburquerque@crcltd.com.do; internet www.centralromana.com.do; f. 1912; agro-industrial and tourism devt; Pres. Alfonso Fanjul; 25,000 employees.

Cerámica Industrial del Caribe, C por A: Autopista Duarte Km 17.5, Apdo 222-9, Santo Domingo, DN; tel. 560-5618; fax 561-2884; e-mail gerenciageneral@cerinca.com.do; f. 1979; manufacturers of ceramic products; sales 450m. pesos (2000); Pres. Dr Jacobo Salas; 450 employees.

Cervecería Nacional Dominicana, C por A: Avda Independencia, Santo Domingo, DN; tel. 487-3802; fax 533-5815; e-mail centro.atencionalcliente@eli.com.do; internet www.cnd.com.do; f. 1929; part of Grupo León Jimenes; manufacturers of beer and malt liquor; Pres. Rafael Menicucci Vila; 2,500 employees.

Delta Comercial, C por A: Avda Luperón, esq. Rómulo Betancourt, Apdo 1376, Santo Domingo, DN; tel. 537-1000; fax 518-1202; e-mail info@deltacomercial.com.do; internet www.deltacomercial.com.do; f. 1962; importers and distributors of Toyota and Lexus cars; Pres. José Antonio Najri; 675 employees.

DuBar & Co, C por A: Avda Ulises Heureaux 20, Villa Duarte, Santo Domingo, DN; tel. 592-2223; fax 593-4209; e-mail info@dubar.com.do; internet www.dubar.com.do; f. 1926 as Barceló & Co, present name adopted 2010; mfrs of distilled alcoholic drinks; Exec. Pres. José Antonio Barceló; Pres. José Antonio Miguel Barceló; 1,400 employees.

Falcondo Xstrata Nickel, C por A: Loma La Peguera, Bonao, Santo Domingo, DN; tel. 682-6041; fax 687-4735; internet www.xstratanickel.com; f. 1971; subsidiary of Xstrata PLC; nickel mining and smelting; Dir, Public Relations Luis Rosado; 600 employees.

Grupo León Jimenes: Autopista 30 de Mayo, Km 6.5, Santo Domingo, DN; tel. 535-5555; fax 533-5845; e-mail empleos@elj.com.do; internet www.glj.com.do; f. 1985; manufacturers of beer and cigars; Pres. José León Asencio; 1,000 employees.

Grupo M: Caribbean Industrial Park, Santiago de los Caballeros; tel. 241-7171; fax 242-7510; e-mail info@grupom.com.do; internet www.grupom.com.do; f. 1986; manufacturers of clothing; Pres. FERNANDO CAPPELLÁN; approx. 12,000 employees.

Grupo Vicini: Isabel la Católica 158, Zona Colonial, Santo Domingo, DN; tel. 221-8021; fax 685-7503; e-mail c.moya@codetel.net.do; internet www.inazucar.gov.do/grupo_vicini.htm; f. 1883; sugar-cane cultivation and processing; Pres. FELIPE VICINI LLUBERES; Vice-Pres. JUAN VICINI LLUBERES.

Industria Textil del Caribe, C por A: Isabel Aguirre, Apdo 2347, Santo Domingo, DN; f. 1957; manufacturers of cotton fabrics; Pres. PEDRO Z. BENDEK; 876 employees.

Industrias Banilejas, C por A: Avda Máximo Gómez 118, Apdo 942, Santo Domingo, DN; tel. 565-3121; fax 541-5465; e-mail i.banilejas@verizon.net.do; internet www.induban.com; f. 1962; coffee roasting and processing; Pres. MANUEL DE JESÚS PERELLO BAEZ; 877 employees.

Industrias Textiles Puig, SA: Anibal Espinosa 303, Villas Agrícolas, Apdo 954, Santo Domingo, DN; tel. 536-5800; fax 536-6579; f. 1958; producers of socks, hosiery, underwear and other clothing; Pres. RAMÓN L. PUIG; Vice-Pres. DINO MARRANZINI PUIG; 343 employees.

Induveca: Avda Máximo Gómez, No 182, Santo Domingo, DN; tel. 793-3000; fax 541-2627; internet www.induveca.com.do; f. 2000 by merger of Industrias Vegas and Mercasid; producer of meat products and edible oils.

Interamericana Products International, SA: Apdo 192-2, Zona Franca Industrial, Santiago de los Caballeros; tel. 575-0007; fax 575-0253; e-mail info@interamericana.com.do; mfrs of clothing; 8,200 employees.

Refinería Dominicana de Petroleo, SA (Refidomsa): Antigua Carretera Sánchez, Km 17.5, Zona Industrial de Haina, Apdo 1439, Santo Domingo, DN; tel. 472-9999; fax 957-2520; e-mail contacto@refidomsa.com.do; internet www.refidomsa.com.do; f. 1973; petroleum refinery; state-owned; sale of 49% stake to PDVSA Petróleo, SA, Venezuela, agreed in mid-2010; Pres. ANGEL ROSARIO VIÑAS; Gen. Man. VIRIATO SÁNCHEZ.

La Tabacalera, C por A: Calle Numa Silverio 1, Villa González, Apdo 758, Santiago de los Caballeros; tel. 535-4448; fax 581-3019; e-mail info@latabacalera.com; internet www.latabacalera.com; f. 1902 as La Habanera; adopted current name 2000; mfrs of cigarettes and tobacco products; Pres. FRANCISCO DURÁN; 1,300 employees.

Tabacalera San Luis, C por A: Calle Gustavo Mejía Ricart 120, Ste 104, Ensanche Piantini, Santo Domingo, DN; tel. 567-2201; fax 547-2862; e-mail info@deverascigars.com.

Tabacos Dominicanos, SA: Carretera Don Pedro, H del Caimito, Apdo 1162, Santiago de los Caballeros; tel. 582-6440; fax 582-9118; mfrs and distributors of cigarettes; Pres. HENDRIK KELNER; 800 employees.

R. J. Zapata and Associates, SA: Marg Sarasota 12, Santo Domingo, DN; tel. 412-2384; fax 683-9992; e-mail rjzasoc@codetel.net.do; waste management; Pres. RAFAEL ZAPATA.

UTILITIES

Regulatory Authority

Superintendencia de Electricidad: Edif. CREP, 5°, Avda Gustavo Mejía Ricart 73, esq. Agustín Lara, Ensanche Serrallés, Apdo 1725, Santo Domingo, DN; tel. 683-2500; fax 544-1637; e-mail sie@sie.gov.do; internet www.sie.gov.do; f. 2001; Pres. FRANCISCO MÉNDEZ.

Electricity

AES Dominicana: Torre Acrópolis, 23°, Santo Domingo, DN; tel. 955–2223; e-mail infoaesdominicana@aes.com; internet www.aesdominicana.com.do; f. 1997; subsidiary of AES Corpn, USA; largest private electricity generator in the Dominican Republic (300MW); Pres. MARCO DE LA ROSA.

Corporación Dominicana de Empresas Eléctricas Estatales (CDEEE): Edif. Principal CDE, Centro de los Héroes, Avda Independencia, esq. Fray C. de Utrera, Apdo 1428, Santo Domingo, DN; tel. 535-9098; fax 533-7204; e-mail info@cdeee.gov.do; internet www.cdeee.gov.do; f. 1955; state electricity co; partially privatized in 1999, renationalized in 2003; Pres. ARMANDO PEÑA CASTILLO; Exec. Vice-Pres. CELSO MARRANZINI.

Empresa de Generación Hidroeléctrica Dominicana (EGEHID): Avda Rómulo Betancourt 303, Bella Vista, Santo Domingo, DN; tel. 533-5555; fax 535-7472; e-mail hidro@hidroelectroca.gov.do; internet www.hidroelectrica.gob.do; distributor of hydroelectricity; Dir VICTOR VENTURA.

Unidad de Electrificación Rural y Suburbana (UERS): Avda José Andrés Aybar Castellanos 136, Ensanche La Esperilla, Santo Domingo, DN; tel. 227-7666; e-mail info@uers.gov.do; internet www.uers.gov.do; f. 2006; manages supply of electricity to rural areas; Dir-Gen. THELMA EUSEBIO.

There are three electricity distribution companies operating in the Dominican Republic. Empresa Distribuidora de Electricidad del Norte (Ede-Norte), responsible for distribution in the north of the country, and Empresa Distribuidora de Electricidad del Sur (Ede-Sur), in the south, are owned by the Government, while Empresa Distribuidora de Electricidad del Este (Ede-Este), in the east, is jointly owned by the Government and AES Dominicana (q.v.), a subsidiary of the US company AES. In November 2004 AES Dominicana divested its 50% stake in Ede-Este, owing to continued problems in the country's power sector, although in 2009 plans to renationalize the company were announced. In 2006 the Government began restructuring Ede-Norte and Ede-Sur, prior to privatization.

Gas

AES Andrés: Santo Domingo, DN; internet www.aes.com; f. 2003; subsidiary of AES Corpn, USA; 319-MW gas-fired plant and liquefied natural gas terminal; Pres. ANDREW VESEY.

Water

As part of the continuing programme of repair to the country's infrastructure, in 2001 construction began on aqueducts, intended to supply water to the provinces of Bahoruco, Barahona, Duarte, Espaillat, Independencia and Salcedo.

Corporación del Acueducto y Alcantarillado de Santo Domingo: Calle Euclides Morillo 65, Arroyo Hondo, Santo Domingo, DN; tel. 562-3500; fax 541-4121; e-mail info@caasd.gov.do; internet www.caasd.gov.do; f. 1973; Dir RAMÓN RIVAS.

Instituto Nacional de Aguas Potables y Alcantarillado (INAPA): Edif. Inapa, Centro Comercial El Millón, Calle Guarocuya, Apdo 1503, Santo Domingo, DN; tel. 567-1241; fax 567-8972; e-mail info@inapa.gob.do; internet www.inapa.gob.do; Exec. Dir MARIANO GERMÁN.

Instituto Nacional de Recursos Hidráulicos: Avda Jiménez de Moya, Centro de los Héroes, Santo Domingo, DN; tel. 532-3271; fax 532-2321; internet www.indrhi.gov.do; f. 1965; Exec. Dir FRANK RODRÍGUEZ.

TRADE UNIONS

Central General de Trabajadores (CGT): Juan Erazo 14, Villa Juana, 5°, Santo Domingo, DN; tel. 688-3932; f. 1972; 13 sections; Sec.-Gen. RAFAEL ABREU; 65,000 mems.

Central de Trabajadores Independientes (CTI): Juan Erazo 133, Santo Domingo, DN; tel. 688-3932; f. 1978; left-wing; Sec.-Gen. RAFAEL SANTOS.

Central de Trabajadores Mayoritarias (CTM): Tunti Cáceres 222, Santo Domingo, DN; tel. 562-3392; Sec.-Gen. NÉLSIDA MARMOLEJOS.

Confederación Autónoma de Sindicatos Clasistas (CASC) (Autonomous Confederation of Trade Unions): Juan Erazo 14, Villa Juana, 4°, Santo Domingo, DN; tel. 687-8533; fax 689-1439; e-mail cascnacional@codetel.net.do; f. 1962; supports PRSC; Sec.-Gen. GABRIEL DEL RÍO.

Confederación Nacional de Trabajadores Dominicanos (CNTD) (National Confederation of Dominican Workers): Calle José de Jesús Ravelo 56, Villa Juana, 2°, Santo Domingo, DN; tel. 221-2117; fax 221-3217; e-mail cntd@codetel.net.do; f. 1988 by merger; 11 provincial federations totalling 150 unions are affiliated; Sec.-Gen. JACOBO RAMOS; c. 188,000 mems.

Confederación de Trabajadores Unitaria (CTU) (United Workers' Confederation): Edif. de las Centrales Sindicales, 3°, Villa Juana, Juan Erazo 14, Santo Domingo, DN; tel. 221-9443; fax 689-1248; e-mail ctu01@codetel.net.do; f. 1991; Sec.-Gen. JULIO CÉSAR BAZÁN.

Transport

RAILWAYS

In April 2001 plans were announced for the construction of a passenger and freight railway from the coastal port of Haina to Santiago, with the possibility of subsequent extension to Puerto Plata and Manzanillo. The Government invested US $50m.–$100m. in 2006 on the installation of an underground railway system in Santo Domingo. Construction of the first line—14 km in length, between Villa Mella and Centro de los Héroes—was completed in early 2008, and the line entered into service in early 2009. Two further lines were being planned, and the completed network was to have a total length of some 60 km.

Ferrocarriles Unidos Dominicanos: Santo Domingo, DN; govt-owned; 142 km of track from La Vega to Sánchez and from Guayubín to Pepillo principally used for the transport of exports.

There are also a number of semi-autonomous and private railway companies for the transport of sugar cane, including:

Ferrocarril Central Río Haina: Apdo 1258, Haina; 113 km open.

Ferrocarril de Central Romana: La Romana; 375 km open; Pres. C. MORALES.

ROADS

In 2005 there were an estimated 17,000 km of roads, of which about 6,225 km were paved. There is a direct route from Santo Domingo to Port-au-Prince in Haiti. The Mejía administration undertook an extensive road-building programme from 2000, aiming primarily to reduce traffic congestion in Santo Domingo. In April 2007 a new road, the 'Cruz del Isleño Macao', was inaugurated in the province of La Altagracia. The road, built at a cost of more than RD $174m., was expected to increase tourism in the region.

Autoridad Metropolitana de Transporte (AMET): Avda Expreso V Centenario, esq. Avda San Martín, Santo Domingo, DN; tel. 686-6520; fax 686-3447; e-mail info@amet.gov.do; internet www.amet.gov.do; Dir-Gen. RAFAEL OSCAR BENCOSME CANDELIER.

Dirección General de Carreteras y Caminos Vecinales: Santo Domingo, DN; fax 567-5470; f. 1987; operated by the Secretary of State for Public Works and Communications; Dir-Gen. ELIZABETH PERALTA BRITO.

SHIPPING

The Dominican Republic has 14 ports, of which Río Haina is by far the largest, handling about 80% of imports in 2005. Other important ports are Boca Chica, Santo Domingo and San Pedro de Macorís on the south coast, and Puerto Plata in the north. The Caucedo port and transshipment centre, near the Las Américas international airport, opened in 2003 and was destined specifically for use by free trade zone businesses.

A number of foreign shipping companies operate services to the island.

Agencias Navieras B&R, SA: Avda Abraham Lincoln 504, Apdo 1221, Santo Domingo, DN; tel. 562-1661; fax 562-3383; e-mail ops@navierasbr.com; internet www.navierasbr.com; f. 1919; shipping agents and export services; Man. JUAN PERICHE PIDAL.

Armadora Naval Dominicana, SA: Isabel la Católica 165, Apdo 2677, Santo Domingo, DN; tel. 689-6191; Man. Dir Capt. EINAR WETTRE.

Autoridad Portuaria Dominicana: Avda Máximo Gómez, Santo Domingo, DN; tel. 687-4772; fax 687-2661; internet www.apordom.gov.do; Exec. Dir JOSÉ FRANCISCO PEÑA GUABA.

Frederic Schad, Inc: José Gabriel García 26, Apdo 941, Santo Domingo, DN; tel. 221-8000; fax 688-7696; e-mail mail@fschad.com; internet www.fschad.com; f. 1922; logistics and shipping agent.

Líneas Marítimas de Santo Domingo, SA: José Gabriel García 8, Apdo 1148, Santo Domingo, DN; tel. 689-9146; fax 685-4654; Pres. C. LLUBERES; Vice-Pres. JUAN T. TAVARES.

CIVIL AVIATION

There are international airports at Santo Domingo, Puerto Plata, Punta Cana, Santiago, La Romana, Samaná and Barahona. A new international airport, Aeropuerto Internacional La Isabela, at El Higuero, near Santo Domingo, was scheduled to become operational in 2004. Construction went ahead, at a cost of over RD $2,000m., without the requisite technical feasibility studies being carried out and despite warnings about the suitability of the chosen site. After a lengthy delay in securing approval from the relevant national and international aviation authorities, the new airport finally commenced operations in mid-2006, replacing the Aeropuerto Internacional de Herrera, which had been closed in February of that year. Another new airport, President Juan Bosch International Airport, in El Catey, in the north of the country, was inaugurated in February 2007. Most main cities have domestic airports.

Instituto Dominicano de Aviación Civil: Avda México, esq. Avda 30 de Marzo, Apdo 1180, Santo Domingo, DN; tel. 221-7909; fax 221-6220; e-mail aeronautica.c@codeltel.net.do; internet www.idac.gov.do; f. 1955; fmrly Dirección General de Aeronáutica Civil; adopted current name 2007; govt supervisory body; Dir-Gen. JOSÉ TOMÁS PÉREZ.

Aerodomca: La Isabela Airport, Santo Domingo, DN; tel. 826-4141; fax 826-4065; e-mail sales@aerodomca.com; internet www.aerodomca.com; f. 1980; operates charter flights to the Caribbean.

Aerolíneas Argo: Santo Domingo, DN; f. 1971; cargo and mail services to the USA, Puerto Rico and the US Virgin Islands.

Aerolíneas Dominicanas (Dominair): El Sol 62, Apdo 202, Santiago de los Caballeros; tel. 581-8882; fax 582-5074; f. 1974; owned by Aeropostal (Venezuela); scheduled and charter passenger services.

Aerolíneas Santo Domingo: Edif. J. P., Avda 27 de Febrero 272, esq. Seminario, Santo Domingo, DN; e-mail reservas@airsantodomingo.com.do; f. 1996; operates scheduled and charter internal, regional and international flights; Pres. HENRY W. AZAR.

Caribbean Atlantic Airlines (Caribair): Aeropuerto Internacional La Isabela, Santo Domingo, DN; tel. 826-4444; e-mail info@caribair.com.do; internet www.caribair.com.do; f. 1962; operates scheduled flights to Aruba, Haiti, and domestic and regional charter flights.

Líneas Aéreas del Caribe (VOLAIR): Dr Joaquín Balaguer International Airport, Santo Domingo, DN; tel. 826-4068; fax 826-4071; e-mail reservas@volair.com.do; internet www.volair.com.do; f. 2003; operates charter flights to domestic destinations and the Caribbean.

Servicios Aéreos Profesionales (SAP): Dr Joaquín Balaguer International Airport, La Isabela, Santo Domingo, DN; tel. 565-2448; e-mail hheyer@sapair.com; internet www.sapair.com; f. 1981; operates charter flights to Central America, the Caribbean and the USA.

Tourism

Strenuous efforts were made to improve the tourism infrastructure, with RD $200m. spent on increasing the number of hotel rooms by 50%, road improvements and new developments. The total number of visitors to the Dominican Republic in 2009 was 4,414,756. In 2007 receipts from tourism, excluding passenger transport, totalled US $4,082m. There were 67,197 hotel rooms in the Dominican Republic in 2009.

Secretaría de Estado de Turismo: Bloque D, Edif. de Ofs Gubernamentales, Avda México, esq. 30 de Marzo, Apdo 497, Santo Domingo, DN; tel. 221-4660; fax 682-3806; internet www.godominicanrepublic.com.

Asociación Dominicana de Agencias de Viajes: Calle Padre Billini 263, Apdo 2097, Santo Domingo, DN; tel. 687-8984; Pres. RAMÓN PRIETO.

Consejo de Promoción Turística: Avda México 66, Santo Domingo, DN; tel. 685-9054; fax 685-6752; e-mail cpt@codetel.net.do; Dir EVELYN PAIEWONSKY.

Defence

As assessed at November 2009, the Dominican Republic's armed forces numbered an estimated 49,910: army 40,140, navy 4,000 (including naval infantry), air force 5,500. There were also paramilitary forces numbering 15,000. Military service is voluntary and lasts for four years.

Defence Expenditure: The budget allocation for 2009 was an estimated RD $11,400m.

Secretary of State for the Armed Forces and General Chief of Staff: Lt-Gen. PEDRO RAFAEL PEÑA ANTONIO.

Army Chief of Staff: Maj.-Gen. JOAQUÍN V. PÉREZ FELIZ.

Navy Chief of Staff: Vice-Adm. HOMERO LUIS LAJARA SOLÁ.

Air Force Chief of Staff: Maj.-Gen. CARLOS RAFAEL MARTÍN ALTUNA TEZANOS.

Education

Education is, where possible, compulsory for children between the ages of six and 14 years. Primary education commences at the age of six and lasts for eight years. Secondary education, starting at 14 years of age, lasts for four years. In 2008 enrolment at primary level included 80% of children in the relevant age-group, while secondary enrolment included 58% of children in the relevant age-group (males 52%, females 63%). In 1997/98 there were 4,001 primary schools and in 1996/97 there were an estimated 1,737 secondary schools. There were eight universities. Budgetary expenditure on education in 2005 was RD $15,650.7m., representing 8.1% of total spending. In 2010 the Government agreed a US $100m. loan with the Inter-American Development Bank for school improvements, as part of its 10-Year Plan for Education.

Bibliography

For works on the Caribbean generally, see Select Bibliography (Books)

Atkins, G. P., and Wilson, L. C. *The Dominican Republic and the United States: From Imperialism to Transnationalism*. Athens, GA, University of Georgia Press, 1998.

Betances, E. *State and Society in the Dominican Republic*. Boulder, CO, Westview Press, 1995.

The Catholic Church and Power Politics in Latin America: The Dominican Case in Comparative Perspective. Lanham, MD, Rowman & Littlefield Publrs, 2007.

Chester, E. T. *Rag-tags, Scum, Riff-raff, and Commies: The US Intervention in the Dominican Republic, 1965–1966*. New York, Monthly Review Press, 2001.

Diederich, B. *Trujillo: The Death of the Dictator*. Princeton, NJ, Markus Wiener Publrs, 2000.

Gregory, S. *The Devil Behind the Mirror: Globalization and Politics in the Dominican Republic*. Berkeley, CA, University of California Press, 2006.

Hall, M. R. *Sugar and Power in the Dominican Republic: Eisenhower, Kennedy and the Trujillos (1958–62)*. Westport, CT, Greenwood Press, 2000.

Hartlyn, J. *The Struggle for Democratic Politics in the Dominican Republic*. Chapel Hill, NC, University of North Carolina Press, 1998.

Hernández, R. *The Mobility of Workers Under Advanced Capitalism: Dominican Migration to the United States*. New York, Columbia University Press, 2002.

Hillman, R. S., and D'Agostino, T. J. *Distant Neighbors: The Dominican Republic and Jamaica in Comparative Perspectives*. New York, Praeger Publrs, 1992.

Howard, D. *Dominican Republic in Focus: A Guide to the People, Politics and Culture*. London, Latin America Bureau, 1999.

Coloring the Nation: Race and Ethnicity in the Dominican Republic. Oxford, Signal Books, 2001.

Itzigsohn, J. *Developing Poverty: The State, Labor Market Deregulation, and the Informal Economy in Costa Rica and the Dominican Republic*. University Park, PA, Pennsylvania State University Press, 2000.

Martinez-Vergne, T. *Nation and Citizen in the Dominican Republic, 1880–1916*. Chapel Hill, NC, University of North Carolina Press, 2005.

Moya Pons, F. *The Dominican Republic: A National History*. Princeton, NJ, Markus Wiener Publrs, 1998.

Peguero, V., and Crawford, L. *Immigration and Politics in the Caribbean: Japanese and Other Immigrants in the Dominican Republic*. Coconut Creek, FL, Caribbean Studies Press, 2008.

Peguero, V., Maslowski, P., and Grimsley, M. (Eds). *Militarization of Culture in the Dominican Republic: From the Captains General to General Trujillo (Studies in War, Society & the Military)*. Lincoln, NE, University of Nebraska Press, 2004.

Roorda, E. P. *The Dictator Next Door: The Good Neighbor Policy and the Trujillo Regime in the Dominican Republic, 1930–1945*. Durham, NC, Duke University Press, 1998.

Sagas, E. *Race and Politics in the Dominican Republic*. Gainesville, FL, University Press of Florida, 2000.

San Miguel, P. L. *The Imagined Island: History, Identity, and Utopia in Hispaniola*. Chapel Hill, NC, University of North Carolina Press, 2005.

Suárez, L. M. *The Tears of Hispaniola: Haitian and Dominican Diaspora Memory*. Gainesville, FL, University Press of Florida, 2006.

Turits, R. L. *Foundations of Despotism: Peasants, the Trujillo Regime and Modernity in Dominican History*. Revised edn. Palo Alto, CA, Stanford University Press, 2004.

Veeser, C. *Improving Paradise: American Capitalists and US Intervention in the Dominican Republic, 1890–1908*. New York, Columbia University Press, 2003.

Vega, B. (Ed.). *Dominican Cultures: The Making of a Caribbean Society*. Princeton, NJ, Markus Wiener Publishing, 2008.

Wucker, M. *Why the Cocks Fight: Dominicans, Haitians and the Struggle for Hispaniola*. New York, Hill and Wang Publishing, 2000.

ECUADOR

Geography

PHYSICAL FEATURES

The Republic of Ecuador is in western South America, straddling the Equator, which gives the country its name. Some 965 km (about 600 miles) to the west of the mainland, but also on the Equator, is the country's Pacific territory on the Islas Galápagos (Galápagos Islands—the observation of whose unique ecosystem was important to the development of the theory of evolution by the 19th-century British scientist Charles Darwin). Continental Ecuador was once rather more extensive, but border disputes and adverse military encounters have reduced Ecuador's territory considerably (notably in 1904–42). There have been occasional clashes subsequently, mainly with Peru—most recently in 1995, although this was resolved in 1999. Ecuador's main border concerns are now not so much territorial as preventing any extension of the conflicts in Colombia. The border with Peru, to the east and south, has been settled at some 1,420 km in extent, and that with Colombia, to the north, is 590 km, giving Ecuador a total area of 272,045 sq km (105,037 sq miles).

Ecuador stretches for 2,237 km along the west coast of South America, extending over the Andes and, in the north-east, down onto the edge of the great Amazonian plains. The country is divided, therefore, into the Costa or coastal plains, the Sierra or central highlands and the Oriente, the forested eastern slopes of the Andes descending to alluvial plains. The Costa covers about one-quarter of the country and is a rich agricultural region, with rolling, forested hills in the north and, generally, a broad lowland basin descending from the Andes to the sea. There is also tropical jungle in the south, climbing the mountain sides as wet, mossy woodland. The Sierra itself is where the chain of the Andes, the Continental Divide, forms a double range of mountains flanking a narrow, inhabited upland plateau. The great cordilleras, Occidental and Oriental, include 22 massive volcanoes among their peaks, including the highest active volcano in the world, Cotopaxi (5,897 m or 19,354 ft), signalling the seismic instability of the region. The highest point in the country is at the summit of Chimborazo (6,310 m), which is also distinguished as being the point on the surface of the earth furthest from its centre (owing to the globe being wider around the Equator). The Oriente, or eastern jungles, consists of the eastern, forested slopes of the Andes and the gently undulating plains, thick with tropical rainforest. In fact, trees cover over one-half of the country, with 15% classed as pastureland. The mountain heights above 3,000 m or so tend to be grassland. Wildlife includes bears, jaguars, otters, skunks and crocodiles, with a huge variety of birds, including a number of North American species that winter here. Perhaps more unique is the isolated ecosystem of the Galápagos (officially, the Archipiélago Colón), the six larger and nine smaller islands of which (mostly extinct volcanic peaks) have been declared a UNESCO World Heritage Site.

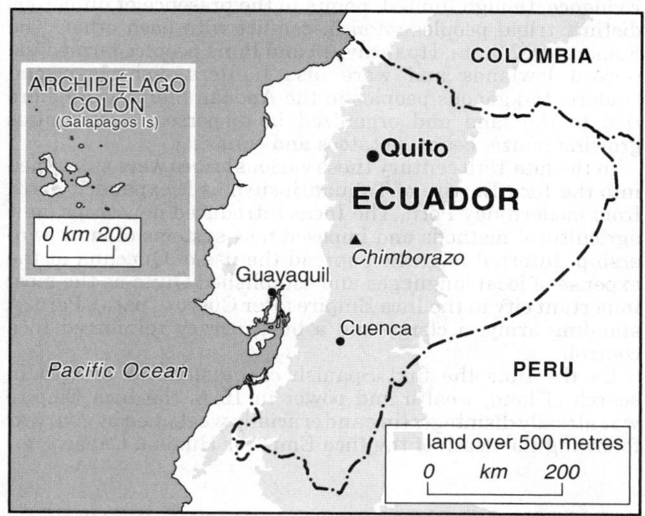

CLIMATE

The climate is tropical at sea level, the Costa being hot and humid, with an average annual temperature of 78°F (26°C). Being on the Equator, there is little seasonal variation in temperature, although there is a wet season from December to April, with particularly heavy rains, but there is no dry season as such. On the Sierra the average temperatures range from 45°F to 70°F (7°C–21°C), depending on the elevation, with Quito at 2,850 m above sea level on 13°C (55°F). However, average figures can obscure the contrast of warm days and chilly nights. The Oriente is even hotter and more humid than the Costa. Temperatures approach nearer 40°C (104°F) and average annual rainfall is about 2,050 mm (80 ins), falling year round.

POPULATION

The white élite, predominantly of Spanish descent, still controls most of the wealth in Ecuador, although those of largely unmixed European descent account for little more than 10% of the population. Blacks amount to about one-half of that, with even smaller groups of Arabs and Asians. The vast bulk of the population, over four-fifths, is either Amerindian or of mixed-Amerindian (Mestizo) descent. Figures vary as to the exact proportions, but indigenous peoples could make up anywhere upward of one-fifth of the entire population. The official language, however, is Spanish, although many speak Quechua, the language of the Incas, in daily life. There are about 700 tribes, the main ones being the Otavalos, the Salasacas, the Saraguros, the Colorados, the Cayapas, the Jivaros, the Aucas, the Yumbos, the Zaparos and the Cofan. Many retain the use of their own dialects or languages. The ancient religions, by contrast, now only persist in the more remote parts of the Oriente, although elements have been maintained in conjunction with the dominant Roman Catholic Christianity (which claims the adherence of about 90% of the population). There is a small, but growing, Protestant Christian (2%) minority.

According to mid-year estimates in 2010, the total population was 14.2m. Almost one-half of the population lives on the Costa (predominantly Mestizos and blacks), and only slightly less on the Sierra (where most people are Amerindians). The capital is Quito, at 2,850 m the second highest capital in South America, but the largest city is Guayaquil, the main port (2.7m. in mid-2010, according to UN estimates—compared to Quito's 1.8m.). Guayaquil is in the south, on the gulf that bears its name, while Quito is in the Sierra, towards the north. The third city, Cuenca, is also in the mountains, but in the south. The country is divided into 22 provinces.

History

SANDY MARKWICK

Archaeologists date the existence of ancient civilization in the area comprising modern-day Ecuador as far back as 3500 BC. Evidence, though limited, points to the presence of numerous distinct tribal peoples often in conflict with each other. The Esmeralda, Manta, Huancavilca and Puná peoples farmed the coastal lowlands and were also hunters, fishermen and traders. Indigenous peoples in the Andean Sierra were more tied to the land and organized in dispersed communities growing maize, beans, potatoes and squash.

In the late 15th century these various tribes were subsumed into the Inca Empire of Tahuantinsuyo as it expanded north from modern-day Peru. The Incas introduced new crops, new agricultural methods and imposed new systems of land ownership. Internal migration spread the use of Quechua at the expense of local languages and established Quito as the most important city in the Inca Empire after Cusco (Cuzco), Peru. A standing army, a clergy and a bureaucracy reinforced Inca control.

By the time the first Spanish *conquistadores* arrived in search of land, wealth and power in 1526, the Inca Empire was already disintegrating and crucially weakened by civil war following the death of the Inca Emperor Huayna Cápac.

SPANISH COLONIAL RULE AND INDEPENDENCE

The Spanish crown sponsored several exploratory voyages southwards along the Pacific coast of South America. Francisco Pizarro led the forces that conquered the Inca territory for the Spanish crown, and in 1534 Quito was captured by Sebastián de Belalcázar. In 1540 Pizarro appointed his brother Gonzalo as Governor of Quito, as the colony was named.

As a result of in-fighting among rival Spanish *conquistadores*, the Spanish crown intervened to establish order by incorporating the territory into the Viceroyalty of Peru in 1544, though it was briefly transferred to the Viceroyalty of Nueva Granada in 1717. Spanish dominance was not uniform as significant areas, particularly of the coastal region and jungle lowlands, remained unconquered.

In Ecuador, the movement for independence from Spain was part of a pan-continental struggle between *criollos* (the local élite of Spanish descent) and the demands of the Spanish crown and the privileges of its local representatives. Following decades of revolts, successfully contained, colonial rule ended when Simón Bolívar's forces, under the command of Venezuelan Gen. José Antonio de Sucre, defeated the Spanish at the battle of Pichincha in 1822. Ecuador was then incorporated into the short-lived Confederación de Gran Colombia. In 1830 Ecuador seceded from the Confederación and attained independence. Gen. Juan José Flores became the country's first President and dominated the politics of the new republic for the first 15 years.

LIBERALISM VERSUS CONSERVATISM

Throughout the 19th century Ecuador endured political instability. In 1851 Gen. José María Urbina seized power. A defining characteristic of Ecuadorean politics began to emerge during his rule, which lasted until 1856: a persistent power struggle between the forces of liberalism, largely based in Guayaquil, and conservatism, based in the Sierra. This bipartisan dichotomy continued to resonate in the modern era.

Liberalism as represented by Urbina and his successor, Gen. Francisco Robles, was a modernizing, anti-clerical and pro-business influence. Urbina ended slavery, and Robles partially abolished the feudal annual tributes that the indigenous population had been required to pay to landowners for centuries. Regional interests reinforced the ideological division, with modern business and trading interests concentrated in the port city of Guayaquil, while Quito was the centre of the old landowning élites of the Sierra. The liberal direction of the Urbina-Robles era provoked regional opposition from local caudillos (provincial rulers), which threatened to undermine the territorial integrity of Ecuador.

In response to the liberal influence of Urbina and Robles emerged the controversial figure of Gabriel García Moreno (President in 1861–65 and 1869–75), the founder of conservatism in Ecuador. He suppressed local rebellions and expelled the Peruvian army from southern Ecuador. The conservatism of García Moreno was rooted in a fanatical adherence to contemporary Catholic theology, which emphasized personal self-discipline, hierarchy and order. In 1869 he founded the Partido Conservador (PC—Conservative Party) and attempted to install a theocratic state. His nation-building vision also took the form of a major road- and railway-building exercise linking the capital Quito with Guayaquil.

Between 1852 and 1890 the value of exports grew from US $1m. to $10m., partly because Ecuador took advantage of trading opportunities that arose while Ecuador's main trading rivals—Peru, Chile and Bolivia—were engaged in the War of the Pacific (1879–83). The economic boom strengthened the Guayaquil business élite, which was then reflected in a period of power for the Liberals between 1895 and 1925.

If García Moreno was the founder of conservatism in Ecuador, Gen. José Eloy Alfaro Delgado was the principal figure behind Ecuadorean liberalism. He seized power and founded the Partido Liberal Radical (PLR—Radical Liberal Party) in 1895, and quickly commenced stripping the Roman Catholic Church of the powers and privileges it had enjoyed under the García Moreno regime. The Government tried to implement social reform to help the poor, but progress was undermined by unfavourable economic conditions. Liberal rule also failed to build and strengthen democratic institutions, and the period was noted for its violent instability, stemming largely from disunity within the PLR.

Political power during the early 20th century was dominated by an oligarchy of agricultural and banking interests based in the coastal region. A spendthrift attitude among money-printing bankers and agriculturalists within this liberal élite (known as *la argolla*—the ring) led to spiralling inflation. Economic conditions were exacerbated by competition from overseas cocoa producers. The authorities ruthlessly suppressed a general strike in Guayaquil in 1922 and a peasant rebellion in the Sierra in 1923. In 1925, with unrest growing, a group of military social reformers, the League of Young Officers, overthrew the Government with the stated aim of ending the corruption of liberal rule.

The post-liberal era proved to be equally unstable. From 1925 to 1948 Ecuador had 22 Governments, each one terminated by unconstitutional means. A new Constitution was introduced in 1929, which shifted the balance of power away from the executive to the legislature, thereby encouraging a plethora of minor political parties and groupings that, in combination with the Wall Street Crash of 1929 and the ensuing Great Depression, increased instability. Nationalist opinion was inflamed by the signing of the Rio Protocol in 1942, in which Ecuador renounced claims to 200,000 sq km of territory to Peru. In 1948 Galo Plaza Lasso came to power at the head of a coalition of liberals and socialists. His victory began an era of 12 years of unbroken constitutional rule.

CONSTITUTIONAL RULE, 1948–60

Plaza aligned himself closely to the USA, which proved a frequent source of tension between the Government and populist opposition politicians. He was credited with attempts to deepen democratic rights and institutions even though the opposition largely frustrated his attempts to reform economic and development policy along pragmatic and technocratic lines. Political frustration was the price for relative stability, which was undoubtedly helped by a banana boom that saw revenue from exports grow from US $2m. in 1948 to $20m. in 1952. During this time the Government succeeded in balancing budgets and slowing inflation.

José María Velasco Ibarra, elected President for the third time (previously in 1934 and 1944), succeeded Plaza in 1952. Encouraged by the relatively healthy state of the economy, Velasco raised public spending on infrastructure projects and the military, but his Government became increasingly authoritarian. He was succeeded by Camilo Ponce Enríquez in 1956, but won another term of office in 1960. However, after 14 months in office and amid a general strike and violent unrest precipitated by worsening economic conditions, the military deposed Velasco and installed Carlos Julio Arosemena Monroy as President. Nevertheless, the military was concerned about Arosemena's pro-Cuban rhetoric and, fearing the emergence of domestic left-wing insurgency, ousted the President in 1963.

MILITARY RULE, 1963–79

The new military Government, led by a four-man junta, intended to stay in power for as long as it took to implement unpopular economic policies while defeating left-wing political activity. However, in 1966, confronted with continued economic problems and growing unrest, the military stepped down. Interim Governments took office while an elected constituent assembly drafted a new constitution. In 1968 the first elections under the new Constitution returned 75-year-old Velasco to the presidency for the fifth time, though he received just one-third of the votes cast. The last Velasco Government was to be hampered by a weak mandate. Frequent resignations from his administration and economic mismanagement fuelled instability and led to an *autogolpe* in 1970, in which Velasco disbanded the Congreso Nacional (Congress) and the Supreme Court and assumed direct powers himself with the support of the military. Velasco implemented various unpopular measures, including a devaluation of the sucre. He introduced more controls on foreign exchange and increased import tariffs. In 1972 he was deposed by a military *coup d'état* led by Gen. Guillermo Rodríguez Lara, who became Head of State.

The military regime had a nationalist outlook that underpinned its heavy investment in infrastructure and industry and the founding of the state petroleum company, Estatal Petrolera Ecuatoriana (which was replaced by PETROECUADOR—Empresa Estatal Petróleos del Ecuador—in 1989). The Government's nationalism was reflected in its petroleum policy: it took Ecuador into the Organization of the Petroleum Exporting Countries (OPEC) in 1973 and renegotiated contracts to develop petroleum concessions with foreign oil companies on more favourable terms.

The military Government tried to control inflation with low tariffs to encourage imports and absorb the spending power of the small, but growing, middle class. However, the strategy fuelled balance of payments problems. When the regime changed policy and imposed a 60% duty on luxury imports it provoked fierce opposition from Ecuador's élite, which had grown accustomed to cheap luxury goods. In 1976 a military faction led a successful and bloodless transfer of power to a three-man military junta, appointed to oversee the return to civilian rule. In 1978 voters approved a new, more progressive Constitution in a referendum. The Constitution acknowledged the role of the state in socio-economic development, established a single-chamber legislature, disallowed immediate re-election for serving presidents and ended the literacy standard for voter eligibility (effectively enfranchising a large proportion of the indigenous population).

In 1979 Jaime Roldós Aguilera, from the Concentración de Fuerzas Populares (CFP—Concentration of Popular Forces), was elected President with over 68% of the second-round votes cast. Doubts that the military would permit Roldós to take office were dispelled when he assumed the presidency in August, although the military had put in place safeguards to prevent any investigations into human rights violations during its period in power.

CIVILIAN GOVERNMENT RESTORED

Many of the weaknesses of civilian politics in Ecuador re-emerged when democracy was restored. Regional and personal rivalries were expressed in the high number of small political parties, groupings and shifting alliances. President Roldós, who came to power with an agenda to promote socio-economic reform, encountered opposition not only from the traditional right, but also from within his own CFP. In May 1981 the President, his wife and the Minister of Defence were killed in a plane crash in the southern province of Loja. The Vice-President, Osvaldo Hurtado, the leader of the Partido Demócratico Cristiano (PDC—Christian Democratic Party), assumed the presidency amid a deteriorating economic situation occasioned by the end of the petroleum boom. Foreign debt totalled some US $7,000m. Despite Hurtado's left-of-centre credentials, his response was to pursue IMF-approved austerity measures. He reduced government subsidies and devalued the sucre. In the 1984 presidential election right-wing interests united behind León Febres Cordero, a Guayaquil businessman of the Partido Social Cristiano (PSC—Social Christian Party), who narrowly defeated Rodrigo Borja Cevallos, who had defected from the PLR to form the Izquierda Democratica (ID—Democratic Left).

Conflict between the executive and the legislature threatened a number of constitutional crises. Febres Cordero's use of executive power was consistent with the long tradition in Ecuador of the caudillo rather than the constitutionally elected politician, and he attempted to implement changes that would grant him additional powers and postpone legislative elections. The President's relationship with the military was tense. His dismissal of the chief of the armed forces, Lt-Gen. Frank Vargas Pazzos, for allegations of corruption he had made against senior defence staff, led to a military revolt at an air base and at Quito's international airport in 1986. Vargas was arrested and Febres Cordero subsequently ignored an amnesty granted to Vargas by the Congreso. In January 1987 paratroopers loyal to Vargas abducted the President. Vargas was given an amnesty in exchange for Febres Cordero's release.

In May 1988 Rodrigo Borja Cevallos won the presidential election, defeating Abdalá Bucaram Ortiz of the Partido Roldosista Ecuatoriano (PRE—Ecuadorean Roldosist Party) in the second round of voting, with 46% of the votes cast. Both candidates had proposed economic nationalism and import substitution. Borja's ID also won the largest number of seats in the Congreso and, by entering into an alliance with fringe leftist and populist parties, could look forward to the prospect of a supportive legislature. Borja pledged to defend human rights and introduce moderate socio-economic reforms while balancing the conflicting interests of the labour movement and Guayaquil's business élite. However, a concurrent programme of economic austerity provoked large public demonstrations and led to disillusion among the electorate. In mid-term legislative elections in June 1990 the ID-led coalition lost its majority in the Congreso, resulting in legislative paralysis for the remainder of Borja's term of office.

During the Borja presidency there was a greater mobilization of social groups representing the indigenous population. Particularly active was the Confederación de Nacionalidades Indígenas del Ecuador (CONAIE—Confederation of Indigenous Nationalities of Ecuador). CONAIE led an uprising in seven Andean provinces in 1990, during which they blocked roads and brought the countryside to a virtual standstill. The trade union movement joined the protests of the increasingly powerful indigenous organization, which fuelled conservative fears of the Borja administration, particularly after the Government had made overtures to left-wing insurgents to end their violent struggle. In 1989 the President had successfully concluded negotiations with Alfaro Vive ¡Carajo! (Alfaro Lives, Damn It!), one of Ecuador's small guerrilla movements, after it agreed to abandon the armed struggle and enter the legal political arena.

PRESIDENT DURÁN BALLÉN, 1992–96

These fears helped the conservative Sixto Durán Ballén of the Partido Unitario Republicano (PUR—Unitary Republican Party) to victory in the second round of the presidential election in July 1992. Durán Ballén defeated another right-wing candidate, Jaime Nebot Saadi of the PSC, with 58% of the ballot. The ID candidate was humiliated, receiving just 8.2% of the votes cast in the first round in May as those associated with the labour unrest and the incumbent Government were unequivocally rejected. Durán Ballén, having promised to accelerate free market reforms and encourage foreign investment, introduced a series of structural reforms within two months of assuming power. The Government took Ecuador into the Andean Pact free trade area and introduced a new, more liberal, foreign investment code. In November 1992 Ecuador withdrew from OPEC to allow it greater freedom in the production and export of oil. Negotiations to restructure the foreign debt led to improved relations with international creditors and a stand-by facility from the IMF in 1994.

During the first half of Durán Ballén's term of office the Government depended on support from an alliance of the PUR and the PC, with additional ad hoc support from the PSC, to secure majority support for legislation in the Congreso. However, this period of relative legislative consensus was short lived. Corruption charges levelled at cabinet members undermined the fragile support of the PSC and slowed the implementation of the Government's legislative agenda. In May 1994 the opposition parties effectively took control of the Congreso, following an emphatic defeat for the PUR and PC in legislative mid-term elections.

Renewed military skirmishes along the border with Peru in January 1995 temporarily stifled domestic political opposition. However, normal political discourse resumed in February after a cease-fire agreement was reached and following revelations that government representatives had paid legislators and judges to help ease the path of legislative proposals. The President survived the scandal, but it highlighted the existence of widespread corruption within the political and judicial élite. There was an increasing mobilization of the population against the policies and practices of the Durán Ballén administration in the wake of the scandal. In late 1995 violence accompanied protests among inhabitants of the Galápagos Islands, who were demanding greater political and financial autonomy, and protests against labour code reform and fuel price increases. Industrial action in the public sector led to a series of one-day national strikes and an energy crisis.

PRESIDENTS BUCARAM AND ALARCÓN, 1996–98

The presidential election of 1996 resulted in victory for the populist Abdalá Bucaram Ortiz, representing the PRE, who unexpectedly won the second round of voting, defeating Nebot Saadi of the PSC. His victory was fuelled both by a widespread disillusion with established party politics and a rejection of the structural-adjustment economic programme initiated by Durán Ballén. Bucaram's electoral platform included anti-poverty measures, such as increased subsidies for basic commodities and wage rises for public sector workers. However, once in power, Bucaram raised the price of utilities as the Government tried to balance its budget. In early 1997 there was a general strike in response to commodity price increases, mass demonstrations and violent clashes between protesters and the security forces.

Charges of 'cronyism' were levelled against the President after family members and close friends were appointed to important cabinet positions. Eventually, Bucaram's undiplomatic style and unpredictable decision-making created such an atmosphere of instability that, on 6 February 1997, the Congreso voted by simple majority to dismiss Bucaram on grounds of mental incapacity (thus avoiding impeachment proceedings, which required a two-thirds' majority). The Congreso elected Fabián Alarcón Rivera to the presidency on 11 February, and scheduled new elections for August 1998.

Alarcón did little to address Ecuador's fiscal crisis. Instead, he reinstated the public sector employees dismissed by his predecessor and built up support for his small, populist Frente Radical Alfarista (FRA—Alfarist Radical Front). Despite his public efforts to tackle corruption and have Bucaram extradited from self-imposed exile in Panama to face charges of misappropriating government funds, Alarcón himself became embroiled in allegations of embezzlement. (After his term ended he spent several months in prison before charges were dismissed.)

Elections to a 70-member Asamblea Nacional (National Assembly) to consider constitutional reform were brought forward to November 1997 under considerable public pressure. In February 1998 the Asamblea agreed a series of reforms designed to ensure greater government stability, including the enlargement of the Congreso from 82 to 121 seats, the abolition of mid-term elections and more limited impeachment powers for the Congreso. Elections to the newly enlarged Congreso were held in May 1998. The Democracia Popular (DP—People's Democracy) became the largest single party with 32 seats, followed by the PSC (27 seats), the PRE (24) and the ID (18). In the second round of the presidential election in July, Quito mayor and DP candidate Jamil Mahuad Witt narrowly defeated the PRE's Alvaro Noboa Pontón. Mahuad took office in August and appointed a Cabinet largely composed of independents.

PRESIDENT MAHUAD, 1998–2000

A peace agreement with Peru in October 1998 increased Mahuad's popular standing. The treaty established a definitive border with Peru and granted Ecuador navigation rights on the Amazon river. Unlike previous agreements, this accord seemed to offer the opportunity of a permanent settlement, which would allow the two countries to normalize relations. However, the new administration quickly encountered Ecuador's familiar economic and political problems. The strength of the political opposition in the Congreso ensured that there was little consensus, and any reforms required a tortuous process of negotiation with a multitude of disparate parties, each aiming to extract policy concessions from the Government.

The introduction of austerity measures led to a general strike in October 1998, followed by a period of violent unrest. By 1999 the economic crisis was in danger of leading to a collapse of the banking system, default on debt repayments, hyperinflation and a rapid decline in investor confidence. Protests against a 'freeze' on bank deposits, decreed in March by Mahuad in response to the decreasing value of the sucre, led to violent demonstrations and the declaration of a 60-day state of emergency. The military was deployed to maintain order while the Government, aiming to secure much-needed loans from international creditors, increased attempts to restructure the public sector in line with IMF prescriptions. The Government achieved mixed results. Ecuador received US $500m. in loans from the World Bank, the Inter-American Development Bank (IDB) and the Andean Development Corporation, but missed the deadline for signing a letter of intent with the IMF that held out the prospect of much larger loans. The threat of debt default compelled the Government to impose fiscal reform. However, under popular pressure, the Congreso rejected privatization legislation that would have allowed the Government to earn windfall revenues. In August Mahuad declared a moratorium on foreign debt repayments, making Ecuador the first country to default on its Brady bond and Eurobond commitments.

Popular protest continued despite the debt moratorium. The President's popularity declined precipitously. In January 2000 Mahuad announced the decision to adopt the US dollar in place of the sucre as the currency of Ecuador, provoking the resignation of the central bank President, Pablo Better. Further protests by indigenous groups received the tacit support of sections of the military, which allowed thousands of protesters to occupy the Congreso building on 21 January. During the occupation, CONAIE President Antonio Vargas, along with a group of army colonels (among them Lucio Gutiérrez Borbua, who would become President three years later), announced the overthrow of Mahuad. The military high command was divided, but the following day supported the transfer of power to Vice-President Gustavo Noboa Bejeramo, who was given the task of completing Mahuad's four-year term.

PRESIDENT NOBOA, 2000–03

Gustavo Noboa was an independent, although he was associated with the PSC and another right-leaning party, the Movimiento de Integración Nacional (MIN—National Integration Movement), which was formed following a split with former President Mahuad's DP. His Cabinet included representatives of several parties and had a strong business influence.

New alliances and splits between the parties undermined the prospect of Noboa forging a consistent consensus within the Congreso. Noboa frequently vetoed congressional amendments to proposed legislation, which caused delays to his reform programme. Noboa, as Mahuad before him, had to secure the approval of legislation with the help of ad hoc alliances to secure congressional approval. Ecuador's history of a political party system, which is only loosely based around strong ideological identification and where regional and personal rivalries are much in evidence, led to a highly fragmented political landscape that undermined the efficiency of government. However, popular weariness of further political instability gave Noboa a degree of flexibility to deepen the economic reform programme. High petroleum prices and pressure from the IMF in the early 21st century further encouraged neoliberal reform.

Noboa was quick to demonstrate his intention to maintain market-orientated policies. In March 2000 he secured congressional approval for the Ley de Transformación Económica (Economic Transformation Law). This latest attempt to introduce structural reforms included dollarization, increased labour market flexibility, and an extended policy of privatization, as well as reductions in government spending and tax reform. Additional measures, including a timetable for the adoption of the Basel standard of capital adequacy for the banking sector, persuaded the IMF in April to extend a one-year stand-by agreement, conditionally approving US $2,000m. in multilateral aid over the following two years. In the same month the Government formally began the process of replacing the sucre with the US dollar as Ecuador's unit of currency, which led to the stabilization of the exchange rate and reduced interest rates. The release of small bank depositor funds, frozen since March 1999 under Noboa's predecessor, helped further to restore public confidence. Opponents of the stabilization programme were partly appeased by an increase in public sector salaries. In July the Government proposed a second round of reforms, which included more liberal rules governing private investment in petroleum, electricity and telecommunications, as well as health and social security. However, the success of the reform package was threatened by a breakdown in relations between the DP and PSC in the legislature, following the defeat of the PSC's candidate for President of the Congreso. An impasse between the executive and the legislature was resolved in August when the Constitutional Tribunal decreed a new vote, which was subsequently won by the PSC.

Opposition to economic liberalization persisted, led by the forces that had been so influential in removing Mahuad from office: CONAIE, trade unions and students. The Government encountered significant unrest over its unpopular policies, which included fuel price increases and privatization plans. Anti-Government protests led by CONAIE escalated following fuel price rises in December 2000. Protests in January and February 2001 were the most serious since similar protests led to the downfall of Mahuad one year earlier. Noboa's Government declared a national state of emergency, giving the security forces extra powers to control unrest. In contrast to Mahuad, however, Noboa maintained the support of most mainstream political parties as well as the business community and the military. His popularity declined in the wake of the protests, but not to the depths of antipathy towards Mahuad.

Opponents of the Government tried to prevent an increase in value-added tax (VAT) and the implementation of other policies imposed as part of an IMF stand-by agreement. In December 2000 the Minister of Finance and Public Credit, Luis Yturralde, resigned in protest against the conditions prescribed in the IMF agreement. The Congreso continued to oppose the VAT increase, particularly as petroleum revenues were rising. In April 2001 the 'Paris Club' of Western creditor nations suspended talks with the Government until the tax issue had been resolved. The IMF subsequently followed suit. When the Government succeeded in securing a 2% increase in VAT in an extraordinary congressional session, the IMF approved a US $48m. disbursement and an extension of the agreement until the end of 2001.

When the Government announced further fuel price increases as part of its budget for 2002, protests ensued, led by CONAIE and the Frente Unitario de los Trabajadores (FUT—Workers' United Front), as well as an umbrella group of Amerindian organizations, student groups and trade unions, the Frente Popular (FP—Popular Front). The Government declared a state of emergency in the Amazon provinces of Sucumbíos and Orellana in February 2002 to counter a regional strike. Protesters blocked petroleum operations and demanded greater regional investment from central government and foreign petroleum companies. In March the conflict was resolved following a pledge from the Government to direct more state funds to local infrastructure development.

PRESIDENT GUTIÉRREZ, 2003–05

Elections to the presidency and the legislature proceeded as scheduled in October 2002, with the two leading presidential candidates competing in a second round of voting in November. Lucio Gutiérrez Borbua, a former army colonel involved in the coup to oust President Mahuad, won 59% of the votes cast in the run-off ballot, defeating a wealthy banana magnate, Alvaro Noboa Pontón (of no relation to former President Gustavo Noboa). Gutiérrez's nationalist and leftist campaign rhetoric, targeting particularly corruption within the political establishment, earned him the support of a loose alliance of indigenous peoples' interests and left-wing groups. Principal among these was the Partido Sociedad Patriótica 21 de Enero (PSP—Patriotic Society Party), which Gutiérrez had formed with former army colleagues, the indigenous Pachakútik movement and the small left-wing Movimiento Popular Democrático (MPD—Popular Democratic Movement).

The new President confronted an opposition-dominated Congreso. Parties of the ruling coalition accounted for just 20 of the Congreso's 100 seats, a figure that had been reduced to 17 by mid-2003. The opposition included the larger established parties such as the PSC and ID, as well as the PRE, the DP and former presidential candidate Noboa's own Partido Renovador Institucional de Acción Nacional (PRIAN—National Action Institutional Renewal Party). This opposition bloc took control of important congressional committees and installed ID leader Guillermo Landazuri as congressional speaker.

On taking office, President Gutiérrez moderated his rhetoric and quickly embarked on a largely orthodox programme of economic management intended to secure an IMF stand-by loan. Although the new Cabinet reflected the diverse forces that supported Gutiérrez, the key position of Minister of Finance and Public Credit went to the market-friendly Quito businessman Mauricio Pozo. A public sector salary freeze was imposed and fuel subsidies were reduced. Gutiérrez also proposed a tax reform to increase revenues and improve the Government's fiscal position. Although not all IMF prescriptions were followed—notably, the politically sensitive subsidy on cooking gas was maintained—the Government's proposals damaged relations with its own supporters. Trade unions and popular and indigenous groups were dissatisfied with what they perceived to be broken promises on the part of the Government, and their reaction called into question the Government's ability to sustain its minority alliance in the Congreso or its support in the country at large. This was borne out in August 2003 when Gutiérrez's electoral campaign ally Pachakútik was expelled from the governing coalition after failing to support his public sector reforms. The traditional parties were not strongly opposed to Gutiérrez's reform efforts on ideological grounds, but they conceived the government alliance of small parties drawn from outside established politics as a threat to their influence.

In March 2003 the IMF approved a US $205m. stand-by loan, which paved the way for further lending. In May the World Bank announced a four-year programme of lending, worth a projected $1,050m. Ambivalence within the Congreso led to several measures being diluted and falling short of IMF demands. The Government missed a 30 April deadline to send a labour reform bill to the Congreso, and the legislature amended measures to reform the customs service. Further proposed legislation to improve supervision of the financial sector was rejected in May. The Government struggled to satisfy IMF requirements on the one hand, while attempting to avoid alienating its campaign supporters on the other.

A cabinet reorganization in December 2003 succeeded in shoring up political support for Gutiérrez and stemmed a deteriorating political environment that threatened his presidency. Gutiérrez appointed several members of the PSC and PRE to cabinet positions, broadening the Government's appeal in the Congreso. Furthermore, with the appointment as Minister of the Interior of Raúl Baca Carbo, a trusted politician who enjoyed good relations with indigenous organizations and trade unions, the Government went some way to appease its former allies. At the same time, Gutiérrez reappointed Mauricio Pozo to the finance portfolio, thereby reconfirming the Government's commitment to structural reform and orthodox fiscal policies agreed with the IMF. Nevertheless, many obstacles remained. Despite their participation in government, the traditional parties were not formally in a coalition with Gutiérrez. As a result, many reforms were delayed or diluted in the face of political opposition. Furthermore, the Government had yet to relinquish control of state electricity and telecommunications companies to private management, and it failed to introduce tax reform at the end of 2003. In the Congreso, recognizing that it was not possible to build a sustainable majority, the Government attempted to garner ad hoc support.

Gutiérrez's political difficulties mounted towards the end of 2004. The ruling PSP won just 7% of the vote in local and provincial elections held in October of that year, while the PSC gained control of several coastal cities and the ID dominated in the Sierra. Emboldened by this strong electoral support the PSC, ID and Pachakútik began impeachment proceedings against Gutiérrez, accusing him of misappropriating public funds during October's elections. The President survived the attempt to depose him, which required a simple majority in the Congreso, by engaging the support of exiled former President Bucaram of the PRE and the PRIAN's Alvaro Noboa, with additional support from smaller parties. Using his new alliance, Gutiérrez launched a counteroffensive against the PSC and the ID, taking control of important congressional committees and replacing the ID President of the Congreso with leading PRE member Omar Quintana Baquerizo. In late November allies of the new governing majority were appointed as justices to the Constitutional Tribunal and the Supreme Electoral Court. More controversial still, in early December the Government called an extraordinary session of the Congreso, during which it voted to expel 27 members of the Supreme Court alleged to be too closely associated with the PSC. They were replaced with new judges with links to the PRE, PRIAN and the Government. Furthermore, any future replacements were to be appointed by other justices. This purge was widely condemned as a gross violation of the judiciary's independence and of the Constitution. In response, the opposition began to mobilize domestic and international support for its accusations of corruption, authoritarianism and 'cronyism' on the part of the governing alliance, which now effectively controlled the judiciary and electoral authorities. Among other allegations, the opposition claimed that the judicial appointments were a step towards suspending fraud charges against former President Bucaram, now a government ally.

In early 2005 the PSC called protest demonstrations against the Government, taking advantage of popular discontent over its record, especially in reducing crime and providing services in Guayaquil, in order to maintain pressure on the Government over its manipulation of the judiciary. Popular protest spread to Quito and elsewhere, and demonstrations were held throughout March and April. As predicted by the opposition, at the end of March the Supreme Court announced that all charges against exiled former President Bucaram had been dismissed. Polls indicated that support for Gutiérrez had declined to below 5%. Following a week of daily protests by thousands in the capital, on 15 April Gutiérrez declared a state of emergency and announced the dissolution of the Supreme Court; however, by this time he had lost the support both of the Congreso, which on 20 April voted to oust him for 'abandoning his post', and of the military, which had allowed protesters to reach the presidential palace on the same day. Gutiérrez (who fled to Brazil, where he claimed asylum) became the third elected President since 1997 to be removed following popular unrest.

INTERIM GOVERNMENT OF PRESIDENT PALACIO, 2005–07

Immediately following the removal of Gutiérrez, his Vice-President, Dr Alfredo Palacio González, was sworn in as President. Palacio, while nominally an independent, had associations with the PSC, and his cabinet appointees similarly had links with the traditional parties. There were doubts over the constitutional legitimacy of Palacio's accession because the vote to remove Gutiérrez from office had not been approved by the required minimum of 67 legislators in the Congreso. Palacio secured initial support with an alliance of the PSC, ID, Pachakútik, DP, MPD and assorted independents. However, active support, beyond simple recognition of Palacio as head of an interim Government, was not forthcoming from any party or legislative bloc, making it difficult for him to govern effectively. Once again, the President confronted the prospect of governing while having to negotiate with a fragmented Congreso in which he enjoyed limited personal support.

Political weakness undermined the ability of the Palacio Government to impose its own legislative agenda. President Palacio attempted to initiate reforms to shore up the institutions of government and improve the country's political stability. His proposals, which included restoring a bicameral legislature and increasing regional autonomy, were rejected by the Congreso in September 2005, prompting the resignation of the Minister of Government and Police, Oswaldo Molestina Zavala, in October, after barely one month in the post. The Government responded to the congressional defeat by announcing it would hold a referendum to seek popular approval for the establishment of a constituent assembly to oversee state and constitutional reform. To proceed with the referendum, the Government tried to bypass the Congreso and instead, in October, sought approval from the Supreme Electoral Court. However, that body rejected the plan on the grounds that any referendum required congressional authorization. The Government and the Congreso failed to reach a compromise solution involving a constitutional assembly with more limited powers.

Meanwhile, the new Government had an important decision to make concerning the composition of the Supreme Court of Justice, which had been suspended since the state of emergency introduced by former President Gutiérrez in mid-April 2005. Rather than reinstate the disbanded Supreme Court, an independent panel was appointed to select new justices. The new Supreme Court was established in December; it was confronted with a long backlog of cases, owing to the institutional vacuum.

Expenditure increased under President Palacio, with the Government under popular pressure to raise public spending. Meanwhile, the interim administration sought to reassure the IMF and the international financial community that higher spending from oil revenues would not lead to economic instability. This approach was broadly maintained under Diego Borja, appointed Minister of Economy and Finance in January 2006, who, despite political links with the left, emphasized his commitment to dollarization and to reducing the fiscal deficit by curbing spending and increasing tax revenues.

Relations with overseas investors deteriorated in April 2006 when President Palacio signed a new hydrocarbons law imposing a 'windfall' tax on foreign oil companies' earnings over a designated threshold. It was hoped that this tax would raise government revenues by some US $500m. Tensions increased in May after the Government announced that the US Occidental Petroleum Corpn (Oxy) had violated the terms of its contract by transferring 40% of its shares to the Canadian firm EnCana. The Government cancelled Oxy's exploration and production contract and transferred its operations to PETROECUADOR. The dispute halted negotiations for a free trade agreement with the USA, and damaged Ecuador's reputation among foreign investors. However, the proposed free trade agreement was bitterly opposed by left-wing and indigenous groupings (the protests of which had led to a state of emergency being declared in three provinces in March), so the suspension of negotiations eased the pressure on the weakened Palacio administration. Opposition attempts to impeach Palacio in late 2005 had raised questions about the ability of his interim

Government to remain in power until legislative and presidential elections scheduled for October 2006.

PRESIDENT CORREA, 2007–

In November 2006 Rafael Correa Delgado, a radical candidate of the left, won a convincing presidential election run-off, with 56.7% of the vote, against Alvaro Noboa, the defeated candidate in the 2003 election and a populist right-wing businessman. The result was a surprise, as Correa had not won the largest share of the vote in the first round, and opinion polls had suggested that supporters of eliminated candidates would transfer their allegiance to Noboa. Correa moderated his rhetoric prior to the second ballot and underplayed his friendship with Venezuela's radical President, Hugo Chávez Frías. This appeared to allay the concerns of undecided voters, who then chose to support him rather than Noboa, a candidate who, it was feared, could have too much power at his disposal, given his business interests, if he secured the presidency.

Elections to the Congreso were held concurrently with the first round of the presidential ballot in October 2006. Correa's Alianza País (AP—Country Alliance) did not campaign in the legislative elections, and the President sought to govern with the informal support of the PSP, the party of former President Gutiérrez, and smaller left-wing parties. However, such support was conditional and pragmatic. Correa could use the widespread popularity he enjoyed among Ecuadoreans to put pressure on the Congreso, but with public opinion notoriously volatile there remained the prospect of encountering a hostile Congreso once the initial 'honeymoon' period of his administration had passed.

Correa took office in January 2007 with a programme of constitutional reform, increasing the state's participation in the oil sector and prioritizing public spending on social services over debt servicing. Correa's stated aim in securing constitutional reform was to depoliticize Ecuador's state institutions, which were controlled by entrenched interests, particularly within the powerful PSC, and to instill greater democracy in the country's party system. President Correa charged the Supreme Electoral Court with preparing a referendum on the establishment of a constituent assembly to rewrite the Constitution. For the referendum to be held, the support of both the Supreme Electoral Court and the Congreso would be required. In March the Court approved a referendum by three votes to two and then expelled 57 legislators from the 100-member Congreso who had voted for the head of the Court to be dismissed. It was his casting vote that had secured support for a referendum. The dismissal of the deputies, who were replaced by only 21 new representatives, helped ensure that the Congreso, aware of the risks of a potential public backlash, approved the referendum. With 81.7% of voters supporting the proposal, Correa secured an overwhelming victory in the referendum, which was held in April. In September 2007 an election to a 130-member Constituent Assembly, tasked with drafting a new constitution in 2008, resulted in a majority for the AP, which obtained a total of 80 seats. At its first session in late November, the Constituent Assembly voted to dissolve the Congreso until a further referendum on the new constitution was held. In the mean time, Correa transferred the Congreso's legislative powers to a commission of the Constituent Assembly. The expulsion of opponents from the Congreso, the referendum victory and the transfer of powers from the Congreso to a legislative commission bolstered Correa's political position. The final text of the draft Constitution was approved by the Assembly on 24 July and in a referendum in September.

President Correa won a second term of office following elections in April 2009. In a comfortable victory, Correa won in the first round of voting with 52.0% of the votes, while his nearest rival, former President Lucio Gutiérrez, polled 28.2%, thereby satisfying the two conditions required for automatic first round victory: a more than 50% vote share for the winner and a minimum 10% margin of victory over the second placed candidate. Correa's victory was the first time since the restoration of civilian democracy in 1979 that a second round had not been required in a presidential contest. Correa also became the first incumbent President to win re-election (President Velasco Ibarra was elected five times between 1934 and 1968, but failed to complete his term on each occasion).

President Correa benefited from particularly weak and fragmented opposition. As well as Gutiérrez, another conservative populist candidate, Alvaro Noboa, a third time losing presidential nominee, polled poorly, winning just 11.4% of the votes. A third candidate, Martha Roldós Bucaram, attracted just 4.3% of votes from supporters of Amerindian groups dissatisfied with the Government's support for large mining projects. Neither of the traditionally powerful parties, the PSC from the right nor the ID from the left, put forward candidates.

President Correa enjoyed broad popular support for his spending increases on health, education, pensions and infrastructure. His defiance in the face of the perceived influence of the USA and international financial institutions garnered further support. Correa defaulted on some of the country's debt commitments in December 2008, claiming that they were 'illegitimate', and in early 2009 ended a lease arrangement with the USA to operate a military base at Manta. However, despite his clear popular mandate, Correa's ability to govern was hampered by a loss of legislative majority. Correa's AP secured 59 seats, four short of a majority, requiring the Government to seek support from smaller parties on the left. The Government was frustrated in its attempt to introduce laws regulating strategic sectors including communications, hydrocarbons and water, while divisions within the AP further complicated the approval of legislation. In particular, several AP legislators were in conflict with the President in the aftermath of a road accident in January 2010 in which the car of the wife of Washington Pesantez, the Prosecutor-General, killed a pedestrian. The President threatened to remove the immunity from prosecution of legislators who demanded the impeachment of Pesantez for allegedly covering up an investigation into the incident. In a cabinet reorganization in April 2010, Minister of Finance María Elsa Viteri Acaiturri was replaced by Patricio Rivera, while Wilson Pastor Morris, hitherto head of PETROECUADOR, took over from Germánico Pinto as Minister of Non-Renewable Natural Resources. The reorganization was designed to reinvigorate the Government rather than support a shift in policy direction. There was speculation that, if the legislative impasse continued, President Correa might invoke the powers given to him by the 2008 Constitution to dissolve the Asamblea Nacional and rule by decree until new elections were held. Correa maintained a broad base of support among low income groups, although in Guayaquil, traditionally antagonistic towards the central Government in Quito, the right-wing mayor Jamie Nebot was gaining in popularity.

CONCLUSION

The history of politics and government in Ecuador has been turbulent. A fragmented party system, based around personalities and regional and ethnic interests, continued to pose a threat to coherent government, rather than providing an effective balance to executive power. The Government's constitutional reforms were a new attempt to tackle this endemic problem. President Correa's second term of office represented a period of stability in government that was untypical in Ecuador, though a fragmented legislature kept up concerns about long-term political stability. As always, the Government's political fortunes were closely related to the performance of the economy. Financial constraints grew due to the Government's difficulty in accessing international funding following the country's December 2008 debt default. Meanwhile, the failure of the Government to implement its radical agenda threatened to lead to social unrest and frustration within the ranks of the ruling AP and among independent supporters in Congreso.

Economy

SANDY MARKWICK

Ecuador comprises a landmass of 272,045 sq km (105,037 sq miles), making it one of the smaller South American countries. Despite its relatively small size, Ecuador has a richly diverse geography. The Andean Sierra runs north to south through the middle of the country forming a natural barrier between the tropical lowlands of the Amazon basin to the east, the Oriente region, and the coastal lowlands, the Costa, to the west. Meanwhile, the Galápagos Islands, 1,500 km off the Pacific coast, contribute a unique range of flora and fauna to the already rich biodiversity of mainland Ecuador.

Climate varies between regions. Most of the country is tropical or subtropical while some 20% is temperate. Ecuador has some 8.29m. ha of land with potential for agricultural use. The fertile soils of the coastal plains and Oriente can support a wide range of crops, while the coastlines, as well as freshwater rivers and lakes, provide abundant opportunity for commercial fishing and seafood production. Ecuador suffers from the regular occurrence of *El Niño*, a periodic warming of the tropical Pacific Ocean that brings heavy rains and damages agricultural output.

Since the 2001 census counted 12.2m. inhabitants, the population rose by approximately 1.7% annually, to an estimated 14.2m. in 2010. Net emigration throughout the 1990s increased from 1998, which, along with improvements in family planning, slowed population growth. It was estimated in 2006 that more than 1m. Ecuadoreans were working outside the country. Emigration peaked in 2000 when an estimated 175,000 people left Ecuador. Although improved job prospects at home and restrictions to immigration abroad slowed the pace of emigration subsequently, it continued to have an important economic impact. Approximately 59,000 Ecuadoreans left in 2006 as growth in the formal economy struggled to absorb young entrants to the labour market. Most emigrants left for Spain, where 420,000 Ecuadoreans were estimated to be living in mid-2007, followed by the USA. In common with other developing countries, Ecuador has a large informal economy. Around 66% of the population lived in cities in 2010, compared with 47% in 1980. The three largest cities—Guayaquil, Quito and Cuenca—accounted for 35% of the population. Almost 50% of Ecuadoreans live in the coastal lowlands, and 45% in the Sierra, while only 4.5% live in the Oriente and less than 1% in the Galápagos Islands. Ecuador has a young population, with approximately 30.3% aged under 15 years.

Most social indicators show Ecuador to be among the poorest countries in South America. Gross domestic product (GDP) per head was US $3,690 in 2008. The proportion of the population considered poor was 36% in 2010. In common with most of the region, income distribution was uneven. The poorest 20% of the population received 4.6% of national income, while 36.1% went to the richest 10%. World Bank indicators suggested that there had been improvements in living standards since 1980. Life expectancy increased to an estimated 75.3 years in 2009 from 63 years in 1980, and infant mortality declined significantly from 74 per 1,000 live births in 1980 to a low of 15 in 2003, before increasing to 20.9 in 2009. This reversal of the long-term trend was probably a result of declining living standards from the late 1990s, owing to economic instability. Public spending on health care has suffered as successive governments have struggled to balance their budgets. The proportion of the urban workforce considered unemployed or underemployed was an estimated 51.3% in March 2010. High rates of emigration and the Government's narrow definition of unemployment tended to restrain official unemployment figures, which reported an average of 9.1% of the total urban labour force out of work in September 2009 and an average of 7.2% in the previous 12 months. Unemployment increased owing to recession in the first half of 2009.

The country's GDP in 2009 was an estimated US $52,021m. at nominal dollar rates, up from $45,789m. in 2007. Ecuador is the seventh largest economy in South America but is in eighth position in terms of GDP per head in the region. In 2009 agriculture and fisheries contributed an estimated 10.4% of GDP; industry, including mining, contributed 38.1% and services 51.5%. Since Ecuador began producing petroleum in the early 1970s, economic growth figures have closely mirrored the performance of the petroleum sector. Following Ecuador's withdrawal from the Organization of the Petroleum Exporting Countries (OPEC) in 1992, oil production increased, leading to a period of strong growth until the mid-1990s. Ecuador's positive, though modest, annual growth after 1994 was interrupted in 1999 when GDP declined by 7.3% as a result of the spiralling effects of a banking crisis, devaluation and political instability, which in turn led to fiscal indiscipline, under-investment in the petroleum sector and depressed domestic demand. Other circumstances exacerbated the situation, such as the devastation wrought by the *El Niño* weather pattern, a credit squeeze stemming from a financial crisis in East Asia and a decrease in petroleum prices. There was a recovery in 2000 when GDP grew by 2.3%, partly because of an increase in oil pipeline capacity and higher petroleum output. GDP increased by an average of 4.5% per year between 2001 and 2008. GDP rose by 7.2% in 2008, led by growth in the petroleum sector. However, reduced expansion in the oil sector combined with the global economic slowdown precipitated a recession in the first half of 2009. By the end of the year, according to the central bank's preliminary figures, the economy had grown by 0.4%.

Petroleum revenues in the 1970s stimulated domestic demand and inflationary pressures. Public sector spending increases led to budget deficits and currency weakness, fuelling inflation from the 1980s. By 1989 inflation reached an annual average of 76%, which, at the time, was the highest rate in Ecuador's history. Inflation in the 1990s averaged 37.4% a year, but increased to an annual average of 96.9% in 2000, far exceeding all other South American economies. The increase stemmed largely from an expanded monetary base as the Government offered financial assistance to banks confronting liquidity crises, which in turn led to a decline in the value of the sucre, further fuelling inflation. Fears of hyperinflation led to the policy of 'dollarization', in which the sucre was replaced with the US dollar as the unit of currency. The policy, which was announced in January 2000 and came into effect in March, had the effect of stabilizing the economy by removing exchange rate instability and reducing the Government's scope for fiscal imprudence. Existing inflationary pressures and reductions in state subsidies meant that the rate of inflation continued to rise after the introduction of the dollarization policy, reaching 107.9% in September. Subsequently, however, as the monetary base contracted and an increase in agricultural products reduced the prices of food and beverages, inflation declined to an annual average of 2.1% in 2005. Strong domestic demand increased inflation to an estimated average of 3.3% during 2006, but the rate reduced slightly to 3.2% in 2007 as import price rises slowed. Annual inflation rose sharply in 2008, ending the year at 8.3%, a result of higher prices for food and imports, exacerbated by the weakness of the US dollar. The rate of inflation increased in 2009 partly owing to poor weather conditions associated with *El Niño* combined with rising international commodity prices, ending the year at 4.3%. Price rises and a fixed exchange rate undermined the competitiveness of Ecuadorean producers. Attempts to increase productivity or to push for privatization or other structural reforms to boost competitiveness could expect opposition from entrenched business interests, as well as trade unions and left-wing groups. The inflation rate was 3.2% in April 2010.

Successive governments came under pressure to generate fiscal surpluses in order to meet burdensome debt obligations. A fiscal deficit equivalent to 4.8% of GDP in 1998 was fuelled by the banking crisis. The deficit was reduced to 3.8% of GDP in 1999 before a surplus equivalent to 1.5% of GDP was achieved in 2000. High international oil prices helped Ecuador maintain a small fiscal surplus during 2001–02, although the position remained unhealthy and was exacerbated by the Government's undisciplined handling of public finances. Overspending in early 2002 was followed by a drastic halt in the latter half of the year, including a failure to pay public sector wages. The Ley Orgánica de Responsibilidad, Estabilización y Transparencia Fiscal (Fiscal Responsibility, Stability and Transparency Law), adopted in June 2002, restricted the Government to annual spending increases of no more than 3.5% in real terms, and directed windfall profits from petroleum production towards debt buy-back. As a result, small fiscal surpluses were recorded from 2004. In January 2003 the new Government of Lucio Gutiérrez Borbua addressed the fiscal shortfall by decreeing reductions in fuel subsidies and other public spending. A stand-by agreement with the IMF, announced in March 2003, was an important first step in gaining access to credit from the other multilateral lending agencies and private creditors required to finance Ecuador's debt. Nevertheless, the Government encountered political and popular opposition to some of the IMF-prescribed restructuring, which raised questions about its ability to fulfil its commitments and maintain access to international credit. IMF approval of the Government's economic policies was a condition for disbursements from the World Bank and the Inter-American Development Bank (IDB). President Alfredo Palacio Gonzáles (2005–07) relaxed fiscal rules by assigning petroleum revenues to social spending. Despite this, and despite higher spending under Palacio's successor, President Rafael Correa Delgado, a fiscal surplus equivalent to 2.2% of GDP was estimated in 2007 because of high oil prices and improvements in tax collection. However, the fiscal balance was estimated to be in deficit in 2008 at 0.8% of GDP, stemming from lower oil earnings weakening demand and sharp increases in spending under the Government of President Correa. In 2009 the fiscal deficit expanded to an estimated 5.2% of GDP.

AGRICULTURE AND FISHERIES

Close to one-third of Ecuador's land mass is used for agricultural purposes. Sectoral output increased by an estimated 1.5% in 2009 following preliminary growth figures of 5.4% in 2008 and 4.1% in 2007. Agriculture's contribution to GDP has been largely stable since the early 1990s. During the previous three decades, however, the importance of agriculture declined dramatically: agriculture accounted for 25% of total output in the 1960s. A combination of poor infrastructure, lack of mechanization, financing difficulties and the effects of *El Niño* limited productivity in the sector.

Ecuador's climatic and geographic diversity supports a wide range of crops and fisheries production. The coastal region features a modern agro-industry where land has been converted for production, largely for export, of bananas and other fruit, coffee, cocoa, rice and shrimps. Another important export is cut flowers, the cultivation of which is concentrated in the Sierra. Staple products for domestic consumption include rice, sugar cane and plantains, grown in coastal areas, while grains, vegetables and dairy products are produced in the Sierra.

Ecuador exports more bananas than any other country in the world. Bananas became the principal crop of Ecuador in the 1940s when disease and hurricanes damaged production in Central America. Banana plantations were principally located in the lowlands of Guayas province, though road construction and improved irrigation expanded the viable area of production. By 1995 the land area given to banana production slowed. Global growth in demand, particularly from the former USSR and Eastern Europe, led to heavy investment in technology. The disease-resistant and higher-yielding Cavendish variety of banana replaced the traditional Gros Michel. However, increased output and reduced demand saw prices decrease from 1997. The steady decline in exports was reversed in 2001, when banana production of 6.1m. metric tons generated exports worth US $847m., equivalent to 18.2% of total export earnings. This increased to $1,099.3m., some 18.2% of export earnings, in 2003. In 2009 bananas accounted for export revenues of $1,995.1m., a rise in revenues during the year of 21.7%. As a proportion of total export value, bananas represented 14.5% in 2009 compared with 9.6% in 2006. In 1999 the World Trade Organization (WTO) ruled in favour of Ecuador in a dispute with the European Union (EU). Ecuador had long protested that the preference for trading with African, Caribbean and Pacific countries, with which parts of the EU maintained post-colonial ties, was contrary to trade regulations. The dispute was exacerbated by the EU's introduction in January 2006 of a levy on banana imports from Latin America to replace a quota system, which imposed a lower tariff on imports over a quota limit. Ecuador and other Latin American producers complained that the new tariff was discriminatory and contrary to the spirit of the 1999 WTO ruling. Ecuador submitted a new complaint to the WTO, which was upheld in April 2008. The dispute was finally settled following an agreement in December 2009 in which the EU agreed to reduce gradually the tariffs on bananas from Latin America by up to one-third.

Before bananas took over in the 1940s, cocoa had been Ecuador's main export crop. In the 19th century coastal plantations had produced cocoa accounting for up to three-quarters of total export earnings. Decline followed disease and the emergence of alternative sources to satisfy global demand. A revival in the sub-sector took place in the 1980s as the Government subsidized production. Production reached record levels of 131,000 metric tons in 1985. The crop is vulnerable to adverse climatic conditions and fluctuations in demand. By 1987 production had decreased to 57,500 tons. Cocoa exports came under threat when the International Cocoa Organization reclassified the quality of Ecuadorean cocoa at a lower level. In the mid-1990s, with the help of EU funds, Ecuador embarked on a programme to improve quality and increase production. In 1996 production increased to 93,800 tons, but damage caused by *El Niño* saw production suffer in subsequent years. In 2008 Ecuador produced 94,300 tons of cocoa, a 9.8% increase during the year. Export earnings benefited from favourable world prices. Ecuadorean cocoa and cocoa products earned an estimated US $393.9m. in 2009, up 50.2% during the year. Plans to focus on high-quality niche markets for cocoa were showing signs of success.

As with other commodities, the importance of coffee to the Ecuadorean economy varied with international prices, supply and climatic conditions. With more than 100,000 small family growers, coffee production is fragmented and inefficient. Intermittent attempts by Latin American coffee producers to support higher international prices by limiting exports have not been sustained. *El Niño* severely affected coffee production in 1997, leading to a 54.2% decline in production volumes to 87,350 metric tons. Production levels continued to decline, reaching an historic low of 43,128 tons in 2005. Revenues from exports of coffee and coffee products amounted to US $139.6m. in 2009 owing to higher international prices.

New agricultural products, including cut flowers, melons, asparagus, artichokes and strawberries, gave a boost to export earnings in the 2000s. Cut flowers earned export revenues estimated at US $545.8m. in 2009, down slightly from $565.7m. in 2008 and up from $469.4m. in 2007. Ecuadorean producers took advantage of the appreciation of the Colombian peso, which ensured more competitive prices in international markets. Colombia was Ecuador's principal competitor in the flower industry. Both countries, however, were vulnerable to the strengthening real exchange rate.

Staple crops such as rice, sugar cane, potatoes, maize, soybeans, wheat, barley and cotton were important for domestic consumption, but contributed insignificant amounts to overall export earnings. Landholdings in the non-export sector tended to be smaller and had lower levels of productivity. Ecuador became self-sufficient in rice cultivation in the early 1990s. In 2004 rice production rose to 1.8m. metric tons (up from 781,000 tons in 1987), before declining to 1.5m. tons in 2005. In 2008 Ecuador produced 1.4m. tons of rice, mostly for export. Production is concentrated in the Guayas lowlands. Ecuador relied on imports to satisfy requirements for wheat and barley. Patterns of land ownership, characterized by a predominance of subsistence smallholdings, contributed to the shortfall in wheat production.

Shrimp production, concentrated in the Guayas and Esmeraldas provinces, increased in the 1990s, and export revenues reached a record US $886m. in 1997. At this time, Ecuador was one of the world's most important suppliers of shrimps, which had become the country's third most important export commodity after petroleum and bananas. Despite this growth, cultivation was dramatically affected in 1998–99 by competition from Asia, environmental damage caused by *El Niño*, interruptions in power supply, lack of investment and disease. Export volumes and earnings were partially restored from 2000, but did not approach 1997 levels. Ecuador's shrimp-fishing sector earned $654m. in 2009, a progressive increase since 2002, when revenues were $253m. Additional revenues came from tuna, sardines, mackerel, anchovies and fishmeal. Processed fish products, including canned fish, earned an estimated $723m. in export revenues in 2009, down from $890m. in 2008.

MINING AND ENERGY

Oil drilling in Ecuador began in 1917 in the Santa Elena peninsula, west of Guayaquil. However, large-scale production dates back to the late 1960s with the discovery of major reserves in Lago Agrio in the Oriente by the US consortium of Texaco-Gulf. The Trans-Andean pipeline was built linking the oilfields to a tanker terminal in the port of Esmeraldas, and exports began in 1972. Ecuador joined OPEC in 1973, but the required production quotas limited exploration and proven reserves.

The Government made it easier for foreign companies to operate in the petroleum sector in 1983, following which several foreign companies signed contracts with the state oil company Corporación Estatal Petrolera Ecuatoriana (CEPE). New reserves were found in the south-eastern Oriente. Ignoring OPEC production quotas, Ecuador increased production to maximize revenues when oil prices were declining. In 1989 President Rodrigo Borja Cevallos formed a new state oil company, Empresa Estatal Petróleos del Ecuador (PETROECUADOR), to replace CEPE and assume greater state control over the process of production and distribution. PETROECUADOR took over the Trans-Andean pipeline, but a decline in export revenues led to a policy that encouraged greater levels of foreign investment. In 1993 President Sixto Durán Ballén introduced a more liberal foreign investment code. The changed rules led to eight new production-sharing agreements with petroleum companies in the mid-1990s.

In 1992 Durán Ballén withdrew Ecuador from membership of OPEC because of its refusal to authorize an increase in Ecuador's production quota. Durán Ballén announced a target of producing 576,000 barrels per day (b/d) by 1996, representing an ambitious 55% increase over the 1992 production volume. In the mid-1990s petroleum discoveries almost tripled Ecuador's proven reserves, and the Government signed several contracts with foreign companies for drilling and exploration. Production increased from 341,774 b/d in 1993 to 386,725 b/d in 1995, still far below government targets. Increased opposition and sensitivities to foreign participation in the petroleum sector slowed development and growth. Under-investment during the administration of President Fabián Alarcón Rivera (1997–98) contributed to a decline in production that occurred concurrently with a decrease in international petroleum prices. At 370,000 b/d, production was at levels lower than any time since 1993. Production increased to 407,000 b/d in 2001, but declined to 393,273 b/d during 2002, largely as a consequence of technical problems and an industrial dispute at the Esmeraldas refinery. Poor infrastructure was another obstacle to increased production. In 2000 work was completed to expand the existing Sistema del Oleoducto Trans-Ecuatoriano (SOTE—Trans-Ecuadorean Oil Pipeline System), which added 60,000 b/d to overall capacity. The Oleoducto de Crudos Pesados, a pipeline that doubled heavy crude petroleum transport capacity to 850,000 b/d, became operational in 2003. As a result, average production for that year increased to 447,000 b/d. However, in March 2004 oil shipments via the SOTE were suspended following a landslide, forcing PETROECUADOR to declare *force majeure* on its contractual obligations. Until 2003 PETROECUADOR had supplied over 50% of national output. A dispute with the US Occidental Petroleum Corporation (Oxy), which led the Government to cancel its exploration and production contract and take over its operations in May 2006, increased the state company's output relative to private sector output. The cancellation of Oxy's contract followed a series of disputes with foreign oil companies over tax payments. However, the takeover undermined the planned expansion of petroleum production. PETROECUADOR found it difficult to maintain production levels at Block 15, formerly operated by Oxy. The Oxy contract cancellation and tax disputes were precipitated by a history of conflict between successive Governments and the US oil firm Texaco (part of Chevron since 2001) over environmental damage dating back to the 1970s. The company argued that its responsibilities were fulfilled following a settlement with the Government in 1998, which included a US $40m. clean-up operation. Chevron argued that most of the pollution was the responsibility of PETROECUADOR, with which Texaco had been a junior partner. Compensation claims against Chevron totalled $27,000m. The dispute was ongoing into 2010, and the company was seeking to have the case heard by the International Court of Arbitration rather than an Ecuadorean court. Relations with foreign oil companies had worsened further under President Correa following the termination of a contract with French firm Perenco in early 2009 and a demand by the Government that the company, along with Spain's Repsol, pay $326m. and $444m., respectively, in disputed taxes. Meanwhile, in 2007 President Correa restored Ecuador's status within OPEC after a 15-year hiatus with a view to strengthening the Government's position in negotiations with oil companies, and in April 2010 President Correa raised the prospect of nationalizing foreign oil operations unless they agreed to new contract terms. Continued under-investment in PETROECUADOR, combined with aversion to risks associated with the legal status of contracts with foreign companies, suggested that Ecuador's oil production potential would remain unrealized in the short term. In 2008 Ecuador produced an average of 501,400 b/d of petroleum, down 2.0% since 2007.

Ecuador is heavily reliant on oil as a source of export revenues. Petroleum and petroleum derivatives were Ecuador's most important export commodities (comprising an estimated 48.6% of total export revenue in 2009), and the sector was one of the largest contributors to the central government treasury, accounting for 19.8% of government revenues in 2009, down from 32.3% in 2008. The significant decline in 2009 stemmed from a 36% decline in average prices of Ecuadorean crude petroleum. Petroleum's share of export earnings has increased since 2000, when it accounted for 49.6% of export earnings, in large part owing to rises in international prices. The average export price of a barrel was US $53.40 in 2009 following an historically high average price of $83.40 in 2008. The USA was the most significant destination for petroleum exports. Proven reserves stood at 6,511m. barrels in 2008. Most Ecuadorean petroleum was medium-heavy crude, although recent discoveries have been of heavy crude. Under President Correa, relations with President Hugo Chávez Frías's Venezuela became closer leading to an agreement in May 2006 whereby Venezuela would help to finance the construction of a 300,000-b/d oil refinery at the port of Manta. The plan followed a 2006 agreement in which Venezuela refined some 100,000 b/d of Ecuadorean crude on preferential terms.

Most mining focuses on non-metals used in construction, including limestone, sand and clay, though there are reserves of metals such as gold, silver, copper, iron, lead, zinc, uranium and magnesium. The Government opened up mining to foreign investment in 1991 in a bid to develop the sector with a more liberal mining law. Subsequently, the bureaucracy associated with investment was reduced, and further reforms were introduced in 2000 granting stronger legal rights to mining companies. However, the risks surrounding exploration rights due to changes in government policy and enforcement have deterred investment.

MANUFACTURING AND CONSTRUCTION

Traditional manufacturing sectors were textiles, food and drink, tobacco, petroleum refining and cement production. Most industrial activity takes place in the Guayas and Pichincha provinces, though other areas occupied important roles in industry. Petroleum refining and wood activity take place in Esmeraldas, iron and steel in Cotopaxi, while ceramics, furniture and tyres are produced in Azuay, and marine and agricultural products are manufactured in Manabí. Ecuador established *maquiladoras* (in-bond assembly plants) at the Guayas Free Zone near Guayaquil, and several other areas have been identified for further free zones.

The petroleum boom of the 1970s fuelled expansion in manufacturing, which the Government encouraged with protectionist trade initiatives designed to substitute imports with domestically produced products. Industrial development was heavily dependent on the import of capital goods. Manufacturing output increased at an average annual rate of 9.5% between 1972 and 1982. The sector was characterized by recession and stagnation in the rest of the decade, but growth was restored in the 1990s. Manufacturing output increased by an average of 1.4% per year during 1995–2004. Excluding construction, manufacturing output declined by 1.5% in 2009 following growth estimated at 8.1% in 2008 and 4.9% in 2007. In 2007 the manufacturing and construction sector's contribution to GDP was a provisional 13.6%. In the 1990s government policy shifted significantly away from protectionism towards a more liberal trade environment in line with regional and global developments. Membership of the WTO and Comunidad Andina de Naciones (CAN—Andean Community of Nations) reinforced this outlook. The elimination and reduction of tariff and non-tariff barriers has exposed domestic producers to foreign competition while, at the same time, presenting opportunities for local industry to serve foreign markets. Exports to the CAN, in particular, led to an expansion in the chemicals, machinery, minerals, paper, printing and wood products industries. Despite new external markets, manufacturing continued to contribute modestly to overall export earnings. Canned fish was the single largest manufacturing export, attracting revenues of an estimated US $671m. in 2007. An underdeveloped stock market was an impediment to businesses seeking investment capital.

The construction sector outpaced the economy as a whole in 2009, growing by 5.4%. This followed rapid growth of 13.8% in 2008, but static output in 2007. The state sector accounted for most of the investment in construction, and major public sector infrastructure projects, such as new oil pipelines and highways, were an important source of employment.

FINANCIAL SERVICES

The regulation of financial services was overhauled in 1994. Inadequate banking sector supervision and risk assessment, as well as the importance of US dollar-denominated lending, made banks vulnerable to recession or devaluation of the sucre. As well as growth, the sector experienced regular crises from the mid-1990s. Poor economic performance, declining commodity prices, exchange rate depreciation and rising interest rates reduced bank deposits and increased bad debts. Banking collapses in 1998–99 led to a halt in banking activity, in an attempt to prevent further bankruptcies, and a deposit freeze lasting one year. Between 1998 and 2001 16 banks closed. By mid-2000 the majority of depositors whose assets had been frozen were reimbursed. A government agency, the Agencia de Garantía de Depósitos (AGD—Deposit Guarantee Agency), was pursuing the assets of former bankers and bank shareholders, many of whom had fled the country to escape criminal investigation, in order to repay remaining creditors and depositors. The influence of powerful debtors curbed the process of debt recovery, and confidence was slow in returning to the sector. Growth in bank deposits began to return in 2001, though most deposits were placed in current accounts and those of short maturity, reflecting the vulnerability of savings deposits to political turbulence and a lack of confidence in the banking system. Financial deposits decreased by US $200m., to $9,700m., in the first three months of the new administration of President Correa, whose plans for the Government to be more interventionist in the financial sector led to fears of a possible account freeze. Intentions to adopt the Bank for International Settlements' Basel Committee on Banking Supervision's standards of capital adequacy in the banking sector were frustrated by a lack of resources. At the end of 2008 $9,721m. was deposited in savings accounts.

TRANSPORT AND COMMUNICATIONS

Under-investment left most of Ecuador's road network in poor condition. The standard of the road network was best near the coast where large-scale reconstruction followed extensive damage caused by *El Niño* in 1997–98. Since 1998 private companies have been able to operate concessions to build and maintain highways. Road traffic has increased dramatically since the 1970s: in 2008 there were some 989,039 registered vehicles, compared with just 76,000 in 1971. Roads were built to open up new areas in the Oriente and Costa regions for agriculture and settlement. There was a road network of about 50,000 km of which just 14.8% was paved compared with a regional average of 22.0%.

The railway network, once nearly 1,000 km in length, fell into disrepair as a consequence of flooding and lack of investment. The main railway line runs between San Lorenzo, on the northern coast, through the Sierra to Cuenca and to the coast at Guayaquil. Limited sections of the track are operational and serve local and tourist traffic. Just 29,758 passenger journeys were made in 2008, and the railway carried no significant freight traffic.

Quito and Guayaquil host Ecuador's two main international airports. In November 2002 a private North American consortium won a 35-year concession to operate Quito's existing Mariscal Sucre airport (an upgrade was completed in March 2004) and to build a new one 25 km east of the capital at Puembo. Construction was scheduled for completion in 2010. An Argentine-based company won a concession to undertake a more limited modernization of Guayaquil's airport, completed in 2006. Restrictions on Ecuadorean carriers serving routes to the USA, imposed by the US Federal Aviation Administration (FAA), were lifted in 2006 following improvements in safety. The principal airline, TAME, Línea Aérea del Ecuador, served Latin American destinations as well as national routes. Ecuatoriana, which was part-privatized in 1995, subsequently went into receivership. The majority of its assets were later acquired by the LAN Chile group, which launched a new airline, LAN Ecuador, in April 2003.

Ecuador had seven ports capable of accommodating petroleum tankers. Of these, Guayaquil was the main trading port, handling approximately 56% of all traffic, and Esmeraldas the most important port serving the petroleum sector. The other principal ports are Manta (through which most coffee and cocoa exports are distributed), Puerto Bolívar (particularly supporting banana exports), Balao, El Salitral and La Libertad.

Ecuador had an average of just 13.3 fixed telephone lines for every 100 inhabitants in 2010, almost 50% below the Latin American regional average. Installed lines are concentrated in urban areas. Foreign investment and management is required to improve services. Plans dating back to 1998 to sell two state companies in the sector—Andinatel, providing services in the Sierra, and Pacifictel, in the coastal region—were frustrated by political opposition and potential bidders' aversion to risks associated with uncertain regulations. Outright privatization plans were suspended under the Government of President Gustavo Noboa Bejeramo (2000–03) in favour of transferring management to the private sector. This commitment became part of the IMF stand-by agreement of March 2003, but continued to be the subject of delays, owing to political opposition. The underdevelopment of fixed-line telecommunications was partially offset by a rapid increase in mobile cellular telephone use. There were 77 mobile phone subscribers per 100 inhabitants in 2008. Mobile penetration had increased rapidly from just 6.6 subscribers per 100 inhabitants in 2001 to overtake Ecuador's neighbours Peru and Colombia. The Government awarded a third mobile telecommunications licence to Andinatel following an auction in February 2006. In November 2008 the Government merged Andinatel and Pacifictel to form the Corporación Nacional de Telecomunicaciones (CNT—National Telecommunications Corporation) with a market share of fixed line telephony in excess of 90%. The CNT planned to invest in fixed-line infrastructure, targeting a 19% penetration rate. The company committed to an estimated US $520m. in investment. Two foreign-controlled mobile network operators dominated the market in 2010: OTECEL and Porta (Conecel, SA), with majority ownership from Spain and Mexico, respectively.

The generally undeveloped telecommunications infrastructure undermined the use of the internet as a tool for business, although measures to provide a legal framework for so-called 'e-commerce' and fixed tariffs on internet connections helped to increase use.

TOURISM

Tourism has been a significant sector of the national economy since the 1960s, with growth in long-haul, international travel. The sector became Ecuador's fourth largest earner of foreign exchange during the 1990s, behind petroleum, bananas and shrimps. Despite its significance as a foreign exchange earner, Ecuadoreans spent more outside Ecuador than visitors spent in the country. The net balance on tourism revenues stood at a deficit of US $114m. in 2009. Ecuador's rich biodiversity and varied climate and landscape—Andean highlands, tropical rainforest, Pacific beaches and the Galápagos Islands—mostly within accessible journey times from main cities, make it a popular destination.

The number of tourists visiting Ecuador increased from 172,000 in 1975 to 859,888 in 2005, up 11% over the previous year. However, visitor numbers declined to 840,555 in 2006. Most international visitors were from Colombia, Peru and the USA. Resolution of the long-running border dispute with Peru led to direct air links between Peru's capital, Lima, and several destinations in Ecuador.

FOREIGN INVESTMENT

Regulations governing foreign investment were liberalized from the 1980s in line with global and regional trends. President León Febres Cordero (1984–88) relaxed ownership restrictions on foreign companies and raised limits on profit remittances. In 1991 President Borja opened up some sectors of the economy that had been restricted to sole or majority domestic ownership only. In 1993 President Durán Ballén introduced a further liberalization of the foreign investment code. This established equal treatment for national and international investors and opened further sectors of the economy to foreign capital. In addition, profits could be freely repatriated and prior government approval for foreign investments was no longer required. In 1998 the remaining restrictions on foreign investment in strategic sectors such as fishing, air transport and media were abolished.

Encouraged by these reforms, together with membership of the CAN, which restricted future governments' ability to return to a less liberal investment environment, foreign direct investment (FDI) increased. From an average annual rate of US $108m. in 1982–92, FDI rose to $589m. in 1993–99. Since the mid-1980s 65% of inflows have come from the USA and Canada. Europe was the source of 18% of foreign investment. Investment in the petroleum sector accounted for more than 90% of FDI, encouraged by the introduction of production-sharing contracts introduced in the mid-1990s. The dispute with US oil company Oxy, which saw its contract cancelled by the Government in May 2006, discouraged foreign investment in the sector. Relations with five other foreign oil companies continued to be difficult into 2009 over tax claims and following last-minute revisions, proposed by the Government, to agreements transferring companies from production-sharing contracts to service provider contracts. While a more liberal foreign investment regime went some way to increasing the confidence of overseas investors, this was offset by the conflict with Peru in the mid-1990s and by the 'tequila effect' (the damage caused to all Latin American economies following the devaluation of the Mexican peso in December 1994). Confidence among investors was also undermined by domestic political scandal and instability during 1997–2000 as two elected Governments failed to complete their terms of office. President Noboa succeeded in securing significant reform in 2000 with the Ley de Transformación Económica (Economic Transformation Law), the most notable feature of which was dollarization, in order to support privatization plans. Under President Correa, Ecuador assumed a more radical profile in terms of relations with foreign investors and international financial institutions.

Despite a perception of increased political risks to foreign investment in Ecuador under Correa, net FDI increased from US $194.2m. in 2007 to $1,000.5m. in 2008. The mining sector largely accounted for the massive increase in FDI during 2008, although there were also significant increases in foreign investment in communications and manufacturing. FDI levels declined after the completion of the heavy crude pipeline. Historically, the USA has been the largest source of FDI into Ecuador of any single country. However, in 2008 there was a net outflow of investment to the USA from Ecuador following a net inflow of $49.8m. in 2007. In 2008 the most important source of net FDI was Mexico, which accounted for $302,567m. or 31.1%. The next most important country in terms of net FDI was Spain, which contributed $127,360m. FDI decreased to $311.7m. in 2009. The contribution of the stock market to the economy was insignificant, both as a source of investment funds for local business and as a destination for portfolio investment. Banks were the principal source of financing available. Around one-third of all transactions involved central bank debt issues. Net portfolio investment represented an outflow of funds.

DEBT

Ecuador rapidly accumulated sizeable debt in the 1970s to finance state-led industrial development. Petroleum reserves were used to finance the debt, but, with a decline in international petroleum prices in 1982 and interest rate increases, the country fell behind in repayments. In the 1980s infrastructure was damaged by earthquakes, which in turn detrimentally affected petroleum revenues. Lending from both commercial banks and the 'Paris Club' of official creditors increased annually between 1987 and 1994 to unsustainable levels.

Persistent difficulties in debt repayment obligations led to the 1995 Brady Plan, in which US $7,580m. of debt with commercial banks was restructured to ensure that Ecuador had access to further commercial lending. However, a combination of a depreciating currency, low petroleum prices and a weak economy led to a further worsening of the debt position. Total public external debt increased to more than 100% of GDP in 1999, making Ecuador the first country to default on Brady and Eurobond obligations. In 2000 the Noboa Government reached an agreement with the IMF and private sector creditors to restructure debt. The IMF provided a $2,000m. loan facility over a two-year period. However, the debt-servicing ratio remained high, and Ecuador had limited access to international lending.

The Government won the confidence of the international financial community by persisting with orthodox fiscal discipline despite political opposition in 2001–02. In December 2001 the IMF released funds to complete an earlier stand-by agreement, following payment of US $55m. in arrears owed to 'Paris Club' creditors. In March 2003 the Gutiérrez Government secured a 13-month stand-by loan of $205m. from the IMF, conditional upon a programme of structural reform. This facility gave Ecuador access to further multilateral lending, including a new Country Assistance Strategy, worth some $1,050m. over four years. In May 2004 this loan was extended to the end of the year. It was hoped that this new credit, in addition to high international petroleum prices, would help Ecuador finance its debt repayments. Indeed, the Gutiérrez Government was committed to placing above-budget oil revenues and those from the new heavy crude oil pipeline into a stabilization fund to repay debt, with a target of reducing the debt/GDP ratio to 40% by the end of 2007 (the ratio was 42.3% in 2006, down from 50.0% in 2005 and 54.6% in 2004). The Gutiérrez administration also embarked on a concerted effort to restrain public spending; its limited successes included a reduction in fuel subsidies and a public sector pay freeze. The Government's IMF-approved fiscal performance target for 2003 was a non-financial primary surplus of 3.3% of GDP, requiring a financial primary surplus equivalent to 6.4% of GDP. Despite being on target during the first three quarters of 2003, the Government fell short, as tax revenues were lower than expected, while public sector wages increased and the Government decided against reducing the subsidy on cooking gas. In December 2008 the Correa Government announced that it was defaulting on $3,200m. of outstanding debt, in the form of global bonds. This was Ecuador's third debt default in 15 years. The Government's offer of 35% on the dollar was accepted by a majority of bondholders, and represented a softening of the Government's position after the December default, in recognition of its need for access to funds. The default made it more difficult for Ecuador to secure external funding to finance fiscal deficits. There was a non-financial public sector deficit equivalent to 0.4% of GDP in 2008. Provisional estimates suggested a similar deficit in 2009 despite a 7.6% increase in tax collection revenue during the year to $6,700m. Total foreign debt was estimated at $13,820m. in 2009, representing debt-service obligations equivalent to 22.9% of exports.

FOREIGN TRADE

Liberalization of trade policy progressively made Ecuador more open in the 1990s, beginning with a reform of the Tariff Law and the elimination of import quotas. The policy shift away from import substitution, which had been favoured in the 1970s, was given institutional support when Ecuador joined the WTO in 1996 and ratified the General Agreement on Trade in Services. Domestic manufacturing—with a few exceptions, such as vehicles, as permitted by the WTO—no longer enjoys the protection of high tariff barriers. Ecuador's standard tariff is below the Andean Community's agreed common external tariff, making it one of the most open in South America.

Trade liberalization, including the burgeoning new CAN markets, encouraged diversification of exports. Manufacturing exports grew significantly from the early 1990s, from 12% of export revenues in 1991 to an estimated 29% in 2002. Food, drink and tobacco was the most important manufacturing subsector, in particular canned fish. Among other growth areas in non-traditional exports were vehicles assembled for export to the rest of the Andean region. However, despite diversification, Ecuador remained vulnerable to the volatility of international commodity markets, as exports remained dominated by primary products.

According to central bank figures, Ecuador registered a trade surplus of just US $75.2m. in 2009 following surpluses of $1,371.3m. in 2008 and $1,823.0m. in 2007. Monthly deficits in the trade balance began from September 2008, resulting from drastic price decreases for crude petroleum. The monthly deficits continued into 2009, undermined further by recession in the USA, Ecuador's main export market. An annual surplus in the calendar year 2009 was achieved as a result of an improved performance in the second half of the year owing to a lower import bill. Ecuador registered a surplus in the first quarter of 2010. Until 2003 the trade account had been in deficit. The shift into a positive trade balance on goods was led by increased volumes and prices of petroleum exports, which outpaced strong import growth. In 2008 consumer goods accounted for an estimated 21.9% of all imports, while capital goods comprised 25.6% and primary goods 31.1%. Crude petroleum (and its derivatives) was the largest export item, accounting for an estimated 48.6% of total exports in 2009, down from 60.1% in 2008 owing to the decline in international petroleum prices. After oil, the most important exports were bananas (including plantains), canned fish and shrimps. In 2009 32.2% of exports were destined for the USA, down from 35.7% in 2008, but still surpassing other export markets. Panama was the second most important recipient, accounting for 14.2% of exports, followed by Peru with 6.8% of the total and Chile with 6.5%. The largest European export destination was Russia, accounting for 4.4%, followed by Italy (4.2%) and Spain (2.3%). In 2009 the USA was also the largest source of imports (25.4%), followed by Colombia (10.6%), China (7.2%) and Venezuela (6.5%). High oil prices had offset repatriation of foreign investors' earnings abroad, as well as Ecuador's large interest obligations on its debt, allowing the country to record current account surpluses from 2005. Remittances from Ecuadoreans living abroad represented the largest source of foreign exchange earnings after petroleum, totalling an estimated $2,822m. in 2008, a 9.4% decline from the figure in 2007, illustrating the vulnerability of remittances to economic slowdowns, particularly in the main host countries, the USA and Spain.

Talks between the USA and Ecuador over a proposed Free Trade Agreement collapsed after the Government's takeover of the operations of Oxy in 2006 (see above). The new President, Rafael Correa, who had been critical of the talks, was disinclined to renew negotiations. Ecuador withdrew from trade talks with the EU in May 2009, claiming that it was being pushed towards accepting liberal free trade principles over Ecuador's preference for trade co-operation including provision for investment and aid.

CONCLUSION

President Correa came to power in January 2007 on a radical platform opposed to IMF-prescribed structural reform designed to boost the non-oil economy, including changes to the tax regime, the introduction of private management in public sector utilities and greater flexibility in labour markets. Once in power, Correa used increased oil revenues to expand social investment significantly. Despite generally high oil prices, the Government confronted an increased fiscal deficit, prompting speculation that it might abandon dollarization, and leading to further economic uncertainty. The fiscal challenge confronting President Correa was exacerbated by difficulties in securing external credit, a legacy of his 2008 default on global bonds and his heterodox policy mix. Weak economic recovery was likely to undermine the Government's plans for social reform and threatened unrest, while a deterioration in the unity of the ruling Alianza País and the support the Government received from independents in the legislature would impair Correa's ability to pursue his policy agenda.

Statistical Survey

Sources (unless otherwise stated): Instituto Nacional de Estadística y Censos, Juan Larrea 534 y Riofrío, Quito; tel. (2) 529-858; e-mail inec1@ecnet.ec; internet www.inec.gov.ec; Banco Central del Ecuador, Casilla 339, Quito; tel. (2) 257-2522; fax (2) 295-5458; internet www.bce.fin.ec; Ministerio de Industrias y Competitividad, Avda Eloy Alfaro y Amazonas, Quito; tel. (2) 254-6690; fax (2) 250-3818; e-mail info@mic.gov.ec; internet www.mic.gov.ec.

Area and Population

AREA, POPULATION AND DENSITY

Area (sq km)	272,045*
Population (census results)†	
25 November 1990	9,648,189
25 November 2001	
Males	6,018,353
Females	6,138,255
Total	12,156,608
Population (official estimates at mid-year)	
2008	13,805,092
2009	14,005,445
2010	14,204,900
Density (per sq km) at mid-2010	52.2

* 105,037 sq miles.

† Excluding nomadic tribes of indigenous Indians and any adjustment for underenumeration, estimated to have been 6.3% in 1990; the 1990 total was subsequently revised to 9,697,979.

POPULATION BY AGE AND SEX

(official estimates at mid-2010)

	Males	Females	Total
0–14	2,196,080	2,109,773	4,305,853
15–64	4,501,523	4,501,117	9,002,640
65 and over	418,380	478,027	896,407
Total	7,115,983	7,088,917	14,204,900

REGIONS AND PROVINCES

(projected population estimates at mid-2007)

	Area (sq km)	Population	Density (per sq km)	Capital
Sierra	63,269	6,111,542	96.6	—
Azuay	8,125	678,746	83.5	Cuenca
Bolívar	3,940	180,293	45.8	Guaranda
Cañar	3,122	226,021	72.4	Azogues
Carchi	3,605	166,116	46.1	Tulcán
Chimborazo	6,072	443,522	73.0	Riobamba
Cotopaxi	6,569	400,411	61.0	Latacunga
Imbabura	4,559	397,704	87.2	Ibarra
Loja	11,027	434,020	39.4	Loja
Pichincha	12,915	2,683,272	207.8	Quito
Tungurahua	3,335	501,437	150.4	Ambato
Costa	67,646	6,720,798	99.4	—
El Oro	5,850	608,032	103.9	Machala
Esmeraldas	15,239	438,576	28.8	Esmeraldas
Guayas	20,503	3,617,504	176.4	Guayaquil
Los Ríos	7,175	742,241	103.4	Babahoyo
Manabí	18,879	1,314,445	69.6	Portoviejo
Amazónica	130,834	662,948	5.1	—
Morona Santiago	25,690	131,337	5.1	Macas
Napo	11,431	96,029	8.4	Tena
Orellana	22,500	110,782	4.9	Puerto Francisco de Orellana (Coca)
Pastaza	29,774	75,782	2.5	Puyo
Sucumbíos	18,328	163,447	8.9	Nueva Loja
Zamora Chinchipe	23,111	85,571	3.7	Zamora
Insular	8,010	22,678	2.8	—
Archipiélago de Colón (Galápagos)	8,010	22,678	2.8	Puerto Baquerizo (Isla San Cristóbal)
Uncharted areas	2,289	87,519	38.2	—
Total	272,045	13,605,485	50.0	

Note: Two new provinces, Santo Domingo de los Tsáchilas and Santa Elena, were created in late 2007.

Source: partly Stefan Helders, *World Gazetteer*.

PRINCIPAL TOWNS

(2001 census)

Guayaquil	1,985,379	Ambato	154,095
Quito (capital)	1,399,378	Riobamba	124,807
Cuenca	277,374	Quevedo	120,379
Machala	204,578	Loja	118,532
Santo Domingo de los Colorados	199,827	Milagro	113,440
Manta	183,105	Ibarra	108,535
Portoviejo	171,847	Esmeraldas	95,124

Mid-2010 ('000, incl. suburbs, UN estimates): Guayaquil 2,690; Quito 1,846 (Source: UN, *World Urbanization Prospects: The 2009 Revision*).

BIRTHS, MARRIAGES AND DEATHS

(excluding nomadic Indian tribes)*

	Registered live births†		Registered marriages		Registered deaths	
	Number	Rate (per 1,000)	Number	Rate (per 1,000)	Number	Rate (per 1,000)
2001	278,170	22.3	67,741	5.4	55,214	4.4
2002	275,300	21.7	66,208	5.2	55,549	4.4
2003	262,004	20.4	65,393	5.1	53,521	4.2
2004	254,362	19.5	63,299	4.9	54,729	4.2
2005	252,725	19.1	66,612	5.0	56,825	4.3
2006	278,591	20.8	74,036	5.5	57,940	4.3
2007	283,984	20.9	76,154	5.6	58,016	4.3
2008	n.a.	n.a.	76,354	5.5	60,023	4.3

* Registrations incomplete.

† Figures include registrations of large numbers of births occurring in previous years. The number of births registered in the year of occurrence was: 202,257 in 2000, 192,786 in 2001, 183,792 in 2002, 178,549 in 2003, 168,893 in 2004, 168,324 in 2005, 185,056 in 2006, 195,051 in 2007 and 206,215 in 2008.

Life expectancy (years at birth, WHO estimates): 73 (males 70; females 76) in 2008 (Source: WHO, *World Health Statistics*).

ECONOMICALLY ACTIVE POPULATION

(ISIC major divisions, urban areas only, '000 persons aged 10 years and over, at November of each year, unless otherwise indicated)

	2004	2005	2006
Agriculture, hunting and forestry	320.8	273.5	285.0
Fishing	37.5	51.1	48.9
Mining and quarrying	16.1	10.7	15.8
Manufacturing	539.0	537.2	555.5
Electricity, gas and water	22.9	18.8	19.4
Construction	248.7	258.7	290.1
Wholesale and retail trade; repair of motor vehicles, motorcycles and personal and household goods	1,096.2	1,099.0	1,151.8
Hotels and restaurants	171.1	190.8	225.4
Transport, storage and communications	264.7	280.1	292.3
Financial intermediation	49.1	51.9	47.9
Real estate, renting and business activities	189.8	199.7	200.7
Public administration and defence; compulsory social security	173.9	168.2	170.3

—continued	2004	2005	2006
Education	263.0	258.9	281.0
Health and social work	137.8	132.0	116.0
Other community, social and personal service activities	176.1	158.7	162.9
Private households with employed persons	150.4	201.7	167.7
Extra-territorial organizations and bodies	1.4	0.7	0.9
Total employed	3,858.5	3,891.9	4,031.6
Unemployed	362.1	333.6	341.8
Total labour force	4,220.6	4,225.5	4,373.4
Males	2,449.2	2,471.1	2,559.9
Females	1,771.5	1,754.3	1,813.5

Source: ILO.

2007 (urban areas only, '000 persons aged 10 years and over, at March): Total employed 4,149,647 (males 2,422,371, females 1,727,276); Unemployed 401,964 (males 172,633, females 229,331); Total labour force 4,551,611 (males 2,595,004, females 1,956,608).

2008 (urban areas only, '000 persons aged 10 years and over, at March): Total employed 4,179,476 (males 2,441,060, females 1,738,416); Unemployed 307,978 (males 156,086, females 151,892); Total labour force 4,487,454 (males 2,597,146, females 1,890,308).

2009 (urban areas only, '000 persons aged 10 years and over, at March): Total employed 4,162,832 (males 2,412,919, females 1,749,913); Unemployed 391,685 (males 180,487, females 211,198); Total labour force 4,554,517 (males 2,593,406, females 1,961,111).

Mid-2010 (estimates in '000): Agriculture, etc. 1,169; Total labour force 6,320 (Source: FAO).

Health and Welfare

KEY INDICATORS

Total fertility rate (children per woman, 2008)	2.6
Under-5 mortality rate (per 1,000 live births, 2008)	25
HIV/AIDS (% of persons aged 15–49, 2007)	0.3
Physicians (per 1,000 head, 2000)	1.5
Hospital beds (per 1,000 head, 2003)	1.7
Health expenditure (2007): US $ per head (PPP)	434
Health expenditure (2007): % of GDP	5.8
Health expenditure (2007): public (% of total)	39.1
Access to water (% of persons, 2008)	94
Access to sanitation (% of persons, 2008)	92
Total carbon dioxide emissions ('000 metric tons, 2006)	31,305.2
Carbon dioxide emissions per head (metric tons, 2006)	2.4
Human Development Index (2007): ranking	80
Human Development Index (2007): value	0.806

For sources and definitions, see explanatory note on p. vi.

Agriculture

PRINCIPAL CROPS
('000 metric tons)

	2006	2007	2008
Rice, paddy	1,501	1,734	1,442
Barley	23	25	18
Maize	734	945	805
Potatoes	361	317	267
Cassava (Manioc)	69	74	74*
Sugar cane	6,996	8,360	9,341
Beans, dry	18	12	15
Soybeans (Soya beans)*	60	61	61
Coconuts*	20	21	21
Oil palm fruit*	2,000	2,100	2,100
Tomatoes	62	70	51
Onions and shallots, green*	93	93	93
Carrots and turnips*	27	27	27
Watermelons*	32	33	33

—continued	2006	2007	2008
Bananas	6,127	6,002	6,701
Plantains	581	595	506
Oranges	58	56	55
Tangerines, mandarins, clementines and satsumas	16	22	22*
Mangoes*	155	157	157
Pineapples*	105	110	110
Papayas*	43	43	43
Coffee, green	31	39	32
Cocoa beans	88	86	94
Abaca (Manila hemp)*	29	29	29

* FAO estimate(s).

Aggregate production ('000 metric tons, may include official, semi-official or estimated data): Total cereals 2,278 in 2006, 2,726 in 2007, 2,285 in 2008; Total roots and tubers 444 in 2006, 408 in 2007, 358 in 2008; Total vegetables (incl. melons) 429 in 2006, 441 in 2007, 425 in 2008; Total fruits (excl. melons) 7,409 in 2006, 7,317 in 2007, 7,928 in 2008.

Source: FAO.

LIVESTOCK
('000 head, year ending September)

	2006	2007	2008
Cattle	5,035	4,727	4,892
Sheep	973	846	743
Pigs	1,912	1,323	1,097
Horses	403	383	364
Goats	156	171	150
Asses	169	162	145
Mules	134	119	220120
Chickens*	105,000	110,000	110,000

* FAO estimates.

Source: FAO.

LIVESTOCK PRODUCTS
('000 metric tons)

	2006	2007	2008
Cattle meat	210.5	233.1	248.1
Sheep meat	9.2	8.4	8.4
Pig meat	163.1	189.1	212.5
Goat meat	1.2	1.3	1.3
Chicken meat	300.0	336.0	330.0*
Cows' milk	5,179.10	4,759.4	5,325.7
Sheep's milk*	6.4	6.4	6.4
Goats' milk*	2.6	2.6	2.6
Hen eggs*	85.0	88.0	88.0
Wool, greasy*	1.7	1.7	1.7

* FAO estimate(s).

Source: FAO.

Forestry

ROUNDWOOD REMOVALS
('000 cubic metres, excluding bark)

	2006	2007	2008
Sawlogs, veneer logs and logs for sleepers	1,121	1,198	1,280
Pulpwood	492	476	364
Other industrial wood*	250	296	296
Fuel wood*	3,977	4,112	4,076
Total	5,840	6,082	6,016

* FAO estimates.

Source: FAO.

SAWNWOOD PRODUCTION
('000 cubic metres, including railway sleepers)

	2006	2007	2008
Coniferous (softwood)	107	107	107
Broadleaved (hardwood)	1,275	1,373	1,300
Total	1,382	1,480	1,407

Source: FAO.

Fishing

('000 metric tons, live weight)

	2006	2007	2008
Capture*	449.5	384.3	434.2
Pacific thread herring	16.9	4.7	1.8
Anchoveta (Peruvian anchovy)	76.6	58.9	53.5
Pacific anchoveta	12.3	1.6	28.4
Frigate and bullet tunas	13.1	24.9	12.5
Skipjack tuna	142.7	100.0	143.0
Yellowfin tuna	28.8	22.3	21.0
Bigeye tuna	31.8	30.7	39.8
Chub mackerel	37.7	42.7	18.5
Aquaculture	169.6	171.0*	172.1*
Whiteleg shrimp	149.2	150.0*	150.0*
Nile tilapia	19.4	20.0*	21.0*
Total catch*	619.0	555.3	606.4

* FAO estimate(s).

Source: FAO.

Mining

	2006	2007	2008
Crude petroleum ('000 barrels)	195,948	186,669	184,746
Natural gas (gross, million cu m)	1,309	1,196	1,200
Gold (kilograms)*	5,168	3,186	800

* Metal content of ore only.

Source: US Geological Survey.

Industry

SELECTED PRODUCTS
('000 barrels unless otherwise indicated)

	2005	2006	2007
Jet fuels	2,500	2,699	2,913
Motor spirit (gasoline)	6,954	7,273	7,311
Distillate fuel oils	13,064	12,677	11,789
Residual fuel oils	21,255	21,969	23,052
Liquefied petroleum gas	2,259	2,311	1,614
Crude steel ('000 metric tons)*	84	85	87
Cement ('000 metric tons)*	3,690	4,110	4,420
Electric energy (million kWh)†	13,404	14,814	17,339

* Preliminary estimates.

† Source: UN Industrial Commodity Statistics Database.

Source: mostly US Geological Survey.

2008 ('000 barrels): Motor spirit (gasoline) 17,090; Distillate fuel oils 8,561; Residual fuel oils 13,251; Liquefied petroleum gas 1,924 (Source: US Geological Survey).

Finance

CURRENCY AND EXCHANGE RATES

Monetary Units

United States currency is used: 100 cents = 1 US dollar ($).

Sterling and Euro Equivalents (31 May 2010)

£1 sterling = US $1.458;
€1 = US $1.238;
US $100 = £68.59 = €80.75.

Note: Ecuador's national currency was formerly the sucre. From 13 March 2000 the sucre was replaced by the US dollar, at an exchange rate of $1 = 25,000 sucres. Both currencies were officially in use for a transitional period of 180 days, but from 9 September sucres were withdrawn from circulation and the dollar became the sole legal tender.

BUDGET
(consolidated central government accounts, US $ million)

Revenue	2006	2007	2008*
Petroleum revenue	1,718.6	1,764.3	4,641.7
Non-petroleum revenue	5,176.3	6,725.9	9,157.2
Taxation	4,243.9	4,749.4	6,569.8
Taxes on goods and services	2,485.6	2,728.6	3,298.5
Value-added tax	2,228.2	2,508.8	2,824.9
Taxes on income	1,068.0	1,268.0	2,338.6
Import duties	618.2	678.6	789.3
Other non-petroleum revenue	452.6	505.3	969.3
Transfers	479.9	1,471.2	1,618.2
Total	6,895.0	8,490.2	13,799.0

Expenditure	2006	2007	2008*
Wages and salaries	2,581.4	2,913.9	3,928.6
Purchases of goods and services	458.5	537.4	844.6
Interest payments	941.8	915.3	796.9
Transfers	776.0	800.0	1,880.6
Other current expenditure	584.3	833.3	1,034.6
Capital expenditure	1,669.0	2,627.5	5,928.6
Total	7,011.0	8,627.3	14,413.9

* Provisional figures.

Note: Data exclude adjustment in treasury accounts for expenditure (US $ million): –28.3 in 2006; –73.4 in 2007; 0.0 in 2008.

INTERNATIONAL RESERVES
(US $ million at 31 December)

	2007	2008	2009
Gold (national valuation)	704.3	734.7	918.6
IMF special drawing rights	24.3	26.2	26.5
Reserve position in IMF	27.1	26.4	26.9
Foreign exchange	2,764.9	3,685.5	2,819.8
Total	3,520.6	4,472.8	3,791.8

Source: IMF, *International Financial Statistics*.

MONEY SUPPLY
(US $ million at 31 December)

	2007	2008	2009
Currency outside depository corporations	71.4	77.3	77.4
Transferable deposits	4,323.4	5,829.7	6,222.3
Other deposits	7,974.2	9,383.4	10,391.0
Broad money	12,369.0	15,290.4	16,690.6

Source: IMF, *International Financial Statistics*.

COST OF LIVING
(Consumer Price Index; base: 2005 = 100)

	2006	2007	2008
Food (incl. non-alcoholic beverages)	105.7	109.1	127.5
Fuel (excl. light)	100.1	100.2	100.3
Clothing	100.6	101.5	107.9
Rent	108.2	114.5	119.7

All items (base: 2000 = 100): 175.4 in 2006; 181.2 in 2007; 200.9 in 2008; 211.3 in 2009.

Source: ILO.

NATIONAL ACCOUNTS
(US $ million at current prices)

Expenditure on the Gross Domestic Product

	2006	2007	2008
Government final consumption expenditure	4,612.5	5,195.9	5,951.2
Private final consumption expenditure	26,911.2	29,138.6	33,267.8
Changes in stocks	475.1	906.5	2,416.5
Gross fixed capital formation	9,300.6	10,129.1	13,022.4
Total domestic expenditure	41,299.4	45,370.1	54,657.9
Exports of goods and services	14,212.8	16,088.1	20,671.2
Less Imports of goods and services	13,749.0	15,668.8	20,643.3
GDP in market prices	41,763.2	45,789.4	54,685.9
GDP in constant 2000 prices	21,553.3	22,090.2	23,529.5

Gross Domestic Product by Economic Activity

	2006	2007	2008
Agriculture, hunting, forestry and fishing	2,790.0	3,027.0	3,448.6
Petroleum and other mining	9,406.8	10,671.1	14,652.7
Manufacturing (excl. petroleum-refining)	3,697.6	4,081.4	5,003.9
Manufacture of petroleum derivatives	−2,867.1	−3,190.2	−4,662.5
Electricity, gas and water	538.5	610.9	611.5
Construction	3,822.0	4,162.0	5,343.7
Wholesale and retail trade	4,822.3	5,357.2	6,399.5
Transport, storage and communications	3,039.4	3,106.8	3,306.8
Financial intermediation	1,086.6	1,121.9	1,290.5
Public administration, defence and other social services	2,147.6	2,396.4	2,773.2
Other services	11,186.8	12,233.0	13,827.8
Private households with domestic services	53.7	60.8	61.1
Sub-total	39,724.1	43,638.4	52,056.7
Less Financial intermediation services indirectly measured	−1,005.4	−1,148.0	−1,316.7
Gross value added in basic prices	38,719.0	42,490.3	50,740.0
Taxes, less subsidies, on products	3,044.3	3,299.1	3,945.9
GDP in market prices	41,763.2	45,789.4	54,685.9

BALANCE OF PAYMENTS
(US $ million)

	2006	2007	2008
Exports of goods f.o.b.	13,176	14,870	19,147
Imports of goods f.o.b.	−11,408	−13,047	−17,776
Trade balance	1,768	1,823	1,371
Exports of services	1,037	1,200	1,313
Imports of services	−2,341	−2,572	−2,954
Balance on goods and services	464	452	−270
Other income received	165	259	187
Other income paid	−2,114	−2,306	−1,785
Balance on goods, services and income	−1,485	−1,595	−1,868
Current transfers received	3,234	3,395	3,150
Current transfers paid	−130	−149	−162
Current balance	1,618	1,650	1,120
Capital account (net)	19	22	23
Direct investment from abroad	271	194	993
Portfolio investment assets	−641	−116	217
Portfolio investment liabilities	−743	−3	−4
Other investment assets	−1,957	−1,485	−1,119
Other investment liabilities	1,146	1,263	−406
Net errors and omissions	213	−119	110
Overall balance	−74	1,407	935

Source: IMF, *International Financial Statistics*.

External Trade

PRINCIPAL COMMODITIES
(distribution by HS, US $ million)

Imports f.o.b.	2007	2008	2009
Mineral fuels, oils, distillation products, etc.	2,824.4	3,255.8	2,670.6
Pharmaceutical products	524.5	628.8	683.4
Plastics and articles thereof	615.7	786.3	646.8
Iron and steel	622.8	1,113.2	526.6
Articles of iron or steel	264.2	364.1	447.7
Nuclear reactors, boilers, machinery, etc.	1,507.7	1,960.2	2,006.4
Electrical, electronic equipment	1,210.4	1,726.5	1,320.4
Vehicles other than railway, tramway	1,365.5	1,858.3	1,590.7
Total (incl. others)	13,565.3	17,415.3	15,093.3

Exports f.o.b.	2007	2008	2009
Fish, crustaceans, molluscs, aquatic invertebrates	743.5	868.9	886.8
Live trees, plants, bulbs, roots, cut flowers etc.	406.2	566.7	510.1
Edible fruit, nuts, peel of citrus fruit, melons	1,378.8	1,716.9	2,086.6
Food preparations of meat, fish and seafood	584.7	815.4	630.8
Mineral fuels, oils, distillation products, etc.	8,279.1	11,672.3	6,963.9
Crude petroleum oils, etc.	7,428.4	10,568.3	6,284.1
Total (incl. others)	13,800.4	18,510.6	13,724.3

Source: Trade Map-Trade Competitiveness Map, International Trade Centre, www.intracen.org/marketanalysis.

PRINCIPAL TRADING PARTNERS
(US $ million)

Imports c.i.f.	2007	2008	2009
Argentina	436.5	510.3	482.9
Brazil	730.9	858.3	690.2
Canada	186.0	227.3	209.6
Chile	503.3	515.5	446.9
China, People's Republic	1,121.7	2,120.9	1,722.8
Colombia	1,488.8	1,652.5	1,452.6
Germany	276.8	382.1	414.3
Italy	159.9	222.4	225.1
Japan	494.7	875.2	766.9
Korea, Republic	404.7	593.5	504.6
Mexico	392.1	770.6	660.1
Netherlands	216.6	104.3	109.2
Panama	489.1	45.6	55.3
Peru	481.1	462.6	564.9
Spain	176.8	190.0	174.5
Thailand	203.4	287.9	171.3
USA	2,794.8	2,592.2	2,495.9
Venezuela	1,318.5	442.6	226.5
Total (incl. others)	13,565.3	17,415.3	15,093.3

Exports f.o.b.	2007	2008	2009
Belgium and Luxembourg	168.0	196.2	189.1
Chile	658.1	1,503.4	897.8
China, People's Republic	36.6	384.7	122.5
Colombia	650.6	775.3	673.1
El Salvador	173.5	309.1	156.4
France	140.5	156.1	155.7
Germany	238.9	300.0	323.1
Guatemala	215.9	170.5	224.3
Italy	448.3	510.3	575.0
Korea, Republic	3.6	6.0	60.9
Malaysia	73.1	0.2	1.9
Netherlands	250.6	250.4	294.8
Netherlands Antilles	336.0	2.8	30.7
Panama	464.9	897.6	1,963.4
Peru	1,491.9	1,702.4	932.1
Russia	405.5	548.6	603.9
Spain	335.4	418.4	314.4
USA	5,977.8	8,379.6	4,582.5
Venezuela	484.1	698.4	535.3
Total (incl. others)	13,800.4	18,510.6	13,724.3

Source: Trade Map-Trade Competitiveness Map, International Trade Centre, www.intracen.org/marketanalysis.

Transport

RAILWAYS
(traffic)

	2002	2003	2004
Passenger-km (million)	33	4	2

Source: UN, *Statistical Yearbook*.

ROAD TRAFFIC
(motor vehicles in use at 31 December)

	2005	2006	2007
Passenger cars	462,175	519,041	507,469
Buses and coaches	10,349	11,164	10,925
Lorries and vans	334,998	346,350	323,480
Motorcycles and mopeds	60,144	85,001	78,323

Source: IRF, *World Road Statistics*.

SHIPPING

Merchant Fleet
(registered at 31 December)

	2006	2007	2008
Number of vessels	220	243	258
Total displacement ('000 grt)	280.5	300.0	318.3

Source: Lloyd's Register-Fairplay, *World Fleet Statistics*.

International Sea-borne Freight Traffic
('000 metric tons; estimates derived from monthly averages)

	2005	2006	2007
Goods loaded	24,636	26,736	24,612
Goods unloaded	5,484	8,832	10,332

Note: For goods unloaded, data include freight movement at ports of El Salitral, Esmeraldas, Guayaquil, La Libertad, Manta and Puerto Bolívar; data for goods loaded also include movements at the port of Balao.

Source: UN, *Monthly Bulletin of Statistics*.

CIVIL AVIATION
(traffic on scheduled services)

	2005	2006	2007
Kilometres flown (million)	11.4	15.9	34.4
Passenger-km (million)	867.1	918.8	3,692.9
Total ton-km (million)	5.4	5.9	139.4

Passengers carried ('000): 1,123 in 2003.

Source: UN, *Statistical Yearbook for Latin America and the Caribbean*.

Tourism

FOREIGN VISITOR ARRIVALS*

Country of residence	2005	2006	2007
Argentina	16,720	16,666	19,226
Chile	18,228	18,341	21,674
Colombia	177,700	179,487	203,326
France	15,363	14,181	16,856
Germany	20,809	18,586	23,302
Peru	191,048	145,410	150,439
Spain	31,956	36,502	46,358
United Kingdom	22,822	22,008	27,014
USA	206,839	205,077	241,018
Venezuela	16,276	16,178	21,110
Total (incl. others)	859,888	840,555	937,487

* Figures refer to total arrivals (including same-day visitors), except those of Ecuadorean nationals residing abroad.

Tourism receipts (US $ million, excl. passenger transport): 490 in 2006; 623 in 2007; 763 in 2008 (provisional).

Source: World Tourism Organization.

Communications Media

	2007	2008	2009
Telephones ('000 main lines in use)	1,823.1	1,904.2	2,004.2
Mobile cellular telephones ('000 subscribers)	9,940.0	11,692.2	13,634.8
Internet users ('000)	1,151.9	1,309.6	2,052.1
Broadband subscribers ('000)	30.0	35.2	241.2

Personal computers: 1,710,000 (129.5 per 1,000 persons) in 2006.

Radio receivers ('000 in use): 5,040 in 1999.

Daily newspapers: 36 in 2000 (average circulation 1,220,000).

Sources: UNESCO, *Statistical Yearbook*; UN, *Statistical Yearbook*; International Telecommunication Union.

Education

(2007/08 unless otherwise indicated)

	Teachers	Students ('000) Males	Females	Total
Pre-primary	16,091	144.5	138.9	283.4
Primary	96,545	896.3	849.2	1,745.5
Secondary	48,272	526.7	512.1	1,038.8
general	37,129	405.6	392.3	797.9
technical/vocational	11,143	121.0	119.8	240.8
Tertiary*	22,714	202.3	241.2	443.5

* 2006/07.

Institutions (2002/03): Pre-primary 5,244; Primary 18,203; Secondary 3,486.

Sources: UNESCO Institute for Statistics; Ministerio de Educación y Cultura.

Pupil-teacher ratio (primary education, UNESCO estimate): 22.6 in 2006/07 (Source: UNESCO Institute for Statistics).

Adult literacy rate: 84.2% (males 87.3%; females 81.7%) in 2007 (Source: UNESCO Institute for Statistics).

Directory

The Constitution

The Constitution of the Republic of Ecuador—the country's 20th—was promulgated on 20 October 2008 following its approval in a referendum held on 28 September. It replaced the Constitution of 1998, which retained many of the provisions of the 1979 Constitution that introduced democratic reforms following a period of military rule.

The first part of the Constitution enshrines certain rights and constitutional guarantees: these include rights relating to *sumak kawsay* ('good living'), disadvantaged people, political participation, freedom, the environment and justice. The other main provisions of the Constitution are summarized below:

LEGISLATIVE POWER

Legislative power is exercised by the unicameral National Assembly (Asamblea Nacional), whose members are elected for a four-year term. The National Assembly is composed of 15 members elected from a nation-wide constituency and two from each province, plus one for every 200,000 inhabitants or the greater fraction thereof in each province. The functions of the National Assembly include: inaugurating the President and Vice-President of the Republic; enacting, codifying, reforming and repealing laws; levying taxes; approving international treaties; authorizing, by means of a two-thirds' majority, criminal proceedings against the President or Vice-President; approving the state budget; and granting amnesties and pardons. The Assembly convenes on 14 May of the year of its election.

The National Assembly may dismiss the President of the Republic for acting contrary to the Constitution (subject to approval by the Constitutional Court) or because of serious political crisis and internal commotion. The dismissal of the President requires a two-thirds' majority vote, and may be carried out once only during a legislative term and only in the first three years of the same. Early legislative and presidential elections shall subsequently be held to cover the remainder of the term. The Assembly may also dismiss government ministers and certain other officials—by means of a two-thirds' majority vote, in the case of ministers—for non-compliance of their functions as determined by the Constitution and the law.

EXECUTIVE POWER

Executive power is exercised by the President and Vice-President of the Republic, the Ministries of State and other bodies created to fulfil that function. The President must be Ecuadorean by birth and at least 35 years of age. The President and Vice-President are elected on the same ballot. If no candidate achieves an absolute majority, a second round of voting is contested by the two candidates with the most votes. A second round is not necessary if the winner achieves at least 40% of valid votes and a difference of at least 10 percentage points over the votes cast for the second-placed candidate. The President serves a four-year term and may be re-elected only once.

The President's functions include: obeying and ensuring the obedience of the Constitution, the law, international treaties and other legal requirements; defining and directing the policies of the executive; presenting the National Development Plan for approval by the National Planning Council; creating, modifying or abolishing ministries and other such bodies, and appointing ministers; reporting the Government's achievements and objectives to the National Assembly once a year; presenting the state budget to the National Assembly for its approval; defining foreign policy; signing and ratifying international treaties; participating in the legislative process by initiating legislation; and exercising supreme authority over the armed forces and national police.

The President may dissolve the National Assembly for acting contrary to the Constitution (subject to approval by the Constitutional Court), or if it repeatedly and unjustifiably obstructs the execution of the National Development Plan, or because of serious political crisis and internal commotion. This right may be exercised once only during a legislative term and only in the first three years of the same. Legislative and presidential elections shall subsequently be held to cover the remainder of the term.

Ministers of state are freely appointed by the President, and represent him in the affairs pertaining to them. They are responsible for the actions they undertake in the exercise of their functions. Close relations of the President, those contracted by the state to undertake public works or services, and serving members of the armed forces and police may not be ministers.

JUDICIAL POWER

The authorities of indigenous communities exercise jurisdiction according to their ancestral traditions and within their territorial limits. They shall apply their own rules and procedures for the resolution of internal conflicts, providing these do not contravene the Constitution or internationally recognized human rights.

The judicial structure comprises the National Court of Justice (Corte Nacional de Justicia), provincial courts of justice, other courts and tribunals as established by law, and courts of the peace. The Council of the Judiciary (Consejo de la Judicatura) regulates and administers the judicial system and is responsible to the National Assembly.

TERRITORIAL ORGANIZATION

The state is organized into regions, provinces, cantons and rural parishes. Autonomous metropolitan districts, the province of Galápagos and indigenous territories constitute special regimes. Contiguous provinces meeting certain requirements of area and population may form an autonomous region, with an elected regional council and governor; similarly, one or more contiguous cantons containing a large conurbation may form an autonomous metropolitan district.

The Constitution defines the powers of the various levels of government. The exclusive powers of the state include: national defence and internal order; foreign relations; economic policy; education, health, social security and housing policy; and natural resources. The exclusive powers of autonomous regional governments, in addition to any other powers that may be granted by law, include: regional planning; the management of water catchment areas; regional transport; and the promotion of regional production and food security.

OTHER PROVISIONS

A part of the Constitution regulates economic affairs, while another concerns social affairs and environmental protection.

The foreign relations of Ecuador are based on principles that include the independence and equality of states, peaceful solutions to conflicts, the condemnation of intervention in the internal affairs of other states, universal citizenship, and the political, cultural and economic integration of the Andean region, South America and Latin America. Foreign military bases and installations are not permitted in Ecuador.

Amendments to one or more articles of the Constitution, providing they do not alter its fundamental structure, may be effected by referendum or by a two-thirds' majority vote of the National Assembly. Any constitutional reform of wider scope must be approved by the National Assembly and subsequently approved by a referendum. The formation of a constituent assembly must receive prior approval in a popular consultation, and the new constitution thereby drafted shall require approval by referendum.

The Government

HEAD OF STATE

President: Rafael Correa Delgado (took office 15 January 2007; re-elected 26 April 2009).

Vice-President: Lenín Moreno Garcés.

CABINET
(July 2010)

The electoral alliance Alianza País formed a Government following the election of April 2009.

Minister of Foreign Relations, Trade and Integration: Ricardo Armando Patiño Aroca.

Minister of Finance: Patricio Rivera.

Minister of Government, Worship, Police and Municipalities: Dr Charbel Gustavo Jalkh.

Minister of Electricity and Renewable Energy: Miguel Calahorrano.

Minister of National Defence: Dr Javier Ponce Cevallos.

Minister of Urban Development and Housing: Walter Solís Valarezo.

Minister of Education: Gloria Vidal.

Minister of Public Health: Dr David Chriboga.

Minister of Agriculture, Livestock, Aquaculture and Fishing: Ramón Leonardo Espinel Martínez.

Minister of the Environment: Marcela Aguiñaga Vallejo.

Minister of Labour Relations: Dr Richard Espinosa Guzmán B. A.

Minister of Tourism: Freddy Ehlers.

Minister of Economic and Social Inclusion: Ximena Ponce León.

Minister of Industry and Competitiveness: Verónica Sión.

Minister of Transport and Public Works: María de los Ángeles Duarte.

Minister of Sport: Sandra Vela Dávila.

Minister of Culture: Érika Sylva Charvet.

Minister of Coastal Affairs: Dr Nicolás Issa Wagner.

Minister of Non-Renewable Natural Resources: Wilson Pástor Morris.

Minister of Justice and Human Rights: José Serrano.

Minister of Information and Telecommunications: Jaime Ruíz Guerrero.

Co-ordinating Ministers

Co-ordinating Minister for Security: Miguel Carvajal Aguirre.

Co-ordinating Minister for Production, Competitiveness and Commercialization: Nathalie Cely.

Co-ordinating Minister for Economic Policy: Katiuska King.

Co-ordinating Minister for Social Development: Jeannette Sánchez Zurita.

Co-ordinating Minister for Policy: Doris Solíz Carrión.

Co-ordinating Minister for Cultural and Natural Heritage: María Fernanda Espinosa.

Co-ordinating Minister for Strategic Sectors: Jorge Glas Espinel.

MINISTRIES

Office of the President: Palacio Nacional, García Moreno 1043, Quito; tel. (2) 221-6300; internet www.presidencia.gov.ec.

Office of the Vice-President: Calle Benalcázar N4-40, entre Calles Espejo y Chile, Quito; tel. (2) 258-4574; internet www.vicepresidencia.gov.ec.

Ministry of Agriculture, Livestock, Aquaculture and Fishing: Avda Eloy Alfaro y Amazonas, Quito; tel. (2) 396-0100; fax (2) 396-0200; e-mail webmaster@magap.gov.ec; internet www.magap.gov.ec.

Ministry of Coastal Affairs: Edif. Gobierno del Litoral, 13°, Avda Francisco de Orellana y Justino Cornejo 106, Ciudadela Kennedy Norte, Guayaquil; tel. (4) 268-3882; fax (4) 268-3878; e-mail comunicaciones@minlitoral.gov.ec; internet www.minlitoral.gov.ec.

Ministry of Culture: Avda Colón E5-34 y Juan León Mera, Quito; tel. (2) 381-4550; e-mail comunicacion@ministeriodecultura.gov.ec; internet www.ministeriodecultura.gov.ec.

Ministry of Economic and Social Inclusion: Edif. Matríz, Robles 850 y Páez, Quito; tel. (2) 254-4136; fax (2) 250-9850; e-mail ris@mies.gov.ec; internet www.mies.gov.ec.

Ministry of Finance: Avda 10 de Agosto 1661 y Bolivia, Quito; tel. (2) 255-9145; fax (2) 250-5256; e-mail mefecuador@mef.gov.ec; internet www.mef.gov.ec.

Ministry of Education: Avda Amazonas N34-451, entre Avda Atahualpa y Juan Pablo Sánz, Quito; tel. (2) 396-1300; e-mail info@educacion.gov.ec; internet www.educacion.gov.ec.

Ministry of Electricity and Renewable Energy: Edif. Correos del Ecuador, 6°, Eloy Alfaro N29-50 y 9 de Octubre, Edif. Correos del Ecuador, Quito; tel. (2) 397-6000; e-mail info@mer.gov.ec; internet www.mer.gov.ec.

Ministry of the Environment: Edif. M.A.G.A.P, 7° y 8°, Avda Eloy Alfaro y Amazonas, Quito; tel. (2) 256-3429; fax (2) 256-3462; e-mail mma@ambiente.gov.ec; internet www.ambiente.gov.ec.

Ministry of Foreign Relations, Trade and Integration: Avda 10 de Agosto y Carrión E1-76, Quito; tel. (2) 299-3284; fax (2) 299-3273; e-mail gabminis@mmrree.gov.ec; internet www.mmrree.gov.ec.

Ministry of Government, Worship, Police and Municipalities: Espejo y Benalcázar N4-24, Quito; tel. (2) 295-5666; fax (2) 295-8360; e-mail informacion@mingobierno.gov.ec; internet www.mingobierno.gov.ec.

Ministry of Industry and Competitiveness: Avda Eloy Alfaro y Amazonas, Quito; tel. (2) 254-6690; fax (2) 250-3818; e-mail info@mic.gov.ec; internet www.mic.gov.ec.

Ministry of Information and Telecommunications: Avda 6 de Diciembre N25-75 y Avda Colón, Quito; tel. (2) 220-0200; fax (2) 222-8950; e-mail info@mintel.gov.ec; internet www.mintel.gov.ec.

Ministry of Justice and Human Rights: Avda Amazonas N34-451 y Atahualpa, Quito; tel. (2) 246-3083; fax (2) 246-4914; e-mail webmaster@minjusticia-ddhh.gov.ec; internet www.minjusticia-ddhh.gov.ec.

Ministry of Labour Relations: Clemente Ponce N15-59 y Piedrahita, Quito; tel. (2) 254-8900; fax (2) 254-2580; e-mail comunicacion_social@mrl.gov.ec; internet www.mrl.gov.ec.

Ministry of Non-Renewable Natural Resources: Edif. MOP, Avda Orellana 26-220 y Juan León Mera (esq.), Quito; tel. (2) 297-7000; e-mail info@minasypetroleos.gov.ec; internet www.recursosnorenovables.gov.ec.

Ministry of National Defence: Calle Exposición 208, La Recoleta, Quito; tel. (2) 295-2043; fax (2) 258-0941; internet www.midena.gov.ec.

Ministry of Public Health: República de El Salvador 950, entre Suecia y Naciones Unidas, Quito; tel. and fax (2) 381-4400; e-mail despacho@msp.gov.ec; internet www.msp.gov.ec.

Ministry of Sport: Avda Shyris 42-31 y Tomás de Berlanga, Quito; tel. (2) 227-0260; fax (2) 245-4418; e-mail arodriguez@ministeriodeldeporte.gov.ec; internet www.ministeriodeldeporte.gov.ec.

Ministry of Tourism: Avda Eloy Alfaro N32-300 y Carlos Tobar, 2°, Quito; tel. (2) 399-9333; fax (2) 222-9330; e-mail info@turismo.gov.ec; internet www.turismo.gov.ec.

Ministry of Transport and Public Works: Avda Juan León Mera N26-220 y Orellana, Quito; tel. (2) 256-0290; e-mail comumicacion@mtop.gov.ec; internet www.mtop.gov.ec.

Ministry of Urban Development and Housing: Avda 10 de Agosto 2270 y Corotero, 6°, Quito; tel. (2) 223-8060; fax (2) 256-6785; e-mail despacho@miduvi.gov.ec; internet www.miduvi.gov.ec.

Office for Public Administration: Palacio Nacional, García Moreno 1043 y Chile, Quito; tel. (2) 258-0716.

President and Legislature

PRESIDENT

Election, 26 April 2009

Candidate	Valid votes	% of valid votes
Rafael Correa Delgado (Alianza País)	3,586,439	51.99
Lucio Gutiérrez Borbua (PSP)	1,947,830	28.24
Alvaro Fernando Noboa Pontón (PRIAN)	786,718	11.40
Martha Roldós Bucaram (RED/MPD)	298,765	4.33
Others	278,160	4.04
Total*	6,897,912	100.00

* In addition, there were 534,149 blank and 496,687 invalid ballots.

ASAMBLEA NACIONAL

President: Fernando Cordero.

Election, 26 April 2009, preliminary results

Political parties	Seats
Alianza País	59
Partido Sociedad Patriótica 21 de Enero (PSP)	19
Partido Social Cristiano (PSC)	11
Partido Renovador Institucional de Acción Nacional (PRIAN)	7
Movimiento Municipalista por la Integridad Nacional	5
Movimiento Popular Democrático (MPD)	5
Movimiento de Unidad Pluriacional Pachakútik—Nuevo País (MNPP—NP)	4
Partido Roldosista Ecuatoriano (PRE)	3
Izquierda Democrática (ID)	2
Others	9
Total	124

Election Commission

Consejo Nacional Electoral (CNE): Avda 6 de Diciembre N33-122 y Bosmediano, Quito; tel. (2) 381-5410; internet www.cne.gov.ec; f. 2008 to replace the Tribunal Supremo Electoral; independent; Pres. Omar Simón Campaña.

Political Organizations

Alianza País (Patria Altiva i Soberana): Of. 501, Edif. Torres Whimper, Diego de Almagro 32-27 y Whimper, Quito; tel. (2) 600-0630; fax (2) 600-1029; internet revolucionciudadana.com.ec; f. 2006; electoral alliance mainly comprising the Movimiento País; left-wing; Pres. Rafael Correa Delgado.

Izquierda Democrática (ID): Polonia N30-83 y Vancouver, Quito; tel. (2) 256-4436; fax (2) 256-4860; e-mail webmaster@partidoizquierdademocratica.com; internet www.partidoizquierdademocratica.com; f. 1977; absorbed Fuerzas Armadas Populares Eloy Alfaro—Alfaro Vive ¡Carajo! (AVC) in 1991; Pres. Daltón Emory Bacigalupo Buenaventura.

Movimiento Municipalista por la Integridad Nacional (MMIN): Quito; tel. (2) 246-9683; fax (2) 246-9769; internet www.movimientomunicipalista.com; f. 2008; left-wing; advocated further provincial autonomy; Leader Paco Moncayo Gallegos; Sec.-Gen. Carlos Villalba.

Movimiento Popular Democrático (MPD): Manuel Larrea N14-70 y Rio Frío, Quito; tel. (2) 250-3580; fax (2) 252-6111; e-mail info@mpd15.org.ec; internet www.mpd15.org.ec; f. 1978; attached to the PCMLE (q.v.); Dir Luis Villacís; Sec. Washintong Alajo.

Movimiento de Unidad Pluriacional Pachakútik—Nuevo País (MUPP—NP): Calle Lugo 13-04 y Avda Ladrón de Guevara, La Floresta, Quito; tel. (2) 322-7259; fax (2) 256-0422; e-mail info@pachakutik.org.ec; internet www.pachakutik.org.ec; f. 1995 as Movimiento Nuevo País—Pachakútik (MNPP); represents indigenous, environmental and social groups; Nat. Co-ordinator Jorge Guamán Coronel; Sec. Patricio Quezada Ortega.

Partido Comunista Marxista-Leninista de Ecuador (PCMLE): e-mail pcmle@bigfoot.com; internet www.pcmle.org; f. 1964; contests elections as the MPD (q.v.).

Partido Renovador Institucional Acción Nacional (PRIAN): Quito; internet www.prian.org.ec; right-wing, populist; Leader Alvaro Fernando Noboa Pontón.

Partido Roldosista Ecuatoriano (PRE): 1 de Mayo 912 y Tulcán, Quito; tel. (2) 229-0542; fax (2) 269-0250; e-mail dalo-por-hecho@hotmail.com; internet www.dalo10.com; f. 1982; populist; Founder and Leader Abdalá Bucaram Ortiz; Nat. Dir Abdalá Bucaram Pulley.

Partido Social Cristiano (PSC): Carrión 548 y Reina Victoria, Casilla 9454, Quito; tel. (2) 254-4536; fax (2) 256-8562; e-mail sugerencias@partidosocialcristiano.org; internet www.partidosocialcristiano.org; f. 1951; centre-right; Pres. Pascual Eugenio del Cioppo Aragundi; Sec. Xavier Eduardo Buitrón Carrera.

Partido Socialista—Frente Amplio (PS—FA): Avda Gran Colombia N15-201 y Yaguachi, Quito; tel. (2) 232-4417; fax (2) 222-2184; e-mail psecuador@andinanet.net; internet www.psecuador17.org; f. 1926; Pres. Silvia Salgado Andrade.

Partido Sociedad Patriótica 21 de Enero (PSP): Quito; internet www.sociedadpatriotica.com; contested the 2002 elections in alliance with the MUPP—NP; Leader Gilmar Gutiérrez.

Red Etica y Democracia (RED): Edif. Alemania, 1°, Alemania y Guayanas, Quito; tel. (2) 222-3348; e-mail info@redeticaydemocracia.com; internet www.redeticaydemocracia.com.ec; Leader León Roldós Aguilera.

Unión Demócrata Cristiana (UDC): Pradera N30-58 y San Salvador, Quito; tel. (2) 250-2995; e-mail cbonilla@udc.com.ec; internet www.udc.com.ec; f. 1978 as Democracia Popular—Unión Demócrata Cristiana (DP—UDC); adopted current name 2006; Christian democrat; Pres. Diego Ordóñez; Sec. Marco Benavides.

OTHER ORGANIZATIONS

Confederación de las Nacionalidades Indígenas de la Amazonia Ecuatoriana (CONFENIAE): Union Base, Apdo 17-01-4180, Puyo; tel. (3) 227-644; fax (2) (3) 227-644; e-mail info_confel@confeniae.org.ec; internet www.confeniae.org.ec; represents indigenous peoples; mem. of CONAIE; Pres. Tito Puanchir.

Confederación de Nacionalidades Indígenas del Ecuador (CONAIE): Avda Los Granados 2553 y 6 de Diciembre, Quito; tel. (2) 245-2335; fax (2) 244-4991; e-mail info@conaie.org; internet www.conaie.org; f. 1986; represents indigenous peoples; MUPP—NP (q.v.) represents CONAIE and related orgs in the legislature; Pres. Marlon Santi; Vice-Pres. Miguel Guatemal.

Confederación de los Pueblos de Nacionalidad Kichua del Ecuador (Ecuarunari): Edif. El Conquistador, 1°, Julio Matovelle 128, entre Vargas y Pasaje San Luis, Quito; tel. (2) 258-0700; fax (2) 258-0713; e-mail ecuarunari@ecuarunari.org; internet www.ecuarunari.org; f. 1972; indigenous movt; Pres. Delfín Tenesaca.

Coordinadora de las Organizaciones Indígenas de la Cuenca Amazónica (COICA): Sevilla N24-358 y Guipuzcoa, La Floresta, Quito; tel. (2) 322-6744; e-mail com@coica.org.ec; internet www.coica.org.ec; f. 1984 in Lima, Peru; moved to Quito in 1993; umbrella group of 9 orgs representing indigenous peoples of the Amazon Basin in Bolivia, Brazil, Colombia, Ecuador, French Guiana, Guyana, Suriname and Venezuela; Gen. Co-ordinator Egberto Tabo Chipunavi; Vice-Co-ordinator Rosa Alvorado.

ARMED GROUPS

The following guerrilla organizations were reported to be active in the mid-2000s.

Ejército de Liberación Alfarista (ELA): f. 2001; extreme left-wing insurrectionist group; formed by fmr mems of disbanded armed groups Alfaro Vive ¡Carajo!, Montoneros Patria Libre and Sol Rojo; Spokesperson Sebastián Sánchez.

Grupos de Combatientes Populares (GCP): Cuenca; internet gcp-ecuador.blogspot.com; communist guerrilla grouping; active since 2000.

Izquierda Revolucionaria Armada (IRA): extreme left-wing revolutionary group opposed to international capitalism.

Milicias Revolucionarias del Pueblo (MRP): extreme left-wing grouping opposed to international capitalism.

Diplomatic Representation

EMBASSIES IN ECUADOR

Argentina: Avda Amazonas 21-147 y Roca, 8°, Of. 812 a la 820, Apdo 17-12-937, Quito; tel. (2) 256-2292; fax (2) 256-8177; e-mail embarge2@uio.satnet.net; Ambassador CARLOS PIÑEIRO IÑIGUEZ.

Bolivia: Avda Eloy Alfaro 2432 y Fernando Ayarza, Apdo 17-210003, Quito; tel. (2) 244-4830; fax (2) 224-4833; e-mail emboliviaquito@andinanet.net; Ambassador JUAN XAVIER ZARATE RIVAS.

Brazil: Edif. España, Avda Amazonas 1429 y Colón, 9° y 10°, Apdo 17-01-231, Quito; tel. (2) 256-3142; fax (2) 250-4468; e-mail ebrasil@embajadadelbrasil.org.ec; internet www.embajadadelbrasil.org.ec; Ambassador ANTONINO MARQUES-PORTO E SANTOS.

Canada: Edif. Eurocenter, 3°, Avda Amazonas 4153 y Unión Nacional de Periodistas, Apdo 17-11-6512, Quito; tel. (2) 245-5499; fax (2) 227-7672; e-mail quito@international.gc.ca; internet www.canadainternational.gc.ca/ecuador-equateur; Ambassador ANDREW SHISKO.

Chile: Edif. Xerox, 4°, Juan Pablo Sanz 3617 y Amazonas, Apdo 17-17-206, Quito; tel. (2) 224-9403; fax (2) 244-4470; e-mail embachileecu@uio.satnet.net; Ambassador JUAN PABLO LIRA BIANCHI.

China, People's Republic: Avda Atahualpa 349 y Amazonas, Quito; tel. (2) 243-3337; fax (2) 244-4364; e-mail embchina@uio.telconet.net; Ambassador CAI RUNGUO.

Colombia: Edif. Digicom, 3°, Atahualpa 955 y República, Apdo 17-07-9164, Quito; tel. (2) 227-0154; fax (2) 246-0054; e-mail cquito@cancilleria.gov.co; Ambassador (vacant).

Costa Rica: Isla San Cristóbal N44-385 y Guepi, Apdo 17-03-301, Quito; tel. (2) 244-0781; fax (2) 225-4087; e-mail embajcr@uio.satnet.net; Ambassador EDGARDO PICADO ARAYA.

Cuba: Mercurio 365, entre La Razón y El Vengador, Quito; tel. (2) 245-6936; fax (2) 243-0594; e-mail embajada@embacuba.ec; internet embacu.cubaminrex.cu/ecuador; Ambassador BENIGNO PÉREZ FERNÁNDEZ.

Dominican Republic: German Alemán E12-80 y Juan Ramírez, Sector Megamaxi, Batan Alto, Quito; tel. (2) 243-4232; fax (2) 243-4275; e-mail info@embajadadominicanaecuador.com; internet www.embajadadominicanaecuador.com; Ambassador NÉSTOR JUAN CERÓN SUERO.

Egypt: Avda Tarqui E4-56 y Avda 6 de Diciembre, Apdo 17-7-9355, Quito; tel. (2) 222-5240; fax (2) 256-3521; e-mail embassy.quito@mfa.gov.eg; Ambassador HICHAM OMAR MARZOUK.

El Salvador: Edif. Gabriela III, 3°, Avda República de El Salvador 733 y Portugal, Quito; tel. (2) 243-3070; fax (2) 224-2829; e-mail embajada@elsalvador.com.ec; internet www.elsalvador.com.ec; Ambassador MARIO JOSÉ AVILA ROMERO.

France: Calle Leonidas Plaza 107 y Avda Patria, Apdo 19-13-536, Quito; tel. (2) 294-3800; fax (2) 294-3809; e-mail chancellerie.quito@ifrance.com; internet www.ambafrance-ec.org; Ambassador DIDIER LOPINOT.

Germany: Edif. Citiplaza, 13° y 14°, Avda Naciones Unidas E10-44 y República de El Salvador, Apdo 17-17-536, Quito; tel. (2) 297-0820; fax (2) 297-0815; e-mail info@quito.diplo.de; internet www.quito.diplo.de; Ambassador CHRISTIAN BERGER.

Guatemala: Edif. Gabriela III, 3°, Of. 301, Avda República de El Salvador 733 y Portugal, Apdo 17-03-294, Quito; tel. (2) 245-9700; fax (2) 226-4228; e-mail embecuador@minex.gob.gt; Ambassador ALFREDO FERNÁNDEZ GRADIS.

Holy See: Avda Orellana 692 E10-03, Apdo 17-07-8980, Quito; tel. (2) 250-5200; fax (2) 256-4810; e-mail nunzec@uio.satnet.net; Apostolic Nuncio Most Rev. GIACOMO GUIDO OTTONELLO (Titular Archbishop of Sasabe).

Honduras: Edif. Suecia, Avda Shyris y calle Suecia 277, 5° Norte, Apdo 17-03-4753, Quito; tel. (2) 243-8820; fax (2) 244-2476; e-mail embhquito@yahoo.com; Ambassador RAFAEL MURILLO SELVA.

Iran: José Queri E14-43 y Avda Los Granados, Quito; tel. (2) 334-3450; fax (2) 245-2824; e-mail embiranecuador@gmail.com; Ambassador MAJID SALEHI.

Israel: Edif. Altana Plaza, 5°, Avda Coruña E26-48 y San Ignacio, Apdo 17-21-038, Quito; tel. (2) 397-1500; fax (2) 397-1555; e-mail info@quito.mfa.gov.il; internet www.quito.mfa.gov.il; Ambassador EYAL SELA.

Italy: Calle La Isla 111 y Humberto Alborñoz, Apdo 17-03-72, Quito; tel. (2) 256-1077; fax (2) 250-2818; e-mail archivio.quito@esteri.it; internet www.ambitalquito.org; Ambassador EMANUELO PIGNATELLI.

Japan: Edif. Amazonas Plaza, 11° y 12°, Avda Amazonas N39-123 y Arízaga, Apdo 17-21-01518, Quito; tel. (2) 227-8700; fax (2) 244-9399; e-mail embapon@embajadadeljapon.org.ec; internet www.ec.emb-japan.go.jp; Ambassador OSAMU IMAI.

Korea, Republic: Edif. World Trade Center, Avda 12 de Octubre 1942 y Cordero, Torre B, 3°, Apdo 17-03-626, Quito; tel. (2) 290-9227; fax (2) 250-1190; e-mail ecuador@mofat.go.kr; internet ecu.mofat.go.kr; Ambassador JANG KEUN-HO.

Mexico: Avda 6 de Diciembre N36-165 y Naciones Unidas, Apdo 17-11-6371, Quito; tel. (2) 292-3770; fax (2) 244-8245; e-mail embajadamexico@embamex.org.ec; internet www.sre.gob.mx/ecuador; Chargé d'affaires a.i. VÍCTOR MANUEL DELGADO TREJO.

Netherlands: Edif. World Trade Center, Torre A, 1°, Avda 12 de Octubre 1942 y Luis Cordero, Quito; tel. (2) 222-9229; fax (2) 256-7917; e-mail qui@minbuza.nl; internet www.mfa.nl/qui; Ambassador KORNELIS SPAANS.

Panama: Edif. Maria Gabriela, 5°, Avda Coruña 601 y Orellana (esq.), Quito; tel. (2) 256-6449; fax (2) 250-8837; e-mail panaembaecuador@hotmail.com; internet www.embajadadepanamaecuador.com; Ambassador ROBERTO NEYROT RUIZ DIAZ.

Paraguay: Edif. Torre Sol Verde, 8°, Avda 12 de Octubre esq. Salazar, Apdo 17-03-139, Quito; tel. (2) 290-9005; fax (2) 290-9006; e-mail embapar@uio.satnet.net; Ambassador JOSÉ MILCIADES MARTÍNEZ LESCANO.

Peru: Avda República de El Salvador N34-361 e Irlanda, Apdo 17-07-9380, Quito; tel. (2) 246-8410; fax (2) 225-2560; e-mail embaperu-quito@rree.gob.pe; internet www.embajadadelperu.org.ec; Ambassador JAVIER LEÓN OLAVARRÍA.

Russia: Reina Victoria 462 y Ramón Roca, Apdo 17-01-3868, Quito; tel. (2) 252-6361; fax (2) 256-5531; e-mail embrusia@accessinter.net; internet www.ecuador.mid.ru; Ambassador YAN A. BURLIAY.

Spain: General Francisco Salazar E12-73 y Toledo (Sector La Floresta), Apdo 17-01-9322, Quito; tel. (2) 322-6296; fax (2) 322-7805; e-mail emb.quito@mae.es; internet www.maec.es/embajadas/quito; Ambassador FEDERICO TORRES MURO.

Switzerland: Edif. Xerox, 2°, Avda Amazonas 3617 y Juan Pablo Sanz, Apdo 17-11-4815, Quito; tel. (2) 243-4949; fax (2) 244-9314; e-mail qui.vertretung@eda.admin.ch; internet www.eda.admin.ch/quito; Ambassador MARKUS-ALEXANDER ANTONIETTI.

United Kingdom: Edif. Citiplaza, 14°, Avda Naciones Unidas y República de El Salvador, Apdo 17-17-830, Quito; tel. (2) 297-0800; fax (2) 297-0809; e-mail britembq@uio.satnet.net; internet ukinecuador.fco.gov.uk; Ambassador LINDA CROSS.

USA: Avigiras 12-170 y Eloy Alfaro, Apdo 17-17-1538, Quito; tel. (2) 398-5000; fax (2) 398-5100; e-mail contacto.usembuio@state.gov; internet ecuador.usembassy.gov; Ambassador HEATHER M. HODGES.

Uruguay: Edif. Josueth González, 9°, Avda 6 de Diciembre 2816 y Paul Rivet, Apdo 17-12-282, Quito; tel. (2) 256-3762; fax (2) 256-3763; e-mail uruguay@embajadauruguay.com.ec; Ambassador GUSTAVO VANERIO BALBELA.

Venezuela: Edif. COMONSA, 8° y 9°, Avda Amazonas N30-240 y Eloy Alfaro, Apdo 17-01-688, Quito; tel. (2) 255-4032; fax (2) 252-0306; e-mail embve.ecqto@mre.gob.ve; internet www.venezuela.org.ec; Ambassador OSCAR NAVAS TORTOLERO.

Judicial System

CONSTITUTIONAL COURT

Corte Constitucional: Avda 12 de Octubre N16-114 y Pasaje Nicolás Jiménez, Quito; tel. (2) 290-1267; e-mail mencalada@tc.gov.ec; internet www.tribunalconstitucional.gov.ec; f. 2008 by reform of fmr Tribunal Constitucional; Pres. Dr PATRICIO PAZMIÑO FREIRE.

NATIONAL COURT OF JUSTICE

The former Supreme Court of Justice was reconstituted as the National Court of Justice in 2008 under the terms of the new Constitution. It is composed of 21 Justices, including the President. Three Justices sit in each of its seven chambers, which comprise two penal law courts, one administrative litigation court, one fiscal law court, one civil law court and two employment law courts.

Corte Nacional de Justicia: Avda Amazonas N37-101, esq. Unión Nacional de Periodistas, Quito; tel. (2) 227-8396; e-mail ramaguai@funcionjudicial-pichincha.gov.ec; internet www.cortesuprema.gov.ec; f. 1830; Pres. JOSÉ VICENTE TROYA JARAMILLO.

Attorney-General: Dr DIEGO GARCÍA CARRIÓN.

OTHER COURTS

Other courts include Higher or Divisional Courts and Provincial Courts. The structure of the judicial system was subject to reform in early 2009.

COUNCIL OF THE JUDICIARY

Consejo de la Judicatura: Jorge Washington E4-157, entre Juan León Mera y Avda Río Amazonas, Quito; internet www.cnj.gov.ec; f. 1998; Pres. XAVIER AROSEMENA CAMACHO.

Religion

There is no state religion, but the vast majority of the population are Roman Catholics. There are representatives of various Protestant Churches and of the Jewish faith in Quito and Guayaquil.

CHRISTIANITY

The Roman Catholic Church

Ecuador comprises four archdioceses, 12 dioceses and eight Apostolic Vicariates. Some 90% of the population are Roman Catholics.

Bishops' Conference

Conferencia Episcopal Ecuatoriana, Avda América 24-59 y La Gasca, Apdo 17-01-1081, Quito; tel. (2) 222-3137; fax (2) 250-1429; e-mail confepec@uio.satnet.net.

f. 1939 statutes approved 1999; Pres. Most Rev. ANTONIO ARREGUI YARZA (Archbishop of Guayaquil).

Archbishop of Cuenca: LUIS GERARDO CABRERA HERRERA, Arzobispado, Manuel Vega 8-66 y Calle Bolívar, Apdo 01-01-0046, Cuenca; tel. (7) 847-234; fax (7) 844-436; e-mail dicuenca@etapaonline.ne.ec.

Archbishop of Guayaquil: ANTONIO ARREGUI YARZA, Arzobispado, Calle Clemente Ballén 501 y Chimborazo, Apdo 09-01-0254, Guayaquil; tel. (4) 232-2778; fax (4) 232-9695; e-mail marregui@q.ecua.net.ec; internet www.iglesiacatolicaguayaquil.org.

Archbishop of Portoviejo: LORENZO VOLTOLINI ESTI, Arzobispado, Avda Universitaria s/n, Entre Alajuela y Ramos y Duarte, Apdo 13-01-0024, Portoviejo; tel. (5) 263-0404; fax (5) 263-4428; e-mail arzobis@ecua.net.ec.

Archbishop of Quito: RAÚL EDUARDO VELA CHIRIBOGA, Arzobispado, Calle Chile 1140 y Venezuela, Apdo 17-01-00106, Quito; tel. (2) 228-4429; fax (2) 258-0973; e-mail raul.vela@andinanet.net; internet www.arquidiocesisdequito.org.

The Anglican Communion

Anglicans in Ecuador are under the jurisdiction of Province IX of the Episcopal Church in the USA. The country is divided into two dioceses, one of which, Central Ecuador, is a missionary diocese.

Bishop of Central Ecuador: Rt Rev. WILFRIDO RAMOS-ORENCH, Avda Amazonas 4430 y Villalengua, 7°, Of. 708, Quito.

Bishop of Littoral Ecuador: Rt Rev. ALFREDO MORANTE, Calle Bogotá 1010, Barrio Centenario, Apdo 5250, Guayaquil; tel. (2) 443-3050; e-mail iedl@gu.pro.ec.

Other Churches

Convención Bautista Ecuatoriana: Casilla 3236, Guayaquil; tel. (4) 237-5673; fax 245-2319; e-mail cbe@telconet.net; f. 1950; Baptist; Pres. Rev. JULIO XAVIER ALVARADO SILVA.

Iglesia Evangélica Metodista del Ecuador: Rumipamba 915, Apdo 17-03-236, Quito; tel. (2) 226-5158; fax (2) 243-9576; Methodist; 800 mems, 2,000 adherents.

BAHÁ'Í FAITH

National Spiritual Assembly of the Bahá'ís: Apdo 869A, Quito; tel. (2) 256-3484; fax (2) 252-3192; e-mail ecua9nsa@uio.satnet.net; mems resident in 1,121 localities.

The Press

PRINCIPAL DAILIES

Quito

El Comercio: Avda Pedro Vicente Maldonado 11515 y el Tablón, Apdo 17-01-57, Quito; tel. (2) 267-0999; fax (2) 267-0214; e-mail contactenos@elcomercio.com; internet www.elcomercio.com; f. 1906; morning; independent; Proprs Compañía Anónima El Comercio; Pres. FABRIZIO ACQUAVIVA MANTILLA; Dir-Gen. GUADALUPE MANTILLA DE ACQUAVIVA; circ. 160,000.

La Hora: Panamericana Norte km 3½, Quito; tel. (2) 247-3724; fax (2) 247-5086; e-mail lahora@uio.satnet.net; internet www.lahora.com.ec; f. 1982; 12 regional edns; Pres. Dr FRANCISCO VIVANCO RIOFRÍO; Gen. Editor JUANA LÓPEZ SARMIENTO.

Hoy: Avda Mariscal Sucre Of. 6-116, Apdo 17-07-09069, Quito; tel. (2) 249-0888; fax (2) 249-1881; e-mail hoy@hoy.com.ec; internet www.hoy.com.ec; f. 1982; morning; independent; Dir JAIME MANTILLA ANDERSON; Editor JUAN TIBANLOMBO; circ. 72,000.

Ultimas Noticias: Avda Pedro Vicente Maldonado 11515 y el Tablón, Apdo 17-01-57, Quito; tel. (2) 267-0999; fax (2) 267-4923; e-mail mivoz@ultimasnoticias.ec; internet www.ultimasnoticias.ec; f. 1938; evening; independent; commercial; Proprs Compañía Anónima El Comercio; Dir JORGE RIBADENEIRA ARAUJO; circ. 60,000.

Guayaquil

Expreso: Avda Carlos Julio Arosemena km 2½, Casilla 5890, Guayaquil; tel. (4) 220-1100; fax (4) 220-0291; e-mail editorgeneral@granasa.com.ec; internet www.diario-expreso.com; f. 1973; morning; independent; Gen. Editor EDWIN ULLOA ARELLANO; circ. 60,000.

Extra: Avda Carlos Julio Arosemena km 2½, Casilla 5890, Guayaquil; tel. (4) 220-1100; fax (4) 220-0291; e-mail matriz@granasa.com.ec; internet www.diario-extra.com; f. 1974; morning; popular; Dir NICOLÁS ULLOA FIGUEROA; Editor HENRY HOLGUÍN; circ. 200,000.

La Razón: Avda Constitución y las Américas, Guayaquil; tel. (4) 228-0100; fax (4) 228-5110; e-mail cartas@larazonecuador.com; internet www.larazonecuador.com; f. 1965; morning; independent; Propr ROBERTO ISAÍAS DASSUM; circ. 35,000.

El Telégrafo: Avda 10 de Agosto 601 y Boyacá, Casilla 415, Guayaquil; tel. (4) 232-6500; fax (4) 232-3265; e-mail contacto@telegrafo.com.ec; internet www.telegrafo.com.ec; f. 1884; acquired by the state in 2008 and refounded; morning; Dir RUBÉN MONTOYA VEGA; Chief Editor PATRICIO GONZÁLEZ.

El Universo: Avda Domingo Comín y Alban, Casilla 09-01-531, Guayaquil; tel. (4) 249-0000; fax (4) 249-1034; e-mail pocha@eluniverso.com; internet www.eluniverso.com; f. 1921; morning; independent; Pres. NICOLÁS PÉREZ LAPENTTI; Dir CARLOS PÉREZ BARRIGA; circ. 174,000 (weekdays), 290,000 (Sundays).

Cuenca

El Mercurio: Avda las Américas Sur y N. Aguilar, Sector El Arenal, Casilla 01-60, Cuenca; tel. (7) 409-5682; fax (7) 409-5685; e-mail redaccion1@elmercurio.com.ec; internet www.elmercurio.com.ec; f. 1924; morning; Dir NICANOR MERCHÁN LUCO.

El Tiempo: Avda Loja y Rodrigo de Triana, Cuenca; tel. (7) 288-2551; fax (7) 288-2555; e-mail redaccion@eltiempo.com.ec; internet www.eltiempo.com.ec; f. 1955; morning; independent; Dir Dr RENÉ TORAL CALLE; circ. 35,000.

PERIODICALS

Quito

Chasqui: Avda Diego de Almagro 32-133 y Andrade Marín, Apdo 17-01-584, Quito; tel. (2) 254-8011; fax (2) 250-2487; e-mail chasqui@ciespal.net; internet chasqui.comunica.org; f. 1997; quarterly; media studies; publ. of the Centro Internacional de Estudios Superiores de Comunicación para América Latina (CIESPAL); Dir EDGAR JARAMILLO; Editor LUIS ELADIO PROAÑO.

Cosas: Avda 12 de Octubre N26-14 y Coruña, Quito; tel. and fax (2) 250-2444; e-mail redaccion@cosas.com.ec; internet www.cosas.com.ec; f. 1994; women's interest; Dir CLAUDIA GONZÁLEZ DE RIZZI; Editor MARTHA DUBRAVCIC.

Criterios: Edif. Las Cámaras, 4°, Avda Amazonas y República, Casilla 17-01-202, Quito; tel. (2) 244-3787; fax (2) 243-5862; e-mail criterios@lacamaradequito.com; internet www.lacamaradequito.com; f. 1996; monthly; organ of the Cámara de Comercio de Quito; commerce; Dir-Gen. LOLO ECHEVERRÍA; Gen. Editor MARÍA UTRERAS.

Gestión: Avda González Suárez 335 y San Ignacio, 2°, Quito; tel. (2) 223-6848; fax (2) 255-9930; e-mail info@dinediciones.com; internet www.gestion.dinediciones.com; f. 1994; monthly; economy and society; Gen. Man. HERNÁN ALTAMIRANO; Editor JUANITA ORDÓÑEZ; circ. 15,000.

Mundo Diners: Avda 12 de Octubre N25-32 y Coruña, Quito; tel. (2) 254-5209; fax (2) 254-5188; e-mail jortiz@dinediciones.com; internet www.dinediciones.com/diners; f. 1986; monthly; culture, politics, society, etc.; Pres. FIDEL EGAS GRIJALVA.

Guayaquil

El Agro: Avda Constitución y Avda de las Américas 11 y Calle A, Casilla 09-01-9686, Guayaquil; tel. (4) 269-0019; fax (4) 269-0555; e-mail elagro@uminasa.com; internet www.elagro.com.ec; f. 1991; monthly; agriculture; Pres. EDUARDO PEÑA; Gen. Editor ALEXANDRA ZAMBRANO DE ANDRIUOLI.

Análisis Semanal: Edif. La Previsora, 30°, Of. 3005, Avda 9 de Octubre 100 y Malecón Simón Bolívar, Guayaquil; tel. (4) 230-7371; fax (4) 232-6842; e-mail wspurrier@ecuadoranalysis.com; internet www.ecuadoranalysis.com; weekly; economic and political affairs; Editor WALTER SPURRIER BAQUERIZO.

El Financiero: Avda Jorge Pérez Concha (Circunvalación Sur) 201 y Única, Casilla 6666, Guayaquil; tel. (4) 261-1000; fax (4) 288-2950; e-mail redacciong@elfinanciero.com; internet www.elfinanciero.com; weekly; business and economic news; f. 1990; Dir XAVIER PÉREZ MACCOLLUM.

Generación XXI: Aguirre 734 y García Avilés, Guayaquil; tel. (4) 232-7200; fax (4) 232-4870; e-mail g21@vistazo.com; internet www.generacion21.com; f. 1996; youth; Dir SEBASTIAN MÉLIÈRES; Editor CHRISTIAN KALIL CARTER.

Revista Estadio: Aguirre 734 y García Avilés, Casilla 09-01-1239, Guayaquil; tel. (4) 232-7200; fax (4) 232-0499; e-mail estadio@vistazo.com; internet www.revistaestadio.com; f. 1962; fortnightly; sport; Dir-Gen. SEBASTIAN MÉLIÈRES; Editor FABRICIO ZAVALA GARCÍA; circ. 40,000.

Revista Hogar: Aguirre 724 y Boyacá, Apdo 09-01-1239, Guayaquil; tel. (4) 232-7200; fax (4) 232-4870; e-mail rbustap@vistazo.com; internet www.revistahogar.com; f. 1964; monthly; women's interest; Dir-Gen. MARÍA GABRIELA GÁLVEZ VERA; Chief Editor ALEXANDRA ZURITA ANDRADE; circ. 47,000.

La Verdad: Malecón 502 y Tomás Martínez, Guayaquil; e-mail laverdad@telconet.net; internet www.revista-laverdad.com; f. 1988; monthly; politics and economics; associated with the Partido Renovador Institucional de Acción Nacional; Pres. ALVARO FERNANDO NOBOA PONTÓN; Dir RODOLFO BAQUERIZO BLUM.

Vistazo: Aguirre 734 y García Avilés, Casilla 09-01-1239, Guayaquil; tel. (4) 232-7200; fax (4) 232-4870; e-mail vistazo@vistazo.com; internet www.vistazo.com; f. 1957; fortnightly; general; Gen. Editor PATRICIA ESTUPIÑÁN DE BURBANO; circ. 85,000.

PRESS ASSOCIATION

Asociación Ecuatoriana de Editores de Periódicos (AEDEP): Edif. World Trade Center, 14°, Of. 14-01, Avda 12 de Octubre y Cordero, Quito; tel. (2) 254-7457; fax (2) 254-7404; e-mail aedep@aedep.org.ec; internet www.aedep.org.ec; f. 1985; Pres. JAIME MANTILLA ANDERSON.

Publishers

Artes Gráficas Ltda: Avda 12 de Octubre 1637, Casilla 456A, Quito; Man. MANUEL DEL CASTILLO.

Casa de la Cultura Ecuatoriana: Avdas 6 de Diciembre y Patria, Quito; tel. (2) 222-3391; e-mail info@cce.org.ec; internet www.cce.org.ec; Dir JAIME PAREDES.

Centro de Educación Popular: Avda América 3584, Apdo 17-08-8604, Quito; tel. (2) 252-5521; fax (2) 254-2369; e-mail centro@cedep.ec; f. 1978; communications, economics; Dir DIEGO LANDÁZURI.

Centro de Planificación y Estudios Sociales (CEPLAES): Sarmiento N39-198 y Hugo Moncayo, Apdo 17-11-6127, Quito; tel. (2) 225-0659; fax (2) 245-9417; e-mail ceplaes@andinanet.net; internet www.ceplaes.org.ec; f. 1978; agriculture, anthropology, education, health, social sciences, women's studies; Exec. Dir GLORIA CAMACHO.

Centro Interamericano de Artesanías y Artes Populares (CIDAP): Hermano Miguel 3-23, Casilla 01-011-943, Cuenca; tel. (7) 282-9451; fax (7) 283-1450; e-mail cidapl@cidap.org.ec; internet www.cidap.org.ec; art, crafts, games, hobbies; Dir CLAUDIO MALO GONZÁLEZ.

Centro Internacional de Estudios Superiores de Comunicación para América Latina (CIESPAL): Avda Diego de Almagro 32-133 y Andrade Marín, Apdo 17-01-584, Quito; tel. (2) 254-8011; fax (2) 250-2487; e-mail ejaramillo@ciespal.net; internet www.ciespal.net; f. 1959; communications, technology; Dir EDGAR JARAMILLO.

Corporación Editora Nacional: Roca E9–59 y Tamayo, Apdo 17-12-886, Quito; tel. (2) 255-4358; fax (2) 256-6340; e-mail cen@cenlibrosecuador.org; internet www.cenlibrosecuador.org; f. 1977; archaeology, economics, education, geography, political science, history, law, literature, management, philosophy, social sciences; Pres. GUILLERMO BUSTOS LOZANO.

Corporación de Estudios y Publicaciones: Acuna E2-02 y J. Agama, Casilla 17-21-0086, Quito; tel. (2) 222-1711; fax (2) 222-6256; e-mail editorial@cep.org.ec; internet www.cep.org.ec; f. 1963; law, public administration.

Ediciones Abya-Yala: Avda 12 de Octubre 1430, Apdo 17-12-719, Quito; tel. (2) 250-6251; fax (2) 250-6267; e-mail editorial@abyayala.org; internet www.abyayala.org; f. 1975; anthropology, environmental studies, languages, education, theology; Pres. Fr JUAN BOTTASSO; Dir-Gen. P. XAVIER HERRÁN.

Editorial Don Bosco: Vega Muñoz 10-68 y General Torres, Cuenca; tel. (7) 283-1745; fax (7) 284-2722; e-mail edibosco@bosco.org.ec; internet www.lns.com.ec; f. 1920; Gen. Man. P. EDUARDO SANDOVAL; Deputy Man. FANNY FAJARDO Z.

Editorial El Conejo: 6 de Diciembre N26-97 y La Niña, Quito; tel. (2) 222-7948; fax (2) 250-1066; e-mail info@editorialelconejo.com; internet www.editorialelconejo.com; f. 1979; non-profit publr of educational and literary texts; Dir ABDÓN UBIDIA.

Editorial Edinacho, SA: Bartolomé Sánchez Lote 6 y Calle C Lotización Muñoz Carvajal, Carcelén, 5932, Quito; tel. (2) 247-0429; fax (2) 247-0430; e-mail edinacho@ecnet.ec; f. 1985; Man. GERMÁN SEGURA; Editor Dr DALIA MARÍA NOBOA.

Grupo Bueno Editores, SA: Selva Alegre 5-287 y la Isla, Quito; tel. (2) 320-0200; fax (2) 320-2177; e-mail buenoeditores@yahoo.com; internet www.grupoedibueno.com; f. 1981; Pres. SEGUNDO BUENO QUICHIMBO; Gen. Man. DIANA BUENO MEJÍA.

Libresa, SA: Murgeon 364 y Ulloa, Quito; tel. (2) 223-0925; fax (2) 250-2992; e-mail info@libresa.com; internet www.libresa.com; f. 1979; education, literature, philosophy; Pres. FAUSTO COBA ESTRELLA; Man. JAIME PEÑA NOVOA.

Libros Técnicos Litesa Cía Ltda: Avda América 542, Casilla 456A, Quito; tel. (2) 252-8537; Man. MANUEL DEL CASTILLO.

Pontificia Universidad Católica del Ecuador, Centro de Publicaciones: Avda 12 de Octubre 1076 y Carrión, Apdo 17-01-2184, Quito; tel. (2) 252-9250; fax (2) 256-7117; e-mail puce@edu.ec; internet www.puce.edu.ec; f. 1974; literature, natural science, law, anthropology, sociology, politics, economics, theology, philosophy, history, archaeology, linguistics, languages and business; Dir Dr MARCO VINICIO RUEDA.

Trama Ediciones: Edif. Marinoar, planta baja, entre Catalina Aldaz y El Batán, Eloy Alfaro 34-85, Quito; tel. (2) 224-6315; fax (2) 224-6317; e-mail trama@trama.ec; internet www.trama.com.ec; f. 1977; architecture, design, art and tourism; Dir-Gen. ROLANDO MOYA TASQUER.

Universidad Central del Ecuador: Departamento de Publicaciones, Servicio de Almacén Universitario, Ciudad Universitaria, Avda América y Avda Pérez Guerrero, Apdo 3291, Quito; tel. (2) 222-6080; fax (2) 250-1207; internet www.uce.edu.ec.

Universidad de Guayaquil: Departamento de Publicaciones, Biblioteca General 'Luis de Tola y Avilés', Apdo 09-01-3834, Guayaquil; tel. (4) 251-6296; internet www.ug.edu.ec; f. 1930; general literature, history, philosophy, fiction; Man. Dir LEONOR VILLAO DE SANTANDER.

Broadcasting and Communications

TELECOMMUNICATIONS

Consejo Nacional de Telecomunicaciones (CONATEL): Avda Diego de Almagro 31-95 y Alpallana, Casilla 17-07-9777, Quito; tel. (2) 294-7800; fax (2) 250-5119; e-mail comunicacion@conatel.gov.ec; internet www.conatel.gov.ec; Pres. JAIME GUERRERO RUIZ.

Secretaría Nacional de Telecomunicaciones (SENATEL): Avda Diego de Almagro 31-95 y Alpallana, Casilla 17-07-9777, Quito; tel. (2) 294-7800; fax (2) 290-1010; e-mail comunicacion@conatel.gov.ec; internet www.conatel.gov.ec/website/senatel/senatel.php; Sec. JAIME GUERRERO RUIZ.

Superintendencia de Telecomunicaciones (SUPERTEL): Edif. Olimpo, Avda 9 de Octubre N27-75 y Berlín, Casilla 17-21-1797, Quito; tel. (2) 294-6400; fax (2) 223-2115; e-mail info@supertel.gov.ec; internet www.supertel.gov.ec; f. 1992; Supt FABIÁN LEONARDO JARAMILLO PALACIOS.

Major Service Providers

Alegro (Telecomunicaciones Móviles del Ecuador, SA—Telecsa): Edif. Vivaldi, Amazonas 3837 y Corea, Quito; tel. and fax (2) 299-0000; e-mail info@alegro.com.ec; internet www.alegro.com.ec; state-owned; cellular telephone provider.

Corporación Nacional de Telecomunicaciones: Edif. Zeta, Avda Veintimilla 1149 y Amazonas, Quito; tel. (2) 297-7100; fax (2) 256-2240; e-mail clara.salazar@cnt.com.ec; internet www.cnt.com.ec; f. 2008 by merger of Andinatel and Pacifictel; state-owned; Pres. JORGE GLAS ESPINEL; Gen. Man. CÉSAR REGALADO IGLESIAS.

Movistar Ecuador: Avda República y esq. La Pradera, Quito; tel. (2) 222-7700; internet www.movistar.com.ec; f. 1997; name changed from BellSouth Ecuador to above in 2005; owned by Telefónica Móviles, SA (Spain); mobile telephone services; CEO JOSÉ LUIS DÍAZ DE MERA.

OTECEL, SA: f. 2004; subsidiary of Movistar Ecuador; mobile cellular telephone network provider.

Porta (Conecel, SA): Avda Francisco de Orellana y Alberto Borgues, Edif. Centrum, Guayaquil; e-mail callcenter@conecel.com; internet www.porta.net; f. 1993; subsidiary of América Móvil group (Mexico); mobile telecommunications provider.

Telmex Ecuador: Edif. Plaza 2000, 2°, Avda Gen. Salazar y 12 de Octubre, Quito; tel. (2) 223-0093; fax (2) 224-0494; e-mail servicios .ec@telmex.com; internet www.telmex.com/ec; part of Teléfonos de México, SA de CV (Mexico).

BROADCASTING

Regulatory Authority

Consejo Nacional de Radiodifusión y Televisión (CONARTEL): Edif. Inglaterra, Amazonas 33275 e Inglaterra, Quito; tel. (2) 226-1000; fax (2) 292-1637; e-mail correo@conartel.gov.ec; internet www.conartel.gov.ec; Pres. Dr Antonio García Reyes.

Radio

There are nearly 300 commercial stations, 10 cultural stations and 10 religious stations. The following are among the most important stations:

Radio Católica Nacional: Avda América 1830 y Mercadillo, Casilla 17-03-540, Quito; tel. (2) 254-1557; fax (2) 256-7309; e-mail buenanoticia@radiocatolica.org.ec; internet www.radiocatolica.org .ec; f. 1985; Dir-Gen. Dr Ramiro Arroyo Ponce.

Radio Centro: Avda República de El Salvador 836 y Portugal, Quito; tel. (2) 244-8900; fax (2) 250-4575; f. 1977; Pres. Edgar Yánez Villalobos.

Radio Colón: Avellanas E5-107 y Avda Eloy Alfaro, Casilla 17-07-9927, Quito; tel. 248-4574; fax (2) 248-5666; e-mail escucha@ radiocolon.ec; internet www.radiocolon.ec; f. 1934; Pres. Dr Gerardo Castro; Dir Bernardo Nussbaum.

Radio CRE Satelital (CORTEL, SA): Edif. El Torreón, 9°, Avda Boyacá 642 y Padre Solano, Apdo 4144, Guayaquil; tel. (4) 256-4290; fax (4) 256-0386; e-mail cre@cre.com.ec; internet www.cre.com.ec; Pres. Rafael Guerrero Valenzuela.

Radio Latina: Quito; internet www.radiolatina.com.ec; f. 1990; Pres. Juan Carlos Isaías.

Radio La Luna: Quito; internet www.radiolaluna.com; Owner Paco Velasco.

Radio Quito: Avda 10 de Agosto 2441 y Colón, Casilla 17-21-1971, Quito; tel. (2) 250-8301; fax (2) 250-3311; e-mail radioquito@ ecuadoradio.com; internet www.elcomercio.com/radio_quito.html; f. 1940; owned by El Comercio newspaper.

Radio Sonorama (HCAEL): Avda Eloy Alfaro 5400 y Los Granados, Casilla 130B, Quito; tel. (2) 244-8403; fax (2) 244-5858; f. 1975; Pres. Santiago Proaño.

Radio Sucre: Joaquín Orrantia y Miguel H. Alcivar (Casa de las Américas Kennedy Norte), Guayaquil; tel. (4) 268-0588; fax (4) 268-0592; e-mail info@radiosucretv.com; internet www.radiosucre.com .ec; f. 1983; Pres. Vicente Arroba Ditto; Dir Yotti Daniel Guerra Avila.

La Voz de los Andes (HCJB): Villalengua 884 y Avda 10 de Agosto, Casilla 17-17-691, Quito; tel. (2) 226-6808; fax (2) 226-7263; e-mail tdltorre@hcjb.org.ec; internet www.vozandes.org; f. 1931; operated by World Radio Missionary Fellowship; programmes in 11 languages (including Spanish and English) and 22 Quechua dialects; Evangelical; Int. Dir, Radio Curt Cole; Gen. Man. John E. Beck.

Television

Corporación Ecuatoriana de Televisión—Ecuavisa Canal 2: Cerro El Carmen, Casilla 1239, Guayaquil; tel. (4) 256-2444; fax (4) 256-2432; internet www.ecuavisa.com; f. 1967; Pres. Xavier Alvarado Roca; Gen. Man. Francisco Arosemena Robles.

TC Televisión: Avda de las Américas, frente al Aeropuerto, Casilla 09-01-673, Guayaquil; tel. (4) 239-7664; fax (4) 228-7544; internet www.tctelevision.com; f. 1969; commercial; seized by the Govt in July 2008; Gen. Man. Jorge Kronfle.

Teleamazonas Cratel, CA: Granda Centeno Oeste 429 y Brasil, Casilla 17-11-04844, Quito; tel. (2) 397-4444; fax (2) 244-1620; e-mail guerrero@teleamazonas.com; internet www.teleamazonas.com; f. 1974; commercial; Gen. Man. Sebastián Corral.

Teleandina Canal 23: Avda de la Prensa 3920 y Fernández Salvador, Quito; tel. (2) 259-9403; fax (2) 259-2600; f. 1991; Pres. Humberto Ortiz Flores; Dir Patricio Aviles.

Televisión del Pacífico, SA—Gamavisión: Avda Eloy Alfaro 5400 y Río Coca, Quito; tel. (2) 226-2222; fax (2) 226-2284; e-mail gerenciageneral@gamavision.com; internet www.gamavision.com; f. 1978; Pres. and Gen. Man. Nicolás Vega.

Televisora Nacional—Ecuavisa Canal 8: Bosmediano 447 y José Carbo, Bellavista, Quito; tel. (2) 244-8100; fax (2) 244-5488; internet www.ecuavisa.com; commercial; f. 1970; Pres. Patricio Jaramillo.

Association

Asociación Ecuatoriana de Radiodifusión (AER): Edif. Atlas, 8°, Of. 802, Calle Justino Cornejo con Francisco de Orellana, Guayaquil; tel. and fax (4) 229-1783; ind. asscn; Pres. Lenín Andrade Quiñónez.

Finance

(cap. = capital; res = reserves; dep. = deposits; m. = million; brs = branches; amounts in US dollars unless otherwise indicated)

SUPERVISORY AUTHORITY

Superintendencia de Bancos y Seguros: Avda 12 de Octubre 1561 y Madrid, Casilla 17-17-770, Quito; tel. (2) 255-4225; fax (2) 250-6812; e-mail webmaster@superban.gov.ec; internet www.superban .gov.ec; f. 1927; supervises national banking system, including state and private banks and other financial institutions; Supt Gloria Sabando García.

BANKING

Central Bank

Banco Central del Ecuador: Avda 10 de Agosto N11-409 y Briceño, Casilla 339, Quito; tel. (2) 257-2522; fax (2) 295-5458; internet www .bce.fin.ec; f. 1927; cap. 2.5m., res 1,944.5m., dep. 5,441.7m. (Dec. 2008); Pres. Diego Borja; Gen. Man. Christian Ruiz; 2 brs.

Other State Banks

Banco Ecuatoriano de la Vivienda: Avda 10 de Agosto 2270 y Luis Cordero, Casilla 3244, Quito; tel. and fax (2) 396-3300; e-mail bevinfo@bevecuador.com; internet www.bevecuador.com; f. 1961; Pres. Walter Solís Valarezo; Gen. Man. Rodrigo González Kelz.

Banco del Estado (BDE): Avda Atahualpa OE1-109 y Avda 10 de Agosto, Casilla 17-17-1728, Quito; tel. (2) 299-9600; fax (2) 225-0320; e-mail secretaria@bancoestado.com; internet www.bancoestado .com; f. 1979; Pres. Patricio Rivera (Minister of Finance); Gen. Man. Diego Aulestia Valencia.

Banco Nacional de Fomento: Ante 107 y Avda 10 de Agosto, Casilla 685, Quito; tel. (2) 257-2049; fax (2) 257-0286; e-mail judithcevallos@bnf.fin.ec; internet www.bnf.fin.ec; f. 1928; Pres. Ramon Espinel; Gen. Man. Roberto Barriga Ayala; 70 brs.

Corporación Financiera Nacional (CFN): Avda Juan León Mera 130 y Avda Patria, Casilla 17-21-01924, Quito; tel. (2) 256-4900; fax (2) 222-3823; e-mail informatica@q.cfn.fin.ec; internet www.cfn.fin .ec; f. 1964; state-owned bank providing export credits, etc.; Pres. Camilo Samán Salem; Gen. Man. Jorge Wated.

Commercial Banks

Quito

Banco Amazonas, SA: Avda Amazonas 4430 y Villalengua, Casilla 121, Quito; tel. (2) 226-0400; fax (2) 225-5123; e-mail bserviciouio@ bancoamazonas.com; internet www.bancoamazonas.com; f. 1976; cap. 9.6m., res 0.4m., dep. 122.6m. (Dec. 2006); affiliated to Banque Paribas; Pres. Rafael Ferretti Benítez; Vice-Pres. Roberto Seminario.

Banco General Rumiñahui: Avda República E6-573 y Avda Eloy Alfaro, Quito; tel. (2) 250-9929; fax (2) 256-3786; e-mail mrodas@bgr .com.ec; internet www.bgr.com.ec; total assets 192.0m. (Dec. 2004); Gen. Man. Alejandro Ribadeneira Jaramillo.

Banco Internacional, SA: Avda Patria E-421 y 9 de Octubre, Casilla 17-01-2114, Quito; tel. (2) 256-5547; fax (2) 256-5758; e-mail baninteronline@bancointernacional.com.ec; internet www .bancointernacional.com.ec; f. 1973; cap. 8,600m. (Dec. 2000); Pres. José Enrique Fuster Camps; CEO Enrique Beltrán Mata; 58 brs.

Banco del Pichincha, CA: Avda Amazonas 4560 y Pereira, Casilla 261, Quito; tel. (2) 298-0980; fax (2) 298-1226; e-mail sugerencias@ pichincha.com; internet www.pichincha.com; f. 1906; cap. 111.0m., res 71.0m., dep. 3,033.2m. (Dec. 2005); 61.82% owned by Exec. Pres. and Chair.; Exec. Pres. and Chair. Dr Fidel Egas Grijalva; Gen. Man. Fernando Pozo Crespo; 218 brs.

Produbanco (Banco de la Producción, SA): Avda Amazonas N35-211 y Japón, Quito; tel. (2) 299-9000; fax (2) 244-7319; e-mail bancaenlinea@produbanco.com; internet www.produbanco.com; f. 1978 as Banco de la Producción; adopted current name in 1996; cap. 80m., res 18.3m., dep. 1,226.6m. (Dec. 2006); part of Grupo Financiero Producción; Exec. Pres. Abelardo Pachano Bertero; Chair. Rodrigo Paz Delgado; 47 brs.

UniBanco (Banco Universal, SA): Avda 10 de Agosto 937 y Buenos Aires, Quito; tel. (2) 290-6555; fax (2) 222-7898; internet www .unibanco.fin.ec; f. 1964 as Banco de Cooperativas del Ecuador; adopted current name 1994; Pres. Andrés Jervis González.

Cuenca

Banco del Austro: Sucre y Borrero (esq.), Casilla 01-01-0167, Cuenca; tel. (7) 283-1646; fax (7) 283-2633; internet www.bancodelaustro.com; f. 1977; total assets 249.8m. (Sept. 2004); Pres. JUAN ELJURI ANTÓN; Gen. Man. GUILLERMO TÁLBOT DUEÑAS; 19 brs.

Guayaquil

Banco Bolivariano, CA: Junín 200 y Panamá, Casilla 09-01-10184, Guayaquil; tel. (4) 230-5000; fax (4) 256-6707; e-mail info@bolivariano.com; internet www.bolivariano.com; f. 1978; cap. 50.0m., res 10.3m., dep. 739.9m. (Dec. 2006); 61.2% owned by Tabos Investment, SA; Pres. JOSÉ SALAZAR BARRAGÁN; CEO MIGUEL BABRA LEÓN; 53 brs.

Banco de Guayaquil, SA: Plaza Ycaza 105 y Pichincha, Casilla 09-01-1300, Guayaquil; tel. (4) 251-7100; fax (4) 251-4406; e-mail servicios@bankguay.com; internet www.bancoguayaquil.com; f. 1923; absorbed the finance corpn FINANSUR in 1990 to become Ecuador's first 'multibanco', carrying out commercial and financial activities; cap. 90.0m., res 23.4m., dep. 1,387.6m. (Dec. 2007); Pres. DANILO CARRERA DROUET; Exec. Pres. GUILLERMO LASSO MENDOZA; 50 brs.

Banco del Pacífico: Francisco de P. Ycaza 200, entre Pichincha y Pedro Carbo, Casilla 09-01-988, Guayaquil; tel. (4) 256-6010; fax (4) 232-8333; e-mail webadmin@pacifico.fin.ec; internet www.bp.fin.ec; f. 2000 by merger of Banco del Pacífico and Banco Continental; 100% owned by Banco Central del Ecuador; cap. 151.7m., res 72.4m., dep. 1,404.1m. (Dec. 2008); Exec. Pres. ANDRÉS BAQUERIZO; 227 brs.

Banco Territorial, SA: P. Icaza 115, entre Malecón y Pichincha, Guayaquil; tel. (4) 256-1950; e-mail informacion@grupozunino.com; internet www.bancoterritorial.com; f. 1886; Gen. Man. JUAN CARLOS CASTAÑEDA ARCHILA.

Loja

Banco de Loja: esq. Bolívar y Rocafuerte, Casilla 11-01-300, Loja; tel. (7) 257-1682; fax (7) 257-3019; internet www.bancodeloja.fin.ec; f. 1968; Pres. STEVE BROWN HIDALGO; Man. LEONARDO BURNEO MULLER.

Machala

Banco de Machala, SA: Avda 9 de Mayo y Rocafuerte, Casilla 711, Machala; tel. (7) 293-0100; fax (7) 292-2744; e-mail jorejuela@bmachala.com; internet www.bmachala.com; f. 1962; cap. 19.5m., res 3.5m., dep. 238.1m. (Dec. 2006); Pres. Dr ESTEBAN QUIROLA FIGUEROA; Exec. Pres. Dr MARIO CANESSA ONETO; 2 brs.

Portoviejo

Banco Comercial de Manabí, SA: Avda 10 de Agosto 600 y 18 de Octubre, Portoviejo; tel. and fax (5) 263-2222; e-mail info@bcmanabi.com; internet www.bcmanabi.com; f. 1980; Gen. Man. ARISTO ANDRADE DÍAZ.

Associations

Asociación de Bancos Privados del Ecuador: Edif. Delta 890, 7°, Avda República de El Salvador y Suecia, Casilla 17-11-6708, Quito; tel. (2) 246-6670; fax (2) 246-6702; e-mail abpe1@asobancos.org.ec; internet www.asobancos.org.ec; f. 1965; 36 mems; Pres. FERNANDO POZO CRESPO; Exec. Pres. CÉSAR ROBALINO GONZAGA.

Asociación de Instituciones Financieras del Ecuador (AIFE): Edif. La Previsora, Torre B, 3°, Of. 308, Avda Naciones Unidas 1084 y Amazonas, Quito; tel. and fax (2) 246-6560; e-mail aife1@punto.net.ec; internet www.aife.com.ec; Pres. GIANNI GARIBALDI; Exec. Dir JULIO DOBRONSKY NAVARRO.

STOCK EXCHANGES

Bolsa de Valores de Guayaquil: 9 de Octubre 110 y Pichincha, Guayaquil; tel. (4) 256-1519; fax (4) 256-1871; e-mail rgallegos@bvg.fin.ec; internet www.mundobvg.com; Pres. RODOLFO KRONFLE AKEL; Dir-Gen. ARTURO BEJARANO ICAZA.

Bolsa de Valores de Quito: Edif. Londres, 8°, Avda Amazonas 21–252 y Carrión, Casilla 17-01-3772, Quito; tel. (2) 222-1333; fax (2) 250-0942; e-mail informacion@bolsadequito.com; internet www.bolsadequito.com; f. 1969; Chair. PATRICIO PEÑA ROMERO; Exec. Pres. MÓNICA VILLAGÓMEZ DE ANDERSON.

INSURANCE

Instituto Ecuatoriano de Seguridad Social: Avda 10 de Agosto y Bogotá, Apdo 2640, Quito; tel. (2) 252-7998; fax (2) 252-1087; internet www.iess.gov.ec; f. 1928; various forms of state insurance provided; directs the Ecuadorean social insurance system; provides social benefits and medical service; Pres. RAMÓN GONZÁLEZ JARAMILLO; Dir-Gen. FERNANDO GUIJARRO CABEZAS.

Principal Companies

Ace Seguros, SA: Edif. Antisana, 4°, Avdas Amazonas 3655 y Juan Pablo Sanz, Quito; tel. (2) 292-0555; fax (2) 244-5817; e-mail serviciocliente@ace-ina.com; internet www.acelatinamerica.com; Exec. Pres. EDWIN ASTUDILLO.

AIG Metropolitana Cía de Seguros y Reaseguros, SA: Avda Brasil 293 y Antonio Granda Centeno, 5°, Quito; tel. (2) 246-6955; fax (2) 292-4434; e-mail servicio.cliente@aig.com; internet www.aig.com.ec; part of American International Group, Inc (USA); Exec. Pres. DIANA PINILLA ROJAS.

Alianza Cía de Seguros y Reaseguros, SA: Avdas 12 de Octubre 24-359 y Baquerizo Moreno, Apdo 17-17-041, Quito; tel. (2) 256-6143; fax (2) 256-4059; e-mail alianzauio@segurosalianza.com; internet www.segurosalianza.com; f. 1982; Gen. Man. CARLOS ROMERO ROMERO.

Atlas Cía de Seguros, SA: Edif. Torre Atlas, 11°, Kennedy Norte, Justino Cornejo y Avda Luis Orrantia, Guayaquil; tel. (4) 269-0430; fax (4) 228-3099; internet www.mapfreatlas.com.ec; f. 1984; Pres. VICTORIA BEJARANO DE LA TORRE; Gen. Man. MARKUS FREY KELLER.

Bolívar Cía de Seguros del Ecuador, SA: Edif. Las Cámaras, 11° y 12°, Avda Francisco de Orellana, Guayaquil; tel. (2) 268-1777; fax (2) 268-3363; e-mail ssanmiguel@seguros-bolivar.com; internet www.seguros-bolivar.com; f. 1957; Pres. FABIÁN ORTEGA TRUJILLO.

Cía Reaseguradora del Ecuador, SA: Edif. Intercambios, 1°, Junín 105 y Malecón Simón Bolívar, Casilla 09-01-6776, Guayaquil; tel. (4) 256-6326; fax (4) 256-4454; e-mail oespinoz@ecuare.fin.ec; f. 1977; Man. Dir Ing. OMAR ESPINOSA ROMERO.

Cía de Seguros Cóndor, SA: Plaza Ycaza 302, Apdo 09-01-5007, Guayaquil; tel. (4) 256-5300; fax (4) 256-0144; e-mail asalame@bonita.com; internet www.seguroscondor.com; f. 1966; Gen. Man. AUGUSTO SALAME ARZUBIAGA.

Cía de Seguros EcuatorianoSuiza, SA: Avda 9 de Octubre 2101 y Tulcán, Apdo 09-01-0937, Guayaquil; tel. (4) 245-2444; fax (4) 245-2971; e-mail ecuasuiza@ecuasuiza.com; internet www.ecuasuiza.com; f. 1954; Pres. JOSÉ SALAZAR BARRAGÁN; Gen. Man. LUIS FERNANDO SALAS RUBIO.

Cía Seguros Unidos, SA: Edif. Metrocar, 2°, 10 de Agosto y Avda Mariana de Jesús, Quito; tel. (2) 252-6466; fax (2) 245-0920; e-mail jribas01@hotmail.com; internet www.segurosunidos.ec; Gen. Man. JUAN RIBAS DOMENECH.

Nacional Cía de Seguros, SA: Panamá 809 y Rendón, Guayaquil; tel. (4) 456-0700; fax (4) 456-6327; f. 1940; Gen. Man. BRUNO ORLANDINI.

Panamericana del Ecuador, SA: Calle Portugal E-12-72 y Avda Eloy Alfaro, Quito; tel. (2) 246-8840; fax (2) 246-9650; e-mail larango@panamericana.com.ec; internet www.panamericana.com.ec; f. 1973; Pres. PATRICIO ALVAREZ PLAZA; Gen. Man. LUIS FELIPE ARANGO PARDO.

Seguros Rocafuerte, SA: Edif. Filanbanco, 15°, Plaza Carbo 505 y 9 de Octubre, Apdo 09-04-6491, Guayaquil; tel. (4) 232-6125; fax (4) 232-9353; e-mail segroca@gye.satnet.net; f. 1967; life and medical; Exec. Pres. NORMAN PICHARDO VAN DER DIJS.

Seguros Sucre, SA: Edif. San Francisco 300, 6°, Pedro Carbo 422 y Avda 9 de Octubre, Apdo 09-01-480, Guayaquil; tel. (4) 256-3399; fax (4) 231-4163; e-mail pespinel@segurossucre.fin.ec; internet www.segurossucre.fin.ec; f. 1944; part of Grupo Banco del Pacífico; Gen. Man. MAXIMILIANO DONOSO VALLEJO.

La Unión Cía Nacional de Seguros: Urb. Los Cedros Solares 1-2, Km 5½, Vía a la Costa, Apdo 09-01-1294, Guayaquil; tel. (4) 285-1500; fax (4) 285-1700; e-mail rgoldbaum@seguroslaunion.com; internet www.seguroslaunion.com; f. 1943; Exec. Pres. ROBERTO GOLDBAUM; Gen. Man. CARLOS LESMES.

Trade and Industry

GOVERNMENT AGENCIES

Consejo Nacional de Modernización del Estado (CONAM): Edif. CFN, 10°, Avda Juan León Mera 130 y Patria, Quito; tel. (2) 250-9432; fax (2) 222-8450; e-mail info@conam.gov.ec; internet www.conam.gov.ec; f. 1994; responsible for overseeing privatizations; Pres. CARLOS VEGA.

Consejo Nacional para la Reactivación de la Producción y la Competitividad (CNPC): Edif. Plaza 2000, Torre B, 1°, Esq. Avda 12 de Octubre 24-593 y Francisco Salazar, Quito; tel. (2) 255-4840; e-mail info@cnpc.gov.ec; internet www.cnpc.gov.ec; promotes competitiveness of Ecuadorean businesses; Exec. Dir VERÓNOCA SIÓN DE JOSSE.

Fondo de Solidaridad: Avda 6 de Diciembre 25–75 y Colón, Edif. Partenón, Quito; tel. (2) 220-0429; internet www.fondodesolidaridad

.gov.ec; f. 1996; govt devt agency; responsibility for overseeing privatization of electricity sector; Pres. JORGE BURBANO.

Instituto Ecuatoriano de Desarrollo Agrario (INDA): León Vivar s/n y Jerónimo Carrión, Quito; tel. (2) 254-5771; e-mail info@inda.gov.ec; internet www.inda.gov.ec; f. 1994; in charge of legalization and adjudication of land ownership; Exec. Dir CARLOS ROLANDO AGUIRRE.

Superintendencia de Compañías del Ecuador: Roca 660 y Amazonas, Casilla 687, Quito; tel. (2) 252-9960; fax (2) 256-6685; e-mail superintcias@q.supercias.gov.ec; internet www.supercias.gov.ec; f. 1964; responsible for the legal and accounting control of commercial enterprises; Supt PEDRO SOLINES CHACÓN; Sec.-Gen. VÍCTOR CEVALLOS VÁSQUEZ.

DEVELOPMENT ORGANIZATIONS

Consejo Nacional de Desarrollo (CONADE): Juan Larrea y Arenas, Quito; fmrly Junta Nacional de Planificación y Coordinación Económica; aims to formulate a general plan of economic and social devt and supervise its execution; also to integrate local plans into national plans; Chair. GALO ABRIL OJEDA; Sec. PABLO LUCIO PAREDES.

Fondo de Desarrollo del Sector Rural Marginal (FODERUMA): f. 1978; allots funds to rural devt programmes in poor areas.

Fondo Nacional de Desarrollo (FONADE): f. 1973; national devt fund.

Organización Comercial Ecuatoriana de Productos Artesanales (OCEPA): Carrión 1236 y Versalles, Casilla 17-01-2948, Quito; tel. (2) 254-1992; fax (2) 256-5961; f. 1964; develops and promotes handicrafts; Gen. Man. MARCELO RODRÍGUEZ.

Programa Nacional del Banano y Frutas Tropicales: Guayaquil; promotes the devt of banana and tropical fruit cultivation; Dir Ing. JORGE GIL CHANG.

Programa Regional de Desarrollo del Sur del Ecuador (PREDESUR): Pasaje María Eufrasia 100 y Mosquera Narváez, Quito; tel. (2) 254-4415; f. 1972; promotes the devt of the southern area of the country; Dir Ing. LUIS HERNÁN EGUIGUREN CARRIÓN.

CHAMBERS OF COMMERCE AND INDUSTRY

Cámara de Comercio de Ambato: Edif. Las Cámaras, Montalvo 03-31, entre Bolívar y Rocafuerte, Ambato; tel. and fax (3) 242-1930; fax (3) 242-4773; e-mail webmaster@ccomercioambato.org; internet www.ccomercioambato.org; Pres. MIGUEL SUÁREZ JARAMILLO.

Cámara de Comercio de Cuenca: Avda Federico Malo 1-90, 2°, Casilla 4929, Cuenca; tel. (7) 282-7531; fax (7) 283-3891; e-mail cccuenca@etapa.com.ec; internet www.cccuenca.com; f. 1919; 5,329 mems; Pres. JUAN PABLO VINTIMILLA.

Cámara de Comercio Ecuatoriano-Americana (Amcham Quito-Ecuador): Quito; tel. (2) 250-7450; fax (2) 250-4571; e-mail info@ecamcham.com; internet www.ecamcham.com; f. 1974; promotes bilateral trade and investment between Ecuador and the USA; brs in Ambato, Cuenca and Manta; Pres. MAURICIO ROBALINO; Vice-Pres. ALBERTO SANDOVAL.

Cámara de Comercio Ecuatoriano Canadiense (Ecuadorean-Canadian Chamber of Commerce): Quito; internet www.ecucanchamber.org; Exec. Dir PATRICIA BUSTAMANTE; Pres. JANIO SÁNCHEZ.

Cámara de Comercio de Guayaquil: Avda Francisco de Orellana y V. H. Sicouret, Centro Empresarial 'Las Cámaras', 2° y 3°, Guayaquil; tel. (4) 268-2771; fax (4) 268-2766; e-mail info@lacamara.org; internet www.lacamara.org; f. 1889; 31,000 affiliates; Pres. MARÍA GLORIA ALARCÓN ALCÍVAR.

Cámara de Comercio de Machala: Edif. Cámara de Comercio, 2°, Rocafuerte y Buenavista, CP 825, Machala, Cuenca; tel. (7) 293-0640; fax (7) 293-4454; e-mail ccomach@ecua.net.ec; Pres. JOSÉ MENDIETA E.

Cámara de Comercio de Manta: Edif. Cámara de Comercio, Avda 2, entre Calles 10 y 11, Apdo 13-05-477, Manta; tel. and fax (5) 262-1306; e-mail cacoma@ccm.org.ec; f. 1927; Pres. LUCÍA FERNÁNDEZ DE DEGENNA; Exec. Dir JOSELIAS SÁNCHEZ RAMOS.

Cámara de Comercio de Quito: Edif. Las Cámaras, 6°, Avda República y Amazonas, Casilla 17-01-202, Quito; tel. (2) 244-3787; fax (2) 243-5862; e-mail ccq@ccq.org.ec; internet www.ccq.org.ec; f. 1906; 12,000 mems; Pres. BLASCO PEÑAHERRERA SOLAH; Exec. Dir GUIDO TOLEDO ANDRADE.

Cámara de Industrias de Cuenca: Edif. Cámara de Industrias de Cuenca, 12° y 13°, Avda Florencia Astudillo y Alfonso Cordero, Cuenca; tel. (7) 284-5053; fax (7) 284-0107; internet www.industriascuenca.org.ec; f. 1936; Pres. Ing. MARCEJO JARAMILLO CRESPO.

Cámara de Industrias de Guayaquil: Avda Francisco de Orellana y M. Alcívar, Casilla 09-01-4007, Guayaquil; tel. (4) 268-2618; fax (4) 268-2680; e-mail caindgye@cig.org.ec; internet www.cig.ec; f. 1936; Pres. ALBERTO DASSUM A.

Federación Nacional de Cámaras de Comercio del Ecuador: Avda Amazonas y República, Edif. Las Cámaras, Quito; tel. (2) 244-3787; fax (2) 292-2084; Pres. BLASCO PEÑAHERRERA SOLAH; Vice-Pres. MARÍA GLORIA ALARCÓN.

Federación Nacional de Cámaras de Industrias: Avda República y Amazonas, 10°, Casilla 2438, Quito; tel. (2) 245-2994; fax (2) 244-8118; e-mail camara@camindustriales.org.ec; internet www.camindustriales.org.ec; f. 1974; Pres. Ing. GUSTAVO PINTO.

INDUSTRIAL AND TRADE ASSOCIATIONS

Asociación de la Industria Hidrocarburífera del Ecuador (AIHE): Edif. Puerta del Sol, 8°, Avda Amazonas 4080 y Calle UNP, Quito; tel. (2) 226-1270; fax (2) 226-1272; e-mail aihe@aihe.org.ec; internet www.aihe.org.ec; f. 1997 as Asociación de Compañías Petroleras de Exploración y Explotación de Hidrocarburos del Ecuador (ASOPEC); name changed as above in 2002; asscn of 24 int. and domestic hydrocarbon cos; Exec. Pres. JOSÉ LUIS ZIRITT.

Centro de Desarrollo Industrial del Ecuador (CENDES): Apdo 2845, Guayaquil; tel. (4) 198-9432; f. 1962; carries out industrial feasibility studies, supplies technical and administrative assistance to industry, promotes new industries, supervises investment programmes; Gen. Man. CLAUDIO CREAMER GUILLÉN.

Corporación de Promoción de Exportaciones e Inversiones (CORPEI): Centro de Convenciones Simón Bolivar, 1°, Avda de las Américas 406, Guayaquil; tel. (4) 228-7123; fax (4) 229-2910; internet www.corpei.org; f. 1997 to promote exports and investment; CEO RICARDO E. ESTRADA.

EMPLOYERS' ORGANIZATIONS

Asociación de Atuneros: Malecón s/n, Muelle Portuario de Manta 1, Manta; tel. and fax (5) 262-6467; e-mail atunec@manta.ecua.net.ec; asscn of tuna producers; Pres. LUCÍA FERNÁNDEZ DE GENNA.

Asociación de Cafecultores del Cantón Piñas: García Moreno y Abdón Calderón, Quito; coffee growers' asscn.

Asociación de Comerciantes e Industriales: Avda Boyacá 1416, Guayaquil; traders' and industrialists' asscn.

Asociación de Compañías Consultoras del Ecuador: Edif. Delta 890, 4°, República de El Salvador y Suecia, Quito; tel. (2) 246-5048; fax (2) 245-1171; e-mail acce@acce.com.ec; asscn of consulting cos; Pres. RODOLFO RENDÓN.

Asociación Ecuatoriana de Industriales de la Madera: Edif. de las Cámaras, 7°, República y Amazonas, Quito; tel. (2) 226-0980; fax (2) 243-9560; e-mail secre@aima.org.ec; internet www.aima.org.ec; wood mfrs' asscn; Pres. CÉSAR ALVAREZ.

Asociación de Industriales Gráficos de Pichincha: Edif. de las Cámaras, 8°, Amazonas y República, Quito; tel. (2) 292-3141; fax (2) 245-6664; e-mail aigquito@aig.org.ec; internet www.aig.org.ec; asscn of the graphic industry; Pres. MAURICIO MIRANDA.

Asociación de Industriales Textiles del Ecuador (AITE): Edif. Las Cámaras, 8°, Avda República y Amazonas, Casilla 2893, Quito; tel. (2) 224-9434; fax (2) 244-5159; e-mail aite@aite.org.ec; internet www.aite.com.ec; f. 1938; textile mfrs' asscn; 40 mems; Pres. FERNANDO PÉREZ.

Asociación Nacional de Empresarios (ANDE): Edif. España, 6°, Of. 67, Avda Amazonas 25–23 y Colón, Casilla 17-01-3489, Quito; tel. (2) 290-2545; fax (2) 223-8507; e-mail info@ande.org.ec; internet www.ande.org.ec; national employers' asscn; Pres. PABLO PINTO; Vice-Pres. DR RENÉ ORTIZ DURÁN.

Asociación Nacional de Exportadores de Cacao y Café (ANECAFE): Casilla 4774, Manta; tel. (2) 229-2782; fax (2) 229-2885; e-mail anacafe@uio.satnet.net; cocoa and coffee exporters' asscn.

Asociación Nacional de Exportadores de Camarones: Pres. LUIS VILLACÍS.

Asociación Nacional de Molineros: 6 de Diciembre 3470 e Ignacio Bossano, Quito; tel. (2) 246-5597; fax (2) 246-4754; Exec. Dir RAFAÉL CALLEJAS.

Asociación de Productores Bananeros del Ecuador (APROBANEC): Avda Jaime Roldós y Décima Octava, Edif. Aprocico, Quevedo; tel. (5) 276-2025; fax (5) 276-2265; e-mail aprobanec@aprobanec.org; internet www.aprobanec.org/es; banana growers' asscn; Pres. WILFREDO MACÍAS; Man. KARINA CAMPUZANO.

Cámara de Agricultura: Casilla 17-21-322, Quito; tel. (2) 223-0195; Pres. ALBERTO ENRÍQUEZ PORTILLA.

Consorcio Ecuatoriano de Exportadores de Cacao y Café: cocoa and coffee exporters' consortium.

Corporación Nacional de Exportadores de Cacao y Café: Guayaquil; cocoa and coffee exporters' corporation.

Federación Nacional de Cooperativas Cafetaleras del Ecuador (FENACAFE): Jipijapa; tel. (4) 260-0631; e-mail orgcafex@mnb.satnet.net; coffee co-operatives' fed.

Unión Nacional de Periodistas: Joaquín Auxe Iñaquito, Quito; national press asscn.

There are several other coffee and cocoa organizations.

STATE HYDROCARBON COMPANIES

EP PETROECUADOR (Empresa Pública de Hidrocarburos del Ecuador): Alpallana E8-86 y Avda 6 de Diciembre, Casilla 17-11-5007, Quito; tel. (2) 256-3060; fax (2) 250-3571; e-mail rin@petroecuador.com.ec; internet www.eppetroecuador.ec; f. 1989; state petroleum co; Exec. Pres. Rear-Adm. MANUEL E. ZAPATER RAMOS.

Petroindustrial: Alpallana E8-86 y Avda 6 de Diciembre, Casilla 17-11-5007, Quito; tel. (2) 323-8821; fax (2) 323-8822; petroleum-refining; Vice-Pres. Capt. EDMUNDO GEOVANNY LERTORA ARAUJO.

Petroproducción (Empresa Estatal de Exploración y Producción de Petróleos del Ecuador): Avda 6 Diciembre 4226 y Gaspar Cañero, Casilla 17-01-1006, Quito; tel. (2) 244-0333; fax (2) 244-0383; e-mail info@petroproduccion.com.ec; internet www.petroproduccion.com.ec; f. 1989; petroleum and natural gas exploration; Vice-Pres. Capt. CAMILO DELGADO MONTENEGRO; 1,300 employees.

MAJOR COMPANIES

The following are some of the leading industrial and commercial companies currently operating in Ecuador.

Acero Comercial Ecuatoriano, SA: Avda La Prensa, No 45-14 y Telégrafo 1, Quito; tel. (2) 245-4333; fax (2) 245-4455; e-mail infouio@acerocomercial.com; internet www.acerocomercial.com; f. 1957; production of construction materials; Gen. Man. FRANK CAÑADAS; 260 employees.

Compañía Azucarera Váldez, SA: Edif. Executive Center Mezanine 1, Avda Joaquín Orrantia y Avda Juan Tanca Marengo, Guayaquil; tel. (4) 256-3966; fax (4) 256-3248; internet www.azucareravaldez.com; f. 1884; processing and refining of sugar; Gen. Man. RALF SCHNEIDEWIND; 3,100 employees.

Compañía de Cervezas Nacionales, CA: Vía a Daule, Km 16½, Calle Cobre, entre Avda Río Daule y Avda Pascuales, Casilla 519, Guayaquil; tel. (4) 289-3088; fax (4) 289-3263; e-mail cerveceria nacional@ccn.com.ec; internet www.cerveceria nacional.com.ec; f. 1921; subsidiary of SABMiller plc (United Kingdom); brewing; Exec. Pres. ROBERTO JARRÍN; 1,154 employees.

Corporación El Rosado Cía Ltda: Avda 9 de Octubre 729, entre García Aviles y Boyacá, Casilla 0901-534, Guayaquil; tel. (4) 232-2000; fax (4) 232-8196; e-mail luchoweb@elrosado.com; internet www.elrosado.com; f. 1954; retailing; Dir-Gen. JOHNNY CZARNINSKI BAIER; 4,000 employees.

Hidalgo e Hidalgo, SA: Avda Galo Plaza Lasso, No 51-127 y Algarrobos, Quito; tel. (2) 240-8038; fax (2) 240-0541; e-mail hidalgo@hehconstructores.com.ec; internet www.hehconstructores.com.ec; f. 1969; civil engineering; Pres. JUAN FRANCISCO HIDALGO; Gen. Man. JULIO HIDALGO GONZÁLEZ; 1,000 employees.

Holcim Ecuador, SA: Edif. El Caimán, 2°, Avda Barcelona, Urb. San Eduardo I, Casilla 09-01-04243, Guayaquil; tel. (4) 287-1900; fax (4) 287-3482; internet www.holcim.com/ec; f. 1934; manufacture of cement; Gen. Man. CARLOS REPETTO; 864 employees.

Industria Ecuatoriana Productora de Alimentos, CA (INEPACA): Calle Malecón, Casilla 4881, Manta; tel. (5) 262-4584; fax (5) 262-4870; e-mail inepaca@inepaca.net; internet www.inepaca.net; f. 1949; fishing and processing of fish; Pres. Dr EDGAR TERÁN; Gen. Man. CARLOS E. ZÁRATE; 987 employees.

Industrias Ales, CA: Avda Calo Plaza N51–23 y Rua Bustamente, Quito; tel. (2) 240-2600; fax (2) 240-8344; e-mail jmalo@ales.com.ec; internet www.ales.com.ec; f. 1943; manufacture of cooking oils, fats and soap; Gen. Man. JOSE MALO DONOSO.

Lafarge Cementos Selva Alegre, SA: Edif. Banco La Previsora, 4°, Of. 402, Amazonas y Naciones Unidas, Casilla 6663, Quito; tel. (2) 245-9140; fax (2) 225-6091; e-mail compras@csa.com.ec; internet www.csa.com.ec; f. 1979; owned by Lafarge Group (France); manufacture of cement; Pres. FERNANDO SANTOS; Gen. Man. PIERRE DELEPLANQUE; 567 employees.

Lanafit, SA: Avda 6 de Diciembre 41–245 y Tomás de Berlanga, Sector El Inca, Pichincha, Quito; tel. (2) 224-9311; fax (2) 246-7049; e-mail lanafit@textilanafit.com; internet www.textilanafit.com; f. 1953; part of Grupo Dassum; manufacture of clothing from synthetic fibres; Gen. Man. FUAD ALBERTO DASSUM ARMÉNDARIZ; 700 employees.

Sociedad Agrícola e Industrial San Carlos, SA: General Elizalde 114, Guayaquil; tel. (4) 232-1280; fax (4) 253-4133; e-mail xmarcos@gu.pro.ec; f. 1897; agriculture, processing and refining of sugar; Pres. MARIANO GONZÁLEZ; Dir XAVIER MARCOS STAGG; 4,000 employees.

Supermercados La Favorita, CA (SUPERMAXI): Avda Gen. Enriquez s/n, Sangolquí, Quito; tel. (2) 299-6623; fax (2) 299-6617; e-mail favorita@favorita.com; internet www.supermaxi.com; f. 1952; Pres. RONALD WRIGHT DURÁN BALLÉN; Exec. Vice-Pres. EDUARDO DONOSO; 2,475 employees.

Tejidos Pintex, SA: Avda de la Prensa 3741 y Manuel Herrera, Quito; tel. (2) 244-8333; fax (2) 244-8335; e-mail pintex@pintex.com; internet www.pintex.com.ec; f. 1959; manufacture of textiles; Pres. CRISTINA PINTO MANCHENO; Gen. Man. SUSANA PINTO; 420 employees.

Textil San Pedro, SA: Avda Napo y Pedro Pinto Guzmán 709, Apdo 17-01-3002, Quito; tel. (2) 266-0918; fax (2) 266-1596; internet sanpedro.accessinter.net; production of cotton textiles; f. 1948; Gen. Man. PEDRO PINTO.

Universal Sweet Industries, SA: Eloy Alfaro 1103, entre Gómez Rendón y Maldonada, Guayaquil; tel. and fax (4) 241-0222; e-mail mmaspons@launiversal.com.ec; internet www.launiversal.com.ec; f. 1889 as La Universal (ceased trading 2001); relaunched under current name in 2005; manufacture of food products; Pres. MAURICIO AYALA; Gen. Man. CÉSAR AUGUSTO GAVIÑO; 400 employees.

UTILITIES

Regulatory Authorities

Agencia de Control y Regulación Hidrocarburífera (ARCH): Quito; f. 2010; responsible for the regulation and control of the hydrocarbons sector; Dir CARLOS LOOR.

Centro Nacional de Control de Energía (CENACE): Panamericana Sur Km 17.5, Sector Santa Rosa de Cutuglagua, Casilla 17-21-1991, Quito; tel. (2) 299-2001; fax (2) 299-2031; e-mail pcorporativo@cenace.org.ec; internet www.cenace.org.ec; f. 1999; co-ordinates and oversees national energy system; Exec. Dir GABRIEL ARGÜELLO RÍOS.

Consejo Nacional de Electricidad (CONELEC): Avda Naciones Unidas E7-71 y Avda De Los Shyris, Apdo 17-17-817, Quito; tel. (2) 226-8746; fax (2) 226-8737; e-mail conelec@conelec.gov.ec; internet www.conelec.gov.ec; f. 1999; supervises electricity industry following transfer of assets of the former Instituto Ecuatoriano de Electrificación (INECEL) to the Fondo de Solidaridad; pending privatization as six generating companies, one transmission company and 19 distribution companies; Exec. Dir CLAUDIO OTERO NARVÁEZ.

Secretaría de Hidrocarburos: Ministerio de Recursos Norenovables, Juan León Mera y Orellana, Quito; f. 2010, fmrly known as the Dirección Nacional de Hidrocarburos; part of the Ministry of Non-Renewable Natural Resources; supervision of the enforcement of laws regarding the exploration and devt of petroleum; also responsible for dispute resolution and imposition of sanctions against oil cos failing industry standards; Dir RAMIRO CAZAR.

Electricity

Corporación para la Administración Temporal Eléctrica de Guayaquil (CATEG): Urb. La Garzota, Sector 3, Manzana 47; tel. (4) 224-8006; fax (4) 224-8040; f. 2003 to administer activities of fmr state-owned Empresa Eléctrica del Ecuador (EMELEC); major producer and distributor of electricity, mostly using oil-fired or diesel generating capacity; Admin. OSCAR ARMIJOS GONZÁLEZ-RUBIO.

Empresa Eléctrica Quito, SA (EEQ): Avda 10 de Agosto y Las Casas, Casilla 17-01-473, Quito; tel. (2) 396-4700; fax (2) 250-3817; e-mail asoeeq@eeq.com.ec; internet www.eeq.com.ec; f. 1955; produces electricity for the region around Quito, mostly from hydroelectric plants; Gen. Man. CARLOS ANDRADE FAINI.

Empresa Eléctrica Regional El Oro, SA (EMELORO): Dir Arízaga 1810 y Santa Rosa, esq. Machala, El Oro; tel. (7) 293-0500; e-mail emeloro@emeloro.gov.ec; internet www.emeloro.gov.ec; electricity production and generation in El Oro province; Chair. GONZALO QUINTANA GALVEZ; Exec. Pres. WASHINGTON MORENO BENITEZ.

Empresa Eléctrica Regional del Sur, SA (EERSSA): internet www.eerssa.com; f. 1973; electricity production and generation in Loja and Zamora Chinchipe provinces; Exec. Pres. WILSON VIVANCO ARIAS.

Empresa Eléctrica Riobamba, SA: Larrea 2260 y Primera Constituyente, Riobamba; tel. (3) 296-0283; fax (3) 296-5257; e-mail e-mail@eersa.com.ec; internet www.eersa.com.ec/eersa.php; state-owned utility; Pres. MARIANO CURICAMA; Gen. Man. JOE RUALES.

Water

Instituto Ecuatoriano de Obras Sanitarias: Toledo 684 y Lérida, Troncal, Quito; tel. (2) 252-2738.

TRADE UNIONS

Frente Unitario de los Trabajadores (FUT): f. 1971; left-wing; 300,000 mems; Pres. JAIME ARCINIEGA AGUIRRE; comprises:

Confederación Ecuatoriana de Organizaciones Clasistas Unitarias de Trabajo (CEDOCUT): Edif. Cedocut 5°, Flores 846 y Manabí, Quito; tel. (2) 295-4551; fax 295-4013; e-mail presicdocut@cedocut.org; internet www.cedocut.org; f. 1938; humanist; Pres. MESÍAS TATAMUEZ MORENO; Vice-Pres. FANNY POZO LITARDO; 1,065 mem. orgs, 86,416 individual mems.

Confederación Ecuatoriana de Organizaciones Sindicales Libres (CEOSL): Avda Tarqui 15-26, 6°, Casilla 17-11-373, Quito; tel. (2) 252-2511; fax (2) 250-0836; e-mail presidencia@ceosl.net; internet ceosl.net; f. 1962; Pres. EDUARDO VALDEZ CUÑAS; dissident leadership (internet ceosl.wordpress.com, Pres. JAIME ARCINIEGA AGUIRRE) emerged in July 2007; 110,000 mems (2007).

Confederación de Trabajadores del Ecuador (CTE) (Confederation of Ecuadorean Workers): 9 de Octubre 26106 y Marieta de Veintimilla, Casilla 17-014166, Quito; tel. (2) 252-0456; fax (2) 252-0445; e-mail presidencia@cte-ecuador.org; internet www.cte-ecuador.org; f. 1944; Pres. SANTIAGO YAGUAL YAGUAL; Vice-Pres. EDGAR SARANGO CORREA.

Central Católica de Obreros: Avda 24 de Mayo 344, Quito; tel. (2) 221-3704; f. 1906; craft and manual workers, and intellectuals; Pres. CARLOS E. DÁVILA ZURITA.

A number of trade unions are not affiliated to the above groups. These include the Federación Nacional de Trabajadores Marítimos y Portuarios del Ecuador (FNTMPE—National Federation of Maritime and Port Workers of Ecuador) and both railway trade unions.

Transport

RAILWAYS

All railways are government controlled. In 2000 the total length of track was 956 km. A programme of rehabilitation of disused lines was begun in 2008.

Empresa de Ferrocarriles Ecuatorianos (EFE): Calle Bolívar 443 y García Moreno, Quito; tel. (2) 295-3034; internet www.efe.gov.ec; Pres. DORIS SOLÍS CARRIÓN (Co-ordinating Minister for Cultural and Natural Heritage); Gen. Man. JORGE EDUARDO CARRERA SÁNCHEZ.

There are divisional state railway managements for the following lines: Guayaquil–Quito, Sibambe–Cuenca and Quito–San Lorenzo.

ROADS

There were 43,197 km of roads in 2004, of which 15.0% were paved. The Pan-American Highway runs north from Ambato to Quito and to the Colombian border at Tulcán, and south to Cuenca and Loja.

SHIPPING

Port Authorities

Autoridad Portuaria de Esmeraldas: Avda Jaime Roldós Aguilera (Recinto Portuario), Esmeraldas; tel. (6) 272-1352; fax (6) 272-1354; e-mail sugerencias@puertoesmeraldas.gov.ec; internet www.puertoesmeraldas.gov.ec; f. 1970; 25-year operating concession awarded to private consortium in 2004; renationalized in 2010; Gen. Man. RAFAEL PLAZA PERDOMO.

Autoridad Portuaria de Guayaquil: Avda 25 de Julio, Vía Puerto Marítimo, Guayaquil; tel. (4) 248-0120; fax (4) 248-4728; internet www.apg.gov.ec; f. 1958; Pres. FRANCISCO ALEMÁN VARGAS; Gen. Man. VICENTE PIGNATARO ECHANIQUE.

Autoridad Portuaria de Manta: Avda Malecón s/n, Manta; tel. (5) 262-7161; fax (5) 262-1861; e-mail gerente@apm.gov.ec; internet www.apmanta.gov.ec; Pres. ROBERTO SALAZAR BRACCO.

Autoridad Portuaria de Puerto Bolívar: Avda Bolívar Madero Vargas, Puerto Bolívar; tel. (7) 292-9999; e-mail appb@eo.pro.ec; internet www.appb.gov.ec; f. 1970; Pres. MONTGOMERY SÁNCHEZ REYES; Gen. Man. JOSÉ ZAMBRANO.

Principal Shipping Companies

Ecuanave, CA: Junín 415 y Córdova, 4°, Casilla 09-01-30H, Guayaquil; tel. (4) 229-3808; fax (4) 228-9257; e-mail ecuanav@ecua.net.ec; Chair. P. ERNESTO ESCOBAR; Man. Dir A. GUILLERMO SERRANO.

Flota Bananera Ecuatoriana, SA: Edif. Gran Pasaje, 9°, Plaza Ycaza 437, Guayaquil; tel. (4) 230-9333; f. 1967; owned by govt and private stockholders; Pres. DIEGO SÁNCHEZ; Gen. Man. JORGE BARRIGA.

Flota Mercante Grancolombiana, SA: Guayaquil; tel. (4) 251-2791; f. 1946 with Colombia and Venezuela; on Venezuela's withdrawal, in 1953, Ecuador's 10% interest was increased to 20%; operates services from Colombia and Ecuador to European, US, Mexican and Canadian ports; Man. Naval Capt. J. ALBERTO SÁNCHEZ.

Flota Petrolera Ecuatoriana (FLOPEC): Edif. FLOPEC, Avda Amazonas 1188 y Cordero, Casilla 535-A, Quito; tel. (2) 255-2100; fax (2) 250-1428; e-mail planificacion@flopec.com.ec; internet www.flopec.com.ec; f. 1972; Gen. Man. Capt. RAÚL SAMANIEGO GRANJA.

Logística Marítima, CA (LOGMAR): Avda Córdova 812 y V. M. Rendón, 1°, Casilla 9622, Guayaquil; tel. (4) 230-7041; Pres. J. COELLOG; Man. IGNACIO RODRÍGUEZ BAQUERIZO.

Naviera del Pacífico, CA (NAPACA): El Oro 101 y La Ría, Casilla 09-01-529, Guayaquil; tel. (4) 234-2055; Pres. LUIS ADOLFO NOBOA NARANJO.

Servicios Oceánicos Internacionales, SA: Avda Domingo Comin y Calle 11, Casilla 79, Guayaquil; Pres. CARLOS VALDANO RAFFO; Man. FERNANDO VALDANO TRUJILLO.

Transfuel, CA: Avda Pedro Menéndez Gilbert s/n, diagonal Hospital Solca, Guayaquil; tel. (4) 229-3808; fax 229-6512; Chair. JORGE JARAMILLO DE LA TORRE, ALFREDO ESCOBAR.

Transportes Navieros Ecuatorianos (Transnave): Edif. Citibank, 4°–7°, Avda 9 de Octubre 416 y Chile, Casilla 4706, Guayaquil; tel. (4) 256-1455; fax (4) 256-6273; transports general cargo within the European South Pacific Magellan Conference, Japan West Coast South America Conference, and Atlantic and Gulf West Coast South America Conference; Pres. Vice-Adm. YÉZID JARAMILLO SANTOS; Gen. Man. RUBÉN LANDÁZURI ZAMBRANO.

CIVIL AVIATION

There are two international airports: Mariscal Sucre, near Quito, and Simón Bolívar, near Guayaquil. A new airport in Quito was scheduled for completion in 2010, while the new José Joaquín de Olmedo airport in Guayaquil opened in August 2006.

LAN Ecuador, SA: Avda de las Américas s/n, Guayaquil; tel. (4) 269-2850; fax (4) 228-5433; internet www.lanecuador.com; f. 2002; commenced operations in April 2003, following acquisition of assets of Ecuatoriana by LAN Chile; scheduled daily flights between Quito, Guayaquil, Miami and New York; Dir BRUNO ARDITO.

TAME Línea Aérea del Ecuador: Avda Amazonas 1354 y Colón, 6°, Casilla 17-07-8736, Sucursal Almagro, Quito; tel. (2) 250-9375; fax (2) 255-4907; e-mail tamejefv@impsat.net.ec; internet www.tame.com.ec; f. 1962; fmrly Transportes Aéreos Mercantiles Ecuatorianos, SA; removed from military control in 1990; state-owned; domestic scheduled and charter services for passengers and freight; Pres. FERNANDO MARTÍNEZ DE LA VEGA.

Tourism

Tourism has become an increasingly important industry in Ecuador, with 937,487 foreign arrivals (including same-day visitors) in 2007. Of total visitors in that year, some 26% were from the USA, 22% came from Colombia and 16% were from Peru. In 2008 receipts from the tourism industry amounted to a provisional US $763m.

Asociación Ecuatoriana de Agencias de Viajes, Operadores de Turismo y Mayoristas (ASECUT): Caldas 340 y Guayaquil, Edif. San Blas, 6°, Ofs 61–62, Quito; tel. (2) 250-0759; fax (2) 250-3669; e-mail asecut@pi.pro.ec; f. 1953; Pres. IRMA UGALDE.

Federación Hotelera del Ecuador (AHOTEC): América 5378 y Diguja, Quito; tel. (2) 244-3425; fax (2) 245-3942; e-mail ahotec@interactive.net.ec; internet www.hotelesecuador.com.ec; Pres. JOSÉ OCHOA; Exec. Dir DIEGO UTRERAS.

Defence

As assessed at November 2009, Ecuador's armed forces numbered 57,983: army 46,500, navy 7,283 (including 2,160 marines and 375 in the naval air force) and air force 4,200. Paramilitary forces included 400 coastguards. Military service lasts for one year and is selective for men at the age of 20.

Defence Budget: US $918m. in 2008.

Chief of the Joint Command of the Armed Forces: Gen. ERNESTO GONZÁLEZ.

Chief of Staff of the Army: PATRICIO CÁRDENAS PROAÑO.

Chief of Staff of the Navy: Rear-Adm. JAVIER MOLESTINA MALTA ALAND.

Chief of Staff of the Air Force: LEONARDO BARREIRO MUÑOZ.

Education

Education in Ecuador is officially compulsory for 10 years, to be undertaken between five and 15 years of age. All public schools are free. Private schools feature prominently in the educational system. Primary education begins at six years of age and lasts for six years. Secondary education, in general and specialized technical or humanities schools, begins at the age of 12 and lasts for up to six years, comprising two equal cycles of three years each. In 2006/07 enrolment at primary schools included 97% of pupils in the relevant age-group, while the comparable ratio for secondary schools in 2007/08, according to UNESCO estimates, was 62%. A 10-year plan to make education universal at primary and secondary levels was begun in 2006. University courses last for up to six years, and include programmes for teacher training. In many rural areas, Quechua and other indigenous Amerindian languages are used in education. Total expenditure on education by the central Government was projected at 3,996,970m. sucres in 2010.

Bibliography

For works on South America generally, see Select Bibliography (Books)

Cruz, H., Castro, A. V., and Arnold, A. *Faith in Service: Developing Credit Unions in Ecuador.* Los Angeles, CA, Writer's Showcase Press, 2001.

Downes, R., and Marcella, G. *Security Cooperation in the Western Hemisphere: Resolving the Ecuador-Peru Conflict*. Boulder, CO, Lynne Rienner Publrs, 1999.

Gerlach, A. *Indians, Oil, and Politics: A Recent History of Ecuador (Latin American Silhouettes)*. Wilmington, DE, Scholarly Resources Inc, 2003.

Herz, M., and João Pontes, N. *Ecuador Vs Peru: Peacemaking Amid Rivalry*. Boulder, CO, Lynne Rienner Publrs, 2002.

Kyle, D. *Transnational Peasants: Migrations, Networks and Ethnicity in Andean Ecuador.* Baltimore, MD, Johns Hopkins University Press, 2000.

Lane, K. *Quito 1599: City and Colony in Transition*. Albuquerque, NM, University of New Mexico Press, 2002.

Lucas, K. *We Will Not Dance on Our Grandparents' Tombs: Indigenous Uprisings in Ecuador*. London, Latin America Bureau, 2000.

Pallares, A. *From Peasant Struggles to Indian Resistance: The Ecuadorian Andes in the Late Twentieth Century.* Norman, OK, University of Oklahoma Press, 2002.

Rival, L. *Trekking Through History: The Huaorani of Amazonian Ecuador*. New York, Columbia University Press, 2002.

Sawyer, S. *Crude Chronicles: Indigenous Politics, Multinational Oil, and Neoliberalism in Ecuador*. Durham, NC, Duke University Press, 2004.

Selverston-Scher, M. *Ethnopolitics in Ecuador: Indigenous Rights and the Strengthening of Democracy.* Boulder, CO, Lynne Rienner Publrs, 2001.

Solimano, A., and Beckerman, P. *Crisis and Dollarization in Ecuador: Stability, Growth, and Social Equity (Directions in Development)*. Washington, DC, World Bank, 2002.

Striffler, S. *In the Shadows of State and Capital: The United Fruit Company, Popular Struggle, and Agrarian Restructuring in Ecuador, 1900–1995.* Durham, NC, Duke University Press, 2002.

Whitten, N. (Ed.). *Millennial Ecuador: Critical Essays on Cultural Transformations and Social Dynamics*. Iowa City, IA, University of Iowa Press, 2003.

EL SALVADOR

Geography

PHYSICAL FEATURES

The Republic of El Salvador is the smallest country in Central America and the only one without a Caribbean shore. It lies on the western or Pacific side of the Central American land bridge, but itself has a southern coast. Guatemala lies to the west, further up the isthmus, beyond a 203-km (126-mile) border. Honduras is to the north and east—a definitive border demarcation, along the 342 km of frontier, was only agreed in 1992, when an International Court of Justice (ICJ) decision was accepted, although the demarcation was not ratified by both countries until 2006. The ICJ referred the issue of the maritime boundary in the Gulf of Fonseca (a line was agreed in 1990 by the Honduras–Nicaragua Mixed Boundary Commission) to tripartite discussion—Nicaragua lies beyond the Gulf, in the south-east. The dispute in the Gulf is also complicated by the Salvadorean claim to the island of Conejo, currently held by Honduras. The country has a total area of 21,041 sq km (8,124 sq miles).

El Salvador is about 260 km in length (east–west) and 140 km wide, with 307 km of coast along the Pacific Ocean. It is a land of volcanoes, and is prone to sometimes devastating earthquakes. This can make the terrain unstable and dangerous, but has also given the country rich volcanic soil suitable for growing coffee, the basis of the Salvadorean economy. The uplands consist of a double row of volcanoes and mountains, the roughly parallel and east–west coastal chain and the further inland Cordillera Apeneca, which reach their highest point in the north-west, at Cerro El Pital (2,730 m or 8,960 ft). There is also a central plateau and, beneath the highlands, falling fairly steeply into the Pacific, is a narrow coastal plain. The three main topographical areas are, therefore: a flat, tropical region in the south, some of it wetlands; the central plateau of mountains, valleys and volcanoes; and the northern lowlands formed by the valleys of the Lempa river and the Sierra Madre. In all there are 150, usually fast-flowing, rivers and three lakes. The terrain still sustains much biological diversity, despite the pressures of the densely settled human population, with, for instance, more species of trees than in all of Western Europe. There are reckoned to be large numbers of species of plants (notably orchids), butterflies, birds and fish, but, nevertheless, there are fewer than in any other Central American country. Woodland covers 17% of El Salvador (only 3% of the country remains with its natural primary forest), most of it secondary forest and scrubland, but there is an additional 9% of territory planted with coffee bushes, which are also provided with trees for shade. El Salvador has the highest rate of deforestation (just over 3% per year) and the least amount of territory protected by national parks (0.5%) in Central America.

CLIMATE

The climate is tropical, but more temperate in the high country. The rainy season is over the summer, in May–October, the wettest month in San Salvador, the inland capital, being June. Rainfall is generally heavier on the coast, however, while the interior remains relatively dry. The average annual rainfall for the whole country is almost 1,800 mm (70 ins). Temperatures in the wet season average about 28°C (82°F), whereas in the cooler dry season they range between 15°C and 23°C (59°–73°F). Greater altitude, of course, moderates these temperatures. The country is susceptible to hurricanes from the Caribbean, as well as to the vagaries of the El Niño weather phenomenon.

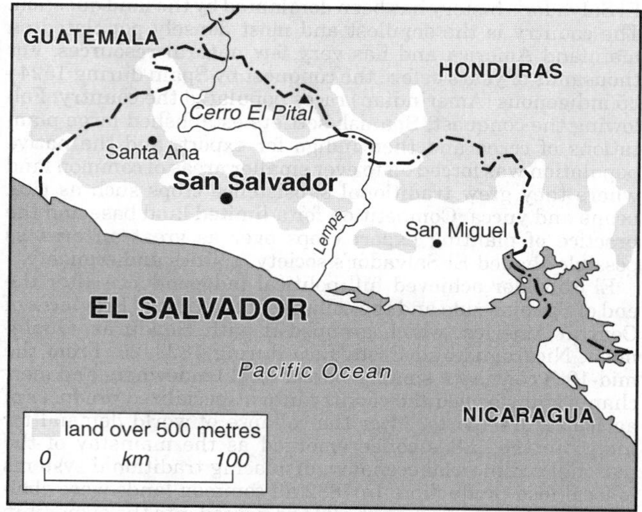

POPULATION

The population is predominantly Mestizo, of mixed-race descent (90%), the rest of the population consisting of those of European stock and of indigenous Amerindians (the latter consisting mainly of the Pipil, descendants of the Aztecs, and the Lenca). A number of nationalities have settled in El Salvador over the years, but nearly all of today's population is of Spanish descent. For this reason it is no surprise to find that around 76% of the country adheres to the Roman Catholic Church, although, as elsewhere in Latin America, evangelical Protestant groups have been very active and have made significant numbers of converts. The official language, and that used by nearly the entire population, is Spanish. Some speak Amerindian tongues, notably Nahua (Pipil). Informally, the people of El Salvador are sometimes known as Guanacos.

The total population was estimated at 6.2m. at mid-2009, about two-fifths of whom live in rural areas and one-third in and around the greater metropolitan area of the capital, San Salvador, which is located in the highlands immediately above the western end of the coastal plains. There are a number of other large urban centres, but probably the two most eminent cities are Santa Ana, to the north-west of the capital, and San Miguel, in the south-east of El Salvador. Although it is the smallest country of Central America, El Salvador is the most densely populated country on the American mainland (292.4 people per sq km at mid-2009). For administrative purposes, the country is divided into 14 departments.

History

DIEGO SÁNCHEZ-ANCOCHEA

Revised for this edition by the editorial staff

El Salvador's history has been dominated by the land question. The country is the smallest and most densely populated on mainland America and has very few natural resources. For thousands of years before the conquest by Spain during 1524–35 indigenous (Amerindian) races populated the country. Following the conquest, Spanish settlers established large plantations of cocoa and then indigo for export, and the native population was forced on to ever smaller areas of common land where they grew traditional subsistence crops such as rice, beans and yucca. Competition for a limited land base and the practice of planting export crops over as great an area as possible shaped El Salvador's society, politics and economy.

El Salvador achieved full political independence after the end of Spanish rule and the collapse of the United Provinces of Central America, which grouped it with Honduras, Guatemala, Nicaragua and Costa Rica during 1823–29. From the mid-19th century a small group of local landowners and merchants transformed the country into a specialized producer of agricultural exports. After the collapse of world demand for indigo in the 1860s coffee emerged as the mainstay of the national commercial economy, displacing traditional systems of local food production. In 1882 all common lands were abolished and three-quarters of all land passed into the ownership of families comprising only about 2% of El Salvador's inhabitants. The majority of the population, displaced from their traditional lands, became permanent wage labourers on the new plantations or migratory seasonal workers.

In contrast to other Central American countries, the agro-export economy of El Salvador was created by domestic, not foreign, capital and expertise. The economy was dominated by an interlocked élite of landowners and merchants (known as the 'Fourteen Families'), who controlled the state, land, capital and markets. The formal democratic procedures of a constitutional republic were maintained, but governments were effectively appointed by the oligarchy to administer power in its own interests.

MILITARY DOMINATION OF GOVERNMENT, 1932–82

The events of 1931–32 challenged the basis of this power structure. In 1931, against a background of national and international economic depression, relatively fair elections brought to office a reformist President, Arturo Araújo. The existence of widespread popular discontent and allegations that the Partido Comunista Salvadoreño (PCS—Salvadorean Communist Party), recently established under the leadership of Agustín Farabundo Martí, was promoting armed insurrection, provoked a conservative reaction. Araújo was deposed by a military coup in December 1931 and replaced by Gen. Maximiliano Hernández Martínez. A large-scale peasant uprising in January 1932 was violently suppressed; 10,000–30,000 people, among them many Amerindians, were killed in reprisals known as *la matanza* (the massacre). Farabundo Martí was arrested and executed. The landowning élite, shaken by these perceived threats to its economic interest, abdicated its control of political power to the army that had saved it.

For the next 50 years the relationship between the armed forces and the civilian oligarchy remained the central reality of the nation's power structure: the former guaranteed the privileges of the latter, while simultaneously promoting their own interests by establishing military rule as an institution. Shifts between 'conservative' and 'progressive' factions within the military led to a pattern of reform and repression. When abuses of presidential power threatened to provoke popular discontent, incumbent Presidents were removed by military coup: Gen. Hernández Martínez in 1944, Lt-Col José María Lemus in 1960 and Gen. Carlos Humberto Romero Mena in 1979. When reformist administrations were considered to be too radical, they were removed by counter-coup, as in the overthrow of the military-civilian juntas of 1944 and 1960.

The economy continued to develop after 1945. A second period of export-led agricultural growth (based mainly on sugar, cotton and cattle) was accompanied by some industrialization. The latter was as a result of the creation of the Central American Common Market (CACM), which increased market size. As in the past, this development was achieved primarily by Salvadorean capital and entrepreneurs, but the benefits accrued to a minority while the needs of the majority continued to be denied. It also benefited food processors and exporters more than producers. This created a new, more progressive class in the oligarchy that was not so dependent on land and bonded labour as the traditional coffee growers.

Between 1961 and 1979 the military leadership attempted to present its own party, the Partido de Conciliación Nacional (PCN—Party of National Conciliation), as the country's unifying force. Other parties were tolerated, but repeated electoral manipulation ensured that PCN candidates—Lt-Col Julio Adalberto Rivera, Gen. Fidel Sánchez Hernández, Col Arturo Armando Molina Barraza and Gen. Romero—gained the presidency, and so retained power in the hands of the army. From 1960 the Partido Demócrata Cristiano (PDC—Christian Democratic Party), under the leadership of José Napoleón Duarte, consistently attracted the largest electoral support for any opposition party and steadily grew in strength.

In July 1969 a 13-day war with Honduras killed 2,000 people. The catalyst for the so-called 'football war' was a disputed decision in the third qualifying round of the football (soccer) World Cup, although the roots of the conflict were territorial disputes and migration pressures. Some 300,000 Salvadoreans had emigrated to Honduras to farm. Honduras decided to expel them as it pressed a boundary claim. The frontier dispute was settled in September 1972 when Honduras was awarded two-thirds of the disputed land by international arbitration.

The return of the emigrants, now refugees, put more pressure on El Salvador's land. The number of landless peasants grew from 30,500 in 1961 (12% of the rural population) to 167,000 in 1975 (41% of the rural population). This combined with an economic depression, caused partly by the 1973 oil shock and its global consequences and partly by the loss of the Honduran market, to put heavy pressure on the regime. In the 1972 presidential election the opposition parties united behind Duarte, but Col Molina unilaterally declared victory. Subsequent protests and an attempted coup were crushed and Duarte exiled. These events not only frustrated the hopes of fundamental reform by democratic means, but also convinced many opponents of military rule that armed insurrection was inevitable.

In 1970 Cayetano Carpio, Secretary-General of the PCS, broke from the party to pursue a campaign of armed insurrection. His lead was followed by a number of distinct guerrilla groups on the extreme left, and in Cuba in 1980 they co-ordinated to form the Frente Farabundo Martí para la Liberación Nacional (FMLN—Farabundo Martí National Liberation Front). The FMLN also established a political wing, the Frente Democrático Revolucionario (FDR—Democratic Revolutionary Front). Reforming politicians, previously strongly opposed to armed struggle, began to support the FMLN as the only available option for the pursuit of democratic change. The Roman Catholic Church, which had been a supporter of the conservative regime, also became more identified with the opposition after the Medellín council of bishops in 1968 appealed for it to transform the lives of the poor and overcome injustice.

Gen. Romero's victory in the presidential election of 1977 followed a campaign characterized by intimidation, fraud and violent suppression of subsequent public protests. Alarmed by the implications of the overthrow of the dictatorship of Gen. Anastasio Somoza Debayle in Nicaragua in July 1979, the military ousted President Romero in October. After a series of abortive civilian-military juntas, Duarte agreed to lead a provisional government, on the condition that fundamental reforms be introduced immediately and be guaranteed by the military and by the USA.

Duarte joined the junta in March 1980. In the same month the Government, assisted by the USA, expropriated one-quarter of all agricultural land, for conversion into peasant co-operatives, and nationalized the banks and major export institutions. This was the first stage of the most important change in the nation's economy since the abolition of common lands a century before. However, civil war was already imminent. Army and 'death squad' human rights abuses were such that the population had little faith in the Government. At the end of March Oscar Romero, Archbishop of San Salvador, whose Sunday homilies had regularly expressed support for the cause of the poor and oppressed, was assassinated in the act of celebrating Mass. At his funeral, without provocation, soldiers fired into the crowd of mourners, which numbered more than 250,000. The Government was also under pressure from the left, which, as in 1932, favoured revolution over reform.

THE CIVIL WAR

The Effects of the War

In January 1981 the FMLN launched its 'Final Offensive', intended to achieve victory before the inauguration of President Ronald Reagan of the USA. It failed, and the civil war continued at an increasing cost in human suffering and economic disruption. By 1992 more than 80,000 combatants and civilians had been killed, the vast majority by the armed forces; an estimated 550,000 (more than 10% of the population) had been displaced from their homes, while in excess of 500,000 had fled the country as refugees. There was military stalemate. The army, relying heavily on US support, was increased in size to 55,000 military and 15,000 paramilitary personnel. However, it was ill-led and relied on a strategy of sporadic infantry attacks, supported by aerial bombings across extensive 'free-fire' zones, thus alienating the civilian population. The FMLN relied on well co-ordinated, dispersed ambush attacks, urban terrorism and economic sabotage, such as the destruction of power lines and crops and the mining of public highways, all of which increased the war's impact on civilians.

The economic cost of the conflict was so high that the collapse of the economy was only averted by direct US economic assistance. One-half of government budgets were committed to defence spending. Reduced export earnings and increased government deficits by 1987 resulted in servicing of the public sector external debt exceeding 50% of annual export income. Unemployment and underemployment affected more than one-half of the adult population and per-head income decreased to levels of the 1960s. The crisis was exacerbated by two natural disasters: the 1986 earthquake that killed 1,500 people and the subsequent drought.

Elections for a constituent assembly in March 1982 divided power between the PDC and two major right-wing parties—the PCN and the Alianza Republicana Nacionalista (ARENA—Nationalist Republican Alliance), founded in 1981. In 1982 Alvaro Magaña Borja, a politically independent banker, was accepted by all parties as interim President. Under his guidance, in 1983 the major parties agreed to a new Constitution. This provided for a democratic political process and incorporated the essential principles of economic reform.

In May 1984 Duarte won the presidency in a direct electoral contest with the ARENA candidate, Maj. Roberto D'Aubuisson Arrieta. Elections in March 1985 gave the PDC an absolute majority in the Asamblea Legislativa (Legislative Assembly). However, Duarte failed to make progress towards a negotiated settlement of the war or social and economic reforms. In the 1988 election ARENA won control of the Asamblea Legislativa and in 1989 its candidate, Alfredo Cristiani Burkard, was elected President.

Progress Towards Peace

Formal and informal contacts between the Government and the FDR-FMLN began as early as 1980. Each attempt at a negotiated peace, however, foundered on two key issues: the future role, control and structure of the military; and the integration of the FDR-FMLN into national political life. Despite his position as Commander-in-Chief of the Armed Forces, President Duarte did not control them and so could not guarantee the FDR-FMLN's conditions. His failure to do so was demonstrated by the terror tactics of the extreme right-wing death squads, which, aided by his senior officers, were responsible for the assassination of church leaders, trade unionists and political activists.

The FDR-FMLN also considered each of the six elections held between 1982 and 1989 as invalid. On each occasion the guerrillas disrupted balloting. From 1989 the FDR leaders accepted that there had been sufficient improvement in electoral conditions to allow them openly to participate in the election, as the Convergencia Democrática (CD—Democratic Convergence), but not until 1991 did one of its five constituent parties contest national elections.

The victory of ARENA in the elections of 1989 and 1991 caused widespread expectation that the conflict would escalate. Many of its senior members were openly committed to a military solution and there was a common belief that some party leaders, such as Roberto D'Aubuisson, were involved in the death squads. After President Cristiani's assumption of power in April 1989, the FMLN launched limited, but effective, offensives in May and June, accompanied by direct attacks against the ARENA leadership, notably the assassination of the Attorney-General in April and the Minister of the Presidency in July. The reaction of the right-wing extremists, orchestrated by groups within ARENA and the military, involved the assassination of trade union leaders and suspected FMLN sympathizers. FMLN–ARENA negotiations in September collapsed almost immediately and were followed by an FMLN nation-wide offensive in November, which posed the most formidable challenge to the Government in 10 years of civil war. The FMLN gained temporary occupation of large areas of the capital. These successes provoked major reactions by right-wing extremists: the assassination of six Jesuit priests; the less-remarked killings of alleged FDR-FMLN sympathizers; and intimidation of church and human rights groups and of left-wing politicians. In April 1990, however, representatives of the Government and the FDR-FMLN met in Geneva, Switzerland, under the chairmanship of the UN Secretary-General. Following a series of difficult negotiations a comprehensive agreement was reached by 31 December 1991, leading to a cease-fire on 1 February 1992.

The cease-fire was brought about by both domestic and international factors. The end of the cold war in 1989 ended US–Soviet confrontation in Central America, and this allowed a regional solution by reviving the Esquípulas Accord, proposed by Costa Rica and endorsed by Central American Presidents in 1987. The Accord committed all five countries to adopting specific measures to achieve regional peace. These measures included: dialogue between Governments and insurgent groups; commitments to democratic and pluralistic political systems; and cessation of support for insurgent groups from whatever source. The end of the cold war also allowed the UN to become actively involved in the task of conflict resolution in El Salvador: first, by sponsorship of negotiations; second, by the establishment of a resident UN Observer Mission in El Salvador (ONUSAL), to verify compliance with negotiated agreements. Finally, within El Salvador, the Government, and especially the military, came under intense US pressure to reach a settlement. The ARENA leadership was dominated by export and consumer-orientated business and financial interests who needed peace to continue to flourish, while the FMLN, appreciating its increasing international and regional isolation, accepted the need for a peace agreement.

This settlement was achieved in the UN-brokered agreement, announced in December 1991, and signed at Chapultepec castle in Mexico City on 16 January 1992. The Chapultepec Accords provided a framework for the reconstruction of Salvadorean society, focusing on the demilitarization and submission of the country to civilian control under the rule of law. On 1 February the formal cease-fire was implemented under the supervision of some 1,000 UN personnel, and the National Commission for the Consolidation of Peace (COPAZ) was formally installed with representatives from government and guerrilla forces and all major political parties.

As well as the immediate measures for the disengagement and demobilization of FMLN guerrillas, and the reform and reduction of the Salvadorean military, the Accords established a range of new civilian institutions and programmes and included the participation of former FMLN members in a new national civilian police force (Policía Nacional Civil—PNC), which replaced the paramilitary national police. A new National Council for the Defence of Human Rights was to be supported by an independent National Judiciary Council. A Land Transfer Programme for demobilized combatants and displaced civilians envisaged the transfer of some 10% of El Salvador's agricultural land to a total beneficiary population of about 47,500 people.

Initial progress was made possible by a widespread desire for reconciliation and a willingness to seek *concertación*, or consensus. However, mutual allegations of failure to comply with the terms of the Accords persisted throughout 1992 and resulted in the negotiation of a revised timetable for disarmament. Nevertheless, the cease-fire was observed by both sides and, on 15 December (declared National Reconciliation Day), the conflict was formally concluded. On the same day the FMLN was officially registered and recognized as a legitimate political party.

POST-ACCORD POLITICS

Expectations over the Chapultepec Accords were only partially fulfilled. In November 1992 the Comisión de la Verdad (Truth Commission) released the names of 103 military personnel alleged to have participated in human rights abuses in the civil war. The Government, however, was at first reluctant to remove from the armed forces those personnel identified by the Commission. The FMLN was prompted to delay the demobilization of its forces. The effective operation of the new civilian police was constrained by a lack of resources. A dramatic decline in political violence and human rights violations was accompanied by increasing criminal violence. The independence and security of the judiciary, reformed on the recommendations of the Commission's report, had not yet been tested. In late 1993, following international pressure, the military personnel identified by the Commission were dismissed.

These issues posed the principal themes in the campaign leading to national elections on 20 March 1994, monitored by ONUSAL. In spite of problems in the organization of the elections, the people of El Salvador were provided with their first opportunity to express their political preferences in elections that were peaceful as well as free and fair. The three major contending parties were ARENA, the PDC and the FMLN, which in September 1993 had confirmed its political alliance with the CD, and later, in December, with the Movimiento Nacional Revolucionario (MNR—National Revolutionary Movement). Following a second-round run-off contest on 24 April, Armando Calderón Sol, the ARENA candidate, was elected President. He took office on 1 June.

Despite its success, serious divisions emerged within the FMLN in 1994. In December two factions, the Resistencia Nacional (RN—National Resistance) and the Expresión Renovadora del Pueblo (ERP—Renewed Expression of the People), left the FMLN because of a difference in political interests. In March 1995 Joaquín Villalobos, the ERP Secretary-General, announced the formation of the Partido Demócrata (PD—Democrat Party), a centre-left grouping consisting of the ERP, the RN, the MNR and a dissident faction of the PDC. The PD co-operated with the ruling ARENA party initially, but later withdrew in protest at the coalition's neo-liberal policies.

Meanwhile, there was increasing dissatisfaction with the Government's failure to honour the terms of the Chapultepec Accords. Former soldiers alleged that they had not received financial compensation and other benefits promised in the 1992 agreement. In September 1994 retired soldiers occupied the parliament building and held a number of deputies hostage. The Government immediately pledged to enter into direct negotiations with the soldiers, and the siege ended peacefully. However, in January 1995 former soldiers again occupied the Asamblea Legislativa and took a number of hostages. Once again the occupation ended swiftly and bloodlessly as the Government reiterated its promise to meet its obligations. However, the spectre of renewed armed conflict remained.

A reduced ONUSAL contingent, known as MINUSAL, remained in El Salvador until the end of 1996. In March 1997, contrary to expectation, the ruling ARENA party lost seats to the FMLN in municipal and legislative elections. The FMLN also experienced a significant increase in support in the capital. However, the party was deeply divided and unable to present a coherent alternative to ARENA nationally. In the presidential elections, held on 7 March 1999, Francisco Flores Pérez, the ARENA candidate, was elected President. The election was characterized by an abstention rate of over 60% of registered voters.

Although in many respects the peace process in El Salvador had opened the country's political arena to wider participation, and judicial and political reforms were planned, most of the population remained too overwhelmed by the daily struggle for economic survival to feel that politics had any relevance to their lives. The neo-liberal reforms adopted from the beginning of the 1990s had delivered neither high rates of growth nor a substantial improvement in the living standards of a majority of the population. Moreover, the levels of criminality in the country were of greater importance to the people than the electoral contest. The number of violent deaths in El Salvador was higher after than during the civil war.

THE FLORES AND SACA ADMINISTRATIONS, 1999–2009

The right-wing ARENA dominated Salvadorean politics during most of the first decade of the 21st century. Although the FMLN was the largest single party in the Asamblea Legislativa in some years, control of the presidency and the creation of coalitions with other right-wing parties allowed ARENA to advance its socio-economic agenda.

The presidency of Francisco Flores was dominated by dollarization and by the response to natural disasters and growing security concerns. In November 2000 Flores unexpectedly announced that, from 1 January 2001, the US dollar would be introduced as an official currency alongside the colón, anchored to the colón at a fixed rate of exchange. The intention was to stabilize the economy, lower interest rates and encourage domestic and foreign investment.

Two severe earthquakes struck El Salvador in January and February 2001, presenting the country with its most serious test since the civil war. More than 1,100 people were killed and damage was estimated at US $1,900m., representing 14% of gross domestic product (GDP) for that year. Around 1.5m. people (one-quarter of the population) were made homeless. The Government initially was overwhelmed; however, international and domestic criticism prompted President Flores to devolve much responsibility to the municipalities. Society grew closer through the national recovery effort and the efficient response of the police and army, which grew in popularity. In March the US immigration authorities granted a one-year protected status to Salvadorean illegal immigrants residing in the USA, releasing those held in custody. This was subsequently extended a number of times until September 2010.

The FMLN did unexpectedly well in regional and congressional elections held in March 2003 and won 31 seats in the Asamblea Legislativa, compared with ARENA's 27. However, ARENA renewed its alliance with the PCN, and Flores announced aggressive policies to reduce insecurity. He introduced the *Mano Dura* (Firm Hand) policy, imposing strict penalties on anyone convicted of being a member of a street gang, blamed by Salvadoreans for the rampant crime rate in the country. However, the law was ruled unconstitutional by the Supreme Court, and judges and lawyers generally declined to take on cases brought under it.

The presidential elections of March 2004 pitted two sharply differing candidates against each other. The FMLN selected Schafik Jorge Handal, a 72-year-old committed Marxist and former guerrilla leader, as its candidate. In contrast, ARENA's candidate, Elias Antonio (Tony) Saca, was a 39-year-old media entrepreneur of middle-class origins. His selection confirmed ARENA's transformation from a party of the old, coffee-producing élite to one dominated by businessmen from services such as banking and retailing. Saca won 57.7% of the vote against 35.7% for Handal. The turn-out was a record high of 66.2% as the public was galvanized by the fierce campaign.

After his election, Saca announced plans to reduce unemployment, poverty and violence. Despite improving economic conditions, the results were mixed on all fronts. During January–November 2006 some 3,609 people were killed in the country—more than 10 a day. The Government responded by introducing legislation to combat organized crime, by selecting members for the National Commission for Public Security and Social Peace and by creating a new Ministry of Justice and Public Security. In 2007 there was a 13% reduction in violent crime, although there were still an average of nine murders per day, a higher number than at the beginning of the term (when there were six or seven). Despite higher rates of economic growth than in previous years, the popularity of the Saca administration declined steadily. High levels of inequality and social polarization and insufficient expansion of social programmes contributed to public dissatisfaction.

Despite these problems, the opposition FMLN was not able to benefit from Saca's ineffective Government, and in the legislative and municipal elections of March 2006 ARENA increased its representation in the Asamblea Legislativa from 27 deputies to 34, and its number of mayors from 111 to 147 (56% of the total in the country). The FMLN succeeded in retaining control of San Salvador's mayoralty, but by only 44 votes. ARENA's new majority, however, did not help Saca to become more successful, and low social spending, mediocre economic performance and high insecurity remained as the main problems of his administration. Moreover, the murder rate remained one of the highest in Latin America.

THE HISTORIC ELECTIONS OF 2009

Saca's relative ineffectiveness in addition to deteriorating global economic conditions contributed to the results of the legislative and presidential elections of January and March 2009, respectively. In the legislative elections, held on 18 January, the FMLN became the largest party in the Asamblea Legislativa with 35 out of 84 deputies, followed by ARENA with 32 and the PCN with 11. In the concurrent municipal elections, ARENA lost 27 mayoralties compared to its performance in 2006, while the FMLN gained 35 (although it lost the capital).

The presidential election on 15 March 2009 was contested by Mauricio Funes Cartagena of the FMLN and Rodrigo Avila of ARENA. A popular journalist with a moderate discourse, Funes helped to modernize and revive the FMLN. Avila, the former Director-General of the Police, was seen by many to be an uninspiring candidate. Despite a tense campaign and some concern about electoral fraud, the elections were relatively peaceful and the results historic. For the first time since the 1992 Chapultepec Accords, the candidate from the left-wing, ex-guerrilla movement FMLN won (with 51.3% of the vote, compared with 48.7% for his opponent). The extraordinary result was expected to open a new era in Salvadorean politics and to herald fresh progress towards the consolidation of democracy.

However, upon taking office on 1 June 2009 Funes was immediately confronted with a hostile legislature. ARENA, the PCN and the PDC had formed an opposition coalition with a combined majority over the FMLN in the Asamblea, allowing the right-wing parties to block Funes' proposed legislation. As an early demonstration of this obstructive power, in July the new President was forced to compromise over the composition of the Supreme Court and the appointment of the Procurator-General, which preserved ARENA's domination of the judiciary, thereby undermining Funes' pledge to prosecute members of the previous administration for corruption. However, in a dramatic manifestation of the growing disharmony within ARENA, in October 12 deputies announced their withdrawal from the party and formed a new legislative bloc, the Gran Alianza por la Unidad Nacional (GANA). The loss of the right-wing coalition's majority in the legislature prompted vicious infighting within ARENA. In the following month GANA, the PCN and the PDC voted with the FMLN to approve Funes' budget, which allocated additional funding for health and education, leaving ARENA politically isolated. Moreover, a fiscal reform bill, approved with the help of the GANA deputies in December, was viewed as a significant victory for Funes. Continuing discord within ARENA, led to the expulsion of former President Saca by party officials who blamed him for 'instigating the defection of the 12 ARENA deputies' and for selecting the lacklustre Avila as ARENA's unsuccessful candidate in the presidential election.

Tensions within the FMLN also became apparent during 2009 with Vice-President Salvador Sánchez Cerén making a number of public statements that appeared to depart from Funes's moderate, left-leaning, but business-friendly agenda. His pronouncements embarrassed Funes and revealed that the party was still dominated by a more radical core of activists. The divisions were highlighted in January 2010 by the adoption by the Asamblea Legislativa of populist, FMLN-led legislation that removed telephone tariffs, undermining the President's efforts to develop a business environment attractive to investors. By mid-2010 it was reported that Funes's relationship with the FMLN had deteriorated to such an extent that he was regularly co-operating with right-wing groups in order to pass legislation. In a further attempt to demonstrate his distinctiveness from the core of the FMLN Funes launched an informal grouping, the Citizens' Movement for Change, in mid-2010.

President Funes declared a state of emergency in November 2009 after flooding and mudslides, concentrated mainly in San Salvador and the surrounding area, caused by Hurricane Ida left some 200 dead and over 10,000 destitute. Transportation infrastructure and agriculture were also badly affected, and the cost of the recovery operation was estimated at US $350m. Funes criticized the previous ARENA Government for failing to put into place appropriate flood-prevention measures.

The legacy of violence committed during the civil war (1980–92) continued to influence the political life of the country. In January 2010 President Funes made the first formal apology for human rights abuses committed by the state during that period. Meanwhile, human rights activists and organizations, including Amnesty International, used the thirtieth anniversary of the murder of Oscar Romero to urge the Government to repeal the controversial law, promulgated in 1992, which exempted all war crimes from prosecution.

In mid-2010 gang-related violent crime remained the most prominent issue for most Salvadoreans. Despite efforts by the Government to address the problem by deploying some 4,000 troops in the capital and granting extended powers to the police, the murder rate continued to rise. By June 2010 it was estimated that an average of 13 people per day were being killed by gangs, the highest rate in more than a decade. The issue received international attention in that month when 14 people were killed in an attack on a bus in San Salvador by one of the capital's most notorious gangs.

DEPENDENCE ON THE USA AND THE ADVENT OF DR-CAFTA

El Salvador has traditionally been a close ally of the USA, and ties between the two countries have strengthened in recent years. El Salvador was an active participant in the negotiations towards what became known as the Dominican Republic-Central American Free Trade Agreement (DR-CAFTA), which began in January 2003 and concluded in May 2004. El Salvador was the first country to ratify the agreement in December, the first to introduce the required legislation to comply with the new rules, and the first country to implement DR-CAFTA in March 2006. El Salvador also supported the US-led invasion of Iraq in March 2003, contributing a small number of troops. One item that remained non-negotiable during discussions towards DR-CAFTA was the free movement of labour. There were more than 1.5m. Salvadoreans living in the USA, who, for historical reasons, found it more difficult to gain US citizenship than did Nicaraguans and Cubans. This was particularly problematic for El Salvador, given its growing dependence on remittances from the USA, which grew steadily from the 1990s. The election of Funes was expected to result in a more diversified approach towards foreign relations and closer relations with Venezuela and Cuba. Nevertheless, the USA would remain the key ally and trade partner for El Salvador.

PROSPECTS FOR THE FUTURE

During 1999–2009 El Salvador consolidated an economic and political model based on three tenets: increasing political and economic links with the USA; the implementation of neo-liberal economic policies; and the growing influence of ARENA in the political domain. Despite having contributed to the expansion of remittances and non-traditional exports, this model has created numerous social tensions. The economy has failed to achieve sustainable growth and improve its level of competitiveness in recent years, while continuing high levels of poverty and social instability have contributed to increasing levels of violence. Meanwhile, according to an opinion poll by Latinobarómetro, the Salvadorean population has lost faith in democracy and economic progress: in 2007 only 38% of Salvadoreans stated that they believed that democracy was the best political system and just 27% that economic conditions would improve in the short run. The presidency of the FMLN's Funes, who took office on 1 June 2009, opened a new era for hope, and could result in a gradual modification of El Salvador's troubled neo-liberal model. None the less, the obstacles were immense, particularly owing to the recession in the USA and the problems in global financial markets.

Economy

DIEGO SÁNCHEZ-ANCOCHEA

Revised for this edition by the editorial staff

With a gross domestic product (GDP) per head of US $6,670 in 2008 on an international purchasing-power parity basis, El Salvador was a middle-income country, according to the classification of the World Bank. At the same time, however, El Salvador was one of the least developed countries in Latin America and the Caribbean: in 2007 the country was ranked 106th in the UN Human Development Index, higher than just five other countries in the entire Latin American region.

Infant mortality in 2007 was 24 per 1,000 live births, life expectancy at birth was 72 years and adult illiteracy was 18.0% in the same year. Human development was constrained by an unequal distribution of land and a high population density. El Salvador has a land area of only 20,721 sq km (8,003 sq miles) and an estimated population of 7.3m. in 2009, resulting in one of the highest population densities in the Western Hemisphere (326.7 people per sq km). A high level of violence is also a problem: El Salvador has one of the highest murder rates in the world.

PHASES OF ECONOMIC DEVELOPMENT

El Salvador, like many of its neighbours in Central America and the Caribbean, has slowly moved from a primary-based economy to one that depends on manufacturing exports from free trade zones and remittances from Salvadoreans abroad. This process of change has taken place in five different phases since independence in 1821. Initially, the dominant products were indigo and cotton. From the mid-19th century coffee superseded these commodities in importance. After the abolition of common land in 1882 vast *haciendas* (plantations) emerged, worked by a seasonal peasant work-force who had lost access to common land. Coffee 'barons' branched out into finance and commerce and in the 1960s their capital helped establish a manufacturing base that exported throughout Central America.

The new process of industrialization based on the Central American Common Market (CACM) contributed to the acceleration of economic growth and opened a third stage of development. However, deterioration in the price of coffee and other commodities, together with negative international conditions and the crisis of the CACM, led to a severe downturn at the end of the 1970s. By 1983 GDP per head had fallen to levels comparable with those of the 1960s. From 1979 to 1982 investment, in real terms, decreased by 68% and consumption by 20%. Unemployment, combined with underemployment, was estimated to affect more than 40% of the total work-force. In an attempt to ease social tensions and avert a left-wing uprising, a new military Government nationalized the banks and the coffee industry and began breaking up large *haciendas* and handing them to worker co-operatives, initiating what can be considered the fourth phase of development. Nevertheless, these attempts failed to prevent a civil war that extended from 1980 to 1992. The war caused more than 80,000 deaths, the internal and external displacement of over 1m. people, a massive flight of capital, and economic damage estimated at more than US $2,000m. During the war external financial assistance, mainly from the USA, helped to keep the economy from sliding into recession. Between 1980 and 1990 total external financial assistance to El Salvador was in excess of $5,000m., with approximately 90% from the USA, making El Salvador the third largest recipient of assistance from the US Government at the time. One of the main purposes of US assistance was to offset economic sabotage by the Frente Farabundo Martí para la Liberación Nacional (FMLN—Farabundo Martí National Liberation Front), which particularly affected the harvesting and export of the country's main export crop, coffee, and severely disrupted transport and power transmission. Coffee exports were also affected by the government monopoly that controlled them, which paid less than market rates.

The latest stage of economic development, which began in 1989, involved a full adoption of the so-called 'Washington Consensus'. El Salvador was one of the most radical reformers in Latin America and the Caribbean, with policies ranging from external liberalization to privatization of key public companies, domestic deregulation and the dollarization of the economy. During the administration of Alfredo Cristiani (1989–94) important sectors of the economy were returned to private ownership, including sugar refineries, distilleries, textile mills, hotels and fish processing plants, as well as most of the banks and financial institutions. Public spending was cut and price controls and subsidies reduced or abolished. The tax system was simplified and tariffs diminished. In 1990 the IMF granted a stand-by loan agreement of US $50m., indicating international approval of the reforms.

Market reforms continued after the peace accords under successive Alianza Republicana Nacionalista (ARENA) Governments. In 1998 the state telecommunications company, Administración Nacional de Telecomunicaciones (ANTEL), was privatized and in 1999 several electricity generating stations were sold. Private pensions were introduced in 1998. While public protests prevented further privatization in the health and banking sectors in the period 1999–2002, other radical reforms were implemented during the administration of Francisco Flores Pérez (1999–2004). The most important was the dollarization of the economy approved in November 2000. From 1 January 2001 the US dollar circulated freely with the colón at a fixed rate of $1 = 8.75 colones. The World Bank and the IMF supported the move, which aimed to reduce real interest rates to close to US levels to encourage investment and integrate El Salvador into the global economy.

The election of ARENA's candidate Elías Antonio (Tony) Saca in March 2004 did not change the direction of economic policy. El Salvador was the first country to approve the Dominican Republic-Central American Free Trade Agreement (DR-CAFTA) with the USA, in December of that year. Despite mass demonstrations, El Salvador was also the first country to implement the institutional changes required to be in full compliance with DR-CAFTA during the second half of 2005;

the accord came into effect in El Salvador in March 2006. The election of Mauricio Funes (from the left-wing FMLN) as President in June 2009 was expected to mark a significant shift in economic policy. Funes was, however, careful to emphasize the moderate nature of his agenda and his desire to develop a business environment attractive to investors.

GENERAL EVOLUTION OF THE ECONOMY SINCE 1990

Cristiani's reforms and demand after the end of the war led to a short-lived economic boom, partly facilitated by the expansion of remittances. Between 1990 and 1995 real GDP per head expanded rapidly, at an average annual rate of 4%. However, in 1995–2005 GDP per head stagnated, increasing at an average annual rate of only 0.7%. The economy did recuperate between 2006 and 2008 (expanding at an average annual rate of 2.3%), but real GDP per head still increased less than in the rest of Central America (where it expanded at an average of 3.2% a year in this period). From 2008 the global financial crisis reduced the opportunities for growth.

Frequent natural disasters were partly responsible for this uneven economic record. Hurricane Mitch, which struck Central America in October 1998, resulted in the loss of an estimated 8% (about US $1,760m.) of El Salvador's GDP in that year. In January and February 2001 two severe earthquakes hit the country, killing more than 1,100 people and leaving a further 1.5m. people homeless. Reconstruction costs were estimated at $1,900m., or 14% of GDP. Donors in March promised $1,300m., mostly in loans, and the Government diverted $150m. from the 2001 budget. The Government was also forced to borrow heavily to finance reconstruction over the following five years. External debt increased from a comparatively low 21.6% of GDP in 2000 to an estimated 29.3% of GDP in 2005. In October 2005 the combination of Hurricane Stan and the eruption of the Ilamatepec volcano resulted in 69 deaths and material losses of some $355m. The external debt was estimated at US $9,313m. in 2009 (compared with US $8,300m. in the previous year).

Low economic growth and ineffective economic reforms were instrumental in maintaining high levels of poverty. According to data from ECLAC, although the poverty rate fell by five percentage points between 1995 and 2001, it was still at 48.9% in the latter year. In 2004 the percentage of Salvadoreans living in poverty remained high at 47.5%, while 19% lived in extreme poverty. In that year some 48% of the population worked in sectors with low productivity—most within the informal economy—representing an increase in five percentage points from 1995. Poor urban, as well as rural, households became increasingly dependent on remittances from family members who had migrated, especially to the USA, which helped to lessen the impact of macro-economic adjustments. Remittances reached a record US $3,787.7m. in 2008, covering almost four-fifths of the growing trade deficit.

AGRICULTURE

Agriculture (including hunting, forestry and fishing) remained an important economic activity in the early 21st century, despite a contraction in the sector, owing to mass migration to the cities. By 2007 an estimated 60% of the population lived in urban areas, an increase from 50% in 1995. Agricultural growth was stagnant between 1996 and 2003, during which time sectoral contribution to real GDP decreased from 13.5% to 11.4%. However, the performance of this sector improved from 2004: in 2007 and 2008 agricultural GDP expanded, in real terms, by 8.3% and 7.3%, respectively (the latter according to preliminary figures), while the sector's contribution to overall GDP was equivalent to a preliminary 13.1% in 2008. Despite the recent upsurge, there was still intense pressure for land in a country with an increasing population density. Uneven rainfall, some 84% of which occurred during May–October, was another problem.

Inequality in the distribution of land was a long-standing problem. During the war the centrist Government attempted substantial, but flawed, agricultural reform. In 1980 all plantations of more than 500 ha (20% of all agricultural land) were expropriated by the state-owned Instituto Salvadoreño de Transformación Agraria (Salvadorean Institute of Agrarian Transformation), for transfer to peasant-run co-operatives. A programme of transfer of freehold titles to tenant smallholders began in 1981, and by 1985 more than 35,000 peasants had benefited. In 1983 a statutory limit of 245 ha was placed upon the amount of land that could be owned by any Salvadorean national. The aim was to provide one-half of the landless rural population with land rights. However, this target was later reduced, and in the end less than one-quarter received rights. As part of the 1992 peace settlement, an estimated 10% of agricultural land was to be distributed among 45,000 families of refugees and combatants. The programme was finally completed at the beginning of 1998, three years after the official deadline. Nevertheless, post-war Governments gave little assistance to the sector, with the exception of coffee, believing that progress lay in industrialization. After the earthquakes of 2001 the Government actively discouraged the replanting of crops, often locating new settlements near export processing zones, which provided jobs in the low-wage *maquila* assembly factories. Hence, land reform was no panacea, with many new landowners lacking the capital and expertise necessary to take full advantage of their land. For example, the share of national coffee production by land reform co-operatives fell from 10% to 7% between 1996 and 2000 in a declining market.

Production of arabica coffee was adversely affected by external and internal shocks in the 1990s and 2000s. The 1992 harvest was 3.2m. quintales (approximately 147,000 metric tons), but natural disasters and then low prices caused by rising exports from non-traditional growers such as Viet Nam adversely affected the sector. Following Hurricane Mitch in 1998 the crop amounted to 117,200 tons. Export income from coffee declined owing to 40-year price lows in 2002 and 2003 and was determined more by the fluctuations of world prices than by output. By 2004 coffee production had fallen to 78,500 tons. Following a small recuperation in international prices, coffee exports increased from US $123m. in 2004 to $259m. in 2008, representing 5.7% of the value of total export earnings. However, this was still well below the $522m. earned in 1997. A survey in 2000 found there were an estimated 22,500 producers of coffee in El Salvador, employing 150,000 people. The leading 6% of producers accounted for 72% of production while 70% of growers produced fewer than 30 bags of 60 kg per year, providing an annual income of less than $800. By 2004 the number of people working in the sector had fallen to an estimated 50,000 as many smaller growers switched to other crops. The Government gave only modest support, in the form of favourable loans to producers, demonstrating the once-powerful industry's loss of influence. El Salvador's future was thought to lie in its mountain-grown, high quality coffee, pitched at the high-margin gourmet market. Organic and fair trade coffee were also on the rise.

Output of sugar cane, another important cash crop, also declined during the civil war, and a recovery in the sector in the late 1990s proved short-lived. In the 2000s annual production fluctuated around 5.6m. metric tons in nominal terms. The value of sugar exports declined to US $37m. in 2004 before recovering to an estimated $72m. in 2006 and 2007, increasing to $76m. in 2008.

The commercial fishing industry expanded considerably after the 1960s. After declines in the mid-1990s, in 1998 the total catch increased to 11,400 metric tons; however, earthquakes, pollution and the changes in weather associated with the El Niño phenomenon reduced the catch to a low of 9,900 tons in 2000. Rapid expansion of industrial fishing of tuna and other pelagic fishes allowed for the recuperation of the sector in the following years. Total catch of pelagic fishes increased from just 120 tons in 2001 to 12,280 tons in 2005. As a result, total catch—both industrial and artesan—was more than 43,300 tons in 2005. In 2003 the Spanish company Grupo Calvo established an important tuna-processing plant in the Gulf of Fonseca; by 2005 export earnings from El Salvador by Grupo Calvo reached some US $54m. Total exports of sea products from El Salvador increased from $18m. in 2001 to $85m. in 2005, but then decreased by 12% in 2006, to $75m.

Non-traditional exports (including animal fodder, melons and pineapples) became more important at the end of the 20th century, particularly exports to the countries of the CACM. Food production for the domestic market was dominated by the cultivation of maize, sorghum, beans and rice, primarily on smallholdings. However, El Salvador imported around 30% of its basic food needs. Production of staples declined after 1979, owing mainly to the security situation and the displacement of the population. Nevertheless, substantial increases were achieved after 1982. The staple food of most Salvadoreans was maize (output of which was an estimated 1m. metric tons in 2008), and beans (120,100 tons in 2008). For most of the 2000s dry weather affected rice production, which more than halved in 2000–05, from 47,204 tons to 17,100 tons, but increased by 21% between 2006 and 2008 owing to higher prices.

MINING AND POWER

Mining was of negligible importance, accounting for an estimated 0.4% of GDP in 2008 and employing just 2,249 employees (less than 0.1% of the total work-force) in 2005. The main minerals produced were limestone, gypsum and salt.

El Salvador still relied significantly on imported petroleum, despite a drive to exploit the hydroelectric and geothermal potential in its rugged terrain and volcanoes. The Lempa river was dammed in 1950, feeding the 180-MW San Lorenzo power station. The development of the sector was impeded by the civil war, and in 1992 installed capacity was 740 MW: 50% hydroelectric, 37% thermal and 13% geothermal. Persistently low rainfall eroded hydroelectric production, however, as did deforestation, leading to erosion and silting up of rivers. In 2007 oil accounted for 40% of the 5,518 GWh generated, and hydroelectric power for 32%. Geothermal sources provided 1,293 GWh, up from only 384 GWh in 1990. Crude petroleum imports rose from just US $87m. in 1998 to an estimated $629m. in 2008, as a result of the sharp increase in world prices. Much was bought on favourable terms from Venezuela under the 2000 Caracas energy accord.

The Government prioritized energy production as a motor of industrialization and economic recovery after the civil war. In 1998 75% of the shares were sold in four state-owned regional electricity distribution companies. The state still owned the nation's hydroelectric dams, but competition was allowed in thermal and geothermal production, in an effort to encourage investment. Modernization of the infrastructure for energy production and distribution received a boost when the 'Plan Puebla–Panamá' (see below) devised the creation of the Sistema de Interconexión Eléctrica de Centroamérica (SIEPAC—Central American Electricity Interconnection System). The SIEPAC included the construction of 282 km of electrical transmission lines in El Salvador in an effort to connect the country with Honduras. Funding for the project, which began later than originally planned, in July 2006, was provided partly by the Inter-American Development Bank. It was envisaged that it would lower energy prices and encourage investment by providing economies of scale. In mid-2006 construction began of a hydroelectric dam known as 'El Tigre' on the Lempa river on the El Salvador–Honduras border.

MANUFACTURING

The rapid growth of the manufacturing sector after 1960, within the CACM, increased the sector's contribution to 15% of GDP by 1979. Although the war reversed this trend temporarily, from 1983 a series of measures was adopted to revitalize the sector, including the promotion of exports within the regional market and the creation of credit lines for industrial companies in the context of the US Government's Caribbean Basin Initiative (CBI). At the same time, consideration was given to combining compensation to previous owners of expropriated agricultural land with reinvestment of this compensation in industrial enterprises. The return of business confidence and the development of regional markets in Central America contributed to the recuperation of the manufacturing sector during the post-war period. Manufacturing production grew at an average annual rate of 4.2% in real terms between 1995 and 2004, making it the strongest performing sector in the economy. In 2004–07, however, the manufacturing sector underperformed in comparison with the rest of the economy, growing at an average annual rate of 2.8% compared to 4.0% for the economy as a whole. In 2008 the sector grew at 2.7%, in line with overall growth of 2.5%.

The *maquila* plants, which mainly assemble apparel products for the US market, have played a central role in the promotion of manufacturing production, exports and jobs in the last two decades. The creation of the CBI, favourable access to the US market and tax incentives in El Salvador contributed to the *maquila* sector's rapid expansion during the 1990s. Between 1991 and 2000 *maquila* exports grew at an average annual rate of 32% and by 2003 the sector employed more than 89,000 people. Nevertheless, the sector suffered two significant limitations: the low level of value added generated in free trade zones, and the declining competitiveness in the US market despite improvements in market access. In 2008 value added totalled just US $647m., equivalent to just 34% of total *maquila* exports. In May 2000 the USA agreed to broaden the terms of the CBI to provide North American Free Trade Agreement (NAFTA) parity to El Salvador and 23 other Latin American countries. The enhanced CBI provided duty-free access to the US market for a number of previously excluded categories of *maquila* garments. Nevertheless, *maquila* exports stagnated from 2004: in 2008 *maquila* exports amounted to an estimated $1,928m., compared with $1,923m. in 2004. By further improving access to the US market and allowing the use of material from any country within Central and North America, it was anticipated that DR-CAFTA would support apparel exports and contribute to the development of the dyeing and cutting industries. After a disappointing first year in 2007 (when *maquila* exports increased by just 1.3%), *maquila* exports accelerated in 2008, expanding by 7.0% in nominal terms. Nevertheless, as in other areas, the global financial crisis jeopardized the long-term survival of the sector.

TRANSPORT AND TOURISM

There were some 10,886 km of roads in 2000, of which 2,827 km were paved. The number of vehicles on the roads tripled from 145,000 to 450,000 between 1997–2001, and continued its expansion in the subsequent years. Improving the quality of existing roads through maintenance, rehabilitation and modernization was a major challenge for post-war El Salvador. The earthquakes of 2001 caused considerable damage to the road system, which, according to government estimates, would cost US $188m. to repair. In 2002 the Government established a road maintenance fund, the Fondo de Conservación Vial (Fovial), financed by a tax on petrol of 20 US cents per gallon, which began to give concessions to private companies to repair the roads.

The Comisión Ejecutiva Portuaria Autónoma (CEPA) is responsible for the administration of El Salvador's only main ports, Acajutla and Cutuco, and the El Salvador International Airport at Comalapa, Cuscatlán. CEPA improved its financial situation in the 1990s, but faced the problem of recovering traffic lost during the civil war, as well as competing with other Central American ports, particularly Puerto Quetzal in Guatemala. In 2001 the Government finalized an agreement to reactivate Cutuco port on the Gulf of Fonseca with support from the Japanese Government. After some delays, construction began in 2005 and concluded in early 2009. A Japanese company was to run the port, renamed Puerto La Unión Centroamericana, in concession. The national railway system, which had some 555 km of track, stopped operating in 2005 owing to the high cost of maintenance, although a limited passenger service resumed in 2007.

El Salvador's recent bloody history and high crime rate has stunted the growth of its tourism industry. Nevertheless, the country has much to offer, with Mayan temples and cities, volcanoes, mountain lakes and sandy beaches. Tourist arrivals rose from 387,052 in 1997 to almost 1.6m. in 2007. Many of the visitors to El Salvador were Salvadoreans living in the USA returning to visit families or their home towns; 37% of all tourists in 2006 went to El Salvador with the primary aim of visiting friends and family. As a result of the expansion in the number of tourists, the foreign exchange generated by the tourism sector increased steadily from US $75m. in 1997 to an estimated $894m. in 2008. In 2004 tourism became the second largest generator of foreign exchange, behind remittances, but surpassing the free trade zones. President Saca also prioritized tourism by creating a Ministry of Tourism when he took office in June 2004.

INVESTMENT AND FINANCE

The cost of reconstruction following the 2001 earthquakes placed a heavy burden on the Government's finances. The public deficit of the central Government as a proportion of GDP in 2001 was 3.6% of GDP. However, the deficit narrowed in subsequent years: in 2007 the deficit was reduced to US $56m., equivalent to 0.6% of GDP. None the less, impending crisis in the privatized pension system, which had witnessed only minor modifications during the Saca administration, was expected to undermine successful management of the public accounts in the medium and long run. The country continued to depend on high levels of foreign aid and concessionary loans to finance much-needed infrastructural development. Public revenue rose from 12.5% of GDP in 2002 to an estimated 14.7% in 2008 following minor tax reform in 2006. The Government took advantage of its low debt and healthy credit rating to borrow internationally. It also increased incentives for foreign investment as part of its programme for economic reactivation and stabilization; however, high crime levels and a violent death rate on a par with that experienced during the civil war deterred foreign investors. Nevertheless, in the early 21st century the introduction of the US dollar as legal tender and the forging of closer links with Mexico contributed to an escalation of foreign direct investment (FDI). In 1991–95 FDI averaged just $263m. per year, compared with an average annual figure of $3,298m. in 2001–05. In 2008 FDI reached a record $6,701m., according to data from the Central Bank.

In 1998–2005 the average annual rate of inflation was 2.8%, a relatively moderate rate, particularly in comparison to the rest of Central America. The annual inflation rate rose to 4.9% in 2006 and 2007 and to 5.5% in 2008, largely owing to rising oil and food prices. By May 2010 the rate stood at -0.2%.

FOREIGN TRADE AND PAYMENTS

The change in the Salvadorean economic model has been particularly reflected in the shift in the export structure. While in 1970 coffee and sugar constituted 91% of non-regional exports, they accounted for only an estimated 7.3% of total exports in 2008. Meanwhile, *maquilas*, tourism and, most importantly, remittances from abroad became the main generators of foreign exchange. The shift in the structure of exports coincided with an expansion of both exports and imports. According to preliminary estimates by the Central Bank, exports (including from the *maquila* zones) in 2008 totalled US $4,549m., while imports were $9,754m. The principal export partner was the USA, which in 2008 was the destination of 48% of Salvadorean exports and the origin of 34% of its imports. While the signing of DR-CAFTA was supposed to increase the link between both countries and contribute to the expansion of El Salvador's exports, the first two years were rather disappointing.

The trade surplus that El Salvador had recorded during most of the 1970s gave way to a deficit from 1981, even though the declines in export revenues were accompanied by rigorous restrictions on 'non-essential' imports. After 1992 the deficit increased. In 2005 the trade deficit stood at a record US $3,008m. Since the 1980s the deterioration in the trade balance has been offset by remittances from abroad and by capital inflows. As a result, international reserves have steadily increased from a low of $72m. in 1981. In March 2009 international reserves amounted to $2,524m.

Between 1990 and 2009 total external debt increased from US $2,148m. to an estimated $9,313m. as the Government borrowed to finance reconstruction following various earthquakes and to increase expenditure on selected social programmes. Almost all of this debt was incurred on a medium- to long-term basis at low interest rates, owing to El Salvador's high credit rating. In 2007 external debt was equivalent to 48% of GDP.

El Salvador has been an active participant in recent processes of regional integration. In March 2001 a free trade agreement (FTA) with Mexico, Guatemala and Honduras came into effect, which, it was hoped, would gradually open up markets for industrial and agricultural products over a 12-year period. In May the Central American countries, including El Salvador, reached the basis of a deal with Mexico, the 'Plan Puebla–Panamá' (restyled the Proyecto de Integración y Desarrollo de Mesoamérica in 2008), to integrate the region through joint transport, industry and tourism projects. In December 2003 El Salvador and its neighbours Costa Rica, Guatemala, Honduras and Nicaragua (and later, the Dominican Republic), concluded negotiations with the USA for the creation of CAFTA (later DR-CAFTA). The agreement entered into force in El Salvador on 1 March 2006. In May of that year El Salvador and Honduras also signed an FTA with Taiwan, a move that threatened to impede trade relations with the People's Republic of China. The country was also a leading proponent of the Association Agreement between Central America and the European Union (a free trade agreement between the European Union and El Salvador, Panama, Nicaragua, Guatemala, Honduras and Costa Rica). Negotiations on the agreement began in 2007 and were concluded in May 2010.

OUTLOOK

El Salvador was financially stable in 2010, having recovered from the economic and political crises of the 1980s and weathered the international financial recession which began in 2008. The country had one of the most liberal economies in Latin America and had established strong links with the US economy. Despite all the reforms, however, many challenges remained, and the global financial crisis made their solution even harder than before. GDP per head grew slowly and was affected by repeated natural disasters. Poverty remained widespread and dollarization eroded some of the country's competitive advantages. High levels of poverty, agricultural stagnation, environmental damage and increasing crime and violence were all issues that the country would need to confront urgently. External conditions helped El Salvador to expand its economy faster between 2006 and 2008 than at any time in the previous decade, but the financial crisis slowed this considerably. The election of Mauricio Funes Cartagena to the presidency in March 2009 promised to result in a more progressive and redistributive policy approach, but the new Government had little room for manoeuvre owing to difficult external conditions.

Statistical Survey

Sources (unless otherwise stated): Banco Central de Reserva de El Salvador, Alameda Juan Pablo II y 17 Avda Norte, Apdo 01-106, San Salvador; tel. 2281-8000; fax 2281-8011; internet www.bcr.gob.sv; Dirección General de Estadística y Censos, Edif. Centro de Gobierno, Alameda Juan Pablo II y Calle Guadalupe, San Salvador; tel. 2286-4260; fax 2286-2505; internet www.digestyc.gob.sv.

Area and Population

AREA, POPULATION AND DENSITY

Area (sq km)	
Land	20,721
Inland water	320
Total	21,041*
Population (census results)†	
27 September 1992	5,118,599
12 May 2007	
Males	2,719,371
Females	3,024,742
Total	5,744,113
Population (official estimates)	
2008	6,124,700
2009	6,152,600
Density (per sq km) at 2009	292.4

* 8,124 sq miles.

† Excluding adjustments for underenumeration.

POPULATION BY AGE AND SEX
(UN estimates at mid-2010)

	Males	Females	Total
0–14	997,159	955,461	1,952,620
15–64	1,722,454	2,065,430	3,787,884
65 and over	242,718	315,231	557,949
Total	2,962,331	3,336,122	6,298,453

Source: UN, *World Population Prospects: The 2008 Revision*.

DEPARTMENTS
(population at 2007 census)

	Area (sq km)	Population	Density (per sq km)
Ahuachapán	1,239.6	319,503	257.7
Santa Ana	2,023.2	523,655	258.8
Sonsonate	1,225.8	438,960	358.1
Chalatenango	2,016.6	192,788	95.6
La Libertad	1,652.9	660,652	399.7
San Salvador	886.2	1,567,156	1,768.4
Cuscatlán	756.2	231,480	306.1
La Paz	1,223.6	308,087	251.8
Cabañas	1,103.5	149,326	135.3
San Vicente	1,184.0	161,645	136.5
Usulután	2,130.4	344,235	161.6
San Miguel	2,077.1	434,003	208.9
Morazán	1,447.4	174,406	120.5
La Unión	2,074.3	238,217	114.8
Total	21,040.8	5,744,113	273.0

PRINCIPAL TOWNS
(official population projections at mid–2009)*

San Salvador (capital)	513,487	Mejicanos	215,528
San Miguel	308,635	Santa Tecla†	208,226
Soyapango	305,729	Ciudad Delgado	178,808
Santa Ana	288,588	Ilopango	165,452
Apopa	229,580	San Martín	155,396

* Figures refer to municipios, which may each contain rural areas as well as an urban centre.

† Formerly Nueva San Salvador.

BIRTHS, MARRIAGES AND DEATHS

	Registered live births		Registered marriages		Registered deaths	
	Number	Rate (per 1,000)	Number	Rate (per 1,000)	Number	Rate (per 1,000)
2001	138,354	21.6	29,216	4.6	29,559	4.6
2002	129,363	19.9	26,077	4.0	27,458	4.2
2003	124,476	18.7	25,071	3.8	29,377	4.4
2004	119,710	17.7	25,240	3.7	30,058	4.4
2005	112,769	16.4	24,475	3.6	30,933	4.5
2006	107,111	15.3	24,500	3.5	31,453	4.5
2007	106,471	15.0	28,675	4.0	31,349	4.4
2008	112,049	15.3	27,714	3.8	31,594	4.4

Life expectancy (years at birth, WHO estimates): 72 (males 68; females 76) in 2008 (Source: WHO, *World Health Statistics*).

ECONOMICALLY ACTIVE POPULATION
(persons aged 16 years and over at 2007 census)

	Males	Females	Total
Agriculture and hunting	251,960	23,496	275,456
Forestry	1,208	74	1,282
Fishing	8,776	987	9,763
Mining and quarrying	1,202	70	1,272
Manufacturing	145,586	126,083	271,669
Electricity, gas and water	6,039	762	6,801
Construction	127,887	3,068	130,955
Wholesale and retail trade; repair of motor vehicles	200,442	185,397	385,839
Hotels and restaurants	17,393	51,666	69,059
Transport, storage and communications	82,070	8,719	90,789
Financing, insurance, real estate and business services	83,089	47,206	130,295
Public administration, defence and social security	53,488	23,656	77,144
Education	25,421	45,143	70,564
Health	18,348	34,580	52,928
Other community, social and personal services	18,640	15,118	33,758
Private households with employed persons	5,580	113,286	118,866
Extra-territorial organizations and bodies	395	319	714
Total employed	1,047,524	679,630	1,727,154
Unemployed	96,916	85,186	182,102
Total labour force	1,144,440	764,816	1,909,256

Health and Welfare

KEY INDICATORS

Total fertility rate (children per woman, 2008)	2.3
Under-5 mortality rate (per 1,000 live births, 2008)	18
HIV/AIDS (% of persons aged 15–49, 2007)	0.8
Physicians (per 1,000 head, 2002)	1.2
Hospital beds (per 1,000 head, 2005)	0.9
Health expenditure (2007): US $ per head (PPP)	402
Health expenditure (2007): % of GDP	6.2
Health expenditure (2007): public (% of total)	58.9
Access to water (% of persons, 2007)	87
Access to sanitation (% of persons, 2007)	87
Total carbon dioxide emissions ('000 metric tons, 2006)	6,456.0
Carbon dioxide emissions per head (metric tons, 2006)	1.1
Human Development Index (2007): ranking	106
Human Development Index (2007): value	0.747

For sources and definitions, see explanatory note on p. vi.

Agriculture

PRINCIPAL CROPS
('000 metric tons)

	2006	2007	2008
Rice, paddy	31.0	31.5	35.2
Maize	742.1	836.7	1,000.0
Sorghum	164.0	181.7	198.6
Yautia (Cocoyam)*	5.2	5.2	5.2
Sugar cane	4,878.0	4,956.5	5,249.9
Beans, dry	90.7	99.3	120.1
Coconuts	57.2	63.1	68.7
Watermelons	86.8	88.5	98.3
Bananas*	65.0	65.0	65.0
Plantains	82.7	88.5	96.5
Oranges	59.7	67.0	73.0
Coffee, green	78.5	95.5	97.7

* FAO estimates.

Aggregate production ('000 metric tons, may include official, semi-official or estimated data): Total cereals 937.1 in 2006, 1,049.9 in 2007, 1,233.8 in 2008; Total vegetables (incl. melons) 222.5 in 2006, 219.2 in 2007, 240.4 in 2008; Total fruits (excl. melons) 345.4 in 2006, 363.6 in 2007, 389.7 in 2008.

Source: FAO.

LIVESTOCK
('000 head, year ending September)

	2006	2007	2008
Horses*	96	96	96
Asses*	32	32	32
Mules*	24	24	24
Cattle	1,319	1,370	1,397
Pigs	436	441	467
Sheep*	5	5	5
Goats*	11	11	11
Chickens	13,706	14,748	14,748*

* FAO estimate(s).

Source: FAO.

LIVESTOCK PRODUCTS
('000 metric tons)

	2006	2007	2008
Cattle meat	30.6	33.9	37.3
Pig meat	14.2	16.7	18.0
Chicken meat	101.4	106.8	96.1
Cows' milk	492.5	535.7	578.5
Hen eggs	69.2	70.0	66.3

Source: FAO.

Forestry

ROUNDWOOD REMOVALS
('000 cubic metres, excl. bark, FAO estimates)

	2006	2007	2008
Sawlogs, veneer logs and logs for sleepers	682	682	682
Fuel wood	4,204	4,210	4,217
Total	4,886	4,892	4,899

Source: FAO.

SAWNWOOD PRODUCTION
('000 cubic metres, incl. railway sleepers, FAO estimates)

	2002	2003	2004
Total (all broadleaved, hardwood)	68.0	68.0	16.3

2005–08: Figures assumed to be unchanged from 2004 (FAO estimates).

Source: FAO.

Fishing

('000 metric tons, live weight)

	2006	2007	2008
Capture	43.2	48.6	48.0
Nile tilapia	0.6	0.8	0.8
Other freshwater fishes	0.7	0.9	0.9
Croakers and drums	1.4	1.8	1.7
Skipjack tuna	7.3	11.1	10.5
Yellowfin tuna	7.5	4.4	5.0
Bigeye tuna	0.4	2.3	2.0
Sharks, rays, skates, etc.	0.8	0.7	0.7
Other marine fishes	6.8	7.8	7.7
Pacific seabobs	0.6	0.6	0.6
Marine molluscs	0.1	0.5	0.5
Aquaculture	3.1	3.7	3.8
Total catch	46.3	52.4	51.8

Source: FAO.

Mining

(metric tons, unless otherwise specified)

	2004	2005	2006
Gypsum*	5,600	5,600	5,500
Steel (crude)*	59,000	48,000	72,000
Limestone ('000 metric tons)	1,161	1,150*	1,200*
Salt (marine)*	31,400	31,400	30,000

* Estimate(s).

2007–08: Figures assumed to be unchanged from 2006 (estimates).

Source: US Geological Survey.

Industry

SELECTED PRODUCTS
('000 metric tons, unless otherwise indicated)

	2005	2006	2007
Raw sugar	633	542	560
Motor gasoline (petrol)	111	112	117
Kerosene	22	16	20
Distillate fuel oil	198	176	229
Residual fuel oil	419	437	477
Liquefied petroleum gas (refined)	16	17	20
Cement	1,131	1,311	1,300
Electric energy (million kWh)	4,788	5,597	5,806

Cement ('000 metric tons): 1,300 in 2008 (estimate).

Source: US Geological Survey and UN Industrial Commodity Statistics Database.

Finance

CURRENCY AND EXCHANGE RATES

Monetary Units
100 centavos = 1 Salvadorean colón.

Sterling, Dollar and Euro Equivalents (31 May 2010)
£1 sterling = 12.758 colones;
US $1 = 8.750 colones;
€1 = 10.836 colones;
100 Salvadorean colones = £7.84 = $11.43 = €9.23.

Note: The foregoing information refers to the principal exchange rate, applicable to official receipts and payments, imports of petroleum and exports of coffee. In addition, there is a market exchange rate, applicable to other transactions. The principal rate was maintained at 8.755 colones per US dollar from May 1995 to December 2000. However, in January 2001, with the introduction of legislation making the US dollar legal tender, the rate was adjusted to $1 = 8.750 colones. Both currencies were to be accepted for a transitional period.

CENTRAL GOVERNMENT BUDGET
(US $ million)

Revenue*	2007	2008†	2009†
Current revenue	2,917.2	3,190.7	2,773.8
Tax revenue	2,724.4	2,885.8	2,609.4
Taxes on earnings	933.2	1,004.1	949.2
Import duties	203.8	178.8	138.0
Value-added tax	1,389.4	1,460.7	1,251.2
Non-tax revenue	192.8	304.9	164.4
Public enterprise transfers	12.0	5.3	25.3
Financial public enterprise transfers	31.0	29.6	28.6
Capital revenue	0	0.1	0.1
Total	2,917.2	3,190.7	2,773.8

Expenditure‡	2007	2008†	2009†
Current expenditure	2,496.6	2,778.9	3,031.4
Remunerations	889.8	973.0	1,069.8
Goods and services	445.7	516.5	538.5
Interest payments	498.2	509.4	518.0
Transfers	662.9	779.9	905.2
To other government bodies	373.3	407.1	448.9
To the private sector	273.0	357.9	444.3
Capital expenditure	531.0	603.3	602.6
Gross investment	233.2	305.4	305.3
Total	3,027.6	3,382.2	3,634.0

* Excluding grants received (US $ million): 55.6 in 2007; 52.2 in 2008 (preliminary); 83.5 in 2009 (preliminary).

† Preliminary figures.

‡ Excluding lending minus repayments (US $ million): –11.3 in 2007; –6.3 in 2008 (preliminary); –4.6 in 2009 (preliminary).

INTERNATIONAL RESERVES
(US $ million at 31 December)

	2007	2008	2009
Gold (national valuation)	88.8	101.9	117.5
IMF special drawing rights	39.5	38.5	256.8
Foreign exchange	2,070.5	2,404.6	2,612.0
Total	2,198.8	2,545.0	2,986.3

Source: IMF, *International Financial Statistics.*

MONEY SUPPLY
(US $ million at 31 December)

	2007	2008	2009
Currency outside depository corporations	33.2	33.0	32.8
Transferable deposits	1,802.0	1,837.0	2,120.4
Other deposits	6,974.8	6,901.0	6,858.0
Securities other than shares	1,453.4	1,432.4	1,405.7
Broad money	10,263.5	10,203.3	10,417.0

Source: IMF, *International Financial Statistics.*

COST OF LIVING
(Consumer Price Index; annual averages; base: December 1992 = 100)

	2007	2008	2009
Food and non-alcoholic beverages	214.9	240.6	231.5
Clothing and footwear	111.7	113.4	115.0
Rent, water, electricity, gas and other fuels	205.9	207.2	224.5
Health	224.5	229.2	237.2
Transport	164.4	178.2	168.2
All items (incl. others)	202.1	216.8	218.0

NATIONAL ACCOUNTS
(US $ million at current prices, preliminary)

Expenditure on the Gross Domestic Product

	2007	2008	2009
Final consumption expenditure	21,525.9	23,789.0	21,602.9
Households	19,675.6	21,790.1	19,395.8
General government	1,850.3	1,998.9	2,207.1
Gross capital formation	3,246.0	3,295.4	2,767.9
Total domestic expenditure	24,771.9	27,084.4	24,370.8
Exports of goods and services	5,168.8	5,651.7	4,696.1
Less Imports of goods and services	9,563.9	10,629.4	7,966.4
GDP in purchasers' values	20,376.7	22,106.8	21,100.5
GDP at constant 1990 prices	9,176.1	9,399.4	9,066.6

Gross Domestic Product by Economic Activity

	2007	2008	2009
Agriculture, hunting, forestry and fishing	2,215.0	2,619.5	2,519.6
Mining and quarrying	62.1	71.0	61.1
Manufacturing	4,202.1	4,524.0	4,318.6
Construction	834.5	876.5	826.3
Electricity, gas and water	341.4	382.2	401.5
Transport, storage and communications	1,759.2	1,841.8	1,720.4
Wholesale and retail trade, restaurants and hotels	4,055.0	4,420.3	4,226.1
Finance and insurance	917.9	968.7	922.3
Real estate and business services	850.6	910.2	877.3
Owner-occupied dwellings	1,335.0	1,382.2	1,414.1
Community, social, domestic and personal services	1,517.2	1,638.9	1,638.7
Government services	1,312.6	1,442.1	1,519.3
Sub-total	19,402.6	21,077.4	20,445.3
Import duties and value-added tax	1,685.7	1,774.3	1,384.5
Less Imputed bank service charge	711.5	744.8	729.4
GDP in purchasers' values	20,376.7	22,106.8	21,100.5

BALANCE OF PAYMENTS
(US $ million)

	2006	2007	2008
Exports of goods f.o.b.	3,758.6	4,039.1	4,610.7
Imports of goods f.o.b.	–7,291.4	–8,143.6	–9,004.2
Trade balance	–3,532.8	–4,104.6	–4,393.5
Exports of services	1,426.2	1,493.9	1,509.9
Imports of services	–1,505.4	–1,746.4	–2,008.0
Balance on goods and services	–3,612.0	–4,357.1	–4,891.6
Other income received	234.3	287.0	222.7
Other income paid	–765.3	–863.0	–758.6
Balance on goods, services and income	–4,142.9	–4,933.1	–5,427.6
Current transfers received	3,548.8	3,819.1	3,900.2
Current transfers paid	–76.7	–69.1	–68.5

—continued	2006	2007	2008
Current balance	–670.8	–1,183.1	–1,595.9
Capital account (net)	96.8	150.5	79.8
Direct investment abroad	26.3	–100.3	–65.3
Direct investment from abroad	241.1	1,508.3	784.2
Portfolio investment assets	62.3	–92.5	193.9
Portfolio investment liabilities	715.1	–103.9	–56.3
Other investment assets	–60.5	–214.1	158.9
Other investment liabilities	84.6	–467.7	618.4
Net errors and omissions	–423.2	783.1	216.1
Overall balance	71.6	280.2	333.8

Source: IMF, *International Financial Statistics*.

External Trade

PRINCIPAL COMMODITIES
(US $ million, preliminary)

Imports c.i.f.*	2007	2008	2009
Live animals and animal products; vegetables, crops and related products, primary	626.5	725.5	682.3
Food, beverages (incl. alcoholic) and tobacco manufactures	499.1	570.4	569.3
Mineral products	1,444.9	1,907.9	1,136.8
Crude petroleum oils	458.4	629.3	367.7
Light oils (gasoline, etc.)	249.2	288.2	193.6
Heavy oils (gas oil, diesel oil, fuel oil, etc.)	400.4	614.7	309.7
Chemicals and related products	918.2	1,150.7	882.6
Therapeutic and preventative medicines	210.2	245.8	245.4
Plastics, artificial resins, rubbers, and articles thereof	471.4	512.0	400.2
Plastics, artificial resins, and articles thereof	404.0	441.3	334.6
Wood pulp, paper, paperboard and articles thereof	312.9	351.3	283.8
Textile materials and articles thereof	314.6	319.9	376.2
Base metals and manufactures thereof	546.4	689.7	350.0
Cast iron and steel	257.0	378.9	140.9
Mechanical and electrical machinery and apparatus	1,317.1	1,230.5	977.2
Mechanical machinery and apparatus	566.5	611.8	487.0
Electrical machinery and appliances	750.6	618.7	490.2
Radio and television transmitters and receivers, and parts thereof	325.2	220.5	186.0
Transport equipment	418.0	349.6	243.8
Total (incl. others)	7,475.2	8,472.7	6,415.7

* Excluding imports into *maquila* zones (US $ million, preliminary): 1,236.5 in 2007; 1,281.7 in 2008; 839.0 in 2009.

Exports f.o.b.*	2007	2008	2009
Vegetables, crops and related products, primary	254.5	332.4	298.9
Coffee, including roasted and decaffeinated	187.2	258.7	230.3
Food, beverages incl. alcoholic) and tobacco manufactures	451.5	508.8	505.8
Unrefined sugar	71.8	75.5	88.4
Mineral products	136.0	188.3	114.0
Chemical products	343.5	430.9	280.2
Therapeutic and preventative medicines	97.2	108.6	97.8
Surgical spirit	142.1	195.2	74.2
Plastics, rubber, and articles thereof	160.3	196.3	180.1
Boxes, bags, bottles, stoppers and other plastic containers	62.7	82.5	85.0
Wood pulp, paper, paperboard and articles thereof	195.8	223.4	225.2
Toilet paper for domestic use	78.6	97.5	96.9
Textile materials and articles thereof	133.9	154.4	229.4
Base metals and manufactures thereof	246.5	282.8	178.8
Iron and steel products, laminated	72.0	88.3	42.7
Other iron and steel products	87.7	121.3	81.3
Electrical machinery, appliances and associated products	70.0	76.4	51.7
Total (incl. others)	2,180.3	2,620.8	2,310.0

* Excluding exports from *maquila* zones (US $ million, preliminary): 1,803.7 in 2007; 1,928.3 in 2008; 1,487.4 in 2009.

PRINCIPAL TRADING PARTNERS
(US $ million, preliminary)

Imports c.i.f.*	2007	2008	2009
Argentina	116.1	77.5	42.9
Brazil	291.2	330.3	171.9
Chile	140.7	163.7	66.1
China, People's Republic	402.4	482.6	333.1
Colombia	83.2	173.9	93.2
Costa Rica	248.5	261.0	224.6
Ecuador	222.6	354.3	223.1
Germany	130.6	154.9	104.7
Guatemala	744.1	826.8	754.1
Honduras	299.5	375.4	343.5
Hong Kong	114.7	74.6	38.0
Japan	180.1	186.9	103.3
Korea, Republic	103.7	118.9	59.3
Mexico	843.1	874.5	540.1
Netherlands Antilles	61.4	117.0	90.1
Nicaragua	164.4	198.9	195.1
Panama	187.7	198.7	177.0
Spain	76.5	94.0	72.4
Taiwan	94.6	118.0	87.4
USA	3,146.5	3,336.6	2,606.2
Venezuela	112.6	193.9	97.5
Total (incl. others)	8,711.7	9,754.4	7,254.7

* Including imports into *maquila* zones (mostly from USA) (US $ million, preliminary): 1,236.5 in 2007; 1,281.7 in 2008; 839.0 in 2009.

Exports f.o.b.*	2007	2008	2009
Costa Rica	137.2	166.2	135.0
Dominican Republic	63.4	62.3	66.9
Germany	105.2	123.1	89.8
Guatemala	539.5	620.6	533.3
Honduras	445.6	589.4	510.6
Mexico	47.5	48.3	56.7
Nicaragua	220.3	251.8	208.7
Panama	90.6	122.8	104.0
Spain	93.6	105.7	65.3
USA	2,028.1	2,184.3	1,763.1
Total (incl. others)	3,984.0	4,549.1	3,797.3

* Including exports from *maquila* zones (mostly to USA) (US $ million, preliminary): 1,803.7 in 2007; 1,928.3 in 2008; 1,487.4 in 2009.

Transport

RAILWAYS
(traffic)

	1999	2000
Number of passengers ('000)	543.3	687.3
Passenger-km (million)	8.4	10.7
Freight ('000 metric tons)	188.6	136.2
Freight ton-km (million)	19.4	13.1

Source: Ferrocarriles Nacionales de El Salvador.

ROAD TRAFFIC
(motor vehicles in use at 31 December)

	1998	1999	2000
Passenger cars	187,440	197,374	207,259
Buses and coaches	34,784	36,204	37,554
Lorries and vans	166,065	177,741	189,812
Motorcycles and mopeds	32,271	35,021	37,139

Source: Servicio de Tránsito Centroamericano (SERTRACEN).

2007 (motor vehicles in use at 31 December): Passenger cars 283,787; Buses and coaches 6,306; Vans and lorries 283,787; Motorcycles and mopeds 44,145 (Sources: IRF, *International Road Statistics*).

SHIPPING

Merchant Fleet
(registered at 31 December)

	2006	2007	2008
Number of vessels	14	14	14
Total displacement ('000 grt)	6.6	6.6	6.6

Source: Lloyd's Register-Fairplay, *World Fleet Statistics*.

CIVIL AVIATION
(traffic on scheduled services)

	2003	2004	2005
Kilometres flown (million)	34	40	40
Passengers carried ('000)	2,271	2,391	2,541
Passenger-km (million)	3,644	4,236	4,419
Total ton-km (million)	339	407	417

Source: UN, *Statistical Yearbook*.

Tourism

TOURIST ARRIVALS BY NATIONALITY
(arrivals of non-resident tourists at national borders)

	2005	2006	2007
Canada	16,042	21,186	33,827
Costa Rica	33,905	33,198	44,782
Guatemala	382,673	519,670	488,453
Honduras	198,333	253,586	189,453
Mexico	24,456	23,255	32,418
Nicaragua	162,377	120,871	113,883
Panama	10,074	9,953	13,319
Spain	9,091	8,512	12,003
USA	231,806	227,576	320,298
Total (incl. others)	1,127,141	1,278,927	1,338,543

Receipts from tourism (US $ million, excl. passenger transport): 793 in 2006; 847 in 2007; 894 in 2008 (provisional).

Source: World Tourism Organization.

Communications Media

	2007	2008	2009
Telephones ('000 main lines in use)	1,080.1	1,077.2	1,099.1
Mobile cellular telephones ('000 subscribers)	6,137.4	6,950.7	7,566.2
Internet users ('000)	421.0*	650.0*	889.0
Broadband subscribers ('000)	89.8	123.5	149.4

* Estimate.

Radio receivers ('000 in use): 2,940 in 1999.

Television receivers ('000 in use): 1,260 in 2000.

Daily newspapers: 5 in 2004 (circulation 250,000).

Non-daily newspapers: 6 in 1996 (circulation 52,000).

Book production: 663 in 1998.

Personal computers: 350,000 (57.8 per 1,000 persons) in 2005.

Sources: UNESCO, *Statistical Yearbook*, International Telecommunication Union.

Education

(2007/08)

	Teachers	Students		
		Males	Females	Total
Pre-primary	9,205	112,662	111,258	223,920
Primary	30,474	515,215	478,580	993,795
Secondary	20,484	269,232	270,045	539,277
Tertiary	8,562	62,951	75,664	138,615

Institutions (2001/02): Pre-primary 4,838; Primary 5,414; Secondary 757; Tertiary 43.

Sources: Ministry of Education and UNESCO Institute for Statistics.

Pupil-teacher ratio (primary education, UNESCO estimate): 32.6 in 2007/08 (Source: UNESCO Institute for Statistics).

Adult literacy rate (UNESCO estimates): 84.0% (males 87.1%; females 81.4%) in 2008 (Source: UNESCO Institute for Statistics).

Directory

The Constitution

The Constitution of the Republic of El Salvador came into effect on 20 December 1983. It has been amended from time to time.

The Constitution provides for a republican, democratic and representative form of government, composed of three Powers—Legislative, Executive, and Judicial—which are to operate independently. Voting is a right and duty of all citizens over 18 years of age. Presidential and congressional elections may not be held simultaneously.

The Constitution binds the country, as part of the Central American Nation, to favour the total or partial reconstruction of the Republic of Central America. Integration in a unitary, federal or confederal form, provided that democratic and republican principles are respected and that basic rights of individuals are fully guaranteed, is subject to popular approval.

LEGISLATIVE ASSEMBLY

Legislative power is vested in a single chamber, the Asamblea Legislativa, whose members are elected every three years and are eligible for re-election. The Asamblea's term of office begins on 1 May. The Asamblea's duties include the choosing of the President and Vice-President of the Republic from the two citizens who shall have gained the largest number of votes for each of these offices, if no candidate obtains an absolute majority in the election. It also selects the members of the Supreme and subsidiary courts; of the Elections Council; and the Accounts Court of the Republic. It determines taxes; ratifies treaties concluded by the Executive with other States and international organizations; sanctions the Budget; regulates the monetary system of the country; determines the conditions under which foreign currencies may circulate; and suspends and reimposes constitutional guarantees. The right to initiate legislation may be exercised by the Asamblea (as well as by the President, through the Cabinet, and by the Supreme Court). The Asamblea may override, with a two-thirds' majority, the President's objections to a Bill that it has sent for presidential approval.

PRESIDENT

The President is elected for five years, the term beginning and expiring on 1 June. The principle of alternation in the presidential office is established in the Constitution, which states the action to be taken should this principle be violated. The Executive is responsible for the preparation of the Budget and its presentation to the Asamblea; the direction of foreign affairs; the organization of the armed and security forces; and the convening of extraordinary sessions of the Asamblea. In the event of the President's death, resignation, removal or other cause, the Vice-President takes office for the rest of the presidential term and, in case of necessity, the Vice-President may be replaced by one of the two Designates elected by the Asamblea.

JUDICIARY

Judicial power is exercised by the Supreme Court and by other competent tribunals. The Magistrates of the Supreme Court are elected by the Legislature, their number to be determined by law. The Supreme Court alone is competent to decide whether laws, decrees and regulations are constitutional or not.

The Government

HEAD OF STATE

President: CARLOS MAURICIO FUNES CARTAGENA (assumed office 1 June 2009).

Vice-President: SALVADOR SÁNCHEZ CERÉN.

CABINET
(July 2010)

The Government is formed by the Frente Farabundo Martí para la Liberación Nacional.

Minister of Finance: JUAN RAMÓN CARLOS ENRIQUE CÁCERES CHÁVEZ.

Minister of Foreign Affairs: HUGO ROGER MARTÍNEZ BONILLA.

Minister of Internal Affairs: HUMBERTO CENTENO NAJARRO.

Minister of Justice and Public Security: JOSÉ MANUEL MELGAR HENRÍQUEZ.

Minister of the Economy: HÉCTOR MIGUEL ANTONIO DADA H.

Minister of Education: SALVADOR SÁNCHEZ CERÉN.

Minister of National Defence: Col (retd) DAVID VICTORIANO MUNGUÍA PAYÉS.

Minister of Labour and Social Security: Dra VICTORIA MARINA DE AVILÉS.

Minister of Public Health and Social Welfare: Dra MARÍA ISABEL RODRÍGUEZ.

Minister of Agriculture and Livestock: GUILLERMO LÓPEZ SUÁREZ.

Minister of Public Works, Transport, Housing and Urban Development: MANUEL ORLANDO QUINTEROS A. (alias Gerson Martínez).

Minister of the Environment and Natural Resources: HERMÁN HUMBERTO ROSA CHÁVEZ.

Minister of Tourism: JOSÉ NAPOLEÓN DUARTE DURÁN.

MINISTRIES

Ministry for the Presidency: Alameda Dr Manuel Enrique Araujo 5500, San Salvador; tel. 2248-9000; fax 2248-9370; internet www.presidencia.gob.sv.

Ministry of Agriculture and Livestock: Final 1a, Avda Norte y Avda Manuel Gallardo, Santa Tecla; tel. 2241-1700; fax 2229-9271; e-mail info@mag.gob.sv; internet www.mag.gob.sv.

Ministry of the Economy: Edif. C1–C2, Centro de Gobierno, Alameda Juan Pablo II y Calle Guadalupe, San Salvador; tel. 2231-5600; fax 2221-5446; e-mail info@minec.gob.sv; internet www.minec.gob.sv.

Ministry of Education: Edif. A, Centro de Gobierno, Alameda Juan Pablo II y Calle Guadalupe, San Salvador; tel. 2281-0044; fax 2281-0077; e-mail educacion@mined.gob.sv; internet www.mined.gob.sv.

Ministry of the Environment and Natural Resources: Edif. MARN 2, Calle y Col. Las Mercedes, Carretera a Santa Tecla, Km 5.5, San Salvador; tel. 2267-6276; fax 2267-9420; e-mail medioambiente@marn.gob.sv; internet www.marn.gob.sv.

Ministry of Finance: Blvd Los Héroes 1231, San Salvador; tel. 2244-3000; fax 2244-6408; e-mail webmaster@mh.gob.sv; internet www.mh.gob.sv.

Ministry of Foreign Affairs: Calle El Pedregal, Blvd Cancillería, Ciudad Merliot, Antiguo Cuscatlán; tel. 2231-1000; fax 2289-8016; e-mail webmaster@rree.gob.sv; internet www.rree.gob.sv.

Ministry of Internal Affairs: Centro de Gobierno, Calle Oriente 9 y Avda Norte 15, San Salvador; tel. 2527-7000; fax 2527-7972; e-mail info@gobernacion.gob.sv; internet www.gobernacion.gob.sv.

Ministry of Justice and Public Security: Centro de Gobierno, Complejo Plan Maestro, Edifs B1, B2 y B3, Alameda Juan Pablo II y 17 Avda Norte, San Salvador; tel. 2526-3000; fax 2526-3105; internet www.seguridad.gob.sv.

Ministry of Labour and Social Security: Centro de Gobierno, Complejo Plan Maestro, Edifs 2 y 3, Alameda Juan Pablo II y 17 Avda Norte, San Salvador; tel. 2209-3700; fax 2209-3756; e-mail informacion@mtps.gob.sv; internet www.mtps.gob.sv.

Ministry of National Defence: Alameda Dr Manuel E. Araújo, Km 5, Carretera a Santa Tecla, San Salvador; tel. 2250-0100; e-mail fuerzaarmada@faes.gob.sv; internet www.fuerzaarmada.gob.sv/index.html.

Ministry of Public Health and Social Welfare: Calle Arce 827, San Salvador; tel. 2221-0966; fax 2221-0991; e-mail webmaster@mspas.gob.sv; internet www.mspas.gob.sv.

Ministry of Public Works, Transport, Housing and Urban Development: Plantel la Lechuza, Carretera a Santa Tecla Km 5.5, San Salvador; tel. 2528-3000; fax 2279-3723; e-mail info@mop.gob.sv; internet www.mop.gob.sv.

Ministry of Tourism: Edif. Carbonel 1, Alameda Dr Manuel Enrique Araujo y Pasaje Carbonel, Col. Roma, San Salvador; tel. 2243-7835; fax 2223-6120; e-mail info@corsatur.gob.sv; internet www.elsalvador.travel.

President and Legislature

PRESIDENT

Election, 15 March 2009

Candidates	Valid votes	% of valid votes
Carlos Mauricio Funes Cartagena (FMLN)	1,354,000	51.32
Rodrigo Avila Avilez (ARENA)	1,284,588	48.68
Total*	2,638,588	100.00

* In addition, there were 20,550 blank or invalid ballots.

ASAMBLEA LEGISLATIVA

President: CIRO CRUZ ZEPEDA (PCN).

General Election, 18 January 2009

Party	Votes	% of valid votes	Seats
Frente Farabundo Martí para la Liberación Nacional (FMLN)	943,936	42.60	35
Alianza Republicana Nacionalista (ARENA)	854,166	38.55	32
Partido de Conciliación Nacional (PCN)	194,751	8.79	11
Partido Demócrata Cristiano (PDC)	153,654	6.94	5
Cambio Democrático (CD)	46,971	2.12	1
Frente Democrático Revolucionario (FDR)	22,111	1.00	—
Total	2,215,589	100.00	84

Election Commission

Tribunal Supremo Electoral (TSE): 15a Calle Poniente 4223, Col. Escalón, San Salvador; tel. 2263-4641; fax 2263-4678; e-mail info@tse.gob.sv; internet www.tse.gob.sv; f. 1992; Pres. WALTER ARAUJO.

Political Organizations

Alianza Republicana Nacionalista (ARENA): Prolongación Calle Arce 2426, Col. Flor Banca, San Salvador; tel. 2260-4400; fax 2260-6260; e-mail infoparena@gmail.com; internet www.arena.com.sv; f. 1981; right-wing; Pres. ALFREDO FÉLIX CRISTIANI BURKARD; Exec. Dir ORLANDO CABRERA CANDRAY.

Cambio Democrático (CD): Casa 197, Calle Héctor Silva, Col. Médica, San Salvador; tel. 2225-5978; fax 2281-9636; e-mail comunicaciones@cambiodemocraticosv.org; internet www.cambiodemocraticosv.org; f. 1987 as Convergencia Democrática (CD); changed name as above in 2005; Sec.-Gen. HÉCTOR DADA HIREZI; Dep. Sec. JUAN JOSÉ MARTEL.

Frente Democrático Revolucionario (FDR): Avda Sierra Nevada 926, Col. Miramonte, San Salvador; tel. 2237-8844; fax 2260-1547; e-mail info@fdr.org.sv; internet www.fdr.org.sv; f. 2005; left-wing, reformist; breakaway faction of FMLN; Co-ordinator-Gen. JULIO HERNÁNDEZ.

Frente Farabundo Martí para la Liberación Nacional (FMLN): 27 Calle Poniente, Col. Layco 1316, San Salvador; tel. 2226-7183; e-mail comision.politica@fmln.org.sv; internet www.fmln.org.sv; f. 1980 as the FDR (Frente Democrático Revolucionario—FMLN) as a left-wing opposition front to the Govt; the FDR was the political wing and the FMLN was the guerrilla front; achieved legal recognition 1992; comprised various factions, including Communist (Leader SALVADOR SÁNCHEZ CERÉN), Renewalist (Leader OSCAR ORTIZ) and Terceristas (Leader GERSON MARTÍNEZ); Co-ordinator-Gen. MEDARDO GONZÁLEZ.

Partido de Conciliación Nacional (PCN): 15 Avda Norte y 3a Calle Poniente 244, San Salvador; tel. 2221-3752; fax 2281-9272; e-mail czepeda@asamblea.gob.sv; internet www.pcn.com.sv; f. 1961; right-wing; Sec.-Gen. CIRO CRUZ ZEPEDA.

Partido Demócrata Cristiano (PDC): Centro de Gobierno, Alameda Juan Pablo II y 11 Avda Norte bis 507, San Salvador; tel. 2281-5498; fax 7998-1526; e-mail pdcsal@navegante.com.sv; internet www.pdc.org.sv; f. 1960; 150,000 mems; advocates self-determination and Latin American integration; Sec.-Gen. RODOLFO ANTONIO PARKER SOTO.

Diplomatic Representation

EMBASSIES IN EL SALVADOR

Argentina: Calle La Sierra 3-I-B, Col. Escalón, San Salvador; tel. 2263-3638; fax 2263-3687; e-mail esalv@mrecic.gov.ar; Ambassador RUBÉN NÉSTOR PATTO.

Belize: Plaza Viscaya, Final Calle La Mascota, 1015 Col. Maquilishuat, San Salvador; tel. 2264-8024; fax 2273-6744; e-mail embsalbel@yahoo.com; Chargé d'affaires a.i. JUANITA CELIE PAZ MARIN DE GONZALEZ.

Brazil: Blvd Sérgio Vieira de Mello 132, Col. San Benito, San Salvador; tel. 2298-3286; fax 2279-3934; e-mail embajada@brasil.org.sv; internet www.brasil.org.sv; Ambassador LUIZ FELIPE MENDONÇA FILHO.

Canada: Centro Financiero Gigante, Torre A, Lobby 2, Alameda Roosevelt y 65 Avda Sur, Col. Escalón, San Salvador; tel. 2279-4655; fax 2279-0765; e-mail ssal@international.gc.ca; internet www.canadainternational.gc.ca/el_salvador-salvador; Ambassador CLAIRE POULIN.

Chile: Pasaje Bellavista 121, 9a Calle Poniente, Col. Escalón, San Salvador; tel. 2263-4285; fax 2263-4308; e-mail embachile@embachile.org.sv; internet www.conchileelsalvador.com.sv; Ambassador MANUEL MATTA ARAGAY.

China (Taiwan): Avda La Capilla 716, Blvd. del Hipódromo, Col. San Benito, Apdo 956, San Salvador; tel. 2263-1330; fax 2263-1329; e-mail sinoemb3@intercom.com.sv; internet www.taiwanembassy.org/sv; Ambassador CARLOS S. C. LIAO.

Colombia: Calle El Mirador 5120, Col. Escalón, San Salvador; tel. 2263-1936; fax 2263-1942; e-mail elsalvador@minrelext.gov.co; Ambassador CARLOS ALBERTO GAMBA.

Costa Rica: 85 Avda Sur y Calle Cuscatlán 4415, Col. Escalón, San Salvador; tel. 2264-3863; fax 2264-3866; e-mail embajada@embajadacostarica.org.sv; internet www.embajadacostarica.org.sv; Ambassador INGRID HERRMANN ESCRIBANO.

Cuba: Calle Arturo Ambrogui 530, esq. Avda el Mirador, Col. Escalón, San Salvador; tel. 2508-0446; Ambassador PEDRO PABLO PRADA QUINTERO.

Dominican Republic: Edif. Colinas, 1°, Blvd El Hipódromo 253, Zona Rosa, Col. San Benito, San Salvador; tel. 2223-4036; fax 2223-3109; e-mail endosal@saltel.net; Ambassador ROBERTO VICTORIA.

Ecuador: Pasaje Los Pinos 241, entre 77 y 79 Avda Norte, Col. Escalón, San Salvador; tel. 2263-5258; fax 2264-2973; e-mail ecuador@integra.com.sv; Ambassador Dr GALO LARENAS SERRANO.

France: 1a Calle Poniente 3718, Col. Escalón, Apdo 474, San Salvador; tel. 2279-4016; fax 2298-1536; e-mail info@embafrancia.com.sv; internet www.embafrancia.com.sv; Ambassador BLANDINE KREISS.

Germany: 7a Calle Poniente 3972, esq. 77a Avda Norte, Col. Escalón, Apdo 693, San Salvador; tel. 2247-0000; fax 2247-0099; e-mail info@san-salvador.diplo.de; internet www.san-salvador.diplo.de; Ambassador Dr CHRISTIAN STOCKS.

Guatemala: 15 Avda Norte 135, entre Calle Arce y 1a Calle Poniente, San Salvador; tel. 2271-2225; fax 2221-3019; e-mail embelsalvador@minex.gob.gt; Ambassador SILVIA ELIZABETH CÁCERES VETTORAZZI DE ALEMÁN.

Holy See: 87 Avda Norte y 7a Calle Poniente, Col. Escalón, Apdo 01-95, San Salvador (Apostolic Nunciature); tel. 2263-2931; fax 2263-3010; e-mail nunels@telesal.net; Apostolic Nuncio Most Rev. LUIGI PEZZUTO (Titular Archbishop of Torre di Proconsolare).

Honduras: 89 Avda Norte 561, entre 7a y 9a Calle Poniente, Col. Escalón, San Salvador; tel. 2263-2808; fax 2263-2296; e-mail embhon@integra.com.sv; internet www.sre.hn/elsalvador.html; Ambassador CÉSAR PINTO.

Israel: Centro Financiero Gigante, Torre B, 11°, Alameda Roosevelt y Avda Sur 63, San Salvador; tel. 2211-3434; fax 2211-3443; e-mail info@sansalvador.mfa.gov.il; internet sansalvador.mfa.gov.il; Ambassador MATTANYA COHEN.

Italy: Calle la Reforma 158, Col. San Benito, Apdo 0199, San Salvador; tel. 2223–5184; fax 2298-3050; e-mail ambasciatore.sansalvador@esteri.it; internet www.ambsansalvador.esteri.it; Ambassador CATERINA BERTOLINI.

Japan: World Trade Center, Torre 1, 6°, 89 Avda Norte y Calle El Mirador, Col. Escalón, Apdo 115, San Salvador; tel. 2528–1111; fax 2528–1110; internet www.sv.emb-japan.go.jp; Ambassador SHISEI KAKU.

Korea, Republic: 5a Calle Poniente 3970, entre 75 y 77 Avda Norte, Col. Escalón, San Salvador; tel. 2263-9145; fax 2263-0783; e-mail embcorea@mofat.go.kr; internet slv.mofat.go.kr; Ambassador MAENG DAL-YOUNG.

Mexico: Calle Circunvalación y Pasaje 12, Col. San Benito, Apdo 432, San Salvador; tel. 2248-9900; fax 2248-9906; e-mail embamex@

intercom.com.sv; internet portal.sre.gob.mx/elsalvador; Ambassador LEANDRO ARELLANO RESÉNDIZ.

Nicaragua: Calle El Mirador y 93 Avda Norte 4814, Col. Escalón, San Salvador; tel. 2263-8770; fax 2263-2292; e-mail embanic@integra.com.sv; Ambassador GILDA MARÍA BOLT GONZÁLEZ.

Panama: Calle los Bambúes, Avda las Bugambilías 21, Col. San Francisco, San Salvador; tel. 2536-0601; fax 2536-0602; e-mail embpan@telesat.net; Chargé d'affaires a.i. EDILMA ALEMÁN.

Peru: Avda Masferrer Norte 17P, Cumbres de la Escalafón, Col. Escalón, San Salvador; tel. 2275-5566; fax 2275-5569; e-mail embperu@telesal.net; Ambassador LUIS JUAN CHUQUIHUARA CHIL.

Spain: Calle La Reforma 164 bis, Col. San Benito, San Salvador; tel. 2257-5700; fax 2257-5712; e-mail emb.sansalvador@mae.es; internet www.maec.es/embajadas/sansalvador; Ambassador JOSÉ JAVIER GÓMEZ-LLERA Y GARCÍA-NAVA.

USA: Blvd Santa Elena Sur, Antiguo Cuscatlán, San Salvador; tel. 2501-2999; fax 2501-2150; internet sansalvador.usembassy.gov; Ambassador MARI CARMEN APONTE (designate).

Uruguay: Edif. Gran Plaza 405, Blvd del Hipódromo 111, Col. San Benito, San Salvador; tel. 2279-1626; fax 2279-1627; e-mail urusalva@telesal.net; Ambassador JULIO CÉSAR BENÍTEZ SÁENZ.

Venezuela: 7a Calle Poniente 3921, entre 75 y 77 Avda Norte, Col. Escalón, San Salvador; tel. 2263-3977; fax 2211-0027; e-mail embajadadevenezuela@telesal.net; Ambassador NORA MARGARITA URIBE TRUJILLO.

Judicial System

Supreme Court of Justice

Frente a Plaza José Simeón Cañas, Centro de Gobierno, San Salvador; tel. 2271-8888; fax 2271-3767; internet www.csj.gob.sv.

f. 1824; composed of 15 Magistrates, one of whom is its President; the Court is divided into four chambers: Constitutional Law, Civil Law, Criminal Law and Litigation; Pres. Dr JOSÉ BELARMINO JAIME.

Courts of First Instance: 201 courts throughout the country.

Courts of Appeal: 26 chambers composed of two Magistrates.

Courts of Peace: 322 courts throughout the country.

Procurator-General: ROMEO BENJAMÍN BARAHONA MELÉNDEZ (acting).

Procurator-General for the Defence of Human Rights: OSCAR HUMBERTO LUNA.

Religion

Roman Catholicism is the dominant religion, but other denominations are also permitted. The Baptist Church, Seventh-day Adventists, Jehovah's Witnesses, and the Church of Jesus Christ of Latter-day Saints (Mormons) are represented.

CHRISTIANITY

The Roman Catholic Church

El Salvador comprises one archdiocese and seven dioceses. Roman Catholics represent some 76% of the total population.

Bishops' Conference

Conferencia Episcopal de El Salvador, 15 Avda Norte 1420, Col. Layco, Apdo 1310, San Salvador; tel. 2225-8997; fax 2226-5330; e-mail cedes.casa@telesal.net; internet www.iglesia.org.sv.

f. 1974; Pres. Most Rev. JOSÉ LUIS ESCOBAR ALAS (Archbishop of San Salvador).

Archbishop of San Salvador: Most Rev. JOSÉ LUIS ESCOBAR ALAS, Arzobispado, Col. Médica, Avda Dr Emilio Alvarez y Avda Dr Max Bloch, Apdo 2253, San Salvador; tel. 2226-0501; fax 2226-4979; e-mail info@arzobispadosansalvador.org; internet www.arzobispadosansalvador.org.

The Anglican Communion

El Salvador comprises one of the five dioceses of the Iglesia Anglicana de la Región Central de América. The Iglesia Anglicana has some 5,000 members.

Bishop of El Salvador: Rt Rev. MARTÍN DE JESÚS BARAHONA PASCACIO, 47 Avda Sur, 723 Col. Flor Blanca, Apdo 01-274, San Salvador; tel. 2223-2252; fax 2223-7952; e-mail martinba@gbm.net; internet www.cristosal.org.

The Baptist Church

Baptist Association of El Salvador: Avda Sierra Nevada 922, Col. Miramonte, Apdo 347, San Salvador; tel. 2226-6287; e-mail asociacionbautistaabes@hotmail.com; internet www.ublaonline.org/paises/elsalvador.htm; f. 1933; Pres. MANUEL ENRIQUE RIVAS; 4,427 mems.

Other Churches

Sínodo Luterano Salvadoreño (Salvadorean Lutheran Synod): Final 49 Avda Sur, Calle Paralela al Bulevar de los Próceres, San Salvador; tel. 2225-2843; fax 2248-3451; Pres. Bishop MEDARDO E. GÓMEZ SOTO; 12,000 mems.

The Press

DAILY NEWSPAPERS

San Miguel

Diario de Oriente: Avda Gerardo Barrios 406, San Miguel; internet www.elsalvador.com/diarios/oriente; Editor ROBERTO VALENCIA.

San Salvador

Co Latino: 23a Avda Sur 225, Apdo 96, San Salvador; tel. 2271-1303; fax 2271-0822; e-mail info@diariocolatino.com; internet www.diariocolatino.com; f. 1890; evening; Editor FRANCISCO ELÍAS VALENCIA SORIANO; circ. 15,000.

El Diario de Hoy: 11 Calle Oriente 271, Apdo 495, San Salvador; tel. 2231–7777; fax 2231-7869; e-mail redaccion@elsalvador.com; internet www.elsalvador.com; f. 1936; morning; independent; Dir ENRIQUE ALTAMIRANO MADRIZ; circ. 115,000.

Diario Oficial: 4a Calle Poniente y 15a, Avda Sur 829, San Salvador; tel. 2555-7829; fax 2222-4936; e-mail diariooficial@imprentanacional.gob.sv; internet www.imprentanacional.gob.sv; f. 1875; govt publ.; Dir LUIS ERNESTO FLORES LÓPEZ; circ. 1,000.

El Mundo: 15 Calle Poniente y 7a Avda Norte 521, San Salvador; tel. 2234-8000; fax 2222-8190; e-mail mercadeo@elmundo.com.sv; internet www.elmundo.com.sv; f. 1967; morning; Exec. Dir ONNO WUELFERS; circ. 40,215.

La Prensa Gráfica: 3a Calle Poniente 130, San Salvador; tel. 2241–2000; fax 2271-4242; e-mail lpg@laprensa.com.sv; internet www.laprensagrafica.com; f. 1915; general information; conservative, independent; Editor RODOLFO DUTRIZ; circ. 97,312 (weekdays), 115,564 (Sundays).

Santa Ana

Diario de Occidente: 1a Avda Sur 3, Santa Ana; tel. 2441-2931; internet www.elsalvador.com/diarios/occidente; f. 1910; circ. 6,000.

PERIODICALS

Cultura: Dirección de Publicaciones e Impresos, 17 Avda Sur 430, San Salvador; tel. 2510-5318; fax 2221-4415; e-mail revistacultura@concultura.gob.sv; internet www.dpi.gob.sv/Revista_Cultura.htm; f. 1955; 3 a year; publ. by the National Council for Culture and the Arts; Pres. LUIS FEDERICO HERNÁNDEZ AGUILAR; circ. 1,000.

El Economista: Grupo Dutriz, Blvd Santa Elena, Antiguo Cuscatlán, La Libertad; tel. 2241-2677; e-mail eleconomista@eleconomista.net; internet www.eleconomista.net; f. 2005; owned by Grupo Dutriz; monthly; business and economics; Chairman JOSÉ ROBERTO DUTRIZ.

Ella: Final blvd Santa Elena, frente a embajada de EUA, Antiguo Cuscatlán, La Libertad; tel. 2241-2000; e-mail ella@laprensa.com.sv; internet www.laprensagrafica.com; publ. by La Prensa Gráfica.

El Salvador Investiga: Proyección de Investigaciones, Edif. A5, 2°, Centro de Gobierno, San Salvador; tel. 2221-4439; e-mail dirección.investigaciones@concultura.gob.sv; internet www.concultura.gob.sv/revistainvestiga.htm; f. 2005; 2 a year; publ. by the National Council for Culture and the Arts; historical and cultural research; Editor MARIO COLORADO.

Motor Magazine: Final blvd Santa Elena, frente a embajada de EUA, Antiguo Cuscatlán, La Libertad; tel. 2241-2000; e-mail motor@laprensa.com.sv; internet www.laprensagrafica.com; publ. by La Prensa Gráfica; Editor ROBERTO FLORES PINTO.

PRESS ASSOCIATION

Asociación de Periodistas de El Salvador (Press Association of El Salvador): Edif. Casa del Periodista, Paseo Gen. Escalón 4130, San Salvador; tel. 2263-5335; e-mail info@apes.org.sv; internet www.apes.org.sv; Pres. RAFAEL DOMÍNGUEZ.

Publishers

Clásicos Roxsil, SA de CV: 4a Avda Sur 2–3, Nueva San Salvador; tel. 2228-1832; fax 2228-1212; e-mail roxanabe@navegante.com.sv; f. 1976; textbooks, literature; Dir ROSA VICTORIA SERRANO DE LÓPEZ; Editorial Dir ROXANA BEATRIZ LOPEZ.

Dirección de Publicaciones e Impresos: Concultura, 17a Avda Sur 430, San Salvador; tel. 2271-1806; fax 2271-1071; e-mail publicaciones.direccion@concultura.gob.sv; internet www.dpi.gob.sv; f. 1953; literary and general; Dir MIGUEL ANGEL RIVERA LARIOS.

Editorial Delgado: Universidad 'Dr José Matías Delgado', Km 8.5, Carretera Panamericana, Antiguo Cuscatlán; tel. 2278-1011; e-mail jalas@ujmd.edu.sv; internet www.ujmd.edu.sv; f. 1984; Dir Dr DAVID ESCOBAR GALINDO.

UCA Editores: Apdo 01-575, San Salvador; tel. 2210–6655; fax 2210-6655; e-mail ucaeditores@gmail.com; internet www.uca.edu.sv/uca; f. 1975; social science, religion, economy, literature and textbooks; Dir RODOLFO CARDENAL.

PUBLISHERS' ASSOCIATION

Cámara Salvadoreña del Libro: Col. Flor Blanca, 47 Avda Norte y 1a Calle Poniente, Apdo 3384, San Salvador; tel. 2275-0231; fax 2261-2231; e-mail camsalibro@integra.com.sv; f. 1974; Pres. ANA MOLINA DE FAUVET; Exec. Dir AMÉRICA DE DOMÍNGUEZ.

Broadcasting and Communications

TELECOMMUNICATIONS

Regulatory Authority

Superintendencia General de Electricidad y Telecomunicaciones (SIGET): 16a Calle Poniente y 37 Avda Sur 2001, Col. Flor Blanca, San Salvador; tel. 2257-4438; fax 2257-4498; e-mail fernado.arguello@siget.gob.sv; internet www.siget.gob.sv; f. 1996; Supt FERNANDO ARGÜELLO TÉLLEZ.

Major Service Providers

Digicel: Edif. Palic, 5°, Alameda Dr Manuel Enrique Araujo y Calle Nueva No 1, Col. Escalón, San Salvador; tel. 2285-5100; fax 2285-5585; e-mail servicioalcliente.sv@digicelgroup.com; internet www.digicel.com.sv; mobile telecommunications; owned by Digicel (USA); CEO JOSÉ ANTONIO RODRÍGUEZ.

Telecom El Salvador: Edif. Palic, 40°, Alameda Manuel E. Araujo y Calle Nueva 1, San Salvador; tel. 2250-5555; e-mail webmaster@telecom.com.sv; internet www.telecom.com.sv; terrestrial telecommunications network, fmrly part of Administración Nacional de Telecomunicaciones (ANTEL), which was divested in 1998; changed name from CTE Antel Telecom in 1999; acquired by América Móvil, SA de CV (Mexico) in 2003; Chair. PATRICK SLIM DOMIT.

Telefónica El Salvador: San Salvador; tel. 2244-0144; e-mail telefonica.empresas@telefonicamail.com.sv; internet www.telefonica.com.sv; fmrly Internacional de Telecomunicaciones (Intel), divested in 1998; controlling interest owned by Telefónica, SA (Spain); Pres. CÉSAR ALIERTA.

Telefónica Movistar: Torre Telefónica (Torre B de Centro Financiero Gigante), Alameda Roosevelt y 63 Avda Sur, Col. Escalón, San Salvador; tel. 2257-4000; internet www.telefonica.com.sv/movistar; mobile telecommunications; 92% owned by Telefónica Móviles, SA (Spain); Pres. ANTONIO VIANA-BAPTISTA; CEO JUAN ANTONIO ABELLÁN RÍOS.

Telemóvil: Centro Financiero, Gigante Torre D, 9°, Avda Roosevelt, San Salvador; tel. 2246-9977; fax 2246-9999; e-mail servicioalcliente@tigo.com.sv; internet www.telemovil.com; mobile telecommunications and internet services; subsidiary of Millicom International Cellular (Luxembourg).

RADIO

Radio Nacional de El Salvador: Dirección General de Medios, Calle Monserrat, Plantel Ex-IVU, San Salvador; e-mail radio.elsalvador@gobernacion.gob.sv; internet www.radioelsalvador.com.sv; f. 1926; non-commercial cultural station; Dir-Gen. JAIME VILANOVA.

TELEVISION

Canal 8 (Agape TV): 1511 Calle Gerardo Barrios, Col. Cucumacuyán, San Salvador; tel. 2281-2828; fax 2271-3419; e-mail dircomunicaciones@agape.com.sv; internet www.agapetv8.com; Catholic, family channel; Pres. FLAVIÁN MUCCI.

Canal 12: Urb. Santa Elena 12, Antiguo Cuscatlán, San Salvador; tel. 2121-1212; fax 2278-0722; internet www.canal12.com.sv; f. 1984; Dir ALEJANDRO GONZÁLEZ.

Grupo Megavisión: Calle Poniente entre 85 y 86 Avda Norte, Apdo 2789, San Salvador; tel. 2283-2121; e-mail serviciosmegavision@salnet.net; internet www.megavision.com.sv; operates Canal 15, 19 and Megavision 21.

Grupo Televisivo Cuscatleco: 6a.10a Calle Poniente 2323, Col. Flor Blanca, San Salvador; tel. 2240-0083; fax 2245-6142; internet www.tecoloco.com.sv; operates Canal 23, 25, 67 and 69 (in the West only).

Tecnovisión Canal 33: Calle Arce 1120, San Salvador; tel. 2275-8888; e-mail nachocastillo@canal33.tv; internet www.canal33.tv; Pres. JOSÉ MAURICIO LOUCEL; Dir-Gen. NARCISO CASTILO.

Finance

(cap. = capital; res = reserves; dep. = deposits; m. = million; brs = branches; amounts in colones unless otherwise stated)

BANKING

Supervisory Bodies

Superintendencia del Sistema Financiero: 7a Avda Norte 240, Apdo 2942, San Salvador; tel. 2281-2444; fax 2281-1621; e-mail webmaster@ssf.gob.sv; internet www.ssf.gob.sv; Pres. VÍCTOR ANTONIO RAMÍREZ NAJARRO.

Superintendencia de Valores: Antiguo Edif. BCR, 2°, 1a Calle Poniente y 7a Avda Norte, San Salvador; tel. 2281-8900; fax 2221-3404; e-mail info@superval.gob.sv; internet www.superval.gob.sv; Supt RENÉ MAURICIO GUARDADO RODRÍGUEZ.

Central Bank

Banco Central de Reserva de El Salvador: Alameda Juan Pablo II, entre 15 y 17 Avda Norte, Apdo 01-106, San Salvador; tel. 2281-8000; fax 2281-8011; e-mail info@bcr.gob.sv; internet www.bcr.gob.sv; f. 1934; nationalized Dec. 1961; entered monetary integration process 1 Jan. 2001; cap. US $115.0m., res $131.7m., dep. $1,695.4m. (Dec. 2008); Pres. CARLOS ACEVEDO; Vice-Pres. MARTA EVELYN DE RIVERA.

Commercial and Mortgage Banks

Banco Agrícola: Blvd Constitución 100, San Salvador; tel. 2267-5000; fax 2267-5930; e-mail info@bancoagricola.com; internet www.bancoagricola.com; f. 1955; merged with Banco Desarrollo in July 2000; acquired Banco Capital in Nov. 2001; cap. US $200.0m., res $196.1m., dep. $2,846.1m. (Dec. 2007); Pres. SERGIO RESTREPO ISAZA; 8 brs.

Banco Citibank de El Salvador, SA: Edif. Pirámide Cuscatlán, Km 10, Carretera a Santa Tecla, Apdo 626, San Salvador; tel. 2212-2000; fax 2228-5700; e-mail info@bancocuscatlan.com; internet www.bancocuscatlan.com/elsalvador; f. 1972; acquired by Citi (USA) in 2008; cap. US $135.0m., res $134.2m., dep. $2,054.1m. (Dec. 2007); Pres. JOSÉ MAURICIO SAMAYOA RIVAS; 31 brs.

Banco Hipotecario de El Salvador: Pasaje Senda Florida Sur, Col. Escalón, Apdo 999, San Salvador; tel. 2223-7713; fax 2298-2071; internet www.bancohipotecario.com.sv; f. 1935; cap. US $14.5m., res $16.3m., dep. $282.6m. (Dec. 2007); Pres. CARLOS ALBERTO ORTIZ; 12 brs.

Banco HSBC Salvadoreño, SA (Bancosal): Edif. Centro Financiero, Avda Manuel E. Araujo y Avda Olímpica 3550, Apdo 0673, San Salvador; tel. 2214-2000; fax 2214-2755; e-mail info@bancosal.com; internet www.hsbc.com.sv; f. 1885 as Banco Salvadoreño, SA; adopted current name 2007; cap. US $150m., res $79.6m., dep. $1,653.9m. (Dec. 2007); CEO GERARDO JOSÉ SIMÁN SIRI; 74 brs.

Banco Promérica: Edif. Promérica, Centro Comercial La Gran Vía, Antiguo Cuscatlan; tel. 2513-5000; e-mail soluciones@promerica.com.sv; internet www.promerica.com.sv; f. 1996; privately owned; Chair. RAMIRO ORTIZ GURDÍAN; Exec. Pres. EDUARDO A. QUEVEDO MORENO.

Public Institutions

Banco de Fomento Agropecuario: Km 10.5, Carretera al Puerto de la Libertad, Santa Tecla, La Libertad, Nueva San Salvador; tel. 2241-0966; fax 2241-0800; internet www.bfa.gob.sv; f. 1973; state-owned; cap. 14.9m., res 5.3m., dep. 153.1m. (Dec. 2007); Pres. NORA MIRANDA DE LÓPEZ; Gen. Man. JOSÉ ANTONIO PEÑATE; 27 brs.

Banco Multisectorial de Inversiones: Edif. World Trade Center II, 4°, San Salvador; tel. 2267-0000; fax 2267-0011; e-mail servicio.cliente@bmi.gob.sv; internet www.bmi.gob.sv; f. 1994; Pres. RICARDO MORA.

Federación de Cajas de Crédito (FEDECREDITO): 25 Avda Norte y 23 Calle Poniente, San Salvador; tel. 2209-9696; fax 2226-7161; e-mail informacion@fedecredito.com.sv; internet www.fedecredito.com.sv; f. 1943; Pres. MACARIO ARMANDO ROSALES ROSA.

Fondo Social para la Vivienda (FSV): Calle Rubén Darío 901, entre 15 y 17 Avda Sur, Apdo 2179, San Salvador; tel. 2231-2000; fax 2271-4011; e-mail comunicaciones@fsv.gob.sv; internet www.fsv.gob.sv; f. 1973; provides loans to workers for house purchases; Pres. JOSÉ TOMÁS CHÉVEZ RUIZ; Gen. Man. FRANCISCO ANTONIO GUEVARA.

Banking Association

Asociación Bancaria Salvadoreña (ABANSA): Pasaje Senda, Florida Norte 140, Col. Escalón, San Salvador; tel. 2298-6959; fax 2223-1079; e-mail info@abansa.net; internet www.abansa.org.sv; f. 1965; Pres. ARMANDO ARIAS; Exec. Dir MARCELA DE JIMÉNEZ.

STOCK EXCHANGE

Mercado de Valores de El Salvador, SA de CV (Bolsa de Valores): Urb. Jardines de la Hacienda, Blvd Merliot y Avda Las Carretas, Antiguo Cuscatlán, La Libertad, San Salvador; tel. 2212-6400; fax 2278-4377; e-mail info@bves.com.sv; internet www.bves.com.sv; f. 1992; Pres. ROLANDO ARTURO DUARTE SCHLAGETER.

INSURANCE

AIG Unión y Desarrollo, SA: Calle Loma Linda 265, Col. San Benito, Apdo 92, San Salvador; tel. 2250-3200; fax 2250-3201; e-mail aig.elsalvador@aig.com; internet www.aigelsalvador.com; f. 1998; following merger of Unión y Desarrollo, SA and AIG; Exec. Dir RAMÓN AVILA QUEHL; Gen. Man. PEDRO ARTANA.

Aseguradora Agrícola Comercial, SA: Alameda Roosevelt 3104, Apdo 1855, San Salvador; tel. 2261-8233; fax 2260-3344; e-mail informacion@acsasal.com.sv; internet www.acsasal.com.sv; f. 1973; Pres. LUIS ALFREDO ESCALANTE SOL; Commercial Man. LUIS ALFONSO FIGUEROA.

Aseguradora Popular, SA: Paseo Gen. Escalón 5338, Col. Escalón, San Salvador; tel. 2263-0700; fax 2263-1246; e-mail aseposapresi@telesal.net; f. 1975; Pres. Dr CARLOS ARMANDO LAHÚD; Gen. Man. HERIBERTO PÉREZ AGUIRRE.

Aseguradora Suiza Salvadoreña, SA (ASESUISA): Alameda Dr Manuel Enrique Araujo, Plaza Suiza, Apdo 1490, Col. San Benito, San Salvador; tel. 2209-5000; fax 2209-5001; e-mail info@asesuisa.com; internet www.asesuisa.com; f. 1969; acquired in 2001 by Inversiones Financieras Banco Agrícola (Panama); Pres. Dr SERGIO RESTREPO ISAZA; Exec. Dir RICARDO COHEN.

La Central de Seguros y Fianzas, SA: Avda Olímpica 3333, Apdo 01-255, San Salvador; tel. 2268-6000; fax 2223-7647; e-mail gerenciafianzas@lacentral.com.sv; internet www.lacentral.com.sv; f. 1983; Pres. EDUARDO ENRIQUE CHACÓN BORJA.

Compañía General de Seguros, SA: Calle Loma Linda 223, Col. San Benito, Apdo 1004, San Salvador; tel. 2279-3777; fax 2223-0719; e-mail cogeseg@cgs.com.sv; internet www.cgs.com.sv; f. 1955; Pres. JOSÉ GUSTAVO BELISMELIS VIDES; CEO ERICK PRADO.

Internacional de Seguros, SA (Interseguros): Edif. Plaza Credicorp Bank, Calle 50, 19°, 20° y 21°, San Salvador; tel. 2206-4000; fax 2210-1900; e-mail interseguros@interseguros.com.sv; internet isweb.iseguros.com/iseguros; f. 1910; merged with Seguros Universales in 2004; Pres. JUAN PABLO FÁBREGA.

Mapfre La Centro Americana, SA: Alameda Roosevelt 3107, Apdo 527, San Salvador; tel. 2257-6666; fax 2223-2687; e-mail lacentro@lacentro.com; internet www.lacentro.com; f. 1915; Pres. ANTONIO PENEDO CASMARTIÑO; Gen. Man. GILMAR NAVARRETE.

Seguros e Inversiones, SA (SISA): 10.5 Km Carretera Panamericana, Santa Tecla; tel. 2229-8888; fax 2229-8187; e-mail informacion@sisa.com.sv; internet www.sisa.com.sv; f. 1962; Pres. JOSÉ EDUARDO MONTENEGRO.

Association

Asociación Salvadoreña de Empresas de Seguros (ASES): Calle Los Castaños 120, Col. San Francisco, San Salvador; tel. 2223-7169; fax 2223-8901; e-mail asesgeneral@ases.com.sv; internet www.ases.com.sv; Pres. Dr PEDRO GEOFFROY CARLETTI; Exec. Dir RAÚL BETANCOURT MENÉNDEZ.

Trade and Industry

GOVERNMENT AGENCIES AND DEVELOPMENT ORGANIZATIONS

Comisión Nacional de la Micro y Pequeña Empresa (CONAMYPE): Of. 41, 1°, Avda Norte y Avda Scout de El Salvador, No 115, San Salvador; tel. 2521-2200; fax 2521-2274; e-mail conamype@conamype.gob.sv; internet www.conamype.gob.sv; f. 1996; micro and small industrial devt; Pres. HÉCTOR DADA HIREZI (Minister of the Economy); Exec. Dir ILEANA ROGEL.

Consejo Nacional de Ciencia y Tecnología (CONACYT): Avda Dr Emilio Alvarez, Pasaje Dr Guillermo Rodríguez Pacas 51, Col. Médica, San Salvador; tel. 2234-8400; fax 2225-6255; e-mail cit@conacyt.gob.sv; internet www.conacyt.gob.sv/drupal; f. 1992; formulation and guidance of national policy on science and technology; Exec. Dir CARLOS ROBERTO OCHOA CÓRDOBA.

Corporación de Exportadores de El Salvador (COEXPORT): Avda La Capilla 359A, Col. San Benito, San Salvador; tel. 2212-0200; fax 2243-3159; e-mail info@coexport.com.sv; internet www.coexport.com.sv; f. 1973 to promote Salvadorean exports; Pres. FRANCISCO BOLAÑOS; Exec. Dir SILVIA M. CUÉLLAR DE PAREDES.

Corporación Salvadoreña de Inversiones (CORSAIN): Avda Bunganbilias, Casa 14, Col. San Francisco, San Salvador; tel. 2224-6070; fax 2224-6877; e-mail info@corsain.gob.sv; internet www.corsain.gob.sv; Pres. RENÉ MAURICIO MENDOZA JÉREZ.

Fondo de Inversión Social para el Desarrollo Local (FISDL): Avda Sur y Calle México, No 10, Barrio San Jacinto, San Salvador; tel. 2505-1200; fax 2505-1370; e-mail webmaster@fisdl.gob.sv; internet www.fisdl.gob.sv; f. 1990; poverty alleviation and development; Pres. HÉCTOR SILVA ARGÜELLO.

Instituto Salvadoreño de Fomento Cooperativo (INSAFOCOOP): Edif. Urrutia Abrego 2, Frente a INPEP, 15 Calle Poniente, No 402, San Salvador; tel. 2222-2563; fax 2222-4119; e-mail insafocoop@insafocoop.gob.sv; internet www.insafocoop.gob.sv; f. 1971; devt of co-operatives; Pres. FÉLIX CÁRCAMO.

Instituto Salvadoreño de Transformación Agraria (ISTA): Final Col. Las Mercedes, Km 5.5, Carretera a Santa Tecla, San Salvador; tel. 2527-2600; fax 2224-0259; e-mail info@ista.gob.sv; internet www.ista.gob.sv; f. 1976 to promote rural devt; empowered to buy inefficiently cultivated land; Pres. PABLO ALCIDES OCHOA.

CHAMBER OF COMMERCE

Cámara de Comercio e Industria de El Salvador: 9a Avda Norte y 5a Calle Poniente, Apdo 1640, San Salvador; tel. 2231–3000; fax 2271-4461; e-mail camara@camarasal.com; internet www.camarasal.com; f. 1915; 2,000 mems; Pres. JORGE JOSÉ DABOUB; brs in San Miguel, Santa Ana, Sonsonate and La Unión.

INDUSTRIAL AND TRADE ASSOCIATIONS

Asociación Azucarera de El Salvador: 103 Avda Norte y Calle Arturo Ambrogi 145, Col. Escalón, San Salvador; tel. 2264-1226; fax 2263-0361; e-mail asosugar@sal.gbm.net; internet www.asociacionazucarera.com; national sugar asscn, fmrly Instituto Nacional del Azúcar; Pres. Dr FRANCISCO ARMANDO ARIAS; Dir JULIO ARROYO.

Asociación Cafetalera de El Salvador (ACES): 67 Avda Norte 116, Col. Escalón, San Salvador; tel. 2223-3024; fax 2298-6261; e-mail ascafes@telesal.net; f. 1930; coffee growers' asscn; Pres. JOSÉ ROBERTO INCLÁN ROBREDO; Exec. Dir AMIR SALVADOR ALABÍ.

Asociación Salvadoreña de Beneficiadores y Exportadores de Café (ABECAFE): 87 Avda Norte, Condominio Fountainblue 4, Col. Escalón, San Salvador; tel. 2263-2834; fax 2263-2833; e-mail abecafe@telesal.net; coffee producers' and exporters' asscn; Pres. CARLOS BORGONOVO.

Asociación Salvadoreña de Industriales: Calles Roma y Liverpool, Col. Roma, Apdo 48, San Salvador; tel. 2279-2488; fax 2267-9253; e-mail medios@asi.com.sv; internet www.industriaelsalvador.com; f. 1958; 400 mems; manufacturers' asscn; Pres. JAVIER ERNESTO SIMAN; Exec. Dir JORGE ARRIAZA.

Cámara Agropecuaria y Agroindustrial de El Salvador (CAMAGRO): Calle El Lirio 19, Col. Maquilishuat, San Salvador; tel. 2264-4622; fax 2263-9448; e-mail contactenos@camagro.com; internet www.camagro.com; Pres. AGUSTÍN MARTÍNEZ.

Consejo Salvadoreño del Café (CSC) (Salvadorean Coffee Council): 1 Avda Norte y 13 Calle Poniente, Nueva San Salvador, La Libertad; tel. 2267-6600; fax 2267-6650; e-mail csc@consejocafe.org.sv; internet www.consejocafe.org; f. 1989 as successor to the Instituto Nacional del Café; formulates policy and oversees the coffee industry; Exec. Dir ANA ELENA ESCALANTE.

Cooperativa Algodonera Salvadoreña, Ltda (COPAL): 49 Avda Norte 161, San Salvador; tel. 2298-9330; fax 2298-9331; f. 1940; 185 mems; cotton growers' asscn; Pres. MARIO LÓPEZ AYALA.

Unión de Cooperativas de Cafetaleras de El Salvador de RL (UCAFES): Avda Río Lempa, Calle Adriático 44, Jardines de Guadalupe, San Salvador; tel. 2243-2238; fax 2298-1504; union of coffee-growing co-operatives; Pres. ERNESTO LIMA.

EMPLOYERS' ORGANIZATION

Asociación Nacional de Empresa Privada (ANEP) (National Private Enterprise Association): 1 Calle Poniente y 71 Avda Norte 204, Col. Escalón, Apdo 1204, San Salvador; tel. 2209-8300; fax 2209-8317; e-mail communicaciones@anep.org.sv; internet www.anep.org

.sv; national private enterprise asscn; Pres. CARLOS ENRIQUE ARAUJO; Exec. Dir RAÚL MELARA MORÁN.

MAJOR COMPANIES

Construction and Metals

Condusal, SA (Conductores Eléctricos Salvadoreños): Km 15 Autopista al Aeropuerto Internacional, Santo Tómas, San Salvador; tel. 2213-5999; fax 2213-5900; e-mail condusal@condusal.com; internet www.condusal.com; f. 1993; manufactures electrical conductors; Dir JAIME FUENTE.

Corporación Industrial Centroamericana, SA de CV (CORINCA): Carretera a Quezaltepeque, Km 25, San Salvador; tel. 2310-2033; fax 2310-2234; internet www.corinca.com.sv; f. 1966; iron rods and wire, construction and building materials; Pres. SÉRGIO CATANI PAPINI; Gen. Man. CARLOS FRANCISCO ALVARADO; 350 employees.

Holcim El Salvador, SA de CV: Avda El Espino, Urb. Madreselva, Antiguo Cuscatlán, La Libertad; tel. 2505-0000; fax 2505-0777; e-mail cessamer@cessa.com.sv; internet www.holcim.com.sv; f. 1949 as Cemento de El Salvador; adopted present name in 2010 following acquisition of 90% stake by Holcim, Switzerland; manufacturers of Portland cement; Chair. ROLF SOIRON; CEO RICARDO CHÁVEZ CAPARROSO; 400 employees.

Food and Beverages

Grupo Calvo: Puerto Cutuco, Punta Gorda; internet www.calvo.es; f. 2003; tuna-processing plant; Pres. JOSÉ LUIS CALVO; 750 employees.

Industrias La Constancia, SA de CV (ILC): Edif. World Trade Center, Torre 1, 2°, Calle El Mirador y 89 Avda Norte, Col. Escalón, San Salvador; tel. 2222-8080; fax 2231-5152; e-mail servicioalcliente@ca.sabmiller.com; internet www.laconstancia.com; f. 1906; subsidiary of SABMiller PLC (United Kingdom); produces and sells beer; Pres. CARLOS HABENCIO FERNÁNDEZ; Corporate Dir ALDO VALLEJO; 950 employees.

Molinos de El Salvador, SA: Blvd del Ejército Nacional y 50 Avda Norte, Apdo 327, San Salvador; tel. 2297-8900; fax 2293-1525; e-mail info@molsa.com.sv; internet www.molsa.com.sv; f. 1959; production of wheat flour and biscuits; Gen. Man. JORGE ARMANDO CARDONA; 121 employees.

Productos Alimenticios Diana, SA de CV: Blvd del Ejercito Nacional, 12 Avda Sur, Soyapango, Apdo 117, San Salvador; tel. 2227-1233; fax 2227-7023; e-mail servicioalcliente@diana.com.sv; internet www.diana.com.sv; f. 1951; food-processing; Pres. ROSY DE PAREDES; Gen. Man. HUGO CÉSAR BARRERA; 2,000 employees.

Sello de Oro, SA, Productos Alimenticios: 2.5 km Carretera a Jayaque, La Libertad, San Salvador; tel. 2317-7777; fax 2317-7704; e-mail info@sellodeoro.com.sv; internet www.sellodeoro.com.sv; f. 1967; food and food-processing; Pres. CARMEN ELENA DEL SOL; Exec. Dir JOSÉ AGUSTÍN MARTÍNEZ; 1,285 employees.

Pharmaceuticals

Droguería Santa Lucía, SA de CV: Calle Roma 238, Col. Roma, Apdo 06-5, San Salvador; tel. 2223-8000; fax 2223-8033; e-mail ventas@drogueria-santalucia.com; internet www.drogueriasantalucia.com; owned by AstraZeneca PLC (United Kingdom); pharmaceutical products.

Laboratorio López, SA de CV: Blvd del Ejército Nacional, Km 5.5, Jurisdicción de Soyapango, San Salvador; tel. 2277-6166; fax 2227-2783; e-mail info@lablopez.com.sv; internet www.lablopez.com; f. 1948; manufacturers of pharmaceutical products; Pres. THELMA DAVIDSON DE LÓPEZ.

Laboratorios Vijosa, SA de CV: Calle L-3, 10 Zona Industrial Merliot, Antiguo Cuscatlán; tel. 2251-9797; fax 2278-3121; e-mail info@vijosa.com; internet www.vijosa.com; manufacturers of pharmaceutical products; Pres. Dr VÍCTOR JORGE SACA; 130 employees.

Textiles and Clothing

Almacenes Simán, SA de CV: Centro Comercial Galerías, Paseo General Escalón 3700, Col. Escalón, San Salvador; tel. 2507-3000; fax 2245-4000; e-mail contacto@siman.com.sv; internet www.siman.com.sv; f. 1921; wholesale and retail sale of clothing; Exec. Pres. RICARDO SIMÁN; Regional Man. ALVARO CORPIÑO; 1,100 employees.

Facalca Hiltex, SA de CV: Calle el Progreso 3440, Col. Roma, Km 99½, Carretera a San Salvador, Ahuachapán; tel. 2413-2000; fax 2443-0461; e-mail webmaster@facalca-hiltex.com; internet www.facalca-hiltex.com; f. 1964; thread mills; Pres. and Man. JORGE BAHAIT GHIA; 980 employees.

Grupo Hilasal: Km 32, Carretera a Santa Ana, San Juan Opico, La Libertad, San Salvador; tel. 2319-1256; fax 2338-4064; e-mail cserviceinfo@hilasal.com; internet www.hilasal.com.sv; manufacturers of cotton goods and towelling; Pres. and CEO RICARDO SAGRERA; 1,000 employees.

Industrias Unidas, SA (IUSA): Km 11.5, Carretera Panamericana Oriente, Ilopango, Apdo 893, San Salvador; tel. 2250-9500; fax 2295-0846; e-mail ventas@iusa.com.sv; internet www.iusa.com.sv; f. 1955; owned by Toyobo-Itochu y Marubeni (Japan); manufacturers of textiles; Pres. EDUARDO MARTÍNEZ; 1,600 employees.

INSINCA, SA (Industrias Sintéticas de Centroamérica): Carretera Troncal del Norte, Km 12½, Apopa, San Salvador; tel. 2216-0055; fax 2216-0062; e-mail info@insinca.com; internet www.insinca.com; f. 1966; manufacturers of synthetic fibres; Pres. FÉLIX CASTILLO MAYORGA; 1,000 employees.

Textufil, SA de CV: 12 Avda Sur, Soyapango, Apdo 1632, San Salvador; tel. 2277-0066; fax 2227-2308; e-mail info@textufil.com; internet www.textufil.com; f. 1972; manufacturers of nylon and polyester textiles; Pres. JORGE ELÍAS BAHAIA; Man. ELÍAS JORGE BAHAIA SAMOUR.

Miscellaneous

British American Tobacco El Salvador: Alameda Roosevelt 2115, Apdo 06-113, San Salvador; tel. 2250-4444; fax 2250-4443; internet www.batcentralamerica.com; manufacture and sale of cigarettes; Gen. Man. GIOVANNI PARADA.

Compañía Química Industrial, SA de CV (COQUINSA): 29 Calle Oriente 73, Col. La Rabida, San Salvador; tel. 2226-0137; fax 2225-8430; e-mail info@coquinsa.com; internet www.coquinsa.com; f. 1979; manufacturers of adhesives, detergents, disinfectants, insecticides; Pres. MANUEL DE J. RODRÍGUEZ.

Empresas Adoc, SA: Blvd Ejército Nacional, Km 4½, Final Col. Montecarlo, Apdo 687, Soyapango, San Salvador; tel. 2277-2277; fax 2277-0352; e-mail adoces@adoc.com.sv; f. 1952; tannery, rubber, plastics, manufacturers of shoes and leather goods; retailers; Gen. Man. WILFREDO ROSALES; 4,370 employees.

Excel Automotriz: Blvd Los Héroes, Edif. DIDEA, San Salvador; tel. 2261-1133; fax 2260-3516; f. 1919; known as DIDEA El Salvador until 2010; distributor of cars and car supplies; Exec. Vice-Pres. (Group) CARLOS BOZA; Vice-Pres. JORGE DÍAZ SALAZAR.

Grupo Monge: Calle El Boqueron 5, Urb. Santa Elena, Antiguo Cuscatlan, La Libertad; tel. 2244-0000; fax 2289-7105; e-mail naguirre@prado.com.sv; internet prado.com.sv; f. 1952 as Muebles Metálicos Prado, SA de CV; bought by Grupo Monge in 2006, name changed 2010; 355 stores in Central America under several brands: El Gallo más Gallo, Monge, Play, El Verdugo and Almacenes Prado; home appliances.

PriceWaterhouseCoopers: Centro Profesional Presidente, Avda La Revolución y Calle Circunvalación, Col. San Benito, Apdo 695, San Salvador; tel. 2243-5844; fax 2243-3546; internet www.pwc.com/sv; accountancy and management consultancy; Pres. MARIO WILFREDO LÓPEZ SALGADO; 150 employees.

Siemens, SA: Calle Siemens 43, Parque Industrial Santa Elena, Antiguo Cuscatlán, Apdo 1525, San Salvador; tel. 2248-7333; fax 2278-3334; e-mail siemens.elsalvador@siemens.co; internet www.siemens-centram.com/index_elsalvador.shtml; owned by Siemens AG (Germany); manufacturers of electrical equipment and machinery; Gen. Man. ARTURO LARA.

SIGMA/Q, SA: 8 Km Blvd del Ejército, Apdo 1096, San Salvador; tel. 2254-2500; fax 2424-3298; e-mail atencionalcliente@sigmaq.com; internet www.sigmaq.com; f. 1973; manufacturers of collapsible packaging; Man. Corporate Affairs CARMEN AIDA DE MEARDI; 957 employees.

Tabacalera de El Salvador, SA de CV: 69 Avda Norte 213, Col. Escalón, San Salvador; tel. 2241-5200; fax 2241-5270; e-mail jorge.zablah@pmintl.com; f. 1976; subsidiary of Philip Morris Inc, USA; manufacturers of cigarettes; Pres. JORGE ZABLAH TOUCHÉ; 186 employees.

UTILITIES

Electricity

Comisión Ejecutiva Hidroeléctrica del Río Lempa (CEL): 9 Calle Poniente 950, entre 15 y 17 Avda Norte, Centro de Gobierno, San Salvador; tel. 2211-6000; fax 2207-1302; e-mail naguilar@cel.gob.sv; internet www.cel.gob.sv; f. 1948; hydroelectric electricity generation; Pres. NICOLÁS ANTONIO SALUME BABÚN.

Superintendencia General de Electricidad y Telecomunicaciones (SIGET): see Broadcasting and Communications—Telecommunications; regulatory authority.

Electricity Companies

AES El Salvador: e-mail consultas@aes.com; internet www.aeselsalvador.com; Exec. Pres. ABRAHAM BICHARA; operates four distribution cos in El Salvador:

CLESA: 23 Avda Sur y 5a Calle Oriente, Barrio San Rafael, Santa Ana; tel. 2429-4000; f. 1892.

Compañía de Alumbrado Electric (CAESS): Calle El Bambú, Col. San Antonio, Ayutuxtepeque, San Salvador; tel. 2529-9999; f. 1890.

Distribuidora Eléctrica de Usulután (DEUSEM): Centro Comercial Puerta de Oriente Local 2, Usulután; tel. 2622-4000; f. 1957.

EEO: Final 8, Calle Poniente, Calle a Ciudad Pacífico, Plantel Jalacatal, San Miguel; tel. 2606-8000; f. 1995.

Distribuidora de Electricidad del Sur (DELSUR): Edif. Corporativo DELSUR, Unidad de Comunicaciones, Final 17 Avda Norte. y Calle El Boquerón, Santa Tecla, La Libertad; tel. 2233-5700; fax 2243-8662; e-mail comunicaciones@delsur.com.sv; internet www.delsur.com.sv; Pres. IVÁN DÍAZ MOLINA; Gen. Man. ALEXIS BUTTO.

La Geo: Final 15, Avda Sur y Blvd Sur, Colonia Utila, Santa Tecla, La Libertad; tel. 2211-6700; fax 2211-6746; e-mail info@lageo.com.sv; internet www.lageo.com.sv; f. 1999; jt venture between state and ENEL Latin America; operates Ahuachapán and Berlin geothermal fields; Dir JORGE JOSÉ SIMÁN.

Water

Administración Nacional de Acueductos y Alcantarillados (ANDA): Edif. ANDA, Final Avda Don Bosco, Col. Libertad, San Salvador; tel. 2247-2700; fax 2225-3152; e-mail sugerencias@anda.gob.sv; internet www.anda.gob.sv; f. 1961; maintenance of water supply and sewerage systems; Pres. MARCO ANTONIO FORTÍN; Exec. Dir CARLOS MANUEL DERAS BARILLAS.

TRADE UNIONS

Central de Trabajadores Democráticos de El Salvador (CTD) (Democratic Workers' Confederation): 1a Avda Norte y 19 Calle Poniente 12, San Salvador; tel. and fax 2235-8043; e-mail comuctd@netcomsa.com; Sec.-Gen. AMADEO GARCÍA ESPINOZA; 50,000 mems (2007).

Central de Trabajadores Salvadoreños (CTS) (Salvadorean Workers' Confederation): Calle Darío González 616, San Jacinto, San Salvador; tel. 2237-2315; fax 2270-1703; e-mail felixblancocts@hotmail.com; f. 1966; Christian Democratic; Pres. FÉLIX BLANCO; 30,000 mems (2007).

Confederación General de Sindicatos (CGS) (General Confederation of Unions): Edif. Kury, 3a Calle Oriente 226, San Salvador; tel. and fax 2222-3527; f. 1958; admitted to ITUC/ORIT; Sec.-Gen. JOSÉ ISRAEL HUIZA CISNEROS; 27,000 mems.

Confederación General del Trabajo (CGT) (General Confederation of Workers): 141 Avda B, Calle 2, Col. El Roble, San Salvador; tel. and fax 2222-6109; f. 1983; 20 affiliated unions; Sec.-Gen. JOSÉ RENÉ PÉREZ; 85,000 mems.

Confederación Sindical de Trabajadores de El Salvador (CSTS) (Salvadorean Workers' Union Federation): Blvd Universitario 2226, Col. San José, San Salvador; e-mail csts-es@navegante.com.sv; conglomerate of independent left-wing trade unions; Sec.-Gen. NEFTALÍ COLOCHO.

Confederación Unitaria de Trabajadores Salvadoreños (CUTS) (United Salvadorean Workers' Federation): 141 Avda A, Col. San José, San Salvador; tel. and fax 2226-2100; e-mail proyectocuts@salnet.net; left-wing; Sec.-Gen. RÓGER GUTIÉRREZ.

Federación Nacional Sindical de Trabajadores Salvadoreños (FENASTRAS) (Salvadorean Workers' National Union Federation): 10a Avda Norte 120, San Salvador; f. 1975; left-wing; 35,000 mems in 16 affiliates; Sec.-Gen. JUAN JOSÉ HUEZO.

Unidad Nacional de Trabajadores Salvadoreños (UNTS) (National Unity of Salvadorean Workers): Centro de Gobierno El Salvador, Calle 27 Poniente 432, Col. Layco, Apdo 2479, San Salvador; tel. 2225-7811; fax 2225-0558; f. 1986; largest trade union conglomerate; Leader MARCO TULIO LIMA.

Unión Comunal Salvadoreña (UCS) (Salvadorean Communal Union): 2a Calle Oriente y Avda Melvyn Jones, Santa Tecla, San Salvador; tel. 2228-2023; fax 2229-1111; peasants' asscn; 100,000 mems; Gen. Sec. GUILLERMO BLANCO.

Transport

Comisión Ejecutiva Portuaria Autónoma (CEPA): Edif. Torre Roble, Blvd de Los Héroes, Apdo 2667, San Salvador; tel. 2224-1133; fax 2224-0907; internet www.cepa.gob.sv; f. 1952; operates and administers the ports of Acajutla and Cutuco and the El Salvador International Airport, as well as Ferrocarriles Nacionales de El Salvador; Pres. GUILLERMO LÓPEZ SUÁREZ.

RAILWAYS

In 2005 there were 554.8 km of railway track in the country. The main track linked San Salvador with the ports of Acajutla and Cutuco (also known as La Unión) and with Santa Ana. The Salvadorean section of the International Railways of Central America ran from Anguiatú on the El Salvador–Guatemala border to the Pacific ports of Acajutla and Cutuco and connected San Salvador with Guatemala City and the Guatemalan Atlantic ports of Puerto Barrios and Santo Tomás de Castilla. Operation of the railway network was suspended in 2005, owing to the high cost of maintenance; however, a passenger service between San Salvador and Apopa (a distance of 12.5 km) resumed in 2007, and the rehabilitation of further sections of track was planned.

Ferrocarriles Nacionales de El Salvador (FENADESAL): Avda Peralta 903, Apdo 2292, San Salvador; tel. 2271-5632; fax 2271-5650; internet www.fenadesal.gob.sv; 555 km of track; in 1975 Ferrocarril de El Salvador and the Salvadorean section of International Railways of Central America were merged and are administered by the Railroad Division of CEPA (q.v.); Gen. Man. SALVADOR SANABRIA.

ROADS

The country's highway system is well integrated with its railway services. There were some 10,886 km of roads in 2000, including the Pan-American Highway (306 km). Following the earthquakes of early 2001, the Inter-American Development Bank pledged some US $106.0m. to the transport sector for the restoration and reconstruction of roads and bridges.

Fondo de Conservación Vial (FOVIAL): Carretera a La Libertad Km 10.5, Antiguo Cuscatlán, San Salvador; tel. 2228-8425; internet www.fovial.com; f. 2000; responsible for maintaining the road network; Pres. MANUEL ORLANDO QUINTEROS A. (alias Gerson Martínez—Minister of Public Works, Transport, Housing and Urban Development); Vice-Pres. GIUSEPPE ANGELUCCI SILVA.

SHIPPING

The port of Acajutla is administered by CEPA (see above). Services are also provided by foreign lines. The port of Cutuco (Puerto La Unión Centroamericana) ceased activity in 1996; however, construction of an expanded port was completed in 2009.

CIVIL AVIATION

The El Salvador International Airport is located 40 km (25 miles) from San Salvador in Comalapa. An expansion of the airport was completed in 1998. The former international airport at Ilopango is used for military and private civilian aircraft; there are an additional 88 private airports, four with permanent-surface runways.

Continental Airlines: Edif. Torre Roble, 9°, Blvd de los Héroes, San Salvador; tel. 2260-3263; fax 2260-3331; e-mail amolina@coair.com; internet www.continental.com.

Delta Airlines: World Trade Center, 3°, Local 304, 89 Avda Norte, Calle El Mirador, Col. Escalón, San Salvador; tel. 2264-2483; fax 2264-5300; e-mail cristina.minervini@delta.com; internet www.delta.com.

TACA International Airlines: Santa Elena, Antiguo Cuscatlán, San Salvador; tel. 2267-8888; internet www.taca.com; f. 1931; in Oct. 2009 a merger with AVIANCA of Colombia was announced; passenger and cargo services to Central America and the USA; Chair. and CEO ROBERTO KRIETE.

United Airlines: Local 14, Centro Comercial Galerías, Paseo Gen. Escalón, San Salvador; tel. 2279-3900; fax 2298-5539; e-mail patricia.mejia@ual.com; internet www.unitedelsalvador.com; f. 1910; Pres. and CEO GLENN F. TILTON.

Tourism

El Salvador was one of the centres of the ancient Mayan civilization, and the ruined temples and cities are of great interest. The volcanoes and lakes of the uplands provide magnificent scenery, while there are fine beaches along the Pacific coast. Following the earthquakes of early 2001, the Inter-American Development Bank pledged some US $3.6m. to the tourism and historical and cultural heritage sectors. In 2008 tourism receipts stood at a provisional $894m. In the previous year the number of tourist arrivals was 1,338,543, while the number of rooms available in 2005 stood at 5,757.

Asociación Salvadoreña de Hoteles: 63 Aveda Sur, Pasaje y Urb. Santa Mónica 12-A, Col. Escalón, San Salvador; tel. 2298-5383; fax 2298-5382; e-mail info@hoteles-elsalvador.com; internet www.hoteles-elsalvador.com; f. 1996; Pres. CARLOS ALBERTO DELGADO Z.; Sec. BELLYNI SIGUENZA.

Buró de Convenciones de El Salvador: Alameda Manuel E. Araujo, Pasaje y Edif. Carbonell 2, Local 3 Colonia Roma, San Salvador; tel. 2245-3304; fax 2245-2683; e-mail buroconvenciones@integra.com.sv; internet www.meetingselsalvador.com.sv; f. 1973;

assists in organization of national and international events; Pres. JOSÉ MIGUEL CARBONELL; Exec. Dir ADRIANA DE GALE.

Cámara Salvadoreña de Turismo (CASATUR): 63 Avda Sur, Pasaje y Urb., Santa Mónica 12-A, Col. Escalón, San Salvador; tel. 2279-2156; fax 2279–2156; e-mail info@casatur.org; internet www.casatur.org; f. 1978; non-profit org. concerned with promotion of tourism in El Salvador; Pres. RAFAEL LARET CASTILLO.

Corporación Salvadoreña de Turismo (CORSATUR): Edif. y Pasaje Carbonel 1, Alameda Doctor Manuel Enrique Araujo, Col. Roma, San Salvador; tel. 2241-3200; fax 2223-6120; e-mail info@corsatur.gob.sv; internet www.corsatur.gob.sv; f. 1996; Dir HUMBERTO CENTENO NAJARRO.

Feria Internacional de El Salvador (FIES): Avda La Revolución 222, Col. San Benito, Apdo 493, San Salvador; tel. 2243-0244; fax 2243-3161; e-mail feria@fies.gob.sv; internet www.fies.gob.sv; f. 1965; Pres. BENJAMÍN TRABANINO LLOBELL.

Instituto Salvadoreño de Turismo (ISTU) (National Tourism Institute): Calle Rubén Darío 619, San Salvador; tel. 2222-5727; fax 2222-1208; e-mail informacion@istu.gob.sv; internet www.istu.gob.sv; f. 1950; Pres. MANUEL AVILÉS; Man. Dir ARTURO HILERMANN.

Defence

As assessed at November 2009, the armed forces totalled 15,500, of whom an estimated 13,850 (including 4,000 conscripts) were in the army, 700 were in the navy and 950 (including some 200 conscripts) were in the air force. There were, in addition, some 9,900 joint reserves. The Policía Nacional Civil numbered some 17,000. Military service is by compulsory selective conscription of males between 18 and 30 years of age and lasts for one year.

Defence Budget: 1,150m. colones in 2009.

Chief of the Joint Command of the Armed Forces: Col FRANCISCO LUIS SILVA AVALOS.

Chief of Staff of the Army: Col CARLOS ANTONIO ZALDÍVAR AGUILAR.

Chief of Staff of the Navy: Capt. GUILLERMO JIMÉNEZ VÁSQUEZ.

Chief of Staff of the Air Force: Col JAIME LEONARDO PARADA GONZÁLEZ.

Education

Education in El Salvador is provided free of charge in state schools and there are also numerous private schools. Pre-primary education, beginning at four years of age and lasting for three years, and primary education, beginning at the age of seven years and lasting for nine years, are officially compulsory. In 2007/08 enrolment at primary schools included 94% of children in the relevant age-group. Secondary education, from the age of 16, lasts for two years for an academic diploma or three years for a vocational one. In 2007/08 enrolment at secondary schools included 55% of students in the relevant age-group. Budgetary expenditure on education in 2009 was US $756.2m., equivalent to 15.7% of total expenditure.

Bibliography

For works on Central America generally, see Select Bibliography (Books)

Almeida, P. D. *Waves of Protest: Popular Struggle in El Salvador, 1925-2005 (Social Movements, Protest and Contention)*. Minneapolis, MN, University of Minnesota Press, 2008.

Brockett, C. D. *Political Movements and Violence in Central America (Cambridge Studies in Contentious Politics)*. Cambridge, Cambridge University Press, 2005.

La Comisión de la Verdad para El Salvador. *De la Locura a la Esperanza: La Guerra de 12 Años en El Salvador*. San Salvador, United Nations, 1993.

Consalvi, C. H. *Broadcasting the Civil War: A Memoir of Guerrilla Radio*. Austin, TX, University of Texas Press, 2010.

Cousens, E. M., et al (Eds). *Peacebuilding as Politics*. Boulder, CO, Lynne Rienner Publrs, 2001.

Eriksson, J. R., et al. *El Salvador: Post Conflict Reconstruction: Country Case Evaluation*. Washington, DC, World Bank, 2000.

Grenier, Y. *The Emergence of Insurgency in El Salvador*. Pittsburgh, PA, University of Pittsburgh Press, 1999.

Hume, M. *The Politics of Violence: Gender, Conflict and Community in El Salvador*. Hoboken, NJ, Wiley-Blackwell, 2009.

Juhn, T. *Negotiating Peace in El Salvador: Civil–Military Relations and the Conspiracy to end the War*. London, Macmillan, 1998.

Ladutke, L. M. *Freedom of Expression in El Salvador: The Struggle for Human Rights and Democracy*. Jefferson NC, McFarland & Co Inc Publrs, 2004.

Lauria-Santiago, A. A. *An Agrarian Republic: Commercial Agriculture and the Politics of Peasant Communities in El Salvador, 1823–1914*. Pittsburgh, PA, University of Pittsburgh Press, 1999.

Lauria-Santiago A. A., and Binford, L. *Landscapes of Struggle: Politics, Society, and Community in El Salvador*. Pittsburgh, PA, University of Pittsburgh Press, 2004.

Lund, L., and Sepponen, C. (Eds). *Lifeline Performance: El Salvador Earthquakes of January 13 and February 13 2001*. Reston, VA, American Society of Civil Engineers, 2002.

Lungo Ucles, M. *El Salvador in the 1980s*. Philadelphia, PA, Temple University Press, 1996.

MacLeod, L. *Constructing Peace: Lessons from UN Peacebuilding Operations in El Salvador and Cambodia*. Lanham, MD, Lexington Books, 2006.

McClintock, C. *Revolutionary Movements in Latin America: El Salvador's FMLN and Peru's Shining Path*. Washington, DC, United States Institute of Peace, 1998.

Miller, A. P. *Military Disengagement and Democratic Consolidation in Post-Military Regimes: The Case of El Salvador*. Ceredigion, Edwin Mellen Press, 2006.

Moodie, E. *El Salvador in the Aftermath of Peace: Crime, Uncertainty and the Transition to Democracy*. Philadelphia, PA, University of Pennsylvania Press, 2010.

Popkin, M. L. *Peace Without Justice: Obstacles to Building the Rule of Law in El Salvador*. University Park, PA, Pennsylvania University Press, 2000.

Reformas Económicas, Régimen Cambiario y Choques Externos: Efectos en el Desarrollo Económico, la Desigualdad y la Pobreza en Costa Rica, El Salvador y Honduras (Estudios y Perspectivas). New York, NY, United Nations Educational, 2005.

Ross, D. G. *Development of Railroads in Guatemala and El Salvador, 1849–1929*. Lewiston, NY, Edwin Mellen Press, 2001.

Studemeister, M. S. *El Salvador: Implementation of the Peace Accords*. Washington, DC, US Institute of Peace, 2000.

Williams, P. J., and Walter, K. *Militarization and Demilitarization in El Salvador's Transition to Democracy*. Pittsburgh, PA, University of Pittsburgh Press, 1998.

THE FALKLAND ISLANDS

Geography

PHYSICAL FEATURES

The Falkland Islands is an Overseas Territory of the United Kingdom, claimed by Argentina as the Islas Malvinas. It is located in the South Atlantic, at the same latitude as southern Argentina and Chile, some 770 km (480 miles) north-east of Cape Horn, but 480 km from the nearest point on the South American mainland. The colony's authorities claim an economic zone around the islands and their waters, so as to regulate fishing and the exploitation of hydrocarbons, but the United Kingdom seeks agreement with Argentina on such issues. The islands cover an area more than one-half the size of Wales (United Kingdom), 12,173 sq km (4,700 sq miles).

There are several hundred islands and many more islets and rocks, with a combined area greater than that of Jamaica, but stretching over a distance of 238 km from east to west. The two main islands of East and West Falkland butterfly on either side of the intervening Falkland Sound. The coastline, 1,288 km in total length, is deeply indented and rugged. The windswept islands are hilly, clad in lichen-covered rocks, low-lying, scrubby vegetation or grassland dotted with heath and dwarf shrubs. There are some undulating and usually boggy plains. The islands reach their heights at Mt Usborne (705 m or 2,314 ft) on East Falkland and Mt Adam (700 m) on West Falkland. The natural environment is rich, despite the harsh conditions, although the last example of the only native mammal, the warrah or Falklands wolf, was killed in 1876. Introduced species of mammal, apart from sheep (of which there are more than 500,000), cattle, horses and, more recently, reindeer, include the Patagonian fox, rats, mice, cats, rabbits and, on Staats Island, the guanaco. There are also breeding colonies of the southern sea lion, leopard, elephant and fur seals, and rockhopper, king, macaroni, gentoo and Magellanic (or jackass) penguins. In fact, over 200 species of birds have been recorded in the islands, from the tiny tussac, through two endemic species, the Falkland flightless steamer duck (logger) and the Cobb's or rock wren, to the mighty black-browed albatross.

CLIMATE

The climate is a cold marine one, cloudy, humid, windy (there are strong westerlies) and seldom hot. Although the Falklands are at a similar latitude to the south as the British capital of London is to the north, there is no Gulf Stream to warm the islands, so temperatures range from –5°C (23°F) in July (winter) to 22°C (72°F) in January (summer). Average annual rainfall is low, but fairly evenly distributed throughout the year, at 626 mm (24 ins). It can snow in any month except the main summer months of January and February, but it seldom sticks for long. It should also be noted that the islands are sometimes directly beneath the 'hole' in the earth's ozone layer.

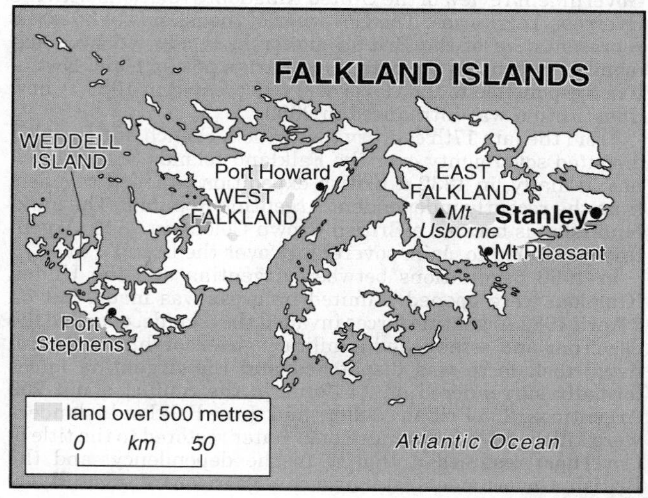

POPULATION

Most of the population are of British descent (there are also some descended from Scandinavian whalers), 96% hold British citizenship and English is the universal language. Spanish names and phrases in use stem from the mid-19th century, when farmers brought in gauchos from the South American mainland to help work the vast livestock holdings. The main religion is Christianity (Anglican, Roman Catholic and some Nonconformist Protestant denominations).

The total population at the 2006 census was 2,562, with most people (2,115) living in the capital, Stanley, in the east of northern East Falkland. There are obviously few people left in the small settlements scattered over the rest of the countryside (known locally as the 'Camp', from the Spanish for countryside). There were also some 1,700 civilians and military personnel located at the Mount Pleasant military base in that year. In compliance with statutes of the Ottawa Convention, adopted under the Landmines Act 1998, the British Government was responsible for clearing the territory of all remaining mine devices by March 2009; however, in November 2008 the British Government was granted a 10-year extension of the deadline. There were 144 people on West Falkland and 38 on other islands (apart from East Falkland). By April 2010 more than 1,100 devices had been cleared, but it was estimated that a further 20,000 landmines remained.

History

The islands are a United Kingdom Overseas Territory. From February 1998 the British Dependent Territories were referred to as the United Kingdom Overseas Territories, following the announcement of the interim findings of a British Government review of the United Kingdom's relations with the Overseas Territories. The Governor of the islands, who is the representative of the British monarch, is advised by a six-member Executive Council; the separate post of Chief Executive (responsible to the Governor) was created in 1983. A new Constitution was introduced in 2009.

From the late 17th century the British, French and Spanish disputed sovereignty over the Falkland Islands (Islas Malvinas). Finally, in 1832 a British expedition expelled colonists from the recently independent Argentine Republic. The Falkland Islands became a British Crown Colony in 1833. Argentina continued to claim sovereignty over the islands.

In 1966 negotiations between Argentina and the United Kingdom were opened. Limited progress was made, but on 2 April 1982 Argentine forces invaded the islands, expelled the Governor and established a military governorship. A British naval task force was dispatched and the Argentine forces formally surrendered on 14 June; in the conflict about 750 Argentines, 255 British soldiers and three Falkland Islanders were killed. A Civil Commissioner (later restored to the title of Governor) resumed authority in the dependency, and the British Government established a garrison of some 4,000 troops (later reduced).

The Argentine military Government refused to declare a formal cessation of hostilities until the United Kingdom agreed to negotiations on sovereignty, while the United Kingdom maintained that sovereignty was not negotiable and that the wishes of the Falkland Islanders were paramount (the Constitution of 1985 guaranteed the islanders' right to self-determination). It was only in October 1989 that the formal cessation of hostilities and the re-establishment of diplomatic relations at consular level were agreed. In February 1990 it was announced that full diplomatic relations were to be re-established and the naval protection zone around the islands was to be ended. Disputes over fishing areas and exclusion zones continued into the 1990s, but did not prevent some agreement between the United Kingdom and Argentina on the allocation of marine resources and the exploitation of hydrocarbons reserves: a joint hydrocarbon exploratory contract was signed by the Argentine President, Carlos Saúl Menem, in 1995 and was regarded as recognizing the United Kingdom's claim to the sea floor surrounding the Falkland Islands.

In May 1999 delegations from the Falkland Islands and Argentina met in the United Kingdom for formal negotiations intended to improve relations. In July an agreement was signed by both Governments that ended a ban on Argentine citizens visiting the islands and re-established direct flights there from Chile. (In March Chile had ended its country's regular air services to the islands in protest at the British Government's continued detention of the former Chilean dictator Gen. Augusto Pinochet.) Furthermore, Argentina and the islands were to co-operate in fishing conservation and in the prevention of poaching in the South Atlantic. The agreement did not affect claims to sovereignty. The arrival of the first flights carrying Argentine passengers in October was greeted by protests.

In February 2000, in a meeting with the British Prime Minister, Tony Blair, the recently elected Argentine President, Fernando de la Rúa, reiterated his country's claim to sovereignty of the islands. In July the de la Rúa Government announced that it would not engage in any dialogue with Falkland Islands councillors that involved the British Government, and the Anglo-Argentine dialogue on joint petroleum and gas exploration was suspended by mutual agreement for an indefinite period of time.

In November 2003 Argentina began to demand that the increasingly frequent air-charter services flying from the Falkland Islands to Chile obtain permission to use Argentine airspace. The decision was intended to exert pressure on the British Government into reversing its policy of not allowing Argentine airlines to fly to the Falkland Islands. The services were suspended in January 2004 after the British Government lodged objections to the Argentine demands; the situation seemed likely to damage the territory's burgeoning tourist trade. Appeals by Falkland Islands councillors to the UN's Special Committee on Decolonization in mid-2005 to be allowed to exercise the right to self-determination proved fruitless: at a Caribbean regional session of the Committee staged in mid-2007, it was determined that territories currently the subject of sovereignty disputes were excluded from self-determination rights on the basis of their contested status. The ruling meant that any ambition within the Falkland Islands for complete self-governance would have to wait until Argentina and the United Kingdom reached a peaceful solution.

The Argentine Government formed a Congressional Observatory in June 2006 with the express function of actively reclaiming the Falkland Islands, which it continued to refer to as Argentine territory. In July, in response to a recent policy change by the British Government in issuing fishing licences for up to 25 years (as opposed to just one, as had been the practice hitherto), the Government of Argentina threatened to adopt sanctions against businesses that engaged in the exploration or extraction of hydrocarbons or in fishing activities in the region. In January 2007 the Argentine Minister of Foreign Affairs, International Trade and Worship, Jorge Taiana, sought to enlist the support of the UN Secretary-General, Ban Ki-Moon, asserting that the United Kingdom had seized the archipelago by illegal means. The Argentine President, Néstor Carlos Kirchner, argued that the present population had displaced indigenous Argentine residents upon settlement in 1833 with the intention of establishing a British colonial state and, consequently, that the islanders possessed no right to self-determination. In February Argentina rejected an invitation by the British Government to participate in joint commemorative celebrations to mark the 25th anniversary of the conflict's end and, in the following month, suspended its 1995 joint hydrocarbon exploratory contract with the United Kingdom. Argentina accused the British of pursuing a 'unilateral' approach to oil exploration initiatives and declared that, until the United Kingdom had agreed to resume negotiations over the islands' sovereignty, the suspension would remain. New legislation was approved by the Argentine Government on 11 April 2007 that effectively politicized the permit-issuing process for fishing companies wishing to operate in the maritime exclusion zone surrounding the islands; companies were now required to choose between Argentine and British issuing authorities, while commercial access to Argentine jurisdictional waters was restricted to holders of Argentine-issued permits. In response to further pressure from the Kirchner administration for the British Government to engage in dialogue over the islands' future, the United Kingdom announced that no amendments to the governance or sovereign allegiance of the Falkland Islands would be considered unless and until a request to this effect was registered by the islanders.

In August 2006 Alan Huckle succeeded Howard Pearce as Governor of the Falkland Islands. Following Attorney-General David Lang's retirement at the end of October, Melanie Chilton—then Principal Crown Counsel—was inaugurated as his replacement on 1 November, but resigned after only a month in office. On 1 September 2007 David Pickup, formerly Director-General of HM Revenue and Customs, assumed the role. In January 2008 Dr Tim Thorogood replaced Chris Simpkins as Chief Executive.

Meanwhile, the Argentine Government continued to seek a favourable resolution with regard to its claims of sovereignty over the Falkland Islands. During her inauguration speech in December 2007 the new President of Argentina, Cristina Fernández de Kirchner, stated that she was not prepared to make concessions in those claims, and her Government once again urged the United Kingdom to relaunch the negotiations process. However, in October 2007 the British Government announced its intention to submit a claim to the UN Commission on the Limits of the Continental Shelf for Atlantic seabed territory around the Falkland Islands. Argentine foreign minister Taiana insisted that his Government would challenge any such claim made by the United Kingdom. Furthermore, tensions between the two countries were exacerbated in May 2008 when Taiana accused the British Government of 'illegitimately' issuing licences for hydrocarbon exploration and extraction activities in an area north of the Falkland Islands, part of the Argentine continental shelf. The British Government refused to concede to any of the claims made by its Argentine counterpart and maintained that it held sovereignty over the disputed area. On 24 April 2009 Argentina lodged a hostile claim before the UN Commission to some 1.7m. sq km (660,000 sq miles) of seabed surrounding the territory, as well as an area north of Antarctica, ahead of a 13 May deadline for demarcating possession of extended continental shelves. This was formally countered by the United Kingdom, which presented its own claim to the disputed region on 11 May. As a result, both claims were frozen, preventing either country from exploiting the areas beyond 200 nautical miles from its respective coastline.

Tensions between Argentina and the United Kingdom rose further in September 2009 after a British company, Desire Petroleum, announced plans to commence drilling in an area north of the Falklands in 2010. In the weeks preceding the start of the operation in February, the Argentine Government asserted that the drilling was illegal, and reiterated its claim on the seabed surrounding the islands. In mid-February President Fernández decreed that all ships sailing through Argentine waters must hold a permit, effectively blockading the area around the islands, and later that month Taiana formally requested the UN to initiate negotiations with the United Kingdom over the sovereignty of the islands. At the end of February US Secretary of State Hillary Clinton appeared to support Argentina's position by pledging to help 'resolve' the sovereignty issue. Despite the escalation of the dispute, drilling went ahead as planned, although only small deposits of hydrocarbons were found in the first well drilled. In May, however, the British company Rockhopper Exploration, which was also involved in drilling north of the Falklands, announced that it had discovered oil in a second well in the area; samples recovered from the well were to undergo further analysis. Later that month, following a change of government in the United Kingdom, President Fernández urged the new Prime Minister, David Cameron, to engage in talks over the sovereignty of the Falkland Islands, but this was rejected by a Minister of State in the British Foreign and Commonwealth Office (FCO), who reaffirmed the British Government's commitment to the islanders' right to self-determination.

A constitutional review process was initiated by the British Government Department of Overseas Territories in 1997, with the aim of according greater self-governance to the islands. A number of changes to the administration of the territory were proposed, most notably the strengthening of the citizens' right to self-determination within the Constitution, the updating of provisions to comply with the United Kingdom's obligations under the European Convention on Human Rights, and clarification of the roles of the Governor and the Chief Executive. A Constitutional Select Committee was convened on 2 February 2007 to complete the review discussions, and its final proposals were submitted to the FCO for deliberation in June. Officials from the FCO held two rounds of talks with the Constitutional Select Committee in December 2007 and February 2008 to discuss the draft new constitution. Following further public consultation, the new Constitution came into force on 1 January 2009. It asserted the islanders' right to self-determination and contained amendments to the rules under which British citizens would be eligible for Falklands Islands status, as well as provisions for a Public Accounts Committee and a Complaints Commissioner to improve transparency in the territory. It also provided further clarification of the division of powers between the Executive Council and the Governor, stating that the Governor must abide by the advice of the Executive Council on domestic policies, though not in matters of external affairs, defence and the administration of justice.

In January 2009 the Speaker of the Falkland Islands Legislative Council, Darwin Lewis Clifton, was found guilty of market abuse in his capacity as director of Desire Petroleum and fined £59,000. He was replaced as Speaker in February by Keith Biles.

Economy

The economy of the Falkland Islands enjoyed a period of strong and sustained growth at the end of the 20th century, notably after the introduction of the fisheries-licensing scheme in 1987. The main economic activity of the islands was sheep-rearing and in the late 1990s annual exports of wool were valued at some £3.5m. From 1987, when a licensing system was introduced for foreign vessels fishing within a 150-nautical-mile conservation and management zone, the islands' annual income tripled. Revenue from licence sales totalled £25m. in 1991, but declined following the Argentine Government's commencement of the sale of fishing licences in 1993. The revenue, amounting to £14.5m. in 2009/10, some 34.2% of total revenue in that year, funds social provisions and economic development programmes, including subsidies to the wool industry, which is in long-term decline, owing to the oversupply of that commodity on the international market. Stocks of squid, for which the waters around the islands are noted, can vary considerably from year to year owing to their one-year life cycle. Catches of *illex* squid reached encouraging levels in 2006–08, following two poor seasons, but in 2009 the catch declined to just 44 metric tons, according to official figures. Owing to the low stocks, companies with licences to fish for *illex* were reimbursed in 2009, resulting in a significant reduction in fishing revenue. According to FAO, in 2008 the total catch reached 81,708 tons, representing a decrease of 4.2% compared with the previous year.

The decline in revenues from the fishing licence sector in the 2000s increased hopes that exploitation of hydrocarbons in the waters around the islands would yield positive results. Licences for petroleum and gas exploration had been issued in October 1996 under an Argentine-British agreement of the previous year, although no commercial quantities of petroleum were found in the initial phase of drilling in 1998. In July 2002 the Falkland Islands Government, without consultation with the Argentine Government, granted 10 petroleum exploration licences to the Falklands Hydrocarbon Consortium (comprising Global Petroleum Ltd, Hardman Resources Ltd and Falkland Islands Holdings)—now known as Falkland Oil and Gas Ltd (FOGL)—for an area covering 57,700 sq km to the south of the islands. In March 2007 Argentina terminated a joint hydrocarbon exploration agreement with the United Kingdom. None the less, amid significant increases in the price of oil, the waters around the Falkland Islands became of increasing interest to oil exploration companies during 2008, with seismic surveys suggesting the area could yield as much as 18,000m. barrels of petroleum. A second phase of exploratory drilling commenced in February 2010, with a well in the North Falkland Basin licensed to a British company, Desire Petroleum. Only small amounts of hydrocarbons were discovered in this first well. More encouraging was the discovery, in May, of oil in a well drilled by the British company Rockhopper Exploration, also in the North Falkland Basin; samples recovered from the well were to undergo further analysis. FOGL, in partnership with Australia's BHP Billiton, drilled the first exploration well in the East Falklands Basin in June, but the results were disappointing. The renewed exploration of hydrocarbons in the area reignited the issue of the sovereignty of the islands (see History). Argentina imposed several economic sanctions on the Falklands, including a ban on oil companies working in that country from any involvement in oil exploration around the Falkland Islands.

The services sector has expanded rapidly during the last decade, while the importance of the agricultural sector has decreased, not least because of its reliance on direct and indirect subsidies. There were some 85 farms on the islands in 2009. In 2001 the Government brought 100 reindeer from the South Georgia Islands (with the aim of increasing the number to 10,000 over the next 20 years) in order to export venison to Scandinavia and Chile. Tourism, and in particular eco-tourism, was developing rapidly in the early 21st century. During 2008/09 almost 69,000 tourists visited the Falklands Islands, with around 62,600 of these arriving on cruise ships. In 2006/07 the majority of visitors came from the USA (41.5%). Tourism numbers were expected to increase by 17% in 2010, following a slight decline in 2009. The sale of postage stamps and coins also represents a significant source of income.

In 2000 the Falkland Islands recorded an estimated trade surplus of £28m. Fish, most of which is purchased by the United Kingdom, Spain and Chile, is the islands' most significant export. The annual rate of inflation averaged 2.5% in 1990–2003; consumer prices increased by 1.2% in 2003. Budgeted overall revenue totalled an estimated £42.4m. in 2009/10, while expenditure was estimated at £47.6m., leaving a deficit of £5.2m. According to government figures, the economy was expected to expand by 5.3% in 2010. This followed a drastic contraction of about 9.0%, according to preliminary estimates, in 2009, mainly owing to the fall in the squid catch and the decline in tourist numbers.

Statistical Survey

Source (unless otherwise stated): The Treasury of the Falkland Islands Government, Stanley, FIQQ 1ZZ; tel. 27143; fax 27144 internet www.falklands.gov.fk.

AREA AND POPULATION

Area: approx. 12,173 sq km (4,700 sq miles): East Falkland and adjacent islands 6,760 sq km (2,610 sq miles); West Falkland and adjacent islands 5,413 sq km (2,090 sq miles).

Population: 2,478 at census of 8 October 2006. Note: Figure excludes military personnel and civilians based at Mount Pleasant military base and the 84 residents absent on the night of the census.

Density (2006 census): 0.20 per sq km.

Population by Age and Sex (at 2006 census): *0–14:* 458 (males 222, females 236); *15–64:* 1,755 (males 903, females 852); *65 and over:* 265 (males 135, females 130); *Total* 2,478 (males 1,260, females 1,218).

Principal Town (2006 census): Stanley (capital), population 2,115.

Births and Deaths (2006): Live births 27; Deaths 20. Source: UN, *Population and Vital Statistics Report*.

Economically Active Population (persons aged 15 years and over, 2001 census): 2,475 (males 1,370, females 1,105).

AGRICULTURE, ETC.

Livestock (2009, official figures at 31 May): Sheep 504,620; Cattle 5,116; Goats 472; Reindeer 169; Horses 567; Poultry 1,770.

Livestock Products (metric tons, 2008, FAO estimates): Cattle meat 156; Sheep meat 810; Cows' milk 1,600; Wool, greasy 2,400. Source: FAO.

Fishing ('000 metric tons, live weight of capture, 2008): Southern blue whiting 1.8; Argentine hake 3.9; Patagonian grenadier 4.1; Patagonian squid 45.7; Argentine shortfin squid 4.0; Total catch (incl. others) 81.7. Source: FAO.

FINANCE

Currency and Exchange Rates: 100 pence (pennies) = 1 Falkland Islands pound (FI £). *Sterling, Dollar and Euro Equivalents* (31 May 2010): £1 sterling = FI £1.00; US $1 = 68.59 pence; €1 = 84.94 pence; FI £100 = £100.00 sterling = $145.80 = €117.73. *Average Exchange Rate* (FI £ per US dollar): 0.4998 in 2007; 0.5412 in 2008; 0.6419 in 2009. Note: The Falkland Islands pound is at par with the pound sterling.

Budget (FI £ million, 2009/10): *Revenue:* Sales and services 9.7; Fishing licences and transsshipment 18.0; Investment income 4.5; Taxes and duties 10.2; Total 42.4 *Expenditure:* Operating expenditure 38.9 (Public works 8.5, Fisheries 5.2, Health care 7.5, Education 5.3, Aviation 2.5, Police and justice 1.5, Agriculture 1.0, Central administration 3.5 Other 3.9); Capital expenditure 8.7; Total 47.6.

Cost of Living (Consumer Price Index for Stanley; base: 2000 = 100): All items 101.3 in 2001; 102.0 in 2002; 103.2 in 2003. Source: ILO.

EXTERNAL TRADE

2000 (estimates): Total imports £18,958,103; Total exports £47,000,000. Fish is the principal export. Trade is mainly with the United Kingdom, Spain and Chile.

TRANSPORT

Shipping: *Merchant Fleet* (at 31 December 2008): Vessels 27; Displacement 47,822 grt. Source: Lloyd's Register-Fairplay, *World Fleet Statistics*.

Road Traffic: 3,065 vehicles in use in 1995.

TOURISM

Day Visitors (country of origin of cruise ship excursionists, 2006/07 season): Canada 4,862; United Kingdom 6,736; USA 21,298; Total (incl. others) 51,282. *2008/09:* Total 62,600 (Source: Falkland Islands Tourist Board).

EDUCATION

2003 (Stanley): *Primary:* Teachers 18; Pupils 203. *Secondary:* Teachers 18; Pupils 160.

Directory

The Constitution

The present Constitution of the Falkland Islands came into force on 1 January 2009 (replacing that of 1985). The Governor, who is the personal representative of the British monarch, is advised by the Executive Council, comprising six members: the Governor (presiding), three elected members of the Legislative Council, and two ex officio members, the Chief Executive and the Director of Finance of the Falkland Islands Government, who are non-voting. The Legislative Council is composed of the Governor, eight elected members and the same two (non-voting) ex officio members. One of the principal features of the Constitution is the reference in the preamble to the islanders' right to self-determination. The separate post of Chief Executive (responsible to the Governor) was created in 1983. The electoral principle was introduced, on the basis of universal adult suffrage, in 1949. The minimum voting age was lowered from 21 years to 18 years in 1977.

The Government

(July 2010)

HEAD OF STATE

Queen: HM Queen ELIZABETH II.

Governor: ALAN HUCKLE (took office 25 August 2006).

Governor-designate: NIGEL HAYWOOD (scheduled to take office in Sept. 2010).

HEAD OF GOVERNMENT

Chief Executive of the Falkland Islands Government: Dr TIM THOROGOOD.

TERRITORIAL ADMINISTRATION

Government Secretary: PETER T. KING.

Attorney-General: DAVID PICKUP.

Commander, British Forces South Atlantic Islands: Cdre PHILIP THICKNESSE.

EXECUTIVE COUNCIL

The Council consists of six members.

GOVERNMENT OFFICES

Office of the Governor: Government House, Stanley, FIQQ 1ZZ; tel. 27433; fax 27434; e-mail gov.house@horizon.co.fk.

London Office: Falkland Islands Government Office, Falkland House, 14 Broadway, London, SW1H 0BH, United Kingdom; tel. (20) 7222-2542; fax (20) 7222-2375; e-mail reception@falklands.gov .fk; internet www.falklands.gov.fk; f. 1983.

LEGISLATIVE ASSEMBLY

Comprises the Governor, two ex officio (non-voting) members and eight elected members. Elections to the Legislative Assembly are held every four years. The last election was held on 5 November 2009.

Speaker: KEITH BILES.

Office of the Legislative Assembly: Legislature Dept, Gilbert House, Stanley, FIQQ 1ZZ; tel. 27455; e-mail assembly@sec.gov.fk; internet www.falklands.gov.fk.

Judicial System

The judicial system of the Falkland Islands is administered by the Supreme Court (presided over by the non-resident Chief Justice), the Magistrate's Court (presided over by the Senior Magistrate) and the Court of Summary Jurisdiction. The Court of Appeal for the Territory sits in England and appeals therefrom may be heard by the Judicial Committee of the Privy Council.

Chief Justice of the Supreme Court: CHRISTOPHER GARDNER, QC.

Judge of the Supreme Court and Senior Magistrate: JOHN TREVASKIS (acting).

Registrar to the Supreme Court and Courts Administrator: CHERILYN KING, Town Hall, Ross Rd, Stanley, FIQQ 1ZZ; tel. 27271; fax 27270.

FALKLAND ISLANDS COURT OF APPEAL

President: Judge BRIAN APPLEBY.

Registrar: MICHAEL J. ELKS.

Religion

CHRISTIANITY

The Anglican Communion, the Roman Catholic Church and the United Free Church predominate. Also represented are the Evangelist Church, Jehovah's Witnesses, the Lutheran Church, Seventh-day Adventists and the Bahá'í faith.

The Anglican Communion

The Archbishop of Canterbury, the Primate of All England, exercises episcopal jurisdiction over the Falkland Islands and South Georgia.

Rector: Rev. Dr RICHARD HINES, The Deanery, Christ Church Cathedral, Stanley, FIQQ 1ZZ; tel. 21100; fax 21842; e-mail deanery@horizon.co.fk.

The Roman Catholic Church

Prefect Apostolic of the Falkland Islands: MICHAEL BERNARD MCPARTLAND, St Mary's Presbytery, 12 Ross Rd, Stanley, FIQQ 1ZZ; tel. 21204; fax 22242; e-mail stmarys@horizon.co.fk; internet www .southatlanticrcchurch.com; f. 1764; 300 adherents (2006).

The Press

Falkland Islands Gazette: Cable Cottage, POB 587, Stanley, FIQQ 1ZZ; tel. 28460; fax 27276; e-mail bsteen@sec.gov.fk; internet www.falklands.gov.fk; govt publ; Editor BARBARA STEEN.

Falkland Islands News Network: POB 141, Stanley, FIQQ 1ZZ; tel. and fax 21182; e-mail finn@horizon.co.fk; internet www .falklandnews.com; relays news daily online and via fax as FINN(COM) Service; Man. JUAN BROCK; publishes *Teaberry Express* (weekly).

Penguin News: Ross Rd, Stanley, FIQQ 1ZZ; tel. 22709; fax 22238; e-mail adverts@penguinnews.co.fk; internet www.penguin-news .com; f. 1979; weekly (Fri.); independent newspaper; Man. Editor TONY CURRAN; circ. 1,450.

Broadcasting and Communications

TELECOMMUNICATIONS

In 1989 Cable & Wireless PLC installed a £5.4m. digital telecommunications network covering the entire Falkland Islands. The Government contributed to the cost of the new system, which provides international services as well as a new domestic network. Further work to improve the domestic telephone system was completed in the late 1990s at a cost of £3.3m. The first mobile telephone network was introduced in 2005 and a broadband internet service in 2006.

Cable & Wireless South Atlantic Ltd: Ross Rd, POB 584, Stanley, FIQQ 1ZZ; tel. 20836; fax 20801; e-mail info@cwfi.co.fk; internet www.cwfi.co.fk; f. 1989; exclusive provider of national and international telecommunications services in the Falkland Islands under a licence issued by the Falkland Islands Govt; CEO JUSTIN MCPHEE.

BROADCASTING

Radio

British Forces Broadcasting Service (BFBS): BFBS Falkland Islands, Mount Pleasant, BFPO 655; tel. 32179; fax 32193; e-mail bfbsfalklands@bfbs.com; internet www.bfbs.com/falklands; 24-hour satellite service from the United Kingdom; Station Man. CHRIS PEARSON; Sr Engineer ADRIAN ALMOND.

Falkland Islands Radio Service: Broadcasting Studios, John St, Stanley, FIQQ 1ZZ; tel. 27277; fax 27279; e-mail cgoss@firs.co.fk; internet www.firs.co.fk; f. 1929; fmrly Falklands Islands Broadcasting Station; 24-hour service, partly financed by local Govt; broadcasts in English; Station Man. CORINA GOSS; Programme Controller LIZ ELLIOT.

Television

British Forces Broadcasting Service (BFBS): BFBS Falkland Islands, Mount Pleasant, BFPO 655; tel. 32179; fax 32193; internet www.bfbs.com/falklands; daily four-hour transmissions of taped broadcasts from BBC and ITV of London, United Kingdom; Sr Engineer COLIN MCDONALD.

KTV: 16 Ross Rd West, Stanley, FIQQ 1ZZ; tel. 22349; fax 21049; e-mail kmzb@horizon.co.fk; internet www.ktv.co.fk; satellite television broadcasting services; Man. MARIO ZUVIC BULIC.

Finance

BANK

Standard Chartered Bank: Ross Rd, POB 597, Stanley, FIQQ 1ZZ; tel. 22220; fax 22219; e-mail bank.info@sc.com; internet www .standardchartered.com/fk; branch opened in 1983; Man. RINO DONOSEPOETRO.

INSURANCE

The British Commercial Union, Royal Insurance and Norman Tremellen companies maintain agencies in Stanley.

Consultancy Services Falklands Ltd: 44 John St, Stanley, FIQQ 1ZZ; tel. 22666; fax 22639; e-mail consultancy@horizon.co.fk; Man. ALISON BAKER.

Trade and Industry

DEVELOPMENT ORGANIZATION

Falkland Islands Development Corporation (FIDC): Shackleton House, West Hillside, Stanley, FIQQ 1ZZ; tel. 27211; fax 27210; e-mail dwaugh@fidc.co.fk; internet www.fidc.co.fk; f. 1983; provides loans and grants; encourages private sector investment, inward investment and technology transfer; Gen. Man. DAVID WAUGH.

CHAMBER OF COMMERCE

Chamber of Commerce: West Hillside, POB 378, Stanley, FIQQ 1ZZ; tel. 22264; fax 22265; e-mail commerce@horizon.co.fk; internet www.falklandislandschamberofcommerce.com; f. 1993; promotes private industry; operates DHL courier service; runs an employment agency; Pres. ROGER SPINK; 87 mems.

TRADING COMPANIES

Falkland Islands Co Ltd (FIC): Crozier Pl., Stanley, FIQQ 1ZZ; tel. 27600; fax 27603; e-mail fic@horizon.co.fk; internet www.the-falkland-islands-co.com; f. 1851; part of Falkland Islands Holding PLC; the largest trading co; retailing, wholesaling, shipping, insurance and Land Rover sales and servicing; operates as agent for Lloyd's of London and general shipping concerns; travel services; wharf owners and operators; Dir and Gen. Man. ROGER KENNETH SPINK.

Falkland Islands Meat Co Ltd: Sand Bay, East Falklands, FIQQ 1ZZ; tel. 27013; fax 27113; e-mail info@falklandmeat.co.fk; internet www.falklands-meat.com; exporters of lamb, mutton and beef meat; Gen. Man. JOHN FERGUSON.

Falkland Oil and Gas Ltd (FOGL): 56 John St, Stanley, F1QQ 1ZZ; e-mail info@fogl.co.uk; internet www.fogl.co.uk; f. 2004; shareholders include Falkland Islands Holdings PLC (16%), Global Petroleum (14%) and RAB Capital PLC (33%); operates an offshore petroleum exploration programme with 8 licences covering 65,354 sq km; Chair. RICHARD LIDDELL; CEO TIM BUSHELL.

EMPLOYERS' ASSOCIATION

Sheep Owners' Association: Coast Ridge Farm, Fox Bay, FIQQ 1ZZ; tel. 42094; fax 42084; e-mail n.knight.coastridge@horizon.co.fk; f. 1967; asscn for sheep station owners; limited liability private co; Company Sec. N. KNIGHT.

TRADE UNION

Falkland Islands General Employees Union: Ross Rd, Stanley, FIQQ 1ZZ; tel. 21151; e-mail geu@horizon.co.fk; f. 1943; Chair. GAVIN SHORT; 100 mems.

Transport

RAILWAYS

There are no railways on the islands.

ROADS

There are 29 km (18 miles) of paved road in and around Stanley. There are 54 km of all-weather road linking Stanley and the Mount Pleasant airport (some of which has been surfaced with a bitumen substance), and a further 37 km of road as far as Goose Green. There are 300 km of arterial roads in the North Camp on East Falkland linking settlements, and a further 197 km of road on West Falkland. Where roads have still not been built, settlements are linked by tracks, which are passable by all-terrain motor vehicles or motorcycles except in the most severe weather conditions.

SHIPPING

There is a ship on charter to the Falkland Islands Co Ltd, which makes the round trip to the United Kingdom four or five times a year, carrying cargo. A floating deep-water jetty was completed in 1984. The British Ministry of Defence charters ships, which sail for the Falkland Islands once every three weeks. There are irregular cargo services between the islands and southern Chile and Uruguay. The Falkland Islands Development Corpn commissioned a port development plan in February 2007 for the upgrade of existing facilities to reflect growth in containerized traffic and cruise ship arrivals, and to accommodate proposed further oil exploration in territorial waters.

The Falkland Islands merchant fleet numbered 27 vessels, with a total displacement of 47,822 grt, at December 2008; the majority of vessels registered are deep-sea fishing vessels.

Stanley Port Authority: c/o Dept of Fisheries, POB 598, Stanley, FIQQ 1ZZ; tel. 27260; fax 27265; e-mail jclark@fisheries.gov.fk; Marine Officer and Harbour Master JON CLARK.

Private Companies

Byron Marine Ltd: 3 H Jones Rd, Stanley, FIQQ 1ZZ; tel. 22245; fax 22246; e-mail info@byronmarine.co.fk; internet www.byronmarine.co.fk; f. 1992; additional activites include oil exploration support services, deep-sea fishing and property; contracted managers of the Falkland Islands Government Port Facility; island-wide pilotage services; vessel agent; Man. Dir LEWIS CLIFTON.

Darwin Shipping Ltd: Stanley, FIQQ 1ZZ; tel. 27600; fax 27603; e-mail darwin@horizon.co.fk; internet www.the-falkland-islands-co.com; subsidiary of the Falkland Islands Co Ltd (q.v.); Man. ANDY WATSON.

Falkland Islands Co Ltd (FIC): see Trade and Industry—Trading Companies.

Seaview Ltd: 37 Fitzroy Rd, POB 215, Stanley, FIQQ 1ZZ; tel. 22669; fax 22670; e-mail seaview.agent@horizon.co.fk; internet www.fis.com/polar; operates subsidiary co, Polar Ltd (f. 1989); Man. Dir ALEX REID.

Sulivan Shipping Services Ltd: Davis St, POB 159, Stanley, FIQQ 1ZZ; tel. 22626; fax 22625; e-mail sulivan@horizon.co.fk; internet www.sulivanshipping.com; f. 1987; provides port-agency and ground-handling services; Man. Dir JOHN POLLARD; Operations Man. MIGS COFRÉ.

CIVIL AVIATION

There are airports at Stanley and Mount Pleasant; the latter has a runway of 2,590 m (8,497 ft), and is capable of receiving wide-bodied jet aircraft. The British Royal Air Force operates two weekly flights from the United Kingdom. The Chilean carrier LAN Airlines operates weekly return flights from Punta Arenas. An 'air bridge', operated by charter carriers subcontracted to the British Ministry of Defence, provides a link via Ascension Island between the Falkland Islands and the United Kingdom.

Falkland Islands Government Air Service (FIGAS): Stanley Airport, Stanley, FIQQ 1ZZ; tel. 27219; fax 27309; e-mail operations@figas.gov.fk; internet www.visitorfalklands.com/contents/view/116; f. 1948 to provide social, medical and postal services between the settlements and Stanley; aerial surveillance for Dept of Fisheries since 1990; operates five nine-seater aircraft to over 35 landing strips across the islands; Gen. Man. SHAUN MINTO.

Tourism

During the 2008/09 season some 62,600 day visitors from cruise ships visited the islands. US citizens constitute the primary visitor group. Wildlife photography, bird-watching and hiking are popular tourist activities. The Falkland Islands Development Corpn (FIDC) plans to develop the sector in collaboration with the Government and tourism operators in the territory.

Falkland Islands Tourist Board: POB 618, Stanley, FIQQ 1ZZ; tel. 22215; fax 27020; e-mail info@visitorfalklands.com; internet www.falklandislands.com; Gen. Man. JAKE DOWNING.

Defence

As assessed at November 2009, there were approximately 1,520 British troops stationed on the islands (420 army, 680 air force and 420 navy). The annual cost of maintaining the garrison is approximately £65m. There is a Falkland Islands Defence Force, composed of 75 islanders.

Education

Education is compulsory, and is provided free of charge, for children between the ages of five and 16 years. Facilities are available for further study beyond the statutory school-leaving age. In 2003 203 pupils were instructed by 18 teachers at the primary school in Stanley, while 160 pupils received instruction from 18 teachers at the secondary school in the capital; further facilities existed in rural areas, with six peripatetic teachers visiting younger children for two out of every six weeks (older children boarded in a hostel in Stanley). Total expenditure on education was estimated at £5.3m. for 2009/10 (equivalent to 11.1% of total government expenditure).

FRENCH GUIANA

Geography

PHYSICAL FEATURES

France's Overseas Department of Guiana is the easternmost and smallest of the three Guianas on the north coast of South America (until 1946 it was administered as a colony, under the name of its capital, Cayenne). Suriname (formerly Dutch Guiana) lies to the west, beyond a frontier of 510 km (317 miles), but it also claims territory in the south-east of the Department, beyond the border-marking Litani (Itany) river, as far as the Marouini (both headwaters of the Lawa and, later, the Maroni—Marowijne—which also help delineate the western border). Brazil is to the south-east and south, beyond a border of 673 km, much of it along the course of the Oiapoque (Oyapock). There are 378 km of north-east-facing Atlantic coastline. French Guiana is the only place on the American mainlands not to be independent, although it is an integral part of France. It covers an area of 83,534 sq km (32,253 sq miles).

Most of French Guiana is fairly low-lying, flat and sometimes marshy along the coast, which has a number of rocky islands off shore (notably the old penal camp of Ile du Diable—Devil's Island). Most of the Department consists of rolling, fertile plains, reaching inland to the lower, northern foothills of the Serra Tumucumaque. Hills occasionally break the monotony of the landscape, with the Chaîne Granitique in the centre of the territory, and low mountains rising in the far south. The highest point is Bellevue de l'Inini, at 851 m (2,793 ft). Most of the terrain is wooded (83%), much of it rainforest, and few people live in the swathes of wilderness inland.

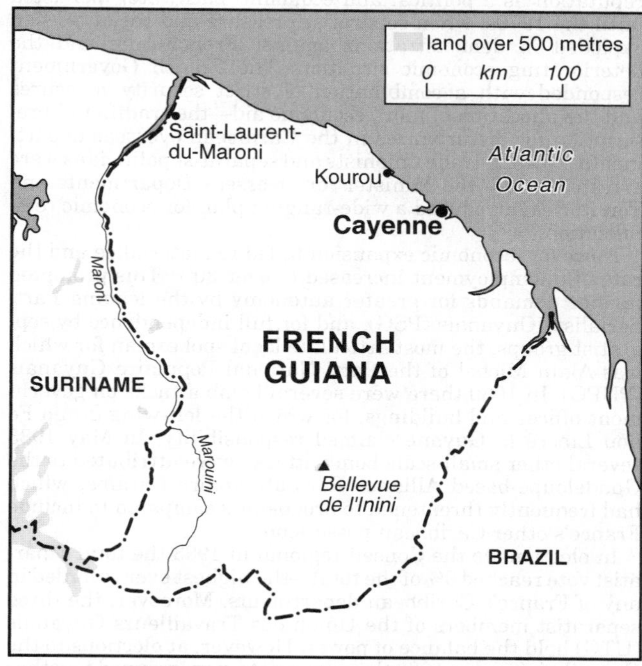

CLIMATE

The climate is tropical, hot and humid, with little seasonal variation in temperature. Average year-round temperatures in Cayenne, on the coast, range between 23°C and 33°C (73°F–91°F). The dry season is in August–October, the wet season December–June. Average annual rainfall is over 2,500 mm (around 100 ins), with frequent heavy showers and thunderstorms able to cause flooding in the generally flat countryside.

POPULATION

The people of the Department are French citizens, and perhaps two-thirds are black or mixed-black (mulatto)—about 17% of the population are of Haitian extraction. Some 12% are white, while the rest are mainly native Amerindian, 'East' Indian or Chinese (the latter two groups arriving when labour was needed after the abolition of slavery in the 19th century). Although there are followers of native, tribal faith systems, as well as adherents of syncretic Afro-American spiritualist groups and some Muslims, most of the population is nominally Christian. About 80% are Roman Catholic and 4% Protestant. French is the official and most widely used language, but there are speakers of Amerindian tongues and of a local Creole patois.

The total population was estimated at 231,000 at mid-2010. Most of the population lives in the coastal areas, and about four-fifths in urban areas. The departmental headquarters and the largest city is Cayenne, a port on the east-central coast. To the west is Kourou, the launching centre for the European Space Agency. In the far north-west is the town of Saint-Laurent-du-Maroni. None of the inland towns is large.

History

PHILLIP WEARNE

Revised for this edition by Dr PETER CLEGG

The land that is now French Guiana (Guyane) was first sighted by Europeans at the end of the 15th century. The French began to settle the territory in 1604, but rumours of its potential gold and diamond wealth led to frequent changes of ownership. The Dutch, British and Portuguese all occupied the area, and there were frequent border disputes before the colony was finally confirmed as French in 1817. Subsequent border disputes were settled by arbitration in 1891, 1899 and 1915. In March 1946 the colony, hitherto known as Cayenne, became an Overseas Department, like Guadeloupe and Martinique, with the same laws and administration as a department of metropolitan France. The head of state is the President of France, represented locally by a Commissioner of the Republic. The Conseil général (General Council) with 19 seats and the Conseil régional (Regional Council) with 31 seats are the two local legislative houses. Both have Presidents, and the territory also sends two deputies to the French Assemblée nationale (National Assembly), one senator to the Sénat (Senate) in Paris and one representative to the European Parliament in Strasbourg.

The discovery of gold in the basin of the Approuague river brought a brief period of prosperity in the mid-19th century, but French Guiana's chief notoriety, until 1937, was as a penal colony. After arriving, prisoners were distributed to camps scattered throughout the territory. Devil's Island became the most infamous. Prisoners mingled freely with other settlers and the indigenous population during a period of exile after serving their sentences, but few could afford to return to France.

The practice of imprisoning convicts and political prisoners in French Guiana ceased in 1937. However, the territory's reputation as a political and economic 'backwater' persisted until the 1970s, when separatist pressure and racial tension exploded in demonstrations against French rule and the deteriorating economic situation. The French Government responded with a combination of strict security measures and the allocation of more economic aid—the traditional prescription for disturbances in the Caribbean overseas departments. Leading trade unionists and separatist politicians were arrested, while the Minister for Overseas Departments and Territories introduced a wide-ranging plan for economic revitalization.

However, economic expansion failed to materialize and the rate of unemployment increased to over 30%. This prompted further demands for greater autonomy by the leading Parti Socialiste Guyanais (PSG), and for full independence by separatist groups, the most articulate legal spokesman for which was Alain Michel of the Parti National Populaire Guyanais (PNPG). In 1980 there were several bomb attacks on government offices and buildings, for which the left-wing group Fo nou Libéré la Guyane claimed responsibility. In May 1983 several other small-scale bomb attacks were attributed to the Guadeloupe-based Alliance Révolutionnaire Caraïbe, which had frequently threatened to broaden its campaign to include France's other Caribbean possessions.

In elections to the Conseil régional in 1983 the total separatist vote reached 9% of the total—the highest ever recorded in any of France's Caribbean departments. Moreover, the three separatist members of the Union des Travailleurs Guyanais (UTG) held the balance of power. However, at elections to the Conseil régional in 1986 the separatists, now grouped together in the PNPG, had their proportion of the vote reduced by 60% to only 3.3% of the total poll. Thereafter, opinion polls repeatedly indicated a majority in favour of greater autonomy, with an average of about 5% of the population favouring complete independence.

In 1989 a split occurred in the PSG when Georges Othily, President of the Conseil régional, was expelled from the party for unauthorized links with the opposition, along with five other senior party figures. Analysts believed that the revolt signified growing discontent with the PSG's increasingly partisan and corrupt 10-year domination of Guianese politics. The PSG split was at least partially responsible for the party's loss of support in the 1992 elections, when it lost two seats in the Conseil général (retaining 10), although Elie Castor, leader of the PSG, remained President of the Conseil général and one of the territory's two representatives in the Assemblée nationale. In the elections to the Conseil régional, the PSG won 16 seats, but Othily supporters secured 10 seats.

Weakened by continued infighting, the decline of the PSG continued. In the 1993 elections to the Assemblée nationale a political newcomer, Christiane Taubira-Delannon of the Walwari movement, a dissident Socialist who once favoured independence, defeated the PSG's candidate, Rodolfe Alexandre, for the Cayenne-Macouria seat. Léon Bertrand of the Rassemblement pour la République (RPR), mayor of the territory's second largest town, Saint-Laurent-du-Maroni, won a convincing 52.5% of the votes cast in the second constituency, Kourou-Saint-Laurent. PSG representation in the Conseil général fell to eight seats after the March 1994 elections. Castor left the party, but a PSG member, Stéphan Phinera-Horth, was elected President of the Conseil général. Taubira-Delannon was ousted by Antoine Karam, the PSG's Secretary-General, but in June she became the first woman from the Department to enter the European Parliament. She took her place as a representative of the Energie Radicale grouping, which led the poll with 36% of the votes.

Bertrand and Taubira-Delannon were both re-elected to the Assemblée nationale in 1997, although candidates from pro-independence parties gained increased support, winning just over 10% of the votes cast in both constituencies. The high rate of abstention in the 1997 legislative and presidential elections and the re-emergence of separatist parties were symptoms of an increasing dissatisfaction with departmental politics and of rising tension between the Department and metropolitan France. These developments precipitated, and were reinforced by, escalating social unrest. In November 1996 protests in Cayenne, in support of secondary school pupils who were boycotting classes to demand improved study conditions, degenerated into rioting and looting. Violent clashes between protesters and anti-riot police sent from metropolitan France provoked a one-day general strike in Cayenne, organized by the UTG. These tensions worsened as pupils' representatives and local politicians criticized the actions of the police, and local officials alleged that separatist groups were working to exploit the crisis for their own ends. The situation was temporarily resolved when the French Government announced administrative reform and additional funding for the education system. However, in April 1997 the arrest of five pro-independence activists suspected of setting fire to the home of the public prosecutor during the disturbances of November 1996, and the subsequent detention of five others, including leading members of the UTG and the PNPG, led to further demonstrations and riots in Cayenne. In August 1997 the release of the five original detainees, who had been held on remand since April, signalled an end to the immediate crisis.

In January 1999 representatives from 10 separatist organizations from French Guiana, Guadeloupe and Martinique, including the PNPG and the Mouvement pour la Décolonisation et l'Emancipation Sociale (MDES), signed a joint declaration denouncing 'French colonialism'. The political and constitutional future of the Overseas Departments generated considerable debate and controversy throughout that year, especially in French Guiana. In February members of the two Councils held a congress, which recommended the replacement of the two Councils with a single body to which added powers and responsibilities in areas such as economic development, health and education would be transferred. In October, however, the French Prime Minister, Lionel Jospin, ruled out the possibility of any such merger. In December Karam co-signed a declaration along with the Presidents of the Conseil régional in both Guadeloupe and Martinique, stating their intention to propose to the French Government legislative and constitutional amendments aimed at creating a new status of Overseas Region (Région d'outre-mer). The amendments would also provide for greater financial autonomy. The declaration and subsequent announcements by Karam and his counterparts were dismissed by Jean-Jack Queyranne, Secretary of State for Overseas Departments and Territories, in February 2000 as unconstitutional and exceeding the mandate of the politicians responsible. In March, during a visit to the Department by Queyranne, rioting broke out following his refusal to meet a delegation of separatist organizations. Later that month the Conseil régional rejected, by 23 votes to seven, the reforms proposed by Queyranne in February, which included the creation of a Congrès (Congress) in French Guiana, as well as the extension of the Departments' powers in areas such as regional co-operation. Nevertheless, the proposals were provisionally accepted by the Assemblée nationale in May, and were subsequently adopted, by a narrow margin, by the Sénat, following a number of modifications. In November the Assemblée nationale approved the changes and in December they were ratified by the Constitutional Council.

In November 2000 riots took place in Cayenne. The demonstrations followed a march, organized by the UTG, demanding greater autonomy for French Guiana, as well as immediate negotiations with the new Secretary of State for Overseas Departments and Territories, Christian Paul. Discussions were held in December in Paris at which Paul, various senior politicians from French Guiana and representatives from the PSG, the RPR, Walwari, and the Forces Démocratiques Guyanaises (FDG) were present. It was agreed that further talks were to be held between the Conseil général and the Conseil régional of French Guiana before the end of 2001, eventually to be followed by a referendum in the Department; however, no constitutional changes were to be effected before the 2002 presidential and parliamentary elections. Following a meeting of members of both councils in June 2001, a series of proposals on greater autonomy, to be presented to the French Government, was agreed upon. These included: the division of the territory into four districts; the creation of a Territorial Collectivity (collectivité territoriale), governed by a 41-member Assembly elected for a five-year term; and the establishment of an independent executive council. Furthermore, the proposals included a request that the territory be given control over legislative and administrative affairs, as well as legislative authority on matters concerning French Guiana alone. In November the French Government announced itself to be in favour of the suggested constitutional developments, and in March 2003 the two houses of the French parliament approved constitutional changes that conferred the status of Overseas Region (région d'outre-mer) on French Guiana; the changes also allowed for a referendum on proposals for greater autonomy, as occurred in Martinique and Guadeloupe. However, the electorate of French Guiana was not consulted in a referendum, a majority of 10 of the 19 members of the Conseil général voting against the proposal, provoking accusations of anti-democratic behaviour from the MDES.

In September 2001 Christian Paul announced the establishment of a number of measures designed to improve security in the Department. Plans included a 20% increase in the police force, the creation of a small 'peace corps' and a continuous police presence in the town of Maripasoula and its surrounding region, following concerns over the security of gold prospectors in the area. In September the gendarmerie, in co-operation with the national police, launched 'Operation Anaconda' in the south of the Department, aimed at stopping the illegal gold trade. Unlicensed gold-mining operations were a chief cause of illegal immigration, and a focus for other criminal activities, such as drug-smuggling and gun-running. They also caused extensive environmental damage, destroying natural habitats, polluting watercourses and spreading disease. In 2006 the number of expulsions rose by more than 50% to 9,711; however, the deportees included a substantial proportion (59%) of recidivists. Official estimates of the total number of illegal immigrants in French Guiana were between 30,000 and 35,000, the majority from Brazil and Suriname. At that time there were some 41,903 registered foreigners living in French Guiana, many attracted by the relative affluence of the Department, where wages were reported to be between four and 10 times higher than other countries in the region. At the 89th conference of the Association des Maires de France, which convened in Paris in November 2006, French Guianese mayors criticized the national Government's lack of political resolution in addressing the issue.

In elections to the Conseil régional held in March 2004, the PSG won 17 of the council's 31 seats with 37.7% of the votes cast, while the FDG and the Union pour un Mouvement Populaire (UMP) each won seven seats with 31.2% and 31.1% of the ballot, respectively. Antoine Karam was duly re-elected as President of the Conseil régional.

In early January 2006 a strike by dockers over working conditions, introduced the previous November, paralysed the port at Dégrad-des-Cannes for 12 days, causing a backlog of more than 200 shipping containers. An agreement was eventually reached with local employers' organizations, but the strike had a serious impact on the local economy, particularly on smaller companies and those dependent on primary materials. It was the fourth such strike since January 2005.

In early December 2006 a week of industrial action by employees in the electricity sector led to long periods without power across the Department. The strike was in protest at proposed plans by the state-owned Eléctricité de France (EdF) to remodel its operations, which employees feared would result in at least a degree of privatization. On 7 December some 200 protesters attended a demonstration in Cayenne to signal their opposition to the blackouts. The industrial action was suspended following an agreement by EdF to schedule negotiations in Paris with trade unions, including the UTG.

At elections to the Assemblée nationale held on 10 and 17 June 2007, Taubira-Delannon, representing the Walwari party, was re-elected with 63.4% of the votes cast, while the PSG nominee Chantal Berthelot was elected with 52.9% of the ballot. Following municipal elections held on 10 March 2008, Alain Tien-Liong replaced Pierre Désert as President of the Conseil général.

In November 2008 protests erupted against high fuel prices, and a damaging blockade was put in place. Protesters closed schools, cut off the airport and severely curtailed commercial activity. The strike and the blockade ended in early December after an agreement was signed between the prefect and local politicians that included a commitment to reduce the price of fuel. It was suggested that the two-week strike cost the economy between €143m. and €165m. Further protests, albeit on a more limited scale, took place in February and March 2009. These were largely inspired by events in Martinque and particularly Guadeloupe (q.v.), where serious labour and civil unrest occurred.

Later in 2009, in light of the perceived dissatisfaction with the existing governance arrangements, the French Government and local representatives agreed that a referendum should be held on the subject of whether French Guiana should become an autonomous territory governed by Article 74, which grants greater autonomy (rather than Article 73), of the French Constitution. The vote took place on 10 January 2010 and, contrary to expectations, some 69.8% of voters rejected the motion. Turn-out was moderate, at 48.2% of the electorate. In a follow-up vote conducted two weeks later, 57.5% of voters cast their ballot in support of the less significant reform of merging the Conseil régional and Conseil général into a single body. Turn-out was disappointing, at 27.4%. The French Government accepted the results of both votes and suggested that a conclusion to the debate over French Guiana's constitutional relationship with France had thus been reached. The restructuring of the legislature was to be effected within two years.

In elections to the Conseil régional held on 14 and 21 March 2010, Guyane 73, the UMP-supported list, secured 21 of the 31 seats, with 56.1% of the ballot, while Deux Ans: Un Marathon pour Bâtir, comprising various left-wing parties led by Walwari and the MDES, won the remaining 10 seats, with 43.9%. The UMP list's electoral prospects had been aided by the leadership of Rodolphe Alexander, the mayor of Cayennes—formerly a member of the PSG but allied to French President Nicolas Sarkozy since 2007—who had been one of the few politicians publicly to oppose greater autonomy prior to the referendum in January 2010. Disunity among the political left and the decision of Antoine Karam to retire from front-line politics had also facilitated the UMP's victory. Alexandre was elected President of the Conseil régional on 26 March.

Economy

PHILLIP WEARNE

Revised for this edition by Dr PETER CLEGG

French Guiana's main exports are gold, road vehicles, capital goods and shrimps. Mineral resources and hydroelectric potential remain unexploited, and, although the tourist sector has expanded, its growth is limited by the lack of infrastructure inland. Like Martinique and Guadeloupe, the Department is highly dependent on France for its foreign trade and for aid transfers, estimated at €855m. in 2007, to reduce the balance of payments deficit. The impact of the aerospace sector on the economy from the 1970s was another unsettling factor. In 2007 French Guiana's gross domestic product (GDP) was estimated at €2,970m., according to official figures, equivalent per head to €14,100. The unemployment rate in 2008 stood at 21.8%, representing a 1.5% increase from 2007, but less than the 27.6% recorded in 2006. GDP growth, meanwhile, was 3.6% in 2005, 6.4% in 2006, and 4.1% in 2007. In 2008 the Department recorded a trade deficit of some €947.1m. The value of exports was €99.9m., about 9.5% of the total value of imports, which stood at €1,051.4m. The main market for exports was France, which received 56.6% of the total in 2008, while the share purchased by the European Union (EU) increased to approximately 24%. France was also the single largest source of imports, accounting for 50.0% of their total value in 2008. Other European countries, Trinidad and Tobago, and Martinique were also important sources of imports. Road vehicles, refined petroleum products and pharmaceuticals were among the Department's principal imports.

According to the 2007 regional budget, expenditure totalled €81.7m., while revenue amounted to €54.6m. The departmental budget for 2007 produced a surplus of €17.0m., with total receipts of €234.1m. and expenditure amounting to €217.0m. The annual rate of inflation averaged 1.6% in 1997–2007, before rising to 3.5% in 2008.The agricultural sector, concentrated in forestry and fisheries, engaged 2.4% of the salaried labour force in 2007, and contributed 4.3% of GDP in 2005. In 2008 agricultural products accounted for about 16.7% of total export earnings, at €16.7m. Shrimps remained the single most important agricultural export, accounting for 7.4% of total export revenue in 2008, at €7.4m. In 2007 shrimp production was recorded at 1,531 metric tons. However, the importance of shrimp exports declined significantly during the mid-2000s owing to increased competition from shrimp producers in Latin America and Asia and high fuel prices.

The main crops grown for local consumption were cassava, vegetables, rice and sugar cane, the last for use in the making of rum. Livestock-rearing was also largely for subsistence. In 2008, according to official data, Guianese abattoirs produced some 281 metric tons of cattle meat and 480 tons of pig meat. Rice, pineapples and citrus fruit continued to be cultivated for export.

Timber exports declined steadily from the mid-1980s to 2001. In 2001 total wood extraction was 48,122 cu m, about one-half of the 1991 figure. However, the figure then stabilized and stood at 55,946 cu m in 2007. In 2008 extraction increased by 27% to reach 71,302 cu m, bolstered by higher demand from the construction sector. There were several sawmills, but exploitation of timber resources was hampered by the lack of infrastructure in the forest. Local mills produced plywood and veneers, while rosewood, satinwood and mahogany were the major hardwood products. According to FAO, by 2008 roundwood removals totalled some 182,200 cu m, while sawnwood production (including railway sleepers) amounted to 15,000 cu m. The value of wood exports in 2007 was €2.2m.

Industry, including construction, engaged 26.9% of the salaried work-force in 2007, and contributed 20.0% of GDP in 2005, according to official sources. There is little manufacturing activity in French Guiana, except for the processing of agricultural or seafood products, mainly shrimp-freezing and rum distillation. A small quantity of sugar cane—5,500 metric tons in 2007—was processed to supply the sole rum distiller, which produced 1,170 hl of rum in 2008. The European Space Agency's satellite-launching centre at Kourou has provided a considerable stimulus to the economy, most notably the construction sector (which engaged an estimated 13.8% of the salaried labour force in 2007). The space centre was estimated to contribute approximately 16% of French Guiana's GDP in 2007 and to employ some 4,000 people (1,500 directly and another 2,500 indirectly) in 2006.

The mining sector is dominated by the extraction of gold, mostly in the Inini region, which involves small-scale alluvial operations and larger local and multinational mining concerns. Exploration activity intensified in the mid-1990s, and the proposed construction of a major new road into the interior of the Department was expected to encourage further development. The first new concession in 70 years was awarded to Cambior in 2004 for a 25-year period. Figures indicated that in 2008 1,504 kg of gold were mined, down from 2,425 kg in the previous year. In 2003 exports of gold were worth €54.1m., accounting for some 49.9% of export earnings; by 2008 the value of gold exported had fallen to €35.7m., comprising 35.7% of export earnings. The illegal gold trade has been a long-standing problem for French Guiana. It is estimated that there are between 3,000 and 14,000 illegal gold-miners in the country, a situation exacerbated by many prospectors crossing the southern border from Brazil. In early 2008 the French President, Nicolas Sarkozy, announced plans to limit the occurrence of such operations. Indeed, the ongoing activity of 'Operation Anaconda' (see History), stricter environmental regulation of the sector, and enhanced co-operation between the Governments of France, Brazil and Suriname have placed limits on the expansion of the mining industry.

Exports of all metals and metal products amounted to €43.9m. in 2008—a 20% decline compared with the previous year. Crushed rock for the construction industry was the only other mineral extracted in significant quantities, but exploratory drilling of known diamond deposits began in 1995. Bauxite, kaolin and columbo-tantalite were also present in commercial quantities, in particular on the Kaw plateau and near Saint-Laurent-du-Maroni. However, low market prices and the high cost of building the infrastructure necessary for the exploitation of such reserves hampered development.

Before the flooding of the Petit-Saut hydroelectric dam on the River Sinnamary in 1994 French Guiana depended heavily on imported fuels for the generation of energy (in 2008 imports of mineral fuels still accounted for 11.6% of total imports). Together with existing plants, the 116-MW dam was expected to supply the Department's energy for 30 years, annually generating around two-thirds of the Department's electricity. However, in response to increasing demand for electricity, plans have been put in place further to increase capacity, including the development of biofuels (particularly ethanol) and other renewables (including biomass and solar power). In June 2001 an Australian hydrocarbons company, Hardman Resources (now known as Tullow Oil), was awarded an exclusive exploration licence for French Guiana's offshore basin. Environmental groups raised concerns that the company had not given due consideration to the impact of seismic surveying on the coastal fauna. None the less, Tullow Oil (in conjunction with the international oil companies Shell and Total) was planning to begin high-impact drilling in late 2010.

French Guiana's economic development was hindered by its location, its poor infrastructure away from the coast and the lack of a skilled indigenous work-force, which left the potential for growth in agriculture, fishing, tourism, forestry and the energy sector largely unexploited. There was also a critically high level of unemployment, especially among younger sectors of the urban work-force, while much agricultural and mining work was carried out by undocumented migrants from Haiti, Suriname and Brazil. French Guiana's geographical characteristics, with large parts of the territory accessible only by river, made it difficult to regulate key sections of the economy, such as gold-mining and forestry. There was considerable concern among environmentalists that this could have severe ecological consequences. Proposals for the creation of a national park, covering 2.5m. ha in the south of French Guiana, were initially made in 1992. However, it was not until February 2007 that the Guiana Amazonian Park was established by the French Government, despite some local opposition to the project. The central area of the park, in which the natural environment is fully protected, encompasses 7,840 sq miles (24% of the surface area of French Guiana), while the outer rim covers a further 5,250 sq miles. The park borders the Tumucumaque National Park in neighbouring Brazil, and together they constitute the largest area of protected rainforest in the world. Pressure to reduce the high budget deficit increased the Department's dependence on metropolitan France, while the high demand for imported consumer goods among the relatively affluent civil servant population tended to undermine any progress. In early 2003 the French Minister of the Overseas Departments, Territories and Country (as the Minister of the Overseas Possessions was then known) announced plans to stimulate the economies of French Guiana, Guadeloupe and Martinique by introducing tax incentives for the hotel sector, to help it remain competitive in the Caribbean region, and by creating jobs, for young people in particular. In 2001 and 2002 some 65,000 visitor arrivals were recorded, while receipts from tourism increased from an estimated US $42m. to $45m. over the same period. In 2003 it was estimated that tourism contributed 3% of GDP. By 2007 tourism numbers had increased to 108,800. In July 2005 the Governments of France and Brazil signed an agreement to build a bridge across the Oiapoque, which, it was hoped, would stimulate trade and tourism between Brazil and French Guiana; construction began in 2008 and was scheduled for completion by the end of 2010.

Statistical Survey

Sources (unless otherwise indicated): Institut National de la Statistique et des Etudes Economiques (INSEE), Service Régional de Guyane, ave Pasteur, BP 6017, 97306 Cayenne Cédex; tel. 5-94-29-73-00; fax 5-94-29-73-01; internet www.insee.fr/fr/insee_regions/guyane; Chambre de Commerce et d'Industrie de la Guyane (CCIG), Hôtel Consulaire, pl. de l'Esplanade, BP 49, 97321 Cayenne Cédex; tel. 5-94-29-96-00; fax 5-94-29-96-34; internet www.guyane.cci.fr.

AREA AND POPULATION

Area: 83,534 sq km (32,253 sq miles).

Population: 157,213 at census of 8 March 1999; 205,954 (males 101,930; females 104,023) at census of 1 January 2006. Note: According to new census methodology, data in 2006 refer to median figures based on the collection of raw data over a five-year period (2004–09). *1 January 2009* (estimate): 229,000. *Mid-2010* (UN estimate): 231,000 (Source: UN, *World Population Prospects: The 2008 Revision*.

Density (at mid-2010): 2.8 per sq km.

Population by Age and Sex (population in '000, UN estimates at mid-2010): *0–14:* 78 (males 40, females 38); *15–64:* 144 (males 71, females 73); *65 and over:* 9 (males 4, females 5); *Total* 231 (males 115, females 116) (Source: UN, *World Population Prospects: The 2008 Revision*).

Principal Towns (population at 1999 census): Cayenne (capital) 50,594; Saint-Laurent-du-Maroni 19,211; Kourou 19,107; Matoury 18,032; Rémire-Montjoly 15,555; Mana 5,445; Macouria 5,050; Maripasoula 3,710. *Mid-2009* (UN estimate, incl. suburbs): Cayenne 62,437 (Source: UN, *World Urbanization Prospects: The 2009 Revision*).

Births, Marriages and Deaths (2008): Registered live births 6,247 (birth rate 28.2 per 1,000); Registered marriages 619 (marriage rate 2.8 per 1,000); Registered deaths 762 (death rate 3.4 per 1,000).

Life Expectancy (years at birth): 76.2 (males 72.8; females 80.1) in 2009. Source: Pan American Health Organization.

Economically Active Population (persons aged 15 years and over, 1999): Agriculture, forestry and fishing 2,888; Construction 3,256; Industry 3,524; Trade 4,573; Transport 1,616; Education, health and social services 8,990; Public administration 10,337; Other services 8,259; Total employed 43,443 (males 25,703; females 17,740). *2007* (provisional estimates at 31 December): Agriculture 803; Industry 4,111; Construction 3,712; Trade 4,426; Services 35,677; Total employed 48,729; Unemployed 11,697; Total labour force 60,426. Note: Figures for employment exclude unsalaried workers. *31 December 2008:* Unemployed 12,834.

HEALTH AND WELFARE

Key Indicators

Total Fertility Rate (children per woman, 2009): 3.2.

Under-5 Mortality Rate (per 1,000 live births, 2009): 14.6.

Physicians (per 1,000 head, c. 2001): 1.4.

Hospital Beds (per 1,000 head, 2005): 3.0.

Access to Water (% of persons, 2004): 84.

Access to Sanitation (% of persons, 2004): 78.

Source: mostly Pan American Health Organization.

For other sources and definitions, see explanatory note on p. vi.

AGRICULTURE, ETC.

Principal Crops ('000 metric tons, 2008, FAO estimates): Rice, paddy 8.7; Cassava 10.3; Sugar cane 5.5; Cabbages and other brassicas 6.3; Tomatoes 3.7; Cucumbers and gherkins 3.7; Beans, green 3.3; Bananas 4.5; Plantains 3.2. *Aggregate Production* ('000 metric tons, may include official, semi-official or estimated data): Total vegetables (incl. melons) 24.5; Total fruits (excl. melons) 15.3.

Livestock ('000 head, 2008, FAO estimates): Cattle 9.3; Pigs 11.0; Sheep 2.7.

Livestock Products (metric tons, 2008, FAO estimates): Cattle meat 283; Pig meat 1,153; Chicken meat 470; Cows' milk 270; Hen eggs 460.

Forestry ('000 cubic metres, 2008, FAO estimates): *Roundwood Removals* (excl. bark): Sawlogs, veneer logs and logs for sleepers 57.0; Other industrial wood 9.0; Fuel wood 116.2; Total 182.2. *Sawnwood Production* (incl. railway sleepers): Total 15.

Fishing (metric tons, live weight, 2008): Capture 3,957 (Marine fishes 2,427; Shrimps 1,530); *Total catch* 3,957. Note: Data for aquaculture were not available.

Source: FAO.

MINING

Production ('000 metric tons unless otherwise indicated, 2008, estimates): Cement 62,000; Gold (metal content of ore, kilograms, reported figure) 2,000; Sand 1,500. Source: US Geological Survey.

INDUSTRY

Production: Rum 1,170 hl in 2008; Electric energy 582 million kWh in 2007 (Source: l'Institut d'Emission des Départements d'Outre-Mer, *Rapport Annuel 2008*).

FINANCE

Currency and Exchange Rates: 100 cent = 1 euro (€). *Sterling and Dollar Equivalents* (31 May 2010): £1 sterling = €1.177; US $1 = €0.807; €10 = £8.49 = $12.38. *Average Exchange Rate* (euros per US dollar): 0.731 in 2007; 0.683 in 2008; 0.720 in 2009. Note: The national currency was formerly the French franc. From the introduction of the euro, with French participation, on 1 January 1999, a fixed exchange rate of €1 = 6.55957 French francs was in operation. Euro notes and coins were introduced on 1 January 2002. The euro and French currency circulated alongside each other until 17 February, after which the euro became the sole legal tender. Some of the figures in this Survey are still in terms of francs.

Budgets (excl. debt rescheduling, € million, 2007 unless otherwise indicated): *Regional Government:* Current revenue 81.7 (Taxes 58.9); Capital revenue 25.3; Total 107.1. Current expenditure 56.8; Capital expenditure 47.5; Total 104.3. *Departmental Government* (2006):

Revenue 263.8; Expenditure 234.1. Source: Département des Etudes et des Statistiques Locales.

Money Supply (million French francs at 31 December 1996): Currency outside banks 3,000; Demand deposits at banks 1,621; Total money 4,621.

Cost of Living (Consumer Price Index; base: 2000 = 100): All items 114.2 in 2007; 118.2 in 2008; 119.0 in 2009. Source: ILO.

Gross Domestic Product (US $ million at constant 1990 prices): 1,668 in 2001; 1,695 in 2002; 1,722 in 2003. Source: UN, *Statistical Yearbook*.

Expenditure on the Gross Domestic Product (€ million at current prices, 2003): Total final consumption expenditure 2,293 (General government and non-profit institutions serving households 1,154, Households 1,139); Changes in inventories –29; Gross fixed capital formation 493; *Total domestic expenditure* 2,757; Exports of goods and services 727; *Less* Imports of goods and services 1,276; *GDP in purchasers' values* 2,207.

Gross Domestic Product by Economic Activity (€ million at current prices, 2003): Agriculture, hunting, forestry and fishing 95; Food industries 39; Manufacturing 180; Energy 40; Construction 163; Services 1,564 (Restaurants and hotels 42, Transport –85, Commerce 223, Other market services 560; Non-market services 824); *Sub-total* 2,081; Financial intermediation services indirectly measured –42; Import duties, less subsidies 169; *GDP in purchasers' values* 2,207.

EXTERNAL TRADE

Principal Commodities (€ million, 2006): *Imports c.i.f.:* Products of agriculture and food industries 144; Pharmaceutical products 51; Home equipment 47; Car industry products 101; Mechanical equipment 73; Electronic equipment 63; Fuels and combustibles 93; Total (incl. others) 756. *Exports f.o.b.:* Products of agriculture and food industries 12.9; Boats, planes, trains, and motorcycles 1.8; Car industry products 19.7; Mechanical equipment 6.3; Electronic equipment 11.1; Metals and products thereof 54.4; Total (incl. others) 112.3.

Principal Trading Partners (€ million, 2006): *Imports c.i.f.:* France (metropolitan) 297; Germany 18; Italy 14; Japan 16; Martinique 18; Netherlands 18; Spain 8; Trinidad and Tobago 90; USA 9; Total (incl. others) 756. *Exports f.o.b.:* Australia 2; Belgium 2; France (metropolitan) 62; Germany 7; Guadeloupe 3; Italy 8; Martinique 4; Portugal 2; Suriname 4; Switzerland 18; Total (incl. others) 112.

TRANSPORT

Road Traffic ('000 motor vehicles in use, 2001): Passenger cars 32.9; Commercial vehicles 11.9 (Source: UN, *Statistical Yearbook*). *2002:* 50,000 motor vehicles in use.

International Sea-borne Shipping (traffic, 2005 unless otherwise indicated): International vessels entered 115; Goods loaded 25,103 metric tons; Goods unloaded 472,567 metric tons (Source: CCIG); Passengers carried 275,300 (1998).

Civil Aviation: Freight carried (incl. post) 6,252 metric tons (2005); Passengers carried 384,168 (2008).

TOURISM

Tourist Arrivals by Country (2007): France 62,016; Guadeloupe 14,362; Martinique 22,739; Total (incl. others) 108,801.

Receipts from Tourism (US $ million, incl. passenger transport): 49 in 2007.

Source: World Tourism Organization.

COMMUNICATIONS MEDIA

Radio Receivers ('000 in use): 104 in 1997.

Television Receivers ('000 in use): 37 in 1998.

Telephones ('000 main lines in use): 48.2 in 2009.

Mobile Cellular Telephones ('000 subscribers): 217.7 in 2009.

Personal Computers ('000 in use): 33 in 2004.

Internet Users ('000): 58.0 in 2009.

Daily Newspaper: 1 in 1996 (average circulation 2,000 copies).

Sources: UNESCO, *Statistical Yearbook*; UN, *Statistical Yearbook*; International Telecommunication Union.

EDUCATION

Pre-primary (2008/09): 40 institutions; 13,571 students (12,755 state, 816 private).

Primary (2008/09): 114 institutions (106 state, 8 private); 26,175 students (24,513 state, 1,662 private).

Specialized Pre-primary and Primary (2008/09): 432 students (427 state, 5 private).

Secondary (2008/09): 42 institutions (37 state, 5 private); 30,814 students (29,102 state, 1,712 private). Source: Rectorat de la Guyane *Enquête 19 (1st degré)* and *Enquête 19 (2nd degré)*.

Higher (2007/08): 2,653 students.

Teachers (2008/09 unless otherwise indicated): *Primary:* 2,243 teachers (2,121 state, 122 private); *Secondary:* 2,433 teachers (2,285 state, 148 private); *Higher* (2004/05): 63 teachers. Source: Ministère de l'Education Nationale, *Repères et références statistiques*.

Adult Literacy Rate: 83.0% (males 83.6%; females 82.3%) in 1998. Source: Pan American Health Organization.

Directory

The Government

(July 2010)

HEAD OF STATE

President: NICOLAS SARKOZY.

Prefect: DANIEL FÉREY, Préfecture, 1 rue Fiedmont, BP 7008, 97307 Cayenne Cédex; tel. 5-94-39-45-00; fax 5-94-30-02-77; e-mail courrier@guyane.pref.gouv.fr; internet www.guyane.pref.gouv.fr.

DEPARTMENTAL ADMINISTRATION

President of the General Council: ALAIN TIEN-LIONG, Hôtel du Département, pl. Léopold Héder, BP 5021, 97397 Cayenne Cédex; tel. 5-94-29-55-00; fax 5-94-29-55-25; e-mail atienliong@cg973.fr; internet www.cg973.fr.

President of the Economic and Social Committee: ROGER-MICHEL LOUPEC, Cité Administrative Régionale, 4179 route de Montabo, Carrefour de Suzini, BP 7025, 97307 Cayenne Cédex; tel. 5-94-28-96-01; fax 5-94-30-73-65; e-mail cesr@cr-guyane.fr.

President of the Culture, Education and Environment Committee: JEAN-PIERRE BACOT, 66 ave du Général de Gaulle, 97300 Cayenne; tel. 5-94-25-66-84; fax 5-94-37-94-24; e-mail ccee@cr-guyane.fr; internet www.cr-guyane.fr.

President of the Regional Council: RODOLPHE ALEXANDRE (UMP), Cité Administrative Régionale, 4179 route de Montabo, Carrefour de Suzini, BP 7025, 97307 Cayenne Cédex; tel. 5-94-29-20-20; fax 5-94-31-95-22; e-mail cabcrg@cr-guyane.fr; internet www.cr-guyane.fr.

Elections, 14 and 21 March 2010

	Seats
Guyane 73*	21
Deux Ans: Un Marathon pour Bâtir†	10
Total	31

* Electoral list comprising the Union pour un Mouvement Populaire (UMP) and allies.

† Electoral list comprising various left-wing parties led by Walwari and the Mouvement de Décolinisation et d'Emancipation Sociale (MDES).

REPRESENTATIVES TO THE FRENCH PARLIAMENT

Deputies to the French National Assembly: CHRISTIANE TAUBIRA-DELANNON (Walwari), CHANTAL BERTHELOT (PSG).

Representatives to the French Senate: GEORGES PATIENT (Groupe Socialiste), JEAN-ETIENNE ANTOINETTE (Groupe Socialiste).

Political Organizations

Forces Démocratiques de Guyane (FDG): 41 rue du 14 Juillet, BP 403, 97300 Cayenne; tel. 5-94-28-96-79; fax 5-94-30-80-66; e-mail g.othily@senat.fr; internet www.fdguyane.com; f. 1989 by a split in the PSG; Pres. ALICK EGOUY; Sec.-Gen. GIL HORTH.

Mouvement de Décolonisation et d'Emancipation Sociale (MDES): 21 rue Maissin, 97300 Cayenne; tel. 5-94-30-55-97; fax 5-94-30-97-73; e-mail mdes.parti@wanadoo.org; internet www.mdes.org; f. 1991; pro-independence; Sec.-Gen. MAURICE PINDARD.

Parti Socialiste (PS): 7 rue de l'Adjudant Pindard, 97300 Cayenne Cédex; tel. 5-94-37-81-33; fax 5-94-37-81-56; e-mail fede973.partisocialiste@wanadoo.fr; departmental br. of the metropolitan party; Leader LÉON JEAN BAPTISTE EDOUARD; Sec. PAUL DEBRIETTE.

Parti Socialiste Guyanais (PSG): 1 Cité Césaire, 97300 Cayenne; tel. 5-94-28-11-44; e-mail contact@psg-guyane.org; internet www.psg-guyane.org; f. 1956; left-wing; Sec.-Gen. ANTOINE KARAM.

Union pour un Mouvement Populaire (UMP): 42 rue du Docteur Barrat, 97300 Cayenne; tel. 5-94-28-80-74; fax 5-94-28-80-75; internet www.u-m-p.org; f. 2002 as Union pour la Majorité Presidentielle by mems of the fmr Rassemblement pour la République and Union pour la Démocratie Française; centre-right; departmental br. of the metropolitan party; Pres., Departmental Cttee RÉMY-LOUIS BUDOC.

Les Verts Guyane: 64 rue Madame Payé, 97300 Cayenne; tel. 5-94-40-97-27; e-mail tamanoir.guyane@wanadoo.fr; internet guyane.lesverts.fr; ecologist; departmental br. of the metropolitan party; Regional Sec. PHILIPPE MÉNARD.

Walwari: 69 bis ave de la Liberté, 97338 Cayenne Cédex; tel. 5-94-30-07-73; fax 5-94-31-84-95; internet www.walwari.com; f. 1993; left-wing; Leader CHRISTIANE TAUBIRA-DELANNON; Sec.-Gen. JEAN-MARIE TAUBIRA.

Judicial System

Courts of Appeal: see Judicial System, Martinique.

Tribunal de Grande Instance: Palais de Justice, 9 ave du Général de Gaulle, 97300 Cayenne; Pres. DOMINIQUE PANNETIER; Procurators-Gen. CLAIRE LANET, YVES-ARMAND FRASSATI (acting).

Religion

CHRISTIANITY

The Roman Catholic Church

French Guiana comprises the single diocese of Cayenne, suffragan to the archdiocese of Fort-de-France, Martinique. Some 80% of the population are Roman Catholics. French Guiana participates in the Antilles Episcopal Conference, currently based in Port of Spain, Trinidad and Tobago.

Bishop of Cayenne: Rt Rev. EMMANUEL M. P. L. LAFONT, Evêché, 24 rue Madame Payé, BP 378, 97328 Cayenne Cédex; tel. 5-94-28-98-48; fax 5-94-30-20-33; e-mail eveche-cayenne@orange.fr; internet diocese.cayenne.free.fr.

The Anglican Communion

Within the Church in the Province of the West Indies, French Guiana forms part of the diocese of Guyana. The Bishop is resident in Georgetown, Guyana. There were fewer than 100 adherents in 2000.

Other Churches

In 2000 there were an estimated 7,000 Protestants and 7,200 adherents professing other forms of Christianity.

Assembly of God: 1051 route de Raban, 97300 Cayenne; tel. 5-94-35-23-04; fax 5-94-35-23-05; e-mail jacques.rhino@wanadoo.fr; internet www.addguyane.fr; Pres. JACQUES RHINO; c. 500 mems.

Church of Jesus Christ of Latter-day Saints (Mormons): Route de la Rocade, 97305 Cayenne; Br. Pres. FRANÇOIS PRATIQUE; c. 250 mems.

Seventh-day Adventist Church: Mission Adventiste de la Guyane, 39 rue Schoëlcher, BP 169, 97324 Cayenne Cédex; tel. 5-94-25-64-26; fax 5-94-37-93-02; e-mail adventiste.mission@orange.fr; f. 1949; Pres. and Chair. ALAIN LIBER; 2,164 mems.

The Jehovah's Witnesses are also represented.

The Press

France-Guyane: 17 rue Lallouette, BP 428, 97329 Cayenne; tel. 5-94-29-70-00; fax 5-94-29-70-02; e-mail france.guyane@media-antilles.fr; internet www.franceguyane.fr; daily; Publishing Dir FRÉDÉRIC AURAND; Local Dir MARC AUBURTIN; Editor-in-Chief JÉRÔME RIGOLAGE; circ. 9,000.

L'Hebdo de Guyane: pl. Léopold Héder, 97300 Cayenne; tel. 5-94-29-55-55; fax 5-94-29-55-54; e-mail communication@cg973.fr; publ. by the Conseil général; 5 a week; Editor-in-Chief TCHISSÉKA LOBELT.

La Semaine Guyanaise: 6 ave Louis Pasteur, 97300 Cayenne; tel. 5-94-31-09-83; fax 5-94-31-95-20; e-mail semaine.guyanaise@nplus.gf; internet www.semaineguyanaise.com; weekly (Thurs.); Dir ALAIN CHAUMET; Editor-in-Chief JÉRÔME VALLETTE.

Oka.Mag': 11 rue Abel Azor, 18 Cité Manil, 97310 Kourou; tel. 5-94-22-01-44; fax 5-94-32-17-66; e-mail oka.mag@wanadoo.fr; internet www.okamag.fr; f. 2001; 6 a year; Amerindian interest; Pres. and Editor-in-Chief DANIEL FRANÇOIS; circ. 15,000.

Ròt Kozé: 21 rue Maissin, 97300 Cayenne; tel. 5-94-30-55-97; fax 5-94-30-97-73; e-mail webmaster@mdes.org; internet www.mdes.org; f. 1990; left-wing organ of the MDES party; monthly; Dir MAURICE PINDARD.

NEWS AGENCY

Agence France Presse (AFP): 17 résidence Saint-Antoine, chemin Saint-Antoine, 97300 Cayenne; tel. and fax 5-94-39-09-42; e-mail rozga@yahoo.com; Correspondent ALEXANDRE ROZGA.

Publishers

Editions Amazone: 2 Centre Commerciale Montjoly, 97354 Montjoly; tel. 6-94-23-18-78; fax 5-94-30-45-00; Dir LÉO MIRA.

Editions Anne C.: 8 Lot Mapaou, route de Baduel, BP 212, 97325 Cayenne; tel. and fax 5-94-35-20-10; e-mail canne@nplus.gf; f. 1998; French-Creole children's and youth literature; Dir NICOLE PARFAIT-CHAUMET.

Ibis Rouge Editions: chemin de la Levée, BP 267, 97357 Matoury; tel. 5-94-35-95-66; fax 5-94-35-95-68; e-mail jlm@ibisrouge.fr; internet www.ibisrouge.fr; f. 1995; general literature, French-Creole, and academic; Gen. Man. JEAN-LOUIS MALHERBE; agencies in Guadeloupe and Martinique.

PUBLISHERS' ASSOCIATION

Promolivres Guyane: BP 96, 97394 Rémire-Montjoly Cédex; tel. 5-94-29-55-56; fax 5-94-38-52-82; e-mail promolivreguyane@wanadoo.fr; f. 1996; asscn mems incl. editors, booksellers, journalists and librarians; promotes French Guianese literature; Pres. TCHISSÉKA LOBELT.

Broadcasting and Communications

TELECOMMUNICATIONS

Digicel Antilles Françaises Guyane: see Martinique—Telecommunications.

France Telecom: 76 ave Voltaire, BP 8080, 97300 Cayenne; tel. 5-94-39-91-15; fax 5-94-39-91-00; e-mail eline.miranda@francetelecom.com.

Orange Caraïbe: see Guadeloupe—Telecommunications.

Outremer Telecom: 112 ave du Général de Gaulle, 97300 Cayenne; tel. 5-94-28-71-15; fax 5-94-23-93-59; e-mail communication@outremer-telecom.fr; internet www.outremer-telecom.fr; f. 1998; mobile telecommunications provider; Group CEO JEAN-MICHEL HEGESIPPE.

ONLY: 112 ave du Général de Gaulle, 97300 Cayenne; tel. 5-94-28-71-15; fax 5-94-23-93-59; e-mail communication@outremer-telecom.fr; internet www.outremer-telecom.fr; f. 2004 as Outremer Telecom Guyane; subsidiary of Outremer Telecom, France; present name adopted following merger of Volubis, ONLY and OOL in 2006; mobile and fixed telecommunications provider.

BROADCASTING

Réseau France Outre-mer (RFO): ave le Grand Boulevard, Z.A.D. Moulin à Vent, 97354 Rémire-Montjoly; tel. 5-94-25-67-00; fax 5-94-25-67-64; internet guyane.rfo.fr; acquired by Groupe France Télévisions in 2004; fmrly Société Nationale de Radio-Télévision Française d'Outre-mer, present name adopted 1998; Radio-Guyane Inter accounts for 46.6% of listeners (2003); Télé Guyane/RFO1 and

RFO (Tempo) account for 52.3% and 7.5% of viewers, respectively (2003); Dir.-Gen. GENEVIÈVE GIARD; Regional Dir FRED AYANGMA.

Radio

KFM: 6 rue François Arago, 97300 Cayenne; tel. 5-94-31-30-38; fax 5-94-37-84-20; f. 1993 as Radio Kikiwi; present name adopted 2003.

NRJ Guyane: 2 blvd de la République, 97300 Cayenne; tel. 5-94-39-54-88; fax 5-94-39-54-79; e-mail wladimir@nrjguyane.com; internet www.nrjguyane.com; f. 2006; commercial radio station; Mans WLADIMIR MANGACHOFF, MARC HO-A-CHUCK.

Radio Joie de Vivre: 39 rue Schoëlcher, 97324 Cayenne Cédex; BP 169, 97300 Cayenne; tel. 5-94-31-29-00; fax 5-94-29-47-26; internet www.advent973.org; f. 1993; operated by the Seventh-day Adventist church; Gen. Man. ESAÏE AUGUSTE.

Radio Littoméga (RLM): 24 blvd Malouet, BP 108, 97320 Saint-Laurent-du-Maroni; tel. 5-94-34-22-09; e-mail centre.cl@wanadoo.fr; internet www.rlm100.com; f. 1994; Dir ARIELLE BERTRAND; Man. ALAIN ACOUCKIA.

Radio Mig: 100 ave du Général de Gaulle, 97300 Cayenne; tel. 5-94-30-77-67; fax 5-94-31-86-81; f. 1995; Creole; affiliated to the MDES party and UTG; Man. YVES ICARE.

Radio Mosaïque: 11 rue Sainte-Catherine, cité Brutus, 97300 Cayenne; tel. 5-94-30-94-76; e-mail guyanes@free.fr; commercial radio station; Man. BÉRIL BELVU.

Radio Ouassailles: rue Maurice Mongeot, 97360 Mana; tel. 5-94-34-80-96; fax 5-94-34-13-89; e-mail radio.ouassailles@wanadoo.fr; f. 1994; French and Creole; Man. RÉMY AUBERT.

Radio Saint-Gabriel: 23 rue Lallouette, BP 372, 97328 Cayenne; tel. 5-94-31-10-28; e-mail radiosaintgabriel@wanadoo.fr; f. 2001; Roman Catholic; Man. ROMAINE ASSARD.

Radio Toucan Fréquence International (TFI): 1 pl. du Vidé, BP 68, 97300 Kourou; tel. 5-94-32-96-11; fax 5-94-39-71-61; e-mail direction@tfifm.com; internet www.tfifm.com; f. 1983; part of Groupe I-Medias Antilles-Guyane; commercial radio station; Dir YVAN DUCOUDRAY-SAINT-PRIX; Man. JEAN-MARC DE CRENY.

Radio UDL (Union Défense des Libertés): ave Félix Eboué, 97323 Saint-Laurent-du-Maroni; tel. 5-94-34-27-90; e-mail redaction973@gmail.com; internet www.udlguyane.com; f. 1982; Man. JEAN GONTRAND.

Radio Vinyle Club: 7 pl. Gaston Monnerville, 97310 Kourou; tel. 5-94-22-02-58; fax 5-94-22-38-69; f. 2001; Man. ARNAUT CHARLE.

Radio Voix dans le Désert: 5 route de Raban, chemin du Château d'Eau, 97300 Cayenne; tel. 5-94-31-27-22; fax ; 5-90-37-90-06; f. 1993; operated by the Assembly of God church; Pres. EDDY LAUTRIC; Man. YVON RAMASSANY.

Other radio stations include: Média Tropique FM; Nostalgie Guyane; Ouest FM; Radio 2000; Radio Bonne Nouvelle Guyane; Radio Gabrielle; Radio JAM; Radio Loisirs Guyane; Radio Merci Seigneur; Radio Pagani; Radio Tour l'Isle; Radio Tout'Moun; Radyo ITG; RFM 90; and Sky FM.

Television

Antenne Créole Guyane: 31 ave Louis Pasteur, 97300 Cayenne; tel. 5-94-28-82-88; fax 5-94-29-13-08; e-mail acg@acg.gf; internet www.acg.gf; f. 1994; sole local private TV station; gen. interest with focus on music and sports; produces 30% of own programmes; received by 95% of the population, accounting for 25% of viewers (2003); Pres. MARC HO-A-CHUCK; Gen. Man. WLADIMIR MANGACHOFF.

Canal+ Guyane: 14 Lotissement Marengo, Z. I. de Collery, 97300 Cayenne; tel. 5-94-29-54-55; fax 5-94-30-53-35; f. 1994; subsidiary of Groupe Canal+, France; satellite TV station.

Finance

(cap. = capital; res = reserves; dep. = deposits; m. = million; brs = branches; amounts in French francs)

BANKING

Central Bank

Institut d'Emission des Départements d'Outre-mer (IEDOM): 8 rue Christophe Colomb, BP 6016, 97306 Cayenne Cédex; tel. 5-94-29-36-50; fax 5-94-30-02-76; e-mail direction@iedom-guyane.fr; internet www.iedom.fr; f. 1959; Dir-Gen. YVES BARROUX; Dir PATRICK BESSE.

Commercial Banks

Banque Française Commerciale Antilles-Guyane (BFC Antilles-Guyane): 8 pl. des Palmistes, BP 111, 97345 Cayenne; tel. 5-94-29-11-11; fax 5-94-30-13-12; e-mail service-client@bfc-ag.com; internet www.bfc-ag.com; f. 1985; Regional Dir PHILIPPE BISSAINTE.

BNP Paribas Guyane SA: 2 pl. Victor Schoëlcher, BP 35, 97300 Cayenne; tel. 5-94-39-63-00; fax 5-94-30-23-08; e-mail bnpg@bnpparibas.com; internet www.bnpparibas.com; f. 1964 following purchase of BNP Guyane (f. 1855); name changed July 2000; 94% owned by BNP Paribas SA, 3% by BNP Paribas Martinique and 3% by BNP Paribas Guadeloupe; cap. 71.7m., res 100.0m., dep. 2,007m. (Dec. 1994); Dir and CEO ANTOINE GARCIA; Gen. Sec. JACQUES SALGE; 2 brs.

BRED-Banque Populaire (BRED-BP): 76 ave du Général de Gaulle, 97300 Cayenne; tel. 5-94-29-68-70; fax 5-94-31-48-01; Pres. STÈVE GENTILI; 3 brs.

Crédit Agricole: see Martinique—Finance.

Development Bank

Société Financière pour le Développement Economique de la Guyane (SOFIDEG): PK 3, 700 route de Baduel, BP 860, 97339 Cayenne Cédex; tel. 5-94-29-94-29; fax 5-94-30-60-44; e-mail sofideg@nplus.gf; f. 1982; bought from the Agence Française de Développement (AFD—q.v.) by BRED-BP in 2003; Dir FRANÇOIS CHEVILLOTTE.

Insurance

AGF Vie & AGF IARD France: Centre Commercial Katoury, BP 933, 97341, Cayenne Cédex; tel. 5-94-28-67-27; fax 5-94-30-99-49; e-mail eagfguyane@wanadoo.fr; internet www.agf.fr; life and short-term insurance.

Groupama Antilles Guyane: see Martinique—Insurance.

Trade and Industry

GOVERNMENT AGENCIES

Direction de l'Agriculture et de la Forêt (DAF): Parc Rebard, BP 5002, 97305 Cayenne Cédex; tel. 5-94-29-63-74; fax 5-94-29-63-63; e-mail daf.guyane@agriculture.gouv.fr; internet daf.guyane.agriculture.gouv.fr.

Direction Régionale et Départementale des Affaires Maritimes (DRAM): 2 bis rue Mentel, BP 6008, 97306 Cayenne Cédex; tel. 5-94-29-36-15; fax 5-94-29-36-16; e-mail stephane.gatto@equipement.gouv.fr; responsible for shipping, fishing and other maritime issues at a nat. and community level; Dir STÉPHANE GATTO.

Direction Régionale de l'Industrie, de la Recherche et de l'Environnement (DRIRE): Pointe Buzaré, BP 7001, 97307 Cayenne Cédex; tel. 5-94-29-75-30; fax 5-94-29-07-34; e-mail drire-antilles-guyane@industrie.gouv.fr; internet www.ggm.drire.gouv.fr; active in industry, business services, transport, public works, tourism and distribution; Regional Dir PHILIPPE COMBE.

DEVELOPMENT ORGANIZATIONS

Agence de l'Environnement et de la Maîtrise de l'Energie (ADEME): 28 ave Léopold Heder, Cayenne Cédex; tel. 5-94-31-73-60; fax 5-94-30-76-69; e-mail ademe.guyane@ademe.fr; internet www.ademe-guyane.fr; Delegate SUZANNE PONS.

Agence Française de Développement (AFD): Lotissement les Héliconias, route de Baduel, BP 1122, 97345 Cayenne Cédex; tel. 5-94-29-90-90; fax 5-94-30-63-32; e-mail afdcayenne@groupe-afd.org; internet www.afd-guyane.fr; fmrly Caisse Française de Développement; Dir ROBERT SATGE.

Agence Régionale de Développement économique (ARD): 1 pl. Schoëlcher, BP 325, 97325 Cayenne Cédex; tel. 5-94-25-66-66; fax 5-94-25-43-19; f. 2009 to replace Agence pour la Création et le Développement des Entreprises en Guyane.

Fédération des Organisations Amérindiennes de Guyane (FOAG): Centre des Cultures, rue Capt. Charles Claude, 97319 Awala Yalirnapo; tel. 6-94-42-27-76; fax 5-94-33-50-06; e-mail foag@nplus.gf; f. 1993; civil liberties org. representing the rights of the indigenous peoples of French Guiana; Sec.-Gen. Chief JEAN AUBÉRIC CHARLES.

CHAMBERS OF COMMERCE

Chambre d'Agriculture: 8 ave du Général de Gaulle, BP 544, 97333 Cayenne Cédex; tel. 5-94-29-61-95; fax 5-94-31-00-01; e-mail chambre.agriculture.973@orange.fr; Pres. CHRISTIAN EPAILLY; Dir (vacant).

Chambre de Commerce et d'Industrie de la Guyane (CCIG): Hôtel Consulaire, pl. de l'Esplanade, BP 49, 97321 Cayenne Cédex; tel. 5-94-29-96-00; fax 5-94-29-96-34; e-mail contact@guyane.cci.fr; internet www.guyane.cci.fr; Pres. JEAN-PAUL LE PELLETIER.

Chambre de Métiers: Jardin Botanique, blvd de la République, BP 176, 97324 Cayenne Cédex; tel. 5-94-25-24-70; fax 5-94-30-54-22;

e-mail m.toulemonde@cm-guyane.fr; internet www.cm-guyane.fr; Pres. SYLVAIN LEMKI; Sec.-Gen. JOCELYN HO-A-CHUCK.

Jeune Chambre Economique de Cayenne: 1 Cité A. Horth, route de Montabo, BP 1094, Cayenne; tel. 5-94-31-62-99; fax 5-94-31-76-13; internet www.jcef.asso.fr; f. 1960; Pres. PAUL-RICHARD VINGADASSALOM; Gen. Sec. RENÉE-LINE SABAS.

EMPLOYERS' ORGANIZATIONS

Coopérative des Céréales et Oléagineux de Guyane (COCEROG): PK 24, chemin départemental 8, Sarcelles, 97360 Mana; tel. 5-94-34-20-82; fax 5-94-34-02-08.

Groupement Régional des Agriculteurs de Guyane (GRAGE): PK 15 route nationale 1, Domaine de Soula, 97355 Macouria; tel. 5-94-38-71-26; e-mail grage@wanadoo.fr; internet www.grage.gf; affiliated to the Confédération Paysanne; Pres. ALBÉRIC BENTH.

MEDEF Guyane: 27A Résidence Gustave Stanislas, Source de Baduel, BP 820, 97338 Cayenne Cédex; tel. 5-94-31-17-71; fax 5-94-30-32-13; e-mail updg@nplus.gf; f. 2005; fmrly Union des Entreprises de Guyane; Pres. ADRIEN AUBIN.

Ordre des Pharmaciens du Département Guyane: ave Hector Berlioz, 97310 Kourou; tel. 5-94-32-17-62; fax 5-94-32-17-66; e-mail delegation_guyane@ordre.pharmacien.fr; internet www.ordre.pharmacien.fr; Pres LILIANE POGNON, EJULIBERTE PAUILLAC MAM LAM FOUCK.

Syndicat des Exploitants Forestiers et Scieurs de Guyane (SEFSG): Macouria; tel. 5-94-35-26-66; fax 5-94-35-29-92; f. 1987; represents timber processors; Man. M. POMIES.

Syndicat des Transformateurs du Bois de Guyane (STBG): Menuisserie Cabassou, PK 4.5, route de Cabassou, 97354 Remire-Montjoly; tel. 5-94-31-34-49; fax 5-94-35-10-51; f. 2002; represents artisans using wood; Pres. YVES ELISE; Sec. FRANÇOIS AUGER.

MAJOR COMPANIES

Air Liquide Spatial Guyane (ALSG): Route de l'Espace, Ensemble de Lancement, BP 826, 97388 Kourou Cedex; tel. 5-94-33-75-69; fax 5-94-33-75-77; f. 1969; subsidiary of Air Liquide Group; mfrs of propellant gases for the space industry; Dir Man. LAURENT DU HAYES; Administrator FRANCOIS MOUTIEZ; c. 40 employees.

Arianespace: BP 809, 97388 Kourou Cedex; tel. 5-94-33-67-07; fax 5-94-33-69-13; e-mail webmaster@arianespace.com; internet www.arianespace.com; f. 1979; local br. of French-based co; satellite launch vehicle operators; 32.53% owned by CNES, France; 15.81% owned by EADS ST SA, France; 10.87% owned by EADS ST Gmbh, Germany; Dir. PATRICK LOIRE; 3 launch vehicles; c. 50 employees.

Auplata: 9 Lotissement Montjoyeux, 97300 Cayenne; tel. 5-94-29-54-40; fax 5-94-29-85-00; e-mail presse@auplata.fr; internet www.auplata.fr; f. 2006; gold-mining; Chair. JEAN-PIERRE GORGÉ; CEO DIDIER TAMAGNO.

Bamyrag-Pétrole: 7 Lotissement Marengo, Z. I. Collery, 97300 Cayenne; tel. 5-94-36-26-00; fax 5-94-35-14-45; subsidiary of Groupe Bernard Hayot, Martinique; distribution of fuels, metal minerals and chemical products; Pres. BERNARD HAYOT.

Cegelec Space: Global Technologies, CIGMA Division, Immeuble Vercors, pl. Newton, 97310 Kourou; BP 819, 97388 Kourou; tel. 5-94-32-05-24; fax 5-94-32-31-39; e-mail mail.space@cegelec.com; internet www.space.cegelec.com/space-kourou.htm; f. 2001; supplier to the space industry; responsible for operation and maintenance of Guiana Space Centre ground infrastructure; subsidiary of Cegelec Germany and Cegelec France; Pres. MICHAEL MARTER; 140 employees.

Ciments Guyanais (CIGU): Z. I. Dégrad-des-Cannes, 97354 Rémire-Montjoly; tel. 5-94-35-54-98; fax 5-94-35-54-99; e-mail accueil@ciments-guyanais.com; f. 1989; owned by Holcim (Switzerland) and Lafarge (France); cement production; Gen. Man. PATRICK VANDRESSE; 25 employees.

Compagnie Guyanaise de Transformation des Produits de la Mer (COGUMER): Port de Pêche du Larivot, 97351 Matoury; tel. 5-94-29-00-00; fax 5-94-30-30-46; e-mail cogumer@wanadoo.fr; f. 1986; as CODEPEG; present name adopted 2003; fish-processing; Pres. CHRISTIAN MADERE; Gen. Man. RENÉ GUSTAVE; 250 employees.

Groupe Rubis Antilles-Guyane: Z. I. Pariacabo, BP 139, 97310 Kourou; tel. 5-94-32-05-00; fax 5-94-32-33-40; internet www.vito-ag.com; f. 2005; fmrly Shell SAGF; subsidiary of GPL Rubis, France; distribution of petroleum products; Chief Financial Officer BRUNO KRIEF.

Hardman Petroleum France SAS (HPF SAS): Parc d'Activite, C. O. Soprim, 97354 Remire Montjoly; affiliate of Tullow Oil; CEO ALAN MARTIN.

Nofrayane: 9 Parc d'Activité Cognot Matoury, BP 1166, 97345 Cayenne; tel. 5-94-35-18-65; fax 5-94-35-18-60; subsidiary of Vinci Construction Grands Projets; construction and civil engineering; Dir OLIVIER MANTEZ; 98 employees.

Régulus (CSG): Centre Spatial Guyanais, BP 73, 97372 Cayenne; tel. 5-94-35-15-00; fax 5-94-32-49-42; f. 1991; space industry; jt subsidiary of Fiat Avio, Italy (60%) and SNPE, France(40%); Plant Dir JEAN-EMMANUEL QUEBRE.

SARA (Société Anonyme de la Raffinerie des Antilles): Dégrad-des-Cannes, BP 227, 97301 Cayenne; tel. 5-94-25-50-50; fax 5-94-35-41-79; internet www.sara.mq; f. 1982; second depot opened in Kourou in 2000; Chair. CHRISITAN CHAMMAS; Regional Gen. Man. FRANÇOIS NAHAN; c. 250 employees regionally (see entry under Martinique).

UTILITIES

Electricity

Electricité de France Guyane (EdF): blvd Jubelin, BP 6002, 97306 Cayenne; tel. 5-94-39-64-00; fax 5-94-30-10-81; electricity producer; Gen. Man. MARC GIRARD.

Water

Société Guyanaise des Eaux: 2738 route de Montabo, BP 5027, 97306 Cayenne Cédex; tel. 5-94-25-59-26; fax 5-94-30-59-60; internet www.suez-environnement.fr; f. 1978; CEO LUC FAUCHER; Gen. Man. RODOLPHE LELIEVRE.

TRADE UNIONS

Centrale Démocratique des Travailleurs de la Guyane (CDTG): 99–100 Cité Césaire, BP 383, 97328 Cayenne Cédex; tel. 5-94-31-02-32; fax 5-94-31-81-05; e-mail sg.cdtg@wanadoo.fr; affiliated to the Confédération Française Démocratique du Travail; Sec.-Gen. JEAN-MARC BOURETTE.

Affiliated unions incl.:

SGEN-CFDT: 99–100 Cité Césaire, BP 383, 97328 Cayenne Cédex; tel. 5-94-31-02-32; fax 5-94-35-71-17; e-mail guyane@sgen.cfdt.fr; affiliated to the Fédération des Syndicats Généraux de l'Education Nationale et de la Recherche; represents teaching staff.

Fédération Syndicale Unitaire Guyane (FSU): Mont Lucas, Bât G, No C37, 97300 Cayenne; tel. 5-94-30-05-69; fax 5-94-38-36-58; e-mail fsu973@fsu.fr; f. 1993; departmental br. of the Fédération Syndicale Unitaire; represents public sector employees in teaching, research and training, and also agriculture, justice, youth and sports, and culture; Sec. ALAIN BRAVO.

Union Départementale Confédération Française des Travailleurs Chrétiens Guyane (UD CFTC): BP 763, 97337 Cayenne Cédex; tel. 5-94-30-14-85; fax 5-94-35-77-30; e-mail lydie.leneveu@wanadoo.fr.

Union Départementale Force Ouvrière de Guyane (FO): 25 Cité Mirza, rue des Acajous, 97300 Cayenne; tel. and fax 5-94-31-62-55; Sec.-Gen. CHRISTIAN DESFLOTS.

Union Régionale Guyane: 52 rue François Arago, BP 807, 97300 Cayenne; tel. 5-94-21-67-61; fax 5-94-30-89-70.

Union des Travailleurs Guyanais (UTG): 40 ave Digue Ronjon, BP 265, 97326 Cayenne Cédex; tel. 5-94-31-26-42; fax 5-94-30-82-46; e-mail utg1@wanadoo.fr; internet www.utg-guyane.com; Sec.-Gen. ALBERT DARNAL.

UNSA Education Guyane: 46 rue Vermont Polycarpe, BP 341, 97327 Cayenne Cédex; tel. and fax 5-94-30-89-70; Sec.-Gen. MARTINE NIVOIX.

Transport

RAILWAYS

There are no railways in French Guiana.

ROADS

In 2004 there were 1,300 km (808 miles) of roads in French Guiana, of which 397 km were main roads. Much of the network is concentrated along the coast, although proposals for a major new road into the interior of the Department were under consideration.

SHIPPING

Dégrad-des-Cannes, on the estuary of the river Mahury, is the principal port, handling 80% of maritime traffic in 1989. There are other ports at Le Larivot, Saint-Laurent-du-Maroni and Kourou. Saint-Laurent is used primarily for the export of timber, and Le Larivot for fishing vessels. There are river ports on the Oiapoque and on the Approuague. There is a ferry service across the Maroni river between Saint-Laurent and Albina, Suriname. The rivers provide the best means of access to the interior, although numerous rapids prevent navigation by large vessels.

Compagnie Guyanaise de Transport Maritime (CGTM): 26 Avenue de la Liberte, 97300 Cayenne; Man. DENIS BLOUIN.

SOMARIG (Société Maritime et Industrielle de la Guyane): Z. I. de Dégrad-des-Cannes, Rémire, BP 81, 97322 Cayenne Cédex; tel. 5-94-35-42-00; fax 5-94-35-53-44; e-mail cay.hrouchon@cma-cgm.com; internet www.cma-cgm.com; f. 1960; owned by Groupe CMA—GGM (France); Man. Dir HERVÉ ROUCHON.

CIVIL AVIATION

Rochambeau International Airport, situated 17.5 km (11 miles) from Cayenne, is equipped to handle the largest jet aircraft. There are also airports at Maripasoula, Saul and Saint Georges. Access to remote inland areas is frequently by helicopter.

Air Guyane: Aéroport de Rochambeau, 97300 Matoury; tel. 5-94-35-03-07; fax 5-94-30-54-37; e-mail resa@airguyane.com; internet www.airguyane.com; f. 1980; 46% owned by Guyane Aéro Invest, 20% owned by Sodetraguy; operates domestic services; Pres. CHRISTIAN MARCHAND.

Tourism

The main attractions are the natural beauty of the tropical scenery and the Amerindian villages of the interior. In 2005 there were 27 hotels with some 1,184 rooms. In 2007 tourist arrivals totalled 108,801. Receipts from tourism were US $49m. in that year.

Comité du Tourisme de la Guyane: 12 rue Lallouette, BP 801, 97338 Cayenne Cédex; tel. 5-94-29-65-00; fax 5-94-29-65-01; e-mail ectginfo@tourisme-guyane.com; internet www.tourisme-guyane.com; Pres. JEAN-ELIE PANELLE; Dir VALÉRIE ROBINEL.

Délégation Régionale au Tourisme, au Commerce et à l'Artisanat pour la Guyane: 9 rue Louis Blanc, BP 7008, 97307 Cayenne Cédex; tel. 5-94-28-92-90; fax 5-94-31-01-04; e-mail drtca973@wanadoo.fr; Delegate DIDIER BIRONNEAU (acting).

L'Ensemble Culturel Régional (ENCRE): 82 ave du Général de Gaulle, BP 6007, 97306 Cayenne Cédex; tel. 5-94-28-94-00; fax 5-94-28-94-04; f. 2004 by merger of Ecole Nationale de Musique et de Danse and Office Culturel de la Région Guyane; fmrly Asscn Régionale de Développement Culturel; Pres. ANTOINE KARAM.

Fédération des Offices de Tourisme et Syndicats d'Initiative de la Guyane: 12 rue Lallouette, 97300 Cayenne; tel. 5-94-30-96-29; fax 5-94-31-23-41; e-mail frguyane@fnotsi.net; Pres. ARMAND HILDAIRE.

Defence

As assessed at November 2009, France maintained a military force of 1,585 in French Guiana. The headquarters is in Cayenne. There was also a gendarmerie of about 700 personnel.

Education

Education is modelled on the French system and is compulsory for children between six and 16 years of age. Primary education begins at six years of age and lasts for five years. Secondary education, beginning at 11 years of age, lasts for up to seven years, comprising a first cycle of four years and a second of three years. Education at state schools is provided free of charge. In 2008/09 there were 40 pre-primary schools, 114 primary schools and 42 secondary schools. In the same period there were 40,178 students in pre-primary and primary education, while in secondary education there were 30,814 students, of whom some 94% were educated in the state sector. Higher education in law, administration and French language and literature is provided by a branch of the Université des Antilles et de la Guyane in Cayenne; there is also a teacher-training college (IUFM), a technical institute at Kourou and an agricultural college. In 2007/08 some 2,653 students were enrolled in higher education in French Guiana. The French Government announced its decision to increase expenditure in the education sector in 2000–06, including €71m. on the construction of new school buildings.

Bibliography

For works on the Caribbean generally, see Select Bibliography (Books)

Crane, J. *French Guiana*. Oxford, ABC Clio, 1999.

Mam-Lam-Fouk, S. *Histoire générale de la Guyane française*. Matoury, Ibis Rouge, 2002.

Plénet, C. *Les fonds structurels européens*. Matoury, Ibis Rouge, 2005.

Redfield, P. *Space in the Tropics: From Convicts to Rockets in French Guiana*. Berkeley, CA, University of California Press, 2000.

Rodway, J. *Guiana: British, Dutch, and French*. Boston, MA, Elibron Classics, 2005.

GRENADA

Geography

PHYSICAL FEATURES

Grenada is in the Windward Islands, in the Lesser Antilles, and is considered to be the most southerly island of the eastern Caribbean. It lies about 145 km (90 miles) north of Trinidad (Trinidad and Tobago). The country includes Carriacou, the largest island of the Grenadines, and a number of smaller islands in the chain that runs north and a little east of the main island. Off shore from Carriacou, to the east, is Petit (often spelt Petite) Martinique, the most northerly of the islands of Grenada and separated from Petit St Vincent (Saint Vincent and the Grenadines) by only a narrow sea channel. Grenada is the second smallest independent state in the Americas (after Saint Christopher and Nevis), with a total area of 344.5 sq km (133 sq miles).

The main island of Grenada is about 34 km long by 19 km wide, aligned along a north–south axis, apart from a southern tapering towards the south-west and a northern tendency to reach towards the chain of the Grenadines in the north-east. The wooded mountains march across the island following this diagonal, the land to the north and west rising (the highest point is at Mt St Catherine—840 m or 2,757 ft), the land to the south and east falling to an indented coast of rias (drowned valleys), which provide deep harbours. Grenada is volcanic in origin, demonstrated by its central highlands and its fertile soil, which give sustenance to tropical forests and mangrove swamps, as well as the crops that have earned it the moniker of the 'spice island of the Caribbean'. Birds and animals thrive, including armadillos and Mona monkeys originally imported from Africa, but the only unique species are the endangered hookbilled kite—a large hawk that eats tree snails and is now, globally, only found in the Levera National Park—and the native Grenada dove. A controversial amendment to the Grenada National Parks and Protected Areas Act in May 2007, however, allowed for the sale for development of the Mount Hartman National Park—the last sanctuary of the Grenada dove—threatening the imminent decline of the already critically endangered species. The 121-km coastline is largely protected by reefs, particularly in the Grenadines.

The southern Grenadines form part of the country of Grenada. These islands include a group around Ronde Island, then, further north, a smaller group located just to the south of the large island of Carriacou, which is 37 km north-east of Grenada itself. Carriacou is almost 34 sq km in extent, an island of low, green hills. About 4 km east of its northern end is the island of Petit Martinique, the next largest of the Grenadian Grenadines.

CLIMATE

The climate is subtropical, tempered by north-eastern trade winds off the Atlantic. Grenada can occasionally be affected by hurricanes, but the country is generally considered to lie just to the south of the hurricane belt (in 1999 a heavy swell from a hurricane to the north caused considerable damage, for instance). There is, though, a rainy season from June to November, followed by the cooler months of December and

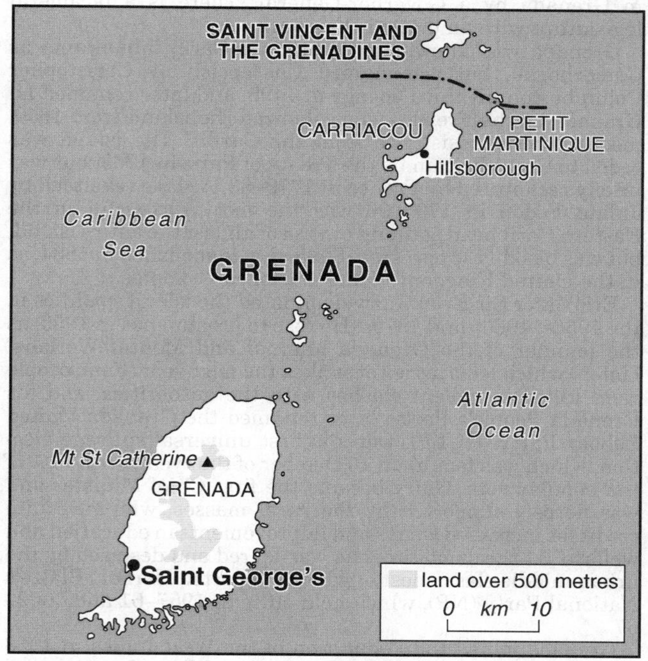

January. Average annual rainfall is about 1,520 mm (60 ins), but in the high forest there can be over 4,000 mm per year. The average annual temperature along the coast is 28°C (82°F).

POPULATION

Racially the population is 85% black, with 11% of mixed black-white ancestry and the rest consisting mainly of whites and 'East' Indians. Some claim to include in their ancestry traces of the original Carib and Arawak Amerindian inhabitants. Although most cultural evidence of early French rule has disappeared, almost one-half of the population is still Roman Catholic, with Nonconformist Protestant denominations (33%) and Anglicans (14%) making up the balance. The official language is English, but a French patois has survived in some areas.

According to mid-year estimates, the total population was 104,342 in mid-2010. Many of these people are young, with almost two-fifths under 15 years of age and a further one-quarter between 15 and 30 years old. More than 4,000 live in the capital, the beautiful harbour city of St George's in the south-west, and over 5,000 on the islands of Carriacou and Petit Martinique. The chief town of the Grenadines is Hillsborough, on the central western shore of Carriacou. Grenada island is divided into six parishes, with Carriacou and Petit Martinique described as a dependency.

History

MARK WILSON

Grenada is a constitutional monarchy within the Commonwealth. Queen Elizabeth II is Head of State, and is represented in Grenada by a Governor-General. There is a bicameral legislature with an elected chamber.

Grenada was known by its original Carib inhabitants as Camerhogue, but was named Concepción by Christopher Columbus on his third voyage in 1498, and later renamed La Grenade by the French, who colonized the island from 1650, meeting fierce resistance from the Caribs. The island was ceded to Great Britain by the Treaty of Paris in 1763, but was briefly recaptured by France in 1779–83. A slave revolt led by Julian Fedon in 1795–96 was the most successful in the Eastern Caribbean, gaining control of almost the entire island, but was bloodily suppressed. Slavery was abolished in 1834, as in the United Kingdom's other Caribbean colonies.

Eric (later Sir Eric) Gairy dominated the island's politics in the 1950s, 1960s and 1970s. He rose to prominence in 1950, as the founder of the Grenada Manual and Mental Workers' Union, which led a series of strikes the next year. Four people were killed in violent clashes with the authorities, and his Grenada People's Party, later renamed the Grenada United Labour Party (GULP), won the first universal suffrage election, which was fought on 10 October of that year, with 71% of the popular vote. Gairy became the first Chief Minister and was fiercely supported by the rural masses, who gave him credit for increased wages and improvements in education and welfare. At the same time, he was feared and despised by the urban middle class, most of whom supported Herbert Blaize's National Party (NP), which held office in 1957–61 and 1962–67.

Grenada joined the Federation of the West Indies in 1958 along with nine other British colonies. When Jamaica and Trinidad left in 1962 the Federation collapsed, and an attempt to unite the remaining colonies as the 'little eight' was unsuccessful, while a proposal for a union with Trinidad and Tobago was not followed through. Along with its neighbours to the north, Grenada became a British Associated State in 1967, responsible for its internal affairs, with the United Kingdom retaining control of external affairs and defence.

Young left-wing opponents of Gairy, led by Maurice Bishop, in 1973 formed the New Jewel Movement (NJM—Joint Endeavour for Welfare, Education and Liberation). Grenada was the first Associated State to gain independence, on 7 February 1974. Gairy's opponents were strongly opposed to separation from the United Kingdom under what they saw as a repressive regime, and the months before were marked by protracted strikes and widespread demonstrations; Bishop's father was shot dead by the police during a demonstration on 21 January.

In elections held in 1976 an opposition alliance won 48% of the popular vote; Bishop became leader of the opposition. On 13 March 1979 the NJM removed Gairy from power, installing a People's Revolutionary Government (PRG), with Bishop as Prime Minister, but retaining the Queen as Head of State. The PRG had close relations with Cuba and the USSR, while the USA saw the regime as a potential security threat. Bishop, in particular, at first enjoyed strong popular support, but this was gradually eroded both by the refusal to call elections and by economic difficulties. An important policy initiative was the construction, with Cuban assistance, of the Point Salines International Airport. Although designed as a civilian facility, the USA feared that Point Salines could be used for military purposes.

In 1983 a militant wing of the NJM and the army became increasingly hostile to Bishop and his immediate supporters. In October these forces organized a coup, led by Gen. Hudson Austin. Bishop and several cabinet ministers were shot, as well as members of a crowd of demonstrators, which gathered in the capital, St George's. The USA led a military intervention, supported by seven Caribbean states, which installed an interim Government, led by Nicholas Brathwaite. In June 2006 Grenada's Truth and Reconciliation Commission submitted a report to Parliament that appealed for fresh trials to be held of 17 people convicted in relation to the 1983 killings. In February 2007 the Privy Council, based in the United Kingdom, ordered that the remaining 13 prisoners be resentenced (following the release of three of their original number in December 2006 on grounds of good behaviour, and the earlier discharge of Phyllis Coard in 2000 in order to seek life-saving medical treatment), and in June of that year a hearing in the Grenada High Court precipitated the immediate acquittal of a further three prisoners. Lawyers for the prosecution had recommended that consecutive fixed-term sentences, providing for eventual release, be considered in respect of the other 10 prisoners. The presiding judge, Justice Francis Belle of Barbados—whose suitability in such a capacity was officially contested by several of the victims' families—subsequently handed down sentences of up to 40 years, although most of the 10 had already served a majority of this term. National responses to the verdict were deeply divided, with many in government expressing incomprehension at the decision while declaring many of the local advocates for the defence to be affiliates of the opposition National Democratic Congress (NDC). Bernard Coard and the remaining prisoners were released in September 2009, having served 26 years in prison.

The NP, still led by Blaize, convincingly won the general election of December 1984. Blaize's Government completed the construction of the international airport and returned the country to a more stable path of development. None the less, splits and defections weakened the NP Government, as did the death of Blaize in 1989. Blaize's successor, Ben Jones, lost a general election in March 1990; the NDC, led by Brathwaite, gained a majority through the defection of individual members from other parties. However, the NP's main successor, the New National Party (NNP), led by Keith Mitchell, regained office in June 1995. After losing his parliamentary majority through further defections, Mitchell called fresh elections in January 1999, in which the NNP won all 15 parliamentary seats.

The NNP had at times been criticized over allegations of impropriety, including lax supervision of the 'offshore' financial sector; moreover, several prominent overseas investors had proved to be undesirable, and departed in controversial circumstances. Four officers of the former First International Bank of Grenada in 2007 received prison sentences in the USA for fraud, after pleading guilty. The bank and its subsidiaries had in 1996–2000 operated a Ponzi scheme, with investors losing an estimated US $170m.

In late 2001 Canada announced that Grenadians travelling to Canada would require visas. This reflected growing international concern, which increased following the terrorist attacks on the USA in September, over Grenada's economic citizenship programme, under which passports were sold to non-citizens. Grenada eventually abandoned the programme in December 2002.

The NNP narrowly won a general election held on 27 November 2003, holding eight of the 15 seats in the House of Representatives; the NDC took the remaining seven seats. The results were contested, however, and the opposition pursued legal challenges to the election results, while in 2006 the Government attempted unsuccessfully to unseat an opposition Member of Parliament on the grounds that he had held dual Grenadian and Canadian citizenship at the time of the 2003 election. Mitchell appointed a new Cabinet in December 2003; the most significant change was the transferral of the agriculture portfolio to Gregory Bowen, the erstwhile Minister of Communications, Works and Public Utilities, as part of a wider plan to revitalize the ailing agricultural sector, in particular the nutmeg industry.

Hurricane Ivan struck Grenada in September 2004, causing widespread devastation. A further storm, Hurricane Emily, struck the island in July 2005. In spite of this, the political climate remained bitterly polarized. Lawyers and trade unions campaigned vigorously in February of that year against a proposal to appoint a controversial Jamaican lawyer, Hugh Wildman, as Attorney-General, successfully persuading the

Judicial and Legal Services Commission of the Organisation of Eastern Caribbean States (OECS) to oppose the appointment. The Government unwillingly accepted the ruling, and in March the position of Attorney-General was added to the other portfolios held by Elvin Nimrod, the Minister of Foreign Affairs and International Trade, of Carriacou and Petit Martinique Affairs, and of Legal Affairs. Wildman remained legal adviser to the Government and launched a legal challenge to the OECS legal commission's refusal to appoint him. A commission of inquiry was established in 2004 to investigate alleged corruption by Mitchell; however, it was unable to start work, as the opposition contested a refusal to grant it the right to examine witnesses, and the subsequent arrival of Hurricane Ivan visited further disruption upon proceedings.

Further controversy was caused by the switching of diplomatic recognition in January 2005 from Taiwan to the People's Republic of China. China had agreed in December 2004 to assist with the construction of a sports stadium, housing and other projects. A broadly similar package had previously been agreed with Taiwan, formerly the island's largest bilateral aid donor, but Mitchell argued that the destruction caused by Hurricane Ivan had forced the Government to reconsider its international relationships. A formal opening ceremony for the China-funded stadium was held in February 2007, ahead of the Cricket World Cup; however, the Grenadian police band caused some consternation by playing the Taiwanese national anthem. Two separate public inquiries were held into the incident.

Grenada is a centre for cocaine and marijuana transshipment, and is a minor marijuana producer. Close co-operation is reported with Trinidadian anti-trafficking organizations; 80% of cocaine transshipped is believed to be destined for the British market. Cocaine seizures fell from 936 kg in 2007 to 46 kg in 2008 and only 6 kg in 2009; a trafficker held with 162 kg of marijuana was fined only EC $10,000, with a boat also confiscated, but avoided a custodial sentence. The per caput murder rate of 16 per 100,000 in 2008 was high by international standards, but fell in 2009 to 7 per 100,000, among the lowest in the Caribbean. Anti-corruption legislation has been passed but the bodies required for implementation have yet to be established.

A general election was held on 8 July 2008, ahead of the April 2009 constitutional deadline. The NNP failed to secure an unprecedented fourth successive term in office, with the NDC winning 11 of the 15 legislative seats and 51.2% of the valid votes cast. The NNP won the remaining four seats and 48.0% of the vote. The United Labour Platform, a coalition of the GULP and the Peoples Labour Movement, failed to have an impact upon the result. Electoral turn-out was high with some 80.3% of eligible voters participating in the poll, and election observers from the Organization of American States reported positively upon the procedure of the election. Thomas was sworn in as Prime Minister on 9 July and the new Cabinet was installed on 13 July: notable appointments included Nazim Burke as Minister of Finance, Planning, Economy, Energy and Co-operatives, and Peter David as Minister of Foreign Affairs. One of the NDC Government's first priorities was to effect measures to counteract the rising cost of living: the party's election manifesto had included proposals to reduce import duties on selected essential goods and to increase the provision of affordable housing.

The International Centre for Settlement of Investment Disputes in Washington, DC, USA, ruled in March 2009 in favour of Grenada in a dispute with petroleum company RSM Production over a 1996 agreement to issue an oil and gas exploration licence. Grenada subsequently announced that maritime boundary talks would be resumed with Trinidad and Tobago; these had been inactive since 1993. An agreed line was fixed by treaty and ratified in April 2010. An agreed south-eastern maritime boundary will allow bidding for oil and gas exploration in parts of Grenada's exclusive economic zone; however, the maritime boundary with other neighbouring states remained unclear.

Economy

MARK WILSON

The three-island state of Grenada, Carriacou and Petit Martinique is the second smallest nation in the western hemisphere in area, with 345 sq km and some 110,821 inhabitants in mid-2009, of whom 4,900 live on Carriacou and 800 on Petit Martinique. Although devastated by Hurricane Ivan in September 2004, the nation had developed a fairly prosperous middle-income economy, with a per-head gross domestic product (GDP) of US $4,650 in 2009. The unemployment rate decreased from 17.0% to 11.5% in 2000–03. Growth has been uneven in recent years. GDP grew by 8.4% in 2004, but contracted by 6.5% in 2005, the year of Ivan. Reconstruction stimulated a recovery, with growth of 12.0% in 2006, but there was a further contraction of 1.9% in 2007. Growth of 4.5% in 2007 slowed to 2.2% in 2008, as a result of the international financial crisis, and GDP contracted by 7.7% in 2009 as investment inflows, tourism and migrant remittances were negatively affected by the next phase of the downturn. Construction output declined by 15% in 2008 and a further 50% in 2009. Reduced government revenue and rising salary costs resulted in an increase in the overall fiscal deficit from 2.9% of GDP in 2000 to 19.0% in 2002, financed mainly through local commercial borrowing and an accumulation of arrears. An IMF report, which followed Article IV consultations in January 2003, more than a year ahead of Hurricane Ivan, noted the need to reverse the sharp and unsustainable increase in public debt (111% of GDP at the end of that year) and to reduce the fiscal deficit. Total public debt outstanding rose to 131% of GDP after Ivan in 2004 and was US $658.4m. in 2006, equivalent to 125% of GDP according to IMF estimates. The fiscal deficit has remained high, and was just over 6% of GDP in each year from 2006 to 2009. The debt-to-GDP ratio improved as a result of restructuring, to 97% by 2008 according to local estimates, but rose again to 114% in 2009, largely because of new domestic borrowing.

Grenada is a member of the Caribbean Community and Common Market, or CARICOM, the larger members of which formed a single market (the Caribbean Single Market and Economy—CSME) at the start of 2006. Grenada, along with five other members of the Organisation of Eastern Caribbean States (OECS)—which links nine of the smaller Caribbean territories—joined this initial stage of the CSME early in July. Grenada is also a member of the Eastern Caribbean Securities Exchange (based in Saint Christopher and Nevis), while its financial affairs are supervised by the Eastern Caribbean Central Bank, also located in Saint Christopher and Nevis.

Agriculture and fishing made up some 6.5% of GDP in 2009, compared with 10.3% in 2002. The major export crops were nutmeg and its by-product, mace, of which Grenada was the world's second most important producer, after Indonesia. However, these and other tree crops were devastated by Ivan, with 70% of nutmeg trees destroyed, and, with replanting proceeding slowly at best, output was expected to remain well below pre-2004 levels for the foreseeable future. There was some prospect of offshore petroleum or gas reserves, and the Government negotiated an Exclusive Economic Zone boundary with Trinidad and Tobago, and intended to pursue similar agreements with Venezuela and other maritime neighbours. Grenada was also one of 13 states to subscribe to Venezuela's PetroCaribe initiative in June 2006, receiving up to 340,000 barrels of gasoline, diesel and fuel oil annually, purchased on favourable terms.

The pleasant climate, white sand beaches and natural beauty of the islands have encouraged the growth of tourism, with the additional benefit of direct air connections to the United Kingdom and North America. Receipts from tourism increased from US $37.5m. in 1990 to an estimated US $109.9m. in 2007, before declining slightly to US $98.8m. in 2009. Following Hurricane Ivan in 2004, the number of stop-over tourists declined to 98,548 in 2005, from 127,904 in the previous year; however, numbers increased by 20.4% in 2006, to 118,653, with most hotels back in operation, and then increased by a further 9.0% to 129,145 in 2007, slipping to 109,407 in 2009 as international demand slowed. There were also 339,752 cruise ship passengers in 2009, who made a smaller contribution to the economy as a result of limited onshore spending. Hotels' and restaurants' contribution to GDP decreased from 8.0% in 2003 to 3.7% in 2005, but recovered to 6.8% in 2008 before slipping to 5.2% in 2009. There are several proposals for major hotel developments; however, progress was set back from mid-2008 with a recession in international tourism demand.

St George's University, which includes an 'offshore' medical school, had close to 3,000 resident students and staff in 2009, most of them from the USA, with direct local spending estimated at US $40m. This institution made a substantial contribution to GDP.

Manufacturing made up some 4.1% of GDP in 2009. Industries such as the assembly of electronic components were oriented entirely to the export market, while others, such as beverages, were produced for the local market, with some exports to other Caribbean islands.

The Government stressed the importance of recent advances in technology for economic development. Grenada is a member of the Eastern Caribbean Telecommunications Authority, which liberalized the regime for local and international communications. Call centres and telemarketing operations have been a source of employment, but performance was uneven.

There is a small 'offshore' financial sector, which included 1,580 international business companies in 2008. The sector, until the late 2000s, failed to meet internationally accepted regulatory standards; Grenada was listed as a 'non-co-operative jurisdiction' by the Organisation for Economic Co-operation and Development (OECD) in 2001, and appeared on a comparable list compiled by the Financial Action Task Force on Money Laundering (FATF, based in Paris, France) in September that same year. Legislation and regulatory standards were subsequently tightened by the Grenada International Financial Services Authority, with the licences of 26 banks and trust companies revoked; as a result, Grenada was de-listed by the FATF in February 2003. None the less, international monitoring of the sector remained strict, and Grenada was listed by the US Department of State as a country of concern, their intermediate category. OECD in April 2008 included Grenada on a 'grey' list of countries that did not yet have a significant number of Tax Information Exchange Agreements in place; however, six agreements had been signed by mid-2010, representing significant progress. Four officers of the former First International Bank of Grenada received prison sentences in the USA in August 2007 after a fraudulent investment scheme lost investors an estimated total of US $170m. Before the appointment of a receiver in August 2000, the bank had operated for an extended period in clear breach of Grenadian capitalization and audit requirements.

The islands contain several volcanic centres, although the only one with a recent history of activity was the underwater volcano of Kick'Em Jenny, to the north of the main island. Earthquakes also represent a threat. Grenada was devastated by Hurricane Ivan on 7 September 2004. The OECS assessed damage at US $815m., equivalent to more than double the country's annual GDP. There was extensive damage to housing stock, infrastructure and public services, particularly in the south of the island. Most notably, of the 1,700 hotel rooms, only 300 were usable in the immediate aftermath of the hurricane, and damage to the agriculture sector included the aforementioned devastation of the nutmeg harvest. The hurricane disabled the main export industries, while increasing the need for reconstruction-related imports as the construction sector expanded from 10.6% of GDP in 2003 to 21.5% in 2005, before contracting to 12.8% of GDP in 2007.

As a consequence of the hurricane, the burden on public finances was dramatically increased, while revenue was sharply reduced. Generous grant aid supported disaster relief and reconstruction efforts, with pledges totalling one-third of annual GDP. Expenditure by the Government was channelled through the new Agency for Reconstruction and Development, in order to improve public and donor confidence in accountability and transparency. Grants peaked at 11.3% of GDP in 2005, but were projected at below 3% of GDP for 2007. The IMF in 2005 projected a financing gap rising to 12%–14% in 2006–10. Most of the external creditors in October 2005, though, agreed a debt restructuring programme, with interest reduced for the period to 2015 and the principal to be repaid in 2025. However, total debt stock increased from 96% of GDP in 2005 to 114% in 2006, in part because of substantial domestic borrowing. In 2006 the Government raised additional revenue from fuel and from a contentious 3% levy on salaries, while curtailing recurrent expenditure and obtaining additional development assistance. The plan was to move from a primary deficit of 2.0% of GDP in 2005 to a primary surplus of 2.5% by 2008, while reducing debt to 60% of GDP by 2015; however, with debt rising to 114% of GDP in 2009 amid an international recession, that target appeared unattainable. In 2006 grant aid allowed the recurrent budget to show a 5.5% surplus, but the overall deficit was 7.1% of GDP as a result of extensive capital spending, in part because of preparations for 2007 Cricket World Cup matches in Grenada. Although debt restructuring reduced interest payments by one-half, and in spite of substantial donor support, there were irregular payments and intermittent arrears on domestic debt. Standard and Poor's reduced its credit rating for Grenada from B- to CCC+ in April 2007, but reverted to B- in August on the basis of a low default risk and improved debt management. For 2007 the overall deficit was estimated at 6.6% of GDP, and was estimated at 6.1% for 2008, with heavy pre-election spending by the former New National Party Government. The IMF made a positive assessment of the fiscal policies of the National Democratic Congress Government elected in July 2008, and a 2008 review of the IMF's three-year Poverty Reduction and Growth Facility approved a one-year extension to 2010 and granted a waiver for missed targets on the government primary balance. In April 2010 the Fund completed a performance review, and agreed a new three-year extended credit facility of US $13.3m. to mitigate the effects of the global financial crisis, and support a reform programme designed to boost growth, reduce poverty, improve the business climate and reduce the vulnerability of the financial sector.

Proposals for recovery included the reduction of tax exemptions, the introduction of a value-added tax from 2010 and extensive public sector reform. Of the main productive sectors, hotel-based tourism was fully functional in time for the 2006–07 winter season; however, the recovery of nutmeg-farming was expected to be slow at best, partly owing to the diversion of labour from agriculture to reconstruction projects that promised more immediate returns. Total exports of goods in 2006 were 42% below the average figure for 2002–03.

Statistical Survey

AREA AND POPULATION

Area: 344.5 sq km (133.0 sq miles).

Population: 94,806 (males 46,637, females 48,169) at census of 12 May 1991 (excluding 537 persons in institutions and 33 persons in the foreign service); 100,895 at census of 25 May 2001 (preliminary). *Mid-2010* (UN estimate) 104,342 (Source: UN, *World Population Prospects: The 2008 Revision*).

Density (mid-2010): 302.9 per sq km.

Population by Age and Sex (UN estimates at mid-2010): *0–14:* 28,648 (males 14,633, females 14,015); *15–64:* 68,453 (males 34,671, females 33,782); *65 and over:* 7,241 (males 2,925, females 4,316); *Total* 104,342 (males 52,229, females 52,113) (Source: UN, *World Population Prospects: The 2008 Revision*).

Principal Town (population at 2001 census, preliminary): St George's (capital) 3,908. *Mid-2009* (UN estimate, incl. suburbs): St George's 40,400 (Source: UN, *World Urbanization Prospects: The 2009 Revision*).

Births and Deaths (registrations, 2001, provisional): Live births 1,899 (birth rate 18.8 per 1,000); Deaths 727 (death rate 7.2 per 1,000); *2009*: Birth rate 19.5 per 1,000; Death rate 6.1 per 1,000 (Source: Pan American Health Organization).

Life Expectancy (years at birth, WHO estimates): 69 (males 67; females 70) in 2008. Source: WHO, *World Health Statistics*.

Employment (employees only, 1998): Agriculture, hunting, forestry and fishing 4,794; Mining and quarrying 58; Manufacturing 2,579; Electricity, gas and water 505; Construction 5,163; Wholesale and retail trade 6,324; Restaurants and hotels 1,974; Transport, storage and communications 2,043; Financing, insurance and real estate 1,312; Public administration, defence and social security 1,879; Community services 3,904; Other services 2,933; *Sub-total* 33,468; Activities not adequately defined 1,321; *Total employed* 34,789 (males 20,733, females 14,056). *Mid-2010* (estimates): Agriculture, etc. 9,000; Total labour force 45,000 (Source: FAO).

HEALTH AND WELFARE

Key Indicators

Total Fertility Rate (children per woman, 2008): 2.3.

Under-5 Mortality Rate (per 1,000 live births, 2008): 15.

Physicians (per 1,000 head, 1998): 1.0.

Hospital Beds (per 1,000 head, 2005): 4.1.

Health Expenditure (2007): US $ per head (PPP): 591.

Health Expenditure (2007): % of GDP: 7.1.

Health Expenditure (2007): public (% of total): 51.1.

Access to Water (% of persons, 2004): 95.

Access to Sanitation (% of persons, 2008): 98.

Total Carbon Dioxide Emissions ('000 metric tons, 2006): 241.8.

Total Carbon Dioxide Emissions Per Head (metric tons, 2006): 2.4.

Human Development Index (2007): ranking: 74.

Human Development Index (2007): value: 0.813.

For sources and definitions, see explanatory note on p. vi.

AGRICULTURE, ETC.

Principal Crops ('000 metric tons, 2008, FAO estimates): Sugar cane 7.2; Pigeon peas 0.5; Coconuts 7.0; Bananas 1.3; Plantains 0.7; Oranges 0.9; Grapefruit and pomelos 2.1; Apples 0.6; Plums and sloes 0.8; Mangoes, mangosteens and guavas 2.0; Avocados 1.6; Cocoa beans 0.2; Nutmeg, mace and cardamom 2.8; *Aggregate Production* ('000 metric tons, may include official, semi-official or estimated data): Roots and tubers 4.1; Vegetables (incl. melons) 2.8; Fruits (excl. melons) 14.6.

Livestock ('000 head, year ending September 2008, FAO estimates): Cattle 4.5; Pigs 2.7; Sheep 13.2; Goats 7.2; Chickens 270.

Livestock Products ('000 metric tons, 2008, FAO estimates): Chicken meat 0.6; Cows' milk 0.5; Hen eggs 0.9.

Fishing (metric tons, live weight, 2008): Red hind 165; Coney 86; Snappers and jobfishes 122; Parrotfishes 114; Blackfin tuna 290; Yellowfin tuna 755; Atlantic sailfish 215; Swordfish 43; Common dolphinfish 146; *Total catch* (incl. others) 2,384.

Source: FAO.

INDUSTRY

Production (1994 unless otherwise indicated): Rum 300,000 litres; Beer 2,400,000 litres; Wheat flour 4,000 metric tons (1996); Cigarettes 15m.; Electricity 182.9 million kWh (2009). Sources: UN, *Industrial Commodity Statistics Yearbook*; Eastern Caribbean Central Bank.

FINANCE

Currency and Exchange Rates: 100 cents = 1 Eastern Caribbean dollar (EC $). *Sterling, US Dollar and Euro Equivalents* (31 May 2010): £1 sterling = EC $3.397; US $1 = EC $2.700; €1 = EC $3.344; EC $100 = £25.40 = US $37.04 = €29.91. *Exchange Rate:* Fixed at US $1 = EC $2.70 since July 1976.

Budget (EC $ million, 2009, preliminary figures): *Revenue:* Tax revenue 379.9 (Taxes on income and profits 87.2, Taxes on property 18.8, Taxes on domestic goods and services 76.0, Taxes on international trade and transactions 197.9); Other current revenue 21.9; Total 401.8 (excluding grants received 29.2). *Expenditure:* Current expenditure 416.6 (Personal emoluments 191.2, Goods and services 86.0, Interest payments 45.3, Transfers and subsidies 94.1); Capital expenditure and net lending 117.1; Total 533.7. Source: Eastern Caribbean Central Bank.

International Reserves (US $ million at 31 December 2009): IMF special drawing rights 16.69; Foreign exchange 112.39; Total 129.08. Source: IMF, *International Financial Statistics*.

Money Supply (EC $ million at 31 December 2009): Currency outside depository corporations 106.66; Transferable deposits 372.97; Other deposits 1,527.80; *Broad money* 2,007.43. Source: IMF, *International Financial Statistics*.

Cost of Living (Consumer Price Index; base: 2005 = 100): 109.2 in 2007; 114.8 in 2008; 112.1 in 2009. Source: IMF, *International Financial Statistics*.

Gross Domestic Product (EC $ million at constant 1990 prices): 1,026.16 in 2007; 1,035.42 in 2008; 965.13 in 2009 (preliminary estimate). Source: Eastern Caribbean Central Bank.

Expenditure on the Gross Domestic Product (EC $ million at current prices, 2008): Government final consumption expenditure 333.77; Private final consumption expenditure 1,654.35; Gross capital formation 602.89; *Total domestic expenditure* 2,591.01; Exports of goods and services 476.64; *Less* Imports of goods and services 1,235.73; *GDP in purchasers' values* 1,831.92. Source: Eastern Caribbean Central Bank.

Gross Domestic Product by Economic Activity (EC $ million at current prices, 2008): Agriculture 83.28; Mining and quarrying 8.66; Manufacturing 71.52; Electricity and water 92.23; Construction 147.80; Wholesale and retail trade 125.32; Hotels and restaurants 103.34; Transport and communications 285.78; Housing and real estate 39.00; Financial and business services 146.17; Government services 279.83; Other services 257.29; *Sub-total* 1,640.20; *Less* Financial intermediation services indirectly measured (FISIM) 121.54; *GDP at factor cost* 1,518.66; Taxes on products, less subsidies 313.26; *GDP in market prices* 1,831.92. Source: Eastern Caribbean Central Bank.

Balance of Payments (EC $ million, 2009, preliminary estimates): Goods (net) –598.60; Services (net) 106.89; *Balance of goods and services* –491.72; Other income (net) –117.58; Current transfers (net) 94.29; *Current balance* –515.01; Capital account (net) 114.45; Direct investment 212.97; Portfolio investment –6.29; Other investments 101.08; Net errors and omissions 51.41; *Overall balance* –41.40. Source: Eastern Caribbean Central Bank.

EXTERNAL TRADE

Principal Commodities (US $ million, 2007): *Imports c.i.f.:* Meat and edible meat offal 11.3; Mineral fuels, oils, distillation products, etc. 61.7; Wood, articles of wood and wood charcoal 14.3; Iron and steel articles 12.6; Nuclear reactors, boilers, machinery, etc. 27.4; Electrical and electronic equipment 33.5; Vehicles other than railway, tramway 19.3; Furniture, lighting, signs, prefabricated buildings 11.9; Total (incl. others) 365.1. *Exports f.o.b:* Fish, crustaceans, molluscs, aquatic invertebrates 4.1; Coffee, tea, mate and spices 2.8; Milling products, malt, starches, etc. 4.5; Residues, wastes of food industry, animal fodder 1.5; Paper, paperboard and pulp, paper and board articles 2.5; Textile articles, sets, worn clothing etc. 4.0; Electrical and electronic equipment 7.5; Total 33.4. (Source: Trade Map-Trade Competitiveness Map, International Trade Centre, www.intracen.org/marketanalysis).*2008* (EC $ million): Total imports c.i.f. 792.60; Total exports f.o.b. 79.90 (Source: Eastern Caribbean Central Bank).

Principal Trading Partners (US $ million, 2007): *Imports c.i.f.:* Barbados 6.7; Brazil 7.9; Canada 8.1; China, People's Republic 10.1; France (incl. Monaco) 4.1; Germany 4.2; Guyana 3.8; Japan 17.9; Netherlands 7.7; Trinidad and Tobago 101.6; United Kingdom 15.4; USA 130.7; Venezuela 8.1; Total (incl. others) 365.1. *Exports f.o.b.:* Antigua and Barbuda 0.7; Barbados 1.7; Belgium 0.6; Canada 0.6; Dominica 2.5; France (incl. Monaco) 4.8; Guyana 0.4; Jamaica 0.7; Japan 6.5; Netherlands 1.6; Saint Christopher and Nevis 1.5; Saint Lucia 2.8; Saint Vincent and the Grenadines 0.9; Trinidad and Tobago 1.3; USA 5.8; Total (incl. others) 33.4. Source: Trade Map-Trade Competitiveness Map, International Trade Centre, www.intracen.org/marketanalysis.

TRANSPORT

Road Traffic ('000 motor vehicles in use, 2001): Passenger cars 15.8; Commercial vehicles 4.2. Source: UN, *Statistical Yearbook*.

Shipping: *Merchant Fleet* (registered at 31 December 2008) 11 vessels (total displacement 2,821 grt) (Source: Lloyd's Register-Fairplay, *World Fleet Statistics*). *International Sea-borne Freight Traffic* (estimates, '000 metric tons, 1995): Goods loaded 21.3; Goods unloaded 193.0. *Ship Arrivals* (1991): 1,254. *Fishing Vessels* (registered, 1987): 635.

Civil Aviation (aircraft arrivals, 1995): 11,310.

TOURISM

Visitor Arrivals: 410,811 (incl. 129,088 stop-over visitors and 270,259 cruise ship passengers) in 2007; 426,900 (incl. 123,770 stop-over visitors and 292,712 cruise ship passengers) in 2008; 455,964 (incl. 109,407 stop-over visitors and 339,752 cruise ship passengers) in 2009.

Tourism Receipts (EC $ million): 293.6 in 2007; 293.2 in 2008; 266.7 in 2009.

Source: Eastern Caribbean Central Bank.

COMMUNICATIONS MEDIA

Radio Receivers (1997): 57,000 in use*.

Television Receivers (1999): 35,000 in use*.

Telephones (2009): 28,600 main lines in use†.

Mobile Cellular Telephones (2009): 64,000 subscribers†.

Personal Computers (2005): 16,000 in use†.

Internet Users (2009): 25,000†.

Broadband Subscribers (2009): 14,000†.

Non-daily Newspapers (2004): 4; circulation 14,000 (1996)*.

* Source: UNESCO, *Statistical Yearbook*.

‡ Source: International Telecommunication Union.

† Source: UN, *Statistical Yearbook*.

EDUCATION

Pre-primary (2007/08 unless otherwise indicated): 74 schools (1994); 255 teachers; 3,808 pupils.

Primary (2007/08 unless otherwise indicated): 57 schools (1995); 615 teachers; 13,873 pupils.

Secondary (2007/08 unless otherwise indicated): 20 schools (2002);751 teachers; 12,469 pupils.

Higher (excl. figures for the Grenada Teachers' Training College, 1993): 66 teachers; 651 students.

Source: partly UNESCO Institute for Statistics.

Pupil-teacher Ratio (primary education, UNESCO estimate): 22.6 in 2007/08 (Source: UNESCO Institute for Statistics).

Adult Literacy Rate: 96.0% in 2003. Source: UN Development Programme, *Human Development Report*.

Directory

The Constitution

The 1974 independence Constitution was suspended in March 1979, following the coup, and almost entirely restored between November 1983, after the overthrow of the Revolutionary Military Council, and the elections of December 1984. The main provisions of this Constitution are summarized below:

The Head of State is the British monarch, represented in Grenada by an appointed Governor-General. Legislative power is vested in the bicameral Parliament, comprising a Senate and a House of Representatives. The Senate consists of 13 Senators, seven of whom are appointed on the advice of the Prime Minister, three on the advice of the Leader of the Opposition and three on the advice of the Prime Minister after he has consulted interests that he considers Senators should be selected to represent. The Constitution does not specify the number of members of the House of Representatives, but the country consists of 15 single-member constituencies, for which representatives are elected for up to five years, on the basis of universal adult suffrage.

The Cabinet consists of a Prime Minister, who must be a member of the House of Representatives, and such other ministers as the Governor-General may appoint on the advice of the Prime Minister.

There is a Supreme Court and, in certain cases, a further appeal lies to Her Majesty in Council.

The Government

HEAD OF STATE

Queen: HM Queen Elizabeth II.

Governor-General: Carlyle Glean, Sr (appointed 27 November 2008).

THE CABINET
(July 2010)

Prime Minister and Minister of National Security, Public Administration, Information, Information Communications Technology, Legal Affairs and Culture: Tillman Thomas.

Minister of Finance, Planning, Economy, Energy and Co-operatives: Nazim Burke.

Minister of Foreign Affairs: Peter David.

Minister of Youth Empowerment and Sports: Patrick Simmons.

Minister of the Environment, Foreign Trade and Export Development: Michael Church.

Minister of Housing, Lands and Community Development: Alleyne Walker.

Minister of Works, Physical Development and Public Utilities: Joseph Gilbert.

Minister of Labour, Social Security and Ecclesiastical Affairs: Karl Hood.

Minister of Social Development: Sylvester Quarless.

Minister of Tourism and Civil Aviation: Glynis Roberts.

Minister of Agriculture, Forestry and Fisheries: Michael Denis Lett.

Minister of Carriacou and Petit Martinique Affairs: George Prime.

Minister of Education and Human Resource Development: Franka Alexis-Bernadine.

Minister of Health: Ann Peters.

Minister of State in the Prime Minister's Office with responsibility for Information, Information Communications Technology and Culture: Arley Gill.

Minister of State in the Ministry of Housing, Lands and Community Development: Glen Noel.

MINISTRIES

Office of the Governor-General: Government House, Bldg 5, Financial Complex, The Carenage, St George's; tel. 440-6639; fax 440-6688; e-mail pato@spiceisle.com.

Office of the Prime Minister and Ministry of National Security, Public Administration, Information, Information Communications Technology, Legal Affairs and Culture: Ministerial Complex, 6th Floor, Botanical Gardens, Tanteen, St George's; tel. 440-2255; fax 440-4116; e-mail pmsec@gov.gd; internet www.pmoffice.gov.gd.

Ministry of Agriculture, Forestry and Fisheries: Ministerial Complex, 3rd Floor, Botanical Gardens, Tanteen, St George's; tel. 440-2708; fax 440-4191; e-mail agriculture@gov.gd; internet www.agriculture.gov.gd.

Ministry of Carriacou and Petit Martinique Affairs: Beauséjour, Carriacou; tel. 443-6026; fax 443-6040; e-mail minccoupm@spiceisle.com.

Ministry of Education and Human Resource Development: Ministry of Education Bldg, Ministerial Complex, Botanical Gardens, Tanteen, St George's; tel. 440-2737; fax 440-6650; internet www.grenadaedu.com.

Ministry of the Environment, Foreign Trade and Export Development: Financial Complex, The Carenage, St George's; tel. 440-2731; fax 440-4115; e-mail michael.church@gov.gd.

Ministry of Finance, Planning, Economy, Energy and Cooperatives: Financial Complex, The Carenage, St George's; tel. 440-2731; fax 440-4115; e-mail finance@gov.gd; internet finance.gov.gd.

Ministry of Foreign Affairs: Ministerial Complex, 4th Floor, Botanical Gardens, Tanteen, St George's; tel. 440-2640; fax 440-4184; e-mail foreignaffairs@gov.gd.

Ministry of Health: Ministerial Complex, Southern Wing, 1st and 2nd Floors, Botanical Gardens, Tanteen, St George's; tel. 440-2649; fax 440-4127; e-mail min-healthgrenada@spiceisle.com.

Ministry of Housing, Lands and Community Development: Ministerial Complex, 2nd Floor, Botanical Gardens, Tanteen, St George's; tel. 440-2103; fax 435-5864; e-mail mofhlcd@gov.gd.

Ministry of Labour, Social Security and Ecclesiastical Affairs: Ministerial Complex, 1st Floor, Botanical Gardens, Tanteen, St George's; tel. 440-2269; fax 440-7990.

Ministry of Social Development: Ministerial Complex, West Wing, 1st Floor, Botanical Gardens, Tanteen, St George's; tel. 440-7952; fax 440-7990; e-mail ministrysod@yahoo.com.

Ministry of Tourism and Civil Aviation: Ministerial Complex, 4th Floor, Botanical Gardens, Tanteen, St George's; tel. 440-0366; fax 440-0443; e-mail tourism@gov.gd; internet www.grenada.mot.gd.

Ministry of Works, Physical Development and Public Utilities: Ministerial Complex, 4th Floor, Botanical Gardens, Tanteen, St George's; tel. 440-2271; fax 440-4122; e-mail ministryofworks@gov.gd.

Ministry of Youth Empowerment and Sports: Ministerial Complex, 3rd Floor, Botanical Gardens, Tanteen, St George's; tel. 440-6917; fax 440-6924; e-mail sports@gov.gd.

Legislature

PARLIAMENT

Houses of Parliament: Parliamentary Office, Botanical Gardens, Tanteen, POB 315, St George's; tel. 440-2090; fax 440-4138; e-mail order.order@caribsurf.com.

Senate

President: Sen. JOAN PURCELL.

There are 13 appointed members.

House of Representatives

Speaker: GEORGE JAMES MCGUIRE.

General Election, 8 July 2008

	Votes	%	Seats
National Democratic Congress (NDC)	28,998	51.15	11
New National Party (NNP)	27,188	47.97	4
United Labour Platform (ULP)*	479	0.85	—
Total (incl. others)	56,677	100.00	15

* A coalition of the Grenada United Labour Party and the People's Labour Movement.

Political Organizations

Grenada United Labour Party (GULP): St George's; tel. 438-1234; e-mail gulp@spiceisle.com; internet www.gulpstar.org; f. 1950; merged with United Labour Congress in 2001; right-wing; formed a coalition with the People's Labour Movt, the United Labour Platform, to contest the 2008 elections; Pres. COLIN FRANCIS.

National Democratic Congress (NDC): NDC Headquarters, Lucas St, St George's; tel. 440-3769; e-mail ndcgrenada@ndcgrenada.org; internet www.ndcgrenada.org; f. 1987 by fmr mems of the NNP and merger of Democratic Labour Congress and Grenada Democratic Labour Party; centrist; Leader TILLMAN THOMAS; Dep. Leader NAZIM BURKE.

New National Party (NNP): Upper Lucas St, Mount Helicon, POB 646, St George's; tel. 440-1875; fax 440-1876; e-mail nnpadmin@spiceisle.com; internet www.nnpnews.com; f. 1984 following merger of Grenada Democratic Movement, Grenada National Party and National Democratic Party; centrist; Chair. ELVIN NIMROD; Leader Dr KEITH MITCHELL; Dep. Leader GREGORY BOWEN.

People's Labour Movement (PLM): St George's; f. 1995 by fmr mems of the NDC; fmrly known as the Democratic Labour Party; formed a coalition with the Grenada United Labour Party, the United Labour Platform, to contest the 2008 elections; Leader Dr FRANCIS ALEXIS.

Diplomatic Representation

EMBASSIES AND HIGH COMMISSION IN GRENADA

Brazil: POB 1226, Grand Anse, St George's; tel. 439-7160; fax 439-7165; e-mail brasembsaintgeorges@mre.gov.br; Ambassador PAULO WANGNER DE MIRANDA.

China, People's Republic: Azar Villa, Calliste St, St George's; tel. 439-6230; fax 439-6231; internet gd.china-embassy.org; Ambassador ZHANG WANHAI.

Cuba: L'Anse aux Epines, St George's; tel. 444-1884; fax 444-1877; e-mail embacubagranada@caribsurf.com; Ambassador ANGEL NARCISO REIGOSA DE LA CRUZ.

USA: L'Ance aux Epines, POB 54, St George's; tel. 444-1173; fax 444-4820; e-mail usembgd@caribsurf.com; Chargé d'affaires a.i. KAREN JO MCISAAC.

Venezuela: Upper Lucas St, Belmont, POB 201, St George's; tel. 440-1721; fax 440-6657; e-mail vennes@caribsurf.com; Ambassador CARLOS AMADA PEREZ SILVA.

Judicial System

Justice is administered by the Eastern Caribbean Supreme Court, formerly styled the West Indies Associated States Supreme Court in Grenada, composed of a High Court of Justice and a Court of Appeal. The Itinerant Court of Appeal consists of three judges and sits three times a year; it hears appeals from the High Court and the Magistrates' Court. Two of the 16 Puisne judges of the High Court are resident in Grenada. The Magistrates' Court administers summary jurisdiction.

Attorney-General: ROHAN PHILLIP.

Puisne Judges: FRANCIS CUMBERBATCH, CLAIRE HENRY, LYLE ST. PAUL.

Registrar of the Supreme Court: ROBERT BRANCH.

Acting Chief Justice of the Court of Appeal: HUGH ANTHONY RAWLINS (resident in Saint Lucia).

Office of the Attorney-General: Communal House, 414 H. A. Blaize St, St George's; tel. 440-2050; fax 435-2964; e-mail legalaffairs@spiceisle.com.

Religion

CHRISTIANITY

The Roman Catholic Church

Grenada comprises the single diocese of Saint George's, suffragan to the archdiocese of Castries (Saint Lucia). The Bishop participates in the Antilles Episcopal Conference (based in Port of Spain, Trinidad and Tobago). Some 45% of the population are Roman Catholics.

Bishop of St George's in Grenada: Rev. VINCENT DARIUS, Bishop's House, Morne Jaloux, POB 375, St George's; tel. 443-5299; fax 443-5758; e-mail bishopgrenada@caribsurf.com; internet www.stgdiocese.org.

The Anglican Communion

Anglicans in Grenada are adherents of the Church in the Province of the West Indies. The country forms part of the diocese of the Windward Islands (the Bishop, the Rt Rev. CALVERT LEOPOLD FRIDAY, resides in Kingstown, Saint Vincent).

Other Christian Churches

The Presbyterian, Methodist, Plymouth Brethren, Baptist, Salvation Army, Jehovah's Witness, Pentecostal and Seventh-day Adventist faiths are also represented.

The Press

NEWSPAPERS

Barnacle: Mt Parnassus, St George's 3530; tel. 435-0981; fax 435-5685; e-mail barnacle@spiceisle.com; internet www.barnaclegrenada.com; f. 1991; business journal; bi-weekly; Editor IAN GEORGE.

Government Gazette: St George's; weekly; official; Man. ERIC BRATHWAITE.

The Grenada Informer: Market Hill, POB 622, St George's; tel. 440-1530; fax 440-4119; e-mail grenadainformer@yahoo.com; f. 1985; weekly; Editor CARLA-RAE A. BRIGGS; circ. 6,000.

The Grenadian Voice: Frequente Industrial Park, Bldg 1B, Maurice Bishop Hwy, POB 633, St George's; tel. 440-1498; fax 440-4117; e-mail gvoice@spiceisle.com; weekly; Man. Editor LESLIE PIERRE; circ. 3,000.

PRESS ASSOCIATION

Press Association of Grenada: St George's; f. 1986; Pres. LESLIE PIERRE.

Publisher

Anansi Publications: Woodlands, St George's; tel. 440-0800; e-mail aclouden@spiceisle.com; f. 1986; Man. Dir ALVIN CLOUDEN.

Broadcasting and Communications

TELECOMMUNICATIONS

Regulatory Authorities

Eastern Caribbean Telecommunications Authority: Vide Boutielle, Castries, POB 1886, Saint Lucia; tel. 458-1701; fax 458-1698; e-mail ectel@ectel.int; internet www.ectel.int; f. 2000 to regulate telecommunications in Grenada, Dominica, Saint Christopher and Nevis, Saint Lucia and Saint Vincent and the Grenadines.

National Telecommunications Regulatory Commission (NTRC): Suite 8, Grand Anse Shopping Centre, POB 854, St George's; tel. 435-6872; fax 435-2132; e-mail gntrc@ectel.int; internet www.ectel.int/grd; Chair. Dr LINUS SPENCER THOMAS; Co-ordinator ALDWYN FERGUSON (acting).

Major Service Providers

Digicel Grenada Ltd: Point Salines, POB 1690, St George's; e-mail grenadacustomercare@digicelgroup.com; internet www.digicelgrenada.com; tel. 439-4463; fax 439-4464; f. 2003; began operating cellular telephone services in Oct. 2003; owned by an Irish consortium; Chair. DENIS O'BRIEN; Gen. Man. GERALDINE PITT (OECS South).

Grenada Postal Corporation (GPC): Burns Point, St George's; tel. 440-2526; fax 440-4271; e-mail grenadapost@grenadapost.net; internet www.grenadapost.net; Chair. ADRIAN FRANCIS; Dir of Post LEO ROBERTS.

LIME: POB 119, The Carenage, St George's; tel. 440-1000; fax 440-4134; e-mail cwcares@candw.gd; internet www.time4lime.com; f. 1989; fmrly Cable & Wireless Grenada Ltd; name adopted as above 2008; until 1998 known as Grenada Telecommunications Ltd (Grentel); 30% govt-owned; CEO DAVID SHAW.

BROADCASTING

Grenada Broadcasting Network (GBN): Observatory Rd, POB 535, St George's; tel. 444-5521; fax 440-4180; e-mail gbn@spiceisle.com; internet www.klassicgrenada.com; f. 1972; 60% owned by One Caribbean Media Ltd, 40% govt-owned; Chair. CRAIG REYNALD; Gen. Man. RUEL EDWARDS.

Radio

City Sound FM: River Road, St George's; tel. 440-9616; e-mail citysound97i5@yahoo.com; internet www.citysoundfm.com; f. 1996.

Grenada Broadcasting Network (Radio): see Broadcasting.

HOTT FM: Observatory Rd, POB 535, St George's; tel. 444-5521; fax 440-4180; e-mail gbn@spiceisle.com; internet www.klassicgrenada.com; f. 1999; contemporary music.

Klassic AM: Observatory Rd, POB 535, St George's; tel. 435-2041; fax 440-4180; e-mail gbn@spiceisle.com; internet www.klassicgrenada.com.

The Harbour Light of the Windwards: Carriacou; tel. and fax 443-7628; e-mail harbourlight@spiceisle.com; internet www.harbourlightradio.org; f. 1991; owned by Aviation Radio Missionary Services; Christian radio station; Station Man. Dr RANDY CORNELIUS; Chief Engineer JOHN MCPHERSON.

KYAK 106: Church St, Hillsborough, Carriacou; tel. 443-6262; e-mail info@kyak106.com; internet www.kyak106.com; f. 1996; Office Man. DOREEN STANISLAUS.

Sister Isle Radio: Fort Hill, Hillsborough, Carriacou; tel. 443-8141; fax 443-8142; e-mail sisterisle@gmail.com; internet www.sisterisleradio.com; f. 2005.

Spice Capital Radio FM 90: Springs, St George's; tel. 440-0162; internet spicecapitalradio.net.

WeeFM: Cross St, POB 555, St George's; tel. 440-4933; e-mail weefmradio@hotmail.com; internet www.weefmgrenada.com.

Television

Television programmes from Trinidad and Tobago and Barbados can be received on the island.

Grenada Broadcasting Network (Television): see Broadcasting; two channels.

Finance

(cap. = capital; res = reserves; dep. = deposits; brs = branches; amounts in Eastern Caribbean dollars)

The Eastern Caribbean Central Bank, based in Saint Christopher, is the central issuing and monetary authority for Grenada.

Eastern Caribbean Central Bank—Grenada Office: Monckton St, St George's; tel. 440-3016; fax 440-6721; e-mail eccbgnd@spiceisle.com; Country Dir LINDA FELIX-BERKLEY.

BANKING

Regulatory Authority

Grenada Authority for the Regulation of Financial Institutions (GARFIN): POB 3973, Queens Park, St George's; tel. 440-6575; fax 440-4780; e-mail garfingda@spiceisle.com; internet www.garfingrenada.org; f. 1999 as Grenada International Financial Services Authority; name changed to above in Feb. 2007; revenue 4.2m. (2002); Chair. TIMOTHY ANTOINE; Exec. Dir ANGUS SMITH.

Commercial Banks

FirstCaribbean International Bank (Barbados) Ltd: Church St, POB 37, St George's; tel. 440-3232; fax 440-4103; internet www.firstcaribbeanbank.com; f. 2002; 83.0% owned by Canadian Imperial Bank of Commerce (CIBC), after Barclays Bank PLC (United Kingdom) sold its 43.7% stake to CIBC in 2006; Chair. MICHAEL MANSOOR; CEO JOHN D. ORR; 4 brs.

Grenada Co-operative Bank Ltd: 8 Church St, POB 135, St George's; tel. 440-2111; fax 440-6600; e-mail info@grenadaco-opbank.com; internet www.grenadaco-opbank.com; f. 1932; Chair. DERICK STEELE; Man. Dir and Sec. RICHARD W. DUNCAN; brs in St Andrew's, St George's, St Patrick's and Hillsborough.

Grenada Development Bank: Melville St, POB 2300, St George's; tel. 440-2382; fax 440-6610; e-mail gdbbank@spiceisle.com; f. 1965; Chair. MICHAEL ARCHIBALD.

RBTT Bank Grenada Ltd: Cnr of Cross and Halifax Sts, POB 4, St George's; tel. 440-3521; fax 440-4153; e-mail RBTTLTD@caribsurf.com; internet www.rbtt.com; f. 1983 as Grenada Bank of Commerce; name changed as above 2002; 10% govt-owned; national insurance scheme 15%; public 13%; RBTT Bank Caribbean Ltd, Castries 62%; cap. 11.1m., res 7.3m., dep. 437.8m. (31 Dec. 2008); Country Man. CYRILLA GEMON; Regional Dir DAVID HACKETT.

Republic Bank (Grenada) Ltd: Republic House, Maurice Bishop Hwy, Grand Anse, POB 857, St George's; tel. 444-2265; fax 444-5500; e-mail republichouse@republicgrenada.com; internet www.republicgrenada.com; f. 1979; fmrly National Commercial Bank of Grenada; name changed as above in 2006; 51% owned by Republic Bank Ltd, Port of Spain, Trinidad and Tobago; cap. 15.0m., res 18.0m., dep. 651.3m. (Sept. 2008); Chair. RONALD HARFORD; Man. Dir DANIEL ROBERTS; 9 brs.

STOCK EXCHANGE

Eastern Caribbean Securities Exchange: based in Basseterre, Saint Christopher and Nevis; tel. (869) 466-7192; fax (869) 465-3798; e-mail info@ECSEonline.com; internet www.ecseonline.com; f. 2001; regional securities market designed to facilitate the buying and selling of financial products for the eight member territories—Anguilla, Antigua and Barbuda, Dominica, Grenada, Montserrat, Saint Christopher and Nevis, Saint Lucia, and Saint Vincent and the

Grenadines; Chair. Sir K. DWIGHT VENNER; Gen. Man. and CEO TREVOR E. BLAKE.

INSURANCE

Several foreign insurance companies operate in Grenada and the other islands of the group. Principal locally owned companies include the following:

Gittens Insurance Brokerage Co Ltd: Benoit Bldg, Grand Anse, POB 1696, St George's; tel. 439-4408; fax 439-4462; CEO PHILLIP A. GITTENS.

Grenada Motor and General Insurance Co Ltd: Scott St, St George's; tel. 440-3379; fax 440-7977; e-mail gmginsurance@spiceisle.com.

Grenadian General Insurance Co Ltd: Cnr of Young and Scott Sts, POB 47, St George's; tel. 440-2434; fax 440-6618; e-mail clingren@caribsurf.com; Dir KEITH RENWICK.

Trade and Industry

CHAMBERS OF COMMERCE

Grenada Chamber of Industry and Commerce, Inc (GCIC): Bldg 11, POB 129, Frequente, St George's; tel. 440-2937; fax 440-6627; e-mail info@grenadachamber.org; internet www.grenadachamber.org; f. 1921; inc 1947; 170 mems; Pres. JUSTIN EVANS; Exec. Dir HAZELANN DERIGGS.

Grenada Manufacturing Council: POB 129, Tempest, St George's; tel. 440-2937; fax 440-4100; f. 1991 to replace Grenada Manufacturers' Asscn; Chair. CHRISTOPHER DEALLIE.

INDUSTRIAL AND TRADE ASSOCIATIONS

Grenada Cocoa Association (GCA): Lagoon Rd, POB 3649, St George's; tel. 440-2234; fax 440-1470; e-mail gca@spiceisle.com; f. 1987 following merger; changed from co-operative to shareholding structure in 1996; Chair. RAMSEY RUSH; Man. ANDREW HASTICK.

Grenada Co-operative Nutmeg Association (GCNA): Lagoon Rd, POB 160, St George's; tel. 440-2117; fax 440-6602; e-mail gcna.nutmeg@caribsurf.com; f. 1947; processes and markets all the nutmeg and mace grown on the island; includes the production of nutmeg oil; Chair. VICTOR ASHBY; Gen. Man. TERRENCE MOORE.

Grenada Industrial Development Corporation (GIDC): Frequenté Industrial Park, Frequente, St George's; tel. 444-1035; fax 444-4828; e-mail gidc@caribsurf.com; internet www.grenadaidc.com; f. 1985; Chair. R. ANTHONY JOSEPH; Gen. Man. SONIA RODEN.

Marketing and National Importing Board (MNIB): Young St, POB 652, St George's; tel. 440-1791; fax 440-4152; e-mail mnib@spiceisle.com; internet www.mnib.gd; f. 1974; govt-owned; imports basic food items, incl. sugar, rice and milk; also exports fresh produce; Chair. BYRON CAMPBELL; Gen. Man. FITZROY JAMES.

EMPLOYERS' ORGANIZATION

Grenada Employers' Federation: Bldg 11, Frequenté Industrial Park, Grand Anse, POB 129, St George's; tel. 440-1832; fax 440-6627; e-mail gef@spiceisle.com; internet www.grenadaemployers.com; Pres. (vacant); Exec. Dir CECIL EDWARDS; 60 mems.

There are several marketing and trading co-operatives, mainly in the agricultural sector.

UTILITIES

Public Utilities Commission: St George's.

Electricity

Grenada Electricity Services Ltd (Grenlec): Halifax St, POB 381, St George's; tel. 440-2097; fax 440-4106; e-mail customersupport@grenlec.com; internet www.grenlec.com; generation and distribution; 90% privately owned, 10% govt-owned; Chair. G. ROBERT BLANCHARD, Jr; Man. Dir and CEO VERNON LAWRENCE.

Water

National Water and Sewerage Authority (NAWASA): The Carenage, POB 392, St George's; tel. 440-2155; fax 440-4107; e-mail nawasa@caribsurf.com; internet www.spiceisle.com/nawasa; f. 1969; Chair. MICHAEL PIERRE; Gen. Man. CHRISTOPHER HUSBANDS.

TRADE UNIONS

Grenada Trade Union Council (GTUC): Green St, POB 411, St George's; tel. and fax 440-3733; e-mail gtuc@caribsurf.com; internet www.grenadatuc.org; Pres. MADONNA HARFORD (acting); Gen. Sec. RAY ROBERTS.

Bank and General Workers' Union (BGWU): Bain's Alley, POB 329, St George's; tel. and fax 440-3563; e-mail bgwu@caribsurf.com; Pres. JUSTIN CAMPBELL; Gen. Sec. EDMOND CALLISTE.

Commercial and Industrial Workers' Union: Bain's Alley, Grand Anse, POB 1791, St George's; tel. and fax 440-3423; e-mail cominwu@caribsurf.com; Pres. GEORGE MASON; Gen. Sec. BARBARA FRASER; 492 mems.

Grenada Manual, Maritime and Intellectual Workers' Union (GMMIWU): c/o Birchgrove, POB 1927, St Andrew's; tel. and fax 442-7724; Pres. BERT LATOUCHE; Gen. Sec. OSCAR WILLIAMS.

Grenada Public Workers' Union (GPWU): Tanteen, POB 420, St George's; tel. 440-2203; fax 440-6615; e-mail gpwu@spiceisle.com; f. 1931 as Civil Service Association; Pres. MADONNA HARFORD; Exec. Sec. WILLAN THOMPSON.

Grenada Technical and Allied Workers' Union (GTAWU): Green St, POB 405, St George's; tel. 440-2231; fax 440-5878; e-mail gtawu@spiceisle.com; f. 1958; Pres.-Gen. Sen. CHESTER HUMPHREY; Gen. Sec. ANDRÉ LEWIS.

Grenada Union of Teachers (GUT): Marine Villa, POB 452, St George's; tel. 440-2992; fax 440-9019; e-mail gut@caribsurf.com; internet gutgrenada.org; f. 1913; Pres. KENNY A. M. JAMES; Gen. Sec. TESSA MCQUILKIN; 1,300 mems.

Media Workers' Association of Grenada (MWAG): St George's; e-mail mwagrenada@yahoo.com; f. 1999; Pres. RAWLE TITUS.

Seamen and Waterfront Workers' Union: Ottway House, POB 154, St George's; tel. 440-2573; fax 440-7199; e-mail swwu@caribsurf.com; f. 1952; Pres. ALBERT JULIEN; Gen. Sec. LYLE SAMUEL; 350 mems.

Transport

RAILWAYS

There are no railways in Grenada.

ROADS

In 1999 there were approximately 1,127 km (700 miles) of roads, of which 61.3% were paved. Public transport is provided by small private operators, with a system covering the entire country.

SHIPPING

The main port is St George's, with accommodation for two ocean-going vessels of up to 500 ft. A number of shipping lines call at St George's. Grenville, on Grenada, and Hillsborough, on Carriacou, are used mostly by small craft. The first phase of a project to expand the port at St George's and enable the harbour to accommodate modern super-sized cruise ships was completed in July 2003, while the Melville Street Cruise Terminal phase became operational in November 2004. Work commenced in November 2006 upon an ambitious EC $1,600m. development at Port Louis, to include a 350-slipway marina with yachting facilities.

Grenada Ports Authority: POB 494, The Carenage, St George's; tel. 440-7678; fax 440-3418; e-mail grenport@caribsurf.com; internet www.grenadaports.com; f. 1981; state-owned; Chair. NIGEL JOHN; Gen. Man. AMBROSE PHILLIP.

CIVIL AVIATION

Maurice Bishop International Airport (formerly Point Salines International Airport), 10 km (6 miles) from St George's, was opened in October 1984, and has scheduled flights to most East Caribbean destinations, including Venezuela, and to the United Kingdom and North America. There is an airfield at Pearls, 30 km (18 miles) from St George's, and Lauriston Airport, on the island of Carriacou, offers regular scheduled services to Grenada, Saint Vincent and Palm Island (Grenadines of Saint Vincent).

Grenada is a shareholder in the regional airline, LIAT (Antigua and Barbuda), which acquired another regional carrier, Caribbean Star, in October 2007.

Grenada Airports Authority: Maurice Bishop Int. Airport, POB 385, St George's; tel. 444-4101; fax 444-4838; e-mail gaa@caribsurf.com; f. 1985; Chair. RODNEY GEORGE; Gen. Man. DONALD MCPHAIL.

Airlines of Carriacou: Maurice Bishop Int. Airport, POB 805, St George's; tel. 444-1475; fax 444-2898; e-mail info@travelgrenada.com; f. 1992; acquired by St Vincent and Grenada Air in 1999; national airline, operates in asscn with LIAT; Man. Dir ARTHUR W. BAIN.

Tourism

Grenada has the attractions of both white sandy beaches and a scenic, mountainous interior with an extensive rainforest. There are also sites of historical interest, and the capital, St George's, is a noted beauty spot. In 2009, according to preliminary figures, there were 109,407 stop-over arrivals and 339,752 cruise ship passengers. In that year tourism earned a preliminary EC $266.7m.

Grenada Board of Tourism: Burns Point, POB 293, St George's; tel. 440-2279; fax 440-6637; e-mail gbt@spiceisle.com; internet www.grenadagrenadines.com; f. 1991; Chair. NIKOYAN ROBERTS; Dir WILLIAM JOSEPH.

Grenada Hotel and Tourism Association Ltd: POB 440, St George's; tel. 444-1353; fax 444-4847; e-mail grenhota@spiceisle.com; internet www.grenadahotelsinfo.com; f. 1961; Pres. RUSSELL FIELDEN; Exec. Dir PANCY CHANDLER CROSS.

Defence

A regional security unit was formed in 1983, modelled on the British police force and trained by British officers. A paramilitary element, known as the Special Service Unit and trained by US advisers, acts as the defence contingent and participates in the Regional Security System, a defence pact with other East Caribbean states.

Commissioner of Police: JAMES CLARKSON.

Education

Education is free and compulsory for children between the ages of five and 16 years. Primary education begins at five years of age and lasts for seven years. Secondary education, beginning at the age of 12, lasts for a further five years. In 2007/08 enrolment at primary schools included 93% of children in the relevant age group; there were 57 primary schools in 1995. There were 20 public secondary schools in 2002, with 12,469 pupils registered in 2007/08; enrolment at all secondary schools included 89% of pupils in the relevant age group in 2007/08. In 2006 there were 2,710 full-time enrolled students at the T. A. Marryshow Community College. Technical Centres have been established in St Patrick's, St David's and St John's, and the Grenada National College, the Mirabeau Agricultural School and the Teachers' Training College have been incorporated into the Technical and Vocational Institute in St George's. The Extra-Mural Department of the University of the West Indies has a branch in St George's. Total budgeted capital expenditure on education was $11.5m. in 2006 (equivalent to 5.0% of total capital expenditure).

Bibliography

For works on the Caribbean generally, see Select Bibliography (Books)

Beck, R. J. *The Grenada Invasion*. Boulder, CO, Westview Press, 1993.

Brizan, G. I. *Grenada: Island of Conflict*. Grand Cayman, Caribbean Publishing, 1998.

Coley, K. 'Grenada Rebuilds: After the Hurricane', in *UN Chronicle*, Vol. 42, No. 3 (2005).

Ferguson, J. *Grenada: Revolution in Reverse*. New York, NY, Monthly Review Press, 1990.

Heine, J. (Ed.). *A Revolution Aborted*. Pittsburgh, PA, University of Pittsburgh Press, 1991.

Pryor, F. L. *Revolutionary Grenada: A Study in Political Economy*. Westport, CT, Praeger Publrs, 1986.

Smith, C. A. *Socialist Transformation in Peripheral Economies*. Brookfield, VT, Avebury Publishing Co, 1995.

Steele, B. A. *Grenada: A History of its People*. Oxford, Macmillan Caribbean, 2003.

GUADELOUPE

Geography

PHYSICAL FEATURES

The Overseas Department of Guadeloupe is an integral part of the French Republic, but lies in the Lesser Antilles. It includes the main islands of Guadeloupe itself (Basse-Terre and Grande-Terre) and a number of surrounding islands, which lie in the Windward Islands. Until 2007 it also included St-Barthélemy and the northern part of the island of St-Martin (Sint Maarten), in the Leewards. All these islands lie in the north-eastern Caribbean. Guadeloupe itself is flanked by two sea lanes from the Atlantic: the Dominica Passage to the south, beyond which lies the Commonwealth of Dominica; and the wider Guadeloupe Passage to the north, beyond which, some 64 km (40 miles) to the north-west, is the southernmost of the Leeward Islands, the British dependency of Montserrat. A similar distance directly north is Antigua and Barbuda, while about one-half that distance south of Marie-Galante is the island of Dominica.

Guadeloupe, a butterfly-shaped landmass is, technically, two islands, separated by a narrow channel, the Rivière Sallée. The name Guadeloupe originally applied only to the larger, mountainous western island, which is now known as Basse-Terre (like the first settlement and the administrative headquarters), after the only 'low shore', on the leeward side of the cliff-edged island. The broad, flat lands of the east, Grande-Terre, soon assumed commercial and agricultural significance and the name of Guadeloupe came to be applied to both 'wings'. Basse-Terre, the largest single island of Guadeloupe (848 sq km), is fertile, mountainous and volcanic, the densely forested central range reaching the highest point in the Department, at the desolate volcano of La Soufrière (1,354 m or 4,444 ft), in the south of the island. About two-thirds of the way up the eastern coast of Basse-Terre a broad peninsula reaches out to its sister island. The lower-lying Grande-Terre (about three-fifths the size of Basse-Terre), essentially a limestone plateau, extends mainly northwards, tapering from a west–east base between the near-isthmus to Basse-Terre and the eastward-pointing Pointe des Châteaux. There are some hills in the south and mangrove swamps along the west coast, but much of the land is given to sugar cane, fruit trees and livestock. The wealth of vegetation throughout Guadeloupe includes native and widely protected forests, but indigenous wildlife has largely been wiped out—a few racoons (*ratons laveurs*) and iguanas survive on the offshore islands. The only other island of any size in the Department is 22 km south of Grande-Terre—the flat, round Marie-Galante (158 sq km). Just east of Grande-Terre is La Désirade, a rather dry island, to the south-west of which, midway to Marie-Galante, are the Îles de la Petite-Terre. West of Marie-Galante and just south of Basse-Terre are the Îles des Saintes (near which an important naval battle took place in 1782). These are the main offshore islands of Guadeloupe and most are hilly, though drier than the mainland.

CLIMATE

The climate is subtropical, tempered by trade winds. All the islands are in the potential path of hurricanes, and Guadeloupe itself is fairly humid. The average temperatures on the coast of the main islands range between 22°C and 30°C (72°F–86°F), but it can be about 3°C cooler inland, particularly in the mountains. Most of this rain falls in September–November, although the wet season (*hivernage*) is reckoned to begin in

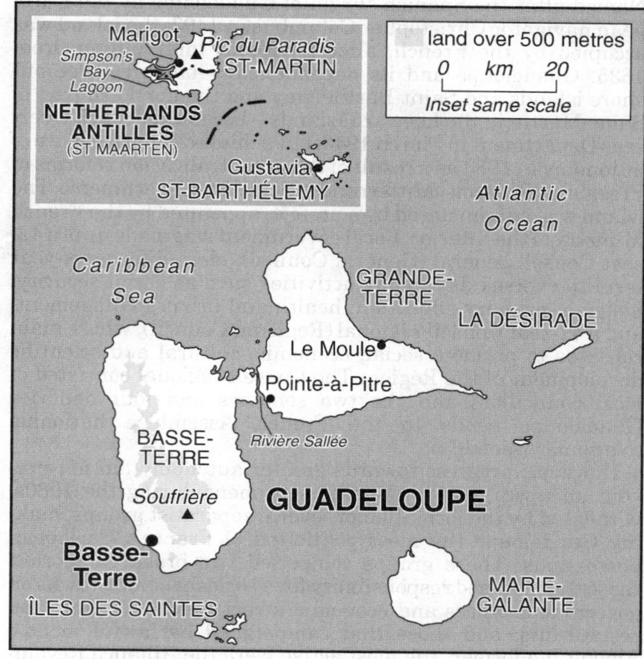

July. The dry season (*carême*) falls in the cooler months of January–April.

POPULATION

Around 90% of the population is black or of mixed race (mulatto), with 5% whites and smaller communities of 'East' Indians, Chinese and Lebanese, similar to many places in the West Indies. Some 76% of the population is Roman Catholic, with only 1% Protestant, and the rest being Hindu or espousing pagan African religions or syncretic versions thereof. The official language is French, which most people speak, but many people generally use the Creole patois that employs West African grammatical structures with a predominantly French-derived vocabulary.

The total population was estimated at 407,205 at 1 January 2010. Most of the population lives on Guadeloupe, with Grande-Terre being the more densely populated. The administrative capital, Basse-Terre, is not a large city—it is on the western coast, at the southern end, of the western 'wing' of the main island. The largest city in the Department, the chief city of Grande-Terre and the commercial capital of Guadeloupe is Pointe-à-Pitre, on the south-west coast of the eastern 'wing', near the Rivière Sallée. There are about 100,000 people living in Pointe-à-Pitre and its environs. Other important centres include: Le Gosier, just to the south-east of Pointe-à-Pitre, and Les Abymes, inland, just to the north-east; Le Moule, a former capital, on Grande-Terre, but on the east coast; and Capesterre-Belle-Eau, on the south-east coast of Basse-Terre. Marie-Galante, with a total population of around 18,000, has three main settlements, the largest being Grand-Bourg, on the south-west coast.

History

PHILLIP WEARNE

Revised for this edition by Dr PETER CLEGG

Named after the Spanish Virgin of Guadeloupe by the European navigator Christopher Columbus in 1493, the island was occupied by the French, almost without interruption, from 1635. Guadeloupe and its dependencies—namely three offshore islands and Saint-Barthélemy and the northern part of Saint-Martin in the Leeward Islands—became a French Overseas Department in March 1946, but achieved some measure of autonomy in 1983 as a result of the decentralization reforms of President François Mitterrand's Socialist Government. The island was administered by a prefect, appointed by the French Ministry of the Interior. Local government was made up of a 42-seat Conseil général (General Council), elected for a six-year term to oversee day-to-day activities such as social security, housing, primary education, health and urban management, and a 41-seat Conseil régional (Regional Council), whose main role was to promote social, economic, cultural and scientific development of the Région. The Conseil régional consisted of local councillors and the two senators and four deputies Guadeloupe sends to the French Assemblée nationale (National Assembly).

However, progress towards greater autonomy did not prevent an upsurge of nationalist sentiment during the 1980s, witnessed by the formation of several separatist groups, making Guadeloupe the most politicized of France's Caribbean possessions. These groups comprised two broad categories: those that claimed responsibility for a series of bomb attacks on government offices and economic targets such as hotels and restaurants; and those that campaigned by lawful means. Among the former, the most active were the Alliance Révolutionnaire Caraïbe (ARC) and, during 1983 and 1984, the Groupe Libération Armée. In 1984 the ARC merged with the Mouvement Populaire pour une Guadeloupe Indépendante (MPGI), but continued its bombing campaign, using the MPGI as a legitimate cover for its activities. In 1984 the leader of the ARC, Luc Reinette, was sentenced to 12 years in prison for possession of arms and conspiracy to carry out more than 20 bomb attacks in 1983–85. He escaped in June 1985, but was recaptured in July 1987 and held in Paris, where he was due to go on trial with 13 other Guadeloupe separatists. In June 1989, however, after demonstrations demanding the release of political prisoners and after hunger strikes by separatist activists, among them Reinette, the Assemblée nationale granted an amnesty to those imprisoned or accused in connection with politically motivated crimes committed before July 1988 in the Overseas Departments.

The amnesty, the failure of the independence groups at the polls and the Mitterrand administration's willingness to cede more autonomy to Guadeloupe's democratic left, in firm control of the island's Conseil général by 1988, formed the basis for a new political *modus vivendi* in Guadeloupe. The bombers, temporarily at least, changed tactics. Pressure from trade unionists, the support base of the socialist movement on the island, who attributed a further decline in the island's economy to the bombing campaign, seems to have played a crucial role.

As in other French possessions (such as New Caledonia, in the Pacific), nationalist pressure had a racial element. The original white planters represented only 5% of the population, yet they owned more than 80% of all land and property until 1945. The position of this group was consolidated, after 1946, by the arrival of French government officials and professionals. They not only altered the racial balance in favour of the whites, at a time when black national consciousness was growing, but also effectively blocked the advancement of the most able blacks and people of mixed descent by monopolizing the most desirable jobs. The problems of change in the racial balance of the island were compounded by the influx of up to 45,000 illegal immigrants from Dominica, Haiti and other neighbouring islands, attracted by the relatively high standard of living that Guadeloupeans enjoyed, and by work opportunities in the agricultural sector. Many native islanders preferred to emigrate or to seek work in the services sector rather than accept wages below the legal minimum on the land. However, salary levels remained high by Caribbean standards, being linked to those of metropolitan France. Emigration, meanwhile, continued at a rate of nearly 20,000 per year, with the result that perhaps 40% of all Guadeloupeans lived abroad by the early 1990s. Their remittances to relatives at home became a vital part of the island's economic structure.

The belief that the separatists had an influence out of all proportion to their numbers was borne out by the French presidential and parliamentary elections, which, along with local elections, took place in 1988. In all three gauges of public opinion, it was the moderate left—the Socialists—that made gains, although the independence movement claimed that the increased rate of abstention reflected growing support for their cause. For the presidency of the Republic, François Mitterrand gained 69.4% of the votes in Guadeloupe in the second round of voting in May 1988. At elections to the Assemblée nationale, held in June 1988, the Socialists made one gain, when Dominique Larifla, President of the Conseil général, defeated the sitting deputy of the conservative Union du Rassemblement du Centre (URC), a local alliance between the main national parties of the right, the Rassemblement pour la République (RPR) and the Union des Démocrates pour la République. One Socialist and one Communist were re-elected, as was Lucette Michaux-Chévry of the URC. In the elections for the Conseil général itself, the Socialist–Communist coalition increased its total by one seat, giving it 26 seats, against the 16 of the right-wing parties. Dominique Larifla was re-elected President of the Conseil général.

In March 1992 Dominique Larifla was returned as President of the Conseil général, but the Socialists suffered some reversal in the elections to the Conseil régional, held simultaneously. The right-wing grouping Objectif Guadeloupe, led by Michaux-Chévry, won 15 of the 41 seats; two Socialist groups obtained 16 seats between them. The split on the Socialist side meant that Michaux-Chévry, with the support of six dissident left--wingers, was able to oust the Socialist Félix Proto from the presidency of the Conseil régional. The decline of the left-wing was consolidated when a repeat of the election to the Conseil régional was required after a complaint was upheld that one party's candidates had been registered after the official deadline. Objectif Guadeloupe took a further seven seats to push its tally up to 22, while the two left-wing parties retained only 10.

At elections to the French Assemblée nationale held in March 1993 the local wing of the national Parti Socialiste (PS) lost more ground when an independent right-wing candidate, Edouard Chammougon, defeated Larifla by just 273 votes. Chammougon, mayor of Baie-Mahault, was elected despite being implicated in several corruption scandals, which involved many leading figures in the Department during the early 1990s. However, further corruption charges and allegations of abuse and misappropriation of public funds led to Chammougon's membership of the Assemblée nationale being revoked by the French Conseil constitutionnel (Constitutional Council) in November 1994, at which time Léo Andy of the 'dissident' PS was elected to his seat. In 1993 Lucette Michaux-Chévry retained her seat at the Assemblée with 79.9% of the poll, while an anti-Larifla Socialist, Frédéric Jalton, and a dissident Communist, Ernest Moutoussamy, retained the other two seats. However, the Socialist–Communist coalition retained control of the Conseil général in March 1994 and Larifla was re-elected its President.

At municipal elections held in May 1995 Michaux-Chévry defeated the Communist incumbent to become mayor of the capital, Basse-Terre. She and Larifla were elected to the French Sénat (Senate) in September and Philippe Chaulet of the RPR was subsequently elected to her seat in the Assemblée nationale. Jean Barfleur became Guadeloupe's first pro-independence mayor when he won Port-Louis.

At elections to the Assemblée nationale in late May and early June 1997, Moutoussamy, Andy and Chaulet all retained their seats, while Daniel Marsin, a candidate of the independent left, was elected in the Les Abymes–Pointe-à-Pitre constituency. In March 1998 the RPR won a majority of seats in the Conseil régional, although the PS increased its representation. Michaux-Chévry was re-elected to the presidency of the Conseil. In concurrent elections to the Conseil général the Socialist–Communist coalition retained a majority, although the RPR increased its representation. Larifla was deposed from the Conseil's presidency and replaced by Marcellin Lubeth of the Parti Progressiste Démocratique Guadeloupéen (PPDG), which had been formed in 1991, following a split in the Parti Communiste Guadeloupéen (PCG).

The issue of Guadeloupe's constitutional status arose in 1999 following a series of meetings between the Presidents of the Conseil régionaux of Guadeloupe, Martinique and French Guiana. In December Michaux-Chévry co-signed a declaration, stating the intention of the three Presidents to propose, to the French Government, legislative and constitutional amendments aimed at creating a new status of Overseas Region (Région d'outre-mer) and providing for greater financial autonomy. The declaration and subsequent announcements by Michaux-Chévry and her counterparts were dismissed by Jean-Jack Queyranne, the French Secretary of State for Overseas Departments and Territories, in February 2000, as unconstitutional and exceeding the mandate of the politicians responsible. However, in May 2000 a number of proposals, including the extension of the Departments' powers in areas such as regional co-operation, were provisionally accepted by the Assemblée nationale; a modified version of the proposals was subsequently adopted, by a narrow margin, by the Sénat. In November the Assemblée nationale approved the changes, and in December they were ratified by the Conseil constitutionnel.

In municipal elections held in March 2001 Michaux-Chévry was re-elected mayor of Basse-Terre, despite corruption charges against her (in January Michaux-Chévry was acquitted of charges of forgery; however, she was still under investigation for charges of embezzlement). Following her election Michaux-Chévry relinquished the post to Pierre-Marti. Henri Bangou of the PPDG was also re-elected to the mayoralty of Pointe-à-Pitre. In the concurrently held election to the presidency of the Conseil général Jacques Gillot of Guadeloupe Unie, Socialisme et Réalité (GUSR) defeated Marcellin Lubeth of the PPDG.

In early June 2001 riots took place in Pointe-à-Pitre in which a number of people were injured, in protest at the arrest of the leader of the UGTG, Michel Madassamy, who had been charged in late May with vandalizing a number of shops that had remained open, in defiance of the UGTG's recommendations. The General Secretary of the UGTG subsequently called for a general strike to be held for the duration of Madassamy's incarceration. A period of severe drought, necessitating the rationing of water supplies, served to exacerbate the deteriorating social situation on the island.

Following a meeting of members of the Conseil régional and the Conseil général in late June 2001, a series of proposals on greater autonomy, to be presented to the French Government, was agreed upon. These included: the division of the territory into four districts; the creation of a Territorial Collectivity (Collectivité territoriale), governed by a 41-member Assembly elected for a five-year term; and the establishment of an independent executive council. Furthermore, the proposals included a request that the territory be given control over legislative and administrative affairs, as well as legislative authority on matters concerning Guadeloupe alone. In November the French Government announced itself to be in favour of the suggested constitutional developments, and in March 2003 the two houses of the French parliament approved constitutional changes which would allow for a referendum on proposals for greater autonomy. In the same month the status of Overseas Region was conferred upon Guadeloupe.

At elections to the Assemblée nationale in June 2002 Chaulet, Marsin, Moutoussamy and Andy were all defeated; Objectif Guadeloupe emerged as the most successful political grouping, with both Gabrielle Louis-Carabin and Joël Beaugendre being elected as deputies; Eric Jalton (son of Frédéric Jalton) of the PCG and Victorin Lurel of the Gauche Plurielle grouping were also successful. In August Dominique Vian replaced Jean-François Carenco as Prefect.

In December 2003 voting took place in the referendum to determine Guadeloupe's constitutional relationship with France. The proposed new arrangement, laid out by Jean-Pierre Raffarin's right-of-centre Government in Paris, foresaw the replacement of the Conseil général and Conseil régional with a single elected council, with the aim of streamlining administrative and political processes. Despite the enthusiastic support of Michaux-Chévry, however, an overwhelming 73.0% voted against the proposal. Supporters of the 'yes' vote claimed that voters had been misled into believing that the new constitutional status would involve cuts in French subsidies and social security payments. In Saint-Barthélemy and Saint-Martin, however, the vote was in favour of the proposed change, by 95.5% and 76.2%, respectively, meaning that the islands would no longer be communes of Guadeloupe but separate Overseas Collectivities (Collectivités d'outre-mer). The reorganization was subsequently approved by the French Sénat on 6 February 2007 and by the Assemblée nationale the following day. Two weeks later, on 21 February, Saint-Barthélemy and the French part of Saint-Martin were formally designated Overseas Collectivities. However, the existing forms of government continued until elections to a local legislative assembly—to be known as the Conseil territorial (Territorial Council)—were held on 1 July 2007, after which the two Overseas Collectivities acceded to administrative independence. Furthermore, each Overseas Collectivity was to elect one representative to the French Sénat (in September 2008) and one deputy to the Assemblée nationale (in 2012). (See the chapters on Saint-Barthélemy and Saint-Martin.)

In elections to the Conseil régional in March 2004 Michaux-Chévry suffered a further defeat when Lurel's left-wing coalition, Guadeloupe pour Tous, won a majority of votes cast. Michaux-Chévry was forced to resign as President of the Conseil régional. In mid-2004 Dominique Vian was replaced as Prefect by Paul Girot de Langlade, who was in turn succeeded by Jean-Jacques Brot in June 2006.

Meanwhile, in early October 2004 the arrest of Michel Madassamy on fresh charges of vandalism led to a deterioration in the social situation. Madassamy was accused of attacking two petrol tankers during the blockade of a service station in Pointe-à-Pitre in November 2003. In March 2004 he was found guilty and sentenced to 10 months' imprisonment. Following a failed appeal process, Madassamy was taken into custody early in October. The UGTG challenged the legality of the arrest, and in conjunction with other unions, urged workers to strike in support of Madassamy's release; Madassamy himself began a hunger strike. While there was no call for a general strike, areas affected included the airport, local shops and service stations. Dock workers at the port of Jarry refused to load or unload containers and ships were diverted to other Caribbean ports. Several hundred protesters took to the streets in Pointe-à-Pitre in late October, leading to a number of arrests. French Prefect Dominique Vian issued a statement in support of the authorities; however, Lurel called for the judge investigating Madassamy's case to bring the hearing forward. Madassamy was granted conditional release in November pending a further hearing in January 2005, when the judge ruled that he should serve a further eight months in prison.

At the first round of the national presidential election, held on 22 April 2007, Nicolas Sarkozy of the Union pour un Mouvement Populaire (UMP) won 42.6% of votes cast in Guadeloupe, ahead of PS candidate Ségolène Royal, who attracted 38.3% of the vote. At the second round, held on 6 May, Royal gained 50.8% to Sarkozy's 49.2%, although Sarkozy emerged victorious overall. Meanwhile, at elections to the Assemblée nationale, held on 10 and 17 June, UMP candidate Gabrielle Louis-Carabin, PS representative Lurel and Eric Jalton of the PCG were re-elected, while Jeanny Marc-Matthiasin of the GUSR was also successful. In November Emmanuel Berthier succeeded Brot as Prefect. At municipal elections held on 10 March 2008 Michaux-Chevry was again elected mayor of Basse-Terre. The PS and GUSR retained control of the Conseil général, and Gillot was subsequently re-elected as its President.

In early 2009 Guadeloupe was badly shaken by a six-week general strike. The unrest began on 20 January with demands that the French authorities address growing inequality and social dislocation within Guadeloupan society. There was particular concern over low wages earned by many employees, which were exacerbated by the high and increasing cost of living that was linked to the significant dependence on imports from the metropole. Initially the demonstrators lacked coherence in their approach, but soon an 'umbrella' group, called the Liyannaj Kont Pwofitasyon (LKP), or 'Collective Against Exploitation', was formed. This grouping contained a large number of trade unions and other civil society organizations, and provided an effective force in calling for change. In the course of laying out their demands the protestors directed some of their dissatisfaction against the *béké* class, the white descendents of colonial plantation owners, for allegedly exploiting their monopoly power in retail and construction in order to maintain high prices and therefore their privileged status. All aspects of society were affected by the general strike. Commercial activity was severely restricted, including at the main shipping and air ports, government business was disrupted, and schools were shut.

After a month of relatively peaceful protest, the strike turned violent amid worsening economic and social conditions and growing frustration over the lack of progress in meeting the protesters' demands. There were several quite serious clashes between the police (several hundred of whom had been drafted in from mainland France) and demonstrators. However, on 18 February 2009 events took a more serious turn when a union activist, Juan Bino, was shot and killed. Although the death was at the hands of fellow demonstrators and most likely an accident, the incident highlighted to all sides the real risk of anarchy in the Department if a solution to the crisis was not found. Indeed, soon after Bino's death serious talks began between the French Government and the LKP in an attempt to end the unrest. The negotiations, however, were protracted, in large part owing to the Government's reluctance to accede to the central demands of the LKP. Nevertheless, on 4 March an accord was signed, prompting the LKP to call off the strike. The agreement met many of the LKP's demands, including a pay rise for the lowest paid workers, a reduction in the cost of basic staples and commodities, and an increase in financial assistance for farmers, fishermen and small businesses.

On 25 and 26 June 2009 President Sarkozy visited Guadeloupe and Martinique. He was joined by his new Minister of the Overseas Possessions, Marie-Luce Penchard, a native of Guadeloupe and the first holder of the office from outside metropolitan France. The intention of the visit was to hold talks with local politicians and members of civil society, and more broadly to assist the French Government's efforts to rebuild relations with the overseas territories. Sarkozy's visit came during a consultation process, initiated in April by the French Government, intended to address the underlying concerns within the Departments. Key issues considered included the development of local production, the pricing mechanisms for goods and services, and the ways in which social dialogue could be improved. A range of groups participated in the discussions, although most unions boycotted them, including those associated with the LKP. Further, the situation on the ground remained tense. The LKP decreed 'a week of mobilization', with strikes and demonstrations to accompany Sarkozy's visit. In order to retain some calm during the presidential visit, some 900 extra police officers were drafted in from mainland France.

The situation remained tense in the ensuing months, and on 24–25 November 2009 the LKP staged a second general strike. A 10,000-strong demonstration was held in Pointe-à-Pitre, during which participants beseeched the French Government to honour the commitments to which it had agreed in the March accord. However, there was a markedly lower level of support for wide-spread civil protest, suggesting to observers that a degree of normality was returning to Guadeloupe. This notion was reinforced by elections to the Conseil régional, held in March 2010. The PS-led list, Tous pour la Guadeloupe, retained power, securing 31 of the 41 council seats, with its share of the vote increasing to 56.5%. The Ensemble pour la Guadeloupe—comprising the UMP, led by Penchard, and other right-wing candidates—won just four seats, with 14% of the vote. The results highlighted Guadeloupeans'continued dissatisfaction with the French Government, but also a strong preference for more moderate and consensual leadership at home. Also in this vein was the decision to retain the existing constitutional relationship with France and not to request a referendum on the issue of greater autonomy (unlike Martinique and French Guiana). By contrast, Tous pour la Guadeloupe, with Lurel at the helm, determined that its focus should remain firmly on economic and social renewal.

Economy

PHILLIP WEARNE

Revised for this edition by Dr PETER CLEGG

The structure of Guadeloupe's economy helps to explain why the separatist movement has not commanded greater support. The penalties that would normally be associated with huge trade deficits and low productivity do not apply in Guadeloupe as French and European Union (EU) aid and subsidies make up the difference, providing one of the highest standards of living in the Caribbean. In 2008 Guadeloupe's gross domestic product (GDP), measured at current prices, was €8,130m., equivalent to €17,912 per head. Between 1997 and 2007 the annual rate of inflation averaged 1.7%, although this rose moderately to 2.2% in 2008. Guadeloupe experienced a sustained period of economic growth prior to 2007; although the rate of unemployment declined as a consequence, this remained in excess of one-fifth of the total work-force. The economic conditions deteriorated with the onset of the global economic crisis from the latter half of 2008. Guadeloupe's economy expanded by just 1% in 2008 as a whole, compared with growth of 2.7% in the previous year, and there was a concomitant increase, albeit modest, in the number of unemployed. In terms of overall economic activity, in 2007 the primary sector (agriculture, fishing and forestry) contributed approximately 2% of GDP, the secondary sector (manufacturing, construction and utilities) contributed some 10%, and the tertiary sector (services, transport, communications and government services) 88%. Compared with a decade earlier the respective contributions of the primary and secondary sectors had declined slightly, while that of the tertiary sector had increased. Guadeloupe's trade deficit rose steadily at the end of the 20th century. In 1980 the value of exports covered 14.5% of imports, but by 1998 that figure had fallen to 6.6%. The deficit rose from 2,628m. francs in 1981 to 9,999.7m. francs by 1998. In 2008 the trade deficit stood at €2,199.5m., with exports representing 6.7% of imports. The principal exports in 2008 were products of its food industries, electronic equipment, and boats, planes, trains and motorcycles. Products of its food industries were also the main imports that year, followed by fuels and combustibles, car industry products and pharmaceutical products. Metropolitan France was the Department's most important trading partner in 2008, accounting for 49.8% of exports and 52.9% of imports. The majority of the remaining trade was conducted with the other French Overseas Departments and the USA (the latter primarily for imports).

Imports of mineral fuels increased from 2.1% of total imports in 1993 to 9.0% in 2003, and rose further to 20.0% of the total in 2008. Much of the increase was due to Guadeloupe's strong economic growth and the higher cost of oil (90% of the Department's energy needs are met through imports); approximately one-third of imported fuel was destined for the production of electricity. In 2008 Guadeloupe's total electricity consumption was 1,661m. kWh., representing a modest decline from the previous year. In 2006 almost 45% of the Department's installed generating capacity was fuelled by diesel and a further 29% provided by steam turbine installations. A mixture of coal and bagasse (a by-product of sugar cane), such as fuels the power plant at Le Moule, accounted for some 15% of energy production. (The remainder was provided by a combination of wind, solar, geothermal and hydraulic power.)

One possible solution to the island's deteriorating trade position was more regional integration. Closer co-operation with the Organisation of Eastern Caribbean States (OECS—a seven-state, Commonwealth-Caribbean group, using a common currency, the Eastern Caribbean dollar), was the most obvious option. At an OECS meeting in Antigua and Barbuda in 1989, it was agreed to establish a committee to examine the possibility of OECS countries using Guadeloupe and Martinique as entrepôts for exporting to Europe. Joint ventures were another possibility. However, the advent of the single market in Europe from 1993 neutralized some of the special advantages the French Overseas Departments and Territories had previously enjoyed, with all three French Caribbean possessions thenceforth being treated simply as less developed areas of Europe.

As in other states in the region, the economy is based on agriculture, tourism and some light industry, mostly the processing of food and beverages. Bananas and raw sugar were traditionally Guadeloupe's principal exports, although the volume of production fluctuated in the early and mid-1990s owing to variable climatic conditions. Production of bananas reached 148,296 metric tons in 1992, but in 1994 a combination of drought and the damage caused to plantations in September by Hurricane Debbie devastated the crop. Banana production in 2006 was, according to FAO estimates, at 54,500 tons, compared with an estimated 123,000 tons in 2004. Production fell again, to 38,000 tons, in 2007 following the destruction of 80% of the island's banana plantations by Hurricane Dean, but recovered slightly in 2008, to 40,200 tons. Meanwhile, banana exports, typically about 120,000 tons per year in the early 1990s, were recorded at just 44,500 tons in 2006, having fallen from more than 96,500 tons in 2002. They decreased again in 2007 to just 37,900 tons, but recovered marginally in 2008. Guadeloupe's banana sector was adversely affected by declining prices on the European market, while a dispute between the USA and four major Latin American producers and the EU over the latter's banana import regime also undermined the sector. The liberalization of EU banana imports from 2006 onwards also led many growers to abandon the crop, fearful of lower prices and increased competition. Since 1998 the number of banana farmers has dropped by about 80%. In 2008 there were only 212 active producers and 1,300 people directly employed by the industry. In conjunction with Martinique, Guadeloupe received €110m. in 2004, and a further €129m. in 2006, in EU aid as compensation for the low market price of bananas. Further assistance was subsequently provided, amounting to approximately €270m. a year. However, production and exports continued to disappoint. Production accounted for only 0.4% of GDP in 2005.

The fall in international sugar prices of the mid-1980s made the production of sugar cane in Guadeloupe uneconomic. A five-year plan to provide subsidies and price guarantees to growers was largely unsuccessful in maintaining production levels, as equipment deteriorated and growers voluntarily reduced production. In 1995 Guadeloupe's worst sugar cane harvest—except for 1990, the year after Hurricane Hugo—saw production fall to less than 376,000 metric tons of cane and 33,000 tons of sugar, though exports of raw sugar still accounted for 11.5% of total export earnings in that year. However, in 1997 production of raw sugar recovered to 57,000 tons, when it accounted for 23.7% of total export earnings, before declining to 38,400 tons in 1998. Thereafter, however, production recovered, and stood at almost 64,000 tons of raw sugar in 2005, from a harvest of around 855,400 tons of sugar cane. Under EU reforms introduced in 2006, which led to a decline of 33% in the reference price, the sugar industry was entitled to a share of aid worth some €90m. as compensation for price reductions and the cost of restructuring. As a result, production increased to 73,700 tons in that year, according to official figures, despite a 5.2% decline in exports. Production increased once more in 2007, to 80,800 tons, and accounted for 29.8% of export earnings. Despite improved production, sugar's contribution to GDP remained low, at around 0.4%. Moreover, in 2008 production declined to its lowest level for five years, largely attributable to adverse weather conditions

The most promising agricultural sector remained non-traditional crops. In 2007, according to FAO estimates, pineapple production totalled 5,700 metric tons, while melon (including cantaloupe) output reached an estimated 7,500 tons in the same year. Nevertheless, their importance remained limited, with production accounting for approximately 6% of total agricultural output. Output of aubergines, avocados, limes and cut flowers also increased from the 1980s, although many non-traditional sectors subsequently experienced problems. Yams, sweet potatoes and plantains were the main subsistence crops. The fishing sector, traditionally underdeveloped, responded to efforts to stimulate output. Fishing, mostly at an artisanal level, fulfilled about two-thirds of domestic requirements. The total fishing catch in 2007 totalled 10,137 tons.

The main industrial activity concerned the processing of the island's agricultural crops, particularly the refining of sugar and the distillation of rum, one of Guadeloupe's major manufactured exports. In 2003 sugar accounted for some 60% of processed agricultural products for consumption and rum some 20%. From February 1996 the quotas of light rum from the African, Caribbean and Pacific states associated with the EU under the Lomé Conventions were abolished; furthermore, the EU proposed that a phased abolition of quotas of traditional rum be in place by the end of the century. The proposals were understood to comply with requests from the French Government, which wanted to pre-empt potential competition with its rum suppliers in the overseas territories. However, by 2006 rum production had fallen from a peak of 79,550 hl in 1989 to just 57,447 hl, although in 2007 production recovered to 74,899 hl, a year-on-year increase of some 30.4%, and this level of production was maintained in 2008 with a total production of 75,679 hl in 2009. Export volumes of rum have grown every year since 2003; volumes increased by 9.9% in 2008 alone. The sector received an added boost in mid-2007 when the EU announced that it would offer €60m. in aid through reduced excise duty on rum produced in the French Overseas Departments, a concession that was expected to remain in place until at least 2012.

There was only limited activity in the textile, furniture, metal, cement, plastics and printing sub-sectors. Despite government efforts to expand the island's industrial base with the establishment of an industrial zone and free port at Jarry, and by the promotion of fiscal incentives, industry and construction continued to employ relatively few people. According to estimates, in 2007 some 6.9% of the salaried work-force was employed in industry and 7.1% in construction (some 2.0% of salaried workers were employed in the agricultural sector, while trade and services accounted for 84.0%).

Tourism remained the major source of foreign exchange. In 1988 tourism replaced sugar production as the Department's principal source of income and the sector continued to expand rapidly in the 1990s. In the 2000s, however, the tourism sector suffered a steady slowdown, with overall passenger arrivals at the main airport falling from 773,400 in 2001 to 623,134 in 2006. Cruise-ship arrivals also decreased, from 361,700 in 2001 to 195,102 in 2006. The Caribbean Tourism Organization has not produced more recent statistics, but data published by the French Government indicate that tourist numbers have continued to decline. Over 90% of arrivals were from France (including Réunion). Despite marketing campaigns funded by the EU targeted at crossing the linguistic barrier between the Overseas Departments and the USA, there continued to be a problem of diversifying away from the French market. Further, because tourism was not Guadeloupe's *raison d'être*, or even its principal activity, there was not a determined attempt to revitalize the sector. As a consequence, tourism expenditure declined from 7% of local GDP in 1995 to 3.2% in 2006.

Most importantly, the economy of Guadeloupe remained heavily underpinned by huge inflows of money from the French state. In 2007 public services—in health, education and social investment—accounted for 34% of GDP in Guadeloupe, representing almost €2,500m. (approximately €6,200 per person) per year. One important change with implications for spending came in 1996 with the alignment of the social security systems of the Overseas Departments with that of metropolitan France. In 2003 it was estimated that social security benefits worth €515m. were paid to over 100,000 claimants, of which 40% took the form of child support. EU funds also became increasingly important for Guadeloupe. For example, assistance from EU Structural Funds during the period 2000–06 amounted to €809m., and was expected to total €729m. during 2007–13.

As the economy was heavily dependent on France, so local commercial activity was largely dependent on the spending power of French civil servants and tourists. More than one-half of the total salary payments made on the island went to civil servants or the French Government's contractors. Civil servants received a 40% bonus on their basic metropolitan earnings, which further increased their economic importance to the Department, in terms of purchasing power. As a result, local investment interest remained concentrated on the import-export business or in the services sector (such as the discount stores that handled imported goods), rather than in productive investment.

Despite large levels of financial support, the underlying reality was that the economic model sustaining Guadeloupe (as well as Martinique and French Guiana) was being challenged as never before, via three processes. First, globalization and neo-liberal economic policies were undermining the idea of trade preferences and government subsidy, both of which were important to the Overseas Departments. Second, the process of EU enlargement meant that funds once allocated to the Departments were being disbursed elsewhere, particularly to the poorer former Communist countries in Central and Eastern Europe. Third, French President Nicolas Sarkozy talked about reducing the amount of central funding for the Departments and 'freeing' them from their dependency by giving them more autonomy and therefore a greater capacity for self-development, although this process was somewhat encumbered by the outbreak of civil unrest in 2009 (see History).

Statistical Survey

Sources (unless otherwise indicated): Institut National de la Statistique et des Etudes Economiques (INSEE), Service Régional de la Guadeloupe, ave Paul Lacavé, BP 96, 97102 Basse-Terre; tel. 5-90-99-02-50; internet www.insee.fr/fr/regions/guadeloupe; Service de Presse et d'Information, Ministère des Départements et Territoires d'Outre-mer, 27 rue Oudinot, 75700 Paris 07 SP, France; tel. 1-53-69-20-00; fax 1-43-06-60-30; internet www.outre-mer.gouv.fr.

AREA AND POPULATION

(Note: In July 2007 Saint-Barthélemy and Saint-Martin seceded from Guadeloupe to become Overseas Collectivities.)

Area: 1,630 sq km (629.3 sq miles), comprising continental Guadeloupe 1,438 sq km (Basse-Terre à l'Ouest 848 sq km, Grande-Terre à l'Est 590 sq km) and dependencies 194 sq km (La Désirade 22 sq km, Iles des Saintes 14 sq km, Marie-Galante 158 sq km).

Population: 422,496 at census of 8 March 1999; 400,736 (males 188,720; females 212,016) at census of 1 January 2006. Note: According to new census methodology, data in 2006 refer to median figures based on the collection of raw data over a five-year period (2004–09). *1 January 2010* (estimate): 407,205.

Density (1 January 2010): 249.8 per sq km.

Population by Age and Sex (provisional estimates at 1 January 2008): *0–14:* 90,150 (males 46,284, females 43,866); *15–64:* 260,224 (males 120,268 females 139,956); *65 and over:* 52,126 (males 22,003, females 30,123); *Total* 402,500 (males 188,555, females 213,945).

Principal Towns (population at 1999 census): Les Abymes 63,054; Saint-Martin 29,078; Le Gosier 25,360; Baie-Mahault 23,389; Pointe-à-Pitre 20,948; Le Moule 20,827; Petit Bourg 20,528; Sainte Anne 20,410; Basse-Terre (capital) 12,410.

Births, Marriages and Deaths (2008): Registered live births 5,758 (birth rate 14.2 per 1,000); Registered marriages 1,502 (marriage rate 3.7 per 1,000); Registered deaths 2,785 (death rate 6.9 per 1,000). *2009:* Crude birth rate 14.1 per 1,000; Crude death rate 8.0 per 1,000. Source: partly Pan American Health Organization.

Life Expectancy (years at birth): 79.3 (males 76.2; females 82.4) in 2009. Source: Pan American Health Organization.

Economically Active Population (persons aged 15 years and over, 1990 census): Agriculture, hunting, forestry and fishing 8,391; Industry and energy 9,630; Construction and public works 13,967; Trade 15,020; Transport and telecommunications 6,950; Financial services 2,802; Other marketable services 26,533; Non-marketable services 34,223; *Total employed* 117,516 (males 68,258, females 49,258); Unemployed 54,926 (males 25,691, females 29,235); *Total labour force* 172,442 (males 93,949, females 78,493). *2007* (provisional estimates at 31 December): Agriculture 2,375; Industry 8,247; Construction 8,562; Trade 17,661; Services 82,828; Total 119,673; Unemployed 44,560; Total labour force 164,233. Note: Figures for employment exclude 21,405 non-salaried workers. *2008* (estimate at 31 December): Unemployed 43,160.

HEALTH AND WELFARE

Key Indicators

Total Fertility Rate (children per woman, 2009): 2.1.

Under-5 Mortality Rate (per 1,000 live births, 2009): 8.6.

Physicians (per 1,000 head, c. 2001): 1.4.

Hospital Beds (per 1,000 head, 2004): 6.1.

Access to Water (% of persons, 2004): 98.

Access to Sanitation (% of persons, 2004): 64.

Source: mainly Pan American Health Organization.

For other sources and definitions, see explanatory note on p. vi.

AGRICULTURE, ETC.

Principal Crops ('000 metric tons, 2008, FAO estimates): Sweet potatoes 4.3; Sugar cane 732.5; Cabbages and other brassicas 2.3; Lettuce and chicory 2.5; Tomatoes 3.0; Cucumbers and gherkins 3.0; Bananas 40.2; Plantains 9.0. *Aggregate Production* ('000 metric tons, may include official, semi-official or estimated data): Total roots and tubers 13.4; Total vegetables (incl. melons) 41.9; Total fruits (excl. melons) 61.8.

Livestock ('000 head, year ending September 2008, FAO estimates): Cattle 75.0; Pigs 30.

Livestock Products ('000 metric tons, 2008, FAO estimates): Cattle meat 3.3; Pig meat 1.2; Chicken meat 1.4; Hen eggs 1.7.

Forestry ('000 cubic metres, 2008, FAO estimates): *Roundwood Removals* (excl. bark): Sawlogs, veneer logs and logs for sleepers 0.3; Fuel wood 31.9; Total 32.2. *Sawnwood Production* (incl. railway sleepers): Total 1.0.

Fishing (metric tons, live weight, 2008, FAO estimates unless otherwise indicated): Capture 10,100 (Common dolphinfish 700; Other mackerel-like fishes 1,600; Marine fishes 7,100; Stromboid conchs 550—official figure); Aquaculture 33; *Total catch* 10,133.

Source: FAO.

MINING

Production ('000 metric tons, 2008, estimates): Cement 230; Pumice 210; Salt 49. Source: US Geological Survey.

INDUSTRY

Production (2009): Sugar 55,600 metric tons; Rum 75,679 hl; Electric energy 1,628 million kWh. Source: Institut d'Emission des Départements d'Outre-mer, *Guadeloupe: Rapport Annuel 2009*.

FINANCE

Currency and Exchange Rates: The French franc was used until the end of February 2002. Euro notes and coins were introduced on 1 January 2002, and the euro became the sole legal tender from 18 February. Some of the figures in this Survey are still in terms of francs. For details of exchange rates, see French Guiana.

Budget: *French Government* (€ million, 2005): Revenue 1,132; Expenditure 1,040. *Regional Budget* (€ million, 2008): Current revenue 261.0 (Taxes 182.3, Other current revenue 78.7); Capital revenues 44.7; Total 305.7. Current expenditure 148.9; Capital expenditure 156.8; Total 305.7 (Source: Département des Etudes et des Statistiques Locales). *Departmental Budget* (excl. debt rescheduling, € million, 2006): Revenue 562.8; Expenditure 562.8 (Source: Département des Etudes et des Statistiques Locales).

Money Supply (million French francs at 31 December 1996): Currency outside banks 1,148; Demand deposits at banks 6,187; Total money 7,335.

Cost of Living (Consumer Price Index; base: 2000 = 100): All items 115.8 in 2007; 118.4 in 2008; 118.7 in 2009. Source: ILO.

Gross Domestic Product (US $ million at constant 1990 prices): 3,543 in 2001; 3,707 in 2002; 3,844 in 2003. Source: UN, *Statistical Yearbook*.

Expenditure on the Gross Domestic Product (€ million at current prices, 2008, estimates): Total final consumption expenditure 8,461; Changes in inventories 35; Gross fixed capital formation 1,863; *Total domestic expenditure* 10,359; Exports of goods and services 498; *Less* Imports of goods and services 2,731; *GDP in purchasers' values* 8,127. Source: Institut d'Emission des Départements d'Outre-mer, *Guadeloupe: Rapport Annuel 2009*.

Gross Domestic Product by Economic Activity (€ million at current prices, 2006): Agriculture, hunting, forestry and fishing 197; Food industries 87; Other manufacturing 265; Energy 37; Construction 713; Services 6,094 (Restaurants and hotels 253, Transport 249, Commerce 948, Other market services 2,269, Non-market services 2,375); *Sub-total* 7,393; Financial intermediation services indirectly measured (FISIM) –325; Import duties, less subsidies 690; *GDP in purchasers' values* 7,758.

EXTERNAL TRADE

Principal Commodities (€ million, 2008): *Imports c.i.f.:* Products of agriculture and food industries 377.0; Pharmaceutical products 185.0; Home equipment 145.2; Car industry products 313.2; Mechanical equipment 169.2; Electronic equipment 153.8; Fuels and combustibles 501.3; Total (incl. others) 2,600.7. *Exports f.o.b.:* Products of agriculture and food industries 56.6; Boats, planes, trains, and motorcycles 4.5; Electronic equipment 10.5; Metals and metallic products 14.8; Total (incl. others) 205.3.

Principal Trading Partners (€ million, 2008): *Imports c.i.f.:* Aruba 98; China, People's Repub. 87; France (metropolitan) 1,355; Germany 110; Italy 65; Martinique 210; Spain 40; USA 146; Total (incl. others) 2,601. *Exports f.o.b.:* France (metropolitan) 79; French Guiana 40; Germany 3; Martinique 44; Poland 5; Portugal 4; USA 4; Total (incl. others) 205.

TRANSPORT

Road Traffic ('000 motor vehicles in use, 2002): Passenger cars 117.7; Commercial vehicles 31.4. Source: UN, *Statistical Yearbook*.

Shipping: *Merchant Fleet* (vessels registered, '000 grt at 31 December 1992): Total displacement 6 (Source: Lloyd's Register-Fairplay, *World Fleet Statistics*). *International Sea-borne Traffic* (1995, unless otherwise indicated): Freight vessels entered 1,257; Freight vessels departed 1,253; Gross freight handled 2,973,169 metric tons; Containers handled 154,263 TEUs; Passengers carried 924,446 (2004).

Civil Aviation (2008): Freight carried 13,799 metric tons; Passengers carried 2,020,042.

TOURISM

Tourist Arrivals by Country (2000): Canada 10,431; France 440,779; Italy 15,670; Switzerland 9,766; USA 92,474; Total (incl. others) 623,134. *2004:* France 391,910; Total (incl. others) 423,172. *2005:* France 406,871; Total (incl. others) 433,358. *2006:* France 352,140; Total (incl. others) 383,518.

Receipts from Tourism (US $ million, incl. passenger transport): 306 in 2005; 299 in 2006; 344 in 2007.

Source: partly World Tourism Organization.

COMMUNICATIONS MEDIA

Radio Receivers ('000 in use): 113 in 1997.

Television Receivers ('000 in use): 118 in 1997.

Telephones ('000 main lines in use): 250.8 in 2009.

Mobile Cellular Telephones ('000 subscribers): 314.7 in 2004.

Personal Computers: 90,000 in 2004.

Internet Users ('000): 109.0 in 2009.

Daily Newspaper: 1 (estimate) in 1996 (estimated average circulation 35,000 copies).

Sources: UNESCO, *Statistical Yearbook*; UN, *Statistical Yearbook*; International Telecommunication Union.

EDUCATION

Pre-primary (2008/09): 22,411 students (20,362 state, 2,049 private).

Primary (2008/09): 37,650 students (33,797 state, 3,853 private).

Specialized Pre-primary and Primary (2005/06): 1,253 students (1,041 state, 212 private).

Secondary (2008/09): 52,547 students (47,134 state, 5,413 private).

Higher (2007/08): 8,718 students. Source: Ministère de l'Education Nationale, de la Recherche et de la Technologie.

Teachers (2007/08 unless otherwise indicated): *Primary:* 3,382 (3,139 state, 243 private); *Secondary:* 4,675 (4,223 state, 452 private); *Higher* (2004/05): 203. Source: Ministère de l'Education Nationale, *Repères et références statistiques*.

Institutions (2002/03): 136 pre-primary; 220 primary. Source: Ministère de l'Education Nationale, de l'Enseignement Supérieur et de la Recherche, *Repères et références statistiques sur les enseignements, la formation et la recherche 2003*.

Adult Literacy Rate: 90.1 (males 89.7; females 90.5) in 1998. Source: Pan American Health Organization.

Directory

The Government

(July 2010)

HEAD OF STATE

President: NICOLAS SARKOZY.

Prefect: JEAN-LUC MICHEL FABRE, Préfecture, Palais d'Orléans, rue Lardenoy, 97109 Basse-Terre Cédex; tel. 5-90-99-39-00; fax 5-90-81-58-32; e-mail webmestre@guadeloupe.pref.gouv.fr; internet www.guadeloupe.pref.gouv.fr.

DEPARTMENTAL ADMINISTRATION

President of the General Council: Dr JACQUES GILLOT (GUSR), Hôtel du Département, blvd Félix Eboué, 97109 Basse-Terre; tel. 5-90-99-77-77; fax 5-90-99-76-00; e-mail info@cg971.fr; internet www.cg971.fr.

President of the Economic and Social Committee: JOCELYN JALTON, 16 rue Peynier, 97100 Basse-Terre; tel. 5-90-41-05-25; fax 5-90-41-05-23; e-mail cr-cesr-guadeloupe@wanadoo.fr; internet www.cr-guadeloupe.fr.

President of the Culture, Education and Environment Committee: JEAN-JACQUES JEREMIE, 16 rue Peynier, 97100 Basse-Terre; tel. 5-90-41-05-15; fax 5-90-41-05-23; e-mail cr-cesr-guadeloupe@wanadoo.fr; internet www.cr-guadeloupe.fr.

President of the Regional Council: VICTORIN LUREL (PS), 1 rue Paul Lacavé, Petit-Paris, 97109 Basse-Terre; tel. 5-90-80-40-40; fax 5-90-81-34-19; internet www.cr-guadeloupe.fr.

Elections, 14 and 21 March 2010

	Seats
Tous pour la Guadeloupe*	31
Ensemble pour la Guadeloupe†	4
Région Autrement‡	4
Pou Gwadloup an nou ay	2
Total	41

* Comprising the Parti Socialiste (PS) and other left-wing candidates.
† Comprising the Union pour un Mouvement Populaire (UMP) and other right-wing candidates.
‡ Comprising smaller left-wing parties and dissident socialists.

REPRESENTATIVES TO THE FRENCH PARLIAMENT

Deputies to the French National Assembly: ERIC JALTON (PCG), GABRIELLE LOUIS-CARABIN (UMP), JEANNY MARC-MATTHIASIN (GUSR), VICTORIN LUREL (PS).

Representatives to the French Senate: Dr JACQUES GILLOT (Groupe Socialiste), DANIEL MARSIN (Rassemblement Démocratique et Social Européen), LUCETTE MICHAUX-CHEVRY (UMP).

Political Organizations

Combat Ouvrier: BP 213, 97156 Pointe-à-Pitre Cédex; tel. 5-90-26-23-58; e-mail redaction@combat-ouvrier.net; internet www.combat-ouvrier.net; Trotskyist; associated with national party Lutte Ouvrière; mem. of the Internationalist Communist Union; Leaders JEAN-MARIE NOMERTIN.

Guadeloupe Unie, Socialisme et Réalité (GUSR): Pointe-à-Pitre; e-mail gusr@ais.gp; internet perso.mediaserv.net/gusr; 'dissident' faction of the Parti Socialiste; Pres. GUY LOSBAR.

Konvwa pou Liberasyon Nasyon Gwadloup (KLNG): Pointe-à-Pitre; f. 1997; pro-independence; Leader LUC REINETTE.

Parti Communiste Guadeloupéen (PCG): 119 rue Vatable, 97110 Pointe-à-Pitre; tel. 5-90-88-23-07; f. 1944; Sec.-Gen. CHRISTIAN CÉLESTE.

Parti Socialiste (PS): 8 Résidence Légitimus, blvd Légitimus, 97110 Pointe-à-Pitre; tel. and fax 5-90-21-65-72; fax 5-90-83-20-51; e-mail fede971@parti-socialiste.fr; internet www.parti-socialiste.fr; divided into 2 factions to contest the March 1992 and March 1993 elections; Regional Sec. OTTO JULES.

Pou Gwadloup an nou ay: Pointe-à-Pitre; youth party; Leader CÉDRIC CORNET.

Union pour un Mouvement Populaire (UMP): Les Portes de Saint Martin Bellevue, 97150 Saint Martin; tel. and fax 5-90-87-50-01; fax 5-90-87-75-72; e-mail ump-sxm@laposte.net; internet www.u-m-p.org; f. 2002; centre-right; local br. of the metropolitan party; Pres., Departmental Cttee PHILIPPE CHAULET.

Les Verts Guadeloupe: 5 rue François Arago, 97110 Pointe-à-Pitre; tel. 5-90-35-41-90; fax 5-90-25-02-62; internet guadeloupe.lesverts.fr; ecologist; departmental br. of the metropolitan party; Regional spokespersons HARRY DURIMEL, MARIE-LINE PIRBAKAS.

Other political organizations included Mouvement pour la Démocratie et le Développement (MDDP), Union Populaire pour la Libération de la Guadeloupe (UPLG), Mouvman Gwadloupéyen (MG), Parti Progressiste Démocratique Guadeloupéen (PPDG), Renouveau Socialiste; and the coalitions Priorité à l'Education et à l'Environnement and Union pour une Guadeloupe Responsable.

Judicial System

Cour d'Appel: Palais de Justice, 4 blvd Félix Eboué, 97100 Basse-Terre; tel. 5-90-80-63-36; fax 5-90-80-63-39; First Pres. HENRY ROBERT; Procurator-Gen. CHRISTINE PENICHON.

There are two Tribunaux de Grande Instance and four Tribunaux d'Instance.

Religion

The majority of the population belong to the Roman Catholic Church.

CHRISTIANITY

The Roman Catholic Church

Guadeloupe comprises the single diocese of Basse-Terre, suffragan to the archdiocese of Fort-de-France, Martinique. Some 76% of the population are Roman Catholics. The Bishop participates in the Antilles Episcopal Conference, based in Port of Spain, Trinidad and Tobago.

Bishop of Basse-Terre: (vacant), Evêché, pl. Saint-Françoise, BP 369, 97100 Basse-Terre Cédex; tel. 5-90-81-36-69; fax 5-90-81-98-23; e-mail eveche@catholique-guadeloupe.info.

OTHER CHURCHES

Seventh-day Adventist Church: Eglise Adventiste de la Guadeloupe, BP 19, 97151 Pointe-à-Pitre Cédex; tel. 5-90-82-79-76; fax 5-90-83-44-24; e-mail adventiste.federation@wanadoo.fr; internet www.adventiste-gpe.org; f. 1931; Pres. ALAIN ANGERVILLE; Sec. DANIEL LOUSSALA; 11,957 members (2007).

Other denominations active in Guadeloupe include the Baptist Church and Jehovah's Witnesses.

The Press

France Antilles: ZAC Moudong Sud, 97122 Baie-Mahault; tel. 5-90-90-25-25; fax 5-90-91-78-31; e-mail f.breland@media-antilles.fr; internet www.guadeloupe.franceantilles.fr; f. 1964; subsidiary of Groupe France Antilles; daily; Chair. PHILIPPE HERSANT; Man. Dir FRÉDÉRIC AURAND; circ. 50,000.

Match: 33 rue Peynier, 97110 Pointe-à-Pitre; tel. 5-90-82-18-68; fax 5-90-82-01-87; fortnightly; Dir MARIE ANTONIA JABBOUR; circ. 6,000.

Nouvelles Etincelles: 119 rue Vatable, 97110 Pointe-à-Pitre; tel. 5-90-91-12-77; fax 5-90-83-69-90; f. 1944 as l'Etincelle, organ of the Parti Communiste Guadeloupéen (q.v.); present name adopted 2005; weekly; Editor-in-Chief DANIK ZANDRONIS; circ. 5,000.

Sept Mag Communication: Immeuble Curaçao, voie Verte, 97122 Baie-Mahault; weekly; Dir JACQUES CANNEVAL; circ. 30,000.

Terre de Guadeloupe: Immeuble Pluriel, 3 rue Ferdinand Forest, 97122 Baie-Mahault; tel. 5-90-25-20-20; fax 5-90-38-29-61; f. 2003; publ. by Groupe Maximini; monthly; local and environmental issues; CEO JEAN-YVES FRIXON; Publ. Dir THIERRY ELFGANG; circ. 60,000; also publ. *Maximini News* (f. 2005, daily, circ. 3,500).

TV Magazine Guadeloupe: 1 rue Paul Lacavé, BP 658, 97169 Pointe-à-Pitre; tel. 5-90-90-25-25; weekly.

Publishers

Editions Caret (Centre Antillais de Recherche et d'Edition de Textes): BP 165, 97190 Le Gosier; tel. and fax 5-90-84-82-29; e-mail caret@wanadoo.fr; French-Creole language, culture and fiction; Dir JACQUELINE PICARD.

Editions Jasor: 46 rue Schoëlcher, 97110 Pointe-à-Pitre; tel. 5-90-91-18-48; fax 5-90-21-07-01; e-mail editionsjasor@orange.fr; French-Creole culture, biography and language, and youth fiction; Dir RÉGINE JASOR.

PLB Editions: route de Mathurin, 97190 Gosier; tel. 5-90-89-91-17; fax 5-90-89-91-05; e-mail plbeditions@wanadoo.fr; f. 1997; regional natural history and French-Creole youth fiction; Dirs CHANTAL MATTET, THIERRY PETIT LE BRUN.

Broadcasting and Communications

TELECOMMUNICATIONS

Digicel Antilles Françaises Guyane: see Martinique—Telecommunications.

Orange Caraïbe: BP 2203, 97196 Jarry Cédex; tel. 5-90-38-45-55; fax 8-10-50-05-59; e-mail webmaster@orange.gp; internet www.orangecaraibe.com; f. 1996; subsidiary of Orange France; mobile cellular telephone operator; network coverage incl. Martinique and French Guiana; Dir-Gen. JEAN-PHILIPPE GAY.

Outremer Telecom: SCI, Brand, voie Verte, Z. I. de Jarry, 97122 Baie-Mahault; e-mail communication@outremer-telecom.fr; internet www.outremer-telecom.fr; f. 1998; mobile telecommunications provider; Group CEO JEAN-MICHEL HEGESIPPE.

ONLY: SCI, Brand, voie Verte, Z. I. de Jarry, 97122 Baie-Mahault; e-mail communication@outremer-telecom.fr; internet www.outremer-telecom.fr; f. 1998 as Outremer Telecom Guadeloupe; present name adopted following merger of Volubis, ONLY and OOL in 2006; subsidiary of Outremer Telecom, France; fixed and mobile telecommunications provider.

BROADCASTING

Réseau France Outre-mer (RFO): Morne Bernard Destrellan, BP 180, 97122 Baie-Mahault Cédex; tel. 5-90-60-96-96; fax 5-90-60-96-82; e-mail rfo@rfo.fr; internet guadeloupe.rfo.fr; f. 1964; acquired by Groupe France Télévisions in 2004; fmrly Société Nationale de Radio-Télévision Française d'Outre-mer, present name adopted in 1998; radio and TV; Dir-Gen. GENEVIÈVE GIARD; Regional Dir LILIANE FRANCIL.

Radio

Kilti FM: Impasse Augustin Fresnel, Immeuble 590, Z. I. de Jarry, 97122 Baie-Mahault; tel. 5-90-32-52-61; fax 5-90-25-66-03; e-mail kiltifm@wanadoo.fr; f. 2006; French and Creole.

NRJ Guadeloupe: 2 blvd de la Marne, 97200 Fort-de-France; tel. 5-96-63-63-63; fax 5-96-73-73-15; e-mail webmaster@nrjantilles.com; internet www.nrjantilles.com; Dir FRANCK FÉRANDIER-SICARD; Dir JEAN-CHRISTOPHE MARTINEZ.

Ouest FM: Immeuble Vivies, rue Thomas Edyson, Z. I. Jarry, 97122 Baie-Mahault; tel. 5-90-32-01-32; fax 5-90-26-02-97; e-mail contact@ouestfm.com; internet www.ouestfm.net; f. 2008; commercial radio station; French.

Radio Caraïbes International (RCI Guadeloupe): Carrefour Grand Camp, BP 40, 97151 Pointe-à-Pitre Cédex; tel. 5-90-83-96-96; fax 5-90-83-96-97; internet gp.rci.fm; f. 1962; Dir FRANK FERANDIER-SICARD; Man. THIERRY FUNDÉRÉ.

Radio Contact: 40 bis, rue Lamartine, 97110 Pointe-à-Pitre; tel. 5-90-82-25-41; fax 5-96-91-56-77; internet www.radio-contact.net; operated by l'Asscn Citoyenne de Sauvegarde et de Défense des Intérêts des Guadeloupéens; Dir OCTAVIE LOSIO; Man. HENRI YOYOTTE.

Radio Gayak Media Delkaribe: BP 535, 97135 Pointe-à-Pitre Cédex; tel. 6-90-55-85-15; fax 5-90-83-12-30; e-mail gaston971@yahoo.fr; internet www.radiogayak.com; operated by the l'Asscn Guadeloupéenne de Défense et de Valorisation du Patrimoine Historique, Culturel et de l'Environnement; French and Creole; Dir JEAN ADÉLAÏDE; Man. DANIK IBRAHIM ZANDWONIS.

Radio Haute Tension: route de Petit Marquisat, Routhiers, 97130 Capesterre Belle Eau; tel. 5-90-99-08-12; e-mail hautetension2@wanadoo.fr; internet www.radiohautetension.fr; f. 1986; Dir HUGUETTE HUBERT; Man. RUDDY CORNELIE.

Radio Inter S'Cool (RIS): Lycée Ducharmoy, 97120 Saint-Claude; tel. and fax 5-90-80-38-40; e-mail contact@gupilvision.com; internet www.radiointerscool.net; educational and school-focused programmes; French and Creole; Pres. JAQUES REMUS.

Radio Tanbou: 153 résidence Espace, 97110 Pointe-à-Pitre; tel. 5-90-21-66-45; fax 5-90-21-66-48; e-mail kontak@radyotanbou.com; internet www.radyotanbou.com; French and Creole; operated by the l'Asscn pour le Développement de l'Information et de la Culture Guadeloupéenne.

Virgin Radio: Pointe-à-Pitre; internet www.virginradio.fr; f. 1987 as Europe 2 Fréquence Alizée; adopted current name 2008; commercial music station; Dir-Gen. JEAN-CHRISTOPHE LESTRA.

Zouk Radio: Immeuble Général Bricolage, Petit Pérou, 97139 Les Abymes; tel. 5-90-89-25-80; fax 5-90-89-26-22; internet www.zoukradio.fr; commercial music station; French and Creole.

Other radio stations include: Média Tropical Guadeloupe; Radio Actif; Radio Arago; Radio Basses Internationale; Radio Bélo; Radio Climax; Radio Cosmique One; Radio Côte sous le Vent; Radio Eclair; Radio Horizon; Radio Karata; Radio Madras; Radio Massabielle; Radio Saint-Martin; Radio Saphir; Radio Sofaïa Altitude; Radio Souffle de Vie; Radio Tonic; and Radio Vie Meilleure.

Television

Antilles Télévision (ATV): see Martinique—Television.

Archipel 4: Immeuble Debs-Montauban, 97190 Gosier; tel. 5-93-21-05-20; f. 2002; Chair. JEAN-CLAUDE THOMASEAU.

Canal Plus Antilles: Immeuble Canal Media, Moudong Centre Jarry, 97122 Baie-Mahault; tel. 5-90-38-09-00; fax 5-90-38-09-04; e-mail mrichol@canalantilles.gp; internet www.canalantilles.com; f. 1993; subsidiary of Groupe Canal Plus, France; satellite TV station; Pres. JEAN-NOËL TRONC.

Canal 10: Immeuble CCL, blvd de Houelbourg, ZI de Jarry, BP 2271, 97122 Baie-Mahault; tel. 5-90-26-73-03; fax 5-90-26-61-25; e-mail contact@canal10-tv.com; internet www.canal10-tv.com; f. 1990; focus on social, economic and cultural issues in Guadeloupe; produces 100% of its programmes; Man. MICHEL RODRIGUEZ.

Eclair TV (ETV): Basse-Terre Télévision, Pintade, 97100 Basse-Terre; tel. 5-90-60-15-30; fax 5-90-60-15-33; e-mail eclairfm.com@orange.fr; f. 1998; community station local to Basse-Terre; Pres. (vacant).

La Une Guadeloupe (L'A1): 20 rue Henri Becquerel, Z. I. de Jarry, 97122 Baie-Mahault; tel. 5-90-38-06-06; fax 5-90-38-06-07; f. 1998; fmrly TCI; gen. interest; purchases 65% of programmes from TF1, France (2003); Pres. JOSÉ GADDARKHAN.

Finance

(cap. = capital; res = reserves; dep. = deposits; m. = million; brs = branches; amounts in euros unless otherwise indicated)

BANKING

Central Bank

Institut d'Emission des Départments d'Outre-mer (IEDOM): Parc d'activité la Providence, ZAC de Dothémare, BP 196, 97139 Les Abymes; tel. 5-90-93-74-00; fax 5-90-93-74-25; e-mail iedom-pap-etudes@iedom-guadeloupe.fr; internet www.iedom.fr; Dir LUC LE CABELLEC.

Commercial Banks

Banque des Antilles Françaises: Parc d'Activités de la Jaille, BP 46, Bâtiments 5 et 6, 97122 Baie-Mahault; tel. 5-90-38-50-38; fax 5-90-38-62-92; internet www.bdaf.fr; f. 1967 by merger of Banque de la Martinique and Banque de la Guadeloupe; subsidiary of Financière Océor, France; cap. 12.2m., res –1.9m., dep. 695.3m. (Dec. 2005); Pres. and Chair. CHRISTIAN CAMUS; Gen. Man. JEAN-MARC VARGEL; 19 brs.

Banque Française Commerciale Antilles-Guyane (BFC Antilles-Guyane): Z. I. de Jarry. ZAC de Moudong Sud, 97122 Baie-Mahault; tel. 5-90-25-19-50; fax 5-90-25-19-49; e-mail f.aujoulat@bfc-ag.com; internet www.bfc-ag.com; f. 1976 as br. of Banque Française Commerciale, SA, separated 1984; total assets 594.6m. (2003); Group Dir ANICETTE LUBIN; Gen. Man. JEAN MARGUIER.

BNP Paribas Guadeloupe: pl. de la Rénovation, BP 161, 97155 Pointe-à-Pitre; tel. 5-90-90-58-58; fax 5-90-90-04-07; internet guadeloupe.bnpparibas.net; f. 1941; subsidiary of BNP Paribas, France; CEO JEAN-PIERRE BAJON-ARNAL; Gen. Sec. JEAN-LUC RIVIERE; 12 brs.

BRED Banque Populaire (BRED-BP): Immeuble Simcar, blvd Marquisat de Houelbourg, Z. I. Jarry, 97122 Baie-Mahault; tel. 5-90-89-67-00; internet www.bred.banquepopulaire.fr; cap. 242m. (Oct. 2005); Regional Man. THIERRY MOREAU.

Caisse d'Epargne de la Guadeloupe: 20 Lotissement Plazza II, Grand Camp-La Rocade, 97142 Abymes, BP 22, 97151 Pointe-à-Pitre Cédex; tel. 5-90-93-12-12; fax 5-90-93-12-13; Pres. DANIEL NUCCIO.

Crédit Agricole de la Guadeloupe: Petit Pérou, 97176 Abymes Cédex; tel. 5-90-90-65-65; fax 5-90-90-65-89; e-mail catelnet@ca-guadeloupe.fr; internet www.ca-guadeloupe.fr; total assets 1,228.1m. (Dec. 2003); Pres. CHRISTIAN FLÉREAU; Gen. Man. ROGER WUNSCHEL; 30 brs.

Crédit Maritime de la Guadeloupe: 36 rue Achille René-Boisneuf, BP 292, 97175 Pointe-à-Pitre; tel. 5-90-21-08-40; fax 5-90-89-52-42; e-mail pointe-a-pitre-agence-cmm@creditmaritime.com; internet www.creditmaritime-outremer.com; Dir GÉRARD CADIC; 4 agencies.

Société Générale de Banque aux Antilles (SGBA): I30 rue Frébault, BP 55, 97152 Pointe-à-Pitre; tel. 5-90-25-49-77; fax 5-90-25-49-78; e-mail sgba@wanadoo.fr; internet www.sgba.fr; f. 1979; cap. 26.6m., res –10.0m., dep. 298.3m. (Dec. 2006); Pres. JEAN-LOUIS MATTEI; Gen. Man. MICHEL PECHEUR; 5 brs in Guadeloupe, 3 brs in Martinique.

Development Banks

Banque de Développement de Petites et Moyennes Entreprises (BDPME): c/o AFD, blvd Légitimus, BP 160, 97159 Pointe-à-Pitre Cédex; tel. 5-90-89-65-58; fax 5-90-21-04-55; Rep. MUGUETTE DAIJARDIN.

Société de Crédit pour le Développement de Guadeloupe (SODEGA): Carrefour Raizet Baimbridge, BP 54, 97152 Pointe-à-Pitre; tel. 5-90-82-65-00; fax 5-90-90-17-91; e-mail credit@sodega.fr; internet www.sodega.fr; f. 1970; bought from the Agence Française de Développement (q.v.) by BRED Banque Populaire (q.v.) in 2003.

INSURANCE

Some 30 of the principal European insurance companies are represented in Pointe-à-Pitre, and another six companies have offices in Basse-Terre.

AGF Vie France: Immeuble AGF, ZAC Houelbourg-Jarry, BP 2458, 97085 Jarry; tel. 5-90-41-13-14; fax 5-90-41-96-91; e-mail guaviel@agfgua.com; life insurance.

Capma & Capmi: blvd Légitimus, (face à Air France), 97110 Pointe-à-Pitre; tel. 5-90-83-27-12; fax 5-90-91-19-40.

GAN Guadeloupe: 59–61 rue A. R. Boisneuf, BP152, 97171 Pointe-à-Pitre Cédex; tel. 5-90-89-32-00; fax 5-90-04-43; subsidiary of Groupama, France.

Trade and Industry

GOVERNMENT AGENCIES

Direction de l'Agriculture et de la Forêt (DAF): Jardin Botanique, 97100 Basse-Terre; tel. 5-90-99-09-09; fax 5-90-99-09-10; e-mail webmestre@agriculture.pref.gouv.fr; internet www.guadeloupe.pref.gouv.fr/daf971; Man. GILBERT GRIVAULT.

Direction Régionale des Affaires Maritimes (DRAM): 1 quai Layrle, BP 473, 97164 Pointe-à-Pitre; tel. 5-90-82-03-13; fax 5-90-90-07-33; responsible for shipping, fishing and other maritime issues at a national and community level.

Direction Régionale du Commerce Extérieur Antilles-Guyane (DRCE): see Martinique—Trade and Industry.

Direction Régionale de l'Industrie, de la Recherche et de l'Environnement (DRIRE): 552 rue de la Chapelle, Z. I. Jarry, 97122 Baie-Mahault; tel. 5-90-38-03-47; fax 5-90-38-03-50; e-mail pierre.juan@industrie.gouv.fr; internet www.ggm.drire.gouv.fr; active in industry, business services, transport, public works, tourism and distribution; Departmental Co-ordinator MICHEL MASSON.

DEVELOPMENT ORGANIZATIONS

Agence de l'Environnement et de la Maîtrise de l'Energie (ADEME): Immeuble Café Center, rue Ferdinand Forest, Z. I. Jarry, 97122 Baie-Mahault; tel. 5-90-26-78-05; fax 5-90-26-87-15; e-mail ademe.guadeloupe@ademe.fr; internet www.ademe.fr; developing energy and waste management; Man. GUY SIMONNOT.

Agence Française de Développement (AFD): blvd Légitimus, BP 160, 97154 Pointe-à-Pitre Cédex; tel. 5-90-89-65-65; fax 5-90-83-03-73; internet www.afd.fr; fmrly Caisse Française de Développement; Man. YVES MALPEL.

Agence pour la Promotion des Investissements en Guadeloupe (APRIGA): 12 Convenance's Center, Lieu-dit Convenance, 97122 Baie-Mahault; tel. 5-90-94-45-40; fax 5-90-95-86-47; e-mail apriga@apriga.com; f. 1979; as Agence pour la Promotion de l'Industrie de la Guadeloupe; Pres. LYLIANE PIQUION SALOME.

CHAMBERS OF COMMERCE

Chambre d'Agriculture de la Guadeloupe: Espace régional Agricole, Convenance BP 35, 97122 Baie-Mahault; tel. 5-90-25-17-17; fax 5-90-26-07-22; e-mail cda_direction@guadeloupe.chambagri.fr; Pres. MAURICE RAMASSAMY.

Chambre de Commerce et d'Industrie de Basse-Terre: 6 rue Victor Hugues, 97100 Basse-Terre; tel. 5-90-99-44-44; fax 5-90-81-21-17; e-mail cci-basse-terre@wanadoo.fr; internet www.basseterre.cci.fr; f. 1832; Pres. GÉRARD THÉOBALD; 32 mems.

Chambre de Commerce et d'Industrie de Pointe-à-Pitre: Hôtel Consulaire, rue Félix Eboué, 97110 Pointe-à-Pitre Cédex; tel. 5-90-93-76-00; fax 5-90-90-21-87; e-mail contact@pointe-a-pitre.cci.fr; internet www.pointe-a-pitre.cci.fr; f. 1832; Pres. COLETTE KOURY; Sec. HENRI NAGAPIN; 34 full mems and 17 assoc. mems.

Chambre de Métiers de la Guadeloupe: route Choisy, BP 61, 97120 Saint-Claude; tel. 5-90-80-23-33; fax 5-90-80-08-93; e-mail sgstc@cmguadeloupe.org; internet www.cmguadeloupe.org; Pres. JOËL LOBEAU; 11,630 mems (2005).

Jeune Chambre Economique de Basse-Terre: BP 316, 97100 Basse-Terre; tel. 5-90-81-13-73; e-mail basseterre@jcef.asso.fr; Pres. FABIENNE BOA.

Jeune Chambre Economique de Pointe-à-Pitre: BP 505, 97168 Pointe-à-Pitre Cédex; tel. 5-90-89-01-30; fax 5-90-91-72-98; e-mail pointeapitre@jcef.asso.fr; internet www.jcepap.fr; Pres. XAVIER FLASON.

EMPLOYERS' ORGANIZATIONS

Association des Moyennes et Petites Industries (AMPI): Z.I. Jarry, BP 2325, 97187 Jarry Cédex; tel. 5-90-25-06-28; fax 5-90-25-06-29; e-mail mpi.guadeloupe@wanadoo.fr; f. 1974; Pres. PATRICK DOQUIN; Gen. Sec JEAN JOACHIM; 116 mem. cos.

Interprofession Guadeloupéenne pour la Canne à Sucre (IGUACANNE): Espace Régional Agricole de Convenance, 97122 Baie-Mahault; f. 2005; represents sugar cane growers, sugar producers and professional bodies; Pres. VICTOR NANETTE.

Ordre des pharmaciens du département Guadeloupe: Rocade Forum de Grand Camp, Bâtiment A, No 1, 97142 Pointe-à-Pitre; tel. 5-90-21-66-05; fax 5-90-21-66-07; Pres. CLAUDIE ESPIAND.

Syndicat des Producteurs-Exportateurs de Sucre et de Rhum de la Guadeloupe et Dépendances: Z. I. Jarry, 97122 Baie-Mahault; BP 2015, 97191 Pointe-à-Pitre; tel. 5-90-23-53-15; fax 5-90-23-52-34; f. 1937; Pres. IVAN DE DIEULEVEULT; 4 mems.

Union des Entreprises-Mouvement des Entreprises de France (UDE-MEDEF): Immeuble SCI BTB, voie Principale de Jarry, Baie-Mahault; tel. 5-90-26-83-58; fax 5-90-26-83-67; e-mail ude.medef@medef-guadeloupe.com; Pres. CHRISTIAN VIVIES.

MAJOR COMPANIES

Chantiers Audebert et Cie, SARL: Z. I. de la Pointe Jarry, 97122 Baie-Mahault; tel. 5-90-26-75-40; fax 5-90-26-75-43; e-mail chantier@chantiers-audebert.com; internet www.chantiers-audebert.com; f. 1904; construction equipment; Chair. JEAN AUDEBERT; Gen. Man. DERRICK AUDEBERT; 100 employees.

Compagnie Frigorifique de la Guadeloupe, SARL (COFRIGO): Z. I. de la Pointe Jarry, 97122 Baie-Mahault; tel. 2-55-25-05-90; fax 5-90-26-80-91; e-mail info@cofrigo.fr; internet www.cofrigo.biz; f. 1973; manufacture of soft drinks; Pres. ALAIN HUYGHUES-DESPOINTES; Gen. Man. THIERRY HUYGHUES-DESPOINTES; 87 employees.

Coopérative des Marins-Pêcheurs de la Guadeloupe (COMAPEGA): Port de Pêche de Bergevin, 97110 Pointe-à-Pitre; tel. 5-90-21-46-60; fax 5-90-91-63-78; f. 1976; fishing co-operative; Pres. JEAN-CLAUDE YOYOTTE.

Gardel SA: Usine de Gardel, 97160 Le Moule; tel. 5-90-23-87-96; fax 5-90-23-44-54; f. 1870; 24.48% owned by Saint-Louis Sucre SNC, France; sole sugar refinery.

Groupe Barbotteau et Compagnie: impasse J. M. Jacquart, Z. I. de Jarry, BP 2121, 97191 Jarry Cédex; tel. 5-90-32-56-78; fax 5-90-26-68-89; volume retail and distribution.

Liquoristerie Madras (LIQUOMA): rue Eugene Freyssinet, 97122 Baie-Mahault; tel. 5-90-26-60-28; fax 5-90-26-76-69; f. 1983; production and bottling of cane syrup, rums and other beverages; Man. Dir RAYMOND BICHARA-JABOUR; 20 employees.

SARA (Société Anonyme de la Raffinerie des Antilles): BP 2039, 97191 Jarry Cédex; tel. 5-90-38-13-13; fax 5-90-26-70-98; e-mail francois.nahan@sara.mq; internet www.sara.gp; f. 1970; owned by TotalFinaElf 50%, Shell 24%, Esso 14.5%, Texaco 11.5%; Regional Gen. Man. FRANÇOIS NAHAN; c. 250 employees regionally (see entry in Martinique).

Severin Industrie SARL: Domaine de Séverin, Cadet, 97115 Sainte-Rose; f. 1929; production of alcoholic beverages; Man. JOSEPH MARSOLLE.

Société Des Eaux Thermales Capes Dolé: Lieu-dit Dolé, 97113 Gourbeyre; tel. 5-90-92-10-92; fax 5-90-92-26-19; f. 1968; bottling of mineral water; Man. PATRICK DOQUIN; 21 employees.

Somatco: Z. I. de la Pointe Jarry, impasse Augustin Fresnel, 97122 Baie-Mahault; tel. 5-90-26-71-67; fax 5-90-26-86-24; f. 1980; industrial manufacture of construction materials; Pres. CHRISTIAN BONNARDEL; 17 employees.

UTILITIES

Electricity

Electricité de France Guadeloupe (EdF): BP 85, 97153 Pointe-à-Pitre; tel. 5-90-82-40-34; fax 5-90-83-30-02; e-mail marie-therese.fournier@edfgdf.fr; internet guadeloupe.edf.fr; electricity producer; Man. MAX BORDELAIS.

Water

Veolia Water—Compagnie Générale des Eaux Guadeloupe: Centre de la Guadeloupe, 7 Morne Vergain, BP 17, 97139 Abymes, Pointe-à-Pitre; tel. 5-90-89-76-76; fax 5-90-91-39-10; e-mail mail-elise@gde-guadeloupe.com; internet www.generaledeseaux.gp; fmrly SOGEA; Dir (Americas) AUGUSTE LAURENT.

TRADE UNIONS

Centrale des Travailleurs Unis de la Guadeloupe (CTU): Logement Test 14, Bergevin, 97110 Pointe-à-Pitre; BP 120, 97153 Pointe-à-Pitre Cédex; tel. 5-90-28-96-36; fax 5-90-28-81-16; e-mail ctu.gpe@wanadoo.fr; f. 1999 by merger of the FASU-G and Centrale Syndicale des Travailleurs de la Guadeloupe; represents public and private sector workers; collegial directorate of 11 Secs-Gen; 3,500 mems.

Confédération Générale du Travail de la Guadeloupe (CGTG): 4 Cité Artisanale de Bergevin, BP 779, 97110 Pointe-à-Pitre Cédex; tel. 5-90-82-34-61; fax 5-90-91-04-00; f. 1961; Sec.-Gen. JEAN-MARIE NOMERTIN; 5,000 mems.

Fédération Départementale des Syndicats d'Exploitants de la Guadeloupe (FDSEA): Chambre d'Agriculture, Rond-Point de Destrellan, 97122 Baie-Mahault; tel. 5-90-26-06-47; fax 5-90-26-48-

82; e-mail fdsea5@wanadoo.fr; affiliated to the Fédération Nationale des Syndicats d'Exploitants; Pres. FIRMIN LODIN NELSON.

Fédération Syndicale Unitaire Guadeloupe (FSU): 2108 Immeuble Cap. Moede, 97142 Grand Camp; tel. 5-90-90-10-21; fax 5-90-90-29-42; e-mail fsu971@fsu.fr; f. 1993; departmental br. of the Fédération Syndicale Unitaire; represents public sector employees in teaching, research and training, and also agriculture, justice, youth and sports, and culture; Sec. JOSÉ SEVERIEN.

SGEN-CFDT: Maison Test 14, BP 676, Bergevin, 97169 Pointe-à-Pitre; tel. 5-90-83-16-50; fax 5-90-91-78-02; e-mail guadeloupe@sgen.cfdt.fr; affiliated to the Fédération des Syndicats Généraux de l'Education Nationale et de la Recherche; represents teaching staff.

Union Départementale de la Confédération Française des Travailleurs Chrétiens (UD CFTC): 29 rue Victor Hugo, BP 245, 97159 Pointe-à-Pitre Cédex; tel. 5-90-82-04-01; f. 1937; Sec.-Gen. ALBERT SARKIS; 3,500 mems.

Union Départementale des Syndicats Force Ouvrière: 59 rue Lamartine, BP 687, 97110 Pointe-à-Pitre; tel. 5-90-82-86-83; fax 5-90-82-16-12; e-mail udfoguadeloupe@force-ouvriere.fr; Gen. Sec. MAX EVARISTE; 1,500 mems.

Union Générale des Travailleurs de la Guadeloupe (UGTG): rue Paul Lacavé, 97110 Pointe-à-Pitre; tel. 5-90-83-10-07; fax 5-90-89-08-70; e-mail ugtg@ugtg.org; internet www.ugtg.org; f. 1973; confederation of pro-independence trade unions incl. Union des Agents de la Sécurité Sociale (UNASS), l'Union des Employés du Commerce (UEC), Union des Travailleurs de l'Etat et du Département (UTED), l'Union des Travailleurs des Collectivités (UTC), l'Union des Travailleurs de l'Hôtellerie, du Tourisme et de la Restauration (UTHTR), l'Union des Travailleurs des Produits Pétroliers (UTPP), l'Union des Travailleurs de la Santé (UTS), and l'Union des Travailleurs des Télécommunications (UTT); Gen. Sec. ELIE DOMOTA; 4,000 mems.

Union des Moyennes et Petites Entreprises de Guadeloupe (UMPEG): 17 Immeuble Patio, Grand Camp, 97142 Abymes, Pointe-à-Pitre; tel. 5-90-91-79-31; fax 5-90-93-09-18.

Union Régionale Guadeloupe: Immeuble Jabol, 5ème étage, rue de l'Assainissement, 97110 Pointe-à-Pitre; tel. 5-90-91-01-15; fax 5-90-83-08-64; e-mail m.alidor@aol.fr; internet www.unsa.org; mem. of l'Union Nationale des Syndicats Autonomes (UNSA).

UNSA Education Guadeloupe: Immeuble Jabol, 5ème étage, rue de l'Assainissement, 97110 Pointe-à-Pitre; tel. 5-90-91-01-15; fax 5-90-83-08-64; e-mail pelage.girard@wanadoo.fr; Sec.-Gen. GIRARD PELAGE.

Transport

RAILWAYS

There are no railways in Guadeloupe.

ROADS

In 1990 there were 2,069 km (1,286 miles) of roads in Guadeloupe, of which 323 km were Routes Nationales.

SHIPPING

The Port Autonome de la Guadeloupe comprises five sites. The two principal seaports are at Pointe-à-Pitre, which offers both cargo-handling and passenger facilities, and the container terminal at Jarry (Baie-Mahault); the smaller port of Basse-Terre caters to freight and inter-island passenger traffic. There is also a sugar terminal at Folle-Anse (Saint-Louis); and a marina at Bas-du-Fort with 1,000 berths for pleasure craft.

Compagnie Générale Maritime Antilles-Guyane: 30 blvd de la Pointe, Z. I. Jarry, BP 92, 97122 Baie-Mahault; tel. 5-90-25-57-00; fax 5-90-26-74-62; e-mail ptp.dhouzard@cma-cgm.com; subsidiary of CMA-CGM, France; shipping agents, stevedoring; Gen. Man. DOMINIQUE HOUZARD.

Port Autonome de la Guadeloupe: Quai Ferdinand de Lesseps, BP 485, 97165 Pointe-à-Pitre Cédex; tel. 5-90-68-61-70; fax 5-90-68-61-71; e-mail v-sene@port-guadeloupe.com; internet www.port-guadeloupe.com; port authority; Pres. GIL THÉMINE; Gen. Man. LAURENT MARTENS.

> **Compagnie Générale Portuaire:** Marina Bas-du-Fort, 97110 Pointe-à-Pitre; tel. 5-90-93-66-20; fax 5-90-90-81-53; e-mail marina@marina-pap.com; internet www.caribbean-marinas.com; port authority; Man. PHILIPPE CHEVALLIER; Harbour Master TONY BRESLAU; 1,000 berths for non-commercial traffic.

Société Guadeloupéenne de Consignation et Manutention (SGCM): 8 rue de la Chapelle, BP 2360, 97001 Jarry Cédex; tel. 5-90-38-05-55; fax 5-90-26-95-39; e-mail gerard.petrelluzzi@sgcm.fr; internet www.sgcm.gp; f. 1994; shipping agents, stevedoring; also operates Navimar Cruises inter-island tour co; Chair. BERNARD AUBERY; Gen. Man. GERARD PETRELLUZZI; 17 berths.

Société de Transport Maritimes Brudey Frères: 78 centre St John Perse, 97110 Pointe-à-Pitre; tel. 5-90-91-60-87; fax 5-90-93-00-79; e-mail brudey.freres@wanadoo.fr; internet www.brudey-freres.fr; f. 1983; inter-island ferry service; Dir DENIS BRUDEY; 6 vessels; c. 400,000 passengers per year.

Transcaraïbes S.A.: BP 2453, 97085 Pointe-à-Pitre; tel. 5-90-26-63-27; fax 5-90-26-67-49; e-mail transcaraibes.gpe@wanadoo.fr; f. 1976; shipping agents, stevedoring; office in Martinique; Gen. Man. PASCAL PEDROSA.

CIVIL AVIATION

Raizet International Airport is situated 3 km (2 miles) from Pointe-à-Pitre and is equipped to handle jet-engined aircraft. There are smaller airports on the islands of Marie-Galante, La Désirade and Saint-Barthélémy.

Air Caraïbes (CAT): ZAC de Dothemare, 97139 Abymes; tel. 5-90-82-47-41; fax 5-90-82-47-49; e-mail drh@aircaraibes.com; internet www.aircaraibes.com; f. 2000 following merger of Air St Martin, Air St Barts, Air Guadeloupe and Air Martinique; owned by Groupe Dubreuil; operates daily inter-island, regional and international services within the Caribbean, and flights to Brazil, French Guiana and Paris; CEO SERGE TSYGALNITZKY; 16 aircraft; 800,000 passengers (2006).

> **Air Caraïbes Atlantique:** Aéroport, 97232 Le Lamentin; f. 2003; subsidiary of Air Caraïbes; services between Pointe-à-Pitre, Fort-de-France (Martinique) and Paris; Pres. FRANÇOIS HERSEN.

Tourism

Guadeloupe is a popular tourist destination, especially for visitors from metropolitan France (who account for some 89% of tourists) and the USA. The main attractions are the beaches, the mountainous scenery and the unspoilt beauty of the island dependencies. In 2006 some 433,358 tourists visited Guadeloupe. Receipts from tourism totalled US $344m. in 2007. In 2005 there were 93 hotels, with some 6,632 rooms.

Comité du Tourisme: 5 sq. de la Banque, BP 555, 97166 Pointe-à-Pitre Cédex; tel. 5-90-82-09-30; fax 5-90-83-89-22; e-mail info@lesilesdeguadeloupe.com; internet www.lesilesdeguadeloupe.com; Pres. JOSETTE BOREL-LINCERTIN; Dir THIERRY GARGAR.

Délégation Régionale au Tourisme: 5 rue Victor Hugues, 97100 Basse-Terre; tel. 5-90-81-10-44; fax 5-90-81-94-82; e-mail drtourisme.guadeloupe@wanadoo.fr; Dir JEAN FRANÇOIS DESBROCHES.

Syndicat d'Initiative de Pointe-à-Pitre: Centre Commercial de la Marina, 97110 Pointe-à-Pitre; tel. 5-90-90-70-02; fax 5-90-90-74-70; e-mail syndicatinitiativedepap@wanadoo.fr; internet www.sivap.gp; Pres. DENYS FORTUNE.

Defence

As assessed at November 2009, France maintained a military force of about 1,225 in Fort-de-France (Martinique).

Education

The education system is similar to that of metropolitan France (see chapter on French Guiana). In 2002/03 there were 136 pre-primary and 220 primary schools. In 2000/01 secondary education was provided at 35 institutions. In 2008/09 there were 22,411 students in pre-primary and 37,650 in primary education, while in secondary education there were 52,547 students, of whom some 90% attended state schools. There were also two teacher-training institutes, and colleges of agriculture, fisheries, hotel management, nursing, midwifery and child care. A branch of the Université des Antilles et de la Guyane, at Pointe-à-Pitre, has faculties of law and economics, sciences, medicine, sports science and humanities. In 2007/08 there was a total of 8,718 students in higher education.

Bibliography

For works on the Caribbean generally, see Select Bibliography (Books)

Bangou, H. (Ed.). *La Guadeloupe et sa décolonisation ou un demi-siècle d'enfantement*. Paris, Editions L'Harmattan, 2003.

Belenus, R. *L'esclave en Guadeloupe et en Martinique du XVIIe au XIXe siècles*. Pointe-à-Pitre, Editions Jasor, 1998.

Cérol, J. (Mazama A.) *Langue et identité en Guadeloupe: Une perspective afrocentrique*. Pointe-à-Pitre, Editions Jasor, 1997.

Destouches, D. *Du statut colonial au statut départemental: l'administration révolutionnaire en Guadeloupe (1787-An X)*. Aix-en-Provence, Presses Universitaires d'Aix-Marseille, 2007.

Feler, A. *Histoire des télécommunications à la Guadeloupe*. Pointe-à-Pitre, Editions Jasor, 2002.

Goslinga, M. *Guadeloupe*. Oxford, ABC Clio, 1999.

Jeangoudoux, A. *Français de Souches*. Pointe-à-Pitre, Editions Jasor, 2005.

Jennings, E. T. *Vichy in the Tropics*. Stanford, CA, Stanford University Press, 2001.

Lefort, J. *Chronique intempestive de la télévision de proximité en Guadeloupe*. Pointe-à-Pitre, Editions Jasor, 2003.

Orizio, R. *Lost White Tribes: The End of Privilege and the Last Colonials in Sri Lanka, Jamaica, Brazil, Haiti, Namibia and Guadeloupe*. Mississauga, ON, Random House of Canada, 2001.

Smeralda, J. *Peau noire, cheveu crépu*. Pointe-à-Pitre, Editions Jasor, 2005.

Valérius, R. *La Guadeloupe d'en-France*. Pointe-à-Pitre, Editions Jasor, 2005.

GUATEMALA

Geography

PHYSICAL FEATURES

The Republic of Guatemala is in Central America, apart from Belize the country furthest north on the isthmus, its territory abutting into the Yucatán peninsula. Its longest border (962 km or 597 miles), therefore, is with the North American country of Mexico, which lies to the north and the north-west (Campeche is to the north, Tabasco in the north-west and Chiapas stretches west). To the south-east, further down the trunk of Central America, are El Salvador (beyond a 203-km frontier) on the Pacific Ocean and, further north, Honduras (with a 256-km border). The long Pacific coast faces south and south-west. Apart from a relatively short, north-facing shore with no natural harbours at the marshy head of the Gulf of Honduras, the country is isolated from the Caribbean coast by Belize, which lies to the east of northern Guatemala. The border with Belize is 266 km long, but Guatemala maintains claims on territory in the south of the former British colony, as well as rights of access to the Caribbean. The Organization of American States is mediating the dispute, which also gave rise to the protocols of 2000 that govern a buffer territory within the 'Lines of Adjacency', a zone 2 km wide bisected by the common border. The area of Guatemala is 108,889 sq km (42,042 sq miles).

The extent of the country is about 450 km (north–south) by 430 km, and it has about 400 km of coastline, mostly on the Pacific. Guatemala is mostly mountainous (66%), with narrow coastal plains and a rolling limestone plateau in the north. It is heavily forested (62%), woodland types varying from warm and humid, through cool and humid to warm and dry, which, together with the altitude and two coasts, contributes to the variety of flora and fauna. The most spectacular of the many bird species in the country is the national bird, the quetzal, but another noteworthy example might be the ocellated turkey, while the largest native mammal is a fresh water sea cow (manatee) found in Lake Izabal, in the east. There are volcanoes in the mountains, indicating that the country is an area prone to seismic activity. A volcano is actually the highest point not only in Guatemala, but in all of Central America—Tajumulco, at 4,211 m or 13,821 ft—and is found at the western end of the main mountain chain, in the south-west of the country. The main mountain range of the high plateau of the south-west is the Sierra Madre, which echoes the line of the Rockies and the Andes in the continents to north and south, and it runs roughly east–west above the Pacific coast. There is a branching range, the Sierra de los Chuchumatanes, which thrusts more to the north-west, and other highlands in this area include the Sierra Chaucus, the Montañas del Mico and the Sierra de Chama. Most of the country's volcanoes are on the central plateau. The three other topographical regions are less lofty. South of the mountains is the Pacific coast, which consists of tropical savannah plains and lagoons, and is traversed by 18 short rivers. North of the central plateau and in the east of the country are the lower slopes and more easterly out-thrusts of the Continental Divide (such as the Sierra de las Minas), giving way to the often swampy Caribbean flatlands. This region is dominated by three deep river valleys (of the Motagua, the Polochic and the Sarstun). Finally, north of here, occupying most of northern Guatemala and mainly beyond the Maya Mountains is the water-eroded limestone plateau of El Petén, dotted with lakes and densely cloaked in tropical forest, watered by heavy, year-round rain. The largest lakes are not in this area, however, with the 800-sq-km Izabal (also known as the Dulce gulf) in the Caribbean lowlands and the famously beautiful, 126-sq-km Atitlán in the central highlands.

CLIMATE

The climate is tropical, hot and humid, especially on the Caribbean coast and in the El Petén lowlands, but it is cooler

in the highlands. The Caribbean coast is also prone to hurricanes and other tropical storms. Average annual rainfall varies from as low as 510 mm (20 ins) in the eastern highlands to 2,540 mm (100 ins) in the north. The average maximum and minimum temperatures in Guatemala City, the capital, which is located on the central plateau, range from 12°–23°C (54°–73°F) in January to 16°–29°C (61°–84°F) in May. May is the end of the dry season and the start of the rainy season.

POPULATION

Guatemala has the largest surviving indigenous population in Central America. The normally dominant Mestizo population of mixed-Spanish descent (including assimilated Amerindians), here known as Ladino, accounts for barely 55% of the total. Often included with the Ladinos are the small populations of more purely Spanish descent and of other non-indigenous origins, such as Syrians and Lebanese, Asians and the Garifuna (Black Caribs, mainly of African descent, with some Amerindian ancestry, settled on the Caribbean coast). Amerindian peoples, however, account for 43% of the population. That they are concentrated in the countryside may obscure the veracity of the figure, with some claiming the Amerindians, the Mayas, account for almost two-thirds of the population. Spanish is the official language and is spoken by 60% of the population, but there is some official status for Garifuna (Carib) and around 20 of the 50 or so Mayan languages spoken in the country. The main Mayan language groups spoken in Guatemala are Quiché (Kiche), Cakchiquel, Mam and Kelchi. It is not only language that survives among the Maya, but also some traditional religious beliefs and practices, although usually syncretized with the dominant Roman Catholic Christianity. Certainly more than three-quarters of the population claim to adhere to the Church, although campaigning Protestant groups from North America gained up to one-fifth of the population over the last decades of the 20th century. There are also small groups of Orthodox Catholics ('Uniates'), Buddhists, Jews, Muslims and 'Moonies' (followers of the Unification Church).

In mid-2010 the people of Guatemala, sometimes informally referred to as 'Chapines', numbered an estimated 14.4m., making Guatemala the most populous nation in Central America. Most of the population lives in the temperate valleys of the highlands, in the south-centre of the country, around the capital. The capital is Guatemala City (which numbered some 1,104,000 residents in mid-2010). The other chief cities of the highlands, to the north-west of the capital, are Quetzaltenango and Sololá. Livingston, on the Caribbean coast, is not a large city, but it is the chief town of the east, while Flores is the main centre of El Petén. The country is divided into 22 departments.

History

DIEGO SÁNCHEZ-ANCOCHEA

Revised for this edition by the editorial staff

PRE-HISPANIC, COLONY AND EARLY REPUBLIC

The territory of modern-day Guatemala was occupied as early as 2000 BC by fishing and farming villages. These gave rise to the Maya civilization, which became one of the most important in the continent. Extending to what is now southern Mexico, Honduras, Belize and El Salvador, the Maya civilization reached its height between AD 600 and 900. When Spanish conquistadors arrived in the early 16th century they encountered fragmented ethnic groups, dispersed between different kingdoms, fighting for political and economic domination. Military superiority, exploitation of political differences, and the devastating effect of diseases of European origin on the indigenous population provided the invaders with the opportunity to secure a swift and decisive victory. Spanish settlers subsequently appropriated both land and labour, which were ruthlessly exploited.

The so-called Capitanía General del Reino de Guatemala—which included the five current Central American countries and Chiapas (now a state of Mexico)—attained independence from Spain peacefully in September 1821. The move towards independent statehood was led by wealthy landowners and businessmen, mainly of Spanish origin (Creoles). The resultant new federal, political and administrative entity, the United Provinces of Central America, was dissolved in 1839, owing to internal conflicts. The current geographical territory of Guatemala was established later in the century, following the loss of Belize to the United Kingdom and Chiapas to Mexico. From the mid-19th century onwards Guatemala invested heavily in the development of coffee plantations, which had become the main source of national income by the end of the century. After the Liberal revolution of 1871, the country was integrated into the global market by the rapid expansion of agro-exports. As a result of the introduction of new legislation and the creation of a national army, Liberal governments institutionalized a more coercive role for the state in promoting agrarian capitalism. Indigenous peoples lost huge swathes of their communal lands, which were incorporated into large landholdings dedicated to the production of coffee exports. Hundreds of European settlers, particularly Germans, were attracted by the prospect of favourable grants of land and labour to aid in the development of agro-exports. The rights and obligations of rural employers and workers were codified in the late 19th century in a series of agricultural laws, which refined and intensified traditional practices of debt peonage. During the first two decades of the 20th century the Government of Manuel Estrada Cabrera opened the country to capital investment from the USA. This monopolized services such as railways, ports, electricity and maritime transport, as well as the international mail service. US monopoly capital was also used to acquire significant land holdings, as the United Fruit Company procured large tracts for the development of banana plantations.

In 1944, after 14 years in power, Gen. Jorge Ubico, the last representative of the Liberal reforms of 1871, was overthrown by a popular uprising led by nationalist members of the army and progressive intellectuals, who were inspired by US President Franklin Delano Roosevelt's 'Four Freedoms' address to the US Congress in 1941. The so-called 'October Revolution' led to presidential elections, which were won by a civilian, Juan José Arévalo. Arévalo introduced a series of economic and social reforms, including universal male suffrage, the establishment of a social security system for state employees and a new labour code. His successor, Col Jacobo Arbenz Guzmán, who acceded to the presidency in 1950, enhanced these measures and initiated a radical agrarian reform, which encouraged the organization of peasant leagues throughout the countryside and benefited some 100,000 families by expropriating uncultivated lands from large landowners and the United Fruit Company. At the height of the Cold War, concerned by the influence of the communist Partido Guatemalteco del Trabajo (PGT) within the Arbenz administration, the recently created US Central Intelligence Agency (CIA) exploited discontent within the Guatemalan army and private sector and organized a military invasion from Honduras, which overthrew the Arbenz Government in June 1954. The counter-revolution reversed most of the reforms of the previous decades, began a systematic process of political persecution of government supporters, and installed a series of anti-communist regimes dominated by the armed forces. During the late 1970s the ability of these military regimes to govern deteriorated, as a result both of splits within the ruling coalition and of their lack of popular legitimacy. Elections held in 1974, 1978 and 1982 were openly fraudulent.

GUERRILLA WARFARE AND COUNTER-INSURGENCY

Beginning in the early 1960s an armed opposition developed, originating from a schism within the army, but later garnering widespread indigenous support in the rural areas. Guerrilla and anti-guerrilla warfare ensued for more than three decades. Some 200,000 Guatemalans were either killed or disappeared during this period, largely as a result of state military operations against civilians, particularly rural Mayan communities suspected of supporting the insurgency. Mass violations of human rights under the military Government of Gen. Fernando Romeo Lucas García (1978–82) led the US Administration of Jimmy Carter (1977–81) to suspend military aid to Guatemala (only resumed in 1985 under President Ronald Reagan). In February 1982 three different guerrilla organizations and the PGT formed a guerrilla coalition, the Unidad Revolucionaria Nacional Guatemalteca (URNG). At their height the guerrillas were operating in 18 of the country's 22 departments. Divisions within the army over the prosecution of the war also facilitated two military coups during this period. The first took place on 23 March 1982 and was led by Gen. Efrain Ríos Montt, a former Christian Democrat candidate and, latterly, evangelical preacher, who was denied the presidency in 1974, owing to electoral fraud. Gen. Ríos Montt's 15 months in office are widely regarded as having been the most violent in the country's modern history. He intensified the counter-insurgency offensive, and in the first year of his regime more than 15,000 Guatemalans were assassinated, mainly among the Mayan rural population, 70,000 fled the country, and some 500,000 were displaced internally. Hundreds of villages were eradicated, destroyed by systematic army massacres. In the rural areas all men between the ages of 16 and 60 were forced to participate in paramilitary civil defence patrols, which, at their height, comprised some 1m. peasants. 'Model villages', under strict army control, were established as detention centres for those across the country who had been displaced by war. The military operations of the guerrilla movement declined dramatically during this period, overwhelmed by the superior firepower and ruthless tactics of the army. In August 1983 Gen. Ríos Montt was overthrown by his Minister of Defence, Gen. Oscar Humberto Mejía Víctores. The new military regime restored the promotional hierarchy that had been disrupted by the former Government, and promised a swift return to constitutional rule, while enforcing a continued programme of counter-insurgency and political repression.

CIVILIAN RULE AND PEACE PROCESS

By the mid-1980s there was a consensus within the higher echelons of the military that Guatemala should shift to civilian rule if it was to change its international status as a pariah. On 1 July 1984 a Constituent Assembly was elected; the promulgation of a new Constitution in 1985 and the holding of general elections in the same year ushered in a period of elected civilian rule and a limited relaxation of the military's control over national affairs. However, the key institutions of the counter-insurgency, such as the civil patrols, were legalized by the new Constitution, which provided a framework for civilian government throughout the 1980s. Although the URNG boycotted the presidential elections held in November 1985, the centre-right Christian Democrat candidate, Vinicio Cerezo, won them by an ample margin. Despite high hopes for the new civilian Government, Cerezo did not challenge the dominance of the military or address the country's acute socio-economic problems. Rising prices for industrial imports, coupled with falling prices for Central America's primary export products, meant that the Guatemalan economy suffered negative growth rates during the 1980s; unemployment and inflation reached unprecedented levels. Overall levels of poverty increased significantly in the second half of the decade, and by the end of the 1980s nearly 90% of the population were living below the poverty line (compared with 79% in 1980); approximately three-quarters of the population were living in extreme poverty. The social and economic crisis led to the re-emergence of social movements and civic protests, despite the harsh repressive measures that this evinced from the military. After the 1985 election the URNG proposed that the armed conflict be settled by negotiation, and in October 1987 representatives of the Government and the URNG met for the first time in Madrid, Spain, to initiate discussions. The meeting was a direct result of the regional 'Esquipulas II Accord', signed two months previously by all six Central American republics in search of a political resolution to the region's armed conflicts. On 30 March 1990 the guerrilla movement and the Government agreed to both a framework for negotiations and to a mediating role for the UN and consultative status for the Comisión Nacional de Reconciliación (CNR—National Commission for Reconciliation), a coalition of national civic groups led by the head of the Guatemalan Bishops' Conference, Rodolfo Quezada Toruño. However, the peace talks stalled within months, owing to the army's insistence upon a full demobilization of the URNG prior to a final settlement and an amnesty on human rights violations.

Presidential and congressional elections held in November 1990 registered abstention rates of 70%. No parties of the left were permitted to participate. Jorge Serrano Elías, an evangelical leader and former member of the 1982–83 Ríos Montt Government, won the second round of voting, held in January 1991. The new Government reinitiated peace negotiations with the guerrilla movement, and meetings were held in Cuernavaca, Mexico, in April. Meanwhile, the domestic political situation deteriorated; human rights organizations reported some 1,750 human rights violations, including 650 extra-judicial executions, during the first nine months of the Serrano Government. The USA once again suspended military aid to Guatemala and, together with the World Bank and the European Parliament, exerted pressure upon the Government to bring an end to the political violence. In October 1992 Rigoberta Menchú, a Guatemalan Maya-K'iche' woman and indigenous human rights activist, won the Nobel Peace Prize, focusing global attention on the perpetuation of human rights violations in the country, and also signalling the emergence of an increasingly organized Mayan, indigenous, popular movement. Facing a mounting crisis of legitimacy, President Serrano, supported by a faction of the military, mounted a so-called *autogolpe* 'self-coup' in May 1993, attempting to suspend significant constitutional guarantees and dissolve the Congreso (Congress) and the Supreme Court. However, in the face of domestic and international opposition the coup ultimately proved unsuccessful, and a few days later Serrano abandoned the country for exile in Panama.

The then ombudsman for human rights, Ramiro de León Carpio, was designated interim President by the Congreso on 6 June 1993 to enable the completion of Serrano's presidential term. His cousin, Jorge Carpio Nicolle, a political leader and newspaper tycoon who had been defeated by Serrano in the second round of the 1991 election, was assassinated shortly after de León assumed power. The end of the Cold War, and the successful negotiation of settlements of conflicts in neighbouring Nicaragua and El Salvador, favoured those sectors supporting a negotiated end to the armed conflict. Yet disenchantment with domestic democratic politics persisted—a referendum to approve a series of constitutional reforms in 1994 registered an abstention rate of 85%. The hardline, populist Frente Republicano Guatemalteco (FRG), headed by the former de facto chief of state, Gen. (retd) Ríos Montt, obtained a congressional majority in elections held in the same year. In January 1994 the Government and the guerrilla movement signed a framework agreement for the resumption of peace talks in Mexico. In March a comprehensive agreement on human rights was signed following discussions held in Oslo, Norway, which was to enter into immediate effect (unlike the other accords, which would be implemented only at the end of the entire peace process) with *in situ* verification by the UN. Before the end of the year the guerrilla movement and the Government had signed an agreement, with UN verification, for the protection of human rights. A further agreement established conditions for the resettlement of displaced populations. Most controversial was the June 1994 accord that delineated the terms of a Commission for Historical Clarification, or truth commission, to investigate human rights violations committed during the armed conflict. Despite the efforts of domestic and international human rights organizations, the final agreement stated that the commission's report would not individualize responsibility for gross violations—this was widely interpreted as being a concession to the hardline element within the military. In March 1995 another wide-ranging agreement relating to the identity and rights of Guatemala's indigenous population (which constitutes 50%–60% of the total population) was signed. This was the only accord in the formulation of which civic groups played a significant role, through the consultative forum of the Civil Society Assembly (ASC), created in 1994 to replace the CNR. By mid-1995 peace negotiations had stalled again, a consequence of the declining strength of the de León Government and a lack of political will on the part of military and civilian élites.

The presidential election held in November 1995 led to a second round of voting, won by Alvaro Enrique Arzú Yrigoyen of the Partido de Avanzada Nacional (PAN), a party representing the interests of the private sector, in January 1996. Arzú, a businessman, former mayor of Guatemala City and Minister of Foreign Affairs during the first months of Serrano's Government, won a close electoral race against Alfonso Portillo of the FRG. The rate of abstention was approximately 63%. The new administration advanced the peace process and gave new impetus to its development. Arzú appointed prominent business leaders to key government posts, securing the private sector's commitment to the peace negotiations. New peace accords, arguably some of the most controversial, were signed in 1996, before a final settlement was reached in December. The accords included an agreement on socio-economic issues and the agrarian situation, committing the Government to increase social spending and to fund a land bank through which landless peasants could acquire land. Another strengthened civilian rule and defined the function of the army in a democratic society, specifying the terms by which military power would be gradually reduced. A number of enabling accords were signed in December, including those referring to: constitutional reform and the electoral regime; the legalization of the URNG; the conclusion of a definitive cease-fire; and the final accord for a firm and lasting peace, which was signed in Guatemala City on 29 December in the presence of UN Secretary-General, Dr Boutros Boutros-Ghali. The rebels disarmed shortly afterwards, under UN supervision, and the URNG subsequently became a legal political party.

POST-ACCORD POLITICS

The period immediately following the achievement of the negotiated settlement was dominated by attempts to implement the reforms promised in the various accords, and by efforts to investigate past violations of human rights. In April 1998 a report by the Roman Catholic Church's Oficina de Derechos Humanos del Arzobispado (ODHA—Archbishopric's Human Rights Office) documenting gross violations of human rights that had occurred during the armed conflict attributed more than 85% of war atrocities to the army and army-controlled paramilitary forces and 10% to the URNG. In February 1999 the UN Report of Historical Clarification, based on over 9,000 testimonies, went further, attributing 93% of atrocities to the army and 3% to the URNG. The UN report demonstrated that the army had committed acts of genocide (as defined by international law) legitimated by state policy during the 1981–83 period. However, the costs of such investigations were high—Juan José Gerardi Conadera, the bishop in charge of the 1998 ODHA report, was murdered just days after its publication. It took three years and the exertion of immense international pressure for domestic courts to find three army officers guilty of his extra-judicial execution. Guatemalan human rights organizations attempting to secure the prosecution of former army officers in domestic and international courts for gross violations of human rights were subject to continuing intimidation and violence.

In March 1999 the peace settlement suffered a serious reverse when a referendum on a package of constitutional reforms agreed by the legislature to implement the peace agreements was rejected with a turn-out of less than 25%, slowing implementation of the settlement almost to a standstill. The FRG candidate, Alfonso Portillo Cabrera, won the 1999 presidential election held in December. Although the FRG was formally committed to the implementation of the peace agreements (a key feature of the prevailing conditions by which international aid was granted), the party lacked the commitment of the Arzú administration to the process, divided as it was between moderates and hardliners, the latter allied with party founder, Ríos Montt, who maintained a powerful position as the President of the Congreso. The weakness of the public security and justice systems and the growth of organized crime meant that the increasing problem of crime and public insecurity had reached unprecedented levels by the end of the decade. The state-orchestrated violence of the 1980s was replaced by a wave of kidnappings, armed assaults and robberies, leading to escalating public alarm about law and order and calls for more stringent penal measures, such as the introduction of the death penalty for kidnappers, which was approved in 1996. Meanwhile, the implementation of the demilitarization agreed in the September 1996 accord met with numerous obstacles; although the size of the armed forces was reduced by one-third as stipulated, the reform of military intelligence institutions was slow. The UN repeatedly raised concerns that the military budget was being expanded and that the new civilian police force was becoming increasingly militarized. Consistently high levels of violence and crime with impunity led the population to resort to private justice; levels of gun ownership and homicide continued to increase and suspected criminals were subjected to mob lynchings.

The Portillo administration was characterized by growing conflict between the Government and the private sector, which opposed the former's attempts to raise taxes—a key demand of the IMF and bilateral donors. Discontent over the Portillo administration's lacklustre record in office, multiple corruption scandals involving high-ranking government officials, and poor fiscal management became increasingly manifest. Relations with the USA were also strained, in large part owing to the growth in drugs-trafficking, which was often linked to government officials. Fiscal weakness and divisions between the Portillo Government and Ríos Montt's faction of the FRG continued to undermine the administration's coherence. Until 2004 the country remained on the so-called 'blacklist' of countries considered to be unco-operative in the fight against money-laundering, drawn up by the Financial Action Task Force on Money Laundering (FATF), based in Paris, France.

THE GOVERNMENT OF OSCAR BERGER PERDOMO

In Guatemala's highly fragmented and unstable political party system, parties have tended to be vehicles for élite interests rather than organizations promoting a coherent programme for government. Politicians often switch their party loyalties once elected, according to their calculations for future electoral advantage. Since the return to democracy in 1985 no incumbent party has ever been re-elected to office. The FRG proved no exception to this rule and the discredited party lost power in the presidential and legislative elections in November 2003. In the first round of voting, Oscar Berger Perdomo of the centre-right Gran Alianza Nacional (GANA—Great National Alliance) won 34.3% of the votes cast, followed by Alvaro Colom Caballeros of the centre-left Unidad Nacional de la Esperanza (UNE—National Unity of Hope). Ríos Montt, the FRG candidate, attracted just 19.3% of the ballot, effectively sealing the end of his presidential ambitions. Following a second round of voting between the two leading candidates Berger emerged victorious, winning 54.1% of the vote.

Confidence in state institutions had been severely eroded during the Portillo Government, and on assuming office in January 2004 Berger launched an anti-corruption campaign, giving rise to dozens of investigations into alleged illicit activities and corrupt practices by former government officials. Although denounced by former government members as a political 'witch-hunt', these measures received strong support from the USA and won some much-needed popular support for the Berger Government. However, the new Government was based on an unstable coalition and lacked a congressional majority, making it far weaker than the previous PAN administration. Because of this Berger's Government pursued a minimalist agenda and made little progress in addressing social and economic inequalities, as mandated by the peace accords.

The Berger Government also witnessed rising social discontent in response to increases in rates of inflation, unemployment and poverty, as well as to worsening domestic security. The rapid increase in violent crime continued to be a major public—and international—concern, threatening to undermine the development agenda. More than 5,500 homicides were committed in 2006, higher than the death rate in the final years of the civil war. Guatemala remained one of the most violent countries in the western hemisphere. Gang violence increased exponentially in the early 21st century: violent killings of alleged gang, or *mara*, members became an almost daily occurrence. Violence against women also increased to unprecedented levels: in 2003 women accounted for 9.0% of all murders, rising to 11.7% and 12.5% in 2004 and 2005, respectively. Very few of these crimes were officially investigated. In March 2007 the UN Special Rapporteur on extra-judicial, summary or arbitrary executions, Philip Alston, presented a damning report that held the Guatemalan state accountable for the rising violence that had afflicted the country since the end of the civil war in 1996. The report found that less than 10% of murders resulted in a criminal conviction, largely owing to corruption and the inefficiency of the justice system. Human rights organizations denounced systematic campaigns of 'social cleansing', involving murder and torture of youths accused of being gang members. A number of violent prison riots involving confrontations between organized *maras* also resulted in a high death toll. Both UN and human rights organizations expressed concern at the rising influence of organized criminal networks on the formal political system. The murder of three Salvadorean congressional deputies in Guatemala in February 2007 and the subsequent assassination in prison of the four Guatemalan policemen arrested in connection with the crime (and therefore due to give evidence in court) pointed to the existence of so-called 'death squads' within the Ministry of the Interior, forcing the resignation of the Minister of the Interior Carlos Vielmann Montes. A special UN Commission to investigate illegal and clandestine groups involved in organized crime (sometimes referred to as 'parallel powers'), the Comisión Internacional contra la Impunidad en Guatemala (CICIG—International Commission against Impunity in Guatemala), was approved by the UN and the Government in December 2006. Despite considerable domestic political opposition, legislation to establish the Commission was overwhelmingly approved by the Congreso Nacional in August 2007, and it was formally constituted in September.

THE 2007 ELECTIONS AND THE TROUBLES OF THE NEW COLOM ADMINISTRATION

Security issues dominated the campaign for the presidential and legislative elections held on 9 September 2007. More than 40 people were killed in the months preceding the vote, including candidates, their relatives and party activists, in the most violent electoral campaign since the end of the civil war. In the presidential ballot, the UNE's Alvaro Colom—contesting his third consecutive presidential election—secured 28.2% of valid votes cast, followed by Gen. (retd) Otto Fernando Pérez Molina, the candidate of the far-right Partido Patriota (PP), with 23.5%, and former prison chief Alejandro Eduardo Giammattei Falla, representing the ruling business-friendly GANA alliance, who received 17.2%. Nobel Peace Prize winner Rigoberta Menchú of the social democratic Encuentro por Guatemala, who was the first indigenous woman to run for President, polled just 3.1%. A second round of voting on 4 November resulted in the election of Colom as President, with 52.8% of valid votes, defeating Pérez Molina.

The Colom administration encountered many problems after taking office, and numerous changes were made to the composition of the Cabinet in 2008 and 2009. While tax revenues and social programmes increased slightly, the global financial crisis impeded real advances. Violence remained high with nearly 6,300 murders in 2008, while gangs became increasingly powerful. In mid-2008 the President of the Congreso, a close ally of Colom, was obliged to resign after being implicated in a financial scandal. In September two high-ranking security officials were dismissed and it was announced that presidential security would be restructured following the discovery of bugging devices in Colom's office. In May 2009 the murder of a prominent lawyer, Rodrigo Rosenberg, resulted in one of the worst political crises since the Peace Accords. After his death a video recording was released in which Rosenberg, filmed days earlier, accused Colom, and others, of plotting his murder. Rosenberg also made allegations concerning widespread corruption in the Government, and in the Banco Rural de Desarrollo. Street protests ensued to demand the resignation of the President, while others demonstrated in his support. By June Colom was under intense pressure from the press to resign. In January 2010, however, CICIG exonerated Colom, concluding that Rosenberg had orchestrated his own assassination, although the commission was to continue examining other claims made by Rosenberg, including alleged corruption at the Banco Rural de Desarrollo.

Meanwhile, CICIG continued to encounter resistance from officials while conducting its investigations. In June 2009 the commission filed a formal complaint against a judge who was seeking to terminate its involvement in the case against former President Portillo. The organization achieved a major victory in January 2010 with the arrest of Portillo, who was widely regarded as the most corrupt of Guatemala's former Presidents. In mid-2010 the UN Secretary-General, Ban Ki-Moon, urged the Guatemalan political and judicial authorities to support CICIG's work and in July the Congreso approved a two-year extension of CICIG's mandate (until September 2011). The release of figures indicating a 37% increase in violent deaths in the first half of 2009, compared with the corresponding period of 2008, served to highlight the urgency of the problems CICIG was seeking to address. Gándara resigned as Minister of the Interior in July 2009, after only six months in office; he was succeeded by Raúl Antonio Velásquez Ramos. Gándara's decision to replace the leadership of the PNC with retired police officials in the previous month had been criticized by human rights groups as representing a step backwards in efforts to reform the police force and in August they were dismissed by Velásquez for alleged involvement in drugs-trafficking. Moreover, following objections by CICIG to several of the Congreso's nominees to the Supreme Court, as well as criticism from UN officials over a lack of transparency in the appointment process, in October the legislature revised the list of new judges.

In August 2009, in the first such conviction since the end of the civil war, Felipe Cusanero Coj, a former member of the PAC, was found guilty of the forced 'disappearances' of six Mayan citizens in 1982–84 and sentenced to 150 years' imprisonment. In December a retired army officer, Marco Antonio Sánchez, received a 53-year prison sentence for the 'disappearances' of eight farm workers.

Further changes were made to the Cabinet and to the leadership of the PNC in February and March 2010. Three ministers were dismissed in late February: the Minister of Agriculture, Livestock and Food, Mario Aldana, owing to irregularities in the tendering process for the supply of fertilizers; the Minister of Education, Bienvenido Argueta, for failing to reveal information about the beneficiaries of Mi Familia Progresa, a social programme that some opposition members suspected had been used to reward government supporters; and Minister of the Interior Velásquez as a result of corruption allegations related to a contract for the provision of fuel to the PNC. Carlos Menocal, hitherto co-ordinator of the presidential anti-impunity commission, was appointed to replace Velásquez, becoming Colom's fifth Minister of the Interior. In early March the PNC Director, Baltázar Gómez Barrios, the head of the PNC's counter-narcotics division, Nelly Bonilla, and Bonilla's deputy were arrested on suspicion of alleged collusion with drugs-traffickers.

The continuing struggle against organized crime in Guatemala suffered a further reversal in June 2010 when the head of CICIG, Carlos Castresana, resigned. Upon leaving the post Castresana expressed frustration with the Government's failure to co-operate in the organization's efforts, particularly where these involved investigating the infiltration of state institutions. He also restated his belief that Colom should dismiss the recently-appointed Attorney-General, Conrado Reyes, who was alleged to have strong links to organized crime in the country. Shortly afterwards, UN Secretary-General Ban Ki-Moon announced that the current Attorney-General of Costa Rica, Francisco Dall'Anesse Ruiz, a well-known anti-corruption campaigner, would assume the role.

PROSPECTS FOR THE FUTURE

Despite significant international support for the peace process in the late 1990s, progress in development has been disappointing. The country has advanced in some areas (tax revenues, and more participation of indigenous groups in the political debate), but the problems are still immense. Guatemala's population and economy were the largest in Central America, yet growth rates have remained sluggish until recently. The country has also suffered from the region's lowest public investment in social services and worst tax collection base from which to support these investments. Massive inequality in incomes, as well as in access to health care and education, reflected the urban/rural, non-indigenous/indigenous divide. The lack of available economic alternatives for the poor majority has resulted in increased emigration and dependence on remittances from Guatemalans working abroad. Drugs-related violence has continued to hamper the economic development of the country and this, together with the associated corruption of state institutions, remained, according to a UN report in early 2010, the most serious problem faced by Guatemala.

Economy

DIEGO SÁNCHEZ-ANCOCHEA

Based on an earlier article by Prof. JENNY PEARCE and revised for this edition by the editorial staff

Guatemala is the largest economy in Central America, in terms of population and total current production, but has one of the lowest levels of human development. In 2008 gross domestic product (GDP) per head stood at just US $2,796, while in 2006 the country was ranked 121st in the UN Human Development Index, the second lowest in the region (after Haiti). Social indicators were poor: in 2007 Guatemala had an adult illiteracy rate of 26.8%, a life expectancy of 69 years and an infant mortality rate of 39 per 1,000 live births. Despite some economic growth in the 1990s, Guatemala's economic development was severely constrained by dependence on the agricultural sector (amounting to an estimated 13.3% of real GDP in 2008) and primary exports, by low levels of human capital and by one of the most unequal distributions in the whole world, with the richest 10% of the population receiving 48 times more than the poorest 10% of the population in 2002.

OVERALL ECONOMIC PERFORMANCE

Economic growth declined in the late 1970s after two decades of expansion, and the economy stagnated in the 1980s as war and violence escalated in Guatemala and the rest of Central America. In 1980–90 annual growth in real quetzals averaged 0.9%, while per-head GDP decreased by an annual average of 0.8%, in real terms. From 1990 better international conditions and a more stable domestic environment contributed to greater economic expansion. Average annual growth in real quetzals in 1990–2006 was 3.6%, reaching its peak in 1998 with 5.0%, while GDP per head grew at an annual average rate of 1.4% in the same period. In 2007 and 2008 Guatemala grew at a similar speed to the rest of Central America, with rates of growth of 5.7% and 4.3%, respectively.

From 1990 growth was stimulated by a sharp rise in infrastructure development and by an increase in non-traditional exports, which in 1990 outperformed the principal traditional export, coffee. Nevertheless, Guatemala continued to show a large trade deficit, which increased from US $521m. in 1991 to an estimated $6,252.0m. in 2008. A weak manufacturing base and the failure to diversify its export base as fast as other Central American countries partly responsible for the growing dependence of the Guatemalan economy.

High levels of poverty remained a major constraint on economic development. It was estimated that Guatemala's poverty rate increased from 63.4% to 89.0% in 1980–90. Extreme poverty, defined as the percentage of people unable to meet basic nutritional requirements, more than doubled, from 31% in 1980, to 67% in 1990, with even higher figures among the country's majority indigenous population. The poverty rate subsequently decreased, but was still 54% in 2007, according to national statistics; however, this figure was thought to underestimate the problem. Remittances from Guatemalans living abroad formed a large part of the economy. From 1996 remittances increased annually, becoming Guatemala's second largest hard currency inflow after commodity exports. In 2007 remittances reached a new record of US $4,314.7m. (more than seven times higher than in 2001), equivalent to 87% of the total exports of goods. However, the expansion of remittances contributed little to the growth of private and public investment, which was necessary to strengthen the productive base of the economy and to improve social indicators. Guatemala was also affected by numerous natural disasters. In early 2002 a severe drought in the Central American region had particularly significant repercussions in Guatemala. Many families engaged in subsistence-level farming lost their crops, and poverty and malnourishment were widespread. In March the UN's World Food Programme announced an emergency plan to feed an estimated 60,000 Guatemalan children under the age of five who were severely malnourished. In October 2005 Hurricane Stan caused material damage and losses estimated at some $983m. The Guatemalan economy was also affected by the high level of horizontal inequality between indigenous peoples and the Ladinos—those of European and Mestizo origin.

AGRICULTURE

Coffee, bananas, sugar and cardamom were the major agricultural exports; however, fluctuating international prices since the 1990s had an adverse effect on primary exports until the mid-2000s. Cardamom prices, for example, fell by more than 50% between 2002 and 2005, leading to a 25% reduction in export earnings from this product (from US $93.0m. to $70.4m.). The situation reversed between 2006 and 2008, when exports of cardamom, bananas and coffee increased rapidly: exports of bananas grew by 47%, while those of cardamom grew by 149% and coffee by 39%. Other exported agricultural products included vegetables, plants (including seeds and flowers) and fish.

Although the suspension of the International Coffee Organization quota system in 1989 was initially beneficial to Guatemala, it severely affected coffee exports in the early 1990s. There was some recovery in the mid-1990s, although Hurricane Mitch, which struck Central America in 1998, contributed to a decline in coffee exports in that year. Revenue from coffee exports fell from $586.5m. in 1998 to $261.8m. in 2002, partly as a result of low coffee prices. Small-scale producers, representing around 100,000 families and contributing 30% of overall national production, were particularly badly affected. Coffee prices recuperated in 2004 and exports earned $327.8m. in that year. The value of coffee exports totalled $582.2m. in 2009.

The question of how best to sustain international coffee prices preoccupied all exporters following the collapse of the International Coffee Agreement. Guatemala opted not to support a Central American plan to withhold coffee exports in an attempt to stimulate growth in falling international prices. The National Coffee Association (Anacafé) adopted a 'hedged' loan programme, under which producers received financial support by selling coffee beans at or above a set minimum price, which would then cover the loan in the event of depressed market conditions. In 2001, with prices at an all-time low, Guatemala joined an agreement negotiated by Mexico, Colombia and the Central American nations in March, to withhold 5% of their lowest quality beans from export and put them to other uses, for example, fertilizer or fuel for industry. The plan coincided with an international scheme to withhold 20% of the export goods that had failed to prevent the plunge in coffee prices. Meanwhile, some of the nation's growers held internet auctions of quality beans.

From the 1980s there was a substantial decline in the area planted with cotton, a trend accelerated by the guerrilla war and high production costs, compounded by competition from other regions and from a rise in the production of synthetic fibres. Conversely, the area planted with sugar cane expanded, and production of sugar rose slowly. Sugar exports in 1999 were worth US $192.1m., compared with $316.6m. in the previous year. Exports fluctuated thereafter, declining to $188.0m. in 2004, then recovering steadily to reach $509.4m. in 2009.

Banana export revenues also fluctuated, but increased from only US $143.1m. in 1999 to $484.6m. in 2009. There was potential for profitable wood production, as more than one-third of the country was covered with forests, including valuable cedar and mahogany. Total roundwood removals in 2008 amounted to 17.8m. cu m, while sawnwood production was estimated at 439,000 cu m.

MINING AND POWER

The mining sector remains small, contributing an estimated 1.6% of GDP in 2009. The largest operation was a copper mine in Alta Verapaz Department, which began production in 1975, but had an unrealized potential of 150,000 metric tons per year. Lead and zinc output fell drastically and a nickel mining project was suspended in 1980, after only three years of production, owing to low world prices and high production costs. Antimony and tungsten were mined and Guatemala had exploitable reserves of sulphur and marble. With the hope that guerrilla violence was over, in 1996 the Government began attempts to attract foreign investment to the mining sector. Australia's Broken Hill Proprietary (BHP) Co was granted a concession to explore for copper, lead, zinc and silver in Quiché and Alta Verapaz in 1996. Mining production has also experienced an erratic trend in the last few years. In 2005 it decreased by 1.3%, before increasing by a combined 31% in 2006 and 2007, owing to a significant expansion in the production of sand and higher commodity prices. In 2008 production stagnated as a result of lower international prices.

The main reserves of petroleum were found in the north of the country, across the border from Mexican production areas. In January 2000 proven reserves totalled 526m. barrels, while potential reserves were believed to be 800m.–1,000m. barrels. Earnings from exports increased during the 1990s, reaching some 25,000 barrels per day (b/d) in 1997, worth US $98.7m. (4.2% of total export earnings). Greater political stability following the final peace accord signed in December 1996 raised hopes that other foreign petroleum companies could be encouraged to become active in Guatemala. Plans for the petroleum sector were, however, confounded by the fall in oil prices in 1998 (from $14.4 to $6.8 per barrel) and the withdrawal of foreign investors. Subsequently, exports increased as prices recuperated and reached more than $125 per barrel in mid-2008. As a result, exports of oil increased steadily in value, from $58.3m. in 1998 to $249m. in 2007 and to $374m. in 2008 (4.8% of the total value of exports).

Energy was generated principally from hydroelectric power (37% in 2007), diesel (34%) and carbon (13%). The energy sector has experienced significant transformations in recent years and was affected by government policy reversals. The privatization of the energy sector had been a major objective of the Government of Alvaro Enrique Arzú Irigoyen (1996–2000): in July 1998 some 80% of the capital of the state-owned Empresa Eléctrica de Guatemala, SA was sold to foreign investors for US $520m., and in December the Instituto Nacional de Electrificación (INDE) was sold for $100m. However, the Government of Alfonso Antonio Portillo Cabrera (2000–04) did much to reverse the privatization policy (see below). The Chixoy watershed is the country's main source of hydroelectric power, and the Portillo Government promoted the creation of a new hydroelectric dam in Quiché. In May 2007 the communities affected voted against the dam's construction, although the Government appealed against the decision. In 2008 the Government of Alvaro Colom Caballeros announced an ambitious plan to expand hydroelectric production and reduce dependence on oil. The Government expected to attract foreign investment to build five hydroelectric plants and several carbon-based electric generating plants before 2014. Meanwhile, in 2006 Guatemala and Mexico linked their electricity grids, the first step in an ambitious project to create an integrated electricity system in Central America.

MANUFACTURING

As in the rest of Central America, the manufacturing sector in Guatemala experienced rapid expansion in the 1960s and 1970s, under the stimulus of the Central America Common Market (CACM) and foreign investment. In the 1980s manufacturing output was adversely affected by the contraction in demand from other Central American countries as a result of the civil wars in the region and a shortage of domestic credit. Real manufacturing output decreased by an annual average rate of 1.7% during 1980–86. Some recovery was experienced during 1987–2001, but the manufacturing sector still grew less than the rest of the economy (by 2.5% per year as opposed to 3.9% for the economy as a whole). By 2008 manufacturing contributed an estimated 18.1% of real GDP. The most significant activities in 2006 were food and beverages (generating an estimated 44% of total industrial production) and textiles (15%). In 2006 the manufacturing sector (including mining) provided 15.4% of total formal employment.

The clothing assembly, or *maquila*, plants contributed to an increase in non-traditional exports from the late 1980s. The sector's dynamism depended considerably on special government incentives to investors and low wages for a non-unionized labour force. The *maquila* sector expanded rapidly through the 1990s and into 2000: between 1995 and 2000 value added from the *maquila* sector increased by an annual average of 16.4%. Following a period of contraction in 2001 apparel exports to the USA (most of which came from *maquilas*) resumed their growth and Guatemala gained market share in the USA. By the mid-2000s, however, increasing Chinese competition led to a reversal of this trend. The approval of the Dominican Republic-Central American Free Trade Agreement (DR-CAFTA), which entered into force in July 2006, did little to stop this downward trend: between 2007 and 2008 Guatemalan exports of textiles and apparel to the USA decreased by 17% and the market share in 2008 was just 1.5%, compared with 2.4% in 2004.

The construction sector underwent a period of rapid expansion during the 1990s, although there were suspicions that the sector was partly funded by money raised from the illegal drugs trade. In the first decade of the 21st century, however, the sector's performance has been rather erratic. In 2002–04 the sector contracted dramatically. After a recuperation in 2005–07 (when construction grew at an annual average of 9.8%), the sector again experienced a contraction of 3.6% in 2008. Some 354,900 people were directly employed by the construction sector (16.6% of the total employed labour force) in 2006. The sector contributed an estimated 4.5% of GDP in 2009.

TRANSPORT AND COMMUNICATIONS

According to government statistics, in 2005 Guatemala had 14,283 km of roads, around 6,500 km of which were paved in 2008. The road system has experienced a significant modernization since 1990, with an increase in kilometres of paved roads of 5% per year during 1990–2005. The Guatemalan section of the Pan-American Highway was 518.7 km long and totally asphalted. Highways are concentrated in the producing areas of the Pacific and Altiplano regions. The main ports are Puerto Barrios and Santo Tomás de Castilla, on the Gulf of Mexico, and San José and Champerico, on the Pacific Ocean. There are several airports, the main international airport being La Aurora, near Guatemala City.

Guatemala had 886 km of rail lines in 2005. The Arzú Government placed much emphasis on the modernization of the country's infrastructure, which included the 1997 sale of the Ferrocarriles de Guatemala (FEGUA) rail network and the 1998 sale of a 50-year concession of the railways to the Railroad Development Corporation (USA). The Portillo Government also attempted to improve Guatemala's infrastructure, announcing several proposals in 2002, including plans to expand La Aurora airport and to construct a new international airport on the outskirts of Guatemala City. Nevertheless, little action was actually taken. The modernization of La Aurora finally began in early 2006, delayed by conflicts between national and local government.

In 1998 95% of the state telecommunications company, Empresa Guatemalteca de Telecomunicaciones (Guatel), was sold for US $700m. to a group of mostly domestic investors and the Mexican operator Teléfonos de México (Telmex). While the telecommunications service in the country improved dramatically, with the number of main telephone lines per 100 people increasing from 2.9 in 1995 to 10.4 in 2006 and the number of mobile cellular subscribers per 100 people rising from just 0.3 in 1995 to 55.1 in 2007, it nevertheless remained inadequate.

INVESTMENT AND FINANCE

Following the transfer of power to the civilian Government of President Vinicio Cerezo in 1986, a programme of austerity measures and financial reform was implemented. As a result, the economy began to show signs of revival after several years of decline. However, these positive developments were adversely affected by the decrease in coffee prices in the late 1980s and the decline in international reserves. A single exchange rate was introduced to deal with the latter in February 1989, followed in November by the flotation of the Guatemalan currency unit, the quetzal. Inflationary pressures increased in the economy as the quetzal was devalued several times, and a series of austerity measures was introduced. Although the general value of the quetzal stabilized, the rate of inflation continued to rise. The level of generalized crisis in the economy was such that by the end of the Cerezo Government, per-head income was estimated to have decreased to its 1969 level. The Government of Jorge Serrano Elías (1990–93) succeeded in stabilizing the currency and in increasing international reserves. A more stable economy and better economic conditions resulted in higher rates of investment. Between 1990 and 1999 gross capital formation grew at an annual average of 9.5%, with private gross capital formation growing by an annual average rate of 10.2%. As a result, investment as a proportion of GDP increased from 8.4% to 13.2% in the same period. Worsening external conditions, together with several natural disasters, resulted in a deterioration in investment levels during the first four years of the 21st century. Between 2001 and 2004 total real gross capital formation decreased; however, during 2005–07 gross capital formation recovered, increasing at an annual average of 9.1%, owing to the improvement in global conditions and the reconstruction effort after Hurricane Stan. The rate of inflation averaged 7.0% annually in 1998–2005. Strict monetary policy in 2006 led to a significant reduction of the annual rate of inflation, to 5.8%, but high international oil and food prices resulted in an acceleration of inflation in 2007 and 2008, to 8.7% and 9.4% respectively

The signing of the final peace accord in December 1996 enabled Guatemala to attract international aid for reconstruction. Some US $1,900m. in grants and loans was finally agreed. The Inter-American Development Bank (IDB) promised $800m., the World Bank $400m. and the European Union (EU) $250m. The Government committed itself to raising the shortfall of the estimated $2,500m. needed to implement the peace accords by raising tax revenues to 50% above the 1995 levels by 2000. Failure to meet their commitment prompted increasing pressure on the Government from international organizations; the EU gave an explicit warning in June 2001. Tax revenues slowly increased from that year and were equal to some 11.3% of GDP in 2007 and 2008.

In an attempt to reduce the fragility of the banking sector, in mid-2001 the Guatemalan Monetary Board initiated a thorough review of the banking system. As a result, the courts were requested to liquidate the three banks that had been subjected to state intervention earlier in the year (following a corruption scandal), as well as two finance companies. Further reforms were enabled in that year when the Congreso Nacional approved four bills creating a legislative framework through which the Central Bank would be able to exercise more effective control over the banking sector. The new legislation also allowed for the supervision of 'offshore' banks, for which previous banking laws had made no provision. The World Bank granted Guatemala two US $155m. loans to strengthen the newly created framework. A licensing system was introduced. Despite all these efforts, the country experienced a new scandal in October 2006, when the Central Bank closed Banco del Café, the country's fourth largest bank. Moreover, in January 2007 Banco de Comercio was suspended, confirming the weakness of the Guatemalan banking sector.

FOREIGN TRADE AND THE BALANCE OF PAYMENTS

In 2009 traditional primary exports (sugar, coffee and bananas) accounted for only 20.9% of total exports, while textiles alone represented 14.2% (despite an annual reduction of 11% in each of the preceding two years). Between 2002 and 2008 growth in exports lagged behind growth in imports. The trade deficit thus increased to an estimated US $3,301.1m. in 2009, compared with $1,707.9m. in 2000. However, largely owing to remittances from citizens working abroad, the deficit on the current account of the balance of payments remained significantly lower; in 2009 it was an estimated $267.1m. The USA was the principal market for Guatemalan exports, taking an estimated 41.7% in 2009. Other significant purchasers were El Salvador, Honduras, Nicaragua, Costa Rica and Mexico. The USA was also the major import source, supplying 36.5% in 2009.

At the end of the 1990s imports from Mexico far exceeded exports in terms of value. In April 2000 El Salvador, Guatemala and Honduras (the so-called CA-3 countries) signed a free trade agreement with Mexico, which promised greater access to the Mexican market for Guatemala, with increased bilateral trade in the future. The agreement became operational in March 2001. As predicted, however, the agreement initially benefited the Mexican economy to the detriment of Guatemala, as in 2001 Guatemalan exports to Mexico decreased by about one-third, while Mexican exports to Guatemala increased. In 2003, however, bilateral trade increased to the benefit of both countries. In 2002 Guatemala also agreed with Costa Rica, El Salvador, Honduras and Nicaragua to eliminate all regional trade barriers. Negotiations on the establishment of a Central American Free Trade Agreement (CAFTA) with the USA were concluded in late 2003; the agreement (renamed the DR-CAFTA following the inclusion of the Dominican Republic in negotiations in 2004) was ratified by the Congreso Nacional in March 2005 and entered into force in July 2006, months after Honduras, Nicaragua and El Salvador had implemented the accord. DR-CAFTA was intended to boost manufacturing exports to the USA, but the first years were disappointing. In May 2004 President Berger, together with the Presidents of El Salvador, Honduras and Nicaragua, signed an agreement creating a Central American customs union. A free trade agreement between Guatemala and Taiwan came into effect in early 2006. Negotiations between Central America and the EU for an association agreement were concluded in May 2010.

In May 2001 the Central American countries, including Guatemala, reached an agreement with Mexico, called the 'Plan Puebla–Panamá' (restyled the Proyecto de Integración y Desarrollo de Mesoamérica in 2008), to establish a series of joint transport, industry and tourism projects intended to integrate the region. In December Guatemala and Mexico agreed that they would link their electricity grids under the terms of the Plan, as part of its initiative on energy integration. Officials from the two nations agreed to co-operate on a project to construct an 80-km power line that would link a substation in Tapachula, Mexico, with a Guatemalan substation situated in Los Brillantes; the cost would be an estimated US $30m. In 2006 construction began on the Central American electricity interconnection system via a transmission line that would span 1,830 km (281 km in Guatemala), linking 15 substations in Costa Rica, El Salvador, Guatemala, Honduras, Nicaragua and Panama. The IDB was partially financing the project, with loans amounting to $170m. towards the estimated total cost of $385m.

PUBLIC REVENUE

In 1998, following the socio-economic component of the peace accords, President Arzú proposed a Fiscal Pact, envisaged as a multi-sectoral, long-term consensus between the principal political, economic and social bodies over the future tax regime and fiscal policies. To this end a Fiscal Pact Preparatory Committee (CPPF) was established to organize a national debate on tax policy. The CPPF's report, presented in late 1999, argued that increasing tax collection was the only means for Guatemala to meet peace accord goals and advance infrastructure development plans; the report contained 66 recommendations to be implemented by 2004. Its proposals included the establishment of mechanisms to audit the Superintendency for Tax Administration, and the creation of a body to curb tax evasion and strengthen the judiciary's capacity to process cases of tax evasion and fraud.

The Government of President Portillo also cited the signing of the Fiscal Pact to be one of its priorities, and in 2001 controversially raised the rate of value-added tax (VAT) to this end. In early 2003 Portillo implemented by decree further unpopular tax rises on fuel, wheat and a number of other items.

One of the main tenets of the Fiscal Pact, to achieve a 12% tax collection goal by 2002, was postponed to 2004 (when tax revenue was equivalent to 10.2% of GDP). In 2007 newly elected President Colom appointed an active proponent of tax reform, Juan Alberto Fuentes, as Minister of Finance, and negotiations for further tax expansion began. Nevertheless, deteriorating economic conditions resulted in a reduction of tax revenues in 2008 and 2009. Low income from tax revenue resulted in increased levels of public debt, which rose from 5.6% of GDP in 2003 to an estimated 11.6% in 2008.

OUTLOOK

Guatemala had a difficult time adapting to globalization and moving forward after the civil war. The early 21st century also presented obstacles to economic recovery, despite an expansion of non-traditional exports and the increasing role of remittances as a source of income. The Portillo administration implemented a number of neo-liberal reforms, but corruption and institutional weakness was endemic. Furthermore, in 2003 a report by the Consultative Group of donor countries was highly critical of the Government's failure to implement the terms of the peace accords. The election of Berger of the centre-right Gran Alianza Nacional (GANA) to the presidency in November of that year gave rise to optimism that the change of government would prompt inflows of much-needed foreign investment; Berger's determination to address endemic corruption at all levels of public office was welcomed by investors, as was the new Cabinet, largely comprising businessmen. However, the performance of the Berger administration in its four years of government was disappointing. GANA did not obtain a majority in the Congreso Nacional, impeding attempts to implement promised economic reforms, while tax reforms failed to increase revenues to the required level.

The election of Colom of the Unidad Nacional de la Esperanza to the presidency created some space for more progressive reforms, particularly in the tax system and social spending. Yet the Colom administration has had to contend with growing internal and external challenges. Ongoing problems with institutionalized corruption and violent crime diminished the Government's ability to promote its economic agenda. More importantly, the global financial crisis created additional problems for the country, with a decline in revenue from exports and remittances triggering a significant reduction of economic growth and a likely increase in poverty.

Statistical Survey

Sources (unless otherwise stated): Banco de Guatemala, 7a Avda 22-01, Zona 1, Apdo 365, Guatemala City; tel. 2429-6000; fax 2253-4035; internet www.banguat.gob.gt; Instituto Nacional de Estadística, Edif. América, 4°, 8a Calle 9-55, Zona 1, Guatemala City; tel. 2232-6212; e-mail info-ine@ine.gob.gt; internet www.ine.gob.gt.

Area and Population

AREA, POPULATION AND DENSITY

Area (sq km)	
Land	108,429
Inland water	460
Total	108,889*
Population (census results)†	
17 April 1994	8,322,051
24 November 2002	
Males	5,496,839
Females	5,740,357
Total	11,237,196
Population (official estimate at mid-year)	
2010	14,361,666
Density (per sq km) at mid-2010	131.9

* 42,042 sq miles.

† Excluding adjustments for underenumeration.

POPULATION BY AGE AND SEX

(official estimates at mid–2010)

	Males	Females	Total
0–14	3,027,304	2,941,373	5,968,677
15–64	3,682,854	4,089,170	7,772,024
65 and over	293,177	327,788	620,965
Total	7,003,335	7,358,331	14,361,666

DEPARTMENTS

(official estimates at mid-2010)

Alta Verapaz	1,078,942	Quetzaltenango	771,674
Baja Verapaz	264,019	Quiché	921,390
Chimaltenango	595,769	Retalhuleu	297,385
Chiquimula	362,826	Sacatepéquez	310,037
El Progreso	155,596	San Marcos	995,742
Escuintla	685,830	Santa Rosa	340,381
Guatemala	3,103,685	Sololá	424,068
Huehuetenango	1,114,389	Suchitepéquez	504,267
Izabal	403,256	Totonicapán	461,838
Jalapa	309,908	Zacapa	218,510
Jutiapa	428,462		
Petén	613,693	**Total**	14,361,666

PRINCIPAL TOWNS

(population at census of November 2002)

Guatemala City	942,348	Cobán	144,461
Mixco	403,689	Quetzaltenango	127,569
Villa Nueva	355,901	Escuintla	119,897
San Juan Sacatepéquez	152,583	Jalapa	105,796
San Pedro Carcha	148,344	Totonicapán	96,392

Mid-2010 ('000, incl. suburbs, UN estimate): Guatemala City 1,104 (Source: UN, *World Urbanization Prospects: The 2009 Revision*).

BIRTHS, MARRIAGES AND DEATHS

	Registered live births		Registered marriages		Registered deaths	
	Number	Rate (per 1,000)	Number	Rate (per 1,000)	Number	Rate (per 1,000)
1999	409,034	36.9	62,034	5.6	65,139	5.9
2000	425,410	37.4	58,311	5.1	67,284	5.9
2001	415,338	35.6	54,722	4.7	68,041	5.8
2002	387,287	32.3	51,857	4.3	66,089	5.5
2003	375,092	31.0	51,247	4.2	66,695	5.5
2004	383,704	31.0	53,860	4.3	66,991	5.4
2005	374,066	29.5	52,186	4.1	71,039	5.6
2006	368,399	28.3	57,505	4.4	69,756	5.4

Sources: partly UN, *Demographic Yearbook* and *Population and Vital Statistics Report*.

Life expectancy (years at birth, WHO estimates): 69 (males 65; females 72) in 2008 (Source: WHO, *World Health Statistics*).

ECONOMICALLY ACTIVE POPULATION
(at census of November 2002)

	Males	Females	Total
Agriculture, forestry, hunting and fishing	1,278,739	178,364	1,457,103
Mining and quarrying	5,313	756	6,069
Manufacturing	301,222	164,725	465,947
Construction	186,611	21,266	207,877
Electricity, gas, water and sanitary services	23,518	10,135	33,653
Commerce	343,586	228,114	571,700
Transport, storage and communications	96,410	16,913	113,323
Financial and property services	82,644	42,839	125,483
Public administration and defence	60,853	25,137	85,990
Education	42,366	59,796	102,162
Community and personal services	68,165	197,794	265,959
Sub-total	2,507,427	927,839	3,435,266
Activities not adequately described	18,256	9,875	28,131
Total	2,525,683	937,714	3,463,397

2006 ('000 persons aged 10 years and over, labour force survey): Agriculture, forestry, hunting and fishing 1,791.4; Mining and quarrying 7.5; Manufacturing 854.8; Electricity, gas and water 12.4; Construction 354.9; Wholesale and retail trade; repair of motor vehicles, motorcycles and personal and household goods; restaurants and hotels 1,226.9; Transport, storage and communications 160.7; Finance, real estate, renting and business activities 176.1; Public administration, defence and compulsory social security 115.5; Education 219.8; Health, social work and other community, social and personal service activities 457.4; Extra-territorial organizations and bodies 13.2; *Total employed*: 5,390.5 (Source: ILO).

Health and Welfare

KEY INDICATORS

Total fertility rate (children per woman, 2008)	4.1
Under-5 mortality rate (per 1,000 live births, 2008)	34
HIV/AIDS (% of persons aged 15–49, 2007)	0.8
Physicians (per 1,000 head, 1999)	0.9
Hospital beds (per 1,000 head, 2005)	0.7
Health expenditure (2007): US $ per head (PPP)	384
Health expenditure (2007): % of GDP	7.3
Health expenditure (2007): public (% of total)	29.3
Access to water (% of persons, 2008)	94
Access to sanitation (% of persons, 2008)	81
Total carbon dioxide emissions ('000 metric tons, 2006)	11,757.8
Carbon dioxide emissions per head (metric tons, 2006)	0.9
Human Development Index (2007): ranking	122
Human Development Index (2007): value	0.704

For sources and definitions, see explanatory note on p. vi.

Agriculture

PRINCIPAL CROPS
('000 metric tons)

	2006	2007	2008*
Maize	1,183.9	1,294.4	1,294.4
Sugar cane	18,721.4	25,436.8	25,436.8
Oil palm fruit*	833.3	866.7	1,233.3
Tomatoes	304.6	355.5	355.5
Watermelons*	128.0	135.0	135.0
Cantaloupes and other melons	384.2	530.7	530.7
Bananas	1,324.2*	1,569.5	1,569.5
Plantains*	325.0	345.0	345.0
Lemons and limes	122.5	123.0	123.0
Guavas, mangoes and mangosteens	105.1	110.6	110.6
Coffee, green	220.5†	252.0†	254.8
Tobacco, unmanufactured*	21.5	21.5	21.5

* FAO estimates.
† Unofficial figure.

Aggregate production ('000 metric tons, may include official, semi-official or estimated data): Total cereals 1,276.0 in 2006, 1,389.9 in 2007–08; Total pulses 177.2 in 2006, 133.3 in 2007–08; Total roots and tubers 455.1 in 2006, 468.3 in 2007–08; Total vegetables (incl. melons) 1,443.5 in 2006, 1,645.1 in 2007–08; Total fruits (excl. melons) 2,649.7 in 2006; 3,016.3 in 2007–08.

Source: FAO.

LIVESTOCK
('000 head, year ending September)

	2006	2007	2008
Horses*	124	125	125
Asses*	9.9	9.9	9.9
Mules*	38.7	38.7	38.7
Cattle	2,796	3,261	3,261*
Sheep*	265	265	265
Pigs	2,701	2,708	2,736
Goats	112*	109	109*
Chickens	36,956	31,430	31,430*

* FAO estimate(s).

LIVESTOCK PRODUCTS
('000 metric tons)

	2005	2006	2007*
Cattle meat*	63.0	65.0	75.6
Pig meat*	66.7	58.0	58.2
Chicken meat	151.0	167.7	151.0
Cows' milk	294.8	336.4*	338.2
Hen eggs*	85.0	85.0	85.0
Honey*	1.5	1.5	1.5

* FAO estimate(s).

2008: Production assumed to be unchanged from 2007 (FAO estimates).

Source: FAO.

Forestry

ROUNDWOOD REMOVALS
('000 cubic metres, excl. bark)

	2006	2007	2008
Sawlogs, veneer logs and logs for sleepers	439	439*	439*
Other industrial wood*	15	15	15
Fuel wood*	16,609	16,960	17,319
Total*	17,063	17,414	17,773

* FAO estimate(s).

Source: FAO.

SAWNWOOD PRODUCTION
('000 cubic metres, incl. railway sleepers)

	2002	2003	2004*
Coniferous (softwood)	180*	251	251
Broadleaved (hardwood)	160	115	115
Total	340	366	366

* FAO estimate(s).

2005–08: Production assumed to be unchanged from 2004 (FAO estimates).

Fishing

('000 metric tons, live weight)

	2006	2007	2008
Capture*	18.7	17.6	22.8
Freshwater fishes	2.3*	2.3*	2.3
Skipjack tuna	6.1	7.5	10.5
Yellowfin tuna	7.5	4.6	5.7
Bigeye tuna	0.9	1.1	2.2
Penaeus shrimps	0.4	0.6	0.5
Pacific seabobs	0.7	0.8	0.8
Aquaculture	16.3	16.4*	18.7
Other tilapias	2.9	2.9	3.0
Penaeus shrimps	13.4	13.5*	15.7
Total catch*	35.0	34.0	41.6

* FAO estimate(s).

Source: FAO.

Mining

('000 metric tons, unless otherwise indicated, estimates)

	2006	2007	2008
Crude petroleum ('000 42-gallon barrels)	5,893	4,630*	4,500
Gold (kg)	5,036	7,068	7,500
Silver (kg)	49,719	88,250	99,900
Limestone	4,938	6,131†	6,000
Sand and gravel ('000 cubic metres)	502	237	250

* Estimate.

† Converted to weight measure from reported volume of production using a conversion factor of 2.611 metric tons per cubic metre.

Source: US Geological Survey.

Industry

SELECTED PRODUCTS
('000 metric tons, unless otherwise indicated)

	2004	2005	2006
Sugar (raw)	2,092	2,015	1,961
Cement*	2,200	2,400	2,500
Electric energy (million kWh)	7,009	7,550	7,916

* Estimates from US Geological Survey.

2000 (million): Cigarettes 4,262.

2002 ('000 metric tons): Motor spirit (petrol) 111.

2007: Electricity (million kWh) 8,755; Cement ('000 metric tons) 2,500 (US Geological Survey estimate).

Source (unless otherwise indicated): UN Industrial Commodity Statistics Database.

Finance

CURRENCY AND EXCHANGE RATES

Monetary Units
100 centavos = 1 quetzal.

Sterling, Dollar and Euro Equivalents (31 May 2010)
£1 sterling = 11.673 quetzales;
US $1 = 8.006 quetzales;
€1 = 9.915 quetzales;
10,000 quetzales = £8.57 = $12.49 = €10.09.

Average Exchange Rate (quetzales per US dollar)

2007	7.6733
2008	7.5600
2009	8.1616

Note: In December 2000 legislation was approved to allow the circulation of the US dollar and other convertible currencies, for use in a wide range of transactions, from 1 May 2001.

GOVERNMENT FINANCE
(budgetary central government operations, cash basis, million quetzales)

Summary of Balances

	2006	2007	2008
Revenue	29,102.5	33,521.5	35,448.3
Less Expense	29,905.5	32,608.3	34,564.5
Net cash inflow from operating activities	–803.0	913.2	883.8
Less Net cash outflow from investments in non-financial assets	3,694.4	4,664.3	5,567.9
Cash surplus/deficit	–4,497.4	–3,751.1	–4,684.1

Revenue

	2006	2007	2008
Taxation	27,251.6	31,566.6	33,356.0
Taxes on income, profits and capital gains	7,646.8	8,653.9	9,698.4
Taxes on goods and services	16,398.3	19,623.4	20,610.2
Social contributions	585.1	658.6	746.5
Grants	370.0	419.7	362.9
Other revenue	895.8	876.6	982.9
Total (incl. grants)	29,102.5	33,521.5	35,448.3

Expense/Outlays

Expense by economic type	2006	2007	2008
Compensation of employees	7,608.7	8,180.0	9,202.1
Use of goods and services	2,876.6	3,447.1	5,255.5
Interest	3,128.2	3,831.3	3,961.8
Subsidies	12.9	78.5	564.9
Grants	9,168.1	9,716.3	9,777.2
Social benefits	1,876.0	2,058.0	2,415.0
Other expense	5,235.0	5,297.1	3,388.0
Total	29,905.5	32,608.3	34,564.5

Outlays by function of government*	2006	2007	2008
General public services	5,834.2	7,183.3	7,442.7
Defence	821.9	868.1	903.8
Public order and safety	3,176.7	3,620.2	4,415.5
Economic affairs	6,039.9	6,853.9	7,047.9
Environmental protection	701.6	649.8	309.0
Housing and community amenities	4,608.5	4,837.8	4,858.4
Health	2,550.8	2,645.7	2,957.1
Recreation, culture and religion	542.1	574.9	600.7
Education	6,406.8	6,925.9	7,848.3
Social protection	2,924.6	3,113.7	3,749.3
Statistical discrepancy	–7.2	–0.7	–0.2
Total	33,599.9	37,272.6	40,132.5

* Including purchases of non-financial assets.

Source: IMF, *Government Finance Statistics Yearbook*.

INTERNATIONAL RESERVES
(US $ million at 31 December)

	2007	2008	2009
Gold*	9.3	9.3	9.4
IMF special drawing rights	4.3	3.5	273.3
Foreign exchange	4,125.6	4,458.4	4,690.3
Total	4,139.2	4,471.2	4,973.0

* Valued at US $42 per troy ounce.

Source: IMF, *International Financial Statistics*.

MONEY SUPPLY
(million quetzales at 31 December)

	2007	2008	2009
Currency outside depository corporations	17,134.1	16,695.1	18,108.5
Transferable deposits	36,460.8	39,737.8	42,557.9
Other deposits	59,167.0	66,382.8	76,172.8
Securities other than shares	4,890.3	4,857.4	5,319.2
Broad money	117,652.2	127,673.0	142,158.4

Source: IMF, *International Financial Statistics*.

COST OF LIVING
(Consumer Price Index; base: 2000 = 100)

	2007	2008	2009
Food and non-alcoholic beverages	195.6	219.7	213.5
Clothing and footwear	132.5	136.4	138.5
Housing, water and power	150.5	157.2	160.2
Health	150.0	157.7	164.7
Transport and communications	154.8	171.0	176.7
Recreation and culture	157.9	166.5	171.3
Education	155.2	163.6	156.4
All items (incl. others)	167.2	183.0	182.4

NATIONAL ACCOUNTS
(million quetzales at current prices)

Expenditure on the Gross Domestic Product

	2007	2008	2009
Government final consumption expenditure	22,663	26,668	30,829
Private final consumption expenditure	228,461	264,272	271,442
Increase in stocks	3,255	–4,409	–15,779
Gross fixed capital formation	51,273	52,827	44,551
Total domestic expenditure	305,652	339,358	331,043
Exports of goods and services	66,920	73,133	74,403
Less Imports of goods and services	110,812	116,596	100,841
GDP in purchasers' values	261,760	295,894	304,604
GDP at constant 2001 prices	186,767	192,929	194,037

Source: IMF, *International Financial Statistics*.

Gross Domestic Product by Economic Activity

	2007	2008*	2009†
Agriculture, hunting, forestry and fishing	29,975.7	32,991.1	35,325.9
Mining and quarrying	4,120.9	5,370.7	4,572.9
Manufacturing	47,885.5	54,628.8	56,615.2
Electricity, gas and water	6,387.9	6,667.6	6,824.2
Construction	13,429.3	15,134.6	13,234.2
Trade, restaurants and hotels	39,967.2	48,858.1	49,756.4
Transport, storage and communications	18,262.3	22,229.9	22,740.7
Finance, insurance and real estate	7,883.4	9,347.7	10,127.8
Ownership of dwellings	24,174.6	26,121.8	27,465.0
General government services	16,970.8	18,500.1	21,887.5
Other community, social and personal services	39,595.2	43,953.1	46,044.5
Sub-total	248,652.8	283,803.5	294,594.3
Less Financial intermediation services indirectly measured (FISIM)	7,030.1	8,218.7	9,101.3
Gross value added in basic prices	241,622.7	275,584.8	285,493.0
Taxes on imports, less subsidies	20,137.4	20,309.4	19,111.2
GDP in purchasers' values	261,760.1	295,894.1	304,604.3

* Preliminary figures.

† Estimated figures.

BALANCE OF PAYMENTS
(US $ million)

	2007	2008	2009
Exports of goods f.o.b.	6,983.0	7,846.4	7,330.7
Imports of goods f.o.b.	–12,470.3	–13,421.2	–10,631.8
Trade balance	–5,487.3	–5,574.8	–3,301.1
Exports of services	1,731.0	1,872.9	1,512.8
Imports of services	–2,041.0	–2,148.4	–1,882.7
Balance on goods and services	–5,797.3	–5,850.3	–3,671.0
Other income received	556.0	544.6	337.9
Other income paid	–1,398.8	–1,471.1	–1,285.9
Balance on goods, services and income	–6,640.1	–6,776.8	–4,619.0
Current transfers received	4,808.0	4,952.9	4,368.8
Current transfers paid	–11.2	–19.0	–16.9
Current balance	–1,843.3	–1,842.9	–267.1
Direct investment abroad	–25.3	–16.4	–24.5
Direct investment from abroad	745.0	753.9	566.0
Portfolio investment assets	16.5	–10.4	10.9
Portfolio investment liabilities	–245.0	–28.5	–15.5
Other investment assets	–597.3	–90.5	63.5
Other investment liabilities	1,657.4	607.7	–706.2
Net errors and omissions	406.2	882.7	780.8
Overall balance	114.2	255.6	407.9

Source: IMF, *International Financial Statistics*.

External Trade

PRINCIPAL COMMODITIES
(US $ million)

Imports c.i.f.	2007	2008	2009
Transmitting and receiving apparatus	364.1	361.7	270.7
Threads and yarns	303.5	336.9	290.1
Paper and cardboard products	360.8	364.9	329.9
Electrical machinery and apparatus	1,259.6	1,179.3	956.3
Plastics and manufactures thereof	770.7	818.4	639.0
Textile materials (cloth or fabric)	735.8	644.6	506.4
Chemical and pharmaceutical products	908.0	1,041.4	911.9
Vehicles and transport equipment	1,151.9	1,084.1	728.8
Diesel oil	873.0	1,027.3	768.1
Motor gasoline	767.8	827.1	707.3
Iron and steel	380.9	556.7	242.8
Total (incl. others)	13,575.7	14,546.5	11,530.5

Exports f.o.b.	2007	2008	2009
Coffee	577.3	646.2	582.3
Sugar	358.1	378.1	507.7
Bananas	300.2	317.1	414.6
Articles of clothing	1,366.1	1,206.0	1,023.0
Plastics and manufactures thereof	190.8	221.7	177.1
Pharmaceutical products	156.2	175.4	169.7
Petroleum	249.1	373.7	191.7
Precious metals and stones	204.4	261.6	345.5
Total (incl. others)	6,897.7	7,737.4	7,213.9

PRINCIPAL TRADING PARTNERS
(US $ million, preliminary)

Imports c.i.f.	2007	2008	2009
Argentina	215.1	142.4	119.9
Brazil	309.1	268.1	233.5
Canada	134.5	174.8	95.8
Chile	282.1	268.2	132.9
China, People's Republic	776.2	839.4	607.7
Colombia	214.8	289.2	325.7
Costa Rica	405.9	422.7	394.2
Ecuador	190.1	124.1	205.2
El Salvador	620.8	692.1	590.0
Germany	236.9	215.0	172.0
Honduras	279.7	353.4	262.3
Hong Kong	144.2	164.3	137.0
Italy	154.0	108.0	75.3
Japan	395.3	365.4	173.9
Korea, Republic	444.0	365.0	317.8
Mexico	1,184.3	1,411.6	1,185.6
Netherlands Antilles	448.6	460.8	300.0
Panama	400.2	412.5	363.9
Puerto Rico	88.0	96.8	30.3
Spain	162.7	183.9	142.2
Taiwan	126.8	110.3	85.9
USA	4,642.6	5,242.4	4,209.3
Total (incl. others)	13,575.7	14,546.5	11,530.5

Exports f.o.b.	2007	2008	2009
Canada	111.3	110.8	110.6
Costa Rica	257.8	318.9	283.7
Dominican Republic	92.0	113.8	107.2
El Salvador	842.1	973.3	817.3
Germany	85.8	78.2	73.5
Honduras	593.5	737.1	606.4
Korea, Republic	74.8	31.8	68.0
Mexico	464.1	509.2	425.7
Netherlands	71.9	107.3	108.3
Nicaragua	267.6	327.6	281.8
Panama	119.6	161.6	184.5
Switzerland	33.1	35.2	13.7
USA	2,903.8	3,014.4	2,941.6
Total (incl. others)	6,897.7	7,737.4	7,213.9

Transport

RAILWAYS
(traffic)

	1994	1995	1996
Passenger-km (million)	991	0	0
Freight ton-km (million)	25,295	14,242	836

Source: UN, *Statistical Yearbook*.

ROAD TRAFFIC
(motor vehicles in use at 31 December)

	1997	1998	1999
Passenger cars	470,016	508,868	578,733
Buses and coaches	9,843	10,250	11,017
Lorries and vans	34,220	37,057	42,219
Motorcycles and mopeds	111,358	117,536	129,664

Source: IRF, *World Road Statistics*.

SHIPPING

Merchant Fleet
(registered at 31 December)

	2006	2007	2008
Number of vessels	10	12	10
Total displacement ('000 grt)	5.5	5.9	3.6

Source: Lloyd's Register-Fairplay, *World Fleet Statistics*.

International Sea-borne Freight Traffic
('000 metric tons)

	1992	1993	1994
Goods loaded	2,176	1,818	2,096
Goods unloaded	3,201	3,025	3,822

CIVIL AVIATION
(traffic on scheduled services)

	1997	1998	1999
Kilometres flown (million)	5	7	5
Passengers carried ('000)	508	794	506
Passenger-km (million)	368	480	342
Total ton-km (million)	77	50	33

Source: UN, *Statistical Yearbook*.

Tourism

TOURIST ARRIVALS BY COUNTRY OF ORIGIN

	2005	2006	2007
Belize	13,112	26,340	34,572
Canada	24,820	32,268	32,206
Costa Rica	34,693	35,842	40,436
El Salvador	497,430	582,676	617,798
France	19,219	18,351	19,835
Germany	18,258	18,178	18,587
Honduras	106,473	122,428	138,944
Italy	16,467	14,960	14,932
Mexico	72,908	79,731	86,466
Nicaragua	46,936	36,478	40,298
Spain	21,182	22,794	24,581
USA	286,871	338,472	377,565
Total (incl. others)	1,315,646	1,502,069	1,627,552

Tourism receipts (US $ million, excl. passenger transport): 919 in 2006; 1,055 in 2007; 1,068 in 2008 (provisional).

Source: World Tourism Organization.

Communications Media

	2007	2008	2009
Telephones ('000 main lines in use)	1,413.7	1,448.9	1,413.2
Mobile cellular telephones ('000 subscribers)	11,897.6	14,948.6	17,307.5
Internet users ('000)	1,640.0	1,960.0	2,280.0
Broadband subscribers ('000)	57.0	79.0	110.0

Personal computers: 262,000 (20.6 per 1,000 persons) in 2005.

Source: International Telecommunication Union.

Radio receivers ('000 in use): 835 in 1997.

Television receivers ('000 in use): 680 in 1999 (Source: UN, *Statistical Yearbook*).

Daily newspapers (number): 7 in 1996.

Education

(2006/07, unless otherwise indicated)

	Institutions	Teachers	Students
Pre-primary	11,859*	18,859	456,541
Primary	17,499*	80,418	2,448,976
Secondary	4,874*	53,630	864,154
Tertiary	1,946†	3,843*	233,885

* 2005/06 data.

† 2003/04 data.

Source: mainly UNESCO Institute for Statistics.

Teachers (2008 unless otherwise indicated): Pre-primary 20,539; Primary 84,980; Secondary 54,498; Tertiary 3,843 (2006) (Source: UNESCO Institute for Statistics).

Pupil-teacher ratio (primary education, UNESCO estimate): 29.4 in 2007/08 (Source: UNESCO Institute for Statistics).

Adult literacy rate (UNESCO estimates): 73.8% (males 79.5%; females 68.7%) in 2008 (Source: UNESCO Institute for Statistics).

Directory

The Constitution

In December 1984 the Constituent Assembly drafted a new Constitution (based on that of 1965), which was approved in May 1985 and came into effect in January 1986. A series of amendments to the Constitution were approved by referendum in January 1994 and came into effect in April 1994. The Constitution's main provisions are summarized below:

Guatemala has a republican, representative, democratic system of government and power is exercised equally by the legislative, executive and judicial bodies. The official language is Spanish. Suffrage is universal and secret, obligatory for those who can read and write and optional for those who are illiterate. The free formation and growth of political parties, with democratic aims, are guaranteed. There is no discrimination on grounds of race, colour, sex, religion, birth, economic or social position, or political opinions.

The State will give protection to capital and private enterprise in order to develop sources of labour and stimulate creative activity.

Monopolies are forbidden and the State will limit any enterprise that might prejudice the development of the community. The right to social security is recognized and it shall be on a national, unitary and obligatory basis.

Constitutional guarantees may be suspended in certain circumstances for up to 30 days (unlimited in the case of war).

CONGRESS

Legislative power rests with Congress, which is made up of 158 deputies, elected according to a combination of departmental and proportional representation. Congress meets on 15 January each year and ordinary sessions last four months; extraordinary sessions can be called by the Permanent Commission or the Executive. All Congressional decisions must be taken by absolute majority of the members, except in special cases laid down by law. Deputies are elected for four years; they may be re-elected after a lapse of one session, but only once. Congress is responsible for all matters concerning the President and Vice-President and the execution of their offices; for all electoral matters; for all matters concerning the laws of the Republic; for approving the budget and decreeing taxes; for declaring war; for conferring honours, both civil and military; for fixing the coinage and the system of weights and measures; and for approving, by two-thirds' majority, any international treaty or agreement affecting the law, sovereignty, financial status or security of the country.

PRESIDENT

The President is elected by universal suffrage, by absolute majority, for a non-extendable period of four years. Re-election or prolongation of the presidential term of office are punishable by law. The President is responsible for national defence and security, fulfilling the Constitution, leading the armed forces, taking any necessary steps in time of national emergency, passing and executing laws, international policy, and nominating and removing Ministers, officials and diplomats. The Vice-President's duties include co-ordinating the actions of Ministers of State and taking part in the discussions of the Council of Ministers.

ARMY

The Guatemalan Army is intended to maintain national independence, sovereignty and honour, and territorial integrity. It is an indivisible, apolitical, non-deliberating body and is made up of land, sea and air forces.

LOCAL ADMINISTRATIVE DIVISIONS

For the purposes of administration, the territory of the Republic is divided into 22 Departments and these into 330 Municipalities, but this division can be modified by Congress to suit the interests and general development of the Nation without loss of municipal autonomy. Municipal authorities are elected every four years.

JUDICIARY

Justice is exercised exclusively by the Supreme Court of Justice and other tribunals. Administration of Justice is obligatory, free and independent of the other functions of State. The President of the Judiciary, judges and other officials are elected by Congress for five years. The Supreme Court of Justice is made up of 13 judges. The President of the Judiciary is also President of the Supreme Court. The Supreme Court nominates all other judges. Under the Supreme Court come the Court of Appeal, the Administrative Disputes Tribunal, the Tribunal of Second Instance of Accounts, Jurisdiction Conflicts, First Instance and Military, and the Extraordinary Tribunal of Protection. There is a Court of Constitutionality presided over by the President of the Supreme Court.

The Government

HEAD OF STATE

President: ALVARO COLOM CABALLEROS (took office 14 January 2008).

Vice-President: Dr RAFAEL ESPADA.

CABINET

(July 2010)

The Government is formed by the Unidad Nacional de la Esperanza.

Minister of Foreign Affairs: ROGER HAROLDO RODAS MELGAR.

Minister of the Interior: CARLOS MENOCAL.

Minister of National Defence: Gen. ABRAHAM VALENZUELA GONZÁLEZ.

Minister of Public Finance: EDGAR BALSELLS.

Minister of the Economy: ERICK COYOY.

Minister of Public Health and Social Welfare: LUDWIG WERNER OVALLE CABRERA.

Minister of Communications, Infrastructure, Transport and Housing: GUILLERMO ANDRÉS CASTILLO RUIZ.

Minister of Agriculture, Livestock and Food: JUAN ALFONSO DE LEÓN.

Minister of Education: DENIS ALONZO MAZARIEGOS.

Minister of Employment and Social Security: EDGAR ALFREDO RODRÍGUEZ.

Minister of Energy and Mines: (vacant).

Minister of Culture and Sport: JERÓNIMO LANCERIO CHINGO.

Minister of the Environment and Natural Resources: LUIS ALBERTO FERRATÉ FELICE.

MINISTRIES

Ministry of Agriculture, Livestock and Food: Edif. Monja Blanca, Of. 306, 3°, 7a Avda 12-90, Zona 13, Guatemala City; tel. 2413-7351; fax 2413-7352; e-mail infoagro@maga.gob.gt; internet www.maga.gob.gt.

Ministry of Communications, Infrastructure, Transport and Housing: Edif. Antiguo Cocesna, 8a Avda y 15 Calle, Zona 13, Guatemala City; tel. 2362-6051; fax 2362-6059; e-mail relpublicas@micivi.gob.gt; internet www.civ.gob.gt.

Ministry of Culture and Sport: Calle 7, entre Avda 6 y 7, Centro Histórico, Palacio Nacional de la Cultura, Zona 1, Guatemala City; tel. 2239-5100; fax 2253-0540; e-mail info@mcd.gob.gt; internet www.mcd.gob.gt.

Ministry of the Economy: 8a Avda 10-43, Zona 1, Guatemala City; tel. 2412-0200; fax 2412-0488; e-mail infonegocios@mineco.gob.gt; internet www.mineco.gob.gt.

Ministry of Education: 6a Calle 1-87, Zona 10, Guatemala City; tel. 2411-9595; fax 2361-0350; e-mail info@mineduc.gob.gt; internet www.mineduc.gob.gt.

Ministry of Employment and Social Security: Edif. Torre Empresarial, 7a Avda 3-33, Zona 9, Guatemala City; tel. 2422-2500; fax 2422-2507; e-mail ministro@mintrabajo.gob.gt; internet www.mintrabajo.gob.gt.

Ministry of Energy and Mines: Diagonal 17, 29-78, Zona 11, Las Charcas, Guatemala City; tel. 2419-6363; fax 2476-2007; e-mail informatica@mem.gob.gt; internet www.mem.gob.gt.

Ministry of the Environment and Natural Resources: Edif. MARN, 20 Calle 28-58, Zona 10, Guatemala City; tel. 2423-0500; e-mail rpublicas@marn.gob.gt; internet www.marn.gob.gt.

Ministry of Foreign Affairs: 2a Avda La Reforma 4-17, Zona 10, Guatemala City; tel. 2410-0010; fax 2410-0011; e-mail webmaster@minex.gob.gt; internet www.minex.gob.gt.

Ministry of the Interior: Antiguo Palacio de la Policía Nacional Civil, 6a Avda 13-71, Zona 1, Guatemala City; tel. 2413-8888; fax 2413-8587; internet www.mingob.gob.gt.

Ministry of National Defence: Antiguas Instalaciones de la Escuela Politécnica, Avda La Reforma 1-45, Zona 10, Guatemala City; tel. 2269-4924; fax 2360-9919; e-mail dip@mindef.mil.gt; internet www.mindef.mil.gt.

Ministry of Public Finance: Centro Cívico, 8a Avda y 21 Calle, Zona 1, Guatemala City; tel. 2248-5005; fax 2248-5054; e-mail info@minfin.gob.gt; internet www.minfin.gob.gt.

Ministry of Public Health and Social Welfare: Escuela de Enfermería, 3°, 6a Avda 3-45, Zona 1, Guatemala City; tel. 2475-2121; fax 2475-1125; e-mail info@mspas.gob.gt; internet www.mspas.gob.gt.

President and Legislature

PRESIDENT

Presidential Election, 9 September and 4 November 2007

Candidate	First round % of votes	Second round % of votes
Alvaro Colom Caballeros (UNE)	28.25	52.81
Gen. (retd) Otto Fernando Pérez Molina (PP)	23.54	47.19
Alejandro Eduardo Giammattei Falla (GANA)	17.23	—
José Eduardo Suger Cofiño (CASA)	7.45	—
Luis Armando Rabbe Tejada (FRG)	7.30	—
Mario Amilcar Estrada Orellana (UCN)	3.16	—
Rigoberta Menchú Tum (EG)	3.06	—
Total valid votes (incl. others)	100.00	100.00

CONGRESO DE LA REPÚBLICA

President: JOSÉ ROBERTO ALEJOS CÁMBARA.

Vice-Presidents: GABRIEL HEREDIA CASTRO, OSWALDO IVÁN ARÉVALO BARRIOS, CARLOS RAFAEL FIÓN MORALES.

General Election, 9 September 2007

	% of votes	Seats
Unidad Nacional de la Esperanza	22.84	50
Gran Alianza Nacional	16.54	36
Partido Patriota	15.66	29
Frente Republicano Guatemalteco	9.71	15
Partido Unionista	6.10	8
Centro de Acción Social	4.88	5
Unión del Cambio Nacionalista	4.06	5
Encuentro por Guatemala	6.18	3
Partido de Avanzada Nacional	4.54	3
Unidad Revolucionaria Nacional Guatemalteca—Movimiento Amplio de Izquierdas	3.56	3
Unión Democrática	1.41	1
Total valid votes (incl. others)	100.00	158

Election Commission

Tribunal Supremo Electoral: 6a Avda 0-32, Zona 2, Guatemala City; tel. 2413-0303; e-mail tse@tse.org.gt; internet www.tse.org.gt; f. 1983; independent; Pres. MARIA EUGENIA VILLAGRÁN DE LEÓN.

Political Organizations

Bienestar Nacional (BIEN): 8a Avda 6-40, Zona 2, Guatemala City; tel. 2254-1458; internet www.bienestarnacional.org; Sec.-Gen. FIDEL REYES LEE.

Centro de Acción Social (CASA): 4 Avda 10-31, Zona 10, Guatemala City; tel. 2362-6980; f. 2003; Sec.-Gen. MARIO RODERICO MAZARIEGOS DE LEÓN.

Encuentro por Guatemala (EG): 9 Avda 0-71, Zona 4, Guatemala City; tel. 2231-9859; fax 2230-6463; e-mail izaveliz@yahoo.es; internet www.encuentroporguatemala.org; f. 2006; centre-left; promotes indigenous interests; Sec.-Gen. NINETH VERENCA MONTENEGRO COTTOM.

Frente Republicano Guatemalteco (FRG): 3a Calle 5-50, Zona 1, Guatemala City; tel. 2238-0826; internet www.frg.org.gt; f. 1988; right-wing group; Sec.-Gen. Gen. (retd) JOSÉ EFRAÍN RÍOS MONTT.

Gran Alianza Nacional (GANA): 6a Avda, 3-44, Zona 9, Guatemala City; tel. 2331-4811; fax 2362-7512; e-mail info@gana.com.gt; internet www.gana.com.gt; f. 2003 as electoral alliance of PP, Movimiento Reformador and Partido Solidaridad Nacional; registered as a party in 2005 following withdrawal of PP; Sec.-Gen. JAIME ANTONIO MARTÍNEZ LOHAYZA.

Partido de Avanzada Nacional (PAN): 3a Avda 18-28, Zona 14, Guatemala City; tel. 2366-1509; fax 2337-2001; e-mail pan.partidodeavanzadanacional@gmail.com; internet www.pan-gt.com; Sec.-Gen. JUAN GUTIÉRREZ.

Partido Patriota (PP): 11 Calle 11-54, Zona 1, Guatemala City; tel. 2311-6886; e-mail comunicacion@partidopatriota.org; internet www.partidopatriota.com; f. 2002; contested 2003 elections as part of GANA (q.v.); withdrew from GANA in May 2004; right-wing; Leader Gen. (retd) OTTO FERNANDO PÉREZ MOLINA; Sec.-Gen. INGRID ROXANA BALDETTI ELÍAS.

Partido Unionista (PU): 5a Avda 'A' 13-43, Zona 9, Guatemala City; tel. 2331-7468; fax 2331-6141; e-mail info@unionista.org; internet www.unionistas.org; f. 1917; Sec.-Gen. FRIEDERICH GARCÍA-GALLONT.

Unidad Nacional de la Esperanza (UNE): 6a Avda 8-72, Zona 9, Guatemala City; tel. 2334-3451; e-mail ideas@une.org.gt; internet www.une.org.gt; f. 2001 following a split within the PAN; centre-left; Founder and Pres. ALVARO COLOM CABALLEROS.

Unidad Revolucionaria Nacional Guatemalteca—Movimiento Amplio de Izquierdas (URNG—MAIZ): 12a Avda 'B' 6-00, Zona 2, Guatemala City; tel. 2254-0704; fax 2254-0572; e-mail prensaurng@guate.net; f. 1982 following unification of principal guerrilla groups engaged in the civil war; formally registered as a political party in 1998, following the end of the civil war in Dec. 1996; Sec.-Gen. HÉCTOR ALFREDO NUILA ERICASTILLA.

Unión del Cambio Nacionalista (UCN): 5a Calle 5-27, Zone 9, Guatemala City; tel. 2361-6729; e-mail ucnguatemala@gmail.com; internet www.ucnguatemala.com; f. 2006; Sec.-Gen. MARIO ESTRADA.

Unión Democrática (UD): Casa 9, 5 Calle 12-00, Zona 14, Guatemala City; tel. 2363-5013; fax 2369-3062; e-mail info@uniondemocratica.info; f. 1983; Sec.-Gen. MANUEL EDUARDO CONDE ORELLANA.

Los Verdes (LV): 3a Avda 3-72, Zona 1, Guatemala City; tel. 570-3420; e-mail losverdesguatemala@gmail.com; Sec.-Gen. RODOLFO ROSALES GARCÍA SALAS.

Diplomatic Representation

EMBASSIES IN GUATEMALA

Argentina: Edif. Europlaza 1703, 17°, Torre I, 5a Avda 5-55, Zona 14, Apdo 120, Guatemala City; tel. and fax 2385-3786; e-mail embajadadeargentina@hotmail.com; Ambassador ERNESTO JUSTO LÓPEZ.

Belize: Edif. Europlaza Torre II, Of. 1502, 5a Avda 5-55, Zona 14, Guatemala City; tel. 2367-3883; fax 2367-3884; e-mail info@embajadabelice.org; internet www.embajadadebelice.org; Ambassador ALFREDO MARTÍN MARTÍNEZ.

Brazil: 18a Calle 2-22, Zona 14, Apdo 196-A, Guatemala City; tel. 2321-6800; fax 2337-3475; e-mail braembs@intelnet.net.gt; internet www.embajadadebrasil.com.gt; Ambassador LUIS ANTONIO FACHINI GOMES.

Canada: Edif. Edyma Plaza, 8°, 13a Calle 8-44, Zona 10, Apdo 400, Guatemala City; tel. 2363-4348; fax 2365-1210; e-mail gtmla@international.gc.ca; internet www.canadainternational.gc.ca/guatemala; Ambassador LEEANN MCKECHNIE.

Chile: 14a Calle 15-21, Zona 13, Guatemala City; tel. 2334-8273; fax 2334-8276; e-mail echilegu@intelnet.net.gt; Ambassador JORGE MARIO SAAVEDRA CANALES.

China (Taiwan): 4a Avda 'A' 13-25, Zona 9, Apdo 897, Guatemala City; tel. 2339-0711; fax 2332-2668; e-mail gtm@mofa.gov.tw; internet www.taiwanembassy.org/gt; Ambassador ADOLFO SUN.

Colombia: Edif. Europlaza, Torre I, Of. 1603, 5a Avda 5-55, Zona 14, Guatemala City; tel. 2385-3432; fax 2385-3438; e-mail embacolombia@intelett.com; Ambassador EDUARDO LÓPEZ SABOGAL.

Costa Rica: 15a Calle 7-59, Zona 10, Guatemala City; tel. 2366-9918; fax 2366-9935; e-mail embarica@intelnet.net.gt; Ambassador LIDIETTE BRENES ARGUEDAS.

Cuba: Avda las Américas 20-72, Zona 13, Guatemala City; tel. 2332-4066; fax 2332-5525; e-mail embagua@intelnet.net.gt; Chargé d'affaires a.i. ELISEO ZAMORA HERNÁNDEZ.

Dominican Republic: Centro Empresarial 'Zona Pradera', Torre II, Of. 1606, 18 Calle 24-69, Zona 10, Guatemala City; tel. 2261-7016; fax 2261-7017; e-mail embardgt@gmail.com; Ambassador OCTAVIO LISTER HENRÍQUEZ.

Ecuador: 4a Avda 12-04, Zona 14, Guatemala City; tel. 2337-2994; fax 2368-1831; e-mail embecuad@itelgua.com; Ambassador VICENTE FÉLIX VÉLIZ BRIONES.

Egypt: Edif. Cobella, 5°, 5a Avda 10-84, Zona 14, Apdo 502, Guatemala City; tel. 2333-6296; fax 2368-2808; e-mail egyptemb@gold.guate.net.gt; Ambassador MOSTAFA MAHMOUD ELREMALY.

El Salvador: Avda las Américas 16-40, Zona 13, Guatemala City; tel. 2360-7660; fax 2332-1228; e-mail emsalva@intelnet.net.gt; Ambassador CLAUDIA CANJURA DE CENTENO.

France: Edif. COGEFAR, 5a Avda 8-59, Zona 14, Apdo 971-A, 01014 Guatemala City; tel. 2421-7370; fax 2421-7407; e-mail ambfrguate@intelnet.net.gt; internet www.ambafrance.org.gt; Ambassador MICHÈLE RAMIS-PLUM.

Germany: Edif. Plaza Marítima, 2°, 20 Calle 6-20, Zona 10, Guatemala City; tel. 2364-6700; fax 2333-6906; e-mail embalemana@intelnet.net.gt; internet www.guatemala.diplo.de; Ambassador PETER LINDER.

Holy See: 10a Calle 4-47, Zona 9, Apdo 3041, Guatemala City (Apostolic Nunciature); tel. 2332-4274; fax 2334-1918; e-mail nuntius@itelgua.com; Apostolic Nuncio Most Rev. PAUL RICHARD GALLAGHER (Titular Archbishop of Hodelm).

Honduras: 19 Avda 'A' 20-19, Zona 10, Guatemala City; tel. 2366-5640; fax 2368-0062; e-mail embhond@intelnet.net.gt; Chargé d'affaires a.i. CARMEN BULNES HERNÁNDEZ.

Israel: 13a Avda 14-07, Zona 10, Guatemala City; tel. 2333-4624; fax 2333-6950; e-mail info@guatemala.mfa.gov.il; internet guatemala.mfa.gov.il; Ambassador ELIYAHU LOPEZ.

Italy: Edif. Santa Bárbara, 12a Calle 6-49, Zona 14, Guatemala City; tel. 2366-9271; fax 2367-3916; e-mail ambasciata.guatemala@esteri.it; internet www.ambguatemala.esteri.it; Ambassador MAINARDO BENARDELLI DE LEITENBURG.

Japan: Edif. Torre Internacional, 10°, Avda de la Reforma 16-85, Zona 10, Guatemala City; tel. 2382-7300; fax 2382-7310; e-mail info@japon.net.gt; internet www.gt.emb-japan.go.jp; Ambassador KAZUMI SUZUKI.

Korea, Republic: Edif. Europlaza, Torre III, 7°, 5a Avda 5-55, Zona 14, Guatemala City; tel. 2382-4051; fax 2382-4057; e-mail korembsy@mofat.go.kr; internet gtm.mofat.go.kr; Ambassador NAM SANG-JUNG.

Mexico: 2a Avda 7-57, Zona 10, Apdo 1455, Guatemala City; tel. 2420-3400; fax 2420-3410; e-mail embamexguat@itelgua.com; internet www.sre.gob.mx/guatemala; Ambassador EDUARDO IBARROLA NICOLÍN.

Netherlands: Edif. Torre Internacional, 13°, 16a Calle 0-55, Zona 10, Guatemala City; tel. 2381-4300; fax 2381-4350; e-mail nlgovgua@intelnet.net.gt; internet www.embajadadeholanda-gua.org; Ambassador TEUNIS KAMPER.

Nicaragua: 13 Avda 14-54, Zona 10, Guatemala City; tel. 2368-2284; fax 2333-4636; e-mail embaguat@terra.com.gt; Ambassador SILVIO MORA MORA.

Norway: Edif. Murano Center, 15°, Of. 1501, 14 Calle 3-51, Zona 10, Apdo 1764, Guatemala City; tel. 2366-5908; fax 2366-5823; e-mail emb.guatemala@mfa.no; internet www.noruega.org.gt; Ambassador LARS OLE VAAGEN.

Panama: 12a Calle 2-65, Zona 14, Apdo 929A, Guatemala City; tel. 2366-3331; fax 2366-3338; e-mail panguate@hotmail.com; Ambassador DIONISIO DE GRACIA GUILLÉN.

Peru: 15a Avda 'A' 20-16, Zona 13, Guatemala City; tel. 2331-7841; fax 2361-8542; e-mail leprugua@concyt.gob.gt; internet www.embajadaperu-guatemala.org; Ambassador GLICERIO VILLANUEVA DÍAZ.

Russia: 2a Avda 12-85, Zona 14, Guatemala City; tel. 2367-2765; fax 2367-2766; e-mail embrusa@guate.net.gt; internet www.guat.mid.ru; Ambassador NIKOLAYI M. VLADIMIR (resident in San José, Costa Rica).

Spain: 6a Calle 6-48, Zona 9, Guatemala City; tel. 2379-3530; fax 2379-3533; e-mail emb.guatemala@maec.es; internet www.maec.es/embajadas/guatemala; Ambassador MARÍA DEL CARMEN DÍEZ OREJAS.

Sweden: Edif. Reforma 10, 11°, Avda de la Reforma 9-55, Zona 10, Apdo 966-A, Guatemala City; tel. 2384-7300; fax 2384-7350; e-mail ambassaden.guatemala@foreign.ministry.se; internet www.swedenabroad.com/guatemala; Chargé d'affaires a.i. EWA NUNES-SÖRENSEN.

Switzerland: Edif. Torre Internacional, 14°, 16a Calle 0-55, Zona 10, Apdo 1426, Guatemala City; tel. 2367-5520; fax 2367-5811; e-mail vertretung@gua.rep.admin.ch; internet www.eda.admin.ch/guatemala; Ambassador JEAN-PIERRE VILLARD.

United Kingdom: Edif. Torre Internacional, 11°, Avda de la Reforma, 16a Calle, Zona 10, Guatemala City; tel. 2380-7300; fax 2380-7339; e-mail embassy@intelnett.com; internet ukinguatemala.fco.gov.uk; Ambassador JULIE CHAPPELL.

USA: Avda de la Reforma 7-01, Zona 10, Guatemala City; tel. 2326-4000; fax 2326-4654; internet guatemala.usembassy.gov; Ambassador STEPHEN MCFARLAND.

Uruguay: Edif. Plaza Marítima, 3°, Of. 342, 6a Avda 20-25, Zona 10, Guatemala City; tel. 2368-0810; fax 2333-7553; e-mail uruguate@gmail.com; Ambassador CARMEN FROS DONINELLI.

Venezuela: Edif. Atlantis, Of. 601, 13a Calle 3-40, Zona 10, Apdo 152, Guatemala City; tel. 2366-9832; fax 2366-9838; e-mail embavene@concyt.gob.gt; Ambassador JENY FIGUEREDO FRÍAS.

Judicial System

Corte Suprema

Centro Cívico, 21 Calle 7-70, Zona 1, Guatemala City; internet www.oj.gob.gt.

The members of the Supreme Court are appointed by Congress.

President of the Supreme Court: Dr ERICK ALFONSO ALVAREZ MANCILLA.

Members: Dr C. R. C. BARRIENTOS PELLECER, Dr G. A. MEDRANO VALENZUELA, G. A. MENDIZÁBAL MAZARIEGOS, H. M. MALDONADO MÉNDEZ, Dr R. ZARCEÑO GAITÁN, T. E. ALDANA HERNÁNDEZ, L. A. PINEDA ROCA, M. C. FRANCO FLORES, E. G. GÓMEZ MÉNDEZ, J. A. SIERRA GONZÁLEZ, A. R. ARCHILA LERAYEES, G. BONILLA.

Civil Courts of Appeal: 20 courts, located in Guatemala City, Quetzaltenango, Jalapa, Zacapa, Antigua Guatemala, Retalhuleu, Cobán and Mazatenango.

Courts of the First Instance: 10 civil and 12 penal in Guatemala City, and at least one civil and one penal in each of the 21 remaining Departments of the Republic.

Attorney-General: CONRADO REYES SAGASTUME.

Religion

Almost all of the inhabitants profess Christianity, with a majority belonging to the Roman Catholic Church. In recent years the Protestant churches have attracted a growing number of converts.

CHRISTIANITY

The Roman Catholic Church

For ecclesiastical purposes, Guatemala comprises two archdioceses, 10 dioceses and the Apostolic Vicariates of El Petén and Izabal. Some 78% of the population are Roman Catholics.

Bishops' Conference

Conferencia Episcopal de Guatemala, Secretariado General del Episcopado, Km 15, Calzada Roosevelt 4-54, Zona 7, Mixco, Apdo 1698, Guatemala City; tel. 2433-1832; fax 2433-1834; e-mail ceguatemala@gmail.com; internet www.iglesiacatolica.org.gt.

f. 1973; Pres. Rev. PABLO VIZCAÍNO PRADO (Bishop of Suchitepéquez-Retalhuleu).

Archbishop of Guatemala City: Cardinal RODOLFO QUEZADA TORUÑO, Arzobispado, 7a Avda 6-21, Zona 1, Apdo 723, Guatemala City; tel. 2232-9707; fax 2251-5068; e-mail curiaarzobispal@intelnet.net.gt.

Archbishop of Los Altos, Quetzaltenango-Totonicapán: OSCAR JULIO VIAN MORALES, Arzobispado, 11a Avda 6-27, Zona 1, Apdo 11, 09001 Quetzaltenango; tel. 7761-2840; fax 7761-6049.

The Anglican Communion

Guatemala comprises one of the five dioceses of the Iglesia Anglicana de la Región Central de América.

Bishop of Guatemala: Rt Rev. ARMANDO ROMÁN GUERRA SORIA, Avda Castellana 40-06, Zona 8, Apdo 58-A, Guatemala City; tel. 2473-6828; fax 2472-0764; e-mail diocesis@infovia.com.gt; diocese founded 1967.

Protestant Churches

The largest Protestant denomination in Guatemala is the Full Gospel Church, followed by the Assembly of God, the Central American Church, and the Prince of Peace Church. The Baptist, Presbyterian, Lutheran and Episcopalian churches are also represented.

The Baptist Church: Convention of Baptist Churches of Guatemala, 12a Calle 9-54, Zona 1, Apdo 322, 01901 Guatemala City; tel. and fax 2232-4227; e-mail cibg@intelnet.net.gt; f. 1946; Pres. JOSÉ MARROQUÍN R.; 43,876 mems.

Church of Jesus Christ of Latter-day Saints: 12a Calle 3-37, Zona 9, Guatemala City; e-mail contactos@mormones.org.gt; internet www.mormones.org.gt; 17 bishoprics, 9 chapels; Pres. THOMAS S. MONSON.

Conferencia de Iglesias Evangélicas de Guatemala (CIEDEG) (Conference of Protestant Churches in Guatemala): 7a Avda 1-11, Zona 2, Guatemala City; tel. 2232-3724; fax 2232-1609; Pres. VITALINO SIMILOX.

Congregación Luterana La Epifanía (Evangelisch-Lutherische Epiphanias-Gemeinde): 2a Avda 15-31, Zona 10, 01010 Guatemala City; tel. 2368-0301; fax 2366-4968; e-mail schweikle@web.de; mem. of Lutheran World Federation; Pres. ROLF MEIER; 200 mems.

Divine Saviour Lutheran Church: Zacapa; tel. 7941-0254; e-mail hogarluterano@hotmail.com; f. 1946; Pastor GERARDO VENANCIO VÁSQUEZ SALGUERO.

Iglesia Evangélica Nacional Presbiteriana de Guatemala: Avda Simeón Cañas 7-13, Zona 2, Apdo 655, Guatemala City; tel. 2288-4441; fax 2254-1242; e-mail ienpg@yahoo.com; f. 1962; mem. of World Alliance of Reformed Churches; Sec. Pastor IVAN HAROLDO PAZ ANDRADE; 25,000 mems.

Iglesia Nacional Evangélica Menonita Guatemalteca: Guatemala City; tel. 2339-0606; e-mail AlvaradoJE@ldschurch.org; Contact JULIO ALVARADO; 210,000 mems (2003).

Union Church: 12a Calle 7-37, Zona 9, 01009 Guatemala City; tel. 2361-2037; fax 2362-3961; e-mail unionchurch@guate.net.gt; internet careministryucg.org; f. 1943; English-speaking church; Pastor DAVID GINTER.

The Press

PRINCIPAL DAILIES

Al Día: Avda de la Reforma 6-64, Zona 9, Guatemala City; tel. 2339-7430; fax 2339-7435; e-mail aldia@notinet.com.gt; f. 1996; Pres. LIONEL TORIELLO NÁJERA; Dir GERARDO JIMÉNEZ ARDÓN; Editor OTONIEL MONROY HERNÁNDEZ.

Diario de Centroamérica: 18a Calle 6-72, Zona 1, Guatemala City; tel. 2222-4418; e-mail info@dca.gob.gt; internet www.diariodecentroamerica.gob.gt; f. 1880; morning; official; Dir ANA MARÍA RODAS; circ. 15,000.

Guía Interamericana de Turismo: Edif. Plaza los Arcos, 3°, 20 Calle 5-35, Zona 10, Guatemala City; tel. 2450-6431; e-mail info@guiainter.org; internet www.guiainter.org; f. 1989; online journal; Dir-Gen. MARIO ORINI; Editor ALFREDO MAYORGA; circ. 5,000.

La Hora: 9a Calle 'A' 1-56, Zona 1, Apdo 1593, Guatemala City; tel. 2423-1800; fax 2423-1837; e-mail lahora@lahora.com.gt; internet www.lahora.com.gt; f. 1920; evening; independent; Dir ÓSCAR CLEMENTE MARROQUÍN; Editor MARIO CORDERO; circ. 18,000.

Nuestro Diario: 15 Avda 24-27, Zona 13, Guatemala City; tel. and fax 2379-1600; fax 2379-1621; e-mail opinion@nuestrodiario.com.gt; internet www.nuestrodiario.com; Gen. Man. JORGE SPRINGMÜHL; Gen. Editor RODRIGO CASTILLO DEL CARMEN.

El Periódico: 15a Avda 24-51, Zona 13, Guatemala City; tel. 2427-2300; fax 2427-2361; e-mail redaccion@elperiodico.com.gt; internet www.elperiodico.com.gt; f. 1996; morning; independent; Pres. JOSÉ RUBÉN ZAMORA; Editor ANA CAROLINA ALPÍREZ; circ. 30,000.

Prensa Libre: 13a Calle 9-31, Zona 1, Apdo 2063, Guatemala City; tel. 2230-5096; fax 2251-8768; e-mail nacional@prensalibre.com.gt; internet www.prensalibre.com.gt; f. 1951; morning; independent; Gen. Man. LUIS ENRIQUE SOLÓRZANO; Editor GONZALO MARROQUÍN GODOY; circ. 120,000.

Siglo Veintiuno: 12a Avda 4-33, Zona 1, Guatemala City; tel. 2423-6101; fax 2423-6346; e-mail buzon21@sigloxxi.com; internet www.sigloxxi.com; f. 1990; morning; Dir GUILLERMO FERNÁNDEZ; Gen. Man. LUCIANA CISNEROS; circ. 65,000.

PERIODICALS

Amiga: 13 Calle 9-31, Zona 1, Guatemala City; tel. 2412-5000; fax 2220-5123; e-mail revistas@prensalibre.com.gt; internet www.revistaamiga.com; health; Dir CAROLINA VÁSQUEZ ARAYA; Editor ALEJANDRA CARDONA.

Crónica Semanal: Guatemala City; tel. 2235-2155; fax 2235-2360; f. 1988; weekly; politics, economics, culture; Publr FRANCISCO PÉREZ.

Especiales: Edif. El Gráfico, 14a Avda 4-33, Zona 1, Guatemala City; e-mail moneda@guate.net; international news magazine; Dir KATIA DE CARPIO.

Gerencia: Torre Citigroup, Of. 402, 3a Avda 13-78, Zona 14, Guatemala City; tel. 2427-4900; fax 2427-4971; e-mail agg@guate.net; internet www.agg.org.gt; f. 1967; monthly; official organ of the Asscn of Guatemalan Managers; Man. ILEANA LÓPEZ AVILA.

Guatemala Business News: 10a Calle 3-80, Zona 1, Guatemala City; monthly; Editor RODOLFO GARCÍA; circ. 5,000.

Inforpress Centroamericana: Calle Mariscal 21, 6-58, Zona 11, Guatemala City; tel. 2473-1704; e-mail inforpre@inforpressca.com; internet www.inforpressca.com; f. 1972; weekly; Spanish and English; regional political and economic news and analysis; Dir ARIEL DE LEÓN.

El Metropolitano: Plaza Morumbi 7 y 8, 2°, 3a Calle 15-29, Zona 8, San Cristóbal, Guatemala City; e-mail info@elmetropolitano.net; internet www.elmetropolitano.net; Editor JORGE GARCÍA MONTENEGRO.

Mundo Motor: 13a Calle 9-31, Zona 1, Guatemala City; tel. 2412-5000; fax 2220-5123; e-mail evasquez@prensalibre.com.gt; internet www.mundoymotor.com; Dir CAROLINA VÁSQUEZ; Editor NÉSTOR A. LARRAZÁBAL B.

Revista D: 13 Calle 9-31, Zona 1, Guatemala City; e-mail revistas@prensalibre.com.gt; internet www.prensalibre.com/pl/domingo/index.shtml; weekly; general interest; Dir CAROLINA VÁSQUEZ; Editor GERARDO JIMÉNEZ.

Revista Data Export: 15 Avda 14-72, Zona 13, Guatemala City; tel. 2422-3431; fax 2422-3434; e-mail portal@agexport.org.gt; internet revistadataexport.com; monthly; foreign trade affairs; organ of the Asociacíon Guatemalteca de Exportadores; Editor FULVIA DONIS; circ. 1,500.

Revista Industria: 6a Ruta 9-21, Zona 4, Guatemala City; tel. 2380-9000; e-mail contactemos@industriaguate.com; internet www.revistaindustria.com; monthly; official organ of the Chamber of Industry; Dir OSCAR VILLAGRÁN.

Revista Mundo Comercial: 10a Calle 3-80, Zona 1, 01001 Guatemala City; e-mail mundo@guatemala-chamber.org; internet www

.negociosenguatemala.com; monthly; business; official organ of the Chamber of Commerce; circ. 11,000.

Tertulia: Guatemala City; e-mail tertulia@intelnett.com; f. 1997; women's affairs; Editor LAURA E. ASTURIAS.

Usuario: 13a Calle 9-31, Zona 1, Guatemala City; computing; Dir CAROLINA VÁSQUEZ.

Viajes: 13a Calle 9-31, Zona 1, Guatemala City; e-mail revistas@prensalibre.com.gt; internet www.viajeaguatemala.com; tourism; Dir CAROLINA VÁSQUEZ.

Vida Médica: Edif. Reforma Montúfar, Torre A, Of. 1006, Avda Reforma 12-01, Zona 10, Guatemala City; tel. 2331-7679; fax 2331-7754; health; Dir SERAPIO ALVARADO; Editorial Dir Dr CARLOS SALAZAR.

PRESS ASSOCIATIONS

Asociación de Periodistas de Guatemala (APG): 14a Calle 3-29, Zona 1, Guatemala City; tel. 2232-1813; fax 2238-2781; e-mail apege@intelnet.net.gt; f. 1947; affiliated to IFEX and FELAP; Pres. JORGE HUMBERTO FONG CROCKER; Sec. RAFAEL HERNÁNDEZ CABRERA.

Cámara Guatemalteca de Periodismo (CGP): Guatemala City; Pres. RICARDO CASTILLO DEL CARMEN.

Círculo Nacional de Prensa (CNP): 2 Avda 10-52, Zona 1, Guatemala City; tel. 2251-4363; internet www.circuloprensa.org; f. 1963; Pres. SERGIO ROBERTO LIMA MORALES; Sec.-Gen. JORGE ROBERTO CHAN PEDRO.

NEWS AGENCY

Inforpress Centroamericana: Calle Mariscal o Diagonal 21, 6-58, Zona 11, 0100 Guatemala City; tel. and fax 2473-1704; e-mail inforpre@guate.net; internet www.inforpressca.com; f. 1972; independent news agency; publishes 2 weekly news bulletins, in English and Spanish.

Publishers

Cholsamaj: 1a Avda 9-18, Zona 1, Apdo 4, Guatemala City; tel. 2232-5417; e-mail cholsamaj@fundacioncholsamaj.org; internet www.cholsamaj.org; Mayan language publs.

Ediciones Legales Comercio e Industria: 12a Avda 14-78, Zone 1, Guatemala City; tel. 2253-5725; fax 2220-7592; Man. Dir LUIS EMILIO BARRIOS.

Editorial Cultura: 10A Calle 10-14, Zona 1, Guatemala City; tel. 2232-5667; fax 2230-0591; e-mail cultuarte@intelnet.net.gt; part of the Ministry of Culture and Sport.

Editorial Nueva Narrativa: Edif. El Patrio, Of. 108, 7a Avda 7-07, Zona 4, Guatemala City; tel. 2360-0732; fax 5704-7895; Man. Dir MAX ARAÚJO A.

Editorial Palo de Hormigo: 0 Calle 16-40, Zona 15, Col. El Maestro, Guatemala City; tel. 2369-3089; fax 2369-8858; e-mail eph_info@palodehormigo.com; f. 1990; Man. Dir RICARDO ULYSSES CIFUENTES.

Editorial Universitaria: Edif. de la Editorial Universitaria, Universidad de San Carlos de Guatemala, Ciudad Universitaria, Zona 12, Guatemala City; tel. and fax 2476-9628; literature, social sciences, health, pure and technical sciences, humanities, secondary and university educational textbooks.

F & G Editores: 31a Avda 'C' 5-54, Zona 7, 01007 Guatemala City; tel. and fax 2439-8358; e-mail informacion@fygeditores.com; internet www.fygeditores.com; f. 1990 as Figueroa y Gallardo; changed name in 1993; law, literature and social sciences; Editor RAÚL FIGUEROA SARTI.

Piedra Santa: 37a Avda 1-26, Zona 7, Guatemala City; tel. 2422-7676; fax 2422-7610; e-mail piperalta@piedrasanta.com; internet www.piedrasanta.com; f. 1947; education, culture; Man. Dir IRENE PIEDRA SANTA.

Broadcasting and Communications

TELECOMMUNICATIONS

Regulatory Authority

Superintendencia de Telecomunicaciones de Guatemala: Avda 3-87, Zona 10, Guatemala City; tel. 2321-1000; e-mail supertel@sit.gob.gt; internet www.sit.gob.gt; f. 1996; Supt OSCAR STUARDO CHINCHILLA.

Major Service Providers

Comunicaciones Celulares (Comcel): Guatemala City; tel. 2428-0000; e-mail sugerencias@comcel.com.gt; internet www.tigo.com.gt; provider of mobile telecommunications; 55% owned by Millicom International Cellular (Luxembourg).

Telecomunicaciones de Guatemala, SA (Telgua): Edif. Central Telgua, 7a Avda 12-39, Zona 1, Guatemala City; internet www.telgua.com.gt; fmrly state-owned Empresa Guatemalteca de Telecomunicaciones (Guatel); name changed as above to facilitate privatization; 95% share transferred to private ownership in 1998; owned by América Móvil, SA de CV (Mexico); Dirs JULIO BELIZARIO MONTEPEQUE, MARVIN EMILIO PAR-GONZÁLEZ LÓPEZ.

Telefónica MoviStar Guatemala, SA: Torre Telefónica, 9°, Blvd Los Próceres 20-09, Zona 10, Guatemala City; tel. 2379-7979; e-mail servicioalcliente@telefonica.com.gt; internet www.telefonica.com.gt; owned by TelefónicaMóviles, SA (Spain); acquired BellSouth Guatemala in 2004; wireless, wireline and radio paging communications services; 298,000 customers; CEO HUMBERTO PATO VINUESA.

Other service providers include: Emergia, FT & T (Telered), Cablenet, Universal de Telecomunicaciones, Telefónica Centroamérica Guatemala, Servicios de Comunicaciones Personales Inalámbricas, A-tel Communications, Cybernet de Centroamérica, Teléfonos del Norte, Americatel Guatemala, Desarrollo Integral, BNA, TTI, Optel and Concert Global Networks.

BROADCASTING

Dirección General de Radiodifusión y Televisión Nacional: Edif. Tipografía Nacional, 3°, 18 de Septiembre 6-72, Zona 1, Guatemala City; tel. 2323-8282; e-mail radiotgw@radiotgw.gob.gt; internet www.radiotgw.gob.gt; f. 1931; govt supervisory body; Dir-Gen. EDGAR FRANCISCO GUDIEL LEMUS.

Radio

There are currently five government and six educational stations, including:

Radio Cultural TGN: 4a Avda 30–09 Zona 3, Apdo 601, Guatemala City; tel. 2471-4378; fax 2440-0260; e-mail tgn@radiocultural.com; internet www.radiocultural.com; f. 1950; religious and cultural station; programmes in Spanish and English, Cakchiquel, Kekchi, Quiché and Aguacateco; Dir Emeritus Dr STEPHEN ROBB SYWULKA BURGESS; Man. ANTHONY WAYNE BERGER WISEMAN.

Radio Nacional TGW (La Voz de Guatemala): 18a Calle 6-72, Zona 1, Guatemala City; tel. 2323-8282; e-mail info@radiotgw.gob.gt; internet www.radiotgw.gob.gt; govt station; Dir EDGAR FRANCISCO GUDIEL LEMUS.

There are some 80 commercial stations, of which the most important are:

Emisoras Unidas de Guatemala: 4a Calle 6-84, Zona 13, Guatemala City; tel. 2421-5353; fax 2475-3870; e-mail patrullajeinformativo@emisorasunidas.com; internet www.emisorasunidas.com; f. 1964; 7 stations: Yo Sí Sideral, EmisorasUnidas, Kiss, Atmósfera, Fabustereo, Radio Estrella and La Grande; Pres. JORGE EDGARDO ARCHILA MARROQUÍN; Vice-Pres. ROLANDO ARCHILA MARROQUÍN.

La Marca: 30a Avda 3-40, Zona 11, Guatemala City; tel. 2410-3150; fax 2410-3151; e-mail lamarca@94fm.com.gt; internet www.94fm.com.gt.

Metro Stereo: 14a Avda 14-78, Zona 10, Guatemala City; tel. 2277-7686; fax 2368-2040; e-mail metrored@metrostereo.net; internet www.metrostereo.net; Dir RUGGIERO MAURO-RHODIO.

Television

Canal 5—Televisión Cultural y Educativa, SA: 4a Calle 18-38, Zona 1, Guatemala City; tel. 2253-1913; fax 2232-7003; f. 1980; cultural and educational programmes; Dir ALFREDO HERRERA CABRERA.

Radio-Televisión Guatemala, SA: 30a Avda 3-40, Zona 11, Apdo 1367, Guatemala City; tel. 2410-3600; e-mail telediario@canal3.com.gt; internet www.canal3.com.gt; f. 1956; commercial; operates channels 3 and 10; Pres. MAX KESTLER FARNÉS; Vice-Pres. J. F. VILLANUEVA.

Teleonce: 20a Calle 5-02, Zona 10, Guatemala City; tel. 2368-2532; fax 2368-2221; e-mail jcof@canalonce.tv; f. 1968; commercial; channel 11; Gen. Dir JUAN CARLOS ORTIZ.

Televisiete, SA: 30a Avda 3-40, Zona 11, Apdo 1242, Guatemala City; tel. 2410-3000; fax 2369-1393; internet www.canal7.com.gt; f. 1988; commercial; channel 7; Dir ABDÓN RODRÍGUEZ ZEA.

Trecevisión, SA: 20a Calle 5-02, Zona 10, Guatemala City; tel. 2368-2221; commercial; channel 13; f. 1978; Dir JUAN CARLOS ORTIZ; Gen. Man. JUAN CARLOS GONZÁLEZ.

Finance

(cap. = capital; res = reserves; dep. = deposits; m. = million; brs = branches; amounts in quetzales)

BANKING

Superintendencia de Bancos: 9a Avda 22-00, Zona 1, Apdo 2306, Guatemala City; tel. 2232-0001; fax 2232-0002; e-mail info@sib.gob.gt; internet www.sib.gob.gt; f. 1946; Supt EDGAR BARQUÍN.

Central Bank

Banco de Guatemala: 7a Avda 22-01, Zona 1, Apdo 365, Guatemala City; tel. 2429-6000; fax 2253-4035; e-mail webmaster@banguat.gob.gt; internet www.banguat.gob.gt; f. 1946; state-owned; cap. and res 3,037.4m., dep. 34,445.9m. (Dec. 2006); Pres. MARÍA ANTONIETA DEL CID NAVAS DE BONILLA; Gen. Man. MANUEL AUGUSTO ALONSO ARAUJO.

State Commercial Bank

Crédito Hipotecario Nacional de Guatemala (CHN): 7a Avda 22-77, Zona 1, Apdo 242, Guatemala City; tel. 2223-0333; fax 2238-2041; e-mail mercadeo@chn.com.gt; internet www.chn.com.gt; f. 1980; govt-owned; Pres. IVÁN DE PAZ; Gen. Man. JOSÉ FIDENCIO GARCÍA BELTETÓN; 44 agencies.

Private Commercial Banks

Banco Agromercantil de Guatemala, SA: 7a Avda 7-30, Zona 9, 01009 Guatemala City; tel. 2338-6565; fax 2388-6566; e-mail agromercantil@bam.com.gt; internet www.agromercantil.com.gt; f. 2000 as Banco Central de Guatemala; changed name to Banco Agrícola Mercantil in 1948; name changed as above in 2000, following merger with Banco del Agro; cap. 345.8m., res 86.1m., dep. 6,675.5m. (Dec. 2006); Pres. JOSÉ LUIS VALDÉS; Man. RAFAEL ANTONIO E. VIEJO RODRÍGUEZ; 78 agencies.

Banco de América Central, SA (BAC): Local 6-12, 1º, 7a Avda 6-26, Zona 9, Guatemala City; tel. 2360-9440; fax 2331-8720; internet www.bac.net; Gen. Man. JUAN JOSÉ VIAUD PÉREZ.

Banco Americano, SA: 11 Calle 7-44, Zona 9, 01009 Guatemala City; tel. 2386-1700; fax 2386-1753; e-mail grufin@infovia.com.gt; internet www.bancoamericano.com.gt; Gen. Man. JUAN JOSÉ VIAUD PÉREZ.

Banco Citibank de Guatemala, SA: Torre Citibank, 1°, 3a Avda 13-78, Zona 10, 01010 Guatemala City; tel. 2333-6574; fax 2333-6860; e-mail info@cuscatlanguate.com; internet www.bancocuscatlan.com; Citi acquired Banco Cuscatlan and Banco Uno in 2007.

Banco Corporativo, SA: 6a Avda 4-38, Zona 9, 01009 Guatemala City; tel. 2279-9999; fax 2279-9990; e-mail mcatalan@corpobanco.com.gt; internet www.corpobanco.com.gt; f. 1990.

Banco de Desarrollo Rural, SA: Avda La Reforma 9-30, Zona 9, Guatemala City; tel. 2339-8888; fax 2360-9740; e-mail internacional4@banrural.com.gt; internet www.banrural.com.gt; f. 1971 as Banco de Desarrollo Agrícola; name changed as above in 1998; cap. 554.1m., res 68.3m., dep. 15,932.7m. (Dec. 2006); Pres. JOSÉ ANGEL LÓPEZ CAMPOSECO; Gen. Man. ADOLFO FERNANDO PEÑA PÉREZ; 450 agencies.

Banco G & T Continental, SA: Plaza Continental, 6a Avda 9-08, Zona 9, Guatemala City; tel. 2338-6801; fax 2332-2682; e-mail subanco@gytcontinental.com.gt; internet www.gytcontinental.com.gt; f. 2000 following merger of Banco Continental and Banco Granai y Townson; total assets 11.4m. (2000); 130 brs.

Banco Industrial, SA (BAINSA): Edif. Centro Financiero, Torre 1, 7a Avda 5-10, Zona 4, Apdo 744, Guatemala City; tel. 2420-3000; fax 2331-9437; e-mail webmaster@bi.com.gt; internet www.bi.com.gt; f. 1964 to promote industrial devt; merged with Banco del Quetzal in 2007; total assets 7.91m. (1999); Gen. Man. DIEGO PULIDO ARAGÓN.

Banco Inmobilario, SA: 7a Avda 11-59, Zona 9, Apdo 1181, Guatemala City; tel. 2339-3777; fax 2332-1418; e-mail info@bcoinmob.com.gt; internet www.bcoinmob.com.gt; f. 1958; cap. 77.6m., res 0.4m., dep. 738.6m. (Dec. 2002); Pres. EMILIO ANTONIO PERALTA PORTILLO; 44 brs.

Banco Internacional, SA: Torre Internacional, Avda Reforma 15-85, Zona 10, Apdo 2588, Guatemala City; tel. 2277-3666; fax 2366-6743; e-mail info@bco.inter.com; internet www.bancointernacional.com.gt; f. 1976; cap. 217.7m., res –21.8m., dep. 1,943.6m. (Dec. 2006); Pres. CARLOS BARTOLOMÉ FERNÁNDEZ; Gen. Man. JUAN MANUEL VENTAS BENÍTEZ; 34 brs.

Banco Privado para el Desarrollo, SA: 7a Avda 8-46, Zona 9, Guatemala City; tel. 2423-6666; fax 2361-7217; e-mail atencionalpublico@bancosol.com.gt; internet www.bancasol.com.gt.

Banco Reformador, SA: 7a Avda 7-24, Zona 9, 01009 Guatemala City; tel. 2362-0888; fax 2362-0847; internet www.bancoreformador.com; cap. 184.1m., res 188.5m., dep. 4,348.9m. (Dec. 2006); merged with Banco de la Construcción in 2000, acquired Banco SCI in 2007; Pres. LUIS MIGUEL AGUIRRE FERNÁNDEZ; Gen. Man. RAYMOND PUCCINI; 86 brs.

Banco de los Trabajadores: Avda Reforma 6-20, Zona 9, 01001 Guatemala City; tel. 2410-2600; fax 2410-2616; e-mail webmaster@bantrab.net.gt; internet www.bantrab.com.gt; f. 1966; deals with loans for establishing and improving small industries as well as normal banking business; cap. 460.4m., dep. 2,119.5m., total assets 2,897.6m. (Dec. 2005); Pres. EDWIN ARIEL PEREIRA; Gen. Man. RONALD GIOVANNI GARCIA NAVARIJO; 52 brs.

Banco Uno: Edif. Unicentro, 1°, Blvd Los Próceres, 18 Calle 5-56, Zona 10, 01010 Guatemala City; tel. 2366-1777; fax 2366-1553; e-mail bancouno@gua.pibnet.com; internet www.bancouno.com.gt.

Finance Corporations

Corporación Financiera Nacional (CORFINA): 11a Avda 3-14, Zona 1, Guatemala City; tel. 2253-4550; fax 2232-5805; e-mail corfina@guate.net; internet www.guate.net/corfina; f. 1973; provides assistance for the devt of industry, mining and tourism.

Financiera Guatemalteca, SA (FIGSA): 1a Avda 11-50, Zona 10, Apdo 2460, Guatemala City; tel. 2338-8000; fax 2331-0873; e-mail figsa@figsa.com; internet www.banexfigsa.com; f. 1962; investment agency; Gen. Man. ROBERTO FERNÁNDEZ BOTRÁN.

Financiera de Inversión, SA: 11a Calle 7-44, Zona 9, Guatemala City; tel. 2332-4020; fax 2332-4320; f. 1981; investment agency; Pres. MARIO AUGUSTO PORRAS GONZÁLEZ; Gen. Man. JOSÉ ROLANDO PORRAS GONZÁLEZ.

Banking Association

Asociación Bancaria de Guatemala: Edif. Margarita 2, Of. 502, Diagonal 6, Zona 10, Guatemala City; tel. 2336-6080; fax 2336-6094; internet www.abg.org.gt; f. 1961; represents all state and private banks; Pres. LUIS FERNANDO SAMAYOA DELGADO.

STOCK EXCHANGE

Bolsa de Valores Nacional, SA: Centro Financiero, Torre II, 2°, 7a Avda 5-10, Zona 4, Guatemala City; tel. 2338-4400; fax 2332-1721; e-mail bvn@bvnsa.com.gt; internet www.bvnsa.com.gt; f. 1987; the exchange is commonly owned (1 share per associate) and trades stocks from private companies, govt bonds, letters of credit and other securities; Pres. JUAN CARLOS CASTILLO; Gen. Man. ROLANDO SAN ROMÁN.

INSURANCE

National Companies

Aseguradora La Ceiba, SA: 20 Calle 15-20, Zona 13, Guatemala City; tel. 2379-1800; fax 2334-8167; e-mail aceiba@aceiba.com.gt; internet www.aceiba.com.gt; f. 1978; Man. ALEJANDRO BELTRANENA.

Aseguradora General, SA: 10a Calle 3-71, Zona 10, Guatemala City; tel. 2285-7200; fax 2334-2093; e-mail servicio@generali.com.gt; internet www.aseguresemejor.com; f. 1968; subsidiary of Grupo Generali, Trieste, Italy; Pres. JUAN O. NIEMANN; Man. ENRIQUE NEUTZE A.

Aseguradora Guatemalteca, SA: Edif. Torre Azul, 10º, 4a Calle 7-53, Zona 9, Guatemala City; tel. 2361-0206; fax 2361-1093; e-mail aseguate@guate.net; internet www.aseguate.com; f. 1974; Pres. Gen. FERNANDO ALFONSO CASTILLO RAMÍREZ; Man. JOSÉ GUILLERMO H. LÓPEZ CORDÓN.

Aseguradora Mundial Guatemala: Edif. Torre Mundial II, 1°, 6° y 9°, 15a Avda 17-30, Zona 13, Guatemala City; tel. 2328-5000; fax 2328-5001; internet www.amundial.com.gt; f. 1967; subsidiary of Grupo Munidal de Panama; Pres. ORLANDO EDMUNDO SÁNCHEZ AVILÉS.

Chartis Seguros Guatemala, SA: Edif. Etisa, 7a Avda 12-23, Plazuela España, Zona 9, Guatemala City; tel. 2285-5900; fax 2361-3026; e-mail servicios.cmg@aig.com; internet www.aig.com; f. 1967 as La Seguridad de Centroamérica; present name adopted 2010; Gen. Man. JUAN MANUEL FRIEDERICH L.

Cía de Seguros El Roble, SA: Torre 2, 7a Avda 5-10, Zona 4, Guatemala City; tel. 2332-1702; fax 2332-1629; e-mail rerales@elroble.com; f. 1973; Gen. Man. HERMANN GIRON.

Departamento de Seguros y Previsión del Crédito Hipotecario Nacional: Centro Cívico, 7a Avda 22-77, Zona 1, Guatemala City; tel. 2223-0333; fax 2253-8584; e-mail vjsc@chn.com.gt; internet www.chn.com.gt; f. 1942; Pres. FREDDY A. MUÑOZ MORAN; Man. HUGO CRUZ MONTERROSO.

Pan-American Life Insurance Group, SA: Edif. Plaza Panamericana, Avda de la Reforma 9-00, Zona 9, Guatemala City; tel. 2338-9800; e-mail servicioalclientegt@panamericanlife.com; internet www.espanol.panamericanlife.com; f. 1968; Regional Pres. SALVADOR ORTEGA.

Seguros G & T, SA: Edif. Mini, 6a Avda 1–73, Zona 4, Guatemala City; tel. 2338-5778; e-mail erodriguez@gyt.com.gt; internet www.segurosgyt.com.gt; f. 1947; Gen. Man. ENRIQUE RODRÍGUEZ MHAR.

Seguros de Occidente, SA: 7a Calle 'A' 7-73, Zona 9, Guatemala City; tel. 2279-7000; e-mail seguros@occidentecorp.com.gt; internet www.occidentecorp.com.gt; f. 1979; Gen. Man. MARIO ROBERTO VALDEAVELLANO MUÑOZ.

Seguros Universales, SA: 4a Calle 7-73, Zona 9, Apdo 1479, Guatemala City; tel. 2277-2727; fax 2332-3372; e-mail info@segurosuniversales.net; internet www.segurosuniversales.net; f. 1962; Man. PEDRO NOLASCO SICILIA.

Insurance Association

Asociación Guatemalteca de Instituciones de Seguros (AGIS): Edif. Torre Profesional I, Of. 703, 4°, 6a Avda 0-60, Zona 4, Guatemala City; tel. 2335-2140; fax 2335-2357; e-mail agis@intelnet.net.gt; internet www.agis.com.gt; f. 1953; 12 mems; Pres. ALEJANDRO BELTRANENA BUFALINO; Exec. Dir MARIO MENDIZABAL VELASCO.

Trade and Industry

DEVELOPMENT ORGANIZATIONS

Comisión Nacional Petrolera: Diagonal 17, 29-78, Zona 11, Guatemala City; tel. 2276-0680; fax 2276-3175; f. 1983; awards petroleum exploration licences.

Corporación Financiera Nacional (CORFINA): see Finance—Finance Corporations.

Instituto de Fomento de Hipotecas Aseguradas (FHA): Edif. Aristos Reforma, 2°, Avda Reforma 7-62, Zona 9, Guatemala City; tel. 2362-9434; fax 2362-9492; e-mail promocion@fha.com.gt; internet www.fha.com.gt; f. 1961; insured mortgage institution for the promotion of house construction; Pres. FRANCISO SANDOVAL; Man. SERGIO IRUNGARAY.

Instituto Nacional de Administración Pública (INAP): 5a Avda 12-65, Zona 10, Apdo 2753, Guatemala City; tel. 2366-3021; fax 2366-2655; e-mail webmaster@inapgt.com; internet www.inapgt.com; f. 1964; provides technical experts to assist the Govt in administrative reform programmes; provides in-service training for local and central govt staff; has research programmes in administration, sociology, politics and economics; provides postgraduate education in public administration; Pres. HARRIS WHITBECK PIÑOL; Man. SANDRA JIMÉNEZ.

Instituto Nacional de Transformación Agraria (INTA): 14a Calle 7-14, Zona 1, Guatemala City; tel. 2228-0975; f. 1962 to carry out agrarian reform; Pres. NERY ORLANDO SAMAYOA; Vice-Pres SÉRGIO FRANCISCO MORALES-JUÁREZ, ROBERTO EDMUNDO QUIÑÓNEZ LÓPEZ.

Secretaría de Planificación y Programación (SEGEPLAN): 9a Calle 10-44, Zona 1, Guatemala City; tel. 2232-6212; fax 2253-3127; e-mail segeplan@segeplan.gob.gt; internet www.segeplan.gob.gt; f. 1954; prepares and supervises the implementation of the national economic devt plan; Sec. Dr KARIN SLOWING UMAÑA.

CHAMBERS OF COMMERCE AND INDUSTRY

Cámara de Comercio de Guatemala: 10a Calle 3-80, Zona 1, Guatemala City; tel. 2417-2700; fax 2220-9393; e-mail info@camaradecomercio.org.gt; internet www.negociosenguatemala.com; f. 1894; Pres. JORGE BRIZ; Exec. Dir RICARDO RODRÍGUEZ AMADO.

Cámara de Industria de Guatemala: 6a Ruta 9-21, 12°, Zona 4, Apdo 214, Guatemala City; tel. 2380-9000; e-mail info@industriaguate.com; internet www.industriaguate.com; f. 1959; Pres. THOMAS DOUGHERTY; Exec. Dir SERGIO DE LA TORRE.

Cámara Oficial Española de Comercio de Guatemala: Edif. Paladium, 4°, Avda 15-70, Zona 10, Guatemala City; tel. 2470-3301; fax 2470-3304; Pres. Dr RAFAEL BRIZ; Gen. Man. SILVIA CAROLINA DE ARDÓN.

Comité Coordinador de Asociaciones Agrícolas, Comerciales, Industriales y Financieras (CACIF): Edif. Cámara de Industria de Guatemala, 6a Ruta 9-21, Zona 4, Guatemala City; tel. 2231-0651; fax 2334-7025; e-mail informacion@cacif.org.gt; internet www.cacif.org.gt; co-ordinates work on problems and organization of free enterprise; 6 mem. chambers; Pres. JOSÉ PIVARAL GUZMÁN.

INDUSTRIAL AND TRADE ASSOCIATIONS

Asociación de Azucareros de Guatemala (ASAZGUA): Edif. Europlaza, 178°, 5a Avda 5-55, Zona 14, Guatemala City; tel. 2386-2299; fax 2386-2020; e-mail asazgua@azucar.com.gt; internet www.azucar.com.gt; f. 1957; sugar producers' asscn; 15 mems; Pres. FRATERNO VILA; Gen. Man. ARMANDO BOESCHE.

Asociación General de Agricultores (AGA): 9a Calle 3-43, Zona 1, Guatemala City; f. 1920; general farmers' asscn; 350 mems.

Asociación Guatemalteca de Exportadores (AGEXPORT): 15a Avda 14-72, Zona 13, Guatemala City; tel. 2422-3400; fax 2422-3434; e-mail portal@export.com.gt; internet www.export.com.gt; f. 1982; fmrly Asociación de Gremiales de Exportadores de Productos No Tradicionales (AGEXPRONT); exporters' asscn; Pres. TULIO GARCÍA.

Asociación Nacional de Avicultores (ANAVI): Edif. El Reformador, Avda La Reforma 1-50, Zona 9, Guatemala City; tel. 2231-1381; fax 2234-7576; e-mail anavig@terra.com.gt; f. 1964; national asscn of poultry farmers; 60 mems; Pres. MARIA DEL ROSARIO DE FALLA.

Asociación Nacional de Fabricantes de Alcoholes y Licores (ANFAL): Guatemala City; tel. 2292-0430; e-mail info@ronesdeguatemala.com; f. 1947; distillers' asscn; Pres. JUAN GUILLERMO BORJA.

Asociación Nacional del Café—Anacafé: 5a Calle 0-50, Zona 14, Guatemala City; tel. 2421-3700; e-mail info@email.anacafe.org; internet www.anacafe.org; f. 1960; national coffee asscn; Pres. CHRISTIAN RASCH.

Cámara del Agro: 15a Calle 3-20, Zona 10, Guatemala City; tel. 2219-9021; e-mail camagro@intelnet.net.gt; internet www.camaradelagro.net; f. 1973; Pres. CARLOS ZÚÑIGA.

Gremial de Huleros de Guatemala: 6a Avda A 12-37, Zona 9, Guatemala City; tel. 2339-1752; fax 2339-1755; e-mail gremhuleger@guate.net.gt; internet www.gremialdehuleros.org; f. 1970; rubber producers' guild; 125 mems; Dir CARLOS NÁJERA.

MAJOR COMPANIES

Construction

Cementos Progreso, SA: Centro Gerencial Las Margaritas, Torre II, 19°, Zona 10, Guatemala City; tel. 2338-9100; fax 2338-9110; e-mail info@cempro.com; internet www.cempro.com; f. 1899; cement manufacturers; sold to the Swiss Holderbank Financiere Glaris Ltd in 2000; Pres. FREDERICK C. E. MELVILLE NOVELLA; Gen. Man. JORGE LEMCKE; 1,550 employees.

Ingenieros Mayorga y Tejada: 4a Avda 8-40, Zona 9, Guatemala City; tel. 2331-6749; fax 2332-0959; f. 1966; heavy construction and civil engineering services; Man. Dir ENRIQUE TEJADA; 800 employees.

Food and Beverages

Central America Beverage Corporation (CABCORP): Guatemala City; f. 1885; mfr and distributor of Pepsi-Cola products; Pres. CARLOS ENRIQUE MATA CASTILLO.

Cervecería Centro Americana, SA: 3a Avda Norte Final, Finca El Zapote, Zona 2, Guatemala City; tel. 2289-1555; fax 2289-1716; internet www.cerveceria.com.gt; f. 1886; brewery; Pres. JORGE CASTILLO LOVE; 440 employees.

Grupo INA, SA: 33 Calle 6-34, Col. Las Charcas, Zona 11, Guatemala City; tel. and fax 2429-8200; e-mail ina@ina.com.gt; internet www.ina.com.gt; manufacturers of pasta; owns Pastas Ina, Galletas GAMA and Distribuidora Interamericana de Alimentos, SA; Man. ALBERTO MORALES.

Industrias Alimenticias Kerns y CIA, SA: Km 7, Carretera al Atlántico, Zona 18, Guatemala City; tel. 2323-7100; fax 2256-2378; e-mail info@alimentoskerns.com; internet www.alikerns.com; f. 1959; manufacturers of canned fruit juices and fruit products; Gen. Man. ALFONSO BOCALETTI; 550 employees.

Ingenio Tululá, SA: 19 Calle 3-97, Zona 10, Guatemala City; tel. 2379-9810; fax 2379-9809; e-mail mail@ingenio-tulula.com.gt; f. 1982; processing sugar cane; Pres. JOSÉ LUIS BOUSCAYROL; 1,600 employees.

Pollo Campero: Guatemala City; tel. 2333-7233; e-mail ebarillas@campero.com.gt; internet www.campero.com; f. 1971; restaurant franchise; Pres. JUAN JOSÉ GUTIÉRREZ.

Metals and Rubber

Hulera Centroamericana, SA: 24 Calle 24-75, Zona 12, Guatemala City; tel. 2476-0364; fax 2442-3890; e-mail silvian@grupocoban.com; f. 1958; part of Grupo Coban; manufacturers of rubber goods; Gen. Man. JUAN IGNACIO TORREBIARTE; 250 employees.

Llantas Vifrio, SA: 42 Calle 20-64, Zona 12, Guatemala City; tel. 2476-1212; fax 2479-3017; e-mail llantas@vifrio.com; internet www.vifrio.com; f. 1967; repair and retreading of tyres; Pres. HUMBERTO SUÁREZ VALDEZ.

SIDASA (Servicios Industriales y Agrícolas, SA): 10a Calle 0-52, Zona 9, Guatemala City; tel. 2323-5555; fax 2334-7149; e-mail info@sidasa.net; internet www.sidasa.net; f. 1979; manufacturers of industrial and agro-industrial equipment.

Pharmaceuticals

Abbott Laboratórios, SA: Apdo 37, 01901 Guatemala City; tel. 2420-9797; fax 2420-9748; internet www.abbott.com; medical equipment manufacturers; Chair. MILES D. WHITE.

Colgate Palmolive Central America, SA: Avda Ferrocarril 49-65, Zona 12, Guatemala City; tel. 2423-9200; fax 2423-9500; internet www.colgatecentralamerica.com; f. 1971; pharmaceuticals and consumer products; Pres. IAN M. COOK; Gen. Man. PEGGY GERICHTER; 465 employees.

Tobacco

British American Tobacco Central America (BATCA): 24 Avda 3581, Zona 120, Calzada Atanacio Tzul, Apdo 316, Guatemala City; tel. 2366-8787; fax 2366-8785; internet www.batca.com; f. 1928; subsidiary of BAT Industries PLC (United Kingdom); manufacturers of cigarettes; Man. SOFÍA OLIVA; 345 employees.

Tabacalera Centroamericana, SA (TACASA): 1a. Avda 1-90, Zona 1, Villa Canales, Aldea Boca del Monte, Apdo 626, Guatemala City; tel. 2449-5555; fax 2448-0154; e-mail pmi.pressoffice@pmintl.com; f. 1945; subsidiary of Philip Morris Int. Finance Corpn of the USA; manufacturers of cigarettes; Pres. (Latin America) JIM MORTENSEN; Man. LEOPOLDO SANZ; 350 employees.

Miscellaneous

Alcatel-Lucent Tecnologías Guatemala, SA: Edif. Lucent, 9a Calle 15-45, Zona 13, Guatemala City; tel. 5278-7098; e-mail mfsegura@alcatel-lucent.com; subsidiary of Alcatel-Lucent (France); manufacturer of telecommunications equipment; Pres. (Americas) ROBERT VRIJ.

Excel Automotriz: Guatemala City; known as Grupo Central Automotriz until 2010; part of the Grupo DIDEA; distributor of cars and car parts; Exec. Vice-Pres. (Group) CARLOS BOZA.

Industria La Popular, SA: Vía 3 5-42, Zona 4, Guatemala City; tel. 2420-0202; fax 2331-0381; e-mail atencionalcliente@ilpsa.com; internet www.industrialapopular.com; f. 1920; producers of soap and detergents; Pres. FEDERICO KONG VIELMAN; 555 employees.

Inyectores de Plástico: Avda Petapa, Calle 56, Zona 12, Guatemala City; tel. 2326-5700; fax 2477-4814; e-mail ventasipsa@icasa.com.gt; internet www.ipsa.com.gt; f. 1974; subsidiary of Grupo Industrial EEC; manufacturers of plastic packaging.

KPMG Guatemala: 7a Avda 5-10, Zona 4, Centro Financiero, Torre 1, 16°, Guatemala City; tel. 2334-2628; fax 2331-5477; e-mail kpmg@guate.net; internet www.kpmg.com; accountants and management consultants; Dir FELIPE GÓMEZ.

Minas de Guatemala, SA: 4a Avda 8-53, Zona 9, Guatemala City; tel. 2336-3976; f. 1969; metal ore mining; Gen. Man. OSCAR ÁLVAREZ MARROQUÍN; 650 employees.

PricewaterhouseCoopers: Edif. Tívoli Plaza, 6a Calle 6-38, Zona 9, Apdo 868, Guatemala City; tel. 2420-7800; fax 2331-8345; internet www.pwcglobal.com; accountants and management consultants; Partners OSCAR CORDÓN, CARLOS E. PARRA.

Proquirsa: Edif. Proquirsa, 19 Avda 12-57, Zona 11, Guatemala City; tel. 2310-6767; fax 2474-5761; e-mail ventas@proquirsa.com; internet www.proquirsa.com; distributors of industrial chemicals.

Vidriera Guatemalteca (VIGUA): Avda Petapa 48-01, Zona 12, Apdo 1759, Guatemala City; tel. 2422-6400; fax 2422-6500; e-mail vigua@grupovical.com; internet www.grupovical.com; f. 1964; subsidiary of Grupo Vidriero Centroamericano (VICAL); producers of glass bottles and containers.

UTILITIES

Electricity

Empresa Eléctrica de Guatemala, SA: 6a Avda 8-14, Zona 1, Guatemala City; tel. 2277-7000; e-mail consultas@eegsa.net; internet www.eegsa.com; f. 1972; state electricity producer; 80% share transferred to private ownership in 1998; Commercial Man. JORGE ALONZO.

Instituto Nacional de Electrificación (INDE): Edif. La Torre, 7a Avda 2-29, Zona 9, Guatemala City; tel. (2) 2422-1800; e-mail gerencia.general@inde.gob.gt; internet www.inde.gob.gt; f. 1959; fmr state agency for the generation and distribution of hydroelectric power; principal electricity producer; privatized in 1998; Pres. ALBERTO DAVID COHEN MORY; Gen. Man. JUAN FERNANDO CASTRO MARTINEZ.

CO-OPERATIVE

Instituto Nacional de Cooperativas (INACOP): 13a Calle 5-16, Zona 1, Guatemala City; tel. 2234-1097; fax 2234-7536; technical and financial assistance in planning and devt of co-operatives.

TRADE UNIONS

Asamblea Nacional del Magisterio (ANM): Guatemala City; teachers' union; Co-ordinator JOVIEL ACEVEDO.

Central de Trabajadores del Campo y la Ciudad (CTC): 12a Calle 'A' 12-44, Zona 1, Guatemala City; tel. and fax 2232-6947; e-mail centracampo@yahoo.com; Sec.-Gen. MIGUEL ANGEL LUCAS GÓMEZ.

Confederación General de Trabajadores de Guatemala (CGTG): 3a Avda 12-22, Zona 1, Guatemala City; tel. 2232-1010; fax 2251-3212; e-mail cgtg@turbonett.com; f. 1987; Sec.-Gen. JOSÉ E. PINZÓN SALAZAR; 60,000 mems (2007).

Federación Sindical de Trabajadores de la Alimentación Agro-Industrias y Similares de Guatemala (FESTRAS): 16a Avda 13-52, Zona 1, Guatemala City; tel. and fax 2338-3075; e-mail festras@terra.com.gt; internet festras.homestead.com; affiliated to International Union of Food, Agricultural, Hotel, Restaurants, Catering, Tobacco and Allied Workers' Asscns; Sec.-Gen. JOSÉ DAVID MORALES C.

Unidad de Acción Sindical y Popular (UASP): 10a Avda 'A' 5-40, Zona 1, Guatemala City; f. 1988; broad coalition of leading labour and peasant orgs; includes:

Comité de la Unidad Campesina (CUC) (Committee of Peasants' Unity): 31a Avda 'A' 14-46, Zona 7, Ciudad de Plata, Apdo 1002, Guatemala City; tel. 2434-9754; fax 2438-1428; e-mail cuc@intelnett.com; internet www.cuc.org.gt; Gen. Co-ordinator DANIEL PASCUAL HERNÁNDEZ.

Confederación de Unidad Sindical de Guatemala (CUSG): 12a Calle 'A', Zona 1, Guatemala City; tel. and fax 2232-8154; e-mail cusg@itelgua.com; f. 1983; mem. of ITUC; Sec.-Gen. CARLOS H. CARBALLO; 30,000 mems (2007).

Federación Nacional de Sindicatos de Trabajadores del Estado de Guatemala (FENASTEG): 10a Avda 5-40, Zona 1, Guatemala City; tel. and fax 2232-2772; Sec. ARTURO MESÍAS.

Sindicato de Trabajadores del Instituto Guatemalteco de Seguridad Social (STIGSS): 7a Avda 22-72, Zona 1, Guatemala City; tel. 2232-6718; fax 2251-2349; f. 1953.

Unión Sindical de Trabajadores de Guatemala (UNSITRAGUA): 9a Avda 1-43, Zona 1, Guatemala City; tel. 2220-4121; fax 2238-2272; e-mail unsitragua02@yahoo.com; internet www.unsitragua.org; f. 1985; mem. unions are mostly from the private industrial sector and include STECSA, SITRALU and SCTM; Co-ordinator BYRON GRAMAJO.

Unión Guatemalteca de Trabajadores (UGT): 13a Calle 11-40, Zona 1, Guatemala City; tel. and fax 2251-1686; e-mail ugt.guatemala@yahoo.com; Sec.-Gen. CARLOS ENRIQUE MANCILLA.

Transport

RAILWAYS

In 2005 there were 886 km of railway track in Guatemala.

Ferrovías Guatemala: 24a Avda 35-91, Zona 12, 01012 Guatemala City; tel. 2412-7200; fax 2412-7205; internet www.rrdc.com/op_guatemala_fvg.html; f. 1968 as Ferrocarriles de Guatemala (FEGUA); 50-year concession to rehabilitate and operate railway awarded in 1997 to the US Railroad Devt Corpn (RDC); 784 km from Puerto Barrios and Santo Tomás de Castilla on the Atlantic coast to Tecún Umán on the Mexican border, via Zacapa, Guatemala City and Santa María; in 2007 services were suspended due to an arbitration claim filed by the RDC under the terms of the DR-CAFTA free trade agreement; Pres. WILLIAM J. DUGGAN.

ROADS

In 2005 there were 14,283 km of roads, of which about 6,500 km were paved in 2008. The Guatemalan section of the Pan-American highway is 518.7 km long and totally asphalted. In 2009 legislation was approved that provided for the long-planned construction of a highway across the north of the country, linking the departments of Huehuetenango and Izabal, under the Proyecto de Integración y Desarrollo de Mesoamérica at an estimated cost of US $240m.

SHIPPING

Guatemala's major ports are Puerto Barrios and Santo Tomás de Castilla on the Gulf of Mexico, San José and Champerico on the Pacific Ocean, and Puerto Quetzal.

Armadora Marítima Guatemalteca, SA (ARMAGUA): Edif. Armagua, 5°, 14a Calle 8-30, Zona 1, Apdo 1008, Guatemala City; tel. 2230-4686; fax 2253-7464; e-mail infoarmagua@armagua.com; internet www.armagua.com; f. 1968; cargo services; Pres. and Gen. Man. L. R. CORONADO CONDE.

Comisión Portuaria Nacional: 6a Avda A 8-66, Zona 9, Apdo 01009, Guatemala City; tel. 2360-5632; fax 2360-5457; e-mail comportn@cpn.gob.gt; internet www.cpn.gob.gt; Exec. Dir MARÍA ISABEL FERNÁNDEZ COLÍNDRES.

Empresa Portuaria Nacional de Champerico: Avda del Ferrocarril, frente a la playa, 1000101 Champerico, Retalhuleu; tel. 7773-7225; fax 7773-7221; internet www.epnac.blogspot.com; Pres. LUIS ENRIQUE PRADO LUARCA.

Empresa Portuaria Nacional Santo Tomás de Castilla: Calle Real de la Villa, 17 Calle 16-43, Zona 10, Guatemala City; tel. 2366-9413; fax 2366-9445; internet www.santotomasport.com.gt; Man. Col OTTO GUILLERMO NOACK SIERRA.

Empresa Portuaria Quetzal: Edif. Torre Azul, 1°, 4a Calle 7-53, Zona 9, Guatemala City; tel. 2334-7101; fax 2334-8172; e-mail mercadeo@puerto-quetzal.com; internet www.puerto-quetzal.com; port and shipping co; Pres. RODOLFO NEUTZE; Gen. Man. EDUARDO GARRIDO.

Transportes Renegado: 49a Calle 16-25, Zona 12, Guatemala City; tel. 2479-2529; e-mail trenegado@intelnet.net.gt; Gen. Man. JORGE GUTIÉRREZ.

Several foreign lines link Guatemala with Europe, the Far East and North America.

CIVIL AVIATION

There are two international airports, La Aurora in Guatemala City and Mundo Maya in Santa Elena, El Petén.

Aeroquetzal: Avda Hincapié, Hangar EH-05, Zona 13, Guatemala City; tel. 2334-7689; fax 2232-1491; scheduled domestic passenger and cargo services, and external services to Mexico.

Aviones Comerciales de Guatemala (Avcom): Aeropuerto 'La Aurora', Avda Hincapié 18, Zona 13, Guatemala City; tel. 2331-5821; fax 2332-4946; domestic charter passenger services.

TACA: Aeropuerto 'La Aurora', Avda Hincapié 12-22, Zona 12, Guatemala City; tel. 2331-0375; fax 2334-7846; internet www.grupotaca.com; f. 1945 as Aerolíneas de Guatemala (AVIATECA); internal services and external services to the USA, Mexico, and within Central America; transferred to private ownership in 1989.

Tourism

Following the end of the civil war in 1996 the number of tourist arrivals rose steadily and were recorded at some 884,190 in 2002. By 2007 arrivals had reached 1,627,552. In the following year receipts from tourism were estimated at US $1,068m.

Instituto Guatemalteco de Turismo (INGUAT) (Guatemala Tourist Institute): Centro Cívico, 7a Avda 1-17, Zona 4, Guatemala City; tel. 2331-1333; fax 2331-4416; e-mail informacion@inguat.gob.gt; internet www.visitguatemala.com; f. 1967; policy and planning council: 11 mems representing the public and private sectors; Dir ROBERTO ROBLES.

Defence

As assessed in November 2009, Guatemala's active armed forces numbered an estimated 15,212: army 13,444, navy 897 and air force 871. Reserve forces totalled 63,863. In addition, there were paramilitary forces of 18,536. Military service is by selective conscription for 30 months.

Defence Budget: 1,300m. quetzales (US $156m.) in 2009.

Chief of Staff of National Defence: Brig.-Gen. JUAN JOSÉ RUIZ MORALES.

Education

Elementary education is free and, in urban areas, compulsory between seven and 14 years of age. Primary education begins at the age of seven and lasts for six years. Secondary education, beginning at 13 years of age, lasts for up to six years, comprising two cycles of three years each. Enrolment at primary schools in 2008 included 95% of children in the relevant age–group (males 97%; females 94%). The comparable ratio for secondary education in that year was 40% (males 41%; females 39%). There are 12 universities, of which 11 are privately run. In 2006 expenditure on education by the central Government was an estimated 6,251.2m. quetzales, equivalent to 18.6% of total spending.

Bibliography

For works on Central America generally, see Select Bibliography (Books)

Afflitto, F., and Jesilow, P. *The Quiet Revolutionaries: Seeking Justice in Guatemala*. Austin, TX, University of Texas Press, 2007.

Barrie, L., and Anson, R. (Eds.) *Prospects for the Textile and Clothing Industry in Guatemala*. Wilmslow, Textiles Intelligence, 2005.

Benson, P., and Fischer E. F. *Broccoli and Desire: Global Connections and Maya Struggles in Postwar Guatemala*. Lanham, MD, Stanford University Press, 2006.

Brockett, C. D. *Political Movements and Violence in Central America (Cambridge Studies in Contentious Politics)*. Cambridge, Cambridge University Press, 2005.

Chase-Dunn, C., Amaro, N., and Jonas, S. (Eds). *Globalization on the Ground: Postbellum Guatemalan Democracy and Development*. Lanham, MD, Rowman & Littlefield Publrs, 2001.

Cullather, N., and Gleijeses, P. *Secret History: The CIA's Classified Account of its Operations in Guatemala, 1952–1954*. Stanford, CA, Stanford University Press, 1999.

Dosal, P. J. *Doing Business with the Dictators: A Political History of United Fruits in Guatemala, 1899–1944*. Wilmington, DE, Scholarly Resources, 1993.

Fischer, E. F. *Cultural Logics and Global Economies: Maya Identity in Thought and Practice*. Austin, TX, University of Texas Press, 2001.

Forster, C. *The Time of Freedom: Campesino Workers in Guatemala's October Revolution*. Pittsburgh, PA, University of Pittsburgh Press, 2001.

Garrard-Burnett, V. *Terror in the Land of the Holy Spirit: Guatemala under General Efrain Rios Montt 1982-1983*. New York, NY, OUP USA, 2010.

Glebbeek, M.-L. *In the Crossfire of Democracy: Police Reform and Police Practice in Post-Civil War Guatemala (Thela Latin America Series)*. Amsterdam, Rozenberg, 2003

Grandin, G. *The Blood of Guatemala: A History of Race and Nation*. Durham, NC, Duke University Press, 2000.

Hawkins, T. *José de Bustamante and Central American Independence: Colonial Administration in an Age of Imperial Crisis*. Tuscaloosa, AL, University of Alabama Press, 2004.

Hererra Robinson, A. *Natives, Europeans and Africans in 16th-century Santiago de Guatemala*. Austin, TX, University of Texas Press, 2003.

Little, W. E. *Mayas in the Marketplace: Tourism, Globalization, and Cultural Identity*. Austin, TX, University of Texas Press, 2004.

Lovell, W. G. *A Beauty that Hurts: Life and Death in Guatemala*. Austin, TX, University of Texas Press, 2001.

McCleary, R. M. *Dictating Democracy: Guatemala and the End of Violent Revolution*. Gainesville, FL, University Press of Florida, 1999.

McCreery, D. *Rural Guatemala 1760–1940*. Stanford, CA, Stanford University Press, 1994.

May, R. A. *Terror in the Countryside*. Athens, OH, Ohio University Press, 2001.

Menchú, R. *Crossing Borders*, (translated and edited by A. Wright). Lewiston, NY, Mellen University Press, 1998.

Montejo, V. *Voices From Exile: Violence and Survival in Modern Maya History*. Norman, OK, University of Oklahoma Press, 1999.

Montgomery, J. *Tikal: An Illustrated History*. New York, NY, Hippocrene Books, 2001.

Neier, A. *Paradise in Ashes: A Guatemalan Journey of Courage, Terror, and Hope*. Berkeley, CA, University of California Press, 2004.

Nolin, C. *Transnational Ruptures: Gender and Forced Migration (Gender in a Global/Local World)*. Stanford, CA, Stanford University Press, 2006.

Poverty in Guatemala. Washington, DC, World Bank, 2003.

Remijnse, S. *Memories of Violence: Civil Patrols and the Legacy of Conflict in Joyabaj, Guatemala*. Amsterdam, Rozenberg, 2002.

Sanford, V. *Buried Secrets: Truth and Human Rights in Guatemala*. New York, Palgrave Macmillan, 2003.

Schirmer, J. *The Guatemalan Military Project*. University Park, PA, University of Pennsylvania Press, 1998.

Schlesinger, S., and Kinzer, S. *Bitter Fruit: The Story of the American Coup in Guatemala*. Cambridge, MA, Harvard University Press, 1999.

Shea, M. E. *Culture and Customs of Guatemala*. Westport, CT, Greenwood Publishing Group, 2000.

Short, N. *The International Politics of Post-Conflict Reconstruction in Guatemala*. Basingstoke, Palgrave Macmillan, 2008.

Sieder, R. (Ed.). *Guatemala after the Peace Accords*. London, Institute of Latin American Studies, 1999.

Siekmeier, J. F. *Aid, Nationalism and Inter-American Relations—Guatemala, Bolivia and the United States 1945–1961*. Lewiston, NY, Edwin Mellen Press, 1999.

Stolen, K. A. *Guatemalans in the Aftermath of Violence: The Refugees' Return (Ethnography of Political Violence Series)*. Philadelphia, PA, University of Pennsylvania Press, 2007.

Stoll, D. *Rigoberta Menchú and the Story of All Poor Guatemalans*. Boulder, CO, Westview Press 1999.

Tovar Siebentritt, G. (Translator) *Guatemala: Never Again! - The Official Report of the Human Rights Office, Archdiocese of Guatemala*. London, Latin America Bureau, 1999.

Yashar, D. J. *Demanding Democracy: Reform and Reaction in Costa Rica and Guatemala, 1870s–1950s*. Stanford, CA, Stanford University Press, 1997.

GUYANA

Geography

PHYSICAL FEATURES

The Co-operative Republic of Guyana is the westernmost and largest of the three Guianas that occupy that part of the north-eastern coast of South America between the Serra Tumucumaque and the Atlantic Ocean. Formerly the United Kingdom's colony of British Guiana, Guyana is bordered to the east by Suriname (formerly Dutch Guiana). The two countries share a border along the Courantyne (Corantijn) river, although Suriname disputes possession of territory between the upper reaches of the Courantyne (or Kutari) and the New River (Upper Courantyne), in the south-eastern corner of Guyana. Venezuela, which lies to the west, claims most of northern Guyana by arguing that its border should run along the Essequibo. Brazil lies beyond the longer, southern part of the western border and in the south (Brazil has 1,119 km—695 miles—of frontier with Guyana, Venezuela has 743 km and Suriname 600 km). Guyana is the third smallest country in South America (after Suriname and Uruguay), with an area of 214,969 sq km (83,000 sq miles).

Guyana consists of a northern block, longer along the coast, with a narrower southern extension into Brazil and along the border with Suriname. Guyana's Atlantic coast, which extends for 459 km, faces north-east. Behind it, protected by a complex system of dams and dykes (except in the east, where more than just a coastal strip is still swampy), is a rich plain of alluvial mud, deposited by the Amazon and other rivers. These coastal plains vary between 8 km and 65 km in width, and are mostly below sea level. Most of the agriculture and population of the country is located here. Inland are rolling highlands, most of it clad in dense woodland. The forest region, which accounts for four-fifths of the country, covers an eroded plateau. From this, in the south-west of northern Guyana, are the Pakaraima Mountains, including the country's highest, Roraima (2,835 m or 9,304 ft), which is on the Venezuelan border, and also just north of the border with Brazil. The forest region extends into the highlands, reaching as far as where the land rises again in the far south. Here, forest tends to be displaced by savannah grasslands, such as in the Rupununi valley in the far south-west. The country is 84% wooded, and has rich farmland along the coast, all of this watered by a number of rivers (Guyana means 'land of many waters'), the main ones being the Essequibo, in the centre of the country, and its tributaries, the Demerara, the Berbice and the Courantyne.

CLIMATE

Although the climate is characteristically hot and humid, it is relatively mild for such a low-lying area in the tropics, being moderated by the north-eastern trade winds off the Atlantic. There are two rainy seasons (May–August and November–January), during which flash floods are always a risk. The average annual rainfall in Georgetown, the capital, on the coast, is 2,280 mm (almost 90 ins). There is less rain on the higher plateau regions, with the savannah of the far south receiving about 1,525 mm per year. The average temperatures in Georgetown range from 23°C (73°F) to 31°C (88°F) all year round.

POPULATION

Guyana has a varied and complex ethnic constitution, the result of different solutions to labour demand during the colonial period. There are some Amerindian peoples (about 9% according to the 2002 census—mainly Caribs) in the interior still, but most of the population (43%) is now 'East' Indian, descended from indentured workers brought from the Indian subcontinent in the 19th century. Some 30% are black, descended from the African slaves whose freedom had required new labour solutions. There are also the descendants of Chinese and Portuguese workers (the latter mainly from Madeira, but who have not maintained the use of their original language), who together comprise less than 1% of the total population. About 17% of the total population are of mixed race; in Guyana they usually form a socially distinct group maintaining closer links to the European community. English is the official language and the one most widely used by all these communities, but an English-based Creole is also spoken, as is (particularly among the older generations) Hindi, Urdu and Chinese. The Amerindians have their own languages too. Almost one-half of the population is Christian, 28% Hindu and 7% Muslim.

The total population, according to official projections for 2010, was 784,894. Around 90% of the population lives on the coast and just over three-fifths reside in rural areas. In mid-2009 it was estimated that some 132,000 people lived in and around the capital, Georgetown, which is located just to the east of the mouth of the Essequibo. To the east of the capital is the port of New Amsterdam, another important town, and inland is the mining town of Linden (formerly Mackenzie), with the nearby centres of Wismar and Christianborg. The country is divided into 10 regions for administrative purposes.

History

CHARLES ARTHUR

Revised for this edition by MARK WILSON

EARLY OCCUPATION

The region of present-day Guyana was originally inhabited by Carib, Arawak, Warao and other Amerindian peoples, and its name derives from Amerindian words meaning '(land of) many waters', because of the numerous rivers and the extensive swamps in the coastal areas. The Dutch were the first Europeans to settle when, in 1616, traders established the fort and settlement of Kyk-Over-Al 25 km upstream from the mouth of the Essequibo river. In 1621 the Government of the Netherlands gave the newly formed Dutch West India Company control of this trading post, which subsequently developed into a colony known as Essequibo. The company established a second colony on the Berbice river, south-east of Essequibo, in 1627, and a third—Demerara, situated between Essequibo and Berbice—was settled in 1741 and recognized as a separate Dutch West India Company colony in 1773. The Dutch West India Company established tobacco and sugar cane plantations using the labour of Amerindian slaves. However, as the agricultural production of the colonies increased, a labour shortage emerged, and in the 1650s the first large-scale importation of African slaves began. By the 1660s the slave population numbered about 2,500, while the number of indigenous people had declined to an estimated 50,000 as a result of disease and poor treatment at the hands of the Dutch. Most of those who survived the encounter with the Europeans retreated into the interior of the territory. During the 18th and early 19th centuries more African slaves were brought to the territory to labour on sugar, cotton and coffee estates, most of them on reclaimed wetlands in the coastal plain. The working conditions were brutal, and there were several slave rebellions. One of the most famous took place in 1763 when slaves led by Cuffy (today the national hero of Guyana) rose up and forced more than half of the European population to flee. The rebel force of 3,000 slaves was eventually defeated with the assistance of troops from the neighbouring French and British colonies.

At various times control of the three colonies fell to the British and the French, while British planters settled in the Guianas even under Dutch rule. The British took permanent control in 1796, and in 1814 British rule was formally recognized by the Netherlands through the London Convention. In 1831 the colonies were consolidated as one administrative unit, named British Guiana. Slavery was abolished in 1834. It was succeeded by a system of 'apprenticeship', originally intended to last for six years; however, this was ended ahead of schedule in 1838, largely because of rebellions, including one in Guyana. From this date, the British began to bring in indentured (contract) labour from other sources, principally from India, but also from China and Madeira. The original intention was that the Indian labourers would return to their homeland once two five-year periods of service had ended, but the authorities were keen to retain labour. Many were asked to pay a proportion of their return passage, while some were offered land. Most stayed in Guyana, and by the end of indentured immigration in 1917, they formed the majority of the rural population of British Guiana, which was often referred to as the land of six peoples, with descendants of African, Chinese, Indian and Portuguese slaves and workers, and of the mainly British colonists, as well as the continuing presence of the Amerindians.

Indo-Guyanese, now universally English-speaking but retaining many of their cultural traditions, made up the largest ethnic group, with 43% of the population at the time of the 2002 census, and formed a clear majority in most of the coastal agricultural belt, particularly in eastern Guyana (Berbice). Most Indo-Guyanese are Hindu, but significant numbers are either Muslim or Christian. However, their proportion of the population has decreased from 52% in 1980, when Indo-Guyanese formed an absolute majority. Afro-Guyanese were 30% of the total in 2002, and formed the largest group in the capital, Georgetown, and in the bauxite-mining town of Linden, while 17% of Guyanese were of mixed race, an increase from 11% in 1980. Amerindians made up 9% of the population, a proportion that had increased from 5% in 1980 as a result of a higher birth rate and lower rate of emigration; most lived in the interior, or in coastal districts of north-western Guyana. Minorities of Chinese, Madeiran Portuguese, British and other European origin formed less than 1% of the total, but played a significant role in business and the professions.

THE BIRTH OF ETHNIC POLITICS

During the 19th century the political system was dominated by the white—mainly British and Dutch—sugar planters, but other groups increasingly pressed for constitutional reform and a more representative political system. Towards the end of the century, disenfranchised elements began to organize themselves to demand greater participation in the colony's affairs. These organizations were mainly composed of members of the small, but articulate, emerging middle class. The demands of the working class were sometimes expressed in the form of protests and riots, as in the Ruimveldt riots around Georgetown in 1905. After the First World War, economic changes brought renewed pressure for political change. With less dependence on sugar, and the growing importance of rice and bauxite, the political dominance of the sugar planters was increasingly questioned. However, the drive for an expansion of democracy was impeded when the British announced a new Constitution in 1928. It made British Guiana a crown colony, with an increased role for the governor and the appointed members of the Executive Council, and a reduced role for representatives who had been elected, albeit on the basis of a restricted franchise. During the Great Depression of the 1930s all of the colony's major exports—sugar, rice and bauxite—were affected by lower international prices. Unemployment increased rapidly, and, as in the rest of the British Caribbean, British Guiana experienced serious labour unrest and violent demonstrations. From 1943 the property qualification for voters was reduced, and elected members formed a majority in the Legislative Council. However, it was not until after the Second World War that political parties were formed that represented the majority of the population and the extension of universal suffrage opened up the possibility of significant political change.

The first modern political party in the colony's history was the People's Progressive Party (PPP), established in January 1950 by Dr Cheddi Jagan, a US-educated Indo-Guyanese dentist. Jagan had been a leading figure in the Political Affairs Committee (PAC), a left-wing discussion group that, through its outspoken criticism of the colony's poor living standards, had developed strong support, particularly from Indo-Guyanese workers. A turning point came in 1948, when five Indo-Guyanese sugar workers were shot by police at Enmore, close to Georgetown, during a strike and demonstration. The PPP aimed to win support from both the Afro-Guyanese and Indo-Guyanese communities, and its initial leadership was multi-ethnic. Forbes Burnham, a British-trained Afro-Guyanese lawyer, was the party's Chairman. In the run-up to the country's first general election held under universal adult suffrage, Jagan and Burnham proposed an anti-imperialist agenda. In the election in April 1953 the PPP won a resounding victory, taking 18 out of the 24 contested seats. However, the PPP's first administration was brief. Conservative forces in the business community were alarmed by the new Government's programme to expand the role of the state, and by its prompt moves to introduce reforms. At the same time, the British Conservative Government viewed the party's Labour Relations Act, which strengthened the position of the Guiana Industrial Workers' Union (GIWU), as a direct challenge to the Governor and to the Constitution. The day the Act was introduced to the legislature, the GIWU went on strike in support of the proposed law. The very next day, 9 October 1953, the British suspended the colony's Constitution and, under pretext of quelling disturbances, sent in troops. Jagan was removed from office and an interim Government was appointed. The demise of the PPP Government exposed and deepened cracks in the party's previously harmonious ethnic relations. Many Afro-Guyanese had viewed Jagan's proposals to overhaul the civil service as a threat to their established dominance of public administration, and in general perceived Jagan's radical approach as detrimental to the drive towards independence from Britain. In 1955 Jagan and Burnham formed rival wings of the PPP, with support for each leader largely, but not totally, divided along ethnic lines. Burnham's wing of the PPP, supported by the Africans, moved to the right, leaving Jagan's wing, supported mainly by the Indians, on the left. Elections were held in 1957 for 15 members of the Legislative Council, with the remaining nine either appointed or sitting ex-officio; Jagan's wing of the PPP won a clear majority of elected seats with 48% of the vote. Burnham's move toward the right was confirmed when his faction of the PPP broke away and formed what eventually became the People's National Congress (PNC).

In elections in 1961, Jagan's PPP, strongly supported by the Indian population, won 20 of the 35 seats in a wholly elected Legislative Assembly, with 43% of the vote; the PNC took eleven, and The United Force (TUF), supported by business interests, and some Amerindian communities, the remaining four. Ethnic tensions grew as the two main parties vied for power in the run-up to expected independence from the United Kingdom. Riots and demonstrations against the PPP administration were frequent, and during disturbances in 1962 and 1963 mobs destroyed part of the capital, Georgetown. The PNC's efforts to destabilize the Government were encouraged by TUF. Following the success of the revolution led by Fidel Castro in Cuba in 1959, the USA as well as the British colonial authorities and local conservative forces feared that independence under the PPP would lead to a second Cuba on the South American mainland. The conflict between the parties was mirrored in the struggle for control of the labour movement. In an attempt to counter the PNC's strong links with organized labour, the PPP formed the Guianese Agricultural and General Workers' Union (GAWU) to organize among Indian sugar cane field workers. In March 1963 the PPP Government published a new Labour Relations Bill favouring the GAWU, and opponents responded with protests and rallies in Georgetown. The anti-PPP movement—encouraged by the US Central Intelligence Agency—increased the intensity of its campaign with a general strike and violent riots, which eventually forced the Government to withdraw the Bill.

At this delicate stage, the colonial authorities in the United Kingdom agreed to opposition parties' demands for a pre-independence election based on proportional representation, rather than the first-past-the-post system traditionally used in the Caribbean colonies. The opposition believed that this system would reduce the number of seats won by the PPP, and prevent it from obtaining a clear majority in parliament. In response the GAWU, which was sympathetic towards the PPP, appealed to sugar workers to strike in January 1964, and Jagan led a protest march by sugar workers from the interior of the country to Georgetown. The protest movement ignited outbursts of violence, and in May the Governor declared a state of emergency. As the situation worsened, in June the Governor assumed full powers, rushed in British troops to restore order, and banned all political activity. During six months of political turmoil more than 160 people were killed, thousands were injured and more than 1,000 homes were destroyed. When order was finally restored, elections were held in October 1964, and, just as the PPP had feared, the new system allowed the opposition to take power. The PPP won 46% of the vote and 24 seats, which made it the largest party, but the PNC, which won 40% of the vote and 22 seats, and TUF, which won 11% of the vote and seven seats, formed a coalition. Jagan refused to resign as Prime Minister, but the Constitution was amended to allow the British Governor to remove Jagan from office, and the PNC's leader Forbes Burnham became Prime Minister in December.

BURNHAM'S RULE OF INDEPENDENT GUYANA

In the early years of the Burnham Government, economic conditions began to improve, with an end to the riots and disturbances, as the coalition administration implemented policies that favoured local investors and foreign industry. Two years of economic growth and relative domestic peace culminated in independence: on 26 May 1966 the colony of British Guiana became the independent nation of Guyana. In a move to ingratiate his Government with the US Administration, Burnham cut trade relations with Cuba, and western aid money began to flow in. In elections held in 1968, which were, however, marred by fraud and coercion, the PNC won 30 seats to the PPP's 19 and TUF's four. Thereafter, governing without the need for a coalition with TUF, Burnham's rule became increasingly statist and authoritarian, and in February 1970 Guyana removed Queen Elizabeth II as head of state and declared itself a Co-operative Republic, initially under a largely ceremonial President, Arthur Chung. Relations with Cuba improved, and Guyana became a voice in the Non-aligned Movement. From the early 1970s electoral fraud became increasingly prevalent and overt. The police and military intimidated the Indo-Guyanese population, and the army was accused of tampering with ballot boxes. Although some Afro-Guyanese voters, especially among the middle class, were uneasy with Burnham's leanings to the left, they continued to support the PNC, viewing it as a bulwark against Indo-Guyanese dominance.

In 1975 the PPP—still under the control of Cheddi Jagan—tried to shift from confrontation to critical support of the PNC Government, but when overtures intended to bring about new elections and PPP participation in the Government were rejected, the largely Indo-Guyanese sugar work-force went on a bitter strike. The strike was broken, and sugar production declined steeply from 1976 to 1977. At the same time a new political force, the Working People's Alliance (WPA), was established with the aim of breaking the pattern of ethnic-based factionalism. The WPA opposed the PNC's authoritarian rule and promoted racial harmony and democratic socialism. When the PNC postponed the 1978 elections, and instead organized a referendum on a proposed new constitution in which an Executive President would hold wide-ranging powers, the WPA joined the PPP and other opposition forces in organizing a boycott, ensuring a low rate of participation of around 10% of the electorate. By 1979 the WPA found itself the target of increasing repression. When one of the party's leaders, Walter Rodney, and several academics at the University of Guyana were arrested on apparently unfounded arson charges, WPA leaders turned the organization into Guyana's most vocal opposition party. In June 1980 Rodney was killed by a bomb allegedly planted by agents of the Burnham regime. Two years later than scheduled, a general election was held in December 1980, with Burnham elected as Executive President. The PNC claimed 77% of the vote and took 41 seats, while the PPP and TUF won 10 and two seats, respectively. The WPA refused to participate in an electoral contest it regarded as fraudulent. International observers upheld opposition claims of extensive electoral fraud. Christian church groups and human rights organizations took up the protest against Burnham, but he clung onto power despite the worsening economic situation in the early 1980s. With sugar, bauxite, and many other sectors of the economy in state ownership, the country was plagued by blatant corruption and mismanagement, while relations with potential aid donors were soured both by Burnham's largely pro-Soviet foreign policy and his record of reneging on debt service. Petty economic controls were tightened, while large numbers of professionals, managers and business people immigrated to the USA, Canada, other Caribbean nations, or elsewhere. Many imported consumer goods were banned or in short supply, to conserve foreign exchange; by 1984 wheat flour, bread and cheese were unobtainable through legal channels. Smuggling and the parallel economy thrived. Controls over newsprint imports were used to create a virtual press monopoly for the state-owned Guyana Chronicle. Domestic and international confidence in the regime had been further shaken in November 1978, when an American evangelist Jim Jones, welcomed to Guyana by Burnham in 1975, led a mass suicide at his Jonestown agricultural settlement in a remote district in north-western Guyana, in which more than 900 people died. Then, in August 1985 Burnham unexpectedly died while recovering from minor surgery for a throat ailment.

THE HOYTE PRESIDENCY, 1985–92

Following Burnham's death, Prime Minister Hugh Desmond Hoyte acceded to the presidency and led the PNC to claim another victory in a general election in December 1985. The party was held to have won 79% of the vote and 42 of the 53 directly elected seats. Eight seats were given to the PPP, two to TUF, and one to the WPA. However, faced with no alternative as the economic collapse continued, Hoyte responded to international pressure and gradually reversed many of Burnham's policies, moving from state socialism and one-party control towards a market economy, and from 1986 allowing an opposition weekly, Stabroek News, which later became a daily newspaper. Under pressure from the USA, Britain and Canada (the ABC group), the Hoyte Government took important moves to clean up the tarnished electoral process by abolishing overseas voting and the provisions for widespread proxy and postal voting, all of them subject to abuse. In 1988 Hoyte launched an Economic Recovery Programme, and made a nationally televised address in which he declared that Guyana's economy and foreign policy would be pro-capitalist, noting that the strengthening of Guyana's relations with the USA was 'imperative'. He renewed relations with the IMF and the World Bank, and in return for implementing policies to promote the private sector and reduce the role of the state, Guyana started to receive loans from the international financial institutions. In the early 1990s Hoyte gradually opened up the political system. After a visit to Guyana by former US President Jimmy Carter in 1990, Hoyte made changes to the electoral rules, appointed an independent chairman for the Elections Commission, and endorsed the compilation of new voters' lists; this was also seen as a reason to delay elections, which had been due in 1990. Conditions of daily life, meanwhile, remained extremely difficult, with real wages eroded by devaluation and rapid price inflation, and daily power and water outages throughout the country.

THE CHEDDI JAGAN PRESIDENCY, 1992–97

At a general election in October 1992, the PPP finally returned to power after 28 years in opposition. In the ballot, deemed free and fair by international observers, the PPP in coalition with Civic, a movement created by members of the private sector, won 28 seats to the PNC's 23. PPP leader Jagan was named President and the Civic leader, Samuel Hinds, was appointed Prime Minister. Over the years, Jagan had moderated his Marxist-Leninist leanings, and on becoming President, he followed a pro-Western foreign policy, adopted free market policies, and pursued sustainable development for Guyana's environment, presiding over a period of steady economic growth and social stability.

THE JANET JAGAN PRESIDENCY, 1997–99

Cheddi Jagan died in March 1997, and was succeeded as President by Hinds. In national elections held in December 1997, the PPP/Civic alliance won 55% of the total votes cast, giving it 29 of the 53 seats in the National Assembly to the PNC's 22. The PPP's candidate—Cheddi Jagan's widow, the US-born Janet Jagan—was declared President. Janet Jagan had been General Secretary of the PPP from 1950 to 1970 and had held several cabinet posts since the 1950s. However, the PNC disputed the results of the election, and racial slurs were aimed at the new white President. There were large demonstrations by PNC supporters, and the situation only partly stabilized when mediators from the Caribbean Community and Common Market (CARICOM) came to Georgetown to broker an accord between the two parties. The Herdmanston Accord in January 1998 followed by the St Lucia Accord in June provided for an international audit of the election results, a redrafting of the Constitution (which had by 2009 produced only minor reforms), and new elections within three years rather than five. In August 1999, as arguments continued about the legitimacy of the PPP/Civic Government, and after a protracted strike by the largely Afro-Guyanese public sector trade unions, which resulted in substantial salary increases, Janet Jagan suffered a mild heart attack and relinquished her role as President. She was replaced by the Minister of Finance, Bharrat Jagdeo, who had been hastily appointed Prime Minister in place of Hinds so that the latter could assume the presidency. Once in office, Jagdeo reappointed Hinds as Prime Minister. Janet Jagan remained a prominent figure in Guyanese life until her death in March 2009, at the age of 88.

THE BHARRAT JAGDEO PRESIDENCY, 1999–

While controversy over the electoral process continued, new elections took place in March 2001. The PPP/Civic alliance won 34 of the 65 parliamentary seats, while the PNC—with independent supporters allied as the Reform group—won 27 seats. The election results were contested by the PNCReform, but although international observers noted some protests, arson and street violence during the election, the process was deemed free and fair, and the nation's High Court upheld the results. As in 1997, the election result sparked numerous public demonstrations and some rioting among the minority Afro-Guyanese community, who claimed that there had been widespread election fraud. The Jagdeo administration immediately initiated moves to improve its relationship with the PNCReform, and Hoyte agreed to a process of dialogue that aimed to develop a more inclusive system of governance. However, within a year the dialogue broke down, with the PNCReform claiming that it was failing to produce any results. On the death of Desmond Hoyte following a heart attack in December 2002, the new PNCReform leader, Robert Corbin, agreed to resume the dialogue with the Government. As a result, Jagdeo and Corbin agreed on a number of confidence-building measures, including the appointment of an Ethnic Relations Committee and a commission to investigate the Disciplined Forces (police and army), which reported in 2004, making recommendations that in 2010 remained under consideration by a parliamentary select committee.

Against the backdrop of simmering ethnic tensions between the Indo- and Afro-Guyanese sections of the population, social tensions were further exacerbated by a sharp increase in violent crime during the early years of the 21st century. After the escape of five high-profile Afro-Guyanese prisoners in February 2002, the number of murders rose by 56% compared to the previous year, and there was a spate of robberies and attacks on businesses, particularly in the area around the capital and around the village of Buxton, which spans the only road connection to eastern Guyana. Human rights groups criticized the police force's heavy-handed response, while the reaction of some prominent PNCReform supporters to the upsurge in violence appeared ambivalent. Adding to the tensions were accusations that the Government was linked to a so-called 'death squad', allegedly responsible for more than 40 extra-judicial killings in 2003. New appointments to the leadership of both the police force and the army in early 2004 failed to ease public concerns. An official inquiry found no evidence of wrongdoing by the Minister of Home Affairs Ronald Gajraj, but he resigned in April 2005.

After some delays, a general election was held on 28 August 2006. The PPP/Civic won 54.3% of the vote and increased its seats in the parliament from 34 to 36. The PNCReform, which had renamed itself the PNCReform-One Guyana (PNCR-1G) ahead of the election, polled 34.0% of the votes cast and lost five seats but remained the second largest political party. Although tensions had been raised in the pre-election period by a continuing crime wave and by the assassination of the Minister of Agriculture, Satyadeow Sawh, in April 2006, the campaign was largely peaceful, but the rate of participation was low at just 69% of the electorate. A new party, the Alliance for Change (AFC), founded prior to the elections by disaffected members of the PPP/Civic and PNCReform, campaigned to end the ethnic divide, and won 8.3% of the vote, securing just five seats; this was the best showing by a 'third party' since the 1960s.

In early 2008 ethnic tensions were again inflamed by a series of killings carried out by members of armed groups in different parts of the country. Eleven Indo-Guyanese, including five children, were shot dead in January in the coastal village of Lusignan, close to Buxton. In a subsequent statement, the authorities claimed that the attack had been an attempt to exacerbate tensions between the Afro- and Indo-Guyanese communities. Angry residents blocked streets and burned tyres after the massacre, venting anger against leading PPP/Civic politicians who were seen as ineffective in controlling violence. Then, in mid-February, armed gunmen attacked a police station and other buildings in the village of Bartica, killing three police officers and nine civilians, while eight diamond miners were massacred at a remote camp in June. Rondell 'Fineman' Rawlins, the last remaining 2002 prison escapee and held responsible for the massacres, was killed in a gun battle with police in August 2008. Ethnic tensions and violent crime remained two of the more urgent issues confronting the authorities. At 15 per 100,000, the murder rate in Guyana is not particularly high by Caribbean standards, but is around three times that of the USA. Assistance has been offered by the United Kingdom, the USA and the Organization of American States for strengthening community security, but implementation of proposed programmes has been delayed by disagreements over policy issues. Counter to international advice, Guyana in 2007 appointed Bernard Kerik, a former police commissioner in New York, USA, as security adviser to the President; he was soon afterwards charged in the USA with tax evasion and corruption, and following his conviction was sentenced in February 2010 to four years' imprisonment. A proposal for a £4.9m. security reform programme, to be implemented with British funding, was agreed in outline in 2007, but the plans were abandoned in 2009 owing to disagreement regarding appropriate management and strategy, and to a lack of progress made by Guyana on key project requirements.

Inter-party hostility and mistrust remained strong, while entrenched ethnic voting brought little prospect of a change in political control, and institutions intended to promote consensus have instead led to further disagreement. The leadership of both main parties remained intolerant of internal criticism and debate. Jagdeo, meanwhile, was limited under the Constitution to two terms in office, and was not therefore expected to stand in the next election, due in 2011. There was no clear indication as to his possible successor, although Jagdeo repeatedly rejected assertions that he intended to seek a constitutional amendment allowing him to stand for a third term, a move that would require approval by a two-thirds' majority and would therefore necessitate opposition support. There were proposals for a broad opposition block, including, *inter alia*, the PNCR-1G and the AFC; however, the AFC announced in 2010 that it would not ally itself with either of the main parties. Local elections, due since 1997, have been repeatedly postponed. The Government stated that they would be held in 2010; however, similar pledges in previous years had gone unheeded.

INTERNATIONAL RELATIONS

Guyana has been involved in long-running border disputes with two of its neighbours, Venezuela and Suriname.

In 1962 Venezuela renewed its claim to 130,000 sq km (50,000 sq miles) of land west of the Essequibo river (more than two-thirds of Guyanese territory). This dispute was unlikely to lead to open conflict, and day-to-day relations were often friendly. However, it delayed offshore petroleum exploration in the large area of Guyana's Exclusive Economic Zone that is claimed by Venezuela, as international oil companies have been threatened with retaliation for activities in the area. The land area claimed by Venezuela was accorded to Guyana in 1899, on the decision of an international tribunal, but Venezuela held that this award resulted from improper pressure by Britain. After Guyanese independence, Venezuela occupied the Guyanese portion of Ankoko island on the Cuyuni river, but the Port of Spain Protocol of 1970 put the issue in abeyance until 1982. Guyana and Venezuela referred the dispute to the UN in 1983, and in August 1989 the two countries agreed to a mutually acceptable intermediary ('good officer'), suggested by the UN Secretary-General; a Jamaican academic, Norman Girvan, was appointed to the post in April 2010, replacing Oliver Jackman of Barbados, who died in 2007. In March 1999 Guyana and Venezuela established a joint commission, the High Level Binational Commission, to expedite resolution of the dispute. However, in October 1999, after the award of Guyanese offshore petroleum exploration licences, President Lt-Col (retd) Hugo Chávez Frías of Venezuela, speaking on the 100th anniversary of the international tribunal, reasserted the Venezuelan claim, as did a new Constitution adopted in December of that year. In 2005 Guyana signed the PetroCaribe energy accord with Venezuela, which offered favourable terms for oil imports, while Venezuela in October 2007 cancelled US $12.5m. in Guyanese debt. However, there have been serious border incidents; the Venezuelan national guard arrested six Guyanese on the Cuyuni river, within Guyanese territory, in October 2006, killing one of them, while in November 2007 a Venezuelan army unit with helicopter support destroyed two Guyanese gold dredges. Venezuela apologized for the latter incident. Meanwhile, in a more positive development, five bilateral energy and trade agreements were signed between the two countries during a visit by Jagdeo to the Venezeulan capital, Caracas, in July 2005.

Relations with Suriname have been hampered by two significant disputes. A disagreement over the maritime boundary became critical in June 2000, when a Surinamese gunboat prevented a rig operated by a small Canadian oil company, CGX Energy, from drilling an exploratory well in waters claimed by both parties. After repeated attempts to negotiate a settlement failed, in February 2004 Guyana referred the dispute to arbitration at the UN's International Tribunal for the Law of the Sea (ITLOS). The Tribunal ruled in favour of Guyana in September 2007, granting sovereignty over 33,152 sq km (12,800 sq miles) including the most promising geological structures for petroleum and gas; Suriname was awarded 17,891 sq km (6,900 sq miles). The second dispute over the 'New River Triangle', an area of uninhabited forest close to the southern border with Brazil, remains unresolved, and hinges on a debate as to which of two tributaries forms the true upstream continuation of the Corentyne border river. Surinamese irregulars built a border camp in the disputed area in 1967 ('Post Tigri'). This was swiftly taken by Guyana, and remains an army post today as Camp Jaguar. After this incident, diplomatic relations were restored only in 1979. By contrast, Guyana's relations with Brazil remain amicable, aided by a long-standing border settlement. In May 2003 the Government approved a request by the Brazilian authorities for a partial abolition of visas for both countries, and a partial scope trade agreement is in force. On a visit to Guyana in February 2005, Brazil's President, Luiz Inácio ('Lula') da Silva, reiterated his Government's commitment to the construction of the bridge across the Takutu river between the two countries, which was opened to vehicular traffic in 2009.

Guyana is a centre for the transshipment of cocaine travelling from Colombia through Venezuela, and onwards through the Caribbean to Europe and North America. There was little police or army presence in the sparsely populated interior, and most of the country's land and river borders were unguarded, while the coast guard in 2010 had no seaworthy vessels, and controls over money-laundering remained weak. Onward drugs shipments have been found in consignments of almost every export commodity, from timber and sugar to rice and vegetables. The economic impact of the drugs trade was thought to be substantial, and there were concerns over the influence of trafficking organizations in Guyanese society. US Department of State analysts believed that counter-narcotics efforts were being hindered by inadequate resources and poor co-ordination among law enforcement agencies, an overburdened and inefficient judiciary, and the lack of a coherent national security strategy. US analysts also contended that drugs-trafficking organizations in Guyana eluded law enforcement through bribes and coercion, with arrests limited mainly to small-scale users and low-level couriers held at the airport, and suggested that North American law enforcement agencies were doing more to combat the problem of Guyanese drugs-trafficking than the authorities in Guyana itself.

Guyana has been vocal in pushing for countries with substantial areas of tropical forest to be compensated for conservation efforts that limit international carbon emissions. As early as in 1989 Guyana made 3,600 sq km of remote forest available for sustainable management as the Iwokrama International Centre for Rainforest Conservation and Development. Jagdeo was one of three world leaders invited by the

UN Secretary-General, Ban Ki-Moon, to participate in an Advisory Group on Climate Change Financing in March 2010. Meanwhile, Guyana secured an environmental agreement with Norway in November 2009, under the terms of which Norway was to provide up to US $280m. in return for an agreement that allows Guyana to increase the rate of deforestation, but within agreed maximum limits, in a scheme linked to the World Bank's Forest Carbon Partnership Facility. Norway was to invest $30m. initially, and would disburse as much as an additional $250m. if this initial investment were to yield a tangible reduction in both emissions and poverty. Jagdeo expressed his 'delight' at Guyana's involvement in the search for 'solutions that align the development aspirations of our people with the urgent need to protect the world's tropical forests'. However, monitoring issues remained unresolved, and some environmental non-governmental organizations have expressed concerns.

Economy

CHARLES ARTHUR

Revised for this edition by MARK WILSON

Guyana has a small economy in a country rich in natural resources, yet it remains one of the poorest nations in the western hemisphere. In 2009 it ranked 114th out of 182 countries in the UN Development Programme's Human Development Index, the lowest ranking in the English-speaking Caribbean. In the same year, according to figures released by the central bank, Guyana had an estimated per caput gross domestic product (GDP) of US $1,634, also the lowest in the region. In recent decades the economic situation has been volatile. In the late 1970s and 1980s there was a severe economic crisis, accompanied by the rapid deterioration of public services, infrastructure and overall quality of life, with basic consumer goods unavailable except on the illegal market, and real wages in steep decline. There was then a period of rapid growth from 1991 to 1997, followed by a decade of relative stagnation.

After years of a state-dominated economy, concerted international pressure and the lack of any viable alternative forced President Hugh Desmond Hoyte in 1987 to launch an Economic Recovery Programme (ERP) bringing market-oriented reforms and liberalization. The move towards an open economy continued after free elections in 1992 brought a change in government, with Cheddi Jagan taking office after 28 years in opposition. In the period 1991–97 average annual growth reached 7%. Reforms introduced by both administrations reduced the Government's role in the economy, encouraged foreign investment, enabled the Government to clear arrears on loan repayments to foreign governments and the multilateral banks, and brought about the sale of 15 of the 41 government-owned businesses. The telephone company and assets in the timber, rice, and fishing industries were privatized. A British firm, Booker Tate, was hired to manage the huge state sugar company, Guyana Sugar Corpn Inc (GuySuCo). Furthermore, a US company was allowed to open a bauxite mine, and two Canadian companies were permitted to develop the Omai gold mine, the largest open-pit gold mine in Latin America. Most price controls were removed, the laws affecting mining and petroleum exploration were improved, and an investment policy receptive to foreign investment was announced. Tax reforms designed to promote exports and agricultural production in the private sector were enacted. Inflation declined to single digits from 1995, and the currency stabilized, while fiscal and external imbalances were reduced. However, by 1998 the recovery was exhausted and long-term structural vulnerabilities made themselves felt, while investor confidence was damaged by political disturbances following the 1997 election. Growth in the economy was also hindered by a lack of private sector activity, the ongoing migration of professionals to North America (the 'brain-drain'), which had continued since the 1970s, large fiscal and external imbalances, and problems in the implementation of structural reforms. While financial stability was broadly maintained, growth averaged a meagre 0.3% from 1998 to 2005, with the economy contracting in four of these eight years. In early 2005 extensive flooding in the coastal areas, where the majority of the population lives, caused considerable damage. Sugar and rice production was badly affected, and GDP contracted by 2.0%.

Emerging from this unpromising backdrop, the economy made a recovery in 2006 and 2007, with GDP growth of 5.1% and 5.4%, respectively. The overall fiscal deficit remained very high, but declined slightly from 13.6% of GDP in 2005 to 11.5% in 2006, narrowing more significantly to 7.6% in 2007 with the introduction of a value-added tax (VAT) from the start of that year. After receiving debt relief totalling US $585m. in 2003 under the Enhanced Heavily Indebted Poor Countries (HIPC) Initiative, Guyana qualified for an additional $189m. under the Multilateral Debt Relief Initiative (MDRI) in 2006. Agriculture recovered from the 2005 floods in 2006 and 2007, while mining and most other sectors performed well, although the external current account deficit widened to 20.9% of GDP in 2006, reflecting high fuel prices and large capital imports for the sugar sector, and the external deficit remained high, at 18.0%, in 2007. GDP growth slackened to 3.1% in 2008, with mining, construction and services still performing well, but sugar production well below target. The economy did well to maintain positive growth of 2.3% in 2009, a year in which most Caribbean and international economies contracted owing to the effects of the global economic downturn; this relative strength was attributable in part to high gold prices and the lack of dependence on leisure-based tourism, unlike many other Caribbean economies. The fiscal deficit was 6.3% of GDP in 2008, modestly above the 6.0% budget target, but fell back to 6.0% in 2009. Meanwhile, the external current account deficit rose again to 25.7% of GDP in 2008, but fell back to 17.6% in 2009, owing in part to lower international oil prices. The Guyana dollar has remained broadly stable in the mid- to late 2000s, depreciating by only 5.4% since 2003, with an exchange rate of G $203.25 = US $1 in April 2010. Inflation rose sharply from 4.2% in 2006 to 14.0% in 2007 with the introduction of VAT, but decreased to 6.4% in 2008, in spite of steep rises in the price of imported fuel and food commodities, and declined further to 3.6% in 2009 as the effects of the global recession took hold.

AGRICULTURE, FORESTRY AND FISHING

Nearly all of Guyana's agricultural production takes place along the country's coastal plains. Originally swamp lands, these areas were reclaimed and converted into fertile estates by the Dutch during the colonial period. Since independence, governments have repeatedly committed considerable resources to maintaining the sea defences and drainage systems in order to guarantee the continuation of one of Guyana's most important economic activities. In 2009 agriculture, fishing and forestry contributed 24.3% of total GDP. Following a 5.8% decline in 2008, agricultural output staged a partial recovery, expanding by 2.8% in 2009, largely as a result of more favourable weather conditions; however, growth was restricted by high input costs and labour unrest in the sugar industry, and a contraction was recorded in the forestry and fishing sectors.

GuySuCo was formed in 1976 as a single state-owned company and grows sugar cane in eight large estates, each with its own factory; four are close to Georgetown, and four are in the eastern part of the coastal belt. Some cane is also grown by independent farmers for sale to GuySuCo. In contrast to the rest of the Caribbean, the climate allows two annual sugar crops, while canals are used for drainage, irrigation, and transport of cane. In 2009 sugar output increased by 3.3%, to 233,736 metric tons, but export earnings were down by 10.2% compared with the previous year. Total export earnings amounted to US $119.8m., representing 15.6% of total export receipts. Traditionally the main export market for Guyana's sugar has been the countries of the European Union (EU), thanks to a preferential agreement between the EU and the former colonies of the African, Caribbean and Pacific (ACP) group of states. With the EU sugar protocol ending in 2009 and guaranteed sugar prices phased out, export prices have declined sharply, although the reduction in the sugar price was offset in the years to 2008 by the appreciation of the euro against the US dollar, to which the Guyanese currency is closely linked. In 2009 some 89.6% of sugar exports went to the EU under the sugar protocol, while exports to the Caribbean Community and Common Market (CARICOM) member states totalled around 4%. Efforts were under way to restructure the sugar sector in order to maintain its competitiveness. Central to the initiative was the construction by Chinese contractors of a new sugar factory at Skeldon in Berbice, eastern Guyana, in production from 2009 with a co-generation plant to produce 30 MW of electricity from sugar cane waste (bagasse) and additional land for large-scale cane cultivation. The target was to produce 110,000 metric tons of sugar annually by 2013; however, the factory was still experiencing ongoing teething problems in the first half of 2010, and cane supply had not yet reached target levels. GuySuCo now also exports packaged and branded sugar, which fetches a much higher price than the bulk commodity, and plans to increase the proportion of the harvest that is fully mechanized from 4% in 2008 to 47% in 2016, eventually phasing out the cutting of cane by hand; however, at mid-2010 the mechanization programme was running behind schedule. As a result of relatively low production costs and the Government's significant investments, Guyana was one of the few sugar producers in the Caribbean region that were expected to survive the changes in the trading relationship with the EU. Guysuco also intends to build an ethanol plant, to be operational from 2012.

The other main component of Guyana's agricultural sector is the rice industry, traditionally dominated by independent farmers who, like the majority of the rural population in the coastal belt, are descendents of indentured labourers from India. Rice farms are distributed throughout the coastlands, and, as with sugar, there are two annual harvests. In 2009 rice production increased by 9.2%; however, prices were down by 27% from 2008 levels, partly reversing a doubling of rice prices in the previous year. The volume exported declined by 27.2% in 2008, but export earnings decreased by 3.3% to US $114m., or 15% of total exports. Rice is sold predominantly to the EU and CARICOM, markets in which Guyana has a tariff advantage, and each of which took 43% of Guyanese exports in 2009. However, the tariff advantage in the European market is likely to be eroded over the coming decade as trade liberalization progresses. Guyana remains the largest rice producer in the Caribbean.

In the late 2000s the Government implemented several initiatives to encourage farmers to increase production in the non-traditional sectors of agriculture, which had achieved some positive effects by 2010, with increased sales of fresh fruits and vegetables to Caribbean and North American markets. Meanwhile, in early 2008 the Ministry of Agriculture announced that a further US $6m. would be allocated to increase the market opportunities available to small-scale food producers.

The production of shrimp for export in the 1980s rejuvenated a dwindling fishing sector, with some exports to the USA and other markets. In the late 2000s, despite government efforts to promote aquaculture, the sector stagnated, mainly as a consequence of the rising cost of fuel. In 2008 the fish catch was 8.1% less than in 2007, and the shrimp catch was down by 56.2% year-on-year. Export sales of fish and shrimp totalled US $45.5m., or 5.9% of total exports, and were down by 24.2% from 2007.

The exploitation of the tropical rainforest that covers approximately 75% of the country's land area increased in the 1990s and 2000s with the granting of concessions to Asian companies. Exports of 122,406 cu m of timber earned US $41.1m. in 2009, but were 43% less than in 2007 with tighter enforcement of forestry regulations, and made up 5.4% of total exports. Forestry policy remained controversial, with loggers pressing for the export of unprocessed timber, and the Government for value-added production of sawn timber and other forest products, while there was an increasing emphasis on conservation objectives. Guyana has lobbied vigorously since 2007 for substantial international compensation for countries that preserve their standing forests, thus reducing global carbon emissions. As early as 1989, Guyana made 3,600 sq km of remote forest available for sustainable management as the Iwokrama International Centre for Rainforest Conservation and Development. Most forests in the southern half of the country are still untouched by commercial forestry. In December 2009 Guyana and Norway signed an agreement under the terms of which Norway would invest up to US $2,850m. in grant aid during 2010–15, almost 20% of annual GDP, in return for an agreement that allows Guyana to increase the rate of deforestation, but within agreed maximum limits. This was a pioneer Reduced Emissions from Deforestation and Forest Degradation (REDD) scheme, linked to the World Bank's Forest Carbon Partnership Facility, and an initial $30m. was expected to be paid into the Guyana REDD Investment Fund (GRIF) by the end of 2010, with up to $250m. additional funding to be disbursed if initial targets regarding the reduction of cardon emissions and the alleviation of poverty within Guyana were met. Monitoring issues remained unresolved, and some environmental non-governmental organizations have expressed concerns; however, successful completion of the scheme would result in a substantial improvement to the balance of payments capital account, the fiscal deficit, and Guyana's economic outlook.

MINING AND ENERGY

Mining, mainly of bauxite, gold and diamonds, was responsible for 6.8% of GDP in 2009. Substantial investment in and restructuring of the bauxite industry in the late 2000s, and increases in the world prices for bauxite and gold, helped the mining sector to register growth of 22% in 2007 and 6% in 2008; however, growth slowed to 0.7% in 2009, as the continued prosperity of gold was outweighed by a contraction in the bauxite industry owing to low international prices. Bauxite is mined around Linden on the Demarara river, and around Aroaima on the Berbice, each mining area somewhat more than 100 km upstream from the river mouth. Mining costs are high, as an overburden of white silica sand must be removed before the bauxite can be extracted, while rivers used to transport bauxite are too shallow for fully loaded bulk carriers, so costs are further increased by transshipment for ocean transport to overseas markets. However, Guyanese bauxite is particularly pure. In addition to metal-grade bauxite, Guyana is one of the few producers of high-value, refractory-grade bauxite (used in the manufacture of firebricks, electrical insulators and anti-skid surfacing) and chemical-grade bauxite (for aluminium sulphate, used in water purification). A number of state-owned and private sector companies have operated the mines; production reached a low point in 1990 under state-owned company Guymine, but has since recovered with varying ownership and management arrangements. Since 2007 the Linden mines have been operated by a Chinese company, Bosai Minerals Group, with the Government retaining a 30% stake, and the Aroaima mines since 2005 by United Company RUSAL. A plant at Linden that processed bauxite to produce alumina (pure aluminium oxide) was closed in 1981, but proposals to build a new alumina plant were under consideration in 2010. Production was 2.09m. metric tons in 2008, and exports totalled US $131m.; however, in 2009 production fell by 33.6% to 1.48m. tons, while exports declined by 39.4% to US $79.5m. (accounting for 10.3% of Guyana's total exports), as a result of low international prices. High-value refractory- and chemical-grade bauxite were affected by the downturn to an even greater extent than lower-value metal-grade ore.

Guyanese gold miners operate on a small scale by international standards, using dredges to extract gold from gravel along the rivers of western Guyana. Diamond miners use similar methods. A Canadian-owned mine at Omai was a much larger operation, producing gold from crushed rock and accounting for up to three-quarters of gold production, but it closed in 2005 with its ore resources depleted. With gold prices high, the smaller-scale miners expanded their operations in the late 2000s, and in 2009 produced 299,822 ounces, an 11.4% increase over 2008. Gold exports earned US $281.7m. in 2009, an 83% increase over 2007, and made up 36.7% of Guyanese exports. A number of Canadian and other overseas companies were prospecting for gold in 2009, or were completing feasibility studies for mining operations. These included IAMGold, successors to the former operators of the Omai mine, which hoped that high prices would justify new activity on and around the former mine site. A Canadian company, Guyana Goldfields Inc, had plans to open a mine at Aurora, on the Cuyuni river, by the end of 2013. Diamond production declined by 37% in 2008 and by a further 15% in 2009, as miners switched their attention to gold.

In 2009 Guyana was dependent for most of its energy needs on imported refinery products from Trinidad and Tobago and from Venezuela. Electricity is generated and distributed by Guyana Power and Light Inc, which moved back into the state sector after an unsuccessful partnership with the Commonwealth Development Corporation and Ireland's Electricity Supply Board from 1999 to 2003. Problems included high generating costs, some antiquated plant, and the loss of up to 45% of power generated in some years, either through theft of power from illegal connections, or through losses from the inadequate transmission and distribution system. Most electricity is generated from petroleum products, but some is now supplied by the Skeldon co-generation plant and there are small hydroelectric plants in the interior. The high cost and poor reliability of electricity continued to constrain profitability and efficient business operations in Guyana and was an ongoing problem for low-income households. There is potential for very large-scale hydroelectric power production in the interior, which could supply existing general demand as well as an alumina plant and aluminium smelter, while also providing a surplus for export to neighbouring countries. However, the capital cost of development would be high. Development of a 150 MW generating station at Amaila Falls was proposed, with a framework agreement signed in July 2010 by Guyana Power and Light, the China Development Bank, the China Railway First Group Co Ltd and Sithe Global Amaila Holdings Ltd (a subsidiary of Sithe Global, a power company majority owned by the Blackstone Group). Financial closure on the project was expected within 12 months of the signing of the deal. The project, the total cost of which was projected at an estimated US $650m., was to include 65 km of transmission lines, 195 km of new or improved access roads and other infrastructure. Development of this site has been under discussion for a decade, with proposals mooted for further expansion, which would increase capacity eventually to 1,060 MW. The project was to be funded in part with GRIF funds, and would substitute hydro-electric power for imported hydrocarbons, although at some cost in terms of rainforest disturbance. Power generated nationally in 2009 was 602 MW, a 5.8% increase over the previous year.

Despite their border dispute (see History), in June 2005 Guyana was one of 13 Caribbean countries that signed the PetroCaribe agreement, under which Venezuela provides low-interest loans to finance a proportion of oil purchases. These totalled US $82m. in 2008, covering 20% of fuel imports, but decreased to $31.5m. in 2009, owing to lower international oil prices; the cumulative total under the PetroCaribe agreement had reached $132.1m. by the end of 2009.

There is strong potential for petroleum exploration, mainly within the Exclusive Economic Zone, but also onshore. A study by the US Geological Survey suggested that Guyana may have offshore reserves of up to 2,200m. barrels of oil and 6,000,000m. cu ft of natural gas. Seismic surveys were completed in 2008 and 2009 in offshore blocks held by international oil companies, with detailed data analysis to be followed by possible drilling in 2011 or at a later date. Onshore prospects with more modest potential were likely to be drilled in 2010–11 by smaller oil companies.

MANUFACTURING AND CONSTRUCTION

The processing of sugar, rice, and other primary products accounted for close to 40% of Guyana's manufacturing activity. A small manufacturing sector producing for the domestic market confronted serious constraints in the form of competition from cheap imports, high energy costs and inadequate infrastructure. The domestic sector's contribution to GDP had declined by 2009 to just 5.8%, as a number of manufacturers had gone out of business from the 1980s. One of the main remaining industries is the production of beverages, including beer, soft drinks and rum; although output of alcoholic beverages decreased in 2009, local firms have in recent years competed effectively with imports, and in the case of rum have been able to develop export markets for branded premium products, while the Banks DIH brewery now has a mutual shareholding with Banks (Barbados) Breweries Ltd. The engineering and construction sector recorded growth of 1.5% in 2009, and contributed 10.9% of GDP, reaching a plateau after rapid growth in the preceding year. This expansion had reflected an increase in public sector investment, much of it funded with international assistance, in the construction of roads, housing, drainage and irrigation, as well as the final stages of the Skeldon sugar plant, and private sector investment in housing and other sectors.

TOURISM

Guyana only began to develop its tourism potential in the 1980s, and despite government attempts to develop this sector, tourism facilities remained limited. The Guyana Tourism Authority was set up in 2003 to market Guyana as a tourist destination, and the accent has been put on efforts to exploit the country's potential for 'eco-tourism'. However, a high proportion of travellers are business visitors or overseas Guyanese on family visits, and most hotel accommodation is in Georgetown. According to the Caribbean Tourism Organization, in 2009 the total number of visitors was 141,053, a 6.2% increase over the previous year; of these, 54% were from the USA, 17% from Canada, and 6% from Europe (primarily the United Kingdom). Of the remaining 23%, the majority were from the English-speaking Caribbean. With several hotels completed in advance of the 2007 Cricket World Cup, occupancy has been low. Nevertheless, Marriott International announced in June 2010 that it was to its first hotel in Guyana, in Georgetown, in 2013. With a low proportion of visitors being leisure tourists, travel to Guyana remained largely unaffected by the global economic downturn that took hold in the second half of 2008.

TRANSPORT AND INFRASTRUCTURE

The poor condition of Guyana's internal transport infrastructure was a major impediment to the country's economic development. Paved roads connected the settlements of the coastal belt, and ran inland to the bauxite-mining town of Linden and some other points. There were bridges over the Demerara and Berbice rivers, but the Essequibo and the Courantyne (which forms the border with Suriname) must be crossed by ferry. There were some unpaved roads in the interior, which were in many cases difficult to use in wet weather. There has since the 1990s been an unpaved road connecting the capital Georgetown to the border with Brazil. A bridge over the Takutu river at the border with Brazil was completed in 2009, providing a continuous road connection to Boa Vista and the Brazilian highway network. The Government would like to see eventual upgrading of the Guyanese road connection to a surfaced all-weather road capable of taking heavy traffic, with construction of a deep-water port allowing the northern provinces of Brazil to send export products into and through Guyana for export to the Caribbean and North America; however, this remained a distant objective.

Guyana's main port is Georgetown, which can take vessels with a draft of up to 6 m and up to 10,000 tons of cargo. There are specialized facilities elsewhere for bauxite and sugar, also with draft limitations, and a number of small river and sea ports. As of 2004 the Berbice, Demerara, and Essequibo rivers were navigable by some vessels for 150 km, 100 km, and 80 km, respectively. The other main method of transport within Guyana is by air, and there are around 120 airstrips, catering for light aircraft. The country's only international airport, the Cheddi Jagan International Airport, is located at Timehri, 42 km outside Georgetown, but the Ogle airport just east of Georgetown has been upgraded to take regional flights, providing services to Suriname from January 2010, and with connections to other destinations due to be added upon completion of the project later in the year. Commercial railway services for both passengers and goods were operated until 1974, but were then closed, with some mineral lines in the interior operating in the 2000s.

SERVICES

The service sector grew by 2.7% in 2009 and accounted for 49% of GDP. Distribution expanded by 6.6% assisted by strong consumer demand. There was also contining growth of 2.0% in transport and communications (although this compared poorly with the 9.9% recorded in 2008), with further investment in mobile services as an Irish-owned provider, Digicel, which entered the market in 2006, competed vigorously with the privatized incumbent, Guyana Telephones and Telegraph Co. There has been some recent growth in call centres, led by a Mexican company, Qualfon, which opened in 2005 and employed 1,200 staff by 2010. Government spending, the largest component of the service sector, grew by 3.4% in 2009, with spending on wages and salaries increasing by 9.5%. Financial services grew by 3.0% in 2009, with slowly expanding private sector credit to individuals and private sector businesses. Concerns over the standard of financial regulation and the ineffectiveness of money-laundering controls were repeatedly expressed in the 2000s by the US State Department and other international observers.

INVESTMENT AND FINANCE

Guyana was heavily in debt in the 1970s and 1980s, and was unable to access further finance after repeated defaults. The Economic Recovery Programme from 1989 brought debt relief through the 'Paris Club' of major international donors, and renewed access to borrowing. Further debt relief of US $529m. was agreed in 1996 by the 'Paris Club', and by Trinidad and Tobago, which was also a major creditor. From 1998 Guyana qualified for further debt relief under the HIPC programme of the IMF and World Bank, supplemented from 2000 by the Enhanced HIPC programme, with Guyana making a commitment to agreed macroeconomic targets and a Poverty Reduction and Growth Facility providing further assistance; however, waivers on some targets were granted, in view of a challenging political and economic environment. Guyana's principal donor, the Inter-American Development Bank (IDB), in March 2007 agreed to 100% debt relief on loans outstanding at the end of 2004, with a total value of $467m., equivalent to 41% of GDP. This brought Guyana's cumulative debt relief since the mid-1990s to $1,300m. Total debt was dramatically reduced from 184% of GDP in 2005 to 92% in 2009, at which point external debt was down to 67% of GDP. However, these figures remain high by international standards, and debt remains an area of considerable macroeconomic concern. Investment was close to one-third of GDP in the mid-2000s, declining slightly to 30.6% in 2008, but increasing to about 43% in 2009. Of this, 22% was public sector investment in roads, bridges, sea defence, drainage and irrigation, much of it donor funded, and the remaining 21% was private investment in mining, transport, and distribution.

TRADE AND BALANCE OF PAYMENTS

Guyana has a large current account balance of payments deficit, which in the mid- to late 2000s was close to 20% of GDP. Six commodities—bauxite, sugar, rice, fish and shrimps, timber and gold—still made up 89% of total exports in 2009. Fuel imports accounted for 24.5% of the import bill in 2009, and had reached as much as 32% in 2008, a year of high oil prices. Exports in 2009 covered 66% of the value of imports, with a resulting merchandise trade deficit of US $401m., 23% less than in 2008 and equivalent to 32% of GDP. Services were a net outflow item, at $101m. in 2009. However, there was a positive flow of $262m. in family remittances from overseas Guyanese, equivalent to 21% of GDP. As in most recent years, the current account deficit was covered by a capital surplus (of $454m. in 2009), with strong inflows of both private investment in telecommunications, mining and forestry, and of official development assistance, which included disbursements of US $46m. by the IDB, $32m. from PetroCaribe and $53m. in balance of payments support. Reserves therefore increased to reach US $626m., in that year or 5.1 months of import cover.

In 2009 Guyana's main trading partners for exports were Canada (26.4% of total exports), the United Kingdom (13.7%) and the USA (12.3%), and for imports, the USA (28.8% of total imports), Trinidad and Tobago (19.6%) and Venezuela (6.9%).

OUTLOOK

In spite of an unfavourable international economic environment, Guyana was able to maintain macroeconomic stability in 2009 and the first half of 2010 with growth continuing, albeit at a relatively slow pace. This was in part the result of recent debt forgiveness, as well as continuing development assistance, resulting from good relations with major aid donors since the 1990s. Capital spending and assistance programmes stimulated the construction sector, and helped maintain reserves at comfortable levels in spite of persistent current account balance of payments deficits. There were continuing forward commitments for grants and loan assistance from the IDB, the EU and other agencies. However, the economic base remained narrow, with six commodities making up the bulk of exports. This left Guyana vulnerable to price fluctuations and weather-related risks. Recent and proposed investment gave the vital sugar industry a good prospect of survival, despite the forthcoming end to the EU sugar protocol, but difficulties remained and good management would be of great importance. Prospects were good for further investment in gold and, if market conditions recovered, in bauxite. Further ahead, there was a reasonably good prospect of significant petroleum finds, which would be of great benefit to the economy, and of development of the large hydroelectric potential in the interior. Substantial grant aid flowing from participation in the REDD scheme was expected to bring significant macroeconomic benefits. In the public sector, there was a continuing need to address issues of management efficiency, transparency and good governance.

Statistical Survey

Sources (unless otherwise stated): Bank of Guyana, 1 Church St and Ave of the Republic, POB 1003, Georgetown; tel. 226-3250; fax 227-2965; e-mail communications@bankofguyana.org.gy; internet www.bankofguyana.org.gy; Bureau of Statistics, Ministry of Finance, Main and Urquhart Sts, Georgetown; tel. 227-1114; fax 226-1284; internet www.statisticsguyana.gov.gy.

AREA AND POPULATION

Area: 214,969 sq km (83,000 sq miles).

Population: 759,567 (males 376,381, females 383,186) at census of 12 May 1980; 723,673 (males 356,540, females 367,133) at census of 12 May 1991; 751,223 (males 376,034, females 375,189) at census of 15 September 2002. *2010* (official projection): 784,894 (males 393,059, females 391,835).

Density (2010): 3.7 per sq km.

Population by Age and Sex (official projections in 2010): *0–14:* 210,823 (males 106,785, females 104,039); *15–64:* 529,809 (males 266,850, females 262,959); *65 and over:* 44,262 (males 19,425, females 24,837); *Total* 784,894 (males 393,059, females 391,835).

Ethnic Groups (at 2002 census): 'East' Indians 326,277; Africans 227,062; Mixed 125,727; Amerindians 68,675; Portuguese 1,497; Chinese 1,396; White 477; Total (incl. others) 751,223.

Regions (population at 2002 census): Barima–Waini 24,275; Pomeroon–Supenaam 49,253; Essequibo Islands–West Demerara 103,061; Demerara–Mahaica 310,320; Mahaica–Berbice 52,428; East Berbice–Corentyne 123,695; Cuyuni–Mazaruni 17,597; Potaro–Siparuni 10,095; Upper Takutu–Upper Essequibo 19,387; Upper Demerara–Berbice 41,112; Total 751,223.

Principal Towns (population at 2002 census): Georgetown (capital) 134,497; Linden 29,298; New Amsterdam 17,033; Corriverton 11,494. *Mid-2009* ('000, incl. suburbs, UN estimate): Georgetown 132 (Source: UN, *World Urbanization Prospects: The 2009 Revision*).

Births, Marriages and Deaths (per 1,000 population): Birth rate 24.2 in 1995–2000, 21.3 in 2000–05, 18.0 in 2005–10; Crude death rate 9.0 in 1995–2000, 8.8 in 2000–05, 8.2 in 2005–10 (Source: UN, *World Population Prospects: The 2008 Revision*). Marriage rate 3.8 per 1,000 in 2002.

Life Expectancy (years at birth, WHO estimates): 65 (males 62; females 68) in 2008. Source: WHO, *World Health Statistics*.

Economically Active Population (persons aged 15 years and over, census of 2002): Agriculture, hunting and forestry 45,378; Fishing 5,533; Mining and quarrying 9,374; Manufacturing 30,483; Electricity, gas and water 2,246; Construction 16,100; Trade, repair of motor vehicles and personal and household goods 37,690; Restaurants and hotels 5,558; Transport, storage and communications 16,790; Financial intermediation 3,074; Real estate, renting and business services 7,384; Public administration, defence and social security 14,995; Education 13,015; Health and social work 5,513; Other community, social and personal service activities 9,599; Private households with employed persons 6,156; Extra-territorial organizations and bodies 477; *Sub-total* 229,365; Activities not adequately defined 1,489; *Total employed* 230,854. *Mid-2010* ('000, estimates): Agriculture, etc. 51; Total labour force 347 (Source: FAO). *2009:* Central government 10,094; Rest of the public sector 17,410; Total public sector employment 27,504.

HEALTH AND WELFARE

Key Indicators

Total Fertility Rate (children per woman, 2008): 2.3.

Under-5 Mortality Rate (per 1,000 live births, 2008): 61.

HIV/AIDS (% of persons aged 15–49, 2007): 2.5.

Physicians (per 1,000 head, 2000): 0.5.

Hospital Beds (per 1,000 head, 2005): 2.8.

Health Expenditure (2007): US $ per head (PPP): 197.

Health Expenditure (2007): % of GDP: 8.2.

Health Expenditure (2007): public (% of total): 87.7.

Access to Water (% of persons, 2008): 94.

Access to Sanitation (% of persons, 2008): 81.

Total Carbon Dioxide Emissions ('000 metric tons, 2006): 1,505.9.

Total Carbon Dioxide Emissions Per Head (metric tons, 2006): 2.0.

Human Development Index (2007): ranking: 114.

Human Development Index (2007): value: 0.729.

For sources and definitions, see explanatory note on p. vi.

AGRICULTURE, ETC.

Principal Crops ('000 metric tons, 2008, FAO estimates): Rice, paddy 507; Cassava (Manioc) 20; Sugar cane 2,767; Coconuts 70; Bananas 59; Plantains 42. *Aggregate Production* ('000 metric tons, may include official, semi-official or estimated data): Total cereals 511.0; Vegetables (incl. melons) 39.4; Fruits (excl. melons) 32.2.

Livestock ('000 head, year ending September 2008, FAO estimates): Horses 2.4; Asses 1.0; Cattle 110; Sheep 130; Pigs 14; Goats 79; Chickens 19,900.

Livestock Products ('000 metric tons, 2008, FAO estimates): Cattle meat 1.8; Sheep meat 0.6; Pig meat 0.8; Chicken meat 23.2; Cows' milk 30; Hen eggs 1.0.

Forestry ('000 cubic metres, 2008, FAO estimates): *Roundwood Removals:* Sawlogs, veneer logs and logs for sleepers 404, Pulpwood 100, Other industrial wood 21, Fuel wood 857; Total 1,382. *Sawnwood Production:* Total (all broadleaved) 74.

Fishing ('000 metric tons, live weight, 2008): Capture 42.2 (Marine fishes 21.7; Atlantic seabob 14.4; Whitebelly prawn 1.3); Aquaculture 0.3; *Total catch* 42.5. Note: Figures exclude crocodiles: the number of spectacled caimans caught in 2008 was 3,355.

Source: FAO.

MINING

Production (2009): Bauxite 1,484,935 metric tons; Gold 9,326 kg; Diamonds 143,982 metric carats.

INDUSTRY

Selected Products (2009, unless otherwise indicated): Raw sugar 233,736 metric tons; Rice 359,789 metric tons; Rum 94,000 hectolitres; Beer and stout 118,000 hectolitres; Logs 266,198 cu. metres; Margarine 2,022 metric tons; Biscuits 685,000 kg; Paint 23,768 hectolitres; Electricity 602.0m. kWh.

FINANCE

Currency and Exchange Rates: 100 cents = 1 Guyana dollar ($ G). *Sterling, US Dollar and Euro Equivalents* (30 April 2010): £1 sterling = $ G311.542; US $1 = $ G203.250; €1 = $ G270.627; $ G1,000 = £3.21 = US $4.92 = €3.70. *Average Exchange Rate* ($ G per US $): 202.347 in 2007; 203.633 in 2008; 203.950 in 2009.

Budget ($ G million, 2008): *Revenue:* Tax revenue 79,134.0 (Income tax 31,460.0; Value-added tax 23,998.4; Trade taxes 7,754.6); Other current revenue 3,350.1; Capital revenue (incl. grants) 16,579.1; Total 99,063.5. *Expenditure:* Current expenditure 76,154.1 (Personnel emoluments 23,911.4, Other goods and services 47,627.0, Interest 4,615.7); Capital expenditure 36,385.3; *Total* (excl. lending minus repayments) 112,539.4.

International Reserves (US $ million at 31 December 2009): IMF special drawing rights 3.90; Foreign exchange 627.51; *Total* 631.41. Source: IMF, *International Financial Statistics*.

Money Supply ($ G million at 31 December 2009): Currency outside depository corporations 38,195; Transferable deposits 41,443; Other deposits 183,741; *Broad money* 263,379. Source: IMF, *International Financial Statistics*.

Cost of Living (Consumer Price Index; base: 2000 = 100): All items 153.6 in 2007; 166.0 in 2008; 170.9 in 2009. Source: ILO.

Expenditure on the Gross Domestic Product ($ G million at current prices, 2009): Government final consumption expenditure 66,811; Private final consumption expenditure 180,644; Gross capital formation 110,056; *Total domestic expenditure* 357,511; Net exports of goods and services –101,688; *GDP in purchasers' values* 255,823.

Gross Domestic Product by Economic Activity ($ G million at current prices, 2009): Agriculture 33,851 (Sugar 10,402; Rice 8,497; Livestock 4,926; Other crops 10,026); Forestry 3,480; Fishing 11,830; Mining and quarrying 22,701; Manufacturing (incl. utilities) 13,285; Engineering and construction 13,925; Distribution 13,133; Transport and communications 26,946; Rented dwellings 9,899; Financial services 9,292; Other services 4,736; Government 39,178; *Sub-total* 202,258; Indirect taxes, less subsidies (incl. deduction for financial intermediation services indirectly measured) 53,565; *GDP in purchasers' values* 255,823.

Balance of Payments (US $ million, 2009): Exports of goods f.o.b. 768.2; Imports of goods f.o.b. −1,169.2; *Trade balance* −401.0; Services (net) −118.3; *Balance on goods and services* −519.3; Transfers (net) 299.6; *Current balance* −219.7; Capital account (net) 454.0; Net errors and omissions 0.1; *Overall balance* 234.4.

EXTERNAL TRADE

Principal Commodities (US $ million, 2009): *Imports c.i.f.:* Capital goods 259.5; Consumer goods 335.9; Fuel and lubricants 286.5; Other intermediate goods 115.7; Total (incl. others) 1,161.0. *Exports f.o.b.:* Bauxite 79.5; Sugar 119.8; Rice 114.1; Gold 281.7; Shrimps 30.5; Timber 41.4; Total (incl. others, excl. re-exports) 768.2.

Principal Trading Partners (US $ million, 2009): *Imports:* Canada 26.0; China, People's Republic 59.3; Finland 28.1; Japan 42.2; Suriname 61.4; Trinidad and Tobago 227.3; United Kingdom 43.5; USA 334.0; Venezuela 79.7; Total (incl. others) 1,161.0. *Exports:* Barbados 15.9; Belgium 13.8; Canada 203.1; Germany 31.9; Jamaica 37.4; Trinidad and Tobago 28.5; Ukraine 48.4; United Kingdom 105.6; USA 94.8; Total (incl. others) 768.2.

TRANSPORT

Road Traffic ('000 vehicles in use, 2002): Passenger cars 61.3; Commercial vehicles 15.5. Source: UN, *Statistical Yearbook*.

Shipping: *International Sea-borne Freight Traffic* ('000 metric tons, estimates, 1990): Goods loaded 1,730; Goods unloaded 673 (Source: UN, *Monthly Bulletin of Statistics*). *Merchant Fleet* (at 31 December 2008): Vessels 120; Displacement 41,154 grt (Source: Lloyd's Register-Fairplay, *World Fleet Statistics*).

Civil Aviation (traffic on scheduled services, 2001): Kilometres flown (million) 1; Passengers carried ('000) 48; Passenger-km (million) 175; Total ton-km (million) 17. Source: UN, *Statistical Yearbook*.

TOURISM

Tourist Arrivals: 116,596 (USA 60,071) in 2005; 113,474 (USA 57,193) in 2006; 131,487 (USA 68,861) in 2007.

Tourism Receipts (US $ million, incl. passenger transport): 35 in 2005; 37 in 2006; 50 in 2007.

Source: World Tourism Organization.

COMMUNICATIONS MEDIA

Radio Receivers (1999): 400,000 in use.

Television Receivers (2000): 70,000 in use.

Telephones (2009): 130,000 main lines in use.

Mobile Cellular Telephones (2009): 281,400 subscribers.

Personal Computers (2005): 29,000 (38.0 per 1,000 persons) in use.

Internet Users (2009): 220,000.

Broadband Users (2009): 2,000.

Daily Newspapers (2000): 2; estimated circulation 56,750.

Non-daily Newspapers (2000): 4; estimated circulation 47,700.

Book Production (1997): 25.

Sources: mainly UNESCO, *Statistical Yearbook*; UN, *Statistical Yearbook*; International Telecommunication Union.

EDUCATION

Pre-primary (1999/2000): Institutions 320; Teachers 2,218 (males 22, females 2,196); Students 36,955 (males 18,768, females 18,187).

Primary (1999/2000): Institutions 423; Teachers 3,951 (males 561, females 3,390); Students 105,800 (males 54,105, females 51,695).

General Secondary (1999/2000): Institutions 70; Teachers 1,972 (males 715, females 1,257); Students 36,055 (males 16,000, females 20,055).

Special Education (1999/2000): Institutions 6; Teachers 64 (males 14, females 50); Students 617 (males 420, females 197).

Technical and Vocational (1999/2000): Institutions 6; Teachers 215 (males 144, females 71); Students 4,662 (males 2,585, females 2,077).

Teacher Training (1999/2000): Institutions 1; Teachers 297 (males 121, females 176); Students 1,604 (males 246, females 1,358).

University (1999/2000): Institutions 1; Teachers 371 (males 256, females 115); Students 7,496 (males 2,455, females 5,041).

Private Education (1999/2000): Institutions 7; Teachers 120 (males 27, females 93); Students 1,692 (males 831, females 861).

Source: Ministry of Education.

2007/08 (estimates): *Pre-primary:* Institutions 425; 27,153 pupils; 1,825 teachers. *Primary:* Institutions 441; 107,456 pupils; 4,204 teachers. *Secondary:* Institutions 332; 74,673 pupils; 3,574 teachers. *Tertiary:* 7,306 students; 816 teachers (Source: mainly UNESCO Institute for Statistics).

Pupil-Teacher Ratio (primary education, UNESCO estimate): 25.6 in 2007/08 (Source: UNESCO Institute for Statistics).

Adult Literacy Rate (UNESCO estimates): 98.6% (males 99.0%; females 98.2%) in 2001. Source: UN Development Programme, *Human Development Report*.

Directory

The Constitution

Guyana became a republic, within the Commonwealth, on 23 February 1970. A new Constitution was promulgated on 6 October 1980, and amended in 1998, 2000 and 2001. Its main provisions are summarized below:

The Constitution declares the Co-operative Republic of Guyana to be an indivisible, secular, democratic sovereign state in the course of transition from capitalism to socialism. The bases of the political, economic and social system are political and economic independence, involvement of citizens and socio-economic groups, such as co-operatives and trade unions, in the decision-making processes of the State and in management, social ownership of the means of production, national economic planning and co-operativism as the principle of socialist transformation. Personal property, inheritance, the right to work, with equal pay for men and women engaged in equal work, free medical attention, free education and social benefits for old age and disability are guaranteed. Additional rights include equality before the law, the right to strike and to demonstrate peacefully, the right of indigenous peoples to the protection and preservation of their culture, and a variety of gender and work-related rights. Individual political rights are subject to the principles of national sovereignty and democracy, and freedom of expression to the State's duty to ensure fairness and balance in the dissemination of information to the public. Relations with other countries are guided by respect for human rights, territorial integrity and non-intervention.

THE PRESIDENT

The President is the supreme executive authority, Head of State and Commander-in-Chief of the armed forces, elected for a five-year term of office, with no limit on re-election. The successful presidential candidate is the nominee of the party with the largest number of votes in the legislative elections. The President may prorogue or dissolve the National Assembly (in the case of dissolution, fresh elections must be held immediately) and has discretionary powers to postpone elections for up to one year at a time for up to five years. The President may be removed from office on medical grounds, or for violation of the Constitution (with a two-thirds' majority vote of the Assembly), or for gross misconduct (with a three-quarters' majority vote of the Assembly if allegations are upheld by a tribunal).

The President appoints a First Vice-President and Prime Minister, who must be an elected member of the National Assembly, and a Cabinet of Ministers, which may include four non-elected members and is collectively responsible to the legislature. The President also appoints a Leader of the Opposition, who is the elected member of the Assembly deemed by the President most able to command the support of the opposition.

THE LEGISLATURE

The legislative body is a unicameral National Assembly of 65 members (66 in special circumstances), elected by universal adult suffrage in a system of proportional representation; 40 members are elected at national level, and a further 25 are elected from regional constituency lists. The Assembly passes bills, which are then presented to the President, and may pass constitutional amendments.

LOCAL GOVERNMENT

Guyana is divided into 10 Regions, each having a Regional Democratic Council elected for a term of up to five years and four months, although it may be prematurely dissolved by the President.

OTHER PROVISIONS

Impartial commissions exist for the judiciary, the public service and the police service. An Ombudsman is appointed, after consultation between the President and the Leader of the Opposition, to hold office for four years.

The Government

HEAD OF STATE

President: BHARRAT JAGDEO (sworn in 11 August 1999, 31 March 2001 and 2 September 2006).

CABINET
(July 2010)

Following the election of Bharrat Jagdeo in September 2006, the PPP/Civic alliance formed a Government.

Prime Minister: SAMUEL A. HINDS.

Minister of Foreign Affairs, Foreign Trade and International Co-operation: Dr CAROLYN RODRIGUES-BIRKETT.

Minister of Finance: Dr ASHNI KUMAR SINGH.

Minister in the Ministry of Finance: JENNIFER WEBSTER.

Minister of Agriculture: ROBERT MONTGOMERY PERSAUD.

Minister of Amerindian Affairs: PAULINE CAMPBELL-SUKHAI.

Minister of Home Affairs: CLEMENT J. ROHEE.

Minister of Legal Affairs and Attorney-General: CHARLES RAMSON.

Minister of Education: SHAIK K. Z. BAKSH.

Minister in the Ministry of Education: Dr DESREY FOX.

Minister of Health: Dr LESLIE RAMSAMMY.

Minister in the Ministry of Health: Dr BHERI RAMSARRAN.

Minister of Housing and Water: IRFAN ALLY.

Minister of Labour: MANZOOR NADIR.

Minister of Human Services and Social Security: PRIYA DEVI MANICKCHAND.

Minister of Local Government and Regional Development: KELLAWAN LALL.

Minister of Public Service Management: Dr JENNIFER WESTFORD.

Minister of Transport and Hydraulics: BRINDLEY H. R. BENN.

Minister of Tourism, Industry and Commerce: MANNIRAM PRASHAD.

Minister of Culture, Youth and Sport: Dr FRANK ANTHONY.

Secretary to the Cabinet: Dr ROGER LUNCHEON.

MINISTRIES

Office of the President: New Garden St, Bourda, Georgetown; tel. 225-3130; fax 227-3050; e-mail opmed@op.gov.gy; internet www.op.gov.gy.

Office of the Prime Minister: Oranapai Towers, Wight's Lane, Kingston, Georgetown; tel. 226-6955; fax 226-7573; e-mail opm@networksgy.gy.

Ministry of Agriculture: Regent and Vlissengen Rds, POB 1001, Georgetown; tel. 226-5165; fax 227-2978; e-mail minister@agriculture.gov.gy; internet www.agriculture.gov.gy.

Ministry of Amerindian Affairs: Thomas and Quamina Sts, Georgetown; tel. 227-5067; fax 225-7072; e-mail ministryofamerindian@networksgy.com.

Ministry of Culture, Youth and Sport: 71–72 Main St, South Cummingsburg, Georgetown; tel. 227-7867; fax 225-5067; e-mail mincys@guyana.net.gy.

Ministry of Education: 26 Brickdam, Stabroek, POB 1014, Georgetown; tel. 226-3094; fax 225-5570; e-mail moegyweb@yahoo.com; internet www.moe.gov.gy.

Ministry of Finance: Main and Urquhart Sts, Kingston, Georgetown; tel. 225-6088; fax 226-1284; e-mail minister@finance.gov.gy; internet www.finance.gov.gy.

Ministry of Foreign Affairs, Foreign Trade and International Co-operation: 254 South Rd and Shiv Chanderpaul Dr., Bourda, Georgetown; tel. 226-1607; fax 225-9192; e-mail minfor@guyana.net.gy; internet www.minfor.gov.gy.

Ministry of Health: Brickdam, Stabroek, Georgetown; tel. 226-5861; fax 225-4505; e-mail moh@sdnp.org.gy; internet www.health.gov.gy.

Ministry of Home Affairs: 60 Brickdam, Stabroek, Georgetown; tel. 225-7270; fax 227-4806; e-mail homemin@guyana.net.

Ministry of Housing and Water: 41 Brickdam, Stabroek, Georgetown; tel. 225-7192; fax 227-3455; e-mail mhwps@sdnp.org.gy.

Ministry of Labour, Human Services and Social Security: 1 Water St and Corhill St, Stabroek, Georgetown; tel. 225-0655; fax 227-1308; e-mail psmlhsss@yahoo.com; internet www.mlhsss.gov.gy.

Ministry of Legal Affairs and Office of the Attorney-General: 95 Carmichael St, North Cummingsburg, Georgetown; tel. 226-2616; fax 226-9721; e-mail legalaffairsps@yahoo.com; internet www.agmla.gov.gy.

Ministry of Local Government and Regional Development: De Winkle Bldg, Fort St, Kingston, Georgetown; tel. 225-8621; fax 226-5070; e-mail mlgrdps@telsnetgy.net.

Ministry of Public Service Management: 164 Waterloo St, North Cummingsburg, Georgetown; tel. 226-6528; fax 225-7899; e-mail psm@sdnp.org.gy; internet www.sdnp.org.gy/psm.

Ministry of Tourism, Industry and Commerce: 229 South Rd, Lacytown, Georgetown; tel. 226-2505; fax 225-9898; e-mail ministry@mintic.gov.gy; internet www.mintic.gov.gy.

Ministry of Transport and Hydraulics: Wights Lane, Kingston, Georgetown; tel. 226-1875; fax 225-6954; e-mail minoth@networksgy.com.

President and Legislature

NATIONAL ASSEMBLY

Speaker: HARI NARAYEN (RALPH) RAMKARRAN.

Deputy Speaker: CLARISSA RIEHL.

Clerk: SHERLOCK ISAACS.

Election, 28 August 2006

Party	% of votes	Seats
People's Progressive Party/Civic	54.3	36
People's National Congress Reform-One Guyana	34.0	22
Alliance for Change	8.3	5
Guyana Action Party/Rise, Organize and Rebuild Guyana Movement	2.5	1
The United Force	0.9	1
Total	100.0	65

Under Guyana's system of proportional representation, the nominated candidate of the party receiving the most number of votes is elected to the presidency. Thus, on 2 September 2006 the candidate of the PPP/Civic alliance, BHARRAT JAGDEO, was inaugurated as President for a further term.

Election Commission

Guyana Elections Commission (GECOM): 41 High and Cowan Sts, Kingston, Georgetown; tel. 225-0277; e-mail gecomfeedback@webworksgy.com; internet www.gecom.org.gy; f. 2000; appointed by the Pres., partly in consultation with the leader of the opposition; Chair. Dr STEVE SURUJBALLY.

Political Organizations

Alliance for Change (AFC): 77 Hadfield St, Werk-en-Rust, Georgetown; tel. 225-0452; fax 225-0455; e-mail alliance4changegy@yahoo.com; internet www.afcguyana.com; f. 2005; Leader RAPHAEL TROTMAN; Chair. KHEMRAJ RAMJATTAN.

Guyana Action Party (GAP): Georgetown; allied with ROAR in 2006 elections; Leader PAUL HARDY.

Guyana Democratic Party (GDP): Georgetown; f. 1996; Leaders ASGAR ALLY.

Guyana National Congress (GNC): Georgetown; Leader SAMUEL HAMER.

Justice For All Party (JFAP): 43 Robb and Wellington Sts, Lacytown, Georgetown; tel. 226-5462; fax 227-3050; e-mail cnsharma@guyana.net.gy; Leader CHANDRANARINE SHARMA.

People's Democratic Party of Guyana (PDP): e-mail admin@guyanapdp.org; internet www.guyanapdp.org; f. 2008.

People's National Congress Reform-One Guyana (PNCR-1G): Congress Place, Sophia, POB 10330, Georgetown; tel. 225-7852; fax 225-2704; e-mail pnc@guyana-pnc.org; internet www.guyanapnc.org; f. 1957 as People's National Congress following split with the PPP; present name adopted in 2006; Reform wing established in 2000; Leader ROBERT H. O. CORBIN; Chair. WINSTON MURRAY; Gen. Sec. OSCAR E. CLARKE.

People's Progressive Party/Civic (PPP/Civic): Freedom House, 41 Robb St, Lacytown, Georgetown; tel. 227-2095; fax 227-2096; e-mail pr@ppp-civic.org; internet www.ppp-civic.org; f. 1950; Marxist-Leninist; Gen. Sec. DONALD RAMOTAR.

Rise, Organize and Rebuild Guyana Movement (ROAR): 186 Parafield, Leonora, West Coast Demerara, POB 101409, Georgetown; tel. 268-2452; fax 268-3382; e-mail guyroar@yahoo.com; f. 1999; allied with GAP in 2006 elections; Leader RAVI DEV; Sec. ROY SINGH.

The United Force (TUF): Unity House, 95 Robb and New Garden Sts, Bourda, Georgetown; tel. 226-2596; fax 225-2973; internet www.tufsite.com; f. 1960; right-wing; advocates rapid industrialization through govt partnership and private capital; allied with the PPP/Civic since 2001 but contested 2006 election under its own auspices; Leader MANZOOR NADIR; Dep. Leader MICHAEL ANTHONY ABRAHAM.

Unity Party: 77 Hadfield St, Georgetown; tel. 227-6744; fax 227-6745; e-mail info@unityparty.net; internet www.unitypartyguyana.com; f. 2005; promotes private enterprise and coalition politics; Pres. CHEDDI (JOEY) JAGAN, Jr.

Working People's Alliance (WPA): Walter Rodney House, 80 Croal St, Stabroek, Georgetown; tel. and fax 225-3679; originally popular pressure group, became political party 1979; independent Marxist; Collective Leadership Dr CLIVE THOMAS, Dr RUPERT ROOPNARINE.

Diplomatic Representation

EMBASSIES AND HIGH COMMISSIONS IN GUYANA

Brazil: 308 Church St, Queenstown, POB 10489, Georgetown; tel. 225-7970; fax 226-9063; e-mail brasemb@networksgy.com; Ambassador LUIZ GILBERTO SEIXAS DE ANDRADE.

Canada: High and Young Sts, POB 10880, Georgetown; tel. 227-2081; fax 225-8380; e-mail grgtn@international.gc.ca; internet www.canadainternational.gc.ca/guyana; High Commissioner FRANCOIS MONTOUR.

China, People's Republic: Lot 2, Botanic Gardens, Mandella Ave, Georgetown; tel. 227-1651; fax 225-9228; e-mail prcemb@networks.gy.com; internet gy.china-embassy.org/eng; Ambassador ZHANG JUNGAO.

Cuba: 46 High St, POB 10268, Kingston, Georgetown; tel. 225-1883; fax 226-1824; e-mail emguyana@networksgy.com; internet www.cubanembassy.org.gy; Ambassador RAUL GORTÁZAR MARRERO.

India: 307 Church St, Queenstown, Georgetown; tel. 226-3996; fax 225-7012; e-mail hoc.georgetown@mea.gov.in; High Commissioner SUBIT KUMAR MANDAL.

Mexico: 44 Brickdam, South Cummingsburg, Georgetown; tel. 226-3987; fax 226-3722; e-mail mexicoembassygy@gmail.com; Ambassador FERNANDO SANDOVAL FLORES.

Russia: 3 Public Rd, Kitty, Georgetown; tel. 226-9773; fax 227-2975; e-mail embrus.guyana@mail.ru; internet www.rusembassyguyana.org.gy; Ambassador PAVEL SERGIEV.

Suriname: 171 Peter Rose and Crown Sts, Queenstown, Georgetown; tel. 226-7844; fax 225-0759; e-mail surnmemb@gol.net.gy; Ambassador MANORMA SOEKNANDAN.

United Kingdom: 44 Main St, POB 10849, Georgetown; tel. 226-5881; fax 225-3555; e-mail bhcguyana@networksgy.com; internet ukinguyana.fco.gov.uk; High Commissioner FRASER WILLIAM WHEELER.

USA: 100 Young and Duke Sts, POB 10507, Kingston, Georgetown; tel. 225-4900; fax 225-8497; e-mail usembassy@hotmail.com; internet georgetown.usembassy.gov; Chargé d'affaires a.i. KAREN WILLIAMS.

Venezuela: 296 Thomas St, South Cummingsburg, Georgetown; tel. 226-1543; fax 225-3241; e-mail embveguy@gol.net.gy; Ambassador DARÍO MORANDY.

Judicial System

The Judicature of Guyana comprises the Supreme Court of Judicature, which consists of the Court of Appeal and the High Court (both of which are superior courts of record), and a number of Courts of Summary Jurisdiction.

The Court of Appeal, which came into operation in 1966, consists of the Chancellor as President, the Chief Justice, and such number of Justices of Appeal as may be prescribed by the National Assembly.

The High Court of the Supreme Court consists of the Chief Justice as President of the Court and Puisne Judges. Its jurisdiction is both original and appellate. It has criminal jurisdiction in matters brought before it on indictment. A person convicted by the Court has a right of appeal to the Guyana Court of Appeal. The High Court of the Supreme Court has unlimited jurisdiction in civil matters and exclusive jurisdiction in probate, divorce and admiralty and certain other matters. Under certain circumstances, appeal in civil matters lies either to the Full Court of the High Court of the Supreme Court, which is composed of no fewer than two judges, or to the Guyana Court of Appeal. On 4 November 2004 the National Assembly approved legislation recognizing the Caribbean Court of Justice (CCJ) as Guyana's highest court of appeal. The CCJ was inaugurated in Port of Spain, Trinidad and Tobago, on 16 April 2005.

A magistrate has jurisdiction to determine claims where the amount involved does not exceed a certain sum of money, specified by law. Appeal lies to the Full Court.

Chancellor of Justice: CARL SINGH (acting).

Chief Justice: CARL SINGH.

Justices of Appeal: CLAUDETTE SINGH, IAN CHANG, NANDRAM KISSOON.

High Court Justices: WINSTON HORATIO PATTERSON, ROXANNE GEORGE, BRASSINGTON REYNOLDS.

Religion

CHRISTIANITY

Guyana Council of Churches: 26 Durban St, Lodge, Georgetown; tel. 227-5126; e-mail bishopedghill@hotmail.com; f. 1967 by merger of the Christian Social Council (f. 1937) and the Evangelical Council (f. 1960); 15 mem. churches, 1 assoc. mem.; Chair. Rev. ALPHONSO PORTER; Sec. Rev. NIGEL HAZEL.

The Anglican Communion

Anglicans in Guyana are adherents of the Church in the Province of the West Indies, comprising eight dioceses. The Archbishop of the Province is the Bishop of the North Eastern Caribbean and Aruba, resident in St John's, Antigua. The diocese of Guyana also includes French Guiana and Suriname. According to the latest available census figures (2002), Anglicans constitute 7% of the population.

Bishop of Guyana: Rt Rev. RANDOLPH OSWALD GEORGE, The Church House, 49 Barrack St, POB 10949, Georgetown 1; tel. and fax 226-4183; e-mail dioofguy@networksgy.com; internet www.anglican.bm/G/01.html.

The Baptist Church

The Baptist Convention of Guyana: POB 10149, Georgetown; tel. 226-0428; 33 mem. churches, 1,823 mems.

The Lutheran Church

The Evangelical Lutheran Church in Guyana: Lutheran Courts, Berbice, POB 88, New Amsterdam; tel. and fax 333-6479; e-mail lcg@guyana.net.gy; internet www.elcguyana.org; f. 1947; 11,000 mems; Pres. Rev. ROY K. THAKURDYAL.

The Roman Catholic Church

Guyana comprises the single diocese of Georgetown, suffragan to the archdiocese of Port of Spain, Trinidad and Tobago. According to the 2002 census, some 8% of the population are Roman Catholics. The Bishop participates in the Antilles Episcopal Conference Secretariat, currently based in Port of Spain, Trinidad.

Bishop of Georgetown: FRANCIS DEAN ALLEYNE, Bishop's House, 27 Brickdam, POB 101488, Stabroek, Georgetown; tel. 226-4469; fax 225-8519; e-mail rcbishop@networksgy.com; internet www.rcdiocese.org.gy.

Seventh-day Adventists

According to the 2002 census, 5% of the population are Seventh-day Adventists. The Guyana Conference is a member of the Caribbean Union Conference and comprises two congregations and 137 churches.

Guyana Conference: 222 Peter Rose and Almond Sts, Queenstown, POB 10191, Georgetown; tel. 226-3313; fax 223-8142; e-mail hgarnett@guyanaconference.org; internet guyanaconference.org; 50,291 mems in 2007; 173 churches in 23 pastoral districts; Pres. Pastor HILTON GARNETT.

Other Christian Churches

According to the 2002 census, 17% of the population are Pentecostal Christians. Other denominations active in Guyana include the African Methodist Episcopal Church, the African Methodist Episcopal Zion Church, the Church of God, the Church of the Nazarene, the Ethiopian Orthodox Church, the Guyana Baptist Mission, the Guyana Congregational Union, the Guyana Presbyterian Church, the Hallelujah Church, the Methodist Church in the Caribbean and the Americas, the Moravian Church and the Presbytery of Guyana.

HINDUISM

According to the 2002 census, Hindus constitute 28% of the population.

Guyana Hindu Dharmic Sabha (Hindu Religious Centre): 162 Lamaha St, POB 10576, Georgetown; tel. 225-7443; f. 1934; Pres. REEPU DAMAN PERSAUD.

ISLAM

Muslims in Guyana comprise 7% of the population, according to the 2002 census.

The Central Islamic Organization of Guyana (CIOG): M.Y.O. Bldg, Woolford Ave, Thomas Lands, POB 10245, Georgetown; tel. 225-8654; fax 227-2475; e-mail contact@ciog.org.gy; internet www.ciog.org.gy; Pres. Haji S. M. NASIR; Dir of Education QAYS ARTHUR.

Guyana United Sad'r Islamic Anjuman: 157 Alexander St, Kitty, POB 10715, Georgetown; tel. 226-9620; e-mail khalid@gusia.org; f. 1936; 120,000 mems; Pres. Haji A. HAFIZ RAHAMAN.

BAHÁ'Í FAITH

National Spiritual Assembly: 220 Charlotte St, Bourda, Georgetown; tel. and fax 226-5952; e-mail secretariat@gy.bahai.org; internet gy.bahai.org; incorporated in 1976; National Sec. PAM O'TOOLE.

The Press

DAILIES

Guyana Chronicle: 2A Lama Ave, Bel Air Park, POB 11, Georgetown; tel. 227-5204; fax 227-5208; e-mail gm@guyanachronicle.com; internet www.guyanachronicle.com; f. 1881; govt-owned; also produces weekly Sunday Chronicle (tel. 226-3243); Editor-in-Chief SHARIEF KHAN; circ. 23,000 (weekdays), 43,000 (Sundays).

Guyana Times: 238 Camp and Quamina Sts, Georgetown; tel. 225-5128; fax 225-5134; e-mail news@guyanatimesgy.com; internet www.guyanatimesgy.com; f. 2008; owned by Queen's Atlantic Investment Inc; Editor NIGEL WILLIAMS.

Kaieteur News: 24 Saffon St, Charlestown, Georgetown; tel. 225-8465; fax 225-8473; e-mail kaieteurnews@yahoo.com; internet www.kaieteurnewsonline.com; f. 1994; independent; Editor-in-Chief ADAM HARRIS; Publr GLENN LALL; daily circ. 19,000, Fridays 25,000, Sundays 32,000.

Stabroek News: E1/2 46–47 Robb St, Lacytown, Georgetown; tel. 227-5197; fax 226-2549; e-mail stabroeknews@stabroeknews.com; internet www.stabroeknews.com; f. 1986; also produces weekly Sunday Stabroek; liberal independent; Editor-in-Chief ANAND PERSAUD; circ. 14,100 (weekdays), 26,400 (Sundays).

WEEKLIES AND PERIODICALS

The Catholic Standard: 222 South & Wellington Sts, Queenstown, POB 10720, Georgetown; tel. 226-1540; e-mail colinsmit@gmail.com; f. 1905; organ of the Roman Catholic church; weekly; Editor COLIN SMITH; circ. 4,000.

Diocesan Magazine: 49 Barrack St, Kingston, Georgetown; e-mail dioofguy@networksgy.com; quarterly.

Guyana Review: 143 Oronoque St, POB 10386, Georgetown; tel. 226-3139; fax 227-3465; e-mail guyrev@networksgy.com; f. 1993; taken over by Guyana Publs Inc in Jan. 2007; monthly.

Mirror: Lot 8, Industrial Estate, Ruimveldt, Greater Georgetown; tel. 226-2471; fax 226-2472; e-mail ngmirror@guyana.net.gy; internet www.mirrornewsonline.com; owned by the New Guyana Co Ltd; Sundays; Editor DAVID DE GROOT; circ. 25,000.

New Nation: Congress Pl., Sophia, Georgetown; tel. 226-7891; f. 1955; organ of the People's National Congress Reform-One Guyana; weekly; Editor FRANCIS WILLIAMS; circ. 26,000.

The Official Gazette of Guyana: Guyana National Printers Ltd, Lot 1, Public Rd, La Penitence; govt-owned; weekly; circ. 450.

Thunder: Freedom House, 41 Robb St, Lacytown, Georgetown; tel. 227-2095; fax 227-2096; e-mail ppp@guyana.net.gy; internet www.ppp-civic.org; organ of the People's Progressive Party/Civic; quarterly; Editor (vacant).

PRESS ASSOCIATION

Guyana Press Association (GPA): 82C Duke St, Kingston, Georgetown; tel. 623-5430; fax 223-6625; e-mail gpaexecutive@gmail.com; internet www.gpa.org.gy; f. 1945; affiliated with the Association of Caribbean Media Workers; Pres. DENIS CHABROL.

NEWS AGENCY

Guyana Information Agency: Area B, Homestretch Ave, D'Urban Backlands, Georgetown; tel. 225-3117; fax 226-4003; e-mail gina@gina.gov.gy; internet www.gina.gov.gy; f. 1993; Dir Dr PREM MISIR.

Publishers

Guyana Free Press: POB 10386, Georgetown; tel. 226-3139; fax 227-3465; e-mail guyrev@networksgy.com; books and learned journals.

Guyana National Printers Ltd: 1 Public Rd, La Penitence, POB 10256, Greater Georgetown; tel. 225-3623; e-mail gnpl@guyana.net.gy; f. 1939; govt-owned printers and publishers; privatization pending.

Guyana Publications Inc: E 1/2 46–47 Robb St, Lacytown, Georgetown; tel. 226-5197; fax 226-3237; e-mail info@stabroeknews.com; internet www.stabroeknews.com; publishers of Stabroek News and Sunday Stabroek; Man. Dir DOREEN DECAIRES.

Broadcasting and Communications

TELECOMMUNICATIONS

The telecommunications sector was restructured and opened to competition in 2002.

Digicel Guyana: 56 High St, POB 101845, Kingston, Georgetown; tel. 669-3444; fax 223-6532; e-mail customercare.guyana@digicelgroup.com; internet www.digicelguyana.com; f. 1999 as Trans-World Telecom; acquired Cel Star Guyana in 2003; acquired by Digicel Group in Nov. 2006; GSM cellular telecommunications network; operates Celstar and U-Mobile brands; Vice-Pres. GREGORY LIBERTINY.

Guyana Telephones and Telegraph Company (GT & T): 79 Brickdam, POB 10628, Georgetown; tel. 226-7840; fax 226-2457; e-mail pubcomm@gtt.co.gy; internet www.gtt.co.gy; f. 1991; fmrly state-owned Guyana Telecommunications Corpn; 80% ownership by Atlantic Tele-Network (USA); Chair. (vacant); CEO Maj.-Gen. (retd) JOSEPH G. SINGH.

BROADCASTING

In May 2001 the Government implemented the regulation of all broadcast frequencies. Two private stations relay US satellite television programmes.

National Communications Network (NCN): Homestretch Ave, D'Urban Park, Georgetown; tel. 227-1566; fax 226-2253; e-mail feedback@ncnguyana.com; internet www.ncnguyana.com; f. 2004 following merger of Guyana Broadcasting Corpn (f. 1979) and Guyana Television and Broadcasting Co (f. 1993); govt-owned; operates three radio channels and six TV channels; Chair. ROBERT PERSAUD; CEO DESMOND MOHAMED SATTAUR; Editor-in-Chief MICHAEL GORDON.

Radio

National Communications Network (NCN): see Broadcasting; operates three channels: Hot FM, Radio Roraima and Voice of Guyana.

Television

CNS Television Six: 43 Robb and Wellington Sts, Lacytown, Georgetown; tel. 226-5462; fax 227-3050; e-mail sharma@cns6.tv; internet www.cns6.tv; f. 1992; privately owned; Man. Dir CHANDRANARINE SHARMA.

National Communications Network (NCN): see Broadcasting; TV network covers channels 8, 11, 13, 15, 21 and 26.

Finance

(cap. = capital; res = reserves; dep. = deposits; m. = million; brs = branches; amounts in Guyana dollars)

BANKING

Central Bank

Bank of Guyana: 1 Church St and Ave of the Republic, POB 1003, Georgetown; tel. 226-3250; fax 227-2965; e-mail communications@bankofguyana.org.gy; internet www.bankofguyana.org.gy; f. 1965; cap. 1,000m., res 4,586.1m., dep. 10,506.5m. (Dec. 2008); central bank of issue; acts as regulatory authority for the banking sector; Gov. LAWRENCE T. WILLIAMS.

Commercial Banks

Bank of Baroda (Guyana) Inc (India): 10 Ave of the Republic and Regent St, POB 10768, Georgetown; tel. 226-6423; fax 225-1691; e-mail bobinc@networksgy.com; f. 1908; Man. Dir V. K. SEHGAL.

Citizens' Bank Guyana Inc (CBGI): 201 Camp St, Lacytown, Georgetown; tel. 226-1705; fax 226-1719; internet www.citizensbankgy.com; f. 1994; 51% owned by Banks DIH; total assets 18,773m. (Sept. 2007); Chair. CLIFFORD B. REIS; Man. Dir ETON M. CHESTER (acting); 4 brs.

Demerara Bank Ltd: 230 Camp and South Sts, POB 12133, Georgetown; tel. and fax 225-0610; e-mail banking@demerarabank.com; internet www.demerarabank.com; f. 1994; cap. 450.0m., res 345.7m., dep. 17,899.9m. (Sept. 2007); Chair. YESU PERSAUD; CEO PRAVINCHANDRA S. DAVE.

Guyana Bank for Trade and Industry Ltd (GBTI): 47–48 Water St, POB 10280, Georgetown; tel. 226-8430; fax 227-1612; e-mail banking@gbtibank.com; internet www.gbtibank.com; f. 1987 to absorb the operations of Barclays Bank; cap. 800m., res 792m., dep. 41,007.2m. (Dec. 2008); Chair. ROBIN STOBY; CEO JOHN TRACEY; 7 brs.

Republic Bank (Guyana): Promenade Court, 155–156 New Market St, Georgetown; tel. 223-7938; fax 227-2921; e-mail email@republicguyana.com; internet www.republicguyana.com; f. 1984; 51% owned by Republic Bank Ltd, Port of Spain, Trinidad and Tobago; acquired Guyana National Co-operative Bank in 2003; name changed from National Bank of Industry and Commerce in 2006; cap. 300m., res 938.8m., dep. 75,719.2m. (Sept. 2008); Chair. DAVID DULAL-WHITEWAY; Man. Dir EDWIN H. GOODING; 5 brs.

Merchant Bank

Guyana Americas Merchant Bank Inc (GAMBI): GBTI Bldg, 138 Regent St, Lacytown, Georgetown; tel. 223-5193; fax 223-5195; e-mail gambi@networksgy.com; f. 2001; fmrly known as Guyana Finance Corpn Ltd; Man. Dir Dr GRAHAM SCOTT.

STOCK EXCHANGE

The Guyana Association of Securities Companies and Intermediaries Inc. (GASCI): Hand-in-Hand Bldg, 1 Ave of the Republic, Georgetown; tel. 223-6176; fax 223-6175; e-mail info@gasci.com; internet www.gasci.com; f. 2001; Chair. NIKHIL RAMKARRAN; Gen. Man. GEORGE EDWARDS.

INSURANCE

Supervisory Body

Office of the Commissioner of Insurance: Privatisation Unit Bldg, 126 Barrack St, Kingston, Georgetown; tel. 225-0318; fax 226-6426; e-mail mvanbeek@insurance.gov.gy; internet www.insurance.gov.gy; regulates insurance and pensions industries; Commr MARIA VAN BEEK.

Companies

CLICO: 191 Camp St, South Cummings, Georgetown; tel. 227-1330; e-mail info@clico.com; internet www.clico.com; Exec. Chair. LAWRENCE A. DUPREY; CEO GEETA SINGH-KNIGHT.

Demerara Mutual Life Assurance Society Ltd: 61–62 Robb St and Ave of the Republic, Georgetown; tel. 225-8991; fax 225-8995; e-mail demlife@demeraramutual.com; internet www.demeraramutual.org; f. 1891; Chair. RICHARD B. FIELDS.

Diamond Fire and General Insurance Inc: 44B High St, Kingston, Georgetown; tel. 223-9771; fax 223-9770; e-mail diamondins@solutions2000.net; f. 2000; privately owned; Man. TARA CHANDRA; cap. 100m.

Guyana Co-operative Insurance Service (GCIS): 47 Main St, Georgetown; tel. 225-9153; f. 1976; 67% owned by the Hand-in-Hand Group; Area Rep. SAMMY RAMPERSAUD.

Guyana and Trinidad Mutual Fire & Life Insurance Co Ltd: 27–29 Robb and Hinck St, Georgetown; tel. 225-7910; fax 225-9397; e-mail gtmgroup@gtm-gy.com; internet www.gtm-gy.com; f. 1925; affiliated co: Guyana and Trinidad Mutual Fire Insurance Co Ltd; Chair. HAROLD B. DAVIS; Gen. Man. ROGER YEE.

Hand-in-Hand Mutual Fire and Life Group: Hand-in-Hand Bldg, 1–4 Ave of the Republic, POB 10188, Georgetown; tel. 225-1865; fax 225-7519; e-mail info@hihgy.com; internet www.hihgy.com; f. 1865; fire and life insurance; Chair. C. A. F. HUGHES; CEO KEITH EVELYN.

Association

Insurance Association of Guyana: South 0.5, 14 Pere St, Kitty, Georgetown; tel. 226-3514; f. 1968.

Trade and Industry

GOVERNMENT AGENCIES

Environmental Protection Agency, Guyana: Lot 1, Broad and Charles Sts, Charlestown, Georgetown; tel. 225-2062; fax 225-5481; e-mail epa@epaguyana.org; internet www.epaguyana.org; f. 1988 as Guyana Agency for the Environment; renamed 1996; formulates, implements and monitors policies on the environment; Exec. Dir DOORGA PERSAUD.

Guyana Energy Agency (GEA): 295 Quamina St, POB 903, Georgetown; tel. 226-0394; fax 226-5227; e-mail ecgea@guyana.net.gy; internet www.sdnp.org.gy/gea; f. 1998 as successor to Guyana National Energy Authority; CEO MAHENDRA SHARMA (acting).

Guyana Marketing Corporation: 87 Robb and Alexander Sts, Lacytown, POB 10810, Georgetown; tel. 226-8255; fax 227-4114; e-mail newgmc@networksgy.com; internet www.newgmc.com; Gen. Man. NIZAM HASSAN.

Guyana Office for Investment (Go-Invest): 190 Camp and Church Sts, Georgetown; tel. 225-0653; fax 225-0655; e-mail goinvest@goinvest.gov.gy; internet www.goinvest.gov.gy; f. 1994; CEO GEOFFREY DA SILVA.

DEVELOPMENT ORGANIZATION

Institute of Private Enterprise Development (IPED): 253 South Rd, Bourda, Georgetown; tel. 225-8949; fax 223-7834; e-mail iped@solutions2000.net; internet www.ipedgy.com; f. 1986 to help establish small businesses; total loans provided $ G1,400m. (2007); Chair. YESU PERSAUD; Exec. Dir Dr LESLIE CHIN.

CHAMBER OF COMMERCE

Georgetown Chamber of Commerce and Industry: 156 Waterloo St, Cummingsburg, POB 10110, Georgetown; tel. 225-5846; fax 226-3519; e-mail info@georgetownchamberofcommerce.org; internet www.georgetownchamberofcommerce.org; f. 1889; Pres. GERALD GOUVEIA; 122 mems.

INDUSTRIAL AND TRADE ASSOCIATIONS

Guyana Rice Development Board: 116–17 Cowan St, Kingston, Georgetown; tel. 225-8717; fax 225-6486; internet www.grdb.gy; f. 1994 to assume operations of Guyana Rice Export Board and Guyana Rice Grading Centre; Gen. Man. JAGNARINE SINGH.

National Dairy and Development Programme (NDDP): c/o Lands and Surveys Bldg, 22 Upper Hadfield St, Durban Backlands, POB 10367, Georgetown; tel. 225-7107; fax 226-3020; e-mail nddp@sdnp.org.gy; internet www.sdnp.org.gy/minagri/nddp/generalinfo.htm; f. 1984; aims to increase domestic milk and beef production; Programme Dir MEER BACCHUS.

EMPLOYERS' ASSOCIATIONS

Consultative Association of Guyanese Industry Ltd: 157 Waterloo St, POB 10730, Georgetown; tel. 225-7170; fax 227-0725; e-mail cagi@guyana.net.gy; f. 1962; Chair. YESU PERSAUD; Exec. Dir DAVID YANKANA; 193 mems, 3 mem. asscns, 159 assoc. mems.

Forest Products Association of Guyana: 157 Waterloo St, Georgetown; tel. 226-9848; fax 226-2832; e-mail fpasect@sdnp.org.gy; internet www.fpaguyana.org; f. 1944; 62 mem. cos; Pres. DAVID PERSAUD; Exec. Officer WARREN PHOENIX.

Guyana Manufacturing and Services Association Ltd (GMSA): National Exhibition Centre, Sophia, Georgetown; tel. 219-0072; fax 219-0073; e-mail gma_guyana@yahoo.com; internet www.gma.org.gy; f. 1967 as the Guyana Manufacturers' Asscn; name changed in 2005 to reflect growth in services sector; 190 mems; Pres. RAMESH DOOKHOO.

Guyana Rice Producers' Association (GRPA): 126 Parade and Barrack St, Georgetown; tel. 226-4411; fax 223-7249; e-mail grpa.riceproducers@networksgy.com; f. 1946; non-govt org.; 18,500 mems; Pres. LEEKHA RAMBRICH; Gen. Sec. DHARAMKUMAR SEERAJ.

MAJOR COMPANIES

The following are some of the major companies operating in Guyana:

Food and Beverages

Banks DIH Ltd: Thirst Park, POB 10194, Georgetown; tel. 226-2491; fax 226-6523; e-mail banks@banksdih.com; internet www.banksdih.com; f. 1848; brewers and soft drinks and snacks manufacturers; revenue $ G14,017m. (2005/06); Chair. and Man. Dir CLIFFORD BARRINGTON REIS; Dir DAN BRYAN STOUTE; 1,500 employees.

Chin's Manufacturing Industries Ltd: Area K, Le Ressouvenir, East Bank, Demerara; tel. 220-2138; fax 220-3592; e-mail chinsagency@yahoo.com; Man. Dir COMPTON CHIN.

Demerara Distillers Ltd: Plantation Diamond, East Bank, Demerara; tel. 265-5019; fax 265-3367; e-mail ddlweb@demrum.com; internet www.demrum.com; f. 1952; producer of alcoholic and non-alcoholic beverages; sales of $ G10.6m. (2003); Pres. and Chair. YESU PERSAUD; 1,165 employees.

Edward B. Beharry & Co Ltd (EBB): 191 Charlotte St, Lacytown, Georgetown; tel. 227-0632; fax 225-6062; internet www.beharrygroup.com; f. 1935; producer of confectionery, condiments and pasta; Chair. EDWARD ANAND BEHARRY.

Guyana Sugar Corpn Inc (GuySuCo): Ogle Estate, POB 10547, East Bank, Demerara; tel. 222-6030; fax 222-6048; e-mail info@guyguco.com; internet www.guysuco.com; f. 1976; from 1990 managed by Booker Tate (United Kingdom); sugar production; US $169m. project to modernize the Skeldon sugar factory and enhance production efficiency was scheduled for completion in 2008; scheduled for privatization; Chair. NANDA KISHORE GOPAUL; Dir KEITH WARD.

National Milling Co of Guyana Inc (NAMILCO): Agricola, East Bank, Demerara; tel. 225-2990; fax 226-9822; e-mail info@namilcoflour.com; internet www.namilcoflour.com; subsidiary of Seaboard Corporation (USA); flour millers; Man. Dir DONALD FRANKE.

Forestry and Timber

A. Mazaharally and Sons Ltd: 22 Wight's Lane, Kingston, Georgetown; tel. 226-0442; fax 226-4151; logs supplier.

Barama Co Ltd: Land of Canaan, East Bank, Demerara; tel. 225-4555; fax 225-8360; e-mail barama@samling.com; internet www.baramaguyana.com; f. 1991; subsidiary of Samling Global Ltd (Malaysia); forestry concession; CEO PETER HO; c. 1,000 employees.

Demerara Timbers Ltd (DTL): 1 Water St and Battery Rd, Kingston, Georgetown; tel. 225-3835; fax 227-1663; e-mail demtim@solutions.net; owned by Prime Group Holdings Ltd (British Virgin Islands); CEO LU KUI SAN.

Toolsie Persaud Ltd: 10–12 Lombard St, Georgetown; tel. 226-4071; fax 226-0793; e-mail tpl@tpl-gy.com; internet www.tpl-gy.com; f. 1949; logging and quarrying co and manufacturer of construction materials; Chair. TOOLSIE PERSAUD; Man. Dir DAVID PERSAUD; 2,000 employees.

Willems Timber and Trading Co Ltd: 7 Water St, Werk-en-Rust, POB 10443, Georgetown; tel. 227-2046; fax 226-5210; e-mail info@willemstimbertrading.com; internet willemstimber.com; production of timber and lumber; Dir JOHN WILLEMS.

Mining

Bauxite Company of Guyana Inc (BCGI): 274 Peter Rose St, Queenstown, Georgetown; tel. 225-0231; e-mail norma.pooran@rusal.ru; internet www.rusal.ru; f. 2004 as jt venture between Govt and Russian Aluminium Company (RUSAL); 90% owned by RUSAL subsidiary, the Bauxite and Alumina Mining Venture (BAMV); acquired assets of the state-owned Aroaima Mining Co on 31 March 2006; commenced devt of bauxite deposit at Kurubuku 22 in Aroaima area in 2007 following agreement with indigenous community and Hururu tribe regarding the territory; Gen. Man. ALEXEY GORDYMOV.

Guyana Oil Company (GUYOIL): 166 Waterloo St, POB 10710, Georgetown; tel. 225-3890; fax 227-1211; e-mail guyoilmd@networksgy.com; internet www.guyoil.com; state-owned; petroleum exploration and production; Man. Dir BADRIE PERSAUD; Marketing Man. ALWYN APPIAH.

Omai Bauxite Mining Inc: POB 32217, Linden; tel. (444) 6415; fax (444) 6103; f. 1992; fmrly state-owned Linden Mining Enterprises Ltd, name changed as above upon full privatization in 2004; mining of bauxite; Chair. C. P. PLUMMER; CEO H. JAMES; 300 employees.

Miscellaneous

A. H. & L. Kissoon Group of Companies: Lot 2, Strand, New Amsterdam, Berbice; tel. 333-2538; fax 333-4174; e-mail sales@kissoon-furniture.com; internet www.kissoon-furniture.com; construction of wooden furniture and housing, rice cultivation, cattle rearing; Man. Dir HEMRAJ KISSOON.

Alesie Guyana (Group Management): 79 Cowan St, Kingston, Georgetown; tel. 226-4601; fax 226-2038; e-mail infoguyana@alesierice.com; internet www.alesierice.com; exporters of rice; CEO TURHANE DOERGA; Gen. Man. HODIA PETERS.

Colgate-Palmolive (Guyana) Ltd: Ruimveldt, East Bank, Georgetown; tel. 226-2663; fax 225-6792; subsidiary of Colgate-Palmolive Co (USA); manufacturer of toothpaste and domestic cleaning products.

Courts Guyana Ltd: 25–26 Main St, POB 10481, Georgetown; tel. 225-5886; fax 227-8751; e-mail fcollins@courtsguyana.com; internet www.courtsguyana.com; f. 1993 as Geddes Grant (Home Furnishers) Ltd; fully owned subsidiary of Courts PLC, United Kingdom; Country Man. LESTER ALIVIS.

Demerara Tobacco Co Ltd: Eping Ave, Bel Air Park, POB 10262, Greater Georgetown; tel. 227-0106; fax 226-9322; f. 1975; subsidiary co of British American Tobacco PLC; importer of cigarettes; Chair. PATRICK SMITH; Man. Dir CHANDRADAT CHINTAMANI; 200 employees.

Denmor Garments (Manufacturers) Inc: 7–9 Coldingen Industrial Estate, East Bank, Demerara; tel. 270-4512; fax 270-4500; e-mail denmor@guyana.net.gy; clothing manufacturer; Man. Dir DENNIS MORGAN MUDLIER; 1,000 employees.

Gafsons Industries Ltd: Lot 1–2, Area X, Plantation Houston, Georgetown; tel. 226-3666; fax 227-8763; e-mail nil@guyana.net.gy; f. 1956; part of the Gafsons Group of Cos; manufacturer and wholesaler of PVC products and construction materials; Chair ABDOOL SATTAUR GAFOOR.

Guyana National Industrial Company (GNIC): 1–9 Lombard St, Charlestown, POB 10520, Georgetown, Demerara-Mahaica; tel. 226-3291; fax 225-8525; e-mail gnicadmin@futurenetgy.com; privatized in 1995; 70% owned by Laparkan Holdings Ltd and 30% owned by National Engineering Company; ship repairs, ship building, aluminium castings, wharf operations, machinery sales; CEO CLINTON WILLIAMS; Gen. Man. M. F. BASCOM; 1,150 employees.

Guyana Refrigerators Ltd: 15A Water and Holmes Sts, POB 10392, Georgetown; tel. 225-4934; fax 227-0302; manufacturer of refrigerators, freezers and ice buckets.

Laparkan Holdings Ltd: 2-9 Lombard St, Georgetown; tel. 226-1095; fax 227-6808; e-mail infoguyana@laparkan.com; internet www.laparkan.com; Chair. and CEO GLEN KHAN; Man. Dir AVINAISH BHAGWANDIN; Gen. Man. OSCAR PHILLIPS.

National Hardware (Guyana) Ltd: 17–19A Water St, South Cummingsburg, Georgetown; tel. 227-1961; fax 226-5280; e-mail natware@guyana.net.gy; internet www.nationalhardwareguyana.com; f. 1971; CEO EDWARD BOYER; Man. Dir MOHAMMED RAZACK.

New GPC Inc: Al Farm, East Bank, Demerara; tel. 265-4261; fax 265-2229; e-mail limacol@newgpc.com; internet www.newgpc.com; fmrly Guyana Pharmaceutical Corpn Ltd, privatized Dec. 1999; manufacturer of pharmaceuticals and cosmetics; Exec. Chair. Dr RANJISINGHI RAMROOP; Company Sec. D. AMANDA PIERRE.

Ram & MacRae: 157C Waterloo St, North Cummingsburg, POB 10148, Georgetown; tel. 226-1301; fax 225-4221; e-mail info@ramandmcrae.com; internet www.ramandmcrae.com; f. 1985; chartered accountants; Man. Partner CHRISTOPHER L. RAM.

G & C Sanata Company Inc: Industrial Site, Ruimveldt, Georgetown; tel. 231-7273-6; fax 227-8197; e-mail Sanata@networksgy.com; fabrics manufacturer; Man. Dir CHEN RONG.

Sol Guyana Inc: Lot BB Rome, POB 10132, Georgetown; tel. 225-8930; fax 227-2249; e-mail info@solpetroleum.com; internet www.solpetroleum.com; f. 1960; acquired Shell's petroleum distribution and marketing businesses in 2005; distributor of fuels, lubricants, bitumen and LPG; Chair. KYFFIN SIMPSON.

Torginol Paints Inc: 9–12 Industrial Site, Ruimveldt, East Bank, Demerara; tel. 226-4041; fax 225-3568; internet www.continentalgy.com/continentalpaints.htm; manufacturer of paints; owned by The Continental Group of Companies.

TSD Lall and Co: 77 Brickdam, Stabroek, POB 10506, Georgetown; tel. 226-3226; fax 225-7578; accountancy and management consultancy; ind. correspondent firm of Deloitte and Touche Tohmatsu (DTT); Sr Partner RAMESTIWAR LAL.

UTILITIES

Electricity

Guyana Power and Light Inc (GPL): 40 Main St, POB 10390, Georgetown; tel. 225-4618; fax 227-1978; e-mail enquiries@gplinc.com; internet www.gplinc.com; f. 1999; fmrly Guyana Electricity Corpn; state-owned; Chair. WINSTON BRASSINGTON; CEO BHARAT DINDYAL; 1,200 employees.

Water

Guyana Water Inc (GWI): Vllissengen Rd and Church St, Bel Air Park, Georgetown; tel. 225-0471; fax 225-0478; e-mail pro@gwi.gy;

internet www.gwiguyana.com; f. 2002 following merger of Guyana Water Authority (GUYWA) and Georgetown Sewerage and Water Comm.; operated by Severn Trent Water International (United Kingdom); Chair. Dr CYRIL SOLOMON; CEO YURI CHANDISINGH (acting).

CO-OPERATIVE SOCIETY

Chief Co-operatives Development Officer: Ministry of Labour, Human Services and Social Security, 1 Water and Cornhill Sts, Stabroek, Georgetown; tel. 225-8644; fax 227-1308; e-mail coopdept@telsnet.gy.net; f. 1948; Dir CLIVE NURSE.

TRADE UNIONS

Federation of Independent Trade Unions of Guyana (FITUG): f. 1988; c. 35,000 mems; Gen. Sec. KENNETH JOSEPH.

Clerical and Commercial Workers' Union (CCWU): Clerico House, 140 Quamina St, South Cummingsburg, POB 101045, Georgetown; tel. 225-2822; fax 227-2618; e-mail ccwu@guyana.net.gy; Pres. ROY HUGHES; Gen. Sec. GRANTLEY L. CULBARD.

Guyana Agricultural and General Workers' Union (GAWU): 59 High St and Wight's Lane, Kingston, Georgetown; tel. 227-2091; fax 227-2093; e-mail gawu@bbgy.com; internet www.gawu.net; f. 1977; Pres. KOMAL CHAND; Gen. Sec. SEEPAUL NARINE; 20,000 mems.

Guyana Labour Union (GLU): 198 Camp St, Cummingsburg, Georgetown; tel. 227-1196; fax 225-0820; e-mail glu@solutions2000.net; Pres. SAMUEL WALKER; Gen. Sec. CARVIL DUNCAN; 6,000 mems.

National Association of Agricultural, Commercial and Industrial Employees (NAACIE): 64 High St, Kingston, Georgetown; tel. 227-2301; f. 1946; Pres. KENNETH JOSEPH; Gen. Sec. KAISREE TAKECHANDRA; c. 2,000 mems.

Guyana Trades Union Congress (GTUC): Critchlow Labour College, Woolford Ave, Non-pareil Park, Georgetown; tel. 226-1493; fax 227-0254; e-mail gtucorg@yahoo.com; f. 1940; national trade union body; 13 affiliated unions; c. 15,000 mems; affiliated to the Internat. Trade Union Confederation; Pres. GILLIAN BURTON.

Amalgamated Transport and General Workers' Union: Transport House, 46 Urquhart St, Georgetown; tel. 226-6243; fax 225-6602; Pres. CLAIRMONT PEARSON; Gen. Sec. VICTOR JOHNSON.

Association of Masters and Mistresses: c/o Critchlow Labour College, Georgetown; tel. 226-8968; Pres. GANESH SINGH; Gen. Sec. T. ANSON SANCHO.

Guyana Bauxite and General Workers' Union: 180 Charlotte St, Georgetown; tel. 225-4654; Pres. CHARLES SAMPSON; Gen. Sec. LEROY ALLEN (acting).

Guyana Local Government Officers' Union: Woolford Ave, Georgetown; tel. 227-7209; fax 227-7376; e-mail daleantford@yahoo.com; f. 1954; Pres. ANDREW GARNETT; Gen. Sec. DALE BERESFORD.

Guyana Mining, Metal and General Workers' Union: 56 Wismar St, Linden, Demerara River; tel. 204-6822; Pres. ERIC TELLO; Gen. Sec. LESLIE GONSALVES; 5,800 mems.

Guyana Postal and Telecommunication Workers' Union: Postal House, 310 East St, POB 10352, Georgetown; tel. 226-7920; fax 225-1633; Pres. MORRIS WALCOTT; Gen. Sec. GILLIAN BURTON.

Guyana Teachers' Union: Woolford Ave, POB 738, Georgetown; tel. 226-3183; fax 227-0403; Pres. SYDNEY MURDOCK; Gen. Sec. SHIRLEY HOOPER.

National Mining and General Workers' Union: 10 Church St, New Amsterdam, Berbice; tel. 203-3496; Pres. CYRIL CONWAY; Gen. Sec. MARILYN GRIFFITH.

National Union of Public Service Employees: 4 Fort St, Kingston, Georgetown; tel. 227-1491; Pres. ROBERT JOHNSON; Gen. Sec. RUDOLPH WELCH.

Printing Industry and Allied Workers' Union: c/o Guyana TUC, Georgetown; tel. 226-8968; Gen. Sec. PATRICIA HODGE (acting).

Public Employees' Union: Regent St, Georgetown; Pres. REUBEN KHAN.

Union of Agricultural and Allied Workers (UAAW): 10 Hadfield St, Werk-en-Rust, Georgetown; tel. 226-7434; Pres. JEAN SMITH; Gen. Sec. SEELO BAICHAN.

University of Guyana Workers' Union: POB 841, Turkeyen, Georgetown; tel. 222-3586; e-mail adeolaplus@yahoo.com; supports Working People's Alliance; Pres. CLIVE Y. THOMAS; Gen. Sec. A. ESOOP.

Guyana Public Service Union (GPSU): 160 Regent and New Garden Sts, Georgetown; tel. 225-0518; fax 226-4811; e-mail gpsu@networksgy.com; internet www.tcionline.biz/gpsu; Pres. PATRICK YARDE; Gen. Sec. LAWRENCE MENTIS; 11,600 mems.

Transport

RAILWAY

There are no public railways in Guyana. Until the early 21st century the 15-km Linmine Railway was used for the transportation of bauxite from Linden to Coomaka.

ROADS

The coastal strip has a well-developed road system. In 1999 there were an estimated 7,970 km (4,952 miles) of paved and good-weather roads and trails. In September 2001 a European Union-funded road improvement programme between Crabwood Creek and the Guyana–Suriname Ferry Terminal was completed; the project was intended to help integrate the region. In 2009 a bridge across the Takutu river, linking Guyana to Brazil, was officially inaugurated. The US $40m. rehabilitation of the Mahaica–Rosignol road, partly funded by the Inter-American Development Bank (IDB), began in 2003. In the same year work began on a complementary project to remove and relocate both the Mahaica and Mahaicony bridges. Construction of a bridge over the Berbice river began in late 2006 and was completed in 2008. The IDB approved a 40-year loan of $24.3m. towards highway infrastructure rehabilitation under the supervision of the Ministry of Public Works and Communications in November 2006. In the 2008 budget some $30.5m. was allocated for the construction and maintenance of roads and bridges.

SHIPPING

Guyana's principal ports are at Georgetown and New Amsterdam. The port at Linden serves for the transportation of bauxite products. A ferry service is operated between Guyana and Suriname. Communications with the interior are chiefly by river, although access is hindered by rapids and falls. There are 1,077 km (607 miles) of navigable rivers. The main rivers are the Mazaruni, the Potaro, the Essequibo, the Demerara and the Berbice. In 2000 the Brazilian Government announced that it was to finance the construction of both a deep-water port and a river bridge.

Transport and Harbours Department: Battery Rd, Kingston, Georgetown; tel. 225-9350; fax 227-8545; e-mail t&hd@solutions2000.net; Gen. Man. KEVIN TRIM; Deputy Gen. Man. DAVID JOHN.

Shipping Association of Guyana Inc (SAG): 10–11 Lombard St, Werk-en-Rust, Georgetown; tel. 226-2169; fax 226-9656; e-mail saginc@networksgy.com; internet www.shipping.org.gy; f. 1952; non-governmental forum; Chair. ANDREW ASTWOOD; Vice-Chair. BERNIE FERNANDES; members:

Guyana National Industrial Company Inc (GNIC): 1–9 Lombard St, Charlestown, POB 10520, Georgetown; tel. 225-5398; fax 226-0432; e-mail gnicadmin@futurenetgy.com; metal foundry, ship building and repair, agents for a number of international transport cos; privatized 1995; CEO CLINTON WILLIAMS; Port Man. ALBERT SMITH.

Guyana National Shipping Corporation Ltd: 5–9 Lombard St, La Penitence, POB 10988, Georgetown; tel. 226-1840; fax 225-3815; e-mail gnsc@guyana.net.gy; internet www.gnsc.com; govt-owned; Man. Dir ANDREW ASTWOOD (acting).

John Fernandes Ltd: 24 Water St, POB 10211, Georgetown; tel. 227-3344; fax 226-1881; e-mail philip@jf-ltd.com; internet www.jf-ltd.com; ship agents, pier operators and stevedore contractors; part of the John Fernandes Group of Cos; Chair. and CEO CHRIS FERNANDES.

CIVIL AVIATION

The main airport, Cheddi Jaggan International Airport, is at Timehri, 42 km (26 miles) from Georgetown.

Roraima Airways: R8 Epring Ave, Bel Air Park, Georgetown; tel. 225-9648; fax 225-9646; e-mail ral@roraimaairways.com; internet www.roraimaairways.com; f. 1992; flights to Venezuela and 4 domestic destinations; Man. Dir Capt. GERALD GOUVEIA.

Trans Guyana Airways: Ogle Aerodrome, Ogle, East Coast Demerara; tel. 222-2525; e-mail commercial@transguyana.com; internet www.transguyana.com; f. 1956; internal flights to 22 destinations; Dir Capt. GERARD GONSALVES.

Tourism

Despite the beautiful scenery in the interior of the country, Guyana has limited tourist facilities, and began encouraging tourism only in the late 1980s. During the 1990s Guyana began to develop its considerable potential as an 'eco-tourism' destination. However, tourist arrivals declined towards the end of the decade. The total number of visitors to Guyana in 2007 was 131,487, of whom 52.4% were from the USA. In that year expenditure by tourists amounted to some US $50m.

Guyana Tourism Authority: National Exhibition Centre, Sophia, Georgetown; tel. 219-0094; fax 219-0093; e-mail info@guyana-tourism.com; internet www.guyana-tourism.com; f. 2003; Chair. BRIAN JAMES.

Tourism and Hospitality Association of Guyana (THAG): 157 Waterloo St, Georgetown; tel. 225-0807; fax 225-0817; e-mail thag@networksgy.com; internet www.exploreguyana.com; f. 1992; Pres. CATHY HUGHES; Exec. Dir MAUREEN PAUL.

Defence

The armed forces are united in a single service, the Combined Guyana Defence Force, which consisted of some 1,100 men (of whom 900 were in the army, 100 in the air force and about 100 in the navy), as assessed at November 2009. In addition there were reserve forces numbering some 670 (army 500, navy 170). The Guyana People's Militia, a paramilitary reserve force, totalled about 1,500. The President is Commander-in-Chief.

Defence Budget: An estimated $ G1,370m. (US $67m.) in 2008.

Chief-of-Staff: Cdre GARY BEST.

Education

Education is free and compulsory for children aged between five years at the beginning of the school year and 15 years of age. Children receive primary education for a period of six years; enrolment at primary schools in 2008 included 95% of children in the relevant age-group. Secondary education, beginning at 12 years of age, lasts for up to seven years in a general secondary school, comprising an initial cycle of five years, followed by a cycle of two years. Higher education is provided by five technical and vocational schools, one teacher-training college, and one school for home economics and domestic crafts. An estimated $ G15,500m. was allocated to the Ministry of Education from the central Government's current expenditure in 2008, equivalent to 13.4% of the total budget.

Bibliography

Bartilow, H. A. *The Debt Dilemma: IMF Negotiations in Jamaica, Grenada and Guyana*. Warwick, Warwick University Caribbean Studies, 1997.

Colchester, M. *Guyana: Fragile Frontier*. Kingston, Ian Randle Publrs, 1997.

Cruickshank, J. G. *Scenes from the History of the Africans in Guyana*. Georgetown, Guyana Free Press, 1999.

Egoume-Bossogo, P., Faal, E., Nallari, R., and Weisman, E. *Guyana: Experience With Macroeconomic Stabilization, Structural Adjustment, and Poverty Reduction*. Ottowa, ON, Renouf Publishing Co Ltd, 2003.

Gafar, J. *Guyana: From State Control to Free Markets*. Hauppauge, NY, Nova Science Publrs Inc, 2003.

Graham Burnett, D. *Masters of All They Surveyed: Exploration, Geography and a British El Dorado*. Chicago, IL, University of Chicago Press, 2001.

Granger, D. G. (Ed.). *Emancipation*. Georgetown, Guyana Free Press, 1999.

Guyana's Military Veterans: Promises, Problems and Prospects. Georgetown, Guyana Free Press, 1999.

Guyana General and Regional Elections, 19 March 2001: the Report of the Commonwealth Observer Group. London, Commonwealth Secretariat Group, 2001.

Hinds, D. *Race and Political Discourse in Guyana*. Georgetown, Guyana-Caribbean Politics Publications, 2004.

Hintzen, P. C., and Campbell, E. Q. (Eds). *Costs of Regime Survival: Racial Mobilization, Elite Domination and Control of the State in Guyana and Trinidad*. Cambridge, Cambridge University Press, 2007.

Hoyte, H. D. *Guyana's Economic Recovery: Leadership, Will-power and Vision. Selected Speeches of Hugh Desmond Hoyte*. Georgetown, Guyana Free Press, 1997.

Irving, B. *Guyana: a Composite Monograph*. Hato Rey, Puerto Rico, Inter American University Press, 1972.

Joseph, C. L. *Anglo-American Diplomacy and the Re-Opening of the Guyana—Venezuela Boundary Controversy, 1961–66*. Georgetown, Guyana Free Press, 1998.

McGowan, W. F., et al (Eds). *Themes in African—Guyanese History*. Georgetown, Guyana Free Press, 1998.

The Demerara Revolt, 1823. Georgetown, Guyana Free Press, 1998.

Mars, J. R. *Deadly Force, Colonialism and the Rule of Law*. Westport, CT, Greenwood Press, 2002.

Mars, P., and Young, A. L. *Caribbean Labor and Politics: Legacies of Cheddi Jagan and Michael Manley*. Detroit, MI, Wayne State University Press, 2004.

Mitchell, W. B., Bibbiana, W. A., DuPre, C. E., et al. *Area Handbook for Guyana*. Washington, DC, US Government Printing Office, 1969.

Mohamed, I. A. *Guyana's Approach: From Singapore to Seattle: World Trade Negotiations: Pushing for a Development Round of Negotiations through Process of Review, Repair and Reform of the World Trade Organization*. Georgetown, Ministry of Foreign Affairs, 2000.

Morrison, A. *Justice: The Struggle for Democracy in Guyana 1952–1992*. Georgetown, Red Thread Women's Press, 1998.

Munslow, B. *Guyana: Microcosm of Sustainable Development Challenges*. Aldershot, Hampshire, Ashgate Publishing Ltd, 1998.

Peake, L., and Peake, A. *Gender, Ethnicity and Poverty in Guyana*. London, Routledge, 1999.

Rabe, S. G. *U.S. Intervention in British Guiana: A Cold War Story (The New Cold War History)*. Chapel Hill, NC, University of North Carolina Press, 2005.

Ramcharan, B. G. *The Guyana Court of Appeal: the Challenges of the Rule in a Developing Country*. London, Cavendish Publishing Ltd, 2002.

Seecomar, J. *Contributions Towards the Resolution of Conflict in Guyana*. Leeds, Peepal Tree Press, 2002.

Democratic Advance and Conflict Resolution in Post-Colonial Guyana. Leeds, Peepal Tree Press, 2005.

Seetahal, D. S. *Commonwealth Caribbean Criminal Practice and Procedure: Second edition*. London, Routledge-Cavendish, 2006.

Singh, J. N. *Guyana: Democracy Betrayed*. Kingston, Jamaica, Kingston Publrs, 1996.

HAITI

Geography

PHYSICAL FEATURES

The Republic of Haiti lies at the western end of the island of Hispaniola, which it shares with the larger Dominican Republic (beyond a 360-km or 224-mile eastern border, partly along the Pedernales river in the south and the Massacre in the north). The land border was first set by treaty between France and Spain at Ryswick (Rijswijk, Netherlands) in 1697, and most recently revised in 1936. Cuba lies 80 km beyond the Windward Passage in the north-west and Jamaica twice that distance to the west of the south-western peninsula. The country includes a number of offshore islands, but also claims Navassa Island. This is a scrubby, uninhabited, 5-sq km (2-sq mile), coral and limestone rock, some 65 km west of Haiti and 160 km south of the USA's Guantánamo Bay naval base in southern Cuba. Navassa is currently administered as an unincorporated territory and wildlife reserve by the USA. To the north, Haiti is less than 100 km from the southernmost Bahamas and about 140 km from the Turks and Caicos Islands, a British dependency. Haiti includes only 190 sq km of inland waters, but has 1,771 km of coastline. At 27,750 sq km (10,714 sq miles), the country is the same size as the US state of Massachusetts and somewhat smaller than Belgium.

Mainland Haiti has a long, westward-extending peninsula in the south of the country, while the centre and the north broaden north-westwards to form the other arm of the Gulf of Gonâve. At the head of the Gulf, in the south-east, lies the capital, Port-au-Prince. The Gulf embraces the barren island of Gonâve, at some 60 km in length and 15 km in width, the largest of Haiti's offshore territories. The next largest is the Ile de la Tortue, or Tortuga, 40 km in length and 12 km off Port-de-Paix on the north coast (it was the main Caribbean pirate centre in the 17th century, then the base for the French acquisition of western Hispaniola). Stretching east of here run the northern coastal plains (about 150 km in length, 30 km wide and covering some 2,000 sq km), the main area of flat land in the country, apart from the drier Cul-de-Sac in the south, which extends eastwards from Port-au-Prince to brackish Lake Saumâtre (20 km long and 6 km–14 km wide) in the south-east. The fertile, well-watered northern plains had attracted the original colonial plantations and, earlier, piratical outcasts and renegades, who hunted the wild cattle roaming the plains, cooking over wood fires known as *boucans*—hence the word buccaneer. The other main areas of flat land in Haiti are in the valley of the Artibonite and on the south coast, the densely populated Léogâne plains. However, it is the highlands that are more typical of the country. Most of Haiti is mountainous and, in fact, it is considered the most mountainous country in the Caribbean. The Massif du Nord lies behind the coastal plains of the north, running north-westwards into the dry and drought-afflicted peninsula and, in the other direction, over the border of the Dominican Republic as the Cordillera Central. The highest point in the country, however, is Morne de la Selle (2,680 m or 8,796 ft), which rises from the south-eastern massif—the mountains then continue westwards, along the peninsula, where, towards the end, is the Massif de la Hotte. The centre of Haiti is dominated by the elevated eastern central plateau and a number of other ranges, extensions of the Massif du Nord or the Dominican Sierra de Neibe. Cleaving through the central highlands is the valley of the Artibonite (some 800 sq km of plains land), the main river of Haiti and the trunk of the largest drainage system. The river, 400 km in length, enters the country from the Dominican Republic (it also forms part of the border), but it arose in Haiti as the Libón. Although deep and strong, and prone to flooding in the wet seasons, at drier times of the year the river can shrink dramatically and even cease to flow in some places. The most important tributary of the Artibonite is the 95-km Guayamouc. The main river of the north, at 150 km in length, is the oddly named Trois Rivières. Flooding of the often swift-

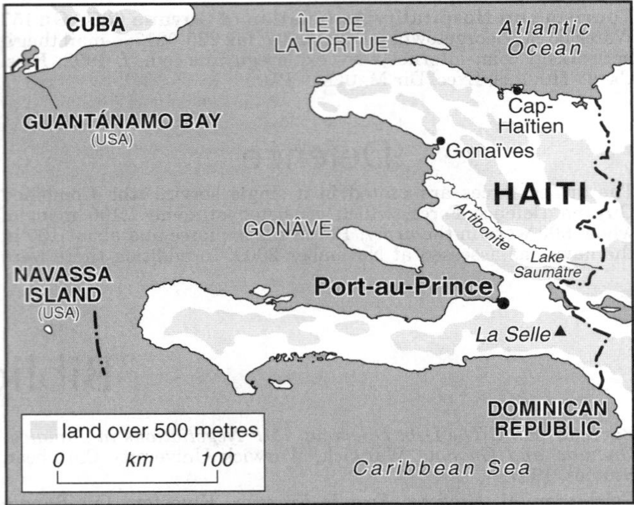

flowing rivers in steep terrain is made worse by the extensive soil erosion caused by deforestation. The widespread poverty in the country has contributed to the wiping out of Haiti's once-extensive tree cover. There are only really two places where woodland survives, both high and inaccessible (one on the Massif de la Selle, the other around the Pic de Macaya, at the end of the south-western peninsula). These places shelter some remnant riches of Haiti's devastated environment, which has been denuded of forest and rendered prone to soil erosion and drought.

CLIMATE

The climate is subtropical, but parts of Haiti are semi-arid, owing to the eastern mountains shadowing the rain brought by the Atlantic trade winds. The northern plains, the mountains of the north-east and the highlands of the south-western peninsula receive the most rain. The driest and most barren areas are the coastal strip east of Port-au-Prince and the north-western peninsula. The recurring problem of drought does not preclude severe storms during the June–October hurricane season, which can bring flooding, and the country also suffers from occasional earthquakes. There are two rainy seasons, April–May and September–October, with average annual rainfall, unevenly distributed, ranging between 1,400 mm (55 ins) and 2,000 mm (79 ins). It is humid on the coast, but the heat is made bearable by morning and evening breezes. Temperatures on the coast vary between about 20°C (68°F) and 35°C (95°F), being slightly hotter in April–September and cooler in the hills at any time of year.

POPULATION

The majority of Haitians are black (95%), the inheritors of the world's only successful slave revolt, which drove out or killed most of its white, planter aristocracy in the early 19th century (the French colony was known as Saint-Domingue). However, there is still a white and mulatto minority, most of whom remain disproportionately wealthy and powerful. Although race and colour have remained important prejudices bedevilling Haitian society, it is language that has had the widest effect. The élite continued to use French after the revolution, and to disparage the lower classes' constant use of Creole (*créole* or *kreyòl*), perpetuating the old colonial tongue as the speech of formal use and as the official language into the present. However, only about 15% of the population speak

French and, although they usually also speak Creole, only about 5% can speak both fluently, crippling a society that has long permitted education and advancement only on the basis of French. Only since the 1990s has Creole begun to make official advances, the culmination of a movement to dignify the native culture that only began in the 1920s. Creole, now also an official language, is a tongue that shares many words with French, but has a very different (West African) grammatical structure, its origins either in a pidgin used between slaves of various African nationalities and their French masters or in a French maritime-trade dialect. Another influence imported from West Africa into Haitian culture is in the field of religion, with Voodoo (vodou), as it is labelled, practised by over one-half of the population. This does not preclude continued adherence to the official religion, Roman Catholic Christianity, as Voodoo adapted the African veneration of family and ancestral spirits with local conditions under the French. The Roman Catholic Church is the main official religious affiliation, and still claims the loyalty of 65% of the population. However, its identity with the ruling establishment helped the growth of Protestant churches, which are now adhered to by 16% (mainly Baptists—10%, and Pentecostalists—4%). The Protestants, in contrast to the uneasy, de facto accommodation by the Roman Catholic Church, tend to be fierce in their rejection of Voodoo.

The population of Haiti totalled approximately 9.9m., according to official projections in mid-2009. It was estimated that as many as 230,000 people were killed as a result of a powerful earthquake that devastated the country's capital, Port-au-Prince, in January 2010. Moreover, about four-fifths of the population live in considerable poverty and Haiti is described as the poorest country in the Western hemisphere (and one of the poorest in the world) under many definitions. Port-au-Prince, the capital, had a projected population of 897,859 in mid-2009. The second city of Haiti, and the largest port, is Cap-Haïtien (as Cap-Français, it was the colonial capital—now usually referred to as Cap or, in Creole, Okap), on the central northern coast. The third city, Gonaïves (known as the 'city of independence'), is also on the Gulf, but in the north-eastern corner. The fourth city is Les Cayes (Okay), on the south coast, towards the end of the south-western peninsula. Haiti is administered as 10 departments.

History

CHARLES ARTHUR

The independent Republic of Haiti was born out of a 12-year revolutionary struggle for freedom from slavery, and against the colonial ambitions of France, Spain and the United Kingdom. The final victory for the revolutionaries came in late 1803 when the united black and mulatto forces defeated the French army, and the new republic was declared on 1 January 1804. Although the 1791–1804 revolution brought an end to slavery and made both blacks and mulattoes free and theoretically equal, racial, social and economic divisions deriving from the colonial regime exerted strong influences on the shaping of post-independence society. The black former slaves, who composed the vast majority of the population, refused to return to work as labourers on the plantations and instead occupied idle or abandoned land or carved new plots out of marginal land on the hillsides. As a result, a minority élite—both mulatto landowners and black officers from the revolutionary armies—was obliged to look for new ways to perpetuate their wealth. They turned away from investment in agricultural production, and instead focused on the distribution and export of the produce grown by peasant farmers and the control of state revenue, in particular the levying of taxes. Within a few decades the new nation of Haiti emerged, deeply divided between a rural population of smallholding peasants and an economic and political élite located in a few coastal towns. The mostly black and poor peasants (and later shanty-town dwellers) communicated in the Creole language, maintained certain African traditions and developed the rituals and ceremonies to serve the spirits of Voodoo (vodou). Meanwhile, a mainly mulatto, urban-based, élite minority wrote and spoke French, saw itself as European, and professed spiritual allegiance to the Roman Catholic Church.

Throughout the 19th century competing élite factions manoeuvred to secure the power of government, giving rise to countless insurrections and coups. A US occupation from 1915–34 failed to alter the fundamental structure of Haitian society but did establish a basic infrastructure and, more significantly, a standing army. Formal politics continued to be marked by the almost complete exclusion of the majority population. In 1957 Dr François ('Papa Doc') Duvalier proposed an alliance between the emerging black middle class and the poor black majority and subsequently won election as President. He swiftly countered the power of the army by creating his own militia force, popularly known as the Tontons Macoutes. Employing indiscriminate violence against all opposition, whether real, potential or imagined, Duvalier established a brutal dictatorship. All major institutions in civil society, including political parties, workers' unions, peasant co-operatives and student associations, were abolished and as many as 30,000 of his opponents were killed. Tens of thousands of educated Haitians chose to go into exile to North America, Europe and Africa. Despite the brutality of his regime, Duvalier had the support of successive US Administrations, which perceived him as a valuable ally in its attempt to isolate the communist revolution in neighbouring Cuba.

Following Duvalier's death in 1971, his son, Jean-Claude, continued the dictatorship. Although some members of the black middle and lower-middle classes prospered through their association with the dictators' power structure, the majority of the population suffered from the exploitation and corruption on which the regime was based. In the mid-1980s, encouraged by the emerging liberation theology branch of the Roman Catholic Church, the increasingly poverty-stricken population began to organize in opposition to the dictatorship. Fearing a descent into revolution, the USA and the Haitian military decided to withdraw their support and, consequently, on 7 February 1986 Jean-Claude Duvalier and his family went into exile in France.

Successive military governments countered an emerging movement for democracy and social change with repression. Elections in November 1987 were abandoned when soldiers and resurgent Tontons Macoutes gunned down voters at polling stations. Free elections, monitored by the UN, were finally held in December 1990, and were won convincingly by the radical Roman Catholic priest Jean-Bertrand Aristide. His campaign, which he called 'Lavalas'—Creole for an avalanche or flood—promised to cleanse Haiti of the Duvalierist legacy, bringing justice, governmental accountability and the opportunity for the populace to participate in determining the nation's future.

President Aristide's programme challenged vested interests, and after less than eight months in office his Government was overthrown by a military coup. Aristide was forced into exile and a military regime embarked on a campaign of repression targeting the country's pro-Lavalas grassroots organizations. For three years summary executions, arbitrary searches and arrests, disappearances, beatings, torture and extortion were systematic and commonplace. An estimated 5,000 people were killed, some 400,000 were internally displaced and tens of thousands attempted to escape the country by boat. From late 1993, much of the repression was carried out by the army-sponsored paramilitary group Front Révolutionnaire pour l'Avancement et le Progrès d'Haïti (FRAPH).

The UN imposed economic sanctions in an attempt to unseat the military regime, but senior military officers and their élite supporters refused to yield and even prospered through the control of a thriving contraband trade. The majority of the population was acutely affected by the economic crisis that resulted from the UN sanctions; nevertheless, support for the exiled Aristide remained high. Continuing political instability and concerns about the continuing refugee exodus finally resulted in decisive action in September 1994 when 20,000 US troops, acting with UN authorization, were dispatched to Haiti. The invasion was unopposed and within four weeks the three principal military leaders went into exile, allowing Aristide to return to serve out the remaining 16 months of his presidency. One of his most significant acts in that short time was to disband the much-detested army.

At the end of March 1995 the US occupation force was succeeded by a UN peace-keeping mission. Later that year parliamentary and local government elections were held, and the result was an overwhelming victory for a three-party coalition dominated by the Organisation Politique Lavalas (OPL). At the presidential election in December, Aristide's ally and former Prime Minister, René Garcia Préval, stood as the pro-Lavalas candidate (Aristide was constitutionally barred from serving a second consecutive term in office) and won convincingly.

The new OPL-led Government began to implement the programme of neo-liberal reforms demanded by international financial institutions, prompting significant civil unrest. In late 1996 political tensions were exacerbated by Aristide's creation of a new party, La Fanmi Lavalas (FL), and his criticism of the Government's structural adjustment programme. The OPL and other political parties grew increasingly concerned at what was perceived as the negative behind-the-scenes influence of former President Aristide. Party leaders accused Aristide of undermining Préval's authority and of attempting to establish control over the newly created police force.

After many delays, elections for a new legislature, urban mayors and local administrative councils were eventually held in May 2000. Contrary to expectations, the turnout was high: over 60% of registered voters participated in the election. According to official results, Aristide's FL won a landslide victory. Although the elections were largely peaceful and well-organized, the unsuccessful parties claimed the results were fraudulent. These claims were bolstered by charges made by international election monitors that the national electoral council had used an incorrect method of calculating the senate vote percentages, thereby giving outright victories to as many as eight FL Senators who should have faced a second round run-off. Despite threats by the USA and the European Union that future development aid would be withheld if the results were not recalculated, the Préval Government—under pressure from Aristide and his supporters—refused to back down. The main opposition parties denounced what they termed a totally flawed election process and joined together to form the Convergence Démocratique (CD) coalition. As well as political parties, the CD included right-wing pro-army and evangelical Christian groupings. In August 2000, amid continuing protests from the CD and the international community, a new legislature, dominated by the FL, was inaugurated.

In November 2000 a further round of elections for a new President and another third of the Sénat (Senate) went ahead, despite the opposition parties' refusal to participate and in the absence of international observers. The opposition claimed that its appeal for a boycott was heeded—a charge that was denied by the electoral authorities. According to official results Aristide won the presidency with 92% of the votes, and in the Sénat his FL party now held 26 of the 27 seats in addition to all but 10 of the 83 seats in the Chambre des Députés (Chamber of Deputies). The CD refused to recognize the legitimacy of the legislature or of Aristide's presidency. When bilateral and multilateral donors suspended their assistance to the central Government, until such time as the dispute was resolved, the CD took an even more intransigent position, believing that a continuation of the deadlock would weaken the Government. This strategy had some success, as the lack of foreign aid increasingly hindered the Government's ability to implement planned social programmes.

With the political impasse continuing, tensions increased when former soldiers mounted sporadic attacks on police stations in remote border areas and even briefly occupied the presidential palace in December 2001. The Government responded by using the police to harass opposition leaders and mobilizing its supporters among the urban youth to repress meetings of opposition parties, credit union members' organizations, women's groups, trade unions and university students. The Government attempted to secure the resumption of foreign aid by implementing the economic reform programme long demanded by international financial institutions. Beginning with the removal of the fuel subsidy—a move that sent living costs spiralling in the first months of 2003—the Government implemented a harsh austerity programme in agreement with the IMF. The programme included measures to reduce the public sector deficit by decreasing expenditure on education and the public sector. The combination of heavy-handed repression with neo-liberal austerity rapidly alienated the small, urban middle class.

During 2003 armed opposition forces grew in strength, and towards the end of the year one group of former soldiers allied itself with disaffected government supporters in the central city of Gonaïves. At the same time, a new anti-Government force emerged on the political scene. The Group of 184 opposition coalition, comprising private sector associations, student groups and non-governmental organizations, took a leading role in galvanizing opposition protests within Haiti and helping to discredit the FL Government abroad. In December 2003, following a violent attack by government supporters on students and staff at the state university in the capital, the Group of 184 organized a series of street demonstrations demanding the Government's resignation.

Although the Government maintained strong support among the inhabitants of the shanty towns in and around Port-au-Prince, it found itself increasingly isolated nationally and internationally. In February 2004 a small armed force headed by former FRAPH leaders and former army officers succeeded in driving the police out of a series of towns in the north and centre of the country. Aristide rejected all suggestions that he resign before the end of his mandate in February 2006; however, in the last days of February 2004 the USA and France withdrew their lingering support for the FL Government, ending hopes of a mediated settlement to the crisis. The armed opposition announced plans to attack Port-au-Prince and a number of high-level government leaders fled into exile. In the early hours of 29 February 2004 Aristide and his family left Haiti on a US Air Force plane in disputed circumstances. The President and his supporters accused the USA of forcing him into exile, while the US authorities maintained that Aristide left Haiti voluntarily.

The UN authorized US and French troops to take control of strategic points in the capital and deter any attempted take-over by the armed insurgents. However, former soldiers assumed power in most urban centres in the rest of the country, while police officers fled and FL officials went into hiding. With the collapse of the Government, Gérard Latortue, a career diplomat, was asked to assume the office of Prime Minister, and he selected a Cabinet composed of technocrats and leading figures from the anti-FL movement. Latortue's Government, tasked with running the country on an interim basis pending new elections, courted the support of the armed insurgents and the private sector. It ordered the police to arrest a large number of leading FL members, and incorporated several hundred former soldiers into the police force—moves that quickly alienated the still significant sector of the population that remained loyal to the ousted Aristide. In June 2004 the UN deployed a peace-keeping force, the UN Stabilization Mission in Haiti (MINUSTAH), predominantly composed of troops from Brazil and other South American countries. The mission initially restricted its operations to patrols in Port-au-Prince, while in many other parts of the country former insurgents and former soldiers assumed responsibility for law and order. Supporters of the ousted Government claimed they were victims of a wave of repression. The interim Government made no effort to achieve reconciliation after the upheavals of previous months and consistently sought to portray the inhabitants of urban slums as criminals and gangsters. At the beginning of October

2004 tense relations between the new Government and FL supporters in the capital erupted into violent conflicts. Hundreds of people were killed as units of the national police force clashed with armed FL supporters in densely populated slum areas. Police and former soldiers were accused of carrying out extra-judicial executions and random killings, while armed FL supporters were accused of a campaign of murder and violent crime intended to destabilize the interim Government. MINUSTAH was severely criticized by foreign human rights organizations for failing to protect the civilian population.

During 2005 MINUSTAH began to take a more proactive stance against the former soldiers and succeeded in wresting control of the provincial towns from them, but in Port-au-Prince it struggled to restore order. The proliferation of arms in preceding years, combined with acute political tensions and crushing poverty, had given rise to an ever-increasing rate of violent crime. Armed gangs, some linked to the ousted Government, others that allegedly received financial support from members of the country's élite, vied for control of the shanty towns. Gun battles between gangs, and between the gangs and the police and MINUSTAH forces, claimed hundreds of lives.

After many delays caused by concerns over security and poor organization of voter registration, a general election was finally held on 7 February 2006. The FL was split over whether to participate in the elections: one faction supported a boycott while another fielded candidates for legislative seats and backed the presidential bid of established politician Marc Bazin. The FL position was further complicated by Aristide's endorsement of the presidential candidacy of Catholic priest Gérard Jean-Juste, who had been detained in prison as a result of dubious allegations of involvement in acts of violence. The party was left in disarray when Jean-Juste was prevented from registering his candidacy from prison. Much FL support was subsequently transferred to former President René Préval, who was standing as the candidate for the newly formed party, Fwon Lespwa (Front de l'Espoir). Préval won by far the largest share of votes in the presidential race, attracting support not just from FL supporters but from a range of social sectors, including some of the more progressive members of the private sector.

Initial results showed Préval narrowly lacked the 50%-plus-one-vote majority required for a first round victory. Amid protests about fraud and manipulation of the vote count, and growing concerns that they might escalate into violence if a second round were deemed necessary, the interim Government and electoral officials agreed to distribute the blank ballots among the candidates in proportion to the number of valid votes that each obtained. This expedient measure resulted in Préval's total being revised to 51.2%. In the legislative elections, Lespwa won the largest number of seats in both the upper and lower houses, but failed to garner a majority in either. In May 2006 Préval nominated the Lespwa leader, Jacques-Edouard Alexis, as Prime Minister, and he in turn named a consensus Cabinet with ministers representing six different parties, including the FL.

Préval and Alexis stressed the need for political dialogue and reconciliation, and reached out to the core FL supporters by ordering the release from prison of FL members who had been detained without trial. The new Government moved to address the serious problem of violence and crime in the capital by negotiating with a number of gang leaders, who indicated they would lay down their weapons if social welfare projects to improve the lives of slum residents were implemented. At the same time, Alexis announced that his Government would spend US $1,200m. over five years to strengthen the police force, increasing it in size from 5,000 to 12,000 officers.

In the first few months after Préval's election victory there was a marked improvement in the security situation, raising hopes of a much-needed period of stability. However, by mid-2006 incidents of gang violence in the capital increased again, reaching a peak in November and December when armed men carried out increasingly brazen crimes, including kidnapping and murder. In December the situation had deteriorated to such an extent that the Government requested that MINUSTAH take a more aggressive approach. In a series of raids into the vast slum area of Cité Soleil, MINUSTAH forces targeted the strongholds of the most powerful gang leaders, and succeeded in arresting some and forcing others to flee. MINUSTAH and the national police force subsequently arrested gang leaders in other slum areas of the capital, and the immediate impact was a sharp decrease in crime during the early months of 2007.

Towards the end of 2007 the number of kidnappings for ransom in Port-au-Prince surged again, and there was criticism of MINUSTAH's inability to combat organized crime. There was growing criticism too of the Government's failure to rebuild the economy, despite high levels of international assistance, and Alexis became the focus of accusations of government inefficiency and corruption. In early 2008 sharp increases in the cost of fuel and food caused public disenchantment with the Government to grow rapidly. In early April street protests against the rising cost of living broke out in the southern city of Les Cayes. Within days the protests spread to other towns, and to Port-au-Prince, where thousands of protestors took to the streets, erecting roadblocks, ransacking several businesses and banks, and attempting to tear down the gates of the presidential palace. Several days of rioting ended when police and MINUSTAH troops intervened. The sudden outburst of protest by poorer sections of society, and the violence that accompanied some of the demonstrations, shocked Haitian politicians and foreign diplomats alike. The fragile stability that had been growing steadily since Préval took office was reversed in the course of just a few days. On 12 April the Sénat approved a motion of no confidence in Alexis on the grounds that he had failed to meet the basic demands of the population.

The repercussions of the April 2008 food riots continued when Préval's first two nominees to assume the post of Prime Minister and form a new government were both rejected by the Chambre des Députés. Finally, in August, both the lower house and the Sénat accepted Préval's third nominee for the post, Michèle Duvivier Pierre-Louis, an economist and the director of a charitable foundation. A new Government was formed in early September. However, just as one crisis was resolved, another much more serious one developed. In August and early September a series of powerful hurricanes inflicted widespread damage and flooding across the country. Gonaïves, the fourth largest city in the country, was completely flooded, and, when the flood waters receded in late September, the city was covered in several feet of mud. More than 800 people were killed during the storms, most of them residents of Gonaïves. Emergency relief agencies estimated that nation-wide around 800,000 people had been left homeless and/or unable to feed themselves. There was also extensive damage to the country's rudimentary infrastructure and communications networks, and to thousands of buildings, including hospitals and schools.

For its first four months in office the new Pierre-Louis Government was obliged to focus on trying to provide relief and co-ordinating repairs and reconstruction in the wake of the weather catastrophe. Meanwhile, although the security situation improved, the Government, international agencies and diplomats of countries involved in Haiti warned that the country's hard-won stability remained in jeopardy because of its precarious socio-economic situation. In response to these warnings, key players in the international community provided strong shows of support for the Government, including pledges of significant amounts of development assistance.

Growing public disenchantment with the political process was reflected in the much-delayed election for 11 Sénat seats held in April 2009. The electorate has traditionally shown little enthusiasm for mid-term, partial elections, but participation in this poll was further diminished by the disqualification of all 16 FL candidates by the Conseil Electoral Provisoire (CEP—Provisional Electoral Council), on the grounds that the party's national representative, Aristide, still in exile in South Africa, had not sanctioned any of them. The decision was widely viewed as a political manoeuvre to remove the FL from the contest, and the party appealed to the electorate to boycott the ballot. Official figures recorded a voter participation rate of just 12%, but even this was probably an exaggeration. Following a second round run-off election in June, in which an even smaller proportion of the electorate participated, Lespwa emerged victorious in five of the 11 contested seats.

In October 2009 a rare period of political stability was brought to an abrupt end when the Sénat approved a vote of no confidence in Prime Minister Pierre-Louis, ostensibly because she had failed to account for the Government's use of US $197m. allocated to hurricane relief and repair projects. Some senators had further accused her administration of failing to combat poverty and revive the economy. Despite these claims, it seemed more probable that the removal of Pierre-Louis was a Lespwa strategy, reflecting an ongoing political realignment ahead of presidential and legislative elections scheduled to be held in 2010. This argument was strengthened when Préval promptly nominated Minister of Planning and External Co-operation Jean-Max Bellerive, an architect of the poverty reduction strategy that underpinned the Government's economic policies, as Prime Minister.

In late 2009 Lespwa was disbanded by its leaders, including Préval, and a new party, Inite (Creole for 'unity'), also known as Unité, was created in its stead. As well as including many of the leading figures from Lespwa, the new party also co-opted a number of prominent members of other parties, including dissidents from the FL. In November the CEP announced that a number of political parties would be excluded from participation in the upcoming legislative election, scheduled for the end of February 2010, on the dubious grounds that they had failed to meet electoral law requirements. The most high-profile party barred from the election was the FL, but others such as the Union Nationale Chrétienne Pour la Reconstruction d'Haïti, which apparently refused invitations to merge with Inite, were also excluded. Opposition party leaders denounced the CEP as a tool of the presidency, and claimed that Préval intended to give Inite complete control of the legislature.

On 12 January 2010 a massive earthquake struck southern Haiti, causing extensive damage, claiming the lives of more than 200,000 people, injuring 250,000 more, destroying much of Port-au-Prince and many provincial towns and villages, and leaving around 1.2m. people homeless or displaced. The Haitian authorities were overwhelmed by the scale of the disaster. The parliament building, the presidential palace, the main police station, and most government ministry buildings were all seriously damaged or destroyed by the earthquake. International humanitarian relief groups were quickly mobilized, but rescue teams and medical aid were slow to arrive in the capital because of the chaos and damage to transport routes and infrastructure. The collapse of the MINUSTAH headquarters also slowed the UN's initial relief efforts. In response, the US Administration of President Barack Obama deployed thousands of US marines in order to secure the airport infrastructure and establish security for the deployment of international aid workers and the distribution of medical and food assistance.

Health care provision for the injured survivors of the earthquake was severely hampered by the fact that, of the 40 state hospitals operating in the three departments most severely affected by the earthquake (Ouest, Sud-Est and Nippes), 23 had sustained significant damage. Thousands of those made homeless established 'tent cities' throughout the Port-au-Prince area. In February 2010 Haiti's Direction de la Protection Civile (Directorate of Civil Protection) reported that at least 1,000 camps for displaced persons had been created around the country, and that nearly 600,000 displaced persons had migrated from Port-au-Prince and its environs to the countryside.

In the aftermath of the earthquake, there was a massive international response to the disaster, but it suffered from poor co-ordination. By early March 2010 the International Federation of Red Cross and Red Crescent Societies, responsible for co-ordinating the effort to provide shelter for earthquake survivors, announced that only around 40% of the estimated 1.2m. homeless and displaced persons had received any sort of shelter materials. The World Food Programme was more successful, stating that by February emergency food distribution had reached nearly 3m. people.

While the Government remained in ostensible control of the country, real authority resided with the UN, owing to the work of its various agencies and the presence of MINUSTAH, and with the USA, as a result of the large number of US troops deployed in Haiti and its position as the largest international aid donor. MINUSTAH's presence was increased, comprising more than 11,500 soldiers and police officers by mid-2010. Initially, the relationship between the USA and the UN showed some signs of discord, largely because of conflicting approaches to the humanitarian operation. In an effort to overcome this tension, the UN Secretary-General, Ban Ki-Moon, promoted a former US President, Bill Clinton (1993–2001), who was already serving as the UN Special Envoy to Haiti, to head the international reconstruction effort. At an international donors' conference in New York, USA, at the end of March 2010, Clinton was named as a Co-Chairman, with Bellerive, of the Interim Haiti Recovery Commission.

The country awaits the impact of the large amounts of international assistance pledged in the months following the earthquake. The displaced population has exacerbated tensions in urban areas and strained the resources of extended families in the countryside, while living conditions in the camps and in many of the capital's slum areas remain deplorable. The escape of over 4,000 prisoners from the main gaol in Port-au-Prince on the day of the earthquake is believed to explain a subsequent rise in criminal activity in the capital, and human rights organizations have also reported an increase in sexual violence, with females in the temporary camps particularly vulnerable.

The earthquake has undermined much of the recent progress made in stabilizing the country's political, economic and security situation. The huge reconstruction effort—at a projected cost of US $11,500m. over the next decade—will dominate the political agenda in both the short and medium term. The Government, which was weak before the earthquake, is now severely debilitated and will rely on international support. Legislative elections scheduled for February 2010 were cancelled, and are expected to be rearranged to coincide with the presidential ballot due to take place before the end of the year. President Préval's five-year term ends in February 2011, and he has announced his attention to step down at that time. Most domestic and international officials agree that elections need to take place, but the process will be difficult to organize.

Economy

CHARLES ARTHUR

The economy of the Republic of Haiti has been in trouble ever since independence was won in 1804. Following 12 years of revolutionary upheaval and the subsequent collapse of the slave-driven plantation economy, a nation of smallholding peasant farmers soon emerged. Throughout the 19th century, national development was held back by the need to pay a massive indemnity in return for France's recognition of the country's independence. An urban élite that grew rich by the control of agricultural exports, and, in particular, by helping itself to government revenue raised by taxation, did nothing to help the country's economic development. Until the 1950s, crops grown by peasant farmers were sufficient to satisfy most of the country's food requirements, but since then the agricultural sector has experienced a deepening crisis. Agro-exports, once the mainstay of the national economy, declined throughout the latter half of the 20th century. Inadequate infrastructure, political instability and violence, inefficient bureaucracy and low standards of education have all contributed to a downward economic spiral that accelerated in the late 20th century. Haiti is the most underdeveloped economy in the Americas, and, for the majority of a population projected at 9.9m. in 2009, extremely low incomes are the norm. Some 76% of the population lives below the US $2 per day poverty line, with 54% living in extreme poverty (less than $1 per day). There is a massive wealth disparity, with 80% of the population controlling a mere 32% of the country's total income, and the wealthiest 2% of the population controlling 26% of total income.

Since the 1960s the country has been a major recipient of foreign aid, yet, while this assistance, in particular the provision of food aid, has saved the country from complete collapse, it has resulted in scant sustainable development. More recently, a massive increase in remittances sent to family members in Haiti by relatives living abroad has developed into one of the mainstays of the everyday economy. Remittances increased steadily during the first decade of the 21st century, and represented around 20% of gross domestic product (GDP) in 2008/09. Following the January 2010 earthquake, it was expected that remittances would increase, to 21% of GDP, as Haitians living abroad responded to the humanitarian crisis.

The only new economic activity of any real significance has been the development since the 1970s of an export assembly industry that has increasingly specialized in garment assembly. At its peak, in the early 1980s, this sector employed 60,000 people, mostly women, assembling light-industrial products for export. During the 1980s this sector too began to decline as US companies began to send orders to countries where better infrastructure allowed a quicker and cheaper turnaround.

By the end of the 20th century deepening poverty in the countryside, and the prospect—however remote—of finding employment in the city, spurred a rural exodus that is still continuing. An estimated 100,000 people relocate each year, most of them to the capital, Port-au-Prince. Nearly all the new arrivals join the estimated 1m. people working in the so-called informal sector, a term that covers a multitude of occupations ranging from self-employed traders and artisans to casual labourers, porters, shoe-shiners and gardeners. By far the most common activities are the buying and reselling of tiny quantities of everyday goods and the provision of basic services.

Nearly all of the approximately 100,000 formal economy jobs that do exist are located in Port-au-Prince. Approximately one-half of these are in public administration, where significant employers are the government ministries, particularly education, health and justice, the state-owned enterprises such as the telephone and electricity companies, the police force and the customs and tax services. Non-governmental organizations (NGOs), both local and foreign, also furnish a small but significant number of employment opportunities. Since 1995 the one area of employment that has really boomed has been the provision of private security, reflecting serious concerns about increased crime.

The huge loss of life and massive destruction to buildings and infrastructure in Port-au-Prince and surrounding areas caused by the 2010 earthquake completely disrupted normal economic activity. The damage was estimated at approximately US $7,900m., equivalent to 120% of Haiti's GDP. With much of Port-au-Prince, Haiti's centre of political and economic activity, destroyed, the domestic authorities and international agencies and donors will be forced to rebuild completely and even reorient the economy.

AGRICULTURE

Although it has undergone a massive decline, agriculture remains the mainstay of the economy. Approximately 70% of the population lives in rural areas, and 65% of the economically active population depends directly or indirectly on the agricultural sector. Typically, a small peasant farm produces maize, millet, bananas and plantains, beans, yams and sweet potato. Any produce that is surplus to the family's needs is sold at the local market. Rice is grown principally in the central Artibonite valley and a few other areas of the country where irrigation systems have been introduced. Over the last 100 years, agricultural output has suffered from a growing population farming a finite area of land. The result has been the division of cultivated land into smaller and smaller holdings. On these tiny plots, the soil has become progressively exhausted and less productive. This problem has been compounded by extensive deforestation, which has in turn led to severe erosion of the fertile topsoil. As yields have declined, peasant farmers have found themselves locked into a self-destructive cycle in which the felling of trees for charcoal production, and the farming of land higher up the mountainsides, can stave off short-term financial disaster, but only creates greater problems for the sector as a whole in the long run.

The extent of the agricultural sector's decline is such that, whereas in the 1970s it accounted for about one-half of the nation's GDP, by the early years of the 21st century it measured around one-quarter. The repercussions at national level are manifold. For example, the central Government, which has long relied on customs charges on exports, has seen its revenue reduced dramatically. At the same time, food production has failed to keep pace with population growth. Today the country must import more than one-half of the food that is consumed, creating a further pressure on the national balance of payments. The social and political ramifications of such a dependence were starkly highlighted in early 2008 when a sudden increase in international food prices made many food items too expensive for poor Haitian families. The resultant demonstrations and riots across the country brought down the Government.

The agricultural sector was negatively affected by the damage and losses resulting from the tropical storms and hurricanes that battered the country in August and September 2008, registering a decline in real terms of 6% compared with 2007/08. The Government, NGOs and the staff of internationally funded projects carried out a joint evaluation of the extent of the damage to the country's agricultural sector, and estimated total losses at US $229m. The central department of Artibonite was the worst affected, with agricultural sector losses totalling $95m. The Ministry of Agriculture, Natural Resources and Rural Development estimated that 4,178 ha of farm land were washed away when rivers burst their banks during the storms. According to the national food security platform, the Coordination Nationale Securité Alimentaire (CNSA), the damage to the 2008 winter season harvest of beans, maize, sorghum and root crops made access to food even more difficult in the first half of 2009. However, abundant rains during the rest of the year brought good harvests, and the sector registered a slight recovery in 2008/09. By the end of 2009 the CNSA estimated that the proportion of the population existing in a condition of food insecurity remained steady at around one-third, amounting to approximately 3.3m. people.

The agricultural sector was largely unscathed by the 2010 earthquake, but environmental degradation, devastation from recent hurricanes and underinvestment were expected to constrain food output and keep the sector vulnerable to natural risks. Following the earthquake, an estimated 600,000 people left the Port-au-Prince area to seek refuge with relatives in the provinces, with almost 50% relocating to the Artibonite department. The economic impact of this exodus was uncertain: although the influx of people from Port-au-Prince to already impoverished rural and agricultural communities was likely to exacerbate economic and environmental strain, their presence may stimulate economic activity as a result of increased spending, funded by remittances, and greater demand for agricultural produce at the local level.

The demise of the rice sector illustrates how local and national factors affect food production. In 1985 Haiti produced 125,000 metric tons of rice, but by 2007 the total had fallen to an estimated 90,000 tons. In part the decline is a consequence of lack of investment in infrastructure, particularly the failure to repair irrigation canals or establish rice-processing facilities. Rice farmers in the Artibonite valley also lack the capital to invest in machinery and fertilizers, and the overwhelming majority of the cultivation is carried out by hand or with rudimentary hand-tools. Rice production has also been hit hard by the effects of structural adjustment policies applied since 1987, resulting in the lowering of import tariffs and a subsequent influx of cheaper, subsidized rice imports from the USA. While national production has declined, the consumption of rice has strongly increased. On average each Haitian currently consumes 50 kg of rice per year, a figure far higher than in the other main rice-consuming countries. This demand has been met by imports, which have risen from between 10,000 tons and 20,000 tons a year in the mid-1980s, to around 400,000 tons in the early years of the 21st century. Almost 80% of the rice consumed in Haiti is now imported.

Agricultural production for export has also undergone a significant decline, partly because peasants have been obliged to shift to growing food crops just to fend off starvation, and partly as a consequence of changes in the international market. Domestic factors have also played a part in the demise of agricultural exports, nowhere more obviously than in the case of the spectacular collapse of sugar production. In 1951 the country produced almost 90,000 metric tons of sugar, but by 1977 it had become a net importer. In the absence of any investment in sugar production, growers were still using the most basic production methods, and as a result were unable to remain competitive with the more advanced sugar industries of other countries. Even so, until the mid-1980s sugar cane was second only to coffee as Haiti's most important cash crop. Then, in 1986, the Haitian owners of the last three cane refineries capable of producing quality sugar found that there were greater profits to be made from the import and sale of foreign sugar, and consequently closed the refineries down. This brought an end to sugar exports altogether, and since then sugar cane has only been grown for use in the production of local products. In 2000 a sugar refinery opened at Darbonne, near Léogane, west of the capital, and by 2005 annual output had reached 2,607 tons. However, this represented just 2% of the country's annual refined sugar consumption. Most of the sugar cane still grown (some 68%) is used by around 500 rudimentary distilleries to produce low-quality rum and sugar-based liqueurs. The rest is used to produce raw sugar and syrup, and a small amount (just 3% of the annual sugar cane crop) is used for the production of high-quality rum by a handful of modern distilleries.

As recently as 1949 Haiti was the third largest coffee exporter in the world, and coffee was by far the country's most important export crop, but since then output has steadily fallen. Haiti is now a marginal producer of coffee in the international market, accounting for just 0.4% of world production between 1995 and 2000. The decline in the coffee sector began in the 1980s when it was hit by low output and weak prices, and was further damaged by the economic sanctions against the military dictatorship in the early 1990s. Production fell dramatically, from 450,000 bags in 1985 to officially only 10,000 bags in 2003. The value of coffee exports has continued to decline in the 21st century.

By the early 21st century the most significant agricultural exports were mangoes, cacao and essential oils. Export earnings from mangoes have increased each year since 2002 and totalled US $8.9m. in 2005/06. Haiti is the biggest mango exporter in the Caribbean region, and the sixth largest source of mango imports to the USA. There is also an informal export trade to the Dominican Republic, where Haitian mangoes are used in the production of chutney for the European market. After a strong performance in the first half of 2006/07, the mango industry suffered a serious setback when in July 2007 the main market country, the USA, temporarily suspended imports from Haiti following the discovery of fruit flies in mango export shipments. The US Department of Agriculture subsequently ordered a further suspension of exports pending the implementation of a pest control programme. During 2008 the Haitian authorities received support from Canada to carry out a programme that successfully detected and controlled fruit flies, and exports to the USA resumed. Export earnings from mangoes totalled $7.9m. in 2006/07 and increased to $10m. in 2007/08. A traditional crop, cacao, experienced a revival, earning $6.9m. in 2006/07 and $7.4m in 2007/08. The once lucrative essential oils sector also made a comeback. A mainstay of this sector is vetiver grass, which, when steam-distilled, produces a red-brown aromatic oil that is used in the manufacture of perfume. In the 1950s and 1960s Haitian vetiver oil was considered a high-quality variety, and it recently became fashionable again. Essential oils earned $7.2m. in 2004/05, rising to $13.1m. in 2006/07 and $17.8m. in 2007/08. A new crop, avocado, grew in significance in the early years of the 21st century, and by 2005 approximately 50,000 metric tons were produced annually. Some 20% of avocado production is exported informally to the Dominican Republic.

Fishing supplements the diet of those peasant farmers who live on Haiti's 1,700 km-long coastline, but, like agriculture, this economic sector is facing serious problems. In the absence of the capital needed to purchase outboard motors and modern fishing boats, all fishing occurs in shallow coastal waters. Over the years, fish stocks in these waters have dwindled as fishermen have used nets with smaller and smaller mesh in an effort to make a catch. However, over-fishing is not the only problem. Just as serious are the effects of the vast quantities of eroded topsoil washed into the sea at times of heavy rainfall. This silt destroys most sea-life, including potentially fish-rich coral reefs.

MINING

The mining of mineral deposits was a significant economic activity in the 1960s and 1970s when the US-owned Reynolds company extracted bauxite from an area around the town of Miragoâne, and the Canadian subsidiary, Sedren, extracted copper from a mine north of Gonaïves. The Sedren mine closed in 1971, and Reynolds ceased its operations in Haiti in 1983 because of low world prices. Prospecting for petroleum and lignite in the 1970s proved fruitless, and, although North American companies did find gold and copper deposits in the late 1990s, they decided against investing in the infrastructure necessary for profitable mining operations. In April 2007 one of them, the Canadian company St. Geneviève Resources Ltd, announced that it would begin mining gold and copper deposits located between Terrier Rouge and Trou-du-Nord in the North-East department. In 2008 the US company Hidalgo Mining International created a Haitian subsidiary to pursue mining projects in the country. Another Canadian company, Eurasian Minerals, was also involved in a major exploration project looking for gold, silver and copper deposits in north-eastern and central Haiti. The company negotiated mineral rights on 30 concessions, covering roughly 282,000 ha. In early 2010 rumours arose surrounding the involvement of foreign companies in Haiti's mining sector as part of the post-earthquake reconstruction phase, but no major discoveries had been announced by mid-2010.

At present, the most important extractive enterprises are those quarrying stone, gravel and sand for use in road and building construction. According to the Government's Office of Mines and Energy, this sector provides employment for 3,000–4,000 people, and central bank data shows that it continues to exhibit remarkable growth, reflecting the continuing boom in the construction sector, particularly in the greater Port-au-Prince region. Following the earthquake, the construction sector was expected to expand further.

MANUFACTURING

The manufacturing sector has been in decline since it peaked in the early 1980s. At that time it accounted for more than 18% of GDP but by 2005/06 it had fallen to 7.8%. Assembly production for export was decimated during the three years of military rule after the 1991 coup when political upheaval, power supply problems, and economic sanctions forced the closure of nearly all the assembly plants. In the second half of the 1990s the garment assembly sub-sector experienced a slight recovery, employing around 20,000 workers in Port-au-Prince on extremely low wages to assemble pyjamas and T-shirts for the North American market.

In late 2003 a new free trade zone in the north-eastern border town of Ouanaminthe opened, and over 1,000 workers were employed by the Dominican Grupo M company to assemble jeans and T-shirts. Political and criminal violence in Port-au-Prince in 2004–05 forced many garment assembly plants to close, and, with the expiry of the duty-free quota system under the Agreement on Textiles and Clothing at the beginning of 2005, there were serious concerns about the viability of the sub-sector. Already lagging far behind the Central American republics and the Dominican Republic in terms of a share of the US market, the removal of the duty-free quotas was a serious blow to Haitian manufacturers who were unable to compete with Chinese and other East Asian producers. Government officials and operators in the garment assembly sector expected that the Haitian Hemispheric Opportunity through Partnership Encouragement (HOPE) Act, which was enacted by the US Congress in December 2006 and which came into effect in June 2007, would provide a significant boost to foreign investment and job creation in the industry. The legislation, which provided duty-free access to the US market for clothing assembled in Haiti from materials sourced from countries with which the USA had free trade agreements or regional preference programme partnerships, was predicted to create some 20,000 new jobs. However, only around 3,000 more workers had been taken on by late 2007, and the total work-force of the garment sector in Haiti still stood at just 20,000. Nearly all the new jobs were created by the expansion of existing assembly operations, and only two new companies set up business in Haiti. In response, the Haitian Government and representatives of the garment assembly sector lobbied the US Congress to amend the HOPE Act, and in mid-2008 the HOPE II Act was approved to increase the quantity of fabric allowed duty-free access to the US and to extend the life of the preference until 2018.

In early 2009 a UN-commissioned report by the British economist Paul Collier proposed that international aid should focus on developing the garment assembly sector as a way of rapidly creating tens of thousands of jobs. The Collier Report was taken up by the international community, and in turn by the Government of President René Garcia Préval and Prime Minister Michèle Pierre-Louis. At the international donors' conference in April 2009, an unspecified amount of assistance was pledged, with the intention of funding the infrastructure that would facilitate the creation of several new free trade zones to accommodate new garment assembly operations. During 2009 a local investment company, the WIN Group, and the Soros Economic Development Fund announced their intention to construct a US $45m. free trade zone in the capital's Cité Soleil slum. However, this project was put on hold in the aftermath of the 2010 earthquake.

Following the earthquake, international donors, meeting to discuss the reconstruction of Haiti, once again identified the garment-manufacturing sector as the key to the country's economic development. The USA, in particular, expressed interest in developing the Haitian garment industry; measures under consideration included the introduction of US trade benefits and additional incentives for investment in Haiti's apparel sector, and a voluntary scheme to urge US apparel and textile companies to source 1% of their production from Haitian factories, the 'Plus One' plan.

Real exports, which grew by a strong 9.9% in 2008/09 owing mostly to increases in garments assembled for the US market under the HOPE II programme, were expected to contract sharply in 2009/10 as many industries, and more importantly transport infrastructure, had suffered from the earthquake.

Manufacturing for domestic consumption, consisting mainly of foodstuffs and beverages, is limited. High poverty rates and the preference of the wealthy élite for imported goods mean that the domestic market is very small in size. Local investors have traditionally shown little interest in developing local production, favouring the import/export business instead.

TRANSPORT AND COMMUNICATIONS

Haiti's road system is rudimentary, constrained by the mountainous terrain, soil erosion and torrential rains. During the US occupation of 1915–34 the basic road network was extended and many bridges were built, and in the 1980s French foreign aid helped to construct a durable road link connecting the southern town of Jacmel with the main road across the south of the country. During the 1991–94 military regime, the main road from the border to Port-au-Prince was modernized in order to receive traffic bringing goods and fuel in circumvention of international sanctions. There are three official border crossing points providing road connections to the Dominican Republic: Malpasse in the south, Belladères in the centre and Ouanaminthe in the north. In the late 1990s foreign aid financed the construction of a main road along the Artibonite Valley. At the time when the interim Government of Gérard Latortue took office in 2004, the existing network of roads was just 3,400 km long, and only 20% of those were covered with asphalt. Around 85% of traffic is concentrated in and around the capital.

On assuming office in 2006, the Government of Préval and Jacques-Edouard Alexis announced a sweeping programme to repair and extend the road network in order to link all areas of the country, including roads to connect the main provincial towns, along much of the coastline, and a north–south route along the border. The Government stated that the proposed road system extension would facilitate the transport of goods—both those imported and those for export—allow the development of tourism, and contribute to the social, political and economic inclusion of previously marginalized citizens. Priority routes included the road from Cap-Haïtien to Ouanaminthe, and road triangles linking Les Cayes, Jérémie and Miragoâne in the south-west, and Port-de-Paix, Cap-Haïtien and Gonaïves in the north-west.

The only airports capable of receiving international flights are in Port-au-Prince and Cap-Haïtien. Facilities are poor, but in March 2007, during an official visit by the Venezuelan President, Hugo Chávez Frías, it was announced that Venezuela would provide US $57m. to rehabilitate both airports. Small airports receiving flights from Port-au-Prince exist in the provincial towns of Jérémie, Les Cayes, Hinche, Port-de-Paix and Jacmel.

Port-au-Prince is the country's major port, with container facilities and berths for cruise-liners, but the 2010 earthquake caused serious damage (including the complete destruction of one of the two piers). In mid-March 2010 the local WIN Group announced a US $70m. joint venture project with the US-based Santé Holding Corpn to redevelop Terminal Varreux, the country's largest privately owned shipping terminal, on the northern outskirts of Port-au-Prince. The terminal was damaged during the earthquake, but was quickly repaired in order to allow crucial fuel shipments to reach Haiti (it receives and stores more than 70% of the country's fuel imports). The redevelopment plans included the construction of a new port, additional jetties and a modern 150-acre terminal. The two other main ports for exports are Miragoâne and Cap-Haïtien. Small ports at Petit-Goâve, St Marc, Gonaïves and Port-de-Paix are also active, and the wharf at Jacmel has recently been enlarged to enable cruise-liners to dock. In early 2008 the US-Norwegian company Royal Caribbean Cruises agreed to construct an 800-ft-long pier costing $27m. that would allow cruise passengers easier access to the secluded beach at Labadee to the west of Cap-Haïtien. Presently, around 500,000 cruise passengers visit Labadee each year, and the new pier will allow an increase in visitors to what is currently the only significant tourist development in the country.

Until 1998 the state telephone company, Télécommunications d'Haïti (Téléco), was the only telephone service provider, and Haiti had by far the lowest telephone density in the Latin American and Caribbean region. Since then, three new service providers have entered the market: Haiti Telecommunications International, SA (HaiTel, part-owned by US-based MCI WorldCom), Communication Céllulaire d'Haïti (Comcel, owned by US-based Western Wireless), and Digicel Haiti (an affiliate of the pan-Caribbean Digicel Group). The competition between these providers has transformed the communications sector, and there has been a recent rapid expansion in mobile phone usage. Comcel (which operates under the Voilà brand) and Haitel had seen limited success, but with the launch of Digicel Haiti in May 2006 there was phenomenal growth. Galvanized by Digicel's low prices, the number of mobile phone users increased to 3.5m. in 2009 from around 600,000 in 2006. Digicel was the market leader with over 2m. customers, but the mobile phone penetration rate, at 37%, remained very low in relation to other countries in the region. The economic importance of the mobile phone companies was highlighted in early 2009 when the Government proposed to include a new tax on telephone calls in its budget. In response, representatives of Digicel, Voilà and HaiTel threatened to curtail their operations in Haiti if the planned new tax was implemented. Acutely aware that the three companies had invested more than US $600m. in the country over the previous 10 years, and provided more than 2,000 jobs, with a further 55,000 people employed indirectly, the Government hastily withdrew the proposed new tax. In April 2010 the long-delayed privatization of Téléco took place when a Vietnamese company, Viettel, formally acquired 60% of the shares in the company, with the Haitian Government maintaining possession of the remaining 40%.

ENERGY PROVISION

Haiti has one of the lowest rates of energy consumption per head in the world, estimated at 30 kWh per person, of which residential consumption accounts for around 60%, industrial consumption 20%, transport 15% and services 5%. The vast majority of the population relies on charcoal for cooking and heating, and kerosene oil for illumination. Less than 15% of the population has access to electricity. The use of charcoal is a significant contributor to the continuing deforestation of the country. Commercial production of energy is limited to electricity, both thermal (fuelled by imported oil) and hydroelectric. The largest hydroelectric facility is located at the Péligre dam, at the head of the Artibonite valley. The plant came into production in 1971 with a potential capacity of some 54 MW, but lack of investment and low water levels have meant that it has never achieved this output. Established thermal generating stations run by the state electricity company, Electricité d'Haïti (Ed'H), are located at Carrefour and Varreux in Port-au-Prince, and in late 2008–early 2009 two new thermal generating stations run by Ed'H began operations in Cap-Haïtien and Gonaïves, each with a capacity to produce 13 MW of power. A third station at Carrefour, with a 30-MW capacity, began operating in mid-2009. The three stations were built and funded through an agreement with Cuba and Venezuela.

The absence of investment in the power sector over the last three decades has created major problems of power supply. In recent years, the combined output of the hydroelectric and thermal generators has fallen to less than 50 MW, and with total demand in the metropolitan region of Port-au-Prince alone reaching more than 150 MW, power outages for those connected to the national grid have become an everyday occurrence. To supplement the erratic electricity supply generated by Ed'H, for a number of years the Government has subcontracted two private companies. Alstom provides an additional 50 MW for the Port-au-Prince area, while Sogener provides electricity for 12 hours a day to the provincial towns of Les Cayes, Gonaïves, St Marc and Petit-Goâve. In early 2006 work to repair and refurbish the Péligre facility and refit the thermal generating stations in Port-au-Prince was carried out, but the rising price of oil on the international market left the Government hard pressed to purchase sufficient fuel. With the national electricity network unable to guarantee even a meagre supply, individual businesses have been forced to invest in their own 'back-up' systems, and this privately owned capacity may amount to as much as 60 MW.

The country is heavily dependent on imported oil, and as such is very vulnerable to international oil price rises. In May 2006 the Government signed up to Venezuela's PetroCaribe initiative to enable it to purchase oil on favourable terms, and in March 2007 Venezuela's President Chávez announced that his country would double the amount of oil that it provided to Haiti under the PetroCaribe agreement to 14,000 barrels per day. The improved terms meant that Venezuela would supply all of Haiti's oil needs, 50% of it at below the market price and the other 50% on favourable credit terms. At the same time, the Préval/Alexis Government responded positively to Brazilian proposals to explore the potential for the production and use of biofuels. A pilot project to produce ethanol from sugar cane, funded by the US Agency for International Development and the Inter-American Development Bank (IDB), is in progress in the Montrouis watershed near St Marc. The weakness of the sugar cane sector means that future biofuel development is likely to focus on the production of biodiesel from crops such as castor beans and jatropha, and in several areas of the country jatropha-growing projects funded by private investors are already under way.

INVESTMENT AND FINANCE

The small amounts of foreign investment that Haiti has received in recent decades have been committed almost exclusively to the assembly sector. Most of this investment has come from US companies, although in recent years some Dominican, Canadian and South Korean companies have also set up operations in Haiti. National private sector investment has traditionally been at very low levels, with Haitian investors favouring the stability and lower risks on offer in the USA and the Dominican Republic.

With little foreign investment and limited access to commercial credit, Haiti is heavily dependent on international development aid and loans. The suspension of economic and development aid in 1991–94 hit the country particularly hard, and, although international donors promised more than US $1,000m. in aid to support the restored democratic Government in 1994, aid flows were repeatedly interrupted by political crises. Following the dispute over the 2000 elections, the flow of aid and loan disbursements decreased sharply, as donors suspended payments pending a resolution of the political deadlock. Private investment also declined, and the result was negative real GDP growth, high inflation, and large fiscal and external deficits. Although the interim Government installed in early 2004 received strong political support from foreign powers, donors proved wary about releasing pledged assistance, because of concerns about the Government's capacity to absorb the aid, and perceptions of high levels of government and public sector corruption.

Following the installation of the Préval/Alexis administration, donors committed to increase the level of assistance, but the rate of disbursement continued to disappoint the Government, and ministers repeatedly claimed that failure to release promised financing for its rapid-impact job creation and social improvement programme would jeopardize political stability. The Government continued to rely heavily on international assistance and worked closely with the IMF to achieve policy objectives, including the maintenance of broadly orthodox fiscal and monetary policies and a host of structural reforms aimed at increasing tax income, raising social spending, strengthening governance, enhancing economic transparency and improving the overall investment climate. In June 2009 the international finance institutions finally recognized the success of the Government's reform programmes by agreeing to long-demanded debt relief. More than US $1,200m. of the estimated total external debt of $1,900m. was cancelled in line with the Heavily Indebted Poor Countries (HIPC) initiative. Following the 2010 earthquake, there was a series of further debt cancellations, in addition to the pledges of aid from foreign donors. Responding to its own data, revealing that damage from the earthquake could total as much as $14,000m., the IDB announced that it was cancelling Haiti's total debt of $479m., and would offer an additional $2,000m. in financing over the next 10 years. Venezuela also cancelled the $295m. that it was owed by Haiti, leaving total external debt at around $420m. (or just 6% of GDP). As a result of the cancellations, combined with additional restructuring, the Government will have few, if any, debt repayments due before 2012, and even thereafter repayments will be much lower than in the past.

Inflows of foreign assistance and improvements in macroeconomic management contributed to continued GDP growth, which reached 3.2% in 2006/07. However, prospects for growth and the authorities' economic strategy in general were undermined by significant developments in late 2007 and early 2008. GDP growth for 2007/08 was 1.2% as a result of the food and fuel price shocks, declining US demand, and the physical destruction and damage to agriculture associated with the August/September hurricanes. During 2008/09 real GDP grew by a modest, but respectable, 2.9%, although the economy was expected to contract by as much as 8.5% during 2009/10 owing to the cessation of economic activity in January and February 2010 following the earthquake.

POST-DISASTER RECONSTRUCTION

The Government's Post-Disaster Needs Assessment (PDNA)—published in March 2010—envisaged a decentralized Haiti, aiming to 'decongest', rather than rebuild as before, the metropolitan area of Port-au-Prince. The plan also provided for the establishment of the Interim Haiti Recovery Commission and a Multi-Donor Trust Fund, to be administered by the World Bank, to organize and disperse reconstruction money. The PDNA suggested that a total of US $11,500m. would be needed to rebuild the country over the three years, with 50% directed towards social programmes, 17% towards infrastructure, and 15% towards environmental and disaster analysis. The Government appealed for $3,900m. by the end of 2011 to reconstruct destroyed infrastructure, government buildings, hospitals and schools. At the end of March 2010 an estimated $5,300m. was pledged for the following two years at an international donors' conference in New York, USA. The impact of these pledges will depend heavily on whether countries actually meet their commitments and on the speed of implementation of reconstruction plans.

OUTLOOK

In the aftermath of the January 2010 earthquake, the extent of the economic downturn and subsequent recovery will depend on the timing and effectiveness of foreign aid, and how soon key economic sectors such as agriculture and garment-manufacturing can be re-established. The significant amounts of foreign assistance pledged for 2010/11 should help to support the economy, but poor organization and inadequate infrastructure will complicate the distribution of aid and limit the impact of efforts to create jobs and stimulate economic activity. Strong inflows of foreign assistance and remittances, and an expansion in construction activity, should provide an impetus to the economy. None the less, the level of economic growth needed to reduce poverty and improve social indicators will require increased investment in key productive sectors and infrastructure. In order to prevent an increase in social unrest and insecurity, Haiti will need a relatively rapid recovery, with priority being given to the rebuilding of homes, offices and factories, and the creation of jobs.

Statistical Survey

Sources (unless otherwise stated): Banque de la République d'Haïti, angle rues du Pavée et du Quai, BP 1570, Port-au-Prince; tel. 2299-1200; fax 2299-1045; e-mail brh@brh.net; internet www.brh.net; Institut Haitien de Statistique et d'Informatique, Ministère de l'Economie et des Finances, 1, angle rue Joseph Janvier et boulevard Harry Truman, Port-au-Prince; tel. 2514-3789; fax 2221-5812; e-mail info@ihsi.ht; internet www.ihsi.ht.

Area and Population

AREA, POPULATION AND DENSITY

Area (sq km)	27,750*
Population (census results)	
30 August 1982†	5,053,792
7 July 2003	
Males	4,039,272
Females	4,334,478
Total	8,373,750
Population (official projections at mid-year)	
2007	9,602,304
2008	9,761,927
2009	9,923,243
Density (per sq km) at mid-2009	357.6

* 10,714 sq miles.

† Excluding adjustment for underenumeration.

Note: It was estimated that as many as 230,000 people were killed as a result of a powerful earthquake that devastated the country's capital, Port-au-Prince, in January 2010.

POPULATION BY AGE AND SEX

(official projections at mid-2009)

	Males	Females	Total
0–14	1,832,933	1,767,764	3,600,697
15–64	2,886,307	3,007,789	5,894,095
65 and over	193,273	235,177	428,451
Total	4,912,513	5,010,730	9,923,243

DEPARTMENTS

(official projections at mid-2009)

	Population	Capital
Ouest	3,664,620	Port-au-Prince
Sud-Est	575,293	Jacmel
Nord	970,495	Cap-Haitien
Grand'Anse	425,878	Jérémie
Nord-Est	358,277	Fort Liberté
L'Artibonit (Artibonite)	1,571,020	Gonaïves
Centre	678,626	Hinche
Sud	704,760	Les Cayes
Nord-Ouest	662,777	Port-de-Paix
Nippes	311,497	Miragoâne
Total	9,923,243	—

PRINCIPAL TOWNS

(official projected population at mid-2009)

Port-au-Prince (capital)	897,859	Delmas	359,451
Carrefour	465,019		

BIRTHS AND DEATHS
(UN estimates)

	1995–2000	2000–05	2005–10
Crude birth rate (per 1,000)	32.7	29.8	27.9
Crude death rate (per 1,000)	10.3	9.8	9.1

Source: UN, *World Population Prospects: The 2008 Revision*.

Life expectancy (years at birth, WHO estimates): 62 (males 60; females 64) in 2008 (Source: WHO, *World Health Statistics*).

ECONOMICALLY ACTIVE POPULATION
(official estimates, persons aged 10 years and over, mid-1990)

	Males	Females	Total
Agriculture, hunting, forestry and fishing	1,077,191	458,253	1,535,444
Mining and quarrying	11,959	12,053	24,012
Manufacturing	83,180	68,207	151,387
Electricity, gas and water	1,643	934	2,577
Construction	23,584	4,417	28,001
Trade, restaurants and hotels	81,632	271,338	352,970
Transport, storage and communications	17,856	2,835	20,691
Financing, insurance, real estate and business services	3,468	1,589	5,057
Community, social and personal services	81,897	73,450	155,347
Sub-total	1,382,410	893,076	2,275,486
Activities not adequately defined	33,695	30,280	63,975
Total employed	1,416,105	923,356	2,339,461
Unemployed	191,333	148,346	339,679
Total labour force	1,607,438	1,071,702	2,679,140

Source: ILO, *Yearbook of Labour Statistics*.

2003 (national survey of living conditions, sample survey of persons aged 10 years and over, primary occupation, percentage distribution): Agriculture 44.6; Fishing 1.2; Mining and quarrying 0.3; Manufacturing 6.5; Electricity, gas and water 0.2; Construction 2.7; Wholesale and retail trade, vehicle repairs 27.7; Hotels and restaurants 1.5; Transport, storage and communications 2.1; Financial intermediation 0.2; Real estate, renting and other business activities 1.4; Public administration and compulsory social security 1.7; Education 3.8; Health and social welfare 1.3; Other community, social and personal services 2.5; Other services 2.4; Total employed 100.0.

Mid-2010 (estimates in '000): Agriculture, etc. 2,317; Total labour force 3,940 (Source: FAO).

Health and Welfare

KEY INDICATORS

Total fertility rate (children per woman, 2008)	3.5
Under-5 mortality rate (per 1,000 live births, 2008)	72
HIV/AIDS (% of persons aged 15–49, 2007)	2.2
Physicians (per 1,000 head, 1998)	0.3
Hospital beds (per 1,000 head, 2000)	0.8
Health expenditure (2007): US $ per head (PPP)	58
Health expenditure (2007): % of GDP	5.3
Health expenditure (2007): public (% of total)	23.3
Access to water (% of persons, 2008)	63
Access to sanitation (% of persons, 2008)	17
Total carbon dioxide emissions ('000 metric tons, 2006)	1,810.0
Carbon dioxide emissions per head (metric tons, 2006)	0.2
Human Development Index (2007): ranking	149
Human Development Index (2007): value	0.532

For sources and definitions, see explanatory note on p. vi.

Agriculture

PRINCIPAL CROPS
('000 metric tons)

	2006	2007	2008
Rice, paddy	110	130	110
Maize	205	270	210
Sorghum	100	120	100
Sweet potatoes	200	220	230
Cassava (Manioc)	400	450	435
Yams	220	230	235
Sugar cane	1,075	1,100	1,110
Bananas	280	295	295*
Plaintains	265*	240	200
Guavas, mangoes and mangosteens	265	295	295*

* Estimate.

Aggregate production ('000 metric tons, may include official, semi-official or estimated data): Total cereals 415 in 2006, 520 in 2007, 420 in 2008; Total roots and tubers 873 in 2006, 955 in 2007, 955 in 2008; Total vegetables (incl. melons) 209 in 2006, 217 in 2007, 208 in 2008; Total fruits (excl. melons) 998 in 2006, 1,039 in 2007, 997 in 2008.

Source: FAO.

LIVESTOCK
('000 head, year ending September, FAO estimates)

	2006	2007	2008
Horses	500	500	500
Asses	210	210	210
Mules	80	80	80
Cattle	1,450	1,450	1,455
Pigs	1,000	1,001	1,001
Sheep	153	153	154
Goats	1,900	1,900	1,910
Chickens	5,500	5,500	5,600
Turkeys	195	195	195
Ducks	190	190	190

Source: FAO.

LIVESTOCK PRODUCTS
('000 metric tons, FAO estimates)

	2004	2005	2006
Cattle meat	42.5	43.5	42.0
Goat meat	6.0	6.0	6.0
Pig meat	33.0	33.1	33.0
Horse meat	5.6	5.7	5.6
Chicken meat	8.0	8.1	8.0
Cows' milk	44.5	44.8	44.5
Goats' milk	25.2	25.6	25.2
Hen eggs	4.4	4.4	4.5

2007–08: Output assumed to be unchanged from 2006 (FAO estimates).

Source: FAO.

Forestry

ROUNDWOOD REMOVALS
('000 cubic metres, excl. bark, FAO estimates)

	2006	2007	2008
Sawlogs, veneer logs and logs for sleepers*	224	224	224
Other industrial wood*	15	15	15
Fuel wood	2,008	2,016	2,024
Total	2,247	2,255	2,263

* Production assumed to be unchanged since 1971.

Source: FAO.

SAWNWOOD PRODUCTION
('000 cubic metres, incl. railway sleepers)

	1969	1970	1971
Coniferous (softwood)	5	8	8
Broadleaved (hardwood)	10	5	6
Total	14	13	14

1972–2008: Annual production as in 1971 (FAO estimates).

Source: FAO.

Fishing

('000 metric tons, live weight, FAO estimates)

	2004	2005	2006
Freshwater fishes	0.3	0.3	0.3
Marine fishes	5.7	6.3	7.2
Marine crabs	0.3	0.4	0.4
Caribbean spiny lobster	1.0	1.0	1.0
Natantian decapods	0.8	0.8	0.9
Stromboid conchs	0.3	0.3	0.3
Total catch	8.3	9.0	10.0

2007–08: Figures assumed to be unchanged from 2006 (FAO estimates).

Note: Figures exclude corals and madrepores (FAO estimates, metric tons): 10 in 2004–08.

Source: FAO.

Industry

SELECTED PRODUCTS
(metric tons, unless otherwise indicated, year ending 30 September)

	1999/2000
Edible oils	38,839.6
Butter	2,972.2
Margarine	2,387.4
Cornflour	104,542.6
Soap	30,069.9
Detergent	4,506.1
Beer ('000 cases of 24 bottles)	784.5
Beverages ('000 cases of 24 bottles)	1,807.7
Rum ('000 750ml bottles)	2,009.5
Electric energy (million kWh)	697.6

Cement ('000 metric tons, estimates): 290.0 in 2004–08 (Source: US Geological Survey).

Electric energy (million kWh): 535 in 2003; 547 in 2004; 556 in 2005; 570 in 2006; 469 in 2007 (Source: UN Industrial Commodity Statistics Database).

Finance

CURRENCY AND EXCHANGE RATES

Monetary Units

100 centimes = 1 gourde.

Sterling, Dollar and Euro Equivalents (31 March 2010)

£1 sterling = 60.018 gourdes;
US $1 = 39.616 gourdes;
€1 = 53.398 gourdes;
1,000 gourdes = £16.66 = $25.24 = €18.73.

Average Exchange Rate (gourdes per US $)

2007	36.861
2008	39.108
2009	41.198

Note: The official rate of exchange was maintained at US $1 = 5 gourdes until September 1991, when the central bank ceased all operations at the official rate, thereby unifying the exchange system at the 'floating' free market rate.

BUDGET
(million gourdes, year ending 30 September)

Current revenue	2007	2008*	2009*
Internal receipts	15,656.9	18,025.5	19,948.2
Customs	6,924.1	7,917.3	9,013.3
Total (incl. others)	23,667.2	26,673.7	31,303.5

Expenditure	2007	2008*	2009*
Current expenditure	22,428.4	24,300.2	33,599.6
Wages and salaries	8,830.8	12,855.6	14,465.0
Capital expenditure	6,043.0	6,066.0	1,955.0
Total	28,471.4	30,366.1	35,554.6

* Provisional figures.

INTERNATIONAL RESERVES
(US $ million at 31 December)

	2007	2008	2009
IMF special drawing rights	7.5	7.0	108.0
Reserve position in IMF	0.1	0.1	0.1
Foreign exchange	444.4	534.3	696.7
Total	452.0	541.4	804.8

Source: IMF, *International Financial Statistics*.

MONEY SUPPLY
(million gourdes at 31 December)

	2007	2008	2009
Currency outside depository corporations	13,633.9	15,304.8	15,854.7
Transferable deposits	43,158.2	49,120.8	55,782.6
Other deposits	45,934.9	50,999.6	54,729.0
Broad money	102,727.1	115,425.2	126,366.3

Source: IMF, *International Financial Statistics*.

COST OF LIVING
(Consumer Price Index, year ending 30 September; base: 2000 = 100, metropolitan areas)

	2006	2007	2008
Food	300.1	324.5	388.6
Clothing and footwear	225.9	250.0	278.4
Rent	272.7	309.6	350.4
All items (incl. others)	286.9	311.3	359.6

2009: All items 354.7.

Source: ILO.

NATIONAL ACCOUNTS
(million gourdes, year ending 30 September)

Expenditure on the Gross Domestic Product
(at current prices)

	2006/07*	2007/08†	2008/09†
Final consumption expenditure	209,590	257,145	273,005
Gross capital formation	67,092	72,281	73,161
Total domestic expenditure	29,142	31,903	37,936
Exports of goods and services	29,142	31,903	37,936
Less Imports of goods and services	85,715	110,739	117,198
GDP in purchasers' values	220,110	250,590	266,904
GDP at constant 1986/87 prices	13,508	13,622	14,015

Gross Domestic Product by Economic Activity
(at constant 1986/87 prices)

	2006/07*	2007/08†	2008/09†
Agriculture, hunting, forestry and fishing	3,378	3,125	3,288
Mining and quarrying	15	16	17
Manufacturing	1,030	1,029	1,067
Electricity and water	57	52	68
Construction	1,031	1,085	1,119
Trade, restaurants and hotels	3,661	3,868	3,911
Transport, storage and communications	910	967	991
Business services	1,602	1,653	1,654
Other services	1,443	1,514	1,518
Sub-total	13,127	13,309	13,633
Less Imputed bank service charge	619	716	689
Taxes, less subsidies, on products.	1,000	1,029	1,071
GDP in purchasers' values	13,508	13,622	14,015

* Provisional figures.
† Estimates.

BALANCE OF PAYMENTS
(US $ million, year ending 30 September)

	2006/07	2007/08	2008/09
Exports of goods f.o.b.	522.1	490.2	551.0
Imports of goods f.o.b.	–1,704.2	–2,107.8	–2,032.1
Trade balance	–1,182.1	–1,617.6	–1,481.1
Exports of services	257.1	342.8	381.8
Imports of services	–680.2	–746.0	–780.6
Balance on goods and services	–1,605.3	–2,020.8	–1,879.9
Other income received	21.8	28.0	31.1
Other income paid	–19.6	–22.5	–18.5
Balance on goods, services and income	–1,603.1	–2,015.3	–1,867.3
Current transfers received	1,222.1	1,369.8	1,375.5
Current transfers paid	–96.4	–117.1	–134.8
Current balance	–477.4	–762.6	–626.6
Direct investment from abroad	74.5	29.8	38.0
Other investment assets	12.9	–90.0	36.0
Other investment liabilities	73.3	339.1	–594.4
Net errors and omissions	126.1	106.5	–177.4
Overall balance	–190.6	–377.2	–1,324.4

Source: IMF, *International Financial Statistics*.

External Trade

PRINCIPAL COMMODITIES
(US$ million, year ending 30 September, provisional figures)

Imports c.i.f.	2006/07	2007/08	2008/09
Food products	369.8	553.6	512.3
Mineral fuels, lubricants, etc.	406.0	618.3	383.0
Basic manufactures	276.3	217.3	243.7
Machinery and transport equipment	224.8	187.0	198.7
Miscellaneous manufactured goods	169.7	173.0	236.3
Total (incl. others)	1,851.7	2,148.2	2,081.9

Exports f.o.b.*	2006/07	2007/08	2008/09
Coffee	2.0	3.7	2.7
Cocoa	6.2	7.4	7.4
Mangoes	7.9	10.0	10.2
Crayfish	4.4	4.8	3.5
Essential oils	13.8	17.2	9.8
Manufactured goods	180.6	158.7	191.1
Total (incl. others)	522.1	472.4	548.8

* Excluding re-export of assembled goods to USA (US $ million, year ending 30 September, provisional figures): 463.4 in 2006/07; 425.1 in 2007/08; n.a. in 2008/09.

Source: Administration Générale des Douanes, Port-au-Prince.

PRINCIPAL TRADING PARTNERS
(US$ million, year ending 30 September)*

Imports c.i.f.	1989/90	1990/91	1991/92
Belgium	3.4	3.7	2.9
Canada	22.0	31.9	15.2
France	24.5	32.4	17.2
Germany, Federal Republic	14.6	19.2	10.0
Japan	23.6	31.2	17.7
Netherlands	11.2	13.9	8.7
United Kingdom	5.6	6.7	4.2
USA	153.1	203.2	126.7
Total (incl. others)	332.2	400.5	277.2

Exports f.o.b.†	1989/90	1990/91	1991/92
Belgium	15.9	19.5	6.0
Canada	4.5	4.7	2.3
France	17.4	21.6	6.1
Germany, Federal Republic	5.4	6.6	2.4
Italy	16.5	20.7	8.7
Japan	2.4	2.9	0.9
Netherlands	3.4	4.3	1.4
United Kingdom	2.3	2.3	0.7
USA	78.3	96.3	39.7
Total (incl. others)	163.7	198.7	74.7

* Provisional figures.
† Excluding re-exports.

Source: Administration Générale des Douanes, Port-au-Prince.

Transport

ROAD TRAFFIC
('000 motor vehicles in use)

	1994	1995	1996
Passenger cars	30.0	49.0	59.0
Commercial vehicles	30.0	29.0	35.0

1999 ('000 motor vehicles in use): Passenger cars 93.0; Commercial vehicles 61.6.

Source: UN, *Statistical Yearbook*.

SHIPPING

Merchant Fleet
(registered at 31 December)

	2006	2007	2008
Number of vessels	5	6	7
Total displacement ('000 grt)	1.3	1.8	2.4

Source: Lloyd's Register-Fairplay, *World Fleet Statistics*.

International Sea-borne Freight Traffic
('000 metric tons)

	1988	1989	1990
Goods loaded	164	165	170
Goods unloaded	684	659	704

Source: UN, *Monthly Bulletin of Statistics*.

CIVIL AVIATION

Traffic (international flights, 1995): Passengers arriving 367,900; Passengers departing 368,330.

Tourism

TOURIST ARRIVALS BY COUNTRY OF ORIGIN

	2005	2006	2007
Canada	9,986	8,733	30,046
Dominican Republic	5,543	2,785	n.a.
France	3,349	2,787	10,246
Jamaica	3,649	1,936	n.a.
USA	77,047	79,247	266,793
Total (incl. others)	112,267	107,783	386,060

Receipts from tourism (US $ million, excl. passenger transport): 80 in 2005; 135 in 2006; 140 in 2007.

Source: World Tourism Organization.

Communications Media

	2007	2008	2009
Telephones ('000 main lines in use)	108.3	108.0	108.3
Mobile cellular telephones ('000 subscribers)	2,500	3,200	3,648
Internet users ('000)	900	1,000	1,000

Personal computers: 16,000 (1.7 per 1,000 persons) in 2005.

Source: International Telecommunication Union.

Radio receivers ('000 in use): 415 in 1997.

Television receivers ('000 in use): 42 in 1999.

Daily newspapers: 4 in 1996 (total circulation 20,000 copies); 2 in 2004.

Book production: 340 titles published in 1995.

Sources (unless otherwise indicated): UNESCO, *Statistical Yearbook*; UN, *Statistical Yearbook*.

Education

(1994/95)

	Institutions	Teachers	Students
Pre-primary	n.a.	n.a.	230,391*
Primary	10,071	30,205	1,110,398
Secondary	1,038	15,275	195,418
Tertiary	n.a.	654*	6,288*

* 1990/91 figure.

Adult literacy rate (UNESCO estimates): 62.1% (males 60.1%; females 64.0%) in 2007 (Source: UNESCO Institute for Statistics).

Directory

The Constitution

The Constitution of the Republic of Haiti, which was approved by the electorate in a referendum held in March 1987, provided for a system of power-sharing between a President (who may not serve two consecutive five-year terms), a Prime Minister, a bicameral legislature (comprising a chamber of deputies elected for four years and a senate whose members serve six-year terms, one-third of whom are elected every two years) and regional assemblies. The army and the police were no longer to be a combined force. The death penalty was abolished. Official status was given to the Creole language spoken by Haitians and to the folk religion, Voodoo (vodou). Fr Jean-Bertrand Aristide was elected President in December 1990, but was deposed in September 1991 by a military coup. The US military returned him to Haiti to begin the restoration of constitutional government. He declared the army dissolved in April 1995, but a constitutional amendment formally abolishing it was never presented to the legislature as required and, after the fall of Aristide in February 2004, there were calls for its revival. The head of the Supreme Court, Boniface Alexandre, succeeded Aristide, and a Council of Elders appointed Gérard Latortue as Prime Minister. Presidential and legislative elections were held in February and April 2006, and constitutional rule was re-established when President René Garcia Préval took office in May. In 2005 the number of seats in both chambers was increased, from 27 to 30 in the Senate and from 83 to 99 in the Chamber of Deputies.

The Government

HEAD OF STATE

President: RENÉ GARCIA PRÉVAL (assumed office on 14 May 2006).

CABINET
(July 2010)

The Government was formed by Inite, the successor party to Fwon Lespwa.

Prime Minister and Minister of Planning and External Co-operation: JEAN-MAX BELLERIVE.

Minister of Agriculture, Natural Resources and Rural Development: JOANAS GUÉ.

Minister of Culture and Communication: MARIE LAURENCE JOCELYN LASSÈGUE.

Minister of the Economy and Finance: RONALD BAUDIN.

Minister of Education and Professional Training: JOËL DESROSIERS JEAN-PIERRE.

Minister of the Environment: JEAN-MARIE CLAUDE GERMAIN.

Minister of Foreign Affairs and Religion: MARIE-MICHÈLE REY.

Minister of Haitians Residing Abroad: EDWIN PARAISON.

Minister of the Interior and Local Government: PAUL ANTOINE BIEN-AIMÉ.

Minister of Justice and Public Security: PAUL DENIS.

Minister of Public Health and the Population: DR ALEX LARSEN.

Minister of Public Works, Transport and Communications: JACQUES GABRIEL.

Minister of Social Affairs and Labour: YVES CRISTALLIN.

Minister of Tourism: PATRICK DELATOUR.

Minister of Trade and Industry: JOCELYNE COLIMON FÉTHIÈRE.

Minister of Women's Affairs and Women's Rights: MARJORIE MICHEL.

Minister of Youth, Sports and Civic Action: EVANS LESCOUFLAIR.

Minister-delegate to the Prime Minister, in charge of Parliamentary Relations: JOSEPH JASMIN.

There are also four Secretaries of State.

MINISTRIES

Many ministerial buildings were destroyed in the earthquake of January 2010.

Office of the President: Palais National, rue de la République, Port-au-Prince; tel. 2222-3024; e-mail webmestre@palaisnational.info.

Office of the Prime Minister: Villa d'Accueil, 1 rue Prosper, Musseau, Port-au-Prince; tel. 2228-6000; e-mail primature@primature.gouv.ht; internet www.primature.gouv.ht.

Ministry of Agriculture, Natural Resources and Rural Development: BP 2162, Route Nationale 1, Damien, Port-au-Prince; tel. 2222-3599; fax 2222-3591; internet www.agriculture.gouv.ht.

Ministry of Culture and Communication: Champ de Mars, Port-au-Prince; tel. 2221-3238; fax 2221-7318; e-mail dg1@haiticulture.org.

Ministry of the Economy and Finance: Palais des Ministères, rue Mgr Guilloux, Port-au-Prince; tel. 2223-7113; fax 2223-1247; e-mail mef@mefhaiti.gouv.ht; internet www.mefhaiti.gouv.ht.

Ministry of Education and Professional Training: rue Dr Audain, Port-au-Prince; tel. 2222-1036; fax 2245-3400; internet www.eduhaiti.gouv.ht.

Ministry of the Environment: 181 ave Jean-Paul II, Port-au-Prince; tel. 2245-7585; fax 2245-7360.

Ministry of Foreign Affairs and Religion: blvd Harry S Truman, Cité de l'Exposition, Port-au-Prince; tel. 2222-8482; fax 2223-1668; e-mail webmaster@maehaitiinfo.org; internet www.mae.gouv.ht.

Ministry of Haitians Residing Abroad: 87 ave Jean-Paul II, Turgeau, Port-au-Prince; tel. 2245-1116; fax 2245-0287; e-mail info@mhave.gouv.ht; internet www.mhave.gouv.ht.

Ministry of the Interior and Local Government: Palais des Ministères, rue Mgr Guilloux, Port-au-Prince; tel. 2222-6490; fax 2222-8057.

Ministry of Justice and Public Security: 19 ave Charles Sumner, Port-au-Prince; tel. 2245-9737; fax 2245-0474; internet www.mjsp.gouv.ht.

Ministry of Planning and External Co-operation: Palais des Ministères, rue Mgr Guilloux, Port-au-Prince; tel. 2228-2512; fax 2222-0226; e-mail info@mpce.gouv.ht; internet www.mpce.gouv.ht.

Ministry of Public Health and the Population: Palais de Ministères, rue Mgr Guilloux, Port-au-Prince; tel. 2223-6248; fax 2222-4066.

Ministry of Public Works, Transport and Communications: Palais des Ministères, rue Mgr Guilloux, Port-au-Prince; tel. 2222-2528; fax 2223-4519; e-mail secretariat.directiongenerale@mtptc.gouv.ht; internet www.mtptc.gouv.ht.

Ministry of Social Affairs and Labour: 16 rue de la Révolution, Port-au-Prince; tel. 2222-1244; fax 2221-0717.

Ministry of Tourism: 8 rue Légitime, Port-au-Prince; tel. 2223-2135; fax 2223-5359; e-mail pdelatour@yahoo.com.

Ministry of Trade and Industry: rue Légitime, Champ de Mars, BP 200, Port-au-Prince; tel. 2222-2125; fax 2223-8402.

Ministry of Women's Affairs and Women's Rights: ave Magny 4, Port-au-Prince; tel. 2224-9152; e-mail contact@mcfdf.gouv.ht; internet www.mcfdf.gouv.ht.

Ministry of Youth, Sports and Civil Action: angle rues Garoute et Pacot, Turgeau, BP 2339, Port-au-Prince; tel. 2245-5794.

Office of the Minister-delegate to the Prime Minister, in charge of Parliamentary Relations: Delmas 48, 5 rue François, Port-au-Prince; tel. 2246-9912.

President and Legislature

PRESIDENT

Election, 7 February 2006*

Candidates	Votes†	%
René Garcia Préval	992,766	51.21
Leslie François Manigat	240,306	12.40
Charles Henri Baker	159,683	8.24
Jean Chavannes Jeune	108,283	5.59
Luc Mesadieu	64,850	3.35
Serge Gilles	50,796	2.62
Paul Denis	50,751	2.62
Evans Paul	48,232	2.49
Guy Philippe	37,303	1.92
Luc Fleurinord	36,912	1.90
Total (incl. others)	1,938,641	100.00

* After 95.8% of the votes had been counted.

† Total votes for each candidate include blank ballots. As no candidate attracted 50% of the valid votes cast, in order to avoid a second round of voting blank ballots were distributed among the candidates in proportion to their share of valid votes cast.

LEGISLATURE

Sénat
(Senate)

President: KELLY C. BASTIEN.

Distribution of Seats, December 2009*

	Seats
Fwon Lespwa	14
Fusion des Sociaux-Démocrates Haïtiens	4
Organisation du Peuple en Lutte (OPL)	3
Latibonit an Aksyon (LAAA)	2
La Fanmi Lavalas (FL)	1
Konbit pou Bati Ayiti (KONBA)	1
Alyans	1
Pont	1
Union Nationale Chrétienne pour la Reconstruction d'Haïti (UNION)	1
Independent	1
Vacant	1
Total	30

* The Sénat has 30 members, three from each province. One-third of these seats are renewable every two years. The last elections to the Sénat were held on 19 April and 21 June 2009.

Chambre des Députés
(Chamber of Deputies)

President: LEVAILLANT LOUIS-JEUNE.

Elections, 7 February and 21 April 2006

	Seats
Fwon Lespwa	24
Fusion des Sociaux-Démocrates Haïtiens	18
Union Nationale Chrétienne pour la Reconstruction d'Haïti (UNCRH)	12
Organisation du Peuple en Lutte (OPL)	11
Alyans	10
Latibonit an Aksyon	5
Mouvement Chrétien pour une Nouvelle Haïti (MOCHRENHA)	3
Mobilization for Haïti's Development (MPH)	3
Co-operative Action to Build Haïti (KONBA)	2
Mouvement Démocratique et Renovateur d'Haïti (MODEREH)	1
Mouvement Indépendant pour la Réconciliation Nationale (MIRN)	1
Mouvement pour la Reconstruction Nationale (MRN)	1
Front de Reconstruction Nationale (FRN)	1
Action Démocratique pour Bâtir Haïti (ADEBHA)	1
La Fanmi Lavalas (FL)	1
Rassemblement des Démocrates Nationaux et Progressistes (RDNP)	1
Total	99

Election Commission

Conseil Electoral Provisoire (CEP): 300 route de Delmas, Port-au-Prince; tel. 2246-1733; e-mail info@cep-ht.org; internet www.cep-ht.org; f. 2004; Pres. GAILLOT DORSINVIL; Dir-Gen. PIERRE LOUIS OPONT.

Political Organizations

Some 52 political parties and movements were registered to contest the legislative elections that were scheduled to take place in February and March 2010 but were postponed following the earthquake in January of that year. Many addresses in Port-au-Prince and surrounding areas were destroyed in the earthquake.

Action Démocratique pour Bâtir Haïti (ADEBHA): 509 route de Delmas, entre Delmas 103 & 105, Port-au-Prince; tel. 2256-6739; fax 3446-6161; e-mail versun_etatdedroit@yahoo.fr; internet www.adebha.populus.org; f. 2004; Pres. RENÉ JULIEN.

Alliance pour la Libération et l'Avancement d'Haïti (ALAH): Haut Turgeau 95, BP 13350, Port-au-Prince; tel. 2245-0446; fax

2257-4804; e-mail reynoldgeorges@yahoo.com; f. 1975; Leader REYNOLD GEORGES.

Alyans (Alliance Démocratique): Port-au-Prince; contested the 2006 elections; centre-left coalition of Konvansyon Inite Demokratik (KID) and Popular Party for the Renewal of Haïti (PPRH); formed an alliance with the Fusion des Sociaux-Démocrates Haïtiens and the OPL in late 2009 to contest the 2010 legislative elections; Leader EVANS PAUL.

Ayiti an Aksyon (AAA): Port-au-Prince; internet ayitianaksyon .net.

Congrès National des Mouvements Démocratiques (KONA-KOM): 101 Bois Verna, Port-au-Prince; tel. 2245-6228; f. 1987; social-democratic; Leader VICTOR BENOÎT.

La Fanmi Lavalas (FL): blvd 15 Octobre, Tabarre, Port-au-Prince; tel. 2256-7208; internet www.hayti.net; f. 1996 by Jean-Bertrand Aristide; formed a coalition with the MOP, the OPL and the PLB.

Front de Reconstruction Nationale (FRN): Gonaïves; f. 2004; Sec.-Gen. GUY PHILIPPE.

Fusion des Sociaux-Démocrates Haïtiens: POB 381056, Miami, FL 33138, USA; e-mail fusion@pfsdh.org; internet www.pfsdh.org; formed an alliance with Alyans and the OPL in late 2009 to contest the 2010 legislative elections; Leader SERGE GILLES.

Grand Front de Centre Droit (GFCD): 21 blvd Harry S. Truman, Cité de l'Exposition, Port-au-Prince; tel. 2245-6251; e-mail hdr@ mdnhaiti.org; internet www.gfcd.org; f. 2003; centre-right alliance; Leader (vacant).

Grand Parti Socialiste Haïtien (GPSH): Port-au-Prince; f. 2004; mem. of the GFCD; contested 2006 elections under Fusion des Sociaux-Démocrates umbrella; Leader SERGE GILLES.

Grand Rassemblement pour l'Evolution d'Haïti (GREH): Port-au-Prince; Leader HIMMLER REBU.

Inite (Unité): Port-au-Prince; f. 2009 to replace Fwon Lespwa (Front de l'Espoir, f. 2005); supports President René Garcia Préval; mems incl. the MIRN, the MOP and the PLB; Nat. Co-ordinator JOSEPH LAMBERT.

Jeunesse Pouvoir Populaire (JPP): 410 rue Tiremasse, Port-au-Prince; tel. 2558-1647; f. 1997; Leader RENÉ CIVIL.

Konbit pou Bati Ayiti (KONBA) (Co-operative Action to Build Haïti): Port-au-Prince; f. 2005; contested the 2006 elections; Leader CHAVANNES JEAN-BAPTISTE.

Koordinasyon Resistans Grandans (KOREGA-ESCANP): regionally based; radical left; Leader Fr JOACHIM SAMEDI.

Latibonit an Aksyon (LAAA) (L'Artibonite en Action): Port-au-Prince; contested the 2006 elections; Leader YOURI LATORTUE.

Mobilisation pour le Développement National (MDN): c/o CHISS, 33 rue Bonne Foi, BP 2497, Port-au-Prince; tel. 2222-3829; e-mail info@mdnhaiti.org; internet www.mdnhaiti.org; f. 1986; Pres. HUBERT DE RONCERAY; Sec.-Gen. MAX CARRE.

Mobilization for Haïti's Development (MPH): Port-au-Prince; Leader SAMIR MOURRA.

Mouvement pour l'Avancement, le Développement, et l'Innovation de la Démocracie en Haïti (MADIDH): Port-au-Prince; Leader MARC ANTOINE DESTIN.

Mouvement Chrétien pour une Nouvelle Haïti (MOCHRENHA): rue M 7 Turgeau, Carrefour, Port-au-Prince; tel. 3443-3120; e-mail mochrenha@hotmail.com; f. 1998; Leaders LUC MÉSADIEU, GILBERT N. LÉGER.

Mouvement Démocratique et Renovateur d'Haïti (MOD-EREH): Port-au-Prince; e-mail modereh@yahoo.com; Leaders DANY TOUSSAINT, PRINCE PIERRE SONSON.

Mouvement Indépendant pour la Réconciliation Nationale (MIRN): Port-au-Prince; contested the 2006 elections; mem. of Inite; Leader LUC FLEURINORD.

Mouvement pour l'Instauration de la Démocratie en Haïti (MIDH): 114 ave Jean Paul II, Port-au-Prince; tel. 2245-8377; f. 1986; centre-right; Pres. MARC BAZIN.

Mouvement National et Patriotique du 28 Novembre (MNP-28): f. 1991; Leader JEAN BAPTISTE DE JEAN BÉLIZAIRE.

Mouvement d'Organisation du Pays (MOP): 9 rue Stella, Delmas 31, Port-au-Prince; tel. 2249-3408; f. 1946; centre party; mem. of Inite; Leader JEAN MOLIÈRE.

Mouvement Patriotique pour le Sauvetage National (MPSN): f. 1998; right-wing coalition comprising 7 parties; Leader HUBERT DE RONCERAY.

Mouvement pour la Reconstruction Nationale (MRN): f. 1991; Leader JEAN-ENOL BUTEAU.

Mouvman Konbit Nasyonal (MKN): Leader VOLVICK RÉMY JOSEPH.

Nouveau Parti Communiste Haïtien (NPCH): Port-au-Prince; e-mail vanialubin@yahoo.fr; internet www.npch.net; Marxist-Leninist.

Organisation pour l'Avancement de d'Haïti et des Haïtiens (OLAHH): Port-au-Prince; Leader JOEL BORGELLA.

Organisation du Peuple en Lutte (OPL): 105 ave Lamartinière, Bois Verna, Port-au-Prince; tel. 2245-4214; e-mail info@oplpeople .com; internet www.oplpeople.com/home.html; f. 1991 as Organisation Politique Lavalas; name changed as above 1998; formed an alliance with Alyans and the Fusion des Sociaux-Démocrates Haïtiens in late 2009 to contest the 2010 legislative elections; Leader PAUL DENIS.

Parti Agricole et Industrie National (PAIN): f. 1956; Spokesman TOUSSAINT DESROSIERS.

Parti du Camp Patriotique et de l'Alliance Haïtienne (PACA-PALAH): Port-au-Prince; Leader FRANCK FRANÇOIS ROMAIN.

Parti des Démocrates Haïtiens (PADEMH): Leader JEAN-JACQUES CLARK PARENT.

Parti Démocratique et Chrétien d'Haïti (PDCH): 127 rue du Magasin de l'Etat, Port-au-Prince; tel. 2550-7282; f. 1979; Christian Democrat party; Leaders OSNER FÉVRY, JOACHIN PIERRE.

Parti pour un Développement Alternatif (PADH): Leader GÉRARD DALVIUS.

Parti pour l'Evolution Nationale d'Haïti (PENH): Port-au-Prince; Leader YVES M. SAINT-LOUIS.

Parti des Industriels, Travailleurs, Commercants et Agents du Développement d'Haïti (PITACH): Port-au-Prince; Leader JEAN JACQUES SYLVAIN.

Parti National Progressiste Révolutionnaire (PANPRA): 5 rue Marcelin, Port-au-Prince; tel. 2257-5359; f. 1989; social-democratic; Leader SERGE GILLES.

Parti National des Travailleurs (PNT): Port-au-Prince.

Parti Nationale Démocratique Progressiste d'Haïti (PNDPH): Port-au-Prince; Pres. TURNEB DELPÉ.

Parti Populaire Nationale (PPN): 11 rue Capois, Port-au-Prince; tel. 2222-6513; f. 1987 as Assemblée Populaire Nationale (APN); name changed as above in 1999; radical left; Sec.-Gen. BEN DUPUY.

Parti Revolutionnaire Démocratique d'Haïti (PRDH): fmrly Mouvement Démocratique pour la Libération d'Haïti (MODELH); Leader FRANÇOIS LATORTUE.

Parti Social Chrétien d'Haïti (PSCH): BP 84, Port-au-Prince; f. 1979; Leader GRÉGOIRE EUGÈNE.

Parti Social Renove (PSR): Port-au-Prince; Leader BONIVERT CLAUDE.

Pati Louvri Baryè (PLB): f. 1992 by Renaud Bernardin; mem. of Inite; Sec.-Gen. HERMOGÈNE DURAND.

Pont (Bridge): Port-au-Prince; contested the 2006 elections.

Rassemblement des Démocrates Chrétiens (RDC): 177 rue du Centre, Port-au-Prince; tel. 2234-4214; Leader EDDY VOLEL.

Rassemblement des Démocrates Nationaux Progressistes (RDNP): 234 route de Delmas, Delmas, Port-au-Prince; tel. 2246-3313; f. 1979; centre party; Sec.-Gen. MIRLANDE MANIGAT.

Regroupement Patriotique pour le Renouveau National (REPAREN): Port-au-Prince; Leader JUDIE C. ROY.

Respè: Port-au-Prince; f. 2005; party of the wealthy élite; Leader CHARLES HENRI BAKER.

Union Démocrates Patriotiques (UDP): 30 rue Geffrard, Port-au-Prince; tel. 2256-1953; Leader ROCKFELLER GUERRE.

Union Nationale Chrétienne pour la Reconstruction d'Haïti (Union): Leader JEAN CHAVANNES JEUNE.

OTHER ORGANIZATIONS

Mouvman Peyizan Papay (MPP): Papaye, Hinche; internet www .mpphaiti.org; f. 1973; peasant org., chiefly concerned with food production and land protection; Leader CHAVANNES JEAN-BAPTISTE.

Diplomatic Representation

EMBASSIES IN HAITI

Many addresses in Port-au-Prince and surrounding areas were destroyed in the earthquake of January 2010.

Argentina: 50 rue Lamarre, Pétionville, BP 1755, Port-au-Prince; tel. and fax 2256-6414; e-mail embarghaiti@hainet.net; Ambassador JOSÉ MARÍA VÁSQUEZ OCAMPO.

Bahamas: 12 rue Goulard, pl. Boyer, Pétionville, Port-au-Prince; tel. 2257-8782; fax 2256-5729; e-mail bahamasembassy@hainet.net; Ambassador (vacant).

Brazil: Immeuble Héxagone, 3ème étage, angle des rues Clerveaux et Darguin, Pétion-Ville, BP 15845, Port-au-Prince; tel. 2256-9662; fax 2256-0900; e-mail haibrem@accesshaiti.com; internet www.bresil-ht.org/site; Ambassador IGOR KIPMAN.

Canada: route de Delmas, entre Delmas 71 et 75, BP 826, Port-au-Prince; tel. 2249-9000; fax 2249-9920; e-mail prnce@international.gc.ca; internet www.canadainternational.gc.ca/haiti; Ambassador CLAUDE BOUCHER.

Chile: 2 rue Coutilien, Musseau, Port-au-Prince; tel. 2256-7960; fax 2257-0623; e-mail embajadachile_haiti@hotmail.com; Ambassador MAURICIO LEONE BRAVO.

China (Taiwan): 16 rue Léon Nau, Pétionville, BP 655, Port-au-Prince; tel. 2257-2899; fax 2256-8067; e-mail haiti888@gmail.com; Ambassador HSU MIEN-SHENG.

Cuba: 18 rue Marion, Peguy Ville, Pétionville, POB 15702, Port-au-Prince; tel. 2256-3812; fax 2257-8566; e-mail embacuba@hughes.net; internet embacu.cubaminrex.cu/haiti; Ambassador RICARDO SOTERO GARCÍA NÁPOLES.

Dominican Republic: rue Panaméricaine 121, BP 56, Pétionville, Port-au-Prince; tel. 3257-9215; fax 3257-0383; e-mail embrepdomhai@yahoo.com; Ambassador RUBÉN SILIÉ VALDEZ.

France: 51 pl. des Héros de l'Indépendance, BP 1312, Port-au-Prince; tel. 2222-0952; fax 2223-8420; e-mail ambafrance@hainet.net; internet www.ambafrance-ht.org; Ambassador DIDIER LE BRET.

Germany: 2 impasse Claudinette, Bois Moquette, Pétionville, BP 1147, Port-au-Prince; tel. 2257-7280; fax 2257-4131; e-mail info@port-au-prince.diplo.de; internet www.port-au-prince.diplo.de; Ambassador JENS-PETER VOSS.

Holy See: rue Louis Pouget, Morne Calvaire, BP 326, Port-au-Prince; tel. 2257-6308; fax 2257-3411; e-mail nonciatureap@hughes.net; Apostolic Nuncio Most Rev. BERNARDITO CLEOPAS AUZA (Titular Archbishop of Suacia).

Japan: Villa Bella Vista, 2 Impasse Tulipe Desprez, BP 2512, Port-au-Prince; tel. 2245-3333; fax 2245-8834; Ambassador vacant (resides in the Dominican Republic).

Mexico: Delmas 60, 2, BP 327, Port-au-Prince; tel. 2257-8100; fax 2256-6528; e-mail embmxhai@yahoo.com; Ambassador EVERARDO LUIS SUÁREZ AMEZCUA.

Panama: blvd 15 Octobre, Tabarre, Capital Coach Line Terminal, Port-au-Prince; tel. 2513-1844; e-mail panaembahaiti@yahoo.com; Chargé d'affaires a.i. EUFEMIO URIHA TAYLOR SALINAS.

Spain: 54 rue Pacot, State Liles, BP 386, Port-au-Prince; tel. 2245-4410; fax 2245-3901; e-mail ampespht@mail.mae.es; internet www.mae.es/embajadas/puertoprincipe; Ambassador JUAN FERNÁNDEZ TRIGO.

USA: Tabarre 41, blvd 15 Octobre, Port-au-Prince; tel. 2229-8000; fax 2229-8028; internet haiti.usembassy.gov; Ambassador KENNETH H. MERTEN.

Venezuela: blvd Harry S Truman, Cité de l'Exposition, BP 2158, Port-au-Prince; tel. 3443-4127; fax 2223-7672; e-mail embavenezhaiti@hainet.net; Ambassador PEDRO ANTONIO CANINO GONZÁLEZ.

Judicial System

Law is based on the French Napoleonic Code, substantially modified during the presidency of François Duvalier.

Courts of Appeal and Civil Courts sit at Port-au-Prince and the three provincial capitals: Gonaïves, Cap-Haïtien and Port de Paix. In principle each commune has a Magistrates' Court. Judges of the Supreme Court and Courts of Appeal are appointed by the President.

Cour de Cassation (Supreme Court): Port-au-Prince; tel. 2222-3212; Pres. (vacant); Vice-Pres. GEORGES MOÏSE.

Citizens' Rights Defender: NECKER DESSABLES.

Religion

Roman Catholicism and the folk religion Voodoo (vodou) are the official religions. There are various Protestant and other denominations.

Many addresses in Port-au-Prince and surrounding areas were destroyed in the earthquake of January 2010.

CHRISTIANITY

The Roman Catholic Church

For ecclesiastical purposes, Haiti comprises two archdioceses and eight dioceses. Some 65% of the population are Roman Catholics.

Bishops' Conference

Conférence Episcopale de Haïti, angle rues Piquant et Lammarre, BP 1572, Port-au-Prince; tel. 222-5194; fax 223-5318; e-mail ceh56@hotmail.com.

f. 1977; Pres. Most Rev. LOUIS KÉBREAU (Archbishop of Cap-Haïtien).

Archbishop of Cap-Haïtien: Most Rev. LOUIS KÉBREAU, Archevêché, rue 19–20 H, BP 22, Cap-Haïtien; tel. 262-0071; fax 262-1278.

Archbishop of Port-au-Prince: JOSEPH SERGE MIOT, Archevêché, rue Dr Aubry, BP 538, Port-au-Prince; tel. 222-2045; e-mail archevechepap@globalsud.com.

The Anglican Communion

Anglicans in Haiti fall under the jurisdiction of a missionary diocese of Province II of the Episcopal Church in the USA.

Bishop of Haiti: Rt Rev. JEAN ZACHÉ DURACIN, Eglise Episcopale d'Haïti, BP 1309, Port-au-Prince; tel. 2257-1624; fax 2257-3412; e-mail epihaiti@hotmail.com; internet www.egliseepiscopaledhaiti.org.

Protestant Churches

Baptist Convention: Route Nationale 1, Cazeau BP 2601, Port-au-Prince; tel. 2262-0567; e-mail conventionbaptiste@yahoo.com; f. 1964.

Evangelical Lutheran Church of Haiti: Eglise Evangélique Luthérienne d'Haiti, 144 rue Capitale, BP 15, Les Cayes; tel. 2286-3398; f. 1975; Pres. THOMAS BERNARD; 9,000 mems.

Other denominations active in Haiti include Methodists and the Church of God 'Eben-Ezer'.

VOODOO

Konfederasyon Nasyonal Vodou Ayisyen (KNVA): f. 2008; Supreme Leader FRANÇOIS MAX GESNER BEAUVOIR.

The Press

Many addresses in Port-au-Prince and surrounding areas were destroyed in the earthquake of January 2010.

DAILY

Le Nouvelliste: Complexe Promenade, Pétionville, Port-au-Prince; internet www.lenouvelliste.com; f. 1898; evening; French; suspended print edn following Jan. 2010 earthquake; recommenced daily edn in April; independent; Chief Editor FRANTZ DUVAL; Publr MAX CHAUVET; circ. 10,000.

PERIODICALS

Ayiti Fanm: Centre National et International de Documentation, d'Information et de Défense des Droits des Femmes en Haiti, 16 rue de La Ligue Féminine (ci devant: 1ère Ave du Travail), Port-au-Prince; tel. 2241-1842; fax 2241-1842; internet www.ayitifanm.org; e-mail ayitifanm@enfofanm.net; f. 1991; monthly; publ. by ENFOFANM; Creole; Founder and Editor-in-Chief CLORINDE ZÉPHIR; Dir MYRIAM MERLET.

Bon Nouvèl: 103 rue Pavée, étage Imprimerie La Phalange, BP 1594, Port-au-Prince; tel. 2223-9186; fax 2222-8105; e-mail bonnouvel@rehred-haiti.net; f. 1967; offices destroyed in the Jan. 2010 earthquake; monthly; Creole; Dir JEAN HOET; circ. 10,000.

Bulletin de Liaison: Centre Pedro-Arrupe, BP 1710, Port-au-Prince; tel. and fax 2245-3132; e-mail gillesbeaucheminsj@hotmail.com; internet liaison.lemoyne.edu; f. 1996; 4 a year; Editors ANDRÉ CHARBONNEAU, GILLES BEAUCHEMIN, DONALD MALDARI.

Haïti en Marche: 74 bis, rue Capois, Port-au-Prince; tel. 2245-2030; e-mail haiti-en-marche@direcway.com; internet www.haitienmarche.com; f. 1987; weekly; Editor MARCUS GARCIA.

Haïti Observateur: 98 ave John Brown, Port-au-Prince; tel. 2228-0782; e-mail contact@haiti-observateur.net; internet www.haiti-observateur.net; f. 1971; weekly; Editor LÉO JOSEPH; circ. 75,000.

Haïti Progrès: 1 Impasse Lavaud, no 22, Port-au-Prince; tel. 2244-3264; fax 2222-7022; e-mail editor@haiti-progres.com; internet www.haiti-progres.com; f. 1983; weekly; French, English and Creole; Dir KIM IVES.

Liaison: Centre Pedro-Arrupe, CP 1710, 6110 Port-au-Prince; tel. 2245-3132; fax 2245-3629; e-mail gillesbeaucheminsj@hotmail.com; internet liaison.lemoyne.edu; French; available in Creole as *Aksyon*; Editors ANDRÉ CHARBONNEAU, DONALD MALDARI, GILLES BEAUCHEMIN.

Le Matin: 3 rue Goulard, Pétionville, Port-au-Prince; tel. 2256-4461; e-mail djoseth@lematinhaiti.com; internet www.lematinhaiti.com; f. 1907; French; suspended daily publication following Jan. 2010 earthquake; publ. every other week from Jan. 2010; independent; Editor JACQUES DESROSIERS; Publr REGINALD BOULOS; circ. 5,000.

Le Messager du Nord-Ouest: Port-de-Paix; weekly.

Le Moniteur: rue du Centre, BP 1746 bis, Port-au-Prince; tel. 2222-1744; fax 2223-1026; e-mail info@pressesnationales-dhaiti.com; internet www.pressesnationales-dhaiti.com; f. 1845; 2 a week; French; official state gazette; circ. 2,000.

Optique: 99 rue Lamartinière, Bois Verna; tel. 2245-7766; monthly; arts.

Le Septentrion: Cap-Haïtien; weekly; independent; Editor NELSON BELL; circ. 2,000.

Superstar Détente: 3 ruelle Chériez, Port-au-Prince; tel. 2245-3450; fax 2222-6329; cultural magazine; Dir CLAUDEL VICTOR.

NEWS AGENCIES

Agence Haïtienne de Presse (AHP): 6 rue Fernand, Port-au-Prince; tel. 2245-7222; fax 2245-5836; e-mail ahp@hotmail.com; internet www.ahphaiti.org; f. 1989; publishes daily news bulletins in French and English; continued to publish following Jan. 2010 earthquake; Dir-Gen. GEORGES VENEL REMARAIS.

AlterPresse: 38 Delmas 8, BP 19211, Port-au-Prince; tel. 2249-9493; e-mail alterpresse@medialternatif.org; internet www.alterpresse.org; f. 2001; independent; owned by Alternative Media Group; still publishing online following Jan. 2010 earthquake; Dir GOTSON PIERRE.

Haiti Press Network: 14 rue Lamarre, Pétionville, Port-au-Prince; tel. 2511-6555; fax 2256-6197; e-mail hpnhaiti@yahoo.fr; internet www.hpnhaiti.com; still online following Jan. 2010 earthquake; Dir CLARENS RENOIS.

Publishers

Many addresses in Port-au-Prince and surrounding areas were destroyed in the earthquake of January 2010.

Editions des Antilles: route de l'Aéroport, Port-au-Prince.

Editions Caraïbes, SA: 57 rue Pavée, BP 2013, Port-au-Prince; tel. 2222-0032; e-mail piereli@yahoo.fr; Man. PIERRE J. ELIE.

Editions du Soleil: rue du Centre, BP 2471, Port-au-Prince; tel. 2222-3147; education.

L'Imprimeur Deux: Le Nouvelliste, 198 rue du Centre, Port-au-Prince.

Maison Henri Deschamps—Les Entreprises Deschamps Frisch, SA: 25 rue Dr Martelly Seïde, BP 164, Port-au-Prince; tel. 2223-2215; fax 2223-4976; e-mail entdeschamps@gdfhaiti.com; f. 1898; education and literature; Man. Dir JACQUES DESCHAMPS, Jr; CEO HENRI R. DESCHAMPS.

Natal Imprimerie: rue Barbancourt, Port-au-Prince; Dir ROBERT MALVAL.

Théodore Imprimerie: rue Dantes Destouches, Port-au-Prince.

Broadcasting and Communications

Many addresses in Port-au-Prince and surrounding areas were destroyed in the earthquake of January 2010.

TELECOMMUNICATIONS

Regulatory Body

Conseil National des Télécommunications (CONATEL): 16 ave Marie Jeanne, Cité de l'Exposition, BP 2002, Port-au-Prince; tel. 2222-0300; fax 2223-9229; e-mail info@conatel.gouv.ht; internet www.conatel.gouv.ht; f. 1969; govt communications licensing authority; Dir-Gen. MONTAIGNE MARCELIN.

Major Operators

Digicel Haiti: angle ave John Paul II et Impasse Duverger, BP 15516, Port-au-Prince; tel. 3711-3444; e-mail customercarehaiti@digicelgroup.com; internet www.digicelhaiti.com; f. 2005; owned by Digicel (Ireland); mobile telephone network provider; bldg badly damaged by Jan. 2010 earthquake; Group Chair. DENIS O'BRIEN.

Haiti Telecommunications International, SA (HaiTel): 17 rue Darguin, 3ème étage, Pétionville, Port-au-Prince; tel. 3510-1201; fax 3510-6273; internet www.haitelonline.com; f. 1999; part-owned by US-based MCI WorldCom; mobile telecommunications provider; Pres. FRANCK CINÉ.

Télécommunications d'Haïti (Téléco): blvd Jean-Jacques Dessalines, BP 814, Port-au-Prince; tel. 2245-2200; fax 223-0002; e-mail info@haititeleco.com; 60% owned by Viettel (Viet Nam), 40% govt-owned; landline provider.

Voilà: Port-au-Prince; internet www.voila.ht; f. 1998 as Communication Céllulaire d'Haïti (ComCEL); fmrly owned by US-based Western Wireless, bought by Trilogy (USA) in 2005; mobile telecommunications provider; CEO JOHN STANTON.

BROADCASTING

Following the earthquake in January 2010, many radio and television stations were unable to broadcast, or to broadcast only at a low capacity. According to the Association of Haitian Journalists, of the approximately 50 radio stations in Port-au-Prince, only around 12 were back on the air by February. Most television stations were still unable to broadcast, although Télé Métropole and Télé Caraïbe were broadcasting via foreign stations.

Radio

La Brise FM 105.3: Camp Perrin, Les Cayes, Sud; internet www.labrisefm.com; music station.

Radio Antilles International: 175 rue du Centre, BP 2335, Port-au-Prince; tel. 2223-0696; fax 2222-0260; f. 1984; independent; Dir-Gen. JACQUES SAMPEUR.

Radio Canal du Christ: 175 rue du Centre, Port-au-Prince; tel. 2223-9917; fax 2222-0260; e-mail canalchrist93.5@mcm.net; f. 1998; Dir JACQUES SAMPEUR.

Radio Caraïbes: 19 rue Chavannes, Port-au-Prince; tel. 2223-0644; e-mail radiocaraibesfm@yahoo.fr; internet www.caraibesfm.com; f. 1949; independent; Dir PATRICK MOUSSIGNAC.

Radio Galaxie: 17 rue Pavée, Port-au-Prince; tel. 2223-9942; e-mail galaxie@radiogalaxiehaiti.com; internet www.radiogalaxiehaiti.com; f. 1990; independent; Dir YVES JEAN-BART.

Radio Ginen: 9 bis, Delmas 31, Port-au-Prince; tel. 2249-1738; e-mail jeffrey.borges@radioteleginenhaiti.com; internet www.radyoginen.com; f. 1994; Dir LUCIEN BORGES.

Radio Ibo: Port-au-Prince; internet radioibo.ht; broadcasting from Dir's private residence following Jan. 2010 earthquake; Dir HEROLD JEAN FRANÇOIS.

Radio Kadans FM: 3 rue Neptune, Delmas 65, Port-au-Prince; tel. 2249-4040; fax 2245-2672; f. 1991; Dir LIONEL BENJAMIN.

Radio Kiskeya: 42 rue Villemenay, Port-au-Prince; tel. 2244-6605; e-mail admin@radiokiskeya.com; internet radiokiskeya.com; f. 1994; Dirs LILIANE PIERRE-PAUL, MARVEL DANDIN.

Radio Lumière: Côte-Plage 16, Carrefour, BP 1050, Port-au-Prince; tel. 2234-0330; fax 2234-3708; e-mail rlumiere@starband.net; internet www.radiolumiere.org; f. 1959; Protestant; independent; Dir VARNEL JEUNE.

Radio Megastar: 106 rue de la Réunion, Port-au-Prince; tel. 2222-4714; fax 2222-6636; f. 1991; Dir JEAN-ELIE CHARLES.

Radio Mélodie: 74 bis, rue Capois, Port-au-Prince; tel. 2221-8567; fax 2221-1323; e-mail melodiefm@hotmail.com; f. 1998; Dir MARCUS GARCIA.

Radio Metropole: 18 Delmas 52, BP 62, Port-au-Prince; tel. 2246-2626; fax 2249-2020; e-mail informations@naskita.com; internet www.metropolehaiti.com; f. 1970; independent; resumed normal programming from 1 Feb. 2010 following Jan. earthquake; Pres. HERBERT WIDMAIER; Dir-Gen. RICHARD WIDMAIER.

Radio Nirvana FM: Cap-Haïtien; tel. 2431-5784; e-mail pdg@radionirvanafm.com; internet www.radionirvanafm.com; Owner RAPHAEL ABRAHAM.

Radio Port-au-Prince Plus: Stade Sylvio Cator, BP 863, Port-au-Prince; tel. 3927-3182; e-mail contactus@radioportauprinceplus.com; internet www.radioportauprinceplus.com; f. 1979; independent; broadcasts in Creole and English; religious programming; Dir-Gen. MAX PRINCE.

Radio Sonic Plus: rue Duplan 42, Saint-Marc; tel. 2279-4943; e-mail sonicplus@peoplepc.com; internet radiosonicplus.com; Dir-Gen. WILSON PAUL.

Radio Superstar: Delmas 68, angle rues Safran et C. Henri, Pétionville, Port-au-Prince; tel. 2257-3444; fax 2257-3015; e-mail info@radiosuperstarhaiti.com; internet www.superstarhaiti.com; f. 1987; independent; Dir ALBERT CHANCY, Jr.

Radio Télé Venus: 106 rue 5 et 6 E, Cap-Haïtien; tel. 2262-2742; fax 3780-8053; internet www.radiotelevenushaiti.com.

Radio Tropic FM: 6 ave John Brown, 3°, Lalue, Port-au-Prince; tel. 2223-6565; e-mail tropicradio@yahoo.fr; internet www.radiotropichaiti.com; f. 1991; independent; Dir GUY JEAN.

Radio Vision 2000: 184 ave John Brown, Port-au-Prince; tel. 2245-4914; e-mail info@radiovision2000.com; internet www.radiovision2000haiti.net; f. 1991; Dir LÉOPOLD BERLANGER.

Sans Souci FM: 25–26 blvd Carénage, Cap-Haïtien; tel. 2262-5430; e-mail sanssoucifm@radiosanssouci.com; internet www.radiosanssouci.com; f. 1998; Dir IVES-MARIE CHANEL.

Signal FM: 127 rue Louverture, Pétionville, BP 391, Port-au-Prince; tel. 2256-4395; fax 2256-4396; e-mail amisignal@yahoo.com; internet www.signalfmhaiti.com; f. 1991; independent; Dir-Gen. ANNE MARIE ISSA.

Television

Galaxy 2: 6 rue Henri Christophe, Jacmel; tel. 2288-2324; f. 1989; independent; Dir MILOT BERQUIN.

PVS Antenne 16: 137 rue Mgr Guilloux, Port-au-Prince; tel. and fax 2222-1277; f. 1988; independent; Dir-Gen. RAYNALD DELERME.

Société Haïtienne de Télévision par Satellites, SA (Télé Haïti): blvd Harry S Truman, BP 1126, Port-au-Prince; tel. 2222-3887; fax 2222-9140; e-mail telehaiti@telehaiti.net; f. 1959; independent; pay-cable station with 38 channels; broadcasts in French, Spanish and English; Dir MARIE CHRISTINE MOURRAL BLANC.

Télé Caraïbe: Port-au-Prince; broadcasts continued following earthquake of Jan. 2010.

Télé Eclair: 526 route de Delmas, Port-au-Prince; tel. 2256-4505; fax 2256-3828; f. 1996; independent; Dir PATRICK ANDRÉ JOSEPH.

Télé Express Continentale: rue de l'Eglise, Jacmel; tel. 2288-2246; fax 2288-2191; f. 1985; independent; Dirs JEAN-FRANÇOIS VERDIER, JACQUES JEAN-PIERRE.

Télé Metropole: 18 Delmas 52, BP 62, Port-au-Prince; tel. 2246-2626; fax 2249-2020; e-mail informations@naskita.com; internet www.metropolehaiti.com; f. 1970; independent; broadcasts continued following Jan. 2010 earthquake; Pres. HERBERT WIDMAIER; Dir-Gen. RICHARD WIDMAIER.

Télé Smart: Hinche; tel. 2277-0347; f. 1998; independent; Dir MOZART SIMON.

Télémax: 3 Delmas 19, Port-au-Prince; tel. 246-2002; fax 2246-1155; f. 1994; independent; Dir ROBERT DENIS.

Télévision Nationale d'Haïti: Delmas 33, BP 13400, Port-au-Prince; tel. 2246-2325; fax 2246-0693; e-mail info@tnh.ht; internet www.tnh.ht; f. 1979; merged with Radio Radio Nationale d'Haïti in 1987; govt-owned; cultural; 4 channels in Creole, French and Spanish; administered by 4-mem. board; Dir PRADEL HENRIQUEZ.

Trans-America: ruelle Roger, Gonaïves; tel. 2274-0113; f. 1990; independent; Dir-Gen. HÉBERT PELISSIER.

TV Magik: 16 rue Conty, Jacmel; tel. 2288-2456; f. 1992; independent; Dirs LOUIS ANTONIN BLAISE, RICHARD CYPRIEN.

TVA: rue Liberté, Gonaïves; independent; cable station with 3 channels; Dir-Gen. GÉRARD LUC JEAN-BAPTISTE.

Finance

(cap. = capital; m. = million; res = reserves; dep. = deposits; brs = branches; amounts in gourdes)

Many addresses in Port-au-Prince and surrounding areas were destroyed in the earthquake of January 2010.

BANKING

Central Bank

Banque de la République d'Haïti: angle rues du Pavée et du Quai, BP 1570, Port-au-Prince; tel. 2299-1200; fax 2299-1045; e-mail brh@brh.net; internet www.brh.net; f. 1911 as Banque Nationale de la République d'Haïti; name changed as above in 1979; bank of issue; administered by 5-mem. board; cap. 50m., res 1,474.9m., dep. 24,705.9m. (Sept. 2006); Gov. CHARLES CASTEL; Dir-Gen. MARC HÉBERT IGNACE.

Commercial Banks

Banque Industrielle et Commerciale d'Haïti: 158 rue Dr Aubry, Port-au-Prince; tel. 2299-6800; fax 2299-6804; f. 1974.

Banque Nationale de Crédit: angle rues du Quai et des Miracles, BP 1320, Port-au-Prince; tel. 2299-4081; fax 2299-4076; internet www.bnconline.com; f. 1979; cap. 25m., dep. 729.9m. (Sept. 1989); Pres. GUITEAU TOUSSAINT; Dir-Gen. JOSEPH EDY DUBUISSON.

Banque Populaire Haïtienne: angle rues des Miracles et du Centre, Port-au-Prince; tel. 2299-6080; fax 2299-6076; e-mail bphinfo@brh.net; f. 1973; state-owned; cap. and res 72.9m., dep. 819m. (31 Mar. 2007); Dir-Gen. ANDRE DAUPHIN; Pres. RODNÉE DESCHINEAUX; 3 brs.

Banque de Promotion Commerciale et Industrielle, SA (PROMOBANK): angle aves John Brown et Rue Lamarre, BP 2323, Port-au-Prince; tel. 2299-8000; fax 2299-8125; e-mail info@promointer.net; internet www.gbgroup.net/pages/promobank; f. 1974 as B.N.P. Haïti; name changed as above in 1994; cap. 60.4m., res 16.4m., dep. 1,183.4m. (Dec. 1998); Pres. and Chair. GILBERT BIGIO; Gen. Man. RUDOLPH BERROUET.

Banque de l'Union Haïtienne: angle rues du Quai et Bonne Foi, BP 275, Port-au-Prince; tel. 2299-8500; fax 2299-8517; e-mail buh@buhsa.com; f. 1973; cap. 30.1m., res 6.2m. (Sept. 1997), dep. 1,964.3m. (Sept. 2004); Pres. RICHARD SASSINE; 12 brs.

Capital Bank: 38 rue Flaubert, BP 2464, Port-au-Prince; tel. 2299-6700; fax 2299-6519; e-mail capitalbank@brh.net; internet www.capitalbankhaiti.com; f. 1985; fmrly Banque de Crédit Immobilier, SA; Pres. BERNARD ROY; Gen. Man. LILIANE C. DOMINIQUE.

Sogebank, SA (Société Générale Haïtienne de Banque, SA): route de Delmas, BP 1315, Port-au-Prince; tel. 2229-5000; fax 2229-5022; internet www.sogebank.com; f. 1986; dep. 16,371.4m. (Dec. 2005); Pres. RALPH PERRY; 35 brs.

Sogebel (Société Générale Haïtienne de Banque d'Espargne et de Logement): route de l'Aéroport, BP 2409, Delmas; tel. 2229-5000; fax 2229-5352; internet www.sogebank.com/groupe/sogebel.html; f. 1988; cap. 15.1m., dep. 249.9m.; Gen. Man. CLAUDE PIERRE-LOUIS; 2 brs.

Unibank: 157 rue Flaubert, Pétionville, BP 46, Port-au-Prince; tel. 2299-2057; fax 2299-2070; e-mail info@unibankhaiti.com; internet www.unibankhaiti.com; f. 1993; cap. 100m., res 17.5m., dep. 3,366m. (Sept. 1999); Pres. F. CARL BRAUN; Dir-Gen. FRANCK HELMCKE; 20 brs.

Development Bank

Banque Haïtienne de Développement: 20 ave Lamartiniére, Port-au-Prince; tel. 2245-4422; fax 2244-3737; f. 1998; Pres. RANDOLPH VOYARD; Dir-Gen. YVES LEREBOURS.

INSURANCE

National Companies

Compagnie d'Assurances d'Haïti, SA (CAH): étage Dynamic Entreprise, route de l'Aéroport, BP 1489, Port-au-Prince; tel. 2250-0700; fax 2250-0236; e-mail info@groupedynamic.com; internet www.groupedynamic.com/cah.php; f. 1978; subsidiary of Groupe Dynamic SA; Group Chair. and CEO PHILIPPE R. ARMAND.

Excelsior Assurance, SA: rue 6, no 24, Port-au-Prince; tel. 2245-8881; fax 2245-8598; Dir-Gen. EMMANUEL SANON.

Générale d'Assurance, SA: Champ de Mars, Port-au-Prince; tel. 2222-5465; fax 2222-6502; f. 1985; Dir-Gen. ROLAND ACRA.

Haïti Sécurité Assurance, SA: 352 Ave John Brown, BP 1754, Port-au-Prince; tel. 2244-8534; fax 2244-8521; e-mail phipps@haiti-securite.com; f. 1985; Dir-Gen. WILLIAM PHIPPS.

International Assurance, SA (INASSA): angle rues des Miracles et Pétion, Port-au-Prince; tel. 2222-1058; Dir-Gen. RAOUL MÉROVÉ-PIERRE.

MAVSA Multi Assurances, SA: étage Dynamic Entreprise, route de l'Aéroport, BP 1489, Port-au-Prince; tel. 2250-0700; fax 2250-0236; e-mail info@groupedynamic.com; internet www.groupedynamic.com/mavsa.php; f. 1992; subsidiary of Groupe Dynamic SA; credit life insurance and pension plans; Group Chair. and CEO PHILIPPE R. ARMAND.

National d'Assurance, SA (NASSA): 25 rue Ferdinand Canapé-Vert, Port-au-Prince, HT6115; tel. 2245-9800; fax 2245-9701; e-mail nassa@nassagroup.com; f. 1989; specializing in property, medical and life insurance; Pres. FRITZ DUPUY.

Office National d'Assurance Vieillesse (ONA): Champ de Mars, rue Piquant, Port-au-Prince (bldg destroyed in Jan. 2010 earthquake); tel. 2223-9034; Dir-Gen. JEAN RONALD JOSEPH.

Société de Commercialisation d'Assurance, SA (SOCOMAS): étage Complexe STELO, 56 route de Delmas, BP 636, Port-au-Prince; tel. 2246-4768; fax 2246-4874; Dir-Gen. JEAN DIDIER GARDÈRE.

Foreign Companies

Les Assurances Léger, SA (ALSA) (France): 40 rue Lamarre, BP 2120, Port-au-Prince; tel. 2222-3451; fax 2223-8634; e-mail alsa@alsagroup.com; f. 1994; Pres. GÉRARD N. LÉGER.

Cabinet d'Assurances Fritz de Catalogne (USA): angle rues du Peuple et des Miracles, BP 1644, Port-au-Prince; tel. 2222-6695; fax 2223-0827; Dir FRITZ DE CATALOGNE.

Groupement Français d'Assurances (France): Port-au-Prince; Agent ALBERT A. DUFORT.

National Western Life Insurance (USA): 13 rue Pie XII, Cité de l'Exposition, Port-au-Prince; tel. 2223-0734; e-mail intlmktg@globalnw.com; internet www.nationalwesternlife.com; Chair. and CEO ROBERT L. MOODY; Agent VORBE BARRAU DUPUY.

Sagicor Capital Life Insurance Company Ltd (Bahamas): angle rues du Peuple et des Miracles, BP 1644, Port-au-Prince; tel. 2222-6695; fax 2223-0827; e-mail capital@compa.net; internet www.sagicor.com; Agent FRITZ DE CATALOGNE.

Insurance Association

Association des Assureurs d'Haïti: 153 rue des Miracles, POB 1754, Port-au-Prince; tel. 2223-0796; fax 2223-8634; Dir Fritz de Catalogne.

Trade and Industry

Many addresses in Port-au-Prince and surrounding areas were destroyed in the earthquake of January 2010.

GOVERNMENT AGENCY

Conseil de Modernisation des Entreprises Publiques (CMEP): Palais National, Port-au-Prince; tel. 2222-4111; fax 2222-7761; f. 1996; oversees modernization and privatization of state enterprises.

DEVELOPMENT ORGANIZATIONS

Fonds de Développement Industriel (FDI): 12 angle rue Butte et impasse Chabrier, BP 2597, Port-au-Prince; tel. 2244-9728; fax 2244-9727; e-mail fdi@fdihaiti.com; internet www.fdihaiti.com; f. 1981; Dir-Gen. Roosevelt Saint-Dic.

Société Financière Haïtienne de Développement, SA (SOFIHDES): 11 blvd Harry S Truman, BP 1399, Port-au-Prince; tel. 2250-1427; fax 2250-1436; e-mail info@sofihdes.com; f. 1983; industrial and agro-industrial project-financing, accounting, data-processing, management consultancy; Chair. Pierre Marie Boisson.

CHAMBERS OF COMMERCE

Chambre de Commerce et d'Industrie Française en Haïti (CCIFH): 5 rue Goulard, Pétionville, 6140 Port-au-Prince; tel. and fax 2510-8965; e-mail haiti@ccife.org; internet www.ccife.org/haiti; f. 1987; Pres. Grégory Brandt; Vice-Pres. Patrick Attie; 109 mems.

Chambre de Commerce et d'Industrie d'Haïti (CCIH): blvd Harry S Truman, Cité de l'Exposition, BP 982, Port-au-Prince; tel. 2222-8661; fax 2222-2081; e-mail mjeanclaude@ccih.ht; f. 1895; Exec. Dir Martine Jean-Claude.

Chambre de Commerce et d'Industrie Haïtiano-Américaine (HAMCHAM): 6 rue Oge, Pétionville, POP 13486, Port-au-Prince; tel. 2511-3024; e-mail hamcham@globelsud.net; f. 1979; Exec. Dir Chantal Salomon-Jean.

Chambre de Commerce et d'Industrie des Professions du Nord et du Nord-Est (CCIPNE): 43a–b rue 17, BP 244, Cap-Haïtien; tel. 2262-2360; fax 2262-2895; Vice-Pres. Marcel Samson.

INDUSTRIAL AND TRADE ORGANIZATIONS

Association des Exportateurs de Café (ASDEC): rue Barbancourt, BP 1334, Port-au-Prince; tel. 2249-2160; e-mail asdec@primexsa.com; Pres. Hubert Duport.

Association des Industries d'Haïti (ADIH): 199 route de Delmas, entre Delmas 31 et 33, étage Galerie 128, BP 2568, Port-au-Prince; tel. 2246-4509; fax 2246-2211; e-mail adih@acn2.net; f. 1980; Pres. Maryse Kedar-Penette.

Association Nationale des Distributeurs de Produits Pétroliers (ANADIPP): Centre Commercial Dubois, route de Delmas, Bureau 401, Port-au-Prince; tel. 2246-1414; fax 2245-0698; e-mail moylafortune@hotmail.com; f. 1979; Pres. Maurice Lafortune.

Association Nationale des Exporteurs de Mangues (ANEM): group of 10 mango exporters; Vice-Pres. Cassandra Reimers.

Association Nationale des Importateurs et Distributeurs de Produits Pharmaceutiques (ANIDPP): blvd Harry S Truman, Port-au-Prince; tel. 2222-0268; fax 2222-7887; e-mail anidpp@direcway.com; Pres. Ralph Edmond.

Association des Producteurs Agricoles (APA): BP 1318, Port-au-Prince; tel. 2246-1848; fax 2246-0356; f. 1985; Pres. Reynold Bonnefil.

MAJOR COMPANIES

Acra Industries: Autoroute De Delmas, Port-au-Prince; mfrs of metal construction sheeting, paper and plastic bags and plastic plumbing pipes; also importers of sugar and rice; operates 4 factories; bldgs destroyed by Jan. 2010 earthquake, but aimed to recommence manufactures in late 2010; Dir Marc-Antoine Acra.

AGA Corporation: 26 angle rue Jean-Gilles et Blvd Toussaint Louverture, Port-au-Prince; tel. 2246-2772; fax 2246-1417; e-mail clifford@agacorp.com; f. 1952; mfrs of textiles; subsidiaries incl. GMC Global Manufacturers & Contractors, SA, and Premium Apparel, SA; Pres. André Apaid; 7,500 employees.

Brasserie Nationale d'Haïti, SA (BRANA): ave Hailé Sélassié, BP 1334, Port-au-Prince; tel. 2250-1501; fax 2250-1300; e-mail brana@branahaiti.com; f. 1973; brewery and soft-drinks bottler; Pres. and CEO Michael Madsen; 900 employees.

Carifresh, SA: Santo 17, Croix-Des-Bouquets, Port-au-Prince; fruit packers and exporters; resumed business in May 2010 following Jan. earthquake; Pres. Wilhelm Reimers.

Cimenterie Nationale, SEM (CINA): Km 25, route Nationale 1, Fond Mombin, Port-au-Prince; tel. 2298-3234; e-mail csantamaria@cinahaiti.com; controlled since 1999 by Cementos Argos (Colombia); packagers of imported cement; Pres. Carlos Esteban Santa Maria; 200 employees.

Etablissement Raymond Flambert, SA: 430 route de Delmas, BP 896, Port-au-Prince; tel. 2246-2605; fax 2246-4908; e-mail erf@erfhaiti.com; internet www.erfhaiti.com; mfrs of building materials; Pres. Alex Flambert; 245 employees.

Groupe Dynamic, SA: étage Dynamic Enterprise, route de l'Aéroport, BP 1489, Port-au-Prince; tel. 2250-0700; fax 2250-0236; e-mail info@groupedynamic.com; internet www.groupedynamic.com; holding co with 12 subsidiaries across the financial, insurance, medical, tourism, transportation and building sectors; Chair. and CEO Philippe R. Armand.

Laboratoires 4C: Delmas 71, BP 44, Port-au-Prince; tel. 2246-2207; fax 2246-5332; e-mail cchti@dnetwork.net; f. 1952; mfrs of pharmaceuticals and paper products; Pres. and Gen. Man. Maurice Acre; 450 employees.

Mima, SA: POB 462, Port-au-Prince; tel. 2222-6388; fax 2222-4030; e-mail info@mima-sa.com; internet www.mima-sa.com; f. 1993; industrial chemical and lubricant mfr and raw materials supplier; Gen. Man. Raphael Boulos.

Les Moulins d'Haïti, SEM: 1 route Nationale, Laffiteau, BP 15509, Pétionville (bldg destroyed in Jan. 2010 earthquake); tel. 2298-3616; fax 2244-8050; e-mail ddaines@lmh-ht.com; fmrly La Minoterie d'Haïti; privatized 1999; now a semi-public co; 70% owned by two US agribusiness cos, 30% state-owned; flour milling; Pres. Christian Fucina.

Pharval Pharmaceuticals: 13 rue Simmonds, Cité Militaire, Port-au-Prince; tel. 2221-3573; fax 2221-3575; mfrs of pharmaceutical products; Dir-Gen. Rudolph Boulos.

SAFICO (SA Filature et Corderia d'Haïti): Diquini 63, Port-au-Prince; tel. 2234-0523; e-mail micama45@yahoo.com; f. 1952; sisal processor, mattress and foam mfr; also produces lighting products; sales US $3m. (2009); Dir-Gen. Thomas Adamson; 150 employees.

Société du Rhum Barbancourt: Port-au-Prince; internet www.barbancourt.net; f. 1862; rum distillery; premises destroyed by Jan. 2010 earthquake, but production recommenced mid-2010; Dir-Gen. Thierry Gardère; 250 employees.

UTILITIES

Electricity

Electricité d'Haïti (Ed'H): rue Dante Destouches, Port-au-Prince; tel. 2222-4600; state energy utility company; recommenced energy production (10 MW) in Feb. 2010 following Jan. earthquake; Gen. Man. Serge Raphael.

Péligre Hydroelectric Plant: Artibonite Valley.

Saut-Mathurine Hydroelectric Plant: Les Cayes.

Water

Service Nationale d'Eau Potable (SNEP): 48 Delmas, Port-au-Prince; tel. 2246-3044; fax 2246-0881; e-mail snep_eau_potable@hotmail.com; Dir-Gen. Pétion Roy.

TRADE UNIONS

Association des Journalistes Haïtiens (AJH): f. 1954; Sec.-Gen. Jacques Desrosiers.

Batay Ouvriye (Workers' Struggle): Delmas, BP 13326, Port-au-Prince; tel. 2222-6719; e-mail batay@batayouvriye.org; internet www.batayouvriye.org; f. 2002; independent umbrella org. providing a framework for various autonomous trade unions and workers' asscns.

Centrale Autonome des Travailleurs Haïtiens (CATH): 37 route Delmas, Port-au-Prince; tel. 3401-5820; e-mail fignole2000@yahoo.fr; f. 1980; Sec.-Gen. Fignole Saint-Cyr.

Confédération Nationale des Educateurs d'Haïti (CNEH): impasse Noë 17, ave Magloire Ambroise, BP 482, Port-au-Prince; tel. 2224-4482; fax 2245-9536; e-mail lana14@caramail.com; f. 1986; Sec.-Gen. Jean Lavaud Frédéric.

Confédération Ouvriers Travailleurs Haïtiens (KOTA): 155 rue des Césars, Port-au-Prince.

Confédération des Travailleurs Haïtiens (CTH): f. 1989; Sec.-Gen. Paul Chéry.

Fédération Haïtienne de Syndicats Chrétiens (FHSC): BP 416, Port-au-Prince; Pres. LÉONVIL LEBLANC.

Fédération des Ouvriers Syndiques (FOS): angle rues Dr Aubry et des Miracles 115, BP 785, Port-au-Prince; tel. 2222-0035; f. 1984; Pres. PIERRE CHARLES JOSEPH.

Organisation Générale Indépendante des Travailleurs et Travailleuses d'Haïti (OGITH): 2–3 étage, 121 angle route Delmas et Delmas 3, BP 1212, Port-au-Prince; tel. 2249-0575; e-mail pnumas@yahoo.fr; f. 1988; Gen. Sec. PATRICK NUMAS.

Syndicat des Employés de l'EDH (SEEH): c/o EDH, rue Joseph Janvier, Port-au-Prince; tel. 2222-3367.

Union Nationale des Ouvriers d'Haïti (UNOH): Delmas 11, 121 bis, Cité de l'Exposition, BP 3337, Port-au-Prince; f. 1951; Pres. MARCEL VINCENT; Sec.-Gen. FRITZNER ST VIL; 3,000 mems from 8 affiliated unions.

A number of unions are non-affiliated and without a national centre, including those organized on a company basis.

Transport

RAILWAYS

The railway service closed in the early 1990s.

ROADS

In 1999, according to International Road Federation estimates, there were 4,160 km (2,585 miles) of roads, of which 24.3% was paved. There are all-weather roads from Port-au-Prince to Cap-Haïtien, on the northern coast, and to Les Cayes, in the south.

SHIPPING

Many European and American shipping lines call at Haiti. The two principal ports are Port-au-Prince and Cap-Haïtien. There are also 12 minor ports.

Autorité Portuaire Nationale: blvd La Saline, BP 616, Port-au-Prince; tel. 2223-2440; fax 2221-3479; e-mail apnpap@hotmail.com; internet www.apn.gouv.ht; f. 1978; Dir-Gen. JEAN EVENS CHARLES.

CIVIL AVIATION

The international airport, situated 8 km (5 miles) outside Port-au-Prince, is the country's principal airport, and is served by many international airlines linking Haiti with the USA and other Caribbean islands. Although the airport was badly damaged by the earthquake of January 2010, it reopened to commercial flights in the following month. There is an airport at Cap-Haïtien, and smaller airfields at Jacmel, Jérémie, Les Cayes and Port-de-Paix.

Office National de l'Aviation Civile (OFNAC): Aéroport International Mais Gate, BP 1346, Port-au-Prince; tel. 2246-0052; fax 2246-0998; e-mail lpierre@ofnac.org; Dir-Gen. JEAN-LEMERQUE PIERRE.

Caribintair: Aéroport International, Port-au-Prince; tel. 2246-0778; scheduled domestic service and charter flights to Santo Domingo (Dominican Republic) and other Caribbean destinations.

Haiti Air Freight, SA: Aéroport International, BP 170, Port-au-Prince; tel. 2246-2572; fax 2246-0848; cargo carrier operating scheduled and charter services from Port-au-Prince and Cap-Haïtien to Miami (USA) and Puerto Rico.

Haiti International Airlines: Delmas 65, rue Zamor 2, Port-au-Prince; tel. 3434-7201; f. 1996; scheduled passenger and cargo services from Port-au Prince to Miami and New York (USA); Pres. and Chair. KHAN RAHMAN.

Tourism

Tourism was formerly Haiti's second largest source of foreign exchange. However, as a result of political instability, the number of cruise ships visiting Haiti declined considerably. In 2007 tourist arrivals totalled 386,060. Receipts from tourism in that year totalled US $140m.

Association Haïtienne des Agences de Voyages (ASHAV): 17 rue des Miracles, Port-au-Prince; tel. 2222-8855; fax 2222-2054; f. 1988; Pres. PIERRE CHAUVET, Fils.

Association Touristique d'Haïti: rue Lamarre, BP 2562, Port-au-Prince; tel. 2257-4647; fax 2257-4134; Vice-Pres. RICHARD BUTEAU; Dir ELIZABETH SILVERA DUCASSE.

Defence

In November 1994, following the return to civilian rule, measures providing for the separation of the armed forces from the police force were approved by the legislature. In 1995 the armed forces were effectively dissolved, although officially they remained in existence pending an amendment to the Constitution providing for their abolition; such an amendment was, however, never presented to the legislature. As assessed at November 2009, the national police force numbered an estimated 2,000. There was also a coastguard of 30. In June 2004, following the resignation of President Aristide, a UN security force—the UN Stabilization Mission in Haiti (MINUSTAH)—assumed peace-keeping responsibilities in the country. Following the presidential and legislative elections of 2006, MINUSTAH remained in the country. In October 2009 its mandate was extended for a further 12 months. Following the earthquake of January 2010, MINUSTAH's authorized capacity was increased, standing at a maximum of 8,940 military personnel and 4,391 police officers in June 2010. At that time MINUSTAH comprised 8,609 troops, 2,969 civilian police, 1,708 international and local civilian staff, and 208 UN Volunteers. The security budget for 2003 was an estimated US $23m.

Director-General of the Police Nationale: MARIO ANDRESOL.

Education

Education is provided by the state, by the Roman Catholic Church and by other religious organizations, but many schools charge for tuition, books or uniforms. Teaching is based on the French model, and French is the language of instruction. Primary education, which normally begins at six years of age and lasts for six years, is officially compulsory. Secondary education usually begins at 12 years of age and lasts for a further six years, comprising two cycles of three years each. In 1997 primary enrolment included only 19% of children in the relevant age-group, while enrolment at secondary schools was equivalent to only 34% of children in the relevant age-group. In 1999 combined enrolment in primary, secondary and tertiary education was 52%. Higher education is provided by 18 technical and vocational centres, 42 domestic science schools, and by the Université d'Etat d'Haïti, which has faculties of law and economics, medicine and pharmacy, dentistry, science, agronomy and veterinary medicine, applied linguistics, human sciences and ethnology. More than 1,300 educational institutions were destroyed in the January 2010 earthquake.

Bibliography

For works on the Caribbean generally, see Select Bibliography (Books)

Avril, P. *Haiti (1995–2000): The Black Book on Insecurity*. Boca Raton, FL, Universal Publrs, 2004.

Brown, G. S. *Toussaint's Clause: The Founding Fathers and the Haitian Revolution*. Jackson, MS, University Press of Mississippi, 2005.

Buss, T. F. *Haiti in the Balance: Why Foreign Aid Has Failed and What We Can Do About It*. Washington, DC, Brookings Institution, 2008.

Catanese, A. *Haitians: Migration and Diaspora*. Boulder, CO, Westview Press, 1999.

Chin, P., Flounders, S., and Dunkel, G. (Eds). *Haiti: A Slave Revolution—200 Years After 1804*. New York, International Action Center, 2004.

Chomsky, N., Farmer, P., and Goodman, A. *Getting Haiti Right This Time: The US and the Coup*. Monroe, ME, Common Courage Press, 2004.

Cousens, E. M., et al. (Eds). *Peacebuilding as Politics*. Boulder, CO, Lynne Rienner Publrs, 2001.

Dash, J. M. *Culture and Customs of Haiti*. London, Greenwood Press, 2001.

Diederich, B., and Burt, A. *Papa Doc: Haiti and Its Dictator*. Princeton, NJ, Markus Wiener Publications, 1998.

Dubois, L. *Avengers of the New World: The Story of the Haitian Revolution*. Cambridge, MA, Belknap Press, 2004.

Fatton, Jr, R. *Haiti's Predatory Republic: The Unending Transition to Democracy*. Boulder, CO, Lynne Rienner Publrs, 2002.

The Roots of Haitian Despotism. Boulder, CO, Lynne Rienner Publrs, 2007.

Ferguson, J. *Papa Doc, Baby Doc*. Oxford, Blackwell Publrs, 1998.

Fischer, S. *Modernity Disavowed: Haiti and the Cultures of Slavery in the Age of Revolution*. Durham, NC, Duke University Press, 2004.

Geggus, D. P. (Ed.). *The Impact of the Haitian Revolution in the Atlantic World*. Columbia, SC, University of South Carolina Press, 2001.

Haitian Revolutionary Studies. Bloomington, IN, Indiana University Press, 2002.

Gibbons, E. D. *Sanctions in Haiti: Human Rights and Democracy under Assault*. New York, Praeger Publrs, 1999.

Girard, P. *Paradise Lost: Haiti's Tumultuous Journey from Pearl of the Caribbean to Third World Hotspot*. Basingstoke, Palgrave Macmillan, 2010.

Gray, O. *Economic Implications of CARICOM for Haiti*. Lewiston, NY, Edwin Mellen Press, 2003.

Hallward, P. *Damming the Flood: Haiti, Aristide and the Politics of Containment*. London and New York, Verso Books, 2008.

Kovats-Bernat, J. C. *Sleeping Rough in Port-au-Prince: An Ethnography of Street Children and Violence in Haiti*. Gainesville, FL, University Press of Florida, 2006.

Kumar, C. *Building Peace in Haiti*. Boulder, CO, Lynne Reinner Publrs, 1998.

Diasporic Citizenship: Haitian Americans in Transnational America. Basingstoke, Palgrave Macmillan, 1998.

Matthewson, T. *A Proslavery Foreign Policy: Haitian-American Relations During the Early Republic*. Westport, CT, Praeger Publrs, 2003.

Pamphile, L. D. *Haitians and African Americans: A Heritage of Tragedy and Hope*. Gainesville, FL, University Press of Florida, 2002.

Renda, M. *Taking Haiti: Military Occupation and the Culture of US Imperialism, 1915–1940*. Chapel Hill, NC, University of North Carolina Press, 2001.

Rhodes, L. *Democracy and the Role of the Haitian Media*. Lewiston, NY, Edwin Mellen Press, 2001.

Robinson, R. *An Unbroken Agony: Haiti, from Revolution to the Kidnapping of a President*. New York, Basic Civitas Books, 2007.

San Miguel, P. L. *The Imagined Island: History, Identity, and Utopia in Hispaniola*. Chapel Hill, NC, University of North Carolina Press, 2005.

Smith, M. J. *Red and Black in Haiti: Radicalism, Conflict and Political Change, 1934–1957*. Chapel Hill, NC, University of North Carolina Press, 2009.

Suárez, L. M. *The Tears of Hispaniola: Haitian and Dominican Diaspora Memory*. Gainesville, FL, University Press of Florida, 2006.

Von Hippel, K. *Democracy by Force*. Cambridge, Cambridge University Press, 1999.

White, A. *Encountering Revolution: Haiti and the Making of the Early Republic*. Baltimore, MD, John Hopkins University Press, 2010.

World Bank Country Study. *Social Resilience and State Fragility in Haiti*. Washington, DC, World Bank Publications, 2007.

Zacair, P. *Haiti and the Haitian Diaspora in the Wider Caribbean*. Gainesville, FL, University Press of Florida, 2010.

HONDURAS

Geography

PHYSICAL FEATURES

The Republic of Honduras is a Central American country, which sits on a north-facing Caribbean coast and, on its east side, tapers southwards to a short Pacific coast, on the Gulf of Fonseca. Its territory includes a number of offshore islands and cays in the Caribbean, but also in the Gulf of Fonseca. El Salvador, which lies in the south-west of the country, occupying the Pacific coast west of the Gulf of Fonseca, has claims on the island of Conejo in the Gulf. Competing maritime claims in the Gulf have been referred to a tripartite commission with Nicaragua. The exact demarcation of the Honduras–El Salvador border (342 km or 212 miles) was the subject of a decision by the International Court of Justice (ICJ) in 1992, although this was not ratified by both countries until 2006. Guatemala lies beyond a 256-km border in the west and north-west. Belize also lies to the north-west, but beyond the Gulf of Honduras (its Sapodilla Cays are claimed by Honduras). The longest border, across the widest part of the country, running south-westwards from the Caribbean (Atlantic) to the Pacific coasts, is the 922-km frontier with Nicaragua, which lies to the south-east. The maritime boundary between the two countries has been the subject of dispute since Nicaragua filed claims with the ICJ in 1999. The demarcation of the maritime boundary with the Cayman Islands, a British dependency in the Caribbean, has not yet been settled. Honduras, which is slightly larger than Guatemala, is the second largest country in Central America (after Nicaragua), covering an area of 112,492 sq km (43,433 sq miles), including about 200 sq km of inland waters.

Honduras is dominated by its central highlands, widest and highest in the west, towering above the narrow Pacific coastal plains and above the broader northern lowlands and plains on the Caribbean. About three-quarters of the country is mountainous, largely consisting of extinct volcanoes and their outflows (the whole country is prone to usually mild earthquakes), while the shores along the southern Gulf of Fonseca amount to only 124 km and the Caribbean coast extends for 644 km. The northern lowlands include out-thrust ranges from the Continental Divide and river valleys, notably those of the Ulua and the Aguan, running down to the coastal plains. The North Coast region is agricultural and well populated. Other important rivers include the Guayape and the Patuca, the latter dominating the second northern topographical region, the flat, hot and humid Mosquito Coast (the name a corruption of the local Miskito people), densely clad in rainforest and sparsely inhabited. This region, in the far north-east of the country, includes extensive wetlands, especially around the Caratasca lagoon. Honduras encompasses only the northern part of the Mosquito Coast (Mosquitia—the rest is Nicaragua's eastern shore), which begins at Cabo Gracias a Dios, named in gratitude by the Genoese (Italian) navigator exploring for the Spanish monarchy, Christopher Columbus, when he rounded it and escaped the 'deep waters' (in Spanish) that gave Honduras its name. The central highlands, crowded in the west and dominating the south, consist of two main ranges, the Central American Cordillera and the Volcanic Highlands. The highest point in Honduras is in the west, at Celaque, the loftiest peak of which is Cerro de las Minas (2,870 m or 9,419 ft). The far south, beneath the heights where the national capital, Tegucigalpa, sprawls, is the fertile strip of coastal plain (only about 24 km in width) along the Gulf of Fonseca. Offshore are a number of islands belonging to Honduras, including the disputed Conejo and volcanic cones of Tigre and Zacate Grande, for instance. Strewn over a wider area are the Caribbean islands and cays of Honduras, notably the Bay Islands (Islas de la Bahía—mostly jungle-clad volcanic cones), just off the North Coast, and, further out, the Swan Islands. This vast territory includes a varied natural environment, little of it free from risk, be it mining damage to part of the country's extensive river system or to Lake Yojoa, an important source of fresh water, or the encroachments of urban expansion and agriculture. Deforestation throughout Honduras is a problem, with the accompanying hazards of soil erosion, etc., but just over one-half of the country is still wooded, more than anywhere else in Central America. The surviving forests host a huge variety of plant, bird and animal life, such as butterflies, jaguars, and white-faced, spider and howler monkeys. The insular environments are often more unusual, with the Bay Islands, for instance, noted for features such as its reef system (the most diverse in the Caribbean after Jamaica), the yellow-naped parrot or the spiny-tailed iguana found only on Utila.

CLIMATE

The climate is tropical in the lowlands and temperate in the mountainous interior. Both climatic zones have a wet season, which is in April–October. In the north of Honduras, on the North Coast and in the hill country between there and the highest uplands, average annual rainfall varies from 1,780 mm (70 ins) to about 2,550 mm, while along the Pacific coastal plains the range is around 1,550 mm–2,050 mm. The Caribbean coasts are very susceptible to hurricanes and flooding. The average minimum and maximum temperatures in Tegucigalpa range from 4°C–27°C (39°F–81°F) in February to 12°C–33°C (54°F–91°F) in May.

POPULATION

The people of Honduras, who refer to themselves as 'Catrachos', are mainly (90%) Mestizo (Ladino), with 7% Amerindian, 2% black and 1% white. Most Ladinos are of predominantly Spanish descent, and Spanish is the official and overwhelmingly the most widely spoken language. Some English is spoken on the North Coast and in the Bay Islands, by blacks and Anglo-Antilleans descended from those arriving in the country from elsewhere in the Caribbean about one century ago. Two centuries ago the main black population had arrived in this part of Central America, when the British deported the Black Caribs (mixed descendants of Amerindians and escaped slaves of African origin) from St Vincent (now part of Saint Vincent and the Grenadines); they speak Garifuna (Carib), originally an Amerindian tongue. Generally, however, such racial identities are preserved in cultural vestiges rather than language; the six dominant Amerindian language groups native to the region are Lenca, Jicaque or Tol, Paya, Chortí, Miskito, and Sumo. Another legacy of the dominant Spanish influence in Honduras is that in 2010 some 82% of the population still adhered to the Roman Catholic Church, although about 10% were Protestant.

Most of the 7.6m. (official estimate at mid-2010) population lives in central and western upland valleys, and on the North Coast. There are considerably fewer people in the north-east and in the south. The people of Honduras are poor—there are very pronounced levels of income inequality—and only two-fifths are urbanized. Moreover, since the civil conflicts in neighbouring countries during the 1970s and 1980s, some 50,000 legal refugees, as well as many illegal migrants, have moved into Honduras. These are split between Salvadorean Mestizos in the west and Sumo and Miskito Amerindians in the north-east. The capital of Honduras is Tegucigalpa, in the centre-south of the country, in the highlands. The second city, in the north-west, is San Pedro Sula, which controls the important Ulea valley. La Ceiba, actually on the North Coast, was famous as the headquarters of the Standard Fruit Co, the US banana company that once dominated the country, whereas the Copán valley, in the far west, was the centre for the even earlier rule of the Mayas. Choluteca is the focus for southern Honduras, the Pacific coast. There are 18 departments.

History

HELEN SCHOOLEY

Revised for this edition by SANDY MARKWICK

The history of Honduras has been strongly influenced by a series of geographical factors. The country has enjoyed relatively few natural resources in proportion to the size of its population, is prone to natural disasters, and at the turn of the 21st century was reckoned to be one of the poorest states in Latin America. It has suffered from endemic political instability, and despite many attempts at regional integration, Honduras has often come into conflict with its Central American neighbours. Its principal economic activity has helped to earn it the epithet 'banana republic', and the cultivation of bananas also provided the basis for another major theme of the country's history in the 20th century, the dominant influence of the USA in the nation's internal politics and regional stance. Major developments in the country's history have often been precipitated as much from events outside its borders as from internal politics.

Before the Spanish conquest Honduras lay on the southern edge of the Mayan civilization, which was already struggling with internal disturbances. Socio-economic pressures caused by famine, disease and soil erosion contributed to political divisions. After the Spanish adventurer Hernán Cortés had established power in Mexico City, he turned his attention south and arrived in Honduras in 1525, enticed by greatly exaggerated rumours of mineral wealth there. The significant deposits of silver were largely exhausted by the 18th century, and the economic mainstay subsequently became subsistence farming. In 1549 Honduras became a province of the Kingdom of Guatemala, which was in turn part of the Viceroyalty of New Spain (Mexico). The existing rivalries between the provinces were fostered by Spain to help it retain its imperial power.

INDEPENDENCE

In 1822 the newly independent Mexico annexed Central America into its short-lived empire. The following year the provinces seceded and formed the Central American Federation. In 1827 internal conflict between the two main political factions, the Liberals, who supported the Federation, and the Conservatives, who opposed it, escalated into civil war. The Liberal Honduran leader, Francisco Morazán, emerged as the President, but in 1838 a peasant revolt in Guatemala, led by the conservative Rafael Guerrera, brought the Federation to an end, and Honduras became an independent state.

The new country had internal divisions of its own, retaining the Liberal–Conservative divide, which continued to dominate political life throughout the 19th and 20th centuries. The Conservatives held power for most of the first four decades of independence, and the first national capital was the city of Comayagua. The Liberals returned to government in 1876 under Marco Aurelio Soto, and remained there for 56 years, consolidating their dominance by relocating the capital to Tegucigalpa. Despite the existence of the political tendencies (not yet fully formalized into parties), government was relatively weak, and was subject to considerable influence from other countries. Soto was both installed and removed in 1881 with the active participation of Guatemala, and in 1907 Nicaraguan forces helped to replace President Policarpo Bonilla with Miguel Dávila. The most powerful foreign influence, however, was that of the USA. In the late 19th and early 20th centuries vast tracts of land were granted to US companies, in particular the United Fruit Company (UFCO), on very advantageous terms, often in exchange for political support. By 1913 UFCO controlled two-thirds of Honduras's banana exports. A political crisis arose in 1911–12, in which President Dávila was overthrown and replaced by Manuel Bonilla in what was essentially a struggle between UFCO and another US banana enterprise.

DICTATORSHIP AND MILITARY RULE, 1932–80

The US Great Depression had a severe impact on the Honduran economy with its dependence on exports to the USA, and, as in Guatemala and El Salvador, contributed to the rise of dictatorship in the 1930s. Gen. Tiburcio Carías Andino, leader of the conservative Partido Nacional (PN), was elected President in 1932, and proceeded to hold office for 16 years without further election. He was persuaded to resign in 1948, and was succeeded by Dr Juan Manuel Gálvez of the PN, the sole candidate. After inconclusive elections in 1954, Vice-President Julio Lozano Díaz dissolved the Congreso Nacional (Congress), abrogated the Constitution and declared himself head of state. Lozano was in turn overthrown in a bloodless coup two years later. After constituent elections in which the Partido Liberal (PL) achieved a substantial majority, the PL leader, Dr José Ramón Villeda Morales, took office in 1957. His moderate social reforms aroused opposition from the traditional ruling class, and he was overthrown in 1963 in a military coup led by Gen. Oswaldo López Arellano. A new Constitution was approved in June 1965 and López Arellano was installed as President.

Elections were held again in 1971, and were won by the PN candidate, Dr Ramón Ernesto Cruz Uclés. This brief return to civilian rule followed a humiliating defeat for the Honduran military in the war against El Salvador in 1969. Triggered by events after two football (soccer) World Cup qualifying matches, it became known as the 'Football War', although it had its roots in long-standing economic grievances between the two countries. Full-scale hostilities lasted less than two weeks, but a final peace agreement was not signed until 1980.

Gen. López Arellano returned to power in a coup in 1972, but in 1975 was overthrown by Col (later Gen.) Juan Melgar Castro. Only a few weeks before the coup López Arellano had been named in a bribery scandal involving United Brands Company (as UFCO had become in 1970), to which the company later admitted. Melgar Castro's attempts to introduce a comprehensive land reform programme provoked opposition from landed interests and he was removed from power in 1978, in a coup led by Gen. Policarpo Paz García.

RETURN TO CIVILIAN GOVERNMENT

During the 1980s Honduras became an important player in US policy in Central America. Ironically, the return to civilian government marked a sharp increase in actual military power, because the armed forces had greater, if not always overt, US support and were consequently better equipped than they had been previously. Under US encouragement, constituent elections were held in 1980, resulting in a surprise victory for the Liberals. PL leader Roberto Suazo Córdova was elected President in 1981 and a new Constitution was promulgated in January 1982; an amendment transferred the post of Commander-in-Chief from the President to the head of the armed forces (then Gen. Gustavo Adolfo Alvarez Martínez). Gen. Alvarez was widely regarded as the most powerful man in the country and, under his command, the army carried out a 'dirty war' against 'subversives'; the attendant allegations of human rights abuses would continue for the next two decades. (In 1993 a human rights commission attributed responsibility for 184 'disappearances' to special units directly answerable to Gen. Alvarez and his successors.) Gen. Alvarez was removed from power in 1984 by a group of junior officers disenchanted with his authoritarian policies, and he was assassinated in 1989.

The presidential election of November 1985 was won by José Simeón Azcona del Hoyo of the PL, under a new system that awarded victory to the leading candidate of the party with the greatest number of votes. (As each party fielded more than one candidate, the winner might not be the most popular individual candidate.) Azcona took office in January 1986, the first time for 55 years in which one freely elected president had succeeded another. The voting procedure was simplified for the 1989 elections, and the presidential ballot was won by Rafael Callejas Romero of the PN (who had polled the highest individual number of votes in 1985).

HUMAN RIGHTS AND SOCIAL ISSUES

Lacking a majority in the Congreso Nacional, the Callejas administration also encountered opposition on many fronts. The armed forces, resenting attempts to prosecute some of its members for human rights abuses, continued to demonstrate that their influence outweighed the country's political and judicial institutions, and made unsuccessful coup attempts in 1991 and 1993. Meanwhile, the Government's economic structural adjustment programme raised vociferous protests not only from trade unions and peasant groups, but also from private business and the Roman Catholic Church. The Church was concerned principally with the matter of land distribution, and denounced the amassing of large estates by foreign companies, a development justified by the Government on the grounds of agricultural modernization. In addition, several indigenous Amerindian groups protested over the Government's failure to fulfil land rights agreements and to improve living and working conditions. A series of accords providing for the return of some 7,000 ha of land to the indigenous communities, along with many infrastructure projects on their land, was reached in 1994, but conflicted with vested interests.

Human rights was a prominent issue in the elections of November 1993, with the two main parties accusing each other of complicity in past abuses. The campaign also exposed the regular practice of purchasing favourable press coverage. The PL retained its majority and its candidate, Carlos Roberto Reina Idiáquez, was elected President. Reina, a former President of the Inter-American Court of Human Rights (part of the Organization of American States—OAS), set out to reform the judicial system, curb the power of the army and combat political corruption. Under Reina the post of Commander-in-Chief was returned to the civilian authority (the defence minister), the Military High Council was abolished and a new national police force was created outside direct military control. Despite these measures, the armed forces generally managed to evade the judicial process, and in 1998 the independent Comité para la Defensa de Derechos Humanos en Honduras (CODEH—Committee for the Defence of Human Rights in Honduras) claimed that paramilitary 'death squad' activity had doubled since 1995.

In the 1997 elections the PL retained power and Carlos Roberto Flores Facussé became President. In 1999 he appointed Edgardo Dumas as the country's first civilian defence minister. Dumas opened an audit of the military pension fund, which had wide-ranging interests through the economy and allegedly operated an extensive network of corruption. The armed forces' economic penetration was so thorough that it constituted one of the principal business interests in the country. In November 2001 an investigation reported that five former Commanders-in-Chief had diverted some US $8m. in government revenues between 1986 and 1997. The appointment of Dumas angered the military command, and in July 1999 President Flores removed four senior officers and redeployed 33 others in an effort to reassert political supremacy over the armed forces. Tension between the civilian and military authorities increased with the announcement in August that a series of graves had been discovered at a former US-built military base at El Aguacate. The camp had been used for training right-wing Nicaraguan counter-revolutionary guerrillas ('Contras') and allegedly for the detention and torture of suspected left-wing activists. The graves were estimated to contain about one-half of the 184 'disappeared'.

Protests over the land rights issue intensified, and were increasingly accompanied by demands from environmental groups. From 1996 regular demonstrations were staged in Tegucigalpa calling for a full investigation into the murders of more than 40 indigenous leaders, who had come into conflict with cattle ranchers, logging interests, energy companies and tourism developers. In March 2000 four leaders of the Chortí people were shot dead by security guards of a landowner in the west of the country, and in September the Chortí held a protest in Copán over the minimal implementation of the 1994 accords.

The country also faced a range of socio-economic problems, and was ranked as one of the poorest in Central America. In 2001 a survey indicated that 79% of the population lived in poverty, and 56% were classified as destitute (according to the UN's Economic Commission for Latin America and the Caribbean), with contingent poor standards of housing and health; there were several outbreaks of cholera in the 1990s. The infant mortality rate was high, and, of surviving children, 43% had no access to school education, with many living precariously. Street children were at risk of summary brutality and execution, with more than 1,500 killed during 1998–2002, mostly by police and security forces. Many street children became involved in child prostitution, allied with a rise in 'sex tourism', and also in criminal gangs and drugs-related crime. The country had a rising rate of violent crime; by 2001 the city of San Pedro Sula had the highest murder rate, with 95 per 100,000 head of population, and the incidence of kidnapping increased sharply in 2001 and 2002, particularly targeted at the business community. The seriously overcrowded prisons often experienced violent riots by inmates, and some 90% of those in detention had not been convicted. The number of Hondurans suffering from AIDS rose from some 2,500 in 1993 to over 14,000 in 1999, with more than 70% of cases occurring in the 19–35 age group.

The country's socio-economic problems were compounded by frequent natural disasters, of which one of the most severe was Hurricane Mitch; in October 1998. There was major damage to infrastructure and the environment, as well as to health and job prospects, prompting an increase in illegal immigration to Mexico and the USA. Furthermore, the arrival of international aid focused attention on the country's inadequate provision of housing and services and on the high level of corruption.

THE GOVERNMENT OF RICARDO MADURO JOEST

The general election held on 25 November 2001 resulted in a surprise victory for the PN. That party's candidate, Ricardo Maduro Joest, was elected President and the party won the largest number of seats in the Congreso Nacional for the first time since the restoration of civilian rule in 1980. A number of smaller parties, previously considered politically irrelevant, also made significant gains. In June 2002 the Partido Demócrata Cristiano de Honduras (PDCH), which had won three seats in the elections, joined the government coalition to give the Maduro administration a majority in the legislature.

Maduro, a prominent businessman and former Governor of the Central Bank, undertook to pursue the reforms advocated by the IMF, including the acceleration of the privatization programme. A number of fiscal reforms were subsequently introduced in 2002 and 2003, including the extension of sales tax to a wider range of basic goods and an increase in income tax. President Maduro was also committed to reducing spending on public sector wages, a policy that led to strikes among teachers and health workers in early 2005.

In March 2003 the Government announced the formation of a special commission to establish responsibility for the murder of street children, and in August increased sentences for crimes by gang members were introduced. There had been a marked rise in violent gang warfare since 1997, when the USA had begun to deport Hondurans convicted of offences; by 2002 the number of such deportees had reached 4,680. The most prominent gang was *Mara 18*, which had grown out of the civil wars of the 1980s and which operated throughout Central America and within the USA. The Honduran police force lacked training and resources and, at only 7,000 strong, proved unequal to combat the rising crime level. The police force was also adjusting to a new penal code, passed in 2002, which introduced the concept of 'innocent until proven guilty'; however, many officers were still unfamiliar with new procedures. Since November 2000 army units had been deployed to help them patrol the streets, a measure that alarmed many human rights groups. Many people died in gun battles between gang members and the police, and there were also numerous reports of innocent bystanders being arrested and killed. The authorities alleged that most of the street children killed by security forces (with 549 such fatalities in 2002 alone) were connected with gangs, but the human rights group Casa Alianza claimed many had been shot indiscriminately. Criminal activity included extortion, with armed robberies in the streets and the levying of an illegal 'tax' to enter areas of the capital, as well as illegal drugs-trafficking. In order to counter the growing links between narcotics and political corruption, President Maduro announced restrictions on parliamentary immunity. There were renewed prison riots, and in April 2003, in a disturbance at La Ceiba prison, 69 inmates were shot dead (61 of whom were members of *Mara 18*) by security forces, some apparently after they had surrendered. Despite the Government's focus on crime, there was a continuing public perception that violence was on the increase.

THE GOVERNMENT OF JOSÉ MANUEL ZELAYA ROSALES

Elections to the presidency and the Congreso Nacional took place on 27 November 2005. The PL candidate, José Manuel (Mel) Zelaya Rosales, the former head of a social investment fund, narrowly defeated PN nominee Porfirio Lobo Sosa, hitherto President of the Congreso Nacional: Zelaya won 49.9% of the votes cast, compared with 46.2% obtained by Lobo. Constitutional rules had prevented Maduro from standing for a successive term of office. Nonetheless, it was widely believed that corruption scandals during Maduro's administration damaged the chances of the PN candidate. The result was also seen as a rejection of Lobo's draconian crime reduction proposals. The PL campaign focused on government accountability, addressing unemployment, improving rates of enrolment in schools and increasing popular participation in public life. However, there was broad consensus between the two leading candidates on continuing the economic programme agreed with the IMF within the Poverty Reduction and Growth Facility (PRGF). President Zelaya took office in January 2006.

The new administration was weakened by its position in the Congreso Nacional. In the November 2005 legislative election the PL won 62 of the 128 seats, while the PN secured 55 seats; the remainder were allocated to the Partido de Unificación Democrática, the PDCH and the Partido Innovación y Unidad—Social Demócrata. Having failed to garner a congressional majority, the Government would have to rely on the support of other parties to pass legislative initiatives. Negotiating the selection of the President of the Congreso Nacional was an early illustration of the political difficulties encountered by the Government. A compromise was reached after opposition parties were awarded control of 26 of the 56 committees responsible for important policy areas.

President Zelaya occupied centre-left territory within the PL, which, in addition to a populist style, raised doubts about the new Government's commitment to fiscal prudence. On taking office, Zelaya promised to create jobs, eliminate corruption and improve domestic security. The Government planned to recruit an additional 4,000 police officers over a four-year period, many of whom would be transferred from the army, which itself would enlist a similar number of new members. However, combating crime required fundamental reform of the justice system to eradicate corruption among public officials, including the police, and Zelaya did not demonstrate sufficient political strength to suggest such state reform was likely. Furthermore, the extra policing had minimal effect on crime levels, which remained a primary concern. Zelaya also announced a package of social measures to increase employment and opportunities for young people in an attempt to promote internal security by reducing gang membership.

The Government pursued campaign pledges to increase teachers' pay and fuel subsidies. In June 2006 the Minister of Finance, Hugo Noé Pino, resigned in protest at presidential interference in spending policy, which he felt undermined the Government's ability to meet fiscal targets. Economic growth and debt relief took some pressure off Zelaya in his bid to fulfil sometimes contradictory commitments to the IMF, on the one hand, and to reduce poverty and create jobs on the other. Zelaya oversaw the successful fulfilment of fiscal targets set out in the PRGF, agreed by the former Government, up to its conclusion in February 2007. A new bridging agreement was signed with the IMF in April 2008 committing the Government to reducing the fiscal deficit and shifting the emphasis of public spending towards longer-term investment. With presidential and parliamentary elections due in November 2009, the Government faced a challenge in overcoming its weak position in the Congreso Nacional while at the same time fulfilling its IMF commitments.

CONSTITUTIONAL CRISIS

On 28 June 2009 the army seized President Zelaya and forced him into exile in Costa Rica. The ousting of Zelaya was the culmination of opposition from the Congreso Nacional, including factions within the ruling PL, and the Supreme Court to the President's plans for a non-binding referendum, due to be held later that day, that would have sought public approval to hold a further referendum for the purpose of reforming the Constitution. Zelaya's opponents accused him of attempting to change the rules to allow him to remain in power after the end of his four-year term in January 2010, a charge that Zelaya denied. On the same day the Congreso installed the speaker of the legislature, Roberto Micheletti Baín, as acting President. Micheletti was himself a member of the PL and a prospective candidate for the forthcoming presidential election, scheduled for 29 November 2009. Violence broke out in early July 2009 when President Zelaya attempted to fly to Tegucigalpa to retake power. The army refused to allow his aircraft to land and opened fire on a crowd of his supporters, killing at least two. The removal of President Zelaya differed from many previous coups in the country's history inasmuch as the army had no stated intention of assuming control of government. Nevertheless, the episode illustrated the fragile nature of Honduras's democratic institutions.

Strong international diplomatic efforts were launched in the immediate aftermath of the coup in an attempt to restore Zelaya to office. Despite Zelaya's strained relationship with the USA (see below), US President Barack Obama led demands from political leaders throughout the Americas for Zelaya's reinstatement. The USA, along with the OAS, the UN and the European Union (EU), refused to recognize Micheletti's de facto Government. The OAS suspended Honduras from the Organization, the first time that it had suspended a member state since Cuba in 1962.

In September 2009 Zelaya returned to Honduras unnoticed by the authorities and immediately sought refuge in the Brazilian embassy. The embassy became a focal point for Zelaya's supporters, but the immediate area around the building was swiftly brought under the control of the police force and army. While diplomatic attempts to resolve the crisis were under way, a microcosm of the constitutional crisis was played out in the form of a stand-off between Zelaya and his opponents. Talks between the two sides, brokered by the USA, led to the Tegucigalpa-San José Accord, under the terms of which both factions agreed to the establishment of a 'Government of Unity and National Reconciliation', which was to remain in force until the winner of the forthcoming presidential election took office. While important differences regarding interpretation of the Accord ensured a continuation of the dispute between the respective supporters of Zelaya and Micheletti, the agreement was a significant step towards Honduras restoring foreign diplomatic relations that had been broken since the June coup.

Presidential and legislative elections went ahead on 29 November 2009 as scheduled. Lobo was again the candidate of the PN. This time he was victorious, garnering 56% of the votes cast to defeat the PL candidate, Elvin Santos, who secured 36% of the ballot. Upon his inauguration on 27 January 2010, Lobo pledged to lead a government of national unity. Among his first acts as President was the signing of an amnesty for Zelaya and the military, and escorting the deposed former President from the Brazilian embassy into exile in the Dominican Republic. Lobo's cabinet included members from the main opposition parties and, as of mid-2010, the new Government was pursuing more fiscally conservative policies than its predecessor. Moreover, Lobo's Government was strengthened by a PN majority in the Congreso Nacional, controlling 71 out of the 128 seats, and by the restoration of multilateral credit. A difficult challenge that Lobo's Government would have to confront was to manage, without reopening social and political divisions, the findings of the Comisión de la Verdad (Truth Commission) tasked with investigating the coup that had deposed Zelaya.

INTERNATIONAL RELATIONS

Honduras was drawn into the Central American conflicts of the 1980s when right-wing Nicaraguan Contras, with US support, began using its territory as a base for military operations and sabotage missions against Sandinista-ruled Nicaragua. The legacy of the conflict was a powerful and arguably over-manned and over-equipped armed forces, which needed to redefine a role in the 1990s, while also facing a drastic cut in US military aid. In addition, the virtual demise of the few and relatively small guerrilla groups formed in the 1980s eliminated an obvious internal threat. Another long-term consequence of the conflict was the presence of some 30,000 landmines along the border with Nicaragua, mostly planted by the Contras. A clearance programme launched in 1995 was disrupted by Hurricane Mitch in 1998, which also caused the large-scale displacement of many of these devices.

The advent of peace in Central America, and the electoral defeat of the Sandinistas in April 1990, led to substantially improved relations between the Central American states, although the traditional sources of conflict resurfaced thereafter. Once again domestic troubles and the economic burdens imposed by natural disasters plagued renewed attempts at regional integration. One notable attempt was the formation of the Central American Integration System in 1991, which helped to foster a rapid expansion of the Central American Common Market (CACM).

The 1980 peace agreement with El Salvador (see above) had left territorial issues unresolved, both along the border and in the Gulf of Fonseca, causing intermittent tension. In 1986 the territorial dispute was referred to the International Court of Justice (ICJ) in The Hague, Netherlands, which, in 1992, awarded about two-thirds of the disputed territories to Honduras. In 1998 the two countries undertook to complete the border demarcation, but relations remained uneasy, and in August 2001 Honduras expelled two Salvadorean diplomats, alleging that they had been involved in naval espionage. In October 2006 the Congreso Nacional voted to stop bilateral talks with El Salvador over a joint project to construct a hydroelectric dam on their mutual border. The vote came after renewed tensions over the uninhabited island of Conejo, which did not form part of the 1992 ICJ ruling.

In November 1999 the Government provoked a new dispute with Nicaragua when it asked the Congreso Nacional to ratify an agreement, signed with Colombia in 1986, delineating maritime boundaries. The Nicaraguan Government protested that this threatened its national maritime claims, and both countries posted troops on their joint border and introduced high tariffs on each other's goods. The border area was demilitarized in February 2000 and, following OAS mediation, the two nations agreed to establish a maritime exclusion zone in the disputed area. After a year of relative calm, relations deteriorated in February 2001 when the Nicaraguan Government accused Honduras of violating the agreement reached the previous year by holding military exercises in the border region. The tension was defused by OAS-mediated talks held in June, but in August Nicaragua again protested, on this occasion accusing Honduras of planning an attack on its territory. In September 2002 the Honduran Government protested over the sale by the Nicaraguan authorities of oil-drilling rights in the disputed region. In March 2003, however, the Nicaraguan legislature voted to suspend import taxes on Honduran goods, imposed in 1999. The dispute appeared definitively resolved following an ICJ ruling in 2007, which delineated the maritime border and awarded sovereignty of four small islands to Honduras.

Honduras was one of 12 Latin American countries, and one of just 23 world-wide, to maintain diplomatic relations with China (Taiwan), an important source of trade and investment, which was boosted by a bilateral free trade agreement signed in 2008. Ties with Taiwan have been a long-standing obstacle to the establishment of full diplomatic relations with the People's Republic of China. Overtures were made by the de facto Government of President Micheletti to forge greater informal diplomatic ties with the People's Republic, and the new Government of President Zelaya was expected similarly to pursue better relations, without damaging relations with Taiwan, in order to maximize the vast investment potential of the two Chinas.

During the 1980s relations with the USA had revolved chiefly around security matters. This issue dwindled in the 1990s, although human rights investigations alleged the involvement of US military advisers in the conduct of the 'dirty war'. Bilateral relations predominantly reverted to economic considerations, among which was the question of the thousands of illegal Honduran immigrants currently living in the USA. Following the devastation caused by Hurricane Mitch in 1998, Honduran immigrants to the USA were granted Temporary Protection Status. There were an estimated 320,000 Hondurans living in the USA without authorization in 2009, with an additional 500,000 legal residents of Honduran origin. Under President Zelaya, diplomatic relations with the USA were strained over the Government's warm relations with Venezuela's radical President Hugo Chávez Frías (offering the potential for cheap oil for Honduras) and by the nomination in February 2007 of a Honduran ambassador to Cuba, the first since diplomatic relations with that country were suspended in 1962. Honduras's accession in October 2008 to the Alternativa Bolivariana para los Pueblos de Nuestra América (ALBA), a Venezuelan-led regional integration project, provoked a further deterioration in relations with the USA, and also attracted considerable domestic opposition. None the less, following the ousting of Zelaya in June 2009, the USA and Venezuela were briefly united in demanding the reinstatement of the democratically elected President. However, divisions developed within the international community over the election of the Government of President Lobo. The USA was satisfied that, with the election and inauguration of the new President, democratic legitimacy had been fully restored. The USA extended the Temporary Protection Status in May 2010 until January 2012, multilateral organizations resumed credit lines with Honduras and it was expected that the OAS would reinstate Honduras after its suspension. However, the countries of ALBA—which included Bolivia, Cuba, Ecuador, Nicaragua and Venezuela—as well as the Southern Common Market (Mercosur) countries—i.e. Argentina, Brazil, Paraguay and Uruguay—were expected to be considerably more reluctant to recognize the Lobo Government.

Economy

PHILLIP WEARNE

Revised for this edition by SANDY MARKWICK

With a national income per head estimated at just US $1,818 in 2009, Honduras remained one of the poorest and least developed nations in Latin America. Over one-half of the population were considered to be living below the poverty line and the country also posted one of the highest inequality ratings in the region. Acute socio-economic problems fuelled significant levels of crime and corruption. Despite some success in efforts to diversify the country's economic base in the 1990s, Honduras remained overly dependent on primary agricultural and fisheries exports such as coffee, bananas, meat, shrimp and lobster, as well as on large quantities of external finance. Dependence on agriculture also made the economy vulnerable in the wake of frequent natural disasters.

Real average annual gross domestic product (GDP) growth in 1980–90 was 2.3%. By 1990 the economy was stagnant. Nevertheless, growth increased in 1991 and the country sustained steady rates of growth thenceforth. Although the devastation caused by Hurricane Mitch in October 1998 interrupted the economic growth trend, GDP increased, in real terms, at an average annual rate of 3.2% in 1995–2004. The economy grew by an average annual rate of 6.4% in 2006–07, the highest rates since the early 1990s. Growth was led by financial services, telecommunications, electricity and water, was fuelled by a sharp increase in credit and foreign direct investment (FDI) and built on confidence stemming from debt reduction and free trade agreements. The economy grew by 4.0% in 2008, but declined by 2.1% in 2009, owing to the decline in investment as a result of a global crisis of liquidity and political instability. The worst-performing sectors were construction, manufacturing and financial services.

However, economic growth could not keep pace with population growth in the last decade of the 20th century, causing a steady rise in unemployment. The population increased by an average annual rate of 2.7% in 1995–2004 and of 2.3% in 2006–08, and stood at an estimated 8.0m. in mid-2010. The unemployment rate in 2009 was 3.0% of the economically active population, down from 3.5% in 2006. However, many more were underemployed. Pressure on land, the increased mechanization of export agriculture, and the seasonal nature of coffee, banana, sugar and fruit production led to high levels of underemployment among the agricultural work-force, up to 60% by some estimates. The maintenance of the fixed exchange rate, at two lempiras per US dollar, and a reduction in the money supply kept the annual inflation rate below 5% between 1984 and 1988. However, massive devaluations of the lempira in 1990–91, combined with more gradual ones thereafter, took the annual inflation rate to a record 34% in 1991. By 2000 the rate had fallen to 6.0%, but progressive devaluation of the lempira increased the pressure on domestic prices, and in 2001–05 annual inflation averaged 8.4%. The annual rate of inflation declined in 2006 to 5.3%, historically a very low rate, helped by a stable exchange rate since mid-2005. However, the rate increased to 10.8% at the end of 2008, above the target range of 8%–10%, mainly as a result of high oil and food prices. Declining energy and food prices from late 2008, coupled with falling demand owing to a contraction of economic activity and lower remittances sent by Hondurans overseas, led to annual inflation of 3.0% in 2009, below the target range of 3.5%–5.5%. By May 2010 inflation had increased to 4.4%, pushed up by reduced energy subsidies, rising commodity prices and a weaker currency. The target rate for inflation in 2010 was 5.0%–7.0%.

After economic decline in the early 1980s, as a result of world recession, rising petroleum prices, falling international agricultural commodity prices and the Central American civil wars, in the mid-1980s a reduction in international oil prices and an increase in coffee revenues, combined with decreases in public sector expenditure and higher inflows of US aid, renewed creditors' confidence in the economy. However, by 1989 the position had been reversed. As imports soared and coffee prices fell drastically, the World Bank declared the country ineligible for further credits. This followed President José Simeón Azcona del Hoyo's (1986–90) unilateral suspension of all interest payments on the country's US $3,200m. foreign debt. The Government of President Rafael Leonardo Callejas Romero (1990–94) steadily recovered the situation, adhering to the economic prescriptions of the US Agency for International Development (USAID) more closely. An effective 100% devaluation of the lempira against the US dollar in March 1990 began the process.

By mid-1990 the credibility of the new Government had been rewarded with a stand-by agreement with the IMF, a second structural adjustment accord with the World Bank and a US $247m. bridging loan. In 1992 Honduras signed an Extended Structural Adjustment Facility (ESAF) loan agreement with the IMF, but deterioration in the fiscal accounts meant that the Government was soon missing targets, and the administration of President Carlos Roberto Reina Idiáquez (1994–98) was forced to repeat the initial measures of its predecessor. In February 1994 the tax base was widened, the lempira was devalued and public expenditure further decreased, in an effort to reduce a fiscal deficit that was equivalent to 10.6% of GDP.

By late 1995 the Honduran economy was recovering. The rise in the rate of inflation was slowing and the fiscal deficit was less than 4% of GDP. As a result, by early 1996 the Inter-American Development Bank (IDB) had made some US $160m. available for the modernization of the economy and the World Bank approved a further $60m. In May 1997 the IMF announced a partial agreement for the third-year disbursement of funds under its ESAF agreement.

Following Hurricane Mitch, the IMF approved a Poverty Reduction and Growth Facility (PRGF) worth US $215m. in March 1999 to aid economic reconstruction. Honduras was further supported by a three-year deferral of bilateral debt service payments to the 'Paris Club' of Western creditor countries. Subsequently, the country was formally approved for debt relief under the IMF and World Bank's initiative for heavily indebted poor countries (HIPC). Under this programme, in July 2000 the IMF and the World Bank announced a reduction in debt service payments, contingent on the Government's economic management. The IMF did not immediately renew the PRGF, which expired in December 2002, dissatisfied as it was with the Government's progress towards IMF targets, a central objective of which was a reduction of the fiscal deficit to below 3% of GDP by 2005. The deficit was reduced to 5.4% in 2003, following which, in February 2004, the IMF approved a three-year $108m. PRGF, while at the same time maintaining pressure on the Government to extend reform. In further support of these structural policies, in April the IDB approved funding totalling almost $600m. The fiscal deficit fell to 2.9% of GDP in 2004, and in April 2005 the IMF announced that Honduras had reached 'completion point' within the HIPC initiative. This entitled Honduras to immediate debt relief worth $1,200m. over 10 years. In June this decision was endorsed by the finance ministers of the Group of Eight (G8) industrialized nations, during a summit in Gleneagles, United Kingdom.

The fiscal deficit improved further, to 2.2% of GDP in 2005, supported by GDP growth, improved tax collection (14.1% more than in 2004), and higher aggregate demand, particularly consumer demand, which boosted sales tax revenues. An increase in government expenditure of 16.6% in 2005 offset the healthy revenue performance, but the deficit remained in line with PRGF targets. The deficit declined to 1.1% of GDP in 2006, driven by strong growth and reforms to improve the efficiency of tax collection, but also by the Government's failure to meet its capital investment target. The fiscal deficit increased to

2.9% of GDP in 2007, but improved in 2008, to 2.4% of GDP, as income outpaced expenditure and lower oil prices in the second half of the year resulted in reduced spending on energy and transport subsidies. The fiscal deficit widened to 6.1% of GDP in 2009. Financing from multilateral organizations was threatened by the political instability that followed the forced removal from office of President José Manuel Zelaya Rosales by the army in June of that year (see History), which was widely denounced internationally as a coup.

The World Bank, the IDB and the US Government restored credit lines to Honduras after the inauguration of President Porfirio Lobo Sosa in January 2010. The renewal of multilateral financing was of paramount importance to the Government's management of the fiscal deficit and paved the way for congressional approval, in March, of a budget that was designed to improve the fiscal position. Talks with the IMF, ongoing at mid-2010, were expected to lead to the provision of further funding to underpin fiscal adjustment.

AGRICULTURE

Agriculture remained the most important sector of the economy. In 2008 the sector (including hunting, forestry and fishing) employed 33.5% of the economically active population. Agriculture accounted for an estimated 11.5% of GDP in 2009, compared with 23% in 1997, a decline that reflected long-term trends and the lasting impact of the devastation caused by Hurricane Mitch. The sector remained underdeveloped—of a total land area of 11.2m. ha, only an estimated 1.7m. ha were utilized for arable farming, with a further 1.5m. ha under pasture. Despite the country's relatively low density of population, land shortages were a persistent problem. As a result, disturbances caused by the unofficial occupation of unused or underutilized agricultural land had become a marked feature of life in rural Honduras.

The rapid development of cash crop farming, most notably coffee and bananas, as well as relatively stable world commodity prices, allowed for an average annual growth in agricultural production of 5.8% during the 1960s. Although the rate of growth was reduced to 2.4% during the 1970s, significant gains were made in livestock farming and sugar production. Adverse weather conditions, falling commodity prices, scarce credit facilities and the onset of world recession reduced the growth rate markedly during the 1980s. In the early 1990s the sector began to recover. However, Hurricane Mitch, which affected the agricultural sector more adversely than any other, ended the revival. Coffee and banana production were particularly badly affected. Losses in the sector were estimated at US $200m. in 1998, and at a further $500m. in 1999, when it contracted by 8.5%. Some 70% of the banana crop was destroyed and coffee production fell markedly at a time when prices were already experiencing record lows. In 2000 the sector increased by an estimated 9.5%, followed by modest growth, averaging 3.0%, in 2001–03. More significant growth, of 7.2% in 2004, was followed by stagnation, largely owing to adverse weather conditions affecting harvests. Coffee, rice and banana production registered the most significant contractions in 2005, offset by growth in the production of corn, sugar and African oil palm fruit. Agricultural output rebounded in 2006, with growth of 7.6% following a recovery in prices of principal commodities, particularly coffee. The sector grew by 5.5% in 2007, but slowed to just 0.5% in 2008. Output was affected by unfavourable weather conditions in 2009 and contracted by 1.7% in that year.

In November 1983 the effective control of the banana industry by two US conglomerates, United Brands Company (formerly the United Fruit Company) and Standard Fruit Company, was broken when agreements were reached for the sale of a large proportion of the national crop to local trading companies. This, combined with a government export incentive scheme in the mid-1980s, an increase in demand following the collapse of the communist bloc in Eastern Europe in the early 1990s, and the implementation of the free market within the European Community (now the European Union) in 1992, acted as a stimulant to banana production. In 1990 the Anglo-Irish banana company Fyffes began financing new, independent banana co-operatives, in a further challenge to the monopoly of the two US companies. Nevertheless, Chiquita Brands International Inc (formerly United Brands Company) and Dole Food Company (formerly Standard Fruit Company) remained the dominant forces in the industry.

In the first half of the 1990s export earnings from bananas experienced a decline. Following a brief recovery in the middle of the decade, in 1997 earnings fell back as export volumes decreased by more than 15%. Figures for 1999 reflected the disastrous consequences of Hurricane Mitch, with the destruction of more than 70% of the total crop. Banana export earnings fell dramatically, to US $38m., compared with $220m. in the previous year. Exports subsequently recovered, but fluctuated thereafter, suffering a slight decline, to $241.9m., in 2006 (down from $260.3m. in 2005), owing to the negative effect on yields of tropical storms at the end of 2005. Exports increased to an estimated $383.3m. in 2008. Export volumes in 2008 stood at an estimated 30.3m. 40-lb boxes, up from 27.3m. in 2006.

In the mid-1980s the volume of coffee exports increased significantly under the combined stimuli of greatly improved international prices and the success of government efforts to eradicate diseases such as coffee rust. However, the improvement was negated by the consequences of the collapse of the International Coffee Agreement in 1989. The subsequent disastrous fall in prices did not begin to be reversed until 1994, when world shortages produced the highest coffee prices in a decade. Although Hurricane Mitch had less impact on the coffee sector than the banana industry, the devastation, combined with low prices, cut earnings to just US $256.1m. in 1999 compared with $429.8m. in the previous year. Earnings partially recovered in 2000, to $339.4m., before falling to just $160.7m. in 2001, as prices declined to their lowest real levels for more than a century. A slight improvement was recorded in 2002 and 2003, when coffee exports earned $182.5m. and $183.3m., respectively. Earnings increased significantly from 2004. In that year Honduras earned $251.8m. from coffee exports, which rose steadily to an estimated $620.3m. in 2008 as both volumes and prices increased. The figure declined to $531.5m. in 2009.

Poor prices and the consequent lower production caused the sugar, cotton and tobacco sectors to decrease dramatically in importance as export crops in the 1980s. By 2002 sugar exports were worth a mere US $15.6m., and they declined further, to $13.2m., in 2003. Subsequent recovery saw exports increase to $29.6m. in 2006; however, export earnings fell sharply, to $19.4m., in 2007, rising only modestly, to $20.9m., in 2008. Growth in some non-traditional agricultural sectors and substantial expansion of the seafood industry during the 1990s helped to offset the deficit in traditional exports. Exports of shellfish, principally lobster and shrimp, more than tripled in little more than a decade. Shellfish exports earned the country $134.1m. in 2008, down 14.9% compared with earnings in 2007.

The timber industry, which was nationalized in 1974 and placed under the control of the Corporación Hondureña de Desarrollo Forestal (COHDEFOR—Honduran Corporation of Forestry Development), encountered a series of problems. Like other state corporations, COHDEFOR incurred huge financial losses and its principal sawmill, the Bonito timber project in Olancho province, was eventually sold to a US citizen for only 5m. lempiras, representing a loss of 18m. lempiras. This followed devastating fires at the beginning of the 1980s, as a consequence of which the value of timber exports declined from US $44.7m. in 1982 to just $19.0m. in 1995, a level at which exports stabilized in the mid-1990s. In 2007 wood exports earned Honduras an estimated $44.5m., but by 2009 this figure had declined to $19.9m. Almost all timber exports were pine and other softwoods. An estimated 2.5m. ha of Honduras were believed to be in need of reforestation, following the loss of more than 30% of the country's forests since 1970.

MINING AND POWER

Although no comprehensive geological survey had been undertaken, Honduras was reported to have substantial reserves of tin, iron ore, coal, pitchblende and antimony, and exploitable reserves of gold. In recent years there has been an increase in interest in the sector from foreign companies, following the liberalization of the mining code. In 2007 gold, silver, zinc and lead exports earned the country an estimated US $174.5m., up from $160.3m. in 2006. However, declining commodity prices contributed to a significant reduction in earnings, to $116.2m., in 2009. Mining and quarrying accounted for only 0.7% of GDP in that year.

Activity focused on the extraction of lead, zinc, silver and gold. Gold transformed from a statistically insignificant export commodity in 1999 to the most important mineral export, earning US $79.9m. in 2006, before declining by 11.5%, to $70.7m., in 2007 and by a further 32.7%, to $47.6m., in 2008 in tandem with falling prices. Such dramatic shifts reflect the limited extent of mineral exploitation in Honduras. Zinc and lead exports increased dramatically in the mid-1990s, more than doubling export revenues in 1997, although this fell at the end of the decade and into the 2000s. Production of both zinc and lead experienced another dramatic increase from 2004, in which year combined earnings amounted to $51m. This figure increased to $84.6m. in 2007, boosted by high international prices. Combined earnings declined to $43.6m. in 2009, owing to a sharp decline in zinc prices. Silver production earnings experienced similar fluctuations. Earnings and production reached new highs in 1998, with Honduras exporting 1.5m. troy oz to earn $7.8m., but had fallen in 2000 to 976,000 troy oz, earning $4.8m. In 2008 silver exports earned $21.4m. In 2001 Entremares Honduras, SA (a subsidiary of Glamis Golds Ltd of the USA), the Canadian company Geomaque Explorations and the Argentine concern Coviasa began mining operations in Honduras, joining the Canadian-owned American Pacific, which worked the El Mochito lead, zinc and copper mines.

Honduras had no exploited oil reserves. Minerals imports, largely composed of petroleum, accounted for 19.3% of imports in 2009. In the 1970s two major hydroelectric systems, the El Cajín dam (capacity 292 MW) and the Río Lindo–Yojoa system (capacity 285 MW), were developed. By the 1990s the combination of under-investment, mismanagement and natural disasters had brought the sector into crisis. Declining levels of water in both hydroelectric systems were blamed on deforestation, caused by logging and the clearing of woodland for agriculture in order to cope with the country's growing land crisis. In 1997–98 a drought caused by the El Niño weather phenomenon reduced El Cajín's generating capacity by 50%. The floods caused by Hurricane Mitch in 1998 then wrought havoc with the power distribution network, despite raising water levels and thus increasing power generation capacity.

From 1994 successive governments attempted, with some success, to resolve the problems of the power sector. Electricity prices were increased several times, and the state-owned Empresa Nacional de Energía Eléctrica (ENEE—National Electrical Energy Company) intensified efforts to collect more than 120m. lempiras in debts. In February 1996 a new 40-MW thermal electricity plant was inaugurated. However, plans for the development of other plants were postponed, and continued under-investment in the transmission network meant that more than 20% of the power generated was lost. The damage caused by Hurricane Mitch proved a major obstacle to efforts to overhaul the distribution network to major cities. In April 1999 the Governments of Honduras and El Salvador agreed to construct a regional electricity grid using a grant of US $30m. from the IDB. The transmission cable came into operation in May 2002. In 2008 the country generated some 6,589.3 GWh of electricity, up 5.2% over the previous year. Hydroelectric plants accounted for 29.8% of the total electricity generating capacity, with thermal plants, largely in the private sector, accounting for the remainder. All electricity generation was produced for the domestic market; demand increased at an average annual rate of 7.8% in 1999–2003. By 2003 this rising demand prompted the ENEE to arrange for an additional 60 MW per day to be imported from Costa Rica in order to ease the strain on domestic supplies. In mid-2003 President Ricardo Maduro Joest commissioned a new authority to develop the country's first new hydroelectric projects since 1985. By April 2009 78% of the households had access to electricity, compared with just 45% in 1995.

MANUFACTURING

Owing to the establishment of *maquila* (offshore assembly) plants producing goods for re-export, the Honduran manufacturing sector underwent a substantial transformation in the 1980s and 1990s. According to the central bank, value-added earnings from *maquila* plants totalled an estimated US $958.1m. in 2008, and the sector employed around 118,000 people. This represented a recovery in the sector, which had been contracting from 2001. In that year some 220 *maquila* plants employed an estimated 94,000 people and accounted for $560.8m. in value-added export earnings. The rate of growth had been slowing in the 1990s, with little diversification taking place from the main industry, textile assembly, and competition from the Caribbean impacting the relative attraction of the country. The manufacturing sector's contribution to GDP remained relatively stable as the decline in traditional industries offset the growth in the offshore assembly plants. Manufacturing GDP increased at an average annual rate of 4.3% during 1995–2004. The extension of North American Free Trade Agreement (NAFTA) privileges to Honduran textiles encouraged growth in manufacturing, though the sector was highly sensitive to demand from the USA, the country's major export market. Output growth in manufacturing was consistent during 2000–08, averaging 5.2% per year during that period. The sector expanded by 14.6% in 2008 but contracted by 1.1% in 2009, in which year the sector's contribution to overall GDP totalled 17.6%.

Traditional manufacturing activity was based largely on agro-forestry products for both export and domestic consumption and included food processing, beverages, textiles, furniture making, cigarettes, sugar refining, seafood and meat processing, and paper and pulp processing. Cement, textile fabric, beer, soft drinks, wheat flour and rum were some of the major products. Despite some initial damage to plants and markets as a result of Hurricane Mitch, much of the domestic manufacturing sector benefited substantially as a result of the reconstruction programme. Cement production, for example, increased from 28.8m. 42.5-kg bags in 2002 to 38.3m. bags in 2009.

In the 1990s it was the free market and privatization policies of the Governments of Presidents Callejas and Reina that dominated prospects in the manufacturing sector. During 1991 several factories, including a cement and textile plant, were sold, following the liquidation of the Corporación Nacional de Inversiones (National Investment Corporation), the state-owned industrial development agency. Reductions in tariff protection in 1991 adversely affected industry, but, for exporters at least, the successive currency devaluations helped to increase competitiveness.

Another major stimulus was the creation of five free trade zones from 1976 onwards. The success of these led to the creation of six private free trade zones from 1987. All of the free trade zones were concentrated near the coastal cities of San Pedro Sula and Puerto Cortés. Textile and assembly companies predominated in the sector. Most companies operated under the customs provisions of the USA's Caribbean Basin Initiative (CBI), which allowed for the duty-free importation of clothes assembled from US cloth. Electronics, furniture and metal-manufacturing assembly plants all increased in number in the 1990s, albeit from a very low base, and the country of origin of the investment diversified.

For the *maquila* sector, 1999 and 2000 were the most successful years in more than a decade. With Hurricane Mitch devastating traditional agricultural exports such as bananas and coffee, export earnings of some US $545m. in 1999, then $662m. in 2000, made the *maquila* sector Honduras's most important foreign exchange earner for the first time. The sector was further boosted in July 2000 by the extension of NAFTA import duty parity to Honduran-assembled goods. The extension of these provisions reduced the import tariff on Honduran-assembled goods into the US market by 15% and allowed the sector to diversify into textile operations such as dyeing and cutting. The move encouraged the Government to target $700m. in new investment into the sector over the subsequent five years, which, it hoped, would create up to 80,000 jobs. In November 2000 the Formosa Industrial Park, financed by Taiwan, opened. However, the US economic slowdown that began in 2001 badly affected the sector, with 32 *maquila* plants closing and employment levels falling, with an estimated 10,000 jobs lost, for the first time in more than a decade.

FOREIGN TRADE AND PAYMENTS

Honduras recorded a persistently large current account deficit, although there was some improvement in the late 1990s. In 2000 the deficit fell to US $276m., from $625m. in the previous year; however, by 2004 it had increased to $678m. In 2005 the deficit fell significantly, to $290m., equivalent to 1.4% of GDP. The rapid improvement was principally a result of bilateral transfers through the HIPC initiative, together with increased remittances from Hondurans living abroad. In 2006 the current account deficit increased to $404m., equivalent to 3.7% of GDP, and then increased significantly to $1,976.7m. in 2008, equivalent to some 15% of GDP, as increases in import costs outpaced increases in export revenues. The deficit was estimated to have fallen to $449m. in 2009, equivalent to 3.1% of GDP. A 21.2% decline in export revenues was outweighed by a 28.1% fall in imports across consumer, intermediate and capital goods.

The trade deficit has always fluctuated in line with the prices of major exports and the demand for imports; however, it increased dramatically after 1990. According to the central bank, in 2001 the trade deficit on the balance of payments stood at US $729.3m. and continued to rise in subsequent years, reaching $4,342m. in 2008, before falling to $2,471m. in 2009. Revenue from the export of commodities rose by more than 10% per year in the mid-1990s, but declined substantially in the wake of Hurricane Mitch. Banana and coffee prices rose significantly from 2005–08 and were accompanied by sizeable price rises in metals, although prices of lead and zinc declined in 2008. Total exports were valued at $2,238.2m. in 2009, reflecting a contraction in global demand. In 2000 imports of goods totalled $3,987.8m., increasing to $8,830.9m. in 2008. The steep rise in the cost of imports reflected higher fuel prices and the strength in consumer demand in the first half of 2008. A reversal of these trends led to total import costs of $6,133.3m. in 2009.

In the mid-1980s the widening trade gap was partially offset by a sharp rise in aid from the USA, but subsequent falls in both aid and export revenue forced the Government to yield to pressure from the IMF for a currency devaluation, which took place in 1990. Throughout the 1990s the fiscal situation continued to deteriorate, and there were further devaluations in 1994 in order to secure a US $500m. loan agreement from the World Bank and the IMF. Multilateral and bilateral creditor support subsequently remained strong, despite the significant weakening of government finances in the wake of Hurricane Mitch. The most obvious demonstration of this was the country's achievement of HIPC status in mid-2000. The agreement promised debt service relief of some $900m. in return for continued economic reform and adherence to an IMF- and World Bank-agreed PRGF programme. The programme allowed for an increase in social spending, subject to a rise in national revenue. The debt relief secured by the Government after reducing the fiscal deficit and reaching 'completion point' within the HIPC initiative in 2005 enabled further investment in poverty reduction.

Improved terms from creditors in the 1990s were contingent upon investment liberalization, which helped dramatically to increase foreign investment inflows during that decade. In 2000 FDI increased to US $381.7m., before falling to $275.2m. in 2002. Since then, FDI increased each year, reaching an estimated $927.5m. in 2007, driven by loans to the private sector in order to exploit opportunities in mobile telecommunications, financial services and the *maquila* sub-sector of manufacturing. Net FDI inflows declined to $877m. in 2008, of which some 44% was directed towards the telecommunications sectors, 23% to the *maquila* sector and 11% to other manufacturing industries. With the onset of a tightening of credit in the global economy, direct investment in Honduras fell significantly, by 44.4%, to $500.4m. in 2009.

External debt more than doubled in the 1980s, reaching US $3,700m. in 1990. However, rescheduling, renegotiation and relief steadily reduced the Honduran debt service ratio (debt service as a percentage of earnings from the export of goods and services) from 35.3% in 1990 to 13.0% 10 years later. Total external debt declined from $5,793m. in 2004 to an estimated $3,317m. in 2009, helped by the Government successfully meeting its targets agreed in the PRGF. The debt-to-GDP ratio decreased from 66.7% of GDP in 2004 to more manageable rates, estimated at 23.0% in 2009, while the debt service ratio was stable at approximately 3.1% in that year.

By 2005 it was increasingly clear that successive Honduran Governments had enjoyed some success in their efforts to diversify the economy and the country's sources of foreign exchange. Non-traditional agricultural and fishery exports soared; earnings from the *maquila* industry exceeded those from both coffee and bananas; and invisibles, such as tourism and remittances from Hondurans living abroad (remittances totalled US $2,476m. in 2009, greater than commodity export earnings), were making increasingly important contributions to the current account. Revenues from tourism grew dramatically, rising from $31.8m. in 1992 to an estimated $621m. in 2008, before declining modestly, to $611m., in 2009. The vast majority of visitors were from other Central American countries and the USA.

There was less success in the diversification of the direction of trade, with dependence on the USA, the country's principal market, remaining strong. In 2009 an estimated 39.8% of the country's exports went to the USA, compared with some 54% a decade earlier. The major trade development was the growth of intra-regional trade; other Central American countries, principally El Salvador and Guatemala, collectively purchased 23.9% of Honduran exports in 2009. Reliance on US imports gradually declined, but still remained strong. In 2009 some 34.0% of the country's total imports came from the USA, compared with 47% a decade earlier. Other important suppliers in that year were regional neighbours, with Guatemala, El Salvador, Mexico and Costa Rica collectively accounting for 23.5% of the total.

Following four years of negotiations, in April 2000 the Central American countries of El Salvador, Guatemala and Honduras signed a free trade agreement with Mexico, which promised greater access to the Mexican market and increased bilateral trade. The 'Plan Puebla–Panamá' of May 2001 provided for regional integration through joint transport, industry and tourism projects. The Plan was restyled the Proyecto de Integración y Desarrollo de Mesoamérica in 2008. Honduras was also party to the establishment of the Central American Free Trade Agreement (CAFTA) with the USA, which was agreed in December 2003 and ratified, as DR-CAFTA (Dominican Republic-Central American Free Trade Agreement), by the Honduran legislature in March 2005. The Agreement, which finally came into effect in April 2006 following ratification by the USA, consolidated trade privileges, which had previously come under the auspices of the CBI, particularly access to the US market. DR-CAFTA was expected to attract investment inflows and boost export earnings, diversification and jobs generated by the *maquila* sector.

Although credit from international lending agencies had resumed following the inauguration in January 2010 of President Lobo, diplomatic relations with regional governments following the ousting in June 2009 of President Zelaya had yet to be fully re-established by mid-2010. In January Honduras had left ALBA, whose other members included Bolivia, Cuba, Ecuador and Venezuela, all of which had left-wing Governments. Honduras had acceded to the grouping during the presidency of Zelaya, and the ALBA countries, along with members of Mercado Común del Sur (Mercosur—Southern Common Market), continued to refuse to recognize the legitimacy of the Lobo Government.

CONCLUSION

The global economic downturn from 2008 undermined the ability of Honduras to meet macroeconomic targets. Furthermore, the ousting of President Zelaya in June 2009, and the ensuing political instability, threatened an extension of the IMF stand-by agreement, although it was hoped that the budget for 2010, which involved an orthodox fiscal adjustment programme, might result in the successful securing of such an extension before the end of that year. Meanwhile, the suspension of diplomatic relations by many regional governments during 2009–10, in response to Zelaya's removal from office, underscored the importance of relations with the USA; the Temporary Protected Status (TPS) covering undocumented Hondurans living in the USA was expected to be renewed during 2010.

Statistical Survey

Sources (unless otherwise stated): Department of Economic Studies, Banco Central de Honduras, Avda Juan Ramón Molina, 1a Calle, 7a Avda, Apdo 3165, Tegucigalpa; tel. 237-2270; fax 238-0376; e-mail jreyes@bch.hn; internet www.bch.hn; Instituto Nacional de Estadística, Edif. Gómez, Blvd Suyapa, Col. Florencia Sur, Apdo 9412, Tegucigalpa; e-mail info@ine.online.hn; internet www.ine-hn.org.

Note: The metric system is in force, although some old Spanish measures are used, including 25 libras = 1 arroba; 4 arrobas = 1 quintal (46 kg).

Area and Population

AREA, POPULATION AND DENSITY

Area (sq km)	112,492*
Population (census results)†	
29 May 1988	4,614,377
1 August 2001	
Males	3,230,958
Females	3,304,386
Total	6,535,344
Population (official estimates at mid-year)	
2007	7,537,952
2008	7,706,907
2009	7,876,662
Density (per sq km) at mid-2009	70.0

* 43,433 sq miles.

† Excluding adjustments for underenumeration, estimated to have been 10% at the 1974 census.

POPULATION BY AGE AND SEX

('000, UN estimates at mid-2010)

	Males	Females	Total
0–14	1,428	1,373	2,802
15–64	2,224	2,262	4,486
65 and over	154	174	328
Total	3,806	3,809	7,616

Source: UN, *World Population Prospects: The 2008 Revision*.

PRINCIPAL TOWNS

('000, official estimates, 2009)

Tegucigalpa—Distrito Central (capital)	990.6	La Lima	67.1
San Pedro Sula	646.3	Danlí	62.1
Choloma	223.9	Villanueva	54.5
La Ceiba	172.9	Siguatepeque	54.1
El Progreso	122.0	Catacamas	53.5
Choluteca	91.0	Tocoa	46.9
Comayagua	78.3	Juticalpa	45.6
Puerto Cortés	68.4		

BIRTHS AND DEATHS

(UN estimates)

	1995–2000	2000–05	2005–10
Birth rate (per 1,000)	33.4	30.1	27.7
Death rate (per 1,000)	5.6	5.3	5.1

Source: UN, *World Population Prospects: The 2008 Revision*.

Life expectancy (years at birth, WHO estimates): 70 (males 67; females 73) in 2008 (Source: WHO, *World Health Statistics*).

EMPLOYMENT

('000 persons)

	2007	2008	2009
Agriculture, hunting, forestry and fishing	979.9	1,048.7	1,161.8
Mining and quarrying	7.1	7.5	8.1
Manufacturing	421.2	425.2	411.5
Electricity, gas and water	12.4	11.9	11.8
Construction	189.2	190.8	205.8
Trade, restaurants and hotels	603.6	642.9	692.8
Transport, storage and communications	106.1	101.1	104.5
Financing, insurance, real estate and business services	94.9	96.9	95.4
Community, social, personal and other services	421.7	427.7	443.7
Total employed	2,836.1	2,952.7	3,135.4

Health and Welfare

KEY INDICATORS

Total fertility rate (children per woman, 2008)	3.3
Under-5 mortality rate (per 1,000 live births, 2008)	31
HIV/AIDS (% of persons aged 15–49, 2007)	0.7
Physicians (per 1,000 head, 2000)	0.6
Hospital beds (per 1,000 head, 2002)	1.0
Health expenditure (2007): US $ per head (PPP)	235
Health expenditure (2007): % of GDP	6.2
Health expenditure (2007): public (% of total)	65.7
Access to water (% of persons, 2008)	86
Access to sanitation (% of persons, 2008)	71
Total carbon dioxide emissions ('000 metric tons, 2006)	7,188.8
Carbon dioxide emissions per head (metric tons, 2006)	1.0
Human Development Index (2007): ranking	112
Human Development Index (2007): value	0.732

For sources and definitions, see explanatory note on p. vi.

Agriculture

PRINCIPAL CROPS
('000 metric tons)

	2005	2006	2007
Maize	468	531	617
Sorghum	41	65	69
Sugar cane	5,625	5,570	5,958
Beans, dry	86	100	108
Oil palm fruit	1,092	1,040	1,112
Tomatoes	153	155*	155*
Melons*	269	282	286
Bananas	887	890*	910*
Plantains	285	287*	290*
Oranges	285	290*	290*
Pineapples	145	147*	154*
Coffee, green	191	199	218

* FAO estimate(s).

Aggregate production ('000 metric tons, may include official, semi-official or estimated data): Total cereals 531.3 in 2005, 618.7 in 2006, 710.7 in 2007; Total vegetables (incl. melons) 658.6 in 2005, 674.3 in 2006, 698.2 in 2007; Total fruits (excl. melons) 1,702 in 2005, 1,715 in 2006, 1,748 in 2007.

2008: Production assumed to be unchanged from 2007 (FAO estimates).

Source: FAO.

LIVESTOCK
('000 head, year ending September)

	2006*	2007*	2008
Cattle	2,550	2,600	2,545
Sheep	15	15	15*
Goats	25	24	24*
Pigs	490	490	490*
Horses	181	181	181*
Mules	70	70	70*
Chickens	32,500	34,000	34,000*

* FAO estimate(s).

Source: FAO.

LIVESTOCK PRODUCTS
('000 metric tons)

	2006	2007	2008
Cattle meat	67.6	70.9	74.4
Pig meat*	9.1	9.5	9.5
Chicken meat*	141.0	145.0	145.0
Cows' milk*	703.0	724.0	724.0
Hen eggs*	41.0	41.0	41.0

* FAO estimates.

Source: FAO.

Forestry

ROUNDWOOD REMOVALS
('000 cubic metres, excl. bark)

	2006	2007	2008
Sawlogs, veneer logs and logs for sleepers	873	822	662
Fuel wood*	8,668	8,641	8,617
Total	9,541	9,463	9,279

* FAO estimates.

Source: FAO.

SAWNWOOD PRODUCTION
('000 cubic metres, incl. railway sleepers)

	2006	2007	2008
Coniferous (softwood)	403	370	342
Broadleaved (hardwood)	9	9	7
Total	412	379	349

Source: FAO.

Fishing

('000 metric tons, live weight)

	2006	2007	2008
Capture*	18.9	14.8	12.9
Marine fishes	3.7	3.7	2.3*
Caribbean spiny lobster	2.9	2.8	3.0
Penaeus shrimps	1.4	1.2	1.7
Stromboid conchs	0.1	0.6	—
Aquaculture	55.4*	54.7	47.1
Nile tilapia	28.4*	28.4	20.5
Penaeus shrimps	27.0	26.3	26.6
Total catch*	74.3	69.5	60.0

* FAO estimate(s).

Source: FAO.

Mining

(metal content)

	2006	2007	2008*
Lead (metric tons)	11,775	11,775	3,300
Zinc (metric tons)	37,646	38,000	7,700
Silver (kilograms)	55,036	50,000	12,000
Gold (kilograms)*	4,100	3,275	2,561

* Reported production from the country's major producer(s); data may not reflect total production.

Source: US Geological Survey.

Industry

SELECTED PRODUCTS

	2007	2008	2009
Raw sugar ('000 quintales)	8,502	8,340	8,531
Cement ('000 bags of 42.5 kg)	41,777	41,966	38,335
Cigarettes ('000 packets of 20)	315,293	307,170	308,942
Beer ('000 12 oz bottles)	293,047	294,958	253,413
Soft drinks ('000 12 oz bottles)	1,489,987	1,604,007	1,867,888
Wheat flour ('000 quintales)	3,000	3,017	3,239
Fabric ('000 yards)	178,847	204,853	171,064
Liquor and spirits ('000 litres)	13,203	13,883	14,267
Vegetable oil and butter ('000 libras)	171,527	213,359	199,057
Electric energy (million kWh)	6,324.6	6,604.8	6,580.6

Finance

CURRENCY AND EXCHANGE RATES

Monetary Units
100 centavos = 1 lempira.

Sterling, Dollar and Euro Equivalents (31 May 2010)
£1 sterling = 27.550 lempiras;
US $1 = 18.895 lempiras;
€1 = 23.400 lempiras;
1,000 lempiras = £36.30 = $52.92 = €43.74.

Average Exchange Rate (lempiras per US $)
2007 18.8951
2008 18.9038
2009 18.8951

GOVERNMENT FINANCE

(general government transactions, non-cash basis, million lempiras, preliminary)

Summary of Balances

	2006	2007	2008
Revenue	48,831.8	56,048.6	68,092.3
Less Expense	41,489.7	50,279.9	57,476.9
Gross operating balance	7,342.2	5,768.7	10,615.5
Less Net acquisition of non-financial assets	6,599.7	8,483.9	11,315.0
Net lending/borrowing	742.5	–2,715.2	–699.5

Revenue

	2006	2007	2008
Taxes	32,696.6	38,867.5	44,007.6
Taxes of income, profits and capital gains	9,256.0	11,845.6	13,163.5
Taxes of goods and services	19,441.0	23,067.8	25,646.7
Social contributions	4,958.4	6,036.6	7,307.6
Grants	3,079.2	3,718.8	5,520.1
Other revenue	8,097.6	7,425.7	11,257.0
Total	48,831.8	56,048.6	68,092.3

Expense by economic type*

	2006	2007	2008
Compensation of employees	21,687.6	25,994.3	30,735.4
Wages and salaries	19,932.8	23,914.4	28,300.5
Social contributions	1,754.8	2,079.9	2,434.9
Use of goods and services	7,821.0	9,048.3	10,016.4
Interest	1,807.3	1,458.5	1,630.6
Subsidies	999.4	3,037.4	857.4
Grants	151.0	256.9	245.6
Social benefits	341.7	262.5	252.7
Other expense	8,681.7	10,222.1	13,738.8
Total	41,489.7	50,279.9	57,476.9

* Including purchases of non-financial assets.

Source: IMF, *Government Finance Statistics Yearbook*.

CENTRAL BANK RESERVES

(US $ million at 31 December)

	2006	2007	2008
Gold (national valuation)	13.95	18.19	19.11
IMF special drawing rights	—	0.09	0.09
Foreign exchange	2,615.50	2,514.30	2,460.00
Reserve position in IMF	12.98	13.63	13.29
Total	2,642.43	2,546.21	2,492.49

2009: Gold (national valuation) 24.04; IMF special drawing rights 164.26; Reserve position in IMF 13.52.

Source: IMF, *International Financial Statistics*.

MONEY SUPPLY

(million lempiras at 31 December)

	2007	2008	2009
Currency outside depository corporations	11,906	11,857	12,971
Transferable deposits	23,585	24,032	24,476
Other deposits	93,764	100,328	100,687
Securities other than shares	3,310	2,796	1,500
Broad money	132,565	139,013	139,634

Source: IMF, *International Financial Statistics*.

COST OF LIVING

(Consumer Price Index, base: 1999 = 100)

	2007	2008	2009
Food and non-alcoholic beverages	164.8	193.1	200.0
Alcohol and tobacco	200.5	214.0	228.7
Rent, water, fuel and power	198.8	217.1	232.0
Clothing and footwear	172.4	181.9	192.8
Health	207.6	220.1	236.7
Transport	202.0	226.6	222.7
Communications	78.2	74.0	72.8
Culture and recreation	147.6	154.1	160.0
Education	267.6	285.6	306.4
Restaurants and hotels	179.4	201.0	222.0
All items (incl. others)	179.0	199.4	210.3

NATIONAL ACCOUNTS

(million lempiras at current prices)

Expenditure on the Gross Domestic Product

	2007	2008*	2009†
Government final consumption expenditure	38,778	44,259	51,145
Private final consumption expenditure	183,112	209,964	216,792
Changes in inventories	3,596	7,779	–7,964
Gross fixed capital formation	74,192	86,033	61,087
Total domestic expenditure	299,678	348,035	321,060
Exports of goods and services	124,980	138,579	113,897
Less Imports of goods and services	190,501	222,543	164,415
GDP in purchasers' values	234,156	264,072	270,543
GDP at constant 2000 prices	151,678	157,701	154,686

Gross Domestic Product by Economic Activity

	2007	2008*	2009†
Agriculture, hunting, forestry and fishing	27,820	32,909	31,192
Mining and quarrying	2,767	2,072	1,990
Manufacturing	41,929	48,058	46,674
Electricity, gas and water	2,469	3,235	3,348
Construction	13,929	16,511	15,943
Wholesale and retail trade	33,274	36,301	34,725
Hotels and restaurants	6,774	7,450	7,966
Transport and storage	7,865	9,299	9,640
Communications	8,009	9,490	10,319
Finance and insurance	13,881	16,663	17,076
Owner-occupied dwellings	12,717	13,819	15,135
Business activities	10,404	11,939	12,927
Education services	16,302	18,327	20,878
Health	6,756	8,180	9,852
Public administration and defence	14,373	16,417	19,257
Other services	6,080	6,919	7,787
Sub-total	225,349	257,589	264,709
Less Financial intermediation services indirectly measured	11,301	13,217	14,407
GDP at factor cost	214,047	244,371	250,302
Indirect taxes, *less* subsidies	20,109	19,701	20,241
GDP in purchasers' values	234,156	264,072	270,543

* Preliminary.
† Estimates.

BALANCE OF PAYMENTS
(US $ million)

	2006	2007	2008
Exports of goods f.o.b.	5,276.6	5,642.2	6,046.3
Imports of goods f.o.b.	–7,303.3	–8,820.3	–10,388.7
Trade balance	–2,026.7	–3,178.1	–4,342.5
Exports of services	744.9	788.1	909.8
Imports of services	–1,035.7	–1,136.7	–1,214.6
Balance on goods and services	–2,317.4	–3,526.7	–4,647.2
Other income received	198.2	264.5	172.0
Other income paid	–735.0	–664.3	–522.4
Balance on goods, services and income	–2,854.2	–3,926.6	–4,997.6
Current transfers received	2,610.0	2,805.9	3,159.7
Current transfers paid	–136.6	–154.0	–138.7
Current balance	–380.8	–1,274.6	–1,976.7
Capital account (net)	1,484.8	1,193.2	56.2
Direct investment abroad	–0.6	–1.5	–1.8
Direct investment from abroad	669.1	929.3	877.0
Portfolio investment assets	–20.9	–25.5	–13.9
Other investment assets	84.4	–59.1	260.2
Other investment liabilities	–1,203.7	–843.8	482.4
Net errors and omissions	–327.6	–106.2	222.2
Overall balance	304.7	–188.2	–94.4

Source: IMF, *International Financial Statistics*.

External Trade

PRINCIPAL COMMODITIES
(US $ million)

Imports c.i.f.*	2007	2008	2009
Vegetables and fruit	302.1	389.3	271.9
Mineral fuels and lubricants	1,344.7	1,990.4	1,183.0
Chemicals and related products	900.2	1,118.4	927.7
Plastic and manufactures	391.0	440.7	348.5
Paper, paperboard and manufactures	322.1	367.8	307.4
Textile yarn, fabrics and manufactures	188.8	194.7	162.3
Metal and manufactures	518.8	708.6	373.7
Food products	627.4	724.2	650.4
Machinery and electrical appliances	1,413.4	1,596.6	992.0
Transport equipment	570.0	611.6	395.7
Total (incl. others)	7,224.4	8,830.9	6,133.3

* Excluding imports destined for the *maquila* sector (US $ million): 2,237.2 in 2007; 2,338.0 in 2008; 1,852.8 in 2009.

Exports f.o.b.*	2007	2008	2009
Bananas	289.3	383.8	327.2
Cigars and cigarettes	89.4	124.6	66.9
Coffee	518.3	620.3	531.5
Lead and zinc	82.1	47.1	43.6
Melons and watermelons	46.2	35.4	42.3
Palm oil	121.2	205.8	125.4
Lobsters and prawns	157.9	143.2	134.3
Soaps and detergents	44.0	52.4	48.4
Tilapia	55.5	63.0	55.8
Wood	44.5	34.0	19.9
Total (incl. others)	2,461.3	2,833.4	2,238.2

* Excluding exports of gold, and of *maquila* goods (US $ million): 3,240.8 in 2007; 3,559.5 in 2008; 2,771.7 in 2009.

PRINCIPAL TRADING PARTNERS
(US $ million, excluding *maquila* goods)

Imports c.i.f.	2007	2008	2009
Brazil	142.6	133.4	104.5
Colombia	68.4	93.8	167.4
Costa Rica	324.4	349.1	281.2
El Salvador	403.9	480.4	380.8
Germany	104.6	163.3	72.6
Guatemala	632.1	764.5	643.7
Japan	198.1	148.6	101.6
Mexico	389.1	494.9	416.5
Nicaragua	127.9	121.6	111.0
Spain	74.0	92.0	62.6
USA	2,903.5	3,540.7	2,070.7
Venezuela	82.2	145.2	132.4
Total (incl. others)	7,224.4	8,830.9	6,133.3

Exports f.o.b.*	2007	2008	2009
Belgium	123.2	157.9	99.6
Canada	11.5	41.1	43.3
Costa Rica	59.1	69.0	56.5
El Salvador	242.9	252.1	197.5
France	14.5	24.4	30.5
Germany	184.3	154.7	160.4
Guatemala	173.8	189.0	165.4
Italy	24.9	20.9	33.8
Japan	20.9	26.9	19.3
Mexico	112.9	183.1	51.1
Netherlands	50.2	32.8	25.1
Nicaragua	134.9	134.8	105.3
Spain	76.8	38.5	53.2
United Kingdom	19.5	47.8	71.0
USA	991.9	1,156.3	872.6
Total (incl. others)	2,461.3	2,833.4	2,238.2

* Excluding exports of gold.

Transport

ROAD TRAFFIC
(licensed vehicles in use)

	2001	2002	2003
Passenger cars	345,931	369,303	386,468
Buses and coaches	20,380	21,814	22,514
Lorries and vans	81,192	86,893	91,230
Motorcycles and bicycles	36,828	39,245	41,852

2007 (vehicles in use): Passenger cars 487,743; Buses and coaches 31,467; Vans and lorries 165,203; Motorcycles and mopeds 94,402 (Source: IRF, *World Road Statistics*).

SHIPPING

Merchant Fleet
(registered at 31 December)

	2006	2007	2008
Number of vessels	1,072	1,052	1,041
Total displacement ('000 grt)	735.3	712.4	704.5

Source: Lloyd's Register-Fairplay, *World Fleet Statistics*.

International Sea-borne Freight Traffic
('000 metric tons)

	1988	1989	1990
Goods loaded	1,328	1,333	1,316
Goods unloaded	1,151	1,222	1,002

Source: UN, *Monthly Bulletin of Statistics*.

CIVIL AVIATION
(traffic on scheduled services)

	1993	1994	1995
Kilometres flown (million)	4	5	5
Passengers carried ('000)	409	449	474
Passenger-km (million)	362	323	341
Total ton-km (million)	50	42	33

Source: UN, *Statistical Yearbook*.

Tourism

TOURIST ARRIVALS BY COUNTRY OF ORIGIN

	2005	2006	2007
Canada	11,002	12,442	18,184
Costa Rica	20,855	23,902	25,031
El Salvador	159,546	158,198	165,901
Guatemala	92,612	106,063	126,645
Italy	11,975	13,762	8,462
Mexico	17,212	20,417	23,412
Nicaragua	76,646	76,874	119,569
Panama	8,394	9,660	9,071
Spain	8,536	9,790	6,260
USA	197,601	228,002	276,547
Total (incl. others)	673,035	738,667	831,433

Receipts from tourism (US $ million, excl. passenger transport): 488 in 2006; 557 in 2007; 621 in 2008 (provisional).

Source: World Tourism Organization.

Total tourist arrivals: 899,300 (excluding 692,500 excursionists) in 2008; 869,500 (excluding 753,900 excursionists) in 2009.

Communications Media

	2007	2008	2009
Telephones ('000 main lines in use)	821.2	825.8	716.3
Mobile cellular telephones ('000 subscribers)	4,184.8	6,210.7	8,390.8
Internet users ('000)	424.2	658.5	n.a.

Radio receivers ('000 in use): 2,450 in 1997 (Source: UN, *Statistical Yearbook*).

Television receivers ('000 in use): 640 in 2001 (Source: UN, *Statistical Yearbook*).

Daily newspapers: 4 in 2002; 4 in 2003.

Weekly newspapers: 3 in 2002; 3 in 2003.

Personal computers: 181,875 (24.9 per 1,000 persons) in 2008 (Source: International Telecommunication Union).

Education

(2006/07, unless otherwise indicated)

	Institutions	Teachers	Students
Pre-primary	8,178	8,925	216,438
Primary (grades 1 to 6)	11,277	45,685	1,272,499
Secondary (grades 7 to 9)			304,959
High school	938	24,048	163,767
Higher (incl. university)*	16	6,457	145,171

* Figures for 2005/06.

Pupil-teacher ratio (primary education, UNESCO estimate): 33.3 in 2007/08 (Source: UNESCO Institute for Statistics).

Adult literacy rate (UNESCO estimates): 83.1% (males 82.4%; females 83.7%) in 2007 (Source: UNESCO Institute for Statistics).

Directory

The Constitution

Following the elections of April 1980, the 1965 Constitution was revised. The new Constitution was approved by the Congreso Nacional (National Congress) in November 1982, and amended in 1995. The following are some of its main provisions:

Honduras is constituted as a democratic Republic. All Hondurans over 18 years of age are citizens.

THE SUFFRAGE AND POLITICAL PARTIES

The vote is direct and secret. Any political party that proclaims or practises doctrines contrary to the democratic spirit is forbidden. A National Electoral Council will be set up at the end of each presidential term. Its general function will be to supervise all elections and to register political parties. A proportional system of voting will be adopted for the election of Municipal Corporations.

INDIVIDUAL RIGHTS AND GUARANTEES

The right to life is declared inviolable; the death penalty is abolished. The Constitution recognizes the right of habeas corpus and arrests may be made only by judicial order. Remand for interrogation may not last more than six days, and no-one may be held incommunicado for more than 24 hours. The Constitution recognizes the rights of free expression of thought and opinion, the free circulation of information, of peaceful, unarmed association, of free movement within and out of the country, of political asylum and of religious and educational freedom. Civil marriage and divorce are recognized.

WORKERS' WELFARE

All have a right to work. Day work shall not exceed eight hours per day or 44 hours per week; night work shall not exceed six hours per night or 36 hours per week. Equal pay shall be given for equal work. The legality of trade unions and the right to strike are recognized.

EDUCATION

The State is responsible for education, which shall be free, lay, and, in the primary stage, compulsory. Private education is liable to inspection and regulation by the State.

LEGISLATIVE POWER

Deputies are obliged to vote, for or against, on any measure at the discussion of which they are present. The Congreso Nacional has power to grant amnesties to political prisoners; approve or disapprove of the actions of the Executive; declare part or the whole of the Republic subject to a state of siege; declare war; approve or withhold approval of treaties; withhold approval of the accounts of public expenditure when these exceed the sums fixed in the budget; decree, interpret, repeal and amend laws, and pass legislation fixing the rate of exchange or stabilizing the national currency. The Congreso Nacional may suspend certain guarantees in all or part of the Republic for 60 days in the case of grave danger from civil or foreign war, epidemics or any other calamity. Deputies are elected in the proportion of one deputy and one substitute for every 35,000 inhabitants, or fraction over 15,000. Congress may amend the basis in the light of increasing population.

EXECUTIVE POWER

Executive power is exercised by the President of the Republic, who is elected for four years by a simple majority of the people. No President may serve more than one term.

JUDICIAL POWER

The Judiciary consists of the Supreme Court, the Courts of Appeal and various lesser tribunals. The nine judges and seven substitute judges of the Supreme Court are elected by the Congreso Nacional for a period of four years. The Supreme Court is empowered to declare laws unconstitutional.

THE ARMED FORCES

The Armed Forces are declared by the Constitution to be essentially professional and non-political. The President exercises direct authority over the military.

LOCAL ADMINISTRATION

The country is divided into 18 Departments for purposes of local administration, and these are subdivided into 298 autonomous Municipalities; the functions of local offices shall be only economic and administrative.

The Government

HEAD OF STATE

President: PORFIRIO LOBO SOSA (took office 27 January 2010).

First Vice-President: MARÍA ANTONIETA GUILLÉN DE BOGRÁN.

Second Vice-President: SAMUEL ARMANDO REYES RENDÓN.

Third Vice-President: VÍCTOR HUGO BARNICA ALVARADO.

CABINET

(July 2010)

A coalition of the Partido Nacional, the Partido Liberal, the Partido de Unificación Democrática and the Partido Demócrata Cristiano de Honduras.

Minister of the Interior and Justice: AFRICO MADRID.

Minister of the Presidency: MARÍA ANTONIETA GUILLÉN DE BOGRÁN.

Minister of Foreign Affairs: MARIO CANAHAUTI.

Minister of Industry and Commerce: OSCAR ESCALANTE.

Minister of Finance: WILLIAM CHONG WONG.

Minister of Labour and Social Welfare: FELÍCITO AVILA.

Minister of Health: ARTURO BENDAÑA.

Minister of Public Security: OSCAR ALVAREZ.

Minister of Public Works, Transport and Housing: MIGUEL PASTOR.

Minister of Education: ALEJANDRO VENTURA.

Minister of Culture, Art and Sports: BERNARD MARTÍNEZ.

Minister of Agriculture and Livestock: JACOBO REGALADO WEIZEMBLUT.

Minister of the National Agrarian Institute: CÉSAR HAM.

Minister of National Defence: MARLON PASCUA CERRATO.

Minister of Natural Resources and the Environment: RIGOBERTO CUÉLLAR.

Minister of Tourism: NELLY JEREZ.

Minister of the Technical Secretariat for Planning and External Co-operation: ARTURO CORRALES.

Minister of Communications and Strategy: MIGUEL ANGEL BONILLA.

Minister of Social Development: HILDA HERNÁNDEZ.

Minister of the National Institute for Women's Affairs: MARÍA ANTONIETA BOTTO.

MINISTRIES

Office of the President: Palacio José Cecilio del Valle, Blvd Juan Pablo II, Tegucigalpa; tel. 232-6282; fax 231-0097; internet www.presidencia.gob.hn.

Ministry of Agriculture and Livestock: Blvd Miraflores, Avda La FAO, Tegucigalpa; tel. 232-4105; fax 231-0051; e-mail infoagro@sag.gob.hn; internet www.sag.gob.hn.

Ministry of Communications and Strategy: Tegucigalpa.

Ministry of Culture, Art and Sports: Col. Palmira, Edif. Castillo y Poujol, Tegucigalpa; tel. 235-4700; fax 235-6717; e-mail binah@sdnhon.org.hn.

Ministry of Education: 1a Avda, entre 2a y 3a Calle, Comayagüela, Tegucigalpa; tel. 238-4325; fax 222-8571; e-mail webmaster@se.gob.hn; internet www.se.gob.hn.

Ministry of Finance: Edif. SEFIN, Avda Cervantes, Barrio El Jazmín, Tegucigalpa; tel. 222-0111; fax 238-2309; e-mail sgeneral@sefin.gob.hn; internet www.sefin.gob.hn.

Ministry of Foreign Affairs: Centro Cívico Gubernamental, Antigua Casa Presidencial, Blvd Kuwait, Contiguo a la Corte Suprema de Justicia, Tegucigalpa; tel. 234-1962; fax 234-1484; e-mail consultas.sre@gmail.com; internet www.sre.hn.

Ministry of Health: 2a Calle, Avda Cervantes, Tegucigalpa; tel. 222-8518; fax 238-6787.

Ministry of Industry and Commerce: Edif. San José, Col. Humuya, Blvd José Cecilio del Valle, Tegucigalpa; tel. 235-3699; fax 235-3686; e-mail info@sic.gob.hn; internet www.sic.gob.hn.

Ministry of the Interior and Justice: Residencia La Hacienda, Calle La Estancia, Tegucigalpa; tel. 232-1373; fax 232-0226; e-mail atencionalpublico@gobernacion.gob.hn; internet www.gobernacion.gob.hn.

Ministry of Labour and Social Welfare: Blvd Hacienda, frente a Auto Excel, Tegucigalpa; tel. 232-3918; fax 235-3456; e-mail info@trabajo.gob.hn.

Ministry of National Defence: Barrio Concepción, Paseo El Obelisco, Comayagüela, Tegucigalpa; tel. 238-2890; fax 238-0238; internet www.ffaah.mil.hn.

Ministry of Natural Resources and the Environment: 100 m al sur del Estadio Nacional, Apdo 1389, Tegucigalpa; tel. 232-1386; fax 232-6250; e-mail sdespacho@yahoo.com; internet www.serna.gob.hn.

Ministry of Public Security: Plantel Casamata, subida al Picacho, Tegucigalpa; tel. 220-5547; fax 237-9070.

Ministry of Public Works, Transport and Housing: Barrio La Bolsa, Comayagüela, Tegucigalpa; tel. 225-2690; fax 225-5003; e-mail info@soptravi.gob.hn; internet www.soptravi.gob.hn.

Ministry of Social Development: Tegucigalpa.

Ministry of Tourism: Edif. Europa, Col. San Carlos, Apdo 3261, Tegucigalpa; tel. and fax 222-2124; e-mail tourisminfo@iht.hn; internet www.iht.hn.

National Agrarian Institute: see Instituto Nacional Agrario (see p. 582), Trade and Industry.

National Institute for Women's Affairs: Tegucigalpa; tel. 221-3637; fax 221-4827; e-mail dtecnica@inam.gob.hn; internet www.inam.gob.hn.

Technical Secretariat for Planning and External Co-operation: Edif. El Sol, Col. Puerta del Sol, Blvd San Juan Bosco, Apdo 1327, Tegucigalpa; tel. 239-5545; fax 239-5277; e-mail a_corrales@seplan.gob.hn; internet www.seplan.gob.hn.

President and Legislature

PRESIDENT

Election, 29 November 2009

Candidate	Valid votes cast	% of valid votes
Porfirio Lobo Sosa (PN)	1,213,695	56.56
Elvin Santos (PL)	817,524	38.09
Bernard Martínez (PINU—SD)	39,960	1.86
Felícito Avila (PDCH)	38,413	1.79
César Ham (PUD)	36,420	1.70
Total	2,146,012	100.00

In addition, there were 61,440 blank votes and 92,604 invalid votes.

CONGRESO NACIONAL

President: JUAN ORLANDO HERNÁNDEZ ALVARADO.

General Election, 29 November 2009

	Seats
Partido Nacional (PN)	71
Partido Liberal (PL)	45
Partido Demócrata Cristiano de Honduras (PDCH)	5
Partido de Unificación Democrática (PUD)	4
Partido Innovación y Unidad—Social Demócrata (PINU—SD)	3
Total	128

Election Commission

Tribunal Supremo Electoral (TSE): Col. El Prado, frente a Edif. Syre, Tegucigalpa; tel. 239-1058; fax 239-3060; e-mail centroinformacion@tse.hn; internet www.tse.hn; f. 2004 as successor to Tribunal Nacional de Elecciones; Pres. JOSÉ SAÚL ESCOBAR.

Political Organizations

Partido Demócrata Cristiano de Honduras (PDCH): Col. San Carlos, Tegucigalpa; tel. 236-5969; fax 236-9941; e-mail pdch@hondutel.hn; internet www.pdch.hn; legally recognized in 1980; Pres. LUCAS EVANGELISTO AGUILERA PINEDA; Sec.-Gen. CARLOS A. TURCIOS M.

Partido Innovación y Unidad—Social Demócrata (PINU—SD): 2a Avda, entre 9 y 10 calles, Apdo 105, Comayagüela, Tegucigalpa; tel. 220-4224; fax 220-4232; e-mail pinusd@amnettgu.com; internet www.pinusd.com; f. 1970; legally recognized in 1978; Pres. JORGE RAFAEL AGUILAR PAREDES; Sec. MARGEN OMELDA DÍAZ SOTO.

Partido Liberal (PL): Col. Miramontes, atrás de Supermercado la Col. No 1, Tegucigalpa; tel. 232-0822; e-mail info@partidoliberaldehonduras.hn; internet www.partidoliberaldehonduras.hn; f. 1891; factions within the party include the Movimiento Pinedista (Leader Dr RAFAEL PINEDA PONCE), the Movimiento LIBRE (Leader JAIME ROSENTHAL OLIVA) and the Movimiento Esperanza Liberal (Leader JOSÉ MANUEL (MEL) ZELAYA ROSALES); has a youth organization called the Frente Central de Juventud Liberal de Honduras (Pres. EDUARDO RAINA GARCÍA); Pres. ROBERTO MICHELETTI BAÍN; Sec.-Gen. BILL O'NEILL SANTOS BRITO.

Partido Nacional (PN): Paseo el Obelisco, Comayagüela, Tegucigalpa; tel. 237-7310; fax 237-7365; e-mail partidonacional@partidonacional.hn; internet www.partidonacional.hn; f. 1902; traditional right-wing party; Pres. PORFIRIO LOBO SOSA; Sec.-Gen. JUAN ORLANDO HERNÁNDEZ.

Partido de Unificación Democrática (PUD): Barrio La Plazuela, Avda Cervantes, Tegucigalpa; tel. and fax 238-2498; e-mail colectivoparlud@hotmail.com; f. 1993; left-wing coalition comprising Partido Revolucionario Hondureño, Partido Renovación Patriótica, Partido para la Transformación de Honduras and Partido Morazanista; Leaders CÉSAR HAM, MARVIN PONCE.

Diplomatic Representation

EMBASSIES IN HONDURAS

Argentina: Calle Palermo 302, Col. Rubén Darío, Apdo 3208, Tegucigalpa; tel. 232-3376; fax 231-0376; e-mail ehond@mrecic.gov.ar; Chargé d'affaires a.i. ALEJANDRO JOSÉ AMURA.

Brazil: Col. Palmira, Calle República del Brasil, Apdo 341, Tegucigalpa; tel. 221-4432; fax 236-5873; e-mail embajada@brasilhonduras.org; internet www.brasilhonduras.org; Chargé d'affaires a.i. FRANCISCO CATUNDA REZENDE.

Chile: Calle Oslo C-4242, Col. Lomas del Guijarro, Tegucigalpa; tel. 232-4106; fax 232-2114; e-mail echilehn@123.hn; internet www.embajadadechilehonduras.com; Ambassador SERGIO VERDUGO NEIRA.

China (Taiwan): Col. Lomas del Guijarro, Calle Eucaliptos 3750, Apdo 3433, Tegucigalpa; tel. 239-5837; fax 232-0532; e-mail hnd@mofa.gov.tw; internet www.taiwanembassy.org/hn; Ambassador LAI CHIEN-CHUNG.

Colombia: Edif. Palmira, 3°, Col. Palmira, Apdo 468, Tegucigalpa; tel. 239-9324; fax 232-9324; e-mail ehonduras@cancilleria.gov.co; Ambassador SONIA MARINA PEREIRA PORTILLA.

Costa Rica: Residencial El Triángulo, Calle 3451, Lomas del Guijarro, Apdo 512, Tegucigalpa; tel. 232-1768; fax 232-1054; e-mail embacori@amnettgu.com; internet www.embajadadecostaricaenhonduras.com; Chargé d'affaires a.i. MARÍA DE LOS ANGELES GUTIÉRREZ VARGAS.

Cuba: Col. Loma Linda Norte, Calle Diangonal Huri 2255, contiguo a Residencial Torres Blancas, Tegucigalpa; tel. 239-3778; fax 235-7624; e-mail embajador@hn.embacuba.cu; internet embacu.cubaminrex.cu/honduras; Ambassador JUAN CARLOS HERNÁNDEZ PADRÓN.

Dominican Republic: Plaza Miramontes, 2°, Local No 6, Col. Miramontes, Tegucigalpa; tel. 239-0130; fax 239-1594; e-mail joacosta@serex.gov.do; Ambassador JOSÉ DEL CARMEN ACOSTA CARRASCO.

Ecuador: Bloque F, Casa 2968, Sendero Senecio, Col. Lomas del Castaños Sur, Apdo 358, Tegucigalpa; tel. 221-4906; fax 221-1049; e-mail mecuahon@multivisionhn.net; Chargé d'affaires a.i. CRISTINA GRANDA MENDOZA.

El Salvador: Col. Altos de Miramontes, Casa 2952, Diagonal Aguan, Tegucigalpa; tel. 232-4947; fax 239-6556; e-mail embasalhonduras@rree.gob.sv; internet www.rree.gob.sv/embajadas/honduras.nsf; Ambassador CARLOS POZO.

France: Col. Palmira, Avda Juan Lindo, Callejón Batres 337, Apdo 3441, Tegucigalpa; tel. 236-6800; fax 236-8051; e-mail info@ambafrance-hn.org; internet www.ambafrance-hn.org; Ambassador LAURENT DOMINATI.

Germany: Avda República Dominicana 925, Callejón Siria, Col. Lomas del Guijarro, Apdo 3145, Tegucigalpa; tel. 232-3161; fax 239-9018; e-mail info@tegucigalpa.diplo.de; internet www.tegucigalpa.diplo.de; Ambassador KARL-HEINZ RODE.

Guatemala: Calle Arturo López Rodezno 2421, Col. Las Minitas, Tegucigalpa; tel. 232-5018; fax 232-1580; Ambassador ANGELA GAROZ CABRERA.

Holy See: Palacio de la Nunciatura Apostólica, Col. Palmira, Avda Santa Sede 412, Apdo 324, Tegucigalpa; tel. 232-6613; fax 239-8869; e-mail nunciature@amnettgu.com; Apostolic Nuncio Most Rev. LUIGI BIANCO (Titular Archbishop of Falerone).

Italy: Edif. Plaza Azul, 4°, Col. Lomas del Guijarro Sur, Apdo U-9093, Tegucigalpa; tel. 239-5790; fax 239-5737; e-mail ambasciata.tegucigalpa@esteri.it; internet www.ambtegucigalpa.esteri.it; Ambassador GIUSEPPE MAGNO.

Japan: Col. San Carlos, Calzada Rep. Paraguay, Apdo 3232, Tegucigalpa; tel. 236-5511; fax 236-6100; e-mail keikyo1@multivisionhn.net; internet www.hn.emb-japan.go.jp; Ambassador OSAMU SHIOZAKI.

Korea, Republic: Edif. Plaza Azul, 5°, Col. Lomas del Guijarro Sur, Tegucigalpa; tel. 235-5561; fax 235-5564; e-mail coreaembajada@mofat.go.kr; internet hnd.mofat.go.kr; Ambassador SUN KIU KIM.

Mexico: Col. Lomas del Guijarro, Avda Eucalipto 1001, Tegucigalpa; tel. 232-4039; fax 232-4719; e-mail embamexhonduras@gmail.com; internet www.sre.gob.mx/honduras; Ambassador TARCISIO NAVARRETE MONTES DE OCA.

Nicaragua: Col. Tepeyac, Bloque M-1, Avda Choluteca 1130, Apdo 392, Tegucigalpa; tel. 231-1966; fax 231-1412; e-mail embanic@amnettgu.com; Ambassador MARIO JOSÉ DUARTE ZAMORA.

Panama: Edif. Palmira, 2°, Col. Palmira, Apdo 397, Tegucigalpa; tel. 239-5508; fax 232-8147; e-mail ephon@multivisionhn.net; Ambassador ROBERT JOVANÉ.

Peru: Col. Linda Vista, Calle Principal 3301, Tegucigalpa; tel. 236-7994; fax 221-4596; e-mail embajadadelperu@cablecolor.hn; Ambassador ALFREDO JOSÉ CASTRO PÉREZ-CANETTO.

Spain: Col. Matamoros, Calle Santander 801, Apdo 3221, Tegucigalpa; tel. 236-6875; fax 236-8682; e-mail emb.tegucigalpa@mae.es; Ambassador IGNACIO RUPÉREZ RUBIO.

USA: Avda La Paz, Apdo 3453, Tegucigalpa; tel. 236-9320; fax 236-9037; internet honduras.usembassy.gov; Ambassador HUGO LLORENS.

Venezuela: Col. Rubén Darío, 2116 Circuito Choluteca, Apdo 775, Tegucigalpa; tel. 232-1879; fax 232-1016; e-mail info@venezuelalabolivariana.com; internet venezuelalabolivariana.com; Chargé d'affaires a.i. ARIEL NICOLAS VARGAS ARDENCO.

Judicial System

Justice is administered by the Supreme Court (which has 15 judges), five Courts of Appeal and departmental courts (which have their own local jurisdiction).

Tegucigalpa has two Courts of Appeal, the first of which has jurisdiction in the department of Francisco Morazán, and the second of which has jurisdiction in the departments of Choluteca Valle, El Paraíso and Olancho.

The Appeal Court of San Pedro Sula has jurisdiction in the department of Cortés; that of Comayagua has jurisdiction in the departments of Comayagua, La Paz and Intibucá; and that of Santa Bárbara in the departments of Santa Bárbara, Lempira and Copán.

Supreme Court: Edif. Palacio de Justicia, contiguo Col. Miraflores, Centro Cívico Gubernamental, Tegucigalpa; tel. 233-9208; fax 233-6784; internet www.poderjudicial.gob.hn; Pres. JORGE RIVERA AVILÉS.

Attorney-General: LUIS ALBERTO RUBÍ.

Religion

The majority of the population are Roman Catholics; the Constitution guarantees toleration to all forms of religious belief.

CHRISTIANITY

The Roman Catholic Church

Honduras comprises one archdiocese and seven dioceses (the diocese of Yoro was created in 2005). Some 82% of the population are Roman Catholics.

Bishops' Conference

Conferencia Episcopal de Honduras, Blvd Estadio Suyapa, Apdo 3121, Tegucigalpa; tel. 229-1111; fax 229-1144; e-mail ceh@unicah.edu.

f. 1929; Pres. Cardinal OSCAR ANDRÉS RODRÍGUEZ MARADIAGA (Archbishop of Tegucigalpa).

Archbishop of Tegucigalpa: Cardinal OSCAR ANDRÉS RODRÍGUEZ MARADIAGA, Arzobispado, 3a y 2a Avda 1113, Apdo 106, Tegucigalpa; tel. 237-0353; fax 222-2337; e-mail orodriguez@unicah.edu.

The Anglican Communion

Honduras comprises a single missionary diocese, in Province IX of the Episcopal Church in the USA.

Bishop of Honduras: Rt Rev. LLOYD EMMANUEL ALLEN, Apdo 586, San Pedro Sula; tel. 556-6155; fax 556-6467; e-mail emmanuel@anglicano.hn.

The Baptist Church

Convención Nacional de Iglesias Bautistas de Honduras (CONIBAH): Apdo 2176, Tegucigalpa; tel. and fax 221-4024; internet www.ublaonline.org/paises/honduras.htm; Pres. Pastor TOMÁS MONTOYA; 24,142 mems.

Other Churches

Iglesia Cristiana Luterana de Honduras (Lutheran): Barrio Villa Adela, 19 Calle entre 5a y 6a Avda, Apdo 2861, Tegucigalpa; tel. and fax 225-4464; e-mail iclh@123.hn; internet www.iglesialuteranadehonduras.com; Pres. Rev. ARMINDO SCHMECHEL; 1,000 mems.

BAHÁ'Í FAITH

National Spiritual Assembly: Sendero de los Naranjos 2801, Col. Castaños, Apdo 273, Tegucigalpa; tel. 232-6124; fax 231-1343; internet www.bahaihon.org; Co-ordinator SOHEIL DOOKI; 40,000 mems resident in more than 500 localities.

The Press

DAILIES

La Gaceta: Empresa Nacional de Artes Gráficas, Col. Miraflores, Tegucigalpa; tel. 230-4956; fax 230-3026; f. 1830; morning; official govt paper; Gen. Man. MARTA GARCÍA CASCO; Co-ordinator MARCO ANTONIO RODRÍGUEZ CASTILLO; circ. 3,000.

El Heraldo: Avda los Próceres, Frente al Pani, Barrio San Felipe, Apdo 1938, Tegucigalpa; tel. 236-6000; e-mail contactos@elheraldo.hn; internet www.elheraldo.hn; f. 1979; morning; independent; Editor FERNANDO BERRÍOS; circ. 50,000.

El Nuevo Día: 3a Avda, 11–12 Calles, San Pedro Sula; tel. 552-4298; fax 557-9457; f. 1994; morning; independent; Pres. ABRAHAM ANDONIE; Editor ARMANDO CERRATO; circ. 20,000.

La Prensa: Guamilito, 3a Avda, 6–7 Calles No 34, Apdo 143, San Pedro Sula; tel. 553-3101; fax 553-0778; e-mail redaccion@laprensa.hn; internet www.laprensahn.com; f. 1964; morning; independent; Editor NELSON GARCÍA; Exec. Dir MARÍA ANTONIA FUENTES; circ. 50,000.

El Tiempo: 1 Calle, 5a Avda 102, Barrio Santa Anita, Cortés, Apdo 450, San Pedro Sula; tel. 553-3388; fax 553-4590; e-mail web.tiempo@continental.hn; internet www.tiempo.hn; f. 1960; morning; left-of-centre; Pres. JAIME ROSENTHAL OLIVA; Editor MANUEL GAMERO; circ. 35,000.

La Tribuna: Col. Santa Bárbara, Carretera al Primer Batallón de Infantería, Comayagüela, Apdo 1501, Tegucigalpa; tel. 234-3206; fax 234-3050; e-mail tribuna@latribuna.hn; internet www.latribuna.hn; f. 1976; morning; independent; Dir ADÁN ELVIR FLORES; Gen. Man. MANUEL ACOSTA MEDINA; circ. 45,000.

PERIODICALS

Comercio Global: Cámara de Comercio e Industrias de Tegucigalpa, Blvd Centroamérica, Apdo 3444, Tegucigalpa; tel. 232-4200; fax 232-0759; f. 1970; monthly; commercial and industrial news; Editor VANESSA BALDASSARRE.

Hablemos Claro: Edif. Torre Libertad, Blvd Suyapa, Residencial La Hacienda, Tegucigalpa; tel. 232-8058; fax 239-7008; e-mail rwa@hablemosclaro.com; internet www.hablemosclaro.com; f. 1990; weekly; Editor RODRIGO WONG ARÉVALO; circ. 9,000.

Hibueras: Apdo 955, Tegucigalpa; Dir RAÚL LANZA VALERIANO.

Honduras Weekly: Centro Comercial Villa Mare, Blvd Morazán, Apdo 1323, Tegucigalpa; tel. 239-0285; fax 232-2300; e-mail editor@hondurasweekly.com; internet www.hondurasweekly.com; f. 1988; weekly; English language; tourism, culture and the environment; Bureau Chief NICOLE MARRDER; Editor MARCO CÁCERES.

El Libertador: Tegucigalpa; internet www.ellibertador.hn; Dir JHONY LAGOS; Editor DELMER MEMBREÑO.

Poder Ciudadano: Residencial Las Lomas del Guijarro Sur, Calle Madrid, Casa 39, Tegucigalpa; tel. 239-4945; e-mail poderciudadanohn@yahoo.com; internet www.poderciudadano.info; f. 2007; weekly; govt-owned.

PRESS ASSOCIATION

Asociación de Prensa Hondureña: Casa del Periodista, Avda Gutemberg 1525, Calle 6, Barrio El Guanacaste, Apdo 893, Tegucigalpa; tel. 239-2970; fax 237-8102; f. 1930; Pres. MIGUEL OSMUNDO MEJÍA; Sec.-Gen. FELA ISABEL DUARTE.

Publishers

Centro Editorial: San Pedro Sula; tel. and fax 558-1282; Dir JULIO ESCOTO.

Ediciones Ramses: Edif. Torres Fiallos, Avda Jerez, Apdo 5600, Tegucigalpa; tel. 220-4248; fax 220-0833; e-mail servicioalcliente@edicionesramses.hn; internet edicionesramses.galeon.com; educational material.

Editora Fuego Nuevo: Col. Florencia Sur, Blvd Suyapa, Tegucigalpa; tel. 232-4638; fax 232-4964.

Editorial Pez Dulce: 143 Paseo La Leona, Barrio La Leona, Tegucigalpa; tel. and fax 222-1220; e-mail pezdulce@yahoo.com.

Editorial Universitaria de la Universidad Nacional Autónoma de Honduras: Blvd Suyapa, Tegucigalpa; tel. and fax 231-4601; f. 1847.

Guaymuras: Apdo 1843, Tegucigalpa; tel. 237-5433; fax 238-4578; e-mail ediguay@123.hn; internet www.guaymuras.hn; f. 1980; Dir ISOLDA ARITA MELZER.

Broadcasting and Communications

TELECOMMUNICATIONS

Regulatory Authority

Comisión Nacional de Telecomunicaciones (Conatel): Col. Modelo, 6a Avda Suroeste, Apdo 15012, Tegucigalpa; tel. 234-8600; fax 234-8611; e-mail conatel@conatel.hn; internet www.conatel.hn; Pres. RASEL ANTONIO TOMÉ.

Major Service Providers

The monopoly of the telecommunications sector by Hondutel ceased at the end of 2005, when the fixed line and international services market was opened to domestic and foreign investment. In 2009 there were, in addition to Hondutel, three private mobile cellular telephone providers in operation.

Claro Honduras: Col. San Carlos, Avda República de Colombia, Tegucigalpa; tel. 205-4222; internet www.claro.com.hn; f. 2003; operated by Servicios de Comunicaciones de Honduras (Sercom Honduras), a subsidiary of América Móvil, SA de CV (Mexico) since July 2004; mobile cellular telephone operator.

Digicel Honduras: Col. Lomas de Guijarro Sur, Edif. Plaza Azul, 6°, Local 69, Tegucigalpa; tel. 216-1800; internet www.digicel.hn; f. 2007; mobile cellular telephone operator; CEO MIGUEL GARCÍA.

Empresa Hondureña de Telecomunicaciones (Hondutel): Apdo 1794, Tegucigalpa; tel. 221-6555; fax 236-7795; e-mail miguel.velez@hondutelnet.hn; internet www.hondutel.hn; scheduled for privatization; Gen. Man. Gen. (retd) ROMEO VÁSQUEZ VELÁSQUEZ.

Multifon: Tegucigalpa; tel. 206-0607; e-mail sac@multifon.net; internet www.multifon.net; f. 2003; subsidiary of MultiData; awarded govt contract with UT Starcom (q.v.) for fixed telephone lines in 2003; Pres. JOSÉ RAFAEL FERRARI; CEO JOSÉ LUIS RIVERA.

Telefónica Celular (CELTEL): Edif. Celtel, contiguo a la Iglesia Episcopal, Blvd Suyapa, Col. Florencia Norte Hondureña, Tegucigalpa; tel. 235-7966; fax 220-7060; e-mail info@mail.celtel.net; internet www.tigo.com.hn; f. 1996; mobile cellular telephone company; 66.7% owned by Millicom International Cellular (Luxembourg).

UT Starcom (USA): Edif. Plaza Azul, 6°, Calle Viena, Avda Berlin, Col. Lomas del Guijarro Sur, Tegucigalpa; tel. 239-8289; fax 239-9161; internet www.utstar.com; awarded govt contract with Multifon (q.v.) for fixed telephone lines in 2003; Pres. and CEO HONG LIANG LU; Gen. Man. JULIO LARIOS.

BROADCASTING

Radio

Estereo McIntosh: La Ceiba, Atlántida; tel. 440-0326; fax 440-0325; commercial channel.

HRN, La Voz de Honduras: Blvd Suyapa, Apdo 642, Tegucigalpa; internet www.radiohrn.hn; commercial station; f. 1933; broadcasts 12 channels; 23 relay stations; Gen. Man. NAHÚN VALLADARES.

Power FM: Edif. Continental, Local 25, Calle Principal, Col. Miramontes, Tegucigalpa; tel. 239-4595; fax 239-7935; e-mail info@powerfm.hn; internet www.powerfm.hn; Gen. Man. XAVIER SIERRA.

Radio América: Col. Alameda, frente a la Droguería Mandofer, Apdo 259, Tegucigalpa; tel. 290-4950; fax 232-2923; internet www.radioamerica.hn; commercial station; broadcasts Radio San Pedro, Radio Continental, Radio Monderna, Radio Universal, Cadena Radial Sonora, Super Cien Stereo, Momentos FM Stereo and 3 regional channels; f. 1948; 13 relay stations; Gen. Man. MARCELO CHIMIRRI.

Radio Club Honduras: Salida Chamelecon, Apdo 273, San Pedro Sula; tel. 556-6173; fax 648-0723; e-mail hr2rch@yahoo.com; internet www.hr2rch.org; amateur radio club; Pres. DANIEL MEJÍA.

Radio Esperanza: La Esperanza, Intibucá; tel. 783-0025; fax 783-0644; internet www.honducontact.com/Radio%20Esperanza.htm; Dir J. M. DEL CID.

Radio Nacional de Honduras: Avda La Paz, contiguo a la Secretaría de Cultura, Artes y Deportes, Tegucigalpa; tel. 236-7551; fax 236-7359; internet www.rnh.hn; f. 1976; official station, operated by the Govt; Exec. Dir MARIO ORLANDO MENDOZA.

Radio la Voz del Atlántico: 12a Calle, 2a–3a Avda, Barrio Copen, Puerto Cortés; tel. 665-5166; fax 665-2401; e-mail atlantico@sescomnet.com; internet radioatlantico.8m.com.

La Voz de Centroamérica: 9a Calle, 10a Avda 64, Apdo 120, San Pedro Sula; tel. 552-7660; fax 557-3257; f. 1955; commercial station.

Television

Televicentro: Edif. Televicentro, Blvd Asuyapa, Apdo 734, Tegucigalpa; tel. 207-5514; internet www.televicentro.hn; f. 1987; 11 relay stations; Pres. JOSÉ RAFAEL FERRARI SAGASTUME.

Canal 5: tel. 232-7835; fax 232-0097; f. 1959; Gen. Man. JOSÉ RAFAEL FERRARI SAGASTUME.

Telecadena 7 y 4: tel. 239-2081; fax 232-0097; f. 1959; Pres. JOSÉ RAFAEL FERRARI SAGASTUME; Gen. Man. RAFAEL ENRIQUE VILLEDA.

Telesistema Hondureño, Canal 3 y 7: tel. 232-7064; fax 232-5019; f. 1967; Gen. Man. RAFAEL ENRIQUE VILLEDA.

VICA Television: 9a Calle, 10a Avda 64, Barrio Guamilito, Apdo 120, San Pedro Sula; tel. 552-4478; fax 557-3257; e-mail info@mayanet.hn; internet www.vicatv.hn; f. 1986; operates regional channels 2, 9 and 13; Pres. BLANCA SIKAFFY.

Finance

(cap. = capital; res = reserves; dep. = deposits; m. = million; brs = branches; amounts in lempiras unless otherwise stated)

BANKING

Central Bank

Banco Central de Honduras (BANTRAL): Avda Juan Ramón Molina, 7a Avda y 1a Calle, Apdo 3165, Tegucigalpa; tel. 237-2270; fax 237-1876; e-mail eanariba@mail.bch.hn; internet www.bch.hn; f. 1950; bank of issue; cap. 223.4m., res 2,148.7m., dep. 43,974m. (Dec. 2006); Pres. MARÍA ELENA MONDRAGÓN; Man. JORGE OVIEDO IMBODEN; 4 brs.

Commercial Banks

Banco Atlántida, SA (BANCATLAN): Plaza Bancatlán, Blvd Centroamérica, Apdo 3164, Tegucigalpa; tel. 232-1050; fax 232-6120; e-mail webmaster@bancatlan.hn; internet www.bancatlan.hn; f. 1913; cap. 2,017.0m., res 162.8m., dep. 23,413.7m. (Dec. 2008); Exec. Pres. GUILLERMO BUESO; Exec. Vice-Pres GUSTAVO OVIEDO, ILDOIRA G. DE BONILLA; 132 brs.

Banco Bac-Bamer, SA: Blvd Suyapa, frente a Emisoras Unidas, Apdo 116, Tegucigalpa; tel. 216-0200; fax 239-4509; internet www.bac.net/honduras; fmrly Banco Mercantil, S.A.

Banco Continental, SA (BANCON): 9–10 Avda NO, Blvd Morazán, San Pedro Sula; tel. 550-0880; fax 550-2750; e-mail imontoya@continental.hn; internet www.bancon.hn; f. 1974; cap. 500.0m., res 5.1m., dep. 2,752.4m. (Dec. 2006); Pres., Chair. and Gen. Man. JAIME ROSENTHAL OLIVA; 41 brs.

Banco Financiera Comercial Hondureña (Banco FICOHSA): Edif. Plaza Victoria, Col. Las Colinas, Blvd Francia, Tegucigalpa; tel. 239-6410; fax 239-6420; e-mail ficobanc@ficohsa.hn; internet www.ficohsa.com; Pres. LEONEL GIANNINI.

Banco de Honduras, SA: Blvd Suyapa, Col. Loma Linda Sur, Tegucigalpa; tel. 232-6122; fax 232-6167; internet www.bancodehonduras.citibank.com; f. 1889; subsidiary of Citibank NA (USA); cap. 250.0m., res 6.8m., dep. 1,940.9m. (2008); Gen. Man. MÁXIMO R. VIDAL; 2 brs.

Banco HSBC Honduras, SA: Intersección Blvd Suyapa y Blvd Juan Pablo II, Apdo 344, Tegucigalpa; tel. 240-0909; internet www.hsbc.com.hn; Exec. Pres. JONATHAN HARTLEY.

Banco de Occidente, SA (BANCOCCI): 6a Avda, Calle 2–3, Apdo 3284, Tegucigalpa; tel. 263-144; fax 263-8240; internet www.bancocci.hn; f. 1951; cap. 800.0m., res 315.1m., dep. 17,297.4m. (2006); Pres. and Gen. Man. JORGE BUESO ARIAS; Vice-Pres. EMILIO MEDINA R.; 146 brs.

Banco del País (BANPAIS): San Pedro Sula; internet www.banpais.hn; f. 1969; acquired Banco Sogerin and client portfolio of Banco de las Fuerzas Armadas in 2003; Pres. JUAN MIGUEL TORREBIARTE.

Banco de los Trabajadores, SA (BANCOTRAB): 3a Avda, 13a Calle, Comayagüela, Apdo 3246, Tegucigalpa; tel. 238-0017; fax 238-0077; internet www.btrab.com; f. 1967; cap. 204.8m. (Dec. 2002); Pres. ROLANDO DEL CID VELÁSQUEZ; 13 brs.

Development Banks

Banco Centroamericano de Integración Económica: Edif. Sede BCIE, Blvd Suyapa, Apdo 772, Tegucigalpa; tel. 240-2243; fax 228-2185; e-mail cmartine@bcie.hn; internet www.bcie.org; f. 1960 to finance the economic devt of the Central American Common Market and its mem. countries; mems: Costa Rica, El Salvador, Guatemala, Honduras, Nicaragua; cap. and res US $1,020.0m. (June 2003); Dir SONIA MARLINA DUBÓN.

Banco Financiera Centroamericana, SA (FICENSA): Edif. FICENSA, Blvd Morazán, Apdo 1432, Tegucigalpa; tel. 238-1661; fax 238-1630; e-mail rrivera@ficensa.com; internet www.ficensa.com; f. 1974; private org. providing finance for industry, commerce and transport; Pres. OSWALDO LÓPEZ ARELLANO.

Banco Hondureño del Café, SA (BANHCAFE): Calle República de Costa Rica, Blvd Juan Pablo II, Col. Lomas del Mayab, Apdo 583, Tegucigalpa; tel. 232-8370; fax 232-8782; e-mail bcaferhu@hondutel.hn; internet www.banhcafe.com; f. 1981 to help finance coffee production; owned principally by private coffee producers; cap. 260.5m., res 69.2m., dep. 2,378.2m. (Dec. 2008); Pres. MIGUEL ALFONSO FERNÁNDEZ RÁPALO; 50 brs.

Banco Nacional de Desarrollo Agrícola (BANADESA): 4a Avda y 5a Avda, 13a y 14a Calles, Barrio Concepción, Apdo 212, Tegucigalpa; tel. 237-2201; fax 237-5187; e-mail banadesa@banadesa.hn; internet www.banadesa.hn; f. 1980; govt devt bank; loans to agricultural sector; cap. 323.0m., res 3.6m., dep. 689.2m. (Dec. 2007); Gen. Man. ENRIQUE ALBERTO CASTELLON; 35 brs.

Banking Associations

Asociación Hondureña de Instituciones Bancarias (AHIBA): Edif. AHIBA, Blvd Suyapa, Apdo 1344, Tegucigalpa; tel. 235-6770; fax 239-0191; e-mail ahiba@ahiba.hn; internet www.ahiba.hn; f. 1957; 21 mem. banks; Pres. ROQUE RIBERA RIVAS; Exec. Dir MARÍA LYDIA SOLANO.

Comisión Nacional de Bancos y Seguros (CNBS): Edif. Santa Fé, Col. Castaño Sur, Paseo Virgilio Zelaya Rubí Bloque C, Apdo 20074, Tegucigalpa; tel. 290-4500; fax 237-6232; e-mail rbarahona@cnbs.gov.hn; internet www.cnbs.gov.hn; Pres. MILTON JIMÉNEZ PUERTO.

STOCK EXCHANGE

Bolsa Centroamericana de Valores: Edif. Sonisa, Costado este Plaza Bancatlán, Apdo 2885, Tegucigalpa; tel. 239-1930; fax 232-2700; internet www.bcv.hn; Pres. JOSÉ ARTURO ALVARADO.

INSURANCE

American Home Assurance Co: Edif. Los Castaños, 4°, Blvd Morazán, Apdo 3220, Tegucigalpa; tel. 232-4671; fax 232-8169; internet www.aig.com; f. 1958; Mans LEONARDO MOREIRA, EDGAR WAGNER.

Aseguradora Hondureña, SA: Edif. El Planetario, 4°, Col. Lomas del Guijarro Sur, Calle Madrid, Avda Paris, Apdo 312, Tegucigalpa; tel. 216-2672; fax 231-0982; e-mail gerencia@asegurahon.hn; internet www.amundial.com.hn; f. 1954; Pres. MANUEL JOSÉ PAREDES LEFEVRÉ.

HSBC Seguros: Edif. Torre Imperial Colonia Palmira, Avda República de Panamá, Tegucigalpa; tel. 237-8219; internet www.hsbc.com.hn; Exec. Dir JONATHAN HARTLEY.

Interamericana de Seguros, SA: Col. Los Castaños, Apdo 593, Tegucigalpa; tel. 232-7614; fax 232-7762; internet www.interamericanadeseguros.com; f. 1957; part of Grupo Financiero Ficohsa; Pres. LEONEL GIANNINI K.

Pan American Life Insurance Co (PALIC): Edif. PALIC, Avda República de Chile 804, Col. Palmira, Apdo 123, Tegucigalpa; tel. 216-0909; fax 239-3437; e-mail servicioalclientehn@panamericanlife.com; internet www.panamericanlife.com; f. 1944; Pres. SALVADOR ORTEGA (Central America); Gen. Man. MARÍA DEL ROSARIO ALVAREZ.

Seguros Atlántida: Tres Caminos, Francisco Morazán, Tegucigalpa; tel. 232-4014; fax 232-3688; e-mail info@seatlan.com; internet www.segurosatlantida.com; f. 1986; Pres. GUILLERMO BUESO; Gen. Man. JUAN MIGUEL ORELLANA.

Seguros Continental, SA: Edif. Continental, 4°, 3a Avda SO, 2a y 3a Calle, Apdo 605, San Pedro Sula; tel. 550-0880; fax 550-2750; e-mail seguros@continental.hn; internet www.continental.hn; f. 1968; Pres. JAIME ROSENTHAL OLIVA; Gen. Man. MARIO R. SOLÍS DACOSTA.

Seguros Crefisa: Edif. Banco Ficensa, 1°, Blvd Morazán, Apdo Postal 3774, Tegucigalpa; tel. 238-1750; fax 238-1714; internet www.crefisa.com; f. 1993; Gen. Man. MARIO BATRES PINEDA.

Seguros del País: Edif. IPM Anexo, 4°, Blvd Centroamérica, Tegucigalpa; tel. 239-7077; fax 232-4216; internet www.segpais.com; f. 2000; Gen. Man. GERARDO RIVERA.

Insurance Association

Cámara Hondureña de Aseguradores (CAHDA): Edif. Casa Metromedia, 3°, Col. San Carlos, Apdo 3290, Tegucigalpa; tel. 221-5354; fax 221-5356; e-mail info@cahda.org; internet www.cahda.org; f. 1974; Pres. MARIO DEL ROSARIO ALVAREZ.

Trade and Industry

GOVERNMENT AGENCIES

Fondo Hondureño de Inversión Social (FHIS): Antiguo Edif. I.P.M., Col. Godoy, Comayagüela, Apdo 3581, Tegucigalpa; e-mail csalgado@fhis.hn; internet www.fhis.hn; tel. 234-5231; fax 534-5255; social investment fund; Dir CARLOS BANEGAS.

Fondo Social de la Vivienda (FOSOVI): Col. Kennedy, 5°, entrada antigua bodega del INVA, Tegucigalpa; tel. 230-2624; fax 230-2245; e-mail fosovi.hn@hotmail.com; social fund for housing, urbanization and devt.

DEVELOPMENT ORGANIZATIONS

Consejo Hondureño de la Empresa Privada (COHEP): Edif. 8, Calle Yoro, Col. Tepeyac, Apdo 3240, Tegucigalpa; tel. 235-3336; fax 235-3345; e-mail consejo@cohep.com; internet www.cohep.com; f. 1968; represents 52 private sector trade asscns; Pres. AMILCAR BULNES.

Dirección Ejecutiva de Fomento a la Minería (DEFOMIN): Edif. DEFOMIN, 3°, Blvd Miraflores, Apdo 981, Tegucigalpa; tel. 232-6721; fax 232-8635; promotes the mining sector; Dir-Gen. SANDRA MARLENE PINTO.

Instituto Hondureño del Café (IHCAFE): Edif. El Faro, Col. las Minitas, Apdo 40-C, Tegucigalpa; tel. 237-3130; fax 238-2368; e-mail gerencia@ihcafe.2hn.com; internet www.cafedehonduras.org; f. 1970; coffee devt programme; Gen. Man. FERNANDO D. MONTES M.

Instituto Hondureño de Mercadeo Agrícola (IHMA): Apdo 727, Tegucigalpa; tel. 235-3193; fax 235-5719; internet ihmahn.org; f. 1978; agricultural devt agency; Gen. Man. TULIO ROLANDO GIRÓN ROMERO.

Instituto Nacional Agrario (INA): Col. La Almeda, 4a Avda, entre 10a y 11a Calles, No 1009, Apdo 3391, Tegucigalpa; tel. 232-4893; fax 232-7398; internet www.ina.hn; agricultural devt programmes; Dir CÉSAR HAM.

Instituto Nacional de Conservación Forestal (INCF): Salida Carretera del Norte, Zona El Carrizal, Comayagüela, Apdo 1378, Tegucigalpa; tel. 223-8810; fax 223-3348; e-mail alvarezlazzaroni@yahoo.com; f. 2008 to replace Corporación Hondureña de Desarrollo Forestal (f. 1974); control of the forestry industry and conservation of forest resources; Dir SUPAYA OTERO CARVAJAL.

CHAMBERS OF COMMERCE

Cámara de Comercio e Industrias de Copán: Edif. Comercial Romero, 2°, Barrio Mercedes, Santa Rosa de Copán; tel. 662-0843; fax 662-1783; e-mail info@camaracopan.com; internet www.camaracopan.com; f. 1940; Pres. EUDOCIO LEIVA AMAYA.

Cámara de Comercio e Industrias de Cortés (CCIC): Barrio Las Brisas, 22 y 24 Calle, Apdo Postal 14, San Pedro Sula; tel. 566-0345; fax 553-3777; e-mail ccic@ccichonduras.org; internet www.ccichonduras.org; f. 1931; 812 mems; Pres. LUIS NAPOLEON LARACH; Dir RAÚL REINA CLEAVES.

Cámara de Comercio e Industrias de Tegucigalpa (CCIT): Blvd Centroamérica, Apdo 3444, Tegucigalpa; tel. 232-4200; fax 232-5764; e-mail asuservicio@ccit.hn; internet www.ccit.hn; Pres. ALINE FLORES (acting).

Federación de Cámaras de Comercio e Industrias de Honduras (FEDECAMARA): Edif. Castañito, 2°, 6a Avda, Col. Los Castaños, Apdo 3393, Tegucigalpa; tel. 232-1870; fax 232-6083; e-mail fedecamara.direccion@amnettgu.com; internet www.fedecamara.org; f. 1948; 1,200 mems; Pres. EDISON CARDENAS; Coordinator JUAN FERRERA LÓPEZ.

Fundación para la Inversión y Desarrollo de Exportaciones (FIDE) (Foundation for Investment and Export Development): Col. La Estancia, Plaza Marte, final del Blvd Morazán, POB 2029, Tegucigalpa; tel. 221-6303; fax 221-6318; internet www.hondurasinfo.hn; f. 1984; private, non-profit agency; Pres. VILMA SIERRA DE FONSECA.

Honduran American Chamber of Commerce (Amcham Honduras): Commercial Area Hotel Honduras Maya, POB 1838, Tegucigalpa; tel. 232-6035; fax 232-2031; e-mail amcham1@quikhonduras.com; internet www.amchamhonduras.org; f. 1981; Pres. ROBERTO ALVAREZ GUERRERO; Exec. Dir JUAN CARLOS CASCO.

INDUSTRIAL AND TRADE ASSOCIATIONS

Consejo Hondureño de la Empresa Privada (COHEP): Edif. 8, Col. Tepeyac, Calle Yoro, Apdo 3240, Tegucigalpa; tel. 235-3336; fax 235-3345; e-mail consejo@cohep.com; internet www.cohep.com; f. 1968; umbrella org. representing 54 industrial and trade asscns; Pres. AMILCAR BULNES.

Asociación Hondureña de Productores de Café (AHPROCAFE) (Coffee Producers' Association): Edif. AHPROCAFE, Avda La Paz, Apdo 959, Tegucigalpa; tel. 236-8286; fax 236-8310; e-mail ahprocafe@amnet.tgu.com; Pres. ASTERIO REYES.

Asociación Nacional de Acuicultores de Honduras (ANDAH) (Aquaculture Association of Honduras): Calle Vicente Williams, Barrio La Esperanza, Apdo 229, Choluteca; tel. 782-0986; fax 782-3848; e-mail andahn@hondutel.hn; f. 1986; 136 mems; Pres. ROBERTO CORRALES BARAHONA.

Asociación Nacional de Exportadores de Honduras (ANEXHON) (National Association of Exporters): Industrias Panavisión, salida nueva a la Lima Frente a Sigmanet, San Pedro Sula; tel. 553-3029; fax 557-0203; e-mail roberto@ipsa.hn; comprises 104 private enterprises; Pres. ROBERTO PANAYOTTI.

Asociación Nacional de Industriales (ANDI) (National Association of Manufacturers): Edif. Fundación Covelo, 3°, Col. Castaño Sur, Blvd Morazán, Apdo 3447, Tegucigalpa; tel. 239-1238; fax 221-5199; e-mail andi@andi.hn; internet www.andi.hn; Pres. ADOLFO FACUSSÉ; Sec. LEONARDO VILLEDA BERMUDEZ.

Federación Nacional de Agricultores y Ganaderos de Honduras (FENAGH) (Farmers' and Livestock Breeders' Association): Col. Miramone, Avda Principal, 7a calle 1447, Tegucigalpa; tel. 239-1303; fax 231-1392; e-mail fenagh@hotmail.com; Exec. Dir MARCO POLO MICHELETTI.

MAJOR COMPANIES

The following are some of the major companies currently operating in Honduras:

Aquacultura Fonseca: Carretera a Orocuina, desvío a Linaca, Apdo 181/255, Choluteca; tel. 782-0099; fax 782-2579; e-mail ismael@seajoy.com; internet www.seajoy.com; f. 1985; seafood exporters; owned by Seajoy, Miami, FL, USA; Gen. Man. ISMAEL WONG C.

Azucarera La Grecia, SA de CV: Municipio de Marcovia, Dept de Choluteca, Apdo 32, Choluteca; tel. 887-3201; fax 887-3203; f. 1976 as Azucarera Central; processing and refining of sugar cane; acquired by Grupo Panataleón in 2008; Man. GUILLERMO LIPPMANN.

Breakwater Resources: Apdo 342, San Pedro Sula; tel. 659-3051; fax 659-3059; e-mail mochito@breakwater.hn; internet www.breakwater.ca; Canadian mining co, owner/operator of El Mochito mine; Chair. and CEO GARTH MACRAE; Vice-Pres. (Latin America) DANIEL GOFFAUX.

Cementos del Norte, SA de CV (CENOSA): Río Bijao, Choloma, Apdo 132, Cortés; tel. 669-1407; fax 669-1411; internet www.cenosa.hn; f. 1958; cement producers; Pres. YANI ROSENTHAL HIDALGO; Gen. Man. EDWIN ARGUETA; 265 employees.

Cervecería Hondureña, SA: Blvd. del Norte, Carretera a Puerto Cortés, Apdo 86, San Pedro Sula; tel. 553-3310; fax 552-2845; e-mail centroinformacion@ca.sabmiller.com; internet www.cerveceriahondurena.com; f. 1915; brewery and soft drink manufacturers; subsidiary of SABMiller PLC (United Kingdom); Pres. MAURICIO LEIVA ARBOLEDA; Dir of Corp. Relations AUGUSTO CHICAS; 1,150 employees.

Compañía Azucarera Choluteca, SA de CV: Municipio de Marcovia, Zona de los Mangos, Apdo 15, Choluteca; tel. 882-0530; fax 882-0554; e-mail achsa@hondudata.hn; f. 1967; sugar-cane refining; Gen. Man. BRAULIO CRUZ ASCENCIO; 180 employees.

Compañía Azucarera Hondureña, SA: 3 Avda 36, Municipio de Villanueva, Búfalo, Apdo 552, Cortés; tel. 574-8092; fax 574-8093; e-mail sugar1@hondutel.hn; f. 1938; cultivation and refining of sugar cane; Pres. SERGIO R. SALINAS S.; Gen. Man. CHARLES HEYER; 560 employees.

Compañía Hulera Sula: 3.5km, Carretera a Puerto Cortés, Frente al Seguro Social, Apdo 202, San Pedro Sula; tel. 551-2832; fax 551-3718; e-mail hulesula@globalnet.hn; internet www.hulerasula.hn; f. 1963; manufacturer of plastics and rubber products; Gen. Man. HÉCTOR GUILLÉN.

Corporación Lady Lee: Centro Comercial Megaplaza 2km, Autopista al Aeropuerto, Apdo 948, San Pedro Sula; tel. 580-1584; fax 580-6161; e-mail info@corporacionladylee.com; internet www.ladylee.com; department stores; Gen. Man. RAYMOND MAALOUF.

Derivados de Metal: 3km después de Choloma, Quebrada Seca Choloma, Apdo 797, Cortés; tel. 612-0515; fax 669-3066; e-mail demesa@sigmanet.hn; steel manufacturer; Gen. Man. MANUEL CASTILLO.

Droguería Pharma Internacional: Casa 1812, Calle 11, 2a Avda, Col. Alameda, Tegucigalpa; tel. 234-8989; fax 234-9292; e-mail info@pharmainternacional.com; internet www.pharmainternacional.com; f. 1994; manufacturers of pharmaceutical products; Gen. Man. AURELIO NEMBRINI.

Excel Automotriz: Tegucigalpa; known as Autoexcel until 2010; part of the Grupo DIDEA; distributor of cars and car parts; Exec. Vice-Pres. (Group) CARLOS BOZA.

Gabriel Kafati, SA: Barrio La Bolsa, Comayaguela, POB 37, Tegucigalpa; tel. 225-1675; fax 225-3792; e-mail sales@cafeelindio.com; internet www.cafeelindio.com; f. 1933; f. 1933; coffee producer; Gen. Man. MIGUEL OSCAR KAFATI.

Hilos y Mechas, SA de CV: Carretera a Puerto Cortés, Apdo 118, San Pedro Sula; tel. 558-8141; fax 558-8142; e-mail himesa@himesa.hn; internet www.himesa.hn; f. 1953; manufacturers of cotton fabrics, twine and thread; Gen. Man. EDUARDO HANDAL; 856 employees.

Lácteos de Honduras, SA de CV (LACTHOSA): Carretera a Puerto Cortés, Apdo 140, San Pedro Sula; tel. 566-3828; fax 566-3917; e-mail servicioalcliente@lacthosa.com; internet www.lacthosa.com; manufacturer of dairy products and fruit juices under the Sula brand; Gen. Man. SHUKRI KAFIE; 1,000 employees.

Leche y Derivados, SA (LEYDE): 8km Carretera a Tela, Apdo 95, La Ceiba; tel. 553-1417; fax 441-0108; f. 1973; milk and dairy products; Pres. JOSÉ BONANO; 1,200 employees.

Minerales Entremares Honduras, SA: Edif. Inmobiliaria Cordillera, Blvd Azocona, Anillo Periferico, Prados Universitarios, Tegucigalpa; tel. 235-5826; internet www.goldcorp.com; subsidiary of Goldcorp Inc. (Canada); mining co; CEO EDUARDO VILLACORTA; Spokesperson HÉCTOR SEVILLA.

Palao Williams & Co: Col. Lomas del Mayab, Calle Hibueras, Avda Cotán 3359, Tegucigalpa; tel. 232-0799; fax 231-3712; e-mail dpca@david.intertel.hn; accountants; Gen. Man. OSCAR HERNAN CASTILLO.

Procesadora de Tabaco, SA: 2506 Blvd del Sur, Apdo 130, San Pedro Sula; tel. 556-9113; fax 556-9410; e-mail protabsa@sulanet.net; f. 1996; tobacco maufacturer; Gen. Man. CÉSAR LÓPEZ PÉREZ; 1,000 employees.

Químicas Handal de Centroamérica, SA de CV: Km 2.6 Autopista a Puerto Cortés, Choloma, Apdo 559, Cortés; tel. 565-2900; fax 565-2909; e-mail info@quimicashandal.com; internet www.quimicashandal.com; f. 1967; manufacturer of shoe care products; Gen. Man. FUAD HANDAL.

Tabacalera Hondureña, SA: Carretera Chamelecon, Zona El Cacao, Apdo 64, San Pedro Sula; tel. 556-6161; fax 556-6189; e-mail graco.paredes@bat.com; f. 1928; subsidiary of British-American Tobacco Ltd, United Kingdom; cigarette manufacturers; Man. EDUARDO CASTAÑEDA; 280 employees.

Tela Railroad Company: Edif. Banco del País, 5°, Blvd Suyapa, Apdo 155, Tegucigalpa; tel. 235-8084; fax 235-8083; banana producers; subsidiary of Chiquita Brands International; Vice-Pres. FERNANDO SÁNCHEZ.

Unilever de Centroamérica, Operación Honduras: Tegucigalpa; internet www.unilever-ancam.com; f. 2000 after Unilever bought Corporación Cressida; manufacturers of detergents, soaps, fats and vegetable oils; subsidiary of Unilever (United Kingdom/Netherlands); Chair. MIGUEL FACUSSÉ BARJUM; 600 employees.

UTILITIES

Electricity

AES Honduras: Tegucigalpa; tel. 556-5563; fax 556-5567; subsidiary of AES Corpn (USA); CEO CARLOS LARACH.

Empresa Nacional de Energía Eléctrica (ENEE) (National Electrical Energy Co): Edif. EMAS, 4°, Bo El Trapiche, Tegucigalpa; tel. 235-2934; fax 235-2969; e-mail informatica@enee.hn; internet www.enee.hn; f. 1957; state-owned electricity co; Pres. RIGOBERTO CUELLAR; Man. ROBERTO MARTÍNEZ LOZANO.

Luz y Fuerza de San Lorenzo, SA (LUFUSSA): Edif. Comercial Los Próceres, Final Avda Los Próceres 3917, Tegucigalpa; tel. 236-6545; fax 236-5826; e-mail lufussa@lufussa.com; internet www.lufussa.com; f. 1994; generates thermoelectric power; Pres. EDUARDO KAFIE.

TRADE UNIONS

Central General de Trabajadores de Honduras (CGTH) (General Confederation of Labour of Honduras): Barrio La Granja, antiguo Local CONADI, Apdo 1236, Comayagüela, Tegucigalpa; tel. 225-2509; fax 225-2525; e-mail cgt@david.intertel.hn; f. 1970; legally recognized from 1982; attached to Partido Demócrata Cristiano de Honduras; Sec.-Gen. DANIEL A. DURÓN; 250,000 mems (2007).

Federación Auténtica Sindical de Honduras (FASH): Barrio La Granja, antiguo Local CONADI, Apdo 1236, Comayagüela, Tegucigalpa; tel. 225-2509.

Federación Sindical del Sur (FESISUR): Barrio La Ceiba, 1 c. al norte del Instituto Santa María Goretti, Apdo 256, Choluteca; tel. 882-0328; Pres. REINA DE ORDÓÑEZ.

Unión Nacional de Campesinos (UNC) (National Union of Farmworkers): antiguo Local CONADI, Barrio La Granja, Comayagüela, Tegucigalpa; tel. 225-1005; Sec.-Gen. VÍCTOR MANUEL CAMPO.

Confederación Hondureña de Cooperativas (CHC): 3001 Blvd Morazán, Edif. I.F.C., Apdo 3265, Tegucigalpa; tel. 232-2890; fax 231-1024; Pres. JOSÉ R. MORENO PAZ.

Confederación de Trabajadores de Honduras (CTH) (Workers' Confederation of Honduras): Edif. Beige, 2°, Avda Juan Ramón Molina, Barrio El Olvido, Apdo 720, Tegucigalpa; tel. 238-3178; fax 237-8575; e-mail cthhn@yahoo.com; f. 1964; Sec.-Gen. (vacant); 55,000 mems (2007).

Asociación Nacional de Campesinos Hondureños (ANACH) (National Association of Honduran Farmworkers): Edif. Chávez Mejía, 2°, Calle Juan Ramón Molina, Barrio El Olvido, Tegucigalpa; tel. 238-0558; f. 1962; Pres. BENEDICTO CÁRCAMO MEJÍA; 80,000 mems.

Federación Central de Sindicatos de Trabajadores Libres de Honduras (FECESITLIH) (Honduran Federation of Free Trade Unions): antiguo Edif. EUKZKADI, 3a Avda, 3a y 4a Calle No 336, Comayagüela, Tegucigalpa; tel. 237-3955; Pres. (vacant).

Federación Sindical de Trabajadores Nacionales de Honduras (FESITRANH) (Honduran Federation of Farmworkers): 10a Avda, 11a Calle, Barrio Los Andes, Apdo 245, Cortés, San Pedro Sula; tel. 557-2539; f. 1957; Pres. MAURO FRANCISCO GONZÁLEZ.

Sindicato Nacional de Motoristas de Equipo Pesado de Honduras (SINAMEQUIPH) (National Union of HGV Drivers): Avda Juan Ramón Molina, Barrio El Olvido, Tegucigalpa; tel. 237-4415; Pres. ERASMO FLORES.

Confederación Unitaria de Trabajadores de Honduras (CUTH): Barrio Bella Vista, 10a Calle, 8a y 9a Avda, Casa 829, Tegucigalpa; tel. and fax 220-4732; e-mail sgeneral@cuth.hn; internet www.cuth.hn; f. 1992; Sec.-Gen. ISRAEL SALINAS; 295,000 mems (2007).

Asociación Nacional de Empleados Públicos de Honduras (ANDEPH) (National Association of Public Employees of Honduras): Barrio Los Dolores, Avda Paulino Valladares, frente

Panadería Italiana, atrás Iglesia Los Dolores, Tegucigalpa; tel. 237-4393; Pres. FAUSTO MOLINA CASTRO.

Federación Unitaria de Trabajadores de Honduras (FUTH): Barrio La Granja, contiguo Banco Atlántida, Casa 3047, frente a mercadito La Granja, Apdo 1663, Comayagüela, Tegucigalpa; tel. 225-1010; f. 1981; Pres. JUAN ALBERTO BARAHONA MEJÍA; 45,000 mems.

Federación de Cooperativas de la Reforma Agraria de Honduras (FECORAH): Casa 2223, antiguo Local de COAPALMA, Col. Rubén Darío, Tegucigalpa; tel. 232-0547; fax 225-2525; f. 1970; legally recognized from 1974; Pres. Ing. WILTON SALINAS.

Transport

RAILWAYS

The railway network is confined to the north of the country and most lines are used for fruit cargo. There are 995 km of railway track in Honduras, of which 349 km are narrow gauge. Only 255 km of track were in use in 2004.

Ferrocarril Nacional de Honduras (National Railway of Honduras): 1a Avda entre 1a y 2a Calle, Apdo 496, San Pedro Sula; tel. and fax 552-8001; f. 1870; govt-owned; Gen. Man. JOAQUÍN MIGUEL SOSA.

ROADS

In 2004 there were an estimated 13,720 km of roads in Honduras, of which 2,970 km were paved. A further 3,156 km of roads have been constructed by the Fondo Cafetero Nacional, and some routes have been built by the Corporación Hondureña de Desarrollo Forestal in order to facilitate access to coffee plantations and forestry development areas. In 2003 the Central American Bank for Economic Integration approved funding worth $22.5m. for the construction of a highway from Puerto Cortés to the Guatemalan border.

Dirección General de Carreteras: Barrio La Bolsa, Comayagüela, Tegucigalpa; tel. 225-1703; fax 225-2469; e-mail dgc@soptravi.gob.hn; internet www.soptravi.gob.hn; f. 1915; highways board; Dir MARCIO ALVARADO ENAMORADO.

SHIPPING

The principal port is Puerto Cortés on the Caribbean coast, which is the largest and best-equipped port in Central America. Other ports include Tela, La Ceiba, Trujillo/Castilla, Roatán, Amapala and San Lorenzo; all are operated by the Empresa Nacional Portuaria. There are several minor shipping companies. A number of foreign shipping lines call at Honduran ports.

Empresa Nacional Portuaria (National Port Authority): Apdo 18, Puerto Cortés; tel. 665-0987; fax 665-1402; e-mail rbabun@enp.hn; internet www.enp.hn; f. 1965; has jurisdiction over all ports in Honduras; a network of paved roads connects Puerto Cortés and San Lorenzo with the main cities of Honduras, and with the principal cities of Central America; Gen. Man. ROBERTO BABUM.

CIVIL AVIATION

Local airlines in Honduras compensate for the deficiencies of road and rail transport, linking together small towns and inaccessible districts. There are four international airports: Golosón airport in La Ceiba, Ramón Villeda Morales airport in San Pedro Sula, Toncontín airport in Tegucigalpa and Juan Manuel Gálvaz airport in Roatán. A new airport being constructed at Copán, near the Copán Ruinas archaeological park, was expected to commence operations in 2011.

Dirección General Aeronáutica Civil: Apdo 30145, Tegucigalpa; tel. 233-1115; fax 233-3683; e-mail soptravi@soptravi.gob.hn; internet www.soptravi.gob.hn; airport infrastucture and security; Dir-Gen. JOSÉ MARIO MALDONADO MUÑOZ.

Isleña Airlines: Centro Financiero, Centro Comercial Megaplaza, La Ceiba; tel. 442-1967; e-mail info@flyislena.com; internet www.flyislena.com; subsidiary of TACA, El Salvador; domestic service and service to the Cayman Islands; Pres. and CEO ARTURO ALVARADO WOOD.

Tourism

Tourists are attracted by the Mayan ruins, the fishing and boating facilities in Trujillo Bay and Lake Yojoa, near San Pedro Sula, and the beaches on the northern coast. There is an increasing eco-tourism industry. Honduras received 869,500 tourists in 2009; in 2008 tourism receipts totalled US $621m.

Asociación Hotelera y Afines de Honduras (AHAH): Hotel Escuela Madrid, Suite 402, Col. 21 de Octubre-Los Girasoles, Tegucigalpa; tel. 221-5805; fax 221-4789; e-mail ahah@123.hn; Pres. LUZ MEJÍA; Exec. Dir KARLA AGUILAR.

Asociación Nacional de Agencias de Viajes y Turismo de Honduras: Blvd Morazán, frente a McDonald's, Tegucigalpa; tel. 232-2308; e-mail scarlethmoncada@yahoo.com; Pres. SCARLETH DE MONCADA.

Asociación de Tour Operadores de Honduras (OPTURH): Col. Juan Lindo, 8 Calle, 32 Avda, Noroeste, Casa 709, San Pedro Sula; tel. 557-8447; e-mail presidencia@opturh.com; f. 1997; Pres. SONIA REGALADO.

Cámara Nacional de Turismo de Honduras: Col. Lomas del Guijarro Sur, Calle Paris 'Da', Casa de lado izquierdo, Tegucigalpa; tel. 232-1937; internet www.canaturh.org; f. 1976; Pres. EPAMINONDAS MARINAKYS.

Instituto Hondureño de Turismo: Edif. Europa, 5°, Col. San Carlos, Apdo 3261, Tegucigalpa; tel. and fax 222-2124; e-mail tourisminfo@iht.hn; internet www.iht.hn; f. 1972; Dir NELLY JEREZ (Minister of Tourism).

Defence

Military service is voluntary. Active service lasts eight months, with subsequent reserve training. As assessed at November 2009, the armed forces numbered 12,000: army 8,300, navy 1,400 and air force some 2,300. Paramilitary public security and defence forces numbered 8,000. In addition, some 421 US troops were based in Honduras.

Defence Budget: 1,930m. lempiras (US $102m.) in 2009.

Chairman of the Joint Chiefs of Staff: Gen. CARLOS ANTONIO CUÉLLAR.

Chief of Staff (Army): Brig.-Gen. CARLOS ALBERTO ESPINOZA URQUÍA.

Chief of Staff (Air Force): Col MARCO VITELIO CASTILLO BROWN.

Chief of Staff (Navy): Rear-Adm. JUAN PABLO RODRÍGUEZ RODRÍGUEZ.

Education

Primary education, beginning at six years of age and comprising three cycles of three years, is officially compulsory and is provided free of charge. Secondary education, which is not compulsory, begins at the age of 15 and lasts for three years. In 2007/08 enrolment at primary schools included 97% of children in the relevant age-group, while enrolment at secondary schools in that year was equivalent to 65% of children (57% of boys; 72% of girls) in the appropriate age-group. There are eight universities, including the Autonomous National University in Tegucigalpa. Estimated spending on education in 2004 was 8,779m. lempiras, representing 34.3% of the total budget.

Bibliography

For works on Central America generally, see Select Bibliography (Books)

Binns, J. R. *The United States in Honduras*. Jefferson, NC, McFarland & Co, 2000.

Bradshaw, S., and Linneker, B. *Challenging Women's Poverty: Perspectives on Gender and Poverty Reduction Strategies from Nicaragua and Honduras (CIIR Briefing)*. London, Catholic Institute for International Relations, 2004.

Chambers, G. A. *Race, Nation and West Indian Immigration to Honduras, 1890-1940*. Baton Rouge, Louisiana State University Press, 2010.

De Coster, J., and Anson R. (Ed.). *Profile of the Maquila Apparel Industry in Honduras*. Wilmslow, Textiles Intelligence Ltd, 2003.

Douglass, J. G. *Hinterland Households: Rural Agrarian Diversity in Northwest Honduras*. Boulder, CO, University of Colorado Press, 2002.

Euraque, D. A. *Reinterpreting the Banana Republic: Region and State in Honduras, 1870–1972*. Chapel Hill, NC, University of North Carolina Press, 1996.

Loker W. M. *Changing Places: Environment, Development and Social Change in Rural Honduras*. Durham, NC, Carolina Academic Press, 2004.

Private Solutions for Infrastructure in Honduras. Washington, DC, World Bank Publications, 2003.

Reformas económicas régimen cambiario y choques externos: efectos en el desarrollo económico, la desigualdad y la pobreza en Costa Rica, El Salvador y Honduras (Estudios y Perspectivas). New York, United Nations Educational, 2005.

Roquas, E. *Stacked Law: Land, Property and Conflict in Honduras*. Amsterdam, Rozenburg Publishers, 2002.

Soluri, J. *Banana Cultures: Agriculture, Consumption, and Environmental Change in Honduras and the United States*. Austin, TX, University of Texas Press, 2006.

Thorpe, A. *Agrarian Modernisation in Honduras*. Lewiston, NY, Edwin Mellen Press, 2001.

Turck, M., and Black, N. J. *Honduras: Hunger and Hope*. Parsippany, NJ, Dillon Press, 1999.

USA Ibp. *Honduras Foreign Policy and Government Guide*. Milton Keynes, Lightning Source UK Ltd, 2003.

Honduras Customs, Trade Regulations and Procedures Handbook. Milton Keynes, Lightning Source UK Ltd, 2005.

JAMAICA

Geography

PHYSICAL FEATURES

Jamaica is in the Caribbean Sea, about 145 km (90 miles) south of eastern Cuba and 160 km west of south-western Haiti. The small, uninhabited US island of Navassa falls midway between Jamaica and Haiti, and the Cayman Islands, a British dependency, lies 290 km (180 miles) to the north-west. Jamaica lies between two of the main sea lanes to Panama, the Cayman Trench to the north and the Jamaica Channel to the east. Jamaica has an area of 10,991 sq km (4,244 sq miles), contained within 1,022 km of coastline and including 160 sq km of inland waters.

Jamaica is the third largest island of the Greater Antilles (after Cuba and Hispaniola), being 235 km from east to west and 82 km from north to south at its widest. The length of the island is dominated by ranges of mountains, reaching their height at Blue Mountain Peak (2,256 m or 7,404 ft) in the east, but falling away in the west. The mountains stretch north and south in a series of spurs and gullies, and the heights are luxuriantly forested. The terrain is, therefore, mainly mountainous, relieved only by narrow and discontinuous coastal plains. The soil is fertile and, although cultivation has made an impact, there are still vast tracts of native vegetation—for instance, some 3,000 species of flowering plant (827 of which are endemic) and 550 varieties of fern. There are several species of reptile (including the crocodile, the Jamaican iguana, which was thought to be extinct until 1990, and five types of snake, all harmless and rare, such as the yellow snake or Jamaican boa) and few large mammals (the mongoose, an introduced pest, wild boar in the mountains and the endangered hutia or coney, as well as the Pedro seal and a small number of sea cows or manatees). Life in the air is obviously more adaptable on Jamaica, with at least 25 species of bat (including a fish-eating one) and many butterflies and birds. There are a number of indigenous creatures, such as the extremely rare Jamaican butterfly (a black-and-yellow swallowtail, the largest butterfly of the Americas and the second largest in the world), the red-billed streamertail hummingbird or doctor bird (the national bird) and some parrots.

CLIMATE

The climate is subtropical, hot and humid on the coast, particularly, but more temperate inland, mainly owing to elevation. The average, annual temperature on the coast is 27°C (81°F). The thermometer can sometimes reach readings of 32°C (90°F) in the height of summer (July–August), but never falls below 20°C (68°F). However, in the mountains winter temperatures can fall as low as 7°C (45°F). The hurricane season is July–November and the rainy season October–November, although rain need not be uncommon from May onwards (average annual rainfall is 78 inches or 1,980 mm) and is more copious in the mountains.

POPULATION

The population is mostly black, 90.9% being of African descent, with those of mixed race at 7.3%, 'East' Indians at 1.3% and

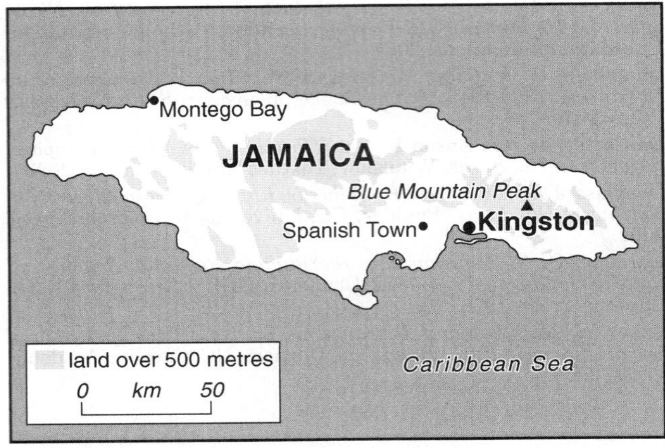

Chinese and whites at 0.2% each. The original settlers from Europe, who displaced the Taino Amerindians, were soon outnumbered by the slaves they brought in as agricultural labour, whose descendants are now Jamaica's dominant ethnic group. The vast majority of these slaves were brought in by the British, the main colonial power, but some earlier groups joined the original Spanish settlers in resisting the British occupation of the island, and their descendants became known as the Maroons, some of whom still maintain a distinct identity in the west. British institutions and culture have, therefore, been influenced by other traditions, notably West African, giving Jamaican culture its modern vibrancy. Thus, English is the official language, but an English patois is generally spoken (using many Ashanti words) and, while most people are Christian, there are influences of other traditions in religion too. Protestant denominations have the largest number of followers (Church of God claims 24% of the total population, Adventists 11% and Pentecostalists 10%), but there are also Anglicans, Roman Catholics and Ethiopian Orthodox adherents, and 35% of people profess other religions (apart from some Jews, Muslims and followers of various Asian belief systems, these are mainly spiritualist cults or the indigenous Rastafarian religion, a pan-Africanist movement). Some adaptations of Christianity, such as Pocomania and Revival, are also found.

Estimates for December 2009 put the total population of Jamaica at almost 2.7m., but there are far more people of Jamaican descent living abroad. About 0.6m. people live in the capital, Kingston, which is found at the eastern end of the southern coast. The second city is Montego Bay, right across the island, in the north-west. For administrative purposes, Jamaica is divided into 14 parishes.

History

CHARLES ARTHUR

Revised for this edition by MARK WILSON

Prior to the arrival of Christopher Columbus in 1494, the island now known as Jamaica was inhabited by the indigenous Amerindians, who lived in simple communities based on fishing, hunting, and the small-scale cultivation of cassava and other crops. They called the island Xaymaca, meaning 'land of wood and springs'. The Spanish began colonizing in 1510, and within 70 years the effects of new diseases, warfare, and enslavement had decimated the Arawak population. Although the Spanish brought the first African slaves to Jamaica in 1517 and tried to build up a sugar and cotton plantation economy, the colony remained under-populated and undeveloped. For nearly 150 years, its main importance was as a stopping point for galleons travelling to and from the more prosperous Spanish colonies on the Latin American mainland. In 1655 an English naval force sent by Oliver Cromwell seized the island. Cromwell increased the island's 3,000-strong white population by transporting indentured servants and prisoners captured in battles with the Irish and Scots, as well as some common criminals, to the territory. Great Britain gained formal possession of Jamaica in 1670, and the introduction of large numbers of African slaves over the following two centuries transformed the colony. At the beginning of the 18th century, the slave population stood at approximately 45,000, but, as the sugar plantation economy boomed, their number rose dramatically, and by 1800 had increased to in excess of 300,000. Over the years escaped slaves—known as Maroons—established communities in remote areas of the interior, and, for several decades during the 18th century, Maroon fighters inflicted heavy casualties on the British troops and local militia despatched to attack them, winning an autonomy from the colonial Government, which the community of Accompong retains to this day.

With the abolition of the slave trade in 1808, followed by that of slavery itself in 1834, the island's slave-based economy faltered. Immigrants from Europe and indentured servants from Africa and Asia were introduced in an attempt to bolster a dwindling plantation labour force, but these were far fewer than in Trinidad or Guyana. Then, in 1846, Jamaican planters, still reeling from the loss of slave labour, suffered a further crushing blow when the United Kingdom adopted legislation eliminating the tariff advantage previously given to its Caribbean colonies. The once immensely rich planter class saw its livelihood undercut by producers in Brazil and Cuba. In 1865 racial and political tensions erupted with the Morant Bay Rebellion, a peasant uprising over land rights. Although the rebellion was violently suppressed, the ensuing instability prompted the British Government to impose direct rule, with a temporary end to the island's assembly, elected on a limited franchise of propertied voters. As a Crown Colony, although elections for nine members of the executive council were restored from 1883, the island's white and mixed-race propertied class continued to hold dominant positions in every societal domain, while the vast majority of the black population remained poor and disenfranchised. Between the world wars the established élite and an emerging middle class grew increasingly dissatisfied with Crown Colony rule, and began to agitate for self-government.

At the same time, in the wake of the world-wide economic depression that began in 1929, economic and political tensions deepened. In 1938 a sugar-workers' strike led to serious social unrest. During this period the two political parties that came to dominate Jamaica's modern political scene were formed. In September 1938 Norman Manley founded the People's National Party (PNP), based on the support of members of the mixed-race middle class and the liberal sector of the business community. The PNP reacted to the 1938 riots by trying to organize workers both in urban areas and in banana-growing rural parishes. In 1942 Manley's cousin, Alexander Bustamante, the founder of the first major Jamaican trade union—that had since evolved into the Bustamante Industrial Trade Union (BITU)—established a rival party, the Jamaica Labour Party (JLP). Although both parties sought the support of the general populace, and both advocated independence from the United Kingdom, there were significant differences between them. The JLP was supported by conservative businessmen and BITU members, mainly dock and sugar plantation workers and other unskilled urban labourers, and over time adopted a strong anti-communist, pro-USA position. By contrast, Manley's PNP embraced the social democratic model espoused by many Western European politicians. Although the PNP developed close links with the National Workers' Union that formed in the 1950s, it was less focused on union-organizing and more interested in access to control over state power and political rights.

Throughout the 20th century, Jamaicans emigrated in search of a better way of life, with an initial wave of migration to work on construction of the Panama Canal, completed in 1914. In the 1930s and 1940s tens of thousands left to live and work in the cities of the eastern USA. After the introduction of more stringent US immigration laws in the 1950s, Britain became the favoured destination, and between 1950 and 1960 some 200,000 Jamaicans moved to the United Kingdom. When the United Kingdom restricted immigration in 1967, the major flow was again to the USA, but also to Canada. Remittances from the expatriate communities in the USA, United Kingdom, Canada and elsewhere were US $1,964m. per year in 2007, constituting a significant contribution to Jamaica's economy.

In 1944 a new Constitution, inaugurating limited self-government (based on the Westminster model) and universal adult suffrage, was introduced. During elections that year the JLP, promising to create jobs and distribute public funds, garnered 22 seats in the 32-member House of Representatives, with five going to the PNP and five to other, transient parties. The following year Bustamante took office as Jamaica's first premier. During the late 1940s and early 1950s the JLP and PNP vied for the uncommitted votes. The JLP narrowly won the general election in 1949, while the PNP won the 1955 election, having abandoned most of its socialist rhetoric. Moves towards independence gathered pace, with the British promoting the idea of a West Indian federation. Manley backed this proposal, believing it would expedite the achievement of independence, whereas Bustamante doubted the benefit for Jamaica of merging with many smaller and (at that time) poorer island states. In January 1958 Jamaica joined nine other British territories in the West Indies Federation. Although the union was not popular with the Jamaican public, Manley won a second term as premier when the PNP secured a decisive victory in the general election of July 1959, taking 30 of the 45 House seats. Bustamante continued to demand Jamaica's withdrawal from the Federation; a referendum on the issue was held in September 1961, when 54% of the electorate voted to withdraw. Jamaica subsequently left the Federation, which collapsed in 1962 when Trinidad and Tobago also seceded. The JLP narrowly won the election of early 1962, and Bustamante assumed the premiership in April. Jamaica's transition to independence was formalized on 6 August 1962, although it retained its membership of the Commonwealth and the British monarch as head of state.

Illness forced Bustamante to retire from politics in 1964; his successor, Donald Sangster, led the JLP to a further narrow victory in the February 1967 election. Political violence had already emerged at this early stage in Jamaica's independent history, with a state of emergency imposed in western areas of the capital, Kingston, in 1966. Sangster died suddenly two months later, and was replaced by Hugh Shearer, the leader of the BITU. The Shearer Government was beset by allegations of corruption and mismanagement, and its conservative positions and policies generated a growing discontent. Following the death of Norman Manley in 1969, his son Michael took over as leader of the PNP; with new leadership, the party built support among the disenchanted middle class, but also placed renewed emphasis on the PNP's socialist roots. Under the eloquent and charismatic Michael Manley, the PNP won 56% of the vote and 36 of the 53 House seats in the February 1972 election. The triumph owed something to Manley's courting of the Rastafarian and youth vote through frequent reference to the revered black nationalist leader Marcus Garvey, and by use of reggae music during his election campaign. Rastafarianism, a 'return to Africa' religious current, had grown in popularity since its foundation in the 1940s.

Michael Manley's PNP Government set out to honour campaign pledges to protect the weaker sections of the population and promote the welfare of those on low incomes. It also attempted to increase the ability of the state to intervene in the economy, and tried to reduce the influence exerted by foreign and local capital. In 1974 the Government imposed a bauxite levy in an effort to extract a better deal from the foreign mining companies operating in Jamaica. However, these initiatives foundered in the unfavourable context of an international economic recession, and, as foreign investment declined, unemployment increased. Another important feature of Manley's move to the left was a new alignment with non-capitalist countries, and a particular emphasis on closer relations with Cuba.

Despite the Government's economic problems, the PNP won 57% of the vote and 47 of the 60 House seats in the December 1976 election. Although it had lost much support among the upper and middle classes, the PNP increased its share of the votes cast by manual labourers and the unemployed. With the voting age for this election reduced from 21 to 18, the PNP also benefited from the youth vote. During Manley's second term he guided the party further to the left, appointing a number of leading left-wingers to cabinet positions, and forging close relations with the new Workers Party of Jamaica (WPJ), a pro-USSR communist party. These developments caused serious rifts in diplomatic relations with the USA. In 1978 a balance of payments crisis obliged the Government to appeal to the IMF for financial assistance. Loans were provided but were conditional upon the Government reducing public spending and social service provisions. By the end of the 1970s economic problems, particularly growing unemployment, had begun to damage the PNP Government's popularity.

During the 1970s the rivalry between the two main parties grew increasingly bitter, and in the slum districts of Kingston gunmen acting in the name of the political parties fought for control of territory; a state of emergency was imposed prior to the 1976 election, and maintained during the succeeding years. In 1978, against a backdrop of politically motivated gang warfare, the reggae music icon Bob Marley staged a reconciliation concert in Kingston. During the concert Manley and Edward Seaga, a conservative technocrat and former Minister of Finance and Planning, were invited on stage to denounce escalating political violence; despite this initiative, however, the violence continued to intensify.

New elections in late 1980 took place in the context of a foreign exchange crisis that translated into shortages in shops and industry. The JLP—now under the leadership of Seaga—had moved away from its union-based origins and enjoyed strong support in the business community. Under Seaga, the JLP took a pro-USA, pro-free enterprise line, portraying the PNP Government as inept in terms of its administration of the economy and dangerously close to communist Cuba. An extremely violent election campaign, in a year when the total number of murders reached close to 900, then an all-time high, ended with a landslide victory for the JLP, which secured 59% of the vote and 51 of the 60 seats in the House.

Under Seaga, the new JLP Government announced a complete reversal of the country's economic policy, espousing the virtues of the free market, emphasizing the role of the private sector and encouraging foreign investment. A major realignment in foreign policy was also effected, involving the severing of relations with Cuba and the forging of close ties with the US Administration of President Ronald Reagan (1981–89). In October 1983 Jamaican forces participated in the US-led invasion to overthrow the left-wing Government in Grenada. Seaga took advantage of the initiative's popularity to hold an early election. The PNP, unable to nominate candidates within the four days allowed, boycotted the December ballot, and, as a result, the JLP won all 60 seats in the House of Representatives. Despite enjoying complete control of the legislature and substantial financial support from the USA and the IMF, the JLP Government struggled to revive the economy: progress was further hindered by a recession in the USA, and the application of austerity measures, demanded by the IMF and the World Bank, failed to produce the expected improvements. The sale of many state-owned enterprises contributed to a rising rate of unemployment, while the removal of price controls on basic food items caused considerable hardship for the poor. In local government elections in July 1986, the opposition PNP soundly defeated the JLP. The result was repeated in the general election postponed until February 1989, following the catastrophic disruption caused by Hurricane Gilbert that had devastated the island the previous September. The PNP returned to power, winning 45 of the 60 seats in the House of Representatives.

Following his defeat in 1980, Manley had sought to moderate the PNP's political image. He broke links with the communist WPJ, and tempered his socialist rhetoric. On returning to power in 1989, Manley cultivated cordial relations with the USA, and honoured existing agreements with the IMF. His Government instituted a number of neo-liberal economic reforms in return for further loans from international financial institutions; however, these measures failed to revitalize the economy. In March 1992 deteriorating health obliged Manley to step down as Prime Minister, and his deputy, Percival J. Patterson, was appointed as his successor. Under Patterson, the economy showed some signs of recovery, and in March 1993 he called an early election. The result was an easy victory for the PNP, which polled 60% of the votes cast. A second defeat for the JLP generated increased internal criticism of Seaga's leadership, and in 1995 the former JLP chairman, Bruce Golding, resigned to form a new centre-right party, the National Democratic Movement (NDM). The split in the JLP helped the PNP return to power for an unprecedented third consecutive term following an election in December 1997, when the party attained 56% of the votes.

The country continued to confront economic and social difficulties throughout the remainder of the decade. There were violent protests in response to a 30% increase in fuel prices in April 1999, and in July of that year the Government ordered the army to patrol the streets of Kingston following a significant increase in crime. Industrial output continued to dwindle and the Government borrowed heavily, but the continuing growth of the tourism industry, particularly in northern coastal towns such as Ocho Rios and Montego Bay, provided some respite.

In legislative elections in October 2002 the PNP recorded yet another victory, taking 34 of the 60 seats. The PNP's success was facilitated by several years of economic growth following years of stagnation, and by the public's continued lack of confidence in the JLP. The efforts of civil society organizations and the presence of international observers helped reduce the violence that had plagued earlier elections, but the process was marred by a low turn-out.

During its fourth consecutive term in office, the PNP Government confronted considerable economic difficulties, and struggled to cope with an increase in violent crime. The JLP won a majority of seats in local government elections in June 2003, but divisions among its leadership impeded the party's attempts to capitalize on growing public dissatisfaction with the Government's performance. The JLP's long-standing leader, Edward Seaga, finally stepped down at the end of 2004, and was replaced by Bruce Golding, the former leader of the NDM, who had rejoined the party in 2001. There was also a change of leadership for the PNP, when Patterson announced his retirement in September 2005. The Minister of Local Government, Community Development and Sport, Portia Simpson-Miller, assumed command of the PNP. Simpson-Miller, a veteran politician with strong grass-roots appeal, became Jamaica's first female Prime Minister in March 2006.

On entering office Prime Minister Simpson-Miller confronted heightened expectations from the electorate, but her

Government was restricted in its ability to fund social programmes as a result of large-scale debts accumulated over previous years, and efforts to expedite economic growth faltered. The JLP rallied support in advance of a general election planned for 27 August 2007 with a focus on boosting the island's economy, tackling national debt, and fighting crime and corruption. The election campaign was marked by violent incidents, and political tensions mounted when the planned voting date was postponed after Hurricane Dean ravaged the island on 18–19 August. In the days before the 3 September election day there was a surge of politically motivated violence, including the killing of seven people on 1 September. On the day of the election itself shots were fired at a polling station in the capital, forcing a temporary two-hour suspension of voting in the district. Turn-out was low, with some 60.5% of the registered electorate participating in the ballot: this partly was due to the chaos and damage caused by Hurricane Dean and concerns about another hurricane. The result was extremely close, with the JLP winning a total of 405,215 votes to the PNP's 402,275. After recounts the JLP, which secured 32 seats compared with the PNP's 28, emerged victorious. The result brought an end to 18 years of PNP government.

The new Prime Minister, Bruce Golding, confronted immediate difficulties caused by rising international oil and food prices. Another cloud over the incoming Government was the court challenge against four JLP members of Parliament accused of holding dual nationality. Court rulings in 2008 and in February and May 2009 forced two of the members affected to fight by-elections, which took place in March and June 2009; both held their seats with increased margins, to the discomfort of the PNP, which also confronted continuing uncertainty over the party leadership and embarrassment over corruption charges filed in February 2008 against the former junior energy minister Kern Spencer, stemming from the administration of a Cuban donation of light bulbs under the PNP Government. (No final ruling on Spencer's case had been made by mid-2010, with hearings delayed by repeated procedural disputes.) Corruption allegations also affected the governing JLP, however; the junior transport minister Joseph Hibbert resigned in July 2009 after allegations that he had, while a civil servant in the 1990s, received bribes from a British bridge construction company, Mabey and Johnson.

Like its predecessors, the Golding administration was attempting to resolve the problem of violent crime; since the beginning of the 21st century a variety of initiatives have been implemented to address the problem and curtail its disruptive impact on daily life for the majority of Jamaicans, as well as on investor confidence, the development of tourism and the country's image abroad, with costs on some estimates equivalent to 5% of GDP. The British Government has been at the forefront of international efforts to enhance the strength and capacity of the local police, the Jamaica Constabulary Force, in order that it might more effectively combat the illegal drugs-trafficking business and related gang feuds in the deprived inner city areas of Kingston, Spanish Town and elsewhere. There were an estimated 150 neighbourhood gangs, which were also involved in extortion and financial scams; many had links to the two main political parties, particularly in the inner-city 'garrison constituencies', originating in some cases from the time of the bitter inter-party conflicts of the 1970s. At the same time Jamaica was a hub for Caribbean cocaine transshipment towards the United Kingdom and North America, with close links between local and overseas drugs gangs, and a lively 'guns for drugs' trade with Haiti. The island also remained a fairly important producer and exporter of marijuana. In October 2004 the authorities launched 'Operation Kingfish', an intelligence-based task force intended to reduce the increasing crime rate by targeting major criminal networks. Although the task force had some success with a number of seizures of illegal drugs and weapons, the murder toll in 2009 increased to 1,690, giving Jamaica the probable distinction of having displaced Colombia and South Africa as the country with the highest rate of murder in the world. International human rights organizations, including Amnesty International, have criticized the police force's aggressive approach to the crime problem, in particular raising concerns over the high number of people killed by police officers: between 2000 and 2008 the Jamaican Constabulary Force killed 1,714 people. The difficulties surrounding police reform and crime were highlighted by the resignation of the Commissioner of Police, Rear-Adm. Hardley Lewin, in November 2009.

The USA in August 2009 requested the extradition of Christopher 'Dudus' Coke, the alleged leader of a large and powerful gang based in the Kingston slum district of Tivoli Gardens. Although Jamaica usually responded promptly to extradition requests, there were delays in this case, and an arrest warrant was not issued until May 2010, by which time Coke was preparing to barricade his Tivoli stronghold. After attacks on six police stations by supporters of Coke in late May the Government declared a state of emergency, and an estimated 2,000 soldiers and police officers moved into Tivoli Gardens. At least 73 residents were killed before or during the operation, as well as three members of the security forces. Coke surrendered to police in late June and was extradited to New York two days later, although the state of emergency remained in place for another month. During the clashes over 4,000 people were detained, and 16 were charged with serious offences. Although opinion polls in April had shown a loss of support for Golding and the JLP Government, later polls indicated broad approval for the state of emergency; a majority of respondents declared that crime and violence were Jamaica's most pressing problems.

During its four terms, the PNP spearheaded efforts to enhance regional integration by supporting the Caribbean Community and Common Market (CARICOM). Jamaica, together with Barbados, Belize, Guyana, Suriname, and Trinidad and Tobago, joined the Caribbean Single Market and Economy (CSME), the single market component of which was inaugurated on 1 January 2006. The CSME sought to convert the 15 CARICOM states into a single, enlarged economic entity, while retaining the individual territories' political autonomy. However, the PNP Government failed in an attempt to replace the Privy Council (based in the United Kingdom) with the newly established regional Caribbean Court of Justice (CCJ), based in Trinidad, as the country's highest appellate body, as the Privy Council ruled that the new court must be protected by an entrenched clause in the Constitution, a process that would have required opposition support.

Economy

CHARLES ARTHUR

Revised for this edition by MARK WILSON

Jamaica's economy has moved on since its heyday as a colony producing sugar and other tropical crops. Tourism, bauxite and remittances from overseas migrants are now the main sources of foreign exchange. However, the island confronted a difficult outlook in the early years of the 21st century, after decades of economic reversal or slow growth. The slow decline of the island's sugar cane industry during the 19th century was a painful process, and it was only with the development of the banana as an export crop from the 1870s that a recovery began. The advent of refrigeration helped the banana industry to prosper, and foreign fruit companies developed substantial interests in Jamaica. Peasant farmers came to rely on the crop as a steady although modest source of income, supplementing subsistence production and the proceeds from the sale of coffee and citrus fruit. In the early 20th century significant deposits of bauxite, the ore that is used to produce aluminium, were discovered, and when bauxite-mining began in 1952 the economy further diversified. In the period following independence in 1962, efforts to develop a manufacturing base both for the domestic market and for export had some success, creating many new jobs and shifting the economy away from reliance on agro-industry. At the same time, with the advent of mass tourism, Jamaica's climate, coastline and natural beauty made it a popular destination. A tourism industry composed of resorts, hotels, restaurants and bars serving foreign visitors quickly developed into an economic mainstay. During the 1960s Jamaica's gross domestic product (GDP) grew by an average of almost 6% per year in real terms, mainly as a result of high prices for bauxite exports and substantial foreign investment. Despite this progress, the economy was vulnerable to external economic factors, such as decreases in international commodity prices, and sudden shifts in patterns of foreign investment. In the 1970s Michael Manley's People's National Party (PNP) Government tried to develop the country's human capital by increasing public expenditure on social services such as education and health. The aim was to try to establish the foundations for an economy less dependent on foreign capital and foreign markets. This attempt to re-orientate the economy failed owing to an international economic recession and the hostility of the USA and the international financial institutions, as well as much of the local business community. From 1974 to 1980 the economy contracted sharply, with GDP declining by 16% overall.

From the 1970s international lending agencies insisted on neo-liberal reforms, including the privatization of state-owned industries, the reduction of public sector employment, the removal of price controls and subsidies, and the liberalization of the financial system, involving the privatization of banks. During the 1980s, following electoral victory in 1980, the Jamaica Labour Party (JLP) Government championed the free market and private sector-led growth, and received extensive support in the form of loans from international institutions. However, overall average annual growth in 1980–90 was 1.6%, a minimal growth rate that left the Government ill-equipped to meet substantial and growing debt repayments. The PNP had during this period abandoned its earlier socialist orientation, and returned to government in 1989, but the overall economic picture remained miserable. GDP growth averaged only 0.3% a year during the 1990s (3% cumulative growth over the decade), and agricultural and manufacturing output contracted. The Government responded to rapid inflation, peaking at 80% in the early part of the decade, with fiscal and monetary tightening; interest rates for borrowers reached over 65% in 1994. This stabilized the exchange rate for the Jamaican dollar, and brought inflation under control, but led to severe problems for most of the real economy, and a period of rapid and unsustainable growth for the financial sector. From 1994 mainstream financial institutions were in obvious difficulties, with growing liquidity problems and an increasing portfolio of non-performing loans (the average non-performing loan ratio reached 27% in 1997). The Government established a Financial Sector Adjustment Company (FINSAC), which was forced to take control of the seven largest locally owned commercial banks, four major life insurers, and close to 100 hotel, property and other businesses, most of which were restructured and divested by 2002. By this point the accumulated costs of the state rescue of the financial sector were equivalent to 40% of annual GDP. Interest payments on public debt rose to 14% of GDP and 50% of government revenue in the financial year ending in March 2002, and have remained high since that date.

After reaching 148% of GDP in March 2003, public debt declined, but by early 2008 it remained prodigious at 128% of GDP (according to IMF estimates), and debt service took up 60% of the annual budget in 2009/10. External government debt was US $5,464m. at the end of 2009, with a further US $1,130m. in government-guaranteed debt and J $754,000m. in domestic debt. Unemployment increased from the mid-1990s, owing to a large decline in formal private sector employment. Negative per-head GDP growth for most of the last 25 years of the 20th century and the early part of the 21st century meant that average incomes in Jamaica failed to improve for more than three decades. Annual growth averaged 1.3% in 2000–05, and was set back in September 2004 by Hurricane Ivan, one of the most destructive of recent Caribbean hurricanes, which was estimated to have cost approximately 8% of the total annual GDP. Growth remained weak at 2.7% in 2006 and 1.4% in 2007, while GDP contracted by 0.9% in 2008 and 2.7% in 2009 as the global financial crisis unfolded. Bauxite exports declined by 70% in 2009, remittances decreased, and hotels were forced to discount room rates heavily to maintain occupancy, while the fiscal deficit widened and the exchange rate depreciated.

The high debt burden created severe difficulties in developing an effective countercyclical response to the economic crisis through further domestic or commercial borrowing. However, the IMF in February 2010 agreed an economic programme supported by a US $1,270m. stand-by loan, of which US $610m. was immediately disbursed, and which was expected to release a further US $1,100m. in funding from other multilateral institutions. The economic programme covered public finance and public sector reform, financial sector regulation, and a strategy for reduction of debt interest. Aims also included increased resources for investment in education and infrastructure, and higher levels of social spending.

A 'Jamaica Debt Exchange' package agreed in January 2010 aimed to lower debt interest payments by 3% of GDP and reduce repayment of maturing debt in 2010–13 by 65%. A total of J $722,000m. in domestic debt, equivalent to 55% of total debt, and carrying interest rates of up to 28%, was swapped for new bonds with maximum interest rates of 13.25% and longer maturities, saving J $40,000m. a year in interest costs. Financial institutions were able to absorb losses stemming from the debt exchange, and the Government's treasury bill borrowing rates were reduced to their lowest levels for 24 years, while the exchange rate appreciated by 4.3% in the first half of 2010. A satisfactory initial review by the IMF allowed disbursement of a further US $94m. in June.

According to the Statistical Institute of Jamaica, the total population of Jamaica at the end of 2009 was 2,698,800. The most recent census, conducted in 2001, recorded that 31% of the population lived in the urban area surrounding the capital, Kingston, which included the parish of St Andrew and the rapidly growing suburb of Portmore. An additional 19% lived in other urban centres such as the former capital of Spanish Town, close to Kingston, and Montego Bay, situated on the north-west coast, which is the third largest city and a centre of tourism activity. Despite Jamaica's poor track record of economic growth over recent decades, many of the country's social indicators were fairly good, and recent trends indicated declining poverty. However, in 2009 Jamaica ranked 100th out of 182 countries in the UN Development Programme's Human Development index, with 11 members of the Caribbean Community and Common Market grouping scoring a higher rank, and only Guyana placed lower. Life expectancy at birth, which has been rising gradually, was 72 years in 2008. Access to safe water and sanitary facilities has been increasing. At the national level, over 80% of the population had access to safe water, while 93% had access to sanitary facilities. At October 2009 the labour force totalled 1,259,200 people. During the economic troubles of the late 20th century unemployment was often extremely high, reaching levels of between 20% and 30%, but during the early years of the 21st century economic growth helped to reduce the rate, although it remained high, at 11.6% in October 2009. Youth unemployment (ages 14–24) remained at above this level, and was 29.8% in 2009.

Despite consistently high levels of unemployment and declining per-head GDP throughout the 1990s, the Inter-American Development Bank (IDB) calculated that the percentage of Jamaicans defined as living in poverty decreased from 28.0% to 14.8% between 1990 and 2005, with the Jamaica Survey of Living Conditions showing a further decline to 9.9% in 2007. This apparent paradox can perhaps be explained by the impact of a decrease in the relative price of food, a contraction in the rate of inflation, a growth in the size of the informal sector and an increase in the level of remittances sent back by Jamaicans living abroad. Tens of thousands of Jamaicans earned a living in the unregulated informal sector, either as casual labourers in the agriculture or service sector, or as street merchants buying and selling tiny quantities of everyday goods. In 2005 the informal sector was estimated to be equivalent to 43% of GDP. Remittance inflows grew from US $184m. in 1990 to US $2,021m. in 2008, a level exceeding earnings from either tourism or bauxite and equivalent to 14% of GDP. This reflected both the success of some emigrants and the high level of emigration during the previous four decades of economic stagnation. However, remittances declined by 11.4% to US $1,792m. in 2009, as earnings of Jamaicans overseas were affected by the international recession, while expatriates resident in the United Kingdom suffered from the depreciation of sterling against the US dollar, to which the Jamaican currency is closely linked. The main source of the remittances was the USA (55%), with the United Kingdom second (21%), followed by Canada and the Cayman Islands with 8% each. An estimated 80% of university graduates emigrated during the 1990s. Approximately as many Jamaicans lived abroad as in Jamaica (depending on definitions used).

The once dominant agricultural sector is no longer a significant pillar of the economy, although it still provided employment to 20.5% of the labour force in 2009. Agriculture's decline gathered pace during the 1990s, and from 2004 to 2008 the sector suffered greatly from a series of weather-related shocks, including Hurricane Ivan in September 2004 and drought conditions in the first four months of 2005. Hurricanes Dennis, Emily and Wilma during 2005, Dean in August 2007, and Tropical Storm Gustav a year later caused further destruction and heavy losses. Both larger-scale farming enterprises and smallholding peasant farmers were affected by extreme weather. However, agricultural output in 2009 recovered to some extent from the damage caused by the poor weather conditions in previous years, growing by 12.1%. Peasant farmers grew a great variety of crops for the local market, but in terms of quantity the main ones were beans, plantains, sweet potatoes, yams and cassava. An additional pressure on domestic farming has been the reduction in import tariffs, which resulted in a large influx of cheaper foreign foodstuffs that have undercut local producers. Agriculture, including forestry and fishing, comprised just 5.0% of GDP in 2008.

After experiencing decades of decline, the sugar industry, historically the most important sector of Jamaica's economy, sank even further in the 2000s. The privatization of part of the state-owned sugar industry in 1993 proved a disaster, and the Government was in 1998 obliged to resume control of loss-making enterprises. Annual sugar production totalled 506,500 metric tons in 1965, but stood at 209,825 tons in 2000, before decreasing further to 127,001 tons in 2005 after Hurricane Ivan, and was only 130,400 tons in 2009. Export earnings from sugar were US $72.3m. in 2009, a decline of 30.6% compared with 2008 and equivalent to 1.7% of goods and services exports. Sugar export earnings were for many decades maintained by agreements guaranteeing preferential access to European markets, but with the expiry in 2009 of the European Union's (EU) sugar protocol, and the phasing out of the guaranteed EU price for sugar imports, the future for the industry looked bleak. The Jamaican sugar industry, which employed 40,000 persons in 2007, was uncompetitive, with production costs that were over three times those of the world's principal sugar exporters. While Jamaica's two private sector firms were still profitable and might be able to survive with lower preferences, the five state-owned companies could not survive without government subsidies or new investment. The Government sold two enterprises to local investors in 2009, while Chinese company COMPLANT International Sugar Industry Company Ltd proposed in July to buy the three remaining firms for US $9m. (deleted because Petrojam and private sector Jamaica Broilers were both processing Braziian ethanol for re-export to US, but have had to cease operations with lack of supply from Brazil and unfavourable price environment – given that we have limited space, easiest to skip the whole thing. The Chinese are talking about an ethanol plant but no firm proposal)

The other main traditional agricultural export crop, bananas, also experienced serious difficulties, with the value of exports declining from US $45m. in 1996 to US $9m. in 2007, and export production coming to a halt in 2008, although some bananas were still grown for the domestic market and for processed snack production. Problems included the high cost of the local industry, repeated hurricane damage, plant disease outbreaks, and most significantly the reduced protection given to traditional African, Caribbean and Pacific suppliers against Latin American rivals in the formerly protected European market. Tropical Storm Gustav in August 2008 delivered a final blow to the industry, destroying 79% of the standing crop a year after the passage of Hurricane Dean. Another important export crop for both small- and large-scale farmers was coffee. The two main varieties grown in Jamaica were lowland coffee, which was generally grown on small farms, and the connoisseur's Blue Mountain coffee, grown on larger highland farms in the island's three eastern parishes, with most exported in recent years to Japan. Production volumes have been in decline since exports reached a record high of almost 3,000 metric tons in 1996; exports were valued at US $35m. in 2009. In common with other agricultural products, the coffee sector suffered greatly from adverse weather and hurricane damage, as well as pest infestation and price fluctuations. Other export crops were citrus, cocoa and pimento (allspice).

Jamaica's most significant mineral resource is bauxite, mined mainly in the parishes of Clarendon, St Elizabeth, St Ann and Trelawny, in west-central Jamaica. Most Jamaican bauxite was processed locally for alumina, or pure aluminium oxide; this was then exported to overseas smelters to produce aluminium. Some bauxite was exported in its raw form to overseas alumina plants. Mining costs were high, as the bauxite was found in scattered pockets, rather than as a continuous deposit. Mining and quarrying comprised an estimated 3.8% of GDP in 2008, but employed only 0.4% of the labour force in 2009. World aluminium demand and prices increased in the early years of the 21st century, and earnings from alumina exports were US $1,235m. in 2008, with an additional US $115m. from unprocessed bauxite, making up 49% of merchandise exports. However, owing to lower prices from mid-2008, export earnings declined in 2009 to US $368m. from alumina and US $85m. from bauxite. Mining GDP contracted by 50.2% in 2009.

The three main bauxite-extracting and alumina-producing companies in Jamaica have been: Jamalco, a joint venture between the Jamaican Government and the US company Alcoa; the West Indies Alumina Co (WINDALCO), until 2007 a joint venture between the Jamaican Government and the Swiss company Glencore Alumina Jamaica Ltd (but bought by the Russian-Swiss concern United Company RUSAL in that year); and Alumina Partners of Jamaica (Alpart), also owned by RUSAL. RUSAL suspended operations at both companies in 2009, although the WINDALCO plant reopened in July 2010, and there were hopes that the two Alpart plants would follow.

Jamaica was heavily dependent on the import of petroleum products, which made up 39% of goods imports in 2008, although this was reduced to 27% in 2009 as oil prices declined. There were good geological prospects off shore, and several small overseas companies were exploring offshore blocks in the Exclusive Economic Zone in 2010. In 2008 a total of 4,123m. kWh of electricity was generated, a 1.1% increase on generation over 2007. In 2009 total generating capacity was 820 MW, with peak demand of 650 MW. The sole distributor and main generator of electricity was the Jamaica Public Service Company (JPSCo), which was in state ownership from 1970 to 2001, and has from 2007 been owned as a 50:50 joint venture between the Marubeni Corporation of Japan and Abu Dhabi National Energy Company of the United Arab Emirates. In 2008 JPSCo accounted for 69.5% of total electricity generated, and in addition to four large fossil fuel plants there were eight small hydroelectric plants, with a 3-MW wind farm under development. JPSCo also bought power from four smaller, independent generating companies. The reliability of the power supply improved in the 2000s, but electricity costs were higher than in many countries.

Approximately 26.2m. barrels of crude petroleum and petroleum products were imported in 2005. About one-third of the fuel was used for bauxite- and alumina-processing. Taking an opportunity to reduce the cost of imported petroleum, in September 2005 the Government signed the PetroCaribe energy accord with Venezuela. Under the terms of the accord, Jamaica and other Caribbean nations received petrol imports from Venezuela under preferential terms, allowing the importer to finance a proportion of the cost with long-term, low-interest loans. The agreement was expected to save Jamaica between US $180m. and US $200m. in annual oil payments. In 2006 Venezuela bought a 49% stake in the refinery operated by the state-owned Petroleum Corporation of Jamaica, and a further 2% stake was purchased in 2010, which, it was thought, might open the way for additional investment.

Jamaica's manufacturing sector expanded in the 1950s, and in subsequent decades the Government intervened to develop the domestic market by providing incentives and erecting protective tariffs. Then, in the 1980s, the JLP Government changed course, removing import restrictions and introducing tax incentives to benefit manufacturing for export. From the mid-1980s the export-orientated manufacturing sector grew rapidly, especially within the free trade zones established in Kingston, Montego Bay and Spanish Town. The free trade zones stimulated foreign investment in garment assembly, light manufacturing and data entry. However, since the late 1980s the manufacturing sector declined in importance, with its share of GDP contracting from 19.6% in 1988 to 8.5% in 2008. Manufacturing output contracted by a further 5.0% in 2009, with the sector employing 6.9% of the labour force. At its height in the mid-1990s, Jamaica's apparel industry, which primarily assembled garments cut in the USA for re-export to that country, employed about 25,000 people and earned around US $550m. in exports. With the advent of the North American Free Trade Agreement (NAFTA) in 1994, and the end of the Multi-fibre Agreement 10 years later, it became increasingly difficult for Jamaica to compete with countries such as China with lower wages and lower operating costs. Annual export earnings from assembled garments declined from US $149m. in 2000, to just US $9.4m. in 2005, and have since virtually ceased. In early 2008 one of the last multinational garment assembly operations in Jamaica announced the impending end of its 24-year presence in the country. Jockey International, the US underwear manufacturer, stated that it would close its last Jamaican plant by the end of the year, leading to a further 575 redundancies. Construction accounted for 8.2% of GDP in 2008, down from 10.9% in 2005.The sector contracted by 4.6% in 2008 and by 6.7% in 2009, as public sector, tourism-related and residential investment slowed. Cement sales decreased by 9.4% in 2009.

Transport infrastructure is fairly well developed by regional standards, particularly with regard to seaports and airports. The principal port at Kingston is a major transshipment centre for the Caribbean region, and the natural harbour is the seventh largest in the world. In the 2000s investment in ports and the privately run airport at Montego Bay continued and facilities have improved. However, shipping has been affected by the international recession. During 2008 the number of ship calls in Jamaican ports was 3,586, a contraction of 12% compared with 2006, with 20.2m. tons of domestic cargo handled. Further decreases were anticipated, not least because of the steep decline in alumina exports. For a country of its size, the national road network is extensive (20,693 km), but, although the whole network is paved with asphalt, only 50% of it is in good condition. Insufficient maintenance, rising traffic volumes, increased overloading of commercial vehicles and, particularly over the past few years, damage caused by flooding associated with the increasing intensity of the hurricane seasons have all taken their toll. A highway along the north coast was completed in the late 2000s, and Highway 2000, a toll road to connect Kingston, Ocho Rios and Montego Bay, was under construction by French contractors in 2010, with the section from Kingston to Spanish Town already open to public traffic. The public passenger railway service ceased operations in October 1992, although private freight transport continued from the alumina plants to the export-shipping facilities. In early 2008 the Minister of Transport and Works announced that China had agreed to help Jamaica to revive its rail network as a way of offsetting rising fuel costs by financing 85% of a US $354m. project through a loan with the state-owned Jamaica Railway Corporation. However, there was no further progress by mid-2010.

Privatization and liberalization of the telecommunications sector from 2000 encouraged significant private sector investment that, in turn, resulted in improvements in coverage and access. Mobile cellular telephone penetration was very high; in 2009 there were 1,196 mobile and 112 fixed line subscriptions per 1,000 people. The cellular sector was dominated by Irish-owned Digicel Jamaica, with Claro Jamaica (owned by América Móvil of Mexico) and the British Cable & Wireless Jamaica Ltd, now operating as LIME (Landline, Internet, Mobile and Entertainment) and historically the main supplier of fixed lines, also in competition. There were 1.6m. internet users in 2010 (56% of the population). Call centres have been a successful growth industry. The largest company, ACS-eServices, grew from a start-up with 35 employees in 2000 to employ 48,600 in Jamaican call centres by 2009, and a further 5,400 in Saint Lucia.

The health of the financial sector improved to some extent after restructuring in 1997–2002. The IMF in 2008 noted generally positive bank soundness indicators, while interest rates declined, although they remained very high by international standards. Weighted average loan rates of commercial banks were 16.2% in April 2009, while the rate on treasury bills was 9.5%, down from 19.2% a year earlier. Weaknesses in supervision were indicated by the ability of several high-profile unregulated foreign exchange trading and investment schemes to flourish in the early years of the 21st century, offering very high purported rates of return, taking on the characteristics of Ponzi schemes, and accumulating deposits estimated at between 12.5% and 25% of GDP. Most collapsed in 2008, with a large number of depositors losing their funds. The US authorities, meanwhile, noted weaknesses in the Financial Investigations Division, which was responsible for controls on money-laundering within the Ministry of Finance and the Public Service. There were proposals in the late 2000s to establish an international financial centre, a move that would appear unwise in view of the weak regulatory environment, the international financial crisis and the high level of regional competition. However, financial regulations were improved as part of the 2010 IMF reform programme.

Tourism began to grow in economic importance in the 1950s, and, with the advent of the long-haul charter flight and the popular package holiday in the late 1960s, the sector made rapid advances, before suffering a downturn with the rest of the economy in the late 1970s. Stop-over tourist arrivals reached 840,777 in 1990, and rose to 1.83m. in 2009. Cruise ships also brought increasing numbers to the island, albeit for short visits and with only 8% of the average spend of stop-over tourists. Cruise ship arrivals increased from 133,400 in 1980 to

1.34m. in 2006, but decreased to 922,000 by 2008, as cruise lines moved to other destinations. Partly because of the high crime rate and visitor harassment, Jamaica from the late 1970s pioneered the 'all-inclusive' resort, and two locally owned companies, Sandals and SuperClubs, operate successfully across the island and in other Caribbean and overseas markets. In the early years of the 21st century several Spanish companies built large resorts in Jamaica, and in 2008 and 2009 additional room stock produced a further increase in tourist arrivals, in contrast to most other Caribbean markets, albeit with decreased percentage room occupancy and following steep discounts in room rates. Tourism was heavily dependent on the US market, which accounted for 64% of arrivals in 2009, with 16% from Canada and 15% from Europe, most of whom were British.

Beginning in the 1970s, successive governments have struggled with fiscal deficits and mounting debts, largely as a consequence of overspending and low levels of tax collection. Despite numerous reform programmes recommended and monitored by the IMF, the situation barely improved by the early years of the 21st century. The fiscal deficit narrowed to 3.5% of GDP in 2004/05, but then rose again to 7.3% in 2008/09. With revenue affected by the economic recession and with interest payments and other spending commitments increasing, the deficit rose to 10.9% in 2009/10, although there was a primary surplus of J $68,000m. In accordance with the IMF programme, the Government increased income tax for high earners and raised the rate of the General Consumption Tax (a value-added tax—VAT) from the start of 2010, to raise revenue equivalent to 2% of GDP, while a two-year wage freeze was introduced for the public sector, after three years in which public sector salary costs had increased by 54%. The Jamaica Debt Exchange was intended to bring the cost of debt-servicing down to 47% of total spending, from 60% in 2009/10. Accordingly, the budget for 2010/11 projected a deficit of 6.5% of GDP, of which two-thirds was to be financed by domestic borrowing; the medium-term target was to achieve a balanced budget by 2013/14. The Government also continued its divestment programme, selling the loss-making national airline Air Jamaica to Caribbean Airlines of Trinidad and Tobago, with privatization of the Kingston port and airport also planned, as well as shareholdings in the bauxite industry.

Efforts to improve on existing low rates of tax collection have been complicated by the difficulties posed by the existence of a growing informal sector and a culture of tax evasion. Following a comprehensive review of the tax system, in 2005 the Government pursued improvements in revenue collection. The reforms aimed to simplify tax administration and improve compliance, and included the modification of personal and corporate income tax, as well as bringing a number of indirect taxes into the VAT system. The IMF programme and the budget for 2010/11 proposed further reforms in tax administration.

Since the 1970s Jamaica has been forced to depend on external financial support, and in the 2000s the World Bank, the IDB, the EU, the Caribbean Development Bank, and bilateral donors, such as Kuwait, Japan and Belgium, provided substantial assistance. In May 2005 the World Bank announced plans for a US $150m. programme of poverty alleviation and development initiatives, scheduled to take place in 2006–09. IDB loans in March 2008 made up 49% of Jamaica's foreign debt, and the IDB in January 2009 agreed further liquidity support of US $300m.

The rate of the Jamaican dollar against the US dollar declined in the 2000s, down from J $47 : US $1 at the end of 2002, to J $72 : US $1 in August 2008. Depreciation accelerated from the last quarter of 2008, with the exchange rate reaching J $89 : US $1 in April 2009. However, external support and debt restructuring prompted a recovery to J $6 : US $1 in July 2010, although the currency remained vulnerable to pressures such as capital flight or loss of confidence in the economy.

Jamaica suffered several bouts of very high inflation, with prices increasing by 80% in 1991 and 40% in 1992, for example, as the currency depreciated. Monetary tightening brought inflation down to single digits by 1997 and brought relative currency stability, but at severe cost to the economy. After a further period of double-digit price rises in 2003–05, inflation was reduced to a low point of 5.7% in 2006. Prices again rose rapidly, with inflation recorded at 16.8% in both 2007 and 2008, in part because of higher import costs for oil, basic foods and other commodities. However, inflation decreased to 10.5% in 2010, as a result of reduced domestic demand and lower international oil prices.

Jamaica's foreign-trade balance has been in deficit since the mid-20th century. Although the level fluctuated when world prices for exports such as bauxite, alumina and sugar and for oil imports changed, the overall trend has been negative, as imports increased more than two-and-a-half times as fast as exports in the period 1994–2008. The deficit in merchandise trade was US $3,123m. in 2009, a reduction of 35% compared with the previous year, as lower oil prices and reduced import demand offset a decline in bauxite and alumina exports. Tourism produced gross earnings of US $1,938m. However, there was a negative balance for other services, and for overseas travel by Jamaican residents, so the net services balance of US $752m. covered only 24% of the trade deficit. Inward remittances of US $1,792m. were offset by outflows including US $526m. of interest payments on foreign debt. There was a resulting current account balance of payments deficit of US $912m., the lowest since 2004 and equivalent to 7.3% of GDP. This showed an improvement from a deficit of US $2,793m. (21.9% of GDP) in 2008. Capital and investment inflows came close to covering the current deficit, despite a dramatic decrease in net private investment inflows to US $609m. from US $2,159m. in 2008, when major tourism-related and other investments were in progress. Reserves were down by US $44m. over the calendar year, and were US $1,729m. at the end of 2009, equivalent to 13.2 weeks' import cover.

CONCLUSION

Jamaica's economy has undergone a profound reorientation over the last 50 years, shifting from reliance on agricultural production for the local and export markets to dependence on bauxite and alumina, tourism, call centres, the informal sector, and remittances from Jamaicans living abroad. However, Jamaica's economy has grown only by a cumulative 25% since 1970, while its Caribbean neighbours expanded on average by 174%, and the world economy by 216%. Jamaica has the fourth lowest per head GDP in the English-speaking Caribbean. Jamaica has more than twice the population of Trinidad and Tobago, but an economy of one-half of the size. The Jamaican economy remained vulnerable to fluctuating international commodity prices both for exports of bauxite and alumina, and for imports of petroleum, as well as to the international borrowing environment and international demand for tourism. After confronting the economic difficulties of 2008–09 with what the Prime Minister Bruce Golding referred to in his May 2009 budget presentation as a 'weak immune system', debt restructuring and an IMF programme provided a basis for stabilizing the economy in 2010. However, the underlying structural problems that had produced the historically anaemic growth rate remained to be addressed. These included the high costs of the tourism industry at a time when it was increasingly challenged by competition from cruise ships and other destinations, the finite extent of remaining bauxite reserves and the great expense required to exploit them, and the apparent lack of growth or new enterprise in manufacturing or agriculture. However, relations with international lending agencies were good, and these were expected to assist Jamaica in surmounting the difficulties of the current economic climate. With social and political stability clearly necessary for economic growth, the continued existence of high levels of crime and youth unemployment underscored the need to translate macroeconomic progress into tangible improvements to the living standards of the poorer sectors of the population.

Statistical Survey

Sources (unless otherwise stated): Statistical Institute of Jamaica, 7 Cecelio Ave, Kingston 10; tel. 926-5311; fax 926-1138; e-mail info@statinja.com; internet www.statinja.com; Jamaica Information Service, 58A Half Way Tree Rd, POB 2222, Kingston 10; tel. 926-3740; fax 926-6715; e-mail jis@jis.gov.jm; internet www.jis.gov.jm; Bank of Jamaica, Nethersole Pl., POB 621, Kingston; tel. 922-0750; fax 922-0854; e-mail info@boj.org.jm; internet www.boj.org.jm.

Area and Population

AREA, POPULATION AND DENSITY

Area (sq km)	10,991*
Population (census results)	
7 April 1991	2,314,479
10 September 2001	
Males	1,283,547
Females	1,324,085
Total	2,607,632
Population (official estimates at 31 December)†	
2007	2,682,100
2008	2,692,400
2009	2,698,800
Density (per sq km) at 31 December 2009	245.5

* 4,243.6 sq miles.

† Figures are rounded to the nearest 100 persons.

POPULATION BY AGE AND SEX

(official estimates at 31 December 2009)

	Males	Females	Total
0–14	378,762	360,906	739,668
15–64	849,073	880,471	1,729,545
65 and over	101,506	128,091	229,597
Total	1,329,341	1,369,469	2,698,810

PARISHES

	Area (sq km)	Population (31 December 2009)	Capitals (with population*)
Kingston and St Andrew	453†	667,778	Kingston M.A. (587,798)
St Thomas	743	94,471	Morant Bay (9,185)
Portland	814	82,442	Port Antonio (13,246)
St Mary	611	114,591	Port Maria (7,651)
St Ann	1,213	173,830	St Ann's Bay (10,518)
Trelawny	875	75,799	Falmouth (7,245)
St James	595	184,854	Montego Bay (83,446)
Hanover	450	70,094	Lucea (6,002)
Westmoreland	807	145,335	Savanna La Mar (16,553)
St Elizabeth	1,212	151,484	Black River (3,675)
Manchester	830	191,378	Mandeville (39,430)
Clarendon	1,196	247,109	May Pen (46,785)
St Catherine	1,192	499,645	Spanish Town (92,383)
Total	10,991	2,698,810	—

* Population at 1991 census.

† Kingston 22 sq km, St Andrew 431 sq km.

PRINCIPAL TOWNS

(population at census of 7 April 1991)

Kingston (capital)	587,798	Montego Bay	83,446
Spanish Town	92,383	May Pen	46,785
Portmore	90,138	Mandeville	39,430

Source: Thomas Brinkhoff, *City Population* (internet www.citypopulation.de).

Mid-2009 ('000, incl. suburbs, UN estimate): Kingston 580 (Source: UN, *World Urbanization Prospects: The 2009 Revision*).

BIRTHS, MARRIAGES AND DEATHS*

	Registered live births†		Registered marriages		Registered deaths
	Number	Rate (per 1,000)	Number	Rate (per 1,000)	Number (estimates)
2000	48,717	18.8	27,028	10.4	15,248
2001	48,065	18.5	22,308	8.6	14,473
2002	44,331	16.9	23,070	8.8	15,711
2003	43,407	16.5	22,476	8.6	15,581
2004	42,448	16.2	21,670	8.2	15,389
2005	41,836	15.7	25,937	9.8	15,523
2006	45,436	17.0	23,148	8.7	15,180
2007	45,590	17.0	n.a.	n.a.	17,048

* Data are tabulated by year of registration rather than by year of occurrence.

† Including births to non-resident mothers.

Sources: UN, *Demographic Yearbook* and *Population and Vital Statistics Report*.

2008: Live births 44,838 (birth rate 16.7 per 1,000); Deaths 17,000 (death rate 6.3 per 1,000); Marriages 21,989 (marriage rate 8.1 per 1,000).

2009: Live births 44,006 (birth rate 16.3 per 1,000); Deaths 17,553 (death rate 6.5 per 1,000); Marriages 21,412 (marriage rate 7.9 per 1,000).

Life expectancy (years at birth, WHO estimates): 72 (males 69; females 74) in 2008 (Source: WHO, *World Health Statistics*).

ECONOMICALLY ACTIVE POPULATION

('000 persons aged 14 years and over, annual averages)

	2006	2007	2008
Agriculture, forestry and fishing	206.1	206.1	222.6
Mining and quarrying	6.4	8.8	9.2
Manufacturing	73.6	71.6	68.6
Electricity, gas and water	7.1	9.3	9.0
Construction	113.1	121.3	106.1
Trade, restaurants and hotels	272.4	262.3	265.2
Transport, storage and communications	79.3	80.6	81.3
Financing, insurance, real estate and business services	59.3	71.1	77.8
Community, social and personal services	310.4	337.2	326.6
Sub-total	1,127.7	1,168.3	1,166.4
Activities not adequately defined	1.8	1.9	1.4
Total employed	1,129.5	1,170.2	1,167.8
Unemployed	119.6	119.4	134.6
Total labour force	1,249.1	1,289.6	1,302.4
Males	697.8	708.2	711.1
Females	551.3	581.4	591.3

Source: ILO.

Health and Welfare

KEY INDICATORS

Total fertility rate (children per woman, 2008)	2.4
Under-5 mortality rate (per 1,000 live births, 2008)	31
HIV/AIDS (% of persons aged 15–49, 2007)	1.6
Physicians (per 1,000 head, 2003)	0.9
Hospital beds (per 1,000 head, 2005)	1.7
Health expenditure (2007): US $ per head (PPP)	357
Health expenditure (2007): % of GDP	4.7
Health expenditure (2007): public (% of total)	50.3
Access to water (% of persons, 2008)	94
Access to sanitation (% of persons, 2008)	83
Total carbon dioxide emissions ('000 metric tons, 2006)	12,142.5
Carbon dioxide emissions per head (metric tons, 2006)	4.6
Human Development Index (2007): ranking	100
Human Development Index (2007): value	0.766

For sources and definitions, see explanatory note on p. vi.

Agriculture

PRINCIPAL CROPS

('000 metric tons)

	2006	2007	2008
Sweet potatoes	27	26	26
Yams	123	113	102
Sugar cane	1,745	1,968	1,968*
Coconuts	311†	311*	311*
Cabbages and other brassicas	26	22	21
Tomatoes	23	20	19
Pumpkins, squash and gourds	36	35	34
Carrots and turnips	23	19	19
Bananas*	125	125	125
Plantains	22	19	15
Oranges*	140	142	142
Lemons and limes*	24	24	24
Grapefruit and pomelos*	44	44	44
Pineapples	21	18	20

* FAO estimate(s).

† Unofficial figure.

Pimento, allspice ('000 metric tons): 10 in 2005.

Aggregate production ('000 metric tons, may include official, semi-official or estimated data): Total cereals 1.9 in 2006, 1.8 in 2007, 1.9 in 2008; Total roots and tubers 194.7 in 2006, 182.5 in 2007, 164.9 in 2008; Total vegetables (incl. melons) 200.7 in 2006, 181.3 in 2007, 177.6 in 2008; Total fruits (excl. melons) 467.3 in 2006, 461.9 in 2007, 458.0 in 2008.

Source: FAO.

LIVESTOCK

('000 head, year ending September, FAO estimates)

	2005	2006	2007
Horses	4	4	4
Mules	10	10	10
Asses	23	23	23
Cattle	360	430	430
Pigs	262	221	186
Sheep	2	1	1
Goats	440	440	440
Poultry	12,500	12,500	12,500

2008: Figures assumed to be unchanged from 2007 (FAO estimates).

Source: FAO.

LIVESTOCK PRODUCTS

('000 metric tons)

	2005	2006	2007
Cattle meat	10.3	6.0	6.0
Goat meat	0.7	0.7	0.6
Pig meat	9.4	7.6	7.2
Chicken meat	101.5	104.6	107.3
Cows' milk	14.6	14.5	14.0
Hen eggs	5.1	8.6	6.3
Honey	1.0	1.0	1.0

2008: Figures assumed to be unchanged from 2007 (FAO estimates).

Source: FAO.

Forestry

ROUNDWOOD REMOVALS

('000 cubic metres, excl. bark, FAO estimates)

	2006	2007	2008
Sawlogs, veneer logs and logs for sleepers	128	127	127
Other industrial wood	150	150	150
Fuel wood	559	556	552
Total	837	833	829

Source: FAO.

SAWNWOOD PRODUCTION

('000 cubic metres, incl. railway sleepers)

	1996	1997	1998
Coniferous (softwood)	3	3	3
Broadleaved (hardwood)	61	62	63
Total	64	65	66

1999–2008: Annual production as in 1998 (FAO estimates).

Source: FAO.

Fishing

('000 metric tons, live weight)

	2006	2007	2008
Capture*	17.8	16.5	13.2
Marine fishes	12.3	11.0	9.5
Freshwater fishes*	0.4	0.4	0.4
Aquaculture	8.0	5.6	5.9
Nile tilapia	7.5	5.6	5.8
Total catch*	25.8	22.2	19.1

* FAO estimates.

Source: FAO.

Mining

('000 metric tons)

	2006	2007	2008*
Bauxite†	14,865	14,568	14,363
Alumina	4,100	3,941	3,996
Crude gypsum	364	228	238
Salt*	19.0	19.0	19.0

* Estimates.

† Dried equivalent of crude ore.

Source: US Geological Survey.

Industry

SELECTED PRODUCTS

	2006	2007	2008
Sugar (metric tons)	143,806	162,039	140,405
Molasses (metric tons)	73,426	77,905	62,654
Rum ('000 litres)	24,468	23,902	26,538
Beer and stout ('000 litres)	86,955	86,948	85,987
Fuel oil ('000 litres)	625,211	680,873	811,792
Gasoline (petrol) ('000 litres)	178,736	170,369	176,512
Kerosene, turbo and jet fuel ('000 litres)	81,762	67,452	87,785
Auto diesel oil ('000 litres)	257,422	236,822	206,536
Cement ('000 metric tons)	762,912	773,570	724,529
Concrete ('000 cu metres)	250,835	164,155	n.a.

Electrical energy (million kWh): 7,576 in 2005; 7,528 in 2006; 7,782 in 2007 (Source: UN Industrial Commodity Statistics Database).

Finance

CURRENCY AND EXCHANGE RATES

Monetary Units

100 cents = 1 Jamaican dollar (J $).

Sterling, US Dollar and Euro Equivalents (29 January 2010)

£1 sterling = J $144.410;
US $1 = J $89.484;
€1 = J $124.974;
J $1,000 = £6.92 = US $11.18 = €8.00.

Average Exchange Rate (J $ per US $)

2007 69.192
2008 72.756
2009 87.894

GOVERNMENT FINANCE

(budgetary central government, non-cash basis, J $ million, year ending 31 March)

Summary of Balances

	2006	2007	2008*
Revenue	214,001	249,512	272,150
Less Expense	230,955	275,223	323,096
Gross operating balance	–16,955	–25,711	–50,946
Less Net acquisition of non-financial assets	14,095	25,191	23,791
Net lending/borrowing	–31,050	–50,902	–74,737

Revenue

	2006	2007	2008*
Tax revenue	188,354	219,518	246,217
Taxes on income, profits and capital gains	85,530	102,887	119,169
Taxes on goods and services	73,280	83,525	94,276
Grants	5,710	5,772	8,935
Other revenue	19,937	24,223	16,999
Total	214,001	249,512	272,150

Expense/Outlays

Expense by economic type	2006	2007	2008*
Compensation of employees	36,445	40,568	52,063
Use of goods and services	12,657	15,905	18,893
Interest	97,054	103,480	124,102
Social benefits	9,585	12,045	13,306
Other expense	75,214	103,225	114,733
Total	230,955	275,223	323,096

Outlays by functions of government†	2006	2007	2008*
General public services	122,790	138,206	139,507
Defence	5,100	6,005	10,677
Public order and safety	22,931	26,519	34,782
Economic affairs	18,776	36,920	51,773
Environmental protection	558	562	690
Housing and community amenities	2,896	7,190	8,220
Health	18,910	23,349	28,859
Recreation, culture and religion	5,777	5,635	3,540
Education	44,066	52,079	63,777
Social protection	3,248	3,948	5,061
Total	245,051	300,414	346,887

* Preliminary.

† Including net acquisition of non-financial assets.

Source: IMF, *Government Finance Statistics Yearbook*.

INTERNATIONAL RESERVES

(excl. gold, US $ million at 31 December)

	2007	2008	2009
IMF special drawing rights	0.3	0.1	346.5
Foreign exchange	1,878.2	1,772.6	1,734.0
Total	1,878.5	1,772.7	2,080.5

Source: IMF, *International Financial Statistics*.

MONEY SUPPLY

(J $ million at 31 December)

	2007	2008	2009
Currency outside depository corporations	39,396	40,565	43,371
Transferable deposits	75,195	71,581	77,139
Other deposits	302,667	328,767	360,411
Securities other than shares	77,641	97,286	86,513
Broad money	494,900	538,199	567,433

Source: IMF, *International Financial Statistics*.

COST OF LIVING

(Consumer Price Index; base: January 1988 = 100)

	2004	2005	2006
Food (incl. beverages)	1,711.0	1,987.9	2,218.2
Fuel and power	1,795.6	2,131.3	2,395.5
Clothing and footwear	1,490.9	1,551.0	1,659.1
Rent and housing	1,813.6	2,034.1	2,435.2
Transport	1,994.2	2,051.9	2,623.6
All items (incl. others)	1,801.8	2,032.8	2,295.7

2007 (base: December 2006 = 100): All items 116.8.

2008 (base: December 2006 = 100): All items 136.5.

2009 (base: December 2006 = 100): All items 150.4.

NATIONAL ACCOUNTS

(J $ million at current prices)

Expenditure on the Gross Domestic Product

	2006	2007	2008
Government final consumption expenditure	105,076.5	124,238.3	155,814.0
Private final consumption expenditure	613,985.7	762,608.5	923,306.8
Increase in stocks	2,803.7	1,734.3	3,855.5
Gross fixed capital formation	220,384.0	235,105.9	245,541.2
Total domestic expenditure	942,249.9	1,123,687.0	1,328,517.5
Exports of goods and services	311,932.5	355,783.9	411,051.0
Less Imports of goods and services	468,051.3	586,324.9	721,340.8
GDP in purchasers' values	786,131.2	893,146.0	1,018,227.7
GDP at constant 2003 prices	501,746	509,249	504,422

Gross Domestic Product by Economic Activity

	2006	2007	2008
Agriculture, forestry and fishing	39,723.9	41,318.5	50,078.5
Mining and quarrying	27,260.4	32,353.2	16,239.5
Manufacturing	60,211.1	68,640.3	83,316.0
Electricity and water	25,960.1	28,814.8	38,126.3
Construction	56,665.7	67,616.3	74,603.7
Wholesale and retail trade; repairs and installation of machinery	138,090.1	155,760.6	191,980.0
Hotels and restaurants	33,353.5	36,178.6	40,419.0
Transport, storage and communication	80,494.1	91,920.7	96,394.5
Finance and insurance services	66,822.8	76,133.7	87,767.4
Real estate, renting and business services	67,511.0	78,216.8	91,612.1
Producers of government services	79,289.7	90,853.1	108,674.5
Other services	43,547.0	48,516.9	56,023.4
Sub-total	718,929.4	816,323.5	935,234.9
Less Financial intermediation services indirectly measured	31,355.5	35,204.9	41,790.0
Gross value added in basic prices	687,573.8	781,118.5	893,444.7
Taxes, less subsidies, on products	98,557.3	112,027.5	124,782.9
GDP in market prices	786,131.2	893,146.0	1,018,227.7

BALANCE OF PAYMENTS
(US $ million)

	2006	2007	2008
Exports of goods f.o.b.	2,133.6	2,362.6	2,499.9
Imports of goods f.o.b.	–5,077.1	–6,203.9	–7,546.8
Trade balance	–2,943.5	–3,841.3	–5,046.9
Exports of services	2,648.7	2,706.6	2,794.6
Imports of services	–2,021.0	–2,286.9	–2,367.1
Balance on goods and services	–2,315.8	–3,421.7	–4,619.4
Other income received	378.4	520.7	487.9
Other income paid	–994.0	–1,182.3	–1,056.2
Balance on goods, services and income	–2,931.4	–4,083.3	–5,187.6
Current transfers received	2,088.5	2,385.7	2,488.7
Current transfers paid	–339.9	–345.8	–339.0
Current balance	–1,182.8	–2,043.4	–3,038.0
Capital account (net)	–27.7	–35.5	18.1
Direct investment abroad	–85.4	–115.0	–75.9
Direct investment from abroad	882.2	866.5	1,436.6
Portfolio investment assets	–506.4	–1,768.6	–813.8
Portfolio investment liabilities	377.9	1,128.1	781.1
Other investment assets	–269.0	–238.3	–242.2
Other investment liabilities	912.7	1,420.8	1,934.2
Net errors and omissions	128.9	345.6	–105.1
Overall balance	230.3	–439.8	–105.0

Source: IMF, *International Financial Statistics*.

External Trade

PRINCIPAL COMMODITIES
(US $ million, preliminary)

Imports c.i.f.	2007	2008	2009
Foods	730.7	886.3	802.3
Beverages and tobacco	93.2	93.5	79.9
Crude materials (excl. fuels)	67.6	73.4	54.9
Mineral fuels and lubricants	2,428.9	3,354.8	1,396.6
Animal and vegetable oils and fats	31.6	53.9	33.9
Chemicals	849.0	951.0	740.3
Manufactured goods	753.4	883.6	555.8
Machinery and transport equipment	1,252.4	1,264.3	820.2
Miscellaneous manufactured articles	591.2	682.0	461.6
Total (incl. others)	6,893.0	8,361.0	5,065.7

Exports f.o.b.	2007	2008	2009
Foods	240.3	259.7	236.9
Beverages and tobacco	98.3	93.6	101.9
Crude materials (excl. fuels)	1,387.8	1,373.4	470.4
Mineral fuels and lubricants	326.0	434.4	213.8
Chemicals	183.8	449.2	203.9
Miscellaneous manufactured articles	10.5	20.2	20.5
Total (incl. others)	2,254.2	2,682.9	1,320.2

PRINCIPAL TRADING PARTNERS
(US $ million)

Imports c.i.f.	2006	2007	2008
Canada	123.7	137.4	131.6
CARICOM*	857.3	1,191.1	1,635.3
Latin America	939.6	1,122.4	1,510.8
United Kingdom	133.1	129.3	105.5
Other European Union	211.7	323.8	404.7
USA	2,165.0	2,699.5	3,294.4
Total (incl. others)	5,650.4	6,893.9	8,467.1

Exports f.o.b.	2006	2007	2008
Canada	309.4	333.3	259.0
CARICOM*	53.0	46.6	65.9
Latin America	13.5	13.7	22.8
United Kingdom	204.7	216.0	225.3
Other European Union	137.9	376.6	496.0
Norway	90.4	54.0	78.6
USA	598.9	824.7	981.8
Total (incl. others)	2,133.6	2,329.9	2,682.9

* Caribbean Community and Common Market.

Transport

RAILWAYS
(traffic)

	1988	1989	1990
Passenger-km ('000)	36,146	37,995	n.a.
Freight ton-km ('000)	115,076	28,609	1,931

Source: Jamaica Railway Corporation.

ROAD TRAFFIC
(motor vehicles in use)

	2004	2005	2006
Passenger cars	357,660	357,810	373,742
Commercial vehicles	128,239	n.a.	n.a.
Motorcycles	26,969	27,038	29,061

Source: IRF, *World Road Statistics*.

SHIPPING

Merchant Fleet
(registered at 31 December)

	2006	2007	2008
Number of vessels	31	36	44
Total displacement ('000 grt)	121.0	174.1	218.0

Source: Lloyd's Register-Fairplay, *World Fleet Statistics*.

International Sea-borne Freight Traffic
('000 metric tons, estimates)

	2007	2008	2009
Goods loaded	16,352	16,013	12,573
Goods unloaded	15,071	14,290	12,413

Source: Port Authority of Jamaica.

CIVIL AVIATION
(traffic on scheduled services)

	2003	2004	2005
Kilometres flown (million)	48	53	53
Passengers carried ('000)	1,838	2,008	1,574
Passenger-km (million)	5,005	5,060	3,855
Total ton-km (million)	484	499	369

Source: UN, *Statistical Yearbook*.

Tourism

VISITOR ARRIVALS BY COUNTRY OF ORIGIN

	2005	2006	2007
Canada	116,862	153,569	190,650
Cayman Islands	15,822	16,901	19,685
Germany	19,860	19,668	19,895
United Kingdom	149,773	175,363	185,657
USA	1,058,317	1,190,721	1,132,532
Total (incl. others)	1,478,663	1,678,905	1,700,785

Tourism revenue (US $ million, excl. passenger transport): 1,870 in 2006; 1,910 in 2007; 1,984 in 2008 (provisional).

Source: World Tourism Organization.

Communications Media

	2007	2008	2009
Telephones ('000 main lines in use)	369.7	316.6	302.3
Mobile cellular telephones ('000 subscribers)	2,684.3	2,723.3	2,971.3
Internet users ('000)	1,500.0	1,540.0	1,581.1
Broadband subscribers ('000)	92.8	97.3	112.2

Personal computers: 179,000 (67.5 per 1,000 persons) in 2005.

Radio receivers ('000 in use): 1,215 in 1997.

Television receivers ('000 in use): 510 in 2001.

Daily newspapers: 3 in 1996 (circulation 158,000).

Sources: International Telecommunication Union; UN, *Statistical Yearbook*; UNESCO, *Statistical Yearbook*.

Education

(2003/04, unless otherwise indicated)

	Institutions*	Teachers	Students
Pre-primary	2,137†	5,955‡	141,856‡
Primary	355	11,793§	310,021‡
Secondary	161	13,006‡	257,186‡
Tertiary	15	1,051	11,600

* Excludes 349 all-age schools and 88 primary and junior high schools.
† Includes 2,008 community-operated basic schools.
‡ 2006/07 data.
§ 2004/05 data.

Source: Ministry of Education and Youth; UNESCO Institute for Statistics.

Pupil-teacher ratio (primary education, UNESCO estimate): 27.7 in 2004/05 (Source: UNESCO Institute for Statistics).

Adult literacy rate (UNESCO estimates): 85.9% (males 80.6%; females 90.8%) in 2008 (Source: UNESCO Institute for Statistics).

Directory

The Constitution

The Constitution came into force at the independence of Jamaica on 6 August 1962. Amendments to the Constitution are enacted by Parliament, but certain entrenched provisions require ratification by a two-thirds' majority in both chambers of the legislature, and some (such as a change of the head of state) require the additional approval of a national referendum.

HEAD OF STATE

The Head of State is the British monarch, who is locally represented by a Governor-General, appointed by the British monarch, on the recommendation of the Jamaican Prime Minister in consultation with the Leader of the Opposition.

THE LEGISLATURE

The Senate or Upper House consists of 21 Senators, of whom 13 will be appointed by the Governor-General on the advice of the Prime Minister and eight by the Governor-General on the advice of the Leader of the Opposition. (Legislation enacted in 1984 provided for eight independent Senators to be appointed, after consultations with the Prime Minister, in the eventuality of there being no Leader of the Opposition.)

The House of Representatives or Lower House consists of 60 elected members called Members of Parliament.

A person is qualified for appointment to the Senate or for election to the House of Representatives if he or she is a citizen of Jamaica or another Commonwealth country, of the age of 21 or more and has been ordinarily resident in Jamaica for the immediately preceding 12 months.

THE PRIVY COUNCIL

The Privy Council consists of six members appointed by the Governor-General after consultation with the Prime Minister, of whom at least two are persons who hold or who have held public office. The functions of the Council are to advise the Governor-General on the exercise of the Prerogative of Mercy and on appeals on disciplinary matters from the three Service Commissions.

THE EXECUTIVE

The Prime Minister is appointed from the House of Representatives by the Governor-General, and is the leader of the party that holds the majority of seats in the House of Representatives. The Leader of the party is voted in by the members of that party. The Leader of the Opposition is voted in by the members of the Opposition party.

The Cabinet consists of the Prime Minister and not fewer than 11 other ministers, not more than four of whom may sit in the Senate. The members of the Cabinet are appointed by the Governor-General on the advice of the Prime Minister.

THE JUDICATURE

The Judicature consists of a Supreme Court, a Court of Appeal and minor courts. Judicial matters, notably advice to the Governor-General on appointments, are considered by a Judicial Service Commission, the Chairman of which is the Chief Justice, members being the President of the Court of Appeal, the Chairman of the Public Service Commission and three others.

CITIZENSHIP

All persons born in Jamaica after independence automatically acquire Jamaican citizenship and there is also provision for the acquisition of citizenship by persons born outside Jamaica of Jamaican parents. Persons born in Jamaica (or persons born outside Jamaica of Jamaican parents) before independence who immediately prior to independence were citizens of the United Kingdom and colonies also automatically become citizens of Jamaica.

Appropriate provision is made which permits persons who do not automatically become citizens of Jamaica to be registered as such.

FUNDAMENTAL RIGHTS AND FREEDOMS

The Constitution includes provisions safeguarding the fundamental freedoms of the individual, irrespective of race, place of origin, political opinions, colour, creed or sex, subject only to respect for the rights and freedoms of others and for the public interest. The fundamental freedoms include the rights of life, liberty, security of the person and protection from arbitrary arrest or restriction of movement, the enjoyment of property and the protection of the law, freedom of conscience, of expression and of peaceful assembly and association, and respect for private and family life.

The Government

HEAD OF STATE

Queen: HM Queen ELIZABETH II.

Governor-General: Sir PATRICK LINTON ALLEN (took office 26 February 2009).

PRIVY COUNCIL OF JAMAICA

KENNETH SMITH, DONALD MILLS, DENNIS LALOR, JAMES KERR, ELSA LEO RHYNIE, HEADLEY CUNNINGHAM.

CABINET
(July 2010)

The Government is formed by the Jamaica Labour Party.

Prime Minister and Minister of Planning and Development and of Defence, Information and Telecommunications: BRUCE GOLDING.

Deputy Prime Minister and Minister of Foreign Affairs and Foreign Trade: Dr KENNETH BAUGH.

Minister of Finance and the Public Service: AUDLEY SHAW.

Minister of National Security: DWIGHT NELSON.

Attorney-General and Minister of Justice: DOROTHY LIGHTBOURNE.

Minister of Education: ANDREW HOLNESS.

Minister of Industry, Commerce and Investment: KARL SAMUDA.

Minister of Tourism: EDMUND BARTLETT.

Minister of Agriculture and Fisheries: Dr CHRISTOPHER TUFTON.

Minister of Energy and Mining: JAMES ROBERTSON.

Minister of Water and Housing: Dr HORACE CHANG.

Minister of Labour and Social Security: PEARNEL CHARLES.

Minister of Health: RUDYARD SPENCER.

Minister of Culture, Youth and Sports: OLIVIA GRANGE.

Minister of Transport and Works: MICHAEL HENRY.

Minister without Portfolio in the Office of the Prime Minister: DARYL VAZ.

MINISTRIES

Office of the Governor-General: King's House, Hope Rd, Kingston 6; tel. 927-6424; fax 927-4561; e-mail kingshouse@kingshouse.gov.jm; internet www.kingshousejamaica.gov.jm.

Office of the Prime Minister: Jamaica House, 1 Devon Rd, POB 272, Kingston 6; tel. 927-9941; fax 968-8229; e-mail pmo@opm.gov.jm; internet www.opm.gov.jm.

Ministry of Agriculture and Fisheries: Hope Gardens, POB 480, Kingston 6; tel. 927-1731; fax 927-1904; e-mail psoffice@moa.gov.jm; internet www.moa.gov.jm.

Ministry of Culture, Youth and Sports: 64 Knutsford Blvd, 3rd and 5th Floor, Kingston 5; tel. 960-6427; fax 968-4511; e-mail info@micys.gov.jm; internet www.micys.gov.jm.

Ministry of Education: 2 National Heroes Circle, Kingston 4; tel. 922-1400; fax 967-1837; e-mail webmaster@moec.gov.jm; internet www.moec.gov.jm.

Ministry of Energy and Mining: PCJ Bldg, 36 Trafalgar Rd, Kingston 10; tel. 929-8990; fax 960-1623; e-mail info@mem.gov.jm; internet www.mem.gov.jm.

Ministry of Finance and the Public Service: 30 National Heroes Circle, Kingston 4; tel. 922-8600; fax 922-7097; e-mail info@mof.gov.jm; internet www.mof.gov.jm.

Ministry of Foreign Affairs and Foreign Trade: 21 Dominica Dr., POB 624, Kingston 5; tel. 926-4220; fax 929-5112; e-mail mfaftjam@cwjamaica.com; internet www.mfaft.gov.jm.

Ministry of Health: Oceana Hotel Complex, 2–4 King St, Kingston 10; tel. 967-1100; fax 967-1643; e-mail webmaster@moh.gov.jm; internet www.moh.gov.jm.

Ministry of Industry, Commerce and Investment (MITEC): 4 St Lucia Ave, Kingston 5; tel. 968-7116; fax 960-7422; e-mail communications@miic.gov.jm; internet www.miic.gov.jm.

Ministry of Justice and Attorney-General's Department: Mutual Life Bldg, NCB Towers, 2 Oxford Rd, Kingston 5; tel. 906-4923; fax 906-1712; e-mail customerservice@moj.gov.jm; internet www.moj.gov.jm.

Ministry of Labour and Social Security: 1F North St, POB 10, Kingston; tel. 922-9500; fax 922-6902; e-mail mlss_perm_sect@yahoo.com; internet www.mlss.gov.jm.

Ministry of National Security: NCB North Tower, 2 Oxford Rd, Kingston 5; tel. 906-4908; fax 906-6807; e-mail information@mns.gov.jm; internet www.mns.gov.jm.

Ministry of Tourism: 64 Knutsford Blvd, Kingston 5; tel. 929-9200; fax 929-9375; e-mail info@visitjamaica.com; internet www.visitjamaica.com.

Ministry of Transport and Works: 138H Maxfield Ave, Kingston 10; tel. 754-1900; fax 960-2886; e-mail ps@mtw.gov.jm; internet www.mtw.gov.jm.

Ministry of Water and Housing: 25 Dominica Dr., Kingston 5; tel. 926-1690; fax 926-0543; e-mail info@mwh.gov.jm; internet www.mwh.gov.jm.

Legislature

PARLIAMENT

Houses of Parliament: Gordon House, 81 Duke St, POB 636, Kingston; tel. 922-0202; fax 967-0064; e-mail clerk@japarliament.gov.jm; internet www.japarliament.gov.jm; Clerk HEATHER COOKE.

Senate

President: OSWALD HARDING.

Deputy-President: NAVEL FOSTER CLARKE.

The Senate has 19 other members.

House of Representatives

Speaker: DELROY CHUCK.

Deputy Speaker: MARISA DALRYMPLE-PHILIBERT.

General Election, 3 September 2007

	% of votes cast	Seats
Jamaica Labour Party (JLP)	50.1	32
People's National Party (PNP)	49.8	28
Total (incl. others)	100.0	60

Election Commission

Electoral Office of Jamaica (EOJ): 43 Duke St, Kingston; tel. 922-0425; fax 967-0728; e-mail eojinfo@eoj.com.jm; internet www.eoj.com.jm; f. 1943; Dir ORRETTE FISHER.

Political Organizations

Jamaica Alliance Movement (JAM): Flamingo Beach, Falmouth, Trelawny, Kingston; tel. 861-5233; e-mail nowjam@gmail.com; internet www.nowjam.org; f. 2001; Rastafarian; Pres. ASTOR BLACK.

Jamaica Labour Party (JLP): 20 Belmont Rd, Kingston 5; tel. 929-1183; e-mail join@jamaicalabourparty.com; internet www.jamaicalabourparty.com; f. 1943; supports free enterprise in a mixed economy and close co-operation with the USA; Leader BRUCE GOLDING; Gen. Sec. KARL SAMUDA.

National Democratic Movement (NDM): 72 Half Way Tree Rd, Kingston 10; tel. 318-4802; fax 995-5912; e-mail ndmjamaica@yahoo.com; internet www.ndm4jamaica.org; f. 1995; advocates a clear separation of powers between the central executive and elected representatives; supports private investment and a market economy; mem. of the New Jamaica Alliance; Chair. PETER TOWNSEND; Gen. Sec. MICHAEL WILLIAMS.

People's National Party (PNP): 89 Old Hope Rd, Kingston 6; tel. 978-1337; fax 927-4389; e-mail information@pnpjamaica.com; internet www.pnpjamaica.com; f. 1938; socialist principles; affiliated with the National Workers' Union; Pres. PORTIA SIMPSON-MILLER; Chair. ROBERT PICKERSGILL; Gen. Sec. PETER BUNTING.

Diplomatic Representation

EMBASSIES AND HIGH COMMISSIONS IN JAMAICA

Argentina: Dyoll Life Bldg, 6th Floor, 40 Knutsford Blvd, Kingston 5; tel. 926-5588; fax 926-0580; e-mail embargen@cwjamaica.com; Ambassador MARIO JOSÉ PINO.

Belgium: 10 Millsborough Crescent, Kingston 6; tel. 978-5543; fax 978-7791; e-mail kingston@diplobel.fed.be; Ambassador FRÉDÉRIC MEURICE.

Brazil: Pan Caribbean Bldg, 10th Floor, 60 Knutsford Blvd, Kingston 5; tel. 929-8607; fax 968-5897; e-mail brasking@infochan.com; Ambassador ALEXANDRE RUBEN MILITO GUEIROS.

Canada: 3 West Kings House Rd, POB 1500, Kingston 10; tel. 926-1500; fax 511-3493; e-mail kngtn@international.gc.ca; internet www.canadainternational.gc.ca/jamaica-jamaique; High Commissioner STEPHEN HALLIHAN.

Chile: Island Life Centre, 5th Floor, South Sixth St, Lucia Ave, Kingston 5; tel. 968-0260; fax 968-0265; e-mail chilejam@cwjamaica.com; Ambassador ALFREDO GARCÍA CASTELBLANCO.

China, People's Republic: 8 Seaview Ave, POB 232, Kingston 10; tel. 927-3871; fax 927-6920; e-mail chinaemb_jm@mfa.gov.cn; internet jm.chineseembassy.org/eng; Ambassador CHEN JINGHUA.

Colombia: Victoria Mutual Bldg, 4th Floor, 53 Knutsford Blvd, Kingston 5; tel. 929-1701; fax 968-0577; e-mail ekingston@cancilleria.gov.co; internet www.embajadaenjamaica.gov.co; Ambassador VENTURA EMILIO DIAZ MEJÍA.

Costa Rica: Belvedere House, Beverley Dr., Kingston 6; tel. 927-5988; fax 978-3946; e-mail cr_emb_jam14@hotmail.com; Chargé d'affaires a.i. MARCIA WATSON LOCKWOOD.

Cuba: 9 Trafalgar Rd, Kingston 10; tel. 978-0931; fax 978-5372; e-mail embacubajam@cwjamaica.com; Ambassador YURI GALA LOPEZ.

Dominican Republic: 32 Earls Court, Kingston 8; tel. 755-4155; fax 755-4156; e-mail domemb@cwjamaica.com; Ambassador FILOMENA ALTAGRACIA NAVARRO TAVAREZ.

France: 13 Hillcrest Ave, POB 93, Kingston 6; tel. 946-4000; fax 946-4020; e-mail frenchembassy@cwjamaica.com; internet www.ambafrance-jm-bm.org; Ambassador MARK-OLIVIER GENDRY.

Germany: 10 Waterloo Rd, POB 444, Kingston 10; tel. 926-6728; fax 620-5457; e-mail germanembassa.kingston@gmail.com; internet www.kingston.diplo.de; Ambassador JÜRGEN ENGEL.

Haiti: 2 Munroe Rd, Kingston 6; tel. 927-7595; fax 978-7638; Chargé d'affaires a.i. MAX ALCE.

Honduras: 7 Lady Kay Dr., Norbrook, Kingston 8; tel. 941-1790; fax 941-6470; e-mail eduardonorris@hotmail.com; Ambassador JOSÉ EDUARDO NORRIS MADRID.

India: 27 Seymour Ave, POB 446, Kingston 6; tel. 927-4270; fax 978-2801; e-mail hicomindkin@cwjamaica.com; internet www.hcikingston.com; High Commissioner MOHINDER GROVER.

Japan: NCB Towers, North Tower, 6th Floor, 2 Oxford Rd, POB 8104, Kingston 5; tel. 929-3338; fax 968-1373; internet www.jamaica.emb-japan.go.jp; Ambassador HIROSHI YAMAGUCHI.

Mexico: PCJ Bldg, 36 Trafalgar Rd, Kingston 10; tel. 926-4242; fax 929-7995; e-mail embamexj@cwjamaica.com; Ambassador ROSAURA LEONORA RUEDA GUTIÉRREZ.

Nigeria: 5 Waterloo Rd, POB 94, Kingston 10; tel. 968-3732; fax 968-7371; e-mail nhckingston@mail.infochan.com; High Commissioner CHARLES EYO (acting).

Panama: 1 Norbrook Close, Kingston 8; tel. 924-3428; fax 924-5235; e-mail panaemba@hotmail.com; Ambassador (vacant).

Peru: 23 Barbados Ave, POB 1818, Kingston 5; tel. 920-5027; fax 920-4360; e-mail embaperu-kingston@rree.gob.pe; Ambassador LUIS SÁNDIGA CABRERA.

Russia: 22 Norbrook Dr., Kingston 8; tel. 924-1048; fax 925-8290; e-mail rusembja@colis.com; Ambassador VICTOR ZOTIN.

Saint Christopher and Nevis: 11A Opal Ave, Golden Acres, Red Hills, St Andrew; tel. 944-3861; fax 945-0105; High Commissioner CEDRIC HARPER.

South Africa: 15 Hillcrest Ave, Kingston 6; tel. 978-3160; fax 978-0339; e-mail sahc-jamaica@cwjamaica.com; High Commissioner FAITH DOREEN RADEBE.

Spain: Island Life Centre, 6th Floor, 8 St Lucia Ave, Kingston 5; tel. 929-5555; fax 929-8965; e-mail emb.kingston@mae.es; Ambassador JESÚS SILVA FERNÁNDEZ.

Trinidad and Tobago: First Life Bldg, 3rd Floor, 60 Knutsford Blvd, Kingston 5; tel. 926-5730; fax 926-5801; e-mail kgnhctt@cwjamaica.com; High Commissioner YVONNE GITTENS-JOSEPH.

United Kingdom: 28 Trafalgar Rd, POB 575, Kingston 10; tel. 510-0700; fax 510-0737; e-mail bhc.kingston@fco.gov.uk; internet ukinjamaica.fco.gov.uk; High Commissioner HOWARD DRAKE.

USA: 142 Old Hope Rd, Kingston 6; tel. 702-6000; e-mail opakgn@state.gov; internet kingston.usembassy.gov; Ambassador PAMELA E. BRIDGEWATER AWKARD.

Venezuela: PCJ Bldg, 3rd Floor, 36 Trafalgar Rd, POB 26, Kingston 10; tel. 926-5510; fax 926-7442; e-mail embavene@n5.com.jm; Ambassador NOEL ENRIQUE MARTÍNEZ OCHOA.

Judicial System

The judicial system is based on English common law and practice. Final appeal is to the Judicial Committee of the Privy Council in the United Kingdom, although in 2001 the Jamaican Government signed an agreement to establish a Caribbean Court of Justice to fulfil this function.

Justice is administered by the Privy Council, Court of Appeal, Supreme Court (which includes the Revenue Court, the Gun Court and, since 2001, the Commercial Court), Resident Magistrates' Court (which includes the Traffic Court), two Family Courts and the Courts of Petty Sessions.

Judicial Service Commission: Office of the Services Commissions, 30 National Heroes Circle, Kingston 4; tel. 922-8600; e-mail communications@osc.gov.jm; advises the Governor-General on judicial appointments, etc.; chaired by the Chief Justice.

Supreme Court

Public Bldg E, 134 Tower St, POB 491, Kingston; tel. 922-8300; fax 967-0669; e-mail webmaster@sc.gov.jm; internet www.sc.gov.jm.

Chief Justice: ZAILA MCCALLA.

Senior Puisne Judge: MARVA MCINTOSH.

Master: AUDRE LINDO.

Registrar: NICOLE SIMMONS.

Court of Appeal

POB 629, Kingston; tel. 922-8300.

President: SEYMOUR PANTON.

Registrar: G. P. LEVERS.

Religion

CHRISTIANITY

Jamaica Council of Churches: 14 South Ave, Kingston 10; tel. and fax 926-0974; e-mail jchurch@cwjamaica.com; f. 1941; 10 mem. churches and three agencies; Gen. Sec. GARY HARRIOT.

The Anglican Communion

Anglicans in Jamaica are adherents of the Church in the Province of the West Indies, comprising eight dioceses. The Archbishop of the Province is the Bishop of the North East Caribbean and Aruba. The Bishop of Jamaica, whose jurisdiction also includes Grand Cayman (in the Cayman Islands), is assisted by three suffragan Bishops (of Kingston, Mandeville and Montego Bay). According to the 2001 census, some 4% of the population are Anglicans.

Bishop of Jamaica: Rt Rev. ALFRED C. REID, Church House, 2 Caledonia Ave, Kingston 5; tel. 926-8925; fax 968-0618; e-mail info@anglicandiocese.com; internet anglicandiocese.dthost.com.

The Roman Catholic Church

Jamaica comprises the archdiocese of Kingston in Jamaica (which also includes the Cayman Islands), and the dioceses of Montego Bay and Mandeville. Some 3% of the population are Roman Catholics. The Archbishop and Bishops participate in the Antilles Episcopal Conference (currently based in Port of Spain, Trinidad and Tobago).

Archbishop of Kingston in Jamaica: Most Rev. DONALD JAMES REECE, Archbishop's Residence, 21 Hopefield Ave, POB 43, Kingston 6; tel. 927-9915; fax 927-4487; e-mail rcabkgn@cwjamaica.com; internet www.archdioceseofkingston.org.

Other Christian Churches

According to the 2001 census, the largest religious bodies are the Church of God (whose members represent 24% of the population),

Seventh-day Adventists (11% of the population), Pentecostalists (10%) and Baptists (7%). Other denominations include Jehovah's Witnesses, the Methodist and Congregational Churches, United Church, the Church of the Brethren, the Ethiopian Orthodox Church, the Disciples of Christ, the Moravian Church, the Salvation Army and the Religious Society of Friends (Quakers).

Assembly of God: Evangel Temple, 3 Friendship Park Rd, Kingston 3; tel. 928-2995; Sec. Pastor WILSON.

Baptist Union: 2B Washington Blvd, Kingston 20; tel. 969-2223; fax 924-6296; e-mail info@jbu.org.jm; internet www.jbu.org.jm; 40,000 mems in 302 churches; Pres. Rev. STEPHEN JENNINGS; Gen. Sec. Rev. KARL JOHNSON.

First Church of Christ, Scientist: 17 National Heroes Circle, Kingston 4; tel. 967-3814.

Methodist Church (Jamaica District): 143 Constant Spring Rd, POB 892, Kingston 8; tel. 925-6768; fax 924-2560; e-mail jamaicamethodist@cwjamaica.com; internet www.jamaicamethodist.org; f. 1789; 15,820 mems; Pres. Rev. Dr BYRON CHAMBERS; Synod Sec. Rev. EVERALD GALBRAITH.

Moravian Church in Jamaica: 3 Hector St, POB 8369, Kingston 5; tel. 928-1861; fax 928-8336; e-mail moravianchurch@cwjamaica.com; internet www.jamaicamoravian.com; f. 1754; 30,000 mems.

New Testament Church of God in Jamaica: New Testament Church of God Convention Centre, Rodons Pen, Old Harbour, St Catherine; 87,965 mems of 337 churches; Overseer Rev. Dr DENNIS MCQUIRE.

United Church in Jamaica and the Cayman Islands: 12 Carlton Cres., POB 359, Kingston 10; tel. 926-6059; fax 929-0826; e-mail churchunited@hotmail.com; internet www.ucjci.netfirms.com; f. 1965 by merger of the Congregational Union of Jamaica (f. 1877) and the Presbyterian Church of Jamaica and Grand Cayman to become United Church of Jamaica and Grand Cayman; merged with Disciples of Christ in Jamaica in 1992 when name changed as above; 20,000 mems; Moderator RODERICK HEWITT; Gen. Sec. Rev. COLLIN COWAN.

West Indies Union Conference of Seventh-day Adventists: 125 Manchester Rd, Mandeville; tel. 962-2284; fax 962-3417; e-mail wiu.president@jmsda.net; internet www.wiunion.org; f. 1903; 205,000 mems; Pres. Dr PATRICK ALLEN.

RASTAFARIANISM

Rastafarianism is an important influence in Jamaican culture. The cult is derived from Christianity and a belief in the divinity of Ras (Prince) Tafari Makonnen (later Emperor Haile Selassie) of Ethiopia. It advocates racial equality and non-violence, but causes controversy in its use of 'ganja' (marijuana) as a sacrament. According to the 2001 census, 1% of the population are Rastafarians. Although the religion is largely unorganized, there are some denominations.

Haile Selassie Jahrastafari Royal Ethiopian Judah Coptic Church: 11 Welcome Ave, Kingston 11; tel. 547-8507; fax 660-8726; e-mail royalethiopian@yahoo.com; internet www.nationofjahrastafari8.ning.com; f. 1966; not officially incorporated; Head Pres. Dr MATT O. MYRIE.

BAHÁ'Í FAITH

National Spiritual Assembly: 208 Mountain View Ave, Kingston 6; tel. 927-7051; fax 978-2344; internet www.jm.bahai.org; incorporated in 1970; Chair. DOROTHY WHYTE.

ISLAM

According to the 2001 census, there are an estimated 5,000 Muslims (less than 1% of the population).

JUDAISM

According to the 2001 census, there are some 350 Jews (less than 1% of the population).

United Congregation of Israelites: K. K. Shaare Shalom Synagogue, 92 Duke St, Kingston 6; tel. and fax 922-5931; e-mail info@ucija.org; internet www.ucija.org; f. 1655; 250 mems; Pres. MICHAEL MATALON.

The Press

DAILIES

Daily Gleaner: 7 North St, POB 40, Kingston; tel. 922-3400; fax 922-6223; e-mail feedback@jamaica-gleaner.com; internet www.jamaica-gleaner.com; f. 1834; morning; independent; Chair. and Man. Dir OLIVER CLARKE; Editor-in-Chief GARFIELD GRANDISON; circ. 50,000.

Daily Star: 7 North St, POB 40, Kingston; tel. 922-3400; fax 922-6223; e-mail feedback@jamaica-gleaner.com; internet www.jamaica-tar.com; f. 1951; evening; Editor-in-Chief GARFIELD GRANDISON; Editor DWAYNE GORDON; circ. 45,000.

Jamaica Observer: 40-42 1/2 Beechwood Ave, Kingston 5; tel. 920-8136; fax 926-7655; e-mail feedback@jamaicaobserver.com; internet www.jamaicaobserver.com; f. 1993; Chair. GORDON 'BUTCH' STEWART.

PERIODICALS

The Anglican: 2 Caledonia Ave, Kingston 5; tel. 920-2714; internet www.anglicandiocesejamaica.com; f. 2004 following cessation of Jamaica Churchman; quarterly; circ. 9,000.

Catholic Opinion: Roman Catholic Chancery Office, 21 Hopefield Ave, POB 43, Kingston 6; tel. 927-9915; fax 927-4487; e-mail rcabkgn@cwjamaica.com; internet www.archdioceseofkingston.org; 6 a year; religious; circulated in the Sunday Gleaner; Editor Mgr MICHAEL LEWIS; circ. 100,000.

Children's Own: 7 North St, POB 40, Kingston; tel. 922-3400; fax 922-6223; e-mail feedback@jamaica-gleaner.com; internet www.jamaica-gleaner.com; weekly during term time; Editor-in-Chief GARFIELD GRANDISON; circ. 120,000.

Jamaica Journal: 10–16 East St, Kingston; tel. 922-0620; fax 922-1147; e-mail ioj.jam@mail.infochan.com; internet www.instituteofjamaica.org.jm; f. 1967; 3 a year; literary, historical and cultural review; publ. by Institute of Jamaica; Chair. of Editorial Cttee KIM ROBINSON.

Mandeville Weekly: 31 Ward Ave, Mandeville, Manchester; tel. 961-0118; fax 961-0119; e-mail mandevilleweekly@flowja.com; internet www.mandevilleweekly.com; f. 1993; Chair. and Editor-in-Chief ANTHONY FRECKLETON; Man. Dir WENDY FRECKLETON.

North Coast Times: 130 Main St, Ocho Rios; tel. 795-4201; fax 974-9306; internet www.northcoasttimes.com; weekly; Publr FRANKLIN MCKNIGHT; Gen. Man. DESRINE PRICE.

Sunday Gleaner: 7 North St, POB 40, Kingston; tel. 922-3400; fax 922-6223; e-mail feedback@jamaica-gleaner.com; internet www.jamaica-gleaner.com; weekly; Editor-in-Chief GARFIELD GRANDISON; circ. 100,000.

Sunday Herald: 17 Norwood Ave, Kingston 5; tel. 906-7572; fax 908-4044; e-mail sunherald@cwjamaica.com; internet www.sunheraldja.com; f. 1997; weekly; Man. Editor DESMOND RICHARDS; Exec. Editor R. CHRISTENE KING.

Sunday Observer: 40-42 1/2 Beechwood Ave, Kingston 5; tel. 920-8136; fax 926-7655; internet www.jamaicaobserver.com; weekly; Chair. GORDON 'BUTCH' STEWART.

The Visitor Vacation Guide: 4 Cottage Rd, POB 1258, Montego Bay; tel. 952-5256; fax 952-6513; Editor LLOYD B. SMITH.

Weekend Star: 7 North St, POB 40, Kingston; tel. 922-3400; fax 922-6223; e-mail feedback@jamaica-gleaner.com; internet www.jamaica-gleaner.com; f. 1951; weekly; Editor-in-Chief GARFIELD GRANDISON; Editor DWAYNE GORDON; circ. 80,000.

Western News: 40-42 1/2, Beechwood Ave, Kingston 5; tel. 920-8136; fax 926-7655; e-mail feedback@jamaicaobserver.com; internet www.jamaicaobserver.com; Chair. GORDON 'BUTCH' STEWART; circ. 20,000.

West Indian Medical Journal: Faculty of Medical Sciences, University of the West Indies, Mona, Kingston 7; tel. 927-1214; fax 927-1846; e-mail wimj@uwimona.edu.jm; internet www.mona.uwi.edu/fms/wimj; f. 1951; quarterly; Editor EVERARD N. BARTON; circ. 2,000.

X-News Jamaica: 86 Hagley Park Rd, Kingston 10; tel. 937-7304; fax 901-7667; e-mail comments@xnewsjamaica.com; internet www.xnewsjamaica.com; f. 1993; weekly; Assistant Editor CECELIA CAMPBELL-LIVINGSTON.

PRESS ASSOCIATION

Press Association of Jamaica (PAJ): Kingston 8; tel. 925-7836; internet pressassociationjamaica.org; f. 1943; Pres. BYRON BUCKLEY.

Publishers

Jamaica Publishing House Ltd: 97B Church St, Kingston; tel. 967-3866; fax 922-5412; e-mail jph@cwjamaica.com; f. 1969; subsidiary of Jamaica Teachers' Asscn; English language and literature, mathematics, history, geography, social sciences, music; Chair. WOODBURN MILLER; Man. ELAINE R. STENNETT.

LMH Publishing Ltd: 7 Norman Rd, Suite 10-11, Sagicor Industrial Complex, POB 8296, Kingston CSO; tel. 938-0005; fax 759-8752; e-mail lmhbookpublishing@cwjamaica.com; internet www.lmhpublishing.com; f. 1970; educational textbooks, general, travel, fiction; Chair. L. MICHAEL HENRY; Man. Dir DAWN CHAMBERS-HENRY.

Ian Randle Publishers (IRP): 11 Cunningham Ave, POB 686, Kingston 6; tel. 978-0745; fax 978-1156; e-mail ian@ianrandlepublishers.com; internet www.ianrandlepublishers.com; f. 1991; history, gender studies, politics, sociology, law, cooking and music; Pres. and Publr IAN RANDLE; Man. Dir CHRISTINE RANDLE.

University of the West Indies Press (UWI Press): 7A Gibraltar Hall Rd, Mona, Kingston 7; tel. 977-2659; fax 977-2660; internet www.uwipress.com; f. 1992; Caribbean history, culture and literature, gender studies, education and political science; Man. Editor SHIVAUN HEARNE; Gen. Man. LINDA SPETH.

Western Publishers Ltd: 4 Cottage Rd, POB 1258, Montego Bay; tel. 952-5253; fax 952-6513; e-mail westernmirror@mail.infochan.com; internet westernmirror.com; f. 1980; CEO and Editor-in-Chief LLOYD B. SMITH.

GOVERNMENT PUBLISHING HOUSE

Jamaica Printing Services: 77 1/2 Duke St, Kingston; tel. 967-2250; fax 967-2225; e-mail jps_1992@yahoo.com; internet jps1992.org; Gen. Man. RALPH BELL.

Broadcasting and Communications

TELECOMMUNICATIONS

The sector was regulated by the Office of Utilities Regulation (see Utilities).

Claro Jamaica Ltd (MiPhone): 30–36 Knutsford Blvd, Kingston 5; tel. 621-1000; fax 906-3486; internet claro.com.jm; mobile cellular telephone operator; Oceanic Digital bought by América Móvil, SA de CV (Mexico) in 2007; adopted current name in 2008; CEO ALEJANDRO GUTIERREZ; 100,000 subscribers.

Digicel Jamaica: 10–16 Grenada Way, Kingston 5; tel. 960-2696; fax 920-0948; internet www.digiceljamaica.com; mobile cellular telephone operator; owned by Irish consortium, Mossel (Jamaica) Ltd; f. 2001; Chair. DENIS O'BRIEN; CEO (Jamaica) MARK LINEHAN.

LIME: 7 Cecilio Ave, Kingston 10; tel. 926-9700; fax 929-9530; e-mail customer.services@cwjamaica.com; internet www.time4lime.com; f. 1989; name changed as above in 2008; 79% owned by Cable & Wireless (United Kingdom); landline, internet and mobile services; Pres. RODNEY DAVIS; Man. Dir (Jamaica and the Cayman Islands) GEOFF HOUSTON.

BROADCASTING

Regulatory Authority

Broadcasting Commission of Jamaica: 5th Floor, Victoria Mutual Bldg, 53 Knutsford Blvd, Kingston 5; tel. 920-9537; fax 929-1997; e-mail info@broadcom.org; internet www.broadcastingcommission.org; Chair. Dr HOPETON DUNN.

Radio

Independent Radio: 6 Bradley Ave, Kingston 10; tel. 968-4880; fax 968-9165; commercial; broadcasts 24 hrs a day on FM; Man. Dir NEWTON JAMES.

Music 99 FM: 6 Bradley Ave, Kingston 10.

Power 106: 6 Bradley Ave, Kingston 10; tel. 968-4880; fax 968-9165; e-mail power106@cwjamaica.com; internet www.go-jamaica.com/power; f. 1992; talk and sports programmes.

IRIE FM: 1B Derrymore Rd, Kingston 10; tel. 968-5023; fax 968-8332; e-mail iriefmmarket@cwjamaica.com; internet www.iriefm.net; f. 1991; owned by Grove Broadcasting Co; reggae music; Man. BRIAN SCHMIDT.

Island Broadcasting Corporation: 17 Haining Rd, Kingston 5; tel. 929-1346; fax 906-7604; commercial; broadcasts 24 hrs a day on FM; Chair. ALSTON STEWART.

KLAS Sports FM 89: 17 Haining Rd, Kingston 5; tel. 929-1344; fax 960-0572; e-mail admin@klassportsradio.com; internet www.klassportsradio.com; f. 1991; sports broadcasting.

Love FM: 81 Hagley Park Rd, Kingston 10; tel. 968-9596; e-mail webmaster@love101.org; internet www.lovefm.com; f. 1993; commercial radio station, religious programming on FM; owned by National Religious Media Ltd; Gen. Man. WINSTON RIDGARD.

Radio Jamaica Ltd (RJR): Broadcasting House, 32 Lyndhurst Rd, POB 23, Kingston 5; tel. 926-1100; fax 929-7467; e-mail rjr@radiojamaica.com; internet www.radiojamaica.com; f. 1947; commercial, public service; 3 channels; Man. Dir GARY ALLEN; Gen. Man. Radio Services FRANCOIS ST JUSTE.

FAME 95 FM: internet www.famefm.fm; broadcasts on FM, island-wide 24 hrs a day.

Hitz 92 FM: internet www.hitz92fm.com; broadcasts on FM, island-wide 24 hrs a day; youth station.

RJR 94 FM: internet www.rjr94fm.com; broadcasts on AM and FM, island-wide 24 hrs a day; Exec. Producer NORMA BROWN-BELL.

ZIP 103 FM: 1B Derrymore Rd, Kingston 10, Jamaica; tel. 819-7699; fax 929-6233; e-mail zip103fm@cwjamaica.com; internet www.ZIPFM.net; f. 2002; commercial radio station; Dir D'ADRA WILLIAMS.

Television

Creative TV (CTV): Kingston; tel. 967-4482; fax 924-9432; internet www.creativetvjamaica.com; operated by Creative Production & Training Centre Ltd (CPTC); local cable channel; regional cultural, educational and historical programming; CEO Dr HOPETON DUNN.

CVM Television: 69 Constant Sprint Rd, Kingston 10; tel. 931-9400; fax 931-9417; e-mail contact@cvmtv.com; internet www.cvmtv.com; Pres. and CEO DAVID MCBEAN.

Love Television: Kingston; internet www.love101.org; f. 1997; religious programming; owned by National Religious Media Ltd.

Television Jamaica Limited (TVJ): 32 Lyndhurst Rd, Kingston 5; tel. 926-1100; fax 929-1029; e-mail tvjadmin@cwjamaica.com; internet www.televisionjamaica.com; f. 1959 as Jamaica Broadcasting Corpn; privatized and adopted current name in 1997; subsidiary of RJR Communications Group; island-wide VHF transmission 24 hrs a day; Gen. Man. KAY OSBORNE.

Finance

(cap. = capital; res = reserves; dep. = deposits; m. = million; brs = branches; amounts in Jamaican dollars)

BANKING

Central Bank

Bank of Jamaica: Nethersole Pl., POB 621, Kingston; tel. 922-0750; fax 922-0854; e-mail info@boj.org.jm; internet www.boj.org.jm; f. 1960; cap. 4.0m., res 5,101.9m., dep.198,334.5m. (Dec. 2008); Gov. and Chair. BRIAN HECTOR WYNTER.

Commercial Banks

Bank of Nova Scotia Jamaica Ltd (Canada): Scotiabank Centre Bldg, cnr Duke and Port Royal Sts, POB 709, Kingston; tel. 922-1000; fax 924-9294; e-mail customercare-jam@scotiabank.com; internet www.scotiabank.com.jm; f. 1967; cap. 2,927.2m., res 11,954.7m., dep. 135,210.4m. (Oct. 2007); Chair. R. H. PITFIELD; Pres. and CEO WILLIAM E. CLARKE; 35 brs.

Citimerchant Bank Ltd: 63–67 Knutsford Blvd, POB 286, Kingston 5; tel. 926-3270; fax 929-3745; internet www.citibank.com/jamaica; owned by Citifinance Ltd; cap. 25.7m., res 128.4m., dep. 87.2m. (Dec. 2003); Vice-Pres EVA LEWIS, PETER MOSES.

FirstCaribbean International Bank (Jamaica) Ltd (Canada): 78 Halfway Tree Rd, POB 762, Kingston 10; tel. 929-9310; fax 926-7751; internet www.firstcaribbeanbank.com; owned by CIBC Investments (Cayman) Ltd; cap. and res 4,738.0m., dep. 35,106.3m. (Oct. 2007); Exec. Chair. MICHAEL MANSOOR; CEO JOHN D. ORR; 12 brs.

National Commercial Bank Jamaica Ltd: 'The Atrium', 32 Trafalgar Rd, POB 88, Kingston 10; tel. 929-9050; fax 929-8399; internet www.jncb.com; f. 1837; merged with Mutual Security Bank in 1996; cap. 6,465.7m., res 8,949.7m., dep. 206,391.6m. (Sept. 2007); Chair. MICHAEL LEE-CHIN; Man. Dir PATRICK HYLTON; 37 brs.

RBTT Bank Jamaica Ltd: 17 Dominica Dr., Kingston 5; tel. 960-2340; fax 960-5120; e-mail rbtt@cwjamaica.com; internet www.rbtt.com; f. 1993 as Jamaica Citizens Bank Ltd; acquired by Royal Bank of Trinidad and Tobago in 2001 and name changed as above; Chair. Dr OWEN JEFFERSON; Man. Dir MICHAEL E. A. WRIGHT; 23 brs.

Development Banks

Development Bank of Jamaica Ltd: 11A–15 Oxford Rd, POB 466, Kingston 5; tel. 929-6124-7; fax 929-6055; e-mail dbank@cwjamaica.com; f. 2000 following merger of Agricultural Credit Bank of Jamaica Ltd and the National Devt Bank of Jamaica Ltd; provides funds for medium- and long-term devt-orientated projects; Man. Dir MILVERTON REYNOLDS.

Jamaica Mortgage Bank: 33 Tobago Ave, POB 950, Kingston 5; tel. 929-6350; fax 968-5428; e-mail jmb@cwjamaica.com; internet www.jamaicamortgagebank.com; f. 1971 by the Jamaican Govt and the US Agency for Int. Devt; govt-owned statutory org. since 1973; functions primarily as a secondary market facility for home mortgages and to mobilize long-term funds for housing devts in Jamaica; also insures home mortgage loans made by approved financial institutions, thus transferring risk of default on a loan to the Govt; Chair. GEORGE THOMAS; Gen. Man. PATRICK THELWALL.

Pan Caribbean Financial Services: 60 Knutsford Blvd, Kingston 5; tel. 929-5583; fax 926-4385; e-mail options@gopancaribbean.com; internet www.gopancaribbean.com; fmrly Trafalgar Devt Bank, name changed as above in Dec. 2002; Chair. RICHARD O. BYLES; Pres. and CEO DONOVAN H. PERKINS.

Other Banks

National Export-Import Bank of Jamaica Ltd: 11 Oxford Rd, Kingston 5; tel. 922-9690; fax 960-5956; e-mail info@eximbankja.com; internet www.eximbankja.com; f. 1986; govt-owned; replaced Jamaica Export Credit Insurance Corpn; finances import and export of goods and services; Chair. GARY CRAIG 'BUTCH' HENDRICKSON; Man. Dir PAMELLA MCLEAN.

National Investment Bank of Jamaica Ltd: 11 Oxford Rd, POB 889, Kingston 5; tel. 960-9691; fax 920-0379; e-mail info@nibj.com; internet www.nibj.com; Chair. AUBYN HILL; Sec. JENNIFER CAMPBELL.

Banking Association

Jamaica Bankers' Association: PSOJ Bldg, 39 Hope Rd, POB 1079, Kingston 10; tel. 927-6238; fax 927-5137; e-mail jbainfo@jba.org.jm; internet www.jba.org.jm; f. 1973; Pres. PATRICK HYLTON.

STOCK EXCHANGE

Jamaica Stock Exchange Ltd: 40 Harbour St, POB 1084, Kingston; tel. 967-3271; fax 922-6966; internet www.jamstockex.com; f. 1968; 55 listed cos (2008); Chair. CURTIS MARTIN; Gen. Man. MARLENE STREET-FORREST.

INSURANCE

Financial Services Commission: 39–43 Barbados Ave, Kingston 5; tel. 906-3010; fax 906-3018; e-mail inquiry@fscjamaica.org; internet www.fscjamaica.org; f. 2001; succeeded the Office of the Superintendent of Insurance; regulatory body; Exec. Dir BRIAN WYNTER.

Jamaica Association of General Insurance Companies: 3–3A Richmond Ave, Kingston 10; tel. 929-8404; e-mail jagic@cwjamaica.com; internet www.jagiconline.com/index.htm; Man. GLORIA M. GRANT; Chair. LESLIE CHUNG.

Principal Companies

British Caribbean Insurance Co Ltd: 36 Duke St, POB 170, Kingston; tel. 922-1260; fax 922-4475; e-mail bricar@cwjamaica.com; internet www.bciconline.com; f. 1962; general insurance; Man. Dir LESLIE W. CHUNG.

General Accident Insurance Co Jamaica Ltd: 58 Half Way Tree Rd, Kingston 10; tel. 929-8451; fax 929-1074; e-mail genac@cwjamaica.com; internet www.genac.com; f. 1981; Gen. Man. SHARON E. DONALDSON.

Globe Insurance Co of Jamaica Ltd: 19 Dominica Dr., POB 401, Kingston 5; tel. 926-3720; fax 929-2727; e-mail info@globeins.com; internet www.globeins.com; f. 1963; subsidiary of Lascelles deMercado Group; Man. Dir EVAN THWAITES.

Guardian Life: 12 Trafalgar Rd, Kingston 5; tel. 978-8815; fax 978-4225; e-mail guardian@ghl.com.jm; internet www.guardianlife.com.jm; subsidiary of Guardian Holdings (Trinidad and Tobago); pension and life policies; Pres. and CEO EARL MOORE.

Insurance Co of the West Indies Ltd (ICWI): 2 St Lucia Ave, POB 306, Kingston 5; tel. 926-9040; fax 929-6641; e-mail direct@icwi.net; internet www.icwi.net; Chair. and CEO DENNIS LALOR.

Jamaica General Insurance Co Ltd: 9 Duke St, POB 408, Kingston; tel. 922-6420; fax 922-2073; acquired by Lascelles deMercado Group in 2003.

Sagicor Life Jamaica Ltd: 28–48 Barbados Ave, Kingston 5; tel. 960-8920; fax 960-1927; internet www.sagicorjamaica.com; f. 1970; owned by Sagicor Group (Barbados); merged with Island Life Insurance Co Ltd in 2001; renamed as above in 2009; Chair. R. DANNY WILLIAMS; Pres. and CEO RICHARD O. BYLES.

NEM Insurance Co (Jamaica) Ltd: NEM House, 9 King St, Kingston; tel. 922-1460; fax 922-4045; e-mail info@nemjam.com; internet www.nemjam.com; fmrly the National Employers' Mutual General Insurance Assn; Chair. GEORGE MAGNUS.

Trade and Industry

GOVERNMENT AGENCY

Jamaica Information Service (JIS): 58A Half Way Tree Rd, POB 2222, Kingston 10; tel. 926-3740; fax 929-6715; e-mail jis@jis.gov.jm; internet www.jis.gov.jm; f. 1963; govt agency; CEO DONNA-MARIE ROWE.

DEVELOPMENT ORGANIZATIONS

Agro-Investment Corpn: Ministry of Agriculture & Fisheries, 188 Spanish Town Rd, Kingston 11; tel. 764-8071; fax 758-7160; e-mail agricultural@cwjamaica.com; internet www.assp.gov.jm; f. 2009; following the merger of Agricultural Devt Corp (ADC) and Agricultural Support Services Productive Projects Fund Ltd (ASSPPFL); agricultural devt, investment facilitation, promotion and management; CEO HERSHELL BROWN.

Jamaica Trade and Invest (JTI): 18 Trafalgar Rd, Kingston 10; tel. 978-7755; fax 946-0090; e-mail info@jamprocorp.com; internet www.jamaicatradeandinvest.org; f. 1988 by merger of Jamaica Industrial Development Corpn, Jamaica National Export Corpn and Jamaica Investment Promotion Ltd; trade and investment promotion agency; Chair. GORDON STEWART; Pres. SANCIA BENNETT-TEMPLER.

Planning Institute of Jamaica: 16 Oxford Rd, Kingston 5; tel. 960-9339; fax 906-5011; e-mail info@pioj.gov.jm; internet www.pioj.gov.jm; f. 1955 as the Central Planning Unit; adopted current name in 1984; formulates policy on and monitors performance in the fields of the economy and social, environmental and trade issues; publishing and analysis of social and economic performance data; Chair. and Dir-Gen. Dr PAULINE KNIGHT.

Urban Development Corpn: The Office Centre, 8th Floor, 12 Ocean Blvd, Kingston; tel. 922-8310; fax 922-9326; e-mail info@udcja.com; internet www.udcja.com; f. 1968; responsibility for urban renewal and devt within designated areas; Chair. WAYNE CHEN; Gen. Man. JOY DOUGLAS.

CHAMBERS OF COMMERCE

American Chamber of Commerce of Jamaica: The Jamaica Pegasus, 81 Knutsford Blvd, Kingston 5; tel. 929-7866; fax 929-8597; e-mail amcham@cwjamaica.com; internet www.amchamjamaica.org; f. 1986; affiliated to the Chamber of Commerce of the USA; Pres. DIANA STEWART; Exec. Dir BECKY STOCKHAUSEN.

Jamaica Chamber of Commerce: UDC Office Centre, Suites 13–15, 12 Ocean Blvd, Kingston 10; tel. 922-0150; fax 924-9056; e-mail info@jamaicachamber.org.jm; internet www.jamaicachamber.org.jm; f. 1779; Pres. MILTON JEFFERSON SAMUDA; Gen. Man PATRICIA PEART; 450 mems.

INDUSTRIAL AND TRADE ASSOCIATIONS

Cocoa Industry Board: Marcus Garvey Dr., POB 1039, Kingston 15; tel. 923-6411; fax 923-5837; e-mail cocoajam@cwjamaica.com; f. 1957; has statutory powers to regulate and develop the industry; owns and operates 4 central fermentaries; Chair. JOSEPH SUAH; Man. and Sec. NAUBURN NELSON.

Coconut Industry Board: 18 Waterloo Rd, Kingston 10; tel. 926-1770; fax 968-1360; e-mail cocindbrd@cwjamaica.com; internet www.j-cib.gov.jm; f. 1945; 9 mems; Chair. Dr TONY HART; Gen. Man. EDGAR WATSON.

Coffee Industry Board: 1 Willie Henry Dr., POB 508, Kingston 13; tel. 758-1259; fax 758-3907; e-mail datacoordinator@ciboj.org; internet www.ciboj.org; f. 1950; 9 mems; has wide statutory powers to regulate and develop the industry; Chair. HOWARD MITCHELL; Dir-Gen. CHRISTOPHER GENTLES.

Jamaica Bauxite Institute: Hope Gardens, POB 355, Kingston 6; tel. 927-2073; fax 927-1159; f. 1975; adviser to the Govt in the negotiation of agreements, consultancy services to clients in the bauxite/alumina and related industries, laboratory services for mineral and soil-related services, Pilot Plant services for materials and equipment testing, research and devt; Chair. CARLTON DAVIS; Exec. Dir PARRIS LYEW-AYEE.

Jamaica Export Trading Co Ltd (JETCO): 188 Spanish Town Rd, AMC Complex, Kingston 11; tel. 923-9379; fax 937-6547; e-mail jetcoja@mail.infochan.com; internet www.exportjamaica.org/jetco; f. 1977; export trading in non-traditional products, incl. spices, fresh produce, furniture, garments, processed foods, minerals, etc.; Man. Dir HERNAL L. HAMILTON.

Sugar Industry Authority: 5 Trevennion Park Rd, POB 127, Kingston 5; tel. 926-5930; fax 926-6149; e-mail sia@cwjamaica.com; internet www.jamaicasugar.org; f. 1970; statutory body under portfolio of Min. of Agriculture and Land; responsible for regulation and control of sugar industry and sugar marketing; conducts research through Sugar Industry Research Institute; Exec. Chair. DERICK HEAVEN.

Trade Board Ltd: Air Jamaica Bldg, 10th Floor, 72 Harbour St, Kingston; tel. 967-0507; fax 948-5441; e-mail info@tradeboard.gov.jm; internet www.tradeboard.gov.jm; Trade Admin. DOUGLAS WEBSTER.

EMPLOYERS' ORGANIZATIONS

All-Island Banana Growers' Association Ltd: Banana Industry Bldg, 10 South Ave, Kingston 4; tel. 922-5492; fax 922-5497; e-mail aibga@cwjamaica.com; f. 1946; 1,500 mems (1997); Chair. BOBBY POTTINGER; Sec. I. CHANG.

Banana Export Co (BECO): 10 South Ave, Kingston Gardens, Kingston 4; tel. 967-0735; fax 967-1936; e-mail beco@cwjamaica.com; f. 1985 to replace Banana Co of Jamaica; oversees the export of bananas; Chair. Dr MARSHALL MCGOWAN HALL; Man. VINCENT EVANS.

Citrus Growers' Association Ltd: Ortanique House, Bog Walk, Linstead; tel. 985-1496; fax 708-2051; internet www.jcgja.com; f. 1944; 13,000 mems; Chair. JOHN THOMPSON; Gen. Man. DENNIS BOOTH.

Jamaica Association of Sugar Technologists: c/o Sugar Industry Research Institute, Kendal Rd, Mandeville; tel. 962-2241; fax 962-1287; e-mail jast@jamaicasugar.org; f. 1936; 275 mems; Chair. EARLE ROBERTS; Pres. GILBERT THORNE.

Jamaica Exporters' Association (JEA): 1 Winchester Rd, Kingston 10; tel. 960-4908; fax 960-9869; e-mail info@exportja.org; internet www.exportjamaica.org; Pres. MICHAEL LUMSDEN; Gen. Man. JEAN SMITH.

Jamaica Gasoline Retailers' Association (JGRA): 38C Spring Rd, Kingston 11; tel. 926-4463; Pres. TREVOR BARNES.

Jamaica Livestock Association: Newport East, POB 36, Kingston; tel. 922-7130; fax 922-8934; e-mail jlapurch@cwjamaica.com; internet www.jlaltd.com; f. 1941; 7,584 mems; Man. Dir and CEO HENRY J. RAINFORD.

Jamaica Manufacturers' Association Ltd (JMA): 85A Duke St, Kingston; tel. 922-8880; fax 922-9205; e-mail jma@cwjamaica.com; internet www.jma.com.jm; f. 1947; 289 mems; Pres. OMAR AZAN.

Jamaica Producers' Group Ltd: 6A Oxford Rd, POB 237, Kingston 5; tel. 926-3503; fax 929-3636; e-mail cosecretary@jpjamaica.com; internet www.jpjamaica.com; f. 1929; fmrly Jamaica Banana Producers' Asscn; Chair. C. H. JOHNSTON; Man. Dir Dr MARSHALL HALL.

Jamaica Sugar Cane Growers' Association (JSCGA): 4 North Ave, Kingston Gardens, Kingston 4; tel. 922-3010; fax 922-2077; e-mail allcane@cwjamaica.com; f. 1941; registered cane farmers; 27,000 mems; fmrly All-Island Cane Farmers' Assn; name changed as above in 2008; Pres. ALLAN RICKARDS; Gen. Man. KARL JAMES.

Private Sector Organization of Jamaica (PSOJ): The Carlton Alexander Bldg, 39 Hope Rd, POB 236, Kingston 10; tel. 927-6957; fax 927-5137; e-mail psojinfo@psoj.org; internet www.psoj.org; f. 1976; federative body of private business individuals, cos and asscns; Pres. JOSEPH MATALON; CEO SANDRA GLASGOW.

Shipping Association of Jamaica: see Transport—Shipping.

Small Businesses' Association of Jamaica (SBAJ): 2 Trafalgar Rd, Kingston 5; tel. 978-0168; fax 927-7071; e-mail dpjam@cwjamaica.com; internet www.sbaj.org.jm; Pres. DALMA JAMES; Man. ALBERT HUIE.

Sugar Manufacturing Corpn of Jamaica Ltd: 5 Trevennion Park Rd, Kingston 5; tel. 926-5930; fax 926-6149; est. to represent the sugar manufacturers in Jamaica; deals with all aspects of the sugar industry and its by-products; provides liaison between the Govt, the Sugar Industry Authority and the Jamaica Sugar Cane Growers' Asscn; 9 mems; Gen. Man. DERYCK T. BROWN.

MAJOR COMPANIES

Food and Beverages

Big City Brewing Company: 7 Pechon St, Kingston; tel. 948-6725; fax 948-6723; e-mail salesandinfo@bigcitybrewing.com; internet www.bigcitybrewing.com; f. 1994; Pres. PETER WONG.

Dairy Industries (Jamaica) Ltd: 111 Washington Blvd, POB 336, Kingston 11; tel. 934-8272; fax 934-1793; e-mail gracekennedy@gkco.com; f. 1964; 50% owned by Grace Kennedy and Co PLC and 50% owned by Fonterra Co-op Group Ltd (New Zealand); manufacturer of dairy products, contract packer of powdered drinks; Chair. DOUGLAS ORANE; Gen. Man. ANDREW HO; 100 employees.

Desnoes and Geddes Ltd: 214 Spanish Town Rd, POB 190, Kingston 11; tel. 923-9291; fax 923-8599; f. 1918; part of Diageo Corpn; brewery and soft-drinks bottlers; producers of Red Stripe lager and Dragon Stout; sales of J $4,615m. (1995); Chair. PATRICK H. O. ROUSSEAU; Pres. JOHN IRVINE; 667 employees.

Grace Kennedy Ltd: 73 Harbour St, POB 86, Kingston; tel. 922-3440; fax 948-3073; e-mail gracekennedy@gkco.com; internet www.gracekennedy.com; f. 1922; holding co concerned with food-processing and wholesale distribution, manufacturing, financial services, maritime activities, hardware, information technology; over 65 subsidiaries and related cos, incl. GK Investments and GK Foods; sales of J $48,750m. (2007); Chair. and CEO DOUGLAS ORANE; 2,200 employees.

Island Spice: 21–23 Bell Rd, Kingston 11; e-mail sales@starlites.com; internet www.islandspice.com; f. 1987; producers of spices, flavourings, sauces and coffee; Contact LAWRENCE SHADEED.

Jamaica Broilers Group Ltd: 15 McCook's Pen, St Catherine, C.S.O; tel. 943-4370; fax 943-4322; e-mail mchristian@jabgl.com; internet www.jamaicabroilersgroup.com; f. 1958; manufacturer of animal feed, producer of poultry, beef, tilapia and hatching eggs; operator of an ethanol distillery; sales of J $11,490m. (2007); cap. J $762m.; Chair. ROBERT E. LEVY; Pres. and CEO CHRISTOPHER LEVY; 1,500 employees.

Jamaica Flour Mills Ltd: 209 Windward Rd, POB 28, Kingston 2; tel. 928-7221; fax 928-7348; e-mail garnett_williams@admworld.com; f. 1966; subsidiary of Archer Daniels Midland Co; milling of grain, incl. flour; Man. Dir DERRICK NEMBHARD; Gen. Man. GARNETT WILLIAMS; 104 employees.

Jamaica Producers' Group Ltd: Producers House, 6A Oxford Rd, POB 237, Kingston 5; tel. 926-3503; fax 926-3636; e-mail headoffice@jpjamaica.com; internet www.jpjamaica.com; f. 1929 as Jamaica Banana Producers Asscn Ltd; owns Eastern Banana Estates Ltd, St Mary Banana Estates Ltd, JP Fresh Produce, JP Snacks, Sunjuice Ltd, Jamaica Producers Shipping Co Ltd and A. L. Hoogesteger Fresh Specialist BV (Netherlands); producers and exporters of bananas and other foodstuffs; Chair. CHARLES H. JOHNSTON; CEO JEFFREY HALL.

Jamaica Standard Products Co Ltd: POB 2, Williamsfield, Manchester; tel. 963-4211; fax 963-4309; e-mail asalmon@jamaicastandardproducts.com; internet www.jamaicastandardproducts.com; f. 1942; production and export of coffee, coffee liqueurs, sauces and spices; Man. Dir JOHN O. MINOTT; 232 employees.

National Rums Jamaica Ltd: 25 Dominica Dr., Kingston; tel. 926-7548; fax 926-7499; f. 1980 by jt venture between the Govt and Seagram Co Ltd; Seagram sold its 49% share to Diageo Group in 2002; manufacturer of distilled alcoholic drinks; Man. Dir R. EVON BROWN; 139 employees.

Nestlé-JMP Jamaica Ltd: Pan Jamaican Bldg, 60 Knutsford Blvd, POB 281, Kingston; tel. 926-1300; fax 926-7388; e-mail consumerservices@ja.nestle.com; f. 1986; subsidiary of Nestlé (Switzerland); manufacturer of milk products; Vice-Pres. (Caribbean) LUIS CANTARELL; Gen. Man. JAMES RAWLE; 456 employees.

Pepsi-Cola Jamaica Bottling Co Ltd: 214 Spanish Town Rd, Kingston; bottling co for PepsiCo Beverages Americas soft drink mfrs; in process of being sold to CABCORP (Guatemala) in 2010; CEO, PepsiCo Beverages Americas MASSIMO D'AMORE; Dir ANDREW REID.

Salada Foods: 20 Bell Rd, POB 71, Kingston 11; tel. 923-7114; fax 923-5336; e-mail info@saladafoodsja.com; internet www.saladafoodsja.com; coffee production and processing; sales of J $342.8m. (2007); Chair. JOHN BELL; Man. Dir JOHN ROSEN.

Sugar Company of Jamaica Ltd: f. 1993 by Govt of Jamaica and private consortium; Govt assumed complete ownership in 1998; Infinity Bio-Energy (Brazil) purchased 75% stake in June 2008; sugar producers; runs five plantations; Pres. RICHARD HARRISON.

Walkerswood Group: Walkerswood PO, St Ann; tel. 917-2318; fax 917-2648; e-mail partners@walkerswood.com; internet www.walkerswood.com; f. 1978; dissolved in 2009 but bought by New Castle Co in 2010 and reformed; manufacturer of food products.

J. Wray and Nephew Ltd: 234 Spanish Town Rd, POB 39, Kingston 11; tel. 923-6141; fax 923-8619; e-mail customerservices@wrayandnephew.com; internet www.appletonestate.com; f. 1960; subsidiary of Lascelles deMercado and Co Ltd; sugar plantation and rum distillery; owns Appleton Estates; Man. Dir PAUL HENRIQUES; Gen. Man. JOYCE SPENCE; 2,400 employees.

Mining and Power

Alumina Partners of Jamaica (Alpart): Spur Tree Post Office, Manchester; tel. 962-3251; fax 962-3332; e-mail lance.neita@alpart-jm.com; internet www.rusal.ru/en/alpart_factory.aspx; f. 1969; 65% owned by Rusal (Russia/Switzerland) and 35% is owned by Norsk Hydro (Norway); bauxite mining and processing, aluminium products; Man. Dir TIMOTHY O'DRISCOLL; 1,400 employees.

Cool Petroleum Holdings: Kingston; f. 2005; jt venture by Cool Corporation and Neal & Massy Holdings, Trinidad and Tobago; distribution of fuels and lubricants to retail, chemical and liquefied petroleum gas sectors; CEO JOE ISSA.

Jamalco (Alcoa Minerals of Jamaica, Inc): Clarendon Parish, Clarendon; tel. 986-2561; fax 986-9637; internet www.alcoa.com/Jamaica; f. 1959 as Alcoa Minerals of Jamaica; 55% owned by Alcoa (USA), 45% by the Govt of Jamaica; alumina and bauxite mining; Man. Dir JEROME T. MAXWELL.

Petroleum Corpn of Jamaica (PCJ): 36 Trafalgar Rd, POB 579, Kingston 10; tel. 929-5380; fax 929-2409; e-mail ica@pcj.com; internet www.pcj.com; f. 1979; state-owned; owns and operates petroleum refinery; holds exploration rights to local petroleum and gas reserves; Chair. KATHRYN PHIPPS; Man. Dir RUTH POTOPSINGH.

Petrojam Ltd: 96 Marcus Garvey Dr., POB 241, Kingston 15; tel. 923-8611; fax 923-0384; e-mail wlw@petrojam.com; internet www.petrojam.com; f. 1964 by Esso, bought by Govt in 1982; 51% owned by PCJ, 49% bought by PDVSA of Venezuela in May 2007; operates sole oil refinery in Jamaica; Chair. PAUL THOMAS; Gen. Man. WINSTON WATSON; 145 employees.

Petroleum Co of Jamaica Ltd (PETCOM): 695 Spanish Town Rd, Kingston 11; tel. 934-6682; fax 934-6690; e-mail petcom@cwjamaica.com; internet www.pcj.com/petcom; f. 1984; wholly owned subsidiary of PCJ; markets gasoline, lubricants and petrochemicals and operates service stations; Chair. EVON BROWN; Gen. Man. ALWYN BROWN.

St Ann Bauxite Ltd: Discovery Bay Post Office, Kingston; tel. 973-2221; fax 973-2568; f. 1953 as Reynolds Jamaica Mines Ltd; name later changed to Kaiser Jamaica Bauxite Co; 51% owned by Century Aluminum and 49% by Noranda Aluminum Holding Corpn; bauxite mining; annual output of 4.5m. metric tons of bauxite; Pres. LARRY HOLLEY; Gen. Man. PANSY JOHNSON; 589 employees.

West Indies Alumina Co (WINDALCO): Kirkvine PO, Manchester; tel. 962-3141; fax 962-0606; internet www.windalco.com; f. 1943 as Alcan Jamaica; bought by United Company RUSAL(Russia/Switzerland) in 2007; bauxite mining, production of calcinated alumina; ended bauxite production in March 2010; operates Kirkvine and Ewarton refineries; Man. Dir ANDREW CURRIE (acting).

Miscellaneous

ACS-eServices: 1 Mangrove Way, Montego Bay; f. 2000 as eServices; sold to Affiliated Computer Services (ACS) in 2009; call centre; CEO PATRICK CASSERLY; 5,000 employees.

Alkali Group of Cos: 259 Spanish Town Rd, POB 200, Kingston 11; tel. 923-6131; fax 923-4947; e-mail abe@alkaligroup.com; internet www.alkaligroup.com; f. 1960; holding co comprising Powertrac, Industrial Chemical Company, Leder Mode Ltd and Tanners Ltd; Chair. A. BARCLAY EWART; Group Administrator ANDREW C. BROWN; 800 employees.

Ashtrom International Ltd Jamaica: Mandela Highway, Central Village, POB 283, Kingston; tel. 984-2395; fax 984-3210; e-mail ashfd@colis.com; internet www.ashtrom-international.com; f. 1970; part of Ashtrom Group Ltd (Israel); production and installation of pre-constructed commercial buildings; Chair. HOWARD HAMILTON; Contact SHMUEL TSEMEL; 455 employees.

Berger Paints Jamaica Ltd: 256 Spanish Town Rd, POB 8, Kingston 11; tel. 923-9116; fax 923-5129; e-mail bergerja@infochan.com; internet www.bergercaribbean.com; f. 1952; subsidiary of UB International Ltd (United Kingdom); manufacturer of paints; Man. Dir WARREN MCDONALD; 125 employees.

Caribbean Brake Products Ltd: 11 Bell Rd, POB 66, Kingston 11; tel. 923-7236; fax 923-6352; e-mail cbpsales@toj.com; f. 1959; production and distribution of automobile components; Chair. GORDON A. STEWART; Man. Dir PHILIP N. CRIMARCO; 170 employees.

Caribbean Cement Co Ltd: Rockfort, POB 448, Kingston 5; tel. 928-6232; fax 928-7381; e-mail info@caribcement.com; internet www.caribcement.com; f. 1947; manufacturer of cement; subsidiary of Trinidad Cement Ltd (TCL); sales of J $6,731m. (2006); Chair. BRIAN YOUNG; Gen. Man. FRANCIS L. A. HAYNES; 250 employees.

Courts Jamaica: 79–81A Slipe Rd, Cross Roads, Kingston 5; tel. 926-2110; fax 929-0887; e-mail charter@courts.com.jm; internet www.courts.com.jm; subsidiary of Courts (Furnishers) Ltd, United Kingdom; furniture retailers; Chair. STUART MILLER; Man. Dir R. HAYDEN SINGH.

Federated Pharmaceutical Co Ltd: 1 Bell Rd, Kingston 11; tel. 932-7236; fax 922-0183; f. 1958; subsidiary of Lascelles deMercado and Co Ltd; manufacturer of pharmaceuticals and cosmetics; Man. Dir (Lascelles) WILLIAM MCCONNELL; Gen. Man. JIMMY LAWRENCE; 70 employees.

Goodyear (Jamaica) Ltd: 230 Spanish Town Rd, Kingston 11; tel. 924-6130; fax 924-6372; internet www.goodyear.com.jm; f. 1945; subsidiary of Goodyear Tire and Rubber Co (USA); manufacturer of automobile tyres; sales of J $717m. (2000); Chair. EDUARDO FORTUNATO; Gen. Man. STEVEN MILLER; 223 employees.

Kingston Wharves Ltd (KWL): Third St, New Port West, Kingston; tel. 923-9211; fax 923-5361; e-mail kingstonwharves@kwljm.com; internet www.kingstonwharves.com.jm; f. 1945; port terminal operators; subsidiaries include Harbour Cold Stores Ltd and Security Administrators Ltd; Chair. and CEO GRANTLEY STEPHENSON.

Multi-Media Jamaica Ltd: 32 Lyndhurst Rd, Kingston 5; tel. 501-2637; fax 929-2576; e-mail info@multimediajamaica.com; internet www.multimediajamaica.com; f. 2000; wholly owned subsidiary of Radio Jamaica Ltd (RJR); technology related products and services; Gen. Man. MAURICE MILLER.

The Original Bamboo Factory: Windsor House, Caymanas Estate, Spanish Town, St Catherine; tel. 746-9906; fax 746-9905; e-mail hamilton1@cwjamaica.com; internet www.originalbamboofactory.com; f. 1990; CEO JOHN HAMILTON.

Seprod Group of Companies: 3 Felix Fox Blvd, Kingston; tel. 922-1220; fax 922-6948; e-mail corporate@seprod.com; internet www.seprod.com; f. 1940; owned by Musson Jamaica Ltd; manufacturer and distributor of soap, detergents, edible oils and fats, animal feeds; processors of grain, cereals, glycerine, etc.; Chair. A. DESMOND BLADES; CEO BRYON E. THOMPSON; 350 employees.

Supreme Ventures Group: Sagicor Centre, 28–48 Barbados Ave, Kingston 5; tel. 754-6526; fax 754-2143; e-mail communications@svlotteries.com; internet www.supremeventures.com; f. 1995, granted lottery licence in 2001; owns the following subsidiaries, Supreme Ventures Lotteries Ltd, Prime Sports (Jamaica) Ltd and Supreme Ventures Financial Services Ltd; Chair. PAUL HOO; Pres. and CEO BRIAN GEORGE.

UTILITIES

Regulatory Authority

Office of Utilities Regulation (OUR): PCJ Resource Centre, 3rd Floor, 36 Trafalgar Rd, Kingston 10; tel. 929-6672; fax 929-3635; e-mail office@our.org.jm; internet www.our.org.jm; f. 1995; regulates provision of services in the following sectors: water, electricity, telecommunications, public passenger transportation, sewerage; Dir-Gen. AHMAD ZIA MIAN.

Electricity

Jamaica Energy Partners (JEP): 10–16 Grenada Way, RKA Bldg, 3rd Floor, Kingston 5; tel. 920-1746; fax 920-1750; e-mail info@jamenergy.com; internet jamenergy.com; owned by Conduit Capital Partners (USA); owns and operates two power barges at Old Harbour Bay, St Catherine; sells electricity to JPSCo; Gen. Man. and CEO WAYNE MCKENZIE.

Jamaica Public Service Co (JPSCo): Dominion Life Bldg, 6 Knutsford Blvd, POB 54, Kingston 5; tel. 926-3190; fax 968-5341; e-mail media@jpsco.com; internet www.jpsco.com; responsible for the generation and supply of electricity to the island; 80% sold to Mirant Corpn (USA) in March 2001; jt venture between the Marubeni Corpn of Japan and Abu Dhabi National Energy Co; the JPSCo operating licence due to expire in 2027; Pres. and CEO DAMIAN OBIGLIO.

Water

National Water Commission: LOJ Centre, 5th Floor, 28–48 Barbados Ave, Kingston 5; tel. 929-5430; fax 926-1329; e-mail pr@nwc.com.jm; internet www.nwcjamaica.com; f. 1980; statutory body; provides potable water and waste water services; Chair. RUSSELL HADEED.

Water Resources Authority: Hope Gardens, POB 91, Kingston 7; tel. 927-0077; fax 977-0179; e-mail info@wra.gov.jm; internet www.wra.gov.jm; f. 1996; manages, protects and controls allocation and use of water supplies; Man. Dir BASIL FERNANDEZ.

TRADE UNIONS

Bustamante Industrial Trade Union (BITU): 98 Duke St, Kingston; tel. 922-2443; fax 967-0120; e-mail bitu@cwjamaica.com; f. 1938; Pres. KAVAN GAYLE; Gen. Sec. GEORGE FYFFE; 60,000 mems.

Jamaica Confederation of Trade Unions (JCTU): 1A Hope Blvd, Kingston 6; tel. 927-2468; fax 977-4575; e-mail jctu@cwjamaica.com; Pres. LLOYD GOODLEIGH.

National Workers' Union of Jamaica (NWU): 130–132 East St, POB 344, Kingston 16; tel. 922-1150; fax 922-6608; e-mail nwyou@cwjamaica.com; f. 1952; affiliated to the International Trade Union Confederation; Pres. VINCENT MORRISON; Gen. Sec. LLOYD GOODLEIGH; 10,000 mems.

Trades Union Congress of Jamaica: 25 Sutton St, POB 19, Kingston; tel. 922-5313; fax 922-5468; affiliated to the Caribbean Congress of Labour and the International Trade Union Confederation; Pres. EDWARD SMITH; Gen. Sec. HOPETON CRAVEN; 20,000 mems.

Principal Independent Unions

Caribbean Union of Teachers: 97 Church St, Kingston; tel. 922-1385; fax 922-3257; e-mail jta@cwjamaica.com; internet www.caribbeanteachers.com; Pres. ROUSTAN JOB; Gen. Sec. Dr ADOLPH CAMERON.

Jamaica Association of Local Government Officers: 15A Old Hope Rd, Kingston 5; tel. 929-5123; fax 960-4403; e-mail jalgo@cwjamaica.com; internet www.jalgo.org; Pres. STANLEY THOMAS; Gen. Sec. HELENE DAVIS-WHITE.

Jamaica Civil Service Association: 10 Caledonia Ave, Kingston 5; tel. 968-7087; fax 926-2042; e-mail jacisera@cwjamaica.com; Pres. WAYNE JONES; Sec. DENHAM WHILBY.

Jamaica Federation of Musicians and Affiliated Artistes Union: 5 Balmoral Ave, Kingston 10; tel. 926-8029; fax 929-0485; e-mail jafedmusic@cwjamaica.com; f. 1958; Pres. DESMOND YOUNG; Sec. CHARMAINE BOWMAN; 1,500 mems.

Jamaica Teachers' Association: 97B Church St, Kingston; tel. 922-1385; fax 922-3257; e-mail jta@cwjamaica.com; internet www.jamaicateachers.org.jm; Pres. MICHAEL STEWART; Sec.-Gen. Dr ADOLPH CAMERON.

Jamaica Union of Public Officers and Public Employees: 4 Northend Pl., Kingston 10; tel. 929-1354; Pres. FITZROY BRYAN; Gen. Sec. NICKELLOH MARTIN.

Jamaica Workers' Union: 3 West Ave, Kingston 4; tel. 922-3222; fax 967-3128; e-mail jamaicaworkersunion@yahoo.com; Pres. CLIFTON BROWN; Gen. Sec. MICHAEL NEWTON.

Union of Schools, Agricultural and Allied Workers (USAAW): 2 Wildman St, Kingston; tel. 967-2970; f. 1978; Pres. DEVON BROWN; Gen. Sec. KEITH COMRIE.

Union of Technical, Administrative and Supervisory Personnel: 108 Church St, Kingston; tel. 922-2086; Pres. ANTHONY DAWKINS; Gen. Sec. REG ENNIS.

United Portworkers' and Seamen's Union (UPWU): Kingston.

United Union of Jamaica: 35A Lynhurst Rd, Kingston; tel. 960-4206; Pres. JAMES FRANCIS; Gen. Sec. WILLIAM HASFAL.

University and Allied Workers' Union (UAWU): 50 Lady Musgrave Rd, Kingston; tel. 927-7968; fax 927-9931; e-mail labpoyh@yahoo.com; Pres. LAMBERT BROWN.

There are also some 30 associations registered as trade unions.

Transport

RAILWAYS

There are about 339 km of railway, all standard gauge, in Jamaica. In 2008 the Government announced that it had reached an agreement with the People's Republic of China, which was to provide assistance in the reconstruction of the railway system between Kingston and Montego Bay, and Spanish Town and Ewarton. The three-year project was to include the construction of 18 new railway stations and the provision of passenger and freight coaches.

Jamaica Railway Corpn (JRC): 142 Barry St, POB 489, Kingston; tel. 922-6443; fax 922-4539; internet www.mtw.gov.jm/dep_agencies/ja_rail.aspx; f. 1845 as Jamaica Railway Co, the earliest British colonial railway; transferred to JRC in 1960; govt-owned, but autonomous, statutory corpn until 1990, when it was partly leased to Alcan Jamaica Co Ltd (subsequently West Indies Alumina Co) as the first stage of a privatization scheme; 215 km of railway; Gen. Man. OWEN CROOKS.

Jamalco (Alcoa Minerals of Jamaica): Clarendon Parish, Clarendon; tel. 986-2561; fax 986-9637; internet www.alcoa.com/jamaica/en/home.asp; 43 km of standard-gauge railway; transport of bauxite; CEO ALAIN BELDA; Man. DAHLIA ALERT (Railroad Operations and Maintenance).

ROADS

Jamaica has a good network of tar-surfaced and metalled motoring roads. According to government statistics, in 2006 there were 20,963 km of roads in Jamaica. In 2004 an estimated 70.1% of roads were paved, according to the International Road Federation.

Transport Authority: 119 Maxfield Ave, Kingston 10; tel. 929-4642; e-mail transauth@infochan.com; internet www.mhtww.gov.jm/dep_agencies/transport_authority.aspx; regulatory body; administers the licensing of public and commercial vehicles; Chair. GEORGE JOHNSON; Man. Dir KEITH GOODISON.

SHIPPING

The principal ports are Kingston, Montego Bay and Port Antonio. The port at Kingston is a major transshipment terminal for the Caribbean area. In July 2008 the fifth phase of an expansion project Kingston was completed, doubling the port's handling capacity. Further plans for the expansion of Jamaica's port facilities, to include the construction of three additional berths and a second terminal at Montego Bay, were under way. There were also plans to expand the transshipment port at Fort Augusta; construction was scheduled to begin in 2011.

Port Authority of Jamaica: 15–17 Duke St, Kingston; tel. 922-0290; fax 924-9437; e-mail paj@portjam.com; internet www.portjam.com; f. 1966; Govt's principal maritime agency; responsible for monitoring and regulating the navigation of all vessels berthing at Jamaican ports, for regulating the tariffs on public wharves, and for the devt of industrial free zones in Jamaica; Pres. and Chair. NOEL A. HYLTON.

Kingston Free Zone Co Ltd: 27 Shannon Dr., POB 1025, Kingston 15; tel. 923-6021; fax 923-6023; e-mail blee@portjam.com; internet www.pajfz.com; f. 1976; subsidiary of Port Authority of Jamaica; management and promotion of an export-orientated industrial free trade zone for cos from various countries; Gen. Man. KARLA HUIE.

Montego Bay Free Zone: POB 1377, Montego Bay; tel. 979-8696-8; fax 979-8088; e-mail clients-mbfz@jadigiport.com; internet www.pajfz.com; Gen. Man. GLORIA HENRY.

Shipping Association of Jamaica: 4 Fourth Ave, Newport West, POB 1050, Kingston 15; tel. 923-3491; fax 923-3421; e-mail saj@jamports.com; internet www.jamports.com; f. 1939; 73 mems; regulates the supply and management of stevedoring labour in Kingston; represents mems in negotiations with govt and trade bodies; Pres. MICHAEL GEORGE BERNARD; Gen. Man. TREVOR RILEY.

Principal Shipping Company

Jamaica Freight and Shipping Co Ltd (JFS): 80–82 Second St, Port Bustamante, POB 167, Kingston 13; tel. 923-9271; fax 923-4091; e-mail jfs@jashipco.com; internet www.jashipco.com; f. 1976; liner and port agents, stevedoring services; Exec. Chair. CHARLES JOHNSTON; Man. Dir MICHAEL BERNARD.

CIVIL AVIATION

There are two international airports linking Jamaica with North America, Europe, and other Caribbean islands. The Norman Manley International Airport is situated 22.5 km outside Kingston. Sangster International Airport is 5 km from Montego Bay. A J $800m. programme to expand and improve the latter was completed in February 2009. In 2010 the national airline Air Jamaica was taken over by the Trinidadian Caribbean Airlines.

Airports Authority of Jamaica: Norman Manley International Airport, Palisadoes; tel. 924-8452; fax 924-8419; e-mail aaj@cwjamaica.com; internet www.aaj.com.jm; Chair. DENNIS E. MORRISON; Pres. EARL A. RICHARDS.

Civil Aviation Authority: 4 Winchester Rd, POB 8998, Kingston 10; tel. 960-3948; fax 920-0194; e-mail info@jcaa.gov.jm; internet www.jcaa.gov.jm; f. 1996; Dir-Gen. Lt Col OSCAR DERBY.

Spirit Airlines: Kingston; internet www.spiritair.com; daily flights to the USA, the Bahamas, and other Caribbean destinations, from Kingston and Montego Bay; Pres. and CEO BEN BALDANZA; Sr Vice-Pres. BARRY BIFFLE.

Tourism

Tourists, mainly from the USA, visit Jamaica for its beaches, mountains, historic buildings and cultural heritage. In 2007 there were 1,700,785 visitor arrivals. In that year there were some 27,231 rooms in all forms of tourist accommodation. In 2008 tourism receipts were estimated to be US $1,984m.

Jamaica Hotel and Tourist Association (JHTA): 2 Ardenne Rd, Kingston 10; tel. 926-3635-6; fax 929-1054; e-mail info@jhta.org; internet www.jhta.org; f. 1961; trade asscn for hoteliers and other cos involved in Jamaican tourism; Pres. WAYNE CUMMINGS; Exec. Dir CAMILLE NEEDHAM.

Jamaica Tourist Board (JTB): 64 Knutsford Blvd, Kingston 5; tel. 929-9200; fax 929-9375; e-mail info@visitjamaica.com; internet www.visitjamaica.com; f. 1955; a statutory body set up by the Govt to promote all aspects of the tourism industry; Chair. and Dir of Tourism JOHN LYNCH.

Defence

As assessed at November 2009, the total strength of the Jamaican Defence Force was 2,830. This included an army of 2,500, a coastguard of 190 and an air wing of 140 members on active service. There were reserves of some 953.

Defence Budget: an estimated J $8,000m. (US $90m.) in 2009.

Chief of Defence Staff: Maj.-Gen. STEWART EMERSON SAUNDERS.

Education

Primary education is compulsory in certain districts, and free education is ensured. The education system consists of a primary cycle of six years, followed by two secondary cycles of three and four years, respectively. In 2007/08 enrolment at primary schools included 80% of children in the relevant age-group. In the same year enrolment at secondary schools included 77% of children in the relevant age-group. Higher education was provided by five institutions, including the University of the West Indies, which had five faculties situated at its Mona campus, in Kingston. Government spending on education in 2008/09 was budgeted at some J $58,000m., representing 11.9% of total planned expenditure.

Bibliography

For works on the Caribbean generally, see Select Bibliography (Books)

Besson, J., and Mintz, S. W. *Martha Brae's Two Histories*. Raleigh, NC, University of North Carolina Press, 2002.

Clarke, C. *Decolonizing the Colonial City: Urbanization and Stratification in Kingston, Jamaica (Oxford Geographical & Environmental Studies)*. Oxford, Oxford University Press, 2006.

Harriott, A. *Understanding Crime in Jamaica*. Kingston, University of the West Indies Press, 2004.

Organizational Crime and Politics in Jamaica. Kingston, University of the West Indies Press, 2007.

Harrison, M. *King Sugar: Jamaica, the Caribbean and the World Sugar Industry*. New York, NY, New York University Press, 2001.

Higman, B. W. *Plantation Jamaica, 1750-1850: Capital and Control in a Colonial Economy*. Kingston, University of the West Indies Press, 2005.

Ingram, K. E. *Jamaica* (World Bibliographical Series). Oxford, ABC Clio, 1997.

Johnson, A. S. *Jamaican Leaders*. Kingston, Teejay, 2001.

King, C. L. *Michael Manley and Democratic Socialism: Political Leadership and Ideology in Jamaica*. San José, CA, Resource Publications, 2003.

Lundy, P. *Debt and Adjustment: Social and Environmental Consequences in Jamaica*. Aldershot, Ashgate, 1999.

Manderson, P., et al. *The Story of the Jamaican People*. Kingston, Ian Randle Publrs, 1997.

Manley, M. *The Politics of Change: A Jamaican Testament*, revised edn. Washington, DC, Howard University Press, 1990.

Jamaica: Struggle in the Periphery. London, Writers' and Readers' Publishing Co-operative Society, 1982.

Mars, P., and Young, A. L. *Caribbean Labor and Politics: Legacies of Cheddi Jagan and Michael Manley*. Detroit, MI, Wayne State University Press, 2004.

Mason, P. *Jamaica in Focus*. London, Latin America Bureau, 2000.

Miller, E. *Jamaica in the Twenty-First Century: Contending Issues*. Kingston, Grace Kennedy Foundation, 2001.

Monteith, K., and Richards, G. (Eds). *Jamaica in Slavery and Freedom: History, Heritage and Culture*. Kingston, University of the West Indies Press, 2001.

Patterson, P. J. *A Jamaica Voice in Caribbean and World Politics*. Kingston, Ian Randle Publrs, 2002.

Persaud, R. B., and Cox, R. W. *Counter-Hegemony and Foreign Policy: The Dialectics of Marginalized and Global Forces in Jamaica*. Albany, NY, SUNY, 2001.

Tafari-Ama, I. *Blood, Bullets and Bodies: Sexual Politics Below Jamaica's Poverty Line (Caribbean Cultural Studies)*. Kingston, University of the West Indies Press, 2006.

MARTINIQUE

Geography

PHYSICAL FEATURES

The Overseas Department of Martinique is an integral part of France, but is located in the Windward Islands, in the Lesser Antilles, 6,856 km (4,261 miles) from the French capital, Paris. Its immediate neighbours are the two anglophone Windward nations of Dominica (25 km to the north—the islands of Guadeloupe, which are also French, lie beyond that) and Saint Lucia (37 km to the south). The Department, comprising the island of Martinique and its few offshore islets, covers an area of 1,100 sq km (425 sq miles), including 40 sq km of inland waters. This makes Martinique the largest single island of the Windwards or the Leewards (though smaller than the combined island of Guadeloupe, Basse-Terre and Grande-Terre together).

Martinique is about 80 km in length and 32 km at its widest, aligned more towards the north-west than along a straight north–south axis, its long, thin shape, broader in the north, distorted by two peninsulas. In the south-west there is a broad abutment of land, the north littoral of which forms the southern shore of the main bay on the leeward coast. The bay is named after the capital, Fort-de-France, which is on the north shore. Further north, but on the more rugged, eastern coast, thrusting out into the Atlantic, is the thinner Caravelle peninsula. South of these two features, the coastline (350 km around the whole island) is deeply indented and eroded, whereas the north is less so, having been more recently added to by volcanic action. The great volcano of Mt Pelée (1,397 m or 4,585 ft) dominates the north, while to its south the twin peaks (*pitons*) of Carbet achieve heights just below its own. The mountains in the south are much lower, with the land tending to fall away southwards, from the central, raised Lamentin plain of low, rounded hills and gentle valleys. The soil is extremely fertile, the north dominated by extensive rainforest (and banana and pineapple plantations) and the Lamentin plain by sugar cane. Native fauna is now scarce, but the flora remains rich and varied (the Carib name for Martinique meant 'island of flowers'—see History), the rainforest consisting of mahogany trees, mountain palms, bamboo and many other types of tree, as well as fostering flowering plants and orchids, and over 1,000 species of fern. This luxuriance flourishes on the productive emissions of former eruptions by Mt Pelée: the last were in 1902, the one on 8 May being the most famously devastating, wiping out the then capital of St-Pierre and all but one of its 26,000 inhabitants.

CLIMATE

The climate is a humid, subtropical one, moderated by the trade winds (*alizés*) from the Atlantic (Antilles means 'breezy islands'). Precipitation is higher in Martinique than in many of the Caribbean islands, owing to its mountains. There is a rainy season from June to November, brought by the same weather conditions that can bring hurricanes to the region—the latter only occasionally hit Martinique. A more usual natural hazard is the risk of flooding, while an unusual one is the volcano, which is now dormant. The average annual temperature is about 26°C (79°F), but it can be much cooler at altitude.

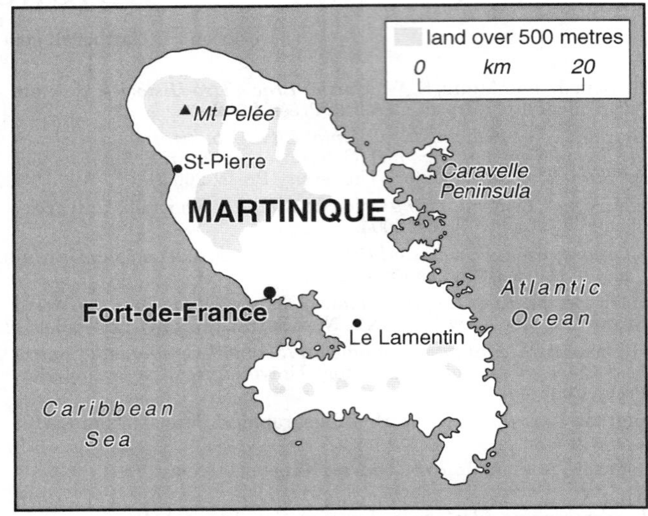

POPULATION

Most of the population are of African descent, some 90% of the population being either black or of mixed descent (mainly black, white and Asian) and only 5% white (the descendants of the original white colonial settlers are known as *békés*). The rest of the population is mainly Asian—Indian or Chinese. The Roman Catholic Church claims the adherence of 80% of the population, with the rest being mainly Hindu or practitioners of pagan rites adapted by those brought from Africa in the 17th and 18th centuries. Everyone speaks French, and many a Creole patois thereof. The hybrid culture, although increasingly French since Martinique became a department, has always flourished and the island has long been considered the most sophisticated part of the French Antilles. Famous products and inhabitants of the island range from the rum invented by a Dominican monk, through the 'three queens' (Madame de Maintenon, mistress of Louis XIV; Marie Rose Tascher de la Pagerie, better known as Napoléon Bonaparte's Empress Josephine; and her cousin, Aimée Dubuc de Rivery, who married an Ottoman sultan and gave birth to his successor) to Aimé Césaire (politician, poet and a pioneer of the literary 'négritude' movement), one of the many writers from Martinique.

The total population was provisionally estimated at 402,000 at the beginning of 2010. The capital and largest city is Fort-de-France (originally Fort-Royale, then République-Ville), on the west coast. The old administrative capital, St-Pierre, is further north up the coast. Inland from Fort-de-France, at the western end of the central plain of the same name, is Le Lamentin. There are also a number of other large towns not too far from Fort-de-France, and others on the east coast. Most people live in the capital or on the central plains.

History

PHILLIP WEARNE

Revised for this edition by Dr PETER CLEGG

Martinique's name is either a corruption of the Amerindian (Carib) name of Madinina ('island of flowers') or a derivation of Saint Martin. The navigator Christopher Columbus sighted the island in 1493 or 1502—the date is disputed. It was first settled by the French in 1635, despite the hostility of the local Caribs, and was occupied with little interruption thereafter. Like Guadeloupe, Martinique was made an Overseas Department of France in 1946, its people becoming French citizens. The island's Governor was replaced with a Prefect and an elected Conseil général (General Council) was constituted. Thereafter, the French Government's policy of assimilation created a strongly French society, bound by linguistic, cultural and economic ties to metropolitan France. The island enjoyed a better infrastructure and a higher standard of living than its immediate Caribbean neighbours, but in consequence it also became heavily dependent on France and more recently the European Union (EU). For many years economic power remained concentrated in the hands of the *békés* (descendants of white colonial settlers), who still owned most of the agricultural land and controlled the lucrative import-export market in the last decade of the 20th century. This led to little incentive for innovation or self-sufficiency and fostered resentment of lingering colonial attitudes.

The evolution of Martinique's political system was based on the French Government's response to the growth in nationalist sentiment during the latter half of the 20th century. In 1960 the mandate of the island's Conseil général was broadened, to permit discussion of political as well as administrative issues. In 1974 Martinique was granted regional status, as were Guadeloupe and French Guiana, and an indirectly elected Conseil régional (Regional Council), whose main role was to promote social, economic, cultural and scientific development of the Région, was established. In the early 1980s the Socialist Government of President François Mitterrand tried to curb the continued growth of nationalist pressure and the threat of civil disturbances by instituting a policy of greater decentralization. The two local Conseils were given increased control over taxation, the local police and the economy.

In the first direct election to the Conseil régional in February 1983 the Department's left-wing parties, which articulated nationalist sentiments while supporting the French Government's policy of decentralization, gained 21 of the 41 seats. That success weakened the threat posed by militant separatist challengers inside and outside the left-wing parties. The most vocal of the separatist parties, the Mouvement Indépendantiste Martiniquais (MIM), won less than 3% of the votes cast.

One of the principal campaigners for greater autonomy, from the 1940s, was the veteran socialist writer and poet Aimé Césaire, leader of the Parti Progressiste Martiniquais (PPM). Mayor of Fort-de-France, Césaire held a seat in the French Assemblée nationale (National Assembly) from 1945 until March 1993, when he was succeeded by Camille Darsières, the General Secretary of the PPM. With Louis-Joseph Dogué of the Fédération Socialiste de la Martinique, the local wing of the national Parti Socialiste (PS), standing down in the same election, the Gaullist Rassemblement pour la République (RPR) was able to increase its representation to three of the four seats reserved for Martinique in the Assemblée nationale, through the election of André Lesueur, mayor of Rivière-Salée, Pierre Petit and Anicet Turinay.

The left wing secured control of the Conseil général in the 1988 elections with a one-seat majority. Emile Maurice, from the conservative RPR, was elected President of the Conseil général, for his seventh term. However, Maurice was defeated in the 1992 elections, and replaced by the PPM candidate, Claude Lise. The left-wing predominance in local politics was further enhanced by the results of elections to the Conseil régional at the same time. Although the right-wing grouping was the largest single list, with 16 of the 41 seats, the parties of the left had a working majority. Elections in March 1994 brought little change in the composition of the Conseil général. However, at elections to the European Parliament in June, the conservative government list secured the greatest proportion of the votes cast. A combined list of the parties of the left, the Rassemblement d'Outre-Mer et des Minorités, came second.

At elections to the Assemblée nationale in May and June 1997, Turinay and Petit of the RPR were re-elected, together with Camille Darsières of the PPM. Alfred Marie-Jeanne, the First Secretary and a founding member of the MIM, was elected in the Le François-Le Robert constituency (hitherto held by the RPR). At elections to the Conseil régional in March 1998 the left retained a majority. The MIM increased its representation to 13 seats, while the PPM held seven seats, the RPR six and the centrist Union pour la Démocratie Française five. Marie-Jeanne was elected to the presidency of the Conseil régional. In concurrent elections to the Conseil général the parties of the left again performed well, increasing their representation to 29 seats, with right-wing candidates securing 14 seats and independents two. Claude Lise was re-elected President of the Conseil général.

Martinique was adversely affected by industrial action in 1998 and 1999, with strikes occurring among banana- and automobile-sector workers. The crisis in the banana industry was caused by falling prices in the European market; however, the two-month strike was ended in January 1999, when a pay agreement was reached. There was further conflict in the sector in October, however, when, prior to a two-day visit by French Prime Minister Lionel Jospin, banana producers occupied the headquarters of the French naval forces for several days, demanding the disbursement of exceptional aid to compensate for the adverse effect on their industry of a dramatic decline in prices on the European market. Marie-Jeanne, who was opposed to the limited nature of the Government's plans for institutional reform, refused to participate in the events organized for Jospin's visit. The Prime Minister announced an emergency plan for the banana sector and agreed, in principle, to a proposal for greater autonomy for the local authorities in conducting relations with neighbouring countries and territories. The dispute at the Toyota motor company, where workers were demanding substantial pay increases and a reduction in working hours, lasted five months and involved secondary action and blockades by trade unionists, but was eventually settled in November 1999.

The issue of Martinique's constitutional status also arose in 1999, following a series of meetings between the Presidents of the Conseils régionaux of Martinique, Guadeloupe and French Guiana. In December Marie-Jeanne co-signed a declaration, stating the intention of the three Presidents to propose, to the French Government, legislative and constitutional amendments aimed at creating a new status of Overseas Region (Région d'outre-mer). The declaration and subsequent announcements by Marie-Jeanne and his counterparts were dismissed by the Secretary of State for Overseas Affairs in February 2000 as unconstitutional and exceeding the mandate of the politicians responsible. However, in May a number of proposals, including the extension of the Departments' powers in areas such as regional co-operation, were provisionally accepted by the Assemblée nationale; a modified version of the proposals was subsequently adopted, by a narrow margin, by the Sénat. In November the Assemblée nationale approved the proposals and in December they were ratified by the Conseil constitutionnel (Constitutional Council). Following a meeting of members of the Conseil régional and the Conseil général in late June 2001, a series of proposals on greater autonomy, to be presented to the French Government, was agreed upon. These included: the division of the territory into four districts; the creation of a Territorial Collectivity (Collectivité territoriale), governed by a 41-member assembly elected for a five-year term; and the establishment of an independent executive council. Furthermore, the proposals included a request that the territory be given control over legislative and administrative affairs, as well as legislative authority on matters concerning Martinique alone. In November the French Government announced itself to be in favour of the suggested constitutional developments, and in March 2003 the two houses of the French parliament approved constitutional changes that would allow for a referendum on proposals for greater autonomy. In the same month the status of Overseas Region was conferred on Martinique.

At municipal elections held in March 2001 the PPM retained control of the majority of municipalities. In the concurrent election to the Conseil général, Claude Lise was re-elected as President. In mid-2001 the French President, Jacques Chirac, rejected a joint request by French Guiana, Guadeloupe and Martinique that they be permitted to join, as associate members, the Association of Caribbean States.

At elections to the Assemblée nationale in June 2002 only the MIM candidate, Marie-Jeanne, was re-elected; the PS representative, Louis-Joseph Manscour, Alfred Almont of the Union pour un Mouvement Populaire (UMP—the new grouping of the centre-right) and Pierre-Jean Samot of the left-wing Bâtir le Pays Martinique were also successful. Samot was ordered to resign by the Conseil constitutionnel in Paris in March 2003 for receiving campaign funds for the 2002 elections from his party, which was not officially registered at the time. He was replaced by Philippe Edmond-Mariette, also of Bâtir le Pays Martinique, who won a by-election in May 2003.

The referendum on Martinique's constitutional status and the proposed new Territorial Collectivity framework was held in December 2003. Despite the explicit support of Marie-Jeanne for the new arrangement, which would have replaced the Conseil général and Conseil régional with a single elected council, 50.5% of those voting opposed the change. The rejection of the reform plan, proposed by the centre-right Government of Jean-Pierre Raffarin, was widely seen as symptomatic of fears that the French Government would seek to reduce subsidies and social security payments under any new constitutional arrangement.

In elections to the Conseil régional held in March 2004 a joint list comprising Marie-Jeanne's MIM won 28 of the 41 seats, with 53.8% of the votes cast, while the PPM and other left-wing candidates won only nine seats and 30.6% of the ballot. Marie-Jeanne was subsequently elected President of the Conseil régional.

n the national referendum on ratification of the proposed constitutional treaty of the EU, conducted on 29 May 2005, Martinique voted overwhelmingly in favour of the proposal (69.0%). At odds with the mainland French rejection of the proposed constitution, Martinique's endorsement was also overshadowed by a massive rate of abstention, with 71.6% of voters ignoring the poll. Neither the pro-constitution centre-right and centre-left, nor Marie-Jeanne's anti-constitution, pro-independence supporters, could claim credit for the outcome.

In early December 2005 it was reported that more than 1,000 protesters took part in demonstrations in Fort-de-France against a law that proposed changing the school syllabus to reflect the 'positive' role of French colonialism. The law had been quietly approved in the previous February, and attempts by left-wing representatives in the Assemblée nationale to repeal it had been defeated in late November. The French Minister of the Interior, Nicolas Sarkozy, who was known to support the law, was forced to cancel a planned visit to Martinique and Guadeloupe. President Chirac intervened, announcing later that month that the law was under review, and in January 2006 the law was removed in accordance with a ruling by the Conseil constitutionnel that it lay outside the competence of the legislature.

At the first round of the national presidential election, held on 22 April 2007, Ségolène Royal of the PS won 48.5% of votes cast on the island, ahead of UMP candidate Sarkozy, who attracted 33.8% of the vote. At the second round, held on 6 May, Royal won 60.5% of the vote in the Department. However, nationally, Sarkozy emerged victorious, securing 53.1% of votes overall. Meanwhile, at elections to the Assemblée nationale, held on 10 and 17 June, MIM candidate Marie-Jeanne, Manscour of the PS and Almont of the UMP were re-elected, while Serge Letchimy of the PPM was also successful. In July Ange Mancini replaced Yves Dassonville as Prefect. Following elections to the Conseil général in March 2008 Lise was again re-elected as the Conseil's President.

From early February 2009 Martinique was affected by a period of serious labour unrest. The trigger was a general strike that had begun two weeks earlier in the neighbouring French Overseas Department of Guadeloupe, which was experiencing the same social and economic problems as Martinique. In particular, there was concern over the low wages faced by many employees, exacerbated by the high and increasing cost of living that was linked to the significant dependence on imports from mainland France. The protests in Martinique, which also took the form of a general strike, were led by the February 5 Collective, a coalition of unions and other social groups named after the day the strike began. The protests centred largely on the capital city, Fort-de-France, but much of Martinique was affected. The demands of the February 5 Collective focused on the need to increase the salaries of those workers earning the minimum wage and to reduce the cost of key utilities such as water and electricity. Also, and as in Guadeloupe, protestors directed some of their dissatisfaction against the *béké* class for allegedly exploiting their monopoly power in retail and construction in order to maintain high prices and, therefore, their privileged status.

In an effort to defuse the worsening crisis, the French Government and local business leaders agreed to reduce the cost of a range of key commodities, including food staples. However, the general strike continued, and violent clashes took place in late February and early March 2009 between demonstrators and the police—some of whom had been drafted in from mainland France. However, on 14 March the strike was called off after a deal was reached with the mainland Government. The agreement gave an extra €200 per month to low wage earners, and small increases to those with higher incomes. Despite a resolution to the dispute much bitterness remained and more fundamentally the strike highlighted long-standing tensions in relation to the political, economic and social arrangements that operated both within Martinique and between Martinique and mainland France.

On 25 and 26 June 2009 President Sarkozy visited Guadeloupe and Martinique. He was joined by his new Minister of the Overseas Possessions, Marie-Luce Penchard, a native of Guadeloupe and the first holder of the office from outside metropolitan France. The intention of the visit was to hold talks with local politicians and members of civil society, and more broadly to assist the French Government's efforts to rebuild relations with the overseas territories. Sarkozy's visit came during a consultation process, initiated in April by the French Government, intended to address the underlying concerns within the Departments. A range of groups participated in the discussions, although most unions boycotted them, including those associated with the February 5 Collective.

Later in 2009, in light of the perceived unhappiness with the existing governance arrangements, the French Government and local representatives agreed that a referendum should be held on the issue of greater autonomy for Martinique and whether or not it should become an autonomous territory governed by Article 74, which grants greater autonomy (rather than Article 73), of the French Constitution. The vote took place on 10 January 2010; contrary to expectation, 79.3% of voters rejected the motion. Turn-out was 55.4%. In a follow-up vote conducted two weeks later, 68.3% of voters cast their ballot in support of the less significant reform of merging the Conseil régional and Conseil général into a single body within two years. Turn-out was low, at 35.8%. The French Government accepted the results of both votes and suggested that a conclusion to the debate over Martinique's constitutional relationship with France had thus been reached.

In elections to the Conseil régional held on 14 and 21 March 2010, Letchimy's PPM secured a convincing victory, securing 48.4% of the ballot and 26 of the 41 seats. Marie-Jeanne's MIM won 12 seats, with 41.0% of the votes cast, while the UMP-led list attained only three seats, with 10.6%. On 23 March Marie-Jeanne announced that, after 18 years in the Conseil régional, and 12 years as its leader, he was to relinquish his seat, with immediate effect. Letchimy was duly elected as the new President of the Conseil régional.

Economy

PHILLIP WEARNE

Revised for this edition by Dr PETER CLEGG

Martinique's economy, like that of Guadeloupe, is closely tied to that of France. Aid and subsidies, in various forms, are necessary to balance a huge deficit between visible exports and imports. In 2008 the trade deficit was €2,356.7m., with export earnings worth 13.5% of the total value of imports. In 2008 approximately one-quarter of total exports went to metropolitan France. However, Guadeloupe and French Guiana were the most significant purchasers, accounting for about 70% of total exports. The main exports in that year were fuels and combustibles and agricultural products. France was the single largest source of imports, accounting for 55.8% of their total value in 2008. The bulk of the remainder came from other members of the European Union (EU), the USA and Asia. The principal imports in that year included fuels and combustibles, products of food industries, car industry products and pharmaceutical products. Agriculture is an important economic activity, with sugar, bananas, fruit, vegetables and some flowers being the principal crops. Some light industry is also significant. The largest export is rum. Tourism is also a major source of convertible currency revenue. Consumer prices increased by an annual average of 1.8% in 1997–2007; consumer prices increased by 2.4% in 2007 and by 2.7% in 2008. The rate of unemployment in 2008 was high, at 22.4%, but, although 1.2% higher than in 2007, this was nevertheless substantially lower than the 2000 figure of 27.5%. Gross domestic product (GDP), measured at current prices, was €7,862m. in 2007, equivalent to around €19,692 per head. In terms of overall economic activity, in 2006 the primary sector (agriculture) contributed 2.4% of GDP; the secondary sector (industry, energy and construction) contributed 15.0%; and the tertiary sector (services, transport, communications and government services) contributed 82.6%. These percentage shares were largely unchanged from a decade earlier.

AGRICULTURE

The sugar industry was Martinique's original source of prosperity. However, it was dealt a devastating blow by the volcanic eruption of Mt Pelée in 1902. Bananas then became the major export. Banana exports grew steadily in the late 1980s to reach 215,980 metric tons by 1990. From the 1990s the volume of exports fluctuated, owing to variable climatic conditions. A significant decline in prices on the European market, and an ongoing dispute between the USA and four Latin American countries and the EU over the latter's banana import regime also threatened Martinique's banana growing sector. By 2000 production had recovered to 316,194 tons, but by 2007 output had fallen to 300,000 tons and was estimated by FAO to have remained unchanged in 2008. Exports in 2003 reached 264,959 tons, accounting for around 40% of total export revenues. In 2007 export volumes declined by 38.2% to reach just 134,000 tons, in large part owing to the impact of Hurricane Dean, which caused widespread destruction in August 2007 and precluded the export of any bananas between September 2007 and March 2008. Export volumes were thus still affected into 2008, but recovered slightly to 147,000 tons for the year as a whole.

Sugar cane remained the island's major agricultural crop, despite low world prices, under-investment and the diversification of some cane-growing land to the cultivation of other crops. By 1982 local production proved insufficient to supply domestic demand, causing a reversal of the policy of neglect and a dramatic increase in the cane harvest, to 217,000 metric tons by 1989. In the early 1990s production declined, but recovered again, to reach 212,000 tons in 1996; despite the effects of Hurricane Dean, the cane harvest totalled 215,000 tons in 2007 and declined only modestly to 208,000 in 2008. Local consumption accounts for virtually all the harvest, with about one-third going on the production of rum, the island's major manufactured product. Output of rum has historically varied according to the supply of sugar, but in the early 1990s it fell precipitously. In 1990 it declined by almost 20%, to 84,828 hl. Production declined further, to 69,458 hl by 1998. By 2002 production levels had recovered to 93,849 hl, but fell again to around 74,500 hl by 2008. Most of the rum exports were destined for France.

In the 1980s agricultural diversification became official government policy and it contributed to efforts to increase export earnings and reduce the cost of food imports. Pineapples, avocados and aubergines became significant export crops, and flowers and citrus fruits, particularly limes, were also shipped abroad. The most dramatic growth was in the cultivation of melons and pineapples; according to FAO estimates, output of the former reached an estimated 3,000 metric tons in 2007, and production of the latter was estimated at 18,000 tons in 2008. However, only melon exports were having a major economic impact by 2003, when 1,654 tons were shipped overseas. In 2007 there was a shift away from domestic food production and towards food imports as a consequence of Hurricane Dean. In response, €144m. in financial aid was provided to compensate local farmers.

Some of the farm practices used in Martinique, as well as in Guadeloupe, were brought into disrepute. In particular, aerial crop spraying of the pesticide chlordecone was a source of controversy. The practice was banned in mainland Europe in the 1990s, and banned in the French Caribbean in 1993, although it continued illicitly until 2002. During the period of chlordecone's prolonged use, it made its way into the food chain and contaminated the water supply. Some medical experts suggested that this contributed to the islands' high incidence of cancer, congenital malformation and infertility. More recently, attempts have been made to establish more sustainable and environmentally friendly forms of agriculture. In 2007, for example, a pilot programme that aimed to promote organic food production was initiated; the scheme was scheduled to run until 2013.

With less land available for pasture than on Guadeloupe, a significant proportion of the island's meat and dairy products had to be imported, although the local administration claimed some success in boosting livestock production. In 2008, according to FAO estimates, some 1,800 metric tons of cattle meat, 1,700 tons of pig meat and 2,200 tons of cows' milk were produced. This was produced from a livestock population put at 25,000 cattle, 15,000 sheep, 20,000 pigs and 13,500 goats. In 2003 it was estimated that 46% of fresh meat consumed was locally produced. The total fishing catch declined sharply in the late 1980s, to only 3,314 tons in 1989, but by the early 2000s had recovered, totalling an estimated 6,300 tons in 2007. However, this was insufficient to meet local consumption demand, which was estimated at 15,000 tons. The shortfall was covered by imports sourced from Europe, Guyana, Venezuela and neighbouring Caribbean islands.

INDUSTRY

Industry (including construction and public works) employed some 13.8% of the salaried labour force in 2007 and accounted for 15.0% of GDP in 2006, but the sector remained underdeveloped. Industry's total contribution to the economy was somewhat inflated by the petroleum refinery, processing crude petroleum imported from Venezuela, Trinidad and Tobago and even Saudi Arabia. In 2008 exports of fuels and combustibles accounted for 57.6% of the total value of exports. Energy was derived mainly from mineral fuels. Imports of fuels and combustibles accounted for 21.9% of the total value of imports in 2008. Martinique generated an estimated 1,530m. kWh of energy in 2008.

Besides sugar refining and the distillation of rum, industrial activity in general was concentrated on food and drink processing, in particular fish and fruit canning and soft-drink manufacture. A polyethelyne plant and a cement factory were in operation, the latter producing an estimated 261,725 metric tons of cement in 2008, virtually all of which was used locally. There were also producers of other construction materials, some small wood-furniture manufacturers and a paper-carton outlet.

TOURISM

Martinique's tourist attractions are its beaches and coastal scenery, its mountainous interior and the historic towns of Fort-de-France and St-Pierre. Tourism has remained one of the most important sources of foreign exchange, and there was a steady growth in the number of arrivals from the early 1990s. Most visitors were from France (75% in 2007). In the last few years, however, the sector has stagnated. In 2009 the number of tourist arrivals, excluding cruise ship passengers and same-day visitors, totalled 443,202, down from 479,933 in 2008 and 501,491 in 2007. A much greater decline has affected the cruise ship sub-sector. In 1995 there were 428,000 cruise visitors; by 2009 the figure had fallen to just 69,749. The decline was primarily caused by a significant reduction in the number of visitors from the USA. In 1998 the USA was the main source market, accounting for 72% of all cruise visitors to the Department, but by 2008 this figure had declined to just 18%; most passengers now come from Europe. As a result of the decline in the sub-sector, during 2004–09 no cruise liners docked in Martinique between May and September. Overall, tourism receipts in 2007 totalled €245.9m., equivalent to 3.1% of GDP.

EMPLOYMENT

As in Guadeloupe, relatively high wages—tied to those of metropolitan France—coupled with the high levels of aid and imports from France served to restrict economic development. The descendants of the original colonial settlers, or *békés*, were reinforced by professionals, whose spending power, together with that of the foreign tourists, simply encouraged the development of the services sector and import businesses. On the other hand, the native black population was reinforced by illegal immigrants from Saint Lucia, Dominica and Haiti.

Thus, as the more labour-intensive agricultural sector contracted, emphasis on the services sector increased and unemployment rose, particularly as more young people entered the job market. The lack of job prospects encouraged extensive emigration to France and other Caribbean islands. Dependency on French subsidies increased in the first years of the 21st century, with social security payments worth €559m. being paid to 95,656 Martinicans in 2008. More generally, in 2008 public services—in health, education and social investment—accounted for 33.8% of Martinique's GDP. If applied to 2007 GDP levels, this contribution represented almost €2,657m. and equated to approximately €6,656 per person, per year.

Statistical Survey

Sources (unless otherwise indicated): Institut National de la Statistique et des Etudes Economiques (INSEE), Service Régional de Martinique, Centre Administratif Delgrès, blvd de la Pointe des Sables, Hauts de Dillon, BP 641, 97262 Fort-de-France Cédex; tel. 5-96-60-73-73; fax 5-96-60-73-50; e-mail antilles-guyane@insee.fr; internet www.insee.fr/fr/regions/martinique; Ministère des Départements et Territoires d'Outre-mer, 27 rue Oudinot, 75700 Paris 07 SP; tel. 1-53-69-20-00; fax 1-43-06-60-30; internet www.outre-mer.gouv.fr.

AREA AND POPULATION

Area: 1,100 sq km (424.7 sq miles).

Population: 381,427 at census of 8 March 1999; 397,732 (males 185,604; females 212,128) at census of 1 January 2006. Note: According to new census methodology, data in 2006 refer to median figures based on the collection of raw data over a five-year period (2004–09). *1 January 2010* (provisional estimate): 402,000.

Density (1 January 2010): 365.4 per sq km.

Population by Age and Sex (official estimates at 1 January 2008): *0–14:* 81,067 (40,715 males, 40,352 females); *15–64:* 261,558 (120,109 males, 141,449 females); *65 and over:* 56,875 (24,106 males, 32,769 females); *Total:* 399,500 (males 184,930, 214,570 females).

Principal Towns (at 2006 census): Fort-de-France (capital) 90,347; Le Lamentin 39,847; Le Robert 23,856; Schoelcher 21,419; Sainte-Marie 19,528; Le François 19,201; Saint-Joseph 17,107; Ducos 15,977. *2007* (official estimates): Fort-de-France (capital) 89,794; Le Lamentin 39,442; Le Robert 24,068; Schoelcher 21,510.

Births, Marriages and Deaths (2008): Registered births 5,333 (birth rate 13.3 per 1,000); Registered marriages 1,395 (marriage rate 3.5 per 1,000); Registered deaths 2,793 (death rate 6.9 per 1,000). *2009:* Birth rate 12.3 per 1,000; Death rate 7.9 per 1,000. Source: partly Pan American Health Organization.

Life Expectancy (years at birth): 79.8 (males 76.8; females 82.5) in 2009. Source: Pan American Health Organization.

Economically Active Population (persons aged 15 years and over, 1998): Agriculture and fishing 7,650; Industry 7,103; Construction and public works 10,405; Trade 16,196; Transport 4,383; Financial services and real estate 3,354; Business services 8,376; Public services 14,179; Education 14,991; Health and social security 10,676; Administrative services 18,742; *Total employed* 116,055 (males 62,198, females 53,857); Unemployed 48,537 (males 22,628, females 25,909); *Total labour force* 164,592 (males 84,826, females 79,766). *2008* (provisional figures at 31 December): Agriculture 4,108; Construction 7,575; Other industry 8,442; Trade 49,193; Other services 10,379; Total employed (incl. others) 119,274 (Source: Institut d'Emission des Départements d'Outre-mer, *Martinique: Rapport Annuel 2009*).

HEALTH AND WELFARE

Key Indicators

Total Fertility Rate (children per woman, 2009): 1.9.

Under-5 Mortality Rate (per 1,000 live births, 2009): 8.2.

Physicians (per 1,000 head, c. 2001): 19.7.

Hospital Beds (per 1,000 head, 2007): 4.1.

Source: mainly Pan American Health Organization.

For definitions and other sources, see explanatory note on p. vi.

AGRICULTURE, ETC.

Principal Crops ('000 metric tons, 2008, FAO estimates): Yams 7.5; Sugar cane 215.0; Lettuce and chicory 5.0; Tomatoes 6.7; Cucumbers and gherkins 4.0; Bananas 300.0; Plantains 18.0; Pineapples 18.0. *Aggregate Production* ('000 metric tons, may include official, semi-official or estimated data): Total vegetables (incl. melons) 30.8; Total fruits (excl. melons) 338.0.

Livestock ('000 head, year ending September 2008, FAO estimates): Cattle 25; Sheep 15; Pigs 20; Goats 13.5.

Livestock Products ('000 metric tons, 2008, FAO estimates): Cattle meat 1.8; Pig meat 1.7; Chicken meat 1.0; Cows' milk 2.2; Hen eggs 1.5.

Forestry ('000 cubic metres, 2008, FAO estimates): *Roundwood Removals* (excl. bark): Sawlogs, veneer logs and logs for sleepers 2; Fuel wood 24.4; Total 26.4. *Sawnwood Production* (incl. railway sleepers): 1.0.

Fishing (metric tons, live weight, 2008): Capture 6,200—FAO estimate (Clupeoids 4,000; Common dolphinfish 210—FAO estimate; Other marine fishes 1,050—FAO estimate; Caribbean spiny lobster 190; Clams, etc. 700); *Total catch* 6,200—FAO estimate. Note: Data for aquaculture were not available.

Source: FAO.

MINING

Production ('000 metric tons, 2008, estimates): Cement 221; Pumice 130; Salt 200. Source: US Geological Survey.

INDUSTRY

Production ('000 metric tons, 2007, unless otherwise indicated): Motor spirit (petrol) 165; Kerosene 144; Gas-diesel (distillate fuel) oils 180; Residual fuel oils 313; Liquefied petroleum gas 28; Electric energy (million kWh) 1,225. Source: UN Industrial Commodity Statistics Database. *2008:* Raw sugar 4,700 metric tons; Rum (hl) 74.5. *2009:* Raw sugar 5,600 metric tons; Rum (hl) 70.6 (Source: Institut d'Emission des Départements d'Outre-mer, *Rapport Annuel 2009*).

FINANCE

Currency and Exchange Rates: The French franc was used until the end of 2001. Euro notes and coins were introduced on 1 January 2002, and the euro became the sole legal tender from 18 February. Some of the figures in this Survey are still in terms of francs. For details of exchange rates, see French Guiana.

Budget: *French Government* (million French francs, 1998): Revenue 4,757; Expenditure 8,309. *Regional Budget* (€ million, 2008): Current revenue 232.2 (Taxes 174.1, Other current revenue 58.1); Capital revenue 61.9; Total 294.1. Current expenditure 165.1; Capital expenditure 143.2; Total 308.3. *Departmental Budget* (forecasts, million French francs, 2001): Tax revenue 836.9 (Departmental taxes 332.0, Fuel tax 295.0, Transfer taxes, etc. 58.0, Motor vehicle tax 68.0, Fiscal subsidy 53.0); Other current revenue 886.6 (Refunds of social assistance 65.0, Operational allowance 315.0, Decentralization allowance 477.0); Capital revenue 499.5 (EU development funds 71.0, Capital allowances 59.0, Other receipts 101.4, Borrowing 270.0); Total 2,223.0. Current expenditure 1,482.2 (Finance service 57.1, Permanent staff 394.7, General administration 65.1, Other indirect services 69.0, Administrative services 108.4, Public health 49.9, Social assistance 503.6, Support costs of minimum wage 99.8, Economic services 114.7); Capital expenditure 740.8 (Road system 139.5, Networks 47.9, Education and culture 111.5, Other departmental programmes 101.6, Other public bodies 83.7, Other programmes 96.3, Non-programme expenditure 162.3); Total 2,223.0. *2008* (€ million, excl. debt rescheduling): Total revenue 667.7; Total expenditure 496.9. Source: partly Département des Etudes et des Statistiques Locales.

Money Supply (million French francs at 31 December 1998): Currency outside banks 924; Demand deposits at banks 6,330; Total money 7,254.

Cost of Living (Consumer Price Index at January; base: 1998 = 100): All items (excluding tobacco) 120.0 in 2008; 121.3 in 2009; 121.7 in 2010.

Gross Domestic Product (€ million at current prices): 6,800 in 2004; 7,210 in 2005; 7,638 in 2006. Source: Institut d'Emission des Départements d'Outre-mer, *Rapport Annuel 2009*.

Expenditure on the Gross Domestic Product (€ million at current prices, 2008, estimates): Total final consumption expenditure 8,024.8 (General government and non-profit institutions serving households 3,101.1, Households 4,923.7); Changes in stocks 157.9; Gross fixed capital formation 1,894.9; *Total domestic expenditure* 10,077.6; Exports of goods and services 670.4; *Less* Imports of goods and services 2,842.2; *GDP in purchasers' values* 7,905.7. Source: Institut d'Emission des Départements d'Outre-mer, *Martinique: Rapport Annuel 2009*.

Gross Domestic Product by Economic Activity (€ million at current prices, 2006): Agriculture 160; Food industries 122; Other manufacturing 282; Energy 164; Construction 453; Services 6,088 (Restaurants and hotels 232, Transport 222, Commerce 852, Other market services 2,387, Non-market services 2,395); *Sub-total* 7,269; *Less* Financial intermediation services indirectly measured 298; Taxes, less subsidies 667; *GDP in purchasers' values* 7,638.

EXTERNAL TRADE

Principal Commodities (€ million, 2008): *Imports c.i.f.:* Products of food industries 391.5; Leather and clothing 90.5; Pharmaceutical products 185.3; Home equipment 151.3; Car industry products 320.2; Mechanical equipment 184.3; Electronics and electrical equipment 147.5; Chemicals, rubber and plastics 195.7; Metals and metal products 123.3; Fuels and combustibles 598.3; Total (incl. others) 2,766.0. *Exports f.o.b.:* Products of agriculture, forestry and fishing 43.3; Products of food industries 51.9; Metals and metal products 11.6; Fuels and combustibles 213.4; Total (incl. others) 367.1. *2009* (€ million): Total imports 2,024.0; Total exports 267.5 (Source: Institut d'Emission des Départements d'Outre-mer, *Martinique: Rapport Annuel 2009*).

Principal Trading Partners (€ million, 2008): *Imports c.i.f.:* Aruba 78; France (metropolitan) 1,519; Germany 72; Guadeloupe 44; Italy 45; Japan 36; Netherlands 54; Spain 26; United Kingdom 326; USA 199; Total (incl. others) 2,766. *Exports f.o.b.:* Antigua 4; France (metropolitan) 90; French Guiana 38; Guadeloupe 210; Netherlands Antilles 3; USA 9; Total (incl. others) 367. *2009* (€ million): Total imports 2,024.0; Total exports 267.5 (Source: Institut d'Emission des Départements d'Outre-mer, *Martinique: Rapport Annuel 2009*).

TRANSPORT

Road Traffic ('000 motor vehicles in use, 1995): Passenger cars 95.0; Commercial vehicles 21.5. Source: UN, *Statistical Yearbook*.

Shipping: *Merchant Fleet* (vessels registered '000 grt at 31 December, 1992): 1 (Source: Lloyd's Register of Shipping). *International Sea-borne Traffic* (2006, provisional figures): Goods loaded 950,000 metric tons (petroleum products 359,000 metric tons); Goods unloaded 2,302,000 metric tons (petroleum products 1,109,000 metric tons).

Civil Aviation (2008): Freight (incl. post) carried 13,052 metric tons; Passengers carried 1,680,256.

TOURISM

Tourist Arrivals by Country (excl. same-day visitors and cruise ship arrivals, 2003): France (metropolitan) 357,726; Guadeloupe 40,668; French Guiana 10,619; Total (incl. others) 453,159. *2007* (excl. same-day visitors and cruise ship arrivals): Total 501,491 (France 379,928; USA 12,366). *2008* (excl. same-day visitors and cruise ship arrivals): Total 479,933. *2009* (excl. same-day visitors and cruise ship arrivals): Total 441,647. Source: partly Institut d'Emission des Départements d'Outre-mer, *Martinique: Rapport Annuel 2009*.

Receipts from Tourism (€ million, incl. passenger transport): 280 in 2005; 306 in 2006; 299 in 2007. Source: World Tourism Organization.

COMMUNICATIONS MEDIA

Radio Receivers ('000 in use): 82 in 1997.

Television Receivers ('000 in use): 62 in 1999.

Telephones ('000 main lines in use): 172.0 in 2009.

Mobile Cellular Telephones ('000 subscribers): 295.4 in 2004.

Personal Computers: 82,000 in 2004.

Internet Users ('000): 170.0 in 2009.

Broadband Subscribers: 6,000 in 2009.

Daily Newspaper: 1 (estimate) in 1996 (estimated average circulation 30,000 copies).

Sources: UNESCO, *Statistical Yearbook*; UN, *Statistical Yearbook*; International Telecommunication Union.

EDUCATION

Pre-primary (2008/09): 17,079 students (16,048 state, 1,031 private).

Primary (2008/09): 29,611 students (27,306 state, 2,305 private).

Specialized Pre-primary and Primary (2008/09): 318 students.

Secondary (2008/09): 44,277 students (40,264 state, 4,013 private).

Higher (2007/08, unless otherwise indicated): 8,985 students. Source: Ministère de l'Education Nationale, de la Recherche et de la Technologie. *Université Antilles-Guyane (Campus de Schoelcher):* 5,344 students in 2003/04. Source: Préfecture de Martinique, *Livret d'accueil des services de l'Etat en Martinique*.

Teachers (2004/05): *Primary:* 3,031 (2,787 state, 244 private); *Secondary:* 4,553 (4,177 state, 376 private); *Higher:* 186. Source: Ministère de l'Education Nationale, *Repères et références statistiques—édition 2005*.

Institutions (2003/04): 258 primary schools; 41 lower secondary schools; 22 state upper secondary schools; 24 private institutions. Source: Préfecture de Martinique, *Livret d'accueil des services de l'Etat en Martinique*.

Adult Literacy Rate: 98.0% (males 97.6%; females 98.3%) in 2005. Source: Pan American Health Organization.

Directory

The Government

(July 2010)

HEAD OF STATE

President: NICOLAS SARKOZY.

Prefect: ANGE MANCINI, Préfecture, 82 rue Victor Sévère, BP 647–648, 97262 Fort-de-France Cédex; tel. 5-96-39-36-00; fax 5-96-71-40-29; e-mail contact.prefecture@martinique.pref.gouv.fr; internet www.martinique.pref.gouv.fr.

DEPARTMENTAL ADMINISTRATION

President of the General Council: CLAUDE LISE (PPM), Conseil général de la Martinique, blvd Chevalier Sainte-Marthe, 97200 Fort-de-France Cédex; tel. 5-96-55-26-00; fax 5-96-73-59-32; internet www.cg972.fr.

President of the Economic and Social Committee: MICHEL CRISPIN, Hôtel de la Région, ave Gaston Deferre, Plateau Roy Cluny, BP 601, 97200 Fort-de-France; tel. 5-96-59-63-00; fax 5-96-59-64-31; e-mail cesr-s@region-martinique.com; internet www.cr-martinique.fr.

President of the Culture, Education and Environment Committee: CLAUDE PETIT, Hôtel de la Région, ave Gaston Deferre, Plateau Roy Cluny, BP 601, 97200 Fort-de-France; e-mail ccee@cr-martinique.fr; fax www.cr-martinique.fr.

President of the Regional Council: SERGE LETCHIMY (PPM), Hôtel de la Région, ave Gaston Deferre, BP 601, 97200 Fort-de-France Cédex; tel. 5-96-59-63-00; fax 5-96-72-68-10; e-mail service.communication@cr-martinique.fr; internet www.cr-martinique.fr.

Elections, 14 and 21 March 2010

	Seats
Parti Progressiste Martiniquais	26
Mouvement Indépendantiste Martiniquais	12
Rassembler la Martinique*	3
Total	41

* Electoral list comprising the Union pour un Mouvement Populaire (UMP) and allies.

REPRESENTATIVES TO THE FRENCH PARLIAMENT

Deputies to the French National Assembly: LOUIS-JOSEPH MANSCOUR (PS), ALFRED ALMONT (UMP), SERGE LETCHIMY (PPM), ALFRED MARIE-JEANNE (MIM).

Representatives to the French Senate: SERGE LARCHER (Rassemblement Démocratique et Social Européen), CLAUDE LISE (PS).

Political Organizations

Bâtir le Pays Martinique: Fort-de-France; f. 1998; left-wing; split from the Parti Communiste Martiniquais; Leader PIERRE-JEAN SAMOT; Nat. Sec. DAVID ZOBDA.

Combat Ouvrier: BP 821, 97258 Fort-de-France Cédex; e-mail redaction@combat-ouvrier.net; internet www.combat-ouvrier.net; Trostskyist; mem. of the Communist Internationalist Union; Leader GHISLAINE JOACHIM-ARNAUD.

Conseil National des Comités Populaires (CNCP): 8 rue Pierre et Marie Curie, Terres Sainville, 97200 Fort-de-France; tel. 5-96-63-75-23; e-mail cncp@netcaraibes.com; internet www.m-apal.com; f. 1983; pro-independence party affiliated to the Union Général des Travailleurs de Martinique; contested the 2004 regional elections in alliance with the MIM; Pres. JOSETTE MASSOLIN; Spokesperson ROBERT SAÉ.

Fédération Socialiste de la Martinique (FSM): 52 rue du Capitaine Pierre-Rose, 97200 Fort-de-France; tel. 5-96-60-14-88; fax 5-96-63-81-06; e-mail federation.socialiste-martinique@wanadoo.fr; internet martinique.parti-socialiste.fr; local br. of the Parti Socialiste (PS); Fed. Sec. LOUIS JOSEPH MANSCOUR; Spokesperson FRÉDÉRIC BUVAL.

Forces Martiniquaises de Progrès (FMP): 12 rue Ernest Deproge, 97200 Fort-de-France; tel. 5-96-57-74-10; fax 5-96-63-36-19; e-mail miguel.laventure@fmp-regionales.org; internet www.jrdmedias.com/laventure/index.html; f. 1998 to replace the local br. of the Union pour la Démocratie Française; Pres. MIGUEL LAVENTURE.

Mouvement des Démocrates et Écologistes pour une Martinique Souveraine (MODEMAS): Fort-de-France; f. 1992; left-wing, pro-independence; Pres. GARCIN MALSA.

Mouvement Indépendantiste Martiniquais (MIM): Fort-de-France; internet www.mim-matinik.org; f. 1978; pro-independence party; First Sec. ALFRED MARIE-JEANNE.

Mouvement Populaire Franciscain: angle des rues Couturier et Holo, 97240 Le François; tel. 5-96-54-20-40; e-mail direction@pont-abel.fr; left-wing; Leader MAURICE ANTISTE.

Osons Oser: Fort-de-France; f. 1998; right-wing; affiliated with the metropolitan Union pour un Mouvement Populaire (UMP); Pres. PIERRE PETIT; Vice-Pres. JENNY DULYS-PETIT.

Parti Communiste Martiniquais (PCM): angle des rues A. Aliker et E. Zola, Terres-Sainville, 97200 Fort-de-France; f. 1957; Sec.-Gen. GEORGES ERICHOT.

Parti Progressiste Martiniquais (PPM): Ancien Réservoir de Trénelle, 97200 Fort-de-France; tel. 5-96-71-88-01; fax 5-96-72-68-56; e-mail contact@ppm-martinique.fr; internet www.ppm-martinique.fr; f. 1958; left-wing; Leader SERGE LETCHIMY; Sec.-Gen. DIDIER LAGUERRE.

Rassemblement Démocratique pour la Martinique (RDM): Résidence Pichevin 2, Bâtiment Hildevert, Les Hauts du Port, 97200 Fort-de-France; tel. 5-96-71-89-97; internet rfdm.e-monsite.com; f. 2006; Sec.-Gen. CLAUDE LISE.

Union pour un Mouvement Populaire (UMP): angle des rues de la République et Vincent Allègre, 97212 Saint Joseph; tel. 5-96-57-96-68; fax 5-96-57-32-68; internet www.u-m-p.org; centre-right; local br. of the metropolitan party; Pres., Departmental Cttee (vacant).

Les Verts Martinique: Lotissement Donatien, 54 rue Madinina, Cluny, 97200 Fort-de-France; tel. and fax 5-96-71-58-21; e-mail louisleonce@wanadoo.fr; ecologist; departmental br. of the metropolitan party; Leader LOUIS-LÉONCE LECURIEUX-LAFFERONNAY.

Judicial System

Cour d'Appel de Fort-de-France: Ave St John Perse, Morne Tartenson, BP 634, 97262 Fort-de-France Cédex; tel. 5-96-70-62-62; fax 5-96-63-52-13; e-mail ca-fort-de-france@justice.fr; highest court of appeal for Martinique and French Guiana; First Pres. HERVÉ EXPERT; Procurator-Gen. JEAN-MICHEL DURAND.

There are two Tribunaux de Grande Instance, at Fort-de-France and Cayenne (French Guiana), and three Tribunaux d'Instance (two in Fort-de-France and one in Cayenne).

Religion

The majority of the population belong to the Roman Catholic Church.

CHRISTIANITY

The Roman Catholic Church

Some 80% of the population are Roman Catholics. Martinique comprises the single archdiocese of Fort-de-France. The Archbishop participates in the Antilles Episcopal Conference, based in Port of Spain, Trinidad and Tobago.

Archbishop of Fort-de-France and Saint-Pierre: Most Rev. GILBERT MARIE MICHEL MÉRANVILLE, Archevêché, 5–7 rue du Révérend Père Pinchon, BP 586, 97207 Fort-de-France Cédex; tel. 5-96-63-70-70; fax 5-96-63-75-21; e-mail archeveche-martinique@wanadoo.fr.

Other Churches

Among the denominations active in Martinique are the Assembly of God, the Evangelical Church of the Nazarene and the Seventh-day Adventist Church.

The Press

Antilla: Le Lamentin, BP 46, 97281 Fort-de-France, Cédex 1; tel. 5-96-75-48-68; fax 5-96-75-58-46; e-mail antilla@orange.fr; f. 1981; weekly; politics and economics; Publ. Dir ALFRED FORTUNE; Editor-in-Chief TONY DELSHAM.

France Antilles: pl. François Mitterrand, 97207 Fort-de-France; tel. 5-96-59-08-83; fax 5-96-60-29-96; e-mail redaction.fa@media-antilles.fr; internet www.martinique.franceantilles.fr; f. 1964; subsidiary of Groupe France Antilles; daily; Editor PAUL-HENRI COSTE; circ. 30,000 (Martinique edn).

Journal Asé Pléré Annou Lité (Journal APAL): 8 rue Pierre et Marie Curie, Terres Sainville, 97200 Fort-de-France; tel. 5-96-63-75-23; fax 5-96-70-30-82; e-mail journ.apal@orange.fr; internet www.m-apal.com; f. 1983; monthly; organ of the Conseil Nat. des Comités Populaires (q.v.) and the Union Général des Travailleurs de Martinique (q.v.); Dir ROBERT SAÉ.

Justice: rue André Aliker, 97200 Fort-de-France; tel. 5-96-71-86-83; fax 5-96-63-13-20; e-mail ed.justice@wanadoo.fr; internet journal-justice-martinique.com; f. 1920; weekly; organ of the Parti Communiste Martinique (q.v.); Dir FERNAND PAPAYA; circ. 8,000.

Lutte Ouvriér: 1111 Rés Matéliane, l'aiguille, 97128 Goyave; e-mail combatouvrier@fr.fm; internet www.lutte-ouvrier.net; f. 1970; fortnightly; communist; Publ. Dir MICHEL RODINSON; circ. 14,000.

Le NAIF-Magazine: Résidence K, Pointe des Nègres, route Phare, 97200 Fort-de-France; tel. 5-96-61-62-55; fax 5-96-61-85-76; e-mail docedouard@yahoo.fr; internet www.wmaker.net/lenaif; weekly; publ. by CIC; Owner CAMILLE CHAUVET.

Le Progressiste: c/o Parti Progressiste Martiniquais, Ancien Réservoir de Trénelle, 97200 Fort-de-France; tel. 5-96-71-88-01; e-mail d.compere@ool.fr; internet www.ppm-martinique.fr; weekly; organ of the PPM; Publ. Dir DANIEL COMPERE; circ. 13,000.

TV Magazine: pl. François Mitterand, 97232 Lamentin; tel. 5-96-42-60-77; fax 5-96-42-98-70; e-mail tv.mag@media-antilles.fr; f. 1989; weekly; Editor-in-Chief RUDY RABATHALY.

Publishers

Editions Desormeaux: Z. I. la Jambette, 97232 Fort-de-France; tel. 5-96-50-30-30; fax 5-96-50-30-70; e-mail info@editions-desomeaux.com; internet www.editions-desormeaux.com; French-Creole history, language, culture, culinaria, natural history, academic and fiction.

Editions Exbrayat: 5 rue des Oisillons, route de Balata, 97234 Fort-de-France; tel. 5-96-64-60-58; fax 5-96-64-70-42; e-mail andre.exbrayat@exbrayat.com; internet commerce.ciel.com/exbrayat; regional art, history, natural history, culinaria, maps and general fiction; 2 brs in Guadeloupe; Commercial Dir PAQUITA EXBRAYAT-SANCHEZ.

Editions Lafontaine: Bâtiment 12, Maniba, 97222 Case Pilote; tel. and fax 5-96-78-87-98; e-mail info@editions-lafontaine.com; internet www.editions-lafontaine.com; f. 1994; Creole, French and English literature, general fiction, culture, history, youth and educational; Dir JEANNINE 'JALA' LAFONTAINE.

Broadcasting and Communications

TELECOMMUNICATIONS

Digicel Antilles Françaises Guyane: Oasis, Quartier Bois Rouge, 97224 Ducos; tel. 8-10-63-56-35; fax 5-96-42-09-01; e-mail contact@digicelgroup.fr; internet www.digicel.fr; f. 2000 as Bouygues Telecom Caraïbe; acquired from Bouygues Telecom, France, in 2006; mobile cellular telephone operator; network coverage incl. Guadeloupe and French Guiana; Group Chair. DENIS O'BRIEN; Gen. Man. (French Caribbean) GHADA GEBARA.

Orange Caraïbe: see Guadeloupe—Telecommunications.

Outremer Telecom: Z. I. la Jambette, BP 280, 97285 Lamentin Cédex 2; e-mail communication@outremer-telecom.fr; internet www.outremer-telecom.fr; f. 1998; mobile telecommunications provider; CEO JEAN-MICHEL HEGESIPPE.

ONLY: Z. I. la Jambette, BP 280, 97285 Lamentin Cédex 2; e-mail communication@outremer-telecom.fr; internet www.outremer-telecom.fr; f. 1998 as Outremer Telecom Martinique; present name adopted following merger of Volubis, ONLY and OOL in 2006; telecommunications provider; subsidiary of Outremer Telecom, France.

BROADCASTING

Réseau France Outre-mer (RFO): La Clairière, BP 662, 97263 Fort-de-France; tel. 5-96-59-52-00; fax 5-96-59-52-26; internet www.rfo.fr; acquired by Groupe France Télévisions in 2004; fmrly Société Nationale de Radio-Télévision Française d'Outre-mer, present name adopted in 1998; Dir-Gen. GENEVIÈVE GIARD; Regional Dir JEAN-PHILIPPE PASCAL.

Radio

Radio Asé Pléré Annou Lité (Radio APAL) (Radio Pèp-la): 8 rue Pierre et Marie Curie, Terres Sainville, 97200 Fort-de-France; tel. 5-96-63-75-23; fax 5-96-70-30-82; e-mail radio.apal@netcaraibes.com; internet www.m-apal.com; f. 1989; affiliated to the Conseil Nat. des Comités Populaires (q.v.) and the Union Général des Travailleurs de Martinique (q.v.); French and Creole; Dir MICHEL NE'DAN; Station Man. JEAN-CLAUDE LOUIS-SYDNEY.

Radio Banlieue Relax (RBR): 107 ave Léona Gabriel, Cité Dillon, 97200 Fort-de-France; tel. 5-96-60-00-90; fax 5-96-73-06-53; e-mail radiorbr@hotmail.fr; internet www.rbrfm.com; f. 1981; regional social and cultural programmes; Pres. FRANCIS CLÉORON.

Radio Canal Antilles (RCA): plateau Fofo, 97233 Schoelcher; tel. 5-96-61-74-19; fax 5-96-61-23-58; internet membres.lycos.fr/canalantilles; f. 1980; fmrly Radio 105; regional social and cultural programmes; Radio France Internationale relay; Pres. SERGE POGNON.

Radio Caraïbes International (RCI Martinique): 2 blvd de la Marne, 97200 Fort-de-France Cédex; tel. 5-96-63-98-70; fax 5-96-63-26-59; internet mq.rci.fm; commercial radio station; Dir JOSÉ ANELKA; Station Man. VINCENT CHRÉTIEN; Editor-in-Chief JEAN-PHILIPPE LUDON.

Radio Fréquence Atlantique (RFA): 10 rue du Docteur Laveran, 97232 Le Lamentin; tel. 5-96-42-35-51; fax 5-96-51-04-26; e-mail r.f.a@wanadoo.fr; internet www.radiorfa.fr; operated by Société Martiniquaise de Communication; Dir JOSEPH LEVI.

Radio Merci Seigneur: 16 rue Pierre et Marie Curie, 97200 Fort-de-France; tel. 5-96-60-44-34; fax 5-96-63-79-73; Evangelical religious programming; Man. JUDES LARCHER.

Other radio stations include: Chérie FM (formerly Campêche FM); Difé Radio; Fun Radio (formerly Maxxi FM); Radio 22; Radio Actif Martinique; Radio Alizés; Radio Archipel; Radio Espérance; Radio Espoir; Radio Inter Tropicale; Radio Solidarité Rurale—La Voix des Mornes; and West Indies Radio.

Television

Antilles Télévision (ATV): 28 ave des Arawacks, Chateauboeuf, 97200 Fort-de-France; tel. 5-96-75-44-44; fax 5-96-75-55-65; e-mail contact@atvweb.fr; internet www.antillestelevision.com; f. 1993; general interest; accounts for 22% of viewers; also broadcasts to French Guiana and Guadeloupe; Chair. JEAN-MAX ELIZÉ; Gen. Man. DANIEL ROBIN; Editor-in-Chief KARL SIVATTE.

Canal Plus Antilles: see Guadeloupe—Television.

Kanal Martinique Télévision (KMT) (Kanal Matinik Télévision): voie 7, Renéville, 97200 Fort-de-France; tel. 5-96-63-64-85; f. 2004; operated by l'Asscn pour le Développement des Techniques Modernes de Communication; Pres. ROLAND LAOUCHEZ.

Finance

(cap. = capital; res = reserves; dep. = deposits; m. = million; brs = branches; amounts in euros)

BANKING

Central Bank

Institut d'Emission des Départements d'Outre-mer (IEDOM): 1 blvd du Général de Gaulle, BP 512, 97206 Fort-de-France Cédex; tel. 5-96-59-44-00; fax 5-96-59-44-04; e-mail agence@iedom-martinique.fr; internet www.iedom.fr; Dir PHILIPPE LA COGNATA.

Commercial Banks

Banque des Antilles Françaises: see Guadeloupe—Finance.

BNP Paribas Martinique: 72 ave des Caraïbes, BP 588, 97200 Fort-de-France; tel. 5-96-59-46-02; fax 5-96-63-71-42; e-mail michel.lafont@bnpparibas.com; internet martinique.bnpparibas.net; f. 1941; subsidiary of BNP Paribas, France; 12 brs; Gen. Man. MICHEL LAFONT.

BRED Banque Populaire: Z. I. la Jambette, 97232 Le Lamentin; tel. 5-96-63-77-63; e-mail courrier-direct@bred.fr; internet www.bred.banquepopulaire.fr; cap. 242m. (Oct. 2005); Regional Man. BRUNO DUVAL; brs in Martinique and French Guiana.

Crédit Agricole: rue Case Nègre, pl. d'Armes, BP 370, 97232 Le Lamentin Cédex 2; tel. 8-20-39-93-10; fax 5-96-51-37-12; internet www.ca-martinique.fr; f. 1950; total assets 1,263m. (Dec. 2004); Pres. GUY RANLIN; Gen. Man. PASCAL DURIEUX; 30 brs in Martinique and French Guiana.

Société Générale de Banque aux Antilles (SGBA): see Guadeloupe—Finance.

INSURANCE

AGF Allianz Vie France: ZAC de l'Etang Z'Abricots, Bâtiment C, 97200 Fort-de-France; tel. 5-96-50-55-61; fax 5-96-50-55-71; e-mail marvie1@agfmar.com; internet www.allianz.fr; life insurance; subsidiary of Allianz Group.

Groupama Antilles Guyane: 10 Lotissement Bardinet Dillon, BP 559, 97242 Fort-de-France Cédex; tel. 5-96-75-33-33; fax 5-96-75-06-78; internet www.groupama.fr; f. 1978; Chair. JEAN JARNAC; Dir-Gen. DIDIER COURIER; 6 brs in Martinique, 7 brs in Guadeloupe, 3 brs in French Guiana.

Groupement Français d'Assurances Caraïbes (GFA Caraïbes): 46–48 rue Ernest Desproges, 97205 Fort-de-France; tel. 5-96-59-04-04; fax 5-96-73-19-72; e-mail contact@gfa-caraibes.fr; internet www.gfa-caraibes.fr; subsidiary of Gruppo Generali, Italy; Chair. JEAN-CLAUDE WULLENS; Man. Dir SERGE CANTIRAN.

Trade and Industry

GOVERNMENT AGENCIES

Direction Régionale du Commerce Extérieur Antilles-Guyane (DRCE): Bureaux 406 et 408, BP 647, 97262 Fort-de-France Cédex; tel. 5-96-39-49-90; fax 5-96-60-08-14; e-mail drceantilles@missioneco.org; internet www.tresor.economie.gouv.fr/region/antilles-guyane; Regional Dir CHRISTIAN BENOIT; Regional Asst. (Martinique) XAVIER BUCHOUX.

Direction Régionale de l'Industrie, de la Recherche et de l'Environnement (DRIRE): see French Guiana—Trade and Industry.

Direction de la Santé et du Développement Social (DSDS): Centre d'Affaires AGORA, l'Etang Z'abricots, Pointe des Grives, BP 658, 97263 Fort-de-France Cédex; tel. 5-96-39-42-43; fax 5-96-60-60-12; e-mail josiane.pinville@sante.gouv.fr; internet www.martinique.sante.gouv.fr; Dir CHRISTIAN URSULET.

DEVELOPMENT ORGANIZATIONS

Agence Française de Développement (AFD): 1 blvd du Général de Gaulle, BP 804, 97244 Fort-de-France Cédex; tel. 5-96-59-44-73; fax 5-96-59-44-88; e-mail afdfortdefrance@groupe-afd.org; internet www.afd.fr; fmrly Caisse Française de Développement; Man. ERIC BORDES.

Secrétariat Général pour les Affaires Régionales (SGAR)—Bureau de la Coopération Régionale: Préfecture, 97262 Fort-de-France; tel. 5-96-39-49-78; fax 5-96-39-49-59; e-mail jean-charles.barrus@martinique.pref.gouv.fr; successor to the Direction de l'Action Economique Régionale (DAER); research, documentation, and technical and administrative advice on investment in industry and commerce; Chief JEAN-CHARLES BARRUS.

CHAMBERS OF COMMERCE

Chambre d'Agriculture: pl. d'Armes, BP 312, 97286 Le Lamentin Cédex 2; tel. 5-96-51-75-75; fax 5-96-51-93-42; e-mail chambagr@ais.mq; Pres. LOUIS-DANIEL BERTOME; Dir NICAIRE MONROSE.

Chambre de Commerce et d'Industrie de la Martinique: 50 rue Ernest Desproge, BP 478, 97200 Fort-de-France Cédex; tel. 5-96-55-28-00; fax 5-96-60-66-68; e-mail dic@martinique.cci.fr; internet www.martinique.cci.fr; f. 1907; Pres. CLAUDE POMPIÈRE; Sec. MARIUS MARTIAL.

Chambre des Métiers et de l'Artesanat de la Martinique: 2 rue du Temple, Morne Tartenson, BP 1194, 97200 Fort-de-France; tel. 5-96-71-32-22; fax 5-96-70-47-30; e-mail cmm972@wanadoo.fr; internet www.cma-martinique.com; f. 1970; Pres. HERVÉ LAUREOTE; Sec.-Gen. JOSEPH THOME; 8,000 mems.

INDUSTRIAL ORGANIZATION

Association Martiniquaise pour la Promotion de l'Industrie (AMPI): Centre d'Affaires de la Martinique, Bâtiment Pierre, 2ème étage, Californie, 97232 Le Lamentin; tel. 5-96-50-74-00; fax 5-96-50-74-37; e-mail info@ampi.mq; internet www.industriemartinique.com; f. 1972 as Association des Moyennes et Petites Industries; 119 mem. cos; Pres. PIERRE MARIE-JOSEPH.

EMPLOYERS' ORGANIZATIONS

Banalliance: Centre d'Affaires le Baobab, rue Léon Gontran Damas, 97232 Le Lamentin; tel. 5-96-57-42-42; fax 5-96-57-35-18; f. 1996; Pres. DANIEL DISER; 220 mems.

Banamart: Quartier Bois Rouge, 97224 Ducos; tel. 5-96-42-43-44; fax 5-96-51-47-70; internet www.banamart.com; f. 2005 by merger of SICABAM and GIPAM; represents banana producers; Pres. NICOLAS MARRAUD DES GROTTES.

Ordre des Médecins de la Martinique: 9 rue du Gouverneur-Ponton, 97200 Fort-de-France; tel. 5-96-63-27-01; fax 5-96-60-58-00; e-mail martinique@972.medecin.fr; Pres. Dr RENÉ LEGENDRI.

Ordre des Pharmaciens de la Martinique: Apt G-01, Immeuble Gaëlle, Résidence Studiotel-Grand Village, BP 587, 97233 Schoelcher; tel. 5-96-52-23-67; fax 5-96-52-20-92; e-mail delegation_martinique@ordre.pharmacien.fr; internet www.ordre.pharmacien.fr; Pres. JEAN BIGON.

MAJOR COMPANIES

Bellonie Bourdillon Successeurs (BBS): Z. I. Génipa, BP 35, 97224 Ducos; tel. 5-96-56-82-82; fax 5-96-56-82-83; e-mail info@rhumdemartinique.com; internet www.rhumdemartinique.com; f. 1919; rum producer, markets other spirits and wines; Pres. XAVIER THIEBLIN; Gen. Dir. FRANÇOIS DE LAVIGNE; 161 employees.

Biometal, SA: Usine de Robert, Parc d'activité du Robert, 97231 Le Robert; tel. 5-96-65-14-44; fax 5-96-65-10-01; e-mail mbellemare@biometal.com; internet www.biometal.com/mq/accueil; f. 1979; manufacture of steel products; Pres. and Dir-Gen. LIONEL DE LAGUARIGUE; Man. GILLES DE REYNAL DE SAINT MICHEL; 70 employees.

Comptoir Martiniquais d'Industrie Alimentaire (COMIA): pl. d'Armes, BP 266, 97232 Le Lamentin; tel. 5-96-66-61-62; fax 5-96-51-40-21; e-mail info@comia.fr; f. 1978; cooked meats; Pres. MARCEL OSENAT; c. 40 employees.

Denel SAS: Usine Dénel, 97213 Gros-Morne; tel. 5-96-67-51-23; fax 5-96-67-67-56; e-mail info@denelmartinique.com; internet www.denelmartinique.com; f. 1932; subsidiary of Groupe Despointes; food processing, fruit juices and preserves; CEO ALAIN HUYGHUES-DESPOINTES; Gen. Man. LAURENT HUYGHUES-DESPOINTES; 49 employees.

Distillerie Dillon, SA: 9 route Chateauboeuf, BP 212, 97257 Fort-de-France Cédex; tel. 5-96-75-20-20; fax 5-96-75-30-33; e-mail info@rhum-dillon.com; f. 1967; rum producer; Man. PASCAL RENARD; 45 employees; 80 planters.

Esso Antilles Guyane, SAS: pl. d'Armes, BP 272, 97285 Le Lamentin Cédex 2; tel. 5-96-66-90-82; fax 5-96-51-17-87; e-mail christian.l.porter@exxonmobil.com; f. 1965; distribution of petroleum and petroleum products; Pres. CHRISTIAN PORTER; 28 employees.

Groupe Bernard Hayot (GBH): Acajou, BP 423, 97232 Le Lamentin Cédex 02; tel. 5-96-50-37-56; fax 5-96-50-11-47; e-mail contact@gbh.fr; internet www.gbh.fr; f. 1960; volume retail and distribution; also operates in French Guiana and Guadeloupe; Chair. BERNARD HAYOT.

Groupe Ho Hio Hen: Hauts de Californie, 97232 Le Lamentin; tel. 5-96-42-70-00; fax 5-96-50-96-28; e-mail col@hohiohen.com; f. 1972; volume retail and distribution; Chair. CHARLES HO HIO HEN; c. 800 employees in Martinique and Guadeloupe.

Groupe SEEN (Société d'Entretien et de Nettoyage): Z. I. de la Lézarde, 97232 Le Lamentin; tel. 5-96-66-65-66; fax 5-96-51-61-25; commercial waste disposal and environmental services; Chair. YANN MONPLAISIR; 360 employees.

Prochimie, SA: Palmiste, BP 233, 97284 Le Lamentin Cédex 2; tel. 5-96-50-32-82; fax 5-96-50-22-48; e-mail contact@prochimie.fr; internet www.prochimie.fr; f. 1972; domestic and sanitary products and paper; Man. ALEX DORMOY; 50 employees.

SAEM Le Galion (Société Anonyme d'Economie Mixte de Production Sucrière et Rhumière de La Martinique): Usine du Le Galion, 97220 La Trinité; tel. 5-96-58-20-65; fax 5-96-58-34-40; e-mail sucrerie@saem-legalion.net; f. 1984; sugar refinery; rum business managed by COFEPP; Man. PHILIPPE ANDRÉ; 91 employees.

SARA (Société Anonyme de la Raffinerie des Antilles): Z. I. Californie, BP 436, 97292 Le Lamentin Cédex 2; tel. 5-96-50-18-94; fax 5-96-50-00-15; e-mail christine.ransay@sara.mq; internet www.sara.mq; f. 1969; TotalFinaElf 50%, Shell 24%, Esso 14.5%, Texaco 11.5%; depots in French Guiana and Guadeloupe; processes 800,000 metric tons of crude oil annually; Dir-Gen. DAVID MARION; c. 260 employees regionally.

Siapoc, SA (Société Industrielle Antillaise de Peintures et de Produits Chimiques): Z. I. Californie, Acajou, 97232 Le Lamentin; tel. 5-96-50-54-14; fax 5-96-50-09-11; e-mail stesiapoc@siapoc.org; f. 1965; paints; Man. BRUNO MENCE; 65 employees.

SMPA: Z. I. pl. d'Armes, 97232 Le Lamentin; tel. 5-96-30-00-14; fax 5-96-51-70-43; e-mail eursulet@sasi.fr; f. 1987; industrial bakery products and frozen foods; Man. EMMANUEL URSULET; 35 employees.

Socara, SARL (Société Caraïbe de Representation Importation Exportation): 2 ave des Arawaks, BP 560, 97242 Fort-de-France Cédex; tel. 5-96-75-04-04; fax 5-96-75-04-76; e-mail socara@wanadoo.fr; f. 1948; distribution of fruit juices, wines, beer, spirits; Dir NICOLAS CHABROL; 32 employees.

Société d'Embouteillage de l'Eau Minérale Didier (SEEMD): 9 km route de Didier, 97200 Fort-de-France; tel. 5-96-64-07-88; fax 5-96-64-01-69; e-mail seemd@fontainedidier.com; internet www.fontainedidier.com; mineral water; CEO JEAN-LUC GARCIN; Dir MIGUEL GOSSELIN; 41 employees.

SOCIPAR: Z. I. pl. d'Armes, 97232 Lamentin; tel. 5-96-51-99-01; fax 5-96-51-52-69; e-mail cv@socipar.com; holding co for Groupe Aubéry; interests in agriculture and the agroalimentary industry, automobile distribution and real estate; Chair. HUBERT AUBÉRY.

SOMES (Société Martiniquaise des Eaux de Source): Quartier Champflore, 97260 Morne Rouge; tel. 5-96-52-52-52; fax 5-96-52-30-55; e-mail somes@wanadoo.fr; f. 1976; carbonated drinks bottler and juice distributor; Pres. BERTRAND CLERC; 49 employees.

UTILITIES

Electricity

Edf Martinique (Electricité de France Martinique): Pointe des Carrières, BP 573, 97242 Fort-de-France Cédex 01; tel. 5-96-59-20-00; fax 5-96-60-29-76; e-mail edf-services-martinique@edfgdf.fr; internet www.edf.fr/martinique; f. 1975; electricity supplier; successor to Société de Production et de Distribution d'Electricité de la Martinique (SPDEM); Chair. and CEO HENRI PROGLIO; 174,753 customers (2006).

Water

Veolia Water-Société Martiniquaise des Eaux (SME): pl. d'Armes, BP 213, 97284 Le Lamentin Cédex 02; tel. 5-96-51-80-51; fax 5-96-51-80-55; internet www.martiniquaisedeseaux.com; f. 1977 as Société Martiniquaise des Eaux.

TRADE UNIONS

Centrale Démocratique Martiniquaise du Travail (CDMT): Maison des Syndicats, Jardin Desclieux, 97200 Fort-de-France; tel. 5-96-70-19-86; fax 5-96-71-32-25; Sec.-Gen. PHILIPPE PIERRE-CHARLES.

Confédération Générale du Travail de la Martinique (CGTM): Maison des Syndicats, blvd Général de Gaulle, 97200 Fort-de-France; tel. 5-96-70-25-89; fax 5-96-70-57-17; e-mail contact@cgt-martinique.fr; internet www.cgt-martinique.fr; f. 1961; affiliated to World Fed. of Trade Unions; Sec.-Gen. GHISLAINE JOACHIM-ARNAUD.

Fédération Départementale des Syndicats d'Exploitants Agricoles de la Martinique (FDSEA): Immeuble Chambre d'Agriculture, pl. d'Armes, 97232 Le Lamentin; tel. 5-96-51-61-46; fax 5-96-57-05-43; e-mail fdsea.martinique@wanadoo.fr; affiliated to the Fédération Nationale des Syndicats d'Exploitants Agricoles; Pres. JOSEPH LUGO; Sec.-Gen. GUY OVIDE-ETIENNE.

Fédération Syndicale Unitaire Martinique (FSU): route des Réligieuses, Bâtiment B, Cité Bon Air, 97200 Fort-de-France; tel. 5-96-63-63-27; fax 5-96-71-89-43; e-mail fsu972@fsu.fr; f. 1993; departmental br. of the Fédération Syndicale Unitaire; represents public sector employees in teaching, research and training, and also agriculture, justice, youth and sports, and culture; Sec. DANIEL OTHILY.

Union Départementale Confédération Française des Travailleurs Chrétiens Martinique (UD CFTC): Maison des Syndicats, Jardin Desclieux, 97200 Fort-de-France; tel. 5-96-71-95-10; fax 5-96-60-39-10; e-mail cftc972@wanadoo.fr; internet www.cftc.fr.

Union Départementale Force Ouvrière Martinique (UD-FO): rue Bouillé, BP 1114, 97248 Fort-de-France Cédex; tel. 5-96-70-07-04; fax 5-96-70-18-20; e-mail udfomartinique@wanadoo.fr; internet www.force-ouvriere.fr; affiliated to the Int. Trade Union Confederation; Sec.-Gen. ERIC BELLEMARE.

Union Générale des Travailleurs de Martinique (UGTM): 8 rue Pierre et Marie Curie, Terres Sainville, 97200 Fort-de-France; tel. 5-96-63-75-23; fax 5-96-70-30-82; e-mail ugtm.centrale@wanadoo.fr; f. 1999; Pres. LÉON BERTIDE; Sec.-Gen. PATRICK DORÉ.

Union Régionale Martinique: Maison des Syndicats, rue de la Sécurité Jardin Desclieux, Salles 5–7, 97200 Fort-de-France; tel. 5-96-72-64-74; fax 5-96-70-16-80; e-mail ur-martinique@unsa.org; internet www.unsa.org.

UNSA Education Martinique (UE): Maison des Syndicats, Salles 4–5, Jardin Desclieux, 97200 Fort-de-France; tel. 5-96-72-64-74; fax 5-96-70-16-80; e-mail unsa972@wanadoo.fr; Sec.-Gen. MIREILLE JACQUES.

Transport

RAILWAYS

There are no railways in Martinique.

ROADS

There were 2,077 km (1,291 miles) of roads in 1998, of which 261 km were motorways and first-class roads.

SHIPPING

CMA-CGM CGM Antilles-Guyane: ZIP de la Pointe des Grives, BP 574, 97242 Fort-de-France Cédex; tel. 5-96-55-32-00; fax 5-96-63-08-87; e-mail fdf.jgourdin@cma-cgm.com; internet www.cma-cgm.com; subsidiary of CMA-CGM, France; also represents other passenger and freight lines; Pres. JACQUES R. SAADÉ; Man. Dir JEAN-CHARLES CREN.

Direction des Concessions Services Portuaires: quai de l'Hydro Base, BP 782, 97244 Fort-de-France Cédex; tel. 5-96-59-00-00; fax 5-96-71-35-73; e-mail port@martinique.cci.fr; port services management; Dir FRANTZ THODIARD; Operations Man. VICTOR EUSTACHE.

Direction Régionale des Affaires Maritimes (DRAM): blvd Chevalier de Sainte-Marthe, BP 620, 97261 Fort-de-France Cédex; tel. 5-96-60-80-30; fax 5-96-60-79-80; e-mail dram-martinique@equipement.gouv.fr.

Horn-Linie: Immeuble La Yole, ZAC L'Etang, Z'Abricots, Pointe de Sables, 97200 Fort-de-France; tel. 5-96-71-27-74; fax 5-96-71-27-83; e-mail fgrancher@wanadoo.fr; internet www.hornlinie.com; owned by Fresh Del Monte Produce, Inc (USA); freight and passenger services between Europe and the Caribbean; Man. FRANCK GRANCHER.

CIVIL AVIATION

Fort-de-France–Le Lamentin international airport is located at Le Lamentin, 12 km from Fort-de-France and is equipped to handle jet-engined aircraft.

Direction des Services Aéroportuaires: BP 279, 97285 Le Lamentin; tel. 5-96-42-16-00; fax 5-96-42-18-77; e-mail thodiard@martinique.cci.fr; Dir FRANTZ THODIARD.

Air Caraïbes: see Guadeloupe—Transport.

Tourism

Martinique's tourist attractions are its beaches and coastal scenery, its mountainous interior, and the historic towns of Fort-de-France and Saint-Pierre. In 2005 there were 97 hotels, with some 4,676 rooms. In 2009 the number of tourists who stayed on the island totalled 443,202, according to preliminary figures. Receipts from tourism were €299m. in 2007.

Comité Martiniquais du Tourisme: Immeuble Beaupré, Pointe de Jaham, 97233 Schoelcher; tel. 5-96-61-61-77; fax 5-96-61-22-72; internet www.welcome2martinique.com; Pres. KARINE ROY-CAMILLE.

Délégation Régionale au Tourisme: 41 rue Gabriel Périé, 97200 Fort-de-France; tel. 5-96-63-00-19; fax 5-96-73-00-96; Delegate JOSÉ DELAUNAY-BELLEVILLE.

Fédération Martiniquaise des Offices de Tourisme et Syndicats d'Initiative (FMOTSI): Maison du Tourisme Vert, 9 blvd du Général de Gaulle, BP 491, 97207 Fort-de-France Cédex; tel. 5-96-63-18-54; fax 5-96-70-17-61; e-mail contact@fmotsi.net; internet www.fmotsi.net; f. 1984; Pres. JOSÉ REINETTE; Sec.-Gen. JEAN-MARC LUSBEC.

Defence

As assessed at November 2009, France maintained a military force of about 1,225 and a gendarmerie, headquartered in Fort-de-France.

Education

The educational system is similar to that of metropolitan France (see chapter on French Guiana). In 2007/08 there were 48,443 pupils in pre-primary and primary education, while in secondary education there were 45,348 students, of whom some 91% attended state schools. Higher education in law, French language and literature, human sciences, economics, medicine and Creole studies is provided in Martinique by a branch of the Université des Antilles et de la Guyane. During 2003/04 some 5,344 students were enrolled at the university in Martinique; in 2007/08 there were 8,985 students enrolled in higher education on the island. There are also two teacher-training institutes, and colleges of agriculture, fisheries, hotel management, nursing, midwifery and childcare. Departmental expenditure on education and culture was estimated at €44.1m. in 2006.

Bibliography

For works on the Caribbean generally, see Select Bibliography (Books)

Abénon, L., and Joseph, H. E. *Les Dissidents des Antilles dans les Forces françaises libres combattantes, 1940–1945*. Fort-de-France, Editions Desormeaux, 1999.

Browne, K. *Creole Economics: Caribbean Cunning under the French Flag*. Austin, TX, University of Texas Press, 2005.

Constant, R. *Quelques affaires de justice à la Martinique*. Case Pilote, Editions Lafontaine, 2003.

Crane, J. *Martinique*. (World Bibliographical Series). Oxford, ABC Clio, 1995.

Darsières, C. *Des origines de la nation martiniquaise*. Fort-de-France, Editions Desormeaux, 1974.

Dévoué, E. *Les Antilles françaises: Les activites informelles, un aspect méconnu*. Paris, Publisud, 2000.

Laguerre, M. S. *Urban Poverty in the Caribbean (French Martinique as a Social Laboratory)*. New York, NY, Palgrave, 1990.

M'Kba, M. *L'Ethiopie-Martinique*. Case Pilote, Editions Lafontaine, 1999.

Scarth, A. *La Catastrophe: The Eruption of Mount Pelée*. Oxford, Oxford University Press, 2002.

MEXICO

Geography

PHYSICAL FEATURES

The United Mexican States is the southernmost of the three great federations of North America, a republic that narrows south and east towards the great land bridge of Central America. Mexico is the smallest of the continental North American countries, being about one-fifth the size of the USA or Canada, but it is the third largest country of Latin America (it is less than one-quarter the size of Brazil and 70% of Argentina, but the next country in area, Peru, is only two-thirds its size) and the most northerly. The longest border (3,152 km or 1,959 miles) is with the USA, which lies to the north and north-east, while its south-eastern frontier is with the Central American countries of Guatemala (956 km), on the Pacific side, and Belize (193 km), on the Caribbean side. The country's nearest insular Caribbean neighbour is Cuba, some 210 km to the east of the Yucatán peninsula, in the south. The eastern coast is along the Gulf of Mexico and on the Caribbean, while the western coast, almost double in length, is on the Pacific Ocean. In total, there are about 11,122 km of coastline. Mexico covers an area of 1,964,375 sq km (758,449 sq miles), including 5,127 sq km of islands (the latter an area almost equivalent in size to Trinidad and Tobago).

Mexico has a diverse and crumpled topography, covering a vast area (it is the 13th largest country in the world). It is at its widest in the north, along the US border, where it is about 2,000 km from east to west. It is at its narrowest, 210 km from north to south, on the Tehuantepec isthmus, where there is a break in the Continental Divide, just before the country broadens westwards into Central America. Some two-thirds of Mexico is mountainous and one-half of it above 1,500 m (about 5,000 ft). Most of it is dry and sere, although the extent and variety of the terrain makes for regional contrasts. The Pacific coast runs roughly from north-west to south-east, before curving into a south-facing shore and continuing into Guatemala. The more northerly section of this western coast is dominated by the lowlands of the Sonora Desert, shielded from the immediate presence of the Pacific by the 1,300-km peninsula of Baja California, joined to the rest of Mexico in the far north-west, then thrusting southwards, parallel to the main coast on the other shore of what is known in Mexico as the Sea of Cortez (Cortés—Gulf of California). On the other side of the country, the western shore curves out of the north-east, circling around the Gulf of Mexico and into the north-thrusting abutment of the Yucatán peninsula, which separates the Gulf from the Caribbean. The flat, forested Yucatán has a relatively short eastern coast on the Caribbean, below which is Belize. Much of the interior of the country is an elevated plateau, the Mesa Central, which occupies about 60% of the territory of Mexico and contains most of its mountains, population and historical remains. A number of other distinct regions can be identified—the narrow coastal plains of the Pacific and of the Gulf of Mexico, the peninsulas of Baja California and Yucatán, and two further areas of upland, the southern highlands and the Chiapas highlands.

The central plateau is flanked, to west and east, by two mountain ranges, each rising steeply from their respective coastal plains, the Sierra Madre Occidental and the Sierra Madre Oriental. The western (Occidental) mountains are generally higher, above narrower coastal plains. Both ranges continue the thrust of the Rockies from the north, and merge some 240 km south of Mexico City (Ciudad de México), the capital, in an area of towering, inactive volcanoes and some of the country's highest peaks—such as Potacatépetl and Ixaticcíhuatl (just south-east of Mexico City) or the highest, Orizaba (5,610 m or 18,412 ft), between there and the Gulf city of Veracruz. The average elevation of the central plateau itself is about 900 m in the north and 2,400 m in the south. The plateau is interrupted by heights and broad basins, consisting of desert in the north (*bolsones*) and areas of settlement amid the rolling

hills of the south. One such basin in the south of the plateau is the site of Mexico City and is known as the Valley of Mexico.

Just as the Sierra Madre is a part of the Continental Divide and a continuation of the Rockies, the mountainous interior of Baja (Lower) California is a continuation of the Coast Ranges in the USA. The northern connection to 'mainland' Mexico is interrupted by a deep cleft (continuing in the Sea of Cortez) in which the Laguna Salada is the lowest point in the country, being 10 m below sea level. Sparsely inhabited and arid, the peninsula most resembles the desert of the northern shores on the other side of the Sea of Cortez. Mid-way down the long inlet of the Pacific begin the coastal plains, about 50 km in width and extending southwards to just below Tepic (which lies north-west of Guadalajara). These plains are extensively irrigated and used for agriculture, being one of the limited fertile areas of the country (only 13% of the national territory is cultivated). Thereafter, the few patches of coastal plain are much narrower, as the southern highlands meet the sea, but widen again beyond Tehuantepec. The southern highlands are the Sierra Madre del Sur, which begin on the coast to the west of the Valley of Mexico and swing south of the central highlands, pushing south-eastwards to tail away at the Tehuantepec isthmus. The terrain consists of steep mountains, deep valleys (hot and dry inland) and high plateaux. The mountains often plunge straight into the Pacific, and the coast is rugged, and sometimes called the 'Mexican Riviera'. Beyond Tehuantepec, the Sierra Madre and the Continental Divide resume in the Chiapas highlands, continuing into Guatemala. The coastal plains also resume here, beneath the mountains, but the landscape is very different here in the south. Chiapas receives more rainfall than anywhere else in Mexico and is thinly inhabited, leaving forest cover still extensive. Beyond the highlands, east of the central plateau, are the limestone lowlands and coastal plains along the Gulf of Mexico. In the north, near the US border along the Río Bravo del Norte (known as the Rio Grande in the USA), there are about 280 km between the sea and the steep mountain wall, but this narrows to only a few kilometres near Veracruz (which is east of Mexico City). Beyond here, the plains widen again into the lowlands of the Isthmus of Tehuantepec, before thrusting north and east beyond Tabasco into the Yucatán peninsula. Much of the plains immediately on the Gulf consist of lagoons and swampy lowlands. Yucatán itself is broad and flat, without surface rivers, being dry and scrubby in the north-west, but much wetter and covered in dense rainforest in the south, the jungle often cloaking the ruins of the old Maya civilization.

The country is largely dry and also has few large rivers. There are the Grijalva and the Usumacinta, for instance, which rise in Guatemala and empty into the Gulf of Mexico. The most important river system is that of the Grande de Santiago and the Lerma, which empty into the Pacific. The two rivers are interrupted by the country's largest lake, Chapala, which is 80 km long and 13 km wide—Mexico has relatively few lakes, although many lagoons and enclosed bodies of salt water contribute to inland waters of 49,510 sq km. This contributes to the variety of ecosystems to be found in the country, which still enjoys a diverse range of living species, both plant and animal. However, human settlement, in the north particularly, has had an adverse effect on the natural environment, with a continuing high rate of deforestation (this and the lack of clean water have both been declared national security issues by the Government: as an example of the seriousness, the depletion of groundwater reserves in the Valley of Mexico is causing subsidence). Nevertheless, about one-quarter of the country is forested (mainly in the south), and this helps to shelter the range of species found in Mexico—30,000 plants, 1,000 birds and 1,500 mammals, reptiles and amphibians. About 15% of these species are reckoned to be unique to Mexico. The human population being less numerous and less widespread in the south, the ecological damage here is considerably less than in the north, with the environment similar to Central America, still inhabited by animals such as tapirs, jaguars and monkeys. Even in the north, in the high Sierra Madre, animals such as bears, deer, coyotes and mountain lions can still be found. The continually rising population and the fact that most of Mexico's profitable natural resources are subsoil, however, means a continuing threat to the environment, even in the hitherto neglected desert areas. It is the north of the country that is dominated by desert foliage, with extensive grasslands and hardwood forests in the highlands, while the wetter south is more typically rainforest.

CLIMATE

The climate is as varied as the topography, ranging from tropical to temperate, mainly depending on altitude. Most of the country is south of the Tropic of Cancer, which crosses the tip of the Baja California peninsula. It is also generally dry, particularly in the north-west, but the south receives copious rainfall. Mexico mostly experiences two seasons, wet and dry, the latter (November–May) being the cooler. The central plateau is milder than the rest of the country, the evenings not only cool but even cold at times during the winter. Most rain is between June and September, ranging from about 300 mm (12 ins) in the north to 500 mm–650 mm in the south. However, the deleterious effects human settlement can have even on weather is amply demonstrated in the disruption to the traditional rainfall patterns in the Valley of Mexico, owing to industrial pollution. The north-west of the country is the driest part, particularly on the Baja California peninsula. The northern part of the peninsula has a climate similar to that of southern California in the USA, with dry, warm summers and mild winters, while the south of the peninsula can get extremely hot. Here and in the Sonora is the area of lowest rainfall (about 130 mm annually). The coastal plains of the Pacific tend to have a little more rain and rather stronger storm patterns. Further down this coast, on the Riviera region, there is a definite tropical monsoon climate, although the southern highlands hinterland tends to be drier. In Chiapas the tropical conditions are even more pronounced, with average annual rainfall reaching 2,030 mm, but many places getting as much as double that amount. The coast of the Gulf of Mexico is muggy, with average rainfall about twice that of Baja California and increasing significantly south of Tampico (midway between Veracruz and the US border). Summer temperatures are high, but rain in autumn and winter (September–February), a slightly different wet season, is helped by brisk, cold northerlies. Yucatán is hot and humid in its jungle interior, alleviated by proximity to the coasts. The north of the peninsula is dry, but precipitation levels in the south approach those of Chiapas. There are two main wet seasons, in April–May and September–January. September–October can bring hurricanes, to which Caribbean, Gulf and Pacific coasts are all prone (natural hazards also come from the earthquakes common in a volcanic region such as this, with tsunamis liable to hit the Pacific coast). The average maximum and minimum temperatures in Mexico City range from 6°C–19°C (43°F–66°F) in January to 12°C–26°C (54°F–79°F) in May.

POPULATION

The population of Mexico is predominantly Mestizo (60%), of mixed Spanish and Amerindian descent, and full-blood Amerindian (anywhere between 15% and 30%, depending on which figures are given credence), the balance made up of whites (9%—of mixed descent from Spanish and other immigrant, mainly European, groups), with small black, mixed-black and Asian groups. The early adoption of Spanish and Roman Catholicism by the native Amerindians has made for a more uniform culture than might otherwise have been the case. Spanish remains the official language, although 7% of the population speak only one of at least 62 indigenous tongues (mainly Nahuatl or, in the south, Mayan languages). English is widely spoken along the northern border. About 88% of the population are at least nominally Roman Catholic, despite the official anti-clericalism of the regime for most of the 20th century, and 6% are Protestant.

At the by-census of 29 October 2005 the total population of Mexico was 103.3m. According to official estimates, this figure had increased to 108.4m. by mid-2010. After decades of rural exodus, about three-quarters of this population is urbanized, with nearly one-fifth of the total living in or around Mexico City. The capital is just north of where the Sierra Madre Occidental and the Sierra Madre Oriental converge, in central Mexico. The population of Mexico City at the time of the 2000 census was 8.61m., although, in addition, some cities on its outskirts are virtually suburbs (such as Ecatepec—1.62m.—and Nezahualcóyotl—1.23m.). According to UN estimates, the population of Mexico City, including suburbs, was 19.5m. in mid-2010. The second city of the country is Guadalajara (4.4m.), to the west-north-west of the capital, about three-quarters of the way to the coast. Monterrey, south-west of the Texas border, on the edge of the Gulf lowlands and the Sierra Madre Oriental, had an estimated population of 3.9m., while Puebla, not far to the south-east of Mexico City, had 2.3m. residents according to mid-2010 estimates. A further eight cities had more than 1m. residents (including Tijuana (in the far north-west, south of California, with 1.7m. people). Mexico is a federal republic, consisting of 31 states and the Federal District (Distrito Federal) encompassing Mexico City.

History

SANDY MARKWICK

SPANISH CONQUEST

The area comprising modern Mexico was home to some of the most advanced pre-Columbian civilizations in the Americas. The most sophisticated societies were those of the Mayans, centred on the Yucatán peninsula, at its height between AD 700 and 900, and the Aztecs, based in the central Valle de México (Valley of Mexico), location of present-day Mexico City, at its height between AD 1300 and 1500.

The meeting of European and indigenous cultures resonates powerfully in Mexico, as it does in much of Latin America. Some commentators see in the authoritarianism of modern Mexico, only recently challenged by genuine multi-party democracy, not just contemporary influences, but a persistent theme that can be traced back to the hierarchical organization of Aztec society. The modern population of Mexico is predominantly of mixed European and indigenous ethnicity (*mestizo*), though large populations of Mexican Amerindians continue to live throughout Mexico, typically occupying the poorest strata of rural and urban society.

Invading Europeans led by Hernán Cortés destroyed the Aztec empire, led by its emperor, Cuauhtémoc, in 1521; following the conquest, diseases brought from Europe severely reduced the indigenous population. Mexico City was subsequently founded on the ruins of the Aztec capital of Tenochtitlan. Mexico was part of the larger territory of New Spain, incorporating much of Central America, the Caribbean and the Philippines, under the nominal control of the King of Spain's viceroy. Colonial society divided along racial and class lines and was built on the wealth derived largely from Mexico's silver resources.

INDEPENDENCE

The liberal philosophies behind the French and American revolutions influenced opinion in favour of independence in Mexico from the late 18th century. Loyalty to the Spanish crown was called into question following Napoleon's invasion of the Iberian peninsula in 1808. The French emperor had ousted Carlos IV and installed his brother, Joseph Bonaparte, as king. The ensuing breakdown in Spanish royal authority in Mexico exacerbated tensions between Mexican-born élites (*criollos*) and their counterparts from Spain (*peninsulares)*, leading to conflict and an 11-year independence struggle. On 16 September 1810 a radical *criollo* priest, Miguel Hidalgo, formally proclaimed independence from his base in Guanajuato. The date is celebrated as Independence Day.

The insurrection met with partial success, but by 1820 had failed to defeat the colonial forces in Mexico City and the two principal leaders of the pro-independence forces, Hidalgo and his successor, José María Morelos, had been executed. However, the seizure of power in Spain by liberals had the effect of provoking conservative loyalists, led by Augustín de Iturbide, to turn against Spain and unite with the rebels behind independence. Spain signed the Treaty of Córdoba in September 1821, recognizing Mexican independence under the rule of a Mexican monarch, with equal privileges for *criollos* and *peninsulares*, and with the Roman Catholic Church afforded privileges as the official religion.

Iturbide was appointed 'emperor' as he forcibly annexed most of Spanish-speaking Central America, though his empire was short-lived. A garrison commander, Antonio López de Santa Ana, led a republican revolt, which received significant support and precipitated Iturbide's abdication. Central American territories subsequently declared their independence from Mexico (the southern state of Chiapas, which had been part of Guatemala, opted to remain part of Mexico).

Federal Republic, 1824–36

A constitutional congress drafted the Constitution of 1824 and established a federal republic of 19 states and four territories. Superficially, the Constitution had the liberal appearance of the US Constitution, with separation of powers between the states, the executive, legislature and judiciary. Where it departed from a liberal influence was in privileges granted to the military and the Roman Catholic Church, concessions secured by conservatives within the constitutional congress.

For a decade political conflict in the Federal Republic set federalists against conservatives. The former received support from liberal *criollos* and *mestizos* and feared control from a conservative Mexico City, while the conservatives were centralists and traditionalists supported by the military and the Roman Catholic Church. Liberal rule under the Federal Republic was brought to an end with the assumption of dictatorial powers by the provincial ruler (*caudillo*) López de Santa Ana. He had been elected President in 1833 after his defeat of earlier conservative revolts, but subsequently abandoned liberalism. López de Santa Ana dominated politics either as President or as the power behind the scenes until 1855.

Santa Ana and Territorial Loss

López de Santa Ana drafted the new Constitution of 1836, with power concentrated in the hands of the President. Regional *caudillos* were appointed to run the former states as military districts. The new regime's authoritarianism and nationalism brought it into conflict with the English-speaking settlers of Texas. Texans declared independence from Mexico in 1836 and, with the support of volunteers from the USA, defeated López de Santa Ana's forces. Texan independence lasted until 1845, when it became the 28th state of the USA.

War between Mexico and the USA erupted in 1846 over the disputed status of Texas (the Mexican legislature had never ratified López de Santa Ana's treaty recognizing Texan independence), culminating in the occupation of Mexico City by US forces. The 1848 Treaty of Guadalupe Hidalgo established the border between Mexico and the USA at the Río Bravo del Norte (Rio Grande), accepted Texas' incorporation into the USA and saw more than one-half of its territory—a large part of present-day south-western USA, including California, Nevada and Utah—ceded to the USA. López de Santa Ana sold further territory to the USA—southern New Mexico and Arizona—in the Gadsden Purchase of 1854. This last episode enraged a group of reformists led by Benito Juárez, a lawyer and Zapotec Amerindian. Inspired by the liberal European political philosophers, such as Jean-Jacques Rousseau and John Stuart Mill, this group planned the overthrow of López de Santa Ana. Support for the conspirators grew and led to López de Santa Ana's resignation in 1855.

The Reform and Emperor Maximilian

A period of liberal rule ensued under the provisional Government of Juan Ruíz de Alvarez, charged with governing until a new constitution could be drafted. A series of reform laws saw the powers of the Church curtailed, slavery abolished and civil liberties guaranteed. These reforms were incorporated into the new Constitution of 1857, but they polarized Mexico, leading to a civil war, known as the War of the Reform (1858–61). Conservatives, supported by the military and the Church, dissolved the Congreso (Congress), while Juárez formed a liberal 'Government-in-exile'. The liberals defeated the conservative forces at the end of 1860 and entered the capital on 1 January 1861. Juárez won a presidential election and, faced with a stagnant economy and the demands of foreign creditors to repay loans, declared a moratorium on foreign debt repayments. In response, Spain, the United Kingdom and France sent a joint military expedition to enforce repayment. The United Kingdom and Spain subsequently withdrew their forces, but the French continued the occupation with the support of the defeated conservatives. The French lost a disastrous battle at Puebla on 5 May 1862, which is commemorated by the Cinco de Mayo national holiday. The French finally captured the capital in 1863 and, with Napoleon III hoping to gain territory in the Americas, imposed Archduke Maximilian of Austria, from the house of Habsburg, as the Emperor of Mexico.

When the French, facing a threat from the Prussians, recalled their forces, Maximilian was left isolated, not just against Juárez and his supporters (which by now included the USA, after its own Civil War had ended), but also against the conservatives, who were disillusioned with Maximilian's refusal to repeal liberal reforms. Liberals and conservatives united to defeat Maximilian in June 1867, after which he was executed, and Juárez returned to power.

Republican forces under the newly elected Juárez restored the Constitution of 1857 and embarked on a programme to develop communications, natural resources and education. Juárez died in 1872 and was replaced by another liberal, Sebastián Lerdo de Tejada. When Lerdo tried to seek re-election he was deposed during an uprising by José de la Cruz Porfirio Díaz, who had earlier staged an unsuccessful revolt against Juárez. Porfirio Díaz was to rule largely uninterrupted from 1876 to 1910, during a period that came to be known as the Porfiriato.

The Porfiriato

Díaz pursued a strategy of modernization and economic development based on the integration of Mexico into the global economy through export-orientated growth, and he created a modern infrastructure, including an expanded railway network, to support the development of agriculture and minerals. The Porfiriato was characterized by economic growth, modernization and political stability, although achieved at the cost of social division and authoritarianism. Wealth was concentrated in the hands of a narrow élite, political opposition was not tolerated and Díaz flouted the clause in the Constitution that prohibited re-election. The Government concentrated land ownership in the hands of a few rich landowners (*hacendados*), creating widespread rural landlessness.

THE MEXICAN REVOLUTION, 1910–20

Díaz's attempt to ensure his re-election (for the seventh time) in 1910 sparked a rebellion led by Francisco Madero, a wealthy northerner who represented the political resentment towards Díaz's monopoly of power. Other revolts broke out against Díaz, including those led by 'Pancho' Villa in the northern state of Chihuahua and Emiliano Zapata, a peasant leader from Morelos state. Zapata expressed the discontent among poor, rural, indigenous Mexicans, particularly in the south. Díaz resigned in the face of the rebellions in May 1911.

Madero became President in November 1911, but found it difficult to satisfy the expectations of those revolutionary forces who appealed for social justice as well as political reform and nationalist rhetoric based on indigenous heritage. Zapata turned his rebellion against Madero, demanding land reform, while other revolutionary and counter-revolutionary forces plotted against the President. A commander formerly loyal to Madero, Victoriano Huerta, joined counter-revolutionary forces under a nephew of Díaz, deposed Madero and installed himself as President. Madero was assassinated in February 1913. Opposition to Huerta stemmed from numerous northern *caudillos*, including Villa in Chihuahua, Alvaro Obregón in Sonora and Venustiano Carranza in Coahuila, and from Zapata in the south. Huerta tried to maintain control through repressive use of federal forces, but the economy was in ruins and conflict continued. Huerta resigned in July 1914.

A conference of military leaders organized by Carranza revealed a broad division between those principally concerned with the restoration of the Constitution, led by Carranza and Obregón, and those fighting for land reform, led by Zapata and Villa. At one point all four leaders established governments and claimed legitimacy: Carranza based in Veracruz; Obregón in Mexico City; Villa in Guanajuato; and Roque González Garza in Cuernavaca, supported by Zapata. This period of civil war ended in victory for Carranza. His Government was recognized by the USA, though Villa continued to resist. Carranza held the Congress of Querétaro on 1 December 1916 to draft a new constitutional settlement. (Mexican Presidents are inaugurated on 1 December to commemorate the Querétaro meeting.) The Constitution of 1917 that emerged from Querétaro was a liberal democratic charter. It departed from the 1857 Constitution by giving greater powers to the executive, although the clause prohibiting re-election was maintained, and by incorporating revolutionary goals: civil liberties; labour rights and land reform; subordination of the military; secularization of education; and strict observance of the electoral calendar. It established a federal system of 31 states and a Distrito Federal (Federal District) comprising Mexico City.

With the new Constitution in place, Carranza took office in May 1917, following electoral victory. Civil war was to continue for another three years. Carranza restored expropriated land to former landowners rather than legally recognize land seizures or extend land reform. This ensured that insurrection persisted, particularly from the Zapatistas in Morelos. Carranza ordered Zapata's assassination in 1919. However, Carranza provoked further military opposition when he tried to install an ally as a successor to allow him to maintain power behind the scenes. Adolfo de la Huerta and Plutarco Elías Calles led an army from the north, invoking the Constitution. Carranza left for exile, but was assassinated en route. Obregón was elected to a new four-year term in 1920. Villa ended resistance in the north by signing a peace treaty with the federal Government.

POST-REVOLUTIONARY SETTLEMENT AND THE FOUNDING OF A STATE PARTY

Under Obregón's presidency (1920–24), land redistribution proceeded cautiously, disappointing radicals in the process, although his Government furthered revolutionary goals through a large-scale education policy in rural areas, in which it sought to integrate indigenous groups into Mexican society. During this time the Government commissioned Diego Rivera and other renowned muralists to teach the history and cultivate the myths of the revolution through visual imagery.

Obregón nominated his interior secretary Calles as his successor in 1924. Calles' presidency was more radical than his predecessor's: he redistributed 3.2m. ha of land, three times as much as had been redistributed under Obregón, and also implemented the anti-clerical provisions of the Constitution in closing Church-run schools, banning religious processions and forcing priests to register with the Government in order to perform duties. The policies provoked fierce revolt among militant supporters of the Roman Catholic Church, violence which was met in kind by government forces. By 1929 the Church had been forced to accept government terms. During this period a religious militant assassinated former President Obregón, who had won elections in 1928 (thereby flouting the constitutional clause prohibiting re-election) and was due to assume office in that year. Calles effectively remained in power behind three weak Presidents until 1934, in a period known as the Maximato.

In 1929 Calles established the Partido Nacional Revolucionario (PNR—National Revolutionary Party) providing institutional support for his political ambitions. The PNR was designed as a permanent organization and as an official institutional expression of the revolution. Under the Maximato, Calles and his Governments shifted to the right, as land redistribution was halted and independent labour organizations suppressed. The President came under pressure from the left within the PNR and, to avoid a split in the party, nominated Lázaro Cárdenas, a populist Governor of Michoacán, as candidate in the 1934 presidential elections.

The Presidency of Lázaro Cárdenas, 1934–40

The Cárdenas presidency gave significant new impetus to the revolutionary vision. Cárdenas redistributed close to 18m. ha of land, eclipsing the combined efforts of all previous Governments, and displayed his independence from Calles by removing many of his supporters from their positions in the federal bureaucracy. The military demonstrated its loyalty in suppressing a rebellion of Calles' conservative supporters in San Luis Potosí. Cárdenas is also noted for his expropriation of foreign oil companies in 1938 and the formation of a national oil company, Petróleos Mexicanos (PEMEX). The initiative damaged relations with the USA and led to under-investment in the industry, but ensured Cárdenas' place in Mexican history as a hero of the nationalist left.

Cárdenas reorganized the PNR into the Partido de la Revolución Mexicana (PRM—Party of the Mexican Revolution) and in doing so integrated key sectors of Mexican society into the party in official 'corporatist' sectors. Labour was represented by the newly formed Confederación de Trabajadores de México (CTM—Confederation of Mexican Workers). Other quasi-official organizations represented rural labourers and small farmers and urban employees of the state bureaucracy. These organizations did not emerge from the grassroots of sectoral organization, but instead were imposed from above by the political hierarchy to distribute benefits while simultaneously controlling and suppressing demands. The corporatist organizations enjoyed the benefits conferred on them as a result of their quasi-official status, which independent organizations did not.

THE MEXICAN 'MIRACLE', 1940–81

The period 1940–81 was one of steady, sustained economic growth. Following Cárdenas, Mexican Presidents over the next half-century focused on ensuring that the state took the lead in economic and industrial development. Domestic industry was sheltered behind protectionist tariff barriers, and governments used their authority through the CTM to suppress workers' wage demands. Public investment was directed towards modernizing infrastructure and developing strategic industries such as oil and petrochemicals. (Mexico had become the 15th largest economy in the world by 1980.) All Mexican Governments up to this time had shared this broad strategy, varying principally in the degree of nationalist tone and their enthusiasm for rural development and land redistribution. Avila Camacho (1940–46), Miguel Alemán (1946–52) and Adolfo Ruiz Cortines (1952–58) were more conservative Presidents than Cárdenas, slowing land reform and promoting private investment by keeping wages low. By contrast, Adolfo López Mateos (1958–64) represented a shift back to the left, with a reinvigoration of land redistribution, while also maintaining strict control of the unions. The combination of economic growth and relative political stability was unique in Latin America during this period and often referred to as the Mexican 'miracle'.

The political system that underpinned the Mexican miracle for half a century and evolved during the post-revolutionary period under Calles, and then Cárdenas, was unique. One of its principal features was the enormous power provided de facto to the President. While the Constitution of 1917 provided for a separation of powers between the executive, legislature and judiciary, in reality the President dominated everything. The Congreso was a pliant body, little more than a rubber stamp for presidential ambitions. The judiciary was nominally independent, but in fact expressed the will of the executive. The 31 state governors were not accountable to an electorate, but to the *gran elector*, the President himself, to whom they had to show loyalty, dependent as they were on the federal treasury. The President controlled state resources and could use them as punishment or reward. The enormous powers of the President were limited only by the fixed electoral calendar and the constitutional clause prohibiting re-election. Even then the incumbent could choose his successor by nominating the ruling party's presidential candidate. The nomination was not the result of any internal party democracy.

The party was a vital feature of the system and a central pillar of Mexico's relative stability in the post-war decades. The Partido Revolucionario Institucional (PRI—Institutional Revolutionary Party), as the party founded by Calles in 1929 came to be known, was not established as a traditional political party, as the term is understood in modern democracies. The aim of the party was not to compete with other parties, but to include all the factions behind the revolution and to provide a mechanism for the peaceful resolution of disputes. The party was a co-ordinator of the electoral process, an election-winning machine dominated by successive Presidents, which ensured victory through privileged access to state resources, patronage and, at times, fraud and repression.

Leaders sought democratic legitimacy through the electoral process, but for most of the post-revolutionary 20th century genuine electoral competition was lacking. The authoritarian reality behind a democratic and constitutional façade inspired the Peruvian novelist Mario Vargas Llosa to refer to the Mexican political system as the 'perfect dictatorship'. The PRI 'won' all elections at state and federal level, and the great majority at municipal level too. The PRI encouraged some semi-official 'opposition' parties and occasionally conceded defeat in municipal elections to the opposition, largely to boost democratic legitimacy. Genuine opposition, for example from the conservative Partido Acción Nacional (PAN—National Action Party), tended to be limited regionally, in this case to the pro-business north and the Roman Catholic south-east. PRI candidates wielded significant advantages over opposition candidates in their proximity to the apparatus and largesse of the state, including funds and police, which they used in pursuit of electoral support. If that was not enough, the executive's dominance over the electoral commission ensured PRI victories unless the regime felt it prudent to concede defeat.

The most important political battles took place in relative obscurity within the PRI itself rather than at the polling stations. The unity of the PRI was maintained by imposing obstacles and disincentives to party resignations, such as electoral failure or repression, and incentives to remain loyal, such as jobs in the state bureaucracy or the promise of political power in the future. The fixed calendar, strictly adhered to, allowed for a circulation of competing governing élites each *sexenio* (six-year presidential term). This encouraged loyalty to the system, but was also a source of weakness. There was a pattern of crises accompanying transitions between Governments, as outgoing administrations, made up of multiple patron-client relationships about to lose power, did not necessarily behave in the national interest.

While presidential power supported by a dominant state party made the Mexican system undoubtedly authoritarian, it was also socially inclusive. Mexican Presidents were heirs of a revolutionary and nationalist struggle. The legacy was not just rhetoric: the economic growth generated was used to pursue social justice (to varying degrees, according to the administration). This included land redistribution to communal landholdings (*ejidos*), subsidies for the poor, job creation, and investment in health and education. The institutional expression of the socially inclusive character of the Mexican system was the PRI-affiliated corporatist sectoral organizations representing labour unions, small farmers, landless peasants and employees of urban public sector bureaucracies. The system distributed benefits to those groups within these sectors that were affiliated with the PRI in return for control, and discriminated against any independent organizations. In this way it secured the loyalty of potential opponents. For example, the Government exercised control over the peasantry by means of land titles, loans, seeds and fertilizer, which it distributed through official agrarian co-operatives, ensuring their dependence and discouraging the emergence of any alternative autonomous organization.

Cracks in the System

Under the presidency of Gustavo Díaz Ordaz (1964–70), the authoritarianism of the system was exposed to the world when the Government countered mounting student unrest with brutal repression. Hundreds of protesters were killed in Tlatelolco Square in October 1968, in response to protests from students and intellectuals, who had been demanding greater openness. Mexican society had changed significantly since the days of Calles and Cárdenas. Steady growth, stability and economic development promoted by PRI Governments transformed Mexico from a predominantly uneducated rural society to a predominantly educated and urban one, and PRI authoritarianism began to appear anachronistic.

In response to the threat of unrest, the Government employed a tactic that previous Governments had used successfully when faced with a threat to stability: it co-opted into the regime the very group that had threatened it. In 1970 Luis Echeverría, who as interior secretary was responsible for the actions of the security forces, became President (1970–76) and defused urban protest by integrating disaffected students into the system and conferring some of its benefits to them. Echeverría released imprisoned students, brought other student leaders into prominent positions in his Government and gave jobs in an expanded bureaucracy to the educated middle-class youth.

Debt Crisis and the End of the 'Miracle'

Under President Luis López Portillo (1976–82), the seeds were sown for a crisis that would change the development model and threaten the system of government. López Portillo benefited from the discovery of massive new oil reserves, particularly in the Gulf of Mexico. By 1981 Mexico had tripled its oil production to become the world's fourth largest producer, earning huge revenues as the price of crude increased. Mexico used these reserves as collateral to borrow extensively from willing foreign banks, the coffers of which were filled with the deposits of oil producers in the Middle East. When the petroleum price slumped in 1981 and interest rates increased, it meant that by 1982 Mexico was faced with a US $10,000m. current account deficit and servicing obligations on a $90,000m. foreign debt, equivalent to 45% of export earnings. The Government devalued the peso and, to control the flight of capital overseas, nationalized the banking sector.

President Miguel de la Madrid Hurtado (1982–88) inherited an economy in crisis, in which the old statist and protectionist development model was no longer appropriate. Instead, the Government chose spending cuts and austerity measures in order to keep credit lines open from the international financial community, as well as trade liberalization. In 1986 Mexico joined the General Agreement on Tariffs and Trade, the forerunner to the World Trade Organization (WTO), and so began a process of progressively reducing tariffs and eliminating non-tariff barriers.

The new economic environment had important political reverberations. The efficiency of the system in co-opting sufficient numbers and interests behind the President came under severe strain. The system was no longer delivering steady economic growth. The austerity measures threw inequality within Mexican society into sharp relief; rising inflation, public spending cuts and devaluation most affected the poor. During de la Madrid's administration, real wages declined by 40%. The crisis opened regional divisions between the pro-business north and Mexico City. Support for the PAN in the north grew. The Government, less able now to use economic policy to shore up loyalty, began tentative moves towards greater political pluralism. The PAN won municipal mayoralties and seats in state legislatures in 1983 and 1985, respectively.

Economic crisis, inequality and the shift towards the free market in government policy resulted in a left-wing breakaway from the PRI, led by Cuauhtémoc Cárdenas (son of nationalist hero and former President Cárdenas). He stood as an independent candidate in the 1988 elections, campaigning for a return to the principles of the Mexican revolution against the PRI candidate, the 'technocrat', Carlos Salinas de Gortari.

THE PRESIDENCY OF CARLOS SALINAS

The year 1988 proved a watershed in Mexican politics. For the first time, a candidate from the PRI faced a serious challenge for the presidency. Salinas was declared the winner with just over 50% of votes cast (PRI presidential candidates had consistently polled over 80%), amid widespread allegations of fraud. For the first time, the PRI held less than a two-thirds' majority in the Congreso, requiring it to negotiate with opposition parties to enact constitutional reform.

President Salinas extended the structural transformation of the Mexican economy through privatization, trade liberalization and modernization of the financial system. There was also a significant political element to his economic policies. The manner of his 'victory' strongly influenced the path of his presidency. The election demonstrated a loss of support for the PRI and the party's system, and the dubious nature of the count called into question the legitimacy of the Government. From the outset, Salinas aimed to regain the support of the middle classes through exchange-rate and price stability; liberalization of trade, together with a fixed, overvalued exchange rate, was designed to reduce inflation through cheaper imports.

The policy opened a trade gap, which, along with debt-servicing requirements, fuelled a current account deficit. Salinas attempted to finance the deficit by attracting capital through privatization. Between 1986 and 1994 the Government sold the state's interest in more than 700 companies, including all its commercial banks, airlines, television networks, telephone companies, ports, industrial processing plants, mines and steel production facilities. The process generated revenues of US $22,000m. The Government lifted the tight restrictions on foreign investment, fuelling a boom in the Mexican stock exchange and in the growth of the *maquiladora* sector (tax-free assembly plants predominantly located along the border with the USA).

President Salinas' policies brought some macroeconomic success, but the benefits were not evenly distributed. Annual inflation fell from 159% in 1987 to 6.7% in 1994, garnering significant support from the urban middle classes, who enjoyed a consumer boom brought about by cheap imports. However, growth rates remained modest, averaging 2.6% in the period 1988–94. Unemployment and underemployment remained high, leading to a significant rate of emigration to the USA. Joining the North American Free Trade Agreement (NAFTA) in 1994 consolidated the radical shift in Mexican trading policy. Salinas turned around decades of nationalist-driven protectionism to direct the economy towards integration into the international economy. He promised political reform, but delivered a highly selective version, which did little to threaten the PRI's hold on power, at least in the short term.

In July 1989 the PRI conceded the governorship of the state of Baja California Norte to the PAN. This was unprecedented, the first time the opposition had won any gubernatorial election. However, it represented only a limited political opening: state governors were reliant on the federal treasury, and Salinas could afford to 'allow' a PAN victory, knowing that it would give the impression of increasing pluralism without being an immediate threat to PRI control. While the PRI allowed a PAN victory in the north, it appeared to be engaging in ballot-rigging and manipulation of the electoral authorities in order to prevent a victory for Cárdenas' party, which had been renamed the Partido de la Revolución Democrática (PRD—Party of the Democratic Revolution), in his home state of Michoacán.

President Salinas had to work with the PAN in the Congreso. He was forced to accept a succession of electoral reform measures—limits were placed on campaign financing and proportional representation was extended in the Cámara Federal de Diputados (Federal Chamber of Deputies). On their own neither measure marked a major watershed in electoral democracy in Mexico, but each brought it a little closer, leaving the Government less bargaining power when negotiating concessions from the opposition. Greater openness encouraged the opposition, and the process of democratization gathered a momentum of its own, no longer under the control of the Government. Meanwhile, the PAN's strategy was to stop questioning the legitimacy of the Government. Instead, it co-operated with Salinas, who had adopted many of the policies that the party had advocated.

Political Instability

President Salinas' neo-liberal policies and the PRI's continued grip on power provoked the emergence of an armed guerrilla group inspired by the revolutionary peasant leader Emiliano Zapata, known as the Ejército Zapatista de Liberación Nacional (EZLN—Zapatista Army of National Liberation). A small but well-organized group, consisting of several hundred indigenous guerrillas, led by the enigmatic 'Subcomandante Marcos', the EZLN briefly assumed control of several municipalities in the southern state of Chiapas on 1 January 1994, the day that Mexico's membership of NAFTA came into force. The modern-day Zapatistas blamed the Government's liberal free-market policies, and NAFTA in particular, for enriching big business and the agricultural industry at the expense of the rural poor.

Another shattering blow to Mexico's image of stability came in March with the assassination of the PRI's presidential candidate, Luis Donaldo Colosio, during a campaign rally in Tijuana. It was the first assassination of a national PRI figure since the killing of President Álvaro Obregón in 1928. Few accepted the official version of events surrounding the killing, which held that a lone gunman was responsible. Following so shortly after the Zapatista uprising, the event raised fears of a breakdown in governance in Mexico. Former education secretary Ernesto Zedillo Ponce de León succeeded Colosio as PRI presidential candidate. Fraud allegations in the 1994 elections were not on the scale of the 1988 ballot, and the vote was considered relatively free and fair, aided by electoral reforms that had recently been put in place.

However, political violence did not subside. Just a month after Zedillo's victory, in September 1994, José Ruiz Massieu, another senior PRI official and former brother-in-law of Salinas, was assassinated. Salinas' brother, Raúl, was subsequently convicted for the murder of Massieu (and for money-laundering on a massive scale), while the victim's own brother and Deputy Attorney-General, Mario Ruiz Massieu, was arrested for obstructing the investigation into the crime. These two crimes were high-profile examples of what many feared was a growing willingness for disputes within élite circles to be settled violently instead of through negotiation. Whoever was behind Colosio's murder (drugs-traffickers and anti-reformist PRI 'dinosaurs' are most often blamed), the fact that the dispute was resolved violently appeared to reflect a breakdown of the system. This was partly ascribed to the new, increasingly liberal economy, which had weakened the basis of authoritarian rule. Many of the state's former assets were now controlled by the private sector (often by close associates of Salinas), reducing the opportunities for patronage and undermining the mechanisms for the peaceful settlement of disputes among élites. An opaque system of authoritarian control was being eroded, but as yet it had not been replaced with a new and transparent democratic order.

The increase in drugs-trafficking activity and the consequent influx of so-called 'narco-dollars' worsened law and order in a country where law enforcement had traditionally been weak or corrupt. Owing to its geography and history of state corruption, Mexico was a conduit for the shipment of cocaine from Colombia to markets in the USA. The opportunities for increased revenues from shipping Colombian cocaine compromised the security forces and state sector further.

ERNESTO ZEDILLO: STABILIZATION AND REFORM

The election of Zedillo to the presidency in 1994 was arguably the first post-authoritarian election in Mexico. Although the PRI continued to enjoy advantages over opposition parties in terms of media coverage, financial resources, state access and organizational strength, there was genuine doubt about the outcome of the ballot, owing to a high rate of participation and greater independent scrutiny of electoral practices.

Zedillo took office in December 1994 and was immediately embroiled in crisis management, lasting into the first half of 1995. Throughout the Salinas presidency an overvalued peso had been maintained to support a political imperative, that of low inflation and a boom in consumer spending. There were few opportunities for a corrective devaluation that would not have had damaging political implications. Salinas had had to consider mid-term elections, state elections and the close US congressional vote on Mexico's entry into NAFTA. In the mean time, Mexico had become highly dependent on short-term, speculative investment from overseas to finance the deficit accumulated under Salinas. Such investment was highly vulnerable to foreign interest rates and political instability, of which there had been no shortage in 1994. With fears of an impending devaluation, many investors switched to US-dollar-denominated short-term treasury bonds (*tesobonos*). When devaluation came on 20 December, the Government found itself unable to meet its US $29,000m. *tesobono* obligations, payable in 1995.

Zedillo's Government was criticized for mishandling the devaluation. Initially, the Government attempted to raise the ceiling at which the peso was traded by 15%, but this merely alarmed investors already nervous with low foreign exchange reserves. Pressure on the peso forced the Government to float it freely against the US dollar. Inflation increased dramatically from 6% to 50%, businesses were forced into bankruptcy and consumers suffered as Mexico descended into deep recession. Many people lost jobs and many more were pushed into poverty. Only international intervention on a massive scale (a US-led rescue package amounting to US $50,000m.) prevented further decline. Zedillo's emergency economic plan involved stricter fiscal and monetary policies and price and wage restraints agreed by business groups and trade unions. With the help of export performance, growth was restored in 1997.

President Zedillo played a significant role in advancing the cause of political reform. In a government system characterized by a divide between the constitutional theory and the informal reality, Zedillo's contribution was not so much in pushing through electoral reform legislation, although among the new rules agreed by the main parties in 1996 was the highly significant establishment of full independence of the federal electoral body. Instead, it was his willingness to step back from using the informal powers at the disposal of the presidency that advanced political reform in Mexico. In doing so he allowed the other institutions and office holders, including municipal mayors, state governors and judges, to realize their potential as alternative sources of power and to begin to accept the accountability that accompanies it. Early in his administration Zedillo appointed an opposition PAN member as Attorney-General, and gave autonomy to the central bank, as part of his vision for greater transparency in public finances. Some saw Zedillo's non-intervention in disputes that previous Presidents would have settled as a sign of weakness. A more generous assessment suggests that Zedillo recognized the need to allow nominally independent institutions to mature, free from interference from the executive.

END OF THE PRI ERA

In the mid-term congressional elections of July 1997, the PRI lost its absolute majority in the lower house for the first time, so beginning the development of the Congreso into a genuine check on executive power. Simultaneously, the PRD's Cuauhtémoc Cárdenas won the mayoral election in the Distrito Federal. Zedillo also agreed to internal reforms to the PRI, allowing party nominations for President to be chosen in primary elections. Zedillo was the first incumbent President to agree to forego his right to nominate the PRI candidate.

In a presidential election held on 2 July 2000, Vicente Fox Quesada, the candidate of the PAN-led Alianza por el Cambio (Alliance for Change), of which the Partido Verde Ecologista de México (PVEM—Green Ecologist Party of Mexico) was also a member, defeated Francisco Labastida Ochoa of the PRI. Fox received 44% of the valid votes cast, while Labastida secured 37%. The result brought 71 years of uninterrupted dominance by the PRI and its predecessor ruling parties to an end. By 2000 some 10 states were controlled by governors belonging to opposition parties.

Vicente Fox was a charismatic agro-industrialist and former President of Coca-Cola México, who had been elected Governor of Guanajuato state in 1995. Fox aimed to apply reforms that he had introduced in Guanajuato state on a national level. Examples included the devolution of powers such as tax collection and responsibility for services to districts and municipalities to encourage local autonomy in a country long accustomed to lobbying for funds from central government. Fox's Government, which took office in December 2000, unlike those of his predecessors, contained secretaries without party affiliations, and from the private sector. Fox himself showed independence from his own party, with which he had an intermittently tense relationship. This approach meant that he was unable automatically to rely on the support of PAN legislators.

VICENTE FOX: FIRST PAN GOVERNMENT

The Alianza por el Cambio formed the largest bloc in the Cámara Federal de Diputados, although its 224 seats fell short of an absolute majority (the PRI secured 209 seats). In the Senado (Senate) the alliance held 51 of the 128 seats, compared with the PRI's 60. Fox was prevented from pursuing a more ambitious agenda because of his minority support in the Congreso and the need to seek consensus with the PRI, still the largest single party in the legislature. In particular, Fox's plans for reform of the labour market and liberalization of the energy sector faced opposition from the Congreso.

While President Fox was experiencing difficulties in implementing his agenda, the Congreso developed significantly from its pliant existence under PRI Governments. In 2001 the legislature blocked two of the Government's key initiatives (on tax reform and indigenous rights). Relations between the executive and the legislature reached a nadir in April 2002, when the Congreso refused permission for President Fox to travel to the USA and Canada—Presidents require congressional permission to travel, but it had never previously been denied. Deputies from the PRI, the PRD and the PVEM were angered at budget cuts and Fox's adversarial approach to Cuba.

In June 2002 the Government published its Programa Nacional de Financiamiento del Desarrollo (Pronafide—National Financing for Development Programme), which outlined its plans for the remainder of its term in office. The main fiscal aim of Pronafide was to reduce the budget deficit and cut the public sector borrowing requirement. It aimed to do this by increasing federal tax revenues, including eradicating certain income tax and value-added tax (VAT) exemptions, as well as increasing state and municipal tax revenues to reduce the federal tax burden; however, attempts to reform the tax system were blocked by the Congreso.

The Fox Government gave new impetus to efforts to improve Mexico's human rights record. In July 2002 the Office of the UN High Commissioner for Human Rights opened an office in Mexico City. Fox had some success in defusing the conflict with the EZLN, although an unresolved stalemate prevailed in Zapatista-dominated areas of Chiapas. The advent of genuine multi-party democracy in recent years has led to much of the support for the EZLN drifting into electoral politics.

The Government's focus on human rights extended into foreign policy. Fox abandoned a policy of non-intervention in foreign affairs that had been pursued for decades by successive PRI Governments. The shift saw Mexico actively promoting human rights and democracy, which, along with closer relations with the USA, led to a deterioration of the historically good relations between Mexico and Cuba. Fox's main foreign-affairs priority was to strengthen relations with Mexico's NAFTA partners, the USA and Canada, while defending the interests of the millions of Mexicans working, legally and illegally, in the USA.

FOX REFORMS STALL

Although presidential elections were not due until 2006, the first signs of unofficial campaigning were placing obstacles in the way of the Government's legislative agenda as early as 2004. President Fox's fiscal proposals to devolve responsibility to the states was frustrated by a failure to forge the necessary consensus in his last year in office. He did succeed in introducing a new fiscal regime for PEMEX, which would pave the way for new investment, and secured passage of a new Federal Law on Budget and Fiscal Responsibility. However, the political parties were entering a long election campaign phase not conducive to cross-party initiatives.

In February 2005 the PRD received an electoral fillip by winning the governorship in the historic PRI stronghold of Guerrero. Political tensions increased in April after the PRI and PAN voted to remove the immunity enjoyed by the PRD mayor of the Distrito Federal, Andrés Manuel López Obrador, who was accused of contempt of court in a 2001 planning dispute. In May all charges against López Obrador were dropped in the face of widespread support for the mayor, a popular figure who was also a leading contender for the PRD's presidential nomination. López Obrador emerged stronger from the episode, while the PAN and the PRI were accused of cynically attempting to remove him from the ballot in 2006 rather than promoting, as both parties claimed, accountability among public officials. López Obrador resigned as mayor in July 2005 to focus on securing the PRD nomination. In September he was formally nominated as the PRD presidential candidate.

Felipe Calderón Hinojosa, a Harvard-trained economist, won the primary election, held in October 2005, for the PAN presidential candidacy. Calderón had served in the Fox administration, as energy secretary, but had resigned in 2004 following a public disagreement with the President over his presidential ambitions. Calderón's ability to distance himself from Fox's administration, which was popularly seen as lacklustre, was important in shoring up his chances in the national election.

PAN NARROWLY WINS CONSECUTIVE TERM

In the presidential election held on 2 July 2006 the PAN's Calderón secured an extremely narrow margin of victory, of just 0.59% (243,934 votes out of almost 42m. cast), over López Obrador. According to official results, Calderón polled 35.89% of the total votes cast, compared with López Obrador's 35.33%. Madrazo, the PRI nominee, trailed in third place with 22.23%, an historic low for the party.

López Obrador did not accept the initial official results, alleging that electoral irregularities undermined their legitimacy and insisting that the votes be recounted. He appealed to his supporters to take to the streets in peaceful protest to put pressure on the electoral authorities; a well-attended rally was held in the capital on 8 July 2006, at which protesters demanded a recount. The close election results were an important test of the autonomy of the Instituto Federal Electoral (IFE—Federal Electoral Institute). Control of the IFE had been removed from the Secretariat of the Interior under President Zedillo, and the IFE had secured an unprecedented degree of popular trust by overseeing the end to the PRI's monopoly on the presidency in 2000. The IFE confirmed the results, and Calderón took office in December 2006. Thereafter, López Obrador's campaign against the results lost support and momentum. Fears that the official election result, with its echoes of Cuauhtémoc Cárdenas's defeat in 1988, would undermine the recent gains in legitimacy and lead to instability and institutional crisis proved unfounded.

In elections to the Congreso, also held on 2 July 2006, the seats were evenly distributed among the three leading parties, ensuring that the new President would encounter an opposition-dominated legislature. The PAN secured 206 of the 500 seats in the Cámara Federal de Diputados, followed by the PRI-led Alianza por México (159 seats) and the PRD's Por el Bien de Todos alliance (122 seats). Of the 128 seats in the Senado, the PAN won 52, the Alianza por México 39 and the Por el Bien de Todos alliance 36. Despite opposition domination of the Congreso, President Calderón achieved some success in building cross-party support, particularly with the PRI, which was more open to co-operation than it had been under President Fox. Calderón's decisions to cut the pay of senior public officials and to deploy 24,000 troops to combat the high level of violence related to drugs-trafficking were popular and helped nurture cross-party support.

THE CALDERÓN PRESIDENCY, 2006–

Calderón had more success than his predecessor in negotiating with the legislature, despite the Congreso being similarly dominated by the opposition. The President succeeded in securing passage of public sector pension reform and fiscal reform in 2007, although the latter was significantly diluted, compared with President Fox's proposals, in not including the introduction of VAT on food and medicine. The concessions required to secure reforms demonstrated the continuing importance of the PRI as the strongest political party in Mexico. Plans to extend reform in, for example, labour and education were not forthcoming as coalition-building efforts in the Congreso were impeded by campaigning for mid-term congressional elections, held in July 2009. Despite hopes that the emergency measures introduced by President Calderón to fight an epidemic of the H1N1 virus ('swine flu') had shored up support for the governing PAN, thus offsetting the negative effects of the contraction in economic growth and rising unemployment to the party's popularity, the PAN suffered a heavy defeat at the mid-term polls on 5 July. The PAN had attempted to shift the emphasis on campaign issues away from the economy towards security, accusing the PRI of failing to provide sufficient support for Calderón in his efforts to fight drugs cartels. Nevertheless, the PAN's representation in the Cámara Federal de Diputados declined from 206 to 143 seats, while the PRI increased its number of deputies to 237. Added to the 21 seats held by its ally, the PVEM, this meant that the PRI enjoyed an absolute majority in the lower house. The Congreso therefore threatened to pose a greater obstacle to the President's legislative programme in the second half of his term than in the first. The PAN's failure to retain at least one-third of seats in July also raised the prospect of opposition parties uniting to overturn the presidential veto, and the scale of its defeat prompted the resignation of the party President, Germán Martínez Cazares; he was replaced by José César Nava Vázquez.

Popular disillusion with the PAN and the Calderón Government ensured that the PRI had the highest approval ratings in opinion polls during mid-2010. Gubernatorial, state and municipal elections were held in 14 states in July of that year. While the PRI secured the largest proportion of the popular vote, the gubernatorial elections suggested that the party's resurgence had to a degree been curbed. Despite retaining six governorships and gaining a further three from the PAN, the PRI lost the governship in Puebla (to the PAN) and in the states of Oaxaca and Sinaloa (to an electoral alliance of the PAN and the PRD). Oaxaca was formerly a PRI stronghold, but the party lost support after the Governor, Ulises Ruíz, was implicated in corruption charges and accused of employing violent tactics to suppress protests in 2006. The success of the PAN-PRD coalition prompted considerable speculation regarding the possibility of the two parties forging a national alliance to contest the presidential election scheduled to be held in 2012.

Escalating levels of drugs-related violence presented a significant challenge to Calderón. The activities of drugs-traffickers had increased in recent years to threaten not only public security but also the integrity of state institutions. Calderón made his strategy to combat drugs-traffickers a centrepiece of his Government. His decision to employ the army in anti-drugs operations was popular, but showed few tangible signs of success. According to official estimates, there were approximately 23,000 drugs-related killings between 2006 and 2009, with the annual rate increasing each year. Among the fatalities in 2010 was Rodolfo Torre Cantú, the PRI candidate for the governorship of Tamaulipas; Torre Cantú, who had pledged to combat drugs-trafficking, was fatally shot during a campaign event. His assassination, widely believed to have been carried out by members of a local drugs cartel, was the most high-profile murder since that of presidential candidate Luis Donaldo Colosio in 1994. In May 2010 US President Barack Obama announced that that an additional 1,200 National Guard troops were to be deployed along the Mexican border and requested additional funds from the US Congress to reinforce border security.

Economy

SANDY MARKWICK

Mexico occupies an area of 1.96m. sq km (758,449 sq miles), sharing a 3,152 km-long border with the USA in the north and bounded by Guatemala and Belize to the south. The Gulf of Mexico and the Caribbean Sea lie to the east, and the Pacific Ocean and the Sea of Cortés (Gulf of California) to the west. The climate and topography are extremely varied: the tropical southern region and coastal lowlands are hot and wet, while the highlands of the centre are temperate and much of the north and west is arid desert. Although conditions are not ideally suited to agriculture, Mexico is among the world's leading producers of a number of crops. By contrast, the country's forestry and fishing resources are underdeveloped. Extensive mineral potential also remains largely unrealized, although this does not apply to petroleum reserves, extraction of which began at the start of the 20th century and accelerated in the 1970s, following important discoveries.

The population of Mexico was an estimated 108.5m. in mid-2010, making it the world's 11th most populous country. A population growth rate of less than 1.0% per year is significantly lower than in recent decades, reflecting improving education and health care. The economy became increasingly industrialized in the second half of the 20th century. Successive governments encouraged this trend with fiscal incentives and protection against imports. Supported by high government spending, considerable overseas investment and massive foreign borrowing, as well as by petroleum discoveries and increases in petroleum prices, the Mexican economy grew by over 6% per year, on average, during 1958–82. However, rapid growth was accompanied by high fiscal deficits, a rising rate of inflation and increasing trade deficits. By 1982 Mexico's external debt totalled US $90,000m. Domestic investors, concerned about the Government's ability to manage the economy, withdrew massive amounts of capital from the country. With its foreign exchange reserves all but exhausted, Mexico was forced to suspend debt-servicing payments. In late 1982 the incoming Government of President Miguel de la Madrid Hurtado was forced to implement austerity measures in order to secure the much-needed support of multilateral lending agencies and thus reschedule the debt. In 1983–88 consumer prices increased by almost 4,000%, while annual gross domestic product (GDP) growth averaged just 0.1%.

The Government of President Carlos Salinas de Gortari (1988–94) continued and advanced the structural adjustment process. Deregulation loosened the constraints on market forces, encouraged foreign investment and reduced the role of the state in numerous sectors of the economy with the sale of state interests to the private sector. In 1992 import licences were required for fewer than 2% of all imports, while the average tariff was 11%, compared with 13% in 1986. Part of President Salinas' motives for trade liberalization were political: cheaper consumer imports restored the support of a significant proportion of the middle classes who had abandoned the ruling Partido Revolucionario Institucional (PRI—Institutional Revolutionary Party) in 1988. Trade liberalization was consolidated when the North American Free Trade Agreement (NAFTA) between Mexico, the USA and Canada came into effect in January 1994. Trade liberalization and an exchange rate band system succeeded in reducing inflation from 114% in 1988 to around 7% in December 1994, when Ernesto Zedillo Ponce de León assumed the presidency. The economy appeared stronger, partly because of a broadening of the tax base and more efficient tax collection, but also because of wage and price restraints, which were the result of a pact with labour and business leaders. Another reason for the economic improvement was a reduction in domestic interest rates. The country's admittance into the Organisation for Economic Co-operation and Development (OECD) in June 1994 was intended to have a similar effect to that of admittance into NAFTA, by committing the Mexican economy to a free market programme and ensuring that capital receipts remained substantial. Encouraged by the new regulatory environment, foreign direct investment increased to US $8,000m. by 1994.

However, President Salinas' economic successes were based on an exchange rate policy that, ultimately, proved unsustainable. The rate at which the peso was traded with the US dollar was allowed to 'float' (i.e., be made freely convertible) within a band, the floor of which was fixed at 3.0562 pesos to US $1, while the ceiling depreciated daily. Salinas maintained this policy in spite of peso appreciation in real terms, rapidly increasing balance of payments problems and a current account deficit that had risen to $29,662m. in 1994 (almost 8% of GDP). To cover the current account shortfall, the Government maintained real interest rates in order to continue to attract capital inflows, which were under threat because of fears of political instability in Mexico and higher interest rates in the USA. In 1994 dollar-linked bonds, *tesobonos*, were introduced to strengthen inflows. The capital account deficit was largely financed by volatile, speculative portfolio inflows. Domestic political instability resulted in a loss of confidence in the currency during 1994. There was a massive withdrawal of investment funds, and a rapid depletion of foreign exchange reserves, from $24,886m. at the end of 1993 to $6,101m. one year later.

Overvaluation of the peso led to a devaluation crisis within just three weeks of President Zedillo assuming power in December 1994. With foreign reserves low, the Government opted for a limited devaluation by lifting the exchange band ceiling to 4.10 pesos to US $1, but this failed to ease pressure on the peso. Two days later the Government allowed the peso to float freely. At the end of 1994 there were 5.33 pesos to $1, and the currency continued to weaken in 1995. Investor nervousness was exacerbated by the Government's delay in producing a credible plan to control devaluation. The crisis led to fears that the Government would be unable to repay $29,000m. of short-term *tesobono* debt due in early 1995 and that the banking system would collapse because of increases in external debt-servicing costs.

In late January 1995 the US Government's announcement of a rescue programme successfully prevented a default on debt payments and supported the Mexican economy until it could develop firmer foundations. The US Government pledged US $20,000m., while the Bank for International Settlements and the IMF agreed to extend a further $17,800m. Other financial institutions also agreed credit facilities. This rescue programme, the largest since the US Marshall Plan (European Reconstruction Program) to aid Europe following the Second World War, was agreed after the Zedillo administration committed itself to emergency stabilization measures, consisting of strict control of the money supply, reductions in public spending in order to create a public sector surplus, increased taxes and wage constraints. The Government maintained its priority of reducing inflation by means of strict monetary policies.

The austerity measures succeeded in improving the balance of payments, but the Mexican economy entered a deep recession, contracting by 6.2% in 1995. The annual rate of inflation increased to 35.0% in 1995. The Government continued its strict monetary policies into 1996, to re-establish credibility and to regain the confidence of the financial markets and the IMF. Mexico began refinancing its public sector external debt, which had increased by US $15,636m. in 1995, to $95,167m. The successful issue of a floating rate note supported by petroleum exports helped to raise $7,000m. towards repaying the US Treasury. Mexico was able to resume borrowing in international financial markets in June 1996.

The economy began to recover in 1996, led by the manufacturing, construction, mining, communications and transport sectors. A trade deficit of US $18,464m. in 1994 became a surplus of $7,089m. in 1995. Mexico maintained a trade surplus until mid-1997. Thereafter it registered consistent deficits as imports accompanied growth and consumer demand. Inflation fell to 15.9% in 1998. After consumer prices increased by 16.6% in 1999, annual inflation declined to 3.8% in 2007. Central bank independence underpinned macroeconomic stability during a year of political uncertainty when a new Government assumed office at the end of 2006, following disputed elections in July. The central bank's annual inflation target range of 2%–4% was set in 2003; in May 2010 annual inflation of 3.9% was recorded. Historically low inflation was supported by lower domestic demand and commodity prices. Additionally, expectations of stable or slowing price increases created a virtuous circle by leading to reduced wage demands. President Zedillo adhered to prudent monetary and fiscal policies throughout his term in office. Public spending was restricted to meet budget targets, and foreign exchange reserves were restored, increasing to $44,384m. in 2001. The current account deficit doubled from 1997 to 1998, declined slightly in 1999, but increased in 2000, fuelled by interest payments on public debt. However, as a proportion of GDP, the deficit was not a cause for alarm. The current account deficit fell after 2000 (see below).

GDP growth slowed to 3.7% in 1999, principally owing to turmoil in Asian markets and currency devaluations in Brazil and Russia, although Mexico benefited from sustained demand from the USA. Strong growth, of 6.6%, was restored in 2000, led by commerce, restaurants and hotels, and again by the transport and communications sector. Fears of traditional fiscal indiscipline on the part of the incumbent Government in an election year proved unfounded, helped partly by the autonomy of the central bank. The new President, Vicente Fox Quesada, was the first head of state to come from outside the traditional ruling PRI. While this marked a watershed in modern Mexican history, the implications for immediate economic policy were few. President Fox, from the conservative Partido Acción Nacional (PAN—National Action Party), renewed the Government's broad commitment to macroeconomic orthodoxy and free market reform. Following strong growth in 2000, GDP contracted in 2001 by an estimated 0.2%, largely owing to reduced demand from the USA, leading to a significant fall in export revenues, as well as lower investment and public spending. Growth was restored in 2002, but remained sluggish, at an overall 0.8%. Sectoral performance was very uneven, with agriculture, mining, manufacturing and commerce still in recession. Exports were the main source of growth in the economy. The economy grew by an average of 3.3% in 2003–07. Output was closely linked to cycles in the US economy. Generally, growth after 2003 was broad-based, stemming from private consumption and investment as well as exports. Declining demand and reduced investment resulted in the rate of growth falling to 1.5% in 2008. Output began contracting in the third quarter of 2008 as a result of recession in the USA and this trend continued into 2009. According to preliminary data, output declined by 6.5% in 2009; GDP stood at US $874,902m. in 2009. Structural reforms to improve education and training, reduce bureaucratic obstacles to business and increase labour market flexibility were widely identified as necessary to raise long-term productivity.

Mexico remained vulnerable to external conditions, particularly to changes in interest and growth rates in the USA, the source of most of the country's trade and investment. The structural reforms of the 1980s caused widespread social hardship, which persisted at the beginning of the 21st century. Nevertheless, Mexico had among the highest levels of poverty and inequality in the OECD. Extreme poverty is concentrated in the rural south.

Job creation accompanied economic recovery in the late 1990s, but underemployment remained a significant issue. As Mexico's population was predominantly a young one—about one-third of the population was under 14 years of age in 2008—the labour market came under intense pressure to absorb new additions to the work-force each year. The fact that the economy consistently did not achieve adequate growth rates for more than a decade was reflected in high unemployment rates and the existence of a thriving informal economy.

The official rate of unemployment averaged 5.5% in 2009, up from 4.0% in 2008. Official unemployment figures concealed the problem of underemployment. An estimated 28.2% of the employed population earned a living in the informal sector.

AGRICULTURE, LIVESTOCK, FORESTRY AND FISHING

Mexico's topography and wide variation of climates restrict the area that could be cultivated to about 21% of its total territory. A total of 27.0% of the country was desert or scrubland, 17.6% was natural forest or jungle, while 14.0% was pasture and 15.8% arable, including managed forestry. In May 2010 the agricultural sector (including livestock, forestry and fishing) engaged 13.4% of the employed work-force. Agriculture accounted for 3.8% of GDP in 2009, compared with 20% in 1950. The decline in its share of GDP was largely a result of post-Second World War industrialization, but it also reflected low growth rates. According to the World Bank, in 1996–2006 the sector achieved an average growth rate of 1.8% per year, in real terms. The sector came out of a recession in 2005 and rebounded with growth of 6.3% in 2006. Agricultural output grew by 1.8% in 2009, following growth of 1.2% in 2008.

Decapitalization, inadequate transport facilities, low international prices, adverse weather conditions and unpaid debts all adversely affected the sector. One fundamental problem was the *ejido* land-holding system, arising from the agrarian reforms of the 1930s, which allowed for individual plots to be cultivated on communally owned land. There was no provision for the individual plots to be sold or leased, although they could be passed on to descendants. In 1992 the Government amended the Constitution in order to allow *ejido* land to be rented or sold, or to be used as collateral security for raising finance. Despite these changes, the land remained uneconomically fragmented.

Other impediments to agricultural growth were trade liberalization and the decrease in subsidies, indebtedness made worse by devaluation and high interest rates. In 1995 President Zedillo introduced a programme of direct cash subsidies for the agricultural sector and followed this with measures designed to stimulate output, including debt-rescheduling for producers and increases in financing and credit from state agencies.

Increased competition from producers in the USA and Canada also placed pressure on the sector. On 1 January 2003 tariffs were lifted on trade in agricultural products representing some 30% of agricultural imports, in accordance with progressive liberalization under NAFTA. While devaluation resulted in a rare surplus being achieved in 1995, Mexico regularly recorded trade deficits in agricultural products. In 2009 the trade deficit for the agriculture and fisheries sector declined to US $813m., from some $3,943m. in 2008, as static exports in the sector were offset by a 27.3% decline in imports.

Sugar cane and maize were the principal crops in terms of the value of harvest. Mexico has produced a stable average annual supply of more than 40.0m. metric tons of sugar cane since the mid-1990s; output in 2008 stood at 51.1m. tons. Annual maize production averaged around 20m. tons, occupying 33.4% of harvested land; output was estimated at 24.3m. tons in 2008. Production of other staples in 2008 included sorghum (6.6m. tons), wheat (4.0m. tons), tomatoes (2.9m.), green chillies (2.1m.) and dry beans (1.1m. tons). Barley, rice and soya beans were also grown. Coffee was the most valuable export crop until 1998, when production in the main coffee-growing state of Chiapas was adversely affected by extensive flooding associated with the El Niño weather phenomenon (a warm ocean current that appears periodically in the Pacific). Coffee production thereafter fluctuated, and stood at 1.4m. tons in 2008. Coffee was surpassed by tomatoes, peppers, melon and avocado in terms of export revenues. Production volumes of tobacco also fluctuated in response to weather conditions. Sales of fruit and vegetables increased substantially in the first half of the 1990s, earning some $2,251.3m. in 1995, compared with $935m. in 1988. The increase came about mainly owing to an expansion in exports to the USA. Mexico's fruit and vegetable production included citrus fruits, strawberries, mangoes, apples, pears, melons, pineapples, chillies and tomatoes.

In the livestock sub-sector, cattle-rearing was the most important activity. Total meat production, including poultry, amounted to some 5.5m. metric tons in 2008. Production of cows' milk steadily increased from the late 1980s and reached an estimated 10.8m. litres in 2008. From the 1980s there was a sharp increase in poultry stocks, which was reflected in greater production of chicken meat (roughly 2.6m. tons in 2008, compared with 399,200 tons in 1980) and eggs (2.3m. tons in 2008, compared with 644,400 in 1980). The contribution of agricultural produce to total export revenues declined steadily after 1995, when revenues of US $4,016m. represented 5.0% of total export revenues. Agricultural exports were valued at $7,916m. in 2008, equivalent to 2.7% of total export revenues.

Neither the transport infrastructure nor the landownership system encouraged long-term investment in forestry. Exploitation depleted Mexico's forested land at an average annual rate of 1.4% in 1981–90. The sector faced further damage to output from poor planning and the lack of infrastructure for effectively tackling the regular problems of El Niño and forest fires. In 2001 the Government established the Comisión Nacional Forestal (CONAFOR—National Forestry Commission) to encourage sustainable development of the forestry sector.

Although it has long Caribbean and Pacific coastlines and extensive inland waters, in the 21st century Mexico had yet to develop a modern fishing industry of any real importance. The annual catch increased gradually until 2003, when it stood at an estimated 1.6m. metric tons. The annual catch was 1.6m. tons in 2008. Leading varieties of fish caught were Californian pilchard (sardines), shrimp, tuna (tunny), squid and mojarra. Exports of fish (including shellfish) earned just US $799.3m. in 2008, up from $692.8m. in 2007.

MINING AND POWER

Petroleum was traditionally by far the most important product of the extractive sector. Mexico was one of the world's largest crude oil-producing countries, and the state oil monopoly, Petróleos Mexicanos (PEMEX), was one of the largest oil companies in the world. However, towards the end of the 20th century its contribution to the Mexican economy declined as world petroleum prices fell. Between 1986 and 1998 petroleum export revenues declined by an estimated 61%, from the equivalent of 5.7% of GDP to just 1.7%. In 1990 petroleum accounted for 35.6% of export earnings. Earnings from petroleum increased after 1999, when total earnings were US $9,605m., as a result of dramatic increases in the oil price. Having declined to their lowest level in two decades in December 1998, at $7.67 per barrel (/b), prices for Mexican crude reached $29.27/b in March 2000; however, prices declined in 2001, to as low as $12/b in December. Another price recovery led to a 13.1% increase in output in 2002 and exports of $14,266m. (8.9% of the value of total exports). Higher prices for Mexican crude, which rose each year during 2001–08, led to further growth in export earnings and enhanced their importance in relation to total exports. In 2001 crude oil exports were valued at $11,928m. (7.5% of total exports). In 2009 Mexico earned $25,666m. from crude oil exports, equivalent to 11.2% of total exports, down from a record $43,324m. (14.9% of total exports) in 2008. Record revenues in 2008 materialized despite lower production and export volumes owing to a 36.9% increase in the average price of Mexican crude to $84.35/b from $61.62/b in 2007. Prices began to fall in October 2008, reaching $33.70/b, a four-year low, in December. The average price in 2009 was an estimated $57.56/b.

Despite the importance of oil to the economy and the monopoly exercised by PEMEX, the company faced financial losses that prevented it from pursuing further investment in exploration and development, which was necessary to maintain current production levels. The tax burden imposed on PEMEX by the Government represented an obstacle to achieving profitability. Although the company recorded its first net profit for a decade in 2006, PEMEX paid 50.2% of its total income as tax in 2009, leading to a net loss of $7,249m. Petroleum production (and liquid gas equivalent) increased from 2.62m. barrels per day (b/d) in 1995 to a record 3.38m. b/d in 2004, a marginal increase over 2003 output. Production decreased steadily to 2.6m. b/d in 2009, reflecting reduced output from the Cantarell oilfield (down 31% in 2008), the largest field in terms of output in Mexico. A decline in proven reserves at Cantarell was set to continue highlighting the need for new investment in exploration. A large, protracted oil leak during offshore drilling by BP in the Gulf of Mexico in 2010 jeopardized the future of oil exploration in the area, the site of most of Mexico's reserves. Although PEMEX enjoyed a monopoly on petroleum production, foreign petroleum companies did operate under service contracts with PEMEX, while US and Canadian concerns had the opportunity to enter into 'performance' contracts with the company. Plans to sell petrochemicals assets proceeded slowly, owing to investor concern and domestic opposition to privatization. According to PEMEX, Mexico's proven hydrocarbons reserves stood at 13,990m. barrels (and equivalent) at the beginning of 2010, a decline over previous years owing, in part, to a change in measuring criteria, but also to a failure of new discoveries to keep pace with extraction. Crude oil represented 74% of proven reserves, with the remainder made up of natural gas. Daily output of natural gas has grown steadily since 2003 when rule changes allowed private participation in gas exploration and production. Daily output averaged 4,423m. cu ft in 2002 but had increased substantially to 7,031m. cu ft by 2009. The first private contracts applied to the Burgos Basin off the north-eastern coast. Despite increased production, output was not sufficient to meet domestic demand. The cost of imported dry gas amounted to $1,424m. in 2008.

Apart from petroleum, Mexico produced an impressive amount of other minerals. It was the largest producer of silver in the world, and was also a leading source of fluorite, celestite and sodium sulphate, as well as bismuth, graphite, antimony, arsenic, barite, sulphur and copper. It also produced iron ore, lead, zinc and coal. However, despite the wealth of resources, the mining sector was not a major force in the economy. In 2009 mining contributed 5.4% of total GDP.

Unlike mining, the utilities sector (electricity, gas and water) expanded relatively rapidly in the 1990s, outstripping GDP growth. Utilities averaged annual growth of 2.0% in 2000–05. The sector contributed 1.4% of GDP in 2009. Electricity production rose steadily, doubling in output between 1987 and 2000. Mexico generated 286,739m. kWh in 2009. Of Mexico's installed capacity of electric power, 68.0% came from thermal plants, fuelled by oil, gas or both, including private sector production, 22.0% from hydroelectric plants, 5.0% from coal-fired plants, 1.9% from geothermal plants and 2.6% from the Laguna Verde nuclear power station. National distribution of electricity was uneven. In March 2003 the state-owned power utility, Comisión Federal de Electricidad (CFE), awarded a contract to build the El Cajón hydroelectric plant to a consortium led by ICA, Mexico's largest construction company. The plant in Nayarit state, which began operations in June 2007, increased generating capacity by 750 MW. As a response to the challenge of expanding output to meet rising demand, from the late 1980s the Government gradually increased the opportunities for private enterprise, including foreign competition, both to collaborate with the CFE in installing new plants, and to produce power on its own account. However, political opposition delayed the introduction of comprehensive measures to increase private sector involvement in the electricity industry.

MANUFACTURING

The manufacturing sector began to be developed after the Second World War, and for four decades it enjoyed a considerable degree of protection from outside competition. However, from the 1980s trade barriers were dismantled. The results were mixed. Manufacturing exports grew quite strongly, but many sectors were unable to meet the challenge of competition in either the export or the domestic market. This was particularly the case with small and medium-sized enterprises, which accounted for the majority of manufacturing businesses and for more than 90% of official employment in the sector. Metal products, machinery and equipment was one of the most important manufacturing sub-sectors and grew at an average annual rate of 10.3% in 1995–2000; the sub-sector was led by the automotive industry, which expanded rapidly from the mid-1990s as transnational corporations established operations in Mexico, in order to take advantage of growth in the Mexican market and of the provisions of NAFTA. Manufacturing contributed 16.7% of GDP in 2009, when the sector generated 82.5% of total export earnings. The manufacturing sector recovered from three years of recession in 2004, recording annual growth of 4.0% in that year. Recovery stemmed from increased US import demand, particularly for machinery and equipment, metals, non-metallic minerals, and wood products. Growth averaged 2.9% during 2005–07, slower than the comparable rate of growth for the economy as a whole. The global economic downturn in 2008, and particularly lower demand from the USA, led to a contraction in manufacturing output of 0.4% during the year. The poor manufacturing performance continued into 2009, with output declining by 10.2% during the year. The decline in sectoral output was most severe in the equipment sub-sector, particularly transportation equipment (down 26.8%), machinery and equipment (down 20.1%), basic metals (down 19.5%) and electronics (down 18.7%). Drinks and tobacco was the only manufacturing sub-sector to record positive growth, of just 0.4%, in 2009.

The most important manufacturing branch in 2008, in terms of its contribution to sectoral GDP and employment, was food products, which accounted for 24.0% of manufacturing output. Key industries drew on domestically produced raw materials, including grain-milling and bakeries, sugar-processing, fruit-and-vegetable-processing, cigarettes, and beers and spirits. Transport equipment manufacturing was the next most important sub-sector, accounting for 14.4% of manufacturing output in 2008. The chemicals industry (10.8% of manufacturing GDP in 2009) was another major sub-sector, of which the petrochemicals division was a particularly dynamic component, but which also encompassed plastics, rubber and pharmaceuticals. One of the main traditional industrial activities was textiles and clothing, developed following the success of locally grown cotton and, later, of petroleum resources. In fact, in the 1990s synthetic fibres output far exceeded that of natural fibres. The industry traditionally had a significant export market, but the domestically orientated segment had suffered considerably from import competition.

Mexico had a significant iron and steel industry, which was privatized in 1989, after which production increased above overall rates of GDP, while the work-force was reduced by 40%. In 2009 Mexico produced an estimated 14.0m. metric tons of steel, down from 17.2m. tons in 2008. There was concern that Mexico's reserves of iron ore would last only a further 25 years at existing rates of steel production.

Mexico also developed silver-, copper-, lead-, zinc- and tin-processing facilities, while non-metallic mineral resources provided the basis for glass and cement industries. Mexico was one of the world's largest manufacturers of cement. The other main industrial activities were paper, printing and publishing, and wood and cork manufactures.

In 1965 the Government began to plan a *maquila* (assembly plant) industry, allowing temporary imports of inputs (parts), which were then assembled for duty-free exports. The provisions initially only covered the northern border areas, but were later extended to the whole country. This sector, which took advantage of Mexico's low wage rates, prospered from the early 1980s. The main activities with which the *maquila* industries were concerned were electrical and electronic machinery and equipment, transport equipment and textiles. The sector generated an appreciable amount of foreign exchange; however, as the sector was orientated towards the processing of imported inputs from the USA, earnings were offset by considerable costs.

The construction industry contracted by 7.5% in 2009, following slow growth in 2008 and growth averaging 5.4% in 2005–07, aided by a combination of public sector investment in house-building and infrastructure, low interest rates and a wider availability of mortgages. The sector contributed 6.4% of GDP in 2009 and employed 8.1% of the active labour force in May of that year.

TRANSPORT AND COMMUNICATIONS

Road transport was the chief means of conveying passengers and freight in Mexico. In 2009 there were 366,341 km (228,963 miles) of roads in the total network, of which 36.3% were paved. In order to support the development of the export trade and to spread the benefits of economic growth more evenly, the Government pursued extensive road-building projects in the 1990s and attempted to encourage private sector involvement by granting concessionaires the right to build, maintain and collect the fees from toll roads. In July 2007 the Government announced a Highways Programme in which it pledged to improve 17,500 km of federal highways in order to bolster trade, in addition to investing in rural roads to combat the marginalization of communities in the countryside.

The railway system, covering 26,717 km in 2009, was owned by the state-owned Ferrocarriles Nacionales de México until 2001, when it was sold. Inadequate investment had resulted in the deterioration of the service, with the volume of freight traffic decreasing by 13% between 1986 and 1992, to 49.8m. metric tons, before recovering to 80.4m. tons by 1999. Freight traffic totalled 70,010m. tons in 2007. Passenger numbers decreased after the mid-1980s into the early 2000s. However, new investment halted the decline, and passenger travel rose significantly from 73m. passenger-kms in 2005 to 399m. in 2010; meanwhile, the total number of passengers carried in 2007 stood at 288,000. The Government had slowly opened the railway system to private sector involvement as it prepared to link the Mexican system with that of the USA and Canada, under NAFTA. In July 2007 the Government pledged new investment, both public and private, to upgrade railways.

In the early 1990s US $700m. was spent on port development, much of it from the private sector. The need for port facilities to meet international standards induced the Government to transport the management of key ports to the private sector in the mid-1990s. Plans were underway to expand capacity at the ports of Manzanillo, on the Pacific coast, Veracruz, in the Gulf of Mexico, and Puerto Morelos, in the Caribbean, as part of a infrastructure investment programme announced by President Felipe Calderón Hinojosa.

Mexico boasts one of the largest networks of airports in the world, with nearly every town or city of over 50,000 inhabitants having its own airport. In 2009 there were 61 international airports. There were numerous national air companies, of which the formerly state-owned Aerovías de México (Aeroméxico) and Compañía Mexicana de Aviación, SA de CV (Mexicana) were the two largest and together controlled a majority of the domestic market. Their share was eroded after 2005 following the emergence of a competitive low-cost airline sector. The Government also planned to allow the private sector to build and operate airports on 50-year renewable contracts. In December 1998 a consortium including Danish, French and Spanish investors successfully bid in the first auction for the management of airports, gaining control of nine southern airports, including Cancún. In August 1999 Mexican and Spanish investors won control of Pacific coast airports, including Guadalajara and Tijuana. A new terminal at Mexico City's Benito Juárez airport became fully operational in 2009, but the airport was still considered by many to be inadequate for the city's needs. Plans to build a second airport outside the city were abandoned by the administration of former President Vicente Fox in response to violent protests.

The state-owned telephone company, Teléfonos de México, SA de CV (Telmex), was privatized in 1990. The number of telephone lines increased from 5.4m. in 1990 to an estimated 20.8m. in 2009. Growth in fixed lines was static after 2005. Further liberalization opened long-distance and cellular services to competition in 1996. In 1997 Telmex received a provisional licence to provide services in the USA, in conjunction with US telecommunications company Sprint. The local market was opened to competition in 1998. However, Mexico and the USA were in dispute over interconnection fees in a market dominated by Telmex. In 2004 the World Trade Organization ruled that Telmex was abusing its dominant position in the market by overcharging companies and consumers. Among mobile cellular telephone operators, América Móvil, operating under the brandname Telcel, was the largest. América Móvil was spun off from Telmex in 2001, but in February 2010 the Comision Federal de Competencia (CFC—Federal Competition Commission) approved the acquisition by América Móvil of its former parent company. Telcel's principal competitor was movistar, owned by Spain's Telefónica group. In 2009 there were 74.2 mobile phone users per 100 inhabitants, up from 36.3 in 2004.

TOURISM

Tourism was an important foreign exchange earner. Mexico recorded net surplus revenue flows from international travel (including tourism and business visitors) of US $4,143m. in 2009. The surplus represented a marked increase from that of just $7m. in 1990, but was slightly down on that recorded in 2008. There were an estimated 86.2m. visits from abroad in 2009 (down by 5.8% on 2008), mainly from the USA and Canada. The year-on-year decline was attributable to the global economic downturn, coupled with an outbreak of a 'swine flu' (the H1N1 virus) pandemic in April 2009, that began in Mexico. Significant travel by Mexicans abroad reduced the beneficial effects of overseas visitors' contribution to Mexico's 'invisible earnings' account. Mexico's attractions range from beach resorts such as Acapulco and Bahías de Huatulco on the Pacific coast and Cancún on the Caribbean coast, to a number of pre-Columbian sites including Teotihuacan and Chichén Itzá, as well as various colonial cities. A significant category of both inbound and outbound tourism was the cross-border day trip. From the late 1980s the Government made a concerted effort to encourage deregulation of the civil aviation market, while investment rules were liberalized for domestic and foreign investors alike.

FINANCE

The financial sector underwent dramatic changes from the early 1980s. In 1982 the Government nationalized the banking sector in an attempt to help overcome the debt crisis. A process of rationalization ensued, with a reduction in the number of commercial banks from 58 to 18. They were reprivatized in 1991–92, and were generally sold for a high price, reflecting their profitability. However, operating systems had become cumbersome and outmoded and the new owners had to invest in modernization.

An added incentive to increase the banking sector's competitiveness came in 1993, when the Government began to authorize the establishment of new domestic banks. Following the ratification of NAFTA in 1994, US and Canadian banks were allowed access to the Mexican financial sector, albeit with certain restrictions. Financial services sectoral GDP declined by 1.2% in 2009 after averaging annual growth of 18.71% in 2005–08. Financial services contributed 4.6% of GDP in 2009, up from 2.6% in 2003.

The object of the financial sector reforms was both to increase domestic savings and to reduce borrowing costs. Before the bank privatizations began, the rules on lending had been relaxed. This, combined with success in reducing the fiscal deficit, lowered interest rates from 95% in 1987 to 14% by the end of 1993. In April 1994 interest rates in particular, and the setting of monetary policy in general, became the preserve of an autonomous central bank, Banco de México (BANXICO), in the expectation that this was the most effective way to achieve price stability. The Government intervened to support ailing commercial banks and to prevent a collapse in the banking sector owing to 'bad' debts, which multiplied following devaluation in late 1994.

The Government established the Fondo Bancario de Protección al Ahorro (Fobaproa—Banking Fund for the Protection of Savings) to assume bad banking debts in exchange for new capital injections from shareholders. By late 1999 Fobaproa had absorbed US $89,000m. of liabilities, of which only an estimated 20% of the value would be recovered. After much debate in the Congreso, in 1999 a new agency was approved, the Instituto de Protección al Ahorro Bancario (IPAB—Bank Savings Protection Institute). IPAB continued to prop up bankrupt banks, notably the third largest bank, Banca Serfin, which it sold to Banco Santander Central Hispano of Spain in May 2000. IPAB also introduced new insurance quotas for banks to cover deposits and auctioned the rights to manage and recover loans accumulated by Fobaproa.

FOREIGN TRADE AND THE BALANCE OF PAYMENTS

The economic adjustments made necessary by the debt crisis of the 1980s led to a distinct improvement in the foreign trade balance, with surpluses being recorded each year during 1982–89. However, from 1990 the balance of trade was in deficit once again. Trade liberalization measures and a foreign exchange policy that tended to allow the peso to become over-valued were partly to blame, as were the recovery in domestic growth rates and weak commodity prices. Following devaluation of the peso in 1994, exports performed better than imports, and a trade surplus of US $6,531m. was recorded in 1996; however in 1997 the surplus declined dramatically to $623m., as the growth in non-petroleum exports stimulated demand for imports of intermediate goods. While the value of exports increased by 22% in 1996–98, the value of imports increased by 40% over the same period, resulting in the trade balance falling into deficit in 1998. Thereafter the deficit increased to $9,955m. in 2001 and remained significant subsequently, fluctuating in line with oil prices and import demand. In 2007 growth of imports outpaced export growth to widen the deficit further to $11,189m., despite the higher oil price. The trend continued into 2008 with the deficit widening to $17,261m. The high price of oil had the effect of increasing the price of intermediate goods imports, offsetting oil export growth. Capital imports were driven by growth in public investment, while domestic demand fuelled consumer imports. However, in 2009 the trade deficit narrowed significantly to $4,677m. as a global economic slowdown reduced overall trade and particularly depressed imports.

Petroleum was traditionally the most important export, but it was surpassed in the mid-1990s by manufactures. Crude petroleum and petroleum products accounted for just 13.4% of the value of total exports in 2009, compared with 82.5% for manufactures (including *maquila* manufactures). Agriculture (including livestock, forestry and fisheries) represented 3.4% of total exports in 2009, down from 5.0% in 1995.

Imports consisted mainly of intermediate products required by the manufacturing sector. In 2009 these products totalled US $170,912m., or 72.9% of total imports. Imports of capital goods, which rose during the 1990s to support the increase in investment activity, amounted to $30,645m. in 2009, equivalent to 13.1% of total imports. Imports of consumer goods represented the remaining 14.0% of imports, valued at $32,828m.

The vast majority of Mexico's foreign trade was, unsurprisingly, with the USA, a pattern that was reinforced by NAFTA. In 2009 the USA was the destination for an estimated 84.1% of Mexico's exports and the origin of 51.1% of imports. In 1997 Mexico displaced Japan as the USA's second most important trading partner. The second largest single export market for Mexican goods was Canada, which received 3.6% of exports in 2009, followed by Germany (1.4%). The next largest source of imports after the USA was the People's Republic of China, accounting for 13.9% in 2009, followed by Japan (4.9%) and the Republic of Korea (4.7%). The largest European source of imports was Germany, which provided 4.2% of total imports in 2009. Although NAFTA would also forge trade flows with Canada, the Mexican Government endeavoured to prevent excessive dependence on its northern neighbours. To this end it entered into free trade agreements with Bolivia, Chile, Colombia, Costa Rica and Venezuela, and also sought to foster closer trading relations with countries outside Latin America.

As well as a trade deficit, Mexico had a perennial shortfall on its 'invisibles' or services account. The largest contributors to this deficit were interest payments on the foreign debt, which led to substantial current account deficits in the balance of payments. At the same time, there was substantial new foreign borrowing by the public and private sector alike. The result was a rapid increase in the size of the foreign debt. During the 1980s the authorities embarked on various debt-rescheduling exercises with commercial bank creditors. The most fruitful was an agreement reached in 1989, adopting the idea of debt relief proposed by Nicholas Brady, the US Treasury Secretary, under the so-called Brady Plan. Although the Brady Plan required new borrowing from the World Bank, the IMF and Japan to provide a certain amount of collateral, it did lead to a reduction in the stock of external debt. However, in the early 1990s the debt increased once more, reaching US $166,000m. in 1999. Meanwhile, the current account deficit declined. A continuing deficit on the invisibles account offset a trade surplus to produce a current account deficit of $2,330m. in 1996, which was covered by new debt and foreign investment. In 1996–2000 the current account deficit increased, reaching $18,185m. in the latter year before decreasing to $13,541m. by 2002, principally owing to improved oil earnings. The current account deficit fell further thereafter, to $2,220m., reflecting increases in remittances from Mexicans working in the USA. These transfers grew in importance, representing 2.5% of GDP in 2009, compared with 1.2% of GDP in 2000. In 2009 the decline in the value of imports relative to exports was the main contributor to a significant decline in the current account deficit to $5,238m., about one-third of the $15,527m. deficit recorded in 2008.

Contributing to the current account deficit along with the trade deficit were the services and income balances, amounting to deficits of US $8,025m. and $14,053m., respectively, in 2009. The bulk of the income deficit comprised net interest on public debt. At the end of 2009 public sector foreign debt amounted to an estimated $96,400m. Mexico registered a capital account surplus of $14,526m. in 2009, down from $21,400m. in 2008. The decrease in the capital account was partly explained by a decrease in foreign direct investment (FDI) inflows to $11,417m. in 2009, down from $23,170m. in 2008, and by an increase in Mexican investments overseas to $7,598m. in 2009, from $1,157m. in 2008. Manufacturing was the principal target of FDI, accounting for 50% of the total from 1999–2007, followed by financial services (representing 25% of FDI inflows during that period). (This reflected a shift in the direction of FDI over the previous decade: in 1990 32% of FDI had been directed towards industrial projects and 59% towards services.) FDI declined sharply in 2008 and 2009, to $11,400m. in the latter year, its lowest level since 1996. Most FDI continued to be directed towards the manufacturing sector (42.3% in 2009), particularly machinery and equipment related to the automotive industry. The principal source of FDI was the USA, which provided 50.9% of the total in 2009.

CONCLUSION

Unquestionably, there was a dramatic transformation in the Mexican economy in the last two decades of the 20th century. The role of the state was steadily reduced, trade was liberalized and opportunities for private and foreign investment increased. While NAFTA and other free trade agreements with Latin American and Pacific countries were expected to continue to provide an impetus to exports and investment, it was the Government's hope that this investment would be increasingly directed to productive, rather than speculative, assets. The maintenance of political calm was crucial to Mexico's economic future. The defeat of the ruling PRI in the presidential elections of 2000 represented a profound watershed in Mexican history. Investor confidence in Mexican political stability was encouraged by an orderly transfer of power in December 2000 and macroeconomic stability. However, political weakness prevented the Government of President Fox from achieving economic and state sector reforms that might have underpinned more dynamic or consistent growth. Fears that political uncertainty following the disputed presidential election in July 2006 would undermine macroeconomic stability proved unfounded following the inauguration of President Calderón, like his predecessors from the PAN, who was committed to fiscal prudence and structural reform to increase productivity. In April 2010 Calderón submitted a proposal to Congreso to expand the power of the CFC in a bid to increase market competition. However, fears of corruption and the growing influence of drug cartels undermined confidence in public institutions. Meanwhile, Mexico, as ever, remained vulnerable to fluctuations in the US economy. The global economic downturn that began in the USA in 2008 started to affect adversely the Mexican economy towards the end of that year, and continued to undermine economic performance into 2009, leading to a significant contraction in output. There were signs of improvement in the first quarter of 2010 in terms of economic activity and its impact on public sector revenue. The main driver of recovery was the external sector, with domestic demand remaining subdued.

Statistical Survey

Sources (unless otherwise stated): Instituto Nacional de Estadística, Geografía e Informática (INEGI), Edif. Sede, Avda Patriotismo 711, Torre A, Piso 10, Col. San Juan Mixcoac, Del. Benito Juárez, 03730 México, DF; tel. (55) 5278-1000 (ext. 1282); fax (55) 5278-1000 (ext. 1523); e-mail comunicacionsocial@inegi.org.mx; internet www.inegi.org.mx; Banco de México, Avda 5 de Mayo 1, Col. Centro, Del. Cuauhtémoc, 06059 México, DF; tel. (55) 5237-2000; fax (55) 5237-2370; internet www.banxico.org.mx.

Area and Population

AREA, POPULATION AND DENSITY

Area (sq km)	
Continental	1,959,248
Islands	5,127
Total	1,964,375*
Population (census and by-census results)†	
14 February 2000	97,483,412
29 October 2005	
Males	50,249,955
Females	53,013,433
Total	103,263,388
Population (projected mid-year estimates)‡	
2008	106,682,518
2009	107,550,697
2010	108,396,211
Density (per sq km) at mid-2010	55.2

* 758,449 sq miles.

† Including adjustment for underenumeration (1,730,016 in 2000).

‡ Source: Consejo Nacional de Población, *Proyecciones de la Población de México 2005–2050.*

POPULATION BY AGE AND SEX

(official estimates at 1 January 2010)

	Males	Females	Total
0–14	15,655,975	15,042,213	30,698,188
15–64	34,547,494	36,432,271	70,979,765
65 and over	2,841,126	3,459,877	6,301,003
Total	53,044,595	54,934,361	107,978,956

Mid-2010: *0–14* 30,489,619; *15–64* 71,493,827; *65 and over* 6,412,765; *Total* 108,396,211 (males 53,229,849, females 55,166,362).

ADMINISTRATIVE DIVISIONS

(at by-census of October 2005)

States	Area (sq km)*	Population	Density (per sq km)	Capital
Aguascalientes (Ags)	5,623	1,065,416	189.5	Aguascalientes
Baja California (BC)	71,540	2,844,469	36.8	Mexicali
Baja California Sur (BCS)	73,937	512,170	6.9	La Paz
Campeche (Camp.)	57,718	754,730	13.1	Campeche
Chiapas (Chis)	73,680	4,293,459	58.3	Tuxtla Gutiérrez
Chihuahua (Chih.)	247,490	3,241,444	13.1	Chihuahua
Coahuila (de Zaragoza) (Coah.)	151,447	2,495,200	16.5	Saltillo
Colima (Col.)	5,629	567,996	100.9	Colima
Distrito Federal (DF)	1,485	8,720,916	587.7	Mexico City
Durango (Dgo)	123,364	1,509,117	12.2	Victoria de Durango
Guanajuato (Gto)	30,617	4,893,812	159.8	Guanajuato
Guerrero (Gro)	63,618	3,115,202	50.0	Chilpancingo de los Bravos
Hidalgo (Hgo)	20,855	2,345,514	112.5	Pachuca de Soto
Jalisco (Jal.)	78,624	6,752,113	85.9	Guadalajara
México (Méx.)	22,332	14,007,495	627.2	Toluca de Lerdo
Michoacán (de Ocampo) (Mich.)	58,672	3,966,073	67.6	Morelia
Morelos (Mor.)	4,894	1,612,899	329.6	Cuernavaca
Nayarit (Nay.)	27,861	949,684	34.1	Tepic
Nuevo León (NL)	64,206	4,199,292	65.4	Monterrey
Oaxaca (Oax.)	93,348	3,506,821	37.6	Oaxaca de Juárez
Puebla (Pue.)	34,246	5,383,133	157.2	Heroica Puebla de Zaragoza
Querétaro (de Arteaga) (Qro)	11,659	1,598,139	137.1	Querétaro
Quintana Roo (Q.Roo)	42,544	1,135,309	26.7	Ciudad Chetumal
San Luis Potosí (SLP)	61,165	2,410,414	39.4	San Luis Potosí
Sinaloa (Sin.)	57,334	2,608,442	45.5	Culiacán Rosales
Sonora (Son.)	179,527	2,394,861	13.3	Hermosillo
Tabasco (Tab.)	24,747	1,989,969	80.4	Villahermosa
Tamaulipas (Tamps)	80,155	3,024,238	37.7	Ciudad Victoria
Tlaxcala (Tlax.)	3,988	1,068,207	267.8	Tlaxcala de Xicohténcatl
Veracruz-Llave (Ver.)	71,856	7,110,214	99.0	Jalapa Enríquez
Yucatán (Yuc.)	39,675	1,818,948	45.8	Mérida
Zacatecas (Zac.)	75,412	1,367,692	18.1	Zacatecas
Total	1,959,248	103,263,388	52.7	—

* Excluding islands.

PRINCIPAL TOWNS

(population at by-census of October 2005)

Ciudad de México (Mexico City, capital)	8,720,916	Saltillo	648,929
Ecatepec de Morelos (Ecatepec)	1,688,258	Torreón	577,477
Guadalajara	1,600,940	Benito Juárez (Cancún)	572,973
Heroica Puebla de Zaragoza (Puebla)	1,485,941	Tlaquepaque	563,006
Tijuana	1,410,687	Villahermosa	558,524
Ciudad Juárez	1,313,338	Reynosa	526,888
León	1,278,087	Victoria de Durango (Durango)	526,659
Zapopan	1,155,790	Santa María Chimalhuacán (Chimalhuacán)	525,389
Nezahualcóyotl	1,140,528	Veracruz Llave (Veracruz)	512,310
Monterrey	1,133,814	Tuxtla Gutiérrez	503,320
Mexicali	855,962	Cuautitlán Izcalli	498,021
Naucalpan de Juárez (Naucalpan)	821,442	San Nicolás de los Garzas	476,761
Culiacán Rosales (Culiacán)	793,730	Tultitlán	472,867
Mérida	781,146	Atizapán de Zaragoza	472,526

Chihuahua	758,791	Irapuato	463,103
Toluca de Lerdo (Toluca)	747,512	Matamoros	462,157
Querétaro	734,139	Iztapaluca	429,033
San Luis Potosí	730,950	Ensenada	413,481
Aguascalientes	723,043	Jalapa Enríquez (Xalapa)	413,136
Acapulco de Juárez (Acapulco)	717,766	Tonalá	408,729
Hermosillo	701,838	Mazatlán	403,888
Guadalupe	691,931	Nuevo Laredo	355,827
Morelia	684,145	Cuernavaca	349,102
Tlalnepantla de Baz (Tlalnepantla)	683,808	Valle de Chalco (Xico)	332,279

Mid-2010 ('000, incl. suburbs, UN estimates): Ciudad de México 19,460,212; Guadalajara 4,402,412; Monterrey 3,895,876; Puebla 2,315,422; Tijuana 1,663,686; Toluca de Lerdo 1,582,142; León de los Aldamas 1,570,650; Ciudad Juárez 1,394,491; Torreón 1,199,084; San Luis Potosí 1,048,903; Querétaro 1,030,679; Mérida 1,015,309 (Source: UN, *World Urbanization Prospects: The 2009 Revision*).

BIRTHS, MARRIAGES AND DEATHS

	Registered live births		Registered marriages		Registered deaths	
	Number	Rate (per 1,000)	Number	Rate (per 1,000)	Number	Rate (per 1,000)
2001	2,767,610	22.9	665,434	6.7	443,127	4.8
2002	2,699,084	21.7	616,654	6.1	459,687	4.8
2003	2,655,894	20.6	584,142	5.7	472,140	4.8
2004	2,625,056	19.8	600,563	5.8	473,417	4.8
2005	2,567,906	19.3	595,713	5.7	495,240	4.8
2006	2,505,939	19.0	586,978	5.6	494,471	4.8
2007	2,655,083	18.6	595,209	5.6	514,420	4.9
2008	2,636,110	18.3	589,352	5.5	539,530	5.1

Life expectancy (years at birth, UN estimates): 76 (males 73; females 78) in 2008 (Source: WHO, *World Health Statistics*).

ECONOMICALLY ACTIVE POPULATION

(sample surveys, '000 persons aged 14 years and over, April–June)

	2006	2007	2008
Agriculture, hunting, forestry and fishing	6,033.0	5,772.4	5,758.6
Mining, quarrying and electricity	350.3	406.3	389.4
Manufacturing	7,000.3	7,041.3	7,150.4
Construction	3,452.5	3,585.8	3,641.2
Trade	8,211.6	8,502.3	8,603.7
Hotels and restaurants	2,514.9	2,670.6	2,836.7
Transport and communications	2,222.7	2,133.1	2,184.7
Finance and business services	2,365.9	2,530.4	2,722.1
Social services	3,413.7	3,531.9	3,578.9
Other services	4,288.2	4,371.9	4,492.3
Public sector	2,034.9	2,048.5	2,175.8
Sub-total	41,888.1	42,594.5	43,533.7
Activities not adequately defined	309.7	312.2	333.0
Total employed	42,197.8	42,906.7	43,866.7
Unemployed	1,377.7	1,505.2	1,593.3
Total labour force	43,575.5	44,411.9	45,460.0
Males	27,409.4	27,726.2	28,329.1
Females	16,166.1	16,685.6	17,130.9

Health and Welfare

KEY INDICATORS

Total fertility rate (children per woman, 2008)	2.2
Under-5 mortality rate (per 1,000 live births, 2008)	17
HIV/AIDS (% of persons aged 15–49, 2007)	0.3
Physicians (per 1,000 head, 2002)	1.5
Hospital beds (per 1,000 head, 2004)	1.0
Health expenditure (2007): US $ per head (PPP)	819
Health expenditure (2007): % of GDP	5.9
Health expenditure (2007): public (% of total)	45.4
Access to water (% of persons, 2008)	94
Access to sanitation (% of persons, 2008)	85
Total carbon dioxide emissions ('000 metric tons, 2006)	435,832.8
Carbon dioxide emissions per head (metric tons, 2006)	4.2
Human Development Index (2007): ranking	53
Human Development Index (2007): value	0.854

For sources and definitions, see explanatory note on p. vi.

Agriculture

PRINCIPAL CROPS

('000 metric tons)

	2006	2007	2008
Wheat	3,378	3,515	4,019
Rice, paddy	337	295	224
Barley	869	653	811
Maize	21,893	23,513	24,320
Oats	152	125	148
Sorghum	5,519	6,203	6,611
Potatoes	1,523	1,751	1,670
Sugar cane	50,676	52,089	51,107
Beans, dry	1,386	994	1,123
Chick peas	163	148	165
Soybeans (Soya beans)	81	88	153
Groundnuts, with shell	68	83	81
Coconuts*	1,132	1,167	1,246
Safflower seed	74	113	96
Cabbages	211	219	215
Lettuce and chicory	274	286	285
Tomatoes	2,899	3,150	2,937
Cauliflower and broccoli	305	326	371
Pumpkins, squash and gourds	547	517	486
Cucumbers and gherkins	496	490	475
Chillies and peppers, green*	1,681	1,890	2,055
Onions, dry	1,238	1,387	1,252
Carrots and turnips	382	404	386
Bananas	2,196	1,965	2,159
Oranges	4,157	4,249	4,307
Tangerines, mandarins, clementines and satsumas	350	469	469*
Lemons and limes	1,867	1,936	2,224
Grapefruit and pomelos	387	313	395
Apples	602	505	525
Peaches and nectarines	222	192	202
Strawberries	192	176	207
Grapes	244	356	307
Watermelons	977	1,059	1,200
Cantaloupes and other melons	570	543	582
Guavas, mangoes and mangosteens	2,046	1,911	1,855
Avocados	1,134	1,143	1,125
Pineapples	634	671	686
Papayas	799	919	638
Coffee, green	280	269	266
Cocoa beans	38	30	28
Tobacco, unmanufactured	19	13	11

* FAO estimate(s).

Aggregate production ('000 metric tons, may include official, semi-official or estimated data): Total cereals 32,154.7 in 2006, 34,311.1 in 2007, 36,141.2 in 2008; Total fruits (excl. melons) 15,776.5 in 2006, 15,825.5 in 2007, 16,122.2 in 2008; Total vegetables (incl. melons) 11,451.8 in 2006, 12,121.1 in 2007, 12,100.9 in 2008.

Source: FAO.

LIVESTOCK

('000 head, year ending September)

	2006	2007*	2008*
Horses	6,300*	6,350	6,350
Asses	3,260*	3,260	3,260
Mules	3,280*	3,280	3,280
Cattle	31,163	31,950	32,565
Pigs	15,257	15,500	15,528
Sheep	7,287	7,500	7,825
Goats	8,890	8,900	8,831
Chickens	481,421	496,500	504,300
Ducks	8,150*	8,200	8,200
Turkeys	4,587	4,300	4,500

* FAO estimate(s).

Source: FAO.

LIVESTOCK PRODUCTS

('000 metric tons)

	2006	2007	2008
Cattle meat	1,613	1,635	1,667
Sheep meat	48	49	51
Goat meat	43	43	43
Pig meat	1,109	1,152	1,161
Horse meat*	79	79	79
Chicken meat	2,464	2,542	2,581
Cows' milk	10,089	10,346	10,766
Goats' milk	164	167	165
Hen eggs	2,290	2,291	2,337
Honey	56	55	55

* FAO estimates.

Source: FAO.

Forestry

ROUNDWOOD REMOVALS

('000 cubic metres, excl. bark)

	2006	2007	2008
Sawlogs, veneer logs and logs for sleepers	4,878	5,210	5,308
Pulpwood	999	882	932
Other industrial wood	254	214	185
Fuel wood*	38,521	38,600	38,676
Total	44,652	44,906	45,101

* FAO estimates.

Source: FAO.

SAWNWOOD PRODUCTION

('000 cubic metres, incl. railway sleepers)

	2006	2007	2008
Coniferous (softwood)	2,324	2,366	2,409
Broadleaved (hardwood)	326	321	405
Total	2,650	2,687	2,814

Source: FAO.

Fishing

('000 metric tons, live weight)

	2006	2007	2008
Capture	1,357.4	1,483.7*	1,588.9*
Tilapias	66.3	78.2	69.0
California pilchard (sardine)	268.9	324.7*	386.0*
Yellowfin tuna	77.8	65.6	83.3
American cupped oyster	42.9	43.8	33.3
Jumbo flying squid	65.6	57.6	84.4
Aquaculture	154.5	128.4*	151.1*
Whiteleg shrimp	112.5	111.8	130.2
Total catch	1,511.8	1,612.1*	1,739.9*

* FAO estimate.

Note: Figures exclude aquatic plants ('000 metric tons, capture only): 4.5 in 2006; 5.1 in 2007; 4.9 in 2008. Also excluded are aquatic mammals and crocodiles (recorded by number rather than by weight), shells and corals. The number of gray whales caught was 1 in 2006. The number of bottlenose dolphins caught was 1 in 2007; 9 in 2008. The number of Morelet's crocodiles caught was: 158 in 2006; 11 in 2007; n.a. in 2008. The catch of marine shells and corals (metric tons) was: 578 in 2006; 581 in 2007 (FAO estimate); 581 in 2008 (FAO estimate).

Source: FAO.

Mining

(metric tons, unless otherwise indicated)

	2006	2007	2008
Antimony*	778	414	380
Arsenic*	1,595	513	—
Barytes	199,605	185,921	140,066
Bismuth*	1,186	1,170	1,132
Cadmium*	1,399	1,605	1,550
Celestite	128,321	96,902	29,621
Coal	10,882,685	11,886,757	10,402,658
Coke	1,569,561	1,536,325	1,547,391
Copper*	327,536	335,502	268,620
Crude petroleum ('000 barrels per day)†	3,256	3,076	2,792
Diatomite	62,948	82,519	128,536
Dolomite	1,282,590	1,123,225	1,233,993
Feldspar	459,209	438,696	445,519
Flourite	936,433	933,361	1,057,649
Gas (million cu ft per day)*	5,356	6,058	6,919
Gold (kg)*	35,899	39,355	50,365
Graphite	11,773	9,900	7,229
Gypsum	5,950,794	5,963,715	5,135,151
Iron*	6,589,586	7,323,121	7,725,959
Kaolin	18,852	86,784	85,092
Lead*	120,450	89,838	100,725
Manganese*	124,417	152,446	169,908
Molybdenum*	2,519	6,491	7,812
Salt	7,987,318	8,032,273	8,808,714
Silica	2,661,770	2,950,438	2,779,075
Silver*	2,413,147	2,351,570	2,668,028
Sulphur	1,076,391	1,029,736	1,040,546
Wollastonite	44,280	50,809	46,844
Zinc*	432,347	426,509	397,306

* Figures for metallic minerals refer to metal content of ores.

† Source: Petróleos Mexicanos, México, DF.

Industry

SELECTED PRODUCTS
('000 metric tons, unless otherwise indicated)

	2005	2006	2007
Wheat flour	2,646	2,689	2,679
Maize (corn) flour	1,617	1,656	1,685
Raw sugar	3,257	3,016	3,200
Beer ('000 hectolitres)	72,030	78,040	80,510
Soft drinks ('000 hectolitres)	141,451	144,608	151,581
Cigarettes (million units)	41,439	44,295	39,763
Cotton yarn (pure and mixed)	44	44	45
Tyres ('000 units)*	11,650	10,825	10,233
Cement	37,452	40,362	41,213
Non-electric, cooking or heating appliances—household ('000 units)	3,962	4,093	4,278
Refrigerators—household ('000 units)	2,844	3,043	2,650
Washing machines—household ('000 units)	988	1,042	962
Lorries, buses, tractors, etc. ('000 units)	501	561	556
Passenger cars ('000 units)	1,128	1,430	1,501
Electric energy (million kWh)	234,895	249,648	257,455

* Tyres for road motor vehicles.

Source: UN Industrial Commodity Statistics Database.

2008 (million kWh, preliminary): Electric energy 195,479t.

Finance

CURRENCY AND EXCHANGE RATES

Monetary Units
100 centavos = 1 Mexican nuevo peso.

Sterling, Dollar and Euro Equivalents (31 May 2010)
£1 sterling = 18.786 nuevos pesos;
US $1 = 12.885 nuevos pesos;
€1 = 15.956 nuevos pesos;
1,000 Mexican nuevos pesos = £53.23 = $77.61 = €62.67.

Average Exchange Rate (nuevos pesos per US $)
2007 10.928
2008 11.130
2009 13.514

Note: Figures are given in terms of the nuevo (new) peso, introduced on 1 January 1993 and equivalent to 1,000 former pesos.

BUDGET*
(million new pesos)

Revenue	2007	2008	2009
Taxation	1,002,670.0	994,552.3	1,129,552.6
Income taxes	527,183.6	562,222.3	534,190.6
Value-added tax	409,012.5	457,248.3	407,795.1
Excise tax	–6,791.8	–168,325.2	50,567.4
Import duties	32,188.0	35,783.1	30,196.4
Other revenue	708,550.5	1,055,384.0	870,895.5
Total revenue	1,711,220.6	2,049,936.3	2,000,448.1

Expenditure	2007	2008	2009
Programmable expenditure	1,392,394.0	1,607,040.7	1,639,602.7
Current expenditure	278,059.1	284,843.0	345,275.5
Wages and salaries	162,791.4	181,455.6	205,441.7
Acquisitions	12,706.4	17,181.7	17,945.4
Other current expenditure	102,561.3	86,205.6	121,888.4
Capital expenditure	134,202.4	170,490.1	101,524.5
Transfers	980,132.5	1,151,707.6	1,192,802.7
Non-programmable expenditure	537,372.5	638,661.1	622,908.7
Interest and fees	188,671.4	200,121.7	231,265.4
Revenue sharing	332,757.7	423,454.9	375,717.3
Total expenditure	1,929,766.5	2,245,701.8	2,262,511.4

* Figures refer to the consolidated accounts of the central Government, including government agencies and the national social security system. The budgets of state and local governments are excluded.

INTERNATIONAL RESERVES
(excl. gold, US $ million at 31 December)

	2007	2008	2009
IMF special drawing rights	466	519	4,525
Reserve position in the Fund	334	613	961
Foreign exchange	86,309	93,994	94,103
Total	87,109	95,126	99,589

Source: IMF, *International Financial Statistics*.

MONEY SUPPLY
(million new pesos at 31 December)

	2007	2008	2009
Currency outside depository corporations	429,854	494,345	536,824
Transferable deposits	695,346	755,947	1,079,210
Other deposits	1,830,063	1,996,329	1,999,716
Securities other than shares	33,971	8,624	14,513
Broad money	2,989,234	3,255,245	3,630,263

Source: IMF, *International Financial Statistics*.

COST OF LIVING
(Consumer Price Index; base: 2000 = 100)

	2006	2007	2008
Food, beverages and tobacco	134.1	142.6	154.1
Clothing and footwear	113.5	115.0	117.0
Electricity, gas and other fuel	173.1	178.2	190.7
Rent	133.2	137.2	141.4
All items (incl. others)	131.8	137.0	144.0

2009: Food, beverages and tobacco 167.5; All items (incl. others) 151.6.

Source: ILO.

NATIONAL ACCOUNTS
('000 million new pesos at current prices)

Expenditure on the Gross Domestic Product

	2007	2008	2009
Government final consumption expenditure	1,180.74	1,248.98	1,375.78
Private final consumption expenditure	7,307.49	7,935.60	7,972.89
Increase in stocks	468.69	513.44	65.93
Gross fixed capital formation	2,394.01	2,678.04	2,578.47
Total domestic expenditure	11,350.93	12,376.06	11,993.07
Exports of goods and services	3,163.02	3,424.22	3,291.67
Less Imports of goods and services	3,337.97	3,689.74	3,461.76
GDP in purchasers' values	11,175.99	12,110.56	11,822.99
GDP at constant 2003 prices	8,818.37	8,928.63	8,345.65

Source: IMF, *International Financial Statistics*.

Gross Domestic Product by Economic Activity
(million new pesos at current prices)

	2008	2009
Agriculture, forestry and fishing	432,989.5	483,726.4
Mining and quarrying	1,204,021.8	1,020,097.8
Manufacturing	2,070,799.5	1,951,770.2
Construction	847,242.2	796,562.0
Electricity, gas and water	183,979.9	176,585.3
Trade	1,866,400.9	1,681,444.3
Restaurants and hotels	274,045.9	259,159.3
Transport, storage and communications	1,147,065.9	1,150,283.0
Finance, insurance, real estate and business services	2,355,668.8	2,308,938.1
Public administration	449,516.5	484,534.4
Community, social and personal services	375,303.9	393,854.1
Education	555,304.5	558,447.7
Other activities	278,536.0	283,994.8
Sub-total	12,040,875.3	11,549,397.4
Less Financial intermediation services indirectly measured	219,081.6	216,653.0
GDP at factor cost	11,821,793.7	11,332,744.5
Indirect taxes, *less* subsidies	309,038.6	490,241.7
GDP in purchasers' values	12,130,832.3	11,822,986.2

BALANCE OF PAYMENTS
(US $ million)

	2007	2008	2009
Exports of goods f.o.b.	271,875	291,343	229,707
Imports of goods f.o.b.	−281,949	−308,603	−234,385
Trade balance	−10,074	−17,261	−4,678
Exports of services	17,609	18,480	15,423
Imports of services	−24,064	−25,235	−23,212
Balance on goods and services	−16,529	−24,016	−12,466
Other income received	7,876	7,397	4,922
Other income paid	−26,161	−24,731	−19,211
Balance on goods, services and income	−34,814	−41,350	−26,755
Current transfers received	26,508	25,575	21,564
Current transfers paid	−108	−128	−60
Current balance	−8,413	−15,903	−5,252
Direct investment abroad	−8,256	−1,157	−7,598
Direct investment from abroad	27,311	23,170	11,418
Portfolio investment liabilities	13,347	4,841	15,253
Other investment assets	−21,776	−7,923	−10,964
Other investment liabilities	9,062	5,616	10,417
Net errors and omissions	−1,024	−914	−7,584
Overall balance	10,250	7,731	5,690

Source: IMF, *International Financial Statistics*.

External Trade

PRINCIPAL COMMODITIES
(distribution by HS, US $ million)

Imports f.o.b.*	2006	2007	2008†
Live animals and products thereof	4,193.9	5,159.1	5,486.8
Vegetable products	6,155.5	7,580.6	10,078.9
Animal and vegetable oils and fats	755.2	1,064.5	1,518.3
Prepared food, beverages, spirits and tobacco	4,479.6	5,147.7	5,600.5
Mineral products	16,217.5	20,990.8	31,747.0
Chemicals and related industries	18,617.9	20,873.7	23,903.6
Plastics, rubber and articles thereof	19,547.1	20,136.2	20,238.8
Raw hides, skins, leather and furs	1,481.7	1,308.9	1,268.5
Wood, charcoal, cork, straw, etc.	1,436.1	1,517.2	1,509.0
Paper-making material; paper and paperboard and articles thereof	6,134.9	6,485.7	6,700.8
Textiles and textile articles	9,062.3	8,677.9	8,512.8
Footwear, headgear, umbrellas, etc.	586.9	643.3	729.4
Articles of stone, plaster, cement, asbestos, etc.; glass and glassware	2,219.6	2,425.6	2,153.6
Pearls, precious stones and metals and articles thereof; imitation jewellery and coins	1,032.4	1,226.6	1,127.7
Base metals and articles thereof	23,752.5	24,714.0	26,888.2
Machinery and mechanical appliances; electrical equipment, parts and accessories	96,375.4	102,371.9	110,245.2
Vehicles, aircraft, vessels and associated transport equipment	26,026.0	28,387.8	27,842.9
Optical, photographic, measuring, precision and medical apparatus; clocks and watches; musical instruments	10,258.5	13,060.1	12,786.9
Arms and ammunitions, parts and accessories	41.0	47.0	52.7
Miscellaneous manufactured articles	4,488.4	6,022.5	6,215.8
Works of art, collectors' pieces, antiques	13.0	19.7	13.8
Total (incl. others)	256,058.4	281,949.0	308,644.7

* Figures include data for the *maquila* sector (US $ million): 86,527.3 in 2006; n.a. in 2007; n.a. in 2008.
† Preliminary.

Exports f.o.b.*	2006	2007	2008†
Live animals and products thereof	1,729.6	1,751.8	1,759.8
Vegetable products	5,774.7	6,498.9	7,237.8
Animal and vegetable oils and fats	91.5	115.8	184.8
Prepared food, beverages, spirits and tobacco	5,982.7	6,303.2	7,101.0
Mineral products	40,042.4	44,419.1	52,211.4
Chemicals and related industries	6,894.3	7,819.7	8,752.1
Plastics, rubber and articles thereof	6,173.5	6,716.0	6,839.2
Raw hides, skins, leather and furs	549.1	565.9	514.4
Wood, charcoal, cork, straw, etc.	491.8	434.6	394.5
Paper-making material; paper and paperboard and articles thereof	1,862.8	1,920.8	1,944.8
Textiles and textile articles	8,451.1	7,258.2	6,862.7
Footwear, headgear, umbrellas, etc.	380.4	394.6	386.3
Articles of stone, plaster, cement, asbestos, etc.; glass and glassware	2,850.8	2,848.9	2,896.0
Pearls, precious stones and metals and articles thereof; imitation jewellery and coins	3,064.1	3,824.9	5,262.7
Base metals and articles thereof	13,267.1	15,073.5	16,163.0
Machinery and mechanical appliances; electrical equipment, parts and accessories	94,340.6	104,177.6	108,888.8
Vehicles, aircraft, vessels and associated transport equipment	40,889.0	43,933.2	45,022.9
Optical, photographic, measuring, precision and medical apparatus; clocks and watches; musical instruments	8,922.9	8,936.5	9,513.4
Arms and ammunitions, parts and accessories	17.5	17.6	20.8
Miscellaneous manufactured articles	7,393.1	8,060.7	8,078.4
Works of art, collectors' pieces, antiques	10.9	8.2	8.1
Total (incl. others)	249,925.1	271,875.3	291,342.6

* Figures include data for the *maquila* sector (US $ million): 111,823.8 in 2006; n.a. in 2007; n.a. in 2008.
† Preliminary.

PRINCIPAL TRADING PARTNERS*
(US $ million)

Imports c.i.f.	2007	2008	2009
Argentina	1,609.7	1,436.4	1,144.6
Brazil	5,575.3	5,182.7	3,495.3
Canada	7,957.4	9,442.5	7,303.7
Chile	2,594.0	2,592.3	1,650.6
China, People's Republic	29,743.7	34,690.3	32,529.0
France	3,097.8	3,511.0	2,502.5
Germany	10,687.7	12,605.7	9,727.3
Italy	5,542.4	5,219.3	3,146.7
Japan	16,343.0	16,282.5	11,397.1
Korea, Republic	12,658.1	13,548.1	10,958.7
Malaysia	4,771.2	4,659.2	4,035.5
Philippines	1,198.3	1,238.4	1,069.7
Singapore	2,086.8	1,697.7	1,377.8
Spain	3,830.5	4,055.8	3,004.0
Switzerland	1,246.1	1,412.9	1,208.0
Taiwan	5,897.1	6,658.5	4,592.1
Thailand	2,105.8	2,207.9	1,983.2
United Kingdom	2,294.3	2,595.5	1,837.8
USA	139,472.8	151,334.6	112,433.8
Total (incl. others)	281,949.0	308,644.7	234,385.0

Exports f.o.b.	2007	2008	2009
Aruba	1,517.8	1,494.6	104.0
Canada	6,491.0	7,102.4	8,310.1
China, People's Republic	1,895.3	2,044.8	2,215.3
Colombia	2,943.2	3,032.4	2,500.1
Germany	4,103.6	5,008.2	3,214.2
Japan	1,912.6	2,064.0	1,607.1
Spain	3,689.8	4,232.9	2,478.3
United Kingdom	1,562.7	1,749.3	1,253.1
USA	223,133.3	233,522.7	184,944.1
Venezuela	2,332.6	2,310.3	1,421.2
Total (incl. others)	271,875.3	291,342.6	229,707.5

* Imports by country of origin; exports by country of destination.

Transport

RAILWAYS
(traffic)

	2005	2006	2007
Passengers carried ('000)	253	261	288
Passenger-kilometres (million)	73	76	84
Freight carried ('000 tons)	89,814	94,713	99,845
Freight ton-kilometres (million)	72,185	73,726	77,170

Source: Dirección General de Planeación, Secretaría de Comunicaciones y Transportes.

ROAD TRAFFIC
('000 vehicles in use at 31 December, estimates)

	2005	2006	2007
Passenger cars	14,075	15,313	17,533
Lorries and vans	7,111	7,563	7,870
Buses and coaches	265	284	283
Motorcycles and mopeds	n.a.	706	869

Source: IRF, *World Road Statistics*.

SHIPPING

Merchant Fleet
(registered at 31 December)

	2006	2007	2008
Number of vessels	753	780	799
Total displacement ('000 grt)	1,161.9	1,217.0	1,278.9

Source: Lloyd's Register-Fairplay, *World Fleet Statistics*.

Sea-borne Shipping
(domestic and international freight traffic, '000 metric tons)

	2006	2007	2008
Goods loaded	181,234	169,870	163,643
Goods unloaded	106,197	103,065	101,594

Source: Coordinación General de Puertos y Marina Mercante.

CIVIL AVIATION
(traffic on scheduled services)

	2005	2006	2007
Passengers carried ('000)	42,176	45,406	52,221
Freight carried ('000 tons)	529	544	572

Source: Dirección General de Planeación, Secretaría de Comunicaciones y Transportes.

Tourism

VISITOR ARRIVALS BY COUNTRY OF ORIGIN
(including cross-border visitors)

	2005	2006	2007
Argentina	78,654	84,583	112,165
Brazil	78,026	31,890	57,834
Canada	675,216	785,457	952,810
Chile	35,543	41,230	54,259
Colombia	33,863	35,955	59,066
France	160,119	173,184	191,855
Germany	129,973	135,251	151,969
Guatemala	36,088	31,444	37,012
Italy	151,565	163,289	166,729
Japan	65,788	68,981	71,857
Korea, Republic	26,219	30,742	37,631
Netherlands	61,813	70,202	73,034
Spain	203,716	261,458	280,089
United Kingdom	231,421	260,146	286,411
USA	17,905,684	17,512,050	17,248,429
Venezuela	32,243	38,015	62,532
Total (incl. others)	21,914,917	21,352,605	21,423,545

Total visitor arrivals ('000): 21,370 in 2007; 22,637 in 2008.

Tourism receipts (excluding excursionists, US $ million): 9,146 in 2005; 9,559 in 2006; 10,340 in 2007; 10,817 in 2008.

Source: mainly World Tourism Organization.

Communications Media

	2007	2008	2009
Telephones ('000 main lines in use)	19,997.9	20,491.4	19,424.9
Mobile cellular telephones ('000 subscribers)	66,559.5	75,303.5	83,527.9
Internet users ('000)	22,104.1*	23,260.3	28,439.2
Broadband subscribers ('000)	4,564.3	7,594.1†	9,921.4

* Estimated figure.
† Preliminary figure.

Personal computers: 15,000,000 (143.9 per 1,000 persons) in 2006.

Radio receivers ('000 in use): 31,000 in 1997.

Television receivers ('000 in use): 28,000 in 2000.

Daily newspapers (2002): Number 300; Average circulation 9,251,000 in 2000.

Non-daily newspapers (2002): Number 11; Average circulation 614,000 in 2000.

Books published (titles): 15,542 in 2002.

Sources: partly International Telecommunication Union; UNESCO Institute for Statistics; UNESCO, *Statistical Yearbook*; UN, *Statistical Yearbook*.

Education

(2007/08 unless otherwise indicated)

	Institutions*	Teachers*	Students ('000)†
Pre-primary	92,753	224,741	4,739.2
Primary	98,332	566,809	14,585.8
Secondary (incl. technical)	34,034	366,731	6,055.5
Intermediate: professional/ technical	1,488	29,267	352.5
Intermediate: Baccalaureate	12,311	241,376	3,390.4
Higher (incl. post-graduate)	5,549	296,729	2,528.7

* Estimates.
† 2006/07.

Pupil-teacher ratio (primary education, UNESCO estimate): 28.0 in 2007/08 (Source: UNESCO Institute for Statistics).

Adult literacy rate (UNESCO estimates): 92.9% (males 94.6%; females 91.5%) in 2008 (Source: UNESCO Institute for Statistics).

Directory

The Constitution

The present Mexican Constitution was proclaimed on 5 February 1917, at the end of the Revolution, which began in 1910, against the regime of Porfirio Díaz. Its provisions regarding religion, education, and the ownership and exploitation of mineral wealth reflect the long revolutionary struggle against the concentration of power in the hands of the Roman Catholic Church and the large landowners, and the struggle that culminated, in the 1930s, in the expropriation of the properties of the foreign petroleum companies. It has been amended from time to time.

GOVERNMENT

The President and Congress

The President of the Republic, in agreement with the Cabinet and with the approval of the Congreso de la Unión (Congress) or of the Permanent Committee when the Congreso is not in session, may suspend constitutional guarantees in case of foreign invasion, serious disturbance, or any other emergency endangering the people.

The exercise of supreme executive authority is vested in the President, who is elected for six years and enters office on 1 December of the year of election. The presidential powers include the right to appoint and remove members of the Cabinet and the Attorney-General and to appoint, with the approval of the Senado (Senate), diplomatic officials, the higher officers of the army, and ministers of the supreme and higher courts of justice. The President is also empowered to dispose of the Armed Forces for the internal and external security of the federation.

The Congreso is composed of the Cámara Federal de Diputados (Federal Chamber of Deputies), elected every three years, and the Senado, whose members hold office for six years. There is one deputy for every 250,000 people and for every fraction of over 125,000 people. The Senado is composed of two members for each state and two for the Distrito Federal (Federal District). Regular sessions of the Congreso begin on 1 September and may not continue beyond 31 December of the same year. Extraordinary sessions may be convened by the Permanent Committee.

The powers of the Congreso include the right to: pass laws and regulations; impose taxes; specify the criteria on which the Executive may negotiate loans; declare war; raise, maintain and regulate the organization of the Armed Forces; establish and maintain schools of various types throughout the country; approve or reject the budget; sanction appointments submitted by the President of the Supreme Court and magistrates of the superior court of the Distrito Federal; approve or reject treaties and conventions made with foreign powers; and ratify diplomatic appointments.

The Permanent Committee, consisting of 29 members of the Congreso (15 of whom are deputies and 14 senators), officiates when the Congreso is in recess, and is responsible for the convening of extraordinary sessions of the Congreso.

The States

Governors are elected by popular vote in a general election every six years. The local legislature is formed by deputies, who are changed every three years. The judicature is specially appointed under the Constitution by the competent authority (it is never subject to the popular vote).

Each state is a separate unit, with the right to levy taxes and to legislate in certain matters. The states are not allowed to levy inter-state customs duties.

The Federal District

The Distrito Federal (DF) consists of Mexico City and several neighbouring small towns and villages. The first direct elections for the Head of Government of the Distrito Federal were held in July 1997; hitherto, a Regent had been appointed by the President.

EDUCATION

According to the Constitution, the provision of educational facilities is the joint responsibility of the federation, the states and the municipalities. Education shall be democratic, and shall be directed to developing all the faculties of the individual students, while imbuing them with love of their country and a consciousness of international solidarity and justice. Religious bodies may not provide education, except training for the priesthood. Private educational institutions must conform to the requirements of the Constitution with regard to the nature of the teaching given. The education provided by the states shall be free of charge.

RELIGION

Religious bodies of whatever denomination shall not have the capacity to possess or administer real estate or capital invested therein. Churches are the property of the nation; the headquarters of bishops, seminaries, convents and other property used for the propagation of a religious creed shall pass into the hands of the state, to be dedicated to the public service of the federation or of the respective state. Institutions of charity, provided they are not connected with a religious body, may hold real property. The establishment of monastic orders is prohibited. Ministers of religion must be Mexican; they may not criticize the fundamental laws of the country in a public or private meeting; they may not vote or form associations for political purposes. Political meetings may not be held in places of worship.

A reform proposal, whereby constitutional restrictions on the Catholic Church were formally ended, received congressional approval in December 1991 and was promulgated as law in January 1992.

LAND AND MINERAL OWNERSHIP

Article 27 of the Constitution vests direct ownership of minerals and other products of the subsoil, including petroleum and water, in the nation, and reserves to the Federal Government alone the right to grant concessions in accordance with the laws to individuals and companies, on the condition that they establish regular work for the exploitation of the materials. At the same time, the right to acquire ownership of lands and waters belonging to the nation, or concessions for their exploitation, is limited to Mexican individuals and companies, although the State may concede similar rights to foreigners who agree not to invoke the protection of their governments to enforce such rights.

The same article declares null all alienations of lands, waters and forests belonging to towns or communities made by political chiefs or other local authorities in violation of the provisions of the law of 25 June 1856*, and all concessions or sales of communally held lands, waters and forests made by the federal authorities after 1 December 1876. The population settlements that lack *ejidos* (state-owned smallholdings), or cannot obtain restitution of lands previously held, shall be granted lands in proportion to the needs of the population. The area of land granted to the individual may not be less than 10 hectares of irrigated or watered land, or the equivalent in other kinds of land.

The owners affected by decisions to divide and redistribute land (with the exception of the owners of farming or cattle-rearing properties) shall not have any right of redress, nor may they invoke the right of *amparo*† in protection of their interests. They may, however, apply to the Government for indemnification. Small properties, the areas of which are defined in the Constitution, will not be subject to expropriation. The Constitution leaves to the Congreso the duty of determining the maximum size of rural properties.

In March 1992 an agrarian reform amendment, whereby the programme of land distribution established by the 1917 Constitution was abolished and the terms of the *ejido* system of tenant farmers were relaxed, was formally adopted.

Monopolies and measures to restrict competition in industry, commerce or public services are prohibited.

A section of the Constitution deals with work and social security.

POLITICAL ORGANIZATIONS AND ELECTORAL PROCEDURE

In December 1977 a Federal Law on Political Organizations and Electoral Procedure was promulgated. It includes the following provisions:

Legislative power is vested in the Congreso de la Unión, which comprises the Cámara Federal de Diputados and the Senado. The Cámara shall comprise 300 deputies elected by majority vote within single-member electoral districts and up to 100 deputies (increased to 200 from July 1988) elected by a system of proportional representation from regional lists within multi-member constituencies. The Senado comprises two members for each state and two for the Distrito Federal, elected by majority vote.

Executive power is exercised by the President of the Republic of the United Mexican States, elected by majority vote.

Ordinary elections will be held every three years for the federal deputies and every six years for the senators and the President of the Republic on the first Sunday of July of the year in question. When a vacancy occurs among members of the Congreso elected by majority vote, the house in question shall call extraordinary elections, and when a vacancy occurs among members of the Cámara elected by proportional representation it shall be filled by the candidate of the same party who received the next highest number of votes at the last ordinary election.

Voting is the right and duty of every citizen, male or female, over the age of 18 years.

A political party shall be registered if it has at least 3,000 members in each one of at least half the states in Mexico or at least 300 members in each one of at least half of the single-member constituencies. In either case, the total number of members must be no fewer than 65,000. A party can also obtain conditional registration if it has been active for at least four years. Registration is confirmed if the party obtains at least 1.5% of the popular vote. All political parties shall have free access to the media.

In September 1993 an amendment to the Law on Electoral Procedure provided for the expansion of the Senado to 128 seats, representing four members for each state and the Distrito Federal, three to be elected by majority vote, and one by proportional representation.

* The Lerdo Law against ecclesiastical privilege, which became the basis of the Liberal Constitution of 1857.

† The Constitution provides for the procedure known as *judicio de amparo*, a wider form of habeas corpus, which the individual may invoke in protection of his constitutional rights.

The Government

HEAD OF STATE

President: FELIPE CALDERÓN HINOJOSA (took office 1 December 2006).

CABINET
(July 2010)

The Government is formed by the Partido de Acción Nacional.

Secretary of the Interior: JOSÉ FRANCISCO BLAKE MORA.

Secretary of Foreign Affairs: PATRICIA ESPINOSA CANTELLANO.

Secretary of Finance and Public Credit: ERNESTO CORDERO ARROYO.

Secretary of National Defence: Gen. GUILLERMO GALVÁN GALVÁN.

Secretary of the Navy: Adm. MARIANO FRANCISCO SAYNEZ MENDOZA.

Secretary of the Economy: BRUNO FERRARI GARCÍA DE ALBA.

Secretary of Social Development: HERIBERTO FÉLIX GUERRA.

Secretary of Public Security: GENARO GARCÍA LUNA.

Secretary of Public Function: SALVADOR VEGA CASILLAS.

Secretary of Communications and Transport: JUAN MOLINAR HORCASITAS.

Secretary of Labour and Social Welfare: JAVIER LOZANO ALARCÓN.

Secretary of the Environment and Natural Resources: JUAN RAFAEL ELVIRA QUESADA.

Secretary of Energy: GEORGINA KESSEL MARTÍNEZ.

Secretary of Agriculture, Livestock, Rural Development, Fisheries and Food: FRANCISCO JAVIER MAYORGA CASTAÑEDA.

Secretary of Public Education: ALONSO LUJAMBIO IRAZÁBAL.

Secretary of Health: JOSÉ ANGEL CÓRDOVA VILLALOBOS.

Secretary of Tourism: GLORIA GUEVARA MANZO.

Secretary of Agrarian Reform: ABELARDO ESCOBAR PRIETO.

Procurator-General: ARTURO CHÁVEZ CHÁVEZ.

SECRETARIATS OF STATE

Office of the President: Los Pinos, Col. San Miguel Chapultepec, 11850 México, DF; tel. (55) 5093-5300; fax (55) 5277-2376; e-mail felipe.calderon@presidencia.gob.mx; internet www.presidencia.gob.mx.

Secretariat of State for Agrarian Reform: Avda Heroica Escuela Naval Militar 669, Col. Presidentes Ejidales, 2a Sección, Del. Coyoacán, 04470 México, DF; tel. (55) 5624-0000; fax (55) 5695-6368; e-mail sra@sra.gob.mx; internet www.sra.gob.mx.

Secretariat of State for Agriculture, Livestock, Rural Development, Fisheries and Food: Avda Municipio Libre 377, Col. Santa Cruz Atoyac, Del. Benito Juárez, 03310 México, DF; tel. (55) 3871-1000; fax (55) 9183-1018; e-mail contacto@sagarpa.gob.mx; internet www.sagarpa.gob.mx.

Secretariat of State for Communications and Transport: Avda Xola y Universidad, Col. Narvarte, Del. Benito Juárez, 03020 México, DF; tel. (55) 5723-9300; fax (55) 5530-0093; e-mail webmaster@sct.gob.mx; internet www.sct.gob.mx.

Secretariat of State for the Economy: Alfonso Reyes 30, Col. Hipódromo Condesa, 06140 México, DF; tel. (55) 5729-9100; fax (55) 5729-9320; e-mail primercontacto@economia.gob.mx; internet www.economia.gob.mx.

Secretariat of State for Energy: Insurgentes Sur 890, 17°, Col. del Valle, Del. Benito Juárez, 03100 México, DF; tel. (55) 5000-6000; fax (55) 5000-6222; e-mail calidad@energia.gob.mx; internet www.energia.gob.mx.

Secretariat of State for the Environment and Natural Resources: Blvd Adolfo Ruíz Cortines 4209, Col. Jardines en la Montaña, Del. Tlalpan, 14210 México, DF; tel. (55) 5628-0600; fax (55) 5628-0643; e-mail contactodgeia@semarnat.gob.mx; internet www.semarnat.gob.mx.

Secretariat of State for Finance and Public Credit: Palacio Nacional, Plaza de la Constitución, Col. Centro, Del. Cuauhtémoc, 06000 México, DF; tel. (55) 9158-2000; fax (55) 9158-1142; e-mail secretario@hacienda.gob.mx; internet www.hacienda.gob.mx.

Secretariat of State for Foreign Affairs: Avda Juárez 20, Col. Centro, Del. Cuauhtémoc, 06010 México, DF; tel. (55) 3686-5100; fax (55) 3686-5582; e-mail comentario@sre.gob.mx; internet www.sre.gob.mx.

Secretariat of State for Health: Lieja 7, 1°, Col. Juárez, Del. Cuauhtémoc, 06600 México, DF; tel. (55) 5286-2383; fax (55) 5553-7917; e-mail portalesweb@salud.gob.mx; internet www.salud.gob.mx.

Secretariat of State for the Interior: Abraham González 48, Col. Juárez, Del. Cuauhtémoc, 06600 México, DF; tel. (55) 5728-7400; fax (55) 5728-7300; e-mail contacto@segob.gob.mx; internet www.gobernacion.gob.mx.

Secretariat of State for Labour and Social Welfare: Periférico Sur 4271, Col. Fuentes del Pedregal, Del. Tlalpan, 14149 México, DF; tel. (55) 3000-2100; fax (55) 5645-5594; e-mail correo@stps.gob.mx; internet www.stps.gob.mx.

Secretariat of State for National Defence: Blvd Manuel Avila Camacho, esq. Avda Industria Militar, 3°, Col. Lomas de Sotelo, Del. Miguel Hidalgo, 11640 México, DF; tel. (55) 2122-8800; fax (55) 5395-2935; e-mail ggalvang@mail.sedena.gob.mx; internet www.sedena.gob.mx.

Secretariat of State for the Navy: Eje 2 oriente, Tramo Heroica, Escuela Naval Militar 861, Col. Los Cipreses, Del. Coyoacán, 04830 México, DF; tel. (55) 5624-6500; e-mail srio@semar.gob.mx; internet www.semar.gob.mx.

Secretariat of State for Public Education: Argentina 28, Centro Histórico, 06029 México, DF; tel. (55) 3601-1000; fax (55) 5329-6873; e-mail educa@sep.gob.mx; internet www.sep.gob.mx.

Secretariat of State for Public Function: Insurgentes Sur 1735, 10°, Col. Guadalupe Inn, Del. Alvaro Obregón, 01020 México, DF; tel. (55) 2000-3000; e-mail contactociudadano@funcionpublica.gob.mx; internet www.funcionpublica.gob.mx.

Secretariat of State for Public Security: Avda Constituyentes 947, Ex Hacienda de Belem, Del. Alvaro Obregón, 01110 México, DF; tel. (55) 1103-6000; e-mail enlace@ssp.gob.mx; internet www.ssp.gob.mx.

Secretariat of State for Social Development: Avda Paseo de la Reforma 116, Col. Juárez, Del. Cuauhtémoc, 06600 México, DF; tel. (55) 5328-5000; e-mail contacto@sedesol.gob.mx; internet www.sedesol.gob.mx.

Secretariat of State for Tourism: Avda Presidente Masaryk 172, Col. Chapultepec Morales, Del. Miguel Hidalgo, 11587 México, DF; tel. (55) 3002-6300; fax (55) 1036-0789; e-mail atencion@sectur.gob.mx; internet www.sectur.gob.mx.

Office of the Procurator-General: Avda Paseo de la Reforma 211–213, Col. Cuauhtémoc, Del. Cuauhtémoc, 06500 México, DF; tel. (55) 5346-0000; fax (55) 5346-0908; e-mail ofproc@pgr.gob.mx; internet www.pgr.gob.mx.

State Governors

(July 2010)

Aguascalientes: LUIS ARMANDO REYNOSO (PAN).
Baja California: JOSÉ GUADALUPE OSUNA MILLÁN (PAN).
Baja California Sur: NARCISO AGÚNDEZ (PRD).
Campeche: FERNANDO ORTEGA BERNÉS (PRI).
Chiapas: JUAN JOSÉ SABINES GUERRERO (PRD).
Chihuahua: JOSÉ REYES BAEZA (PRI).
Coahuila (de Zaragoza): HUMBERTO MOREIRA VALDES (PRI).
Colima: MARIO ANGUIANO MORENO (PRI).
Durango: ISMAEL HERNÁNDEZ DERAS (PRI).
Guanajuato: JUAN MANUEL OLIVA RAMÍREZ (PAN).
Guerrero: CARLOS ZEFERINO TORREBLANCA GALINDO (PRD).
Hidalgo: MIGUEL ANGEL OSORIO CHONG (PRI).
Jalisco: EMILIO GONZÁLEZ MÁRQUEZ (PAN).
México: ENRIQUE PEÑA NIETO (PRI).
Michoacán (de Ocampo): LEONEL GODOY RANGEL (PRD).
Morelos: MARCO ANTONIO ADAME CASTILLO (PAN).
Nayarit: NEY GONZÁLEZ SÁNCHEZ (PRI).
Nuevo León: RODRIGO MEDINA DE LA CRUZ (PRI).
Oaxaca: ULISES RUÍZ ORTIZ (PRI).
Puebla: MARIO MARÍN TORRES (PRI).
Querétaro (de Arteaga): JOSÉ CALZADA ROVIROSA (PRI).
Quintana Roo: FÉLIX GONZÁLEZ CANTO (PRI).
San Luis Potosí: FERNANDO TORANZO (PRI).
Sinaloa: JESÚS AGUILAR PADILLA (PRI).
Sonora: GUILLERMO PADRÉS ELÍAS (PAN).
Tabasco: ANDRÉS RAFAEL GRANIER MELO (PRI).
Tamaulipas: EUGENIO HERNÁNDEZ FLORES (PRI).
Tlaxcala: HECTOR ISRAEL ORTIZ ORTIZ (PAN).
Veracruz-Llave: FIDEL HERRERA (PRI).
Yucatán: IVONNE ORTEGA PACHECO (PRI).
Zacatecas: AMALIA GARCÍA MEDINA (PRD).

Head of Government of the Distrito Federal: MARCELO LUIS EBRARD CASAUBÓN (PRD).

President and Legislature

PRESIDENT

Election, 2 July 2006

Candidate	Number of votes	% of votes
Felipe Calderón Hinojosa (PAN)	14,916,927	35.89
Andrés Manuel López Obrador (Por el Bien de Todos*)	14,683,096	35.33
Roberto Madrazo Pintado (Alianza por México†)	9,237,000	22.23
Patricia Mercado Castro (PASC‡)	1,124,280	2.71
Roberto Campa Cifrián (Nueva Alianza)	397,550	0.96
Total§	41,557,430	100.00

* An alliance of the PRD, the PT and Convergencia.
† An alliance of the PRI and the PVEM.
‡ The Partido Alternativa Socialdemócrata y Campesina, subsequently renamed the Partido Socialdemócrata.
§ Including 900,373 invalid votes and 298,204 votes for unregistered candidates.

CONGRESO DE LA UNIÓN

Senado

Senate: Xicoténcatl 9, Centro Histórico, 06010 México, DF; tel. (55) 5130-2200; internet www.senado.gob.mx.

President: SANTIAGO CREEL MIRANDA (PAN).

Elections, 2 July 2006

Party	Seats
Partido Acción Nacional (PAN)	52
Partido Revolucionario Institucional (PRI)*	33
Partido de la Revolución Democrática (PRD)†	29
Partido Verde Ecologista de México (PVEM)*	6
Convergencia†	5
Partido del Trabajo (PT)†	2
Nueva Alianza	1
Total	128

* Part of the Alianza por México.
† Part of the Por el Bien de Todos alliance.

Cámara Federal de Diputados

Federal Chamber of Deputies: Avda Congreso de la Unión 66, Col. El Parque, Del. Venustiano Carranza, 15969 México, DF; tel. (55) 5628-1300; internet www.diputados.gob.mx.

President: RUTH ZAVALETA SALGADO (PRD).

Elections, 5 July 2009

Party	Seats
Partido Revolucionario Institucional (PRI)*	237
Partido Acción Nacional (PAN)	143
Partido de la Revolución Democrática (PRD)†	71
Partido Verde Ecologista de México (PVEM)*	22
Partido del Trabajo (PT)†	13
Nueva Alianza	8
Convergencia†	6
Total	500

* Part of the Alianza por México.
† Part of the Por el Bien de Todos alliance.

Election Commission

Instituto Federal Electoral (IFE): Viaducto Tlalpan 100, Col. Arenal Tepepan, Del. Tlalpan, 14610 México, DF; e-mail info@ife.org.mx; internet www.ife.org.mx; f. 1990; independent; Pres. LEONARDO VALDÉS ZURITA; Sec. EDMUNDO JACOBO MOLINA.

Political Organizations

To retain legal political registration, parties must secure at least 1.5% of total votes at two consecutive federal elections. Following the 2009 mid-term elections eight national political parties were registered.

Convergencia: Louisiana 113, Col. Nápoles, esq. Nueva York, Del. Benito Juárez, 03810 México, DF; tel. (55) 1167-6767; e-mail gestionsocial@convergencia.org.mx; internet www.convergencia.org.mx; f. 1995 as Convergencia por la Democracia; part of the Por el Bien de Todos alliance formed to contest 2006 presidential election, later renamed the Frente Amplio Progresista; Pres. LUIS WALTON ARBURTO; Sec.-Gen. ARMANDO LÓPEZ VELARDE CAMPA.

Nueva Alianza: Durango 199, Col. Roma, Del. Cuauhtémoc, 06700 México, DF; tel. (55) 3685-8485; fax (55) 3685-8455; e-mail contacto@nueva-alianza.org.mx; internet www.nueva-alianza.org.mx; f. 2005 by dissident faction of the PRI; includes mems of the Sindicato Nacional de Trabajadores de la Educación (SNTE, see Trade Unions) and supporters of Elba Esther Gordillo Morales; Pres. JORGE KAHWAGI MACARI; Sec.-Gen. FERMÍN TRUJILLO FUENTES.

Partido Acción Nacional (PAN): Avda Coyoacán 1546, Col. del Valle, Del. Benito Juárez, 03100 México, DF; tel. (55) 5200-4000; e-mail correo@cen.pan.org.mx; internet www.pan.org.mx; f. 1939; democratic party; 150,000 mems; Pres. JOSÉ CÉSAR NAVA VÁZQUEZ; Sec.-Gen. JOSÉ GONZÁLEZ MORFIN.

Partido Popular Socialista (PPS): Avda Alvaro Obregón 185, Col. Roma, Del. Cuauhtémoc, 06797 México, DF; tel. (55) 5208-5063; fax (55) 2454-6593; e-mail info@partidopopularsocialista.org.mx; internet www.partidopopularsocialista.org.mx; f. 1948; Marxist-Leninist, Lombardist; Sec.-Gen. JESÚS ANTONIO CARLOS HERNÁNDEZ; Org. Sec. HÉCTOR MARÍN REBOLLO.

Partido de la Revolución Democrática (PRD): Avda Benjamín Franklin 84, Col. Escandón, Del. Miguel Hidalgo, 11800 México, DF; tel. (55) 1085-8000; fax (55) 1085-8144; e-mail comunicacion@prd.org.mx; internet www.prd.org.mx; f. 1989; centre-left; leading mem. of the Por el Bien de Todos alliance formed to contest 2006 presidential election, later renamed the Frente Amplio Progresista; factions include Izquierda Unida (radical faction supporting Andrés Manuel López Obrador's claim to the presidency) and Nueva Izquierda (moderate); Pres. JESÚS ORTEGA MARTÍNEZ; Sec.-Gen. HORTENSIA ARAGÓN CASTILLO.

Partido Revolucionario Institucional (PRI): Edif. 2, Insurgentes Norte 59, Col. Buenavista, Del. Cuauhtémoc, 06359 México, DF; tel. (55) 5729-9600; internet www.pri.org.mx; f. 1929 as the Partido Nacional Revolucionario; regarded as the natural successor to the victorious parties of the revolutionary period; broadly based and centrist; formed Alianza por México alliance with PVEM to contest 2006 presidential election; Pres. BEATRIZ ELENA PAREDES RANGEL; Sec.-Gen. JESÚS MURILLO KARAM; groups within the PRI include: the Corriente Crítica Progresista, the Corriente Crítica del Partido, the Corriente Constitucionalista Democratizadora, Corriente Nuevo PRI XIV Asamblea, Democracia 2000, México Nuevo and Galileo.

Partido del Trabajo (PT): Avda Cuauhtémoc 47, Col. Roma Norte, Del. Miguel Hidalgo, 06700 México, DF; tel. and fax (55) 5525-2727; internet www.partidodeltrabajo.org.mx; f. 1990; labour party; part of the Por el Bien de Todos alliance formed to contest 2006 presidential election, later renamed the Frente Amplio Progresista; Leader ALBERTO ANAYA GUTIÉRREZ.

Partido Verde Ecologista de México (PVEM): Loma Bonita 18, Col. Lomas Altas, Del. Miguel Hidalgo, 11950 México, DF; tel. and fax (55) 5257-0188; internet www.partidoverde.org.mx; f. 1987; ecologist party; formed Alianza por México alliance with PRI to contest 2006 presidential election; Pres. JORGE EMILIO GONZÁLEZ MARTÍNEZ; Sec.-Gen. MARCO ANTONIO DE LA MORA TORREBLANCA.

The following parties are not officially registered but continue to be politically active:

Fuerza Ciudadana: Rochester 94, Col. Nápoles, 03810 México, DF; tel. (55) 5534-4628; e-mail info@fuerzaciudadana.org.mx; internet www.fuerzaciudadana.org.mx; f. 2002; citizens' asscn; Pres. JORGE ALCOCER VILLANUEVA; Sec. ALBERTO CONSEJO VARGAS.

Partido Democrático Popular Revolucionario: f. 1996; political grouping representing the causes of 14 armed peasant orgs, including the EPR and the PROCUP.

Partido Revolucionario Obrerista y Clandestino de Unión Popular (PROCUP): peasant org.

Partido Socialdemócrata (PSD): Tejocotes 164, Col. Tlacoquemécatl del Valle, Del. Benito Juárez, 03200 México, DF; tel. (55) 5488-1520; fax (55) 5488-1598; internet www.psd.org.mx; f. 2005 as Partido Alternativa Socialdemócrata y Campesina; adopted current name 2008; progressive and peasants' rights; lost political registration following 2009 mid-term elections; Pres. JORGE CARLOS DÍAZ CUEVOS.

Illegal organizations active in Mexico include the following:

Ejército Popular Revolucionario (EPR): e-mail pdprepr@hotmail.com; f. 1994; left-wing guerrilla group active mainly in southern states, linked to the Partido Democrático Popular Revolucionario (q.v.).

Ejército Revolucionario Popular Insurgente (ERPI): f. 1996; left-wing guerrilla group active in Guerrero, Morelos and Oaxaca; Leader JACOBO SILVA NOGALES.

Ejército Zapatista de Liberación Nacional (EZLN): e-mail laotra@ezln.org.mx; internet www.ezln.org.mx; f. 1993; left-wing guerrilla group active in the Chiapas region; Leader 'Subcomandante MARCOS'.

Frente Democrático Oriental de México Emiliano Zapata (FDOMEZ): peasant org.

Other armed groups include the Tendencia Democrática Revolucionaria-Ejército del Pueblo and the Comando Popular Revolucionario—La Patria es Primero.

Diplomatic Representation

EMBASSIES IN MEXICO

Algeria: Sierra Madre 540, Col. Lomas de Chapultepec, Del. Miguel Hidalgo, 11000 México, DF; tel. (55) 5520-6950; fax (55) 5540-7579; e-mail embajadadeargelia@yahoo.com.mx; Ambassador MERZAK BELHIMEUR.

Angola: Gaspar de Zúñiga 226, Col. Lomas de Chapultepec, Sección Virreyes, Del. Miguel Hidalgo, 11000 México, DF; tel. (55) 5202-4421; fax (55) 5540-5928; e-mail info@embangolamex.org; Ambassador JOSÉ JAIME FURTADO GONÇALVEZ.

Argentina: Avda Palmas 910, Col. Lomas de Chapultepec, Del. Miguel Hidalgo, 11000 México, DF; tel. (55) 5520-9430; fax (55) 5540-5011; e-mail embajadaargentina@prodigy.net.mx; Ambassador PATRICIA VACA NARVAJA.

Australia: Rubén Darío 55, Col. Polanco, Del. Miguel Hidalgo, 11580 México, DF; tel. (55) 1101-2200; fax (55) 1101-2201; e-mail embaustmex@yahoo.com.mx; internet www.mexico.embassy.gov.au; Ambassador KATRINA ANNE COOPER.

Austria: Sierra Tarahumara 420, Col. Lomas de Chapultepec, Del. Miguel Hidalgo, 11000 México, DF; tel. (55) 5251-0806; fax (55) 5245-0198; e-mail mexiko-ob@bmaa.gv.at; internet www.embajadadeaustria.com.mx; Ambassador ALFRED LANGLE.

Azerbaijan: Avda Virreyes 1015, Col. Lomas de Chapultepec, Del. Miguel Hidalgo, 11000 México, DF; tel. (55) 5540-4109; fax (55) 5540-1366; Ambassador ILGAR MUKHTAROV.

Belgium: Alfredo Musset 41, Col. Polanco, Del. Miguel Hidalgo, 11550 México, DF; tel. (55) 5280-0758; fax (55) 5280-0208; e-mail mexico@diplobel.org; internet www.diplomatie.be/mexico; Ambassador BOUDEWIJN E. G. DEREYMAEKAR.

Belize: Bernardo de Gálvez 215, Col. Lomas de Chapultepec, Del. Miguel Hidalgo, 11000 México, DF; tel. (55) 5520-1274; fax (55) 5520-6089; e-mail embelize@prodigy.net.mx; Ambassador ROSENDO URBINA.

Bolivia: Goethe 104, Col. Anzures, Del. Miguel Hidalgo, 11590 México, DF; tel. and fax (55) 5255-3620; e-mail embajada@embol.org.mx; internet www.embol.org.mx; Ambassador JORGE MANSILLA TORRES.

Brazil: Lope de Armendáriz 130, Col. Lomas Virreyes, Del. Miguel Hidalgo, 11000 México, DF; tel. (55) 5201-4531; fax (55) 5520-4929; e-mail embrasil@brasil.org.mx; internet www.brasil.org.mx; Ambassador SERGIO AGOSTO DE ABREU E LIMA FLORENCIO SOBRINHO.

Bulgaria: Paseo de la Reforma 1990, Col. Lomas de Chapultepec, Del. Miguel Hidalgo, 11000 México, DF; tel. (55) 5596-3283; fax (55) 5596-1012; e-mail ebulgaria@yahoo.com; Ambassador SERGEY PENCHEV MICHEV.

Canada: Schiller 529, Col. Polanco, Del. Miguel Hidalgo, 11560 México, DF; tel. (55) 5724-7900; fax (55) 5724-7980; e-mail mxico@international.gc.ca; internet www.canadainternational.gc.ca/mexico-mexique; Ambassador GUILLERMO E. RISHCHYNSKI.

Chile: Andrés Bello 10, 18°, Col. Polanco, Del. Miguel Hidalgo, 11560 México, DF; tel. (55) 5280-9681; fax (55) 5280-9703; e-mail echilmex@prodigy.net.mx; internet www.embajadadechile.com.mx; Ambassador GERMÁN GUERRERO PAVEZ.

China, People's Republic: Avda San Jerónimo 217B, Del. Alvaro Obregón, 01090 México, DF; tel. (55) 5616-0609; fax (55) 5616-0460; e-mail embchina@data.net.mx; internet www.embajadachina.org.mx; Ambassador YIN HENGMIN.

Colombia: Paseo de la Reforma 379, 5°, Col. Cuauhtémoc, Del. Cuauhtémoc, 06500 México, DF; tel. (55) 5525-0277; fax (55) 5208-2876; e-mail emcol@colombiaenmexico.org; internet www.embajadaenmexico.gob.co; Ambassador LUIS CAMILO OSORIO ISAZA.

Costa Rica: Río Po 113, Col. Cuauhtémoc, Del. Cuauhtémoc, 06500 México, DF; tel. (55) 5525-7764; fax (55) 5511-9240; e-mail embajada@embajada.decostaricaenmexico.org; internet www.embajada.decostaricaenmexico.org; Ambassador GABRIELA JIMÉNEZ CRUZ.

Côte d'Ivoire: Tennyson 67, Col. Polanco, Del. Miguel Hidalgo, 11560 México, DF; tel. 5280-8573; fax 5282-2954; Ambassador ANNE GNAHOURET TATRET.

Cuba: Presidente Masaryk 554, Col. Polanco, Del. Miguel Hidalgo, 11560 México, DF; tel. (55) 5280-8039; fax (55) 5280-0839; e-mail embajada@embacuba.com.mx; internet www.embacuba.com.mx; Ambassador MANUEL FRANCISCO AGUILERA DE LA PÁZ.

Cyprus: Sierra Gorda 370, Col. Lomas de Chapultepec, Del. Miguel Hidalgo, 11000 México, DF; tel. (55) 5202-7600; fax (55) 5520-2693; e-mail chipre@att.net.mx; Ambassador VASILIOS PHILIPPOU.

Czech Republic: Cuvier 22, esq. Kepler, Col. Nueva Anzures, Del. Miguel Hidalgo, 11590 México, DF; tel. (55) 5531-2777; fax (55) 5531-1837; e-mail mexico@embassy.mzv.cz; internet www.mzv.cz/mexico; Ambassador JIŘÍ HAVLÍK.

Denmark: Tres Picos 43, Col. Chapultepec Morales, Del. Miguel Hidalgo, 11580 México, DF; tel. (55) 5255-3405; fax (55) 5545-5797; e-mail mexamb@um.dk; internet www.ambmexicocity.um.dk; Ambassador JOHANNES DAHL-HANSEN.

Dominican Republic: Prado Sur 755 (entre Monte Blanco y Monte Everest), Col. Lomas de Chapultepec, Del. Miguel Hidalgo, 11000 México, DF; tel. (55) 5540-3841; fax (55) 5520-0779; e-mail embajada@embadom.org.mx; internet www.embadom.org.mx; Ambassador FERNANDO ANTONIO PÉREZ MEMÉN.

Ecuador: Tennyson 217, Col. Polanco, Del. Miguel Hidalgo, 11560 México, DF; tel. (55) 5545-3141; fax (55) 5254-2442; e-mail mecuamex@prodigy.net.mx; Ambassador GALO GALARZA DÁVILA.

Egypt: Alejandro Dumas 131, Col. Polanco, Del. Miguel Hidalgo, 11560 México, DF; tel. (55) 5281-0823; fax (55) 5282-1294; e-mail embofegypt@prodigy.net.mx; Ambassador IBRAHIM AHDY KHAIRAT.

El Salvador: Temístocles 88, Col. Polanco, Del. Miguel Hidalgo, 11560 México, DF; tel. (55) 5281-5725; fax (55) 5280-0657; e-mail embesmex@webtelmex.net.mx; Ambassador HUGO ROBERTO CARRILLO CORLETO.

Finland: Monte Pelvoux 111, 4°, Col. Lomas de Chapultepec, Del. Miguel Hidalgo, 11000 México, DF; tel. (55) 5540-6036; fax (55) 5540-0114; e-mail finmex@prodigy.net.mx; internet www.finlandia.org.mx; Ambassador ULLA MARIANNA VAISTO.

France: Campos Elíseos 339, Col. Polanco, Del. Miguel Hidalgo, 11560 México, DF; tel. (55) 9171-9893; fax (55) 9171-9703; e-mail prensa@ambafrance-mx.org; internet www.ambafrance-mx.org; Ambassador DANIEL PARFAIT.

Germany: Horacio 1506, Col. Los Morales, Del. Miguel Hidalgo, 11530 México, DF; tel. (55) 5283-2200; fax (55) 5281-2588; e-mail info@mexi.diplo.de; internet www.mexiko.diplo.de; Ambassador Dr ROLAND MICHAEL WEGENER.

Greece: Sierra Gorda 505, Col. Lomas de Chapultepec, Del. Miguel Hidalgo, 11010 México, DF; tel. (55) 5520-2070; fax (55) 5202-4080; e-mail grem.mex@mfa.gr; Ambassador VASSILIS KARANTONIS.

Guatemala: Explanada 1025, Col. Lomas de Chapultepec, Del. Miguel Hidalgo, 11000 México, DF; tel. (55) 5540-7520; fax (55) 5202-1142; e-mail embaguatemx@minex.gob.gt; Ambassador JOSÉ LUIS CHEA URRUELA.

Haiti: Presa Don Martín 53, Col. Irrigación, Del. Miguel Hidalgo, 11500 México, DF; tel. (55) 5557-2065; fax (55) 5395-1654; e-mail ambadh@mail.internet.com.mx; Ambassador ROBERT MANUEL.

Holy See: Juan Pablo II 118, Col. Guadalupe Inn, Del. Alvaro Obregón, 01020 México, DF; tel. (55) 5663-3999; fax (55) 5663-5308; Apostolic Nuncio Most Rev. CHRISTOPHE PIERRE (Titular Archbishop of Gunela).

Honduras: Alfonso Reyes 220, Col. Condesa, Del. Cuauhtémoc, 06170 México, DF; tel. (55) 5211-5747; fax (55) 5211-5425; e-mail emhonmex@prodigy.net.mx; Ambassador ROSALINDA BUESO ASFURA.

Hungary: Paseo de las Palmas 2005, Col. Lomas de Chapultepec, Del. Miguel Hidalgo, 11000 México, DF; tel. (55) 5596-0523; fax (55) 5596-2378; internet www.mfa.gov.hu/kulkepviselet/MX/hu; Ambassador TEREZ DÖRÖMBÖZI DE DEHELAN.

India: Musset 325, Col. Polanco, Del. Miguel Hidalgo, 11550 México, DF; tel. (55) 5531-1050; fax (55) 5254-2349; e-mail indembmx@prodigy.net.mx; internet www.indembassy.org; Ambassador DINESH KUMAR JAIN.

Indonesia: Julio Verne 27, Col. Polanco, Del. Miguel Hidalgo, 11560 México, DF; tel. (55) 5280-6363; fax (55) 5280-7062; e-mail kbrimex@prodigy.net.mx; Chargé d'affaires a.i. LINGGA SETIAWAN.

Iran: Paseo de la Reforma 2350, Col. Lomas Altas, Del. Miguel Hidalgo, 11950 México, DF; tel. (55) 9172-2691; fax (55) 9172-2694; e-mail iranembmex@hotmail.com; Ambassador MOHAMMAD HASSAN GHADIRI ABYANEH.

Iraq: Paseo de la Reforma 1875, Col. Lomas de Chapultepec, Del. Miguel Hidalgo, 11000 México, DF; tel. (55) 5596-0933; fax (55) 5596-0254; e-mail mxcemb@iraqfamail.com; Chargé d'affaires a.i. SABIR MAHMOUD ABDULRAZZAK AL-ANI.

Ireland: Cerrada Blvd Manuel Avila Camacho 76, 3°, Col. Lomas de Chapultepec, Del. Miguel Hidalgo, 11000 México, DF; tel. (55) 5520-5803; fax (55) 5520-5892; e-mail emexicoembassy@dfa.ie; internet www.irishembassy.com.mx; Ambassador EAMONN HICKEY.

Israel: Sierra Madre 215, Col. Lomas de Chapultepec, Del. Miguel Hidalgo, 11000 México, DF; tel. (55) 5201-1500; fax (55) 5201-1555; e-mail publicaffairs@mexico.mfa.gov.il; internet mexico-city.mfa.gov.il; Ambassador YOSEF LIVNE.

Italy: Paseo de las Palmas 1994, Col. Lomas de Chapultepec, Del. Miguel Hidalgo, 11000 México, DF; tel. (55) 5596-3655; fax (55) 5596-2472; e-mail segreteria.messico@esteri.it; internet www.ambcittadelmessico.esteri.it; Ambassador ROBERTO SPINELLI.

Jamaica: Schiller 326, 8°, Col. Chapultepec Morales, Del. Miguel Hidalgo, 11570 México, DF; tel. (55) 5250-6804; fax (55) 5250-6160; e-mail embajadadejamaica@prodigy.net.mx; Ambassador SHEILA IVOLINE SEALY-MONTEITH.

Japan: Paseo de la Reforma 395, Apdo 5-101, Col. Cuauhtémoc, Del. Cuauhtémoc, 06500 México, DF; tel. (55) 5211-0028; fax (55) 5207-7743; e-mail embjapmx@mail.internet.com.mx; internet www.mx.emb-japan.go.jp; Ambassador MASAAKI ONO.

Korea, Democratic People's Republic: Calle Halley 12, Col. Anzures, Del. Miguel Hidalgo, 11590 México, DF; tel. (55) 5250-0263; fax (55) 5545-8775; e-mail dpkoreaemb@prodigy.net.mx; Ambassador AN KUN SONG.

Korea, Republic: Lope de Armendáriz 110, Col. Lomas Virreyes, Del. Miguel Hidalgo, 11000 México, DF; tel. (55) 5202-9866; fax (55) 5540-7446; e-mail coremex@prodigy.net.mx; internet mex.mofat.go.kr; Ambassador CHO WHAN-BOK.

Lebanon: Julio Verne 8, Col. Polanco, Del. Miguel Hidalgo, 11560 México, DF; tel. (55) 5280-5614; fax (55) 5280-8870; e-mail embalibano@embajadadelibano.org.mx; internet www.embajadadelibano.org.mx; Ambassador NOUHAD MAHMOUD.

Libya: Horacio 1003, Col. Polanco, Del. Miguel Hidalgo, 11550 México, DF; tel. (55) 5545-5725; fax (55) 5545-5677; e-mail libia.mexico@yahoo.com; Chargé d'affaires a.i. KHALID A. A. DAHAN.

Malaysia: Sierra Nevada 435, Col. Lomas de Chapultepec, Del. Miguel Hidalgo, 11000 México, DF; tel. (55) 5282-5166; fax (55) 5282-4910; e-mail mwmexico@prodigy.net.mx; Ambassador NAFISAH BINTI MOHAMED.

Morocco: Paseo de las Palmas 2020, Col. Lomas de Chapultepec, Del. Miguel Hidalgo, 11000 México, DF; tel. (55) 5245-1786; fax (55) 5245-1791; e-mail sifamex@infosel.net.mx; internet www.marruecos.org.mx; Ambassador MAHMOUD RMIKI.

Netherlands: Edif. Calakmul, 7°, Avda Vasco de Quiroga 3000, Col. Santa Fe, Del. Alvaro Obregón, 01210 México, DF; tel. (55) 5258-9921; fax (55) 5258-8138; e-mail mex-info@minbuza.nl; internet www.paisesbajos.com.mx; Ambassador CORA MINDERHOUD.

New Zealand: Edif. Corporativo Polanco, 4°, Jaime Balmes 8, Col. Los Morales Polanco, Del. Miguel Hidalgo, 11510 México, DF; tel. (55) 5283-9460; fax (55) 5283-9480; e-mail kiwimexico@prodigy.net.mx; internet www.nzembassy.com/mexico; Ambassador CECILE HILLYER.

Nicaragua: Prado Norte 470, Col. Lomas de Chapultepec, Del. Miguel Hidalgo, 11000 México, DF; tel. (55) 5540-5625; fax (55) 5520-6961; e-mail embanic@prodigy.net.mx; Ambassador HORACIO BRENES ICABALCETA.

Nigeria: Paseo de las Palmas 1880, Col. Lomas de Chapultepec, Del. Miguel Hidalgo, 11000 México, DF; tel. (55) 5245-1487; fax (55) 5245-0105; e-mail nigembmx@att.net.mx; Ambassador LAWRENCE NWANCHO NWURUKU.

Norway: Avda de los Virreyes 1460, Col. Lomas Virreyes, Del. Miguel Hidalgo, 11000 México, DF; tel. (55) 5540-3486; fax (55) 5202-3019; e-mail emb.mexico@mfa.no; internet www.noruega.org.mx; Ambassador ARNE AASHEIM.

Pakistan: Hegel 512, Col. Chapultepec Morales, Del. Miguel Hidalgo, 11570 México, DF; tel. (55) 5203-3636; fax (55) 5203-9907; e-mail parepmex@hotmail.com; Ambassador ZEHRA AKBARI.

Panama: Sócrates 339, Col. Polanco, Del. Miguel Hidalgo, 11560 México, DF; tel. (55) 5280-7857; fax (55) 5280-7586; e-mail informes@embpanamamexico.com; internet www.embpanamamexico.com; Ambassador FRANCISCO TROYA AGUIRRE.

Paraguay: Homero 415, 1°, esq. Hegel, Col. Polanco, Del. Miguel Hidalgo, 11570 México, DF; tel. (55) 5545-0405; fax (55) 5531-9905; e-mail embapar@prodigy.net.mx; Ambassador CARLOS HERIBERTO RIVEROS SALCEDO.

Peru: Paseo de la Reforma 2601, Col. Lomas Reforma, Del. Miguel Hidalgo, 11000 México, DF; tel. (55) 1105-2270; fax (55) 1105-2279; e-mail embaperu@prodigy.net.mx; Ambassador LUIS ALVARADO CONTRERAS.

Philippines: Río Rhin 56, Cuauhtemoc, Del. Cuauhtemoc, 06500 México, DF; tel. (55) 5202-8456; fax (55) 5202-8403; e-mail ambamexi@yahoo.com.mx; Ambassador FRANCISCO ORTIGAS MIRANDA.

Poland: Cracovia 40, Col. San Angel, Del. Alvaro Obregón, 01000 México, DF; tel. (55) 5481-2051; fax (55) 5481-2056; e-mail embajadadepolonia@prodigy.net.mx; internet www.meksyk.polemb.net; Ambassador ANNA ELZBIETA NIEWIADOMSKA.

Portugal: Avda Alpes 1370, Lomas de Chapultepec, Del. Miguel Hidalgo, 11000 México, DF; tel. (55) 5520-7897; fax (55) 5520-4688; e-mail embpomex@prodigy.net.mx; internet embpomex.wordpress.com; Ambassador FRANCISCO DOMINGOS GARCÍA FALCÃO MACHADO.

Romania: Sófocles 311, Col. Polanco, Del. Miguel Hidalgo, 11560 México, DF; tel. (55) 5280-0197; fax (55) 5280-0343; e-mail secretariat@rumania.org.mx; internet www.rumania.org.mx; Ambassador MANUELA VULPE.

Russia: José Vasconcelos 204, Col. Hipódromo Condesa, Del. Cuauhtémoc, 06140 México, DF; tel. (55) 5273-1305; fax (55) 5273-1545; e-mail embrumex@hotmail.com; internet www.embrumex.com.mx; Ambassador VALERY I. MOROZOV.

Saudi Arabia: Paseo de las Palmas 2075, Col. Lomas de Chapultepec, Del. Miguel Hidalgo, 11000 México, DF; tel. (55) 5596-0173; fax (55) 5020-3160; e-mail saudiemb@prodigy.net.mx; Ambassador MUNEER IBRAHIM AL-BENJABI.

Serbia: Montañas Rocallosas Oeste 515, Col. Lomas de Chapultepec, Del. Miguel Hidalgo, 11000 México, DF; tel. (55) 5520-0524; fax (55) 5520-9927; e-mail embajadaserbia@alestra.net.mx; Ambassador ZORAN STANOJEVIĆ.

Slovakia: Julio Verne 35, Col. Polanco, Del. Miguel Hidalgo, 11560 México, DF; tel. (55) 5280-6669; fax (55) 5280-6294; e-mail eslovaquia@prodigy.net.mx; Ambassador JOZEF ADAMEC.

South Africa: Edif. Forum, 9°, Andrés Bello 10, Col. Polanco, Del. Miguel Hidalgo, 11560 México, DF; tel. (55) 1100-4970; fax (55) 5282-9259; e-mail safrica@prodigy.net.mx; Ambassador MPHAKAMA NYANGWENI MBETE.

Spain: Galileo 114, esq. Horacio, Col. Polanco, Del. Miguel Hidalgo, 11550 México, DF; tel. (55) 5282-2271; fax (55) 5282-1520; e-mail embaes@prodigy.net.mx; internet www.mae.es/embajadas/mexico; Ambassador MANUEL ALABART FERNANDEZ-CAVADA.

Sweden: Paseo de las Palmas 1375, Col. Lomas de Chapultepec, Del. Miguel Hidalgo, 11000 México, DF; tel. (55) 9178-5010; fax (55) 5540-3253; e-mail suecia@prodigy.net.mx; internet www.suecia.com.mx; Ambassador ANNA LINDSTEDT.

Switzerland: Paseo de las Palmas 405, 11°, Torre Óptima, Col. Lomas de Chapultepec, Del. Miguel Hidalgo, 11000 México, DF; tel. (55) 9178-4370; fax (55) 5520-8685; e-mail vertretung@mex.rep.admin.ch; internet www.eda.admin.ch/mexico; Ambassador URS BREITER.

Thailand: Paseo de las Palmas 1610, Col. Lomas de Chapultepec, Del. Miguel Hidalgo, 11000 México, DF; tel. (55) 5540-4551; fax (55) 5540-4817; e-mail thaimex@prodigy.net.mx; internet www.thaiembmexico.co.nr; Ambassador CHARUWAN THIEMTHAD.

Turkey: Monte Líbano 885, Col. Lomas de Chapultepec, Del. Miguel Hidalgo, 11000 México, DF; tel. (55) 5282-4277; fax (55) 5282-4894; e-mail turkishembassy@hotmail.com; internet www.turkembmex.org; Ambassador ALEV KILIC.

Ukraine: Paseo de la Reforma 730, Col. Lomas de Chapultepec, Del. Miguel Hidalgo, 11000 México, DF; tel. (55) 5282-4085; fax (55) 5282-4768; e-mail ucraniaemb@prodigy.net.mx; Ambassador OLEKSIY V. BRANASHKO.

United Kingdom: Río Lerma 71, Col. Cuauhtémoc, Del. Cuauhtémoc, 06500 México, DF; tel. (55) 5242-8500; fax (55) 5242-8517; e-mail ukinmex@att.net.mx; internet www.embajadabritanica.com.mx; Ambassador JUDITH ANNE MACGREGOR.

USA: Paseo de la Reforma 305, Del. Cuauhtémoc, 06500 México, DF; tel. (55) 5080-2000; fax (55) 5080-2150; internet www.usembassy-mexico.gov; Ambassador CARLOS ENRIQUE PASCUAL.

Uruguay: Hegel 149, 1°, Col. Chapultepec Morales, Del. Miguel Hidalgo, 11560 México, DF; tel. (55) 5531-0880; fax (55) 5545-3342; e-mail uruguaymex@prodigy.net.mx; Ambassador JOSÉ IGNACIO KORZENIAK PASTORINO.

Venezuela: Schiller 326, Col. Chapultepec Morales, Del. Miguel Hidalgo, 11570 México, DF; tel. (55) 5203-4233; fax (55) 5254-1457; e-mail venezmex@prodigy.net.mx; Ambassador TRINO ALCIDES DÍAZ.

Viet Nam: Sierra Ventana 255, Col. Lomas de Chapultepec, Del. Miguel Hidalgo, 11000 México, DF; tel. (55) 5540-1632; fax (55) 5540-1612; e-mail vietnam.mx@mofa.gov.vn; internet www.vietnamembassy-mexico.org/vi; Ambassador PHAM VAN QUE.

Judicial System

The principle of the separation of the judiciary from the legislative and executive powers is embodied in the 1917 Constitution. The judicial system is divided into two areas: the federal, dealing with federal law, and the local, dealing only with state law within each state.

The federal judicial system has both ordinary and constitutional jurisdiction, and judicial power is exercised by the Supreme Court of Justice, the Electoral Court, Collegiate and Unitary Circuit Courts and District Courts. The Supreme Court comprises two separate chambers: Civil and Criminal Affairs, and Administrative and Labour Affairs. The Federal Judicature Council is responsible for the administration, surveillance and discipline of the federal judiciary, except for the Supreme Court of Justice.

In 2006 there were 172 Collegiate Circuit Courts (Tribunales Colegiados), 62 Unitary Circuit Courts (Tribunales Unitarios) and 285 District Courts (Juzgados de Distrito). Mexico is divided into 29 judicial circuits. The Circuit Courts may be collegiate, when dealing with the *derecho de amparo* (protection of constitutional rights of an individual), or unitary, when dealing with appeal cases. The Collegiate Circuit Courts comprise three magistrates with residence in the cities of México, Toluca, Naucalpan, Guadalajara, Monterrey, Hermosillo, Puebla, Boca del Río, Xalapa, Torreón, Saltillo, San Luis Potosí, Villahermosa, Morelia, Mazatlán, Oaxaca, Mérida, Mexicali, Guanajuato, León, Chihuahua, Ciudad Juárez, Cuernavaca, Ciudad Victoria, Ciudad Reynosa, Tuxtla Gutiérrez, Tapachula, Acapulco, Chilpancingo, Querétaro, Zacatecas, Aguascalientes, Tepic, Durango, La Paz, Cancún, Tlaxcala and Pachuca. The Unitary Circuit Courts comprise one magistrate with residence mostly in the same cities as given above.

SUPREME COURT OF JUSTICE

Suprema Corte de Justicia de la Nación: Pino Suárez 2, Col. Centro, 06065 México, DF; tel. (55) 5522-0096; fax (55) 5522-0152; e-mail administrator@mail.scjn.gob.mx; internet www.scjn.gob.mx.

Chief Justice: GUILLERMO I. ORTÍZ MAYAGOITIA.

First Chamber—Civil and Criminal Affairs

President: SERGIO ARMANDO VALLS HERNÁNDEZ.

Second Chamber—Administrative and Labour Affairs

President: JOSÉ FERNANDO FRANCO GONZÁLEZ SALAS.

ELECTORAL TRIBUNAL OF THE FEDERAL JUDICIARY

Tribunal Electoral del Poder Jucicial de la Federación (TEPJF): Carlota Amero 5000, Col. Culhuacán, Del. Coyoacán, 04480 México, DF; tel. (55) 5728-2300; fax (55) 5728-2400; internet www.trife.gob.mx; Pres. MARÍA DEL CARMEN ALANIS FIGUEROA.

Religion

CHRISTIANITY

The Roman Catholic Church

The prevailing religion is Roman Catholicism, but the Church, disestablished in 1857, was for many years, under the Constitution of 1917, subject to state control. A constitutional amendment, promulgated in January 1992, officially removed all restrictions on the Church. For ecclesiastical purposes, Mexico comprises 18 archdioceses, 68 dioceses, five territorial prelatures and two eparchies (both directly subject to the Holy See). According to the latest available census figures (2000), some 88% of the population are Roman Catholics.

Bishops' Conference

Conferencia del Episcopado Mexicano (CEM), Edif. S. S. Juan Pablo II, Prolongación Ministerios 26, Col. Tepeyac Insurgentes, Apdo 118-055, 07020 México, DF; tel. (55) 5781-8462; fax (55) 5577-5489; e-mail segcem@cem.org.mx; internet www.cem.org.mx; Pres. CARLOS AGUIAR RETES (Archbishop of Tlalnepantla); Sec.-Gen. JOSÉ LEOPOLDO GONZÁLEZ GONZÁLEZ.

Archbishop of Acapulco: FELIPE AGUIRRE FRANCO, Arzobispado, Quebrada 16, Apdo 201, Centro, 39300 Acapulco, Gro; tel. and fax (744) 482-0763; e-mail arzobispadoaca@aca.cableonline.com.mx; internet www.arquidiocesisacapulco.org.mx.

Archbishop of Antequera, Oaxaca: JOSÉ LUIS CHÁVEZ BOTELLO, García Virgil 600, Anexos de Catedral, Col. Centro, 68000 Oaxaca, Oax.; tel. (951) 516-4822; fax (951) 514-1348; e-mail arzobispadoaxaca@hotmail.com; internet arquidiocesisoaxaca.org.mx.

Archbishop of Chihuahua: CONSTANCIO MIRANDA WECKMANN, Arzobispado, Avda Cuauhtémoc 1828, Apdo 7, Col. Cuauhtémoc, 31020 Chihuahua, Chih.; tel. (614) 410-3202; fax (614) 410-5621; e-mail ferar@megalink.com.mx; internet www.arquichi.org.mx.

Archbishop of Durango: HÉCTOR GONZÁLEZ MARTÍNEZ, Arzobispado, 20 de Noviembre 306, Poniente Centro, 34000 Durango, Dgo; tel. (618) 811-4242; fax (618) 812-8881; e-mail arqdgo@prodigy.net.mx.

Archbishop of Guadalajara: Cardinal JUAN SANDOVAL IÑIGUEZ, Arzobispado, Liceo 17, Apdo 1-331, Col. Centro, 44100 Guadalajara, Jal.; tel. (33) 3614-5504; fax (33) 3658-2300; e-mail arzgdl@arquinet.com.mx; internet www.arquidiocesisgdl.org.mx.

Archbishop of Hermosillo: JOSÉ ULISES MACÍAS SALCEDO, Arzobispado, Dr Paliza y Ocampo, Ala Sur de la Catedral, Col. Centenario, 83260 Hermosillo, Son.; tel. (662) 213-2138; fax (662) 213-1327; e-mail arzohmo@hotmail.com; internet www.iglesiahermosillo.com.mx.

Archbishop of Jalapa: HIPÓLITO REYES LARIOS, Arzobispado, Avda Manuel Avila Camacho 73, Apdo 359, Col. Centro, 91000 Jalapa, Ver.; tel. (228) 812-0579; fax (228) 817-5578; e-mail arzobispadoalxal@prodigy.net.mx.

Archbishop of León: JOSÉ GUADALUPE MARTÍN RÁBAGO, Arzobispado, Pedro Moreno 312, Apdo 108, 37000 León, Gto; tel. (477) 713-2747; fax (477) 713-1286; e-mail canciller@arquidiocesisleon.org.mx; internet www.arquidiocesisdeleon.org.mx.

Archbishop of Mexico City: Cardinal NORBERTO RIVERA CARRERA, Curia del Arzobispado de México, Durango 90, 5°, Col. Roma, Apdo 24433, 06700 México, DF; tel. (55) 5208-3200; fax (55) 5208-5350; e-mail arzobisp@arquidiocesismexico.org.mx; internet www.arzobispadomexico.org.mx.

Archbishop of Monterrey: Cardinal FRANCISCO ROBLES ORTEGA, Zuazua 1100 Sur con Ocampo Centro, Apdo 7, 64000 Monterrey, NL; tel. (81) 1158-2450; fax (81) 1158-2488; e-mail cancilleria@arquidiocesismty.org; internet www.arquidiocesismty.org.mx.

Archbishop of Morelia: ALBERTO SUÁREZ INDA, Arzobispado, Costado Catedral, Frente Avda Madero, Apdo 17, 58000 Morelia, Mich.; tel. (443) 313-2493; fax (443) 312-0919; e-mail asuarexi@prodigy.net.mx; internet www.arquimorelia.org.mx.

Archbishop of Puebla de los Angeles: VÍCTOR SÁNCHEZ ESPINOSA, Avda 2 Sur 305, Apdo 235, Col. Centro, 72000 Puebla, Pue.; tel. (222) 232-4591; fax (222) 246-2277; e-mail rhuesca@mail.cem.org.mx.

Archbishop of San Luis Potosí: LUIS MORALES REYES, Arzobispado, Francisco Madero 300, Apdo 1, Col. Centro, 78000 San Luis Potosí, SLP; tel. (444) 812-4555; fax (444) 812-7979; e-mail arqsanluis@iglesiapotosina.org; internet www.iglesiapotosina.org.

Archbishop of Tijuana: RAFAEL ROMO MUÑOZ, Arzobispado, Calle Décima y Avda Ocampo 8525, Apdo 226, 22000 Tijuana, BC; tel. (664) 684-8411; fax (664) 684-7683; internet www.iglesiatijuana.org.

Archbishop of Tlalnepantla: CARLOS AGUIAR RETES, Arzobispado, Avda Juárez 42, Apdo 268, Col. Centro, 54000 Tlalnepantla, Méx.; tel. (55) 5565-3944; fax (55) 5565-2751; e-mail curia@arqtlalnepantla.org; internet www.arqtlalnepantla.org.

Archbishop of Tulancingo: DOMINGO DÍAZ MARTÍNEZ, Arzobispado, Plaza de la Constitución, Apdo 14, 43600 Tulancingo, Hgo; e-mail sgamitra@netpac.net.mx.

Archbishop of Tuxtla Gutiérrez: ROGELIO CABRERA LÓPEZ, Uruguay 500A, Col. El Retiro, Apdo 365, 29040 Tuxtla Gutiérrez, Chis; e-mail casaepiscopal@prodigy.net.mx.

Archbishop of Yucatán: EMILIO CARLOS BERLIE BELAUNZARÁN, Arzobispado, Calle 58 501, Col. Centro, 97000 Mérida, Yuc.; tel. (999) 924-7777; fax (999) 923-7983; e-mail aryu@prodigy.net.mx; internet www.arquidiocesisdeyucatan.org.

The Anglican Communion

Mexico is divided into five dioceses, which form the Province of the Anglican Church in Mexico, established in 1995.

Bishop of Cuernavaca: RAMIRO DELGADO VERA, Minerva 1, Col. Delicias, 62431 Cuernavaca, Mor.; tel. and fax (777) 315-2870; e-mail adoc@cableonline.com.mx; internet www.cuernavaca-anglican.org.

Bishop of Mexico City and Primate of the Anglican Church in Mexico: CARLOS TOUCHÉ PORTER, La Otra Banda 40, Avda San Jerónimo 117, Col. San Angel, 01000 México, DF; tel. and fax (55) 5616-2205; e-mail contacto@iglesiaanglicanademexico.org; internet www.iglesiaanglicanademexico.org.

Bishop of Northern Mexico: MARCELINO RIVERA DELGADO, Simón Bolívar 2005 Nte, Col. Mitras Centro, 64460 Monterrey, NL; tel. (81) 8333-0922; fax (81) 8348-7362; e-mail diocesisdelnorte@att.net.mx.

Bishop of South-Eastern Mexico: BENITO JUÁREZ MARTÍNEZ, Avda de las Américas 73, Col. Aguacatl, 91130 Jalapa, Ver.; tel. and fax (228) 814-6951; e-mail dioste99@aol.com.

Bishop of Western Mexico: LINO RODRÍGUEZ-AMARO, Francisco Javier Gamboa 255, Col. Barrera, 45150 Guadalajara, Jal.; tel. (33) 3615-5070; fax (33) 3615-4413; e-mail iamoccidente@prodigy.net.mx; internet www.iamoccidente.org.mx.

Protestant Churches

According to the 2002 census, some 5% of the population are Protestant or Evangelical Christians.

Iglesia Luterana Mexicana: POB 1-1034, 44101 Guadalajara, Jal.; tel. (33) 3639-7253; e-mail dtrejocoria@hotmail.com; f. 1951; Pres. DANIEL TREJO CORIA; 1,500 mems.

Iglesia Metodista de México, Asociación Religiosa: Miravelle 209, Col. Albert, 03570 México, DF; tel. (55) 5539-3674; e-mail prenapro@iglesia-metodista.org.mx; internet www.iglesia-metodista.org.mx; f. 1930; 55,000 mems; Pres. Rev. MOISÉS VALDERRAMA GÓMEZ; 370 congregations; comprises six episcopal areas.

National Baptist Convention of Mexico: Tlalpan 1035-A, Col. Américas Unidas, 03610 México, DF; tel. (55) 5539-7720; fax (55) 5539-2302; e-mail comunicacion@cnbm.org.mx; internet www.cnbm.org.mx; f. 1903; Pres. Rev. JOSÉ TRINIDAD BONILLA MORALES.

BAHÁ'Í FAITH

National Spiritual Assembly of the Bahá'ís of Mexico: Emerson 421, Col. Chapultepec Morales, 11570 México, DF; tel. (55) 5545-2155; fax (55) 5255-5972; e-mail info@bahaimexico.org; internet www.bahaimexico.org; mems resident in 978 localities.

JUDAISM

According to the 2000 census, the Jewish community numbers 45,260 (less than 1% of the population).

Comité Central de la Comunidad Judía de México: Cofre de Perote 115, Lomas Barrilaco, 11010 México, DF; tel. (55) 5520-9393; fax (55) 5540-3050; e-mail comitecentral@prodigy.net.mx; internet www.tribuna.org.mx; f. 1938; Pres. OSCAR GORODZINSKY.

The Press

DAILY NEWSPAPERS

México, DF

La Afición: Ignacio Mariscal 23, Apdo 64 bis, Col. Tabacalera, 06030 México, DF; tel. (55) 5546-4780; fax (55) 5546-5852; internet www.laaficion.com; f. 1930; sport; Pres. FRANCISCO A. GONZÁLEZ; circ. 85,000.

La Crónica de Hoy: Londres 36, Col. Juárez, 06600 México, DF; tel. and fax (52) 5512-3429; e-mail suscripciones@cronica.com.mx; internet www.cronica.com.mx; Pres. JORGE KAHWAGI GASTINE; Editorial Dir PABLO HIRIART LE BERT.

Cuestión: Laguna de Mayrán 410, Col. Anáhuac, 11320 México, DF; tel. (55) 5260-0499; fax (55) 5260-3645; internet www.cuestion.com.mx; f. 1980; midday; Dir-Gen. Lic. ALBERTO GONZÁLEZ PARRA; circ. 48,000.

Diario de México: Chimalpopoca 38, Col. Obrera, 06800 México, DF; tel. (55) 5442-6501; fax (55) 5588-4289; e-mail redaccion@diariodemexico.com.mx; internet www.diariodemexico.com.mx; f. 1949; morning; Dir-Gen. FEDERICO BRACAMONTES BAZ; Editorial Dir ABEL MAGAÑA CAMPUZANO; circ. 76,000.

El Economista: Avda Coyoacán 515, Col. del Valle, 03100 México, DF; tel. (55) 5326-5454; fax (55) 5687-3821; e-mail jppadilla@eleconomista.com.mx; internet www.economista.com.mx; f. 1988; financial; Pres. JOSÉ GÓMEZ CAÑIBE; Editor-in-Chief DAVID CUEN; circ. 37,448.

Esto: Guillermo Prieto 7, 1°, Col. San Rafael, Del. Cuauhtémoc, 06470 México, DF; tel. and fax (55) 5566-1511; e-mail esto@oem.com.mx; internet www.esto.com.mx; f. 1941; published by Organización Editorial Mexicana; morning; sport; Dir MARIO VÁZQUEX RAÑA; circ. 400,000, Mondays 450,000.

Excélsior: Paseo de la Reforma 18 y Bucareli 1, Apdo 120 bis, Col. Centro, 06600 México, DF; tel. (55) 5705-4444; fax (55) 5566-0223; e-mail foro@excelsior.com.mx; internet www.excelsior.com.mx; f. 1917; morning; independent; Pres. OLEGARIO VÁZQUEX RAÑA; Dir ERNESTO RIVERA AGUILAR; circ. 200,000.

El Financiero: Lago Bolsena 176, Col. Anáhuac entre Lago Peypus y Lago Onega, 11320 México, DF; tel. (55) 5227-7600; fax (55) 5254-6427; internet www.elfinanciero.com.mx; f. 1981; financial; Dir-Gen. PILAR ESTANDÍA DE CÁRDENAS; circ. 119,000.

El Heraldo de México: Dr Lucio, esq. Dr Velasco, Col. Doctores, 06720 México, DF; tel. (55) 5578-7022; fax (55) 5578-9824; e-mail heraldo@iwm.com.mx; internet www.heraldo.com.mx; f. 1965; morning; Dir-Gen. GABRIEL ALARCÓN VELÁZQUEZ; circ. 209,600.

La Jornada: Avda Cuauhtémoc 1236, Col. Santa Cruz Atoyac, Del. Benito Juárez, 03310 México, DF; tel. (55) 9183-0300; internet www .jornada.unam.mx; f. 1984; morning; Dir-Gen. CARMEN LIRA SAADE; Gen. Man. JORGE MARTÍNEZ JIMÉNEZ; circ. 86,275.

Milenio Diario: México, DF; internet www.milenio.com; publishes Mexico City and regional edns, and a weekly news magazine, *Milenio Semanal*; Pres. FRANCISCO A. GONZÁLEZ; Dir-Gen. FRANCISCO D. GONZÁLEZ A.

Novedades: Balderas 87, esq. Morelos, Col. Centro, 06040 México, DF; tel. (55) 5518-5481; fax (55) 5521-4505; internet www.novedades .com.mx; f. 1936; morning; independent; Pres. and Editor-in-Chief ROMULO O'FARRILL, Jr; Vice-Pres. JOSÉ ANTONIO O'FARRILL AVILA; circ. 42,990, Sundays 43,536.

Ovaciones: Lago Zirahuén 279, 20°, Col. Anáhuac, 11320 México, DF; tel. (55) 5328-0700; fax (55) 5260-2219; e-mail ovaciones@ova .com.mx; internet www.ovaciones.com; f. 1947; morning and evening editions; Pres. and Dir-Gen. MAURICIO VÁZQUEZ RAMOS; circ. 130,000; evening circ. 100,000.

La Prensa: Basilio Vadillo 40, Col. Tabacalera, 06030 México, DF; tel. (55) 5228-9977; fax (55) 5521-8209; e-mail bmedina@la-prensa .com.mx; internet www.la-prensa.com.mx; f. 1928; published by Organización Editorial Mexicana; morning; Pres. and Dir-Gen. MARIO VÁZQUEZ RAÑA; Dir MAURICIO ORTEGA CAMBEROS; circ. 270,000.

Reforma: Avda México Coyoacán 40, Col. Santa Cruz Atoyac, 03310 México, DF; tel. (55) 5628-7100; fax (55) 5628-7188; internet www .reforma.com; f. 1993; morning; Pres. and Dir-Gen. ALEJANDRO JUNCO DE LA VEGA ELIZONDO; circ. 94,000.

El Sol de México: Guillermo Prieto 7, 20°, Col. San Rafael, 06470 México, DF; tel. (55) 5566-1511; fax (55) 5535-5560; e-mail enlinea@ elsoldemexico.com.mx; internet www.elsoldemexico.com.mx; f. 1965; published by Organización Editorial Mexicana; morning and midday; Pres. and Dir-Gen. MARIO VÁZQUEZ RAÑA; Man. EDGAR FIERRO GRANADOS; circ. 76,000.

El Universal: Bucareli 8, Apdo 909, Col. Centro, Del. Cuauhtémoc, 06040 México, DF; tel. (55) 5709-1313; fax (55) 5510-1269; e-mail rdirgral@eluniversal.com.mx; internet www.eluniversal.com.mx; f. 1916; morning; independent; centre-left; Pres. JUAN FRANCISCO EALY ORTIZ; Dir-Gen. JUAN FRANCISCO EALY, Jr; circ. 165,629, Sundays 181,615.

Unomásuno: Gabino Barreda 86, Col. San Rafael, México, DF; tel. (55) 1055-5500; fax (55) 5598-8821; e-mail cduran@servidor.unam .mx; internet www.unomasuno.com.mx; f. 1977; morning; left-wing; Pres. NAIM LIBIEN KAUI; Dir JOSÉ LUIS ROJAS RAMÍREZ; circ. 40,000.

PROVINCIAL DAILY NEWSPAPERS

Baja California

El Sol de Tijuana: Rufino Tamayo 4, Zona del Río, 22320 Tijuana, BC; tel. (664) 634-3232; fax (664) 634-2234; e-mail soltij@oem.com .mx; internet www.oem.com.mx/elsoldetijuana; f. 1989; published by Organización Editorial Mexicana; morning; Gen. Man. MARIO VALDÉS HERNÁNDEZ; Dir MIGUEL ANGEL TORRES PONCE; circ. 50,000.

La Voz de la Frontera: Avda Madero 1545, Col. Nueva, Apdo 946, 21100 Mexicali, BC; tel. (686) 562-4545; fax (686) 562-6912; e-mail ramondiaz@lavozdelafrontera.com.mx; internet www.oem.com.mx/ lavozdelafrontera; f. 1964; morning; published by Organización Editorial Mexicana; Dir FELIPE DE JESÚS LÓPEZ RODRÍGUEZ; Gen. Man. Lic. MARIO VALDÉS HERNÁNDEZ; circ. 65,000.

Chihuahua

El Diario: Publicaciones Paso del Norte, Avda Paseo Triunfo de la República 2505, Zona Pronaf, 32310 Ciudad Juárez, Chih.; tel. (656) 629-6900; internet www.diario.com.mx; f. 1976; Pres. OSVALDO RODRÍGUEZ BORUNDA.

El Heraldo de Chihuahua: Avda Universidad 2507, Apdo 1515, 31240 Chihuahua, Chih.; tel. (614) 432-3800; fax (614) 413-5625; e-mail elheraldo@buzon.online.com.mx; internet www.oem.com.mx/ elheraldodechihuahua; f. 1927; published by Organización Editorial Mexicana; morning; Dir Lic. JAVIER H. CONTRERAS; circ. 27,520, Sundays 31,223.

El Mexicano de Ciudad Juárez: Ciudad Juárez, Chih.; e-mail director@pesquisasenlinea.org; f. 1959; published by Organización Editorial Mexicana; morning; Dir RAFAEL NAVARRO; Editor-in-Chief JAIME NÚÑEZ; circ. 80,000.

Coahuila

El Siglo de Torreón: Avda Matamoros 1056 Pte, Col. Centro, 27000 Torreón, Coah.; tel. (871) 759-1200; e-mail internet@elsiglodetorreon .com.mx; internet www.elsiglodetorreon.com.mx; f. 1922; morning; Pres. OLGA DE JUAMBELZ Y HORCASITAS; Dir-Gen. ANTONIO IRAZOQUI Y DE JUAMBELZ; circ. 38,611, Sundays 38,526.

Vanguardia: Blvd Venustiano Carranza 1918, esq. con Chiapas, República Oriente, 25280 Saltillo, Coah.; tel. (844) 450-1000; e-mail hola@vanguardia.com.mx; internet www.vanguardia.com.mx; Dir-Gen. DIANA MARÍA GALINDO DE CASTILLA.

Colima

Diario de Colima: Avda 20 de Noviembre 380, 28060 Colima, Col.; tel. (312) 312-5688; internet www.diariodecolima.com; f. 1953; Dir-Gen. HÉCTOR SÁNCHEZ DE LA MADRID; Man. Dir ENRIQUE ZÁRATE CANSECO.

Guanajuato

Correo de Guanajuato: Carreterra Guanajuato—Juventino Rosas Km 9.5, 36260 Guanajuato, Gto; tel. (477) 733-1253; fax (477) 733-0057; e-mail correo@correo-gto.com.mx; internet www.correo-gto .com.mx; Dir-Gen. ARNALDO CUÉLLAR.

El Sol de Salamanca: Faro de Oro 800, 36700 Salamanca, Gto; tel. (464) 647-0144; e-mail aherrera@elsoldeirapuato.com.mx; internet www.elsoldesalamanca.com.mx; published by Organización Editorial Mexicana; Dir-Gen. ALEJANDRO HERRERA SÁNCHEZ.

Jalisco

El Informador: Independencia 300, Apdo 3 bis, 44100 Guadalajara, Jal.; tel. (33) 3678-7700; e-mail webmanager@informador.com.mx; internet www.informador.com.mx; f. 1917; morning; Editor JORGE ÁLVAREZ DEL CASTILLO; circ. 50,000.

El Occidental: Calzada Independencia Sur 324, Apdo 1-699, 44100 Guadalajara, Jal.; tel. (33) 3613-0690; fax (33) 3613-6796; e-mail silvia@eloccidental.com.mx; internet www.eloccidental.com.mx; f. 1942; published by Organización Editorial Mexicana; morning; Pres. and Dir-Gen. MARIO VÁSQUEZ RAÑA; Dir JAVIER VALLE CHÁVEZ; circ. 49,400.

México

ABC: Avda Hidalgo Oriente 1339, Centro Comercial, Col. Ferrocarriles Nacionales, 50070 Toluca, Méx.; tel. (722) 217-9880; fax (722) 217-8402; e-mail miled1@mail.miled.com; internet www.miled.com; f. 1984; morning; Pres. and Editor MILED LIBIEN KAUI; circ. 65,000.

Diario de Toluca: Allende Sur 209, 50000 Toluca, Méx.; tel. (722) 215-9105; fax (722) 214-1523; f. 1980; also publishes *Siete Días* and *El Noticiero*; morning; Pres. ANUAR MACCISE DIB; circ. 22,200.

El Heraldo de Toluca: Salvador Díaz Mirón 700, Col. Sánchez Colín, 50150 Toluca, Méx.; tel. (722) 217-3542; fax (722) 212-2535; e-mail editotol@prodigy.net.mx; internet www.heraldotoluca.com; f. 1955; morning; Editor ALBERTO BARRAZA SÁNCHEZ; circ. 90,000.

El Sol de Toluca: Santos Degollado 105, Apdo 54, Col. Centro, 50050 Toluca, Méx.; tel. (722) 214-7077; fax (722) 215-2564; internet www .oem.com.mx/elsoldetoluca; f. 1947; published by Organización Editorial Mexicana; morning; Dir RAFAEL VILCHIS GIL DE ARÉVALO; circ. 42,000.

Michoacán

La Voz de Michoacán: Blvd del Periodismo 1270, Col. Arriaga Rivera, Apdo 121, 58190 Morelia, Mich.; tel. (443) 327-3712; fax (443) 327-3728; e-mail jcgonzalez@voznet.com.mx; internet www .vozdemichoacan.com.mx; f. 1948; morning; Dir-Gen. MIGUEL MEDINA ROBLES; circ. 50,000.

Morelos

El Diario de Morelos: Morelos Sur 132, Col. Las Palmas, 62050 Cuernavaca, Mor.; tel. and fax (777) 362-0220; e-mail redaccion@ diariodemorelos.com; internet www.diariodemorelos.com; f. 1978; morning; Propr Grupo BRACA de Comunicación; CEO and Editor-in-Chief MIGUEL BRACAMONTES; circ. 35,000.

Nayarit

Meridiano de Nayarit: Independencia 335, Fracc. Las Aves, Tepic, Nay.; tel. (311) 210-3211; e-mail ventas@meridiano.com.mx; internet meridiano.nayaritpuntocom.com; f. 1942; morning; Dir Dr DAVID ALFARO; circ. 60,000.

Nuevo León

ABC: Platón Sánchez Sur 411, 64000 Monterrey, NL; tel. (81) 8344-2510; fax (81) 8344-5990; f. 1985; morning; Dir-Gen. GONZALO ESTRADO TORRES; circ. 40,000, Sundays 45,000.

El Norte: Washington 629 Oeste, Apdo 186, 64000 Monterrey, NL; tel. (81) 8150-8100; fax (81) 8343-2476; internet www.elnorte.com .mx; f. 1938; morning; Man. Dir ALEJANDRO JUNCO DE LA VEGA; circ. 133,872, Sundays 154,951.

El Porvenir: Galeana Sur 344, Apdo 218, 64000 Monterrey, NL; tel. (81) 8345-4080; fax (81) 8345-7795; internet www.elporvenir.com .mx; f. 1919; morning; Dir-Gen. JOSÉ GERARDO CANTÚ ESCALANTE; circ. 75,000.

Oaxaca

El Imparcial: Armenta y López 312, Apdo 322, 68000 Oaxaca, Oax.; tel. (951) 516-2812; fax (951) 514-7020; e-mail subdireccion@imparcialenlinea.com; internet www.imparoax.com.mx; f. 1951; morning; Dir-Gen. BENJAMÍN FERNÁNDEZ PICHARDO; circ. 17,000, Sundays 20,000.

Puebla

La Opinión: 3 Oriente 1207, Barrio del Analco, 238 Puebla, Pue.; tel. (222) 246-4358; fax (222) 232-7772; internet www.opinion.com.mx; f. 1924; morning; Dir-Gen. OSCAR LÓPEZ MORALES; circ. 40,000.

El Sol de Puebla: Avda 3 Oriente 201, Col. Centro, 72000 Puebla, Pue.; tel. (222) 514-3300; fax (222) 246-0869; e-mail elsoldepuebla@elsoldepuebla.com.mx; internet www.oem.com.mx/elsoldepuebla; f. 1944; published by Organización Editorial Mexicana; morning; Dir SERAFÍN SALAZAR ARELLANO; circ. 67,000.

San Luis Potosí

El Heraldo: Villerías 305, 78000 San Luis Potosí, SLP; tel. (444) 812-3312; fax (444) 812-2081; e-mail redaccion@elheraldoslp.com.mx; internet www.elheraldoslp.com.mx; f. 1954; morning; Dir-Gen. ALEJANDRO VILLASANA MENA; circ. 60,620.

Pulso: Galeana 485, Centro, 78000 San Luis Potosí, SLP; tel. (444) 812-7575; fax (444) 812-3525; internet www.pulsoslp.com.mx; morning; Dir-Gen. PABLO VALLADARES GARCÍA; circ. 60,000.

El Sol de San Luis: Avda Universidad 565, Apdo 342, 78000 San Luis Potosí, SLP; tel. and fax (444) 812-4412; internet www.oem.com.mx/elsoldesanluis; f. 1952; published by Organización Editorial Mexicana; morning; Dir JOSÉ ANGEL MARTÍNEZ LIMÓN; circ. 60,000.

Sinaloa

El Debate de Culiacán: Madero 556 Pte, 80000 Culiacán, Sin.; tel. (667) 716-6353; fax (667) 715-7131; e-mail andrea.miranda@lai.com.mx; internet www.debate.com.mx; f. 1972; morning; Dir ROSARIO I. OROPEZA; circ. 23,603, Sundays 23,838.

Noroeste Culiacán: Grupo Periódicos Noroeste, Angel Flores 282 Oeste, Apdo 90, 80000 Culiacán, Sin.; tel. (667) 759-8100; fax (667) 712-8006; e-mail direccion@noroeste.com.mx; internet www.noroeste.com.mx; f. 1973; morning; Dir-Gen. BEATRIZ BECERRA GONZÁLEZ; Editor RODOLFO DIAZ; circ. 35,000.

El Sol de Sinaloa: Blvd G. Leyva Lozano y Corona 320, Apdo 412, 80000 Culiacán, Sin.; tel. (667) 713-1621; fax (667) 713-1800; internet www.elsoldesinaloa.com.mx; f. 1956; published by Organización Editorial Mexicana; morning; Dir JORGE LUIS TÉLLEZ SALAZAR; circ. 30,000.

Sonora

Expreso: Hermosillo, Son.; tel. (662) 108-3000; e-mail holguin@expreso.com.mx; internet www.expreso.com.mx; Dir-Gen. MARTÍN HOLGUÍN ALATORRE; circ. 17,000, Sundays 18,000.

El Imparcial: Sufragio Efectivo y Mina 71, Col. Centro, Apdo 66, 83000 Hermosillo, Son.; tel. (662) 259-4700; fax (662) 217-4483; e-mail lector@elimparcial.com; internet www.elimparcial.com; f. 1937; morning; Pres. and Dir-Gen. JUAN F. HEALY; circ. 32,083, Sundays 32,444.

Tabasco

Tabasco Hoy: Avda de los Ríos 206, Col. Tabasco 2000, 86035 Villahermosa, Tab.; tel. (993) 316-2135; internet www.tabascohoy.com.mx; f. 1987; morning; Dir-Gen. MIGUEL CANTÓN ZETINA; circ. 50,000.

Tamaulipas

El Bravo: Morelos y Primera 129, Apdo 483, 87300 Matamoros, Tamps; tel. (871) 816-0100; fax (871) 816-2007; e-mail comenta@elbravo.com.mx; f. 1951; morning; Pres. and Dir-Gen. JOSÉ CARRETERO BALBOA; circ. 60,000.

El Diario de Nuevo Laredo: González 2409, Apdo 101, 88000 Nuevo Laredo, Tamps; tel. (867) 711-5500; fax (867) 712-8221; internet www.diario.net; f. 1948; morning; Editor RUPERTO VILLARREAL MONTEMAYOR; circ. 68,130, Sundays 73,495.

Expresión: Calle 3 y Novedades 3, Col. Periodistas, 87457 Matamoros, Tamps; tel. (868) 817-9555; fax (868) 817-3307; e-mail xpresion@prodigy.net.mx; morning; Dir-Gen. MIGUEL GARAY AVILA; circ. 50,000.

El Mañana: Juárez y Perú, Col. Juárez, Nuevo Laredo, Tamps; tel. (867) 711-9900; fax (867) 715-0405; e-mail mauricio.deleon@elmanana.com.mx; internet www.elmanana.com.mx; f. 1932; morning; Pres. NINFA DEÁNDAR MARTÍNEZ; Editor HERIBERTO CANTÚ DEÁNDAR; circ. 16,473, Sundays 20,957.

El Mañana de Reynosa: Calle Matías Canales 504, Apdo 14, Col. Ribereña, 88620 Ciudad Reynosa, Tamps; tel. (899) 921-9950; fax (899) 924-9348; internet www.elmananarey.com.mx; f. 1949; morning; Chief Editors HERIBERTO DEÁNDAR ROBINSON, HILDEBRANDO DEÁNDAR AYALA; circ. 52,000.

Prensa de Reynosa: Matamoros y González Ortega, Zona Centro, 88500 Reynosa, Tamps; tel. (899) 922-0299; fax (899) 922-2412; e-mail prensa_88500@yahoo.com; internet www.prensadereynosa.com; f. 1963; morning; Dir-Gen. FÉLIX GARZA ELIZONDO; circ. 60,000.

El Sol de Tampico: Altamira 311 Pte, Apdo 434, 89000 Tampico, Tamps; tel. (833) 212-1067; fax (833) 212-6821; internet www.oem.com.mx/elsoldetampico; f. 1950; published by Organización Editorial Mexicana; morning; Dir-Gen. RUBÉN DÍAZ DE LA GARZA; circ. 77,000.

Veracruz

Diario del Istmo: Avda Hidalgo 1115, Col. Centro, 96400 Coatzacoalcos, Ver.; tel. (921) 211-8000; e-mail info@istmo.com.mx; internet www.diariodelistmo.com; f. 1979; morning; Dir-Gen. HÉCTOR ROBLES BARAJAS; circ. 64,600.

El Dictamen: 16 de Septiembre y Arista, 91700 Veracruz, Ver.; tel. (229) 931-1745; fax (229) 931-5804; e-mail dovali@hotmail.com; internet www.eldictamen.com.mx; f. 1898; morning; Pres. BERTHA ROSALIA MALPICA DE AHUED; circ. 25,000, Sundays 28,000.

La Opinión: Poza Rica de Hidalgo, Ver.; e-mail publicidad@laopinion.com.mx; internet www.laopinion.com.mx; Dir ABEL ANDRADE LICONA.

Yucatán

Diario de Yucatán: Calle 60 521, 97000 Mérida, Yuc.; tel. (999) 942-2222; fax (999) 942-2204; internet www.yucatan.com.mx; f. 1925; morning; Dir-Gen. CARLOS R. MENÉNDEZ NAVARRETE; circ. 54,639, Sundays 65,399.

Por Esto!: Calle 60, No 576 entre 73 y 71, 97000 Mérida, Yuc.; tel. (999) 24-7613; fax (999) 28-6514; e-mail redaccion@poresto.net; internet www.poresto.net; f. 1991; morning; Dir-Gen. MARIO RENATO MENÉNDEZ RODRÍGUEZ; circ. 26,985, Sundays 28,727.

Zacatecas

Imagen: Calzada Revolución 24, Col. Tierra y Libertad, 98600 Guadalupe, Zac.; tel. and fax (492) 923-8898; e-mail buzon@imagenzac.com.mx; internet www.imagenzac.com.mx; Dir-Gen. EUGENIO MERCADO.

SELECTED WEEKLY NEWSPAPERS

El Heraldo Bajio: Hermanos Aldama 222, Apdo 299, Zona Centro, 37000 León, Gto; tel. (477) 719-8800; e-mail heraldo@el-heraldo-bajio.com.mx; internet www.el-heraldo-bajio.com.mx; f. 1957; Pres. and Dir-Gen. MAURICIO BERCÚN LÓPEZ; circ. 85,000.

Segundamano: Insurgentes Sur 619, Col. Nápoles, Del. Benito Juárez, 03810 México, DF; tel. (55) 5350-7070; e-mail soporte@segundamano.com.mx; internet www.segundamano.com.mx; f. 1986; Dir-Gen. LUIS MAGAÑA MAGAÑA; circ. 105,000.

Zeta: Avda las Américas 4633, Fraccionamiento El Paraíso, Tijuana, BC; e-mail zeta@zetatijuana.com; internet www.zetatijuana.com; f. 1980; news magazine; Editor ADELA NAVARRO.

SELECTED PERIODICALS

Boletín Industrial: Luis Khune 55-B, Col. Las Águilas, 01710 México, DF; tel. (55) 5337-2200; fax (55) 5337-2230; e-mail hvalades@boletinindustrial.com; internet www.boletinindustrial.com; f. 1983; publ. by Editorial Nova SA de CV; monthly; Pres. HUMBERTO VALADÉS; circ. 37,200.

Casas & Gente: Amsterdam 112, Col. Hipódromo Condesa, 06100 México, DF; tel. (55) 5286-7794; fax (55) 5211-7112; e-mail informac@casasgente.com; internet www.casasgente.com; 10 a year; interior design; Dir-Gen. IGNACIO DÍAZ SÁNCHEZ.

Contenido: Darwin 101, Col. Anzures, 11590 México, DF; tel. (55) 5531-3162; fax (55) 5545-7478; e-mail contenido@contenido.com.mx; internet www.contenido.com.mx; f. 1963; monthly; popular appeal; Editor-in-Chief MARIANA CHAVEZ RODRÍGUEZ; circ. 124,190.

Cosmopolitan México: Vasco de Quiroga 2000, Col. Santa Fe, Del. Alvaro Obregón, 01210 México, DF; tel. (55) 5261-2600; fax (55) 5261-2704; internet www2.esmas.com/cosmopolitan; f. 1973; fortnightly; women's magazine; Dir SARA MARÍA CASTANY; circ. 300,000.

Expansión: Avda Constituyentes 956, Col. Lomas Altas, 11950 México, DF; tel. and fax (55) 9177-4100; e-mail quien@expansion.com.mx; internet www.expansion.com.mx; fortnightly; business and financial; Editor ARMANDO TALAMANTES.

Fama: Avda Eugenio Garza Sada 2245 Sur, Col. Roma, Apdo 3128, 64700 Monterrey, NL; tel. (81) 8359-2525; internet www.revistafama

.com; fortnightly; show business; Pres. JESÚS D. GONZÁLEZ; Dir RAÚL MARTÍNEZ; circ. 350,000.

Gaceta Médica de México: Academia Nacional de Medicina, Unidad de Congresos del Centro Médico Nacional Siglo XXI, Bloque B, Avda Cuauhtémoc 330, Col. Doctores, 06725 México, DF; tel. (55) 5578-2044; fax (55) 5578-4271; internet www.medigraphic.com; f. 1864; every 2 months; journal of the Academia Nacional de Medicina de México; Editor ALFREDO ULLOA AGUIRRE; circ. 20,000.

Kena Mensual: Río Balsas 101, Col. Cuauhtémoc, 06500 México, DF; tel. (55) 5442-9600; e-mail corporativo@grupoarmonia.com.mx; f. 1977; fortnightly; women's interest; Editor GINA URETA; circ. 100,000.

Letras Libres: Chilaque 9, Col. San Diego Churubusco, 04120 México, DF; tel. (55) 9183-7800; fax (55) 9183-7836; e-mail revista@letraslibres.infonegocio.com; internet www.letraslibres .com; monthly; culture; Dir ENRIQUE KRAUZE.

Manufactura: Avda Constituyentes 956, esq. Rosaleda, Col. Lomas Altas, 11950 México, DF; tel. (55) 9177-4369; e-mail valcantara@ expansion.com.mx; internet www.manufacturaweb.com; f. 1994; monthly; industrial; Dir-Gen. DAVID LUNA ARELLANO; circ. 25,000.

Marie Claire: Editorial Televisa, SA de CV, Avda Vasco de Quiroga 2000, Edif. E, 3°, Col. Santa Fe, 01210 México, DF; tel. (55) 5261-2622; fax (55) 5261-2733; e-mail mmartinezgom@editorial.televisa .com.mx; internet www.esmas.com/editorialtelevisa; f. 1990; monthly; women's interest; Editor MÓNICA MARTÍNEZ GÓMEZ; circ. 145,000.

Mecánica Popular (Popular Mechanics en Español): Vasco de Quiroga 2000, Col. Santa Fe, Del. Alvaro Obregón, 01210 México, DF; tel. (55) 5447-4711; fax (55) 5261-2705; internet www .mimecanicapopular.com; f. 1947; monthly; crafts and home improvements; Dir ANDRÉS JORGE; circ. 55,000.

Men's Health: Vasco de Quiroga 2000, Col. Santa Fe, Del. Alvaro Obregón, 01210 México, DF; tel. (55) 5261-2645; fax (55) 5261-2733; internet www.menshealth.com.mx; f. 1994; monthly; health; Editor JUAN ANTONIO SEMPERE; circ. 130,000.

Muy Interesante: Vasco de Quiroga 2000, Col. Santa Fe, Del. Alvaro Obregón, 01210 México, DF; tel. (55) 5261-2600; fax (55) 5261-2704; internet www.esmas.com/editorialtelevisa; f. 1984; monthly; scientific devt; Dir PILAR S. HOYOS; circ. 250,000.

Negocios y Bancos: Bolívar 8-103, Apdo 1907, Col. Centro, 06000 México, DF; tel. (55) 5510-1884; fax (55) 5512-9411; e-mail nego_bancos@mexico.com; f. 1951; fortnightly; business, economics; Dir ALFREDO FARRUGIA REED; circ. 10,000.

Proceso: Fresas 7, Col. del Valle, 03100 México, DF; tel. (55) 5636-2028; e-mail buzon@proceso.com.mx; internet www.proceso.com.mx; f. 1976; weekly; news analysis; Dir RAFAEL RODRÍGUEZ CASTAÑEDA; circ. 98,784.

Quién: Avda Constituyentes 956, Col. Lomas Altas, CP 11950, México, DF; tel. (55) 9177-4100; e-mail quien@expansion.com.mx; internet www.quien.com; fortnightly; celebrity news, TV, radio, films; Editor BLANCA GÓMEZ MORERA.

La Revista Peninsular: Calle 35, 489 x 52 y 54, Zona Centro, Mérida, Yuc.; tel. and fax (999) 926-3014; e-mail direccion@larevista .com.mx; internet www.larevista.com.mx; f. 1988; weekly; news and politics; Dir-Gen. RODRIGO MENÉNDEZ CÁMARA.

Selecciones del Reader's Digest: Avda Prolongación Paseo de la Reforma 1236, 10°, Col. Santa Fe, Del. Alvaro Obregón, 05348 México, DF; tel. (55) 5351-2200; internet www.selecciones.com.mx; f. 1940; monthly; Editor AUDÓN CORIA; circ. 611,660.

Siempre!: Vallarta 20, Col. Tabacalera, 06030 México, DF; tel. and fax (55) 5566-1804; e-mail suscripciones@siempre.com.mx; internet www.siempre.com.mx; f. 1953; weekly; left of centre; Dir Lic. BEATRIZ PAGÉS REBOLLAR DE NIETO; circ. 100,000.

Tele-Guía: Vasco de Quiroga 2000, Col. Santa Fe, Del. Alvaro Obregón, 01210 México, DF; tel. (55) 5261-2600; fax (55) 5261-2704; internet www.esmas.com/editorialtelevisa; f. 1952; weekly; television guide; Editor MARÍA EUGENIA HERNÁNDEZ; circ. 375,000.

Tiempo Libre: Holbein 75 bis, Col. Nochebuena Mixcoac, Del. Benito Juárez, 03720 México, DF; tel. (55) 5611-2884; fax (55) 5611-3982; e-mail buzon@tiempolibre.com.mx; internet www .tiempolibre.com.mx; f. 1980; weekly; entertainment guide; Dir JUAN ALBERTO BECERRA; Editor ALICIA LABRA GÓMEZ; circ. 95,000.

Tú: Vasco de Quiroga 2000, Col. Santa Fe, Del. Alvaro Obregón, 01210 México, DF; tel. (55) 5261-2600; fax (55) 5261-2730; internet www.esmas.com/editorialtelevisa; f. 1980; monthly; teenage; Editor MARÍA ANTONIETA SALAMANCA; circ. 250,000.

TV y Novelas: Vasco de Quiroga 2000, Col. Santa Fe, Del. Alvaro Obregón, 01210 México, DF; tel. (55) 5261-2600; fax (55) 5261-2704; f. 1982; weekly; television guide and short stories; Dir JESÚS GALLEGOS; circ. 460,000.

Ultima Moda: Morelos 16, 6°, Col. Centro, 06040 México, DF; tel. (55) 5518-5481; fax (55) 5512-8902; e-mail revista_ultimamoda@ yahoo.com.mx; f. 1966; monthly; fashion; Pres. ROMULO O'FARRILL, Jr; Gen. Man. Lic. SAMUEL PODOLSKY RAPOPORT; circ. 110,548.

Vanidades: Vasco de Quiroga 2000, Col. Santa Fe, Del. Alvaro Obregón, 01210 México, DF; tel. (55) 5261-2600; fax (55) 5261-2704/ e-mail vanidades@editorialtelevisa.com; internet www.esmas.com/ vanidades; f. 1961; fortnightly; women's magazine; Dir JAQUELINE BLANCO; circ. 290,000.

Vogue (México): Condé Nast México, México, DF; tel. (55) 5095-8076; fax (55) 5245-7109; f. 1999; monthly; women's fashion; circ. 208,180.

ASSOCIATIONS

Asociación Nacional de Periodistas y Comunicadores, A.C.: Luis G. Obregón 17, Of. 209, Col. Centro, 06020 México, DF; tel. (55) 5341-1523; Pres. MOISÉS HUERTA.

Federación de Asociaciones de Periodistas Mexicanos (Fapermex): Humboldt 5, Col. Centro, 06030 México, DF; tel. (55) 5510-2679; e-mail fapermexmail@gmail.com; internet www .fapermex.com; Pres. ROBERTO PIÑÓN OLIVAS; 88 mem. asscns; c. 9,000 mems.

Federación Latinoamericana de Periodistas (FELAP): Nuevo Leon 144, 1°, Col. Hipódromo Condesa, 06170 México, DF; tel. (55) 5286-6055; fax (55) 5286-6085; internet www.ciap-felap.org; Pres. JUAN CARLOS CAMAÑO; Sec.-Gen. JOSÉ RAFAEL VARGAS.

Fraternidad de Reporteros de México (FREMAC): Avda Juárez 88, Col. Centro, Del. Cuauhtémoc, México, DF; e-mail info@fremac .org.mx; internet www.fremac.org.mx; f. 1995; Sec.-Gen. MARCELA YARCE VIVEROS.

NEWS AGENCIES

Agencia de Información Integral Periodística (AIIP): Tabasco 263, Col. Roma, Del. Cuauhtémoc, 06700 México, DF; tel. and fax (55) 5440-5284; e-mail aiipmx@aiip.com.mx; internet www.aiip.com.mx; f. 1987; Dir-Gen. MIGUEL HERRERA LÓPEZ.

Agencia Mexicana de Información (AMI): Avda Cuauhtémoc 16, Col. Doctores, 06720 México, DF; tel. (55) 5761-9933; e-mail info@ red-ami.com; internet www.ami.com.mx; f. 1971; Dir-Gen. JOSÉ LUIS BECERRA LÓPEZ; Gen. Man. EVA VÁZQUEZ LÓPEZ.

Notimex, SA de CV: Morena 110, 3°, Col. del Valle, 03100 México, DF; tel. (55) 5420-1163; fax (55) 5420-1188; e-mail ventas@notimex .com.mx; internet www.notimex.com.mx; f. 1968; services to press, radio and television in Mexico and throughout the world; Dir-Gen. SERGIO UZETA MURCIO.

Publishers

MÉXICO, DF

Aguilar, Altea, Taurus, Alfaguara, SA de CV: Avda Universidad 767, Col. del Valle, 03100 México, DF; tel. (55) 5688-8966; fax (55) 5604-2304; f. 1965; general literature; Dir SEALTIEL ALATRISTE.

Arbol Editorial, SA de CV: Avda Cuauhtémoc 1430, Col. Santa Cruz Atoyac, 03310 México, DF; tel. (55) 5688-4828; fax (55) 5605-7600; e-mail editorialpax@maxis.com; f. 1979; health, philosophy, theatre; Man. Dir GERARDO GALLY TEOMONFORD.

Artes de México y del Mundo, SA de CV: Cordoba 69, Col. Roma, 06700 México, DF; tel. (55) 5525-5905; fax (55) 5525-5925; e-mail artesdemexico@artesdemexico.com; internet www.artesdemexico .com; f. 1988; art, design, poetry; Dir-Gen. ALBERTO RUY SÁNCHEZ LACY.

Editorial Avante, SA de CV: Luis G. Obregón 9, 1°, Apdo 45-796, Col. Centro, 06020 México, DF; tel. (55) 5510-8804; fax (55) 5521-5245; e-mail didactips@editorialavante.com.mx; internet www .editorialavante.com.mx; f. 1948; educational, drama, linguistics; Man. Dir Lic. MARIO A. HINOJOSA SAENZ.

Editorial Azteca, SA: Calle de la Luna 225–227, Col. Guerrero, 06300 México, DF; tel. (55) 5526-1157; fax (55) 5526-2557; internet www.circuloeditorialazteca.com.mx; f. 1956; religion, literature and technical; Man. Dir ALFONSO ALEMÓN JALOMO.

Cía Editorial Continental, SA de CV (CECSA): Renacimiento 180, Col. San Juan Tlihuaca, Azcapotzalco, 02400 México, DF; tel. (55) 5561-8333; fax (55) 5561-5231; e-mail info@patriacultural.com .mx; f. 1954; business, technology, general textbooks; Pres. CARLOS FRIGOLET LERMA.

Ediciones de Cultura Popular, SA: Odontología 76, Copilco Universidad, México, DF; f. 1969; history, politics, social sciences; Man. Dir URIEL JARQUÍN GALVEZ.

Editorial Diana, SA de CV: Arenal 24, Edif. Norte, Ex-Hacienda Guadalupe, Chimalistac, Del. Álvaro Obregón, 01050 México, DF; tel. (55) 5089-1220; fax (55) 5089-1230; internet www.editorialdiana

.com.mx; f. 1946; general trade and technical books; Pres. and CEO JOSÉ LUIS RAMÍREZ.

Ediciones Era, SA de CV: Calle del Trabajo 31, Col. La Fama, Tlalpan, 14269 México, DF; tel. (55) 5528-1221; fax (55) 5606-2904; e-mail edicionesera@laneta.apc.org; internet www.edicionesera.com.mx; f. 1960; general and social science, art and literature; Gen. Man. NIEVES ESPRESATE XIRAU.

Editorial Everest Mexicana, SA: Calzada Ermita Iztapalapa 1631, Col. Barrio San Miguel del Iztapalapa, 09360 México, DF; tel. (55) 5685-1966; fax (55) 5685-3433; f. 1980; general textbooks; Gen. Man. JOSÉ LUIS HUIDOBRO LEÓN.

Fernández Editores, SA de CV: Eje 1 Pte México-Coyoacán 321, Col. Xoco, 03330 México, DF; tel. (55) 5605-6557; fax (55) 5688-9173; f. 1943; children's literature, textbooks, educational toys; Man. Dir LUIS GERARDO FERNÁNDEZ PÉREZ.

Editorial Fondo de Cultura Económica, SA de CV: Carretera Picacho-Ajusco 227, Col. Bosques del Pedregal, 14200 México, DF; tel. (55) 5227-4672; fax (55) 5227-4640; e-mail juan.cortes@fondodeculturaeconomica.com; internet www.fondodeculturaeconomica.com; f. 1934; economics, history, philosophy, children's books, science, politics, psychology, sociology, literature; Dir JUAN FRANCISCO CORTÉS GONZÁLEZ.

Nueva Editorial Interamericana, SA de CV: Cedro 512, Col. Atlampa, Apdo 4-140, 06450 México, DF; tel. (55) 5541-6789; fax (55) 5541-1603; f. 1944; medical publishing; Man. Dir RAFAEL SÁINZ.

Distribuidora Intermex, SA de CV: Lucio Blanco 435, Azcapotzalco, 02400 México, DF; tel. (55) 5230-9500; fax (55) 5230-9516; f. 1969; romantic fiction; Gen. Dir Lic. ALEJANDRO PAILLÉS.

Editorial Jus, SA de CV: Avda Constituyentes 647, 3°, Col. 16 de Septiembre, 11810 México, DF; tel. (55) 5093-1925; fax (55) 5529-0951; internet www.jus.com.mx; f. 1938; history of Mexico, law, philosophy, economy, religion; Man. TOMÁS G. REYNOSO.

Ediciones Larousse, SA de CV: Londres 247, Col. Juárez, Del. Cuauhtémoc, 06600 México, DF; tel. (55) 1102-1300; fax (55) 5208-6225; e-mail psala@larousse.com.mx; internet www.larousse.com.mx; f. 1965; Dir-Gen. GERARDO GUERRERO (acting).

Libros para Todos (EDAMEX): Heriberto Frias 1104, Col. del Valle, 03100 México, DF; tel. (55) 5559-8588; fax (55) 5575-0555; e-mail octaviocolmenares@edamex.com; internet www.edamex.com; arts and literature, sport, journalism, education, philosophy, food, history, children's, health, sociology.

Editorial Limusa, SA de CV: Balderas 95, 1°, Col. Centro, 06040 México, DF; tel. (55) 5521-2105; fax (55) 5510-9415; internet www.noriega.com.mx; f. 1962; science, general, textbooks; Pres. CARLOS NORIEGA MILERA.

McGraw-Hill Interamericana de México, SA de CV: Torre A, 17°, Paseo de la Reforma 1015, Col. Santa Fé, 01376 México, DF; tel. (55) 1500-5000; internet www.mcgraw-hill.com.mx; education, business, science; Man. Dir CARLOS RIOS.

Medios Publicitarios Mexicanos, SA de CV: Eugenia 811, Eje 5 Sur, Col. del Valle, 03100 México, DF; tel. (55) 5523-3342; fax (55) 5523-3379; e-mail editorial@mpm.com.mx; internet www.mpm.com.mx; f. 1958; advertising media rates and data; Gen. Man. FERNANDO VILLAMIL.

Editorial Nuestro Tiempo, SA: Avda Universidad 771, Despachos 103–104, Col. del Valle, 03100 México, DF; tel. (55) 5688-8768; fax (55) 5688-6868; f. 1966; social sciences; Man. Dir ESPERANZA NACIF BARQUET.

Editorial Oasis, SA: Avda Oaxaca 28, 06700 México, DF; tel. (55) 5528-8293; f. 1954; literature, pedagogy, poetry; Man. MARÍA TERESA ESTRADA DE FERNÁNDEZ DEL BUSTO.

Editorial Orión: Sierra Mojada 325, 11000 México, DF; tel. (55) 5520-0224; f. 1942; archaeology, philosophy, psychology, literature, fiction; Man. Dir SILVIA HERNÁNDEZ BALTAZAR.

Editorial Patria, SA de CV: Renacimiento 180, Col. San Juan Tlihuaca, Del. Azcapotzalco, 02400 México, DF; tel. (55) 5354-9100; fax (55) 5354-9109; e-mail info@editorialpatria.com.mx; internet www.patriacultural.com.mx; f. 1933; fiction, general trade, children's books; Pres. CARLOS FRIGOLET LERMA.

Editorial Planeta Mexicana, SA de CV: Clavijero 70, Col. Esperanza, México, DF; tel. (55) 5533-1250; internet www.editorialplaneta.com.mx; general literature, non-fiction; part of Grupo Planeta (Spain); Grupo Planeta incorporates Ariel, Crítica, Destino, Deusto, Ediciones del Bronce, Editorial Joaquín Mortiz, Emecé, Espasa, Martínez Roca, Seix Barral and Temas de Hoy; Man. Dir JOAQUIN DIEZ-CANEDO.

Editorial Porrúa Hnos, SA: Argentina 15, 5°, 06020 México, DF; tel. (55) 5704–7578; fax (55) 5702-6529; e-mail servicios@porrua.com; internet www.porrua.com; f. 1944; general literature; Dir JOSÉ ANTONIO PÉREZ PORRÚA.

Editorial Posada, SA de CV: Eugenia 13, Despacho 501, Col. Nápoles, 03510 México, DF; tel. (55) 5682-0660; f. 1968; general; Dir-Gen. CARLOS VIGIL ZUBIETA.

Editorial Quetzacoatl, SA: Medicina 37, Local 1 y 2, México, DF; tel. (55) 5548-6180; Man. Dir ALBERTO RODRÍGUEZ VALDÉS.

Random House Mondadori, SA de CV: Homero 544, Col. Chapultepec Morales, 11570, México, DF; tel. (55) 3067-8400; e-mail diredit@grijalbo.com.mx; internet www.randomhousemondadori.com.mx; f. 1954; owned by Mondadori (Italy); general fiction, history, sciences, philosophy, children's books; Man. Dir AGUSTÍN CENTENO RÍOS.

Reverté Ediciones, SA de CV: Río Pánuco 141A, Col. Cuauhtémoc, 06500 México, DF; tel. (55) 5533-5658; fax (55) 5514-6799; e-mail reverte@reverte.com.mx; internet www.reverte.com; f. 1955; science, technical, architecture; Man. RAMÓN REVERTÉ MASCÓ.

Salvat Mexicana de Ediciones, SA de CV: Presidente Masaryk 101, 5°, 11570 México, DF; tel. (55) 5250-6041; fax (55) 5250-6861; medicine, encyclopaedic works; Dir GUILLERMO HERNÁNDEZ PÉREZ.

Siglo XXI Editores, SA de CV: Avda Cerro del Agua 248, Col. Romero de Terreros, Del. Coyoacán, 04310 México, DF; tel. (55) 5658-7999; fax (55) 5658-7599; e-mail informes@sigloxxieditores.com.mx; internet www.sigloxxieditores.com.mx; f. 1966; art, economics, education, history, social sciences, literature, philology and linguistics, philosophy and political science; Dir-Gen. Dr JAIME LABASTIDA OCHOA; Gen. Man. JOSÉ MARÍA CASTRO MUSSOT.

Editorial Trillas, SA: Avda Río Churubusco 385 Pte, Col. Xoco, Apdo 10534, 03330 México, DF; tel. (55) 5688-4233; fax (55) 5601-1858; e-mail ftrillas@trillas.com.mx; internet www.trillas.com.mx; f. 1954; science, technical, textbooks, children's books; Man. Dir FRANCISCO TRILLAS MERCADER.

Universidad Nacional Autónoma de México: Dirección General de Fomento Editorial, Avda del Imán 5, Ciudad Universitaria, 04510 México, DF; tel. (55) 5622-6572; internet www.unam.mx; f. 1935; publications in all fields; Dir-Gen. ARTURO VELÁZQUEZ JIMÉNEZ.

ESTADO DE MÉXICO

Pearson Educación de México, SA de CV: Atlacomulco 500, 4°, Industrial Atoto, Naucalpan de Juárez, Méx.; tel. (55) 5387-0700; fax (55) 5358-6445; internet www.pearsoneducacion.net; f. 1984; educational books under the imprints Addison-Wesley, Prentice Hall, Allyn and Bacon, Longman and Scott Foresman; Pres. STEVE MARBAN.

ASSOCIATIONS

Cámara Nacional de la Industria Editorial Mexicana: Holanda 13, Col. San Diego Churubusco, 04120 México, DF; tel. (55) 5688-2011; fax (55) 5604-3147; e-mail consejodirectivo@caniem.com; internet www.caniem.com; f. 1964; Pres. JUAN LUIS ARZOZ ARBIDE; Sec. PATRICIA VAN RHIJN ARMIDA.

Instituto Mexicano del Libro, AC: México, DF; tel. (55) 5535-2061; Pres. KLAUS THIELE; Sec.-Gen. ISABEL RUIZ GONZÁLEZ.

Broadcasting and Communications

TELECOMMUNICATIONS

Regulatory Authorities

Comisión Federal de Telecomunicaciones (Cofetel): Bosque de Radiatas 44, 4°, Col. Bosques de las Lomas, Del. Cuajimalpa, 05120 México, DF; tel. and fax (55) 5015-4000; e-mail nuevaimagen@cft.gob.mx; internet www.cofetel.gob.mx; Pres. HÉCTOR OSUNA.

Dirección General de Política de Telecomunicaciones: Avda Xola y Universidad s/n, Col. Narvarte, Del. Benito Juárez, 03020 México, DF; tel. (55) 5723-9369; fax (55) 5723-9300; e-mail holavarr@sct.gob.mx; internet www.sct.gob.mx; part of Secretariat of State for Communications and Transport; Dir HECTOR OLAVARRÍA TAPIA.

Principal Operators

Alestra: Paseo de las Palmas 405, Col. Lomas de Chapultepec, 11000 México, DF; tel. (55) 8503-5000; internet www.alestra.com.mx; 49% owned by AT&T; Dir-Gen. ROLANDO ZUBIRÁN SHETLER.

América Móvil, SA de CV: Edif. Telcel 2, Lago Alberto 366, Col. Anáhuac, 11320 México, DF; tel. (55) 2581-3947; fax (55) 2581-3948; e-mail patricia.ramirez@americamovil.com; internet www.americamovil.com; f. 2000 as a spin off from Telmex; subsidiaries operate mobile telephone services in 18 countries in the Americas; CEO DANIEL HAJJ ABOUMRAD.

Telcel: internet www.telcel.com; f. 1978, present name adopted 1989; subsidiary of above, providing mobile services in Mexico; COO PATRICIA RAQUEL HEVIA COTO.

AT&T México: Montes Urales 470, Col. Lomas de Chapultepec, 11000 México, DF; internet www.att.com.

Avantel: Liverpool 88, Col. Juárez, 06600 México, DF; e-mail servicioaclientes@avantel.com.mx; internet www.avantel.net.mx; f. 1994; Dir-Gen. OSCAR RODRÍGUEZ MARTÍNEZ.

Axtel: Blvd Díaz Ordáz Km 3.33, Zona Industrial, 66215 San Pedro Garza García, NL; tel. (81) 8114-0000; e-mail contacto@axtel.com .mx; internet www.axtel.com.mx; f. 1993; fixed-line operator.

Grupo Iusacell, SA de CV: Avda Prolongación Paseo de la Reforma 1236, Col. Santa Fe, 05438 México, DF; tel. (55) 5109-0611; e-mail webmaster@iusacell.com.mx; internet www.iusacell.com.mx; f. 1992; a merger with Unefon was announced in Sept. 2006; operates mobile cellular telephone network; 74% owned by Móvil Access; Dir-Gen. GUSTAVO GUZMÁN SEPÚLVEDA.

Maxcom Telecomunicaciones, SAB de CV: Guillermo González Camarena 2000, Col. Centro Ciudad Santa Fe, 01210 México, DF; tel. (55) 5147-1111; internet www.maxcom.com; f. 1996; fixed-line operator; Pres. ADRIÁN AGUIRRE GÓMEZ; Dir-Gen. RENÉ SAGASTUY FERRANDIZ.

Telecomunicaciones de México (TELECOMM): Torre Central de Telecomunicaciones, Eje Central Lázaro Cárdenas 567, 11°, Ala Norte, Col. Narvarte, Del. Benito Juárez, 03020 México, DF; tel. (55) 5090-1166; fax (55) 1035-2408; e-mail figueroa@telecomm.net.mx; internet www.telecomm.net.mx; govt-owned; Dir-Gen. ANDRÉS FIGUEROA COBIÁN.

Telefónica México: Prolongación Paseo de la Reforma 1200, Lote B-2, Col. Santa Fe, Cruz Manca, 05348 México, DF; tel. (55) 1616-5000; internet www.telefonicamoviles.com.mx; f. 1924 (in Spain); owned by Telefónica, SA (Spain); fixed, mobile and broadband services; operates telephone service Telefónica Móviles México (movistar), call centre co Atento, and research and devt co Telefónica I+D; Pres. FRANCISCO GIL DÍAZ; Dir FRANCISCO DE ASIS CABALLERO FERNÁNDEZ.

Teléfonos de México, SA de CV (Telmex): Parque Vía 190, Col. Cuauhtémoc, 06599 México, DF; tel. (55) 5222-1212; fax (55) 5545-5500; e-mail ri@telmex.com; internet www.telmex.com.mx; majority-owned by Carso Global Telecom; Pres. CARLOS SLIM DOMIT; Dir-Gen. HÉCTOR SLIM SEADE.

Unefon: Periférico Sur 4119, Col. Fuentes del Pedregal, 14141 México, DF; tel. (55) 8582-5000; e-mail ainfante@unefon.com.mx; internet www.unefon.com.mx; mobile operator; a merger with Grupo Iusacell was announced in Sept. 2006.

BROADCASTING

Regulatory Authority

Dirección General de Sistemas de Radio y Televisión (DGSRT): Roma 41, Col. Juaréz, Del. Cuauhtémoc, 06600 México, DF; tel. (55) 5723-9300; fax (55) 5530-4315; e-mail jrodrigc@sct.gob .mx; internet www.rtc.gob.mx; Dir-Gen. JORGE ALBERTO RODRIGUEZ CASTAÑEDA.

Radio

There were 1,423 radio stations in Mexico in 2004. Among the most important commercial networks are:

ARTSA: Avda de Los Virreyes 1030, Col. Lomas de Chapultepec, 11000 México, DF; tel. (55) 5202-3344; fax (55) 5202-6940; Dir-Gen. Lic. GUSTAVO ECHEVARRÍA ARCE.

Corporación Mexicana de Radiodifusión: Tetitla 23, esq. Calle Coapa, Col. Toriello Guerra, 14050 México, DF; tel. (55) 5424-6380; fax (55) 5666-5422; e-mail comentarios@cmr.com.mx; internet www .cmr.com.mx; Pres. ENRIQUE BERNAL SERVÍN; Dir-Gen. OSCAR BELTRÁN.

Firme, SA: Gauss 10, Col. Nueva Anzures, 11590 México, DF; tel. and fax (55) 5250-7788; Dir-Gen. LUIS IGNACIO SANTIBÁÑEZ.

Grupo Acir, SA: Monte Pirineos 770, Col. Lomas de Chapultepec, 11000 México, DF; tel. (55) 5201-1700; fax (55) 5201-1771; e-mail chernandez@fundacionacir.org.mx; internet www.grupoacir.com .mx; f. 1965; comprises 140 stations; Exec. Pres. MARI CARMEN IBARRA FARIÑA; Dir CECILIA HERNÁNDEZ AVALOS.

Grupo Radio Centro, SA de CV: Constituyentes 1154, Col. Lomas Atlas, Del. Miguel Hidalgo, 11950 México, DF; tel. (55) 5728-4947; fax (55) 5259-2915; e-mail rcentro@grc.com.mx; internet radiocentro .com.mx; f. 1965; comprises 100 radio stations; Pres. ADRIÁN AGUIRRE GÓMEZ; Dir-Gen. Ing. GILBERTO SOLIS SILVA.

Grupo Siete Comunicación: Montecito 38, 31°, Of. 33, México, DF; tel. (55) 9000-0787; fax (55) 9000-0747; e-mail jch@gruposiete.com .mx; internet www.gruposiete.com.mx; f. 1997; Pres. Lic. FRANCISCO JAVIER SÁNCHEZ CAMPUZANO.

Instituto Mexicano de la Radio (IMER): Mayorazgo 83, 2°, Col. Xoco, 03330 México, DF; tel. (55) 5628-1704; internet www.imer.com .mx; f. 1983; Dir-Gen. ANA CECILIA TERRAZAS VALDÉS.

MVS Radio Stereorey y FM Globo: Mariano Escobedo 532, Col. Anzures, 11590 México, DF; tel. (55) 5203-4574; fax (55) 5255-1425; e-mail vargas@data.net.mx; f. 1968; Pres. Lic. JOAQUÍN VARGAS G.; Vice-Pres. Lic. ADRIÁN VARGAS G.

Núcleo Radio Mil: Prolongación Paseo de la Reforma 115, Col. Paseo de las Lomas, Santa Fe, 01330 México, DF; tel. (55) 5258-1200; e-mail radiomil@rnm.com.mx; internet www.nrm.com.mx; f. 1942; comprises seven radio stations; Pres. and Dir-Gen. Lic. E. GUILLERMO SALAS PEYRÓ.

Organización Radio Centro: Artículo 123, No 90, Col. Centro, 06050 México, DF; tel. (55) 5709-2220; fax (55) 512-8588; nine stations in Mexico City; Pres. MARÍA ESTHER GÓMEZ DE AGUIRRE.

Organización Radiofónica de México, SA: Tuxpan 39, 8°, Col. Roma Sur, 06760 México, DF; tel. (55) 5264-2025; fax (55) 5264-5720; Pres. JAIME FERNÁNDEZ ARMENDÁRIZ.

Radio Cadena Nacional, SA (RCN): Lago Victoria 78, Col. Granada, 11520 México, DF; tel. (55) 2624-0401; e-mail loregonzalez@rcn.com.mx; internet www.rcn.com.mx; f. 1948; Pres. RAFAEL C. NAVARRO ARRONTE; Dir-Gen. SERGIO FAJARDO ORTIZ.

Radio Educación: Angel Urraza 622, Col. del Valle, 03100 México, DF; tel. (55) 4155-1050; e-mail direccion@radioeducacion.edu.mx; internet www.radioeducacion.edu.mx; f. 1968; Dir-Gen. VIRGINIA BELLO MÉNDEZ.

Radio Fórmula, SA: Privada de Horacio 10, Col. Polanco, 11560 México, DF; tel. (55) 5282-1016; internet www.radioformula.com .mx; Dir ROGERIO AZCARRAGA.

Radiodifusoras Asociadas, SA de CV (RASA): Durango 341, 2°, Col. Roma, 06700 México, DF; tel. (55) 5286-1222; fax (55) 5211-6159; e-mail rasa@rasa.com.mx; internet www.rasa.com.mx; f. 1956; Exec. Pres. JOSÉ LARIS RODRÍGUEZ.

Radiodifusores Asociados de Innovación y Organización, SA: Emerson 408, Col. Chapultepec Morales, 11570 México, DF; tel. (55) 5203-5577; fax (55) 5545-2078; Dir-Gen. Lic. CARLOS QUIÑONES ARMENDÁRIZ.

Radiópolis, SA de CV: owned by Grupo Televisa and Grupo Prisa; owns 5 radio stations; affiliated to Radiorama, SA de CV (q.v.) in 2004; Dir-Gen. RAÚL RODRÍGUEZ GONZÁLEZ.

Radiorama, SA de CV: Reforma 2620, 2°, Col. Lomas, 11950 México, DF; tel. (55) 1105-0000; fax (55) 1105-0002; e-mail grupo@ radiorama.com.mx; internet www.radiorama.com.mx; Dir JOSÉ LUIS C. RESÉNDIZ.

Representaciones Comerciales Integrales: Avda Chapultepec 431, Col. Juárez, 06600 México, DF; tel. (55) 5533-6185; Dir-Gen. ALFONSO PALMA V.

Sistema Radio Juventud: Pablo Casals 567, Prados Providencia, 44670 Guadalajara, Jal.; tel. (33) 3641-6677; fax (33) 3641-3413; f. 1975; network of several stations including Estereo Soul 89.9 FM; Dirs ALBERTO LEAL A., J. JESÚS OROZCO G., GABRIEL ARREGUI V.

Sistema Radiofónico Nacional, SA: Baja California 163, Of. 602, 06760 México, DF; tel. (55) 5574-0298; f. 1971; represents commercial radio networks; Dir-Gen. RENÉ C. DE LA ROSA.

Sociedad Mexicana de Radio, SA de CV (SOMER): Paseo de la Reforma 115, 4°, Col. Lomas, Santa Fé, 01330 México, DF; tel. (55) 9177-6660; fax (55) 9177-6671; e-mail somer@somer.com.mx; internet www.somer.com.mx; Dir-Gen. EDILBERTO HUESCA PERROTIN.

Radio Insurgente, the underground radio station of the Ejército Zapatista de Liberación Nacional (EZLN—Zapatistas), is broadcast from south-eastern Mexico. Programmes can be found on www.radioinsurgente.org.

Television

There were 658 television stations in 2004. Among the most important are:

Asesoramiento y Servicios Técnicos Industriales, SA (ASTISA): México, DF; tel. (55) 5585-3333; commercial; Dir ROBERTO CHÁVEZ TINAJERO.

MVS (Multivisión): Blvd Puerto Aéreo 486, Col. Moctezuma, 15500 México, DF; tel. (55) 5764-8100; e-mail orivas@mvs.com; internet www.mvs.com; subscriber-funded; Pres. JOAQUÍN VARGAS GUAJARDO; Vice-Pres. ERNESTO VARGAS.

Once TV: Carpio 475, Col. Casco de Santo Tomás, 11340 México, DF; tel. (55) 5166-4000; e-mail info@mail.oncetv.ipn.mx; internet www .oncetv.ipn.mx; f. 1959; Dir FERNANDO SARIÑANA MÁRQUEZ.

Tele Cadena Mexicana, SA: Avda Chapultepec 18, 06724 México, DF; tel. (55) 5535-1679; commercial, comprises about 80 stations; Dir JORGE ARMANDO PIÑA MEDINA.

Televisa, SA de CV: Edif. Televicentro, Avda Chapultepec 28, Col. Doctores, 06724 México, DF; tel. (55) 5709-3333; fax (55) 5709-3021; e-mail webmaster@televisa.com.mx; internet www.televisa.com; f. 1973; commercial; began broadcasts to Europe via satellite in

Dec. 1988 through its subsidiary, Galavisión; 406 affiliated stations; Chair. and CEO EMILIO AZCÁRRAGA JEAN.

Televisión Azteca, SA de CV: Anillo Periférico Sur 4121, Col. Fuentes del Pedregal, 14141 México, DF; tel. (55) 5447-8844; fax (55) 5645-4258; e-mail webtva@tvazteca.com; internet www.tvazteca.com; f. 1992; assumed responsibility for fmr state-owned channels 7 and 13; Pres. RICARDO B. SALINAS PLIEGO; CEO PEDRO PADILLA LONGORIA.

Televisión de la República Mexicana: Mina 24, Col. Guerrero, México, DF; tel. (55) 5510-8590; cultural; Dir EDUARDO LIZALDE.

Association

Cámara Nacional de la Industria de Radio y Televisión (CIRT): Avda Horacio 1013, Col. Polanco Reforma, Del. Miguel Hidalgo, 11550 México, DF; tel. (55) 5726-9909; fax (55) 5545-6767; e-mail cirt@cirt.com.mx; internet www.cirt.com.mx; f. 1942; Pres. ENRIQUE PEREDA GÓMEZ; Dir-Gen. ANDRÉS MASSIEU FERNÁNDEZ.

Finance

(cap. = capital; res = reserves; dep. = deposits; m. = million; brs = branches; amounts in new pesos unless otherwise stated)

BANKING

The Mexican banking system is comprised of the Banco de México (the central bank of issue), multiple or commercial banking institutions and development banking institutions. Banking activity is regulated by the Federal Government.

Commercial banking institutions are constituted as *Sociedades Anónimas*, with wholly private social capital. Development banking institutions exist as *Sociedades Nacionales de Crédito*; participation in their capital is exclusive to the Federal Government, notwithstanding the possibility of accepting limited amounts of private capital. In 2005 there were 34 commercial and development banks operating in Mexico, and 71 foreign banks maintained offices.

All private banks were nationalized in September 1982. By July 1992, however, the banking system had been completely returned to the private sector. Legislation removing all restrictions on foreign ownership of banks received congressional approval in 1999.

Supervisory Authority

Comisión Nacional Bancaria y de Valores (CNBV) (National Banking and Securities Commission): Avda Insurgentes Sur 1971, Torre Norte, Sur y III, Col. Guadalupe Inn, Del. Alvaro Obregón, 01020 México, DF; tel. and fax (55) 1454-6000; e-mail info@cnbv.gob.mx; internet www.cnbv.gob.mx; f. 1924; govt commission controlling all credit institutions in Mexico; Pres. GUILLERMO ENRIQUE BABATZ TORRES.

Central Bank

Banco de México (BANXICO): Avda 5 de Mayo 2, Col. Centro, Del. Cuauhtémoc, 06059 México, DF; tel. (55) 5237-2000; fax (55) 5237-2070; e-mail comsoc@banxico.org.mx; internet www.banxico.org.mx; f. 1925; currency issuing authority; became autonomous on 1 April 1994; cap. 6.3m., res –77.2m., dep. 704.9m. (Dec. 2007); Gov. AGUSTÍN CARSTENS CARSTENS; Dir-Gen. DAVID AARON MARGOLÍN SCHABES; 6 brs.

Commercial Banks

Banco del Bajío, SA: Avda Manuel J. Clouthier 508, Col. Jardines del Campestre, 37128 León, Gto; tel. (477) 710-4600; fax (477) 710-4693; e-mail internacional@bancobajio.com.mx; internet www.bancobajio.com.mx; f. 1994; cap. 2,141m., res 5,195m., dep. 55,895m. (Dec. 2008); Pres. SALVADOR OÑATE.

Banco Mercantil del Norte, SA (BANORTE): Avda Revolución 3000, Col. Primavera, 64830 Monterrey, NL; tel. (81) 3319-7200; fax (81) 3319-5216; internet www.banorte.com; f. 1899; merged with Banco Regional del Norte in 1985; cap. 13,409.0m., res 17,379.0m., dep. 308,198.0m. (Dec. 2008); Chair. ROBERTO GONZÁLEZ BARRERA; Dir-Gen. ALEJANDRO VALENZUELA; 457 brs.

Banco Nacional de México, SA (Banamex): Avda Isabel la Católica 44, 06089 México, DF; tel. (55) 5720-7091; fax (55) 5920-7323; e-mail prensa@banamex.com; internet www.banamex.com; f. 1884; transferred to private ownership in 1991; merged with Citibank México, SA in 2001; cap. 30,248.0m., res 53,010.0m., dep. 400,191.0m. (Dec. 2007); CEO MANUEL MEDINA MORA; 1,260 brs.

Banca Santander, SA: Mod 401, 4°, Prolongación Paseo de la Reforma 500, Col. Lomas de Santa Fe, Del. Alvaro Obregon, 01219 México, DF; tel. (55) 5261-1543; fax (55) 5261-5549; internet www.santander.com.mx; f. 1864 as Banco Serfin; acquired by Banco Santander Central Hispano (Spain) in Dec. 2000; adopted current name 2006; cap. 11,091.0m., res 49,053.0m., dep. 407,119.0m. (Dec. 2008); Exec. Pres. and Dir-Gen. MARCOS MARTÍNEZ GAVICA; 554 brs.

BBVA Bancomer, SA: Centro Bancomer, Avda Universidad 1200, Col. Xoco, 03339 México, DF; tel. (55) 5621-3434; fax (55) 5621-3230; internet www.bancomer.com.mx; f. 2000 by merger of Bancomer (f. 1864) and Mexican operations of Banco Bilbao Vizcaya Argentaria (Spain); privatized in 2002; cap. 21,430.0m., res 40,754.0m., dep. 1,009,367.0m. (Dec. 2008); Pres. IGNACIO DESCHAMPS GONZÁLEZ.

Dresdner Bank Mexico, SA: Blvd M. A. Camacho 164, 4°, Col. Lomas de Barrilaco, 11010 México, DF; tel. (55) 5258-3170; fax (55) 5258-3199; e-mail mexico@dbla.com; f. 1995; Man. Dir LUIS NIÑO DE RIVERA.

HSBC México: Paseo de la Reforma 156, Col. Juárez, Del. Cuauhtémoc, 06600 México, DF; tel. (55) 5721-2222; fax (55) 5721-2393; internet www.hsbc.com.mx; f. 1941; bought by HSBC (United Kingdom) in 2002; name changed from Banco Internacional, SA (BITAL) in 2004; cap. 4,271.6m., res 22,040.6m., dep. 359,574.3m. (Dec. 2008); Dir-Gen. LUIS JAVIER PEÑA KEGEL; 1,400 brs.

Scotiabank Inverlat, SA: Blvd Miguel Avila Camacho 1, 18°, Col. Lomas de Chapultepec, Del. Miguel Hidalgo, 11009 México, DF; tel. (55) 5728-1000; fax (55) 5229-2019; internet www.scotiabankinverlat.com; f. 1977 as Multibanco Comermex, SA; changed name to Banco Inverlat, SA in 1995; 55% holding acquired by Scotiabank Group (Canada) and adopted current name 2001; cap. 7,451.0m., surplus and res 14,833.0m., dep. 121,321.0m. (Dec. 2008); Pres. PETER C. CARDINAL; 476 brs.

Development Banks

Banco Nacional de Comercio Exterior, SNC (BANCOMEXT): Periférico Sur 4333, Col. Jardines en la Montaña, Del. Tlalpan, 14210 México, DF; tel. (55) 5449-9100; fax (55) 5652-9342; e-mail bancomext@bancomext.gob.mx; internet www.bancomext.com; f. 1937; cap. 15,040.0m., res -6,471.0m., dep. 77,920.0m. (Dec. 2008); Dir-Gen. HÉCTOR RANGEL DOMENE.

Banco Nacional del Ejército, Fuerza Aérea y Armada, SNC (BANJERCITO): Avda Industria Militar 1055, Col. Lomas de Sotelo, Del. Miguel Hidalgo, 11200 México, DF; tel. and fax (55) 5626-0500; e-mail info@banjercito.com.mx; internet www.banjercito.com.mx; f. 1947; Dir-Gen. Maj.-Gen. FERNANDO MILLÁN VILLEGAS.

Banco Nacional de Obras y Servicios Públicos, SNC (BANOBRAS): Avda Javier Barros Sierra 515, Col. Lomas de Santa Fe, Del. Álvaro Obregón, 01219 México, DF; tel. (55) 5270-1552; fax (55) 5270-1564; internet www.banobras.gob.mx; f. 1933; govt-owned; cap. 11,765.0m., res 1,963.0m., dep. 123,406.0m. (Dec. 2008); Dir-Gen. ALONSO GARCÍA TAMÉS.

Compartamos Banco: Insurgentes Sur 552, Col. Escandón, 11800 México, DF; tel. (55) 5276-7250; fax (55) 5276-7299; e-mail servicioalcliente@compartamos.com; internet www.compartamos.com; f. 1990; Dir-Gen. FERNANDO ALVAREZ TOCA.

Financiera Rural: Agrarismo 227, Col. Escandón, Del. Miguel Hidalgo, CP 11800, México, DF; tel. (55) 5230-1600; internet www.financierarural.gob.mx; f. 2004; state-run devt bank, concerned with agricultural, forestry and fishing sectors; Dir-Gen. ENRIQUE DE LA MADRID CORDERO.

Nacional Financiera, SNC (NAFIN): Insurgentes Sur 1971, Torre IV, 13°, Col. Guadalupe Inn, 01020 México, DF; tel. (55) 5325-6700; fax (55) 5661-8418; e-mail info@nafin.gob.mx; internet www.nafin.com; f. 1934; cap. 7,952.0m., res 4,222.0m., dep. 148,386.0m. (Dec. 2008); Dir-Gen. HÉCTOR RANGEL DOMENE; 32 brs.

BANKERS' ASSOCIATION

Asociación de Bancos de México: 16 de Setiembre 27, 3°, Col. Centro Histórico, 06000 México, DF; tel. (55) 5722-4300; internet www.abm.org.mx; f. 1928; Pres. IGNACIO DESCHAMPS GONZÁLEZ; Dir-Gen. JUAN CARLOS JIMÉNEZ ROJAS; 52 mems.

STOCK EXCHANGE

Bolsa Mexicana de Valores, SA de CV: Paseo de la Reforma 255, Col. Cuauhtémoc, 06500 México, DF; tel. (55) 5726-6000; fax (55) 5726-6836; e-mail cinforma@bmv.com.mx; internet www.bmv.com.mx; f. 1894; Pres. and CEO LUIS TÉLLEZ KUENZLER.

INSURANCE

México, DF

ACE Seguros: Bosques de Alisos, 47A, 1°, Col. Bosques de las Lomas, 5120 México, DF; tel. (5) 258-5800; fax (5) 258-5899; e-mail info@acelatinamerica.com; f. 1990; fmrly Seguros Cigna; Pres. and Gen. Man. ROBERTO FLORES.

Aseguradora Cuauhtémoc, SA: Manuel Avila Camacho 164, 11570 México, DF; tel. (55) 5250-9800; fax (55) 5540-3204; f. 1944; general; Exec. Pres. JUAN B. RIVEROLL; Dir-Gen. JAVIER COMPEÁN AMEZCUA.

Grupo Nacional Provincial, SAB: Avda Cerro de las Torres 395, Col. Campestre Churubusco, Del. Coyoacán, 04200 México, DF; tel. (55) 5227-3999; internet www.gnp.com.mx; f. 1936; member of Grupo BAL; general; Chair. ALBERTO BAILLÈRES; CEO ALEJANDRO BAILLÈRES.

ING Mexico: Avda Paseo de la Reforma 222, 4°, 5° y 6°, Col. Juárez 06600, México, DF; tel. (55) 5169-2500; internet www.ing.com.mx; f. 1936 as La Comercial; acquired by ING Group in 2000; life, etc.; CEO JAN HOMMEN.

La Nacional, Cía de Seguros, SA: México, DF; f. 1901; life, etc.; Pres. CLEMENTE CABELLO; Chair. Lic. ALBERTO BAILLERES.

MetLife: Blvd Manuel Avila Camacho 32, SKY 14-20 y PH, Col. Lomas de Chapultepec, Del. Miguel Hidalgo, 11000 México, DF; tel. (55) 5328-7000; e-mail contacto@metlife.com.mx; internet www.metlife.com.mx; f. 1931 as Aseguradora Hidalgo, acquired by MetLife Inc in 2002; life; CEO ALBERTO VILAR.

Pan American de México, Cía de Seguros, SA: Reforma 355, 8°, Cuauhtemoc, 06500 México, DF; tel. (55) 5525-7024; f. 1940; Pres. Lic. JESS N. DALTON; Dir-Gen. GILBERTO ESCOBEDA PAZ.

Royal & SunAlliance Mexico: Blvd Adolfo López Mateos 2448, Col. Altavista, 01060 México, DF; tel. (55) 5723-7999; fax (55) 5723-7941; e-mail direccion.general@mx.rsagroup.com; internet www.royalsun.com.mx; f. 1941; acquired Seguros BBV-Probursa in 2001; general, except life; Chair. JOHN NAPIER.

Seguros Azteca, SA: Insurgentes Sur 3579, Tlalpan La Joya, 14000 México, DF; tel. (55) 1720-9854; e-mail infoseguros@segurosazteca.com.mx; internet www.segurosazteca.com.mx; f. 1933, renamed as above in 2003; general including life; Dir-Gen. ALFREDO HONSBERG.

Seguros Banamex, SA: Venustiano Carranza 63, Col. Centro Histórico, Del. Cuauhtémoc, 06000 México, DF; tel. (55) 1226-8100; e-mail sbainternet@banamex.com; internet www.segurosbanamex.com; f. 1994; life, accident and health; Dir-Gen. DANIEL GARDUÑO GUTIÉRREZ.

Seguros Constitución, SA: Avda Revolución 2042, Col. La Otra Banda, 01090 México, DF; tel. (55) 5550-7910; f. 1937; life, accident; Pres. ISIDORO RODRÍGUEZ RUIZ; Dir-Gen. ALFONSO DE ORDUÑA Y PÉREZ.

Seguros el Fénix, SA: México, DF; f. 1937; Pres. VICTORIANO OLAZÁBAL E.; Dir-Gen. JAIME MATUTE LABRADOR.

Seguros Internacional, SA: Abraham González 67, México, DF; f. 1945; general; Pres. Lic. GUSTAVO ROMERO KOLBECK.

Seguros La República, SA: Paseo de la Reforma 383, México, DF; f. 1966; general; 43% owned by Commercial Union (United Kingdom); Pres. LUCIANO ARECHEDERRA QUINTANA; Gen. Man. JUAN ANTONIO DE ARRIETA MENDIZÁBAL.

Seguros de México, SA: Insurgentes Sur 3496, Col. Peña Pobre, 14060 México, DF; tel. (55) 5679-3855; f. 1957; life, etc.; Dir-Gen. Lic. ANTONIO MIJARES RICCI.

Seguros Monterrey New York Life: Presidente Mazaryk 8, Bosques de Chapultepec, Del. Miguel Hidalgo, México, DF; tel. (55) 5326-9000; fax (55) 5536-9610; e-mail clientes@monterrey-newyorklife.com.mx; internet www.monterrey-newyorklife.com.mx; f. 1940 as Monterrey Cía de Seguros; acquired by New York Life in 2000; casualty, life, etc.; Dir-Gen. MARIO VELA BERRONDO.

Monterrey, NL

Seguros Monterrey del Círculo Mercantil, SA, Sociedad General de Seguros: Padre Mier Pte 276, Monterrey, NL; f. 1941; life; Gen. Man. CARMEN G. MASSO DE NAVARRO.

Insurance Association

Asociación Mexicana de Instituciones de Seguros, AC (AMIS): Francisco I Madero 21, Col. Tlacopac, San Angel, 01040 México, DF; tel. (55) 5480-0646; fax (55) 5662-8036; e-mail amis@mail.internet.com.mx; internet www.amis.com.mx; f. 1946; all insurance cos operating in Mexico are mems; Pres. JUAN IGNACIO GIL ANTÓN; Dir-Gen. RECAREDO ARIAS JIMÉNEZ.

Trade and Industry

GOVERNMENT AGENCIES

Comisión Federal de Protección Contra Riesgos Sanitarios (COFEPRIS): Monterrey 33, esq. Oaxaca, Col. Roma, Del. Cuauhtémoc, 06700 México, DF; tel. (55) 5080-5200; fax (55) 5207-5521; e-mail mdiosdado@salud.gob.mx; internet www.cofepris.gob.mx; f. 2003; pharmaceutical regulatory authority; Sec.-Gen. (vacant).

Comisión Nacional Forestal (CONAFOR): Carretera a Nogales s/n, esq. Periférico Poniente 5360, 5°, San Juan de Ocotán, 45019 Zapopan, Jal.; tel. (33) 3777-7000; fax (33) 3777-7012; e-mail conafor@conafor.gob.mx; internet www.conafor.gob.mx; f. 2001; Dir-Gen. JUAN MANUEL TORRES ROJO.

Comisión Nacional de Inversiones Extranjeras (CNIE): Dirección General de Inversión Extranjera, Insurgentes Sur 1940, 8°, Col. Florida, 01030 México, DF; tel. (55) 5229-6100; fax (55) 5229-6507; e-mail gcanales@economia.gob.mx; f. 1973; govt commission to co-ordinate foreign investment; Exec. Sec. GREGORIO MANUEL CANALES RAMÍREZ.

Comisión Nacional de los Salarios Mínimos (CNSM): Avda Cuauhtémoc 14, 2°, Col. Doctores, Del. Cuauhtémoc, 06720 México 7, DF; tel. (55) 5998-3800; fax (55) 5578-5775; e-mail cnsm1@conasami.gob.mx; internet www.conasami.gob.mx; f. 1962, in accordance with Section VI of Article 123 of the Constitution; national commission on minimum salaries; Pres. Lic. BASILIO GONZÁLEZ NÚÑEZ.

Instituto Nacional de Investigaciones Nucleares (ININ): Centro Nuclear de México, Carretera México–Toluca Km 36.5, La Marquesa, 52750 Ocoyoacac, Méx.; tel. (55) 5329-7200; fax (55) 5329-7296; e-mail hernan.rico@inin.gob.mx; internet www.inin.mx; f. 1979 to plan research and devt of nuclear science and technology; also researches the peaceful uses of nuclear energy, for the social, scientific and technological devt of the country; administers the Secondary Standard Dosimetry Laboratory and the Nuclear Information and Documentation Centre, which serves Mexico's entire scientific community; operates a tissue culture laboratory for medical treatment; the 1-MW research reactor, which came into operation in 1967, supplies part of Mexico's requirements for radioactive isotopes; also operates a 12-MV Tandem van de Graaff; Mexico has two nuclear reactors, each with a generating capacity of 654 MW; the first, at Laguna Verde, became operational in 1989 and is administered by the Comisión Federal de Electricidad (CFE); Dir-Gen. RAÚL ORTÍZ MAGAÑA.

Instituto Nacional de Pesca (INAPESCA) (National Fishery Institute): Pitágoras 1320, Col. Santa Cruz Atoyac, Del. Benito Juárez, 03310 México, DF; tel. (55) 3871-9517; fax (55) 5604-9169; e-mail gerardo.garcia@inapesca.sagarpa.gob.mx; internet www.inapesca.gob.mx; f. 1962; Dir MIGUEL ANGEL CISNEROS MATA.

Procuraduría Federal del Consumidor (Profeco): Avda José Vasconcelos 208, Col. Condesa, Del. Cuauhtémoc, 06140 México, DF; tel. (55) 5625-6700; internet www.profeco.gob.mx; f. 1975; consumer protection; Procurator ANTONIO MORALES DE LA PEÑA.

Servicio Geológico Mexicano (SGM): Blvd Felipe Angeles, Carretera México–Pachuca, Km 93.50-4, Col. Venta Prieta, 42080 Pachuca de Soto, Hgo; tel. (771) 711-4266; fax (771) 711-4204; e-mail gintproc@sgm.gob.mx; internet www.coremisgm.gob.mx; f. 1957; govt agency for the devt of mineral resources; Dir-Gen. RAFAEL ALEXANDRI RIONDA.

DEVELOPMENT ORGANIZATIONS

Centro de Investigación para el Desarollo, AC (CIDAC) (Centre of Research for Development): Jaime Balmes 11, Edif. D, 2°, Col. Los Morales Polanco, 11510 México, DF; tel. (55) 5985-1010; fax (55) 5985-1030; e-mail info@cidac.org.mx; internet www.cidac.org; f. 1984; researches economic and political devt; Pres. LUIS RUBIO.

Comisión Nacional de las Zonas Aridas (CONAZA): Blvd Isidro López Zertuche 2513, Col. Los Maestros, 25260 Saltillo, Coah.; tel. and fax (844) 450-5200; e-mail contacto@conaza.gob.mx; internet www.conaza.gob.mx; f. 1970; commission to co-ordinate the devt and use of arid areas; Dir-Gen. LUIS CARLOS FIERRO GARCÍA.

Fideicomiso de Fomento Mineiro (FIFOMI): Puente de Tecamachalco 26, 2°, Col. Lomas de Chapultepec, Del. Miguel Hidalgo, 11000 México, DF; tel. (55) 5249-9500; e-mail pguerra@fifomi.gob.mx; internet www.fifomi.gob.mx; trust for the devt of the mineral industries; Dir-Gen. ALBERTO ORTIZ TRILLO.

Fideicomisos Instituídos en Relación con la Agricultura (FIRA): Km 8, Antigua Carretera Pátzcuaro 8555, 58341 Morelia, Mich.; tel. (443) 322-2399; fax (443) 327-6338; e-mail webmaster@correo.fira.gob.mx; internet www.fira.gob.mx; a group of devt funds to aid agricultural financing, under the Banco de México, comprising Fondo de Garantía y Fomento para la Agricultura, Ganadería y Avicultura (FOGAGA); Fondo Especial para Financiamientos Agropecuarios (FEFA); Fondo Especial de Asistencia Técnica y Garantía para Créditos Agropecuarios (FEGA); Fondo de Garantía y Fomento para las Actividades Pesqueras (FOPESCA); Dir RODRIGO SÁNCHEZ MÚJICA.

Fondo de Operación y Financiamiento Bancario a la Vivienda (FOVI): Ejército Nacional 180, Col. Anzures, 11590 México, DF; tel. (55) 5263-4500; fax (55) 5263-4541; e-mail jmartinez@fovi.gob.mx; internet www.fovi.gob.mx; f. 1963 to promote the construction of low-cost housing through savings and credit schemes; devt fund under the Banco de México; Dir-Gen. MANUEL ZEPEDA PAYERAS.

Instituto Mexicano del Petróleo (IMP): Eje Central Lázaro Cárdenas 152, Col. San Bartolo Atepehuacan, Del. Gustavo A.

Madero, 07730 México, DF; tel. (55) 9175-6000; fax (55) 9175-8000; e-mail gdgarcia@imp.mx; internet www.imp.mx; f. 1965 to foster devt of the petroleum, chemical and petrochemical industries; Dir JOSÉ ENRIQUE VILLA RIVERA.

CHAMBERS OF COMMERCE

Chambers of Commerce exist in the chief town of each state as well as in the larger centres of commercial activity. There are also other international Chambers of Commerce.

American Chamber of Commerce of Mexico (Amcham): Lucerna 78, Col. Juárez, 06600 México, DF; tel. (55) 5141-3800; fax (55) 5141-3833; e-mail amchammx@amcham.com.mx; internet www.amcham.com.mx; f. 1917; brs in Guadalajara and Monterrey; Exec. Vice-Pres. and Dir-Gen. GUILLERMO WOLF.

Cámara de Comercio, Servicios y Turismo Ciudad de México (CANACO) (Chamber of Commerce, Services and Tourism of Mexico City): Paseo de la Reforma 42, 3°, Col. Centro, Apdo 32005, Del. Cuauhtémoc, 06048 México, DF; tel. (55) 3685-2269; fax (55) 5592-2279; e-mail sos@ccmexico.com.mx; internet www.ccmexico.com.mx; f. 1874; 50,000 mems; Pres. ARTURO MENDICUTI NARRO; Dir-Gen. RICARDO CASADO GUZMÁN.

Cámara Nacional de la Industria de Transformación (CANACINTRA): Avda San Antonio 256, Col. Ampliación Nápoles, Del. Benito Juárez, 06849 México, DF; tel. (55) 5482-3000; fax 5598-8044; e-mail direcciongeneral@canacintra.org.mx; internet www.canacintra.org.mx; represents majority of smaller manufacturing businesses; Pres. SERGIO ENRIQUE CERVANTES RODILES.

Confederación de Cámaras Nacionales de Comercio, Servicios y Turismo (CONCANACO-SERVYTUR) (Confederation of National Chambers of Commerce, Services and Tourism): Balderas 144, 3°, Col. Centro, 06070 México, DF; tel. (55) 5722-9300; e-mail comentarios@concanacored.com; internet www.concanaco.com.mx; f. 1917; Pres. JORGE E. DÁVILA FLORES; Dir-Gen. EDUARDO GARCÍA VILLASEÑOR; comprises 283 regional Chambers.

CHAMBERS OF INDUSTRY

The 47 national chambers, 15 regional chambers, 3 general chambers and 42 associations, many of which are located in the Federal District, are representative of the major industries of the country.

Central Confederation

Confederación de Cámaras Industriales de los Estados Unidos Mexicanos (CONCAMIN) (Confed. of Industrial Chambers): Manuel María Contreras 133, 4°, Col. Cuauhtémoc, Del. Cuauhtémoc, 06500 México, DF; tel. (55) 5140-7800; fax 5140-7831; e-mail webmaster@concamin.org.mx; internet www.concamin.org.mx; f. 1918; represents and promotes the activities of the entire industrial sector; Pres. ISMAEL PLASCENCIA NÚÑEZ; Dir-Gen. FRANCISCO JAVIER JIMÉNEZ ROJAS; 108 mem. orgs.

INDUSTRIAL AND TRADE ASSOCIATIONS

Asociación Nacional de Importadores y Exportadores de la República Mexicana (ANIERM) (National Association of Importers and Exporters): Monterrey 130, Col. Roma, Del. Cuauhtémoc, 06700 México, DF; tel. (55) 5584-9522; fax (55) 5584-5317; e-mail anierm@anierm.org.mx; internet www.anierm.org.mx; f. 1944; Pres. JOSÉ OTHÓN RAMÍREZ GUTTIÉREZ; Exec. Vice-Pres. HUMBERTO SIMONEEN ARDILA.

Asociación Nacional de la Industria Química (ANIQ): Angel Urraza 505, Col. del Valle, 03100 México, DF; tel. (55) 5230-5100; internet www.aniq.org.mx; f. 1959; chemicals asscn; Dir-Gen. MIGUEL BENEDETTO; c. 200 mem. cos.

Comisión Nacional de Seguridad Nuclear y Salvaguardias (CNSNS): Dr José María Barragán 779, Col. Narvarte, Del. Benito Juárez, 03020 México, DF; tel. (55) 5095-3200; fax (55) 5095-3295; e-mail swaller@cnsns.gob.mx; internet www.cnsns.gob.mx; f. 1979; nuclear regulatory agency; Dir-Gen. JUAN EIBENSCHUTZ HARTMAN.

Comisión Petroquímica Mexicana: México, DF; promotes the devt of the petrochemical industry; Tech. Sec. Ing. JUAN ANTONIO BARGÉS MESTRES.

Consejo Mexicano de Asuntos Internacionales (COMEXI): Oficina 502, Torre Magnum, Sierra Mojada 620, Col. Lomas de Chapultepec, 11000 México, DF; tel. (55) 5202-3776; e-mail info@consejomexicano.org; internet www.consejomexicano.org; Pres. FERNANDO SOLANA.

Consejo Mexicano del Café (CMCAFE): José María Ibarrarán 84, 1°, Col. San José Insurgentes, Del. Benito Juárez, 03900 México, DF; tel. and fax (55) 5611-9075; e-mail cmc@sagar.gob.mx; f. 1993; devt of coffee sector; Pres. JAVIER USABIAGA.

Consejo Mexicano de Comercio Exterior (COMCE): Lancaster 15, 2° y 3°, Col. Juárez, 06600 México, DF; tel. (52) 5231-7100; fax (55) 5321-7109; e-mail direccion@comce.org.mx; internet www.comce.org.mx; f. 1999 to promote international trade; Pres. VALENTÍN DIEZ MORODO.

Consejo Nacional de la Industria Maquiladora de Exportación (CNIME): Ejército Nacional 418, 12°, Of. 1204, Col. Chapultepec Morales, Del. Miguel Hidalgo, 11570 México, DF; tel. and fax (55) 5250-6093; e-mail dirgral@cnimme.org.mx; internet www.cnime.org.mx; f. 1975; Pres. CÉSAR CASTRO; Dir-Gen. CARLOS PALENCIA ESCALANTE.

Instituto Nacional de Investigaciones Forestales y Agropecuarios (INIFAP) (National Forestry and Agricultural Research Institute): Avda Progreso No 5, Col. Barrio de Santa Catarina, Del. Coyoacán, 04010 México, DF; tel. (55) 3871-8700; e-mail brajcich.pedro@inifap.gob.mx; internet www.inifap.gob.mx; f. 1985; conducts research into plant genetics, management of species and conservation; Dir-Gen. PEDRO BRAJCICH GALLEGOS.

EMPLOYERS' ORGANIZATIONS

Consejo Coordinador Empresarial (CCE): Lancaster 15, Col. Juárez, 06600 México, DF; tel. (55) 5229-1100; fax (55) 5592-3857; e-mail sistemas@cce.org.mx; internet www.cce.org.mx; f. 1976; co-ordinating body of private sector; Pres. ARMANDO PAREDES ARROYO; Dir-Gen. LUIS MIGUEL PANDO.

Consejo Mexicano de Hombres de Negocios (CMHN): México, DF; f. 1963; represents leading businesspeople; affiliated to CCE; Pres. CLAUDIO GONZÁLEZ LAPORTE.

STATE HYDROCARBONS COMPANY

Petróleos Mexicanos (PEMEX): Avda Marina Nacional 329, Col. Huasteca, 11311 México, DF; tel. (55) 1944-2500; fax (55) 5531-6354; e-mail petroleosmexicanos@pemex.com; internet www.pemex.com; f. 1938; govt agency for the exploitation of Mexico's petroleum and natural gas resources; Dir-Gen. JUAN JOSÉ SUÁREZ COPPEL; 106,900 employees.

MAJOR COMPANIES

Mining and Metals

Altos Hornos de México, SA: Prolongación Juárez s/n, Edif. GAN Modulo II, Col. La Loma, Monclova, 25770 Coah.; tel. (866) 649-3400; fax (866) 633-2390; e-mail ventas@ahmsa.com; internet www.ahmsa.com.mx; f. 1942; fmr state-owned iron and steel foundry and rolling mill; privatized in the early 1990s; subsidiary of Grupo Imsa; Pres. ALONSO ANCIRA; Dir-Gen. LUIS ZAMUDIO MIECHIELSEN; 17,000 employees (incl. subsidiaries).

Carso Infraestructura y Construcción (CICSA): Miguel de Cervantes Saavedra 255, Col. Granada, 11520 México, DF; internet www.gcarso.com.mx; f. 1980; civil engineering, mining, services and infrastructure for petrochemical industry; part of Grupo Carso, SA de CV; Dir Gen. ANTONIO GÓMEZ; Gen. Man. GUILLERMO BARBOSA.

Grupo Industrial Saltillo, SA de CV: Chiapas 375, Col. República, 25280 Saltillo, Coah.; tel. (844) 4111-000; fax (844) 4111-034; e-mail jorge.verastegui@gis.com.mx; internet www.gis.com.mx; f. 1966; ceramics, iron, autoparts, water heaters; CEO JOSÉ ANTONIO LÓPEZ MORALES; 10,928 employees (2007).

Grupo México, SA de CV: Campos Eliseos 400, Col. Lomas de Chapultepec, Del. Miguel Hidalgo, 11000 México, DF; tel. (55) 1103-5000; fax (55) 5574-7677; internet www.gmexico.com; f. 1901; began operations in Mexico as Asarco (USA); holding co with interests in extraction and processing of metallic ores, and transportation; Chair. and CEO GERMAN LARREA MOTA VELASCO; 21,110 employees (2005).

Industrias Cobre, SA de CV (Nacobre): Poniente 134, No 719, Col. Industria Vallejo, 02300 México, DF; tel. (55) 5728-5300; fax (55) 5728-5391; internet www.nacobre.com.mx; f. 1951; copper, brass, aluminium, plastics producers; part of Grupo Carso, SA de CV; Gen. Man. ALEJANDRO OCHOA ABARCA; 6,500 employees.

Industrias Peñoles, SA de CV: Moliere 222, Col. Polanco, 11540 México, DF; tel. (55) 5279-3000; fax (55) 5279-3514; internet www.penoles.com.mx; f. 1969; silver, gold, lead, zinc mining; sodium sulphate plant; part of Grupo BAL; Chair. ALBERTO BAILLÈRES; CEO FERNANDO ALANÍS ORTEGA; 9,081 employees.

TenarisTamsa (Tubos de Acero de México, SA): Campos Eliseos 400, 17°, Col. Chapultepec, Polanco, 11560 México, DF; tel. (55) 5282-9919; fax (55) 5282-9966; e-mail elenah@tamsa.com.mx; internet www.tenaris.com; f. 1952; manufacturers of seamless steel tubes and fittings, services for petroleum industry; Chair. and CEO PAOLO ROCCA; Area Man. (North America) GERMÁN CURÁ; 2,500 employees.

Ternium, SA: Avda Bernardo Reyes 5616, Col. Ferrocarrilera, Monterrey, Nueva León; tel. (81) 8865-2828; internet www.ternium.com.mx; in 2007 Ternium obtained full control of Grupo Imsa; steel; Chair. PAOLO ROCCO; CEO DANIEL NOVEGIL; 16,000 employees (2006).

Tubacero, SA de CV: Avda Guerrero 3729 Norte, Col. del Norte, 64500 Monterrey, Nuevo León; tel. (81) 8305-5555; fax (81) 8305-5550; e-mail sistemas@tubacero.com; internet www.tubacero.com; f. 1943; manufacturers of piping; Dir-Gen. LEÓN GUTIÉRREZ VELA; 299 employees.

Motor Vehicles

BMW de México, SA: Paseo de los Tamarindos 100, 5°, Of. 501, Col. Bosque de las Lomas, 05120 México, DF; tel. (55) 9140-8700; fax (55) 9140-8777; e-mail crm@bmw.com.mx; internet www.bmw.com.mx; f. 1994; subsidiary of BMW AG of Germany; motor vehicles and parts; Man. Dir GERD DRESSLER.

DACOMSA, SA de CV: Calzada San Bartolo Naucalpan 136, Col. Argentina Poniente, Delegación Miguel Hidalgo, 11230 México, DF; tel. (555) 726-8230; e-mail servicio.clientes@kuoafmkt.com; internet www.dacomsa.com.mx; makers of motor vehicle components; Dir BENJAMÍN CENTURIÓN.

Chrysler de México, SA (DCM): Paseo de la Reforma 1240, Col. Santa Fe, Cuajimalpa, 05109 México, DF; tel. (55) 5081-3000; fax (55) 5729-7568; internet chrysler.com.mx; f. 1972; subsidiary of the Chrysler Corpn, USA; automobile assembly; CEO SERGIO MARCHIONNE; 9,000 employees.

Ford Motor Company, SA de CV: Guillermo González Camarena 1500, 6°, Col. Centro de Ciudad Santa Fe, 01210 México, DF; tel. (55) 5899-7594; internet www.ford.com.mx; f. 1925 in Mexico; subsidiary of Ford Motor Co, USA; manufacturers of motor-vehicle, truck and tractor parts; Pres. and Dir-Gen. EDUARDO SERRANO; 7,765 employees.

General Motors de México, SA de CV: Avda Ejército Nacional 843, Col. Granada, 11520 México, DF; tel. (55) 5329-0800; fax (55) 5625-3335; internet www.gm.com.mx; f. 1931 in Mexico; subsidiary of General Motors Corpn of the USA; automobile assembly; Pres. and Dir-Gen. GRACE LIEBLEIN; 11,250 employees.

Nissan Mexicana, SA de CV: Avda Insurgentes Sur 1958, Col. Florida, 01030 México, DF; tel. (55) 5628-2727; fax (55) 5628-2695; e-mail comunicacioncorporativa@nissan.com.mx; internet www.nissan.com.mx; f. 1961 in Mexico; subsidiary of Nissan Motors Co Ltd, Japan; automobile assembly plant; Pres. and Dir-Gen. JOSÉ MUÑOZ; 9,000 employees.

Volkswagen de Mexico, SA de CV: Autopista México–Puebla Km 116, San Lorenzo Almecatla, 72008 Cuautlancingo, Pue.; tel. (222) 308-111; fax (222) 308-468; e-mail contacto@vw.com.mx; internet mx.volkswagen.com; f. 1964; subsidiary of Volkswagen AG of Germany; manufacture of motor vehicles; Exec. Pres. OTTO LINDNER; 16,000 employees.

Food and Drink, etc.

Coca-Cola Femsa, SA de CV: Guillermo González Camarena 600, Centro de Cuidad Santa Fe, Delegación Alvaro Obregón, 01210 México, DF; tel. (55) 5081-5100; fax (55) 5292-3474; e-mail krelations@kof.com.mx; internet www.coca-colafemsa.com; f. 1991; subsidiary of Coca-Cola Export Co, USA, and FEMSA, SA de CV; soft-drink manufacturer; CEO CARLOS SALAZAR LOMELÍN; 55,635 employees (2005).

Embotelladoras Arca, SA de CV: Avda San Jerónimo 813, 64640 Monterrey, Nuevo León; tel. (81) 8151-1400; e-mail info@e-arca.com.mx; internet www.e-arca.com.mx; f. 2001; bottling plant; Dir-Gen. FRANCISCO GARZA EGLOFF.

Fomento Económico Mexicano, SA de CV (FEMSA): General Anaya 601 Pte., Col. Bella Vista, 64410 Monterrey, NL; tel. (81) 8328-6000; fax (81) 8328-6080; e-mail comunicacion@femsa.com; internet www.femsa.com; f. 1991; convenience stores, beer and soft-drink producers; Pres. and Dir-Gen. JOSÉ ANTONIO FERNÁNDEZ CARBAJAL; 120,000 employees (2008).

Gruma, SA: Rio de la Plata, 407 Oeste, Col. Calzada del Valle, 66220 San Pedro Garza García, Nueva León; tel. (81) 8399-3349; fax (81) 8399-3359; e-mail ir@gruma.com; internet www.gruma.com; f. 1949; tortilla and cornflour products manufacturers and distributors; Pres. and CEO ROBERTO GONZÁLEZ BARRERA; 17,000 employees (2006).

Grupo Bimbo, SA: Paseo de la Reforma 1000, Col. Peña Blanca, Santa Fe, Del. Alvaro Obregón, 01210 México, DF; tel. (55) 5268-6585; fax (55) 5258-6697; e-mail prensa@grupobimbo.com; internet www.grupobimbo.com; f. 1945; bread, confectionery and canned food manufacturers; CEO DANIEL SERVITJE MONTULL; 9,000 employees (2008).

Grupo Modelo, SA de CV: Avda Javier Barros Sierra 555, Col. Zedec Santa Fe, 01210 México, DF; tel. (55) 2266-0000; fax (55) 5280-6718; e-mail comunica@gmodelo.com.mx; internet www.gmodelo.com.mx; f. 1925; beer producers; Pres. and CEO CARLOS FERNÁNDEZ GONZÁLEZ; 38,402 employees (2008).

Grupo Sanborns: Calvario 106, Col. Tlalpan, 14000 México, DF; tel. (55) 5325-9900; fax (55) 5325-9941; internet www.sanborns.com.mx; operates a chain of restaurants, department stores, pharmacies; operates in retail, music promotion; part of Grupo Carso, SA de CV; Dir-Gen. CARLOS SLIM HELÚ; Gen. Man. GERMÁN HERNÁNDEZ; 18,500 employees (2008).

Molinos Azteca y Juper, SA de CV: Calle 7, No 1057, Zona Industrial, 44940 Guadalajara, Jal.; tel. (33) 3645-6980; fax (33) 3645-2393; e-mail informacion@molinosazteca.com; internet www.molinosazteca.com; f. 1950; agro-industrial subsidiary of Gruma, SA; Gen. Man. GERARDO GÓMEZ; 250 employees.

Savia, SA de CV: Río Sena 500, Col. del Valle Oriente, 66220 San Pedro Garza García, NL; tel. (81) 8173-5500; fax (81) 8173-5509; e-mail rherrera@savia.com.mx; internet www.savia.com.mx; produces and markets seeds for fruit and vegetables through its Seminis and Bionova subsidiaries; develops real estate projects through Desarrollo Inmobiliario Omega; Chair. and CEO ALFONSO ROMO GARZA; 8,000 employees.

Electrical Goods

Grupo Condumex, SA de CV: Miguel de Cervantes Saavedra 255, Col. Ampliación Granada, 11520 México, DF; tel. (55) 5328-5800; fax (55) 5255-1026; internet www.condumex.com.mx; f. 1954; automotive parts, cables, electronics, mining; part of Grupo Carso, SA de CV; Gen. Man. ALFREDO GUTIÉRREZ; 20,000 employees.

IBM de México, SA de CV: Alfonso Napoles Gandara 3111, Parque Corporativo de Peña Blanca, Col. Santa Fe, 01210 México, DF; tel. (55) 5270-3000; internet www.ibm.com.mx; f. 1927; manufacturers of computers and office equipment; Pres. and Dir-Gen. HUGO SANTANA; 2,100 employees.

Teleindustria Ericsson, SA de CV: Prolongación Paseo de la Reforma 1015, 5°–14°, Col. Santa Fe, Del. Alvaro Obregón, 01210 México, DF; tel. (55) 1103-0000; fax (55) 5726-2333; internet www.ericsson.com.mx; f. 1904; subsidiary of Telefonaktiebolaget L. M. Ericsson of Sweden; makers of telecommunications equipment; Man. Dir GERHARD SKLADAL; 3,565 employees.

Cement and Construction

Cemex, SA de CV: Avda Ricardo Margáin Zozaya 325, 66265 San Pedro Garza García, NL; tel. (81) 8888-8888; fax (81) 8888-4417; internet www.cemexmexico.com; f. 1906; manufacturers and distributors of cement, concrete and building materials; Pres. and CEO LORENZO H. ZAMBRANO; 64,585 employees (2008).

Concretos Cruz Azul: Insurgentes Sur 670, Col. del Valle, Del. Benito Juárez, 03100 México, DF; tel. (55) 5340-4040; fax (55) 5340-4041; e-mail atencion.clientes@concretoscruzazul.com.mx; internet www.concretoscruzazul.com; f. 1881; co-operative manufacturers of cement; Dir-Gen. GUILLERMO ALVAREZ CUEVAS.

Corporación GEO, SA de CV: Margaritas 433, Col. Guadalupe Chimalistac, 01050 México, DF; tel. (55) 5480-5000; fax (55) 5554-6064; e-mail comunicacionsocial@casasgeo.com; internet www.casasgeo.com; f. 1973; construction and real estate; Pres. and Dir-Gen. LUIS ORVAÑANOS LASCURAIN; 4,906 employees (2005).

Empresas ICA Sociedad Controladora, SA: Minería 145, Col. Escandón, 11800 México, DF; tel. (55) 5272-9991; fax (55) 5271-1607; e-mail comunicacion@ica.com.mx; internet www.ica.com.mx; f. 1947; holding co with interests in the construction industry; Pres. BERNARDO QUINTANA; CEO JOSÉ LUIS GUERRERO ALVAREZ; 17,902 employees (2007).

Holcim Apasco, SA de CV: Campos Eliseos 345, Col. Polanco Chapultepec, Del. Miguel Hidalgo, 11560 México, DF; tel. (55) 5724-0000; fax (55) 5724-0299; internet www.holcim.com/mx; f. 1963; manufacture and distribution of construction materials; part of Holcim Group, Switzerland; Dir EDUARDO KRETSCHMER; 4,500 employees.

Pharmaceutical

Bayer de México, SA de CV: Blvd Miguel de Cervantes Saavedra 259, Col. Ampliación Granada, 11520 México, DF; tel. (55) 5728-3000; fax (55) 5728-3111; internet www.bayer.com.mx; f. 1921; 2,500 employees; Pres. KURT SOLAND.

Boehringer Ingelheim Promeco, SA de CV: Maíz 49, Barrio Xaltocan, Xochimilco, 16090 México, DF; tel. (55) 5629-8300; e-mail contacto.mex@boehringer-ingelheim.com; internet www.boehringer-ingelheim.com.mx; f. 1971; subsidiary of Boehringer Ingelheim Pharmaceuticals, Germany; Pres. ANDREAS BARNER.

Bristol-Myers Squibb México: Avda Revolución 1267, Col. Tlacopac, 01040 México, DF; tel. (55) 5337-2800; fax (55) 5651-2092; internet www.bms.com.mx; f. 1947; Pres. and Dir-Gen. ULRICH STEUER.

Eli Lilly de México, SA de CV: Barranca del Muerto 329, Col. San José Insurgentes, 03900 México, DF; tel. (55) 1719-4500; e-mail infomed@lilly.com; internet www.lilly.com.mx; f. 1943; Pres. and Dir-Gen. CARLOS BAÑOS.

Grupo Casa Saba, SA de CV: Paseo de la Reforma 215, Col. Lomas de Chapultepec, Del. Miguel Hidalgo, 11000 México, DF; tel. (55) 5284-6600; e-mail info@casasaba.com; internet www.casasaba.com; f. 1944; name changed from Grupo Casa Autrey in 2000; pharmaceutical co; Pres. ISAAC SABA RAFFOUL; Dir-Gen. MANUEL SABA ADES; 5,700 employees.

Grupo Roche Syntex de México, SA de CV: Cerrada de Bezares 9, Col. Lomas de Bezares, 11910 México, DF; tel. (55) 5258-5000; fax (55) 5258-5472; e-mail mexico.comunicacion@roche.com; internet www.roche.com.mx; Chair. SEVERIN SCHWAN.

Laboratorios Liomont: Adolfo López Mateos 68, Del. Cuajimalpa, 05000 México, DF; tel. (55) 5814-1200; fax (55) 5812-1074; e-mail direccioncomercial@liomont.com.mx; internet www.liomont.com; f. 1938; Dir-Gen. JAQUELINE CIRCUIT; 1,500 employees (2009).

Laboratorios Sanfer: Blvd Adolfo Lópaz Mateos, 1° A, Col. Tlacopac, Del. Alvaro Obregón, 01049 México, DF; tel. (55) 5639-5400; fax (55) 5639-5519; internet www.sanfer.com.mx; f. 1941; Commercial Dir LUIS SERRANO.

Merck Sharp & Dohme—MSD, SA de CV: Avda San Jerónimo 369, 8°, Col. Tizapán San Angel, 01090 México, DF; tel. (55) 5481-9708; e-mail comunicaciones1@merck.com; internet www.msd.com.mx; f. 1932; prescription medications and vaccinations; Pres. JOSÉ LUIS ROMÁN PUMER.

Pisa Farmaceutica Mexicana: Avda España 1840, Col. Moderna, 44190 Guadalajara, Jal.; tel. (33) 3678-1600; fax (33) 3810-1609; e-mail saq@pisa.com.mx; internet www.pisafarmaceutica.com.mx; f. 1945; Pres. CARLOS ALVAREZ BERMEJILLO.

Sanofi-aventis México: Avda Universidad 1738, Col. Coyoacán, 04000 México, DF; tel. (55) 5484-4400; fax (55) 5872-0433; internet www.sanofi-aventis.com.mx; CEO JUAN CARLOS VALDÉS.

Teva Mexico: Pasaje Interlomas 16, 5°, Col. San Fernando la Herradura, 52784 Huixquilucan, Méx.; tel. (55) 5950-0200; fax (55) 5950-0201; e-mail servicio.cliente@tevamexico.com; internet www.tevamexico.com; part of Teva Parmaceutical Industries Ltd.

Retail

Controladora Comercial Mexicana, SA de CV (CCM): Avda Revolucion 780, Modulo 2, Col. San Juan, 03730 Mexico, DF; tel. (55) 5270-9312; fax (55) 5371-9302; e-mail comercial.mexicana@centrodecontacto.com.mx; internet www.comerci.com.mx/inicio.html; f. 1944; retail traders; Chair. GUILLERMO GONZÁLEZ NOVA; CEO CARLOS GONZÁLEZ ZABALEGUI; 39,191 employees (2009).

El Puerto de Liverpool, SA de CV: Mario Pani 200, Col. Santa Fe, Del. Cuajimalpa de Morelos, 05109 México, DF; tel. (55) 5262-9999; fax (55) 5254-5688; e-mail ventasd@liverpool.com.mx; internet www.liverpool.com.mx; f. 1847; retail traders; Chair. MAX DAVID; CEO JOSÉ CALDERÓN MUÑOZ DE COTE; 24,156 employees (2005).

Far-Ben, SA de CV (Farmacias Benavides): Avda Fundadores 935, Col. Valle del Mirador, 64750 Monterrey, NL; tel. and fax (81) 8389-9900; e-mail inversionistas@benavides.com.mx; internet www.benavides.com.mx; f. 1917; retail chemists (pharmacies); Chair. JAIME M. BENAVIDES POMPA; CEO FERNANDO BENAVIDES SAUCEDA; 5,036 employees.

Grupo Corvi: Pico de Tolima 29, Jardines en la Montaña, 14210 México, DF; tel. (55) 5628-5100; fax (55) 5645-1581; e-mail bvillasenor@infosel.net.mx; internet www.grupocorvi.com; retail distribution and confectionery; Pres. BENJAMÍN VILLASEÑOR COSTA.

Grupo Elektra, SA de CV: Avda Insurgentes Sur 3579, Col. Tlalpan La Joya, 14000 México, DF; tel. (55) 1720-7000; fax (55) 1720-7822; e-mail jrangelk@elektra.com.mx; internet www.grupoelektra.com.mx; f. 1950; retail and consumer finance; Chair. RICARDO B. SALINAS PLIEGO; Dir-Gen. CARLOS SEPTIÉN; 28,510 employees.

Grupo Gigante, SA de CV: Ejército Nacional 769A, Col. Nueva Granada, Del. Miguel Hidalgo, 11520 México, DF; tel. (55) 5269-8000; fax (55) 5269-8308; e-mail buzongigante@gigante.com.mx; internet www.gigante.com.mx; f. 1962; retail traders; Chair. and Dir-Gen. ANGEL LOSADA MORENO; 33,215 employees (2005).

Organización Soriana, SA de CV: Alejandro de Rodas 3102A, Col. Las Cumbres, 8 Sector, 64610 Monterrey, NL; tel. (81) 8329-9000; fax (81) 8329-9003; e-mail comunicacion@soriana.com.mx; internet www.soriana.com.mx; f. 1968; holding co with interests in the grocery, general merchandise and clothing trade; Pres. FRANCISCO J. MARTÍN BRINGAS; CEO RICARDO MARTÍN BRINGAS; 83,000 employees (2008).

Sears Roebuck de México, SA de CV: San Luis Potosí 214, Col. Romao, 06700 México, DF; tel. (55) 5247-7500; fax (55) 5584-6848; internet www.sears.com.mx; f. 1947; part of Grupo Carso, SA de CV; department stores; Pres. CARLOS HAJJ; Gen. Man. AGUSTÍN MAGAÑA; 50,100 employees.

Wal-Mart de México, SA de CV: Blvd Manuel Avila Camacho 647, Col. Periodistas, Del. Miguel Hidalgo, 11220 México, DF; tel. (55) 5328-3500; fax (55) 5328-3557; e-mail relutamiento@wal-mart.com; internet www.walmartmexico.com.mx; subsidiary of Walmart Inc of the USA; retail traders; Chair. EDUARDO SOLÓRZANO MORALES; Exec. Pres. and Dir-Gen. SCOT RANK CRAWFORD; 124,295 employees.

Miscellaneous

Alfa, SA de CV: Avda Gómez Morín 1111 Sur, Col. Carrizalejo, 66254 San Pedro Garza García, NL; tel. (81) 8748-1111; fax (81) 8748-2552; internet www.alfa.com.mx; holding co with interests in steel, petrochemicals, food products and telecommunications; Chair. ARMANDO GARZA SADA; 50,992 employees (2008).

Berol, SA de CV: Vía Dr Gustavo Baz 309, Col. La Loma, 54060 Tlalnepantia, Méx.; tel. (55) 5729-3400; fax (55) 5729-3433; internet www.berol.com.mx; f. 1970; stationery manufacturers; part of Sandford Group; Pres. CARLOS MORENO RIVAS; 600 employees.

CYDSA, SAB de CV y Subsidarias: Avda Ricardo Margáin Zozaya 565-B, Parque Corporativo Santa Engracia, 66267 San Pedro Garza García, NL; tel. (81) 8152-4500; fax (81) 8152-4813; e-mail informeanual@cydsa.com; internet www.cydsa.com; f. 1945; manufacturers of textiles, chemicals and plastic products; Pres. and Dir-Gen. Ing. TOMÁS GONZÁLEZ SADA; Dir ALEJANDRO VON ROSSUM GARZA; 2,513 employees.

Empaques Ponderosa, SA de CV: José Santos Chocano 970, Col. Anahuác, 66220 San Nicolás de los Garza, NL; tel. and fax (81) 8158-1702; fax (81) 8158-1706; e-mail info@ponderosa.com.mx; internet www.ponderosa.com.mx; f. 1989; cardboard manufacturers; Chair. MARIO VÁZQUEZ RAÑA; 858 employees.

Grupo Carso, SA de CV: Insurgentes 3500, POB 03, Col. Pena Pobre, 14060 México, DF; tel. (55) 5202-8838; fax (55) 5238-0601; internet www.gcarso.com.mx; f. 1980; holding co with interests in retail, food, mining, electricals, tobacco; Dir-Gen. JOSÉ HUMBERTO GUTIÉRREZ OLVERA; Gen. Man. JOSÉ LUIS OCAÑA; 30,840 employees.

Grupo Celanese, SA de CV: Insurgentes Sur 2453, 2°, Col. Tizapán San Angel, 01090 México, DF; tel. (55) 5480-9100; fax (55) 5480-9145; e-mail info@celanese.com.mx; internet www.celanese.com.mx; f. 1944; subsidiary of Celanese Corpn of USA; holding co with interests in production of speciality materials and chemicals; Dir IGNACIO BRAVO; 800 employees.

Grupo Kuo, SA de CV (KUO): Paseo de los Tamarindos 400B, 31°, Col. Bosque de las Lomas, 05120 México, DF; tel. (55) 5261-8000; fax (55) 5261-8361; e-mail ir@kuo.com.mx; internet www.kuo.com.mx; f. 1973; adopted current name 2007; holding co with interests in auto parts, food, chemicals and real estate; Pres. and CEO FERNANDO SENDEROS MESTRE; 13,168 employees (2005).

Industrias John Deere de México, SA de CV: Blvd Díaz Ordáz 500, San Pedro Garza García, NL; tel. (81) 8288-1212; internet www.deere.com/es_MX; f. 1955; subsidiary of Deere and Co of the USA; farming machinery and equipment makers; Pres. AGUSTÍN SANTAMARINA VÁZQUEZ; 1,215 employees.

Internacional de Cerámica, SA de CV: Avda Carlos Pacheco 7200, 31060 Chihuahua, Chih.; tel. (614) 429-1111; fax (614) 429-1124; internet www.interceramic.com/mx/main.asp; f. 1978; makers of floor tiles; Chair. OSCAR E. ALMEIDA CHABRE; Dir-Gen. VÍCTOR D. ALMEIDA GARCÍA; 2,900 employees.

Kimberly-Clark de México, SA de CV: José Luis Lagrange 103, 3°, Col. Los Morales, 11510 México, DF; tel. (55) 5282-7300; fax (55) 5282-7282; e-mail kcm.informacion@kcc.com; internet www.kimberly-clark.com.mx; f. 1955; subsidiary of Kimberly Clark Corpn of the USA; paper manufacturers; Chair. CLAUDIO XAVIER GONZÁLEZ LAPORTE; CEO PABLO GONZÁLEZ GUAJARDO; 7,700 employees.

Nadro, SA de CV: Vasco de Quiroga 3100, Col. Centro de Ciudad Santa Fe, Del. Alvaro Obregón, 01210 México, DF; tel. (55) 5292-4343; internet www.nadro.com.mx; f. 1943 as Nacional de Drogas; distribution of pharmaceuticals and beauty products; Chair. and CEO PABLO ESCANDÓN CUSI.

Química Magna: Blvd Jesús Valdez Sánchez 130, La Aurora, Saltillo, Coah.; tel. (844) 431-1127; fax (844) 135-2697; e-mail ventas@quimicamagna.com; internet www.quimicamagna.com; f. 1986; industrial cleaning products; Gen. Man. JORGE VARELA PINALES.

Vitro, SA de CV: Roble 660, Col. Valle del Campestre, 66265 San Pedro Garza García, NL; tel. (81) 8863-1200; fax (81) 8863-7839; e-mail rriva@vitro.com; internet www.vitro.com; f. 1909; manufacturers of glass, glass bottles and containers; Chair. ADRIÁN SADA GONZÁLEZ; Pres. and CEO HUGO LARA GONZÁLEZ; 24,637 employees (2005).

UTILITIES

Regulatory Authorities

Comisión Nacional del Agua (CONAGUA): Avda Insurgentes Sur 2416, Col. Copilco el Bajo, Del. Coyoacán, 04340 México, DF; tel. (55) 5174-4000; fax (55) 5550-6721; e-mail direccion@cna.gob.mx;

internet www.cna.gob.mx; commission to administer national water resources; Dir-Gen. José Luis Luege Tamargo.

Comisión Reguladora de Energía (CRE): Avda Horacio 1750, Col. Los Morales Polanco, Del. Miguel Hidalgo, 11510 México, DF; tel. (55) 5283-1500; e-mail calidad@cre.gob.mx; internet www.cre.gob.mx; f. 1994; commission to control energy policy and planning; Pres. Francisco Xavier Salazar Diez de Sollano; Exec. Sec. Carlos Hans Valadez Martínez.

Secretariat of State for Energy: see section on The Government (Secretariats of State).

Electricity

Comisión Federal de Electricidad (CFE): Avda Reforma 64, Col. Juárez México, México, DF; tel. (55) 5229-4400; fax (55) 5553-5321; e-mail servicioalcliente@cfe.gob.mx; internet www.cfe.gob.mx; state-owned power utility; Dir-Gen. Alfredo Elías Ayub.

Gas

Gas Natural México (GNM): Jaime Blames 8-703, Col. Los Morales Polanco, 11510 México, DF; e-mail sugerencias@gnm.com.mx; internet www.gasnaturalmexico.com.mx; f. 1994 in Mexico; distributes natural gas in the states of Tamaulipas, Aguascalientes, Coahuila, San Luis Potosí, Guanajuato, Nuevo León and México and in the Distrito Federal; subsidiary of Gas Natural (Spain); Pres. Angel Larraga.

Petróleos Mexicanos (PEMEX): see State Hydrocarbons Company; distributes natural gas.

TRADE UNIONS

Confederación Regional Obrera Mexicana (CROM) (Regional Confederation of Mexican Workers): República de Cuba 60, México, DF; f. 1918; Sec.-Gen. Ignacio Cuauhtémoc Paleta; 120,000 mems, 900 affiliated syndicates.

Confederación Revolucionaria de Obreros y Campesinos de México (CROC) (Revolutionary Confederation of Workers and Farmers): Hamburgo 250, Col. Juárez, Del. Cuauhtémoc, 06600 México, DF; tel. (55) 5208-5449; e-mail crocmodel@hotmail.com; internet www.croc.org.mx; f. 1952; Sec.-Gen. Isias González Cuevas; 4.5m. mems in 32 state federations and 17 national unions.

Confederación Revolucionaria de Trabajadores (CRT) (Revolutionary Confederation of Workers): Dr Jiménez 218, Col. Doctores, México, DF; f. 1954; Sec.-Gen. Mario Suárez García; 10,000 mems; 10 federations and 192 syndicates.

Confederación de Trabajadores de México (CTM) (Confederation of Mexican Workers): Vallarta 8, Col. Tabacalera, Del. Cuauhtémoc, 06030 México, DF; tel. (55) 5141-1730; e-mail ctmorganizacion@prodigy.net.mx; internet ctmorganizacion.org.mx; f. 1936; admitted to ICFTU; Sec.-Gen. Joaquín Gamboa; 5.5m. mems.

Congreso del Trabajo (CT): Avda Ricardo Flores Magón 44, Col. Guerrero, 06300 México 37, DF; tel. (55) 5583-3817; internet www.congresodeltrabajo.org.mx; f. 1966; trade union congress comprising trade union federations, confederations, etc.; Pres. Joaquín Gamboa Pascoe.

Federación Nacional de Sindicatos Independientes (National Federation of Independent Trade Unions): Isaac Garza 311 Oeste, 64000 Monterrey, NL; tel. (81) 8375-6677; e-mail fnsi@prodigy.net.mx; internet www.fnsi.org.mx/esp; f. 1936; Sec.-Gen. Jacinto Padilla Valdez; 230,000 mems.

Federación Obrera de Organizaciones Femeniles (FOOF) (Workers' Federation of Women's Organizations): Vallarta 8, México, DF; f. 1950; women workers' union within CTM; Sec.-Gen. Hilda Anderson Nevárez; 400,000 mems.

Federación de Sindicatos de Trabajadores al Servicio del Estado (FSTSE) (Federation of Unions of Government Workers): Gómez Farías 40, Col. San Rafael, 06470 México, DF; internet www.fstse.com; f. 1938; Sec.-Gen. Joel Ayala Almeida; 2.5m. mems; 80 unions.

Frente Unida Sindical por la Defensa de los Trabajadores y la Constitución (United Union Front in Defence of the Workers and the Constitution): f. 1990 by more than 120 trade orgs to support the implementation of workers' constitutional rights.

Unión General de Obreros y Campesinos de México, Jacinto López (UGOCM-JL) (General Union of Workers and Farmers of Mexico, Jacinto López): José María Marroquí 8, 2°, 06050 México, DF; tel. (55) 5518-3015; f. 1949; admitted to WFTU/CSTAL; Sec.-Gen. José Luis González Aguilera; 7,500 mems, over 2,500 syndicates.

Unión Nacional de Trabajadores (UNT) (National Union of Workers): Villalongen 50, Col. Cuauhtémoc, México, DF; tel. (55) 5140-1425; fax (55) 5703-2583; e-mail secretariageneral@strm.org.mx; internet www.unt.org.mx; f. 1998; Sec.-Gen. Francisco Hernández Juárez.

A number of major unions are non-affiliated, including:

Federación Democrática de Sindicatos de Servidores Públicos (Democratic Federation of Public Servants): México, DF; f. 2005.

Frente Auténtico de los Trabajadores (FAT): Godard 20, Col. Guadalupe Victoria, México, DF; tel. (55) 5556-9314; fax (55) 5556-9316; internet www.fatmexico.org.

Pacto de Unidad Sindical Solidaridad (PAUSS): comprises 10 independent trade unions.

Sindicato Nacional de Trabajadores de la Educación (SNTE) (Education Workers): Venezuela 44, Col. Centro, México, DF; tel. (55) 5702-0005; fax (55) 5702-6303; e-mail info@snte.org.mx; internet www.snte.org.mx; f. 1943; Pres. Elba Esther Gordillo Morales; Sec.-Gen. Rafael Ochoa Guzmán; 1.4m. mems.

Coordinadora Nacional de Trabajadores de la Educación (CNTE): dissident faction; Leader Teodoro Palomino.

Sindicato Nacional de Trabajadores Mineros, Metalúrgicos y Similares de la República Mexicana (SNTMM) (Mine, Metallurgical and Related Workers): Avda Dr Vertiz 668, Col. Narvarte, 03020 México, DF; tel. (55) 5519-5690; f. 1933; Sec.-Gen. Napoleón Gómez Urrutia; 86,000 mems.

Sindicato de Trabajadores Ferrocarrileros de la República Mexicana (STFRM) (Railway Workers): Avda Ricardo Flores Magón 206, Col. Guerrero, México 3, DF; tel. (55) 5597-1133; e-mail secretarianacional@stfrm.org; internet www.stfrm.org; f. 1933; Sec.-Gen. Víctor F. Flores Morales; 100,000 mems.

Sindicato de Trabajadores Petroleros de la República Mexicana (STPRM) (Union of Workers): Zaragoza 15, Col. Guerrero, 06300 México, DF; tel. (55) 5546-0912; close links with PEMEX; Sec.-Gen. Carlos Romero Deschamps; 110,000 mems; includes:

Movimiento Nacional Petrolero: reformist faction; Leader Hebraícaz Vásquez.

Sindicato Unico de Trabajadores Electricistas de la República Mexicana (SUTERM) (Electricity Workers): Río Guadalquivir 106, Col. Cuauhtémoc, 06500 México, DF; tel. (55) 5207-0578; internet www.suterm.org.mx; Sec.-Gen. Victor Fuentes del Villar.

Sindicato Unico de Trabajadores de la Industria Nuclear (SUTIN) (Nuclear Industry Workers): Viaducto Río Becerra 139, Col. Nápoles, 03810 México, DF; tel. (55) 5523-8048; fax (55) 5687-6353; e-mail exterior@sutin.org.mx; internet www.sutin.org.mx; Sec.-Gen. Arturo Delfín Loya.

Unión Obrera Independiente (UOI) (Independent Workers' Union): non-aligned.

The major agricultural unions are:

Confederación Nacional Campesina (CNC) (National Peasant Confederation): Mariano Azuela 121, Col. Santa María de la Ribera, México, DF; tel. (55) 5547-8042; internet www.cnc.org.mx; Sec.-Gen. Cruz Lopez Aguilar.

Confederación Nacional de Organizaciones Ganaderas (National Confederation of Stockbreeding Organizations): Calzada Mariano Escobedo 714, Col. Anzures, México, DF; tel. (55) 5203-3506; e-mail teresa.hernandez@cnog.com.mx; internet www.cnog.com.mx; Pres. Oswaldo Cházaro Montalvo; 300,000 mems.

Consejo Agrarista Mexicano (Mexican Agrarian Council): 09760 Iztapalapa, México, DF; Sec.-Gen. Humberto Serrano.

Unión Nacional de Trabajadores Agriculturas (UNTA) (National Union of Agricultural Workers).

Transport

Road transport accounts for about 98% of all public passenger traffic and for about 80% of freight traffic. Mexico's terrain is difficult for overland travel. As a result, there has been an expansion of air transport, and there were 61 international and national airports in 2009. In 2002 plans to build a new airport in the capital were postponed after conflict over the proposed site. International flights are provided by a large number of national and foreign airlines. Mexico has 140 seaports, 29 river docks and a further 29 lake shelters. More than 85% of Mexico's foreign trade is conducted through maritime transport. In the 1980s the Government developed the main industrial ports of Tampico, Coatzacoalcos, Lázaro Cárdenas, Altamira, Laguna de Ostión and Salina Cruz in an attempt to redirect growth and to facilitate exports. The port at Dos Bocas, on the Gulf of Mexico, was one of the largest in Latin America when it opened in 1999. A 300-km railway link across the isthmus of Tehuantepec connects the Caribbean port of Coatzacoalcos with the Pacific port of Salina Cruz.

Secretariat of State for Communications and Transport: see section on The Government (Secretariats of State).

Caminos y Puentes Federales (CAPUFE): Calzada de los Reyes 24, Col. Tetela del Monte, 62130 Cuernavaca, Mor.; tel. (55) 5200-2000; e-mail contacto@capufe.gob.mx; internet www.capufe.gob.mx; Dir-Gen. MANUEL ZUBIRIA MAQUEO.

RAILWAYS

In 2009 there were 26,717 km of main line track. In 2007 the railway system carried 288,000 passengers and 70,010m. freight ton-km. Ferrocarriles Nacionales de México (FNM), government-owned since 1937, was liquidated in 2001 following a process of restructuring and privatization. A suburban train system for the Valle de México began operations in 2008. In that year plans were under way for the construction of a high-speed rail link between Mexico City and Guadalajara, and a new line from Manzanillo, Aguascalientes, to Mexico City.

Ferrocarril Mexicano, SA de CV (Ferromex): Bosque de Ciruelos 99, Col. Bosques de la Loma, 11700 México, DF; tel. (55) 5246-3700; e-mail webmaster@ferromex.com.mx; internet www.ferromex.com.mx; 50-year concession awarded to Grupo Ferroviario Mexicano, SA, (GFM) commencing in 1998; owned by Grupo México, SA de CV; 8,500 km of track and Mexico's largest rail fleet; links from Mexico City to Guadalajara, Hermosillo, Monterrey, Chihuahua and Pacific ports; Exec. Pres. ALFREDO CASAR PÉREZ; Dir-Gen. ROGELIO VÉLEZ LÓPEZ DE LA CERDA.

Ferrocarril del Sureste (Ferrosur): Bosque de Ciruelos 180, 1°, Col. Bosques de las Lomas, 11700 México, DF; tel. (55) 5387-6500; e-mail magarcia@ferrosur.com.mx; internet www.ferrosur.com.mx; 50-year concession awarded to Grupo Tribasa in 1998; 66.7% sold to Empresas Frisco, SA de CV, in 1999, owned by Grupos Carso, SA de CV; Dir MIGUEL ANGEL GARCÍA.

Kansas City Southern de México (KCSM): Avda Manuel L. Barragán 4850, Col. Hidalgo, 64420 Monterrey, NL; tel. (81) 8305-7800; fax (81) 8305-7766; e-mail werdman@kcsouthern.com; internet www.kcsouthern.com; formerly Ferrocarril del Noreste; 4,242 km of line, linking Mexico City with the ports of Lázaro Cárdenas, Veracruz, Tampico/Altamira and north-east Mexico; Pres. HENRY R. DAVIES; Chair. MICHAEL R. HAVERTY.

Servicio de Transportes Eléctricos del Distrito Federal (STE): Avda Municipio Libre 402, Col. San Andrés Tetepilco, México, DF; tel. (55) 2595-0000; fax (55) 5672-4758; e-mail sugiere@ste.df.gob.mx; internet www.ste.df.gob.mx; suburban tram route with 17 stops upgraded to light rail standard to act as a feeder to the metro; also operates bus and trolleybus networks; Pres. MARCELO LUIS EBRARD CASAUBÓN (Head of Govt of the Distrito Federal); Dir-Gen. RUFINO H. LEÓN TOVAR.

Sistema de Transporte Colectivo (Metro) (STC): Delicias 67, 06070 México, DF; tel. (55) 5709-1133; fax (55) 5512-3601; internet www.metro.df.gob.mx; f. 1967; the first stage of a combined underground and surface railway system in Mexico City was opened in 1969; 10 lines, covering 158 km, were operating, in 1998, and five new lines, bringing the total distance to 315 km, are to be completed by 2010; the system is wholly state-owned and the fares are partially subsidized; Dir-Gen. FRANCISCO BOJÓRQUEZ HERNÁNDEZ.

ROADS

In 2009 there were 366,341 km of roads, of which 36.3% were paved. Long-distance buses form one of the principal methods of transport in Mexico, and there are some 600 lines operating services throughout the country.

Dirección General de Autotransporte Federal: Calzada de las Bombas 411, 11°, Col. Los Girasoles, Del. Goyoacán, 04920 México, DF; tel. (55) 5677-3561; internet dgaf.sct.gob.mx; co-ordinates long-distance bus services; Dir Dr LUIS TÉLLEZ KUENZLER.

SHIPPING

At the end of 2008 Mexico's registered merchant fleet numbered 799 vessels, with a total displacement of 1,278,900 grt. The Government operates the facilities of seaports.

Coordinación General de Puertos y Marina Mercante (CGPMM): Avda Nuevo León 210, Col. Hipódromo, 03310 México, DF; tel. (55) 5723-9300; fax (55) 5265-3108; e-mail egarciai@sct.gob.mx; internet cgpmm.sct.gob.mx; Co-ordinator ALEJANDRO CHACÓN DOMÍNGUEZ; Dir-Gen. de Puertos (vacant); Dir-Gen. de Marina Mercante ADOLFO XAVIER ZAGAL OLIVARES.

Port of Acapulco: Puertos Mexicanos, Malecón Fiscal s/n, Acapulco, Gro; Harbour Master Capt. RENÉ F. NOVALES BETANZOS.

Port of Coatzacoalcos: Administración Portuaria Integral de Coatzacoalcos, SA de CV, Interior Recinto Portuario s/n, Coatzacoalcos, 96400 Ver.; tel. (921) 211-0270; fax (921) 211-0272; e-mail dirgral@puertocoatzacoalcos.com.mx; internet www.apicoatza.com; Dir-Gen. Ing. GILBERTO RIOS RUÍZ.

Port of Dos Bocas: Administración Portuaria Integral de Dos Bocas, SA de CV, Carretera Federal Puerto Ceiba–Paraíso 414, Col. Quintín Arzuz, 86600 Paraíso, Tab.; tel. (933) 353-2744; e-mail dosbocas@apidosbocas.com; internet www.apidosbocas.com; Dir-Gen. ROBERTO DE LA GARZA LICÓN.

Port of Manzanillo: Administración Portuaria Integral de Manzanillo, SA de CV, Avda Tte Azueta 9, Col. Burócrata, 28250 Manzanillo, Col.; tel. and fax (314) 331-1400; e-mail gcomercial@puertomanzanillo.com.mx; internet www.puertomanzanillo.com.mx; Dir-Gen. JOSÉ JULIÁN DIP LEOS.

Port of Tampico: Administración Portuaria Integral de Tampico, SA de CV, Edif. API de Tampico, 1°, Recinto Portuario, 89000 Tampico, Tamps; tel. (833) 241-1400; fax (833) 212-5744; e-mail contacto@puertodetampico.com.mx; internet www.port-of-tampico.com.mx; Gen. Dir MANUEL FLORES GUERRA.

Port of Veracruz: Administración Porturia Integral de Veracruz, SA de CV, Avda Marina Mercante 210, 7°, Col. Centro, 91700 Veracruz, Ver.; tel. (229) 932-2170; fax (229) 932-3040; e-mail mespinosa@puertodeveracruz.com; internet www.puertodeveracruz.com.mx; privatized in 1994; Dir-Gen. JUAN IGNACIO FERNÁNDEZ CARBAJAL.

Transportación Marítima Mexicana, SA de CV (TMM): Avda de la Cúspide 4755, Col. Parque del Pedregal, Del. Tlalpan, 14010 México, DF; tel. (55) 5629-8866; fax (55) 5629-8899; e-mail grupotmm@tmm.com.mx; internet www.tmm.com.mx; f. 1955; cargo services to Europe, the Mediterranean, Scandinavia, the USA, South and Central America, the Caribbean and the Far East; Pres. JOSÉ F. SERRANO SEGOVIA; Sec. IGNACIO RODRÍGUEZ PULLEN.

CIVIL AVIATION

There were 61 international airports in Mexico in 2009. Of these, México, Cancún, Guadalajara, Monterrey and Tijuana registered the highest number of operations.

Aeropuertos y Servicios Auxiliares (ASA): Edif. B, Avda 602 161, Col. San Juan de Aragón, Del. Venustiano Carranza, 15620 México, DF; tel. (55) 5133-1000; fax (55) 5133-2985; e-mail glmeyer@asa.gob.mx; internet www.asa.gob.mx; oversees airport management and devt; Gen. Man. GILBERTO LÓPEZ MEYER.

Dirección General de Aeronáutica Civil (DGAC): Providencia No 807, Col. Del Valle, 03100 México, DF; tel. (55) 5523-6642; fax (55) 5523-7207; e-mail hgonzalw@sct.gob.m; internet dgac.sct.gob.mx; subdivision of Secretariat of State for Communications and Transport; regulates civil aviation; Dir-Gen. HECTOR GONZALEZ WEEKS.

Aerocalifornia: Aquiles Serdán 1955, 23000 La Paz, BCS; e-mail aeroll@aerocalifornia.uabcs.mx; f. 1960; services suspended in 2006 over safety concerns; regional carrier with scheduled passenger and cargo services in Mexico and the USA; Chair. PAUL A. ARECHIGA.

Aeromar, Transportes Aeromar: Hotel María Isabel Sheraton, Paseo de la Reforma 325, Local 10, México, DF; tel. (55) 5514-2248; e-mail web.aeromar@aeromar.com.mx; internet www.aeromar.com.mx; f. 1987; scheduled domestic passenger and cargo services; Dir-Gen. JUAN I. STETA.

Aeromexpress Cargo: Avda Texococo s/n esq., Avda Tahel, Col. Peñón de los Baños, 15620 México, DF; tel. (55) 5133-0203; internet www.aeromexpress.com.mx; owned by state holding co Consorcio Aeroméxico, SA; cargo airline.

Aerovías de México (Aeroméxico): Paseo de la Reforma 445, 3°, Torre B, Col. Cuauhtémoc, 06500 México, DF; tel. (55) 5133-4000; fax (55) 5133-4619; internet www.aeromexico.com; f. 1934 as Aeronaves de México, nationalized 1959; sold by state holding co Consorcio Aeroméxico, SA, to private investors in 2007; services between most principal cities of Mexico and the USA, Chile, Brazil, Peru, France and Spain; Pres. and Dir-Gen. ANDRÉS CONESA LABASTIDA.

Aviacsa: Aeropuerto Internacional, Zona C, Hangar 1, Col. Aviación General, 15520 México, DF; tel. (55) 5716-9005; fax (55) 5758-3823; internet www.aviacsa.com; f. 1990; operates internal flights, and flights to the USA; Pres. EDUARDO MEGA.

Click Mexicana: Avda Xola 535, Col. del Valle, 03100 México, DF; tel. (55) 5284-3132; e-mail servicio.cliente@clickmx.com; internet www.clickmx.com; f. 2005; owned by Mexicana; fmrly known as Aerocaribe; budget airline operating internal flights; CEO ISAAC VOLIN BOLOK.

Interjet (ABC Aerolíneas, SA de CV): Aeropuerto Internacional de Toluca, Toluca, Méx.; tel. (55) 1102-5555; e-mail atencionaclientes@interjet.com.mx; internet www.interjet.com.mx; f. 2005; budget airline operating internal flights; Pres. MIGUEL ALEMÁN MAGNANI.

Mexicana (Compañía Mexicana de Aviación, SA de CV): Avda Xola 535, Col. del Valle, 03100 México, DF; tel. (55) 5448-3000; fax (55) 5448-3129; e-mail dirgenmx@mexicana.com.mx; internet www.mexicana.com; f. 1921; fmrly state-owned; sold to Grupo Posadas in 2005; international services between Mexico City and the USA, Central America and the Caribbean; domestic services; CEO MANUEL BORJA CHICO.

Volaris: Aeropuerto Internacional de la Ciudad de Toluca, 50500 Toluca, Méx.; tel. (55) 1102-8000; e-mail comentarios@volaris.com.mx; internet www.volaris.com.mx; f. 2006; operated by Vuela Compañía de Aviación; budget airline operating internal flights; Pres. PEDRO ASPE ARMELLA; Dir-Gen. ENRIQUE BELTRANENA.

Tourism

Tourism remains one of Mexico's principal sources of foreign exchange. Mexico received 22.6m. foreign visitors in 2008, and receipts from tourism in that year were US $10,817m. More than 90% of visitors come from the USA and Canada. The country is famous for volcanoes, coastal scenery and the great Sierra Nevada (Sierra Madre) mountain range. The relics of the Mayan and Aztec civilizations and of Spanish Colonial Mexico are of historic and artistic interest. Zihuatanejo, on the Pacific coast, and Cancún, on the Caribbean, were developed as tourist resorts by the Government. The government tourism agency, FONATUR, encourages the renovation and expansion of old hotels and provides attractive incentives for the industry. FONATUR is also the main developer of major resorts in Mexico.

Secretariat of State for Tourism: see section on The Government (Secretariats of State).

Asociación Mexicana de Agencias de Viajes (AMAV): Guanajuato 128, México, DF; tel. (55) 5584-9300; e-mail amavcun@prodigy.net.mx; internet www.amavnacional.com; f. 1945; asscn of travel agencies; Pres. JORGE HERNÁNDEZ DELGADO.

Fondo Nacional de Fomento al Turismo (FONATUR): Tecoyotitla 100, Col. Florida, 01030 México, DF; tel. (55) 5090-4200; fax (55) 5090-4469; e-mail jrbusquets@fonatur.gob.mx; internet www.fonatur.gob.mx; f. 1956 to finance and promote the devt of tourism; Dir-Gen. MIGUEL GÓMEZ-MONT URUETA.

Defence

As assessed at November 2009, Mexico's regular armed forces numbered 267,506: army 200,000, navy 55,961 (including naval air force—1,250—and marines—19,328) and air force 11,545. There were also 39,899 reserves. Paramilitary forces numbered 36,500, comprising a federal preventive police force of 14,000, a federal ministerial police force of 4,500 and a rural defence militia numbering 18,000. Military service, on a part-time basis, is by a lottery and lasts for one year.

Defence Budget: 58,400m. new pesos in 2010.

Chief of Staff of National Defence: Gen. CARLOS DEMETRIO GAYTAN OCHOA.

Superintendant and Comptroller of the Army and Air Force: Gen. ROBERTO MIRANDA SÁNCHEZ.

Commander of the Air Force: Gen. LEONARDO GONZÁLEZ GARCÍA.

Chief of Staff of the Navy: Adm. JORGE H. PASTOR GÓMEZ.

Education

State education in Mexico is free and compulsory at primary and secondary level. Primary education lasts for six years between the ages of six and 11. Secondary education lasts for up to six years. Children aged four years and over may attend nursery school. In 2008 enrolment at primary schools included 98% of pupils in the relevant age-group, while in the same year enrolment at secondary schools included 72% of pupils in the relevant age-group. In 2007/08 nursery schools numbered 92,753 and there were 98,332 primary schools. There were 34,034 secondary schools in the same year, attended, in 2006/07, by 6.1m. pupils. In spite of the existence of more than 80 indigenous languages in Mexico, there were few bilingual secondary schools. In 2007/08 there were an estimated 5,549 institutes of higher education, attended, in 2006/07, by some 2.5m. students. Federal expenditure on education in 2003 was an estimated 265,238.1m. new pesos (equivalent to 21.4% of total central government expenditure).

Bibliography

Ashbee, E., Balslev Clausen, H., and Pedersen, C. (Eds). *The Politics, Economics, and Culture of Mexican-U.S. Migration: Both Sides of the Border*. Basingstoke, Palgrave Macmillan, 2007.

Babb, S. L. *Managing Mexico: Economists from Nationalism to Neoliberalism*. Princeton, NJ, Princeton University Press, 2002.

Bartra, R. *Blood, Ink and Culture: Miseries and Splendours of the Post-Mexican Condition*. Raleigh, NC, Duke University Press, 2002.

Beatty, E. *Institutions and Investment: The Political Basis of Industrialization in Mexico before 1911*. Stanford, CA, Stanford University Press, 2001.

Bortz, J., and Haber, S. (Eds). *The Mexican Economy, 1870–1930*. Stanford, CA, Stanford University Press, 2002.

Bruhn, K. *Urban Protest in Mexico and Brazil*. Cambridge, Cambridge University Press, 2008.

Cameron, M. A., and Tomlin, B. W. *The Making of NAFTA*. Ithaca, NY, Cornell University Press, 2002.

Caneque, A. *The King's Living Image: The Culture and Politics of Viceregal Power in Colonial Mexico*. London, Routledge, 2004.

Castaneda, J. G. *Perpetuating Power: How Mexican Presidents are Chosen*. New York, New Press, 2000.

Chappell Lawson, J. *Building the Fourth Estate: Democratization and the Rise of a Free Press in Mexico*. Berkeley, CA, University of California Press, 2002.

Corchabo, A., and Schwartz, G. *Mexico: Experiences with Pro-Poor Expenditure*. Washington, DC, International Monetary Fund, 2002.

Dawson, A. *First World Dreams: Mexico since 1989*. London, Zed Books, 2006.

Day, S. A. *Staging Politics in Mexico: The Road to Neoliberalism*. Lewisburg, PA, Bucknell University Press, 2004.

Diez, J. *Political Change and Environmental Policymaking in Mexico*. Abingdon, Routledge, 2006.

Domínguez, J. I., de Castro, R. F. *United States and Mexico: Between Partnership and Conflict*. 2nd edn, Abingdon, Routledge, 2009.

Eisenstadt, T. A. *Courting Democracy in Mexico: Party Strategies and Electoral Institutions*. Cambridge, Cambridge University Press, 2007.

Ellingwood, K. *Hard Line: Life and Death on the US–Mexico Border*. New York, Pantheon, Random House, 2004.

Flores de la Pena, H., *et al. Bases para la planeación económica y social de México*. Madrid, Editores Siglo XXI, 2002.

Greene, K. F. *Why Dominant Parties Lose: Mexico's Democratization in Comparative Perspective*. Cambridge, Cambridge University Press, 2007.

Guardino, P. F. *Peasants, Politics and the Formation of Mexico's National State*. Stanford, CA, Stanford University Press, 2001.

Hernández Chávez, A. *Mexico: A Brief History*. Berkeley, CA, University of California Press, 2006.

Hodges, D. C., and Gandy, R. *Mexico: The End of the Revolution*. New York, Praeger Publrs, 2001.

Jung, C. *The Moral Force of Indigenous Politics: Critical Liberalism and the Zapatistas*. Cambridge, Cambridge University Press, 2008.

Kusnetsov, Y., and Dahlman, C. J. (Eds). *Mexico's Transition to a Knowledge-based Economy: Challenges and Opportunities*. Washington, DC, World Bank Publications, 2007.

Levy, D. C., Bruhn, K., and Zebadúa, E. *Mexico: The Struggle for Democratic Development*. Berkeley, CA, University of California Press, 2006.

Mentinis, M. *Zapatistas: The Chiapas Revolt and What it Meant for Radical Politics*. London, Pluto Press, 2006.

Murphy, R. D., and Feltenstein, A. *Private Costs and Public Infrastructure: The Mexican Case*. Washington, DC, International Monetary Fund, 2001.

Nevins, J. *Operation Gatekeeper and Beyond: The War on 'Illegals' and the Remaking of the US–Mexico Boundary*. 2nd edn, Abingdon, Routledge, 2010.

Otero, G. (Ed.). *Mexico in Transition: Neoliberal Globalism, the State and Civil Society*. London, Zed Books, 2004.

O'Toole, G. *The Reinvention of Mexico: National Ideology in a Neoliberal Era*. Liverpool, Liverpool University Press, 2010.

Prescott, W. H. *History of the Conquest of Mexico*. London, Phoenix Press, 2002.

Preston, J., and Dillon, S. *Opening Mexico: The Making of a Democracy*. New York, Farrar, Straus and Giroux, 2004.

Richmond, D. W. *The Mexican Nation: Historical Continuity and Modern Change*. Paramus, NJ, Prentice Hall, 2001.

Rubio, L. *Políticas económicas del México contemporáneo*. México, DF, Fondo de Cultura Económica, 2001.

Russell, P. *The History of Mexico: From Pre-Conquest to Present*. Abingdon, Routledge, 2010.

Schlefer, J. *Palace Politics: How the Ruling Party Brought Crisis to Mexico*. Austin, TX, University of Texas Press, 2008.

Selee, A., and Peschard, J. (Eds). *Mexico's Democratic Challenges: Politics, Government, and Society*. Washington, DC, Woodrow Wilson Press, 2010.

Snyder, R. *Politics after Neoliberalism: Reregulation in Mexico*. New York, Cambridge University Press, 2006.

Suchlicki, J. *Mexico: From Montezuma to the Rise of the PAN*. 3rd revised edn, Dulles, VA, Potomac Books Inc, 2007.

Terry, E. D., Fallaw, B., Joseph, G. M., and Moseley, E. H. (Eds). *Peripheral Visions: Politics, Society and the Challenges of Modernity in Yucatan*. Tuscaloosa, AL, University of Alabama Press, 2010.

Uildriks, N. *Mexico's Unrule of Law: Implementing Human Rights in Police and Judicial Reform under Democratization*. Lanham, MD, Lexington Books, 2010.

Vincent, T. G. *The Legacy of Vincente Guerrero, Mexico's First Black Indian President*. Gainesville, FL, University Press of Florida, 2002.

Washbrook, S. (Ed.). *Rural Chiapas Ten Years after the Zapatista Uprising*. Abingdon, Routledge, 2006.

Weintraub, S. *Unequal Partners: The United States and Mexico*. Pittsburgh, PA, University of Pittsburgh Press, 2010.

Wise, T. A., Salazar, H., and Carlsen, L. (Eds). *Confronting Globalization: Economic Integration and Popular Resistance in Mexico*. Bloomfield, CT, Kumarian Press, 2003.

MONTSERRAT

Geography

PHYSICAL FEATURES

The devastated island of Montserrat is a United Kingdom Overseas Territory located in the Leeward Islands, in the eastern Caribbean. The nearest other polity to the colony is Antigua and Barbuda, with Antigua island some 43 km (27 miles) to the north-east, although its uninhabited outpost of Redonda is only 24 km to the north-west. Beyond Redonda lies Nevis, the smaller unit of the federation of Saint Christopher (St Kitts) and Nevis. The main islands of the French department of Guadeloupe lie 64 km to the south-east, where the arc of the Lesser Antilles continues. Montserrat is 102 sq km (39.5 sq miles) in extent, only slightly larger than Anguilla (but much more mountainous). Volcanic activity has increased its area somewhat since the mid-1990s.

Montserrat is a roughly pear-shaped island about 19 km long (north–south) and 11 km wide, with a mountainous terrain provided by three groups of highlands, steadily rising towards the south: Silver Hill in the far north; the Centre Hills; and the great Soufrière Hills, which dominate the south. This last range reaches its height at Chance's Peak (914 m—3,000 ft) and now also dominates the island because of the renewed volcanic activity centred here. Previously distinguished by verdant, forest-clad heights, occasionally scarred by areas of sulphurous springs (soufrières), the Soufrière Hills resumed a more active volcanic state for the first time in over 350 years on 18 July 1995. The series of eruptions resulted in the removal of government from the capital, Plymouth (on the south-western coast), and the evacuation of other towns (including the airport, across the island from Plymouth) from an Exclusion Zone covering over one-half of the island by April 1996. People remain generally forbidden to visit this Zone, although a Daytime Entry Zone (volcanic conditions permitting) now moderates this, operating in the west, as far as just to the north of the site of Plymouth.

Eruptions in the Soufrière Hills steadily increased in seriousness up to September 1996, but the deadly pyroclastic flows took their worst toll in June 1997 (19 people died in the Exclusion Zone despite official warnings, and the air and sea ports were finally closed) and, thereafter, the flows destroyed the centre of the abandoned capital. The largest flow occurred on 26 December 1997. Pyroclastic flows are a particularly fast-moving and deadly form of volcanic emission, making the Exclusion Zone a fundamental safety feature during eruptions. Dome collapses fuel the most devastating flows, and these have continued into the 2000s. The largest dome collapse of the eruption was on 27 July 2000, but most of the flow was down the Tar River (a seasonal stream before 1995), in the east of the Zone. Another major conduit is the valley of the White River, the delta of which is also expanding the south of the island, on the south-west coast. A further significant eruption on 12 July 2003, reportedly the largest since 1995, prompted an extension of the Exclusion Zone to embrace the Salem region—formerly on the periphery of the 'safe zone'—which had suffered severe damage from the resultant pyroclastic outflows. A subsequent extension to the Exclusion Zone, since re-designated the Unsafe Area, was necessitated following outflow incursions into safe zones in the south of the island in May 2006. Close monitoring of continuing volcanic activity at the site enabled the authorities more accurately to predict future eruption threats and instigate measures to prevent a repeat of the human tragedy which occurred in 1997. The south of Montserrat is now dominated by seven active volcanoes, which have devastated the landscape, emptying it of life and rendering it uninhabitable for at least one decade more. Additionally, three Maritime Exclusion Zones identified as liable to volcanic activity exist to the south and east of the Territory.

Prior to the eruption of the Soufrière Hills, the richest land was in the south, and most people lived in the south-west. The greenery on the hills and coasts had confirmed the sobriquet of the 'Emerald Isle of the Caribbean', earned by Montserrat's Irish heritage. Its forestland sheltered a rich bird and animal life, including the unique black and gold Montserrat oriole and the terrestrial frog ('mountain chicken'), the latter being only otherwise found in Dominica, where it is known as the crapaud. It is as yet uncertain quite how devastating or prolonged the effect of the eruptions has been on Montserrat's natural environment, but, as about one-third of the island has been rendered into a bleak and desolate rockscape, it is severe. The central and northern highlands retain their vegetation, but the north was always drier than the south and woodland less extensive. The mountainous nature of the island has contributed to a rugged coastline, particularly on the Atlantic or weather coast, and there are no natural harbours, although the more sheltered western coast offers some anchorages (port facilities at Plymouth were finally destroyed by the volcanic activity of the mid-1990s and Little Bay now serves as the main port).

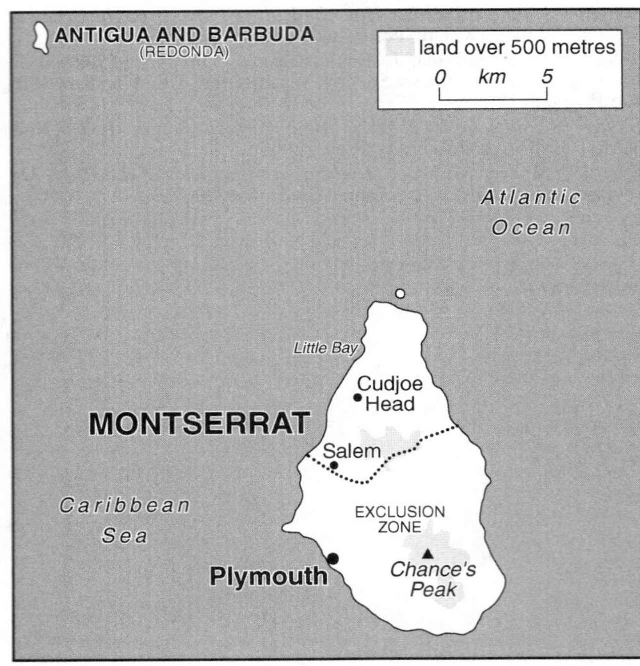

CLIMATE

The climate is subtropical, tempered by the trade winds and by altitude. There is little seasonal variation in temperature, with average monthly maximums ranging between 24°C and 31°C (76°F–88°F). Rainfall averages some 1,530 mm (60 ins) per year, or more with altitude, and most occurs in November–January. Humidity is low, but the island lies in the hurricane belt; the last time it was seriously affected being in 1989.

POPULATION

The population is now predominantly black or of mixed race, but Montserrat was originally noted as the only centre of Roman-Catholic Irish settlement in the West Indies (in the 17th century). Other white families joined the Irish ones, but the main addition to the population was African slaves, whose descendants now preserve the legacy of Irish names, phrases and, allegedly, a touch of brogue in the local accent (English is the official language). There is still a large Roman Catholic community in Montserrat, although the Anglican Church is also well represented and there are many other Christian denominations in a traditionally religious society.

Owing to volcanic activity from 1995 and the evacuation of the south, the total population declined from its normal level of about 11,000 (10,639 at the 1991 census) to less than 3,000 in 1998. A mid-year estimate in 2009 put the population at 4,932. The largest emigrant communities are in Antigua and Barbuda and in the United Kingdom. The capital is still officially Plymouth, but this has been largely destroyed by the volcano and lies within the Exclusion Zone. Government buildings have been established at Brades in the Carr's Bay area, in the north-west. This is on the coastal lowlands, just south of the new port facilities at Little Bay and to the north of Cudjoe Head Village, on the heights above. Cudjoe Head and Salem were the original two settlements of any size in the north of the island, in the area now outside the Exclusion Zone. Salem is just north of the boundary, also on hills near the west coast. Montserrat was originally divided into three parishes, but virtually the entire Parish of St Anthony (in the south and south-west) is now in the Exclusion Zone, as is most of the eastern Parish of St George. This leaves only the northern, hillier (and originally more sparsely populated) parts of St George's and the Parish of St Peter in the north and north-west.

History

MARK WILSON

Montserrat is a United Kingdom Overseas Territory. A Governor, who is the representative of the British monarch, has important reserve powers, including responsibility for national security and defence, the civil service, the judiciary and certain financial matters. A Chief Minister is responsible to the Legislative Council, similar in function to a parliament, which contains a majority of elected members. The Governor presides over an Executive Council, similar in function to a cabinet, which includes the Chief Minister and the other ministers. A constitutional review commission reported in 2002. Talks with the United Kingdom regarding possible reforms were ongoing in mid-2010, with the adoption of a draft constitution order expected in September.

Few traces remain of the original Amerindian inhabitants, who knew the island as Alliougana, or land of the prickly bush. Christopher Columbus sighted the island in 1493, and named it after the Spanish monastery of St Ignatius of Loyola. The first British settlers arrived in 1632, most of them Irish Catholics, resettling from Saint Christopher (St Kitts) or from the North American colony of Virginia. To this day, Montserrat is sometimes known as the 'Emerald Isle of the Caribbean', and has received some limited reconstruction assistance from the Irish Government. For most of its colonial history small slave plantations grew sugar and other crops, Montserrat being most famous for its limes and its cotton; however, the island was never an economic powerhouse.

From 1871 to 1956 Montserrat formed part of the Leeward Islands Federation. Unlike the larger islands of the eastern Caribbean, it did not join the short-lived Federation of the West Indies in 1958–62, and did not progress to associated statehood, retaining instead its status as a United Kingdom Dependent Territory, at first under an Administrator and then under a Governor.

In the first universal suffrage elections, held in 1952, all the seats were won by the Montserrat Labour Party, linked to the Montserrat Trades and Labour Union. This pattern was repeated in 1955, but broken in 1958. Since then, party allegiances in this small community have been fluid, overridden on most occasions by personal loyalties. The People's Liberation Movement, led by John Osborne, won all seven elected seats in a 1978 election, and remained the majority party with five seats in 1983 and four in 1987, when Osborne sought a fresh mandate during a dispute with the British authorities. Osborne's relations with the United Kingdom and with the Governor had deteriorated sharply as the result of a dispute over the management of the island's 'offshore' financial sector. Several hundred 'offshore' banks had been allowed to operate with no physical presence on the island and no effective supervision; most of these were later closed down, one of them run by Allen Stanford, who later played a prominent role in the affairs of neighbouring Antigua (see separate chapter). There was also some concern over Osborne's proposal to introduce casino gambling. In response, the British Government proposed a revised constitution, with increased powers of control over the financial sector for the Governor.

While this dispute was in progress, the island was devastated in September 1989 by Hurricane Hugo. Most of the housing stock was severely damaged, many public buildings were destroyed, and telephone and overhead electricity-distribution systems had to be completely reconstructed. The disaster underlined the advantages of a continuing link with the United Kingdom, and somewhat weakened Osborne's internal political position. Along with his three ministers, British police detectives questioned him in June in connection with a fraud investigation. He lost his majority in September 1991, and the National Progressive Party (NPP), whose leader, Reuben Meade, became Chief Minister, won elections on 8 October.

The Soufrière Hills volcano, which had been inactive since before the time of European settlement, came to life in July 1995. The southern part of the island was temporarily evacuated in August and December of that year, and what turned out to be a permanent evacuation was ordered on 1–3 April 1996. Twenty-three emergency shelters were established in the north of the island, initially housing 1,381; the last residents moved out of emergency accommodation only in 2001. By the time of the April 1996 evacuation, around 3,000 residents had left the island; soon afterwards, the British Government agreed Montserratians would be granted two years' stay in the United Kingdom, with the right to work or to obtain income support and housing benefits; however, no assistance with travel was offered to low-income islanders.

A general election was held in November 1996, despite the volcanic emergency. With a low turn-out, the NPP held one seat, with two each for the People's Progressive Alliance and the Movement for National Reconstruction, and two for independent candidates. Bertrand Osborne formed a coalition Government, and, in contrast to some of Montserrat's previous Chief Ministers, enjoyed consistently good relations with the United Kingdom.

In March and April 1997 the pace of volcanic activity quickened. There were flows of hot ash from the volcano, and ash clouds extended up to 12.5 km into the atmosphere. The remaining inhabitants of the southern part of the island, including the former capital, Plymouth, were forced to leave their homes. Most of the south has since been covered by a thick layer of volcanic ash, while volcanic deposits have in one location extended the coastline out to sea by 1.5 km. However, not everyone complied with instructions to stay out of the danger area at all times, and 19 people were killed on 25 June, some of whom were visiting closed areas to tend crops or livestock. The port was destroyed, while the airport lay within the danger zone. Some emergency accommodation was provided in the north, but two-thirds of the population left the island altogether, moving either to the United Kingdom, to Antigua and Barbuda or to other Caribbean islands.

There was considerable public disquiet both locally and in the United Kingdom at what was seen as a lack of assistance from the British Government. After public protests over conditions in emergency accommodation, Osborne resigned in August 1997, and was replaced as Chief Minister by the more vociferous David Brandt, who had been a key member of John Osborne's Government during the 'offshore' banking crisis. Brandt immediately moved into a bitter dispute with the British authorities, which escalated after remarks perceived as insensitive were made by the British Secretary of State for International Development, Clare Short, about Montserratian demands for 'golden elephants'.

Since the entire population now lived in the north of the island, the old constituency system was no longer relevant. Brandt's Government lost its majority in February 2001, and elections were held in April under a new 'at-large' voting system, without constituencies. John Osborne returned to office as Chief Minister, as leader of the New People's Liberation Movement (NPLM), which won seven of the nine elective seats, with the NPP taking the remaining two seats. In contrast to his earlier period in office, Osborne in general enjoyed a harmonious relationship with the British Government and its local representatives.

In February 2002 the Organisation of Eastern Caribbean States (OECS) countries, including Montserrat, agreed to allow nationals of member states to travel freely within the OECS area and to remain in a foreign territory within the area for up to six months. It was also planned to introduce a common OECS passport. In May 2002 the British Overseas Territories Act, having received royal assent in the United Kingdom in February, came into force and granted British citizenship to the people of its Overseas Territories, including Montserrat. Under the new law, Montserratians would be able to hold British passports and work in the United Kingdom and elsewhere in the European Union.

The Government's majority was reduced to a single seat in February 2003, when the Minister of Communications and Works, Dr Lowell Lewis, resigned his post, and, along with a party colleague, crossed the floor of the Legislative Council to sit as an independent. A former government backbencher, John Wilson, was appointed to the Executive Council in his place.

The level of volcanic activity increased again from September 2002, and a small area containing 300 houses was taken out of the 'safe' zone. Most of those affected were wealthy expatriates with winter homes; however, 80 Montserratians were placed in emergency accommodation. A further massive eruption, reported to be the largest since 1995, occurred in July 2003, causing damage to the supply of water and electricity, and the destruction of numerous buildings in the Salem area, which is on the periphery of the 'safe' zone. In July 2004 the USA informed the 200 Montserratians granted emergency residence during the volcanic emergency that they should plan to return home. However, the volcano was far from quiet, with renewed activity occurring in May 2006. Construction work on housing for the 48 people remaining in evacuation shelters began in that same month and it was intended that all shelters should close by the end of that year. However, a further phase of lava dome growth commenced in later months, continuing into early 2007, which prompted the USA in November 2006 to consider an extension to its programme of Temporary Protected Status for Montserratians imperilled by the renewed volcanic threat. A series of ash eruptions in January 2007 resulted in the addition of two small areas to the existing exclusion zone. Although the authorities remained on moderately high alert in subsequent months, by mid-April volcanic activity had reportedly abated and plans for further evacuations were suspended. Intermittent volcanic activity has continued since that date.

Although the crime rate remains relatively low, drugs-trafficking is a concern. Five Vincentians were arrested in June 2010 with 300 kg of cannabis on a beach within the exclusion zone; a separate 90-kg shipment had been intercepted in Montserrat waters in May.

At a general election held on 31 May 2006, allegations of corruption and mismanagement were made against candidates from both Government and opposition. As no party won a clear majority, Lowell Lewis, the sole elected member for the Montserrat Democratic Party, formed a coalition Government with the three members elected from the NPLM (including former Chief Minister John Osborne) and Brandt, who was elected as an independent. The Movement for Change and Prosperity (MCP), the largest single party represented, with four seats, formed the opposition. The new Government was sworn into office on 2 June, although some doubted the stability of its composition. This administration lasted until 21 February 2008, when Lewis announced an alliance with the MCP, three of whose members took ministerial portfolios. John Osborne became a government backbencher, along with the fourth elected member of the MCP. Two former NPLM cabinet ministers formed the opposition, along with Brandt, and in mid-2008 stated their intention to form a new party. To head off a vote of no confidence by Brandt, in November Lewis handed the economic development portfolio to Reuben Meade, who in addition to his experience as a former chief minister has also worked with the Caribbean Development Bank. However, Lewis retained responsibility for finance, and in March presented the annual budget for 2009. Tensions within the coalition increased during 2009, and Lewis called a fresh poll for 8 September, with two years of the current term still to run. The MCP took six of the nine seats under the at-large voting system, led by Reuben Meade, who became Chief Minister. Lewis retained his seat and sits as one of three independents who form the opposition.

Peter Andrew Waterworth succeeded Deborah Barnes-Jones as Governor in July 2007, following the conclusion of her tenure in office. Waterworth had some previous experience of Montserrat and had participated in a 1988 constitutional review. He is expected to retire in April 2011, with Adrian Derek Davis named in June 2010 as his successor, to be transferred from the United Kingdom's Department for International Development where he has worked since 1974.

Following preliminary consultations, draft proposals for a new constitution were discussed in 2009. After further local consultation, in May 2010 discussions with representatives from the United Kingdom were held; proposals included replacing the post of Chief Minister with that of premier, and the establishment of a national advisory council (including the opposition leader as well as senior government figures) to advise the Governor on matters of defence, external affairs, security and emergency powers. These, however, would remain, however, under the Governor's direct control. After an additional round of discussions, a final decision on the proposed constitution was expected in September.

Economy

MARK WILSON

Montserrat is an Overseas Territory of the United Kingdom in the eastern Caribbean, with an area of 102 sq km and a population of 4,932 in mid-2009; this figure is much lower than the total of 11,581 in 1994, just before the volcano became active, but considerably more than the low point of 2,850 reached in 1998. A proportion of the increased population were migrant workers, however (and some of the money earned by them was therefore sent abroad in the form of remittances). In spite of the volcanic emergency, the island is reasonably prosperous, with a per-head gross domestic product (GDP) of some US $9,099 in 2009, and an economy supported by substantial grant aid from the United Kingdom. GDP has been erratic, moving, for example, from a 5.9% contraction in 2006 to 6.7% growth in 2008, and slowing to growth of 3.6% in 2009. Construction was estimated to contribute some 10.5% of GDP in 2009, down from 16.7% in 2002.

Montserrat is a member of the Caribbean Community and Common Market, or CARICOM, whose members formed a single market in 2006. It is also a member of the Organisation of Eastern Caribbean States, which links nine of the smaller Caribbean territories, while the Eastern Caribbean Central Bank, headquartered in Saint Christopher (St Kitts) and Nevis, supervises its financial affairs. The Territory also uses the services of the regional stock exchange, the Eastern Caribbean Securities Exchange (also based in Saint Christopher and Nevis), established in 2001.

The southern two-thirds of the island forms an Exclusion Zone around the Soufrière Hills volcano, which has been active since July 1995, and is expected to remain active for several decades. Before the recent volcanic devastation, there was a small manufacturing sector, including a rice mill and an electronics assembly plant. These, as well as most tourist accommodation and much of the transport, utilities and infrastructure, were in what is now the Unsafe Area. Since 1997 there has been no significant manufacturing or commercial agriculture. There is a small 'offshore' financial sector, now better regulated than in the mid-1980s. In mid-2005 the first major export was made since the volcanic eruption: a quantity of aggregate from a quarry in Little Bay was shipped to Antigua. Since then, shipments of volcanic ash have been exported to the Virgin Islands, the Netherlands Antilles and Anguilla for use in construction, generating some employment and government revenue. The contribution of the mining and quarrying sector to GDP expanded from 0.1% in 2004 to 1.4% in 2009. Thus, the economy has been able to capitalize on by-products from volcanic activity.

Economic activity has centred since 1997 on the construction of new facilities in the north of the island, supported largely by British development grants. The Government's own recurrent revenue in 2009 was expected to contribute only EC $42.7m. to a total current expenditure of $95.2m. The remainder of the current budget and the entire EC $42.8m. capital programme were funded by grants from the United Kingdom (67%), the European Union (EU) (23%) and other sources; United Kingdom budgetary assistance was £20m. for the financial year 2010/11. Depreciation of sterling against the US dollar, to which the local currency is linked, substantially reduced the local value of programmed British assistance from the second half of 2008. A Sustainable Development Plan for 2008–10 was completed for the Ministry of Finance and Economic Development in March 2008. Goals included a diversified economy, sustained economic growth and graduation from British budgetary support by 2017, with a population of 9,000 by that date. The plan proposed private sector-led growth with improved infrastructure and transport facilities, renewed expansion in tourism, and development of geothermal energy, quarrying and food production. Problems noted include a shortage of entrepreneurial talent, with costly telecommunications services and physical access.

The temporary capital is at Brades, formerly a small village with few services. The Montserrat Development Corporation was established in 2007 to oversee the construction of a new capital at Little Bay. Facilities completed in the north include a small port, a housing development, fuel-storage facilities, a power plant, a water supply system, schools, a small hospital, a police headquarters, a fire station, sheltered housing for the elderly and a new building for the volcanic observatory. An airport at Gerald's with a 600-m runway was completed in 2005, funded by the EU and the United Kingdom; a new airline, Montserrat Airways, began service in November 2009, and a ferry service to Antigua began in December. Privately funded projects have included a small shopping centre and a 700-seat cultural centre opened in May 2007, funded by the British record producer Sir George Martin. A new power station building was completed in 2005. For the longer term, proposals for the use of geothermal power to generate electricity were under consideration in 2009.

A number of interesting proposals were made with the intention of revitalizing the island's economy. There is a small and specialized tourism industry based on the volcano itself, with facilities for visiting scientists, students and the merely curious. A number of visitors already make day trips while staying in Antigua and Barbuda or on other islands; there were 1,190 excursionist visitors in 2009. For stop-over visitors, there were 60 rooms in hotels and guest houses in mid-2006; there were 5,332 stop-over tourist arrivals in 2009, a reduction of 27.6% from a 2004 peak of 10,110. There were also 1.353 yachting visitors. Receipts from tourism totalled some EC $13.9m. in 2009. Further hotel and scuba-diving developments were under discussion, with a yachting marina and cruise ship facilities also proposed; at present, most cruise ships pause offshore, allowing passengers a distant view. A Cable and Wireless telecommunications monopoly expired in March 2007, and the Government passed legislation in 2009 in preperation for liberalization. By 2010 Cable and Wireless was still the only operator, although Digicel had expressed interest in gaining a presence on the island. Another proposal was a graduate school of disaster studies, to be operated in collaboration with British and US universities. Besides volcanic activity and hurricanes, the island is at some risk from earthquakes, landslides and tsunamis.

Statistical Survey

Sources (unless otherwise stated): Government Information Service, Media Centre, Chief Minister's Office, Old Towne; tel. 491-2702; fax 491-2711; Eastern Caribbean Central Bank, POB 89, Basseterre, Saint Christopher; internet www.eccb-centralbank.org; OECS Economic Affairs Secretariat, *Statistical Digest*.

AREA AND POPULATION

Area: 102 sq km (39.5 sq miles).

Population: 10,639 (males 5,290, females 5,349) at census of 12 May 1991; 4,491 at census of 12 May 2001 (Source: UN, *Population and Vital Statistics Report*). *2009* (projected estimate at mid-year): 4,932.

Population by Age and Sex (at 2001 census): *0–14:* 869 (males 454, females 415); *15–64:* 2,910 (males 1,599, females 1,311); *65 and over:* 689 (males 344, females 345); *Total* 4,468 (males 5,628, females 5,802). Note: Total includes persons of unknown age.

Density (mid-2009): 48.4 per sq km.

Principal Towns: Plymouth, the former capital, was abandoned in 1997. Brades is the interim capital.

Births and Deaths (1999): 45 live births (birth rate 9.4 per 1,000); 59 deaths (death rate 12.4 per 1,000) (Source: UN, *Population and Vital Statistics Report*). *2003:* Crude birth rate 9.6 per 1,000; Crude death rate 12.3 per 1,000 (Source: Caribbean Development Bank, *Social and Economic Indicators*). *2009:* Crude birth rate 12.4 per 1,000; Crude death rate 8.4 per 1,000 (Source: Pan American Health Organization).

Life Expectancy (years at birth, estimates): 72.8 (males 74.7; females 70.7) in 2009. Source: Pan American Health Organization.

Employment (1992): Agriculture, forestry and fishing 298; Mining and manufacturing 254; Electricity, gas and water 68; Wholesale and retail trade 1,666; Restaurants and hotels 234; Transport and communication 417; Finance, insurance and business services 242; Public defence 390; Other community, social and personal services 952; *Total* 4,521 (Source: *The Commonwealth Yearbook*). *1998* (estimate): Total labour force 1,500.

HEALTH AND WELFARE

Physicians (per 1,000 head, 1999): 0.18.

Hospital Beds (per 1,000 head, 2007): 3.0.

Health Expenditure (public, % of GDP, 2000): 7.7.

Health Expenditure (public, % of total, 1995): 67.0.

Source: Pan American Health Organization.

For sources and definitions, see explanatory note on p. vi.

AGRICULTURE, ETC.

Principal Crops (metric tons, 2008, FAO estimates): Vegetables 495; Fruit (excl. melons) 735.

Livestock ('000 head, 2008, FAO estimates): Cattle 9.9; Sheep 4.8; Goats 7.1; Pigs 1.2.

Livestock Products ('000 metric tons, 2008, FAO estimates): Cattle meat 0.7; Cows' milk 2.3.

Fishing (metric tons, live weight, 2008, FAO estimate): Total catch 50 (all marine fishes).

Source: FAO.

INDUSTRY

Electric Energy (million kWh): 11.6 in 2007; 11.7 in 2008; 11.8 in 2009.

FINANCE

Currency and Exchange Rates: 100 cents = 1 East Caribbean dollar (EC $). *Sterling, US Dollar and Euro Equivalents* (31 May 2010): £1 sterling = EC $3.937; US $1 = EC $2.700; €1 = EC $3.344; EC $100 = £25.40 = US $37.04 = €29.91. *Exchange Rate*: Fixed at US $1 = EC $2.70 since July 1976.

Budget (EC $ million, 2009): *Revenue:* Revenue from taxation 35.8 (Taxes on income and profits 16.8, Taxes on property 1.1, Taxes on domestic goods and services 3.7, Taxes on international trade and transactions 14.2); Non-tax revenue 4.3; Total 40.1 (excl. grants 100.2). *Expenditure:* Current expenditure 97.3 (Personal emoluments 41.4, Goods and services 23.9, Interest payments 0.1, Transfers and subsidies 31.9); Capital expenditure 37.1; Total 134.4.

International Reserves (US $ million at 31 December 2009): Foreign exchange 14.30. Source: IMF, *International Financial Statistics*.

Money Supply (EC $ million at 31 December 2009): Currency outside depository corporations 14.86; Transferable deposits 41.80; Other deposits 131.29; *Broad money* 187.96. Source: IMF, *International Financial Statistics*.

Cost of Living (Consumer Price Index; base: previous year = 100): All items 99.2 in 2003; 104.3 in 2004; 101.76 in 2005. Source: partly Caribbean Development Bank, *Social and Economic Indicators*.

Gross Domestic Product (EC $ million at constant 1990 prices): 67.18 in 2006; 68.16 in 2007; 72.71 in 2008.

Expenditure on the Gross Domestic Product (EC $ million at current prices, 2008): Government final consumption expenditure 75.82; Private final consumption expenditure 126.49; Gross fixed capital formation 36.78; *Total domestic expenditure* 239.09; Export of goods and services 48.42; *Less* Imports of goods and services 152.35; *GDP at market prices* 135.16.

Gross Domestic Product by Economic Activity (EC $ million at current prices, 2008): Agriculture, forestry and fishing 1.60; Mining and quarrying 1.62; Manufacturing 0.87; Electricity and water 7.80; Construction 10.43; Wholesale and retail trade 5.76; Restaurants and hotels 1.40; Transport 9.26; Communications 3.90; Banks and insurance 13.97; Real estate and housing 15.86; Government services 48.14; Other services 9.11; *Sub-total* 129.72; *Less* Financial intermediation services indirectly measured 12.47; *Gross value added at basic prices* 117.28; Taxes, less subsidies, on products 17.87; *GDP at market prices* 135.16.

Balance of Payments (EC $ million, 2009): Goods (net) –63.80; Services (net) –18.21; *Balance on goods and services* –82.01; Income (net) –13.00; *Balance on goods, services and income* –95.01; Current transfers (net) 60.66; *Current balance* –34.34; Capital account (net) 17.00; Direct investment (net) 18.55; Public sector long-term investment –0.62; Commercial banks 1.36; Other investment assets 0.12; Other investment liabilities –4.21; Net errors and omissions –1.09; *Overall balance* –3.21.

EXTERNAL TRADE

Principal Commodities (US $ '000, 2009): *Imports c.i.f.:* Meat and edible meat offal 914; Beverages, spirits and vinegar 1,285; Mineral fuels, oils, distillation products, etc. 7,943 (Petroleum oils, not crude 7,444); Nuclear reactors, boilers, machinery, etc. 2,067; Electrical, electronic equipment 1,295; Vehicles other than railway, tramway 2,432 (Cars, incl. station wagon 1,445); Total (incl. others) 29,605. *Exports f.o.b.:* Salt, sulphur, earth, stone, plaster, lime and cement 1,404; Nuclear reactors, boilers, machinery, etc. 957; Electrical, electronic equipment 189; Optical, photo, technical, and medical apparatus 299;; Total (incl. others) 3,148.

Principal Trading Partners (US $ '000, 2009): *Imports c.i.f.:* Barbados 128; Canada 415; China, People's Repub. 237; Dominican Republic 237; Jamaica 654; Japan 1,520; Netherlands 309; St. Vincent and the Grenadines 295; Trinidad and Tobago 1,803; United Kingdom 1,666; USA 20,272; Total (incl. others) 29,605. *Exports f.o.b.:* Anguilla 480; Antigua and Barbuda 77; British Virgin Islands 208; Dominica 381; France (incl. Monaco) 133; Netherlands Antilles 211; New Zealand 247; St. Christopher and Nevis 366; Trinidad and Tobago 481; United Kingdom 153; USA 384; Total (incl. others) 3,148.

Source: UN, *International Trade Statistics Yearbook*.

TOURISM

Tourist Arrivals (2009, preliminary): Stay-over arrivals 5,332 (USA 1,327, Canada 328, United Kingdom 1,508, Caribbean 1,978, Others 191); Excursionists 1,190; Total visitor arrivals (incl. others) 7,875.

Tourism Receipts (EC $ million): 20.1 in 2007; 19.0 in 2008; 13.9 in 2009 (preliminary).

TRANSPORT

Road Traffic (vehicles in use, 1990): Passenger cars 1,823; Goods vehicles 54; Public service vehicles 4; Motorcycles 21; Miscellaneous 806.

Shipping: ('000 metric tons, 1990): *International Freight Traffic:* Goods loaded 6; Goods unloaded 49. Source: UN, *Monthly Bulletin of Statistics*.

Civil Aviation (1985): Aircraft arrivals 4,422; passengers 25,380; air cargo 132.4 metric tons.

COMMUNICATIONS MEDIA

Radio Receivers (1997): 7,000 in use.

Television Receivers (1999): 3,000 in use.

Telephones (2009): 2,700 main lines in use.

Mobile Cellular Telephones (2000): 3,000 subscribers.

Broadband Subscribers: 600 in 2009 (estimate).

Non-daily Newspapers (1996): 2 (estimated circulation 3,000).

Sources: UNESCO, *Statistical Yearbook*; International Telecommunication Union.

EDUCATION

Pre-primary: 11 schools (1999); 11 teachers (2006/07); 116 pupils (2006/07).

Primary: 2 schools (1999); 31 teachers (2006/07); 497 pupils (2006/07).

Secondary: 1 school (1999); 29 teachers (2006/07); 347 pupils (2006/07).

Sources: UNESCO, *Statistical Yearbook*; UNESCO Institute for Statistics.

Directory

The Constitution

The present Constitution came into force on 19 December 1989 and made few amendments to the constitutional order established in 1960. The Constitution now guarantees the fundamental rights and freedoms of the individual and grants the Territory the right of self-determination. Montserrat is governed by a Governor and has its own Executive and Legislative Councils. The Governor retains responsibility for defence, external affairs (including international financial affairs) and internal security. The Executive Council consists of the Governor as President, the Chief Minister and three other Ministers, the Attorney-General and the Financial Secretary. The Legislative Council consists of the Speaker (chosen from outside the Council), nine elected, two official and two nominated members. Owing to the disruption caused by evacuation from the south of the island, both the 2001 and 2006 general elections were conducted according to a new 'at large' voting system, without constituencies, but still choosing nine members of the legislature. Following a constitutional review process, a final decision on a new Constitution was expected in late 2010.

The Government

HEAD OF STATE

Queen: HM Queen ELIZABETH II.

Governor: PETER ANDREW WATERWORTH (took office in July 2007).

Governor-designate: ADRIAN DEREK DAVIS (scheduled to take office in April 2011).

Deputy Governor: SARITA FRANCIS (acting).

EXECUTIVE COUNCIL

(July 2010)

The Government is formed by the Movement for Change and Prosperity.

President: PETER ANDREW WATERWORTH (The Governor).

Official Members:

Attorney-General: JAMES WOOD.

Financial Secretary: JOHN SKERRITT.

Chief Minister and Minister of Finance with responsibility for Local Government, Immigration, Information Communication, Regional and International Affairs, Economic Development, Tourism and Trade: REUBEN T. MEADE.

Minister of Agriculture, Lands, Housing, the Environment, Consumer Affairs and Ecclesiastical Affairs: EASTON TAYLOR-FARRELL.

Minister of Communication, Works and Labour: CHARLES KIRNON.

Minister of Education, Health, Community Services, Youth Affairs, Sports and Culture: COLLIN RILEY.

Clerk to the Executive Council: JUDITH JEFFERS.

MINISTRIES

Office of the Governor: Unit 8, Farara Plaza, Brades; tel. 491-2688; fax 491-8867; e-mail govoffice.montserrat@fco.gov.uk; internet ukinmontserrat.fco.gov.uk.

Office of the Deputy Governor: No. 3, Farara Plaza, Brades; tel. 491-6524; fax 491-9202; e-mail odg@gov.ms; internet odg.gov.ms.

Office of the Attorney-General: POB 129, Valley View; tel. 491-4686; fax 491-4687; e-mail legal@gov.ms; internet agc.gov.ms.

Office of the Chief Minister: Govt HQ, POB 292, Brades; tel. 491-3378; fax 491-6780; e-mail ocm@gov.ms; internet ocm.gov.ms.

Ministry of Agriculture, Lands, Housing and the Environment: Govt HQ, POB 272, Brades; tel. 491-2546; fax 491-9275; e-mail malhe@gov.ms; internet www.malhe.gov.ms.

Ministry of Communications and Works: Woodlands; tel. 491-2521; fax 491-3475; e-mail comworks@gov.ms.

Ministry of Education: Govt HQ, POB 103, Brades; tel. 491-2541; fax 491-6941; e-mail deped@gov.ms.

Ministry of Finance: Govt HQ, POB 292, Brades; tel. 491-2777; fax 491-2367; e-mail minfin@gov.ms; internet www.finance.gov.ms.

Ministry of Health and Community Services: Govt HQ, POB 24, Brades; tel. 491-2880; fax 491-3131; e-mail mehcs@gov.ms; internet moh.gov.ms.

LEGISLATIVE COUNCIL

Speaker: TERESINA BODKIN.

Election, 8 September 2009

Party	Seats
Movement for Change and Prosperity	6
Independent	3
Total	9

There are also two ex officio members (the Attorney-General and the Financial Secretary).

Political Organizations

Montserrat Democratic Party (MDP): c/o Kelsick & Kelsick, Woodlands Main Rd, POB 185, Brades; tel. 491-2102; e-mail lowell@mdp.ms; internet www.mdp.ms; f. 2006; Leader Dr LOWELL LEWIS; Chair. JEAN KELSICK.

Montserrat Labour Party (MLP): Brades; f. 2009 by fmr mems of the NPLM (q.v.); Leaders MARGARET DYER-HOWE, IDABELLE MEADE.

Montserrat Reformation Party (MRP): Brades; f. 2009; Leaders ADELINA TUITT, ALRIC TAYLOR.

Movement for Change and Prosperity (MCAP): POB 419, Brades; e-mail mail@mcap.ms; internet www.mcap.ms; f. 2005 by fmr mems of the National Progressive Party (NPP); Leader REUBEN T. MEADE; Chair. RANDOLPH RILEY.

New People's Liberation Movement (NPLM): f. 1997 as successor party to People's Progressive Alliance and the Movement for National Reconstruction (MNR); opposition party; Leader JOHN OSBORNE.

Judicial System

Justice is administered by the Eastern Caribbean Supreme Court (based in Saint Lucia—comprised of the Court of Appeal and the High Court), the Court of Summary Jurisdiction and the Magistrate's Court. A revised edition of the Laws of Montserrat came into force on 15 April 2005, following five years of preparation by a Law Revision Committee.

Puisne Judge (Montserrat Circuit): JANICE MESADIS GEORGE-CREQUE (concurrently accredited to Anguilla).

Magistrate: CLIFTON WARNER, Govt HQ, Brades; tel. 491-4056; fax 491-8866; e-mail magoff@gov.ms.

Religion

CHRISTIANITY

The Montserrat Christian Council: St Peter's, POB 227; tel. 491-4864; fax 491-2139; Chair. Rev. B. RUTH ALLEN.

The Anglican Communion

Anglicans are adherents of the Church in the Province of the West Indies, comprising eight dioceses. Montserrat forms part of the diocese of the North Eastern Caribbean and Aruba. The Bishop is resident in The Valley, Anguilla.

The Roman Catholic Church

Montserrat forms part of the diocese of St John's-Basseterre, suffragan to the archdiocese of Castries (Saint Lucia). The Bishop is resident in St John's, Antigua and Barbuda.

Other Christian Churches

There are Baptist, Methodist, Pentecostal and Seventh-day Adventist churches and other places of worship on the island.

The Press

Montserrat Newsletter: Farara Plaza, Unit 8, Brades; tel. 491-2688; fax 491-8867; e-mail richard.aspin@fco.gov.uk; f. 1998; quarterly; govt information publ; Publicity Officer RICHARD ASPIN.

The Montserrat Reporter: POB 306, Davy Hill; tel. 491-4715; fax 491-2430; e-mail editor@themontserratreporter.com; internet www

.themontserratreporter.com; weekly on Fridays; circ. 2,000; Editor BENNETTE ROACH.

Broadcasting and Communications

TELECOMMUNICATIONS

Cable & Wireless (West Indies) Ltd: POB 219, Sweeney's; tel. 491-1000; fax 491-3599; e-mail venus.george@cwni.cwplc.com; internet www.cwmontserrat.com.

BROADCASTING

Radio

Radio Antilles: POB 35/930, Plymouth; tel. 491-2755; fax 491-2724; f. 1963; in 1989 the Govt of Montserrat, on behalf of the OECS, acquired the station; has 1 of the most powerful transmitters in the region; commercial; regional; broadcasts in English and French; Chair. Dr H. FELLHAUER; Man. Dir KRISTIAN KNAACK; Gen. Man. KEITH GREAVES.

Radio Montserrat (ZJB): POB 51, Sweeney's; tel. 491-2885; fax 491-9250; e-mail zjb@gov.ms; internet www.zjb.gov.ms; f. 1952; first broadcast 1957; govt station; CEO LOWELL MASON.

Television

Television services can also be obtained from Saint Christopher and Nevis, Puerto Rico and from Antigua and Barbuda.

Cable Television of Montserrat Ltd: POB 447, Olveston; tel. 491-2507; fax 491-3081; Man. SYLVIA WHITE.

People's Television (PTV): POB 82, Brades; tel. 491-5110; Man. DENZIL EDGECOMBE.

Finance

The Eastern Caribbean Central Bank, based in Saint Christopher and Nevis, is the central issuing and monetary authority for Montserrat.

Eastern Caribbean Central Bank—Montserrat Office: 2 Farara Plaza, POB 484, Brades; tel. 491-6877; fax 491-6878; e-mail eccbmni@candw.ms; internet www.eccb-centralbank.org; Resident Rep. CHARLES T. JOHN.

Financial Services Commission: Phoenix House, POB 188, Brades; tel. 491-6887; fax 491-9888; e-mail fscmrat@candw.ms; internet fscmontserrat.org; f. 2001; the Commission consists of the Commissioner and 3 other mems appointed by the Governor; Head DULCIE JAMES.

BANKING

Bank of Montserrat Ltd: Hilltop, POB 10, St Peters; tel. 491-3843; fax 491-3163; e-mail bom@candw.ag; Man. ANTON DOLDRON.

Montserrat Building Society: POB 101, Brades Main Rd, Brades; tel. 491-2391; fax 491-6127; e-mail mbsl@candw.ms.

St Patrick's Co-operative Credit Union Ltd: POB 337, Brades; tel. 491-3666; fax 491-6566; e-mail monndf@candw.ms; Exec. Dir ROSELYN CASSELL-SEALY.

STOCK EXCHANGE

Eastern Caribbean Securities Exchange: based in Basseterre, Saint Christopher and Nevis; tel. (869) 466-7192; fax (869) 465-3798; e-mail info@ecseonline.com; internet www.ecseonline.com; f. 2001; regional securities market designed to facilitate the buying and selling of financial products for the 8 mem. territories—Anguilla, Antigua and Barbuda, Dominica, Grenada, Montserrat, Saint Christopher and Nevis, Saint Lucia and Saint Vincent and the Grenadines; Chair. Sir K. DWIGHT VENNER; Gen. Man. and CEO TREVOR E. BLAKE.

INSURANCE

British American Insurance Co Ltd: POB 77, St Peter's; tel. 491-2361; fax 491-9361.

Insurance Services (Montserrat) Ltd: POB 185, Brades; tel. 491-2103; fax 491-6013; e-mail ismcall@candw.ag; Gen. Man. STEPHEN FRANCOIS.

NAGICO: Ryan Investments, Brades; tel. 491-3403; fax 491-7307; e-mail talicj@yahoo.com.

N. E. M. (West Indies) Insurance Ltd (NEMWIL): POB 287, Brades; tel. 491-3813; fax 491-3815.

United Insurance Co Ltd: Jacquie Ryan Enterprises Ltd, POB 425, Brades; tel. 491-2055; fax 491-3257; e-mail united@candw.ms; CEO JACQUIE RYAN.

Trade and Industry

GOVERNMENT AGENCIES

Montserrat Development Corporation (MDC): Brades; internet www.mdc.ms; f. 2007; overseeing plans for new capital in Little Bay; promotes private sector investment and economic growth; Chair. KENNETH SCOTLAND; CEO COLIN HEARTWELL.

Montserrat Economic Development Unit: Govt HQ, POB 292, Brades; tel. 491-2066; fax 491-4632; e-mail devunit@gov.ms; internet www.devunit.gov.ms.

CHAMBER OF COMMERCE

Montserrat Chamber of Commerce and Industry (MCCI): Vue Pointe Hotel, Old Towne, POB 384, Brades; tel. 491-3640; fax 491-6602; e-mail chamber@candw.ms; refounded 1971; 31 company mems, 26 individual mems; Pres. KENNY CASSELL; Sec.-Treas. ROSELYN CASSELL-SEALY.

UTILITIES

Electricity and Water

Montserrat Utilities Ltd (MUL): POB 324, Davy Hill; tel. 491-2538; fax 491-4904; e-mail mul@mul.ms; internet www.mul.ms; f. 2008 by merger of Montserrat Electricity Services Ltd and Montserrat Water Authority; domestic electricity generation and supply; domestic water supply; Man. Dir PETER WHITE; Man. of Water and Sewerage EMILE DUBERRY.

Gas

Grant Enterprises and Trading: POB 350, Brades; tel. 491-9654; fax 491-4854; e-mail granten@candw.ms; domestic gas supplies.

TRADE UNIONS

Montserrat Allied Workers' Union (MAWU): POB 245, Dagenham, Plymouth; tel. 491-5049; fax 491-6145; e-mail bramblehl@candw.ag; f. 1973; private sector employees; Pres. CHARLES RYAN; Gen. Sec. HYLROY BRAMBLE; 1,000 mems.

Montserrat Civil Service Association: POB 468, Plymouth; tel. 491-6797; fax 491-5655; e-mail lewisp@gov.ms; Pres. PAUL LEWIS.

Montserrat Union of Teachers: POB 460, Plymouth; tel. 491-4382; fax 491-5779; f. 1978; Pres. HERMAN FRANCIS; Gen. Sec. HYACINTH BRAMBLE-BROWNE; 46 mems.

Transport

The eruption in 1997 of the Soufrière Hills volcano, and subsequent volcanic activity, destroyed much of the infrastructure in the southern two-thirds of the island, including the country's principal port and airport facilities, as well as the road network.

ROADS

Prior to the 1997 volcanic eruption, Montserrat had an extensive and well-constructed road network. There were 203 km (126 miles) of good surfaced main roads, 24 km of secondary unsurfaced roads and 42 km of rough tracks. Government expenditure on road rehabilitation works in 2006 amounted to more than US $3m., while a further US $0.5m. was allocated to the maintenance budget of the Public Works Department for surfacing of the secondary road network. The 2007 budget allocated funds of over US $5m. for continued road and infrastructure improvements, particularly in areas to become more densely populated through housing developments carried out under the Emergency Resettlement Strategy. A five-year roads development project proposal, to cost $20m., was also submitted to the British Department for International Development in that year.

SHIPPING

The principal port at Plymouth was destroyed by the volcanic activity of June 1997. An emergency jetty was constructed at Little Bay in the north of the island. Regular transshipment steamship services are provided by Harrison Line and Nedlloyd Line. The Bermuth Line and the West Indies Shipping Service link Montserrat with Miami, USA, and with neighbouring territories. A ferry service with Antigua, which had been suspended in 2005, was reinstated in December 2008.

Port Authority of Montserrat: Little Bay, POB 383, Plymouth; tel. 491-2791; fax 491-8063; e-mail monpa@candw.ms; Man. SHAWN O'GARRO.

Montserrat Shipping Services: POB 46, Carr's Bay; tel. 491-3614; fax 491-3617.

CIVIL AVIATION

The main airport, Blackburne at Trants, 13 km (8 miles) from Plymouth, was destroyed by the volcanic activity of 1997. A helicopter port at Gerald's in the north of the island was completed in 2000. A new, temporary international airport at Gerald's, financed at a cost of EC $51.95m. by the European Union and the British Department for International Development, was completed in 2005, to be serviced by Windward Islands Airways International (Winair). In the longer term, the Government intended to construct a permanent international airport at Thatch Valley. Montserrat is linked to Antigua by a helicopter service, which operates three times a day. The island is also a shareholder in the regional airline, LIAT (based in Antigua and Barbuda), which acquired its troubled rival, Caribbean Star Airlines, in October 2007. In July 2008, upon termination of Winair's contract, LIAT and Carib Aviation (also based in Antigua and Barbuda) entered into an agreement to operate scheduled flights into and out of the airport at Gerald's, renamed the John A. Osborne Airport in the same month.

Montserrat Airways Ltd: John A. Osborne Airport, POB 225, Gerald's; tel. 491-3434; e-mail info@flymontserrat.com; internet www.flymontserrat.com; charter services; subsidiary of Love Air, United Kingdom; Chair. Capt. NIGEL HARRIS.

FlyMontserrat: John A. Osborne Airport, POB 225, Gerald's; tel. 491-3434; e-mail info@flymontserrat.com; internet www.flymontserrat.com; f. 2009; flights between Montserrat and Antigua; subsidiary of Montserrat Airways; Chair. Capt. NIGEL HARRIS.

Tourism

Since the 1997 volcanic activity, Montserrat has been marketed as an eco-tourism destination. Known as the 'Emerald Isle of the Caribbean', Montserrat is noted for its Irish connections, and for its range of flora and fauna. In 2009 there were a preliminary 5,332 stay-over tourist arrivals. In that year some 37% of total tourist arrivals were from Caribbean countries, 28% from the United Kingdom and 25% from the USA. In addition there were 1,190 excursionists. A large proportion of visitors are estimated to be Montserrat nationals residing overseas. Tourism earnings totalled EC $13.9m. in 2009.

Montserrat Tourist Board: 7 Farara Plaza, POB 7, Brades; tel. 491-2230; fax 491-7430; e-mail info@montserrattourism.ms; internet www.visitmontserrat.com; f. 1993; Chair. JOHN PONTEEN; Dir of Tourism ERNESTINE CASSELL.

Defence

The United Kingdom is responsible for the defence of Montserrat.

Education

Education, beginning at five years of age, is compulsory up to the age of 14. In 1993 there were 11 primary schools, including 10 government schools, but this was reduced to just two in 1999. Secondary education begins at 12 years of age, and comprises a first cycle of five years and a second, two-year cycle. In 1999 there was one government secondary school. In 2007 enrolment in primary education included an estimated 92% of children in the relevant age-group, while the comparable ratio for secondary education was an estimated 96%. In 1999 there were 11 nursery schools, sponsored by a government-financed organization, and a Technical College, which provided vocational and technical training for school-leavers. There was also an extra-mural department of the University of the West Indies in Plymouth. Construction of the Montserrat Community College was completed in 2003. Three 'offshore' medical schools were licensed in 2003. The Ministry of Education was allocated a total of EC $8.3m. in the 2008 budget.

THE NETHERLANDS ANTILLES

Geography

PHYSICAL FEATURES

The Netherlands Antilles is part of the tripartite Kingdom of the Netherlands. The dependency has been known informally as the 'Antilles of the Five' since Aruba separated in 1986, and is now composed of the island territories of Curaçao and Bonaire in the southern Caribbean and, in the north-eastern Caribbean, of Sint Maarten, the Dutch (southern) half of the island of Saint Martin, Sint Eustatius (Statia—from the original Spanish name, St Anastasia) and Saba. An agreement signed in The Hague, Netherlands, on 12 October 2006 confirmed the redesignation of Saba, Bonaire and St Eustatius as Dutch municipalities, while a further accord, ratified by St Maarten on 2 November, and by Curaçao on 9 July 2007, awarded the two latter territories powers of independent governance as associated states of the Kingdom of the Netherlands. Formal dissolution of the five-island federation was scheduled for 15 December 2008, but later postponed until 10 October 2010. The Netherlands Antilles' Caribbean colleague in the Kingdom, Aruba, is 68 km (42 miles) to the west of Curaçao. These two islands, together with Bonaire known as the 'ABC islands', lie off the coast of Venezuela, and are the westernmost extension of the southern Lesser Antilles. The Venezuelan mainland is about 55 km south of Curaçao and 80 km south of Bonaire (Bonaire is actually closer to the offshore Venezuelan Antilles, specifically, the Islas Las Aves, to the east). Curaçao and Bonaire, themselves only about 35 km apart, together with Aruba, are known as the *Benedenwindse Eilands* ('Leeward Islands'). The other islands of the Dutch Caribbean, about 900 km to the north-east, are grouped in the *Bovenwindse Eilands* ('Windward Islands'—the Dutch adopted this terminology from the Spanish, at variance with the anglophone tradition, which terms the surrounding islands in the north-eastern Caribbean as the Leeward Islands). The *Bovenwindse Eilands* are sometimes known as the 'three Ss' (Saba, St Eustatius or Statia, and St Maarten). St Eustatius is about 20 km north-west of St Kitts (Saint Christopher and Nevis). Saba lies 27 km to the north-west of St Eustatius. St Maarten lies 56 km to the north of St Eustatius and 45 km from Saba. On St Maarten is the only land border (10.2 km) in the Lesser Antilles. The north of the island (St-Martin—as well as the island of St-Barthélemy, some 20 km to the south-east) lies in France and is part of the Overseas Department of Guadeloupe. The British dependency of Anguilla lies just to the north of the Franco-Dutch island, with the Virgin Islands some distance to the west. The five island territories of the Netherlands Antilles, formerly known as Curaçao and Dependencies (then including Aruba), together cover an area of 800 sq km (309 sq miles).

Curaçao is the largest island of the Netherlands Antilles, with an area of 444 sq km. It is about 61 km long, undulating in width (at most, 14 km) south-eastwards from the north-western tip (North Point) to East Point. Volcanic in origin, reef development has added to the island, which remains surrounded by coral barriers. The northern coasts face the weather, while a complex littoral of drowned valleys and inlets, still home to some mangrove wetlands, is more characteristic of the leeward shore. The largest enclosed bay is the Schottegat, on the south coast, which is where the port of Willemstad, the capital, has its Annabaai harbour, inland from the original site of the city. The interior (cunucu) is hilly (the highest point being St Christoffelberg, at 345 m or 1,132 ft, in the north-west), but dry, with vegetation being scrubby and drought resistant. The natural environment is similar to that in Aruba and Bonaire, but has eroded more from human development, although it is distinguished by fauna such as the blue iguana and the small Curaçao deer (a white-tail deer believed to have been imported by the original Amerindian Arawaks in the 14th century).

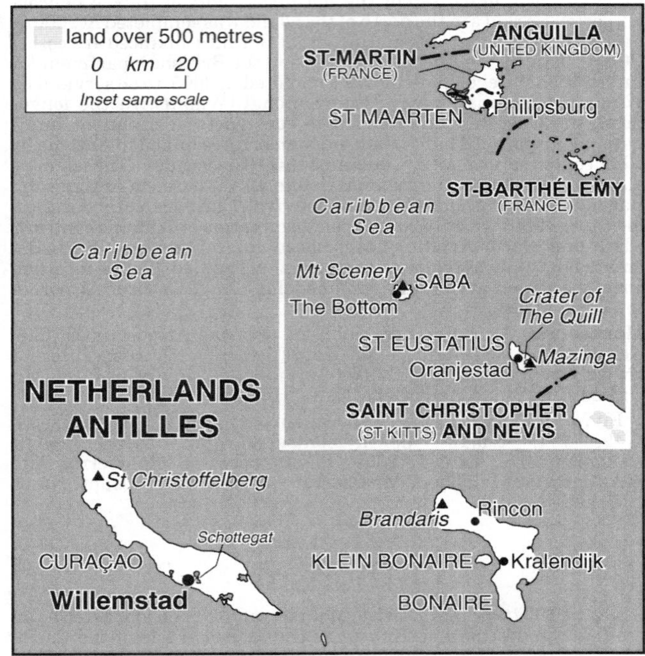

Bonaire pushes south-eastwards, before thrusting south, the gentler, south-western, leeward shore forming a rough crescent, which shelters the small limestone island of Klein Bonaire, some 750 m off the west coast. Bonaire covers an area of 288 sq km, and is about 40 km long and 11 km at its widest. Like Curaçao, Bonaire is a reef-fringed island originally of volcanic origin, but it is much lower, most of the south being only about 2 m above sea level. Hills are confined to the north (reaching their height at Mt Brandaris—238 m). Water retention of the soil is poor and this, combined with low rainfall, has added the feature of salinas (extremely saline lakes separated from the sea by coral-rubble barriers), which attracted the original Dutch settlers, who wished to harvest the salt. The saltpans also shelter one of the largest colonies of Caribbean flamingos in the Americas. The island's natural environment, including its economically important marine environment (Bonaire is considered to be one of the world's three leading diving destinations), has been long and extensively protected. Among the multitude of other bird species found on the island are the indigenous Bonaire green parrot and the rare yellow-shouldered amazon, while the only native mammal is also airborne—the bat, of which eight species have been identified. Reptiles include the iguana and the anolis. Bonaire is the Dutch island least densely populated by people.

The island of St Martin (Sint Maarten or Saint-Martin) is of volcanic origin, but is fairly flat and comprised primarily of a coralline limestone base. The dry, often scrubby landscape is dotted with salt ponds and other inland waters, notably the great Simpson's Bay Lagoon, which dominates the low-lying, west-pointing peninsula that extends the island in the south-west. The highest point is in the centre of the hillier, eastern bulk of the island, at Pic du Paradis (424 m), and lies in the French sector. At 86 sq km, Saint Martin is the smallest island in the world to be divided between two nations—the southern part of the island is Dutch, covers 34 sq km (as finally agreed in the 1839 revision of the original 1648 Franco-Dutch Treaty of Mount Concordia) and is known as Sint Maarten. St Maarten has a slightly larger population than Saint-Martin and is heavily developed.

St Eustatius (Statia) covers 21 sq km and, like Saba, is of a more explicit volcanic origin than the other three islands. In the south it rises to the rainforest-filled crater of an extinct volcano, The Quill. The highest point of the crater rim, Mazinga, is 600 m above sea level. To the north-west are less lofty heights, culminating in the Boven at the northern end of Statia, with central plains connecting the two highlands. Although much of the native forest disappeared during the period of economic expansion that ended towards the end of the 18th century, when the island was known as the 'Golden Rock' and slave-worked plantations added to its immense entrepôt wealth, Statia still has a diverse plant life and hosts a number of bird species. Butterflies abound and animal life includes the threatened Antilles iguana, land crabs and tree frogs. The island is rich in historical remains.

At 13 sq km, Saba is the smallest of the Dutch West Indian islands, but reaches their highest point (indeed, the highest point in the whole Kingdom of the Netherlands), at Mt Scenery (866 m). Rising steeply from the sea, the island is the peak of a single, composite dormant volcano that rears up from a base some 600 m below sea level, the main peak surrounded by subsidiary peaks and domes. The green hillsides, scored by drainage valleys known locally as guts (ghauts), have a hugely varied vegetation, dependent upon altitude (although a hurricane in 1999 severely damaged much woodland), and shelter numerous birds and some animals, mainly reptilian, among them the green iguana, the endemic anole lizard and a non-poisonous red-bellied racer snake (only otherwise known on Statia). The mountain terrain permits only one inlet at which it is possible to land from the sea, and prevented the construction of a road (which, hitherto, was believed to be unachievable) until 1943. There is no human settlement on the coast as such.

CLIMATE

The climate of Curaçao and Bonaire is tropical and the two islands are south of the main hurricane belt. The islands also receive little rain, while the fairly constant Atlantic breezes contribute to a high evaporation rate, ensuring that the climate is defined as semi-arid. On Curaçao average annual rainfall is 570 mm (22 ins), although this varies considerably from year to year, and there is more in November–December than in other months. The mean annual air temperature is 27.5°C (81.5°F), with a nocturnal minimum of about 26°C and a daytime maximum of 30°C. January is the coolest month. Temperatures, and most weather conditions, are similar in Bonaire, but there is even less precipitation (an annual average of just over 490 mm) and it falls far more unevenly, with much more in the north.

The northern islands have a more subtropical climate, so are slightly cooler. The islands receive more rainfall, but lie firmly in the hurricane belt. Average annual rainfall in all three island territories is about 1,100 mm, but the loftier altitudes of Saba and St Eustatius can receive considerably more. Temperature, too, can vary with altitude, with averages most affected on Saba, which is higher than the other islands and where settlement begins at a greater altitude. Saba is used to 25°C–28°C during the day, but thermometric readings can fall as low as 16°C at night. The other two islands are warmer, but remain milder, though more humid, than the southern islands.

POPULATION

Most of the population are of a mixed black descent (85%), including some claiming descent from the original Amerindians, while the rest are other mestizos, whites and Asians. Roman Catholicism is the largest of the Christian denominations, but Protestants are also well represented, with proportions varying from island to island and the Roman Catholics more dominant on the southern islands. There are also some Jews in the Netherlands Antilles, with Curaçao boasting the oldest synagogue in continuous use in the Americas. Curaçao and Bonaire are also where the cosmopolitan islanders developed the native Papiamento dialect, an eclectic mix of Portuguese, Spanish, Dutch and English evolved from a slave pidgin. In the northern islands English tends to be more generally spoken, and is the first language for many, while Spanish is spoken widely in the south and mainly by immigrant workers from the Dominican Republic in the north. Dutch, however, is the official language of the dependency.

The total population was estimated at 199,926 at 1 January 2009. About 70.9% of the total population lived in Curaçao, 20.5% in St Maarten, 6.4% in Bonaire, 1.4% in St Eustatius and 0.8% in Saba. St Maarten is the most densely populated part of the Netherlands Antilles and Bonaire the least. The capital of the Netherlands Antilles is Willemstad, on Curaçao, where most of that island's population lives (123,355 at mid-2009). The second city of the dependency is Philipsburg, the chief town of St Maarten, where it is located in the south-west of the island, between an inland lake and the Great Bay on the southern coast. The government headquarters and main settlement on Bonaire is Kralendijk (known locally as Playa), on the coast opposite Klein Bonaire, while the second town of the island is the older and more northerly inland settlement of Rincon. Oranjestad, on the west coast of St Eustatius, just to the north-west of The Quill, was once the main port of the entire region, but remains the chief town of Statia. The main settlement on Saba is The Bottom, with fewer than 400 residents.

History

CHARLES ARTHUR

EARLY OCCUPATION

The six island territories known as the Netherlands Antilles were originally inhabited by Arawak Amerindians. Spanish explorers claimed the islands in 1499, but largely ignored the 'three Ss' in the centre of the Caribbean island chain: St Maarten, St Eustatius, and Saba. Conversely, the three 'ABC islands'—Aruba, Bonaire and Curaçao, just 70 km off the coast of Venezuela—were colonized by the Spanish for over 100 years. Early Spanish involvement in the 'ABC islands' consisted mainly of rounding up the Arawak people and transporting them to work as slaves in Hispaniola, and using the islands as a location for rearing livestock. The Dutch took control of Curaçao in 1634 and of Bonaire in 1636, and, after a series of conflicts between the Spanish and the Dutch, Aruba finally passed to Dutch control in 1648. St Maarten, St Eustatius, and Saba were captured by the Dutch in 1630, 1635 and 1640, respectively. As was the case in much of the Caribbean region, control of all the islands frequently changed hands as the colonial powers fought for supremacy, but it was the Dutch who eventually established uncontested sovereignty.

UNDER THE RULE OF THE WEST INDIAN COMPANY

Curaçao became the hub of the Dutch Caribbean empire. It was a strategically important point for Dutch military and naval campaigns against the Spanish, and from 1648 it became the centre of the Dutch slave trade. By the end of the 17th century the majority of slaves transported from Africa to the Caribbean passed through Curaçao. Under the administration of the Dutch West-Indische Compagnie (WIC—West Indian Company), the flourishing trade in slaves, as well as a range of goods, made Curaçao immensely wealthy. In the early 18th century St Eustatius also thrived as a trading centre and transshipment location for African slaves bound for the plantations in the territories today known as Guyana and Suriname. Aruba, Bonaire and Curaçao attracted a range of immigrants from Europe who set up small plantations despite the difficult terrain and climate. The majority came from the Protestant south-west of the Netherlands but significant numbers of Jews escaping persecution in Spain and Portugal also migrated to these islands. Jewish immigrants were particularly successful in the agriculture and banking sectors in Curaçao. The 'S islands' also attracted Dutch Protestant immigrants as well as other white Europeans, particularly Scottish and Irish, and in St Maarten some French. Saba remained sparsely populated because of its difficult terrain, and many of its inhabitants left to find work as sailors. The island of St Maarten was divided between the Dutch and the French in 1648, but conflicts over ownership continued for many decades before finally, in 1817, the current partition line between the Dutch and French territories was established. The Dutch part of the island then prospered as a slave-based plantation economy and a major exporter of salt.

THE SEARCH FOR A NEW DIRECTION

The demise of the transatlantic slave trade during the first decades of the 19th century brought big changes to the islands. The disappearance of the lucrative trade initiated a slow economic decline, and in 1828 the Dutch WIC ceded responsibility for the Netherlands Antilles to the Dutch Crown. In 1845 the islands were consolidated as one colony, named Curaçao and Dependencies, with a Governor appointed by the monarchy (and later by the Dutch Government). When slavery in the Dutch territories was finally abolished in 1863, the plantation system entered a further decline. Although some former slaves continued to work in the plantations, many squatted or rented land and set up as small-scale farmers. Following the commercialization of sugar beet in Europe, the sugar cane sector went into decline in the colony, as it did across the Caribbean. The islands' fortunes did not start to pick up until the early years of the 20th century with the discovery of oil in Venezuela, the South American country neighbouring the 'ABC islands'. In 1915 the Royal Dutch Shell Company set up an oil refinery in Curaçao as a way of avoiding the consequences of expected political instability in Venezuela. Then, in 1929, a subsidiary of the US oil company Exxon opened a refinery in Aruba, also a decision based on the fear of possible nationalization of the oil industry in Venezuela itself. The refineries, and the various businesses that sprung up to serve them, provided economic opportunities and jobs for the inhabitants of Curaçao and the other Antillean islands. There was further economic progress for Curaçao during the Second World War when an influx of US troops—sent to protect oil installations—created the basis for a tourism industry. Even more importantly, Dutch businesses, anticipating the German invasion of the Netherlands, transferred their assets to Curaçao, and gave the impetus to what was to become a thriving 'offshore' finance industry.

AGITATING FOR INDEPENDENCE

In the aftermath of the Second World War, elements within the colony became more vocal in calls for independence from the Netherlands. The Democratische Partij (DP—Democratic Party), founded in 1944, was particularly active on this question. However, greater autonomy was not granted until 1954 when the Dutch Government agreed to allow self-government except in relation to foreign affairs, defence, security and migration. The status of the islands was promoted from that of a colonial territory to part of the Kingdom of the Netherlands as an associated state within a federation. Willemstad in Curaçao became the seat of government of the Netherlands Antilles. In 1986 Aruba left the federation and was granted *status aparte*, meaning that it became a self-governing part of the Kingdom of the Netherlands.

The status of the other islands in relation to the Netherlands has been the main political issue over recent decades. Referendums asking the population for their preferred option were held in the 1990s and produced a conclusive vote in favour of maintaining the federation. However, subsequent ballots held between 2000 and 2005 produced markedly different results, beginning in June 2000 when 69% of voters in St Maarten expressed a preference for obtaining *status aparte* within the Kingdom of the Netherlands. In October 2004 a commission established by the Dutch and Antillean Governments recommended the dissolution of the federation on the grounds that public support for it had more or less evaporated. A further set of referendums held between September 2004 and April 2005 found that a majority of participants in Bonaire (59%) and Saba (86%) were in favour of becoming part of the Netherlands, while 68% of voters in Curaçao favoured *status aparte*. However, in St Eustatius the vote was overwhelmingly in favour of continuing with the federation, receiving the support of 76% of those who participated. On the basis of these results, an inter-island constitutional conference held in late April 2005 recommended the abolition of the federation by July 2007. Curaçao and St Maarten would be granted *status aparte*, and Bonaire, St Eustatius and Saba (the 'BES islands') would come under more direct control of the Netherlands, as *koninkrijkseilanden* (kingdom islands).

DISSOLVING THE FEDERATION

In February 2007 the central Government of the Netherlands Antilles, the Island Councils of Bonaire, Saba and St Eustatius, and the Dutch Government agreed an accord to complete the new relationships by 15 December 2008. However, Curaçao's Island Council did not take part in the agreement, and negotiations continued throughout 2007, centring on Curaçao's acceptance of new judicial arrangements and the Dutch Government's provision of debt relief for all the federation. While the Dutch Government pushed for Curaçao's unequivocal agreement to the new justice, security and administration measures, Curaçao, the most heavily indebted island, insisted on its inclusion in the original Dutch government pledge to assume liability for 85% of the federation's public debt.

Negotiations concerning the details of the transition were marred by controversy, with opposition leaders, in particular in Curaçao, accusing the Dutch authorities of acting in bad faith. As a result, it came as little surprise when the Dutch Secretary of State for the Interior and Kingdom Relations confirmed in early 2008 that the deadline of 15 December for the break-up of the Federation of the Netherlands Antilles was unattainable. A new date—January 2010—was agreed by all parties when a new accord was signed in December 2008. Curaçao and St Maarten would become self-governing (except in matters of defence, foreign policy, judicial and financial matters), and Bonaire, St Eustatius and Saba would gain new status equivalent to that of Dutch municipalities.

However, despite the best efforts of the Dutch and Antillean authorities to further the transition process, including the creation of a specially convened financial supervision body, the College financieel toezicht (CFT), there were further delays. The main problems concerned the cancellation of the debt owed by the Netherlands Antilles to the Netherlands; the establishment of sound financial management; and responsibility for law and order. The CFT began supervising the finances of the respective island councils of Bonaire, St Eustatius and Saba in early 2008, and those of St Maarten and Curaçao at the end of 2008. Some progress was made in resolving the outstanding issues during 2009, and the impetus for the dissolution of the federation was boosted by the results of a referendum vote in Curaçao in May; 52% of voters cast their ballot in support of autonomy for the island. However, while the process of preparing the BES islands for independence progressed well, preparations for Curaçao and St Maarten proved much more difficult and the deadline for the dissolution of the federation was again postponed, until 10 October 2010. New preparatory legislation in advance of the major constitutional changes was approved by the Dutch parliament, but the collapse of the Dutch Government in February 2010 caused fresh delays. Two seminal pieces of legislation yet to be passed concerned pivotal issues regarding the granting of authority to judicial institutions and the police force in Curaçao and St Maarten. Although the authorities in the Netherlands Antilles remained optimistic about the transition process, at mid-2010 a further postponement of the date for final dissolution was under discussion.

THE DOMESTIC SITUATION

Political parties in the Netherlands Antilles are generally based on the individual islands, and few of them have federation-wide appeal. The two parties that have developed the widest appeal are the Partido Antía Restrukturá (PAR—Restructured Antilles Party) and the Partido Nashonal di Pueblo (PNP—National People's Party), both of them based in Curaçao. The fact the Curaçao-based parties regularly control the majority of the Staten's 22 seats causes some resentment from the other islands. The large number of parties winning representation in the Staten means that it is nearly always necessary to put together a coalition in order to form a government.

Following the elections in 1998, a coalition Government comprising the PNP and the Partido Laboral Krusado Popular (Popular Workers' Crusade Party) formed and attempted to implement stringent austerity measures in an effort to revitalize the economy. The measures failed to produce the expected results, and the Government was replaced by a new coalition of nine parties under PAR leadership that took office in late 1999. This Government negotiated a structural adjustment programme with the IMF. In elections in January 2002 the populist Frente Obrero i Liberashon 30 di mei (FOL—Workers' Liberation Front of 30 May), which campaigned against the IMF agreement, made substantial headway, winning 23% of the vote and five of the 22 seats in the Staten. Despite its success, the FOL failed to agree on a coalition and instead the PAR agreed to share power with the PNP and three other parties. The FOL then became mired in controversy when its leader, Anthony Godett, was imprisoned in 2003 on charges of bribery and corruption. Other members of the FOL were also convicted. Godett had been barred from holding public office following the 2002 election win while under investigation on the charges, and when, after the FOL won local elections in May 2003, it succeeded in forming a coalition, his sister, Myrna Godett, was named Prime Minister. However, the FOL-led coalition proved unstable, and Myrna Godett stepped down in April 2004 when four parties withdrew from the alliance, rescinding its majority and leading to another PAR-led coalition Government. In the general election held on 27 January 2006, corruption scandals counted against the FOL and its share of the vote dropped to only 11%, giving it just two seats. The PAR, with 21% of the vote, increased its total by one to five. Its leader, Emily de Jongh-Elhage, took office as Prime Minister at the head of a seven-party coalition with representatives from all five islands. The main coalition partners were the PNP and the St Maarten-based National Alliance (NA). Another Curaçao-based party, the Movimentu Antiyas Nobo (Movement for a New Antilles), was part of the coalition until it was ousted in November 2007, following its opposition to the transition accord with the Netherlands.

In the general election on 22 January 2010 the governing coalition was re-elected with an increased majority, securing 14 of the 22 seats. Opposition parties that had opposed the dissolution plan failed to win crucial cabinet positions. The PAR further increased its total number of seats by one to six, while the NA also gained one seat, giving it a total of three seats. The composition of the new coalition Government remained largely unchanged from that of its predecessor, with only one amendment, namely the absence of the FOL, which lost its two seats.

During the first years of the 21st century drugs-trafficking and associated violent crime developed into a serious issue for the Antillean authorities. The introduction of direct flights between the islands' main airports and Amsterdam, Netherlands, in 2002 was quickly followed by evidence that traffickers were using couriers on the flights to deliver large quantities of cocaine. The islands subsequently became an important transshipment location for cocaine trafficked from producer countries on the South American mainland to markets in North America and Europe. The influx of traffickers and the transshipment of cocaine in large quantities were blamed for a sudden increase in violent crime. The authorities estimated that 75% of all crime on the islands was drugs-related. As the economies of most of the islands depended on tourism, the increase in violent crime was a particular source of concern. A concerted effort to combat the twin scourges of drugs-trafficking and violent crime was taken in conjunction with the Dutch authorities. In particular, the introduction of screening of air passengers to detect couriers produced impressive results—resulting in the apprehension of 6,147 drugs-traffickers between 1 January 2004 and 1 April 2006—and within a short time the number of couriers using air routes out of the Netherlands Antilles was estimated to have dropped significantly.

Economy

CHARLES ARTHUR

In the early 20th century the Netherlands Antilles was heavily reliant on the economic stimulus provided by the construction and operation of foreign oil refineries, but since the 1970s the islands have made some movement towards economic diversification with the development of tourism and financial services sectors. Poor soils and inadequate water supplies have seriously restricted the development of agriculture. The islands possess few natural resources and are dependent to a large extent upon imports, particularly of food and manufactures. According to official estimates prepared in early 2008 as part of calculations to divide the islands' assets and liabilities prior to the projected break-up of the Netherlands Antilles federation, Curaçao accounted for 73.3% of the islands' gross domestic product (GDP), St Maarten 18.8% of GDP, Bonaire 5.8% of GDP, St Eustatius 1.5% of GDP and Saba 0.7% of GDP. In Curaçao, oil-refining, free zone exports, financial services and tourism are the economic mainstays; for the other four islands, tourism is by far the most important economic sector. Despite this lack of economic diversification, the islands enjoy a high per caput income and a well-developed infrastructure compared with other countries in the region.

The secession of Aruba from the federation in 1986 led to political instability and consequent negative economic repercussions, including capital flight. The remaining five islands endured a period of serious recession throughout the 1990s. During this decade the central Government and island administrations made two attempts at fiscal consolidation on the advice of the IMF, but both initiatives failed owing to a lack of political commitment and financing constraints. From the beginning of the 21st century the economy began a slow recovery: in 2001–05 annual GDP growth averaged just 0.4%. Higher growth was impeded by a number of external shocks—including uncertainty over a tax treaty with the USA that depressed activity in the financial sector—as well as a decline in tourism following the terrorist attacks in the USA in September 2001 and the collapse of the national air carrier, Dutch Caribbean Airlines, in 2004. By 2006 the rate of recovery improved, with GDP growing by 2.4%, largely driven by an increase in tourism revenues. St Maarten in particular made a strong recovery from the decline in tourism following the terrorist attacks in 2001, and significantly expanded its hotel capacity. The more encouraging GDP growth rate also reflected positive developments in the private and public sectors, led by the construction, wholesale and retail, and financial services sectors. In 2007 GDP growth climbed to 3.8% as a result of solid domestic demand in the form of higher consumer spending, which in turn reflected increased employment (the unemployment rate fell to 11.5% in 2007, from 18.2% in 2005) and rising wages.

During 2008 the strong increase in commodity and food prices in the first half of the year, and the international financial crisis and its effect on the global economy in the second half of the year, brought the accelerating economy of the Netherlands Antilles to a stuttering halt. GDP growth declined to 2.0% for the year as a whole, as both private and public demand slowed. Private consumption fell as soaring inflation eroded consumers' purchasing power. The inflation rate for 2008 increased to 6.8%, from 2.8% in 2007, driven by the sharp increase in food and fuel prices. During 2009 the impact of the global economic crisis was felt more keenly and consequently economic growth was even weaker, at an estimated 0.6%. Private investment declined, reflecting a downturn in activity across many sectors, including construction, wholesale and retail trade, hotels and restaurants and financial services. The muted economic growth was matched by a sharp decline in inflation; although prices began to rise towards the end of 2009, the annual average rate stood at just 1.8%

TOURISM

Although the Netherlands Antilles has little to offer in the way of marketable natural resources—with the exception of popular diving sites off the coast of Bonaire—tourism is the economic mainstay. It is a major source of foreign exchange earnings and an important provider of employment. In recent years there have been major investment projects, including several large hotel complexes in St Maarten and Curaçao, a 'mega-pier' at the entrance to the Curaçao harbour, and new terminals at Curaçao's Hato International Airport and St Maarten's Princess Juliana Airport. The most popular destination in the federation is St Maarten, the main attractions of which are its fine beaches and duty-free shopping opportunities; the island also benefits from a recently upgraded international airport and a number of US hotel chains. By contrast, the neighbouring islands of Saba and St Eustatius have small tourism industries. The main sources of tourist visitors to the Netherlands Antilles are the USA, the Netherlands and Venezuela.

In 2008, despite concerns about the sector's prospects in the context of the escalating cost of aviation fuel and a steadily rising crime rate, tourist arrivals continued to increase, with the number of stay-over passengers reaching 970,680, representing a year-on-year expansion of some 12.6%. Curaçao was the main contributor to this growth, recording a massive year-on-year increase of 34%, mainly as a result of more tourists from Venezuela and Europe. The vast increase in the number of Venezuelan tourists reflected the great disparity between the 'black market' exchange rate and the rate in Venezuela, while the rise in the number of European visitors can be explained by appreciation of the euro against the Netherlands Antillean gilder. Cruise tourism recorded only a moderate increase in 2008, with large growth in Bonaire, slight growth in Curaçao, and a decline in St Maarten. In 2009 the tourism sector experienced a decline but weathered the economic storm more successfully than other Caribbean destinations. A decline in tourist arrivals from North America and the rest of the Caribbean tempered an increase in arrivals from Europe and South America. In December the inaugural arrival of the world's largest cruise liner—Royal Caribbean International's *Oasis of the Seas*—in Philipsburg, St Maarten, provided a welcome break for the cruise sector. With the average per caput spend of cruise passengers visiting St Maarten estimated at US $148, the island authorities were confident that a recent $100m. investment in a new pier to receive the 5,400-passenger ship would soon pay dividends.

FINANCIAL SERVICES

The early 1990s brought steady growth of the 'offshore' financial sector—driven partly by the deregulation of the financial services industry—and many foreign banks set up in Curaçao to offer specialized 'offshore' banking facilities. The majority of transactions in the 'offshore' financial sector were legal, but in the mid-1990s there was growing concern on the international level about the prevalence of money-laundering operations, many of them involving drugs-traffickers. From 1997 a central reporting centre to monitor large financial transactions was put into operation in an effort to deter money-launderers. Despite this and other supervisory and regulatory moves, in June 2000 the Organisation for Economic Co-operation and Development (OECD) included the Netherlands Antilles on a list of countries deemed to be operating 'un-co-operative tax havens'. Action by the authorities to improve accountability and transparency of the financial services sector resulted in OECD removing the federation from the list in 2002. It was anticipated that as a result of the elimination of 'harmful tax practices' new business would develop, but progress has been slow. In April 2009 OECD published a report that included the Netherlands Antilles on a 'grey list' of countries that it deemed to have failed to meet international standards in the supervision of their financial services sector, despite co-operating with efforts to improve transparency. The Netherlands Antilles signed information-sharing agreements with 14 other countries in the second half of the year and thus secured removal from the 'grey list' in September. In 2008 the federation's international financial services sector registered a decline, related mainly to the impact of the international financial crisis.

PETROLEUM INDUSTRY

The refining industry peaked in the mid-20th century when refineries processed crude petroleum from Venezuela and shipped the refined products to the USA. In the 1970s the sector diversified into transshipment and oil storage. The transshipment sector revolved around the construction of terminals to handle the huge oil tankers that, because of their size, could not deliver direct to the USA. In the 1980s the terminal at Bullen Bay in Curaçao, then one of the world's largest, and the smaller ones in Bonaire and St Eustatius, made as much revenue as the refineries. However, in the mid-1980s the construction of large offshore terminals in the Gulf of Mexico and on the eastern US seaboard, the drop in oil prices, and the lowering of Venezuelan oil output made the Antillean oil-processing industry unprofitable. In 1985 the Government took ownership of the Curaçao-based refinery, originally built by the Royal Dutch-Shell Company, and it was eventually leased to the Venezuelan state oil producer, Petróleos de Venezuela, SA (PDVSA), which adapted it to process Venezuelan heavy crude oil. The refinery, known as Refinería Isla, has succeeded in increasing efficiency in recent years through extensive reductions in the number of workers on the payroll. Average production levels increased from 208,000 barrels per day (b/d) in 1999 to 335,000 b/d in 2004, before slipping back again in 2005 to 320,000 b/d as investment, which was deemed necessary to upgrade the refinery's products and meet new international environmental standards, stalled owing to uncertainty over the long-term leasehold.

During 2008 frequent plant shut-downs, partly owing to the obsolete state of the refinery, resulted in a decline in production. The urgent need for sizeable investments to upgrade the refinery was underlined in May 2009 when a local court ruled that the excessive emissions of sulphur dioxide from the refinery were damaging local people's health and that the PDVSA must reduce these emissions or face multi-million dollar fines. There were further problems in early 2010 when a strike by the refinery's 1,000 workers forced the closure of the facility for 10 days. The strike was in protest at the poor state of the refinery's power supply and to register their concerns that the PDVSA would end its lease and that the refinery would be closed down.

TRANSPORT AND INFRASTRUCTURE

The transport sector, a major contributor to the economy, is based around the port of Willemstad in Curaçao, one of the largest harbours in the world. The port houses most of the shipping facilities available on the island. Cruise ships dock at various cruise terminals on the side of the bay, at the end of which lie the port's main facilities, including the largest oil refinery in the Caribbean, a dry dock, an economic free zone area, a modern container terminal and cargo wharves. There are a further six ports on Curaçao, whose amenities include an oil terminal, deep-water facilities, and yachting facilities. Prospects for Curaçao's ship repair company, the Curaçao Drydock Company (CDM), have improved since 1999, when it decided to focus activities on the repair of large vessels and cruise ships. An average of 700–800 employees work at the CDM at any one time, with the level rising occasionally to 1,000 workers. Although an increase in activities in the ship-repair industry helped the CDM to prosper in 2008, it requires significant investment in order to upgrade its facilities if it is to remain viable. St Maarten, which is one of the Caribbean's leading ports for visits by cruise ships, has new pier facilities that can accommodate up to four cruise liners at the same time. It also has a large cargo port facility. Bonaire also has a cruise port, and St Eustatius and Saba have small cargo ports.

There are no railways on any of the islands, but the road network is generally in good condition. As of 2004 there were 845 km of roadway, of which 31% was paved. In terms of air travel, there are international airports on Curaçao, Bonaire and St Maarten. Dutch Antilles Express, a regional airline based at Hato International Airport, Curaçao, operates scheduled services in the Dutch Caribbean and to Venezuela. There are two small companies providing charter flights to and from St Eustatius and Saba.

As in many Caribbean islands, the telecommunications sector has been transformed by the rapid increase in the widespread use of mobile phones and the internet. As plans to privatize the state-owned telecommunications company, United Telecom Services, have long been delayed, other private companies have entered the market. Digicel in particular has made significant inroads into the mobile phone sector. The company launched itself in Aruba in 2002, and acquired Curaçao Telecom in March 2005. Then, in April 2006, Digicel acquired a majority shareholding in Antilliano Por NV, the entity that holds a business licence to operate telecommunications in Bonaire, and it became the first operator to connect all three of the 'ABC islands'.

AGRICULTURE AND MANUFACTURING

Owing to the scarcity of arable land, an unsuitable climate, and poor soil quality, the agriculture sector is very small. Locally produced crops, mainly fruit and vegetables, are consumed domestically, and the islands are heavily dependent on food imports. On Bonaire and Curaçao fresh water is in short supply and is manufactured, at a price, at desalination plants. As a result, irrigation is prohibitively expensive. St Maarten is the only island with a commercial, albeit small, fishing sector. Agriculture and fishing (there is no mining in the Netherlands Antilles) usually contributes less than 1% to annual GDP. Manufacturing is also a small-scale concern, contributing just 5.5% to annual GDP in 2008. The main sectors are food-processing, the production of the Curaçao liqueur, and the manufacture of paper, plastics and textiles.

TRADE AND BALANCE OF PAYMENTS

Other than refined oil products and a free zone specializing in semi-processing and re-exports, the Netherlands Antilles does not have much by way of an export sector. As on most Caribbean islands, the need for imported food and manufactures heavily outweighs export earnings and the merchandise trade balance always registers a large deficit. Almost all consumer and capital goods are imported, with Venezuela, the USA, and Mexico being the major suppliers. In recent years exports have benefited from solid growth in the USA, the strong recovery in Venezuela, and increased attractiveness in European tourism markets owing to the euro appreciation. However, at the same time, imports have risen sharply, partly owing to higher oil prices, but also as a result of the import of merchandise by companies operating in the free zone. In 2008 the balance of payments deficit continued to increase as a result of a strong growth in imports, which in turn resulted from sharp increases in commodity and food prices, continued strong investment growth, the favourable performance of tourism, and increased imports to the free zones. In 2009 the trade deficit narrowed again as declining private investment and consumption slowed import demand, outpacing the decline in demand for exports.

FINANCES

In 2005 public finances started to show signs of improvement, but the reduction in the overall budget deficit was entirely due to a one-off windfall (dividend tax revenues from the Netherlands), while the underlying fiscal situation had not improved. The debt ratio of the general Government (including island governments) reached 86% of GDP. In 2006 the budgets of the central Government and the island Government of Curaçao fell short of what was necessary to make an impact upon public debt, and in 2007, although the islands took on little new external debt, the public debt ratios rose, owing to euro appreciation against the US dollar. Public debt rose by NA Fl. 438m. (US $245m.) in that year, reaching NA Fl. 5,400m. ($3,000m., equivalent to 84% of GDP). The federation's central bank expects debt relief, provided by the Netherlands under the plan to dissolve the federation in 2010, to have a significant beneficial effect on the public finances, enabling the Netherlands Antilles Government to reduce the budget deficit significantly as a result of lower interest payments on outstanding public debt. Debt cancellation began in February 2009, and, in accordance with agreements reached, 100% of the capital and 70% of the interest payable on the public debt was to be met by the Netherlands. This led to a marked improvement in the fiscal balance, and a surplus was recorded in 2009.

OUTLOOK

The economic future of the Netherlands Antilles is closely connected to the projected disbanding of the federation, which is now expected to occur in late 2010 or, more likely, in 2011. Curaçao and St Maarten will become fully self-governing, except in matters of defence, foreign policy, and judicial and financial matters, which will be the responsibility of the Dutch Government, while the three smaller islands—Bonaire, St Eustatius and Saba—will become Dutch municipalities. The economy contracted in 2009 as falling global demand hit trade and tourism, and investment flows decreased in the context of the global financial crisis. While there were signs that the economic downturn might have bottomed out in late 2009, with only modest economic recoveries forecast for the USA and Europe in 2010, the growth prospects for the Netherlands Antilles are not bright. Tourism is unlikely to make a strong recovery owing to concerns regarding job security in North America and Europe, and this will continue to deter further investment in the sector.

Statistical Survey

Sources (unless otherwise stated): Centraal Bureau voor de Statistiek, Fort Amsterdam, Willemstad, Curaçao; tel. (9) 461-1031; fax (9) 461-1696; internet www.central-bureau-of-statistics.an; Bank van de Nederlandse Antillen, Simon Bolivar Plein 1, Willemstad, Curaçao; tel. (9) 434-5500; fax (9) 461-5004; e-mail info@centralbank.an; internet www.centralbank.an.

AREA AND POPULATION

Area (sq km): Curaçao 444; Bonaire 288; St Maarten (Dutch sector) 34; St Eustatius 21; Saba 13; Total 800 (309 sq miles).

Population: 189,474 at census of 27 January 1992 (excluding adjustment for underenumeration, estimated at 3.2%); 175,653 (males 82,521, females 93,132) at census of 29 January 2001; 199,926 at 1 January 2009 (official estimate). *By Island* (official estimates at 1 January 2009): Curaçao 141,766; Bonaire 12,877; St Maarten (Dutch sector) 40,917; St Eustatius 2,768; Saba 1,601.

Density (per sq km at 1 January 2009): 249.9. *By Island:* Curaçao 319.3; Bonaire 44.7; St Maarten (Dutch sector) 1,203.4; St Eustatius 131.8; Saba 123.2.

Population by Age and Sex (official estimates at 1 January 2009): *0–14:* 43,578 (males 22,105, females 21,472); *15–64:* 136,582 (males 63,116, females 73,467); *65 and over:* 19,766 (males 8,118, females 11,648); *Total* 199,926 (males 93,339, females 106,587).

Principal Town: Willemstad (capital), population (incl. suburbs, UN estimate) 123,355 at mid-2009. Source: UN, *World Urbanization Prospects: The 2009 Revision*.

Births, Marriages and Deaths (2008 unless otherwise indicated): Registered live births 2,765 (birth rate 14.2 per 1,000); Registered marriages 1,104 (marriage rate 5.8 per 1,000) in 2006; Registered deaths 1,453 (death rate 7.3 per 1,000).

Life Expectancy (years at birth): 76.4 (males 72.9; females 79.6) in 2009. Source: Pan American Health Organization.

Economically Active Population (sample survey, Curaçao only, persons aged 15 years and over, average 2006–08): Agriculture, forestry, fishing and mining 727; Manufacturing 3,958; Electricity, gas and water 839; Construction 4,691; Wholesale and retail trade, repairs 9,718; Hotels and restaurants 4,546; Transport, storage and communications 3,885; Financial intermediation 4,194; Real estate, renting and business activities 5,929; Public administration, defence and social security 5,093; Education 2,730; Health and social work 4,631; Other community, social and personal services 3,529; Private households with employed persons 2,008; Extra-territorial organizations and bodies 57; *Total employed* 56,535; Unemployed 6,486; *Total labour force* 63,021.

HEALTH AND WELFARE

Total Fertility Rate (children per woman, 2009): 2.0.

Under-5 Mortality Rate (per 1,000 live births, 2009): 13.8.

Physicians (per 1,000 head, 1999): 1.4.

Hospital Beds (per 1,000 head, 2002): 7.24.

Health Expenditure (% of GDP, 2005): 4.8.

Total Carbon Dioxide Emissions ('000 metric tons, 2006): 4,308.9.

Total Carbon Dioxide Emissions Per Head (metric tons, 2006): 22.8.

Source: mostly Pan American Health Organization.

For other sources and definitions, see explanatory note on p. vi.

AGRICULTURE, ETC.

Livestock ('000 head, year ending September 2008, FAO estimates): Cattle 0.7; Pigs 2.6; Goats 13.6; Sheep 9.1; Chickens 140.

Livestock Products (metric tons, 2008, FAO estimates): Pig meat 189; Chicken meat 300; Cows' milk 450; Hen eggs 530.

Fishing (metric tons, live weight, 2008): Skipjack tuna 6,436; Yellowfin tuna 7,351; Bigeye tuna 1,721; *Total catch* (incl. others) 16,698 (FAO estimate).

Source: FAO.

MINING

Production ('000 metric tons, estimate): Salt 500 in 2003–08. Source: US Geological Survey.

INDUSTRY

Production ('000 metric tons, 2007, unless otherwise indicated): Jet fuel 783; Kerosene 46 (2004); Residual fuel oils 4,056; Lubricating oils 327; Petroleum bitumen (asphalt) 1,128; Liquefied petroleum gas, refined 83; Motor spirit (petrol) 1,987; Aviation gasoline 18; Distillate fuel oils (gas-diesel oil) 2,350; Sulphur (recovered) 23 (2008); Electric energy (million kWh) 1,294.

Sources: mainly UN Industrial Commodity Statistics Database and Yearbook, and US Geological Survey.

FINANCE

Currency and Exchange Rates: 100 cents = 1 Netherlands Antilles gulden (guilder) or florin (NA Fl.). *Sterling, Dollar and Euro Equivalents* (31 May 2010): £1 sterling = NA Fl. 2.610; US $1 = NA Fl. 1.790; €1 = NA Fl. 2.217; NA Fl. 100 = £38.32 = $55.87 = €45.11. *Exchange Rate:* In December 1971 the central bank's mid-point rate was fixed at US $1 = NA Fl. 1.80. In 1989 this was adjusted to $1 = NA Fl. 1.79. The US dollar also circulates on St Maarten. In December 2009 it was announced that the US dollar would replace the Netherlands Antilles guilder and florin in Bonaire, St Eustatius and Saba from 1 January 2011, following the planned dissolution of the existing federation of the Netherlands Antilles in October 2010.

Central Government Budget (NA Fl. million, 2009): *Revenue:* Tax revenue 788.8 (Taxes on property 40.4, Taxes on goods and services 559.2, Taxes on international trade and transactions 179.9, Other taxes 9.3); Non-tax revenue 105.6 (Entrepreneurial and property income 90.1, Administrative fees and charges, non-industrial and incidental sales 10.3, Other 5.2); Grants (from other levels of government, excluding overseas development aid) 571.5; Total 1,465.9. *Expenditure:* Wages and salaries 342.4; Other goods and services 123.5; Interest payments 170.9; Subsidies 0.0; Current transfers 427.4; Capital expenditure (incl. transfers and net lending) 37.2; Total 1,101.4.

International Reserves (US $ million at 31 December 2009): Gold (national valuation) 356; Foreign exchange 867; Total 1,223. Source: IMF, *International Financial Statistics*.

Money Supply (NA Fl. million at 31 December 2009): Currency outside banks 334.1; Demand deposits at commercial banks 2,106.0; Total (incl. others) 2,440.1. Source: IMF, *International Financial Statistics*.

Cost of Living (Consumer Price Index; base: 2005 = 100): All items 106.3 in 2007; 113.6 in 2008; 115.6 in 2009. Source: IMF, *International Financial Statistics*.

Gross Domestic Product (US $ million at constant 1990 prices): 2,385 in 2006; 2,449 in 2007; 2,504 in 2008. Source: UN Statistics Division, National Accounts Main Aggregates Database.

Expenditure on the Gross Domestic Product (million NA Fl. at current prices, 2008): Final consumption expenditure 5,208 (Government 1,302, Households and non-profit institutions serving households 3,905); Gross fixed capital formation 1,934; Change in inventories –53; *Total domestic expenditure* 7,089; Exports of goods and services 5,302; *Less* Imports of goods and services 5,613; Statistical discrepancy 41; *GDP in market prices* 6,819. Source: UN Statistics Division, National Accounts Main Aggregates Database.

Gross Domestic Product (million NA Fl. at current prices, 2008): Agriculture, hunting, forestry and fishing 46.0; Mining, electricity, gas and water 278.4; Manufacturing 381.5; Construction 357.7; Trade, restaurants and hotels 1,106.4; Transport, storage and communications 630.1; Other activities 3,563.4; *Sub-total* 6,363.7; Net of indirect taxes 455.9 (obtained as a residual); *GDP in purchasers' values* 6,819.4. Source: UN National Accounts Main Aggregates Database.

Balance of Payments (US $ million, 2007): Exports of goods f.o.b. 676.5; Imports of goods f.o.b. –2,543.2; *Trade balance* –1,866.7; Exports of services 2,099.7; Imports of services –802.6; *Balance on goods and services* –569.6; Other income received 175.8; Other income paid –165.6; *Balance on goods, services and income* –559.4; Current transfers received 296.4; Current transfers paid –326.8; *Current balance* –589.7; Capital account (net) 121.6; Direct investment abroad 3.2; Direct investment from abroad 231.8; Portfolio investment assets –67.9; Portfolio investment liabilities –9.6; Financial derivatives assets –4.2; Other investment assets 427.7; Other investment liabilities –66.2; Net errors and omissions 82.4; *Overall balance* 129.2. Source: IMF, *International Financial Statistics*.

EXTERNAL TRADE

Principal Commodities (US $ million, distribution by HS, 2008): *Imports c.i.f.:* Meat and edible meat offal 43.3; Beverages, spirits and vinegar 43.6; Pharmaceutical products 56.2; Products of iron or steel 57.7; Nuclear reactors, boilers, machinery, etc. 171.2; Electrical and electronic equipment 136.3; Vehicles other than railway, tramway 128.8; Total (incl. others) 1,437.0. *Exports f.o.b.:* Cocoa and cocoa preparations 16.0; Miscellaneous edible preparations 10.4; Salt, sulphur, earth, stone, etc. 6.5; Soaps, lubricants, waxes, candles and modelling pastes 4.8; Pearls, precious stones, metals, coins, etc. 15.3; Nuclear reactors, boilers, machinery, etc. 16.1; Electrical and electronic equipment 5.2; Vehicles other than railway, tramway 6.7; Aircraft, spacecraft, and parts thereof 18.8; Optical, photo, technical and medical apparatus 4.7; Total (incl. others) 146.2. Source: Trade Map-Trade Competitiveness Map, International Trade Centre, www.intracen.org/marketanalysis.

Principal Trading Partners (US $ million, 2008): *Imports c.i.f.:* Aruba 24.1; Brazil 30.0; China, People's Republic 30.5; Colombia 37.3; Germany 17.0; Hong Kong 14.4; Japan 39.0; Korea, Republic 20.7; Netherlands 332.3; Panama 51.8; USA 566.1; Venezuela 51.6; Total (incl. others) 1,437.0. *Exports f.o.b.:* Antigua and Barbuda 2.1; Aruba 14.9; Belgium 1.5; Canada 1.7; France 1.7; Germany 4.0; Namibia 2.2; Netherlands 50.0; USA 33.6; Venezuela 3.7; Total (incl. others) 146.2. Source: Trade Map-Trade Competitiveness Map, International Trade Centre, www.intracen.org/marketanalysis.

TRANSPORT

Road Traffic (Curaçao and Bonaire, motor vehicles registered, excl. government-owned vehicles, 2008): Passenger cars 82,281; Lorries 18,458; Buses 460; Taxis 220; Other cars 296; Motorcycles 2,457.

Shipping: *International Sea-borne Freight Traffic* (Curaçao, TEUs moved, 2008): 102,082. *Merchant Fleet* (registered at 31 December 2008): Number of vessels 201; Total displacement 1,564,166 grt (Source: Lloyd's Register-Fairplay, *World Fleet Statistics*).

Civil Aviation (aircraft landings, 2008): *Bonaire* 16,908 (Commercial 14,843). *Curaçao* 22,373 (Commercial 18,461).

TOURISM

Tourist Arrivals: *Stop-overs*: 782,249 in 2006; 862,102 in 2007; 970,680 in 2008. *Cruise ship passengers* (Bonaire, Curaçao and St Maarten only): 1,805,040 in 2006; 1,860,448 in 2007; 1,873,411 in 2008.

Tourism Receipts (NA Fl. million, incl. passenger transport): 1,683.5 in 2002; 1,761.0 in 2003; 1,906.5 in 2004.

COMMUNICATIONS MEDIA

Radio Receivers (1997): 217,000 in use.

Television Receivers (1999): 71,000 in use.

Telephones (2009): 89,000 main lines in use.

Mobile Cellular Telephones (2008): 200,000 subscribers.

Internet Users (1999, UN estimate): 2,000.

Daily Newspapers: 6 titles (estimated circulation 70,000 copies per issue) in 1996; 5 in 2004.

Sources: UNESCO, *Statistical Yearbook*; UNESCO Institute for Statistics; UN, *Statistical Yearbook*; International Telecommunication Union.

EDUCATION

Pre-primary (2002/03): 5,972 pupils; 309 teachers.

Primary (2002/03): 22,667 pupils; 1,145 teachers.

General Secondary (2002/03): 9,180 pupils; 639 teachers.

Vocational (2002/03): 6,088 pupils; 542 teachers.

Tertiary (2001/02): 2,285 students; 340 teachers.

English Language Secondary (2000/01): 377 pupils.

Special Education (2000/01): 2,337 pupils; 178 teachers.

Teacher Training (2000/01): 133 students; 22 teachers.

Pupil-teacher Ratio (primary education, UNESCO estimate): 19.8 in 2002/03.

Adult Literacy Rate (2008, UNESCO estimates): 96.3% (males 96.3%; females 96.3%).

Source: partly UNESCO Institute for Statistics.

Directory

The Constitution

The form of government for the Netherlands Antilles is embodied in the Charter of the Kingdom of the Netherlands, which came into force on 20 December 1954. The Netherlands, the Netherlands Antilles and, since 1986, Aruba each enjoy full autonomy in domestic and internal affairs and are united on a basis of equality for the protection of their common interests and the granting of mutual assistance.

The monarch of the Netherlands is represented in the Netherlands Antilles by the Governor, who is appointed by the Dutch Crown for a term of six years. The central Government of the Netherlands Antilles appoints a Minister Plenipotentiary to represent the Antilles in the Government of the Kingdom. Whenever the Netherlands Council of Ministers is dealing with matters coming under the heading of joint affairs of the realm (in practice mainly foreign affairs and defence), the Council assumes the status of Council of Ministers of the Kingdom. In that event, the Minister Plenipotentiary appointed by the Government of the Netherlands Antilles takes part, with full voting powers, in the deliberations.

A legislative proposal regarding affairs of the realm and applying to the Netherlands Antilles as well as to the 'metropolitan' Netherlands is sent, simultaneously with its submission, to the Staten Generaal (the Netherlands parliament) and to the Staten (parliament) of the Netherlands Antilles. The latter body can report in writing to the Staten Generaal on the draft Kingdom Statute and designate one or more special delegates to attend the debates and furnish information in the meetings of the Chambers of the Staten Generaal. Before the final vote on a draft the Minister Plenipotentiary has the right to express an opinion on it. If he disapproves of the draft, and if in the Second Chamber a three-fifths' majority of the votes cast is not obtained, the discussions on the draft are suspended and further deliberations take place in the Council of Ministers of the Kingdom. When special delegates attend the meetings of the Chambers this right devolves upon the delegates of the parliamentary body designated for this purpose.

The Governor has executive power in external affairs, which he exercises in co-operation with the Council of Ministers. He is assisted by an advisory council, which consists of at least five members appointed by him.

Executive power in internal affairs is vested in the nominated Council of Ministers, responsible to the Staten. The Netherlands Antilles Staten consists of 22 members, who are elected by universal adult suffrage for four years (subject to dissolution). Each island forms an electoral district. Curaçao elects 14 members, Bonaire three members, St Maarten three members and Saba and St Eustatius one member each. In the islands where more than one member is elected, the election is by proportional representation. Inhabitants have the right to vote if they have Dutch nationality and have reached 18 years of age. Voting is not compulsory. Each island territory also elects its Island Council (Curaçao 21 members, Bonaire 9, St Maarten 7, St Eustatius and Saba 5), and its internal affairs are managed by an executive council, consisting of the Gezaghebber (Lieutenant-Governor), and a number of commissioners. The central Government of the Netherlands Antilles has the right to annul any local island decision which is in conflict with the public interest or the Constitution. Control of the police, communications, monetary affairs, health and education remain under the jurisdiction of the central Government.

On 1 January 1986 Aruba acquired separate status (*status aparte*) within the Kingdom of the Netherlands. However, in economic and monetary affairs there is a co-operative union between Aruba and the Antilles of the Five, known as the 'Union of the Netherlands Antilles and Aruba'.

The islands of Saba, Bonaire and St Eustatius ratified an agreement with the Government of the Netherlands on 12 October 2006 under which they would be redesignated as 'special municipalities' of the Kingdom of the Netherlands. A further accord was signed by St Maarten and Curaçao on 28 November 2006 and 9 July 2007, respectively, confirming these islands' secession from the federation to achieve a degree of independent governance and status similar to that enjoyed by Aruba. The transition process was ongoing in mid-2010, with final dissolution of the Netherlands Antilles scheduled to take place on 10 October.

The Government

HEAD OF STATE

Queen of the Netherlands: HM Queen BEATRIX.

Governor: Dr FRITZ M. DE LOS SANTOS GOEDGEDRAG.

COUNCIL OF MINISTERS
(July 2010)

The Government is formed by a coalition of the Partido Antía Restrukturá (PAR), the National Alliance (NA), the Unión Patriótico Bonairiano (UPB), the Democratic Partij—Statia (DP—StE), the Partido Nashonal di Pueblo (PNP) and the Windward Islands People's Movement (WIPM).

Prime Minister and Minister of General Affairs and Foreign Relations: EMILY DE JONGH-ELHAGE (PAR).

First Deputy Prime Minister and Minister of Constitutional Affairs and the Interior: ROLAND E. DUNCAN (NA).

Second Deputy Prime Minister and Minister of Economic Affairs and Labour: ELVIS E. J. TJIN ASJOE (UPB).

Minister of Finance: ERSILIA T. M. DE LANNOOY (PNP).

Minister of Justice: MAGALI JACOBA (PAR).

Minister of Education and Culture and of Public Health and Social Development: OMAYRA VICTORIA ELISABETH LEEFLANG (PAR).

Minister of Transport and Telecommunications: PATRICK ILLIDGE (NA).

State Secretary of the Interior: FELIX THOMAS (UPB).

State Secretary of Constitutional Affairs: SHAMARA NICHOLSON-LINZEY (WIPM).

State Secretary of Justice, with responsibility for Police Affairs and the Penal Institution of the Windward Isles: ERNIE C. SIMMONS (DP—StE).

Minister Plenipotentiary and Member of the Council of Ministers for the Realm of the Netherlands Antilles in the Netherlands: MARCEL VAN DER PLANK (PAR).

Minister Plenipotentiary for the Realm of the Netherlands Antilles in Washington, DC (USA): ANN GROOT-PHILIPPS.

Attorney-General of the Netherlands Antilles: DICK A. PIAR.

MINISTRIES

Office of the Governor: Fort Amsterdam 2, Willemstad, Curaçao; tel. (9) 461-1289; fax (9) 461-1412; e-mail rojer@kgna.an; internet www.gouverneur.an.

Ministry of Constitutional Affairs and the Interior: Fort Amsterdam 1, Willemstad, Curaçao.

Ministry of Economic Affairs and Labour: Directorate of Labour, Schouwburgweg 22, Willemstad, Curaçao; tel. (9) 461-9999; fax (9) 461-5553; e-mail info@diraz.an; internet www.diraz.an.

Ministry of Education and Culture: Schouwburgweg 24–26 (APNA Bldg), Willemstad, Curaçao; tel. (9) 434-3711; fax (9) 462-4471; e-mail minoc@gov.an; internet www.minoc.an.

Ministry of Finance: Pietermaai 17, Willemstad, Curaçao; tel. (9) 432-8242; fax (9) 461-3339; e-mail g.d.dirfin@curinfo.an.

Ministry of Foreign Relations: 4 Fort Amsterdam, Willemstad, Curaçao; tel. (9) 461-3933; fax (9) 461-7123; e-mail verdragen.dbb@gov.an.

Ministry of Justice: Willhelminaplein, Willemstad, Curaçao; tel. (9) 463-0650; fax (9) 465-8083.

Ministry of Public Health and Social Development: Fort Amsterdam 1, Willemstad, Curaçao; Dept of Health, Santa Rosaweg 122, Willemstad, Curaçao; tel. (9) 736-3530; e-mail vornil@cura.net; Dept of Social Devt, Kaya Flamboyan 22, Willemstad, Curaçao; tel. (9) 736-7266; fax (9) 736-7479; e-mail dwghz@attglobal.net.

Ministry of Transport and Telecommunications: Fort Amsterdam 17, Willemstad, Curaçao; tel. (9) 463-0461; fax 461-5420; e-mail mhpadriaens@yahoo.com.

Office of the Minister Plenipotentiary for the Netherlands Antilles: Kabinet van de Gevolmachtigde Minister van de Nederlanse Antillen, Badhuisweg 175, POB 90706, 2509 LS The Hague, Netherlands; tel. (70) 3066111; fax (70) 3066110; e-mail info@antillenhuis.nl; internet www.antillenhuis.nl.

GEZAGHEBBERS
(Lieutenant-Governors)

Bonaire: GLENN A. E. THODE, Bestuurskantoor, Wilhelminaplein 1, Kralendijk, Bonaire; tel. 717-5330; fax 717-8416; e-mail gezag@bonairelive.com.

Curaçao: LIZANNE M. RICHARDS-DINDIAL, Breedestraat 39C, Willemstad, Curaçao; tel. (9) 433-3131; fax (9) 433-3130; e-mail info@curacao-gov.an; internet www.curacao-gov.an.

Saba: JONATHAN JOHNSON, 1 Power St, The Bottom, Saba; tel. 416-3311; fax 416-3274; e-mail lt.gov@sabagov.com; internet www.sabagovernment.com.

St Eustatius: GERARD BERKEL, Oranjestad, St Eustatius; tel. 318-2552; fax 318-2324; e-mail lt.governor@statiagovernment.com; internet www.statiagovernment.com.

St Maarten: FRANKLYN E. RICHARDS, Government Administration Bldg, Clem Labega Sq., POB 943, Philipsburg, St Maarten; tel. 542-6085; fax 542-4172; e-mail dircab@governorsxm.com; internet www.governorsxm.com.

Legislature

STATEN

Speaker: PEDRO ATACHO.

General Election, 22 January 2010

Party	Seats
Partido Antía Restrukturá	6
Lista di Kambio*	5
National Alliance	3
Unión Patriótico Bonairiano	2
Pueblo Soberano	2
Partido Nashonal di Pueblo	1
Windward Islands People's Movement	1
Democratische Partij—Statia	1
Democratische Partij—Bonaire	1
Total	22

* Comprising the Movimentu Antiyas Nobo, the Forsa Kòrsou and Niun Paso Atras.

Political Organizations

Democratische Partij—Bonaire (DP—B) (Democratic Party—Bonaire): Kaya America 13A, POB 294, Kralendijk, Bonaire; tel. 717-8903; fax 717-5923; f. 1954; also known as Partido Democratico Boneriano; liberal; Leader JOPIE ABRAHAM.

Democratische Partij—Curaçao (DP—C) (Democratic Party—Curaçao): Neptunusweg 28, Willemstad, Curaçao; f. 1944; Leader NORBERT GEORGE.

Democratische Partij—Sint Maarten (DP—StM): Tamarind Tree Dr. 4, Union Rd, Cole Bay, St Maarten; tel. 543-1166; fax 542-4296; Leader SARAH WESCOTT-WILLIAMS.

Democratische Partij—Statia (DP—StE): Oranjestad, St Eustatius; Leader JULIAN WOODLEY.

Frente Obrero i Liberashon 30 di mei (FOL) (Workers' Liberation Front of 30 May): Mayaguanaweg 16, Willemstad, Curaçao; tel. (9) 461-8105; f. 1969; socialist; Leader ANTHONY GODETT.

Lista di Kambio (LdK) (List of Change): Willemstad, Curaçao; electoral alliance; Leader CHARLES COOPER.

Forsa Kòrsou: F. D. Rooseveltweg 347, Willemstad, Curaçao; tel. (9) 888-3041; fax (9) 888-3504; e-mail forsakorsou@onenet.an; internet www.forsakorsou.com; Pres. NELSON NAVARRO; Leader GREGORY DAMOEN.

Movimentu Antiyas Nobo (MAN) (Movement for a New Antilles): Landhuis Morgenster, Willemstad, Curaçao; tel. (9) 468-4781; internet www.new.partidoman.org; f. 1971; socialist; Pres. EUGENE CLEOPA; Sec.-Gen. GIOVANNI ATALITA.

Niun Paso Atras: Willemstad, Curaçao; Leader NELSON PIERRE.

National Alliance (NA): Philipsburg, St Maarten; internet www.sxmnationalalliance.org; comprises the Sint Maarten Patriotic Alliance and the National Progressive Party; Leader WILLIAM MARLIN.

Partido Antía Restrukturá (PAR) (Restructured Antilles Party): Fokkerweg 26, Unit 3, Willemstad, Curaçao; tel. (9) 465-2566; fax (9) 465-2622; e-mail omi7@ibm.net; internet www.cura.net/archives/par/frame.html; f. 1993; social-Christian ideology; Leader MIGUEL ARCHANGEL POURIER; Pres. GLENN SULVARAN.

Partido Laboral Krusado Popular (PLKP): Winston Churchillweg 57, Willemstad, Curaçao; tel. (9) 868-1924; internet www.plkp.an; f. 1997; progressive; Leader ERROL A. COVA.

Partido Nashonal di Pueblo (PNP) (National People's Party): Winston Churchillweg 133, Willemstad, Curaçao; tel. (9) 869-6777; fax (9) 869-6688; f. 1958; also known as Nationale Volkspartij; social-Christian party; Pres. FAROE METRY; Leader HUMPHREY DAVELAAR.

People's Democratic Party (PDP): Philipsburg, St Maarten; tel. 542-2696; Leader MILLICENT DE WEEVER.

People's Progressive Alliance: Philipsburg, St Maarten; Leader GRACITA ARRINDELL.

Pueblo Soberano: Willemstad, Curaçao; Leader HERMAN WIELS.

Unión Patriótico Boneriano (UPB) (Patriotic Union of Bonaire): Kaya Sabana 22, Kralendijk, Bonaire; tel. 717-8906; fax 717-5552; 2,134 mems; Christian democratic; Leader RAMONSITO T. BOOI; Sec.-Gen. C. V. WINKLAAR.

Windward Islands People's Movement (WIPM): Windwardside, POB 525, Saba; tel. 416-2244; Chair. and Leader RAY HASSELL; Sec.-Gen. DAVE LEVENSTONE.

Judicial System

Legal authority is exercised by the Court of First Instance (which sits in all the islands) and in appeal by the Joint High Court of Justice of the Netherlands Antilles and Aruba. The members of the Joint High Court of Justice sit singly as judges in the Courts of First Instance. The Chief Justice of the Joint High Court of Justice, its members (a maximum of 30) and the Attorneys-General of the Netherlands Antilles and of Aruba are appointed for life by the Dutch monarch, after consultation with the Governments of the Netherlands Antilles and Aruba. The Supreme Court of the Netherlands (based in The Hague) is the court of Final Instance for any appeal. Under a provision of the agreement for the eventual dissolution of the five-island federation, reforms to the judicial system were to be implemented from 2007.

Joint High Court of Justice

Wilhelminaplein 4, Willemstad, Curaçao; tel. (9) 463-4111; fax (9) 461-8341; e-mail hofcur@cura.net.

Chief Justice of the Joint High Court: LISBETH HOEFDRAAD.

Secretary-Executive of the Joint High Court: M. E. N. ROJER-DE FREITAS (acting).

Religion

CHRISTIANITY

Most of the population are Christian, the predominant denomination being Roman Catholicism. There are also small communities of Jews, Muslims and Bahá'ís.

Curaçaose Raad van Kerken (Curaçao Council of Churches): Periclesstraat 6, Willemstad, Curaçao; tel. (9) 465-3207; fax (9) 461-0733; e-mail ddtic@yahoo.com; f. 1958; six mem. churches; Chair. IDA VISSER; Exec. Sec. PAUL VAN DER WAAL.

The Roman Catholic Church

According to the latest available census figures (2001), some 72% of the population are adherents of the Roman Catholic Church. Roman Catholics form the largest single group on Bonaire, Curaçao, Saba and St Maarten. The Netherlands Antilles and Aruba together form the diocese of Willemstad, suffragan to the archdiocese of Port of Spain (Trinidad and Tobago). The Bishop participates in the Antilles Episcopal Conference, currently based in Trinidad and Tobago.

Bishop of Willemstad: Rt Rev. LUIGI ANTONIO SECCO, Bisdom, Breedestraat 31, Otrobanda, Willemstad, Curaçao; tel. (9) 462-5857; fax (9) 462-7437; e-mail bisdomwstad@curinfo.an.

The Anglican Communion

According to the 2001 census, around 1% of the population are Anglicans. Saba, St Eustatius and St Maarten form part of the diocese of the North Eastern Caribbean and Aruba, within the Church in the Province of the West Indies. The Bishop is resident in The Valley, Anguilla.

Other Churches

The largest of the other churches, according to the 2001 census, are the Pentecostal (5% of the population), Protestant (3%), Seventh-day Adventist (3%) and Methodist (3%). On St Eustatius the Methodists form the largest single denomination. Other denominations active in the islands include the Moravian, Apostolic Faith, Wesleyan Holiness and Norwegian Seamen's Churches, the Baptists, Calvinists, Jehovah's Witnesses, Evangelists, the Church of Christ, and the New Testament Church of God.

Iglesia Protestant Uni (United Protestant Church): Fortkerk, Fort Amsterdam, Willemstad, Curaçao; tel. (9) 461-1139; fax (9) 465-7481; e-mail vpg-cur@curlink.com; internet www.vpg-curacao.com; f. 1825 by union of Dutch Reformed and Evangelical Lutheran Churches; associated with the World Council of Churches; Pres. MARITZA BEAUJON-BAKHUIS; 3 congregations; 11,280 adherents; 3,200 mems.

Methodist Church: Oranjestad, St Eustatius.

JUDAISM

According to the 2001 census, around 1% of the population are Jews.

Congregation 'Shaarei Tsedek' Ashkenazi Orthodox Jewish Community: 37 Magdalenaweg, Willemstad, Curaçao; tel. and fax (9) 738-5949; e-mail rel_yes@yahoo.com; 140 mems; Rabbi ARIEL YESHURUN.

Reconstructionist Shephardi Congregation Mikvé Israel-Emanuel: Hanchi di Snoa 29, POB 322, Willemstad, Curaçao; tel. (9) 461-1067; fax (9) 465-4141; e-mail information@snoa.com; internet www.snoa.com; f. 1732 on present site; about 350 mems.

The Press

Algemeen Dagblad: ABCourant NV, Prof. Kernkampweg z/n, POB 725, Willemstad, Curaçao; tel. (9) 747-2200; fax (9) 747-2257; e-mail algemeen@antilliaansdagblad.com; internet www.antilliaansdagblad.com; daily; Dutch; Editor NOUD KÖPER.

Amigoe: Kaya Fraternan di Skèrpènè z/n, POB 577, Curaçao; tel. (9) 767-2000; fax (9) 767-4084; e-mail management@amigoe.com; internet www.amigoe.com; f. 1884; Christian; daily; evening; Dutch; Dir ERNEST VOGES; Editor-in-Chief WILLEM DA COSTA GOMEZ; circ. 12,000.

Bala: Noord Zapateer nst 13, Willemstad, Curaçao; tel. (9) 467-1646; fax (9) 467-1041; e-mail bala@cura.net; daily; Papiamento.

Beurs en Nieuwsberichten: A. M. Chumaceiro Blvd 5, POB 741, Willemstad, Curaçao; tel. (9) 465-4544; fax (9) 465-3411; f. 1935; daily; evening; Dutch; Editor L. SCHENK; circ. 8,000.

Bonaire Holiday: POB 569, Curaçao; tel. (9) 767-1403; fax (9) 767-2003; f. 1971; tourist guide; English; 3 a year; circ. 95,000.

Bonaire Reporter: Kaya Gob. Debrot 200-6, POB 407, Bonaire; tel. and fax 717-8988; e-mail info@bonairereporter.com; internet bonairereporter.com; English; weekly.

The Business Journal: Indjuweg 30A, Willemstad, Curaçao; tel. (9) 461-1367; fax (9) 461-1955; monthly; English.

Curaçao Holiday: POB 569, Curaçao; tel. (9) 767-1403; fax (9) 767-2003; f. 1960; tourist guide; English; 3 a year; circ. 300,000.

De Curaçaosche Courant: Frederikstraat 123, POB 15, Willemstad, Curaçao; tel. (9) 461-2766; fax (9) 462-6535; f. 1812; weekly; Dutch; Editor J. KORIDON.

Daily Herald: Bush Rd 22, POB 828, Philipsburg, St Maarten; tel. 542-5253; fax 542-5913; e-mail editorial@thedailyherald.com; internet www.thedailyherald.com; daily; English.

Extra: W. I. Compagniestraat 41, Willemstad, Curaçao; tel. (9) 462-4595; fax (9) 462-7575; e-mail redactie@extra.an; daily; morning; Papiamento; Man. R. YRAUSQUIN; Editor MIKE OEHLERS; circ. 20,000.

Newsletter of Curaçao Trade and Industry Association: Kaya Junior Salas 1, POB 49, Willemstad, Curaçao; tel. (9) 461-1210; fax (9) 461-5422; f. 1972; monthly; English and Dutch; economic and industrial paper.

Nobo: Scherpenheuvel w/n, POB 323, Willemstad, Curaçao; tel. (9) 467-3500; fax (9) 467-2783; daily; evening; Papiamento; Editor CARLOS DAANTJE; circ. 15,000.

Nos Isla: Refineria Isla (Curazao) SA, Emmastad, Curaçao; 2 a month; Papiamento; circ. 1,200.

La Prensa: W. I. Compagniestraat 41, Willemstad, Curaçao; tel. (9) 462-3850; fax (9) 462-5983; e-mail webmaster@laprensacur.com; internet news.laprensacur.com; f. 1929; daily; evening; Papiamento; Man. R. YRAUSQUIN; Editor SIGFRIED RIGAUD; circ. 10,750.

Saba Herald: The Level, Saba; tel. 416-2244; f. 1968; monthly; news, local history; Editor WILL JOHNSON; circ. 500.

St Maarten Guardian: Vlaun Bldg, Pondfill, POB 1046, Philipsburg, St Maarten; tel. 542-6022; fax 542-6043; e-mail guardian@sintmaarten.net; f. 1989; daily; English; Man. Dir RICHARD F. GIBSON; Man. Editor JOSEPH DOMINIQUE; circ. 4,000.

St Maarten Holiday: POB 569, Curaçao; tel. (9) 767-1403; fax (9) 767-2003; f. 1968; tourism guide; English; 3 a year; circ. 175,000.

Teen Times: c/o The Daily Herald, Bush Rd 22, POB 828, Philipsburg, St Maarten; tel. 542-5597; e-mail info@teentimes.com; for teenagers by teenagers; sponsored by The Daily Herald; English; Editor-in-Chief MICHAEL GRANGER.

Ultimo Noticia: Frederikstraat 123, Willemstad, Curaçao; tel. (9) 462-3444; fax (9) 462-6535; daily; morning; Papiamento; Editor A. A. JONCKHEER.

La Unión: Rotaprint NV, Willemstad, Curaçao; weekly; Papiamento.

NEWS AGENCY

Algemeen Nederlands Persbureau (ANP) (Netherlands): Panoramaweg 5, POB 439, Willemstad, Curaçao; tel. (9) 461-2233; fax (9) 461-7431; Representative RONNIE RENS.

Publishers

Drukkerij Scherpenheuvel NV: Lindberghweg 28A, Curaçao; tel. (9) 465-6801.

Drukkerij de Stad NV: W. I. Compagniestraat 41, POB 3011, Willemstad, Curaçao; tel. (9) 462-3566; fax (9) 462-2175; e-mail management@destad.an; internet www.destad.an; f. 1929; Dir KENRICK A. YRAUSQUIN.

Ediciones Populares: W. I. Compagniestraat 41, Willemstad, Curaçao; f. 1929; Dir RONALD YRAUSQUIN.

Broadcasting and Communications

TELECOMMUNICATIONS

Digicel Curaçao: Biesheuvel 24–25, Curaçao; tel. (9) 736-1056; fax (9) 736-1057; e-mail customercare@digicelcuracao.com; internet www.digicelcuracao.com; f. 1999; bought by Digicel (Ireland) in 2005; bought into Bonaire market through majority shareholding of Antilliano Por NV in April 2006; known as Curaçao Telecom until 2006; telephone and internet services; Digicel acquired mobile business of TELBO (Bonaire) in Dec. 2006; also operates in Aruba; Chair. DENIS O'BRIEN; CEO (Dutch Caribbean) HANS LUTE.

East Caribbean Cellular NV (ECC): 13 Richardson St, Philipsburg, St Maarten; tel. 542-4100; fax 542-5678; e-mail info@eastcaribbeancellular.com; internet www.eastcaribbeancellular.com; f. 1989.

Scarlet: Fokkerweg 26, Suite 106, Willemstad, Curaçao; tel. (9) 766-0000; fax (9) 461-8301; internet www.scarlet.an; telecommunications provider in Curaçao and St Maarten; CEO ERIC E. STAKLAND.

St Maarten Telecommunications Group: Soualiga Blvd 5, Philipsburg, St Maarten; tel. 542-0200; fax 543-0101; e-mail info@telemgroup.an; internet www.telemgroup.an; f. 1975; comprises TelEm (providing local services), TelCell NV (digital mobile services), TelNet Communications NV (internet services) and SMITCOMS NV (international services); 15,000 subscribers (TelEm); Chair. RAFAEL BOASMAN; CEO PIETER DRENTH.

Telefonia Bonairiano NV (TELBO NV): Kaya Libertador Simon Bolivar 8, POB 94, Bonaire; tel. 717-7000; fax 717-5007; e-mail telbo@telbo.an; internet www.telbo.net; f. 1983; fixed line telecommunications and internet service provider; TELBO's mobile operations on Bonaire were purchased by Digicel in Dec. 2006; Gen. Man. GILBERT DE BREE.

United Telecom Services (UTS): UTS Headquarters, Rigelweg 2, Willemstad, Curaçao; tel. (9) 777-0101; fax (9) 777-1284; e-mail info@uts.an; internet www.uts.an; f. 1999 following merger of Antelecom NV (f. 1908) and SETEL (f. 1979); Antelecom and SETEL still operate under own names; Chair. DAVID DICK; CEO PAUL DE GEUS.

Servicio de Telekomunikashon (UTS Wireless Curaçao) (SETEL): UTS Headquarters, Rigelweg 2, Willemstad, Curaçao; tel. (9) 777-0101; fax (9) 777-1284; e-mail info@uts.an; internet www.uts.an; f. 1979; telecommunications equipment and network provider; forms part of UTS; state-owned, but privatization pending; Pres. ANGEL R. KOOK; Man. Dir JULIO CONSTANCIA; 400 employees.

BROADCASTING

Radio

Curom Broadcasting Inc: Roodeweg 64, POB 2169, Willemstad, Curaçao; tel. (9) 462-2020; fax (9) 462-5796; e-mail z86@curom.com; internet www.curom.com; f. 1933; broadcasts in English, Papiamento, Dutch and Spanish; Dir ORLANDO CUALES.

Mi 95: f. 1988; FM; music station, aimed at adults.

Z-86: news station.

88 Ròckòrsou: rock music station, aimed at young people.

Easy 97.9 FM: Arikokweg 19A, Willemstad, Curaçao; tel. (9) 462-3162; fax (9) 462-8712; e-mail radio@easyfm.com; internet www.easyfm.com; f. 1995; Dir KEVIN CARTHY.

Gold 91.5 FM Curaçao: De Rouvilleweg 7, Ingang Klipstraat, POB 6103, Curaçao; tel. (9) 426-1803; fax (9) 461-9103; e-mail info@gold915.com; internet gold915.an; music station.

Laser 101 (101.1 FM): Suite 2, 106 A. T. Illidge Rd, Philipsburg, St Maarten; tel. 543-2200; fax 543-2229; e-mail master@laser101.com; internet www.laser101.fm; 24 hours a day; music; English and Papiamento.

Paradise FM: De Rouvilleweg 7, Ingang Klipstraat, POB 6103, Curaçao; tel. (9) 426-1803; fax (9) 461-9103; e-mail studio@paradisefm.an; internet paradisefm.an; news station.

Radio Caribe: Ledaweg 35, Brievengat, Willemstad, Curaçao; tel. (9) 736-9564; fax (9) 736-9569; f. 1955; commercial station; programmes in Dutch, English, Spanish and Papiamento; Dir-Gen. C. R. HEILLEGGER.

Radio Exito: Julianaplein 39, Curaçao; tel. (9) 462-5577; fax (9) 462-5580.

Radio Hoyer NV: Plasa Horacio Hoyer 21, Willemstad, Curaçao; tel. (9) 461-1678; fax (9) 461-6528; e-mail hoyer1@radiohoyer.com; internet www.radiohoyer.com; f. 1954; commercial; two stations: Radio Hoyer I (mainly Papiamento, also Spanish) and II (mainly Dutch, also English) in Curaçao; Man. Dir HELEN HOYER.

Radio Korsou FM: Bataljonweg 7, POB 3250, Willemstad, Curaçao; tel. (9) 737-3012; fax (9) 737-2888; e-mail studio@korsou.com; internet www.korsou.com; f. 1976; 24 hrs a day; programmes in Papiamento and Dutch; Gen. Man. ALAN H. EVERTSZ.

Radio Tropical: Kaya W. F. G. Mensing, Willemstad, Curaçao; tel. (9) 465-0190; fax (9) 465-2470; e-mail tropi@cura.net; Dir DWIGHT RUDOLPHINA.

Radiodifusión Boneriana NV: Kaya Gobernador Debrot 2, Kralendijk, Bonaire; tel. 717-7220; fax 717-6659; e-mail vozdibonaire@gmail.com; internet www.vozdibonaire.com; f. 1980; Owner FELICIANO DA SILVA PILOTO.

Alpha FM: broadcasts in Spanish.

Mega FM: internet www.megahitfm.com; broadcasts in Dutch.

Voz di Bonaire (PJB2) (Voice of Bonaire): broadcasts in Papiamento.

Trans World Radio (TWR): Kaya Gobernador N. Debrot 64, Kralendijk, Bonaire; tel. 717-8800; fax 717-8808; e-mail 800am@twr.org; internet www.twr.org; f. 1964; religious, educational and cultural station; programmes to South, Central and North America, and Caribbean in five languages; Pres. LAUREN LIBBY; Station Dir JOSEPH BARKER.

Voice of Saba (PJF1): The Bottom, POB 1, Saba; studio in St Maarten; tel. 546-3213; internet www.mannelli.com/saba; also operates The Voice of Saba FM; Man. MAX W. NICHOLSON.

Voice of St Maarten (PJD2 Radio): Plaza 21, Backstreet, POB 366, Philipsburg, St Maarten; tel. 542-2580; fax 542-4905; also operates PJD3 on FM (24 hrs); commercial; programmes in English; Gen. Man. DON R. HUGHES.

There is a relay station for Radio Nederland on Bonaire.

Television

Antilliaanse Televisie Maatschappij NV (TeleCuraçao): Berg Ararat z/n, POB 415, Willemstad, Curaçao; tel. (9) 461-1288; fax (9) 461-4138; e-mail web@telecuracao.com; internet www.telecuracao.com; f. 1960; fmrly operated Tele-Aruba; commercial; owned by United Telecommunication Services; also operates cable service, offering programmes from US satellite television and two Venezuelan channels; Dir PAUL DE GEUS; Gen. Man. HUGO LEW JEN TAI.

Leeward Broadcasting Corporation—Television: Postbus 375, Philipsburg, St Maarten; tel. (5) 23491; transmissions for approx. 10 hours daily.

Five television channels can be received on Curaçao in total. Relay stations provide Bonaire with programmes from Curaçao, St Maarten with programmes from Puerto Rico, and Saba and St Eustatius with programmes from St Maarten and neighbouring islands. Curaçao has a publicly owned cable television service, TDS.

Finance

(cap. = capital; res = reserves; dep. = deposits; m. = million; br.(s) = branch(es); amounts in Netherlands Antilles guilders unless otherwise stated)

BANKING

Central Bank

Bank van de Nederlandse Antillen (Bank of the Netherlands Antilles): Simon Bolivar Plein 1, Willemstad, Curaçao; tel. (9) 434-5500; fax (9) 461-5004; e-mail info@centralbank.an; internet centralbank.an; f. 1828 as Curaçaosche Bank, name changed as above Jan. 1962; cap. 30.0m., res 519.9m., dep. 2,447.4m. (Dec. 2008); Chair. RALPH PALM; Pres. Dr EMSLEY D. TROMP; 2 brs on St Maarten and Bonaire.

Commercial Banks

Banco di Caribe NV: Schottegatweg Oost 205, POB 3785, Willemstad, Curaçao; tel. (9) 432-3000; fax (9) 461-5220; e-mail info@bancodicaribe.com; internet www.bancodicaribe.com; f. 1973; cap. 4.7m., res 120.1m., dep. 1,028.2m. (Dec. 2008); Chair. HUSHANG ANSARY; CEO and Gen. Man. Dir IDEFONS D. SIMON; Man. Dirs EDUARDO A. DE KORT, PERCIVAL VIRGINIA; 5 brs.

Banco Industrial de Venezuela, SA: Handeiskade N-12, Punda, Curaçao; tel. (9) 461-6534; subsidiary of state-owned Banco Industrial de Venezuela, SA.

CITCO Banking Corporation NV: De Ruyterkade 62, POB 707, Willemstad, Curaçao; tel. (9) 732-2322; fax (9) 732-2330; e-mail curacao-bank@citco.com; internet www.citco.com; f. 1980 as Curaçao Banking Corpn NV; Man. Dir and Gen. Man. SCOTT CASE; Man. Dirs GLENDA E. C. LALLJEE-TRAPENBERG, RUPERT E. WALLÉ.

FirstCaribbean International Bank (Curaçao) NV: De Ruyterkade 61, POB 3144, Willemstad, Curaçao; tel. (9) 433-8338; fax (9) 433-8198; e-mail bank.curacao@firstcaribbeanbank.com; internet www.firstcaribbeanbank.com/curacao; f. 1964 as ABN AMRO Bank NV; part of FirstCaribbean Group, based in Barbados; 91.5% owned by CIBC, Canada; Exec. Chair. MICHAEL MANSOOR; Man. Dir (Dutch Caribbean) W. M. (PIM) VAN DER BERG; 6 brs.

Girobank NV: Scharlooweg 35, Willemstad, Curaçao; tel. (9) 433-9999; fax (9) 461-7861; e-mail info@gironet.com; internet www.girobank.net; Man. Dirs ERIC GARCIA, MANUEL SUENO.

Maduro & Curiel's Bank NV: Plaza Jojo Correa 2–4, POB 305, Willemstad, Curaçao; tel. (9) 466-1100; fax (9) 466-1122; e-mail info@mcb-bank.com; internet www.mcb-bank.com; f. 1916 as NV Maduro's Bank; merged with Curiel's Bank in 1931; affiliated with Bank of Nova Scotia NV, Toronto, Canada; br. in Bonaire; cap. 50.7m., res 168.6m., dep. 4,762.2m. (Dec. 2008); Pres. and CEO LIONEL CAPRILES; Man. Dir RONALD GOMES CASSERES; 31 brs.

Meespierson (Curaçao) NV: Berg Arrarat 1, POB 3889, Willemstad, Curaçao; tel. (9) 463-9200; fax (9) 461-3769; e-mail privatebanking_curacao@meespierson.com; internet www.meespierson.an; f. 1952 as Pierson, Heldring and Pierson (Curaçao) NV; became Meespierson (Curaçao) NV in 1993; name changed to Fortis Bank (Curaçao) NV in 2000, and reverted to Meespierson (Curaçao) NV in 2009; international banking/trust co; Man. Dir WILLIE BEUMER; Gen. Man. FRANK LAMMERS.

Orco Bank NV: Dr Henry Fergusonweg 10, POB 4928, Willemstad, Curaçao; tel. (9) 737-2000; fax (9) 737-6741; e-mail info@orcobank.com; internet www.orcobank.com; f. 1986; cap. 7.8m., res 11.1m., dep. 393.6m. (Dec. 2008); Man. Dirs M. N. S. SPROCK, K. R. CANWORD; 1 br.

Rabobank Curaçao NV: Zeelandia Office Park, Kaya W. F. G. (Jombi), Mensing 14, POB 3876, Willemstad, Curaçao; tel. (9) 465-2011; fax (9) 465-2066; e-mail l.an.curacao.ops@rabobank.com; internet www.rabobank.com; f. 1978; cap. US $53.0m., res $17.8m., dep. $4,535.2m. (Dec. 2003); Chair. BERT HEEMSKERK; Gen. Man. J. S. KLEP.

RBTT Bank NV: Kaya Flamboyan 1, Rooi Catootje, Willemstad; tel. (9) 763-8438; fax (9) 737-0620; e-mail info@tt.rbtt.com; internet www.rbtt.com; f. 1997 as Antilles Banking Corpn; name changed to RBTT Bank Antilles in 2001; name changed as above in 2002; cap. 114.5m., res 132.6m., dep. 3,393.2m. (Dec. 2008); Pres. and Country Head (Curaçao) DAISY A. TYROL-CAROLUS; Man. Dir RICHARD RAJACK; 4 brs.

Windward Islands Bank Ltd: Clem Labega Sq. 7, POB 220, Philipsburg, St Maarten; tel. 542-2313; fax 542-4761; e-mail info@wib-bank.net; internet www.wib-bank.net; affiliated to Maduro & Curiel's Bank NV; f. 1960; cap. and res 53.2m., dep. 662.2m. (Dec. 2006); Man. Dir JAN J. BEAUJON.

'Offshore' Banks

Abu Dhabi International Bank NV: Kaya W. F. G. (Jombi), Mensing 36, POB 3141, Willemstad, Curaçao; tel. (9) 461-1299; fax (9) 461-5392; internet www.nbad.com; f. 1981; cap. US $20.0m., res $30.0m., dep. $112.2m. (Dec. 2006); Pres. QAMBAR AL MULLA; Man. Dir NAGY S. KOLTA.

FirstCaribbean International Wealth Management (Curaçao) NV: De Ruyterkade 61, Curaçao; tel. (9) 433-8000; fax (9) 433-8198; f. 1976 as ABN AMRO Bank Asset Management (Curaçao) NV; acquired by FirstCaribbean Bank in Dec. 2005; Man. Dir E. J. W. HERMENS.

F. Van Lanschot Bankiers (Curaçao) NV: Schottegatweg Oost 32, POB 4799, Willemstad, Curaçao; tel. (9) 737-1011; fax (9) 737-1086; e-mail info@vanlanschot.an; internet www.vanlanschot.nl; f. 1962; wholly owned by F. Van Lanschot Bankiers NV (Netherlands); Man. A. VAN GEEST.

Development Banks

Ontwikkelingsbank van de Nederlandse Antillen NV: Schottegatweg Oost 3C, POB 267, Willemstad, Curaçao; tel. (9) 747-3000; fax (9) 747-3320; e-mail obna@obna-bank.com; f. 1981; Man. Dir DENNIS CIJNTJE.

Stichting Korporashon pa Desaroyo di Korsou (Curaçao Development Corporation—KORPODEKO): Schottegatweg Oost 36, Willemstad, Curaçao; tel. (9) 738-1799; fax (9) 738-1766; e-mail info@korpodeko.an; internet www.korpodeko.an.

Savings Banks

Postspaarbank van de Nederlandse Antillen: Waaigatplein 1, Willemstad, Curaçao; tel. (9) 433-1100; fax (9) 461-7561; e-mail info@postpaarbank.com; internet www.postspaarbank.com/English; f. 1905; post office savings bank; Chair. H. J. J. VICTORIA; cap. 21m.; 20 brs.

Spaar- en Beleenbank van Curaçao NV: MCB Salinja Bldg, Schottegatweg Oost 130, Willemstad, Curaçao; tel. (9) 466-1585; fax (9) 466-1590; e-mail chbsbb@mcb-bank.com.

There are also several mortgage banks and credit unions.

Banking Associations

Association of International Bankers in the Netherlands Antilles (IBNA): A. M. Chumaceiro Blvd 3, POB 3369, Willemstad, Curaçao; tel. (9) 461-5367; fax (9) 461-5369; e-mail info@ibna.an; internet www.ibna.an; f. 1980; 32 mems; Pres. ARTHUR ADAMS; Sec. ANTONIO TORRES.

Bonaire Bankers' Association: Maduro & Curiel's Bank (Bonaire) NV, Kaya L. D. Gerharts 1, POB 366, Kralendijk, Bonaire; tel. 717-5520; fax 717-5884; Vice-Pres. R. GOMEZ.

Curaçao Bankers' Association (CBA): Girobank NV, Scharlooweg 35, Willemstad, Curaçao; tel. (9) 433-9999; fax (9) 461-7861; e-mail florisela.bentoera@an.rbtt.com; f. 1972; Pres. E. GARCIA; Sec. FLORISELA BENTOERA.

Federashon di Kooperativanan di Spar i Kredito Antiyano (Fekoskan): Curaçaostraat 50, Willemstad, Curaçao; tel. (9) 462-3676; fax (9) 462-4995; e-mail fekoskan@attglobal.net; Pres. W. DE LIMA.

International Bankers' Association in the Netherlands Antilles: A. M. Chumaceiro Blvd 3, Willemstad, Curaçao; tel. (9) 461-5367; fax (9) 461-5369; Pres. F. GIRIGORI.

St. Maarten Bankers' Association: Clem Labega Sq. 7, Philipsburg, St Maarten; tel. 542-2313; fax 542-6355; Pres. J. BEAUJON.

INSURANCE

Amersfoortse Antillen NV: Kaya W. F. G. Mensing 19, Willemstad, Curaçao; tel. (9) 461-6399; fax (9) 461-6709.

Aseguro di Kooperativa Antiyano (ASKA) NV: Scharlooweg 15, Willemstad, Curaçao; tel. (9) 461-7765; fax (9) 461-5991; accident and health, motor vehicle, property.

Ennia Caribe Schaden NV: J. B. Gorsiraweg 6, POB 581, Willemstad, Curaçao; tel. (9) 434-3800; fax (9) 434-3873; e-mail mail@ennia.com; f. 1948; general; life insurance as Ennia Caribe Leven NV; Pres. DONALD BAKHUIS; Man. Dir ALBARTUS WILLEMSEN.

ING Fatum: Cas Coraweg 2, Willemstad, Curaçao; tel. (9) 777-7777; fax (9) 461-2023; f. 1904; property insurance.

MCB Group Insurance NV: MCB Bldg Scharloo, Scharloo, Willemstad, Curaçao; tel. (9) 466-1370; fax (9) 466-1327.

Netherlands Antilles and Aruba Assurance Company (NA&A) NV: Pietermaai 135, Willemstad, Curaçao; tel. (9) 465-7146; fax (9) 461-6269; accident and health, motor vehicle, property.

Seguros Antilliano NV: S. b. N. Doormanweg/Reigerweg 5, Willemstad, Curaçao; tel. (9) 736-6877; fax (9) 736-5794; general.

A number of foreign companies also have offices in Curaçao, mainly British, Canadian, Dutch and US firms.

Insurance Association

Insurance Association of the Netherlands Antilles (NAVV): c/o ING Fatum, Cas Coraweg 2, POB 3002, Willemstad, Curaçao; tel. (9) 777-7777; fax (9) 736-9658; Pres. R. C. MARTINA-JOE.

Trade and Industry

DEVELOPMENT ORGANIZATIONS

Curaçao Industrial and International Trade Development Company NV (CURINDE): Emancipatie Blvd 7, Landhuis Koningsplein, Curaçao; tel. (9) 737-6000; fax (9) 737-1336; e-mail info@curinde.com; internet www.curinde.com; f. 1980; state-owned; manages the harbour free zone, the airport free zone and the industrial zone; Man. Dir ERIC R. SMEULDERS.

Foreign Investment Agency Curaçao (FIAC): Luchthavenweg 55, 5657 EA Eindhoven, Netherlands; tel. (40) 2518674; fax (40) 2572098.

World Trade Center Curaçao: POB 6005, Piscadera Bay, Curaçao; tel. (9) 463-6132; fax (9) 463-6573; e-mail info@wtccuracao.com; internet www.worldtradecentercuracao.com; Man. Dir LUIS E. BELTRAN M.

CHAMBERS OF COMMERCE

Bonaire Chamber of Commerce and Industry: Princess Mariestraat, POB 52, Kralendijk, Bonaire; tel. 717-5595; fax 717-8995.

Curaçao Chamber of Commerce and Industry: Kaya Junior Salas 1, Pietermaai, World Trade Centre Bldg, Piscadera Bay, POB 10, Willemstad, Curaçao; tel. (9) 461-1451; fax (9) 461-5652; e-mail management@curacao-chamber.an; internet www.curacao-chamber.an/info; f. 1884; Chair. RUUD THUIS; Exec. Dir JOHN H. JACOBS.

St Maarten Chamber of Commerce and Industry: Cannegieterstraat 11, POB 454, Philipsburg, St Maarten; tel. 542-3590; fax 542-3512; e-mail info@sxmcoci.org; internet www.sxmcoci.org; f. 1979; Pres. GLEN CARTY; Exec. Dir LUDWIG OUENNICHE (acting).

INDUSTRIAL AND TRADE ASSOCIATIONS

Curaçao Exporters' Association (CEA): c/o Seawings NV, Maduro Plaza z/n CEA, POB 6049, Curaçao; tel. (9) 733-1591; fax (9) 733-1599; e-mail albert.elens@seawings-curacao.com; f. 1993; Dir ALBERT ELENS.

Curaçao International Financial Services Association (CIFA): Chumaceiro Blvd 3, POB 220, Curaçao; tel. (9) 461-5371; fax (9) 461-5378; e-mail info@cifa-curacao.com; internet www.cifa-curacao.com; Chair. ETIENNE YS.

Curaçao Trade and Industry Association (Vereniging Bedrijfsleven Curaçao—VBC): Kaya Junior Salas 1, POB 49, Willemstad, Curaçao; tel. (9) 461-1210; fax (9) 461-5422; e-mail info@vbc.an; internet www.vbc.an; f. 1944; Pres. BASTIAN KOOYMAN; Exec. Dir JOHAN LIEUW.

St Maarten Hospitality and Trade Association (SHTA): 33A WJA Nisbeth Rd, POB 486, Philipsburg, St Maarten; tel. 542-0108; fax 542-0107; e-mail info@shta.com; internet www.shta.com; Pres. EMIL LEE.

MAJOR COMPANIES

The following are some of the leading industrial and commercial companies currently operating in the Netherlands Antilles:

Antillean Paper and Plastic Co NV: Industrial Park Brievengat, POB 3505, Curaçao; tel. (9) 737-6422; fax (9) 737-2424; f. 1976; plastics, paper; subsidiaries produce plastic containers and soaps; Mans HUBERT VAN GRIEKEN, E. J. HALABI, J. B. M. KOOL; 56 employees.

Antillean Soap Co BV: Industrial Park Brievengat, Willemstad, Curaçao; tel. (9) 737-7177; fax (9) 737-7191; e-mail ansoap@carib-online.net; f. 1976; manufactures powder and liquid soap, disinfectants, abrasives, industrial cleaners; Man. Dir EDOUARD J. HALABI; 70 employees.

Antilliaanse Brouwerij NV: Rijkseenheid Blvd w/n, POB 465, Willemstad, Curaçao; tel. (9) 434-1500; fax (9) 434-1599; e-mail r_voorn@heineken.nl; f. 1958; manufacture and distribution of beer and soft drinks; acquired by Parera Group Holding NV in Jan. 2010; Man. YORICK GELDOLPH TEN HOUTE DE LANGE; 121 employees.

Antilliaanse Verffabriek NV: Asteroidenweg z/n, POB 3944, Curaçao; tel. (9) 736-5866; fax (9) 736-5048; e-mail info@avfpaint.com; internet www.avfpaint.com; f. 1960; manufactures paint products; Man. Dir FRANK BRANDAO; 40 employees.

BOPEC (Bonaire Petroleum Corporation NV): Kralendijk, POB 117, Bonaire; tel. 717-8177; fax 717-8266; e-mail bopec@bonairelive.com; oil terminal with storage capacity of 10.1m. barrels; bought by PDVSA (Venezuela) in 1989; Gen. Man. HUMBERTO NIEVES.

Cargill Salt Bonaire NV: Bonaire; internet www.cargillsalt.com; salt production and export; has operated the Solar Salt Works since 1997 when Cargill Salt acquired the North American assets of Akzo Nobel Salt Inc; Man. BRET SCHUTTPELZ.

Caribbean Bottling Co Ltd (CBC–Pepsi Curaçao): Kaminda André F. E. Kusters 6, Zeelandia, POB 302, Willemstad, Curaçao; tel. (9) 461-2488; fax (9) 465-1377; e-mail info@pepsicuracao.com; internet www.pepsicuracao.com; f. 1948; produces carbonated drinks; owned by Pepsi; Man. ALAN F. MADURO; 110 employees.

Caribbean Food Products: 3 Bombardiersweg, Willemstad, Curaçao; tel. (9) 736-4277; fax (9) 736-4262; e-mail info@caribbeanfoodproducts.com; internet www.caribbeanfoodproducts.com; refiners and exporters of sugar products and distributor of cereals; Man. Dir ANDRE J. W. BLAAUW; 15 employees.

Carnefco Curaçao BV: Pletterijweg z/n, POB 3121, Willemstad, Curaçao; tel. (9) 4650221; fax (9) 465-2586; e-mail info@carnefco.com; f. 1973; ship maintenance, grit-blasting, wet-blasting, high-pressure water blasting, internal coatings, etc.; part of Carnefco Group; Man. Dir ROBERT MATTHES; 60 employees.

Curaçao Beverage Bottling Co NV: Rijkseenheid Blvd 1, POB 95, Willemstad, Curaçao; tel. (9) 463-3311; fax (9) 461-1310; e-mail info@fria.com; internet www.fria.com; f. 1938; bottlers and manufacturers of soft drinks, many under licence; Man. Dir TIBOR LUCKMANN; 105 employees.

Curaçao Oil NV (CUROIL): A. Mendes Chumaceiro Blvd 15, POB 3927, Curaçao; tel. (9) 432-0000; fax (9) 461-3335; e-mail curoil@curoil.com; internet www.curoil.com; f. 1985; fuel and petroleum lubricants marketing company; supplies automotive, marine, aviation and industrial fuels and lubricants; Man. Dir GENSLEY J. CAPELLA; 80 employees.

CurAloe: Curaçao Ecocity Projects, Aloë Vera Plantage, Groot Sint Joris West z/n, Curaçao; tel. (9) 767-5507; fax (9) 767-5577; e-mail ecocity@cura.net; internet www.aloecuracao.com; f. 2002; jt venture between BioClin, Netherlands, and local shareholders; produces range of aloe vera skin-care and health products.

Danella NV: Pletterijweg z/n, Curaçao; tel. (9) 461-6300; fax (9) 471-3727; e-mail info@danella-nv.com; internet www.danella-nv.com; f. 1973; manufactures scaffolding, galvanized pipes, steel fittings, valves and ductile iron; Man. LUCIEN P. LIEUW-SJONG.

Janssen de Jong Caribbean: Fort Nassauweg z/n, Willemstad, Curaçao; tel. (9) 433-8500; fax (9) 465-8500; e-mail info@caribbean.jajo.com; internet www.janssendejongcaribbean.com; subsidiary of Janssen de Jong Group BV, Netherlands; operates construction cos in the Netherlands Antilles covering mining, concrete industry, infrastructure, maritime and civil construction activities; Man. Dir PIETER VAN GULIK.

Curacaose Wegenbouw Maatschappij: Fort Nassauweg z/n, Willemstad, Curaçao; tel. (9) 433-8500; fax (9) 465-8500; e-mail info@cwm.jajo.com; internet www.curacaosewegenbouw.com; f. 1953; infrastructure, road building and trenching; part of Janssen de Jong Caribbean.

Harbour and Civil Construction Curaçao (HCCC): Parera, POB 431, Willemstad, Curaçao; tel. (9) 461-1807; fax (9) 461-1146; e-mail info@hccc.jajo.com; internet www.harbourcivil.com; construction of civil and marine devts; part of Janssen de Jong Caribbean.

Mijnmaatschappij Curaçao: POB 3078, Newport, Willemstad, Curaçao; tel. (9) 767-3400; fax (9) 767-6721; e-mail info@mmc.jajo.com; internet www.miningcompanycuracao.com; part of Janssen de Jong Caribbean; 70 employees.

Kooyman NV: Kaya W. F. G. (Jombi) Mensing 44, POB 3062, Zeelandia, Willemstad, Curaçao; tel. (9) 461-3333; fax (9) 465-5428; e-mail info-headoffice@kooymanbv.com; internet www.kooymanbv.com; f. 1939; building supplies, hardware, steel/aluminium goods, glass, timber goods, etc.; Pres. BASTIAAN KOOIJMAN; CEO HERBERT VAN DER WOUDE; over 400 employees.

Lovers Industrial Corporation NV: Industrial Park Brievengat JII 1–2, Curaçao; tel. (9) 737-0499; fax (9) 737-1747; e-mail lovers@loversglobal.com; internet www.loversglobal.com; f. 1984; produces fruit juices, ice cream, frozen yoghurt; purchased Otto Senior ('Ritz') juice and dairy business in 2003; Man. OSWALD C. VAN DER DIJS; 180 employees.

Plastico NV: Pletterijweg z/n, Parera, Curaçao; tel. (9) 461-3060; fax (9) 461-9329; e-mail pipe@plastico-nv.com; internet www.plastico-nv.com; f. 1985; manufactures polythene pipes for water-distribution and irrigation purposes; Man. L. LIEUW-SJONG; 10 employees.

Refinería Isla (Curaçao) BV: Margrietlaan, Emmastad, POB 3843, Curaçao; tel. (9) 466-2273; fax (9) 466-2488; e-mail info@refineriaisla.com; f. 1985; refinery established in 1915 by Royal

Dutch-Shell Co, but from 1985 operated by PDVSA (Venezuela); petroleum products; Pres. ASDRUBAL JOSE CHAVEZ JIMENEZ; Man. Dir EUDOMARIO CARRUYO RONDON; 1,360 employees.

Refinería di Korsou NV: Ara Hilltop Office Complex, Pletterijweg 1, POB 3627, Curaçao; tel. (9) 461-1050; fax (9) 461-3377; internet info@refineriadikorsou.com; internet www.refineriadikorsou.com; f. 1985; owner co of the fmr Shell Curaçao Refinery and the former Curaçao Oil Terminal; leased to Venezuela's PDVSA; Man. HERBERT MENSCHE; 16 employees.

Softex Products NV: Industrial Park Brievengat, POB 3795, Curaçao; tel. (9) 737-7811; fax (9) 737-7903; e-mail softex@cura.net; f. 1976; produces paper towels, napkins, etc.; Man. PAUL L. M. LIEUW; 40 employees.

Vasos Antillanos NV: Industrial Park Brievengat AI 4–6, Curaçao; tel. (9) 737-7082; fax (9) 737-2424; e-mail eelzimm@cura.net; f. 1986; produces plastic cold-drink cups; Man. CHARLES HAROLD VAN GRIEKEN; 55 employees.

West India Mercantile Co (WIMCO): Saliña, POB 74, Willemstad, Curaçao; tel. (9) 461-1833; fax (9) 461-1627; e-mail info@wimco-nv.com; internet www.wimco-nv.com; f. 1928; wholesale and retail of electrical household and commercial appliances; Man. Dir ANTHONY COHEN HENRÍQUEZ; 90 employees.

UTILITIES

Electricity and Water

Aqualectra Production NV (KAE): Rector Zwijsenstraat 1, POB 2097, Curaçao; tel. (9) 463-2200; fax (9) 463-2228; e-mail info@aqualectra.com; internet www.aqualectra.com; present name adopted in 2001 following the restructuring of Curaçao's energy sector; CEO ANTHON CASPERSON.

EcoPower Bonaire BV: Bonaire; f. 2007; consortium of Econcern (Germany), MAN (Germany) and Enercon (Netherlands); sustainable energy producer; Project Man. HANS VAN HEEL.

GEBE NV: Pond Fill, W. J. A. Nisbeth Rd 35, POB 123, St Maarten; tel. 542-2213; fax 542-4810; e-mail gebesxm@nvgebe.com; internet www.nvgebe.com; f. 1961; generates and distributes electricity via island network; operates island water supply system; Man. Dir WILLIAM GODFREY BROOKS.

Water & Energiebedrijf Bonaire (WEB) NV: Carlos Nicolaas 3, POB 381, Kralendijk, Bonaire; tel. 715-8244; e-mail web@web.an; internet www.web.an.

TRADE UNIONS

Algemene Bond van Overheidspersoneel (ABVO) (General Union of Civil Servants): POB 3604, Willemstad, Curaçao; tel. (9) 737-6097; fax (9) 737-3145; e-mail abvo_na@cura.net; internet www.abvo-informa.org; f. 1936; Pres. ROLAND H. IGNACIO; Sec. R. C. SAEZ; 4,000 mems.

Central General di Trahado di Corsow (CGTC) (General Headquarters for Workers of Curaçao): POB 2078, Willemstad, Curaçao; tel. (9) 737-6097; fax (9) 737-3145; e-mail abvo_na@cura.net; f. 1949; Sec.-Gen. ROLAND H. IGNACIO.

Curaçaosche Federatie van Werknemers (Curaçao Federation of Workers): Schouwburgweg 44, Willemstad, Curaçao; tel. (9) 737-6300; fax (9) 737-1426; f. 1964; Pres. WILFRED SPENCER; Sec.-Gen. GILBERT POULINA; 204 affiliated unions; about 2,000 mems.

Federashon Bonaireana di Trabou (FEDEBON): Kaya Krabè 6, Nikiboko, POB 324, Bonaire; tel. and fax 717-8845; Pres. GEROLD BERNABELA.

Petroleum Workers' Federation of Curaçao: Willemstad, Curaçao; tel. (9) 737-0255; fax (9) 737-5250; affiliated to Int. Petroleum and Chemical Workers' Federation; f. 1955; Pres. R. G. GIJSBERTHA; approx. 1,500 mems.

Sentral di Sindikatonan di Korsou (SSK) (Central Trade Unions of Curaçao): Schouwburgweg 44, POB 3036, Willemstad, Curaçao; tel. (9) 737-0255; fax (9) 737-5250; Pres. PABLO COVA; 6,000 mems.

Sindikato di Trahado den Edukashon na Korsou (SITEK) (Curaçao Schoolteachers' Trade Union): Landhuis Stenen Koraal, POB 3545, Willemstad, Curaçao; tel. (9) 468-2902; fax (9) 469-0552; 1,234 mems.

Windward Islands' Federation of Labour (WIFOL): Pond Fill, Long Wall Rd, POB 1097, St Maarten; tel. 542-2797; fax 542-6631; e-mail wifol@sintmaarten.net; Pres. THEOPHILUS THOMPSON.

Transport

RAILWAYS

There are no railways.

ROADS

All the islands have a good system of all-weather roads. There were 845 km of roads in 2004, of which 31% were paved.

SHIPPING

Curaçao is an important centre for the refining and transshipment of Venezuelan and Middle Eastern petroleum. Willemstad is served by the Schottegat harbour, set in a wide bay with a long channel and deep water. A Mega Cruise Facility, with capacity for the largest cruise ships, has been constructed on the Otrobanda side of St Anna Bay. Ports at Bullen Bay and Caracas Bay also serve Curaçao. St Maarten is one of the Caribbean's leading ports for visits by cruise ships, and in 2001 new pier facilities were opened that could accommodate up to four cruise ships and add more cargo space. Each of the other islands has a good harbour, except for Saba, which has one inlet, equipped with a large pier.

Curaçao Ports Authority: Werf de Wilde z/n, POB 689, Willemstad, Curaçao; tel. (9) 434-5999; fax (9) 461-3907; e-mail info@curports.com; internet curports.com; Man. Dir AGUSTÍN DÍAZ.

Curaçao Shipping Association (SVC): c/o Dammers & van der Heide (Antilles) Inc, Kaya Flamboyan 11, Willemstad, Curaçao; tel. (9) 737-0600; fax (9) 737-3875; Pres. K. PONSEN.

St Maarten Ports Authority: J. Yrausquin Blvd, POB 146, Philipsburg, St Maarten; tel. 542-2307; fax 542-5048; e-mail kfranca@smpanv.com; internet www.portofstmaarten.com; Man. Dir KEITH FRANCA.

Principal Shipping Companies

Anthony Veder & Co NV: Zeelandia z/n, POB 3677, Curaçao; tel. (9) 461-4700; fax (9) 461-2576; e-mail anveder@vrshipping.com; Man. Dir JOOP VAN VLIET.

Caribbean Moving Services NV: Caracasbaaiweg 328, POB 442, Willemstad, Curaçao; tel. (9) 767-2588; fax 747-1155; internet www.ccs.an; fmrly Caribbean Cargo Services NV; Man. Dir LOES VAN DER WOUDE.

Curaçao Dry-dock Co Inc: POB 3012, Curaçao; tel. (9) 733-0000; fax (9) 736-5580; e-mail info@cdmnv.com; f. 1958; Man. Dir MARIO RAYMOND EVERTSZ.

Curaçao Ports Services Inc NV (CPS): Curaçao Container Terminal, POB 170, Curaçao; tel. (9) 461-5177; fax (9) 461-6536; e-mail cps@cps.an; Man. Dir KAREL JAN O. ASTER.

Dammers Ship Agencies Inc: Dammers Bldg, Kaya Flamboyan 11, POB 3018, Willemstad, Curaçao; tel. (9) 737-0600; fax (9) 737-3875; e-mail directorate@dammers-curacao.com; internet www.dammers-curacao.com; f. 1964; fmrly Dammers & van der Heide, Shipping and Trading (Antilles) Inc; Man. Dir (Finance) PETER GOVERS; Man. Dir (Marketing and Sales) ROBERT VAN HEULEN.

Gomez Transport NV: Zeelandia z/n, Willemstad, Curaçao; tel. (9) 461-5900; fax (9) 461-3358; e-mail info@gomezshipping.an; Man. FERNANDO DA COSTA GÓMEZ.

Hal Antillen NV: De Ruyterkade 63, POB 812, Curaçao.

Intermodal Container Services NV: Salinja Galleries, 1st Floor Unit 201, POB 3747, Curaçao; tel. (9) 461-3330; fax (9) 461-3432; Mans A. R. BEAUJON, N. N. HARMS.

Lagendijk Maritime Services: POB 3481, Curaçao; tel. (9) 465-5766; fax (9) 465-5998; e-mail ims@ibm.net.

S. E. L. Maduro Shipping: Dokweg 19, Maduro Plaza, Curaçao; tel. (9) 733-1510; fax (9) 733-1538; e-mail maduroship@madurosons.com; internet www.madurosons.com; f. 1837; Vice-Pres. RONALD CORSEN.

St Maarten Port Services: POB 270, Philipsburg, St Maarten; tel. 542-2304.

CIVIL AVIATION

There are international airports at Curaçao (or Hato, 12 km from Willemstad), Bonaire (Flamingo Airport) and St Maarten (Princess Juliana, 16 km from Philipsburg), and airfields for inter-island flights at St Eustatius and Saba. In 1998 a free trade zone was inaugurated at the international airport on Curaçao. The second phase of a US $118m. project to expand Princess Juliana Airport was completed in 2006. The development comprised a new terminal, enhancing the airport's passenger-handling capacity by 2.5m. A new passenger terminal building was opened at Curaçao International Airport in 2006.

Dutch Antilles Express: Pietermaai 33–35, POB 4101, Willemstad, Curaçao; tel. 461-2502; fax 461-2508; e-mail curacao@flydae.com; internet www.flydae.com; f. 2005; scheduled passenger flights within the Netherlands Antilles and to other Caribbean and South American destinations.

Windward Express Airways: Princess Juliana International Airport, St Maarten; tel. 545-2001; fax 545-2224; e-mail windwardexpressreservations@hotmail.com; internet www.windwardexpress.com; domestic and limited Caribbean island charter flights, incl. destinations with restricted access; passenger and cargo flights; Man. Dir CURLETTA HALLEY.

Windward Islands Airways International (WIA—Winair) NV: Princess Juliana Airport, POB 2088, Philipsburg, St Maarten; tel. 545-4237; fax 545-2002; e-mail info@fly-winair.com; internet www.fly-winair.com; f. 1961; govt-owned since 1974; scheduled and charter flights throughout north-eastern Caribbean; Man. Dir EDWIN HODGE.

Tourism

Tourism is a major industry on all the islands. The principal attractions for tourists are the white, sandy beaches, marine wildlife and diving facilities. There are marine parks in the waters around Curaçao, Bonaire and Saba. The numerous historic sites are of interest to visitors. The largest number of tourists visit St Maarten, Curaçao and Bonaire. In 2008 stop-over visitors on all five islands totalled 970,680. In the same year 1,873,411 cruise ship passengers visited St Maarten, Curaçao and Bonaire. Tourism generated earnings of NA Fl. 1,906.5m. in 2004.

Curaçao Tourist Board: Pietermaai 19, POB 3266, Willemstad, Curaçao; tel. (9) 434-8200; fax (9) 461-5017; e-mail ctdbcur@ctdb.net; internet www.ctb.an; f. 1989; supervised by the Curaçao Tourism Development Bureau; Marketing Dir E. NITA.

Saba Tourist Office: Windwardside, POB 527, Saba; tel. 416-2231; fax 416-2350; e-mail tourism@sabagov.com; internet www.sabatourism.com; Dir GLENN C. HOLM.

St Eustatius Tourist Office: St Eustatius Tourism Development Foundation, Fort Oranje, Oranjestad, St Eustatius; tel. and fax 318-2433; e-mail euxtour@goldenrocknet.com; internet www.statiatourism.com; Dir ALIDA FRANCIS.

St Maarten Tourist Bureau: Vineyard Office Park, W. G. Buncamper Rd 33, Philipsburg, St Maarten; tel. 542-2337; fax 542-2734; e-mail info@travelsxm.com; internet www.st-maarten.com; Commr ROY MARLIN; Dir REGINA LA BEGA.

Tourism Corporation Bonaire (TCB): Kaya Grandi 2, Kralendijk, Bonaire; tel. 717-8322; fax 717-8408; e-mail info@tourismbonaire.com; internet www.infobonaire.com; Commr JEFFREY LEVENSTONE.

HOTEL ASSOCIATIONS

Bonaire Hotel and Tourism Association (BONHATA): Kaya Soeur Bartola 15B, Kralendijk, Bonaire; tel. 717-5134; fax 717-8534; e-mail info@bonhata.org; internet www.ilovebonaire.com; f. 1980; Pres. SARA MATERA; Vice-Pres. JACK CHALK.

Curaçao Hospitality and Tourism Association (CHATA): Kaya Junior Salas 01, Curaçao; tel. (9) 465-1005; fax (9) 465-1052; e-mail info@chata.org; internet www.chata.org; f. 1967 as Curaçao Hotel Asscn; Pres. JEANETTE BONET.

St Maarten Hospitality and Trade Association: W. J. A. Nisbeth Rd 33A, POB 486, Philipsburg, St Maarten; tel. 542-0108; fax 542-0107; e-mail info@shta.com; internet www.shta.com; Pres. EMIL LEE; Exec. Project Man. ROBERT DUBOURCQ.

Defence

Although defence is the responsibility of the Netherlands, compulsory military service is laid down in an Antilles Ordinance. The Governor is the Commander-in-Chief of the armed forces in the islands, and a Dutch contingent is stationed in Willemstad, Curaçao. The Netherlands also operates a Coast Guard Force (to combat organized crime and drugs-smuggling), based at St Maarten and Aruba; a joint Coast Guard of the Netherlands Antilles and Aruba commenced operations in 2001. In May 1999 the US air force and navy began patrols from a base on Curaçao to combat the transport of illegal drugs.

Commander of the Navy: Commodore PETER W. LENSELINK.

Education

Education was made compulsory in 1992. The islands' educational facilities are generally of a high standard. The education system is the same as that of the Netherlands. Dutch is used as the principal language of instruction in schools on the Leeward Islands, while English is used in schools on the Windward Islands. Instruction in Papiamento (using a different spelling system from that adopted by Aruba) has been introduced in primary schools. Primary education begins at six years of age and lasts for six years. Secondary education lasts for a further five years. In 2003, according to UNESCO estimates, enrolment at primary schools included 97% of pupils in the relevant age-group, while the comparable ratio at secondary schools was 81%. The University of the Netherlands Antilles, sited on Curaçao, had 2,104 students in 2008/09. In 2001 the budgetary allocation to education by the central Government represented 12.8% of total expenditure.

Bibliography

For works on the Caribbean generally, see Select Bibliography (Books)

Brown, E. *Suriname and the Netherlands Antilles*. Lanham, MD, Scarecrow Press, 1992.

Ferguson, J. *Eastern Caribbean*. New York, NY, Latin American Bureau, 1997.

Greey, M. *Aruba, Bonaire and Curaçao*. Northampton, MA, Interlink, 2007.

Keinders, A. *Politieke Geschiedenis van de Nederlandse Antillen en Aruba, 1950–93*. Zutphen, Walburg Press, 1993.

Klomp, A. *Politics on Bonaire*. Assen, Van Gorcum, 1986.

Koulen, I. *Netherlands Antilles and Aruba: A Research Guide*. London, ICP Publishing Ltd, 1987.

Schaap, C. D. *Fighting Money Laundering*. Dordrecht, Kluwer Law International, 1998.

Schoenhais, K. *Netherlands Antilles and Aruba*, World Bibliographical Series. Oxford, ABC Clio, 1993.

NICARAGUA

Geography

PHYSICAL FEATURES

The Republic of Nicaragua spans the Central American isthmus and is the largest country lying between Mexico and Colombia. Nicaragua tapers westwards from its long eastern coast on the Caribbean, to a south-west-facing Pacific coast, but also southwards from the long, north-western border (922 km) with Honduras, to the shorter, more east–west border (309 km) with Costa Rica (on the latter frontier, the question of Costa Rican navigation rights on the San Juan River has currently become vexatious). In the far north-west Nicaragua looks across the mouth of the Gulf of Fonseca at El Salvador—the two countries and Honduras are holding tripartite discussions on the delimitation of maritime boundaries in the Gulf. Such boundaries also concern Nicaragua in the Caribbean, where it has challenged Honduras and Colombia over some 50,000 sq km (19,300 sq miles) of maritime territory, owing to the Colombian possession of a number of islands and cays lying to the east of the Nicaraguan coast (San Andrés lies 180 km off shore, included administratively with Providencia and a number of other satellites). Nicaraguan territory also includes some islands and islets, notably the Corn Islands, some 70 km off the Caribbean coast near Bluefields, and the Miskito Cays further north. The total area of the country is 130,373 sq km (50,337 sq miles), including 10,034 sq km of inland waters.

Nicaragua is about 440 km from north to south and 450 km, at its widest, from east to west. Like most of the Central American countries, it consists of a central highlands divide between a Pacific coastal region and a wider Caribbean (Atlantic) coastal region. Nicaragua is dominated by the great lake that bears its name in the south-west of the country, where the Pacific lowlands are rather more involved topographically. Rising immediately above the narrow plains along the shore are the Coastal or Diriamba Highlands, which are volcanic and, mainly in the north, still active. These heights subside into the Rivas isthmus as they head south, separating Lake Nicaragua from the ocean (by no more than 17 km at one point). Between this line and the central mountain uplands lies the Great Rift, fertile central lowlands dominated by two great lakes—Managua, on the south-western shores of which is the eponymous national capital, and, to the south of it, the 8,157-sq-km Nicaragua, one of the largest freshwater lakes in the world. The Pacific lowlands broaden southwards around the lakes, following the Rift, sufficient to allow Lake Nicaragua actually to empty into the Caribbean (along the San Juan). This is possible because the central mountain region tapers southwards, as the main thrust of the Continental Divide becomes more diffuse. The highlands, therefore, mainly rise in the north-centre of the country, the highly dissected region contrasting forested ranges with fertile basins and valleys. The highest point is Mogotón (2,438 m—8,002 ft), in the north-west. Finally, the eastern or Caribbean region is dominated by the Mosquito Coast (Costa de Mosquitos—an erroneous adaptation of the name of the local Amerindians, the Miskitos) and its hinterland. This involves the lower slopes of the central uplands merging into an extensive, alluvial plain with gentle valleys, giving way to an often marshy coast of shallow bays, lagoons and salt marshes. The eastern lowlands tend to be savannah, but the coast is dominated by dense rainforest. In fact, about 27% of Nicaragua is forested, and 46% is classified as pastureland. This terrain is well watered, not just by copious rainfall in most places, but by many rivers—the longest is the 780-km Coco, which forms much of the eastern part of the Honduran border. The varied ecosystems common to the countries of Central America (owing to the contrasting topography and its position as the land bridge between two continents) shelter in Nicaragua the usual array of wildlife—numerous bird species, big cats, a variety of reptiles, anteaters, monkeys, etc.—but the country's wide maritime shelf also allows it to boast the richest marine fauna in the Caribbean.

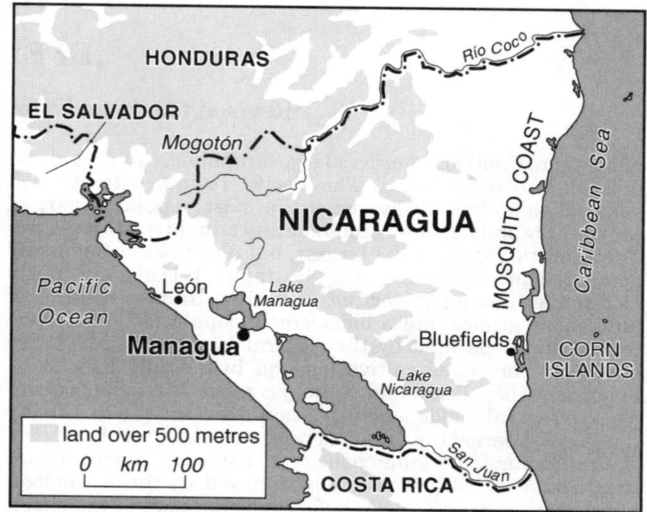

CLIMATE

The climate is tropical in the lowlands and cooler in the highlands. Nicaragua is very susceptible to hurricanes, with volcanoes and earthquakes adding to nature's destructive potential, so the country is particularly prone to landslides. This is not helped by deforestation and the consequent soil erosion. Generally, it is slightly cooler and much wetter in the east than in the Pacific west. The rainy season is May–January, and average annual rainfall in Managua, located in the western lowlands, is 1,140 mm (44 ins). This figure can be more than doubled in the east. The average temperatures in Managua range from 20°C (68°F) to 34°C (93°F) over the year.

POPULATION

Most Nicaraguans ('Nicas') are Mestizo (77%), of mixed race, but there are fairly substantial white (10%) and black (9%) communities, with the balance consisting of indigenous Amerindians (who may be underenumerated). The black population, which is concentrated in the east, mainly along the Caribbean coast, is generally of Jamaican descent or 'Black Carib' (escaped African slaves who married into a Carib Amerindian population, preserving a Carib or Garifuna language, but who were deported from St Vincent island—now in Saint Vincent and the Grenadines—in 1797 to an island off the Honduran coast). Most of the population (96%) use Spanish, the official language, but, as well as Garifuna, a Creole dialect and English are also used in the east (apart from those descended from an anglophone background, there are traces of the time when the United Kingdom claimed a protectorate over the Mosquito Coast). The indigenous languages of the country are mainly of the Miskito, Sumo and Rama groups, in the east, with others spoken by the small numbers of Amerindians in the west, the Monimbo and Subtiaba. The majority of the population are Roman Catholic and the remainder mostly Evangelical Protestant.

According to the census undertaken in mid-2005, the total population numbered 5.1m. Almost one-half of this population is under 15 years of age, 56% are urbanized (the highest rate of urbanization in Central America—the same as Panama) and it is one of the poorest populations in the Western hemisphere. Most people live in the Pacific lowlands and in the adjacent high country. At the 2005 census the capital, Managua, had an estimated population of 937,489, with the second city, León, to the north-west, totalling 174,051 inhabitants. According to official estimates, the population at mid-2010 stood at 5.8m. The country is divided into 15 departments, with the Mosquito Coast now consisting of two autonomous regions (Atlántico Norte and Atlántico Sur).

History

Dr ED BROWN

Revised for this edition by KATHARINE MURISON

Nicaragua, Central America's largest republic, can roughly be divided into three zones. The Pacific region, with its rich volcanic soils, has always been the most populated part of the country and forms its economic and administrative centre. The Atlantic region is the largest, but also the most sparsely populated and isolated, part of Nicaragua. It is also culturally distinctive, having important minorities from a variety of indigenous groups and a black/creole population. These two regions are separated by the Central Highlands, which are important for coffee cultivation and historically have been major zones of political and military conflict. Nicaragua did not emerge as a fully independent nation state until 1838. During the colonial period the area had been a relatively isolated part of the Guatemalan Audiencia and, following independence from Spain in 1821, was briefly annexed by the Iturbidean Mexican Empire (1821–23) before forming part of the short-lived United Provinces of Central America (1823–38). The country's boundaries have undergone a number of alterations since independence: Guanacaste was ceded to Costa Rica in 1858; in a treaty signed in 1928 the islands of San Andrés, Providencia and Santa Catalina (the San Andrés archipelago) were ceded to Colombia; and a large piece of territory in north-eastern Nicaragua was granted to Honduras by the International Court of Justice (ICJ) in the 1960s.

NICARAGUA, 1838–1936

The first decades of Nicaraguan independence are known as the 'Age of Anarchy', owing to successive civil wars between the Liberal élites of León and the Conservatives of Granada. With these two cities acting like autonomous states, the emergence of a national state apparatus was severely impeded. In 1854 Leonese Liberals recruited a group of North American mercenaries, led by William Walker, to fight their Granadan rivals. After defeating the Conservatives, Walker turned on his Liberal patrons, declared himself President, reintroduced slavery and established English as the official language of the republic. However, his ambitions of regional domination united the rest of Central America against him, and he was eventually removed from office. The Liberals, weakened by their association with Walker, compromised with Conservative Presidents over the next 30 years. The stability that this brought saw the first coherent nation-building project of Nicaragua's history as the country's infrastructure began to be developed and the judicial and institutional basis of the state was enhanced.

While the foundations of the modern Nicaraguan state were laid in the 30 years of Conservative hegemony, it was the Liberal regime of José Santos Zelaya (1893–1909) that marked the definitive insertion of the Nicaraguan economy into the international division of labour as a supplier of primary commodities (mainly coffee, but also bananas, gold and timber). Zelaya introduced a Constitution separating the Church from the state, modernized the army, gained control of the Atlantic Coast from the United Kingdom and encouraged overseas capital investment. However, the courting of European and Japanese capital for the construction of an inter-oceanic canal in southern Nicaragua provoked a US-supported rebellion by Nicaragua's Conservatives, which forced Zelaya into exile in 1909 and ushered in 25 years of intermittent US occupation. US marines were stationed in Nicaragua in 1912–25 and again in 1926–33 in order to protect a series of Conservative Presidents from Liberal rebellions. During this period Nicaragua virtually became a colony of the USA. The incipient Nicaraguan state became enmeshed within a financial system where profligate loans were guaranteed by turning over Nicaragua's customs revenues, the national railroads and the national bank to US interests. Meanwhile, the Bryan-Chamorro Treaty of 1916 granted the USA exclusive rights to the construction of any canal within Nicaraguan territory (thereby safeguarding the Panamanian canal from any rival Nicaraguan project).

The second period of occupation saw the USA modify its support for the Conservatives in a bid to allow the USA to continue to dominate Nicaragua without the constant need to have troops on the ground. In 1927 an agreement between the Liberals and the Conservatives included provisions for US-supervised elections to be held in that year, while allowing the continued presence of US troops in Nicaragua until a new 'non-partisan' National Guard could be trained. Only one Liberal lieutenant, Augusto César Sandino, rejected these measures and, with a 300-strong 'Defending Army of National Sovereignty', continued to fight a sustained guerrilla war against the US forces, their Conservative puppets and the Liberal leadership. Sandino and his followers quickly developed very successful guerrilla tactics and the US forces became embroiled in a protracted conflict.

The US marines eventually left following the election of the Liberal Juan Bautista Sacasa in 1932, leaving the National Guard to carry on the struggle against Sandino. In February 1933, however, Sandino signed a peace accord with the Sacasa Government, which guaranteed that US troops would not return, granted an amnesty to Sandino's followers and created a new department in the north of the country, which they would settle in and police themselves. The Sandinistas, however, continued to be harassed by an uncontrollable National Guard, and in February 1934 Sandino was murdered on the orders of the Guard's director, Anastasio Somoza García. Somoza overthrew Sacasa in May 1936. A highly dubious presidential election was held in December, and on 1 January 1937 Somoza was installed as President of Nicaragua. He and his sons were to stay in control of Nicaragua until 1979.

THE SOMOZA DYNASTY

Anastasio Somoza García proved to be a skilful manipulator of successive US Administrations. He utilized his control of the National Guard, clever political manoeuvring and strategies of accommodation with the traditional oligarchy to sustain his position within Nicaragua. Following his assassination in 1956 by the poet Rigoberto López Pérez, Somoza García was succeeded as President by his son, Luís Somoza Debayle, while his youngest son, Anastasio Somoza Debayle (or 'Tachito'), became Commander-in-Chief of the National Guard. Luís pursued a much lower profile and more humanitarian style of leadership, opening up the political system, at least ostensibly, and instigating a range of social programmes under the US-sponsored Alliance for Progress. On the death of Luís in 1967, his brother assumed the presidency and, in spite of lacking the political skill of his father, operated a more repressive form of dictatorship.

Under the Somozas, the Nicaraguan economy expanded considerably as they facilitated the successive evolution of a series of further agro-export crops (including beef, sugar and especially cotton, although coffee continued to be important) and a certain level of industrial development. However, their control of the National Guard, their close ties with the US

Administration, as well as rampant nepotism and cronyism enabled the Somozas to ensure that the state essentially acted to service their own business interests (and those of their closest allies), rather than national economic and social development. It is estimated that by 1979 the Somozas owned around 40% of Nicaragua's economy.

The regime finally began to fragment in the 1970s as the brutality, corruption and political weakness of 'Tachito' grew increasingly apparent. Somoza's abuse of humanitarian aid, following an earthquake that destroyed Managua in 1972, and the assassination of the Conservative opposition leader, Pedro Joaquín Chamorro, in 1978 helped to unite internal opposition to the regime (see below). Moreover, the dictator's excesses also prompted international condemnation and, most importantly, the partial withdrawal of support from the Administration of US President Jimmy Carter (1977–81). Facing international isolation, a growing popular insurrection and a disintegrating National Guard, Somoza resigned the presidency in July 1979. He fled to Paraguay, where he was assassinated in September 1980.

THE SANDINISTA NATIONAL LIBERATION FRONT

The overthrow of the Somoza dictatorship represented one of the most broadly based and popular insurrections in Latin America's history. Its origins lay in 1961 when, inspired by the Cuban revolution, a group of students from the University of León (together with surviving members of Sandino's Defending Army) formed the Frente Sandinista de Liberación Nacional (FSLN—Sandinista National Liberation Front). Despite the fact that many of its founders were Marxists, the FSLN rapidly broadened its ideological base, and its politics represented a mix of nationalism, radical Christianity and a brand of socialism that owed more to cultural practices peculiar to Latin America than to the USSR. By the end of the 1970s the FSLN had become the hegemonic group within an extremely broad revolutionary alliance (which also included the non-Somocista business élite, sections of the Roman Catholic Church, left-wing activists and intellectuals) and had succeeded in mobilizing large numbers of the urban poor and the rural peasantry.

The Somoza regime, however, inflicted serious losses on the FSLN in the late 1960s and early 1970s. By 1974 most of the FSLN's founders were dead or imprisoned, many of its underground networks had been destroyed, and the organization was internally divided. However, the dictator's increasingly brutal and arbitrary repression over the ensuing years contributed to growing public unrest, which enabled the FSLN to attract increasing numbers of new recruits. The murder of Chamorro in January 1978 provoked mass demonstrations against Somoza and was followed by a national strike and a series of uprisings in the major cities in September. Following the Government's brutal suppression of these demonstrations, the FSLN launched a final offensive in mid-1979. By late July Somoza had been removed and Nicaragua was ruled by a Government of National Reconstruction dominated by the FSLN.

THE SANDINISTA GOVERNMENT, 1979–90

The guiding principles of the new regime were the pursuit of political pluralism, a mixed economy, popular participation, and a non-aligned foreign policy. The state was to function according to the 'logic of the majority', with priority given to the interests of the poor, and wide-ranging agricultural, health and educational reforms were subsequently introduced. The five-member governing junta consisted of two members of the anti-Somoza bourgeoisie and three Sandinistas, among them the General Secretary of the FSLN, José Daniel Ortega Saavedra, who became de facto President of Nicaragua. The 1974 Constitution was abrogated, the bicameral Congreso Nacional (National Congress) was dissolved and the National Guard was replaced with the Sandinista People's Army. In May 1980 a 47-seat Council of State was convened (increased to 51 seats in May 1981) to act as a legislative body. The new assembly consisted of representatives of various mass organizations active within civil society. Although the Sandinistas enjoyed an institutionalized parliamentary majority, the non-Sandinista business sectors and constitutional opposition parties were also represented. The new Constitution guaranteed a range of civil liberties common to liberal democracies, abolished the death penalty and established an independent judiciary.

Elections to the presidency and to a new 96-seat Asamblea Nacional (National Assembly) were held on 4 November 1984. The FSLN presidential candidate, Ortega, received 67% of the votes cast, and the FSLN won 61 seats in the Asamblea Nacional. Most national and international observers endorsed the legitimacy of the elections (with the significant exception of the USA).

Under the Sandinista Government, Nicaragua was characterized by a series of popular consultations and legislative debates, which led to the promulgation of a new Constitution on 9 January 1987. Prominent among its provisions was the granting of autonomy to the indigenous population of the Atlantic coast. Initially, the Sandinistas had promoted innovative forms of governance across the country, organized at a local community level, but the management demands of the intensifying military conflict against the Contras (counter-revolutionary forces) gradually led to more authoritarian tendencies from the mid-1980s.

Economically, the Sandinista regime pursued a number of redistributive policies, which included subsidies on basic goods and nationalization (although the public sector never accounted for more than 40% of the economy during the Sandinista period and the private sector was directly encouraged through incentives). An agrarian reform programme was also undertaken, which gradually redistributed lands taken first from the Somozas and later from other large landowners deemed not to be using their land productively. Initially, a significant proportion of this occurred through the creation of large state farms but, as the policy progressed, the majority was granted to landless peasants. By the end of the 1980s more than 50% of Nicaragua's agricultural land had been affected by the land reform programme.

For the first few years of the Sandinista regime the economy performed relatively well, especially given the debt crisis experienced by the whole continent. By 1988, however, the effects of the US trade embargo, imposed in 1985, and the ongoing conflict with the Contras had severely undermined the original Sandinista economic model. Production levels and earnings from the agricultural export sector collapsed, leading to unsustainable increases in the national debt. The combination of this worsening external situation with rapidly expanding budget deficits caused by the escalating costs of defence (over one-half of the national budget was spent on defence by 1985) gradually developed into a severe economic crisis. An economic adjustment plan was instituted, which reduced public sector employment and state subsidies and devalued the currency, while the initiation of peace negotiations also resulted in significant reductions in military expenditure. These measures had some success, but by the elections in early 1990 the parlous state of the economy remained a key problem.

OPPOSITION AND THE WAR

The period of relative political stability following the FSLN's insurrection was short-lived. Ronald Reagan's inauguration as US President in 1981 marked the beginning of a US campaign to destabilize the revolution. The US Government claimed that the Sandinistas were totalitarian communists who directly threatened US security interests and other countries in the region, as well as the liberties of the Nicaraguan people. Reagan adopted an active policy of resourcing, arming and training the Contras. The most important of these, initially consisting of around 2,000 former National Guards, were based in Honduras and were organized into the Movimiento Democrático Nicaragüense (MDN—Nicaraguan Democratic Movement) and the Fuerzas Democráticas Nicaragüenses (FDN—Nicaraguan Democratic Forces). A smaller force, the Alianza Revolucionaria Democrática (ARDE—Democratic Revolutionary Alliance), was based in Costa Rica.

By 1985 the Contras had recruited up to 10,000 members, including a significant number of peasants disaffected by the Sandinistas' agrarian reform programme. With the support of the Honduran army and financial aid from the USA (as well as the direct involvement of US personnel in some operations), the Contras were able to organize numerous incursions into Nicaragua from the early 1980s. It was estimated that nearly 45,000 Nicaraguans were killed, wounded or abducted in the war and about 250,000 people displaced. In 1986 increasing US congressional opposition to the funding of the Contras and growing international censure provoked elements of the Reagan Administration to become involved in the illegal transfer to the Contras of the proceeds of clandestine sales of military equipment to Iran. The eventual exposure of these actions contributed to the strengthening of a congressional ban on aid to the Contras.

Despite their destructive impact on the Sandinista economic project, the failure of the Contras to achieve a decisive military victory, combined with the end of US aid, prompted them to enter into peace negotiations. The first in a series of agreements, known as the Esquipulas Peace Accords, was signed in 1987. These accords laid the foundations for a general disarmament process, with international observation by the Organization of American States (OAS). Subsequent accords (Esquipulas II and III) led to further disarmament and provided the framework for the 1990 elections.

THE 1990 ELECTIONS

The presidential, legislative and municipal elections of February 1990 were a landmark in Nicaraguan history. Recognized to have been free and fair by international observers, the Sandinistas abided by the results. The ballot produced an unexpected victory for the Unión Nacional Opositora (UNO—National Opposition Union), a hastily prepared coalition of 14 anti-Sandinista parties. The UNO's presidential candidate, Violeta Barrios de Chamorro, widow of the assassinated Pedro Joaquín Chamorro, won 55% of the votes cast, compared with Ortega's 41%. The opposition alliance also gained an absolute majority in the Asamblea Nacional and control of 101 of 132 municipal councils. The belief that a Sandinista victory would mean the continuation of war and economic hardship, the unpopularity of military conscription and the increasingly hierarchical attitude of the Sandinista leadership were the principal causes of the Government's electoral defeat.

Violeta Chamorro, a former member of the Government of National Reconstruction in the 1980s, was seen as a figure of national reconciliation. On assuming the presidency she avoided confrontation with the FSLN by reappointing Sandinista Gen. Humberto Ortega as Commander-in-Chief of the Armed Forces, and by agreeing to uphold the 1987 Constitution. Chamorro's actions prompted tensions with more extremist factions within the UNO, led by the Vice-President, Virgilio Godoy Reyes, and the newly elected mayor of Managua, Arnoldo Alemán Lacayo. This infighting led to the collapse of the UNO as a coherent political force in early 1993. A new consensus subsequently was reached between a number of former UNO deputies, the FSLN, the Partido Conservador (PC—Conservative Party), and the President.

THE UNO GOVERNMENT

Although the victory of the UNO coalition generated fears of revenge-taking and political chaos, owing to the extremism of some of its component parties, government policy quickly dispelled such concerns. The architect of government policy was the Minister to the Presidency, Antonio Lacayo Oyanguren, the son-in-law of Chamorro. Lacayo represented Nicaragua's modernizing bourgeoisie and sought pragmatically to implement a range of market-orientated economic reforms, while recognizing the continued influence of the FSLN. However, Chamorro's conciliatory stance towards the Sandinistas led to the suspension of US aid, while economic measures demanded by the IMF provoked industrial action. By mid-1991 Lacayo's strategic policy of market-led modernization had been replaced by short-term crisis management.

THE FSLN IN OPPOSITION

Despite its electoral defeat, the FSLN remained the largest single party in the Asamblea Nacional, and continued to exert considerable influence over the police and the army, both of which were led by prominent Sandinistas, as well as over the trade unions and civil associations. However, the party's popularity among the wider population suffered considerably from what became known as 'la piñata', a process whereby large amounts of state and government property were transferred to the leadership of the FSLN during the two-month transition period between the FSLN and UNO Governments.

In 1994 internal divisions within the FSLN over its co-operation with the Chamorro Government led to the formation of two factions. The Izquierda Democrática Sandinista (Sandinista Democratic Left), led by Daniel Ortega, which advocated a more orthodox revolutionary outlook and was supported by mass organizations, the trade unions and the urban and rural poor, was opposed by the more socio-democratic, 'renewalist' faction, led by a former Vice-President and leader of the FSLN in the Asamblea Nacional, Sergio Ramírez Mercado. The Ortega faction emerged successful from the ensuing political struggle, and in January 1995 Ramírez left the FSLN to form the Movimiento de Renovación Sandinista (MRS—Sandinista Renewal Movement). The majority of the Sandinista deputies moved to the MRS, leaving the FSLN with just eight deputies. However, the overwhelming majority of the grassroots membership remained loyal to the FSLN.

OPPOSITION TO THE CHAMORRO GOVERNMENT

As well as constitutional opposition, the Chamorro presidency was challenged by an increasing number of armed groups. Following the 1990 elections, the OAS supervised a progressive demobilization of Contra forces, and the Nicaraguan army was reduced from 90,000 to 15,000 troops. The resettlement into civilian life of both former Contras and former Sandinista soldiers proved problematic, however, and promises guaranteed in the Esquipulas Accords to provide land, social services and credit to facilitate this process were not fulfilled.

As a result, the Government faced its first major military crisis in July 1993, following the occupation of the town of Estelí by a pro-Sandinista armed group. The security forces recaptured the town by force, resulting in 22 deaths. In August a rearmed group of former Contras, Frente Norte 3-80 (FN—Northern Front 3-80), kidnapped a number of deputies who had gone to the northern town of Quilalí to negotiate its disarmament. The FN demanded the resignations of Gen. Humberto Ortega and Antonio Lacayo. In response, former Sandinista soldiers kidnapped a group of right-wing deputies in Managua, including Vice-President Godoy. A peaceful resolution was negotiated by the OAS and a general amnesty was granted. In late 1993 Gen. Ortega was replaced as Commander-in-Chief of the Armed Forces by Gen. Joaquín Cuadra Lacayo, also a Sandinista. Nevertheless, rearmed groups continued to be a serious problem in parts of northern Nicaragua until as late as 2001.

A further source of tension for the UNO Government arose from the political question of how to address the unconsolidated legal status of the buildings and land that had been nationalized or redistributed during the revolutionary years. Many owners who had fled to the USA following the revolution had returned to Nicaragua since the 1990 elections and were demanding the return of their property. The Government sought to respond to these sometimes violent demands without invalidating the redistribution processes of the 1980s, which would have precipitated a descent into further social and political instability. Eventually, following mediation from former US President Carter, a compromise law of property stability was adopted. Despite the legal protection that this gave to those who had benefited from redistribution, the lack of access of the poorest sectors to legal assistance contributed to a gradual reconcentration of property ownership in the country.

THE 1996 ELECTIONS

Presidential and legislative elections were held on 20 October 1996. Owing to a constitutional amendment adopted in the previous year that prohibited close relatives of a serving President from contesting a presidential election, Lacayo was unable to stand. In the absence of a prominent UNO nominee, the anti-Sandinista platform was filled by the

Alianza Liberal (AL—Liberal Alliance). This coalition, under the candidacy of Arnoldo Alemán Lacayo, mayor of Managua, brought together a range of liberal parties, including Somoza's former Partido Liberal Nacionalista (PLN—Nationalist Liberal Party) and Alemán's Partido Liberal Constitutionalista (PLC—Constitutional Liberal Party), although the PLC would eventually come to dominate the coalition. The FSLN and several other parties claimed the provisional results of the presidential contest, which indicated a victory for Alemán, were fraudulent, although international observers declared the ballot to have been generally free and fair. Many of the provisional results were subsequently revised, but the Consejo Supremo Electoral (CSE—Supreme Electoral Council) declared that these anomalies had not affected the overall result. Alemán was declared the winner, with 51% of the valid votes cast, compared with 38% for the FSLN candidate, former President Ortega. The AL also gained a majority of seats in the Asamblea Nacional and control of 92 municipalities.

THE ALEMÁN ADMINISTRATION

In contrast to the conciliatory stance of Violeta Chamorro, Arnoldo Alemán had an openly anti-Sandinista agenda. His more abrasive style of government had somewhat predictable consequences. The eviction of families occupying land granted to them by the Sandinistas, as part of the new Government's desire to return land to its former owners, prompted the FSLN to organize national protests in April 1997. The issue was eventually settled via direct negotiations between the FSLN and the Government, resulting in the adoption in November of the definitive law of urban and rural reformed property. Meanwhile, unemployment continued to increase, despite Alemán's campaign promise to create 100,000 jobs per year, and the establishment of a multi-party commission to seek solutions to social hardship produced few tangible benefits.

From 1998 the work of the Comptroller-General, Agustín Jarquín Anaya, was systematically obstructed by Alemán, who was, together with members of his family, the subject of a number of investigations by Jarquín's office. In February 1999 a report published by the Comptroller-General's office revealed that Alemán's personal wealth had increased by some 900% during his terms of office as mayor of Managua and as President. However, the campaign of obstruction against Jarquín was aided by senior figures from the FSLN, who were also under investigation concerning their acquisition of former state assets during the transition to the UNO Government in 1990. This culminated in Jarquín being briefly imprisoned in November 1999 on charges of illegal use of state funds to employ an investigative journalist to examine Alemán's finances.

HURRICANE MITCH

The weakness of Nicaragua's public institutions was amply illustrated following Hurricane Mitch in October 1998. The hurricane devastated the north-western parts of the country, killing almost 3,000 people and causing massive infrastructural damage. Initially, Alemán refused to declare a state of emergency and questioned the severity of the disaster. When the full consequences of the disaster became known, international donors adopted a strategy of delivering humanitarian aid directly to non-governmental organizations (NGOs), owing to concerns over the possible misappropriation of funds by the Government. In response, the President threatened to impose a tax of up to 40% on all aid entering the country, a threat universally condemned and subsequently withdrawn.

The confused response to this disaster and the subsequent inefficiency of the Government's reconstruction plans brought criticism from various quarters. The Stockholm Consultative Group, established by international donors to co-ordinate reconstruction efforts in consultation with the Nicaraguan Government and NGOs, approved the Government's plans for post-hurricane reconstruction in April 1999, but became increasingly critical of the Alemán administration's repeated inability to present more detailed proposals on how aid would be spent. Growing accusations of corruption and incompetence in the allocation of reconstruction funds, as well as the attacks on the Comptroller-General's office, led some donors to suspend a number of aid programmes.

THE PLC-FSLN PACT

During 1998 the FSLN maintained strong vocal opposition to Alemán's Government, but the party's apparent lack of long-term strategy, combined with failure in the March Atlantic Coast local elections, led to renewed divisions within the FSLN leadership. Although Ortega was re-elected Secretary-General of the party in May, opposition to his leadership intensified when he subsequently entered into negotiations with President Alemán on political co-operation with the PLC. These negotiations, concluded in October 1999, centred on changes to the Constitution and the electoral system. It was agreed that the PLC and FSLN would appoint their own members to institutions such as the CSE and the Supreme Court, and that elaborate procedures for the granting of legal status to political parties would be established in order to make it more difficult for smaller parties to function, thereby institutionalizing a two-party system, consisting of the PLC and the FSLN. The principal changes to the electoral laws included the following provisions: each party must obtain 75,000 signatures in order to gain legal recognition (in the case of an alliance, 75,000 signatures must be collected for each party included in the alliance); each party must gain 4% of the popular vote in order to retain legal status after an election; and all parties must have a presence in all 150 municipalities. Moreover, the threshold for a first-round victory in the presidential election was reduced from 45% to 35%, albeit on the condition that the victor should have a 5% lead over the second-placed candidate, and all former Presidents were granted a life seat in the Asamblea Nacional (and, with it, comprehensive parliamentary immunity). Other reforms transformed the Comptroller-General's office into a collegiate body of five Comptrollers, chosen by the PLC and FSLN, thus effectively marginalizing the existing Comptroller-General, Jarquín, who, as a result, resigned in June 2000.

The PLC-FSLN pact was initiated in the context of a growing crisis within both parties. In March 1998 Daniel Ortega's stepdaughter, Zoilamérica Narváez Murillo, accused him of having abused her as a child. Ortega claimed that the accusations were politically motivated and that Narváez was manipulated by his political rivals within the FSLN. In March 2000 Narváez finally took the matter to the Nicaraguan courts. Ortega's decision to avoid trial by invoking his parliamentary immunity deepened the divisions in the FSLN. Also in early 2000 Alemán was implicated in the 'narcojet scandal', a complex affair involving a stolen plane, drugs-trafficking and the falsification of government documents. He similarly refused to respond to these accusations. Meanwhile, the PLC lost the support of several of its deputies in the Asamblea Nacional as a result of the pact.

The European Union (EU), Scandinavian Governments and the USA all expressed concern regarding the impact of the PLC-FSLN pact on the transparency of government administration. In June 2000 the Stockholm Consultative Group informed the Alemán Government that although existing aid commitments would be fulfilled, no additional aid would be forthcoming, indicating that the failure of the new Comptroller-General's office to investigate cases of corruption involving government officials played a significant part in its decision.

The impact of the constitutional changes was first explicitly felt in the municipal elections of November 2000, when the CSE caused outrage by denying legal status to all political parties except for the FSLN, the PLC, the PC, the Camino Cristiano Nicaragüense (CCN—Nicaraguan Christian Way), and two small Atlantic Coast indigenous parties. The municipal elections were marked by a high rate of abstention. The FSLN won in 11 of the 17 departmental capitals, including Managua, while the PLC secured control of more municipalities (97, compared with the FSLN's 49).

THE 2001 ELECTIONS

The PLC was again victorious in the presidential and legislative elections of 4 November 2001. In the presidential ballot, former Vice-President Enrique Bolaños Geyer secured 56.3%

of votes cast, compared with the 42.3% polled by the FSLN candidate, Daniel Ortega. The PLC won 47 seats in the Asamblea Nacional, the FSLN 42 seats, and the PC one seat. A higher than expected turn-out (some 92% of the electorate) and the decisive margin of the PLC's victory helped the legitimacy of the electoral process, despite the adverse impacts of the constitutional changes. In accordance with the electoral reforms resulting from the PLC-FSLN pact, Alemán and Ortega, as outgoing President and second-placed presidential candidate, were both given seats in the Asamblea Nacional. The PLC was also successful in elections to the Atlantic Coast Regional Councils, which were held in March 2002, winning a majority of seats in the South Atlantic Regional Council, and an equal number of seats as the FSLN in the northern assembly. The indigenous party Yatama also made significant gains, to become the third largest party on the Coast.

Having been excluded from participating in the 2001 elections as a result of the PLC-FSLN pact, many of the smaller parties had given their support to the FSLN (including demobilized Contras and the MRS, which returned to the Sandinista mainstream for the first time since the split in 1995). Ortega's third successive defeat, despite the support of such a broad alliance, was attributed by some to a heightened awareness of terrorism following the attacks on the USA on 11 September 2001. His opponents made much of his connections with the Libyan leader, Col Muammar al-Qaddafi, who was suspected by the US Government of maintaining links with terrorist networks. The final weeks of the election campaign also saw direct expressions of support for Bolaños from the US Administration of George W. Bush (2001–09). Ortega's continued reluctance to answer the sexual abuse charges against him (he finally surrendered his immunity in December 2001), as well as his close association with the Alemán administration through the PLC-FSLN pact, also damaged his political reputation.

THE BOLAÑOS PRESIDENCY

President Enrique Bolaños Geyer's Government faced a considerable number of challenges after taking office in January 2002, the first being how to deal with Alemán, who seemingly intended to dominate the Government through his former Vice-President. Bolaños' position was particularly weak because most PLC deputies owed their positions to Alemán's control of party structures and later proved fiercely loyal to him. The extent of Alemán's influence over the PLC was demonstrated by his election to the presidency of the Asamblea Nacional as soon as Bolaños took office. Nevertheless, from the outset, Bolaños exerted his independence from Alemán, resolutely pursuing his own political agenda. Key to this agenda was a sustained effort to address the problem of corruption. The first step in this direction was the appointment of a Cabinet composed of party members with few direct links to the Alemán faction of the PLC, many of whom had been critical of the former President's poor record on corruption.

Bolaños' campaign to distance himself from his predecessor intensified in March 2002 when the Attorney-General issued charges against Alemán in connection with fraud involving the state television company (Sistema Nacional de Televisión Canal 6) and, in May, in connection with the state telecommunications company, Enitel (Empresa Nicaragüense de Telecomunicaciones). Several attempts by Bolaños to remove Alemán's parliamentary immunity were thwarted by Alemán loyalists within the Asamblea Nacional. However, this was finally achieved in December, and the former President was placed under house arrest. Nevertheless, the case proved to be protracted and highly politicized, which was compounded by the fact that the presiding Supreme Court judge in the case, Juana Méndez, was an Ortega loyalist. In August 2003, under Méndez's direction, Alemán was moved to a prison in Managua, before being released back to house arrest on his ranch in November. In December, however, he was finally sentenced to 20 years' imprisonment on charges of money-laundering, fraud and theft of state property. Although he was initially allowed to serve this sentence at his ranch, he was once more confined to prison in March 2004 after the Supreme Court rejected his appeal to serve his sentence under house arrest on grounds of ill health. In December, however, a court of appeal overturned Alemán's conviction on fraud charges in connection with Canal 6, allowing him to serve his sentence for money-laundering under house arrest.

The convoluted process of Alemán's trial and imprisonment reflected the complex political interplay between Alemán loyalists in the PLC and Bolaños, as well as between the Government and the FSLN, and the Bush Administration in the USA. In the initial months of Bolaños' administration Alemán's continued control of the PLC votes in the legislature meant that the new President was forced to negotiate with the FSLN in order to pursue the case against his predecessor. This alienated the pro-Alemán legislative bloc of the PLC still further, leading eventually to its definitive break with the Government in March 2003. Meanwhile, the US Administration urged Bolaños to adopt a more hardline, anti-Sandinista stance, even if it meant some sort of rehabilitation for Alemán (although it was also made clear that there could be no return to politics for the latter). Bolaños, whose main remaining claim to legitimacy had been the clear international support for his Government's fight against corruption, appeared to support the US stance. One of his main strategies to this end was an attempt in mid-2003 to depoliticize the system by which judges were appointed, a move designed to break Ortega's power in the judiciary. To do this, he needed the support of Alemán loyalists in the legislature. However, US intervention seemed to unite, albeit temporarily, Alemán loyalists and Sandinistas against the Bolaños Government. The pro-Alemán PLC and the FSLN continued to block the proposed judicial reforms throughout most of 2004. Nevertheless, in October the Asamblea Nacional finally approved the creation of an independent judicial council to appoint judges.

In essence, the central difficulty of Bolaños' presidency was his need, despite the rhetoric from the USA about anti-Sandinista unity, to reach some sort of rapprochement with the FSLN if he was to have any hope of delivering effective government or of developing a liberal alternative free from the influence of Alemán. As a result, in April 2004 Ortega and Bolaños announced that they had reached a new understanding. Bolaños agreed to the restructuring of the directorate of the Asamblea, from which the FSLN had initially been excluded. The President also made attempts to mould a new political alternative to the PLC and the FSLN, launching an electoral alliance, the Alianza por la República (APRE—Alliance for the Republic), in May. Meanwhile, some of the worst elements of the constitutional changes resulting from the PLC-FSLN pact were reversed. For example, in January 2003 the CSE recognized that the removal of the legal status of most political parties under the 2000 electoral law had been unconstitutional.

Nevertheless, President Bolaños' political woes worsened in 2004. In March the President, the Vice-President, José Rizo Castellón, and 31 other senior members of the PLC were accused of illegal campaign financing during the 2001 presidential election. Seven PLC members were arrested, including the party's President, Jorge Castillo Quant. In October the Comptroller-General requested that Bolaños be removed from power and fined two months' wages for withholding information regarding the financing of his electoral campaign. Supporters of the President claimed the request was politically motivated, as the office of the Comptroller-General was controlled by the FSLN and the PLC.

The FSLN won a decisive victory in the local elections of 7 November 2004, securing control of 84 of the 151 municipalities, including Managua, while the PLC won power in 57 municipalities and the APRE obtained control of six local councils. The following day a two-thirds' majority in the Asamblea Nacional voted in support of constitutional amendments limiting presidential powers and increasing legislative ones. The reforms would require the President to seek legislative ratification of key appointments, such as ministers, ambassadors, the chief prosecutor and banking superintendent, and would also enable the Asamblea to remove officials deemed to be incompetent. Furthermore, later that month the PLC and the FSLN approved a law to transfer control of the state energy, water and telecommunications services from the President to one regulatory body, the Superintendencia de Servicios Públicos (Sisep). President Bolaños appealed to the

Supreme Court in December, contending that the proposed reforms were unconstitutional and that such an attempt to redefine the powers of the executive and legislative branches of government exceeded the remit of the Asamblea Nacional. Nevertheless, in January 2005 the Asamblea ratified the amendments. Bolaños agreed to promulgate the reforms in return for a pledge from the opposition that it would work towards a consensus with the executive on such matters as the budget and social security reform. At the end of March the Supreme Court ruled that the reforms were valid, despite the Central American Court of Justice (CCJ) declaring that they were illegal and could only be approved by a specially convened constituent assembly.

Internal divisions within the FSLN arose in early 2005, ahead of the presidential and legislative elections that were scheduled for November 2006. In January 2005 the FSLN ruled that any prospective presidential nominees must have been party members for at least 10 years. The rule was intended to prevent Herty Lewites, the popular former mayor of Managua, from challenging Ortega in the party's primary election. Lewites had represented another party in the 1996 mayoral elections. Lewites and a number of his supporters were expelled from the party in February, accused of 'abandoning anti-imperialist principles'. In March the FSLN's national congress duly selected Ortega as its presidential candidate.

Political tensions were heightened in June 2005 when Bolaños issued a presidential decree compelling the police to comply with the CCJ ruling that invalidated the transfer of control of the public utilities from the President to the newly created Sisep. In response to the decree, the Comptroller-General once more called for President Bolaños to be impeached. In late June an OAS mission arrived in Managua to facilitate dialogue between the President and the Asamblea Nacional. However, Bolaños refused to engage in direct discussions with the PLC and the FSLN. Meanwhile, the USA increased diplomatic pressure on the PLC to break its pact with the FSLN and to unite its factions in order to prevent the Sandinistas from returning to power in the November 2006 elections.

In July 2005 a court released Alemán on probation on the grounds of ill health, but he was returned to house arrest three days later, on the orders of a court of appeal. The court of appeal's decision angered the pro-Alemán faction of the PLC, which threatened to refuse to approve the proposed Dominican Republic-Central American Free Trade Agreement (DR-CAFTA, between Nicaragua, Costa Rica, the Dominican Republic, El Salvador, Guatemala, Honduras and the USA) and to support the removal of Bolaños' immunity from prosecution to allow him to be charged in connection with alleged illegal campaign financing during the 2001 presidential election. In August, however, the Supreme Court overturned the court of appeal's ruling, ordering Alemán's release from house arrest. The Supreme Court also ratified the constitutional reforms adopted by the Asamblea Nacional in January. In September the Asamblea Nacional voted to remove the immunity from prosecution of three cabinet ministers and three deputy ministers.

In October 2005 the political conflict between the President and the legislature was largely resolved, following mediatory efforts by the OAS and the intervention of the US Deputy Secretary of State, Robert Zoellick, who, during a two-day visit to Managua earlier that month, condemned the PLC-FSLN pact and threatened to exclude Nicaragua from DR-CAFTA unless the Asamblea Nacional swiftly approved the agreement. Zoellick also welcomed the presidential candidacies of Herty Lewites and Eduardo Montealegre Rivas, a former government minister who had been effectively forced out of the PLC for remaining in the Cabinet after Bolaños decided to pursue Alemán on corruption charges. Within a week of Zoellick's visit DR-CAFTA had been approved by the Asamblea Nacional, after the FSLN withdrew its opposition to the agreement, and Ortega and Bolaños had agreed to delay the implementation of the constitutional reforms until the end of the latter's term of office in January 2007; legislation providing for their postponement was subsequently adopted. Furthermore, the Asamblea Nacional rejected a proposal to remove Bolaños' immunity from prosecution. All charges against the six ministers whose immunity had been lifted in September were dismissed in December. Meanwhile, in October the US Administration decided to resume military aid to Nicaragua after a seven-month suspension imposed as a result of US dissatisfaction with a lack of progress in the destruction of Nicaragua's remaining 1,051 surface-to-air missiles (around 1,000 had been destroyed in 2004).

THE 2006 ELECTIONS

Following the resolution of the institutional dispute, the presidential and legislative elections scheduled for 5 November 2006 became the main focus of political attention. In early 2006 opinion polls indicated that Montealegre, representing a right-wing coalition of the Alianza Liberal Nicaragüense (ALN—Nicaraguan Liberal Alliance) and the PC, and Lewites, standing for the MRS, enjoyed greatest public support, and a number of PLC deputies defected to the ALN-PC coalition. However, the PLC secured the largest share of the vote in elections to the Atlantic Coast Regional Councils held in March, followed by the FSLN. Yatama retained its position as the third largest party on the Coast. In early April the PLC formally selected former Vice-President Rizo, a close ally of Alemán, as its presidential candidate; Rizo had resigned as Vice-President in September 2005 in order to seek the party's nomination. José Antonio Alvarado was elected to contest the presidency for the APRE at the end of April 2006, but decided to accept an offer from Rizo in May to stand as his vice-presidential candidate, prompting the APRE to declare its support for Montealegre. In May the formation was announced of a broad-based coalition led by the FSLN, the Unidad Nicaragua Triunfa, which included Yatama and several small conservative parties. In June the historically anti-Sandinista PLN announced that it would support the FSLN in the forthcoming elections. By this time Ortega had overtaken Montealegre and Lewites in most opinion polls, with Rizo (who had sought to distance himself from Alemán in response to criticism of the PLC's continued allegiance to the former President) lying in fourth place. Following the death of Lewites from a heart attack in July, the MRS nominated his running mate, Edmundo Jarquín Calderón, an economist and son-in-law of former President Chamorro, as its candidate.

With the right wing still divided, Ortega was elected President on 5 November 2006, winning 38.0% of the votes cast. His nearest rivals, Montealegre and Rizo, secured 28.3% and 27.1%, respectively. Benefiting from the changes to the electoral law introduced under the PLC-FSLN pact (see above), which reduced the share of votes required for an outright victory from 45% to 35%, Ortega avoided the need to contest a second round of voting. The poorer than expected performance of Jarquín, who received only 6.3% of the votes cast, indicated that significant numbers of hitherto dissident Sandinistas had opted to support Ortega. In the concurrent elections to the Asamblea Nacional the FSLN won 38 seats, while the PLC took 25 (compared with 47 in the 2001 elections), the ALN 22 and the MRS five. Bolaños and Montealegre were also allocated seats in the Asamblea. An estimated 69% of the electorate participated in the polls.

Both during the electoral campaign and following his victory, Ortega sought to reassure voters and business leaders that he had renounced the more radical policies of his previous period in office, vowing to respect private property rights and free enterprise, to maintain economic stability, to encourage foreign investment, to co-operate with the IMF and to support the implementation of DR-CAFTA. The eradication of poverty was identified as a priority of the new administration, as was the promotion of national reconciliation. This message of reconciliation was perhaps best exemplified by the choice of Jaime Morales Carazo, a former Contra leader and PLC deputy, as Ortega's vice-presidential candidate.

ORTEGA'S RETURN TO POWER

Ortega was inaugurated as President on 10 January 2007. His new Cabinet was dominated by Sandinista allies, including Samuel Santos López, mayor of Managua during the 1980s, as Minister of Foreign Affairs and Ortega's wife, Rosario Murillo

Zambrana, as Co-ordinator of the Communication and Citizenship Council. Later that month the Asamblea Nacional adopted 'urgent' reforms, proposed by Ortega and supported by the PLC, which increased the President's control over the police force and the military and allowed the President to create 'Citizen Power Councils' by decree. Opposition parties expressed concern regarding the potential power of these Councils, which were to make proposals on government policy and monitor the performance of the authorities, while co-ordinating the work of NGOs and public institutions at a departmental level. In addition, despite opposition from the PLC, the Asamblea approved the further postponement of the controversial constitutional amendments limiting presidential powers that had been due to take effect that month. This measure was proposed by the ALN, which advocated a more thorough revision of the Constitution. In February the four parties represented in the legislature appointed a seven-member commission to draft constitutional amendments. The FSLN was in favour of allowing a President to serve two consecutive terms.

Alemán was granted complete freedom of movement within Nicaragua in March 2007, having been hitherto confined to Managua since his release on probation in mid-2005. Although the decision was ostensibly made by the national prison service, observers speculated that Ortega had ordered the restrictions on Alemán to be eased in an attempt to maintain the FSLN's influence over the PLC, citing continued co-operation over judicial appointments as evidence that the controversial power-sharing pact between the two parties had been renewed. It was also suggested that a newly created Commission for Verification, Peace, Reconciliation and Justice had been established with the intention of annulling Alemán's sentence altogether. Headed by Cardinal Miguel Obando y Bravo, the former Archbishop of Managua, who had been a vocal opponent of the Sandinista regime during the 1980s but was now regarded as an ally of Ortega, the Commission's stated role was to co-ordinate social welfare programmes for veterans of the civil war. (In December 2007 the Managua Appeals Court ordered Alemán's return to house arrest, but this ruling was later overturned, and in January 2009 he was definitively absolved from his conviction by the Supreme Court.)

In May 2007 the Government launched a 'zero hunger' programme aimed at lifting 75,000 families out of poverty by 2012 by granting them each agricultural aid valued at US $2,000. It was envisaged that 20% of the aid received would eventually be returned by the beneficiaries for the establishment of a rural credit bank to guarantee the continuity of the programme.

The establishment of the controversial Citizen Power Councils, which were central to Ortega's plan to introduce a new political system of 'direct democracy', was postponed from July 2007 until September. In early September, however, the President suffered a reverse when the ALN, the PLC and the MRS united in the Asamblea Nacional to adopt legislation stipulating that the Councils could not form part of the executive branch of government, nor implement government programmes. The opposition parties feared that the FSLN intended to consolidate its power by controlling the Councils. Ortega subsequently vetoed the legislation and delayed the inauguration of the Councils further, until November, ostensibly owing to the need to focus on addressing the destruction recently caused by Hurricane Felix, which had killed more than 100 people in the north of the country. In late November the votes of the ALN, PLC and MRS deputies ensured the rejection of the presidential veto by the Asamblea Nacional. However, in response to an appeal by several proposed members of the Councils, the Managua Appeals Court (dominated by FSLN-affiliated magistrates) ordered the Asamblea not to publish the legislation in the official gazette (which was required to render it valid), a ruling with which the President of the Asamblea, the FSLN's René Núñez Téllez, complied. Ortega proceeded to create the Citizen Power Councils by decree at the end of the month, prompting condemnation from opposition parties and civil society organizations, which accused the President of violating institutional procedure. Also established by decree was a National Cabinet of Citizen Power, comprising 272 representatives from the departments and autonomous regions, of which Ortega was to serve as President and Murillo as General Co-ordinator. In addition, Murillo was appointed as Executive Secretary of the Consejo Nacional de Planificación Económica y Social (National Council of Economic and Social Planning), which was reformed, again by presidential decree, with the stated aim of further increasing popular participation in the formulation of policy. In early December the Supreme Court upheld the validity of the presidential veto, prompting the ALN, the MRS, the PLC and the newly established Bancada por la Unidad to form the Bloque Contra la Dictadura (Bloc Against the Dictatorship). Meanwhile, constitutional reforms being mooted by the FSLN and the PLC in late 2007, which would introduce a parliamentary system of government and create a new post of Prime Minister, were strongly opposed by the ALN, the APRE, the PC and some members of the PLC itself.

In January 2008 the ALN and the PLC announced the formation of a coalition to contest the forthcoming municipal elections, naming Montealegre as their joint mayoral candidate for Managua. Also that month the Supreme Court annulled the legislation postponing the implementation of the constitutional amendments curtailing presidential powers that were adopted in 2005 (see above), which duly entered into force, but declared the law establishing Sisep to be invalid. Despite their recent attempts at unity, continued divisions between the ALN and the PLC were evident in mid-February 2008, when the latter voted with the FSLN to approve the budget. Later that month the disarray in the opposition was exacerbated by the CSE's decision to oust Montealegre from the leadership of the ALN and bar him from standing as the party's candidate for mayor of Managua; Montealegre's predecessor as party President, Eliseo Núñez Hernández, was reinstated to the position. The FSLN-controlled CSE cited irregularities during Montealegre's election to the position in 2006 to justify its ruling, but there was speculation that it had in fact been motivated by Montealegre's apparent refusal to enter into a new pact with Ortega to replace that between Ortega and Alemán. In March 2008, having received the support of 17 of the ALN's deputies, Montealegre announced the formation of a new liberal alliance between his personal political movement, Movimiento Vamos con Eduardo (MVCE), and the PLC to contest the municipal elections in November. The CSE provoked further controversy in mid-June by removing the legal status of the MRS and the PC, claiming that the former had failed to submit certain party documentation, while the latter had failed to comply with a requirement to field candidates in at least 80% of the country's municipalities for the November elections; both parties rejected the charges against them. Civil rights groups and opposition parties criticized the decision, as did a number of foreign diplomats.

The FSLN won 105 of the 146 contested mayoralties, including Managua, in the municipal elections held in November 2008, while the PLC secured 37 mayoralties and the ALN four. Allegations of widespread electoral fraud led to a recount in Managua, although demands for monitoring by independent observers were rejected; the FSLN candidate, Alexis Argüello, a former professional boxer, was subsequently confirmed as winner, ahead of Montealegre of the PLC-MVCE alliance. Riots and demonstrations across the country ensued, but a PLC-proposed bill to annul the elections failed to generate sufficient support in the Asamblea Nacional. In late November the Asamblea was suspended by its President, René Núñez Téllez, in response to the election crisis. When the Asamblea reconvened in January 2009 Núñez was re-elected as its President. PLC candidates elected in the municipal elections refused to attend their inauguration ceremonies in an attempt to avoid legitimizing the results. The final report by the election observation group Ética y Transparencia (EyT) issued in March indicated that fraud took place in at least 40 of the 146 municipalities. Although the Government had refused to accredit the EyT, some 30,000 volunteers had been sent by the group to observe the elections.

In January 2009, meanwhile, municipal elections were held in the North Atlantic autonomous region. At the elections, which had been postponed ostensibly owing to the damage caused by Hurricane Felix, the FSLN retained Bonanza and won control of Bilwi, Waspam and Rosita, leaving Yawata with just one municipality and the PLC with two.

The apparent suicide of Argüello in July 2009, just six months into his post as Mayor of Managua, led to criticism of the way in which his duties had been reorganized while he had been out of the country, amid speculation that he had felt humiliated by the changes. Three days of national mourning were declared. In August Núñez Hernández was replaced as President of the ALN by Alejandro Mejía Ferreti.

At celebrations held in Managua in July 2009 to mark the 30th anniversary of the Sandinista revolution, President Ortega confirmed his desire to amend the Constitution to end the ban on consecutive presidential terms. Unable to secure the two-thirds' legislative majority required to effect constitutional change, Ortega turned to the judiciary for support. In October, responding to a petition submitted by Ortega and a group of more than 100 mayors, the constitutional panel of the Supreme Court ruled that the constitutional provision prohibiting presidential re-election was 'unenforceable'. The CSE swiftly endorsed this ruling, which was condemned by opposition parties as being illegal, on the grounds that only the Asamblea Nacional could approve amendments to the Constitution, and also criticized by civil society and business groups and by the US Department of State. Well-attended pro- and anti-Government demonstrations took place in Managua in the following month.

Ortega provoked further controversy in January 2010, when he issued a decree indefinitely extending the terms of incumbent electoral and judicial officials in defiance of the Constitution, according to which the Asamblea Nacional is responsible for appointments to these posts. The President insisted that the decree was necessary in order to ensure 'institutional stability' owing to the legislature's failure to agree on successors. Opposition parties boycotted the Asamblea in protest against the decree. Political tensions escalated in April, after two FSLN-aligned Supreme Court judges refused to leave their posts following the expiry of their terms. Violence broke out as government supporters forcibly prevented opposition legislators from convening in an attempt to overturn the decree, prompting expressions of concern from the US Department of State and the OAS.

Elections to the Atlantic Coast Regional Councils on 7 March 2010 were marked by a high rate of abstention and a lack of independent observers. The FSLN remained the largest party in the North Atlantic Regional Council, as did the PLC in the southern assembly, although neither managed to secure a majority of seats. Later that month Alemán declared his interest in seeking the PLC candidacy for the presidential election due to take place in 2011.

FOREIGN RELATIONS UNDER ORTEGA

Following Ortega's election as President in November 2006, he initially adopted a conciliatory approach towards the USA, stating his intention to develop a 'respectful' bilateral relationship. However, the first confirmation of expectations that relations would be strained came in February 2007, when Ortega declared his continued opposition to the destruction of Nicaragua's remaining surface-to-air missiles, an issue that had led to the suspension of US military aid to Nicaragua during April–October 2005 (see above). Moreover, in May 2007 Ortega accused the USA of encouraging and funding domestic opposition efforts to unite against his Government. Meanwhile, US-Nicaraguan relations were also jeopardized by Ortega's apparent determination to forge strong ties with regimes of which the US Administration disapproved. Shortly after taking office in January 2007, Ortega and the Iranian President, Mahmoud Ahmadinejad, who was on a tour of several Latin American countries, signed a co-operation agreement providing for Iranian investment in Nicaraguan industry and announced plans to open embassies in their respective capitals. Ortega reciprocated Ahmadinejad's visit in June, during a tour of several countries, which also included Libya, Algeria and Cuba, and in August a series of further bilateral accords were signed, under which Iran would provide funding for various infrastructure projects in Nicaragua in return for Nicaraguan agricultural products. Prior to the tour in June Ortega had signed an agreement on enhancing political and economic co-operation with the visiting Deputy Minister of Foreign Affairs of the Democratic People's Republic of Korea. The Nicaraguan Government rejected suggestions that such alliances would damage Nicaragua's relations with the USA. In July Ortega proposed the destruction of 651 of Nicaragua's 1,051 remaining surface-to-air missiles in exchange for the provision of medical equipment and medicines by the USA. Several rounds of discussions on Ortega's proposal took place between the Nicaraguan and US authorities in late 2007 and 2008, although no agreement had been reached by mid-2010.

Ortega also sought to strengthen his already close links with other Latin American left-wing leaders. Flanked by the Presidents of Bolivia and Venezuela at his inauguration, on 10 January 2007, on the following day Ortega confirmed Nicaragua's participation in the Bolivarian Alternative for the Americas—renamed the Bolivarian Alliance for the Peoples of our America (Alianza Bolivariana para los Pueblos de Nuestra América—ALBA) in June 2009—which had been devised by Venezuela as an alternative model to the US-promoted Free Trade Area of the Americas and was also supported by Bolivia and Cuba. Venezuelan President Lt-Col (retd) Hugo Chávez Frías offered significant financial assistance to Nicaragua, signing a series of bilateral economic agreements with Ortega, most of which focused particularly on the energy sector, with Venezuela proposing the construction of a petroleum refinery in Nicaragua, capable of processing 100,000–150,000 barrels of oil per day (b/d), and pledging to supply Nicaragua with 10,000 b/d of petroleum at preferential rates and a number of electricity generators. Nicaraguan opposition parties criticized the Government for a lack of transparency over the details of these agreements with Venezuela. This criticism was renewed in May 2010, following Ortega's announcement, some two weeks after a visit to Managua by Chávez, that ALBA funds would be used to finance the provision of monthly bonuses of US $25 for some 120,000 public sector workers and gas and fuel subsidies for 22,000 transport workers.

Nicaragua's relations with neighbouring Costa Rica were less cordial during Ortega's first few months in office; it was not until August 2007 that the new President held his first talks with his Costa Rican counterpart, Oscar Arias Sánchez, at an event to mark the 20th anniversary of the signing of the Esquipulas Peace Accords (see above). Despite holding differing views on issues such as trade, Central American integration and the Peace Accords themselves, the two Presidents agreed to revive a bilateral commission that had been suspended in the late 1990s amid tensions over Nicaraguan immigrants in Costa Rica and a dispute concerning navigational rights on the San Juan River (which was ended in July 2009 following a ruling by the ICJ). In October 2007 the ICJ ruled on a long-standing territorial dispute between Nicaragua and its other neighbour, Honduras, demarcating a new maritime border approximately midway between the two countries; both Governments accepted the judgment.

Nicaragua's claim to sovereignty over the San Andrés archipelago was effectively rejected in December 2007 when the ICJ upheld Colombia's assertion that the matter had been legitimately resolved by the 1928 treaty (see above). However, the Court was to continue deliberating the sovereignty of several other islands disputed by Nicaragua and Colombia, as well as the general delimitation of their maritime border. Relations between the two countries deteriorated in February 2008 when the Nicaraguan Government accused Colombia of increasing military operations in disputed waters and intimidating Nicaraguan fishermen. A decree issued by Ortega in mid-March authorizing the establishment of a special Nicaraguan fishing zone in the disputed area further exacerbated tensions. Earlier that month Nicaragua had followed Venezuela's lead in briefly suspending diplomatic relations with Colombia in protest at an incursion into Ecuador by Colombian forces targeting rebels of the Fuerzas Armadas Revolucionarias de Colombia—Ejército del Pueblo (FARC). Ortega also joined his Venezuelan counterpart, Chávez, in strongly condemning a Colombian-US agreement signed in October 2009 granting the USA access to military bases in Colombia.

The controversy regarding the results of the November 2008 elections strained relations with the USA and the EU. Both the USA and the EU temporarily suspended budgetary assistance to Nicaragua as a result of the Government's inability to resolve the dispute. In June 2009 the US Government's Millennium Challenge Corporation announced the 'definitive' cancellation of US $62m. (of a total $175m.) of funds to Nicaragua. Ortega criticized the decision and declared that the shortfall would in part be compensated by assistance from ALBA. In June 2010 budgetary assistance of $10m. was promised to Nicaragua by the Russian Government at the first meeting of a recently established bilateral inter-governmental commission on trade, economic, scientific and technical co-operation. Relations between Nicaragua and Russia had been strengthened by the former's recognition, in September 2008, of the separatist Georgian territories of Abkhazia and South Ossetia as independent sovereign states.

Economy

PHILLIP WEARNE

Revised for this edition by KATHARINE MURISON

Nicaragua experienced a period of gradual economic recovery from the mid-1990s, despite the huge set-back of the devastation caused by Hurricane Mitch in October 1998. However, few Nicaraguans shared in the fruits of that recovery, and the economy contracted in 2009, amid a global downturn. Real gross domestic product (GDP) increased by 4.2% in 2006, by 3.1% in 2007, and by 2.8% in 2008, according to official preliminary figures, but declined by an estimated 1.5% in 2009, with the most substantial decreases recorded in the mining, financial services and construction sectors. The average annual rate of inflation in 2001–08 was 9.5%. Consumer prices increased by annual averages of 11.1% in 2007 and 19.9% in 2008, but were estimated by the International Labour Organization (ILO) to have risen by just 3.7% in 2009. Exports nearly doubled in the six years to 2000 (rising from US $351.7m. in 1994 to $642.8m. in 2000). After a slight decline in the early 2000s, they had recovered to $866.0m. by 2005 and increased to $1,049.9m. in 2006. Export revenues rose to $1,224.8m. in 2007 and to $1,488.7m. in 2008, before declining to $1,390.9m. in 2009.

Nicaragua's recovery in the latter half of the 1990s followed one of the most extended and profound economic crises ever witnessed in Latin America. Between the late 1970s and the early 1990s the Nicaraguan economy was beset by a prolonged civil war, the international depression of the early 1980s, the imposition of economic sanctions by the USA and a certain amount of government mismanagement. After the revolution of 1979, which overthrew the dictator Anastasio Somoza Debayle, the size of the state sector increased dramatically. However, the Sandinista Government also actively encouraged the expansion of the private sector, which continued to account for more than 50% of economic activity throughout its time in office. The early revolutionary years saw an attempt to restructure Nicaraguan society and a series of important social reforms were embarked upon, including a wide-ranging agrarian reform programme. Despite the onset of world recession and the downward pressure on agricultural export prices, the initial restructuring and rehabilitation of the economy following the revolution led to a small increase in growth in the early 1980s. However, the subsequent US-funded Contra war against the Sandinista Government and the economic boycott by multilateral lending agencies caused great damage to the Nicaraguan economy, resulting in a decrease in agricultural output, growing trade and budget deficits and, eventually, spiralling inflation levels (which peaked at a staggering 38,000% in 1988). GDP decreased, in real terms, at an average annual rate of 6.1% between 1985 and 1994 (with a particularly severe contraction of 18.6% in the two years from 1988). It was not until 1992 that positive growth, of 0.3%, was recorded. The cumulative impact of the economic contraction of the late 1980s and early 1990s was devastating. By 1994 economic output was more than 60% below what it had been in 1977.

All these factors served to accentuate a traditional dependence on imports and external financing (after 1990 the flows of international aid into Nicaragua expanded markedly) and, productively, economic performance remained excessively reliant on the country's narrow range of traditional agricultural commodity exports, the most important of which were bananas, coffee, cotton, meat and sugar. By 1994 GDP per head in Nicaragua was just US $638, measured at constant 2000 prices, making the country the second poorest in the Western hemisphere, after Haiti. By 2008 Nicaraguan GDP per head, at $905 in constant 2000 prices, remained low.

AGRICULTURE

Nicaragua's agricultural sector was, along with the rest of the economy, deeply depressed in the 1980s and early 1990s. In addition to all of the normal variables affecting agricultural production in Central America (weather, labour shortages, fluctuating world commodity prices and crop disease), Nicaragua had the additional burden of the impact of war in the country's most important agricultural zones, the effects of which lasted long beyond the cessation of hostilities. Immediately after the revolution the state took over more than 1m. ha of land, of which some 70% was converted into state farms, with the remainder transferred to peasant co-operatives. Large areas of underutilized and idle land were then expropriated during the second stage of the Government's land reform programme in mid-1981. From 1986 the emphasis was increasingly placed upon production from co-operatives, or individual smallholders, with the Government continuing to exercise considerable control of the sector through its monopoly purchases of export crops.

The Government of President Violeta Barrios de Chamorro (1990–97) adopted a pragmatic approach, privatizing a number of large state farms, but declining to reverse the Sandinista land reforms. However, the demands of resettling former Contras, who were given land from former state farms, took priority. The administration of President Arnoldo Alemán Lacayo (1997–2002) endorsed this flexibility, reaching an agreement with the Sandinista opposition, which sanctioned the land and property distribution to legitimize beneficiaries of the Sandinista reforms. At the same time, the new Government reinforced an arbitration mechanism to adjudicate the claims of many larger property owners who insisted that they had been victims of asset seizures by senior Sandinistas. Instead of returning properties to these claimants, both the Chamorro and Alemán Governments generously compensated those who had been expropriated. These individuals received approximately US $900m. in government funding between 1990 and 2003. The payments had a massive impact upon the country's internal debt, representing more than one-half of total internal debt in 2003. The property question continued to be a major political and economic issue in Nicaragua, and some saw it as a major disincentive to significant private investment in agriculture. Although the Sandinistas were returned to power in the elections of November 2006, President Daniel Ortega sought to distance himself from the more extreme policies of the 1980s, pledging to respect free enterprise, to protect private property and to encourage investment.

With the exception of the obvious impact of Hurricane Mitch on the sector in 1998 and 1999, agricultural production showed a modest recovery from the mid-1990s, although it was impeded by a scarcity of inputs and credit and continuing political instability in many rural areas. Hurricane Felix, which struck Nicaragua in September 2007, also severely damaged the agricultural sector, destroying an estimated 50% of planted crops. Nevertheless, the sector (including hunting, forestry and fishing) remained the mainstay of the economy, engaging 29.1% of the employed labour force in 2006 and accounting for an estimated 17.8% of GDP in 2009. Despite the negative impact of Hurricane Mitch, the recovery became more consistent after 1999. According to figures issued by FAO, production levels in 2008 were, for example, 45.8% higher than in 1999 in the case of maize, 31.3% higher for beans and 56.5% higher for rice. These increases did not, however, simply reflect an expansion in the area harvested of these crops, but also improvements in productivity. For example, the areas harvested of rice, maize and sorghum all decreased in 2001, but overall production levels of sorghum and maize still grew in that year.

The output and exchange earnings of export crops have been similarly variable. During the revolutionary years, production of the country's major export crop, coffee, declined steadily from 1984, reaching a nadir in 1990. From that point, however, there was throughout the 1990s a reasonably consistent expansion in the total area of coffee harvested, which continued in the 21st century (with the exception of the Mitch-affected year of 1999). Production levels, however, were more variable. Production increased in every year (with the exception of 1996) in the 1990s, reaching a peak of 91,791 metric tons in 1999. A further record crop was reported in 2005, when total output reached 95,455 tons; however, output fell by 26.2% in 2006, to 70,455 tons, highlighting the continued vulnerability of this sector to adverse conditions. Production recovered in 2007, reaching a record 100,000 tons, but declined to 72,727 tons in 2008.

Coffee producers and workers have faced considerable difficulties in recent years. Coffee export earnings reflected not only production levels, but also fluctuations in the commodity's international price. An improvement in earnings, to US $173m., in 1998 was the result of recovering production levels, yielded by the expansion programme begun several years earlier, rather than any rise in international prices. By 2002 international coffee prices had reached their lowest ever level, and export earnings fell to $73.6m., their lowest level for 10 years. Earnings recovered thereafter, however, to $126.8m. in 2004 and $125.9m. in 2005, and in 2006 earnings reached $200.7m. Export revenues declined to $188.1m. in 2007, reflecting the poor harvest of the previous year, but rose to $278.3m. in 2008, before decreasing again slightly, to $236.7m., in 2009.

Cotton fared even worse than coffee, and by 1998 the industry had virtually ceased to exist. In 1991 export earnings from cotton had been as high as US $44.4m., representing the production of 30,000 metric tons of cotton lint. In just two years that figure had fallen to as little as $400,000. By 1998 cotton exports had fallen to $300,000, less than one-10th the level of the previous year; by 2000 earnings from cotton stood at less than $100,000, and production levels did not increase thereafter. In 2006 just 1,050 tons were produced, according to estimates by FAO. Cotton dominated the best agricultural lands of the North Pacific region from the end of the Second World War, and the decline of the industry left many of the communities in the regions around León and Chinandega, areas harshly affected by Hurricane Mitch, with considerable economic problems.

The other major traditional agricultural exports were sugar and bananas (and beef, which is considered separately below). Sugar cane production generally increased from the early 1990s, reaching a peak of 4.51m. metric tons in 2006, before declining slightly, to 4.48m. tons in 2007 and to 4.30m. tons in 2008. Despite this relatively stable level of output, the volatility of international prices produced a fluctuating pattern of sugar export earnings over this period. Earnings steadily increased to reach US $53.2m. by 1997, but fell back to $30.4m. in 1999. They subsequently fluctuated, reaching a low of $25.7m. in 2003, before recovering in 2005 and 2006 when export revenues held firm at $60.3m. Sugar prices rose considerably during 2007, owing to renewed global interest in ethanol production, and earnings from this commodity increased to $74.3m. as a result; earnings declined to $50.4m. in 2008 and to $50.0m. in 2009. The performance of Nicaragua's banana exports vacillated in a similar fashion. There was a precipitous decline in the late 1990s, with earnings reaching a mere $10.1m. in 2000 (this reflected a fall in production from 96,797 tons in 1996 to just 48,359 tons in 2000). There was some recovery after 2000, with production averaging around 56,000 tons and earnings some $11.4m. in 2001–05. Banana production stood at 42,649 tons in 2006 and increased to 44,391 tons in 2007, but output of 36,285 tons in 2008 represented the lowest level recorded since the early 1970s. Banana export receipts amounted to $9.6m. in 1996, increasing to $9.9m. in 2007, but falling back to $9.6m. in 2008. Export earnings recovered in 2009, to reach $11.7m., mainly owing to rising international prices.

The increasing export of less traditional products has been one of the success stories of the Nicaraguan economy in recent years. Groundnut exports became an important source of foreign exchange earnings, contributing US $56.0m. in 2007. Receipts from groundnut exports soared to $90.2m. in 2008, before declining to $65.9m. in 2009. Similarly, the export of beans, for many years seen as merely a staple of the peasant sector, expanded rapidly. Earnings from bean exports to neighbouring countries more than doubled from $13.0m. in 2001 to $39.9m. in 2007, and then rose to $79.8m. in 2008, before decreasing to $61.3m. in 2009.

In the mid-2000s the livestock industry, like other sectors, had yet to recover fully from the shortage of foreign exchange for new machinery and other essential products it had suffered during the Contra war. Compounding this, the sector was excluded from government credit schemes in the early 1990s, and it seemed unlikely to recover its former position in terms of export importance. Some sub-sectors did, none the less, gradually show some improvement. From 1998 beef and veal export earnings increased annually, with earnings reaching US $210.7m. in 2008 and $230.6m. in the following year. Furthermore, the export of meat products has been complemented in recent years by the expanded export of cattle to neighbouring countries, which generated earnings of around $42.2m. in 2007. According to FAO, however, around 6,000 head of livestock were lost to Hurricane Felix. The export of cattle declined in 2008 and 2009, with earnings representing $26.8m. and $17.7m., respectively.

Nicaragua possessed substantial supplies of timber, including considerable reserves of hardwoods such as mahogany, cedar, rosewood, caoba and oak. In the 2000s roundwood production averaged about 6m. cu m annually, an increase on the 4m. cu m averaged in the 1990s. Concern about over-exploitation in the mid-1990s led the Asamblea Nacional (National Assembly) to ban further logging concessions in 1996, although many environmental organizations remained seriously concerned about illegal logging.

The development of the fishing industry was a major priority around the turn of the 21st century. Three fish-processing plants were rehabilitated and commercial fishing of crab, crayfish, shrimp, lobster and tuna was encouraged. By 2000 the total shrimp catch had more than doubled in just seven years, to 9,505 metric tons, while total lobster production peaked at 6,534 tons in that year. Production of lobster subsequently decreased slightly, amounting to 4,337 tons in 2008, while shrimp output steadily increased, reaching 16,459 tons in 2008. Export earnings from lobster and shrimp, which reached US $118.8m. in 2000, fell back to just $69.1m. in 2003, but made a modest recovery thereafter, totalling $88.6m. in 2006, and reaching $92.9m. in 2007 (equivalent to 7.6% of total export earnings). Earnings from the export of lobster and shrimp declined to $87.8m. in 2008 and to $69.5m. (5.0% of total export earnings) in 2009.

MINING AND POWER

The mining sector was completely nationalized in 1979. However, following the end of the Sandinista regime in 1990, successive governments ceded the rights of exploitation to private companies under long-term lease agreements. This policy met with some success: an estimated US $70m. of private investment was directed into the sector in the 1990s. The contribution of the mining sector to overall GDP reflected the investment, rising from 0.6% in 1994 to an estimated 1.2% in 2009. However, the sector's GDP decreased by 5.6% in 2008 and by an estimated 10.5% in 2009. The sector encompasses salt, marble and quarried stone, but the real export value lies in Nicaragua's nine gold and silver mines, three of which were in production. Increases in gold production were in line with sectoral performance, a 50% expansion resulting in output of 123,300 troy oz in 1998. The sector recorded a further rise in 1999, with output of 143,000 troy oz. Output subsequently fluctuated, declining overall to an estimated 109,300 troy oz in 2007. Silver production increased by almost 50% in 1997, to 34,600 troy oz, before rising by a further 81%, to 62,500 troy oz, in 1998. By 2007 output had risen to 96,500 troy oz. Some forecasts saw exports trebling in the coming years, as closed gold and silver mines returned to production. In 2009 gold accounted for 5.8% of export earnings.

Dependence on imported energy sources, particularly petroleum, proved a major problem for successive Nicaraguan governments. The Sandinista Government in power during 1979–90 relied on cheap or bartered petroleum from Mexico or the former USSR for much of its time in office. However, Mexico suspended supplies when even 'soft-term' payments became overdue, and in 1987 the USSR announced large reductions in supplies, causing severe energy problems, compounding the general economic malaise of the time. In the early 2000s, as the country's credit rating was somewhat restored, much of Nicaragua's petroleum needs were met by Venezuela and Mexico, under the concessionary terms of the 1980 San José Agreement. Despite ambitious diversification efforts, in particular the inauguration of the Momotombo geothermal plant in 1984 and the Asturias hydroelectric scheme five years later, imports of petroleum, mineral fuels and lubricants remained crucial at the beginning of the 21st century, costing the country as much as US $1,000.2m. in 2008, representing 23.1% of the total value of imports. The cost of petroleum and fuel imports declined to $684.1m. in 2009 (19.7% of total imports). In March 2007 the new Government of President Daniel Ortega signed several co-operation agreements with the Venezuelan Government of Lt-Col (retd) Hugo Chávez Frías. Venezuela agreed to supply discounted oil to Nicaragua under its PetroCaribe initiative, as well as to build a refinery in the country. In 2006 hydroelectricity provided less than 10% of Nicaragua's total production of 3,137.2 GWh, down from as much as nearly 25% in 1996. Geothermal generation has followed a similar pattern, falling from as much as 15% of total output in 1996 to some 5% in 2006. In 2008 Nicaragua produced an estimated 3,327.4 GWh of electrical energy.

Net electrical generating capacity was estimated to be about 546 MW in 2001, an increase of almost 40% on what had been available in 1997–98, largely a result of a number of new private power plants coming on stream. The new capacity was expected to alleviate the frequent power shortages so common in the 1990s when supply covered just one-half of consumer demand. Foreign companies had been required to restrict output to 30 MW per year until 1999, but in that year the US company Amfels was given permission to increase capacity at its Puerto Sandino plant to 57 MW. At the same time, Ormat Industries of Israel signed a 15-year operating contract for the Momotombo geothermal plant with the state power company, Empresa Nicaragüense de Electricidad (ENEL). The Israeli firm pledged to invest an initial US $15m., with up to $30m. to follow, and announced plans to increase the plant's capacity from 13 MW to 70 MW. In 1999 ENEL was divided into three generating companies (one hydroelectric and two thermal plants) and two distribution companies, in preparation for privatization, for which tenders were solicited in May 2000. Meanwhile, ENEL continued to increase spending on the rehabilitation and repair of existing plants, transmission lines and a regional electricity grid, the core of which already existed in the import and export of power to Honduras and Panama. The dilapidated state of the power distribution system in Nicaragua was responsible for the loss of up to 25% of all power generated during the 1990s. The distribution companies were sold to the Spanish company Unión Fenosa in 2000, which came under intense scrutiny from sectors of civil society unhappy with its pricing policies and failure to fulfil promised infrastructural investments. However, government attempts to sell the generating companies failed when, in July 2003, the Supreme Court annulled the sale of power company HIDROGESA in the previous year, owing to alleged irregularities. Parts of the country continued to suffer prolonged power cuts in 2006 and 2007 as Unión Fenosa struggled with rising oil prices and a concomitant increase in production costs. There remained considerable support for renationalization of the energy sector. Unión Fenosa remained heavily subsidised (with additional tariffs applied incrementally during 2006–07 in tandem with rising oil prices), and in May 2008 the Government signalled that nationalization would ensue if the company failed to cede 16% of its shares to the state as planned. Since becoming a signatory to a number of co-operation agreements with Venezuela the energy sector has benefited from the import of discounted petroleum, additional financing and the provision of capital goods. In late 2008 ENEL announced that, thanks to assistance primarily from Venezuela and Cuba, and the recent installation of 120 MW, prolonged power cuts in Nicaragua would be prevented. Plans were announced to expand generating capacity by an additional 40 MW.

MANUFACTURING AND INDUSTRY

Traditionally, manufacturing activity in Nicaragua centred on the processing and packing of local agricultural produce, although some heavy industries, such as chemical and cement production, also existed. In 2009 manufacturing accounted for an estimated 18.7% of GDP. The origins of the sector lie in the rapid expansion of import substitution industries that occurred during the 1960s. This was, however, short-lived, and the average annual rate of manufacturing growth decreased from 11.4% between 1960 and 1970 to 2.5% between 1970 and 1982. The situation worsened during the 1980s as political strife, hyperinflation, and shortages of raw materials, imported machinery and skilled personnel took full effect. The Contra war seriously disrupted manufacturing activity in that, while the shifting of the economy onto a permanent war footing stimulated the production of consumer goods for the armed forces and of construction materials for the repair of roads and buildings, other import-dependent industries suffered from the reduction in consumer spending and from Nicaragua's chronic shortage of foreign exchange caused by the US trade embargo. By 1985 the private sector had contracted by about 20% and was operating at little more than 50% of capacity, while ambitious state enterprises had failed to yield the hoped-for production levels. After a brief respite in 1986–87, manufacturing was again badly affected by the 1988–89 recession. Industrial production was estimated to have decreased by some 20% in 1989 alone.

The Chamorro Government privatized some of the state agro-business projects initiated by the Sandinistas, including the US $500m. Malacatoya sugar mill, the Chiltepe dairy project and a fruit- and vegetable-processing and canning factory in the Sebaco valley. The end of the war, a sharp fall in import tariffs and renewed access to the US market provided new opportunities in manufacturing, with many Nicaraguan exiles returning to take advantage of them. However, new export opportunities could not counteract continued contraction in the domestic market, particularly in production sectors such as beverages, processed foods and cigarettes. As Nicaragua entered the new millennium, sector-wide figures improved, and manufacturing output grew by 2.8% in 2000 and 2.6% in 2001 (with the building materials sub-sector expanding by nearly 40%, owing to post-Mitch reconstruction activities). The pace of growth slowed in 2002, with sectoral growth of 1.6%. However, economic expansion improved thereafter, with growth of 2.5% in 2003, and robust increases of 9.0% in 2004—which reflected a 35.7% increase in sugar-refining—and 5.6% in 2005. Manufacturing GDP increased by 6.4% in 2006 and by 6.8% in 2007, but growth in the sector slowed to 1.1% in 2008 and a contraction of 2.7% was estimated in 2009. Average growth in manufacturing GDP was 4.9% per year in 2000–08. A glance at the experiences of particular sub-sectors, however, suggested a more complex picture. In 2000–04 certain foodstuffs (meat, biscuits, milk), beer, leather goods, construction materials and certain plastics underwent a considerable expansion. Some of these improvements reflected the acceleration of existing trends, but in other cases they followed prior decreases. Other industries, however, contracted over the same period (examples included rum, some canned goods and most paper goods). The varied performance reflected a major restructuring of the Nicaraguan manufacturing sector, following economic liberalization efforts. An importation tariff reform brought cheap imports and, unable to compete, some traditional manufacturing businesses closed, diversified or formed joint ventures with foreign firms or returning exiles attracted into the country by a more favourable foreign investment environment. The textile, clothing and leather goods sub-sector notably suffered in 2009, its GDP contracting by 7.0% in that year.

The most sustained expansion in the sector has been seen in the *maquila*, or 'offshore' assembly, sector. The Las Mercedes free trade zone, the country's first, doubled its total exports to US $80m. in 1995, although subsequent growth was more modest. However, in 2000 and 2001 the country's free trade zones replicated some of their earlier spectacular growth, with value added rising from $203m. to $300m. and $380m., respectively. Although the principal product was clothing assembled from US-imported textiles, plants also produced footwear, aluminium frames and jewellery, with companies from Hong Kong and Taiwan augmenting those from the USA. The number of jobs in the free trade zones expanded from around 20,000 in 1999 to over 50,000 in 2003. The attraction of more of these enterprises formed the key component of the Government's national economic development plan, with an assumption that more US companies would be attracted to Nicaragua following the implementation of the Dominican Republic-Central American Free Trade Agreement (DR-CAFTA), ratified by the Nicaraguan legislature in October 2005 and implemented in April 2006. Analysts remained divided as to the probability of sustained growth in this area and the ability of the sector to generate sufficient employment to offset the likely agricultural losses that DR-CAFTA would produce. The main concern was that any economic growth that free trade would promote would disproportionately benefit a very small group of people.

Much of the investment in the construction sector during the 1980s was strategic. By the end of the decade, however, the industry contracted as external assistance ended. The Chamorro Government's reconstruction programme reversed the decline in the early 1990s, although sectoral growth fluctuated in the rest of the decade. The assistance given to the sector by reconstruction efforts in the wake of Hurricane Mitch, combined with several large-scale projects in the tourism and transport sectors, dramatically expanded construction in 1999–2001, when it accounted for more than 6.2% of annual GDP. In 2006 the sector engaged some 100,800 people, equivalent to 4.8% of the employed labour force. In 1999 the sector had expanded by more than 60%, with a further expansion of more than 10% the following year. Growth slowed in 2000–03, before rising to 12.1% in 2004 and 7.3% in 2005. However, the sector contracted by 3.2% in 2006, by 4.8% in 2007, by 6.7% in 2008 and by an estimated 4.1% in 2009. In 2009 construction contributed an estimated 5.0% of GDP.

PUBLIC FINANCE AND PAYMENTS

The Governments of Presidents Violeta Chamorro and Arnoldo Alemán Lacayo had some success in controlling what had become one of the most chronic current account budget deficits of any state. Access to external funds from the USA and multilateral lending agencies, a dramatic decrease in inflation, severe reductions in public spending, as well as privatization of state enterprises, improved tax collection and the retirement or renegotiation of some of the country's massive foreign debt combined to help reduce the budget deficit from the average 25% of GDP it had reached in the 1980s. By 1998 the budget deficit (before grants) had fallen to the equivalent of 4.8% of GDP. The next year, however, saw an increase to 13.2% of GDP and by 2001 it had reached around 19.0%, as election year spending and the consequences of Hurricane Mitch took a particularly heavy toll. Much of this deficit was financed by foreign grants and concessionary loans, which, in turn, contributed substantially to an expenditure programme that, by 2001, had reached nearly 40% of GDP. In 2002 and 2003, however, the budget deficit was dramatically reduced to 4.1% and 2.3% of GDP, respectively, as a result of the severe fiscal measures that the administration of Enrique Bolaños Geyer (2002–07) was forced to impose in order to be eligible for access to the World Bank and IMF's heavily indebted poor countries (HIPC) initiative. In 2008 the overall budget deficit (after grants) was 1,438m. gold córdobas, equivalent to 1.2% of GDP. This widened to 2,854m. gold córdobas, or 2.3% of GDP, in 2009, according to preliminary figures.

Many of the policies of the Chamorro Government were in fact implemented by the previous administration. Although the Sandinista Government had attempted to offset the increase in state spending on defence in the 1980s by increasing taxation on profits, workers' remittances and non-essential imports, the Government was forced to implement a number of austerity measures in 1988–89 in an attempt to solve the growing budget crisis. The measures included large devaluations, the creation of new currencies, wide-ranging price increases and budget reductions that involved a large number of job losses in the public sector. There were also job losses under the Chamorro Government, as attempts were made to reduce the deficit as part of its stabilization programme of 1991. This trend continued during the Alemán Government (1997–2002), as well as during the Bolaños administration. As a result, the number of public sector workers in Nicaragua fell from 218,703 in 1990 to only 111,453 by 2001. However, in the early 21st century public sector salaries expanded beyond private sector wages. A labour survey completed as part of the 2005 housing and population census revealed that employment in government services had increased substantially, representing 22.9% of the employed population, equivalent to 383,212 people. Compensation expenditure on central government employees decreased from an estimated 7.6% of GDP in 2000 to some 6.7% of GDP in 2007.

During the 1980s the growing budget deficits produced by the war effort and growing balance of payments deficits had forced the Sandinista Government to increase its foreign borrowing. The main problem was Nicaragua's restricted access to multilateral loans, owing to US opposition. Consequently, Nicaragua became dependent on bilateral credits from Western states and countries that were members of the Council for Mutual Economic Assistance (CMEA). Following initial rescheduling, a moratorium on public sector debt service payments had, by September 1982, become inevitable. In 1983 Nicaragua failed to repay US $45m. and requested the renegotiation of $180m. in interest payments due in 1984. Unable to pay either interest or principal on its debt, Nicaragua entered a state of 'passive default'. However, in 1988–89 the Sandinista Government implemented many of the measures traditionally demanded by the IMF as part of its own austerity programme.

These measures prepared the way for the implementation of the new policies of the Chamorro Government, which was able to take advantage of much more favourable circumstances. Thus, in 1992, with the USA agreeing to waive payment of US $259.5m. in bilateral debt and the 'Paris Club' of Western creditor nations reducing an $830m. debt to $207m., the new Government was able to pay arrears to the World Bank and the Inter-American Development Bank (IDB). This, in turn, opened a series of loan opportunities. The IMF ended its 12-year boycott of Nicaragua by approving a $55.7m. stand-by loan and the IDB approved a loan to support adjustment programmes in the trade and financial sectors. Restructuring of debt payments with various major bilateral creditors such as Mexico, Russia (as the principal successor state of the USSR) and several European countries followed in 1992. However, in 1993 Nicaragua again defaulted on repayment.

In 1994 the Government reached agreement with the IMF on an enhanced structural adjustment loan and redoubled its efforts to secure debt renegotiation and cancellation. The following year the Government secured the purchase of more than 80% of its commercial debt at eight cents in the dollar, effectively paying US $112m. to cancel $1,400m. in debt. This followed the restructuring of debts owed to the Paris Club. In 1998 the Club agreed to a further two-year postponement of

$201m. in debt service payments. In April 1996 Nicaragua finally reached agreement with Russia over its $3,500m. debt to the former USSR, with 95% of the outstanding amount being forgiven. Later that year Mexico followed suit, agreeing to waive 91% of the $1,100m. that it was owed. Agreement was also reached with the IMF in 1998 on a second enhanced structural adjustment loan. In November 1998 a number of countries pardoned or softened terms on bilateral debt they were owed, in the wake of Hurricane Mitch. Cuba, Austria and France, in particular, waived a total of $157m. in bilateral debt. France then waived a further $90m. in outstanding debt in February 2000. In March 2001 Spain assumed most of Nicaragua's $500m. debt to Guatemala, writing off some $399m. of the total in the process. In April 2003 France, Germany and Spain cancelled a further $263m. in bilateral debt.

In September 1999 Nicaragua was declared eligible for inclusion in the HIPC debt relief initiative, which would eventually make the cancellation of 80%–90% of the country's foreign debt possible. In December 2000 the IMF and World Bank declared that the country had fulfilled the necessary conditions to enter the initiative. In 2002 debt service waivers reached US $206m., almost double the amount of the previous year, following the implementation of a severe fiscal programme by the Bolaños Government, while in 2003 the total relief was $214m. In January 2004, after the fulfilment of all obligations, Nicaragua finally attained HIPC status, which included the forgiveness of 80% of the country's public external debt (totalling $6,400m. in 2003). In addition, the country only had to pay 10% of the total servicing of all World Bank loans contracted between 2001 and 2003, and would also receive a debt release of some $106m. on servicing IMF loans entered into between 2002 and 2009. The institutions were also encouraging Nicaragua's bilateral creditors to follow suit. In 2004 Nicaragua obtained a $21m. loan from the IMF and a $70m. loan from the World Bank, both under preferential terms. Then, in June 2005, Nicaragua was among 18 countries to be granted 100% debt relief on multilateral debt agreed by the Group of Eight (G8) leading industrialized nations, subject to the approval of the lenders. This cancellation was approved by the IMF in December, under the Multilateral Debt Relief Initiative. The relief totalled some $201m. ($132m., excluding the remaining HIPC funding) and became available from January 2006. In October 2007 a further agreement was finalized with the IMF, ensuring the release of some $111.3m. to the Ortega Government over three years. (The provision of an additional $10m. was approved by the IMF in September 2008 in view of the adverse effects of Hurricane Felix in 2007.) However, the Fund raised concerns over the Government's burgeoning relationship with Venezuela (which had cancelled $32.5m. of Nicaragua's outstanding debt in 2007) as well as plans to raise the country's minimum wage. From late 2006 onwards Venezuela had made significant contributions to the Ortega administration. However, ongoing questions over the propriety and transparency of these transactions had the effect of undermining the Government during 2007–10. In May 2010 the IMF suspended talks on the fourth review of its arrangment with the Nicaraguan Government, citing concerns regarding the potential impact on inflation of recently announced bonuses for public sector workers and gas and fuel subsidies for transport workers (to be funded by Venezuela).

FOREIGN TRADE

Until the early 1990s Nicaragua's export trade remained dominated by agricultural commodities, mainly coffee, cotton, sugar, beef, bananas and, increasingly, seafood. Import trade was (and continued to be) dominated by petroleum, other raw materials, non-durable consumer goods and machinery. The enormous cost of the war, increased purchases of petroleum and reduced income from exports (chiefly owing to low prices for coffee, sugar and cotton and the loss of the US market because of the embargo) resulted in an increasingly bleak trade deficit by the end of the 1980s. From the early 1990s, however, there was substantial improvement, with revenue from merchandise exports (f.o.b.) rising steadily to reach US $576.7m. by 1997. The damage caused to export crops by Hurricane Mitch resulted in a fall in revenues, to an estimated $546.1m. in 1999; however, export revenues recovered to $642.8m. in 2000, before falling again to $558.7m. in 2002. Export earnings then increased, reaching $866.0m. in 2005, $1,049.9m. in 2006, $1,224.8m. in 2007 and to $1,488.7m. in 2008, before declining to $1,390.9m. in 2009. At the beginning of the 21st century there was a significant transformation in the relative composition of export trade. In 2000 traditional exports (coffee, cotton, sugar, bananas, meat, etc.) represented 63.5% of total earnings; by 2008, these products represented only 36.9% (of which cotton made no contribution). Non-traditional exports, led by industrial production in the *maquila* zones and non-traditional agricultural exports such as groundnuts and beans, increased dramatically in importance over the same period.

Imports increased in the 1990s, fuelled at the end of that decade by the reconstruction and repair needs resulting from Hurricane Mitch. In 1999 merchandise imports (c.i.f) stood at US $1,723.1m., falling slightly, to $1,720.6m., in 2000. The imports bill remained static in 2001 and 2002, but increased thereafter, to $3,026.4m. in 2006, $3,597.8m. in 2007 and $4,337.8m. in 2008, before declining to $3,477.4m. in 2009. These levels of importation, coupled with the lack of dynamism in the export sector, produced a burgeoning overall trade deficit, which had reached $2,211.3m. by 2008. The deficit narrowed to $1,540.4m. in 2009, according to preliminary figures, as import costs declined much more sharply than export revenues.

The only major new sources of income that helped to offset the generally growing trade deficit were income from tourism and remittances from Nicaraguan citizens living abroad, mainly in the USA and Costa Rica. By 2008 income from tourism had reached US $276m., while tourist arrivals increased to 857,901. The sector remained robust in 2009, despite the global economic downturn: income and arrivals rose to $346m. and 931,904, respectively, with a 16.1% increase in arrivals by land compensating for a 0.8% decrease in arrivals by air. There was a massive increase in remittances in the early 21st century. Remittances totalled $818m. in 2008; a decline of 6.1%, to $768m. (equivalent to 12.4% of GDP), was recorded in 2009, although this fall was less severe than that experienced by most other countries in the region.

Fighting in the border regions disrupted Nicaragua's trade with neighbouring Central American countries during the 1980s. Non-traditional exports to the Central American Common Market (CACM) suffered most, decreasing by more than 75% between 1982 and 1985. The irregular availability of foreign exchange was the principal problem, although economic recession throughout the region also had an impact. Trade with Argentina and Brazil increased, owing to the extension of trade credits for Nicaragua's prime agricultural exports. In 2009 exports to the USA represented 29.5% of total exports, while the value of goods from the USA was equivalent to 19.9% of total imports. A significant proportion of trade was carried out with Nicaragua's Central American neighbours: in 2009 CACM states accounted for 32.2% of Nicaragua's exports and 23.9% of the country's imports. El Salvador became Nicaragua's second largest export market, taking 14.3% of export goods in 2009. Previously, in 2005, the member countries of the CACM had made substantial progress in the harmonization of common external tariffs. In that year some 5,861 tariffs were harmonized, representing 94.6% of total tariffs.

CONCLUSION

In 2010 Nicaragua remained the second poorest country in Latin America (after Haiti), heavily dependent on international aid, despite advances made since 1990 in reducing inflation and in increasing foreign reserves. Although the Bolaños administration succeeded in meeting the IMF's criteria for inclusion in the HIPC initiative, the fiscal and trade deficits remained unsustainable and social deprivation was still at an unacceptably high level. An accord reached between the Government and the opposition in October 2005 facilitated the legislative approval of a number of economic reforms required for the extension of the IMF's Poverty Reduction and Growth Facility (PRGF). In January 2006 the IMF completed the seventh, eighth and ninth reviews of the PRGF, extending the arrangement to December 2006. A further arrangement was reached in October 2007 (see above). Daniel Ortega's administration, which took office in January 2007, pledged to promote fiscal prudence, while also focusing on social policies. Advances were made in reducing maternal mortality rates, increasing school enrolment (and literacy rates) and improving access to safe water. Small-scale farmers were offered microcredits as part of an initiative to stimulate agricultural productivity, and the minimum wage was raised. However, donor support was threatened in late 2008 by the legislative impasse that followed disputed municipal elections in November (see History), with the USA announcing in December that it would withhold some $62m. in development aid (this aid was definitively cancelled in June 2009) and the European Union also suspending budgetary assistance. Although Ortega had pledged to further reconciliation with the USA, this endeavour had been undermined by allegations of corruption within his administration, together with his pursuit of closer relations with Iran and Venezuela.

Longer-term economic strategies revolved around an attempt to attract foreign investment through Nicaragua's integration into regional trade initiatives. It had been anticipated that the implementation of DR-CAFTA and the Central American customs union would advance such an aim, although the ratification of DR-CAFTA failed to precipitate a significant expansion in the textile industry. The economy remained vulnerable to external shocks, notably to natural disasters and fluctuations in the international price of commodities (especially petroleum). The aftermath of the global financial crisis also adversely affected the economy in 2009. GDP contracted for the first time since 1993, by an estimated 1.5%, as remittances from workers abroad, foreign aid, investment and export earnings all declined, while the fiscal deficit widened substantially, despite government efforts to curtail spending. Amid improving international conditions, there were indications of a return to growth in the Nicaraguan economy in the first half of 2010. Notably, export revenue increased by 34% in the first quarter of the year compared with the same period of 2009. GDP growth of between 1% and 2% was projected for 2010.

Statistical Survey

Sources (unless otherwise stated): Banco Central de Nicaragua, Carretera Sur, Km 7, Apdos 2252/3, Zona 5, Managua; tel. 265-0500; fax 265-2272; e-mail bcn@cabcn.gob.ni; internet www.bcn.gob.ni; Instituto Nacional de Información de Desarrollo, Los Arcos, Frente Hospital Fonseca, Managua; tel. 266-6178; e-mail webmaster@inide.gob.ni; internet www.inide.gob.ni.

Area and Population

AREA, POPULATION AND DENSITY

Area (sq km)	
Land	120,340
Inland water	10,034
Total	130,373*
Population (census results)	
25 April 1995	4,357,099
28 May–11 June 2005	
Males	2,534,491
Females	2,607,607
Total	5,142,098
Population (official estimates at mid-year)	
2008	5,668,877
2009	5,742,309
2010	5,815,524
Density (per sq km) at mid-2010	44.6

* 50,337 sq miles.

POPULATION BY AGE AND SEX

(official estimates at mid-2010)

	Males	Females	Total
0–14	1,024,450	984,664	2,009,114
15–64	1,733,454	1,813,383	3,546,837
65 and over	120,619	138,954	259,573
Total	2,878,523	2,937,001	5,815,524

ADMINISTRATIVE DIVISIONS

(land area only, population estimates at mid-2010)

	Area (sq km)	Population	Density (per sq km)	Capital
Departments:				
Chinandega	4,822.4	412,731	85.6	Chinandega
León	5,138.0	394,512	76.8	León
Managua	3,465.1	1,401,272	404.4	Managua
Masaya	610.8	336,877	551.5	Masaya
Carazo	1,081.4	179,108	165.6	Jinotepe
Granada	1,039.7	193,065	185.7	Granada
Rivas	2,161.8	168,594	78.0	Rivas
Estelí	2,229.7	218,660	98.1	Estelí
Madriz	1,708.2	149,983	87.8	Somoto
Nueva Segovia	3,491.3	235,381	67.4	Ocotal
Jinotega	9,222.4	393,356	42.7	Jinotega
Matagalpa	6,803.9	518,699	76.2	Matagalpa
Boaco	4,176.7	167,270	40.0	Boaco
Chontales	6,481.3	177,279	27.4	Juigalpa
Río San Juan	7,540.9	109,353	14.5	San Carlos
Autonomous Regions:				
Atlántico Norte (RAAN)	32,819.7	407,397	12.4	Bilwi
Atlántico Sur (RAAS)	27,546.3	351,987	12.8	Bluefields
Total	120,339.5	5,815,524	48.3	—

PRINCIPAL TOWNS

(population at 2005 census)

Managua (capital)	937,489	Chinandega	121,793
León	174,051	Estelí	112,084
Masaya	139,582	Granada	105,171
Matagalpa	133,416	Tipitapa	101,685

BIRTHS, MARRIAGES AND DEATHS
(annual averages, UN estimates)

	1995–2000	2000–05	2005–10
Birth rate (per 1,000)	30.1	26.3	24.8
Death rate (per 1,000)	5.6	5.0	4.7

Source: UN, *World Population Prospects: The 2008 Revision*.

2005: Registered live births 121,380; Registered marriages 23,069; Registered deaths 16,770. Note: Registration believed to be incomplete.

2006: Registered live births 123,886; Registered marriages 23,320; Registered deaths 16,595. Note: Registration believed to be incomplete.

2007: Registered live births 128,171; Registered marriages 20,918; Registered deaths 17,288. Note: Registration believed to be incomplete.

Life expectancy (years at birth, WHO estimates): 74 (males 71; females 77) in 2008 (Source: WHO, *World Health Statistics*).

EMPLOYMENT
(population aged 10 years and over, 2005 census)

	Male	Female	Total
Agriculture, forestry and fishing	537,209	33,611	570,820
Mining and quarrying	5,005	503	5,508
Manufacturing	118,919	89,074	207,993
Electricity, gas and water	3,830	954	4,784
Construction	86,574	2,182	88,756
Trade, restaurants and hotels	166,863	150,580	317,443
Transport and communications	60,346	5,338	65,684
Financial services	7,104	7,320	14,424
Government services	150,992	232,220	383,212
Other activities	9,817	7,109	16,926
Total employed	1,146,659	528,891	1,675,550

2006 (economically active population aged 10 years and over, '000): Agriculture, hunting, forestry and fishing 609.1; Mining and quarrying 6.7; Manufacturing 289.2; Electricity, gas and water supply 6.5; Construction 100.8; Wholesale and retail trade; repair of motor vehicles, motorcycles and personal and household goods 409.1; Hotels and restaurants 72.0; Transport, storage and communications 89.0; Financial intermediation 15.9; Real estate, renting and business activities 54.0; Public administration and defence; compulsory social security 73.7; Education 94.5; Health and social work 54.3; Other community, social and personal service activities 89.2; Households with employed persons 117.4; Extra-territorial organizations and bodies 8.1; *Total employed* 2,089.8; Unemployed 114.5; *Total labour force* 2,204.3 (Source: ILO).

Mid-2010 (estimates in '000): Agriculture, etc. 353; Total labour force 2,395 (Source: FAO).

Health and Welfare

KEY INDICATORS

Total fertility rate (children per woman, 2008)	2.7
Under-5 mortality rate (per 1,000 live births, 2008)	27
HIV/AIDS (% of persons aged 15–49, 2007)	0.2
Physicians (per 1,000 head, 2003)	0.4
Hospital beds (per 1,000 head, 2005)	0.9
Health expenditure (2007): US $ per head (PPP)	232
Health expenditure (2007): % of GDP	8.3
Health expenditure (2007): public (% of total)	54.9
Access to water (% of persons, 2008)	85
Access to sanitation (% of persons, 2008)	52
Total carbon emissions ('000 metric tons, 2006)	4,330.8
Carbon dioxide emissions per head (metric tons, 2006)	0.8
Human Development Index (2007): ranking	124
Human Development Index (2007): value	0.699

For sources and definitions, see explanatory note on p. vi.

Agriculture

PRINCIPAL CROPS
('000 metric tons)

	2006	2007	2008
Rice, paddy	319.6	269.9	321.9
Maize	501.9	486.7	423.9
Sorghum	73.2	107.6	74.6
Cassava (Manioc)*	105.0	115.0	115.0
Sugar cane	4,505.0	4,480.9	4,304.9
Beans, dry	179.7	170.4	176.7
Groundnuts, in shell	145.7†	156.8†	139.3
Oil palm fruit*	58.7	60.0	60.0
Bananas	42.6	44.4	36.3
Plantains*	55.0	55.0	55.0
Oranges*	72.0	85.0	85.0
Pineapples*	50.0	51.0	51.0
Coffee, green	70.5	100.0	72.7

* FAO estimates.
† Unofficial figure.

Aggregate production ('000 metric tons, may include official, semi-official or estimated data): Total cereals 894 in 2006, 864 in 2007, 820 in 2008; Total roots and tubers 149 in 2006, 163 in 2007–08; Total vegetables (incl. melons) 36 in 2006–08; Total fruits (excl. melons) 232 in 2006, 248 in 2007, 240 in 2008.

Source: FAO.

LIVESTOCK
('000 head, year ending September)

	2003	2004	2005*
Cattle	3,500	3,400†	3,500
Pigs*	462	461	463
Goats*	7	7	7
Horses*	260	265	268
Asses*	9	9	9
Mules*	47	48	48
Poultry*	16,000	16,500	18,000

* FAO estimates.
† Unofficial figure.

2006–08: Figures assumed to be unchanged from 2005 (FAO estimates).

Source: FAO.

LIVESTOCK PRODUCTS
('000 metric tons)

	2006	2007	2008
Cattle meat	84.3	92.8	96.1
Pig meat	6.8	6.9	7.1
Horse meat*	2.1	2.1	2.1
Chicken meat	83.6	89.8	91.0
Cows' milk	664.5	691.1	718.9
Hen eggs	21.1	21.5	21.6

* FAO estimates.

Source: FAO.

Forestry

ROUNDWOOD REMOVALS
('000 cubic metres, excl. bark, FAO estimates)

	2006	2007	2008
Sawlogs, veneer logs and logs for sleepers	93	93	93
Fuel wood	5,975	6,003	6,033
Total	6,068	6,096	6,126

Source: FAO.

SAWNWOOD PRODUCTION

('000 cubic metres, incl. railway sleepers, FAO estimates)

	2003	2004	2005
Coniferous	16.0	24.0	19.5
Broadleaved	29.0	42.8	34.6
Total	45.0	66.8	54.1

2006–08: Production assumed to be unchanged from 2005 (FAO estimates).

Source: FAO.

Fishing

('000 metric tons, live weight)

	2006	2007	2008
Capture	29.6	27.1	29.8
Snooks	1.1	1.1	1.1
Snappers	0.7	2.6	1.6
Yellowfin tuna	7.6	5.9	5.5
Skipjack tuna	5.3	2.4	6.0
Common dolphinfish	0.2	0.2	0.4
Caribbean spiny lobsters	3.6	3.7	4.2
Penaeus shrimp	2.3	2.5	1.8
Aquaculture	11.2	11.5	16.1
Whiteleg shrimp	10.9	11.1	14.7
Total catch	40.8	38.6	45.9

Source: FAO.

Mining

	2005	2006	2007
Gold (kg)	3,674	3,395	3,400
Silver (kg)	2,999	2,929	3,000
Gypsum and anhydrite (metric tons)	36,456	42,191	40,000

2008: Figures assumed to be unchanged from 2007 (estimates).

Source: US Geological Survey.

Industry

SELECTED PRODUCTS

('000 barrels, unless otherwise indicated)

	2006	2007	2008*
Liquid gas	178	185	110
Motor spirit	774	721	714
Kerosene	211	239	201
Diesel	1,486	1,515	1,398
Fuel oil	2,691	2,633	2,305
Bitumen (asphalt)	73	92	74
Electric energy (million kWh)	3,137.2	3,208.8	3,327.4

* Preliminary figures.

Cement ('000 metric tons, estimates): 530 in 2006–08 (Source: US Geological Survey).

Finance

CURRENCY AND EXCHANGE RATES

Monetary Units

100 centavos = 1 córdoba oro (gold córdoba).

Sterling, Dollar and Euro Equivalents (30 April 2010)

£1 sterling = 32.461 gold córdobas;
US $1 = 21.178 gold córdobas;
€1 = 28.198 gold córdobas;
1,000 gold córdobas = £30.81 = $47.22 = €35.46.

Average Exchange Rate (gold córdobas per US dollar)

2007	18.4485
2008	19.3719
2009	20.3395

Note: In February 1988 a new córdoba, equivalent to 1,000 of the former units, was introduced, and a uniform exchange rate of US $1 = 10 new córdobas was established. Subsequently, the exchange rate was frequently adjusted. A new currency, the córdoba oro (gold córdoba), was introduced as a unit of account in May 1990 and began to be circulated in August. The value of the gold córdoba was initially fixed at par with the US dollar, but in March 1991 the exchange rate was revised to $1 = 25,000,000 new córdobas (or 5 gold córdobas). On 30 April 1991 the gold córdoba became the sole legal tender.

BUDGET

(million gold córdobas)

Revenue*	2007	2008	2009†
Taxation	18,984.2	21,730.3	22,175.2
Income tax	5,746.0	7,001.9	7,817.7
Value-added tax	8,025.3	9,005.6	8,924.3
Taxes on petroleum products	2,107.6	2,162.2	2,276.6
Taxes on imports	1,093.3	1,183.2	970.2
Other revenue	1,594.6	1,737.8	1,684.1
Total	20,578.8	23,468.0	23,859.3

Expenditure‡	2007	2008	2009†
Compensation of employees	7,247.3	9,050.6	10,177.9
Goods and services	2,526.5	3,947.6	3,313.1
Interest payments	1,579.8	1,447.4	1,711.3
Current transfers	3,863.8	4,498.8	5,084.2
Capital transfers	3,211.3	3,528.7	3,013.7
Social security contributions	528.7	903.8	1,324.0
Other expenditure	1,166.5	1,654.9	1,534.0
Total	20,124.0	25,031.8	26,158.3

* Excluding grants received (million gold córdobas): 3,912.1 in 2007; 3,573.9 in 2008; 3,079.5 in 2009.

† Preliminary figures.

‡ Excluding net acquisition of non-financial assets (million gold córdobas): 3,926.2 in 2007; 3,448.1 in 2008; 3,634.4 in 2009.

INTERNATIONAL RESERVES

(excluding gold, US $ million at 31 December)

	2007	2008	2008
IMF special drawing rights	0.12	0.14	164.48
Foreign exchange	1,103.20	1,140.70	1,408.60
Total	1,103.32	1,140.84	1,573.08

Source: IMF, *International Financial Statistics*.

MONEY SUPPLY

(million gold córdobas at 31 December)

	2007	2008	2009
Currency outside banks	5,537.2	5,498.8	6,157.7
Transferable deposits	7,842.3	10,711.1	13,967.4
Other deposits	29,473.3	29,784.0	32,463.8
Broad money	42,852.8	45,993.9	52,589.0

Source: IMF, *International Financial Statistics*.

COST OF LIVING
(Consumer Price Index; base: 1999 = 100)

	2007	2008	2009
Food	188.9	242.8	252.4
Clothing	129.5	140.0	149.5
Rent, fuel and light	189.7	219.3	213.8
All items (incl. others)	178.8	214.2	222.2

Source: ILO.

NATIONAL ACCOUNTS
(million gold córdobas at current prices)

Expenditure on the Gross Domestic Product

	2007*	2008*	2009†
Final consumption expenditure	104,844.3	127,226.9	128,324.4
Gross capital formation	34,245.6	40,687.5	29,324.3
Total domestic expenditure	139,090.0	167,914.4	157,648.6
Exports of goods and services	35,517.2	42,719.9	43,867.0
Less Imports of goods and services	71,318.2	89,608.0	76,447.1
GDP in purchasers' values	103,289.0	121,026.3	125,068.6
GDP at constant 1994 prices	33,951.7	34,888.7	34,382.0

* Preliminary figures.
† Estimates.

Gross Domestic Product by Economic Activity

	2007*	2008*	2009†
Agriculture, hunting, forestry and fishing	16,669.0	20,700.4	21,003.5
Mining and quarrying	1,211.4	1,479.4	1,433.9
Manufacturing	17,584.0	21,112.2	22,085.9
Electricity, gas and water	2,730.7	3,356.4	3,257.5
Construction	5,169.0	5,848.7	5,893.6
Wholesale and retail trade	14,594.5	17,087.3	17,713.3
Transport and communications	5,914.9	6,589.0	6,835.2
Finance, insurance and business services	5,469.4	6,420.7	6,372.0
General government services	11,882.2	14,580.9	15,750.5
Other services	14,560.4	16,337.8	17,604.4
Sub-total	95,785.4	113,512.9	117,949.7
Net taxes on products	13,285.9	14,788.5	14,368.0
Less Imputed bank service charge	5,782.3	7,275.1	7,249.2
GDP in purchasers' values	103,289.0	121,026.3	125,068.6

* Preliminary figures.
† Estimates.

BALANCE OF PAYMENTS
(US $ million)

	2006	2007	2008
Exports of goods f.o.b.	2,034.1	2,335.7	2,537.6
Imports of goods f.o.b.	–3,485.1	–4,094.3	–4,748.9
Trade balance	–1,451.0	–1,758.6	–2,211.3
Exports of services	343.7	373.1	399.1
Imports of services	–477.7	–555.1	–608.2
Balance on goods and services	–1,585.0	–1,940.6	–2,420.4
Other income received	41.4	48.2	22.9
Other income paid	–169.9	–182.8	–183.5
Balance on goods, services and income	–1,713.5	–2,075.2	–2,581.0
Current transfers (net)	1,003.3	1,074.6	1,068.1
Current balance	–710.2	–1,000.6	–1,512.9
Capital (net)	348.3	416.2	375.0
Direct investment from abroad	286.8	381.7	626.1
Portfolio investment	–9.6	–12.2	–0.3
Other investment assets	4.9	–186.3	–129.6
Other investment liabilities	232.5	284.1	173.0
Net errors and omissions	–119.7	20.4	297.1
Overall balance	33.0	–96.7	–171.6

Source: IMF, *International Financial Statistics*.

External Trade

PRINCIPAL COMMODITIES
(US $ million)

Imports c.i.f.	2007	2008	2009
Consumer goods	1,072.5	1,255.9	1,125.8
Non-durable consumer goods	843.5	1,009.1	940.6
Durable consumer goods	229.0	246.8	185.2
Petroleum, mineral fuels and lubricants	813.4	1,000.2	684.1
Crude petroleum	403.5	503.1	346.8
Mineral fuels and lubricants	409.9	497.1	337.2
Intermediate goods	1,009.5	1,226.3	824.6
Primary materials and intermediate goods for agriculture and fishing	113.9	172.2	138.4
Primary materials and intermediate goods for industry	678.5	808.5	686.2
Construction materials	217.2	245.7	161.6
Capital goods	695.2	846.0	670.6
For agriculture and fishing	35.6	44.0	28.2
For industry	405.5	536.7	436.1
For transport	254.0	265.3	206.2
Miscellaneous	7.2	9.4	10.8
Total	3,597.8	4,337.8	3,477.4

Exports f.o.b.	2007	2008	2009
Coffee	188.1	278.3	236.7
Groundnuts	56.0	90.2	65.9
Cattle on hoof	42.2	26.8	17.7
Beans	39.9	79.8	61.3
Bananas	9.9	9.6	11.7
Lobster	46.8	39.5	31.2
Fresh fish	14.1	14.0	13.4
Shrimp	46.1	48.3	38.3
Tobacco (leaf)	4.8	5.4	5.1
Gold	61.4	78.2	81.2
Meat and meat products	179.5	210.7	230.6
Refined sugars, etc.	74.3	50.4	50.0
Cheese	49.7	66.2	76.9
Wood products	6.3	4.9	4.7
Chemical products	49.6	63.8	66.9
Refined petroleum	10.1	15.7	11.3
Porcelain products	12.1	10.0	4.5
Total (incl. others)	1,224.8	1,488.7	1,390.9

PRINCIPAL TRADING PARTNERS
(US $ million)

Imports c.i.f.	2007	2008	2009
Canada	27.5	37.9	24.2
Costa Rica	303.9	341.1	319.5
Ecuador	136.0	107.0	41.4
El Salvador	172.4	229.3	170.0
Germany	42.6	50.8	42.4
Guatemala	222.8	264.6	217.4
Honduras	108.4	135.3	125.4
Japan	121.5	124.3	80.2
Mexico	492.8	361.7	243.6
Panama	16.0	19.7	12.1
Spain	36.9	46.9	51.7
Sweden	21.0	19.3	12.9
Taiwan	15.4	21.0	13.6
USA	781.3	899.9	692.9
Venezuela	255.8	625.2	586.6
Total (incl. others)	3,597.8	4,337.8	3,477.4

Exports f.o.b.	2007	2008	2009
Belgium	25.2	28.6	15.7
Canada	69.4	75.0	42.3
Costa Rica	87.6	102.97	86.0
El Salvador	168.1	217.2	199.4
France	10.3	12.6	19.0
Germany	24.0	26.8	14.8
Guatemala	65.6	74.9	61.7
Honduras	111.1	101.4	100.6
Italy	11.3	14.6	7.4
Mexico	57.9	78.9	56.8
Spain	43.3	43.3	36.2
USA	353.6	439.0	410.4
Total (incl. others)	1,224.8	1,488.7	1,390.9

Transport

RAILWAYS
(traffic)

	1990	1991	1992
Passenger-km (million)	3	3	6

Freight ton-km (million): 4 in 1985.

Source: UN, *Statistical Yearbook*.

ROAD TRAFFIC
(motor vehicles in use)

	2002	2003	2004
Passenger cars	83,168	86,020	94,998
Buses and coaches	6,947	13,782	16,139
Lorries and vans	111,797	120,408	136,674
Motorcycles and mopeds	28,973	42,153	47,547

Source: IRF, *World Road Statistics*.

2007 (motor vehicles in use): Passenger cars 115,432; Buses and coaches 18,668; Lorries and vans 156,295; Motorcycles and mopeds 56,525.

SHIPPING

Merchant fleet
(registered at 31 December)

	2006	2007	2008
Number of vessels	28	28	29
Total displacement ('000 grt)	5.7	5.7	6.5

Source: Lloyd's Register-Fairplay, *World Fleet Statistics*.

International Sea-Borne Freight Traffic
('000 metric tons)

	1997	1998	1999
Imports	1,272.7	1,964.7	1,180.7
Exports	329.3	204.5	183.6

Total International Cargo Movements ('000 metric tons): 2,831.5 in 2009.

CIVIL AVIATION
(traffic on scheduled services)

	1998	1999	2000
Kilometres flown (million)	1.2	0.8	0.8
Passengers carried ('000)	52	59	61
Passenger-km (million)	93	67	72
Freight ton-km (million)	n.a.	0.5	0.5

Source: UN Economic Commission for Latin America and the Caribbean.

2006: 1,047,000 passengers carried; 19,240 metric tons of cargo carried.

Tourism

TOURIST ARRIVALS BY COUNTRY OF ORIGIN

	2005	2006	2007
Canada	18,068	19,319	16,800
Costa Rica	108,598	80,009	71,370
El Salvador	100,574	103,537	118,252
Guatemala	58,019	56,662	69,629
Honduras	139,134	153,168	173,816
Panama	17,591	15,412	15,479
USA	147,331	164,273	170,662
Total (incl. others)	712,444	749,184	799,996

Tourism receipts (US $ million, excl. passenger transport): 231 in 2006; 255 in 2007; 276 in 2008 (provisional).

Source: World Tourism Organization.

Communications Media

	2007	2008	2009
Telephones ('000 main lines in use)	249.0	252.0	255.0
Mobile cellular telephones ('000 subscribers)	2,502.3	3,108.0	3,204.4
Internet users ('000)	170.0	185.0	200.0
Broadband subscribers ('000)	27.6	36.1	47.0

Personal computers: 220,000 (40.3 per 1,000 persons) in 2005.

Radio receivers ('000 in use): 1,240 in 1997.

Television receivers ('000 in use): 350 in 2000.

Daily newspapers: 6 in 2004 (average circulation 135,000 copies in 1996).

Sources: UNESCO, *Statistical Yearbook*; International Telecommunication Union.

Education

(2007/08, unless otherwise indicated)

	Institutions*	Teachers	Students		
			Males	Females	Total
Pre-primary	5,980	11,032	111,938	108,591	220,529
Primary	8,251	32,349	486,898	457,443	944,341
Secondary: general	1,249	16,164	212,449	234,419	446,868
Tertiary: university level	35	3,630†	47,683‡	51,222‡	98,905‡
Tertiary: other higher	73	210†	1,902‡	2,770‡	4,672‡

* 2002/03 figures.
† 2001/02 figure.
‡ 2003/04 figure.

Sources: UNESCO, *Statistical Yearbook*; Ministry of Education, Culture and Sports.

Pupil-teacher ratio (primary education, UNESCO estimate): 29.2 in 2007/08 (Source: UNESCO Institute for Statistics).

Adult literacy rate (UNESCO estimates): 80.5% (males 79.7%; females 81.4%) in 2007 (Source: UNESCO Institute for Statistics).

Directory

The Constitution

Shortly after taking office on 20 July 1979, the Government of National Reconstruction abrogated the 1974 Constitution. On 22 August 1979 the revolutionary junta issued a 'Statute on Rights and Guarantees for the Citizens of Nicaragua', providing for the basic freedoms of the individual, religious freedom and freedom of the press and abolishing the death penalty. The intention of the Statute was formally to re-establish rights that had been violated under the deposed Somoza regime. A fundamental Statute took effect from 20 July 1980 and remained in force until the Council of State drafted a political constitution and proposed an electoral law. A new Constitution was approved by the National Constituent Assembly on 19 November 1986 and promulgated on 9 January 1987. Amendments to the Constitution were approved by the Asamblea Nacional (National Assembly) in July 1995 and January 2000. The following are some of the main points of the Constitution.

Nicaragua is an independent, free, sovereign and indivisible state. All Nicaraguans who have reached 16 years of age are full citizens.

POLITICAL RIGHTS

There shall be absolute equality between men and women. It is the obligation of the State to remove obstacles that impede effective participation of Nicaraguans in the political, economic and social life of the country. Citizens have the right to vote, to be elected at elections and to offer themselves for public office. Citizens may organize or affiliate with political parties, with the objective of participating in, exercising or vying for power. The supremacy of civilian authority is enshrined in the Constitution.

SOCIAL RIGHTS

The Nicaraguan people have the right to work, to education and to culture. They have the right to decent, comfortable and safe housing, and to seek accurate information. This right comprises the freedom to seek, receive and disseminate information and ideas, both spoken and written, in graphic or any other form. The mass media are at the service of national interests. No Nicaraguan citizen may disobey the law or prevent others from exercising their rights and fulfilling their duties by invoking religious beliefs or inclinations.

LABOUR RIGHTS

All have a right to work, and to participate in the management of their enterprises. Equal pay shall be given for equal work. The State shall strive for full and productive employment under conditions that guarantee the fundamental rights of the individual. There shall be an eight-hour working day, weekly rest, vacations, remuneration for national holidays and a bonus payment equivalent to one month's salary, in conformity with the law.

EDUCATION

Education is an obligatory function of the State. Planning, direction and organization of the secular education system is the responsibility of the State. All Nicaraguans have free and equal access to education. Private education centres may function at all levels.

LEGISLATIVE POWER

The Asamblea Nacional exercises Legislative Power through representative popular mandate. The Asamblea Nacional is composed of 90 representatives elected by direct secret vote by means of a system of proportional representation, of which 70 are elected at regional level and 20 at national level. The number of representatives may be increased in accordance with the general census of the population, in conformity with the law. Representatives shall be elected for a period of five years. The functions of the Asamblea Nacional are to draft and approve laws and decrees; to decree amnesties and pardons; to consider, discuss and approve the General Budget of the Republic; to elect judges to the Supreme Court of Justice and the Supreme Electoral Council; to fill permanent vacancies for the Presidency or Vice-Presidency; and to determine the political and administrative division of the country.

EXECUTIVE POWER

The Executive Power is exercised by the President of the Republic (assisted by the Vice-President), who is the Head of State, Head of Government and Commander-in-Chief of the Defence and Security Forces of the Nation. The election of the President (and Vice-President) is by equal, direct and free universal suffrage in a secret ballot. Should a single candidate in a presidential election fail to secure the necessary 35% of the vote to win outright in the first round, a second ballot shall be held. Close relatives of a serving President are prohibited from contesting a presidential election. The President shall serve for a period of five years and may not serve for two consecutive terms. (In October 2009 the constitutional panel of the Supreme Court ruled that the provision prohibiting consecutive presidential re-election was 'unenforceable'; however, this ruling required ratification by a majority of the Court's magistrates to become effective.) All outgoing Presidents are granted a seat in the Asamblea Nacional.

JUDICIAL POWER

The Judiciary consists of the Supreme Court of Justice, Courts of Appeal and other courts of the Republic. The Supreme Court is composed of at least seven judges, elected by the Asamblea Nacional, who shall serve for a term of six years. The functions of the Supreme Court are to organize and direct the administration of justice. There are 12 Supreme Court justices, appointed for a period of seven years.

LOCAL ADMINISTRATION

The country is divided into regions, departments and municipalities for administrative purposes. The municipal governments shall be elected by universal suffrage in a secret ballot and will serve a six-year term. The communities of the Atlantic Coast have the right to live and develop in accordance with a social organization that corresponds to their historical and cultural traditions. The State shall implement, by legal means, autonomous governments in the regions inhabited by the communities of the Atlantic Coast, in order that the communities may exercise their rights.

The Government

HEAD OF STATE

President: José Daniel Ortega Saavedra (took office 10 January 2007).

Vice-President: Jaime René Morales Carazo.

CABINET

(July 2010)

The Government is formed by the Frente Sandinista de Liberación Nacional.

Minister of Foreign Affairs: Samuel Santos López.

Minister of the Interior: Ana Isabel Morales Mazún.

Secretary-General of Defence with Ministerial Rank: Ruth Esperanza Tapia Roa.

Minister of Finance and Public Credit: Alberto José Guevara Obregón.

Minister of Development, Industry and Trade: Dr Orlando Solórzano Delgadillo.

Minister of Labour: Jeannette Chávez Gómez.

Minister of the Environment and Natural Resources: Juana Argeñal Sandoval.

Minister of Transport and Infrastructure: Pablo Fernando Martínez Espinoza.

Minister of Agriculture and Forestry: Ariel Bucardo Rocha.

Minister of Health: Dr Sonia Castro González.

Minister of Education: Miriam Ráudez.

Minister of the Family, Adolescence and Childhood: Marcia Ramírez Mercado.

Minister of Energy and Mines: Emilio Rappaccioli Baltodano.

Secretary to the Presidency: Salvador Vanegas Guido.

Co-ordinator of the Communication and Citizenship Council: Rosario Murillo Zambrana.

MINISTRIES

Office of the President: Casa Presidencial, Managua; e-mail daniel@presidencia.gob.ni; internet www.presidencia.gob.ni.

Ministry of Agriculture and Forestry: Km 8½, Carretera a Masaya, Managua; tel. 276-0200; fax 276-0204; e-mail ministro@magfor.gob.ni; internet www.magfor.gob.ni.

Ministry of Defence: De los semáforos el Redentor, 4 c. arriba, donde fue la casa 'Ricardo Morales Aviles', Managua; tel. 222-2201; fax 222-5439; e-mail prensa.midef@midef.gob.ni; internet www.midef.gob.ni.

Ministry of Development, Industry and Trade: Edif. Central, Km 6, Carretera a Masaya, Apdo 8, Managua; tel. 278-8702; fax 270-095; internet www.mific.gob.ni.

Ministry of Education: Complejo Cívico Camilo Ortega Saavedra, Managua; tel. 265-1451; fax 265-1595; e-mail webmaster@mined.gob.ni; internet www.mined.gob.ni.

Ministry of Energy and Mines: Hospital Bautista, 1 c. al oeste, 1 c. al norte, Managua; tel. 280-9500; fax 280-9516; e-mail informacion@mem.gob.ni; internet www.mem.gob.ni.

Ministry of the Environment and Natural Resources: Km 12½, Carretera Norte, Apdo 5123, Managua; tel. 233-1111; fax 263-1274; e-mail jargenal@marena.gob.ni; internet www.marena.gob.ni.

Ministry of the Family, Adolescence and Childhood: De donde fue ENEL Central, 100 m al sur, Managua; tel. 278-1620; e-mail webmaster@mifamilia.gob.ni; internet www.mifamilia.gob.ni.

Ministry of Finance and Public Credit: Frente a la Asamblea Nacional, Apdo 2170, Managua; tel. 222-6530; fax 222-6430; e-mail webmaster@mhcp.gob.ni; internet www.hacienda.gob.ni.

Ministry of Foreign Affairs: Del Antiguo Cine González 1 c. al sur, sobre Avda Bolívar, Managua; tel. 244-8000; fax 228-5102; e-mail despacho.ministro@cancilleria.gob.ni; internet www.cancilleria.gob.ni.

Ministry of Health: Complejo Nacional de Salud 'Dra Concepción Palacios', costado oeste Colonia Primero de Mayo, Apdo 107, Managua; tel. 289-7164; e-mail webmaster@minsa.gob.ni; internet www.minsa.gob.ni.

Ministry of the Interior: Apdo 68, Managua; tel. 228-2284; fax 222-2789; e-mail webmaster@migob.gob.ni; internet www.migob.gob.ni.

Ministry of Labour: Estadio Nacional, 400 m al norte, Apdo 487, Managua; tel. 222-2115; fax 228-2103; e-mail info@mitrab.gob.ni; internet www.mitrab.gob.ni.

Ministry of Transport and Infrastructure: Frente al Estadio Nacional, Apdo 26, Managua; tel. 228-2061; fax 222-5111; e-mail webmaster@mti.gob.ni; internet www.mti.gob.ni.

President and Legislature

PRESIDENT

Election, 5 November 2006

Candidate	Votes	% of total
José Daniel Ortega Saavedra (FSLN)	930,862	37.99
Eduardo Montealegre Rivas (ALN)	693,391	28.30
José Rizo Castellón (PLC)	664,225	27.11
Edmundo Jarquín Calderón (MRS)	154,224	6.29
Edén Pastora Gómez (AC)	7,200	0.29
Total	2,449,902	100.00

ASAMBLEA NACIONAL
(National Assembly)

Asamblea Nacional

Avda Bolívar, Contiguo a la Presidencia de la República, Managua; e-mail webmaster@correo.asamblea.gob.ni; internet www.asamblea.gob.ni.

President: RENÉ NÚÑEZ TÉLLEZ.

First Vice-President: OSCAR MONCADA REYES.

Second Vice-President: CARLOS GARCÍA.

Third Vice-President: JUAN RAMÓN JIMÉNEZ.

Election, 5 November 2006

Party	Votes	% of total	Seats
Frente Sandinista de Liberación Nacional (FSLN)	1,837,901	37.47	38
Partido Liberal Constitucionalista (PLC)	1,355,594	27.63	25
Alianza Liberal Nicaragüense (ALN)	1,279,859	26.09	22
Movimiento Renovador Sandinista (MRS)	405,149	8.26	5
Alternativa por el Cambio (AC)	27,135	0.55	—
Total	4,905,638*	100.00	90†

* Each elector had two votes: one for representatives at regional level (for which there were 70 seats) and one for representatives at national level (20 seats). The total number of votes cast at regional level was 2,487,448, while at national level 2,418,190 votes were cast.

† In addition to the 90 elected members, supplementary seats in the Asamblea Nacional are awarded to the unsuccessful candidates at the presidential election who were not nominated for the legislature but who received, in the presidential poll, a number of votes at least equal to the average required for one of the 70 legislative seats decided at a regional level. On this basis, the ALN obtained one additional seat in the Asamblea Nacional. A legislative seat is also awarded to the outgoing President, bringing the total number of seats in the Asamblea Nacional to 92.

Election Commission

Consejo Supremo Electoral (CSE): Iglesia Las Palmas, 1 c. al sur, Apdo 2241, Managua; tel. 268-7948; e-mail info@cse.gob.ni; internet www.cse.gob.ni; Pres. ROBERTO JOSÉ RIVAS REYES.

Political Organizations

Alianza Liberal Nicaragüense (ALN): Managua; fmrly Movimiento de Salvación Liberal; adopted current name in 2006; formed alliance with Partido Conservador (q.v.) ahead of 2006 elections; Pres. ALEJANDRO MEJÍA FERRETI; Sec.-Gen. CARLOS GARCÍA.

Alianza por la República (APRE): Casa 211, Col. Los Robles, Funeraria Monte de los Olivos 1.5 c. al norte, Managua; f. 2004 by supporters of President Enrique Bolaños Geyer; Pres. MIGUEL LÓPEZ BALDIZÓN.

Movimiento Democrático Nicaragüense (MDN): Casa L-39, Ciudad Jardín Bnd, 50 m al sur, Managua; tel. 243-898; f. 1978; Leader ROBERTO SEQUEIRA GÓMEZ.

Partido Social Cristiano (PSC): Ciudad Jardín, Pizza María, 1 c. al lago, Managua; tel. 222-026; f. 1957; 42,000 mems; Pres. ABEL REYES TELLEZ.

Alternativa por el Cambio (AC): Managua; f. as Alternativa Cristiana; fmr faction of Frente Sandinista de Liberación Nacional (q.v.); name changed as above in 2006; Pres. Dr ORLANDO J. TARDENCILLA ESPINOZA.

Camino Cristiano Nicaragüense (CCN): Managua; Pres. GUILLERMO ANTONIO OSORNO MOLINA.

Frente Sandinista de Liberación Nacional (FSLN) (Sandinista National Liberation Front): Costado oeste Parque El Carmen, Managua; tel. and fax 266-8173; internet www.fsln.org.ni; f. 1960; led by a 15-mem. directorate; embraces Izquierda Democrática Sandinista 'orthodox revolutionary' faction, led by Daniel Ortega Saavedra; leads Nicaragua Triunfa electoral alliance; 120,000 mems; Gen. Sec. JOSÉ DANIEL ORTEGA SAAVEDRA.

Movimiento Renovador Sandinista (MRS): De los semáforos del Ministerio de Gobernación, 1/2 cuadra al norte, Managua; tel. 250-9461; fax 278-0268; e-mail info@partidomrs.com; internet www.partidomrs.com; f. 1995; fmr faction of Frente Sandinista de Liberación Nacional (q.v.); formed the Alianza Patriótica in advance of the 2011 elections; Pres. ENRIQUE SÁENZ; Sec. ANA MARGARITA VIJIL.

Movimiento de Unidad Cristiana (MUC): Managua; mem. of Convergencia Nacional alliance; Pres. Pastor DANIEL ORTEGA REYES.

Movimiento Vamos con Eduardo (MVCE): Managua; internet www.vamosconeduardo.org; f. 2005; merged with the Partido Liberal Independiente in Feb. 2009; Pres EDUARDO MONTEALEGRE.

Partido Conservador (PC): Colegio Centroamérica, 500 m al sur, Managua; tel. 267-0484; e-mail contactenos@partidoconservador.org.ni; f. 1992 following merger between Partido Conservador Demócrata and Partido Socialconservadurismo; formed alliance with Alianza Liberal Nicaragüense (q.v.) ahead of 2006 elections; legal status annulled by the Consejo Supremo Electoral in June 2008; Pres. AZALIA AVILÉS.

Partido Indígena Multiétnico (PIM): Residencial Los Robles, de Farmacentro 1 c. al este, 80 varas al sur, Managua; Pres. CARLA WHITE HODGSON.

Partido Liberal Constitucionalista (PLC): Semáforos Country Club 100 m al este, Apdo 4569, Managua; tel. 278-8705; fax 278-1800; f. 1967; Pres. JORGE CASTILLO QUANT; Nat. Sec. Dr NOEL RAMÍREZ SÁNCHEZ.

Partido Liberal Nacionalista (PLN): Managua; f. 1913; Pres. CONSTANTINO VELÁSQUEZ ZEPEDA.

Partido Movimiento de Unidad Costeña (PAMUC): Bilwi Puerto Cabeza; Pres. KENNETH SERAPIO HUNTER.

Partido Neo-Liberal (Pali): Cine Dorado, 2 c. al sur, 50 m arriba, Managua; tel. 266-5166; f. 1986; Pres. ADOLFO GARCÍA ESQUIVEL.

Partido Resistencia Nicaragüense (PRN): Edif. VINSA, frente a Autonica, Carretera Sur, Managua; tel. and fax 270-6508; e-mail salvata@ibw.com.ni; f. 1993; nationalist party; Pres. JULIO CÉSAR BLANDÓN SÁNCHEZ (KALIMÁN).

Partido Socialista (PS): Hospital Militar, 100 m al norte, 100 m al oeste, 100 m al sur, Managua; tel. 266-2321; fax 266-2936; f. 1944; social democratic party; Sec.-Gen. Dr GUSTAVO TABLADA ZELAYA.

Partido Unionista Centroamericano (PUCA): Cine Cabrera, 1 c. al este, 20 m al norte, Managua; tel. 227-472; f. 1904; Pres. BLANCA ROJAS ECHAVERRY.

Unión Demócrata Cristiana (UDC): De Iglesia Santa Ana, 2 c. abajo, Barrio Santa Ana, Apdo 3089, Managua; tel. 266-2576; f. 1976 as Partido Popular Social Cristiano; name officially changed as above in Dec. 1993; mem. of Convergencia Nacional alliance; Pres. AGUSTÍN JARQUÍN ANAYA.

Yatama (Yapti Tasba Masraka Nanih Aslatakanka): Of. de Odacan, Busto José Martí, 1 c. al este y ½ c. al norte, Managua; tel. 228-1494; Atlantic coast Miskito org.; mem. of FSLN-led electoral alliance, Nicaragua Triunfa; Leader BROOKLYN RIVERA BRYAN.

Diplomatic Representation

EMBASSIES IN NICARAGUA

Argentina: Reparto Las Colinas, Calle Prado Ecuestre 235B (intersección con Calle los Mangos), Apdo 703, Managua; tel. 283-7066; fax 270-2343; e-mail embargentina@amnet.com.ni; Ambassador JORGE TELESFORO PEREIRA.

Brazil: Km 7¾, Carretera Sur, Quinta los Pinos, Apdo 264, Managua; tel. 265-0035; fax 265-2206; e-mail ebrasil@ibw.com.ni; Ambassador FLAVIO HELMOLD MACIEIRA.

Chile: Entrada principal los Robles, Semáforos Hotel Milton Princess, 1 c. abajo, 1 c. al sur, Apdo 1289, Managua; tel. 278-0619; fax 270-4073; e-mail echileni@cablenet.com.ni; Ambassador NATACHA MOLINA GARCÍA.

China (Taiwan): Optica Matamoros, 2 c. abajo, ½ c. al lago, Carretera a Masaya, Planes de Altamira, Apdo 4653, Managua; tel. 277-1333; fax 267-4025; e-mail nic@mofa.gov.tw; internet www.roc-taiwan.org.ni; Ambassador WU CHIN-MU.

Colombia: 2da Entrada a Las Colinas, 1 c. arriba, ½ c. al lago, Casa 97, Apdo 1062, Managua; tel. 276-2149; fax 276-0644; e-mail emanagua@cancilleria.gov.co; Ambassador ANTONIO GONZÁLEZ CASTAÑO.

Costa Rica: Reparto Las Colinas, Calle Prado Ecuestre 304, 1°, Managua; tel. 276-1352; fax 276-0115; e-mail infembcr@cablenet.com.ni; Ambassador MELVIN SÁENZ BIOLLEY.

Cuba: 3a Entrada a Las Colinas, 400 varas arriba, 75 al sur, Managua; tel. 276-0742; fax 276-0166; e-mail embacuba@embacuba.net.ni; internet embacu.cubaminrex.cu/nicaragua; Chargé d'affaires a.i. RENÉ CEBALLO PRATS.

Denmark: De la Plaza España, 1 c. abajo, 2 c. al lago, ½ c. abajo, Apdo 4942, Managua; tel. 268-0250; fax 266-8095; e-mail mgaambu@um.dk; internet www.ambmanagua.um.dk; Ambassador SØREN VØHTZ.

Dominican Republic: Reparto Las Colinas, Prado Ecuestre 100, con Curva de los Gallos, Apdo 614, Managua; tel. 276-2029; fax 276-0654; e-mail embdom@cablenet.com.ni; Ambassador PEDRO DESIDERIO BLANDINO CANTO.

Ecuador: Barrio Bolonia, Sede Central Los Pipitos, 1½ c. oeste, Managua; tel. 268-1098; fax 266-8081; e-mail ecuador@ibw.com.ni; Ambassador ANTONIO EUTIMIO PRECIADO BEDOYA.

El Salvador: Reparto Las Colinas, Avda del Campo y Pasaje, Los Cerros 142, Apdo 149, Managua; tel. 276-0712; fax 276-0711; e-mail embelsa@cablenet.com.ni; internet www.embelsanica.org.ni; Ambassador ALFREDO FRANCISCO UNGO RIVAS LAGUARDIA.

Finland: Sucursal Jorge Navarro, Apdo 2219, Managua; tel. 278-1216; fax 278-2840; e-mail sanomat.mgu@formin.fi; internet www.finlandia.org.ni; Ambassador EIJA ROTINEN.

France: Iglesia el Carmen 1½ c. abajo, Apdo 1227, Managua; tel. 222-6210; fax 268-5630; e-mail info@ambafrance-ni.org; internet www.ambafrance-ni.org; Ambassador THIERRY PIERRE FRAYSSÉ.

Germany: Bolonia, de la Rotonda El Güegüense, 1½ c. al lago, contiguo a Optica Nicaragüense, Apdo 29, Managua; tel. 266-3917; fax 266-7667; e-mail alemania@cablenet.com.ni; internet www.managua.diplo.de; Ambassador ANNA BETINA KERN.

Guatemala: Km 11½, Carretera a Masaya, Apdo E-1, Managua; tel. 279-9609; fax 279-9610; e-mail embnic@minex.gob.gt; Ambassador EDGAR RUANO NAJARRO.

Holy See: Apostolic Nunciature, Km 10.8, Carretera Sur, Apdo 506, Managua; tel. 265-8657; fax 265-7416; e-mail nuntius@cablenet.com.ni; Apostolic Nuncio Most Rev. HENRYK JÓZEF NOWACKI (Titular Archbishop of Blera).

Honduras: Reparto Las Colinas, Prado Ecuestre 298, frente a Residencia de la Embajada de China (Taiwán), Apdo 321, Managua; tel. 276-2406; fax 276-1998; e-mail embhonduras@cablenet.com.ni; Chargé d'affaires a.i. VICTORIA MARGARITA RODAS AMAYA.

Iran: Del Club Terraza, 300 m al este, de la principal entrada de las Cumbres, 3 c. al sur, No E4, Managua; tel. 270-0954; fax 255-0565; e-mail embirannic@cablenet.com.ni; Chargé d'affaires a.i. AKBAR ESMAEIL POUR.

Italy: Residencial Bolonia, Rotonda El Güegüense, 1 c. al norte, ½ c. al oeste, Apdo 2092, Managua 4; tel. 266-2961; fax 266-3987; e-mail ambasciata.managua@esteri.it; internet www.ambmanagua.esteri.it; Ambassador OMBRETTA PACILIO.

Japan: Plaza España, 1 c. abajo y 1 c. al lago, Bolonia, Apdo 1789, Managua; tel. 266-8668; fax 266-8566; e-mail embjpnic@ibw.com.ni; internet www.ni.emb-japan.go.jp; Ambassador SHINICHI SAITO.

Korea, Republic: De la Rotonda El Güegüense 3. al Oeste, ½ c. al sur, casa A-45, Apdo LV101, Managua; tel. 254-8107; fax 254-8131; e-mail nicaragua@mofat.go.kr; Ambassador LEE SANG-PAL.

Libya: Del portón principal del Hopsital Militar 1 c. al lago, 1 c. abajo y ½ al lago, Reparto Bolonia, Managua; tel. 266-8540; fax 266-8542; e-mail ofilibia@ibw.com.ni; Sec. of the People's Bureau ABDULLAH MUHAMMAD MATOUG.

Luxembourg: Residencial Bolonia del Hospital Militar, 1c. al lago y 1 1/2 abajo, Contiguo al Hotel Maracas Inn, Apdo 969, Managua; tel. 268-1881; fax 266-7965; e-mail secretariat.managua@mae.etat.lu; Chargé d'affaires a.i. RENÉ LAUER.

Mexico: Contiguo a Optica Matamoros, Km 4½, Carretera a Masaya, 25 varas Arriba, Altamira, Apdo 834, Managua; tel. 278-4919; fax 278-2886; e-mail embamex@turbonett.com.ni; Ambassador RAÚL LÓPEZ-LIRA NAVA.

Netherlands: Calle Erasmus de Rotterdam, Carretera a Masaya Km 5, del Colegio Teresiano 1 c. al sur, 1 c. abajo, Apdo 3688, Managua; tel. 276-8630; fax 276-0399; e-mail mng@minbuza.nl; internet www.embajadaholanda-nic.com; Ambassador LAMBERTUS CHRISTIAAN GRIJNS.

Norway: Rotonda El Güegüense, 100 m el Oeste, Apdo 2090, Correo Central, Managua; tel. 266-4199; fax 266-3303; e-mail emb.managua@mfa.no; internet www.noruega.org.ni; Ambassador TOM TYRIHJELL.

Panama: Casa 93, Reparto Mántica, del Cuartel General de Bomberos 1 c. abajo, Apdo 1, Managua; tel. 266-8633; fax 266-2224; e-mail embdpma@enitel.com.ni; Ambassador OLIMPO ANIBAL SÁENZ MARCUCI.

Peru: Del Hospital Militar, 1 c. al norte, 2 c. hacia oeste, casa 325, Apdo 211, Managua; tel. 266-8678; fax 266-8679; e-mail embajada@peruennicaragua.com.ni; internet www.peruennicaragua.com.ni; Ambassador CARLOS BÉRNINZON DEVÉSCOVI.

Russia: Reparto Las Colinas, Calle Vista Alegre 214, Apdo 249, Managua; tel. 276-0374; fax 276-0179; e-mail rossia@cablenet.com.ni; internet www.nicaragua.mid.ru; Ambassador IGOR S. KONDRASHEV.

Spain: Avda Central 13, Las Colinas, Apdo 284, Managua; tel. 276-0966; fax 276-0937; e-mail emb.managua@mae.es; internet www.mae.es/embajadas/managua; Ambassador ANTONIO PÉREZ-HERNÁNDEZ TORRA.

USA: Km 5½, Carretera Sur, Apdo 327, Managua; tel. 252-7100; fax 252-7300; e-mail consularmanagua@state.gov; internet nicaragua.usembassy.gov; Ambassador ROBERT J. CALLAHAN.

Venezuela: Costado norte de la Iglesia Santo Domingo, Las Sierritas, Casa 27, Apdo 406, Managua; tel. 272-0267; fax 272-2265; e-mail embaveneznica@cablenet.com.ni; Chargé d'affaires a.i. PEDRO LUIS PENSO SÁNCHEZ.

Judicial System

The Supreme Court

Km 7½, Carretera Norte, Managua; tel. 233-0083; fax 233-0581; e-mail webmaster@csj.gob.ni; internet www.poderjudicial.gob.ni.

Deals with both civil and criminal cases, acts as a Court of Cassation, appoints Judges of First Instance, and generally supervises the legal administration of the country.

President: Dr ALBA LUZ RAMOS VANEGAS (acting).

Vice-President: Dr RAFAEL SOLÍS CERDA.

Attorney-General: Dr HERNÁN ESTRADA.

Religion

All religions are tolerated. Almost all of Nicaragua's inhabitants profess Christianity, and the majority belong to the Roman Catholic

Church. The Moravian Church predominates on the Caribbean coast.

CHRISTIANITY

The Roman Catholic Church

Nicaragua comprises one archdiocese, six dioceses and the Apostolic Vicariate of Bluefields. According to the latest available census figures (2005), some 58% of the population aged five years and above are Roman Catholics.

Bishops' Conference

Conferencia Episcopal de Nicaragua, Ferretería Lang 1 c. al norte, 1 c. al este, Zona 3, Las Piedrecitas, Apdo 2407, Managua; tel. 266-6292; fax 266-8069; e-mail cen@tmx.com.ni.

f. 1975; statute approved 1987; Pres. LEOPOLDO JOSÉ BRENES SOLÓRZANO (Archbishop of Managua).

Archbishop of Managua: LEOPOLDO JOSÉ BRENES SOLÓRZANO, Arzobispado, Apdo 2008, Managua; tel. 276-0129; fax 276-0130; e-mail mob@unica.edu.ni.

The Anglican Communion

Nicaragua comprises one of the five dioceses of the Iglesia Anglicana de la Región Central de América.

Bishop of Nicaragua: Rt Rev. STURDIE W. DOWNS, Apdo 1207, Managua; tel. 222-5174; fax 222-6701; e-mail episcnic@tmx.com.ni.

Protestant Churches

Some 22% of the population aged five years and above are members of evangelical churches, according to the last census (2005).

Baptist Convention of Nicaragua: Apdo 2593, Managua; tel. 225-785; fax 224-131; f. 1917; 135 churches, 20,000 mems (2006); Pres. ABEL MENDOZA; Sec. DALIA NAVARRETE.

The Moravian Church in Nicaragua: Iglesia Morava, Bilwi; tel. and fax 282-2222; 199 churches, 83,000 mems; Leader Rt Rev. JOHN WILSON.

The Nicaraguan Lutheran Church of Faith and Hope: Apdo 151, Managua; tel. 266-4467; fax 266-4609; e-mail luterana@turbonett.com.ni; f. 1994; 7,000 mems (2007); Pres. Rev. VICTORIA CORTEZ RODRÍGUEZ.

The Press

NEWSPAPERS AND PERIODICALS

Bolsa de Noticias: Col. Centroamérica, Grupo L 852, Apdo VF-90, Managua; tel. 270-0546; fax 277-4931; e-mail prensa@bolsadenoticias.com.ni; internet www.bolsadenoticias.com.ni; f. 1974; daily; Dir MARÍA ELSA SUÁREZ GARCÍA; Editor-in-Chief MARÍA ELENA PALACIOS.

Confidencial: De Pharoahs Casino, 2 c. abajo, 2 c. al sur, Managua; tel. 277-5134; fax 270-7017; e-mail info@confidencial.com.ni; internet www.confidencial.com.ni; weekly; political analysis; Dir CARLOS F. CHAMORRO; Editors IVÁN OLIVARES, CARLOS SALINAS.

La Gaceta, Diario Oficial: De la Rotonda de Plaza Inter, 1 c. arriba, 2 c. al lago, Managua; tel. 228-3791; fax 228-4001; e-mail lagaceta@presidencia.gob.ni; internet www.lagaceta.gob.ni; f. 1912; morning; daily; official; Dir Dr LEOPOLDO CASTRILLO.

Novedades: Pista P. Joaquín Chamorro, Km 4, Carretera Norte, Apdo 576, Managua; evening; daily.

Nuevo Diario: Pista P. Joaquín Chamorro, Km 4, Carretera Norte, Apdo 4591, Managua; tel. 249-0499; fax 249-0700; e-mail info@elnuevodiario.com.ni; internet www.elnuevodiario.com.ni; f. 1980; morning; daily; independent; Dir FRANCISCO CHAMORRO; Editor-in-Chief ROBERTO COLLADO; circ. 45,000.

El Observador Económico: De Pricesmart, 2 c. al lago, Apdo 2074, Managua; tel. 266-8708; fax 266-8711; e-mail info@elobservadoreconomico.com; internet www.elobservadoreconomico.com; Dir-Gen. ALEJANDRO MARTÍNEZ CUENCA.

La Prensa: Km $4\frac{1}{2}$, Carretera Norte, Apdo 192, Managua; tel. 249-8405; fax 249-6926; e-mail info@laprensa.com.ni; internet www.laprensa.com.ni; f. 1926; morning; daily; independent; Pres. JAIME CHAMORRO CARDENAL; Editor F. POTOY; circ. 30,000.

Prensa Proletaria: Managua; tel. 222-594; fortnightly; official publ. of the Movimiento de Acción Popular Marxista-Leninista.

Revista 7 Días: Altamira de lo Vicky, $5\frac{1}{2}$ al lago, Managua; tel. 270-6509; e-mail 7dias@ibw.com.ni; internet www.7dias.com.ni.

Revista Encuentro: Universidad Centroamericana, Apdo 69, Managua; tel. 278-3923; fax 267-0106; e-mail ucapubli@ns.uca.edu.ni; internet www.uca.edu.ni:8080/encuentro; f. 1968; termly; academic publ. of the Universidad Centroamericana; Dir JORGE ALBERTO PÉREZ HUETE.

Revista Envío: Edif. Nitlapán, 2°, Campus Universidad Centroamericana, Apdo A-194, Managua; tel. 278-2557; fax 278-1402; e-mail info@envio.org.ni; internet www.envio.org.ni; f. 1981; 11 a year; political analysis; edns in Spanish, English and Italian; Dir JUAN RAMIRO MARTÍNEZ; Chief Editor MARÍA LÓPEZ VIGIL.

Tiempos del Mundo: Apdo 3525, Managua; tel. 270-3418; fax 270-3419; e-mail tiempos@tdm.com.ni; f. 1996; weekly; Gen. Man. TAKUYA ISHII; circ. 5,000.

La Tribuna: Detrás del Banco Mercantil, Plaza España, Apdo 1469, Managua; tel. 266-9282; fax 266-5167; e-mail tribuna@latribuna.com.ni; f. 1993; morning; daily; Dir HAROLDO J. MONTEALEGRE; Gen. Man. MARIO GONZÁLEZ.

Trinchera de la Noticia: Managua; tel. 240-0114; e-mail info@trinchera.com.ni; internet www.trinchera.com.ni; daily; Dir XAVIER REYES ALBA; Man. EMILIO NÚÑEZ TENORIO.

Visión Sandinista: Costado este, Parque El Carmen, Managua; tel. and fax 268-1565; internet www.visionsandinista.com; f. 1980; weekly; official publ. of the Frente Sandinista de Liberación Nacional; Dir MAYRA REYES SANDOVAL.

Association

Unión de Periodistas de Nicaragua (UPN): Apdo 4006, Managua; tel. 271-2436; e-mail uperiodistasnic@yahoo.com; internet www.aquinicaragua.com/periodistas2.html; Pres. RÓGER SUÁREZ.

Publishers

Academia Nicaragüense de la Lengua: Calle Central, Reparto Las Colinas, Apdo 2711, Managua; f. 1928; languages; Dir JORGE EDUARDO ARELLANO.

Editora de Arte SA: 53 Reparto Los Robles III, Managua; tel. 278-5854; e-mail editarte@editarte.com.ni; internet www.editarte.com.ni.

Editorial Nueva Nicaragua: Paseo Salvador Allende, Km $3\frac{1}{2}$, Carretera Sur, Apdo 073, Managua; fax 266-6520; f. 1981; Pres. Dr SERGIO RAMÍREZ MERCADO; Dir-Gen. ROBERTO DÍAZ CASTILLO.

Editorial Unión: Avda Central Norte, Managua; travel.

Librería Hispanoamericana (HISPAMER): Costado este de la UCA, Apdo A-221, Managua; e-mail hispamer@hispamer.com.ni; internet www.hispamer.com.ni; f. 1991.

UCA Publicaciónes: Rectoría de la Universidad Centroamericana, Apdo 69, Managua; tel. 278-3923; fax 267-0106; e-mail ucapubli@ns.uca.edu.ni; internet www.uca.edu.ni/publicaciones; academic publishing dept of the Universidad Centroamericana.

Universidad Nacional Agraria: Km $12\frac{1}{2}$ Carretera Norte, Apdo 453, Managua; tel. 233-1950; e-mail info@una.edu.ni; internet www.una.edu.ni; sciences.

Broadcasting and Communications

TELECOMMUNICATIONS

Regulatory Body

Instituto Nicaragüense de Telecomunicaciones y Correos (Telcor): Edif. Telcor, Avda Bolívar diagonal a Cancillería, Apdo 2264, Managua; tel. 222-7350; fax 222-7554; e-mail mgutierrez@telcor.gob.ni; internet www.telcor.gob.ni; Exec. Pres. ORLANDO CASTILLO.

Major Service Providers

Claro: Villafontana 2°, Apdo 232, Managua; tel. 277-3057; fax 270-2128; e-mail cliente@claro.com.ni; internet www.claro.com.ni; f. 2006 by merger of ALÓ PCS (f. 2002) and Empresa Nicaragüense de Telecomunicaciones (Enitel, f. 1925); subsidiary of América Móvil, SA de CV (Mexico); Chair. PATRICIO SLIM DOMIT; CEO DANIEL HAJJ ABOUMRAD.

Telefónica SA Nicaragua: Km $6\frac{1}{2}$, Carretera a Masaya, Managua; tel. 277-0731; internet www.movistar.com.ni; fmrly BellSouth; owned by Grupo Telefónica Móviles (Spain); mobile cellular telephone provider; Vice-Pres. HUMBERTO PATO-VINUESA; Gen. Man. MARÍA JOSEFINA PERALTA.

BROADCASTING

Radio

La Nueva Radio Ya: Pista de la Resistencia, Frente a la Universidad Centroamericana, Managua; tel. 278-8336; fax 278-8334; e-mail info@nuevaya.com.ni; internet www.nuevaya.com.ni; f. 1990 as Radio Ya; restyled as above in 1999; operated by Entretenimiento Digital, SA; Dir-Gen. DENNIS SCHWARTZ.

Radio Católica: Altamira D'Este 621, 3°, Apdo 2183, Managua; tel. 278-0836; fax 278-2544; e-mail oramos@radiocatolica.org; internet www.radiocatolica.org; f. 1961; controlled by Conferencia Episcopal de Nicaragua; Dir Fr ROLANDO ÁLVAREZ; Gen. Man. ALBERTO CARBALLO MADRIGAL.

Radio Corporación, Gadea y Cía: Avda Ponciano Lombillo, Ciudad Jardín Q-20, Apdo 24242, Managua; tel. 249-1619; fax 244-3824; e-mail rc540@radio-corporacion.com; internet www.radio-corporacion.com; f. 1995; Gen. Man. FABIO GADEA MANTILLA; Asst Man. CARLOS GADEA MANTILLA.

Radio Estrella: Sierritas de Santo Domingo, Frente al Cementerio, Apdo UNICA 104, Managua; tel. 276-0241; fax 276-0062; e-mail radiosm@radioestrelladelmar.com; internet www.radioestrelladelmar.com; f. 1997; Catholic.

Radio Mundial: 36 Avda Oeste, Reparto Loma Verde, Apdo 3170, Managua; tel. 266-6767; fax 266-4630; f. 1948; commercial; Dir-Gen. ALMA ROSA ARANA HARTIG.

Radio Nicaragua: Villa Fontana, Contiguo a Enitel, Apdo 4665, Managua; tel. 227-2330-1; fax 267-1448; e-mail director@radionicaragua.com.ni; internet www.radionicaragua.com.ni; f. 1960; govt station; Dir-Gen. ALBERTO CARBALLO MADRIGAL.

Radio Ondas de Luz: Costado Sur del Hospital Bautista, Apdo 607, Managua; tel. and fax 249-7058; f. 1959; religious and cultural station; Pres. GUILLERMO OSORNO MOLINA.

Radio Sandino: Paseo Tiscapa Este, Contiguo al Restaurante Mirador, Apdo 4776, Managua; tel. 228-1330; fax 262-4052; internet www.lasandino.com.ni; f. 1977; station controlled by the Frente Sandinista de Liberación Nacional; Pres. RAFAEL ORTEGA MURILLO.

Radio Segovia: Ocotal, Nueva Segovia; tel. 732-2870; fax 732-2271; e-mail info@radiosegovia.net; internet www.radiosegovia.net; f. 1980; commercial.

Radio Tiempo: Reparto Pancasan 217, 7°, Apdo 2735, Managua; tel. 278-2540; f. 1976; Dir DANILO LACAYO LANZAS.

Radio Universidad: Avda Card, 3 c. abajo, Apdo 2883, Managua; tel. 278-4743; fax 277-5057; f. 1984; Dir LUIS LÓPEZ RUIZ.

There are some 50 other radio stations.

Television

Canal 4: Montoya, 1 c. al sur, 2 c. arriba, Managua; tel. 228-1310; fax 222-4067; internet www.multinoticias.tv; owned by Radio y Televisión de Nicaragua, SA (RATENSA).

Nicavisión, Canal 12: Bolonia Dual Card, 1 c. abajo, ½ c. al sur, Apdo 2766, Managua; tel. 266-0691; fax 266-1424; f. 1993; Dir MARIANO VALLE PETERS.

Televicentro de Nicaragua, SA, Canal 2: Casa del Obrero, 6½ c. al sur, Apdo 688, Managua; tel. 268-2222; fax 266-3688; e-mail tvnoticias@canal2.com.ni; internet www.canal2.com.ni; f. 1965; Pres. OCTAVIO SACASA RASKOSKY; Gen. Man. ALEJANDRO SACASA PASOS.

Televisión Internacional, Canal 23: Casa L-852, Col. Centroamérica, Managua; tel. 268-7466; fax 266-0625; e-mail canal23@ibw.com.ni; f. 1993; Pres. CÉSAR RIGUERO.

Televisora Nicaragüense, SA (Telenica 8): De la Mansión Teodolinda, 1 c. al sur, ½ c. abajo, Bolonia, Apdo 3611, Managua; tel. 266-5021; fax 266-5024; internet www.telenica.com.ni; f. 1989; sold to private buyer in 2010; Pres. (vacant).

Ultravisión de Nicaragua, SA: Casa 567, Rotonda los Cocos, Altamira, Managua; tel. 277-3524; Pres. CRISEYDA OLIVAS VEGA.

Finance

(cap. = capital; res = reserves; dep. = deposits; m. = million; amounts in gold córdobas)

BANKING

All Nicaraguan banks were nationalized in July 1979. Foreign banks operating in the country are no longer permitted to secure local deposits. All foreign exchange transactions must be made through the Banco Central or its agencies. Under a decree issued in May 1985, the establishment of private exchange houses was permitted. In 1990 legislation allowing for the establishment of private banks was enacted.

Supervisory Authority

Superintendencia de Bancos y de Otras Instituciones Financieras: Edif. SIBOIF, Km 7, Carretera Sur, Apdo 788, Managua; tel. 265-1555; fax 265-0965; e-mail correo@sibiof.gob.ni; internet www.superintendencia.gob.ni; f. 1991; Supt Dr VICTOR M. URCUYO VIDAURRE.

Central Bank

Banco Central de Nicaragua: Carretera Sur, Km 7, Apdos 2252/3, Zona 5, Managua; tel. 255-7171; fax 265-0561; e-mail oaip@bcn.gob.ni; internet www.bcn.gob.ni; f. 1961; bank of issue and govt fiscal agent; cap. and res –1,142.0m., dep. 42,382.0m. (Dec. 2008); Pres. Dr ANTENOR ROSALES BOLAÑOS; Gen. Man. JOSÉ DE JESÚS ROJAS RODRÍGUEZ.

Private Banks

Banco de América Central (BAC): Km 4½, Carretera a Masaya, Managua; tel. 274-4444; fax 274-4620; e-mail serviciocliente@bac.com.ni; internet www.bancodeamericacentral.com; f. 1991; total assets 10,516m. (1999); Pres. CARLOS PELLAS CHAMORRO; Gen. Man. CARLOS MATUS TAPIA.

Banco de Crédito Centroamericano (BANCENTRO): Edif. BANCENTRO, Km 4½ Carretera a Masaya, Managua; tel. 278-2777; fax 278-6001; e-mail info@bancentro.com.ni; internet www.bancentro.com.ni; f. 1991; total assets 282m. (2005); Pres. ROBERTO J. ZAMORA LLANES; Gen. Man. CARLOS A. BRICEÑO RÍOS.

Banco Uno, SA: Plaza España, Rotonda el Güegüense 20 m al oeste, Managua; tel. 278-7171; fax 277-3154; e-mail info@bancouno.com.ni; internet www.bancouno.com.ni; dep. 2,372m. (Dec. 2002); fmrly Banco de la Exportación (BANEXPO), present name adopted in Nov. 2002; acquired by Citibank in 2007; Dir ADOLFO ARGÜELLO LACAYO.

STOCK EXCHANGE

Bolsa de Valores de Nicaragua: Edif. Oscar Pérez Cassar, Centro BANIC, Km 5½, Carretera Masaya, Apdo 121, Managua; tel. 278-3830; fax 278-3836; e-mail info@bolsanic.com; internet bolsanic.com; f. 1993; Pres. Dr RAÚL LACAYO SOLÓRZANO; Gen. Man. GERARDO ARGÜELLO LEIVA.

INSURANCE

State Company

Instituto Nicaragüense de Seguros y Reaseguros (INISER): Centro Comercial Camino de Oriente, Km 6, Carretera a Masaya, Apdo 1147, Managua; tel. (2) 66-6772; fax (2) 66-5636; e-mail iniser@iniser.com.ni; internet www.iniser.com.ni; f. 1979 to assume the activities of all the pre-revolution national private insurance cos; Exec. Pres. EDUARDO HALLESLEVENS; Vice-Pres GUILLERMO JIMÉNEZ, JUAN JOSÉ UBEDA.

Private Companies

Aseguradora Mundial Nicaragua: Edif. Invercasa, 1°, Managua; tel. 276-8890; fax 278-6358; e-mail lucia.ramirez@amundial.com.ni; internet www.amundial.com.ni; Pres. ORLANDO EDMUNDO SÁNCHEZ AVILÉS; Gen. Man. LUCÍA RAMÍREZ.

Metropolitana Compañía de Seguros, SA: Reparto Serrano Plaza El Sol, 400 m al norte, Managua; tel. 276-9000; fax 276-9002; e-mail metroseg@metroseg.com; internet www.metroseg.com; Pres. Dr LEONEL ARGÜELLO RAMÍREZ; Sec. HORACIO ARGÜELLO CARAZO.

Seguros América, SA: Centro BAC, Km 5½ Carretera a Masaya, Apdo 6114, Managua; tel. 274-4200; fax 274-4202; e-mail sergioulvert@segamerica.com.ni; internet www.segurosamerica.com.ni; f. 1996; Pres. CARLOS F. PELLAS CHAMORRO; Man. SERGIO ULVERT SÁNCHEZ.

Seguros Lafise, SA: Centro Financiero Lafise, Km 5½ Carretera a Masaya, Managua; tel. 270-3505; fax 270-3558; e-mail seguros@seguroslafise.com.ni; internet www.seguroslafise.com.ni; fmrly Seguros Centroamericanos (Segurossa); Pres. ROBERTO ZAMORA LLANES; Gen. Man. CLAUDIO TABOADA RODRÍGUEZ.

Trade and Industry

GOVERNMENT AGENCIES

Empresa Nicaragüense de Alimentos Básicos (ENABAS): Salida a Carretera Norte, Apdo 1041, Managua; tel. 248-1640; e-mail direccion.administrativa@enabas.gob.ni; internet www.enabas.gob.ni; f. 1979; controls trading in basic foodstuffs; Exec. Dir HERMINIO ESCOTO GARCÍA.

Instituto de Desarrollo Rural (IDR) (Institute of Rural Development): B3, Camino de Oriente, Apdo 3593, Managua; tel. 255-8777; e-mail divulgacion@idr.gob.ni; internet www.idr.gob.ni; f. 1995; Exec. Dir PEDRO HASLAM MENDOZA.

Instituto Nicaragüense de Apoyo a la Pequeña y Mediana Empresa (INPYME): De la Shell Plaza el Sol, 1 c. al sur, 300 m abajo, Apdo 449, Managua; tel. 278-7836; e-mail bcantillo@inpyme.gob.ni; internet www.inpyme.gob.ni; supports small and medium-sized enterprises; Exec. Dir MARÍA LIDIA ESPINALES.

Instituto Nicaragüense de Tecnología Agropecuaria (INTA): Col. Centroamérica, contiguo al Distrito 5, Apdo 1247, Managua; tel. 227-2290; fax 278-0373; e-mail bayserfe@inta.gob.ni; internet www.inta.gob.ni; f. 1993; Dir-Gen. EVA ACEVEDO GUTIÉRREZ.

Instituto de la Vivienda Urbana y Rural (INVUR): Km 4.5, Carretera Sur, contiguo a INISER, Managua; tel. 226-6112; e-mail gmartinez@invur.gob.ni; internet www.invur.gob.ni; housing devt; Pres. JUDITH SILVA.

DEVELOPMENT ORGANIZATIONS

Asociación de Productores y Exportadores de Nicaragua (APEN): Del Hotel Intercontinental, 2 c. al sur y 2 c. abajo, Bolonia, Managua; tel. 268-6053; fax 266-5160; internet www.apen.org.ni; Pres. ENRIQUE ZAMORA LLANES; Gen. Man. AZUCENA CASTILLO.

Cámara de Industrias de Nicaragua: Rotonda el Güegüense, Plaza España 300 m al sur, Apdo 1436, Managua; tel. 266-8847; fax 266-1891; e-mail cadin@cadin.org.ni; internet www.cadin.org.ni; Pres. ALFREDO MARÍN XIMÉNEZ; Vice-Pres. LUZ ARGENTINA CANO ZAMBRANA.

Cámara Nacional de la Mediana y Pequeña Industria (CONAPI): Plaza 19 de Julio, Frente a la UCA, Apdo 153, Managua; tel. 278-4892; fax 267-0192; e-mail conapi@nicarao.org.ni; Pres. FLORA VARGAS LOAISIGA; Gen. Man. URIEL ARGEÑAL C.

Cámara Nicaragüense de la Construcción (CNC): Bolonia de Aval Card, 2 c. abajo, 50 varas al sur, Managua; tel. 226-3363; fax 266-3327; e-mail info@construccion.org.ni; internet www.construccion.org.ni; f. 1961; construction industry; Pres. MARIO ZELAYA BLANDÓN; Gen. Man. BRUNO VIDAURRE.

Instituto Nicaragüense de Fomento Municipal (INIFOM): Edif. Central, Carretera a la Refinería, entrada principal residencial Los Arcos, Apdo 3097, Managua; tel. and fax 266-6050; e-mail eduardo.centeno@inifom.gob.ni; internet www.inifom.gob.ni; Pres. EDUARDO CENTENO GADEA.

CHAMBERS OF COMMERCE

Cámara de Comercio Americana de Nicaragua: Plaza España, Rotonda el Güegüense 400 m al sur, 75 m al este, detrás de American Airlines, Managua; tel. and fax 266-2758; e-mail amcham@ns.tmx.com.ni; internet www.amcham.org.ni; f. 1974; Pres. ROGER ARTEAGA CANO.

Cámara de Comercio de Nicaragua (CACONIC): Rotonda el Güegüense 400 m al sur, 20 m al oeste, Managua; tel. 268-3505; fax 268-3600; e-mail comercio@caconic.org.ni; internet www.caconic.org.ni; f. 1892; 530 mems; Pres. MARIO GONZÁLES LACAYO; Exec. Dir EDUARDO FONSECA.

Cámara Oficial Española de Comercio de Nicaragua: Restaurante la Marseilleisa, $\frac{1}{2}$ c. arriba, Los Robles, Apdo 4103, Managua; tel. 278-9047; fax 278-9088; e-mail camacoesnic@cablenet.com.ni; internet www.camacoesnic.com.ni; Pres. JOSÉ DE LA JARA AHLERS; Sec.-Gen. MARÍA AUXILIADORA MIRANDA DE GUERRERO.

EMPLOYERS' ORGANIZATIONS

Asociación de Café Especiales de Nicaragua (ACEN): Oficentro Norte, Km 5, Carretera Panamericana Norte, Managua; tel. 249-0180; fax 249-0182; internet www.acen.org.ni; coffee producers and exporters; Pres. JULIO PERALTA; Sec. LEANA FERREY.

Consejo Superior de la Empresa Privada (COSEP): De Telcor Zacarías Guerra, 1 c. abajo, Apdo 5430, Managua; tel. 276-3333; fax 276-1666; e-mail cosep@cablenet.com.ni; internet www.cosep.org.ni; f. 1972; private businesses; consists of Cámara de Industrias de Nicaragua (CADIN), Unión de Productores Agropecuarios de Nicaragua (UPANIC), Cámara de Comercio, Cámara de la Construcción, Confederación Nacional de Profesionales (CONAPRO), Instituto Nicaragüense de Desarrollo (INDE); mem. of Coordinadora Democrática Nicaragüense; Pres. Dr JOSÉ ADÁN AGUERRI; Exec. Dir MARÍA GERMANIA CARRIÓN SOTO.

Instituto Nicaragüense de Desarrollo (INDE): Col. Los Robles, del Hotel Colón 1 c. al sur, 1 c. abajo, mano izquierda, frente a Funeraria Reñazco, Managua; tel. 252-5800; fax 270-9866; e-mail inde@inde.org.ni; internet www.inde.org.ni; f. 1963; private business org.; 650 mems; Pres. MARCO ZAVALA; Sec. LIGIA ROBLETO.

Unión Nacional de Agricultores y Ganaderos (UNAG): Managua; tel. 268-7429; fax 266-1675; e-mail unag@unag.org.ni; internet www.unag.org.ni; f. 1981; Pres. ALVARO FIALLOS OYANGUREN; Sec. DOUGLAS ALEMÁN.

Unión de Productores Agropecuarios de Nicaragua (UPANIC): Edif. Jorge Salazar, Reparto Serrano, DGI Central, 1 c. al norte $\frac{1}{2}$ c. al este, Apdo 2351, Managua; tel. 251-0340; fax 251-0307; e-mail upanic@ibw.com.ni; internet www.upanic.org.ni; private agriculturalists' asscn; Pres. MANUEL ALVAREZ SOLÓRZANO; Sec. FERNANDO MANSELL VILLANUEVA.

MAJOR COMPANIES

AMANCO Tubosistemas de Nicaragua, SA (Mexichem—Amanco): Km $3\frac{1}{2}$, Carretera Sur, desvío a Batahola, Apdo 2964-1069, Managua; tel. 266-1551; fax 266-4074; e-mail info.nicaragua@amanco.com; internet www.amanco.com; f. 1967 as NICALIT; fmrly AMANCO; subsidiary of Mexichem, SAB de CV (Mexico); producers of asbestos products, pvc pipes and resin; Pres. ANTONIO DEL VALLE RUIZ; Dir-Gen. RICARDO GUTIÉRREZ MUÑOZ; 300 employees.

British American Tobacco: Km $7\frac{1}{2}$, Carretera Norte, Apdo 1049, Managua; tel. 263-1900; fax 263-1642; internet www.batca.com; f. 1934; cigarette manufacturers; Gen. Man. HUGO ABELLO; 1,100 employees.

Café Soluble, SA (CSSA): Km $8\frac{1}{2}$, Carretera Norte, Apdo 429, Managua; tel. 233-1122; fax 233-1110; e-mail info@cafesoluble.com; internet www.cafesoluble.com; f. 1959; instant coffee manufacturers; Pres. JOSÉ ANTONIO BALTODANO; Man. GABRIEL PASOS; 200 employees.

Compañía Cervecera de Nicaragua, SA: Km $6\frac{1}{2}$, Carretera Norte, de Cruz Lorena 600 m al Lago, Managua; tel. 255-7700; fax 255-7811; e-mail webmaster@victoria.com.ni; internet www.ccn.com.ni; brewery; f. 1926; Gen. Man. JAIME ROSALES; 1,200 employees.

Compañía Licorera de Nicaragua, SA: Centro BAC, 8°, Carretera a Masaya km 4.5, Managua; tel. 274-4040; fax 274-4041; e-mail sales@clnsa.com; internet www.clnsa.com; f. 1890; subsidiary of Grupo Pellas; producers of rum; Chair. CARLOS PELLAS.

Embotelladora Nacional, SA (ENSA): Km $7\frac{1}{2}$, Carretera Norte, Apdo 471, Managua; tel. 233-1300; fax 263-1320; e-mail mcaldera@pepsicentroamerica.com; f. 1944; bottlers of Pepsi brand carbonated beverages; Pres. CARLOS ENRIQUE CASTILLO MONGE; Gen. Man. MILTON CALDERA; 700 employees.

Excel Automotriz: Managua; known as Poma Automotriz until 2010; part of the Grupo DIDEA; distributor of cars and car parts; Exec. Vice-Pres. (Group) CARLOS BOZA.

Industria Centroamericana Sociedad Anónima (INCASA): Km 30, Carretera Managua–Granada, Masaya; tel. 522-2260; fax 522-2431; f. 1960 as Industria Nacional de Clavos y Alambres, SA; producers of nails, wire and meshwork; Man. Dir MARCOS A. CARBALLO QUINTANILLA; 560 employees.

Metales y Estructuras, SA (METASA): Km 28, Carretera Norte, Tipitapa, Managua; tel. 221-1124; f. 1958; production of metals; Pres. PEDRO BLANDÓN MORENO; 498 employees.

Molinos de Nicaragua, SA (MONISA): Km 13.2, Carretera Managua, Masaya; tel. 279-6250; fax 279-9941; e-mail info@monisa.com; internet www.monisa.com; f. 1964; flour producers, animal food; Exec. Dir ALAN CHAMORRO.

Monte Rosa: Km $148\frac{1}{2}$, Carretra El Viejo-Potosí, El Viejo, Chinandega; tel. 342-9040; fax 342-9043; e-mail fbaltodano@pantaleon.com; internet www.pantaleon.com; sugar production; owned by Pantaleon Sugar Holdings, Guatemala; Gen. Man. FRANCISCO BALTODANO.

Narciso Salas y Asociados: Iglesia Católica Las Palma, 1 c. al oeste, 50 varas al sur, Apdo 2446, Managua; tel. 226-4591; fax 266-0436; internet www.mginsalas.com.ni; f. 1972; accountants; Man. Partner NARCISO SALAS CHÁVEZ.

Nicaragua Sugar Estate Ltd: Km $4\frac{1}{4}$, c. Masaya Centro BAC, 8°, Apdo 1494, Managua; tel. 274-4150; fax 274-4152; e-mail rrhh@nicaraguasugar.com.ni; internet www.nicaraguasugar.com; f. 1890; sugar refinery; part of Pellas Group; Pres. CARLOS PELLAS CHAMORRO; Gen. Man. XAVIER ARGÜELLO BARILLAS; 3,500 employees.

Plásticos de Nicaragua, SA (PLASTINIC): Km $44\frac{1}{2}$, Carretera Sur, Dolores, Carazo; tel. 532-2575; fax 532-2579; e-mail servicliente@plastinic.com; internet www.plastinic.com; f. 1963; plastic bag manufacturers; Gen. Man. MIRIAM LACAYO; 245 employees.

PriceWaterhouseCoopers: Km $6\frac{1}{2}$, Carretera a Masaya, Edif. Cobirsa II, 3°, Apdo 2697, Managua; tel. 270-9950; fax 270-9450; e-mail david.urcuyo@ni.pwc.com; internet www.pwc.com; accountants and management consultants; Partners FRANCISCO CASTRO, DAVID URCUYO.

Sacos Macen (MACEN): Contiguo Edif. Rosalinda, Matagalpa; tel. 772-6576; e-mail macen@interlink.com.ni; f. 1957; producers of sacking, string, linings and hammocks; Mans ALBERTO MACGREGOR, ADOLFO MACGREGOR, DONALD SPENCER; 200 employees.

Siemens, SA: Carreterra Norte Km 6, Apdo 1049, Managua; tel. 249-1111; fax 249-1540; e-mail siemens.nic@siemens.com.mx; manufacturer of electrical equipment and machinery; subsidiary of Siemens AG, Germany; Man. Dir LUIS ADOLFO GABUARDI.

UTILITIES

Regulatory Bodies

Comisión Nacional de Energía y Minas (CNEM): Hospital Bautista, 1 c. al oeste, 1 c. al norte, Managua; Pres. EMILIO RAPPACCIOLI BALTODANO (Minister of Energy and Mines).

Instituto Nicaragüense de Acueductos y Alcantarillados (INAA): De la Mansión Teodolinda, 3 c. al sur, Bolonia, Apdo 1084, Managua; tel. 266-7882; fax 266-7917; e-mail inaa@inaa.gob.ni; internet www.inaa.gob.ni; f. 1979; water regulator; Exec. Pres. CARLOS SCHUTZE SUGRAÑES.

Instituto Nicaragüense de Energía (INE): Edif. Petronic, 4°, Managua; tel. 277-5317; fax 228-3104; e-mail dac@ine.gob.ni; internet www.ine.gob.ni; Pres. JOSÉ DAVID CASTILLO SÁNCHEZ; Exec. Sec. MARIELA DEL CARMEN CERRATO VÁSQUEZ.

Electricity

Empresa Nicaragüense de Electricidad (ENEL): Ofs Centrales, Pista Juan Pablo II y Avda Bolívar, Managua; tel. 277-4160; fax 267-2683; e-mail relapub@ibw.com.ni; internet www.enel.gob.ni; responsible for planning, organization, management, administration, research and development of energy resources; split into a transmission co, 2 distribution businesses and 4 generation cos in 1999; Pres. EMILIO RAPPACCIOLI BALTODANO (Minister of Energy and Mines); Sec. RAÚL CASTRO CASCO.

Empresa Nacional de Transmisión Eléctrica, SA (ENATREL): Intersección Avda Bolívar y Pista Juan Pablo II, Apdo 283, Managua; tel. 277-4159; fax 267-4379; internet www.enatrel.gob.ni; operates the electricity transmission network; Exec. Pres. SALVADOR MANSELL CASTRILLO.

Generadora Eléctrica Central, SA (GECSA): electricity generation co; 79 MW capacity thermal plant; almost obsolete and therefore difficult to privatize, GECSA was likely to be retained for emergency purposes.

Generadora Eléctrica Occidental, SA (GEOSA): electricity generation co; 112 MW capacity thermal plant; sold to Coastal Power International (USA) in Jan. 2002.

HIDROGESA: electricity generation co; 94 MW capacity hydroelectric plant; privatized in 2002; Gen. Man. JUSTO SANDINO.

ORMAT Momotombo Power Co: Momotombo; internet www.ormat.com; f. 1999 on acquisition of 15-year concession to rehabilitate and operate Momotombo power plant; 30 MW capacity geothermal plant; subsidiary of ORMAT International, Inc; CEO YEHUDIT (DITA) BRONICKI; Gen. Man. RÓGER ARCIA LACAYO.

Unión Fenosa DISSUR y DISNORTE: Managua; tel. 274-4700; e-mail comunicacion@ni.unionfenosa.com; internet www.disnorte-dissur.com.ni; electricity distribution co; privatized in 2000; distributes some 1460 GWh (DISSUR 658 GWh, DISNORTE 802 GWh); Country Man. CARLOS HERNÁNDEZ.

Water

Empresa Nicaragüense de Acueductos y Alcantarillados Sanitarios (ENACAL): Km 5, Carretera Sur 505, Asososca; tel. 266-7875; e-mail ccomunicacion@enacal.com.ni; internet www.enacal.com.ni; Exec. Pres. (vacant).

TRADE UNIONS

Asociación Nacional de Educadores de Nicaragua (ANDEN): Managua; tel. 517-0018; e-mail anden@guegue.com.ni; Sec.-Gen. JOSÉ ANTONIO ZEPEDA; 19 affiliates, 15,000 mems.

Asociación de Trabajadores del Campo (ATC) (Association of Rural Workers): Rotonda Metrocentro, 120 m al oeste, Complejo el CIPRES, Apdo A-244, Managua; tel. 278-4576; fax 278-4575; e-mail atcnic@ibw.com.ni; internet www.movimientos.org/cloc/atc-ni; f. 1977; Gen. Sec. EDGARDO GARCÍA; 52,000 mems.

Central Sandinista de Trabajadores (CST): Iglesia del Carmen, 1 c. al oeste, ½ c. al sur, Managua; tel. 265-1096; fax 240-1285; Sec.-Gen. ROBERTO GONZÁLEZ GAITÁN; 40,000 mems.

Central de Trabajadores de Nicaragua (CTN) (Nicaraguan Workers' Congress): De la Iglesia del Carmen, 1 c. al sur, ½ c. arriba y 75 varas al sur, Managua; tel. 268-3061; fax 265-2056; f. 1962; mem. of Coordinadora Democrática Nicaragüense; Pres. ANTONIO JARQUÍN.

Confederación de Acción y Unidad Sindical (CAUS) (Confederation for Trade Union Action and Unity): Semáforos de Rubenia, 2 c. abajo y 2 c. al lago, Barrio Venezuela, Managua; tel. and fax 244-2587; f. 1973; trade union wing of Partido Comunista de Nicaragua; Sec.-Gen. EMILIO MÁRQUEZ.

Confederación General de Trabajadores Independientes (CGT-i) (Independent General Confederation of Labour): Centro Comercial Nejapa, 1 c. arriba y 3 c. al lago, Managua; tel. 222-5195; fax 228-7505; f. 1953; Sec.-Gen. NILO M. SALAZAR AGUILAR; 4,843 mems (est.) from 6 federations with 40 local unions, and 6 non-federated local unions.

Confederación de Unificación Sindical (CUS) (Confederation of United Trade Unions): Casa Q3, del Colegio la Tenderi 2½ c. arriba, Ciudad Jardín, Managua; tel. 248-3681; fax 240-1330; f. 1972; affiliated to the Inter-American Regional Organization of Workers, etc.; mem. of Coordinadora Democrática Nicaragüense; Sec.-Gen. JOSÉ ESPINOZA NAVAS.

Enrique Schmidt Cuadra Federation (FESC): Managua; e-mail fschmidt@tmx.com.ni; communications and postal workers' union.

Federación de Trabajadores Nicaragüenses (FTN): workers' federation; Leader DOMINGO PÉREZ.

Federación de Trabajadores de la Salud (FETSALUD) (Federation of Health Workers): Optica Nicaragüense, 2 c. arriba ½ c. al sur, Apdo 1402, Managua; tel. and fax 266-3065; e-mail fntsid@ibw.com.ni; Sec.-Gen. GUSTAVO PORRAS; 25,000 mems.

Federación de Transportistas de Carga de Nicaragua (FETRACANIC) (Cargo Transport Workers' Federation of Nicaragua): Avda del Ejército del Arbolito, 2½ c. al sur, Casa 410, Managua; tel. 266-5255; fax 254-7381; e-mail fetracanic@hotmail.com; internet www.fetracanic.com; f. 1986; part of Consejo Centroamericano del Transporte (CONCETRANS); Pres. JOSÉ FRANCISCO GUERRA CABRERA.

Frente Nacional de los Trabajadores (FNT) (National Workers' Front): Residencial Bolonia, de la Optica Nicaragüense, 2 c. arriba, 30 varas al sur, Managua; tel. 266-3065; fax 266-7457; e-mail prensa@fnt.org.ni; internet www.fnt.org.ni; f. 1979; affiliated to Frente Sandinista de Liberación Nacional; Leader Dr GUSTAVO PORRAS CORTÉS.

Unión Nacional de Caficultores de Nicaragua (UNCAFENIC) (National Union of Coffee Growers of Nicaragua): Reparto San Juan, Casa 300, Apdo 3447, Managua; tel. 782-2225; fax 772-3330; Pres. FREDDY TORRES.

Unión Nacional de Empleados (UNE): Managua; e-mail cocentrafemenino@xerox.com.ni; f. 1978; public sector workers' union; Sec.-Gen. DOMINGO PÉREZ; 18,000 mems.

Transport

RAILWAYS

There are no functioning railways. The state-owned rail operator, Ferrocarril de Nicaragua, which formerly operated a network of 287 km, ceased operations in 1994, and the only remaining private line closed in 2001.

ROADS

In 2006 there were an estimated 19,641 km of roads, of which 5,448 km were highways and 6,662 km were secondary roads. Of the total, only some 12,500 km were accessible throughout the entire year. Some 8,000 km of roads were damaged by Hurricane Mitch, which struck in late 1998. The Pan-American Highway runs for 384 km in Nicaragua and links Managua with the Honduran and Costa Rican frontiers and the Atlantic and Pacific Highways, connecting Managua with the coastal regions.

SHIPPING

Corinto, Puerto Sandino and San Juan del Sur, on the Pacific, and Puerto Cabezas, El Bluff and El Rama, on the Caribbean, are the principal ports. Corinto deals with about 60% of trade. In 2001 the US-based company Delasa was given a 25-year concession to develop and modernize Puerto Cabezas port. It was to invest some US $200m.

Empresa Portuaria Nacional (EPN): Residencial Bolonia, de la Optica Nicaragüense ½ c. al norte, 1 c. al oeste, Managua; tel. 266-3039; fax 266-3488; e-mail epn_puertos@epn.com.ni; internet www.epn.com.ni; Pres. VIRGILIO SILVA MUNGÜIA.

CIVIL AVIATION

The principal airport is the Augusto Sandino International Airport, in Managua. There are some 185 additional airports in Nicaragua.

Empresa Administradora de Aeropuertos Internacionales (EAAI): POB 5179, 11 Km Carretera Norte, Managua; tel. 233-1624; fax 263-1072; e-mail czamora@eaai.com.ni; internet www.eaai.com.ni; autonomous govt entity; operates Managua International Airport and 3 national airports: Bluefields, Puerto Cabezas and Corn Island; Pres. DANILO LACAYO RAPPACIOLI; Gen. Man. ORLANDO CASTILLO GUERRERO.

La Costeña: Managua International Airport, Managua; tel. 263-2142; fax 263-1281; e-mail info@lacostena.com.ni; internet www.lacostena.com.ni; Gen. Man. ALFREDO CABALLERO.

Tourism

In 2007 tourist arrivals totalled 799,996, while receipts from tourism totalled US $255m. In the following year receipts totalled a provisional $276m.

Asociación Nicaragüense de Agencias de Viajes y Turismo (ANAVYT): Edif. Policlínica Nicaragüense, Reparto Bolonia, Apdo 1045, Managua; tel. 266-9742; fax 266-4474; e-mail aeromund@cablenet.com.ni; f. 1966; Pres. ANA MARÍA ROCHA C.

Cámara Nacional de Turismo (CANATUR): Contiguo al Ministerio de Turismo, Apdo 2105, Managua; tel. 278-9971; e-mail direccion@canaturnicaragua.org; internet www.canaturnicaragua.org; f. 1976; Exec. Dir GRETHEL COLLINS.

Instituto Nicaragüense de Turismo (INTUR): Del Hotel Crowne Plaza, 1 c. al sur, 1 c. al oeste, Apdo 5088, Managua; tel. 254-5191; fax 222-6610; e-mail promocion@intur.gob.ni; internet www.intur.gob.ni; f. 1998; Pres. MARÍA NELLY RIVAS BLANCO; Sec.-Gen. IAN CORONEL.

Defence

As assessed at November 2009, Nicaragua's professional armed forces numbered an estimated 12,000: army 10,000, navy 800 and air force 1,200. Conscription was introduced in September 1983, but was abolished in April 1990. In 1995 the armed forces were renamed the Ejército de Nicaragua, following a constitutional amendment removing their Sandinista affiliation. There is a voluntary military service which lasts 18–36 months.

Defence Budget: 837m. gold córdobas (US $40m.) in 2009.

Commander-in-Chief: Gen. JULIO CÉSAR AVILÉS.

Education

Primary and secondary education in Nicaragua is provided free of charge. Primary education, which is officially compulsory, begins at seven years of age and lasts for six years. Secondary education, beginning at the age of 13, lasts for up to five years, comprising a first cycle of three years and a second of two years. In 2007/08 enrolment at primary schools included 92% of children in the relevant age-group. Secondary enrolment in that year included 45% of children in the relevant age-group, according to UNESCO estimates. There are many commercial schools and eight universities. In 2003/04 some 103,577 students attended universities and other higher education institutes. In the same year expenditure on education accounted for 15.0% of total government expenditure.

Bibliography

For works on Central America generally, see Select Bibliography (Books)

Agriculture in Nicaragua: Promoting Competitiveness and Stimulating Broad-based Growth. Washington, DC, World Bank, 2003.

Babb, F. E. *After Revolution: Mapping Gender and Cultural Politics in Neoliberal Nicaragua*. Austin, TX, University of Texas Press, 2002.

Bickham Mendez, J. *From the Revolution to the Maquiladoras: Gender, Labor, and Globalization in Nicaragua*. Durham, NC, Duke University Press, 2005.

Binational Study: The State of Migration Flows Between Costa Rica and Nicaragua—An Analysis of Economic and Social Implications for Both Countries. Geneva, Intergovernmental Committee for Migration, 2003.

Blakemore, S. *Voices Against the State: Nicaraguan Opposition to the FSLN*. Boulder, CO, Lynne Rienner Publrs, 2006.

Charlip, J. A. *Cultivating Coffee*. Columbus, OH, Ohio University Press, 2002.

Chavez Metoyer, C. *Women and the State in Post-Sandinista Nicaragua*. Boulder, CO, Lynne Rienner Publrs, 1999.

Close, D. *Nicaragua: The Chamorro Years*. Boulder, CO, Lynne Rienner Publrs, 1998.

Undoing Democracy: The Politics of Electoral Caudillismo. Lanham, MD, Lexington Books, 2004.

Cruz, C. *Political Culture and Institutional Development in Costa Rica and Nicaragua: World-Making in the Tropics*. Cambridge, Cambridge University Press, 2005.

Diederich, B. and Burt, A. *Somoza and the Legacy of U.S. Involvement in Central America*. Princeton, NJ, Markus Wiener, 2007.

Dye, D. R. *Observing the 2001 Nicaraguan Elections: Final Report*. Atlanta, GA, Carter Center, 2002.

Field, L. W. *The Grimace of MacHo Raton: Artisans, Identity and Nation in Late Twentieth-Century Western Nicaragua*. Durham, NC, Duke University Press, 1999.

Gambone, M. D. *Eisenhower, Somoza and the Cold War in Nicaragua*. New York, Praeger Publrs, 1997.

Gobat, M. D. *Confronting the American Dream: Nicaragua Under U.S. Imperial Rule*. Durham, NC, Duke University Press, 2005.

Hendrix, S. E. *The New Nicaragua: Lessons in Development, Democracy, and Nation-Building for the United States*. Westport, CT, Praeger Publishers, 2009.

Isbester, K. *Still Fighting: The Nicaraguan Women's Movement, 1977–2000*. Pittsburgh, PA, University of Pittsburgh Press, 2001.

Kodrich, K. *Tradition and Change in the Nicaraguan Press: Newspapers and Journalists in a New Democratic Era*. Lanham, MD, University Press of America, 2002.

Leiken, R. S. *Why Nicaragua Vanished: A Story of Reporters and Revolutionaries*. Lanham, MD, Rowman and Littlefield Publrs, 2003.

MacAulay, N. *The Sandino Affair*. Micanopy, FL, Wacahoota Press, 1998.

Marti i Puig, S. *The Origins of the Peasant-Contra Rebellion in Nicaragua, 1979–87*. London, Institute of Latin American Studies, 2001.

Moltaván Belliz, C. A. *Hurricane Mitch and the Impact of the NGOs on Indigenous Miskito Communities in Río Coco, North Atlantic Autonomous Region, Nicaragua*. Managua, Universidad de las Regiones Autónomas de la Costa Caribe Nicaragüense, 2002.

Morley, M. H. *Washington, Somoza and the Sandinistas*. Cambridge, Cambridge University Press, 2002.

Morris, K. E. *Unfinished Revolution: Daniel Ortega and Nicaragua's Struggle for Revolution*. Chicago, IL, Chicago Review Press, 2010.

Murphy, J. W. *Uriel Molina and the Sandinista Popular Movement in Nicaragua*. Jefferson, NC, McFarland & Co, 2006.

Orzoco, M. *International Norms and Mobilization of Democracy: Nicaragua in the World*. Burlington, VA, Ashgate, 2002.

Pastor, R. *Not Condemned to Repetition: The United States and Nicaragua*. Boulder, CO, Westview Press, 2002.

Pineda, L. *Shipwrecked Identities: Navigating Race on Nicaragua's Mosquito Coast*. Chapel Hill, NC, Rutgers University Press, 2006.

Prevost, G., and Vanden, H. E. (Eds). *The Undermining of the Sandinista Revolution*. New York, Palgrave Macmillan, 1999.

Sánchez, M. V., and Vos, R. *DR-CAFTA: ¿Panacea o fatalidad para el desarrollo económico y social en Nicaragua?* New York, United Nations Publications, 2007.

Walker, T. W. (Ed.). *Nicaragua Without Illusions: Regime Transition and Structural Adjustment in the 1990s*. Wilmington, DE, Scholarly Resources, 1997.

Nicaragua: Living in the Shadow of the Eagle. Boulder, CO, Westview Press, 2008.

Weber, C. M. *Visions of Solidarity: U.S. Peace Activists in Nicaragua from War to Women's Activism and Globalization*. Lanham, MD, Lexington Books, 2006.

PANAMA

Geography

PHYSICAL FEATURES

The Republic of Panama is often not included with Central America, its early history being related to Colombia rather than to the countries of the isthmus, but, geographically, it does occupy the narrowest part of the great land bridge connecting South and North America. In shape, Panama is a sinuous east–west land corridor, with the Caribbean to the north and the Pacific to the south. To the east is the South American country of Colombia, from which Panama was hewn in 1903, and to the west Costa Rica. The Costa Rican border is about 330 km (205 miles) in length and the Colombian border 225 km, but the country has an even more extensive coastline, of 2,490 km. From 1903 the USA held 'sovereign rights' over 1,432 sq km (553 sq miles) of Panamanian territory, the Canal Zone that flanked the route of the transisthmian waterway for 8 km (5 miles) on either side. However, the lease was negotiated to an early end on 31 December 1999, when Panama resumed full sovereignty over all of its national territory. The country covers 75,517 sq km (29,157 sq miles), making it larger than El Salvador, Belize or Costa Rica, and a little smaller than Scotland (United Kingdom).

The shape of Panama contributes to its irregular coast, dotted with many islands and islets off shore. In the east, a northward loop encloses the Gulf of Panama, while the southward loop defines the Mosquito Gulf in the Caribbean. On the south coast, a great promontory of land jutting further into the Pacific from the southernmost part of the arc is split into the semi-arid Azuero peninsula and the much smaller Las Palmas peninsula to the west, forming the eastern arm of the Gulf of Chiriquí. The largest Pacific islands are Coiba (used as a prison island), just south-west of the Las Palmas peninsula, and Isla del Rey in the Archipiélago de las Perlas (Pearl Islands), in the Gulf of Panama. The San Blas chain of coral atolls in the north-east, parallel to the coast, are the abode of the indigenous Kuna (Kuna Yala). The bulk of the country consists of a discontinuous spine of steep, rugged mountains, interspersed with upland plains and rolling hills, flanked by coastal plains of varying width. From west to east the country measures about 650 km, but it narrows to as little as 48 km from north to south, at roughly the point where the Canal crosses. There are 2,210 sq km of inland waters, many of them artificially restrained, including the Bayono lake on Chepo river and Gatún lake, one of the largest artificial reservoirs in the world, built as part of the Canal. The Canal, built between 1904 and 1914 by the USA, is about 82 km in length, raising and lowering vessels 26 m by means of six pairs of locks. It crosses a low seat of land, situated in a gap between the western and eastern mountain ranges that form the backbone of the country. This region is known as the central isthmus or the transit zone, and consists of coastal plains and a highland interior. About one-half of the population, 90% of Panama's industry and all the transisthmian links are situated here.

To the east of the transit zone is the sparsely populated and barely developed territory of Darién, covering one-third of Panama with the largest area of rainforest in the Americas outside the Amazon basin. The central mountains here continue nearer the north coast of the isthmus, as the Serranía de San Blas and the Serranía del Darién, with more mountains to the south. Densely wooded and containing the Tuira river, the longest in Panama, Darién is the home of the Choco and other Amerindians. The region contributes the bulk of the country's woodland (most of the northern coast of Panama is also densely forested), which in all accounts for about 44% of the nation's total area. Despite problems of deforestation (immediate concerns with this are focused on soil erosion and the consequent threat of silting in the Canal) and of mining, Panama is still home to a considerable variety of flora and fauna, with more than 2,000 species of tropical plants, numerous native and migratory birds, and many animals common to both South and

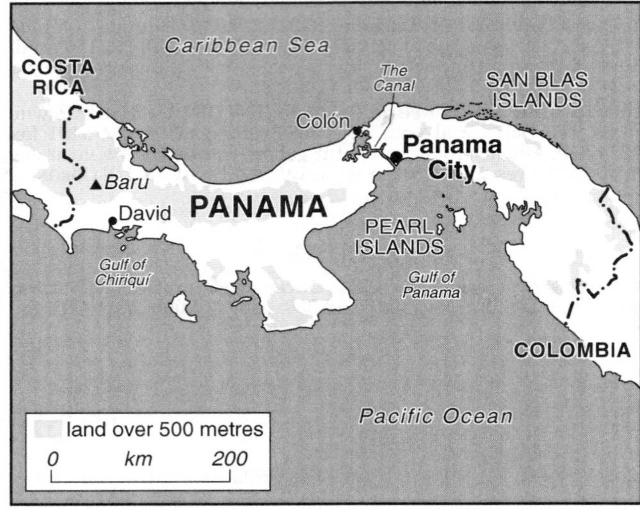

Central America, as well as some unique species (such as the golden tree frog or the giant tree sloth). Biodiversity is less rich west of the Canal and south of the mountains, much of this area having long been cleared for arable farming or ranching. The Continental Divide here forms higher mountains than in the east, where the Cordillera Central reaches its heights in the Serranía de Tabasará, and the highest peak in Panama, here and not in Darién, is the Baru volcano of Chiriquí (3,475 m or 11,405 ft), in the west. Such volcanoes, none now active in the country, have produced the fertile soil that is so widely cultivated in the west of the country. Agriculture dominates Chiriquí—generally the area south of the mountains and extending onto the rolling hills of Las Palmas. Between here and the Canal, along the north-western shores of the Gulf of Panama and in the lowlands west of the transit zone, is the old, settled heartland of central Panama. The final topographical area is the forested north-west, the Atlantic region, between the mountains and the north coast. This region, centred on Bocas del Toro, is the indigenous home of the Guaymí (Ngöbe-Buglé) and of the mainly black descendants of West Indian immigrants, who came to work the banana plantations that once flourished along the Caribbean.

CLIMATE

Panama has a tropical maritime climate, making it hot, humid and cloudy, with a prolonged rainy season (May–January) over the summer and autumn. Prevailing winds are off the Atlantic for most of the year, but change to south-westerlies during the autumn. The Caribbean side of the country is wetter, with Azuero the driest part. The northern mountain slopes receive average rainfall of 2,970 mm (117 ins) per year, with the drier Pacific coast generally on about 1,650 mm annually. The average temperatures in Colón, at the northern, Caribbean end of the Canal, range from the lowest minimum of 20°C to the highest maximum of 32°C (68°F–90°F). At greater altitudes the average temperature can be about 19°C (66°F). Panama falls outside either the Atlantic hurricane belt or the Eastern Pacific one.

POPULATION

The people of Panama (Panameños) are mainly of mixed Spanish and Amerindian race, the Mestizos; they constitute some 63% of the population. There are also large communities of predominantly black descent (14%) and Spanish descent

(10%), as well as some of mixed-black descent (mulatto—5%) and a number of Amerindian peoples (5%). There are also some of Middle Eastern and Asian descent. More recently, there has been a largely illegal influx of Colombians, either seeking employment or political refuge, particularly in the deserted borderlands. The official language, and the one in general use, is Spanish, but, after long years of US rule along the Canal and immigration from North America and the West Indies, English is widely spoken (being the main language for up to 14% of the population), and many Panamanians are reckoned to be bilingual. There is also an English-based Creole still used, while a French-based Creole (San Miguel Creole) is virtually extinct. Some indigenous Amerindian languages are also spoken, by the Choco and Chibchan groups. The vast majority of people are still Roman Catholic, but in recent years membership of Protestant groups has increased, while the largest non-Christian community is Muslim. There are also some Jews. Traditional, indigenous belief systems have usually syncretized with Roman Catholic practice.

According to preliminary results of the census conducted in mid-2010, the total population numbered 3.3m. Most of these people live in the region of the Canal, in the transit zone of the central isthmus, and 64% of the national total is urbanized (as high a rate as in Nicaragua, the most urbanized country of Central America proper). The largest city and the national capital is Panama City (Panamá), the greater metropolitan area of which had a population of around 1.4m. Panamá lies at the southern end of the Canal, on the Gulf that bears its name, and was an early viceregal capital for the Spanish (until replaced by Bogotá, Colombia) in the Americas. The second city of the country, Colón, with its own collection of suburbs, lies at the northern end of the Canal and constitutes the world's second largest free zone for trade and industry. David, the capital of the agricultural, western province of Chiriquí, located on the Pacific coastal plains, is the most populous city outside the central isthmus. The country is divided into nine provinces, with the more recent formation of three territories constituted for various Amerindian groups.

History

HELEN SCHOOLEY

Revised for this edition by KATHARINE MURISON

Geographically, Panama is part of Central America, but, as a result of Spanish colonial divisions and the construction of the Panama Canal through its territory, its history was very different from that of its northern neighbours. The question of the Canal dominated the country's history and, as a result, Panama gained political independence, first from Spain and then from Colombia, only to experience 150 years of US involvement in its national life. The USA was concerned less with the country's internal politics than with the protection of US interests in the operation of the Canal, and with US security policy throughout Latin America. The cession of the Canal to Panama on 31 December 1999 marked a decline in US involvement in Panama.

The Spanish arrived in Panama in 1502, and made it the centre of viceregal government over an area stretching as far south as Peru from 1533 to 1751, when the seat of government was moved to Santafé de Bogotá (Colombia, now Bogotá). In 1821, along with the rest of Central America, Panama declared independence from Spain, but instead of joining the Central American Federation (1823–38), it opted for incorporation into the Federation of Gran (Greater) Colombia, which also included Venezuela and Ecuador, both of which seceded in 1830, while Panama, despite a number of revolts, continued under Colombian rule for a further 70 years.

CONSTRUCTION OF THE CANAL

The idea of constructing a transisthmian route was originated by the Spanish, who hoped to build a trading passage for Peruvian silver. The idea gained renewed prominence in the 1840s as a result of the California gold-rush, and led to the construction of the Panama railway in 1850–55 by a US company. The USA directly intervened in the country's internal politics on five occasions between 1860 and 1902, to protect the railway under the terms of a US-Colombian treaty of 1846. The original contract to build a canal was held by the French Panama Canal Co, but the work begun in 1879 proved so much more complex and costly, in terms of human lives, than anticipated that it was suspended in 1888. The Canal was finished by US interests and finally opened in 1914.

INDEPENDENCE

In 1903 Panama achieved independence from Colombia, largely at the instigation of the USA. Earlier in that year the US Government had negotiated a treaty with Colombia, gaining the canal concession for the sum of US $10m., together with a 100-year lease on a 1,432-sq km strip of Panamanian territory (known as the Canal Zone), extending for 8 km on either side of the Panama Canal route. The Colombian Congress raised objections to the treaty, causing a revolt in Panama, which then received US assistance in declaring independence in November. The USA concluded a similar treaty with the new Panamanian Government, according Panama sovereignty and the USA 'sovereign rights', creating an ambiguity that was to cause considerable disagreement between the two countries in the following years. The USA retained the right to military intervention to protect the Canal, and, within the Zone, it had its own military bases, police force, laws, currency and postal service; it also maintained a direct role in Panama's internal political life until 1918. After more than two decades of relative stability in Panama, constitutional government was disrupted in the 1940s with a progression of bloodless coups and disputed elections. Adolfo de la Guardia (President in 1941 and in 1949–50) pursued a series of right-wing policies, and was impeached and banned from public life in 1950. Antonio Remón was elected President in 1952 and enacted a programme of moderate reforms until his assassination in 1955.

THE TORRIJOS ERA, 1968–81

After 12 years of uninterrupted elected government, political turbulence erupted again in 1968. Dr Arnulfo Arias Madrid won the presidential election, but after 11 days in office he was deposed in a military coup led by the National Guard under the command of Col (later Gen.) Omar Torrijos Herrera. (The National Guard functioned as a defence force, since the formation of an army had been proscribed in the 1904 Constitution.) Freedoms of the press, speech and assembly were suspended for one year, and party political activity was banned from February 1969 until October 1978. The National Guard retained power, first with military, and subsequently with civilian, appointees. Torrijos took the executive title of Chief of Government in 1972, and legislative power was vested in a 505-member Asamblea Nacional de Representantes de Corregimientos (National Assembly of Community Representatives), elected in August on a non-party basis. Under Torrijos, Panama enjoyed a greater degree of internal stability. His Government's most important achievement was the negotiation of a new Canal Treaty with the USA.

The Revision of the Canal Treaty

Despite revisions of the Canal Treaty in 1936 and 1955, which included an increase in the annual rent paid by the USA, the 1903 Treaty continued to be a focus for anti-US sentiment. After repeated pressure from Panama and a number of other Latin American countries, negotiations on a new treaty began in 1973. Two draft treaties were signed in September 1977, in which the USA agreed to cede the Canal to the Government of Panama at noon on 31 December 1999. Prior to that, there would be a phased withdrawal of US troops, with Panama eventually taking control of all US military bases in the Canal Zone. The Zone was to be abolished and renamed the Canal Area. The Panama Canal Co would be replaced by a nine-member Panama Canal Commission, a non-profit US government agency with a board of Panamanian and US directors approved by the US Senate, on which the USA was to retain majority representation until 1989. In addition, Panama and the USA were to be jointly responsible for guaranteeing the Canal's permanent neutrality. The treaties were approved by a national referendum in Panama in October 1977, but opposition within the US Congress delayed their ratification in the USA until October 1979.

In 1978 Gen. Torrijos announced plans to return Panama to elected government. He resigned as Chief of Government in October (retaining the post of National Guard Commander), when a newly elected Asamblea Nacional endorsed his nominee, Dr Arístides Royo Sánchez, as President for a six-year term. However, Gen. Torrijos maintained his hold on power when, at elections in August to the 19-seat Consejo Nacional de Legislación (National Legislative Council—an upper house that also contained 38 members nominated by the Asamblea Nacional), his Partido Revolucionario Democrático (PRD) won 10 seats. The elections were boycotted by Arias Madrid's Partido Panameñista Auténtico (PPA). In July 1981 Gen. Torrijos was killed in an aeroplane crash.

THE RISE AND FALL OF NORIEGA

After the death of Gen. Torrijos, relations between the presidency and the National Guard deteriorated, especially after the appointment as Commander, in March 1982, of Gen. Rubén Darío Paredes, a much keener advocate of pro-US foreign policy than President Royo. In July Gen. Paredes forced Royo from office, and the First Vice-President, Ricardo de la Espriella, became President. In the following year Paredes withdrew from the National Guard in order to contest the 1984 presidential election and was replaced by Gen. Manuel Antonio Noriega Morena. Dr Jorge Illueca, who took over as President in February 1984, was also highly critical of the USA and its alleged violations of the new Canal Treaties.

Constitutional amendments introduced in 1983 provided for the direct election of the President and Consejo Nacional de Legislación, replaced the 505-member Asamblea Nacional de Representantes de Corregimientos with a 67-seat Asamblea Legislativa (Legislative Assembly), reduced the presidential term of office to five years, and prevented members of the National Defence Forces (as the National Guard was renamed) from standing as political candidates. In the May 1984 elections the PRD, in coalition with five other parties, won a majority in the Asamblea Legislativa, and its candidate, Nicolás Ardito Barletta, was elected President. President Ardito resigned in September 1985, however, amid rumours that the National Defence Forces had assisted his election; it was then alleged that Gen. Noriega had removed him in order to disrupt an investigation into the murder, in the same month, of a leading politician, Hugo Spadafora, in which the armed forces' command was implicated. Ardito was succeeded by the First Vice-President, Eric Arturo Delvalle, whose main problems were the growing power of Gen. Noriega and Panamanian claims that the USA was trying to renege on its commitment to withdraw from the Canal Area and also failing to hand over Panama's rightful share of profits.

In February 1988 President Delvalle attempted to dismiss Noriega, following his indictment in the USA on drugs-trafficking charges. Instead, Noriega deposed Delvalle and replaced him with Manuel Solís Palma. Delvalle went into hiding, but continued to be recognized as head of state by the opposition and the US Administration. The May 1989 elections were contested entirely on the issue of Noriega's continuance in power, between two hastily formed coalitions: the government Coalición de Liberación Nacional (COLINA) and the Alianza Democrática de Oposición Civilista (ADOC). There were reports of substantial fraud on the part of COLINA, and, when the ADOC presidential candidate, Guillermo Endara Galimany, claimed victory, the counting was suspended and the whole election annulled. As ADOC refused to accept the annulment, COLINA formed a provisional Government.

US Military Intervention

In December 1989 Gen. Noriega was declared Head of Government. He announced that Panama was at war with the USA, and on 20 December US forces intervened to overthrow him. Endara was installed as President, US economic sanctions (in force since 1987) were ended and full diplomatic relations restored. Although Noriega himself had few allies abroad, the US action was condemned by most Latin American countries, and by the UN General Assembly, as a violation of Panamanian sovereignty. According to US government estimates, 314 Panamanian troops and about 200 civilians were killed, in addition to 23 US troops; the economic cost to Panama was estimated to be at least US $2,000m.

Noriega eventually gave himself up in return for an assurance that he would receive a fair trial and would not face the death penalty. He was flown to the USA, found guilty on charges relating to drugs-trafficking and money-laundering, and in July 1992 was sentenced to 40 years' imprisonment (later reduced to 30 years, after an appeal by his lawyers that he had given years of service to the USA as an 'asset' of the US Central Intelligence Agency). By August 2001 he had received prison sentences in Panama totalling 98 years, on charges that included murder, corruption and drugs-trafficking. Noriega completed his prison term early, in September 2007, having had his sentence reduced on the grounds of good behaviour, but he remained in custody in the USA pending consideration of an extradition request from France. In April 2009 the US federal Court of Appeal ruled that Noriega could be extradited to France, where he had been convicted *in absentia* in 1999 on money-laundering charges. In February 2010 the US Supreme Court refused to hear an appeal by Noriega against his extradition to France, which was effected in April. In July, following a retrial, a French court sentenced Noriega to seven years' imprisonment and ordered the seizure of €2.3m. of his assets.

RESTORATION OF THE DEMOCRATIC PROCESS

In order to regain the confidence of the international community, a new Asamblea Legislativa was formed in February 1990, based on the results of the May 1989 elections; ADOC was awarded 51 seats and COLINA six, while fresh elections were held for the remaining seats. The National Defence Forces were dissolved and a new Public Force created, consisting of the National Police, the National Air Service and the National Maritime Service. However, President Endara's Government lacked domestic confidence.

The PRD returned to power after the May 1994 elections, although it failed to secure an outright majority in either the presidential or legislative polls. The party's presidential candidate, Ernesto Pérez Balladares, won 33.2% of the votes cast, ahead of Mireya Moscoso de Gruber (widow of former President Arias Madrid) of the Partido Arnulfista (PA—the leading member of the ADOC coalition) with 29.1%. In the enlarged 72-seat legislature, the PRD reached an agreement with minority parties to command just 36 seats. President Pérez's social and economic policies were highly controversial. The unions opposed the Government's attempts to liberalize the labour market and to implement a privatization programme, and the President's apparent endorsement of a system of political favours damaged public confidence in the administration.

TRANSFER OF THE CANAL TO PANAMANIAN SOVEREIGNTY

The Canal was formally transferred to Panamanian sovereignty on 31 December 1999, becoming a fully commercial operation; under US control it had been run on a non-profit basis. The administration of the Canal was assumed by an 11-member Autoridad del Canal de Panamá (ACP—Panama Canal Authority). In early 2000 a five-year canal-modernization project was announced, including the development of technology to raise capacity, a general improvement of facilities, the construction of a second bridge, the widening of the narrowest section, at Culebra Cut, and work to deepen certain sections.

THE MOSCOSO PRESIDENCY, 1999–2004

At the presidential election of 2 May 1999, Mireya Moscoso de Gruber, standing for the PA-led Unión por Panamá (UPP) alliance, defeated PRD nominee Martín Torrijos Espino, son of Gen. Torrijos, the candidate of its Nueva Nación (NN) grouping. Her unexpected victory was perceived as an endorsement of her more populist style and greater emphasis on social justice. Moscoso was inaugurated as the country's first female President in September, and formed a new 'Government of national unity', comprising members of the Partido Solidaridad (PS), the Partido Liberal Nacional (PLN), the Partido Demócrata Cristiano (PDC) and the Partido Renovación Civilista (PRC). In the Asamblea Legislativa, the largest group was the NN, with 41 seats, obliging Moscoso to negotiate with six minority parties to achieve a working parliamentary majority, albeit of just one seat. The majority was eliminated in September 2000, but was re-established in September 2002, by which time Moscoso needed the majority in order to introduce fiscal and social security reforms.

Moscoso's election campaign included pledges to increase social spending, suspend the privatization programme and increase tariffs on agricultural imports. However, an economic downturn in 2000–01 triggered increasing public discontent and a series of civilian protests over a range of issues.

Following the discovery of human remains in a former military barracks in Tocumen, in December 2000 President Moscoso announced the establishment of a Truth Commission to investigate human rights abuses under former military leaders. Human rights groups estimated the number of 'disappearances' under the military dictatorships during 1968–89 to be some 160. Little effort had been made to investigate these cases, and there were allegations that the US authorities wished to avoid further scrutiny of their association with Noriega. In March 2004 the Asamblea Legislativa approved the creation of a Special Prosecutor's Office to investigate crimes committed during the military dictatorships. The Truth Commission had reportedly documented 110 cases of 'disappearances' and murders during the period of military rule, and had located the remains of 40 victims.

THE TORRIJOS PRESIDENCY, 2004–09

The presidential election held on 2 May 2004 resulted in a decisive victory for Martín Torrijos Espino of the PRD, with 47% of the votes cast. The PS candidate, former President Endara, won 31% of the ballot, while José Miguel Alemán, representing the PA-led Visión de País alliance, only received 16% of the votes cast. It appeared that Torrijos had succeeded in attracting much of the younger electorate with his promises to address corruption and human rights abuses, to introduce judicial reform, and to improve free trade with the USA. His appeal rested on both the enduring popularity of his father, Gen. Omar Torrijos, and his image as representing a change from the traditional elements of the country's political scene. The PRD also performed well in concurrent elections to the enlarged Asamblea Legislativa, securing 42 of the 78 seats, while the PA won 16 seats and the PS nine seats.

Torrijos succeeded in securing legislative approval for various constitutional reforms even before assuming the presidency on 1 September 2004. The amendments, adopted in July, included a reduction in the number of seats in the legislature to 71 from 2009, the shortening of the transitional period following elections from four months to two, the abolition of parliamentary immunity from prosecution, and the creation of a constitutional assembly to consider future changes to the Constitution.

During his inaugural address President Torrijos was severely critical of Moscoso's administration, pledging to ensure that those guilty of corruption would be brought to justice. In November 2004 the Government announced that it was pursuing the former Minister of Finance and the Treasury, Norberto Delgado, on charges of illicit enrichment and corruption. Meanwhile, a Consejo Nacional de Transparencia contra la Corrupción (National Transparency Council against Corruption) was formed within the Ministry of the Presidency, and audits of major government offices and other public institutions were initiated.

In October 2004 some 5,000 people participated in a march organized by the newly created Frente Nacional por la Defensa de la Seguridad Social (FRENADESSO) to protest against the mooted privatization of the social security fund, the Caja de Seguro Social (CSS). The Government denied that it was considering fully privatizing the CSS, which was burdened by an estimated deficit of at least US $2,500m.

In May 2005 the Government presented its plans to address the CSS's financial difficulties. The proposals, which included increasing the retirement age (from 57 to 62 for women and from 62 to 65 for men) and raising employers' and employees' pension contributions, prompted a series of demonstrations, led by FRENADESSO, which claimed that the Government had failed to consult the trade unions about the reforms. After the Government had made a number of concessions to opponents of the proposals, the reforms to the CSS were approved by the Asamblea Nacional at the beginning of June, despite ongoing protests. However, in late June Torrijos agreed to suspend the pension reform law pending negotiations with representatives of FRENADESSO, industrial organizations and the Roman Catholic Church. In December the Asamblea Nacional approved revised legislation, which extended the minimum period required to contribute to a pension from 15 years to 20 years (instead of the 25 years initially envisaged), but maintained the existing retirement age.

The death from poisoning of Franklin Brewster, the head of the counter-terrorism and -narcotics unit of the Technical Judicial Police, in July 2006 raised concerns regarding corruption within the country's law enforcement institutions. Following an investigation assisted by the US Federal Bureau of Investigation, at the end of October three police officers were charged in connection with Brewster's killing. It was suggested that members of drugs-trafficking organizations had orchestrated the murder.

In November 2006 Torrijos announced reforms to the public health system in response to a number of deaths caused by medicines contaminated with an industrial solvent. The President ordered the closure of the CSS laboratory where the medicines had been manufactured and the establishment of an independent national authority to oversee the production of drugs. The deaths (which numbered 51, according to official figures) had led to demands for the resignation of Camilo Alleyne, the Minister of Health, and the members of the CSS executive board. In January 2007 the Government announced that compensation would be paid to the families of 72 official and suspected victims, as well as to 41 people who had survived the poisoning. However, 403 possible cases had been registered by March, 353 of which were fatal. Alleyne was replaced as Minister of Health by Dr Rosario Turner in early September in a major cabinet reorganization, which also included the appointment of Daniel Delgado Diamante, hitherto Director-General of the customs authority, to succeed Olga Gólcher as Minister of the Interior and Justice.

Amid concerns over rapidly rising consumer prices, the Frente Nacional por la Defensa de los Derechos Económicos y Sociales (FRENADESO, as FRENADESSO had been renamed after expanding its focus) organized a protest march in November 2007, urging the Government to respond to its demands for a freeze on prices of basic goods and services and an increase in the minimum wage. Meanwhile, a six-week strike by doctors seeking higher salaries and assurances that the Government's plans for health care reform would not involve privatization caused significant disruption to health services in November and December. In February 2008 the fatal shooting of a construction worker in Colón during a protest against working conditions provoked several days of nation-wide demonstrations organized by the construction workers' trade union, the Sindicato Único Nacional de Trabajadores de la Industria de la Construcción y Similares (SUNTRACS). Some 30 members of SUNTRACS were injured in clashes with the police, while more than 500 protesters were arrested. The adoption of a government decree aimed at improving health and safety standards for construction workers failed to appease union leaders, who demanded the resignation of Minister of the Interior and Justice Delgado and the Director of the National Police, Rolando Mirones, as well as increased wages and measures to reduce the cost of living. (Mirones resigned in May.) FRENADESO organized a further day of mass demonstrations in August in protest at both the rising cost of living and the Government's intention to implement controversial reforms to the security forces by decree. The reforms, which were enacted later in August (under extraordinary powers granted to the President by the Asamblea Nacional in June), created several new security bodies, including a National Aero-Naval Service (by merger of the Air and Maritime Services) and a National Intelligence and Security Service. High inflation and the security reforms were also the motive for a national one-day strike in September organized by a recently constituted alliance of trade unions.

In October 2008 Delgado temporarily relinquished his position of Minister of the Interior and Justice after the Procurator-General's office opened an investigation into allegations that, as an officer in the National Guard in 1970, he had murdered a corporal. (Delgado admitted the killing, but maintained that he had been investigated and cleared of murder by the military authorities.) In the following month President Torrijos dismissed Delgado from his post as part of a wider cabinet reorganization, appointing Dilio Arcia Torres—hitherto Minister of the Presidency—in his stead.

Expansion of the Canal

In April 2006 the ACP's detailed plans for the expansion of the Panama Canal were announced by President Torrijos. The proposed project, which would involve the construction of a new set of three-chamber locks at either end of the Canal by 2014, at a cost of US $5,250m., was to be financed through increased toll charges, rather than taxation, according to Torrijos, and was to be subject to a referendum, following a national debate. The new locks would allow the Canal to accommodate vessels with container capacities of up to 12,000 20-ft equivalent units (TEUs) rather than the current maximum limit of 5,000 TEUs. The ACP estimated that by 2011 37% of the world's shipping fleet would consist of ships that were too large to use the existing Canal. However, although the country relied heavily on the revenue from the Canal, environmental groups expressed concern regarding the impact of its enlargement and the accompanying relocation of communities required. Other critics, including former President Endara, claimed that the project was an unnecessary expense, while the Partido Panameñista (PP, as the PA had been renamed in 2005) opposed the ACP's proposals on both environmental and financial grounds. Draft legislation on the expansion of the Canal was approved by the Asamblea Nacional in July. The referendum was held on 22 October, when 78.3% of those who participated voted in favour of the plan to widen the Canal. This clear endorsement was to some extent regarded as a victory for Torrijos, who had strongly advocated the expansion. None the less, the turn-out, at 43.3% of the electorate, was much lower than predicted. The expansion project was officially launched at a ceremony held in September 2007. In July 2009 the contract for the construction of the new locks was awarded to a consortium led by a Spanish construction company.

THE 2009 ELECTIONS

Three candidates contested the presidential election of 3 May 2009. Ricardo Martinelli Berrocal, a successful retail businessman and the President of Cambio Democrático, secured a comfortable victory with 60.0% of the valid votes cast; contributing to his success was the decision of Juan Carlos Varela Rodríguez of the PP, who had previously intended to contest the election in his own right, to ally his party with Martinelli's campaign and stand as his vice-presidential candidate. The PRD's candidate, former Minister of Housing Balbina del Carmen Herrera Araúz (whose campaign had been tainted by allegations that it had received US $3m. from a convicted Colombian fraudster, David Murcia Guzmán), received 37.7% of the votes, while former President Endara, in his second consecutive failed bid for the presidency, took just 2.3%. A turn-out of 74.0% was recorded. Martinelli's Alianza por el Cambio also won a majority in the Asamblea Nacional, securing a total of 42 of the 71 seats (reduced from 78), compared with 27 seats for Herrera's PRD-led alliance, Un País para Todos. The resulting shift to the right in Panamanian politics confirmed a pattern of regular alternation between left- and right-wing Governments that had developed since the overthrow of military rule. The leadership of the PRD resigned in October as part of efforts to renew the party following its electoral defeat; Francisco Sánchez Cárdenas and Mitchell Constantino Doens were elected to succeed Herrera and Torrijos as PRD President and Secretary-General, respectively.

President Martinelli was sworn in on 1 July 2009. On taking office, he announced immediate plans to effect three of his major campaign pledges: a US $100 monthly salary increase for police officers, monthly payments to the elderly, and the establishment of a government agency to oversee construction of a metro system in Panama City. Martinelli's administration also sought to demonstrate its commitment to addressing government corruption. A judicial investigation into allegations that the Moscoso Government had bribed PRD deputies in December 2001 was reopened in July 2009, and two former PRD Ministers of Education in the Torrijos Government, Belgis Castro and Salvador Rodríguez, were arrested on charges of embezzlement in September and December. In January 2010, moreover, former President Pérez Balladares was placed under house arrest after being charged with money-laundering. However, Martinelli's appointment of two close allies to fill vacant positions in the Supreme Court of Justice in December 2009 provoked criticism, particularly from civil society groups, as did his suspected involvement in the following month in the Court's decision to suspend the PRD-appointed Ana Matilde Gómez from the post of Procurator-General pending an investigation into her alleged abuse of office.

FRENADESO was reported to be contemplating its transformation into a political party in early 2010, and in March some 10,000 people participated in protests organized by the group against recently approved tax reforms, most notably an increase in the rate of value-added tax from 5% to 7%. Meanwhile, the merger of Cambio Democrático with two other parties in the Alianza por el Cambio—the Movimiento Liberal Republicano Nacionalista and the Unión Patriótica (which had been formed in 2007 by the merger of the PLN and the Partido Solidaridad)—was also under consideration.

In April 2010 the creation was approved of a Ministry of Public Security, which was to be responsible for the police force, border security and migration. José Raúl Mulino, then Minister of the Interior and Justice, was to become the new Minister of Public Security, while Roxana Méndez, the Deputy Mayor of Panama City, was to join the Government as Minister of the Interior. The restructuring, which took effect in June, formed part of wider government efforts to reduce crime.

Swiftly approved legislation, reforming regulations on civil aviation, the environment, the police and labour, *inter alia*, provoked controversy in June 2010. Environmental activists expressed concern regarding the abolishment of the requirement for environmental impact studies for projects declared to be 'in the social interest', while trade unions criticized an amendment to the labour code permitting the dismissal of strikers.

INTERNATIONAL RELATIONS

Political wrangling over the possibility and benefits of a continued US military presence from 2000 shaped Panama's relations with the USA in the 1990s, and relations between the two countries were further complicated by developments in Panama's relationship with Colombia. One legacy of the Central American civil wars of the 1980s was a vast surplus of arms and ammunition in the region, and Panama became a point of passage for arms-trafficking to Colombia and drugs-trafficking to the USA. The presence of left-wing Colombian guerrillas just inside the Panamanian border, in the province of Darién, had been tacitly accepted since 1993, although under President Pérez, Panama appeared to offer more assistance to Colombia's right-wing paramilitary groups. In September 1999 there was a sharp increase in activity by these groups, which some Panamanians alleged were part of an orchestrated scheme to strengthen the case for a continued US military presence. Cross-border incursions continued, and there were death threats against the local population. Colombian efforts to contain the guerrillas and the drugs trade tended to increase the number of refugees fleeing to Panama (estimated at some 8,000 between 1996 and 2000), although by the end of 2001 a series of repatriation initiatives had reduced the number to around 1,700. Investigating reports that some refugees had been forcibly repatriated by Panamanian security forces, the human rights organization Amnesty International expressed concern in 2003 for the safety of the refugees once in Colombia. In January 2010, a day after reporting that three suspected Colombian guerillas had been killed in a clash with Panamanian police officials in Darién Province, the Panamanian Government announced plans to strengthen security co-operation with Colombia.

Although plans were announced to turn a number of former US bases in Panama into tourist developments, some of these were affected by the presence of US chemical and biological weapons and munitions left behind. US forces had tested chemical and biological weapons in Panama during 1930–68, including napalm and 'Agent Orange' (the defoliant used by the USA during the Viet Nam War). In February 2000 the USA maintained that there were insufficient technological resources available to them at that time to ensure the safe removal of the weapons. The Panamanian Government declared its intention to pursue the matter through the machinery of the Chemical Weapons Convention, to which both countries were signatories. Nevertheless, the two Governments subsequently concluded an agreement regarding stricter military patrols of air and maritime borders to combat trafficking of illegal drugs.

Both the staging of the 10th Ibero-American Summit in Panama in November 2000, and the establishment in Panama in 2001 of the temporary headquarters for negotiations regarding the creation of a Free Trade Area of the Americas, were regarded as an indication of the country's growing independence from the USA. Although the USA remained the Canal's principal customer, Panama sought to strengthen trading links with the rest of Latin America and with Europe, while moderating its relations with Asia. Like other Central American countries, Panama accorded diplomatic recognition to Taiwan, receiving considerable investment in return; however, the country also extended links to the People's Republic of China, which was the third greatest user of the Canal, and actively encouraged Panama to end its recognition of Taiwan. None the less, President Moscoso and the Taiwanese President, Chen Shui-bian, signed a bilateral free trade agreement in August 2003, and subsequent administrations maintained diplomatic relations with Taiwan.

President Torrijos made clear his intention to enhance Panama's trading relations within Latin America, and in November 2004 Panama was invited to join the Group of Three, comprising Colombia, Mexico and Venezuela, which sought to abolish trade barriers between its members. Furthermore, in June 2005 Panama was officially invited to become an associate member of the Mercado Común del Sur (Mercosur—Southern Common Market). A free trade agreement with El Salvador entered into force in April 2003, while similar accords with Chile, Costa Rica, Honduras, Guatemala and Nicaragua took effect successively between March 2008 and November 2009. Negotiations towards a free trade agreement between Panama and Colombia commenced in March 2010.

Protracted negotiations on a free trade agreement with the USA were finally concluded in December 2006; the accord was signed in June 2007 and ratified by the Panamanian Asamblea Nacional in the following month. However, the agreement was subject to ratification by the US legislature, and further negotiations on labour laws were also to be held. In June 2009 the outgoing Torrijos Government announced the adoption of US-advocated amendments to labour legislation, which, *inter alia*, facilitated the formation of trade unions, but opponents of the trade agreement within the US Congress asserted that ratification of the trade agreement should be made conditional on efforts by Panama to reduce international tax evasion (see below). After taking office in July, President Martinelli declared that securing US congressional approval of the free trade accord was a priority for his administration, but at mid-2010 the agreement had still not been ratified. In May 2010 Panama signed a free trade agreement with Canada, and was party to a Central American association agreement concluded with the European Union.

Panama's foreign relations were adversely affected by a reputation for political corruption, money-laundering and providing shelter to allegedly corrupt or ruthless foreign politicians. There was also particular concern in the USA over apparent use of Panama as a conduit for illegal drugs and immigrants bound for North America. Moreover, it was widely suspected that the practice of allowing foreign vessels to sail under the Panamanian 'flag of convenience' was used as a cover for illegal activity; Panama had the largest shipping registry in the world. In May 2004 the Panamanian authorities agreed to permit US officials to board any ships sailing under the Panamanian flag that they suspected of carrying weapons of mass destruction. In April 2009 the Organisation for Economic Co-operation and Development (OECD) included Panama on its 'grey list' of territories that had yet substantially toimprove the transparency of its financial sector. President Martinelli sought Panama's removal from the list by concluding seven bilateral agreements by May 2010, although it was uncertain whether the provisions of these treaties conformed fully with OECD standards regarding the exchange of tax information.

Relations between Panama and Cuba were severely strained in August 2004 when outgoing President Moscoso issued a pardon to four prisoners who had been convicted by a Panamanian court of charges related to an alleged plot to assassinate the Cuban leader, Fidel Castro Ruz, during his visit to Panama in November 2000. In response, the Cuban Government, which had sought the extradition of the four, severed diplomatic ties with Panama. On the following day the Venezuelan Government, which had requested the extradition of one of the men, Luis Posada Carriles, in connection with the bombing of a Cuban aeroplane in 1976, also suspended diplomatic relations with Panama. Following the inauguration of President Torrijos in September 2004, the new Minister of Foreign Affairs, Samuel Lewis Navarro, denounced the pardons granted by Moscoso and successfully normalized relations with Venezuela. Achieving a reconciliation with Cuba proved more difficult, however, and it was not until August 2005, during a visit to that country by Torrijos, that full diplomatic ties were restored.

In late 2009 Panama unilaterally withdrew from the Central American Parliament (Parlacen), a regional political forum with its headquarters in Guatemala, fulfilling a pre-election pledge made by President Martinelli, who claimed that membership of the body had been of no benefit to Panama. However, in March 2010 the President of Parlacen announced that he had formally protested against the Panamanian Government's decision to the Central American Court of Justice, maintaining that Panama required the consent of the Presidents of the other member states to withdraw from Parlacen, and that the country owed the organization some US $1.1m. in outstanding dues.

Economy

PHILLIP WEARNE

Revised for this edition by KATHARINE MURISON

Panama's geographic location enabled it to develop as one of the most important shipping crossroads and entrepôts in the world. The country's most famous asset is the 82-km-long Panama Canal, which traverses the Darién isthmus, thus linking the Pacific Ocean with the Caribbean Sea and enabling shipping to avoid the lengthy Cape Horn route around the South American landmass. The Canal diminished in importance with the advent of supertankers and freighters, as the largest of the modern oil and bulk-cargo tankers could not use it. However, with the completion of the widening of the narrowest part of the Canal in 2001 and the rapid growth in cruise ship traffic in both the Caribbean and the Pacific, the Panama Canal regained prominence in terms of income and strategic importance; moreover, a major expansion of the Canal's capacity, scheduled for completion in 2014, would permit the transit of significantly larger vessels. Panama's continued role as a 'land bridge' was also reinforced with the opening, in October 1982, of a transisthmian pipeline to carry petroleum deemed economically impractical for transit in the usual way.

For a relatively small country, Panama possessed abundant natural resources, including high-quality fishing grounds, mineral deposits, forests and, above all, a topography and climate that were ideal for the development of hydroelectric and thermoelectric power. Substantial reserves of gold, copper and coal were underexploited and, apart from some manufacturing in the Colón Free Zone (CFZ—the second largest free trade zone in the world, after Hong Kong), the primary and secondary sectors of the productive economy were also grossly underdeveloped. Panama was thus traditionally a services-based economy, reliant on revenues from the Canal, ship registration, free trade zone transactions and contributions from 'offshore' banking activities. In 2009 services accounted for an estimated 77.4% of gross domestic product (GDP), measured in constant 1996 prices; some of the largest individual sub-sectors were transport, storage and communications (which accounted for some 23.7% of GDP), and renting, real estate and business services (which contributed an estimated 15.5% of GDP). In the same year agriculture (including hunting, forestry and fishing) and industry (including manufacturing) together accounted for only 22.6% of GDP.

Panama's currency was, effectively, the US dollar, although a nominal local currency, the balboa, existed at par with the dollar. The country's banknote supply was thus determined exclusively by trading relations and capital flows. Balance of payment surpluses automatically increased the money supply, while deficits caused it to dwindle. The country's central bank, the Banco Nacional de Panamá, could only influence the credit-creation constituent of the money supply (although it could issue local coinage), and the Government was unable to use currency devaluation or revaluation as an instrument of economic management.

The Government's economic policies were largely dictated by the IMF, the World Bank and the Inter-American Development Bank (IDB), all of which were involved in structural readjustment programmes from 1985. One of the principal aims of these programmes was to correct Panama's lack of international competitiveness by removing distortions and inefficiencies in the tax regime and labour market. Import substitution in industry and agriculture was considered an important means of closing the gap between an over-regulated domestic economy and an under-regulated international services sector. To this end, Panama joined the World Trade Organization in September 1997 and began to dismantle its protective import tariff regime. From the mid-1980s there was some effort to diversify the Panamanian services-orientated economic model. Revenues from the Panama Canal were by no means guaranteed, and the credibility of the 'offshore' banking sector was damaged by its perceived association with drugs-traffickers. Furthermore, the CFZ's exclusive advantages were being increasingly challenged by the creation of free trade ports and zones all over Latin America. It seemed clear, therefore, that the Panamanian economic base had to adapt to avoid a steady decline. From the mid-1980s the contribution of the services sector to the Panamanian economy remained fairly steady; however, there was considerable diversification within the sector itself, with tourism a particularly robust growth area.

Economic policies originating in the 1980s were designed to curb the budget deficit by reducing subsidies, rationalizing employment in the public sector and stimulating export growth, particularly in agriculture, by eliminating bureaucracy and offering better incentives. The initial implementation of such policies, however, produced a high level of political instability in Panama. This led to the resignation of President Nicolás Ardito Barletta in September 1985 and the ousting of his successor, Eric Arturo Delvalle, by the then Commander of the National Defence Forces, Gen. Manuel Antonio Noriega Morena, in February 1988. There could be little doubt that the economic situation, worsened immeasurably by the US economic boycott of 1988–89, also played a crucial role in the downfall of Noriega himself, who was ousted by, and surrendered to, US troops during a brief but devastating invasion of the country in December 1989.

Panama withstood the general global recession of the early 1980s fairly well, and a recovery in the services sector and manufacturing output from the CFZ stimulated growth in 1985–87. US economic sanctions provoked a precipitous 15.6% decline in 1988, and there was a contraction of 0.4% in 1989, before the lifting of US sanctions and a more realistic economic policy in 1990 and 1991 stimulated economic growth. The recovery was maintained in the early 1990s, before growth slowed to just 1.8% in 1995. There was, however, a subsequent revival, and steady progress was maintained until 2000. However, the growth rate declined in 2001, as elsewhere in the region, to just 0.6%, before recovering slightly, to 2.2%, in 2002. Improved economic expansion of 7.5%, 7.2% and 8.5% was recorded in 2004, 2005 and 2006, respectively. According to official figures, the economy grew by an estimated 12.1% and 10.7% in 2007 and 2008, respectively. Growth slowed substantially in 2009, to 2.4%, as a result of the impact of the global economic downturn. The rate of increase in consumer prices was low in the early 2000s: annual inflation was just 0.5% in 2004. Consumer prices increased slightly in 2005 and 2006, by 2.9% and 2.5%, respectively. They increased by 4.2% in 2007 and by 8.7% in 2008, largely owing to steep rises in the prices of electricity, oil and food, but by only 2.4% in 2009.

Panama had one of the highest foreign debts per head of population in the world (partly because it needed to borrow the money that it could not print). At the end of 2007 total external debt was an estimated US $9,862m., of which $8,267m. was long-term public debt. In that year the cost of debt-servicing was equivalent to 5.3% of the value of exports of goods and services. High real interest rates significantly increased the debt-service ratio (annual amortization and interest, expressed as a proportion of foreign exchange earnings on goods and non-factor services) on Panama's external debt during the 1980s, and in 1988 the country suspended all debt-service payments. Despite a series of financial reforms in 1991–92, total arrears to the IMF, the World Bank and the IDB were estimated at $3,000m. in early 1994, before the Government intensified its efforts to reach an agreement with commercial and multilateral creditors.

In May 1995 a Brady Plan debt-restructuring agreement was announced (the initiative on debt relief originally proposed by the then US Treasury Secretary, Nicholas Brady, in 1989), which covered a total of US $3,230m. in principal and interest arrears. The agreement, whereby Panama exchanged debt for new bonds with virtually all its commercial creditors, reduced the country's debt by more than $400m. and opened the way for fresh credit. In 1997 the country further reduced its debt by renegotiating more than $300m. in petroleum-supply debts incurred with Mexico and Venezuela under the San José Agreement of 1980. This restructuring gave Panama access to concessionary finance from the IMF, the World Bank and the IDB and allowed the country access to international capital markets. Panama took full advantage of this and since March 1999, when it sold $500m. worth of 30-year global bonds, using 40% of the receipts to buy back more foreign debt, has raised money to cancel debt. In January 2001 the country sold $750m. worth of 10-year global bonds, and in July and November 2002 it issued a total of $580m. worth of paper in its Global 2012 bond series.

AGRICULTURE, FORESTRY AND FISHING

Agriculture and fishing were vitally important to the success of the economic diversification effort in Panama. In August 2008 13.9% of the working population were employed in agriculture, forestry and fishing, but in 2009 the sector contributed only an estimated 5.7% of GDP. In 2007 about 9.3% of Panama's 7.4m. ha of land was cultivated on a permanent basis, while another 20.6% was permanent pasture land and 57.7% was forest and woodland (more than one-half of which has been declared protected park, woodland and forest in the past 25 years).

Melons, bananas and pineapples are the principal export crops. Melon cultivation increased substantially in the early 21st century. In 2001 melons overtook sugar as the second highest-earning export crop, and in 2005 became the leading export crop. Export earnings from melons increased to US $214.0m. in 2008, equivalent to 18.7% of total export revenue, but declined dramatically in 2009, to $81.9m. (10.0% of total revenue); this decrease was attributed to a lack of financing for producers, flooding, European customs restrictions and reduced demand resulting from the global economic downturn. Panama's exports of bananas, formerly the country's leading export commodity, earned $98.6m. in 2008, compared with $111.6m. in the previous year, and decreased to $61.2m. in 2009. The relative importance of banana exports had been in decline since the 1990s; in 1992 bananas accounted for 44.2% of total export earnings, but in 2009 they represented just 7.5%. The decline was variously attributed to falling international prices, industrial action in the sector, the adverse effects of the El Niño weather phenomenon (the warm current that periodically appears in the Pacific Ocean, altering normal weather patterns) and, perhaps most crucially, the quotas imposed by the European Union (EU) on banana exports from Latin America. However, from 2006 the EU quota system was replaced by an increase in import tariffs from €75 per metric ton to €176 per ton. Representatives of the industry claimed that the new tariffs would destabilize the economy and substantially increase unemployment. In 2000 the sector employed some 15,000 people directly, with a further 60,000 people dependent on the industry. In December 2009, following a protracted dispute with several Latin American countries (including Panama), the EU agreed to reduce import tariffs on bananas from €176 per ton to €114 per ton by 2017.

Traditionally, sugar was one of the principal agricultural export earners. However, revenues declined dramatically from the late 1980s as a result of depressed world prices and drastic annual reductions in the USA's sugar import quota. In 2008 its export revenue was overtaken by that of coffee. Revenue decreased from US $41.3m. in 1983 to $10.2m. in 1989, although it recovered thereafter, reaching $28.7m. in 1997, following significant increases in Panama's share of the US sugar import quota in the mid-1990s. In 1999 export revenue declined dramatically, to $14.5m., when it accounted for just 2.0% of export revenue. Export earnings from sugar subsequently fluctuated, declining to $10.4m. in 2004, before a steep rise in 2005 to an estimated $23.7m. (equivalent, however, to just 2.3% of total earnings). In 2009 it declined to just $13.3m. (equivalent to 1.6% of total earnings). Coffee production increased to 13,900 metric tons in 2002, after remaining stable at about 11,000 tons throughout the 1990s; 12,960 tons were harvested in 2008. Earnings fluctuated owing to international price movements. In 2002 earnings declined to just $9.3m. Coffee revenue made a modest recovery in subsequent years, and in 2009 was recorded at $15.3m., or 1.9% of total exports.

Successive governments recognized the urgent need to increase agricultural production in their agreements with the IMF and the World Bank. A five-year agricultural development plan announced in 1985 intended to counteract the effects of underinvestment resulting from price controls on rice, meat, potatoes and dairy products. Diversification of both crops and markets was given a high priority, and new crops were promoted. However, the need to boost production was somewhat undermined by the move to abolish the high import tariffs that had protected Panamanian farmers for many years, which caused many of those who catered for domestic consumption to be forced out of business from the mid-1980s. Growth did, however, increase thereafter, but average annual expansion of 4.3% in 2000–08 masked some fundamental structural changes in favour of export-driven production. According to official figures, the sector's GDP increased by 7.9% in 2008, but declined by an estimated 6.5% in 2009. The livestock sector, the epitome of the new export-driven policy, underwent particularly rapid expansion, averaging 4.0% annual growth in the late 1980s and early 1990s. However, the sector subsequently suffered from credit problems and export restrictions, and export earnings from livestock products fell dramatically as a result. None the less, the sector recovered after the mid-1990s, with meat exports totalling US $21.4m. in 2002, of which beef exports contributed almost three-quarters. In 2009 meat from cattle raised $14.0m. in export revenue.

Panama was one of the world's largest exporters of shrimps, with exports of shellfish more than doubling in the 1990s. In 2001 exports of shrimps earned US $70.1m. (equivalent to 8.6% of total export earnings); however, this figure fluctuated in subsequent years; in 2006 it decreased to $50.2m. (4.9% of earnings). Export revenue fell significantly in 2008, to just $40.6m. (3.5% of total export revenue), before rising to $43.9m. in 2009 (5.4% of revenue). In the same period fresh and frozen fish and fillets, including yellowfin tuna, increased substantially in importance before declining somewhat: exports reached $280.7m. in 2004 (29.9% of exports), then fell to an estimated $231.7m. in 2006 (equivalent to 22.7% of total exports). However, by 2008 export revenue from fresh and frozen fish and fillets, including yellowfin tuna, had increased to $346.9m. (equivalent to 30.3% of total exports).

MINING AND ENERGY

Despite valuable mineral deposits, which included gold, silver, copper and coal, mineral extraction was traditionally limited to clay, limestone and salt for local consumption. Mining contributed only an estimated 1.5% of GDP in 2009, engaging 0.2% of the employed labour force in August 2008. With a return to political and economic stability in the mid-1990s, and studies indicating potential export earnings from gold, silver and copper of some US $500m. per year, Panama's mining potential began to attract the interest of foreign investors. In 2010 Canada's Inmet Mining Corpn was at an advanced stage in the development of its Cobre (formerly Petaquilla) concession in the district of Donoso, in Colón province, which was estimated to contain 2,143m. metric tons of proven and probable reserves of 0.41% grade copper ore. The GDP of the mining sector increased by an average of 18.9% per year in 2005–09, according to official estimates; the sector expanded by 30.9% in 2008 and by 4.9% in 2009.

Gold-mining in Panama tended to be small scale, but gold-mining concessions were attractive to foreign investors owing to the lower capital costs. Following an initial investment of US $25m. in 1995, the Santa Rosa mine in Veraguas province yielded some 57,000 troy oz in 1997, producing $20m. in export revenue. However, output fell steadily thereafter, with export earnings put at just $12m. in 2000, and work at the mine was subsequently abandoned. In mid-2010 Canada's Bellhaven Copper and Gold, Inc, was preparing to develop the Cerro Quema gold- and silver-mining concession, where measured and indicated resources of gold had been estimated at 451,400 troy oz. Meanwhile, commercial production at the Molejón

Gold Project in Donoso commenced in January 2010; measured and indicated resources were estimated at 756,586 troy oz.

Panama had enormous hydroelectric and thermoelectric potential and aimed eventually to eliminate petroleum-powered electricity generation. By 2009 56.1% of the country's total electricity output was water-generated. In 2003 the Estí hydroelectric project increased installed capacity by 120 MW, while the thermoelectric Pedregal power installation added a further 53.4 MW of generating capacity. AES Panama initiated construction of a new hydroelectric power station, Changuinola 75, in the Bocas del Toro province in early 2008. The new facility was scheduled to become operational in 2011 and had a projected capacity of 223 MW. The hydroelectric sector was to be further augmented by the expansion of the La Estrella and Los Valles facilities. In 2009 electricity generation totalled some 6,397 GWh.

During periods of low hydroelectric output Panama was dependent on power generated from imported petroleum products. The cost of petroleum imports, which had been as high as US $350m. in the early 1980s, fell to less than $125m. by 1994, owing to increased hydroelectric capacity and lower world petroleum prices. However, the subsequent poor performance of the hydroelectricity sector and a rise in the price of crude petroleum resulted in the cost of fuel imports rising in the 2000s. In 2009 fuels and lubricants accounted for some 18.1% of total import expenditure.

MANUFACTURING AND CONSTRUCTION

Manufacturing accounted for an estimated 6.3% of GDP in 2009 and engaged 8.6% of the country's employed labour force in August 2008. The sector was based on agricultural-processing and light manufacturing, particularly food and beverages, clothing, household goods, and construction materials. Growth in the sector fluctuated considerably, successively depressed by a stagnant internal market, political instability and foreign competition, and then buoyed by the removal or neutralization of such impediments. In 2000–08, according to the World Bank, manufacturing GDP increased at an average annual rate of 0.8%; according to official figures, it expanded by 4.0% in 2008, but declined by an estimated 0.3% in 2009. Industrial activity was concentrated in the CFZ, a corridor of land running between Panama City and Colón (roughly following the line of the Canal). This was by far the most important manufacturing area in Panama, covering 400 ha and accommodating some 2,000 companies, with net exports of goods from the CFZ accounting for an estimated 8.7% of GDP in 2009. Most of the imports were from the Far East, destined for markets in South and Central America.

Ambitious expansion plans for the CFZ, costing more than US $65m., were initiated by the Government of President Guillermo Endara Galimany (1989–94). There was a corresponding increase in confidence and private sector investment, with total trade—the sum of imported and re-exported goods—increasing from $5,100m. in 1990 to $11,197m. in 1998. Nevertheless, in the late 1990s competition from other free trade zones and the increasing removal of trade barriers within the region, combined with the severe financial crises that crippled Latin America and Asia, threatened the long-term competitiveness of the CFZ, which responded by emphasizing its geographical location and seeking to reposition itself in the free trade zone market as a transshipment hub. In 2008 total trade in the CFZ amounted to $18,667m., increasing by 15.5% in that year.

In 2005–09 the construction sector expanded at an average annual rate of 17.1%, owing, in part, to the conversion or restoration of a large number of buildings in the Canal Area (known as the Canal Zone until 1979) and to the start of work on a second bridge over the Canal. The sector increased by 22.1% in 2007 and a preliminary 31.2% in 2008 as a result of new infrastructure works; a more moderate rise, of an estimated 4.6%, was recorded in 2009, when the sector contributed an estimated 6.3% of GDP. In August 2008 some 10.2% of the employed labour force were engaged in construction. Despite some concerns that the sector might have peaked, it was expected to be boosted by the enlargement of the Canal and by the construction of a metro system in Panama City, which was planned by the Government of Ricardo Martinelli Berrocal that took office in July 2009.

TRANSPORT AND TOURISM

Economic sanctions against the Noriega regime severely damaged Panama's ship registration industry; however, despite competition, it subsequently recovered well. Panama's open registry fleet grew by 4.5%–5.0% per year in the 1980s, and by 1990 the number of vessels registered, including tankers, was 12,149. However, although the country's shipping registry remained the largest in the world, by 2005 this figure had fallen to 6,838, owing to fierce competition from other countries. By 2008 the number of vessels had increased slightly, to 8,065. Earnings from ship-registration fees also declined. Nevertheless, this represented a recovery from the disastrous US sanctions of the late 1980s, when Panamanian ships were banned from US ports. Thousands of ships transferred to other registers before the Endara Government waived re-registration fees for a year in 1990, in an effort to recover market share. Further measures enacted in 1995 included offering volume discounts of up to 50% in fees to shipowners whose registry was over 100,000 grt in total. Most shipping remained foreign-owned, reflecting the preferential tax treatment available to shipping companies in Panama. Cristóbal and Balboa, ports in the Canal Area, could accommodate ocean-going freighters and passenger ships, following their redevelopment in 1996. Such investment made Panama one of the busiest container transshipment locations in the world. The Manzanillo International Terminal, Evergreen and Panamá ports were the three largest container ports in Latin America. Late 2000 saw the successful inauguration of Panama's first cruise ship terminals, at both ends of the Canal. Meanwhile, in late 2007 it was announced that the Manzanillo Terminal would be expanded at a cost of US $210m.

In 2008, according to preliminary figures, the road network totalled 13,267 km, of which 38.1% was paved, and there were an estimated 412,625 vehicles in use. The Pan-American Highway ran for 545 km in Panama, from the Costa Rican border through Panama City, to Chepo. Three railways served the banana plantations and other agricultural areas in the western parts of Bocas del Toro and Chiriquí, which bordered Costa Rica. On ratification of the 1977 Canal Treaties, Panama also acquired control of the Panama Railroad, which connected Panama City and Colón. The 83-km railroad reopened on 1 July 2001, operating daily passenger and cargo container services. It was operated by Ferrocarril de Panamá, a subsidiary of Kansas City Southern Railway (USA). The Tocumen (formerly Omar Torrijos) International Airport was officially opened in 1978, and, as a consequence of increased tourist arrivals, a project to expand the facilities at a cost of US $20m. was completed in 2006.

Two long, varied coastlines with good beaches and 800 tropical islands offered vast tourism potential. The southern (Pacific) coast of Panama provided some of the best deep-sea fishing in the world. Other tourist attractions included the mountains and volcanic scenery, the ruins of the original Panama City, and the Panama Canal. Although tourism declined steadily throughout the 1980s, the number of tourist arrivals in 1990–95 rose by an average of 10.0% per year. The sector continued to grow thereafter, although more moderately; visitor arrivals in 1995–2005 rose at an average annual rate of 4.8%. Strong growth was recorded in 2007 and 2008, of 34.9% and 19.7%, respectively, with visitor arrivals reaching 1,136,079 in the latter year, before declining to a preliminary 1,054,663 in 2009. Receipts from tourism rose steadily from US $538m. in 1999 to a provisional $1,483m. in 2009. The most spectacular growth in recent years has been in cruise ship arrivals, following the completion of two new cruise ship terminals (see above).

The GDP of the services sector overall grew at an average annual rate of 6.9% in 2000–08, according to the World Bank. It increased by a preliminary 10.7% in 2008 and by an estimated 2.8% in 2009. Strong growth in the sector was attributed primarily to the transport industry. However, in light of the global economic downturn, and particularly the US recession, the transport sector was weakened by a fall in exports brought about by lower demand, in the USA and elsewhere. Growth in transport, storage and communications GDP slowed from 18.5% in 2008 to an estimated 8.3% in 2009.

THE CANAL AREA

The Canal Area (known as the Canal Zone until 1979) is a strip of land, 16 km wide, between the Pacific and Caribbean coasts, running north-west to south-east. The Canal itself is 82 km long, and raises or lowers ships through 26 m by means of six pairs of locks. An average passage takes about nine hours. The Canal can accommodate ships with a maximum draught of 12.0 m and beams of 32.3 m. Improvements to the Canal in the early 21st century increased the transit capacity to 43 vessels per day. In 2008/09 (October to September) traffic in the Canal declined by 2.4% compared with the previous year, while the amount of cargo transported decreased by 5.6%. Canal operations—tolls, transit-related services and sales of surplus water and electricity—accounted for an estimated 8.1% of Panama's GDP in 2009.

Almost 70% of all cargo transported through the Canal either originated from, or was destined for, the USA (moving between Asia and the east coast of the USA). The People's Republic of China was the second most regular user of the Canal in 2008/09, followed by Chile and Japan. In 1996, following a report by the US Army Corps of Engineers that listed more than 1,000 maintenance repairs and equipment upgrades requiring immediate attention, the Panama Canal Commission (PCC, replaced by the Autoridad del Canal de Panamá, ACP—Panama Canal Authority—in December 1999) initiated a six-year modernization programme. The programme, which was to cost US $1,000m. and to increase capacity by one-fifth, was financed entirely from the Canal's revenue, and significantly increased employment in the area. The Culebra Cut widening project—the expansion of the narrowest part of the Canal from 152 m to 192 m—was completed in December 2001. The project allowed two vessels to pass at the same time and increased the capacity of the Canal by some 20%. New lock configurations were also commissioned, and two new tugboats were added to the Canal's fleet in December 2001. In April 2006 the Government announced detailed plans for the expansion of the Panama Canal. While widely considered to be vital to the future of the Canal and therefore the country's commercial sector, concerns were raised relating to the environmental consequences of the expansion and the possible relocation of farmers in communities bordering the Canal. The proposed project would involve the construction of two new sets of locks at either end of the Canal by 2014, at a cost of $5,250m. The proposed expansion was approved by the Asamblea Nacional in July 2006 and then by the public via a referendum held on 22 October. Following a presidential election in May 2009, new President Ricardo Martinelli Berrocal highlighted the expansion of the Canal as an important stimulant of growth, and pledged to push forward with the project. Under the Canal Treaties of 1977, which came into force in October 1979, the neutrality of the Canal Area was guaranteed, so as to ensure the continuous and clear transit of traffic. Panama administered the Canal from January 2000, although the USA reserved the right to protect the Canal by military force if necessary.

The vessels that used the Canal were predominantly bulk cargo carriers carrying grain, petroleum and related products. The number of transits and the cargo figures remained virtually static from 1995. However, revenue from the Canal rose, owing to increases in transit charges that were introduced in 1995 and 2003. The ACP increased toll charges on the Canal in July 2007, despite criticism from shipping companies that the new prices were excessive. The new charges represented an increase of 47% on the previous tariff for large containers and of 20%–30% for other vessels. In 2008/09 canal transit fees earned Panama some US $1,817.4m. (compared with US $460m. in 1995), derived from some 14,342 commercial transits of 198.0m. long tons. Other services, notably the sale of surplus electricity and water from the Canal Area, earned a further $144.6m. in 2008/09.

EXTERNAL TRADE AND FINANCE

Panama regularly incurred a large deficit on its merchandise trade account as a result of its heavy dependence on imported fuel and 'invisibles' (banking, ship registration, Canal fees and re-exports). This was, however, partially offset by a surplus on transactions in services. The trade deficit grew inexorably from the late 1980s, reaching US $1,340.0m. in 1999. After decreasing in 2000 and 2001, to $696.2m. in the latter year, the deficit rose steadily in 2002–06 and more substantially in 2007 and 2008, when it amounted to $3,190.1m. and $4,545.9m., respectively. In 2009, however, the trade deficit narrowed to $2,026.3m., principally owing to significantly lower prices for some imports, notably mineral products, the cost of which declined by 31.3% in that year. The principal imports in 2008 were mineral products, which amounted to $2,003.6m., machinery and apparatus ($1,768.6m.), food and live animals ($990.8m.) and transport materials ($932.8m.).

Panama tended to be heavily dependent on capital inflows, such as IMF assistance. This was partly because its unusually liberal economic system made it particularly vulnerable to lower world-trading activity during periods of recession. Furthermore, because of its use of the US dollar, Panama was unable to resort to currency devaluation in order to correct trading imbalances. Between 1981 and 1986 the debt-service ratio (debt-servicing compared with the total value of exports of goods and services) fluctuated between 43% and 55%, but declined steadily thereafter following renegotiation and rescheduling. Nearly a decade of debt-restructuring, including debt forgiveness, repurchasing and exchanging commercial bank debt for bonds, beginning with a Brady bond deal in 1995, enabled the country to reduce its liabilities steadily. With access to concessionary loans and international capital markets, the Panamanian Government was able to issue bonds worth more than $1,500m. to buy back debt in 1998–2003.

Panama traditionally encouraged foreign investment, a policy that was intensified after 1990, as part of efforts to improve the economy and counterbalance the legacy of sanctions and the US invasion. Many restrictions were ended as part of the Endara Government's privatization programme. Panama exercised no exchange controls, and transfers of funds were never prevented. There were no restrictions on the transfer of profits, dividends, interest, royalties or fees, nor on the repatriation of capital nor the repayment of principal. A 10% withholding tax was levied on dividends from operations in Panama (excluding the CFZ), but Panama did not levy tax on income earned in 'offshore' financial dealings. In 1997–98 foreign capital inflows increased to an annual average of more than US $1,200m. Although this figure was somewhat distorted by the purchase of a 49% stake in the state telecommunications monopoly, Instituto Nacional de Telecomunicaciones (INTEL), by Cable & Wireless (United Kingdom) for $652m., the incidence of such major investments was increasing. For example, the sale of toll-road concessions to two Mexican companies in 1998 secured future inward investment in excess of $600m., while the sale of electricity assets in the same year yielded $603m. Other important sales and joint-venture investments, including many tourism and infrastructure developments linked to redevelopment of military and Canal sites following the withdrawal of US personnel, were expected to help maintain a healthy level of capital investment. However, the completion of a number of major investment projects caused a decline in foreign direct investment from $755.6m. in 1999 to $623.9m. in 2000. After a decrease to just $98.6m. in 2002, the level of investment generally recovered, reaching $917.6m. in 2005. Foreign direct investment rose to an extraordinary $2,557.1m. in 2006, largely owing to the purchase of the Primer Banco del Istmo, which was sold for an estimated $1,700m. to HSBC Bank in July. Investment declined to $1,776.5m. in 2007, before increasing to $2,401.7m. in 2008. A decrease to $1,772.8m. in 2009 was attributed to the effects of the global economic downturn.

From the late 1960s onwards Panama developed its potential as an international finance centre, based on the full transferability of its currency, its favourable tax laws and the absence of state controls. The 'offshore' business, foreign exchange, money and reinsurance markets expanded in the early 1980s, and in 2001 the sector accounted for an estimated

11% of GDP. However, the 'offshore' banking sector experienced difficulties caused by political and economic instability and radical changes in business in the late 20th century. In 2009 the financial services sector accounted for an estimated 8.6% of GDP. Following the onset of the banking crisis, precipitated by a sharp contraction in credit markets in late 2008, the financial services sector in Panama saw its real GDP contract by 7.3% year on year in the third quarter of 2008. In response to the growing global economic crisis, the Government created a banking fund worth some US $1,100m. in order to protect capitalization of the Panamanian banking sector.

By December 2009 the net consolidated assets of the banking sector were estimated to be US $77,841m., representing a substantial increase from the $35,651m. recorded in 2003. In 2010 the number of banks registered was 78, significantly fewer than the 118 registered in 1982. As general financial liberalization eroded Panama's competitiveness in the 1990s, competitors in Latin American and the Caribbean were establishing themselves. The relaxation of financial restrictions globally meant that many banks in the USA and Europe began to deal direct with clients in Latin America, denying Panama's banks one of their principal roles. In June 2000 the Organisation for Economic Co-operation and Development (OECD, based in Paris, France) identified Panama as meeting the technical criteria for being a tax haven. Furthermore, in the same month the Financial Action Task Force on Money Laundering (FATF, also based in Paris) included the country on a list of those jurisdictions considered to be 'non-co-operative' in international efforts to prevent money-laundering and the financing of terrorist organizations. Panama protested against its inclusion on both lists and subsequently modified its legislation to introduce greater legal and administrative transparency in the financial sector. In June 2001 the country was removed from the FATF list, and in April 2002 Panama met OECD criteria in committing to improve the transparency of its tax and regulatory systems and establish effective exchange of information for tax matters by 31 December 2005. In April 2009, however, OECD included Panama on its 'grey list' of territories that had committed to improving financial transparency but had yet substantially to implement reform. In an effort to be removed from the list, the Government of Panama subsequently began concluding bilateral agreements on the avoidance of double taxation with certain countries, signing seven such accords by May 2010, although it was uncertain whether the provisions of these treaties conformed fully with OECD standards regarding the exchange of tax information.

From 1983 Panama's fiscal policies required IMF approval. However, such approval was difficult to secure, principally owing to the Government's difficulty in achieving IMF targets for the budget deficit. Successful rescheduling and negotiations of new loans from the IMF were achieved in the mid-1980s. However, these were gained not only as a result of budgetary austerity, but also because of the Government's commitment to certain reforms opposed by the trade unions and by the private sector. Satisfaction with the Government's efforts at economic restructuring was signalled by the resumption of lending to the country by the World Bank in December 1986. However, in 1987 the Government began to withhold payments to bilateral creditors, and by March 1988 the country's IMF agreement had lapsed, with no new accord negotiated to replace it. By the end of that year accumulated interest and principal arrears on public sector debt were estimated at US $1,400m.

In 1991 the Endara Government had rescheduled US $520m. in bilateral debts with the 'Paris Club' of Western creditor nations. After paying part of the $610m. in arrears to the IMF, the World Bank and the IDB, the country became eligible for further credits during 1992–93. In February 1992 the IMF disbursed $50.4m. in support of the Government's economic programme. The trend was consolidated in April 1995 when Panama signed a debt-rescheduling agreement based on the Brady Plan. The accord covered $2,000m. in principal arrears and $1,500m. in interest arrears, offering creditors a variety of options with the IMF, the World Bank and the IDB, which were all actively supporting the agreement.

Thereafter, Panama repurchased or exchanged US $1,220m. of this Brady bond debt for its own 30-year government bonds. In December 1997 the IMF approved a credit of $162m., under the Extended Fund Facility, in support of the Government's economic programme for 1998–2000. In March 2000 Panama began negotiations with other Central American countries on a free trade accord. In May 2001, following further extensive discussions, the Central American countries, including Panama, reached an agreement with Mexico to establish the 'Plan Puebla–Panamá' (restyled the Proyecto de Integración y Desarrollo de Mesoamérica in 2008). Free trade agreements with El Salvador, Taiwan and Chile entered into force in April 2003, January 2004 and March 2008, while similar accords with Costa Rica, Honduras, Guatemala and Nicaragua took effect successively between November 2008 and November 2009. In June 2007 Panama signed a bilateral free trade agreement with the USA; the accord was ratified by the Asamblea Nactional in July, but as of mid-2010 it still had not received US congressional approval. A contributing factor was Panama's status as an 'offshore' tax haven—it remained on the USA's blacklist—and although the free trade agreement remained important, Panama's financial sector continued to be a significant area of economic growth. Panama's officials were thus unlikely to concede to US demands for more transparency in the near future. In May 2010 Panama signed a free trade agreement with Canada, and was party to a Central American association agreement concluded with the European Union.

In January 2005, despite opposition from the business sector, the Asamblea Nacional approved legislation that aimed to reduce the fiscal deficit from 5% to 1% of GDP by 2009, by increasing the tax yield, rationalizing public spending and reducing expenditure on salaries. The Asamblea Nacional approved the Fiscal Responsibility Law in May 2008 in order to limit the deficit to 1% of GDP for the non-financial public sector, excluding the Panama Canal Authority, and achieve a debt target of 40% of GDP by 2015. In June 2009 the Asamblea Nacional approved a rise in the deficit limit to 2.5% in light of the global economic downturn.

CONCLUSION

Panama's exceptional economic performance in 2006–08, when successive growth rates of 8.5%, 12.1% and 10.7% were recorded, was driven by foreign investment and by the expansion of the construction sector, which was stimulated by a number of real estate and infrastructure developments, most notably the project to expand the Canal. Once enlarged, the Canal was expected to increase GDP growth by 1%–2% per year until 2025. Although growth slowed substantially in 2009, to an estimated 2.4%, as a result of the impact of the global economic downturn, Panama's economic performance remained relatively strong compared with that of other countries within the region, and the fiscal deficit was contained at 1% of GDP. Economic prospects remained good, although much depended on the continued Canal expansion project and on the US Congress ratifying the bilateral free trade agreement, which would remove trade tariffs and, it was hoped, reduce the trade deficit. Furthermore, the new President, Ricardo Martinelli, elected in May 2009, supported the ongoing Canal expansion and aimed to secure US approval of the free trade agreement as soon as possible. Plans for the construction of a metro system for Panama City were also announced. In March 2010 Martinelli enacted taxation reforms intended to increase annual revenue by US $200m.: notably, value-added tax was raised from 5% to 7%, while income tax rates for low-income workers were reduced. The Government forecast growth of 5.0% in 2010; in the first quarter of the year GDP increased by 4.9% compared with the same period of 2009.

Statistical Survey

Sources (unless otherwise stated): Dirección de Estadística y Censo, Contraloría General de la República, Avda Balboa y Federico Boyd, Apdo 5213, Panamá 5; tel. 210-4800; fax 210-4801; e-mail cgrdec@contraloria.gob.pa; internet www.contraloria.gob.pa; Ministry of the Economy and Finance, Edif. Ogawa, Vía España, Apdo 5245, Panamá 5; e-mail webmaster@mef.gob.pa; internet www.mef.gob.pa.

Note: The former Canal Zone was incorporated into Panama on 1 October 1979.

Area and Population

AREA, POPULATION AND DENSITY

Area (sq km)	75,517*
Population (census results)	
13 May 1990	2,329,329
14 May 2000	
Males	1,432,566
Females	1,406,611
Total	2,839,177
Population (official estimates at mid-year)	
2008	3,395,346
2009	3,450,349
2010	3,504,483
Density (per sq km) at mid-2010	46.4

* 29,157 sq miles.

POPULATION BY AGE AND SEX
(official estimates at mid-2010)

	Males	Females	Total
0–14	521,964	500,306	1,022,270
15–64	1,133,405	1,119,093	2,252,498
65 and over	110,365	119,350	229,715
Total	1,765,734	1,738,749	3,504,483

ADMINISTRATIVE DIVISIONS
(official estimates at mid-2010)

Province	Population	Capital (and population)*
Bocas del Toro	118,405	Bocas del Toro (13,686)
Chiriquí	426,790	David (146,094)
Coclé	237,840	Penonomé (84,494)
Colón	250,802	Colón (215,821)
Comarca Emberá	9,497	—
Comarca Kuna Yala	37,545	—
Comarca Ngöbe-Buglé	150,550	—
Darién	46,011	Chepigana (31,656)
Herrera	112,538	Chitré (49,209)
Los Santos	90,984	Las Tablas (27,254)
Panamá	1,796,674	Panamá (894,565)
Veraguas	226,847	Santiago (84,432)
Total	3,504,483	—

* Population of district in which capital is located.

Note: Population figures include the former Canal Zone.

PRINCIPAL TOWNS
(population at 2000 census)

Panamá (Panama City, capital)	463,093	Pacora	57,232
San Miguelito	291,769	Santiago	55,146
Tocumen	81,250	La Chorrera	54,823
David	76,481	Colón	52,286
Nuevo Arraiján	63,753	Changuinola	45,063
Puerto Armuelles	60,102	Pedregal	45,033

Mid-2010 (incl. suburbs, UN estimate): Panama City 1,378,470 (Source: UN, *World Urbanization Prospects: The 2009 Revision*).

BIRTHS, MARRIAGES AND DEATHS

	Registered live births		Registered marriages*		Registered deaths	
	Number	Rate (per 1,000)†	Number	Rate (per 1,000)†	Number	Rate (per 1,000)†
2001	63,900	21.3	9,687	3.6	12,442	4.1
2002	61,671	20.2	9,558	3.1	12,428	4.1
2003	61,753	19.8	10,310	3.3	13,248	4.3
2004	62,743	19.8	10,290	3.2	13,475	4.2
2005	63,645	19.7	10,512	3.3	14,180	4.4
2006	65,764	20.0	10,747	3.3	14,358	4.4
2007	67,364	20.2	11,516	3.4	14,775	4.4
2008	68,759	20.3	11,508	3.4	15,115	4.5

* Excludes tribal Indian population.

† Based on official mid-year population estimates.

Life expectancy (years at birth, WHO estimates): 76 (males 74; females 79) in 2008 (Source: WHO, *World Health Statistics*).

ECONOMICALLY ACTIVE POPULATION
('000 persons aged 15 years and over, August of each year)

	2006	2007	2008
Agriculture, hunting and forestry	183.1	176.5	176.5
Fishing	9.9	9.8	9.1
Mining and quarrying	2.3	3.6	3.3
Manufacturing	105.2	109.6	114.1
Electricity, gas and water supply	8.4	8.1	6.9
Construction	102.8	122.4	136.7
Wholesale and retail trade; repair of motor vehicles, motorcycles and personal and household goods	229.6	240.7	258.6
Hotels and restaurants	64.5	69.5	70.8
Transport, storage and communications	90.8	91.9	100.9
Financial intermediation	26.4	28.8	28.4
Real estate, renting and business activities	62.6	67.0	71.7
Public administration and defence; compulsory social service	70.3	79.6	78.7
Education	62.7	65.3	74.6
Health and social work	48.3	50.6	55.1
Other community, social and personal service activities	68.0	63.8	70.0
Private households with employed persons	74.9	76.1	77.4
Extra-territorial organizations and bodies	0.8	0.7	0.9
Total employed	1,210.7	1,264.0	1,333.8
Unemployed	121.4	92.0	82.9
Total labour force	1,332.1	1,355.9	1,416.7

Source: ILO.

Health and Welfare

KEY INDICATORS

Total fertility rate (children per woman, 2008)	2.5
Under-5 mortality rate (per 1,000 live births, 2008)	23
HIV/AIDS (% of persons aged 15–49, 2007)	1.0
Physicians (per 1,000 head, 2000)	1.5
Hospital beds (per 1,000 head, 2005)	1.8
Health expenditure (2007): US $ per head (PPP)	773
Health expenditure (2007): % of GDP	6.7
Health expenditure (2007): public (% of total)	64.6
Access to water (% of persons, 2008)	93
Access to sanitation (% of persons, 2008)	69
Total carbon dioxide emissions ('000 metric tons, 2006)	6,423.0
Carbon dioxide emissions per head (metric tons, 2006)	2.0
Human Development Index (2007): ranking	60
Human Development Index (2007): value	0.840

For sources and definitions, see explanatory note on p. vi.

Agriculture

PRINCIPAL CROPS

('000 metric tons)

	2006	2007	2008
Rice, paddy	232.4	237.0	231.3
Maize	84.4	86.1	83.9
Sugar cane	1,771.5	1,797.5	1,822.7
Watermelons	92.3	120.7	100.0
Cantaloupes and other melons	100.3	116.6	101.5
Bananas	538.9	544.6	357.9
Plantains	110.0	108.1	105.0
Oranges	44.7	46.1	46.3
Coffee, green	12.8	13.8	13.0
Tobacco, unmanufactured*	2.6	2.8	2.8

* FAO estimates.

Aggregate production ('000 metric tons, may include official, semi-official or estimated data): Total cereals 324.7 in 2006, 332.0 in 2007, 324.0 in 2008; Total roots and tubers 81.4 in 2006, 83.7 in 2007, 78.4 in 2008; Total vegetables (incl. melons) 294.5 in 2006, 361.3 in 2007, 322.7 in 2008; Total fruits (excl. melons) 782.2 in 2006, 809.0 in 2007, 589.4 in 2008.

Source: FAO.

LIVESTOCK

('000 head, year ending September)

	2006	2007	2008
Horses*	185	190	190
Mules*	4	4	4
Cattle	1,562	1,526	1,603
Pigs	278	325	318
Goats*	6	6	6
Chickens	14,535	15,141	17,484
Ducks*	230	235	235
Turkeys*	35	40	40

* FAO estimates.

Source: FAO.

LIVESTOCK PRODUCTS

('000 metric tons)

	2006	2007	2008
Cattle meat	67.1	67.1	69.7*
Pig meat	25.0	27.3	31.2*
Chicken meat	95.9	97.4	110.2
Cows' milk	178.6	180.2	181.5
Hen eggs	25.7	27.3	28.2

* FAO estimate.

Source: FAO.

Forestry

ROUNDWOOD REMOVALS

('000 cubic metres, excluding bark)

	2006	2007	2008
Sawlogs, veneer logs and logs for sleepers	69	70	60
Other industrial wood	1	1	1
Fuel wood*	1,189	1,173	1,158
Pulp wood*	90	90	90
Total*	1,349	1,334	1,309

* FAO estimates.

Source: FAO.

SAWNWOOD PRODUCTION

('000 cubic metres, incl. railway sleepers, FAO estimates)

	2006	2007	2008
Total (all broadleaved)	30	30	9

Source: FAO.

Fishing

('000 metric tons, live weight)

	2006	2007	2008
Capture	227.0	208.5	222.5*
Snappers and jobfishes	8.8	6.7	6.5
Pacific thread herring	30.3	17.7	36.8
Pacific anchoveta	53.4	62.2	47.4
Skipjack tuna	56.7	39.8	50.8
Yellowfin tuna	38.0	39.7	33.9
Bigeye tuna	12.0	10.8	11.0
Marine fishes	8.7	7.7	10.3
Aquaculture	8.7	8.8	8.2
Whiteleg shrimp	8.1	8.2	7.8
Total catch	235.7	217.3	230.7*

* FAO estimate.

Note: Figures exclude crocodiles. The number of spectacled caimans caught was: 2,210 in 2006; 2,752 in 2007; 1,155 in 2008.

Source: FAO.

Industry

SELECTED PRODUCTS

('000 metric tons, unless otherwise indicated)

	2006	2007	2008*
Salt	19	20	21
Sugar	168	164	151
Beer (million litres)	180	195	214
Wines and spirits (million litres)	12	13	14
Evaporated, condensed and powdered milk	21	19	23
Fish oil	7	7	6
Footwear ('000 pairs)	8	14	26
Electricity (million kWh, net)	5,731	6,156	6,171

* Preliminary.

Finance

CURRENCY AND EXCHANGE RATES

Monetary Units
100 centésimos = 1 balboa (B).

Sterling, Dollar and Euro Equivalents (31 May 2010)
£1 sterling = 1.458 balboas;
US $1 = 1.000 balboas;
€1 = 1.238 balboas;
100 balboas = £68.59 = $100.00 = €80.75.

Exchange Rate: The balboa's value is fixed at par with that of the US dollar.

BUDGET

(consolidated general government budget, '000 balboas)

Revenue	2005	2006	2007*
Central government revenue	3,438,186	3,783,081	4,433,157
Current revenue	2,328,211	3,158,010	3,682,164
Tax revenue	1,378,673	1,813,549	2,132,803
Direct taxes	708,181	1,020,263	1,134,342
Income tax	583,901	878,407	985,184
Taxes on property and inheritance	88,037	91,715	109,316
Educational insurance	36,243	50,141	39,842
Indirect taxes	670,492	793,286	998,461
Non-tax revenue	866,506	1,281,780	1,460,182
Panama Canal	200,000	334,181	463,414
Transfers from balance of public sector	2,626	2,522	2,754
Other current revenue	83,032	62,681	89,179
Surplus on cash account	22,265	12,564	357
Capital revenue	1,087,710	612,507	750,636
Decentralized institutional revenue	1,796,600	1,971,100	2,369,000
Department of social security	1,388,900	1,494,300	—
University of Panama	114,800	116,900	—
State enterprises	1,412,000	1,683,800	2,150,300
Non-financial	532,300	568,200	792,000
Financial	879,700	1,115,600	1,358,300
Municipalities	101,400	111,600	129,500
Total revenue	6,748,200	7,549,600	9,081,900

Expenditure	2005	2006	2007*
Central government expenditure	3,408,186	3,772,692	4,432,114
Current expenditure	3,020,194	3,041,525	3,462,913
National Assembly	45,245	50,722	56,305
State treasury	34,122	38,106	40,688
Ministry of the Presidency	41,299	51,863	60,607
Ministry of the Interior and Justice	210,398	224,806	247,908
Ministry of Foreign Affairs	30,807	33,498	39,326
Ministry of Social Development	15,507	16,774	15,384
Ministry of the Economy and Finance	154,515	138,825	112,053
Ministry of Education	533,327	594,516	639,408
Ministry of Commerce and Industry	37,067	33,050	29,660
Ministry of Public Works	22,454	36,003	26,439
Ministry of Agricultural Development	33,755	39,280	42,792
Ministry of Public Health	358,734	473,234	598,101
Ministry of Labour and Social Welfare	8,719	7,197	8,649
Ministry of Housing	11,177	12,147	13,627
Judiciary	36,553	40,474	43,068
Ombudsman	42,244	45,581	49,486
Electoral tribunal	23,237	32,247	29,031
Other expenditures of administration	11,148	11,314	11,478
Debt-servicing	1,333,411	1,115,816	1,362,504
Education fund	36,475	46,072	639,408
Ministerial development expenditure	387,992	731,167	969,201
Decentralized institutional expenditure	1,617,900	1,745,100	1,996,800
Department of social security	1,261,100	1,312,600	—
State enterprises	1,316,400	1,623,800	1,896,300
Municipalities	94,000	102,400	119,800
Total	6,436,500	7,244,000	8,445,000

* Preliminary figures.

Note: Totals may not be equal to the sum of component parts, owing to partial rounding.

2008 (million balboas, preliminary): *Revenue:* Central government revenue 5,204.1; Decentralized institutional revenue 2,786.7; State enterprises 2,451.0; Municipalities 140.3; Total revenue 10,582.1. *Expenditure:* Central government expenditure 5,171.7; Decentralized institutional expenditure 2,453.3; State enterprises 2,298.9; Municipalities 135.0; Total expenditure 10,058.9.

INTERNATIONAL RESERVES

(US $ million at 31 December*)

	2007	2008	2009
IMF special drawing rights	0.9	0.8	268.2
Reserve position in IMF	18.7	18.3	18.6
Foreign exchange	1,915.4	2,404.7	2,741.5
Total	1,935.1	2,423.8	3,028.3

* Excludes gold, valued at US $476,000 in 1991–93.

Note: US treasury notes and coins form the bulk of the currency in circulation in Panama.

Source: IMF, *International Financial Statistics*.

MONEY SUPPLY

(million balboas at 31 December)

	2007	2008	2009
Transferable deposits	3,054.2	3,763.6	4,403.5
Other deposits	14,052.0	15,837.2	17,378.7
Securities other than shares	224.5	179.4	29.9
Broad money	17,330.7	19,780.2	21,812.1

Source: IMF, *International Financial Statistics*.

COST OF LIVING

(Consumer Price Index, base: 2000 = 100)

	2005	2006	2007
Food (incl. beverages)	105.6	107.0	114.2
Rent, fuel and light	104.0	109.3	114.3
Clothing (incl. footwear)	97.1	96.3	94.9
All items (incl. others)	103.3	105.9	110.3

2008: Food (incl. beverages) 131.3; All items (incl. others) 119.9.

2009: Food (incl. beverages) 138.8; All items (incl. others) 122.8.

Source: ILO.

NATIONAL ACCOUNTS

National Income and Product

(million balboas at current prices)

	2006	2007	2008*
Compensation of employees	5,675.5	6,405.5	6,951.8
Operating surplus	6,655.4	7,788.7	9,716.5
Net mixed income	2,207.8	2,602.8	3,094.3
Domestic factor incomes	14,538.7	16,797.0	19,762.6
Consumption of fixed capital	1,254.0	1,369.7	1,556.6
Gross domestic product (GDP) at factor cost	15,792.7	18,166.7	21,319.2
Indirect taxes	1,506.3	1,801.0	2,084.7
Less Subsidies	162.0	174.1	220.0
GDP in purchasers' values	17,137.0	19,793.7	23,183.9
Less Net factor income paid to the rest of the world	1,546.0	1,741.2	2,044.3
Gross national product	15,591.0	18,052.5	21,139.6
Less Consumption of fixed capital	1,254.0	1,369.7	1,556.6
National income in market prices	14,337.0	16,682.8	19,583.0
Other current transfers from abroad (net)	153.7	150.3	122.8
National disposable income	14,490.7	16,833.0	19,705.8

* Preliminary figures.

Expenditure on the Gross Domestic Product

(million balboas at current prices)

	2006	2007	2008*
Government final consumption expenditure	2,116.3	2,236.3	2,389.0
Private final consumption expenditure	10,445.6	11,345.4	13,097.3
Increase in stocks	200.0	221.0	254.7
Gross fixed capital formation	3,134.9	4,554.7	6,100.5
Total domestic expenditure	15,896.8	18,357.4	21,841.5
Exports of goods and services	13,146.6	16,071.9	18,812.0
Less Imports of goods and services	11,906.4	14,635.6	17,469.6
GDP in purchasers' values	17,137.0	19,793.7	23,183.9
GDP at constant 1996 prices	15,238.6	17,084.4	18,917.6

* Preliminary figures.

Gross Domestic Product by Economic Activity

(million balboas at constant 1996 prices)

	2007	2008*	2009†
Agriculture, hunting, forestry and fishing	1,045.0	1,127.9	1,054.8
Mining and quarrying	197.8	259.0	271.8
Manufacturing	1,126.7	1,171.9	1,168.2
Electricity, gas and water	484.3	501.2	536.9
Construction	857.2	1,120.3	1,170.4
Wholesale and retail trade, repair of vehicles, motorcycles and other household goods	2,517.7	2,704.6	2,603.8
Hotels and restaurants	494.9	531.9	542.7
Transport, storage and communications	3,417.5	4,050.6	4,388.1
Financial intermediation	1,414.7	1,636.7	1,600.8
Renting, real estate and business services	2,607.8	2,771.4	2,877.9
General government services	1,272.7	1,321.0	1,353.3
Social services and private education and health	269.0	279.5	290.7
Other community, social and personal services	513.1	555.5	580.6
Private households with employed persons	112.6	114.7	113.6
Sub-total	16,331.0	18,146.2	18,553.6
Less Financial intermediation services indirectly measured	379.8	403.9	430.4
Gross value added in basic prices	15,951.2	17,742.3	18,123.2
Import duties and other taxes, less subsidies	1,133.2	1,175.3	1,251.0
GDP in market prices	17,084.4	18,917.6	19,374.2

* Preliminary figures.

† Estimates.

BALANCE OF PAYMENTS

(US $ million)*

	2007	2008	2009
Exports of goods f.o.b.	9,333.7	10,323.2	10,904.3
Imports of goods f.o.b.	–12,523.8	–14,869.1	–12,930.6
Trade balance	–3,190.1	–4,545.9	–2,026.3
Exports of services	4,958.1	5,825.9	5,438.2
Imports of services	–2,121.8	–2,621.2	–2,165.9
Balance on goods and services	–353.8	–1,341.2	1,246.0
Other income received	1,864.2	1,891.9	1,504.6
Other income paid	–3,170.6	–3,465.7	–2,964.5
Balance on goods, services and income	–1,660.2	–2,915.0	–213.9
Current transfers received	416.4	449.5	463.1
Current transfers paid	–163.2	–211.6	–252.7
Current balance	–1,407.0	–2,677.1	–3.5
Capital account (net)	43.7	56.9	23.1
Direct investment from abroad	1,776.5	2,401.7	1,772.8
Portfolio investment assets	–1,081.6	–464.3	–864.1
Portfolio investment liabilities	450.0	–62.3	1,323.0
Other investment assets	–5,118.5	–3,000.6	–1,106.7
Other investment liabilities	6,432.8	4,034.7	116.5
Net errors and omissions	–476.0	296.3	–652.3
Overall balance	619.9	585.3	608.8

* Including the transactions of enterprises operating in the Colón Free Zone.

Source: IMF, *International Financial Statistics*.

External Trade

PRINCIPAL COMMODITIES

('000 balboas)

Imports c.i.f.	2006	2007	2008
Food and live animals	556,660	737,830	990,839
Mineral products	919,126	1,331,529	2,003,609
Chemicals and chemical products	522,161	643,643	780,094
Plastics, rubber and articles thereof	210,454	282,982	343,952
Textiles and articles thereof	169,953	223,895	276,245
Metals and manufactures of metal	388,368	530,211	826,700
Machinery and apparatus	878,577	1,415,090	1,768,606
Transport materials	531,824	813,776	932,841
Total (incl. others)	4,817,655	6,869,921	9,009,934

Exports f.o.b.*	2006	2007	2008†
Sugar	21,285	17,637	15,149
Bananas	109,437	111,615	98,581
Melons	166,431	202,523	213,994
Pineapples	36,922	42,855	36,503
Coffee	13,363	16,303	15,399
Shellfish	50,239	56,367	40,624
Fresh and frozen fish and fillets (incl. yellowfin tuna)	250,148	286,820	346,923
Meat from cattle	14,246	11,636	13,161
Standing cattle	30,590	16,429	—
Total (incl. others)	1,021,820	1,126,799	1,144,714

* Including re-exports.

† Preliminary.

PRINCIPAL TRADING PARTNERS*
('000 balboas)

Imports c.i.f.†	2006	2007	2008
Brazil	150,047	140,703	140,285
China, People's Republic	166,844	358,725	454,407
Colombia	169,910	192,109	240,779
Costa Rica	246,243	326,226	456,011
El Salvador	59,077	72,337	93,309
Germany	56,828	87,350	125,560
Guatemala	84,859	107,372	145,125
Japan	229,243	328,945	385,137
Korea, Republic	165,674	267,671	263,550
Mexico	173,017	212,027	312,615
Netherlands Antilles‡	488,250	489,156	50,881
Peru	n.a.	69,029	107,026
Spain	73,925	106,958	142,131
USA	1,295,624	2,079,584	2,683,527
Venezuela	51,504	55,401	44,957
Total (incl. others)	4,817,655	6,869,921	9,009,934

Exports f.o.b.	2006	2007	2008§
Belgium-Luxembourg	38,646	42,347	11,688
China, People's Republic	13,449	68,032	49,113
Colombia	18,813	19,138	12,142
Costa Rica	45,608	57,101	65,983
Dominican Republic	16,030	13,440	16,960
El Salvador	9,305	8,022	7,521
Guatemala	33,018	16,712	8,147
Honduras	17,914	20,923	17,152
Hong Kong	n.a.	5,337	n.a.
India	n.a.	7,791	6,671
Italy	26,384	18,309	29,598
Mexico	10,453	9,252	8,901
Netherlands	68,306	114,640	122,756
Nicaragua	17,248	12,879	13,462
Portugal	11,731	13,076	n.a.
Puerto Rico	13,871	9,045	13,062
Spain	83,435	55,792	56,926
Sweden	56,856	62,150	62,689
Taiwan	23,664	38,920	46,665
United Kingdom	34,650	61,239	61,326
USA	393,512	391,402	435,116
Total (incl. others)	1,021,820	1,126,799	1,144,714

* Including trade with the Colón Free Zone (CFZ) ('000 balboas): *Imports:* 573,479 in 2006; 714,614 in 2007; 823,952 in 2008. *Exports:* 16,341 in 2006; 20,229 in 2007; 19,748 in 2008 (preliminary).

† Including imports to the Petroleum Free Zone ('000 balboas): 162,690 in 2006; 360,009 in 2007; 1,381,650 in 2008.

‡ Curaçao only.

§ Preliminary.

Transport

RAILWAYS
(traffic)

	2002*	2003	2004
Passenger-km (million)	35,693	52,324	53,377
Freight ton-km (million)	20,665	41,863	52,946

* Panama Railway only.

Source: UN, *Statistical Yearbook*.

ROAD TRAFFIC
(motor vehicles in use)

	2000	2001	2002
Cars	223,433	219,372	224,504
Buses and coaches	16,865	15,558	16,371
Lorries and vans	75,454	73,139	74,247

2007: Cars 436,205; Buses and coaches 20,133; Lorries and vans 174,482; Motorcycles and mopeds 20,133.

Source: IRF, *World Road Statistics*.

SHIPPING

Merchant Fleet
(registered at 31 December)

	2006	2007	2008
Number of vessels	7,183	7,605	8,065
Total displacement ('000 grt)	154,964.6	168,165.5	183,503.5

Source: Lloyd's Register-Fairplay, *World Fleet Statistics*.

International Sea-borne Freight Traffic
('000 metric tons)

	2001	2002	2003
Goods loaded	108,456	110,556	99,516
Goods unloaded	84,864	99,288	76,152

Panama Canal Traffic

	2006/07	2007/08	2008/09
Transits	14,721	14,702	14,342
Cargo ('000 long tons)	208,220.2	209,763.1	198,014.3

Source: Panama Canal Authority.

CIVIL AVIATION
(traffic on scheduled services)

	2005	2006	2007
Kilometres flown (million)	55	67	81
Passenger-km (million)	5,206	6,078	7,940
Total ton-km (million)	37	36	36

Source: UN Economic Commission for Latin America and the Caribbean, *Statistical Yearbook*.

Tourism

VISITOR ARRIVALS BY COUNTRY OF ORIGIN
(arrivals at Tocumen International Airport)

	2005	2006	2007
Argentina	11,629	14,230	19,093
Canada	19,660	29,392	39,097
Chile	8,150	9,985	13,478
Colombia	108,628	129,418	174,476
Costa Rica	25,455	31,248	42,158
Dominican Republic	7,396	9,049	11,917
Ecuador	25,903	35,024	47,387
El Salvador	9,279	11,545	15,567
France	7,289	9,396	11,752
Germany	4,745	6,275	8,517
Guatemala	14,349	17,361	23,494
Honduras	6,584	8,143	10,950
Italy	6,617	10,584	14,952
Jamaica	5,593	6,890	9,636
Mexico	29,280	34,507	46,787
Nicaragua	6,056	7,332	9,903
Peru	12,592	15,416	20,761
Puerto Rico	8,625	10,585	14,920
Spain	10,838	12,267	16,555
USA	160,288	191,094	258,249
Venezuela	18,892	23,113	31,157
Total (incl. others)	576,050	703,745	948,946

Tourism receipts (US $ million, excl. passenger transport): 960 in 2006; 1,185 in 2007; 1,408 in 2008 (provisional).

Source: World Tourism Organization.

Communications Media

	2007	2008	2009
Telephones ('000 main lines in use)	495.2	524.0	537.1
Mobile cellular telephones ('000 subscribers)	3,010.6	3,915.2	5,677.1
Internet users ('000)	745.3	936.5	959.9
Broadband subscribers ('000)	150.3	196.2	201.1

Personal computers: 96,823 (28.5 per 1,000 persons) in 2008.

Radio receivers ('000 in use): 815 in 1997.

Television receivers ('000 in use): 550 in 2000.

Daily newspapers: 8 in 2004.

Sources: UNESCO, *Statistical Yearbook*; UN, *Statistical Yearbook*; International Telecommunication Union.

Education

(2007/08 unless otherwise indicated, provisional)

	Institutions*	Teachers	Students		
			Males	Females	Total
Pre-primary	1,662	5,315	48,356	46,572	94,928
Primary	3,116	18,364	230,645	214,462	445,107
Secondary	442	17,337	130,846	135,914	266,760
General	n.a.	13,814	108,793	115,124	223,917
Vocational	n.a.	3,523	22,053	20,790	42,843
Tertiary†	24	12,209	52,287	80,373	132,660

* 2001/02 figures.

† 2006/07.

Sources: Ministry of Education; UNESCO, *Statistical Yearbook*; UNESCO Institute for Statistics.

Pupil-teacher ratio (primary education, UNESCO estimate): 24.2 in 2007/08 (Source: UNESCO Institute for Statistics).

Adult literacy rate (UNESCO estimates): 93.5% (males 94.1%; females 92.8%) in 2008 (Source: UNESCO Institute for Statistics).

Directory

The Constitution

Under the terms of the amendments to the Constitution, implemented by the adoption of Reform Acts No. 1 and No. 2 in October 1978, and by the approval by referendum of the Constitutional Act in April 1983, the 67 (later 71) members of the unicameral Asamblea Nacional (National Assembly) are elected by popular vote every five years. Executive power is exercised by the President of the Republic, who is also elected by popular vote for a term of five years. Two Vice-Presidents are elected by popular vote to assist the President. The President appoints the Cabinet. The armed forces are barred from participating in elections. In July 2004 further amendments to the Constitution were adopted, including a reduction (to 71) in the number of members of the renamed Asamblea Nacional (National Assembly) from 2009, the abolition of parliamentary immunity from prosecution, and the creation of a constitutional assembly to consider future changes to the Constitution.

The Government

HEAD OF STATE

President: Ricardo A. Martinelli Berrocal (took office 1 July 2009).

Vice-President: Juan Carlos Varela Rodríguez.

THE CABINET
(July 2010)

The Government is formed by a coalition, comprising representatives of Cambio Democrático (CD), the Partido Panameñista (PP) and the Unión Patriótica (UP), several Independents (Ind.) and a dissident member of the Partido Revolucionario Democrático (PRD).

Minister of Foreign Affairs: Juan Carlos Varela Rodríguez (PP).

Minister of Public Security: José Raúl Mulino (UP).

Minister of the Interior: Roxana Méndez (CD).

Minister of Public Works: Federico José Suárez (Ind.).

Minister of the Economy and Finance: Alberto Vallarino Clement (PP).

Minister of Agricultural Development: Emilio Kieswetter (CD).

Minister of Commerce and Industry: Roberto Henríquez (CD).

Minister of Health: Franklin Vergara J. (Ind.).

Minister of Labour and Social Welfare: Alma Lorena Cortés Aguilar (CD).

Minister of Education: Lucinda Molinar (Ind.).

Minister of Housing: Carlos Alberto Duboy Sierra (PP).

Minister of the Presidency: Demetrio Papadimitriu (CD).

Minister of Social Development: Guillermo Antonio Ferrufino Benítez (CD).

Minister of Canal Affairs: Rómulo Roux (Ind.).

Minister of Tourism: Salomón Shamah Zuchin (Ind.).

Minister of Micro-, Small and Medium Enterprises: GISELLE BURILLO SÁIZ (PRD dissident).

MINISTRIES

Office of the President: Palacio de Las Garzas, Corregimiento de San Felipe, Panamá 1; tel. 527-9600; fax 527-7693; e-mail web@presidencia.gob.pa; internet www.presidencia.gob.pa.

Ministry of Agricultural Development: Edif. 576, Calle Manuel E. Melo, Altos de Curundú, Apdo 5390, Panamá 5; tel. 507-0600; e-mail infomida@mida.gob.pa; internet www.mida.gob.pa.

Ministry of Commerce and Industry: Plaza Edison, Sector El Paical, 2° y 3°, Apdo 0815-0111, Panamá 4; tel. 560-0600; fax 560-0663; e-mail contactenos@mici.gob.pa; internet www.mici.gob.pa.

Ministry of the Economy and Finance: (Economy) Edif. Ogawa, Vía España, Calle del Santuario Nacional, Apdo 5245, Panamá 5; (Finance) Antiguo Edif. de Hacienda y Tesoro, Calle 34 y 35, Avda Perú, Calidonia, Panamá; tel. (Economy) 507-7000; tel. (Finance) 507-7600; e-mail prensa@mef.gob.pa; internet www.mef.gob.pa.

Ministry of Education: Villa Cárdenas, Ancón, Apdo 0816-04049, Panamá 3; tel. 511-4400; fax 511-4440; e-mail meduca@meduca.gob.pa; internet www.meduca.gob.pa.

Ministry of Foreign Affairs: Edif. 26, Palacio Bolívar, Calle 3, San Felipe, Panamá 4; tel. 511-4100; fax 511-4022; e-mail prensa@mire.gob.pa; internet www.mire.gob.pa.

Ministry of Health: Apdo 2048, Panamá 1; tel. and fax 512-9202; e-mail saludaldia@minsa.gob.pa; internet www.minsa.gob.pa.

Ministry of Housing: Edif. Plaza Edison, 4°, Avda Ricardo J. Alfaro, Apdo 5228, Panamá 5; tel. 579-9200; fax 579-9651; e-mail info@mivi.gob.pa; internet www.mivi.gob.pa.

Ministry of the Interior: Avda 7 y Calle 3, Central San Felipe, Apdo 1628, Panamá 1; tel. 512-7600; fax 512-2126; e-mail despachosuperior@mingob.gob.pa; internet www.mingob.gob.pa.

Ministry of Labour and Social Welfare: Plaza Edison, 5°, Avda Ricardo J. Alfaro (Tumba Muerto) Betania, Apdo 2441, Panamá 3; tel. 560-1100; fax 560-1117; e-mail mitradel@mitradel.gob.pa; internet www.mitradel.gob.pa.

Ministry of the Presidency: Palacio de Las Garzas, Corregimiento de San Felipe, Apdo 2189, Panamá 1; tel. 527-9600; e-mail ofasin@presidencia.gob.pa; internet www.presidencia.gob.pa.

Ministry of Public Security: Avda 7 y Calle 3, Central San Felipe, Apdo 1628, Panamá 1; tel. 512-7600; internet www.minseg.gob.pa.

Ministry of Public Works: Edif. Principal 1019, Curundú, Zona 1, Apdo 1632, Panamá 1; tel. 507-9400; fax 507-9419; e-mail info@mop.gob.pa; internet www.mop.gob.pa.

Ministry of Social Development: Plaza Edison, 4°, Avda Ricardo J. Alfaro, Apdo 680-50, El Dorado, Panamá; tel. 500-6001; fax 500-6020; e-mail mides@mides.gob.pa; internet www.mides.gob.pa.

President and Legislature

PRESIDENT

Election, 3 May 2009

Candidate	Votes	% of valid votes
Ricardo A. Martinelli Berrocal (Alianza por el Cambio*)	952,333	60.03
Balbina del Carmen Herrera Araúz (Un País para Todos†)	597,227	37.65
Guillermo Endara Galimany (Vanguardia Moral de la Patria)	36,867	2.32
Total valid votes‡	1,586,427	100.00

* Electoral alliance comprising Cambio Democrático, the Partido Panameñista, the Movimiento Liberal Republicano Nacionalista and the Unión Patriótica.

† Electoral alliance comprising the Partido Revolucionario Democrático, the Partido Popular and the Partido Liberal.

‡ In addition, there were 19,105 blank and 30,976 invalid ballots.

ASAMBLEA NACIONAL
(National Assembly)

President: JOSÉ LUIS VARELA RODRÍGUEZ.

General Election, 3 May 2009

Affiliation/Party	% of votes	Seats
Alianza por el Cambio	56.0	42
Partido Panameñista	22.2	22
Cambio Democrático	23.4	14
Unión Patriótica	5.7	4
Movimiento Liberal Republicano Nacionalista	4.7	2
Un País para Todos	40.6	27
Partido Revolucionario Democrático	35.7	26
Partido Popular	3.7	1
Partido Liberal	1.2	—
Vanguardia Moral de la Patria	1.0	—
Independents	2.4	2
Total	100.0	71

Election Commission

Tribunal Electoral: Edif. del Tribunal Electoral-Dirección Superior, Avda Ecuador y Calle 33, Apdo 5281, Panamá 5; tel. 507-8000; e-mail secretaria-general@tribunal-electoral.gob.pa; internet www.tribunal-electoral.gob.pa; f. 1956; independent; Pres. ERASMO PINILLA CASTILLERO.

Political Organizations

Cambio Democrático (CD): Parque Lefevre, Plaza Carolina, arriba de la Juguetería del Super 99, Panamá; tel. 217-2643; fax 217-2645; e-mail cambio.democratico@hotmail.com; formally registered 1998; contested the 2009 elections as part of the Alianza por el Cambio; Pres. RICARDO A. MARTINELLI BERROCAL; Sec.-Gen. GIACOMO TAMBURELLI.

Movimiento Liberal Republicano Nacionalista (MOLIRENA): Calle 66 (Calle Belén), Casa Duplex 46-A, Corregimiento de San Francisco, Panamá; tel. 399-5280; fax 399-5288; formally registered 1982; conservative; contested the 2009 elections as part of the Alianza por el Cambio; Pres. SERGIO GONZÁLEZ RUIZ; Sec.-Gen. CLAUDIO LACAYO ALVAREZ.

Partido Liberal: Edif. Torre Universal, 11°, Avda Federico Boyd, Panamá; tel. 209-2574; fax 209-2575; e-mail partidoliberal@elveloz.com; f. 2005; Pres. JOAQUÍN F. FRANCO VÁSQUEZ; Sec.-Gen. AUGUSTO C. AROSEMENA.

Partido Panameñista (PP): Avda Perú y Calle 37, No 37–41, al lado de Casa la Esperanza, Apdo 9610, Panamá 4; tel. 227-0028; fax 227-0951; e-mail partidopanamenista@hotmail.com; f. 1990 by Arnulfista faction of the Partido Panameñista Auténtico as Partido Arnulfista (PA); name changed as above in Jan. 2005; contested the 2009 elections as part of the Alianza por el Cambio; Pres. JUAN CARLOS VARELA RODRÍGUEZ; Sec.-Gen. FRANCISCO ALEMÁN MENDOZA.

Partido Popular: Avda Perú, frente al Parque Porras, Apdo 6322, Panamá 5; tel. 225-2381; fax 227-3944; e-mail pdc@cwpanama.net; f. 1960 as Partido Demócrata Cristiano; name changed as above in 2001; contested the 2009 elections as part of the Un País para Todos alliance; Pres. MILTON COHEN-HENRÍQUEZ; Sec.-Gen. ROBERTO MÉNDEZ MOREIRA.

Partido Revolucionario Democrático (PRD): Avda México, entre Calle 27 y 28, Apdo 3-85, Panamá 3; tel. 225-8460; fax 225-8476; e-mail prdpanama@yahoo.com; f. 1979; supports policies of late Gen. Omar Torrijos Herrera; combination of Marxists, Christian Democrats and some business interests; contested the 2009 elections as part of the Un País para Todos alliance; Pres. FRANCISCO SÁNCHEZ CÁRDENAS; Sec.-Gen. MITCHELL CONSTANTINO DOENS.

Unión Patriótica (UP): Edif. Maheli, Avda Ramón Arias, esq. con la Vía Transístmica, Panamá; tel. 261-2294; fax 261-5083; e-mail administracion@partidosolidaridad.com; f. 2007 following merger of Partido Liberal Nacional and Partido Solidaridad; contested the 2009 elections as part of the Alianza por el Cambio; Pres. ANÍBAL GALINDO N.; Sec.-Gen. JORGE RICARDO FÁBREGA.

Vanguardia Moral de la Patria (VMP): Edif. Río Plaza, No 10, planta baja, Calle Décima, esq. con Calle La Pulida, Corregimiento de Río Abajo, Panamá; tel. 221-9337; f. 2004; Pres. (vacant); Gen. Sec. ANA MAE DÍAZ DE ENDARA.

Diplomatic Representation

EMBASSIES IN PANAMA

Argentina: PH Torre Global, 24°, Calle 50, Apdo 832-0458, Panamá 1; tel. 302-0005; fax 302-0004; e-mail embajada@embargen.org; internet www.embargen.org; Ambassador JORGE ALBERTO ARGUINDEGUI.

Belize: Villa de la Fuente 1, F-32, Calle 22, POB 0819-12255, Panamá; tel. 236-3762; fax 236-4132; e-mail nmusag@cwpanama.net; Ambassador ALFREDO MARTÍNEZ.

Bolivia: Calle G, Casa 3, El Cangrejo, Apdo 0823-05603, Panamá; tel. 269-0274; fax 264-3868; e-mail emb_bol_pan@cwpanama.net; internet embolivia-panama.com.pa; Ambassador EDGAR SOLIZ MORALES.

Brazil: Edif. El Dorado 24, 1°, Calle Elvira Méndez y Avda Ricardo Arango, Urb. Campo Alegre, Apdo 4287, Panamá 5; tel. 263-5322; fax 269-6316; e-mail embrasil@embrasil.org.pa; internet www.embrasil.org.pa; Ambassador EDUARDO PRISCO PARAÍSO RAMOS.

Canada: Edif. World Trade Center, Torres de las Américas, Torre A, 11°, Punta Pacífica, Apdo 0832-2446, Panamá; tel. 294-2500; fax 294-2514; e-mail panam@international.gc.ca; internet www.canadainternational.gc.ca/panama; Ambassador PATRICIA LANGAN-TORELL.

Chile: Torres de las Américas, 7°, Punta Pacífica, Apdo 7341, Panamá 5; tel. 294-8901; fax 294-8904; e-mail echilepa@cw.panama.net; internet www.embachilepanama.com; Ambassador ALBERTO LABBÉ GALILEA.

China (Taiwan): Edif. Torre Hong Kong Bank, 10°, Avda Samuel Lewis, Apdo 7492, Panamá 5; tel. 269-1347; fax 264-9118; e-mail panama@mail.gio.gov.tw; internet www.taiwanembassy.org/pa; Ambassador SHEN-YEAW KO.

Colombia: Edif. World Trade Center, Of. 1801, 18°, Calle 53, Urb. Marbella, Panamá; tel. 264-9513; fax 223-1134; e-mail epanama@cancilleria.gov.co; internet www.embajadaenpanama.gov.co; Ambassador GINA BENEDETTI DE VÉLEZ.

Costa Rica: Edif. Plaza Omega, 3°, Calle Samuel Lewis, Apdo 0816-02038, Panamá; tel. 264-2980; fax 264-4057; e-mail embajadacr@cwpanama.net; Ambassador EKHART PETERS SEVEERS.

Cuba: Avda Cuba y Ecuador 33, Apdo 6-2291, Bellavista, Panamá; tel. 227-5277; fax 225-6681; e-mail respanama@sinfo.net; Ambassador REINALDO CARLOS CALVIAC LAFERTÉ.

Dominican Republic: Torre Delta, 16°, Calle Elvira Méndez, Área Bancaria, Apdo 6250, Panamá 5; tel. 263-6324; fax 263-7725; e-mail embajadadompa.zlg@cableonda.net; Ambassador GRECIA FIORDALICIA PICHARDO POLANCO.

Ecuador: Edif. Torre 2000, 6°, Calle 50, Marbella, Bellavista, Panamá; tel. 264-2654; fax 223-0159; e-mail ecuador@cwpanama.net; Ambassador ELSA BEATRIZ VILLACÍS ROCA.

Egypt: Calle 55, No 15, El Cangrejo, Apdo 7080, Panamá 5; tel. 263-5020; fax 264-8406; e-mail egempma@hotmail.com; Ambassador REDA HALIM FAHMY IBRAHIM.

El Salvador: Edif. ADR, 8°, Avda Samuel Lewis y Calle 58, Apdo 0823-05432, Panamá; tel. 223-3020; fax 264-6148; e-mail embasalva@cwpanama.net; Ambassador EFRÉN BERNAL.

France: Plaza de Francia 1, Las Bovedas, San Felipe, Apdo 0816-07945, Panamá 1; tel. 211-6200; fax 211-6201; e-mail cad.panama-amba@diplomatie.gouv.fr; internet www.ambafrance-pa.org; Ambassador HUGUES GOISBAULT.

Germany: Edif. World Trade Center, 20°, Calle 53E, Marbella, Apdo 0832-0536, Panamá 5; tel. 263-7733; fax 223-6664; e-mail germpanama@cwp.net.pa; internet www.panama.diplo.de; Ambassador MICHAEL GRAU.

Guatemala: Edif. World Trade Center, 2°, Of. 203, Calle 53, Urb. Marbella, Panamá 9; tel. 269-3475; fax 223-1922; e-mail embpanama@minex.gob.gt; Ambassador STELLA RIEGER DE GARCÍA-GRANADOS.

Haiti: Edif. Dora Luz, 2°, Calle 1, El Cangrejo, Apdo 442, Panamá 9; tel. 269-3443; fax 223-1767; e-mail embhaitipan@cableonda.net; Chargé d'affaires a.i. BOCCHIT EDMOND.

Holy See: Punta Paitilla, Avda Balboa y Vía Italia, Apdo 0816-00457, Panamá 5 (Apostolic Nunciature); tel. 269-2102; fax 264-2116; e-mail nuncio@cableonda.net; Apostolic Nuncio Most Rev. ANDRÉS CARRASCOSA COSO (Titular Archbishop of Elo).

Honduras: Edif. Bay Mall, 1°, Avda Balboa 112, Apdo 0816-03427, Panamá 5; tel. 264-5513; fax 264-4628; e-mail info@embajadadehonduras.com.pa; internet www.embajadadehonduras.com.pa; Ambassador NERY M. FÚNES PADILLA.

India: Avda Federico Boyd y Calle 51, Bella Vista, Apdo 0823-05815, Panamá 7; tel. 264-3043; fax 209-6779; e-mail ambassador@indempan.org; internet www.indempan.org; Ambassador VISHNU NAMDEO HADE.

Israel: Edif. Torre Banco General, 17°, Calle Aquilino De La Guardia, Urb. Marbella, Panamá; tel. 208-4700; fax 208-4755; e-mail info@panama.mfa.gov.il; internet panama.mfa.gov.il; Ambassador YOED MAGEN.

Italy: Torre Banco Exterior, 25°, Avda Balboa, Apdo 0816-04453, Panamá 9; tel. 225-8950; fax 227-4906; e-mail ambpana.mail@esteri.it; internet www.ambpanama.esteri.it; Ambassador PLACIDO VIGO.

Japan: Calle 50 y 60E, Urb. Obarrio, Apdo 0816-06807, Panamá 1; tel. 263-6155; fax 263-6019; e-mail taiship2@cwpanama.net; internet www.panama.emb-japan.go.jp; Ambassador MAKOTO MISAWA.

Korea, Republic: Edif. Victoria Plaza, 4°, Calle 53, Urb. Obarrio, Apdo 8096, Panamá 7; tel. 264-8203; fax 264-8825; e-mail panama@mofat.go.kr; internet pan.mofat.go.kr; Ambassador DOO JUNG-SOO.

Libya: Avda Balboa y Calle 32 (frente al Edif. Atalaya), Apdo 6-894, El Dorado, Panamá; tel. 227-3342; fax 227-3886; Chargé d'affaires a.i. NAGI A. S. KSUDA.

Mexico: Edif. Torre ADR, 10°, Avda Samuel Lewis y Calle 58, Urb. Obarrio, Corregimiento de Bella Vista, Apdo 0823-05788, Panamá; tel. 263-4900; fax 263-5446; e-mail embamexpan@cwpanama.net; internet www.sre.gob.mx/panama; Ambassador YANERIT CRISTINA MORGAN SOTOMAYOR.

Nicaragua: Edif. De Lessep's, 3°, Calle Manuel Maria Icaza, Urb. Obarrio, Panamá; tel. 264-3080; fax 264-5425; e-mail embapana@sinfo.net; Ambassador ANTENOR ALBERTO FERREY PERNUDI.

Paraguay: Edif. Galerías Balboa, 3°, Of. 45, Avda Balboa y Aquilino de la Guardia, Bella Vista, Panamá; tel. 263-4782; fax 269-4247; e-mail embapar_pa@cwpanama.net; Ambassador. JUAN CARLOS RAMIREZ MONTALBETTI.

Peru: Edif. World Trade Center, 12°, Calle 53, Urb. Marbella, Apdo 4516, Panamá 5; tel. 223-1112; fax 269-6809; e-mail embaperu@cableonda.net; Ambassador GABRIEL GARCÍA PIKE.

Russia: Torre IBC, 10°, Avda Manuel Espinosa Batista, Apdo 6-4697, El Dorado, Panamá; tel. 264-1408; fax 264-1588; e-mail emruspan@sinfo.net; internet www.panama.mid.ru; Ambassador ALEXEI A. ERMAKOV.

Spain: Plaza de Belisario Porras, entre Avda Perú y Calle 33A, Apdo 0816-06600, Panamá 1; tel. 227-5122; fax 227-6284; e-mail emb.panama@mae.es; Ambassador JOSÉ MANUEL LÓPEZ-BARRÓN DE LABRA.

United Kingdom: MMG Tower, 4°, Calle 53, Urb. Marbella, Apdo 0816-07946, Panamá 1; tel. 269-0866; fax 263-5138; e-mail britemb@cwpanama.net; internet ukinpanama.fco.gov.uk; Ambassador RICHARD AUSTEN.

USA: Edif. 783, Avda Demetrio Basilio Lakas, Apdo 0816-02561, Clayton, Panamá 5; tel. 207-7000; fax 317-5568; e-mail panamaweb@state.gov; internet panama.usembassy.gov; Ambassador PHYLLIS MARIE POWERS.

Uruguay: Edif. Los Delfines, Of. 8, Avda Balboa, Calle 50E Este, Apdo 0816-03616, Panamá 5; tel. 264-2838; fax 264-8908; e-mail urupanam@cwpanama.net; internet www.urupana.org; Ambassador FRANCISCO HEBER PURIFICATTI GAMARRA.

Venezuela: Torre HSBC, 5°, Avda Samuel Lewis, Apdo 661, Panamá 1; tel. 269-1244; fax 269-1916; e-mail info@venezuela.org.pa; internet www.venezuela.org.pa; Ambassador JORGE LUIS DURÁN CENTENO.

Viet Nam: 52 José Gabriel Duque, La Cresta, Apdo 12434-6A, El Dorado, Panamá; tel. 264-2551; fax 265-6056; e-mail convietnam@cwpanama.net; Ambassador HOANG CONG THUY.

Judicial System

The judiciary in Panama comprises the following courts and judges: Corte Suprema de Justicia (Supreme Court of Justice), with nine judges appointed for a 10-year term; 10 Tribunales Superiores de Distrito Judicial (High Courts) with 36 magistrates; 54 Jueces de Circuito (Circuit Judges), and 89 Jueces Municipales (Municipal Judges).

Panama is divided into four judicial districts and has seven High Courts of Appeal. The first judicial district covers the provinces of Panamá, Colón, Darién and the region of Kuna Yala and contains two High Courts of Appeal, one dealing with criminal cases, the other dealing with civil cases. The second judicial district covers the provinces of Coclé and Veraguas and contains the third High Court of Appeal, located in Penonomé. The third judicial district covers the provinces of Chiriquí and Bocas del Toro and contains the fourth High Court of Appeal, located in David. The fourth judicial district covers the provinces of Herrera and Los Santos and contains the fifth High Court of Appeal, located in Las Tablas. Each of these courts deals with civil and criminal cases in their respective provinces. There are two additional special High Courts of Appeal. The first hears maritime, labour, family and infancy cases; the second deals with anti-trust cases and consumer affairs.

Corte Suprema de Justicia

Edif. 236, Calle Culebra, Ancón, Apdo 1770, Panamá 1; tel. 262-9833; e-mail prensa@organojudicial.gob.pa; internet www.organojudicial.gob.pa.

President of the Supreme Court of Justice: ANÍBAL SALAS.

Procurator-General: GIUSEPPE BONISSI.

Religion

The Constitution recognizes freedom of worship and the Roman Catholic Church as the religion of the majority of the population.

CHRISTIANITY

The Roman Catholic Church

For ecclesiastical purposes, Panama comprises one archdiocese, five dioceses, the territorial prelature of Bocas del Toro and the Apostolic Vicariate of Darién. Some 83% of the population are Roman Catholics.

Bishops' Conference

Conferencia Episcopal de Panamá, Secretariado General, Apdo 870933, Panamá 7; tel. 223-0075; fax 223-0042; internet www.iglesia.org.pa.

f. 1958; statutes approved 1986; Pres. Rt Rev. JOSÉ LUIS LACUNZA MAESTROJUAN (Bishop of David).

Archbishop of Panamá: Most Rev. JOSÉ DIMAS CEDEÑO DELGADO, Arzobispado Metropolitano, Calle 1a Sur Carrasquilla, Apdo 6386, Panamá 5; tel. 261-0002; fax 261-0820; e-mail ascn4@keops.utp.ac.pa.

The Baptist Church

The Baptist Convention of Panama (Convención Bautista de Panamá): Apdo 0816-01761, Panamá 5; tel. and fax 259-5485; e-mail convencionbautistadepanama@hotmail.com; f. 1959; Pres. FRANCISCO MEDINA; Sec. ESMERALDA DE TUY; 7,573 mems.

The Anglican Communion

Panama comprises one of the five dioceses of the Iglesia Anglicana de la Región Central de América.

Bishop of Panama: Rt Rev. JULIO MURRAY, Edif. 331A, Calle Culebra, Apdo R, Balboa; tel. 212-0062; fax 262-2097.

BAHÁ'Í FAITH

National Spiritual Assembly of the Bahá'ís: Apdo 850-625, Las Cumbres, Panamá 15; tel. 231-1191; fax 231-6909; e-mail panbahai@cwpanama.net; internet panamabahai.net; mems resident in 529 localities; Nat. Sec. YOLANDA RODRÍGUEZ VILLAREAL.

The Press

DAILIES

Crítica Libre: Vía Fernández de Córdoba, Apdo B-4, Panamá 9A; tel. 261-0575; fax 230-0132; e-mail esotop@epasa.com; internet www.critica.com.pa; f. 1925; morning; Pres. ROSARIO ARIAS DE GALINDO; Dir JUAN PRITSIOLAS; circ. 40,000.

DIA a DIA: Vía Ricardo J. Alfaro, al lado de la USMA, Apdo B-4, Panamá 9A; tel. 230-7777; fax 230-2279; e-mail editor.diaadia@epasa.com; internet www.diaadia.com.pa; Pres. FRANCISCO ARIAS V.; Gen. Man. RAMÓN R. VALLARINO A.

La Estrella de Panamá: Calle Alejandro Duque, Vía Transistmica y Frangipani, Panamá; tel. 227-0555; fax 227-1026; e-mail laestre@estrelladepanama.com; internet www.estrelladepanama.com; f. 1853; morning; Pres. EBRAHIM ASVAT; Editor GERARDO BERROA; circ. 10,000.

El Panamá América: Vía Ricardo J. Alfaro, al lado de la USMA, Apdo 0834-02787, Panamá 9A; tel. 230-7777; fax 230-7773; e-mail director@epasa.com; internet pa-digital.com.pa; f. 1925; morning; independent; affiliated to Interamerican Press Asscn; Pres. FRANCISCO ARIAS V.; Dir GUIDO RODRÍGUEZ LUGARI; circ. 25,000.

La Prensa: Avda 12 de Octubre y Calle C, Hato Pintado, Pueblo Nuevo, Apdo 0819-05620, Panamá; tel. 222-1222; fax 221-7328; e-mail editor@prensa.com; internet www.prensa.com; f. 1980; morning; independent; Pres. RICARDO ALBERTO ARIAS; Editor FERNANDO BERGUIDO; circ. 38,000.

El Siglo: Calle 58 Obarrio, Panamá; tel. 264-3921; fax 269-6954; e-mail redaccion@elsiglo.com; internet www.elsiglo.com; f. 1985; morning; acquired by Geo-Media, SA, in 2001; Pres. Dr NIVIA ROSSANA CASTRELLÓN; Editor OCTAVIO COGLEY; circ. 30,000.

PERIODICALS

Dirección de Estadística y Censo: Avda Balboa y Federico Boyd, Apdo 0816-01521, Panamá 5; tel. 210-4800; fax 210-4801; e-mail cie_dec@contraloria.gob.pa; internet www.contraloria.gob.pa/dec; f. 1941; published by the Contraloría General de la República; statistical survey in series according to subjects; Controller-Gen. CARLOS A. VALLARINO R.; Dir of Statistics and Census DIMAS QUIEL.

FOB Colón Free Zone: Apdo 0819-06908, El Dorado, Panamá; tel. 225-6638; fax 225-0466; e-mail focusint@sinfo.net; internet www.colonfreezone.com; annual; bilingual trade directory; publ. by Focus Publications (Int.), SA; Editor ISRAEL ARGUEDAS; circ. 60,000.

Focus Panama: 742 Calle 2A, Perejil, Panamá; tel. 225-6638; fax 225-0466; e-mail focusint@sinfo.net; internet www.focuspublicationsint.com; f. 1970; 2 a year; publ. by Focus Publications; visitors' guide; separate English and Spanish editions; Dir KENNETH J. JONES; circ. 100,000.

Informativo Industrial: Apdo 6-4798, El Dorado, Panamá 1; tel. 230-0482; fax 230-0805; monthly; organ of the Sindicato de Industriales de Panamá; Pres. GASPAR GARCÍA DE PAREDES.

Mi Diario, La Voz de Panamá: Avda 12 de Octubre y Calle C, Hato Pintado, Pueblo Nuevo, Apdo 0819-05620, Panamá; tel. 222-9000; fax 222-9090; e-mail midiario@midiario.com; internet www.midiario.com; f. 2003 by La Prensa (q.v.); Dir LORENZO ÁBREGO.

Revista SIETE: Vía Ricardo J. Alfaro, al lado de la USMA, Apdo B-4, Panamá 9A; tel. 230-7777; fax 230-1033; e-mail revista.siete@epasa.com; internet www.epasa.com/siete; weekly; Editor NAYLA G. MONTENEGRO.

PRESS ASSOCIATION

Sindicato de Periodistas de Panamá: Avda Gorgas 287, Panamá; tel. 214-0163; fax 214-0164; e-mail sindiperpana@yahoo.com; f. 1949; Sec.-Gen. FILEMÓN MEDINA RAMOS.

Publishers

Editora Panamá América (EPASA): Vía Ricardo J. Alfaro, al lado de la USMA, Apdo B-4, Panamá 9A; tel. 230-7777; fax 230-0136; e-mail gerente.general@epasa.com; internet www.epasa.com; Pres. FRANCISCO ARIAS V.; Gen. Man. RAMÓN R. VALLARINO A.

Editora Sibauste, SA: Panamá; tel. 229-4577; fax 229-4582; e-mail esibauste@cwpanama.net; Editor DENIS DE SIBAUSTE.

Focus Publications: Calle 2a 742, Perejil, Apdo 0819-06908, El Dorado, Panamá; tel. 225-6638; fax 225-0466; e-mail focusint@sinfo.net; internet www.focuspublicationsint.com; f. 1970; guides, trade directories, yearbooks and maps; Gen. Man. KENNETH J. JONES.

Ruth Casa Editorial: Edif. Los Cristales, Of. No 6, Calle 38 y Avda Cuba, Apdo 2235, Zona 9A, Panamá; e-mail webmaster@forumdesalternatives.org; internet www.forumdesalternatives.org/Ruth_publicaciones.htm; Pres. FRANÇOIS HOUTART.

GOVERNMENT PUBLISHING HOUSE

Editorial Mariano Arosemena: Instituto Nacional de Cultura, Apdo 662, Panamá 1; tel. 211-4000; fax 211-4016; e-mail comunicacion@inac.gob.pa; internet www.inac.gob.pa; f. 1974; division of National Institute of Culture; literature, history, social sciences, archaeology; Dir LESLIE MOCK.

Broadcasting and Communications

REGULATORY AUTHORITY

Autoridad Nacional de los Servicios Públicos: Vía España, Edif. Office Park, Apdo 4931, Panamá 5; tel. 278-4500; fax 278-4600; e-mail webmaster@ersp.gob.pa; f. 1996 as Ente Regulador de los Servicios Públicos; name changed as above in 2006; state regulator with responsibility for television, radio, telecommunications, water and electricity; Deputy Dir HORACIO HOQUEE.

TELECOMMUNICATIONS

Dirección Nacional de Medios de Comunicación Social: Avda 7A Central y Calle 3A, Apdo 1628, Panamá 1; tel. 262-3197; fax 262-9495.

Major Service Providers

Cable & Wireless Panama: Box 0834-00659, Panamá; e-mail cwp@cwpanama.com; internet www.cwpanama.com.pa; 49% govt-owned,

49% owned by Cable & Wireless; major telecommunications provider; Pres. JORGE NICOLAU.

Movistar: Edif. Magna, Area Bancaria, Calle 51 Este y Manuel M. Icaza, Panamá; tel. 265-0955; internet www.movistar.com.pa; f. 1996 as BellSouth Panamá, SA; acquired by Telefónica Móviles, SA (Spain) in Oct. 2004; name changed as above in April 2005; mobile telephone services; Gen. Man. CLAUDIO HIDALGO.

Optynex Telecom, SA: Edif. Aliado, 2°, Calle 50 y 56, Urb. Obarrio, Apdo 0832-2650, Panamá; tel. 380-0000; fax 380-0099; e-mail info@optynex.com; internet www.optynex.com; f. 2002; Gen. Man. ERIC MEYER.

BROADCASTING

Radio

In 2004 there were 109 AM (Medium Wave) and 181 FM stations registered in Panama. Most stations are commercial.

La Mega 98.3 FM: Casa 35, Calle 50 y 77 San Francisco, Panamá; tel. 270-3242; fax 226-1021; e-mail ventas@lamegapanama.com; internet www.lamegapanama.com; f. 2000.

Omega Stereo: Calle G, El Cangrejo 3, Panamá; e-mail omegaste@omegastereo.com; internet www.omegastereo.com; f. 1981; Pres. GUILLERMO ANTONIO ADAMES.

RPC Radio: Avda 12 de Octubre, Panamá; tel. 390-6700; e-mail mtalessandria@medcom.com.pa; internet www.rpcradio.com; f. 1949; broadcasts news, sports and commentary; Man. MARÍA TERESA ALESSANDRÍA.

SuperQ: Edif. Dominó, Via España, Panamá; tel. 263-5298; fax 263-0362; e-mail info@superqpanama.com; internet www.superqpanama.com; f. 1984; Pres. G. ARIS DE ICAZA.

WAO 97.5: Edif. Plaza 50, 2°, Calle 50 y Vía Brasil, Panamá; tel. 223-8348; fax 223-8351; Gen. Man. ROGELIO CAMPOS.

Television

In 2005 there were 133 authorized television channels broadcasting in Panama.

Fundación para la Educación en la Televisión—FETV (Canal 5): Vía Ricardo J. Alfaro, Apdo 0819-02874, Panamá; tel. 230-8000; fax 230-1955; e-mail comentarios@fetv.org; internet www.fetv.org; f. 1992; Pres. JOSÉ DIMAS CEDEÑO DELGADO; Dir MANUEL SANTIAGO BLANQUÈR I PLANELLS; Gen. Man. TERESA WONG DE FONG.

Medcom: Avda 12 de Octubre, Hato Pintado, Apdo 0827-00116, Panamá 8; tel. 390-6802; fax 390-6895; e-mail murrutia@medcom.com.pa; internet www.rpctv.com; f. 1998 by merger of RPC Televisión (Canal 4) and Telemetro (Canal 13); commercial; also owns Cable Onda 90 and RPC Radio; Pres. FERNANDO ELETA; CEO NICOLÁS GONZÁLEZ-REVILLA.

Sistema Estatal de Radio y Televisión (Canal 11): Curundu, Panamá; tel. 507-1500; e-mail contactenos@sertv.gob.pa; internet www.sertv.gob.pa; f. 1978 as Radio y Televisión Educativa; was restructured and assumed present name in 2005; educational and cultural; Dir-Gen. CARLOS AGUILAR NAVARRO.

Televisora Nacional—TVN (Canal 2): Vía Bolívar, Apdo 6-3092, El Dorado, Panamá; tel. 279–3700; fax 236-2987; e-mail tvn@tvn-2.com; internet www.tvn-2.com; f. 1962; Dir JAIME ALBERTO ARIAS.

Broadcasting Association

Asociación Panameña de Radiodifusión: Apdo 7387, Estafeta de Paitilla, Panamá; tel. 263-5252; fax 226-4396; Pres. ALESSIO GRONCHI; Vice-Pres. RICARDO A. BUSTAMANTE.

Finance

(cap. = capital; res = reserves; dep. = deposits; m. = million; br.(s) = branch(es); amounts in balboas, unless otherwise stated)

BANKING

Superintendencia de Bancos (Banking Superintendency): Torre HSBC, 18°, Avda Samuel Lewis, Apdo 0832-2397, Panamá 1; tel. 506-7800; fax 506-7706; e-mail superbancos@superbancos.gob.pa; internet www.superbancos.gob.pa; f. 1970 as Comisión Bancaria Nacional (National Banking Commission); licenses and controls banking activities within and from Panamanian territory; Comisión Bancaria Nacional superseded by Superintendencia de Bancos in June 1998 with enhanced powers to supervise banking activity; Supt ALBERTO DIAMOND.

National Bank

Banco Nacional de Panamá: Casa Matriz, Vía España, Apdo 5220, Panamá 5; tel. 505-2000; fax 269-0091; e-mail sugerencia@banconal.com.pa; internet www.banconal.com.pa; f. 1904; govt-owned; cap. 500.0m., res –2.9m., dep. 4,911.0m. (Dec. 2008); Pres. CARLOS R. HENRÍQUEZ LÓPEZ; Gen. Man. DARIO ERNESTO BERBEY DE LA ROSA; 53 brs.

Savings Bank

Caja de Ahorros: Vía España y Calle Thays de Pons, Apdo 1740, Panamá 1; tel. 205-1000; fax 269-3674; e-mail atencionalcliente@cajadeahorros.com.pa; internet www.cajadeahorros.com.pa; f. 1934; govt-owned; cap. 150.7m., res 47.9m., dep. 170.9m. (Dec. 2006); Pres. RICCARDO FRANCOLINI AROSEMENA; Gen. Man. JAYSON E. PASTOR; 37 brs.

Domestic Private Banks

Banco Continental de Panamá, SA: Calle 50 y Avda Aquilino de la Guardia, Apdo 135, Panamá 9A; tel. 215-7000; fax 215-7134; e-mail bcp@bcocontinental.com; internet www.bbvabancocontinental.com; f. 1972; merged with Banco Internacional de Panamá in 2002; took over Banco Atlántico (Panamá), SA in 2006; cap. 126.7m., res 29.0m., dep. 3,079.8m. (Dec. 2006); Chair. PEDRO BRESCIA CAFFERATA; Gen. Man. EDUARDO TORRES-LLOSA VILLACORTA; 36 brs.

Banco Cuscatlán de Panamá: Edif. Panabank, Casa Matriz, Calle 50, Apdo 1828, Panamá 1; tel. 208-8300; fax 269-1537; e-mail gerencia@panabank.com; internet www.bancocuscatlan.com/panama; f. 1983; acquired Banco Panamericano (Panabank) in 2004; acquired by Citi in 2007; Chair. MAURICIO SAMAYOA; Gen. Man. GUIDO J. MARTINELLI, Jr.

Banco General, SA: Calle Aquilino de la Guardia, Apdo 0816-00843, Panamá 5; tel. 227-3200; fax 265-0210; e-mail info@bgeneral.com; internet www.bgeneral.com; f. 1955; purchased Banco Comercial de Panamá (BANCOMER) in 2000; cap. 500.0m., res 62.7m., dep. 5,719.9m. (Dec. 2008); Chair. and CEO FEDERICO HUMBERT; Exec. Vice-Pres. and Gen. Man. RAÚL ALEMÁN Z.; 36 brs.

Banco Panameño de la Vivienda (BANVIVIENDA): Edif. Grupo Mundial, Avda Balboa, Calle 41 E, Bella Vista, Apdo 0816-03366, Panamá 5; tel. 300-4700; fax 300-1133; e-mail bpvger@pty.com; internet www.banvivienda.com; f. 1981; cap. 12.4m., dep. 128.0m., total assets 150.3m. (2004); Pres. FERNANDO LEWIS NAVARRO; Gen. Man. JUAN RICARDO DE DIANOUS; 3 brs.

Banco Pichincha Panamá: Edif. PH Parque Urraca, entre Avda Federico Boyd y Avda Balboa, Panamá; tel. 297-4500; fax 264-6129; e-mail banco@pichinchapanama.com; internet wwwp2.pichinchapanama.com; f. 2006; Gen. Man. FRANCISCO JAVIER LEJARRAGA LÓPEZ DE ARROYABE.

Banco Universal: Edif. Miguel A. Brenes, Calle B Norte y Avda 1ra, Apdo 0426-00564, David, Chiriquí; tel. 775-4394; fax 775-2308; e-mail cosorio@bancouniversal.com; internet www.bancouniversal.com; f. 1970 as Asociación Chiricana de Ahorros y Préstamos para la Vivienda; present name adopted 1994; Pres. JOSÉ ISAAC VIRZI LÓPEZ; Gen. Man. CARLOS RAÚL BARRIOS ICAZA.

Global Bank Corporation: Torre Global Bank, Calle 50, Apdo 0831-01843, Paitilla, Panamá; tel. 206-2000; fax 263-3518; e-mail global@pan.gbm.net; internet www.globalbank.com.pa; f. 1994; Pres. LAWRENCE MADURO; Gen. Man. JORGE VALLARINO S.

Multibank: Edif. Prosperidad, planta baja, Vía España 127, Apdo 8210, Panamá 7; tel. 294-3500; fax 264-4014; e-mail banco@grupomulticredit.com; internet www.multibank.com.pa; f. 1990 as Multi Credit Bank; current name adopted 2008; total assets 536.1m. (Dec. 2005); Pres. ALBERTO S. BTESH; Gen. Man. RAFAEL SÁNCHEZ GARRÓS.

Towerbank International Inc: Edif. Tower Plaza, Calle 50 y Beatriz M. de Cabal, Apdo 0819-04318, Panamá; tel. 269-6900; fax 269-6800; e-mail towerbank@towerbank.com; internet www.towerbank.com; f. 1971; cap. 68.0m., res –3.1m., dep. 498.2m. (Dec. 2008); Pres. FRED KARDONSKI; Gen. Man. JOSÉ CAMPA.

Foreign Banks

Principal Foreign Banks with General Licence

BAC International Bank (Panamá), Inc (USA): Edif. BAC Credomatic, Calle Aquilino de la Guardia, Apdo 6-3654, Panamá; tel. 213-0822; fax 269-3879; e-mail infobac@pa.bac.net; internet www.bac.net/panama; f. 1995; Chair. CARLOS PELLAS; Gen. Man. RODOLFO TABASH.

Balboa Bank & Trust Corpn: Torre Generali, 19°, Avda Samuel Lewis y Calle 54, Urb. Obarrio, Panamá; tel. 208-7300; fax 263-4165; e-mail customerservice@balboabanktrust.com; internet www.balboabanktrust.com; f. 2003 as Stanford Bank (Panamá), SA; taken over by the Superintendencia de Bancos de Panamá in 2009; renamed in April 2010; Pres. GEORGE FRANCIS NOVEY DE LA GUARDIA.

BANCAFE (Panamá), SA (Colombia): Avda Manuel María Icaza y Calle 52E, No 18, Apdo 0834-00384, Panamá 9A; tel. 264-6066; fax 263-6115; e-mail bancafe@bancafe-pa.com; internet www.bancafe-pa.com; f. 1966 as Banco Cafetero; current name adopted in

1995; Pres. JORGE CASTELLANOS RUEDA; Gen. Man. JAIME DE GAMBOA GAMBOA; 2 brs.

Banco Aliado, SA: Calle 50 y 56, Urb. Obarrio, 0831-02109 Paitilla, Panamá; tel. 302-1555; fax 302-1556; e-mail bkaliado@bancoaliado.com; internet www.bancoaliado.com; f. 1992; Pres. MOISÉS CHREIM; Gen. Man. ALEXIS A. ARJONA.

Banco Bilbao Vizcaya Argentaria (Panama), SA (Spain): Torre BBVA, Avda Balboa, Calles 42 y 43, Apdo 8673, Panamá 5; tel. 227-0973; fax 227-3663; e-mail fperezp@bbvapanama.com; internet www.bbvapanama.com; f. 1982; cap. 28.7m., res 56.7m., dep. 1,383.0m. (Dec. 2008); Chair. MANUEL ZUBIRÍA PASTOR; Gen. Man. FELIX PEREZ PARRA; 15 brs.

Banco Delta, SA (BMF): Edif. Torre Delta, planta baja, Vía España 122 y Calle Elvira Méndez, Apdo 0816-07831, Panamá; tel. 340-0000; fax 340-0019; e-mail mguerra@bandelta.com; internet www.bandelta.com; f. 2006; Pres. ARTURO MÜLLER; Gen. Man. ARIEL ANTONIO SANMARTÍN MÉNDEZ.

Banco Internacional de Costa Rica, SA: Casa Matriz, Calle Manuel M. Icaza 25, Apdo 0816-07810, Panamá 1; tel. 208-9500; fax 208-9581; e-mail informacion@bicaspan.net; internet www.bicsa.com; f. 1976; Gen. Man. FEDERICO CARRILLO ZURCHER.

Banco Latinoamericano de Comercio Exterior SA (BLADEX) (Multinational): Casa Matriz, Calles 50 y Aquilino de la Guardia, Apdo 0819-08730, El Dorado, Panamá; tel. 210-8500; fax 269-6333; e-mail infobla@blx.com; internet www.blx.com; f. 1979 as Banco Latinoamericano de Exportaciones; name changed as above in 2009; groups together 254 Latin American commercial and central banks, 22 international banks and some 3,000 New York Stock Exchange shareholders; cap. US $415.6m., res $–109.7m., dep. $2,396.1m. (Dec. 2008); CEO JAIME RIVERA; Chair. GONZALO MENÉNDEZ DUQUE.

Citibank Panamá (USA): Edif. Banco Cuscatlán, Calle Aquilino de la Guardia, Apdo 555, Panamá 9A; tel. 210-5900; fax 210-5901; internet www.citibank.com.pa; f. 1904; Gen. Man. FRANCISCO CONTO; 4 brs.

Credicorp Bank, SA: Edif. Plaza Credicorp Bank, Nicanor de Obarrio, Calle 50, Apdo 833-0125, Panamá; tel. 210-1111; fax 210-0100; internet www.credicorpbank.com; f. 1992; cap. 34.1m., res –0.2m., dep. 659.5m. (Dec. 2008); Pres. RAYMOND HARARI; Gen. Man. MAX J. HARARI.

Helm Bank (Panama), SA: Edif. World Trade Center, 19°, Calle 53, Urb. Marbella, Apdo 0819-07070, Panamá; tel. 265-2820; fax 214-9715; e-mail servicioalcliente@helmpanama.com; internet www.helmpanama.com; f. as Banco de Credito (Panama) SA, renamed in 2002 as Banco de Credito Helm Financial Sevices (Panama), and as above in 2009; owned by Helm Bank SA (Colombia); cap. 25.0m., res 1.5m., dep. 386.8m. (Dec. 2009); Gen. Man. CARLOS HUMBERTO ROJAS M.

HSBC Bank (Panama), SA: Plaza HSBC, Calle Aquilino de La Guardia, Urb. Marbella, Panamá; tel. 263-5855; fax 263-6009; e-mail panama_investrel@hsbc.com.pa; internet www.hsbc.com.pa; cap. US $1,293.7m., dep. $11,137.7m. (Dec. 2009); acquired the Panama operations of Chase Manhattan Bank in 2000 and Primer Banco del Istmo (Banistmo) in 2006; CEO ERNESTO FERNANDES; 62 brs.

Principal Foreign Banks with International Licence

Austrobank Overseas (Panamá), SA: Torre Morgan y Morgan, planta baja, Calle 53, Este Marbella, Apdo 0819-07030, El Dorado, Panamá 6; tel. 223-5105; fax 264-6918; e-mail gerencia@austrobank.com; internet www.austrobank.com; f. 1995; Gen. Man. GUILLERMO WILLIS.

Banco Agrícola (Panamá), SA: Edif. Global Bank, 17°, Local E y F, Calle 50, Apdo 6-2637, Panamá; tel. 263-5762; fax 263-5626; e-mail info@bancoagricola.com; internet www.bancoagricolapanama.com; f. 2002; Exec. Pres. JOSÉ ROBERTO ORELLANA MILLA.

Banco de la Nación Argentina: Edif. World Trade Center 501, Calle 53, Urb. Marbella, Panamá; tel. 269-4666; fax 269-6719; e-mail bnapanama@bna.com.pa; internet www.bna.com.ar; f. 1977; Pres. JUAN CARLOS FABREGA; Gen. Man. RUBÉN DARÍO NOCERA.

Banco de Occidente (Panama), SA: Edif. American International, Calle 50 y Aquilino de la Guardia, Apdo 6-7430, El Dorado, Panamá; tel. 263-8144; fax 269-3261; internet www.bancoccidente.com.pa; f. 1982; cap. US $8.0m., res $5.9m., dep. $345.8m. (Dec. 2007); Pres. EFRAÍN OTERO ALVAREZ; Gen. Man. OSCAR LUNA GORDILLO.

Banco del Pacífico (Panama), SA: Calle Aquilino de la Guardia y Calle 52, esq. Edif. Banco del Pacifico, Apdo 0819-07070, El Dorado, Panamá; tel. 263-5833; fax 263-7481; e-mail bpacificopanama@pacifico.fin.ec; internet www.bancodelpacifico.com.pa; f. 1980; Pres. and Gen. Man. ANA ESCOBAR.

Bancolombia (Panama), SA: Edif. Bancolombia, Plaza Marbella, Calle Aquilino de la Guardia y Calle 47, Apdo 0816-03320, Panamá; tel. 263-6955; fax 269-1138; e-mail bancolombiapanama@allus.com.co; internet www.bancolombiapanama.com; f. 1973; current name adopted in 1999; cap. US $14.0m., res $4.3m., dep. $5,622.5m. (Dec. 2007); Gen. Man. MARÍA ISABEL URIBE RAMÍREZ.

FPB International Bank Inc: Ofs A y C, 16°, Calle 50 y Aquilino de la Guardia, Panamá; tel. 210-6600; fax 263-0919; f. 2005; Gen. Man. JOSÉ APARECIDO PAULUCCI.

GNB Sudameris Bank, SA: Area Bancaria, Calle Manuel María Icaza 19, Panamá; tel. 206-6900; fax 206-6901; internet www.gnbsudameris.com; f. 1970; Gen. Man. ANGELMIRO CASTILLO H.

Popular Bank Ltd Inc: Edif. Torre Banco General, Calle 47E y Avda Aquilini de la Guardia, Marbella, Apdo 0816-00265, Panamá; tel. 269-4166; fax 269-1309; e-mail contactenos@popularbank.com.pa; internet www.popularbank.com.pa; f. 1983 as Banco Popular Dominicano (Panama), SA; current name adopted in 2003; cap. 50.4m., res 0.1m., dep. 487.9m. (Dec. 2008); Pres. RAFAEL A. RODRÍGUEZ; Gen. Man. GIANNI VERSARI.

Banking Association

Asociación Bancaria de Panamá (ABP): Torre Hong Kong Bank, 15°, Avda Samuel Lewis, Apdo 4554, Panamá 5; tel. 263-7044; fax 223-5800; e-mail abp@orbi.net; internet www.asociacionbancaria.com; f. 1962; 79 mems; Pres. MOISÉS D. COHEN M.; Exec. Vice-Pres. and Gen. Man. ALBERTO CONDE.

STOCK EXCHANGE

Bolsa de Valores de Panamá: Edif. Vallarino, planta baja, Calles Elvira Méndez y 52, Apdo 87-0878, Panamá; tel. 269-1966; fax 269-2457; e-mail bvp@pty.com; internet www.panabolsa.com; f. 1960; Pres. RICARDO ARANGO; Gen. Man. ROBERTO BRENES PÉREZ.

INSURANCE

Arca Internacional de Reaseguros, SA: Edif. Bolsa de Valores, 1°, Avda Federico Boyd, Frente al Restaurante Rinos, Panamá; tel. 300-2858; fax 300-2859; f. 1996; Gen. Man. CARLOS G. DE LA LASTRA.

Aseguradora Ancón, SA: Avda Samuel Lewis y Calle 54, Urb. Obarrio, Panamá; tel. 210-8700; fax 210-8790; e-mail info@aseguranc on.com; internet www.aseguranc on.com; f. 1992; Pres. TOBIAS CARRERO NACAR; Gen. Man. CARLOS G. CHAMORRO.

Aseguradora Mundial, SA: Edif. Aseguradora Mundial, Avda Balboa y Calle 41, Apdo 8911, Panamá 5; tel. 207-6600; fax 207-8787; e-mail info@mundial.com; internet www.amundial.com; f. 1937; general; Pres. ORLANDO EDMUNDO SÁNCHEZ AVILES.

ASSA Cía de Seguros, SA: Edif. ASSA, Avda Nicanor de Obarrio (Calle 50), Apdo 0816-01622, Panamá 5; tel. 300-2772; fax 300-2729; e-mail assamercadeo@assanet.com; internet www.assanet.com; f. 1973; Pres. STANLEY MOTTA.

Assicurazioni Generali, Spa: Torre Generali, Avda Samuel Lewis y Calle 54, Urb. Obarrio, Apdo 0816-02206, 507 Panamá; tel. 206-9100; fax 206-9101; e-mail mercadeo@generali.com.pa; internet www.generali.com.pa; f. 1977; Gen. Man. GABRIEL R. DE OBARRIO, III.

Cía Interoceánica de Seguros, SA: Plaza Margella, Frente Banco HSBC, Calle Alquilino de la Guardia, Panamá; tel. 205-0700; fax 264-7668; e-mail info@interoceanica.com; internet www.interoceanica.com; f. 1978; Gen. Man. SALVADOR MORALES BACA.

Empresa General de Seguros, SA: Edif. Bancomer, Enre Piso, Calles 50 y 53, Panamá; tel. 269-1896; fax 264-1107; internet www.asecomer.com; f. 1987; Gen. Man. LUIS E. BANDERA.

HSBC Seguros (Panamá), SA (CONASE): Edif. HSBC, No 62, Calle 50, Apdo 5303, Panamá 5; tel. 205-0300; fax 223-1146; e-mail ines.m.arosemena@hsbc.com.pa; f. 1957 as Cía Nacional de Seguros, SA; current name adopted July 2007; Pres. JOSEPH SALTERIO.

Internacional de Seguros, SA: Avda Cuba y Calles 35 y 36, Apdo 1036, Panamá 1; tel. 227-4000; e-mail conase@conase.net; internet www.iseguros.com; f. 1910; Pres. RICHARD A. FORD.

Mitsui Sumitomo Insurance Co Ltd: Of. 701, 7°, Plaza Credicorp Bank Panamá, Panamá; tel. 210-0133; fax 210-0122; internet www.msilm.com; f. 1979; Gen. Man. TA KASHI MORIMOTO.

Provincial Re Panamá, SA: Edif. Alexandra, Of. 3A, Avda Octavio de Icaza, Panamá; tel. 260-5078; fax 260-5055; f. 1984; Gen. Man. FRANK CASTAGNET.

QBE del Istmo Cía de Reaseguros, Inc: Costa del Este, Avda Paseo del Mar y Calle Vista del Pacífico, Apdo 51, Panamá; tel. 301-0610; fax 223-0479; internet www.istmore.com; f. 1979; Pres. and CEO RAMÓN E. FERNÁNDEZ.

La Seguridad de Panamá, Cía de Seguros, SA: Edif. American International, Calle 50, esq. Aquilino de la Guardia, Apdo 5306, Panamá 5; tel. 263-6700; f. 1986; Gen. Man. MARIELA OSORIO.

Trade and Industry

Colón Free Zone (CFZ): Avda Roosevelt, Apdo 1118, Colón; tel. 445-1033; fax 445-2165; e-mail zonalibre@zolicol.org; internet www.zonalibredecolon.com.pa; f. 1948 to manufacture, import, handle and re-export all types of merchandise; some 1,800 companies were established in 2005; well-known international banks operate in the CFZ, where there are also customs, postal and telegraph services; the main exporters to the CFZ are Japan, the USA, Hong Kong, Taiwan, the Republic of Korea, Colombia, France, Italy and the United Kingdom; the main importers from the CFZ are Brazil, Venezuela, Mexico, Ecuador, the Netherlands Dependencies, Bolivia, the USA, Chile, Argentina and Colombia; the total area of the CFZ was 485.3 ha; Gen. Man. LEOPOLDO BENEDETTI.

GOVERNMENT AGENCIES

Autoridad de la Micro, Pequeña y Mediana Empresa: Calle Maritza Alabarca, Edif. 1005 y 1010, Clayton, Panamá; tel. 500-5602; e-mail atencionalcliente@ampyme.gob.pa; internet www.ampyme.gob.pa; f. 2000; promotes the devt of micro-, small and medium enterprises; Dir-Gen. GISELLE BURILLO SÁIZ.

CHAMBERS OF COMMERCE

American Chamber of Commerce and Industry of Panama: POB 0843-00152, Panamá; tel. 301-3881; fax 301-3882; e-mail amcham@panamcham.com; internet www.panamcham.com; Pres. DONALD N. ELDER; Exec. Dir DAVID HUNT.

Cámara de Comercio, Industrias y Agricultura de Panamá: Avda Cuba y Ecuador 33A, Apdo 74, Panamá 1; tel. 207-3440; fax 207-3422; e-mail infocciap@cciap.com; internet www.panacamara.com; f. 1915; Pres. FERNANDO ARANGO; Exec. Dir RAFAEL ZUÑIGA BRID; 1,300 mems.

Cámara Oficial Española de Comercio: Avda Balboa, Edif. Banco BBVA, Torre Menor, 7°, Apdo 1857, Panamá 1; tel. 225-1487; fax 225-6608; e-mail caespan@cwpanama.net; internet www.caespan.com.pa; Pres. NOEL RIANDE; Exec. Dir MARÍA JESÚS ALONSO ROS.

INDUSTRIAL AND TRADE ASSOCIATIONS

Asociación Panameña de Exportadores (APEX): Edif. Ricardo Galindo Quelquejeu, Avda Ricardo J. Alfaro, Urb. Sara Sotillo, Panamá; tel. 230-0169; e-mail apex@cableonda.net; internet www.apexpanama.org; f. 1971; export asscn; Pres. MANUEL FERNÁNDEZ; Sec. JAIME ORTIZ.

Cámara Panameña de la Construcción: Calle Aquilino de la Guardia y Calle 52, Área Bancaria, diagonal al Hotel Ejecutivo, Apdo 0816-02350, Panamá 5; tel. 265-2500; fax 265-2571; e-mail informacion@capac.org; internet www.capac.org; represents interests of construction sector; Pres. JAIME A. JOVANÉ C.; Dir-Gen. EDUARDO RODRÍGUEZ.

Corporación Azucarera La Victoria: Transístmica, San Miguelito; tel. 229-4794; state sugar corpn; scheduled for transfer to private ownership; Dir Prof. ALEJANDRO VERNAZA.

Corporación para el Desarrollo Integral del Bayano: Avda Balboa, al lado de la estación del tren, Estafeta El Dorado, Panamá 2; tel. 232-6160; f. 1978; state agriculture, forestry and cattle-breeding corpn.

Dirección General de Industrias: Edif. Plaza Edison, 3°, Apdo 9658, Panamá 4; tel. 360-0720; govt body that undertakes feasibility studies, analyses and promotion; Dir-Gen. LUCÍA FUENTES DE FERGUSON; Nat. Dir of Business Devt FRANCISCO DE LA BARRERA.

Sindicato de Industriales de Panamá: Vía Ricardo J. Alfaro, Entrada Urb. Sara Sotillo, Apdo 6-4798, Estafeta El Dorado, Panamá; tel. 230-0169; fax 230-0805; e-mail sip@cableonda.net; internet www.industriales.org; f. 1945; represents and promotes activities of industrial sector; Pres. JUAN F. KIENER; Sec.-Gen. MÁXIMO GALLARDO.

EMPLOYERS' ORGANIZATIONS

Asociación Panameña de Ejecutivos de Empresas (APEDE): Avda Justo Arosemena, Calle 31, frente a la Piscina Adán Gordón, Apdo 0816-06785, Panamá; tel. 204-1500; fax 204-1510; e-mail apede@apede.org; internet www.apede.org; Pres. RUBÉN M. CASTILLO GILL; Exec. Dir JACKELINE AIZPURÚA.

Consejo Nacional de la Empresa Privada (CONEP): Avda Morgan, Balboa, Ancón, Casa 302A-B, Zona 1, Apdo 0816-07197, Panamá 1; tel. 211-2672; fax 211-2694; e-mail conep1@cwpanama.net; internet www.conep.org.pa; Pres. ANTONIO FLETCHER; Exec. Dir ALFREDO BURGOS.

MAJOR COMPANIES

Beverages and Tobacco

Cervecería Nacional, SA: Costa del Este, Business Park, Torre Oeste, 2°, El Dorado, Apdo 6-1393, Panamá 1; tel. 305-6000; fax 279-5861; internet www.cerveceria-nacional.com; f. 1909; subsidiary of Grupo SABMiller; production and distribution of beverages, incl. beer and soft drinks; Pres. JULIO MARIO SANTO DOMINGO; Exec. Pres. FERNANDO ZAVALA LOMBARDI; 400 employees.

Coca-Cola FEMSA, SA: Parque Industrial San Cristóbal, Calle Santa Rosa, Panamá 9A; tel. 236-0700; fax 260-3504; e-mail krelations@kof.com.mx; internet www.coca-colafemsa.com; f. 1913; 53.7% owned by Fomento Económico Mexicano, SA de CV (FEMSA), 31.6% by The Coca-Cola Company, and 14.7% by the public; bottlers of soft drinks; CEO CARLOS SALAZAR LOMELÍN; 500 employees.

TANASEC Panama: La Rinconada, Vía Tocumen, Apdo 0839-0714, Panamá 13; tel. 340-4503; fax 340-4521; e-mail haydee.mudarra@pmintl.com; internet www.philipmorris.com; f. 1955; manufacture of cigarettes; merged with Tabacalera Nacional in 2001; Dir ELOY COLLADO; Gen. Man. DENNIS GORKUN; 200 employees.

Varela Hermanos, SA: Vía Tocumen La Pulida, Calle La Cantera, Apdo 0819-07757, Panamá; tel. 217-3777; fax 217-6046; e-mail varela@varehelahermanos.com; internet www.varelahermanos.com; f. 1950; distillation and bottling of liquors; Dir JOSÉ LUIS VARELA; Gen. Man. MANUEL SOSSA; 300 employees.

Food Products

Compañía Azucarera La Estrella, SA: Apdo 0201-000-49 Aguadulce, Prov. de Coclé; tel. 236-1150; fax 236-1079; e-mail info@grupocalesa.com; internet www.grupocalesa.com; f. 1949; sugar mill and refinery; part of Grupo Calesa; Pres. GASPAR GARCÍA DE PAREDES CHIARI; Gen. Man. HANS H. HAMMERSCHLAG; 1,069 employees.

Industrias Lácteas, SA: Vía Simón Bolívar, Apdo 4362, Panamá 5; tel. 29-1122; fax 229-1846; e-mail evenutolo@estrellaazul.com; f. 1956; dairy products; Gen. Man. ENRIQUE VENUTOLO; 1,300 employees.

Nestlé Panamá, SA: Calle 69, 74D, Urb. La Loma, Apdo 0834-00368, Panamá 9A; tel. 229-1333; fax 229-1982; internet www.nestle-centroamerica.com; f. 1937; subsidiary of Nestlé Co, SA (Switzerland); manufacture and wholesale of food products; Gen. Man. LEO LEIMAN; 760 employees.

Productos Alimenticios Pascual, SA: Avda José Agustín Arango, Apdo 8422, Panamá 7; tel. 217-2133; fax 233-2825; e-mail ventas@pascual.com.pa; internet www.pascual.com.pa; f. 1946; acquired by Casa Luker de Colombia in 2004; food and food-processing; Pres. VICENTE ESTEVEZ PASCUAL; Gen. Man. JUAN ALBERTO PASCUAL; 600 employees.

Textile Manufactures

Promedias, SA: 111 Pueblo Nuevo, Panamá; tel. 261-3649; fax 261-5548; e-mail ventas@promedias.com.pa; internet www.promedias.com.pa; manufacturers of socks and tights.

Tejidos y Confecciones, SA: Edif. Durex Carrasquilla, Calle 2A, Apdo 0834-02775, Panamá; tel. 209-8888; fax 209-8889; e-mail sales@teyco.com; internet www.teyco.com; f. 1964; part of Attie Group; manufacturers of men's and children's clothing; Pres. MAYER ATTIE CHAYO; Dir RAMY ATTIE; 500 employees.

Miscellaneous

Aceti-Oxigeno, SA: Boca La Caja, Avda Principal, Paitilla, Panamá; tel. 270-1977; fax 226-4789; e-mail gerencia@acetioxigeno.com.pa; internet acetioxigeno.com.pa; producer and importer of clinical and industrial gases; Man. ROGELIO SALADO A.

BASF Construction Systems Panamá: Torre Global Park, 12°, Of. 12-04, Calle 50, San Francisco, Panamá; tel. 300-1360; e-mail marbella.escobar@basf.com; owned by BASF, AG (Germany); chemicals; Man. MARBELLA ESCOBAR.

Cemento Panamá, SA: Edif. Cemento Panamá, Calle Jorge Zarak Las Sabanas 2, Apdo 1755, Panamá 1; tel. 366-1690; fax 366-1682; e-mail contactenos@cementopanama.com; internet www.cementopanama.com; f. 1943; manufacturers of portland cement; acquired by Holcim (Switzerland) and Argos (Colombia); Pres. JUAN MANUEL RUISECO; Gen. Man. ENRIQUE TOMÁS OLARTE; 90 employees.

Compañía Atlas, SA: Edif. 40, Calle 16½, Apdo 6-1092, El Dorado, Panamá; tel. 236-0066; fax 236-0044; e-mail info@ciatlas.com; internet www.atlastore.com; f. 1949; holding co with interests in the wholesale manufacture, import and distribution of stationery; Gen. Man. ROBERTO C. HENRÍQUEZ; 110 employees.

Deloitte & Touche (Deloitte LATCO): Edif. Capital Plaza, 7°, Paseo Roberto Motta, Costa del Este, Apdo 0816-01558, Panamá; tel. 303-4100; fax 264-7124; e-mail infopanama@deloitte.com; internet www

.deloitte.com; accountancy and management consultancy; Chair. César Cheng Vargas; Dir-Gen. Carlos Haehnel.

Excel Automotriz: Panamá; known as Poma Automotriz until 2010; part of the Grupo DIDEA; distributor of cars and car parts; Exec. Vice-Pres. (Group) Carlos Boza.

Grupo Calesa: Apdo 0823-058-19, Panamá 5; tel. 236-1150; fax 236-1079; e-mail info@grupocalesa.com; internet www.grupocalesa.com; f. 1918; agroindustrial producer; 3,200 employees.

Grupo Corcione: Duplex 10, Calle 59, San Francisco, Apdo 0816-05715, Zona 5, Panamá; tel. 215-0011; fax 269-6057; e-mail sales@grupocorcione.com; internet www.grupocorcione.com; f. 1992; construction contractors; Pres. Nicolás Corcione.

KPMG: Torre KPMG, Calle 50 No 54, Apdo 0816–01089, Panamá 5; tel. 208-0700; fax 215-7863; e-mail pa-fminformation@kpmg.com.pa; internet www.kpmg.com.pa; f. 1958; accountancy and management consultancy; CEO Carlos Karamañites.

Lindo y Maduro, SA: Apdo 0816-01083, Panamá 5; tel. 301-0100; fax 301-0099; e-mail linduro@linduro.com; manufacturers and distributors of non-durable goods and perfumery; Pres. Alfredo Maduro; Man. Karina Jaén; 60 employees.

Melo y Cía, SA: Apdo 333, Panamá 1; tel. 221-0033; fax 224-2311; e-mail grupomelo@grupomelo.com; internet www.grupomelo.com.pa; vendors of veterinary, agricultural and agrochemical products, building materials, and household goods; Pres. Arturo Donaldo Melo S.; Gen. Man. Federico Melo K.; 400 employees.

Petroterminal de Panamá, SA: World Trade Center Bldg, 9°, Marbella, Apdo 0832-0920, Panamá; tel. 263-7777; fax 269-9949; e-mail info@petroterminal.com; internet www.petroterminal.com; f. 1977; petroleum and gasfield services and petroleum storage facilities; Dir-Gen. Luis Roquebert; 80 employees.

H. Tzanetatos Inc: Casa Matriz, Vía Tocumen; tel. 220-1977; fax 220-5122; e-mail grupotza@tzanetatos.com; internet www.htzanetatos.com; general wholesaler; Gen. Man. Alberto Paz Rodríguez; 400 employees.

UTILITIES

Regulatory Authority

Autoridad Nacional de los Servicios Públicos: see Broadcasting and Communications—Regulatory Authority.

Electricity

The partial divestment of generation and distribution services was completed in December 1998. The restructuring of the state-owned Instituto de Recursos Hidráulicos y Electrificación (IRHE) resulted in the sale of four generation and three distribution companies. However, transmission operations remained under state control.

AES Panama: Torre Banco Continental, 25°, Calle 50 y Aquilino de la Guardia, CP 0816-01990, Panamá; tel. 206-2600; fax 206-2645; e-mail aespanama@aes.com; internet www.aespanama.com; f. 1998 upon acquisition by AES Corpn of 49% interest in Empresa de Generación Electrica Bayano and Empresa de Generación Electrica Chiriquí; operates three hydroelectric facilities in Bayano (248 MW), Estí (120 MW) and Chiriquí (90 MW) and one 43-MW thermal facility; Pres. Jaime Tupper; Gen. Man. Javier Giorgio.

Elektra Noreste, SA (ENSA): Costa del Este, Business Park-Torre Oeste, 3°, Panamá; tel. 340-4600; internet www.ensa.com.pa; electricity distribution; Gen. Man. Javier Pariente.

Empresa de Transmisión Eléctrica, SA (ETESA): Plaza Sun Tower, 3°, Avda Ricardo J. Alfaro, El Dorado, Panamá; tel. 501-3800; fax 501-3506; e-mail gerinfo@etesa.com.pa; internet www.etesa.com.pa; f. 1998; state-owned transmission co; Pres. Frank de Lima; Gen. Man. René E. Rivera.

Unión FENOSA—EDEMET EDECHI: Albrook, Panamá; internet www.ufpanama.com; f. 1998 by acquisition from IRHE of Empresa de Distribución Eléctrica Metro Oeste (EDEMET) and Empresa de Distribución Eléctrica Chiriquí (EDECHI) by Unión FENOSA, Spain; Exec. Pres. Ricardo Barranco.

Water

Instituto de Acueductos y Alcantarillados Nacionales (IDAAN) (National Waterworks and Sewage Systems Institute): Apdo 5234, Panamá; tel. 523-8567; e-mail relaciones.publicas@idaan.gob.pa; internet www.idaan.gob.pa; Pres. José Antonio Díaz; Exec. Dir Manuel González Ruíz.

TRADE UNIONS

Central General Autónoma de Trabajadores de Panamá (CGTP): Edif. CGTP, Calle 3a Perejil, detrás del Colegio Javier, Panamá; tel. 269-9741; fax 223-5287; e-mail cgtpan@cwpanama.net; internet www.cgtp.org.pa; fmrly Central Istmeña de Trabajadores; Sec.-Gen. Mariano E. Mena.

Confederación Nacional de Unidad Sindical Independiente (CONUSI): 0421B Calle Venado, Ancón, Apdo 830344, Zona 3, Panamá; tel. 212-3865; fax 212-2565; e-mail conusipanama@hotmail.com; Sec.-Gen. Genaro López.

Confederación de Trabajadores de la República de Panamá (CTRP) (Confederation of Workers of the Republic of Panama): Calle 31, entre Avdas México y Justo Arosemena 3-50, Apdo 0816-03647, Panamá 5; tel. 225-0293; fax 225-0259; e-mail ctrp@cableonda.net; f. 1956; admitted to ITUC/ORIT; Sec.-Gen. Guillermo Puga; 62,000 mems from 13 affiliated groups.

Consejo Nacional de Trabajadores Organizados (CONATO) (National Council of Organized Labour): Edif. 777, 2°, Balboa-Ancón, Panamá; tel. and fax 228-0224; e-mail conato@cwpanama.net; Co-ordinator Miguel Edwards; 150,000 mems.

Convergencia Sindical: Casa 2490, Balboa-Ancón, Calle Bomparte Wise, Apdo 0815-00863, Panamá 4; tel. and fax 314-1615; e-mail conversind@cwpanama.net; f. 1995; Sec.-Gen. Victor Manuel Torres.

Federación Nacional de Servidores Públicos (FENASEP) (National Federation of Public Employees): Galerías Alvear, 2°, Of. 301, Vía Argentina, Apdo 66-48, Zona 5, Panamá; tel. and fax 269-1316; e-mail fenasep@sinfo.net; f. 1984; Sec.-Gen. Alfredo Berrocal.

A number of unions exist without affiliation to a national centre.

Transport

RAILWAYS

In 1998 there was an estimated 485 km of track in Panama. In 2000 a US $75m. project to modernize the line between the ports at either end of the Panama Canal began. In July 2001 the 83-km transisthmian railway, originally founded in 1855, reopened. The construction of an underground railway (metro) system in Panama City was planned by the Government of Ricardo Martinelli Berrocal that took office in July 2009.

Ferrocarril Nacional de Chiriquí: Apdo 12B, David City, Chiriquí; tel. 775-4241; fax 775-4105; 126 km linking Puerto Armuelles and David.

Panama Canal Railway Company: Edif. T-376, Corozal Oeste, Apdo 0843-02448, Balboa Ancón, Panamá; tel. 317-6070; fax 317-6061; e-mail info@panarail.com; internet www.panarail.com; private investment under 50-year govt concession; 83 km linking Panama City and Colón, running parallel to Panama Canal; operation on concession by Kansas City Southern (KS, USA) and Mi-Jack Products (IL, USA); modernization programme completed in 2001; operates daily passenger and cargo service; Marketing Dir Thomas Kenna.

ROADS

In 2008, according to preliminary figures, there were 13,267 km of roads, of which some 5,235 km were paved. The two most important highways are the Pan-American Highway and the Boyd-Roosevelt, or Trans-Isthmian, linking Panama City and Colón. The Pan-American Highway to Mexico City runs for 545 km in Panama and was being extended towards Colombia. There is also a highway to San José, Costa Rica.

SHIPPING

The Panama Canal opened in 1914. Some 5% of all the world's seaborne trade passes through the waterway. It is 82 km long, and ships take an average of nine hours to complete a transit. In 2008/09 some 14,342 transits were recorded. The Canal can accommodate ships with a maximum draught of 12 m (39 ft), beams of up to approximately 32.3 m (106 ft) and lengths of up to about 290 m (950 ft), roughly equivalent to ships with a maximum capacity of 65,000–70,000 dwt. In 2000 a five-year modernization project was begun. The project included: a general improvement of facilities; the implementation of a satellite traffic-management system; the construction of a bridge; and the widening of the narrowest section of the Canal, the Culebra Cut (which was completed in 2001). Plans were also announced to construct a 203-ha international cargo-handling platform at the Atlantic end of the Canal, including terminals, a railway and an international airport. Terminal ports are Balboa, on the Pacific Ocean, and Cristóbal, on the Caribbean Sea. Proposals to expand the Canal's capacity to allow the passage of larger commercial container vessels, by constructing a third set of locks at either end of the waterway, were announced in 2006; the enlargement project was expected to be completed in 2014.

Autoridad del Canal de Panamá (ACP): Administration Bldg, Balboa, Ancón, Panamá; tel. 272-7602; fax 272-7693; e-mail info@pancanal.com; internet www.pancanal.com; f. 1997; manages, operates and maintains the Panama Canal; succeeded the Panama

Canal Commission, a US govt agency, on 31 December 1999, when the waterway was ceded to the Govt of Panama; the ACP is the autonomous agency of the Govt of Panama; there is a Board of 11 mems; Chair. RÓMULO ROUX; Administrator ALBERTO ALEMÁN ZUBIETA; Dep. Administrator JOSÉ BARRIOS NG.

Autoridad Marítima de Panamá: Edif. PanCanal Albrook, Diablo Heights, Balboa, Ancón, Apdo 0843-0533, Panamá 7; tel. 501-5196; fax 501-5406; e-mail ampadmin@amp.gob.pa; internet www.amp.gob.pa; f. 1998 to unite and optimize the function of all state institutions with involvement in the maritime sector; Administrator ROBERTO LINARES TRIBALDOS.

Panama City Port Authority and Foreign Trade Zone 65: Apdo 15095, Panamá; FL 32406, USA; tel. 767-3220; e-mail wstubbs@portpanamacityusa.com; internet www.portpanamacityusa.com; Chair. THOMAS NEUBAUER; Exec. Dir WAYNE STUBBS.

There are deep-water ports at Balboa and Cristóbal (including general cargo ships, containers, shipyards, industrial facilities); Coco Solo (general cargo and containers); Bahía Las Minas (general bulk and containers); Vacamonte (main port for fishing industry); Puerto Armuelles and Almirante (bananas); Aguadulce and Pedregal (export of crude sugar and molasses, transport of fertilizers and chemical products); and Charco Azul and Chiriquí Grande (crude petroleum).

The Panamanian merchant fleet was the largest in the world in December 2008, numbering 8,065 vessels with total displacement of 183.5m. gross registered tons. In November 2000 construction was completed on the largest container terminal in Latin America, in Balboa.

CIVIL AVIATION

Tocumen (formerly Omar Torrijos) International Airport, situated 19 km (12 miles) outside Panamá (Panama City), is the country's principal airport and is served by many international airlines. A project to expand the airport's facilities, at a cost of US $20m., was completed in 2006. The France Airport in Colón and the Rio Hato Airport in Coclé province have both been declared international airports. There are also 11 smaller airports in the country.

Aerolíneas Pacífico Atlántico, SA (Aeroperlas): Apdo 6-3596, El Dorado, Panamá; tel. 315-7500; fax 315-0331; e-mail info@aeroperlas.com; internet www.aeroperlas.com; f. 1970; fmrly state-owned, transferred to private ownership in 1987; operates scheduled regional and domestic flights to 16 destinations; initiated international flights in 2000; Dir JAN ROHDE.

Air Panama: Marcos A. Gelabert Airport, Albrook, Panamá; tel. 316-9000; e-mail info@flyairpanama.com; internet www.flyairpanama.com; operates flights throughout Panama and to Costa Rica; Gen. Man. EDUARDO STAGG.

Compañía Panameña de Aviación, SA (COPA): Avda Justo Arosemena 230 y Calle 39, Apdo 1572, Panamá 1; tel. 227-2522; fax 227-1952; e-mail proquebert@mail.copa.com.pa; internet www.copaair.com; f. 1947; scheduled passenger and cargo services from Panamá (Panama City) to Central America, South America, the Caribbean and the USA; Chair. ALBERTO MOTTA; CEO PEDRO O. HEILBRON.

Tourism

Panama's attractions include Panamá (Panama City), the ruins of Portobelo and 800 sandy tropical islands, including the resort of Contadora, one of the Pearl Islands in the Gulf of Panama, and the San Blas Islands, lying off the Atlantic coast. In 2007 the number of visitor arrivals at Tocumen International Airport stood at 948,946. Income from tourism was some US $1,408m. in 2008, according to provisional figures.

Asociación Panameña de Agencias de Viajes y Turismo (APAVIT): Edif. Balmoral, Vía Argentina, diagonal a la Universidad de Panamá, Panamá; tel. 264-9171; fax 264-5355; e-mail apavit@cableonda.net; f. 1957; Pres. ERNESTO REINA.

Autoridad de Turismo Panamá (IPAT): Centro de Convenciones ATLAPA, Vía Israel, Apdo 4421, Panamá 5; tel. 526-7000; fax 526-7100; e-mail gerencia@atp.gob.pa; internet www.atp.gob.pa; f. 1960; Dir-Gen. SALOMÓN SHAMAH ZUCHIN.

Defence

In 1990, following the overthrow of Gen. Manuel Antonio Noriega Morena, the National Defence Forces were disbanded and a new Public Force was created. The new force was representative of the size of the population and affiliated to no political party. As assessed at November 2009, the Public Force numbered an estimated 12,000, comprising the National Police (11,000) and the National Aero-Naval Service (an estimated 1,000), the latter having been formed in late 2008 by the merger of the National Air Service and the National Maritime Service.

Security Expenditure: budgeted at an estimated US $269m. in 2009.

Director of National Civil Protection System: ARTURO ALVARADO DE ICAZA.

Director of National Police: GUSTAVO PÉREZ.

Director of National Aero-Naval Service: JACINTO TOM.

Education

The education system in Panama is divided into elementary, secondary and university schooling, each of six years' duration. Education is free up to university level and is officially compulsory between six and 15 years of age. Primary education begins at the age of six and secondary education, which comprises two three-year cycles, at the age of 12. In 2007/08 enrolment at primary schools included 98% of children in the relevant age-group, while secondary enrolment included 66% of children in the relevant age-group. There are four public universities and 11 private ones, including one that specializes in distance learning. Budgetary expenditure on education by the central Government in 2007 amounted to a preliminary 639.4m. balboas (equivalent to 18.5% of total current expenditure).

Bibliography

For works on Central America generally, see Select Bibliography (Books)

Clymer, A. *Drawing the Line at the Big Ditch: The Panama Canal Treaties and the Rise of the Right*. Lawrence, KS, University Press of Kansas, 2008.

Coniff, M. L. *Panama and the United States*. Atlanta, GA, University of Georgia Press, 2001.

Diaz Espino, O. *How Wall Street Created a Nation: J. P. Morgan, Teddy Roosevelt and the Panama Canal*. New York, Four Walls Eight Windows, 2001.

Dinges, J. *Our Man in Panama: How General Noriega Fooled the United States and Made Millions in Drugs and Arms*. New York, Random House, 1990.

Dudley Gold, S. *The Panama Canal Transfer: Controversy at the Crossroads*. Austin, TX, Raintree/Steck Vaughn, 1999.

Greene, J. *The Canal Builders: Making America's Empire of the Panama Canal*. London, Penguin Books, 2010.

Guevara Mann, C. *Panamanian Militarism: A Historical Interpretation*. Athens, OH, Ohio University Press, 1996.

Harding, II, R. C. *Military Foundations of Panamanian Politics*. Piscataway, NJ, Transaction Publrs, 2001.

Kempe, F. *Divorcing the Dictator: America's Bungled Affair with Noriega*. New York, G. P. Putnam's Sons, 1990.

Langstaff, E. *Panama*. Oxford, ABC Clio, 2000.

McCullough, D. *Path Between the Seas: Creation of the Panama Canal, 1870–1914*. New York, Simon and Schuster, 1999.

Major, J. *Prize Possession: The United States and the Panama Canal, 1903–1979*. Cambridge, Cambridge University Press, 1993.

O'Reggio, T. *Between Alienation and Citizenship: The Evolution of Black West Indian Society in Panama, 1914-1964*. Lanham, MD, University Press of America, 2006.

Pearcy, T. L. *We Answer Only to God: Politics and the Military in Panama, 1903–1947*. Albuquerque, NM, University of New Mexico Press, 1998.

Pérez, O. J. (Ed.). *Post-Invasion Panama*. Lexington, MA, Lexington Books, 2000.

Rodríguez, J. C. *The Panama Canal: Its History, Its Political Aspects, and Financial Difficulties*. Honolulu, HI, University Press of the Pacific, 2002.

Rudolf, G. *Panama's Poor: Victims, Agents and Historymakers*. Gainesville, FL, University Press of Florida, 1999.

Sanchez, P. *Panama Lost?: U.S. Hegemony, Democracy, and the Canal*. Gainesville, FL, University Press of Florida, 2007.

Sandoval Forero, E. A., and Salazar Pérez, R. *Lectura Crítica del Plan Puebla Panama*. Buenos Aires, Libros en Red, 2002.

Singh Gill Díaz, G. *La Evolución Jurídica del Poder Constituyente en el Istmo de Panamá*. Panamá, Instituto de Estudios Políticos e Internacionales, 2005.

Snapp, J. S. *Destiny by Design: The Construction of the Panama Canal*. Pacific Heritage Press, 2000.

Sosa, J. B. *In Defiance: The Battle Against Gen. Noriega Fought from Panama's Embassy in Washington*. Washington, DC, The Francis Press, 1999.

Taw, J. M. *Operation Just Cause: Lessons for Operations Other than War*. Skokie, IL, Rand McNally, 1996.

USA Ibp. *Doing Business and Investing in Panama*. Milton Keynes, Lightning Source UK Ltd, 2005.

Panama Canal Handbook: Organization And Business Activity. Milton Keynes, Lightning Source UK Ltd, 2005.

Ward, C. *Imperial Panama: Commerce and Conflict in Isthmian America, 1550–1800*. Alberquerque, NM, University of New Mexico Press, 1993.

PARAGUAY

Geography

PHYSICAL FEATURES

The Republic of Paraguay is one of only two land-locked countries in South America—although, unlike Bolivia, it has never had a coastline. The country did, however, suffer immense loss from war in the 1860s, although in the 1930s it secured control over much of the Chaco after war with Bolivia. Paraguay is located in the south-central part of the continent, with Bolivia to the north-west, beyond a 750-km (466-mile) border. Argentina lies to the south-west, behind a 1,880-km frontier which abuts its neighbour in south-eastern Paraguay, while Brazil (1,290 km) is to the north-east. Paraguay is about the same size as the US state of California, covering an area of 406,752 sq km (157,048 sq miles).

Paraguay consists of two rough rectangles of territory on either side of the north–south river of the same name. The slightly larger block (with the south-west corner sliced off), covering about 60% of the territory, is to the west of the river. Offset slightly to the south is the smaller, original block of territory (a block with a much smaller block removed from the north-east corner), east of the Paraguay river. The two regions, known as Paraguay Occidental and Paraguay Oriental or Paraguay proper, have very different landscapes. The west is dominated by the Gran Chaco, an infertile alluvial plain extending through Paraguay and into Bolivia and Argentina. The region receives little rain, but is poorly drained and prone to flooding, so the rough prairie of dry grass and shadeless trees is patched with reedy marshes or thorny scrub. To the south and east, in the Oriental region, are some grassy plains, although broad, fertile valleys and rolling, wooded hills predominate. The Paraná plateau thrusts down from the north, to create a highland of between 300 m (985 ft) and 600 m, its sharp crest running down the centre of Paraguay proper, highest in the west, but dropping abruptly to the fertile grassy foothills that roll down to the Paraguay river, while descending more gently in the east towards the River Paraná. The Paraná forms the entire eastern (much of it through the reservoir behind the Itaipú dam) and southern border of Paraguay Oriental. Its tributary, the Paraguay, joins the Paraná only after cutting across the country and then forming a west-facing border with Argentina. The confluence of the Paraguay and the Paraná, at 46 m above sea level, is the lowest point in Paraguay. The highest point is in the centre of south-eastern Paraguay. It is Cerro Pero (or Cerro Tres Kandu), at 842 m. In total, just over one-half of the country is pastureland, while almost one-third is forested. The terrain is not favourable to many of the larger mammals, although there are jaguars, tapirs, armadillos and anteaters, for instance, but exotically plumaged birds are common (parrots, toucans, black ducks, etc.), and the grasslands are the natural habitat of the rhea or American ostrich.

CLIMATE

Paraguay is bisected by the Tropic of Capricorn, and about two-thirds of the country experiences a mild, subtropical climate. On the Chaco plains of the Occidental region it is hotter, more humid and drier; temperatures can often reach 38°C (100°F). The far north and west is semi-arid. Rainfall on the plains averages about 815 mm (32 ins) per year, falling heavily in the summer (November–May) and virtually not at all in winter. By contrast, the eastern forests receive about 1,525 mm annually, with Asunción, the national capital, on the Paraguay river, getting 1,120 mm. The average temperatures range from 17°C (63°F) in July to 27°C (81°F) in January. The prevailing summer wind is the hot, north-eastern sirocco, while in winter it is the cold pampero from the south.

POPULATION

Paraguay has one of the more homogenous populations of South America, 95% of them being Mestizos. Otherwise, there are some unassimilated Amerindians (notably Guaraní of the eastern forests), some full-blood Spanish (mainly in the cities) and small groups originating from Japan, Italy, Portugal, Canada and Germany (the last mainly the religious minority the Mennonites). Spanish is joined by Guaraní as an official language, as the latter is commonly spoken by about 90% of the population. Spanish is spoken by about three-quarters of the population, with almost one-half of Paraguayans being completely bilingual. Guaraní was the official language for many of the early years of independence. However, the overwhelming majority of people, and most Mestizos, remain at least nominally Roman Catholic. There are other Christians, with the Evangelical Protestants active here as elsewhere in South America, but the largest Protestant minority is that of the Mennonites (based near Filadelfia, in the heart of the Chaco plains).

The total population, according to UN estimates at mid-2010, was 6.5m. Two-thirds of the population are urban and most live in western Paraguay proper. The east is very sparsely populated. The capital and largest city is Asunción, a port on the Paraguay, located where the river flows out of the north, having bisected the country that bears its name, and continues south, forming the border with Argentina. Asunción, which, together with its suburbs had an estimated population of 2.0m. in mid-2010, is in a capital district, which, together with 17 departments, forms the local administration of the country. The next largest city, not even one-quarter of the size, is Ciudad del Este (formerly Puerto Presidente Stroessner), on the Paraná, near the Itaipú dam.

History

Prof. PETER CALVERT

Paraguay was already well populated when the Spanish first arrived in 1524. In 1537 the Spanish founded Asunción. The city enjoyed a brief period of importance until the foundation of Buenos Aires, in what is now Argentina, in 1580, when the seat of regional government was moved to the new port city. In the absence of important resources that were of interest to the Spanish, Paraguay remained economically undeveloped throughout the colonial period, and was politically and economically dependent on Buenos Aires. The indigenous Indians (Amerindians) established good relations with the Spanish and many intermarried; however, they retained their own language, Guaraní.

Jesuit missionaries soon arrived in the country. Indians converted to Christianity were resettled in missions, each farming the surrounding land. They built churches and created a unique, theocratic society. In 1767 the Jesuits were expelled and, for the first time, the Indians were directly exposed to Spanish rule. In 1810 Buenos Aires declared self-government, and on 14 May 1811 Paraguay became the first Spanish territory in the Americas to achieve independence.

The newly independent country was governed by Dr José Gaspar Rodríguez de Francia. Dr Francia, known as 'El Supremo', closed Paraguay's borders to the outside world, thus ensuring Paraguayan sovereignty, despite Argentine plans for annexation. He proclaimed Guaraní the sole language and ruled alone until his death in 1840. His successor, Carlos Antonio López (President, 1842–62), reopened Paraguay's borders. No less a dictator than his predecessor, López encouraged trade, built Paraguay's first railway and abolished slavery. He also gave Paraguay the institution that was to dominate its politics from then on, the army. López's son, Francisco Solano López, succeeded him as President-for-life, and during his rule Paraguay was defeated in the War of the Triple Alliance (1865–70) by the combined forces of Argentina, Brazil and Uruguay. The War, which became known in Paraguay as the 'National Epic' (*Epopeya Nacional*), resulted in the loss of 90% of the country's male population and left the economy devastated. Marshal López himself perished and was buried on the battlefield of Cerro Cora.

International rivalry for control of a defeated Paraguay began with the emergence of national political parties; Anglo-Argentine capital supported the Partido Liberal (Liberal Party), while Brazilian interests supported the Partido Colorado (Red Party), forerunner of the present Asociación Nacional Republicana—Partido Colorado (National Republican Association—Colorado Party). The conservative Colorados remained in power between 1870 and 1904. The 1883 Law of Sale of Public Land enclosed land that had previously been accessible to all and turned it into vast private estates. Peasants were either forced to leave or to work for a pittance. In 1904 a revolution brought the Liberals to power, but achieved little else. The period from 1870 to 1940 was marked by a tumultuous series of coups and counter-coups, as rival groups within each party vied for political control of the riches to be gained from widespread foreign ownership of the national territory.

Of the 45 Presidents who governed between 1870 and 1979, all achieved power by force or by fraud and most were ousted by violence or the threat of it. Factionalism, inability to compromise and the relative weakness of the parties in government left the army as the central institution in Paraguayan politics. Paraguay's historic need to defend its borders justified the role of the armed forces and led to one of the highest ratios in the world of military and police to population.

THE CHACO WAR AND ITS AFTERMATH

Paraguay gradually extended its control west of the River Paraguay, into the arid Chaco region. In response, Bolivia, which also claimed possession of the region, sent troops into the disputed territory. In the ensuing Chaco War (1932–35), Paraguay defeated Bolivia and, under the terms of a 1938 peace treaty, brokered by Argentina, was awarded three-quarters of the disputed territory.

Dissatisfaction with the Liberal war effort, however, led to the overthrow, by a military coup, of the Government of Eusebio Ayala in February 1936. The coup, led by Col Rafael Franco and supported by war veterans, brought to power the reformist Government of the Partido Revolucionario Febrerista (PRF—February Revolution Party). Although the Government managed to seize and redistribute some land, its tenure was short-lived and the Febreristas, as Franco's followers soon became known, were overthrown in 1937 by army officers loyal to the Liberals.

Following a two-year interim presidency, Marshal José Félix Estigarribia (the Liberal leader in the Chaco War) became President. Estigarribia was a reformist nationalist, popular with both the military and peasants. Nevertheless, his restoration of political freedoms was met with generalized unrest, including strikes, attacks by the press and conspiracies by some military cliques, among which the Febrerista movement survived. Estigarribia therefore declared himself a temporary dictator, repressed opposition and announced a developmentalist land programme which included land expropriation. A new corporatist Constitution, which came into force in August 1940, strengthened executive powers and permitted the President to serve a second term. Estigarribia did not benefit from these constitutional changes, however, as both he and his wife were killed in an aeroplane crash only three weeks after the Constitution was approved.

Estigarribia's former Minister of War, Gen. Higinio Morínigo, assumed power following his death. Initially, Morínigo was regarded as a reasonably benevolent autocrat who had the unenviable task of balancing opposing political forces to retain control of the nation. However, he soon assumed absolute powers, banning all political parties, repressing the activities of the trade union movement and dissolving the legislature. Eminent Liberals were forced into exile and Febrerista uprisings were suppressed.

The Allied victory in the Second World War, however, gave rise to a military movement in 1946, which was directed against the Axis sympathizers behind Morínigo. Exiles were allowed to return, and some conservative Colorados—as well as young, developmentalist Febrerista officers—were invited to join a Colorado-PRF coalition Government, under Morínigo's nominal control. From 1946 there was an increase in public unrest. Threatened by a growth in popular political activity and the emergence of a strong left-wing movement, Morínigo excluded the PRF from the Government and openly supported the Colorados. An attempted coup late in 1946 was followed by the disintegration of the coalition Government. Declaring a state of siege, Morínigo formed a new military cabinet in 1947; on the rebel side, Liberals and Communists joined Febrerista forces, led by Col Rafael Franco, in a civil war that erupted in March 1947 and divided the armed forces, with some four-fifths of officers defecting to the rebels. The Colorados triumphed, partly owing to support from the Argentine Government of Gen. Juan Domingo Perón Sosa.

The defeat of the rebels gave the Colorados control of the army and thus of the country. A number of coups followed, the first of which, in 1948, removed Morínigo from power. A presidential election was held in the same year, but the only candidate was a Colorado, Juan Natalicio González. President González was supported by an all-Colorado legislature; thus Paraguay had become a one-party state. Although Morínigo went into exile, factional infighting continued. There were uprisings by Colorado officers against the González Government. Eventually, González also fled abroad. Another Colorado faction, led by Dr Federico Chávez, assumed power.

In October 1951 President Chávez appointed Gen. Alfredo Stroessner Mattiauda, a veteran of the Chaco War, as Commander-in-Chief of the Armed Forces. Paraguay's economy began to deteriorate, however, and as inflation rose, so did political opposition. On 4 May 1954 Stroessner deposed Chávez in a military coup and in the July presidential election Stroessner, a Colorado candidate, was elected unopposed to complete Chávez's term of office.

THE RULE OF GENERAL STROESSNER

Gen. Stroessner immediately established a personal dictatorship. Restrictions were placed on all political activities and the Febrerista and Liberal opposition groups were ruthlessly suppressed. In 1956 Stroessner forced his principal rival within the Partido Colorado, Epifanio Méndez Fleitas, into exile. A state of siege was imposed. For over 30 years, until 1987, this state of siege was renewed every 60 days to comply with constitutional requirements. The unaccustomed sense of order that existed during Stroessner's dictatorship was advantageous to both domestic and foreign companies, and his commitment to IMF austerity measures contributed to the stabilization of the national currency, the guaraní, by 1957. In 1958 Stroessner, as the sole candidate of the only permitted party, was re-elected President and continued to be re-elected in this way every five years until 1988. Opposition continued, but it originated mostly from outside Paraguay; attacks from Argentina by exiles were repelled in 1959 and 1960.

Stroessner's command of the armed forces and of the economy contributed to the strength of his position. Increasing confidence in the economy in the 1960s led to the encouragement of some limited political activity. Stroessner encouraged the pretence of democracy by allowing a dissident wing of the Partido Liberal, the Renovación (Renovation) wing, to participate in controlled legislative elections, in which it received one-third of the seats in the legislature. This did not in any way diminish the President's personal dominance of Paraguayan politics, since he controlled the ruling Partido Colorado, which held the remaining two-thirds of the parliament. In 1959 some 400 Colorado politicians who opposed Stroessner had been imprisoned or had fled into exile, where they formed the Movimiento Popular Colorado (MOPOCO—Colorado Popular Movement), under the leadership of Méndez Fleitas. The President then reorganized the purged Partido Colorado in order to facilitate the entrenchment of an authoritarian style of government. By 1967 the Partido Colorado constituted only members loyal to Stroessner. In that year the President changed the Constitution of 1940 to permit his legal re-election to a fourth term of office.

In the late 1960s the overtly autocratic nature of Stroessner's regime encouraged criticism from the Roman Catholic Church in Paraguay, which, in turn, resulted in popular unrest. However, the upturn in the economy experienced in the 1970s contained much of the opposition. The majority of opposition parties boycotted the presidential and legislative elections of February 1983, enabling Stroessner to obtain more than 90% of the votes cast in the presidential poll, and in August he formally took office for a seventh five-year term. In the mid-1980s the question of who would succeed Stroessner became increasingly important; his son was considered a likely candidate. In April 1987 the President announced that the state of siege was to be ended, since extraordinary security powers were no longer necessary to maintain peace. His decision to seek re-election in February 1988, for an eighth consecutive term as President, precipitated the final crisis of Stroessner's regime. Although it was announced that he had received 89% of the votes cast, opposition leaders complained of electoral malpractice, and denounced his re-election as fraudulent. On 3 February 1989 Stroessner was overthrown in a coup, led by his son-in-law, Gen. Andrés Rodríguez, the second-in-command of the armed forces. (In September 2004 arrest warrants were issued for Stroessner and some 30 retired military personnel, including former Chief of Staff Alejandro Fretes Davalos. The warrants related to three Paraguayan nationals who 'disappeared' in Argentina, allegedly as a result of 'Plan Condor'—an intelligence operation to eliminate opponents of the Latin American military dictatorships in the 1970s. However, Stroessner died in August 2006.)

DEMOCRATIZATION

On 1 May 1989 Gen. Rodríguez was elected President, as the official candidate of the Partido Colorado, with 74% of the votes cast. The Partido Colorado, having won 73% of the votes in the congressional elections, automatically took two-thirds of the seats in both the lower house of the legislature, the Cámara de Diputados (Chamber of Deputies), and the Senado (Senate—48 and 24 seats, respectively). However, the process of democratization continued. In Paraguay's inaugural municipal elections, which took place on 26 May 1991, the Colorados won only 43% of the votes cast in 154 of the 206 municipalities, compared with 29% taken by the opposition Partido Liberal Radical Auténtico (PLRA—Authentic Radical Liberal Party). The Government's liberalizing austerity programme accelerated the formation of both new trade union and peasant movements, which carried out a series of illegal land occupations. On 20 June 1992 a new Constitution was promulgated.

Luis María Argaña Ferraro, leader of the conservative Movimiento de Reconciliación Colorado (MRC—Movement of Colorado Reconciliation) faction, was nominated in December 1992 as the Partido Colorado's candidate for the presidential election due in August 1993. His nomination, however, was reversed following pressure from President Rodríguez and from the Commander of the First Corps, Gen. Lino César Oviedo Silva, who had political ambitions of his own. Argaña took refuge in Brazil, urging his supporters not to vote for his rival. On 9 May 1993, however, the new official candidate, Juan Carlos Wasmosy, a former business associate of President Rodríguez but a political novice, won the presidential election with 40% of the votes cast. International observers agreed that the election was generally fair, despite the partisanship of Gen. Oviedo, and Wasmosy thus became the first civilian President of Paraguay for 39 years.

THE GOVERNMENT OF PRESIDENT WASMOSY

Wasmosy was inaugurated as President on 15 August 1993. There was widespread concern over the composition of his first Council of Ministers, many of whom had served in the administrations of Rodríguez and Stroessner. Despite the new President's apparent desire to restrict the influence of the military, the appointment on 18 August of Gen. Oviedo as Commander of the Army provoked further criticism. As a result, the PLRA refused to co-operate with the Colorados and there were violent demonstrations outside the Congreso Nacional (Congress) building. In September 1994 Wasmosy carried out a reshuffle of the command of the armed forces, strengthening the position of Gen. Oviedo, but tensions remained high between the two men and, on 22 April 1996, the President finally requested that Oviedo resign. Oviedo had begun to campaign for the leadership of the Partido Colorado and hoped to succeed Wasmosy as President in 1998. Oviedo refused to step down and, with the support of some 5,000 troops, in turn demanded the resignation of the President, who sought asylum in the US embassy. On 24 April the President agreed to a compromise by which Oviedo would retire from active service in exchange for the offer of the post of defence minister. The Congreso, however, refused to ratify Oviedo's appointment, which was retracted. The new Commander of the Army, Gen. Oscar Díaz Delmas, did not intervene, and three days later Argaña was again elected President of the Partido Colorado.

A purge of senior military commanders followed. In June 1996 Oviedo was arrested and detained on a charge of sedition, of which he was cleared by the Courts of Appeal in August and freed. In September he narrowly defeated Argaña in the election to become the Partido Colorado's presidential candidate. Following Oviedo's victory in the primary election, the President attempted to exclude him from the presidential contest. In October an arrest order was issued against Oviedo on charges of making inflammatory public statements. Nevertheless, the general eluded capture until mid-December, when he surrendered.

In March 1998 the Special Military Tribunal convened by President Wasmosy found Oviedo guilty of rebellion and sentenced him to 10 years' imprisonment and dishonourable discharge. In April the Supreme Electoral Tribunal annulled Oviedo's presidential candidacy. The nomination of the Partido Colorado was assumed by Raúl Cubas Grau, a wealthy engineer. Argaña was to be the new candidate for the vice-presidency. Despite public protests, the election was held as planned on 10 May 1998. Cubas Grau obtained 55% of the votes cast, ahead of the candidate of the Alianza Democrática (Democratic Alliance), Domingo Laíno, who received 44%.

DEMOCRATIZATION FALTERS

Cubas Grau assumed office on 15 August 1998 and a new Council of Ministers, including two pro-Oviedo generals, was sworn in on the same day. On 18 August the President issued a decree commuting Oviedo's prison sentence to time already served. The new Congreso immediately voted to condemn the decree and to initiate proceedings to impeach the President for unconstitutional behaviour. In December the Supreme Court ruled the decree unconstitutional; shortly afterwards the Argaña faction-controlled central apparatus of the Colorados expelled Oviedo from the party. While the Congreso was unable to muster the two-thirds' majority support necessary to impeach President Cubas Grau, the country remained in effective political deadlock, a situation exacerbated by the fact that the economy had been in recession since 1997.

The political impasse ended dramatically on 23 March 1999 when Vice-President Argaña was assassinated in the capital, Asunción, by three men in military uniform. The 66-year-old Vice-President and his supporters had just succeeded in regaining control of the Colorado headquarters, from which they had been expelled on 14 March by supporters of Oviedo and President Cubas Grau, who were immediately accused by supporters of Argaña of being at least the 'moral instigators' of the assassination. Large crowds took to the streets to demand the President's resignation, and the situation was further inflamed when six protesters, demonstrating outside the Congreso building on 25 March, were killed, apparently by an official at the finance ministry who was filmed firing at the crowds from a building near the Congreso.

On 28 March 1999, hours before the Congreso was due to vote on his impeachment, President Cubas Grau resigned and fled to Brazil, where he was granted political asylum. (In February 2002 Cubas Grau surrendered to the Paraguayan authorities to face trial for the killings of the protesters.) At the same time, Oviedo was granted asylum in Argentina. The President of the Congreso, pro-Argaña Colorado senator Luis González Macchi, became Head of State for the remainder of Cubas Grau's presidential term (which was scheduled to end in 2003). Hoping to overcome the disagreements existing within the Partido Colorado and between the Government and opposition in the legislature, on 30 March 1999 he announced the composition of a multi-party Government of National Unity. In July Oviedo was officially expelled from the Partido Colorado. His arrest was ordered three days later, but the Argentine authorities twice refused to extradite him, and in December he left Argentina to avoid being extradited by the new Government of Fernando de la Rúa.

On 18 May 2000 rebellious soldiers thought to be sympathetic to Oviedo seized the First Cavalry Division barracks and other strategic points. The coup was swiftly suppressed by the Government, which declared a 30-day nation-wide state of emergency, assuming extraordinary powers which resulted in the arrest of more than 70 people, mostly members of the security forces. (The subsequent trial of 18 military officials accused of involvement in the attempted coup collapsed, in judicially controversial circumstances, in May 2003.) However, in June Oviedo was arrested in Foz do Iguaçu, Brazil, by the Brazilian authorities. In March 2001 the Brazilian chief prosecutor ruled that Oviedo could be extradited; however, in December Brazil's Supreme Court rejected the ruling, stating that Oviedo was a victim of political persecution, and released him from imprisonment.

The PLRA withdrew from the governing coalition in February 2000 when it became clear that, contrary to the national unity agreement, the Partido Colorado would contest the election for a new Vice-President. In April the Colorados nominated Félix Argaña, son of the late Vice-President, to be their party's candidate. However, at the election, which was held on 13 August, the 53-year Colorado monopoly on power was ended when Argaña was narrowly defeated (by less than 1% of the votes cast) by the PLRA candidate, Julio César Franco.

In February 2001 the Minister of Education and Culture, Oscar Nicanor Duarte Frutos, resigned in order to campaign for the presidency of the Partido Colorado, which he secured, with almost 50% of the votes, in an election in May. Meanwhile, the Government was further undermined by tensions between the President and the Vice-President; Franco, as the most senior elected government official, demanded the resignation of President González Macchi in the interest of democratic legitimacy. In an attempt to restore confidence, in March González Macchi carried out a cabinet reshuffle in which José Antonio Moreno Rufinelli was appointed to the post of Minister of Foreign Affairs, replacing Juan Esteban Aguirre. On the same day, some 10,000 farmers marched through Asunción to protest against the Government's economic policy and to demand greater action on rural issues. Furthermore, at the end of March several thousand rural workers who had been camping outside the parliament building in protest at depressed cotton prices returned home after securing government concessions. In May the President of the Central Bank of Paraguay, Washington Ashwell, was forced to resign over his alleged involvement in the fraudulent transfer of US $16m. to a US bank account. Later that month, in response to allegations that the President had been a beneficiary of the misappropriated funds, opposition parties launched a bid to impeach him. However, the PLRA was forced to abandon the charges when, on 6 September, it failed to secure the necessary two-thirds' majority in the Congreso. In April 2002 González Macchi was formally charged with involvement in the corruption scandal and in June 2006 he was convicted of charges of false testimony and embezzlement. Following an unsuccessful appeal against the verdict, in December he was sentenced to eight years' imprisonment. Three other officials were each sentenced to terms of 10 years.

In late January 2002 the credibility of the Government was further undermined after two leaders of the left-wing party Movimiento Patria Libre (MPL—Free Homeland Movement) alleged that they had been illegally detained for 13 days and tortured by the police, with the knowledge of government ministers, as part of an investigation into a kidnapping case. In response to the allegations, the head of the national police force and his deputy, as well as the head of the judicial investigations department, were dismissed. Following sustained public and political pressure, the Minister of the Interior, Julio César Fanego, and the Minister of Justice and Labour, Silvio Ferreira Fernández, resigned soon afterwards, although both protested their innocence. In addition, the national intelligence agency, the Secretaría Nacional de Informaciones, was disbanded. The Cámara de Diputados issued a statement assigning some responsibility for the detention of the MPL leaders to the President and the Attorney-General, and describing the event as 'state terrorism'. Later that month 2,000 police officers were deployed to prevent a demonstration by peasants protesting against such 'state terrorism' from reaching government buildings.

During the first half of 2002 an alliance of farmers, trade unions and left-wing organizations staged mass protests throughout the country, demanding an end to the Government's free-market economic policies. The protests succeeded in reversing some of the Government's policies; most notably, the planned privatization of the telecommunications company Corporación Paraguaya de Comunicaciones (COPACO) was suspended in June. Nevertheless, the protests continued, and in July González Macchi declared a state of emergency, which was lifted two days later, after clashes between anti-Government protesters and the security forces resulted in two fatalities in Ciudad del Este. A further mass demonstration in September, organized by opposition parties, including Oviedo's Unión Nacional de Ciudadanos Éticos (UNACE—National Union of Ethical Citizens) grouping, resulted in more clashes with the security forces.

No sooner was the state of emergency lifted than dissident legislators of the ruling Partido Colorado were reported to have initiated impeachment proceedings against President González Macchi on corruption charges. Meanwhile, despite limited attempts to bring the economy under control, both the fiscal deficit and, in consequence, government borrowing had continued to rise. In late June 2002 the Congreso had to raise the state guarantee of private bank deposits when Banco Alemán, the second largest private bank in the country, appeared to be in difficulties. (The bank was liquidated in September.) Furthermore, the IMF refused to give assistance until the Congreso had agreed to increase the standard rate of value-added tax (VAT) and introduced a special tax on luxury items. However, the legislature failed to approve the necessary reforms, postponing the tax reform package until December; as a result, in late October James Spalding resigned as Minister of Finance.

On 5 December 2002 the Cámara de Diputados approved a proposal to impeach President González Macchi on five charges of corruption and failure to fulfil the duties of the presidency. Supported by the pro-Oviedo faction of the Partido Colorado and by the opposition PLRA, this was the third such proposal since July. González Macchi found his position as President ever more tenuous ahead of the presidential election that was due to be held in April 2003. In an attempt to avoid proceedings against him, Macchi offered to leave office early, immediately following the April election (instead of in August, when the inauguration of the new head of state would take place). However, on 11 February the Senado voted against approving the charges against him, by 25 votes to 18, with one abstention and one absence, thus falling short of the two-thirds' majority required by the Constitution.

THE GOVERNMENT OF PRESIDENT DUARTE

The legislative and presidential elections of 27 April 2003 passed off without incident. The ruling Asociación Nacional Republicana—Partido Colorado extended its unbroken 56-year hold on power as its candidate, the 46-year-old lawyer and former minister Oscar Nicanor Duarte Frutos, won 37.1% of the votes cast in the presidential ballot, compared with the 24.0% secured by the PLRA candidate and former Vice-President, Julio César Franco Gómez. A businessman, Pedro Nicolás Fadul, of the Patria Querida (Beloved Fatherland) movement, came third, with 21.3% of the votes, and Guillermo Sánchez Guffanti, a radical populist representing Oviedo's UNACE party, came fourth, with 13.5% of the ballot. Concurrent elections to the 80-seat Cámara de Diputados gave the Colorados 37 seats, the PLRA 21 seats, the Patria Querida 10 seats, UNACE 10 seats and the Partido País Solidario (Party for a Country of Solidarity) two seats. The Colorados also won the most seats in the 45-seat Senado (16), followed by the PLRA (12) and the Patria Querida (eight).

The new President, who took office on 15 August 2003, advocated free-market policies and pledged to address corruption, renegotiate Paraguay's external debt and restore the country's credibility internationally. Duarte promised to take personal charge of the customs service and declared that the sale of state-owned assets would remain a lesser priority than other measures to improve the Government's finances. The IMF initially remained reluctant to revive its lending programme to Paraguay, in view of the Congreso's record of hostility towards reform measures, raising fears that the incoming administration risked an early financial crisis. However, the President soon demonstrated his determination to address the problem of corruption, announcing his intention to reform the judiciary in August. Furthermore, in October the Minister of the Interior, Roberto Eudez González Segovia, a close ally of the President, was forced to resign after being accused of corrupt practices. As a result of the new Government's policies, in December the World Bank granted the country a structural adjustment loan worth US $30m. to fund the proposed reforms, and in the same month the IMF approved a stand-by loan of $73m. on condition that structural reform continue.

Together with measures to overhaul the unpopular Supreme Court, the anti-corruption campaign won President Duarte unprecedented popularity. However, in January 2004 the President returned from holiday in Brazil surrounded by heavy security, reportedly because an assassination attempt had been planned. Later in the same month farmers' organizations demanded the resignation of the Minister of the Interior after police had opened fire on a group of people demonstrating against crop-spraying, killing two farmers; a large number of officials were later disciplined. The President continued to encounter congressional opposition to his reform measures, although in March reform of the Supreme Court was achieved with the replacement of two-thirds of its nine justices (observers noted that the new appointments were simply distributed between the three main political parties). Later in the year a proposed amendment to the Constitution to allow presidential re-election failed, and by the end of 2004 the President's popularity had fallen, although at 44% it was still high compared with many of his predecessors.

Meanwhile, in June 2004, Oviedo returned from exile in Brazil, apparently hoping both to avoid conviction for the various charges he faced, including sedition against the Wasmosy administration, and to relaunch his political career. Instead, he was arrested at the airport and taken to military prison to begin a 10-year sentence. However, in October he was provisionally acquitted of charges of sedition, and in January 2005 he was found not guilty of charges relating to the discovery of an arms cache. Nevertheless, several other charges were still pending against him, and in April 2005 the Supreme Court ruled that he would have to serve his 10-year term of imprisonment. In June several thousand of his supporters protested in Asunción against his detention.

A spate of kidnappings in 2004 led to the replacement of the Minister of the Interior, Orlando Fiorotto Sánchez, with Nelson Mora, hitherto the Attorney-General, following the kidnap and murder in October of the 11-year-old son of a businessman. The head of the national police was also dismissed. Previously, in September Cecilia Cubas, the 32-year-old daughter of former President Cubas Grau, was abducted in a paramilitary-style operation, apparently by a large criminal syndicate. Despite the alleged payment of a ransom, in February 2005 her body was found in a house near Asunción. Six people subsequently arrested in connection with the kidnap and murder were alleged to have connections to the MPL and to the Fuerzas Armadas Revolucionarias de Colombia—Ejército del Pueblo (FARC), which was believed to be using Paraguay as a transshipment centre for drugs-trafficking. Allegations of serious investigative shortcomings by the authorities prompted the dismissal of Nelson Mora, who was replaced by the popular Rogelio Benítez, a former mayor of Encarnación. Thirty-two senior police officials were also dismissed amid criticism of the deteriorating security situation. In March Colombia and Paraguay signed an agreement to co-operate on security and drugs-trafficking issues, in support of the new three-year security plan for Paraguay announced by Duarte in February. The plan met with vociferous and occasionally violent protests by peasants' groups, owing primarily to fears that a greater military presence in rural areas would lead to increased repression of their campaign for agrarian reform, which had involved illegal land occupations since 2003. By the late 2000s kidnapping remained a significant problem, especially in the Triple Border region, where drugs-trafficking and smuggling was rife. In May 2007 Duarte met his Brazilian counterpart, Luiz Inácio Lula da Silva, in Asunción and agreed to increase legitimate trade and strengthen cross-border co-operation to reduce smuggling. They also signed an agreement to build another bridge across the River Paraná, which separates the two countries.

Meanwhile, amid considerable controversy, in February 2006 President Duarte was elected leader of the Partido Colorado, defeating his rival, Osvaldo Domínguez Dibb, who represented the pro-Stroessner ('Stronista') faction of the party. However, also in February, the Electoral Court ruled that the President of the Republic could not hold an additional office. None the less, in the following month the Supreme Court overturned the lower court's decision and, consequently, Duarte assumed the leadership of his party in March. On the same day he announced a proposed referendum to seek approval for amendments to the Constitution to allow presidential re-election. Opposition to Duarte's leadership of the Colorados continued unabated, with the opposition initiating impeachment proceedings against the President and five Supreme Court justices. Confronted with such resistance, Duarte relinquished the party presidency and José Alderete

Rodríguez, hitherto Minister of Public Works and Communications, assumed the post.

The ruling Partido Colorado performed well in local government elections in November 2006, winning control of 150 of 231 municipalities. The Colorados retained control of Asunción, where their candidate, Evangelista de Gallegos, a popular former Minister of Tourism and a television presenter, became the first female mayor of the capital, with 46% of the votes cast. With the opposition divided, the PLRA also made gains, albeit with the aid of Oviedo supporters.

THE GOVERNMENT OF PRESIDENT LUGO

In February 2007 more than 30 social and labour groups joined opposition parties in signing an accord to form the Concertación Nacional, subsequently restyled the Alianza Patriótica para el Cambio (APC—Patriotic Alliance for Change), in the hope of defeating the Partido Colorado in the forthcoming elections. During 2007, moreover, a new candidate emerged who seemed capable of winning the presidency in April 2008, namely Fernando Lugo Méndez, a former Roman Catholic bishop of San Pedro, who had resigned from the priesthood in late 2006 in order to become more actively involved in politics. The Partido Colorado unsuccessfully attempted to disqualify Lugo from standing as a presidential candidate, on the grounds that his resignation had not at that stage been accepted by the Vatican, which regarded entry to the priesthood as a lifelong commitment.

On the other hand, even though President Duarte was forced to abandon his attempt to secure re-election, the Colorados remained divided over their choice of presidential nominee: Duarte favoured the Minister of Education and Culture, Blanca Margarita Ovelar de Duarte, but in June 2007 Vice-President Luis Castiglioni Soria and Partido Colorado President José Alderete Rodríguez also announced their intention to contest the party primaries and later in the year retired Gen. Oviedo was acquitted by the Supreme Court of involvement in the 1996 coup, opening the way for his candidature. Hence at the party primaries in December 2007 Ovelar only narrowly defeated Castiglioni, and, although in late January 2008 the state election commission confirmed Ovelar as the winner (with 45.0% of the votes cast, compared with the 44.5% obtained by Castiglioni), the defeated candidate refused to accept its decision.

Partly as result of these divisions within the Partido Colorado, in the presidential election, held on 20 April 2008, Fernando Lugo, standing for the APC, ended 60 years of Colorado rule, securing 40.9% of the votes cast, followed by Ovelar, with 30.6%, and Oviedo, representing UNACE, with 21.9%; the remaining votes were divided between four minority candidates. In the concurrent legislative elections, however, the Partido Colorado remained the largest party in both congressional chambers, winning 30 of the 80 seats in the Cámara de Diputados and 15 of the 45 seats in the Senado. The PLRA and UNACE obtained 27 and 15 seats in the lower chamber, respectively, and 14 and nine seats in the Senado. Lugo, who was sworn in on 15 August, advocated agrarian reform, increased support for the indigenous population, and negotiations to secure more revenue from the Itaipú Dam, the joint hydroelectric project with Brazil from which, to date, Brazil had been by far the main beneficiary.

Lugo's support base had included those on both the left and the right, and, notably, the traditional opposition PLRA. However, in Lugo's first year in office at least, the entrenched position of the Partido Colorado enabled it successfully to frustrate the hopes of his supporters of real change. The biggest problem arose within the area of agrarian reform, not least because records showed that title had been granted to some 125% of the national territory. Brazil's armed forces were deployed to the border area between the two countries on 20 October 2008, ostensibly for drug interdiction, but the operation followed more than 80 land occupations and evictions in the first 100 days of the new administration, one resulting in the death of Bienvenido Melgarejo, a member of the Farmers' Association in Alto Paraná. Many of those advocating land invasions objected to the settlement of Brazilians in Paraguayan territory. Although the actual number of invasions was reported to be relatively low, they were symbolic of resentment at the overwhelming influence of absentee landlords.

In late April 2010 some 1,000 additional troops and police officers were sent to the border area to combat a small rural guerrilla movement, the Ejército del Pueblo Paraguayo (EPP—Paraguayan People's Army), which was reported to have links to the FARC. The Congreso granted special powers to the authorities in the troubled area, which was also a haven for drugs smugglers. In early May the President Lugo met with his Brazilian counterpart, Luiz Inácio Lula da Silva. After protracted negotiations, in 2009 President da Silva had finally agreed to make some concessions regarding the cost of electricity from the Itaipú Dam, located on the Paraná river along the Paraguay–Brazil border. The attainment of these concessions, which allowed for a fairer system of payment and enabled Paraguay to sell power directly to Brazilian companies, represented a significant political victory for Lugo. A major power distribution failure in November 2009, which had resulted in a blackout across the whole of Paraguay and most of south-eastern Brazil, had been quickly resolved but served as a timely reminder of the dam's strategic importance.

Economy

Prof. PETER CALVERT

Paraguay is an agricultural country but its economy is determined to a large extent by its geographical position, which enables a relatively large informal sector to benefit from smuggling. This informal sector is reputed to be as large as the formal sector. In recent years Paraguay has also suffered greatly from overspill from the periodic economic crises in Argentina, and more recently from the world recession. The country has a land area of 406,752 sq km (157,048 sq miles) and is one of the smaller republics of South America. Together with Bolivia, it is one of the continent's two land-locked countries, with Brazil to the north and east, Argentina to the south and Bolivia to the west. According to mid-2010 estimates, the country had a population of 6,451,122 and, therefore, a population density of approximately 15.9 persons per sq km, making it one of the least densely populated countries in the world.

The country is divided into two distinct geographical regions by the River Paraguay, which joins the River Paraná at an altitude of 46 m above sea level. The majority of the population lives within 160 km of the capital, Asunción, to the east of the river. This region consists of grassy plains and low hills and has a temperate climate. It is divided into two zones by a ridge of hills, to the east of which lies the Paraná plateau, which ranges from 600 m to 2,300 m in height. West of the ridge lie gently rolling hills. To the west of the Paraguay river is the Chaco region, an arid, marshy plain extending to the foothills of the Andes and to the country's border with Bolivia. The Chaco accounts for 61% of Paraguay's land area but is inhabited by less than 2% of the population.

In the 1980s Paraguay had one of the highest population growth rates in Latin America. It was still high, at 2.4%, in 2009. At that time the birth rate was reported by the US Central Intelligence Agency to be 28.17 births per 1,000 inhabitants and the death rate 4.46 deaths per 1,000. The infant mortality rate per 1,000 live births was 24.68 in 2009, compared with 24 in 2004, but estimates of life expectancy at birth had improved steadily in recent years to 75.77 years in

2009. Public sanitation was generally good, although water pollution presented a health risk for many urban residents. Some 23% of the population, mainly in rural areas, had no access to an improved water source. In 2002 there was a ratio of 1.1 doctors to every 1,000 inhabitants. Literacy, at 95%, is high by regional standards.

Owing to the fertility of eastern Paraguay, economic activity was widespread but unevenly distributed. Historically, the main concentration of activity was around Asunción, with a secondary, more recent, economic zone based in the industrial park, Parque Industrial Oriente, 23 km from Ciudad del Este (formerly Puerto Presidente Stroessner). The Chaco region accounted for less than 3% of economic activity. In 2005 the percentage of the population below the national poverty line was estimated at 32%, representing almost one in every three Paraguayans. However, according to the evidence of a survey published by the Government's own statistical service, this figure would include some 70% of Paraguayans in rural areas (only 60.3% of the population was urban in 2008) living on or near the margin of subsistence. Spending on social welfare in the Stroessner era (1954–89) was very low, resulting in a poorly funded education system, inadequate health care and limited sanitation that persisted in the 2000s. The literacy rate, however, was relatively impressive in 2007, estimated at 94.6%, most Paraguayans being bilingual in Spanish and the indigenous official language, Guaraní.

In 2009 the World Bank estimated gross national income (GNI) at US $13,610m. and GNI per head at $1,710 ($4,100 by purchasing-power parity—PPP), ranking Paraguay 121st in the world by PPP, and among the World Bank's lower middle-income countries. In the UN Development Programme's Human Development Index, updated in 2009 and based on 2007 figures, Paraguay ranked 101st in the world, a fall of three places but with a slightly increased score.

AGRICULTURE

Agriculture (including hunting, forestry and fishing) was fundamental to the Paraguayan economy, accounting for 22.3% of gross domestic product (GDP) in 2009 and virtually all export earnings. Agricultural GDP increased at an average annual rate of 2.7% in 1995–2005; real agricultural GDP increased by 4.0% in 2007. In 2006/07 the sector (including forestry) engaged an estimated 31.2% of the employed labour force. Some 9m. ha of land was classified as arable (7.5% of the total land area), of which only some 30% was cultivated. The ownership of land remained one of the most unequal in Latin America. The 1991 agricultural census showed that 351 landowners controlled some 40% of the country's arable land. There was a large subsistence sector, including more than 200,000 families. A further 200,000 rural families were 'landless'. Land reform was a key electoral promise of President Fernando Lugo Méndez, who was elected in April 2008. A year later, however, conservative forces had been able to stifle reform, and growing unrest had led to widespread land occupations, especially in the Eastern region bordering Brazil.

Paraguay is largely self-sufficient in basic foodstuffs and has expanded production in export crops. Maize, cassava (manioc) and wheat are the main food crops. According to the latest available FAO figures, in 2007 the largest area, 2.8m. ha, was planted with oil crops, of which 836,320 metric tons were harvested. In the same year 833,300 ha of cereal crops were planted, yielding a total of 1.85m. tons, of which wheat accounted for 675,000 tons and maize 1.0m. tons. Some 320,000 ha was cultivated with cassava, of which 5.1m. tons were produced in 2007 and 4.8m tons in 2008.

The main products grown for export were soybeans, oilseeds, cotton and sugar cane. Production of soya and cotton increased dramatically with the colonization of the eastern border region in the 1970s, and the area planted continued to expand up to the beginning of the 21st century. Paraguay is the world's sixth largest producer of soybeans. Output was 6.0m. tons in 2007, according to FAO, and 6.8m. tons in 2008. The area planted was 2,845,000 ha. The value of exports rose from US $59m. in 2002 to an estimated $890m. in 2007. In order to increase productivity and the pest- and drought-resistance of their crops, Paraguayan farmers agreed in March 2005 to pay royalties in the 2004/05 crop year to a US-based corporation, Monsanto, for its genetically modified (GM) soybeans, at a rate of $2.82 per sack of seed, sufficient to plant roughly 1 ha. All these developments, and the generally harmful impact of soybean cultivation on the countryside and ecosystems, are strongly opposed by the supporters of agrarian reform.

Paraguay is the world's eighth largest producer of sesame seeds, growing 100,000 metric tons in 2008. Government aid to sesame farmers was extended in early 2009.

Production of seed cotton lint increased to an estimated 330,000 metric tons in 2004, compared with an estimated 172,260 tons in the previous year. However, in 2005 output declined to an estimated 198,000 tons and remained at about 180,000 tons thereafter. Cotton export earnings similarly declined, to an estimated US $34.3m. in 2006. Following a slight recovery in 2007, to $47.1m., cotton export earnings fell dramatically, to a preliminary $19.2m. in 2008, when 185,000 tons were produced. In that year oilseed exports earned a preliminary $1,502.5m., consolidating its position as the country's most valuable export crop. According to FAO estimates, in 2008 sugar cane covered 90,000 ha and its production totalled 4.5m. tons. Among tree crops, three were of particular note: in 2008 46,000 tons of tung nuts were grown on 12.000 ha of land; 3,100 tons of green coffee were produced on 2,600 ha of land; and 32,000 ha of land yielded some 87,500 tons of maté (sometimes known as Paraguayan tea, although Paraguay is now only the world's third largest producer), almost all of which was for domestic consumption.

The gently undulating plains of eastern Paraguay are good ranching country and beef exports make up the largest remaining part of the formal sector. Beef, pork, eggs and milk are produced for domestic consumption. Stocks recorded by FAO in 2008 included 10.6m. head of cattle, 560,000 sheep, 168,000 goats and 21.0m. chickens. The stock of pigs rose slightly from 1.5m. in 2004 to an estimated 1.7m. in 2008. Some 400,000 horses and 35,000 asses were still employed. As with land ownership, possession of livestock in Paraguay was unevenly distributed, with 58% of cattle owned by 1% of the producers. Cattle-ranching used to be the most important sector of the Paraguayan economy, but all meat-packing plants were closed in 1981 as a result of the European Union (EU)'s Common Agricultural Policy and the Lomé Convention (which was succeeded by the Cotonou Agreement in 2000), which excluded Paraguay. Exports of meat and meat preparations totalled only a preliminary US $621.4m. in 2008, equivalent to 14.0% of the total value of exports.

River fishing forms a significant part of the domestic diet. The fishing catch in 2006 totalled an estimated 22,100 metric tons.

Paraguay's once abundant forest resources continue to be severely depleted by competitive logging for export. The damage has been most extreme in eastern Paraguay, which had lost more than three-quarters of its forest cover by the late 1990s. Transport costs acted as a deterrent in the Chaco region, where some 10.5m. ha of primary forest cover remained. Given the continued illegal logging trade and the absence of a systematic reforestation programme, it was not surprising that, between 1990 and 2005, Paraguay lost 12.7% of its forest cover, or around 2.7m. ha, and in the latter year forest cover was officially given as 18.5m. ha. Official figures almost certainly understated the deforestation; FAO forestry statistics showed that in 2008 the country produced 4.04m. cu m of industrial roundwood and 6.35m. cu m of fuelwood, including charcoal, for domestic consumption. In 2008 sawnwood production was an estimated 550,000 cu m, of which 82,066 cu m was exported. Exports of wood and wood products totalled some US $111.3m. in 2008, equivalent to 2.5% of total export earnings.

MINING AND ENERGY

Paraguay has few proven mineral resources. Gypsum, limestone and clays found near the Paraguay river are used locally for building purposes. From 1964 limestone has been mined for the manufacture of Portland cement by the state-owned Industria Nacional de Cemento at Vallemí, in the department of Concepción. Deposits of bauxite, copper, iron ore and manganese are known to exist but have been utilized only on a small scale. Deposits of uranium have been found in both the east and west of the country.

Total electricity consumption in 2009 was estimated by the US Energy Information Administration at 85,000m. kWh. In 2007 53,190m. kWh were generated, of which 45,140m. kWh was exported, primarily to Brazil. Paraguay, bordered by two of the great rivers of South America (the Paraguay and Paraná), has abundant potential hydroelectric generating capacity, which has been developed to create substantial revenue. Installed hydoelectric generating capacity in 2005 was 7,410 MW. The most important source of power was the Paraguayan-Brazilian Itaipú project on the River Paraná, with an installed generating capacity of 14,000 MW. Under the terms of the agreement, Paraguay and Brazil were each to receive one-half of the energy generated; any that they could not consume was then to be offered to the other country at a preferential rate. However, under an outdated agreement not due for revision until 2023, Brazil only paid Paraguay $2.70 per MWh for electricity against a international market price of nearly $60 in 2009.

Following the Chaco War (1932–35), there were repeated hopes that petroleum deposits might be found in that part of the Chaco plain adjoining the southern Bolivian oilfields. These hopes were reactivated by the discovery of petroleum deposits in the northern Argentine province of Formosa in 1984. However, exploratory wells in the Chaco proved to be dry, and in July 1996 the US company Phillips Petroleum abandoned its search. During 2009 Paraguay consumed some 25,100 barrels per day (b/d) of petroleum products, all of which were imported. The Petróleos Paraguayos (PETROPAR) refinery at Villa Elisa had a capacity of only 7,500 b/d. In June 2005 the Presidents of the four Mercosur (Mercado Común del Sur—Southern Common Market) member countries (Paraguay, Argentina, Brazil and Uruguay) signed an agreement creating an 'energy ring' (anillo energético), which would facilitate the supply and storage of natural gas from the Camisea field in Peru. Given the negative impact of rapidly rising oil and gas prices, the Lugo Government, which took office in August 2008, was expected to try to negotiate a more favourable price for its electricity exports.

MANUFACTURING

During 1995–2005 the manufacturing sector decreased by an average of 0.3% per year. According to provisional figures, industry accounted for 18.3% of GDP in 2008 and manufacturing for 12.7%. Manufacturing (including mining and quarrying) employed 10.6% of the economically active population, while total industry, including energy and construction, employed 18.5% in 2007. Industry was dominated by the processing of agricultural inputs, including sugar and wood products. There were also many small companies engaged in import substitution for the domestic market, particularly in the cement, textiles and beverages sub-sectors. From 1995 the country's membership of Mercosur brought significant export advantages, but also increased competition from Argentine and Brazilian imports.

There were two steel mills. The formerly state-owned Aceros del Paraguay (ACEPAR) was privatized in 1997; a second, built by a Brazilian company, Ioscape, to process ore from Corumbá (Brazil), began operations in 1994. There was some production of metal goods and machinery. In the 1990s there was substantial investment in the production of cotton yarn and paper. However, Paraguayan industry has not found it easy to compete within Mercosur, despite the organization's benefit to the country in other respects.

COMMERCE

The main feature of the economic upturn of the 1970s was the joint development with Brazil of the Itaipú hydroelectric project on the River Paraná, which involved a good deal of construction work and attracted many Brazilian settlers. The opening of road links with Brazil stimulated trade, both legal and illegal. Although inflation was high, the second half of the 1970s generated annual GDP growth rates of more than 10%. This growth ended abruptly, however, when the Brazilian economy entered a period of crisis in 1982. GDP growth fell to 1.6% per year, and although work continued at Itaipú, the huge revenues anticipated from the sale of Paraguay's share of its power to Brazil's developing south did not materialize.

In the late 1980s Paraguay, taking advantage of its geographical position, was able to re-establish itself as an entrepôt for intra-regional trade. A busy commercial sector was well established, engaged in the import of consumer goods from the USA, Japan and other Asian countries for re-export to neighbouring countries. The services sector increased by an average of 0.9% per year in 1995–2005 and continued to grow, accounting for 59.6% of GDP in 2009. Services employed 55% of the economically active population in 2008. Commerce was, however, impeded by excessive bureaucracy to such an extent that it was estimated to take an average of 74 days to start a new small business.

Paraguay's informal economy was believed to be as extensive as its formal one. Vastly improved road links with Brazil contributed to Paraguay becoming a major centre for contraband activities. Much of the informal economy consisted of profit from the smuggling of genuine and counterfeit clothing, valuable electronic goods and luxury items such as watches, perfume, spirits and tobacco into Argentina and Brazil. Paraguay was also a major illicit producer of marijuana (cannabis) for the international market, and in recent years played an increasingly significant role in the transshipment of cocaine from Colombia to the USA and Europe.

One of the consequences of this 'black' economy was inflation. Between 2006 and 2007 consumer price inflation rose from 9.6% to 12% and was estimated to be 11% in 2008, with a central bank discount rate of 20%. Since the Brazilian devaluation in 1998, Paraguay has operated a 'managed float' of its currency. At the end of December 2006 the exchange rate to the US dollar was 5,190 guaraníes. Although owing to the weakening of the dollar this had fallen to 4,104 guaraníes by mid-June 2008, the value of the dollar had risen to 4,911 guaraníes by early June 2010.

TRANSPORT AND COMMUNICATIONS

Historically, waterways provided the main mode of transport for foreign trade in Paraguay, although from the 1980s road transport became more important and by 1999 the leading point of exit for exports of cereals and vegetables was Ciudad del Este. The country had 3,100 km of waterways in 2007, with ports at Asunción, Villeta, San Antonio and Encarnación. At the end of 2008 the merchant fleet consisted of 47 vessels, with a total displacement of some 53,600 grt. The country had free-port facilities at Nueva Palmira in Uruguay, although in the 1990s services on the Paraguay–Paraná network became both irregular and expensive. From 1994 Paraguay was linked with the Brazilian port of Santos on the Atlantic Ocean by the Hidrovía project, a network of canals and waterways sponsored by Mercosur.

Paraguay's principal road network was a triangle linking Asunción, Encarnación and Ciudad del Este. The Trans-Chaco Highway linked Asunción to the Bolivian border and there were links with Argentina and Brazil via the international bridge over the River Paraná at Ciudad del Este. In 1999, of the estimated 29,500 km of roads, 14,986 km were paved; however, most roads are of only two lanes and interrupted by tolls and police checks. Excessive reliance on road-hauled container traffic continued to cause congestion on the bridge at Ciudad del Este, despite the opening, in 1995, of a new container port at Hernandarias on the banks of Lake Itaipú.

The state-owned railway, Ferrocarriles del Paraguay, SA, owned a 374-km line (the Ferrocarril Presidente Carlos Antonio López) linking Asunción with Encarnación, on the Argentine border, but regular services operated only as far as Ypacaraí, 36 km from Asunción. A number of other lines, mostly privately owned, made up the remainder of the nominally operated 971 km (441 km standard gauge) of track.

There were more than 800 airports in the country, 13 with paved runways, three of which had runways of more than 3,047 m. The main international airport, Aeropuerto Internacional Silvio Pettirossi, is situated 15 km from Asunción. The state-owned international airline, Líneas Aéreas Paraguayas (LAPSA), was privatized in 1994; in 1997 its name changed to

Transportes Aéreos del Mercosur and 80% of ownership was transferred to TAM Linhas Aéreas of Brazil. Aerolíneas Paraguayas (ARPA) operates daily flights between Paraguay's major cities. In 2008 some 465,911 passengers were carried.

The state-owned telephone service, the Corporación Paraguaya de Comunicaciones (COPACO), had a long history of overstaffing and low productivity. In November 1995 (when the number of people waiting for telephone lines was twice as many as the number of existing subscribers) the Administración Nacional de Telecomunicaciones (as COPACO was then known) signed an agreement with the German company Siemens to modernize the telephone system. By 2006, however, the network, covering 331,100 subscribers or 6% of the population, was still inadequate, but in the mean time two mobile cellular telephone companies had rapidly expanded to reach an estimated 3.2m. mobile subscribers. In 2008 there were 491,000 fixed line subscribers. In 2007 there were five television broadcast stations and a reported 990,000 televisions, although given Paraguay's central role in the regional smuggling of electrical goods, this figure seemed rather low. In 2008 there were 894,212 internet users, a penetration rate of only 14%.

GOVERNMENT FINANCE AND INVESTMENT

Real GDP rose steadily from 2003 to 2007. Total public-sector expenditure in 2007 was 10,244,000m. guaraníes, representing about 13% of GDP. The tax burden stood at 11.7% of GDP in 2007 and tax evasion was estimated at 60%–70%. Despite this, in 2007 an estimated surplus of 593m. guaraníes was recorded.

Unlike many lower middle-income countries, Paraguay was not heavily indebted. Reserves had fallen significantly from 1997, as the Central Bank was obliged to sell foreign exchange to arrest speculative attacks on the local currency, but later stabilized. Total foreign exchange reserves, including gold, were US $3,431m. at the end of 2009, representing some 27% of GDP. At the end of 2008 the country's external debt, then $3,487m., was still low by world standards and the cost of debt-servicing amounted to $459m.

FOREIGN TRADE AND BALANCE OF PAYMENTS

Paraguay's most important trading partner has traditionally been Brazil, and it has benefited considerably from its membership of Mercosur. However, there were substantial differences both between exports and imports and from one year to the next. The main exports in 2009 were soya beans, animal feed, cotton, meat, edible oils, electricity, and wood and leather. The main destinations for exports in 2009 were Brazil (21%), Uruguay (17.0%), Chile (12%), Argentina (11%), and Russia (4%). Paraguay imported road vehicles, consumer goods, tobacco (much of which was illegally re-exported), fuels, electrical machinery, tractors and vehicle parts. The main sources of imports in 2008 were the People's Republic of China (30%), Brazil (23%), Argentina (16%) and the USA (5%).

In 2009 the trade deficit was estimated at US $289m., a significant improvement compared with $509.5m in 2008. In 1992–2000 the trade balance followed a trend of gently rising export levels being overtaken by a steep and continuing increase in the value of imports, a pattern that led to a widening deficit on the balance of trade. From 2001–04 the trade balance fell, and fluctuated thereafter. Despite the improvement in the trade deficit, the current account surplus fell in 2007, to $126.1m., (from $219.1m. in 2006). In 2008 total imports increased by 44.6%, compared with a rise in exports of 37.5%, contributing to a deficit of $345.0m. on the current account in that year (equivalent to 3.8% of GDP). However, these fluctuations also impacted on the other Mercosur countries. By the time of the G-20 Summit in April 2009 Argentina had unilaterally imposed tariffs on a variety of goods including shoes, appliances, farm machinery, processed food, steel, iron and textiles. As a result, Paraguay announced on 1 March that to protect its economy it would have to levy increased tariffs on goods from both Argentina and Brazil. The Minister of Finance, Dionisio Borda, also launched a 'Buy Paraguayan' campaign.

CONCLUSION

Paraguay's geographical position places its economy at a competitive disadvantage, while also offering opportunities, upon which the informal sector has been quick to seize. The country's main economic problems remain the extent of its informal sector, a lack of confidence among investors, the vagaries of climate, a dependency on agriculture and the low intrinsic value of the country's principal agricultural exports. Successive governments attempted to resolve at least some of these problems and Paraguay benefited substantially from its incorporation into Mercosur. Although in July 2006 President Nicanor Duarte Frutos threatened to withdraw Paraguay from the trading bloc, arguing that Mercosur's largest two partners, Brazil and Argentina, exerted undue influence over economic policy and terms of trade, in reality he had no choice but to remain within the organization. In that year Paraguay began a new stand-by agreement with the IMF for SDR 30m. (US $44.1m.). This came to an end in August 2008. Though no money was requested or given, the agreement obliged the Government to meet certain IMF guide-lines, and in a final review in August 2008 the IMF expressed approval of the Government's efforts in reaching these criteria.

However, in the latter part of 2008 the country began to suffer from a prolonged drought, and in October the impact of the world banking crisis forced the new Lugo administration to cut interest rates and ease economic policy. At the same time, owing to a sudden collapse in export demand for meat and soybeans, Paraguay was the first country in the region to be affected by the combined effects of the downturn. That its Government maintained a fiscal surplus, debt was low and inflation—at 7.5% at the end of 2008—was within the IMF target range was, however, viewed abroad as positive, although in March 2009 the IMF noted that the main challenge remained to improve financial supervision. During 2009 political infighting prevented the Congreso from enacting radical legislation, with the consequence that economic policy hardly changed from that of the preceding Government. The economy contracted by 3.5% in 2009, as a result of a fall in world prices and lower demand for primary exports, and Paraguay's economy remained vulnerable to both the international economic crisis and short-term changes in neighbouring states.

Statistical Survey

Sources (unless otherwise stated): Dirección General de Estadística, Encuestas y Censos, Naciones Unidas, esq. Saavedra, Fernando de la Mora, Zona Norte; tel. (21) 51-1016; fax (21) 50-8493; internet www.dgeec.gov.py; Banco Central del Paraguay, Avda Federación Rusa y Marecos, Casilla 861, Barrio Santo Domingo, Asunción; tel. (21) 61-0088; fax (21) 60-8149; e-mail ccs@bcp.gov.py; internet www.bcp.gov.py; Secretaría Técnica de Planificación, Presidencia de la República, Iturbe y Eligio Ayala, Asunción.

Area and Population

AREA, POPULATION AND DENSITY

Area (sq km)	406,752*
Population (census results)	
26 August 1992	4,152,588
28 August 2002	
Males	2,627,831
Females	2,555,249
Total	5,183,080
Population (official estimates at mid-year)	
2008	6,230,143
2009	6,340,639
2010	6,451,122
Density (per sq km) at mid-2010	15.9

* 157,048 sq miles.

DEPARTMENTS

(official population estimates at mid-2008)

	Area (sq km)	Population	Density (per sq km)	Capital
Alto Paraguay (incl. Chaco)	82,349	11,487	0.1	Fuerte Olimpo
Alto Paraná	14,895	720,225	48.4	Ciudad del Este
Amambay	12,933	124,354	9.6	Pedro Juan Caballero
Asunción	117	518,792	4,434.1	—
Boquerón (incl. Nueva Asunción)	91,669	54,575	0.6	Doctor Pedro P. Peña
Caaguazú	11,474	476,437	41.5	Coronel Oviedo
Caazapá	9,496	150,533	15.9	Caazapá
Canindeyú	14,667	175,645	12.0	Salto del Guairá
Central	2,465	1,929,918	782.9	Asunción
Concepción	18,051	190,179	10.5	Concepción
Cordillera	4,948	270,267	54.6	Caacupé
Guairá	3,846	195,230	50.8	Villarrica
Itapúa	16,525	523,203	31.7	Encarnación
Misiones	9,556	114,747	12.0	San Juan Bautista
Ñeembucú	12,147	83,175	6.8	Pilar
Paraguarí	8,705	238,524	27.4	Paraguarí
Presidente Hayes	72,907	99,875	1.4	Pozo Colorado
San Pedro	20,002	352,978	17.6	San Pedro
Total	406,752	6,230,143	15.3	—

PRINCIPAL TOWNS

(population at 2002 census, incl. rural environs)

Asunción (capital)	510,910	Lambaré	119,830
Ciudad del Este*	222,109	Fernando de la Mora	113,990
San Lorenzo	203,150	Caaguazú	100,132
Luque	185,670	Encarnación	97,000
Capiatá	154,520	Pedro Juan Caballero	88,530

* Formerly Puerto Presidente Stroessner.

Mid-2010 ('000, incl. suburbs, UN estimate): Asunción 2,030 (Source: UN, *World Urbanization Prospects: The 2009 Revision*).

BIRTHS, MARRIAGES AND DEATHS

	Live births		Marriages		Deaths	
	Number	Rate (per 1,000)	Number	Rate (per 1,000)	Number	Rate (per 1,000)
2002	46,012	8.3	16,100	2.9	19,416	3.5
2003	45,669	8.0	17,717	3.1	19,593	3.4
2004	49,857	8.6	17,763	3.1	20,283	3.5
2005	51,444	8.7	19,826	3.4	17,360	2.9
2006	49,473	8.2	19,476	3.2	19,298	3.2
2007	49,879	8.2	19,726	3.2	21,049	3.4

Note: Rates were derived from estimates of mid-year population.

Life expectancy (years at birth, WHO estimates): 74 (males 71; females 77) in 2008 (Source: WHO, *World Health Statistics*).

ECONOMICALLY ACTIVE POPULATION

(household survey, '000 persons aged 10 years and over, October–December unless otherwise indicated)

	2006*	2007	2008
Agriculture, hunting, forestry and fishing	797,677	800,577	745,248
Mining and quarrying	} 271,905	8,617	} 346,803
Manufacturing		319,250	
Electricity, gas and water	18,714	8,799	10,769
Construction	149,445	154,915	174,096
Trade, restaurants and hotels	584,255	639,523	673,821
Transport, storage and communications	98,931	101,453	118,415
Financing, insurance, real estate and business services	84,028	104,225	120,802
Community, social and personal services	548,057	578,426	619,950
Sub-total	2,553,012	2,715,785	2,809,904
Activities not adequately described	628	580	602
Total employed	2,553,640	2,716,365	2,810,506
Unemployed	182,006	161,165	170,620
Total labour force	2,735,646	2,877,530	2,981,126

* November 2006–February 2007.

Health and Welfare

KEY INDICATORS

Total fertility rate (children per woman, 2008)	3.0
Under-5 mortality rate (per 1,000 live births, 2008)	28
HIV/AIDS (% of persons aged 15–49, 2007)	0.6
Physicians (per 1,000 head, 2002)	1.1
Hospital beds (per 1,000 head, 2006)	1.3
Health expenditure (2007): US $ per head (PPP)	253
Health expenditure (2007): % of GDP	5.7
Health expenditure (2007): public (% of total)	42.4
Access to water (% of persons, 2008)	86
Access to sanitation (% of persons, 2008)	70
Total carbon dioxide emissions ('000 metric tons, 2006)	3,982.8
Carbon dioxide emissions per head (metric tons, 2006)	0.7
Human Development Index (2007): ranking	101
Human Development Index (2007): value	0.761

For sources and definitions, see explanatory note on p. vi.

Agriculture

PRINCIPAL CROPS
('000 metric tons)

	2006	2007	2008
Wheat	800	800	800*
Rice, paddy	126	130	132*
Maize	2,000	1,900	1,900*
Sorghum	25	35*	35*
Sweet potatoes	165	166*	166*
Cassava (Manioc)	4,800	4,800	4,800*
Sugar cane	3,200	4,100	4,500*
Beans, dry	70	70	70*
Soybeans (Soya beans)	3,800	6,000	6,808†
Oil palm fruit*	126	143	143
Sunflower seed	68	190	200†
Tomatoes	88	89*	89*
Onions, dry*	29	29	30
Carrots and turnips	24	27	27*
Watermelons*	115	118	118
Cantaloupes and other melons*	29	29	29
Bananas	45	46*	46*
Oranges	296	300*	190*
Tangerines, mandarins, clementines and satsumas	19	19*	19*
Grapefruit and pomelos	38	39*	39*
Guavas, mangoes and mangosteens*	29	29	29
Pineapples	72	73*	73*
Maté	86	88*	88*

* FAO estimate(s).
† Unofficial figure.

Aggregate production ('000 metric tons, may include official, semi-official or estimated data): Total cereals 2,951 in 2006, 2,865 in 2007, 2,867 in 2008; Total roots and tubers 4,967 in 2006–08; Total vegetables (incl. melons) 332 in 2006, 344 in 2007, 349 in 2008; Total fruits (excl. melons) 578 in 2006, 586 in 2007, 476 in 2008.

Source: FAO.

LIVESTOCK
('000 head, year ending September)

	2006	2007	2008
Cattle	9,983	10,464	10,562
Horses*	370	380	400
Pigs*	1,650	1,680	1,700
Sheep*	550	550	560
Goats*	165	167	168
Chickens*	19,000	20,000	21,000
Ducks*	750	760	770
Geese and guinea fowls*	105	110	115
Turkeys*	110	115	120

* FAO estimates.

Source: FAO.

LIVESTOCK PRODUCTS
('000 metric tons)

	2006	2007	2008*
Cattle meat	300	265	276
Pig meat	156*	160*	168
Chicken meat	45*	47*	48
Cows' milk	372*	375*	375
Hen eggs	114*	120*	120

* FAO estimate(s).

Source: FAO.

Forestry

ROUNDWOOD REMOVALS
('000 cubic metres, excluding bark, FAO estimates)

	2006	2007	2008
Sawlogs, veneer logs and logs for sleepers	3,515	3,515	3,515
Other industrial wood	529	529	529
Fuel wood	6,149	6,252	6,358
Total	10,193	10,296	10,402

Source: FAO.

SAWNWOOD PRODUCTION
('000 cubic metres, including railway sleepers)

	1995	1996	1997
Total (all broadleaved)	400	500	550

1998–2008: Annual production as in 1997 (FAO estimates).

Source: FAO.

Fishing

('000 metric tons, live weight, FAO estimates)

	2004	2005	2006
Capture	22.0	21.0	20.0
Characins	7.8	7.5	7.0
Freshwater siluroids	10.8	10.3	10.0
Other freshwater fishes	3.4	3.2	3.0
Aquaculture	2.1	2.1	2.1
Total catch	24.1	23.1	22.1

2007–08: Figures assumed to be unchanged from 2006 (FAO estimates).

Source: FAO.

Industry

SELECTED PRODUCTS
('000 metric tons)

	2006	2007	2008
Soya bean oil	246	260*	260
Total sugars†	119	n.a.	n.a.
Hydraulic cement‡§	600	600	600

* Unofficial figure.
† FAO estimates.
‡ Data from US Geological Survey.
§ Estimates.

Source (unless otherwise indicated): FAO.

Finance

CURRENCY AND EXCHANGE RATES

Monetary Units
100 céntimos = 1 guaraní (G).

Sterling, Dollar and Euro Equivalents (30 April 2010)
£1 sterling = 7,244.6 guaraníes;
US $1 = 4,726.4 guaraníes;
€1 = 6,293.2 guaraníes;
100,000 guaraníes = £13.80 = $21.16 = €15.89.

Average Exchange Rate (guaraníes per US dollar)

2007	5,030.3
2008	4,363.2
2009	4,965.4

BUDGET

(central government operations, '000 million guaraníes)

Revenue	2007	2008
Taxation	7,019	8,656
Corporate taxes	1,229	1,531
Value-added tax	3,318	4,428
Import duties	853	1,058
Non-tax revenue and grants	3,794	4,063
Capital revenues	55	62
Total	10,868	12,781

Expenditure	2007	2008
Current expenditure	7,964	8,962
Personal	4,456	5,263
Other	3,508	3,699
Capital expenditure	2,311	1,989
Total	10,275	10,950

INTERNATIONAL RESERVES

(excl. gold, US $ million at 31 December)

	2007	2008	2009
IMF special drawing rights	43.65	44.19	173.00
Reserve position in IMF	33.94	33.08	33.67
Foreign exchange	2,383.89	2,767.29	3,631.97
Total	2,461.47	2,844.56	3,838.64

Source: IMF, *International Financial Statistics*.

MONEY SUPPLY

('000 million guaraníes at 31 December)

	2007	2008	2009
Currency outside depository corporations	3,804.17	3,997.14	4,418.03
Transferable deposits	7,851.48	9,026.60	12,333.36
Other deposits	4,485.80	5,082.18	5,987.74
Securities other than shares	3,805.95	5,951.05	6,888.16
Broad money	19,947.40	24,056.97	29,527.28

Source: IMF, *International Financial Statistics*.

COST OF LIVING

(Consumer Price Index for Asunción; base: 2000 = 100)

	2007	2008	2009
Food (incl. beverages)	213.2	246.1	247.5
Housing (incl. fuel and light)	159.7	172.0	175.2
Clothing (incl. footwear)	141.5	146.0	150.6
All items (incl. others)	178.8	196.9	202.1

Source: ILO.

NATIONAL ACCOUNTS

('000 million guaraníes at current prices, preliminary figures)

Expenditure on the Gross Domestic Product

	2007	2008	2009
Final consumption expenditure	52,849.9	64,147.3	64,100.4
Households*	46,450.7	57,027.4	56,017.5
General government	6,399.2	7,119.9	8,082.9
Gross capital formation	11,095.9	13,289.3	11,203.4
Gross fixed capital formation	10,695.3	12,977.8	10,904.8
Changes in inventories†	400.6	311.6	298.6
Total domestic expenditure	63,945.8	77,436.6	75,303.8
Exports of goods and services	30,129.9	37,092.5	33,503.0
Less Imports of goods and services	32,564.0	40,907.4	36,162.9
GDP in purchasers' values	61,511.7	73,621.7	72,644.0
GDP at constant 1994 prices	17,451.6	18,468.4	n.a.

* Including non-profit institutions serving households.
† Including acquisitions, less disposals, of valuables.

Gross Domestic Product by Economic Activity

	2007	2008	2009
Agriculture, hunting, forestry and fishing	13,533.4	17,379.3	14,615.4
Mining and quarrying	68.9	9,330.0	9,464.6
Manufacturing	7,901.7		
Construction	3,269.5	4,498.0	4,027.6
Electricity and water	1,048.0	1,058.5	1,264.8
Trade	11,982.5	34,432.8	36,452.4
Transport and communications	4,863.5		
Financial intermediation	1,540.0		
Government services	5,640.0		
Real estate, renting and business activities	2,073.3		
Hotels and restaurants	659.0		
Other services	3,263.4		
Gross value added in basic prices	55,843.2	66,698.7	65,824.7
Net taxes on products	5,668.4	6,923.0	6,819.2
GDP in market prices	61,511.7	73,621.7	72,644.0

BALANCE OF PAYMENTS

(US $ million)

	2007	2008	2009
Exports of goods f.o.b.	5,652.1	7,772.2	5,783.7
Imports of goods f.o.b.	–6,185.0	–8,945.9	–6,835.5
Trade balance	–532.9	–1,173.7	–1,051.7
Exports of services	961.9	1,141.7	1,232.9
Imports of services	–463.3	–595.5	–531.1
Balance on goods and services	–34.4	–627.5	–350.0
Other income received	336.7	390.1	300.7
Other income paid	–491.4	–552.2	–646.1
Balance on goods, services and income	–189.0	–789.7	–695.3
Current transfers received	374.8	406.4	501.2
Current transfers paid	–1.5	–1.4	–1.4
Current balance	184.2	–384.7	–195.6
Capital account (net)	28.0	33.0	55.0
Direct investment abroad	–7.2	–8.4	–8.0
Direct investment from abroad	206.3	179.2	289.4
Other investment assets	470.4	–123.1	107.4
Other investment liabilities	53.1	449.0	451.8
Net errors and omissions	–309.8	235.4	268.3
Overall balance	625.0	380.4	968.3

Source: IMF, *International Financial Statistics*.

External Trade

PRINCIPAL COMMODITIES
(US $ million, preliminary)

Imports f.o.b.	2006	2007	2008
Food and live animals	192.7	233.9	363.0
Beverages and tobacco	129.9	157.4	209.3
Mineral fuels	691.1	715.1	1,307.7
Chemical products	328.7	378.2	496.2
Road vehicles	139.5	186.6	335.5
Transport equipment and accessories	302.7	405.8	738.0
Electrical appliances	125.4	144.6	189.3
Motors, general industrial machinery equipment and parts	1,347.0	2,050.9	2,508.4
Total (incl. others)	4,489.0	5,576.8	8,470.7

Exports f.o.b.	2006	2007	2008
Meat and derivatives	422.1	368.0	621.4
Cereals	n.a.	376.2	378.5
Oleaginous seeds	439.1	890.3	1,502.5
Soybean oil	92.4	244.5	n.a.
Flour	n.a.	218.7	562.6
Wood and wooden products	99.3	116.0	111.3
Cotton fibres	34.3	47.1	19.2
Total (incl. others)	1,906.4	2,784.7	4,433.7

PRINCIPAL TRADING PARTNERS
(US $'000)

Imports f.o.b.	2005	2006*	2007*
Argentina	639,188	677,181	799,692
Brazil	883,944	959,795	1,587,833
Chile	38,208	56,744	70,586
China, People's Republic	667,440	1,196,593	1,566,789
Germany	50,683	64,514	102,091
Japan	93,401	187,087	238,744
Korea, Republic	35,453	86,575	68,079
Malaysia	30,540	65,134	57,654
Switzerland-Liechtenstein	136,981	176,183	48,056
Taiwan	53,711	64,613	49,661
USA	169,299	331,904	292,652
Uruguay	52,987	51,810	73,720
Venezuela	5,697	139,922	141,776
Total (incl. others)	3,251,429	4,488,972	5,576,794

Exports f.o.b.	2005	2006*	2007*
Argentina	107,304	168,499	551,785
Brazil	325,528	327,983	557,925
Cayman Islands	169,329	180,228	145,462
Chile	64,787	79,038	206,465
Germany	13,864	19,438	30,548
Italy	16,335	21,198	66,630
Japan	18,478	24,699	30,946
Netherlands	47,194	41,661	34,661
Russia	101,084	227,802	143,302
Switzerland-Liechtenstein	14,565	34,127	83,369
USA	51,561	62,376	66,570
Uruguay	479,290	420,243	264,221
Total (incl. others)	1,687,823	1,906,367	2,784,728

* Preliminary figures.

2008 (US $'000, preliminary): *Imports:* Argentina 1,215,638; Brazil 2,262,402; China, People's Republic 2,346,400; Uruguay 100,408; Total (incl. others) 8,470,668. *Exports:* Argentina 712,026; Brazil 619,979; China, People's Republic 93,155; Uruguay 771,779; Total (incl. others) 4,433,706.

Transport

RAILWAYS
(traffic)

	1988	1989	1990
Passengers carried	178,159	196,019	125,685
Freight (metric tons)	200,213	164,980	289,099

Source: UN, *Statistical Yearbook*.

Passenger-kilometres: 3.0 million per year in 1994–96.

Freight ton-kilometres: 5.5 million in 1994.

Source: UN Economic Commission for Latin America and the Caribbean.

ROAD TRAFFIC
(vehicles in use)

	1999	2000
Cars	267,587	274,186
Buses	8,991	9,467
Lorries	41,329	42,992
Vans and jeeps	134,144	138,656
Motorcycles	6,872	8,825

Source: Organización Paraguaya de Cooperación Intermunicipal.

SHIPPING

Merchant Fleet
(registered at 31 December)

	2006	2007	2008
Number of vessels	43	45	47
Total displacement ('000 grt)	44.1	49.3	53.6

Source: Lloyd's Register-Fairplay, *World Fleet Statistics*.

CIVIL AVIATION
(traffic)

	2006	2007	2008
Passengers carried ('000)	458.1	659.5	604.1
Freight carried ('000 metric tons)	13.7	15.8	16.4

Tourism

ARRIVALS BY NATIONALITY

	2005	2006	2007
Argentina	209,130	194,532	184,745
Brazil	56,036	98,480	126,592
Chile	9,941	14,238	12,707
Germany	7,622	9,324	10,362
Uruguay	9,287	10,295	10,623
USA	13,044	13,262	14,540
Total (incl. others)	340,845	388,465	415,702

Tourism receipts (US $ million, incl. passenger transport): 96 in 2005; 112 in 2006; 121 in 2007.

Source: World Tourism Organization.

Communications Media

	2007	2008	2009
Telephones ('000 main lines in use)	394.4	370.4	387.3
Mobile cellular telephones ('000 subscribers)	4,694.4	5,954.4	5,618.6
Personal computers ('000 in use)	n.a.	n.a.	
Internet users ('000)	687.0*†	890.2†	1,000.0
Broadband subscribers ('000)	51.7‡	89.0	140.9

* Refers only to internet users aged 10 years and over.
† Estimate.
‡ Broadband defined as 64 kbps or more.

Personal computers: 460,000 (77.9 per 1,000 persons) in 2005.

Television receivers ('000 in use): 1,200 in 1997.

Radio receivers ('000 in use): 925 in 1997.

Daily newspapers (estimates): 5 in 1996 (average circulation 213,000 copies).

Non-daily newspapers (estimates): 2 in 1988 (average circulation 16,000 copies).

Book production (estimates): 152 titles (incl. 23 pamphlets) in 1993.

Sources: UNESCO, *Statistical Yearbook*; UN, *Statistical Yearbook*; International Telecommunication Union.

Education

(2006/07, unless otherwise indicated)

	Institutions*	Teachers	Students
Pre-primary schools	4,071	5,671†	152,363
Primary	7,456	33,434†	894,422
Secondary	2,149	44,440†	532,103
Tertiary: university level	111	1,844‡	180,637

* 1999.
† 2003/04, estimate.
‡ 1999/2000.

Source: partly UNESCO Institute for Statistics.

Pupil-teacher ratio (primary education, UNESCO estimate): 27.8 in 2003/04 (Source: UNESCO Institute for Statistics).

Adult literacy rate (UNESCO estimates): 94.6% (males 95.7%; females 93.5%) in 2007 (Source: UNESCO Institute for Statistics).

Directory

The Constitution

A new Constitution for the Republic of Paraguay came into force on 22 June 1992, replacing the Constitution of 25 August 1967.

FUNDAMENTAL RIGHTS, DUTIES AND FREEDOMS

Paraguay is an independent republic whose form of government is representative democracy. The powers accorded to the legislature, executive and judiciary are exercised in a system of independence, equilibrium, co-ordination and reciprocal control. Sovereignty resides in the people, who exercise it through universal, free, direct, equal and secret vote. All citizens over 18 years of age and resident in the national territory are entitled to vote.

All citizens are equal before the law and have freedom of conscience, travel, residence, expression, and the right to privacy. The freedom of the press is guaranteed. The freedom of religion and ideology is guaranteed. Relations between the State and the Catholic Church are based on independence, co-operation and autonomy. All citizens have the right to assemble and demonstrate peacefully. All public and private sector workers, with the exception of the Armed Forces and the police, have the right to form a trade union and to strike. All citizens have the right to associate freely in political parties or movements.

The rights of the indigenous peoples to preserve and develop their ethnic identity in their respective habitat are guaranteed.

LEGISLATURE

The legislature (Congreso Nacional—National Congress) comprises the Senado (Senate) and the Cámara de Diputados (Chamber of Deputies). The Senado is composed of 45 members, the Cámara of 80 members, elected directly by the people. Legislation concerning national defence and international agreements may be initiated in the Senado. Departmental and municipal legislation may be initiated in the Cámara. Both chambers of the Congreso are elected for a period of five years.

GOVERNMENT

Executive power is exercised by the President of the Republic. The President and the Vice-President are elected jointly and directly by the people, by a simple majority of votes, for a period of five years. They may not be elected for a second term. The President and the Vice-President govern with the assistance of an appointed Council of Ministers. The President participates in the formulation of legislation and enacts it. The President is empowered to veto legislation sanctioned by the Congreso, to nominate or remove ministers, to direct the foreign relations of the Republic, and to convene extraordinary sessions of the Congreso. The President is Commander-in-Chief of the Armed Forces.

JUDICIARY

Judicial power is exercised by the Supreme Court of Justice and by the tribunals. The Supreme Court is composed of nine members who are appointed on the proposal of the Consejo de la Magistratura, and has the power to declare legislation unconstitutional.

The Government

HEAD OF STATE

President: FERNANDO ARMINDO LUGO MÉNDEZ (took office 15 August 2008).

Vice-President: LUIS FEDERICO FRANCO GÓMEZ.

COUNCIL OF MINISTERS

(July 2010)

The Government is formed by a coalition, comprising members of the constituent parties of the Alianza Patriótica para el Cambio and of the Partido Liberal Radical Auténtico, and several independents.

Minister of the Interior: RAFAEL FILIZZOLA.

Minister of Foreign Affairs: HÉCTOR LACOGNATA.

Minister of Finance: DIONISIO BORDA.

Minister of Industry and Commerce: FRANCISCO JOSÉ RIVAS ALMADA.

Minister of Public Works and Communications: PEDRO EFRAÍN ALEGRE SASIAIN.

Minister of National Defence: Gen. (retd) LUIS BAREIRO SPAINI.

Minister of Public Health and Social Welfare: ESPERANZA MARTÍNEZ.

Minister of Justice and Labour: HUMBERTO BLASCO.

Minister of Agriculture and Livestock: ENZO CARDOZO JIMÉNEZ.

Minister of Education and Culture: LUIS ALBERTO RIART MONTANER.

MINISTRIES

Office of the President: Palacio de los López, Asunción; tel. (21) 414-0200; internet www.presidencia.gov.py.

Ministry of Agriculture and Livestock: Edif. San Rafael, Yegros, entre 25 de Mayo y Cerro Corá 437, Asunción; tel. (21) 45-0937; fax (21) 49-7965; e-mail prensa@mag.gov.py; internet www.mag.gov.py.

Ministry of Education and Culture: 15 de Agosto, esq. Gral Díaz y Eduardo V. Haedo, Edif. del ex-BNT, Asunción; tel. (21) 44-3078; fax (21) 44-3919; internet www.mec.gov.py.

Ministry of Finance: Chile 252, entre Palma y Presidente Franco, Asunción; tel. (21) 44-0010; fax (21) 44-8283; e-mail info@hacienda.gov.py; internet www.hacienda.gov.py.

Ministry of Foreign Affairs: Edif. Benigno López, Palma, esq. 14 de Mayo, Asunción; tel. (21) 49-3872; fax (21) 49-3910; e-mail sistemas@mre.gov.py; internet www.mre.gov.py.

Ministry of Industry and Commerce: Avda Marescal López 3333, esq. Dr Wiss, Villa Morra, Casilla 2151, Asunción; tel. (21) 616-3012; fax (21) 616-3000; e-mail sprivada@mic.gov.py; internet www.mic.gov.py.

Ministry of the Interior: Chile 1002, esq. Manduvira, Asunción; tel. (21) 415-2000; fax (21) 44-6448; e-mail ministro@mdi.gov.py; internet www.mdi.gov.py.

Ministry of Justice and Labour: Avda Dr José Gaspar Rodríguez de Francia, esq. Estados Unidos, Asunción; tel. (21) 49-3209; fax (21) 20-8469; e-mail info@mjt.gov.py; internet www.mjt.gov.py.

Ministry of National Defence: Avda Mariscal López, esq. Vicepresidente Sánchez y 22 de Septiembre, Asunción; tel. (21) 21-0052; fax (21) 21-1815; e-mail ministro@mdn.gov.py; internet www.mdn.gov.py.

Ministry of Public Health and Social Welfare: Avda Pettirossi, esq. Brasil, Asunción; tel. (21) 20-4601; fax (21) 20-6700; internet www.mspbs.gov.py.

Ministry of Public Works and Communications: Oliva y Alberdi 411, Casilla 1221, Asunción; tel. (21) 414-9000; fax (21) 44-4421; e-mail comunicaciones@mopc.gov.py; internet www.mopc.gov.py.

President and Legislature

PRESIDENT

Election, 20 April 2008

Candidate	Votes	% of votes
Fernando Armindo Lugo Méndez (APC)	766,502	40.90
Blanca Ovelar de Duarte (ANR—PC)	573,995	30.63
Gen. (retd) Lino César Oviedo Silva (UNACE)	411,034	21.93
Pedro Nicolás Fadul Niella (PPQ)	44,060	2.35
Others	12,233	0.65
Total	1,874,127*	100.00

* Including 38,485 blank and 27,818 invalid ballots.

CONGRESO NACIONAL
(National Congress)

President of the Senado and the Congreso Nacional: MIGUEL CARRIZOSA GALIANO (PPQ).

President of the Cámara de Diputados: CÉSAR ARIEL OVIEDO VERDÚN (UNACE) (acting).

General Election, 20 April 2008

Party	Seats: Cámara de Diputados	Seats: Senado
Asociación Nacional Republicana—Partido Colorado	30	15
Partido Liberal Radical Auténtico	27	14
Unión Nacional de Ciudadanos Eticos	15	9
Partido Patria Querida	3	4
Others	5	3
Total	80	45

Election Commission

Tribunal Superior de Justicia Electoral (TSJE): Avda Eusebio Ayala 2759 y Santa Cruz de la Sierra, Casilla 1209, Asunción; tel. and fax (21) 618-0111; e-mail protocolo@tsje.gov.py; internet www.tsje.gov.py; f. 1995; Pres. Dr JUAN MANUEL MORALES SOLER.

Political Organizations

Alianza Patriótica para el Cambio (APC): República Argentina, esq. Fernando de la Mora, Asunción; tel. (21) 55-9400; f. 2007 to support the presidential campaign of Fernando Lugo Méndez; alliance of parties and other orgs; mems incl. Partido Encuentro Nacional, Partido Demócrata Cristiano, Partido Frente Amplio, Partido País Solidario and Partido Revolucionario Febrerista.

Asociación Nacional Republicana—Partido Colorado (ANR—PC): Casa de los Colorados, 25 de Mayo 842, Asunción; tel. (21) 45-2543; fax (21) 45-4136; internet www.anr.org.py; f. 19th century; factions include Movimiento Vanguardia Colorada, led by LUIS CASTIGLIONI; Pres. LILIAN SAMANIEGO.

Convergencia Popular Socialista (CPS): Avda Brasil 663, entre Azara y Herrera, Asunción; tel. (21) 21-2850; e-mail prensapcps@gmail.com; internet convergenciapopular.blogspot.com; f. 2009; Leader ELVIO BENÍTEZ.

Frente Guasú: Asunción; f. 2010; a coalition of 22 political orgs and social movts supportive of President Fernando Lugo Méndez, incl. the constituent parties of the ACP.

Movimiento 20 de Abril: Asunción; f. 2010 by supporters of President Fernando Lugo Méndez; Leader MIGUEL ANGEL LÓPEZ PERITO; Sec.-Gen. LIZ TORRES.

Partido Comunista Paraguayo (PCP): Brasil 228, Asunción; internet www.pcparaguay.org; f. 1928; banned 1928–46, 1947–89; Leader ANANÍAS MAIDANA; Sec.-Gen. NAJEEB AMADO.

Partido Demócrata Cristiano (PDC): Dupuis 962, entre Montevideo y Colón, Asunción; tel. (21) 42-0434; e-mail info@pdc.org.py; internet www.pdc.org.py; f. 1960; 20,500 mems; Pres. GERARDO ROLÓN POSE.

Partido Democrático Progresista (PDP): Avda 25 de Mayo, entre Constitución y Brasil, Asunción; tel. (21) 22-5354; e-mail info@pdp.org.py; internet www.pdp.org.py; f. 2007; democratic socialist; Pres. DESIRÉE MASI.

Partido Encuentro Nacional (PEN): Fulgencio R. Moreno 1048, entre Estados Unidos y Brasil, Asunción; tel. (21) 60-3935; fax (21) 61-0699; e-mail parenac@pla.net.py; f. 1991 as Movimiento Encuentro Nacional; Pres. FERNANDO CAMACHO PAREDES.

Partido Frente Amplio: Antequera 764, esq. Fulgencio R. Moreno, Asunción; tel. (21) 44-1389; e-mail arevalovicente@hotmail.com; internet www.partidofrenteamplio.org; Pres. PEDRO ALMADA; Sec.-Gen. VÍCTOR BAREIRO ROA.

Partido Humanista Paraguayo: San Francisco 1318, San Antonio, Barrio Jara, Asunción; tel. (21) 23-3085; e-mail tere_notario@hotmail.com; f. 1985; recognized by the Tribunal Superior de Justicia Electoral in March 1989; campaigns for the protection of human rights and environmental issues; Sec.-Gen. SERGIO MARTÍNEZ.

Partido Liberal Radical Auténtico (PLRA): Iturbe 936, entre Manuel Domínguez y Teniente Fariña, Asunción; tel. (21) 49-8442; fax (21) 49-8443; e-mail prensa@plra.org.py; internet www.plra.org.py; f. 1978; centre party; 806,000 mems; Pres. AMANDA ROSALIA NUÑEZ DE FIGUEREDO (acting); Sec.-Gen. EMILIO GUSTAVO FERREIRA SAGGIORATO.

Partido del Movimiento al Socialismo (PMAS): 15 de agosto 1660, entre Nuestra Señora de la Asunción 4 y 5, Asunción; tel. (21) 39-1525; e-mail info@pmas.org.py; internet www.pmas.org.py; f. 2006; Sec.-Gen. ROCÍO CASCO.

Partido País Solidario: Avda 5, esq. Méjico, Asunción; tel. (21) 39-1271; e-mail presidencia@paissolidario.org.py; internet www.paissolidario.org.py; f. 2000; mem. of Socialist International; Pres. Dr CARLOS FILIZZOLA PALLARÉS; Exec. Sec. MARÍA TERESA FERREIRA.

Partido Patria Libre (PPL): 15 de Agosto 1939, Asunción; tel. (21) 37-2384; f. 1990 as Corriente Patria Libre; renamed Movimiento Patria Libre in 1992; renamed as above and regd as a political org. in 2002; Marxist.

Partido Patria Querida (PPQ): Padre Cardozo 469, Asunción; tel. 21-3300; e-mail comunicaciones@patriaquerida.org; internet www.patriaquerida.org; f. 2002; recognized by the Tribunal Superior de Justicia Electoral in March 2004; Leader PEDRO NICOLÁS FADUL NIELLA; Sec.-Gen. ARSENIO OCAMPOS VELÁZQUEZ.

Partido Popular Tekojojá: Carios, esq. Médicos del Chaco, Asunción; tel. and fax (21) 55-4104; e-mail tekojoja@tekojoa.org.py; internet www.tekojoja.org.py; f. 2006 to support the presidential campaign of Fernando Lugo Méndez; left-wing, mainly comprising social and indigenous groups; Pres. SIXTO PEREIRA; Sec. FIDELINA ROJAS.

Partido Revolucionario Febrerista (PRF): Casa del Pueblo, Manduvira 522, Asunción; tel. (21) 49-4041; e-mail partyce@mixmail.com; f. 1951; social democratic; mem. of Socialist International; Pres. CARLOS MARÍA LJUBETIC.

Partido Social Demócrata (PSD): 25 de Mayo, esq. Tacuarí, Asunción; tel. (21) 45-3293; e-mail partidosocialdemocrata.paraguay@gmail.com; f. 2007; Pres. MANUEL DOLDÁN DEL PUERTO.

Partido de los Trabajadores (PT): Hernandarias y Piribebuy 890, Asunción; tel. (21) 44-5009; e-mail info@ptparaguay.org; internet www.ptparaguay.org; f. 1989; Socialist; Pres. GLORIA BAREIRO.

Partido de la Unidad Popular (PUP): Palma 571, entre 14 de Mayo y 15 de Agosto, Planta Alta, Asunción; tel. (21) 21-5059; recognized by the Tribunal Superior de Justicia Electoral in March 2004; Pres. BELARMINO BALBUENA.

Unión Nacional de Ciudadanos Eticos (UNACE): Avda Mariscal López, Saturio Ríos, Asunción; tel. (21) 59-1900; e-mail loviedo@unace.org.py; internet www.unace.org.py; f. 1996 as Unión Nacional de Colorados Eticos, a faction of the Partido Colorado; f. 2002 as political party under current name; left-wing; Pres. Gen. (retd) LINO CÉSAR OVIEDO SILVA; Exec. Sec. HERMINIO CHENA VALDEZ.

OTHER ORGANIZATIONS

Federación Nacional Campesina (FNC): Nangariry 1196, esq. Cacique Cará Cará, Asunción; tel. (21) 51-2384; grouping of militant peasants' orgs; Sec.-Gen. ODILÓN ESPÍNOLA; Asst Sec.-Gen. MARCIAL GÓMEZ.

Frente en Defensa de los Bienes Públicos y el Patrimonio Nacional: Asunción; left-wing grouping of orgs opposed to privatization; Co-ordinator GABRIEL ESPÍNOLA.

Frente Nacional de Lucha por la Soberanía y la Vida: Asunción; left-wing grouping of orgs campaigning for agrarian reform and opposed to privatization; Co-ordinator LUIS AGUAYO.

Diplomatic Representation

EMBASSIES IN PARAGUAY

Argentina: Avda España, esq. Avda Perú, Casilla 757, Asunción; tel. (21) 21-2320; fax (21) 21-1029; e-mail contacto@embajada-argentina.org.py; internet www.embajada-argentina.org.py; Ambassador RAFAEL EDGARDO ROMÁ.

Bolivia: Campos Cervera 6421, Barrio Villa Aurelia, Asunción; tel. (21) 61-4984; fax (21) 60-1999; e-mail emboliviapy@tigo.com.py; Ambassador FREDDY MARCEL QUEZADA GAMBARTE.

Brazil: Coronel Irrazábal, esq. Eligio Ayala, Casilla 22, Asunción; tel. (21) 248-4000; fax (21) 21-2693; e-mail parbrem@embajadabrasil.org.py; internet www.embajadabrasil.org.py; Ambassador EDUARDO DOS SANTOS.

Chile: Capital Emilio Nudelman 351, esq. Campos Cervera, Asunción; tel. (21) 61-3855; fax (21) 66-2755; e-mail echilepy@tigo.com.py; Ambassador CRISTIÁN MAQUIEIRA ASTABURUAGA.

China (Taiwan): Avda Mariscal López 1133 y Vicepresidente Sánchez, Casilla 503, Asunción; tel. (21) 21-3362; fax (21) 21-2373; e-mail embroc01@rieder.net.py; internet www.taiwanembassy.org/py; Ambassador HUANG LIEN-SHENG.

Colombia: Coronel Francisco Brizuela 3089, esq. Ciudad del Vaticano, Asunción; tel. (21) 22-9888; fax (21) 22-9703; e-mail easuncio@cancilleria.gov.co; Ambassador MAURICIO GONZÁLEZ LÓPEZ.

Cuba: Luis Morales 757, esq. Luis de León y Luis de Granada, Barrio Jara, Asunción; tel. (21) 22-2108; fax (21) 21-3879; e-mail embajada@embacuba.org.py; internet www.embacuba.org.py; Ambassador ROLANDO ANTONIO GÓMEZ GONZÁLEZ.

Dominican Republic: Edif. Asturias, 9°, Suite C, Avda Mariscal López, esq. Dr Pane 127, Asunción; tel. (21) 21-3143; e-mail embajadadominicanapy@hotmail.com; Ambassador RODOLFO RINCÓN MARTÍNEZ.

Ecuador: Dr Bestard 861, esq. Juan XXIII, Barrio Manorá, Casilla 13162, Asunción; tel. (21) 61-4814; fax (21) 61-4813; e-mail eecuparaguay@mmree.gov.ec; Ambassador JULIO CÉSAR PRADO ESPINOSA.

France: Avda España 893, esq. Padre Pucheu, Casilla 97, Asunción; tel. (21) 21-2449; fax (21) 21-1690; e-mail chancellerie@ambafran.gov.py; internet www.ambafrance-py.org; Ambassador GILLES BIENVENU.

Germany: Avda Venezuela 241, Casilla 471, Asunción; tel. (21) 21-4009; fax (21) 21-2863; e-mail info@asuncion.diplo.de; internet www.asuncion.diplo.de; Ambassador DIETMAR BLAAS.

Holy See: Ciudad del Vaticano 350, casi con 25 de Mayo, Casilla 83, Asunción (Apostolic Nunciature); tel. (21) 21-5139; fax (21) 21-2590; e-mail nunciatura@tigo.com.py; Apostolic Nuncio Most Rev. ELISEO ANTONIO ARIOTTI (Titular Archbishop of Vibiana).

Italy: Quesada 5871 con Bélgica, Asunción; tel. (21) 61-5620; fax (21) 61-5622; e-mail ambitalia@cmm.com.py; internet www.embajadadeitalia.org.py; Ambassador PIETRO PORCARELLI.

Japan: Avda Mariscal López 2364, Casilla 1957, Asunción; tel. (21) 60-4616; fax (21) 60-6901; e-mail embajaponpy@rieder.net.py; internet www.py.emb-japan.go.jp; Ambassador KAZUO WATANABE.

Korea, Republic: Avda Rep. Argentina Norte 678, esq. Pacheco, Casilla 1303, Asunción; tel. (21) 60-5606; fax (21) 60-1376; e-mail paraguay@mofat.go.kr; internet pry.mofat.go.kr; Ambassador PARK DONG-WON.

Lebanon: San Francisco 629, esq. República Siria y Juan de Salazar, Asunción; tel. 22-9375; fax 23-2012; e-mail embajadadelibano@tigo.com.py; Ambassador FARES EID.

Mexico: Avda España 1428, casi San Rafael, Casilla 1184, Asunción; tel. (21) 618-2000; fax (21) 618-2500; e-mail embamex@embamex.com.py; internet www.embamex.com.py; Ambassador ERNESTO CAMPOS TENORIO.

Panama: Carmen Soler 3912, esq. Radio Operadores del Chaco, Barrio Seminario, Asunción; tel. and fax (21) 21-1091; e-mail embapana@gmail.com.py; Ambassador SABRINA DEL CARMEN GARCÍA BARRERA.

Peru: Edif. Santa Teresa, Dept 8B, Avda Santa Teresa 2415, Aviadores del Chaco, Casilla 433, Asunción; tel. (21) 60-0226; fax (21) 60-0901; e-mail embperu@embperu.com.py; Ambassador JORGE ANTONIO LÁZARO GELDRES.

Russia: Edif. Las Palmas, Molas López, esq. Dr C. Caceres y Julio Correa, Barrio Las Lomas, Asunción; tel. (21) 62-3733; fax (21) 62-3735; e-mail reshchikov@inbox.ru; Ambassador IGOR I. EZHOV.

Spain: Edif. S. Rafael, 5° y 6°, Yegros 437, Asunción; tel. (21) 49-0686; fax (21) 44-5394; e-mail emb.asuncion@maec.es; internet www.mae.es/embajadas/asuncion; Ambassador MIGUEL ANGEL CORTIZO NIETO.

Switzerland: Edif. Parapití, 4°, Ofs 419–423, Juan E. O'Leary 409, esq. Estrella, Casilla 552, Asunción; tel. (21) 44-8022; fax (21) 44-5853; e-mail asu.vertretung@eda.admin.ch; internet www.eda.admin.ch/asuncion; Ambassador EMANUEL JENNI.

USA: Avda Mariscal López 1776, Casilla 402, Asunción; tel. (21) 21-3715; fax (21) 21-3728; e-mail paraguayusembassy@state.gov; internet asuncion.usembassy.gov; Ambassador LILIANA AYALDE.

Uruguay: Edif. Maria Luisa, 3°, Avda Boggiani 5832, esq. Alas Paraguayas, Asunción; tel. (21) 66-4244; fax (21) 60-1335; e-mail uruasun@embajadauruguay.com.py; internet www.embajadauruguay.com.py; Ambassador JUAN ENRIQUE FISCHER.

Venezuela: Soldado Desconocido 348, Avda España, Barrio Manorá, Asunción; tel. (21) 66-4682; fax (21) 66-4683; e-mail despacho2@embaven.org.py; internet www.embaven.org.py; Ambassador JAVIER ARRÚE DE PABLO.

Judicial System

The Corte Suprema de Justicia (Supreme Court of Justice) is composed of nine judges appointed on the recommendation of the Consejo de la Magistratura (Council of the Magistracy).

Corte Suprema de Justicia: Palacio de Justicia, Asunción; internet www.pj.gov.py; Ministers Dr JOSÉ RAÚL TORRES KIRMSER (President), Dr VÍCTOR MANUEL NÚÑEZ (First Vice-President), Dr SINDULFO BLANCO (Second Vice-President), Dra ALICIA BEATRIZ PUCHETA DE CORREA, Dr ANTONIO FRETES, Dr CÉSAR ANTONIO GARAY ZUCCOLILLO, Dr MIGUEL O. BAJAC; two vacancies.

Attorney-General: RUBÉN CANDIA AMARILLA.

Under the Supreme Court are the Courts of Appeal, the Tribunal of Jurors and Judges of First Instance, the Judges of Arbitration, the Magistrates (Jueces de Instrucción), and the Justices of the Peace.

Religion

The Roman Catholic Church is the established religion, although all sects are tolerated.

CHRISTIANITY

The Roman Catholic Church

For ecclesiastical purposes, Paraguay comprises one archdiocese, 11 dioceses and two Apostolic Vicariates. Some 91% of the population are Roman Catholics.

Bishops' Conference

Conferencia Episcopal Paraguaya, Calle Alberdi 782, Casilla 1436, 1209 Asunción; tel. (21) 49-0920; fax (21) 49-5115; e-mail cep@infonet.com.py; internet www.episcopal.org.py.

f. 1977, statutes approved 2000; Pres. Most Rev. EUSTAQUIO PASTOR CUQUEJO VERGA (Archbishop of Asunción).

Archbishop of Asunción: Most Rev. EUSTAQUIO PASTOR CUQUEJO VERGA, Arzobispado, Avda Mariscal López 130 esq. Independencia Nacional, Casilla 654, Asunción; tel. (21) 44-5551; fax (21) 44-4150; e-mail asa@pla.net.py.

The Anglican Communion

Paraguay constitutes a single diocese of the Iglesia Anglicana del Cono Sur de América (Anglican Church of the Southern Cone of

America). The Presiding Bishop of the Church is the Bishop of Northern Argentina.

Bishop of Paraguay: Rt Rev. JOHN ELLISON, Iglesia Anglicana, Avda España casi Santos, Casilla 1124, Asunción; tel. (21) 20-0933; fax (21) 21-4328; e-mail iapar@sce.cnc.una.py.

The Baptist Church

Baptist Evangelical Convention of Paraguay: Casilla 1194, Asunción; tel. (21) 22-7110; fax (21) 21-0588; e-mail cebp@sce.cnc.una.py; internet www.ublaonline.org/paises/paraguay.htm; Exec. Sec. AUGUSTO VEGA.

BAHÁ'Í FAITH

National Spiritual Assembly of the Bahá'ís of Paraguay: Eligio Ayala 1456, Apdo 742, Asunción; tel. (21) 22-5747; e-mail bahai@highway.com.py; internet www.bahai.org.py; Sec. MIRNA LLAMOSAS DE RIQUELME.

The Press

DAILIES

ABC Color: Yegros 745, Apdo 1421, Asunción; tel. (21) 49-1160; fax (21) 415-1310; e-mail azeta@abc.com.py; internet www.abc.com.py; f. 1967; independent; Propr ALDO ZUCCOLILLO; circ. 45,000.

La Nación: Avda Zavala Cué entre 2da y 3ra, Fernando de la Mora, Asunción; tel. (21) 51-2520; fax (21) 51-2535; e-mail redaccion@lanacion.com.py; internet www.lanacion.com.py; f. 1995; Dir ALEJANDRO DOMÍNGUEZ WILSON-SMITH; circ. 10,000.

Noticias: Avda Artigas y Avda Brasilia, Casilla 3017, Asunción; tel. (21) 29-2721; fax (21) 29-2716; e-mail alebluth@diarionoticias.com; f. 1985; independent; Dir ALEJANDRO BLUTH; circ. 20,000.

Popular: Avda Mariscal López 2948, Asunción; tel. (21) 60-3401; fax (21) 60-3400; e-mail popular@mm.com.py; internet www.diariopopular.com.py; Dir JAVIER PIROVANO PEÑA; circ. 28,000.

Ultima Hora: Benjamín Constant 658, Asunción; tel. (21) 49-6261; fax (21) 44-7071; e-mail ultimahora@uhora.com.py; internet www.ultimahora.com; f. 1973; independent; Dir OSCAR AYALA BOGARÍN; circ. 30,000.

PERIODICALS

Acción: CEPAG, Vicepresidente Sánchez 612, casi Azara, Asunción; tel. (21) 23-3541; e-mail revistaaccion@cepag.org.py; internet www.montoya.com.py/revista_accion.php; f. 1923; monthly; published by the Centro de Estudios Paraguayos Antonio Guasch (CEPAG—Jesuit org.); Dir JOSÉ MARÍA BLANCH.

Revista Zeta: Eligio Ayala 2002, esq. Gral Bruguez, Asunción; tel. (21) 61-3392; fax (21) 61-3393; e-mail zeta@revistazeta.com.py; internet www.revistazeta.com.py; f. 2000; monthly; general interest; Dir ZUNI CASTIÑEIRA.

TVO: Santa Margarita de Youville 250, Santa María, Asunción; tel. (21) 67-2079; fax (21) 21-1236; e-mail sugerencias@teveo.com.py; internet www.teveo.com.py; f. 1992; fmrly TeVeo; weekly; news and society; Commercial Dir MARTINA LECLERCQ.

NEWS AGENCY

Información Pública Paraguay (IP Paraguay): Palacio de los López, Asunción; e-mail ipparaguay@gmail.com; internet www.ipparaguay.com.py; f. 2009; attached to the Office of the President.

Jaku'éke Paraguay—Agencia Nacional de Noticias: Itapúa y Río Monday, Asunción; tel. (21) 29-7806; fax (21) 28-1950; internet www.jakueke.com; f. 2002; independent.

Publishers

La Colmena, SA: Asunción; tel. (21) 20-0428; Dir DAUMAS LADOUCE.

Dervish SA, Editorial: Avda Mariscal López 1735, CP 1584, Asunción; tel. (21) 21-1729; fax (21) 22-2580; e-mail dervish@dervish.com.py; f. 1989; Co-ordinator JORGELINA MIGLIORISI; Vice-Pres. and Dir JANINE GIANI PATTERSON.

Ediciones Diálogo: Brasil 1391, Asunción; tel. (21) 20-0428; f. 1957; fine arts, literature, poetry, criticism; Man. MIGUEL ANGEL FERNÁNDEZ.

Ediciones Nizza: Eligio Ayala 1073, Casilla 2596, Asunción; tel. (21) 44-7160; medicine; Pres. Dr JOSÉ FERREIRA MARTÍNEZ.

Editorial Comuneros: Cerro Corá 289, Casilla 930, Asunción; tel. (21) 44-6176; fax (21) 44-4667; e-mail rolon@conexion.com.py; f. 1963; social history, poetry, literature, law; Man. OSCAR R. ROLÓN.

Librería Intercontinental: Caballero 270, Calle Mariscal, Estigarribia, Asunción; tel. (21) 49-6991; fax (21) 44-8721; e-mail agatti@libreriaintercontinental.com.py; internet www.libreriaintercontinental.com.py; political science, law, literature, poetry; Dir ALEJANDRO GATTI VAN HUMBEECK.

R. P. Ediciones: Eduardo Víctor Haedo 427, Asunción; tel. (21) 49-8040; Man. RAFAEL PERONI.

ASSOCIATION

Cámara Paraguaya del Libro: Nuestra Señora de la Asunción 697, esq. Eduardo Víctor Haedo, Asunción; tel. (21) 44-4104; fax (21) 44-7053; Pres. PABLO LEÓN BURIAN; Sec. EMA DE VIEDMA.

Broadcasting and Communications

REGULATORY AUTHORITY

Comisión Nacional de Telecomunicaciones (CONATEL): Edif. San Rafael, 2°, Yegros 437 y 25 de Mayo, Asunción; tel. (21) 44-0020; fax (21) 49-8982; e-mail presidencia@conatel.gov.py; internet www.conatel.gov.py; Pres. JORGE ANTONIO SEALL SASIAIN.

TELECOMMUNICATIONS

Claro (AMX Paraguay, SA): Avda Mariscal López 1730, Asunción; tel. (21) 249-9000; fax (21) 249-9099; internet www.claro.com.py; subsidiary of América Móvil, SA de CV (Mexico); fmrly CTI Móvil; mobile cellular telephone services.

Corporación Paraguaya de Comunicaciones, SA (COPACO): Edif. Morotí, 1°–2°, esq. Gen. Bruguez y Teodoro S. Mongelos, Casilla 2042, Asunción; tel. (21) 20-3800; fax (21) 20-3888; e-mail infoweb@copaco.com.py; internet www.copaco.com.py; fmrly Administración Nacional de Telecomunicaciones (ANTELCO); adopted current name in Dec. 2001 as part of the privatization process; privatization suspended in June 2002; Pres. ARNULFO RECALDE.

BROADCASTING

Radio

Radio Arapysandú: Avda Mariscal López y Capitán del Puerto San Ignacio, Misiones; tel. (82) 2374; fax (82) 2206; f. 1982; AM; Dir HECTOR BOTTINO.

Radio Asunción: Avda Artígas y Capitán Lombardo 174, Asunción; tel. and fax (21) 28-2662; fax (21) 28-2661; e-mail radioasuncion@cmm.com.py; internet www.radioasuncion.com.py; AM; Propr MIGUEL GERÓNIMO FERNÁNDEZ; Dir-Gen. BIBIANA LANDO MEYER.

Radio Cáritas: Kubitschek 661 y Azara, Asunción; tel. (21) 21-3570; fax (21) 20-4161; e-mail pedroportillo@caritas.com.py; internet www.caritas.com.py; f. 1936; station of the Archdiocese of Asunción and the Universidad Católica Nuestra Señora de la Asunción; AM; Dir-Gen. JORGE BAZÁN; Dir of Operations PEDRO PORTILLO.

Radio Cardinal: Comendador Nicolás Bó 1334 y Guaraníes, Casilla 2532, Lambaré, Asunción; tel. (21) 31-0555; fax (21) 31-0557; e-mail info@cardinal.com.py; internet www.cardinal.com.py; f. 1991; AM and FM; Pres. ALFREDO CHENA; Man. ANDREA BITTAR.

Radio City: Edif. Líder III, Antequera 652, 9°, Asunción; tel. (21) 44-3324; fax (21) 44-4367; e-mail direccion@fmradiocity.com; internet www.fmradiocity.com; f. 1950; FM; Dir GREGORIO RAMAN MORALES.

Radio Concepción: Coronel Panchito López 241, entre Schreiber y Profesor Guillermo A. Cabral, Casilla 78, Concepción; tel. (31) 42318; fax (31) 42254; f. 1963; AM; Dir SERGIO E. DACAK.

Radio Emisoras del Paraguay, SRL: Teniente Martínez Ramella 1355, Calle Avda Eusebio Ayala, Asunción; tel. (21) 22-0132; e-mail administracion@emisorasparaguay.com.py; internet www.desdeparaguay.com/emisoras; FM; Dir FRANCISCO JAVIER BOSCARINO BÁEZ.

Radio Guairá: Presidente Franco 788 y Alejo García, Villarica; tel. (541) 42130; fax (541) 42385; e-mail administracion@fmguaira.com; internet www.fmguaira.com; f. 1950; AM and FM; Dir LÍDICE RODRÍGUEZ DE TRAVERSI.

Radio Itapiru SRL: Avda San Blás esq. Coronel Julián Sánchez, Ciudad del Este; tel. (61) 57-2206; fax (61) 57-2210; internet www.radioitapiru.com; f. 1969; AM and FM; Dir-Gen. FABIÁN ARANDA.

Radio La Voz de Amambay: 14 de Mayo y Cerro León, Pedro Juan Caballero, Amambay; tel. (36) 72537; f. 1959; AM and FM; Gen. Man. DANIEL ROLÓN DANTAS P.

Radio Nacional del Paraguay: Blas Garay 241, esq. Iturbe y Yegros, Asunción; tel. (21) 39-0374; fax (21) 39-0375; e-mail direccion@radionacionaldelparaguay.com.py; internet www.radionacionaldelparaguay.com.py; f. 1957; AM and FM; Dir JUDITH MARIA VERA.

Radio Ñandutí: Choferes del Chaco y Carmen Soler, Asunción; tel. (21) 60-4308; fax (21) 60-6074; e-mail prensaam@holdingderadio.com.py; internet www.nanduti.com.py; f. 1962; FM; Dir HUMBERTO LEÓN RUBÍN.

Radio Nuevo Mundo: Coronel Romero 1181 y Flórida, San Lorenzo, Asunción; tel. (21) 58-6258; fax (21) 58-2424; f. 1972; AM; Dir JULIO CÉSAR PEREIRA BOBADILLA.

Radio Primero de Marzo: Avda General Perón y Concepción, Casilla 1456, Asunción; tel. (21) 31-1564; fax (21) 33-3427; internet www.780am.com.py; AM and FM; Dir-Gen. ANGEL R. GUERREÑOS.

Radio Santa Mónica FM: Avda Boggiani y Herrera, 3°, Asunción; tel. (21) 50-7501; fax (21) 50-9494; f. 1973; FM; Dir RICARDO FACCETTI.

Radio Uno: Avda Mariscal López 2948, Asunción; tel. (21) 61-2151; internet www.radiouno.com.py; f. 1968 as Radio Chaco Boreal; AM; Dir JAVIER MARÍA PIROVANO SILVA.

Radio Venus: Avda República Argentina y Souza, Asunción; tel. (21) 61-0151; fax (21) 60-6484; e-mail 105.1@venus.com.py; internet www.venus.com.py; f. 1987; FM; Dir ANGEL AGUILERA.

Radio Ysapy: Independencia Nacional 1260, 1°, Asunción; tel. (21) 44-4037; e-mail secretaria@radioysapy.com.py; internet www.radioysapy.com.py; FM; Dir JOSÉ TOMÁS CABRIZA SALVIONI.

Television

Paravision: Belgica 4498, casi Mariscal López, Asunción; tel. (21) 66-4380; e-mail info@paravision.com.py; internet www.paravision.com.py.

Red Guaraní (Canal 2): Complejo Textilia, General Santos 1024, casi Concordia, Asunción; tel. (21) 20-5444; e-mail oescobar@redguarani.com.py; internet www.redguarani.com.py; Exec. Dir Dr ARNOLDO WIENS; Gen. Man. OSCAR ESCOBAR.

Sistema Nacional de Televisión Cerro Corá—Canal 9 (SNT): Avda Carlos A. López 572, Asunción; tel. (21) 42-4222; fax (21) 48-0230; e-mail snt@snt.com.py; internet www.snt.com.py; f. 1965; commercial; Dir Gen. ISMAEL HADID.

Teledifusora Paraguaya—Canal 13: Comendador Nicolás Bó y Guaraníes, Lambaré, Asunción; tel. (21) 33-2823; fax (21) 33-1695; e-mail prensa@rpc.com.py; internet www.rpc.com.py; f. 1981; Pres. ALFREDO CHENA; Dir-Gen. GUSTAVO CUBILLA.

Telefuturo (TV Acción, SA): Andrade 1499 y O'Higgins, Asunción; tel. (21) 618-4000; fax (21) 618-4166; e-mail telefuturo@telefuturo.com.py; internet www.telefuturo.com.py; Gen. Man. MARCO GALANTI.

Finance

(cap. = capital; res = reserves; dep. = deposits; m. = million; brs = branches; amounts in guaraníes, unless otherwise indicated)

BANKING

Superintendencia de Bancos: Edif. Banco Central del Paraguay, Avda Federación Rusa y Avda Marecos, Barrio Santo Domingo, Asunción; tel. (21) 60-8148; fax (21) 419-2403; e-mail supban@bcp.gov.py; internet www.bcp.gov.py/supban; Supt EDGAR ANDRÉS LEGUIZAMON CARMONA.

Central Bank

Banco Central del Paraguay: Avda Federación Rusa y Cabo 1° Marecos, Casilla 861, Barrio Santo Domingo, Asunción; tel. (21) 60-8011; fax (21) 619-2328; e-mail informaciones@bcp.gov.py; internet www.bcp.gov.py; f. 1952; cap. 828,145m., res 454,695m., dep. 4,605,137m. (Dec. 2005); Pres. JORGE RAÚL CORVALÁN MENDOZA; Gen. Man. JORGE AURELIO VILLALBA LEGUIZAMON.

Development Banks

Banco Nacional de Fomento: Independencia Nacional, entre Cerro Cora y 25 de Mayo, Asunción; tel. (21) 44-4440; fax (21) 44-6056; e-mail correo@bnf.gov.py; internet www.bnf.gov.py; f. 1961 to take over the deposit and private banking activities of the Banco del Paraguay; cap. 293,585m., res –135,556m., dep. 1,849,758m. (Dec. 2008); Pres. AGUSTÍN SILVERA ORUE; Sec.-Gen. CÉSAR LEONARDO FURIASSE ROLÓN; 52 brs.

Crédito Agrícola de Habilitación (CAH): Caríos 362 y Willam Richardson, Asunción; tel. (21) 569-0100; fax (21) 55-4956; e-mail info@cah.gov.py; internet www.cah.gov.py; f. 1943; Pres. JOSÉ MARCELO BRUSTEIN ALEGRE.

Fondo Ganadero: Avda Mariscal López 1669 esq. República Dominicana, Asunción; tel. (21) 22-7288; fax (21) 22-7378; e-mail info@fondogan.gov.py; internet www.fondogan.gov.py; f. 1969; govt-owned; Pres. JUAN FERNANDO PERONI CAZAL RIBEIRO.

Commercial Banks

Banco Amambay, SA: Avda Aviadores del Chaco, entre San Martín y Pablo Alborno, Asunción; tel. (21) 60-8831; fax (21) 60-8813; e-mail bcoama@bancoamambay.com.py; internet www.bancoamambay.com.py; f. 1992; cap. US $10.9m., res $5.9m., dep. $125.7m. (Dec. 2008); Pres. and Gen. Man. HUGO JAVIER PORTILLO SOSA; 6 brs.

Banco Bilbao Vizcaya Argentaria Paraguaya, SA: Yegros 435, esq. 25 de Mayo, Casilla 824, Asunción; tel. (21) 417-6000; fax (21) 44-8103; e-mail info@bbva.com.py; internet www.bbva.com.py; f. 1961 as Banco Exterior de España, SA; present name adopted in 2000; cap. 40,052m., res 187,103m., dep. 3,327,164m. (Dec. 2008); Pres. VICENTE LUIS BOGLIOLO DEL RÍO; 5 brs.

Banco Continental, SAECA: Estrella 621, Calle 15 de Agosto, Casilla 021-442002, Asunción; tel. (21) 44-2002; fax (21) 44-2001; e-mail contil@connexion.com.py; internet www.bancontinental.com.py; f. 1980; cap. US $4.2m., res $2.5m., dep. $44.6m. (Dec. 2001); Pres. CARLOS ESPÍNOLA; 28 brs.

Interbanco, SA: Oliva 349, esq. Chile y Alberdi, Asunción; tel. (21) 617-1000; fax (21) 41-71372; e-mail sac@interbanco.com.py; internet www.interbanco.com.py; f. 1978; owned by Unibanco (Brazil); cap. 25,923m., res 330,969m., dep. 3,627,798m. (Dec. 2008); Pres. CLAUDIO YAMAGUTI; 17 brs.

Sudameris Bank, SAECA: Independencia Nacional y Cerro Corá, Casilla 1433, Asunción; tel. (21) 44-8670; fax (21) 44-4024; e-mail gerencia@sudameris.com.py; internet www.sudamerisbank.com.py; f. 1961; savings and commercial bank; cap. 42,991m., surplus and res 34,391m., dep. 970,480m. (Dec. 2007); Chair. CONOR MCENROY; Vice-Chair. and Gen. Man. JUAN LUIS KOSTNER; 8 brs.

Banking Associations

Asociación de Bancos del Paraguay: Jorge Berges 229, esq. Estados Unidos, Asunción; tel. (21) 214-9513; fax (21) 20-5050; e-mail abp.par@pla.net.py; mems: Paraguayan banks and foreign banks with brs in Asunción; Pres. PEDRO DANIEL MIRAGLIO.

Cámara de Bancos Paraguayos: 25 de Mayo, esq. 22 de Setiembre, Asunción; tel. (21) 22-2373; fax (21) 20-5050; Pres. MIGUEL ANGEL LARREINEGABE.

STOCK EXCHANGE

Bolsa de Valores y Productos de Asunción, SA: 15 de Agosto 640, esq. General Díaz y Víctor Haedo, Asunción; tel. (21) 44-2445; fax (21) 44-2446; internet www.bvpasa.com.py; f. 1977; Pres. RODRIGO CALLIZO LÓPEZ.

INSURANCE

Supervisory Authority

Superintendencia de Seguros: Edif. Banco Central del Paraguay, 1°, Federación Rusa y Sargento Marecos, Asunción; tel. (21) 619-2637; fax (21) 619-2542; e-mail dmarti@bcp.gov.py; internet www.bcp.gov.py; Supt DIEGO ARTURO MARTÍNEZ SÁNCHEZ.

Principal Companies

La Agrícola SA de Seguros Generales: Mariscal López 5377 y Concejal Vargas, Asunción; tel. (21) 60-9509; fax (21) 60-9606; e-mail sagricola@tigo.com.py; f. 1982; general; Pres. CARLOS ALBERTO LEVI SOSA.

ALFA SA de Seguros y Reaseguros: Yegros 944 esq. Tte Fariña, Asunción; tel. (21) 44-9992; fax (21) 44-9991; e-mail alfa.seg@conexion.com.py; Pres. NICOLÁS SARUBBI ZAYAS.

Aseguradora del Este SA de Seguros: Avda República Argentina 778, entre Pacheco y Souza, Asunción; tel. (21) 60-5015; e-mail dcespedes@aesaseguros.com.py; Pres. VÍCTOR ANDRÉS RIBEIRO ESPÍNOLA.

Aseguradora Paraguaya, SA (ASEPASA): Israel 309 esq. Rio de Janeiro, Casilla 277, Asunción; tel. (21) 21-5086; fax (21) 22-2217; e-mail asepasa@asepasa.com.py; internet www.asepasa.com.py; f. 1976; life and risk; Pres. and Gen. Man. GERARDO TORCIDA CONEJERO.

Aseguradora Yacyretá SA de Seguros y Reaseguros: Oliva 685, esq. Juan E. O'Leary y 15 de Agosto, Asunción; tel. (21) 45-2374; fax (21) 44-5070; e-mail spalomar@yacyreta.com.py; internet www.yacyretasa.com; f. 1980; Pres. OSCAR HARRISON JACQUET; Vice-Pres. NORMAN HARRISON PALEARI; Gen. Man. EDUARDO BARRIOS PERINI; 5 brs.

Atalaya SA de Seguros Generales: Independencia Nacional 565, 1°, esq. Azara y Cerro Corá, Asunción; tel. (21) 49-2811; fax (21) 49-6966; e-mail ataseg@telesurf.com.py; f. 1964; general; Pres. KARIN M. DOLL.

Cenit de Seguros, SA: Ayolas 1082, esq. Ibáñez del Campo, Asunción; tel. (21) 49-4972; fax (21) 44-9502; e-mail cenit@cenit.com.py; internet www.cenit.com.py; Pres. OSCAR CÁCERES CARDOZO.

Central SA de Seguros: Edif. Betón I, 1° y 2°, Eduardo Víctor Haedo 179, Independencia Nacional, Casilla 1802, Asunción; tel. (21) 49-4654; fax (21) 49-4655; e-mail censeg@conexion.com.py; f. 1977; general; Pres. MIGUEL JACOBO VILLASANTI; Gen. Man. Dr FÉLIX AVEIRO.

El Comercio Paraguayo SA Cía de Seguros Generales: Alberdi 453 y Oliva, Asunción; tel. (21) 49-2324; fax (21) 49-3562; e-mail elcomercioparaguayo@elcomercioparaguayo.com.py; internet www.elcomercioparaguayo.com.py; f. 1947; life and risk; Dir VICTORIA MARTÍNEZ DE ELIZECHE.

La Consolidada SA de Seguros y Reaseguros: Chile 719 y Eduardo Víctor Haedo, Casilla 1182, Asunción; tel. (21) 49-5174; fax (21) 44-5795; internet www.consolidada.com.py; f. 1961; life and risk; Pres. JUAN CARLOS DELGADILLO ECHAGÜE.

Fénix SA de Seguros y Reaseguros: Iturbe 823 y Fulgencio R. Moreno, Asunción; tel. (21) 49-5549; fax (21) 44-5643; e-mail fenixsa@pla.net.py; internet www.fenixseguros.com.py; Pres. VÍCTOR MARTÍNEZ YARYES.

Garantía SA de Seguros y Reaseguros: 25 de Mayo 640, Asunción; tel. (21) 44-3748; fax (21) 49-0678; e-mail garantia@rieder.net.py; Pres. GERALDO CRISTALDO JURE.

Grupo General de Seguros y Reaseguros, SA: Edif. Grupo General, Jejuí 324 y Chile, 2°, Asunción; tel. (21) 49-7897; fax (21) 44-9259; e-mail general_de_seguros@ggeneral.com.py; Pres. JORGE OBELAR LAMAS.

La Independencia de Seguros y Reaseguros, SA: Edif. Parapatí, 1°, Juan E. O'Leary 409, esq. Estrella, Casilla 980, Asunción; tel. (21) 44-7021; fax (21) 44-8996; e-mail liseguros@laindependencia.com.py; f. 1965; general; Pres. EDMUNDO EMILIO RICHER BÉCKER.

Intercontinental SA de Seguros y Reaseguros: Iturbe 1047 con Teniente Fariña, Altos, Asunción; tel. (21) 49-2348; fax (21) 49-1227; e-mail intercontinentalseguros@flash.com.py; f. 1978; Pres. Dr JUAN MÓDICA LUCENTE; Gen. Man. LUIS SANTACRUZ.

Mapfre Paraguay, SA: Avda Mariscal López 910 y General Aquino, Asunción; tel. (21) 44-1983; fax (21) 49-7441; e-mail sac@mapfre.com.py; internet www.mapfre.com.py; Pres. LUIS MARÍA ZUBIZARRETA.

La Meridional Paraguaya SA de Seguros: Iturbe 1046, Teniente Fariña, Asunción; tel. (21) 49-8827; fax (21) 49-8826; e-mail meridian@conexion.com.py; Pres. TITO LIVIO MUJICA VARELA.

La Paraguaya SA de Seguros: Estrella 675, 7°, Asunción; tel. (21) 49-1367; fax (21) 44-8235; e-mail lps@laparaguaya.com.py; internet www.laparaguaya.com.py; f. 1905; life and risk; Pres. JUAN BOSCH BEYNEN.

Patria SA de Seguros y Reaseguros: General Santos 715 esq. Siria, Asunción; tel. (21) 22-5250; fax (21) 21-4001; e-mail patria@tigo.com.py; f. 1967; general; Pres. Dr ERNESTO GOBERMAN.

El Productor SA de Seguros y Reaseguros: Ind. Nacional 811 esq. Fulgencio R. Moreno, 8°, Asunción; tel. (21) 49-1577; fax (21) 49-1599; e-mail ncabanas@elproductor.com.py; Pres. REINALDO PAVÍA MALDONADO.

Regional SA de Seguros y Reaseguros: Roque González 390 y Dr Hassler, Asunción; tel. (21) 61-0692; fax (21) 22-4447; e-mail regisesa@itacom.com.py; Pres. JUAN A. DIAZ DE VIVAR PRIETO.

Rumbos SA de Seguros: Estrella 851, Ayolas, Casilla 1017, Asunción; tel. (21) 44-9488; fax (21) 44-9492; e-mail rumbos@conexion.com.py; f. 1960; general; Pres. MIGUEL A. LARREINEGABE LESME; Man. Dir ROBERTO GÓMEZ VERLANGIERI.

La Rural SA de Seguros: Avda Mariscal López 1082, esq. Mayor Bullo, Casilla 21, Asunción; tel. (21) 49-1917; fax (21) 44-1592; e-mail larural@larural.com.py; internet www.larural.com.py; f. 1920; general; Pres. JUAN CARLOS MANEGLIA; Gen. Man. EDUARDO BARRIOS PERINI.

Seguros Chaco SA de Seguros y Reaseguros: Mariscal Estigarribia 982, Casilla 3248, Asunción; tel. (21) 44-7118; fax (21) 44-9551; e-mail seguroschaco@pla.net.py; f. 1977; general; Pres. EMILIO VELILLA LACONICH; Exec. Dir ALBERTO R. ZARZA TABOADA.

Seguros Generales, SA (SEGESA): Edif. SEGESA, 1°, Oliva 393 esq. Alberdi, Casilla 802, Asunción; tel. (21) 49-1362; fax (21) 49-1360; e-mail segesa@conexion.com.py; f. 1956; life and risk; Pres. CÉSAR AVALOS.

El Sol del Paraguay, Cía de Seguros y Reaseguros, SA: Cerro Corá 1031, Asunción; tel. (21) 49-1110; fax (21) 21-0604; e-mail elsol@elsol.com.py; internet www.elsol.com.py; f. 1978; Pres. MIGUEL ANGEL BERNI CENTURIÓN; Vice-Pres. CAROLINA VEGA DE ONETTO.

Universo de Seguros y Reaseguros, SA: Edif. de la Encarnación, 9°, 14 de Mayo esq. General Díaz, Casilla 788, Asunción; tel. (21) 44-8530; fax (21) 44-7278; f. 1979; Pres. ZENÓN AGÜERO MIRANDA.

Insurance Association

Asociación Paraguaya de Cías de Seguros: 15 de Agosto, esq. Lugano, Casilla 1435, Asunción; tel. (21) 44-6474; fax (21) 44-4343; e-mail apcs@activenet.com.py; f. 1963; Pres. Dr EMILIO VELILLA LACONICH; Gen. Man. RUBÉN RAPPENECKER COSCIA.

Trade and Industry

GOVERNMENT AGENCIES

Instituto Nacional de Tecnología, Normalización y Metrología (INTN): Avda General Artigas 3973 y General Roa, Casilla 967, Asunción; tel. (21) 29-0160; fax (21) 29-0873; e-mail intn@intn.gov.py; internet www.intn.gov.py; national standards institute; Dir-Gen. MARIO GUSTAVO LEIVA ENRIQUE.

Instituto de Previsión Social: Edif. de la Caja Central, Constitución y Luis Alberto de Herrera, Casilla 437, Asunción; tel. (21) 22-3141; fax (21) 22-3654; e-mail secretaria_general@ips.gov.py; internet www.ips.gov.py; f. 1943; responsible for employees' welfare and health insurance scheme; Pres. JORGE STEVAN GIUCICH GREENWOOD.

DEVELOPMENT ORGANIZATIONS

Alter Vida (Centro de Estudios y Formación para el Ecodesarrollo): Itapúa 1372, esq. Primer Presidente y Río Monday, Barrio Trinidad, Asunción; tel. (21) 29-8842; fax (21) 29-8845; e-mail info@altervida.org.py; internet www.altervida.org.py; f. 1985; ecological devt; Exec. Dir VÍCTOR BENÍTEZ INSFRÁN.

Centro de Información y Recursos para el Desarrollo (CIRD): Avda Mariscal López 2029, esq. Acá Carayá, Casilla 1580, Asunción; tel. (21) 22-6071; fax (21) 21-2540; e-mail cird@cird.org.py; internet www.cird.org.py; f. 1988; information and resources for devt orgs; Exec. Pres. AGUSTÍN CARRIZOSA.

Centro de Cooperación Empresarial y Desarrollo Industrial (CEDIAL): Edif. UIP, 2°, Cerro Corá 1038, esq. Estados Unidos y Brasil, Asunción; tel. and fax (21) 23-0047; e-mail cedial@cedial.org.py; internet www.cedial.org.py; f. 1991; promotes commerce and industrial devt; Gen. Man. HERNÁN RAMÍREZ.

Instituto de Biotecnología Agrícola (INBIO): Avda Brasilia 939, Calle Ciancio, Asunción; tel. (21) 23-3892; e-mail info@inbio-paraguay.org; internet www.inbio-paraguay.org; bio-technological research for agricultural devt; Pres. RICARDO WOLLMEISTER; Sec. HUMBERTO PÁEZ.

Instituto Paraguayo de Artesanía (IPA): Asunción; tel. (21) 61-4896; fax (21) 60-0035; e-mail ipa@artesania.gov.py; internet www.artesania.gov.py; f. 2004; promotes handicraft industries; Pres. FREDDY GERARDO OLMEDO COLMAN.

Instituto Paraguayo del Indígena (INDI): Edif. Sudamérica, 2°, Iturbe 891, esq. Manuel Dominguez, Asunción; tel. (21) 44-5818; fax (21) 44-7154; e-mail informes@indi.gov.py; internet www.indi.gov.py; f. 1981; responsible for welfare of Indian population; Pres. LIDA ACUÑA.

Red de Inversiones y Exportaciones (REDIEX): Avda Mariscal López 3333, CP 1892, Asunción; tel. (21) 616-3028; fax (21) 616-3034; e-mail info@rediex.gov.py; internet www.rediex.gov.py; replaced ProParaguay in 2007; responsible for promoting investment in Paraguay and the export of national products; Dir OSCAR STARK ROBLEDO.

Red Rural de Organizaciones Privadas de Desarrollo (Red Rural): Manuel Domínguez 1045, entre Brasil y Estados Unidos, Asunción; tel. (21) 22-9740; e-mail redrural@redrural.org.py; internet www.redrural.org.py; f. 1989; co-ordinating body for rural devt orgs; Gen. Co-ordinator HERMES GARCÍA; Sec. JOSÉ LARROZA.

Secretaría Técnica de Planificación: Estrella 505, esq. 14 de Mayo, Asunción; tel. (21) 45-0422; fax (21) 49-6510; e-mail stp@stp.gov.py; internet www.stp.gov.py; govt body responsible for overall economic and social planning; Minister BERNARDO ESQUIVEL VAESKEN; Co-ordinator Gen. VICTOR SEBASTIÁN URIARTE.

CHAMBERS OF COMMERCE

Cámara Nacional de Comercio y Servicios de Paraguay: Estrella 540, esq. 14 de Mayo y 15 de Agosto, Asunción; tel. (21) 49-3321; fax (21) 44-0817; e-mail info@ccparaguay.com.py; internet www.ccparaguay.com.py; f. 1898; fmrly Cámara y Bolsa de Comercio; adopted current name 2002; Pres. BELTRÁN MACCHI SALIN; Gen. Man. MIGUEL RIQUELME OLAZAR.

Cámara de Comercio Paraguayo-Americana (Paraguayan-American Chamber of Commerce): 25 de Mayo 2090, esq. Mayor Bullo, Asunción; tel. (21) 22-2160; fax (21) 22-1926; e-mail pamcham@pamcham.com.py; internet www.pamcham.com.py; f. 1981; Pres. VÍCTOR GONZÁLEZ ACOSTA; Exec. Dir GERALD MCCULLOCH; c. 120 mem. cos.

Cámara de Comercio Paraguayo-Argentina: Banco de la Nación Argentina, entre Palma y Alberdi (al lado del Consulado Argentino), Asunción; tel. (21) 49-7804; fax (21) 49-7805; e-mail administracion@campyarg.org.py; internet www.campyarg.org.py; f. 1991; Pres. GERARDO DURÉ-PERONI; Man. MARCELA ESCOBAR.

Cámara de Comercio Paraguayo-Británica: Avda Boggiani 5848, Asunción; tel. 61-2611; fax 60-5007; e-mail britcham@conexion.com.py; Pres. GUILLERMO ALONSO.

Cámara de Comercio Paraguayo-Francesa (CCPF): Yegros 837, 1°, Of. 12, CP 3009, Asunción; tel. 49-7852; fax 44-6324; e-mail info@ccpf.com.py; internet www.ccpf.com.py; Pres. ANTONIO LUIS PECCI MILTOS; Man. IRIS FELIU DE FLEITAS.

Cámara de Industria y Comercio Paraguayo-Alemana: Independencia Nacional 811, Casilla 919, Asunción; tel. (21) 44-6594; fax (21) 44-9735; e-mail logisticaahkasu.com.py; internet www.ahkparaguay.com; f. 1956; Pres. JAN HOECKLE; Gen. Man. HELMUT L. ZAGEL.

AGRICULTURAL, INDUSTRIAL AND EMPLOYERS' ORGANIZATIONS

Asociación de Empresas Financieras del Paraguay (ADEFI): Edif. Ahorros Paraguayos, Torre II, 6°, Of. 05, General Díaz 471, Asunción; tel. (21) 44-8298; fax (21) 49-8071; e-mail adefi@adefi.org.py; internet www.adefi.org.py; f. 1975; grouping of financial cos; Pres. SILVIA MURTO DE MÉNDEZ; Sec. MILCIADES FRETES RUBIANI.

Asociación Paraguaya de la Calidad: Eduardo Victor Haedo 680, O'Leary, Asunción; tel. (21) 44-7348; fax (21) 45-0705; e-mail apc@apc.org.py; internet www.apc.org.py; f. 1988; grouping of cos to promote quality of goods and services; Pres. JORGE MIGUEL BRUNOTTE; Sec. SANTIAGO LLANO CAVINA.

Asociación de Productores de Soja, Oleaginosas y Cereales del Paraguay (APS): Asunción; internet www.aps.org.py; soya and grain producers' asscn; Pres. REGIS MERELES.

Asociación Rural del Paraguay (ARP): Ruta Transchaco, Km 14, Mariano Roque Alonso; tel. (21) 75-4412; e-mail ania@arp.org.py; internet www.arp.org.py; grouping of agricultural cos and farmers; Pres. JUAN NÉSTOR NÚÑEZ; Exec. Dir EDUARDO RUIZ DÍAZ.

Cámara Paraguaya de Exportadores de Cereales y Oleaginosas (CAPECO): Avda Brasilia 840, Asunción; tel. (21) 20-8855; fax (21) 21-3971; internet www.capeco.org.py; f. 1980; grain exporters' asscn; Pres. ULRICH BAUER; Gen. Man. IGNACIO SANTIVIAGO.

Centro de Importadores del Paraguay (CIP): Avda Brasilia 1947, casi Artigas, Casillas 2609, Asunción; tel. (21) 29-9800; e-mail cip@cip.org.py; internet www.cip.org.py; f. 1939; importers' asscn; Pres. MAX HABER NEUMANN; Man. JULIO SÁNCHEZ LASPINA.

Federación de la Producción, Industria y Comercio (FEPRINCO): Edif. Union Club, Palma 751, 3°, esq. O'Leary y Ayolas, Asunción; tel. (21) 44-6634; fax (21) 44-6638; e-mail feprinco@quanta.com.py; org. of private-sector business execs; Pres. GERMÁN RUIZ.

Unión Industrial Paraguaya (UIP): Cerro Corá 1038, entre Estados Unidos y Brasil, Casilla 782, Asunción; tel. (21) 21-2556; fax (21) 21-3360; e-mail uip@uip.org.py; internet www.uip.org.py; f. 1936; org. of business entrepreneurs; Pres. GUSTAVO VOLPE; Sec. RAÚL HOECKLE.

MAJOR COMPANIES

Azucarera Paraguaya, SA (AZPA): Avda General Artigas 552, Casi San Jose, Casilla 43, CP 1404, Asunción; tel. (21) 21-3778; fax (21) 21-3150; e-mail informes@azpa.com.py; internet www.azpa.com.py; f. 1905; refining and wholesale distribution of cane sugar, alcohol and carbon dioxide; Pres. RAÚL HOECKLE; Dir-Gen. JAN MARC BOSCH; 700 employees.

Consorcio de Ingeniería Electromecanica, SA (CIE): Avda General Artigas 3443, Casilla 2078, Asunción; tel. (21) 64-2850; fax (21) 64-4130; e-mail ventas@cie.com.py; internet www.cie.com.py; f. 1978; manufacture of sheet metal work; Pres. HUGO ARANDA NÚÑEZ; 800 employees.

Empresa Distribuidora Especializada, SA (EDESA): Prof. Conradi 1690, esq. Avda Eusebio Ayala, Asunción; tel. (21) 50-1652; fax (21) 50-8549; e-mail edesa@edesa.com.py; internet www.edesa.com.py; f. 1981; wholesale distribution of durable goods; Pres. RAÚL ALBERTO DÍAZ DE ESPADA; Gen. Man. ALFREDO SCHIAPPACASSEE; 450 employees.

Fenix, SA: Iturbe 823, esq. Fulgencio R. Moreno, Asunción; tel. and fax (21) 49-5549; e-mail fenixsa@fenixseguros.com.py; internet www.fenixseguros.com.py; f. 1976; import and manufacture of clothing and general merchandise; Pres. JAIME LAUFER; Dir-Gen. GABRIELA GAONA DE VAN HUMBEECK; 1,800 employees.

Grandes Tiendas La Riojana, SA: Avda Mariscal Estigarribia 171, esq. Yegros, Asunción; tel. (21) 49-2211; fax (21) 44-6698; e-mail info@lariojana.com.py; department stores; CEO (vacant); 480 employees.

Grupo A. J. Vierci: Avda Oliva 845, Calle Montevideo, Asunción; tel. (21) 414-1111; fax (21) 414-1116; e-mail contacto@aj.com.py; internet www.grupovierci.com; f. 1967; multiple interests incl. import, retail, media and real estate; Pres. ANTONIO J. VIERCI.

Industria Nacional de Cemento: Teniente Alcorta, esq. Avda Fernando de la Mora, Asunción; tel. (21) 55-7417; e-mail gerencia_general@inc.gov.py; internet www.inc.gov.py; f. 1969 following collapse of private co Vallemi, SA; state-owned; cement manufacturers; Pres. GÓMEZ VERLANGIERI; Gen. Man. EULOGIO MARIÑO ROA.

IRIS, SAIC: Gobernador Irala 1952, Barrio Sajonia, Asunción; tel. (21) 42-0031; fax (21) 48-0172; e-mail iris@iris.com.py; internet www.iris.com.py; f. 1936; manufacture and marketing of cleaning and insecticide products; 50% owned by Chemopharma SA (Chile); Pres. FRANCISCO COSP; Gen. Man. CARMEN COSP.

La Mercantil Guarani, SA: Avda República Argentina, esq. Carios, Asunción; tel. and fax (21) 55-2600; e-mail buzon@mguarani.com.py; internet www.mguarani.com.py; f. 1957; imports alcoholic beverages and food; CEO EMILIO DARÉ.

Petróleos Paraguayos, SA (PETROPAR): Edif. Oga Rape, 9°, Avda Chile 753, Casi Eduardo V. Haedo, Asunción; tel. (21) 44-8503; fax (21) 45-2306; e-mail contactenos@petropar.gov.py; internet www.petropar.gov.py; f. 1986; govt-owned; petroleum refining; Pres. JUAN ALBERTO GONZÁLEZ MEYER; 400 employees.

Scavone Hermanos, SA: Santa Ana 431 y Avda España, Asunción; tel. (21) 60-8171; fax (21) 66-1480; e-mail preshsa@scavonehnos.com.py; internet www.scavonehnos.com.py; f. 1905; manufacture and retail distribution of pharmaceuticals; Pres. FELIPE C. RESCK B.; Gen. Man. CARLOS SÍRTORI; 530 employees.

Tecno Electric, SA: Teniente Primero Demetrio Araujo Miño, Calle Sacramento, Asunción; tel. (21) 29-0080; fax (21) 29-2863; e-mail tesa@tecnoelectric.com.py; internet www.tecnoelectric.com.py; f. 1962; manufacture of electrical equipment and construction of electric installations; Pres. GUIDO BOETTNER BALANSA; Dir JAVIER MEZA BARTRINA; 200 employees.

Vargas Peña Apezteguia y Compañía, SAIC: Avda Boggiani 6777, esq. Teniente Victor Heyn, Casilla 1176, Asunción; tel. (21) 60-2841; fax (21) 60-0262; e-mail administracionvm3@vargaspena.com.py; internet www.vargaspena.com.py; f. 1977; production of cotton and edible oils; Pres. JOSÉ MARÍA HERNAN VARGAS PEÑA APEZTEGUIA; Dir MARÍA CRISTINA VARGAS PEÑA ADAMEK; 600 employees.

UTILITIES

Electricity

Administración Nacional de Electricidad (ANDE): Avda España 1268, Casi Padre Cardozo, Asunción; tel. (21) 21-1001; fax (21) 21-2371; e-mail luis_rojas@ande.gov.py; internet www.ande.gov.py; f. 1949; national electricity board; Pres. GERMÁN FATECHA; Sec.-Gen. LUIS RAMÓN ROJAS IBARRA.

Entidad Binacional Yacyretá: General Díaz 831 esq. Ayolas y Montevideo, Edif. Héroes de Marzo, Asunción; tel. and fax (21) 44-5611; internet www.eby.gov.py; owned jtly by Paraguay and Argentina; operates the hydroelectric dam at Yacyretá on the Paraná river, completed in 1998; installed capacity of 3,200 MW; 14,673 GWh of electricity produced in 2007; Dir (Paraguay) ELBA RECALDE.

Itaipú Binacional: Centro Administrativo, Ruta Internacional Km 3.5, Avda Monseñor Rodríguez 150, Ciudad del Este, Depto Alto Paraná; tel. (61) 599-8989; e-mail itaipu@itaipu.gov.br; internet www.itaipu.gov.py; f. 1974; jtly owned by Paraguay and Brazil; hydroelectric power station on Brazilian-Paraguayan border; 91,652 GWh of electricity produced in 2008; Dir-Gen. (Paraguay) GUSTAVO CODAS FRIEDMANN.

Water

Empresa de Servicios Sanitarios del Paraguay, SA (ESSAP): José Berges 516, entre Brasil y San José, Asunción; tel. (21) 21-0330; fax (21) 21-2624; e-mail secretaria@essap.com.py; internet www.essap.com.py; fmrly Corporación de Obras Sanitarias (CORPOSANA); responsible for public water supply, sewage disposal and drainage; privatization plans suspended in 2002; Pres. EMILIANO INSFRÁN ROLÓN.

TRADE UNIONS

Central Nacional de Trabajadores (CNT): Piribebuy 1078, Asunción; tel. (21) 44-4084; fax (21) 49-2154; e-mail cnt@telesurf.com.py; Sec.-Gen. MIGUEL ZAYAS; 120,840 mems (2007).

Central Sindical de Trabajadores del Estado Paraguayo (Cesitep): Asunción; comprises public sector workers; Pres. REINALDO BARRETO MEDINA.

Central Unitaria de Trabajadores (CUT): San Carlos 836, Asunción; tel. (21) 44-3936; fax (21) 44-8482; f. 1989; Pres. JORGE ALVARENGA; Sec.-Gen. MIRTHA ARIAS.

Confederación Paraguaya de Trabajadores (CPT): Yegros 1309–33 y Simón Bolívar, Asunción; tel. 981878479 (mobile); e-mail cpt_paraguay@yahoo.com; f. 1951; Pres. GERÓNIMO LÓPEZ GÓMEZ; Sec.-Gen. FRANCISCO BRITEZ RUIZ; 43,500 mems from 189 affiliated groups.

Coordinadora Agrícola de Paraguay (CAP): Juan B. Flores y Tacuary, Hernandarias; tel. (983) 52-7003; e-mail bhjca@tigo.com.py; farmers' org.; Pres. GERÓNIMO SÁNCHEZ; Sec. GERARDO BERTÓN.

Organización de Trabajadores de Educación del Paraguay (OTEP): Avda del Pueblo 845 con Ybyra Pyta, Barrio Santa Lucía, Lambaré; tel. and fax (21) 55-5525; e-mail otepsn@highway.com.py; Sec. GABRIELA ESPÍNOLA.

Transport

RAILWAYS

Ferrocarriles del Paraguay, SA (FEPASA): México 145, Casilla 453, Asunción; tel. (21) 44-6789; fax (21) 44-3273; e-mail cultura@ferrocarriles.com.py; internet www.ferrocarriles.com.py; f. 1854; state-owned since 1961; scheduled for privatization; 376 km of track; Pres. EDUARDO LATERZA RIVAROLA.

ROADS

In 1999 there were an estimated 29,500 km of roads, of which 14,986 km were paved. The Pan-American Highway runs for over 700 km in Paraguay and the Trans-Chaco Highway extends from Asunción to Bolivia.

SHIPPING

Administración Nacional de Navegación y Puertos (ANNP) (National Shipping and Ports Administration): Colón y El Paraguayo Independiente, Asunción; tel. (21) 49-5086; fax (21) 49-7485; e-mail gciacomercial@annp.gov.py; internet www.annp.gov.py; f. 1965; responsible for ports services and maintaining navigable channels in rivers and for improving navigation on the Paraguay and Paraná rivers; Pres. ALBINO GONZÁLEZ VILLALBA.

Ocean Shipping

Compañía Paraguaya de Navegación de Ultramar, SA (Copanu): Presidente Franco 625, 2°, Casilla 77, Asunción; tel. (21) 49-2137; fax (21) 44-5013; f. 1963 to operate between Asunción, US and European ports; 10 vessels; Exec. Pres. ROBERT BOSCH B.

Navemar, SA: Avda Republica Argentina 1412, Casilla 273, Asunción; tel. (21) 61-2527; fax (21) 61-2526; e-mail navemar@navemar.com.py; internet www.navemar.com.py; f. 1969; shipping agency, stowage, fleet operations and management; 5 vessels.

Transporte Fluvial Paraguayo SACI: Edif. de la Encarnación, 13°, 14 de Mayo 563, Asunción; tel. (21) 49-3411; fax (21) 49-8218; e-mail tfpsaci@tm.com.py; Admin. Man. DANIELLA CHARBONNIER; 1 vessel.

CIVIL AVIATION

The major international airport, Aeropuerto Internacional Silvio Pettirossi, is situated 15 km from Asunción. A second international airport, Aeropuerto Internacional Guaraní, 30 km from Ciudad del Este, was inaugurated in 1996.

National Airline

Transportes Aéreos del Mercosur (TAM Mercosur): Aeropuerto Internacional Silvio Pettirossi, Hangar TAM/ARPA, Luque, Asunción; tel. (21) 49-1039; fax (21) 64-5146; e-mail tammercosur@uninet.com.py; internet www.tam.com.py; f. 1963 as Líneas Aéreas Paraguayas (LAP); name changed as above in 1997; services to destinations within South America; 80% owned by TAM Linhas Aéreas (Brazil); Pres. LÍBANO MIRANDA BARROSO.

Tourism

Tourism is undeveloped, but, with recent improvements in infrastructure, efforts were being made to promote the sector. Tourist arrivals in Paraguay in 2007 totalled 415,702 (of whom some 45% came from Argentina). In that year tourism receipts were US $121m.

Secretaría Nacional de Turismo: Palma 468, Asunción; tel. (21) 49-4110; fax (21) 49-1230; e-mail ministra@senatur.gov.py; internet www.senatur.gov.py; f. 1998; Exec. Sec. LIZ ROSANNA CRÁMER CAMPOS.

Defence

As assessed at November 2009, Paraguay's armed forces numbered 10,650, of which 2,550 were conscripts. There was an army of 7,600 and an air force of 1,100. The navy, which is largely river-based, had 1,950 members, including 900 marines and a naval air force of 100. There is also a 14,800-strong paramilitary police force, including 4,000 conscripts. Military service, which is compulsory, lasts for 12 months in the army and for two years in the navy.

Defence Budget: 625,000m. guaraníes in 2009.

Commander-in-Chief of the Armed Forces: President of the Republic.

Commander of the Armed Forces: Gen. JUAN OSCAR VELÁZQUEZ.

Commander of the Army: Brig.-Gen. BARTOLOMÉ RAMÓN PINEDA.

Commander of the Air Force: Brig.-Gen. HUGO GILBERTO ARANDA CHAMORRO.

Commander of the Navy: Rear-Adm. EGBERTO EMÉRITO ORUÉ BENEGAS.

Education

Education is, where possible, compulsory for six years, to be undertaken between six and 12 years of age, but there are insufficient schools, particularly in the remote parts of the country. Primary education begins at the age of six and lasts for six years. Secondary education, beginning at 12 years of age, lasts for a further six years, comprising two cycles of three years each. In 2007 enrolment at primary schools included 90% of children in the relevant age-group, while enrolment at secondary schools included 58% of those in the relevant age-group. There are 12 universities in Paraguay. Public expenditure by all levels of government on education was equivalent to 10.0% of total government spending in 2004, according to UNESCO estimates.

Bibliography

For works on South America generally, see Select Bibliography (Books)

Alexander, R. *A History of Organized Labor in Uruguay and Paraguay*. Westport, CT, Praeger Publrs, Inc, 2005.

Cooney, J. W., and Mora, F. O. *Paraguay and the United States: Distant Allies*. Athens, GA, University of Georgia Press, 2007.

Franks, J. *Paraguay, Corruption, Reform, and the Financial System*. Washington, DC, IMF Publications, 2005.

Hernandez, R. E., and Henderson, J. D. *Paraguay*. Broomall, PA, Mason Crest Publrs, 2003.

Horst, R. H. *The Stroessner Regime and Indigenous Resistance in Paraguay*. Gainesville, FL, University Press of Florida, 2010.

Jermyn, L. *Paraguay*. New York, Benchmark Books, 2000.

Kolinsky, C., and Nickson, R. A. *Historical Dictionary of Paraguay*. Lanham, MD, Rowman & Littlefield Publrs, 2000.

Kraay, H., and Whigham, T. *I Die with My Country: Perspectives on the Paraguayan War, 1864–1870*. Lincoln, NE, University of Nebraska Press, 2005.

Leuchars, C. *To the Bitter End: Paraguay and the War of the Triple Alliance*. Westport, CT, Greenwood Publishing Group, 2002.

Nickson, R. A. *Paraguay*. Oxford, ABC Clio, 1999.

O'Shaughnessy, H. *The Priest of Paraguay: Fernando Lugo and the Making of a Nation*. London, Zed Books, 2009.

Paraguay: Addressing the Stagnation and Instability Trap. Washington, DC, International Monetary Fund, 2010.

Paraguay Country Study Guide (World Country Study Guide Library). Washington, DC, International Business Publications, USA, 2000.

Paraguay Foreign Policy and Government Guide. Washington, DC, International Business Publications, USA, 2000.

PERU

Geography

PHYSICAL FEATURES

The Republic of Peru is the third largest country in South America and is located on the west coast of the continent, astride the Andes and descending into the Amazonian plains. The country's longest border is with Brazil (1,560 km or 969 miles), which lies to the east of central Peru. Colombia (1,496 km of border) lies to the north-east, and Ecuador (1,420 km) to the north. Peru has 2,414 km of Pacific coastline, which includes the westernmost bulge of the South American continent, but then runs generally south-eastwards. In the south-east, there is a short southern border with Chile (160 km) and a much longer eastern border with Bolivia (900 km). Only in the late 1990s did Peru settle its outstanding border disputes with Ecuador and Chile, although the maritime boundary with the latter remains unresolved. Slightly smaller than the US state of Alaska, in total Peru covers 1,285,216 sq km (496,225 sq miles), including 5,130 sq km of inland waters.

Apart from some offshore islands, Peru consists of the Costa (the Pacific littoral and the foothills of the Continental Divide), the Sierra of the high Andes and the north-eastern Montaña or Selvas (the wooded lower slopes of the mountains, the high Selvas, and the rainforests of the Amazonian plains, the low Selvas). The coastal plains and lowlands stretch the length of the country, some 65 km–160 km in width, accounting for some 10% of the country. There are few natural harbours, while inland are dry, flat plains and sand dunes near the Sechura Desert, rising to the foothills. This country is an extension of the extremely arid Atacama Desert of Chile, and is so dry that only 10 of the 52 rivers that leave the Andes for the Pacific have sufficient flow to make it to the sea. Dotted along its length are about 40 'oases' suitable for farming. Parallel to the coast, and covering about 30% of the country, is the broad Sierra region. The Andes here consist of three ranges, the main one being the one closest to the sea, the Cordillera Occidental. The mountain ranges, which narrow in width from about 400 km in the south to 240 km in the north, are interspersed with lofty plateaux and deep valleys and gorges. The average height of the region is 3,660 m (about 1,180 ft), but in the mountains north of Lima, the coastal capital of Peru, Nevada de Huascarán reaches 6,768 m (22,213 ft). In the south-east, the interior plateau is broad enough to contain Lake Titicaca, the highest navigable lake in the world, which is shared with Bolivia. Directly west of here, but rather closer to the Pacific seashore to the south-west, is the source of the Amazon (which drains into the Atlantic, far to the east, 6,516 km later), which is usually cited as Lake McIntyre. Those rivers that do not drain into the Amazon or directly into the Pacific drain into Lake Titicaca, which drains through Desaguadero into Lake Poopó in Bolivia. On the rainier eastern slopes of the Andes the rivers have carved deep valleys and sharp crests, and it is this that forms the main barrier between the highlands and the Amazon basin. These forested slopes of the high Selvas in the north-east broaden into the flat, tropical jungle of the Amazon basin, the region (60% of the country's land area) collectively being known as the Montaña. The Montaña, the eastern strip of foothills and the north-east, is largely unexplored and reaches a maximum width of 965 km in the north, where the rainforest continues into Brazil. About one-half of the country is wooded and one-fifth is pasture, the dense rainforest dominating the east, but with more varied tropical vegetation in the centre and west (and still greater variety at altitude). There is some volcanic activity in the mountains, which are prone to earthquakes and landslides, with tsunamis and flooding occurring at lower levels.

CLIMATE

The climate is tropical in the lowlands, but it can be arctic on the highest mountains—there is permanent snow and ice on heights over 5,000 m. Agriculture is possible up to 4,400 m, with the country able to grow a great range of crops and vegetation types at different altitudes. The Costa has an equable climate (temperatures averaging about 20°C—68°F—all year round), cooled by a major offshore sea current, but little rainfall gets past the mountains. For much of the coastal region average rainfall can be only about 50 mm (2 ins) per year, with slightly more in the north and less in the south. The grasslands of the foothills or the western slopes of the Andes survive, when there is no rain, in the mists of the clouds that often cloak the heights. The interior and eastern parts of the Sierra, however, can receive heavy rainfall in October–April. The south-east Sierra, in Cusco (Cuzco), for instance, gets average annual rainfall of 815 mm, but it is the exposed eastern slopes that get most (more than 2,500 mm in places). Minimum and maximum temperatures, on average, range seasonally between −7°C and 21°C (20°F–70°F). Although it is much hotter than the other two major regions of Peru, as is to be expected for a region concentrated in the north and east, it is the Montaña that gets most rainfall (mainly November–April). Here, it is very hot, particularly lower down, and very humid. Total rainfall where the land is beginning to rise can be as much as 3,800 mm per year, although much of the water drains back into the lower Montaña from which it was originally evaporated by the prevailing north-easterlies. Normal patterns can, of course, be disrupted, notably during that periodic feature of the climate known as El Niño. This weather phenomenon can have severe repercussions for Peru, as it brings the heavy rainfall normally delivered to the western Pacific to the east, to a region unsuited to such conditions, which can result in widespread destruction.

POPULATION

There are pronounced class and ethnic divisions, originating in the colonial period, that persist to this day, with the white, urban élite dominating the largely Amerindian and Mestizo countryside. Most of the indigenous natives are descendants of the imperial Incas, who were based in the Peruvian highlands.

About 45% of the population are Amerindian, mainly Quechua-speaking, with some Aymará in the south and about 100 other, isolated groups in the east. A further 37% are of mixed Amerindian and white (mainly Spanish) stock, the Mestizos. About 15% are of unmixed white descent, mainly living in Lima and elsewhere along the Costa, with the rest being black, mixed-black or of Arab, Japanese or Chinese ancestry. Spanish, the principal language of 70% of the population, was the sole official language until 1975, when it was joined by Quechua (of which 28 dialects are spoken in Peru), followed by Aymará. According to the latest census, 81% of Peruvians are Roman Catholic, which was the established religion of the state for much of the 20th century. About 12% belong to the Iglesia Evangélica del Perú, with a number of other religious or non-faith minorities.

According to UN estimates, the total population at mid-2010 was 29.5m. About three-quarters of these people are urbanized, the largest city by far being the national capital, Lima (with over 8.9m. inhabitants), which is on the central coast. Other important centres include Callao, the port of Lima, and the larger cities of Arequipa (the country's second city, but with only about one-10th the population of Lima), to the south and inland from the coast, and Trujillo, to the north. High in the Sierra, to the north of Arequipa, is the ancient Inca city of Cusco (Cuzco). The country is divided into 24 regions and one province (Callao).

History

SANDY MARKWICK

In 1532, when Francisco Pizarro began the conquest of modern-day Peru on behalf of the Spanish, the Inca empire was already endangered through civil war. The territory of the Inca empire, Tahuantinsuyo, had grown too large to control, stretching, at its peak, 5,000 km, from modern-day Colombia to central Chile. Imperial expansion had accelerated as neighbouring societies and cultures were subjugated by the military might and despotism of the Incas. Centred on the fertile Cusco region, Inca control was based on a strong pyramidal system of government. A sophisticated network of stone roads, bridges and tunnels, and intensive systems of irrigation and agriculture, based on a communal productive unit known as the ayllu, supported a high-density population (estimates vary between 12m. and 32m.). Maize and potatoes were the principal crops. The metals worked were gold, silver and bronze.

Pizarro's forces captured the Inca leader, Atahualpa, (subsequently executing him) and killed some 7,000 of his troops, after luring them into a trap in Cajamarca. The Cusco region fell to Pizarro's forces in 1533, and in 1544 the Viceroyalty of Peru was formally established, with its capital in Lima. Sporadic resistance continued until the Incas were finally defeated in 1572, when Tupac Amarú I, the last Inca emperor, was captured at the fall of Vilcabamba, taken to Cusco and beheaded. The Spanish colonial administration, having completed its military conquest (despite intermittent uprisings), embarked on a repressive programme of Christianization. Indigenous Indian (Amerindian) religious traditions survived, however, either assimilated into the new Roman Catholic order or concealed from the Church hierarchy. During the colonial period the Andean tradition of communalism was weakened, as mining for export became the dominant economic activity, and the new Criollo (Creole) élite of Spanish origin established large agricultural estates (haciendas) on the most fertile lands to supply produce for mining and coastal towns. The defeat of the Incas by the Spanish greatly influenced the character of modern Peru, where sharp divisions follow ethnic lines and long-established resentments occasionally escalate into violence.

INDEPENDENCE

At the end of the 18th century an independence movement grew among the Criollos, who resented their inferior status, as well as the restrictive trade regulations and high taxes imposed by the Spanish Government. Peru declared independence from Spain on 28 July 1821, helped by the republican forces of the Argentine General José de San Martín, and its army defeated Spain at the decisive Battle of Ayacucho in 1824. Political instability characterized the first half-century of independence. In the aftermath of the war, political office was held by regional military leaders (caudillos) who, having fought against a common enemy—the Spanish—now fought each other in the contest for central power. After independence Peru was highly regionalized, with economic power vested in the haciendas and political control exercised by hacienda owners in alliance with local caudillos. The weakness of the central state prevented successive Governments from consolidating national political control and forced them to work in co-operation with regional leaders to rule at local level. Between 1826 and 1865 some 34 Presidents, including 27 military officers, held office. One such contender for power was a Bolivian President, Gen. Andrés Santa Cruz, who, allied with southern Peruvian landowners, proclaimed the Peruvian-Bolivian Confederation in 1836, with its capital in Lima. Chile, viewing the Confederation as a threat to its interests in the Pacific, declared war. The Confederation was finally defeated and, subsequently, dissolved by Chilean forces in 1839.

THE GUANO YEARS

The emergence of the guano trade ended a period of economic stagnation. International demand for the fertilizing properties of guano (the accumulated nitrate-rich deposits of bird colonies on the offshore islands) escalated with the development of capital-intensive commercial agriculture in Europe. The Peruvian Government established a state monopoly over the exploitation of guano. However, despite strong economic growth during 1840–78, resulting largely from the trade, the success of the guano industry was not exploited fully. Revenue from guano was spent on the expansion of the bureaucracy, the military and the servicing of the Government's foreign debt, which had accumulated to finance imports. The sharp distinction remained intact between the colonial character of production on large estates and the self-sufficient nature of peasant economies, perpetuating deep ethnic and class divisions and preventing the emergence of a strong internal market, which would have provided Peru's productive sectors with the domestic stimulus for growth. Internal demand among élite consumers, which developed after the dramatic expansion of guano exports, could not be satisfied by the domestic productive sector and resulted in increased imports. The most lucrative years of the guano trade came to an end in the 1870s, as the result of competition from cheaper nitrates and synthetic fertilizers. Peru was under threat of bankruptcy, with a huge external debt of US $35m. and no access to foreign loans. The crisis culminated in another military defeat of Peru and Bolivia by Chile, in the War of the Pacific (1879–83), which resulted from a dispute over nitrate resources in the Atacama desert. Chile occupied much of Peru, including Lima, in 1881. Under the terms of the peace settlement, Chile annexed the province of Tarapacá as well as the Bolivian department of Antofagasta.

THE RISE OF A COASTAL OLIGARCHY

Post-war reconstruction led to the expansion of coastal haciendas and the rise of an oligarchy of merchants, financiers and landowners, better adapted to a new capitalist age, whose interests centred on the production and export of primary products. The coastal oligarchy, allied to foreign capital and semi-feudal landowners of the Sierra, exercised widespread influence and control over government (until as late as 1968, when a modernizing military regime seized power—see below). Raw material prices grew at an average of 7% per year between 1890 and 1929. Peru's reconstruction after the War of the Pacific also received substantial support from the so-called Grace Contract, which was finally approved in 1889. The Contract, negotiated by a British businessman, Michael Grace, provided for the cancellation of Peru's national debt in return for the Government ceding control over its railway network to the largely British-owned Peruvian Corporation. Sugar and cotton became the principal exports, although wool, rubber, silver, copper and petroleum each accounted for more than 15% of total export earnings at various times between 1890 and 1929.

Peru's first modern political party, the Partido Civil (Civil Party), was created in 1871 to represent the interests of the new oligarchy. The *civilistas*, as the party's sympathizers were known, opposed military government and rejected the unproductive use of resources from guano. In 1872 Manuel Pardo was elected as the first *civilista* President. The Partido Civil, guided by liberal, *laissez-faire* doctrines, and the rival Partido Democrático (Democratic Party), which was more pro-Church and conservative, led Peru through a period of export-orientated development and rapid economic and social change during the next half-century. Formal parliamentary democracy was, in practice, extremely limited, with no more than some 3% of the total population enfranchised. During this period, however, the military was professionalized and, at least between 1895 and 1919, was brought under civilian control. The Government was reorganized to conform better to the demands of a modern export economy. Democratic government was interrupted by the dictatorship of Augusto Bernardino Legua, which lasted from 1919 until 1930. From this period, marked by economic prosperity and relative political stability, the structure of contemporary Peru emerged. The advance of capitalism saw peasants migrate to the cities, while traditional haciendas and small-scale mining operations were transformed into more modern agro-industrial or mining complexes. During this export-led expansion, which was allied to foreign capital, the USA replaced the United Kingdom as Peru's main trading partner and source of direct investment.

THE RISE OF APRA

The export-led model of the Peruvian economy was seriously affected by the collapse of world commodity prices in 1929. From this time there was a growing realization that export dependency was fundamental to the country's underdevelopment. The debate over methods of resolving the problem of development was led by the reformist Víctor Raúl Haya de la Torre and the revolutionary José Carlos Mariátegui. De la Torre founded the Alianza Popular Revolucionaria Americana (APRA—American Popular Revolutionary Alliance). (Although the party was officially renamed the Partido Aprista Peruano in 1930, it continued to be known generally as APRA.) Mariátegui founded the Partido Comunista Peruano (PCP—Peruvian Communist Party) in 1928. The emergence of APRA reflected the increasing radicalism among the Peruvian masses as world economic crisis in 1929 led to depression. APRA was a left-wing, populist and anti-imperialist organization claiming to represent peasants, workers and the progressive middle classes whose interests were not being served by the governing élite. When Legua's regime was deposed by a military coup led by Col Luis Sánchez Cerro, a popular military caudillo, the oligarchical élite, conscious of the threat from APRA, gave its support to the military. The takeover inaugurated a period of political instability in national politics between the 1930s and the 1960s, as an emerging national industrial bourgeoisie and Peru's popular sectors challenged the old alliance of the Peruvian agrarian oligarchy and foreign capital that had dominated the Peruvian state. This was reflected in the increase in popularity of APRA, which became an important political force and often had the largest representation in the Congreso (Congress). APRA was prevented from forming a government by an alliance of old oligarchical and military forces whose tactics included electoral fraud, repression (APRA was declared illegal in 1931–45 and in 1948–56) and finally, in July 1962, a pre-emptive *coup d'état* (which annulled the elections of the previous month).

MILITARY GOVERNMENT, 1968–80

In October 1968 a left-wing military regime led by the army Chief of Staff, Gen. Juan Velasco, supplanted President Fernando Belaúnde Terry of the reformist Acción Popular (AP—Popular Action). Belaúnde had been elected President in June 1963, as the candidate of both the AP and of the Partido Demócrata Cristiano (PDC—Christian Democratic Party). A developmentalist ideology had emerged from within the Peruvian armed forces, which coincided more closely with the priorities of industrial interests rather than those of the traditional export-orientated élites. Velasco and other ranking officers in the army assumed the role of modernizers. The military Government introduced land reform and nationalized banks, telecommunications, the railways, electricity production, fisheries and heavy industry. Large haciendas were partitioned and converted into agricultural co-operatives. This policy of nationalization was presented as a nationalist, socialist and anti-imperialist struggle, partly in order to inspire popular support for the reforms.

As opposition to the Velasco regime increased, attention focused on the Government's restrictions on education, its controls on currency and imports, and the failure of its agrarian reform. Agricultural co-operatives proved to be poorly conceived, corrupt and badly managed, resulting in rebellions in rural areas. Velasco was replaced, in August 1975, by Gen. Francisco Morales Bermúdez, in an internal military coup. The new Government abandoned the former regime's anti-imperialist image and pledged a return to civilian democracy. A new Constitution, which, for the first time, granted universal adult suffrage, was adopted in July 1979. In May 1980 military rule came to an end and Belaúnde was elected President for a second term, winning 45% of the votes cast. The Constitution came into effect in July.

SENDERO LUMINOSO AND THE GUERRILLA WAR

On the eve of the presidential election in May 1980 the Maoist insurgent group Sendero Luminoso (Shining Path) initiated a strategy of 'people's war', with the burning of ballot boxes in the rural community of Chuschi, in Ayacucho department. Subsequently, Sendero Luminoso extended its influence to most other departments. By the mid-1990s the movement's destructive campaign and the army's counter-insurgency were estimated to have caused some 30,000 deaths. The origins of Sendero Luminoso lay in a schism in communist ideology as practised in the USSR and the People's Republic of China under Mao Zedung. Sendero Luminoso left the pro-Soviet PCP in 1970, under the leadership of its founder and ideological force, Abimael Guzmán Reynoso (also known as 'Chairman Gonzalo'). Sendero Luminoso won endorsement from some sectors of the peasantry by exploiting Amerindian traditions and centuries-old resentment against the central Government and foreign conquerors. It went on to penetrate shanty-town civic groups, trade unions, universities and teacher-training colleges, and expanded its influence through Huamanga University in Ayacucho, the underdeveloped region chosen for the group's inception as a peasant movement.

The rise of Sendero Luminoso was assisted by the incomplete and largely unsuccessful land reform under Velasco, and by a fragmentation among the parties of the left over the issue of reform. Sendero Luminoso emphasized revolutionary violence as the fundamental mechanism for obtaining political change. Its use of extreme brutality brought a response in kind from the army. Sendero Luminoso's strategy was to mobilize the peasantry initially, and only focus on urban areas once its power and influence in the countryside was consolidated. It grew to represent a genuine threat to the country's internal security, particularly since it increased the risk of a military takeover.

GARCÍA LEADS APRA TO GOVERNMENT

The Belaúnde Government became increasingly unpopular, owing, in particular, to the measures it imposed to deal with Peru's considerable economic problems and its ineffectiveness in combating Sendero Luminoso. The presidential election of April 1985 was won by the Aprista candidate, Alan García Pérez, with 46% of the votes cast. The army accepted García's victory and demonstrated that it was prepared to adhere to the Constitution. President García introduced radical economic policies, including a limit on debt repayments, in order to control inflation. However, the economy continued to deteriorate and guerrilla violence from Sendero Luminoso and a second insurgent group, the Movimiento Revolucionario Tupac Amarú (MRTA—Tupac Amarú Revolutionary Movement), continued to increase. Support for the Izquierda Unida (IU—United Left, a coalition of seven left-wing parties formed in 1980) grew, and trade unions organized a series of general strikes in 1987 and 1988. Right-wing opposition to the Government also increased as a result of the decision, announced in July 1987, to nationalize the financial sector. A 'freedom movement', Libertad (Liberty), expressing opposition to the nationalization plans, was formed under the leadership of the novelist Mario Vargas Llosa.

INFLUENCE OF THE MILITARY RESTORED UNDER FUJIMORI

Alberto Fujimori, an independent candidate, was the unexpected victor in the presidential election of June 1990. An economist of Japanese descent, he had never previously held political office. Fujimori's main rival in the election was Vargas Llosa, representing the centre-right Frente Democrático alliance (FREDEMO—Democratic Front, established in early 1988 by the AP, Libertad and the Partido Popular Cristiano—Popular Christian Party). Fujimori's victory in a second round of voting, in which he secured 57% of the votes cast, reflected a widespread disillusionment with traditional party politics. Fujimori lacked the benefit of a party machine when he entered politics, and therefore established the Cambio 90 (C90—Change 90) party to contest the election. The party consisted largely of members of Protestant movements and centrists dissatisfied with the inefficiency and corruption of APRA and other traditional parties. Although C90 lacked a coherent ideology or programme, Fujimori represented a more populist alternative to Vargas Llosa, who was identified with the Lima-based élite. During the election campaign Fujimori had advocated an economic-reform programme that was markedly less austere than the one proposed by Vargas Llosa. However, shortly after taking office, he broke his campaign pledges and introduced an uncompromisingly orthodox reform programme, which became known as the 'Fujishock'. He reduced state subsidies, freed the exchange rate, and, in December 1990, began negotiations with international lending agencies. In addition, Fujimori liberalized the economy to encourage foreign investment and embarked on an ambitious privatization programme involving all the state's productive ventures.

The lack of a coherent organizational support base meant that the army's loyalty was crucial. As soon as Fujimori came to power he attempted to win the support of the army in order to reduce the risk of a military coup and to secure a powerful political ally in the event of widespread unrest. He gave the army increased powers and autonomy in the counter-insurgency campaign and appointed army generals to his cabinet (Consejo de Ministros—Council of Ministers). On 5 April 1992 Fujimori launched an autogolpe, an incumbent's coup, when he suspended the 1979 Constitution, dissolved parliament, suspended the authority of the judiciary and assumed wide powers of decree, with the endorsement of the armed forces. He justified his actions by claiming that the traditional political élite was blocking the reforms necessary to combat the economic crisis and ultra-leftist insurgencies. When Fujimori suspended the legislature he appealed for, and received, mass popular approval, although the political class in Peru denounced his shift towards authoritarianism, unconstitutionality and demagoguery. Opponents maintained that he had forfeited his position and, in accordance with the 1979 Constitution, declared First Vice-President Máximo San Román Cáceres to be the new President. Similarly, the USA and other foreign powers urged the early restoration of democratic government.

Following the suspension of international financial aid to Peru, which threatened Fujimori's radical economic-reform programme, the President was forced to hold elections to the Congreso Constituyente Democrático (CCD—Democratic Constituent Congress), a constituent assembly, in November 1992. The pro-Fujimori alliance of C90 and the Nueva Mayoría (NM—New Majority) received some 40% of the votes cast, and won 44 seats in the 80-seat chamber. APRA and the AP boycotted the CCD elections, as did Libertad and several small leftist parties. Of the significant political parties, only the Partido Popular Cristiano participated, winning eight seats. The assembly was inaugurated in December. In early January 1993 the CCD exonerated Fujimori for his coup and confirmed him as head of state.

The final draft of the proposed new Constitution was approved by the CCD in early September 1993. It was endorsed by the electorate, with 52% of the votes cast, in a national referendum held in October. The new Constitution consolidated President Fujimori's position by at least partially restoring his democratic legitimacy and by permitting him to be re-elected for a successive five-year term. All presidential decrees issued during the interim period were declared ratified until revised or revoked by the CCD. Foreign aid to Peru, which had been withdrawn in protest against the coup, was largely restored. The CCD acted as the legislature until the end of President Fujimori's existing term of office.

President Fujimori consistently protected the armed forces from accusations of human rights abuses. The extent to which the military influenced government policy was revealed by an amnesty law in June 1995, which covered human rights offences committed during the previous 15 years of counter-insurgency. The protection given to the military by Fujimori was motivated, in part, by a desire to avert any threat of a coup, although the President was not a weak party in the relationship. The President's power vis-à-vis the military was consolidated by a change in the law, granting him the power to appoint all generals and admirals, whereas, under previous Governments, the armed forces had always appointed their own high command.

The armed forces' support for President Fujimori was tested by a short, undeclared border war with Ecuador in January–February 1995, in which more than 100 soldiers were killed. A cease-fire was brokered in Montevideo, Uruguay, in March by the guarantors of the 1942 Rio Protocol (Argentina, Brazil, Chile and the USA), which ended an earlier war with Ecuador in 1941. A short stretch of unmarked border remained a source of tension between Peru and Ecuador, with occasional accusations from both sides of incursions and skirmishes, until a peace agreement to end the long-standing dispute was signed in October 1998. The accord recognized Peruvian claims regarding the delineation of the border, but granted Ecuador navigation rights in Peruvian Amazonia.

CAPTURE OF GUZMÁN

The capture, on 12 September 1992, of Abimael Guzmán and other members of Sendero Luminoso's Central Committee (the organization's highest decision-making body) and, subsequently, many others from among its senior leaders inflicted serious damage on the movement, from which it would not recover. Guzmán's arrest came at a crucial time, when Sendero Luminoso had been escalating its terrorist campaign in Lima and planning further offensives as part of its 'sixth military plan'. A large car bomb in the Lima suburb of Miraflores in July had killed 21 and injured 250 in the worst single terrorist incident in 12 years of guerrilla war. The bombing was designed to cause indiscriminate civilian casualties and to intimidate the wealthy and the middle class of Lima, which had largely escaped the worst effects of terrorism. After Guzmán's arrest the overall scale of guerrilla violence decreased by approximately 50% in the latter half of 1992, and violence continued to decline before stabilizing at a significantly reduced rate. Sendero Luminoso experienced a devastating decline in the geographical extent of its influence, which became confined to shanty towns in Lima and coca-growing areas in the Huallaga valley and central Sierra, and other isolated areas. An extremist faction, under the leadership of Oscar Ramírez Durand, continued to wage guerrilla insurgency, although attacks were smaller and less frequent than in previous years. Despite intermittent violence, Sendero Luminoso was no longer considered to represent a serious threat to the stability of the Government or to the state long before the capture of Durand by the security forces in July 1999.

FUJIMORI'S SECOND TERM

President Fujimori was re-elected in April 1995 for a second five-year term of office, with 64% of the votes cast. His main challenger, former UN Secretary-General Javier Pérez de Cuéllar, supported by an independent movement, Unión por el Perú (UPP—Union for Peru), received 21% of the ballot and conceded the popular mandate that the vote gave to Fujimori. The restoration of economic growth and success against the insurgencies in Fujimori's first term of office ensured the President's popularity. Meanwhile, the traditional parties had lost their support base, and the opposition was divided. Fujimori intended to pursue the liberal, free-market reforms introduced since his accession to the presidency in 1990, although he pledged to use funds from privatization to alleviate poverty. However, divisions within the administration over economic policy widened as a result of the contraction of Peru's economy and a rise in inflation, after three years of rapid economic growth.

The threat of left-wing insurgency re-emerged dramatically in December 1996, with the seizure of the Japanese ambassador's residence in Lima and some 600 hostages by 14 MRTA guerrillas. The guerrillas, led by Néstor Cerpa Cartolini, released most of the hostages within days, but continued to hold 72, among them high-level government officials, foreign diplomats and businessmen, until the residence was stormed by Peruvian commandos in April 1997, resulting in the deaths of all 14 guerrillas and one hostage. Cerpa had demanded the release of MRTA prisoners, including the group's leader, Víctor Polay Campos, a ransom payment and safe passage; the raid appeared to mark an end to MRTA insurgent activity.

President Fujimori's style of government continued to be personal and autocratic, with little in the way of checks and balances to his rule. His NM/C90 supporters enjoyed an absolute majority in the new 120-seat Congreso, which made the passage of legislation and even constitutional reform straightforward. In addition, opposition political parties were in disarray, the trade unions largely defeated, regional and municipal authorities powerless and the Council of Ministers generally weak and subservient. The judiciary and prosecution services were widely accused of becoming tools of the executive. Civilian democracy was weakened, moreover, by the lack of engaging political parties and civic organizations through which popular demands could be articulated. The President's approach was populist, to appeal directly to the public, rather than seek agreement and compromise with rival political groups. He travelled widely throughout Peru, personally addressing problems at local level.

Disaffection with President Fujimori's authoritarian tendencies was growing, but was not strong enough to prevent a pliant Congreso, in August 1996, voting to allow him to stand for re-election to a third presidential term in 2000, despite the Constitution's statute against third consecutive terms of office.

During 1998 President Fujimori repeatedly altered the composition of his administration in an attempt to consolidate his position and restore public confidence in his leadership. In August the President moved to reinforce his control of the levers of state power and strengthen his democratic credentials with the unexpected dismissal of Gen. Nicolás Hermoza Ríos, who had come to be seen as one of a ruling triumvirate, along with President Fujimori and his security chief, Vladimiro Montesinos. President Fujimori's popularity continued to wane, and the administration was increasingly perceived as authoritarian in attitude and dogmatic in its handling of a deteriorating economy.

FUJIMORI WINS DISCREDITED ELECTION FOR THIRD TERM

The first round of presidential voting was held on 9 April 2000. Official results gave Fujimori just under the 50% of the votes required for an outright victory. Fujimori's main rival was an economist, Alejandro Toledo Manrique, of Perú Posible (PP—Possible Peru), who received slightly more than 40% of the votes cast. Toledo's campaign focused on what he referred to as Fujimori's record of authoritarianism and abuse of power, rather than on any significant economic or political differences. Toledo came from relative obscurity to eclipse the challenges of the mayor of Lima, Alberto Andrade, and Luis Casteñeda Lossio, the former head of the Social Security Institute, of Solidaridad Nacional (SN—National Solidarity), who failed to muster nation-wide support. Toledo's mestizo (mixed race) ethnicity and impoverished background attracted support from many poor Peruvians. The vote was marred by allegations, made by the opposition candidates, of large-scale irregularities in the vote count. These allegations received widespread support from international observers and representatives of foreign governments, including, in particular, the USA. Suspicions of electoral fraud provoked protests by opposition supporters. Legislative elections, also held on 9 April, resulted in 52 seats for Fujimori's Perú 2000 alliance, less than the 61 needed for an absolute majority. Toledo's PP was the second largest group, with 29 seats.

A second presidential ballot, between Fujimori and Toledo, was scheduled for 28 May 2000, despite efforts by Toledo and the Organization of American States (OAS) to postpone the vote for 10 days to ensure that the conditions for fair elections were in place. Toledo withdrew from the election and appealed to his supporters to spoil their ballot papers in protest at electoral fraud. The Jurado Nacional Electoral (JNE—National Electoral Board) refused the request for a postponement and, as a result, the OAS issued a statement that the elections could not be considered free and fair. The OAS and other international observers from the US-based Carter Center and the European Union (EU) withdrew their missions. Fujimori won an uncontested election (although the JNE ruled that Toledo remained a candidate and refused to remove his name from the ballot papers), with 51% of the votes cast, while Toledo received 18%, and 31% of voters either spoiled their ballot papers or left them blank. The result was denounced as invalid by the political opposition. The OAS decided against the imposition of economic sanctions, instead dispatching a mission to Peru to explore options for strengthening democracy. Fujimori's inauguration on 28 July was accompanied by violent protests in Lima.

However, Fujimori's term of office was prematurely curtailed by the disclosure, in September 2000, of hundreds of videos, recorded covertly, that showed Vladimiro Montesinos, Fujimori's controversial security adviser, bribing, among others, an opposition member of the Congreso, a Supreme Court judge, television executives and an election official. In response, Fujimori declared that new elections would be organized, in which he would not participate, and that the national intelligence service, which Montesinos headed, would be disbanded. Montesinos' close links with the military high command led to fears of a military coup, but these concerns subsided after the military publicly supported Fujimori's decision. Demonstrations, led by Toledo, demanded the immediate resignation of Fujimori and the arrest of Montesinos, who fled to Panama. At the same time, 10 congressional representatives of Perú 2000 defected, thus depriving Fujimori of his majority in the legislature. In October the Congreso approved OAS-mediated proposals preparing the way for power to be transferred from Fujimori to his successor (as well as the dissolution of the Congreso to make way for a newly elected legislature) in mid-2001. The political crisis deepened in late October 2000, when Montesinos returned from Panama, after failing to secure political asylum there. At the same time, the first Vice-President, Francisco Tudela, resigned in protest at government attempts to link new elections to a military amnesty, and middle-ranking officers in southern Peru staged an isolated rebellion demanding the resignation of Fujimori. Under pressure, the Government launched an investigation into

Montesinos' activities, considering allegations including torture and murder, as well as corruption, 'gun-running' and money-laundering. By this time Montesinos had again gone into hiding. Fujimori's attempts to consolidate political support focused on distancing himself from Montesinos, and included the staging of a highly public operation, led in person by Fujimori, to arrest the former intelligence chief and to dismiss his allies in the military high command. Despite his efforts, he failed to assuage his critics and, with Montesinos' whereabouts still unknown, a number of Fujimori's supporters defected, leading to a shift in power in the Congreso, which appointed Valentín Paniagua, a moderate opposition legislator, as President of the legislature. Paniagua immediately reinstated judges dismissed for challenging the constitutionality of Fujimori's third consecutive term of office.

PRESIDENT ALEJANDRO TOLEDO, 2001–06

Fujimori resigned from the presidency during a visit to Japan in November 2000, prompting speculation that he would live there in self-imposed exile. The Japanese authorities confirmed that Fujimori was entitled to Japanese citizenship and could stay indefinitely. The Congreso, meanwhile, rejected his resignation, and instead voted to dismiss him, declaring him 'morally unfit' to hold office. It appointed Paniagua as interim President of Peru, and he immediately named former UN Secretary-General and former presidential candidate Javier Pérez de Cuéllar as prime minister. The new President, lacking a democratic mandate to pursue a legislative agenda, pledged to act only as an 'administrator' overseeing new elections in April 2001. Paniagua continued the process of purging the military of Montesinos' influence in order to ensure the impartiality of the military in the transition towards a newly elected Government. In June Paniagua set up a Comisión de Verdad y Reconciliación (CVR—Truth and Reconciliation Commission) to investigate political violence in the preceding two decades. When the CVR delivered its final report in August 2003, it estimated that some 69,000 people had been killed during the insurgency and counter-insurgency, 30% of whom had died at the hands of the security forces. The end of the Fujimori era was widely embraced as an opportunity to restore the rule of law and the integrity of democratic institutions.

The principal candidates for the election on 8 April 2001 were Alejandro Toledo, former President Alan García, who had returned from exile to contest the poll, and the conservative Lourdes Flores Nano of the Unidad Nacional (National Unity) alliance. Toledo won 37% of the votes in the first round, while García received 26% and Flores 24%. In the second round of voting, held on 3 June, Toledo emerged victorious, securing 53% of the votes, ahead of García's 47%. The PP won 45 seats in the concurrently held legislative elections but, together with allied parties, failed to secure a majority in the 120-seat Congreso, leaving the prospect of coalition government. Two days before his inauguration, President-elect Toledo announced a new, broad-based, 15-member cabinet, which represented a shift in the balance of the Government towards 'technocrats', and away from Toledo's political allies in the PP. The fiscal orthodoxy of the administration provided a balance to Toledo's populist tendencies, as a result of which the Government was regarded with greater confidence by international investors.

Meanwhile, in June 2001 Venezuelan military intelligence officers, assisted by the US Federal Bureau of Investigation and the Peruvian police force, arrested Montesinos in Caracas, Venezuela. (In July 2002 Montesinos was convicted of abuse of authority and sentenced to nine years' imprisonment. His sentence was increased following further convictions of abuse of power and corruption.)

During his first year in office President Toledo's initially high popularity began to decline. Economic growth was insufficient to deliver on the Government's populist election promises to create jobs. Owing to the unpopularity of plans for a series of major privatizations, anti-Government demonstrations were frequent in 2002, and in June, following a week of violent demonstrations in Arequipa, which left more than 100 people wounded, a state of emergency was declared. The unrest was the first serious episode of protest in what was to become a common feature under Toledo's presidency. In May 2003 the President declared a 30-day state of emergency following violent unrest by public sector workers demanding improved pay and conditions. Toledo's attempts to build a broad cross-party consensus in the Congreso in support of his policy of structural reform and combating corruption were seriously undermined by a series of scandals throughout that year, which cast doubt on his credibility.

The Government's loss of popularity was reflected in poor results for the PP in regional and municipal elections in November 2002. Toledo's promise of decentralization led to the creation of 25 new regional authorities. The results indicated that Toledo was unable to draw on a political base with a nation-wide presence. Aprista success in the regional elections raised the prospect of its leading figure, Alan García, launching another presidential campaign for the election scheduled for 2006.

The tension between satisfying President Toledo's political constituency in the PP and appointing the most capable, often independent, ministers became a theme of his presidency. Cabinet reshuffles during Toledo's administration were generally attempts to shore up political support in response to popular unrest and, therefore, tended to represent a shift to the left, at the expense of capable technocrats. Following the June 2002 unrest the Minister of Economy and Finance, Pedro Pablo Kuczynski, resigned and the privatization process was suspended. Wide-ranging cabinet changes in July, after the unrest of the previous two months, failed to improve Toledo's political fortunes.

The Government's stated objectives continued to focus on promoting economic growth through pro-market management of the economy, including structural reform and fiscal prudence. A new IMF stand-by agreement setting fiscal targets for 2004–06 looked set to underpin this policy for the remainder of President Toledo's term. The inauguration of a fifth new cabinet in February 2004, in contrast to earlier reshuffles, was designed to bring greater technical expertise and independence to the Government, as well as to distance President Toledo from a scandal involving his former legal adviser and intelligence chief, César Almeyda. Kuczynski was reappointed to the economy and finance ministry; it was hoped that his return would give renewed impetus to the administration's privatization efforts.

Despite favourable economic indicators, the Government's political weaknesses were exacerbated in July 2004 when the Congreso elected Antero Flores-Aráoz, of the opposition Unidad Nacional, as its new speaker, defeating the governing PP's candidate, Luis Solari. The defeat prevented President Toledo from controlling the legislative agenda. Popular support for Toledo remained very low in 2004–06. Although there had been impressive economic growth, significant job creation remained elusive and his political and personal integrity had been undermined by a series of damaging allegations. Charges that Toledo was closely involved in the fraudulent collection of signatures as part of the process to register the PP for the 2000 legislative elections continued to undermine his authority. The President appeared before a congressional commission to answer questions on the matter in March 2005 and was judged culpable in early April. The Congreso, however, ruled in May not to impeach the President on the basis of this judgment. Other sources of unrest included coca growers in Cusco and Puno, whose violent protests in late 2004 were aimed at the Government's coca-eradication programme, and cotton farmers demanding compensation for losses incurred as a result of lower trade tariffs attracting cheaper US imports. In January 2005 a retired army major, Antauro Igor Humala Tasso, led a revolt by around 150 army recruits in the southern Andes. The uprising resulted in the death of seven people, including four police officers. Although the insurgents' demand for Toledo's resignation might have received some sympathy from the wider population, their recourse to violence was widely condemned.

In a cabinet reorganization in February 2005 President Toledo attempted to strengthen his position by appointing three new PP ministers, but his popularity remained low. Meanwhile, the opposition itself was deeply divided and had no clear leadership. In August Toledo's appointment of the FIM leader, Fernando Olivera, as Minister of Foreign Affairs prompted the resignation of prime minister Carlos Ferrero Costa and of the housing minister, Bruce Montes de Oca. Considering his position untenable, Olivera, who, controversially, had supported the legalization of coca cultivation in several provinces, resigned two days later. In the ensuing cabinet reshuffle, Kuczynski was appointed President of the Council of Ministers. Kuczynski's appointment received broad congressional and popular approval.

From late 2004 former President Fujimori made public his intention to contest the presidency in 2006, despite the sustained efforts of the Peruvian authorities to extradite him from Japan to stand trial on charges of corruption and other abuses of power. In February 2005 the Government announced its intention to seek Fujimori's extradition through the International Court of Justice. In the same month the Constitutional Court ruled that Fujimori was ineligible to stand in the presidential election. In June the Japanese authorities announced that the extradition process against Fujimori would not proceed in the absence of further evidence against the former head of state. However, in November Fujimori arrived unannounced in Santiago, Chile, where he was immediately placed in custody. In September 2007 Fujimori was extradited to stand trial in Peru.

THE RETURN OF PRESIDENT GARCÍA

In the first round of the presidential election held on 9 April 2006, Lt-Col (retd) Ollanta Moisés Humala Tasso, a left-wing nationalist and brother of Antauro, leader of the January 2005 revolt, received the most votes (30.6%), followed by former President Alan García (24.3%), the APRA candidate. Lourdes Flores Nano, again representing the Unidad Nacional alliance, came third, with 23.8% of the ballot. Humala was the nominee of the UPP coalition, which included his own party, the Partido Nacionalista Peruano (PNP—Peruvian Nationalist Party). Humala was a central figure in the nationalist Cacerist movement, inspired by the 19th-century military leader and President, Andrés Avelino Cáceres Dorregaray, who fought Chilean occupation after the War of the Pacific. Controversially, Humala's candidacy—a mixture of left-wing nationalism and support for indigenous peoples—received support from Venezuela's President Hugo Chávez. Although distrusted by many middle-class voters because of his record in office, García was able, nevertheless, to cast himself as the moderate alternative and exploit fears that Humala would damage Peru's economy and isolate it from markets, foreign investors and credit. García continued to advocate state participation in the economy, but claimed to have learned lessons from the past and to have accepted much of liberal economic orthodoxy. In the run-off ballot between the two leading candidates, on 4 June, García secured the presidency, with 52.6% of the votes cast.

García's new administration took office on 28 July 2006. His new cabinet comprised mainly independents: notable among the appointments were Luis Carranza Ugarte, a fiscal conservative who was appointed Minister of Economy and Finance, and experienced diplomat José Antonio García Belaúnde, who became Minister of Foreign Affairs. The appointment of independents to principal positions to some extent alleviated concern within business circles and was designed to secure sufficient cross-party support of the Government's legislative programme. García's ruling APRA held just 36 of the 120 seats in the Congreso, although the opposition was divided. The President pledged to maintain the fiscal discipline established under Toledo, but economic growth and high commodity prices allowed García to increase public spending, focusing on basic infrastructure, including improvements in water supply and sewerage provision. Despite this, it remained a challenge to manage popular expectations of improving living standards.

In July 2007 protests led by teachers and farm workers escalated into violent clashes with police, and brought much of Peru to a standstill. Among the protesters were coca farmers angry at the Government's support for the UN's Vienna Convention, which criminalizes the cultivation of coca.

By mid-2008 President García's approval ratings had declined significantly as a result of rising prices and a popular perception that the poor were not sharing the benefits of economic growth. Levels of support for the President were lowest in the poorest areas of Peru, particularly in the southern and Amazon regions, as well as among the *pueblos jóvenes* (slums) of Lima. Poverty eradication was one of the issues on the agenda at the fifth summit of EU, Latin American and Caribbean leaders, which was hosted by Peru in May. Disagreement among Andean Pact member states over proposals for a free trade agreement with the EU led President García to announce his intention of negotiating a trade agreement unilaterally. Opponents of the Government's trade policies held demonstrations during the summit. In June 2009 there was violent opposition to free trade talks with the EU among indigenous groups, which claimed the deal, along with the similar free trade agreement (Peru Trade Promotion Agreement—PTPA) with the USA, would further impoverish their communities. The PTPA came into effect in February 2009.

Violence from indigenous groups escalated during June 2009 in response to government plans to to allocate large areas of Peru's protected rainforests to petroleum exploration, mining and farming. Dozens of police and protesters were killed in clashes in the northern Amazonas department in the most serious social unrest in Peru for many years. Opposition to the plans, along with unpopular free trade talks and corruption scandals involving allegations of misuse of public funds by officials in state-run organizations, fuelled anti-Government unrest in the form of protests and strikes. In response, the Government agreed to revoke two decrees that would have opened up 45m. ha of rainforest to development, close to 50% of the Peruvian Amazon, and transferred authority for granting exploration permits from local communities to the central Government. The crisis led to the resignation of the Prime Minister Yehude Simon Munaro and a weakened García administration. García appointed a new cabinet in July in a bid to shore up his damaged Government. Javier Velásquez Quesquén, who replaced Simon as Prime Minister, was one of a number of APRA members who now formed a majority in the Council of Ministers. Meanwhile, García appointed the former national police chief Octavio Salazar as Minister of the Interior, replacing Mercedes Cabanillas Bustamente, who had faced intense criticism for the Government's handling of the crisis.

Presidential and congressional elections were scheduled for 2011. Although President García was constitutionally unable to stand for a consecutive term, there was speculation that he would be anxious to retain support in his remaining period in office in order to enable him to launch a re-election campaign in 2016. Regional and municipal elections in October 2010 were expected to provide an indication of the parties' prospects in the presidential and legislative ballots the following year. Campaigning for the 2010 elections was likely to complicate García's task of governing nationally, as the political parties would focus on the campaign at the expense of compromise in the legislature. Nevertheless, the opposition in 2010 was fragmented with no clear leader.

The trial of former President Fujimori ended in April 2009 with a guilty verdict and a 25-year sentence. Although observers agreed that the trial took place without political interference from either pro- or anti-Fujimori sources, the episode polarized opinion in Peru between sympathizers and opponents. The ex-President's daughter, Keiko Fujimori, was among the leading figures manoeuvring for support for a possible presidential bid in 2011.

With the approach of elections in 2011, the increasing difficulties of securing political support for new legislation reduced expectations of reform to state institutions, which was widely considered to be pressing in view of numerous controversies in the state sector, particularly the judiciary. Persistent scandals involving the judiciary have led to low levels of confidence in the justice system; these included allegations of bribery against a member of the Consejo Nacional de la Magistratura (National Magistrates Council) and claims of political interference by a ruling APRA party official in the appointment of a public prosecutor. The credibility of President Garcia himself was damaged by another scandal, after he pardoned a former television executive, José Enrique Crousillat, who had been sentenced for taking bribes from Vladimiro Montesinos Torres, Fujimori's former head of security, in return for providing editorial support to the former President. The pardon was revoked when it emerged that Crousillat was not gravely ill as had been claimed. The ensuing controversy resulted in the dismissal of Minister of Justice Aurelio Pastor Valdivieso. Despite long-standing problems of corruption and political interference in the judiciary, successive Governments have introduced limited changes rather than the more fundamental reform widely considered to be necessary.

Economy

SANDY MARKWICK

Peru is the third largest country in South America in terms of geographical area (1.29m. sq km, or just under 500,000 sq miles) and, with a population estimated at 29.5m., the fourth most populous. Population growth rates declined from 1.8% in 1995–2000 to an annual average of 1.1% subsequently. Peru's economy was ranked sixth in South America, both in terms of gross domestic product (GDP), at an estimated US $128,750m. in 2009, and also in terms of GDP per head (calculated at purchasing power parity), estimated by the IMF at $8,825 in the same year.

While Peru's population remains young, the proportion of those under 15 years old declined from about 37% in 1993 to 30.5% in 2007 as population growth slowed. The birth rate fell from 46 per 1,000 in 1960 to an estimated 20.3 per 1,000 in 2010. Health and nutritional standards reflected Peru's developing world conditions, but have improved significantly in recent decades. The average rate of infant mortality was 19.5 per 1,000 live births in 2010, down from 50 in 1996, though there were marked regional variations. Life expectancy in 2010 was 74 years, up from 47 years in 1960. The geographical distribution of the population shifted dramatically in favour of the coastal region after 1940, as migrants sought improved standards of living, better employment prospects and access to infrastructure in the cities concentrated along the coastal strip. The proportion of Peruvians living in cities rose from 46% in 1960 to an estimated 76% by mid-2007. The process of urbanization accelerated as guerrilla insurgency intensified in the 1980s, and slowed as the conflict in the countryside all but disappeared in the mid-1990s. Economic activity was highly concentrated in the capital city, Lima.

From the 1950s successive Governments pursued a strategy of state-sponsored industrialization, replacing the prevailing *laissez-faire* economy characterized by little direct government participation and few regulations. Thereafter, Governments attempted to nurture domestic manufacturing by preventing an influx of cheap foreign goods through the imposition of high import tariffs. Industry grew at a faster pace than other sectors of the economy. Broadly, Peru experienced positive growth in GDP until the late 1970s. Real GDP increased at an average annual rate of 5.3% in the 1960s and 4.5% in the 1970s. Between 1980 and 1985 GDP fell, in real terms, at an average annual rate of 0.5%, signalling the worst economic performance since the 1930s. Average annual inflation doubled from 51% in 1975–80 to 102% in 1980–85. The first presidency of Alan García Pérez (1985–90) stimulated demand-led growth by increasing real wages and extending import controls to encourage import substitution. However, by 1988 a balance of payments deficit, an overvalued exchange rate, fiscal difficulties and rising inflation led the Government to adopt a more orthodox free-market approach to economic management until President García, concerned about the outcome of the April 1990 elections, allowed wages to rise, causing an increase in inflation.

On taking office in 1990, President Alberto Fujimori (1990–2000) implemented a rigid stabilization policy aimed at combating inflation by reducing the fiscal deficit. Subsidies were eliminated, causing the rate of inflation to rise in the short term, by dramatically increasing the prices of public services. However, the measures resulted in a reduced annual inflation rate of 11.1% by 1995; the rate decreased steadily, to 3.5% in 1999. Historically low inflation rates continued after the end of the Fujimori Government. Inflation averaged 2.4% during 2000–05. The Central Bank introduced an annual inflation target of 1.5%–3.5% in 2002, which was reduced to 1%–3% in 2007. Annual inflation, 1.1% at the end of 2006, was one of the lowest in Latin America. Lower energy costs, as a result of output from the huge Camisea gas project, and reduced costs of imports, owing to a weak US dollar, helped keep inflation down. The annual inflation rate rose to an average of 3.9% in 2007 and to 6.9% in 2008 as a result of increased fuel and food prices and consumer demand. Annual inflation declined markedly during 2009, as a result of lower international commodity prices as well as reduced domestic demand that stemmed from low growth associated with the global economic downturn. The rate averaged just 0.2% during 2009. The annual rate rose to 0.8% after the first quarter of 2010, as demand increased.

High growth rates were recorded in the mid-1990s, but stringent economic stabilization policies, implemented in response to a widening current account deficit on the balance of payments, led to reduced demand and slower growth rates for the remainder of the decade. The decline was partly owing to high interest rates and weakened demand in international markets brought about by El Niño (a warm surface current from the western Pacific that periodically replaces cold water and brings heavy rains, causing considerable damage to crops) in 1997–98 and financial crises in Asia, Brazil and Russia. In 2001 the economy went into recession as a result of depressed global demand. Recovery later in the year, aided by the opening of the Antamina copper and zinc mine for commercial production in October, led to GDP growth of 0.3% in that year. The economy grew at an average annual rate of 5.1% in 2002–05, fuelled by the Antamina mine as well as an expansion of exports and investment. Construction was another sector that performed well, but growth was spread throughout the economy. A rise in real incomes, private consumption, investment and exports underpinned growth of 7.7% in 2006, 9.0% in 2007 and 9.8% in 2008. From September 2008 into 2009 monthly year-on-year growth rates in Peru declined as the global economic downturn had an effect domestically. Annual output in 2009 registered growth of just 0.9%, according to the Central Bank. Urban unemployment increased during the first quarter of 2009, but ended the year with an average rate of 8.4%, the same rate as in 2007–08. A much higher percentage, estimated at around 40%, was thought to be underemployed. A large proportion of the urban work-force, around 60% by some estimates, was employed in the informal sector, living a hand-to-mouth existence beyond the reach of the tax authorities and unable to take advantage of benefits available to workers in the formal economy.

AGRICULTURE

Irrigation and a temperate climate along Peru's arid coastline supported traditional crops of rice, sugar and cotton from the 1860s, but they increasingly allowed a modern and varied agro-industrial sector of non-traditional agricultural produce such as asparagus, cocoa and fruit. There are extensive pasture lands in the Andean Sierra, although some crops, notably maize, barley and potatoes, are cultivated in deeper valley basins, while tea, coffee and coca are grown on lower eastern-facing slopes. The tropical forests east of the Andes have enormous agricultural potential, but a lack of transport and infrastructure meant that they remained largely unexploited. Of the 1.8m. ha under cultivation in Peru, 53% was in the Andean Sierra, 30% in the coastal region and 17% in the eastern rainforests. There is little room for expansion in the Sierra.

Land reform introduced under the regime of Gen. Juan Velasco between 1968 and 1975 turned huge privately owned coastal haciendas into co-operatives alongside single family smallholdings (*minifundios*). The reforms, however, were largely unsuccessful. Increasing inefficiency and growing demand converted Peru into a net importer of cotton, sugar and rice, which it had traditionally exported in large quantities. Attempts by subsequent Presidents to reactivate agriculture were limited, owing to a lack of resources to provide credit to farmers and the overvaluation of the currency. President Fujimori introduced free-market reforms into the sector by declaring land to be a freely tradable commodity, exchanged under market conditions. Strict landholding limits were relaxed, and subsidized credit, tax rebates and export credits were removed. Foreign investors in agriculture faced the same rules as Peruvian nationals. President Fujimori's policy favoured medium-sized commercial farms producing for export, at the expense of traditional smallholdings.

The contribution of agriculture to GDP declined after the 1950s, when it accounted for more than 20% of GDP. In 2009 the sector (including livestock and forestry) accounted for 7.8% of GDP. Agriculture in Peru, particularly production on non-irrigated land, was vulnerable to unpredictable weather conditions, particularly associated with El Niño, the warm water current affecting the tropical Pacific ocean, which can cause widespread rainfall and flooding resulting in reduced output. Agricultural growth was stimulated by the introduction of the Andean Trade Promotion and Drug Eradication Act (ATPDEA, the successor agreement to the Andean Trade Preference Act), which came into effect in October 2002. This reduced tariffs on Peruvian products entering the US market and gave a particular boost to production in non-traditional agricultural subsectors. Furthermore, access to new technologies and the expansion of cultivated areas helped increase production, although these benefits were not felt uniformly across the agricultural sector. Strong growth of 7.2% in 2006 was assisted by favourable weather, boosting harvests in many key crops. Poorer weather conditions saw growth slow to 3.1% in 2007, led by mango, asparagus and cane sugar. The sector grew by 7.2% in 2008, boosted by improved weather during the year, high food prices and international demand. In 2009 sectoral output grew only by 2.3%, despite a strong increase in production for domestic consumption and livestock, following small harvests in some staple crops and an overall decline in output for export.

Modern productive commercial agro-industry in Peru was located in the coastal region, where irrigation projects enhanced the agricultural potential of the coast. The cultivation of high-price export crops could be maintained all year: mangoes, bananas, passion fruit, and lemons and limes on the northern coast; asparagus, broccoli, green beans, snow-peas (mange-touts) and grapes in the central coastal area; and beans, garlic, onions and oregano in the south. Sugar estates, concentrated in the northern coastal area, were able to produce all year round with careful control of irrigation. Cotton required less water and could be grown where supplies were seasonal. The importance of cotton and sugar as export crops diminished, although they continued to rank second and third in terms of legal agricultural export earnings. Peru became a net importer of sugar because of rising domestic consumption, inefficient methods of production, weak prices and a reduction in the US sugar quota. A dramatic fall in the export earnings of traditional crops saw non-traditional crops overtake sugar, cotton and rice for the first time in 1992. During 1990–2005 it was estimated that cultivation began of some 400 new export crops. In 2009 non-traditional crops earned 74.2% of total agricultural export revenue. The best performers in the new range of crops were asparagus, mangoes, mandarin oranges, grapes, apples and bananas. In 2006 Peru and the USA signed a free trade agreement, the Peru Trade Promotion Agreement (PTPA), to replace the ATPDEA, which would develop free trade with the USA by further phasing out tariffs. The PTPA finally came into full effect in February 2009. Agricultural production in the Sierra was based predominantly on subsistence-orientated smallholdings and large estates for livestock. The major crops were maize, potatoes, barley and wheat. Low productivity, scarce capital and limited land resources perpetuated rural poverty. In the eastern rainforests new road construction was followed by internal migration and agricultural colonization. In this area a variety of agricultural products were destined for the domestic market, including cassava, rice, bananas, oranges, tea, cacao (cocoa plant), beef, rubber and oil palm. Coffee, Peru's most valuable legal agricultural export commodity, was produced in this region. The land area devoted to coffee increased from 76,000 ha in 1960, producing an output of 32,000 metric tons, to an estimated 313,000 ha in 2006. Peru produced 231,000 tons in 2009, a decline of 0.6% during the year, of which 80.5% was exported and earned US $584m. Earnings fell by 9.2% in 2009.

Coca, a traditional crop used for centuries in its leaf form as a stimulant by Amerindians of the Sierra, is grown on lower, eastern-facing slopes where the Sierra descends to meet the eastern rainforests. The role of coca as the raw material for cocaine resulted in a dramatic increase in cultivation after the 1960s, as world demand for cocaine expanded. Peru was the world's second largest supplier, after Colombia, of coca for the production of cocaine. Production increased in 2000–07, in spite of the destruction of an estimated 15% of the coca crop under cultivation in 2003. The total area under coca cultivation was estimated by the UN Office on Drugs and Crime to have increased to more than 59,500 ha in 2009, despite the Government's eradication campaigns.

FISHING

An abundance of fish in the cold Humboldt current, and investment since the 1960s in industrial processing plants, made Peru one of the world's largest exporters of fish products. The anchoveta (Peruvian anchovy) was used to produce fishmeal for animal feed and fertilizers and was the most important species fuelling the fishmeal industry. Other species, principally sardines and pilchards, were caught for human consumption. Peru's main fishing ports are Chimbote, Tambo de Mora, Pisco, Callao, Supe and Ilo.

Owing to fears of over-exploitation, the Government from time to time imposed restrictions on fishing in order to replenish stocks, most recently for a brief period in May 2009. Sectoral output grew by 6.2% in 2008, but declined by 7.8% in 2009. Fisheries exports were equivalent to 8.2% of total exports in 2009, compared with 7.7% in 2008. Exports of non-traditional fisheries products, particularly farmed mackerel, increased from US $322m. in 2005 to $621m. in 2008, boosted by new investment, before falling to $517m. in 2009. Growth in traditional fishmeal production was restored in 2007 following fishing bans imposed in 2006. In 2009 fishing accounted for 0.4% of total GDP.

Unexploited stocks of mackerel, shrimp, trout and turbot, as well as frozen fish, provided opportunities for diversification in the industry. Foreign investment increased in specific areas of fisheries, and Peru granted concessions to foreign fishing operations to exploit Peruvian waters for species not consumed locally. Japanese and Korean boats fished for giant squid. Fishing contracts were awarded on the basis of open and competitive international tender. Furthermore, in 1995 the Government sold fishmeal plants belonging to the state fishing concern, PescaPerú.

MINING AND ENERGY

Mining is an important contributor to export earnings, owing to Peru's varied and considerable mineral wealth. In 2009 traditional mining products accounted for 60.4% of Peru's total export revenue, earning some US $16,509m. Gold, copper and zinc ranked, respectively, as first, second and fourth most significant export earners across all sectors in 2009 (crude petroleum and derivatives was the third biggest export earner). Copper had regained its position as the most important export in 2008, having been second to gold since 1998, but in 2009 gold export earnings of $6,801m. exceeded earnings from copper amounting to $5,933m. In 2009 the mining sector (including hydrocarbons) contributed 5.7% of GDP, compared with 8.6% in 2004. Despite the importance of mining, there was potential for even greater production. Peru was among the world's leading mining countries, yet less than one-fifth of its reserves were under exploitation.

The US-owned mining companies Southern Peru Copper Corporation (SPCC), Cerro de Pasco Corporation and Marcona Mining Company played the major role in the expansion of the mining industry, helped by the 1950 Mining Code, which fostered a favourable investment climate. However, by the 1970s the mining industry had begun to stagnate. The state mining company, MineroPerú (Empresa Minera del Perú), was created in 1970 to participate directly in areas of production where foreign investment was not forthcoming. Those foreign mining companies that failed to invest and were considered to form part of the old power bloc were nationalized. In 1974 Peru took over the Cerro de Pasco complex under its new name, Centromín. The Marcona Mining Company was nationalized in 1975 and its name changed to HierroPerú (known as Shougang Hierro Perú following its reprivatization in 1992). At the same time, the Government negotiated terms with SPCC for one of the world's largest investments in the copper industry.

Until the early 1990s foreign investment in the mining sector was relatively limited. Best estimates indicate that total foreign investment in Peru over the 15 years to 1992 amounted to only US $700m. The most important foreign company in the mining sector was the Southern Copper Corporation (SCC), formerly the SPCC, which consistently produced around two-thirds of Peru's copper. The SCC owned and operated two huge open-pit mines in southern Peru, at Cuajone and Toquepala. However, from the early 1990s the sector was opened to foreign investment, and many large companies subsequently entered into discussions to explore joint-venture possibilities.

In 2009 Peru produced a record 1,040,600 metric tons of copper, up marginally compared with 2008. Output doubled between 1998 and 2004, when it produced 812,900 tons. Copper production was boosted in 2002 by the first full year of production of the Antamina mine.

Peru was one of the world's largest suppliers of zinc. In 2009 output of 1.29m. metric tons represented a fall of 5.8% compared with production volumes in 2008. Most production was destined for export. Centromín dominated zinc production in the early 1990s, accounting for 35% of the total, which was extracted largely from its Cerro de Pasco mine. Despite slow growth in zinc output, higher prices ensured that revenues from zinc sales in 2006 increased by an estimated 147.3%, to US $1,991.3m. and by a further 27.3% to $2,535m. in 2007. As prices fell, export earnings from zinc declined to just $1,041m. in 2008, 41% of the total of the year before. Prices recovered slightly in 2009, resulting in a rise in export earnings from zinc, amounting to $1,225m., despite lower export volumes. Centromín was also the main producer of lead. In 2009 Peru's total lead output was 278,500, significantly less than the 317,800 tons produced in 2008. Export earnings fell by 2.1% in 2009, to $1,112m. In May 1999 a Peruvian-owned zinc producer, Volcán Compañía Minera, bid successfully for the huge Cerro de Pasco zinc and lead mine, which had been renamed Paragsha, one of the largest zinc operations in Latin America. In 2002 Antamina offset lower production from the SPCC and the Tintaya mine to give a boost to overall annual national copper and zinc production by 16% and 15%, respectively. The sole producer of iron ore was Shougang Hierro Perú of the People's Republic of China. Investment in the mine resulted in record production of 4.5m. tons in 2009, compared with 5.2m. tons in 2008. Exports of iron ore in 2009 amounted to $298m., a 3.6% decrease compared with 2008. Shougang Hierro Perú was expected to expand its iron ore operations in Peru with an investment of more than $1,000m., following feasibility studies in 2010.

In 2009 Peru produced 177,194 kg of gold, slightly higher than the figure in 2008, but a significant decrease compared with the 209,700 kg mined in 2005. Supply was interrupted intermittently owing to protests within the local community at the Yanacocha mine. Expansion of the Yanacocha mine, which accounted for 40% of Peru's gold output, had fuelled growth in gold output until 2005. Peru was the world's most important source of silver. Silver production in 2009 declined marginally, to 3.6m. kg, ending a sequence of 10 consecutive years of production volume increases. Silver production contrasted with other major minerals, as the sector was dominated by small and medium-sized mines. The price of silver increased every year during 2001–08, before declining by 2.0% in 2009. Export earnings declined sharply to US $214m. in 2009, compared with $595m. in 2008.

Peru produced 145,280 barrels per day (b/d) of petroleum in 2009, an increase of 21.0% compared with the level in 2008, following a largely uninterrupted growth trend from output averaging 91,350 b/d in 2003. However, output had fallen from a peak of 190,000 b/d in 1980. The long-term decline in production stemmed from the depletion of light crude reserves in the northern jungle, which had the further effect of making production of some heavy crudes no longer economical. Peru was a net petroleum importer from 1992, when it was forced to import increasing amounts of light crude petroleum because of rising domestic demand, declining production and a lower quality of extracted crude.

Encouraged by President Fujimori's liberal hydrocarbons law, the petroleum sector, like mining, expanded in the 1990s. Most of the output stemmed from the operations of four companies: Occidental Petroleum Corporation (Oxy) and Petrotech Peruana of the USA, the Brazilian company Petrobras and the predominantly Argentine Pluspetrol Corporation. New investment in the sector was slow initially, but the pace increased in the mid-1990s; 20 exploration and drilling contracts were signed in 1996. In 2007 a record 24 new contracts were signed, representing an estimated US $800m. investment. In April 2009 the Government signed an additional 13 new licence contracts worth an estimated $660m. for the exploration and exploitation of hydrocarbons. A total of 101 contracts were in force, covering exploration, exploitation and technical evaluation. In June 2010 the Government launched a further tender for 25 new exploration blocks.

Petroleum was drilled in three principal areas: approximately two-thirds of crude was extracted from fields in the eastern jungle, with the remainder coming from fields offshore and in the north-west. In the early 21st century petroleum production continued to be dominated by the state company, Petroperú (Petróleos del Perú), and Oxy, although new investments were diversifying the operators. The Fujimori Government initiated the gradual privatization of Petroperú in 1996. The first parts to be sold were the La Pampilla petroleum refinery, which was purchased by a consortium comprising Repsol of Spain, Yacimientos Petrolíferos Fiscales (YPF) of Argentina and Mobil.

In February 2000 the contract for first-phase exploration of natural gas and hydrocarbon deposits at Camisea was won by a consortium of Pluspetrol, Hunt Oil of the USA and SK Corporation of the Republic of Korea. The consortium had the right to develop the field for 40 years. The second and third phases of the project for transport and distribution were awarded, respectively, to Techint of Argentina and Tractebel of Belgium. The state-owned electricity company, Electroperú, guaranteed a domestic market for the fuel. Gas flows to Lima began on schedule in August 2004. Exports of surplus gas were expected to begin in 2010.

Peru has a huge potential to secure hydroelectric power because of its abundance of steep running rivers. Electricity generation rose steadily in the latter half of the 1990s, from production of 17,440m. kWh in 1995 to an estimated 32,700m. kWh in 2009. However, installed hydroelectric capacity represented only a fraction of the potential. Hydroelectric plants at Santa Eulalia, Marcapomachocha and the Mantaro valley produced Lima's electricity supplies. Installed capacity was evenly split between hydroelectric and thermal sources, but, owing to the higher variable cost of thermal electricity generation, hydroelectricity accounted for 58% of total electricity generated in mid-2010. The reliance on hydroelectricity rendered the electricity supply vulnerable to climatic conditions. In 2006 an estimated 6m. Peruvians, predominantly in poor rural areas, had no access to electricity despite new investment. The Government introduced progressive electricity pricing to benefit the poor. The costs of delivering electricity to low-use households was, in part, subsidized by higher-use consumers. The Fujimori Government embarked on the privatization of electricity assets in 1995, beginning with Cahua, a 40-MW hydroelectric plant, and Edegel, the 700-MW generating unit of former state company Electrolima. Violent protests followed the sale by the administration of President Alejandro Toledo Manrique (2001–06) of two Arequipa-based generating companies, Egasa and Egesur, to Tractebel in June 2002. The protests led Tractebel to withdraw from the purchase and forced the Government to cancel plans for additional private sector participation in electricity generation and supply.

MANUFACTURING AND CONSTRUCTION

In the early 1970s manufacturing output grew at an annual rate of 10%, although at a long-term cost to efficiency, as industry was protected by high tariff barriers. In the late 1970s growth slowed. When protectionism was reduced under President Fernando Belaúnde Terry from 1980, manufacturing output declined dramatically. The Government returned to its policy of protectionist growth in 1984. Under President Fujimori's leadership, manufacturing was exposed to greater foreign competition and underwent a process of restructuring. However, there was a wide divergence in performance between industries and volatility year on year. Average annual growth in 1995–2004 was 2.0%. The manufacturing sector declined by 1.4% in 2009, as global recession adversely affected demand. The sector began to recover towards the end of the year, particularly parts of the sector not based on primary raw materials. The contraction in 2009 followed growth of 9.1% in 2008, which had been fuelled by rising domestic demand. The best performing sub-sectors were those outside primary resource-processing, particularly pharmaceuticals, electrical equipment, vehicles, machinery and metallic products. Textiles and leather exports were boosted by ATPDEA. Manufacturing contributed 14.3% to GDP in 2009, representing a decline from a contribution to GDP during the mid-1990s that averaged more than 20%.

Prior to the military regime, manufacturing largely comprised the processing of agricultural and mineral products. A policy of import-substitution industrialization, introduced under the Velasco regime, encouraged the development of domestic industry by raising the cost of imports. The military's developmentalist outlook saw the beginnings of heavy industry, including petroleum-refining, chemicals, non-ferrous metals and electrical industries.

The principal manufacturing sectors in Peru were food, metalworking, steel, textiles, chemicals, cement, automobile assembly, fish-processing and petroleum-refining. The food industry was heavily dependent on agricultural performance. The main products were processed fish, coffee, cocoa and sugar. The textile industry was the most significant non-traditional exporter, accounting for 24.2% of non-traditional exports and 5.6% of total exports.

The construction sector averaged 8.0% growth in 2002–06, outpacing the economy as a whole. Growth was driven by investment in the mining sector and by the Government's investment in Mivivienda, a low-cost housing programme. The rate of construction growth increased in 2007, to 16.6%. This rapid growth continued in 2008, before slowing to 6.1% in 2009. Growth in the construction sector was fuelled by a US $5,606m. government stimulus package, introduced in mid-2009, which included investment in roads, education and health, as well as a programme to finance low-cost housing. Year-on-year growth in the construction sector continued into early 2010.

TRANSPORT AND COMMUNICATIONS

In 2010 Peru had 2,020 km of railway track. The state national railway enterprise, Empresa Nacional de Ferrocarriles del Perú (Enafer-Perú), was sold off in 1999. The railways were largely used for transporting minerals. The Central Railway (Ferrocarril del Centro del Perú) connected Lima to Huancayo (Junín), with a branch to the mining operations at Cerro de Pasco. The Southern Railway (Ferrocarril del Sur del Perú Enafer, SA) ran from Matarani, through Arequipa, to Juliaca, with branches to Puno and Cusco (Cuzco). The Cusco line ran through the Urubamba valley, bypassing Machu Picchu, to Quillabamba. Passenger use declined in the 1990s. However, in the late 1990s the Government began offering concessions to run Enafer's more commercially viable routes to private operators. In 1999 a private consortium, Consorcio Ferrocarriles del Perú, won a 30-year concession to manage the Southern, Central and South-eastern railways. Private investment and improved services doubled passenger numbers from 793,000 in 1999 to 1.6m. by 2007; passenger numbers remained at that level in 2009. The use of railways for cargo also increased to 9m. metric tons transported in 2007, compared with 5m. tons in 1999. In June 2005 it was announced that the world's first train powered by compressed natural gas had been inaugurated by Ferrovías Central Andina, SA.

The road system was greatly improved after 1960. Until the early 1990s the network lacked adequate investment to ensure basic maintenance or expansion; however, from 1993, as a result of new investment from the Inter-American Development Bank (IDB) and the Government, road repairs were begun. The major road links were: the coastal Pan-American Highway, which linked Peru to Ecuador and Chile; the Central Highway from Lima to Pucallpa, which ran alongside the Ucayali river via Oroya, Huánuco and Tingo María; the northern Trans-Andean Highway from Olmos to Yurimaguas on the Huallaga river; and the Carretera Marginal de la Selva, which was built to provide access to new settlements in the east. The Fujimori Government declared road-building to be central to its aims of integration, development and means to combat insurgency. It was hoped that repairs to the Central Highway between Huánuco, Tingo María and Pucallpa would reduce transport costs and encourage coca-growers to cultivate alternative crops. About 30% of Peru's 78,500-km road network was paved or semi-paved, though much of it was in poor condition. The Government was encouraging private sector investment to extend and improve the road network. In 2005 three concessions were awarded to private consortia to build and maintain sections of the Interoceanic Highway stretching from the ports of Marcona, Matarani and Ilo into southern Brazil. Further concessions were awarded in the latter half of 2007.

There were 29 maritime ports in Peru, of which Lima's neighbouring port of Callao was by far the most important, and dozens of river ports. The deregulation of ports under President Fujimori reduced costs and increased competitiveness with ports in neighbouring Ecuador and Chile. River transport was important in the Amazon region. The port of Iquitos was accessible to ocean-going shipping from the Atlantic Ocean. River traffic extended from there as far as Pucallpa and Yurimaguas, where new ports were constructed in the 1980s. In September 2004 the Autoridad Portuaria Nacional (National Port Authority) approved a development plan including private sector investment. Callao became the first beneficiary in 2006 when the Government awarded a concession to Dubai Ports World to build a new container terminal. Air services were well developed and particularly important in eastern Peru, where the road and railway networks were less extensive than those in other areas. Peru has five international airports and a further 50 domestic airports, in addition to hundreds of airfields. The Government awarded a contract to manage the largest airport, the Jorge Chávez Airport in Lima, to a consortium including Frankfurt Airport (Germany) and US construction firm Bechtel. In 2006 the Government granted a concession to part Spanish-owned Swissport Peru to develop and operate 12 regional airports.

Telefónica of Spain bought a controlling interest in Peru's two former state telecommunications companies, Empresa Nacional de Telecomunicaciones del Perú (ENTEL PERU) and Compañía Peruana de Teléfonos (CPT), in 1994. The Government's objective was to modernize the service and to expand the provision of telephone lines, which, at 2.5 lines per 100 inhabitants in 1994, was the worst in Latin America. Improved communications were considered to be a fundamental requirement for developing poor provincial communities. In 2009 there were 10 lines per 100 inhabitants. In 1996 the telecommunications market regulator also obliged Telefónica to provide a cellular communications infrastructure in the provinces. In the late 1990s the sector was opened to greater competition. The new entrants into the mobile telecommunications market improved services and reduced prices, leading to a rapid increase in users, from 820,700 in 1999 to an estimated 23.5m. in 2009, representing an 80.4% penetration rate of the population. Internet access in the home is limited to a small minority of households. However, a large number of Peruvians, estimated at more than 6m. in 2008, used the internet regularly at home, work or via public access points.

GOVERNMENT FINANCE AND INVESTMENT

Investment declined in the 1980s, particularly under the first García administration, when there was virtually no foreign investment, owing to restrictions on profit remittances, and little external funding. In that decade domestic savings were the main source of investment, with loans to the Government making up most of the remainder. Under President Fujimori foreign investment increased dramatically. A new liberal foreign investment regime lifted restrictions on remittances and provided foreign investors with the same opportunities as national investors. In addition, the Government began an ambitious privatization programme, which aimed to sell virtually all of the state's productive ventures. The sale of the state iron company, HierroPerú, to the Chinese Shougang Corporation in 1992 was the first major privatization. The Government intended to use a proportion of the revenue received for anti-poverty programmes and job-creation schemes, although a large part was to be used for debt-servicing. The sale of state-owned assets generated US $7,180m. in 1991–97. Foreign direct investment (FDI) inflows accelerated thereafter, with annual average flows of $3,026m. in 2000–09, compared with $1,576m. in the previous 10-year period. With economic growth and capital accumulation, inflows were offset by investment overseas, particularly since 2008 when $1,132m. was invested abroad, following investment of only $200m. during 2000–07. Much of this new outward investment was directed towards enterprises and assets in other South American economies, reflecting increased regional integration. FDI inflows amounted to $4,760m. in 2009, these mostly consisting of reinvestments (profits repatriated to firms from oversea investments). Spain was the main source of accumulated foreign investment, accounting for 23.1% in 2008, followed by the United Kingdom (19.4%), the USA (15.4%), the Netherlands (7.8%), Chile (6.1%) and Panama (5.0%). Spanish investment has predominantly been channelled into the Telefónica business while the other principal recipients were the mining, industry, energy, retail and finance sectors. The Camisea gas project, the Antamina copper and zinc mine and other mining and energy projects were expected to support stable overall FDI levels. Net foreign exchange reserves, which were negative in 1988, totalled $33,135m. at the end of 2009, increasing by 6.2% in that year to a record level.

The first García administration's policy of extending subsidies while reducing taxes required the Government to finance a wide public sector deficit and gave rise to hyperinflation at the end of the 1980s. President Fujimori's policy of maintaining fiscal equilibrium as part of a wider monetarist policy of reducing public sector wages, delaying payments and decreasing investments lowered the public sector deficit. In addition, Fujimori introduced reforms to increase revenues and simplify tax collection. When Fujimori assumed office, tax collection amounted to 4.4% of GDP. Following improvements in the efficiency of the tax authority as well as increases in consumption, this figure increased through the 1990s. In 2009 taxes represented 13.8% of GDP. The Government enacted a Fiscal Responsibility and Transparency Law (FRTL) in 2003, which made an explicit commitment to keep the fiscal deficit below 1%. Improved tax collection as well as economic growth helped to create a fiscal surplus equivalent to an estimated 2.1% of GDP in 2008, down from 3.1% in 2007, because of the highest level of public investment for nine years. The fiscal balance went into deficit in 2009 for the first time since 2005, as the Government invested accumulated savings to stimulate economic recovery. The deficit was estimated at 2.1% of GDP, higher than the limit set by the FRTL. There were expectations that the stimulus would successfully return the fiscal balance to the level originally set by the FRTL.

Consistently high inflation resulted in the introduction of two new currencies between 1985 and 1991. First, the inti replaced the sol in 1985 at a rate of one inti per 1,000 sols. In 1991 the new sol replaced the inti at a rate of one new sol per 1m. intis. Between 1978 and 1985 the sol had been gradually devalued by means of a 'crawling-peg' mechanism of mini-devaluations (i.e. the exchange rate changed in response to market pressure, but only by limited amounts over set periods). Multiple exchange rates, designed to favour priority imports and manufacturing exports over traditional exports, were introduced in the mid-1980s. These were simplified to a two-rate system under the first García Government, with a series of crawling-peg mini-devaluations for the official rate and a floating rate for all other transactions. President Fujimori further simplified the exchange-rate mechanism by adopting a free-floating, single-rate system. The new sol appreciated in real terms against the US dollar from 1993 as capital inflows maintained a balance of payments surplus. The exchange rate was affected by the inflow of dollars from the illegal drugs trade. High real interest rates tended to maintain the overvaluation of the new sol. The strength of the sol helped control inflation, but weakened exports. A lack of confidence in the new sol, along with fears that the problem of inflation had not yet been fully solved, encouraged the 'dollarization' of the economy, made possible by Fujimori's deregulation of the financial system. In 1993 more than 80% of bank deposits were made in dollars. Financial reform implemented by the Fujimori Government gave foreign commercial banks equal status with local private banks. In 2009 the average rate at which the new sol was traded for the dollar was 3.01, a depreciation of 2.9%. In June 2010 the new sol was trading at a rate of 2.82 to the dollar. The Central Bank intervened intermittently to reduce currency volatility.

FOREIGN DEBT

Heavy public spending in the mid-1970s resulted in a rapid accumulation of foreign debt. Foreign debt increased further in the 1980s, because of the need to meet considerable debt-service payments and finance large public sector deficits. Peru's failure to meet its debt-servicing commitments to the IMF and 'Paris Club' creditor nations, culminating in President García's decision to designate a maximum of 10% of export earnings for debt-servicing, led to a deterioration in relations with the international financial community. The IMF declared Peru ineligible for further lending in 1986, closely followed by the IDB and the World Bank. Foreign creditor banks ruled Peru ineligible for rescheduling negotiations.

On taking office, President Fujimori immediately sought to re-establish good relations with the international financial organizations; in September 1990 he agreed to resume debt repayments and introduced a programme of economic-restructuring. A support group, including the USA and Japan, provided a US $2,000m. 'bridging' loan to enable Peru to clear part of its arrears. In 1991 Peru rescheduled payment of $6,660m. in principal debts, interest and arrears owed to the Paris Club. The IMF agreed to support the Government's economic reforms, thereby enabling credits from the World Bank and the IDB. In October 1995 Peru announced a debt-restructuring scheme for debts amounting to $10,560m. ($4,400m. principal and $6,160m. interest and arrears) with commercial-bank creditors. The scheme, implemented in March 1997, normalized relations between Peru and the international financial community and reopened private and public sector access to international capital markets. By 2001 the proportion of more costly short-term debt to long-term debt had declined, making Peru less vulnerable to external shocks. In 2004 the IMF approved a two-year stand-by credit for Peru until August 2006, committing the Government to reducing the non-financial public sector deficit to 1% of GDP, which was achieved in 2005. A further stand-by agreement was approved in January 2007 and concluded in February 2009, to the broad satisfaction of the IMF. Relations with the IMF consolidated the credibility of Peru's macro-economic management in the perception of international financial institutions. At the end of 2009 Peru's total external debt amounted to an estimated $33,500m., or 26.4% of GDP, much reduced from 2003, when debt was close to 50% of GDP.

FOREIGN TRADE AND BALANCE OF PAYMENTS

The slow increase in the value of exports from the 1970s reflected Peru's vulnerability to international prices of raw materials. Exports declined and stagnated in the 1980s. An overvalued new sol, recession and weak commodity prices retarded export growth during the early 1990s, but buoyancy returned in 1994 because of larger volumes and higher commodity prices. However, the value of exports declined in 1998, owing to the effects of El Niño, low commodity prices and diminished overseas demand. Annual export revenue growth of 8.2% in 2002, fuelled by a 17% rise in mineral exports, had helped Peru record its first trade surplus (of US $306m.) since 1990 in that year. Exports grew consistently since 2003, assisted initially by the start of the Antamina mine's operations, high gold production and gold price increases. Traditional fisheries, non-traditional agriculture, livestock, textiles and oil and derivatives were also good earners in this period. Continued strong demand, notably for copper from the People's Republic of China, underpinned high commodity prices. Non-traditional exports were led by agriculture and textiles, which benefited from greater competitiveness in the US market as a result of the ATPDEA, and exports of artichokes, asparagus and livestock. In 2009 the trade surplus was $5,874m., a 90.1% increase compared with the surplus in 2008 (the lowest since 2004), but significantly lower than the surpluses in 2006–07, which averaged $8,636m. The growth of the surplus in 2009 followed a $7,428m. decline in imports (of 26.1%), outpacing a decline in exports amounting to $4,644m. (14.7%). Weak domestic consumption associated with economic stagnation had contributed to the fall in imports, while commodity prices rises offset the lower global demand for Peruvian exports.

In 1970 primary products (excluding fuel) accounted for 98% of all exports. Manufacturing amounted to only 1.3% and fuels 0.7%. The composition of exports thereafter shifted away from traditional commodities to non-traditional exports, principally finished and agro-industrial products. In 2009 traditional exports contributed 76.5% of total export revenues. In the same year raw materials and intermediate goods accounted for 51.2% of total import costs, representing the largest share. This was followed by capital goods, which accounted for 32.5%. The relative importance of consumer product imports increased, owing to the Government's trade liberalization policies. Consumer imports were valued at US $2,616m. in 2006, equivalent to 17.6% of total imports; their share was 11% in 1988. Consumer imports were worth $4,257m. in 2009, representing 19.5% of total imports.

In the early 2000s the USA continued to be Peru's main trading partner, although its importance had declined over several decades. In 1970 the USA was the source of just under one-third of all imports and the destination for just over one-third of exports. The USA accounted for 19.7% of imports and 17.0% of exports in 2009. In October 2002 tariffs on the export of 6,000 products to the USA from Peru and other Andean countries had been removed as part of the ATPDEA. After the USA, the next most important export markets in 2009 were the People's Republic of China (15.3% of exports) and Switzerland (14.8%). Trade with Asia increased in 1997, following an agreement with the Asia-Pacific Economic Co-operation (APEC). From 1970 Peru diversified trading partners, creating a greater role for other Latin American countries as sources of imports. In 2009 China, accounting for 15.0% of imports, Brazil (7.7%) and Ecuador (4.7%) were the next most important sources of imports, after the USA. An agreement with the USA, the PTPA, and a trade agreement between Peru and China came into effect in February 2009 and March 2010, respectively.

An improved trade balance converted regular current account deficits into surpluses from 2004. In 2008 the current account was once again in deficit, which amounted to US $4,180m. or 3.3% of GDP. The 2008 deficit was a result of a 45.1% rise in the cost of imports, a consequence of increased prices of imported oil, food and industrial inputs, but also of investment in capital goods associated with Peru LNG, a project designed to stimulate economic development through the export of liquefied natural gas (and one of the largest industrial projects to be undertaken in Peru). A small current account surplus (of $247m., or 0.2% of GDP) was restored in 2009, principally since the cost of imports declined faster than export revenue, although an improved services balance during that year was also a contributory factor.

CONCLUSION

There was initial uncertainty surrounding the economic and social policies of the Government of Alan García, who took office in June 2006. García had been President in the late 1980s when his heterodox economic policies led Peru into a disastrous episode of hyperinflation and isolation from sources of international finance. In 2006, however, García reflected a political shift that had taken place in Latin America in the previous two decades by advocating economically liberal policy commitments during his election campaign for which he received the support of business interests. During his first year in power President García continued the fiscal discipline of his predecessor, Toledo, and gave a clear signal of his intent by appointing the conservative Luis Carranza Ugarte as Minister of Economy and Finance. García's Government had minority support in the legislature, but the opposition was divided. Healthy public finances and significant international reserves left Peru relatively well positioned to pursue a more expansionary fiscal policy to manage the effects of the international economic downturn on the domestic economy. The success of a bond issue in March 2009, in which the Government raised US $1,000m., reflected confidence in the economy. The bond issue followed an investment-grade rating awarded to Peru the previous year by the credit ratings agency Standard & Poor's. Only three other countries in South America attained this rating. President Garcia remained committed to large infrastructure projects, which formed part of a fiscal stimulus programme. Financing problems were not anticipated, owing to the Government's strong credit position. Monetary policy was expected to tighten as demand returned in 2010, accompanied by inflationary pressures. Political considerations were likely to dominate the Government's economic management increasingly, as presidential and legislative elections approached in 2011.

Statistical Survey

Sources (unless otherwise stated): Banco Central de Reserva del Perú, Jirón Antonio Miró Quesada 441–445, Lima 1; tel. (1) 4267041; fax (1) 4275880; e-mail webmaster@bcrp.gob.pe; internet www.bcrp.gob.pe; Instituto Nacional de Estadística e Informática, Avda General Garzón 658, Jesús María, Lima; tel. (1) 2218990; fax (1) 4417760; e-mail infoinei@inei.gob.pe; internet www.inei.gob.pe.

Area and Population

AREA, POPULATION AND DENSITY

(excluding Indian jungle population)

Area (sq km)	
Land	1,280,086
Inland water	5,130
Total	1,285,216*
Population (census results)†‡	
11 July 1993	22,048,356
21 October 2007	
Males	13,626,717
Females	13,792,577
Total	27,419,294
Population (UN estimates at mid-year)§	
2008	28,837,000
2009	29,165,000
2010	29,496,000
Density (per sq km) at mid-2010	23.0

* 496,225 sq miles.

† Excluding adjustment for underenumeration, estimated at 2.35% in 1993.

‡ An additional census was compiled, according to different methodology, during 18 July–20 August 2005. The total population was recorded at 27,219,264 in that year, including adjustment for an estimated 3.92% underenumeration (when the enumerated total was 26,152,265).

§ Source: UN, *World Population Prospects: The 2008 Revision*.

POPULATION BY AGE AND SEX

(UN estimates at mid-2010)

	Males	Females	Total
0–14	4,493,530	4,331,109	8,824,639
15–64	9,482,432	9,426,136	18,908,568
65 and over	805,597	957,316	1,762,913
Total	14,781,559	14,714,561	29,496,120

Source: UN, *World Population Prospects: The 2008 Revision*.

REGIONS

(2007 census)

	Area (sq km)	Population	Density (per sq km)	Capital
Amazonas	39,249	375,993	9.6	Chachapoyas
Ancash	35,915	1,063,459	29.6	Huaraz
Apurímac	20,896	404,190	19.3	Abancay
Arequipa	63,345	1,152,303	18.2	Arequipa
Ayacucho	43,815	612,489	14.0	Ayacucho
Cajamarca	33,318	1,387,809	41.7	Cajamarca
Callao*	147	876,877	5,965.1	Callao
Cusco	71,987	1,171,403	16.3	Cusco (Cuzco)
Huancavelica	22,131	454,797	20.6	Huancavelica
Huánuco	36,849	762,223	20.7	Huánuco
Ica	21,328	711,932	33.4	Ica
Junín	44,197	1,232,611	27.9	Huancayo
La Libertad	25,500	1,617,050	63.4	Trujillo
Lambayeque	14,231	1,112,868	78.2	Chiclayo
Lima	34,802	8,445,211	242.7	Lima
Loreto	368,852	891,732	2.4	Iquitos
Madre de Dios	85,301	109,555	1.3	Puerto Maldonado
Moquegua	15,734	161,533	10.3	Moquegua
Pasco	25,320	280,449	11.1	Cerro de Pasco
Piura	35,892	1,676,315	46.7	Piura
Puno	71,999	1,268,441	17.6	Puno
San Martín	51,253	728,808	14.2	Moyabamba
Tacna	16,076	288,781	18.0	Tacna
Tumbes	4,669	200,306	42.9	Tumbes
Ucayali	102,411	432,159	4.2	Pucallpa
Total	1,285,216	27,419,294	21.3	—

* Province.

PRINCIPAL TOWNS

(population of towns and urban environs at 21 October 2007)

Lima (capital)	8,472,935*	Iquitos	370,962
Arequipa	749,291	Cusco (Cuzco)	348,935
Trujillo	682,834	Chimbote	334,568
Chiclayo	524,442	Huancayo	323,054
Callao	515,200†	Tacna	242,451
Piura	377,496	Ica	219,856

* Metropolitan area (Gran Lima) only.

† Estimated population of town, excluding urban environs, at mid-1985.

Mid-2010 ('000, incl. suburbs, UN estimate): Lima (capital) 8,940,555; Arequipa 789,490 (Source: UN, *World Urbanization Prospects: The 2009 Revision*).

BIRTHS AND DEATHS*

	Live births		Deaths	
	Number	Rate (per 1,000)	Number	Rate (per 1,000)
1996	656,435	27.1	160,045	6.6
1997	652,467	26.4	160,830	6.5
1998	648,075	25.8	161,615	6.4
1999	642,874	25.2	162,457	6.4
2000	636,064	24.5	163,263	6.3
2001	630,947	24.0	164,296	6.2
2002	626,714	23.4	165,467	6.2
2003	623,521	23.0	166,777	6.1

* Data are estimates and projections based on incomplete registration, but including an upward adjustment for under-registration.

2007 (registrations, assumed to be incomplete): Live births 508,384; Deaths 82,620 (Source: UN, *Population and Vital Statistics Report*).

2008 (registrations, assumed to be incomplete): Live births 457,033; Deaths 108,100 (Source: UN, *Population and Vital Statistics Report*).

Marriages: 82,277 in 2005 (marriage rate 3.0 per 1,000); 89,162 in 2006 (marriage rate 3.2 per 1,000); 117,551 in 2007 (marriage rate 4.1 per 1,000) (Source: UN, *Demographic Yearbook*).

Life expectancy (years at birth, WHO estimates): 76 (males 74; females 77) in 2008 (Source: WHO, *World Health Statistics*).

EMPLOYMENT

('000 persons aged 14 and over, urban areas)

	2006	2007	2008
Agriculture, hunting and forestry	857.3	698.5	710.7
Fishing	42.0	58.7	59.0
Mining and quarrying	94.2	97.2	98.8
Manufacturing	1,135.7	1,292.2	1,316.6
Electricity, gas and water	26.3	21.1	35.8
Construction	431.6	469.8	512.0
Wholesale and retail trade; repair of motor vehicles, motorcycles and personal and household goods	2,035.2	2,087.6	2,101.4
Hotels and restaurants	631.1	680.5	730.2
Transport, storage and communications	750.7	840.5	907.0
Financial intermediation	74.5	69.5	92.3
Real estate, renting and business activities	426.8	483.0	486.4
Public administration and defence; compulsory social security	396.5	437.6	423.2
Education	545.7	650.3	641.5
Health and social work	201.1	248.4	270.5
Other services	568.7	587.1	634.5
Private households	476.0	474.3	423.4
Extra-territorial organizations	0.7	1.5	2.2
Total employed	8,694.0	9,197.8	9,445.5

Source: ILO.

2007 (persons aged 14 years and over, census figures): Total employed 10,166,179 (males 6,563,384, females 3,602,795); Unemployed 474,464 (males 316,021, females 158,443); *Total labour force* 10,640,643 (males 6,879,405, females 3,761,238).

Health and Welfare

KEY INDICATORS

Total fertility rate (children per woman, 2008)	2.6
Under-5 mortality rate (per 1,000 live births, 2008)	24
HIV/AIDS (% of persons aged 15–49, 2007)	0.5
Physicians (per 1,000 head, 1999)	1.2
Hospital beds (per 1,000 head, 2004)	0.9
Health expenditure (2007): US $ per head (PPP)	327
Health expenditure (2007): % of GDP	4.3
Health expenditure (2007): public (% of total)	58.4
Access to water (% of persons, 2008)	82
Access to sanitation (% of persons, 2008)	68
Total carbon dioxide emissions ('000 metric tons, 2006)	38,614.9
Carbon dioxide emissions per head (metric tons, 2006)	1.4
Human Development Index (2007): ranking	78
Human Development Index (2007): value	0.806

For sources and definitions, see explanatory note on p. vi.

Agriculture

PRINCIPAL CROPS

('000 metric tons)

	2006	2007	2008
Wheat	191.1	181.6	206.9
Rice, paddy	2,362.3	2,435.1	2,794.0
Barley	191.6	177.5	177.5*
Maize	1,262.4	1,361.7	1,361.7*
Potatoes	3,248.4	3,388.0	3,388.0*
Sweet potatoes	198.6	184.8	184.8*
Cassava (Manioc)	1,139.9	1,158.0	1,158.0*
Sugar cane	7,251.3	8,228.6	8,228.6*
Beans, dry	83.0	81.8	81.8*
Oil palm fruit	236.4	238.4	238.4*
Cabbages	29.8	32.2	32.2*
Asparagus	260.0	284.1	284.1*
Tomatoes	169.7	173.3	173.3*
Pumpkins, squash and gourds	132.3	121.6	121.6*
Chillies and peppers, green*	4.6	10.0	10.0
Onions, dry	576.7	634.4	634.4*
Garlic	73.5	80.9	80.9*
Peas, green	86.5	98.5	98.5*
Broad beans, dry	57.6	61.3	61.3*
Carrots and turnips	176.2	161.8	161.8*
Maize, green	360.6	332.3	332.3*
Plantains	1,778.2	1,834.5	1,834.5*
Oranges	353.8	344.3	344.3*
Tangerines, mandarins, clementines and satsumas	187.3	190.4	190.4*
Lemons and limes*	226.0	227.0	227.0
Apples	136.4	136.7	136.7*
Grapes	191.6	196.6	196.6*
Watermelons	65.1	67.5	67.5*
Guavas, mangoes and mangosteens	320.3	294.4	294.4*
Avocados	113.3	121.7	121.7*
Pineapples	234.3	212.1	212.1*
Papayas	175.4	157.8	157.8*
Coffee, green	231.2	226.0	226.0*

* FAO estimate(s).

Aggregate production ('000 metric tons, may include official, semi-official or estimated data): Total cereals 4,057.0 in 2006, 4,205.2 in 2007, 4,589.4 in 2008; Total roots and tubers 4,867.1 in 2006, 5,009.6 in 2007–08; Total vegetables (incl. melons) 2,298.0 in 2006, 2,403.7 in 2007–08; Total fruits (excl. melons) 4,087.8 in 2006, 4,088.5 in 2007–08.

Source: FAO.

LIVESTOCK

('000 head, year ending September)

	2005	2006	2007
Horses*	730	730	730
Asses*	910	620	630
Mules*	29	29	30
Cattle	5,241	5,241	5,421
Pigs	3,005	3,074	3,116
Sheep	14,822	14,675	14,580
Goats	1,957	1,937	1,926
Chickens	99,255	117,977	120,228

* FAO estimates.

2008: Figures assumed to be unchanged from 2007 (FAO estimates).

Source: FAO.

LIVESTOCK PRODUCTS

('000 metric tons)

	2005	2006	2007
Cattle meat	153.1	162.6	163.2
Sheep meat	33.7	33.9	33.8
Pig meat	102.9	108.7	114.5
Chicken meat	733.2	710.4	770.4
Cows' milk	1,329.3	1,482.9	1,579.8
Hen eggs	182.3	245.5	257.6
Wool, greasy	10.9	10.3	10.9

2008: Figures assumed to be unchanged from 2007 (FAO estimates).

Source: FAO.

Forestry

ROUNDWOOD REMOVALS

('000 cubic metres, excluding bark)

	2006	2007	2008*
Sawlogs, veneer logs and logs for sleepers	1,657	1,810	2,150
Other industrial wood	147	161	190
Fuel wood	7,454	7,454*	10,209
Total	9,258	9,425	12,549

* FAO estimate(s).

Source: FAO.

SAWNWOOD PRODUCTION
('000 cubic metres, including railway sleepers)

	2006	2007	2008*
Coniferous (softwood)	16	16*	16
Broadleaved (hardwood)	840	932	1,124
Total	856	948	1,140

* FAO estimate(s).

Source: FAO.

Fishing

('000 metric tons, live weight)

	2006	2007	2008
Capture	7,017.5	7,210.5	7,362.9
Chilean jack mackerel	277.6	254.4	169.5
Anchoveta (Peruvian anchovy)	5,935.3	6,159.8	6,256.0
Jumbo flying squid	434.3	427.6	533.4
Aquaculture	28.4	39.5	43.1
Total catch	7,045.9	7,250.1	7,406.0

Note: Figures exclude aquatic plants ('000 metric tons, all capture): 3.4 in 2006; 10.8 in 2007; 13.8 in 2008.

Source: FAO.

Mining

('000 metric tons, unless otherwise indicated, preliminary figures)*

	2006	2007	2008
Crude petroleum ('000 barrels)	42,187.2	41,562.2	43,930.4
Natural gas (million cubic feet)	62,691.1	94,485.5	119,955.8
Copper	818.5	952.8	1,036.7
Lead	288.4	303.0	317.7
Molybdenum	16.5	16.1	16.1
Tin	33.4	33.9	33.9
Zinc	1,029.9	1,236.1	1,371.5
Iron ore	4,861.2	5,185.3	5,243.3
Gold (kg)	197.0	165.4	174.7
Silver (kg)	3,263.0	3,291.9	3,465.4

* Figures for metallic minerals refer to metal content only.

Industry

SELECTED PRODUCTS
('000 metric tons, unless otherwise indicated)

	2005	2006	2007
Canned fish	55.5	107.3	84.3
Wheat flour	1,034	1,088	1,056
Raw sugar	695.0	805.1	910.1
Beer ('000 hectolitres)	7,916	9,634	10,535
Motor spirit (petrol, '000 barrels)*	8,968	12,777	13,948
Kerosene ('000 barrels)*	2,501	960	818
Distillate fuel oils ('000 barrels)*	15,287	17,598	19,018
Residual fuel oils ('000 barrels)*	20,740	14,713	14,669
Portland cement	4,535	5,052	5,335
Crude steel*†	750	750	750
Copper (refined)	189.5	205.7	188.4
Zinc (refined)	164.7	177.5	162.7
Electric energy (million kWh)	25,509.9	27,402.5	29,856.5

* Source: US Geological Survey.

† Estimate.

2008 ('000 barrels, unless otherwise indicated): Residual fuel oils 13,874; Motor spirit 13,355; Kerosene 598; Distillate fuel oils 19,519; Crude steel ('000 metric tons) 750 (Source: US Geological Survey).

Finance

CURRENCY AND EXCHANGE RATES

Monetary Units
100 céntimos = 1 nuevo sol (new sol).

Sterling, Dollar and Euro Equivalents (30 April 2010)
£1 sterling = 4.359 new soles;
US $1 = 2.844 new soles;
€1 = 3.787 new soles;
100 new soles = £22.94 = $35.16 = €26.41.

Average Exchange Rate (new soles per US $)
2007 3.1280
2008 2.9244
2009 3.0115

Note: On 1 February 1985 Peru replaced its former currency, the sol, by the inti, valued at 1,000 soles. A new currency, the nuevo sol (equivalent to 1m. intis), was introduced in July 1991.

CENTRAL GOVERNMENT BUDGET
(million new soles, preliminary figures)

Revenue	2007	2008	2009
Taxation	52,454	58,242	52,564
Taxes on income, profits, etc.	22,847	24,146	20,346
Taxes on imports (excl. VAT)	2,198	1,911	1,493
Value-added tax	25,258	31,583	29,519
Domestic	13,586	15,749	17,322
Imports	11,672	15,834	12,197
Excises	4,291	3,461	4,146
Fuel duty	2,419	1,457	2,255
Other taxes	3,848	4,371	4,400
Less Refunds	5,989	7,230	7,341
Other current revenue	8,368	9,716	8,147
Capital revenue	385	394	386
Total	61,207	68,352	61,097

Expenditure	2007	2008	2009
Current non-interest expenditure	42,292	46,100	48,516
Compensation of employees	13,017	13,871	15,168
Goods and non-labour services	10,130	10,854	13,362
Transfers	19,145	21,375	19,987
Interest payments	5,525	5,128	4,863
Internal	1,279	1,814	1,801
External	4,247	3,314	3,062
Capital expenditure	7,206	8,883	14,764
Gross capital formation	5,878	6,968	10,068
Total	55,023	60,111	68,143

General Budget (million new soles, preliminary figures): *2006:* Total revenue 60,416 (current 60,055, capital 361); Total expenditure 54,912 (current non-interest 40,833, capital 8,485, interest payments 5,593). *2007:* Total revenue 69,842 (current 69,456, capital 386); Total expenditure 59,538 (current non-interest 43,504, capital 10,100, interest payments 5,934). *2008:* Total revenue 78,105 (current 77,710, capital 395); Total expenditure 70,078 (current non-interest 49,264, capital 15,065, interest payments 5,749).

INTERNATIONAL RESERVES
(US $ million at 31 December)

	2007	2008	2009
Gold	927.8	982.6	1,217.7
IMF special drawing rights	3.7	9.0	821.6
Foreign exchange	26,852.7	30,262.5	30,999.8
Total	27,784.2	31,254.1	33,039.1

Source: IMF, *International Financial Statistics*.

MONEY SUPPLY
(million new soles at 31 December)

	2007	2008	2009
Currency outside banks	14,985	17,508	19,497
Demand deposits at commercial and development banks	25,586	28,385	30,194
Total money (incl. others)	43,983	48,594	50,511

Source: IMF, *International Financial Statistics*.

COST OF LIVING
(Consumer Price Index, Lima metropolitan area; base: 2000 = 100)

	2005	2006	2007
Food (incl. beverages)	107.6	110.2	113.0
Rent	120.3	123.3	124.5
Electricity, gas and other fuels	129.7	132.5	132.9
Clothing (incl. footwear)	107.5	109.1	111.9
All items (incl. others)	110.1	112.3	114.3

2008: Food (incl. beverages) 123.3; All items (incl. others) 120.9.

2009: Food (incl. beverages) 128.5; All items (incl. others) 124.4.

Source: ILO.

NATIONAL ACCOUNTS
(million new soles at current prices)

Expenditure on the Gross Domestic Product

	2007	2008	2009
Government final consumption expenditure	30,148	33,312	39,452
Private final consumption expenditure	206,187	237,340	249,891
Gross capital formation	77,185	102,856	88,192
Total domestic expenditure	313,520	373,508	377,535
Exports of goods and services	97,815	102,831	92,462
Less Imports of goods and services	74,996	98,776	77,432
GDP in purchasers' values	336,339	377,562	392,565
GDP at constant 1994 prices	174,348	191,367	192,994

Gross Domestic Product by Economic Activity

	2007	2008	2009
Agriculture, hunting and forestry	19,342	22,352	23,945
Fishing	2,183	2,569	2,605
Mining and quarrying	38,413	39,267	38,354
Manufacturing	49,035	54,921	50,897
Electricity and water	6,011	6,539	7,413
Construction	20,395	24,112	27,082
Wholesale and retail trade	42,104	48,602	52,319
Restaurants and hotels	11,694	13,511	14,628
Transport and communications	28,622	32,210	34,811
Government services	21,630	23,922	27,108
Other services	68,584	76,633	83,484
Gross value added at basic prices	308,012	344,640	362,646
Import duties	26,129	31,012	28,426
Taxes on products	2,198	1,911	1,493
GDP in purchasers' values	336,339	377,562	392,565

BALANCE OF PAYMENTS
(US $ million)

	2007	2008	2009
Exports of goods f.o.b.	27,882	31,529	26,885
Imports of goods f.o.b.	−19,595	−28,439	−21,011
Trade balance	8,287	3,090	5,873
Exports of services	3,152	3,649	3,653
Imports of services	−4,343	−5,611	−4,765
Balance on goods and services	7,095	1,128	4,761
Other income received	1,587	1,837	1,432
Other income paid	−9,945	−10,611	−8,803
Balance on goods, services and income	−1,263	−7,646	−2,609
Current transfers received	2,636	2,929	2,863
Current transfers paid	−10	−7	−7
Current balance	1,363	−4,723	247
Capital account (net)	−136	−121	−78
Direct investment abroad	−66	−736	−396
Direct investment from abroad	5,491	6,924	4,760
Portfolio investment assets	−390	462	−3,590
Portfolio investment liabilities	4,030	−1	1,247
Other investment assets	−443	860	531
Other investment liabilities	534	1,510	169
Net errors and omissions	−38	−717	−986
Overall balance	10,343	3,457	1,902

Source: IMF, *International Financial Statistics*.

External Trade

PRINCIPAL COMMODITIES
(distribution by SITC, US $ million)

Imports c.i.f.	2005	2006	2007
Food and live animals	1,158.1	1,249.6	838.8
Cereals and cereal preparations	514.5	555.3	249.7
Vegetables and fruits	73.1	72.2	328.7
Mineral fuels, lubricants and related materials	2,471.1	2,959.7	0.6
Petroleum, petroleum products and related materials	2,2992.7	2,837.4	0.6
Chemicals and related products	2,012.6	2,333.8	3,287.7
Medicinal and pharmaceutical products	263.0	305.0	3,033.9
Plastics in primary forms	551.8	640.7	0.0
Basic manufactures	1,928.4	2,461.4	795.1
Iron and steel	507.9	770.9	10.8
Machinery and transport equipment	3,541.5	4,732.9	4,335.4
Machinery specialized for particular industries	500.4	738.4	307.7
General industrial machinery, equipment, etc.	621.6	759.3	133.5
Office machines and automatic data processing machines	352.0	429.9	494.5
Telecommunications, sound recording and reproducing equipment	659.5	857.3	80.0
Road vehicles	652.9	981.9	2,828.6
Miscellaneous manufactured articles	835.9	965.6	7,417.2
Professional, scientific and controlling instruments	140.4	187.8	1,685.8
Total (incl. others)	12,501.8	15,311.6	20,464.2

Exports f.o.b.	2005	2006	2007
Food and live animals	2,729.8	3,278.1	3,571.8
Fish, crustaceans, molluscs and preparations thereof	326.7	433.7	488.3
Coffee	306.2	151.0	427.0
Crude materials	4,114.9	6,676.8	9,363.9
Iron ore and concentrates	216.1	256.0	285.4
Copper ores and concentrates	1,410.0	2,863.8	4,600.5
Lead ores and concentrates	312.4	449.6	649.4
Zinc ores and concentrates	683.2	1,759.3	2,318.6
Molybdenum ores and concentrates (excl. roasted)	1,149.4	847.1	984.1
Mineral fuels and lubricants	1,595.9	1,901.8	2,409.6
Petroleum, petroleum products and related materials	1,508.2	1,875.3	2,407.5
Basic manufactures	3,482.3	5,550.3	5,386.5
Non-ferrous metals	2,976.7	4,923.2	4,633.4
Copper	2,130.1	3,540.4	2,947.1
Miscellaneous manufactured articles	1,381.2	1,553.6	1,804.6
Total (incl. others)	17,114.3	23,764.9	27,800.1

2008 (US $ million): Total exports f.o.b. 31,162.7.

Source: UN, *International Trade Statistics Yearbook*.

PRINCIPAL TRADING PARTNERS
(US $ million)

Imports c.i.f.	2005	2006	2007
Argentina	724.5	802.4	791.7
Brazil	1,028.4	1,597.2	1,236.2
Canada	210.4	292.4	284.6
Chile	615.6	864.0	149.6
China, People's Republic	1,057.9	1,583.7	467.1
Colombia	772.6	950.7	2,807.8
Ecuador	914.2	1,092.1	14.4
France (incl. Monaco)	146.5	172.2	101.3
Germany	400.9	506.6	558.5
India	122.0	146.0	672.1
Italy	195.3	227.5	1,494.0
Japan	445.6	563.7	547.6
Korea, Republic	347.5	391.6	685.7
Mexico	363.9	518.8	43.3
Nigeria	115.1	271.5	0.0
Spain	193.4	255.8	1,172.0
United Kingdom	96.7	105.2	126.5
USA	2,220.1	2,515.7	6,746.4
Venezuela	528.3	544.9	0.0
Total (incl. others)	12,501.8	15,311.6	20,464.2

Exports f.o.b.	2005	2006	2007
Belgium	227.0	509.5	558.3
Bolivia	154.9	189.5	223.9
Brazil	453.2	814.5	934.6
Canada	1,021.8	1,611.6	1,834.2
Chile	1,129.4	1,429.9	1,694.3
China, People's Republic	1,860.9	2,268.7	3,034.7
Colombia	346.6	505.8	616.6
Ecuador	295.0	327.3	379.1
Germany	515.0	812.3	928.5
Italy	389.0	777.9	817.3
Japan	604.5	1,230.8	2,181.6
Korea, Republic	227.4	548.5	887.9
Mexico	332.1	390.4	269.9
Netherlands	534.7	737.8	630.8
Panama	265.2	337.5	397.2
Spain	558.1	765.8	982.5
Switzerland-Liechtenstein	786.3	1,687.6	2,335.3
United Kingdom	232.9	331.3	229.6
USA	5,257.3	5,707.5	5,383.4
Venezuela	298.5	412.0	765.3
Total (incl. others)	17,114.3	23,764.9	27,800.1

2008 (US $ million): Total exports f.o.b. 31,162.7.

Source: UN, *International Trade Statistics Yearbook*.

Transport

RAILWAYS
(traffic)*

	2003	2004	2005
Passenger-km (million)	103	119	126
Freight ton-km (million)	1,117	1,147	1,115

* Including service traffic.

Source: UN, *Statistical Yearbook*.

ROAD TRAFFIC
(motor vehicles in use)

	2002	2003	2004
Passenger cars	781,751	812,978	824,613
Buses and coaches	44,576	44,486	43,919
Lorries and vans	425,679	415,206	418,884
Motorcycles	231,148	248,395	268,125

2007 (motor vehicles in use): Passenger cars 917,110; Buses and coaches 44,401; Lorries and vans 480,876.

Source: IRF, *World Road Statistics*.

SHIPPING

Merchant Fleet
(registered at 31 December)

	2006	2007	2008
Number of vessels	749	751	759
Total displacement ('000 grt)	235.3	272.5	285.1

Source: Lloyd's Register-Fairplay, *World Fleet Statistics*.

International Sea-borne Freight Traffic
('000 metric tons)

	2004*	2005*	2006
Goods loaded	6,600	6,800	6,329
Goods unloaded	10,100	8,900	9,490

* Approximate figures extrapolated from monthly averages.

Source: UN, *Monthly Bulletin of Statistics*.

CIVIL AVIATION
(traffic on scheduled services)

	2005	2006	2007
Kilometres flown (million)	67	47	60
Passenger-km (million)	5,298	5,752	6,472
Total ton-km (million)	139	112	149

Source: UN Economic Commission for Latin America and the Caribbean, *Statistical Yearbook*.

Tourism

ARRIVALS BY NATIONALITY

	2005	2006	2007
Argentina	61,686	69,256	82,722
Bolivia	72,910	85,365	87,399
Brazil	44,543	45,265	53,558
Canada	35,196	41,443	43,992
Chile	344,296	420,801	470,443
Colombia	49,143	54,505	62,825
Ecuador	101,489	112,100	119,471
France	52,876	54,311	59,781
Germany	43,661	43,760	50,445
Italy	33,640	33,872	34,622
Japan	35,522	36,827	39,864
Mexico	29,558	29,820	31,639
Spain	68,595	75,976	72,180
United Kingdom	59,218	60,277	67,067
USA	330,358	330,845	381,828
Total (incl. others)	1,570,566	1,720,746	1,916,400

Tourism receipts (US $ million, excl. passenger transport): 1,570 in 2006; 1,723 in 2007; 1,991 in 2008 (provisional).

Source: World Tourism Organization.

Communications Media

	2007	2008	2009
Telephones ('000 main lines in use)	2,673.4	2,878.2	2,965.3
Mobile cellular telephones ('000 subscribers)	15,417.2	20,951.8	24,700.4
Internet users ('000)	7,000.0	7,128.3*	8,084.9*
Broadband subscribers ('000)	570.2	725.6	813.0

* Estimate.

Television receivers ('000 in use): 3,800 in 2000.

Radio receivers ('000 in use): 6,650 in 1997.

Book production (titles): 612 in 1996.

Daily newspapers: 73 in 2004.

Personal computers: 2,800,000 (100.6 per 1,000 persons) in 2005.

Sources: UNESCO, *Statistical Yearbook*; International Telecommunication Union.

Education

(2008 unless otherwise indicated, incl. adult education)

	Institutions	Teachers	Pupils
Nursery	19,055	52,448	971,715
Primary	35,893	191,738	3,803,453
Secondary	11,378	162,861	2,504,299
Higher: universities*	78	33,177	435,637
Higher: other tertiary	1,054	25,347	343,321
Special	429	3,351	20,472
Vocational	2,078	13,271	286,677

* Figures for 2000.

Source: Ministerio de Educación del Perú.

Pupil-teacher ratio (primary education, UNESCO estimate): 20.9 in 2007/08 (Source: UNESCO Institute for Statistics).

Adult literacy rate (UNESCO estimates): 89.6% (males 94.9%; females 84.6%) in 2008 (Source: UNESCO Institute for Statistics).

Directory

The Constitution

In 1993 the Congreso Constituyente Democrático (CCD) began drafting a new constitution to replace the 1979 Constitution. The CCD approved the final document in September 1993, and the Constitution was endorsed by a popular national referendum that was conducted on 31 October. The Constitution was promulgated on 29 December 1993.

EXECUTIVE POWER

Executive power is vested in the President, who is elected for a five-year term of office by universal adult suffrage; this mandate is renewable once. The successful presidential candidate must obtain at least 50% of the votes cast, and a second round of voting is held if necessary. Two Vice-Presidents are elected in simultaneous rounds of voting. The President is competent to initiate and submit draft bills, to review laws drafted by the legislature (Congreso) and, if delegated by the Congreso, to enact laws. The President is empowered to appoint ambassadors and senior military officials without congressional ratification, and retains the right to dissolve parliament if two or more ministers have been censured or have received a vote of no confidence from the Congreso. In certain circumstances the President may, in accordance with the Council of Ministers, declare a state of emergency for a period of 60 days, during which individual constitutional rights are suspended and the armed forces may assume control of civil order. The President appoints the Council of Ministers.

LEGISLATIVE POWER

Legislative power is vested in a single-chamber Congreso (removing the distinction in the 1979 Constitution of an upper and lower house) consisting of 120 members (to increase to 130 following the 2011 elections, in accordance with a constitutional amendment adopted in September 2009). The members of the Congreso are elected for a five-year term by universal adult suffrage. The Congreso is responsible for approving the budget, for endorsing loans and international treaties, and for drafting and approving bills. It may conduct investigations into matters of public concern, and question and censure the Council of Ministers and its individual members. Members of the Congreso elect a Standing Committee, to consist of not more than 25% of the total number of members (representation being proportional to the different political groupings in the legislature), which is empowered to make certain official appointments, approve credit loans and transfers relating to the budget during a parliamentary recess, and conduct other business as delegated by parliament.

ELECTORAL SYSTEM

All citizens aged 18 years and above, including illiterate persons, are eligible to vote. Voting in elections is compulsory for all citizens aged 18–70, and is optional thereafter.

JUDICIAL POWER

Judicial power is vested in the Supreme Court of Justice and other tribunals. The Constitution provides for the establishment of a National Council of the Judiciary, consisting of nine independently elected members, which is empowered to appoint judges to the Supreme Court. An independent Constitutional Court, comprising seven members elected by the Congreso for a five-year term, may interpret the Constitution and declare legislation and acts of government to be unconstitutional.

The death penalty may be applied by the Judiciary in cases of terrorism or of treason (the latter in times of war).

Under the Constitution, a People's Counsel is elected by the Congreso with a five-year mandate, which authorizes the Counsel to defend the constitutional and fundamental rights of the individual. The Counsel may draft laws and present evidence to the legislature.

According to the Constitution, the State promotes economic and social development, particularly in the areas of employment, health, education, security, public services and infrastructure. The State recognizes a plurality of economic ownership and activity, supports free competition, and promotes the growth of small businesses. Private initiative is permitted within the framework of a social market economy. The State also guarantees the free exchange of foreign currency.

The Government

HEAD OF STATE

President: ALAN GABRIEL LUDWIG GARCÍA PÉREZ (took office 28 July 2006).

First Vice-President: LUIS ALEJANDRO GIAMPIETRI ROJAS.

Second Vice-President: LOURDES MENDOZA DEL SOLAR.

COUNCIL OF MINISTERS
(July 2010)

The Government was formed by the PAP, UPP, PNP and several independent members.

President of the Council of Ministers: ANGEL JAVIER VELÁSQUEZ QUESQUÉN.

Minister of Foreign Affairs: JOSÉ ANTONIO GARCÍA BELAÚNDE.

Minister of Defence: RAFAEL REY REY.

Minister of the Interior: OCTAVIO EDILBERTO SALAZAR MIRANDA.

Minister of Justice: VÍCTOR GARCÍA TOMA.

Minister of Economy and Finance: MERCEDES ROSALBA ARÁOZ FERNÁNDEZ.

Minister of Labour and Employment: MANUELA ESPERANZA GARCÍA COCHAGNE.

Minister of International Trade and Tourism: MARTÍN PÉREZ MONTEVERDE.

Minister of Transport and Communications: ENRIQUE JAVIER CORNEJO RAMÍREZ.

Minister of Housing, Construction and Sanitation: JUAN SARMIENTO SOTO.

Minister of Health: OSCAR UGARTE UBILLÚS.

Minister of Agriculture: DANTE ADOLFO DE CÓRDOVA VELEZ.

Minister of Energy and Mines: PEDRO SÁNCHEZ GAMARRA.

Minister of Production: JOSÉ NICANOR GONZALES QUIJANO.

Minister of Education: JOSÉ ANTONIO CHANG ESCOBEDO.

Minister of Women and Social Development: NIDIA RUTH VILCHEZ YUCRA.

Minister of the Environment: ANTONIO BRACK EGG.

MINISTRIES

Office of the President of the Council of Ministers: Jirón Carabaya, cuadra 1 s/n, Anexo 1105-1107, Lima; tel. (1) 7168600; fax (1) 4449168; e-mail atencionciudadana@pcm.gob.pe; internet www.pcm.gob.pe.

Ministry of Agriculture: Avda La Universidad 200, La Molina, Lima; tel. (1) 6135800; e-mail postmaster@minag.gob.pe; internet www.minag.gob.pe.

Ministry of Defence: Edif. Quiñones, Avda de la Peruanidad s/n, Jesús María, Lima 1; tel. (1) 625-5959; e-mail webmaster@mindef.gob.pe; internet www.mindef.gob.pe.

Ministry of Economy and Finance: Jirón Junín 319, 4°, Circado de Lima, Lima 1; tel. (1) 3115930; e-mail postmaster@mef.gob.pe; internet www.mef.gob.pe.

Ministry of Education: Biblioteca Nacional del Perú, Avda de la Poesía 160, San Borja, Lima 41; tel. (1) 6155800; fax (1) 4370471; e-mail webmaster@minedu.gob.pe; internet www.minedu.gob.pe.

Ministry of Energy and Mines: Avda Las Artes Sur 260, San Borja, Lima 41; tel. (1) 6188700; e-mail webmaster@minem.gob.pe; internet www.minem.gob.pe.

Ministry of the Environment: Avda Javier Prado Oeste 1440, San Isidro, Lima; tel. (1) 6116000; fax (1) 2255369; e-mail minam@minam.gob.pe; internet www.minam.gob.pe.

Ministry of Foreign Affairs: Jirón Lampa 535, Lima 1; tel. (1) 2042400; e-mail informes@rree.gob.pe; internet www.rree.gob.pe.

Ministry of Health: Avda Salaverry 801, Jesús María, Lima 11; tel. (1) 3156600; fax (1) 6271600; e-mail webmaster@minsa.gob.pe; internet www.minsa.gob.pe.

Ministry of Housing, Construction and Sanitation: Avda Paseo de la República 3361, San Isidro, Lima; tel. (1) 2117930; e-mail webmaster@vivienda.gob.pe; internet www.vivienda.gob.pe.

Ministry of the Interior: Plaza 30 de Agosto 150 s/n, Urb. Córpac, San Isidro, Lima 27; tel. (1) 5180000; fax (1) 2242405; e-mail ministro@mininter.gob.pe; internet www.mininter.gob.pe.

Ministry of International Trade and Tourism: Calle Uno Oeste 50, Urb. Córpac, San Isidro, Lima 27; tel. (1) 5136100; fax (1) 2243362; e-mail webmaster@mincetur.gob.pe; internet www.mincetur.gob.pe.

Ministry of Justice: Scipión Llona 350, Miraflores, Lima 18; tel. (1) 4404310; fax (1) 4223577; e-mail webmaster@minjus.gob.pe; internet www.minjus.gob.pe.

Ministry of Labour and Employment: Avda Salaverry 655, cuadra 8, Jesús María, Lima 11; tel. (1) 6306000; fax (1) 6306060; e-mail webmaster@mintra.gob.pe; internet www.mintra.gob.pe.

Ministry of the Presidency: Plaza de Armas s/n, Lima 1; tel. (1) 3113900; internet www.presidencia.gob.pe.

Ministry of Production: Calle Uno Oeste 60, Urb. Córpac, San Isidro, Lima 27; tel. (1) 6162222; e-mail portal@produce.gob.pe; internet www.produce.gob.pe.

Ministry of Transport and Communications: Avda Jirón Zorritos 1203, Lima 1; tel. (1) 6187800; e-mail atencionalciudadano@mtc.gob.pe; internet www.mtc.gob.pe.

Ministry of Women and Social Development: Jirón Camaná 616, Lima 1; tel. (1) 6261600; fax (1) 4261665; e-mail postmaster@mimdes.gob.pe; internet www.mimdes.gob.pe.

Regional Presidents
(July 2010)

Amazonas: OSCAR RAMIRO ALTAMIRANO QUISPE.

Ancash: (vacant).

Apurímac: DAVID ABRAHAM SALAZAR MOROTE.

Arequipa: JUAN MANUEL GUILLÉN BENAVIDES.

Ayacucho: ISAAC ERNESTO MOLINA CHÁVEZ.

Cajamarca: JESÚS CORONEL SALIRROSAS.

Callao: VÍCTOR AUGUSTO ALBRECHT RODRÍGUEZ.

Cusco: HUGO EULOGIO GONZALES SAYÁN.

Huancavelica: LUIS FEDERICO SALAS GUEVARA SCHULTZ.

Huánuco: JORGE ESPINOZA EGOÁVIL.

Ica: RÓMULO TRIVEÑO PINTO.

Junín: VLADIMIRO HUAROC PORTOCARRERO.

La Libertad: JOSÉ HUMBERTO MURGIA ZANNIER.

Lambayeque: NERY ENNI SALDARRIAGA DE KROLL.

Lima: LUIS CUSTODIO CALDERÓN.

Loreto: YVÁN ENRIQUE VÁSQUEZ VALERA.

Madre de Dios: SANTOS KAWAY KOMORI.

Moquegua: JAIME ALBERTO RODRÍGUEZ VILLANUEVA.

Pasco: FÉLIX RIVERA SERRANO.

Piura: CÉSAR TRELLES LARA.

Puno: PABLO HERNÁN FUENTES GUZMÁN.

San Martín: WILIAN ALBERTO RÍOS TRIGOZO.

Tacna: HUGO FROILÁN ORDOÑEZ SALAZAR.

Tumbes: WILMER FLORENTINO DIOS BENITES.

Ucayali: JORGE VELÁSQUEZ PORTOCARRERO.

President and Legislature

PRESIDENT

Election, 9 April and 4 June 2006

Candidate	First round % of votes	Second round % of votes
Alan Gabriel Ludwig García Pérez (PAP)	24.32	52.63
Lt-Col (retd) Ollanta Moisés Humala Tasso (UPP*)	30.62	47.38
Lourdes Flores Nano (Unidad Nacional)	23.81	—
Martha Gladys Chávez Cossío de Ocampo (Alianza por el Futuro†)	7.43	—
Valentín Paniagua Corazao (Frente de Centro)	5.75	—
Humberto Lay Sun (Restauración Nacional)	4.38	—
Others	3.68	—
Total	100.00	100.00

* In coalition with the Partido Nacionalista Peruano.

† A coalition of Cambio 90 and Nueva Mayoría formed to contest the 2006 elections under the leadership of Keiko Fujimori, the daughter of former President Fujimori.

CONGRESO

President: César Alejandro Zumaeta Flores.

General Election, 9 April 2006

Parties	% of votes	Seats
Unión por el Perú (UPP)	21.15	45
Partido Aprista Peruano (PAP)	20.59	36
Unidad Nacional	15.33	17
Alianza por el Futuro	13.09	13
Frente de Centro	7.07	5
Perú Posible (PP)	4.11	2
Restauración Nacional	4.02	2
Others	14.64	—
Total	100.00*	120

* Excluding 1,682,768 blank votes and 2,188,789 spoiled votes.

Election Commission

Oficina Nacional de Procesos Electorales (ONPE): Jirón Washington 1894, Lima 1; tel. (1) 4170630; e-mail informes@onpe.gob.pe; internet www.onpe.gob.pe; f. 1995; independent; Nat. Dir Dra Magdalena Chú Villanueva.

Political Organizations

The following parties were officially registered by the Oficina Nacional de Procesos Electorales in 2010.

Acción Popular (AP): Paseo Colón 218, Lima 1; tel. and fax (1) 3321965; e-mail webmaster@accionpopular.pe; internet www.accionpopular.pe; f. 1956; 1.2m. mems; liberal; contested the presidential and legislative elections of April 2006 as part of the Frente de Centro coalition; Pres. Javier Alva Orlandini; Sec.-Gen. Yonhy Lescano Ancieta.

Agrupación Independiente Sí Cumple (Sí Cumple): Jirón Lampa 974, Lima; tel. (1) 5392235; f. 2003; supporters of fmr President Fujimori; Sec.-Gen. Carlos Orellana Quintanilla.

Alianza para el Progreso: Avda de la Policía 643, entre Cuadra 8 y 9 de Gregorio Escobedo, Jesús María, Lima; tel. (1) 4613197; e-mail app@app-peru.org.pe; internet www.app-peru.org.pe; f. 2001; Founder and Pres. César Acuña Peralta; Sec.-Gen. Juan Pablo Horna Santa Cruz; Nat. Exec. Sec. Gloria Edelmira Montenegro Figueroa.

APRA: see entry for PAP.

Cambio 90 (C90): Avda Jorge Aprile 312, San Borja; tel. (1) 3461853; f. 1990; part of Alianza por el Futuro coalition formed with Nueva Mayoría in order to contest the 2006 presidential and legislative elections; Pres. Andrés Reggiardo Sayán; Sec.-Gen. Reggio Reggiardo.

Coordinadora Nacional de Independientes (CNI): Las Moreras 293, San Isidro, Lima; tel. (1) 2644089; f. 2003; contested the presidential and legislative elections of April 2006 as part of the Frente de Centro coalition; Pres. Drago Kisic Wagner; Sec.-Gen. Raquel Liliana Lozada Valentín.

Fuerza 2011: Paseo Colón 422, Cercado de Lima, Lima; tel. 999383300 (mobile); e-mail contacto@fuerza2011.com; internet www.fuerza2011.com; Pres. Keiko Sofia Fujimori Higuchi; Sec.-Gen. Clemente Jaime Yoshiyama Tanaka.

Nueva Mayoría: Avda Almirante Guisse 2149, Lince, Lima; tel. (1) 2654302; f. 1992; Pres. Martha Gladys Chávez Cossío de Ocampo; Sec.-Gen. Demetrio Patsias Mella.

Partido Aprista Peruano (PAP): Avda Alfonso Ugarte 1012, Breña, Lima 5; tel. (1) 4250218; internet www.apra.org.pe; f. in Mexico 1924, in Peru 1930; legalized 1945; democratic left-wing party; although legally known as PAP, the party is commonly known as APRA; Pres. Alan Gabriel Ludwig García Pérez; Secs-Gen. Carlos Arana Vivar, Omar Quezada Martínez; 700,000 mems.

Partido Nacionalista Peruano (PNP): Avda Arequipa 3410, Lima 27; tel. (1) 4223592; internet www.partidonacionalistaperuano.com; f. 2005 to support presidential candidacy of Lt-Col (retd) Ollanta Moisés Humala Tasso; contested the 2006 elections in coalition with the Unión por el Perú; Pres. Lt-Col (retd) Ollanta Moisés Humala Tasso.

Partido Político Adelante: Jirón Ricardo Palma 120, San Isidro, Lima; tel. (1) 2212563; e-mail 2004adelante@gmail.com; internet www.adelante.org.pe; f. 2004; Sec.-Gen. Rafael Belaunde Aubry.

Partido Popular Cristiano (PPC): Avda Alfonso Ugarte 1484, Breña, Lima; tel. (1) 4238722; fax (1) 4238721; e-mail estflores@terra.com.pe; internet www.ppc.pe; f. 1967; 250,000 mems; Pres. Lourdes Flores Nano; Sec.-Gen. Raúl Castro Stagnaro.

Perú Posible (PP): Avda Faustino Sánchez Carrión 601, Jesús María, Lima 11; tel. (1) 4602493; fax (1) 2612418; e-mail sgpp@mixmail.com; internet www.peruposible.org.pe; f. 1994; Leader Alejandro Toledo Manrique; Sec.-Gen. Javier Reátegui Rosselló.

Renovación Nacional: Avda Camino Real 1206, 2°, San Isidro, Lima; tel. (1) 5673798; f. 1992; Sec.-Gen. Wilder Ruiz Silva.

Restauración Nacional: Avda Arequipa 3750, San Isidro, Lima; tel. (9) 3117546; internet www.restauracionnacional.org; f. 2005; evangelical Christian party; Pres. Humberto Lay Sun; Sec.-Gen. Juan David Perry Cruz.

Solidaridad Nacional (SN): Amador Merino Reyna 140, San Isidro, Lima 27; tel. (1) 4213348; e-mail fsandoval@psn.org.pe; internet www.psn.org.pe; f. 1999; centre-left; Pres. Luis Castañeda Lossio; Sec.-Gen. Marco Antonio Parra Sánchez.

Somos Perú (SP): Mariscal Las Heras 393, Lince, Lima 14; tel. (1) 4714484; e-mail postmaster@somosperu.org.pe; internet www.somosperu.org.pe; f. 1998; contested the April 2006 elections as part of the Frente de Centro coalition; Pres. Fernando Andrade Carmona; Sec.-Gen. Yuri Vilela Seminario.

Unidad Nacional: Calle Ricardo Palma 1111, Miraflores, Lima; tel. (1) 2242773; f. 2000; centrist alliance comprising Partido Popular Cristiano and Solidaridad Nacional; Leader Lourdes Flores Nano.

Unión por el Perú (UPP): Avda Cuba 543, Jesús María, Lima; tel. (1) 4271941; e-mail ivega@partidoupp.org; internet www.partidopoliticoupp.org; f. 1994; ind. movt; contested 2006 elections in coalition with Partido Nacionalista Peruano, led by Lt-Col (retd) Ollanta Moisés Humala Tasso; Pres. Eduardo Espinoza Ramos; Sec.-Gen. José Vega Antonio.

ARMED GROUPS

Movimiento Nacionalista Peruano (MNP) (Movimiento Etnocacerista): Pasaje Velarde 188, Of. 204, Lima; tel. (1) 4338781; e-mail movnacionalistaperuano@yahoo.es; internet mnp.tripod.com.pe; ultra-nationalist paramilitary group; Pres. Dr Isaac Humala Núñez; Leader of paramilitary wing Maj. (retd) Antauro Igor Humala Tasso (arrested Jan. 2005 following an armed uprising in Andahuaylas).

Sendero Luminoso (SL) (Shining Path): f. 1970; began armed struggle 1980; splinter group of PCP; active in the Apurímac-Ene and Upper Huallaga valleys; advocated the policies of Mao Zedong in the People's Republic of China; from the mid-2000s it became increasingly involved in the illegal drugs trade; founder Dr Abimael Guzmán Reynoso (alias 'Chairman Gonzalo'—arrested Sept. 1992); leaders Víctor Quispe Palomino (alias 'Comrade José'—commander of the Apurímac-Ene contingent), 'Comrade Artemio' (identified as Filomeno Cerrón Cardoso—commander of the Upper Huallaga contingent).

Diplomatic Representation

EMBASSIES IN PERU

Algeria: Miguel de Cervantes 504–510, San Isidro, Lima; tel. 421-7582; fax 421-7580; e-mail embarg@embajadadeargelia.com; Ambassador Muhammad Bensabri.

Argentina: Avda Arequipa 121, Cercado de Lima, Lima 1; tel. (1) 4339966; fax (1) 4330769; e-mail contacto@embajadaargentinaenperu.org; internet www.embajadaargentinaenperu.org; Ambassador DARÍO PEDRO ALESSANDRO.

Australia: Lima; Ambassador JOHN M. L. WOODS (from Sept. 2010).

Austria: Edif. de las Naciones, Avda República de Colombia 643, 5°, San Isidro, Lima 27; tel. (1) 4420503; fax (1) 4428851; e-mail lima-ob@bmeia.gv.at; Ambassador ANDREAS MEIÁN.

Belgium: Avda Angamos Oeste 380, Miraflores, Lima 18; tel. (1) 2417566; fax (1) 2416379; e-mail lima@diplobel.fed.be; internet www.diplomatie.be/lima; Ambassador BEATRIX VAN HEMELDONCK.

Bolivia: Los Castaños 235, San Isidro, Lima 27; tel. (1) 4402095; fax (1) 4402298; e-mail embajada@boliviaenperu.com; Ambassador FRANZ SOLANO CHUQUIMIA.

Brazil: Avda José Pardo 850, Miraflores, Lima; tel. (1) 5120830; fax (1) 4452421; e-mail embajada@embajadabrasil.org.pe; internet www.embajadabrasil.org.pe; Ambassador JORGE D'ESCRAGNOLLE TAUNAY FILHO.

Canada: Calle Bolognesi 228, Miraflores, Casilla 18-1126, Lima; tel. (1) 3193200; fax (1) 4464912; e-mail lima@international.gc.ca; internet www.canadainternational.gc.ca/peru-perou; Ambassador RICHARD LECOQ.

Chile: Avda Javier Prado Oeste 790, San Isidro, Lima; tel. (1) 7102211; fax (1) 7102223; e-mail contacto@chileabroad.gov.cl; internet chileabroad.gov.cl/peru; Ambassador FAVIO VIO UGARTE.

China, People's Republic: Jirón José Granda 150, San Isidro, Apdo 375, Lima 27; tel. (1) 2220841; fax (1) 4429467; e-mail chinaemb_pe@mfa.gov.cn; internet www.embajadachina.org.pe; Ambassador ZHAO WUYI.

Colombia: Avda J. Basadre 1580, San Isidro, Lima 27; tel. (1) 4410954; fax (1) 4419806; e-mail elima@cancilleria.gov.co; internet www.embajadaenperu.gov.co; Ambassador ÁLVARO PAVA CAMELO.

Costa Rica: Baltazar La Torre 828, San Isidro, Lima; tel. (1) 2642999; fax (1) 2642799; e-mail embcr.peru@gmail.com; Ambassador SARA FAIGENZICHT WEISLEDER.

Cuba: Coronel Portillo 110, San Isidro, Lima; tel. (1) 5123400; fax (1) 2644525; e-mail embacuba@pe.embacuba.cu; internet embacu.cubaminrex.cu/peru; Ambassador LUIS DELFÍN PÉREZ OSORIO.

Czech Republic: Baltazar La Torre 398, San Isidro, Lima 27; tel. (1) 2643374; fax (1) 2641708; e-mail lima@embassy.mzv.cz; internet www.mfa.cz/lima; Ambassador VĚRA ZEMANOVÁ.

Dominican Republic: Calle Tudela y Varela 360, San Isidro, Lima 27; tel. (1) 4219765; fax (1) 4219763; e-mail embdomperu@speedy.com.pe; internet www.embajadadominicanaperu.org; Ambassador RAFAEL JULIÁN CEDANO.

Ecuador: Las Palmeras 356 y Javier Prado Oeste, San Isidro, Lima 27; tel. (1) 2124171; fax (1) 4220711; e-mail embajada@mecuadorperu.org.pe; internet www.mecuadorperu.org.pe; Ambassador DIEGO RIBADENEIRA ESPINOSA.

Egypt: Avda Jorge Basadre 1470, San Isidro, Lima 27; tel. (1) 4222531; fax (1) 4402369; e-mail egipto@sspeedy.com.pe; Ambassador HISHAM MUHAMMAD ABAS KHALIL.

El Salvador: Avda Javier Prado 2108, San Isidro, Lima 27; tel. (1) 4403500; fax (1) 2212561; e-mail embajadasv@terra.com.pe; Ambassador RAÚL SOTO-RAMÍREZ.

Finland: Edif. Real Tres, Of. 502, 5°, Avda Víctor Andrés Belaúnde 147, San Isidro, Lima; tel. (1) 2224466; fax (1) 2224463; e-mail sanomat.lim@formin.fi; internet www.finlandia.org.pe; Ambassador PEKKA ORPANA.

France: Avda Arequipa 3415, Lima 27; tel. (1) 2158400; fax (1) 2158410; e-mail france.consulat@ambafrance-pe.org; internet www.ambafrance-pe.org; Ambassador CÉCILE MOUTON-BRADY DE POZZO DI BORGO.

Germany: Avda Arequipa 4202–4210, Miraflores, Lima 18; tel. (1) 2125016; fax (1) 4226475; e-mail info@lima.diplo.de; internet www.lima.diplo.de; Ambassador CHRISTOPH MÜLLER.

Greece: Avda Principal 190, Urb. Santa Catalina, La Victoria, Lima 13; tel. (1) 4761548; fax (1) 2232486; e-mail gremb.lim@mfa.gr; internet www.mfa.gr/lima; Ambassador IONNIS PAPADOPOULOS.

Guatemala: Inca Ripac 309, Jesús María, Lima 11; tel. (1) 4602078; fax (1) 4635885; e-mail embperu@minex.gob.gt; Ambassador BAUDILIO PORTILLO MERLOS.

Holy See: Avda Salaverry, 6a cuadra, Lima 11 (Apostolic Nunciature); tel. (1) 7174897; fax (1) 7174896; e-mail nunciaturaperu@inbox.com; Apostolic Nuncio Most Rev. BRUNO MUSARÒ (Titular Archbishop of Abari).

Honduras: Avda Las Camelias 491, Of. 202, San Isidro, Lima; tel. (1) 4228111; fax (1) 2211677; e-mail info@embhonpe.org; internet www.embhonpe.org; Ambassador JUÁN JOSÉ CUEVA MEMBREÑO.

India: Avda Salaverry 3006, San Isidro, Lima 27; tel. (1) 4602289; fax (1) 4610374; e-mail hoc@indembassy.org.pe; internet www.indembassy.org.pe; Ambassador APPUNNI RAMESH.

Indonesia: Avda Las Flores 334-336, San Isidro, Lima; tel. (1) 2220308; fax (1) 2222684; e-mail kbrilima@indonesia-peru.org.pe; internet www.indonesia-peru.org.pe; Ambassador IGDE DJELANTIK.

Israel: Edif. El Pacifico, 6°, Plaza Washington, Natalio Sánchez 125, Santa Beatriz, Lima; tel. (1) 4180500; fax (1) 4180555; e-mail info@lima.mfa.gov.il; internet lima.mfa.gov.il; Ambassador YOAV BAR-ON.

Italy: Avda Giuseppe Garibaldi 298, Apdo 0490, Lima 11; tel. (1) 4632727; fax (1) 4635317; e-mail ambasciata.lima@esteri.it; internet www.amblima.esteri.it; Ambassador FRANCESCO RAUSI.

Japan: Avda San Felipe 356, Apdo 3708, Jesús María, Lima 11; tel. (1) 2181130; fax (1) 4630302; e-mail cultjapon@embajadajapon.org.pe; internet www.pe.emb-japan.go.jp; Ambassador SHUICHIRO MEGATA.

Korea, Democratic People's Republic: Los Nogales 227, San Isidro, Lima; tel. (1) 4411120; fax (1) 4409877; e-mail embcorea@hotmail.com; Ambassador RI MUN GYU.

Korea, Republic: Avda Principal 190, 7°, Urb. Santa Catalina, La Victoria, Lima; tel. (1) 4760815; fax (1) 4760950; e-mail peru@mofat.go.kr; internet per.mofat.go.kr; Ambassador HAN BYUNG-KIL.

Malaysia: Avda Daniel Hernández 350, San Isidro, Lima 27; tel. (1) 4220297; fax (1) 2210786; e-mail mallima@kln.gov.my; internet www.kln.gov.my/perwakilan/lima; Ambassador AHMAD IZLAM BIN IDRIS.

Mexico: Avda Jorge Basadre 710, esq. Los Ficus, San Isidro, Lima; tel. (1) 6121600; fax (1) 6121627; e-mail info@mexico.org.pe; internet www.mexico.org.pe; Chargé d'affaires a.i. JORGE CICERO FERNÁNDEZ.

Morocco: Calle Tomás Edison 205, San Isidro, Lima; tel. (1) 4403117; fax (1) 4404391; e-mail sifa@embajadamarruecoslima.com; internet www.embajadamarruecoslima.com; Ambassador OUMAMA AOUAD.

Netherlands: Torre Parque Mar, 13°, Avda José Larco 1301, Miraflores, Lima; tel. (1) 2139800; fax (1) 2139805; e-mail info@nlgovlim.com; internet www.nlgovlim.com; Ambassador BAREND VAN DER HEIJDEN.

Nicaragua: Avda Alvarez Calderón 738, San Isidro, Lima 27; tel. (1) 4223892; fax (1) 4223895; e-mail embanic@telefonica.net.pe; Ambassador TOMÁS WIGBERTO BORGE MARTÍNEZ.

Panama: Avda Trinidad Morán 1426, Lince, Lima; tel. (1) 4228084; fax (1) 4227871; e-mail secretaria@panaembaperu.com.pe; internet www.panaembaperu.com.pe; Ambassador CARLOS LUIS LINARES BRIN.

Paraguay: Alcanfores 1286, Miraflores, Lima; tel. (1) 4474762; fax (1) 4442391; e-mail embaparpe@infonegocio.net.pe; Ambassador MODESTO LUIS GUIGGIARI ZAVALA.

Poland: Avda Salaverry 1978, Jesús María, Lima 11; tel. (1) 4713920; fax (1) 4714813; e-mail lima.amb.sekretariat@msz.gov.pl; internet www.lima.polemb.net; Ambassador JAROSŁAW SPYRA.

Portugal: Calle Antequera 777, 3°, San Isidro, POB 3692, Lima 100; tel. (1) 4409905; fax (1) 4215979; e-mail limaportugal@hotmail.com; Ambassador NUNO BESSA LÓPES.

Romania: Avda Jorge Basadre 690, San Isidro, Lima; tel. (1) 4224587; fax (1) 4210609; e-mail ambrom@terra.com.pe; Ambassador ŞTEFAN COSTIN.

Russia: Avda Salaverry 3424, San Isidro, Lima 27; tel. (1) 2640036; fax (1) 2640130; e-mail embrusa@infonegocio.net.pe; internet www.embajada-rusa.org; Ambassador MIKHAIL G. TROYANSKII.

Serbia: Carlos Porras Osores 360, Apdo 18-0392, San Isidro, Lima 27; Apdo 0392, Lima 18; tel. (1) 4212423; fax (1) 4212427; e-mail serbiaembperu@rcp.com.pe; Ambassador GORAN MESIĆ.

South Africa: Edif. Real Tres, Avda Víctor Andres Belaúnde 147, Of. 801, Lima 27; tel. (1) 6124848; fax 4223881; e-mail general.peru@foreign.gov.za; Ambassador ALBERT LESLIE MANLEY.

Spain: Jorge Basadre 498, San Isidro, Lima 27; tel. (1) 2125155; fax (1) 4402020; e-mail embesppe@correo.mae.es; Ambassador FRANCISCO JAVIER SANDOMINGO NÚÑEZ.

Switzerland: Avda Salaverry 3240, San Isidro, Lima 27; tel. (1) 2640305; fax (1) 2641319; e-mail lim.vertretung@eda.admin.ch; internet www.eda.admin.ch/lima; Ambassador ANNE-PASCALE KRAUER MÜLLER.

Thailand: Avda Los Incas 255-275, San Isidro, Lima 27; tel. (1) 2216442; fax (1) 4229895; e-mail thailim@mfa.go.th; Ambassador UDOMPHOL NINNAD.

Ukraine: José Dellepiani 470, San Isidro, Lima; tel. (1) 2642884; fax (1) 2642892; e-mail emb_pe@mfa.gov.ua; internet www.mfa.gov.ua/peru; Chargé d'affaires a.i. VICTOR KHARAMINSKYI.

United Kingdom: Torre Parque Mar, 22°, Avda José Larco 1301, Miraflores, Lima; tel. (1) 6173000; fax (1) 6173100; e-mail belima@fco.gov.uk; internet www.ukinperu.fco.gov.uk; Ambassador JAMES DAURIS.

USA: Avda La Encalada 17, Surco, Lima 33; tel. (1) 6182000; fax (1) 6182397; internet lima.usembassy.gov; Ambassador ROSE M. LIKINS.

Uruguay: José D. Anchorena 84, San Isidro, Lima 27; tel. (1) 7192550; fax (1) 7192865; e-mail uruinca@americatelnet.com.pe; Ambassador JUAN JOSÉ ARTEAGA SÁENZ DE ZUMARÁN.

Venezuela: Avda Arequipa 298, Lima; tel. (1) 4334511; fax (1) 4331191; e-mail consulve@millicom.com.pe; Ambassador ARÍSTIDES MEDINA (recalled in April 2009).

Judicial System

The Supreme Court consists of a President and 17 members. There are also Higher Courts and Courts of First Instance in provincial capitals. A comprehensive restructuring of the judiciary was implemented during the late 1990s.

SUPREME COURT

Corte Suprema

Palacio de Justicia, 2°, Avda Paseo de la República, Lima 1; tel. (1) 4284457; fax (1) 4269437; internet www.pj.gob.pe.

President: Dr JAVIER VILLA STEIN.

Attorney-General: Dra GLADYS MARGOT ECHAÍZ RAMOS.

Religion

CHRISTIANITY

The Roman Catholic Church

For ecclesiastical purposes, Peru comprises seven archdioceses, 19 dioceses, 10 territorial prelatures and eight Apostolic Vicariates. According to the latest census (2007), some 81% of the population are Roman Catholics.

Bishops' Conference

Conferencia Episcopal Peruana, Jirón Estados Unidos 838, Apdo 310, Lima 100; tel. (1) 4631010; fax (1) 4636125; e-mail sgc@iglesiacatolica.org.pe; internet www.iglesia.org.pe.

f. 1981; Pres. HÉCTOR MIGUEL CABREJOS VIDARTE (Archbishop of Trujillo).

Archbishop of Arequipa: JAVIER AUGUSTO DEL RIO ALBA, Arzobispado, Moral San Francisco 118, Apdo 149, Arequipa; tel. (54) 234094; fax (54) 242721; e-mail arzobispadoaqp@planet.com.pe.

Archbishop of Ayacucho or Huamanga: LUIS ABILIO SEBASTIANI AGUIRRE, Arzobispado, Jirón 28 de Julio 148, Apdo 30, Ayacucho; tel. and fax (64) 812367; e-mail arzaya@mail.udep.edu.pe.

Archbishop of Cusco: JUAN ANTONIO UGARTE PÉREZ, Arzobispado, Herrajes, Hatun Rumiyoc s/n, Apdo 148, Cusco; tel. (84) 225211; fax (84) 222781; e-mail arzobisp@terra.com.pe.

Archbishop of Huancayo: PEDRO RICARDO BARRETO JIMENO, Arzobispado, Jirón Puno 430, Apdo 245, Huancayo; tel. (64) 234952; fax (64) 239189; e-mail arzohyo@hotmail.com.

Archbishop of Lima: Cardinal JUAN LUIS CIPRIANI THORNE, Arzobispado, Jirón Carabaya, Plaza Mayor, Apdo 1512, Lima 100; tel. (1) 4275980; fax (1) 4271967; e-mail arzolim@terra.com.pe; internet www.arzobispadodelima.org.

Archbishop of Piura: JOSÉ ANTONIO EGUREN ANSELMI, Arzobispado, Libertad 1105, Apdo 197, Piura; tel. and fax (74) 327561; e-mail ocordova@upiura.edu.pe.

Archbishop of Trujillo: HÉCTOR MIGUEL CABREJOS VIDARTE, Arzobispado, Jirón Mariscal de Orbegozo 451, Apdo 42, Trujillo; tel. (44) 256812; fax (44) 231473; e-mail arztrujillo@terra.com.pe.

The Anglican Communion

The Iglesia Anglicana del Cono Sur de América (Anglican Church of the Southern Cone of America), formally inaugurated in April 1983, comprises seven dioceses, including Peru. The Presiding Bishop of the Church is the Bishop of Northern Argentina.

Bishop of Peru: Rt Rev. HAROLD WILLIAM GODFREY, Apdo 18-1032, Miraflores, Lima 18; tel. and fax (1) 4229160; e-mail diocesisperu@anglicanperu.org; internet www.peru.anglican.org.

The Methodist Church

There are an estimated 4,200 adherents of the Iglesia Metodista del Perú.

President: Rev. JORGE BRAZO CABALLERO, Baylones 186, Lima 5; Apdo 1386, Lima 100; tel. (1) 4245970; fax (1) 4318995; e-mail iglesiamp@computextos.com.pe; internet www.iglesiametodista.org.pe.

Other Protestant Churches

Among the most popular are the Iglesia Evangélica del Perú (accounting for some 12% of the population at the 2007 census), the Asamblea de Dios, the Iglesia del Nazareno, the Alianza Cristiana y Misionera and the Iglesia de Dios del Perú.

BAHÁ'Í FAITH

National Spiritual Assembly of the Bahá'ís of Peru: Horacio Urteaga 827, Jesús María, Apdo 11-0209, Lima 11; tel. (1) 4316077; fax (1) 4333005; e-mail bahai@pol.com.pe; mems resident in 220 localities.

The Press

DAILIES

Lima

El Bocón: Jirón Jorge Salazar Araoz 171, Urb. Santa Catalina, Apdo 152, Lima 1; tel. (1) 6908090; fax (1) 6908127; internet www.elbocon.com.pe; f. 1994; football; Editorial Dir JORGE ESTÉVES ALFARO; circ. 90,000.

El Comercio: Empresa Editora 'El Comercio', SA, Jirón Antonio Miró Quesada 300, Lima; tel. (1) 3116310; fax (1) 4260810; e-mail editorweb@comercio.com.pe; internet www.elcomercioperu.com.pe; f. 1839; morning; Editor JUAN CARLOS LUJÁN; Dir-Gen. FRANCISCO MIRÓ QUESADA G.; circ. 150,000 weekdays, 220,000 Sundays.

Expreso: Jirón Antonio Elizalde 753, Lima; tel. (1) 6124000; fax (1) 6124024; e-mail luis.garciamiro@expreso.com.pe; internet www.expreso.com.pe; f. 1961; morning; conservative; Dir LUIS GARCÍA MIRÓ; circ. 100,000.

Extra: Jirón Libertad 117, Miraflores, Lima; tel. (1) 4447088; fax (1) 4447117; e-mail extra@expreso.com.pe; f. 1964; evening edition of Expreso; Dir CARLOS SÁNCHEZ; circ. 80,000.

Gestión: Miró Quesada 247, 8°, Lima 1; tel. (1) 3116370; fax (1) 3116500; e-mail gestion2@diariogestion.com.pe; internet www.gestion.pe; f. 1990; Gen. Editor JULIO LIRA; Gen. Man. ERNESTO CORTES ROJAS; circ. 131,200.

Ojo: Jirón Jorge Salazar Araoz 171, Urb. Santa Catalina, Apdo 152, Lima; tel. (1) 4709696; fax (1) 4761605; internet www.ojo.com.pe; f. 1968; morning; Editorial Dir AGUSTÍN FIGUEROA BENZA; circ. 100,000.

Perú 21: Jirón Miró Quesada 247, 6°, Lima; tel. (1) 3116500; fax (1) 3116391; e-mail director@peru21.com; internet www.peru21.com; independent; Editors CLAUDIA IZAGUIRRE, MANUEL TUMI.

El Peruano (Diario Oficial): Avda Alfonso Ugarte 873, Lima 1; tel. (1) 3150400; fax (1) 4245023; e-mail gbarraza@editoraperu.com.pe; internet www.elperuano.com.pe; f. 1825; morning; official State Gazette; Dir DELFINA BECERRA GONZÁLEZ; circ. 27,000.

La República: Jirón Camaná 320, Lima 1; tel. (1) 7116000; fax (1) 2511029; e-mail otxoa@larepublica.com.pe; internet www.larepublica.pe; f. 1982; left-wing; Dir GUSTAVO MOHME SEMINARIO; circ. 50,000.

Arequipa

Arequipa al Día: Santa Marta 103, Arequipa; tel. (54) 215515; fax (54) 217810; internet www.ucsm.edu.pe/arequipa; f. 1991; Dir CARLOS MENESES CORNEJO; Editor-in-Chief ENRIQUE ZAVALA CONCHA.

Correo de Arequipa: Calle Bolívar 204, Arequipa; tel. (54) 235150; e-mail diariocorreo@epensa.com.pe; internet www.correoperu.com.pe; Dir ALDO MARIÁTEGUI; circ. 70,000.

El Pueblo: Sucre 213, Arequipa; tel. and fax (54) 205086; internet www.elpueblo.com.pe; f. 1905; morning; independent; Pres. DANIEL MACEDO GUTIÉRREZ; Dir CARLOS MENESES CORNEJO; circ. 70,000.

Chiclayo

La Industria: Tacna 610, Chiclayo; tel. (74) 237952; fax (74) 227678; f. 1952; Dir JULIO ALBERTO ORTIZ CERRO; circ. 20,000.

Cusco

El Diario del Cusco: Centro Comercial Ollanta, Avda El Sol 346, Cusco; tel. (84) 229898; fax (84) 229822; e-mail buzon@diariodelcusco.com; internet www.diariodelcusco.com; morning; independent; Exec. Pres. WASHINTON ALOSILLA PORTILLO; Gen. Man. JOSÉ FERNANDEZ NÚÑEZ.

Huacho

El Imparcial: Avda Grau 203, Huacho; tel. (34) 2392187; fax (34) 2321352; e-mail elimparcial1891@hotmail.com; f. 1891; evening; Dir ADÁN MANRIQUE ROMERO; circ. 5,000.

Huancayo

Correo de Huancayo: Jirón Cusco 337, Huancayo; tel. (64) 235792; fax (64) 233811; evening; Editorial Dir RODOLFO OROSCO.

La Opinión Popular: Huancayo; tel. (64) 231149; f. 1922; Dir MIGUEL BERNABÉ SUÁREZ OSORIO.

Ica

La Opinión: Avda Los Maestros 801, Apdo 186, Ica; tel. (56) 235571; f. 1922; evening; independent; Dir GONZALO TUEROS RAMÍREZ.

La Voz de Ica: Castrovirreyna 193, Ica; tel. and fax (56) 232112; e-mail lavozdeica1918@infonegocio.net.pe; f. 1918; Dir ATILIO NIERI BOGGIANO; Man. MARIELLA NIERI DE MACEDO; circ. 4,500.

Pacasmayo

Diario Ultimas Noticias: 2 de Mayo 33, Pacasmayo; tel. and fax (44) 523022; e-mail escribanos@ultimasnoticiasdiario.com; internet www.ultimasnoticiasdiario.com; f. 1973; morning; independent; Editor MARÍA DEL CARMEN BALLENA RAZURI; circ. 3,000.

Piura

Correo: Zona Industrial Manzana 246, Lote 6, Piura; tel. (74) 321681; fax (74) 324881; Editorial Dir ROLANDO RODRICH ARANGO; circ. 12,000.

El Tiempo: Ayacucho 751, Piura; tel. (74) 325141; fax (74) 327478; e-mail lmhelguero@eltiempo.com.pe; internet www.eltiempo.com.pe; f. 1916; morning; independent; Dir LUZ MARÍA HELGUERO; circ. 18,000.

Tacna

Correo: Jirón Hipólito Unanue 636, Tacna; tel. (54) 711671; fax (54) 713955; Editorial Dir RUBÉN COLLAZOS ROMERO; circ. 8,000.

Trujillo

La Industria: Gamarra 443, Trujillo; tel. (44) 295757; fax (44) 427761; e-mail phidalgo@laindustria.com; internet www.laindustria.com; f. 1895; morning; independent; Dir ERNESTO BARREDA ARIAS; circ. 8,000.

PERIODICALS

Business: Avda La Molina 1110, Of. 203, La Molina, Lima 12; tel. (1) 2500596; fax (1) 2500597; e-mail correo@businessperu.com.pe; internet www.businessperu.com.pe; f. 1994; monthly; Dir DANIEL VALERA LOZA.

Caretas: Jirón Huallaya 122, Portal de Botoneros, Plaza de Armas, Lima 1; Apdo 737, Lima 100; tel. (1) 4289490; fax (1) 4262524; e-mail info@caretas.com.pe; internet www.caretas.com.pe; weekly; current affairs; Dir MARCO ZILERI DOUGALL; circ. 90,000.

Cosas: Calle Recaveren 111, Miraflores, Lima 18; tel. (1) 2023000; fax (1) 4473776; internet www.cosasperu.com; weekly; society; Editor ELIZABETH DULANTO.

Debate Agrario: Avda Salaverry 818, Lima 11; tel. (1) 4336610; fax (1) 4331744; e-mail fegurenl@cepes.org.pe; f. 1987 by Centro Peruano de Estudios Sociales; every 4 months; rural issues; Dir FERNANDO EGUREN L.

Gente Peru: Calle Las Margaritas, San Eugenio, Lince, Lima 14; tel. (1) 2217997; fax (1) 4413646; internet www.genteinternacional.com; f. 1958; weekly; circ. 25,000; Dir HÉCTOR ESCARDÓ.

Industria Peruana: Los Laureles 365, San Isidro, Apdo 632, Lima 27; tel. (1) 6164444; fax (1) 6164412; e-mail industriaperuana@sni.org.pe; internet www.sni.org.pe/servicios/publicaciones; monthly publication of the Sociedad Nacional de Industrias; Dir BORIS ROMERO OJEDA.

Orbita: Parque Rochdale 129, Lima; tel. (1) 4610676; weekly; f. 1970; Dir LUZ CHÁVEZ MENDOZA.

Perú Económico: Apdo 671, Lima 100; tel. (1) 2425656; fax (1) 4455946; internet www.apoyopublicaciones.com/perueconomico; f. 1978; monthly.

The Peruvian Times: Paseo de la República 291, Of. 702, Lima 1; tel. (1) 4676609; e-mail egriffis@peruviantimes.com; internet www.peruviantimes.com; f. 1940, successor to West Coast Leader (f. 1912); refounded 2007 as an online publ; general news, analysis and features; English; daily; Publr ELEANOR GRIFFIS.

QueHacer: León de la Fuente 110, Lima 17; tel. (1) 6138300; fax (1) 6138308; e-mail qh@desco.org.pe; internet www.desco.org.pe/quehacer; f. 1979; 6 a year; supported by Desco research and devt agency; Editor-in-Chief MARTÍN PAREDES; Dir ABELARDO SÁNCHEZ-LEÓN; circ. 5,000.

Revista Agraria: Avda Salaverry 818, Lima 11; tel. (1) 4336610; fax (1) 4331744; internet www.cepes.org.pe/revista/agraria.htm; f. 1987 by Centro Peruano de Estudios Sociales; monthly review of rural problems; Dir FERNANDO EGUREN; circ. 100,000.

Semana Económica: Juan de la Fuente 625, Miraflores, Lima 18; tel. (1) 2130600; fax (1) 4445240; e-mail se@apoyopublicaciones.com; internet www.semanaeconomica.com; f. 1985; weekly; Exec. Dir GONZALO ZEGARRA MULANOVICH.

NEWS AGENCY

Andina—Agencia de Noticias Peruana: Jirón Quilca 556, Lima; tel. (1) 3306341; fax (1) 4312849; e-mail bbecerra@editoraperu.com.pe; internet www.andina.com.pe; f. 1981; state-owned; Pres. MARÍA DEL PILAR TELLO LEYVA; Dir of Media DELFINA BECERRA GONZÁLEZ.

PRESS ASSOCIATIONS

Asociación Nacional de Periodistas del Perú: Jirón Huancavélica 320, Apdo 2079, Lima 1; tel. (1) 4270687; fax (1) 4278493; internet www.anp.org.pe; f. 1928; 8,800 mems; Pres. ROBERTO MARCOS MEJÍA ALARCÓN.

Federación de Periodistas del Perú (FPP): Avda Abancay 173, 3°, Lima; tel. (1) 4261806; e-mail fpp@omco.org; internet www.omco.org/fpp; f. 1950; Pres. JESÚS GERMÁN LLANOS CASTILLO.

Publishers

Asociación Editorial Bruño: Avda Arica 751, Breña, Lima 5; tel. (1) 4237890; fax (1) 4240424; e-mail federico@brunoeditorial.com.pe; internet www.brunoeditorial.com.pe; f. 1950; educational; Man. FEDERICO DÍAZ PINEDO.

Biblioteca Nacional del Perú: Avda de la Poesia 160, San Borja, Lima 41; tel. (1) 5136900; fax (1) 5137060; e-mail contactobnp@bnp.gob.pe; internet www.bnp.gob.pe; f. 1821; general non-fiction, directories; Dir HUGO NEIRA SAMANAZ.

Ediciones PEISA: Avda 2 de Mayo 1285, San Isidro, Lima; tel. (1) 4410473; fax (1) 2215988; internet www.peisa.com.pe; f. 1968; fiction and scholarly; Dir GERMÁN CORONADO.

Editora Normas Legales, SA: Angamos Oeste 526, Miraflores, Lima; tel. and fax (1) 4861410; e-mail ventas@normaslegales.com; internet www.normaslegales.com; law textbooks; Man. JAVIER SANTA MARÍA SILVE.

Editorial Casatomada: Avda 28 de Julio 228, 31°, Lima 11; tel. (1) 4331352; e-mail ecasatomada@gmail.com; internet rcasatomada.blogspot.com; fiction, folklore; Dir GABRIEL RIMACHI SIALER.

Editorial Cuzco, SA: Calle 5 Marzo, Jirón Lote 3, Urb. Las Magnolias, Surco, Lima; tel. (1) 4453261; e-mail ccuzco@camaralima.org.pe; law; Man. SERGIO BAZÁN CHACÓN.

Editorial Horizonte: Avda Nicolás de Piérola 995, Lima 1; tel. (1) 4279364; fax (1) 4274341; e-mail damonte@terra.com.pe; f. 1968; social sciences, literature, politics; Man. HUMBERTO DAMONTE.

Editorial Milla Batres, SA: Lima; f. 1963; history, literature, art, archaeology, linguistics and encyclopaedias on Peru; Dir-Gen. CARLOS MILLA BATRES.

Editorial Océano Peruana, SA: Ricardo Angulo 795, 5°, Urb. Corpac, San Isidro, Lima; tel. (1) 7190777; fax (1) 2257592; e-mail oceanoperuana@oceano.com.pe; general interest and reference; Gen. Man. JORGE A. DAVELOUIS SARTORI.

Editorial Salesiana: Avda Brasil 218, Apdo 0071, Lima 5; tel. (1) 4235225; internet www.libreriasalesiana.com; f. 1918; religious and general textbooks; Man. Dir Dr FRANCESCO VACARELLO.

Editorial San Marcos: Jirón Dávalos Lissón 135, Lima; tel. (1) 3311535; fax (1) 3302405; e-mail informes@editorialsanmarcos.com; internet www.editorialsanmarcos.com; educational, academic, legal; Gen. Man. ANÍBAL JESÚS PAREDES GALVÁN.

Editorial Santillana: Avda Primavera 2160, Santiago de Surco, Lima; tel. (1) 3134000; fax (1) 3134001; e-mail santillana@santillana.com.pe; internet www.gruposantillana.com.pe; literature, scholarly and reference; Man. ANA CECILIA HALLO.

Grijley: Jirón Lampa 1221, Lima; tel. (1) 4273147; e-mail info@grijley.com; internet www.grijley.com; law.

Grupo Editorial Mesa Redonda: Pedro Venturo 234, Miraflores, Lima 18; tel. (1) 2557150; e-mail editoramesaredonda@gmail.com; internet editoramesaredonda.blogspot.com; f. 2005; literature, humanities; imprints incl. Mesa Redonda and Calcomanía; Dir JUAN MIGUEL MARTHANS.

Pontificia Universidad Católica del Perú, Fondo Editorial: Avda Universitaria 1801, San Miguel, Lima 32; tel. (1) 6262650; fax (1) 6262913; e-mail feditor@pucp.edu.pe; internet www.pucp.edu.pe; Dir-Gen. ANA PATRICIA ARÉVALO MAJLUF.

Sociedad Bíblica Peruana, AC: Avda Petit Thouars 991, Apdo 14-0295, Lima 100; tel. (1) 4336608; fax (1) 4336389; internet www

.casadelabiblia.org; f. 1821; Christian literature and bibles; Gen. Sec. Pedro Arana-Quiroz.

Universidad Nacional Mayor de San Marcos: Of. General de Editorial, Avda República de Chile 295, 5°, Of. 508, Lima; tel. (1) 4319689; internet www.unmsm.edu.pe; f. 1850; textbooks, education; Man. Dir Jorge Campos Rey de Castro.

PUBLISHING ASSOCIATIONS

Alianza Peruana de Editores (ALPE): Lima; tel. (1) 2759081; e-mail alianzaeditores@gmail.com; internet alpe.wordpress.com; f. 2007; independent publrs' asscn; Pres. Germán Coronado.

Cámara Peruana del Libro: Avda Cuba 427, esq. Jesús María, Apdo 10253, Lima 11; tel. (1) 4729516; fax (1) 2650735; e-mail cp-libro@amauta.rep.net.pe; internet www.cpl.org.pe; f. 1946; 102 mems; Pres. Carlos A. Benvides Aguije; Exec. Dir Loyda Morán Bustamante.

Broadcasting and Communications

TELECOMMUNICATIONS

Regulatory Authorities

Dirección General de Regulación y Asuntos Internacionales de Telecomunicaciones: Avda Jirón Zorritos 1203, Lima 1; tel. (1) 6185800; Dir-Gen. Patricia Carreño Ferré.

Instituto Nacional de Investigación y Capacitación de Telecomunicaciones (INICTEL): Avda San Luis 1771, esq. Bailetti, San Borja, Lima 41; tel. (1) 3461808; fax (1) 3464354; e-mail informes@inictel.gob.pe; internet www.inictel.gob.pe; Pres. Manuel Adrianzen.

Organismo Supervisor de Inversión Privada en Telecomunicaciones (OSIPTEL): Calle de la Prosa 136, San Borja, Lima 41; tel. (1) 2251313; fax (1) 4751816; e-mail sid@osiptel.gob.pe; internet www.osiptel.gob.pe; f. 1993; established by the Peruvian Telecommunications Act to oversee competition and tariffs, to monitor the quality of services and to settle disputes in the sector; Pres. Dr Guillermo Thornberry Villarán.

Major Service Providers

Claro Perú: Lima; internet www.claro.com.pe; f. 2005; owned by América Móvil, SA de SV (Mexico); mobile cellular telecommunications services; Gen. Dir Humberto Chávez.

Telefónica MoviStar: Juan de Arona 786, San Isidro, Lima; tel. (1) 9817000; internet www.telefonicamoviles.com.pe; f. 1994; 98% bought by Telefónica Móviles, SA (Spain) in 2000; mobile telephone services; 1.8m. customers.

Telefónica del Perú, SA: Avda Arequipa 1155, Santa Beatriz, Lima 1; tel. (1) 2101013; fax (1) 4705950; e-mail mgarcia@tp.com.pe; internet www.telefonica.com.pe; Pres. Antonio Carlos Valente.

Telmex: Torre Parque Mar, Avda Larco 1301, Miraflores, Lima; tel. (1) 6105555; internet www.telmex.com/pe.

BROADCASTING

Regulatory Authorities

Asociación de Radio y Televisión del Perú (AR&TV): Avda Roma 140, San Isidro, Lima 27; tel. (1) 4703734; Pres. Humberto Maldonado Balbín; Dir Daniel Linares Bazán.

Coordinadora Nacional de Radio: San Felipe 943, Jesús María, Lima 11; tel. (1) 4725252; fax (1) 4715808; e-mail postmaster@cnr.org.pe; internet www.cnr.org.pe; f. 1978; Pres. Hugo Ramírez Huamán; Exec. Dir Jorge Acevedo Rojas.

Instituto Nacional de Comunicación Social: Jirón de la Unión 264, Lima; Dir Hernán Valdizán.

Unión de Radioemisoras de Provincias del Perú (UNRAP): Mariano Carranza 754, Santa Beatriz, Lima 1.

State Corporation

Instituto Nacional de Radio y Televisión Peruana (IRTP): Avda Paseo de la República 1110, Lima 1; tel. (1) 471-8200; internet www.irtp.com.pe; f. 1996; Exec. Pres. Alfonso Salcedo Rubio; runs the following stations:

Radio Nacional del Perú: Avda Petit Thouars 447, Santa Beatriz, Lima 1; tel. (1) 4331404; fax (1) 4338952; internet www.radionacional.com.pe; state broadcaster; Man. Felipe Tomás Granados Vásquez.

Televisión Nacional del Perú (TV Perú): Lima; tel. (1) 6190707; internet www.tnp.gob.pe; f. 1958 as Radio y Televisión Peruana; state broadcaster; 22 stations; Commercial Man. Rodolfo Rusca Levano.

Radio

Radio Agricultura del Perú, SA—La Peruanísima: Casilla 625, Lima 11; tel. (1) 4246677; e-mail radioagriculturadelperu@yahoo.com; internet www.laperuanisima.com; f. 1963; Gen. Man. Luz Isabel Dextre Núñez.

Radio América: Montero Rosas 1099, Santa Beatriz, Lima 1; tel. (1) 2653841; fax (1) 2653844; f. 1943; Dir-Gen. Karen Crousillat.

Cadena Peruana de Noticias: Gral Salaverry 156, Miraflores, Lima; tel. (1) 4461554; fax (1) 4457770; e-mail webmastercpn@gestion.com.pe; internet www.cpnradio.pe; f. 1996; Pres. Manuel Romero Caro; Gen. Man. Oscar Romero Caro.

Radio Cutivalú, La Voz del Desierto: Jirón Ignacio de Loyola 300, Urb. Miraflores, Castilla, Piura; tel. (73) 343370; internet www.radiocutivalu.org; f. 1986; Pres. Francisco Muguiro Ibarra; Dir Rodolfo Aquino Ruiz.

Emisoras 'Cruz del Perú': Victorino Laynes 1402, Urb. Elio, Lima 1; tel. (1) 4521028; Pres. Fernando Cruz Mendoza; Gen. Man. Marco Cruz Mendoza M.

Emisoras Nacionales: León Velarde 1140, Lince, Lima 1; tel. (1) 4714948; fax (1) 4728182; Gen. Man. César Coloma R.

Radio Inca del Perú: Pastor Dávila 197, Lima; tel. (1) 2512596; fax (1) 2513324; f. 1951; Gen. Man. Abraham Zavala Chocano.

Radio Panamericana: Paseo Parodi 340, San Isidro, Lima 27; tel. (1) 4226787; fax (1) 4221182; internet www.radiopanamericana.com; f. 1953; Dir Raquel Delgado de Alcántara.

Radio Programas del Perú (GRUPORPP): Avda Paseo de la República 3866, San Isidro, Lima; tel. (1) 2150200; fax (1) 2150264; Pres. Hugo Delgado Nachtigal; Gen. Man. Manuel Delgado Parker.

Radio Santa Rosa: Jirón Camaná 170, Apdo 206, Lima; tel. (1) 4277488; fax (1) 4269219; f. 1958; Dir P. Juan Sokolich Alvarado.

Sonograbaciones Maldonado: Mariano Carranza 754, Santa Beatriz, Lima; tel. (1) 4715163; fax (1) 4727491; Pres. Humberto Maldonado B.; Gen. Man. Luis Humberto Maldonado.

Television

América Televisión, Canal 4: Jirón Montero Rosas 1099, Santa Beatriz, Lima; tel. (1) 2657361; fax (1) 2656979; e-mail web@americatv.com.pe; internet www.americatv.com.pe; Gen. Man. Marisol Crousillat.

ATV, Canal 9: Avda Arequipa 3570, San Isidro, Lima 27; tel. (1) 2118800; fax (1) 4427636; e-mail jdewerpe@atv.com.pe; internet www.atv.com.pe; f. 1983; Gen. Man. Marcello Cúneo Lobiano.

Frecuencia Latina, Canal 2: Avda San Felipe 968, Jesús María, Lima; tel. (1) 2191000; fax (1) 2656660; internet www.frecuencialatina.com.pe; Pres. Baruch Ivcher.

Global Televisión, Canal 13: Gen. Orbegoso 140, Breña, Lima; tel. (1) 3303040; fax (1) 4238202; f. 1989; Pres. Genaro Delgado Parker; Gen. Man. Rafael Leguía.

Nor Peruana de Radiodifusión, SA: Avda Arequipa 3520, San Isidro, Lima 27; tel. (1) 403365; fax (1) 419844; f. 1991; Dir Franco Palermo Ibarguengoitia; Gen. Man. Felipe Berninzón Vallarino.

Panamericana Televisión SA, Canal 5: Avda Alejandro Tirado 217, Santa Beatriz, Lima; tel. (1) 4113201; fax (1) 4703001; internet www.24horas.com.pe; Pres. Rafael Ravettino Flores; Gen. Man. Frederico Anchorena Vásquez.

Cía Peruana de Radiodifusión, Canal 4 TV: Mariano Carranza y Montero Rosas 1099, Santa Beatriz, Lima; tel. (1) 4728985; fax (1) 4710099; f. 1958; Dir José Francisco Crousillat Carreño.

RBC Televisión, Canal 11: Avda Manco Cápac 333, La Victoria, Lima; tel. (1) 4310169; fax (1) 4331237; Pres. Fernando González del Campo; Gen. Man. Juan Sáenz Marón.

Cía de Radiodifusión Arequipa SA, Canal 9: Centro Comercial Cayma, R2, Arequipa; tel. (54) 252525; fax (54) 254959; f. 1986; Dir Enrique Mendoza Núñez; Gen. Man. Enrique Mendoza del Solar.

Uranio, Canal 15: Avda Arequipa 3570, 6°, San Isidro, Lima; e-mail agamarra@atv.com.pe; Gen. Man. Adela Gamarra Vásquez.

Finance

In April 1991 a new banking law was introduced, relaxing state control of the financial sector and reopening the sector to foreign banks (which had been excluded from the sector by a nationalization law promulgated in 1987).

BANKING

(cap. = capital; res = reserves; dep. = deposits; m. = million; brs = branches; amounts in new soles unless otherwise indicated)

Superintendencia de Banca y Seguros: Los Laureles 214, San Isidro, Lima 27; tel. (1) 2218990; fax (1) 4417760; e-mail mostos@sbs.gob.pe; internet www.sbs.gob.pe; f. 1931; Supt FELIPE TAM FOX; Sec.-Gen. NORMA SOLARI PRECIADO.

Central Bank

Banco Central de Reserva del Perú: Jirón Antonio Miró Quesada 441-445, Lima 1; tel. (1) 4267041; fax (1) 4273091; e-mail webmaster@bcrp.gob.pe; internet www.bcrp.gob.pe; f. 1922; refounded 1931; cap. 295.7m., res 110.3m., dep. 39,030.5m. (Dec. 2006); Chair. JULIO VELARDE FLORES; Gen. Man. RENZO ROSSINI MIÑÁN; 7 brs.

Other Government Banks

Banco de la Nación: Avda República de Panamá 3664, San Isidro, Lima 1; tel. (1) 5192164; fax (1) 5192217; e-mail dep_ccorporativa@bn.com.pe; internet www.bn.com.pe; f. 1966; cap. 866.5m., res 336.4m., dep. 10,928.0m. (Dec. 2006); conducts all commercial banking operations of official govt agencies; Exec. Pres. HUMBERTO ORLANDO MENESES ARANCIBIA; Gen. Man. JULIO DEL CASTILLO VARGAS; 391 brs.

Corporación Financiera de Desarrollo (COFIDE): Augusto Tamayo 160, San Isidro, Lima 27; tel. (1) 6154000; fax (1) 4423374; e-mail postmaster@cofide.com.pe; internet www.cofide.com.pe; f. 1971; also owners of Banco Latino; Pres. AURELIO LORET DE MOLA BÖHME; Gen. Man. MARCO CASTILLO TORRES; 11 brs.

Commercial Banks

Banco de Comercio: Avda Paseo de la República 3705, San Isidro, Lima; tel. (1) 5136000; fax (1) 4405458; e-mail postmaster@bancomercio.com.pe; internet www.bancomercio.com; f. 1967; fmrly Banco Peruano de Comercio y Construcción; cap. 54.6m., res 0.3m., dep. 548.8m. (Dec. 2005); Chair. WILFREDO JESÚS LAFOSSE QUINTANA; Gen. Man. CARLOS ALBERTO MUJICA CASTRO; 23 brs.

Banco de Crédito del Perú: Calle Centenario 156, Urb. Las Laderas de Melgarejo, Apdo 12-067, Lima 12; tel. (1) 3132000; internet www.viabcp.com; f. 1889; cap. 1,286.5m., res 1,037.9m., dep. 37,071.7m., total assets 43,713.7m. (Dec. 2007); Pres. and Chair. DIONISIO ROMERO SEMINARIO; Gen. Man. WALTER BAYLY; 217 brs.

Banco Interamericano de Finanzas, SA: Avda Rivera Navarrete 600, San Isidro, Lima 27; tel. (1) 6133000; fax (1) 2212489; e-mail gchang@bif.com.pe; internet www.bif.com.pe; f. 1991; cap. 156.3m., res 11.7m., dep. 2,813.1m. (Dec. 2007); Pres. FRANCISCO ROCHE; Gen. Man. and CEO JUAN IGNACIO DE LA VEGA; 37 brs.

BBVA Banco Continental: Avda República de Panamá 3055, San Isidro, Lima 27; tel. (1) 2111000; fax (1) 2111788; internet www.bbvabancocontinental.com; f. 1951; merged with BBVA of Spain in 1995; 92.01% owned by Holding Continental, SA; cap. 852.9m., res 369.6m., dep. 16,445.2m. (Dec. 2006); Pres. and Chair. PEDRO BESCIA CAFFERATA; Gen. Man. JOSÉ ANTONIO COLOMER GUIU; 190 brs.

INTERBANK (Banco Internacional del Perú): Carlos Villarán 140, Urb. Santa Catalina, Lima 13; tel. (1) 2192347; fax (1) 2192336; e-mail krubin@intercorp.com.pe; internet www.interbank.com.pe; f. 1897; commercial bank; cap. 478.6m., res 117.6m., dep. 8,691.7m. (Dec. 2007); Chair. and Pres. CARLOS RODRÍGUEZ-PASTOR; Gen. Man. JORGE FLORES ESPINOZA; 90 brs.

Scotiabank Perú, SAA: Avda Dionisio Derteano 102, San Isidro, Apdo 1235, Lima; tel. (1) 2116060; fax (1) 4407945; e-mail scotiaenlinea@scotiabank.com.pe; internet www.scotiabank.com.pe; f. 2006 by merger of Banco Sudamericano (owned by Scotiabank, Canada) and Banco Wiese Sudameris; cap. 502.6m., res 1,353.6m., dep. 10,671.7m. (Dec. 2006); Chair. JIM MEEK; Vice-Pres. and CEO CARLOS GONZÁLEZ-TABOADA.

Banking Association

Asociación de Bancos del Perú: Calle 41, No 975, Urb. Córpac, San Isidro, Lima 27; tel. (1) 6123333; fax (1) 6123316; e-mail estudioseconomicos@asbanc.com.pe; internet www.asbanc.com.pe; f. 1929; refounded 1967; Pres. OSCAR JOSÉ RIVERA; Gen. Man. ENRIQUE ARROYO RIZO PATRÓN.

STOCK EXCHANGE

Bolsa de Valores de Lima: Pasaje Acuña 106, Lima 100; tel. (1) 6193333; fax (1) 4267650; internet www.bvl.com.pe; f. 1860; Pres. ROBERTO HOYLE.

Regulatory Authority

Comisión Nacional Supervisora de Empresas y Valores (CONASEV): Santa Cruz 315, Miraflores, Lima; tel. (1) 6106300; fax (1) 6106325; e-mail cendoc@conasev.gob.pe; internet www.conasev.gob.pe; f. 1968; regulates the securities and commodities markets; responsible to Ministry of Economy and Finance; Pres. NAHIL LILIANA HIRSH CARRILLO.

INSURANCE

ACE Seguros, SA: Avda Paseo de la República 3587, 10°, San Isidro, Lima; tel. (1) 4428228; fax (1) 422717; Chair. and CEO EVAN G. GREENBERG.

Interseguro Cía de Seguros, SA: Avda Pardo y Aliaga 640, 2°, San Isidro, Lima; tel. (1) 6114730; fax (1) 2223222; e-mail juan.vallejo@interseguro.com.pe; internet www.interseguro.com.pe; f. 1998; life; owned by Intergroup Financial Services (IFS); Chair. FELIPE MORRIS GUERINONI; CEO JUAN CARLOS VALLEJO BLANCO.

Invita Seguros de Vida, SA: Torre Wiese, Canaval y Moreyra 532, San Isidro, Lima; tel. (1) 2222222; fax (1) 2211683; e-mail dcosta@invita.com.pe; internet www.invita.com.pe; f. 2000; life; fmrly Wiese Aetna, SA; Pres. CARIDAD DE LA PUENTE WIESE; Gen. Man. JAVIER FREYRE TRIVELLI.

Mapfre Perú Cía de Seguros: Avda 28 de Julio 873, Miraflores, Apdo 323, Lima 100; tel. (1) 2137373; fax (1) 2433131; e-mail fmarco@mapfreperu.com; internet www.mapfreperu.com; f. 1994; general; fmrly Seguros El Sol, SA; Pres. RENZO CALDA GIURATO.

Pacífico, Cía de Seguros y Reaseguros: Avda Juan de Arona 830, San Isidro, Lima 27; tel. (1) 5184000; fax (1) 5184295; e-mail arodrigo@pps.com.pe; internet www.pacificoseguros.com; f. 1943; general; Pres. DIONISIO ROMERO SEMINARIO; Gen. Man. DAVID SAETTONE WATMOUGH.

La Positiva Cía de Seguros y Reaseguros, SA: San Francisco 301, Arequipa; tel. (54) 214130; fax (54) 214939; e-mail jaimep@lapositiva.com.pe; internet www.lapositiva.com.pe; f. 1947; Pres. JUAN MANUEL PEÑA ROCA; Gen. Man. GUILLERMO ZARAK.

Rimac Internacional, Cía de Seguros: Las Begonias 475, 3°, San Isidro, Lima; tel. (1) 4218383; fax (1) 4210570; e-mail jortecho@rimac.com.pe; internet www.rimac.com.pe; f. 1896; acquired Seguros Fénix in 2004; Pres. Ing. PEDRO BRESCIA CAFFERATA; Gen. Man. PEDRO FLECHA ZALBA.

SECREX, Cía de Seguro de Crédito y Garantías: Avda Angamos Oeste 1234, Miraflores, Lima; Apdo 0511, Lima 18; tel. (1) 4424033; fax (1) 4423890; e-mail ciaseg@secrex.com.pe; internet www.secrex.com.pe; f. 1980; Pres. Dr RAÚL FERRERO COSTA; Gen. Man. JUAN A. GIANNONI MURGA.

Insurance Association

Asociación Peruana de Empresas de Seguros (APESEG): Arias Araguez 146, Miraflores, Lima 18; tel. (1) 4442294; fax (1) 4468538; e-mail rda@apeseg.org.pe; internet www.apeseg.org.pe; f. 1904; Pres. RENZO CALDA GIURATO; Gen. Man. RAÚL DE ANDREA DE LAS CARRERAS.

Trade and Industry

GOVERNMENT AGENCIES

Agencia de Promoción de la Inversión Privada (ProInversión): Avda Paseo de la República 3361, 9°, San Isidro, Lima 27; tel. (1) 6121200; fax (1) 2212941; e-mail contact@proinversion.gob.pe; internet www.proinversion.gob.pe; f. 2002 to promote economic investment; Exec. Dir JORGE LEÓN BALLÉN; Sec.-Gen. GUSTAVO VILLEGAS DEL SOLAR.

Empresa Nacional de la Coca, SA (ENACO): Avda Arequipa 4528, Miraflores, Lima; tel. (1) 4442292; fax (1) 4471667; e-mail jjara@enaco.com.pe; internet www.enaco.com.pe; f. 1949; agency with exclusive responsibility for the purchase and resale of legally produced coca and the promotion of its derivatives; Pres. JULIO BALTAZAR JARA LADRÓN DE GUEVARA; Gen. Man. RAÚL CAMPANA RAMOS.

Fondo Nacional de Compensación y Desarrollo Social (FONCODES): Avda Paseo de la República 3101, San Isidro, Lima; tel. (1) 4212102; fax (1) 4214128; e-mail consultas@foncodes.gob.pe; internet www.foncodes.gob.pe; f. 1991; responsible for social devt and eradicating poverty; Exec. Dir CARLOS GERARDO ARANA VIVAR.

Instituto de Investigaciones de la Amazonía Peruana (IIAP): Avda Abelardo Quiñones Km 2.5, Apdo 784, Loreto; tel. (65) 265516; fax (65) 2265527; e-mail info@iiap.org.pe; internet www.iiap.org.pe; promotes sustainable devt of Amazon region; Pres. LUIS CAMPOS BACA.

Perúpetro, SA: Luis Aldana 320, San Borja, Lima; tel. (1) 6171800; fax (1) 6171801; e-mail mcobena@perupetro.com.pe; internet www.perupetro.com.pe; f. 1993; responsible for promoting investment in hydrocarbon exploration and exploitation; Chair. DANIEL SABA DE ANDREA; CEO ISABEL TAFUR MARÍN.

DEVELOPMENT ORGANIZATIONS

ACP Inversiones y Desarrollo: Avda Domingo Orue 165, 5°, Surquillo, Lima 34; tel. (1) 2220202; fax (1) 2224166; e-mail accion@accion.org.pe; f. 1969; fmrly Acción Comunitaria del Perú; promotes economic, social and cultural devt through improvements in service provision.

Asociación de Exportadores (ADEX): Avda Javier Prado Este 2875, San Borja, Lima 41; Apdo 1806, Lima 1; tel. (1) 6183333; fax (1) 6183355; e-mail prensa@adexperu.org.pe; internet www.adexperu.org.pe; f. 1973; exporters' asscn; Pres. JUAN MANUEL VARILIAS VELÁSQUEZ; Gen. Man. ALBERTO INFANTO ANGELES; 600 mems.

Asociación Kallpa para la Promoción Integral de la Salud y el Desarrollo: Pasaje Capri 140, Urb. Palomar Norte, La Victoria, Lima 13; tel. (1) 2243344; fax (1) 2429693; e-mail peru@kallpa.org.pe; internet www.kallpa.org.pe; health devt for youths; Pres. ALEJANDRINA ZAMORA PARIONA.

Asociación Nacional de Centros de Investigación, Promoción Social y Desarrollo: Belisario Flores, Lince, Lima 14; tel. (1) 4728888; fax (1) 4728962; e-mail postmaster@anc.org.pe; internet www.anc.org.pe; umbrella grouping of devt orgs; Pres. FRANCISCO SOBERÓN GARRIDO; Exec. Sec. IRIS CASTRO ORDÓÑEZ.

Asociación para la Naturaleza y Desarrollo Sostenible (ANDES): Calle Ruinas 451, Casilla 567, Cusco; tel. (8) 4245021; fax (8) 4232603; e-mail andes@andes.org.pe; internet www.andes.org.pe; devt org. promoting the culture, education and environment of indigenous groups; Exec. Dir CESAR ARGUMEDO.

Sociedad Nacional de Industrias (SNI) (National Industrial Association): Los Laureles 365, San Isidro, Apdo 632, Lima 27; tel. (1) 6164444; fax (1) 6164433; e-mail sni@sni.org.pe; internet www.sni.org.pe; f. 1896; comprises permanent commissions covering various aspects of industry including labour, integration, fairs and exhibitions, industrial promotion; its Small Industry Cttee groups over 2,000 small enterprises; Pres. PEDRO OLAECHEA; Gen. Man. FEDERICO DE APARICI; 90 dirs (reps of firms); 2,500 mems; 60 sectorial cttees.

Centro de Desarrollo Industrial (CDI): Los Laureles 365, San Isidro, Lima; tel. (1) 2158888; fax (1) 2158877; e-mail cdi@sni.org.pe; internet www.cdi.org.pe; f. 1986; supports industrial devt and programmes to develop industrial cos; Exec. Dir LUIS TENORIO PUENTES.

CHAMBERS OF COMMERCE

Cámara de Comercio de Lima (Lima Chamber of Commerce): Avda Giuseppe Garibaldi 396, Jesús María, Lima 11; tel. (1) 4633434; fax (1) 2191674; e-mail secreceex@camaralima.org.pe; internet www.camaralima.org.pe; f. 1888; Pres. CARLOS DURAND CHAHUD; Gen. Man. JOSÉ ROSAS BERNEDO; 5,500 mems.

Cámara Nacional de Comercio, Producción y Servicios (PERUCAMARAS): Giuseppe Garibaldi 396, 6°, Jesús María, Lima 11; tel. (1) 2191580; fax (1) 2191586; e-mail cnadministracion@perucam.com; internet www.perucam.com; national asscn of chambers of commerce; Pres. GUILLERMO VEGA ALVEAR; Gen. Man. MÓNICA M. WATSON ARAMBURÚ.

There are also Chambers of Commerce in Arequipa, Cusco, Callao and many other cities.

EMPLOYERS' ORGANIZATIONS

Asociación Automotriz del Perú: Avda Dos de Mayo 299, Apdo 1248, San Isidro, Lima 27; tel. (1) 6403636; fax (1) 4428865; e-mail aap@aap.org.pe; internet www.aap.org.pe; f. 1926; asscn of importers of motor cars and accessories; 360 mems; Pres. ARMANDO NEGRI PIÉROLA; Gen. Man. ENRIQUE PRADO REY.

Asociación de Ganaderos del Perú (Agalep) (Association of Stock Farmers of Peru): Pumacahua 877, 3°, Jesús María, Lima; f. 1915; Gen. Man. HÉCTOR GUEVARA.

Confederación Nacional de Instituciones Empresariales Privadas (CONFIEP): Edif. Real Tres, Of. 401, Avda Victor Andrés Belaúnde 147, San Isidro, Lima; tel. (1) 4223311; e-mail postmaster@confiep.org.pe; internet www.confiep.org.pe; f. 1984; federation of 20 employers' orgs; Pres. RICARDO BRICEÑO VILLENA; Gen. Man. XIMENA ZAVALA LOMBARDI.

Consejo Nacional del Café: Lima; reps of govt and industrial coffee growers; Pres. ENRIQUE ALDAVE.

Sociedad Nacional de Minería y Petróleo: Francisco Graña 671, Magdalena del Mar, Lima 17; tel. (1) 2159250; fax (1) 4601616; e-mail postmaster@snmpe.org.pe; internet www.snmpe.org.pe; f. 1940; asscn of cos involved in mining, petroleum and energy; Pres. HANS FLURY ROYLE; Gen. Man. CATERINA PODESTÁ MEVIUS.

Sociedad Nacional de Pesquería (SNP): Avda Javier Prado Oeste 2442, San Isidro, Lima 27; tel. (1) 2612970; fax (1) 2617912; e-mail snpnet@terra.com.pe; internet www.snp.org.pe; f. 1952; private sector fishing interests; Pres. RAÚL ALBERTO SÁNCHEZ SOTOMAYOR; Gen. Man. RICHARD INURRITEGUI BAZÁN.

STATE HYDROCARBONS COMPANY

Petroperú (Petróleos del Perú, SA): Avda Enrique Canaval Moreyra 150, Lima 27; tel. (1) 2117800; fax (1) 6145000; internet www.petroperu.com; f. 1969; state-owned petroleum-refining co; Pres. LUIS REBOLLEDO SOBERÓN; Gen. Man. MIGUEL CELI RIVERA.

MAJOR COMPANIES

The following is a selection of the principal industrial companies operating in Peru.

Metals, Mining and Petroleum

Compañía Barrick Misquichilca, SA: Avda Víctor Andrés Belaunde 171, 2°, San Isidro, Lima 27; tel. (1) 6124100; e-mail informacion@barrick.com; internet www.barrick.com; runs Lagunas Norte and Pierina gold mines; Chair. IGOR GONZÁLES.

Compañía de Minas Buenaventura, SA: Avda Carlos Villarán 790, Santa Catalina, La Victoria, Lima 13; tel. (1) 4192500; fax (1) 4717349; e-mail recursos@buenaventura.com.pe; internet www.buenaventura.com; f. 1953; mining of silver ores; sales of US $819m. (2009); Chair. ALBERTO BENAVIDES DE LA QUINTANA; Pres. and CEO ROQUE BENAVIDES; 1,400 employees.

Compañía Minera Antamina, SA: Avda el Derby 55, Santiago de Surco, Lima; tel. (1) 2173000; fax (1) 2173095; e-mail ascorp@antamina.com; internet www.antamina.com; mine produces copper, lead, zinc and molybdenum; owned by Xstrata (33.75%), BHP Biliton PlC (33.75%), Teck-Cominco Ltd (22.5%), Mitsubishi Corpn (10%); Pres. and CEO IAN KILGOUR; 1,528 employees world-wide (2007).

Compañía Minera del Madrigal, SA: Uno 950, Urb. Córpac, San Isidro, Lima 41; tel. (1) 2242382; fax (1) 4210012; f. 1967; copper-mining; Man. MIGUEL ACLEN; 760 employees.

Compañía Minera San Juan (Perú), SA (Nyrstar Coricancha): Baltazar La Torre 915, San Isidro, Lima 27; tel. (1) 2190500; fax (1) 2642942; internet www.nyrstar.com/nyrstar/en/operations/peru/coricancha; f. 1912; 85% owned by Nyrstar (Belgium); lead-, zinc- and arsenic-mining; CEO ROLAND JUNCK; 550 employees.

Compañía Rex, SA: Avda Alfreo Mendiola 1879, San Martín de Porres, Lima 31; tel. (1) 5342143; fax (1) 5342295; e-mail informes@ladrillosrex.com; internet www.ladrillosrex.com; f. 1958; brick production; Gen. Man. HUMBERTO ROSALES; 445 employees.

Corporación Aceros Arequipa, SA: Avda Enrique Meiggs 297, Parque Internacional de la Industria y Comercio, Callao, Lima; tel. (1) 5171800; fax (1) 4520059; internet www.acerosarequipa.com; f. 1966; iron and steel manufacturer; fmrly ACERSA; sales of 379m. new soles (2001); Exec. Pres. RICARDO CILLÓNIZ OBERTI; 792 employees.

Doe Run Peru: Torre Real 3, 9°, Avda Victor Andrés Belaúnde 147, Centro Camino Real, Lima 27; tel. (1) 2151200; internet www.doerun.com.pe; f. 1997 in Peru, after Doe Run Co bought Complejo Metalúrgico de La Oroya; subsidiary of Renco Holding Co (USA); Pres. and Gen. Man. JUAN CARLOS HUYHUA.

Empresa Siderúrgica del Perú (SIDERPERU): Avda Los Rosales 245, Santa Anita, Lima; tel. (1) 6186868; fax (1) 6186873; e-mail marketing@sider.com.pe; internet www.sider.com.pe; f. 1971; part of Gerdau Group; processing of steel; Exec. Man. ROBERTO DE BARROS; 4,195 employees.

Grupo Milpo, SA: San Borja Norte 523, Lima 41; tel. (1) 7105500; e-mail comunicaciones@milpo.com; internet www.milpo.com; f. 1946; lead-, silver- and zinc-mining; operates five mining units; sales of US $211.2m. (2008); Pres. IVO UCOVICH DORSNER; Gen. Man. ABRAHAM CHAHUAN A.; 314 employees.

Compañía Minera Atacocha, SA: Avda Javier Prado Oeste 980, San Isidro, Lima; tel. (1) 7105500; fax (1) 7105544; internet www.atacocha.com.pe; f. 1936; acquired by Grupo Milpo in 2008; lead- and zinc-mining; 1,270 employees.

Inca Pacific Resources Inc.: Comandante Jimenez 128, Magdalena Del Mar, Lima 17; tel. (1) 2641230; fax (1) 2640274; e-mail contact@incapacific.com; internet www.incapacific.com; exploits Magistral mine in Ancash; copper and molybdenum projects; Chair. ANTHONY FLOYD; Pres. and CEO JAMES ROTHWELL.

Pan American Silver Corporation: Avda La Floresta 497, Of. 301, Charcarilla del Estanque, San Borja, Lima; tel. (1) 6189700; fax (1) 6189729; e-mail info@panamericansilver.com; internet www.panamericansilver.com; f. 1994; silver- and zinc-mining; exploits Quiruvilca, Huarón and Morococha mines and the silver-rich stockpiles of Cerro de Pasco owned by Volcán Compañía Minera, SA (q.v.); Man. ENRIQUE RAMÍREZ.

Pluspetrol Perú Corporation, SA: Avda República de Panamá 3055, 8°, San Isidro, Lima; tel. (1) 4117100; fax (1) 4117120; e-mail rrhh-cv-peru@pluspetrol.net; internet www.pluspetrol.net; oil and gas exploration and production; Chair. and Pres. LUIS ALBERTO REY; Exec. Man. ROBERTO RAMALLO.

SAVIA Perú: Avda Rivera Navarrete 501, 11°, San Isidro, Lima; tel. (1) 5137500; fax (1) 4414217; e-mail ptp@petro-tech.com.pe; internet www.saviaperu.com; fmrly Petro-tech Peruana; renamed as above in 2009, following acquisition by Korean National Oil Corpn (Knoc) and Ecopetrol (Colombia); petroleum exploration and production; f. 1993, in Peru; Pres. BUM SUK-POO.

Shougang Hierro Perú, SA: Avda República de Chile 262, Jesús María, Lima 1; tel. (1) 7145200; fax (1) 3305136; e-mail lima@shp.com.pe; internet www.shougang.com.pe; f. 1993; owned by Shougang Corpn, People's Republic of China; mining, processing and shipment of iron ore; Pres. JHU ZIMIN; Gen. Man. WANG BAO JUN; 1,988 employees.

Southern Peru Copper Corporation (SPCC): Avda Caminos del Inca 171, Urb. Chacarilla del Estanque, Santiago de Surco, Lima 33; tel. (1) 5120440; fax (1) 5120492; internet www.southernperu.com; f. 1952; copper-mining; owned by Grupo México (54.1%), Cerro Trading Co, and Phelps Dodge; Chair. and CEO GERMÁN LARREA MOTA-VELASCO; 3,554 employees.

Volcán Compañía Minera, SA: Avda Giuseppe Garibaldi 710, Jésus María, Lima; tel. (1) 2194000; fax (1) 2619716; e-mail contact@volcan.com.pe; internet www.volcan.com.pe; f. 1943; lead-, zinc- and silver-mining; owns 495 mining concessions; Chair. ROBERTO LETTS COLMENARES; Gen. Man. JUAN JOSÉ HERRERA; 3,000 employees.

Food and Drink

Alicorp, SA: Calle Chinchón 980, San Isidro, Lima; tel. (1) 4422552; fax (1) 4216642; e-mail web@alicorp.com.pe; internet www.alicorp.com.pe; f. 1946; manufacturers of edible oils, lard and soaps; fmrly Compañía Oleaginosa del Perú, SA; part of Grupo Romero; Pres. DIONISIO ROMERO; Gen. Man. LESLIE PIERCE DIEZ CANSERO; 2,500 employees.

Alimentos Procesados, SA (Alprosa): Avda Pérez Aranibar, Variante de Uchumayo Km 1.5, Sachaca, Arequipa; tel. (54) 449473; fax (54) 449498; e-mail comercializacion@alprosa.com.pe; internet www.alprosa.com.pe; f. 1988; part of Corporación Cervesur; production and exportation of processed foods; Gen. Man. CARLOS PAREDES RODRÍGUEZ.

Coorporación Cervesur: Avda Alfonso Ugarte 521, Cercado, Arequipa; tel. (54) 205783; fax (54) 205784; internet www.corporacioncervesur.com.pe; f. 1898; agro-industrial products, foods, real estate, services, textiles, tourism, transport; Pres. ANDRÉS VON WEDEMEYER; 3,838 employees.

Empresa de la Sal, SA (EMSAL): Avda Nestor Gambetta, Km 8.5 Carretera Ventanilla, Callao; tel. (1) 5770669; fax (1) 5770685; internet www.quimpac.com.pe; f. 1969; acquired in 1994 by Quimpac; salt production; Chair. MARCOS FISHMAN; Gen. Man. JOSÉ CARLOS DE LOS RÍOS; 500 employees.

Flota Pesquera Peruana, SA (FLOPESCA): Avda Argentina 4090, Callao; tel. (1) 4299808; fax (1) 4640170; f. 1986; fishing co; Gen. Man. JORGE LAINES DE LA CRUZ; 564 employees.

Kraft Foods Perú: Avda Venezuela 2470, Lima 1; tel. (1) 3153000; fax (1) 4312093; e-mail alokraft.peru@kraftla.com; internet kraft.peru.com; f. 1864 as Arturo Field y La Estrella Ltda; adopted current name 2000; production of confectionery; Gen. Man. JULIÁN BALUK; 800 employees.

Nestlé Perú, SA (Perulac): Avda Los Castillos, Cuadra 3, Urb. Ind. Santa Rosa, Apdo 1457, Lima 1; tel. (1) 4364040; fax (1) 4361414; internet www.nestle.com.pe; wholly owned subsidiary of Nestlé Corpn (Switzerland); various foodstuffs; Chair. PETER BRABECK-LEMATHE; Exec. Vice-Pres. LUIS CANTARELL.

Unión de Cervecerías Peruanas Backus y Johnston, SA (Backus): Avda Nicolás Ayllón 3986, Ate Vitarte, Lima; tel. (1) 3113000; fax (1) 3113166; e-mail comunicaciones.externas@backus.sabmiller.com; internet www.backus.com.pe; f. 1879 as The Backus & Johnson Brewery Ltd; beverages and bottling corpn; subsidiary of SABMiller PLC (United Kingdom); Pres. ALEJANDRO SANTO DOMINGO DÁVILA; Gen. Man. ROBERT DAMIAN PRIDAY WOODWORTH; 1,457 employees.

Rubber and Cement

Cementos Lima, SA: Avda Atocongo 2440, Villa María del Triunfo, Lima; tel. (1) 2170200; fax (1) 2171496; e-mail info@cementoslima.com.pe; internet www.cementoslima.com.pe; f. 1967; cement producers; Pres. JAIME RIZO-PATRÓN; Gen. Man. CARLOS UGAS D.; 500 employees.

Lima Caucho, SA: Carretera Central 345–349, Km 1, Zona Industrial de Santa Anita, Lima 3; tel. (1) 3170500; fax (1) 3624069; e-mail spalomino@limacaucho.com.pe; internet www.limacaucho.com.pe; f. 1955; manufacturers of tyres and industrial rubber products; Dir CARLOS URIBE; 300 employees.

Textiles and Clothing

Compañía Industrial Nuevo Mundo, SA: Jirón José Celendón 750, Lima; tel. (1) 4154000; fax (1) 3366880; e-mail ventas@nuevomundosa.com; internet www.nuevomundosa.com; f. 1949; manufacturers of corduroy, denim and industrial fabrics; Pres. NISSIM MAYO; Gen. Man. JACQUES MAYO; 870 employees.

Creditex: Calle Los Hornos 185, Ate Vitarte, Urb. Vulcano, Casilla 2652, Lima 3; tel. (1) 3480491; fax (1) 3480488; e-mail postmaster@creditex.com.pe; internet www.creditex.com.pe; formed by merger of Hilanderías Pimafine, Textil Trujillo-Trutex, Credisa and Textil El Progreso; part of Corporación Cervesur; 8 textile production plants; Pres. ANDRÉS VON WEDEMEYER; Gen. Man. JOSÉ IGNACIO LLOSA.

Michell y Compañía, SA: Avda Juan de la Torre 101, San Lázaro, Arequipa; tel. (54) 202525; fax (54) 202626; e-mail michell@michell.com.pe; internet www.michell.com.pe; f. 1931; yarn mills; Exec. Pres. MICHAEL MICHELL STAFFORD; Gen. Man. MAURICIO CHIRINOS; 419 employees.

Universal Textil, SA: Avda Venezuela 2505, Apdo 554, Lima 1; tel. (1) 3375260; fax (1) 3375270; e-mail postmaster@unitex.com.pe; internet www.universaltextil.com.pe; f. 1952; manufacturers of synthetic fabrics for outerwear; part of Romero group; sales of 66.0m. nuevo soles (2003); Chair. DIONISIO ROMERO PAOLETTI; Gen. Man. FRANCISCO JAVIER SEMINARIO DE LA FUENTE; 850 employees.

Miscellaneous

Bayer, SA: Avda Paseo de la República 3074, 10°, San Isidro, Lima; tel. (1) 2113800; fax (1) 4213381; internet www.bayerandina.com; f. 1969; chemicals, plastics and pharmaceuticals manufacturer; sales of 121m. new soles (2001); Pres. DOMINIQUE DORISON; Gen. Man. CARLOS ENRIQUE CORNEJO DE LA PIEDRA; 150 employees.

Indeco, SA: Avda Universitaria 583, Lima 1; tel. (1) 2054800; fax (1) 2054802; e-mail ventas@indeco.com.pe; internet www.indeco.com.pe; f. 1952; manufacturers of electrical cables; Pres. JORGE ANDRÉS TAGLE OVALLE; Gen. Man. JUAN ENRIQUE RIVERA; 247 employees.

Industrias Eletro Químicas, SA (IEQSA): Avda Elmer Faucett 1920, Callao, Lima; tel. (1) 5724444; fax (1) 5720118; e-mail export@ieqsa.com.pe; internet www.ieqsa.com.pe; f. 1963; zinc production; sales of US $140m. (2006); Gen. Man. RAÚL MUSSO; Pres. CARLOS GLIKSMAN; 400 employees.

Ingenieros Constratistas Cosapi, SA: Nicolás Arriola 740, Lima 13; tel. (1) 2113500; fax (1) 2248665; e-mail postmaster@cosapi.com.pe; internet www.cosapi.com.pe; f. 1967; engineering and construction; Dir-Gen. WALTER PIAZZA TANGUIS; 4,350 employees.

Nissan Motors del Perú, SA: Avda Tomás Valle 601, San Martín de Porres, Lima 31; tel. (1) 5342248; fax (1) 5342326; e-mail webmaster@maquinarias.com.pe; internet www.nissan.com.pe; f. 1957 as Maquinarias, SA; subsidiary of Nissan Motors (Japan); automobile assembly plant; Man. CARLOS CHIAPPORI; 435 employees.

Procesos Agroindustriales, SA (Proagro): Avda Rivera Navarrete 525, 2°, Lima 27; tel. (1) 2218282; fax (1) 2213233; internet www.proagro.com.pe; f. 1990; part of Corporación Cervesur; agro-industrial manufacturers; Gen. Man. ANDRÉS JUAN JOCHAMOWITZ STAFFORD.

Químico-Papelero de Paramonga: Avda Nestor Gambetta 8585, Callao; tel. (1) 6142000; fax (1) 6142020; e-mail quimpac@quimpac.com.pe; internet www.quimpac.com.pe; f. 1898 as W. A. Grace—Sociedad Paramonga Ltda; pulp mills; Man. FERNANDO CARRANZA; 3,000 employees.

Tabacalera Nacional, SA: Avda Sancho de Rivera 1184, Monserrate, Lima 1; tel. (1) 3151060; fax (1) 3151067; internet www.batperu.com; f. 1964; acquired by British American Tobacco Peru Holdings Ltd in 2003; cigarette manufacturers; Country Man. DANTE ALBERTO CONETTA VIVANCO; 300 employees.

Unilever Andina Perú: Francisco Graña 155, Urb. Santa Catalina, La Victoria, Lima 13; tel. (1) 4111600; fax (1) 4111743; e-mail renzo.muente@unilever.com; internet www.unilever.com.pe; f. 1971; manufacturers of detergents, soaps, fats and vegetable oils; subsidiary of Unilever (United Kingdom/Netherlands); Gen. Man. RENZO MUENTE BARZOTTI; 675 employees.

UTILITIES

Regulatory Authority

Gerencia Adjunta de Regulación Tarifaria (GART): Avda Canadá 1470, San Borja, Lima 41; tel. (1) 2240487; fax (1) 2240491; internet www2.osinerg.gob.pe/gart.htm; autonomous agency controlling tariffs.

Electricity

Distriluz: Edif. Torre el Pilar, 13°, Avda Camino Real 348, San Isidro, Lima 27; tel. (1) 2115500; e-mail central@distriluz.com.pe; internet www.distriluz.com.pe; operates 4 energy distribution cos:

Enosa, Ensa, Hidrandina and Electrocentro; Dir GENARO VÉLEZ CASTRO; Gen. Man. MANUEL SUÁREZ MENDOZA.

Edegel (Empresa de Generación Eléctrica de Lima): Lima; e-mail comunicacion@edegel.com; internet www.edegel.com; privatized in 1995; generates electricity; Pres. BLANCO FERNÁNDEZ; Gen. Man. CARLOS ALBERTO LUNA CABRERA.

Electroperú: Prolongación Pedro Miotta 421, San Juan de Miraflores, Lima 29; tel. (1) 2170600; fax (1) 2170621; internet www.electroperu.com.pe; state-owned; Pres. LUIS ALEJANDRO BEDOYA WALLACE; Gen. Man. RAÚL TENGAN MATSUTAHARA.

EnerSur: Avda República de Panamá 3490, San Isidro, Lima 27; tel. (1) 6167979; fax (1) 6167878; e-mail contacto@enersur.com.pe; internet www.enersur.com.pe; f. 1996; part of Grupo GDF SUEZ; electricity generation and transmission; Gen. Man. PATRICK EECKELERS.

Sociedad Eléctrica del Sur-Oeste, SA (SEAL): Consuelo 310, Arequipa; tel. (54) 212946; fax (54) 213296; e-mail seal@seal.com.pe; internet www.seal.com.pe; f. 1905; Pres. MAURICIO CHIRINOS CHIRINOS; Gen. Man. JOSÉ OPORTO VARGAS.

Water

Autoridad Nacional del Agua: Calle Diecisiete 355, Urb. El Palomar, San Isidro, Lima; tel. (1) 2243298; fax (1) 2243298; e-mail comunicaciones@ana.gob.pe; internet www.ana.gob.pe; Dir FRANCISCO PALOMINO GARCÍA.

TRADE UNIONS

Central Unica de Trabajadores Peruanos (CUTP): Lima; f. 1992; Pres. JULIO CÉSAR BAZÁN; includes:

Confederación General de Trabajadores del Perú (CGTP): Plaza 2 de Mayo 4, Lima 1; tel. (1) 4242357; e-mail cgtp@cgtp.org.pe; internet www.cgtp.org.pe; f. 1968; Pres. CARMELA SIFUENTES INOSTROZA; Sec.-Gen. MARIO HUAMÁN RIVERA.

Confederación Intersectorial de Trabajadores Estatales (CITE) (Union of Public Sector Workers): Lima; tel. (1) 4245525; f. 1978; Sec.-Gen. ALAVARO COLE; Asst Sec. OMAR CAMPOS; 600,000 mems.

Confederación Nacional de Trabajadores (CNT): Avda Iquitos 1198, Lima; tel. (1) 4711385; affiliated to the PPC; c. 12,000 mems; Sec.-Gen. ANTONIO GALLARDO EGOAVIL.

Confederación de Trabajadores del Perú (CTP): Jirón Ayacucho 173, CP 3616, Lima 1; tel. (1) 4261310; e-mail ctp7319@hotmail.com; affiliated to PAP; Sec.-Gen. ELÍAS GRIJALVA ALVARADO.

Federación de Empleados Bancarios (FEB) (Union of Bank Employees): Jirón Miró Quesada 260, 7°, Lima; tel. (1) 7249570; e-mail febperu@terra.com.pe; Sec.-Gen. HÉCTOR PÉREZ PÉREZ.

Federación Nacional de Trabajadores Mineros, Metalúrgicos y Siderúrgicos (FNTMMS) (Federation of Peruvian Mineworkers): Jirón Callao 457, Of. 311, Lima; tel. (1) 4277554; Sec.-Gen. PEDRO ESCATE SULCA; 70,000 mems.

Movimiento de Trabajadores y Obreros de Clase (MTOC): Lima.

Sindicato de Estibadores: Callao; stevedores' union; Sec.-Gen. WILMER ESTÉVEZ.

Sindicato Unitario de los Trabajadores en la Educación del Perú (SUTEP) (Union of Peruvian Teachers): Camaná 550, Lima; tel. (1) 4276677; fax (1) 4268692; e-mail suteperu@yahoo.es; internet www.sutep.org.pe; f. 1972; Sec.-Gen. LUIS MUÑOZ.

Independent unions, representing an estimated 37% of trade unionists, include the Comité para la Coordinación Clasista y la Unificación Sindical, the Confederación de Campesinos Peruanos (CCP) and the Confederación Nacional Agraria (Pres. MIGUEL CLEMENTE ALEGRE).

Confederación Nacional de Comunidades Industriales (CONACI): Lima; co-ordinates worker participation in industrial management and profit-sharing.

The following agricultural organizations exist:

Confederación Nacional de Productores Agropecuarios de las Cuencas Cocaleras del Perú (CONPACCP): Lima; coca-growers' confederation; Sec.-Gen. NELSÓN PALOMINO.

Consejo Unitario Nacional Agrario (CUNA): f. 1983; represents 36 farmers' and peasants' orgs, including:

Confederación Campesina del Perú (CCP): radical left-wing; Pres. ANDRÉS LUNA VARGAS; Sec. HUGO BLANCO.

Organización Nacional Agraria (ONA): org. of dairy farmers and cattle breeders.

Transport

RAILWAYS

In 2010 there were some 2,020 km of track.

Ministry of Transport and Communications: see section on The Government (Ministries).

Consorcio Ferrocarriles del Perú: in July 1999, following the privatization of the state railway company, Empresa Nacional de Ferrocarriles (ENAFER), the above consortium won a 30-year concession to operate the following lines:

Empresa Minera del Centro del Perú SA—División Ferrocarriles (Centromín-Perú SA) (fmrly Cerro de Pasco Railway): Edif. Solgas, Avda Javier Prado Este 2175, San Borja, Apdo 2412, Lima 41; tel. (1) 4761010; fax (1) 4769757; acquired by Enafer-Perú in 1997; 212.2 km; Pres. HERNÁN BARRETO; Gen. Man. GUILLERMO GUANILO.

Ferrocarril Transandino, SA (Southern Railway): Avenida Tacna y Arica 200, Arequipa; tel. (54) 215350; fax (54) 231603; internet www.ferrocarriltransandino.com; 915 km open; operates Ferrocarril del Sur y Oriente; also operates steamship service on Lake Titicaca; Man. RÓMULO GUIDINO.

Ferrovías Central Andina, SA: Avda José Galvez Barrenechea 566, 5°, San Isidro, Lima; tel. (1) 2266363; e-mail ferroviasperu@fcca.com.pe; internet www.ferroviasperu.com.pe; f. 1999; operates Ferrocarril del Centro del Perú.

Tacna–Arica Ferrocarril (Tacna–Arica Railway): Avda Aldarracín 484, Tacna; 62 km open.

Private Railways

Ferrocarril Ilo–Toquepala–Cuajone: Apdo 2640, Lima; 219 km open, incl. five tunnels totalling 27 km; owned by the Southern Peru Copper Corpn for transporting copper supplies and concentrates only; CEO OSCAR GONZÁLEZ ROCHA; Gen. Dir, Operations MAURICIO PERÓ.

Ferrocarril Supe–Barranca–Alpas: Barranca; 40 km open; Dirs CARLOS GARCÍA GASTAÑETA, LUIS G. MIRANDA.

ROADS

There are an estimated 78, 500 km of roads in Peru, of which approximately 30% are paved or semi-paved. The most important highways are: the Pan-American Highway (3,008 km), which runs southward from the Ecuadorean border along the coast to Lima; Camino del Inca Highway (3,193 km) from Piura to Puno; Marginal de la Selva (1,688 km) from Cajamarca to Madre de Dios; and the Trans-Andean Highway (834 km), which runs from Lima to Pucallpa on the River Ucayali via Oroya, Cerro de Pasco and Tingo María.

SHIPPING

Most trade is through the port of Callao, but there are 13 deep-water ports, mainly in northern Peru (including Salaverry, Pacasmayo and Paita) and in the south (including the iron-ore port of San Juan). There are river ports at Iquitos, Pucallpa and Yurimaguas, aimed at improving communications between Lima and Iquitos, and a further port is under construction at Puerto Maldonado.

Agencia Naviera Maynas, SA: Avda San Borja Norte 761, San Borja, Lima 41; tel. (1) 4752033; fax (1) 4759680; e-mail lima@navieramaynas.com.pe; internet www.peruvianamazonline.com.pe; f. 1970; owned by the Naviera Yacu Puma, SA; liner services to and from Amazon river ports and Gulf of Mexico; Pres. LUIS VARGAS V.; Gen. Man. ROBERTO MELGAR B.

Asociación Marítima del Perú: Avda Javier Prado Este 897, Of. 33, San Isidro, Apdo 3520, Lima 27; tel. and fax (1) 4221904; internet www.asmarpe.org.pe; f. 1957; asscn of 20 int. and Peruvian shipping cos; Pres. JUAN JOSÉ SALMÓN BALESTRA; Gen. Man. GUILLERMO E. ACOSTA RODRÍGUEZ.

Consorcio Naviero Peruano, SA: Avda República de Colombia 643, 7° y 8°, San Isidro, Lima 27; tel. (1) 4116500; fax (1) 4116599; e-mail cnp@cnpsa.com; internet www.cnpsa.com; f. 1959.

Empresa Nacional de Puertos, SA (Enapu): Avda Contralmirante Raygada 110, Callao; tel. (1) 4299210; fax (1) 4691010; e-mail enapu@inconet.net.pe; internet www.enapu.com.pe; f. 1970; govt agency administering all coastal and river ports; Pres. MARIO ARBULÚ MIRANDA; Gen. Man. JOSE PABLO MEJÍA GONZALO.

Naviera Humboldt, SA: Edif. Pacífico–Washington, 9°, Natalio Sánchez 125, Apdo 3639, Lima 1; tel. (1) 4334005; fax (1) 4337151; e-mail postmast@sorcomar.com.pe; internet www.humboldt.com.pe; f. 1970; cargo services; Pres. AUGUSTO BEDOYA CAMERE; Man. Dir LUIS FREIRE R.

Naviera Universal, SA: Calle 41 No 894, Urb. Corpac, San Isidro, Apdo 10307, Lima 100; tel. (1) 4757020; fax (1) 4755233; Chair. HERBERT C. BUERGER.

Petrolera Transoceánica, SA (PETRANSO): San Isidro, Lima 27; tel. (1) 5139300; fax (1) 5139322; e-mail petranso@petranso.com; internet www.petranso.com; Gen. Man. JUAN VILLARÁN.

CIVIL AVIATION

Of Peru's 294 airports and airfields, the major international airport is Jorge Chávez Airport near Lima. Other important international airports are Coronel Francisco Secada Vignetta Airport, near Iquitos, Velasco Astete Airport, near Cusco, and Rodríguez Ballón Airport, near Arequipa.

Corporación Peruana de Aeropuertos y Aviación Comercial: Aeropuerto Internacional Jorge Chávez, Callao; tel. (1) 7081000; fax (1) 5745578; e-mail sugerencias@corpac.gob.pe; internet www.corpac.gob.pe; f. 1943; Pres. WALTER HUGO TELLO CASTILLO; Gen. Man. LUIS FELIPE VALLEJO LEIGH.

Domestic Airlines

Aero Condor: Juan de Arona 781, San Isidro, Lima; tel. (1) 4425215; fax (1) 2215783; internet www.aerocondor.com.pe; domestic services; Pres. CARLOS PALACÍN FERNÁNDEZ.

LAN Perú, SA: Lima; tel. (1) 2138200; internet www.lan.com; f. 1999; operations temporarily suspended in Oct. 2004; Exec. Vice-Pres. ENRIQUE CUETO P.

Star Peru: Avda Comandante Espinar 331, Miraflores, Lima 18; tel. (1) 7059000; fax (1) 3324789; e-mail atencionalcliente@starperu.com; internet www.starperu.com; f. 1997; operates services to eight domestic destinations; Gen. Man. ROMÁN KASIANOV.

Tourism

Tourism is centred on Lima, with its Spanish colonial architecture, and Cusco, with its pre-Inca and Inca civilization, notably the 'lost city' of Machu Picchu. Lake Titicaca, lying at an altitude of 3,850 m above sea level, and the Amazon jungle region to the north-east are also popular destinations. From the mid-1990s there was evidence of a marked recovery in the tourism sector, which had been adversely affected by health and security concerns. In 2007 Peru received 1,916,400 visitors. Receipts from tourism in 2008 generated an estimated US $1,991m.

Comisión de Promoción del Perú (PromPerú): Edif. Mitinci, Calle Uno Oeste, 13°, Urb. Corpac, San Isidro, Lima 27; tel. (1) 2243279; fax (1) 2243323; e-mail postmaster@promperu.gob.pe; internet www.peru.info; f. 1993; Head of Tourism MARÍA DEL PILAR LAZARTE CONROY; Gen. Man. MARÍA M. SEMINARIO MARÓN.

Defence

As assessed at November 2009, Peru's armed forces numbered 114,000: army 74,000, navy 23,000, air force 17,000. Paramilitary police forces numbered 77,000. There were 188,000 army reserves. Military service was selective and lasted for two years.

Defence Budget: 4,510m. new soles for defence and domestic security in 2009.

President of the Joint Command of the Armed Forces: Gen. FRANCISCO JAVIER CONTRERAS RIVAS.

Commander of the Army: Gen. OTTO NAPOLEÓN GUIBOVICH ARTEAGA.

Commander of the Air Force: Gen. CARLOS EDUARDO SAMAMÉ QUIÑONES.

Commander of the Navy: Adm. ROLAND ANTONIO NAVARRETE SALOMÓN.

Education

Education in Peru is based on a series of reforms introduced after the 1968 revolution. The educational system is divided into three levels: the first level is for children up to six years of age in either nurseries or kindergartens. Basic education is provided at the second level. It is free and, where possible, compulsory between six and 15 years of age. Primary education lasts for six years. Secondary education, beginning at the age of 12, is divided into two stages, of two and three years, respectively. In 2008 enrolment at primary schools included 94% of pupils in the relevant age-group, while secondary enrolment included 75% of students in the relevant age-group. Higher education includes the pre-university and university levels. There were 78 universities in 2000. There is also provision for adult literacy programmes and bilingual education. Total central government expenditure on education was estimated at 2.9% of GDP in 2000. Budget proposals for 2005 allocated some US $2,600m. to education.

Bibliography

For works on South America generally, see Select Bibliography (Books)

Alcade, M. C. *The Woman in the Violence: Gender, Violence, Poverty, and Resistance in Peru*. Nashville, TN, Vanderbilt University Press, 2010.

Arce, M. *Market Reform in Society: Post-crisis Politics and Economic Change in Authoritarian Peru*. University Park, PA, Pennsylvania State University Press, 2005.

Burt, J. M. *Political Violence and the Authoritarian State in Peru: Silencing Civil Society*. Basingstoke, Palgrave Macmillan, 2008.

Caistor, N., and Villaran, S. *Picking Up the Pieces: Corruption and Democracy in Peru*. London, Latin America Bureau, 2006.

Carrion, J. *The Fujimori Legacy: The Rise of Electoral Authoritarianism in Peru*. University Park, PA, 2006.

Conaghan, C. *Fujimori's Peru: Deception in the Public Sphere*. Pittsburgh, PA, University of Pittsburgh Press, 2005.

Cook, N. C. *Demographic Collapse: Indian Peru 1520–1620*. Cambridge, Cambridge University Press, 2002.

Crabtree, J., and Thomas, J. (Eds). *Making Institutions Work in Peru: Democracy, Development and Inequality Since 1980*. London, Institute for the Study of the Americas, 2006.

Gagliano, J. A. *Coca Prohibition in Peru: The Historical Debates*. Tucson, AZ, University of Arizona Press, 2010.

García-Bryce, I. *Crafting the Republic: Lima's Artisans and Nation-building in Peru, 1821–1879*. Albuquerque, NM, University of New Mexico Press, 2004.

Herz, M., and João Pontes, N. *Ecuador vs Peru: Peacemaking Amid Rivalry*. Boulder, CO, Lynne Rienner Publrs, 2002.

McClintock, C., and Vallas, F. *The United States and Peru*. London, Routledge, 2002.

Paredes, C., and Sachs, J. *Peru's Path to Recovery: A Plan for Economic Stabilization and Growth*. Washington, DC, Brookings Institution Press, 2004.

Parodi, J., and Conaghan, C. *To Be A Worker: Identity and Politics in Peru*. Chapel Hill, NC, University of North Carolina Press, 2000.

Peru Foreign Policy and Government Guide. New York, NY, International Business Publications, 2000.

Prescott, W. H. *History of the Conquest of Peru*. London, Phoenix Press, Revised edn, 2005.

Roberts, K. *Deepening Democracy?: The Modern Left and Social Movements in Chile and Peru*. Stanford, CA, University of California Press, 1999.

Rousseau, S. *Women's Citizenship in Peru: The Paradoxes of Neopopulism in Latin America*. Basingstoke, Palgrave Macmillan, 2009.

Silverblatt, I. *Modern Inquisitions: Peru and the Colonial Origins of the Civilized World*. Durham, NC, Duke University Press, 2004.

Skuban, W. E. *Lines in the Sand: Nationalism and Identity on the Peruvian-Chilean Frontier*. Albuquerque, NM, University of New Mexico Press, 2007.

Starn, O., Degregori, C., and Kirk, R. *The Peru Reader: History, Culture, Politics*. Durham, NC, Duke University Press, Revised edn, 2005.

Stern, S. *Shining and Other Paths: War and Society in Peru, 1980–95*. Durham, NC, Duke University Press, 1998.

Thorp, R., and Paredes, M. *Ethnicity and the Persistence of Inequality: The Case of Peru*. Basingstoke, Palgrave Macmillan, 2010.

Walter, R. J. *Peru and the United States, 1960-1975: How Their Ambassadors Managed Foreign Relations in a Turbulent Era*. University Park, PA, Pennsylvania State University Press, 2010.

PUERTO RICO

Geography

PHYSICAL FEATURES

The Commonwealth (Estado Libre Asociado) of Puerto Rico is a US territory based on the smallest and easternmost island of the Greater Antilles. Puerto Rico and its offshore islands comprise a Commonwealth Territory in voluntary association with the USA since 1952, but a colonial possession of the North American country since its military victory against Spain in 1898. Puerto Rico was also known as Borinquén by the Spanish, after the Amerindian name for the island, Boriquén or Boriken. To the east is more US territory, the island of St Thomas in the Virgin Islands being 64 km from the main island of Puerto Rico, although the Isla de Culebra and its own offshore islands lie mid-way between the two. About 15 km to the south-west of Culebra is Vieques, which itself only lies 11 km off the south-eastern coast of Puerto Rico island. In the west, Puerto Rico lies on the strategic Mona Passage, which separates it from the Dominican Republic on the island of Hispaniola. The two islands are only 120 km apart at the narrowest part of this sea lane from the Atlantic into the Caribbean. Their territories come closer only owing to Puerto Rico possessing the small, now uninhabited island of Mona (80 km west of the port of Mayagüez). Puerto Rico, which has 501 km of coastline and a number of fine, natural harbours, has an area about the same as that of Cyprus, at 8,959 sq km (3,459 sq miles), including about 145 sq km of inland waters.

The island of Puerto Rico is roughly rectangular in shape, with a missing south-eastern corner. It is almost 180 km in length (east–west) and nearly 60 km wide, an island of high, central peaks, surrounded by coastal lowlands, except in the west, where the mountains are sheer to the sea. The rugged mountain range, running from east to west, is known as the Cordillera Central and reaches 1,338 m (4,391 ft) at Cerro de Punta, north of the city of Ponce. Parts of the mountains are densely vegetated and there are fairly extensive protected woodland areas; for instance, there is the unique dry-forest vegetation at Guánica (700 plant species, of which 48 are endangered and 16 exist only there), or the main reserve on the island, the El Yunque tropical rainforest, which is a bird sanctuary and the home of the few remaining Puerto Rican parrots. In the 1930s about 90% of Puerto Rico was devoted to agriculture but, as a result of post-war industrialization, the rural population migrated and forest coverage grew from 10% in the 1940s to more than 40% at the turn of the 21st century; urban areas occupied 14% of the island. To the north of the Cordillera Central is a coastal belt, where the limestone has been formed into karst country of conical hills and holes by water erosion, very different to the ancient volcanic peaks. There are also many rock caverns, with the Camuy underground river system, the third largest such in the world. Rain-catching highlands, from which many small rivers spring (falling steeply to the sea, as waterfalls over cliffs in the more rugged terrain), ensure that the island is well watered.

The largest offshore island of Puerto Rico, and the first leading east into the chain of the Lesser Antilles, is Vieques. It is about 34 km long and 6 km wide, and in the past has also been called Graciosa and then Crab Island. Two-thirds of the hilly island was owned until May 2003 by the US Navy; upon the withdrawal of naval personnel, the land was ceded to the US Department of the Interior. To the north of the eastern end of Vieques, and directly east of north-eastern Puerto Rico, is Culebra and its cluster of smaller satellites, much of which is a nature reserve. Culebra, which bears a closer resemblance to the Virgin Islands, is some 11 km long and 5 km wide.

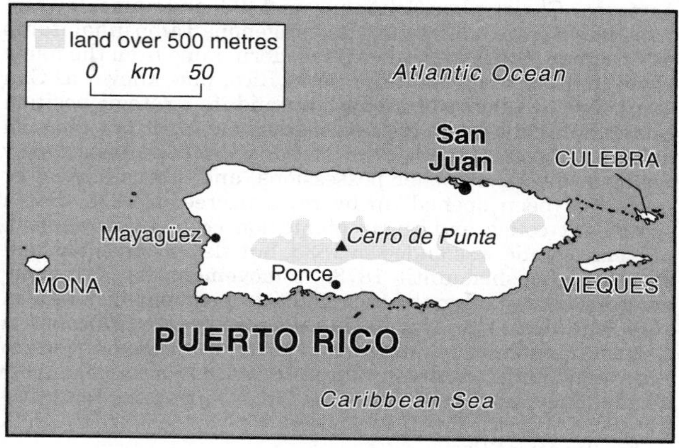

CLIMATE

The climate is a mild, subtropical marine one. The south of the island is often in the rain shadow of the central highlands, making it drier. Average annual rainfall is good, being about 2,300 mm (90 ins) on the north coast, and about one-half that on the south coast. Rain falls regularly from May, but mostly in July–October, which also coincides with the hurricane season—the word hurricane is derived from the name of the local Amerindian weather god, Juracan. There is little seasonal variation in temperature. Atlantic trade winds moderate the heat of the higher summer (July–August) averages of up to 30°C (86°F), while in winter the thermometer readings drop to a range of 21°C–26°C (70°F–79°F).

POPULATION

Racially, Puerto Rico has more in common with Latin America than the anglophone black West Indies. White people account for 80.5% of the total population, most of them being of Spanish descent, with blacks representing 8.0%, Amerindians 0.4% and Asians 0.2%; the remaining population is of mixed race. Another sign of the island's Spanish past is that Roman Catholics make up almost three-quarters of the total population, and there are few non-Christian religions on the island. Over one century of rule by the USA, however, has had a significant impact on the culture, not least that English has joined Spanish as an official language.

The total population of 4.0m. at mid-2010 (UN estimate) was about 80% urbanized. The capital, San Juan (with an estimated population of 420,326 in mid-2009), has one of the best natural harbours in the Caribbean. It is located in the north-east of Puerto Rico, about one-third of the way along the northern coast. Traditionally, the second city is Ponce (named for Juan Ponce de León, the Spanish nobleman who led the colonization of the island and who sought the mythical fountain of eternal youth here), on the south coast, and the third city Mayagüez, on the west coast. The territory is divided into 78 municipalities for local administration.

History

Prof. PETER CALVERT

INTRODUCTION

Puerto Rico was discovered by a Spanish expedition, led by the navigator Christopher Columbus, in 1493, and named by him San Juan Bautista. Known to its indigenous Taino inhabitants as Boriquén, the island takes its modern name from the name given in 1509 to its capital, Puerto Rico, now known as San Juan. The excellence of its harbour and its strategic position commanding the Mona Passage made it an important Spanish military outpost. However, the island tended to be neglected by Spain in favour of richer possessions, and it was only after trade had been opened up by royal decree in 1815 that a significant coffee and sugar plantation economy developed. The slave trade was ended in 1835, but slavery on the island was not abolished until 1873. A movement for autonomy emerged slowly after the change of government in Spain in 1868, but it was not until 1897 that Spain granted its colony a Carta Autonómica (Autonomy Charter). However, Puerto Rico's new-found autonomy abruptly ended just a year later when, following its capture by US forces during the Spanish–American War, the Caribbean possession was ceded to the USA by the Treaty of Paris.

In 1900 the island was reorganized as a US Territory and a civil government replaced the military government that had ruled since 1898. As a Territory, Puerto Rico became subject to most laws of the US Congress, and the US President appointed the Governor and members of the island's Executive Council, which functioned as an upper house of the legislative branch, the lower house being elected by popular vote. In 1917 Congress extended US citizenship to the island's inhabitants over the objections of the island's lower house, and provided for the popular election of the members of an upper house or Senate. The island's Governor, however, continued to be appointed by the US President.

Further internal self-government was achieved under President Harry S Truman in 1947, when Congress approved a law giving the people of Puerto Rico the right to elect their own Governor; a year later they chose as their first elected Governor the charismatic Luis Muñoz Marín. Now recognized as the 'father of modern Puerto Rico', it was he who persuaded the US Government to approve and in large measure to fund 'Operation Bootstrap' (see Economy), a programme to industrialize Puerto Rico and raise its standard of living. In 1950, in yet another move towards greater internal autonomy, Congress approved Public Law 600, allowing Puerto Rico to draft its own constitution, although this was subject to congressional review. This process culminated in 1952, when, in a special referendum, the people of Puerto Rico approved the island's first Constitution under US rule. Puerto Rico was given the status of a Commonwealth (in Spanish Estado Libre Asociado, or associated free state) in its relation to the USA, and the following year, 1953, the island became self-governing. Although Puerto Rico gained wide powers of organization over its internal affairs, it has remained US sovereign territory and most federal laws have continued to apply to it, with the important exception of taxation. Critics maintain that Commonwealth status, although more liberal than earlier forms of US rule, affords fewer powers of self-government than Puerto Rico enjoyed under Spain's Carta Autonómica.

DOMESTIC POLITICS

Since 1898 Puerto Ricans have been divided on the question of the island's political relationship with the USA. The island's two dominant parties both favour continued strong links with the USA. The Partido Popular Democrático (PPD—Popular Democratic Party) supports the existing Commonwealth status with 'enhancements', such as greater autonomy, while the Partido Nuevo Progresista (PNP—New Progressive Party) favours Puerto Rico's inclusion as a US state. The island's third party, the smaller Partido Independentista Puertorriqueño (PIP—Puerto Rican Independence Party) campaigns for independence, which in recent years has commanded the support of only some 3% of the population.

Historically, various clandestine, pro-independence forces have operated in Puerto Rico outside the electoral process. During the 1940s and 1950s the most influential of these groups was the Partido Nacionalista (Nationalist Party), led by the charismatic Pedro Albizu Campos. The Partido Nacionalista was responsible for an uprising in Puerto Rico in 1950, involving an armed attack on La Fortaleza, and a simultaneous, but unsuccessful attempt on the life of President Truman in Washington, DC. It also launched an armed attack during a session of the US House of Representatives on 1 March 1954. In the 1970s another pro-independence group, the Partido Socialista Puertorriqueño (PSP—Puerto Rican Socialist Party) succeeded in raising the question of Puerto Rico's status before the UN's Decolonization Committee and the Conference of Non-Aligned Nations. With the active participation of Cuba, the Decolonization Committee approved a resolution recognizing Puerto Rico's inalienable right to self-determination and independence. However, the USA was able to prevent the UN General Assembly from returning Puerto Rico to the list of political dependencies from which it had been removed in 1953, following the approval of the Commonwealth Constitution. In the early 1980s the most important clandestine pro-independence group was the Ejército Popular Boricua (Puerto Rican Popular Army), known as 'Los Macheteros'. This group claimed responsibility for armed attacks in the USA and Puerto Rico against military targets. However, in 1985 the group fragmented, following a series of raids by the US Federal Bureau of Investigation (FBI), in both Puerto Rico and the USA. Seventeen members of Los Macheteros, including most of its leadership, were arrested and imprisoned. Its most important leader, Filiberto Ojeda Ríos, escaped, but was killed by FBI agents in an exchange of gunfire in September 2005, although his group had not been active recently. Other insurgent and dissident groups active from time to time have included the Armed Forces for National Liberation (FALN), the Armed Forces of Popular Resistance and the Volunteers of the Puerto Rican Revolution.

The PPD, under the leadership of Muñoz Marín, dominated Puerto Rican electoral politics from 1940 to 1968; he voluntarily retired from the leadership of the party in 1964, after serving four terms as Governor. He nominated his successor, Roberto Sánchez Vilella, who was elected Governor in 1964. A division in the PPD allowed the gubernatorial candidate of the newly formed PNP, Luis A. Ferré, to win the governorship in 1968. In the 1972 gubernatorial election the PPD returned to power under the leadership of Senate President Rafael Hernández Colón. He was defeated in 1976 by the PNP Mayor of San Juan, Carlos Romero Barceló. Romero Barceló won again in 1980. The PPD, however, won a majority in both the House of Representatives and the Senate, thus preventing Romero Barceló from holding a referendum to determine whether people favoured US statehood for Puerto Rico.

During 1981 dissatisfaction with Romero Barceló's leadership developed. The murder of two independence activists, allegedly by Puerto Rican police, brought into question the role of Governor Romero Barceló in the affair. He faced additional problems from his own party when the Mayor of San Juan, Hernán Padilla Ramírez, left the PNP over the issue of internal party democracy and formed a new political grouping, the Partido de Renovación Puertorriqueño (PRP—Puerto Rican Renewal Party). Padilla entered the 1984 gubernatorial election as the PRP candidate and received about 4% of the total votes cast. The division in the PNP was enough to ensure the election of former Governor Hernández Colón, the PPD candidate.

The Mayor of San Juan, Baltasar Corrada del Río, assumed control of the PNP following Romero Barceló's electoral defeat in 1984. He was the party's candidate in the 1988 election, but was defeated by Hernández Colón. For the first time in 20 years the PNP lost its traditional bastion of power, the island's capital city of San Juan, to the PPD candidate, Héctor Luis Acevedo. At his third gubernatorial inauguration, Hernández Colón announced that he would seek congressional approval for a status referendum to be held in mid-1991; subsequently, the leaders of the island's three political parties formally petitioned the US Congress to approve legislation to authorize and implement such a referendum. In late 1989, after the US House of Representatives had approved a non-binding status plebiscite bill for Puerto Rico, the US Senate's Energy and Natural Resources Committee, which had jurisdiction in the Senate over territorial matters, defeated the proposed legislation in a dramatic tied vote, thus ending the decolonization initiative. In Puerto Rico the defeat of the plebiscite measure was attributed to the reluctance of the US Congress to approve legislation that could lead to statehood for Puerto Rico.

Following the defeat of the status legislation in the US Congress, Hernández Colón's administration, which held a majority in both legislative chambers, introduced legislation establishing a charter of 'democratic rights'. The charter included guarantees of US citizenship regardless of future changes in the island's constitutional status, and made Spanish the only official language of Puerto Rico, abrogating a 1902 law that had established both Spanish and English as the island's official languages—by this time one-fifth of the inhabitants had English as their first language. The PPD also approved legislation, opposed by the PNP, to hold a plebiscite to amend the island's Constitution by adding six 'principles of self-determination'. The electorate rejected the proposed amendment with 54% voting against. The referendum represented a major defeat for Governor Hernández Colón, and a victory for the new PNP leader, Dr Pedro J. Rosselló, a 48-year-old physician and formerly prominent tennis player. On 8 January 1992, one year before his gubernatorial term expired, Hernández Colón resigned as leader of the PPD, a position that he had occupied almost continuously since 1969. He was succeeded by Victoria Muñoz Mendoza, the daughter of former Governor Luis Muñoz Marín.

In the 1992 election campaign the pro-statehood PNP candidate, Rosselló, pledged to hold a referendum on the three traditional status options: statehood, enhanced Commonwealth or independence. Rosselló secured 50% of the votes cast in the November ballot, defeating Muñoz Mendoza, who won 46% of the ballot. At the same time, the PNP won control of both the Senate and the House of Representatives, as well as 58 of the island's 78 municipalities. The PPD had suffered a major political reverse.

THE STATUS ISSUE

Upon taking office in January 1993, the first bill passed by the PNP-dominated legislature restored English as an official language. Rosselló strove to fulfil his promise to reduce crime by mobilizing the National Guard in several low-income residential areas of San Juan with high crime rates. He also moved to privatize the island's public health system by subsidizing private health insurance for the poor and selling or renting out the Government's health care facilities. Legislation presented by Rosselló to enable a status plebiscite to be held was overwhelmingly endorsed in the island legislature: on 14 November, 48.6% of the electorate voted for the retention of Commonwealth status, 46.3% supported statehood and 4% advocated independence; some 73% of registered voters participated. The results were disappointing for the governing PNP, which had hoped to win a mandate to urge the US Congress to grant the island statehood. Those in favour of continued Commonwealth status, which included the PPD, were equally disappointed that their formula had not received a clear majority and shocked to see their share of the vote, approximately 60% in the 1967 plebiscite, decline to less than 50%. In the 1996 election Rosselló was re-elected by an even greater margin than in 1992, with 51% of the votes cast, compared with 44% for the PPD's Héctor Acevedo. The PNP retained control of both houses of the island legislature and won 54 of the 78 island municipalities.

In November 1994 the Republicans won control of both the US House of Representatives and the Senate. In the following year a bill was introduced that required Puerto Rico to hold periodic plebiscites until the issue of the island's status was resolved. The legislation was withdrawn in 1996 at the insistence of the Resident Commissioner, Romero Barceló, after it had been amended to make English the sole official language of a future US state of Puerto Rico. It was revived in 1997, but was opposed by the PPD, owing to the bill's categorization of the Commonwealth as a territory of the USA. The PPD argued that when the Commonwealth was established in 1952, Puerto Rico ceased to be a colonial dependency of the USA, an interpretation that has been continually challenged by both the PNP and the PIP. In 1998, however, the US House of Representatives passed the bill by one vote. The law authorized a plebiscite to be held that year to allow Puerto Rico to choose between Commonwealth status, independence and statehood. In the event of the electorate voting for the Commonwealth formula, a plebiscite was to be held every 10 years until the island chose either independence or statehood. However, the US Senate leadership opposed the plebiscite and the bill was not voted on in the upper house. Subsequently, Governor Rosselló held another Puerto Rican-sponsored plebiscite in December, which allowed a choice between five options: maintaining the existing Commonwealth status, defined as territorial; independence; statehood; free association with the USA (whereby the USA would yield sovereignty over Puerto Rico); or 'none of the above'. The PPD campaigned for the last of the five options, 'none of the above', which won the plebiscite with 50.2% of the vote, compared with 46.5% in favour of statehood, 2.5% in favour of independence, and less than 1% supporting free association or the existing Commonwealth status.

In June 2000, at the insistence of Rosselló, US President Bill Clinton (1993–2001) met with representatives of the island's three major political parties to discuss a new formula for resolving the status issue. However, the Republican congressional leadership boycotted the meeting. In November Sila María Calderón Serra of the PPD, who had been elected mayor of San Juan in 1996, became the first woman to be elected Governor of Puerto Rico. Aníbal Acevedo Vilá of the PPD was elected to the post of Resident Commissioner with 49% of the votes cast, defeating the incumbent, Romero Barceló. The PPD also gained control of the Senate, the House of Representatives and 46 of the island's 78 municipalities. The simultaneous election of the Republican President George W. Bush and a Republican majority in both houses of the US Congress blocked further moves on the status issue. In July 2002 Governor Calderón announced the creation of a 'status committee' to resolve the issue; the committee was to consist of representatives of the PPD, PNP and PIP, including former Governors Hernández Colón and Romero Barceló. However, the PNP leadership rejected the proposal and the status issue continued to divide local politicians.

VIEQUES

In April 1999 a US navy bomb accidentally fell on an observation tower on the small island of Vieques, which lies off the eastern coast of Puerto Rico, killing a Puerto Rican civilian who worked for the US Navy. Since the end of the Second World War the US Navy had been using most of Vieques as a live firing range, although it was also home to some 10,000 civilian inhabitants. (It was also used as the scene of military exercises, notably those that preceded the US intervention in Grenada in 1983.) The death prompted angry public protests in Puerto Rico, which ultimately led to the illegal occupation of the firing range and widespread demands for the Navy to leave Vieques. In January 2000 Rosselló reached an agreement with President Clinton to allow the Navy to continue bombing practice with inert or dummy ordnance until a referendum had been held on Vieques to determine whether the Navy should stay and renew live bombing practice, or leave the island altogether by May 2003. The US Administration was also to provide immediate development aid to Vieques of US $40m., which would increase to $90m. if residents agreed to the resumption of live ammunition testing. In return, Rosselló promised to help the federal authorities remove the protesters, who had been occupying the firing range since the bombing incident. In May 2000, in anticipation of the recommencement of (dummy) ammunition testing, protests were held on Vieques. US Federal Government agents were deployed to forcibly remove the protesters. Further protests were held throughout that year.

Governor Calderón owed her success in 2000 in part to denouncing corruption in the Rosselló administration and also to her promise to resolve the Vieques question. While mayor of San Juan, Calderón had questioned Rosselló's Vieques agreement with President Clinton and, following her election as Governor, she renounced the agreement and called for the immediate withdrawal of the US Navy from the island, claiming that bombing over the years had caused serious health problems for the residents.

Military exercises resumed on the island in May 2001. Following legal challenges and protests, operations were suspended, but they resumed in June, prompting further protests. In July President Bush announced that the US Navy would leave the island by May 2003, as planned. However, a non-binding referendum on the issue, organized by the Calderón Government, took place on 29 July, in which 68% of islanders voted for an immediate cessation of bombing. The US Navy's activities received endorsement from only 2% of voters. The binding referendum, agreed by Rosselló and Clinton in 2000, was still scheduled to take place in November, but was eventually cancelled by the US Congress, which ordered the US military to remain on the island, claiming that further tests were necessary as part of the Bush Administration's 'war on terror'.

Tests resumed in April 2002, amid protests from members of the PIP. The US Navy carried out its final bombing exercises in February 2003 and withdrew from Vieques on 1 May, as promised. On that date, the Navy announced the end of its tenure on Vieques, ceding the land it owned to the US Department of the Interior to become a wildlife reserve. The Puerto Rican Government subsequently negotiated with the US Navy over cleaning up the island: after decades of bombing, contamination by heavy metals and other pollutants was identified in some two dozen sites. The base had provided jobs for around 2,000 people locally and contributed some US $300m. to the Puerto Rican economy. To compensate for the loss in tax revenue, the US Government was to pay $1.2m. per year to each of the municipalities during a period of redevelopment. The establishment of a local redevelopment authority meant that Vieques also qualified for federal redevelopment aid. Beyond more general proposals to encourage recreation and ecotourism, there were also plans to convert the base hospital and airport facilities for civilian use. The last remaining base, at Ceiba, was closed on 31 March 2004. The US Navy budgeted $76m. to clean Vieques up during 2006–09.

THE STATUS ISSUE REVIVES

In the gubernatorial election of November 2004, the PPD's candidate was Aníbal Acevedo Vilá, the island's delegate to the US Congress, while the PNP's nominee was former Governor Rosselló. The result was as close as the election of 1980. It led to a recount and a court challenge, but on 2 January 2005 Acevedo Vilá was officially declared the winner, taking office the same day. However, in the ballot to elect Puerto Rico's non-voting delegate in the US Congress, the pro-statehood PNP candidate, Luis G. Fortuño Burset, won. Rosselló's PNP also took control of the legislature from the PPD. Rosselló himself won a seat in the Senate.

Governor Acevedo Vilá initially promised to co-operate with opposition leaders. Then, in mid-March 2005, he presented budget proposals for 2006 that included a spending reduction of US $370m. and the elimination of some 23,000 government jobs. The proposals were rejected by the House of Representatives. After some delay, an alternative budget was proposed by the legislature, but was vetoed by the Governor in August, the first time that this had happened in the history of the Commonwealth. Consequently, by April 2006 the Governor had to announce that there were insufficient funds to continue the business of government. When the House rejected his request to raise a temporary loan of $500m. in May, Acevedo Vilá closed schools and government agencies, leading to popular protest. Within two weeks a temporary agreement was negotiated with legislative leaders. However, the ongoing confrontation, which had led to the Commonwealth's debt being downgraded, had done nothing to resolve the dilemma faced by successive governments of a stagnant economy where most residents were directly or indirectly dependent on the Government (see Economy).

Meanwhile, in March 2005 there had been widespread opposition to the decision by the US Territorial District Court of Puerto Rico (a Federal Court) to impose the death sentence on two convicted murderers. Capital punishment had been banned in the Territory in 1930, a decision that had been upheld in 2000 by a ruling of the Supreme Court of Puerto Rico that it violated the island's Constitution. However, the ruling was subsequently overturned by the US Court of Appeals, which found that Puerto Rico was subject to US federal law and that the death penalty was applicable in certain cases; this decision was upheld by the US Supreme Court. In April 2005 Acevedo Vilá wrote to the US Attorney-General requesting that the death penalty should not apply to residents of Puerto Rico. In May the jury serving on the trial moved to sentence the two men to life imprisonment. Social violence remained a problem in the island, which, according to official figures, had 802 murders in 2008.

Acevedo Vilá had promised to summon a constitutional assembly to discuss Puerto Rico's status in 2005. He favoured maintaining the Commonwealth system with changes to allow for greater autonomy, particularly in economic development. Following the 2004 election members of the island's main political parties agreed a tripartite status bill. The proposed legislation scheduled a referendum for 10 July 2005, when Puerto Rican voters would vote for or against a petition urging the US Congress and President to provide Puerto Rico with 'non-colonial and non-territorial' status options and to pledge that the results would be honoured. Although the legislation was approved by both chambers, Acevedo Vilá refused to sign it. A hastily prepared substitute bill included an amendment stating that the US Congress was fully committed to legislation that would allow the Puerto Rican electorate to choose a mechanism to determine status, either by means of a constituent assembly or through a request for a direct congressionally binding referendum, in the event that the US Government did not commit itself to a process of free self-determination before the end of 2006. Although it was unanimously approved by the Puerto Rican congress on 10 April, that legislation was also vetoed by Acevedo Vilá as 'deceptive', because it did not guarantee that the method favoured by the Governor would be adopted.

In December 2005 a US presidential task force called for the US Congress to authorize a binding referendum on the status of Puerto Rico. At the time, this proposal was not accepted and in March 2006 Congress also rejected an appeal to allow the island's inhabitants to vote in US presidential elections. However, following the 2006 elections, the US House of Representatives again took up the status issue, under pressure as it was to address the problem of an estimated 12m. illegal immigrants in the USA. Sponsored by José Serrano, a New York Democratic representative, and Luis Fortuño, the Republican Resident Commissioner for Puerto Rico, the proposed Puerto Rico Democracy Act of 2007 would establish a two-stage plebiscite process. Islanders would choose first between maintaining their current Commonwealth status or assuming a 'permanent non-territorial status' and, in a second vote, between statehood and some form of independence. Ratification of Acevedo Vilá's preferred option, a permanent, 'enhanced Commonwealth' status, was considered improbable, since it would allow Puerto Ricans to enter into trade and tax agreements with third party countries and even waive certain federal laws. The Puerto Rico Self-Determination Act of 2007, that would empower Puerto Ricans from both the territory and diaspora to formulate their own system for determining Puerto Rico's future status, was submitted for consideration by the US Congress simultaneously with the Puerto Rico Democracy Act.

In February 2008 Acevedo Vilá endorsed Senator Barack Obama as Democratic candidate for the US presidency, giving the candidate key support from one of the island's super-delegates in a close fight for the Democratic presidential nomination. The Governor said he chose Obama because the Illinois senator supported a process of resolving Puerto Rico's relationship to the USA that was also favoured by the PPD. The presidential nominee had already promised to respect Puerto Ricans' decisions about their own future and accepted Commonwealth status, statehood and independence as valid options.

In March 2008 Governor Acevedo Vilá and 12 associates were accused of improper financial dealings and tax fraud, following an FBI investigation. The Governor denied the 19 criminal charges brought against him, which related to electoral campaigns during 1999–2004, and reiterated his plan to seek re-election in November. However, the charges were still outstanding at the time of the gubernatorial election in November 2008, in which Luis Fortuño (PNP) was elected Governor with 1,025,945 (52.8%) votes against only 801,053 (41.3%) for the incumbent. Rogelio Figueroa García of Partido Puertorriqueños por Puerto Rico (PPR—Puerto Ricans for Puerto Rico), received 53,690 votes (2.8%) and there were 12,215 write-in votes for former Governor Pedro Rosselló. He had been defeated in his party's primary election by Fortuño. The post of Resident Commissioner in Washington was won in the concurrently held general election by Pedro Pierluisi, also of the PNP. In March 2009 a federal jury found former Governor Acevedo Vilá not guilty on nine counts of conspiracy, giving false statements and wire fraud.

On 29 April 2009 Governor Fortuño presented his first budget in which he proposed to address the Commonwealth's growing financial crisis by cutting US $1,800m. from the $9,480m. of government spending in the current fiscal year. The cuts were to be implemented by the Fiscal Restructuring and Stabilization Board (FRSB) and the deficit for 2009 was expected to be $3,490m. A major drain was the high price of imported fuels. However, during the course of the year the recession in the USA abated, and in 2011 Puerto Rico was expected to benefit by increased revenues against an enlarged budget gap in 2010.

In May 2009 Pierluisi introduced a bill in the US Congress, which became known as the Puerto Rico Democracy Act of 2010 (not to be confused with the 2007 bill submitted by Luis Fortuño), to authorize a 'fair, impartial and democratic process of self-determination' for the island. It would provide for a referendum asking islanders if they wanted to change their political status. If the answer was no, eight years would elapse before the same question would be asked again. However, if the answer was yes, a second referendum would be held, offering a choice between statehood, independence, or 'sovereignty in association with the United States', the precise meaning of which remains unclear. On 29 April 2010 the bill (as HR 2499) was passed by the US House of Representatives by 223 votes to 169. In the Senate it was referred to the Senate Committee on Energy and Natural Resources and hearings were held on 19 May. Meanwhile, on 21 May, Carlos Alberto Torres, imprisoned for 30 years for seditious conspiracy as a member of the FALN and not released under President Clinton's 1999 amnesty, was approved for parole. Nevertheless, it was unlikely that the islanders, facing the imminent loss of important government subsidies and tens of thousands of jobs (see Economy), would want to endanger their present relationship with the USA by seeking independence.

Economy

Prof. PETER CALVERT

INTRODUCTION

Puerto Rico has been a US territory since 1898, and, though it has full internal self-government, its economy is intimately bound to that of the USA. It is a mountainous island measuring 177 km (110 miles) long by 56 km (35 miles) wide, with a relatively flat and narrow coastal belt. It is the smallest of the three Caribbean islands making up the Greater Antilles. At mid-2010 Puerto Rico's population was estimated at 3.98m. inhabitants, with a population density of over 444 per sq km, making the island one of the most densely populated areas on earth. The UN Population Division forecast that the island would be 98.8% urbanized in 2010, with an urban annual growth rate of 0.78%. In 2008 the total labour force stood at 1,458,544, with a participation rate of 47% (female 37%, male 56%).

Until the 1950s Puerto Rico's economy was based on agriculture; in the 19th and early 20th centuries its principal cash crops were coffee, sugar and tobacco. However, following the Second World War the Government planned to encourage economic growth through industrialization. The governing Partido Popular Democrático (PPD—Popular Democratic Party) decided to seek external capital, mainly from the USA, to spur economic growth. US capital was encouraged to invest in manufacturing facilities on the island through a unique combination of low wages supported by massive local and federal tax exemptions. The results of Operation Bootstrap were immediate and astonishing, and soon became known throughout the world. Real gross national product (GNP) increased by 68% in the 1950s and by 90% in the 1960s. The average annual growth in GNP was approximately 6% during these two decades. Living standards rose accordingly, with personal income per head rising from US $342 per year in 1950, to $1,511 per year in 1971 and to $16,320 per year in 2001. By 1970 manufacturing constituted approximately 40% of the island's gross domestic product (GDP). By 2005/06 manufacturing accounted for an estimated 42.4% of GDP, but only about 10.9% of the active work-force. At that time services constituted 55.1% of GDP and employed about 75.5% of the engaged work-force. In 1970 unemployment declined to 10% of the labour force—astonishing progress given the island's traditional agricultural economy with its massive seasonal unemployment and widespread underemployment.

The extraordinary growth produced by Operation Bootstrap ended following the petroleum crisis of 1973. The dramatic increases in world oil prices imposed by the Organization of the Petroleum Exporting Countries (OPEC) severely impeded Puerto Rico's capacity to sustain high economic growth, dependent as it was on imported oil and gas to meet all but a tiny fraction of its energy needs. At the same time, wage increases and reduced US tariffs on foreign products hampered Puerto Rico's ability to attract US capital, compared with other low-wage economies. Governor Rafael Hernández Colón, during his first term in office (1973–77), attempted to combat the economic slowdown through aggressive government intervention in the economy. Under his leadership, the Government purchased the Puerto Rico Telephone Company, the two major shipping lines serving Puerto Rico and US ports, and most of the island's sugar mills. Nevertheless, these efforts did not slow the relative economic decline and Puerto Rico's growth rate dropped to an annual average of 1.8% between 1974 and 1984. For the first time since Operation Bootstrap began, the island experienced a decline in real GNP in 1975, 1982 and 1983. Economic disaster was avoided only by a massive increase in federal (US Government) funds, which offset the decline in the productive sectors.

Governor Hernández Colón won his second term in office in 1984 on the strength of his pledge to make job creation his main priority. His new term of office coincided with the recovery of the USA from the 1981 recession, which was accompanied by a fall in world petroleum prices. Nevertheless, he was faced with a serious challenge from the US Administration of President Ronald Reagan (1981–89), which sought to eliminate the special federal tax incentives for US investment in Puerto Rico. In response, Hernández Colón proposed an ambitious 'twin-plant' programme to promote industrial development in the Caribbean. His idea was to use the capital generated by the operations of US companies in Puerto Rico to invest in secondary

Caribbean plants that would feed the companies' Puerto Rico operations. His programme won the approval of the Reagan Administration, which was deeply committed to assisting the Caribbean region under the Caribbean Basin Initiative, and efforts to eliminate the federal tax incentives for Puerto Rico were subsequently postponed. The success of Hernández Colón's policies was reflected in an annual average growth rate in real GDP of 3.8% in 1984–88. However, economic growth slowed considerably during Hernández Colón's third term in office (1989–93), mainly because of the advent of another world recession. Puerto Rico's real GDP grew by only 2.0% per year during this term, which in turn led to an increase in unemployment which remained high throughout the early 1990s.

In 1993 the incoming administration of Governor Pedro J. Rosselló (1993–2001) structured a new economic development programme in which the private sector was to be the primary vehicle for economic development. In 1994 the Governor introduced his 'new economic model', advocating reduced government regulation of businesses, the privatization of public enterprises and greater promotion of tourism, and the encouragement of local investment and local industry. In 1996–2004 Puerto Rico's GDP grew, in real terms, by an average of 3.7% per year, as the island mirrored the general success of the US economy over the same period.

In keeping with its privatization policy, the Rosselló administration sold the government-owned shipping company, a major state-owned hotel property, the public sugar corporation and majority control of the state-owned Puerto Rico Telephone Company. However, in 1996, in a major reversal for the island, the US Congress approved legislation ending the island's tax credit (see below), the same federal tax incentive—used to attract manufacturing investment from US corporations to Puerto Rico—that the Reagan Administration had tried to eliminate in the 1980s. The PPD administration of Governor Sila María Calderón (2001–05) inherited the resulting economic problems of low growth, which averaged 1.9% in 2000–06, coupled with rising inflation ('stagflation'). GDP expanded by just 0.6% in both 2004/05 and 2005/06, before declining by 1.8% in 2007, by 2.5% in 2008 and by 4.5% in 2009. The unemployment rate rose sharply from 7.7% in 2007 to 15.3% in 2009, according to US official statistics, primarily owing to the impact of the global economic downturn on, *inter alia*, the construction and housing markets. The financial crisis prevented the Government from resorting to the usual remedy of increasing the size of the state sector. Net migration in 2009 was negative, estimated at 0.96 per 1,000 people. Inflation reached 9.6% in 2008, before slowing to 4.2% in 2009, a year in which inflation-adjusted wages fell by 1.6%.

Nevertheless, Puerto Rico was still well off compared with the rest of the Caribbean. In 2009 GDP was estimated at US $87,790m. and GDP per head at $17,200, ranking Puerto Rico with the world's higher-income countries, though placing it well below the poorest US state, Mississippi, in terms of GDP per head.

AGRICULTURE

Only 3.7% of the land area of the country was regarded by FAO as arable in 2008, with a further 5.6% under permanent crops and 15.2% permanent pasture. Some 400 sq km of arable land were irrigated. In 2005/06 only 1.8% of the active work-force worked on the land and agriculture contributed only an estimated 0.4% of GDP. Sugar had declined to insignificance; in 2004 an estimated 773 metric tons were produced on 8,300 ha, compared with 40,000 tons in 2002, and virtually nothing since. Some 8,100 tons of green coffee were grown in 2008 on 22,500 ha. Bananas and plantain production totalled 53,500 tons and 80,000 tons, respectively, in 2008. Ranching and dairy farming (with a total of 380,000 head of cattle and 13.2m. chickens in 2008) had become the mainstay of the agricultural sector. Other farm animals included 50,000 pigs, 3,300 goats, 4,600 mules and asses, and 6,600 horses. In 2008 some 350,000 tons of fresh milk and 11,500 tons of eggs were produced. The total fish catch in 2008 amounted to only 1,837 tons, much of which was processed for export.

MANUFACTURING

The growth of manufacturing in Puerto Rico was almost entirely the result of special tax benefits from both the US and Puerto Rican Governments. Under US law (Section 936 of the US Tax Code), the income of a subsidiary of a US corporation operating a manufacturing facility in Puerto Rico was eligible to receive a federal tax credit, which practically exempted the corporation from the payment of US income taxes on its Puerto Rican earnings. The Puerto Rican Government in 1948 matched the federal possessions tax credit with its own equally generous tax incentive programme. The combined incentives created a powerful lure to attract US corporate investment to Puerto Rico. In the early years of Operation Bootstrap the island attracted the labour-intensive textiles and apparel industries. However, over the years, and as the federal incentive grew more generous, Puerto Rico manufacturing became more capital intensive and diversified, marked by substantial investment in sectors such as pharmaceuticals and medical products, scientific instruments, computers, microprocessors, and electrical goods.

After 1996, when the US Congress repealed Section 936, Puerto Rico's industrialization programme began to decline. Nevertheless, the full impact of the credit's elimination came only in December 2005, at the scheduled end of the 10-year 'grace' period, granted to companies operating in Puerto Rico at the time of the repeal of the tax credit. Growth in the manufacturing sector in the late 1990s resulted mainly from the expansion of those US companies (largely from the pharmaceutical sector) that were converting their legal structures to become Controlled Foreign Corporations (CFCs). Under US tax law, a CFC does not have to pay federal taxes on income earned in a foreign jurisdiction as long as the money remains outside the USA. For the purpose of US tax law, Puerto Rico is considered a foreign tax jurisdiction, so CFCs pay only royalties to their parent companies plus 10% in local taxes. This provision has been particularly attractive to pharmaceutical companies and other large corporations with global manufacturing and distribution networks. Since 1996 some 57 large manufacturing firms operating in Puerto Rico have reincorporated as CFCs; the majority engaged, however, not in manufacturing but in services (31.4%), information technology (25.9%) and the distribution and transportation of goods (21.7%).

Governor Calderón committed her administration to securing new tax incentives from the US Congress, at a time when Congress remained committed to phasing out existing support by 2006. In 2001 Calderón sought US congressional approval to allow Puerto Rican CFCs to repatriate their earnings to their US corporate shareholders at a preferential 10% tax rate. The Republican-controlled Congress was not receptive to any change until February 2004, when Puerto Rico's then Resident Commissioner in the USA, Aníbal Acevedo Vilá (who was elected Governor in November 2004), supported a 'compromise' bill to provide companies in the USA with a one-year period of a very low income tax rate on CFC funds. The 35% corporate income tax rate would be reduced to 5.25% for the year in the case of 'repatriated' funds. There was, however, a serious risk involved in providing a strong incentive for US-based companies to move capital out of the Commonwealth quickly.

COMMERCE

Wholesale and retail trade played a significant role in Puerto Rico's economy. In 2005/06 the sector contributed an estimated 12.4% of total GDP. With some 271,000 workers in 2005/06, commerce represented the third largest source of employment (21.6% of the active population) on the island, after services and government. In that year trade generated US $10,716.5m. in total revenues. Large-scale shopping complexes or 'malls' dominated the retail trade.

FINANCE

Finance, insurance and real estate contributed an estimated 17.1% of the island's GDP in 2005/06. This thriving industry is represented by a broad spectrum of financial services, from large commercial banks and investment brokerage houses, to small loan companies and money transfer outlets. In 2005/06 the finance, insurance and real-estate sector employed a total of 47,000 workers, some 3.8% of the active work-force. Banco Popular de Puerto Rico, the largest firm in the country, was a financial conglomerate with assets of US $26,000m. in mid-2008 before consolidation; after consolidation it had assets of $38,900m. Other major banks were FirstBank Puerto Rico ($17,000m.) and Westernbank Puerto Rico ($17,000m.). All Puerto Rican banks were eligible for support from the US Federal Government under the Troubled Assets Recovery Program (TARP). Investment and brokerage companies include UBS Financial Services of Puerto Rico, Santander Securities and Popular Securities. Although the commercial bank sector has suffered from the impact of the recession, the issue of sub-prime mortgages—which triggered the US recession—has not been a factor.

However, in May 2010 a massive intervention by the US Federal Deposit Insurance Corporation (FDIC) was needed to stave off the collapse of the Commonwealth's banking sector. On 7 May the assets of three local depositary institutions—Eurobank, RG Premier Bank and Westernbank—were seized with a view to recapitalization by sale. This followed the closure at the end of April of all branches of Westernbank, Puerto Rico's oldest and second largest bank, and the transfer of its business to Banco Popular de Puerto Rico. Oriental Bank and Trust took over the assets of Eurobank, while Scotiabank de Puerto Rico acquired those of RG Premier bank.

TOURISM AND TRANSPORTATION

Tourism forms an increasingly important, albeit still small, part of Puerto Rico's economy. In 2002 the tourism industry constituted approximately 5.5% of GDP. Some 14,000 people, or 1.2% of the work-force, are employed by the tourism industry. During the early years of Operation Bootstrap the Government utilized a combination of direct government and private investment to create the necessary infrastructure for tourism. It invested directly in the construction of hotels, but contracted with US corporations for their management. In 1959 the industry was favourably affected by the Cuban Revolution, which led to the US economic embargo and the diversion of much of Cuba's US tourism to other Caribbean destinations. The island's traditional emphasis has been on relatively expensive casinos and hotels located along the beaches. However, in the late 1970s the Government developed a unique system of country 'inns' to move tourism out of San Juan, and improved transportation facilities, including the expansion of the airport and new tourism piers in San Juan's harbour.

The development of tourism was a priority for the Rosselló administration, which extended additional tax credits to the sector to encourage hotel construction. At the same time, Rosselló created a new subsidiary of the Government Development Bank to encourage and promote investment in new hotels. As a result, the number of hotel rooms increased every year—except in 1998, when Hurricane Georges resulted in the closure of several major hotels—under his administration, reaching 11,915 by mid-2000. Tourism received a further set-back owing to the general impact of the terrorist attacks on the USA of 11 September 2001, but subsequently recovered.

The Rosselló administration was particularly successful in decentralizing tourism outside San Juan. New projects were built or planned east of San Juan, extending along the coast to Fajardo, and new tourism enclaves appeared along the west coast between San Juan and Aguadilla. In 1999 the Government announced plans to create an ambitious tourism and trade centre, to be known as the Golden Triangle, on the Isla Grande peninsula in San Juan. The Calderón administration continued with the project, signing a US $200m. agreement with LCOR, Inc., for the construction of two hotels, a trade centre and a retail and entertainment area, but work proceeded slowly. In March 2004 Hotel Sol Melía, one of Europe's largest hotel chains, inaugurated the first all-inclusive resort on the island, the Paradisus, in Rio Grande, and further resorts and hotels under construction throughout the island brought the total number of rooms to 13,000 in that year. Construction of new hotels elsewhere was ongoing in 2009. However, other Caribbean states, which used Puerto Rico as a critical bridge to the lucrative US market, expressed concern at the significant reduction in air access to the island after the US airlines American Airlines and American Eagle announced in mid-2008 that they were cutting flights between Puerto Rico, the USA and other Caribbean destinations.

In 2008/09 receipts from tourism totalled an estimated US $3,473m. and in that year some 3.6m. tourists visited the island. San Juan is the world's second largest home port for cruise ship passengers; it has seven piers and can dock 12 ships at one time, including the very largest ships afloat. In 2007 the tourist industry accounted for an encouragingly high 7% of the island's GNP as cruise ship arrivals and hotel occupancy remained unaffected by the fiscal crisis. However, in 2008/09 the number of excursionists and cruise ship arrivals at San Juan had declined by 17.7% compared with the previous year, numbering 1.23m. in total. Stop-over arrivals in 2008/09 declined by some 4.5% on the previous year.

The island's transport facilities are excellent. The Luis Muñoz Marín International Airport, in San Juan, was served by 45 US and international airlines. In 2009 the airport served approximately 8.2m. passengers and moved 521.4m. lbs of freight in 2006/07. The airport offered daily direct air services between San Juan and more than seven US cities, and regular scheduled services to other Caribbean islands and major Latin American and European cities, though it suffered a reverse in late 1997, when American Airlines, the island's biggest passenger carrier, transferred its Caribbean hub. In June 2009 the US Federal Aviation Administration approved the privatization of the airport as part of its programme of cost-cutting measures. Three highway projects were also due to be transformed into public-private partnerships. There are 26,186 km of roads, 94% of which are paved, 96 km of narrow-gauge railway and 10 major ports apart from San Juan itself, regarded by many as the finest in the Caribbean.

In 1996 construction began of a 'super-aqueduct' to bring water from the western part of the island to the San Juan metropolitan area, where traditional water supplies were insufficient to handle the city's growing population. In the same year the Government also began the construction of a 16.6-km (10.3-mile) mass transit system for the San Juan area. The first phase of the Urban Train (Tren Urbano) was inaugurated in 2005 but as yet has made little impact on the city's traffic congestion. The US $2,150m. project was made possible by an initial $300m. commitment by the US Government, and the Urban Train's corridor, Ciudad Red, was expected to bring in $400m. in public and private sector investment, 16,000 direct jobs, 1,080 housing units and 373,000 sq ft of commercial and office space. The Calderón administration broadened the reach of the port at Guayanilla to include the neighbouring ports of Ponce and Peñuelas. A planned Port of the Americas at Ponce would provide world-class, deep-water docking and onshore warehouse space and factory sites for assembly and re-export of semi-finished goods. Construction of the port was expected to be completed in 2011, at a total cost of $84.4m. (there were four planned construction phases). In February 2010 the port authority took delivery of two Post-Panamax cranes intended to facilitate its plans to achieve an annual throughput capacity of 2.2m. containers and to capture a significant part of the Caribbean transshipment market. Despite optimism surrounding the project, however, the Government has not fully implemented its ambitious infrastructure proposals, construction has been subject to delays and funds have contracted as the Government has run short of revenue.

THE PUBLIC SECTOR

The government sector was the second largest area of employment in 2005/06, employing approximately 278,000 people, or 22.2% of the total labour force. The sector accounted for US $8,424.2m., or an estimated 9.8%, of Puerto Rico's GDP, in the same period. One major reason for Puerto Rico's ability to maintain such a high level of public sector employment was the economic aid it received from the USA, which also meant that a vast number of residents were indirectly dependent on Government. Net federal disbursements to Puerto Rico were estimated to have increased from $2,900m. in 1979 to $8,900m. in

2002, the latter an increase of 3.7% over the previous year. Three-quarters of this (75.8%) consisted of earned benefits, e.g. social security, Medicare and veterans payments; the balance consisted of the National Assistance Program and scholarships. Consequently, in 2002 Puerto Ricans paid $1,724.19 per person in taxes, compared with an average of $6,702.42 for other US citizens.

The Rosselló administration opened the Government-owned and -operated electricity system, the Puerto Rico Electric Power Authority (PREPA—Autoridad de Energía Eléctrica de Puerto Rico), to private co-generators. In 2001 a 507-MW, liquefied natural gas (LNG) co-generation plant, a desalination plant and an LNG storage facility, located on the southern coast of the island, became operational. The water from the desalination plant was used to cool the turbines and the excess sold as fresh water to the Government's Aqueduct and Sewer Authority. In early 2002 the French utilities group Suez won a contract worth US $4,100m. to supply the island's water and treat its waste water over a 10-year period. Water prices on the island have, however, not been raised since 1986 so a substantial increase was long overdue and was already causing concern.

Following the onset of recession in 2007, it soon became clear that such a high level of public sector employment could not be maintained for long. Immediate efforts focused on inviting voluntary redundancies. In May 2009 Governor Fortuño followed the example of his predecessor and dismissed almost 8,000 workers, mostly temporary workers in the education, health and treasury departments. As part of the cost-cutting process, Fortuño agreed to take a 10% cut in salary and the salaries of his cabinet officials were to be reduced by 5% over the next two years. In September the Governor announced the loss of a further 13,700 jobs as the Commonwealth came under increasing pressure from ratings agencies to forestall the downgrading of the Government's credit to 'junk' status. More redundancies were expected to follow as the Governor sought to cut as many as 30,000 jobs in order to meet congressional requirements to balance the budget.

ENERGY

In mid-2001 the USA's AES Corporation opened a US $850m. coal-burning co-generation plant. Like the LNG co-generation plant, it has a contract with PREPA to sell its output to the government network. Construction of the plants was encouraged by the Government, in an attempt to diversify the island's electrical generation, which hitherto had been completely dependent on imported petroleum as its fuel source.

In 2007 Puerto Rico was still the largest importer of energy in the Caribbean area. In 2007 oil consumption was estimated at 215,000 barrels per day (b/d); refining capacity, however, was only 114,400 b/d. Puerto Rico produces a small amount of petroleum (1,254 b/d in 2008), but no natural gas, of which 806.6m. cu m were imported and consumed in 2008. Electricity consumption in that year was 23,720m. kWh, 99.2% of which came from the burning of fossil fuels and 0.8% from hydropower. In April 2005 PREPA announced that it was to build two new gas-fired power-stations with a combined capacity of 971 MW, but global energy prices subsequently rose steeply and complaints were numerous.

PUBLIC FINANCE

Puerto Rico is constitutionally required to operate within a balanced budget. The island's Constitution provided for a limitation on the amount of general debt that could be issued, equal to 15% of the average annual revenues raised over the previous two years. Historically, Puerto Rico kept within its constitutional bounds; in mid-2002 the Commonwealth had a 6.7% borrowing margin, well within its 15% limit. At 30 June 2006 the provisional figure for total public debt—including the debt of the central Government, public corporations and municipalities—amounted to US $39,933.3m. The island suffered a reverse in early 2002 when its bonds were reclassified at a lower level; a further downgrade was announced in 2005. This meant that the Commonwealth would have to pay a higher interest rate on outstanding debts, resulting from operational budget deficits for two years, which the former administration had concealed. In August 2005 the Partido Nuevo Progresista (PNP—New Progressive Party) proposed the introduction of a general sales tax of between 5% and 10%, coupled with reductions in income tax.

However, the impact of the economic downturn in the USA led to a budget crisis in the island in May 2008, when the Government ran out of money two months before the end of the fiscal year. This forced Governor Acevedo Vilá to close down 43 government agencies and lay off 95,000 government employees, resulting in an immediate negative impact on the economy. His proposal of a 7% sales tax to fund a loan was opposed by the PNP, which was, however, soon pressured into even more severe measures upon assuming power (see The Public Sector).

TRADE

Although Puerto Rico for import/export purposes is a distinct entity, the Commonwealth lies within the customs barrier of the USA. Consequently, exports and imports are dominated by that country. Puerto Rico is the fifth largest exporter in the western hemisphere in terms of the total value of its exports, ahead of such larger economies as Chile, Argentina, Colombia and Venezuela. Between 1997 and 2005 exports doubled in value. In 2008/09 the island exported goods valued at US $60,806.6m. Imports grew more slowly, reaching $40,651.0m. that year, giving the island a positive balance of trade, much of which was accounted for by exports of pharmaceuticals. Imports were driven mainly by raw materials used by the island's factories. Since 1982 the island has operated with an annual trade surplus, which stood at an estimated $15,564.7m. in 2007/08. The percentage of exports to the USA remained relatively constant from the 1950s to the end of the 1990s, at around 90% of the total. However, goods shipped from the USA to Puerto Rico decreased from 92% of total imports in 1950 to 55% in 2006.

After the USA (77.2%), Puerto Rico's biggest export markets in 2006/07 were the United Kingdom (4.6%), Netherlands (3.4%) and the Dominican Republic (also 3.4%). Principal exports were chemicals, electronics, apparel, canned tuna, rum, beverage concentrates and medical supplies. With respect to imports, after the USA (50.1%) in 2006/07 came Ireland (21.0%) and Japan (3.7%). Principal imports were chemicals, machinery and equipment, clothing, food and petroleum products.

Efforts continued to increase trade to five target areas: Florida and the east coast of the USA; the US Hispanic/Latino market (constituting some 39m. people); Mexico (a North American Free Trade Agreement—NAFTA—trading partner); the Dominican Republic, the island's fourth largest trading partner; and the Greater Caribbean area. The island Government believed that it was competitive internationally in food and beverage production, contract manufacturing, technology, construction and associated services—particularly engineering and architecture—environmental engineering and finance. Puerto Rico intended to strengthen bilateral relations with other important economies, including Costa Rica, Panama, Chile and the European Union, and to become more active in regional economic organizations.

Statistical Survey

Source (unless otherwise stated): Puerto Rico Planning Board, POB 41119, San Juan, 00940-1119; tel. (787) 723-6200; internet www.jp.gobierno.pr.

Area and Population

AREA, POPULATION AND DENSITY

Area (sq km)	8,959*
Population (census results)	
1 April 1990	3,522,037
1 April 2000	
Males	1,833,577
Females	1,975,033
Total	3,808,610
Population (estimates at mid-year)†	
2008	3,954,553
2009	3,967,288
2010	3,978,702
Density (per sq km) at mid-2010	444.1

* 3,459 sq miles.

† Source: Population Division, US Census Bureau.

POPULATION BY AGE AND SEX

(population estimates at mid-2010)

	Males	Females	Total
0–14	392,531	375,649	768,180
15–64	1,266,497	1,364,890	2,631,387
65 and over	249,332	329,803	579,135
Total	1,908,360	2,070,342	3,978,702

Source: Population Division, US Census Bureau.

PRINCIPAL TOWNS

(population estimates at mid-2009)

San Juan (capital)	420,326	Caguas	143,274
Bayamón	218,949	Guaynabo	103,073
Carolina	187,209	Arecibo	102,770
Ponce	178,346		

Source: Population Division, US Census Bureau.

BIRTHS, MARRIAGES AND DEATHS

	Registered live births		Registered marriages		Registered deaths	
	Number	Rate (per 1,000)	Number	Rate (per 1,000)*	Number	Rate (per 1,000)
2000	59,460	15.5	25,980	8.9	28,550	7.6
2001	55,983	14.6	28,598	7.4	28,794	7.5
2002	52,871	13.7	25,645	6.6	28,098	7.3

* Rates calculated using estimates of population aged 15 years and over.

Source: Department of Health, Commonwealth of Puerto Rico.

2003: Births 50,803 (birth rate 13.1 per 1,000); Deaths 28,356 (death rate 7.3 per 1,000).

2004: Births 51,239 (birth rate 13.2 per 1,000); Deaths 29,066 (death rate 7.5 per 1,000).

2005: Births 50,687 (birth rate 13.0 per 1,000); Deaths 29,702 (death rate 7.6 per 1,000).

2006: Births 48,744 (birth rate 12.4 per 1,000); Deaths 28,589 (death rate 7.2 per 1,000).

2007: Births 46,744 (birth rate 11.9 per 1,000); Deaths 29,292 (death rate 7.4 per 1,000).

2008 (preliminary): Births 45,687 (birth rate 12.1 per 1,000); Deaths 29,024 (death rate 7.3 per 1,000).

2009 (preliminary): Births 44,080 (birth rate 12.1 per 1,000); Deaths 28,173 (death rate 7.3 per 1,000).

Source: Department of Health, Commonwealth of Puerto Rico.

Life expectancy (years at birth): 79.0 (males 75.0; females 82.9) in 2009 (Source: Pan American Health Organization).

ECONOMICALLY ACTIVE POPULATION

('000 persons aged 16 years and over)

	2006/07	2007/08	2008/09
Agriculture, forestry and fishing	16	15	19
Mining	1	1	—
Manufacturing	135	129	112
Construction	94	82	68
Trade	260	257	244
Transportation, communication and other public utilities	53	54	58
Finance, insurance and real estate	45	43	43
Services	364	359	353
Government	296	279	271
Total employed	1,263	1,218	1,168
Unemployed	147	151	181
Total labour force	1,409	1,368	1,349

Health and Welfare

KEY INDICATORS

Total fertility rate (children per woman, 2009)	1.8
Under-5 mortality rate (per 1,000 live births, 2009)	8.4
Physicians (per 1,000 head, *c.* 2007)	2.2
Hospital beds (per 1,000 head, 2006)	3.1
Health expenditure (public, 2004): % of GDP	3.5

Source: mainly Pan American Health Organization.

For other sources and definitions see explanatory note on p. vi.

Agriculture

PRINCIPAL CROPS

('000 metric tons)

	2005	2006*	2007*
Tomatoes	18.7	18.7	18.8
Pumpkins, squash and gourds	14.3	14.3	14.3
Bananas	52.2	52.3	53.5
Plantains	76.4	77.0	80.0
Oranges	18.8	18.9	19.5
Guavas, mangoes and mangosteens	12.9	13.1	13.5
Pineapples	15.3	15.6	17.0
Coffee, green	7.9	8.0	8.1

* FAO estimates.

Aggregate production (may include official, semi-official or estimated data): Total fruits (excl. melons) 193.4 in 2005, 194.7 in 2006, 202.1 in 2007; Total roots and tubers 10.8 in 2005, 10.9 in 2006, 11.3 in 2007; Total vegetables (incl. melons) 45.5 in 2005, 45.5 in 2006, 45.8 in 2007.

Source: FAO.

2008: Figures assumed to be unchanged from 2007 (FAO estimates).

LIVESTOCK
('000 head, year ending September, FAO estimates)

	2006	2007	2008
Asses	2	2	2
Cattle	378.0	380.0	380.0
Sheep	6.1	6.2	6.3
Goats	3.2	3.2	3.3
Pigs	48.7	50.0	50.0
Horses	6.5	6.5	6.6
Chickens	12,500	13,000	13,200

Source: FAO.

LIVESTOCK PRODUCTS
('000 metric tons, FAO estimates)

	2006	2007	2008
Cattle meat	9.8	10.0	10.2
Pig meat	11.0	11.2	11.5
Chicken meat	50.0	50.0	50.0
Cows' milk	350.0	350.0	350.0
Hen eggs	11.2	11.5	11.5

Source: FAO.

Fishing

(metric tons, live weight)

	2006	2007	2008
Capture	2,042	1,675	1,793
Groupers	24	20	19
Snappers and jobfishes	370	311	374
Seerfishes	53	35	32
Caribbean spiny lobster	148	123	142
Stromboid conchs	1,005	829	829
Aquaculture	266	44	44*
Tilapias	12	32	30*
Penaeus shrimps	237	0	0*
Total catch	2,308	1,719	1,837*

* FAO estimate.

Source: FAO.

Industry

SELECTED PRODUCTS
(year ending 30 June)

	1995/96	1996/97	1997/98*
Distilled spirits ('000 proof gallons)	25,343	36,292	33,471

* Preliminary.

Electric energy (million kWh): 25,082.3 in 2006/07; 23,935.2 in 2007/08; 22,650.9 in 2008/09.

Cement ('000 94-lb sacks): 37,173 in 2004; 36,847 in 2005; 36,910 in 2006 (Source: US Geological Survey).

Beer ('000 hectolitres): 317 in 1997; 263 in 1998; 259 in 1999 (Source: UN, *Industrial Commodity Statistics Yearbook*).

Finance

CURRENCY AND EXCHANGE RATES

Monetary Units

United States currency: 100 cents = 1 US dollar (US $).

Sterling and Euro Equivalents (31 December 2009)

£1 sterling = US $1.619;
€1 = US $1.441;
US $100 = £61.75 = €69.42.

BUDGET
(US $ '000, general government operations, year ending 30 June)

Revenue*	2005/06	2006/07	2007/08
Income tax	6,181,995	6,389,973	5,493,881
Excise tax	2,013,998	1,475,311	1,306,416
Sales and use tax	—	583,639	910,609
Other taxes	15,145	4,663	11,356
Charges for services	828,993	757,724	664,505
Intergovernmental transfers	4,663,422	5,166,604	4,569,457
Interest	117,080	176,674	160,926
Other revenue	334,591	434,024	455,439
Total	14,155,224	14,988,612	13,572,589

Expenditure	2005/06	2006/07	2007/08
General government services	2,489,093	2,537,999	1,769,498
Public safety	2,108,152	1,864,256	2,134,919
Health	1,429,888	1,948,201	2,345,650
Public housing and welfare	3,130,373	3,048,585	3,098,684
Education	4,101,980	4,400,321	4,432,880
Economic development	516,444	533,253	415,976
Intergovernmental transfers	409,727	593,247	470,395
Capital outlays	502,348	512,824	429,238
Principal on debt servicing	446,281	904,604	2,163,704
Interest	822,234	814,723	1,037,136
Total	15,956,520	17,158,013	18,298,080

* Excluding net financing (US $ '000): 1,819,389 in 2005/06; 1,865,572 in 2006/07; 3,704,835 in 2007/08.

Source: Department of the Treasury, Commonwealth of Puerto Rico.

COST OF LIVING
(Consumer Price Index; base: 2000 = 100)

	2006	2007	2008
Food (incl. beverages)	257.1	281.0	331.5
Fuel and light	157.2	171.8	206.6
Rent	110.9	114.0	134.6
Clothing (incl. footwear)	95.5	100.7	106.5
All items (incl. others)	178.9	191.1	209.4

2009: Food (incl. beverages) 377.5; All items (incl. others) 218.5.

Source: ILO.

NATIONAL ACCOUNTS
(US $ million at current prices, year ending 30 June)

Expenditure on the Gross Domestic Product

	2006/07	2007/08	2008/09*
Government final consumption expenditure	10,512.4	10,518.1	11,132.7
Private final consumption expenditure	51,949.3	54,561.0	55,564.6
Gross domestic investment	11,987.8	11,373.6	10,204.9
Net sales to the rest of the world	−14,929.0	−14,925.7	−14,143.3
Gross national product	59,520.5	61,527.0	62,758.9
Exports of goods and services } *Less* Imports of goods and services	28,884.0	31,398.9	32,949.3
GDP in purchasers' values	88,404.5	92,925.9	95,708.2

* Preliminary.

Gross Domestic Product by Economic Activity

	2006/07	2007/08	2008/09*
Agriculture	430.2	612.9	633.5
Mining†	61.4	62.0	54.6
Manufacturing	37,636.6	40,548.0	43,548.0
Utilities	2,214.4	2,114.6	2,123.1
Construction	1,965.4	1,928.7	1,727.1
Transportation	968.3	998.5	978.0
Trade	7,223.0	7,343.3	7,469.2
Finance, insurance and real estate	18,380.0	18,845.4	18,205.3
Other services	11,404.6	11,925.1	12,252.7
Government	8,584.9	8,762.2	9,254.2
Sub-total	88,868.4	93,140.7	96,245.7
Statistical discrepancy	−464.2	−214.9	−537.6
Total	88,404.5	92,925.9	95,708.2

* Preliminary.

† Mining includes only quarries.

BALANCE OF PAYMENTS

(US $ million, year ending 30 June)

	2006/07	2007/08	2008/09*
Merchandise exports	64,203.2	68,551.0	66,077.6
Merchandise imports	−51,040.5	−52,986.3	−48,045.6
Trade balance	13,162.7	15,564.7	18,032.0
Exports of services	6,696.4	6,941.4	6,569.1
Imports of services	−4,957.7	−5,033.4	−4,672.5
Balance on goods and services	14,901.4	17,472.7	19,928.6
Other income received	1,668.2	1,763.7	1,371.2
Other income paid	−31,498.6	−34,162.1	−35,443.1
Balance on goods, services and income	−14,929.0	−14,925.7	−14,143.3
Net transfers and interest	11,020.0	12,754.3	14,210.7
Current balance	−3,909.0	−2,171.4	67.4
Net capital movements	5,119.7	1,883.0	−32.5
Overall balance	1,210.7	−288.4	34.9

* Preliminary.

External Trade

PRINCIPAL COMMODITIES

(US $ million, year ending 30 June)

Imports	2006/07	2007/08	2008/09
Mining products	1,510.0	2,457.3	546.1
Manufacturing products	42,259.4	40,779.0	38,605.5
Food	2,440.6	2,627.7	2,955.6
Products of petroleum and coal	4,152.8	5,169.8	4,714.0
Chemical products	21,675.9	19,337.5	18,146.4
Basic chemicals	4,150.3	3,286.5	3,282.4
Pharmaceuticals and medicines	16,494.7	15,065.9	13,591.2
Machinery, except electrical	1,266.0	1,199.1	1,122.4
Computer and electronic products	2,932.8	2,986.2	2,829.2
Transport equipment	1,922.3	1,909.3	1,478.2
Motor vehicles	1,608.7	1,647.8	1,204.9
Miscellaneous manufacturing	1,617.9	1,605.6	1,512.0
Total (incl. others)	45,265.8	44,928.3	40,651.0

Exports	2006/07	2007/08	2008/09
Manufacturing products	59,378.1	63,229.9	60,098.4
Food	3,751.5	4,468.2	3,597.5
Chemicals	39,587.8	45,662.2	45,762.8
Pharmaceuticals and medicines	36,567.9	42,182.7	41,983.5
Computer and electronic products	6,885.0	4,083.5	3,197.2
Computers and peripheral equipment	4,023.0	2,274.0	1,596.6
Electrical equipment, appliances and components	1,281.4	1,558.3	1,241.7
Miscellaneous manufacturing	4,788.6	3,809.7	3,701.8
Medical equipment and supplies	4,675.2	3,732.6	3,649.6
Total (incl. others)	60,010.8	63,953.6	60,806.6

PRINCIPAL TRADING PARTNERS

(US $ million, year ending 30 June)

Imports	2004/05	2005/06	2006/07
Brazil	689.9	676.4	672.9
China, People's Republic	n.a.	566.7	644.9
Dominican Republic	643.9	596.4	485.7
Germany	828.0	903.0	871.9
Ireland	7,716.8	7,950.2	9,492.6
Japan	1,554.8	1,834.9	1,661.3
Nigeria	n.a.	n.a.	903.4
Singapore	956.7	592.7	612.2
United Kingdom	524.5	513.4	n.a.
USA	19,133.7	21,502.9	22,662.4
US Virgin Islands	1,264.7	1,486.1	1,377.5
Total (incl. others)	38,905.2	42,629.5	45,265.8

Transport

ROAD TRAFFIC

(motor vehicles registered at 31 December)

	2004	2006*	2007
Passenger cars	2,210,998	2,341,820	2,421,055
Buses and coaches	3,308	3,503	3,698
Lorries (trucks) and vans	36,063†	100,841	106,446
Motorcycles	31,770	91,082	115,865

* Data for 2005 were not available.

† Privately owned vehicles only.

Source: Federal Highway Administration, US Department of Transportation, *Highway Statistics*.

SHIPPING

(Port of San Juan, year ending 30 June)

	2005/06	2006/07	2007/08
Cruise passenger movements	1,299,323	1,374,379	1,496,853
Cruise ship calls	550	563	581
Cargo movements ('000 short tons)	9,707.3	9,609.5	9,395.9

Source: Puerto Rico Ports Authority.

CIVIL AVIATION

(year ending 30 June)

	2005/06	2006/07	2007/08
Luis Muñoz Marín International Airport			
Passenger movements ('000)	10,680.8	10,321.2	n.a.
Freight (million lbs)	541.0	521.4	n.a.
Regional airports			
Passenger movements ('000)	1,008.1	1,129.5	1,294.7
Freight (million lbs)	266.3	255.5	243.2

Source: Puerto Rico Ports Authority.

Tourism

(year ending 30 June)

	2006/07	2007/08	2008/09*
Total visitors ('000)	3,687.0	3,716.2	3,550.5
From USA	2,867.3	2,894.8	3,002.2
From US Virgin Islands	19.4	17.2	14.5
From elsewhere	800.3	804.3	533.8
Excursionists (incl. cruise passengers)	1,375.4	1,496.9	1,232.0
Expenditure (US $ million)	3,413.9	3,535.0	3,472.8

* Preliminary figures.

Communications Media

	2007	2008	2009
Telephones ('000 main lines in use)	1,012.9	949.4	870.1
Mobile cellular telephones ('000 subscribers)	2,431.5	2,543.6	2,716.0
Internet users ('000)	1,100.0	1,000.0	1,000.0
Broadband subscribers ('000)	182.2	426.3	426.3

Personal computers: 33,000 (8.4 per 1,000 persons) in 2005.

Television receivers ('000 in use): 1,270 in 1999.

Radio receivers ('000 in use): 2,840 in 1997.

Daily newspapers (1996): 3; average circulation ('000 copies) 475.

Non-daily newspapers (1988 estimates): 4; average circulation ('000 copies) 106.

Sources: UNESCO, *Statistical Yearbook*; UN, *Statistical Yearbook*; International Telecommunication Union.

Education

(public education at fall 2005, unless otherwise indicated)

	Institutes	Teachers	Enrolment
Elementary and secondary	1,523*	42,036	563,490
Post-secondary†	17‡	14,557§	67,990

* 2005/06.

† Excluding adult (enrolment 33,463 in 2005) and vocational education.

‡ 2006/07.

§ Four-year full-time equivalent teaching staff.

Adult and vocational education: 80 institutes (private only); 33,463 students enrolled (public only).

Source: National Center for Education Statistics, US Department of Education.

Private education (accredited private institutions, 2009/10 unless otherwise indicated): Institutes 145 (2003/04); Pre-primary enrolment 25,460; Elementary and secondary enrolment 99,817; Post-secondary enrolment 29,773 (Source: Consejo General de Educacíon, San Juan).

Adult literacy rate (UNESCO estimates): 94.1% (males 93.9%; females 94.4%) in 2002 (Source: UNESCO Institute for Statistics).

Directory

The Constitution

RELATIONSHIP WITH THE USA

On 3 July 1950 the Congress of the United States of America adopted Public Law No. 600, which was to allow 'the people of Puerto Rico to organize a government pursuant to a constitution of their own adoption'. This Law was submitted to the voters of Puerto Rico in a referendum and was accepted in the summer of 1951. A new Constitution was drafted in which Puerto Rico was styled as a Commonwealth, or Estado Libre Asociado, 'a state which is free of superior authority in the management of its own local affairs', though it remained in association with the USA. This Constitution, with its amendments and resolutions, was ratified by the people of Puerto Rico on 3 March 1952, and by the Congress of the USA on 3 July 1952; and the Commonwealth of Puerto Rico was established on 25 July 1952.

Under the terms of the political and economic union between the USA and Puerto Rico, US citizens in Puerto Rico enjoy the same privileges and immunities as if Puerto Rico were a member state of the Union. Puerto Rican citizens are citizens of the USA and may freely enter and leave that country.

The Congress of the USA has no control of, and may not intervene in, the internal affairs of Puerto Rico.

Puerto Rico is exempted from the tax laws of the USA, although most other federal legislation does apply to the island. Puerto Rico is represented in the US House of Representatives by a non-voting delegate, the Resident Commissioner, who is directly elected for a four-year term. The island has no representation in the US Senate.

There are no customs duties between the USA and Puerto Rico. Foreign products entering Puerto Rico—with the single exception of coffee, which is subject to customs duty in Puerto Rico, but not in the USA—incur the same customs duties as would be paid on their entry into the USA.

The US social security system is extended to Puerto Rico, except for unemployment insurance provisions. Laws providing for economic co-operation between the Federal Government and the States of the Union for the construction of roads, schools, public health services and similar purposes are extended to Puerto Rico. Such joint programmes are administered by the Commonwealth Government.

Amendments to the Constitution are not subject to approval by the US Congress, provided that they are consistent with the US federal Constitution, the Federal Relations Act defining federal relations with Puerto Rico and Public Law No. 600. Subject to these limitations, the Constitution may be amended by a two-thirds' vote of the Puerto Rican Legislature and by the subsequent majority approval of the electorate.

BILL OF RIGHTS

No discrimination shall be made on account of race, colour, sex, birth, social origin or condition, or political or religious ideas. Suffrage shall be direct, equal and universal for all over the age of 18. Public property and funds shall not be used to support schools other than State schools. The death penalty shall not exist. The rights of the individual, of the family and of property are guaranteed. The Constitution establishes trial by jury in all cases of felony, as well as the right of habeas corpus. Every person is to receive free elementary and secondary education. Social protection is to be afforded to the old, the disabled, the sick and the unemployed.

THE LEGISLATURE

The Legislative Assembly consists of two chambers, the members of which are elected by direct vote for a four-year term. The Senate is composed of 27 members, who must be over 30 years of age. The House of Representatives is composed of 51 members, of whom 40 are elected on a constituency basis, and a further 11 are at large members, elected by proportional representation. Representatives must be over 25 years of age. The Constitution guarantees the minority parties additional representation in the Senate and the House of Representatives, which may fluctuate from one-quarter to one-third of the seats in each House.

The Senate elects a President and the House of Representatives a Speaker from their respective members. The sessions of each house are public. A majority of the total number of members of each house constitutes a quorum. Either house can initiate legislation, although bills for raising revenue must originate in the House of Representatives. Once passed by both Houses, a bill is submitted to the Governor, who can either sign it into law or return it, with his reasons for refusal, within 10 days. If it is returned, the Houses may pass it again by a two-thirds' majority, in which case the Governor must accept it.

The House of Representatives, or the Senate, can impeach one of its members for treason, bribery, other felonies and 'misdemeanours involving moral turpitude'. A two-thirds' majority is necessary before an indictment may be brought. The cases are tried by the Senate. If a Representative or Senator is declared guilty, he is deprived of his office and becomes punishable by law.

THE EXECUTIVE

The Governor, who must be at least 35 years of age, is elected by direct suffrage and serves for four years. Responsible for the execution of laws, the Governor is Commander-in-Chief of the militia and has the power to proclaim martial law. At the beginning of every regular session of the Assembly, in January, the Governor presents a report on the state of the treasury, and on proposed expenditure. The Governor chooses the Secretaries of Departments, subject to the approval of the Legislative Assembly. These are led by the Secretary of State, who replaces the Governor at need.

LOCAL GOVERNMENT

The island is divided into 78 municipal districts for the purposes of local administration. The municipalities comprise both urban areas and the surrounding neighbourhood. They are governed by a mayor and a municipal assembly, both elected for a four-year term.

The Government

HEAD OF STATE

President: Barack Hussein Obama (took office 20 January 2009).

EXECUTIVE
(July 2010)

The Government is formed by the Partido Nuevo Progresista (PNP).

Governor: Luis G. Fortuño (took office 2 January 2009).

Secretary of State: Kenneth D. McClintock Hernández.

Secretary of the Interior: Marcos Rodríguez Emma.

Secretary of Justice: Guillermo Somoza.

Secretary of the Treasury: Juan Carlos Puig Morales.

Secretary of Education: Odette Piñeiro Caballero.

Secretary of the Family: Yanitsia Irizarry Méndez.

Secretary of Labour and Human Resources: Miguel Romero Lugo.

Secretary of Transportation and Public Works: Rubén A. Hernández Gregorat.

Secretary of Health: Lorenzo González.

Secretary of Agriculture: Javier Rivera Aquino.

Secretary of Housing: Yesef Y. Cordero.

Secretary of Natural and Environmental Resources: Daniel José Galán Kercado.

Secretary of Consumer Affairs: Luis Geraldo Rivera Marín.

Secretary of Recreation and Sports: Henry Newmann.

Secretary of Economic Development and Commerce: José R. Pérez Riera.

Secretary of Correction and Rehabilitation: Carlos Molina Rodríguez.

Secretary of Organization and Public Policy: Alejandro J. Figueroa.

Attorney-General: Irene S. Soroeta Kodesh.

Resident Commissioner in Washington: Pedro Pierluisi Urrutia.

GOVERNMENT OFFICES

Office of the Governor: La Fortaleza, POB 9020082, PR 00902-0082; tel. (787) 721-7000; fax (787) 724-1472; e-mail secretariomail@fortaleza.gobierno.pr; internet www.fortaleza.gobierno.pr.

Department of Agriculture: Avda Fernández Juncos 1309, 2°, Parada 19 1/2, PR 00908-1163; POB 10163, Santurce, PR 00909; tel. (787) 721-2120; fax (787) 723-8512; e-mail enegron@da.gobierno.pr; internet www.agricultura.gobierno.pr.

Department of Consumer Affairs: Edif. Norte, 4°, Avda José de Diego, Parada 22, Centro Gubernamental Minillas, San Juan, PR 00940-1059; POB 41059, Minillas Station, Santurce, PR 00940; tel. (787) 722-7555; fax (787) 726-5707; e-mail confidencia@daco.gobierno.pr; internet www.daco.gobierno.pr.

Department of Correction and Rehabilitation: Avda Teniente Cesar Gonzalez, esq. Calle Juan Calaf 34, Urb. Industrial Tres Monjitas, San Juan, PR 00917; POB 71308, Río Piedras, PR 00936; tel. (787) 273-6464; fax (787) 792-7677; internet www.ac.gobierno.pr.

Department of Economic Development and Commerce: Avda Roosevelt 355, Suite 401, San Juan, PR 00936-2350; POB 362350, Hato Rey, PR 00918; tel. (787) 758-4747; fax (787) 753-6874; internet www.ddec.gobierno.pr.

Department of Education: Avda Teniente César González, esq. Calaf, Urb. Industrial Tres Monjitas, Hato Rey, PR 00919-0759; POB 190759, San Juan, PR 00917; tel. (787) 759-2000; fax (787) 250-0275; internet www.de.gobierno.pr.

Department of the Family: POB 11398, Santurce, San Juan, PR 00910-1398; tel. (787) 294-4900; fax (787) 294-0732; internet www.familia.gobierno.pr.

Department of Health: Edif. E altos, Área Centro Médico, Calle Maga, San Juan, PR 00936-8184; POB 70184, Rio Piedras, PR 00936; tel. (787) 765-2929; e-mail webmaster@salud.gov.pr; internet www.salud.gov.pr.

Department of Housing: Edif. Juan C. Cordero, Avda Barbosa 606, Rio Piedras, PR 00928-1365; Apdo 21365, San Juan, PR 00928-1365; tel. (787) 274-2527; fax (787) 758-9263; e-mail mcardona@vivienda.gobierno.pr; internet www.vivienda.gobierno.pr.

Department of Justice: Edif. Principal del Depto de Justicia, 11°, Calle Olimpo, esq. Axtmayer, Parada 11, No 601, Miramar, San Juan, PR 00902-0192; POB 9020192, San Juan, PR 00907; tel. (787) 721-2900; fax (787) 724-4770; e-mail aalamo@justicia.gobierno.pr; internet www.justicia.gobierno.pr; incl. the Office of the Attorney-General.

Department of Labour and Human Resources: Edif. Prudencio Rivera Martínez, Avda Muñoz Rivera 505, Hato Rey, PR 00918; POB 191020, San Juan, PR 00919-1020; tel. (787) 754-5353; fax (787) 756-1149; e-mail webmaster@dtrh.gobierno.pr; internet www.dtrh.gobierno.pr.

Department of Natural and Environmental Resources: Carretera 8838, Km 6.3, Sector El Cinco, Río Piedras, PR 00906-6600; POB 366147, San Juan, PR 00936; tel. (787) 999-2200; fax (787) 999-2303; e-mail webmaster@drna.gobierno.pr; internet www.drna.gobierno.pr.

Department of Recreation and Sports: Parque de Santurce, Calle Los Ángeles, San Juan, PR 00902-3207; POB 9023207, Santurce, PR 00909; tel. (787) 721-2800; fax (787) 728-0313; e-mail mraffaele@drd.gobierno.pr; internet www.drd.gobierno.pr.

Department of State: Calle San José, esq. San Francisco, San Juan, PR 00902-3271; Apdo 9023271, San Juan, PR 00901; tel. (787) 722-2121; fax (787) 725-7303; e-mail estado@gobierno.pr; internet www.estado.gobierno.pr.

Department of Transportation and Public Works: Edif. Sur, 17°, Avda de Diego, Santurce, PR 00940-1269; POB 41269, Minillas Station, Santurce, PR 00940; tel. (787) 722-2929; fax (787) 725-1620; e-mail servciud@act.dtop.gov.pr; internet www.dtop.gov.pr.

Department of the Treasury: Edif. Intendente Ramírez, Parada 1, Paseo Covandonga 10, San Juan, PR 00902-4140; POB 9024140, San Juan, PR 00902; tel. (787) 722-0216; fax (787) 723-6213; e-mail infoserv@hacienda.gobierno.pr; internet www.hacienda.gobierno.pr.

Gubernatorial Election, 4 November 2008

Candidate	Votes	%
Luis G. Fortuño Burset (PNP)	1,025,945	52.84
Aníbal Acevedo Vilá (PPD)	801,053	41.26
Rogelio Figueroa García (PPR)	53,690	2.77
Edwin Irizarry Mora (PIP)	39,590	2.04
Total (incl. others)*	1,941,663	100.00

* Including 13,215 votes for write-in candidates, 3,282 blank votes and 4,888 invalid votes.

Legislature

LEGISLATIVE ASSEMBLY

Senate

President of the Senate: THOMAS RIVERA SCHATZ.

Election, 4 November 2008

Party	Seats
PNP	22
PPD	5
Total	27

House of Representatives

Speaker of the House: JENNIFFER GONZÁLEZ COLÓN.

Election, 4 November 2008

Party	Seats
PNP	37
PPD	14
Total	51

Election Commission

Comisión Estatal de Elecciones de Puerto Rico (CEE): Edif. Administrativo, Avda Arterial B 550, Hato Rey, San Juan, PR 00940-5552; POB 19555, San Juan, PR 00919; tel. (787) 777-8682; fax 296-0173; e-mail comentarios@cee.gobierno.pr; internet www.ceepur.org; f. 1977; independent; Pres. RAMÓN. E. GÓMEZ-COLÓN; Dir YVONNE RIVERA PICORELLI.

Political Organizations

Frente Socialista: Buzón 69, POB 71325, San Juan, PR 00936; tel. (787) 617-7105; e-mail fs@frentesocialistapr.org; internet www.frentesocialistapr.org; f. 1990; mem. orgs incl. the Partido Revolucionario de los Trabajadores Puertorriqueños (PRTP—Los Macheteros) and Movimiento Socialista de Trabajadores; Spokesperson GUILLERMO DE LA PAZ VÉLEZ.

Movimiento Socialista de Trabajadores (MST): POB 123, Río Piedras, PR 00123; e-mail info@bandera.org; internet www.bandera.org; f. 1982 by merger of the Movimiento Socialista Popular and Partido Socialista Revolucionario; pro-independence; mainly composed of workers and university students; Spokesperson SCOTT BARBÉS CAMINERO.

Movimiento Independentista Nacional Hostosiano (MINH): Of. Central, C25 NE339, San Juan, PR 00920; f. 2004 by merger of the Congreso Nacional Hostosiano and Nuevo Movimiento Independentista (fmr mems of the Partido Socialista Puertorriqueño); pro-independence; Co-Pres JULIO MURIENTE PÉREZ, NOEL COLÓN MARTÍNEZ.

Partido Independentista Puertorriqueño (PIP) (Puerto Rican Independence Party): Avda Roosevelt 963, San Juan, PR 00920-2901; tel. (787) 782-1430; fax (787) 782-2000; e-mail pipnacional@independencia.net; internet www.independencia.net; f. 1946; advocates full independence for Puerto Rico as a socialist-democratic republic; Leader RUBÉN BERRÍOS MARTÍNEZ; Exec. Pres. FERNANDO MARTÍN; Sec.-Gen. JUAN DALMAU RAMÍREZ; c. 6,000 mems.

Partido Nuevo Progresista (PNP) (New Progressive Party): POB 1992, Fernández Zuncos Station, San Juan 00910-1992; tel. (787) 289-2000; e-mail dannyls@caribe.net; internet www.pnp.org; f. 1967; advocates eventual admission of Puerto Rico as a federated state of the USA; Pres. LUIS G. FORTUÑO BURSET; c. 225,000 mems.

Partido Popular Democrático (PPD) (Popular Democratic Party): Avda Constitución 403, San Juan, PR 00906; POB 9065788, San Juan, PR 00906-5788; tel. (787) 725-7001; e-mail info@ppdpr.net; internet ppdpr.net; f. 1938; supports continuation and improvement of the present Commonwealth status of Puerto Rico; Pres. and Leader HÉCTOR J. FERRER RÍOS; c. 950,000 mems.

Partido Puertorriqueños por Puerto Rico (Puerto Ricans for Puerto Rico—PPR): Calle Palma 1112, esq. con RH Tood, Santurce; POB 9858, San Juan, PR 00908; tel. (787) 340-4476; fax (787) 725-0001; e-mail contacto@popuertorico.com; internet www.porpuertorico.com; f. 2003 as an ecological ('green') party; formally registered as political party in 2007; promotes citizen participation, sustainable devt and quality of life; Pres. ROGELIO FIGUEROA.

Puerto Rican Republican Party: Suite 203, Avda Piñero 1629, San Juan, PR 00920; tel. (787) 462-7474; e-mail cchardon@goppr.org; internet www.goppr.org; Chair. CARLOS MÉNDEZ MARTÍNEZ; Exec. Dir RICARDO APONTE.

Puerto Rico Democratic Party: POB 19328, San Juan, PR 00910-3939; tel. (787) 274-2921; fax (787) 759-9075; Chair. ROBERTO PRATS.

Refundación Comunista Puerto Rico: Organización RC, POB 13362, San Juan, PR 00908-3362; e-mail refundacionpcp@yahoo.es; internet www.refundacioncomunistapr.com; f. 2001; Marxist-Leninist; pro-independence; maintains close relations with the Frente Socialista; Contact ABALLARDE ROJO.

Judicial System

The Judiciary is vested in the Supreme Court and other courts as may be established by law. The Supreme Court comprises a Chief Justice and up to six Associate Justices, appointed by the Governor with the consent of the Senate. The lower Judiciary consists of Superior and District Courts and Municipal Justices equally appointed.

There is also a US Federal District Court, the judges of which are appointed by the President of the USA. Judges of the US Territorial District Court are appointed by the Governor.

Supreme Court of Puerto Rico

POB 2392, Puerta de Tierra, San Juan, PR 00902-2392; tel. (787) 724-3551; fax (787) 725-4910; e-mail buzon@tribunales.gobierno.pr; internet www.tribunalpr.org.

Chief Justice: FEDERICO HERNÁNDEZ DENTON.

Justices: FEDERICO HERNÁNDEZ DENTON, EFRAÍN E. RIVERA PÉREZ, LIANA FIOL MATTA, ANABELLE RODRÍGUEZ RODRÍGUEZ, ERICK V. KOLTHOFF CARABALLO, MILDRED G. PABÓN CHARNECO, RAFAEL L. MARTÍNEZ TORRES.

US Territorial District Court for Puerto Rico

Clemente Ruiz-Nazario US Courthouse & Federico Degetau Federal Bldg, 150 Carlos Chardón St, Hato Rey, PR 00918; tel. (787) 772-3011; fax (787) 766-5693; internet www.prd.uscourts.gov.

Judges: JOSÉ A. FUSTÉ, CARMEN C. CEREZO, DANIEL R. DOMÍNGUEZ, JAY A. GARCÍA-GREGORY, AIDA M. DELGADO-COLÓN, GUSTAVO A. GELPÍ, FRANCISCO A. BESOSA, JUAN M. PÉREZ GIMÉNEZ, JAIME PIERAS, Jr, RAYMOND L. ACOSTA, SALVADOR E. CASELLAS.

Religion

CHRISTIANITY

The Roman Catholic Church

Puerto Rico comprises one archdiocese and five dioceses. Some 73% of the population are Roman Catholics.

Bishops' Conference of Puerto Rico

POB 40682, San Juan, PR 00940-0682; tel. (787) 728-1650; fax (787) 728-1654; e-mail ceppr@coqui.net.

f. 1960; Pres. Mgr RUBÉN ANTONIO GONZÁLEZ MEDINA (Bishop of Caguas).

Archbishop of San Juan de Puerto Rico: Rt Rev. ROBERTO OCTAVIO GONZÁLEZ NIEVES, Arzobispado, Calle San Jorge 201, Santurce, POB 00902-1967; tel. (787) 725-4975; fax (787) 723-4040; e-mail cancilleria@arqsj.org.

Other Christian Churches

The Protestant churches active in Puerto Rico include the Episcopalian, Baptist, Presbyterian, Methodist, Seventh-day Adventist, Lutheran, Mennonite, Salvation Army and Christian Science.

Episcopal Church of Puerto Rico: POB 902, St Just, PR 00978; tel. (787) 761-9800; fax (787) 761-0320; e-mail iep@episcopalpr.org; internet www.episcopalpr.org; f. 1872; diocese of the Episcopal Church in the USA, part of the Anglican Communion; Leader Bishop Rt Rev. DAVID ANDRÉS ALVAREZ; 42,000 baptized mems.

Puerto Rico Council of Churches: Calle El Roble 54, Apdo 21343, Río Piedras, San Juan, PR 00928; tel. (787) 765-6030; fax (787) 765-5977; f. 1954 as the Evangelical Council of Puerto Rico; Pres. Rev. HÉCTOR SOTO; Exec. Sec. Rev. CRUZ A. NEGRÓN TORRES; 8 mem. churches.

BAHÁ'Í FAITH

National Spiritual Assembly: POB 11603, San Juan, PR 00910-2703; tel. (787) 763-0982; fax (787) 753-4449; e-mail bahaipr@prtc.net; internet www.bahaipr.org.

JUDAISM

There is a small Jewish community numbering around 2,500 adherents (less than 1% of the population).

Sha'are Zedek Synagogue-Community Center: 903 Avda Ponce de León, Santurce, San Juan, PR 00907; tel. (809) 724-4157; fax (809) 722-4157; f. 1942; conservative congregation with 250 families; Rabbi GABRIEL FRYDMAN.

There is also a reform congregation with 60 families.

The Press

Puerto Rico has high readership figures for its few newspapers and magazines, as well as for mainland US periodicals. Several newspapers have a large additional readership among the immigrant communities in New York.

DAILIES

(m = morning; s = Sunday)

El Nuevo Día: Parque Industrial Amelia, Carretera 165, Guaynabo; POB 9067512, San Juan, PR 00906-7512; tel. (787) 641-8000; fax (787) 641-3924; e-mail laferre@elnuevodia.com; internet www.elnuevodia.com; f. 1970; Chair. and Editor MARÍA LUISA FERRÉ RANGEL; Pres. MARÍA EUGENIA FERRÉ RANGEL; Dir LUIS ALBERTO FERRÉ RANGEL; circ. 202,212 (m), 254,769 (s).

Primera Hora: Parque Industrial Amelia, Calle Diana Lote 18, Guaynabo, PR 00966; POB 2009, Cataño, PR 00963-2009; tel. (787) 641-5454; fax (787) 641-4472; e-mail servicios@primerahora.com; internet www.primerahora.com; Pres. and Editor ANTONIO LUIS FERRÉ; Dir JORGE CABEZAS; Gen. Man. JUAN MARIO ALVAREZ CARTAÑA; circ. 133,483 (m), 92,584 (Sat.).

The San Juan Star: POB 364187, San Juan, PR 00936-4187; tel. (787) 782-4200; fax (787) 783-5788; internet www.thesanjuanstar.com; f. 1959; English; Pres. and Publr GERRY ANGULO; Gen. Man. SALVADOR HASBÚN; circ. 50,000.

El Vocero de Puerto Rico: Apdo 7515, San Juan, PR 00906-7515; tel. (787) 721-2300; fax (787) 722-0131; e-mail opinion@vocero.com; internet www.vocero.com; f. 1974; Publr and Editor GASPAR ROCA; circ. 143,150 (m), 123,869 (Sat.).

PERIODICALS

BuenaVIDA: 1700 Fernández Juncos Ave, San Juan, PR 00909; tel. (787) 728-7325; f. 1990 as *Buena Salud*; monthly; health and fitness; Editor IVONNE LONGUEIRA; circ. 61,000.

Caribbean Business: 1700 Fernández Juncos Ave, San Juan, PR 00909-2938; POB 12130, San Juan, PR 00914-0130; tel. (787) 728-9300; fax (787) 726-1626; e-mail cbeditor@casiano.com; internet www.casiano.com/html/cb.html; f. 1973; weekly; business and finance; Man. Editor RAQUEL ROMÁN; circ. 45,000.

Educación: c/o Dept of Education, POB 190759, Hato Rey Station, San Juan, PR 00919; f. 1960; 2 a year; Spanish; Editor JOSÉ GALARZA RODRÍGUEZ; circ. 28,000.

La Estrella de Puerto Rico: 140 Roosevelt Bldg, Ave F. D. Roosevelt, Hato Rey, PR 00917; tel. (787) 754-4440; fax (787) 754-4457; e-mail myrna.lopez@periodicolaestrella.com; internet www.periodicolaestrella.com; f. 1983; weekly; Spanish and English; Editor-in-Chief FRANK GAUD; circ. 123,500.

Imagen: 1700 Fernández Juncos Ave, Stop 25, San Juan, PR 00909-2999; tel. (787) 728-4545; fax (787) 728-7325; e-mail imagen@casiano.com; internet www.casiano.com/html/imagen.html; f. 1986; monthly; women's interest; Editor ANNETTE OLIVERAS; circ. 80,000.

¡Qué Pasa!: Loiza St Station, POB 6338, San Juan, PR 00914; tel. (787) 728-3000; fax (787) 728-1075; e-mail manoly@casiano.com; internet www.casiano.com/html/quepasa.html; f. 1948; quarterly; English; publ. by Puerto Rico Tourism Co; official tourist guide; Editor RONALD FLORES; circ. 120,000.

Resonancias: Instituto de Cultura Puertorriqueña, Oficina de Publicaciones, Ventas y Mercadeo, POB 9024184, San Juan, PR 00902-4184; tel. (787) 724-4215; fax (787) 723-0168; e-mail revista@icp.gobierno.pr; internet www.icp.gobierno.pr; f. 2000; 2 a year; Spanish; Puerto Rican and general culture and music; Editor GLORIA TAPIA; circ. 3,000.

Revista Colegio de Abogados de Puerto Rico: POB 9021900, San Juan, PR 00902-1900; tel. (787) 721-3358; fax (787) 725-0330; e-mail carlosgil@prtc.net; f. 1914; quarterly; Spanish; law; Editor Lic. CARLOS GIL AYALA; circ. 10,000.

Revista del Instituto de Cultura Puertorriqueña: Oficina de Publicaciones, Ventas y Mercadeo, POB 9024184, San Juan, PR 00902-4184; tel. (787) 721-0901; e-mail revista@icp.gobierno.pr; internet www.icp.gobierno.pr; f. 1958; 2 a year; Spanish; arts, literature, history, theatre, Puerto Rican culture; Editor GLORIA TAPIA; circ. 3,000.

La Semana: Calle Cristóbal Colón, esq. Ponce de León, Casilla 6537, Caguas 00726-6537; tel. (787) 743-6537; e-mail gerentegeneral@lasemana.com; internet www.lasemana.com; weekly; f. 1963; Spanish; regional interest; Gen. Man. MARJORIE M. RIVERA RIVERA.

TeVe Guía: San Juan, PR; weekly; TV listings; circ. 470,000 (monthly).

La Torre: POB 23322, UPR Station, San Juan, PR 00931-3322; tel. (787) 758-0148; fax (787) 753-9116; e-mail ydef@hotmail.com; f. 1953; publ. by University of Puerto Rico; quarterly; literary criticism, linguistics, humanities; Editor YUDIT DE FERDINANDY; circ. 1,000.

Vea: POB 190240, San Juan, PR 00919-0240; tel. (787) 721-0095; fax (787) 725-1940; f. 1969; weekly; Spanish; TV, films and celebrities; Editor ENRIQUE PIZZI; circ. 92,000.

El Visitante: POB 41305, San Juan, PR 00940-1305; tel. (787) 728-3710; fax (787) 268-1748; e-mail director@elvisitante.biz; internet www.elvisitante.net; f. 1975; weekly; Roman Catholic; Dir JOSÉ R. ORTIZ VALLADARES; Editor Rev. EFRAÍN ZABALA; circ. 59,000.

Publishers

Ediciones Huracán Inc: 874 Baldorioty de Castro, San Juan, PR 00925; tel. (787) 763-7407; fax (787) 753-1486; e-mail edhucan@caribe.net; f. 1975; textbooks, literature, social studies, history; Pres. CARMEN RIVERA-IZCOA.

Editorial Académica, Inc: 67 Santa Anastacia St, El Vigía, Río Piedras, PR 00926; tel. (787) 760-3879; f. 1988; regional history, politics, government, educational materials, fiction; Dir FIDELIO CALDERÓN.

Editorial Cordillera, Inc: 1500 Ponce de León Local 2, El Cinco, POB 3148, San Juan, PR 00926; tel. (787) 767-6188; fax (787) 767-8646; e-mail info@editorialcordillera.com; internet www.editorialcordillera.com; f. 1962; Puerto Rican history, culture and literature, educational, trade; Pres. PATRICIA GUTIÉRREZ; Sec. and Treas. ADOLFO R. LÓPEZ.

Editorial Cultural Inc: POB 21056, Río Piedras, San Juan, PR 00928; tel. (787) 765-9767; f. 1949; general literature and political science; Dir FRANCISCO M. VÁZQUEZ.

Instituto de Cultura Puertorriqueña: Oficina de Publicaciones, Ventas y Mercadeo, POB 9024184, San Juan, PR 00902-4184; tel. (787) 724-0700; fax (787) 723-0168; e-mail revista@icp.gobierno.pr; internet www.icp.gobierno.pr; f. 1955; literature, history, poetry, music, textbooks, arts and crafts; Dir GLORIA TAPIA.

University of Puerto Rico Press (EDUPR): POB 23322, UPR Station, Río Piedras, San Juan, PR 00931-3322; tel. (787) 250-0435; fax (787) 753-9116; e-mail edupr@upr.edu; internet www.laeditorialupr.com; f. 1947; general literature, children's literature, Caribbean studies, law, philosophy, science, educational; Exec. Dir MANUEL G. SANDOVAL BAÉZ.

Broadcasting and Communications

TELECOMMUNICATIONS

Junta Reglamentadora de Telecomunicaciones de Puerto Rico: Avda Roberto H. Todd 500, Parada 18, Santurce, San Juan, PR 00907-3981; tel. (787) 756-0804; fax (787) 756-0814; e-mail correspondencia@jrtpr.gobierno.pr; internet www.jrtpr.gobierno.pr; telecommunications regulator; Pres. SANDRA E. TORRES LÓPEZ.

Puerto Rico Telephone Co (PRTC): Avda Juan Ponce de León 562, Hato Rey; POB 360998, San Juan, PR 00936-0998; tel. (787) 782-8282; fax (787) 774-0037; internet www.telefonicapr.com; provides all telecommunications services in Puerto Rico; fmrly state-owned; acquired by America Móvil in 2007; Pres. and CEO ENRIQUE ORTIZ DE MONTELLANO RANGEL.

BROADCASTING

There were 120 radio stations and 15 television stations operating in 2002. The only non-commercial stations are the radio station and the two television stations operated by the Puerto Rico Department of Education. The US Armed Forces also operate a radio station and three television channels.

Asociación de Radiodifusores de Puerto Rico (Puerto Rican Radio Broadcasters' Asscn): Caparra Terrace, Calle Delta 1305, San Juan, PR 00920; tel. (787) 783-8810; fax (787) 781-7647; e-mail prbroadcasters@centennialpr.net; internet radiodifusores.info/portal; f. 1947; Pres. MANUEL SANTIAGO SANTOS; Exec. Dir JOSÉ A. RIBAS DOMINICCI; 102 mems.

Finance

(cap. = capital; res = reserves; dep. = deposits; brs = branches; amounts in US dollars)

BANKING

Government Bank

Government Development Bank for Puerto Rico (Banco Gubernamental de Fomento para Puerto Rico—BGF): Roberto Sánchez Vilella Government Centre, Avda De Diego, Stop 22, Santurce, PR 00907; POB 42001, San Juan, PR 00940-2001; tel. (787) 722-2525; fax (787) 721-1443; e-mail gdbpr@bgf.gobierno.pr; internet www.gdb-pur.com; f. 1942; independent govt agency; acts as fiscal (borrowing) agent to the Commonwealth Govt and its public corpns and provides long- and medium-term loans to private businesses; equity 2,271.2m., dep. 9,447.9m. (June 2007); Pres. CARLOS M. GARCÍA; Chair. RAFAEL F. MARTÍNEZ MARGARIDA.

Autoridad para el Financiamiento de la Vivienda de Puerto Rico: Edif. Juan C. Cordero, Avda Barbosa 606, Río Piedras, PR 00919-0345; POB 71361, San Juan, PR 00936-8461; tel. (787) 765-7577; fax (787) 620-3521; f. 1961; fmrly Banco y Agencia de Financiamiento de la Vivienda de Puerto Rico; present name adopted in 2001; subsidiary of the Government Development Bank for Puerto Rico; finance agency; helps low-income families to purchase houses; Exec. Dir GEORGE R. JOYNER KELLY.

Commercial Banks

Banco Bilbao Vizcaya Argentaria Puerto Rico: 15th Floor, Torre BBVA, 258 Muñoz Rivera Ave, San Juan 00918; POB 364745, San Juan, PR 00936-4745; tel. (787) 777-2000; fax (787) 777-2999; internet www.bbvapr.com; f. 1967 as Banco de Mayagüez; taken over by Banco Occidental in 1979; merged with Banco Bilbao Vizcaya, S.A. in 1988; named changed from BBV Puerto Rico in 2000; cap. 138.7m., res, surplus and profits 387.5m., dep. 5,849.8m. (Dec. 2007); Pres. ANTONIO UGUINA; 65 brs.

Banco Popular de Puerto Rico: POB 362708, San Juan, PR 00936-2708; tel. (787) 724-3659; e-mail internet@bppr.com; internet www.bppr.com; f. 1893; cap. 7.0m., res, surplus and profits 1,811.0m., dep. 23,965.0m. (Dec. 2007); Chair. and CEO RICHARD L. CARRIÓN; Pres. DAVID H. CHAFEY, Jr; 195 brs.

Banco Santander Puerto Rico: Avda Ponce de León 207, Hato Rey, PR 00919; POB 362589, San Juan, PR 00936-0062; tel. (787) 759-7070; fax (787) 767-7913; e-mail jdiaz@bspr.com; internet www.santanderpr.com; f. 1976; cap. 106.2m., res, surplus and profits 504.6m., dep. 7,484.0m. (Dec. 2007); Pres. and CEO JUAN MORENO BLANCO; Chair. GONZALO DE LAS HERAS; 67 brs.

Citibank NA: Ochoa Bldg, 500 Tanca St, San Juan, PR 00901; tel. (787) 766-2323; internet www.latam.citibank.com/puertorico; 14 brs.

Doral Bank: Galería Paseos Mall, Grand Blvd Paseos, Suite 107, San Juan, PR 00926; tel. (787) 725-6060; fax (787) 725-6062; e-mail dbcw@doralbank.com; internet www.doralbank.com; cap. 400m., dep. 2,730m., assets 6,726m. (Dec. 2003); subsidiary of local bank-holding co, Doral Financial Corpn, which completed buyout negotiations with financial group, led by Bear Stearn Cos Inc (USA), in July 2007; 90% investor-owned, through Doral Holdings Delaware, LLC, since July 2007; CEO GLEN R. WAKEMAN; Chair. CALIXTO GARCÍA VELEZ; 37 brs.

FirstBank Puerto Rico: First Federal Bldg, 1519 Ponce de León Ave, POB 9146, Santurce, PR 00908-0146; tel. (787) 729-8200; fax (787) 729-8139; internet www.firstbankpr.com; f. 1948, adopted current name in 1998; part of First BanCorp; cap. and res 368.3m., dep. 3,363.0m. (Dec. 2000); Chair. LUIS M. BEAUCHAMP; 45 brs.

Scotiabank de Puerto Rico: Plaza Scotiabank, 273 Ponce de León Ave, esq. Calle Méjico, Hato Rey, PR 00918; POB 362230, San Juan, PR 00936-2230; tel. (787) 758-8989; fax (787) 766-7879; internet www.scotiabankpr.com; f. 1910; cap. 23.2m., res, surplus and profits 140.5m., dep. 1,354.1m. (Dec. 2007); Chair. PETER CARDINAL; Pres. and CEO TROY K. WRIGHT; 19 brs.

Savings Banks

Oriental Bank and Trust: Ave Fagot, esq. Obispado M-26, Ponce; tel. (787) 259-0000; fax (787) 259-0700; e-mail ofg@anreder.com; internet www.orientalonline.com; total assets 2,039m. (June 2001); Pres. and CEO JOSÉ ENRIQUE FERNÁNDEZ; Chair. JOSÉ J. GIL DE LAMADRID.

R & G Financial Corporation: POB 2510, Guaynabo, PR 00970; tel. (787) 766-6677; fax (787) 766-8175; internet www.rgonline.com; total assets 4,676m. (Dec. 2001); Pres. and CEO ROLANDO RODRÍGUEZ; Chair. JUAN AGOSTO-ALICEA.

Banking Organization

Puerto Rico Bankers' Association: 208 Ponce de León Ave, Suite 1014, San Juan, PR 00918-1002; tel. (787) 753-8630; fax (787) 754-6022; e-mail info@abpr.com; internet www.abpr.com; Pres. RAFAEL BLANCO; Vice-Pres. JOSÉ DÍAZ.

INSURANCE

Atlantic Southern Insurance Co: POB 362889, San Juan, PR 00936-2889; tel. (787) 767-9750; fax (787) 764-4707; internet www.atlanticsouthern.com; f. 1945; Chair. DIANE BEAN SCHWARTZ; Pres. RAMÓN L. GALANES.

Caribbean American Life Assurance Co: 273 Ponce de Léon Ave, Suite 1300, Scotiabank Plaza, San Juan, PR 00917; tel. (787) 250-1199; fax (787) 250-7680; internet www.calac.com; Pres. IVÁN C. LOPÉZ.

Cooperativa de Seguros Multiples de Puerto Rico: POB 363846, San Juan, PR 00936-3846; internet www.segurosmultiples.coop; general insurance; Pres. RENÉ A. CAMPOS CARBONELL.

La Cruz Azul de Puerto Rico: Carretera Estatal 1, Km 17.3, Río Piedras, San Juan, PR 00927; POB 366068, San Juan, PR 00936-6068; tel. (787) 272-9898; fax (787) 272-7867; e-mail scliente@cruzazul.com; internet www.cruzazul.com; Exec. Dir MARKS VIDAL.

FirstBank Insurance Agency, Inc: Las Vistas Shopping Village, Suite 36, 300 Felisa Rincón de Gautier, POB 9146, San Juan, PR 00908-0146; tel. (787) 292-4380; fax (787) 292-4355; e-mail lymarie.torres@firstbankpr.com; internet www.firstbankpr.com; f. 2003; owned by First BanCorp; Pres. VICTOR SANTIAGO.

Great American Life Assurance Co of Puerto Rico: POB 363786, San Juan, PR 00936-3786; tel. (787) 758-4888; fax (787) 766-1985; e-mail galifepr@galifepr.com; known as General Accident Life Assurance Co until 1998; Pres. ARTURA CARIÓN; Sr Vice-Pres. EDGARDO DIAZ.

National Insurance Co: POB 366107, San Juan, PR 00936-6107; tel. (787) 758-0909; fax (787) 756-7360; internet www.nicpr.com; f. 1961; subsidiary of National Financial Group; Chair., Pres. and CEO CARLOS M. BENÍTEZ, Jr.

Pan American Life Insurance Co: POB 364865, San Juan, PR 00936-4865; tel. (787) 620-1414; fax (787) 999-1250; e-mail jortega@panamericanlife.com; internet www.panamericanlife.com; Regional Pres. JUAN A. ORTEGA; Gen. Man. MAITE MUÑOZGUREN.

Puerto Rican-American Insurance Co: POB 70333, San Juan, PR 00936-8333; tel. (787) 250-5214; fax (787) 250-5371; f. 1920; total assets 119.9m. (1993); Chair. and CEO RAFAEL A. ROCA; Pres. RODOLFO E. CRISCUOLO.

Security National Life Insurance Co: POB 193309, Hato Rey, PR 00919; tel. (787) 753-6161; fax (787) 758-7409; Pres. CARLOS FERNÁNDEZ.

Universal Insurance Group: Calle 1, Lote 10, 3°, Metro Office Park, Guaynabo; POB 2145, San Juan, PR 00922-2145; tel. (787) 793-7202; fax (787) 782-0692; internet www.universalpr.com; f. 1972; comprises Universal Insurance Co, Eastern America Insurance Agency and Caribbean Alliance Insurance Co; Chair. and CEO LUIS MIRANDA CASAÑAS.

There are numerous agents, representing Puerto Rican, US and foreign companies.

Trade and Industry

DEVELOPMENT ORGANIZATION

Puerto Rico Industrial Development Co (PRIDCO): POB 362350, San Juan, PR 00936-2350; Avda Roosevelt 355, Hato Rey, San Juan, PR 00918; tel. (787) 758-4747; fax (787) 764-1415; internet www.pridco.com; public agency responsible for the govt-sponsored industrial devt programme; Exec. Dir JAVIER VASQUÉZ MORALES.

CHAMBERS OF COMMERCE

Chamber of Commerce of Puerto Rico: 100 Calle Tetuán, Viejo San Juan, PR 00901; POB 9024033, San Juan, PR 00902-4033; tel. (787) 721-6060; fax (787) 723-1891; e-mail camarapr@camarapr.net; internet www.camarapr.org; f. 1913; Pres. JORGE GALLIANO; Exec. Vice-Pres. EDGARDO BIGAS VALLADARES; 1,800 mems.

Chamber of Commerce of the South of Puerto Rico: 65 Calle Isabel, POB 7455, Ponce, PR 00732-7455; tel. (787) 844-4400; fax (787) 844-4705; e-mail camarasur@prtc.net; internet www.camarasur.org; f. 1885; Pres. MARIO R. SILVAGNOLI GUZMÁN; Exec. Dir HÉCTOR E. LÓPEZ PALERMO; 550 mems.

Chamber of Commerce of the West of Puerto Rico, Inc: Edif. Doral Bank, Of. 905, 101 Calle Méndez Vigo Oeste, POB 9, Mayagüez, PR 00680; tel. (787) 832-3749; fax (787) 832-4287; e-mail info@ccopr.com; internet www.ccopr.com; f. 1962; Pres. JOSE A. JUSTINIANO; 300 mems.

Puerto Rico/United Kingdom Chamber of Commerce: 1509 Lopez Landron, Suite 1100, San Juan, PR 00911; tel. (877) 721-0160; fax (787) 721-7333; e-mail iancourt1@cs.com; internet users.bivapr.net/iancourt; Chair. Dr IAN COURT; 120 mems.

INDUSTRIAL AND TRADE ASSOCIATIONS

Home Builders' Association of Puerto Rico: 1605 Ponce de León Ave, Condominium San Martín, Santurce, San Juan, PR 00909; tel. (787) 723-0279; Exec. Dir MARÍA ELENA CRISTY; 150 mems.

Pharmaceutical Industry Association of Puerto Rico (PIA-PR): City View Plaza, Suite 407, Guaynabo, PR 00968; tel. (787) 622-0500; fax (787) 622-0503; e-mail contact@piapr.com; internet www.piapr.com; Chair. DANERIS FERNÁNDEZ; 19 mem. cos.

Puerto Rico Farm Bureau: 1605 Ponce de León Ave, Suite 403, Condominium San Martín, San Juan, PR 00909-1895; tel. (787) 721-5970; fax (787) 724-6932; f. 1925; Pres. ANTONIO ALVAREZ; over 1,500 mems.

Puerto Rico Manufacturers' Association (PRMA): Centro Internacional de Mercadeo, Torre II, Suite 702m, Carretera 165, Guaynabo, PR 00968; POB 195477, San Juan, PR 00919-5477; tel. (787) 759-9445; fax (787) 756-7670; e-mail prma_info@prma.com; internet www.prma.com; Pres. JOSEN ROSSI; Exec. Vice-Pres. WILLIAM RIEFKOHL.

Puerto Rico United Retailers Center: POB 190127, San Juan, PR 00919-0127; tel. (787) 641-8405; fax (787) 641-8406; e-mail cud@centrounido.com; internet www.centrounido.org; f. 1891; represents small and medium-sized businesses; Pres. PEDRO L. MALAVE AGUILÓ; 20,000 mems.

MAJOR COMPANIES

The following is a selection of some of the principal industrial and commercial companies operating in Puerto Rico.

Construction

Aireko General Construction: Las Casas St, Lot 20, Bairoa Industrial Park, Caguas, PR 00725; POB 2128, San Juan, PR 00922-2128; tel. (787) 653-6300; fax (787) 653-0121; e-mail anazario@aireko.com; internet www.aireko.com; f. 1963; principal co of Aireko Enterprises (group of cos), Puerto Rico; management and construction of commercial, industrial and institutional buildings; sales of US $105.5m. (2003); Pres. PAULINO LÓPEZ; 1,000 employees.

Bermúdez, Longo, Díaz-Massó S.E.: Rd 845, Km 0.5, Cupey Bajo Ward, San Juan, PR 00926; POB 191213, San Juan, PR 00919-1213; tel. (787) 761-3030; fax (787) 760-0855; e-mail lfeliciano@bermudez-longo.com; internet www.bldmpr.com; f. 1962; electrical and mechanical contractors; sales of US $108.3m. (2004); Pres. FRANCISCO DÍAZ-MASSÓ; 1,300 employees.

Cemex Puerto Rico: POB 364487, San Juan, PR 00936-4487; tel. (787) 783-3000; fax (787) 781-8850; internet www.cemexpuertorico.com; f. 2002; cement hydraulics; subsidiary of Cemex, SA, Mexico; fmrly Puerto Rican Cement Co, Inc; Country Pres. LEOPOLDO NAVARRO; Dir VLADIMIR TOVAR; 1,060 employees.

F. & R. Construction Group, Inc: Urb. University Gardens, 1010 Harvard St, San Juan, PR 00927; POB 9932 San Juan, PR 00908-9932; tel. (787) 753-7010; fax (787) 763-0269; e-mail ito@frcg.net; internet www.frcg.net; f. 1972; sales of US $230m. (2006); Pres. JAIME FULLANA OLIVENCIA; 1,072 employees.

Electronics and Computers

Hewlett-Packard Puerto Rico Co: Torre Chardón, Suite 801, Avda Chardón 350, esq. Calle Teniente Cesár Gonzales, San Juan, PR 00918; tel. (787) 474-8900; fax (787) 474-8925; internet welcome.hp.com/country/pr/es; f. 1980; subsidiary of Hewlett-Packard Co, USA; mfrs of computer hardware; Gen. Man. LUCY CRESPO; 1,700 employees.

Microsoft Puerto Rico, SA: Metro Office Park, St 1, No 18, Suite 5000, Guaynabo, PR 00968; tel. (787) 273-3600; fax (787) 273-3634; internet www.microsoft.com/puertorico; f. 1990; subsidiary of Microsoft Corpn, USA; mfrs of computer software; Pres. RODOLFO ACEVEDO; 100 employees.

Food and Beverages

Bacardi Caribbean Corpn: Carretera 165, Km 2.6, Cataño, PR 00962; tel. (787) 788-1500; fax (787) 788-0340; internet www.bacardi.com; f. 1992; distillers and distributors of rum; Pres. ANGEL O. TORRES; 1,200 employees.

Ballester Hermanos, Inc: POB 364548, San Juan, PR 00936-4548; tel. (787) 788-4110; fax (787) 788-6460; e-mail contact@bhipr.com; internet www.ballesterhermanos.com; f. 1914; food and beverage distributors; sales of US $156.5m. (2004); Chair., Pres. and CEO ALFONSO F. BALLESTER; 200 employees.

La Enoteca: Carretera 869, Parque Industrial Westgate, Barrio Palmas, Cataño, PR; tel. (787) 788-4110; fax (787) 788-7470; e-mail laenoteca@ballesterhermanos.com; internet www.laenotecapr.com; wholly owned subsidiary of Ballester Hermanos, Inc; wine distributors; Gen. Man. JOSEPH MAGRUDER.

Bumble Bee Food, LLC: 3075 Carretera 64, POB 3268, Mayaguez, PR 00681-3268; tel. (787) 834-3450; fax (787) 265-6130; internet www.bumblebee.com; f. 1960 as Bumble Bee Seafoods, Inc; name changed as above in 2005; subsidiary of Connors Bros, USA; bought by Centre Partners in 2008; seafood and meat cannery; Gen. Man. ZULMA RIVERA; 300 employees.

Destilería Serrallés, Inc: 1 Calle La Esperanza, POB 198, Mercedita, PR 00715; tel. (787) 840-1000; fax (787) 840-1155; e-mail dgadmin@donq.com; internet www.destileriaserralles.com; f. 1949; mfrs of distilled alcoholic beverages; sales of US $118.9m. (2004); Pres. FÉLIX J. SERRALLÉS; 376 employees.

B. Fernández & Hermanos Group: POB 363629, San Juan PR00936-3629; tel. (787) 288-7272; fax (787) 288-7291; e-mail info@bfernandez.com; internet www.bfernandez.com; f. 1888; holding co; food and beverage manufacture and distribution; real estate; sales of US $300m. (8); Pres. and CEO JOSÉ TEIXIDOR; Gen. Man. ANGEL VÁZQUEZ; 240 employees.

Goya Foods of Puerto Rico, Inc: Carretera 28, esq. Carretera 5, Urb. Industrial Luchetti, Bayamón, PR 00961; POB 601467 Bayamón, PR 00960-6067; tel. (787) 740-4900; fax (787) 740-5040; e-mail nramos@goyapr.com; internet www.goyapr.com; f. 1949; mfrs of canned fruit and vegetables; subsidiary of Goya Foods, USA; sales of US $105m. (2004); Pres. CARLOS UNANUE; 500 employees.

Holsum de Puerto Rico, Inc: Carretera 2, Km 20.1, Barrio Candelaria, Toa Baja, PR 00949; tel. (787) 798-8282; e-mail contacto@holsumpr.com; internet www.holsumpr.com; f. 1958; sales of US $107.5m. (2004); mfrs and distributors of bakery products; Pres RAMÓN CALDERÓN RIVERA; 840 employees.

José Santiago, Inc: Marginal Carretera 5, Km 4.4, Urb. Industrial Luchetti, Bayamón; POB 191795, San Juan, PR 00919-1795; tel. (787) 288-8835; fax (787) 288-8809; internet www.josesantiago.com; f. 1902; food and beverage distributors; sales of US $101m. (2004); Pres. JOSÉ E. SANTIAGO; 300 employees.

Méndez & Co, Inc: Carretera 20, Km 2.4, Guaynabo, PR 00969; tel. (787) 793-8888; fax (787) 783-4085; e-mail mdz@mendezcopr.com; internet www.mendezcopr.com; f. 1912; food and beverage distributors; sales of US $246.0m. (2004); Chair. SALUSTIANO 'TITO' ALVAREZ MÉNDEZ; Pres. and CEO JOSÉ ARTURO ALVAREZ; 503 employees.

Northwestern Selecta, Inc: Caparra Heights Station, POB 10718, San Juan, PR 00922-0718; tel. (787) 781-1012; fax (787) 781-1125; e-mail peteynunez@northwesternselecta.com; f. 1980; meat and fish processors and distributors; affiliate of Northwestern Meat, Inc, USA; sales of US $210.0m. (2004); Pres. ELPIDIO NUÑEZ, Jr; 300 employees.

Plaza Provision Co: Carretera 165, esq. Carretera 28, Avda El Caño, Guyanabo, PR 00965; POB 363328, San Juan, PR 00936-3328; tel. (787) 781-2070; fax (787) 781-2210; internet www.plazaprovision.com; f. 1907; food and beverage distributors; sales of US $266.0m. (2004); Chair. JAMES N. CIMINO; Pres. and CEO ROBERT CIMINO; 410 employees.

Puerto Rico Supplies Co, Inc: Lot 22–23, Luchetti Industrial Park, Bayamón, PR 00959-4390; POB 11908, San Juan, PR 00922-1908; tel. (787) 780-4043; fax (787) 780-4390; e-mail oficina@prsupplies.com; internet www.prsupplies.com; f. 1945; tobacco and food distributors; sales of US $183.2m. (2004); Chair. and CEO STANLEY PASARELL; Pres. EDWIN PÉREZ; 220 employees.

V. Suárez & Co, Inc: El Horreo de V. Suárez, Highway 165 and Buchanan, Guaynabo, PR 00968; POB 364588, San Juan, PR 00936; tel. (787) 792-1212; fax (787) 474-0735; e-mail jorge.rivera@vsuarez.com; internet www.vsuarez.com; f. 1943; investment management; food and beverage distribution; real estate; sales of US $800m. (2008); Chair. DIEGO SUÁREZ SÁNCHEZ; Pres. and CEO DIEGO SUÁREZ, Jr; 494 employees.

Packers Provision Co of Puerto Rico: Mercado Central, Edif. C, Zona Portuaria, Puerto Nuevo, PR 00920; tel. (787) 783-0011; fax (787) 782-7134; e-mail packers@packersprovision.com; f. 1974; acquired by V. Suárez & Co, Inc in 2004; meat packers, distributors of frozen and refrigerated products; sales of US $195.0m. (2004); Gen. Man. FRANCISCO JAVIER ARANGO; c. 600 employees.

Pharmaceuticals, Biotechnology and Medical Supplies

Abbott (Puerto Rico), Inc: Montehiedra Office Centre, Suite 700, 9615 Avda Los Romeros, San Juan, PR 00926-7038; tel. (787) 750-5454; fax (787) 276-3016; internet www.abbott.com; f. 1968; subsidiary of Abbott Laboratories, USA; mfrs of pharmaceuticals; Man. THOMAS FREYMAN; sales of US $500m. (2008); 2,400 employees.

Amgen Manufacturing, Ltd: POB 4060, Juncos, PR 00777; tel. (787) 656-2000; fax (787) 734-6161; internet www.amgen.com; mfrs of biotechnology and pharmaceuticals; subsidiary of Amgen, Inc, USA; Vice-Pres. and Gen. Man. MADHU BALACHANDRAN; sales of US $2,000m. (2004); c. 1,000 employees at 2 locations.

IPR Pharmaceuticals, Inc: South Main St, Sabana Gardens Industrial Park, POB 1967, Carolina, PR 00984-1967; tel. (787) 750-5353; fax (787) 750-5332; internet www.astrazeneca.com; subsidiary of AstraZeneca, United Kingdom; Pres. and Gen. Man. RUBÉN FREIRE; 2 locations.

Johnson & Johnson: c/o Ethicon LLC, Carretera 183, Km 8.3, POB 982, San Lorenzo, PR 00754; tel. (787) 783-7070; fax (787) 273-6838; e-mail cdiaz4@psgapr.jnj.com; comprises 14 subsidiaries of Johnson & Johnson, USA; mfrs of pharmaceuticals, biotechnology and medical supplies; Gen. Man. RUBEN CARDONA.

Lilly del Caribe, Inc: 65th Infantry Rd, Carretera 3, Km 12.6, POB 1198, Carolina, PR 00986-1198; tel. (787) 257-5561; fax (787) 251-5429; f. 1985; subsidiary of Eli Lilly & Co, USA; mfrs of pharmaceuticals; inaugurated new biotech facility on the island in October 2006, creating 550 new jobs; Pres. and Gen. Man. SEAMUS MALONE; sales of US $850m. (2008); 1,4900 employees in 3 locations (2008).

Medtronic Puerto Rico Operations Co (MPROC): Citibank Towers, 10th Floor, 252 Avda Ponce de Leon, POB 363829, San Juan, PR 00936-3829; tel. (787) 753-5270; fax (787) 753-2640; f. 1974; subsidiary of Medtronic, Inc, USA; medical supplies mfrs, particularly electrodes for use in pacemakers; operates 5 plants on the island; Gen. Man. MANUEL SANTIAGO; 2,250 employees in 6 locations.

Merck Sharp & Dohme (I.A) Corpn (Merck Sharp & Dohme Química de Puerto Rico): Puerto Rico Industrial Park, 65th Infantry Rd, Km 12.6, Carolina, PR 00985; POB 3689, Carolina, PR 00984-3689; tel. (787) 474-8094; internet www.msd.com.pr; f. 1953; subsidiary of Merck & Co, Inc, USA; mfrs of pharmaceuticals; Vice-Pres. and Gen. Man. DANERIS FERNÁNDEZ; over 2,000 employees in 4 locations.

Patheon, Inc: Puerto Rico Industrial Park, 65th Infantry Rd, Km 13, Carolina, PR 00984; tel. (787) 701-0010; fax (787) 258-6405; e-mail info@patheon.com; internet www.patheon.com; f. 2004 following the purchase of MOVA Pharmaceutical Corpn (f. 1986) by Patheon, Canada; mfrs and distributors of pharmaceuticals; Pres. and CEO JOAQUÍN B. VISO; c. 1,600 employees at 3 sites.

Pfizer Global Manufacturing: Carretera 689, Km 1.9, Barrio Carmelita, Vega Baja, PR 00693; POB 786, Vega Baja, PR 00694; tel. (787) 858-2323; fax (787) 855-447; subsidiary of Pfizer, Inc, USA; Vice-Pres. and Gen. Man. IVÁN DEL RÍO ROMÁN; over 5,500 employees in 5 locations.

Schering-Plough del Caribe, Inc: Carretera 865, Int. Expreso de Diego, Bo. Candelaria Arenas, Toa Baja, PR 00949; tel. (787) 261-2222; fax (787) 854-2715; internet www.schering-plough.com; subsidiary of Schering-Plough Corpn, USA; Gen. Man. RICARDO ZAYAS; c. 1,300 employees in 3 locations.

Miscellaneous

AKM Sheet Metal, Inc: Urb. Industrial Mario Julia, 418 Carretera A, Suite 1, San Juan, PR 00920-2012; tel. (787) 620-4950; fax (787) 620-4956; e-mail amarcano@akmmfg.com; internet www.akmmfg.com; f. 1997; subsidiary of AKM Corpn; mfrs of sheet metal parts and electrical products; Vice-Pres. PEDRO A. ARVESÚ; Gen. Man. ANGEL L. MARCANO.

Almacenes Pitusa, Inc: Urb. Valencia, 359 Calle Guipuzcoa, San Juan 00927; tel. (787) 641-8200; fax (787) 641-8278; f. 1976; department stores; sales of US $249.1m. (2006); Pres. ISRAEL KOPEL; 3,500 employees.

Bella Group Corpn: POB 190816, San Juan, PR 00918-0816; tel. (787) 620-7010; fax (787) 783-5265; internet www.bellainternational.com; f. 1963; sales of US $212.9m. (2004); motor vehicle distributors; Pres. and CEO CARLOS A. LOPÉZ-LAY; 421 employees.

Borschow Hospital & Medical Supplies, Inc: Centro Internacional de Distribución, Edif. 10, Carretera 869, Km 4.2, Guaynabo, PR 00962; POB 366211, San Juan, PR 00936-6211; tel. (787) 625-4100; fax (787) 625-4395; e-mail bhms@borschow.com; internet www.borschow.com; f. 1951; pharmaceutical product and medical supplies distributors; sales US $410.6m. (2006); Pres. and CEO JONATHAN BORSCHOW; 320 employees.

Chevron Phillips Chemical Puerto Rico Core, Inc: Ruta 710, Km 1.3, Barrio Las Mares, POB 10003, Guayama, PR 00785; tel. (787) 864-1515; fax (787) 864-1545; internet www.cpchem.com; f. 1967; subsidiary of Chevron Phillips Co, USA; mfrs of chemicals, chiefly paraxylene; Pres. RICHARD C. KLETT; 66 employees.

Colgate-Palmolive (Puerto Rico), Inc: Puente de Jobos, POB 540, Guayama, PR 00784; tel. (787) 723-5625; fax (787) 864-5053; f. 1988; subsidiary of Colgate-Palmolive Co, USA; mfrs of toiletries and cleaning products; Vice-Pres. and Gen. Man. JOSUÉ MUÑOZ; 90 employees.

Empresas Cordero Badillo, Inc: Avda Ponce de Léon 56, Barrio Amelia, Guaynabo, PR 00962; POB 458, Cataño, PR 00963-0458; tel. (787) 749-1400; fax (787) 749-1500; f. 1967; supermarkets; sales of US $365.0m. (2004); Chair., Pres. and CEO ATILANO CORDERO BADILLO; 2,100 employees.

Empresas Fonalledas, Inc: POB 71450, San Juan, PR 00936-8550; tel. (787) 474-7474; f. 1890; retail and property devt; sales of US $300.0m. (2006); Pres. and CEO JAIME FONALLEDAS, Jr.

Hilton International of Puerto Rico (Caribe Hilton International Hotel): Los Rosales, San Geronimo Grounds, San Juan, PR 00901; tel. and fax (787) 721-0303; fax (787) 725-8849; e-mail sjnhi_sales@hilton.com; internet hiltoncaribbean.com/sanjuan; f. 1981; hotel management; Gen. Man. JOSE CAMPO; 875 employees.

NYPRO PR, Inc: Ave. Luis Muñoz Marín, Ruta 15, Km 25.4, POB 8000, Cayey, PR 00737-8000; tel. (787) 738-4211; fax (787) 263-5738; e-mail rey.encarnacion@nypropr.com; internet www.nypro.com; f. 1973; subsidiary co of Nypro, Inc, USA; mfrs of plastics and associated products; Gen. Man. PEDRO MARTINEZ.

Supermercados Mr Special, Inc: Carretera 114, Km 0.3, Avda Santa Teresa Jornet, POB 3389, Mayaguez, PR 00681; tel. (787) 834-2695; fax (787) 833-9843; f. 1966; supermarket chain; sales of US $245.1m. (2006); Pres. SANTOS ALONSO MALDONADO; 1,082 employees.

UTILITIES

Electricity

Autoridad de Energía Eléctrica (AEE): POB 364267, San Juan, PR 00936-4267; tel. (787) 521-3434; fax (787) 521-4120; e-mail prensa@prepa.com; internet www.prepa.com; f. 1979; govt-owned electricity corpn; monopoly on power transmission and distribution ended in 2009; installed capacity of 4,404 MW; Exec. Dir MIGUEL CORDERO LÓPEZ.

TRADE UNIONS

American Federation of Labor–Congress of Industrial Organizations (AFL–CIO): San Juan; internet www.afl-cio.org; Regional Dir AGUSTÍN BENÍTEZ; c. 60,000 mems.

Central Puertorriqueña de Trabajadores (CPT): POB 364084, San Juan, PR 00936-4084; tel. (787) 781-6649; fax (787) 277-9290; f. 1982; Pres. FEDERICO TORRES MONTALVO.

Confederación General de Trabajadores de Puerto Rico: 620 San Antonio St, San Juan, PR 00907; f. 1939; Pres. FRANCISCO COLÓN GORDIANY; 35,000 mems.

Federación del Trabajo de Puerto Rico (AFL-CIO): POB S-1648, San Juan, PR 00903; tel. (787) 722-4012; f. 1952; Pres. HIPÓLITO MARCANO; Sec.-Treas. CLIFFORD W. DEPIN; 200,000 mems.

Puerto Rico Industrial Workers' Union, Inc: POB 22014, UPR Station, San Juan, PR 00931; Pres. DAVID MUÑOZ HERNÁNDEZ.

Sindicato Empleados de Equipo Pesado, Construcción y Ramas Anexas de Puerto Rico, Inc (Construction and Allied Trades Union): Calle Hicaco 95, Urb. Milaville, Río Piedras, San Juan, PR 00926; f. 1954; Pres. JESÚS M. AGOSTO; 950 mems.

Sindicato de Obreros Unidos del Sur de Puerto Rico (United Workers' Union of South Puerto Rico): POB 106, Salinas, PR 00751; f. 1961; Pres. JOSÉ CARABALLO; 52,000 mems.

Unión General de Trabajadores de Puerto Rico: Apdo 29247, Estación de Infantería, Río Piedras, San Juan, PR 00929; tel. (787) 751-5350; fax (787) 751-7604; f. 1965; Pres. JUAN G. ELIZA-COLÓN; Sec.-Treas. OSVALDO ROMERO-PIZARRO.

Unión de Trabajadores de la Industría Eléctrica y Riego de Puerto Rico (UTIER): POB 13068, Santurce, San Juan, PR 00908; tel. (787) 721-1700; e-mail utier@coqui.net; internet www.utier.org; Pres. RICARDO SANTOS RAMOS; 6,000 mems.

Transport

RAILWAYS

In January 2004 a 17-km urban railway (Tren Urbano), capable of carrying some 300,000 passengers per day, was inaugurated in greater San Juan. The railway took eight years to build and cost some US $2,150m. In 2007 plans were announced for a light-rail line to connect the urban area of Caguas with the Tren Urbano system, at a cost of US $450m. As of mid-2010 construction was yet to begin.

Alternativa de Transporte Integrado (ATI) (Integrated Transportation Alternative): San Juan; internet www.ati.gobierno.pr; govt agency; operates the Tren Urbano railway system.

Ponce and Guayama Railway: Aguirre, PR 00608; tel. (787) 853-3810; owned by the Corporación Azucarera de Puerto Rico; transports sugar cane over 96 km of track route; Exec. Dir A. MARTÍNEZ; Gen. Supt J. RODRÍGUEZ.

ROADS

The road network totalled 26,186 km (16,271 miles) in 2009, of which some 94% was paved. A modern highway system links all cities and towns along the coast and cross-country. A highways authority oversees the design and construction of roads, highways and bridges. In April 2002 it was announced that some US $585.6m. was to be invested in projects to improve or expand the road network.

Autoridad de Carreteras: Centro Gobierno Roberto Sanchez Vilella, Edif. Sur Avda de Diego 328, POB 42007, Santurce, San Juan, PR 00940-2007; tel. (787) 721-8787; fax (787) 727-5456; internet www.dtop.gov.pr/act; Exec. Dir LUIS TRINIDAD GARAY.

SHIPPING

There are 11 major ports on the island, the principal ones being San Juan, Ponce and Mayagüez. Other ports include Guayama, Guayanilla, Guánica, Yabucoa, Aguirre, Aguadilla, Fajardo, Arecibo, Humacao and Arroyo. San Juan, one of the finest and longest all-weather natural harbours in the Caribbean, is the main port of entry for foodstuffs and raw materials and for shipping finished industrial products. In 2007/08 it handled 9.4m. short tons of cargo. Under US cabotage laws all maritime freight traffic between the USA and Puerto Rico must be conducted using US-registered vessels. Passenger traffic is limited to tourist cruise vessels. Work on the US $84.4m. Port of the Americas 'megaport' was ongoing in 2010. In April 2005 a high-speed ferry service was launched, connecting San Juan to the islands of Vieques and Culebra.

Autoridad de los Puertos (Puerto Rico Ports Authority): Calle Lindbergh, 64 Antigua Base Naval Miramar, San Juan, PR 00907; POB 362829, San Juan, PR 00936-2829; tel. (787) 723-2260; fax (787) 722-7867; e-mail webmaster@prpa.gobierno.pr; internet www.prpa.gobierno.pr; f. 1942 as the Autoridad de Transporte de Puerto Rico; present name adopted in 1955; manages and administers all ports and airports; Exec. Dir FERNANDO J. BONILLA.

CIVIL AVIATION

There are two international airports on the island (Luis Muñoz Marín at Carolina, San Juan, and Rafael Hernández at Aguadilla) and nine regional airports. There are also six heliports.

Tourism

An estimated 3.6m. tourists visited Puerto Rico in 2008/09, when revenue from this source was estimated at US $3,473m. Almost 85% of all tourist visitors were from the US mainland. In 2010 there were approximately 12,000 guest rooms.

Compañía de Turismo (Puerto Rico Tourism Co): Edif. La Princesa, 2 Paseo La Princesa, POB 9023960, San Juan, PR 00902-3960; tel. (787) 721-2400; fax (787) 722-6238; e-mail drodriguez2@prtourism.com; internet www.gotopuertorico.com; f. 1970; Exec. Dir TERESTELLA GONZÁLEZ DENTON.

Puerto Rico Hotel & Tourism Association (PRHTA): 165 Ponce de León, Suite 301, San Juan, PR 00917-1233; tel. (787) 758-8001; fax (787) 758-8091; e-mail mtosses@prhta.org; internet www.prhta.org; more than 550 corporate mems; Pres. and CEO CLARISA JIMÉNEZ.

Defence

The USA is responsible for the defence of Puerto Rico. In 2003 the US Navy withdrew from Puerto Rico closing its bases at Roosevelt Roads and on the island of Vieques. Puerto Rico has a paramilitary National Guard of some 11,000 men, which is funded mainly by the US Department of Defense. The National Guard has served under US command in Iraq and has also been deployed to support domestic police operations.

Education

The public education system is centrally administered by the Department of Education. Education is compulsory for children between six and 16 years of age. In 2005/06 there were an estimated 563,490 pupils attending public day schools, and in 2009/10 there were an estimated 99,817 pupils attending private schools. The 12-year curriculum, beginning at five years of age, is subdivided into six grades of elementary school, three years at junior high school and three years at senior high school. Vocational schools at the high-school level and kindergartens also form part of the public education system. Instruction is conducted in Spanish, but English is a required subject at all levels. In 2004 there were five universities. The State University system consists of three principal campuses and six regional colleges. In 2005/06 there were some 67,990 students enrolled in higher education at public institutes (plus a further 33,463 were attending adult education courses), while 29,773 pupils were enrolled in private post-secondary institutions in 2009/10. In 2007/08 some US $4,432.9m. of general government expenditure was allocated to education (24.2% of total expenditure).

Bibliography

For works on the Caribbean generally, see Select Bibliography (Books)

Barreto, A. A. *Vieques, the Navy and Puerto Rican Politics*. Gainesville, FL, University Press of Florida, 2002.

Bosque-Pérez, R. and Colón Morera, J. (Eds). *Puerto Rico Under Colonial Rule: Political Persecution and the Quest for Human Rights*. Albany, NY, State University of New York Press, 2006.

Briggs, L. *Reproducing Empire: Race, Sex, Science and U.S. Imperialism in Puerto Rico*. Berkeley, CA, and London, University of California Press, 2002.

Caban, P. A. *Constructing a Colonial People: Puerto Rico and the United States, 1898–1932*. Boulder, CO, Westview Press, 1999.

Cámara Fuentes, L. R. *The Phenomenon of Puerto Rican Voting (New Directions in Puerto Rican Studies)*. Gainesville, FL, University Press of Florida, 2004.

Carrasquillo, R. E. *Our Landless Patria: Marginal Citizenship and Race in Caguas, Puerto Rico, 1880–1910*. Lincoln, NE, University of Nebraska Press, 2006.

Chinea, J. L. *Race and Labor in the Hispanic Caribbean: the West Indian Immigrant Worker Experience in Puerto Rico, 1800–1850*. Gainesville, FL, University Press of Florida, 2005.

Collins, S. M., Bosworth, B., and Sotoclass, M. A. (Eds). *The Economy of Puerto Rico: Restoring Growth*. Washington, DC, Brookings Institution Press, 2006.

Curet Cuevas, E. *Economía Política de Puerto Rico: 1950–2000*. San Juan, Ediciones M.A.C., 2003.

Dietz, J. L. *Puerto Rico: Negotiating Development and Change*. Boulder, CO, Lynne Rienner Publrs, 2003.

Duany, J. *The Puerto Rican Nation on the Move*. Chapel Hill, NC, University of North Carolina Press, 2002.

Duffy Burnett, C., and Marshall, B. (Eds). *Foreign in a Domestic Sense: Puerto Rico, American Expansion, and the Constitution*. American Encounters/Global Interactions, Durham, MC, Duke University Press, 2001.

Fernández, R., Méndez Méndez, S., and Cueto, G. *Puerto Rico Past and Present: An Encyclopedia*. Westport, CT, Greenwood Press, 1998.

Figueroa, L. A. *Sugar, Slavery, and Freedom in Nineteenth-century Puerto Rico*. Chapel Hill, NC, University of North Carolina Press, 2005.

Garcia-Colon, I. *Land Reform in Puerto Rico: Modernizing the Colonial State, 1941-1969*. Gainesville, FL, University Press of Florida, 2009.

Grosfoguel, R. *Colonial Subjects: Puerto Ricans in a Global Perspective*. Berkeley, CA, University of California Press, 2003.

Lewis, G. K. *Puerto Rico: Freedom and Power in the Caribbean*. Oxford, James Currey Publrs, and Kingston, Ian Randle Publrs, 2004.

McCaffrey, K. T. *Military Power and Popular Protest: the U.S. Navy in Vieques, Puerto Rico*. New Brunswick, NJ, and London, Rutgers University Press, 2002.

Malavet, P. A. *America's Colony: The Political and Cultural Conflict Between the United States and Puerto Rico*. New York, NY, New York University Press, 2004.

Monge, J. T. *Puerto Rico: the Trials of the Oldest Colony in the World*. New Haven, CT, Universal Press, 1999.

Negrón-Muntaner, F. *Boricua Pop: Puerto Ricans and the Latinization of American Culture*. New York, NY, and London, New York University Press, 2004.

Pedreira, A. S. (translated by Rivera Serrano, A.). *Insularismo*. New York, NY, Ausubo Press, 2005.

Picó, F. *A General History of Puerto Rico*. Princeton, NJ, Markus Wiener Publrs, 2005.

Rivera Ramos, E. *The Legal Construction of Identity: The Judicial and Social Legacy of American Colonialism in Puerto Rico*. Washington, DC, American Psychological Association, 2001.

Rivero, Y. M. *Tuning Out Blackness: Race and Nation in the History of Puerto Rican Television*. Durham, NC, Duke University Press, 2005.

Romberg, R. *Witchcraft and Welfare: Spiritual Capital and the Business of Magic in Modern Puerto Rico*. Austin, TX, University of Texas Press, 2003.

Schmidt-Nowara, C. *Empire and Antislavery: Spain, Cuba and Puerto Rico, 1833–1874*. Pittsburgh, PA, University of Pittsburgh Press, 1999.

Schmidt-Nowara, C., and Nieto-Phillips, J. M. (Eds). *Interpreting Spanish Colonialism: Empires, Nations, and Legends*. Albuquerque, NM, University of New Mexico Press, 2005.

Siegel, P. (Ed.). *Ancient Borinquen: Archaeology and Ethnohistory of Native Puerto Rico*. Tuscaloosa, AL, University of Alabama Press, 2005.

Villaronga, G. *Toward a Discourse of Consent: Mass Mobilization and Colonial Politics in Puerto Rico, 1932–1948*. Westport, CT, Praeger Publrs, 2004.

Whalen, C. T., and Vazquez-Hernandez, V. (Eds). *The Puerto Rican Diaspora: Historical Perspectives*. Philadelphia, PA, Temple University Press, 2005.

Zilkia, J. *Puerto Rican Nation-building Literature: Impossible Romance*. Gainesville, FL, University Press of Florida, 2005.

SAINT-BARTHÉLEMY

Saint-Barthélemy is one of the Leeward Islands in the Lesser Antilles. The volcanic island lies in the Caribbean Sea, 230 km north-west of Guadeloupe and 20 km south-east of Saint-Martin. St-Barthélemy occupies only 21 sq km, but has green-clad volcanic hillsides, as well as white beaches and surrounding reefs and islets. The climate is tropical, moderated by the sea, with an annual average temperature of 27.5°C (81°F) and a more humid and wet season between May and November. The island normally receives about 1,100 mm (43 ins) of rain annually. Saint-Barthélemy has a permanent population of little more than 5,000, which is predominantly white, inhabited by people of Breton, Norman and Poitevin descent. There are fewer descendants of the Swedish, who ruled Saint-Barthélemy for almost one century (until a referendum in 1878). French is the official language, but English and two Creole patois are widely spoken. A Norman dialect of French is also still sometimes in use. The majority of the population professes Christianity and belongs to the Roman Catholic Church. The principal town is Gustavia, its main port, in the south-west.

On 7 December 2003 the Guadeloupean dependency of Saint-Barthélemy participated in a Department-wide referendum on Guadeloupe's future constitutional relationship with France. Although the proposal to streamline administrative and political processes was defeated, an overwhelming majority of those participating in Saint-Barthélemy, 95.5%, voted in favour of secession from Guadeloupe to form a separate Overseas Collectivity (Collectivité d'outre-mer). The reorganization was subsequently approved by the French Sénat on 6 February 2007 and by the Assemblée nationale the following day. Two weeks later, on 21 February, the island was formally designated an Overseas Collectivity.

Legislative elections to form a 19-member legislative assembly, the Conseil territorial (Territorial Council), were held in July 2007. At the first round of elections, held on 1 July, the Saint-Barth d'abord/Union pour un Mouvement Populaire (UMP) list, headed by Bruno Magras, won a clear majority of 72.2% of the total votes cast, thereby obviating the need for a second round. The election was also contested by three other groupings: the Tous unis pour St-Barthélemy list, lead by Karine Miot-Richard, the Action Equilibre et Transparence list headed by Maxime Desouches—each of which secured 9.9% of the ballot—and Benoît Chauvin's Ensemble pour St-Barthélemy, which attracted the remaining 7.9% of the votes cast. Some 70.6% of the electorate participated in the election. The Saint-Barth d'abord/UMP list obtained 16 of the 19 legislative seats, while the three other contenders were allocated one seat each. On 15 July Magras assumed the presidency of the Territorial Council and Saint-Barthélemy was officially installed as an Overseas Collectivity.

At an election held on 21 September 2008 Michel Magras of the UMP was elected as the territory's representative to the French Sénat. Pending the election of one deputy to the Assemblée nationale (in 2012), the territory was to continue to be represented by Victorin Lurel of the Parti Socialiste, one of the deputies for Guadeloupe.

Prefect-Delegate: JACQUES SIMONNET.

Conseil Territorial

Hôtel de la Collectivité, BP 133, Gustavia; e-mail contact@comstbarth.fr; internet www.comstbarth.fr.

President: BRUNO MAGRAS (Saint-Barth d'abord/UMP).

Election, 1 July 2007

	Seats
Saint-Barth d'abord/Union pour un Mouvement Populaire	16
Tous unis pour St-Barthélemy	1
Action Equilibre et Transparence	1
Ensemble pour St-Barthélemy	1
Total	19

SAINT CHRISTOPHER* AND NEVIS

Geography

PHYSICAL FEATURES

Saint Christopher and Nevis, a federation of two of the Leeward Islands, is in the Lesser Antilles. The larger island, St Christopher (usually known as St Kitts), is separated from Nevis to the south-east by a 3-km (2-mile) channel called The Narrows. Rather more distance (20 km) separates Saint Christopher from the next island in the chain, St Eustatius (Netherlands Antilles), to the north-west. South-east of Nevis, about 40 km away, is Redonda, a small and uninhabited island dependency of Antigua and Barbuda (the main islands of which are to the east), and 24 km beyond that is Montserrat. All of these islands lie in the Caribbean Sea. Saint Christopher covers 176.1 sq km (68 sq miles) and Nevis 93.3 sq km, giving a total area of 269.4 sq km, the smallest for any sovereign state in the Americas.

Saint Christopher is 37 km (23 miles) long and tapers south-eastwards, forming a low-lying peninsula (which widens at the end and is dotted with salt ponds) pointing towards the more globular island of Nevis. Both islands are of volcanic origin, with mountainous interiors. The main landmass of Saint Christopher is dominated by mountains grouped in three ranges, highest in the north-west, where Mt Liamuiga (formerly Mt Misery, but now renamed with the old Carib name for the island) reaches 1,156 m (3,794 ft). A narrow, sea-flanked ridge connects the main part of the island to the flat lands around the Great Salt Pond. Nevis is also lofty, and cone-shaped, with its central Nevis Peak rising to 985 m. Both islands are fertile and green, although much of the original forest has long since disappeared, except on the higher slopes. Native wildlife suffered not only from the intensive cultivation of sugar cane, but also from the introduction of the mongoose, which has had a serious effect in several Caribbean islands. Other immigrants include green vervet monkeys, originally imported by the French from West Africa (also found in Barbados), and some deer on Saint Christopher. Monkeys are said to outnumber Kittitians, and donkeys Nevisians. Fauna as well as flora is expected to benefit from the recent expansion in woodland, as agriculture contracts and the authorities make efforts to enhance the environment.

CLIMATE

The climate is subtropical marine and falls within the hurricane belt. The average annual temperature is 26°C (79°F), with sea breezes keeping the islands relatively cool, particularly during the driest months of December–March. Temperatures rarely exceed 33°C (91°F) or fall below 17°C (63°F), even in the cooler heights—or on Nevis (despite its name, derived from the Spanish for snow). The hurricane season is in July–October. There is relatively little humidity. Average annual rainfall on Saint Christopher is about 1,400 mm (55 ins) and on Nevis some 1,220 mm (48 ins).

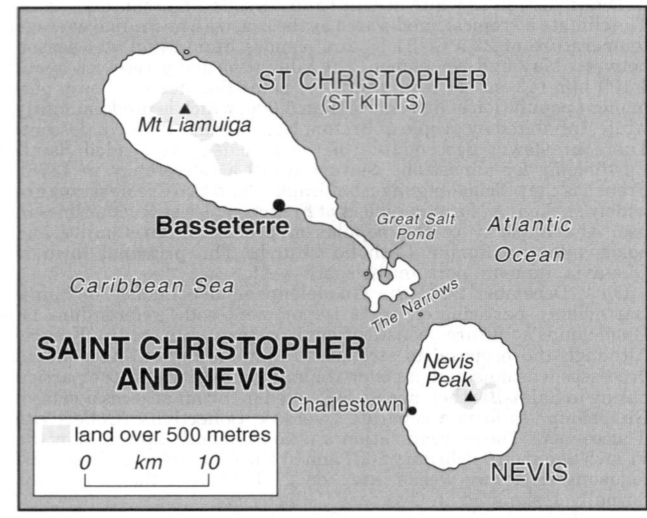

POPULATION

Saint Christopher and Nevis is important in the history of the old British West Indies, with Saint Christopher the 'mother' colony and Nevis long one of the wealthiest. There are still some traces of the French influence on Saint Christopher (the island was at one time partitioned), notably military ruins built in an age of great-power competition—and to protect against the doomed struggle of the native Caribs resisting European encroachment. However, the cultural legacy on both islands is predominantly British, although most of the population (more than 90%) is now black, descended from the African slaves brought to work the plantations. The official language is English and the leading Christian denomination is Anglican. Roman Catholics and Nonconformist Protestants (Methodists established themselves in the islands early) are also represented, and there is a small contingent of Orthodox Christians, as well as some Rastafarians.

The total population of Saint Christopher and Nevis was estimated to be 51,697 in mid-2009. About five-sixths of the people live on Saint Christopher, and almost one-third of these in or around the capital city, Basseterre, in the south-west of the island. The chief town of Nevis, located on the central western coast, is the old settlement of Charlestown (even so, it was preceded as the capital by Jamestown, to the north, which was completely destroyed in 1690 by an earthquake and tidal wave). The country is split into 14 parishes for administrative purposes.

---

*While this island is officially called Saint Christopher as part of the state, the name is usually abbreviated to St Kitts.

History

MARK WILSON

Saint Christopher (also known as St Kitts) and Nevis is a constitutional monarchy within the Commonwealth. Queen Elizabeth II is Head of State, and is represented in Saint Christopher and Nevis by a Governor-General. There is a bicameral legislature with an elected chamber representing both islands, to which the federal Government is responsible. Nevis has a five-member Assembly, and an administration, headed by a Premier, which manages the island's affairs; Saint Christopher, on the other hand, is managed directly by the federal Government.

Few traces remain of the islands' original Amerindian inhabitants. The islands were visited and named by Christopher Columbus in 1493 as San Cristóbal and Nieves. British settlement on Saint Christopher dates from 1623, making the island the first British possession in the Caribbean; Nevis was settled five years later. However, the larger island was later partitioned, with France taking the centre, and Great Britain the extreme north and south, an arrangement that came to an end with the Treaty of Utrecht in 1713. The islands were administered together with Anguilla and the British Virgin Islands from 1816 until 1871, and then as part of the Leeward Islands Federation.

Poverty among the rural working class was extreme in the first part of the 20th century, and in 1935 resulted in a bitter sugar workers' strike; several strikers were killed by police. Political life on the island of Saint Christopher was dominated in the 1950s, 1960s and 1970s by Robert Llewellyn Bradshaw, leader of the St Kitts-Nevis Labour Party (SKNLP), which, in spite of its name, has never had a substantial following outside the larger island. Bradshaw's most solid political support was among the sugar workers of Saint Christopher, who benefited under his leadership from increased wages and improved education and welfare services. However, his relations with the urban middle class and with the populations of Nevis and Anguilla were in general very poor.

With the Leeward Islands Federation disbanded in 1957, Saint Christopher-Nevis-Anguilla joined the Federation of the West Indies in 1958, along with nine other British colonies. When Jamaica and Trinidad and Tobago left in 1962, the Federation collapsed, and an attempt to unite the remaining colonies as the 'little eight' was unsuccessful. Along with its neighbours, Saint Christopher-Nevis-Anguilla became a British Associated State in 1967, responsible for its internal affairs, with the United Kingdom retaining control of external affairs and defence. However, this arrangement was fiercely resisted by Anguilla, which feared domination by its larger neighbour, and broke forcibly away from the three-island grouping in 1967; a British commissioner administered that island separately from 1969.

The Bradshaw Government's poor relations with the island of Nevis led to the smaller island delaying the move to full independence, originally scheduled for 1980. In an election held that year, the SKNLP lost its overall majority, and a new Government was formed by a coalition of the People's Action Movement on Saint Christopher (PAM) and the Nevis Reformation Party (NRP), which took the three Nevis seats. Together, they agreed an arrangement which granted a high degree of autonomy to Nevis, while Saint Christopher, where the SKNLP retained a local majority, remained under the direct control of a federal Government. On this basis, the islands moved to independence on 19 September 1983.

The PAM remained in office for 15 years. However, the latter part of this period was overshadowed by widespread reports that the Government had failed to control major cocaine-traffickers, who had established powerful positions in local politics and business.

On Nevis, the leading position of the NRP came under challenge from the Concerned Citizens Movement (CCM), led by Vance Amory, which won island Assembly elections on 1 June 1992, taking three of the five seats. The CCM has in general favoured independence for Nevis, a position about which the NRP has, in recent years, been ambivalent.

In a general election held on 29 November 1993 the SKNLP, led by Dr Denzil Douglas, gained four of the eight seats on the main island, with the remainder taken by the PAM. On Nevis, one seat was taken by the NRP while the CCM, which was not willing to form an alliance with either of the Saint Christopher parties, won two seats. The leader of the PAM, Dr Kennedy A. Simmonds, remained in office with a minority Government, an arrangement that was fiercely opposed by SKNLP supporters on Saint Christopher. There was rioting in the capital, Basseterre, in December, which was countered by a state of emergency and a curfew, but was controlled after intervention by the Barbados-based Regional Security System. In November 1994 the two parties agreed that fresh elections should be held within a year.

Vincent Morris, the son of Deputy Prime Minister Sidney Morris, disappeared on 2 October 1994, and was found dead in a burnt-out car on 12 November; this incident was believed to be linked to narcotics-trafficking. A police superintendent who was leading the investigation was shot dead while driving to work in the previous month. Two other sons of Sidney Morris were arrested on firearms charges in November. Although Sidney Morris resigned from his post, the complex scandal that ensued further damaged the standing of the PAM Government. Four police officers from the United Kingdom took control of the local force in May 1995.

Elections were held on 3 July 1995, and resulted in a clear victory for the SKNLP, which took seven of the eight seats on Saint Christopher, with PAM retaining one Saint Christopher seat, and the Nevis seats split as they had been the previous year. The SKNLP, still led by Douglas, was returned for a second term on 6 March 2000, winning all eight of that island's seats.

On Nevis, the CCM won a second term of office in 1997. A proposal to secede from the federation received unanimous support in the Nevis assembly, although the NRP later changed its position. The island administration exercised its constitutional option to call a referendum on secession, which was held on 10 August 1998. On a 58% voter turn-out, the proposal received 62% of the votes cast, fewer than the required two-thirds' majority. The federal Government has also proposed constitutional reforms, including replacement of the Queen as Head of State with a President, and a separate assembly and island administration for Saint Christopher. However, any change would require a two-thirds' majority on each island, a difficult target in view of the strongly partisan nature of political debate in Saint Christopher and Nevis. In 2003 a parliamentary select committee on constitutional reform was asked to undertake further consultations. In April Amory announced that the CCM would seek to hold a second referendum on the issue of separation.

In elections to the Nevis Island Assembly in September 2001 the CCM, still led by Amory, strengthened its control of the legislature, gaining a total of four elective seats. The NRP, under the leadership of Joseph Parry, took the remaining seat. The island assembly voted in June 2003 to hold another secession referendum; this initiative was opposed, however, both by the Caribbean Community and Common Market (CARICOM) and the USA, and no further progress was made before the CCM lost office in July 2006 (see below).

At a general election on 25 October 2004 the SKNLP won seven of the eight seats on Saint Christopher, with 60.4% of the popular vote on that island; the PAM took the remaining seat. On Nevis the CCM again secured two of the three seats in the National Assembly, with 54.0% of the votes cast on the smaller island; the remaining seat was won by the NRP. Commonwealth and CARICOM observer teams made several criticisms of the electoral process. The Government subsequently promised reforms, and in June 2006 the National Assembly agreed a consultative process to finalize proposals for voter registration and reform of constituency boundaries. A consultative committee, appointed in August, reported in February 2007. In 2008 some reforms were implemented, including a full revision of the electoral list that eliminated the names of 15,000 dead or absent voters and added 3,500 new electors, thus reducing the overall total to 26,542 from 38,865 in 2004. A commission was appointed in September 2008 to propose new constituency boundaries. The PAM, however, had not participated in the reforms and remained sharply critical of the electoral process.

At an election to the Nevis Island Assembly on 10 July 2006, the NRP secured three of the five elective seats, while the CCM won the remaining two seats. The NRP's leader, Joseph Parry, took office as Nevis Island Premier later in the same month and developed a more constructive relationship with the federal Government than that achieved by his predecessor. Joint meetings of the federal and Nevis Governments have been held occasionally. Following the death in July 2007 of Malcolm Guishard, the CCM leader of the opposition in Parliament, Mark Brantley of the CCM won a by-election, receiving 50.4% of the votes cast (a winning margin of 30 votes), and succeeded Guishard as parliamentary opposition leader.

Denzil Douglas won a fourth successive parliamentary term for the SKNLP at a general election on 25 January 2010, taking six of the eight seats on Saint Christopher (with 47.0% of the popular vote), while two seats were secured by the PAM (with 32.2%). The three Nevis seats in the federal Parliament remained as before, with two being held by the CCM (with 11.0% of the overall vote), and one by the NRP (with 9.8%). The CCM's Mark Brantley remained as leader of the federal opposition. The NRP, however, remained in control of the island administration. Election observers from the Commonwealth and the Organization of American States again noted the need for reforms, including the creation of more equal constituencies and introduction of equal access to state media, a preliminary count at the polling station to increase transparency, and moves to ensure confidence in the independence of election officials.

Saint Christopher and Nevis, along with its CARICOM partners Saint Lucia, Saint Vincent and the Grenadines and Belize, remains one of the few countries to recognize the Republic of China (Taiwan), and has received significant Taiwanese aid. Libya announced in 2010 that it intends to open an investment bank on Saint Christopher to serve the Eastern Caribbean. In common with many of its neighbours in the Organisation of Eastern Caribbean States, Saint Christopher and Nevis has repeatedly supported Japanese proposals for renewed commercial whaling, receiving substantial Japanese assistance.

Narcotics-trafficking and violent crime remained serious concerns for the SKNLP Government, with local gangs working closely with resident representatives of South American criminal groups. The US state department reported in February 2008 that the Royal Saint Christopher and Nevis Police Force Drug Unit had been largely ineffective, with insufficient political will and a lack of complete operational independence. There are no drug rehabilitation centres on the islands. A contribution of US $200,000 to the Government's Sugar Industry Diversification Foundation is sufficient to secure citizenship. The US Government maintained that the islands were at major risk from corruption and money-laundering, and called for sufficient resources and training to create an effective control regime.

In 2009 there were 27 murders, making the per-head murder rate (of 54 per 100,000—more than three times the rate recorded for 2005) and 10 times that of the USA and ahead of much larger Caribbean countries such as Trinidad and Tobago or Guyana. With rising concern over violent crime and an election approaching, in August 2008 Douglas took direct responsibility for this issue by adding national security to his portfolio and delegating finance elsewhere. The former Minister of National Security, Dwyer Astaphan, subsequently became sharply critical of the Government, calling for the resignation of Dr Douglas. Charles Laplace was hanged in December 2008 for the murder of his wife in 2004; by mid-2009 there were 10 convicts on death row. However, the hanging and other crime control measures appeared to have had no deterrent effect as there were 16 murders in the first half of 2010, equivalent to an annualized 64 per 100,000.

Economy

MARK WILSON

Saint Christopher and Nevis is the smallest country in the Western hemisphere in terms of both area and population, with an area of 269.4 sq km and 51,967 inhabitants in mid-2009, of whom approximately 10,000 lived on Nevis. The islands have developed a prosperous middle-income economy, with an estimated per-head gross domestic product (GDP) of US $8,400 in 2009. GDP growth picked up from an average rate of 0.7% in 2002–03 to an average of 5.2% in 2004–07 and, in contrast to most of its neighbours, maintained a brisk pace of 4.6% in 2008 as the tourism and construction sectors expanded. However, the effects of the international recession on investment, construction and tourism were felt in 2009 as the economy contracted by 9.6%.

Since the 1990s there has been concern over the overall fiscal deficit, which at is peak was equivalent to 16.6% of GDP in 2002, and over the level of external debt service payments, which reached 26% of goods and services exports in 2004. Total government and government-guaranteed debt, including borrowing by Nevis, was estimated by the IMF at 195% of GDP at the end of 2004. The Government adopted a stabilization programme in 2003, and brought the overall fiscal deficit down to 4.1% of GDP by 2005, achieving a small surplus of 0.7% in 2009 with the assistance of grant inflows equivalent to 5% of GDP. There was improved revenue collection, fuel pricing reform and higher electricity charges; losses from the Government's electricity department had previously reached 2.5% of GDP. A property tax reform was in progress in 2007 and 2008; the Government also intended to introduce a value-added tax from November 2010. Other measures announced in the aftermath of the January 2010 election included expenditure cuts and a freeze on public sector salaries and recruitment. Debt remained extremely high, and was estimated by the Eastern Caribbean Central Bank (ECCB) at 180% of GDP in 2009. Debt-servicing remained a heavy burden, and was close to one-half of recurrent expenditure in 2009, exceeding the combined total of health and education spending.

Saint Christopher and Nevis is a member of the Caribbean Community and Common Market, or CARICOM, whose larger members formed a single market at the start of 2006, with Saint Christopher and Nevis joining on 3 July. It is also a member of the Organisation of Eastern Caribbean States, which links nine of the smaller Caribbean territories. The ECCB, which has its headquarters just outside the capital, Basseterre, supervises its financial affairs. In June 2006 Saint Christopher and Nevis joined Venezuela's PetroCaribe initiative, which offered Venezuelan petroleum products on preferential terms to its 13 members.

The natural beauty, beaches and climate of both islands provide the basis for a prosperous tourism industry, which grew rapidly to a peak of 140,504 stop-over visitors in 2005, with visitor spending reaching EC $355.4m. in 2006. On both islands, there are large modern resorts, but several former plantation houses have also been converted to small luxury hotels, while historic sites such as the Brimstone Hill Fortress National Park are important tourist attractions. A 900-room hotel with a casino and golf course opened in February 2003 and was followed by several other large tourism projects. However, the number of stop-over visitors declined after 2006, falling to 127,705 in 2008 and 93,081 in 2009, with spending down to EC $225.41m. in the latter year. Cruise ship passenger numbers have continued to increase, reaching 450,553 in 2009, but because of low per-head spending, they have made a much lower contribution to the economy, equivalent in 2006 to only 6% of total tourist expenditure. Hotels and restaurants accounted for 7.4% of GDP in 2009. Agriculture and fishing made up only 2.8% of GDP in 2009, down from 5.5% in 1997, with the fishing industry alone accounting for 1.4%. The sugar industry, which dominated the economy of Saint Christopher until the 1960s, closed after the July 2005 harvest. Output in that year was 10,700 metric tons, well below the 2003 figure of 31,375 tons. In spite of a guaranteed European Union sugar price, which in recent years had been at least three times world market levels, the sugar industry survived only as a result of government subsidies, which were equivalent to 4.0% of GDP by 2004, with accumulated debts equal to 30% of GDP. Large areas formerly used for sugar were redesignated for tourism, and the Government made provision for the retraining of the 1,400 sugar industry employees, who in the main were able to find other employment.

With sugar long since replaced by tourism as the principal industry, there is a continuing need for infrastructural improvement within the country; to this end an agreement was signed in July 2006 with the Export-Import Bank of the Republic of China in Taiwan for US $14m. to facilitate the expansion of the international airport, with completion in December of that year. Taiwan also financed the construction of the Warner Park Cricket Stadium, opened in May 2006, ahead of the 2007 Cricket World Cup, which Saint Christopher and Nevis hosted jointly with other Caribbean nations. It was hoped the tournament would raise the profile of the country as an international tourism destination, but its impact on arrivals was disappointing.

Manufacturing comprised 8.4% of GDP in 2009. Industries such as brewing produce mainly for the local market, while others, including the assembly of electronic components, are orientated entirely to exports. The telecommunications sector has been liberalized; the Government viewed call centres and telemarketing as important growth areas for the economy. The construction sector made up 11.2% of GDP in 2009, down from 14.9% in the previous year.

There is an 'offshore' financial sector on Nevis, which, by October 2008, had registered 13,257 International Business Companies, 4,495 limited liability companies, 109 insurance companies and 1,001 international trusts, with 40 registered agents. On Saint Christopher, the separate 'offshore' sector included 1,592 exempt companies and exempt foundations, 70 captive insurance companies, 28 corporate service providers and four internet gambling companies. The division of regulatory powers between the island administration on Nevis and the federal Government has at times been unclear. Partly for this reason, Saint Christopher and Nevis was, in June 2000, listed as a 'non-co-operative jurisdiction' by the Financial Action Task Force on Money Laundering (FATF, based in Paris, France); the country was removed from this list in 2002 after instituting stricter regulatory controls, and is now listed by the US state department as a country of concern for money-laundering, an intermediate category. In April 2003 a report indicated that the islands' 'offshore' banking operations had been halved as a result of the FATF action and the subsequent financial reforms. However, in March 2006 the island of Nevis was implicated in reports identifying the use of 'offshore' accounts by international criminals, most notoriously paedophiles. Income is also derived from the sale of citizenship, a programme that has received considerable criticism, both locally and internationally. A sufficient number of Tax Information Exchange Agreements were signed by March 2010 for the Organization for Economic Co-operation and Development to remove Saint Christopher and Nevis from its 'grey' list of jurisdictions which did not meet international reporting standards.

There are nine medical, veterinary and nursing schools, of which the best-known is the Ross University School of Veterinary Medicine. These cater mainly to students from the USA, and make a substantial contribution to the economy. However, net earnings from services are not sufficient to cover the deficit on merchandise trade, and the current account balance of payments deficit rose to 22.0% of GDP in 2007 from 22.6% in 2005. This was covered by a capital account surplus, stemming mainly from foreign direct investment inflows.

The islands are in the heart of the hurricane belt, and have been damaged by several storms in recent years, most recently by Georges in September 1998, José and Lenny in 1999, and Omar in 2008. Following the destruction caused by Omar, the largest hotel on Nevis, the Four Seasons, remained closed in mid-2010, as disputed bankruptcy and foreclosure proceedings delayed rehabilitation work. This left most of the 650 staff unemployed and thus had a serious negative impact on the economy of the smaller island, although reports in July indicated that the hotel would reopen in December, in time for the 2010/11 tourist season. The IMF in May 2009 approved US $3.4m. in Emergency Natural Disaster Assistance for Saint Christopher and Nevis. There is also a risk of earthquakes. Mt Liamuiga (on Saint Christopher) and Nevis Peak are both volcanic centres, although they are not presently active. Development of a 10-MW geothermal power station was proposed for development on Nevis in 2011, with another plant to follow on Saint Christopher. There was also a proposal for an 8-MW wind power plant on the latter island.

Statistical Survey

Source (unless otherwise stated): St Kitts and Nevis Information Service, Government Headquarters, Church St, POB 186, Basseterre; tel. 465-2521; fax 466-4504; e-mail skninfo@caribsurf.com; internet www.stkittsnevis.net.

AREA AND POPULATION

Area (sq km): 269.4 (Saint Christopher 176.1, Nevis 93.3).

Population: 40,618 (males 19,933, females 20,685) at census of 12 May 1991; 45,841 (males 22,784, females 23,057) at census of 14 May 2001. *2009:* 51,967 (mid-year estimate). Sources: UN, *Population and Vital Statistics Report* and Eastern Caribbean Central Bank.

Density (mid-2009): 192.9 per sq km.

Population by Age and Sex (at mid-2000): *0–14:* 12,390 (males 6,390, females 6,000); *15–64:* 24,450 (males 12,340, females 12,110); *65 and over:* 3,570 (males 1,670, females 1,900); *Total* 40,410 (males 20,400, females 20,010) (Source: UN, *Demographic Yearbook*).

Principal Town (estimated population incl. suburbs, mid-2009): Basseterre (capital) 12,847. Source: UN, *World Urbanization Prospects: The 2009 Revision*.

Births and Deaths (2001): Registered live births 803 (birth rate 17.4 per 1,000); Registered deaths 352 (death rate 7.6 per 1,000). *2009:* Crude birth rate 17.7 per 1,000; Crude death rate 8.1 per 1,000 (Source: Pan American Health Organization).

Life Expectancy (years at birth, WHO estimates): 73 (males 70; females 76) in 2008. Source: WHO, *World Health Statistics*.

Employment (labour force survey, 1994): Sugar cane production/manufacturing 1,525; Non-sugar agriculture 914; Mining and quarrying 29; Manufacturing (excl. sugar) 1,290; Electricity, gas and water 416; Construction 1,745; Trade (except tourism) 1,249; Tourism 2,118; Transport and communications 534; Business and general services 3,708; Government services 2,738; Other statutory bodies 342; *Total* 16,608 (Saint Christopher 12,516, Nevis 4,092). Source: IMF, *St Kitts and Nevis: Recent Economic Developments* (August 1997).

HEALTH AND WELFARE

Key Indicators

Total Fertility Rate (children per woman, 2008): 1.8.

Under-5 Mortality Rate (per 1,000 live births, 2008): 15.

Physicians (per 1,000 head, 2000): 1.1.

Hospital Beds (per 1,000 head, 2005): 5.5.

Health Expenditure (2007): US $ per head (PPP): 863.

Health Expenditure (2007): % of GDP: 6.0.

Health Expenditure (2007): public (% of total): 57.8.

Access to Sanitation (% of persons, 2008): 96.

Total Carbon Dioxide Emissions ('000 metric tons, 2006): 135.6.

Carbon Dioxide Emissions Per Head (metric tons, 2006): 2.8.

Human Development Index (2007): ranking: 62.

Human Development Index (2007): value: 0.838.

For sources and definitions, see explanatory note on p. vi.

AGRICULTURE, ETC.

Principal Crops ('000 metric tons, 2008, FAO estimates): Sugar cane 105.0; Coconuts 1.3. *Aggregate Production* ('000 metric tons, may include official, semi-official or estimated data): Roots and tubers 1.3; Vegetables (incl. melons) 0.9; Fruits (excl. melons) 1.4.

Livestock ('000 head, 2008, FAO estimates): Cattle 7.0; Sheep 7.0; Goats 9.0; Pigs 6.0.

Livestock Products ('000 metric tons, 2008, FAO estimates): Pig meat 0.1; Chicken meat 0.2; Cattle meat 0.1; Hen eggs 0.2.

Fishing (metric tons, live weight, 2008, FAO estimates): Groupers 25; Snappers 70; Grunts, sweetlips 15; Goatfishes, red mullets 80; Parrotfishes 45; Surgeonfishes 40; Triggerfishes, durgons 20; Caribbean spiny lobster 40; Stromboid conchs 90; *Total catch* (incl. others) 450.

Source: FAO.

INDUSTRY

Production: Raw sugar 10,700 metric tons in 2005; Electric energy 223.4 million kWh in 2009. Sources: IMF, *St Kitts and Nevis: Statistical Appendix* (April 2008) and Eastern Caribbean Central Bank.

FINANCE

Currency and Exchange Rates: 100 cents = 1 Eastern Caribbean dollar (EC $). *Sterling, US Dollar and Euro Equivalents* (31 May 2010): £1 sterling = EC $3.937; US $1 = EC $2.700; €1 = EC $3.344; EC $100 = £25.40 = US $37.04 = €29.91. *Exchange Rate*: Fixed at US $1 = EC $2.70 since July 1976.

Budget (EC $ million, 2009, preliminary): *Revenue:* Revenue from taxation 380.7 (Taxes on income 134.9, Taxes on property 9.0, Taxes on domestic goods and services 71.2, Taxes on international trade and transactions 165.4); Other current revenue 140.5; Capital revenue 26.5; Foreign grants 59.3; Total 606.9. *Expenditure:* Current expenditure 521.7 (Personal emoluments and wages 219.9, Goods and services 130.3, Interest payments 117.3, Transfers and subsidies 54.2); Capital expenditure and net lending 75.7; Total 597.4. Source: Eastern Caribbean Central Bank.

International Reserves (US $ million at 31 December 2009): Reserve position in IMF 0.13; IMF special drawing rights 13.35; Foreign exchange 122.93; Total 136.41. Source: IMF, *International Financial Statistics*.

Money Supply (EC $ million at 31 December 2009): Currency outside depository corporations 78.33; Transferable deposits 599.45; Other deposits 1,546.39; *Broad money* 2,224.17. Source: IMF, *International Financial Statistics*.

Cost of Living (Consumer Price Index; base: 2005 = 100): All items 110.1 in 2007; 118.5 in 2008; 117.6 in 2009. Source: IMF, *International Financial Statistics*.

Gross Domestic Product (EC $ million at constant 1990 prices): 800.78 in 2006; 817.01 in 2007; 854.87 in 2008. Source: Eastern Caribbean Central Bank.

Expenditure on the Gross Domestic Product (EC $ million at current prices, 2008): Government final consumption expenditure 263.20; Private final consumption expenditure 1,149.43; Gross capital formation 627.00; *Total domestic expenditure* 2,039.63; Exports of goods and services 591.60; *Less* Imports of goods and services 1,091.85; *GDP at market prices* 1,539.38. Source: Eastern Caribbean Central Bank.

Gross Domestic Product by Economic Activity (EC $ million at current prices, 2008): Agriculture, hunting, forestry and fishing 34.57; Mining and quarrying 2.72; Manufacturing 110.56; Electricity and water 30.00; Construction 188.18; Wholesale and retail trade 163.10; Restaurants and hotels 103.31; Transport 155.75; Communications 60.37; Finance and insurance 226.63; Real estate and housing 28.12; Government services 228.84; Other community, social and personal services 59.72; *Sub-total* 1,391.87; *Less* Financial intermediation services indirectly measured 128.21; *Total in basic prices* 1,263.66; Taxes, less subsidies, on products 275.72; *GDP at market prices* 1,539.38. Source: Eastern Caribbean Central Bank.

Balance of Payments (EC $ million, 2009): Exports of goods 156.95; Imports of goods –666.76; *Trade balance* –509.81; Services (net) 65.70; *Balance on goods and services* –444.11; Other income received (net) –89.50; *Balance on goods, services and income* –533.61; Current transfers received (net) 103.91; *Current balance* –429.70; Capital account (net) 55.57; Direct investment (net) 374.61; Portfolio investment (net) –32.23; Other investment (net) 195.42; Net errors and omissions –23.31; *Overall balance* –140.36. Source: Eastern Caribbean Central Bank.

EXTERNAL TRADE

Principal Commodities (US $ million, 2007): *Imports c.i.f.:* Food and live animals 42.7; Mineral fuels, lubricants, etc. 18.6 (Refined petroleum products 16.3); Chemicals 19.0; Basic manufactures 49.3 (Iron and steel manufactures 8.3); Machinery and transport equipment 84.6 (Road vehicles 18.3); Total (incl. others) 271.7. *Exports f.o.b.:* Food and live animals 0.7; Beverages and tobacco 2.6; Basic manufactures 0.8 (Metal manufactures 0.6); Machinery and transport equipment 28.5 (Electrical machinery 14.3); Miscellaneous manufactures 1.3 (Printed matter 0.4); Total (incl. others) 34.1. Source: UN, *International Trade Statistics Yearbook*.

Principal Trading Partners (US $ million, 2007): *Imports:* Antigua and Barbuda 2.1; Barbados 4.4; Canada 8.2; China, People's Rep. 3.5; Denmark 4.2; Dominican Republic 4.6; France 2.0; Germany 4.7; Grenada 1.5; Jamaica 2.0; Japan 10.1; Netherlands Antilles 3.2; Trinidad and Tobago 29.3; United Kingdom 9.7; USA 159.8; Total (incl. others) 271.7. *Exports* (excl. re-exports): Antigua and Barbuda 0.6; Dominica 0.4; Netherlands Antilles 0.5; Trinidad and Tobago 0.2; United Kingdom 0.8; USA 29.5; Total (incl. others) 34.1. Source: UN, *International Trade Statistics Yearbook*.

TRANSPORT

Road Traffic (registered motor vehicles): 11,352 in 1998; 12,432 in 1999; 12,917 in 2000.

Shipping: *Arrivals* (2000): 1,981 vessels. *International Sea-borne Freight Traffic* ('000 metric tons, 2000): Goods loaded 24.7; Goods unloaded 234.2. *Merchant Fleet* (vessels registered at 31 December 2008): Number 267; Total displacement 938,759 grt (Source: Lloyd's Register-Fairplay, *World Fleet Statistics*).

Civil Aviation (aircraft arrivals): 24,800 in 1998; 23,500 in 1999; 19,400 in 2000.

TOURISM

Visitor Arrivals: 379,473 (123,062 stop-over visitors, 5,177 excursionists, 1,911 yacht passengers, 249,323 cruise ship passengers) in 2007; 533,353 (127,705 stop-over visitors, 3,920 excursionists, 812 yacht passengers, 400,916 cruise ship passengers) in 2008; 547,561 (93,081 stop-over visitors, 3,718 excursionists, 209 yacht passengers, 450,553 cruise ship passengers) in 2009. *Stop-over Visitors by Country* (2009): Canada 6,413; Caribbean 22,410; United Kingdom 6,496; USA 54,410; Other 3,352.

Tourism Receipts (EC $ million): 336.92 in 2007; 297.17 in 2008; 225.41 in 2009.

Source: Eastern Caribbean Central Bank.

COMMUNICATIONS MEDIA

Radio Receivers ('000 in use, 1997): 28.

Television Receivers ('000 in use, 1999): 10.

Telephones ('000 main lines in use, 2009): 20.5.

Mobile Cellular Telephones (subscribers, 2009): 83,000.

Personal Computers: 11,000 (234.1 per 1,000 persons) in 2004.

Internet Users (2009): 17,000.

Broadband Subscribers (2009): 13,000.

Non-daily Newspapers (2004, unless otherwise indicated): Titles 4; Circulation 34,000 (1996).

Sources: mainly UNESCO, *Statistical Yearbook*; UN, *Statistical Yearbook*; International Telecommunication Union.

EDUCATION

Pre-primary (2007/08 unless otherwise indicated): 77 schools (2003/04); 118 teachers; 1,608 pupils.

Primary (2007/08 unless otherwise indicated): 23 schools (2003/04); 401 teachers; 6,474 pupils.

Secondary (2007/08 unless otherwise indicated): 7 schools (2003/04); 417 teachers; 4,396 pupils.

Tertiary (2003/04): 1 institution; 79 teachers; 751 students.

Pupil-teacher Ratio (primary education, UNESCO estimate): 16.1 in 2007/08.

Adult Literacy Rate: 97.8% in 2004 (Source: UN Development Programme, *Human Development Report*).

Source: mostly UNESCO Institute for Statistics.

Directory

The Constitution

The Constitution of the Federation of Saint Christopher and Nevis took effect from 19 September 1983, when the territory achieved independence. Its main provisions are summarized below:

FUNDAMENTAL RIGHTS AND FREEDOMS

Regardless of race, place of origin, political opinion, colour, creed or sex, but subject to respect for the rights and freedoms of others and for the public interest, every person in Saint Christopher and Nevis is entitled to the rights of life, liberty, security of person, equality before the law and the protection of the law. Freedom of conscience, of expression, of assembly and of association is guaranteed, and the inviolability of personal privacy, family life and property is maintained. Protection is afforded from slavery, forced labour, torture and inhuman treatment.

THE GOVERNOR-GENERAL

The Governor-General is appointed by the British monarch, whom the Governor-General represents locally. The Governor-General must be a citizen of Saint Christopher and Nevis, and must appoint a Deputy Governor-General, in accordance with the wishes of the Premier of Nevis, to represent the Governor-General on that island.

PARLIAMENT

Parliament consists of the British monarch, represented by the Governor-General, and the National Assembly, which includes a Speaker, three (or, if a nominated member is Attorney-General, four) nominated members (Senators) and 11 elected members (Representatives). Senators are appointed by the Governor-General: one on the advice of the Leader of the Opposition, and the other two in accordance with the wishes of the Prime Minister. The Representatives are elected by universal suffrage, one from each of the 11 single-member constituencies.

Every citizen over the age of 18 years is eligible to vote. Parliament may alter any of the provisions of the Constitution.

THE EXECUTIVE

Executive authority is vested in the British monarch, as Head of State, and is exercised on the monarch's behalf by the Governor-General, either directly or through subordinate officers. The Governor-General appoints as Prime Minister that Representative who, in the Governor-General's opinion, appears to be best able to command the support of the majority of the Representatives. Other ministerial appointments are made by the Governor-General, in consultation with the Prime Minister, from among the members of the National Assembly. The Governor-General may remove the Prime Minister from office if a resolution of no confidence in the Government is passed by the National Assembly and if the Prime Minister does not resign within three days or advise the Governor-General to dissolve Parliament.

The Cabinet consists of the Prime Minister and other Ministers. When the office of Attorney-General is a public office, the Attorney-General shall, by virtue of holding that office, be a member of the Cabinet in addition to the other Ministers. The Governor-General appoints as Leader of the Opposition in the National Assembly that Representative who, in the Governor-General's opinion, appears to be best able to command the support of the majority of the Representatives who do not support the Government.

CITIZENSHIP

All persons born in Saint Christopher and Nevis before independence who, immediately before independence, were citizens of the United Kingdom and Colonies automatically become citizens of Saint Christopher and Nevis. All persons born in Saint Christopher and Nevis after independence automatically acquire citizenship, as do those born outside Saint Christopher and Nevis after independence to a parent possessing citizenship. There are provisions for the acquisition of citizenship by those to whom it is not automatically granted.

THE ISLAND OF NEVIS

There is a Legislature for the island of Nevis, which consists of the British monarch, represented by the Governor-General, and the Nevis Island Assembly. The Assembly consists of three nominated members (one appointed by the Governor-General in accordance with the advice of the Leader of the Opposition in the Assembly, and two appointed by the Governor-General in accordance with the advice of the Premier) and such number of elected members as corresponds directly with the number of electoral districts on the island.

There is a Nevis Island Administration, consisting of a premier and two other members who are appointed by the Governor-General. The Governor-General appoints the Premier as the person who, in the Governor-General's opinion, is best able to command the support of the majority of the elected members of the Assembly. The other members of the Administration are appointed by the Governor-General, acting in accordance with the wishes of the Premier. The Administration has exclusive responsibility for administration within the island of Nevis, in accordance with the provisions of any relevant laws.

The Nevis Island Legislature may provide that the island of Nevis is to cease to belong to the Federation of Saint Christopher and Nevis, in which case this Constitution would cease to have effect in the island of Nevis. Provisions for the possible secession of the island contain the following requirements: that the island must give full and detailed proposals for the future Constitution of the island of Nevis, which must be laid before the Assembly for a period of at least six months prior to the proposed date of secession; and that a two-thirds' majority has been gained in a referendum, which is to be held after the Assembly has approved the motion.

The Government

HEAD OF STATE

Queen: HM Queen ELIZABETH II.

Governor-General: Sir CUTHBERT MONTROVILLE SEBASTIAN (took office 1 January 1996).

CABINET

(July 2010)

The Cabinet consists of members of the St Kitts-Nevis Labour Party and one member of the Nevis Reformation Party.

Prime Minister and Minister of Finance, Sustainable Development and Human Resource Development: Dr DENZIL LLEWELLYN DOUGLAS.

Deputy Prime Minister and Minister of Foreign Affairs, National Security, Labour, Immigration and Social Security: SAM TERRENCE CONDOR.

Minister of International Trade, Industry, Commerce, Agriculture, Marine Resources, Consumer Affairs and Constituency Empowerment: Dr TIMOTHY SYLVESTER HARRIS.

Minister of Public Works, Housing, Energy and Utilities: Dr EARL ASIM MARTIN.

Attorney-General and Minister of Justice and Legal Affairs: PATRICE NISBETT (NRP).

Minister of Health, Social Services, Community Development, Culture and Gender Affairs: MARCELLA LIBURD.

Minister of Youth Empowerment, Sports, Information Technology and Telecommunications and Post: GLEN PHILLIP.

Minister of Education: NIGEL ALEXIS CARTY.

Minister of Tourism and International Transport: RICHARD OLIVER SKERRITT.

MINISTRIES

Office of the Governor-General: Government House, Basseterre; tel. 465-2315.

Government Headquarters: Church St, POB 186, Basseterre; tel. 465-2521; fax 466-4505; e-mail infocom@sisterisles.kn; internet www.gov.kn.

Prime Minister's Office: Government Headquarters, Church St, POB 186, Basseterre; tel. 465-9698; fax 465-9997; e-mail sknpmpresssec@cuopm.com; internet www.cuopm.org.

Attorney-General's Office and Ministry of Justice and Legal Affairs: Church St, POB 164, Basseterre; tel. 465-2521; fax 465-5040; e-mail attorneygeneral@gov.kn.

Ministry of Education: Church St, POB 333, Basseterre; tel. 465-2521.

Ministry of Finance, Sustainable Development and Human Resource Development: Church St, POB 186, Basseterre; tel. 465-2521; fax 465-0198; e-mail adminskbmof@caribsurf.com.

Ministry of Foreign Affairs, National Security, Labour, Immigration and Social Security: Church St, POB 186, Basseterre; tel. 465-2521; fax 465-5202; e-mail foreigna@sisterisles.kn; internet www.mofa.gov.kn.

Ministry of Health, Social Services, Community Development, Culture and Gender Affairs: Church St, POB 186, Basseterre; tel. 465-2521.

Ministry of International Trade, Industry, Commerce, Agriculture, Marine Resources, Consumer Affairs and Constituency Empowerment: Basseterre.

Ministry of Public Works, Housing, Energy and Utilities: Basseterre.

Ministry of Tourism and International Transport: Basseterre.

Ministry of Youth Empowerment, Sports, Information Technology and Telecommunications and Post: Basseterre.

NEVIS ISLAND ADMINISTRATION

Premier: JOSEPH W. PARRY.

There are also two appointed members.

Administrative Centre: Main St, POB 689, Charlestown, Nevis; tel. 469-1469; fax 469-0039; e-mail nevfin@caribsurf.com; internet www.gisnevis.com.

Legislature

NATIONAL ASSEMBLY

Speaker: CURTIS MARTIN.

Elected members: 11. Nominated members: 3. Ex officio members: 1.

Election, 25 January 2010

Party	Seats
St Kitts-Nevis Labour Party	6
Concerned Citizens' Movement	2
People's Action Movement	2
Nevis Reformation Party	1
Total	11

NEVIS ISLAND ASSEMBLY

Elected members: 5. Nominated members: 3.

Elections to the Nevis Island Assembly took place in July 2006. The Nevis Reformation Party took three seats and the Concerned Citizens' Movement secured the remaining two seats.

Political Organizations

Concerned Citizens' Movement (CCM): Charlestown, Nevis; tel. 469-3519; e-mail partyorganiser@myccmparty.com; internet myccmparty.com; f. 1986; Leader VANCE W. AMORY; Sec. LIVINGSTONE HERBERT.

Nevis Reformation Party (NRP): Government Rd, POB 480, Charlestown, Nevis; tel. 469-0630; e-mail JosephParry@VoteNRP.com; internet www.votenrp.com; f. 1970; Pres. JOSEPH W. PARRY; Gen. Sec. LLEWELYN PARRIS.

People's Action Movement (PAM): POB 1294, Basseterre; tel. 466-2726; fax 466-3854; e-mail pamdemocrat@pamdemocrat.org; internet www.pamdemocrat.org; f. 1965; Political Leader LINDSAY GRANT; Deputy Leaders SHAWN RICHARDS, EUGENE HAMILTON.

St Kitts-Nevis Labour Party (SKNLP): Masses House, Church St, POB 239, Basseterre; tel. 465-5347; fax 465-8328; e-mail wanda.connor@sknlabourparty.com; f. 1932; socialist party; Chair. Dr TIMOTHY HARRIS; Leader Dr DENZIL LLEWELLYN DOUGLAS.

Diplomatic Representation

EMBASSIES IN SAINT CHRISTOPHER AND NEVIS

Brazil: St Kitts Marriott, Suite 17-206, 858 Frigate Bay Rd, Frigate Bay, Basseterre; tel. 465-1054; fax 465-2015; e-mail central@brazilskn.org; internet www.brazilskn.org; Ambassador MIGUEL JUNIOR FRANÇA CHAVES DE MAGALHÃSE.

China (Taiwan): Taylor's Range, POB 119, Basseterre; tel. 465-2421; fax 465-7921; e-mail rocemb@caribsurf.com; Ambassador RONG-CHUEN WU.

Cuba: 34 Bladen Housing Devt, POB 600, Basseterre; tel. 466-3374; fax 465-8072; e-mail embacubask@sisterisles.kn; Ambassador JORGE DESIDERIO PAYRET ZURBIAUR.

Venezuela: Delisle St, POB 435, Basseterre; tel. 465-2073; fax 465-5452; e-mail frontado@caribsurf.com; Ambassador CRUZ DE JESÚS BELLO.

Diplomatic relations with other countries are maintained at consular level, or with ambassadors and high commissioners resident in other countries of the region, or directly with the other country.

Judicial System

Justice is administered by the Eastern Caribbean Supreme Court (ECSC), based in Saint Lucia and consisting of a Court of Appeal and a High Court. Two of the 16 puisne judges of the High Court are responsible for Saint Christopher and Nevis and preside over the Court of Summary Jurisdiction. One of two ECSC Masters, chiefly responsible for procedural and interlocutory matters, is also resident in the territory. The Magistrates' Courts deal with summary offences and civil offences involving sums of not more than EC $5,000. Saint Christopher and Nevis acceded to the International Criminal Court, administered in The Hague, Netherlands, in September 2006. In 2008 the death penalty was employed in Saint Christopher and Nevis for the first time since 2000.

Puisne Judges: FRANCIS BELLE, IANTHEA LEIGERTWOOD-OCTAVE (acting).

Master: PEARLETTA LANNS.

Registrar: CLAUDETTE JENKINS.

Magistrates' Office: Losack Rd, Basseterre; tel. 465-2170.

Religion

CHRISTIANITY

St Kitts Christian Council: Victoria Rd, POB 48, Basseterre; tel. 465-2167; e-mail stgeorgessk@hotmail.com; Chair. Archdeacon VALENTINE HODGE.

The Anglican Communion

Anglicans in Saint Christopher and Nevis are adherents of the Church in the Province of the West Indies. The islands form part of the diocese of the North Eastern Caribbean and Aruba. The Bishop is resident in The Valley, Anguilla.

The Roman Catholic Church

The diocese of Saint John's-Basseterre, suffragan to the archdiocese of Castries (Saint Lucia), includes Anguilla, Antigua and Barbuda, the British Virgin Islands, Montserrat and Saint Christopher and Nevis. The Bishop participates in the Antilles Episcopal Conference (currently based in Port of Spain, Trinidad and Tobago).

Bishop of Saint John's-Basseterre: (vacant), POB 836, St John's, Antigua; e-mail djr@candw.ag.

Other Churches

There are also communities of Methodists, Moravians, Seventh-day Adventists, Baptists, Pilgrim Holiness, the Church of God, Apostolic Faith and Plymouth Brethren.

The Press

The Democrat: Cayon St, POB 30, Basseterre; tel. 466-2091; fax 465-0857; e-mail thedemocrat@caribsurf.com; internet www.pamdemocrat.org/Newspaper; f. 1948; weekly (Sat.); organ of PAM; Man. Editor DENIECE ALLEYNE; circ. 3,000.

The Labour Spokesman: Masses House, Church St, POB 239, Basseterre; tel. 465-2229; fax 466-9866; e-mail sknunion@sisterisles.kn; internet www.labourspokesman.com; f. 1957; Wed. and Sat.;

organ of St Kitts-Nevis Trades and Labour Union; Editor DAWUD ST LLOYD BYRON; Man. WALFORD GUMBS; circ. 6,000.

The Leewards Times: Pinneys Industrial Site, POB 146, Nevis; tel. 469-1049; fax 469-0662; e-mail hbramble@caribsurf.com; internet www.leewardstimes.net; weekly (Fri.); Editor HOWELL BRAMBLE.

The St Kitts and Nevis Observer: Cayon St, POB 657, Basseterre; tel. 466-4994; fax 466-4995; e-mail observsk@caribsurf.com; internet www.thestkittsnevisobserver.com; weekly (Fri.); independent; Publr and Editor-in-Chief KENNETH A. WILLIAMS.

Publishers

Caribbean Publishing Co (St Kitts-Nevis) Ltd: Dr William Herbert Complex, Frigate Bay Rd, POB 745, Basseterre; tel. 465-5178; fax 466-0307; e-mail sbrisban@caribpub.com; internet www.caribpub.com.

MacPennies Publishing Co: 10A Cayon St East, POB 318, Basseterre; tel. 465-2274; fax 465-8668; e-mail mcpenltd@macpennies.com; internet www.macpennies.com; f. 1969.

St Kitts-Nevis Publishing Association Ltd: 1 Observer Plaza, Observer Dr., POB 510, Charlestown, Nevis; tel. 469-5907; fax 469-5891; e-mail observnv@sisterisles.kn; internet www.thestkittsnevisobserver.com; f. 1994; Publr and Editor-in-Chief KENNETH A. WILLIAMS.

Broadcasting and Communications

TELECOMMUNICATIONS

Regulatory Authority

Eastern Caribbean Telecommunications Authority: Miriam House, Lozack Rd, POB 450, Basseterre; tel. 465-2900; fax 465-1147; e-mail ectel@ectel.int; internet www.ectel.int; f. 2000; based in Castries, Saint Lucia; regulates telecommunications in Saint Christopher and Nevis, Dominica, Grenada, Saint Lucia and Saint Vincent and the Grenadines; Dir (Saint Christopher and Nevis) JASON HAMILTON.

Service Providers

Caribbean Cable Communications (CCC): Charlestown, Nevis; tel. 469-5601; e-mail customersupport@caribcable.com; internet ccc2.caribcable.com; provides internet and cable television services to Nevis; nationalized by Nevis Island Assembly in 2009 and ownership transferred to Nevis Cable Communications Corpn.

Digicel St Kitts and Nevis: Wireless Ventures (Saint Kitts and Nevis) Ltd, Bldg 16, Of. 4, POB 1033, Basseterre; tel. 762-4000; fax 466-4194; e-mail customercarestkittsandnevis@digicelgroup.com; internet www.digicelstkittsandnevis.com; acquired Cingular Wireless' Caribbean operations and licences in 2005; owned by an Irish consortium; Chair. DENIS O'BRIEN; Gen. Man. (St Kitts and Nevis) SEAN LATTY.

LIME (St Kitts and Nevis): Cayon St, POB 86, Basseterre; tel. 465-1000; fax 465-1106; e-mail support@cw.kn; internet www.time4lime.com; f. 1985 as St Kitts and Nevis Telecommunications Co Ltd (SKANTEL); fmrly Cable & Wireless St Kitts and Nevis; name changed as above 2008; CEO DAVID SHAW; Exec. Vice-Pres. (Leeward Islands) DAVIDSON CHARLES.

BROADCASTING

Radio

Radio One (SKNBC): Bakers Corner, POB 1773, Basseterre; tel. 466-0941; fax 465-1141; e-mail radio1941fm@yahoo.com; internet www.radioone941fm.com; owned by St Kitts & Nevis Broadcasting Corpn; music and commentary; Man. Dir GUS WILLIAMS.

Radio Paradise: Bath Plains, POB 508, Charlestown, Nevis; tel. 469-1994; fax 469-1642; e-mail info@radioparadiseonline.com; internet www.radioparadiseonline.com; owned by Trinity Broadcasting Network (USA); Christian; Gen. Man. ANDRE GILBERT.

Sugar City Roc FM: Greenlands, Basseterre; tel. 466-1113; e-mail sugarcityroc903fm@hotmail.com; internet sugarcityscr903.com; Gen. Man. VAL THOMAS.

Voice of Nevis (VON) Radio 895 AM: Bath Plains, POB 195, Charlestown, Nevis; tel. 469-1616; fax 469-5329; e-mail gmanager@vonradio.com; internet www.vonradio.com; f. 1988; owned by Nevis Broadcasting Co Ltd; Gen. Man. EVERED (WEBBO) HERBERT.

WINN FM: Unit C24, The Sands, Newtown Bay Rd, Basseterre; tel. 466-9586; fax 466-7904; e-mail info@winnfm.com; internet www.winnfm.com; owned by Federation Media Group; Chair. MICHAEL KING.

ZIZ Radio and Television: Springfield, POB 331, Basseterre; tel. 465-2622; fax 465-5624; e-mail info@zizonline.com; internet www.zizonline.com; f. 1961; television from 1972; commercial; govt-owned; Gen. Man. WINSTON MCMAHON.

Television

ZIZ Radio and Television: see Radio.

Finance

(cap. = capital; res = reserves; dep. = deposits; brs = branches)

BANKING

Central Bank

Eastern Caribbean Central Bank (ECCB): Headquarters Bldg, Bird Rock, POB 89, Basseterre; tel. 465-2537; fax 465-9562; e-mail info@eccb-centralbank.org; internet www.eccb-centralbank.org; f. 1965 as East Caribbean Currency Authority; expanded responsibilities and changed name 1983; responsible for issue of currency in Anguilla, Antigua and Barbuda, Dominica, Grenada, Montserrat, Saint Christopher and Nevis, Saint Lucia and Saint Vincent and the Grenadines; res EC $248.3m., dep. EC $1,302.5m., total assets EC $2,383.0m. (March 2009); Gov. and Chair. Sir K. DWIGHT VENNER; Country Dir WENDELL LAWRENCE.

Other Banks

Bank of Nevis Ltd: Main St, POB 450, Charlestown, Nevis; tel. 469-5564; fax 469-5798; e-mail info@thebankofnevis.com; internet www.thebankofnevis.com; dep. EC $0.3m., total assets EC $0.4m. (Dec. 2006); Chair. RAWLINSON ISAAC; Gen. Man. L. EVERETTE MARTIN.

FirstCaribbean International Bank (Barbados) Ltd: The Circus, POB 42, Basseterre; tel. 465-2449; fax 465-1041; internet www.firstcaribbeanbank.com; f. 2002 following merger of Caribbean operations of Barclays Bank PLC and CIBC; Barclays relinquished its stake to CIBC in 2006; res EC $0.8m. (March 2006); Exec. Chair. MICHAEL MANSOOR; CEO JOHN D. ORR.

RBTT Bank (SKN) Ltd: Chappel St, POB 60, Charlestown, Nevis; tel. 469-5277; fax 469-1493; internet www.rbtt.com; f. 1955 as Nevis Co-operative Banking Co Ltd; acquired by Royal Bank of Trinidad and Tobago (later known as RBTT) in 1996; Group Chair. PETER J. JULY.

St Kitts-Nevis-Anguilla National Bank Ltd: Central St, POB 343, Basseterre; tel. 465-2204; fax 466-1050; e-mail webmaster@sknanb.com; internet www.sknanb.com; f. 1971; Govt of St Kitts and Nevis owns 51%; cap. EC $81.0m., res EC $325.5m., dep. EC $1,380.3m. (June 2008); Chair. WALFORD GUMBS; Man. Dir EDMUND LAURENCE; 5 brs.

Development Bank

Development Bank of St Kitts and Nevis: Church St, POB 249, Basseterre; tel. 465-2288; fax 465-4016; e-mail info@skndb.com; internet www.skndb.com; f. 1981; cap. EC $10.8m., res EC $5.8m., dep. EC $34.0m. (Dec. 2007); Chair. ELVIS NEWTON; Gen. Man. LENWORTH HARRIS.

STOCK EXCHANGE

Eastern Caribbean Securities Exchange: Bird Rock, POB 94, Basseterre; tel. 466-7192; fax 465-3798; e-mail info@ecseonline.com; internet www.ecseonline.com; f. 2001; regional securities market designed to facilitate the buying and selling of financial products for the eight member territories—Anguilla, Antigua and Barbuda, Dominica, Grenada, Montserrat, Saint Christopher and Nevis, Saint Lucia and Saint Vincent and the Grenadines; Chair. Sir K. DWIGHT VENNER; Gen. Man. and CEO TREVOR E. BLAKE.

INSURANCE

British American Insurance Company Ltd: 4 Cayon St, Basseterre; tel. 465-2348; fax 465-7838; internet www.baico-intl.com; f. 1958 as Industrial Insurance Co; owned by CL Financial Group (Trinidad and Tobago); Gen. Man. LISA TAYLOR.

National Caribbean Insurance Co Ltd: Central St, POB 374, Basseterre; tel. 465-2694; fax 465-3659; internet www.nci-biz.com; f. 1973; subsidiary of St Kitts-Nevis-Anguilla National Bank Ltd; Gen. Man. JUDITH ATTONG.

St Kitts-Nevis Insurance Co Ltd (SNIC): Central St, POB 142, Basseterre; tel. 465-2845; fax 465-5410; e-mail snic@tdcltd.com; internet www.tdclimited.com/snic; subsidiary of St Kitts Nevis Anguilla Trading & Devt Co Ltd (TDC); Chair. DENNIS MICHAEL ARTHUR MORTON; Gen. Man. AUSTIN DA SILVA.

Several foreign companies also have offices in Saint Christopher and Nevis.

Trade and Industry

GOVERNMENT AGENCIES

Central Marketing Corpn (CEMACO): Pond's Pasture, POB 375, Basseterre; tel. 465-2628; fax 465-7823; Man. VERNA HERBERT.

Frigate Bay Development Corporation (FBDC): Frigate Bay, POB 315, Basseterre; tel. 465-8339; fax 465-4463; promotes tourist and residential devts; Chair. JANET HARRIS; Man. Dir RANDOLPH MORTON.

Nevis Investment Promotion Agency (NIPA): Charlestown, Nevis; f. 2008.

St Kitts Investment Promotion Agency: Pelican Mall, Bay Rd, POB 132, Basseterre; tel. 465-4040; fax 465-6968; f. 1987.

Social Security Board: Robert Llewellyn Bradshaw Bldg, Bay Rd, POB 79, Basseterre; tel. 465-2535; fax 465-5051; e-mail pubinfo@socialsecurity.kn; internet www.socialsecurity.kn; f. 1977; Dir SEPHLIN LAWRENCE.

CHAMBER OF COMMERCE

St Kitts-Nevis Chamber of Industry and Commerce: Horsford Rd, Fortlands, POB 332, Basseterre; tel. 465-2980; fax 465-4490; e-mail sknchamber@sisterisles.kn; internet www.stkittsnevischamber.org; incorporated 1949; 137 mems (2006); Pres. FRANKLIN BRAND; Exec. Dir WENDY PHIPPS.

EMPLOYERS' ORGANIZATIONS

Building Contractors' Association: Anthony Evelyn Business Complex, Paul Southwell Industrial Park, POB 1046, Basseterre; tel. 465-6897; fax 465-5623; e-mail sknbca@caribsurf.com; Pres. ANTHONY E. EVELYN.

Nevis Cotton Growers' Association Ltd: Charlestown, Nevis; Pres. IVOR STEVENS.

Small Business Association: Anthony Evelyn Business Complex, Paul Southwell Industrial Park, POB 367, Basseterre; tel. 465-8630; fax 465-6661; e-mail sb-association@caribsurf.com; Pres. EUSTACE WARNER.

UTILITIES

Nevis Electricity Company Ltd (Nevlec): POB 852, Charlestown, Nevis; tel. 469-7245; fax 469-7249; e-mail info@nevlec.com; internet www.nevlec.com; owned by the Nevis Island Administration; Gen. Man. CARTWRIGHT FARRELL.

TRADE UNIONS

Nevis Teachers' Union: POB 559, Charlestown, Nevis; tel. 469-8465; fax 469-5663; e-mail nevteach@caribsurf.com; Pres. WAKELY DANIEL; Gen. Sec. BERNELLA CAINES HAMILTON.

St Kitts-Nevis Trades and Labour Union (SKTLU): Masses House, Church St, POB 239, Basseterre; tel. 465-2229; fax 466-9866; e-mail sknunion@caribsurf.com; f. 1940; affiliated to Caribbean Maritime and Aviation Council, Caribbean Congress of Labour, International Federation of Plantation, Agricultural and Allied Workers, and International Trade Union Confederation; associated with St Kitts-Nevis Labour Party; Pres. CLIFFORD THOMAS; Gen. Sec. BATUMBA TAK; c. 3,000 mems.

St Kitts Teachers' Union: Green Tree Housing Devt, POB 545, Basseterre; tel. 465-1921; e-mail stkittsteachersunion@hotmail.com; Pres. CLYDE CHRISTOPHER; Gen. Sec. CARLENE HENRY-MORTON.

Transport

RAILWAYS

There are 58 km (36 miles) of narrow-gauge light railway on Saint Christopher, serving the sugar plantations. The railway, complete with new trains and carriages, was restored and developed for tourist excursions and opened in late 2002.

St Kitts Scenic Railway: Sands Unit A6, Bay Rd, POB 191, Basseterre; tel. 465-7263; e-mail scenicreservations@sisterisles.kn; internet www.stkittsscenicrailway.com; f. 2002; Gen. Man. THOMAS A. WILLIAMS.

St Kitts Sugar Railway: St Kitts Sugar Manufacturing Corpn, POB 96, Basseterre; tel. 465-8099; fax 465-1059; e-mail agronomy@caribsurf.com; Gen. Man. J. E. S. ALFRED.

ROADS

In 1999 there were 320 km (199 miles) of road in Saint Christopher and Nevis, of which approximately 136 km (84 miles) were paved. In July 2001 the Caribbean Development Bank loaned US $3.75m. to the Nevis Government for a road improvement scheme. Further improvements were undertaken in 2006 in preparation for the Cricket World Cup, principally the construction of the West Basseterre Bypass Road, at an estimated cost of EC $20m. However, only certain sections had been completed as the cricket tournament commenced. The collapse of a bridge in May 2008 delayed construction, but in December 2009 it was reported that traffic was flowing on the full length of the road for the first time.

SHIPPING

The Government maintains a commercial motorboat service between the islands, and numerous regional and international shipping lines call at the islands. A deep-water port, Port Zante, was opened at Basseterre in 1981. In June 2003 the Government of Kuwait agreed to provide a loan of EC $15m. to help fund the development of the cruise ship facilities at Port Zante.

St Christopher Air and Sea Ports Authority: Bird Rock, POB 963, Basseterre; tel. 465-8121; fax 465-8124; e-mail info@scaspa.com; internet www.scaspa.com; f. 1993 to combine St Kitts Port Authority and Airports Authority; Chair. LINKON MAYNARD; CEO and Gen. Man. ERROL DOUGLAS; Airport Man. DENZIL JONES; Sea Port Man. ROSEVELT TROTMAN.

Shipping Companies

Delisle Walwyn and Co Ltd: Liverpool Row, POB 44, Basseterre; tel. 465-2631; fax 465-1125; e-mail info@delislewalwyn.com; internet www.delislewalwyn.com; f. 1951; Chair. KISHU CHANDIRAMANI; Man. Dir DENZIL V. CROOKE.

Tony's Ltd: Main St, POB 564, Charlestown, Nevis; tel. 469-5413.

CIVIL AVIATION

Robert Llewellyn Bradshaw (formerly Golden Rock) International Airport, 4 km (2.5 miles) from Basseterre, is equipped to handle jet aircraft and is served by scheduled links with most Caribbean destinations, the United Kingdom, the USA and Canada. A US $17m. expansion and development project at the airport, financed by Taiwan and the St Kitts-Nevis-Anguilla National Bank Ltd, was completed in December 2006. Saint Christopher and Nevis is a shareholder in the regional airline, LIAT (see chapter on Antigua and Barbuda), which began operating a joint flight schedule with its troubled rival, Caribbean Star Airlines (also headquartered in Antigua and Barbuda) in February 2007; LIAT's full acquisition of Caribbean Star was completed in October 2007. Vance W. Amory International Airport (formerly Newcastle Airfield), 11 km (7 miles) from Charlestown, Nevis, has regular scheduled services to St Kitts and other islands in the region. A new airport, Castle Airport, was opened on Nevis in 1998.

St Christopher Air and Sea Ports Authority: see Shipping.

Private Airlines

Air St Kitts-Nevis: Vance W. Amory International Airport, Newcastle, Nevis; tel. 465-8571.

LIAT (1974) Ltd: Robert Llewellyn Bradshaw International Airport; tel. 465-2098; fax 466-3168; e-mail customerrelations@liatairline.com; internet www.liatairline.com; f. 1956 as Leeward Islands Air Transport Services, jtly owned by 11 regional Govts; privatized in 1995; shares are held by the Govts of Antigua and Barbuda, Montserrat, Grenada, Barbados, Trinidad and Tobago, Jamaica, Guyana, Dominica, Saint Lucia, Saint Vincent and the Grenadines and Saint Christopher and Nevis (30.8%), Caribbean Airlines (29.2%), LIAT employees (13.3%) and private investors (26.7%); merger negotiations with Caribbean Star Airlines were finalized in March 2007; deal was abandoned in July in favour of a buyout arrangement in which LIAT would acquire all remaining shares in Caribbean Star; scheduled passenger and cargo services to 19 destinations in the Caribbean; charter flights are also undertaken; Chair. JEAN STEWART HOLDER; CEO MARK DARBY.

Tourism

The introduction of regular air services to the US cities of Miami and New York has opened up the islands as a tourist destination. Visitors are attracted by the excellent beaches and the historical Brimstone Hill Fortress National Park on Saint Christopher, the spectacular mountain scenery of Nevis and the islands' associations with Lord Nelson and Alexander Hamilton. Many hotels and other tourist accommodation were constructed or refurbished in advance of the 2007 Cricket World Cup, hosted by several Caribbean nations, including Saint Christopher and Nevis. In 2009 there were 450,553 cruise ship passengers and 93,081 stop-over visitors. Receipts from tourism were EC $225.41m. in 2009.

Nevis Tourism Authority: Main St, POB 917, Charlestown, Nevis; tel. 469-7550; fax 469-7551; e-mail info@nevisisland.com; internet www.nevisisland.com; Chair. CHRIS MARTIN; Dir TIMOTHY HOFFMAN.

Nevis Tourism Bureau: Main St, Charlestown, Nevis; tel. 469-1042; fax 469-1066; e-mail nevtour@caribsurf.com; Dir ELMEADER BROOKES.

St Kitts-Nevis Hotel and Tourism Association: Liverpool Row, POB 438, Basseterre; tel. 465-5304; fax 465-7746; e-mail stkitnevhta@caribsurf.com; f. 1972; Pres. KISHU CHANDIRAMANI; Man. MICHAEL HEAD.

St Kitts Tourism Authority: Pelican Mall, Bay Rd, POB 132, Basseterre; tel. 465-4040; fax 465-8794; e-mail ceo@stkittstourism.kn; internet www.stkittstourism.kn; Chair. RICHARD OLIVER SKERRITT.

Defence

The small army was disbanded by the Government in 1981, and its duties were absorbed by the Volunteer Defence Force and a special tactical unit of the police. In July 1997 the National Assembly approved legislation to re-establish a full-time defence force. Coastguard operations were to be brought under military command; the defence force was also to include cadet and reserve forces. Saint Christopher and Nevis participates in the US-sponsored Regional Security System, comprising police, coastguards and army units, which was established by independent Eastern Caribbean states in 1982. According to the 2008 budget address, the Ministry of National Security, Immigration and Labour was to receive an allocation of EC $40.3m. in that year.

Education

Education is compulsory for 12 years between five and 17 years of age. Primary education begins at the age of five, and lasts for seven years. Secondary education, from the age of 12, generally comprises a first cycle of four years, followed by a second cycle of two years. In 2004/05 enrolment at primary schools included 93.4% of children in the relevant age-group, according to UNESCO estimates, while comparable enrolment at secondary schools included 86.1% of pupils. There are 30 state, eight private and five denominational schools. There is also a technical college. In September 2000 a privately financed 'offshore' medical college, the Medical University of the Americas, opened in Nevis with 40 students registered. The Ross University School of Veterinary Medicine and the International University of Nursing also operated on Saint Christopher. Budgetary expenditure on education, training and youth development by the central Government in 2008 was projected to total EC $72.6m. A Basic Education Project funded by the Caribbean Development Bank was in 2003 complemented by a EC $18.8m. Secondary Education Project, which was to include the construction of a new school in Saddlers.

SAINT LUCIA

Geography

PHYSICAL FEATURES

Saint Lucia is the second largest of the Windward Islands, and is located in the eastern Caribbean, between the French department of Martinique and the fellow Commonwealth state of Saint Vincent and the Grenadines. Martinique lies 34 km away, north of the Saint Lucia Channel (a sealane from the Atlantic into the Caribbean), while the main island of Saint Vincent lies 42 km to the south, across the Saint Vincent Passage. The total area of the country is 616.3 sq km (238 sq miles), most of which consists of the main island itself, although there are a few small islands offshore, such as the uninhabited Maria Islands in the south-east.

The island of Saint Lucia is rugged and volcanic, bulked around a great barrier range of mountains along the backbone of the island, the Barre de l'Isle. The highlands are loftiest towards the south, reaching their highest point at Morne Gimie (950 m or 3,118 ft) in the south-west, although the peaks considered most emblematic of the island lie still further to the south-west. Here twin mountain horns rear above the spa town of Soufrière, jungle-clad volcanic plugs known as the Pitons (Petit Piton and, to its south, Gros Piton), steep cones plunging straight into the sea. Elsewhere on the island there are places where the highland terrain gives way to broad, fertile valleys, while the rich soil generally makes for a verdant landscape. The native rainforest has suffered since European colonization, particularly in the later 20th century, but is now protected and is still home to a rich variety of flora and fauna (deforestation was also affecting water supply). Like other islands in the Windwards, Saint Lucia is home to animals such as the iguana, the fer de lance (the only poisonous snake on the island), the manicou, the rarely seen agouti and the historically introduced mongoose. There are some endemic species, such as nine types of flamboyant tree, the pygmy gecko, the Saint Lucia tree lizard and, on the protected Maria Islands, a ground lizard and a grass snake. Bird species include the Saint Lucia parrot, the endangered Saint Lucia oriole and Saint Lucia black finch, and the Semper's warbler, which may now be extinct. On the rougher Atlantic coast turtles lay their eggs and other birds nest.

CLIMATE

The climate is subtropical marine, moderated by the eastern and north-eastern trade winds. The island lies within the hurricane belt, and storms can cause flooding and mudslides in the steep terrain. Most rain falls between May and November, with annual averages varying considerably in different parts of the island, mainly owing to altitude. The range is between 1,540 mm and 3,540 mm (60–138 ins). Temperatures are fairly constant at around 27°C (80°F), though are sometimes slightly lower in the drier months or in the heights.

POPULATION

The long years of alternating French and British rule have contributed to a rich cultural legacy, and the indigenous

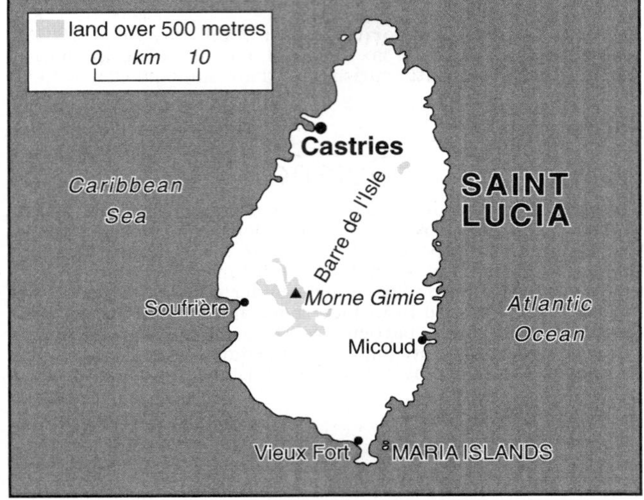

product flourishes with hybrid vigour. The descendants of the black slaves employed under both colonial powers (about 90% of the population is now black—the rest are of mixed race, 'East' Indian or white) use English as their official language, but a French patois or Creole (known as Kweyol locally) is widespread. Some even claim descent from the original Carib residents. Similarly, the system of government and law follows the British model, but about 68% of the population are Roman Catholic. About 9% of the population are Seventh-day Adventists, 6% are Pentecostalists, 2% are Evangelical Christians, 2% are Baptists and 2% are Anglican. There a few Hindu, Muslim and Jewish residents too. Certainly the island has produced some of the Caribbean's foremost writers, artists and thinkers—the country has the highest per-head rate of Nobel laureates ever (Sir Arthur Lewis, Economics, 1979, and Derek Walcott, Literature, 1992).

Estimates put the total population of Saint Lucia at about 174,000 in mid-2010. About two-fifths of this total live in and around the island's capital, Castries, which is sited on the north-western coast. Other important towns include Micoud, on the south-eastern coast, across the island from Soufrière, and Vieux Fort, the main industrial centre, by the airport, near the southern tip of the island. Gros Islet is north of Castries, towards the end of the island, and Dennery is north of Micoud, where the road across the Barre de l'Isle reaches the east coast. For administrative purposes the island is divided into quarters, although, confusingly, there are 11 of these.

History

MARK WILSON

Saint Lucia is a constitutional monarchy within the Commonwealth. Queen Elizabeth II is Head of State, and is represented in Saint Lucia by a Governor-General. There is a bicameral legislature with an elected chamber.

A small number of Saint Lucians trace their ancestry to the island's original Amerindian inhabitants, who knew the island as Hiwanarau or Hewanorra. There is no mention of Saint Lucia in Christopher Columbus's logbook, although a local tradition holds that he discovered and named the island on 13 December 1502, St Lucy's day. The first successful European settlement was French. The island changed hands on 14 occasions before passing to British rule in 1814, but extended periods of French rule in the 17th and 18th centuries established a French Creole as the main spoken language, and the Roman Catholic religion as the faith of the majority of the population. The island's hybrid legal code also contains elements of the pre-Revolutionary French legal tradition.

As in the United Kingdom's other Caribbean colonies, slavery was abolished in 1834. After this date, some former slaves established small peasant farms. Saint Lucia received significant numbers of Indian indentured labourers in the 19th century; their descendants form a significant minority in some parts of the island.

During the Second World War the USA built an important airbase at Vieux Fort in the south of the island, part of which was later developed as Hewanorra International Airport. After the war the introduction of banana cultivation brought a modest increase in rural living standards. The Saint Lucia Labour Party (SLP) was formed in March 1949, won the first universal suffrage election in 1951, and remained in office until its 1964 defeat at the hands of the United Workers' Party (UWP), which then retained power until 1979, with John (later Sir John) Compton as Prime Minister.

Saint Lucia joined the Federation of the West Indies in 1958, along with nine other British colonies. When Jamaica and Trinidad and Tobago left in 1962, the Federation collapsed, and an attempt to unite the remaining colonies as the 'little eight' was unsuccessful. Along with its neighbours, Saint Lucia became a British Associated State in 1967, responsible for its internal affairs, with the United Kingdom retaining control of external affairs and defence. Independence was granted on 22 February 1979.

The SLP won a general election held in July 1979, but the new Government was torn apart by fierce factional rivalries between the Prime Minister, Allan Louisy, and a populist faction led by George Odlum. The Government was further damaged by allegations of mismanagement. After a Government defeat in Parliament, Winston Cenac replaced Louisy as Prime Minister. However, factional struggles continued; a series of protests, including an organized short-term closure of private sector businesses in 1982, led to the formation of an interim Government led by Michael Pilgrim, which presided over fresh elections in that year. The UWP regained power with a convincing majority; Odlum fought the election as leader of the newly formed Progressive Labour Party, but was beaten into third place by the mainstream SLP.

Compton's majority was reduced to a single seat in the 1987 elections. Another election held immediately afterwards produced exactly the same result; however, the Government's position was strengthened when an SLP member crossed the floor.

After a total of 29 years in office, Compton resigned as Prime Minister in March 1996, in preparation for retirement. He was succeeded as Prime Minister by Dr Vaughan Lewis, a former Director-General of the Organisation of Eastern Caribbean States. The SLP at the same time chose a new leader, Dr Kenny Anthony, a lawyer with an academic post in the University of the West Indies. An election in May 1997 resulted in an overwhelming victory for the SLP, which took 16 of the House of Assembly's 17 seats and 60% of the popular vote. A disunited UWP did not perform well in opposition, and was not strengthened by the return of Compton from retirement, nor the formation of an alliance with Odlum, who had, for the second time in his career, broken with an SLP Government. In spite of the continuing troubles of the banana industry and in a poor year for tourism, the SLP won a second comfortable election victory in December 2001, winning 14 of the 17 parliamentary seats, although its share of the popular vote fell to 54.2%; the UWP increased its strength to three seats.

The opposition remained chronically divided in the early years of the new Parliament. Marius Wilson resigned as opposition leader in February 2003 and sat in Parliament as an independent, leaving the UWP with only two seats. He was replaced by Arsene James, who was not considered to be a particularly effective parliamentary performer.

The removal of the Minister of Home Affairs and Gender Relations, Sarah Flood-Beaubrun, in January 2004 over her vehement opposition to a liberalization of abortion law—and her subsequent move to the opposition benches as an independent—had little initial impact on the Government. However, the disruption provoked a further split in the opposition in April, when Arsene James was replaced by Marcus Nicholas, his former deputy. Nicholas enjoyed the support of Flood-Beaubrun and Wilson, but not of the UWP itself, leaving the former party of government with James as its sole loyal supporter in the legislature. Concerned by the deteriorating position of the UWP, Sir John Compton emerged from retirement in March 2005, now aged 79 years, to replace his chosen successor, Dr Vaughn Lewis, as party leader; like Lewis, however, he did not hold a parliamentary seat.

At a general election held in December 2006 the UWP took 11 of the 17 seats, some by a very narrow margin, with 50.06% of the overall vote. The SLP retained only six seats, which, although surprising to most observers, appeared to reflect the view of many voters that the party had become arrogant and élitist in its approach. Allen Chastenet, a successful hotelier who had also served on the board of the regional airline LIAT, was chosen as Minister of Tourism, while Guy Mayers, a former President of the Chamber of Commerce, Industry and Agriculture, was named Minister of Trade and Industry.

The Minister of Foreign Affairs, Rufus Bousquet, announced in April 2007 that Saint Lucia would resume diplomatic relations with the Republic of China (Taiwan). There were, however, deep divisions on the issue within the Cabinet, with Compton reportedly among those expressing grave doubts. Saint Lucia had entered into diplomatic relations with Taiwan soon after independence, but switched to the People's Republic of China following the election of the SLP Government in 1997; in return, China had funded the construction of an 8,000-seat stadium and designated a free trade zone, with further plans announced for a national cultural complex and the construction of a US $10m. psychiatric hospital, work on which had begun in 2007. Compton had held discussions on behalf of his party with a Taiwanese representative in Saint Vincent before the 2006 election, but was believed to favour a restoration of trade and technical relations, rather than full recognition and a split from China. Taiwan offered to complete projects initiated by China, but with construction in progress, a change in sponsor was not straightforward. Following the establishment of relations with Taiwan, China suspended diplomatic relations with Saint Lucia and closed its embassy in Castries. In 2007 Taiwan had diplomatic relations with four other Caribbean Community and Common Market (CARICOM) member states, namely Saint Vincent and the Grenadines, Saint Christopher and Nevis, Belize and Haiti; Dominica and Grenada had switched their recognition to China in 2004.

Compton suffered a series of strokes in late April 2007, and on 1 May departed Saint Lucia in order to seek medical treatment in New York. Stephenson King, the Minister of Health and UWP Chairman, was appointed acting Prime Minister, and remained in the post after Compton's return on 19 May. Upon the latter's advice, on 6 June King assumed responsibility for foreign affairs, finance, home affairs, labour, national security, information and broadcasting, while relinquishing the health portfolio. Compton died on 7 September at the age of 82. On 9 September King was sworn in as Prime Minister, having won the support, after some intra-party manoeuvring, of nine of the UWP's remaining 10 representatives in the House of Assembly. This was a bare majority of the 16 sitting members of the House, with Compton's seat at that point vacant. In a by-election in November Compton's daughter Jeannine Compton-Rambally was elected, restoring the UWP's strength in the House to 11. Divisions within the governing party persisted, however, and Compton-Rambally's by-election opponents included two dissident members of the UWP who had sought the nomination.

Stephenson King's Government remained deeply divided, with continuing disputes between party factions. In June 2007 Rufus Bousquet was removed from his post as Minister of External Affairs, International Financial Services, Information and Broadcasting during the period that King was acting Prime Minister and diplomatic relations with Taiwan had resumed. Bousquet repeatedly questioned the circumstances of his removal, and pressed strongly for readmission to the Cabinet. He abstained on the budget vote in April 2008, and wrote formally to the Governor-General in May to withdraw his support for King as Prime Minister, as did the Deputy Speaker, Marcus Nicholas. In response to this pressure, Bousquet was in June 2008, after a year on the back benches, appointed Minister for External Affairs, International Trade and Investment.

The Minister for Physical Development, Housing, Urban Renewal, Local Government and the Environment, Richard Frederick, was briefly placed under arrest in July 2007 and questioned over alleged under-invoicing of vehicles imported for his private use. The vehicles were not released by customs, and the matter was referred to the Director of Public Prosecutions. However, in May 2008 the Prime Minister made a controversial request to the customs department to treat it on an administrative rather than criminal basis; Frederick then initiated legal action contesting the seizure of his vehicles.

Dr Keith Mondesir was appointed Minister of Home Affairs and National Security after the 2006 election, but in June 2007, after a controversial six months in office, was moved to the more junior position of Minister for Physical Development and National Mobilisation. In September he was given responsibility for Health Wellness, Family Affairs, National Mobilisation, Human Services and Gender Relations.

Ausbert d'Auvergne, an appointed government Senator, resigned in May 2008 from his post of Minister of Economic Affairs, Economic Planning, Investment and National Development, under strong pressure from party colleagues, particularly Bousquet and Frederick, who complained that he had excessive influence. D'Auvergne had been strongly criticized in 1999 in the report of a commission of inquiry by a British Queen's Counsel, Louis Blom-Cooper. The report noted serious conflicts of interest in his role as Permanent Secretary in the Ministry of Planning, Development and the Environment in the early 1990s during the sale of a valuable parcel of state land to a company of which he was Chairman and Managing Director. D'Auvergne had formed the small National Development Movement in 2004, but rejoined the UWP to manage its 2006 election campaign.

A commission of inquiry was appointed in February 2009 under the Guyanese attorney Fenton Ramsahoye into allegations of corruption under the Anthony Government. As part of the investigation the commission examined a road development project, which cost close to three times the original estimate, the affairs of the National Conservation Authority, and a government debt guarantee for a company linked to the construction of the Hyatt Hotel. The report was completed on 6 May and made public in October; it indicated serious mismanagement of public funds, but not corruption. Accusations of corruption, meanwhile, continued to be levelled against the current administration by its political opponents, while a June 2010 judgment of the Eastern Caribbean Court of Appeal was sharply critical of duty concessions granted to a cabinet minister in connection with a resort development.

Drugs transshipment and violent crime remained serious concerns for the Government. Marijuana is imported from Saint Vincent for local use, and is also grown within Saint Lucia. Cocaine is transshipped from Venezuela; according to the US State Department, around 40% of the shipment moves on to the French overseas departments, 25% to the United Kingdom and 25% to the USA or Canada; most of the local marijuana market is supplied from Saint Vincent and the Grenadines. The estimated per-head murder rate of 23 per 100,000 in both 2008 and 2009 was high by international standards. A British woman resident in Saint Lucia was murdered in August 2006, with some resulting adverse publicity in the British media underlining the potential threat to tourism, while there was an attempt in 2006 on the life of the Roman Catholic Archbishop, Kelvin Felix; among those murdered in 2007 was the former Permanent Secretary in the Ministry of Physical Development, Marcia Philbert-Jules.

In November 2006 the outgoing SLP Government recruited 10 former British police officers on two-year contracts as part of a drive to reform the police force. Several incoming UWP ministers had previously developed a sour relationship with elements in the police leadership regarded as being sympathetic to the SLP. Soon after his appointment as Minister of Home Affairs and National Security, Keith Mondesir ordered Deputy Police Commissioner Hermangild Francis to take mandatory leave for 144 days from January 2007, while the Police Commissioner, Ausbert Regis, together with two other senior officers, was sent on leave from early June. A former British police officer, John Broughton, was appointed acting Police Commissioner, but he developed a difficult relationship with many of his colleagues. In May 2008 the Police Welfare Association (PWA) organized a march by police officers to demand his dismissal, claiming that the security of the country had been compromised. Tensions between the PWA and Broughton subsequently subsided to some extent, but by the end of May three of the 10 British officers had tendered their resignation. Broughton's contract ended in October 2008, with his remaining British colleagues leaving at around the same time, after which Regis resumed his post as Commissioner. However, Regis was unexpectedly removed from the post in May 2010 and replaced by Vernon Francois; he subsequently launched a legal challenge to his reassignment.

Economy

MARK WILSON

With an estimated 174,000 inhabitants on 616.3 sq km in mid-2010, Saint Lucia has a larger population than its neighbours in the Organisation of Eastern Caribbean States (OECS). With a per-head gross domestic product (GDP) of US $4,498 in 2008, it was a reasonably prosperous middle-income economy. GDP grew at an annual rate of only 1.9% in 1995–2000, largely because of the severe problems of the banana industry, and contracted by 5.9% in 2001. However, in spite of continuing banana problems, growth averaged 4.0% in 2002–07, falling back to 0.7% in 2008 as a result of weak performance in the tourism sector and hurricane damage to the banana crop. The economy contracted by 5.2% in 2009, as the international economic recession led to a decline in investment inflows, tourism and migrant remittances. In 2010 the IMF noted an increase in non-performing loans and regulatory weaknesses in the non-bank financial sector.

The fiscal position deteriorated from 1999, with an overall surplus equivalent to 3.4% of GDP declining to a deficit that reached more than 6% of GDP in 2005 and 2006; there was a recovery to a more sustainable 2.2% in 2007, followed by an out-turn close to fiscal balance in 2008. In July 2009 the IMF approved a US $10.7m. disbursement under the rapid-access component of the Exogenous Shocks Facility. The Government at that time proposed introduction of a value-added tax in 2010, property tax reform and tight control of spending. However, in the event the deficit increased again, to 2.5% of GDP, in 2009 as the Government increased its capital expenditure, financed by local borrowing, and in March 2010 the IMF noted a lack of progress on earlier commitments. Meanwhile, the unemployment rate stood at 20.5% in 2009, up from 16.8% in 2008, with the construction and tourism sectors suffering a downturn. Total public sector debt was estimated at 79% of GDP at the end of 2009, an increase from 59% in 2006; none the less, the ratio was still below levels recorded in most neighbouring islands.

Saint Lucia is a member of the Caribbean Community and Common Market, or CARICOM, whose larger members formed the Caribbean Single Market and Economy (CSME) at the start of 2006, with Saint Lucia joining on 3 July following the resolution of economic and regional development concerns. The CSME was intended to enshrine the free movement of goods, services and labour throughout the CARICOM region. Saint Lucia also houses the secretariat of the OECS, which links nine of the smaller Caribbean territories, while the Eastern Caribbean Central Bank, based in Saint Christopher and Nevis, supervises its financial affairs.

Agriculture (including hunting, forestry and fishing) comprised only 3.8% of GDP in 2009, down from 14.7% in 1990; however, the sector still employed some 12.2% of the working population in 2007. Banana exports to the United Kingdom under protected market access arrangements were an economic mainstay from the 1950s, but the industry suffered a steep decline from the 1990s as the trade privileges of Caribbean producers in the European market were eroded. In 1992 income from banana exports was US $68.1m., equivalent to 53.6% of merchandise exports and 21.2% of foreign exchange earnings. However, in 2004 banana exports were equivalent only to an estimated 3.2% of foreign exchange earnings, and in 2007 exports totalled only US $16.1m., with damage from Hurricane Dean in August compounding the structural problems of the industry; nevertheless, production recovered by 26.5% in 2008, with exports at US $21.8m. in that year and US $20.5m. in 2009. Significant grant aid from the European Union was available for irrigation and technical support, as well as for economic diversification and social support. Small farmers produced a wide variety of fruits, vegetables and livestock products for the local market, with some produce being exported to neighbouring islands.

Saint Lucia's natural attractions and direct air links to North America and the United Kingdom have encouraged the development of tourism, which is the principal source of foreign exchange. Tourism receipts increased from EC $415.3m. in 1990 to EC $1,030.5m. in 2005, slipping back, however, to an average of EC $811.9 m. for the next four years. In 2008 the island attracted some 295,761 stop-over tourists, 7.0% fewer than in the peak year of 2005, but more than any of its OECS neighbours; the total fell to 278,491 in 2009 as international demand weakened. There were also some 699,306 cruise ship passengers, a 94% increase over 2006, although this group had much lower per-head spending. The US-Norwegian company Royal Caribbean International collaborated with the Government on waterfront development in the capital, Castries, with proposed expansion of more lucrative home port activity. In 2009 some 45.7% of tourist arrivals were from North America and 25.8% were from the United Kingdom. Tourism in Saint Lucia is reliant to a great extent on all-inclusive properties, where meals and other facilities are pre-paid; one Jamaican all-inclusive group had three properties in operation in 2008. These and other hotel and residential development investments provided strong support to the construction industry. However, major hotel and resort investments were placed on hold in 2008, in some cases in mid-construction, as credit conditions tightened and the second-home market stagnated. Yachting is an important sub-sector of tourism with 31,997 passenger arrivals in 2009. The Jazz Festival in May is also a significant attraction, as is the annual Carnival, now held in July in place of its traditional pre-Lenten date. However, the high rate of violent crime, much of it drugs-related, was a potential threat to tourism; the per head murder rate of 24 per 100,000 in 2009 was high by world standards and close to four times that of the USA.

Manufacturing comprised 6.3% of GDP in 2009, down from 8.2% in 1990. A brewery exports some of its products to the regional market. Another major enterprise—a cardboard box manufacturer—has been severely damaged by the decline in the banana industry, which had been its major market. On a much larger scale, a proposal was floated in 2008 to develop an oil refinery at a cost of US $7,000m., extending a transshipment facility operated by the US-based Hess Corporation at Cul de Sac, south of Castries. Saint Lucia houses the headquarters of the Eastern Caribbean Telecommunications Authority; the telecommunications sector has been liberalized, and the Government regarded telemarketing and informatics as areas with great potential for economic growth.

The 'offshore' financial services sector was only established in 2000 and was better regulated than those of most other OECS members. In 2008 there were six 'offshore' banks, 2,851 international business companies, nine mutual funds, 29 'offshore' insurance companies and 15 registered agents. Saint Lucia, in contrast to several of its neighbours, was not listed in 2000 by the Financial Action Task Force on Money Laundering (based in Paris, France) as 'non-co-operative' in the control of money-laundering, but is classed by the US state department as a country of concern, an intermediate category. In May 2010 Saint Lucia was removed from the Organization for Economic Co-operation and Development's 'grey' list of jurisdictions which did not meet international reporting standards, after signing a number of Tax Information Exchange Agreements with the United Kingdom, France and other partners.

The island is at some risk from hurricanes, as well as from less powerful tropical storms, which can cause serious damage to the banana industry. There is a volcanic centre at Soufrière in the south of the island, which has no recent history of threatening activity and has some importance as a tourist attraction. The 2008 budget speech proposed the development of geothermal power in order to reduce the country's dependency on oil.

Statistical Survey

Source (unless otherwise indicated): St Lucian Government Statistics Department, Block A, Government Bldgs, Waterfront, Castries; tel. 452-7670; fax 451-8254; e-mail statsdept@candw.lc; internet www.stats.gov.lc.

AREA AND POPULATION

Area: 616.3 sq km (238 sq miles).

Population: 135,685 (males 65,988, females 69,697) at census of 12 May 1991; 162,982 (males 79,877, females 83,105) at census of 22 May 2001 (including estimate for underenumeration). *2006:* 166,838 (mid-year estimate). *By District* (estimates at mid-2006): Castries 68,209; Anse La Raye 6,468; Canaries 1,920; Soufrière 8,037; Choiseul 6,376; Laborie 7,705; Vieux Fort 15,942; Micoud 16,794; Dennery 13,458; Gros Islet 21,929. *Mid-2010* (UN estimate): 174,000 (Source: UN, *World Population Prospects: The 2008 Revision*).

Density (mid-2010): 282.3 per sq km.

Population by Age and Sex ('000, UN estimates at mid-2010): *0–14:* 45 (males 23, females 22); *15–64:* 117 (males 57, females 60); *65 and over:* 12 (males 5, females 7); *Total* 174 (males 85, females 89) (Source: UN, *World Population Prospects: The 2008 Revision*).

Principal Town (population incl. suburbs, mid-2006): Castries (capital) 14,509. *Mid-2009* (estimates): Castries 15,395. Source: UN, *World Urbanization Prospects: The 2009 Revision*.

Births, Marriages and Deaths (2005, provisional): Registered live births 2,904 (birth rate 19.0 per 1,000); Registered marriages 655; Registered deaths 941 (death rate 6.0 per 1,000).

Life Expectancy (years at birth, WHO estimates): 75 (males 71; females 78) in 2008. Source: WHO, *World Health Statistics*.

Economically Active Population (persons aged 15 years and over, labour survey for October–December 2007): Agriculture, hunting and forestry 7,670; Fishing 600; Manufacturing 4,160; Electricity, gas and water 420; Construction 8,940; Wholesale and retail trade, repair of motor vehicles, motorcycles and personal and household goods 11,210; Hotels and restaurants 8,870; Transport, storage and communications 4,370; Financial intermediation 1,090; Real estate, renting and business activities 2,950; Public administration and compulsory social security 12,200; Education 890; Health and social work 280; Other community, social and personal service activities 2,080; Private households with employed persons 2,280; *Sub-total* 68,010; Activities not adequately defined 420; Not reported 4,350; *Total employed* 72,780; Unemployed 12,480; *Total labour force* 85,260 (males 45,510, females 39,750).

HEALTH AND WELFARE

Key Indicators

Total Fertility Rate (children per woman, 2008): 2.0.

Under-5 Mortality Rate (per 1,000 live births, 2008): 15.

Physicians (per 1,000 head, 1999): 5.2.

Hospital Beds (per 1,000 head, 2005): 3.

Health Expenditure (2007): US $ per head (PPP): 608.

Health Expenditure (2007): % of GDP: 6.3.

Health Expenditure (2007): public (% of total): 54.2.

Access to Water (% of persons, 2008): 98.

Access to Sanitation (% of persons, 2004): 89.

Total Carbon Dioxide Emissions ('000 metric tons, 2006): 381.1.

Carbon Dioxide Emissions Per Head (metric tons, 2006): 2.3.

Human Development Index (2007): ranking: 69.

Human Development Index (2007): value: 0.821.

For sources and definitions, see explanatory note on p. vi.

AGRICULTURE, ETC.

Principal Crops ('000 metric tons, 2008, FAO estimates): Cassava 1.0; Yams 0.5; Coconuts 14.0; Bananas 54.0; Plantains 0.8; Citrus fruits 2.2. *Aggregate Production* ('000 metric tons, may include official, semi-official or estimated data): Roots and tubers 7.1; Vegetables (incl. melons) 1.2; Fruits (excl. melons) 62.9.

Livestock ('000 head, 2008, FAO estimates): Cattle 12.6; Sheep 13.0; Goats 9.0; Pigs 15.5; Horses 1.1; Poultry 290.

Livestock Products ('000 metric tons, 2008, FAO estimates): Pig meat 1.1; Chicken meat 1.2; Cows' milk 1.1; Hen eggs 1.1.

Fishing (metric tons, live weight, 2008): Capture 1,713 (Wahoo 180; Skipjack tuna 168; Blackfin tuna 179; Yellowfin tuna 106; Common dolphinfish 341; Stromboid conchs 40); Aquaculture 0; Total catch 1,713. Figures exclude aquatic plants.

Source: FAO.

INDUSTRY

Production (2006, unless otherwise indicated): Electric energy 355.9 million kWh (2009); Copra 1,094 metric tons (2004); Coconut oil (unrefined) 1.2m. litres; Coconut oil (refined) 88,700 litres; Coconut meal 499,300 kg; Rum 191,900 proof gallons (Source: partly Eastern Caribbean Central Bank).

FINANCE

Currency and Exchange Rates: 100 cents = 1 Eastern Caribbean dollar (EC $). *Sterling, US Dollar and Euro Equivalents* (31 May 2010): £1 sterling = EC $3.937; US $1 = EC $2.700; €1 = EC $3.344; EC $100 = £25.40 = US $37.04 = €29.91. *Exchange Rate:* Fixed at US $1 = EC $2.70 since July 1976.

Budget (EC $ million, 2009): *Revenue:* Tax revenue 724.0 (Taxes on income and profits 226.3; Taxes on property 4.2; Taxes on domestic goods and services 107.4; Taxes on international trade and transactions 386.1); Other current revenue 29.7; Capital revenue 0.1; Total 753.9 (excl. grants 25.9). *Expenditure:* Current expenditure 644.8 (Personal emoluments 309.0; Goods and services 117.9; Interest payments 89.8; Transfers and subsidies 127.9); Capital expenditure and net lending 200.2; Total 845.0. Source: Eastern Caribbean Central Bank.

International Reserves (US $ million at 31 December 2009): IMF special drawing rights 24.19; Reserve position in IMF 0.01; Foreign exchange 150.60; Total 174.80. Source: IMF, *International Financial Statistics*.

Money Supply (EC $ million at 31 December 2009): Currency outside depository corporations 142.46; Transferable deposits 664.21; Other deposits 2,145.88; *Broad money* 2,952.55. Source: IMF, *International Financial Statistics*.

Cost of Living (Consumer Price Index; base: 2005 = 100): All items 105.5 in 2007; 114.1 in 2008; 115.2 in 2009. Source: IMF, *International Financial Statistics*.

Gross Domestic Product (EC $ million at constant 1990 prices): 1,723.61 in 2006; 1,742.85 in 2007; 1,783.23 in 2008.

Expenditure on the Gross Domestic Product (EC $ million at current prices, 2008): Government final consumption expenditure 508.87; Private final consumption expenditure 2,490.06; Gross capital formation 695.51; *Total domestic expenditure* 3,694.44; Exports of goods and services 1,355.09; *Less* Imports of goods and services 2,387.13; *GDP at market prices* 2,662.40. Source: Eastern Caribbean Central Bank.

Gross Domestic Product by Economic Activity (EC $ million in current prices, 2008): Agriculture, hunting, forestry and fishing 103.38; Mining and quarrying 7.22; Manufacturing 126.93; Electricity and water 110.09; Construction 142.01; Wholesale and retail trade 299.67; Restaurants and hotels 292.48; Transport 267.69; Communications 180.45; Banking and insurance 244.70; Real estate and housing 204.53; Government services 323.71; Other services 67.29; *Sub-total* 2,370.15; *Less* Imputed bank service charge 198.61; *Total in basic prices* 2,171.54; Taxes, less subsidies, on products 490.86; *GDP at market prices* 2,662.40. Source: Eastern Caribbean Central Bank.

Balance of Payments (EC $ million, 2009): Exports of goods 416.01; Imports of goods –1,253.15; *Trade balance* –837.14; Services (net) 408.32; *Balance on goods and services* 428.82; Other income received (net) –195.59; *Balance on goods, services and income* –624.41; Current transfers received (net) 35.29; *Current balance* –589.13; Capital account (net) 41.69; Direct investment (net) 449.93; Portfolio investment (net) –8.21; Other investment 130.15; Net errors and omissions 34.58; *Overall balance* 59.01. Source: Eastern Caribbean Central Bank.

EXTERNAL TRADE

Principal Commodities (US $ million, 2008): *Imports c.i.f.:* Food and live animals 108.6 (Meat and preparations thereof 25.0; Cereals and preparations thereof 22.1); Beverages and tobacco 27.7 (Beverages 23.5); Mineral fuels, lubricants, etc. 169.9 (Refined petroleum products 169.9); Chemicals 40.7; Basic manufactures 88.3 (Metal manufactures 17.4); Machinery and transport equipment 127.1

(Telecommunications equipment 8.5; Road vehicles 60.3); Miscellaneous manufactured articles 78.4; Total (incl. others) 655.7. *Exports f.o.b.* (incl. re-exports): Food and live animals 26.6 (Bananas 21.8); Beverages and tobacco 20.4 (Beer 13.4); Mineral fuels, lubricants, etc. 31.2 (Refined petroleum products 31.2); Basic manufactures 11.4 (Paper products 5.7); Machinery and transport equipment 27.3 (Telecommunications equipment 5.0; Electric machinery, etc. 3.1; Road vehicles 3.9); Miscellaneous manufactured articles 32.8; Total (incl. others) 164.0. Source: UN, *International Trade Statistics Yearbook*.

Principal Trading Partners (US $ million, 2008): *Imports c.i.f.:* Barbados 23.1; Canada 11.9; China, People's Repub. 7.1; Finland 0.4; France (incl. Monaco) 8.4; Germany 5.9; Japan 28.2; Netherlands 7.0; Panama 8.8; Saint Vincent and the Grenadines 5.4; Thailand 11.4; Trinidad and Tobago 156.0; United Kingdom 26.8; USA 279.1; Total (incl. others) 655.7. *Exports f.o.b.* (excl. re-exports): Antigua and Barbuda 3.7; Barbados 13.9; Dominica 4.6; France (incl. Monaco) 1.9; Grenada 3.0; Saint Vincent and the Grenadines 4.9; Trinidad and Tobago 38.1; United Kingdom 24.8; USA 55.8; Total (incl. others) 164.0. Source: UN, *International Trade Statistics Yearbook*.

TRANSPORT

Road Traffic (registered motor vehicles, 2002): Goods vehicles 9,554; Taxis and hired vehicles 1,880; Motorcycles 797; Private vehicles 21,421; Passenger vans 3,439; Total (incl. others) 38,572.

Shipping: *Arrivals* (2006): 1,557 vessels. *International Sea-borne Freight Traffic* (at Castries and Vieux Fort, metric tons, 2009): Goods loaded 88,683; Goods unloaded 491,696. Source: Saint Lucia Air and Sea Ports Authority.

Civil Aviation (traffic at George F. L. Charles and Hewanorra airports, 2009): Aircraft movements 32,287; Passenger departures 358,851; Passenger arrivals 349,421; Cargo loaded (metric tons) 1,341.7; Cargo unloaded (metric tons) 1,451.5. Source: Saint Lucia Air and Sea Ports Authority.

TOURISM

Visitor Arrivals: 931,685 (287,518 stop-over visitors, 7,841 excursionists, 26,163 yacht passengers, 610,163 cruise ship passengers) in 2007; 947,445 (295,761 stop-over visitors, 9,582 excursionists, 22,422 yacht passengers, 619,680 cruise ship passengers) in 2008; 1,014,761 (278,491 stop-over visitors, 4,967 excursionists, 31,997 yacht passengers, 699,306 cruise ship passengers) in 2009. *Stop-over Visitors by Country* (2009): USA 98,685; Canada 28,563; United Kingdom 71,853; Caribbean 60,179; Other 19,211.

Tourism Receipts (EC $ million): 814.5 in 2007; 839.7 in 2008; 799.7 in 2009.

Source: Eastern Caribbean Central Bank.

COMMUNICATIONS MEDIA

Radio Receivers ('000 in use, 1997): 111.

Television Receivers ('000 in use, 1999): 56.

Telephones ('000 main lines in use, 2009): 41.0.

Mobile Cellular Telephones ('000 subscribers, 2009): 176.0.

Personal Computers: 26,000 (160.1 per 1,000 persons) in 2004.

Internet Users ('000 subscribers, 2009): 142.9.

Broadband Subscribers (2009, estimate): 15,500.

Non-daily Newspapers (2004 unless otherwise indicated): Titles 5; Circulation 34,000 (1996).

Sources: UN, *Statistical Yearbook*; UNESCO, *Statistical Yearbook*; International Telecommunication Union; Eastern Caribbean Telecommunications Authority, *Annual Telecommunications Sector Review 2006*.

EDUCATION

Pre-primary (state institutions only, 2005/06): 148 schools; 480 teachers; 5,062 pupils.

Primary (state institutions only, 2007/08): 75 schools; 922 teachers; 20,164 pupils.

General Secondary (state institutions only, 2007/08): 23 schools; 924 teachers; 15,630 pupils.

Special Education (state institutions only, 2007/08): 4 schools; 47 teachers; 227 students.

Adult Education (state institutions only, 2006/07 unless otherwise indicated): 13 centres; 70 facilitators; 1,395 learners.

Tertiary (state institutions, including part-time, 2000/01): 127 teachers; 1,403 students.

Source: partly Caribbean Development Bank, *Social and Economic Indicators*.

Pupil-teacher Ratio (primary education, UNESCO estimate): 21.4 in 2007/08. Source: UNESCO Institute for Statistics.

Adult Literacy Rate (UNESCO estimate): 94.8% in 2004. Source: UN Development Programme, *Human Development Report*.

Directory

The Constitution

The Constitution came into force at the independence of Saint Lucia on 22 February 1979. Its main provisions are summarized below:

FUNDAMENTAL RIGHTS AND FREEDOMS

Regardless of race, place of origin, political opinion, colour, creed or sex but subject to respect for the rights and freedoms of others and for the public interest, every person in Saint Lucia is entitled to the rights of life, liberty, security of the person, equality before the law and the protection of the law. Freedom of conscience, of expression, of assembly and of association is guaranteed, and the inviolability of personal privacy, family life and property is maintained. Protection is afforded from slavery, forced labour, torture and inhuman treatment.

THE GOVERNOR-GENERAL

The British monarch, as Head of State, is represented in Saint Lucia by the Governor-General.

PARLIAMENT

Parliament consists of the British monarch, represented by the Governor-General, the 11-member Senate and the House of Assembly, composed of 17 elected Representatives. Senators are appointed by the Governor-General: six on the advice of the Prime Minister, three on the advice of the Leader of the Opposition and two acting on his own deliberate judgement. The life of Parliament is five years.

Each constituency returns one Representative to the House who is directly elected in accordance with the Constitution.

At a time when the office of Attorney-General is a public office, the Attorney-General is an ex officio member of the House.

Every citizen over the age of 21 is eligible to vote.

Parliament may alter any of the provisions of the Constitution.

THE EXECUTIVE

Executive authority is vested in the British monarch and exercisable by the Governor-General. The Governor-General appoints as Prime Minister that member of the House who, in the Governor-General's view, is best able to command the support of the majority of the members of the House, and other Ministers on the advice of the Prime Minister. The Governor-General may remove the Prime Minister from office if the House approves a resolution expressing no confidence in the Government, and if the Prime Minister does not resign within three days or advise the Governor-General to dissolve Parliament.

The Cabinet consists of the Prime Minister and other Ministers, and the Attorney-General as an ex officio member at a time when the office of Attorney-General is a public office.

The Leader of the Opposition is appointed by the Governor-General as that member of the House who, in the Governor-General's view, is best able to command the support of a majority of members of the house who do not support the Government.

CITIZENSHIP

All persons born in Saint Lucia before independence who immediately prior to independence were citizens of the United Kingdom and Colonies automatically become citizens of Saint Lucia. All persons born in Saint Lucia after independence automatically acquire Saint Lucian citizenship, as do those born outside Saint Lucia after independence to a parent possessing Saint Lucian citizenship. Provision is made for the acquisition of citizenship by those to whom it is not automatically granted.

The Government

HEAD OF STATE

Queen: HM Queen ELIZABETH II.

Governor-General: Dame PEARLETTE LOUISY (took office 17 September 1997).

CABINET
(July 2010)

The Government is formed by the United Workers' Party.

Prime Minister and Minister for Finance (International Financial Services), and for Economic Affairs, Economic Planning and National Development: STEPHENSON KING.

Minister for Social Transformation, Public Service, Human Resource Development, Youth and Sports: LENARD SPIDER MONTOUTE.

Minister for Health Wellness, Family Affairs, National Mobilisation, Human Services and Gender Relations: Dr KEITH MONDESIR.

Minister for Physical Development, Housing, Urban Renewal, Local Government and the Environment: RICHARD FREDERICK.

Minister for Education and Culture: ARSENE VIGIL JAMES.

Minister for Agriculture, Lands, Fisheries, and Forestry: EZECHIEL JOSEPH.

Minister for Home Affairs and National Security: GEORGE GUY MAYERS.

Minister for External Affairs, International Trade and Investment: RUFUS GEORGE BOUSQUET.

Minister for Communications, Works, Transport and Public Utilities: GUY EARDLEY JOSEPH.

Minister for Tourism and Civil Aviation: ALLEN M. CHASTANET.

Minister for Labour, Information and Broadcasting: EDMUND ESTEPHANE.

Minister of Commerce, Industry and Consumer Affairs: CHARLOTTE ELIZABETH THERESA TESSA MANGAL.

Attorney-General and Minister for Justice: Dr NICHOLAS FREDERICK.

Minister in the Ministry of Education and Culture: GASPARD PETER DAVID CHARLEMAGNE.

MINISTRIES

Office of the Prime Minister: Greaham Louisy Administrative Bldg, 5th Floor, Waterfront, Castries; tel. 468-2111; fax 453-7352; e-mail admin@pm.gov.lc; internet www.pm.gov.lc.

Attorney-General's Office and Ministry of Justice: Francis Compton Bldg, 2nd Floor, Waterfront, Castries; tel. 468-3200; fax 458-1131; e-mail atgen@gosl.gov.lc.

Ministry of Agriculture, Lands, Fisheries and Forestry: Sir Stanislaus James Bldg, 4th and 5th Floor, Waterfront, Castries; tel. 468-4104; fax 453-6314; e-mail adminag@candw.lc; internet www.maff.egov.lc.

Ministry of Commerce, Industry and Consumer Affairs: Ives Heraldine Rock Bldg, 4th Floor, Block B, Waterfront, Castries; tel. 468-4202; fax 453-7347; e-mail mitandt@candw.lc; internet www.commerce.gov.lc.

Ministry of Communications, Works, Transport and Public Utilities: Williams Bldg, Bridge St, Castries; tel. 468-4300; fax 453-2769; e-mail min_com@gosl.gov.lc.

Ministry of Economic Affairs, Economic Planning and National Development: American Drywall Bldg, POB 929, Vide Boutielle, Castries; tel. 468-2180; fax 451-9706; e-mail projects@candw.lc.

Ministry of Education and Culture: Francis Compton Bldg, 4th Floor, Waterfront, Castries; tel. 468-5203; fax 453-2299; e-mail mineduc@candw.lc; internet www.education.gov.lc.

Ministry of External Affairs, International Trade and Investment: Conway Business Centre, 7th Floor, Waterfront, Castries; tel. 468-4501; fax 452-7427; e-mail foreign@candw.lc.

Ministry of Finance (International Financial Services): Financial Centre, 2nd Floor, Bridge St, Castries; tel. 468-5500; fax 451-9231; e-mail minfin@gosl.gov.lc.

Ministry of Health Wellness, Family Affairs, National Mobilisation, Human Services and Gender Relations: Sir Stanislaus James Bldg, 2nd Floor, Castries; tel. 468–5300; fax 452-5655; e-mail health@candw.lc.

Ministry of Home Affairs and National Security: Sir Stanislaus James Bldg, 1st Floor, Waterfront, Castries; tel. 468-3600; fax 456-0228; e-mail pshans@gosl.gov.lc.

Ministry of Housing, Urban Renewal and Local Government: Cox Bldg, 2nd Floor, Jeremie St, POB 602, Castries; tel. 468-2600; fax 453-1530; e-mail minphul@gosl.gov.lc.

Ministry of International Trade and Investment: Heraldine Rock Bldg, 4th Floor, Waterfront, Castries; tel. 468-4202; fax 451-6986.

Ministry of Labour, Information and Broadcasting: Conway Business Centre, 5th Floor, Waterfront, Castries; tel. 468-2701; fax 453-7347; e-mail agencyadmin@gosl.gov.lc.

Ministry of Physical Development and the Environment: Greaham Lousiy Administrative Bldg, 3rd Floor, Waterfront, Castries; tel. 468-4419; fax 452-2506; internet www.planning.gov.lc.

Ministry of Social Transformation, Public Service, Human Resource Development, Youth and Sports: Greaham Louisy Administrative Bldg, 2nd and 4th Floors, Waterfront, Castries; tel. 468-5101; fax 453-7921; e-mail most@gosl.gov.lc; e-mail minpet@candw.lc (Public Service).

Ministry of Tourism and Civil Aviation: Heraldine Rock Bldg, 4th Floor, Waterfront, Castries; tel. 453-6644; fax 451-7414; e-mail psmot@gosl.gov.lc.

Legislature

PARLIAMENT

Senate

The Senate has nine nominated members and two independent members.

President: LEONNE THEODORE-JOHN.

House of Assembly

Speaker: Dr HILDA ROSE MARIE HUSBANDS-MATHURIN.

Clerk: KURT THOMAS.

Election, 11 December 2006

Party	Seats
United Workers' Party	11
Saint Lucia Labour Party	6
Total	17

Election Commission

Election Commission: St Lucia Electoral Dept, 23 High St, POB 1074, Castries; tel. 452-3725; fax 451-6513; e-mail info@electoral.gov.lc; internet www.electoral.gov.lc; Election Commr CARSON RAGGIE.

Political Organizations

Organization for National Empowerment (ONE): POB 1496, Castries; tel. 484-9424; fax 452-9574; e-mail aziea99@yahoo.com; f. 2004; Leader PETER ALEXANDER; Chair. ROSEMUND CLERY.

Saint Lucia Labour Party (SLP): Tom Walcott Bldg, 2nd Floor, Jeremie St, POB 427, Castries; tel. 451-8446; fax 451-9389; e-mail slp@candw.lc; f. 1946; socialist party; Leader Dr KENNY DAVIS ANTHONY; Chair. JULIAN HUNTE; Gen. Sec. LEO CLARKE.

United Workers' Party (UWP): 9 Coral St, POB 1550, Castries; tel. 451-9103; fax 451-9207; e-mail unitworkers@netscape.net; f. 1964; right-wing; Chair. and Leader STEPHENSON KING; Gen. Sec. GERTRUDE GEORGE.

Diplomatic Representation

EMBASSIES AND HIGH COMMISSION IN SAINT LUCIA

Brazil: 1 Bella Rosa Rd, 3rd Floor, POB 6136, Gros Islet; tel. 450-1671; fax 450-4733; e-mail brasemb.castries@itamaraty.gov.br; Ambassador JOÃO BATISTA CRUZ.

China (Taiwan): Reduit Beach Ave, Rodney Bay; tel. 452-8105; fax 452-0441; e-mail luciaemb@gmail.com; internet www.taiwanembassy.org/lc; Ambassador TOM CHOU.

Cuba: Rodney Heights, Gros Islet, POB 2150, Castries; tel. 458-4665; fax 458-4666; e-mail embacubasantalucia@candw.lc; internet embacu.cubaminrex.cu/santaluciaing; Ambassador HUGO RUIZ CABRERA.

France: French Embassy to the OECS, GPO Private Box 937, Vigie, Castries; tel. 455-6060; fax 455-6056; e-mail frenchembassy@candw.lc; internet www.ambafrance-lc.org; Ambassador MICHÈL PROM.

Mexico: Nelson Mandela Dr., POB 6096, Vigie, Castries; tel. 453-1250; fax 451-4252; e-mail mexicanembassy@candw.lc; internet www.sre.gob.mx/santalucia; Ambassador GERARDO LOZANO ARREDONDO.

United Kingdom: Francis Compton Bldg, Waterfront, POB 227, Castries; tel. 452-2484; fax 453-1543; e-mail postmaster.castries@fco.gov.uk; High Commissioner PAUL BRUMMELL.

Venezuela: Casa Santa Lucía, POB 494, Castries; tel. 452-4033; fax 453-6747; e-mail vembassy@candw.lc; Ambassador EDUARDO ALFONZO BARRANCO HERNÁNDEZ.

Judicial System

SUPREME COURT

Eastern Caribbean Supreme Court: Heraldine Rock Bldg, Block B, Waterfront, POB 1093, Castries; tel. 452-7998; fax 452-5475; e-mail appeal@candw.lc; the West Indies Associated States Supreme Court was established in 1967 and was known as the Supreme Court of Grenada and the West Indies Associated States from 1974 until 1979, when it became the Eastern Caribbean Supreme Court. Its jurisdiction extends to Anguilla, Antigua and Barbuda, the British Virgin Islands, Dominica, Grenada (which rejoined in 1991), Montserrat, Saint Christopher and Nevis, Saint Lucia and Saint Vincent and the Grenadines. It is composed of the High Court of Justice and the Court of Appeal. The High Court is composed of the Chief Justice, who is head of the judiciary, and 16 High Court Judges, three of whom are resident in Saint Lucia. The Court of Appeal is itinerant and presided over by the Chief Justice and three other Justices of Appeal. Additionally, there are two Masters whose principal responsibilities extend to procedural and interlocutory matters. Jurisdiction of the High Court includes fundamental rights and freedoms, membership of the parliaments, and matters concerning the interpretation of constitutions. The Caribbean Court of Justice, inaugurated in April 2005, was intended to replace the Judicial Committee of the Privy Council, based in the United Kingdom, as Saint Lucia's final court of appeal, although by 2010 only Barbados and Guyana were officially under the jurisdiction of the new regional court.

Chief Justice: HUGH ANTHONY RAWLINS.

Justices of Appeal: OLA MAE EDWARDS, JANICE MESADIS GEORGE-CREQUE, DAVIDSON BAPTISTE.

Managing Judge: ESBON ANTHONY ROSS.

Chief Registrar: KIMBERLY CENAC PHULGENCE.

Puisne Judges: KENNETH ANDREW CHARLES BENJAMIN, ROSALYN E. WILKINSON, EPHRAIM FRANCIS GEORGES (acting).

Registrar: CYBELLE CENAC-MARAGH.

Religion

CHRISTIANITY

The Roman Catholic Church

Saint Lucia forms a single archdiocese. The Archbishop participates in the Antilles Episcopal Conference (currently based in Port of Spain, Trinidad and Tobago). According to the latest census (2001), some 68% of the population are Roman Catholics

Archbishop of Castries: ROBERT RIVAS, Archbishop's House, Nelson Mandela Dr., POB 267, Castries; tel. 452-2416; fax 452-3697; e-mail secretaries@archdioceseofcastries.org; internet www.archdioceseofcastries.org.

The Anglican Communion

Anglicans in Saint Lucia are adherents of the Church in the Province of the West Indies, comprising eight dioceses. The Archbishop of the West Indies is the Bishop of Nassau and the Bahamas. Saint Lucia forms part of the diocese of the Windward Islands (the Bishop is resident in Kingstown, Saint Vincent). Some 2% of the population are Anglicans, according to the 2001 census.

Other Christian Churches

According to the 2001 census, 9% of the population are Seventh-day Adventists, 6% are Pentecostalists, 2% are Evangelical Christians and 2% are Baptists.

Seventh-day Adventist Church: St Louis St, POB 117, Castries; tel. 452-4408; e-mail khansamuel@hotmail.com; internet www.tagnet.org/cacoasda; Pastor THEODORE JARIA.

Trinity Evangelical Lutheran Church: Gablewoods Mall, POB 858, Castries; tel. 458-4638; e-mail spiegelbergs@candw.lc; Pastor Rev. TOM SPIEGELBERG.

The Press

The Catholic Chronicle: POB 778, Castries; f. 1957; monthly; Editor Rev. PATRICK A. B. ANTHONY; circ. 3,000.

The Crusader: 19 St Louis St, Castries; tel. 452-2203; fax 452-1986; f. 1934; weekly (Sat.); circ. 4,000.

The Mirror: Bisee Industrial Estate, POB 1782, Castries; tel. 451-6181; fax 451-6197; e-mail webmaster@stluciamirror.com; internet www.stluciamirroronline.com; f. 1994; weekly (Fri.); Man. Editor GUY ELLIS; circ. 3,900.

One Caribbean: POB 852, Castries; e-mail dabread@candw.lc; weekly; Editor D. SINCLAIR DABREO.

She Caribbean: Rodney Bay Industrial Estate, Massade, Gros Islet, POB 1146, Castries; tel. 450-7827; fax 450-8694; e-mail shanna.h@stluciastar.com; internet www.shecaribbean.com; quarterly; Publr and Editor-in-Chief MAE WAYNE.

The Star: Rodney Bay Industrial Estate, Gros Islet, POB 1146, Castries; tel. 450-7827; fax 450-8694; e-mail shanna.h@stluciastar.com; internet www.stluciastar.com; f. 1987; 3 a week (Mon., Wed. and weekend edns); circ. 8,000; Propr RICK WAYNE; Man. Editor NICOLE MCDONALD.

Tropical Traveller: Rodney Bay Industrial Estate, Massade, Gros Islet, POB 1146, Castries; tel. 450-7827; fax 450-8694; e-mail infostar@stluciastar.com; internet www.tropicaltraveller.com; f. 1989; monthly; Editorial Dir MAE WAYNE; Man. Editor NANCY ATKINSON.

Visions of St Lucia Island Guide: 7 Maurice Mason Ave, Sans Soucis, POB 947, Castries; tel. 453-0427; fax 452-1522; e-mail visions@candw.lc; internet www.visionsofstlucia.com; f. 1989; official tourist guide; publ. by Island Visions Ltd; annual; Chair. and Man. Dir ANTHONY NEIL AUSTIN; circ. 120,000.

The Weekend Voice: Odessa Bldg, Darling Rd, POB 104, Castries; tel. 452-2590; fax 453-1453; weekly (Sat.); circ. 8,000.

PRESS ORGANIZATION

Eastern Caribbean Press Council (ECPC): Castries; f. 2003; independent, self-regulating body designed to foster and maintain standards in regional journalism, formed by 14 newspapers in the Eastern Caribbean and Barbados; Chair. Lady MARIE SIMMONS.

NEWS AGENCY

Caribbean Media Corporation: Bisee Rd, Castries; tel. 453-7162; e-mail admin@cmccaribbean.com; internet www.cananews.com; f. 2000 by merger of Caribbean News Agency and Caribbean Broadcasting Union.

Publishers

Caribbean Publishing Co Ltd: American Drywall Bldg, Vide Bouteille Highway, POB 104, Castries; tel. 452-3188; fax 452-3181; e-mail publish@candw.lc; f. 1978; publr of telephone directories and magazines.

Crusader Publishing Co Ltd: 19 St Louis St, Castries; tel. 452-2203; fax 452-1986.

Island Visions Ltd: 7 Maurice Mason Ave, Sans Soucis, POB 947, Castries; tel. 453-0472; fax 452-1522; e-mail visions@candw.lc; internet www.visionsofstlucia.com; f. 1989; Chair. and Man. Dir ANTHONY NEIL AUSTIN.

Mirror Publishing Co Ltd: Bisee Industrial Estate, POB 1782, Castries; tel. 451-6181; fax 451-6503; e-mail mirror@candw.lc; f. 1994; Man. Editor GUY ELLIS.

Star Publishing Co: Rodney Bay Industrial Estate, Massade, Gros Islet, POB 1146, Castries; tel. 450-7827; fax 450-8694; e-mail infostar@stluciastar.com; internet www.stluciastar.com; Propr RICK WAYNE.

Voice Publishing Co Ltd: Odessa Bldg, Darling Rd, POB 104, Castries; tel. 452-2590; fax 453-1453.

Broadcasting and Communications

TELECOMMUNICATIONS

Regulatory Authorities

Eastern Caribbean Telecommunications Authority (ECTEL): Vide Bouteille, POB 1886, Castries; tel. 458-1701; fax 458-1698; e-mail ectel@ectel.int; internet www.ectel.int; f. 2000 to regulate telecommunications in Saint Lucia, Dominica, Grenada, Saint Christopher and Nevis and Saint Vincent and the Grenadines; Chair. ISAAC SOLOMON; Man. Dir EMBERT CHARLES.

National Telecommunications Regulatory Commission (NTRC): S & S Bldg, Suite 1, 35 Chisel St, POB GM 690, Castries; tel. 458-2035; fax 453-2558; e-mail slufeedback@ectel.int; internet www.ntrc.org.lc; f. 2000; regulates the sector in conjunction with ECTEL; Chair. ELMA GENE ISAAC.

Major Service Providers

Digicel St Lucia: Rodney Bay, Gros Islet, POB GM 791, Castries; tel. 456-3400; fax 450-3872; e-mail customercare.stlucia@digicelgroup.com; internet www.digicelstlucia.com; f. 2003; owned by an Irish consortium; acquired operations of Cingular Wireless in Saint Lucia in 2006; Chair. DENIS O'BRIEN; Eastern Caribbean CEO KEVIN WHITE.

LIME: Bridge St, POB 111, Castries; tel. 453-9720; fax 453-9700; e-mail talk2us@candw.lc; internet www.time4lime.com; fmrly Cable & Wireless St Lucia; name changed as above 2008; provides fixed-line, mobile, internet and cable television services; CEO RICHARD DODD.

Saint Lucia Boatphone Ltd: Gros Islet, POB 2136, Castries; tel. 452-0361; fax 452-0394; e-mail boatphone@candw.lc; wholly owned subsidiary of Cable & Wireless Caribbean Cellular.

BROADCASTING

Radio

Radio Caribbean International: 11 Mongiraud St, POB 121, Castries; tel. 452-2636; fax 452-2637; e-mail rci@candw.lc; internet www.rcistlucia.com; operates Radio Caraïbes; English and Creole services; broadcasts 24 hrs; Station Mans PETER EPHRAIM, PET GIBSON.

Saint Lucia Broadcasting Corporation: Morne Fortune, POB 660, Castries; tel. 452-2337; fax 453-1568; govt-owned; Man. KEITH WEEKES.

Radio 100-Helen FM: Morne Fortune, POB 621, Castries; tel. 451-7260; fax 453-1737; e-mail radio@htsstlucia.com; internet www.htsstlucia.com; Gen. Man. STEPHENSON ANIUS.

Radio Saint Lucia Co Ltd (RSL): Morne Fortune, POB 660, Castries; tel. 452-2337; fax 453-1568; e-mail info@rslonline.com; internet www.rslonline.com; f. 1972; English and Creole services; Chair. LINDELL GUSTAVE; Man. Dir MARY POLIUS.

Television

Cablevision: George Gordon Bldg, Bridge St, POB 111, Castries; tel. 453-9311; fax 453-9740.

Catholic Broadcasting TV Network (CBTN): Micoud St, Castries; tel. 452-7050.

Daher Broadcasting Service Ltd (DBS): Vigie, POB 1623, Castries; tel. 453-2705; fax 452-3544; e-mail dbstv@candw.lc; internet dbstelevision.com; Man. Dir LINDA DAHER.

Helen Television System (HTS): National Television Service of St Lucia, POB 621, The Morne, Castries; tel. 452-2693; fax 454-1737; e-mail hts@candw.lc; internet www.htsstlucia.com; f. 1967; commercial station; Gen. Man. STEPHENSON ANIUS.

National Television Network (NTN): Castries; f. 2001; operated by the Government Information Service; provides information on the operations of the public sector.

Finance

(cap. = capital; dep. = deposits; m. = million; brs = branches)

BANKING

The Eastern Caribbean Central Bank, based in Saint Christopher, is the central issuing and monetary authority for Saint Lucia.

Eastern Caribbean Central Bank—Saint Lucia Office: Colony House, Unit 5, John Compton Hwy, POB 295, Castries; tel. 452-7449; fax 453-6022; e-mail eccbslu@candw.lc; internet www.eccb-centralbank.org; Country Dir ISAAC ANTHONY; Rep. GREGOR FRANKLIN.

Local Banks

Bank of Saint Lucia Ltd: Financial Centre, 5th Floor, 1 Bridge St, POB 1860, Castries; tel. 456-6000; fax 456-6702; e-mail info@bankofsaintlucia.com; internet www.bankofsaintlucia.com; f. 2001 by merger of National Commercial Bank of St Lucia Ltd and Saint Lucia Devt Bank; total assets EC $1,600m. (Dec. 2007); 35% state-owned; parent co is East Caribbean Financial Holding Co Ltd; Chair. VICTOR A. EUDOXIE; Gen. Man. RYAN DEVEAUX; 7 brs.

1st National Bank Saint Lucia Ltd: 21 Bridge St, POB 168, Castries; tel. 455-7000; fax 453-1630; e-mail manager@1stnationalbankslu.com; internet www.1stnationalbankonline.com; inc. 1937 as Saint Lucia Co-operative Bank Ltd; name changed as above Jan. 2005; commercial bank; share cap. EC $5m., asset base EC $221.4m. (Dec. 2004); Chair. and Pres. CHARMAINE GARDNER; Man. Dir G. CARLTON GLASGOW; 4 brs.

FirstCaribbean International Bank (Barbados) Ltd: Bridge St, POB 335, Castries; tel. 456-2422; fax 452-3735; internet www.firstcaribbeanbank.com; f. 2002 following merger of Caribbean operations of Barclays Bank PLC and CIBC; CIBC acquired Barclays' 43.7% stake in 2006; Exec. Chair. MICHAEL MANSOOR; CEO JOHN D. ORR.

RBTT Bank Caribbean Ltd: 22 Micoud St, POB 1531, Castries; tel. 452-2265; fax 452-1668; e-mail rbttslu.isd@candw.lc; internet www.rbtt.com; f. 1985 as Caribbean Banking Corpn Ltd, name changed as above in March 2002; owned by R and M Holdings Ltd; Chair. PETER JULY; Country Man. EARL P. CRICHTON; 4 brs.

STOCK EXCHANGE

Eastern Caribbean Securities Exchange: based in Basseterre, Saint Christopher and Nevis; e-mail info@ecseonline.com; internet www.ecseonline.com; f. 2001; regional securities market designed to facilitate the buying and selling of financial products for the eight member territories—Anguilla, Antigua and Barbuda, Dominica, Grenada, Montserrat, Saint Christopher and Nevis, Saint Lucia and Saint Vincent and the Grenadines; Chair. Sir K. DWIGHT VENNER; Gen. Man. and CEO TREVOR E. BLAKE.

INSURANCE

Local companies include the following:

Caribbean General Insurance Ltd: Laborie St, POB 290, Castries; tel. 452-2410; fax 452-3649.

Eastern Caribbean Insurance Ltd: Laborie St, POB 290, Castries; tel. 452-2410; fax 452-3393; e-mail cgi.ltd@candw.lc.

Saint Lucia Insurances Ltd: 48 Micoud St, POB 1084, Castries; tel. 452-3240; fax 452-2240; e-mail sl.ins@candw.lc; principal agents of Alliance Insurance Co Ltd.

Saint Lucia Motor and General Insurance Co Ltd: 38 Micoud St, POB 767, Castries; tel. 452-3323; fax 452-6072.

Trade and Industry

DEVELOPMENT ORGANIZATION

National Development Corporation (NDC): 1st Floor, Heraldine Rock Bldg, The Waterfront, POB 495, Castries; tel. 452-3614; fax 452-1841; e-mail info@investstlucia.com; internet www.investstlucia.com; f. 1971 to stimulate, facilitate and promote investment opportunities for foreign and local investors and to promote the economic devt of Saint Lucia; owns and manages seven industrial estates; br. in Miami, FL, USA; Exec. Chair. VERN GILL; CEO WAYNE VITALIS.

CHAMBER OF COMMERCE

Saint Lucia Chamber of Commerce, Industry and Agriculture: American Drywall Bldg, 2nd Floor, Vide Bouteille, POB 482, Castries; tel. 452-3165; fax 453-6907; e-mail info@stluciachamber.org; internet www.stluciachamber.org; f. 1884; Pres. CHESTER HINKSON; Exec. Dir BRIAN LOUISY; 150 mems.

INDUSTRIAL AND TRADE ASSOCIATIONS

Saint Lucia Banana Corporation (SLBC): 7 Manoel St, POB 197, Castries; tel. 452-2251; f. 1998 following privatization of Saint Lucia Banana Growers' Asscn (f. 1967); Chair. EUSTACE MONROSE; Sec. DURAND DORSEIDE.

Saint Lucia Industrial and Small Business Association: Cnr Chaussee and Victoria Sts, POB 585, Castries; tel. 452-7616; fax 453-1023; e-mail slisbaslu@gmail.com; internet www.slisbastlucia.com; Pres. FLAVIA CHERRY.

Small Enterprise Development Unit (SEDU): Ministry of Commerce, Industry and Consumer Affairs, Heraldine Rock Bldg, 4th

Floor, Waterfront, Castries; tel. 468-4220; fax 453-2891; f. 2000; Dir PETER LORDE.

EMPLOYERS' ASSOCIATIONS

Saint Lucia Agriculturists' Association Ltd: Mongiraud St, POB 153, Castries; tel. 452-2494; fax 453-2693; distributor and supplier of agricultural, industrial and organic products; exporter of cocoa; Chair. CUTHBERT PHILLIPS; CEO KERDE M. SEVERIN.

Saint Lucia Coconut Growers' Association Ltd: Palmiste Rd, POB 269, Castries; tel. 459-7227; fax 459-7216; e-mail slcga1@candw.lc; f. 1939; Gen. Man. GERALD MORRIS.

Saint Lucia Employers' Federation: c/o The Morgan Bldg, L'Anse Rd, POB 160, Castries; tel. 452-2190; fax 452-7335; e-mail slefslu@candw.lc; Pres. CALLISTUS VERN GILL.

Saint Lucia Fish Marketing Corpn: POB 891, Castries; tel. 452-1341; fax 451-7073; e-mail slfmc@candw.lc.

Saint Lucia Marketing Board (SLMB): Conway, POB 441, Castries; tel. 452-3214; fax 453-1424; e-mail slmb@candw.lc; Gen. Man. THERESA DESIR (acting).

Windward Islands Banana Development and Exporting Co (Wibdeco): Manoel St, POB 115, Castries; tel. 452-2411; fax 453-1638; e-mail wibdeco@candw.lc; internet www.wibdeco.com; f. 1994 in succession to the Windward Islands Banana Growers' Asscn (WINBAN); regional org. dealing with banana devt and marketing; jtly owned by the Windward govts and island banana asscns; CEO BERNARD CORNIBERT.

UTILITIES

Electricity

Caribbean Electric Utility Services Corpn (CARILEC): Desir Ave, Sans Soucis, POB CP 5907, Castries; tel. 452-0140; fax 452-0142; e-mail info@carilec.org; internet www.carilec.com; f. 1989; Exec. Dir. NIGEL HOSEIN.

St Lucia Electricity Services Ltd (LUCELEC): Sans Soucis, POB 230, Castries; tel. 457-4400; fax 457-4409; e-mail lucelec@candw.lc; internet www.lucelec.com; f. 1964; Canadian energy co Emera acquired a 19% share in LUCELEC in Jan. 2007; Chair. MARIUS ST ROSE; Man. Dir TREVOR LOUISY.

Water

Water and Sewerage Company (WASCO): L'Anse Rd, POB 1481, Castries; tel. 452-5344; fax 452-6844; e-mail wasco@candw.lc; f. 1999 as the Water and Sewerage Authority (WASA); planned privatization under review; Chair. GORDON CHARLES; Man. Dir JOHN C. JOSEPH.

TRADE UNIONS

National Workers' Union (NWU): Bour Bon St, POB 713, Castries; tel. 452-3664; fax 453-2896; e-mail natwork3@hotmail.com; f. 1973; represents daily-paid workers; affiliated to World Federation of Trade Unions; Pres.-Gen. TYRONE MAYNARD; Sec.-Gen. GEORGE GODDARD, Jr; 3,200 mems (2005).

Saint Lucia Civil Service Association: Sans Soucis, POB 244, Castries; tel. 452-3903; fax 453-6061; e-mail csa@candw.lc; internet www.csastlucia.org; f. 1951; Pres. MARY ISAAC; Gen. Sec. SIMONIA ALTINOR; 2,381 mems.

Saint Lucia Medical and Dental Association: POB 691, Castries; tel. 451-8441; fax 458-1147; e-mail slmdaoffice@gmail.com; internet www.slmda.org; f. 1969; Pres. Dr TANYA DESTANG-BEAUBRUN; Gen. Sec. Dr KIMBERLY JOHNNY.

Saint Lucia Nurses' Association: Victoria Hospital, Nurses' Home, 2nd Floor, POB 819, Castries; tel. 452-1403; fax 456-0121; e-mail slna1970@gmail.com; internet www.stlucianursesassociation.org; f. 1947; Pres. ALICIA BAPTISTE; Gen. Sec. LYDIA LEONCE.

Saint Lucia Seamen, Waterfront and General Workers' Trade Union: L'Anse Rd, POB 166, Castries; tel. 452-1669; fax 452-5452; e-mail seamen@candw.lc; f. 1945; affiliated to Int. Trade Union Confed., Int. Transport Fed. and Caribbean Congress of Labour; Pres. ESTHER ST MARIE (acting); Sec. CELICA ADOLPH; 1,000 mems.

Saint Lucia Teachers' Union: La Clery, POB 821, Castries; tel. 452-4469; fax 453-6668; e-mail sltu@candw.lc; f. 1934; Pres. JULIAN MONROSE; Gen. Sec. WAYNE CUMBERBATCH.

Saint Lucia Trade Union Federation: c/o Saint Lucia Teachers' Union, La Clery, POB 821, Castries; tel. 452-4469; fax 453-6668; e-mail cumbatch42@gmail.com; f. 2005; comprises nine trade unions of Saint Lucia, including the Saint Lucia Civil Service Asscn, Saint Lucia Teachers' Union, Saint Lucia Medical and Dental Asscn, Saint Lucia Nurses' Asscn, Saint Lucia Seamen and Waterfront General Workers' Union, National Farmers' Asscn, Police Welfare Asscn, Saint Lucia Fire Service Asscn and Vieux Fort General and Dock Workers' Union; Pres. JULIAN MONROSE; Gen. Sec. WAYNE CUMBERBATCH.

Saint Lucia Workers' Union: Reclamation Grounds, Conway, Castries; tel. 452-2620; f. 1939; affiliated to International Trade Union Confederation; Pres. GEORGE LOUIS; Sec. TITUS FRANCIS; 1,000 mems.

Vieux Fort General and Dock Workers' Union: New Dock Rd, POB 224, Vieux Fort; tel. 454-5128; e-mail dockworkersunion@hotmail.com; f. 1954; Pres. ATHANATIUS DOLOR; Gen. Sec. CLAUDIA AUGUSTE (acting); 846 mems (1996).

Transport

RAILWAYS

There are no railways in Saint Lucia.

ROADS

In 2000 there was an estimated total road network of 910 km, of which 150 km were main roads and 127 km were secondary roads. In that year only 5.2% of roads were paved. The main highway passes through every town and village on the island. The construction of a coastal highway, to link Castries with Cul de Sac Bay, was completed in February 2000. Improvements to the road infrastructure outlined in the 2008/09 budget address included the construction of 20.2 km of tunnels under the Barre de l'Isle and the rehabilitation of 28.1 km of community and agricultural feeder roads, at a cost of EC $12.9m. The total allocation for the Ministry of Communications, Works, Transport and Public Utilities was EC $72.9m. in that financial year. Internal transport is handled by private concerns and controlled by the Government.

SHIPPING

The ports at Castries and Vieux Fort have been fully mechanized. Castries has six berths with a total length of 2,470 ft (753 m). The two dolphin berths at the Pointe Seraphine cruise ship terminal have been upgraded to a solid berth of 1,000 ft (305 m) and one of 850 ft (259 m). The port of Soufrière has a deep-water anchorage, but no alongside berth for ocean-going vessels. There is a petroleum transshipment terminal at Cul de Sac Bay. In 2009 699,306 cruise ship passengers called at Saint Lucia. Regular services are provided by a number of shipping lines, including ferry services to neighbouring islands. In January 2007 Island Global Yachting Facilities Ltd (New York, USA) acquired the marina at Rodney Bay, and plans for substantial upgrade work to enhance facilities and operations were announced. There were plans to develop and expand the waterfront area at Castries in order for it to become a dedicated cruise ship port; the port at Vieux Fort was also to be expanded in order to handle all commercial cargo.

Saint Lucia Air and Sea Ports Authority (SLASPA): Manoel St, POB 651, Castries; tel. 452-2893; fax 452-2062; e-mail info@slaspa.com; internet www.slaspa.com; f. 1983; Chair. ISAAC ANTHONY; Gen. Man. SEAN MATTHEW; Dir of Airports PETER F. JEAN.

Saint Lucia Marine Terminals Ltd: POB VF 355, Vieux Fort; tel. 454-8742; fax 454-8745; e-mail slumarterm@candw.lc; f. 1995; private port management co.

CIVIL AVIATION

There are two airports in use: Hewanorra International (formerly Beane Field near Vieux Fort), 64 km (40 miles) from Castries, which is equipped to handle large jet aircraft and underwent expansion works in 2006 in preparation for the anticipated increase in traffic ahead of the Cricket World Cup in 2007; and George F. L. Charles Airport, which is at Vigie, in Castries, and which is capable of handling medium-range jets. Saint Lucia is served by scheduled flights to the USA, Canada, Europe and most destinations in the Caribbean. The country is a shareholder in the regional airline LIAT (see chapter on Antigua and Barbuda), which in late 2006 announced that it was to merge with its troubled rival Caribbean Star Airlines (headquartered in Antigua and Barbuda); the two airlines began operating a joint flight schedule from February 2007 under LIAT's airline designation code. The planned merger was subsequently abandoned in favour of negotiations towards LIAT's full acquisition of Caribbean Star, which were completed in October 2007.

Saint Lucia Air and Sea Ports Authority: see Shipping.

Air Antilles: Laborie St, POB 1065, Castries; f. 1985; designated as national carrier of Grenada in 1987; flights to destinations in the Caribbean, the United Kingdom and North America; charter co.

Eagle Air Services Ltd: George F. L. Charles Airport, POB 838, Castries; tel. and fax 452-9683; e-mail eagleairslu@candw.lc; charter flights; Man. Dir Capt. EWART F. HINKSON.

Tourism

Saint Lucia possesses spectacular mountain scenery, a tropical climate and sandy beaches. Historical sites, rich birdlife and the sulphur baths at Soufrière are other attractions. Visitor arrivals totalled 1,014,761 in 2009. Tourism receipts in that year were EC $799.7m. The USA is the principal market (35.4% of total stop-over visitors in 2009), followed by the United Kingdom (with 25.8%).

Saint Lucia Hotel and Tourism Association (SLHTA): John Compton Hwy, POB 545, Castries; tel. 452-5978; fax 452-7967; e-mail slhta@candw.lc; internet www.slhta.org; f. 1963; Pres. Anthony Bowen; Exec. Gen. Man. Silvanius Fontenard.

Saint Lucia Tourist Board: Sureline Bldg, Top Floor, Vide Bouteille, POB 221, Castries; tel. 452-4094; fax 453-1121; e-mail slutour@candw.lc; internet www.stlucia.org; f. 1981; 2 brs overseas; Chair. Laurie Barnad; Dir Louis Lewis.

Defence

The Royal Saint Lucia Police Force, which numbers about 300 men, includes a Special Service Unit for purposes of defence. This Unit was increased to 100 men in 2006, with a further 60 cadets in training. Saint Lucia participates in the US-sponsored Regional Security System, comprising police, coastguards and army units, which was established by independent East Caribbean states in 1982. There are also two patrol vessels for coastguard duties. Some EC $69.0m. (equivalent to 9.9%) of total planned recurrent expenditure was allocated to the Ministry of Home Affairs and National Security in the 2007/08 budget.

Education

Education is compulsory for 10 years between five and 15 years of age. Primary education begins at the age of five and lasts for seven years. Secondary education, beginning at 12 years of age, lasts for five years, comprising a first cycle of three years and a second cycle of two years. Enrolment at primary schools in 2007/08 included 91% of children in the relevant age-group, while comparable enrolment in secondary level education, according to UNESCO estimates, included 80% of pupils in the relevant age category. Free education is provided in more than 90 government-assisted schools. Facilities for industrial, technical and teacher-training are available at the Sir Arthur Lewis Community College at Morne Fortune, which also houses an extra-mural branch of the University of the West Indies. In May 2002 it was announced that an additional US $19m. would be invested in the education system during September 2002–September 2006. The project, to build two new secondary schools and renovate existing ones, was to be partially funded by the World Bank and UNESCO. Some EC $127.2m. of government recurrent expenditure was allocated to the Ministry of Education and Culture in the 2007/08 budget (equivalent to 18.3% of total planned recurrent expenditure).

SAINT-MARTIN

The French Overseas Collectivity (Collectivité d'outre-mer) of Saint-Martin forms the northern half of the island of Saint Martin (the remainder, Sint Maarten, being part of the Netherlands Antilles). The small volcanic island lies among the Leeward group of the Lesser Antilles in the Caribbean Sea, 8 km south of the British Overseas Territory of Anguilla and 265 km north-west of the French Overseas Department of Guadeloupe, of which Saint-Martin was formerly a dependency. The 10.2-km border between the French and the Dutch territories of the island is the only land frontier in the Lesser Antilles. Saint-Martin occupies about 60% of the island (51 sq km or 20 sq miles). The climate is tropical and moderated by the sea. Saint-Martin normally receives about 1,000 mm (43 ins) of rain annually. Saint-Martin has a population of about 30,000. French is the official language, but a Creole patois is widely spoken, as well as English, Dutch and Spanish. The majority of the population professes Christianity and belongs to the Roman Catholic Church. The principal town is Marigot, in the south-west of the territory, on the north coast of the island, between the sea and the Simpson Bay Lagoon.

On 7 December 2003 the Guadeloupean dependency of Saint-Martin participated in a Department-wide referendum on Guadeloupe's future constitutional relationship with France. Although the proposal to streamline administrative and political processes was defeated, a majority of those participating in Saint-Martin, 76.2%, elected to secede from Guadeloupe to form a separate Overseas Collectivity. The reorganization was subsequently approved by the French Sénat on 6 February 2007 and by the Assemblée nationale the following day. Two weeks later, on 21 February, the territory of Saint-Martin was formally designated an Overseas Collectivity.

Legislative elections to form a 23-member legislative assembly to be known as the Conseil territorial (Territorial Council) were held in July 2007. At the first round ballot, held on 1 July, the Union pour le Progrès/Union pour un Mouvement Populaire (UPP/UMP) list, headed by Louis-Constant Fleming, won 40.4% of the total votes cast, while the Rassemblement, responsabilité et réussite (RRR) list, lead by Alain Richardson, secured 31.9%, and Jean-Luc Hamlet's Réussir Saint-Martin obtained 10.9% of the vote. The Alliance list, headed by Dominque Riboud, received 9.1%, and Wendel Cocks's Alliance démocratique pour Saint-Martin attracted the remaining 7.8% of the ballot. Some 46.4% of the electorate exercised their right to vote. As no list emerged with an absolute majority, a further round of voting was contested by the three parties that had secured more than 10% of the vote. At this second round, held on 8 July, the UPP/UMP list won 49.0% of the vote and obtained 16 of the 23 legislative seats, the RRR received 42.2% of the vote (six seats), and Réussir Saint-Martin 8.9% (one seat). Voter participation was slightly higher, at 50.8%. Fleming assumed the presidency of the Conseil territorial on 15 July, and Saint-Martin was officially installed as an Overseas Collectivity. However, in July 2008 Fleming was forced to resign the presidency after the French Conseil d'Etat disqualified him from his seat on the Conseil territorial for one year, owing to irregularities in his financial accounts for the 2007 election campaign. In August the Conseil territorial elected Frantz Gumbs as its new President; however, in April 2009 the Conseil d'Etat annulled the election of Gumbs due to voting irregularities. First Vice-President Daniel Gibbs was installed as interim President pending a re-run of the election, which was to be held within 30 days. On 5 May Gumbs was re-elected as President with 16 votes, defeating Alain Richardson, who received six votes, and Marthe Ogoundélé, who gained one vote.

Meanwhile, at an election held on 21 September 2008 Fleming, representing the UMP, was elected as Saint-Martin's representative to the French Sénat. Pending the election of a deputy to the Assemblée nationale (scheduled for 2012), the territory was to continue to be represented therein by Victorin Lurel of the Parti Socialiste, one of the deputies for Guadeloupe.

Prefect-Delegate: JACQUES SIMONNET.

Conseil territorial

Hôtel de la Collectivité, rue de Hôtel de Ville, BP 374, Marigot; tel. 5-90-87-50-04; fax 5-90-87-88-53; internet www.com-saint-martin.fr.

President: FRANTZ GUMBS.

Elections, 1 and 8 July 2007

	Seats
Union pour le Progrès/Union pour un Mouvement Populaire (UPP/UMP)	16
Rassemblement, responsabilité et réussite (RRR)	6
Réussir Saint-Martin	1
Total	23

Two other lists contested the elections: Alliance, and Alliance démocratique pour Saint-Martin.

SAINT VINCENT AND THE GRENADINES

Geography

PHYSICAL FEATURES

Saint Vincent and the Grenadines is in the Windward Islands and consists of the main island of Saint Vincent itself and 32 other islands and cays to its south. The country is surrounded by other Commonwealth states on the Antillean chain that separates the Caribbean Sea, to the west, from the Atlantic Ocean, to the east. The Lesser Antilles here begin to arc more towards the south-west as they head towards the South American mainland. Saint Lucia lies 47 km (29 miles) to the north, and a little east, while yet another Commonwealth country, Grenada, is southwards along the chain. The large islands of Saint Vincent and Grenada, which are about 100 km apart, are connected by the many smaller islands of the Grenadines, which are split between the two countries. Only a narrow channel separates Petit St Vincent from Petit Martinique, the northernmost island of Grenada. About 160 km to the east, beyond the main arc of the Lesser Antilles, lies Barbados. Saint Vincent and the Grenadines is the third smallest independent state in the Western hemisphere, with an area of 389.3 sq km (150 sq miles), 88% of which is accounted for by the main island of Saint Vincent itself.

The main island of Saint Vincent is 29 km from north to south and almost 18 km at its widest. Like the rest of the Windwards, Saint Vincent has rugged eastern Atlantic coasts and gentler western and south-western shores. The interior, however, is generally mountainous and steep, formed on the largely sunken volcanic ridge that runs north from Grenada and through the connecting archipelago. The Grenadines are largely coralline, although the larger ones are hilly, while the main island is steep and lofty. Saint Vincent is dominated by the central mass of the precipitous Morne Garu range, which runs from south to north and thrusts side spurs to the east and west coasts, but the highest point is to the north, in the Waterloo mountains, where the Soufrière volcano reaches 1,234 m (4,050 ft). This is an active volcano, which last erupted in April 1979, but without the loss of life that accompanied the eruptions of 1902 or 1812. Apart from land in the immediate vicinity of the volcano, the island is fertile and productive, the central mountains being covered in rainforest and the lower hillsides and few flatter areas planted with crops, notably bananas and arrowroot (the island is the world's leading producer of the latter, while economic dependence on the fluctuating prices of the former has led to the alternative, but illicit, cultivation of marijuana). The woodland areas are home to a number of plant, animal and bird species, most notable among the last being the protected Saint Vincent parrot and the whistling warbler, both of which are unique to the island. Marine life is especially rich among the reefs and islands of the Grenadines.

The largest of the Grenadines, and the closest to Saint Vincent itself (14 km), is Bequia, which covers about 18 sq km, its hills wooded with fruit and nut trees. There are a number of smaller islands to the south, such as Isle à Quatre, while to the east of them are Baliceaux and the smaller Battowia, which stand at the end of the main chain of the Grenadines running south-west from here towards Union Island. The main islands in this chain are Mustique (5 km in length and over 2 km wide), then, beyond some smaller islands and an unusually wide sea channel, Canouan (almost 8 sq km in area, and 40 km south of Saint Vincent), followed by Mayreau and the Tobago Cays, and Union Island (the main island of the south, 64 km from Saint Vincent—5 km in length and almost 2 km in width, or just over 8 sq km). Union Island has hills that reach 305 m. To the east, and a little south, the Vincentian Grenadines end at Petit St Vincent, a resort island.

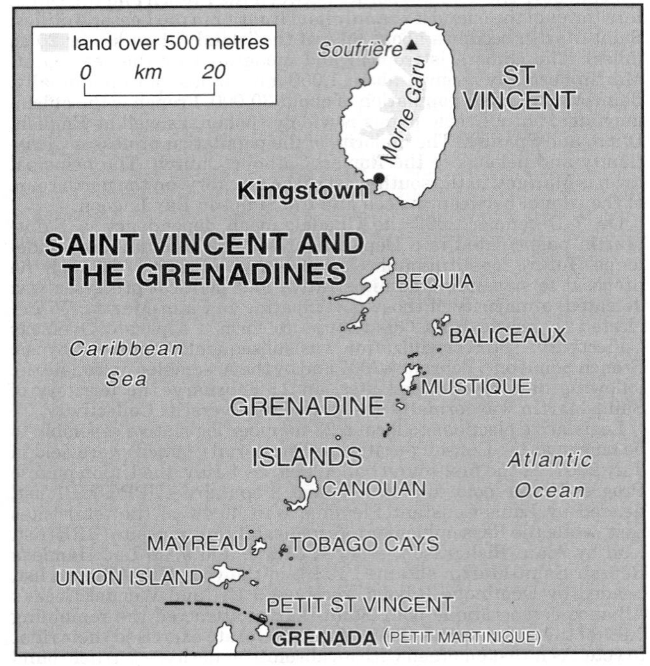

CLIMATE

The climate is subtropical, and the country is on the edge of the hurricane belt, although swell from storms passing to the north can still cause damage on the coasts. The hurricane season coincides with the rainy season (roughly July–October), which contributes substantially to the high annual rainfall, averaging some 2,050 mm (80 ins) on the coast, but up to 3,850 mm in the hilly interior of the main island. The Grenadines, being lower and less forested than Saint Vincent, receive slightly less rainfall than the main island (around 1,500 mm). Average temperatures range between about 25°C and 27°C (77°F–81°F).

POPULATION

The population is a heterogeneous mix, but of predominantly black African descent. Some 66% are counted as black, 19% as mixed race (mainly black-white), 6% as 'East' Indian, 4% as white and 2% as Carib Amerindian. The Caribs are so-called Black Caribs, descended from the union of escaped black slaves with native Caribs, the latter also fiercely resisting the British and French, but more susceptible to disease and cultural isolation. Some 5,000 of the continuously rebellious Black Caribs were deported to an island off Honduras in 1797, and the descendants of the remainder are now generally confined to the north of the island. The main religion is Christianity, with the Church in the Province of the West Indies being the largest single denomination (with somewhere between one-third and one-half of the population being Anglican), followed by the Methodist (around one-quarter) and Roman Catholic (just over one-10th) Churches. The city of Kingstown is the seat of both the Anglican and Roman Catholic bishops. There are also a number of other Protestant groups, including the Seventh-day Adventists, and some adherents of non-Christian traditions. A local blend of African and Christian traditions produced a faith the observers of which were known as Spiritual Baptists. These 'Shakers' (not to be confused with the millenarian sect founded in the United Kingdom in the 18th century), like the 'Shouters' of Trinidad (Trinidad and Tobago), emerged in the 1830s in the aftermath of emancipation, but were banned between 1912 and 1965. English is both the official and the spoken tongue, although a French patois or Creole is still used in some areas.

In mid-2010 the total population of Saint Vincent and the Grenadines was an estimated 109,284. About 25% (28,199 in mid-2009) of the population lives in and around Kingstown, the capital on the south-western coast. Some 8% of the population lives on the Grenadines. The main towns of the smaller islands are Port Elizabeth on Bequia, Charlestown on Canouan and Ashton (and, to a lesser extent, Clifton) on Union Island. The Grenadines are described as dependencies, while Saint Vincent itself is divided into six administrative parishes.

History

MARK WILSON

Saint Vincent and the Grenadines is a constitutional monarchy within the Commonwealth. Queen Elizabeth II is Head of State, and is represented by a Governor-General. There is a bicameral legislature with an elected chamber. A constitutional review process, inaugurated in 2003 with the convening of a dedicated committee, culminated in proposed reforms which were, however, rejected at a referendum held in 2009 (see below).

Saint Vincent's Amerindian inhabitants knew the island as Hairoun. It was given its present name by Christopher Columbus in 1498, although fierce Amerindian resistance delayed European settlement. In 1675 a Dutch ship carrying African slaves was shipwrecked to the south of the island. The human cargo reached land, where they intermarried with the local population, producing a mixed-race Black Carib community. There was fierce resistance to European colonization and when settlements were established, the island changed hands on several occasions between the United Kingdom and France, finally passing to the United Kingdom in 1783. A rebellion by the Black Caribs in 1795–96 succeeded in gaining control of most of the island, but was eventually suppressed. Most of the Black Caribs were deported in 1797 to the island of Roatan, off the coast of Honduras. Their descendants now form the Garifuna community of Belize. Smaller groups of Black Caribs remain in Saint Vincent, and are concentrated in the north-east of the island. As in the rest of the British Caribbean, slavery was abolished in 1834. Poverty remained extreme, and there was some immigration of indentured Portuguese and Indian labourers after emancipation.

The first universal suffrage elections were in 1951, and were won by the loosely organized Workers', Peasants' and Ratepayers' Union. After the elections Ebenezer Joshua founded the People's Political Party (PPP), while Milton Cato formed the Saint Vincent Labour Party (SVLP) in 1954. The SVLP won a general election in 1967, holding office with Cato as Prime Minister until 1972, and again during 1974–84. In the 1972 election, each of the main parties won six seats on the main island. James Mitchell took the Grenadines seat as an independent, and persuaded the PPP to join a Government in which he was Prime Minister, an arrangement which lasted for two years. However, in 1974 the PPP and SVLP joined forces to bring down the Government. In the election that followed, Mitchell again won a single seat, but Cato became Prime Minister, with Joshua as Minister of Finance. Joshua's wife, Ivy, sat on the opposition benches, and she, rather than Mitchell, was appointed Leader of the Opposition.

Saint Vincent and the Grenadines joined the Federation of the West Indies in 1958, along with nine other British colonies. When Jamaica and Trinidad and Tobago left in 1962, the Federation collapsed, and an attempt to unite the remaining colonies as the 'little eight' was unsuccessful. In 1969, two years later than its neighbours, Saint Vincent and the Grenadines became a British Associated State, responsible for its internal affairs, with the United Kingdom retaining control of external affairs and defence, before moving to full independence on 27 October 1979.

James (Sir James from 1995) Mitchell, won a general election in July 1984 as leader of the National Democratic Party (NDP), which took 12 of the 15 parliamentary seats, with the Cato Government by then widely perceived to be tainted by corruption. The NDP Government won all 15 seats in a May 1989 election, and 12 in February 1994, with an alliance of the opposition Labour Party and Movement for National Unity taking three. By 1998 the opposition parties had merged to form the Unity Labour Party (ULP) and were able to mount a strong challenge to the NDP Government, which was itself by now widely accused of corruption, and was further damaged by the serious problems facing the banana industry. The ULP took 54.6% of the vote in an election on 15 June, but the NDP held onto eight of the 15 legislative seats, some with very narrow minorities and amid accusations of electoral malpractice.

The political climate became confrontational thereafter and a serious controversy developed over a move in April 2000 to increase the pensions paid to retired politicians. In May the Caribbean Community and Common Market (CARICOM) brokered an agreement under which fresh elections were to be held by March 2001, giving Mitchell time to retire as Prime Minister in October 2000 at the age of 69; in August his party chose Arnhim Eustace as his successor. At a general election duly held on 28 March 2001 the ULP took 12 of the 15 legislative seats; its leader, Dr Ralph Gonsalves, thus became Prime Minister.

In June 2001 Gonsalves announced his intention to establish a commission to review the Constitution. A 25-member body was appointed in December 2002, and was due to complete its work by the end of 2004; a referendum was expected to be held on any proposed reforms. The commission submitted its report, to be used as a basis for further discussion, in February 2005. Its proposals included: replacing the Queen as Head of State with an indirectly elected President; the establishment of a non-legislative National Advisory Council of Elders; and the introduction of a revamped single-chamber National Assembly, to include three appointed senators and seven civil society representatives. Meanwhile, in June 2002 the Governor-General, Sir Charles Antrobus, died and was succeeded in September by Sir Frederick Ballantyne.

At a general election held on 7 December 2005, the ULP again won 12 of the 15 seats, although its share of the popular vote was marginally reduced, to 55%, compared with 57% in the 2001 election. Observers noted the need to revise the electoral list by removing voters who had died or migrated, as it contained 91,000 names, equivalent to 87% of the all-age population.

Tensions between the Government and opposition parties intensified during 2007, as reciprocal controversies developed that challenged the political integrity of each. An inquiry into the failed Ottley Hall marina and dockyard development project, financially underwritten by the former NDP Government, had been launched in 2003, but was delayed by repeated procedural challenges; the losses incurred under the scheme, according to sources, accounted for more than one-quarter of Saint Vincent's total external debt. The NDP, meanwhile, was attempting to increase its popularity by protesting against government plans to increase taxation by the introduction of a value-added tax. Eustace further argued that the Government had failed adequately to enforce penal law in the islands, resulting in the escalation of violent and drugs-related crime.

Moreover, the discovery of a ballot box containing voting papers from the 2005 general election further reinforced the opposition's argument for the removal of the ULP from power before the expiry (in 2010) of its term in office.

A referendum on constitutional reform in Saint Vincent and the Grenadines was held on 25 November 2009, with 55.6% of the votes cast against the proposals and 43.1% in favour. A new constitution, if approved, would have replaced the Queen as Head of State with a President, the Privy Council in London with the Caribbean Court of Justice in Trinidad as final court of appeal, and have established an Integrity Commission to investigate and control corruption in public life, as well as an ombudsman to look into apparent administrative abuse. In order to gain popular and church support, the new constitution would have defined marriage as between a man and a woman, reinforcing a legal code under which homosexual relations remain subject to imprisonment. In March 2010 the ULP used its parliamentary majority to approve an increase in the number of electoral seats in the House of Assembly from 15 to 17 in time for the anticipated December election. The move was opposed by the NDP.

In mid-2010 there was continuing concern in Saint Vincent and the Grenadines over violent crime. The murder rate of 36 per 100,000 inhabitants in 2007 was second only to Jamaica's within the English-speaking Caribbean, and more than six times that of the USA; the murder rate fell back to 20 per 100,000 in 2009, although at this level it remained higher than any year before 2005. Saint Vincent is a centre for cocaine transshipment and is also the main marijuana producer in the eastern Caribbean, with an estimated 50% of exports going to other Caribbean markets, almost 25% to Europe, 15% to the USA and 10% to Canada. The US State Department lists Saint Vincent as a 'country of concern' for money-laundering, and advocates tighter supervision and regulation of the offshore financial sector.

Defeat in the constitutional referendum of 2009, together with the continuing high crime rate and economic difficulties, weakened the standing of the Gonsalves Government during that year and the early months of 2010.

Saint Vincent has been a member of the PetroCaribe initiative since its inception in 2005, under which Venezuela supplies oil products to Caribbean neighbours on preferential terms, and, in June 2009, formally joined the Venezuelan-led ALBA grouping to encourage regional unity, along with Bolivia, Cuba, Ecuador, Honduras, Nicaragua, Dominica, and Antigua and Barbuda.

A potential embarrassment for the Government arose after Japan pledged to provide US $7m. for the construction of a fisheries complex at Owia, to commence in late 2006. It was claimed that, in return for Japanese financial aid, Saint Vincent and the Grenadines would support the pro-whaling bloc at meetings of the International Whaling Commission (IWC); Gonsalves denied the allegation, pointing out that the Government had abstained on crucial votes relating to the provision of whale sanctuaries in the South Atlantic and the Pacific. However, at an IWC meeting in June 2006, the island, in accordance with several other members of the Organisation of Eastern Caribbean States, endorsed Japan's proposal to end the moratorium on whaling, invoking the criticism of prominent international trading partners and raising a potential threat to the region's crucial tourism economy. Saint Vincent maintained its support for commercial whaling during 2010.

Economy

MARK WILSON

Saint Vincent and the Grenadines is the third smallest country in the western hemisphere in terms of area, with 389.3 sq km, and had an estimated 109,284 inhabitants in mid-2010. Most of the population live on the main island. Of the Grenadine islands to the south, the most significant are Bequia, Mustique and Union Island. The islands have developed a modest middle-income economy, with a per-head gross domestic product (GDP) of US $4,650 in 2009. GDP grew at an average rate of 3.1% per year in 1995–2000, and by an annual average of 3.6% in 2002–05. Growth accelerated to 9.5% in 2006 and 8.4% in 2007, stimulated in part by a recovery in tourism and public sector spending. However, GDP contracted by 0.8% in 2008 and by a further 11% in 2009, according to the Eastern Caribbean Central Bank (ECCB), as the tourism, construction and banana production industries contracted, while migrant remittances were also negatively affected by the international economic recession.

The current account deficit on the balance of payments widened from 9.2% of GDP in 2000 to 34.2% in 2009, while public sector debt increased from the equivalent of 49% of GDP in 1998 to 77.5% in 2006 (declining slightly, to 75%, in 2009). With the Government adopting a policy of counter-cyclical spending, the overall fiscal balance moved from a surplus of 0.1% of GDP in 2000 to a deficit estimated at 4.2% in 2005 and averaging 3.5% in 2006–07. The capital budget is financed in part by grants from the European Union (EU), the Republic of China (Taiwan) and Trinidad and Tobago; and from external and domestic borrowing. A fiscal consolidation plan was developed in 2004 by the Ministry of Finance, the ECCB and the Barbados-based Caribbean Technical Assistance Centre. A value-added tax was implemented in May 2007, with the income tax threshold raised in partial compensation. Fuel prices were increased at the same time, as existing subsidies had risen to unsustainable levels. With these measures in place, the overall fiscal deficit declined an estimated 0.8% of GDP in 2008, but rose again to 3.1% as a result of the economic difficulties experienced in 2009. International donor agencies urged the Government strictly to maintain its restraint of current expenditure and to widen the tax base with the aim of protecting its capital investment programme. In 2009 the IMF projected a debt-to-GDP ratio of 87% by 2014 or, with additional financing for the proposed international airport calculated in, as much as 110%, and proposed measures to improve the primary fiscal balance by 3.5% of GDP. Meanwhile, the Unity Labour Party Government in 2007 had succeeded in a write-off and restructuring of the debt incurred by the previous administration for the failed Ottley Hall marina, which had been equivalent to 11.5% of GDP in 2005. This helped reduce the total level of debt to 67.5% of GDP at the end of 2008; however, debt increased sharply, to 75% of GDP, according to IMF estimates for 2009.

Saint Vincent and the Grenadines is a member of the Caribbean Community and Common Market (CARICOM), whose larger members formed a single market at the start of 2006; Saint Vincent and the Grenadines joined in July, with the proposed establishment of a regional development fund to protect the interests of the smaller member economies. It is also a member of the Organisation of Eastern Caribbean States (OECS), which links nine of the smaller Caribbean territories, while the ECCB, based in Saint Christopher and Nevis, supervises its financial affairs.

Agriculture (including hunting, forestry and fishing) comprised some 7.5% of GDP in 2009, down from 21.2% in 1990. Banana exports to the United Kingdom under protected market access arrangements were an economic mainstay from the 1950s, but the industry suffered a steep decline in the 1990s, as the trade privileges of Caribbean producers in the European market were eroded. In 1990 income from banana exports was US $45.5m., equivalent to 52.2% of merchandise exports. By 2007 exports had diminished to an estimated $7.3m., equivalent to 18% of merchandise exports, and export volume decreased by a further 40.4% in 2008. However, significant grant aid from the EU was available for irrigation and technical support, as well as for economic diversification and social assistance, and there were some hopes that the industry would survive. Small farmers produce a wide variety of fruits, vegetables and livestock products for the local market, and significant quantities are exported to Trinidad and Tobago, and Barbados. Illegal cultivation of marijuana for export to other islands plays a significant role in the parallel economy.

The E. T. Joshua Airport on Saint Vincent cannot accommodate intercontinental flights, and inbound passengers must transfer by short-haul flight from Barbados or Saint Lucia. This lack of direct air connections impeded the growth of tourism, and in August 2005 the Government proposed an international airport at Argyle, in south-eastern Saint Vincent, which was originally intended for completion by 2011. The cost of the project was put at US $225m. (equivalent to 38% of GDP), with financial assistance agreed by Taiwan, Venezuela, Cuba, Trinidad and Tobago, and other donors; the IMF has raised concerns over a funding gap, which the Government intends to compensate for with land sales. Preliminary work was under way in mid-2010. Improvements to E. T. Joshua Airport were meanwhile facilitated principally by overseas loans, in particular the Kuwaiti Fund for Arab Economic Development. The runway of the airport on Canouan island, which serves a major hotel development, was extended in 2008 from 550 m to 1,800 m, allowing direct flights from North America. The main island has few white sand beaches, and most tourism development has taken place on the Grenadines, where a dry climate, clear water and fine beaches have proved powerful attractions for luxury development, and difficulty of public access has been turned into an asset for those who seek seclusion. Yachting is an important sub-sector, but yacht passenger arrivals fell from 93,638 in 2006 to 42,277 in the following year, and have since remained at around this level, with 44,009 arrivals in 2009. A failed marina project at Ottley Hall on the main island was responsible for up to 25% of government debt (EC $156m.); an inquiry was undertaken into the project in 2007. Tourism receipts increased from EC $111m. in 1992 to a peak value of EC $306m. in 2006, but fell back to EC $236m. by 2009. In that year the islands attracted 72,632 stop-over tourists, which was a significant decline compared with previous years, with international demand weakening as a result of the global economic downturn. There were also 163,340 cruise ship passengers in 2009, although this group had much lower per-head spending. In 2009 some 26.3% of stop-over tourists were from the USA and 18.0% were from the United Kingdom.

Manufacturing comprised some 4.1% of GDP in 2009, down from 9.5% in 1992. The most important facility is a mill, which produces flour, milled rice and animal feed for the local and Eastern Caribbean markets. Flour exports totalled some US $4.9m. in 2004 and comprised 13.6% of total merchandise exports. The flour trade was protected from non-OECS imports even after the commencement of the CARICOM single market, but Antigua and other importers obtained permission in 2008 to seek lower-cost imports from other regional sources. Other enterprises include a brewery, and 'enclave' industries producing electronic components for export.

Saint Vincent and the Grenadines is a member of the Eastern Caribbean Telecommunications Authority (based in Saint Lucia) and has liberalized its telecommunications regime. The Government sees telemarketing and informatics as a potentially important source of employment. However, call centres opened from 2001 did not appear to have been as successful as had originally been anticipated.

There is a small 'offshore' financial services sector: six offshore banks, 8,498 International Business Companies, 13 external insurance companies, nine mutual funds, 19 registered agents and 138 international trusts were registered in 2008. Saint Vincent and the Grenadines was in 2000 listed as a 'non-co-operative jurisdiction' by the Financial Action Task Force on Money Laundering (FATF, based in Paris, France). Following some regulatory and legislative reforms, including the establishment of a Financial Intelligence Unit in May 2002, Saint Vincent and the Grenadines was delisted by the FATF in June 2003, and is currently classed by the US Department of State as a country of concern, an intermediate category; the US Government has called for a registry of beneficial owners, immobilization of bearer shares, and proper supervision and regulation of the offshore sector. In April 2009 the Organisation for Economic Co-operation and Development included Saint Vincent and the Grenadines on a 'grey' list of countries with inadequate provision for tax information exchange; however, enough treaties had been signed by March 2010 to allow the country to be removed from this list. In November 2001 the island's leading offshore banker, Thierry Nano, was able to leave the island in time to evade a US request for his extradition on money-laundering charges. Opposition politicians accused the Government of failing to prevent Nano's escape and, in February 2002, Arnhim Eustace, the opposition leader, criticized the Government's decision to take control of the two banks owned by Nano, instead of liquidating them. As an indication of continuing problems within the sector, the Swiss-owned and Saint Vincent-based Millennium Bank was placed in receivership in March 2009 after US allegations that it was running a US $68m. fraudulent investment (Ponzi) scheme.

Saint Vincent and the Grenadines is in the southern fringe of the hurricane belt, and was affected by Hurricane Allen in 1980, Hurricane Emily in 1987 and by the fringe of Hurricane Ivan in 2004. The Soufrière volcano in the north of the island erupted in 1902 and 1979, causing several thousand deaths on the first occasion. There are other volcanic centres in the Grenadines, and there is some long-term risk from the underwater volcano of Kick'Em Jenny, just north of Grenada. There is also a risk of earthquakes.

Statistical Survey

Source (unless otherwise stated): Statistical Office, Ministry of Finance and Economic Planning, Administrative Centre, Bay St, Kingstown; tel. 456-1111; e-mail statssvg@vincysurf.com.

AREA AND POPULATION

Area: 389.3 sq km (150.3 sq miles). The island of Saint Vincent covers 344 sq km (133 sq miles).

Population: 97,914 at census of 12 May 1980; 106,499 (males 53,165, females 53,334) at census of 12 May 1991; 109,202 at preliminary census count of May 2001. *Mid-2010* (UN estimate): 109,284. Source: UN, *World Population Prospects: The 2008 Revision*.

Density (mid-2010): 280.7 per sq km.

Population by Age and Sex (UN estimates at mid-2010): *0–14:* 28,992 (males 14,638, females 14,354); *15–64:* 72,960 (males 37,212, females 35,748); *65 and over:* 7,332 (males 3,321, females 4,011); *Total* 109,284 (males 55,171, females 54,113) (Source: UN, *World Population Prospects: The 2008 Revision*).

Principal Town: Kingstown (capital) population 13,526 at preliminary census count of May 2001. *Mid-2009* (population incl. suburbs, UN estimate): Kingstown 28,199. Source: UN, *World Urbanization Prospects: The 2009 Revision*.

Births, Marriages and Deaths (registrations, 2005): Live births 1,779 (birth rate 17.1 per 1,000); Marriages 576 (marriage rate 5.6 per 1,000); Deaths 813 (death rate 7.8 per 1,000). Source: UN, *Demographic Yearbook*.

Life Expectancy (years at birth, WHO estimates): 71 (males 66; females 76) in 2008. Source: WHO, *World Health Statistics*.

Economically Active Population (persons aged 15 years and over, 1991 census): Agriculture, hunting, forestry and fishing 8,377; Mining and quarrying 98; Manufacturing 2,822; Electricity, gas and water 586; Construction 3,535; Trade, restaurants and hotels 6,544; Transport, storage and communications 2,279; Financing, insurance, real estate and business services 1,418; Community, social and personal services 7,696; *Total employed* 33,355 (males 21,656, females 11,699); Unemployed 8,327 (males 5,078, females 3,249); *Total labour force* 41,682 (males 26,734, females 14,948). Source: ILO, *Yearbook of Labour Statistics*.

HEALTH AND WELFARE

Key Indicators

Total Fertility Rate (children per woman, 2008): 2.1.

Under-5 Mortality Rate (per 1,000 live births, 2008): 13.

Physicians (per 1,000 head, 2000): 0.8.

Hospital Beds (per 1,000 head, 2005): 4.5.

Health Expenditure (2007): US $ per head (PPP): 474.

Health Expenditure (2007): % of GDP: 5.4.

Health Expenditure (2007): public (% of total): 61.3.

Access to Water (% of persons, 2000): 93.

Access to Sanitation (% of persons, 2000): 96.

Total Carbon Dioxide Emissions ('000 metric tons, 2005): 190.5.

Carbon Dioxide Emissions Per Head (metric tons, 2005): 1.8.

Human Development Index (2007): ranking: 91.

Human Development Index (2007): value: 0.772.

For sources and definitions, see explanatory note on p. vi.

AGRICULTURE, ETC.

Principal Crops ('000 metric tons, 2008, FAO estimates): Maize 0.7; Cassava 0.8; Sweet potatoes 2.3; Yams 2.3; Sugar cane 20.0; Coconuts 4.6; Bananas 51.0; Plantains 3.6; Oranges 1.7; Lemons and limes 1.3; Apples 1.3; Mangoes 1.6. *Aggregate Production* ('000 metric tons, may include official, semi-official or estimated data): Roots and tubers 15.3; Vegetables (incl. melons) 4.9; Fruits (excl. melons) 61.3.

Livestock ('000 head, year ending September 2008, FAO estimates): Cattle 5.1; Sheep 12.5; Goats 7.3; Pigs 9.2; Chickens 130.

Livestock Products ('000 metric tons, 2008, FAO estimates): Pig meat 0.6; Chicken meat 0.3; Cows' milk 13.0; Hen eggs 0.7.

Fishing (capture production, metric tons, live weight, 2008): Albacore 201; Skipjack tuna 83; Wahoo 24; Yellowfin tuna 2,547; Other tuna-like fishes 124; Other marine fishes 600; *Total catch* (incl. others) 3,828.

Source: FAO.

INDUSTRY

Selected Products ('000 metric tons, 2005 unless otherwise stated): Copra 2 (FAO estimate); Raw sugar 1.6; Rum 9,000 hectolitres (2003); Electric energy 139.1 million kWh (2008). Sources: FAO, Eastern Caribbean Central Bank and UN Industrial Commodity Statistics Database.

FINANCE

Currency and Exchange Rates: 100 cents = 1 Eastern Caribbean dollar (EC $). *Sterling, US Dollar and Euro Equivalents* (31 May 2010): £1 sterling = EC $3.937; US $1 = EC $2.700; €1 = EC $3.344; EC $100 = £25.40 = US $37.04 = €29.91. *Exchange Rate:* Fixed at US $1 = EC $2.70 since July 1976.

Budget (EC $ million, 2008): *Revenue:* Revenue from taxation 448.0 (Taxes on income 110.4, Taxes on goods and services 245.8, Taxes on property 2.2, Taxes on international trade and transactions 89.5); Other current revenue 41.6; Capital revenue 15.7; Foreign grants 45.2; Total 550.5. *Expenditure:* Current expenditure 431.3 (Personal emoluments 206.8, Other goods and services 91.0, Interest payments 46.8, Transfers and subsidies 86.7); Capital expenditure and net lending 131.0; Total 562.3. *2009* (EC $ million, provisional figures): Total revenue 522.5; Total expenditure 571.5. Source: Eastern Caribbean Central Bank.

International Reserves (US $ million at 31 December 2009): IMF special drawing rights 11.84; Reserve position in IMF 0.78; Foreign exchange 75.20; *Total* 87.82. Source: IMF, *International Financial Statistics*.

Money Supply (EC $ million at 31 December 2009): Currency outside depository corporations 63.50; Transferable deposits 349.37; Other deposits 786.96; *Broad money* 1,199.83. Source: IMF, *International Financial Statistics*.

Cost of Living (Consumer Price Index; base: 2005 = 100): All items 113.5 in 2007; 123.4 in 2008; 121.4 in 2009. Source: IMF, *International Financial Statistics*.

Gross Domestic Product (EC $ million at constant 1990 prices): 1,028.51 in 2007; 1,040.03 in 2008. Source: Eastern Caribbean Central Bank.

Expenditure on the Gross Domestic Product (EC $ million at current prices, 2008): Government final consumption expenditure 300.91; Private final consumption expenditure 1,346.95; Gross capital formation 555.35; *Total domestic expenditure* 2,203.21; Exports of goods and services 552.74; *Less* Imports of goods and services 1,185.3; *GDP at market prices* 1,570.65. Source: Eastern Caribbean Central Bank.

Gross Domestic Product by Economic Activity (EC $ million at current prices, 2008): Agriculture, hunting, forestry and fishing 91.31; Mining and quarrying 3.09; Manufacturing 52.49; Electricity and water 69.42; Construction 192.70; Wholesale and retail trade 256.18; Restaurants and hotels 24.21; Transport 159.43; Communications 72.94; Banking and insurance 127.51; Real estate and housing 24.12; Government services 251.48; Other services 26.86; *Sub-total* 1,351.74; *Less* Financial intermediation services indirectly measured 109.59; *Total in basic prices* 1,242.15; Taxes, less subsidies, on products 328.50; *GDP at market prices* 1,570.65. Source: Eastern Caribbean Central Bank.

Balance of Payments (EC $ million, 2009): Exports of goods 156.30; Imports of goods –816.50; *Trade balance* –660.20; Services (net) 90.65; *Balance on goods and services* –569.55 Other income received (net) –59.88; *Balance on goods, services and income* –629.43; Current transfers (net) 63.00; *Current balance* –566.44; Capital account (net) 178.64; Direct investment (net) 338.84; Portfolio investment (net) –11.04; Other investment (net) 35.83; Net errors and omissions 0.46; *Overall balance* –23.70. Source: Eastern Caribbean Central Bank.

EXTERNAL TRADE

Principal Commodities (US $ million, 2008): *Imports c.i.f.:* Food and live animals 73.5; Beverages and tobacco 11.0; Crude materials 10.0; Mineral fuels, lubricants, etc. 55.1; Chemicals and related products 28.8; Basic manufactures 67.2; Machinery and transport equipment 86.1; Total (incl. others) 373.2. *Exports f.o.b.:* Food and live animals 30.0 (Rice 6.3, Vegetables and fruit 12.9); Beverages and tobacco 2.2; Basic manufactures 4.7 (Iron and steel 1.7); Machinery and transport equipment 12.0; Miscellaneous manufactured articles 1.8; Total (incl. others) 52.2. Source: UN, *International Trade Statistics Yearbook*.

Principal Trading Partners (US $ million, 2008): *Imports c.i.f.:* Barbados 10.1; Brazil 4.1; Canada 7.9; China, People's Rep. 10.0; France (incl. Monaco) 8.6; Germany 8.0; Guyana 4.0; Italy 5.9; Japan 10.3; Trinidad and Tobago 81.0; United Kingdom 22.1; USA 138.2; Total (incl. others) 373.2. *Exports f.o.b.:* Antigua and Barbuda 4.4; Barbados 5.6; Dominica 2.6; Jamaica 1.3; Saint Lucia 7.7; Trinidad and Tobago 9.1; United Kingdom 4.7; USA 2.0; Total (incl. others) 52.2. Source: UN, *International Trade Statistics Yearbook*.

TRANSPORT

Road Traffic (motor vehicles in use, 2008): Private cars 9,247; Buses and coaches 122; Lorries and vans 12,897; Motorcycles 1,217. Source: International Road Federation, *World Road Statistics*.

Shipping: *Arrivals* (2000): Vessels 1,007. *International Sea-borne Freight Traffic* ('000 metric tons, 2000): Goods loaded 54; Goods unloaded 156. *Merchant Fleet* (vessels registered at 31 December 2008): Number 1,009; Total displacement 5,203,419 grt (Source: Lloyd's Register-Fairplay, *World Fleet Statistics*).

Civil Aviation (visitor arrivals): 99,657 in 2004; 104,432 in 2005; 106,466 in 2006 (estimate). Source: IMF, *St Vincent and the Grenadines: Statistical Appendix* (April 2009).

TOURISM

Visitor Arrivals: 283,161 (89,532 stop-over visitors, 6,797 excursionists, 42,277 yacht passengers, 144,555 cruise ship passengers) in 2007; 249,868 (84,101 stop-over visitors, 5,781 excursionists, 43,277 yacht passengers, 116,709 cruise ship passengers) in 2008; 287,118 (72,632 stop-over visitors, 7,137 excursionists, 44,009 yacht passengers, 163,340 cruise ship passengers) in 2009. *Stop-over Visitors by Country* (2009): Canada 6,810; Caribbean 25,358; United Kingdom 13,087; USA 19,069; Other 8,308.

Tourism Receipts (EC $ million): 297.0 in 2007; 259.3 in 2008; 236.4 in 2009.

Source: Eastern Caribbean Central Bank.

COMMUNICATIONS MEDIA

Radio Receivers ('000 in use, 2000): 100.

Television Receivers ('000 in use, 2000): 50.

Telephones ('000 main lines in use, 2009): 23.0.

Mobile Cellular Telephones (subscribers, 2009): 121,100.

Personal Computers: 16,500 (151.8 per 1,000 persons) in 2005.

Internet Users ('000, 2009): 76.

Broadband Subscribers ('000, 2009): 11.5.

Daily Newspapers (2005): Titles 3.

Non-daily Newspapers (2000): Titles 8; Circulation 50,000.

Sources: mainly UNESCO, *Statistical Yearbook*; UN, *Statistical Yearbook*; and International Telecommunication Union.

EDUCATION

Pre-primary (2004/05 unless otherwise indicated): 97 schools (1993/94); 340 teachers; 3,894 pupils.

Primary (2007/08 unless otherwise indicated): 60 schools (2000); 916 teachers; 15,532 pupils.

Secondary (2007/08 unless otherwise indicated): 21 schools (2000); 598 teachers; 11,641 pupils.

Teacher Training (2000): 1 institution; 10 teachers; 107 students.

Technical College (2000): 1 institution; 19 teachers; 187 students.

Community College (2000): 1 institution; 13 teachers; 550 students.

Nursing College (2000): 1 institution; 6 teachers; 60 students.

Pupil-teacher Ratio (primary education, UNESCO estimate): 17.0 in 2008/09.

Sources: partly Caribbean Development Bank, *Social and Economic Indicators*, and UNESCO Institute for Statistics.

Adult Literacy Rate: 88.1% in 2004. Source: UN Development Programme, *Human Development Report*.

Directory

The Constitution

The Constitution came into force at the independence of Saint Vincent and the Grenadines on 27 October 1979. The following is a summary of its main provisions.

FUNDAMENTAL RIGHTS AND FREEDOMS

Regardless of race, place of origin, political opinion, colour, creed or sex, but subject to respect for the rights and freedoms of others and for the public interest, every person in Saint Vincent and the Grenadines is entitled to the rights of life, liberty, security of the person and the protection of the law. Freedom of conscience, of expression, of assembly and of association is guaranteed, and the inviolability of a person's home and other property is maintained. Protection is afforded from slavery, forced labour, torture and inhuman treatment.

THE GOVERNOR-GENERAL

The British Monarch is represented in Saint Vincent and the Grenadines by the Governor-General.

PARLIAMENT

Parliament consists of the British monarch, represented by the Governor-General, and the House of Assembly, comprising 15 elected Representatives (increased from 13 under the provisions of an amendment approved in 1986) and six Senators. Senators are appointed by the Governor-General—four on the advice of the Prime Minister and two on the advice of the Leader of the Opposition. The life of Parliament is five years. Each constituency returns one Representative to the House who is directly elected in accordance with the Constitution. The Attorney-General is an ex officio member of the House. Every citizen over the age of 18 is eligible to vote. Parliament may alter any of the provisions of the Constitution.

THE EXECUTIVE

Executive authority is vested in the British monarch and is exercisable by the Governor-General. The Governor-General appoints as Prime Minister that member of the House who, in the Governor-General's view, is the best able to command the support of the majority of the members of the House, and selects other Ministers on the advice of the Prime Minister. The Governor-General may remove the Prime Minister from office if a resolution of no confidence in the Government is adopted by the House and the Prime Minister does not either resign within three days or advise the Governor-General to dissolve Parliament.

The Cabinet consists of the Prime Minister and other Ministers and the Attorney-General as an ex officio member. The Leader of the Opposition is appointed by the Governor-General as that member of the House who, in the Governor-General's view, is best able to command the support of a majority of members of the House who do not support the Government.

CITIZENSHIP

All persons born in Saint Vincent and the Grenadines before independence who, immediately prior to independence, were citizens of the United Kingdom and Colonies automatically become citizens of Saint Vincent and the Grenadines. All persons born outside the country after independence to a parent possessing citizenship of Saint Vincent and the Grenadines automatically acquire citizenship, as do those born in the country after independence. Citizenship can be acquired by those to whom it would not automatically be granted.

The Government

HEAD OF STATE

Queen: HM Queen Elizabeth II.

Governor-General: Sir Frederick Nathaniel Ballantyne (took office 2 September 2002).

CABINET
(July 2010)

The Government was formed by the Unity Labour Party.

Prime Minister and Minister of Finance and Economic Planning, National Security, Legal Affairs, Grenadines Affairs and Energy: Dr Ralph E. Gonsalves.

Deputy Prime Minister and Minister of Foreign Affairs, Commerce and Trade: Louis Straker.

Minister of Tourism: Glen Beache.

Minister of National Mobilization, Social Development, Local Government, Non-Governmental Organizations (NGOs), Family Affairs, Gender Affairs and Persons with Disabilities: Michael Browne.

Minister of Education: Girlyn Miguel.

Minister of Rural Transformation, Information, Public Service and Ecclesiastical Affairs: Selmon Walters.

Minister of Health and the Environment: Dr Douglas Slater.

Minister of Telecommunications, Science, Technology and Industry: Dr Jerrol Thompson.

Minister of Urban Development, Labour, Culture and Electoral Matters: Reneé Mercedes Baptiste.

Minister of Transportation and Works: Clayton Burgin.

Minister of Agriculture, Forestry and Fisheries: Montgomery Daniel.

Minister of Housing, Informal Human Settlements, Physical Planning, and Lands and Surveys: Julian Everard Francis.

Minister of State in the Office of the Prime Minister: Conrad Sayers.

Attorney-General: Judith S. Jones-Morgan.

MINISTRIES

Office of the Governor-General: Government House, Kingstown; tel. 456-1401; fax 457-9701.

Office of the Prime Minister: Administrative Bldg, 4th Floor, Bay St, Kingstown; tel. 456-1703; fax 457-2152; e-mail pmo.svg@caribsurf.com.

Office of the Attorney-General and Ministry of Legal Affairs: New Methodist Church Bldg, 3rd Floor, Granby St, Kingstown; tel. 456-1762; fax 457-2848; e-mail att.gen.chambers@caribsurf.com.

Ministry of Agriculture, Forestry and Fisheries: Richmond Hill, Kingstown; tel. 456-1410; fax 457-1688; e-mail office.agriculture@mail.gov.vc.

Ministry of Education: Halifax St, Kingstown; tel. 457-1104; fax 457-1114; e-mail office.education@mail.gov.vc.

Ministry of Finance and Economic Planning: Halifax St, Kingstown; tel. 456-1111; fax 457-2943.

Ministry of Foreign Affairs, Commerce and Trade: Administrative Bldg, 3rd Floor, Bay St, Kingstown; tel. 456-2060; fax 456-2610; e-mail office.foreignaffairs@mail.gov.vc.

Ministry of Health and the Environment: Ministerial Bldg, 1st Floor, Bay St, Kingstown; tel. 456-1111; fax 457-2684; e-mail office.health@mail.gov.vc.

Ministry of Housing, Informal Human Settlements, Physical Planning, and Lands and Surveys: Methodist Church Bldg, Granby St, Kingstown; tel. 456-2050; e-mail minister.housing@mail.gov.vc.

Ministry of National Mobilization, Social Development, Local Government, Non-Governmental Organizations (NGOs), Family Affairs, Gender Affairs and Persons with Disabilities: Egmont St, Kingstown; tel. 450-0395; fax 457-2476; e-mail office.socialdevelopment@mail.gov.vc.

Ministry of National Security: Ministerial Bldg, 3rd Floor, Halifax St, Kingstown; tel. 451-2707; fax 451-2820; e-mail office.natsec@mail.gov.vc.

Ministry of Rural Transformation, Information, Public Service and Ecclesiastical Affairs: Ministerial Bldg, 2nd Floor, Halifax St, Kingstown; tel. 451-2707; fax 451-2820; e-mail office.rutrans@mail.gov.vc.

Ministry of Telecommunications, Science, Technology and Industry: Egmont St, Kingstown; tel. 456-1223; fax 457-2880; e-mail office.telecom@mail.gov.vc.

Ministry of Tourism: NIS Bldg, 2nd Floor, Upper Bay St, POB 834, Kingstown; tel. 456-6222; fax 451-2425; e-mail svgta@discoversvg.com; internet www.discoversvg.com.

Ministry of Transportation and Works: Halifax St, Kingstown; tel. 457-2039; fax 456-2168; e-mail office.transport@mail.gov.vc.

Ministry of Urban Development, Labour, Culture and Electoral Matters: Marion House Bldg, Ground Floor, Murray's Rd, Kingstown; tel. 457-1789; fax 485-6737; e-mail labourdpt@vincysurf.com.

Legislature

HOUSE OF ASSEMBLY

Senators: 6.

Elected Members: 15.

Speaker: HENDRICK ALEXANDER.

Clerk: NICOLE HERBERT, House of Assembly, Kingstown; tel. 457-1872; fax 457-1825.

Election, 7 December 2005

Party	Votes	% of votes	Seats
Unity Labour Party	31,848	55.26	12
New Democratic Party	25,748	44.68	3
Saint Vincent and the Grenadines Green Party	34	0.06	—
Total	57,630	100.00	15

Election Commission

Electoral Office: Administrative Centre, Bay St, Kingstown; tel. 457-1762; fax 485-6844; e-mail electoraloffice@gov.vc; Supervisor of Elections SYLVIA FINDLAY SCRUBB.

Political Organizations

New Democratic Party (NDP): Democrat House, Murray Rd, POB 1300, Kingstown; tel. 451-2845; fax 457-2647; e-mail ndp@caribsurf.com; internet www.ivotingndp.com; f. 1975; democratic party supporting political unity in the Caribbean, social devt and free enterprise; Leader ARNHIM ULRIC EUSTACE; Gen. Sec. DANIEL E. CUMMINGS; 7,000 mems.

Saint Vincent and the Grenadines Green Party: POB 1707, Kingstown; tel. and fax 456-9579; e-mail mail@svggreenparty.org; internet www.svggreenparty.org; f. 2005; Leader IVAN O'NEAL; Gen. Sec. ORDAN O. GRAHAM.

Unity Labour Party (ULP): Beachmont, Kingstown; tel. 457-2761; fax 456-2811; e-mail ulpweb@aol.com; f. 1994 by merger of Movement for National Unity and the Saint Vincent Labour Party; moderate, social-democratic party; Leader Dr RALPH E. GONSALVES.

Diplomatic Representation

EMBASSIES IN SAINT VINCENT AND THE GRENADINES

China (Taiwan): Murray Rd, POB 878, Kingstown; tel. 456-2431; fax 456-2913; e-mail rocemsvg@caribsurf.com; Ambassador LEO LEE.

Cuba: Ratho Mill, Kingstown; tel. 458-5844; fax 456-9344; e-mail embajador@vc.embacuba.cu; internet www.embacu.cubaminrex.cu/sanvicenteing; Ambassador OLGA CHAMERO TRÍAS.

Venezuela: Baynes Bros Bldg, Granby St, POB 852, Kingstown; tel. 456-1374; fax 457-1934; e-mail embavenezsanvicente@vincysurf.com; Ambassador YOEL PÉREZ MARCANO.

Judicial System

Justice is administered by the Eastern Caribbean Supreme Court, based in Saint Lucia and consisting of a Court of Appeal and a High Court. Three Puisne Judges are resident in Saint Vincent and the Grenadines. There are five Magistrates, including the Registrar of the Supreme Court, who acts as an additional Magistrate.

Puisne Judges: FREDERICK BRUCE-LYLE, GERTEL THOM, JENNIFER REMY.

Office of the Registrar of the Supreme Court

Registry Dept, Court House, Kingstown; tel. 457-1220; fax 457-1888; e-mail svgregistry@caribsurf.com; Registrar TAMARA GIBSON-MARKS.

Chief Magistrate: SIMONE CHURAMAN.

Magistrates: DONALD BROWNE, ZOILA ELLIS-BROWNE, LESTER CAESAR.

Director of Public Prosecutions: COLIN WILLIAMS.

Religion

CHRISTIANITY

Saint Vincent Christian Council: Melville St, POB 445, Kingstown; tel. 456-1408; f. 1969; four mem. churches; Chair. Mgr RENISON HOWELL.

The Anglican Communion

Anglicans in Saint Vincent and the Grenadines are adherents of the Church in the Province of the West Indies, comprising eight dioceses. The Archbishop of the West Indies is the Bishop of Nassau and the Bahamas, and is resident in Nassau. The diocese of the Windward Islands includes Grenada, Saint Lucia and Saint Vincent and the Grenadines.

Bishop of the Windward Islands: Rt Rev. CALVERT LEOPOLD FRIDAY, Bishop's Court, POB 502, Kingstown; tel. 456-1895; fax 456-2591; e-mail diocesewi@vincysurf.com.

The Roman Catholic Church

Saint Vincent and the Grenadines comprises a single diocese (formed when the diocese of Bridgetown-Kingstown was divided in October 1989), which is suffragan to the archdiocese of Castries (Saint Lucia). The Bishop participates in the Antilles Episcopal Conference, currently based in Port of Spain, Trinidad and Tobago. Some 13% of the population are Roman Catholics.

Bishop of Kingstown: (vacant), Bishop's Office, POB 862, Edinboro, Kingstown; tel. 457-2363; fax 457-1903; e-mail rcdok@caribsurf.com.

Other Christian Churches

The Methodists, Seventh-day Adventists, Baptists and other denominations also have places of worship.

BAHÁ'Í FAITH

National Spiritual Assembly: POB 1043, Kingstown; tel. 456-4717.

The Press

SELECTED WEEKLIES

The News: Frenches Gate, POB 1078, Kingstown; tel. 456-2942; fax 456-2941; e-mail thenews@caribsurf.com; weekly; Man. Dir SHELLEY CLARKE.

Searchlight: Interactive Media Ltd, POB 152, Kingstown; tel. 456-1558; fax 457-2250; e-mail search@caribsurf.com; internet www.searchlight.vc; weekly on Fri.; Chair. CORLITA OLLIVERRE; CEO and Acting Man. Editor CLAIRE KEIZER.

The Vincentian: St George's Pl., Kingstown; tel. 456-1123; fax 457-2821; e-mail info@thevincentian.com; internet www.thevincentian.com; f. 1919; weekly; owned by the Vincentian Publishing Co; Man. Dir EGERTON M. RICHARDS; Editor-in-Chief TERRANCE PARRIS; circ. 6,000.

The Westindian Crusader: Kingstown; tel. 458-0073; fax 456-9315; e-mail crusader@caribsurf.com; weekly; Editor ELSEE CARBERRY; Man. Editor LINA CLARKE.

SELECTED PERIODICALS

Caribbean Compass: POB 175, Bequia; tel. 457-3409; fax 457-3410; e-mail tom@caribbeancompass.com; internet www.caribbeancompass.com; marine news; monthly; free distribution in Caribbean from Puerto Rico to Panama; circ. 11,000; Man. Dir TOM HOPMAN; Editor SALLY ERDLE.

Government Gazette: Govt Printery, Campden Park St, POB 12, Kingstown; tel. 457-1840; fax 453-3240; e-mail govprint@vincysurf.com; f. 1844; Govt Printer OTHNIEL WHITE; circ. 492.

Unity: Middle and Melville St, POB 854, Kingstown; tel. 456-1049; fortnightly; organ of the Unity Labour Party.

Publishers

CJW Communications: POB 1078, Frenches Gate, Kingstown; tel. 456-2942; fax 456-2941.

Great Works Depot: Commission A Bldg, Granby St, POB 1849, Kingstown; tel. 456-2057; fax 457-2055; e-mail gwd@caribsurf.com.

The Vincentian Publishing Co Ltd: St George's Pl., Kingstown; tel. 456-1123; fax 457-2821; e-mail info@thevincentian.com; internet www.thevincentian.com; Man. Dir EGERTON M. RICHARDS.

Broadcasting and Communications

TELECOMMUNICATIONS

Regulatory Authorities

Eastern Caribbean Telecommunications Authority (ECTEL): based in Castries, Saint Lucia; f. 2000 to regulate telecommunications in Saint Vincent and the Grenadines, Dominica, Grenada, Saint Christopher and Nevis and Saint Lucia.

National Telecom Regulatory Commission (NTRC): NIS Bldg, 2nd Floor, Upper Bay St, Kingstown; tel. 457-2279; fax 457-2834; e-mail ntrc@ntrc.vc; internet www.ntrc.vc; f. 2001 by the Telecommunications Act to regulate the sector in collaboration with ECTEL (q.v.); Chair K. DOUGLAS.

Major Service Providers

Digicel: Suite KO59, cnr Granby and Sharpe Sts, Kingstown; tel. 453-3000; fax 453-3010; e-mail customercaresvg@digicelgroup.com; internet www.digicelsvg.com; f. 2003; mobile cellular phone operator; owned by an Irish consortium; Chair. DENIS O'BRIEN; Eastern Caribbean CEO KEVIN WHITE.

LIME: Halifax St, POB 103, Kingstown; tel. 457-1901; fax 457-2777; e-mail support@vincysurf.com; internet www.time4lime.com; fmrly Cable & Wireless (St Vincent and the Grenadines) Ltd; name changed as above 2008; CEO DAVID SHAW; Exec. Vice-Pres. (Windward Islands) MICHAEL IAN BLANCHARD.

BROADCASTING

National Broadcasting Corporation of Saint Vincent and the Grenadines (NBC): Richmond Hill, POB 705, Kingstown; tel. 457-1111; fax 456-2749; e-mail nbcsvgadmin@nbcsvg.com; internet www.nbcsvg.com; govt-owned; Chair. ELSON CRICK; Gen. Man. CORLITA OLLIVERRE.

Radio

NBC Radio: National Broadcasting Corpn, Richmond Hill, POB 705, Kingstown; tel. 457-1111; fax 456-2749; e-mail nbcsvgadmin@nbcsvg.com; internet www.nbcsvg.com; commercial; broadcasts BBC World Service (United Kingdom) and local programmes.

Nice Radio FM: BDS Company Ltd, Dorcetshire Hill, POB 324, Kingstown; tel. 458-1013; fax 456-5556; e-mail bdsnice@caribsurf.com; internet www.niceradio.org; Man. Dir DOUGLAS DE FREITAS.

Television

National Broadcasting Corporation of Saint Vincent and the Grenadines: see above.

SVG Television (SVGTV): Dorsetshire Hill, POB 617, Kingstown; tel. 456-1078; fax 456-1015; e-mail svgbc@vincysurf.com; internet www.svgbc.com/svgtv.htm; f. 1980; broadcasts local, regional and international programmes; Man. Dir R. PAUL MACLEISH.

Television services from Barbados can be received in parts of the islands.

Finance

(cap. = capital; res = reserves; dep. = deposits; m. = million; br. = branch)

BANKING

The Eastern Caribbean Central Bank, based in Saint Christopher, is the central issuing and monetary authority for Saint Vincent and the Grenadines.

Eastern Caribbean Central Bank—Saint Vincent and the Grenadines Office: Frenches House, POB 839, Frenches; tel. 456-1413; fax 456-1412; e-mail eccbsvg@vincysurf.com; Country Dir ELRITHA DICK.

Regulatory Authority

International Financial Services Authority (IFSA): Upper Bay St, POB 356, Kingstown; tel. 456-2577; fax 457-2568; e-mail info@svgifsa.com; internet www.svgifsa.com; f. 1996; Chair. CLAUDE SAMUEL; Exec. Dir SHARDA SINANAN-BOLLERS.

Financial Intelligence Unit (FIU): POB 1826, Kingstown; tel. 451-2070; fax 457-2014; e-mail svgfiu@vincysurf.com; internet www.svgifsa.com/fin_intl_unit.htm; f. 2002; Dir GRENVILLE WILLIAMS.

Local Banks

Bank of Nova Scotia Ltd (Canada): 76 Halifax St, POB 237, Kingstown; tel. 457-1601; fax 457-2623; e-mail bruce.sali@scotiabank.com; Man. BRUCE SALI.

FirstCaribbean International Bank (Barbados) Ltd: Lower Halifax St, POB 212, Kingstown; tel. 457-1587; e-mail Earl.Crichton@firstcaribbeanbank.com; internet www.firstcaribbeanbank.com; f. 2002 following merger of Caribbean operations of Barclays Bank PLC and CIBC; CIBC acquired Barclays' 43.7% stake in 2006; Exec. Chair. MICHAEL MANSOOR; CEO JOHN D. ORR; Man. EARL CRICHTON.

National Commercial Bank (SVG) Ltd: Cnr Halifax and Egmont Sts, POB 880, Kingstown; tel. 457-1844; fax 456-2612; e-mail natbank@caribsurf.com; internet www.svgncb.com; f. 1977; govt-owned; share cap. EC $14.0m., res EC $19.1m., dep. EC $520.7m. (June 2006); CEO PHILIP H. HERNANDEZ; Chair. DESMOND MORGAN.

RBTT Bank Caribbean Ltd: 81 South River Rd, POB 81, Kingstown; tel. 456-1501; fax 456-2141; internet www.rbtt.com; f. 1985 as Caribbean Banking Corpn Ltd, name changed as above in 2002; Chair. PETER J. JULY.

'OFFSHORE' FINANCIAL SECTOR

Legislation permitting the development of an 'offshore' financial sector was introduced in 1976 and revised in 1996 and 1998. International banks are required to have a place of business on the islands and to designate a licensed registered agent. International Business Companies registered in Saint Vincent and the Grenadines are exempt from taxation for 25 years. Legislation also guarantees total confidentiality. In 2009 the 'offshore' financial sector comprised 8,855 International Business Companies, 149 trusts and four banks.

Saint Vincent Trust Service: Trust House, 112 Bonadie St, POB 613, Kingstown; tel. 457-1027; fax 457-1961; e-mail info@st-vincent-trust.com; internet www.jeeves-group.com; br. in Liechtenstein; Pres. BRYAN JEEVES.

'Offshore' Banks

European Commerce Bank: The Financial Services Centre, Paul's Ave, POB 1822, Kingstown; tel. 456-1460; fax 456-1455; e-mail info@eurocombank.com; internet www.eurocombank.com.

Loyal Bank Ltd: Cedar Hill Crest, POB 1825, Kingstown; tel. 485-6705; fax 451-2757; e-mail ceo@loyalbank.com; internet www.loyalbank.com; f. 1997; owned by Ost West Stiftung; CEO Adrian Baron.

Safe Harbor Bank Ltd: Nanton's Bldg, Egmont St, POB 2630, Kingstown; tel. 451-2030; fax 451-2031; e-mail info@safeharborbank.com; internet www.safeharborbank.com; f. 2000; Contact Grahame Bollers.

Trend Bank Ltd: The Financial Services Centre, Paul's Ave, POB 1823, Kingstown; tel. 457-0548; fax 451-2672; internet www.trendb.com; Pres. Adolpho J. Silva Mello Neto.

STOCK EXCHANGE

Eastern Caribbean Securities Exchange: based in Basseterre, Saint Christopher and Nevis; tel. (869) 466-7192; fax (869) 465-3798; e-mail info@ecseonline.com; internet www.ecseonline.com; f. 2001; regional securities market designed to facilitate the buying and selling of financial products for the eight mem. territories—Anguilla, Antigua and Barbuda, Dominica, Grenada, Montserrat, Saint Christopher and Nevis, Saint Lucia, and Saint Vincent and the Grenadines; Chair. Sir K. Dwight Venner; Gen. Man. and CEO Trevor E. Blake.

INSURANCE

A number of foreign insurance companies have offices in Kingstown. Local companies include the following:

Abbott's Insurance Co: Cnr Sharpe and Bay St, POB 124, Kingstown; tel. 456-1511; fax 456-2462.

BMC Agencies Ltd: Sharpe St, POB 1436, Kingstown; tel. 457-2041; fax 457-2103.

Durrant Insurance Services: South River Rd, Kingstown; tel. 457-2426.

Haydock Insurances Ltd: Granby St, POB 1179, Kingstown; tel. 457-2903; fax 456-2952.

Metrocint General Insurance Co Ltd: St George's Pl., POB 692, Kingstown; tel. 456-1821.

Saint Hill Insurance Co Ltd: Bay St, POB 1741, Kingstown; tel. 457-1227; fax 456-2374.

Saint Vincent Insurances Ltd: Lot 69, Grenville St, POB 210, Kingstown; tel. 456-1733; fax 456-2225; e-mail vinsure@caribsurf.com.

Trade and Industry

DEVELOPMENT ORGANIZATIONS

Invest SVG: POB 608, Kingstown; tel. 457-2159; fax 456-2688; e-mail info@investsvg.com; internet www.investsvg.com; f. 2003 as National Investment Promotions Inc; assumed DEVCO's (q.v.) responsibilities for investment promotion and foreign direct investment; reports to the Office of the Prime Minister; board mems appointed from both public and private sectors by the Cabinet; Exec. Dir Cleo Huggins; Chair. Edmond A. Jackson.

Saint Vincent Development Corporation (DEVCO): Grenville St, POB 841, Kingstown; tel. 457-1358; fax 457-2838; e-mail devco@caribsurf.com; f. 1970; finances industry, agriculture, fisheries, tourism; Chair. Samuel Goodluck; Man. Claude M. Leach.

CHAMBER OF COMMERCE

Saint Vincent and the Grenadines Chamber of Industry and Commerce (Inc): Corea's Bldg, 3rd Floor, Halifax and Hillsborough Sts, POB 134, Kingstown; tel. 457-1464; fax 456-2944; e-mail svgchamber@svg-cic.org; internet svg-cic.org; f. 1925; Pres. Angus Steele; Exec. Dir Shafia London.

INDUSTRIAL AND TRADE ASSOCIATION

Saint Vincent Marketing Corporation: Upper Bay St, POB 873, Kingstown; tel. 457-1603; fax 456-2673; e-mail svmc@caribsurf.com; f. 1959; CEO Sonny Williams.

EMPLOYERS' ORGANIZATIONS

Saint Vincent Arrowroot Industry Association: Upper Bay St, POB 70, Kingstown; tel. 457-1511; fax 457-2151; e-mail info@svgarrowroot.com; f. 1930; producers, manufacturers and sellers; 186 mems; Chair. George O. Walker.

Saint Vincent Banana Growers' Association: Sharpe St, POB 10, Kingstown; tel. 457-1605; fax 456-2585; f. 1955; over 7,000 mems; Chair. Lesline Best; Gen. Man. Henry Keizer.

Saint Vincent Employers' Federation: Corea's Bldg, 3rd Floor, Middle St, POB 348, Kingstown; tel. 456-1269; fax 457-2777; e-mail svef@caribsurf.com; Pres. Noel Dickson; Exec. Dir Phyllis John-Primus.

Windward Islands Farmers' Association (WINFA): Paul's Ave, POB 817, Kingstown; tel. 456-2704; fax 456-1383; e-mail winfa@winfacaribbean.org; internet www.winfacaribbean.org; f. 1982; Chair. Julius Polius; Co-ordinator Renwick Rose.

UTILITIES

Electricity

Saint Vincent Electricity Services Ltd (VINLEC): Paul's Ave, POB 865, Kingstown; tel. 456-1701; fax 456-2436; e-mail vinlec@vinlec.com; internet www.vinlec.com; 100% state-owned; country's sole electricity supplier; Chair. Douglas Cole; CEO Thornley O. A. O. Myers; 275 employees.

Water

Central Water and Sewerage Authority (CWSA): New Montrose, POB 363, Kingstown; tel. 456-2946; fax 456-2552; e-mail cwsa@vincysurf.com; internet www.cwsasvg.com; f. 1961; Chair. Richard MacLeish; Gen. Man. Garth Saunders.

CO-OPERATIVES

There are 26 Agricultural Credit Societies, which receive loans from the Government, and five Registered Co-operative Societies.

TRADE UNIONS

Commercial, Technical and Allied Workers' Union (CTAWU): Lower Middle St, POB 245, Kingstown; tel. 456-1525; fax 457-1676; e-mail ctawu@vincysurf.com; f. 1962; affiliated to CCL, ICFTU and other international workers' orgs; Pres. Cheryl Bacchus; Gen. Sec. Lloyd Small; 2,500 mems.

National Labour Congress: POB 875, Kingstown; tel. 457-1801; fax 457-1705; five affiliated unions; Pres. Noel Jackson.

National Workers' Movement: Burkes Bldg, Grenville St, POB 1290, Kingstown; tel. 457-1950; fax 456-2858; e-mail natwok@karicable.com; Gen. Sec. Noel C. Jackson.

Public Services Union of Saint Vincent and the Grenadines: McKie's Hill, POB 875, Kingstown; tel. 457-1950; fax 456-2858; e-mail psuofsvg@caribsurf.com; f. 1943; Pres. Aubrey Burgin; Gen. Sec. Elroy Boucher; 738 mems.

Saint Vincent and the Grenadines Teachers' Union: McKies Hill, POB 304, Kingstown; tel. 457-1062; fax 456-1098; e-mail svgtu@caribsurf.com; f. 1952; Pres. Elvis Charles; Gen. Sec. Joy Matthews; 1,250 mems.

Transport

RAILWAYS

There are no railways in the islands.

ROADS

In 2003 there was an estimated total road network of 829 km (515 miles), of which 580 km (360 miles) were paved. A government plan to extend and rehabilitate the Windward Highway was ongoing, while the first stage of a three-phase project to link Troumaca with Fergusson Gap was completed in 2007, at a cost of EC $2.5m.

SHIPPING

The deep-water harbour at Kingstown can accommodate two ocean-going vessels and about five motor vessels. There are regular motor-vessel services between the Grenadines and Saint Vincent. Geest Industries, formerly the major banana purchaser, operated a weekly service to the United Kingdom. Numerous shipping lines also call at Kingstown harbour. Some exports are flown to Barbados to link up with international shipping lines. A new dedicated Cruise Terminal opened in 1999, permitting two cruise ships to berth at the same time.

Saint Vincent and the Grenadines Port Authority: POB 1237, Kingstown; tel. 456-1830; fax 456-2732; e-mail pkirby@svgpa.com; internet www.svgpa.com; Port Dir Paul Kirby.

CIVIL AVIATION

There is a civilian airport, E. T. Joshua Airport, at Arnos Vale, situated about 3 km (2 miles) south-east of Kingstown, that does not accommodate long-haul jet aircraft. The island of Canouan has a small airport with a recently upgraded runway and passenger terminal; construction of a jet airport was completed in May 2008, at a reported cost of US $21.5m. In March 2009 LIAT began scheduled flights from Grenada and Barbados to Canouan. Mustique island has a landing strip for light aircraft only. Construction of an international airport at Argyle, 13 miles east of Kingstown, began in 2008 and was due to be completed in 2011. The cost of the project was estimated at EC $589m. Cuba, Taiwan, Iran and Venezuela were committed to providing funding for the project, and several other countries had been approached for assistance.

American Eagle: POB 1232, E. T. Joshua Airport, Arnos Vale; tel. 456-5555; fax 456-5616.

Leeward Islands Air Transport (LIAT): tel. 456-6333; fax 456-6111; e-mail pattersond@liatairline.com; internet www.liatairline.com; f. 2009; Station Man. DOMINIQUE PATTERSON; CEO MARK DARBY.

Mustique Airways: POB 1232, E. T. Joshua Airport, Arnos Vale; tel. 458-4380; fax 456-4586; e-mail info@mustique.com; internet www.mustique.com; f. 1979; charter and scheduled flights; Chair. JONATHAN PALMER.

Saint Vincent and the Grenadines Air Ltd (SVG Air): POB 39, Arnos Vale; tel. 457-5124; fax 457-5077; e-mail info@svgair.com; internet www.svgair.com; f. 1990; charter and scheduled flights; CEO MARTIN BARNARD.

Tourism

The island chain of the Grenadines is the country's main tourism asset. There are superior yachting facilities, but the lack of major air links with countries outside the region has resulted in a relatively slow development for tourism. In 2009 Saint Vincent and the Grenadines received 163,340 cruise ship passengers and 72,632 stop-over tourists. Tourism receipts totalled EC $236.4m. in 2009, which represented a decline of 20.4% compared with 2007. In early 2008 the Government announced it would invest €5m. in a Tourism Development Project. The plan would involve an upgrade of tourism and airport facilities.

Department of Tourism: Cruise Ship Terminal, Upper Bay St, POB 834, Kingstown; tel. 457-1502; fax 451-2425; e-mail tourism@caribsurf.com; internet www.svgtourism.com; CEO YVONNE ARMOUR-SHILLINGFORD.

Saint Vincent and the Grenadines Hotel and Tourism Association (SVGHTA): E. T. Joshua International Airport, Arnos Vale; tel. 458-4379; fax 456-4456; e-mail office@svghotels.com; internet www.svghotels.com; f. 1968 as Saint Vincent Hotel Asscn; renamed as above in 1999; non-profit org.; mem. of the Caribbean Hotels Asscn; Pres. LEROY LEWIS; Exec. Dir DAWN SMITH; 71 mems.

Defence

Saint Vincent and the Grenadines participates in the US-sponsored Regional Security System, comprising police, coastguards and army units, which was established by independent Eastern Caribbean states in 1982. Since 1984, however, the paramilitary Special Service Unit has had strictly limited deployment. The recurrent budget for 2008 allocated some 10.3% of total expenditure (projected at EC $423m.) for defence purposes.

Education

Free primary education, beginning at five years of age and lasting for seven years, is available to all children in government schools, although it is not compulsory and attendance is low. There are 61 government, and five private, primary schools. Secondary education, beginning at 12 years of age, comprises a first cycle of five years and a second, two-year cycle. However, government facilities at this level are limited, and much secondary education is provided in schools administered by religious organizations, with government assistance. There are also a number of junior secondary schools. Enrolment at primary schools during the 2008/09 academic year included 95% of children in the relevant age-group, while comparable enrolment in secondary schools in 2007/08 included 90% of pupils. There is a teacher-training college and a technical college. Total budgetary expenditure on education by the central Government was a projected EC $126.5m. in 2008 (17% of the total budget). The Government announced in 2005 that it had achieved its objective of instituting universal secondary education.

SOUTH GEORGIA AND THE SOUTH SANDWICH ISLANDS

South Georgia, an island of 3,592 sq km (1,387 sq miles), lies in the South Atlantic Ocean, about 1,300 km (800 miles) east-south-east of the Falkland Islands. The South Sandwich Islands, which have an area of 311 sq km, lie about 750 km south-east of South Georgia.

The United Kingdom annexed South Georgia and the South Sandwich Islands in 1775. With a segment of the Antarctic mainland and other nearby islands (now the British Antarctic Territory), they were constituted as the Falkland Islands Dependencies in 1908. Argentina made formal claim to South Georgia in 1927, and to the South Sandwich Islands in 1948. In 1955 the United Kingdom unilaterally submitted the dispute over sovereignty to the International Court of Justice (based in the Netherlands), which decided not to hear the application in view of Argentina's refusal to submit to the Court's jurisdiction. South Georgia was the site of a British Antarctic Survey base (staffed by 22 scientists and support personnel) until it was invaded in April 1982 by Argentine forces, who occupied the island until its recapture by British forces three weeks later. The South Sandwich Islands were uninhabited until the occupation of Southern Thule in December 1976 by about 50 Argentines, reported to be scientists. Argentine personnel remained until removed by British forces in June 1982.

Under the provisions of the South Georgia and South Sandwich Islands Order of 1985, the islands ceased to be governed as dependencies of the Falkland Islands on 3 October 1985. The Governor of the Falkland Islands is, ex officio, Commissioner for the territory.

In May 1993, in response to the Argentine Government's decision to commence the sale of fishing licences for the region's waters, the British Government announced an extension, from 12 to 200 nautical miles, of its territorial jurisdiction in the waters surrounding the islands, in order to conserve crucial fishing stocks.

In September 1998 the British Government announced that it would withdraw its military detachment from South Georgia in 2000, while it would increase its scientific presence on the island with the installation of a permanent team from the British Antarctic Survey to investigate the fisheries around the island for possible exploitation. The small military detachment finally withdrew in March 2001. The British garrison stationed in the Falkland Islands would remain responsible for the security of South Georgia and the South Sandwich Islands.

Increased volcanic activity on Montagu Island, in the South Sandwich Islands, previously thought to be dormant, had been monitored closely by the British Antarctic Survey since 2001. In late 2005 Mount Belinda erupted, adding some 50 acres to the island's land area in just one month. The island is largely ice-covered and the eruption allowed scientists the rare opportunity to make direct observations of volcanic activity under ice sheets.

Budget revenue for 2008 amounted to £6.0m., while expenditure totalled £4.7m. The main sources of revenue are the sale of fishing licences £4.1m.), incomes from visitor landing charges (£1.0m.), customs and harbour duties, and philatelic and commemorative coin sales.

At the close of the 2007/08 cruise ship season on 31 March 2008, South Georgia had recorded a total of 64 ship calls and some 8,000 passengers to the island. Greater numbers of visitors to this inhospitable territory—coupled with a growing recognition of the climate change phenomenon—prompted the Government to review its existing biosecurity policy in an effort to prevent the introduction, or translocation, of potentially destructive species of flora and fauna to the island. Furthermore, a major legislative review was begun in 2008, as a result of which the Government expected to implement changes to legislation governing tourism and visitor management.

The British Antarctic Survey maintains two research stations on South Georgia, at King Edward Point (winter personnel 8, summer personnel 12 in 2008/09) and Bird Island (winter personnel 4, summer personnel 10 in 2008/09). In 2008/09 there were eight personnel wintering at King Edward Point and four at Bird Island; summer personnel at the two bases and the Signy research station in the South Orkney Islands amounted to 38.

Commissioner: Alan Huckle (took office on 25 August 2006).

Commissioner-designate: Nigel Haywood (scheduled to take office in Sept. 2010).

Senior Executive Officer and Director of Fisheries: Dr Martin Collins (Stanley, Falkland Islands).

SURINAME

Geography

PHYSICAL FEATURES

The Republic of Suriname is on the north coast of South America and is the smallest country on the continent. Until independence in 1975 Suriname (usually rendered Surinam in English) was known as Dutch or Netherlands Guiana, and it is flanked by the smaller territory of French Guiana (part of France) on the east and Guyana (formerly British Guiana) on the west. Brazil lies beyond a 597-km (371-mile) border in the south. The Atlantic coast is 386 km in extent, while the border with French Guiana is 510 km and that with Guyana is 600 km. However, Suriname disputes the current course of the western and eastern borders and maintains territorial claims on its neighbours on the Guianese coast. Suriname claims part of south-western French Guiana, between the Itany (Litani—the current border) and the Marowijne (Marouini) rivers. In the west, the country claims territory in south-eastern Guyana as far as the New River and not along the current upper reach of the Corantijn (Courantyne) used as a border (Koetari or Kutari). The country covers an area of 163,820 sq km (63,251 sq miles).

The north of Suriname consists of a typically Guianan coastal strip, with rich, alluvial soil made usable and habitable by extensive dykes and irrigation systems. These plains can be as much as 2 m below sea level, so, where not protected or reclaimed, the coastlands tend to be swampy mangrove country. The Atlantic littoral, up to 80 km in width, accounts for about 16% of the country, and is where most of the population lives. Between the plains and the densely forested interior is an intermediate plateau with a landscape alternating tracts of savannah with dunes or woodland. This gives way to a more solid forest cover, a region that accounts for about three-quarters of the country, as rolling hills climb into more mountainous terrain. The highlands of the forest region rear relatively abruptly once away from the coastal belt and its immediate hinterland, so that the country's highest point, at Juliana Top (1,230 m or 4,037 ft) is located near the centre of Suriname. The mountain is just beyond the north end of the Eilerts de Haan Gebergste (a ridge thrusting up from the south and marking off the south-west) and to the west of the Wilhelmina Gebergste; the main range of the south-east is the Oranje Gebergste. Much of this territory is dense tropical rainforest, which hosts a considerable diversity of flora and fauna (although deforestation and the pollution from small-scale mining threaten the environment—the country's timber and mineral reserves, notably bauxite, are the most lucrative natural resources). The discovery of 24 previously undocumented species of fauna—including a frog with fluorescent purple markings and a number of other amphibians, insects and fish—announced in June 2007, foregrounded the importance of Suriname as a rare example of untouched tropical rainforest. The international scientific community strenuously promoted the protection of such regions, and urged a halt to illegal mining activities which jeopardized the security of these species' natural habitat. Finally, in the far south-west, there is a region of high savannah. This entire landscape is laced with numerous rivers, some feeding large reservoirs. For instance, the Professor W. J. van Blommestein Meer, in the north-east, on the edge of the forested region, is one of the largest reservoirs in the world. Dams contain a number of other lakes, and inland waters cover 1,800 sq km of the country's territory. The main rivers, apart from the Corantijn (700 km in length—most of it marking the border with Guyana) and the Marowijne (720 km—also defining much of a border, but with French Guiana, and including its upper reaches, such as the Lawa and its tributaries), are the Suriname, the Coppename, and the Saramacca.

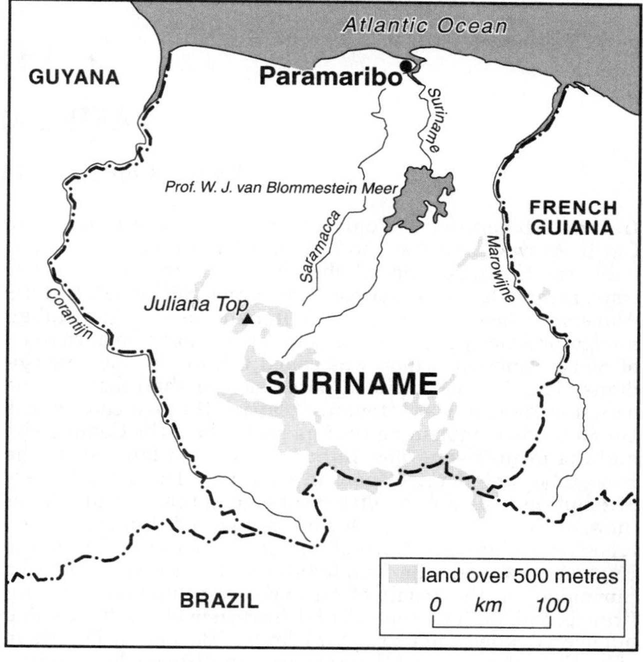

CLIMATE

Suriname experiences high rainfall, humidity and temperatures, although its tropical climate is tempered by the Atlantic trade winds. There are two wet seasons, April–August and November–February, although neither wet nor dry seasons are absolute. The average annual precipitation in Paramaribo, the capital, which is on the coast, is over 2,200 mm (86 ins). Inland, rainfall is more like 1,500 mm per year. Average temperatures range between 23°C and 32°C (73°F–90°F), but there is little seasonal variation.

POPULATION

Suriname is one of the most racially diverse countries in the Americas or, indeed, in the world. Recent estimates put the 'Hindustani' (descendants of indentured workers brought from the Indian subcontinent in the 19th century, generally referred to as 'East' Indians in the Caribbean) population at 37% of the total, Creoles (of black and mixed-black descent) 31%, the Indonesian-descended 'Javanese' 15%, the predominantly black Boschnegers (Bush Negroes or Maroons—descendants of slaves who escaped into freedom in the mountainous interior in the 17th and 18th centuries, preserving more of their African heritage than the Creoles) 10%, indigenous Amerindians 3%, Chinese 2% and whites 1%. Dutch is the official language for all these groups, but many others are also still spoken—not only a Hindi dialect (known as Hindustani—Sarnami Hindi) and Javanese, but also some English-based Creoles, the main dialect being known as Sranan Tongo or Taki-Taki (Djukka and Saramaccan are others); English itself is widely known in the cities or among the better educated. The cosmopolitan nature of Surinamese society is also seen in the country's variety of religious affiliations—while in 2004 just under one-half the people were Christian (the largest denominations were the Roman Catholics, with 25% of the population, and the Moravian Brethren, with 15%, followed by the Dutch Reformed and other Protestants), 24% are Hindu and 16% Muslim. Others practise native or adapted African tribal beliefs, although these are often not considered incompatible with more orthodox faiths.

Most of the population live on the coast and about 65% are classed as urban, with somewhere between one-third and one-half in or around the capital city. Creoles tend to dominate the urban areas and Hindustanis the countryside. However, over recent decades many people have emigrated to the Netherlands. The total population was estimated at 524,345 in mid-2010. Paramaribo, the country's only major urban area, its main seaport and the national capital, is east of centre on the coast, in the north of Suriname. There are 10 districts.

History

JAMES MCDONOUGH

Revised for this edition by the editorial staff

In the 15th century the only inhabitants of Suriname were Carib, Arawak and Awarao Indians (Amerindians). Another tribe, the Surinas, who inhabited the country at an earlier time, is considered the source of the name Suriname. In 1499 Alonso de Ojeada, a Spanish lieutenant serving the Italian navigator Amerigo Vespucci, landed on the north-eastern coast of South America, which was called Guiana by the Amerindians. The Spanish claimed possession of the coast, but no actual settlement was attempted. During the next century the Dutch began establishing trading posts along the Commewijn and Corantijn rivers (now in Suriname), and later along the Essequibo and Berbice (now in Guyana). The French were attempting to establish settlements along the Cayenne River (now in French Guiana). During this period, lumbering and tobacco farming were the chief commercial activities. It was the English, however, who founded the first successful colony in Suriname, as the result of an expedition financed by Lord Francis Willoughby, the colonial Governor of the flourishing but overcrowded English sugar island of Barbados. The group of English planters and their slaves established a large settlement on the Suriname River, near what is now Paramaribo. The British Crown ceded its Suriname colony to the Netherlands in the Treaty of Breda (1667), in exchange for the colony of Nieuw Amsterdam (now New York, USA). The colony remained under Dutch rule for the next 300 years, except for two brief periods of British control in 1799–1802 and 1804–14, during the Napoleonic wars.

The territory became known as Dutch Guiana, and was flanked to the west by British Guiana (now Guyana) and to the east by French Guiana. The colony was administered by a Governor, with the assistance of the Political Council, the members of which were appointed by the Governor, following nomination by the colonial planter class. In 1828 the administration of all Dutch West Indies colonies was centralized under a Governor-General, stationed in Suriname, who reported directly to the Colonial Office in the Netherlands. During this early period the colony flourished on the basis of large, Dutch-owned sugar plantations, worked by African slave labour. Between 1650 and 1820 some 300,000 West African slaves were brought into Suriname. Nevertheless, the plantations suffered a continual labour drain owing to escaping slaves, who would seek refuge from the authorities in the vast and underdeveloped interior of the country. By 1728 these runaway slaves, known as 'Boschnegers' (Bush Negroes) or maroons, had established a number of settlements based on African tribal customs and were warring with the white plantation owners and the colonial authorities. Expeditions were sent into the jungle to subdue them, but without success. Finally, in 1761 the Dutch signed a treaty with the Boschnegers, guaranteeing their liberty and supplying them with yearly shipments of arms. In return, the Boschnegers promised to return all future runaway slaves and never to appear in Paramaribo in armed groups of more than six persons. From that time, the Boschnegers led an isolated, independent life in the Suriname interior.

The abolition of slavery in neighbouring British Guiana in 1834 and in French Guiana in 1848 produced a period of unrest among Suriname's slaves. These events led King William III of the Netherlands finally to abolish slavery in 1863. To solve the problem of labour shortage created by the abolition of slavery, the Dutch turned to overseas contract or indentured labour. Between 1873 and 1917 some 37,000 indentured labourers were brought to Suriname from India. A similar influx of contract labourers, numbering about 33,000, were brought from the Dutch East Indies (now Indonesia) between 1893 and 1939. Furthermore, the Dutch encouraged the immigration of Chinese, Portuguese and, later, Lebanese workers. Suriname's ethnic and racial make-up reflected the plantation colony's historic need for cheap labour. The census in 1980 recorded that 34.7% of Suriname's population were Creole (urban dwellers of African descent), 33.5% were of Indian descent (known locally as Hindustani), 16.3% were Indonesian-descended 'Javanese', 9.6% Boschneger, 3.1% Amerindian and 1.6% Chinese. The country also had European and other minorities, amounting to about 1.3% of the population. Suriname comprised seven different ethnic groups, speaking more than 15 languages. It was the most fragmented country in the Latin American and Caribbean region and among the 20 most fragmented countries in the world. This ethnic fragmentation also existed in the political arena, where the majority of political parties were organized along ethnic lines.

INDEPENDENCE AND POLITICAL DEVELOPMENT

In 1866 the Koloniale Staten (Colonial Assembly, also known as the Staten van Suriname), was established. A representative body with limited local power, its members were elected from a small group of colonial planters, who were extended the franchise on the basis of a poll tax. While ultimate power continued to reside in the Netherlands, the Koloniale Staten remained the principal administrative body in Suriname until the colony gained independence. In the 20th century the exploitation of Suriname's large bauxite reserves and the cultivation of rice replaced sugar as the principal foreign exchange earner, although the Dutch Government found it necessary to subsidize an ever-increasing share of the colony's budget. In 1950 the Dutch Government granted Suriname internal self-government. Then in 1954 Suriname became an overseas territory of the Dutch 'Tripartite Kingdom', composed of the Netherlands, the Netherlands Antilles (now the Netherlands Antilles and Aruba) and Suriname. Full and complete independence was granted to Suriname by the Dutch on 25 November 1975.

Local political parties began forming during the Second World War, at the time of the promise of local autonomy. Further political participation was stimulated by the introduction of universal suffrage for the general election of 1949. The Nationale Partij Suriname (NPS—Suriname National Party), representing the country's Creole population, won the majority of the seats in the Koloniale Staten, under the leadership of Johan Pengel. During the 1950s the Verenigde Hindostaanse Partij (VHP—United Hindustani Party), representing the Hindustani population, gained prominence under the leadership of Jaggernath Lachmon. The NPS and VHP formed an alliance during the 1960s, which gave Suriname a long period of stability under the principle of ethnic *verbroedering* (fraternization). In the 1973 general election the NPS formed the Nationale Partij Kombinatie (NPK—Combined National Party) alliance with three other parties and won 22 of 39 seats in the Koloniale Staten. Henck Arron, who had replaced Pengel as party leader upon the latter's death in 1970, was named Prime Minister and was in power when the country gained independence in 1975.

Dutch aid, worth 3,500m. guilders, gave considerable support to the economy of the new republic. However, the international economic recession of the mid-1970s, brought on by the petroleum crisis, and the fall of the world price of bauxite, caused growing concern that Suriname would be unable to promote economic development, despite the country's large natural resources and relatively small population. Moreover, more than 40,000 persons, mostly the well-educated and well-trained, emigrated to the Netherlands on the eve of independence, in order to qualify for Dutch citizenship. A series of strikes underlined the growing dissatisfaction of the people, while corruption scandals involving cabinet ministers undermined the Government. Nevertheless, in the general election of 1977, the NPK again won 22 seats, with the remaining 17 seats going to a left-wing opposition front, led by Lachmon and the VHP.

MILITARY TAKE-OVER, 1980–87

On 25 February 1980 the Armed Forces took control of government in a *coup d'état*. The coup followed the civilian Government's refusal to recognize demands of members of the military to form a trade union. The take-over was led by a junior army officer, Sgt-Maj. (later Lt-Col) Desiré (Desi) Bouterse, who seized power in alliance with the left-wing Partij Nationalistiche Republiek (PNR—Nationalist Republican Party). Dr Henk Chin-A-Sen, a PNR leader, was chosen as Prime Minister, presiding over a PNR-assembled Government and the eight-member Nationale Militaire Raad (NMR—National Military Council) named by Bouterse. In August 1980, following a disagreement over policy, Bouterse strengthened his control over the Government by dissolving the legislature and declaring a state of emergency. In March 1981 Sgt-Maj. Wilfred Hawker led an unsuccessful Hindustani-inspired, right-wing coup against Bouterse. In December Bouterse launched the Revolutionaire Volksfront (Revolutionary People's Front) and in February 1982 Chin-A-Sen, who earlier had been named President, was dismissed along with his civilian Government. In March a second coup attempt by Sgt-Maj. Hawker failed, resulting in his execution.

As a result of the coup attempt, Bouterse declared a state of siege and imposed martial law. However, to prevent the Netherlands from suspending aid under the terms of the independence treaty, the military regime appointed a 12-member Council of Ministers with a civilian majority, and Henry Neyhorst, a moderate economist, became Prime Minister. The failure to solve Suriname's economic difficulties lost Bouterse the support of the left-wing groups and the trade unions, and soon the country was plagued by strikes, demonstrations, and calls for an end to military rule. Bouterse promised to hold elections for a constituent assembly to draft a new constitution. On 8 December 1982 members of the armed forces burned down Paramaribo offices of the Bouterse opposition. In the ensuing disturbances some 15 leading politicians, trade unionists, lawyers, journalists and academics were killed, in what became known as the 'December Murders'.

In response to the December Murders, the Dutch Government suspended its large aid programme to the country. The USA and the European Union (EU—then known as the European Community) immediately followed suit and the Council of Ministers resigned. Bouterse, however, retained the loyalty of the 3,000-man military by dismissing two-thirds of the officer corps. In February 1983 he formed a new civilian-military Council of Ministers, with Dr Errol Alibux (a former Minister of Social Affairs) as Prime Minister. The new Government was composed of two left-wing parties, the Progressieve Arbeiders en Landbouwers Unie (PALU—Progressive Workers' and Farm Labourers' Union) and the Revolutionaire Volkspartij (Revolutionary People's Party).

In foreign affairs, the Bouterse Government followed a non-alignment policy, establishing close relations with Cuba and Libya, to balance the historically close links with the USA and the Netherlands. These moves alarmed both the French and the US authorities. The French saw potential danger to its Kourou space centre, the launching site for the European Ariane rocket, which was located close to the Surinamese border in French Guiana. The USA, determined to stop the spread of 'Communist' governments in the western hemisphere, was very wary of Suriname's growing ties with Cuba and the large presence of Cuban advisers in the country. George Schultz, former US Secretary of State under President Ronald Reagan (1981–89), revealed in a 1993 memoir that the US Administration had been ready to intervene militarily as a result of the 1982 December Murders; however, US plans for the military overthrow of the Bouterse regime were abandoned after the Netherlands refused to participate.

CIVILIAN RESTORATION

In August 1984 the state of emergency imposed in 1982 was lifted, as the military Government began to move the country towards civilian rule. In December 1984 plans were announced for the formation of a supreme deliberating council, the Topberaad, consisting of representatives of the trade unions, the business sector and Standvaste, a new movement Bouterse had established in November 1983 as a political power base. The Topberaad met in January 1985, with the main task of drafting a new constitution. In March 1987 a draft document consisting of some 186 articles was completed. The Constitution was approved by referendum in September of that year, and a general election was held in November, for the first time in eight years.

In July 1987 Standvaste was reconstituted as the Nationale Democratische Partij (NDP—National Democratic Party), under the leadership of Jules Wijdenbosch. Wijdenbosch was Prime Minister in the last Bouterse-appointed Cabinet of Ministers prior to the November election. In August the three major opposition parties, the Creole NPS, the Hindustani VHP and the Kaum-Tani Persuatan Indonesia (KTPI—Javanese Indonesian Farmers' Union), formed an electoral alliance, the Front voor Demokratie en Ontwikkeling (FDO—Front for Democracy and Development). With the restoration of electoral politics Suriname's ethnic parties, which had dominated the political scene prior to the 1980 military coup, returned to prominence. At the November election the FDO won a decisive victory, taking 40 seats in the new 51-seat National Assembly, with the PALU, the Progressieve Bosneger Partij (PBP—Progressive Boschneger Party) and the NDP sharing out the remaining seats. The National Assembly took over political control in January 1988 and unanimously elected Ramsewak Shankar of the VHP to the presidency. Henck Arron of the NPS was elected Vice-President and Prime Minister, heading a 14-member Cabinet of Ministers.

THE BOSCHNEGER REVOLT

The return to constitutional rule did not end Suriname's internal conflicts. From 1986 the military was fighting against a Boschneger insurgency in the interior of the country, which threatened the successful move to constitutional government. The insurgency was led by Ronnie Brunswijk, a Boschneger who was once a member of the presidential bodyguard. He claimed that plans to develop the interior of the country violated the autonomy of the Boschneger society, which had been guaranteed by the 1761 treaty and subsequent agreements signed between the Boschneger and the colonial Dutch. In 1987 Brunswijk's Surinamese Liberation Army (SLA—popularly known as the Jungle Commando) attacked economic targets, causing severe disruption, including the closure of the main bauxite smelting and refining plants.

Bouterse retaliated against the insurgency with raids into the interior; the rebels claimed that the army massacred Boschnegers in several interior villages. The army also moved to arm about 1,000 Amerindians, leading to armed clashes between the Boschneger and the Tucayana Amerindians. As a result of the fighting, some 10,000 Boschnegers took refuge in French Guiana and the French reinforced the border with Suriname with paratroopers and legionnaires, refusing to let the Suriname military pursue the insurgents across the border.

In June 1988 negotiations began between the Government and representatives of the SLA. Bouterse's willingness to negotiate was attributed by many to the announcement that there would be an amnesty for personnel from both sides involved in the conflict, which the SLA claimed would prevent investigation of alleged abuses of human rights by the army. Nevertheless, in July 1989 the SLA and the Suriname Government signed a peace accord at Kourou, French Guiana. The provisions of the so-called Kourou Accord included a general amnesty for those involved in the conflict, the ending of the state of emergency established in December 1986, the incorporation of members of the SLA into the national police and measures to provide for the safe return of the Surinamese refugees in French Guiana. However, the Accord failed when Bouterse vetoed the clause demanding the integration of Brunswijk's fighting force into the national police, and the Amerindians refused to abide by its terms. In addition, the Boschneger refugees refused to move back to Suriname, fearing reprisals by either the army or the Amerindians once they left the protection of French territory.

The Kourou Accord included proposals for a Consultative Council for the Development of the Interior. Much of the interior's infrastructure had been destroyed and development suspended during the insurgency. The Council was finally appointed in 1995. However, the Government failed to consult the Boschneger and Amerindian representatives about the granting of gold and timber concessions on their land. These communities were concerned about the impact of mining activity on their way of life and, in particular, about the damaging effects on the food chain by the gold miners' widespread use of mercury.

THE MILITARY INTERREGNUM

In 1990 the US Department of State noted, in its annual report to the US Congress on human rights, that the Surinamese military had 're-established itself as the dominant political force in the country'. Only a few of the 120 new laws required to implement the Constitution had been passed by the Assembly, and the Constitutional Court, which was to interpret the Constitution and rule on human rights issues, had not been established. Moreover, the Government had not taken steps to deprive the military of such powers as the investigation and detention of civilians, the issue of visas and the supervision of customs and immigration at airports and harbours. Of concern to the USA was the growing military involvement in the international trafficking of illicit drugs. Western intelligence sources reported that Suriname had become a major centre of the illegal drugs trade, serving as a transshipment point for increasing quantities of cocaine intended for Europe and the USA. The country also served as a transshipment point for the sale of illegal arms to the Colombian drugs cartels. Sources in the USA and in Suriname alleged that Bouterse and the army were behind the illegal trade in drugs and arms.

In early 1990 President Shankar's Government renewed contacts with the SLA, following the failure of the Kourou Accord. With a presidential guarantee of safety, Ronnie Brunswijk travelled to Paramaribo to negotiate. However, Bouterse violated the guarantee and arrested Brunswijk. Although Brunswijk was later released on the insistence of President Shankar, the action of the military showed the weakness of the civilian Government and eventually led to its downfall. On 24 December the military overthrew the Shankar Government and installed leaders of the NDP in the executive. Jules Wijdenbosch held the posts of Vice-President, Prime Minister and Minister of Finance until the elections of May 1991. In August 1992 the new administration signed an accord with the SLA, finally ending the insurgency. The former rebels recognized the Government's authority over the entire country, while the Government promised to honour the rights of the Boschnegers, including their right to engage in gold prospecting and forestry, and to join the army. Nevertheless, in March 2005 former guerrillas claimed that the Government had not fulfilled its pledge to provide them with jobs and medical care, and in April 2007 peaceful demonstrations were staged outside the National Assembly in continuing protest at the Government's perceived failure to implement the provisions agreed under the 1992 accord.

THE FIRST VENETIAAN GOVERNMENT

A general election was held on 25 May 1991, monitored by a delegation from the Organization of American States (OAS). The Nieuw Front coalition (NF—New Front, formerly the FDO), consisting of the dominant NPS, the VHP, the KTPI and the Surinaamse Partij van de Arbeid (SPA—Suriname Labour Party), won a majority of seats in parliament. The NPS leader, Runaldo Ronald Venetiaan, was elected President and Jules Adjodhia, Prime Minister.

In March 1992 the Government requested that the National Assembly remove references in the Constitution that allowed the army to act in a way that contravened the proper democratic functioning of the State. The action to curb the military was taken as a measure designed to improve relations with the Netherlands, Suriname's main international benefactor. With the restoration of democracy in 1987, the Dutch Government had renewed aid to Suriname, but under more restrictive conditions than those imposed at the time of independence. In 1990 some US $700m., which had accumulated over the period of outright military control, had yet to be disbursed by the Netherlands. In 1992 the Netherlands agreed to renew economic assistance, but required the Surinamese Government to implement the IMF's structural adjustment programme, a stringent monetary policy that included reduced public spending, increased taxes and the removal of food and fuel subsidies. The structural adjustment programme, implemented in 1994, proved highly successful and by 1995 the depreciation of the Suriname guilder had been halted and Central Bank reserves had reached a healthy $100m. However, the economic reforms caused widespread hardship and the Government became increasingly unpopular.

THE WIJDENBOSCH GOVERNMENT

The results of the elections to the National Assembly, held on 23 May 1996, represented a reverse for the ruling NF, winning, as it did, fewer seats than in 1991, while Bouterse's NDP increased its legislative representation. The election was also important because Amerindians were elected to the Assembly for the first time. In an attempt to secure broader support, the NDP chose Jules Wijdenbosch, instead of Bouterse, as its candidate to contest the presidency. In the National Assembly's first vote for President, Venetiaan gained more support than Wijdenbosch, but not the two-thirds' majority necessary to win the election outright. Responsibility for electing the President then passed to the United People's Assembly (Vereinigde Volksvergadering), a body comprising national, regional and local representatives. With only a simple majority required, Wijdenbosch was elected President. He was inaugurated in September. The NF alliance disintegrated, with the VHP and the KTPI joining an NDP-led coalition, on condition that Bouterse should not hold office in the new administration. The new coalition Government, appointed later that month, comprised representatives of four different political groupings.

The Wijdenbosch Government soon became characterized by internal political crisis and increasing pressure from diverse opposition groups. In August 1997 the dismissal of the finance minister, Motilal Mungra, following his outspoken criticism of the President's extravagant use of public funds prompted Mungra's Beweging voor Vernieuwing en Democratie (BVD—Movement for Renewal and Democracy) and two other small parties to announce their withdrawal from the governing coalition. Wijdenbosch managed to secure sufficient support to maintain his Government's parliamentary majority. However, the Government's instability was apparent. President Wijdenbosch also drew accusations of political corruption when he revealed, under considerable pressure from local and international human rights groups, that a five-member committee, appointed to investigate past human rights abuses, in particular the 1982 December Murders, was being led by a former Bouterse lawyer. Moreover, the Government's mismanagement of the economy caused increasing public unrest during 1998 and widespread industrial action took place in June demanding the resignation of the Government in favour of a non-political administration.

THE RE-ELECTION OF VENETIAAN

In early 1999 the economic situation became extremely grave, with spiralling inflation caused by an ever-widening budget deficit and a decline in the international price of bauxite, by far Suriname's most important source of foreign exchange earnings. The Dutch Government continued to withhold the US $300m. in aid that had accumulated after it suspended payments in 1998, stating that the beneficial use of the funds by the Surinamese Government could not be assured. Under pressure from the Netherlands, in April 1999 President Wijdenbosch dismissed Bouterse, a precursor to his dismissal of his entire Cabinet of Ministers in the following month in an attempt to avoid demands for his own resignation. However, on 31 May some 30,000 protesters gathered in Paramaribo to demand President Wijdenbosch's removal, while a general strike paralysed the country. On 1 June the National Assembly passed a vote of no confidence in the Government by 27 votes to 14 (with 10 abstentions). The vote, however, fell short of the two-thirds' majority needed to remove the President from office. President Wijdenbosch refused to resign, but did agree to hold new elections on 25 May 2000, one year earlier than was constitutionally required.

In the election of 25 May 2000 the NF, led by Venetiaan, secured a majority of seats in the National Assembly. Bouterse, as an NDP candidate, won a seat in the National Assembly, even as a Dutch appeals court upheld an earlier drugs-trafficking conviction (see below). As the NF narrowly failed to win the two-thirds' majority to appoint a new President directly, it immediately began coalition negotiations with smaller parties. Following the conclusion of these negotiations, on 4 August Venetiaan was elected to the presidency.

In its electoral campaign, the NF had pledged to revitalize the faltering economy; soon after taking office, the new administration instituted a series of economic reforms aimed at reversing the failed economic policies of the Wijdenbosch administration. However, while the Venetiaan administration made progress in stabilizing the economy, tensions within the coalition and the impatience of the populace impeded its efforts.

DECEMBER MURDERS INVESTIGATION

Following the election of Venetiaan, there were calls for the new Government to investigate the December Murders, before the 18-year statute of limitations expired in December 2000. In October the country's highest court, the Court of Justice, began hearings on the December Murders, in response to a request by relatives of the victims. Following an order from the Court of Justice, an examining judge called for a full investigation into the Murders, including the involvement of 36 individuals. In addition, in late 2002 the Court ordered the exhumation of the remains of 15 of the murder victims. A series of burglaries at the homes of the Minister of Justice and a leading judge in April 2003 were thought to be connected to the investigation. In December 2004, following a four-year investigation, a military court indicted Bouterse and 25 other suspects for the December Murders.

Requests from the opposition NDP that an amnesty be offered in respect of the December Murders, by means of an extension to existing legislation exempting from prosecution perpetrators of crimes committed during the 1985–92 military conflict, were formally submitted for consideration by parliament in April 2007. (The party contended that the current Amnesty Act compromised the national unity and future development of Suriname by applying to such an exclusive period.) The President of the Pertijajah Luhur (PL—Full Confidence Party) component of the ruling NF coalition, Paul Somohardjo, declared that his party was in favour of a public referendum on the matter, eliciting strong criticism from fellow coalition members who accused Somohardjo of political opportunism. It was speculated that the PL leader's concession to the controversial amnesty debate, and perceived sympathy with the NDP's proposal, represented a possible intention to ally with the opposition party in the event that the coalition was disbanded. However, discussions on the matter appeared to have closed in June when a local court ruled that 10 of the 26 defendants who had been pursuing appeals to be exempted from trial would face prosecution together with the remaining suspects, now numbering 15 since the acquittal of former Minister of Justice Ivan Graanoogst during the same proceedings. At a preliminary hearing of the military tribunal on 30 November 2007, the judge rejected an appeal by Bouterse's lawyer that, as a former head of state, his client was entitled to stand trial in a civilian court. However, the lawyer did successfully challenge the impartiality of the judge in July 2008, as a result of which the trial was suspended indefinitely. Bouterse's lawyer proceeded to seek a court order to prohibit further media coverage of the trial, claiming that there was a 'deep animosity' between the media and his client.

Meanwhile, in August 2005 the OAS's Inter-American Court of Human Rights instructed the Government to investigate a massacre that occurred in the Maroon village of Moiwana in 1986, during Bouterse's presidency, to pay US $13,000 in compensation to the 130 survivors and to establish a $1.2m. development fund for the region. President Venetiaan formally apologized for the massacre at a ceremony in Moengo in July 2006.

THE 2005 ELECTIONS

In March 2005, in advance of the indirect presidential ballot in June that was to follow the legislative election in May, the NDP formally nominated Bouterse as its candidate. The nomination prompted the USA to threaten to sever diplomatic relations with Suriname in the event of Bouterse being re-elected President. The other main contenders for the presidency were former President Jules Wijdenbosch of the Democratisch Nationaal Platform 2000 (DNP 2000—National Democratic Platform 2000) and the incumbent, Venetiaan, who was seeking a third term in office. At the legislative election of 25 May, in which some 74% of the electorate participated, the NF, which enjoyed the support of the Governments of the Netherlands and the USA, retained its position as the largest party in the National Assembly, securing 23 of the 51 seats and 39.4% of the total votes cast. However, this was 10 seats fewer than in the previous legislature. The NDP performed well, obtaining 15 seats and 22.2% of the votes, while the Volksalliantie Voor Vooruitgang (VVV)—an alliance forged by the DNP 2000—secured just five seats and 13.8% of the votes cast. The A-Combinatie, a coalition including the Algemene Bevrijdings- en Ontwikkelingspartij, led by former guerrilla leader Ronnie Brunswijk, also secured five seats (7.2%), while the A1, a pro-business grouping containing the Democratisch Alternatief 1991, the Democraten van de 21 and the Politieke Vleugel van de FAL obtained the remaining three seats (5.9%).

The major parties subsequently entered into negotiations to form alliances with smaller groupings in an attempt to garner the two-thirds' parliamentary majority needed directly to appoint a presidential nominee. Bouterse and Brunswijk were both elected to the National Assembly. (In January 2009 Bouterse was expelled from the legislature for persistent non-attendance.) However, in June 2005 Bouterse withdrew his presidential candidacy in favour of the NDP's vice-presidential candidate, Rabin Parmessar. At the first vote in the National Assembly no candidate garnered the requisite two-thirds' majority (34 votes); Venetiaan secured 27 votes and Parmessar obtained 20 votes. The second round was similarly unsuccessful, each candidate securing the same number of votes as previously. Responsibility for electing the new head of state subsequently passed to the 891-member United People's Assembly. With only a simple majority required, on 3 August Venetiaan won 560 votes, compared with 315 votes for Parmessar. Venetiaan was inaugurated for a third term in office in August.

VENETIAAN'S THIRD TERM IN OFFICE

The steep increases in petroleum prices, and, consequently, in transport costs, led to civil unrest in the latter half of 2005 and early 2006 when bus drivers and teachers initiated industrial action. Power shortages in the west of the country in February prompted further protests.

In January 2006 a Brazilian congressional investigation heard allegations that senior members of the Surinamese armed forces were involved in trading illegal weapons with

Brazilian drugs-traffickers. The following month the disappearance of 181 hand grenades and ammunition from an army facility near Paramaribo prompted an investigation that reportedly found evidence of illegal arms-trafficking between Guyana and Suriname. Six soldiers and 19 civilians were detained in Suriname in relation to the missing weapons. Four officers of the Surinamese army were arrested in May 2007 following the reported theft of seven hand grenades from the Stoelsmanseiland military post.

Venetiaan's Cabinet of Ministers underwent a number of changes during 2006 and early 2007, precipitated by numerous incidents of corruption and misconduct that threatened irretrievably to undermine the Government's integrity. In mid-January 2006 the Minister of Trade and Industry, Siegfried Gilds, resigned following accusations of money-laundering and membership of a criminal organization. (He was convicted of money-laundering charges in May 2009 and sentenced to 12 months' imprisonment.) Meanwhile, in March 2007 the Minister of Transport, Communications and Tourism, Alice H. Amafo, tendered her own resignation following allegations of financial misconduct related to an official expenses claim for her birthday celebrations (totalling US $13,000).

There was further evidence of civil unrest in late 2007 and early 2008 when workers from four different sectors staged strikes, causing disruption and drawing attention to their poor working conditions. Teachers, air traffic controllers, banana plant workers and bauxite workers all undertook industrial action in support of demands for salary increases.

Violent clashes between local residents and Brazilian mine-workers in the town of Albina in December 2009 highlighted the issue of ethnic tensions connected with the presence of large numbers of migrant workers in Suriname. An initial incident which resulted in the murder of a Surinamese national led to violence in which many people were injured and buildings and local businesses were set alight, leaving some 100 people homeless (most of whom were Brazilian, Chinese or Javanese).

THE RE-ELECTION OF BOUTERSE

A total of 20 parties, mostly grouped into coalitions, contested the general election on 25 May 2010. Former President Desi Bouterse formed the Megacombinatie (an alliance that included the NDP, Nieuw Suriname, PALU and the KTPI) to challenge the ruling NF alliance. At the election the Megacombinatie secured 23 of the 51 seats, the NF alliance secured 14, the A-Combinatie (headed by former rebel leader Ronnie Brunswijk) won seven and the Volksallientie (a grouping of smaller parties) won six. As no single group had secured the two-thirds' majority necessary to elect a President a period of intense negotiations followed. Initial attempts by the Megacombinatie to form an alliance with the A-Combinatie failed and the latter was reported to have joined forces with the NF and Volksallientie. However, A-Combinatie rejoined the Megacombinatie after striking a deal, in which the group was apparently promised three cabinet positions in any future government. On 19 July, therefore, and with the support of most of the smaller parties, Bouterse was elected President with the votes of 36 of the 51 members of the National Assembly. His election was greeted with dismay by his opponents and by many international commentators. Bouterse, who at the time of his election remained on trial for his role in the December Murders, was thought to be the first convicted drugs-trafficker to be elected to the presidency of any country in the region. The Dutch Government issued a statement to say that the former dictator would not be welcome in the Netherlands unless he had travelled there to serve his 11-year prison sentence (a penalty he had received but not served, owing to the absence of an extradition treaty between the two countries, *in absentia* following his conviction for drugs-trafficking in that country in 1999—see below).

INTERNATIONAL RELATIONS

Relations with the Government of the Netherlands deteriorated rapidly under President Wijdenbosch, principally owing to his administration's continued links with Bouterse. In 1997 the President appointed Bouterse an adviser to the Government of Suriname, a cabinet-level position, despite an ongoing investigation by the Dutch Government into drugs-trafficking allegations against the former dictator. In March 1999 the Dutch authorities began legal proceedings against Bouterse, and in July a Dutch court convicted Bouterse *in absentia* of leading a Surinamese cartel that had attempted to smuggle about two metric tons of cocaine seized at Dutch and Belgian ports and airports in 1989–97. Bouterse received a sentence of 16 years' imprisonment (later reduced to 11 years) and a US $2.2m. fine. The Dutch Government secured a warrant from the International Criminal Police Commission (Interpol) for Bouterse's arrest on drugs-trafficking charges with hopes of detaining him in a third country, since the Surinamese Constitution barred extradition of its nationals. The Attorney-General of the Netherlands filed further charges (this time for torture resulting in death) against Bouterse in January 2000. The new suit concerned the December Murders in 1982 and arose because of a complaint filed by relatives of the victims. As a result of the efforts shown by Venetiaan's Government to investigate the murders committed during the Bouterse military regime, in October 2000 the Dutch Government agreed to resume aid to Suriname, suspended since 1998.

In February 2001 President Venetiaan announced his intention to seek the amendment of an article in the Constitution that banned the extradition of Surinamese citizens to other countries for trial. Following a series of meetings in early 2002 between the Minister of Foreign Affairs, Marie Levens, and her Dutch counterpart, a Returned Emigration Committee was established to oversee the voluntary repatriation of Surinamese with Dutch nationality without the loss of social benefits. Proposals to make it easier for Dutch senior citizens to visit Suriname by ending temporary visa requirements for visitors over 60 years of age were also discussed. In May 2007 the Surinamese parliament voted unanimously to ratify the European Convention relating to the transfer of prisoners—which provides for the repatriation of convicted offenders to serve their sentences—so obviating the need for further bilateral agreements with EU member states, such as those previously signed with the Netherlands and the United Kingdom. Minister of Justice Chandrikapersad Santokhi advised that some 100 Surinamese citizens were detained in Dutch prisons at that time, while 84 foreign nationals were accommodated in Surinamese detention facilities; it was thought that, owing to better prison conditions afforded by European states, most convicted Europeans imprisoned in Suriname would apply for transfer under the Convention.

Successive governments made efforts to combat illegal drugs-trafficking, in order to appease both its European and US allies. In June 1997 the President installed a commission to monitor the drugs trade. In June 1998 the Government signed the Anti-Drugs Strategy for the Western Hemisphere that had been prepared by the OAS. New legislation was passed in January 1999, providing for heavier sentences for drugs-trafficking. Finally, the Government prepared a 'Drugs Masterplan 1997–2002', which, among other things, proposed that money-laundering be made a criminal offence. Notwithstanding these and other measures, the Government was unable effectively to stem the tide of drugs-trafficking; according to official estimates, roughly 26,000 kg of cocaine, with a street value of slightly over US $1,000m., were shipped to Europe each year. In March 2001 Surinamese police made the largest ever seizure of drugs, confiscating a consignment of 1,198 kg of cocaine; three Surinamese, three Brazilians and a Colombian were sentenced to 14 years' imprisonment in the following March after being convicted on charges relating to the seizure. In 2004 the Dutch and Surinamese Governments agreed to co-operate on intelligence-gathering and to increase security on both passenger and cargo flights from Suriname and customs officials in the two countries reached an agreement to share information in an attempt to reduce tax evasion on imports from the Netherlands. In March 2008 the country's acceded to the Inter-American Convention Against Illicit Manufacturing of and Trafficking in Firearms, Ammunition, Explosives and Similar Devices; it was hoped the measure would facilitate the delivery of an enhanced security programme for Suriname through regional co-operation and intelligence-sharing. Suriname and Guyana declared their joint commitment to reducing the movement of criminals, and trafficking of drugs and firearms across the countries' border in May 2008, when they signed the 'Nieuw-Nickerie Declaration'.

Relations with France deteriorated in early 2007 when the French Government designated a 2m.-ha region along the disputed border with French Guiana, encompassing land between the Marowijne (Marouini) and Itany (Litani) Rivers, as a national park. Under its new protected status, the traditional hunting and fishing practices of the indigenous Surinamese communities were strictly prohibited in the park. In response, the Organisatie van Inheemsen in Suriname (Organization of Indigenous People in Suriname) submitted a petition to the outgoing French Ambassador, Jean-Marie Bruno, expressing its rejection of the newly instituted park and averring that the development contravened the native groups' human rights. While no official legislation was yet in existence recognizing the indigenous people's rights to land-ownership, the French maintained that the course of the Itany River delineated French Guiana's official border with Suriname and contended that French military operatives were thus entitled to police the river in accordance with French law. Clarification on the issue of border rights and the status of Suriname's indigenous and tribal population in the disputed region was sought by the Surinamese Government in 2007. In February 2008 it was reported that Suriname and France were due to resume talks, although France was seeking to expand its maritime boundary by lodging a claim with the UN Convention on the Law of the Sea.

A number of international agreements were reached in 2007 that would afford significant aid resources to the country, facilitating the development of its infrastructure and economy and enhancing integration with other regional states: following 18 months of preparatory negotiations, in April the Surinamese Government acceded to the UN Development Assistance Framework agreement, under which US $40m. would be made available for social development initiatives in the country in 2008–11. Suriname also benefited from the assistance of the EU which, in July 2007, approved various contracts for the upgrade and development of the country's tourism and transport sectors, totalling allocations of €1.5m. and €3.2m., respectively.

Since 1976 Suriname has maintained diplomatic relations with the People's Republic of China, but in mid-2007 renewed efforts by Taiwan to secure long-sought diplomatic recognition in the country, in return for significant development assistance funding, provoked outrage on the part of the Chinese Government. While Venetiaan's Government had rejected the proffered assistance, declaring adherence to the 'one China' policy promoted by the Chinese Government, the decision of a contingent of Surinamese parliamentarians and business leaders to engage in further negotiations towards enhanced bilateral relations provoked controversy. The Speaker of the House, Paul Somohardjo, was anxious to emphasize that the delegation did not constitute an official government delegation; however, members of parliament participating in the visit declared that they undertook discussions with Taiwan in order to ascertain the most beneficial relationship for the Surinamese people and, further, favoured reunification of the disparate regions of China. Subsequently, the Chinese Government pledged vehicles and military equipment to the value of US $600,000, and discussions towards the acquisition of a number of passenger aircraft by the national carrier from China demonstrated Suriname's commitment to bolster relations with its long-standing diplomatic ally.

Maritime Border Dispute

The Wijdenbosch administration came into conflict with Guyana over the two countries' common border. The present boundary between Guyana and Suriname was based on a draft treaty agreed, but never ratified, between the United Kingdom and the Netherlands in 1939. Under the draft treaty the boundary between the two countries was established on the left bank of the Corantijn and Kutari rivers. In 1962 the Netherlands questioned Guyana's sovereignty over an area of land that protrudes from Guyana into Suriname. The Dutch proposed a modification of the treaty, favouring a boundary that followed the Thalweg, instead of the left bank of the Corantijn, and the westerly New River, instead of the Kutari. The British Government, however, refused to reopen discussions on the issue.

In June 1998 a new border dispute erupted when Guyana granted the Canadian-based CGX Energy Inc a concession to explore for petroleum and gas along the continental shelf off its coastline. Part of the area, designated the Corantijn block, lay within waters claimed by Suriname. The Surinamese Government made a formal protest against the CGX concession in May 2000, claiming it violated Suriname's sovereignty and territorial integrity. The Guyanese Government maintained that the exploration activities were being conducted in Guyanese territory, but indicated its willingness to attend talks. In early June gunboats of the Suriname navy forced CGX to remove the drill rig from the disputed waters. At a meeting held in June in Port of Spain, Trinidad and Tobago, representatives from the two countries agreed that a Joint Technical Committee be established to resolve the dispute, but both sides remained at an impasse. Further talks, held later in the month in Jamaica, also ended in deadlock, and, with an agreement between the two countries unlikely, CGX withdrew from the area. In September Guyana reported an alleged intrusion into its territory by Surinamese soldiers.

Negotiations made new progress following the election of Venetiaan in 2000, and in 2001 the Presidents of both countries made a declaration of their commitment to peace and co-operation. In January 2002 President Bharrat Jagdeo of Guyana addressed the Surinamese National Assembly on the possibility of a joint oil exploration project in the disputed territory; however, opposition members boycotted the speech in protest at the proposals. A decree issued by Venetiaan's Government in March 2003, which stated that maps of the country circulated by diplomatic missions in Paramaribo should include the disputed territory, once again jeopardized the negotiations. Guyana responded with a formal protest and dispatched a naval patrol to the Corantijn river. In February 2004 Guyana referred the maritime boundary dispute to arbitration under the provisions of Article 287 of the UN Convention on the Law of the Sea. Representatives of the two countries participated in talks with the President of the International Tribunal on the Law of the Sea in Hamburg, Germany, in May. Guyana also requested a number of interim measures that would allow gas and oil exploration to continue. In December, at Suriname's behest, the Netherlands denied Guyana access to its archived documents on the border issue. The British Government made its archives available to both Guyana and Suriname. Guyana subsequently filed a protest with the International Tribunal for the Law of the Sea and the case was submitted to court in March 2005. In September 2007 the Tribunal ruled in favour of Guyana, granting sovereignty over 33,152 sq km (12,800 sq miles) of coastal waters; Suriname was awarded 17,891 sq km (6,900 sq miles). Guyana's subsequent claims for compensation of US $34m. for damage arising from the expulsion of the oil rig were dismissed by the UN Permanent Court of Arbitration, which ruled that Suriname had not used armed force. CGX resumed exploration in the area in October 2008. The dispute rumbled on, however, and in the same month the temporary seizure by the Surinamese authorities of a Guyanese boat on the river prompted diplomatic protests by Guyana.

In late 2009 Suriname proposed the creation of a legitimate route across the Corantijn River, used illegally by some 400 people per day to cross between Suriname and Guyana. Guyana agreed to undertake negotiations on the proposal, which would involve the establishment of customs and immigration points along the route.

Economy

JAMES MCDONOUGH

Revised for this edition by the editorial staff

Suriname occupies 163,820 sq km (63,251 sq miles) on the north-east coast of South America, lying between Guyana to the west and French Guiana to the east. Suriname's economy is based on bauxite and agriculture. Bauxite, or rather its derivative, alumina, from which aluminium is made, generally accounts for some 70% of the total value of Suriname's exports and about 15% of gross domestic product (GDP). As a result, Suriname's economy was susceptible to 'boom and bust' cycles caused by variations in the international price of alumina. The tax receipts that Suriname received from the export of alumina and aluminium (hardly any unrefined bauxite was exported from Suriname) provided the revenue to support the large civil service, which employed close to 50% of the working population of about 100,000 in 2000. Both the civil service and the system of public enterprises required reform. Both were large and unwieldy, and the largely unprofitable public enterprises impeded private sector development. Exacerbating the country's economic problems were the poor fiscal policies adopted by the Wijdenbosch administration in 1996–2000. Inflation soared during those years, reaching 98.9% in 1999. While the IMF welcomed the Venetiaan Government's attempts to restore fiscal policy, in 2010 the economic structure of the country was still in need of rationalization. In 2000–08, according to the World Bank, the economy grew at an average annual rate of 5.5%. In 2008 Suriname's gross national income per head was approximately US $4,990. It was estimated that some 70% of the population was living in poverty in the 2000s.

AGRICULTURE

In the 18th century Suriname's economy was based on the sugar industry, but by the 19th century coffee, cocoa and cotton were the country's main commodities. With the decline of large-scale plantation agriculture in the 20th century the former contract labourers from India and Indonesia were induced to remain in Suriname by the offer of free land. The Government distributed small plots of land for the growing of rice along the country's rich coastal plain. In the 1990s rice was the country's principal agricultural export, followed by bananas. The coastal polders (land that had been drained) remained the country's focus of agricultural activity and settlement. At least 70% of Suriname's population, totalling some 492,829 at the census of August 2004, lived on the estuarine lands of the Suriname River, within 25 km of the capital, Paramaribo, while a further 15% lived along the coastal plain.

The majority of Suriname's 58,000 ha of cultivated land, which represented only 0.4% of the country's total land area, was on the coastal plain. One-half of the cultivated area was in the polders close to Paramaribo, between the Commewijne and Saramacca estuaries. The country's agricultural potential was far from being realized, partly because of the inaccessibility of the interior savannahs, but also because of the unequal pattern of land tenure. In the 1980s, of the total number of land holdings, 46% were less than 2 ha in area and a further 27% were between 2 ha and 4 ha. At the other end of the scale, one-half of the agricultural land was occupied by 139 large holdings averaging 370 ha. Nevertheless, during 1980–85 agricultural production increased by an average of 6.1% per year. From 1986–90, as a result of the disruption caused by guerrilla activity, production declined by 6.4% per year. There was a brief recovery at the start of the 1990s, but the agricultural sector registered a decline of 5.6% in 1998, owing to a fall in paddy-rice prices, which led to a sharp reduction in the cultivated acreage. In 2000–06 the sector increased by an average of 2.0% per year, with growth of 0.9% estimated in 2006. In 2008 agriculture (including hunting, forestry and fishing) contributed 5.9% of GDP and employed an estimated 8.0% of the working population in 2004.

In the early 21st century rice remained the crop of greatest commercial value in Suriname. About 50% of all cultivated land was devoted to rice, chiefly in the western polders of the Nickerie district. Much of the rice was produced by Hindustanis and Javanese on plots of less than 1 ha, located on the older polders. On the new polders, land holdings were typically of 80 ha or more and cultivation was mechanized and well managed. The fully mechanized rice farm at Wageningen was one of the largest in the world. The cultivated land area dedicated to rice stood at 45,563 ha in 2005. The annual output of paddy rice declined after 1985, however, owing to a lack of government resources to rebuild and expand the country's decaying canal system. Rice production reached a low of 163,400 metric tons in 2002, but had recovered to an estimated 183,000 tons by 2008 following a US $3.4m. grant from the Inter-American Development Bank (IDB) and a further $15m. from the European Union (EU), intended to aid the restructuring of the drainage and irrigation system. In 2007 rice export earnings, valued at $18.1m., contributed 1.3% of total earnings.

Bananas and plantains (in Suriname usage, an eating banana is referred to as a *bacove*, while *banaan* is a cooking variety), which together comprised the next most important export crop, were grown on plantations in the Paramaribo region. In April 2002 the Government closed its banana plantation company, Surland, claiming that it could no longer afford to pay the workers' wages. Consequently, banana production in 2003 declined to an estimated 1,278 metric tons, from 43,139 tons in 2001. However, Surland was subsequently restructured with the aid of a US $6m. loan from the IDB and production and exports resumed in 2004. Banana production recovered strongly; by 2008 FAO estimated that output was 89,000 tons.

In 2007 Enhanced Biofuels Technologies of India (ECB) submitted a bio-energy investment plan to the Surinamese Government. The company hoped to invest as much as US $150m. in Surinamese agriculture, cultivating crops to be used in the production of biofuels overseas.

Livestock received little attention and the output of livestock products was insufficient for local needs. The few cattle that were reared by small-scale farmers were not of high quality and were used more as draught animals than for the production of either beef or milk. In 2008 there were some 50,000 head of cattle, according to FAO estimates. Some efforts were made by the Government to breed stock of better quality and there were experiments to cross the Holstein breed of cattle with the Santa Gertrudi. On the initiative of the Suriname Aluminium Company (Suralco), a scientifically operated dairy farm was established at Moengo. The ideal location for cattle would have been the interior savannah, but the lack of access roads prevented such development. FAO estimated that the country produced 2,000 tons of beef in 2008.

Fishing played a small, though significant, role in the economy. There was a modern fishing industry, located in Paramaribo. This industry was dominated by Japanese and Korean companies, which exported most of their catch to the USA and Canada. Shrimps were the most important single fisheries export. In 2007 shrimps and fish contributed US $99.2m. in export revenues, equivalent to 7.3% of total earnings. In that year, according to FAO, the total catch measured 29,700 tons.

More than 80% of Suriname is covered by forest, making it one of the most densely forested countries in the world. In 2007 lumber contributed US $1.5m. to export revenue, equivalent to 0.1% of total exports by value. This represented a significant decrease from 2002, when lumber exports totalled $5.4m.

MINING

Mining, dominated by the extraction of bauxite, was the single most important economic activity in Suriname. In 2004 mining employed 5.9% of the population—a substantial increase from the 3.5% employed in 2003—and in 2006 contributed 13.0% of GDP. Bauxite was mined from deposits found along the northern edge of the central plateau, close to the Cottica river (the Moengo deposit) and the Suriname river (the Paranam and Onverwacht deposits). In Suriname the mining of bauxite and its refining into alumina and aluminium was controlled by two multinational companies, one US and the other Dutch. Mining began in 1915, by Suralco, a wholly owned subsidiary of the Aluminum Company of America (Alcoa), the world's largest producer of aluminium. In 1939 Billiton Maatschappij Suriname (BMS), a subsidiary of the Royal Dutch Shell-owned Billiton Company, initiated bauxite mining operations in Suriname's Para District, some 35 km south of Paramaribo. In 1983 BMS bought 46% of Suralco's Paranam refinery on the bank of the Suriname river, 100 km from its mouth, and Suralco purchased 24% of BMS's bauxite mining operations. In 1997 BMS opened the Lelydorp III deposit in the Paranam area. The Paranam refinery included installations for the extraction of alumina (1.7m. metric tons per year) from bauxite ore, as well as a smelter for the production of aluminium using alumina. However, in 1999 Suralco closed the smelter, which had a capacity of 30,000 tons per year. The closure was influenced by the high relative cost of the smelter and low rainfall affecting power generation. The company used hydroelectric power generated by the Brokopondo-Afobaka dam on the Suriname river to run the manufacturing operations. The dam was built by Suralco in the 1960s at a cost of US $150m., creating a 1,560-sq km lake, one of the largest artificial lakes in the world. BMS estimated that it would have enough bauxite for the Paranam refinery until 2006. In the early 2000s BHP Billiton, as BMS became known following a merger with an Australian natural resources company, sought more sites in and outside Suriname to continue to supply the Paranam facility beyond the depletion of its current bauxite reserves. In 2005 Alcoa World Alumina and Chemicals (AWAC) completed a project to increase production at the refinery in Paranam by 250,000 tons, to 2.2m. tons per year.

The bauxite industry was heavily taxed and traditionally accounted for over 40% of the Government's revenue. Suriname's traditional markets for bauxite derivatives were the USA, Canada and Norway. Suriname's annual bauxite output remained fairly constant in the early to mid-2000s, at just over 4.0m. metric tons, but production increased from 2005 and in 2007 totalled 5.3m. tons, a 7.8% increase on the previous year. Suriname's alumina production also increased from 2005, but less dramatically; annual output stood at 2.2m. tons in 2007, compared with 1.9m. tons two years earlier. In the latter year alumina constituted 47.5% of the value of Suriname's exports, generating income of US $645.7m. In mid-2008 it was reported that government officials wanted to establish a state-owned aluminium company in order to increase revenue from the sector.

Other mineral resources included iron ore, nickel, platinum, tin, copper, manganese, diamonds and gold. Gold and diamonds were extracted in small quantities from the river beds by private prospectors. A Canadian company, Cambior, began construction at the Gross Rosebel gold mine in 2002 and commercial production began there in 2004. Rosebel was scheduled to process 4.6m. metric tons of ore in 2004, for production of 245,000 troy oz of gold, at an average mine operating cost of US $184 per oz. The total reserves of the mine area were estimated at 42.9m. tons of ore. Exports of gold increased dramatically in the early 2000s, from 218,900 troy oz in 2001 to 711,400 troy oz in 2007. As a result, export earnings from gold also rose, contributing 35.9% of total export revenues, $488.8m., in 2007, compared with $140.3m., or 25.1%, in 2003.

Petroleum was discovered in the Saramacca district in 1981 by the Gulf Oil Corporation of the USA. As a result, a Suriname State Oil Company (Staatsolie) was formed to exploit the reserves. Suriname exported small quantities of crude petroleum and imported refined petroleum products, as the country lacked refining capacity. Output in the early 2000s was 12,000 barrels per day (b/d), and regional geology suggested additional potential. Staatsolie was actively seeking international joint-venture partners, but with little success. However, in 2004 Staatsolie signed a 30-year contract for joint exploration and production for an offshore block in the Guyana basin with Repsol YPF. In March 2006 Staatsolie launched production at a second onshore oilfield. It was estimated that the new Calcutta field held 23m. barrels of crude oil, which were expected to be extracted over 20 years at a rate of 5,000 b/d. In 2006 an estimated 4.8m. barrels of oil were produced at the Calcutta and Tambaredjo oil fields. In June 2007 Staatsolie entered into partnership with the US-based Murphy Oil Corporation. The Government agreed to subsidize 20% of the costs of offshore oil exploration in exchange for tax revenue on production and exports in the event of a substantial discovery. This contract was scheduled to expire on 31 December 2032. In 2002–06 GDP of the mining sector grew at an average annual rate of 1.6%. Driven by higher global prices for aluminium, gold and oil, the sector grew by 11.0% in 2006.

MANUFACTURING

The industrial sector was dominated by the production of alumina. However, the country manufactured some foodstuffs (flour, margarine, cattle fodder), tobacco products, beverages, construction materials, clothing and furniture, using chiefly local raw materials, but imported machinery. Manufacturing, aside from alumina, grew only marginally in the 1990s owing to shortages caused by lack of foreign exchange, and increased competition from the Caribbean Community and Common Market (CARICOM) countries. In February 1995 Suriname was granted full membership of CARICOM. Suriname accepted CARICOM economic obligations on 1 January 1996 and on 1 January 1997 CARICOM's maximum common external tariff was reduced to 25%. Manufacturing employed an estimated 7.0% of the working population in 2004 and contributed 22.0% of GDP in 2008. The sector grew by an average annual rate of 11.1% in 2000–06, according to World Bank figures. It increased by an estimated 1.6% in 2006.

TRANSPORT AND COMMUNICATIONS INFRASTRUCTURE

Infrastructure remained only minimally developed in Suriname. In 2003 there were an estimated 4,304 km of roads, mainly in the north of the country. A ferry link between Suriname and Guyana, across the Corantijn, operates, as does one between Suriname and French Guiana, across the Marowijne. In July 2007 the EU pledged some €3.2m. to facilitate developments in Suriname's transport infrastructure. In the same year the People's Republic of China agreed to finance the resurfacing of the Afobakka road; a key route linking the southern district of Brokopondo with the capital Paramaribo. In March 2008 it was reported that China had agreed to finance the building and maintenance of 500 km of new roads in Suriname, at an estimated cost of US $214m. Construction on the project began in mid-2008 and was expected to be completed by 2010. Relative to Suriname's population and level of economic development, there were 81,500 telephones in use in 2008.

FOREIGN TRADE AND BALANCE OF PAYMENTS

Exports were dominated by alumina and gold, which accounted for over 80% of Suriname's total export earnings in 2007. The remaining exports included rice, crude petroleum, shrimps and timber products. Imports consisted largely of machinery and transport equipment, as well as manufactured goods, and mineral fuels and lubricants. Owing to an increase in commodity prices, and an expansion in the volume of exports, the trade balance was in surplus from 2003. The trade surplus stood at US $358.4m. in 2008, while there was a surplus of $353.0m. on the current account of the balance of payments. Total public external debt declined to $161.1m. by the end of 2007, from $319.8m. at the end of 2002. In December 2009 public debt was equivalent to some 19% of GDP. Meanwhile, the country's international reserves rose from $127.4m. in 2000 to $473.3m. by the end of 2008. In 2005 the principal destinations for Suriname's exports were Norway (23.9% of the total), the USA (16.8%) and France (8.1%). In the same year imports came chiefly from the USA (24.4%), the Netherlands (14.5%) and Trinidad and Tobago (10.5%).

Suriname was one of 13 Caribbean countries to approve an Economic Partnership Agreement (EPA) with the EU in October 2008. The accord eased restrictions on Caribbean exports and gave European businesses greater freedom to expand into the region. The EPA was intended to stimulate trade and investment in the Caribbean, although critics believed it was more beneficial to EU producers.

INVESTMENT AND FINANCE

Suriname's economy began to decline in the 1980s after the military regime came to power. Official capital imports came to a virtual halt in 1982, when the Netherlands suspended its development co-operation because of the political murders. A reduction in foreign capital investment and in exports, owing to the weakness of the world market for alumina and aluminium products, was reflected in a 20% fall in government revenues. Nevertheless, the military Government increased expenditure excessively, doubling the level of spending during the 1980s. The number of public employees increased by one-fifth, with the result that by 1994 nearly one-half of the active labour force consisted of civil servants. By contrast, spending on development projects collapsed. Over 50% of total government spending in the early 1990s was estimated to go on wages, with another 30% used to buy materials. The Government was able to devote a mere 2% to development projects.

Suriname's budget deficit increased from the equivalent of barely 5% of gross national product in 1980 to over 25% in 1992. The Government financed its expenditures first with international reserves and then by printing money, which by 1994 had precipitated a 'hyperinflationary' crisis, with the annual rate of inflation at 368.5%. Subsequently, the implementation of a stringent austerity programme and an increase in revenues caused by a rise in the world price of bauxite derivatives brought about a dramatic improvement in the country's economic situation. By 1996 the depreciation of the Surinamese guilder had been halted, international reserves had reached almost US $100m. and the country was experiencing deflation. However, in the late 1990s a decline in revenues from exports of alumina and aluminium, along with increased government spending and a relaxation of fiscal controls by the Wijdenbosch administration, combined to recreate the conditions of an economic crisis. In 1998 the budget deficit increased to the equivalent of 11.1% of GDP, financed mainly through domestic borrowing. The deficit was eradicated in the early 2000s and by 2007 the surplus increased to 196.5m. Surinamese dollars, equivalent to 3.0% of GDP, largely owing to a rise in export revenues and commodity prices.

Inflation, which had been brought under control in 1996, increased to 98.9% in 1999. This figure fell to 59.3% in 2000 and continued to fall, reaching 15.5% in 2002, owing to the new Government's ending of central bank credit. In 2003 consumer prices increased by an average of 23.0%, before declining to 9.1% in 2004. Owing to the continued increase in global oil prices, the annual inflation rate rose to 9.9% in 2005 and 11.3% in 2006, but declined, to 6.4%, in 2007. In response to the growing concern over higher food prices, the Government created a fund for low-income families in early 2008 worth around US $20m. It also lowered or removed taxes on flour and sugar, which was expected to lead to revenue losses of around $6.5m. Consumer prices remained virtually constant in 2009.

The guilder depreciated rapidly, despite a 43% devaluation on 1 January 1999. The differential between the official and parallel exchange rate, which had all but been eliminated with the devaluation, reached an average of 82% in 1999–2000. In an attempt to halt the economic decline, the second Venetiaan administration, which assumed power in August 2000, devalued the official exchange rate by 89%. As well as ending government borrowing from the Central Bank, the new Government also eliminated subsidies on petroleum products, substantially increased electricity and water rates, rationalized the list of price controls on 12 basic food items, and increased the tax on cigarettes, alcohol and soft drinks. President Venetiaan also dismissed the President of the Central Bank for financing the previous administration's budget deficits. A new banking supervisory act was passed in January 2003 that aimed to strengthen the powers of the Central Bank. One key measure was the introduction of a formal licensing system that gave the Central Bank the exclusive authority to issue bank licences. In July of that year the Government announced that the Surinamese guilder (Sf) was to be replaced with the Surinamese dollar (SRD). The Surinamese dollar was introduced in January 2004 at an initial exchange rate of 2.8 to the US dollar. In December 2009 the exchange rate stood at 2.7 Surinamese dollars to the US dollar.

OUTLOOK

Suriname's economic prospects improved in the early 21st century. The economy grew by an estimated 6.0% in 2008. This was in part owing to a €1.5m. grant from the EU, which was intended to boost capacity in the tourism sector, and in part to strong growth in the minerals sector. However, the economy was over-reliant on its minerals exports, and, following the sharp fall in commodity prices from mid-2008, growth fell by 0.5% in 2009. An IMF report in March 2009 commended the stabilizing policies instituted by the Venetiaan Government, which had helped to attract increased foreign investment in the economy. However, although government responses to potential economic disasters had improved since the 1990s, the report observed that the policy-making structures and institutions had changed little, which rendered the country still vulnerable to economic shocks. The report also highlighted the significant obstacles to the development of the non-traditional agricultural sector. GDP growth was put at 4.3% in 2008, but, according to official estimates GDP declined by 0.5% in 2009 and was forecast to increase by 2.4% in 2010. At the same time, consumer prices were forecast to continue to rise, reaching an estimated 5.0% in 2010 as a result of significant rises in global food and fuel prices and increased domestic demand.

Statistical Survey

Sources (unless otherwise stated): Algemeen Bureau voor de Statistiek, Kromme Elleboogstraat 10, POB 244, Paramaribo; tel. 473927; fax 425004; e-mail info@statistics-suriname.org; internet www.statistics-suriname.org; Ministry of Trade and Industry, Havenlaan 3, POB 9354, Paramaribo; tel. 402080; fax 402602.

AREA AND POPULATION

Area: 163,820 sq km (63,251 sq miles).

Population: 355,240 (males 175,814, females 179,426) at census of 1 July 1980; 492,829 (males 247,846, females 244,618, not known 365) at census of 2 August 2004. *Mid-2010* (estimate): 524,345. Source: UN, *World Population Prospects: The 2008 Revision*.

Density (at mid-2010): 3.2 per sq km.

Population by Age and Sex (UN estimates at mid-2010): *0–14:* 149,853 (males 76,378, females 73,475); *15–64:* 340,633 (males 171,856, females 168,777); *65 and over:* 33,859 (males 14,490, females 19,369); *Total* 524,345 (males 262,724, females 261,621) (Source: UN, *World Population Prospects: The 2008 Revision*).

Ethnic Groups (1980 census, percentage): Creole 34.70; Hindustani 33.49; Javanese 16.33; Bush Negro 9.55; Amerindian 3.10; Chinese 1.55; European 0.44; Others 0.84.

Administrative Districts (population at census of 2 August 2004): Paramaribo 242,946; Wanica 85,986; Nickerie 36,639; Coronie 2,887; Saramacca 15,980; Commewijne 24,649; Marowijne 16,642; Para 18,749; Brokopondo 14,215; Sipaliwini 34,136; *Total* 492,829.

Principal Towns (census of 2 August 2004): Paramaribo (capital) 205,000; Lelydorp 15,600; Nieuw Nickerie 11,100. Source: Thomas Brinkoff, *City Population* (internet www.citypopulation.de).

Births, Marriages and Deaths (2004): Registered live births 9,062 (birth rate 18.6 per 1,000); Marriages 1,951 (4.0 per 1,000); Registered deaths 3,319 (death rate 6.8 per 1,000). *2007:* Birth rate 19.3 per 1,000; Death rate 7.6 per 1,000. *2008:* Birth rate 19.0 per 1,000; Death rate 7.6 per 1,000. *2009:* Birth rate 18.7 per 1,000; Death rate 7.6 per 1,000. Sources: UN, *Demographic Yearbook*; Pan American Health Organization.

Life Expectancy (years at birth): 69.2 (males 65.7; females 72.9) in 2009. Source: Pan American Health Organization.

Economically Active Population ('000 persons aged 15–64 years, census of 2004): Agriculture, hunting, forestry and fishing 12,593; Mining and quarrying 9,308; Manufacturing 10,971; Utilities 1,659; Construction 14,031; Trade 25,012; Hotels, restaurants and bars 4,833; Transport, storage and communication 8,711; Financial intermediation 2,723; Real estate, renting and business activities 6,350; Public administration and defence 27,995; Education 8,355; Health and social work 6,797; Other community, social and personal service activities 9,911; *Sub-total* 149,249; Unknown 7,456; *Total employed* 156,705 (males 101,919, females 54,768, unknown 18); Unemployed 16,425; *Total labour force* 173,130.

HEALTH AND WELFARE

Key Indicators

Total Fertility Rate (children per woman, 2008): 2.4.

Under-5 Mortality Rate (per 1,000 live births, 2008): 27.

HIV/AIDS (% of persons aged 15–49, 2007): 2.4.

Physicians (per 1,000 head, 2000): 0.5.

Hospital Beds (per 1,000 head, 2004): 3.1.

Health Expenditure (2007): US $ per head (PPP): 527.

Health Expenditure (2007): % of GDP: 7.6.

Health Expenditure (2007): public (% of total): 47.4.

Access to Water (% of persons, 2008): 93.

Access to Sanitation (% of persons, 2008): 84.

Total Carbon Dioxide Emissions ('000 metric tons, 2006): 2,436.6.

Carbon Dioxide Emissions Per Head (metric tons, 2006): 4.8.

Human Development Index (2007): ranking: 89.

Human Development Index (2007): value: 0.770.

For sources and definitions, see explanatory note on p. vi.

AGRICULTURE, ETC.

Principal Crops ('000 metric tons, 2008, FAO estimates): Rice, paddy 183; Roots and tubers 4; Sugar cane 120; Coconuts 9; Vegetables 14; Bananas 89; Plantains 9; Oranges 13; Other citrus fruit 2.

Livestock ('000 head, 2008, FAO estimates): Cattle 50; Sheep 6; Goats 4; Pigs 27; Chickens 5,010.

Livestock Products ('000 metric tons, 2008, FAO estimates): Cattle meat 2; Pig meat 2; Chicken meat 8; Cows' milk 6; Hen eggs 1.

Forestry ('000 cu metres, 2008, FAO estimates): *Roundwood Removals:* Sawlogs, veneer logs and logs for sleepers 188; Other industrial wood 3; Fuel wood 46; Total 237. *Sawnwood Production:* Total (incl. railway sleepers) 60.

Fishing ('000 metric tons, 2008): Capture 23.8 (FAO estimate—Marine fishes 17.2; Penaeus shrimps 0.2; Atlantic seabob 6.0); Aquaculture 0.0; *Total catch* 23.8 (FAO estimate).

Source: FAO.

MINING

Selected Products (2008, estimates): Crude petroleum ('000 barrels) 5,400; Bauxite 5,230; Gold (Au content, kg) 10,300. Sources: US Geological Survey.

INDUSTRY

Selected Products ('000 metric tons, 2007 unless otherwise indicated): Gold-bearing ores 300 (kg, 2004); Gravel and crushed stone 85 (2002); Distillate fuel oil 41; Residual fuel oils 360; Cement 65 (2004); Alumina 1,929 (2005); Beer of barley 21 (2008); Coconut oil 0.87 (2008); Palm oil 0.22 (2008); Cigarettes 483 (million, 1996); Plywood 1 ('000 cubic metres, 2008); Electricity 1,618 (million kWh). Sources: mainly UN Industrial Commodity Statistics Database and FAO.

FINANCE

Currency and Exchange Rates: 100 cents = 1 Surinamese dollar. *Sterling, Dollar and Euro Equivalents* (31 May 2010): £1 sterling = 4.002 Surinamese dollars; US $1 = 2.745 Surinamese dollars; €1 = 3.399 Surinamese dollars; 100 Surinamese dollars = £24.99 = US $36.43 = €29.42. *Average Exchange Rate* (Surinamese dollars per US $): 2.745 in 2007; 2.745 in 2008; 2.745 in 2009. *Note:* Between 1971 and 1993 the official market rate was US $1 = 1.785 guilders. A new free market rate was introduced in June 1993, and a unified, market-determined rate took effect in July 1994. A mid-point rate of US $1 = 401.0 guilders was in effect between September 1996 and January 1999. A new currency, the Surinamese dollar, was introduced on 1 January 2004, and was equivalent to 1,000 old guilders. Some data in this survey are still presented in terms of the former currency.

Budget (million Surinamese dollars, 2007, estimates): *Revenue:* Direct taxation 778.8; Indirect taxation 804.0 (Domestic taxes on goods and services 368.8, Taxes on international trade 430.9, Other taxes (incl. bauxite levy) 4.3); Non-tax revenue 319.7; Total 1,902.5 (excl. grants 99.5). *Expenditure:* Wages and salaries 678.4; Subsidies and transfers 217.0; Goods and services 590.1; Interest payments 94.5; Capital 225.4; Total 1,805.4 (excl. net lending 1.1). Source: IMF, *Suriname: Statistical Appendix* (August 2008).

International Reserves (US $ million at 31 December 2009): Gold (national valuation) 59.66; IMF special drawing rights 126.46; Reserve position in IMF 9.60; Foreign exchange 522.90; Total 718.62. Source: IMF, *International Financial Statistics*.

Money Supply ('000 Surinamese dollars at 31 December 2009): Currency outside depository corporations 568,401; Transferable deposits 2,097,897; Other deposits 2,257,186; Securities other than shares 61,094; *Broad money* 4,984,577. Source: IMF, *International Financial Statistics*.

Cost of Living (Consumer Price Index for Paramaribo area; base: October–December 2000 = 100): 210.0 in 2007; 240.9 in 2008; 240.6 in 2009.

Gross Domestic Product ('000 Surinamese dollars at constant 1990 prices, preliminary figures): 5,430 in 2005; 5,675 in 2006; 5,981 in 2007.

Expenditure on the Gross Domestic Product ('000 Surinamese dollars at current prices, 2008): Government final consumption expenditure 378,447; Private final consumption expenditure 1,319,635; Gross capital formation 6,263,155; *Total domestic expenditure* 7,961,237; Exports of goods and non-factor services 4,940,517; *Less* Imports of goods and non-factor services 4,921,958; Statistical discrepancy –104,796; *GDP in purchasers' values* 7,875,000. Source: UN National Accounts Main Aggregates Database.

Gross Domestic Product by Economic Activity ('000 Surinamese dollars at current prices, 2008): Agriculture, hunting, forestry and fishing 368,054; Mining, quarrying and utilities 1,095,603; Manufacturing 1,384,217; Construction 271,475; Wholesale, retail trade, hotels and restaurants 826,781; Transport, storage and communications 499,792; Other services 1,837,836; *Sub-total* 6,283,758; Net of indirect taxes 1,591,242 (obtained as residual); *GDP in purchasers' values* 7,875,000. Source: UN National Accounts Main Aggregates Database.

Balance of Payments (US $ million, 2008): Exports of goods f.o.b. 1,708.1; Imports of goods f.o.b. –1,349.7; *Trade balance* 358.4; Exports of services 284.6; Imports of services –398.1; *Balance on goods and services* 244.9; Other income received 42.2; Other income paid –21.5; *Balance on goods, services and income* 265.6; Current transfers received 137.9; Current transfers paid –50.5; *Current balance* 353.0; Capital account (net) 31.9; Direct investment from abroad –233.6; Portfolio investment liabilities –16.9; Other investment assets 170.0; Other investment liabilities –10.3; Net errors and omissions –241.7; *Overall balance* 52.4. Source: IMF, *International Financial Statistics*.

EXTERNAL TRADE

Principal Commodities (US $ million, 2008): *Imports c.i.f.:* Food and live animals 144.8; Mineral fuels, lubricants, etc. 190.4; Chemicals 124.2; Basic manufactures 249.4; Machinery and transport equipment 399.6; Total (incl. others) 1,304.4. *Exports (excl. re-exports) f.o.b.:* Crude materials (inedible) except fuels 714.8; Mineral fuels, lubricants, etc. 185.4; Total (incl. others) 1,689.0. *Re-exports:* Beverages and tobacco 14.5; Total (incl. others) 54.4. *2007:* Total exports 1,360.8 (Alumina 645.7; Gold 488.8; Shrimp and fish 99.2; Crude oil 107.5; Rice 18.1) (Source: IMF, *Suriname: Statistical Appendix* —August 2008).

Principal Trading Partners (US $ million, 2005): *Imports c.i.f.:* Belgium 23.6; Brazil 39.3; Canada 10.1; China, People's Repub. 59.5; Germany 23.9; Japan 47.5; Netherlands 160.0; Trinidad and Tobago

116.0; United Kingdom 18.3; USA 267.9; Total (incl. others) 1,099.9. *Exports f.o.b.:* Barbados 6.6; France 74.8; Iceland 26.9; Japan 10.7; Netherlands 24.2; Norway 222.4; Trinidad and Tobago 20.7; USA 155.6; Total (incl. others) 929.1. Source: IMF, *Suriname: Statistical Appendix* (May 2007).

TRANSPORT

Road Traffic (registered motor vehicles, 2006): Passenger cars 81,778; Buses and coaches 3,029; Lorries and vans 25,745; Motorcycles and mopeds 40,889 (Source: IRF, *World Road Statistics*).

Shipping: *International Sea-borne Freight Traffic* (estimates, '000 metric tons, 2001): Goods loaded 2,306; Goods unloaded 1,212. *Merchant Fleet* (registered at 31 December 2008): Number of vessels 16; Total displacement 5,792 grt. Source: Lloyd's Register-Fairplay, *World Fleet Statistics*.

Civil Aviation (traffic on scheduled services, 2005): Kilometres flown (million) 6; Passengers carried ('000) 315; Passenger-km (million) 1,746; Total ton-km (million) 214. Source: UN, *Statistical Yearbook*.

TOURISM

Tourist Arrivals (number of non-resident arrivals at national borders, '000): 160.0 in 2005; 152.9 in 2006; 165.5 in 2007.

Tourism Receipts (US $ million, incl. passenger transport): 96 in 2005; 109 in 2006; 73 in 2007.

Source: World Tourism Organization.

COMMUNICATIONS MEDIA

Radio Receivers (1997): 300,000 in use.

Television Receivers (2000): 110,000 in use.

Telephones (2009): 83,700 main lines in use.

Mobile Cellular Telephones (2009): 763,900 subscribers.

Personal Computers: 20,000 (40.0 per 1,000 persons) in 2005.

Internet Users (2009): 163,000.

Broadband Subscribers (2009): 8,600.

Daily Newspapers (2005): 4.

Non-daily Newspapers (2005): 4.

Sources: mainly UNESCO, *Statistical Yearbook*; UN, *Statistical Yearbook*; International Telecommunication Union.

EDUCATION

Pre-primary (2007/08): 813 teachers; 17,467 pupils.

Primary (2007/08 unless otherwise stated, incl. special education): 308 schools (2001/02); 4,354 teachers; 69,604 pupils.

Secondary (2007/08 unless otherwise stated, incl. teacher-training): 141 schools (2001/02); 3,373 teachers (2006/07); 48,134 pupils.

University (2001/02): 1 institution; 350 teachers; 3,250 students.

Other Higher (2001/02): 3 institutions; 200 teachers; 1,936 students.

Pupil-teacher Ratio (primary education, UNESCO estimate): 16.0 in 2007/08.

Adult Literacy Rate (UNESCO estimates): 90.4% (males 92.7%; females 88.1%) in 2007.

Source: mainly UNESCO Institute for Statistics.

Directory

The Constitution

The 1987 Constitution was approved by the National Assembly on 31 March and by 93% of voters in a national referendum in September.

THE LEGISLATURE

Legislative power is exercised jointly by the National Assembly and the Government. The National Assembly comprises 51 members, elected for a five-year term by universal adult suffrage. The Assembly elects a President and a Vice-President and has the right of amendment in any proposal of law by the Government. The approval of a majority of at least two-thirds of the number of members of the National Assembly is required for the amendment of the Constitution, the election of the President or the Vice-President, the decision to organize a plebiscite and a People's Congress and for the amendment of electoral law. If it is unable to obtain a two-thirds' majority following two rounds of voting, the Assembly may convene a United People's Assembly (Vereinigde Volksvergadering) and supplement its numbers with members of local councils. The approval by a simple majority is sufficient in the United People's Assembly.

THE EXECUTIVE

Executive authority is vested in the President, who is elected for a term of five years as Head of State, Head of Government, Head of the Armed Forces, Chairman of the Council of State, the Cabinet of Ministers and the Security Council.

The Government comprises the President, the Vice-President and the Cabinet of Ministers. The Cabinet of Ministers is appointed by the President from among the members of the National Assembly. The Vice-President is the Prime Minister and leader of the Cabinet, and is responsible to the President.

In the event of war, a state of siege, or exceptional circumstances to be determined by law, a Security Council assumes all government functions.

THE COUNCIL OF STATE

The Council of State comprises the President (its Chairman) and 14 additional members, composed of two representatives of the combined trade unions, one representative of the associations of employers, one representative of the National Army and 10 representatives of the political parties in the National Assembly. Its duties are to advise the President and the legislature and to supervise the correct execution by the Government of the decisions of the National Assembly. The Council may present proposals of law or of general administrative measures to the Government. The Council has the authority to suspend any legislation approved by the National Assembly which, in the opinion of the Council, is in violation of the Constitution. In this event, the President must decide within one month whether or not to ratify the Council's decision.

The Government

HEAD OF STATE

President: DESIRÉ (DESI) DELANO BOUTERSE (took office 12 August 2010).

Council of State: Chair. DESIRÉ (DESI) DELANO BOUTERSE (President of the Republic); 14 mems; 10 to represent the political parties in the National Assembly, one for the Armed Forces, two for the trade unions and one for employers.

CABINET OF MINISTERS
(August 2010)

The current Government is formed by members of the Megacombinatie (MC), A-Combinatie (AC) and Volksalliantie (VA) alliances.

Vice-President: ROBERT AMEERALI (Ind.).

Minister of Finance: WINNIE BOEDHOE (MC).

Minister of Foreign Affairs: WINSTON LACKIN (MC).

Minister of Defence: LAMURÉ LATOUR (MC).

Minister of Home Affairs: SOEWARTO MOESTADJA (VA).

Minister of Justice and the Police: LAMURÉ LATOUR (acting).

Minister of Sport and Youth Affairs: PAUL ABENA (AC).

Minister of Agriculture, Animal Husbandry and Fisheries: HENDRIK SETROWIDJOJO (VA).

Minister of Transport, Communications and Tourism: VALISI PINAS (AC).

Minister of Public Works: RAMON ABRAHAMS (MC).

Minister of Social Affairs and Housing: ALICE AMAFO (AC).

Minister of Trade and Industry: MICHAEL MISKIN (MC).

Minister of Regional Development: LINUS DIKO (AC).

Minister of Education and Community Development: RAYMOND SAPOEN (VA).

Minister of Health: CELCIUS WALDO WATERBERG (AC).

Minister of Labour, Technological Development and the Environment: GINMARDO KROMOSOETO (MC).

Minister of Natural Resources: JIM HOK (MC).

Minister of Physical Planning, Land and Forestry Management: MARTINUS SASTROREDJO (MC).

MINISTRIES

Office of the President: Kleine Combéweg 2–4, Centrum, Paramaribo; tel. 472841; fax 475266; e-mail kabpressur@sr.net; internet www.kabinet.sr.org.

Office of the Vice-President: Dr Sophie Redmondstraat 118, Paramaribo; tel. 474805; fax 472917; e-mail office_vicepres@sr.net.

Ministry of Agriculture, Animal Husbandry and Fisheries: Letitia Vriesdelaan 7, Paramaribo; tel. 477698; fax 470301; e-mail minlvvv@sr.net.

Ministry of Defence: Kwattaweg 29, Paramaribo; tel. 474244; fax 420055; e-mail defensie@sr.net.

Ministry of Education and Community Development: Dr Samuel Kafiluddistraat 117–123, Paramaribo; tel. 498383; fax 495083; e-mail minond@sr.net.

Ministry of Finance: Tamarindelaan 3, Paramaribo; tel. 472610; fax 476314; e-mail financien@sr.net; internet www.minfin.sr.

Ministry of Foreign Affairs: Lim A. Postraat 25, POB 25, Paramaribo; tel. 471209; fax 410411; e-mail buza@sr.net.

Ministry of Health: Henck Arronstraat 64, POB 201, Paramaribo; tel. 477601; fax 473923; e-mail info@volksgezondheid.gov.sr; internet www.volksgezondheid.gov.sr.

Ministry of Home Affairs: Wilhelminastraat 3, Paramaribo; tel. 476461; fax 421170; e-mail minbiza@sr.net.

Ministry of Justice and the Police: Henck Arronstraat 1, Paramaribo; tel. 473033; fax 412109; e-mail min.jus-pol@sr.net; internet www.juspolsuriname.org.

Ministry of Labour, Technological Development and the Environment: Wageswegstraat 22, POB 911, Paramaribo; tel. 475241; fax 410465; e-mail voorlichting@atm.sr.org; internet www.atm.sr.org.

Ministry of Natural Resources: Dr J. C. de Mirandastraat 11–13, Paramaribo; tel. 410160; fax 472911; e-mail minnh@sr.net.

Ministry of Physical Planning, Land and Forestry Management: Cornelis Jongbawstraat 10–12, Paramaribo; tel. 470728; fax 473316; e-mail mpjong@datsunsuriname.com.

Ministry of Public Works: Verlengde Jagernath Lachmonstraat 167, Paramaribo; tel. 462500; fax 464901; e-mail minow@sr.net.

Ministry of Regional Development: Van Rooseveltkade 2, Paramaribo; tel. 471574; fax 424517; e-mail regon@sr.net.

Ministry of Social Affairs and Housing: Waterkant 30, Paramaribo; tel. 472340; fax 470516; e-mail soza@sr.net.

Ministry of Sport and Youth Affairs: Paramaribo.

Ministry of Trade and Industry: Havenlaan 3, POB 9354, Paramaribo; tel. 402080; fax 402602; e-mail hi.voorlichting@minhi.gov.sr; internet www.minhi.gov.sr.

Ministry of Transport, Communications and Tourism: Prins Hendrikstraat 24–26, Paramaribo; tel. 411951; fax 420425; e-mail odc@mintct.sr; internet www.mintct.sr.

Legislature

NATIONAL ASSEMBLY

Chairman: JENNIFER GEERLINGS-SIMONS.

General Election, 25 May 2010

Party	% of votes cast	Seats
Megacombinatie*	40.22	23
Nieuw Front†	31.65	14
A-Combinatie‡	4.70	7
Volksalliantie§	12.98	6
Partij voor Demokratie en Ontwikkeling in Eenheid	5.09	1
Basispartij voor Vernieuwing en Democratie/ Politieke Vleugel van de FAL	5.07	—
Other parties	0.29	—
Total	100.00	51

* An alliance of the Kerukunan Tulodo Pranatan Inggil (KTPI), the Nationale Democratische Partij (NDP), the Nieuw Suriname (NS) and the Progressieve Arbeiders en Landbouwers Unie (PALU).

† An alliance of the Nationale Partij Suriname (NPS), the Surinaamse Partij van de Arbeid (SPA) and the Vooruitstrevende Hervormings Partij (VHP).

‡ Including candidates of the Algemene Bevrijdings- en Ontwikkelingspartij (ABOP) and the Broederschap en Eenheid in Politiek (BEP).

§ An alliance of the Democraten van de 21, Pertijajah Luhur (PL), the Progressieve Surinaamse Volkspartij (PSV) and the Unie van Progressieve Surinamers (UPS).

Election Commission

Centraal Hoofdstembureau (CHS) (Central Polling Authority): Wilhelminastraat 3, Paramaribo; tel. 410362; independent; Chair. LOTHAR BOKSTEEN.

Political Organizations

A-Combinatie (AC): Paramaribo; electoral alliance including:

Algemene Bevrijdings- en Ontwikkelingspartij (ABOP) (General Liberation and Development Party): Jaguarstraat 15, Paramaribo; e-mail webmaster@abop-suriname.net; internet www.abop-suriname.net; f. 1990; Pres. RONNIE BRUNSWIJK; Sec. C. ADA.

Broederschap en Eenheid in Politiek (BEP): Theodorusstraat 55, Land van Dijk, Paramaribo; tel. 402509; fax 422996; e-mail info@bep.sr; internet beppartij.org; f. 1957 as Maroon Party Suriname (MPS); name changed as above in 1987; Chair. CAPRINO ALLENDY; Sec. WENSLEY MISIEDJAN.

Seeka: Paramaribo; Chair. PAUL ABENA.

Basispartij voor Vernieuwing en Democratie (BVD) (Base Party for Renewal and Democracy): Hoogestraat 28–30, Paramaribo; tel. 422231; e-mail info@bvdsuriname.org; internet www.bvdsuriname.org; contested the 2010 election in coalition with the Politiek Vleugel van de FAL (PVF—q.v.); Chair. DILIPKOEMAR SARDJOE; Sec. JERREL CASTLE ROCK.

Democratisch Alternatief 1991 (DA '91) (Democratic Alternative 1991): Gladiolenstraat 17, POB 91, Paramaribo; tel. 432342; fax 493121; e-mail info@da91.sr; internet da91.org; f. 1991 as the Alternatief Forum (AF); social democratic; Chair. WINSTON JESSERUN; Sec. WILFRIED MEYER.

Hernieuwde Progressieve Partij (HPP) (Renewed Progressive Party): Tourtonnelaan 51, Paramaribo; tel. 426965; e-mail hpp@cq-link.sr; f. 1986; Chair. PRIM RAMTAHALSING.

Megacombinatie (MC) (Mega Combination): Paramaribo; Leader DESIRÉ (DESI) DELANO BOUTERSE; alliance formed to contest the 2010 election, comprising:

Kerukunan Tulodo Pranatan Inggil (KTPI) (Party for National Unity and Solidarity): Bonistraat 64, Geyersvlijt, Paramaribo; tel. 456116; f. 1949 as the Kaum Tani Persatuan Indonesia; largely Indonesian; Leader WILLY SOEMITA; Sec. ROBBY DRAGMAN.

Nationale Democratische Partij (NDP) (National Democratic Party): Dr H. D. Benjaminstraat 38, Paramaribo; tel. 499183; fax 432174; e-mail ndpsur@sr.net; internet www.ndp.sr; f. 1987 by Standvaste (the 25 February Movt); army-supported; Chair. DESIRÉ (DESI) DELANO BOUTERSE; Sec. DENNIS MENZO.

Nieuw Suriname (NS) (New Suriname): Paramaribo; f. 2003; Pres. JOHN NASIBDAR; Sec. SAFIEK JAHANGIER.

Progressieve Arbeiders en Landbouwers Unie (PALU) (Progressive Workers' and Farm Labourers' Union): Dr S. Kafiluddistraat 27, Paramaribo; tel. 400115; e-mail palu@sr.net; internet palu-suriname.org; f. 1977; socialist party; Chair. JIM K. HOK; Vice-Chair. HENK RAMNANDANLAL.

Nationale Unie (NU): Postbus 5193, Paramaribo; tel. 476958; fax 499678; e-mail info@nationaleunie.net; internet www.nationaleunie.net; f. 1991; Leader PAUL VAN LEEUWAARDE; Sec.-Gen. MAHIN JANKIE.

Naya Kadam (New Step): Naarstraat 5, Paramaribo; tel. 482014; fax 481012; e-mail itsvof@sr.net; Chair. INDRA DJWALAPERSAD; Sec. WALDO RAMDIHAL.

Nieuw Front (NF) (New Front): Paramaribo; f. 1987 as Front voor Demokratie en Ontwikkeling (FDO—Front for Democracy and Devt); name changed as above in 1991; Pres. RUNALDO R. VENETIAAN; an alliance comprising:

Nationale Partij Suriname (NPS) (Suriname National Party): Grun Dyari, Johan Adolf Pengelstraat 77, Paramaribo; tel. 477302; fax 475796; e-mail nps@sr.net; internet www.nps.sr; f. 1946; predominantly Creole; Pres. RUNALDO VENETIAAN; Sec. S. OEMRAWSINGH.

Surinaamse Partij van de Arbeid (SPA) (Suriname Labour Party): Rust en Vredestraat 64, Paramaribo; tel. 425912; fax 420394; f. 1987; affiliated with C-47 trade union; social democratic party; joined NF in 1991; Chair. GUNO CASTELEN; Sec.-Gen. ROY ADEMA.

Vooruitstrevende Hervormings Partij (VHP) (Progressive Reformation Party): Jagernath Lachmonstraat 130, Paramaribo; tel. 425912; fax 420394; internet www.parbo.com/vhp; f. 1949 as Verenigde Hindostaanse Partij (United Indian Party); name changed as above in 1973; leading left-wing party; predominantly Indian; Leader RAMDIN SARDJOE; Sec. MAHINDER RATHIPAL.

Partij voor Demokratie en Ontwikkeling in Eenheid (DOE) (Party for Democracy and Development in Unity): Prinsenstraat 47, Hoek Waaldijkstraat, Paramaribo; tel. 491701; e-mail info@doepartij.org; internet www.doepartij.org; f. 1999; Chair. CARL BREEVELD; Sec. PAUL BRANDON.

Pendawa Lima: Bonistraat 115, Geyersvlij, Paramaribo; tel. 551802; f. 1977; predominantly Indonesian; Chair. RAYMOND SAPOEN; Sec. RANDY KROMODIHARDJO.

Permanente Voorspoed Republiek Suriname (PVRS) (Lasting Prosperity Party of Suriname): Engelslootstraat 8, Projectsloot, Paramaribo; tel. 493928; e-mail info@nieuwpvrs.com; internet www.nieuwpvrs.com; Chair. CHAS MIJNALS.

Politieke Vleugel van de FAL (PVF): Keizerstraat 150, Paramaribo; f. 1995; political wing of farmers' org. Federatie van Agrariërs en Landarbeiders; contested the 2010 election in coalition with the Basispartij voor Vernieuwing en Democratie (BVD—q.v.); Chair. SOEDESCHAND JAIRAM; Sec. RADJOE BIKHARIE.

Progressieve Bosneger Partij (PBP): f. 1968; resumed political activities 1987; represents members of the Bush Negro (Boschneger) ethnic group; associated with the Pendawa Lima (see above); Chair. ARMAND KANAPE.

Volksalliantie (People's Alliance): Paramaribo; alliance formed to contest the 2010 election; Leader PAUL SALAM SOMOHARDJO.

Democraten van de 21 (D21) (Democrats of the 21st Century): Goudstraat 22, Paramaribo; f. 1996; Chair. SOEWARTO MOESTADJA; Sec. KANIMAN PASIRAN.

Pertijajah Luhur (PL) (Full Confidence Party): Hoek Gemenlandsweg-Daniel Coutinhostraat, Paramaribo; tel. 401087; fax 420394; internet www.pertjajahluhur.org; f. 1998; left Nieuw Front alliance in 2010; Pres. PAUL SALAM SOMOHARDJO.

Progressieve Surinaamse Volkspartij (PSV) (Suriname Progressive People's Party): Keizerstraat 122, Paramaribo; tel. 472979; internet www.middenblok.com; f. 1947; resumed political activities 1987; contested the 2010 election in coalition with the Unie van Progressieve Surinamers (UPS—q.v.); Christian democratic party; Chair. RONALD GRUNBERG.

Unie van Progressieve Surinamers (UPS): Keizerstraat 122, Paramaribo; tel. 472979; internet www.middenblok.com; f. 2004; contested the 2010 election in coalition with the Progressieve Surinaamse Volkspartij (PSV—q.v.); Chair. HENRI ORI.

Diplomatic Representation

EMBASSIES IN SURINAME

Brazil: Maratakkastraat 2, Zorg en Hoop, POB 925, Paramaribo; tel. 400200; fax 400205; e-mail brasemb@sr.net; internet www2.mre.gov.br/suriname/index.asp; Ambassador JOSÉ LUIZ MACHADO E COSTA.

China, People's Republic: Anton Dragtenweg 131, POB 3042 Paramaribo; tel. 451570; fax 452540; e-mail chinaemb_sr@mfa.gov.cn; internet sr.chineseembassy.org; Ambassador YUAN NANSHENG.

Cuba: Brokopondolaan 4, Paramaribo; tel. 434917; fax 432626; e-mail embacubasuriname@parbo.net; internet embacu.cubaminrex.cu/surinaming; Ambassador ANDRÉS MARCELO GONZÁLEZ GARRIDO.

France: Henck Arronstraat 5–7, POB 2648, Paramaribo; tel. 476455; fax 471208; e-mail ambafrance.paramaribo@diplomatie.gouv.fr; internet www.ambafrance-sr.org; Ambassador RICHARD BARBEYRON.

Guyana: Gravenstraat 82, POB 785, Paramaribo; tel. 477895; fax 472679; e-mail guyembassy@sr.net; Ambassador MERLIN UDHO.

India: Dr Sophie Redmondstraat 221, POB 1329, Paramaribo; tel. 498344; fax 491106; e-mail india@sr.net; internet www.indembassysuriname.com; Ambassador KANWAL JIT SINGH SODDHI.

Indonesia: Van Brussellaan 3, Uitvlugt, POB 157, Paramaribo; tel. 431230; fax 498234; e-mail indonemb@sr.net; internet www.paramaribo.deplu.go.id; Ambassador SUPRIJANTO MUHADI.

Japan: Henck Arronstraat 23–25, POB 2921, Paramaribo; tel. 474860; fax 412208; e-mail eojparbo@sr.net; Ambassador TASUAKI IWATA (resident in Venezuela).

Netherlands: Van Roseveltkade 5, POB 1877, Paramaribo; tel. 477211; fax 477792; e-mail prm@minbuza.nl; internet www.nederlandseambassade.sr; Ambassador AART JACOBI.

Russia: Anton Dragtenweg 7, POB 8127, Paramaribo; tel. and fax 472387; Ambassador PAVEL SERGIEV.

USA: Dr Sophie Redmondstraat 129, POB 1821, Paramaribo; tel. 472900; fax 425690; e-mail embuscen@sr.net; internet suriname.usembassy.gov; Ambassador JOHN R. NAY.

Venezuela: Henck Arronstraat 23–25, POB 3001, Paramaribo; tel. 475401; fax 475602; e-mail embajador@suriname.gob.ve; internet www.embavenezsuriname.com; Ambassador FRANCISCO DE JESÚS SIMANCAS.

Judicial System

The administration of justice is entrusted to a Court of Justice, the six members of which are nominated for life, and three Cantonal Courts. Suriname recognized the Caribbean Court of Justice (CCJ) on matters of original jurisdiction pertaining to international trade. The CCJ was inaugurated in Port of Spain, Trinidad and Tobago, on 16 April 2005.

President of the Court of Justice: EWALD OMBRE.

Attorney-General: SUBHAAS PUNWASI.

Religion

CHRISTIANITY

According to the latest census (2004), Christians represent approximately 48% of the population.

Committee of Christian Churches: Paramaribo; tel. 476306; Chair. Rev. WILHELMUS DE BEKKER (Bishop of Paramaribo).

The Roman Catholic Church

For ecclesiastical purposes, Suriname comprises the single diocese of Paramaribo, suffragan to the archdiocese of Port of Spain (Trinidad and Tobago). The Bishop participates in the Antilles Episcopal Conference (currently based in Port of Spain, Trinidad and Tobago). Some 25% of the population are Roman Catholics.

Bishop of Paramaribo: WILHELMUS ADRIANUS JOSEPHUS MARIA DE BEKKER, Bisschopshuis, Henck Arronstraat 12, POB 1230, Paramaribo; tel. 425918; fax 471602; e-mail cabisdom@sr.net.

The Anglican Communion

Within the Church in the Province of the West Indies, Suriname forms part of the diocese of Guyana. The Episcopal Church is also represented.

Anglican Church: St Bridget's, Hoogestraat 44, Paramaribo.

Protestant Churches

Evangelisch Lutherse Kerk in Suriname: Waterkant 102, POB 585, Paramaribo; tel. 425503; fax 425503; e-mail elks@sr.net; f. 1741; Pres. LINDA PROFIJT-DEL PRADO; 3,500 mems.

Moravian Church in Suriname (Evangelische Broeder Gemeente): Maagdenstraat 50, POB 1811, Paramaribo; tel. 473073; fax 475794; e-mail ebgs@sr.net; f. 1735; Praeses MAARTEN MINGOEN; 40,000 mems (2004).

Adherents to the Moravian Church constitute some 15% of the population. Also represented are the Christian Reformed Church, the Dutch Reformed Church, the Baptist Church, the Evangelical Methodist Church, Pentecostal Missions, the Seventh-day Adventists and the Wesleyan Methodist Congregation.

HINDUISM

According to the 2004 census, 24% of the population are Hindus.

Arya Dewaker: Johan Adolf Pengelstraat 210, Paramaribo; tel. 400706; e-mail aryadewaker@sr.net; members preach the Vedic Dharma; disciples of Maha Rishi Swami Dayanand Sarswati, the founder of the Arya Samaj in India; f. 1929; Chair. INDERDATH TILAKDHARIE.

Sanatan Dharm: Koningstraat 31–33, POB 760, Paramaribo; tel. 404190; f. 1930; Pres. Dr R. M. NANNAN PANDAY; over 150,000 mems.

ISLAM

Some 16% of the population are Muslims, according to the 2004 census.

Federatie Islamitische Gemeenten in Suriname: Paramaribo; Indonesian Islamic org.; Chair. K. KAAIMAN.

Stichting der Islamitische Gemeenten Suriname: Verlengde Mahonielaan 39, Paramaribo; Indonesian Islamic org.

Surinaamse Islamitische Organisatie (SIO): Watermolenstraat 10, POB 278, Paramaribo; tel. 475220; fax 472075; e-mail ijamaludin@hotmail.com; f. 1978; Pres. Dr I. JAMALUDIN; Sec. Dr K. M. MOENNE; 6 brs.

Surinaamse Moeslim Associatie: Kankantriestraat 55–57, Paramaribo; Javanese Islamic org.

JUDAISM

The Dutch Jewish Congregation and the Dutch Portuguese-Jewish Congregation are represented in Suriname.

Jewish Community: The Synagogue Neve Shalom, Keizerstraat, POB 1834, Paramaribo; tel. 400236; fax 402380; e-mail rene-fernandes@cq-link.sr; internet www.ujcl.org; f. 1854; mem. of Union of Jewish Congregations of Latin America and the Caribbean (UJCL); Officiant JACQUES VAN NIEL; 300 mems (2005).

The Press

DAILIES

Dagblad Suriname: Zwartenhovenbrugstraat 154, POB 975, Paramaribo; tel. 426336; fax 471718; e-mail general@dbsuriname.com; internet www.dbsuriname.com; f. 2002; Dir FARIED PIERKHAN; Editor LAL MAHOMED JAMES.

De Ware Tijd: Malebatrumstraat 9, POB 1200, Paramaribo; tel. 472833; fax 411169; e-mail infodwt@dwt.net; internet www.dwtonline.com; f. 1957; morning; Dutch; independent/liberal; Dir STEVE JONG TJIEN FA; Editor-in-Chief RICARDO CARROT.

De West: Dr J. C. de Mirandastraat 2–6, POB 176, Paramaribo; tel. 473327; fax 470322; e-mail dewest@cq-link.sr; internet www.dewestonline.cq-link.sr; f. 1909; midday; Dutch; liberal; Editor GEORGE D. C. FINDLAY; circ. 15,000–18,000.

PERIODICALS

Advertentieblad van de Republiek Suriname: Henck Arronstraat 120, POB 56, Paramaribo; tel. 473501; fax 454782; f. 1871; 2 a week; Dutch; govt and official information bulletin; Editor E. D. FINDLAY; circ. 1,000.

CLO Bulletin: Gemenelandsweg 95, Paramaribo; f. 1973; irreg.; Dutch; labour information publ. by civil servants' union.

Kerkbode: Burenstraat 17–19, POB 219, Paramaribo; tel. 473079; fax 475635; e-mail stadje@sr.net; f. 1906; weekly; religious; circ. 2,000.

Omhoog: Henck Arronstraat 21, POB 1802, Paramaribo; tel. 425992; fax 426782; e-mail rkomhoog@sr.net; f. 1952; Dutch; weekly; Catholic bulletin; Editor S. MULDER; circ. 5,000.

Xtreme Magazine: Uranusstraat 49, Paramaribo; tel. 456969.

Publishers

Afaka International NV: Residastraat 23, Paramaribo; tel. and fax 530640; e-mail info@afaka.biz; internet www.afaka.biz; f. 1996; Dir GERRIT BARRON.

Educatieve Uitgeverij Sorava NV: Latourweg 10, POB 8382, Paramaribo; tel. and fax 480808.

IMWO, Universiteit van Suriname: Universiteitscomplex, Leysweg 1, POB 9212, Paramaribo; tel. 465558; fax 462291; e-mail bmhango@yahoo.com.

Ministerie van Onderwijs en Volksontwikkeling (Ministry of Education and Community Development): Dr Samuel Kafilludistraat 117–123, Paramaribo; tel. 498850; fax 495083.

Okopipi Publ. (Publishing Services Suriname): Van Idsingastraat 133, Paramaribo; tel. 472746; e-mail pssmoniz@sr.net; fmrly I. Krishnadath.

Papaya Media Counseling: Plutostraat 30, POB 8304, Paramaribo; tel. and fax 454530; e-mail roy_bhikharie@sr.net; f. 2002; Man. Dir ROY BHIKHARIE.

Stichting Wetenschappelijke Informatie (Foundation for Information and Development): Prins Hendrikstraat 38, Paramaribo; tel. 475232; fax 422195; e-mail swin@sr.net; f. 1977.

Tabiki Productions: Weidestraat 34, Paramaribo; tel. 478525; fax 478526; e-mail insightsuriname@yahoo.com.

VACO, NV: Domineestraat 26, POB 1841, Paramaribo; tel. 472545; fax 410563; f. 1952; Dir EDUARD HOGENBOOM.

PUBLISHERS' ASSOCIATION

Publishers' Association Suriname: Domineestraat 32, POB 1841, Paramaribo; tel. 472545; fax 410563.

Broadcasting and Communications

TELECOMMUNICATIONS

Regulatory Authority

Telecommunications Authority Suriname (TAS): Dr J. F. Nassylaan 23, Paramaribo; tel. 421464; fax 421465; e-mail tasur@sr.net; f. 2007; Dir JETTIE OLFF.

Major Service Providers

Digicel Suriname: Henck Arronstraat 27–29, POB 1848, Paramaribo; tel. 473169; fax 551533; mobile operating licence granted in Aug. 2006; operations commenced Dec. 2007; Dir MITCHELL TJIN A. DJIE; Country Man. PHILIP VAN DALSEN.

International Telecommunication Suriname NV (IntelSur NV): Paramaribo; mobile operating licence granted in August 2006 formalized in April 2007; CEO ERIC LELIENHOF.

Telecommunication Corporation Suriname (Telesur): Heiligenweg 1, POB 1839, Paramaribo; tel. 473944; fax 404800; internet www.telesur.sr; liberalization of the telecommunications sector ended Telesur's monopoly in April 2007; supervisory function of Telesur assumed by new regulatory body, Telecommunication Authority Suriname (q.v.); Man. Dir DIRK M. R. CURRIE.

BROADCASTING

Radio

ABC Radio (Ampie's Broadcasting Corporation): Maystraat 57, Paramaribo; tel. 464609; fax 464680; e-mail info@abcsuriname.com; internet www.abcsuriname.com; f. 1975; re-opened in 1993; commercial; Dutch and some local languages.

Radio Apintie: Verlengde Gemenelandsweg 37, POB 595, Paramaribo; tel. 498855; fax 400684; e-mail apintie@sr.net; internet www.apintie.sr; f. 1958; commercial; Dutch and some local languages; Gen. Man. CHARLES VERVUURT.

Radio Bersama: Bonniestraat 115, Paramaribo; tel. 551804; fax 551803; f. 1997; Dir AJOEB MOENTARI.

Radio Boskopou: Roseveltkade 1, Paramaribo; tel. 410300; govt-owned; Sranang Tongo and Dutch; Head Mr VAN VARSEVELD.

Radio Garuda: Goudstraat 14–16, Paramaribo; tel. 422422; Dir TOMMY RADJI.

Radio Nickerie (RANI): Waterloostraat 3, Nieuw Nickerie; tel. 231462; commercial; Hindi and Dutch.

Radio Paramaribo (Rapar): Verlengde Jagernath Lachmonstraat 34, POB 975, Paramaribo; tel. 499995; fax 493121; e-mail rapar@sr.net; f. 1957; commercial; Dutch and some local languages; Dir FARIED PIERKHAN.

Radio Radika: Indira Gandhiweg 165, Paramaribo; tel. 482800; fax 482910; e-mail radika@sr.net; re-opened in 1989; Dutch and Hindi; Dir ROSHNI RADHAKISHUN.

Radio Sangeet Mala: Indira Gandhiweg 73, Paramaribo; tel. 485893; Dutch and Hindi; Dirs RADJEN SOEKHRADJ, SOEDESH RAMSARAN.

Radio SRS (Stichting Radio Omroep Suriname): Jacques van Eerstraat 20, POB 271, Paramaribo; tel. 498115; fax 498116; e-mail radiosrs@sr.net; f. 1965; commercial; govt-owned; Dutch and some local languages; Dir LEOPOLD DARTHUIZEN.

Radio Ten: Letitia Vriesdelaan 5, Paramaribo; tel. 410881; fax 410885; e-mail radio10@cq-link.sr; internet www.radio10.cq-link.sr.

Other stations include: Radio KBC, Radio Koyeba, Radio Pertjaya, Radio Shalom, Radio Zon, Ramasha Radio, Rasonic Radio and Trishul Radio.

Television

ABC Televisie (Ampie's Broadcasting Corporation): Maystraat 57, Paramaribo; tel. 464555; fax 464680; e-mail info@abcsuriname.com; internet www.abcsuriname.com; Channel 4.

Algemene Televisie Verzorging (ATV): Adrianusstraat 55, POB 2995, Paramaribo; tel. 404611; fax 402660; e-mail info@atv.sr; internet www.atv.sr; f. 1985; govt-owned; commercial; Dutch, English, Portuguese, Spanish and some local languages; Channel 12; Man. GUNO COOMAN.

STVS (Surinaamse Televisie Stichting): Letitia Vriesdelaan 5, POB 535, Paramaribo; tel. 473031; fax 477216; e-mail adm@stvs.info.sr; internet www.parbo.com/stvs; f. 1965; govt-owned; commercial; local languages, Dutch and English; Channel 8; Dir KENNETH OOSTBURG.

Finance

(cap. = capital; res = reserves; dep. = deposits; m. = million; brs = branches; amounts in Surinamese dollars unless otherwise specified)

BANKING

Central Bank

Centrale Bank van Suriname: 18–20 Waterkant, POB 1801, Paramaribo; tel. 473741; fax 476444; e-mail info@cbvs.sr; internet www.cbvs.sr; f. 1957; Gov. GILMORE HOEFDRAAD (designate).

Commercial Banks

Finabank NV: Dr Sophie Redmondstraat 59–61, Paramaribo; tel. 472266; fax 422672; e-mail finabank@sr.net; internet www.finabanknv.com; f. 1991; Gen. Man. MERLEEN ATMODIKROMO.

Handels-Krediet- en Industriebank (Hakrinbank NV): Dr Sophie Redmondstraat 11–13, POB 1813, Paramaribo; tel. 477722; fax 472066; e-mail hakrindp@sr.net; internet www.hakrinbank.com; f. 1936; cap. 0.1m., res 33.2m., dep. 552.5m. (Dec. 2006); Pres. and Chair. A.K.R. SHYAMNARAIN; Man. Dirs M. TJON-A-TEN, J.D. BOUSAID; 6 brs.

Landbouwbank NV: FHR Lim A Postraat 34, POB 929, Paramaribo; tel. 475945; fax 411965; e-mail lbbank@sr.net; f. 1972; govt-owned; agricultural bank; Chair. D. FERRIER; Pres. R. MERHAI; 5 brs.

RBTT Bank NV: Kerkplein 1, Paramaribo; tel. 471555; fax 411325.

De Surinaamsche Bank NV: Henck Arronstraat 26–30, POB 1806, Paramaribo; tel. 471100; fax 411750; e-mail info@dsbbank.sr; internet www.dsbbank.sr; f. 1865; cap. 0.8m., res 93.5m., dep. 1,178.3m. (Dec. 2007); Chair. S. SMIT; 8 brs.

Surinaamse Postspaarbank: Knuffelsgracht 10–14, POB 1879, Paramaribo; tel. 472256; fax 472952; e-mail spsbdir@sr.net; f. 1904; savings and commercial bank; cap. and res Sf 1,044m., dep. Sf 66,533m. (Dec. 2004); Man. ALWIN R. BAARH (acting); 2 brs.

Surinaamse Volkscredietbank: Waterkant 104, POB 1804, Paramaribo; tel. 472616; fax 473257; e-mail btlsvcb@sr.net; f. 1949; cap. and res Sf 170.3m. (Dec. 1997); Man. Dir THAKOERDIEN RAMLAKHAN; 3 brs.

Development Bank

Nationale Ontwikkelingsbank van Suriname NV: Jagernath Lachmonstraat 160–162, POB 677, Paramaribo; tel. 465000; fax 497192; f. 1963; govt-supported; cap. and res Sf 34m. (Dec. 1992).

INSURANCE

Assuria NV: Grote Combeweg 37, POB 1501, Paramaribo; tel. 477955; fax 472390; e-mail assuria@sr.net; internet www.assuria.sr; f. 1961; life and indemnity insurance; Man. Dir Dr S. SMIT.

Assuria Schadeverzekering NV: Henck Arronstraat 5–7, POB 1030, Paramaribo; tel. 473400; fax 476669; e-mail assuria@sr.net; internet www.assuria.sr; Chair. J. J. HEALY; Man. Dir Dr S. SMIT.

CLICO Life Insurance Company Ltd: Klipstenenstraat 29, POB 3026, Paramaribo; tel. 472525; fax 476777; e-mail clicosur@sr.net; internet www.clico.com/suriname; CEO CLAUDIUS DACON; Dir KAREN-ANN GARDIER.

Fatum Levensverzekering NV: Noorderkerkstraat 5–7, Paramaribo; tel. 471541; fax 410067; e-mail fatum@sr.net; internet www.fatum-suriname.com.

Hennep Verzorgende Verzekering NV: Dr Sophie Redmondstraat 246, Paramaribo; tel. 425205; fax 425209; e-mail hennep@sr.net; internet www.uitvaarthennep.com; f. 1896; Man. Dir H. J. HENNEP.

Parsasco NV: Henck Arronstraat 117, Paramaribo; tel. 421212; fax 421325; e-mail parsasco@sr.net; internet www.parsasco.com; f. 1995; Man. Dir AMAR RANDJITSING.

Self Reliance: Heerenstraat 48–50 en Henck Arronstraat 69–71, Paramaribo; tel. 472582; fax 472475; e-mail self-reliance@sr.net; internet www.self-reliance.sr; f. 1980; general and life insurance; Pres. MAURICE L. ROEMER.

Trade and Industry

DEVELOPMENT ORGANIZATIONS

Centre for Industry and Export Development: Rust en Vredestraat 79–81, POB 1275, Paramaribo; tel. 474830; fax 476311; f. 1981; Man. R. A. LETER.

Stichting Planbureau Suriname (National Planning Office of Suriname): Dr Sophie Redmondstraat 118, POB 172, Paramaribo; tel. 447408; fax 475001; e-mail dirsps@sr.net; internet www.planbureau.net; f. 1951; responsible for regional and socio-economic long- and short-term planning; Man. Dir LILIAN J. M. MONSELS-THOMPSON.

CHAMBERS OF COMMERCE

Kamer van Koophandel en Fabrieken (Chamber of Commerce and Industry): Dr J. C. de Mirandastraat 10, POB 149, Paramaribo; tel. 474536; fax 474779; e-mail chamber@sr.net; f. 1910; Pres. ROBERT AMEERALI; 16,109 mems.

Surinaams–Nederlandse Kamer voor Handel en Industrie (Suriname–Netherlands Chamber of Commerce and Industry): Jagernath Lachmonstraat 158, Paramaribo; tel. and fax 476909.

INDUSTRIAL AND TRADE ASSOCIATIONS

Associatie van Surinaamse Fabrikanten (ASFA) (Suriname Manufacturers' Asscn): Jaggernath Lachmonstraat 187, POB 3046, Paramaribo; tel. 434014; fax 439798; e-mail info@asfasuriname.com; internet www.asfasuriname.com; f. 1980; Chair. RAHID DOEKHIE; 317 mems.

Vereniging Surinaams Bedrijfsleven (Suriname Trade and Industry Association): Prins Hendrikstraat 18, POB 111, Paramaribo; tel. 475286; fax 475287; e-mail info@vsbstia.org; internet www.vsbstia.org; Pres. MARCEL A. MEYER; 290 mems.

MAJOR COMPANIES

The following are some of the major enterprises operating in Suriname:

British American Tobacco Company Ltd Suriname: Kristalstraat 1, Ma Retraite, Paramaribo; tel. 451339; fax 454002; internet www.batca.com; subsidiary of BAT Industries, United Kingdom; cigarette manufacturers and distributors.

Bruynzeel Suriname Houtmaatschappij NV: Slangenhoutstraat 1, POB 1831, Paramaribo; tel. 402824; fax 404421; e-mail bruynzeel@sr.net; internet housefactory.org; subsidiary of House Factory International (Romania); timber merchants; producers of sawnwood, plywood and precut and prefabricated houses; Chair. ROBBY NESLO.

CHM Suriname NV: Dr Sophie Redmondstraat 2–14, POB 1819, Paramaribo; tel. 471166; fax 471534; e-mail chmbuy@sr.net; internet www.chmsuriname.com; f. 1888; subsidiary of Handelen Industrie Mij Ceteco NV (Netherlands); electrical appliances, televisions and radios; importer of Toyota automobiles; Gen. Man. EDMUND KASIMBEG; 160 employees.

NV Consolidated Industries Corporation: Industrieweg-zuid 34, POB 635, Paramaribo; tel. 482050; fax 481431; e-mail info@cicsur.com; internet www.cicsur.com; f. 1967; manufacturers of detergents and disinfectants, packaging materials and cosmetics and toiletries; Man. Dir JAMES J. HEALY, Jr; 130 employees.

Fernandes Concern Beheer NV (The Fernandes Group): Klipstenenstraat 2–10, POB 1834, Paramaribo; tel. 471313; fax 471154; e-mail postmaster@fernandesconcern.com; internet fernandesconcern.com; holding co; Chair. MICHEL BRAHIM; 800 employees.

Fernandes Autohandel NV (Fernandes Automotive Ltd): Keizerstraat 105–117, Paramaribo; tel. 475046; fax 473891; e-mail automotive@fernandesautomotive.com; f. 1963; sole importer and distributor for Honda, Isuzu cars; also agricultural equipment, bicycles, fire extinguishers, auto paints; Gen. Man. J. J. F. TJANG-A-SJIN; 105 employees.

Fernandes Bakkerij NV (Fernandes Bakery Ltd): Kernkampweg 84, POB 1834, Paramaribo; tel. 430757; fax 492177; e-mail bakery@fernandesbakery.com; f. 1963; bread, pastry, biscuits; rice, potato and corn snacks; Gen. Man. OSCAR TJON KIE SIM; 350 employees.

Fernandes Bottling Company NV: Indira Gandhiweg 12, Ephraimszegen, POB 1834, Paramaribo; tel. 482121; fax 483091; e-mail postmaster@fernandesbottling.com; internet www.fernandesbottling.com; franchise for Coca-Cola; Gen. Man. BRYAN RENTEN; 175 employees.

Fernandes Handelmaatschappij NV (Fernandes Trading Co, Ltd): Klipstenenstraat 2–10, POB 1834, Paramaribo; tel. 471313; fax 474306; f. 1957; incl. aluminium doors and windows, household, hardware and building materials, wholesale and distribution; Gen. Man. ERNIE DE VRIES.

Fernandes Ice Cream NV: Kernkampweg 82–84, Paramaribo; tel. 439711; fax 49718; e-mail ifsice@sr.net; f. 1999; Gen. Man. GEORGE CHENG; 40 employees.

H. J. de Vries Beheersmaatschappij NV: Waterkant 92–96, POB 1849–1850, Paramaribo; tel. 471222; fax 475718; e-mail devries@hj-devries.com; internet www.hj-devries.com; f. 1903; holding co: import, wholesale, retail and distribution of food and durable goods and mfr of paints, household chemicals and claybricks; CEO KWOK KEUNG CHOY; over 250 employees.

Chemco NV: Indira Gandhiweg, Paramaribo; tel. 481661; fax 481880; e-mail chemco@hj-devries.com; f. 1982; import, wholesale, retail and distribution of chlorine and bleach.

Esuverfa NV (Eerste Surinaamse Verffabriek NV): Indira Gandhiweg, Paramaribo; tel. 483084; fax 483082; e-mail esuverfa@hj-devries.com; f. 1979; paint manufacturer; 19 employees.

H. J. de Vries Agro NV: Indira Gandhiweg, Paramaribo; tel. 482733; fax 480731; e-mail agro@hj-devries.com; importer of pesticides and agricultural products; Supervisor MARJORIE BRANDON.

H. J. de Vries Engros NV: Indira Gandhiweg, Paramaribo; tel. 482733; fax 480731; e-mail engros@hj-devries.com; f. 1903; wholesale and distribution of quality food and non-food products, alcoholic and non-alcoholic beverages and tobacco products.

H. J. de Vries Motors NV: Slangenhoutstraat 46–48, Paramaribo; tel. 402169; e-mail motors@hj-devries.com; official dealer for Suzuki, Mazda, Kia cars.

H. J. de Vries Nickerie NV: G. G. Maynardstraat 25, Nieuw Nickerie; tel. 231832; fax 231220; e-mail nickerie@hj-devries.com; internet www.nickerie.com; chemicals and machinery for the rice sector.

H. J. de Vries Retail NV: Indira Gandhiweg, Paramaribo; tel. 482733; fax 480731; e-mail retail@hj-devries.com; operates retail outlets in Paramaribo, Lelydorp, Tamanredjo and Nickerie.

Keram: Indira Gandhiweg, Paramaribo; fax 475718; e-mail keram@hj-devries.com; brick manufacturer.

Jong A. Kiem NV: Jagernath Lachmonstraat 203, POB 272, Paramaribo; tel. 491600; fax 491855; e-mail info@jongakiem.com; internet www.jongakiem.com; manufacturer of pharmaceutical products; owned by AstraZeneca PLC, United Kingdom.

C. Kersten en Co NV (CKC): Domineestraat 36–38, Paramaribo; tel. 471150; fax 478524; e-mail holding@kersten.sr; internet www.kersten.sr; holding co for distributors of durable goods; operates 12 cos; CEO SHIRLEY SOWMA-SUMTER; COO RICK TJON A. JOE; 648 employees.

Kirpalani's Kleding Industrie NV: Domineestraat 52–56, POB 251 and 1917, Paramaribo; tel. 471400; fax 410527; e-mail kirpa@sr.net; internet www.kirpalani.com; textile and clothing producers; Gen. Man. JHAMATMAL T. KIRPALANI; 636 employees.

Kuldipsingh Group: Anamoestraat, POB 8089, Paramaribo; tel. 551204; fax 550669; e-mail hkanamoe@kuldipsingh.net; internet www.kuldipsingh.net; f. 1979; consists of eight companies; manufactures and distributes metal and building products; Man. Dir SWITRANG KULDIPSINGH; 500 employees.

Nationale Metaal & Constructie Maatschappij NV (Nameco): Industrial Park Behesda, Hallen 5–6, POB 1560, Paramaribo; tel. 482014; f. 1975; construction and civil engineering projects.

Rosebel Gold Mines NV: Heerenstraat 8, Paramaribo; tel. 422741; 95% owned by IAMGold (Canada), 5% state-owned; Man. MATHIEU GIGNAC.

Shell Suriname Verkoopmaatschappij NV: POB 849, Paramaribo; tel. 482027; fax 482569; f. 1975; producers of fuel oil and lubricants; CEO PETER VOSER; 190 employees.

Stichting Behoud Bananensector Suriname (SBBS): Jarikaba, Saramacca; tel. 328170; banana-producers' and exporters' co-operative; fmrly known as Surland until closure in 2002, restructured and reopened under present name in 2004; scheduled for privatization; CEO ANDRÉ BRAHIM.

Suriname Aluminium Company (Suralco): van 't Hogerhuysstraat 13, POB 1810, Paramaribo; tel. 323281; fax 323314; internet www.alcoa.com/suriname; subsidiary of Alcoa, USA; bauxite mining and refining, alumina production; bought bauxite and alumina refining interests of BHP Billiton Maatschappij Suriname (q.v.) in 2009; Man. Dir WARREN PEDERSEN; Gen. Man. GEORGE BIJNOE.

Surinaams-Amerikaanse Industrie Maatschappij NV (SAIL): Cornelis Jongbawstraat 48, POB 3045, Paramaribo; tel. 474014; fax 473521; e-mail sail@sr.net; f. 1955; processors and exporters of marine and farm-raised shrimps and fish; Dir TIELAK SHARMAN; 137 employees.

NV Suriname Food and Flavor Industries: Rossignollaan 3, POB 863, Paramaribo; tel. 442090; fax 464889; f. 1982; food processors; sauces, flavourings and spices; Man. Dir HANS SINGH.

Varossieau Suriname NV: van 't Hogerhuysstraat 21, POB 995, Paramaribo; tel. 402988; fax 402141; e-mail info@varossieau-paints.com; internet www.varossieau-paints.com; f. 1959; manufacturers of industrial paints and enamels; Chair. R. POPPELAARS; Man. Dir R. G. DWARKASING; 66 employees (2003).

UTILITIES

Electricity

NV Energie Bedrijven Suriname (EBS): Noorderkerkstraat 2–14, POB 1825, Paramaribo; tel. 471045; fax 474866; e-mail g.lau@nvebs.com; internet www.nvebs.com; f. 1932 as Nederlands-Indische Gas Maatschappij; present name adopted in 1968; electricity and gas distribution; owns and operates Electricity Co of Paramaribo (EPAR) and Ogane Paramaribo (OPAR); Dir GERARD LAU.

Staatsolie Maatschappij Suriname NV: Dr Ir H. S. Adhinstraat 21, POB 4069, Paramaribo; tel. 499649; fax 491105; e-mail mailstaatsolie@staatsolie.com; internet www.staatsolie.com; f. 1980; state petroleum exploration and exploitation co; electricity and steam generation and supplies; produces 7,000 barrels per day of Saramacca Crude oil; Man. Dir Dr MARC C. H. WAALDIJK; 650 employees.

Paradise Oil Company: Dr Ir H. S. Adhinstraat 21, POB 4069, Paramaribo; tel. 439781; fax 530093; e-mail madaal@staatsolie.com; f. 2003; 100% owned by Staatsolie Maatschappij Suriname NV; oil exploration co; Operations Man. PATRICK BRUNINGS.

Water

NV Surinaamsche Waterleiding Maatschappij (SWM): Henck Arronstraat 9–11, POB 1818, Paramaribo; tel. 471414; fax 476343; e-mail swmsecretariaat@swm.sr; internet www.swm.sr; f. 1932; govt-owned; Dir SCEN SJAUW KOEN SA; 465 employees (2008).

TRADE UNIONS

Council of the Surinamese Federation of Trade Unions (RAVAKSUR) (Raad van Vakcentrales Suriname): f. 1987; Sec. MICHAEL MISKIN; comprises:

Algemeen Verbond van Vakverenigingen in Suriname 'De Moederbond' (AVVS) (General Confederation of Trade Unions): Verlengde Jagernath Lachmonstraat 134, POB 2951, Paramaribo; tel. 465118; fax 463116; e-mail avvsmoederbond51@hotmail.com; right-wing; Pres. ERROLL G. SNIJDERS; Gen. Sec. ALESSANDRO SPRONG; 15,000 mems.

Centrale Landsdienaren Organisatie (CLO) (Central Organization for Civil Service Employees): Gemenelandsweg 743, Paramaribo; tel. 499839; Pres. RONALD HOOGHART; 13,000 mems.

Organisatie van Samenwerkende Autonome Vakbonden (OSAV): Noorderkerkstraat 2–10, Paramaribo; fax 478548; Pres. SONNY CHOTKAN.

Progressieve Werknemers Organisatie (PWO) (Progressive Workers' Organization): Limesgracht 80, POB 406, Paramaribo; tel. 475840; fax 477814; f. 1948; covers the commercial, hotel and banking sectors; Pres. ANDRE KOORNAAR; Sec. EDWARD MENT; 4,000 mems.

Progressive Trade Union Federation (C-47): Wanicastraat 230, Paramaribo; tel. 401120; fax 401149; e-mail c47@sr.net; Pres. ROBBY BERENSTEIN; Gen. Sec CLAUDETTE ETNEL.

Federation of Farmers and Agrarians (FAL): Keizerstraat 150, Paramaribo; tel. 420833; fax 474517; Pres. JIWAN SITAL; Gen. Sec. ANAND DWARKA.

Nickerie Banana Workers' Union (BABN): Paramaribo; f. 2008; Pres. DAYANAND DWARKA.

Transport

RAILWAYS

There are no public railways operating in Suriname.

ROADS

In 2003 Suriname had an estimated 4,304 km (2,674 miles) of roads, of which 26.3% were paved. The principal east–west road, 390 km in length, links Albina, on the eastern border, with Nieuw Nickerie, in the west.

SHIPPING

Suriname is served by many shipping companies and has about 1,500 km (930 miles) of navigable rivers and canals. There are two ferry services linking Suriname with Guyana, across the Corantijn river, and with French Guiana, across the Marowijne river.

Maritieme Autoriteit Suriname (Suriname Maritime Authority): Cornelis Jongbawstraat 2, POB 888, Paramaribo; tel. 476733; fax 472940; e-mail info@mas.sr; internet www.mas.sr; fmrly Dienst voor de Scheepvaart; govt authority supervising and controlling shipping in Surinamese waters; Man. of Maritime Operations A. T. EDENBURG.

Scheepvaart Maatschappij Suriname NV (SMS) (Suriname Shipping Line Ltd): Waterkant 44, POB 1824, Paramaribo; tel.

472447; fax 474814; e-mail surinam_line@sr.net; f. 1936; state-owned; passenger services in the interior; Chair. A. T. EDENBURG.

Suriname Coast Traders NV: Flocislaan 4, Industrieterrein Flora, POB 9216, Paramaribo; tel. 463040; fax 463831; internet www.pasonsgroup.com; f. 1981; subsidiary of Pasons Group.

NV VSH United Suriname Shipping Company: van 't Hogerhuysstraat 9–11, POB 1860, Paramaribo; tel. 402558; fax 403515; e-mail sales@vshunited.com; internet www.vshunited.com/shipping.html; shipping agents and freight carriers; Man. RICHARD STEENLAND.

CIVIL AVIATION

The main airport is Johan Adolf Pengel International Airport (formerly Zanderij International Airport), 45 km from Paramaribo. Domestic flights operate from Zorg-en-Hoop Airport, located in a suburb of Paramaribo. There are 35 airstrips throughout the country.

Surinaamse Luchtvaart Maatschappij NV (SLM) (Suriname Airways): Mr Jagernath Lachmonstraat 136, POB 2029, Paramaribo; tel. 465700; fax 491213; e-mail publicrelations@slm.firm.sr; internet www.slm.nl; f. 1962; services to Amsterdam (Netherlands) and to destinations in North America, South America and the Caribbean; Vice-Pres. CLYDE CAIRO.

Gonini Air Service Ltd: Doekhiweg 1, Zorg-en-Hoop Airport, POB 1614, Paramaribo; tel. 499098; fax 498363; f. 1976; privately owned; licensed for scheduled and unscheduled national and international services (charters, lease, etc.); Man. Dir GERARD BRUNINGS.

Gum Air NV: Doekhieweg 3, Zorg-en-Hoop Airfield, Paramaribo; tel. 498888; fax 497670; e-mail info@gumair.com; internet www.gumair.com; privately owned; unscheduled domestic and regional flights; Man. HENK GUMMELS.

Tourism

Efforts were made to promote the previously undeveloped tourism sector in the 1990s. Attractions include the varied cultural activities, a number of historical sites and an unspoiled interior with many varieties of plants, birds and animals. There are 13 nature reserves and one nature park. There were an estimated 165,509 stop-over arrivals in 2007, of which a majority came from the Netherlands. In that year tourism receipts totalled US $73m.

Suriname Tourism Foundation: Dr J. F. Nassylaan 2, Paramaribo; tel. 424878; fax 477786; e-mail info@suriname-tourism.org; internet www.suriname-tourism.org; f. 1996; Exec. Dir ARMAND LI-A-YOUNG.

Defence

The National Army numbered an estimated 1,840 men and women, as assessed at November 2009. There is an army of 1,400, a navy of 240 and an air force of some 200.

Defence Budget: an estimated 134,000m. Surinamese dollars in 2010.

Commander-in-Chief: Col ERNST MERCUUR.

Education

Education is compulsory for children between the ages of seven and 12. Primary education lasts for six years, and is followed by a further seven years of secondary education, comprising a junior secondary cycle of four years followed by a senior cycle of three years. All education in government and denominational schools is provided free of charge. In 2007/08 enrolment in primary education included 90% of children in the relevant age-group, while in 2004/05, according to UNESCO estimates, enrolment in secondary education included 65% of children in the relevant age-group. Higher education was provided by four technical and vocational schools and by the University of Suriname at Paramaribo. In 2003 the Inter-American Development Bank approved a US $12.5m. loan to fund the reform of the basic education system into a single 10-year cycle. It was hoped that the funds would result in a 10% increase in the number of pupils who finished sixth grade and a 20% reduction in drop-out and repetition rates. A further $13m. grant for the sector was approved by the Dutch Government in 2005.

Bibliography

For works on the region generally, see Select Bibliography (Books)

Carlin, E., and Arends, J. (Eds). *Atlas of the Languages of Suriname*. Kingston, Jamaica, Ian Randle Publishers, 2003.

Colchester, M. *Forest Politics in Suriname*. Chicago, IL, International Books, 1996.

Dew, E. M. *The Trouble in Suriname, 1975–1993*. New York, Praeger Publrs, 1995.

Hoefte, R., and Meel, P. (Eds). *Twentieth Century Suriname: Continuities and Discontinuities in a New World Society*. Kingston, Jamaica, Ian Randle Publishers, 2001.

Kambel, E.-R., and MacKay, F. *The Rights of Indigenous Peoples and Maroons in Suriname*. Copenhagen, International Work Group for Indigenous Affairs, 2000.

Mackenzie, G. A. (Ed.). *Suriname*. Washington, DC, International Monetary Fund, 1999.

Meel, P. *Tussen autonomie en onafhankelijkheid: Nederlands-Surinaamse betrekkingen 1954–1961*. Leiden, KITLV Uitgeverij, 1999.

Norton, A. *U da sembe fa aki (we are people of this place): Place-attachment and belonging. A Saramaka response to globalization*. Ann Arbor, MI, ProQuest, 2006.

Schultz, G. *Turmoil and Triumph: Diplomacy, Power and the Victory of the American Ideal*. New York, Touchstone, 1996.

Sizer, N., and Rice, R. *Backs to the Wall in Suriname: Forest Policy in a Country in Crisis*. Washington, DC, World Resources Institute, 1995.

Suparlan, P. *The Javanese in Suriname: Ethnicity in an Ethnically Plural Society*. Tempe, AZ, Arizona State University Program for Southeast Asian Studies, 1995.

Thoden van Velzen, H. U. E., and van Wetering, W. *In the Shadow of the Oracle: Religion as Politics in a Suriname Maroon Society*. Prospect Heights, IL, Waveland Press Inc, 2004.

USA Ibp. *Suriname Central Bank and Financial Policy Handbook*. Milton Keynes, Lightning Source UK Ltd, 2005.

TRINIDAD AND TOBAGO

Geography

PHYSICAL FEATURES

Trinidad and Tobago lies in the West Indies, its constituent parts being considered the southernmost islands of the Caribbean, although, geologically, they are extensions of the South American continent. Venezuela (specifically, the Paria peninsula) lies only 11 km (seven miles) from the island of Trinidad, the two countries embracing the Gulf of Paria. The Gulf is entered by sea channels known as the Bocas, in the north by the Dragon's Mouths and in the south by the slightly broader Serpent's Mouth, which joins the eastward-widening Columbus Channel between the southern coast of Trinidad and the delta lands of the Orinoco in Venezuela. Some 145 km (90 miles) to the north of Trinidad is Grenada, the next nearest neighbour. Tobago, which accounts for only 300 sq km (116 sq miles) of the country's total area of 5,128 sq km, lies some 32 km to the north-east of Trinidad island.

Trinidad (80 km by 60 km in extent) is an anvil-shaped island, with tapering extensions in both the south-west and the north-west that reach further westward towards the coast of Venezuela and help enclose the Gulf of Paria. This provides a vast sheltered anchorage in the lee of Trinidad island, and it is on this shore that the capital, Port of Spain, is located (in the north). West of here, near the tip of the north-western peninsula, is the only natural harbour, Chaguaramas (central): the northern coast is rocky, the eastern coast exposed to heavy seas directly off the Atlantic and the southern coast steep. Three ranges of highlands cross the island from east to west, the highest being in the north, where El Cerro del Aripo reaches 940 m (3,085 ft), amid the densely forested slopes of the Northern Range. There are also the Central Range and the Trinity Hills in the south-east. Mid-way along the northern coast of the south-western peninsula is the 47 ha (116 acre) Pitch Lake near La Brea, the largest natural asphalt reservoir in the world, which testifies to the country's hydrocarbons wealth, while another geographical oddity, mud volcanoes, indicates the volcanic origins of the island. Plains dominate the rest of the south and the land along the Caroni river between the Central and Northern Ranges. Here the landscape is predominantly agricultural, giving way to wetlands near the coast, such as the Caroni Swamp (the roosting ground for the scarlet ibis and the egret) in the west and the Nariva Swamp (the largest freshwater swamp on the island, and home to the weeping or Trinidad capuchin, the red howler monkey and 32 species of bat) on the east coast. Still-extensive natural habitats such as these, as well as the dense northern rainforest, are widely protected, as both Trinidad and Tobago, once attached separately to the continental landmass, host probably the greatest ecological diversity in the insular Caribbean.

Tobago, the summit of a single mountain mass rising from the sea floor, is aligned from south-west to north-east, its northerly shores, facing the Caribbean, bearing the leeward beaches protected from the Atlantic weather. The island is about 42 km in length and up to 14 km wide, with plains of a coralline origin in the south rising towards the backbone of a central 29-km Main Ridge range, rising towards the north-east and reaching its highest point at Pigeon Peak (594 m). At this end of the island the peaks are cloaked with the oldest protected rainforest region in the Americas (since 1764). Tobago boasts an even greater variety of bird and animal life than the more developed Trinidad, claiming to be home to 210 bird species (notably the beautiful crowned blue mot mot), 123 butterfly species, 24 types of snake, 16 lizard kinds, 14 species of frog and a variety of spectacled cayman (the smallest alligator species). The country as a whole is reckoned to have 433 species of birds and 622 of butterflies, more than any other Caribbean island nation. Wildlife also thrives on the motley collection of smaller islands and islets, mostly north of Tobago, that the country also has under its jurisdiction. The marine environment is also flourishing, encouraged by the confluence of Atlantic currents with the warmer Caribbean and the rich discharge of the Orinoco.

CLIMATE

The climate is tropical, with a rainy season from June to November and a slightly cooler season between December and April. The islands are not in the hurricane belt, but fairly constant breezes off the Atlantic keep the temperatures from becoming too hot. The average maximum temperature is 32°C (89°F), although Tobago is slightly cooler, owing to its more constant exposure to the trade winds. Average annual rainfall is about 2,050 mm (80 ins) over most of the country, being higher in the mountains.

POPULATION

The population is one of the most varied in the Caribbean, a complex colonial history of competing Spanish, French and, finally, British rule augmented by the immigration of black Africans (originally as slaves), Indians (mainly from north India as indentured labour) and many others. The largest single ethnic group is now 'East' Indian, followed closely by those of African descent (each constituting about 40% of the population), with 18% of mixed heritage and the rest consisting of whites, Chinese, Lebanese and others. The East Indians tend to dominate agriculture still, but are also important in business. Blacks are more dominant on Tobago. Culturally, there are two folk traditions in the country, the Creole (black and colonial) and the East Indian, the latter including the presence of Hindus and Muslims, resulting in the official celebration of those religious holidays as well as the Christian ones. Christianity remains the main religion, with Roman Catholicism the leading denomination (26%), but Hindus represent 22% of the population, while Anglican Christians claim the adherence of 8% and various Protestant groups 21% (Orthodox Baptists and Pentecostalists each have 7%). Muslims account for 6% of the population. This diversity is reflected in the variety of languages spoken by the populace, with a French Creole patois surviving in some areas, Hindi being widely spoken among East Indians, and others using Chinese or Spanish. However, the most widely spoken tongue and the official language of the country is English.

In mid-2009 the total population was put at 1,310,100, with only some 4% living on Tobago. The capital, Port of Spain (including its suburbs), had a population of some 54,000 in 2001, while San Fernando, at the southern end of the west coast, is also a major population centre, followed by Arima, inland to the east of Port of Spain. These are the three administrative municipalities of Trinidad, which also has eight counties. Tobago, which has some autonomy within the republic, is constituted as a ward. Its chief town is Scarborough, on the southern coast at the south-western end of the island. The other important towns are Plymouth, across on the north coast from Scarborough, and Roxborough, towards the northern end of the south-facing coast.

History

MARK WILSON

Based on an earlier article by ROD PRINCE

The two islands that constitute the modern state of Trinidad and Tobago were both first settled by Carib and other Amerindian populations from the South American mainland. Contact with Europe and North America dates from the third voyage of the Spanish navigator Christopher Columbus, in 1498. Small Spanish settlements were established from 1592, which formed an insignificant part of the Viceroyalty of New Granada, based in Bogotá, Colombia.

Larger-scale settlement began from 1776, when Spain began to encourage settlers from Grenada and other former French possessions that had passed to British rule. Later, settlers came from Martinique and Guadeloupe, where slavery had been temporarily abolished as a result of the French Revolution. A Spanish cedula of 1783 established a system of land grants for French planters, with additional allocations for those who brought slaves. Coffee, cocoa and sugar plantations were established, and there was considerable growth in trade. Until the late 19th century French creole remained the main spoken vernacular. In the early 21st century Roman Catholicism remained the main Christian denomination.

Trinidad was captured by the United Kingdom in 1797 and was formally ceded to that country by Spain in 1802. Tobago was colonized by the Dutch in 1628, but then claimed by a succession of European countries until the British took possession in 1762, following 100 years of French occupation; France ceded the island to the United Kingdom in the following year. However, it was not until 1814 that the British gained the island in perpetuity. Throughout the 19th century in Trinidad there remained a latent conflict between the British administration and a mainly French planter and commercial class. For this reason, Trinidad, unlike most West Indian colonies, had no elected Assembly.

The abolition of slavery in 1834 was followed by four years in which slaves were forced to remain on the plantations under a system of indentureship. From 1838 many former slaves moved to Port of Spain or established peasant farms on unoccupied land; as did a large number of immigrants from other West Indian colonies. With a labour shortage developing on the plantations, from 1845 the Government encouraged the immigration of indentured labourers, mainly Indian, but also Chinese and Madeiran. On the expiry of a 10-year period, of which the first five were contracted to a single employer, the workers received either their passage home or title to a small plot of land. This form of immigration continued until 1917 and the majority of the rural population in modern Trinidad was descended from Indian indentured labourers. Tobago's sugar industry performed badly after emancipation, and was close to collapse by the 1880s. For this reason, the smaller colony was attached to Trinidad from 1889.

Agitation for increased political rights began in Trinidad from the 1880s, earlier than in most other West Indian colonies. From 1896 the Trinidad Workingmen's Association played an important role in political life. Against this background, in 1899 the colonial authorities unwisely abolished the elected Borough Council in Port of Spain. In 1914 the Council was re-established and, from 1925, there were elected members on the Legislative Council, although the electoral roll was limited by property qualifications.

THE MOVE TO INDEPENDENCE

Disturbances resulting from the depressed economic situation of the 1930s provided propitious conditions for the foundation of the labour movements. These, in turn, evolved into political movements, particularly after the introduction of universal adult suffrage in 1946. The People's National Movement (PNM), founded in 1956 by Dr Eric Williams, won 39% of the votes cast in legislative elections held in 1956, and gained control of the Legislative Council (securing 13 of the 24 elected seats), under the provision of the new constitutional arrangements that provided for self-government. Williams became Trinidad and Tobago's Chief Minister.

Along with most other British Caribbean colonies, Trinidad and Tobago joined the Federation of the West Indies in 1958. However, when Jamaica left the grouping in 1961 in order to seek independence individually, Trinidad and Tobago also withdrew, reluctant to take financial responsibility for the other, and, at that time, poorer, islands, in the north of the region, and the Federation collapsed. Internal self-government for Trinidad and Tobago in 1961 was followed by independence on 31 August 1962.

THE PNM AND PARTY POLITICS

Elective politics in Trinidad and Tobago mostly ran along racial lines, although there was some attempt by all parties to win at least token support from other groups. The PNM was mainly urban and Afro-Trinidadian, with some backing from Muslim and Christian Indians. Its early opponent, the Democratic Labour Party (DLP), led by Rudranath Capildeo, was based in the Hindu section of the Indian-origin community. Although Indo- and Afro-Trinidadians were roughly equal numerically, support from minority and mixed-race voters, together with the pattern of constituency boundaries, was enough to give the PNM a secure parliamentary majority over the DLP and its ethnically based successor parties until 1986. Dr Williams remained Prime Minister until his death in 1981.

The PNM's strongest challenge in this period came from the 'Black Power' movement, which came to prominence on the islands in 1970. Influenced to some extent by African-American radicalism, support for the movement stemmed mainly from a well-established perception that, eight years after independence, there was significant discrimination against Afro-Trinidadians in private sector employment, and that insufficient respect was given to black people and their culture. A series of demonstrations in 1970 was accompanied by some violence, and a state of emergency was declared. Unrest extended to junior army officers, who unsuccessfully attempted to overthrow the Government. The leaders of the Black Power movement were imprisoned without trial, and marches were banned. Nevertheless, many of their aims were achieved in the 1970s, when there were broader economic opportunities and more attention to cultural development.

Political difficulties persisted for some time, however, and there was an opposition boycott of the 1971 elections. In September 1973 Williams announced his resignation, but was persuaded to rescind it. A new Constitution came into effect on 1 August 1976, making Trinidad and Tobago a republic within the Commonwealth. In elections to the House of Representatives in the following month, the PNM won 24 of the 36 seats, while an alliance of petroleum and sugar workers within the newly formed United Labour Front (ULF), a mainly Indian party with trade-union support led by Basdeo Panday, secured 10 seats. The two Tobago seats were won by the Democratic Action Congress (DAC), led by Arthur N. R. Robinson, a former PNM cabinet minister. The former Governor-General, Ellis Clarke, was sworn in as the islands' first President in December.

At this time, the PNM was presiding over a buoyant economy, following steep rises in the world price of petroleum in 1973 and 1974 that transformed Trinidad and Tobago's relatively small reserves of petroleum into a major financial and political asset. Petroleum prices remained high until 1981, by which time the PNM's dominance of national politics was such that, at the time of his death in March of that year, Williams was without serious rivals.

THE RISE OF THE NATIONAL ALLIANCE FOR RECONSTRUCTION

Dr Williams was succeeded as Prime Minister by George Chambers, one of the three deputy leaders of the PNM. Chambers was seen as moderate and generally fair, but failed to command enthusiastic support. He presided over another election victory for the PNM in November 1981, winning 26 seats in the Parliament. The DAC and the ULF, as well as an intellectual pressure group, the Tapia House Movement, formed the National Alliance and took the two Tobago seats and eight, mainly Indian, rural seats, gaining 20.7% of the votes cast. The middle-class, conservative, Organization for National Reconstruction (ONR), led by another former PNM minister, Karl Hudson-Phillips, won 22.3% of the ballot but took no seats, because its mainly middle-class support was evenly spread across a large number of constituencies.

In August 1983 the four opposition parties formed an alliance to contest local elections and won 66 of the 120 local council seats. A united opposition party, the National Alliance for Reconstruction (NAR), was formed a year later. The NAR aimed to offer a credible alternative to the Government, at a time when stagnant and then decreasing petroleum prices were severely reducing government revenues and highlighting the defects of the policies pursued during the increase in prices of the previous decade. In the November 1984 elections to the Tobago House of Assembly, which had been formed in 1980, the DAC (part of the NAR) reduced the PNM's share of the 12 elective seats from four to one. Prime Minister Chambers was increasingly losing political respect, and his position was not strengthened by his failure to support the US-led military intervention in Grenada in October 1983. A 33% devaluation of the currency in December 1985 was deeply unpopular, and was seen as further eroding purchasing power in what was still an import-dependent economy.

Accusations of government economic mismanagement and corruption increased in the months preceding the December 1986 general election, intensified by the Government's failure to publish an official report on drugs-trafficking. The NAR, led by Robinson, won an overwhelming victory, winning 33 of the 36 seats in the House of Representatives, and 67% of the votes. The PNM's parliamentary representation was reduced to just three seats, owing to residual support in urban strongholds in eastern Port of Spain and in San Fernando. The party retained 33% of the popular vote, nevertheless, which formed the basis for a later recovery under the former energy minister, Patrick Manning, who was appointed PNM leader in January 1987. Robinson was appointed Prime Minister.

THE GOVERNMENT OF A. N. R. ROBINSON

The NAR Government was an unwieldy coalition of the ULF, the ONR, the DAC and the Tapia House Movement, a grouping of university radicals. Divisions emerged almost immediately over the allocation of cabinet portfolios and positions on state boards, and extended to policy matters, as the Government was forced to implement unpopular measures in response to a deepening economic crisis. There were also accusations that Indo-Trinidadians, who formed a majority of NAR voters, were being excluded from positions of real power.

The small Tapia House Movement left the NAR in June 1987, while John Humphrey, a former ULF member, was removed from his post as Minister of Public Works and Settlement in November. The external affairs minister and former ULF leader, Basdeo Panday, was dismissed in February 1988, along with one cabinet colleague and a junior minister. All three accused the NAR leadership of racism and were expelled from the party in October. In April 1989 Panday announced the formation of a new party, the United National Congress (UNC), which became the official opposition in September 1990, by virtue of holding six seats to the PNM's three. The UNC at this time was widely perceived to be a rural, Indo-Trinidadian party with strong links to the sugar workers' trade union.

The Government's unpopularity increased as it was forced to take further austerity measures. A compensatory financing agreement with the IMF was followed by stand-by agreements in 1989 and 1990. There was a further 15% currency devaluation in August 1988, which increased retail-price levels. Government expenditure was cut, and the budget of January 1989 imposed a 10% reduction on public sector pay. This last measure aroused the hostility of the trade unions, which successfully challenged its legality.

In July 1990 a group of insurgents from the Jamaat al Muslimeen, a sect of mainly Afro-Trinidadian Muslim converts led by Yasin Abu Bakr, a former policeman, stormed the parliament building during a session of the House of Representatives, taking 46 hostages including the Prime Minister and most of the Cabinet. At the same time, they blew up the police headquarters building and took over what was then the sole television station, using it to broadcast their demands that the Prime Minister should resign, and his deputy lead an interim government into elections within 90 days. Widespread looting and fires began almost immediately in the capital and some suburban centres. The siege lasted for five days, during which time 23 people were killed and 500 wounded, most of them looters shot by the police. The Prime Minister was shot in the leg by the rebels after refusing to sign a letter of resignation. However, the acting President was induced to sign an amnesty for the rebels, which was delivered to them in the parliament building.

Following the surrender of the Jamaat al Muslimeen, the Government announced that the amnesty agreement had been made under duress and was therefore invalid. Abu Bakr and 113 others were charged with murder and treason. The Judicial Committee of the Privy Council (the country's final court of appeal, based in London, United Kingdom) ruled, in November 1991, that the validity of the presidential amnesty should be determined before the case came to trial. In June 1992 the High Court ruled that the pardon was valid, and ordered the release of the accused. In October 1993 the Government lost an appeal against the ruling, but a year later the Privy Council ruled that the Jamaat al Muslimeen had invalidated the pardon by failing to surrender as soon as it was agreed, instead continuing the siege in an attempt to win further concessions. However, it was also ruled that it would be an abuse of process for the accused to be rearrested and tried. In January 2000 the Jamaat al Muslimeen was ordered to pay TT $20m. for damage incurred during the insurrection. In May 2001, however, the High Court awarded TT $625,000 in compensation to the group for damage done to its headquarters, in addition to an earlier payment of TT $1.5m. In 2005 Abu Bakr remained a prominent figure, and was reputedly linked to much of the island's violent crime, as well as to lucrative quarrying operations in north-eastern Trinidad. After a preliminary magistrates' court hearing in July 2004, he was committed to stand trial for conspiracy to murder a former member of the Jamaat al Muslimeen, who had been shot dead in mid-2003. The trial jury was unable in March 2005 to agree a verdict, and a retrial was expected. In 2004 another leading figure of the Jamaat was extradited to the USA to face arms-smuggling charges. In July–October 2005 a series of five bombs exploded in Port of Spain. Following the fourth explosion in mid-October, five people, including Abu Bakr, were arrested, but were subsequently released without being charged. The Jamaat al Muslimeen denied responsibility for the attacks. In November Abu Bakr was re-arrested and charged with seditious speech, incitement and terrorism, after allegedly preaching a sermon that called for a war on affluent Muslims who refused to pay *zakat*, a tithe for the poor, to his organization. In February 2006 the Attorney-General sought high court authorization for the state to confiscate 12 properties from members of the Jamaat al Muslimeen in compensation for damage caused during the attempted coup in 1990.

THE RETURN OF THE PNM

One member of Parliament was killed in the 1990 siege, and the NAR lost the by-election for his successor. This highlighted the Government's loss of support, but there was some surprise at the scale of the NAR's rout in the general election that followed in December 1991, when the party secured only 24% of the valid votes cast and only the two seats on Robinson's home island, Tobago. The PNM won 21 legislative seats and 45% of the popular vote, mainly in urban areas with an Afro-Trinidadian majority, while the UNC took 29% of the ballot and 13, mainly rural, seats in central and southern Trinidad.

The new PNM Government, led by Patrick Manning, contained few members of previous PNM administrations. Economic policies reversed many aspects of the party's previous policies, focusing on financial and trade liberalization, divestment of state enterprises and foreign investment, particularly in heavy industries based on offshore natural gas resources.

In April 1993 the Trinidad and Tobago dollar was made convertible, in a strictly managed float against the US dollar. In contrast with Jamaica and Guyana, the currency remained stable, in spite of occasional shortages on the foreign-exchange markets. The fiscal current account was in surplus from 1993 and the economy moved back into steady growth from 1994. A protracted dispute with trade unions over repayment of the TT $3,000m. in salary arrears incurred through the NAR's attempt in 1991 to reduce public sector salaries was settled in 1995 for teachers, and in the following year for other public servants.

A state of emergency was briefly declared on 3 August 1995, in order to allow the Government to remove from office the Speaker of the House of Representatives, Occah Seapaul, who was the subject of damaging financial allegations. This, in turn, led to the defection from the Government, on the following day, of her brother, Ralph Maraj, the Minister of Public Utilities (and former Minister of Foreign Affairs). With only a narrow majority now remaining, the Prime Minister responded by announcing that a general election was to be held on 6 November 1995, one year earlier than was necessary.

THE ELECTION OF THE UNC

In the election, although the PNM increased its share of the votes to 49%, its support was concentrated heavily in its urban strongholds. The UNC received enthusiastic backing from some important members of the business community (three of the most prominent of these supporters were formally charged in 2002 with corruption-related offences), and raised its share of the ballot to 46%. The UNC secured control of three marginal constituencies, which left each party with 17 of the 34 Trinidad seats. The NAR's remaining support in Trinidad had collapsed, but with the support of the two Tobago members, the UNC was able to form a Government and Basdeo Panday became Prime Minister. In spite of the electoral defeat, Manning resisted continuing demands from within the PNM for his resignation as party leader, winning a further five-year term in the post in 1996. However, he lost the support of important sections of the PNM, which weakened his ability to organize an effective opposition to Panday's Government.

The new administration continued most of the economic policies of its predecessor. The new finance minister, Brian Kuei Tung, and the foreign minister, Ralph Maraj, had both been members of the previous Cabinet. In February 1997 the Government's parliamentary position was strengthened by the defection of two PNM members, who subsequently sat as independents and were appointed junior ministers. The Government presided over a period of strong economic growth, but there were persistent and widespread reports of corruption and mismanagement. On 14 February an electoral college of both houses of Parliament elected Robinson as President. He immediately relinquished his parliamentary and cabinet seats, as well as the leadership of the NAR. The PNM was opposed to a head of state who had, until his nomination, played an active role in party politics, and for the first time a presidential election was contested. However, the PNM candidate, a serving high court judge, received 18 votes to Robinson's 46. The NAR retained President Robinson's former seat at a by-election in May. However, in April the representative of the other Tobago seat, Pamela Nicholson, resigned from the Government and from the NAR to sit as an independent. As a result of these changes, from mid-1997 the Government could command the support of 20 members of the House of Representatives.

A serious dispute between the Government and the Chief Justice, Michael de la Bastide, began in September 1999 when he claimed that the independence of the judiciary was threatened by an attempt by the Attorney-General, Ramesh Lawrence Maharaj, to tighten administrative and financial controls. The Chief Justice was supported by 28 of the country's 29 judges, but not by the President of the Bar Association, Karl Hudson-Phillips. The Government responded in December by announcing that a former British Lord Chancellor, Lord Mackay of Clashfern, would lead a three-member Commission of Inquiry into the administration of justice on the islands. President Robinson, clearly unhappy with this decision, did not appoint the Commission until February 2000, signalling an unprecedented breach between the largely ceremonial head of state and the Cabinet. This was all the more surprising owing to the fact that President Robinson had himself been a senior member of Panday's Cabinet in 1995–97 and had been nominated as President by Panday's Government. The Commission announced its findings and recommendations in October 2000, clearing the Attorney-General of seeking to undermine the independence of the judiciary, but apparently failing to settle the fundamental disagreement between de la Bastide and Maharaj.

The conflict between Prime Minister Panday and President Robinson intensified in 2000 and 2001; both the President and the Chief Justice were alleged by Panday to be 'enemies' of his administration, along with Ken Gordon, Chairman of the Caribbean Communications Network media group, who, as a consequence, won damages of TT $600,000 in a libel suit against Panday in October 2000.

In early January 2000 Hansraj Sumairsingh, a member of the UNC and leader of one of Trinidad's nine regional corporations, was found murdered. It was subsequently reported that Sumairsingh had written to the Prime Minister several times regarding threats made to him by the Minister of Local Government, Dhanraj Singh, following Sumairsingh's revelation of alleged corruption in the unemployment relief programme administered by Singh's ministry. Although Panday said that he could not remember having received such letters, a copy of one was later produced by a PNM member. A full investigation was initiated and in October Singh was dismissed from his government post. Singh left unexpectedly for the USA for medical treatment for stress and high blood pressure. However, he returned to Trinidad in January 2001 and was charged with corruption in the unemployment relief programme and, in February, with the murder of Sumairsingh. In April 2002 Singh was committed for trial, but was acquitted in October 2003.

THE RE-ELECTION OF THE UNC

The general election of 11 December 2000 was won by the UNC with 52% of the votes cast, compared to 46% for the PNM. The UNC gained two marginal seats on Trinidad, bringing its total in the 36-seat House of Representatives to 19, while the PNM won 16 seats and the NAR held one of the two Tobago seats. Panday was appointed Prime Minister for the second time.

At elections to the Tobago House of Assembly, held on 29 January 2001, the PNM took control of the Assembly for the first time, winning eight of the 12 seats. The NAR secured the remaining four seats, while the UNC, contesting the election for the first time, won minimal support, as did the

People's Empowerment Party, formed by former NAR dissidents.

The December 2000 general election was marred by allegations of fraud. Opposition charges that the electoral list had been manipulated were highlighted by police investigations of prominent government supporters and arrests were made following attempted manipulation of the electoral register. In January 2001 Panday announced his Cabinet and his nominations to the Senate. However, President Robinson at first refused to approve the senate nominations of seven UNC members, declaring them to be unconstitutional, as they had been defeated as candidates in the congressional election. His refusal was widely felt to be outside the President's discretionary powers under the Constitution.

Despite its election victory and the continuing growth of the economy, the UNC Government continued to be dogged by allegations of corruption in early 2001, including alleged fraud within the North West Regional Health Authority and irregularities at the state-owned Petroleum Company of Trinidad and Tobago Ltd (Petrotrin). In March, owing to health problems, Panday reduced his workload, relinquishing parts of his portfolio.

Relations between Panday and UNC deputy leader (and Attorney-General) Maharaj began to deteriorate in 2001. Panday pointedly failed to appoint Maharaj to act as Prime Minister when he travelled overseas. During the September budget debate, Maharaj and two cabinet colleagues, Ralph Maraj and Trevor Sudama, were sharply critical of the Government on corruption and other issues. Although the three dissidents did vote in favour of the budget proposals, Maharaj resigned as Attorney-General on 1 October, and his two supporters subsequently resigned their posts. They formed a temporary alliance with the PNM, proposing to form a new Government; however, President Robinson instead agreed to a request by Panday on 10 October to dissolve Parliament and hold a general election on 10 December. Maharaj and his majority on the UNC executive were unable to establish their right to the party's name and symbol, and fought the election as a new grouping, Team Unity.

A HUNG PARLIAMENT

Following a long and bitter electoral campaign, Panday's fiercely loyal ethnic Indian support was barely diminished in the legislative elections of 10 December 2001, despite the divisions within the UNC and the allegations of corruption. The UNC retained 50% of the popular vote, with 46% for the PNM. However, the PNM narrowly gained a marginal seat in Trinidad from the UNC, as well as the NAR's remaining Tobago seat. This left each main party with 18 legislative seats.

As a result, on 16 December 2001 the UNC and PNM leaders signed the so-called 'Crowne Plaza Accord' in a Port of Spain hotel, which, if implemented, would have allowed Parliament to function. They agreed on the choice of Speaker for the House of Representatives and to accept the choice of President Robinson for Prime Minister. Following several days' deliberation, on 24 December the President announced that Manning should be Prime Minister. Panday immediately declared the choice illegal and unconstitutional, and maintained that the candidate for Speaker previously agreed in the Crowne Plaza Accord was closely linked to the PNM. With no Speaker, Parliament could not function, nor could an electoral college be convened to choose a successor for President Robinson, whose term in office was due to expire on 19 March 2002.

In spite of deep political polarization, society continued to function more or less as normal. The budget passed in September 2001 provided a financial basis for administration to continue. Panday's threats to launch a mass campaign of 'civil disobedience' were not enacted, possibly because of pressure from his business supporters. Robinson agreed to remain in office for up to one year, or until an electoral college could be convened. In line with normal practice in Trinidad and Tobago, the PNM replaced UNC appointees with its own supporters in key positions in the state sector; but with both parties agreeing on most points of economic and social policy, there were few other changes. According to the Constitution, a six month interval is allowed between meetings of Parliament. Close to this deadline, on 5 April 2002, an attempt was made to convene the House of Representatives. The UNC voted against the PNM's nominees for Speaker, further complicating the issue by nominating several thousand nominees of its own, while at the same time voting against them, in case any were acceptable to the Government. After two days Parliament was prorogued.

The new Government appointed Commissions of Inquiry to investigate some of the allegations of corruption made against the UNC Government. In March 2002 Brian Kuei Tung, Panday's Minister of Finance in 1995–2000, and five associates were charged with corruption, conspiracy and misbehaviour in public office. The charges were brought in connection with contracts for a new airport terminal, and carried a maximum sentence of 10 years' imprisonment. Further charges were laid in May 2004 against Kuei Tung, former UNC Minister of Works, Sadiq Baksh, and 11 others. Panday himself was charged in September 2002 with failure to note large deposits made to a bank account in the United Kingdom in his statutory declaration of financial assets. However, defence lawyers in these and other cases raised a series of procedural issues, delaying the progress of the cases. Furthermore, a magistrate's ruling on whether the airport terminal charges should be heard in the High Court was still subject to continuing procedural disputes in 2010, even before possible hearings in the High Court, the Court of Appeal and the Privy Council. A final verdict in this case was most unlikely before 2014 at the earliest.

THE SECOND MANNING ADMINISTRATION

Government was able to continue to function on the basis of the 2001 budget until the end of October 2002, but not beyond. The parliamentary impasse over the appointment of a Speaker eventually forced Prime Minister Manning to announce on 28 August that a further general election would be held on 7 October—the third in 22 months. At the October election the PNM gained 50.7% of the popular vote and 20 seats, compared with 46.6% for the UNC (and the remaining 16 seats). In February 2003 the PNM's majority enabled an electoral college of the members of both houses of Parliament to elect George Maxwell Richards, a former principal of the local campus of the University of the West Indies, as President, allowing Robinson to retire.

In an election to the Tobago House of Assembly in January 2005, the PNM increased its legislative strength from eight to 11 of the 12 seats; the remaining seat was taken by the Democratic Action Congress, a group formed by a former NAR Chairman of the island assembly, Hochoy Charles. With little local support, the UNC did not contest the island election.

The UNC's parliamentary presence was reduced to 14 in April 2005, when two members of Parliament realigned themselves as independents in protest at Panday's handling of an incident in which a UNC member of Parliament, Chandresh Sharma, alleged that the Minister of Housing, Keith Rowley, had thrown a teacup at him in September 2004. Sharma was suspended from the House in May 2005 for failing to apologize for his allegations. In the same month further corruption charges were filed against Panday, his wife Oma, his former Minister of Works and Transport, Carlos John, and a business associate. Panday initially refused to pay bail, spending eight days in prison as a result, but later relented and was released. Tensions between Panday's hardline supporters and the UNC's moderate wing increased, and elections were held for a new party leadership in October. Panday remained Chairman, but stood aside as political leader in favour of the moderate Winston Dookeran, who had been Minister of Planning and Mobilization in the 1986–91 NAR Government (serving as acting Prime Minister on several occasions during that period), and subsequently Governor of the Central Bank during 1997–2002. However, Panday supporters took most party executive positions, and Dookeran was effectively marginalized from decision-making.

In April 2006 Panday was sentenced to the maximum penalty of two years' imprisonment, in addition to a fine of TT $60,000 and a forfeiture of TT $1.6m., for failing to declare monies held in a bank account in London. He was released on bail pending an appeal, on health grounds, but under the terms of the Constitution was suspended as member of Parliament, and removed as constitutional Leader of the Opposition. He was replaced as opposition leader, not by Dookeran but by Kamla Persad-Bissessar, a former Attorney-General and Minister of Education in the 1995–2001 Panday Government. Dookeran and four other members of Parliament left the UNC in September 2006 to form the Congress of the People (COP). With one other former UNC legislator remaining as an independent, and Panday's seat declared vacant in October, this reduced the UNC's parliamentary presence to nine.

An appeal by Panday against his conviction was upheld in March 2007, on the basis that the Chief Magistrate Sherman McNicolls, who heard the case, had failed to make public his concerns over alleged improper interference in the case by the Chief Justice, Satnarine Sharma, and over a suspicious cheque received from a company owned by one of Panday's defence witnesses. The Court of Appeal ordered a retrial to be held 'expeditiously'; however, this was delayed by further procedural appeals from the defence, and was not yet under way in mid-2010. Magistrates' court hearings on unrelated corruption charges against Panday, his wife, John and a businessman started in June 2007, but hearings were also subject to repeated procedural delays. Panday was reinstated as UNC leader in April 2007, but Persad-Bissessar remained parliamentary Leader of the Opposition as Panday's parliamentary seat remained vacant under a July 2007 court ruling.

Panday's trial brought to the fore a dispute concerning Chief Justice Sharma. Allegations that the Chief Justice had attempted to interfere in 2004 with the prosecution for murder of a prominent Indo-Trinidadian medical academic and his wife were made public in February 2005. Measures to initiate procedures in April for the removal of Sharma were held back by a legal challenge and subsequent attempts at mediation were unsuccessful. However, in May 2006 it was further alleged by the Chief Magistrate that Sharma had endeavoured to lobby against a guilty verdict in the Panday trial. This prompted a new attempt to remove the Chief Justice, as well as a police investigation into his conduct. A high court ruling that he could not be charged with the criminal offence of attempting to pervert the course of justice was overturned by the Court of Appeal and Privy Council, but the subsequent prosecution collapsed in March 2007, as the Chief Magistrate refused to testify in court. The President in May appointed a tribunal under Section 137 of the Constitution to consider the possible removal of Sharma; this held public hearings in September and reported in December that there was not sufficient evidence to justify his removal. Sharma was briefly reinstated, having been twice suspended from office, but stepped down permanently on reaching retirement age in January 2008. He was replaced by Ivor Archie, who at 49 was younger than previous holders of the office, and was expected to take an energetic and reformist approach to management of the judiciary. The episode was deemed to have severely damaged public perception of the independence and impartiality of the senior judiciary.

Meanwhile, in June 2004 the Elections and Boundaries Commission proposed boundary changes, which were agreed by Parliament in the following June: the changes enlarged the number of constituencies from 36 to 41, thereby preventing the recurrence of a hung parliament and increasing the number of marginal seats, while reducing the influence of the two Tobago members.

A general election was held on 5 November 2007. The PNM took 26 of the 41 seats, with 46.0% of the popular vote, while the UNC secured 15 seats and 29.8% of the vote. The COP won 22.7% of the votes cast, but no seats. Only six of the PNM's 16 sitting members contested the election; with three appointed senators from the previous parliament, 17 of the party's 26 lower house representatives and 13 of the 23-member Cabinet were new to Parliament. The PNM's share of the vote was down from 50.7% in 2002, in part because of concerns over violent crime and apparent mismanagement in certain policy areas.

The UNC, along with four very small groups, contested the election as the UNC-Alliance, led by Panday, who remained party leader in mid-2008 at the age of 75, and resumed the position of Leader of the Opposition after the poll. Of its 15 seats, nine were won with less than 50% of the popular vote, as a large number of former party supporters voted for the COP.

Maxwell Richards was elected to a second five-year presidential term in February 2008. In elections to the Tobago House of Assembly, held on 19 January 2009, the PNM lost ground to a newly formed opposition coalition, the Tobago Organisation of the People (TOP), which took four of the 12 seats; the TOP did not include the UNC, which had no significant presence in Tobago. Elections for local government bodies in Trinidad were scheduled for October 2006 but were postponed three times, and then again in July 2009 while the Government proposed reform of the local government system. Meanwhile, opinion polls in 2009 indicated a low level of support for both government and opposition parties, and for their political leaders.

From the early part of 2003 political attention was focused on the rate of murders and kidnappings, which had accelerated since 2001. The number of murders rose from an average of 108 per year in 1991–99 to a peak of 547 in 2008, with a per head murder rate of 42 per 100,000, an extremely high figure by international standards but lower than that of some other Caribbean countries, including Jamaica, in which the rate was 60 per 100,000 in the same year. Much of the violence stemmed from feuding between rival drugs gangs in lower-income districts within the urbanized east–west corridor running through Port of Spain. There was also a sharp increase in kidnappings for ransom in 2002–03, and again in 2005, with a high proportion apparently also drugs-related. The authorities viewed the control of drugs-transshipment as an essential element of the control of crime. Installation of a new coastal radar system was completed in 2005, and the Government also planned to double the strength of the Defence Force and coast guard and purchase new patrol and interception vessels. Companies in the United Kingdom and Australia were commissioned to deliver offshore patrol vessels; six Austal craft were delivered in 2009. A Special Anti-Crime Unit (SAUTT) established in 2003 included former members of the police, Defence Force and other services. Kidnapping was sharply reduced from 56 cases in 2005 to 17 in 2006 and 12 in 2007, owing to improved surveillance and to legislation enacted in December 2005, under which alleged members of dismantled kidnapping gangs were refused bail. From 2006 some 39 former police officers from the United Kingdom began two-year contracts in Trinidad and Tobago, largely to be dedicated to forensic and intelligence work and training for local officers; with initial contracts completed but some additional recruitment needed, 55 were in place in mid-2010, working with SAUTT on gang-related murders. Police training programmes were upgraded and modernized. These and other measures were expected to have a medium- and long-term effect, rather than an immediate impact on gang violence. There was no clear explanation for the increase in violent crime, although contributory factors included the import and distribution of illegal guns by narcotics traffickers, the growth of youth gangs in low-income areas, the continuing ineffectiveness of police methods and delays in judicial hearings, which, in turn, facilitated the killing or intimidation of witnesses. There were widespread allegations that the Government has allowed criminal gangs to infiltrate urban job-creation schemes. Opinion polls demonstrated that crime was the primary issue of concern for the general public, and the polls also indicated low public confidence in the ability of the police, Government and other institutions to bring criminality under control.

Corruption allegations against the PNM persisted from 2005. In April of that year the UNC raised allegations against the Minister of Works and Transport, Franklyn Khan, and the Minister of Energy and Energy Industries, Eric Williams (no relative of former premier Dr Eric Williams). Khan submitted his resignation in May and was formally charged on six counts of corruption in November. In December Khan also tendered his resignation from his post as Chairman of the PNM. Williams was charged with accepting bribes from a potential contractor and resigned from office in January 2006. A magistrates' court ruled in December 2007 that the evidence against Williams did not merit a high court trial; however, no ruling had been made on Khan's case by mid-2010. Neither stood as a candidate in the 2007 general election. A more serious dispute surfaced in 2008. Dr Keith Rowley, a fiercely outspoken senior member of the Cabinet, was removed from his post as Minister of Trade and Industry in April after forcefully objecting to what he saw as a lack of transparency or accountability in the management of the Urban Development Corporation of Trinidad and Tobago (UDECOTT), a state-owned company responsible for the management of several large government construction projects. The leading private sector organizations in April joined Rowley in calling for a public inquiry into the affairs of UDECOTT. A Commission of Inquiry was established in July 2008, under the leadership of a British lawyer and civil engineer, Prof. John Uff, sitting with three local members, and published its report in March 2010, despite attempts by UDECOTT and others to derail the proceedings through legal actions alleging bias by the commissioners. The so-called Uff Commission identified several apparent instances of mismanagement or corruption on the part of UDECOTT, and noted that procedures and accountability were not clearly defined. Among a long list of serious concerns, it was noted that the construction (managed by UDECOTT) of a stadium intended for use in the 2007 Cricket World Cup remained unfinished in 2010, by which time its estimated cost had increased from TT $272m. to TT $885m. Furthermore, a TT $368m. contract for the construction of an office building had been awarded to a company headed by the Malaysian brother-in-law of UDECOTT Chairman Calder Hart, which did not appear to meet the formal terms to qualify as a bidder. Hart, a Canadian by origin but granted citizenship of Trinidad and Tobago in 2004, resigned from his post in March 2010, and left Trinidad soon afterwards for Florida, USA, while a criminal enquiry into issues raised by the Commission was in progress.

Meanwhile, concerns over the scale of corruption were heightened in February 2009, when the members of the Integrity Commission (a body established under the 1976 Constitution to promote integrity in public life) resigned over judicial findings that an investigation into Rowley had been conducted in bad faith. A new Commission was appointed in April 2009 but immediately collapsed after the majority of its members were deemed ineligible or were suspected of personal corruption; a replacement Commission was not announced until March 2010.

In addition to more general allegations of corruption and incompetence in the public sector, there was also widespread disquiet over perceived extravagance in government spending—for example, in the construction of a TT $175m. diplomatic centre and Prime Minister's residence, and in the priority given to government offices and cultural centres within the Government's capital spending plans. Moreover, provisions suggested in 2008 for a new constitution were seen as proposing too much power for a newly envisaged position of Executive President.

New divisions within the UNC emerged in 2008, with three high-profile members of parliament calling for elections to choose a new party leadership. This faction comprised former Attorney-General Ramesh Lawrence Maharaj, Jack Warner, a Vice-President of Fédération Internationale de Football Association (FIFA), and the prominent calypsonian musician Winston 'Gypsy' Peters. They were threatened repeatedly with disciplinary action, and Maharaj was removed from his post as chief whip for the opposition. A party leadership election was scheduled for 24 January 2010. Kamla Persad-Bissessar, hitherto a loyal ally of Panday, stood against him, and, with the support of Warner, Peters and others, won by a convincing margin, securing 13,932 votes compared with 1,359 for Panday and 1,072 for Maharaj. Panday initially retained the support of the majority of UNC members of Parliament and the post of Leader of the Opposition, but was replaced in this capacity by Persad-Bissessar in late February, who thereby became the first female opposition leader in Trinidad and Tobago's history.

PERSAD-BISSESSAR ASSUMES THE PREMIERSHIP

On 8 April 2010 Prime Minister Manning advised President Maxwell Richards to dissolve Parliament, subsequently calling an election for 24 May. No official reason was offered for the decision. Manning retained a clear majority, and there was no constitutional requirement to call an election before March 2013. Possible concerns he may have had included a motion of no confidence due to have been debated on 9 April, which would have allowed damaging allegations to be reported under parliamentary privilege, and which, in the view of some observers, he risked losing despite the PNM's parliamentary majority. With the election called, Persad-Bissessar swiftly formed an alliance with the COP, the TOP and two minor parties, and fought a vigorous campaign, under the banner of the People's Partnership, in which she pledged to combat crime, corruption and mismanagement, also opposing a proposed increase in property tax, and promising to raise state pensions and other spending commitments. The People's Partnership coalition won a convincing victory at the polls on 24 May, securing 29 of the 41 seats with 59.8% of the popular vote, and taking many seats hitherto regarded as PNM strongholds as well as both seats in Tobago; turn-out was recorded at 69.4% of the registered electorate. Persad-Bissessar was inaugurated as Prime Minister on 26 May, whereupon she pledged to strive for 'a safer, more prosperous and just Trinidad and Tobago'. Dookeran was appointed Minister of Finance, while Warner was awarded the influential works and transport portfolio, and a former Chief of Defence Staff, Brig. John Sandy, a widely respected non-partisan figure, was appointed Minister of National Security.

Although the PNM reacted quickly to the electoral defeat by replacing Manning with Dr Rowley as party Leader in June 2010, the strength of the Partnership's victory was further reinforced at local government elections in July. The ousted party retained only three of the 14 authorities, won no seats in five authorities, and took only a single seat in two others, while the Partnership seized control of Diego Martin, in which the PNM had won all three parliamentary seats two months previously.

Among the first tasks of the new Parliament was to vote on a proposal submitted by the Police Service Commission for a new police commissioner, a matter of some importance in view of public concern over violent crime. The Commission's first two nominees were Canadian; amid expressions of reservation, by Persad-Bissessar, Sandy and the influential Police Social and Welfare Association, among others, with regard to the appointment of a non-national, Parliament rejected the first of these nominees, but appointed the second, Dwayne Gibbs, with another Canadian selected to serve as one of his three deputies.

In July 2010, with the fiscal outlook now believed to be more dismal than initially anticipated, Persad-Bissessar announced a review of the purchase of three offshore patrol vessels, at a combined cost of £150m., from the major British aerospace and defence manufacturer BAE Systems, with delivery scheduled for late 2010 or early 2011; however, the existing contractual commitment was believed to be difficult to cancel without incurring a severe financial penalty. Meanwhile, the Prime Minister's security adviser also voiced concerns regarding the cost of the British police officers currently working with SAUTT (see above).

INTERNATIONAL RELATIONS

In April 2000 Trinidad and Tobago received widespread international condemnation following a government announcement that the country was to withdraw from the first optional protocol to the International Covenant on Civil and Political Rights, owing to its continued support of capital punishment. The Government stated that the withdrawal was intended to prevent condemned murderers from addressing lengthy appeals. Both major parties, while in office, pressed for the use of capital punishment, but, in most cases, were unsuccessful in overcoming the legal obstacles.

Talks were held from 1995 to demarcate the maritime boundary between Trinidad and Tobago and Barbados and to revise a 1991 agreement granting Barbados limited fishing rights. Although fishing issues were prominently reported, oil and gas-bearing geological structures close to the probable boundary line were believed to be of great interest to both sides. Differences escalated sharply from January 2004; in mid-February Barbados imposed limited licensing requirements on some imports from Trinidad and Tobago, and then, two days later, referred the maritime dispute for arbitration under the

UN Law of the Sea. A tribunal ruled in April 2006 on an Exclusive Economic Zone boundary that followed the line of equidistance for most of its length. This allocated a large area to the north-east of Tobago, thought to have some deep-water oil and gas potential, to Barbados. Trinidad and Tobago retained an area of similar size to the north of Tobago, where Barbados had claimed fishing rights, but was instructed to negotiate a fisheries agreement; no tangible progress had been made on this issue by mid-2010. Meanwhile, a maritime boundary agreement with Grenada was signed in April of that year. Barbados and Trinidad and Tobago were the only Caribbean Community and Common Market (CARICOM) members to remain outside Venezuela's 2005 PetroCaribe initiative, which offered oil concessions and favourable financing terms to Caribbean nations. This was expected to threaten the regional market of the state-owned oil company, Petrotrin. However, in April 2006 Trinidad and Tobago agreed to the waiver of CARICOM rules, allowing PetroCaribe to proceed. Progress was subsequently reported in negotiations with Venezuela for the use of cross-border oil and gas reserves, with a framework agreement signed in March 2007 providing a basis for detailed proposals. However, there had been little further progress by mid-2010, and the Government of Venezuelan President Lt-Col Hugo Chávez Frías was not thought to favour an agreement.

In April 2005 the Caribbean Court of Justice was officially inaugurated. The regional Court, based in Port of Spain, was to replace the Privy Council in the United Kingdom as the final court of appeal, and was also to adjudicate on disputes relating to the implementation of CARICOM agreements. An agreement to establish the Court had been signed by the leaders of 11 Caribbean states in February 2001, at a CARICOM summit in Barbados. However, by mid-2010 only Barbados, Belize and Guyana had adopted the appellate jurisdiction of the Court, which had, by that time, delivered 43 judgments, with other member states intending initially to use it only to settle CARICOM matters. The Manning administration had been in favour of the Court; however, while in opposition, the UNC had stated that it would not support the Court, reversing the position that it adopted while in office prior to 2001; at mid-2010 it was not immediately clear which position would be adopted by the new People's Partnership Government. Legislation to make the change would require a three-quarters' parliamentary majority. Former President Robinson had played a prominent role in the establishment, in 2002, of the International Criminal Court; along with most of its CARICOM associates, Trinidad and Tobago remained a strong supporter of this body, and refused to sign an 'Article 98' agreement exempting US military personnel from its proceedings.

Economy

MARK WILSON

At the beginning of the 21st century the economy of Trinidad and Tobago contrasted sharply with those of its Caribbean neighbours. Although no longer dependent on the extraction and refining of petroleum, it was increasingly underpinned by the energy sector, with the extraction of natural gas and crude oil providing the basis for processing and manufacturing industries. Tourism, 'offshore' finance, and agriculture, by contrast, were less well developed.

A phase of rapid economic development began when petroleum prices rose from US $1.30 per barrel in 1970 to US $33.50 in 1982. This led to rapid growth in gross domestic product (GDP) in this period, at an average annual rate of 5.5%. Expansion of GDP, in turn, had strong positive effects on foreign exchange earnings and on government revenue, which grew from TT $888m. in 1974 to TT $4,253m. in 1981. The Government attempted to spread the benefits of the increase in petroleum prices through spending on infrastructure, investment in state-owned, heavy industries and other capital projects. Imports were restricted in an effort to encourage local manufacturing, while protection also extended to services such as insurance.

World oil prices fell sharply in the 1980s, adversely affecting domestic petroleum production, while new facilities for crude petroleum imports to the USA had already prompted the removal of that country's strategically motivated tax incentives for petroleum products refined in the Caribbean. Production declined from 230,000 barrels per day (b/d) in 1978 to an average of 150,000 b/d in 1988–90, with a further decline to 113,500 b/d in 2001. However, there were also some important discoveries, including, in January 1998, the largest newly identified reservoir for 25 years and another large oilfield in 2001; there were also substantial amounts of condensate associated with recent gas finds. Production rose to 144,500 b/d in 2005, with newly developed reserves coming on-stream, but fell back to 107,261 b/d in 2009, in part because of operational difficulties. At the most recent full audit, in early 2004, proven oil reserves were 990m. barrels, with 324m. barrels of probable reserves and 2,000m. barrels of possible reserves. BP (formerly British Petroleum) estimated proven reserves at 800m. barrels in 2010.

Owing to an economic recession, in 1986 the National Alliance for Reconstruction (NAR) Government adopted a structural-adjustment programme and negotiated two successive stand-by agreements with the IMF. This was followed in 1990 by debt-rescheduling agreements with lending agencies and a US $850m. loan agreement with the Inter-American Development Bank (IDB). These measures, along with enhanced use of natural gas resources, overseas investment in energy industries and increased activity in other manufacturing industries and the financial sector, contributed to a general economic recovery in the 1990s. According to the Central Bank of Trinidad and Tobago, GDP grew at an average annual rate of 3.9% in 1996–2001 and exceeded 5% each year from 2001, with energy-derived peaks of 14.4% in 2003 and 13.5% in 2006, slipping back to a still brisk growth rate of 4.6% in 2007, and then to 2.3% in 2008; however, there was a reversal in 2009, with the economy contracting by 3.0% as energy prices fell and the effects of the global economic downturn took hold. Import restrictions were gradually liberalized from the early 1990s, while foreign exchange controls were abolished in April 1993 as the Trinidad and Tobago dollar moved from a fixed rate against the US currency to a strictly managed float. The currency moved sharply from a rate of TT $4.25 to TT $5.74, but remained stable thereafter, with the rate at or close to TT $6.30 from early 1997 to mid-2010 (at which point it stood at TT $6.35), in spite of capital outflows that caused intermittent shortages of foreign exchange at the commercial banks. Unemployment fell to 3.9% in the final quarter of 2008, but increased moderately to 5.1% at the end of 2009 as a result of the economic downturn.

From mid-1999 to mid-2008 a strong upward trend in international petroleum prices had a positive effect on government revenues. Chemicals and steel prices also recovered from declines in the late 1990s. Methanol, a key product, decreased from US $268 per metric ton in 1995 to a low point of US $94 per ton in mid-1999, but recovered to an average of US $434 per ton by 2007, rising further to US $729 per ton in the first quarter of 2008. The price of ammonia declined from US $199 per ton in 1995 to US $88 per ton in the first quarter of 2002, but averaged US $291 per ton in 2007 and US $732 per ton in the third quarter of 2008.

However, the economy came under some pressure from the second half of 2008 as the global economic downturn affected energy commodity prices and, as a result, the economy moved from rapid growth to contraction of 3.0% in 2009. The average West Texas Intermediate oil price in 2009 was 38% lower than that in 2008, at US $61.7 per barrel; ammonia prices declined to US $228 per metric ton, while methanol prices fell to US $241 per ton. Export prices of liquefied natural gas (LNG) also declined substantially, with the Henry Hub (the pricing point for natural gas futures contracts traded on the New York (USA) Mercantile Exchange) gas price averaging US $4.00 in 2009, representing a year-on-year decline of 55%. Although there had been some recovery in energy prices by the early months of 2010, these price trends placed considerable pressure on government finances, and public spending plans were scaled back from late 2008. Major private sector energy investment projects were placed on hold, and the construction sector contracted after working at or above full capacity for several years. The index of retail sales revealed a 7.9% decline in 2009, in sharp contrast to consumer spending growth of 20.1% in 2007 and 13.7% in 2008. Indicating the weakness of consumer confidence, sales of building materials and hardware declined by 21.1% in 2009, and that of motor vehicles and parts fell by 28.6%.

The population stood at 1,310,000 in mid-2009, with a population density (per sq km) of 255.5. Approximately one-half of the population lived in an urbanized 'east–west corridor', stretching from Diego Martin in the west, through Port of Spain to Arima in the east. One-sixth of the population lived in other urban areas, principally the San Fernando conurbation in southern Trinidad and Chaguanas in the centre of the country, with 54,100 in the smaller island of Tobago. The average annual population growth rate was 0.3% in 1995–2009.

AGRICULTURE

The strength of the energy-based economy led to the relative neglect of agriculture from the 1950s, while agricultural wage rates could not compete with other areas of employment. As a result, in 2009 the sector contributed only 0.4% of GDP (down from 6.9% in 1972), but employed 3.9% of the employed labour force. However, the mainly Indo-Trinidadian political parties in office during 1995-2001 and from 2010 placed a greater emphasis on small-scale agriculture than the mainly urban and Afro-Trinidadian People's National Movement (PNM).

The principal commercial crop until 2007 was sugar, which generated 2.0% of total employment in the first half of 2002 (including seasonal employees). Until mid-2003 the main producer was a state-owned company, Caroni (1975) Ltd, which operated two sugar factories. The Government wrote off the company's accumulated debts of TT $2,400m. in 1994, but by 2002 continuing losses had increased the debt again, to TT $2,300m. In July 2003 the Government closed the company down, offering its 10,000 mainly Indo-Trinidadian staff redundancy payments totalling some US $145m. and opportunities to retrain or lease land for their own use. One of Caroni's successors, the state-owned Sugar Manufacturing Company, operated the remaining sugar factory at Sainte Madeleine until 2007, but did not grow sugar cane, buying the crop from independent farmers. Exports, which went mainly to Europe at the preferential price agreed under the European Union's (EU) Cotonou Agreement, totalled 60,900 metric tons in 2002, but fell to 26,600 tons in 2007. With the EU about to phase out its preferential sugar prices, the closure of the Sainte Madeleine factory was announced in 2007. Sugar used on the local market from 2008 was imported from Guyana, Belize and other suppliers.

Premium-quality cocoa was a traditional export, but production fell from 7,542 metric tons in 1972 to just 686 tons in 2008. Low-grade robusta coffee was grown: production was 4,586 tons in 1968, but had fallen to 325 tons in 2008. A wide variety of vegetables and fruits was grown mainly for the local market, as well as some rice. In 2001–08 citrus production ranged from 167 tons to 7,495 tons (standing at 1,933 tons in 2008). Local producers supplied virtually the entire domestic market with eggs and broiler chicken (some 33.1m. birds in 2008).

Teak was the main forestry product, and was used extensively in the yacht repair industry. However, most lumber requirements were imported. The fishing sector was also small in scale, employing approximately 3,140 people in 2000; most of the catch was used locally, but frozen shrimps were exported. Trinidad was also used as a base by Asian vessels for deep-sea fishing in the Caribbean and mid-Atlantic.

PETROLEUM AND GAS

Energy-based industries were of central importance to the Trinidad and Tobago economy. Commercial petroleum production started in 1908, although the first oil well was sunk as early as 1857. Refining of local and imported petroleum was well established by the 1930s, and the sector accounted for 29.2% of GDP by 1955, in which year offshore petroleum production began; most petroleum and gas was produced on the east coast continental shelf. The energy sector's contribution to GDP increased to 42.8% in 1980, owing to higher petroleum prices, but fell to 21.8% in 1986. After a long and powerful recovery, by 2008 the petroleum sector (including mining, refining and petrochemicals) accounted for 48.0% of GDP, assisted by record-high petroleum prices, which peaked in July, but the sector's contribution to GDP fell back to 35.9% in 2009, as a result of markedly lower energy prices. However, the sector's contribution to employment was much lower, at only 3.4% of the working population in 2009.

In 2010 a wide range of international companies were involved in petroleum and gas exploration and production in Trinidad and Tobago's offshore areas. The state-owned Petroleum Company of Trinidad and Tobago Ltd (Petrotrin) and the National Gas Company of Trinidad and Tobago Ltd (NGC), as well as small, local, privately owned producers, operated both onshore and offshore. The leading producer was BP Energy Company of Trinidad and Tobago (70% owned by BP and 30% by Repsol-YPF of Spain). However, from 2005 the Australian company BHP Billiton became an increasingly significant producer, with its Angostura field coming on-stream, while BP in 2005 sold three mature oil fields to its minority partner, Repsol-YPF, with minority interests taken by Petrotrin and the NGC. Following the closure of two smaller plants, by the mid-1990s there was just one refinery, at Pointe-à-Pierre, owned by Petrotrin, which refined local and imported crude petroleum. The plant was upgraded in the mid-1990s, with a further US $1,300m. redevelopment nearing completion in 2010. Most of BP's local crude was refined overseas, although from 1999 some was processed by Petrotrin.

Natural gas use increased at an average annual rate of 19% in 1997–2005 and by a further 21% in 2006, but by an average annual rate of only 1.2% in 2007–09, with only one major new petrochemicals plant commencing operations during that period. A major LNG plant, the Atlantic LNG Company of Trinidad and Tobago came on-stream in April 1999, initially purchasing 450m. cu ft per day of natural gas directly from BP, equivalent to some 30% of total national gas production. The plant was owned by a consortium of BP, British Gas (BG) Trinidad and Tobago Ltd, Repsol-YPF, Tractebel (now Suez-Tractebel) of Belgium, and the NGC, which had a 10% shareholding. The capital cost of the first-phase project was US $950m. An expansion project completed in April 2003 increased gas consumption to approximately 1,400m. cu ft per day, with 62.5% of gas used by the LNG plant supplied by BP and 37.5% by BG and its partners, using a new pipeline that allowed Trinidad's north coast gas fields to be exploited for the first time. Sales contracts were with the USA, Spain, Puerto Rico and the Dominican Republic. A further US $1,160m. expansion was completed in December 2005 by BP, BG, Repsol and the NGC, making Trinidad a leading LNG producer, with additional daily gas usage for LNG of 800m. cu ft (bringing the total for the plant to 2,350m. cu ft) and annual output of 15m. metric tons. After presenting a tough stance on project benefits in negotiations, the Government projected an annual revenue of TT $58,000m. over 20 years from the latest expansion, assuming a natural gas price in the USA of US $5 per million British thermal units (Btu); in spite of weak prices in 2009, this appeared a conservative assumption, with realized prices likely to be higher. With US imports of LNG likely to rise from 2%–5% of gas demand in 2004 to 15%–25% by 2025, proposals for a fifth LNG train were mooted; however, such proposals were unlikely to come to fruition unless any significant new gas discoveries were made.

Concerns centred on the likely extent of gas reserves, and the most prudent depletion rate. Some new discoveries were made in recent years and the potential for new deep-water finds was thought to be good, although several exploration wells drilled in 2006 proved disappointing. Proven reserves were 14,400,000m. cu ft at the end of 2009, an amount that would be exhausted in 9.5 years at 2009 usage rates. This represented a sharp decrease from a reserves-to-production ratio of 58 years in 2001, and prompted concern that reserves were being exploited too rapidly. However, there was a further 13,700,000m. cu ft in probable and possible reserves, which would be sufficient for a further nine years at 2009 usage rates. Moreover, industry estimates based on seismic and other geological data suggest exploration potential of 31,200,000m. cu ft, which, if confirmed, would bring the total to a level that would comfortably accommodate the proposed level of production. However, the proven reserves total of 14,400,000m. cu ft includes cross-border resources whose exploitation requires an agreement with Venezuela, on which there had been no significant progress by mid-2010 despite many years of intermittent talks. There was some optimism in Trinidad and Tobago government circles that Venezuela would agree to the processing of its own otherwise inaccessible gas reserves in Trinidad, but the Venezuelan Government had by mid-2010 offered no indication that this was likely.

In 2009 some 41% of the natural gas produced in Trinidad and Tobago was purchased by the NGC, which operated a 620-km pipeline system, supplying the needs of all end-users except the LNG plant. Natural gas production averaged 4,151m. cu ft per day in 2009, with utilization at 3,810m. In that year some 59% of gas use was in the manufacture of LNG, 30% for petrochemicals, and 7% in electric power generation, with most of the remainder used in the iron and steel industry and cement manufacturing. There were no plans to establish a piped gas supply system for domestic household use. A committee was established in April 2004 to develop proposals to increase the local content of energy sector projects, a strategic aim of the Government. The first locally constructed oil-drilling platform was inaugurated in the same month; a total of eight had been completed by 2010. Further proposals included increased use of local service companies in engineering, fabrication or instrumentation.

MANUFACTURING

Energy-based manufacturing expanded rapidly, and the Government proposed three new industrial estates, with a total area of 38 sq km, be established to cater for expansion up to the year 2050. Trinidad and Tobago became the world's largest methanol exporter in 2000, and in 2005 accounted for an estimated 14% of world production. The first methanol plant was established in 1984, under state ownership, and was sold in 1997 to Methanol Holdings (Trinidad) Ltd, a consortium of a local financial company, CL Financial (which was in severe difficulties from January 2009), and two German companies, Ferrostaal AG and Helm AG. In 2010 these companies owned five methanol plants with a total capacity of 4m. metric tons, including the 'M5000' plant at Point Lisas, the world's largest methanol plant at the time of its opening in October 2005. This took Trinidad and Tobago's total to seven plants with a combined capacity of 6.5m. tons, up from 963,000 tons in 1995.

Trinidad and Tobago was also the world's principal exporter of ammonia, with the Russian Federation a close rival; production started in 1959, and in 2005 a total of nine plants were owned by both local and overseas investors. From 2004 the Government no longer welcomed proposals for stand-alone methanol or ammonia plants without a further downstream component. At the same time, limitations on gas supply were among the factors delaying final agreement for large chemical projects. Several major projects were proposed and under discussion in 2007, but most of them were placed on hold from 2008 as international credit markets tightened and energy and chemicals prices moved sharply down. However, in October 2009 Methanol Holdings commissioned a major component of a US $1,700m. ammonia-urea ammonium nitrate-melamine (AUM) complex.

The state-owned Iron and Steel Company of Trinidad and Tobago, established in 1981, made large losses until the commencement of a lease arrangement with the local subsidiary of an Indian company, Ispat, in 1989. Caribbean Ispat Ltd subsequently acquired the plant in 1994; it comprised three directly reduced iron units with a total capacity of 2.2m. metric tons, as well as mills for billets and wire rods. An Indian conglomerate, Essar, was scheduled to begin construction in 2008 of a US $1,100m. complex producing steel slabs and hot rolled coils, but this project remained on hold in mid-2010. A proposal from Alutrint, a Trinidadian state venture, for a 125,000-ton aluminium smelter with Chinese technology, construction and finance was favoured by the PNM Government, in spite of the withdrawal of Venezuelan joint venture partners. However, the proposal met with strong opposition from lobby groups, both on environmental grounds, and as a result of concerns over their gas demand, and, with a change of government in May 2010 (see History), the plans were not expected to move ahead.

Low-cost natural gas assisted the development of other manufacturing industries. Trinidad Cement Ltd (TCL) used locally quarried limestone in gas-fired kilns; in 2009 cement production declined by 9% to 869,900 metric tons, of which 26.8% was exported to regional markets. The company also owned cement plants in Barbados and Jamaica. Carib Glassworks was another manufacturing concern to benefit from cheap energy, producing bottles for national and export markets, while low-cost electricity from gas-powered generating stations allowed local soft-drink manufacturers to operate competitively for export to the wider Caribbean and beyond. There was also a wide range of consumer goods, food and other industries.

In contrast to Jamaica and some other Caribbean islands, there were very few labour-intensive export industries in Trinidad and Tobago, and the teleservices sector was underdeveloped. In 2009 the manufacturing sector, excluding petroleum, contributed 6.3% of GDP and employed 8.7% of the employed labour force.

TRANSPORT AND COMMUNICATIONS

In 1999 there were 7,900 km (4,910 miles) of roads in Trinidad and Tobago. Major routes were covered by four-lane highways, which, however, suffered from heavy congestion, with an estimated 515,000 vehicles in use by 2008, a 53% increase since 2000. The road system had to accommodate a huge increase in use after the growth of the petroleum sector from the 1970s, and there were plans for a major highway construction programme.

The main international ports were at Port of Spain (container, cargo and cruise ships), run since 2006 by Portia Management Services of the United Kingdom on a three-year contract, which was extended in 2009 for a further two years; and Point Lisas (private sector, handling mainly specialized bulk cargo piers, but also container cargo). The smaller port of Scarborough in Tobago handled general cargo, ferry services and cruise ships. There were also specialized port facilities at Point Fortin (LNG), Pointe-à-Pierre (crude petroleum and refinery products), Claxton Bay (cement) and Tembladora (transshipment of bauxite and alumina). In 2009 a further five specialized port facilities were proposed for metals and chemicals plants, but at mid-2010 it remained to be seen how many, if any, would materialize.

Trinidad's airport at Piarco offered direct connections to North America, Europe, most other Caribbean islands, Guyana, Suriname and Venezuela. A far-reaching but controversial US $250m. improvement project was completed in May 2001. In 2008 some 1.73m. international passengers used the airport. There was a frequent service to Crown Point airport in Tobago, carrying some 650,000 passengers per year; Tobago was also served by direct connections to the United Kingdom, Puerto Rico and some neighbouring Caribbean islands. These services carried 113,000 passengers in 2008. The state-owned airline, BWIA International Airways Ltd, was partly privatized in 1996, with the Government retaining a 33.5% share. However, owing to ongoing financial difficulties, a rights issue was announced in April 2004, allowing the conversion to equity of US $40m. of BWIA's debt to the Government, effectively returning the airline to government control. With losses continuing, the airline was closed, and reopened as Caribbean Airlines at the start of 2007, with a reduced fleet, staffing and route network. Caribbean Airlines was expected to complete the purchase of Air Jamaica before the end of 2010.

Trinidad and Tobago was linked to the Americas I and II fibre-optic systems, with others connected from 2007, and also benefited from international satellite telecommunications links. The landline telecommunications sector was a monopoly until mid-2008, controlled by Telecommunication Services of Trinidad and Tobago (TSTT) Ltd, 51% of which was owned by the Government and 49% by a British company, Cable & Wireless. After repeated delays, a competing cellular telephone operator, Digicel, launched operations in April 2006, gaining a market share of around 30% by early 2007. The monopoly cable television company, Columbus Communications, launched landline services in competition with TSTT from May 2008, but achieved only a small share of the market.

TOURISM

For many years the tourism potential of Trinidad and Tobago was not fully developed. From the early 1980s, however, successive governments placed greater emphasis on the sector, providing new facilities, including a cruise ship terminal in Port of Spain, and conducting more effective promotional campaigns. Stop-over arrivals increased to a peak of 463,191 in 2005, falling to 449,453 in 2007, of whom 40% were from the USA, 13% from the United Kingdom and 11% from Canada. The industry remained significantly less developed than that of other Caribbean islands: 21.2% of 2006 stop-over arrivals on Trinidad were business travellers, while 30.7% were visiting friends and relatives and only 23.3% were vacation tourists staying in hotels and guest houses; for Tobago, the proportion of leisure tourists was higher, at 74.0%, although hoteliers complained of poor occupancy and inadequate air connections. Net earnings from tourism were a negative balance of payments item until 1996, but were equivalent to 3.2% of merchandise imports in 2008. Hotels and guest houses accounted for 0.3% of GDP in 2006. Tourism receipts (excluding passenger transport) totalled US $464m. in 2007. The number of cruise passenger arrivals peaked at 104,061 in 2000, a year with hurricane damage to ports on neighbouring islands, but had declined to just 44,042 by 2008, with few local attractions for day visitors and cruise lines reverting to more northerly routes.

The officially reported number of hotel rooms stood at 3,815 in 2008, of which some 42.4% were on Tobago. On Trinidad the main hotels catered principally for business visitors, with 628 rooms added in three major properties in 2006–08, although the annual pre-Lenten Carnival was a major attraction. There was an important yacht- and powerboat-service industry based at marinas on the north-west peninsula of the island. For insurance purposes, Trinidad lies outside the hurricane belt. This factor, as well as a combination of competitive wage rates and engineering skills, has produced an attractive environment for repair services, which generate an estimated US $24m. per year. Yacht arrivals increased from 637 in 1990 to 3,249 in 2000, but declined to 1,407 in 2007.

PUBLIC FINANCE

From a very strong fiscal position in the 1970s, government finances deteriorated sharply from 1983. Successive austerity and emergency budgets reduced expenditure and increased taxation, while the Government made use of IMF compensatory financing and stand-by credit. The 1989 budget announced a 10% reduction in public sector pay, which was later ruled illegal by the courts. Value-added tax was introduced at the rate of 15% from January 1990. This was followed, in April 1990, by a further stand-by agreement with the IMF, providing US $111m. over 11 months. In the same month the IDB agreed to lend US $850m. over four years for housing, infrastructure development and major energy investments, including a full upgrade of the Pointe-à-Pierre petroleum refinery. The IDB's conditions emphasized relaxation of import and foreign exchange controls, reduced tariffs, currency liberalization and privatization of state-owned industries.

The overall fiscal account was in deficit from 1982 to 1994. The fiscal balance oscillated between modest deficit and surplus over the course of the next decade, influenced primarily by energy price fluctuations, before moving firmly into positive territory—there was an overall surplus of 5.2% of GDP by 2004/05, which increased further to 6.9% in 2005/06, with strong energy prices and rising production. The overall surplus declined to 1.8% of GDP in 2006/07, but recovered to 7.8% in 2007/08 as a rise in energy revenue more than compensated for increased capital spending. However, the fiscal balance moved sharply into a deficit of 5.3% of GDP in 2008/09 as energy prices fell significantly below budget forecasts; the non-energy deficit rose to 18.3% of GDP in that year, indicating a level of dependence on energy revenue that was a source of some concern. There were concerns over the fiscal and inflationary implications of increased spending on infrastructural projects, as well as the use of extra-budgetary expenditure by state-owned implementation companies to fund capital programmes. There was apparent consensus on the need for increased transparency and efficiency in the award of public sector contracts; however, views differed greatly with regard to the means by which these sometimes contradictory objectives could be achieved, with widespread criticism of the operations of state-owned companies used for project implementation, particularly the Urban Development Corporation of Trinidad and Tobago (UDECOTT). A Commission of Inquiry, headed by British legal academic Prof. John Uff, into the recent activities of UDECOTT published its final report, in which it was severely critical of the company, in March 2010 (see History). Meanwhile, an interim Revenue Stabilization Fund was established in 2000, before being placed on a firm statutory footing in March 2007 as the Heritage and Stabilization Fund; in August 2009 the Fund held a balance of US $2,974m., close to 14% of GDP.

The inflation rate remained moderate in the early 2000s, ranging from 3.4% to 5.6% in 1998–2004, but increased from late 2004 to reach a high of 15.4% in October 2008, at which point food price inflation reached 33.4%: this was as a result of strong growth in public sector spending, high food and commodity prices, and strong consumer demand. With tighter monetary policy and a stabilization of international commodity prices, inflation declined to 1.5% in December 2009. However, inflationary pressures subsequently resurged, with inflation rising to 13.7% for the year to June 2010, driven predominantly by steep increases in the price of locally produced foods; excluding food prices, the inflation rate remained at 4.3%. Real estate prices have also increased sharply, but are not reflected in the price index; in the middle- and upper-income property market house prices more than tripled in the three years to mid-2007, although they declined significantly from 2008 onwards.

FINANCIAL SERVICES

Trinidad and Tobago had a large domestic banking sector. Of the six main commercial banks Republic Bank Ltd was in local private sector ownership; RBTT Ltd was purchased in 2008 by Royal Bank of Canada; Scotiabank Trinidad and Tobago Ltd was the local subsidiary of the Canadian Bank of Nova Scotia; First Citizens Bank Ltd was state-owned; and Citibank (Trinidad and Tobago) Ltd and the local operation of First Caribbean International Bank specialized in services for corporate clients. In the late 1990s and 2000s there was increased activity in the commercial banking and finance sector.

Trinidad and Tobago was a regional centre for some financial services. Royal Bank of Canada moved its regional centre of operations to Trinidad and Tobago, while Republic Bank had subsidiaries in Grenada, Guyana, Barbados, Saint Lucia and the Dominican Republic. In 2003 First Citizens established a subsidiary in Saint Lucia. All major Trinidad and Tobago banks provided public and private sector merchant-banking services throughout the region. In 2007 financial institutions based in Trinidad and Tobago led 37 bond issues with a total value of TT $2,592m. in local currency and US $357m. in US currency for the local and regional private and public sectors;

however, as the international financial crisis took hold the emphasis shifted, with TT $5,500m. and US $97m. in issues for the local public sector in 2009, and TT $537m. for the local private sector and US $120m. for the Government of Barbados. Some losses had, meanwhile, been incurred from increased exposure to country risk in Caribbean markets.

At mid-2010 the Trinidad and Tobago Stock Exchange listed 21 local and 10 other Caribbean companies. Against international trends, the stock index for Trinidad companies had fallen by 30.7% between May 2005 and September 2006, before rising by 45%, with strong growth in the five months to July 2008 at a time when major international indices were in steep decline. The index then declined by 26% in the two years to July 2010 as the local economy experienced difficulties. As part of its move to diversify the economy away from the energy sector, from 2008 the former PNM Government energetically promoted proposals for an international financial services centre, building a new waterfront office complex in which to house it. However, with increased international financial instability and the ensuing regulatory pressure on Caribbean offshore centres, this project was unlikely to come to fruition.

A small number of private sector companies played a dominant role in the local economy. The largest publicly quoted local conglomerate, ANSA McAL, had life- and general-insurance subsidiaries, as well as interests in brewing and glass-making, importing, distribution and media sectors. Guardian Holdings, also insurance-based, had important real estate interests in Trinidad and Tobago and, in 1999, bought three insurance companies in Jamaica. Neal & Massy Holdings Ltd held important regional interests, and in 2008 acquired control of the dominant Barbados conglomerate, Barbados Shipping and Trading Company Ltd. One Caribbean Media, formed as a merger with Barbadian interests in 2006, controlled newspapers in each island, and radio stations in seven Caribbean countries.

Another large local conglomerate was CL Financial, an unlisted company under the effective control of a dominant shareholder and chairman, Lawrence Duprey. The conglomerate grew out of the Colonial Life Insurance Company, and by 2008 held a majority shareholding in Republic Bank and interests in property, supermarkets, media, rum, foods and methanol and ammonia plants. It also had subsidiaries in several other Caribbean countries, as well as property companies in the USA, wine and spirits companies in the United Kingdom, France and elsewhere, and a methanol plant in Oman. Its operations had expanded rapidly as a result of very high leveraging and extensive related-party lending, and by early 2009 the group was in severe financial difficulties resulting, in part, from a tighter credit environment and falling methanol prices. The Trinidad and Tobago operation of Colonial Life, which held 55% of the country's insurance sector assets, along with several financial sector subsidiaries were taken into public sector control in January 2009. In June the Central Bank appointed the majority of members to a new CL Financial board, which did not include Duprey. The full cost of these operations had not been established by mid-2010, but announced government support had reached TT $4,000m. or 4% of GDP, by early 2010. The authorities hoped to offset some of the cost from the eventual sale of group subsidiaries and other assets. However, the outlook was complicated by the pledging of substantial assets to third parties and agreements with minority shareholders as well as large-scale related-party lending. A further concern was the possibility of significant financial requirements for Petrotrin.

FOREIGN TRADE, DEBT AND BALANCE OF PAYMENTS

The trade balance was in surplus from the mid-1980s until the late 1990s, albeit a fluctuating one, with deficits in 1997 and 1998 resulting from the import of capital goods for investments in heavy manufacturing. With the completion of these and other projects, combined with strong energy prices, the balance of trade moved strongly into surplus, rising from US $63.6m. in 1999 to US $969m. in 2000 and, buoyed by record-high energy prices, to US $9,064m. in 2008; the current account surplus in 2008 stood at US $8,519m., equivalent to 32.6% of GDP.

However, there was a marked deterioration in 2009. Exports declined by 51%, with a sharp fall in energy prices; although imports also decreased, by 28%, the surplus on merchandise trade shrank to US $2,202m., or 10.4% of GDP. There was a positive services balance of US $721m., sufficient to cover 17.5% of non-energy merchandise imports. Income flows were a strong outflow item in 2009, equivalent to 13.3% of merchandise exports, largely owing to remittances of energy company profits. The current account balance in 2009 declined to US $1,759m., or 8.3% of GDP.

In 2009 the principal merchandise exports were: LNG (41.9%), crude and refined petroleum (34.0%) and petrochemicals (9.6%), down from 22.8% in 2008 because of lower chemical prices and plant shutdowns. Crude oil for local refining made up 40.8% of merchandise imports; capital goods made up a further 27.6%.

External debt increased through the 1980s, reaching US $2,510m. in 1990. As a result of amortization, this figure was reduced to US $1,281m. at the end of 2009, equivalent to 6.0% of GDP. Borrowing for capital projects in 1998–2001 increased total domestic and foreign public debt to 59.3% of GDP at the end of 2002; however, with GDP expanding steadily, this figure decreased to 29.0% at the end of 2009. Debt-servicing peaked in 1993, with total debt service equivalent to 49.2% of current government revenue and foreign debt service equivalent to 30.6% of exports of goods and services in that year. By 2008, however, the external debt service ratio had declined to 1.0%, while interest payments made up 9.4% of current government expenditure in 2009.

The capital and financial account on the balance of payments was in deficit by US $2,472m. in 2009, equivalent to 11.7% of GDP, leaving the overall balance of payments in deficit by US $713m. or 3.4% of GDP. There were mainly short-term private sector capital outflows of US $2,786m. but in contrast to 2008 there were no outward investments by the Heritage and Stabilization Fund. Public and private sector outflows outpaced inward direct investment of US $511m., a figure which was down from US $2,800m. in the previous year. As a result, and despite a strong positive current account balance, there were intermittent shortages of foreign exchange at the commercial banks in 2005–10. Notwithstanding these outflows, exports and foreign direct investment inflows increased gross official reserves to US $9,380m. by the end of December 2008, although this figure had slipped to US $8,652m. at the end of 2009.

CONCLUSION

Trinidad and Tobago's natural gas resources provided the basis for strong economic growth from 1994, with falling unemployment, a stable exchange rate, high investment inflows and increasing foreign exchange reserves. High energy prices from 1999 to mid-2008 greatly improved the fiscal position, allowing an increase in both current and capital spending. Nevertheless, there were concerns at this time regarding economic overheating, rising inflation and weakness in non-energy sectors of the economy, while inefficient state enterprises, including some, such as telecommunications, that were partially divested, remained a burden on the economy. Also of concern was the standard of public services and infrastructure, including health, education, water supply and sewerage, as well as the performance of the police force and the rising crime rate, with increasing evidence of mismanagement in public sector construction, and weaknesses in financial sector supervision. From late 2008 continuing weakness in energy and chemicals prices placed government spending under pressure, while further difficulties stemmed from the collapse of the CL Financial conglomerate. However, the overall economy remained stable, and a recovery in energy prices appeared likely to maintain stability. In the longer term, the major questions relate to the sustainability of projected levels of natural gas use, given the fairly limited local resource base; at mid-2010 major new investments in LNG, petrochemicals or metals were unlikely unless significant new discoveries were made. Government efforts to diversify the economy into sectors such as financial services, information and communications technology, and tourism have hitherto met with only limited success.

Statistical Survey

Sources (unless otherwise stated): Central Statistical Office, National Statistics Bldg, 80 Independence Sq., POB 98, Port of Spain; tel. 623-6945; fax 625-3802; e-mail info@cso.gov.tt; internet www.cso.gov.tt; Central Bank of Trinidad and Tobago, POB 1250, Port of Spain; tel. 625-4835; fax 627-4696; e-mail info@central-bank.org.tt; internet www.central-bank.org.tt.

Area and Population

AREA, POPULATION AND DENSITY

Area (sq km)	5,128*
Population (census results)	
2 May 1990	1,213,733
15 May 2000	
Males	633,051
Females	629,315
Total	1,262,366
Population (official estimates at mid-year)	
2007	1,303,200
2008	1,308,600
2009	1,310,100
Density (per sq km) at mid-2009	255.5

* 1,980 sq miles. Of the total area, Trinidad is 4,828 sq km (1,864 sq miles) and Tobago 300 sq km (116 sq miles).

POPULATION BY AGE AND SEX

(UN estimates at mid-2010)

	Males	Females	Total
0–14	139,957	136,123	276,080
15–64	477,494	497,218	974,712
65 and over	35,109	57,824	92,933
Total	652,560	691,165	1,343,725

Source: UN, *World Population Prospects: The 2008 Revision*.

POPULATION BY ETHNIC GROUP

(1990 census*)

	Males	Females	Total	%
African	223,561	221,883	445,444	39.59
Chinese	2,317	1,997	4,314	0.38
'East' Indian	226,967	226,102	453,069	40.27
Lebanese	493	441	934	0.08
Mixed	100,842	106,716	207,558	18.45
White	3,483	3,771	7,254	0.64
Other	886	838	1,724	0.15
Unknown	2,385	2,446	4,831	0.43
Total	560,934	564,194	1,125,128	100.00

* Excludes some institutional population and members of unenumerated households, totalling 44,444.

ADMINISTRATIVE DIVISIONS

(population at 2000 census)

	Population	Capital
Trinidad	1,208,282	Port of Spain
Port of Spain (city, capital)	49,031	—
San Fernando (city)	55,419	—
Arima (borough)	32,278	Arima
Chaguanas (borough)	67,433	Chaguanas
Point Fortin (borough)	19,056	Point Fortin
Diego Martin	105,720	Petit Valley
San Juan/Laventille	157,295	Laventille
Tunapuna/Piarco	203,975	Tunapuna
Couva/Tabaquite/Talparo	162,779	Couva
Mayaro/Rio Claro	33,480	Rio Claro
Sangre Grande	64,343	Sangre Grande
Princes Town	91,947	Princes Town
Penal/Debe	83,609	Penal
Siparia	81,917	Siparia
Tobago	54,084	Scarborough

BIRTHS AND DEATHS

(annual averages, UN estimates)

	1995–2000	2000–05	2005–10
Birth rate (per 1,000)	15.1	14.5	14.8
Death rate (per 1,000)	7.2	7.9	8.0

Source: UN, *World Population Prospects: The 2008 Revision*.

Life expectancy (years at birth, WHO estimates): 70 (males 66; females 73) in 2008 (Source: WHO, *World Health Statistics*).

ECONOMICALLY ACTIVE POPULATION

('000 persons aged 15 years and over)

	2006	2007	2008
Agriculture, forestry, hunting and fishing	25.8	22.4	22.9
Mining and quarrying	20.4	22.8	21.1
Manufacturing	55.5	54.1	55.1
Electricity, gas and water	7.7	7.2	7.9
Construction	96.7	103.0	108.5
Wholesale and retail trade, restaurants and hotels	106.6	108.3	108.2
Transport, storage and communication	42.7	41.5	41.2
Finance, insurance, real estate and business services	48.1	49.6	52.5
Community, social and personal services	181.1	178.6	179.5
Sub-total	584.6	587.5	596.9
Activities not adequately defined	1.6	0.3	0.7
Total employed	586.2	587.8	597.6
Unemployed	39.0	34.5	29.0
Total labour force	625.2	622.3	626.6
Males	364.9	368.6	n.a.
Females	260.3	253.7	n.a.

Source: ILO.

2009 ('000 persons aged 15 years and over): Total employed 588.3 (Agriculture 23.0; Petroleum and gas 19.3; Construction and utilities 113.4; Manufacturing 53.1); Unemployed 32.6; Total labour force 620.9.

Health and Welfare

KEY INDICATORS

Total fertility rate (children per woman, 2008)	1.6
Under-5 mortality rate (per 1,000 live births, 2008)	35
HIV/AIDS (% of persons, aged 15–49, 2007)	1.5
Physicians (per 1,000 head, 1997)	0.8
Hospital beds (per 1,000 head, 2005)	2.6
Health expenditure (2007): US $ per head (PPP)	1,178
Health expenditure (2007): % of GDP	4.8
Health expenditure (2007): public (% of total)	56.1
Access to water (% of persons, 2008)	94
Access to sanitation (% of persons, 2008)	92
Total carbon dioxide emissions ('000 metric tons, 2006)	33,576.9
Carbon dioxide emissions per head (metric tons, 2006)	25.4
Human Development Index (2007): ranking	64
Human Development Index (2007): value	0.837

For sources and definitions, see explanatory note on p. vi.

Agriculture

PRINCIPAL CROPS
('000 metric tons)

	2005	2006*	2007*
Rice, paddy	2.1	2.3	2.5
Maize*	3.1	3.0	3.0
Taro (Cocoyam)*	4.9	4.9	4.9
Sugar cane	420.0	420.0	475.0
Pigeon peas	1.0	1.0	1.1
Coconuts*	18.0	18.0	18.0
Cabbages*	1.1	1.1	1.1
Lettuce*	1.5	1.5	1.5
Tomatoes	1.6	1.7	1.8
Pumpkins, squash and gourds	2.2	2.2	2.2
Cucumbers and gherkins*	2.0	2.0	2.1
Aubergines*	3.0	3.0	3.0
Watermelons*	1.2	1.2	1.5
Bananas*	7.0	7.0	7.0
Plantains*	4.7	4.7	5.0
Oranges*	5.3	5.3	5.3
Lemons and limes*	1.7	1.7	1.7
Grapefruit and pomelo*	2.8	2.8	2.8
Pineapples*	4.5	4.5	4.5
Coffee, green*	0.4	0.4	0.4
Cocoa beans*	1.4	1.4	1.4

* FAO estimates.

Aggregate production ('000 metric tons, may include official, semi-official or estimated data): Total cereals 5 in 2005–07; Total roots and tubers 9 in 2005–06, 10 in 2007; Total vegetables (incl. melons) 18 in 2005, 19 in 2006–07; Total fruits (excl. melons) 69 in 2005–07.

2008: Production assumed to be unchanged from 2007 (FAO estimates).

Source: FAO.

LIVESTOCK
('000 head year ending September, FAO estimates)

	2005	2006	2007
Horses	1.3	1.3	1.3
Asses	2.2	2.2	2.2
Mules	1.9	1.9	1.9
Cattle	29.0	29.0	30.0
Buffaloes	5.7	5.7	5.7
Pigs	43.0	43.0	45.0
Chickens	28,200	28,200	28,500
Sheep	3.4	3.4	3.5
Goats	59.3	59.3	60.0

Source: FAO.

2008: Figures assumed to be unchanged from 2007 (FAO estimates).

LIVESTOCK PRODUCTS
('000 metric tons, FAO estimates)

	2005	2006	2007
Cattle meat	0.8	0.8	0.8
Pig meat	2.9	2.9	3.0
Chicken meat	57.6	57.6	60.0
Cows' milk	10.5	10.5	11.0
Hen eggs	3.8	3.8	3.9

2008: Production assumed to be unchanged from 2007 (FAO estimates).

Source: FAO.

Forestry

ROUNDWOOD REMOVALS
('000 cubic metres, excl. bark)

	2006	2007	2008
Sawlogs, veneer logs and logs for sleepers	65.0	65.0	47.0
Fuel wood*	34.1	33.8	33.4
Total	99.1	98.8	80.4

* FAO estimates.

Source: FAO.

SAWNWOOD PRODUCTION
('000 cubic metres, incl. railway sleepers)

	2006	2007	2008
Total (all broadleaved)	41	41	30

Source: FAO.

Fishing

('000 metric tons, live weight of capture)

	2006	2007	2008
Demersal percomorphs	1.9	1.7	2.0
King mackerel	0.7	0.6	1.0
Serra Spanish mackerel	1.8	1.4	1.5
Tuna-like fishes	0.1	0.1	0.2
Sharks, rays, skates, etc.	0.4	0.4	0.3
Other marine fishes	6.1	6.2	6.3
Penaeus shrimps	0.8	0.7	0.8
Total catch (incl. others)	13.1	13.1	13.8

Source: FAO.

Mining

('000 barrels, unless otherwise indicated)

	2006	2007	2008*
Crude petroleum	52,105	43,600	45,000
Natural gas liquids	11,251	12,500*	12,500
Natural gas (million cu m)†	40,082	41,766*	40,000

* Estimate(s).
† Figures refer to the gross volume of output.

Source: US Geological Survey.

Industry

SELECTED PRODUCTS
('000 metric tons, unless otherwise indicated)

	2007	2008	2009
Sugar	67	38	32
Beer ('000 litres)	51,770	50,206	50,377
Fertilizers	5,617	5,186	3,942*
Methanol	5,933	5,686	4,455*
Cement	902	953	869
Iron (direct reduced)	2,063	1,601	805*
Steel:			
billets	695	490	290*
wire rods	510	272	174*
Electric energy (million kWh)	7,704.8	7,759.8	7,873.3

* Provisional figure.

Finance

CURRENCY AND EXCHANGE RATES

Monetary Units

100 cents = 1 Trinidad and Tobago dollar (TT $).

Sterling, US Dollar and Euro Equivalents (31 May 2010)

£1 sterling = TT $9.251;
US $1 = TT $6.345;
€1 = TT $7.858;
TT $100 = £10.8 = US $15.76 = €12.73.

Average Exchange Rate (TT $ per US $)

2007	6.3280
2008	6.2894
2009	6.3249

CENTRAL GOVERNMENT BUDGET

(TT $ million)

Revenue	2004/05	2005/06	2006/07
Energy sector	13,961.3	21,416.0	20,079.2
Corporation tax	10,805.6	17,614.8	16,206.2
Withholding tax (oil)	429.2	614.3	928.7
Royalties	1,228.5	1,679.3	1,681.0
Unemployment levy	820.4	1,311.3	1,111.0
Oil impost	42.7	65.9	63.9
Excise duties	634.8	130.4	88.4
Non-energy sector	15,677.4	17,490.9	19,955.6
Taxes	13,878.2	15,414.3	17,266.8
Taxes on income	8,141.2	7,922.5	8,888.1
Taxes on property	62.7	64.4	83.7
Taxes on goods and services	4,200.8	5,591.1	6,288.5
Value-added tax	2,962.5	4,184.2	4,829.0
Taxes on international trade	1,473.5	1,836.3	2,006.5
Non-tax revenue of non-oil sector	1,799.1	2,076.6	2,688.8
Capital revenue and grants	9.1	4.0	29.6
Total	29,647.9	38,910.9	40,064.4

Expenditure	2004/05	2005/06	2006/07
Current expenditure	21,842.4	26,582.6	29,984.0
Wages and salaries	5,309.2	5,455.6	6,221.3
Goods and services	3,170.1	3,843.2	4,283.8
Interest payments	2,541.5	2,453.3	2,698.1
Domestic	1,875.5	1,825.5	2,094.0
External	666.0	600.8	604.1
Transfers and subsidies	10,821.6	14,830.4	16,780.8
Households	2,601.2	4,341.2	8,455.9
Loans and grants to statutory boards and state enterprises	2,481.6	3,805.5	4,916.8
Capital expenditure and net lending	2,798.6	4,615.3	7,781.9
Total	24,641.0	31,197.9	37,765.9

2007/08 (TT $ million): *Revenue:* Energy sector 32,444.3; Non-energy sector 24,403.5; Total 56,847.8. *Expenditure:* Current expenditure 35,030.6; Capital expenditure and net lending 9,684.5; Total 44,715.1.

2008/09 (TT $ million): *Revenue:* Energy sector 18,183.0; Non-energy sector 19,927.6; Total 38,110.6. *Expenditure:* Current expenditure 37,611.0; Capital expenditure and net lending 7,973.2; Total 45,584.2.

2009/10 (TT $ million, projections): *Revenue:* Energy sector 13,609.0; Non-energy sector 23,035.7; Total 36,644.7. *Expenditure:* Current expenditure 37,250.1; Capital expenditure and net lending 7,097.2; Total 44,347.3.

INTERNATIONAL RESERVES

(US $ million at 31 December)

	2007	2008	2009
Gold (national valuation)	51.2	52.9	67.9
IMF special drawing rights	0.9	1.1	431.9
Reserve position in IMF	35.4	61.1	94.4
Foreign exchange	6,657.4	9,380.4	8,651.6
Total	6,744.9	9,495.5	9, 245.8

Source: IMF, *International Financial Statistics*.

MONEY SUPPLY

(TT $ million at 31 December)

	2006	2007	2008
Currency outside banks	2,654.4	3,182.8	3,433.7
Demand deposits at commercial banks	10,219.2	11,083.6	12,399.9
Total money (incl. others)	14,994.5	16,777.2	19,197.2

Source: IMF, *International Financial Statistics*.

COST OF LIVING

(Consumer Price Index; base: January 2003 = 100)

	2007	2008	2009
Food (incl. non-alcoholic beverages)	217.6	274.0	308.7
Clothing	93.3	95.8	95.3
Transport	114.4	117.8	125.6
Housing and utilities	113.5	119.8	125.2
All items (incl. others)	132.0	147.9	158.2

NATIONAL ACCOUNTS

(TT $ million at current prices)

Expenditure on the Gross Domestic Product

	2006	2007	2008*
Government final consumption expenditure	12,801.9	14,328.1	16,665.2
Private final consumption expenditure	56,339.4	65,690.9	68,668.1
Gross capital formation	18,146.0	17,666.0	19,418.0
Total domestic expenditure	87,287.3	97,685.0	104,751.3
Exports of goods and services	79,417.6	88,792.1	111,688.1
Less Imports of goods and services	44,596.9	49,050.5	64,324.1
GDP in purchasers' values	122,108.0	137,426.7	152,115.2

* Provisional.

Gross Domestic Product by Economic Activity

(revised figures)

	2006	2007	2008
Agriculture, hunting, forestry and fishing	657.3	490.5	576.9
Mining and hydrocarbons	54,517.9	56,833.8	78,412.9
Manufacturing	6,444.6	7,494.1	7,642.6
Electricity and water	981.5	1,534.4	1,526.3
Construction	8,576.9	11,711.2	14,069.5
Transport, storage and communication	4,186.4	7,142.5	7,533.5
Distribution	15,081.2	16,925.1	21,140.0
Finance, insurance and real estate	13,351.5	15,561.8	15,494.7
Government	6,987.5	9,038.3	10,132.6
Other services	4,500.9	4,891.6	5,258.5
Sub-total	115,258.7	131,623.3	161,787.5
Less Financial intermediation services indirectly measured	3,658.6	4,677.8	5,090.7
Value-added tax	4,324.1	5,335.3	6,628.1
GDP in purchaser's values	115,951.2	132,280.8	163,324.9

BALANCE OF PAYMENTS
(US $ million)

	2005	2006	2007
Exports of goods f.o.b.	9,672	14,217	13,391
Imports of goods f.o.b.	–5,725	–6,517	–7,670
Trade balance	3,948	7,700	5,721
Exports of services	897	814	924
Imports of services	–541	–363	–377
Balance on goods and services	4,304	8,151	6,268
Other income received	84	262	267
Other paid	–844	–1,198	–1,231
Balance on goods, services and income	3,544	7,215	5,304
Current transfers received	102	105	121
Current transfers paid	–52	–49	–61
Current balance	3,594	7,271	5,364
Direct investment (net)	599	513	830
Portfolio investment assets	–258	–200	–272
Other investment (net)	–1,894	–5,679	–3,808
Net errors and omissions	–653	–808	–593
Overall balance	1,388	1,096	1,521

Source: IMF, *International Financial Statistics*.

2008 (US $ million): Exports of goods f.o.b. 18,686.4; Imports of goods f.o.b. -9,622.0; *Trade balance* 9,064.4; Services (net) 614.4; *Balance on goods and services* 9,678.8; Income (net) -897.1; *Balance on goods, services and income* 8,781.7; Transfers (net) 10.2; *Current balance* 8,791.9; Capital account (net) -6,086.3; *Overall balance* 2,705.6.

External Trade

PRINCIPAL COMMODITIES
(TT $ million)

Imports c.i.f.	2008	2009
Food and live animals	4,224.8	3,806.1
Beverages and tobacco	324.3	340.2
Crude materials except fuels	3,458.9	1,353.3
Mineral fuels and lubricants	20,897.7	14,481.4
Animal and vegetable oils and fats	290.9	207.3
Chemicals	4,851.1	3,442.5
Manufactured goods	8,272.3	5,744.8
Machinery and transport equipment	14,600.4	12,119.5
Miscellaneous manufactured articles	2,941.0	2,383.5
Total (incl. others)	59,914.8	43,935.7

Exports f.o.b.*	2008	2009
Food and live animals	1,279.3	965.0
Beverages and tobacco	999.8	881.2
Crude materials except fuels	3,214.1	1,750.7
Mineral fuels and lubricants	81,746.4	43,744.9
Animal and vegetable oils and fats	10.7	16.2
Chemicals	21,368.5	5,542.3
Manufactured goods	5,285.6	2,702.2
Machinery and transport equipment	2,241.7	1,661.0
Miscellaneous manufactured articles	513.2	441.8
Miscellaneous transactions and commodities	2.7	2.7
Total	116,662.0	57,708.0

* Including ships' stores and bunkers.

PRINCIPAL TRADING PARTNERS
(TT $ million)

Imports c.i.f.	2006	2007	2008
Barbados	204.1	280.5	n.a.
Canada	911.4	1,981.3	1,636.1
Central and South America*	11,040.0	12,695.8	15,719.6
Venezuela	1,755.0	1,887.3	1,445.5
European Free Trade Association (EFTA)	159.3	162.8	228.2
European Union (EU)†	3,241.1	4,353.0	6,603.3
Guyana	117.5	160.5	n.a.
Jamaica	110.2	99.7	n.a.
United Kingdom	1,072.8	1,342.8	1,368.7
USA	11,152.5	12,000.7	14,299.5
Total (incl. others)	40,934.2	48,329.5	60,197.9

Exports f.o.b.‡	2006	2007	2008
Barbados	2,915.2	1,782.6	n.a.
Canada	1,076.0	854.5	1,205.0
Central and South America*	4,370.3	5,558.8	10,216.8
European Free Trade Association (EFTA)	110.0	505.0	136.7
European Union (EU)†	8,357.2	8,560.3	13,271.8
Guyana	2,089.0	1,466.4	n.a.
Jamaica	5,055.0	3,818.6	n.a.
United Kingdom	759.3	1,348.2	2,093.0
USA	50,553.3	47,338.1	51,832.7
Total (incl. others)	88,275.5	83,897.4	115,093.5

* Excluding Belize, French Guiana, Guyana and Suriname.
† Excluding the United Kingdom, listed separately.
‡ Excluding ships' stores and bunkers.

2008 (TT $ million, revised figures): Total imports 59,914.8; Total exports 116,662.0.

2009 (TT $ million): Total imports 43,935.7; Total exports 57,708.0.

Transport

ROAD TRAFFIC
(motor vehicles in use)

	1997	1998	1999
Passenger cars	194,300	213,400	229,400
Commercial vehicles	47,700	51,100	53,900

Source: UN, *Statistical Yearbook*.

Total number of registered vehicles: 441,541 in 2006; 468,255 in 2007; 471,749 in 2008.

SHIPPING

Merchant Fleet
(registered at 31 December)

	2006	2007	2008
Number of vessels	104	111	119
Total displacement ('000 grt)	38.8	51.1	54.3

Source: Lloyd's Register-Fairplay, *World Fleet Statistics*.

International Sea-borne Freight Traffic
(estimates, '000 metric tons)

	1988	1989	1990
Goods loaded	7,736	7,992	9,622
Goods unloaded	4,076	4,091	10,961

Source: UN, *Monthly Bulletin of Statistics*.

1998: Port of Spain handled 3.3m. metric tons of cargo.

CIVIL AVIATION
(traffic on scheduled services)

	2003	2004	2005
Kilometres flown (million)	31	28	27
Passengers carried ('000)	1,084	1,132	1,055
Passenger-km (million)	2,671	3,013	3,100
Total ton-km (million)	276	314	328

Source: UN, *Statistical Yearbook*.

Tourism

FOREIGN TOURIST ARRIVALS

Country of origin	2005	2006	2007
Barbados	35,319	31,218	21,491
Canada	47,702	49,242	51,411
Germany	8,666	6,706	5,422
Grenada	19,501	14,814	10,169
Guyana	22,208	23,673	25,668
Saint Lucia	8,823	8,902	6,006
Saint Vincent and Grenadines	12,658	12,288	8,860
United Kingdom	63,523	58,612	58,660
USA	167,985	170,893	180,557
Venezuela	10,191	9,906	12,392
Total (incl. others)	463,191	457,434	449,453

Tourism receipts (US $ million, incl. passenger transport): 593 in 2005; 517 in 2006; 621 in 2007.

Source: World Tourism Organization.

Total tourist arrivals: 449,863 in 2008; 430,631 in 2009 (estimate).

Communications Media

	2007	2008	2009
Telephones ('000 main lines in use)	307.3	314.8	314.8
Mobile cellular telephones ('000 subscribers)	1,509.8	1,806.1	1,970.0
Internet users ('000)	429.0	456.4	485.0
Broadband subscribers ('000)	35.5	85.4	105.0

Radio receivers (1997, '000 in use): 680.

Personal computers: 175,500 (132.1 per 1,000 persons) in 2007.

Daily newspapers: 4 in 1997 (average circulation: 191,000 in 2001); 3 in 2004 (average circulation: 196,000 in 2003).

Non-daily newspapers: 5 in 1997 (average circulation 167,000 in 2001); 7 in 2004 (average circulation: 170,000 in 2003).

Television receivers ('000 in use): 449 in 2001.

Sources: International Telecommunication Union; UN, *Statistical Yearbook*; UNESCO, *Statistical Yearbook*.

Education

(2007/08 unless otherwise indicated)

	Institutions	Teachers	Students		
			Males	Females	Total
Pre-primary	50*	2,186	15,021†	14,564†	29,585†
Primary	480‡	7,628	67,460	63,420	130,880
Secondary	101‡	7,045	46,613	48,662	95,275
Tertiary	3§	1,800‖	7,515‖	9,405‖	16,920‖

* Government schools and assisted schools only, in 1992/93.
† 2006/07.
‡ 2001/02.
§ 2003/04; university and equivalent institutions.
‖ 2004/05.

Source: UNESCO Institute for Statistics.

Pupil-teacher ratio (primary education, UNESCO estimate): 17.2 in 2007/08 (Source: UNESCO Institute for Statistics).

Adult literacy rate (UNESCO estimates): 98.7% (males 99.1%; females 98.2%) in 2008 (Source: UNESCO Institute for Statistics).

Directory

The Constitution

Trinidad and Tobago became a republic, within the Commonwealth, under a new Constitution on 1 August 1976. The Constitution provides for a President and a bicameral Parliament comprising a Senate and a House of Representatives. The President is elected by an Electoral College of members of both the Senate and the House of Representatives. The Senate consists of 31 members appointed by the President: 16 on the advice of the Prime Minister, six on the advice of the Leader of the Opposition and nine at the President's own discretion from among outstanding persons from economic, social or community organizations. The House of Representatives consists of 41 members who are elected by universal adult suffrage. The duration of a Parliament is five years. The Cabinet, presided over by the Prime Minister, is responsible for the general direction and control of the Government. It is collectively responsible to Parliament.

The Government

HEAD OF STATE

President: Prof. GEORGE MAXWELL RICHARDS (took office 17 March 2003; re-elected by vote of the Electoral College of the Parliament 11 February 2008).

THE CABINET
(July 2010)

The Government is formed by the People's Partnership coalition, comprising the United National Congress, the Congress of the People and the Tobago Organisation of the People.

Prime Minister: KAMLA PERSAD-BISSESSAR.

Minister of Works and Transport: AUSTIN JACK WARNER.

Minister of Finance: WINSTON DOOKERAN.

Minister of National Security: Brig. JOHN SANDY.

Minister of Energy and Energy Industries: CAROLYN SEEPERSAD-BACHAN.

Minister of Foreign Affairs: Dr SURUJATTAN RANBACHAN.

Minister of Public Administration: RUDRAWATEE NAN RAMGOOLAM.

Minister of Science, Technology and Tertiary Education: FAZAL KARIM.

Minister of Health: THERESE BAPTISTE-CORNELIS.

Minister of Public Utilities: EMMANUEL GEORGE.

Minister of Food Production: VASANT BHARATH.

Minister of Planning, Economics and Social Restructuring and Gender Affairs: MARY KING.

Minister of Local Government: CHANDRESH SHARMA.

Minister of Housing and the Environment: Dr ROODAL MOONILAL.

Minister of Trade and Industry: STEPHEN CADIZ.

Minister of Tourism: Dr RUPERT GRIFFITH.

Minister of Justice: HERBERT VOLNEY.

Minister of the People and Social Development: Dr GLEN RAMADHARSINGH.

Minister of Education: Dr TIM GOPEESINGH.

Minister of Community Development: NIZAM BAKSH.

Minister of Legal Affairs: PRAKASH RAMADHAR.

Minister of Labour and Small and Micro Enterprise Development: ERROL MCLEOD.

Minister of Sport and Youth Affairs: ANIL ROBERTS.

Minister of Tobago Development: VERNELLA ALLEYNE TOPPIN.

Minister of the Arts and Culture: WINSTON PETERS.

Minister in the Ministry of Works and Transport: RUDRANATH INDARSINGH.

Minister in the Ministry of Education: CLIFTON DECOTEAU.

Minister in the Ministry of Tourism: DELMON DEXTER-BAKER.

Ministers of State in the Office of the Prime Minister: COLIN JEFFERSON PARTAP, RODGER DOMINIC SAMUEL.

MINISTRIES

Office of the President: President's House, Circular Rd, St Ann's, Port of Spain; tel. 624-1261; fax 625-7950; e-mail presoftt@carib-link.net.

Office of the Prime Minister: Whitehall, 13–15 St Clair Ave, St Clair, Port of Spain; tel. 622-1625; fax 622-0055; e-mail permsec@opm.gov.tt; internet www.opm.gov.tt.

Ministry of the Arts and Culture: Port of Spain.

Ministry of Community Development: ALGICO Bldg, Cnr Jerningham Ave and Queens Park East, Belmont, Port of Spain; tel. 623-6621; fax 623-6979; e-mail cdcga@tstt.net.tt; internet www.cdcga.gov.tt.

Ministry of Education: 18 Alexandra St, St Clair; tel. 622-2181; fax 622-4892; e-mail mined@tstt.net.tt; internet www.moe.gov.tt.

Ministry of Energy and Energy Industries: Levels 22–26, Energy Tower, International Waterfront Centre, 1 Wrightson Rd, Port of Spain; tel. 623-6708; fax 625-6878; e-mail info@energy.gov.tt; internet www.energy.gov.tt.

Ministry of Finance: Level 18, Eric Williams Finance Bldg, Independence Sq., Port of Spain; tel. 627-9700; fax 627-5882; e-mail comm.finance@gov.tt; internet www.finance.gov.tt.

Ministry of Food Production: Port of Spain.

Ministry of Foreign Affairs: Levels 10–14, Tower C, Waterfront Complex, 1 Wrightson Rd, Port of Spain; tel. 623-4116; fax 623-5853; e-mail communications@foreign.gov.tt; internet www.foreign.gov.tt.

Ministry of Health: 63 Park St, Port of Spain; tel. 627-0010; fax 623-9528; e-mail suggestions@health.gov.tt; internet www.health.gov.tt.

Ministry of Housing and the Environment: NHA Bldg, 44–46 South Quay, Port of Spain; tel. 623-4663; fax 625-2793; e-mail info@housing.gov.tt; internet www.mphe.gov.tt.

Ministry of Justice: Cabildo Chambers, 23–27 St Vincent St, Port of Spain; tel. 623-7010; fax 625-0470.

Ministry of Labour and Small and Micro Enterprise Development: Level 11, Riverside Plaza, Cnr Besson and Piccadilly Sts, Port of Spain; tel. 623-4241; fax 624-4091; e-mail rplan@tstt.net.tt; internet www.labour.gov.tt.

Ministry of Legal Affairs: Registration House, Huggins Bldg, 72–74 South Quay, Port of Spain; tel. 624-1660; fax 625-9803; e-mail info@legalaffairs.gov.tt; internet www.legalaffairs.gov.tt.

Ministry of Local Government: Kent House, Long Circular Rd, Maraval, Port of Spain; tel. 622-1669; fax 628-7283; e-mail localgovminister@gov.tt; internet www.localgov.gov.tt.

Ministry of National Security: Temple Court, 31–33 Abercromby St, Port of Spain; tel. 623-2441; fax 627-8044; e-mail info@mns.gov.tt; internet www.nationalsecurity.gov.tt.

Ministry of the People and Social Development: St Vincent Court, 45A–C, St Vincent St, Port of Spain; tel. 624-5319; fax 625-5258; e-mail thenry@ssd.gov.tt; internet www.socialservices.gov.tt.

Ministry of Planning, Economics and Social Restructuring and Gender Affairs: Port of Spain.

Ministry of Public Administration: Level 7, National Library Bldg, Cnr Hart and Abercromby Sts, Port of Spain; tel. 625-6724; fax 623-6027; e-mail communicationsdivision@mpa.gov.tt; internet www.mpa.gov.tt.

Ministry of Public Utilities: Sacred Heart Bldg, 16–18 Sackville St, Port of Spain; tel. 623-4853; fax 625-7003; e-mail cgeorge@mpu.gov.tt; internet www.mpu.gov.tt.

Ministry of Science, Technology and Tertiary Education: Level 3, Nahous Bldg, Cnr Agra and Patna Sts, St James; tel. 622-9922; fax 622-7640; e-mail communicationstte@gov.tt; internet www.stte.gov.tt.

Ministry of Sport and Youth Affairs: 12 Abercromby St, Port of Spain; tel. 625-5622; fax 623-0174; internet www.msya.gov.tt.

Ministry of Tobago Development: Port of Spain.

Ministry of Tourism: Clarence House, 127–129 Duke St, Port of Spain; tel. 624-1403; fax 625-3894; e-mail mintourism@tourism.gov.tt; internet www.tourism.gov.tt.

Ministry of Trade and Industry: Levels 11–17, Nicholas Tower, 63-65 Independence Sq., Port of Spain; tel. 623-2931; fax 627-8488; e-mail info@tradeind.gov.tt; internet www.tradeind.gov.tt.

Ministry of Works and Transport: Main Administrative Bldg, Cnr Richmond and London Sts, Port of Spain; tel. 625-1225; fax 625-8070; internet www.mowt.gov.tt.

Legislature

PARLIAMENT

Senate

President: TIMOTHY HAMEL-SMITH.

The Senate consists of 31 members appointed by the President of the Republic.

House of Representatives

Speaker: WADE MARK.

Election, 24 May 2010

Party	Valid votes	% of valid votes cast	Seats
People's Partnership*	432,026	60.03	29
People's National Movement	285,354	39.65	12
Others	2,347	0.32	—
Total†	719,727	100.00	41

* An electoral alliance comprising the United National Congress, the Congress of the People, the Tobago Organisation of the People, the National Joint Action Committee and the Movement for Social Justice.

† In addition, there were 2,595 invalid votes.

TOBAGO HOUSE OF ASSEMBLY

The House is elected for a four-year term of office and consists of 12 elected members and three members selected by the majority party.

Chief Secretary: ORVILLE LONDON.

Election, 19 January 2009

Party	Seats
People's National Movement	8
Tobago Organisation of the People	4
Total	12

Election Commission

Elections and Boundaries Commission (EBC): Scott House, 134–138 Frederick St, Port of Spain; tel. 623-4622; fax 627-7881; e-mail ebc.research@gmail.com; internet www.ebctt.com; Chair. Dr NORBERT J. MASSON; Chief Election Officer HOWARD CAYENNE.

Political Organizations

Congress of the People: 2 Broome St, Woodbrook, Cnr Tragarete Rd, Port of Spain; tel. 622-5817; e-mail secretariat@coptnt.com; internet www.coptnt.com; f. 2006; contested the 2010 general election as a mem. of the People's Partnership coalition; Leader WINSTON DOOKERAN; Chair. ROY AUGUSTUS.

Democratic Action Congress: Scarborough; f. Jan. 2003 by faction of National Alliance for Reconstruction (q.v.); only active in Tobago; Leader HOCHOY CHARLES.

Democratic National Assembly (DNA): Port of Spain; f. 2006; Chair. DARA HEALY; Leaders Dr KIRK MEIGHOO (Trinidad), COLLIN COKER (Tobago).

Democratic Party of Trinidad and Tobago (DPTT): Port of Spain; f. 2001; Chair. WAYNE RODRIGUES; Leader STEVE ALVAREZ.

Movement for Social Justice: Port of Spain; contested the 2010 general election as a mem. of the People's Partnership coalition; Chair. ERROL MCLEOD.

National Alliance for Reconstruction (NAR): 37 Victoria Sq. South, Port of Spain; tel. 627-6163; fax 627-4627; e-mail alliancehouse37@gmail.com; f. 1983 as a coalition of moderate opposition parties; reorganized as a single party in 1986; Leader Dr CARSON CHARLES; Chair. HILDA GOODIAL.

National Democratic Party (NDP): Port of Spain; f. 2005; Leader MICHAEL SIMS.

National Joint Action Committee (NJAC): Port of Spain; internet www.njactt.org; f. 1969; contested the 2010 general election as a mem. of the People's Partnership coalition; Leader MAKANDAL DAAGA.

National Transformation Movement (NTM): Port of Spain; f. 2006; Leader LLOYD ELCOCK.

New National Vision (NNV): Port of Spain; Leader FUAD ABU BAKR.

People's National Movement (PNM): Balisier House, 1 Tranquility St, Port of Spain; tel. 625-1533; fax 627-3311; e-mail info@pnmtt.org; internet www.pnm.org.tt; f. 1956; moderate nationalist party; Leader Dr KEITH ROWLEY.

Tobago Organisation of the People (TOP): Tobago; internet www.toptobago.com; f. 2007; only active in Tobago; contested the 2010 general election as a mem. of the People's Partnership coalition; Leader ASHWORTH JACK.

United National Congress (UNC): Rienzi Complex, 78–81 Southern Main Rd, Couva; tel. 636-8145; e-mail info@unc.org.tt; internet www.unc.org.tt; f. 1988; contested the 2010 general election as a mem. of the People's Partnership coalition; social democratic; Leader KAMLA PERSAD-BISSESSAR; Chair. JACK WARNER.

Diplomatic Representation

EMBASSIES AND HIGH COMMISSIONS IN TRINIDAD AND TOBAGO

Argentina: TATIL Bldg, 4th Floor, 11 Maraval Rd, POB 162; Port of Spain; tel. 628-7557; fax 628-7544; e-mail etrin@mrecic.gov.ar; internet www.trinidadytobago.embajada-argentina.gov.ar; Chargé d'affaires EDGARDO GARLOTTI.

Brazil: 18 Sweet Briar Rd, St Clair, POB 382, Port of Spain; tel. 622-5779; fax 622-4323; e-mail brasil@tstt.net.tt; internet www.brazilembtt.org; Ambassador HAROLDO TEIXEIRA VALLADÃO FILHO.

Canada: Maple House, 3–3A Sweet Briar Rd, St Clair, POB 1246, Port of Spain; tel. 622-6232; fax 628-1830; e-mail pspan@international.gc.ca; internet www.portofspain.gc.ca; High Commissioner KAREN L. MCDONALD.

China, People's Republic: 39 Alexandra St, St Clair, Port of Spain; tel. 622-6976; fax 622-7613; e-mail chinaembtt@mfa.gov.cn; internet tt.chineseembassy.org; Ambassador YANG YOUMING.

Cuba: 92 Tragarete Rd, 2nd Floor, POB 1779, Port of Spain; tel. 622-6075; fax 628-4186; e-mail embacubatrinidad@tstt.net.tt; internet embacu.cubaminrex.cu/trinidadtobagoing; Ambassador HUMBERTO RIVERO ROSARIO.

Dominican Republic: Suite 101, 10B Queen's Park West, Port of Spain; tel. 624-7930; fax 623-7779; e-mail embdomtrinidadytobago@serex.gov.do; Ambassador JOSÉ A. SERULLE RAMIA.

El Salvador: 29 Long Circular Rd, St James, Port of Spain; tel. 628-4454; fax 622-8314; e-mail jgarciaprieto@rree.gob.sv; Chargé d'affaires a.i. JOSÉ ROBERTO GARCÍA PRIETO LEMUS.

France: TATIL Bldg, 6th Floor, 11 Maraval Rd, POB 1242, Port of Spain; tel. 622-7447; fax 628-2632; e-mail cad.port-d-espagne-amba@diplomatie.gouv.fr; internet www.ambafrance-tt.org; Ambassador MICHEL TRINQUIER.

Germany: 7–9 Marli St, Newtown, POB 828, Port of Spain; tel. 628-1630; fax 628-5278; e-mail info@ports.diplo.de; internet www.port-of-spain.diplo.de; Ambassador Dr ERNST KLAUS KONRAD MARTENS.

Guatemala: Regents Towers, Apt 701, Westmoorings-by-the-Sea, Westmoorings; tel. and fax 632-7629; e-mail embtrintobago@minex.gob.gt; Ambassador GUISELA ATALIDA GODÍNEZ SAZO.

Holy See: 11 Mary St, St Clair, POB 854, Port of Spain; tel. 622-5009; fax 628-5457; e-mail apnuntt@googlemail.com; Apostolic Nuncio Most Rev. THOMAS EDWARD GULLICKSON (Titular Archbishop of Bomarzo).

India: 6 Victoria Ave, POB 530, Port of Spain; tel. 627-7480; fax 627-6985; e-mail hc@hcipos.org; internet www.hcipos.org; High Commissioner MALAY MISHRA.

Jamaica: 2 Newbold St, St Clair, Port of Spain; tel. 622-4995; fax 628-9043; e-mail jhctnt@tstt.net.tt; High Commissioner SHARON SAUNDERS.

Japan: 5 Hayes St, St Clair, POB 1039, Port of Spain; tel. 628-5991; fax 622-0858; e-mail embassyofjapan@tstt.net.tt; internet www.tt.emb-japan.go.jp; Ambassador TATSUAKI IWATA.

Korea, Republic: 60 Eagle Crescent, Fairways, Maraval, Port of Spain; tel. 622-9081; fax 627-6317; e-mail koremb.tt@gmail.com; internet tto.mofat.go.kr; Ambassador YONG-KYN KWON.

Mexico: 12 Hayes St, St Clair, Port of Spain; tel. 622-1422; fax 628-8488; e-mail info@mexico.tt; internet www.mexico.tt; Ambassador RICARDO VILLANUEVA-HALLAL.

Netherlands: 69–71 Edward St, POB 870, Port of Spain; tel. 625-1210; fax 625-1704; e-mail por@minbuza.nl; internet www.holland.tt; Ambassador HANS PETER PAUL MARIA HORBACH.

Nigeria: 3 Maxwell-Phillip St, St Clair, POB 140, Newtown, Port of Spain; tel. 622-4002; fax 622-7162; e-mail contact@nigerianhighcommission-tt.org; internet www.nigerianhighcommission-tt.org; High Commissioner MUSA JOHN JEN.

Panama: Suite 6, 1A Dere St, Port of Spain; tel. 623-3435; fax 623-3440; e-mail embapatt@wow.net; Ambassador ARLINE GONZÁLEZ COSTA.

South Africa: 4 Scott St, St Claire, POB 7111, Port of Spain; tel. 622-9869; fax 622-7089; e-mail betsie.erasmus@southafrica.org.tt; Chargé d'affaires a.i. ROY SETLHAPELO.

Spain: TATIL Bldg, 7th Floor, 11 Maraval Rd, Port of Spain; tel. 625-7938; fax 624-4983; e-mail emb.trinidad@mae.es; Ambassador JOAQUÍN DE ARÍSTEGUI.

Suriname: TATIL Bldg, 5th Floor, 11 Maraval Rd, Port of Spain; tel. 628-0704; fax 628-0086; e-mail surinameembassy@tstt.net.tt; Ambassador FIDELIA GRAAND-GALON.

United Kingdom: 19 St Clair Ave, St Clair, POB 778, Port of Spain; tel. 350-0444; fax 350-0425; e-mail generalenquiries.ptofs@fco.gov.uk; internet ukintt.fco.gov.uk; High Commissioner ERIC JENKINSON.

USA: 15 Queen's Park West, POB 752, Port of Spain; tel. 622-6371; fax 625-5462; e-mail usispos@trinidad.net; internet trinidad.usembassy.gov; Ambassador BEATRICE WILKINSON WELTERS.

Venezuela: 16 Victoria Ave, POB 1300, Port of Spain; tel. 627-9821; fax 624-2508; e-mail embaveneztt@tstt.net.tt; Ambassador MARÍA EUGENIA MARCANO CASADO.

Judicial System

The Chief Justice, who has overall responsibility for the administration of justice in Trinidad and Tobago, is appointed by the President after consultation with the Prime Minister and the Leader of the Opposition. The President appoints and promotes judges on the advice of the Judicial and Legal Service Commission. The Judicial and Legal Service Commission, which comprises the Chief Justice as chairman, the chairman of the Public Service Commission, two former judges and a senior member of the bar, appoints all judicial and legal officers. The Judiciary comprises the higher judiciary (the Supreme Court) and the lower judiciary (the Magistracy). In February 2005 Parliament voted to accept the authority of the Caribbean Court of Justice to settle international trade disputes. The Court was formally inaugurated in Port of Spain on 16 April 2005.

Chief Justice: IVOR ARCHIE.

Supreme Court of Judicature: Knox St, Port of Spain; tel. 623-2417; fax 627-5477; e-mail ttlaw@wow.net; internet www.ttlawcourts.org; the Supreme Court consists of the High Court of Justice and the Court of Appeal. The Supreme Court is housed in three locations: Port of Spain, San Fernando and Tobago. There are 23 Supreme Court Puisne Judges who sit in criminal, civil, and matrimonial divisions; Registrar EVELYN ANN PETERSEN.

Court of Appeal: The Court of Appeal hears appeals against decisions of the Magistracy and the High Court. Further appeals are directed to the Judicial Committee of the Privy Council of the United Kingdom, sometimes as of right and sometimes with leave of the Court. The Court of Appeal consists of the Chief Justice, who is President, and six other Justices of Appeal.

The Magistracy and High Court of Justice

The Magistracy and the High Court exercise original jurisdiction in civil and criminal matters. The High Court hears indictable criminal matters, family matters where the parties are married, and civil matters involving sums over the petty civil court limit. High Court judges are referred to as either Judges of the High Court or Puisne Judges. The Masters of the High Court, of which there are four, have the jurisdiction of judges in civil chamber courts. The Magistracy (in its petty civil division) deals with civil matters involving sums of less than TT $15,000. It exercises summary jurisdiction in criminal matters and hears preliminary inquiries in indictable matters. The Magistracy, which is divided into 13 districts, consists of a Chief Magistrate, a Deputy Chief Magistrate, 13 Senior Magistrates and 29 Magistrates.

Chief Magistrate: PATRICK MARK WELLINGTON (acting), Magistrates' Court, St Vincent St, Port of Spain; tel. 625-2781.

Director of Public Prosecutions: ROGER GASPARD.

Religion

CHRISTIANITY

Caribbean Conference of Churches: POB 876, Curepe; tel. 662-2979; fax 662-1303; e-mail ccchq@tstt.net.tt; internet www.ccc-caribe.org; f. 1973; Pres. Rev. Dr LESLEY G. ANDERSON; Gen. Sec. GERARD A. J. GRANADO.

Christian Council of Trinidad and Tobago: Hayes Court, 21 Maraval Rd, Port of Spain; tel. 637-9329; f. 1967; church unity org. formed by the Roman Catholic, Anglican, Presbyterian, Methodist, African Methodist, Spiritual Baptist and Moravian Churches, the Church of Scotland and the Salvation Army, with the Ethiopian Orthodox Church and the Baptist Union as observers; Pres. The Rt Rev. CALVIN WENDELL BESS (Anglican Bishop of Trinidad and Tobago); Sec. GRACE STEELE.

The Anglican Communion

Anglicans are adherents of the Church in the Province of the West Indies, comprising eight dioceses. The Archbishop of the West Indies is the Bishop of Nassau and the Bahamas. According to figures from the latest available census (2000), some 8% of the population are Anglicans.

Bishop of Trinidad and Tobago: The Rt Rev. CALVIN WENDELL BESS, Hayes Court, 21 Maraval Rd, Port of Spain; tel. 622-7387; fax 628-1319; e-mail bessc@tstt.net.tt; internet www.trinidad.anglican.org.

Protestant Churches

According to the 2000 census, 7% of the population are (Orthodox) Baptists, 7% are Pentecostalists, 4% are Seventh-day Adventists and 3% are Presbyterians.

Baptist Union of Trinidad and Tobago: 104 High St, Princes Town; tel. 655-2291; e-mail baptuni@tstt.net.tt; f. 1816; Pres. Rev. EDWIN H. LEWIS; Gen. Sec. Rev. JOHN S. C. BRAMBLE; 24 churches, 3,300 mems.

Presbyterian Church of Trinidad and Tobago: POB 187, Paradise Hill, San Fernando; tel. and fax 652-4829; e-mail pctt@tstt.net.tt; internet www.presbyterianchurchtt.org; f. 1868; Moderator Rt Rev. ELVIS ELAHIE; Gen. Sec. ALVIN SEEREERAM; 40,000 mems.

The Roman Catholic Church

For ecclesiastical purposes, Trinidad and Tobago comprises the single archdiocese of Port of Spain. According to the 2000 census, 26% of the population are Roman Catholics.

Antilles Episcopal Conference: 9A Gray St, Port of Spain; tel. 622-2932; fax 628-3688; e-mail aec@carib-link.net; internet www.catholiccaribbean.org; f. 1975; 21 mems from the Caribbean and Central American regions; Pres. Most Rev. DONALD JAMES REECE (Archbishop of Kingston, Jamaica); Gen. Sec. Rev. GERARD E. FARFAN.

Archbishop of Port of Spain: EDWARD JOSEPH GILBERT, 27 Maraval Rd, Port of Spain; tel. 622-1103; fax 622-1165; e-mail abishop@carib-link.net.

HINDUISM

Hindu immigrants from India first arrived in Trinidad and Tobago in 1845. The vast majority of migrants, who were generally from Uttar Pradesh, were Vishnavite Hindus, who belonged to sects such as the Ramanandi, the Kabir and the Sieunaraini. The majority of Hindus currently subscribe to the doctrine of Sanathan Dharma, which evolved from Ramanandi teaching. According to the 2000 census, 22% of the population are Hindus.

Arya Pratinidhi Sabha of Trinidad Inc (Arya Samaj): Seereeram Memorial Vedic School, Old Southern Main Rd, Montrose Village, Chaguanas; tel. 663-1721; e-mail president@trinidadaryasamaj.org; Pres. LAKHRAM VIJAY BACHAN.

Pandits' Parishad (Council of Pandits): Maha Sabha Headquarters, Eastern Main Rd, St Augustine; tel. 645-3240; works towards the co-ordination of temple activities and the standardization of ritual procedure; affiliated to the Maha Sabha; 200 mems.

Sanathan Dharma Maha Sabha of Trinidad and Tobago Inc: Maha Sabha Headquarters, Eastern Main Rd, St Augustine; tel. 645-3240; e-mail mahasabha@ttemail.com; f. 1952; Hindu pressure group and public org.; organizes the provision of Hindu education; Pres. Dr D. OMAH MAHARAJH; Sec. Gen. SATNARAYAN MAHARAJ.

ISLAM

According to the 2000 census, 6% of the population are Muslims.

Muslims of Trinidad and Tobago: Port of Spain; Chair. IMTIAZ MOHAMMED.

The Press

DAILIES

Newsday: 23A Chacon St, Port of Spain; tel. 623-2459; fax 657-5008; internet www.newsday.co.tt; f. 1993; CEO and Editor-in-Chief THERESE MILLS; circ. 2,200,000.

Trinidad Guardian: 22 St Vincent St, POB 122, Port of Spain; tel. 623-8871; fax 625-5702; e-mail letters@ttol.co.tt; internet guardian.co.tt; f. 1917; morning; independent; Editor-in-Chief ANTHONY WILSON; circ. 52,617.

Trinidad and Tobago Express: 35 Independence Sq., Port of Spain; tel. 623-1711; fax 627-1451; e-mail express@trinidadexpress.com; internet www.trinidadexpress.com; f. 1967; morning; CEO KEN GORDON; Editor ALAN GEERE; circ. 55,000.

PERIODICALS

The Boca: Crews Inn Marina and Boatyard, Village Sq., Chaguaramas; tel. 634-2055; fax 634-2056; e-mail enquiry@boatersenterprise.com; internet www.theboca.com; monthly; magazine of the sailing and boating community; Man. Dir JACK DAUSEND.

The Bomb: Southern Main Rd, Curepe; tel. 645-2744; weekly; Publr SAT MAHARAJ.

Caribbean Beat Magazine: 6 Prospect Ave, Maraval, Port of Spain; tel. 622-3821; fax 628-0639; e-mail info@meppublishers.com; internet www.caribbean-beat.com; f. 1991; 6 a year; distributed by Caribbean Airlines; Publr JEREMY TAYLOR; Editor JUDY RAYMOND.

Catholic News: 31 Independence Sq., Port of Spain; tel. 623-6093; fax 623-9468; e-mail cathnews@trinidad.net; internet www.catholicnews-tt.net; f. 1892; weekly; Editor JUNE JOHNSTON; circ. 16,000.

Economic Bulletin: Eric Williams Plaza, Independence Sq., POB 1250, Port of Spain; tel. 625-4835; fax 627-4696; e-mail info@central-bank.org.tt; internet www.central-bank.org.tt; f. 1950; issued 3 times a year by the Central Bank; Information Man. KAREN CAMPBELL.

Energy Caribbean: 6 Prospect Ave, Maraval, Port of Spain; tel. 622-3821; fax 628-0639; e-mail dchin@meppublishers.com; internet www.meppublishers.com; f. 2002; bi-monthly; Editor DAVID RENWICK.

Showtime: Cnr 9th St and 9th Ave, Barataria; tel. 674-1692; fax 674-3228; circ. 30,000.

Sunday Express: 35 Independence Sq., Port of Spain; tel. 623-1711; fax 627-1451; e-mail express@trinidadexpress.com; internet www.trinidadexpress.com; f. 1967; circ. 51,405.

Sunday Guardian: 22 St Vincent St, POB 122, Port of Spain; tel. 623-8870; fax 625-7211; e-mail esunday@ttol.co.tt; internet www.guardian.co.tt; f. 1917; independent; morning; Editor-in-Chief DOMINIC KALIPERSAD; circ. 48,324.

Sunday Punch: Cnr 9th St and 9th Ave, Barataria; tel. 674-1692; fax 674-3228; weekly; Editor ANTHONY ALEXIS; circ. 40,000.

Tobago News: Milford Rd, Scarborough; tel. 639-5565; fax 625-4480; e-mail ccngroupc@tstt.net.tt; internet www.thetobagonews.com; f. 1985; weekly; Editor COMPTON DELPH.

Trinidad and Tobago Gazette: 2–4 Victoria Ave, Port of Spain; tel. 625-4139; weekly; official govt paper; circ. 3,300.

Trinidad and Tobago Mirror: Cnr 9th St and 9th Ave, Barataria; tel. 674-1692; fax 674-3228; 2 a week; Editors KEN ALI, KEITH SHEPHERD; circ. 35,000.

Tropical Agriculture: Faculty of Agriculture and Natural Sciences, University of the West Indies, St Augustine; tel. and fax 645-3640; e-mail tropicalagri@fans.uwi.tt; f. 1924; journal of the School of Agriculture (fmrly Imperial College of Tropical Agriculture); quarterly; Editor-in-Chief Prof. FRANK A. GUMBS.

Publishers

Caribbean Children's Press: 1A Lazare St, St James; tel. and fax 628-4248; f. 1987; educational publishers for primary schools.

Caribbean Educational Publishers: Gulf View Link Rd, La Romaine; tel. 657-9613; fax 652-5620; e-mail mbscep@tstt.net.tt; Pres. TEDDY MOHAMMED.

Charran Publishing House Ltd: Wrightson Road, POB 126, Port of Spain; tel. 625-9821; fax 623-6597; e-mail charran_pub@yahoo.com; internet www.charranpublishers.com; Man. Dir REGINALD CHARRAN.

Lexicon Trinidad Ltd: Lot 87, Frederick Settlement Industrial Estate, Caroni; tel. 662-1863; fax 663-0081; e-mail lexiconadmin@gmail.com; Dir KEN JAIKARANSINGH.

Morton Publishing: 97 Saddle Rd, Maraval; tel. 348-3777; fax 762-9923; e-mail morton@morton-pub.com; internet www.morton-pub.com; f. 1977; educational books; Pres. DOUG MORTON; Dir JULIE MORTON.

Royards Publishing Co: 7A Macoya Industrial Estate, Macoya; tel. 663-6002; fax 663-6316; e-mail royards@aol.com; internet www.royards.com; f. 1984; educational publishers; Dirs CLIFFORD NARINESINGH, DWIGHT NARINESINGH.

Trinidad Publishing Co Ltd: 22–24 St Vincent St, Port of Spain; tel. 623-8870; fax 625-7211; e-mail business@ttol.co.tt; internet guardian.co.tt; f. 1917; Man. Dir GRENFELL KISSOON.

Broadcasting and Communications

TELECOMMUNICATIONS

Regulatory Body

Telecommunications Authority of Trinidad and Tobago (TATT): 5 Eighth Ave Ext., off Twelfth St, Barataria; tel. 675-8288; fax 674-1055; e-mail info@tatt.org.tt; internet www.tatt.org.tt; f. 2001 to oversee the liberalization of the telecommunications sector; Chair. WINSTON PARMESAR.

Major Service Providers

bmobile: 52 Jerningham Ave, Belmont; fax 625-5807; e-mail service@tstt.co.tt; internet www.bmobile.co.tt; f. 1991 as TSTT Cellnet; name changed as above 2006; 51% state-owned, 49% by Cable & Wireless (United Kingdom); mobile cellular telephone operator; Vice-Pres. GARY BARROW.

Columbus Communications Trinidad Ltd (CCTL): Nicholas Towers, Ground Floor, Independence Sq., Port of Spain; tel. 223-3569; fax 624-9584; e-mail getflow@columbustrinidad.com; internet www.flowtrinidad.com; f. 2005; digital cable television, internet and local telephone service providers; mobile cellular telephone licence granted in 2006; Pres. and CEO JOHN REID; 250 employees (2007).

Digicel Trinidad and Tobago: Ansa Centre, 11C Maraval Rd, Port of Spain; tel. 628-7000; fax 628-9540; e-mail tt.customer.care@digicelgroup.com; internet www.digiceltrinidadandtobago.com; owned by an Irish consortium; mobile cellular telephone licence granted in 2005; Chair. DENIS O'BRIEN; CEO NIALL DORRIAN.

One Caribbean Media Ltd (OCM): 35 Independence Sq., Port of Spain; tel. 623-1711; fax 625-5712; e-mail tjohnson@trinidadexpress.com; internet www.onecaribbeanmedia.net; f. 2006 by merger of Caribbean Communications Network (CCN) and The Nation Corpn (Barbados); Chair. Sir FRED GOLLOP; CEO TERRENCE FARRELL.

Open Telecom Ltd: 88 Edward St, Port of Spain; tel. 627-6559; e-mail sales@opentelecom.com; internet www.opentelecomtt.com; f. 1992; Chair. PETER GILLETTE; Chief Operations Man. NICHOLAS LOOK HONG.

Telecommunication Services of Trinidad and Tobago (TSTT) Ltd: 1 Edward St, POB 3, Port of Spain; tel. 625-4431; fax 627-0856; e-mail tsttceo@tstt.net.tt; internet www.tstt.co.tt; 51% state-owned, 49% by Cable & Wireless (United Kingdom); 51% privatization pending; CEO ROBERTO PEÓN.

BROADCASTING

Radio

The Caribbean New Media Group (CNMG): 11A Maraval, Port of Spain; tel. 622-4141; fax 628-2043; e-mail webmaster@ctntworld.com; internet www.ctntworld.com; state-owned; operates three radio stations: Talk City 91.1 FM, Next 99.1 FM and Sweet 100.1 FM; and three television channels: 6 (cable), 9 and 13; CEO INGRID ISAAC.

Power 102 FM: Radio Vision Ltd, 88–90 Abercromby St, Port of Spain; tel. 627-6937; fax 627-9320; e-mail power102fm@gmail.com; internet www.power102fm.com; CEO O'BRIAN HAYNES; Man. SHARON PITT.

Radio Jaagriti 102.7 FM: Cnr Pasea Main Rd Ext. and Churchill Roosevelt Hwy, Tunapuna; tel. 645-0613; fax 663-8961; e-mail comments@jaagriti.com; internet www.jaagriti.com; f. 2007; Hindu broadcasting network; Man. Dir SAT MAHARAJ; CEO DEVANT MAHARAJ.

Soca 91.9 FM (Trini Bashment): 56 A, Maraval Rd, Port of Spain; tel. 628-3460; fax 622-7674; e-mail info@soca919.com; internet www.919socafm.com; Man. Dir ANTHONY DEVON GEORGE.

Telemedia Ltd: Long Circular Mall, 4th Floor, Long Circular Rd, St James; tel. 622-4124; fax 622-6693; operates three commercial radio stations: Music Radio 97 FM (www.musicradio97.com), Ebony Radio 104 FM (www.ebony104.com) and Heartbeat 103.5 FM (www.heartbeatradiott.com); Gen. Man. KIRAN MAHARAJ.

Trinidad Broadcasting Co Ltd: Guardian Bldg, 2nd Floor, 22–24 St Vincent St, Port of Spain; tel. 623-9202; fax 623-8972; e-mail tbcnews@ttol.co.tt; operates five radio stations: Inspirational Radio 730 AM, Mix 95.1 FM, Vibe CT 105 FM, Sangeet 106 FM and Aakash Vani 106.5 FM; Gen. Man. BRANDON KHAN.

Trinidad and Tobago Radio Network: 153 Tragarete Rd, Port of Spain; tel. 628-6937; internet www.1077musicforlife.com; operates two stations: 96.1 WEFM and 107.7 FM.

Wack Radio 90.1 FM: 129C Coffee St, San Fernando; tel. 652-9774; fax 657-1888; e-mail contact@wackradio901fm.com; internet www.wackradio901fm.com; CEO KENNY PHILLIPS; Man. Dir DIANNE PHILLIPS.

Television

ieTV Channel 1: 76 Tragarete Rd, Port of Spain; tel. 622-3541; fax 622-3097; e-mail ietv@tstt.net.tt; internet www.ietv1.com; owned by CL Communications Group; Indian entertainment programming; CEO ANTHONY MAHARAJ.

TV6: 35 Independence Sq., Port of Spain; tel. 627-8806; fax 623-0785; e-mail enquiries@tv6tnt.com; internet www.tv6tnt.com; f. 1991; operates channels 6 and 18; owned by One Caribbean Media Ltd (OCM); Chair. Sir FRED GOLLOP; Gen. Man. SHIDA BOLAI.

Finance

(cap. = capital; res = reserves; dep. = deposits; m. = million; brs = branches; amounts in TT $)

BANKING

Central Bank

Central Bank of Trinidad and Tobago: Eric Williams Plaza, Brian Lara Promenade, POB 1250, Port of Spain; tel. 625-4835; fax 627-4696; e-mail info@central-bank.org.tt; internet www.central-bank.org.tt; f. 1964; cap. 100.0m., res 100.0m., dep. 29,044.2m. (Sept. 2006); Gov. EWART S. WILLIAMS.

Commercial Banks

Citibank (Trinidad and Tobago) Ltd: 12 Queen's Park East, POB 1249, Port of Spain; tel. 625-1046; fax 627-6128; internet www.citicorp.com; f. 1983; fmrly The United Bank of Trinidad and Tobago Ltd; name changed as above 1989; owned by Citicorp Merchant Bank Ltd; cap. 30.0m., res 14.7m., dep. 455.5m. (Dec. 1996); Chair. SURESH MAHARAJ; Country Man. DENNIS EVANS; 2 brs.

Citicorp Merchant Bank Ltd: 12 Queen's Park East, POB 1249, Port of Spain; tel. 623-3344; fax 624-8131; cap. 57.1m., res 28.5m., dep. 473.6m. (Dec. 2002); owned by Citibank Overseas Investment Corpn; Chair. SURESH MAHARAJ; Man. Dir KAREN DARBASIE.

First Citizens Bank Ltd: 9 Queen's Park East, Port of Spain; tel. 624-3178; fax 627-4548; e-mail enquiries@simplyfirst.net; internet www.firstcitizenstt.com; f. 1993 following merger of National Commercial Bank of Trinidad and Tobago Ltd, Trinidad Co-operative Bank Ltd and Workers' Bank of Trinidad and Tobago; state-owned; cap. 340.0m., res 253.4m., dep. 8,472.1m. (Sept. 2006); Chair. SAMUEL A. MARTIN; CEO LARRY HOWAI; 22 brs.

RBTT Ltd: Royal Court, 19–21 Park St, POB 287, Port of Spain; tel. 623-1322; fax 625-3764; e-mail royalinfo@rbtt.co.tt; internet www.rbtt.com; f. 1972 as Royal Bank of Trinidad and Tobago to take over local brs of Royal Bank of Canada; present name adopted April 2002; bought by Royal Bank of Canada in 2007; cap. 404.0m., res 215.4m., dep. 10,083.1m. (March 2006); Chair. PETER J. JULY; CEO SURESH SOOKOO; 21 brs.

Republic Bank Ltd: 9–17 Park St, POB 1153, Port of Spain; tel. 623-1056; fax 624-1323; e-mail email@republictt.com; internet www.republictt.com; f. 1837 as Colonial Bank; became Barclays Bank in 1972; name changed as above 1981; merged with Bank of Commerce Trinidad and Tobago Ltd 1997; cap. 537.1m., res 951.8m., dep. 28,549.4m. (Sept. 2006); Chair. RONALD F. HARFORD; Man. Dir DAVID DULAL-WHITEWAY; 34 brs.

Republic Finance & Merchant Bank Ltd: 9–17 Park St, POB 1153, Port of Spain; tel. 623-1056; fax 624-1323; e-mail email@republictt.com; internet www.republictt.com; f. 1965; owned by Republic Bank Ltd (q.v.); cap. 30.0m., res 44.5m., dep. 1,836.5m. (Sept. 2004); Chair. RONALD F. HARFORD; Man. Dir CHERYL F. GREAVES.

Scotiabank Trinidad and Tobago Ltd: 56–58 Richmond St, POB 621, Port of Spain; tel. 625-3566; fax 627-5278; e-mail scotiamain@tstt.net.tt; internet www.scotiabanktt.com; cap. 267.6m., res 301.2m., dep. 9,588.4m. (Oct. 2007); Chair. ROBERT H. PITFIELD; Man. Dir RICHARD P. YOUNG; 23 brs.

Development Banks

Agricultural Development Bank of Trinidad and Tobago: 87 Henry St, POB 154, Port of Spain; tel. 623-6261; fax 624-3087; e-mail adbceo@tstt.net.tt; f. 1968; provides long-, medium- and short-term loans to farmers and the agri-business sector; Chair. NOEL GARCIA; CEO JACQUELINE RAWLINS.

DFL Caribbean: 10 Cipriani Blvd, POB 187, Port of Spain; tel. 623-4665; fax 624-3563; e-mail dfl@dflcaribbean.com; internet www.dflcaribbean.com; provides short- and long-term finance, and equity financing for projects in manufacturing, agro-processing, tourism, industrial and commercial enterprises; total assets US $84.2m. (Dec. 1998); Chair. AUDLEY WALKER; Man. Dir GERARD M. PEMBERTON.

Credit Unions

Co-operative Credit Union League of Trinidad and Tobago Ltd: 32–34 Maraval Rd, St Clair; tel. 645-6943; fax 645-3130; e-mail culeague@tstt.net.tt; internet www.ccultt.org; Pres. BRIAN MOORE; Chair. CALVIN MOSES.

STOCK EXCHANGE

Trinidad and Tobago Stock Exchange Ltd: Nicholas Tower, 10th Floor, 63–65 Independence Sq., Port of Spain; tel. 625-5107; fax 623-0089; e-mail ttstockx@tstt.net.tt; internet www.stockex.co.tt; f. 1981; 30 cos listed (2008); electronic depository system came into operation in 2003; Chair. ANDREW MCEACHRANE; CEO WAIN ITON.

INSURANCE

American Life and General Insurance Co (Trinidad and Tobago) Ltd: ALGICO Plaza, 91–93 St Vincent St, POB 943, Port of Spain; tel. 625-4425; fax 623-6218; e-mail algico@wow.net; Man. Dir GORDON DEANE.

Bankers Insurance Co of Trinidad and Tobago Ltd: 177 Tragarete Rd, Port of Spain; tel. 622-4613; fax 628-6808; e-mail bankersinsurance@hcu.co.tt; internet www.hinducreditunion.com; subsidiary of Hindu Credit Union.

Barbados Mutual Life Assurance Society: The Mutual Centre, 16 Queen's Park West, POB 356, Port of Spain; tel. 628-1636; Gen. Man. HUGH MAZELY.

Capital Insurance Ltd: 38–42 Cipero St, San Fernando; tel. 657-8077; fax 652-7306; f. 1958; motor and fire insurance; 10 brs and 9 agencies.

CLICO (Colonial Life Insurance Co (Trinidad) Ltd): Colonial Life Bldg, 29 St Vincent St, POB 443, Port of Spain; tel. 623-1421; fax 627-3821; e-mail info@clico.com; internet www.clico.com; f. 1936; Central Bank assumed control of CLICO in Jan. 2009; Chair. MARLON HOLDER; CEO (vacant).

Colonial Fire & General Insurance Co Ltd (COLFIRE): e-mail info@colfire.com; internet www.colfire.com; f. 1995; mem. of CL Financial Group; Chair. ROBERT NG CHOW; Man. Dir WILLARD P. HARRIS.

CUNA Caribbean Insurance Society Ltd: 37 Wrightson Rd, POB 193, Port of Spain; tel. 623-7963; fax 623-6251; e-mail cunains@trinidad.net; internet www.cunacaribbean.com; f. 1991; marine aviation and transport; motor vehicle, personal accident, property; Gen. Man. ANTHONY HALL; 3 brs.

Furness Anchorage General Insurance Ltd: 11–13 Milling Ave, Sea Lots, POB 283, Port of Spain; tel. 623-0868; fax 625-1243; e-mail furness@wow.net; internet www.furnessgroup.com; f. 1979; general; Chair. IGNATIUS SEVEIRANO FERREIRA; Exec. Chair. WILLIAM A. FERREIRA.

GTM Fire Insurance Co Ltd: 95–97 Queen St, Port of Spain; tel. 623-1525; e-mail gtmis@tstt.net.tt.

Guardian General Insurance Ltd: Princes Court, Keate St, Port of Spain; tel. 623-4741; fax 623-4320; e-mail info@guardiangenerallimited.com; internet www.guardiangenerallimited.com; founded by merger of NEMWIL and Caribbean Home; Chair. HENRY PETER GANTEAUME; CEO RICHARD ESPINET.

Guardian Life of the Caribbean: 1 Guardian Dr., West Moorings, Port of Spain; tel. 625-5433; internet www.guardianlife.co.tt; Chair. ARTHUR LOK JACK; Pres. and CEO DOUGLAS CAMACHO.

Gulf Insurance Ltd: 1 Gray St, St Clair, Port of Spain; tel. 622-5878; fax 628-0272; e-mail info@gulfinsuranceltd.com; internet www.gulfinsuranceltd.com; f. 1974; general; Exec. Chair. GERRARD LEE-INNISS.

Maritime Financial Group: Maritime Centre, 10th Ave, POB 710, Barataria; tel. 674-0130; fax 638-6663; f. 1978; property and casualty; CEO JOHN SMITH.

Motor and General Insurance Co Ltd: 1–3 Havelock St, St Clair, Port of Spain; tel. 622-2637; fax 622-5345.

New India Assurance Co (T & T) Ltd: 22 St Vincent St, Port of Spain; tel. 623-1326; fax 625-0670; e-mail newindia@wow.net; tel. www.newindia.co.in.

Presidential Insurance Co Ltd: 54 Richmond St, Port of Spain; tel. 625-4788; e-mail pic101@tstt.net.tt.

Trinidad and Tobago Export Credit Insurance Co Ltd: 30 Queen's Park West, Port of Spain; tel. and fax 628-2762; e-mail eximbank@wow.net; internet www.eximbanktt.com; state-owned; CEO BRIAN AWANG; Gen. Man. JOSEPHINE IBLE.

Trinidad and Tobago Insurance Ltd (TATIL): 11 Maraval Rd, POB 1004, Port of Spain; tel. 622-5351; fax 628-0035; e-mail info@tatil.co.tt; internet www.tatil.co.tt; acquired by ANSA McAL in 2004; Chair. JOHN JARDIM; CEO RELNA VIRE.

United Insurance Co: 30 O'Connor St, Woodbrook, Port of Spain; tel. 628-8343; fax 628-6575; e-mail trinidad@unitedinsure.com; internet unitedinsure.com; 95.0% owned by Barbados Shipping and Trading Co; Gen. Man. DENNIS BENISAR.

INSURANCE ORGANIZATIONS

Association of Trinidad and Tobago Insurance Companies: 28 Sackville St, Port of Spain; tel. 624-2817; fax 625-5132; e-mail jsc-attic@trinidad.net; internet www.attic.org.tt; Chair. INEZ SINANAN.

National Insurance Board: Cipriani Pl., 2A Cipriani Blvd, Port of Spain; tel. 625-2171-8; fax 627-1787; e-mail nib@nibtt.co.tt; internet www.nibtt.co.tt; f. 1971; statutory corporation; Chair. CALDER HART; Exec. Dir JEFFREY MCFARLANE.

Trade and Industry

GOVERNMENT AGENCIES

Cocoa and Coffee Industry Board: 27 Frederick St, POB 1, Port of Spain; tel. 625-0298; fax 627-4172; e-mail ccib@tstt.net.tt; f. 1962; marketing of coffee and cocoa beans, regulation of cocoa and coffee industry; Man. BARRY JOEFIELD.

Export-Import Bank of Trinidad and Tobago Ltd (EXIMBANK): 30 Queen's Park West, Port of Spain; tel. 628-2762; fax 622-3545; e-mail eximbank@wow.net; internet www.eximbanktt.com; Chair. CLARRY BENN; CEO BRIAN AWANG.

Trinidad and Tobago Forest Products Ltd (TANTEAK): Connector Rd, Carlsen Field, Chaguanas; tel. 665-0078; fax 665-6645; f. 1975; harvesting, processing and marketing of state plantation-grown teak and pine; privatization pending; Chair. RUSKIN PUNCH; Man. Dir CLARENCE BACCHUS.

DEVELOPMENT ORGANIZATIONS

National Energy Corporation of Trinidad and Tobago Ltd: PLIPDECO House, Orinoco Dr., POB 191, Point Lisas, Couva; tel. 636-4662; fax 679-2384; e-mail infocent@carib-link.net; internet www.ngc.co.tt; owned by the Nat. Gas Co of Trinidad and Tobago Ltd (q.v.); f. 1979; Chair. KENNETH BIRCHWOOD; Pres. FRANK LOOK KIN.

National Housing Authority: 44–46 South Quay, POB 555, Port of Spain; tel. 627-1703; fax 625-3963; e-mail info@housing.gov.tt; internet www.housing.gov.tt; f. 1962; Chair. ANDRE MONYEIL; CEO NOEL GARCIA.

Point Lisas Industrial Port Development Corporation Ltd (PLIPDECO): PLIPDECO House, Orinoco Dr., POB 191, Point Lisas, Couva; tel. 636-2201; fax 636-4008; e-mail plipdeco@plipdeco.com; internet www.plipdeco.com; f. 1966; privatized in the late 1990s; deep-water port handling general cargo, liquid and dry bulk, to serve adjacent industrial estate, which now includes iron and steel complex, methanol, ammonia, urea and related downstream industries; Chair. Commdr KAYAM MOHAMMED; Pres. ROGER TRABOULAY.

CHAMBERS OF COMMERCE

South Trinidad Chamber of Industry and Commerce: Suite 313, Cross Crossing Shopping Centre, Lady Hailes Ave, San Fernando; tel. 652-5613; fax 653-4983; e-mail execoffice@stcic.org;

internet www.stcic.org; f. 1956; Pres. CHARLES PERCY; CEO Dr THACKWRAY DRIVER.

Trinidad and Tobago Chamber of Industry and Commerce (Inc): Chamber Bldg, Columbus Circle, Westmoorings, POB 499, Port of Spain; tel. 637-6966; fax 637-7425; e-mail chamber@chamber.org.tt; internet www.chamber.org.tt; f. 1891; Pres. IAN WELCH; CEO JOAN FERREIRA; 600 mems.

INDUSTRIAL AND TRADE ASSOCIATIONS

Agricultural Society of Trinidad and Tobago: 1st Floor, Henry St, Port of Spain; tel. 623-7797; fax 623-3087; e-mail agrisoc@tstt.net.tt.

Coconut Growers' Association (CGA) Ltd: Eastern Main Rd, POB 229, Laventille, Port of Spain; tel. 623-5207; fax 623-2359; e-mail cgaltd@tstt.net.tt; f. 1936; 354 mems; Exec. Chair. PHILIPPE AGOSTINI.

Co-operative Citrus Growers' Association of Trinidad and Tobago Ltd: Eastern Main Rd, POB 174, Laventille, Port of Spain; tel. 623-2255; fax 623-2487; e-mail ccga@wow.net; internet www.ccga.co.tt; f. 1932; Pres. FELIX CLARK; Gen. Man. KENNETH DEBIQUE; 437 mems.

Pan Trinbago Inc: Victoria Park Suites, 14–17 Park St, Port of Spain; tel. 623-4486; fax 625-6715; e-mail admin@pantrinbago.co.tt; internet www.pantrinbago.co.tt; f. 1971; official body for Trinidad and Tobago steelbands; Pres. KEITH DIAZ; Sec. RICHARD FORTEAU.

Shipping Association of Trinidad and Tobago: 15 Scott Bushe St, Port of Spain; tel. 623-3355; fax 623-8540; e-mail gm@shipping.co.tt; internet www.shipping.co.tt; f. 1938; Pres. HAYDN JONES; Gen. Man. E. JOANNE EDWARDS-ALLEYNE.

Sugar Association of the Caribbean: Brechin Castle, Couva; tel. 636-2449; fax 636-2847; f. 1942; promotes and protects sugar industry in the Caribbean; Chair. IAN MCDONALD; Sec. A. MOHAMMED; 6 mem. asscns.

Trinidad and Tobago Contractors' Association: The Professional Centre, Unit B 203, 11–13 Fitzblackman Dr., Wrightson Rd Extension, Port of Spain; tel. 627-1266; fax 623-2949; e-mail ttcaservice@rave-tt.net; internet www.ttca.com; f. 1968; represents contractors, manufacturers and suppliers to the sector; Pres. MIKEY JOSEPH.

Trinidad and Tobago Manufacturers' Association: 1TTMA Bldg, 42 Tenth Ave, Barataria; tel. 675-8862; fax 675-9000; e-mail info@ttma.com; internet www.ttma.com; f. 1956; Pres. KAREN DE MONTBRUN; 260 mems.

EMPLOYERS' ORGANIZATION

Employers' Consultative Association of Trinidad and Tobago (ECA): 23 Chacon St, Port of Spain; tel. 625-4723; fax 625-4891; e-mail ecatt@tstt.net.tt; internet www.ecatt.org; f. 1959; Chair. CLARENCE RAMBHARAT; CEO LINDA BESSON; 500 mems.

STATE HYDROCARBONS COMPANIES

National Gas Co of Trinidad and Tobago Ltd (NGC): Orinoco Dr., Point Lisas Industrial Estate, POB 1127, Port of Spain; tel. 636-4662; fax 679-2384; e-mail ngc@ngc.co.tt; internet www.ngc.co.tt; f. 1975; purchases, sells, compresses, transmits and distributes natural gas to consumers; Chair. KEITH AWONG; Pres. S. ANDREW MCINTOSH.

Petroleum Co of Trinidad and Tobago Ltd (Petrotrin): Petrotrin Administration Bldg, Cnr Queen's Park West and Cipriani Blvd, Port of Spain; tel. 625-5240; fax 624-4661; e-mail kharnanan@petrotrin.com; internet www.petrotrin.com; f. 1993 following merger between Trinidad and Tobago Oil Co Ltd (Trintoc) and Trinidad and Tobago Petroleum Co Ltd (Trintopec); govt-owned; petroleum and gas exploration and production; operates refineries and a manufacturing complex, producing a variety of petroleum and petrochemical products; Chair. MALCOLM JONES; Pres. KENNETH ALLUM.

Petrotrin Trinmar Operations: Petrotrin Administration Bldg, Point Fortin; tel. 648-2127; fax 648-2519; f. 1962; owned by Petrotrin; marine petroleum and natural gas co; Gen. Man. ALLAN RUSSELL; 705 employees.

Trintomar Ltd: Petrotrin Administration Bldg, Pointe-à-Pierre; tel. 647-8861; fax 647-3193; e-mail lisle.ramyad@petrotrin.com; f. 1988; 80% owned by EOG Resources, 20% owned by NGC; develops offshore petroleum sector; Man. LISLE RAMYAD.

MAJOR COMPANIES

The following is a selection of major industrial and commercial companies operating in Trinidad and Tobago:

Food and Beverages

Angostura Holdings Ltd: Cnr Eastern Main Rd and Trinity Ave, POB 62, Port of Spain; tel. 623-1841; fax 623-1847; e-mail glarondew@angostura.com; internet www.angostura.com; f. 1921; manufacturers of rum, Angostura aromatic bitters and other alcoholic beverages; gross sales of TT $683m. (2006); Chair. SHAFEEK SULTAN-KHAN; Dirs WAYNE YIP CHOY, JOSEPH TEIXEIRA; 35 employees.

Bermudez Biscuit Co Ltd: 6 Maloney St, POB 885, Mount Lambert; tel. 638-3336; fax 638-4445; e-mail bermudez@bermudezcaribbean.com; f. 1950; producers of biscuits and other food products; Man. Dir NOBLE PHILIP; Gen. Man. INGRID LLOYD; 367 employees.

Kiss Baking Co Ltd: 12–14 Gaston St, POB 776, Lange Park, Chaguanas; tel. 671-2253; fax 672-3840; e-mail kissbaking@cariblink.net; f. 1975; bakery; Man. RENE DE GANNES; 2,890 employees.

National Flour Mills Ltd: 27–29 Wrightson Rd, POB 1154, Port of Spain; tel. 625-2416; fax 625-4389; e-mail nfm@nfm.co.tt; internet www.nfm.co.tt; f. 1972; milling of flour and grains; manufacturers of rice, edible oils and animal feed; sales of TT $738.3m. (1996); CEO GILLIAN POLLIDOR (acting); 384 employees.

Nestlé Trinidad and Tobago Ltd: Churchill Roosevelt Highway Valsayn, POB 172, Port of Spain; tel. and fax 663-6832; manufacture and distribution of dairy products, canned vegetables, fruit juices, pasta products; subsidiary of Nestlé SA, Switzerland.

Catelli Primo Ltd: Churchill Roosevelt Highway, Valsayn; tel. 625-1414; fax 625-3915; fruit and vegetable canners; subsidiary of Nestlé Trinidad and Tobago Ltd; Gen. Man. MICHAEL HACKSHAW.

Metals

ArcelorMittal Point Lisas Ltd: Mediterranean Dr., Point Lisas Industrial Estate, POB 476, Couva; tel. 636-2211; fax 636-5696; internet www.arcelormittal.com; f. 2005; owned by ArcelorMittal, Luxembourg; fmrly Iron and Steel Co of Trinidad and Tobago Ltd; name changed to Caribbean Ispat Ltd in 1998; name changed to Mittal Steel Point Lisas Ltd in 2005 and as above in 2006; acquired International Steel Group (USA) in April 2005; production of iron and steel wire and rods; Chair. and CEO LAKSHMI MITTAL; 732 employees.

Bhagwansingh's Hardware and Steel Industries Ltd: 1 Development Circular Rd, Sea Lots, Port of Spain; tel. 627-8335; fax 623-0804; e-mail bhsil@trinidad.net; f. 1974; manufacturers of aluminium products; wholesale of steel and electrical products; Man. Dir HELEN BHAGWANSINGH; 310 employees.

Central Trinidad Steel Ltd (CENTRIN): Mediterranean Dr., Point Lisas Industrial Estate, Point Lisas; tel. 679-2996; fax 636-2940; e-mail centrin@tstt.net.tt; internet www.centrintt.com; f. 1983; owned by Bhagwansingh's Hardware and Steel Industries Ltd; manufacturers of steel and bldg materials; Man. Dir HELEN BHAGWANSINGH.

Petroleum, Natural Gas and Asphalt

(see also State Hydrocarbons Companies)

Atlantic LNG Co of Trinidad and Tobago: POB 1337, Port of Spain; tel. 624-2916; fax 624-8057; e-mail atlanticinfo@atlanticlng.com; internet www.atlanticlng.com; f. 1995; operates 4 natural gas trains; production of liquefied natural gas; run by Atlantic Group, three companies owned by subsidiaries of BP plc, BG Group, GDF Suez, National Gas Company of Trinidad and Tobago Ltd; CEO OSCAR PRIETO.

BG T&T (British Gas Trinidad and Tobago Ltd): BG House, 5 St Clair Ave, Port of Spain; tel. 628-0888; fax 622-6520; e-mail wendell.constantine@bg-group.com; internet www.bg-group.com; extraction of natural gas; operating in Trinidad and Tobago since 1989; Pres. and Asst Gen. Man. DEREK HUDSON.

BP Energy Company of Trinidad and Tobago: 5–5A Queen's Park West Plaza, Port of Spain; tel. 623-2862; fax 627-7863; internet www.bptt.com; f. 1960; exploration and extraction of natural gas and petroleum; CEO ROBERT RILEY; 800 employees.

Lake Asphalt of Trinidad and Tobago (1978) Ltd: Brighton, La Brea; tel. 648-7556; fax 648-7433; e-mail sjagmohan@trinidadlakeasphalt.com; internet www.trinidadlakeasphalt.com; state-owned; manufacturers of asphalt; Dep. Chair. ANTHONY RICHARDSON; CEO WAYNE WOOD.

Mora Oil Ventures (MORAVEN): Suite 405, Long Circular Mall, Port of Spain; tel. 622-0427; fax 628-3708; e-mail mail@moraven.com; internet www.moraven.com; oil production; Chair. TREVOR BOOPSINGH; CEO GEORGE NICHOLAS.

Petrochemicals

Conoco Trinidad B.V.: POB 225, Port of Spain; tel. 636-1522; fax 623-6025; natural gas liquid processing; Pres. EUGENE TIAH; Man. Dir PAUL WARWICK.

EthylChem: Pointe-à-Pierre; tel. 681-1372; ethanol dehydration plant; scheduled to begin operations in 2009; Denham (USA) is major shareholder; Man. Dir NAMDEO MAHARAJ.

Methanex: Maracaibo Dr., Point Lisas, POB 723, Couva; tel. 679-4400; fax 679-2400; e-mail mxtrinidad@methanex.com; internet www.methanex.com; operates Trinidad and Tobago's largest methanol plant; Pres. BRUCE AITKEN; Vice-Pres. JORGE YANEZ.

Methanol Holdings (Trinidad) Ltd: Atlantic Ave, POB 457, Point Lisas Industrial Estate, Couva; tel. 636-2906; fax 636-4501; e-mail mhtlweb@ttmethanol.com; internet www.ttmethanol.com; f. 1999 to consolidate the overall management of the Trinidad and Tobago Methanol Co Ltd (TTMC), the Caribbean Methanol Co Ltd (CMC) and the Methanol IV Co Ltd (MIV); CL Financial Ltd (56.53%) Consolidate Energy Ltd (43.47%); 7 methanol production plants in operation in 2005; new complex to produce urea ammonium nitrate and melamine to open in 2010; CEO RAMPERSAND MOTILAL; 300 employees.

PCS (Potash Corpn of Saskatchewan) Nitrogen Ltd: Atlantic Ave, POB 201, Point Lisas, Couva; tel. 636-2205; fax 636-2052; e-mail iewelch@pcsnitrogen.co.tt; internet www.potashcorp.com; f. 1977; fmrly state-owned Fertilizers of Trinidad and Tobago (Fertrin) Ltd, bought by Arcadian Partners (USA) in 1993; Arcadian Partners bought by PCS in 1997; manufacturers of fertilizers; Man. Dir IAN E. WELCH; 395 employees.

Pt Lisas Nitrogen Ltd: North Caspian Dr., PO Bag 38, Point Lisas, Couva; tel. 679-4045; fax 679-2452; e-mail fmcl@fmcl.tt.com; fmrly Farmland MissChem; renamed as above in 2002; 50% owned by Koch Minerals; ammonia production; Pres. DAVID D'ANDRADE.

Miscellaneous

Agostini's Ltd: 4 Nelson St, POB 191, Port of Spain; tel. 623-2236; fax 624-6751; e-mail marketing@agostini-mktg.com; internet www.agostini-mktg.com; f. 1925; importers and wholesale distributors of construction materials, foodstuffs and pharmaceuticals; sales of TT $385m. (2006); Chair. JOSEPH P. ESAU; Man. Dir ANTHONY J. AGOSTINI; 650 employees.

Automotive Components Ltd: O'Meara Rd, POB 1298, Arima; tel. 642-4236; fax 642-7807; e-mail autocomp@neal-and-massy.com; internet www.acl-tt.com; f. 1964; manufacturers of automobile batteries; owned by Neal & Massy Holdings Ltd (q.v.).

Berger Paints Trinidad Ltd: 11 Concessions Rd, Sea Lots, POB 546, Port of Spain; tel. 623-2231; fax 623-1682; e-mail berger@tstt.net.tt; internet www.bergercaribbean.com; f. 1760; manufacturers of paint, wood stains, wood preservatives, auto refinishes; Man. Dir KISHORE S. ADVANI; 100 employees.

A. S. Bryden and Sons (Trinidad) Ltd: Ibis Ave, San Juan; tel. 674-9191; fax 674-0781; e-mail info@brydenstt.com; internet www.brydenstt.com; f. 1928; importers and distributors of alcoholic beverages, food products, household goods and pharmaceuticals; Chair. KEITH G. MAINGOT; Man. Dir IAN P. FITZWILLIAM; 225 employees.

Carib Glassworks Ltd: Eastern Main Rd, POB 1287, Champs Fleurs, Port of Spain; tel. 662-2231; fax 663-1779; e-mail marketing@caribglass.com; internet www.caribglass.com; f. 1948; part of ANSA McAL Group; glass manufacturers; Man. Dir ROGER MEW; 420 employees.

Conglomerates ANSA McAL: 11 Maraval Rd, Port of Spain; tel. 625-3670; fax 624-8753; internet www.ansamcal.com; activities include glass making, construction, finance, media; owns Caribbean Devt Co brewery; Group Chair. A. NORMAN SABGA; Dir GERRY C. BROOKS.

Fujitsu Transaction Solutions (Trinidad) Ltd: 6th Ave South Extension and Ibis Ave, Barataria; tel. 223-2826; fax 675-1956; e-mail services@fj-icl.com; internet www.fujitsu.com/caribbean; subsidiary of Fujitsu Ltd of Japan; manufacturers of computers and telecommunications equipment; Pres. MERVYN EYRE; Vice-Pres. IAN GALT.

Lever Brothers (West Indies) Ltd: Eastern Main Rd, POB 295, Champ Fleurs, Port of Spain; tel. 663-1787; fax 662-1780; e-mail carla.chang@unilever.com; internet www.unilevercaribbean.com; f. 1964; subsidiary of Unilever PLC of the United Kingdom; manufacturers of soaps, detergents, cosmetic products and foods; Man. Dir and Chair. PABLO GARRIDO; 600 employees.

Neal & Massy Holdings Ltd: 63 Park St, POB 544, Port of Spain; tel. 625-3426; fax 627-9061; e-mail info@neal-and-massy.com; internet www.neal-and-massy.com; f. 1923; industrial, trading and financial group involved in metals, engineering and automobile assembly; revenue of TT $1,464m. (2004); Chair. ARTHUR LOK JACK; CEO E. GERVASE WARNER; 6,500 employees.

Thomas Peake and Co Ltd: 177 Western Main Rd, Cocorite, Port of Spain; tel. 662-0404; fax 622-4580; e-mail peake@peakeind.com; internet www.peakeind.com; manufacturers and repairers of air conditioning equipment; Dir PAUL PEAKE.

Trinidad Cement Ltd (TCL): Southern Main Rd, Claxton Bay; tel. 659-2381; fax 659-2540; e-mail tclinfo@tclgroup.com; internet www.tclgroup.com; f. 1951; manufacture and sale of Portland, sulphate-resisting and oil-well cement and paper sacks and bags; owned by TCL Group; Chair. ANDY J. BHAJAN; Group CEO ROLLIN BERTRAND; 400 employees.

Trinidad and Tobago National Petroleum Marketing Co Ltd: National Dr., POB 666, Sea Lots, Port of Spain; tel. 625-1364; fax 627-4028; e-mail ttnpmc@np.co.tt; internet www.np.co.tt; marketing of petroleum products; state-owned; Chair. LAWFORD DUPRÉS; CEO RICHARD CALLENDER.

L. J. Williams Ltd: POB 339, 5B S. Keys, Port of Spain; tel. 623-2865; fax 625-6782; e-mail sales@ljw.co.tt; f. 1925; manufacturers of glues and sealants; distribution of groceries and beverages; Chair. J. G. FURNESS-SMITH; Man. Dir P. J. WILLIAMS; 500 employees.

West Indian Tobacco Co Ltd (WITCO): Eastern Main Rd, POB 177, Champ Fleurs, Port of Spain; tel. 662-2271; fax 645-3660; internet www.westindiantobacco.com; f. 1904; subsidiary of British-American Tobacco Co Ltd of the United Kingdom; cigarette manufacturers; Man. Dir ANTHONY PHILLIP; 200 employees.

UTILITIES

Regulatory Authority

Regulated Industries Commission: Furness House, 90 Independence Sq., Port of Spain; tel. 625-5384; fax 624-2027; e-mail complaints@ric.org.tt; internet www.ric.org.tt; Chair. IAN WELCH; Exec. Dir HARJINDER S. ATWAL.

Electricity

Power Generation Co of Trinidad and Tobago (PowerGen): 6A Queen's Park West, Port of Spain; tel. 624-0383; fax 625-3759; f. 1994; 51% owned by Trinidad and Tobago Electricity Commission; 39% owned by MaruEnergy Trinidad LLC; 10% owned by Amoco Trinidad Power Resources Corpn; operates 3 generation plants in Point Lisas, Port of Spain and Penal; Gen. Man. GARTH CHATOOR.

Trinidad and Tobago Electricity Commission (T&TEC): 63 Frederick St, Port of Spain; tel. 623-2611; fax 623-3759; e-mail comments@ttec.co.tt; internet www.ttec.co.tt; state-owned electricity transmission and distribution co; Chair. Prof. CLEMENT IMBERT; Gen. Man. INDARJIT SINGH.

Trinity Power Ltd: Railway Rd, Dow Village, Couva; tel. 679-4542; fax 679-4463; e-mail gthompson@trinitypm.com; f. 1999; fmrly Inncogen Ltd; owned by Trinidad Generation Unlimited; Gen. Man. JACQUELINE LOOK LOY.

Gas

National Gas Co of Trinidad and Tobago Ltd: see State Hydrocarbons Companies.

Water

Water and Sewerage Authority (WASA): Farm Rd, St Joseph; tel. 662-2302; fax 652-1253; e-mail contact@wasa.gov.tt; internet www.wasa.gov.tt; Chair. Dr ROLLIN BERTRAND; CEO ERROL GRIMES.

TRADE UNIONS

Federation of Independent Trade Unions and NGOs (FITUN): Paramount Bldg, 99A Circular Rd, San Fernando; tel. 652-2701; fax 652-7170; e-mail fitun_tt@yahoo.com; f. 2003; Pres. DAVID ABDULLAH; Gen. Sec. MORTON MITCHELL.

National Trade Union Centre (NATUC): 16 New St, Port of Spain; tel. 625-3023; fax 627-7588; e-mail natuc@carib-link.net; f. 1991 as umbrella org. unifying entire trade-union movt, incl. former Trinidad and Tobago Labour Congress and Council of Progressive Trade Unions; Pres. ROBERT GIUSEPPI; Gen. Sec. VINCENT CARBERA.

Principal Affiliates

Airline Superintendents' Association: c/o Data Centre Bldg, Piarco International Airport, Port of Spain; tel. 664-3401; fax 664-3303; Pres. JEFFERSON JOSEPH; Gen. Sec. THEO OLIVER.

All-Trinidad Sugar and General Workers' Trade Union (ATSGWTU): Rienzi Complex, Exchange Village, Southern Main Rd, Couva; tel. 636-2354; fax 636-3372; e-mail atsgwtu@tstt.net.tt; f. 1937; Pres. RUDRANATH INDARSINGH; Gen. Sec. SYLVESTER MARAJH; 2,000 mems.

Amalgamated Workers' Union: 16 New St, Port of Spain; tel. 627-6717; fax 627-8993; f. 1953; Pres.-Gen. CYRIL LOPEZ; Sec. FLAVIUS NURSE; c. 7,000 mems.

Association of Technical, Administrative and Supervisory Staff: Brechin Castle, Couva; Pres. Dr WALLY DES VIGNES; Gen. Sec. ISAAC BEEPATH.

Aviation, Communication and Allied Workers' Union: Aero Services Bldg, Orange Grove Rd, Tacarigua; tel. and fax 640-6518; f. 1982; Pres. CHRISTOPHER ABRAHAM; Gen. Sec. SIEUNARINE BALROOP.

Banking, Insurance and General Workers' Union: 85 Eight Street, Barataria, Port of Spain; tel. 675-9135; fax 675-4664; e-mail union@bigwu.org; internet www.bigwu.org; f. 1974 as Bank and General Workers' Union; name changed as above following merger with Bank Employees' Union in 2003; Pres. VINCENT CABRERA; Gen. Sec. TREVOR JOHNSON.

Communication, Transport and General Workers' Trade Union: Aero Services Credit Union Bldg, Orange Grove Rd, Tacarigua; tel. and fax 640-8785; e-mail cattu@tstt.net.tt; Pres. JAGDEO JAGROOP; Gen. Sec. RAYMOND SMALL.

Communication Workers' Union: 146 Henry St, Port of Spain; tel. 623-5588; fax 625-3308; e-mail cwutdad@tstt.net.tt; f. 1953; Pres. PATRICK HALL; Gen. Sec. LYLE TOWNSEND; c. 2,100 mems.

Contractors' and General Workers' Trade Union (CGWTU): 37 Rushworth St, San Fernando; tel. 657-8072; fax 657-6834; Pres. OWEN HINDS; Gen. Sec. AINSLEY MATTHEWS.

Customs and Excise Extra Guard Association: Nicholas Court, Abercromby St, Port of Spain; tel. 625-3311; Pres. ALEXANDER BABB; Gen. Sec. NATHAN HERBERT.

Trinidad and Tobago Fire Service Association (Second Division) (FSA): 127 Edward St, Port of Spain; tel. 627-6700; fax 627-6701; e-mail fsa2@tstt.net.tt; Pres. CHARLES RAMSARROP; Sec. SHARON NICHOLSON-CHARLES.

National General Workers' Union: c/o 143 Charlotte St, Port of Spain; tel. 623-0694; Pres. JIMMY SINGH; Gen. Sec. CHRISTOPHER ABRAHAM.

National Union of Domestic Employees (NUDE): 53 Wattley Circular Rd, Mount Pleasant Rd, Arima; tel. 667-5247; fax 664-0546; e-mail domestic@tstt.net.tt; f. 1982; Gen. Sec. IDA LE BLANC.

National Union of Government and Federated Workers: 145–147 Henry St, Port of Spain; tel. 623-4591; fax 625-7756; e-mail headoffice@nugfw.org.tt; internet nugfw.org.tt; f. 1937; Pres.-Gen. ROBERT GUISEPPI; Gen. Sec. JACQUELINE JACK; c. 20,000 mems.

Oilfield Workers' Trade Union (OWTU): Paramount Bldg, 99A Circular Rd, San Fernando; tel. 652-2701; fax 652-7170; e-mail owtu@owtu.org; internet www.owtu.org; f. 1937; Pres. ANCEL ROGET; Gen. Sec. DAVID ABDULLAH; 9,000 mems.

Public Services Association: 89–91 Abercromby St, POB 353, Port of Spain; tel. 623-7987; fax 627-2980; e-mail psa@tstt.net.tt; f. 1938; Pres. JENNIFER BAPTISTE-PRIMUS; Sec. KAREN FERREIRA; c. 15,000 mems.

Seamen and Waterfront Workers' Trade Union: 1D Wrightson Rd, Port of Spain; tel. 625-1351; fax 625-1182; e-mail swwtu@tstt.net.tt; f. 1937; Pres.-Gen. MICHAEL ANNISETTE; Sec.-Gen. ROSS ALEXANDER; c. 3,000 mems.

Steel Workers' Union of Trinidad and Tobago: c/o ISPAT, Point Lisas, Couva; tel. 679-4666; fax 679-4175; e-mail swutt@tstt.net.tt; Pres. LEX LOVELL; Gen. Sec. PHILIP SANCHO.

Transport and Industrial Workers' Union: 114 Eastern Main Rd, Laventille, Port of Spain; tel. 623-4943; fax 623-2361; e-mail tiwu@tstt.net.tt; f. 1962; Pres. ROLAND SUTHERLAND; Gen. Sec. JUDY CHARLES; c. 5,000 mems.

Trinidad and Tobago Airline Pilots' Association (TTALPA): 35A Brunton Rd, St James; tel. 628-6556; fax 628-2418; e-mail info@ttalpa.org; internet www.ttalpa.org; Chair. Capt. ANTHONY WIGHT; Man. CHRISTINE DAVIS.

Trinidad and Tobago Postal Workers' Union: c/o General Post Office, Wrightson Rd, POB 692, Port of Spain; tel. 625-2121; fax 642-4303; Pres. (vacant); Gen. Sec. EVERALD SAMUEL.

Trinidad and Tobago Unified Teachers' Association: Cnr Fowler and Southern Main Rd, Curepe; tel. 645-2134; fax 662-1813; e-mail generalsecretary@ttuta.org; Pres. ROUSTAN JOB; Gen. Sec. PETER WILSON.

Union of Commercial and Industrial Workers: TIWU Bldg, 114 Eastern Main Rd, POB 460, Port of Spain; tel. and fax 626-2285; f. 1951; Pres. KELVIN GONZALES; Gen. Sec. ROSALIE FRASER; c. 1,500 mems.

Transport

RAILWAYS

In 2005 the Ministry of Works and Transport announced plans to reintroduce a railway service, which had been discontinued in 1968. The design phase of the project began in 2008 and construction was expected to take 10–15 years, costing an estimated TT $15,000m. Services on the first section of railway line, connecting Port of Spain, St Joseph and Chaguanas, were expected to commence in 2010.

ROADS

In 1999 there were 8,320 km (5,170 miles) of roads in Trinidad and Tobago, of which 51.1% were paved. In 2005 the US Agency for International Development allocated US $3.2m. to fund the repair of roads damaged by Hurricane Ivan in 2004. The construction of a new highway from San Fernando to Mayaro was expected to commence in 2010 as part of a TT $15,000m. highway development programme.

Public Transport Service Corporation: Railway Bldgs, South Quay, POB 391, Port of Spain; tel. 623-2341; fax 625-6502; f. 1965; national bus services, operates a fleet of buses; CEO EDISON ISAAC.

SHIPPING

The chief ports are Port of Spain, Pointe-à-Pierre and Point Lisas in Trinidad and Scarborough in Tobago. Port of Spain handles 85% of all container traffic, and all international cruise arrivals. In 1998 Port of Spain handled 3.3m. metric tons of cargo. Port of Spain and Scarborough each have a deep-water wharf. Port of Spain possesses a dedicated container terminal, with two large overhead cranes. Plans were put in place in 2002 for an expansion of operations, through the purchase of an additional crane, the computerization of operations, and the deepening of the harbour (from 9.75 m to 12 m).

Caribbean Drydock Ltd: Port Chaguaramas, Western Main Rd, Chaguaramas; tel. 634-4226; fax 625-1215; ship repair, marine transport, barge and boat construction.

Point Lisas Industrial Port Development Corporation Ltd (PLIPDECO): see Trade and Industry—Development Organizations.

Port Authority of Trinidad and Tobago: Dock Rd, POB 549, Port of Spain; tel. 623-2901; fax 627-2666; e-mail vilmal@patnt.com; internet www.patnt.com; f. 1962; Chair. DEREK HUDSON; CEO CHRISTOPHER MENDEZ.

Shipping Association of Trinidad and Tobago: 15 Scott Bushe St, Port of Spain; tel. 623-3355; fax 623-8570; e-mail satt@wow.net; internet shipping.co.tt; Pres. HAYDN JONES; Gen. Man. JENNIFER GONZÁLEZ.

CIVIL AVIATION

Piarco International Airport is situated 25.7 km (16 miles) south-east of Port of Spain and is used by numerous airlines. The airport was expanded and a new terminal was constructed in 2001. Piarco remains the principal air transportation facility in Trinidad and Tobago. However, following extensive aerodrome development at Crown Point Airport (located 13 km from Scarborough) in 1992 the airport was opened to jet aircraft. It is now officially named Crown Point International Airport. There is a domestic service between Trinidad and Tobago.

Airports Authority of Trinidad and Tobago (AATT): Airport Administration Centre, Caroni North Bank Rd, Piarco; tel. 669-5311; fax 669-2319; e-mail aatt@tntairports.com; internet www.tntairports.com; administers Piarco and Crown Point International Airports; Chair. JOHN ECKSTEIN; Gen. Man. SANDRA PERKINS (acting).

Caribbean Airlines: Sunjet House, 30 Edward St, Port of Spain; tel. 625-7200; e-mail mail@caribbean-airlines.com; internet www.caribbean-airlines.com; f. 2007 as successor to BWIA (f. 1940); operates scheduled passenger and cargo services linking destinations in the Caribbean region, South America, North America and Europe; CEO PHILIP SAUNDERS; Chair. ARTHUR LOK JACK.

Tourism

The climate and coastline attract visitors to Trinidad and Tobago. The latter island is generally believed to be the more beautiful and is less developed. The annual pre-Lenten carnival is a major attraction. Total tourist arrivals numbered an estimated 430,631 in 2009. Tourism receipts were estimated at US $621m. in 2007. In that year there were 76,741 cruise ship passenger arrivals. There were 3,815 hotel rooms in Trinidad and Tobago in 2008, of which 57.5% were on Tobago.

Tourism Development Co of Trinidad and Tobago (TDC): Maritime Centre, Level 1, 29 Tenth Ave, Barataria; tel. 675-7034; fax 675-7722; e-mail info@tdc.co.tt; internet www.tdc.co.tt; f. 1993 as Tourism and Industrial Devt Co of Trinidad and Tobago; restructured and renamed as above in 2005; Chair. DAVID LEWIS; Pres. ERNEST M. LITTLES.

Trinidad Hotels, Restaurants and Tourism Association (THRTA): c/o Trinidad & Tobago Hospitality and Tourism Institute, Airway Rd, Chaguaramas; tel. 634-1174; fax 634-1176; e-mail info@tnthotels.com; internet www.tnthotels.com; Pres. KEVIN KENNY; Exec. Dir GREER ASSAM.

Tobago Hotel and Tourism Association: Apt 1, Lambeau Credit Union Bldg, Auchenskeoch, Carnbee; tel. and fax 639-

9543; e-mail tthtatob@tstt.net.tt; Pres. CAROL ANN BIRCHWOOD-JAMES.

Defence

As assessed at November 2009, the Trinidad and Tobago Defence Force consisted of an army of an estimated 3,000 men and a coastguard of 1,063. Included in the coastguard was an air wing of 50.

Defence Budget: TT $1,000m. (US $158m.) in 2009.

Chief of Defence Staff: Brig.-Gen. EDMUND DILLON.

Education

Primary and secondary education is provided free of charge. Many schools are run jointly by state and religious bodies. Attendance at school is officially compulsory for children between five and 12 years of age. Primary education begins at the age of five and lasts for seven years. In 2008 92% of children in this age group (males 92%; females 91%) were enrolled at primary schools. Secondary education, beginning at 12 years of age, lasts for up to five years, comprising a first cycle of three years and a second of two years. The ratio for secondary enrolment in 2008 was 74% of those in the relevant age-group (males 71%; females 76%), according to UNESCO estimates. Entrance to secondary schools is determined by the Common Entrance Examination.

Free tertiary tuition was introduced in 2006. The Trinidad campus of the University of the West Indies (UWI), at St Augustine, offers undergraduate and postgraduate programmes and includes an engineering faculty. The UWI Institute of Business offers postgraduate courses and develops programmes for local companies. Other institutions of higher education are the Eric Williams Medical Sciences Complex, the Polytechnic Institute and the Eastern Caribbean Institute of Agriculture and Forestry. In the late 1990s the Government established the Trinidad and Tobago Institute of Technology and the College of Science, Technology and Applied Arts of Trinidad and Tobago. The University of Trinidad and Tobago was established in 2004. The country has one teacher-training college and three government technical institutes and vocational centres, including the Trinidad and Tobago Hotel School. Budgeted expenditure on education by the central Government in 2009 was TT $7,121.6m., equivalent to some 14.4% of total government expenditure.

Bibliography

For works on the Caribbean generally, see Select Bibliography (Books)

Anthony, M. *Historical Dictionary of Trinidad and Tobago*. Lanham, MD, Scarecrow Press, 1997.

Harrison, P. *The Impact of Macroeconomic Policies in Trinidad and Tobago*. New York, Palgrave Macmillan, 2002.

Hintzen, P. C., and Campbell, E. Q. (Eds). *Costs of Regime Survival: Racial Mobilization, Elite Domination and Control of the State in Guyana and Trinidad*. Cambridge, Cambridge University Press, 2007.

Khan, A. *Callaloo Nation: Metaphors of Race and Religious Identity Among South Asians in Trinidad*. Durham, NC, Duke University Press, 2004.

Klass, M. *Singing with Sai Baba: Politics of Revitalization in Trinidad*. Prospect Heights, IL, Waveland Press, 1996.

Maharaj, P. D. *Clash of Cultures: The Indian–African Competition in Trinidad*. Arima, Indian Free Press, 2002.

Meighoo, K. P. *Politics in a Half Made Society: Trinidad and Tobago, 1925–2002*. New York, Markus Wiener Publrs, 2003.

Munasinghe, V. *Callaloo or Tossed Salad? East Indians and the Cultural Politics of Identity in Trinidad*. Ithaca, NY, Cornell University Press, 2001.

Palmer, C. A. A. *Eric Williams and the Making of the Modern Caribbean*. Chapel Hill, NC, University of North Carolina Press, 2006.

Purdy, J. M. *Common Law and Colonised Peoples*. Aldershot, Ashgate Publishing Ltd, 1997.

Regis, L. *The Political Calypso: True Opposition in Trinidad and Tobago*. Gainesville, FL, University Press of Florida, 1999.

Seerattan, D. *Tax Reform and Financial Development in Trinidad and Tobago*. St Augustine, Caribbean Centre for Monetary Studies, University of the West Indies, 2002.

THE TURKS AND CAICOS ISLANDS

Geography

PHYSICAL FEATURES

The Turks and Caicos Islands is an Overseas Territory of the United Kingdom, a former British crown colony, and once a dependency of Jamaica, until the latter's independence in 1962. The two groups of islands, the Caicos to the west and the Turks to the east, form the south-eastern extremity of the Atlantic archipelago dominated by the Bahamas. The territory continues the main chain some 63 km (39 miles) to the south-east of Mayaguana, although it lies directly east from the two more isolated Inagua islands. There is only about 45 km between West Caicos and Little Inagua. The Turks and Caicos Islands lies 145 km north of the island of Hispaniola. Some 40 islands, islets and cays, with a total coastline of 389 km, cover 948 sq km (366 sq miles) of territory (this figure includes area at low water level for all islands, but excludes area to high water mark).

The two groups of islands are separated by the Columbus or Turks Island Passage (35 km long and reaching a depth of some 7,000 ft—over 2,130 m) between the Atlantic and the Caribbean. The islands are low and coralline, with thin, poor soil on limestone bases, but this dry and semi-barren surface (particularly in the east) belies the submarine luxuriance of the third largest coral reef system in the world. Moreover, the flat terrain, prone to marshiness and mangrove swamps, and dotted with salt pans and salinas, is attractive to birds and hardy wildlife. Although the rocky interiors, generally covered in scrub, cacti and thorny acacias, remain bleak, the creeks, flats, marshlands and sand flats have delicate and unique ecosystems, teeming with attractions for resident and migratory birds. As a result, the natural and historical environment of the islands and their reefs is protected by over 30 reserves (including wildlife such as the endemic rock iguana or the pygmy boa). All the islands tend to higher terrain, with limestone cliffs and sand dunes, on the northern or north-eastern weather sides. The highest point on the islands is unclear, but is about 49 m (161 ft), be it the peak of the Ridge on Grand Turk or the only recently named Blue Hills on Providenciales. Flamingo Hill (48 m), on East Caicos, is also sometimes quoted as the highest point in the territory.

The Turks Islands (named for the fez-like Turks Head cactus) define the south-eastern edge of the territory, forming an arc of mainly small islands heading from the south-west and culminating in the northward-pointing, and much larger, Grand Turk. Although only 18 sq km in area, the island is the second largest population centre and the site of the capital, Cockburn Town. The only other one of the Turks of any size or population is Salt Cay, a designated UNESCO World Heritage Site, 11 km southwards from Grand Turk.

South Caicos (sometimes known as East Harbour or the Rock) is 35 km west of Grand Turk. It is the eastern-most bulge of the Caicos Islands (named for the Lucayan—Taino—word for a chain of islands), which box in the infamous Caicos Banks, where the sea depth goes from some 2,000 m to less than 10 m in under 1 km. The main landmasses define the northern edge, while South Caicos and a line of cays (such as the Ambergris and Seal Cays) facing the Turks form the eastern edge. There are more islands and cays to the west, but only treacherous reefs mark the south, with dry land rarely breaching the sea surface. The main islands are East Caicos, Middle Caicos and North Caicos, stretching north-westwards, before another chain of islets heads south-westwards to the hooked island of Providenciales ('Provo'). The more isolated and uninhabited West Caicos is just south-west of Providenciales. East Caicos covers about 47 sq km, and is typical with a northern ridge protecting wetlands of creeks, mudflats and mangrove swamp. Middle or Grand Caicos is the largest island in the territory

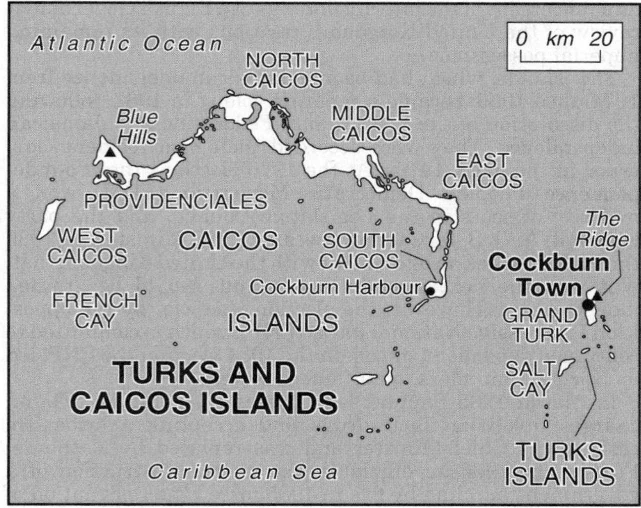

(124 sq km), with more dry land and dramatic coasts than most. North Caicos, at the north-western apex of the territory, has relatively good tree cover and good rainfall and it is known as a sanctuary for flamingos and the West Indian whistling duck. Providenciales, about 40 km in length and 5 km wide, has grown to be the leading population centre only since tourism development began in the late 1960s.

CLIMATE

The climate is subtropical marine, relatively dry and sunny, and exposed to the trade winds off the Atlantic. There are frequently hurricanes. The average annual temperature is 27°C (81°F), with little seasonal variation. Rainfall annually averages about 530 mm (21 ins) in the Turks and eastern Caicos, but reaches almost 1,000 mm in the west.

POPULATION

Almost all of the native population (known as 'belongers') is black and Christian, and officially speaks English, although there is also a local Creole in use. Most belongers are Protestants, while many of the recent immigrants are Roman Catholics, having come from Haiti or the Dominican Republic. According to the 2001 census, some 36% of the total population are Baptists, 12% belong to the Church of God, 11% are Roman Catholics, 10% are Anglicans, 9% are Methodists and 6% are Seventh-day Adventists.

The total population at the 2001 census was 19,886, of whom some 52% were belongers. About 40% of the belongers live on Grand Turk and Salt Cay. Most of the rest of the population resides in the Caicos Islands. The estimated population in 2010 was 40,357, giving a population density of 42.6 per sq km. Six islands are permanently inhabited: Grand Turk and Salt Cay, and South Caicos, Middle Caicos, North Caicos and the tourist-dominated Providenciales. There are also resorts on Parrot Cay and Pine Cay. The main towns are Cockburn Town, which only has a population of about 5,000, and Cockburn Harbour on South Caicos. In addition to the many immigrants who work legally, particularly on Provo, the islands also suffer from illegal immigration (and drugs-transshipping), as Haitians, in particular, use them as a transit point for reaching the Bahamas and, thence, the USA.

History

The Turks and Caicos Islands constitute a United Kingdom Overseas Territory and the British monarch is represented locally by a Governor who presides over the Executive Council. From February 1998 the British Dependent Territories were referred to as the Overseas Territories, following the announcement of the interim findings of a British Government review of the United Kingdom's relations with its remaining imperial possessions.

The islands, which had been a Jamaican dependency from 1874 until 1959, became a separate colony in 1962, following the dissolution of the West Indian Federation and Jamaican independence. They were accorded their own resident Governor in the early 1970s. At the 1976 elections the pro-independence People's Democratic Movement (PDM) won a majority of seats in the Legislative Council, and the party leader, J. A. G. S. McCartney, became Chief Minister. In 1980 the PDM reached an agreement with the United Kingdom that, if it won the next election, the islands would be granted independence. However, the election was won by the opposition Progressive National Party (PNP), which is committed to continued dependent status. In the 1984 election the PNP, led by Norman Saunders, maintained its lead.

In March 1985 Saunders was arrested in Miami, FL, on charges involving illicit drugs and accepting a bribe. He resigned as Chief Minister and was replaced by Nathaniel Francis. In 1986 an official report on the destruction of a government building by fire in 1985 forced the resignation of Francis and two other ministers and discredited the Government amid allegations of unconstitutional behaviour and ministerial malpractice. The Governor proceeded to dissolve the Government and an Order-in-Council authorized him to replace the Executive Council with an interim Advisory Council. In March 1987 the British Government announced that it had accepted a constitutional commission's central recommendations and a general election was held in March 1988, after which there was a return to ministerial government.

The PDM won 11 of the 13 seats on the Legislative Council in the 1988 elections and Oswald Skippings, the leader of the PDM, was appointed Chief Minister. In the April 1991 general election the PNP secured eight seats and Washington Misick, the PNP leader, replaced Skippings as Chief Minister. In January 1995 the PDM, now led by Derek Taylor, gained eight seats. The PDM increased its representation in the Legislative Council to nine seats in March 1999 elections. In the same month the British Government published draft legislation on its future relationship with its overseas dependencies. The Government announced that in future citizens of Overseas Territories would have the right to reside in the United Kingdom, provided they meet international standards in the areas of human rights and the regulation of the financial services sector.

In May 2002 the British Overseas Territories Act, having received royal assent in the United Kingdom in February, came into force and granted British citizenship rights to the people of the Overseas Territories, including the Turks and Caicos Islands. Under the new law Turks and Caicos Islanders were able to hold British passports and work in the United Kingdom and anywhere else in the European Union. In October capital punishment for treason and piracy, the only remaining capital crimes in the United Kingdom Overseas Territories, was abolished in the Turks and Caicos Islands. In December James Poston replaced Mervyn Jones as Governor.

At a general election held on 24 April 2003 the PDM won seven of the 13 seats in the Legislative Council. The PNP took the remaining six seats, but challenged the results in two constituencies. The election was largely fought over Chief Minister Taylor's claims of economic progress, which Michael Misick, leader of the PNP, argued had benefited expatriates rather than Turks and Caicos 'belongers'.

In June 2003 the Supreme Court ruled in favour of the defeated PNP candidates in the two disputed constituencies; Chief Justice Ground found evidence of bribery by supporters of the PDM in one constituency and irregularities in voter-registration lists in the other. Following the judicial ruling, by-elections, in which the PNP secured victory and therefore wrested overall control of the Legislative Council from the PDM, were held in the two constituencies on 7 August. Taylor resigned as Chief Minister on 15 August and Misick was sworn in as his replacement on the same day. Misick's first Executive Council included Floyd Hall as Deputy Chief Minister and Minister of Finance, Health and National Insurance.

In April 2006 the UN Special Committee on Decolonization visited the territory in order to participate in the public education process on self-determination; the Committee presented three routes to independence. In the same month a consultation process took place over a draft constitution for the islands, following the achievement of agreement between local and United Kingdom representatives in the previous October, allowing for greater self-government. The draft constitution was endorsed by the Legislative Council on 28 June 2006, before final submission to the British Foreign and Commonwealth Office (FCO). An Order in Council adopted the new Constitution on 19 July and it came into force on 9 August, which was declared a public holiday. On the same day Chief Minister Misick and Deputy Chief Minister Hall were sworn in as Premier and Deputy Premier, respectively. Mahala Wynns, hitherto the Chief Secretary, was also inaugurated as the territory's first Deputy Governor as part of the new administrative structure; according to the new Constitution, this office was to be fulfilled by a 'belonger'. A unicameral system of parliament was to be instituted, comprising a 21-member House of Assembly, replacing and enlarging upon the former Legislative Council, and a nine-member Cabinet (formerly the Executive Council) over which the Governor would preside. The legislature also approved the enactment of the Electoral District Boundaries 2006 Bill, under constitutional statute, that sanctioned the creation of two new constituencies—to reflect the two additional elected members of the House of Assembly—and which was ratified by the House of Assembly on 8 January 2007.

The PNP was returned to power for a second term at the 9 February 2007 general election, securing 13 of the 15 elected seats in the House of Assembly; the remaining two seats went to the PDM. Misick was reappointed Premier. The ballot was preceded by a bitterly fought election campaign, in which the PDM levelled allegations of corruption against the ruling party.

In July 2007 it was alleged that the Premier had assaulted an opposition member of Parliament, Arthur Robinson, in response to criticism of Misick's despatch of his governmental responsibilities. It was claimed that Misick spent a significant proportion of time away from the islands, provoking PDM accusations that he had become an 'absentee premier'. The leader of the PDM, Floyd Seymour, subsequently demanded Misick's resignation.

In December 2008 Misick avoided a debate on a motion of no confidence submitted by the PDM, as a result of a dispute over parliamentary procedure. Parliament was subsequently prorogued by the Governor, Gordon Wetherell, to be reconvened in April 2009. Later in that month Lillian Boyce, Minister of Health and Human Services, and eight other PNP members, drafted a letter to the Governor requesting that Misick resign, citing a loss of confidence from legislators. Boyce was dismissed by Misick in January 2009 and replaced by Royal Robinson.

Deputy Premier Floyd Hall resigned in February 2009, citing the legislative stalemate caused by the ongoing suspension of Parliament. Galmore 'Galmo' Williams, the Minister for Home Affairs, had resigned the previous day. Following the resignations Misick reorganized his Cabinet; Boyce notably returned to office as Deputy Premier and Minister for Home Affairs only a month after her dismissal. Misick also announced that he would resign as Premier by the end of March, and that he would not be seeking re-election as leader of the PNP. At a special PNP convention held on 28 February, Williams was elected to succeed Misick. Misick stood down on 23 March, at which point Williams was sworn in as Premier. Williams promptly announced the formation of a new Cabinet.

The United Kingdom's House of Commons Foreign Affairs Committee (FAC) published a report in July 2008 regarding the administration of its Overseas Territories, in which it detailed claims of corruption and intimidation made by residents of the Turks and Caicos Islands. The Committee had received evidence from some 50 individuals, much of which had been submitted anonymously. The allegations of corruption referred to the sale of Crown land for unsustainable developments or for the personal gain of government members; nepotism in the distribution of development contracts and irregularities in the purchase of property for government use; the granting of 'belonger' status to individuals who were ineligible under the current law; and the misuse of public funds. The report criticized the Governor, who had failed to investigate the allegations of corrupt practice. The Premier denied the allegations and drew attention to anti-corruption legislation that had been introduced by his Government. However, the Committee's recommendation of the establishment of a Commission of Inquiry was heeded by the Governor and the body began its investigations later that month. Applications made by some members of the legislature to limit the Commission's terms of reference were refused by the Supreme Court. The publication of the report led to a truculent dialogue between the two main parties as Misick blamed opposition opponents for the inception of the allegations; in response, the PDM accused Misick of trying to intimidate members of the public to prevent them from revealing further information to the Commission. In February 2009 Sir Robin Auld issued the Commission of Inquiry's interim report, which referred to a 'high probability of systemic corruption and serious dishonesty', 'political amorality and general incompetence' and contained 24 recommendations, including the partial or full suspension of the Constitution and direct rule of the islands by the United Kingdom, acting through the Governor, with the advice of an Advisory Council. The report also recommended that criminal investigations be instigated against Misick and four of his former cabinet ministers. The Commission's final report, which was submitted to the Governor at the end of May, confirmed the findings and recommendations of the interim document. Following a delay in the implementation of these recommendations, owing to an ultimately unsuccessful legal challenge, on 14 August the British Government announced the imposition of direct rule from the United Kingdom, the partial suspension of the Constitution and the removal of the Premier and Cabinet. The House of Assembly was also dissolved. The FCO announced its intention to hold elections in the territory no later than July 2011 and stated that its aim was to establish a lasting basis for good governance, sound financial management and sustainable development.

The Advisory Council immediately instituted a Stabilization Plan to reduce expenditure, increase revenue and lower the national debt, which was estimated at £135m. In late August 2009 12 'belongers' were appointed as members of a Consultative Forum, which was to make recommendations on proposed legislation and policies refered to it by the Governor. A Special Prosecutor, Helen Garlick, was also appointed to examine possible criminal charges against the former PNP Government arising from the Commission of Inquiry's report. Former Premier Williams denounced the imposition of direct rule as a *coup d'état*. The decision by Governor Wetherell not to appoint a successor to Mahala Wynns following her retirement as Deputy Governor at the end of September further inflamed tensions between the Advisory Council and the former administration. The Constitution stated that the post be held by a 'belonger' and the fact that it remained vacant was perceived as an insult to the islanders. In February 2010 the FCO's Director of Overseas Territories indicated that following the election in 2011, British government representatives would maintain an increased presence in the territory to ensure continuing good governance. The announcement called into question the plan to end direct rule following the ballot. Continued political discontent over the imposition of direct rule was evident in March, when the PNP and the PDM held a joint protest march. Moreover, the resignation that month of local lawyer Carlos Simons as President of the Consultative Forum, ostensibly to contest the PNP leadership at a party convention scheduled for August, followed his criticism of the interim administration's recent decision to reduce public sector salaries by 10%.

At the end of March 2010 the FAC issued a report describing the FCO's plan to hold elections in July 2011 as 'unrealistic', citing the slow pace of political reform, inadequate funding arrangements for the work of the Special Investigation and Prosecution Team, and a consequent lack of progress in the investigation of those suspected of corruption. Sir Robin Auld had earlier raised similar concerns in a letter to the British Foreign Secretary. In April Special Prosecutor Garlick announced that criminal investigations into between six and 10 people had been initiated and could take up to 18 months to complete, and that campaign financing to both the PNP and the PDM was also to be probed.

Economy

Agriculture is not practised on any significant scale in the Turks Islands or on South Caicos (the most populous island of the territory). The other islands of the Caicos group grow some beans, maize and a few fruits and vegetables. There is some livestock-rearing, but the islands' principal natural resource is fisheries, which account for almost all commodity exports, the principal species caught being the spiny lobster (380 metric tons in 2008) and the conch (5,693 tons in that year). Conchs are now being developed commercially (on the largest conch farm in the world), and there is potential for larger-scale fishing. Exports of lobster and conch earned US $4.3m. in 2008, according to provisional (unrounded) figures. However, agricultural possibilities were limited and most foodstuffs were imported. Industrial activity consists mainly of construction (especially for the tourism industry) and fish-processing. Construction of both tourism resorts and residential housing led to large-scale growth in the sector in the mid-2000s (estimated sectoral growth was 48.7% in 2006, slowing to a preliminary 19.9% in 2007), bringing consequent beneficial effects for employment and import levels. Construction contributed 16.4% of gross domestic product (GDP) in 2007.

The principal economic sector is the service industry. This is dominated by the expanding tourism sector, which is concentrated on the island of Providenciales. The market is for wealthier visitors, most of whom come from the USA. Stop-over tourist arrivals increased from 120,898 in 1999 to 264,887 in 2007. Visitor expenditure totalled US $355.1m. in 2005. The number of tourist arrivals from the USA increased significantly in 2006, representing 68.3% of total arrivals that year, although a decline was feared following the introduction, in January 2007, of new US legislation requiring all passengers travelling between the Caribbean and the USA to hold valid passports. As a result of the growth in tourism throughout the last decade many new hotels and resorts have been developed. However, concern has been expressed that the islands are in danger of becoming overdeveloped, thereby damaging their reputation as an unspoilt tourist location. In 2005 plans were announced for the construction of a resort on the largely undeveloped West Caicos, which was to include a 125-room hotel, 75 villas, an airfield and marina, but construction work on the resort was suspended following the bankruptcy, in September 2008, of Lehman Brothers, the company that was financing the project. In 2006 a new US $40m. cruise ship terminal, constructed by Carnival Cruise Lines (USA), was opened on Grand Turk, enabling, for the first time, large passenger liners to stop in the territory. The terminal itself was equipped with extensive leisure facilities and the company invested further in the island's infrastructure and attractions in order to help prepare for the large volume of visitor arrivals. The number of cruise ship passengers visiting the islands rose from just 17,052 (on 14 ships) in 2004 to 379,936 (on 185 ships) in 2007. However, the tourism industry suffered in 2008 and

2009 as a result of the global financial crisis and subsequent economic downturn, which particularly affected the USA.

New regulatory legislation to develop an 'offshore' financial sector was ratified in 1989. In 2008 there were some 15,000 overseas companies registered in the islands. However, in June 2000 the Turks and Caicos Islands were included in the list of so-called 'unco-operative tax havens' compiled by the Organisation for Economic Co-operation and Development (OECD). OECD urged the jurisdictions included on the list to improve their legal and administrative transparency to prevent companies using the jurisdictions' tax systems in an attempt to launder money or avoid paying income tax. The Turks and Caicos Islands were removed from the list in March 2002, when OECD declared that the Government had made sufficient commitments to improve transparency and to achieve effective exchange of information on tax matters by the end of 2005. As part of its regulatory overhaul, the Government established a Financial Services Commission in 2002. In early 2004 the financial sector faced further regulatory disruption when the territory came under pressure to implement the European Union's Savings Tax Directive, which would involve the Government disclosing the identities and account details of Europeans holding private savings accounts on the islands. In April 2009 the territory was included in OECD's so-called 'grey list' of jurisdictions that had yet substantially to improve transparency in the financial sector, but in December the islands succeeded in securing their removal from the list, after concluding international tax information sharing agreements with 12 other nations. The financial intermediation sector grew by 29.6% in 2006. It increased again in 2007, by 13.2% according to preliminary figures, contributing 11.5% of GDP in that year. There is no direct taxation in the country. The main sources of government revenue are derived from import duty (36.3% of recurrent revenue in 2007/08) and stamp duty on land transactions (17.5%), as well as indirect taxes on the tourism industry (accommodation tax, airport departure tax), the 'offshore' sector (business licence fees) and immigrant workers' permits and residence fees.

During 1994–2002 the islands' GDP increased, in real terms, by 5.8% per year. Following a recovery in the tourism sector, GDP increased at an average annual rate of 10.0% in 2003–07, according to official estimates. GDP grew by 17.9% and an estimated 11.2% in 2006 and 2007, respectively. Overall, the economy, and also the population, were estimated to have doubled in size since the early 1990s, making the islands one of the region's most dynamic economies. However, it was estimated that the economic situation of the majority of 'belongers' improved only marginally in that period, as newly created jobs were often taken by low-wage migrant workers or by highly skilled expatriate workers. Although the rate of unemployment declined steadily from 9.9% in 2004 to 5.4% in 2007, the inactivity rate (the proportion of the population not participating in the labour force) rose from 19.9% to 24.6% over the same period. The rate of immigration was likely to become a significant issue for the islands. In addition, the islands' growth is highly dependent on external factors, and the pressure exerted by OECD, Europe and the USA on the 'offshore' financial services sector is therefore of particular concern. Current revenue increased to US $206.8m. in 2007/08; current expenditure was some $235.8m. There was an overall budget deficit of $33.4m. in that year. Consultation over a 10-year National Development Plan was launched in October 2005, and was finalized in the following year.

Following the imposition of direct rule from the United Kingdom in August 2009 (see History), the Advisory Council that replaced the Cabinet identified the containment and rescheduling of the national debt (estimated at £135m.) and fiscal stabilization as its main economic priorities. Government revenue had declined in 2009 owing to the destruction caused by Hurricane Ike in late 2008 (an estimated 80% of homes were damaged), as well as the adverse effects of the global economic downturn, notably on the tourism and construction sectors. In January 2010 the Council secured a loan of US $85m., intended to pay off debts to the business sector, but in March the arrangement, with a syndicate of local banks, collapsed. The loss of this expected revenue led to the announcement of further measures to reduce expenditure, including a 10% cut in public sector salaries. The closure of the indigenous TCI Bank in April, after a number of significant withdrawals of funds left it unable to operate, represented a further reverse for the Turks and Caicos Islands.

Statistical Survey

Source: Department of Economic Planning and Statistics, Ministry of Finance, South Base, Grand Turk; tel. 946-2801; fax 946-2557; e-mail info@depstc.org; internet www.depstc.org.

AREA AND POPULATION

Area: 948 sq km (366 sq miles). Note: Area includes low water level for all islands, but excludes area to high water mark.

Population: 7,413 at census of 12 May 1980; 11,465 at census of 31 May 1990; 19,886 (males 9,897, females 9,989) at census of 20 August 2001; *2010* (estimate): 40,357. *By Island* (2006, estimates): Grand Turk 5,718; South Caicos 1,118; Middle Caicos 307; North Caicos 1,537; Salt Cay 114; Parrot Cay 60; Providenciales 24,348.

Density (2010 estimate): 42.6 per sq km.

Population by Age and Sex (at 2001 census): *0–14:* 5,693 (males 2,736, females 2,957); *15–64:* 13,436 (males 6,826, females 6,610); *65 and over:* 758 (males 335, females 423); *Total* 19,886 (males 9,897, females 9,989) (Source: UN, *Demographic Yearbook*).

Principal Towns: Cockburn Town (capital, on Grand Turk), population 2,500 (1987 estimate); Cockburn Harbour (South Caicos), population 1,000. *Mid-2009* (UN estimate, incl. suburbs): Grand Turk 6,195 (Source: UN, *World Urbanization Prospects: The 2009 Revision*).

Births, Marriages and Deaths (2008): Live births 453 (birth rate 12.4 per 1,000); Marriages 486; Deaths 65 (death rate 1.8 per 1,000). *2009:* Crude birth rate 20.8; Crude death rate 4.2 (Source: Pan American Health Organization).

Life Expectancy (years at birth, 2009): 75.4 (males 73.1; females 77.8). Source: Pan American Health Organization.

Economically Active Population (2007, preliminary): Agriculture and fishing 237; Mining and quarrying 16; Manufacturing 246; Utilities 192; Construction 4,306; Wholesale and retail trade 1,729; Hotels and restaurants 4,065; Transport, storage and communications 846; Financial intermediation 515; Real estate, renting and business services 2,384; Public administration 2,298; Education, health and social work 771; Other community, social and personal services 1,190; Private household employment 376; *Sub-total* 19,171; Activities not adequately defined 416; *Total employed* 19,587; Unemployed 1,124; *Total labour force* 20,711.

HEALTH AND WELFARE

Total Fertility Rate (children per woman, 2009): 3.0.

Under-5 Mortality Rate (per 1,000 live births, 1997): 22.0.

Hospital Beds (per 1,000 head, 2008): 1.4.

Physicians (per 1,000 head, 2001): 7.3.

Health Expenditure (public, % of total, 2004): 12.6.

Health Expenditure (US $ per head, 2004): 741.2.

Access to Water (% of persons, 2008): 98.

Access to Sanitation (% of persons, 2004): 96.

Source: partly Pan American Health Organization.

For other sources and definitions see explanatory note on p. vi.

AGRICULTURE, ETC.

Fishing (metric tons, live weight, 2008): Capture 6,133 (Caribbean spiny lobster 380; Stromboid conchs 5,693); Aquaculture 0; *Total catch* 6,133.

Source: FAO.

INDUSTRY

Electric Energy (production, million kWh): 132 in 2005; 158 in 2006; 182 in 2007. Source: UN Industrial Commodity Statistics Database.

FINANCE

Currency and Exchange Rate: United States currency is used: 100 cents = 1 US dollar ($). *Sterling and Euro Equivalents* (31 May 2010): £1 sterling = US $1.458; €1 = US $1.238; $100 = £68.59 = €80.75.

Budget (US $ million, 2007/08): Total revenue and grants 280.31 (Current revenue 206.79, Capital revenue and grants 73.52); Total expenditure 313.73 (Current expenditure 235.85, Capital expenditure 77.89).

Gross Domestic Product (US $ million at constant 2000 prices): 481.9 in 2005; 568.1 in 2006; 632.0 in 2007 (preliminary).

Expenditure on the Gross Domestic Product (US $ million, 2007, preliminary): Government final consumption expenditure 143.0; Private final consumption expenditure 458.3; Gross capital formation 392.6; *Total domestic expenditure* 993.9; Exports of goods and services 522.6; *Less* Imports of goods and services 687.9; *GDP in market prices* 828.6.

Gross Domestic Product by Economic Activity (US $ million, 2007, preliminary): Agriculture and fishing 7.5; Mining and quarrying 10.0; Manufacturing 13.4; Utilities 26.4; Construction 125.5; Wholesale and retail trade 31.4; Hotels and restaurants 222.1; Transport, storage and communications 61.4; Financial intermediation 88.2; Real estate, renting and business activities 59.7; Public administration, defence and social security 61.8; Education 22.0; Health and social work 18.1; Other community, social and personal services 19.4; *Sub-total* 766.9; *Less* Financial intermediation services indirectly measured 59.3; *Gross value added in basic prices* 707.6; Taxes, *less* subsidies, on products 121.0; *GDP in market prices* 828.6.

Balance of Payments (US $ million, 2002): Exports of goods f.o.b. 8.7; Imports of goods f.o.b. −177.5; *Trade balance* −168.8; Exports of services 163.1; Imports of services −81.8; *Balance on goods and services* −87.5. Source: Caribbean Development Bank, *Social and Economic Indicators*.

EXTERNAL TRADE

Principal Commodities (US $ million, 2008, provisional): *Imports:* Food and live animals 63.3; Beverages and tobacco 17.7; Crude materials (inedible) except fuels 18.0; Mineral fuels, lubricants, etc. 71.6 (Petroleum and petroleum products 69.6); Chemicals and related products 37.5; Basic manufactures 126.1; Machinery and transport equipment 145.2 (Road vehicles 39.4); Miscellaneous manufactured articles 110.1; Total (incl. others) 591.3. *Exports:* Food and live animals 4.6 (Conchs 3.1; Lobsters 1.1); Machinery and transport equipment 16.8; Total exports 24.5. Note: Figures for exports exclude re-exports valued at 0.3.

Principal Trading Partners (US $ million, 2008, provisional): *Imports c.i.f.:* Bahamas 3.2; USA 587.3; Total (incl. others) 591.3. *Exports f.o.b.:* USA 24.5; Total (incl. others) 24.5. Note: Figures for exports exclude re-exports valued at 0.3.

TRANSPORT

Road Traffic (1984): 1,563 registered motor vehicles.

Shipping: *International Freight Traffic* (estimates in '000 metric tons, 1990): Goods loaded 135; Goods unloaded 149. *Merchant Fleet* (vessels registered at 31 December 2008): 5; Total displacement 975 grt. Sources: UN, *Monthly Bulletin of Statistics*; Lloyd's Register-Fairplay, *World Fleet Statistics*.

TOURISM

Tourist Arrivals ('000): 176.1 (of which USA 123.3) in 2005; 248.3 (of which USA 169.7) in 2006; 264.9 in 2007.

Tourism Receipts (US $ million, estimates): 275.6 in 2003; 317.9 in 2004; 355.1 in 2005.

Source: Caribbean Development Bank, *Social and Economic Indicators*.

COMMUNICATIONS MEDIA

Radio Receivers (1997): 8,000 in use.

Telephones (2009): 3,700 main lines in use.

Mobile Cellular Telephones (2008): 25,100 subscribers.

Non-daily Newspapers (1996): 1 (estimated circulation 5,000).

Internet Subscribers (2008): 3,000.

Sources: UNESCO, *Statistical Yearbook*; UN, *Statistical Yearbook*; International Telecommunication Union.

EDUCATION

Pre-primary (2005/06, unless otherwise indicated): 9 schools; 87 teachers (2004/05, estimate); 335 pupils.

Primary (2005/06): 14 schools; 126 teachers (state schools only); 2,353 pupils.

General Secondary (2005/06): 8 schools; 135 teachers (state schools only); 1,539 pupils. Note: In addition, 6 further private schools offered both primary and secondary education to 674 pupils in 2005/06.

Tertiary Education (2005/06): 2 schools; 257 pupils.

Special Education (2005/06): 2 schools; 99 pupils.

Pupil-teacher Ratio (primary education, UNESCO estimate): 15.0 in 2004/05. Source: UNESCO Institute for Statistics.

Adult Literacy Rate (UNESCO estimates): 99% (males 99%; females 98%) in 1998.

Sources: partly UNESCO Institute for Statistics; Caribbean Development Bank, *Social and Economic Indicators*.

Directory

The Constitution

A revised Constitution was passed by a resolution of the Legislative Council on 28 June 2006 and formally adopted on 19 July. The Turks and Caicos Islands Constitution Order 2006 became effective from 9 August.

The revised Constitution of 2006 provides for a Cabinet (formerly the Executive Council) and a House of Assembly (formerly the Legislative Council). Executive authority is vested in the British monarch and is exercised by the Governor (the monarch's appointed representative), who also holds responsibility for external affairs, internal security, defence, the appointment of any person to any public office and the suspension and termination of appointment of any public officer.

The Cabinet comprises: one ex officio member (the Attorney-General); the Premier (formerly the Chief Minister—appointed by the Governor) who is, in the judgement of the Governor, the leader of the political party represented in the House of Assembly that commands the support of a majority of the elected members of the House; and six other ministers from among the elected or nominated members of the House of Assembly, appointed by the Governor on the advice of the Premier. The Cabinet is presided over by the Governor.

The House of Assembly consists of the Speaker, the ex officio member of the Cabinet, 15 members elected by residents aged 18 and over, and four nominated members (appointed by the Governor, two on the advice of the Premier, one on the advice of the Leader of the Opposition and one at the Governor's discretion).

Provision was also included under the revised Constitution for the establishment of an Advisory National Security Council, mandated to advise the Governor on matters relating to defence and internal security, external affairs, and international financial services regulation. The Council would also make recommendations for the dispatch of the Governor's responsibilities in the event of a public emergency.

For the purposes of elections to the enlarged House of Assembly, an Electoral District Boundaries (Amendment) Bill was ratified on 8 January 2007, dividing the islands into 15 electoral districts. In 1988 and 1991 a multiple voting system was used, whereby three districts elected three members each, while the remaining five districts each elected two members. However, from the 1995 election a single-member constituency system was used.

The Government

HEAD OF STATE

Queen: HM Queen ELIZABETH II.

Governor: GORDON WETHERELL (sworn in 5 August 2008).

Deputy Governor: (vacant).

Chief Executive: MARK CAPES.

ADVISORY COUNCIL

On 14 August 2009 the Government of the United Kingdom announced the imposition of direct rule on the Turks and Caicos Islands. This followed publication of the findings of a commission of inquiry charged with investigating allegations of widespread and systemic corruption and mismanagement in the governance of the territory. The islands were henceforth to be governed by the United Kingdom acting through the Governor and assisted by an Advisory Council. It was stated that elections would be held no later than July 2011.

Members: JOSEPH CONNOLLY, EDITH COX, THEOPHILUS DURHAM, EUGENE OTUONYE, DOREEN QUELCH-MISSICK, JOHN SMITH.

Ex officio Members: Gov. GORDON WETHERELL, MARK CAPES (Chief Executive), KURT DE FREITES (Attorney-General, until Sept. 2010), DELTON JONES (Permanent Sec. of Finance).

GOVERNMENT OFFICES

Office of the Governor: Govt House, Waterloo, Grand Turk; tel. 946-2308; fax 946-2903; e-mail govhouse@tciway.tc.

Office of the Premier: Govt Sq., Grand Turk; tel. 946-2801; fax 946-2777.

Office of the Deputy Governor: South Base, Grand Turk; tel. 946-2702; fax 946-2886; e-mail cso@gov.tc.

Office of the Permanent Secretary: South Base, Grand Turk; tel. 946-2801; fax 946-2557; e-mail DJones@gov.tc.

Attorney-General's Chambers: South Base, Grand Turk; tel. 946-2096; fax 946-2588; e-mail attorneygeneral@tciway.tc; internet www.lawsconsolidated.tc.

HOUSE OF ASSEMBLY

Following the imposition of direct rule on the Turks and Caicos Islands in August 2009 (see above), the House of Assembly was suspended and plans were announced for the holding of fresh elections no later than July 2011.

Speaker: CLAYTON GREENE.

Clerk to the Councils: RUTH BLACKMAN.

Election, 9 February 2007

Party	Seats
Progressive National Party (PNP)	13
People's Democratic Movement (PDM)	2
Total	15

There is one ex officio member (the Attorney-General), four appointed members, and a Speaker (assisted by a Deputy Speaker).

Political Organizations

People's Democratic Movement (PDM): POB 309, Providenciales; tel. 231-6898; internet www.votepdm.com; f. 1975; favours internal self-govt and eventual independence; Chair. SHARLENE ROBINSON; Leader DOUGLAS PARNELL; Sec.-Gen. WILBUR CALEY.

Progressive National Party (PNP): Progress House, Airport Rd, Providenciales; tel. 941-8267; fax 946-8206; e-mail pnptci@gmail.com; internet www.mypnp.tc; supports full internal self-govt; Chair. DONHUE GARDINER; Leader CLAYTON GREENE.

United Democratic Party (UDP): Grand Turk; f. 1993; Leader WENDAL SWANN.

Judicial System

Justice is administered by the Supreme Court of the islands, presided over by the Chief Justice. There is a Chief Magistrate resident on Grand Turk, who also acts as Judge of the Supreme Court. There are also three Deputy Magistrates.

The Court of Appeal held its first sitting in February 1995. Previously the islands had shared a court of appeal in Nassau, Bahamas. In certain cases, appeals are made to the Judicial Committee of the Privy Council (based in the United Kingdom).

Judicial Department

Grand Turk; tel. 946-2114; fax 946-2720.

Chief Justice: GORDON WARD.

Supreme Court Judge: (Providenciales) RICHARD WILLIAMS.

Chief Magistrate: (Providenciales) JOAN JOYNER.

Religion

CHRISTIANITY

The Anglican Communion

Within the Church in the Province of the West Indies, the territory forms part of the diocese of Nassau and the Bahamas. The Bishop is resident in Nassau. According to the latest census (2001), around 10% of the population are Anglicans.

Anglican Church: St Mary's Church, Front St, Grand Turk; tel. 946-2289; internet bahamas.anglican.org; Archbishop Rev. LAISH Z. BOYD.

The Roman Catholic Church

The Bishop of Nassau, Bahamas (suffragan to the archdiocese of Kingston in Jamaica), has jurisdiction in the Turks and Caicos Islands as Superior of the Mission to the Territory (founded in June 1984). According to the 2001 census, around 11% of the population are Roman Catholics.

Roman Catholic Mission: Leeward Hwy, POB 340, Providenciales; tel. and fax 941-5136; e-mail info_rcm@catholic.tc; internet www.catholic.tc; churches on Grand Turk, South and North Caicos, and on Providenciales; 132 adherents in 1990 (according to census results); Chancellor Fr PETER BALDACCHINO.

Other Christian Churches

According to the 2001 census, some 36% of the population are Baptists, 12% belong to the Church of God, 9% are Methodists, 6% are Seventh-day Adventists and 2% are Jehovah's Witnesses.

Baptist Union of the Turks and Caicos Islands: South Caicos; tel. 946-3220; Gen. Sec. Rev. GOLDSTONE WILLIAMS.

Jehovah's Witnesses: Kingdom Hall, Intersection of Turtle Cove and Bridge Rd, POB 400, Providenciales; tel. 941-5583; e-mail englishprovo@yahoo.com.

Methodist Church: The Ridge, Grand Turk; tel. 946-2115.

New Testament Church of God: POB N-1708, Orea Alley, Grand Turk; tel. 324-2582; fax 324-7891; e-mail info@churchofgodbtci.org; internet www.churchofgodbtci.org.

Seventh-day Adventists: Grand Turk; tel. 946-2065; Pastor PETER KERR.

The Press

Times of the Islands Magazine: Lucille Lightbourne Bldg 7, POB 234, Providenciales; tel. and fax 946-4788; e-mail timespub@tciway.tc; internet www.timespub.tc; f. 1988; quarterly; circ. 10,000; Man. Editor KATHY BORSUK.

Turks and Caicos Free Press: Market Pl., POB 179, Providenciales; tel. 332-5615; fax 941-3402; e-mail freepress@tciway.tc; internet tcfreepress.com; f. 1991; Vox-Global Télématique; weekly; circ. 3,000; Editor Dr GILBERT MORRIS; Man. BARBARA SMITH.

Turks & Caicos Islands Real Estate Association Real Estate Magazine: Southwind Plaza, POB 234, Providenciales; tel. and fax 946-4788; e-mail timespub@tciway.tc; internet www.tcrea.com; publ. by Times Pub. Ltd; 3 a year; circ. 15,000; Man. Editor KATHY BORSUK.

Turks and Caicos Sun: Airport Plaza, Suite 5, POB 439, Providenciales; tel. 946-8542; fax 941-3281; e-mail turksandcaicossun@express.tc; internet www.suntci.com; f. 2005; publ. by Island Publishing Co Ltd; weekly; Publr and Editor-in-Chief HAYDEN BOYCE.

Turks and Caicos Weekly News: Leeward Hwy, Cheshire House, POB 52, Providenciales; tel. 946-4664; fax 946-4661; e-mail tcnews@

tciway.tc; internet www.tcweeklynews.com; f. 1982; Editor W. BLYTHE DUNCANSON.

Where, When, How: Ad Vantage Ltd, J105 Regent Village, Grace Bay, Providenciales; tel. 946-4815; fax 941-3497; e-mail info@wwhtci.com; internet www.wherewhenhow.com; f. 1994; 5 a year; travel magazine; Co-Editor CHARLES ZDENEK; Co-Editor BRENDA ZDENEK; circ. 70,000 a year.

Broadcasting and Communications

TELECOMMUNICATIONS

Telecommunication Commission: Business Solutions Bldg, Leeward Hwy, Providenciales; tel. 946-1900; fax 946-1119; e-mail sales@tcitelecom.com; internet www.tcitelecom.com; f. 2004; regulates telecommunications; Telecommunications Officer JOHN WILLIAMS.

Digicel: Graceway House, Unit 207, Leeward Hwy, Providenciales; tel. 941-7600; fax 941-7601; e-mail tcicustomercare@digicelgroup.com; internet www.digiceltci.com; owned by an Irish consortium; granted licence in 2006 to provide mobile telecommunications services in Turks and Caicos; Chair. DENIS O'BRIEN; Country Man. KEVIN WHITE.

LIME: Cable & Wireless (TCI) Ltd, Leeward Hwy, POB 78, Providenciales; tel. 946-2200; fax 941-3051; e-mail cwtci@tciway.tc; internet www.time4lime.com; f. 1973; monopoly ended in Jan. 2006; fmrly Cable & Wireless; name changed as above 2008; CEO DAVID SHAW; Exec. Vice-Pres. (Turks and Caicos Islands) JOEL ABDINOOR.

Radio

Power 92.5 FM: Providenciales; tel. 628-9391; e-mail kenny@power925fm.com; internet www.power925fm.com.

Radio Providenciales: Leeward Hwy, POB 32, Providenciales; tel. 946-4496; fax 946-4108; commercial.

Radio Turks and Caicos (RTC): POB 69, Grand Turk; tel. 946-2010; fax 946-1600; e-mail rtcdirector@rtc107fm.com; internet www.rtc107fm.com; govt-owned; commercial; broadcasts 105 hrs weekly; Asst Dir LYNETTE THOMAS.

Radio Visión Cristiana Internacional: North End, South Caicos; tel. 946-6601; fax 946-6600; e-mail radiovision@tciway.tc; internet www.radiovision.net; commercial; Man. WENDELL SEYMOUR.

Television

Television programmes are available from a cable network, and broadcasts from the Bahamas can be received in the islands.

TCI New Media Network: Leeward Hwy, Providenciales; e-mail news@tcinewmedianetwork.tc; internet tcinewmedianetwork.tc; f. 2008; govt-owned; Gen. Man. AVA-DAYNE KERR.

Turks and Caicos Television: Pond St, POB 80, Grand Turk; tel. 946-1530; fax 946-2896.

WIV Cable TV: Tower Raza, Leeward Hwy, POB 679, Providenciales; tel. 946-4273; fax 946-4790; Chair. ROBERT BLANCHARD.

Finance

(cap. = capital; res = reserves; dep. = deposits; br(s). = branch(es); amounts in US $ unless otherwise indicated)

REGULATORY AUTHORITY

Financial Services Commission (FSC): Harry E. Francis Bldg, Pond St, POB 173, Grand Turk; tel. 946-2791; fax 946-2821; e-mail fsc@tciway.tc; f. 2002; regulates local and 'offshore' financial services sector; Man. Dir NEVILLE CADOGAN.

BANKING

Bordier International Bank and Trust Ltd: Caribbean Pl., Leeward Hwy, POB 5, Providenciales; tel. 946-4535; fax 946-4540; e-mail enquiries@bibt.com; internet www.bibt.com; Chair. FRANÇOIS BOHN; Man. ELISE HARTSHORN.

British Caribbean Bank: Governors Rd, POB 270, Providenciales; tel. 941-5028; fax 941-5029; e-mail info@bcbtci.com; internet www.bcbtci.com; fmrly Belize Bank, Turks & Caicos; Man. Dir ANDREW ASHCROFT.

FirstCaribbean International Bank (Bahamas) Ltd: Leeward Hwy, POB 698, Providenciales; tel. 946-2831; fax 946-2695; e-mail care@firstcaribbeanbank.com; internet www.firstcaribbeanbank.com; f. 2002 following merger of Caribbean operations of Barclays Bank PLC and CIBC; Barclays relinquished its stake to CIBC in June 2006; Exec. Chair. MICHAEL MANSOOR; CEO JOHN D. ORR.

Scotiabank (Canada): Cherokee Rd, POB 15, Providenciales; tel. 946-4750; fax 946-4755; e-mail bns.turkscaicos@scotiabank.com; Man. Dir DAVID TAIT; br. on Grand Turk.

Turks and Caicos Banking Co Ltd: Duke St North, Cockburn Town, POB 123, Grand Turk; tel. 946-2368; fax 946-2365; e-mail services@tcbc.tc; internet www.turksandcaicos-banking.com; f. 1980; cap. 2.7m., dep. 9.7m.; Man. Dir ANTON FAESSLER; COO STEFAN O. STOTZ.

TRUST COMPANIES

Berkshire Trust Co Ltd: Caribbean Pl., POB 657, Providenciales; tel. 946-4324; fax 946-4354; e-mail berkshire.trust@tciway.tc; internet www.berkshire.tc; Pres. GORDON WILLIAMSON.

Chartered Trust Co: Town Centre Bldg, Mezzanine Floor, Butterfield Sq., POB 125, Providenciales; tel. 946-4881; fax 946-4041; e-mail reception@chartered-tci.com; internet www.chartered-tci.com; Man. Dir PETER A. SAVORY.

Meridian Trust Co Ltd: Caribbean Pl., Leeward Hwy, POB 599, Providenciales; tel. 941-3082; fax 941-3223; e-mail mtcl@tciway.tc; internet www.meridiantrust.tc; Man. Dir KEITH BURANT.

M & S Trust Co Ltd: Butterfield Sq., POB 260, Providenciales; tel. 946-4650; fax 946-4663; e-mail mslaw@tciway.tc; internet www.mslaw.tc/trusts.htm; Man. Dir TIMOTHY P. O'SULLIVAN; Man. STEVE ROSS.

Temple Trust Co Ltd: 228 Leeward Hwy, Providenciales; tel. 946-5740; fax 946-5739; e-mail info@templefinancialgroup.com; internet www.templefinancialgroup.com; f. 1985; CEO DAVID C. KNIPE.

INSURANCE

Turks and Caicos Islands National Insurance Board: Misick's Bldg, POB 250, Grand Turk; tel. 946-1048; fax 946-1362; internet www.tcinib.tc; f. 1992; 4 brs.

Turks and Caicos Association of Insurance Managers (TC-AIM): Southwinds Pl., Unit 6, Leeward Hwy, Providenciales; tel. 946-4987; fax 946-4621; internet turksandcaicos.tc/aim; f. 2000 as Asscn of Insurance Managers; name changed as above in 2003 when registered as a non-profit asscn; protects interests of domestic and 'offshore' insurance cos in the islands; Pres. GARY BROUGH; Treas. ROSS BLUMENTRITT.

Trade and Industry

GOVERNMENT AGENCIES

Financial Services Commission (FSC): see Finance.

General Trading Company (Turks and Caicos) Ltd: PMBI, Cockburn Town, Grand Turk; tel. 946-2464; fax 946-2799; shipping agents, importers, air freight handlers; wholesale distributor of petroleum products, wines and spirits.

Turks Islands Importers Ltd (TIMCO): Front St, POB 72, Grand Turk; tel. 946-2480; fax 946-2481; f. 1952; agents for Lloyds of London, importers and distributors of food, beer, liquor, building materials, hardware and appliances; Dir HUBERT MAGNUS.

DEVELOPMENT ORGANIZATION

Turks and Caicos Islands Investment Agency (TC Invest): Hon. Headley Durham Bldg, Church Folly, POB 105, Grand Turk; tel. 946-2058; fax 946-1464; e-mail tcinvest@tciway.tc; internet www.tcinvest.tc; f. 1974 as Devt Bd of the Turks and Caicos Islands; statutory body; devt finance for private sector; promotion and management of internal investment; Chair. LILLIAN MISICK; Pres. and CEO COLIN R. HEARTWELL.

CHAMBERS OF COMMERCE

Grand Turk Chamber of Commerce: POB 148, Grand Turk; tel. 946-2043; fax 946-2504; e-mail gtchamberofcomm@tciway.tc; f. 1974; 57 mem. cos; Pres. and Exec. Dir GLENNEVANS CLARKE; Hon. Sec. SHERLIN WILLIAMS.

North Caicos Chamber of Commerce: tel. 231-1232; Pres. FRANKLYN ROBINSON; Sec. LLEWYN HANDFIELD.

Providenciales Chamber of Commerce: POB 361, Providenciales; tel. 242-6418; fax 946-4582; e-mail provochamber@gmail.com; internet www.provochamber.com; f. 1991; 131 mems (2006); Pres. TINA FENIMORE; Vice-Pres. ALLAN HUTCHISON.

UTILITIES

Electricity and Gas

Atlantic (Fortis Turks and Caicos) Ltd: New Airport Rd, Airport Area, South Caicos; tel. and fax 946-3201; Fortis Inc (Bermuda) completed its acquisition of 100% shares in the co in Aug. 2006; sole provider of electricity in South Caicos; Pres. and CEO EDDINTON POWELL.

Provo Power Company (PPC) Ltd: Town Centre Mall, POB 132, Providenciales; tel. 946-4313; fax 946-4532; internet www.provopowercompany.com; Fortis Energy (Bermuda) completed its acquisition of 100% shares in the co, together with those of its sister co Atlantic Equipment and Power (Turks and Caicos) Ltd, in Aug. 2006; cos referred to collectively as Fortis Turks and Caicos; sole supplier of electricity to Providenciales, North Caicos and Middle Caicos; Pres. and CEO EDDINTON POWELL.

Turks and Caicos Utilities Ltd: Pond St, POB 80, Grand Turk; tel. 946-2402; fax 946-2896; e-mail ewiggins@wrbenterprises.com.

Water

Provo Water Co: Grace Bay Rd, POB 39, Providenciales; tel. and fax 946-5205; e-mail provowater@tciway.tc; owned by HAB Group.

Turks and Caicos Water Co: Provo Golf Clubhouse, Grace Bay Rd, POB 124, Providenciales; tel. 946-5126; fax 946-5127.

TRADE UNION

Turks and Caicos Service Workers Union: POB 369, Blue Mountain, Providenciales; tel. 3360; fax 8516; Pres. E. CONRAD HOWELL.

Transport

ROADS

There are 121 km (75 miles) of roads in the islands, of which 24 km, on Grand Turk, South Caicos and Providenciales, are surfaced with tarmac. A causeway linking the North and Middle Caicos islands was completed in 2007.

SHIPPING

There are regular freight services from Miami, Florida, USA. The main sea ports are Grand Turk, Providenciales, Salt Cay and Cockburn Harbour on South Caicos. A new US $40m. cruise ship terminal in Grand Turk, with capacity for large passenger liners, opened in 2006.

Cargo Express Shipping Service Ltd: South Dock Rd, Providenciales; tel. 941-5006; fax 941-5062.

Seacair Ltd: Churchill Bldg, Front St, POB 170, Grand Turk; tel. 946-2591; fax 946-2226.

Tropical Shipping: c/o Cargo Express Services Ltd, South Dock Rd, Providenciales; tel. 941-5006; fax 941-5062; e-mail nbeen@tropical.com; internet www.tropical.com; Pres. RICK MURRELL.

CIVIL AVIATION

There are international airfields on Grand Turk, South Caicos, North Caicos and Providenciales, the last being the most important; there are also landing strips on Middle Caicos, Pine Cay, Parrot Cay and Salt Cay. An expansion project at Providenciales airport was under way in 2010 and included a new terminal building and the lengthening of the runway in order to accommodate transatlantic flights. The project was scheduled for completion in 2013.

Civil Aviation Authority: Hibiscus Sq., POB 1120, Grand Turk; tel. 946-2137; fax 946-1659; e-mail cad@tciway.tc; Man. Dir THOMAS SWANN.

Air Turks and Caicos (2003) Ltd: 1 InterIsland Plaza, Old Airport Rd, POB 191, Providenciales; tel. 946-4181; fax 946-4040; e-mail info@flyairtc.com; internet www.airturksandcaicos.com; also operates *SkyKing Ltd*.

Caicos Caribbean Airlines: South Caicos; tel. 946-3283; fax 946-3377; freight to Miami (FL, USA).

Cairsea Services Ltd: Old Airport Rd, POB 138, Providenciales; tel. 946-4205; fax 946-4504; e-mail caisea@tciway.tc; internet www.cairsea.com; Man. Dir RODNEY THOMPSON.

Global Airways Ltd: POB 359, Providenciales; tel. 941-3222; fax 946-7290; e-mail global@tciway.tc; internet www.globalairways.tc; operates inter-island connections and Caribbean charter flights; Man. Dir LINDSEY GARDINER.

Turks Air Ltd: Providenciales; tel. and fax 946-4504; e-mail turksair@earthlink.net; twice weekly cargo service to and from Miami (USA); Grand Turk Local Agent CRIS NEWTON.

Turks and Caicos Airways Ltd: Providenciales International Airport, POB 114, Providenciales; tel. 946-4181; fax 946-4438; f. 1976 as Air Turks and Caicos; privatized 1983; scheduled daily inter-island service to each of the Caicos Islands, charter flights; Chair. ALBRAY BUTTERFIELD; Dir-Gen. C. MOSER.

Turks and Caicos Islands Airport Authority (TCIAA): Providenciales International Airport, Providenciales; tel. 946-4420; fax 941-5996; e-mail info@tciairports.com; internet www.tciairports.com/web; CEO JOHN T. SMITH.

Tourism

The islands' main tourist attractions are the numerous unspoilt beaches, and the opportunities for diving. Salt Cay has been designated a World Heritage site by UNESCO. Hotel accommodation is available on Grand Turk, Salt Cay, South Caicos, Parrot Cay, Pine Cay and Providenciales. In 2007 there were some 264,887 stop-over tourist arrivals and 379,936 cruise ship passengers visited the islands. In 2006 68.3% of stop-over tourists were from the USA. In 2007 there were 2,632 hotel rooms (some 87% of which were on Providenciales). Revenue from the sector in 2005 totalled an estimated US $355.1m.

Turks and Caicos Hotel and Tourism Association: POB 251, Ports of Call, Providenciales; tel. 941-5787; fax 946-4001; e-mail manager@turksandcaicoshta.com; internet www.turksandcaicoshta.com; fmrly Turks and Caicos Hotel Asscn; over 90 mem. orgs; Pres. KAREN WHITT; CEO CAESAR CAMPBELL.

Turks and Caicos Islands Tourist Board: Front St, POB 128, Grand Turk; tel. 946-2321; fax 946-2733; e-mail provo@turksandcaicostourism.com; internet www.turksandcaicostourism.com; f. 1970; to be replaced by The Tourism Authority from late 2010; br. in Providenciales; Dir LINDSEY MUSGROVE.

Defence

The United Kingdom is responsible for the defence of the Turks and Caicos Islands.

Education

Primary education, beginning at seven years of age and lasting seven years, is compulsory, and is provided free of charge in government schools. Secondary education, from the age of 14, lasts for five years, and is also free. In 2004/05, according to UNESCO estimates, 78% of children in the relevant age-group were enrolled in primary education, while the comparable ratio for secondary education was 70%. In 2005/06 there were 14 government primary schools and eight government secondary schools. In 2003 government budgetary recurrent expenditure on scholarships, education, grants and contributions was US $8.2m. (8.8% of total recurrent expenditure). According to the 2007/08 government budget communication, $19.3m. was to be allocated to tertiary education in the territory during that fiscal year.

THE UNITED STATES VIRGIN ISLANDS

Geography

PHYSICAL FEATURES

The United States Virgin Islands is an unincorporated territory of the USA, a Caribbean colony formerly known as the Danish West Indies (purchased in 1917). The Virgin Islands are the first main group of the Lesser Antilles and are divided between two sovereignties, that of the USA and of the United Kingdom. The main island of the British Virgin Islands, Tortola, lies across a narrow sea channel, to the north-east of St John. About 64 km (40 miles) to the west is the mainland of the US commonwealth territory of Puerto Rico (its offshore island of Culebra lying about mid-way between it and St Thomas). St Thomas is about 8 km to the west of St John, while the third main island of the US Virgins, St Croix, is some distance to the south (64 km from St Thomas and 56 km from St John), making it, geographically, not truly part of the Virgin Islands. St Croix is also the largest of the islands, covering 215 sq km (83 sq miles), out of a total area for the territory of 347 sq km (including about 3 sq km of inland waters).

There are 68 islands in all, but only the main islands are permanently inhabited. All the main islands are mountainous, fertile and of volcanic origin, but much territory has been added by reef action, and there are numerous coralline islands, islets and cays (keys). St Croix (Santa Cruz to the Spanish, but first decisively settled by the Knights of St John of Malta for the French—there were also Dutch and British attempts at colonization) is the largest island, with a less indented coast than the other islands and rolling green hills. St Croix is rockier and more arid in the east, but with wetter, wooded heights in the west. St Thomas (80 sq km) is dominated by an east–west central ridge running the length of the island and towards the west reaching the highest point in the territory, Crown Mountain (474 m or 1,556 ft). Numerous smaller islands surround St Thomas, the largest being Water Island, to the south of the central coast, which is the other inhabited island of the territory and sometimes called the 'fourth Virgin Island'. East of St Thomas is St John, similarly steep and island- and reef-fringed, but covering only 52 sq km. Two-thirds of the island is national park, forming the main part of the wide-ranging protected areas in the islands. Marine ecology is generally of the highest priority in the US Virgin Islands (the area is important for leatherback turtles, for instance, and has extensive reefs), as development has long since damaged the land environment. Thus, as happened in several other islands of the West Indies, the introduction of the mongoose (supposedly to deal with rats—although rats are usually nocturnal and the mongoose is not), which is partial to eggs, severely affected many parrot and snake species, although iguanas have survived in places.

CLIMATE

The climate is subtropical marine, as the heat and humidity is tempered by the Atlantic trade winds. There is little seasonal variation in temperature, with the cooler 'winter' months (December–March) averaging about 25°C (77°F), rising to 28°C (82°F) in summer. There is a rainy season from May to November, average annual precipitation being 1,030 mm (40 ins). The islands can suffer from hurricanes and the afflictions of both drought and flood.

POPULATION

Ethnically, the local population is 80% black and 15% white. By place of birth, 74% are West Indian (49% born in the Virgin Islands, the remaining 29% from elsewhere in the West Indies), 13% are from the US mainland and 5% are from Puerto Rico. The high level of immigration is illustrated on St Croix, where the population is described as either native Crucian or North American 'Continentals'. In terms of religion, most people are Christian, with 42% claiming to be Baptist, 28% Roman Catholic and 17% Episcopalian (Anglican Communion). The longest established denomination is the Dutch Reformed Church (17th century), and there are also groups of Lutherans and other Protestants. The Jewish congregation is also venerable, having been established in the late 18th century. The cosmopolitan history and nature of the islands is visually apparent, particularly the long period of Danish rule, but, culturally, US rule has proved decisive. The official language is English, which is generally spoken, although there are some Spanish-speakers (some on St Croix and Hispanic immigrants) and a local patois—St Croix Creole or Crucian—has survived.

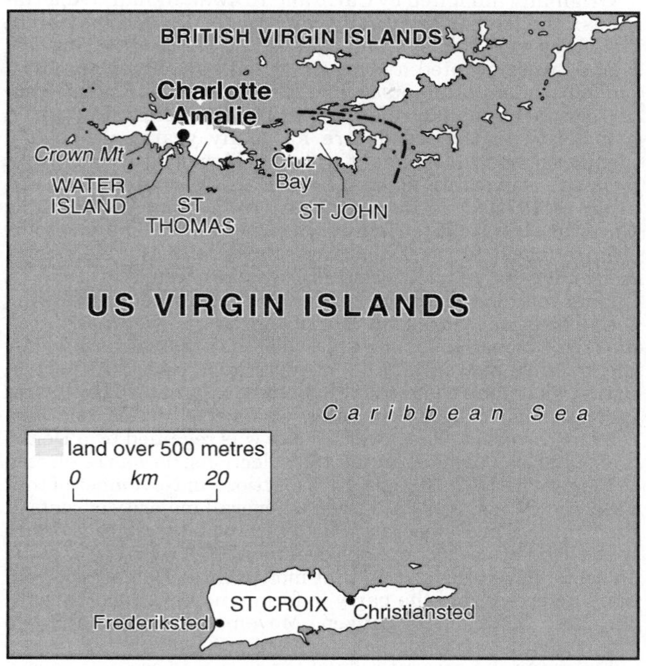

The total population was estimated at 115,431 in 2008, the most populous island being St Croix (56,576 in 2008), closely followed by St Thomas (including Water Island—54,394). St John had only 4,461 inhabitants in that year. However, the islands also host some 2m. visitors annually, with the territorial capital, Charlotte Amalie, the most-visited port in the Caribbean. The town, with just over 11,000 residents, is located on the central south coast of St Thomas and was originally named for the consort of the then Danish king. The main towns of St Croix are Christiansted, the island headquarters (on the north coast, where the island begins to narrow towards the east), and Frederiksted (on the west coast). Cruz Bay, at the western end of St John, is the centre of activity on that island.

History

The Virgin Islands constitute a US External Territory. Executive power is vested in the popularly elected Governor and there is a legislature of 15 Senators; the islands send a non-voting delegate to the US House of Representatives.

Originally inhabited by Carib and Arawak Indians (Amerindians), the islands eventually came under Danish control. In 1917 they were sold by Denmark to the USA for US $25m. The islands were granted a measure of self-government in 1954, but subsequent attempts to give them greater autonomy were all rejected by popular referendum. The Democratic Party held a majority in the legislature for many years, although a member of the Independent Citizens' Movement (which split from the Democratic Party), Cyril E. King, was elected Governor in 1974. On King's death in 1978, Juan Luis became Governor, being elected in his own right in 1982. The governorship returned to the Democratic Party with the election of Alexander Farrelly in 1986; he was re-elected in 1990. A further referendum on the islands' status, postponed following the disruption caused by Hurricane Hugo, eventually took place in October 1993; however, the result was invalidated by the low turn-out: only 27.4% of voters took part (50% participation was required for the referendum to be valid). In 1994 an independent, Dr Roy Schneider, was elected to succeed Farrelly as Governor. The governorship was regained by a Democrat, Charles Turnbull, in the 1998 elections; he was re-elected to the post in 2002. At legislative elections in November of that year, the Democratic Party won an overall majority of seats in the Senate. The Democratic Party retained its senate majority in the legislative elections of November 2004, winning 10 of the 15 seats; however, later in that month three Democratic senators defected from the party to form a narrow majority with the three Independent Citizens Movement senators and two independent senators.

Following the presentation of legislation to create a constitutional convention of the US Virgin Islands Senate, in May 2000 a committee of the US House of Representatives was considering a range of measures to enlarge the scope of local self-government in the territory. In November 2004 Governor Turnbull approved legislation allowing the creation of a further constituent assembly to redraft the Constitution.

In February 2005 a 7,000-signature petition was submitted to the US Congress by residents of St Croix, in support of making the island a separate US External Territory from St Thomas and St John. Organizers of the petition claimed that such a move would generate more federal funding for the island, which was affected by a higher unemployment rate than the other two islands, despite being the location for one of the world's largest petroleum refineries. In May the territorial Government brought a court case against the owners of the Hovensa LLC oil refinery and the defunct St Croix Alumina plant for contaminating the sole groundwater supply on St Croix. Both companies had reached an agreement with the US Environmental Protection Agency (EPA) in 2001 to clean up petroleum spillages; according to the EPA some 2m. gallons of petroleum leaked into the local aquifer between 1978 and 1991.

An inconclusive outcome in the election of a new Governor of the US Virgin Islands' Senate on 7 November 2006 necessitated a run-off election between the two leading candidates, John deJongh of the Democratic Party and independent Kenneth Mapp on 21 November; deJongh defeated Mapp—by 16,644 votes to 12,402—to secure the governorship and, together with Lieutenant-Governor Gregory Francis, was sworn into office on 1 January 2007. Outgoing Governor Turnbull was constitutionally precluded from standing for a third term in office. Donna M. Christensen's re-election as the territory's Delegate to the US Congress for a sixth consecutive term was formalized during a ceremony in Washington, DC, USA on 4 January. Notable appointments to the new Executive included Beverly Nicholson-Doty—former President of the US Virgin Islands Hotel and Tourism Association—as Commissioner of Tourism, James H. McCall as Commissioner of Police, and Robert S. Mathes as Commissioner of Planning and Natural Resources.

Combating crime and terrorism was a stated objective of Governor deJongh's administration. An anti-crime initiative was announced in February 2007; measures included an increase in the size of the police force and establishment of a forensic facility. In his 2008 State of the Territory Address, deJongh reiterated his commitment to reducing crime and in March he submitted legislation to abolish the Drug Enforcement Bureau and to redirect funding to the police department, which had proved to be more successful in targeting drugs-trafficking, having seized 20,000 kg of marijuana plants and 20 kg of cocaine in 2007. Despite the enhanced crime prevention measures, the murder rate continued to rise, reaching 59 in 2009.

Under the provisions of a US Congress amendment to the Revised Organic Act in 1984, ratified by Governor Turnbull in October 2004, the US Virgin Islands Government elected to establish a territorial appellate court in November 2006, becoming the last US sovereign jurisdiction to exercise this entitlement. From 1 January 2007 a Supreme Court would administer all appeals transferred from the Superior Court without the need for recourse to the federal judiciary, in concurrence with the islands' state and territorial counterparts. The first judicial officers of the new Court were inaugurated in December 2006, with a former presiding judge of the Superior Court, Rhys Hodge, being appointed Chief Justice.

Advances towards formulating a new constitution for the territory accelerated in April 2007 when petitions became available for prospective delegate candidates to register their participation in a Special Election on 12 June to enact the US Virgin Islands' Fifth Constitutional Convention; four previous such Conventions had been appointed in 1964, 1971, 1977 and 1980, but had failed to generate proposals regarded as suitable for adoption. The 12 June election was intended to determine the composition of a 30-member constitutional development committee, formed of delegates representing the territory's four constituent islands: 13 were to be elected from St Croix district, 13 from St Thomas-St John, with four at-large representatives (two each from the former electoral districts), as elected by the entire eligible Virgin Islands electorate, completing the committee. Despite concerted government and Elections Office efforts to promote the importance of the ballot, turn-out was very low—with initial estimates indicating only 20% voter participation—provoking concerns that voting on the new constitution in 2008 might fall short of the minimum 50% plus one required to guarantee its passage. After a number of delays, the Fifth Constitutional Convention was assembled on 29 October 2007 to commence work upon the drafting of a new constitution. A final draft document would require the approval of two-thirds of all delegates. Assuming such an endorsement, the document would then have to be approved by the Governor of the US Virgin Islands, the President of the USA and US Congress before being put to a public referendum in the territory. The Convention submitted a proposed constitution in June 2009, although this version was rejected by the Governor for apparently not complying with local and federal laws. In a statement Governor deJongh asserted that any proposed constitution must recognize the US Constitution as the supreme law of the land or adhere to its basic rights and protections. It had been hoped that the constitutional development process would facilitate the US Virgin Islands' transition from a US Constitution- and Organic Act-governed state to one enjoying greater autonomy, and that a greater distinction between the legislative, executive and judicial branches of government might be achieved. Despite deJongh's objections, the constitution was forwarded to the US Congress, which began discussion of the document in March 2010.

Economy

The islands are heavily dependent on links to the US mainland; more than 90% of trade is conducted with Puerto Rico and the USA. St Croix has the world's second largest petroleum refinery, Hovensa LLC (a joint venture between the US oil company Amerada Hess and Petróleos de Venezuela, SA), which produced some 500,000 barrels per day (b/d) in 2009 and is the territory's largest private-sector employer. In 2008 exports of refined petroleum products to the USA were worth US $13,592m. In mid-2009 some 270 workers were dismissed after the company reported serious losses earlier in the year, as a result of the global economic downturn. Efforts have been made to introduce labour-intensive and non-polluting manufacturing industries. An alumina-processing plant on St Croix, closed in 1994, was acquired by the US company Alcoa in 1995 and reopened briefly before closing again in 2001; the plant site was subsequently redeveloped as an eco-industrial business and recreation park that operated on a 'zero-waste' policy, aiming to reduce, eliminate or recycle its waste emissions. Rum is an important product; in 2009 construction began in St Croix on a distillery for Diageo that was expected to produce 20m. proof gallons annually for its Captain Morgan brand from 2012. The project was part of an agreement reached between the Government and Diageo in 2009: the US Virgin Islands authorities agreed to finance construction of the plant in return for receiving an estimated US $3,000m. in additional excise revenue over the 30-year duration of the contract. The agreement prompted protests from Puerto Rico where Diageo's operations had previously been located. In 2009 the Government also agreed to fund expansion of the existing Cruzan Rum distillery in exchange for a guarantee that the rum producer would maintain a presence in the territory for 30 years. Federal excise taxes collected on rum exports to the USA (the so-called 'cover over' programme) returned $86.7m. of revenue in 2007. Some fruit and food crops (notably sorghum) are grown for local consumption, but the land is unsuitable for large-scale cultivation.

According to the 2000 census figures, 0.7% of the economically active population was engaged in agriculture, forestry, fishing and mining. According to FAO estimates, however, the sector engaged around 18.0% of the labour force in mid-2010. Industry (including construction and mining) engaged some 8.9% of the non-agricultural labour force in 2004, according to official figures. Around 28% of the non-agricultural labour force was employed in public administration in 2007.

The major source of income and employment is tourism, with the emphasis on the visiting cruise ship business and the sale of duty-free products to visitors from the US mainland. Major expansion of hotel and resort facilities began in 2002 on St Croix and St Thomas, at a cost of more than US $1,000m. However, the number of rooms and units available has fallen, from 5,138 in 2002 to 4,757 in 2007. The tourism sector is estimated to account for more than 60% of gross domestic product (GDP), although storm damage can cause visitor numbers to fluctuate, as in 1995 when Hurricane Marilyn saw tourist arrivals decrease by some10% on the previous year. Hurricane Marilyn caused considerable damage in that year, destroying an estimated 80% of houses on St Thomas. Similar storms again wreaked havoc in the late 1990s and in 2003, when a week-long storm caused damage amounting to more than $5m. In 2009 tourist arrivals (excluding excursionists and cruise ship passengers) were estimated at 664,200, while tourist expenditures amounted to $961.2m. in that year. Total visitor arrivals in 2009, including day-trippers and cruise ship passengers, totalled over 2.2m., while some $1.5m. was earned in visitor expenditure. In late 2005 an agreement was signed to build a $500m. casino and resort on St Croix; construction was scheduled for completion by 2022. In 2010 work was ongoing on a number of construction projects related to the tourism industry, including a $150m. hotel and marina complex and a $63m. recreation centre on St Thomas, and the addition of a cruise ship dock at St Croix harbour.

The budget deficit, which reached an estimated US $305m. by December 1999, was reduced to $14.1m. in 2003/04 following the introduction of a Five-Year Strategic and Financial Operating Plan in 2001 to cut government expenditure and enhance the effectiveness of procedures for revenue collection; total tax collection was estimated to have increased by 19% in 2001. In 2005/06 the islands' debt amounted to some $1,150m. The average rate of unemployment rose from 2.8% in 1990 to 9.4% in 2003; the rate was estimated at 8.5% in September 2009. The islands were expected to continue to receive grants and other remittances from the US Government, although greater efforts towards achieving improved financial accountability were demanded.

Owing to the islands' heavy reliance on imported goods, local prices and inflation are higher than on the mainland, and the islands' economy, in contrast to that of the USA, remained in recession for most of the 1990s. The level of inflation increased from 3.0% in 2006 to 4.9% in 2007. In 2008 the territory recorded a trade surplus of US $611.9m. In that year the USA provided 6.8% of imports and took 84.0% of exports. Venezuela was also a major source of imports. Other major sources of imports included the United Arab Emirates, the Republic of the Congo and Nigeria. Of total exports to the USA in 2008, 78.8% were refined petroleum products. Crude petroleum accounted for 67.4% of the islands' total imports in that year.

In 1999 the islands' administration successfully negotiated the suspension of debt repayments to the US Federal Emergency Management Agency, and in 2001 the US Congress repaid the balance in full, after the territory had applied for tax relief under the Federal Credit Reform Act. In March 2002 the US Virgin Islands was removed from the Organisation for Economic Co-operation and Development's list of 'unco-operative tax havens', after the Government pledged to improve the transparency of its financial services sector by the end of 2005.

In mid-2009 the administration announced measures to counter increasing levels of tax evasion on the islands, following a dramatic decline in revenue owing to the economic downturn and the inefficient collection of property taxes.

Statistical Survey

Sources (unless otherwise stated): Office of Public Relations, Office of the Governor, Charlotte Amalie, VI 00802; tel. (340) 774-0294; fax (340) 774-4988; Bureau of Economic Research, Dept of Economic Development and Agriculture, 1050 Norre Gade No. 5, Suite 301, Charlotte Amalie, VI 00802; POB 6400, Charlotte Amalie, VI 00804; tel. (340) 774-8784; e-mail dhazell@usviber.org; internet www.usviber.org.

AREA AND POPULATION

Area: 347.1 sq km (134 sq miles): St Croix 215 sq km (83 sq miles); St Thomas 80.3 sq km (31 sq miles); St John 51.8 sq km (20 sq miles).

Population: 101,809 at census of 1 April 1990; 108,612 (males 51,684, females 56,748) at census of 1 April 2000. *By Island* (2000 census): St Croix 53,234, St Thomas 51,181, St John 4,197. Source: US Bureau of the Census. *2004* (official figures): St Croix 54,629; St Thomas 52,523; St John 4,307; Total 111,459. *2008* (resident population): St Croix 56,576; St Thomas 54,394; St John 4,461; Total 115,431.

Density (2008): 332.6 per sq km.

Population by Age and Sex ('000, UN estimates at mid-2010): *0–14:* 23 (males 12, females 11); *15–64:* 71 (males 33, females 38); *65 and over:* 16 (males 7, females 9); *Total* 110 (males 52, females 58) (Source: UN, *World Population Prospects: The 2008 Revision*).

Principal Towns (population at census of 1 April 2000): Charlotte Amalie (capital) 11,004; Christiansted 2,637; Frederiksted 732. Source: Thomas Brinkhoff, *City Population* (internet www.citypopulation.de).

Births and Deaths (2006, preliminary): Registered live births 1,431 (birth rate 13.2 per 1,000); Registered deaths 629 (death rate 5.8 per 1,000) (Source: US National Center for Health Statistics). *2009:* Birth rate 13.2 per 1,000; Death rate 7.2 per 1,000 (Source: Pan American Health Organization).

Life Expectancy (years at birth, estimates): 79.2 (males 76.1; females 82.2) in 2009. Source: Pan American Health Organization.

Economically Active Population (persons aged 16 years and over, 2000 census): Agriculture, forestry, fishing, hunting and mining 324; Manufacturing 2,754; Construction 4,900; Wholesale trade 912; Retail trade 6,476; Transportation, warehousing and utilities 3,321; Information 931; Finance, insurance, real estate, rental and leasing 2,330; Professional, scientific, management, administrative and waste management services 3,058; Educational, health, and social services 6,742; Arts, entertainment, recreation, accommodation and food services 7,351; Public administration 4,931; Other services 2,535; *Total employed* 46,565 (Source: US Bureau of the Census). *2008* (number of waged and salaried jobs, official figures): Construction and mining 2,463; Manufacturing 2,361; Transportation, warehouses and utilities 1,648; Wholesale and retail trade 7,076; Financial activities 2,491; Leisure and hospitality 7,520; Information 787; Other services 9,225; Federal government 978; Territorial government 12,031. *2009* (civilian employment, annual average): 48,280.

HEALTH AND WELFARE

Total Fertility Rate (children per woman, 2009): 2.1.

Under-5 Mortality Rate (per 1,000 live births, 2009): 10.0.

Physicians (per 1,000 head, 2003): 1.47.

Hospital Beds (per 1,000 head, 1996): 18.7.

Source: Pan American Health Organization.

For definitions, see explanatory note on p. vi.

AGRICULTURE, ETC.

Livestock (2008, FAO estimates): Cattle 8,100; Sheep 3,250; Pigs 2,650; Goats 4,100; Chickens 40,000.

Fishing (metric tons, live weight, 2008): Total catch (all capture) 1,075 (Groupers 36; Snappers, jobfishes, etc. 127; Grunts, sweetlips, etc. 38; Parrotfishes 170; Surgeonfishes 36; Triggerfishes, durgons, etc. 49; Caribbean spiny lobster 121; Stromboid conchs 327).

Source: FAO.

INDUSTRY

Production ('000 metric tons unless otherwise indicated, 2002, estimates): Jet fuels 1,745; Motor spirit (petrol) 2,654; Kerosene 91; Gas-diesel (distillate fuel) oil 5,725; Residual fuel oils 3,550; Liquefied petroleum gas 164; Electric energy (2007) 1,070 million kWh. Source: UN, *Industrial Commodity Statistics Yearbook* and Database.

FINANCE

Currency and Exchange Rates: 100 cents = 1 United States dollar (US $). *Sterling and Euro Equivalents* (31 May 2010): £1 sterling = US $1.4580; €1 = US $1,2384; US $100 = £68.59 = €80.75.

Budget (US $ million, 2008): Operating budget 687.9 (Net revenues from taxes, duties and other sources 732.2); Rum excise taxes (Federal remittance) 91.9; Direct Federal expenditures 682.

Cost of Living (Consumer Price Index; base: 2001 = 100): All items 117.6 in 2006; 123.3 in 2007; 132.1 in 2008.

Gross Domestic Product (US $ million at current prices): 4,240 in 2005; 4,298 in 2006; 4,580 in 2007 (Source: Bureau of Economic Analysis, US Department of Commerce).

EXTERNAL TRADE

Total Trade (US $ million): *Imports:* 11,614.8 in 2006; 12,251.0 in 2007; 17,861.3 in 2008. *Exports:* 11,626.6 in 2006; 12,961.8 in 2007; 17,249.4 in 2008. Note: The main import is crude petroleum (12,045.8m. in 2008), while the principal exports are refined petroleum products (13,591.9m. in 2008).

Trade with the USA (US $ million): *Imports:* 1,321.4 in 2006; 1,261.0 in 2007; 1,214.6 in 2008. *Exports:* 11,047.4 in 2006; 12,182.1 in 2007; 14,496.3 in 2008.

TRANSPORT

Road Traffic (registered motor vehicles, 2008): 64,469.

Shipping: *Freight Imports* ('000 metric tons) 1,056 in 2002; 879 in 2003; 979 in 2004. *Cruise Ship Arrivals:* 782 in 2006; 752 in 2007; 687 in 2008. *Passenger Arrivals:* 1,903,533 in 2006; 1,917,878 in 2007; 1,757,067 in 2008.

Civil Aviation (visitor arrivals): 693,373 in 2007; 678,140 in 2008; 664,249 in 2009.

TOURISM

Visitor Arrivals ('000): 2,606.2 (arrivals by air 688.3, cruise ship passengers 1,917.9) in 2007; 2,435.2 in 2008 (arrivals by air 678.1, cruise ship passengers 1,757.1); 2,246.5 in 2009 (arrivals by air 664.2, cruise ship passengers 1,582.3).

Visitor Receipts (US $ million, 2009): Total receipts 1,467.5 (tourists 961.2, excursionists 506.2).

COMMUNICATIONS MEDIA

Radio Receivers (1997): 107,100 in use.

Television Receivers (1999): 71,000 in use.

Telephones (2009): 75,000 main lines in use.

Personal Computers: 3,000 (27.4 per 1,000 persons) in 2005.

Mobile Cellular Telephones (2009): 80,300 subscribers.

Internet Users (2009): 30,000.

Broadband Subscribers (2009, estimate): 9,000.

Daily Newspapers (1996): 3 titles; average circulation 42,000 copies.

Non-daily Newspapers (1988, estimates): 2; average circulation 4,000 copies.

Sources: UNESCO, *Statistical Yearbook*; International Telecommunication Union.

EDUCATION

Pre-primary (1992/93, unless otherwise indicated): 62 schools; 121 teachers; 4,714 students (2000).

Elementary (1992/93, unless otherwise indicated): 62 schools; 790 teachers (public schools only); 11,728 students (2005).

Secondary: 541 teachers (public schools only, 1990); 5,022 students (2005).

Higher Education: 266 teachers (2003/04); 2,610 students (2004).

Sources: UNESCO, *Statistical Yearbook*; US Bureau of the Census.

Directory

The Constitution

The Government of the US Virgin Islands is organized under the provisions of the Organic Act of the Virgin Islands, passed by the Congress of the United States in 1936 and revised in 1954 and 1984. Subsequent amendments provided for the popular election of the Governor and Lieutenant-Governor of the Virgin Islands in 1970 and, since 1973, for representation in the US House of Representatives by a popularly elected Delegate. The Delegate has voting powers only in committees of the House. Executive power is vested in the Governor, who is elected for a term of four years by universal adult suffrage and who appoints, with the advice and consent of the legislature, the heads of the executive departments. The Governor may also appoint administrative assistants as his representatives on St John and St Croix. Legislative power is vested in the legislature of the Virgin Islands, a unicameral body comprising 15 Senators, elected for a two-year term by popular vote. Legislation is subject to the approval of the Governor, whose veto can be overridden by a two-thirds vote of the Legislature. All residents of the islands who are citizens of the USA and at least 18 years of age have the right to vote in local elections, but not in national elections. In 1976 the Virgin Islands were granted the right to draft their own constitution, subject to the approval of the US President and Congress. A constitution permitting a degree of autonomy was drawn up in 1978 and gained the necessary approval, but was then rejected by the people of the Virgin Islands in a referendum in March 1979. A fourth draft, providing for greater autonomy than the 1978 draft, was rejected in a referendum in November 1981. At a further attempt, in October 1993, the referendum was invalidated by the insufficient turn-out of registered voters. In November 2004 legislation was approved to allow the creation of a constituent assembly to redraft the Constitution. A constitutional convention, composed of 30 publicly elected delegates, was convened in October 2007 with a view to drafting a new constitution during 2009. The subsequent proposed constitution, however, was deemed not to comply with local and federal laws and was therefore not expected to be put to the electorate in a referendum.

The Government

HEAD OF STATE

President: BARACK HUSSEIN OBAMA (took office 20 January 2009).

EXECUTIVE
(July 2010)

The Government is formed by the Democratic Party of the Virgin Islands.

Governor: JOHN DEJONGH, Jr.

Lieutenant-Governor: GREGORY FRANCIS.

Commissioner of Agriculture: LOUIS E. PETERSON, Jr.

Commissioner of Education: Dr LAVERNE TERRY.

Commissioner of Finance: ANGEL DAWSON, Jr.

Commissioner of Health: JULIA SHEEN-AARON.

Commissioner of Housing, Parks and Recreation: ST CLAIRE N. WILLIAMS.

Commissioner of Human Services: CHRISTOPHER FINCH.

Commissioner of Labor: ALBERT BRYAN, Jr.

Commissioner of Licensing and Consumer Affairs: WAYNE L. BIGGS, Jr.

Commissioner of Planning and Natural Resources: ROBERT S. MATHES.

Commissioner of Police: NOVELLE E. FRANCIS, Jr.

Commissioner of Property and Procurement: LYNN A. MILLIN.

Commissioner of Public Works: DARRYL SMALLS.

Commissioner of Tourism: BEVERLY NICHOLSON-DOTY.

Attorney-General: VINCENT FRAZER.

US Virgin Islands Delegate to the US Congress: DONNA M. CHRISTENSEN.

GOVERNMENT OFFICES

Office of the Governor: Government House, 21–22 Kongens Gade, Charlotte Amalie, VI 00802; tel. (340) 774-0001; fax (340) 774-1361; e-mail contact@governordejongh.com; internet www.governordejongh.com.

Office of the Lieutenant-Governor: Government Hill, 18 Kongens Gade, Charlotte Amalie, VI 00802; tel. (340) 774-2991; fax (340) 774-6953; internet www.ltg.gov.vi.

Department of Agriculture: Estate Lower Love, Kingshill, St Croix, VI 00850; tel. (340) 774-5182; fax (340) 774-1823; e-mail lpeters@uvi.edu.

Department of Education: 1834 Kongens Gade, Charlotte Amalie, VI 00802-6746; tel. (340) 774-0100; fax (340) 779-7153; e-mail lterry@doe.vi; internet www.doe.vi.

Department of Finance: GERS Bldg, 2nd Floor, 76 Kronprindsens Gade, Charlotte Amalie, VI 00802; tel. (340) 774-4750; fax (340) 776-4028; e-mail aedawson@dof.gov.vi.

Department of Health: 1303 Hospital Ground Suite 10, Charlotte Amalie, St Thomas, VI 00802; tel. (340) 774-0117; fax (340) 777-4001; e-mail julia.sheen@usvi-doh.org; internet www.healthvi.org.

Department of Housing, Parks and Recreation: Property & Procurement Bldg No. 1, Sub Base, 2nd Floor, Rm 206, Charlotte Amalie, VI 00802; tel. (340) 774-0255; fax (340) 774-4600; e-mail info@dspr.vi; internet www.dspr.vi.

Department of Human Services: Knud Hansen Complex, Bldg A, 1303 Hospital Ground, Charlotte Amalie, VI 00802; tel. (340) 774-0930; fax (340) 774-3466; internet www.dhs.gov.vi.

Department of Justice: GERS Bldg, 2nd Floor, 34–38 Kronprindsens Gade, Charlotte Amalie, VI 00802; tel. (340) 774-5666; fax (340) 774-9710; e-mail vfrazer@doj.vi.gov; internet doj.vi.gov.

Department of Labor: 53A–54AB Kronprindsens Gade, St Thomas, VI 00803-2608; tel. (340) 776-3700; fax (340) 774-5908; e-mail customersupport@vidol.gov; internet www.vidol.gov.

Department of Licensing and Consumer Affairs: Property & Procurement Bldg, 1 Sub Base, Rm 205, Charlotte Amalie, St Thomas, VI 00802; tel. (340) 774-3130; fax (340) 776-0675; e-mail dlcacommissioner@dlca.gov.vi; internet www.dlca.gov.vi.

Department of Planning and Natural Resources: Cyril E. King Airport, Terminal Bldg, 2nd Floor, Suite 6, 8100 Lindberg Bay, St Thomas, VI 00802; tel. (340) 774-3320; fax (340) 775-5706; e-mail robertmathes@dpnr.gov.vi; internet www.dpnr.gov.vi.

Department of Police: Alexander Farrelly Criminal Justice Center, Charlotte Amalie, St Thomas, VI 00802; tel. (340) 774-2211; fax (340) 715-5517; e-mail police.commissioner@vipd.gov.vi; internet www.vipd.gov.vi.

Department of Property and Procurement: Property & Procurement Bldg No. 1, 3rd Floor, Sub Base, Charlotte Amalie, VI 00802; tel. (340) 774-0828; fax (340) 777-9587; e-mail lmillin@pnpvi.org; internet www.pnpvi.org.

Department of Public Works: Bldg No. 8, Sub Base, Charlotte Amalie, VI 00802; tel. (340) 776-4844; fax (340) 774-5869; e-mail darryl.smalls@dpw.vi.gov.

Department of Tourism: POB 6400, St Thomas, VI 00804; tel. (340) 774-8784; fax (340) 774-4390; e-mail info@usvitourism.vi; internet www.usvitourism.vi.

Legislature

LEGISLATIVE ASSEMBLY

Senate
(15 members)

President of the Senate: LOUIS PATRICK HILL.

Election, 4 November 2008

Party	Seats
Democrats	10
Independent Citizens' Movement	2
Independent	3
Total	15

Election Commission

Election Board: Election Systems of the Virgin Islands, POB 1499, Kingshill, St Croix, VI 00851-1499; tel. (340) 773-1021; fax (340) 773-4523; e-mail electionsys@unitedstates.vi; internet www.vivote.gov; Supervisor of Elections JOHN ABRAMSON, Jr; brs on St Thomas and St John.

Political Organizations

Democratic Party of the Virgin Islands: POB 502578, St Thomas Democratic District, VI 00805-2578; tel. (340) 643-4600; affiliated to the Democratic Party of the USA; Chair. CECIL R. BENJAMIN, Jr.

Independent Citizens' Movement (The ICM Party, VI): POB 305188, St Thomas, VI 00803-5188; tel. (340) 772-9524; f. 1968; Chair. Sen. TERRENCE NELSON.

Republican Party of the Virgin Islands: 6067 Questa Verde, Christiansted, St Croix, VI 00820-4485; tel. (340) 332-2579; e-mail info@virepublicanwomen.com; internet www.vigop.com; f. 1948; affiliated to the Republican Party of the USA since 1952; Chair. HERBERT SCHOENBOHM; Exec. Dir WARREN COLE.

Judicial System

Supreme Court of the Virgin Islands: No. 161B, Crown Bay, St Thomas, VI 00802; tel. (340) 774-2237; fax (340) 774-2258; e-mail administrative.services@visupremecourt.org; internet www.visupremecourt.org; f. Jan. 2007, pursuant to legislation passed in Oct. 2004; assumed jurisdiction for all appeals formerly administered by the Superior Court; highest local appellate body, established to administer justice independently of the US federal justice system; judges are appointed by the Governor.

Judges: RHYS S. HODGE (Chief Judge), IVE ARLINGTON SWAN, MARIA M. CABRET.

Superior Court of the Virgin Islands: Alexander A. Farrelly Justice Center, 5400 Veteran's Dr., St Thomas, VI 00802; tel. (340) 774-6680; fax (340) 776-9889; e-mail court.administrator@visuperiorcourt.org; internet www.visuperiorcourt.org; f. 1976 as the Territorial Court of the Virgin Islands; name officially changed in 2004; jurisdiction over all local civil actions and criminal matters; court in St Croix also; judges are appointed by the Governor.

Judges: DARRYL DEAN DONOHUE (Presiding), ISHMAEL A. MEYERS, BRENDA J. HOLLAR, AUDREY L. THOMAS, PATRICIA D. STEELE, JULIO A. BRADY, JAMES S. CARROLL, MICHAEL C. DUNSTON, HAROLD W. L. WILLCOCKS, ADAM G. CHRISTIAN.

US Federal District Court of the Virgin Islands: Division of St Thomas/St John: 5500 Veteran's Dr., Charlotte Amalie, St Thomas, VI 00802-6424; Division of St Croix: 3013 Estate Golden Rock, Christiansted, St Croix, VI 00820-4355; tel. (340) 774-0640; fax (340) 774-1293; internet www.vid.uscourts.gov; jurisdiction in civil, criminal and federal actions; judges are appointed by the President of the USA with the advice and consent of the Senate.

Judges: CURTIS V. GOMEZ (Chief Judge), RAYMOND L. FINCH.

Religion

The population is mainly Christian. The main churches with followings in the islands are Baptist, Roman Catholic, Episcopalian, Lutheran, Methodist, Moravian and Seventh-day Adventist. There is also a small Jewish community, numbering around 900 adherents.

CHRISTIANITY

The Roman Catholic Church

The US Virgin Islands comprises a single diocese, suffragan to the archdiocese of Washington, DC, USA. Some 28% of the population are Roman Catholics.

Bishop of St Thomas: Most Rev. HERBERT A. BEVARD, Bishop's Residence, 29A Princesse Gade, POB 301825, Charlotte Amalie, VI 00803-1825; tel. (340) 774-3166; fax (340) 774-5816; e-mail chancery@islands.vi; internet www.catholicvi.com.

The Anglican Communion

Episcopal Church of the Virgin Islands: Bishop: Rt Rev. AMBROSE GUMBS, 13 Commandant Gade, Charlotte Amalie, POB 10437, St Thomas, VI 00801; tel. (340) 776-1797; fax (340) 777-8485; e-mail episcopal@vipowernet.net; internet www.episcopaldioceseofthevirginislands.com.

The Press

Pride Magazine: 22A Norre Gade, POB 7908, Charlotte Amalie, VI 00801; tel. (340) 776-4106; f. 1983; monthly; Editor JUDITH WILLIAMS; circ. 4,000.

St Croix Avis: La Grande Princesse, Christiansted, St Croix, VI 00820; tel. (340) 773-2300; f. 1944; morning; Editor RENA BROADHURST-KNIGHT; circ. 10,000.

St John Tradewinds: The Marketplace, Office Suites II, Office 104, POB 1500, Cruz Bay, St John, VI 00831; tel. (340) 776-6496; fax (340) 693-8885; e-mail editor@tradewinds.vi; internet www.stjohnnews.com; f. 1972; weekly; Publr MALINDA NELSON; circ. 2,500.

Virgin Islands Daily News: 9155 Estate Thomas, VI 00802; tel. (340) 774-8772; fax (340) 776-0740; e-mail dailynews@vipowernet.net; internet www.virginislandsdailynews.com; f. 1930; acquired from Innovative Communication Corpn by Times-Shamrock Communications, USA in 2008; morning; CEO and Exec. Editor JASON ROBBINS; circ. 15,000.

Virgin Islands Source: St Thomas; tel. (340) 777-8144; fax (340) 777-8136; e-mail source@viaccess.net; internet www.visource.com; f. 1998; comprises the *St Thomas Source*, *St Croix Source* and *St John Source*; daily; digital; Publr SHAUN A. PENNINGTON.

Broadcasting and Communications

TELECOMMUNICATIONS

Innovative Telephone: Bjerget House, POB 1730, St Croix, VI 00821; tel. (340) 777-7700; fax (340) 777-7701; e-mail webmaster@iccvi.com; internet www.innovativetelephone.com; f. 1959 as Virgin Islands Telephone Corpn (Vitelco); acquired by Innovative Communication Corpn in 1987; present name adopted in 2001; provides telephone services throughout the islands; launched internet service, Innovative PowerNet, in 1999; Pres. and CEO CLARKE GARNETT (acting).

Innovative Wireless: 4006 Estate Diamond, Christiansted, St Croix, VI 00820; fax (340) 778-6011; internet www.vitelcellular.com; f. 1989 as VitelCellular; subsidiary of Innovative Communication Corpn; mobile cellular telecommunications; Man. Dir BEULAH JONIS (acting).

RADIO

WDHP 1620 AM, WRRA 1290 AM, WAXJ 103.5 FM: 79A Castle Coakley, Christiansted, St Croix, VI 00820; tel. (340) 719-1620; fax (340) 778-1686; e-mail wrra@islands.vi; internet www.reefbroadcasting.com; operated by Reef Broadcasting, Inc; commercial; English; broadcasts to the US and British Virgin Islands, Puerto Rico and the Eastern Caribbean; Owner and Gen. Man. HUGH PEMBERTON.

WEVI (Power 101.7 WeVi-FM): 2C Hogensborg, Frederiksted, St Croix, VI 00840; POB 892, Christiansted, VI 00821; tel. (340) 719-9384; e-mail aw@frontlinemissions.org; internet www.wevifm.net; operated by FrontLine Missions International, Inc; non-commercial; Christian programming; English, Spanish and Creole/Patois.

WGOD: 22A, Estate Dorothea, POB 305012, Charlotte Amalie, St Thomas, VI 00803; tel. (340) 774-4498; fax (340) 777-9978; internet wgodradio.org; operated by Moody Broadcasting Network, USA; commercial; Christian religious programming; Pres. Rev. REYNALD CHARLES; Gen. Man. MARIE RHYMER-MARTIN.

WIUJ: POB 2477, St Thomas, VI 00803; e-mail information@wiuj.com; internet www.wiuj.com; operated by V. I. Youth Development Radio, Inc; non-commercial; educational and public service programmes; Gen. Man. LEO MORONE.

WJKC (Isle 95-FM), WMNG (Mongoose), WVIQ (Sunny): 5020 Anchor Way, POB 25680, Christiansted, St Croix, VI 00824; tel. (340) 773-0995; fax (340) 770-9093; e-mail jkc@viradio.com; internet www.isle95.com; f. 1982; commercial; Gen. Man. JONATHAN K. COHEN.

WSTA (Lucky 13): 121 Sub Base, POB 1340, St Thomas, VI 00804; tel. (340) 774-1340; fax (340) 776-1316; e-mail addie@wsta.com; internet www.wsta.com; f. 1950; acquired by Ottley Communications Corpn in 1984; commercial; Owner and Gen. Man. ATHNIEL C. OTTLEY.

WVGN: 8000 Nisky Centre, Suite 714, St Thomas, VI 00802; tel. (800) 275-6437; e-mail info@wvgn.org; internet www.wvgn.org; f. 2002; operated by Caribbean Community Broadcasting Co; non-commercial; news and public affairs programming; affiliated to NBC, USA; CEO KEITH BASS; Gen. Man. LORRAINE BAA-ELISHA.

WVWI (Radio One), WVJZ (Jamz), WWKS (Kiss), WIVI (Hitz) (Ackley Media Group Stations): POB 302179, St Thomas, VI 00803-2179; tel. (340) 776-1000; fax (340) 776-5357; e-mail info@amg.vi; internet www.amg.vi; f. 1962; acquired from Knight Quality Stations by Ackley Media Group in 2006; commercial; Pres. and CEO GORDON P. ACKLEY.

WZIN (Buzzrocks): Nisky Mall Center, PMB 357, St Thomas, VI 00802; tel. (340) 776-1043; fax (340) 775-446; e-mail cristy@buzzrocks.com; internet www.buzzrocks.com; operated by Pan Caribbean Broadcasting, Inc; commercial; Gen. Man. ALAN FRIEDMAN.

Other radio stations include: WIVH, WMYP (Latino 98.3 FM), WSTX (Magic 97X), and WYAC (Voice of the Virgin Islands).

TELEVISION

Innovative Cable Television (St Croix, St Thomas, St John): 4006 Estate Diamond, Christiansted, St Croix, VI 00820; POB 6100, St Thomas, VI 00804; fax (340) 778-6011; e-mail info@iccvi.com; internet www.innovativecable.com; f. 1997 following acquisition of St Croix Cable TV (f. 1981); subsidiary of Innovative Communication Corpn; acquired Caribbean Communication Corpn in 1998; comprises TV2 (f. 2000); broadcasts to seven Caribbean islands and France; Pres. and Gen. Man. JENNIFER MATARANGAS-KING.

WSVI-TV8 (Channel 8): Sunny Isle Shopping Center, POB 6000, Christiansted, St Croix, VI 00823; tel. (340) 778-5008; fax (340) 778-5011; e-mail channel8@wsvitv.com; internet www.wsvi.tv; f. 1965; operated by Alpha Broadcasting Corpn; affiliated to ABC, USA; one satellite channel and one analogue translator.

WTJX-TV (Public Television Service): POB 808, St Croix, VI 00820; tel. (340) 773-3337; fax (340) 773-4555; e-mail pphipps@wtjxtv.org; internet www.wtjxtv.org; f. 1968; educational and public service programmes; affiliated to PBS, USA; broadcasts on one terrestrial and four digital (cable) channels; broadcasts to the US and British Virgin Islands and Puerto Rico; Chair. RAUL CARRILLO; Exec. Dir OSBERT POTTER.

Finance

BANKING

Banco Popular of the Virgin Islands: 193 Altona and Welgunst, Charlotte Amalie, VI 00802; tel. (340) 693-2702; fax (340) 693-2782; e-mail internet@bppr.com; internet www.bancopopular.com; Chair. RICHARD L. CARRIÓN; 8 brs.

Bank of Nova Scotia (Scotiabank): 214C Altona and Welgunst, POB 420, Charlotte Amalie, VI 00804; tel. (340) 774-0037; fax (340) 693-5994; e-mail lawrence.aqui@scotiabank.com; internet www.usvi.scotiabank.com; Vice-Pres. LAWRENCE AQUI; Man. ALLAN TOBIN; 10 brs.

Bank of St Croix: POB 24240, Gallows Bay, St Croix 00824; tel. (340) 773-8500; fax (340) 773-8508; e-mail info@bankofstcroix.com; internet www.bankofstcroix.com; f. 1994; CEO JAMES BRISBOIS; 1 br.

FirstBank of Puerto Rico: POB 3126, St Thomas, VI 00803; tel. (340) 774-2022; fax (340) 776-1313; acquired First Virgin Islands Federal Savings Bank in 2000 and Virgin Islands Community Bank in Jan. 2008; Pres. and CEO JAMES E. CRITES; 2 brs.

Virgin Islands Community Bank: 12–13 King St, Christiansted, St Croix, VI 00820; tel. (340) 773-0440; fax (340) 773-4028; internet www.vibank.org/vicbank.html; acquired by FirstBank of Puerto Rico in Jan. 2008; Pres. and CEO MICHAEL J. DOW; 3 brs.

INSURANCE

A number of mainland US companies have agencies in the Virgin Islands.

Trade and Industry

GOVERNMENT AGENCY

US Virgin Islands Economic Development Authority: Government Development Bank Bldg, 1050 Norre Gade No. 5, POB 305038, St Thomas, VI 00803; tel. (340) 774-8104; e-mail edc@usvieda.org; internet www.usvieda.org; semi-autonomous body comprising Government Devt Bank, Economic Devt Commission, Industrial Park Devt Corpn, Small Business Devt Agency and the Enterprise Zone programme; offices in St Thomas and St Croix; Chair. ALBERT BRYAN, Jr; CEO PERCIVAL CLOUDEN.

CHAMBERS OF COMMERCE

St Croix Chamber of Commerce: 3009 Orange Grove, Suite 12, Christiansted, St Croix, VI 00820; tel. (340) 718-1435; fax (340) 773-8172; e-mail info@stxchamber.org; internet www.stxchamber.org; f. 1924; Pres. SCOT F. MCCHAIN; Exec. Dir MICHAEL DEMBECK; 300 mems.

St Thomas-St John Chamber of Commerce: 6–7 Dronningens Gade, POB 324, Charlotte Amalie, VI 00804; tel. (340) 776-0100; fax (340) 776-0588; e-mail chamber@islands.vi; Pres. THADDEUS BAST; Exec. Dir JOSEPH S. AUBAIN; c. 700 mems.

UTILITIES

Regulatory Authority

Virgin Islands Energy Office: 4101 Estate Mars Hill, Frederiksted, St Croix, VI 00840; tel. (340) 713-8436; fax (340) 772-0063; e-mail dbuchanan@vienergy.org; internet www.vienergy.org; Dir BEVAN R. SMITH, Jr.

Electricity and Water

Virgin Islands Water and Power Authority (WAPA): POB 1450, Charlotte Amalie, VI 00804-1450; tel. (340) 774-3552; fax (340) 774-3422; internet www.viwapa.vi; f. 1964; public corpn; manufactures and distributes electric power and desalinated sea water; Chair. CHERYL BOYNES-JACKSON; CEO HUGO HODGE, Jr; c. 50,000 customers.

Transport

ROADS

The islands' road network totals approximately 855.5 km (531.6 miles).

SHIPPING

The US Virgin Islands are a popular port of call for cruise ships. The bulk of cargo traffic is handled at a container port on St Croix. A passenger and freight ferry service provides frequent daily connections between St Thomas and St John and between St Thomas and Tortola (British Virgin Islands). In 2004 the Port Authority approved a US $9.3m. project to expand freight, vehicle and passenger facilities at Red Hook. A $150m. marina restoration project on St Thomas, completed in 2006, included provision for 'mega-yacht' docking facilities in addition to conventional moorings, which, it was hoped, would invigorate the cruise ship industry.

Virgin Islands Port Authority: POB 301707, Charlotte Amalie, VI 00803-1707; tel. (340) 774-1629; fax (340) 774-0025; e-mail info@viport.com; internet www.viport.com; f. 1968; semi-autonomous govt agency; maintains, operates and develops marine and airport facilities; Exec. Dir KENN HOBSON (acting).

CIVIL AVIATION

There are airports on St Thomas and St Croix, and an airfield on St John. Seaplane services link the three islands. The runways at Cyril E. King Airport, St Thomas, and Alexander Hamilton Airport, St Croix, can accommodate intercontinental flights.

Tourism

The islands have a well-developed tourism infrastructure, offering excellent facilities for fishing, yachting and other aquatic sports. A National Park covers about two-thirds of St John. There were 4,948 guest rooms in 2009, 3,809 of which were in hotels. Visitors from the US mainland comprised 83.7% of hotel guests in that year. In 2009 there were some 2.2m. visitors to the islands, of whom 664,200 were stop-over tourists and 1.6m. were cruise ship passengers. Visitor expenditure amounted to US $1,467.5m. in that year.

St Croix Hotel Association: POB 24238, St Croix, VI 00824; tel. (340) 773-7117; fax (340) 773-5883.

US Virgin Islands Hotel and Tourism Association: POB 2300, Charlotte Amalie, St Thomas, VI 00803; tel. (340) 774-6835; fax (340) 774-4993; e-mail stsjhta@vipowernet.net; internet www.virgin-islands-hotels.com; Chair. MARC LANGEVIN.

Defence

The USA is responsible for the defence of the United States Virgin Islands.

Education

The public education system in the US Virgin Islands comprises a State Education Agency and two Local Education Agencies, serving the St Thomas/St John District and the St Croix District. Education is compulsory up to the age of 16 years. It generally comprises eight years at primary school and four years at secondary school. There are two high schools, three middle schools and 13 elementary schools in St Thomas/St John District, while the district of St Croix has two high schools, three middle schools, 10 elementary schools and an alternative and a vocational school. In 2009 there were 15,493 students enrolled at public elementary and secondary schools, while in 2008 6,907 students were enrolled at private schools. The University of the Virgin Islands, with campuses on St Thomas and St Croix, had 2,602 full- and part-time students in 2009. The proposed budget for 2010/11 allocated US $40.9m. in federal funds to the Department of Education.

URUGUAY

Geography

PHYSICAL FEATURES

The Eastern Republic of Uruguay is in south-eastern South America, on the east bank of the River Uruguay (hence described as Eastern). On the other side of the Uruguay is Argentina, which also faces the country across the great estuary of the Río de la Plata (River Plate) to the south. Originally the east-bank (Banda Oriental) territory of the Argentine possessions of Spain, it proclaimed independence in 1825 and was recognized in 1828. There remains only a dispute, unresolved but uncontested, over some river islands along the border with Brazil to the north-east (which stretches for about 1,000 km—620 miles; the Argentine border is almost 60% this length). Uruguay is the second smallest country in South America (after Suriname), with an area of 176,215 sq km (68,037 sq miles). There are 1,199 sq km of inland waters, mainly from coastal lagoons and lakes and the great reservoirs along the Río Negro.

Uruguay sits on the Plate, the estuary formed where the Uruguay and the Paraná rivers enter the Atlantic, although it also has a stretch of south-east-facing coastline running up into Brazil. The country has 660 km of seashore and 813 km of river boundaries (435 km along the Uruguay alone). It is roughly triangular in shape, extending for over 560 km north–south and 480 km east–west. Although the defining feature of Uruguay is the river from which it takes its name, the central feature is its tributary, the Negro, which traverses the middle of the country from east to west, ending in the south-west. Its basin lies between two low ranges, the Cuchilla Grande, to the south, and the Cuchilla de Haedo, striking down from the north to bisect the northern part of the country. These ranges rise from plateau uplands of rolling hills, which occupy most of the country. The coastal plains, which only account for 15% of Uruguay's territory, lie along a shore of lagoons, and sandy beaches and dunes that can extend inland for up to 8 km. Beyond this sandy coast the land is very fertile, supporting the vast pasturelands of tall, bluish-tinted prairie grass (which gives way to shorter, scrubbier grasses on the ridges). Pastureland, most of it ideal for ranching, accounts for three-quarters of the country, while woodland can only be found on about 3% (the lowest proportion in South America). In the eastern third of the country the uplands mount into a gentle arc of low mountains (Serranas) and the Cuchilla Grande forms a watershed between the narrow river valleys that drain into the Uruguay and the shorter, steeper valleys heading directly for the Atlantic. In this region is the country's highest point, Cerro Catedral (only 514 m or 1,687 ft). The highlands of the north and east are continuations of the basaltic plateau underlying the Brazilian highlands, while the plains begin the landscape of the Argentine Pampas. Once the plains, hills and coasts were rich with wildlife, but subsequent to European colonization they have become scarcer, although there are deer, rheas, alligators, seals, armadillos, wild pigs and many birds.

CLIMATE

Uruguay is the only country in Latin America to lie completely outside the tropics. The maritime influence also ensures warm summers and mild winters, although the flatness of the country makes flooding likely during the heavy rains to which a country without significant mountains can be exposed. Droughts are also not uncommon. In winter (June–September) there can be cold wind currents, pamperos, blowing from the south-west, but there is seldom frost. The summer features the hot zonda wind from the north. While the climate overall is temperate, average figures can obscure the experience of actual day- and night-time temperatures, and the interior has more of these extremes. The average temperature for the mid-summer months of January and February is 22°C (72°F), and for the coldest month, June, 10°C (50°F). It is hotter in the north-west, where it is also wetter. It is slightly less wet in the south. Generally, rainfall is well distributed and totals about 1,000 mm (about 40 ins) per year.

POPULATION

Unlike in most Latin American countries, most of the population of Uruguay is white, with very few Mestizos (about 8%) and no indigenous Amerindians. A large number of people are foreign-born. Most originate from Spain (54%), but there are significant numbers originating from Italy (22%), Brazil, Argentina and France, with some coming from Eastern Europe after the Second World War. Apart from those of Spanish and Italian descent, perhaps a further 12% originate in Europe, the rest of the population being Mestizo, mulatto, black (4%), Arab or Asian. About 71% of Uruguayans are nominally Roman Catholic. Only about 2% are Protestant, with Jews as the largest non-Christian minority (almost 2%), and many people are professedly non-believers. The official and most widely spoken language is Spanish, although there are some speakers of a Spanish–Portuguese patois, Brazilero, near the eastern borders. English and French are the most popular second languages.

The total population was estimated at 3.4m. in mid-2010. Despite the importance of agriculture to the economy, the population is very urbanized—only 9% live in the countryside (most of whom are very poor). Uruguayans are well educated, and the country is one of the few territories in the western hemisphere where all education is free. Most people live near the coast and almost one-half in Greater Montevideo alone. By far the largest city, port and economic centre, Montevideo is the national capital. It is located on the south coast near the mouth of the Plate. The next largest cities are both on the River Uruguay, Salto and Paysandú. The main city on the Brazilian border is Rivera, mid-way along the frontier, in the north of Uruguay. The country is divided into 19 departments.

History

HELEN SCHOOLEY

Revised for this edition by Dr FRANCISCO PANIZZA

During the early 20th century Uruguay acquired a reputation as 'the Switzerland of South America'—one of the most stable, prosperous and democratic countries in the region. That image, albeit tarnished by a period of military rule in 1973–85, was at variance with the country's early history. From the 16th century to the early 19th century the Banda Oriental, the territory of the east bank of the Uruguay, changed hands between the Spanish and Portuguese several times. In 1776 it became part of the newly created Spanish Viceroyalty of Río de la Plata, but when in 1814 under the leadership of José Artigas it rebelled against the dominance of Buenos Aires it was soon conquered by the Portuguese. Uruguay's independence from both Brazil and Argentina, proclaimed in 1825 and recognized in 1828, was supported by the British Government to provide a buffer state. Both countries continued to influence domestic affairs through their support of rival military rulers (*caudillos*). The first 50 years of nationhood was a period of anarchy, as the rival bands of Blancos ('Whites') and Colorados ('Reds'), the respective forerunners of the modern conservative and liberal political groupings, struggled for land and power.

The transition from anarchy to stability began in the 1870s, with the creation of the apparatus of a modern state. As world demand for wool and hides increased, Uruguayan landowners sought protection from the damage to livestock caused by persistently warring factions. Trading interests, strong in the capital, Montevideo, because of the port's natural advantages in the River Plate region, also sought peace. The replacement of weak civilian government by a military regime (1876–86) and the introduction of modern armaments, railways and telegraph services secured the dominance of central authority in Montevideo over regional *caudillos*. Public utilities received substantial British capital investment, and foreign trade expanded. Ironically, the modernization of the rural export economy displaced much of the labour force, many of whom were to form the armies of the Blanco rebels and the Colorado Government, which fought each other in Uruguay's last civil war, in 1904.

THE RULE AND INFLUENCE OF JOSÉ BATLLE Y ORDÓÑEZ

The Colorados' victory confirmed the authority of José Batlle y Ordóñez, twice President (1903–07 and 1911–15) and the dominant figure in Uruguayan politics until his death in 1929. Under his leadership, Uruguay became South America's first welfare state. Women were given the vote, the Church was disestablished and the death penalty was abolished. The country's social structure was transformed by immigrants from the Mediterranean countries of Europe, and its economic prosperity was founded on export growth. Batlle y Ordóñez tried to limit the power of British capital in the country by encouraging domestic investment in manufacturing and cultivating closer relations with the USA as a counter-weight.

Although Batlle y Ordóñez's radicalism drew support from the middle and working classes, it antagonized foreign and domestic investors and alarmed his own Partido Colorado (Colorado Party). His proposals for constitutional reform, which, in modified form, were embodied in the 1919 Constitution, led to the emergence of the Batllistas and other factions in the party. The Constitution, which divided the executive branch of government between a President and eight other members of a National Council of Government based on the Swiss model, remained in force until the overthrow of the Government by a coup, led by Gabriel Terra, in 1933. Terra claimed he was acting against the inadequacies of the Council, but the coup was more probably a reflection of the anxiety of landowners to maintain access to the British market for their beef exports.

Terra attempted to follow the policies of Benito Mussolini, the Fascist leader of Italy. For most of the Second World War Uruguay was formally neutral, although its political sympathies (and commercial advantage) lay with the Allies, led by the USA and the United Kingdom. In 1942 political and constitutional change led to the restoration to power of the Batllistas, who represented the interests of the urban economy, rather than those of rural exporters. As in the First World War, Uruguay found easy markets for its exports, and commercial relations were strengthened with the USA. After the War the United Kingdom regained its importance as an export market, although the special relationship between the two countries declined with the sale of the mainly British-built railways to the Uruguayan Government in 1948.

THE DEMISE OF TWO-PARTY DOMINANCE

The manufacturing sector expanded rapidly in the decade following the Second World War, although export earnings did not keep pace with industrial growth, and from 1956 until the early 1970s the country experienced economic stagnation. Political parties proved to be adept at staying in power by distributing rewards to their political clientele, and Colorado dominance was maintained by the use of the unique Uruguayan voting system of 'lemas' (otherwise known as the 'double simultaneous vote'). The votes of all the factions were given to the party (lema) to which they belonged, and the presidency went to the candidate of the sub-lema that received the most votes within the winning party. Thus, even if a given ticket garnered more votes than any other running for election, it could not win unless its party also won.

In 1951 the collegiate executive was reintroduced (whereby the presidency was rotated annually among the nine members of the National Council of Government), rendering decision-making even more tortuous. In 1959, however, the Partido Nacional (PN—National Party, the Blancos) defeated the increasingly divided Colorados, and by securing a majority in the National Council took power for the first time in the 20th century. Although the Government adopted an IMF-sponsored austerity programme, economic decline continued. Political and social frustration intensified in the 1960s, and the political left, small in electoral terms but strong in the trade union movement, became more militant.

A new Constitution in 1966 reintroduced the presidential system of government. The presidential election was won by a sporting hero, Gen. Oscar Daniel Gestido of the Colorados, who took office in March 1967 but died in December. His successor, Vice-President Jorge Pacheco Areco, a former pugilist, lacked both Gestido's charisma and his political skills. He used emergency powers to confront students and organized labour and to reduce the influence of professional politicians. With political life radicalized, an urban guerrilla movement, the Movimiento de Liberación Nacional (MLN—National Liberation Movement, known popularly as the Tupamaros), turned to violence, beginning a series of kidnappings and other spectacular operations. The movement peaked in 1970–71 with the arrest and torture of its leader, Raúl Sendic, and the Government's use of 'death squads', but remained active until the armed forces took control of internal security in 1972.

MILITARY DICTATORSHIP, 1973–85

In the 1971 presidential election, Juan María Bordaberry Arocena, a Colorado candidate, was declared victorious, even though Wilson Ferreira Aldunate of the Blancos was the most popular individual candidate. Bordaberry took office in March 1972, but was little more than a figurehead President: in February 1973 he accepted the armed forces' demand for military participation in political affairs. In June both chambers of the elected Congreso (Congress) were dissolved, and in December Bordaberry appointed a new legislature, the Council of State, comprising 25 (later 35) nominated members. Left-wing groups were banned and political activity was suspended. With an estimated 6,000 political prisoners detained by 1976, the military-supported regime came to be regarded as one of the most repressive in South America. In June 1976 Bordaberry was deposed by the army because of his refusal to consider any return to constitutional rule. The newly formed Council of the Nation, comprising the Council of State and the 21-member Joint Council of the Armed Forces, chose Dr Aparicio Méndez Manfredini (a former Minister of Health) as the new President, and he took office in September. Under military rule, economic growth resumed, but real wages declined sharply and some 10% of the population emigrated, for economic or political reasons. Close political and commercial links developed with Brazil and Argentina, but relations with the USA became strained during US President Jimmy Carter's Administration (1977–81), as a result of his criticism of the Uruguayan regime's flagrant violations of human rights.

In November 1980 the military leadership submitted a draft constitution to a referendum. Large sections of the Colorado and Blanco parties campaigned against the military's proposals, on the grounds that they institutionalized the army's role in security matters. When the proposed document was rejected, by 57.8% of those voting, the military leadership was forced to consult with leaders of the recognized parties on the constitutional future of the country.

THE RETURN TO CIVILIAN RULE

The Joint Council of the Armed Forces appointed Lt-Gen. Gregorio Álvarez Armellino to the presidency in September 1981. Restrictions on political activity were eased, and in June 1982 the Partido Colorado, the Partido Nacional and the smaller Unión Cívica (Civic Union) were allowed to operate, although left-wing parties remained banned, and censorship increased. Constitutional negotiations foundered in 1983 over attempts by the military leaders to preserve their authority in future governments, and in August the authorities suspended all political activity. Distinctions between the two main parties, the liberal Colorados and the more conservative Blancos, gradually eroded, and pro- and anti-military tendencies developed within each of them. Two national days of protest were organized by the opposition in November, two months after the Plenario Intersindical de Trabajadores—Convención Nacional de Trabajadores (PIT—CNT, Intersyndical Plenary of Workers—National Convention of Workers), the country's main trade union federation, had organized the first industrial action in the country for 10 years. The PIT—CNT was banned in January 1984, following a 24-hour strike protesting against continued political repression and a 28% increase in prices.

Negotiations between the Government and the Partido Colorado, the still-proscribed Frente Amplio (FA, Broad Front, a left-wing coalition) and the Unión Cívica resumed in July 1984. The Partido Nacional refused to participate while its leader, Ferreira Aldunate, was detained (he had been arrested in June, on returning from an 11-year exile). In August the Government withdrew its suspension of political activity and began to release some political prisoners (at that time numbering 600–900), but Ferreira Aldunate and Gen. Líber Seregni Mosquera, the FA leader, were banned from political activity. In November the presidential election was won by Dr Julio María Sanguinetti Cairolo of the Colorado's Unidad y Reforma (Unity and Reform) faction. In the legislative elections, however, the Partido Colorado did not gain an absolute majority in either congressional chamber. In preparation for the full restoration of civilian rule, most remaining political prisoners, including Ferreira Aldunate, were released in November, and the Tupamaro leader, Raúl Sendic, was freed in March 1985. In December the MLN formally agreed to become a political party and voted to join the FA.

THE AMNESTY LAW

President Sanguinetti was inaugurated in March 1985, and formed a Council of Ministers including two members of the Partido Nacional and one of the Unión Cívica. The Partido Comunista (Communist Party) and other previously outlawed organizations were legalized, and remaining restrictions on press freedom were lifted.

The most controversial issue for the Sanguinetti administration was the introduction in August 1986 of a draft amnesty law, protecting all members of the security forces from prosecution for alleged violations of human rights during the period of military rule. After considerable debate, a revised version of the original proposals was approved by both congressional chambers in December, despite violent outbursts in the streets of Montevideo and within the Cámara de Representantes (Chamber of Representatives) itself. The Ley de Caducidad de la Pretensión Punitiva del Estado (Law of Expiry of the Punitive Powers of the State) ended current military trials and made President Sanguinetti responsible for any further investigations into the whereabouts of the 'disappeared'. By this time it was known that under military rule more than 170 Uruguayan citizens had been seized and subsequently murdered by the military; 33 had 'disappeared' within Uruguay, 132 in Argentina and the remainder in Paraguay and Chile. Public opposition to the legislation increased, and during 1988 a sufficient number of signatures (a minimum of 25% of the electorate) was gathered to force a referendum, which was held in April 1989. For the first time in a national referendum, voting was declared compulsory, and the law was confirmed by a vote of 57% in favour.

ECONOMIC LIBERALIZATION

With the resolution of the amnesty question, economic policy again became the Government's chief concern. Trade unions criticized the Government for adhering to the dictates of international monetary agencies at the expense of the domestic work-force, and organized general strikes in late 1987 and mid-1988. The Government's economic performance cost the Colorados the elections, held in November 1989 (the first free elections since 1972), even though there was little material difference between the economic manifestos of the two leading presidential candidates. Luis Alberto Lacalle de Herrera of the Blancos won 37% of the votes cast, compared with 30% for Jorge Batlle Ibáñez of the Colorados; Líber Seregni of the FA secured 21% of the votes.

The Partido Nacional could form only a minority Government, with 39 out of 99 seats in the Cámara de Representantes and 13 of the 31 seats in the Cámara de Senadores (Senate). Although Lacalle reached a power-sharing agreement with the Colorados, taking office in March 1990, the Partido Colorado publicly expressed its opposition to parts of the Government's economic policy, as did a number of Blanco deputies. The most contentious issue was the proposed privatization programme, which was suspended in 1992. Lacalle remained committed to privatization, however, and the process of eroding the country's large state sector was set in motion, albeit at a far gentler pace than in many neighbouring countries.

The Government provoked further outcry in 1992 when it attempted to impose a programme of wage restraint on public sector workers, but exempted the police and the armed forces. In March 1993 two Blanco factions withdrew their congressional support, and in May the Government was defeated in a vote on finance policy, leaving President Lacalle to rely on his own faction of the Partido Nacional and a right-wing Colorado faction for support in the Congreso. Lacking reliable political support, Lacalle's Government became more sympathetic to the armed forces: legislation extending military powers was prepared, and the Government appeared reluctant to pursue investigations into past violent incidents implicating members of the military.

ELECTORAL REFORM

The presidential and legislative elections of November 1994 marked an end to traditional two-party politics. The vote was almost evenly split between the Partido Colorado (32.5%), the Partido Nacional (31.4%) and a predominantly left-wing electoral alliance, the Encuentro Progresista (EP—Progressive Congress)—FA, which secured 30.8% of the ballot. In the Cámara de Representantes, the Colorados won 32 seats; the Blancos and EP—FA took 31 seats each. Sanguinetti, the leading Colorado presidential candidate, was re-elected President, and was obliged to form a coalition administration with the Partido Nacional, leaving the EP—FA as the main opposition force. The principal member of this alliance, the FA, reportedly gave an undertaking to co-operate with the new administration in return for government consideration of its views when determining social policy.

The new Government immediately tackled electoral reform. The existing system had been criticized both for promoting factionalism and for yielding an unclear result. Under the proposed reform, each party would present a single candidate and, in the event of no candidate securing an absolute majority, a second round of voting would take place (the single-member, second-ballot system). FA members claimed that the change was a deliberate attempt to deny any left-wing group the chance to win the presidency. The amendment was adopted by the Congreso in October 1996, was narrowly approved (by 50.5%) in a plebiscite held in December and came into effect in January 1997.

In March 1995 President Sanguinetti commenced restructuring the social-security system, his fifth attempt at such a reform (see also Economy). The fiscal burden of the pension system was growing to such an extent that on this occasion the proposed reform received support from the two larger parties. The new system proved to have far greater appeal than expected, and within a year of its introduction nearly one-third of the work-force had subscribed.

In May 1996 the Colorados and the Blancos strengthened their 'governability pact'. The attempt to establish a common political agenda was the first such occurrence in 160 years and underlined the shift away from the traditional two-party rivalry. Ironically, this move was accompanied by the emergence of divisions within the FA. In September 1997 the Front's leader, Dr Tabaré Ramón Vázquez Rosas, threatened to resign after party in-fighting concerning privatization. Although his grouping generally opposed privatization, the FA-controlled authorities in Montevideo had begun to offer contracts to private tender, antagonizing the more left-wing member organizations.

In April 1997 FA senator Felipe Michelini, whose father was among the 'disappeared', demanded an investigation into allegations that 32 of the victims of the dictatorship had been interred in the grounds of military property and covertly removed from the burial sites in 1985–86. A judicial ruling in the same month promised to facilitate such an inquiry, and in May 20,000 people attended a rally in Montevideo to demand that the Government and the armed forces acquiesce. However, in June a court of appeal overturned the ruling on the grounds that it contravened the Ley de Caducidad. In October the Government conceded that it had not kept its undertaking in the 1986 amnesty to ascertain where the 'disappeared' had been buried. Nevertheless, no investigations into human rights abuses during military rule were launched during the Sanguinetti administration.

The human rights issue continued to be prominent. In May 1998 the country's principal religious and human rights groups published a National Reconciliation Declaration, making explicit their opposition to the amnesty law. In July a former intelligence chief, Rear-Adm. (retd) Eladio Moll, caused a diplomatic crisis when he alleged that US military officers had instructed the Uruguayan security forces on the detention and torture of Tupamaro suspects. He even claimed that Uruguayan officers had resisted US demands that the suspects be killed after interrogation.

BATLLE IBÁÑEZ VERSUS TABARÉ VÁZQUEZ

In accordance with the Sanguinetti administration's electoral reforms, a presidential primary election was held in April 1999. The Partido Colorado nomination was won by Jorge Batlle Ibáñez. The EP—FA leader, Tabaré Vázquez, was selected as the coalition's candidate. The Partido Nacional's campaign for the primary election was seriously divisive. During the campaign the Blanco candidate, former President Lacalle, had been accused of corruption, and in the months preceding the elections it became clear that the presidential election would be, in effect, a contest between Batlle and Vázquez. The Colorados and Blancos attempted to portray Vázquez (an eminent oncologist) as a Marxist firebrand, claiming that he would destroy the country's economy. His main manifesto promises were government-led job creation, and the rather less popular introduction of an income-tax system.

In presidential and legislative elections held in October 1999 the EP—FA won a plurality in both the Cámara de Representantes (40 of the 99 seats) and in the Cámara de Senadores (12 of the 30 seats). The Partido Colorado secured 33 and 10 seats, respectively, and the Partido Nacional obtained only 22 seats in the lower house and seven in the Cámara de Senadores (although the party performed well in local and regional elections in May 2000, taking control of 13 of the 19 departments). In the presidential ballot, Vázquez won 38.5% of the vote, ahead of Batlle (31.3%) and Lacalle (21.3%). Under the system operating until 1995, Vázquez would have been elected President, but the new electoral law required a second round of voting, which was held on 28 November. Most of the Blanco support was transferred to the Colorado candidate, and Batlle won with 51.6% of the votes cast.

Batlle's inauguration speech in March 2000 included undertakings to reduce public spending, address the farming crisis, investigate the fate of the 'disappeared' and institutionalize the Southern Common Market (Mercado Común del Sur—Mercosur, see Economy). His new cabinet comprised eight Colorados and five Blancos. In April he dismissed Gen. Manuel Fernández, a senior army official who had sought to justify the military repression of the 1970s and had spoken of a renewed struggle against left-wing extremists, and in August a six-member Commission for Peace was formed to investigate 'disappearances' during the military dictatorship. In May 2001 the bodies of two Uruguayan exiles were found in Argentine soil. The Commission released its first report in October 2002, detailing instances of collusion between Argentine and Uruguayan armed forces. It was reported that many of Uruguay's 'disappeared' had been killed in Argentina by members of that country's armed forces.

ECONOMIC CRISIS

The new Government inherited a prolonged economic crisis, which had begun in 1998. Protests ensued, including two general strikes in June 2000 and July 2001 led by the PIT—CNT, over public spending reductions and privatization proposals. Farmers also appealed for aid to mitigate the disastrous effects on the rural economy of the outbreak of foot-and-mouth disease in April 2001. In January 2002 the problems escalated with the impact of the Argentine financial crisis. In May Argentine withdrawals from deposits held in Uruguay increased sharply, prompting a 'run' on Uruguayan banks by Uruguayan nationals, and the Government introduced highly unpopular austerity measures. The competence of the Government inevitably became the dominant issue for the left-wing opposition and the trade unions. In July the Minister of Economy and Finance, Alberto Bensión, resigned. In the last week of July the Government temporarily closed the banks (see Economy), and there were fears that the country might be obliged to default on the national debt.

The economic crisis deepened the rift between the two governing parties, and an opinion poll in August 2002 gave the FA more than 50% of public approval. The Blancos became increasingly critical of government policy, objecting to what they termed the 'high social cost' of financing the national debt. All five Blanco ministers resigned from the Council of Ministers in November; President Batlle reorganized the cabinet and reduced the number of ministerial posts from 13 to 11. In early 2003 the opposition was more conciliatory and did not obstruct the Government's negotiations with the IMF and its efforts to restructure debt payments.

The advent of presidential and legislative elections in October 2004 brought the Batlle administration under further pressure, and broad support for the IMF programme began to wane. By mid-2003 various elements of the Government's economic policy were being criticized, and in August trade unions and opposition groups held a one-day general strike in protest against the Government's reform programme, in particular against plans to increase private sector participation in the economy. In December, following a campaign by the FA, a referendum was held regarding controversial legislation enacted in 2001 allowing private sector involvement in the petroleum, cement and alcohol monopoly, the Administración Nacional de Combustibles, Alcohol y Portland (ANCAP); 62% voted to repeal the law.

Traditionally, Uruguay had enjoyed relative prosperity, more equal distribution of income, a lower rate of poverty, and well-funded education, social security and health systems compared with other South American countries. It also had a reputation for more liberal legislation on social issues, and Batlle advocated a measured decriminalization of certain illegal drugs. An opinion poll conducted in 2001 indicated that support for the principle of democratic governance ran at one of the highest levels on the continent, despite criticism of the current Government. By 2002, however, an increasing number of citizens were unable to meet the cost of health insurance and, in common with other countries in the region, there was a marked rise in street violence and organized crime. Although Uruguay retained the lowest incidence of poverty in Latin America, living standards were in decline even before the 2002 crisis. The poverty index rose from 9.4% in 1999 to 11.4% in 2001, while the extreme poverty index rose from 1.8% to 2.4% in that year and emigration accelerated markedly.

THE 2004 ELECTIONS

In the presidential primary election held in June 2004, the EP—FA joined forces with another party, Nuevo Espacio, and adopted the name EP—FA—Nueva Mayoría (NM), and Vázquez was confirmed as its candidate. In the Blanco party, Jorge Larrañaga defeated Lacalle to secure the party's nomination, while the Colorado party choose former interior minister Guillermo Stirling as its candidate.

Vázquez was elected to the presidency in the first round of voting on 31 October 2004, narrowly securing an absolute majority, with 50.7% of the votes cast. His nearest rival, Larrañaga, won 34.1% of the vote, while Stirling received 10.3%, the worst ever result for the Partido Colorado. Vázquez's victory brought an end to more than 170 years of rule by the Blancos and Colorados. The left-wing coalition was also successful in concurrent legislative elections, winning an absolute majority in both chambers: 52 of the 99 seats in the Cámara de Representantes and 16 of the 30 seats in the Cámara de Senadores. The Partido Nacional won 35 and 11 seats, respectively, and the Partido Colorado's congressional representation declined from 33 to 10 seats in the lower house and from 10 to three seats in the Cámara de Senadores.

Also on 31 October 2004 a constitutional reform guaranteeing that the supply of water and sanitation services would remain under state control was approved by 64.5% of voters in a referendum. The proposal was supported by the leaders of the winning coalition and the Partido Nacional, but opposed by the Colorados. President-elect Vázquez gave assurances during the campaign that the reform would not be retroactive and would therefore not affect existing private sector involvement in the water sector; a decree to that effect was issued in May 2005.

Prior to taking office Vázquez sought co-operation with other parties represented in the Congreso, and in February 2005 an agreement was signed on cross-party support for the incoming Government's policies on the economy, foreign affairs and education. Although opposition parties agreed to Vázquez's offer of a number of positions in state institutions, later in February the Partido Colorado withdrew from this arrangement after the opposition was allocated only one seat on the five-member board of the education directorate. The Partido Nacional followed suit in March when it was offered only one place on the board of a state-owned bank. Members of the opposition had traditionally occupied two seats in every five-strong governing board.

THE VÁZQUEZ PRESIDENCY, 2005–10

Vázquez took office in March 2005 as the country's first left-wing President. His new Council of Ministers largely comprised members of the various factions of the EP—FA—NM, although two independents received posts, including Jorge Lepra, a former executive of a US energy company, who became Minister of Industry, Energy and Mining. Reforming ANCAP, the privatization of which the EP—FA—NM had opposed, was expected to be a priority for Lepra. Danilo Astori, the leader of Asamblea Uruguay (the most centrist party in the ruling coalition), was appointed Minister of Economy and Finance, inheriting an economy that, although recovering, remained burdened by a large external debt. The appointments of Lepra and Astori, apparently aimed at strengthening investor confidence, proved controversial with some of the more leftist parties in the coalition. The portfolios of the interior, foreign affairs and national defence were all allocated to members of Vázquez's own Partido Socialista del Uruguay (PS), while former Tupamaro guerrilla José 'Pepe' Mujica, the leader of the Movimiento de Participación Popular (MPP), which had won some 30% of the EP—FA—NM's vote in the elections, became Minister of Livestock, Agriculture and Fishing.

Investigations into the fate of those who 'disappeared' during the military dictatorship began shortly after Vázquez's inauguration, and in August 2005 the President received a report from the heads of Uruguay's armed forces admitting the kidnap, torture and murder of political detainees. In November information from the report led to the exhumation of the bodies of two dissidents murdered by members of the air force, and in the following month 35 unidentified corpses were exhumed from a cemetery near the border with Brazil. Also in November the Government presented draft legislation to the Congreso, 'interpreting' the Ley de Caducidad (see above). The bill would enable the judiciary to commence investigating a case until it became apparent whether it was covered by the amnesty, and allow for the trial of former senior officers for crimes committed before and after the dictatorship ('disappearances' could be considered as crimes continuing beyond 1985). In order to reduce tensions between the Government and the armed forces, Vázquez made it clear that there were no plans to repeal the Ley de Caducidad.

In March 2005 Vázquez announced the introduction of the Plan de Atención Nacional de Emergencia Social, a two-year social welfare programme aimed at reducing poverty, in which the Government was expected to invest some US $200m. over two years. In April, however, the President was criticized by the MPP for commitments made to the IMF on the fiscal balance and external debt: it was claimed that financial stability was being prioritized at the expense of the social welfare programme in order to satisfy the Fund.

The EP—FA—NM performed well in municipal elections held in May 2005, securing control of eight of the 19 departments, comprising some 70% of the country's population, previously having held only Montevideo. The mayoralty of Montevideo was won by Ricardo Ehrlich of the MPP, which took 25% of the coalition's vote nation-wide. The Partido Nacional retained 10 departments but lost three, while the Partido Colorado held onto only one. At the end of June the PIT—CNT led a one-day strike in support of demands for increased wages, emphasizing that its action was targeted at employers, not at the Government.

Despite the damage done to the economy in 2005–06 by Argentine protests against plans to construct two pulp mills near Fray Bentos (see below), good rates of growth were achieved thereafter, and in 2007 per head income returned to pre-crisis levels. In November the Cámara de Senadores adopted a bill on reproductive rights that would decriminalize abortions carried out within the first 12 weeks of pregnancy, in certain circumstances. Although subsequently the bill was approved by the Cámara de Representantes, it was vetoed by President Vázquez on ethical grounds. His action was strongly criticized by the PS, prompting his resignation from the party shortly afterwards. A law allowing same-sex couples living together to formalize their union went into effect on 1 January 2008; the first ceremony under the new law, unprecedented in Latin America, took place in April.

Preparations for the presidential and legislative elections began in early 2009, ahead of the primary elections to determine the candidates who would contest the presidency in October. In late 2008 the ruling coalition, renamed the FA in November 2005, had nominated José Mujica (an outspoken senator and erstwhile Tupamaro) of the MPP as its official candidate, although Vázquez openly favoured the more orthodox Danilo Astori, former Minister of Economy and Finance, as his successor. (A third candidate, Marcos Carámbula, a doctor and mayor of Canelones, also entered the contest.) The selection procedure proved divisive within the FA: there was concern that Mujica's radicalism might alienate voters, while Astori's neo-liberalism could also deter those with more left-wing sympathies. Support expressed for Mujica by former Argentine President Néstor Carlos Kirchner in April 2009, and Mujica's overtures towards the Argentine administration, also proved controversial, given the ongoing dispute regarding the pulp mills (see below). Nevertheless, a primary election held in late June confirmed Mujica as the FA's candidate, while Lacalle reversed the outcome of the 2004 primary election by defeating Larrañaga to secure the PN's nomination, and Pedro Bordaberry Herrán won the support of the Partido Colorado. After tense negotiations, the defeated Astori agreed to stand as the FA's vice-presidential candidate; similarly, Larrañaga also accepted the PN's invitation to campaign alongside Lacalle for the position of Vice-President.

The main candidates in the presidential election ran largely negative campaigns with few specific policy proposals. Mujica sought to reassure his doubters by stressing that his government would offer significant continuity with that of President Vázquez and underlining that Astori would be in charge of economic policy. Lacalle, the main opposition candidate, failed to impress the electorate during a lack-lustre and error-prone campaign in which he focused on criticizing Mujica's character and drawing attention to his rival's often erratic and contradictory statements. Lacalle also emphasized that Mujica's political sympathies lay further to the left that those of President Vázquez. In the first round of the presidential election on 25 October 2009, Mujica narrowly failed to win an overall majority, securing 48.0% of the votes compared with the 29.1% won by Lacalle. Nevertheless, Mujica won the consequent run-off election on 29 November with 52.4% of the votes. In the legislative elections, held concurrently with the first round of the presidential ballot, the FA secured a narrow but vital majority in both chambers of the Congreso, winning 50 of the 99 seats in the Cámara de Representantes and 16 of the 30 seats in the Cámara de Senadores. A referendum to consider whether to repeal the Ley de Caducidad was also held simultaneously with the national elections. It followed the presentation of some 325,000 signatures (far exceeding the requisite 250,000) to the Congreso in April. (In March the FA had won a non-binding vote in the Congreso declaring the Ley de Caducidad to be unconstitutional; however, it remained for the Supreme Court to decide on its constitutionality.) The referendum, however, failed to achieve the required majority of over 50%; an additional referendum on whether to allow Uruguayan emigrants to vote in elections from 2014 was also unsuccessful (some 600,000 Uruguayans were estimated to live abroad, of whom the majority were believed to be FA supporters).

THE MUJICA PRESIDENCY, 2010–

After a three-month transition period, José Mujica was sworn in as President on 1 March 2010. Cabinet positions were assigned according to the share of the votes won by the FA's different factions. As promised in the electoral campaign, Mujica appointed Fernando Lorenzo, a close ally of Vice-President Astori, as Minister of Economy and Finance. Mujica's conciliatory inaugural speech set the tone for the first 100 days of his administration. The new President reaffirmed the continuity of his administration with that of President Vázquez, stressing that education was to be his Government's main priority, with immediate attention also to be given to the reform of the state and an emergency social housing programme, and he appealed to the opposition for cross-party agreement on key policy objectives. Mujica stated that his Government would focus on macroeconomic equilibriums and openness in the economy while promoting technological change in the agricultural sector and seeking to develop tourism and logistics as strategic areas for economic growth. In February, before taking office, he met with domestic and Argentine entrepreneurs to promote further investment in the country and to stress that there would be no tax increases or unexpected changes to the business environment under his administration. Also during the transition period Mujica established four multiparty working groups to seek policy agreement in the areas of education, security, the environment and energy. In his first days in office, President Mujica appointed representatives of the opposition to the boards of state-owned enterprises and other public bodies, and he also attempted to improve relations with the military, which had imprisoned him for 12 years in the 1970s and 1980s, by proposing that former officers serving prison sentences for human rights abuses during the military dictatorship could serve the remainder of their sentences at home when reaching the age of 70. President Mujica's political initiatives were warmly received by the opposition and resulted in high rates of popular approval. However, his conciliatory approach created some uneasiness within the more radical sections of the FA, which blocked the President's proposal regarding military officers' prison conditions. A more demanding test of the President's ability to mediate between conflicting political interests was to come later in 2010, with public and private sector wage negotiations and congressional debate of the five-year budget law.

Municipal elections in May 2010 represented a political setback for the ruling FA. In spite of President Mujica's popularity, the FA only won control of five departmental administrations, a net loss of three, with the party's share of the vote also declining. The main opposition party, the PN, secured control of 13 departments, while the Partido Colorado obtained one. The FA, however, maintained control of Montevideo, where just under one-half of the country's population lived, and of the two politically and economically significant departments of Canelones and Maldonado.

FOREIGN RELATIONS

Traditionally, relations with Argentina have been close. However, a serious dispute emerged in late 2005 when Argentine ecological demonstrators blockaded a bridge between the two countries in protest against the construction of a cellulose-manufacturing plant on the Uruguayan side of the River Uruguay, alleging that this would damage the River's ecosystem as well as territory in Argentina. Uruguayan officials asserted that fears that the mill would damage the environment were unfounded. The mill, originally installed by the Finnish consortium Botnia and later sold to UPM, represented an investment of US $1,800m (the most significant investment in Uruguay's history) and provided vital employment opportunities. In May 2006 the Argentine Government filed a claim against Uruguay with the UN International Court of Justice (ICJ), alleging breaches of the Statute of the River Uruguay, signed by the two States in 1975, concerning the utilization of the River, and requesting preventive measures to halt construction of the mill. In July 2006 the ICJ ruled that the current circumstances did not require the Court to exercise its power to indicate provisional measures, and thus it was not necessary for Uruguay to suspend construction of the mill. The ICJ noted that there was insufficient evidence that their construction would cause irrevocable damage to the environment. The blockade of the bridge between the two countries (albeit with a reduced following by 2009) resulted in a sharp decline in Argentine tourist arrivals and adversely affected the Uruguayan economy. Bilateral relations remained tense, and in October 2008 Uruguay vetoed the nomination of former Argentine President Néstor Kirchner as a candidate for the first Secretary-General of the newly created Union of South American Nations (Unión de Naciones Suramericanas—UNASUR). On assuming office President Mujica confirmed that ameliorating relations with Argentina was one of his main priorities. Consequently, he held several meetings with Argentine President Cristina Fernández de Kirchner and removed Uruguay's veto on the appointment of her husband as Secretary-General of UNASUR. In April 2010 the ICJ ruled that, although Uruguay had breached the Statue of the River Uruguay in not consulting Argentina before authorizing the construction of the mill, there was no evidence to support Argentina's claim that discharges from the plant had caused environmental damage to the River Uruguay. Following the Court's ruling, the two countries reached a preliminary agreement to monitor jointly the quality of the water along the River, while the Argentine Government, originally supportive of the protesters, threatened to initiate civil and criminal actions against the leaders of the blockade if they refused to remove it. In response, the ecological activists agreed in June to remove temporarily the blockade pending the finalization of the joint monitoring negotiations, a result perceived as a major diplomatic triumph for President Mujica.

The administration of President Vázquez emphasized the importance of strengthening relations with other Latin American countries, particularly within Mercosur. On the day after his inauguration, Vázquez signed agreements on trade and the supply of energy with his Venezuelan counterpart, President Hugo Chávez Frías, and an accord on human rights with Argentina's President Kirchner, which was aimed at facilitating the exchange of information on abuses stemming from both countries' military dictatorships. Vázquez's first foreign visit was to Brazil in April 2005, when he signed six agreements on co-operation with Brazilian President Luiz Inácio Lula da Silva. In one of his first official acts, in March, Vázquez had restored full diplomatic ties with Cuba. Uruguay had severed diplomatic relations with Cuba (established in 1986) in 2002, after Cuba had taken exception to Uruguayan support for a UN resolution demanding greater respect for human rights in Cuba. In June 2008 Vázquez made an official visit to Cuba, where he held discussions with his counterpart, Raúl Castro Ruz, and also with recently retired leader Fidel Castro Ruz. President Vázquez, however, became increasingly disenchanted with Mercosur, which he regarded as being dominated by the interests of Brazil and Argentina.

A bilateral investment treaty with the USA, first signed by outgoing President Batlle in December 2004, was renegotiated by the Vázquez administration and approved in December 2005, despite criticism from members of the ruling EP—FA—NM. In May 2006 Vázquez visited the USA, and, following a meeting with President George W. Bush, confirmed his desire to forge closer bilateral trade relations. President Bush's visit to Montevideo in March 2007 attracted protests in Brazil, and some 5,000 protesters gathered in Uruguay for the visit, while Venezuelan President Chávez, conducting his alternative tour of the region, addressed 40,000 anti-Bush protesters in Argentina, across the River Plate.

President Mujica renewed the Vázquez administration's original priority to strengthen Mercosur and other Latin American integration initiatives. During the first months of his presidency he visited Chile, Bolivia and Venezuela, and aligned the country closely to Brazil's regional leadership. However, his Government also intended to seek closer economic ties with the USA and other economies outside the region.

Economy

HELEN SCHOOLEY

Revised for this edition by Dr FRANCISCO PANIZZA

Uruguay is an interesting test case, a country that developed a modern economy with a strong social security system on an almost exclusively agricultural base. From the late 19th century Uruguay developed as an agricultural export economy by selling wool, beef and hides, mainly to European countries. With favourable natural conditions and a low density of population, export values per head were high, and under the leadership of José Batlle y Ordóñez Uruguay was transformed into a stable democratic welfare state. Government policy encouraged domestic manufacturing, and protection was intensified in the 1930s and after the Second World War. However, the rate of growth of exports was low and the small size of the domestic market meant that the strategy of industrialization by import substitution was exhausted by the mid-1950s. A period of economic stagnation followed and continued into the early 1970s, when the prevailing social unrest led to the army assuming power (see History). The economic policies of the military regime after 1973, based on a reduction of the public sector and incentives to non-traditional exports, helped stimulate growth in the gross domestic product (GDP), averaging 4.5% per year in 1974–80. However, attempts to control inflation and the general effects of the world recession halted economic expansion. Overall, GDP expanded at an average annual rate of only 0.3% in 1980–90.

As with politics, the performance of the economy was negatively affected by events in Uruguay's large neighbouring countries. GDP growth resumed in the 1990s, but the economy then entered a decline towards the end of the decade. Real GDP contracted by 2.7% in 1999, under the influence of a devaluation of the Brazilian currency, and by a further 1.4% in 2000, because of the recession in Argentina and continued low world prices for agricultural exports. In 2001 production was drastically affected by an outbreak of foot-and-mouth disease, and the economy contracted by 3.4%.

In 2002 the country experienced a major economic crisis due to Argentina's debt default. The banking chaos in Argentina precipitated a run on Uruguayan banks that resulted in a loss of almost one-half of their deposits in a six-month period. In 2002–03 the economy contracted by 11.2%, unemployment reached almost 20% and the gross public sector debt-to-GDP ratio increased to over 100%. External debt restructuring and financial assistance from the US Government and the international financial institutions led to a swift recovery, with growth of 2.4% in 2003. Effective macroeconomic policies, a favourable environment for investment, rising real wages and the international boom in agricultural prices contributed to average economic growth of 7% between 2004 and 2008. While the country was not immune to the 2009 global financial crisis, Uruguay proved to be remarkably resilient to the adverse economic conditions. Real GDP contracted by 2.3% during the first quarter of the year, but expansion resumed in the second quarter and continued to accelerate in the second half of the year, with overall GDP growth of 2.9% in 2009. During the same year unemployment declined to 6.3%.

Although the economy was always closely linked to the economies of neighbouring countries, the establishment in 1995 of the Southern Common Market (Mercado Común del Sur—Mercosur, or, in Portuguese, Mercado Comum do Sul—Mercosul) accentuated the influence of markets in Brazil and Argentina. Uruguay maintained one of the highest levels of GDP per head in Latin America, registered at US $13,268 in 2009, and was the only country in Latin America where the gap between the wealthiest and the poorest did not increase during the early and mid-1990s. Owing principally to the economic crisis in Argentina, poverty grew dramatically between 2002 and 2004, affecting almost 40% of the population in 2003 before declining to 22.6% in 2008.

A relatively small country, with an area of 176,215 sq km (68,037 sq miles), Uruguay had an estimated population of 3.33m. in mid-2008. Average annual population growth of 0.1% in 2000–08 was the lowest in Latin America. The proportion of people living in urban areas in 2008 was 94% of the total, the highest in the region, with 39.2% of the population living in the capital, Montevideo. Some 85% of the national territory was devoted to sheep- and cattle-raising, with an estimated 7.8% used for arable land in 2005. In many places, the soils are thin, and in recent years the country has seen a significant erosion in top-soil.

AGRICULTURE

Agriculture has traditionally formed the basis of the Uruguayan economy, and still accounts (directly or indirectly) for almost all commodity export earnings. Some 4.5% of the working population were employed in the sector in 2003, compared with 20% in 1965. The sector performed strongly in the 2000s, largely owing to substantial investment in infrastructure and new technology. Agricultural GDP increased at an average annual rate of 2.8% between 1998 and 2008, according to the World Bank. In 2008 agriculture (including forestry and fishing) accounted for 10.8% of GDP, according to the same source. The strong recovery in international agricultural prices since 2003 has led to a marked increase in linked investment and record prices for land. Between the second half of 2008 and early 2009 the agricultural sector was adversely affected by a period of severe drought, leading the Government to announce an 'agricultural emergency' and provide special funds to assist farmers. Intensive farming, dairy and cereal production all suffered, and livestock losses were reported. However, the sector recovered in the second half of 2009, and agricultural production grew by 2.9% in that year.

Uruguay's two main export products were historically meat (especially beef) and wool. However, during the 2000s external demand led to an expansion in arable crops and a consequent decline in cattle- and sheep-raising, and there was also a significant increase in the production of timber and timber products. Meat was also an important item of the local diet, with consumption rising from 48 kg per head in 2004 to 52 kg per head in 2008. In mid-2009 the cattle herd was estimated at 11.7m. head, and cattle meat production totalled 962,000 metric tons. Beef exports have risen steadily since 2003 prompted by high prices and international demand. The value of beef exports was estimated to have reached US $1,220m. in 2009. The main market for Uruguayan beef in 2009 was the Russian Federation, followed by the European Union (EU). Uruguay has also been promoting the sale of 'organic' beef, exports of which totalled 600 tons in 2005. Since then Uruguay (with Argentina) has been certified by the World Organisation of Animal Health as being in the lowest-risk category for bovine spongiform encephalopathy (BSE), as it bans the use of meat and bone-meal in all products used for animal consumption. The dairy sector, centred in the south-western departments of San José and Colonia and in the southern departments of Florida and Canelones, grew rapidly in the 1990s and 2000s, becoming a significant source of export revenues. Milk yields more than doubled between 1981 and 1997. In 2007/08 Uruguay produced 1,582,000 tons of fresh milk utilizing 849,000 ha of land. Sheep stocks declined from 9.7m. head in 2005 to 8.6m. head in 2009. Although exports of live sheep, particularly to the Middle East, became significant, between late January 2008 and February 2009 sales declined to $2.5m., 83.8% lower than in the previous 12-month period. Exports of ovine meat rose, however, with revenue of $64m. recorded in that period (an increase of 28.5% compared with the previous year); the principal purchasers were the EU and Brazil. In 1988–94 Uruguay's share of wool production in the Southern Cone region increased from 32% to 41%, although the region's total output declined by 30% in the same period. Revenue from wool exports between late January 2008 and February 2009 totalled $159.7m., a decline of 19.3% compared with the previous year. The principal purchaser was the People's Republic of China.

A regional problem in the livestock sector is the recurrence of outbreaks of foot-and-mouth disease. One, in October 2000, resulted in a temporary halt of meat exports and the loss of 6,500 jobs in the meat and dairy industry. Although exports resumed following the slaughter of some 20,000 animals, they were suspended again in April 2001, when there was a second outbreak. The Government was forced to adopt a mass vaccination programme, thereby reducing the value of future meat exports but averting further damage to the industry. Exports to the EU and Israel did not resume until November, and during that period the meat share of export earnings contracted from 20% to 12.8%. Exports of beef to the USA resumed in 2003 after the US Department of Agriculture accepted Uruguayan certification procedures as meeting US guidelines. Exports of beef to Mexico and Japan resumed only in January and June 2006, respectively.

The main crops by output in 2008–09 were wheat, rice, soya beans, barley, maize, sugar cane and potatoes, with cereal production based in the west of the country and rice in the east. Soya bean production in particular has expanded rapidly, increasing from 66,700 tons in 2001–02 to 1.0m. tons in 2008–09. Citrus fruit was grown mainly in the department of Salto, while other fruits in production included grapes, apples, pears, peaches and nectarines. Some 128,930 tons of oranges were produced in 2008, and 112,883 tons of grapes. Flowers and vines were grown around Montevideo and Canelones to the north. The wine industry in Uruguay has developed considerably in recent years; in 2008 79.9m. litres of wine were produced of which 13.5m. litres were exported, resulting in revenue of US $10.6m. Brazil remained the principal market for Uruguayan wine in 2008 by both value and volume, followed by the USA and Canada (in terms of value), and by Russia and the USA (by volume). In 2008 exports of wine increased by 36% and 12% by volume and value, respectively. In 2007 Uruguay commenced exports of wine to China.

Successive governments strove to increase timber production with a view to making forestry one of Uruguay's main economic sectors; plans to construct two pulp mills near Fray Bentos on the banks of the River Uruguay, which forms the boundary between Argentina and Uruguay, proved controversial. In 2005 plans by the Spanish company ENCE and the Finnish consortium Botnia for the two plants were opposed by Argentine environmentalists and the Argentine Government, which alleged that they would contaminate the River Uruguay and were therefore contrary to the binational Statute of the River Uruguay. These allegations were denied by the Uruguayan authorities, but popular protests continued, and it was not until early 2010 that the International Court of Justice ruled that the UPM (formerly Botnia) plant, which commenced production in November 2007, was not polluting the river waters. Meanwhile, ENCE withdrew its initial plan as a result of Argentine protests, and later announced proposals for a pulp mill at a different location. By mid-2009 ENCE's Punta Pereira mill was on hold as the company sought an associate for the project. It had been expected that exports of cellulose, timber and related products would increase from US $206m. in 2005 to $720m. in 2010, making it the largest export sector after meat products. Production of timber rose from 3.0m. cu m in 2001 to 9.4m. cu m in 2008.

Although small scale, the fishing industry grew rapidly from the late 1970s before stabilizing in the mid-2000s. However, with the opening of the South Atlantic to factory fishing, stocks began to decline. The total catch in 2008 was 110,675 metric tons. In 2008 exports to the EU were resumed after a brief suspension to verify the hygiene of processing plants. Uruguay has also been involved in the international debate over the conservation of the Patagonian toothfish. Concern over dwindling fishery reserves prompted attempts at diversification, and beluga caviar is now traded from sturgeon farmed in the Baygorria reservoir, 200 km north of Montevideo, using eggs imported from Siberia. Approximately 4 tons of caviar are produced per year.

MINING AND MANUFACTURING

Industry (including mining, manufacturing, construction and power) accounted for 26.6% of GDP in 2008, according to the World Bank. However, almost all basic resources had to be imported. Apart from quarrying for marble (of which Uruguay has 27 varieties), sand, clay, gravel and other construction materials, raw materials for ceramics and glass manufacture, and a limited extraction of semi-precious stones such as agates and amethysts, there was little mining activity. The GDP of the mining sector increased by 15.0% in 2006, and by 1.1% in 2007, but mining and quarrying still employed only 0.1% of the economically active population in 2003 and accounted for 0.3% of GDP in 2007. In the financial year ending 31 May 2009 the Canadian company, Uruguay Mineral Exploration Inc, produced 70,147 troy oz of gold at its Arenal and San Gregorio mines. Prospection activities for iron ore were been carried out in the department of Tacuarembó, in the centre of the country.

From the 1970s manufacturing became an important sector of the Uruguayan economy. Between 1973 and 1980 industrial output increased by 36%. Adversely affected by the recession of the early 1980s, the sector grew rapidly in the latter part of the decade, chiefly as a result of an increase in car-manufacturing and, to a lesser degree, in textiles and parts for the petroleum industry. In the early 1990s the country's widening trade deficit prompted a programme of investment and reorganization in the sector, followed by expansion in the food-processing and textile sectors in 1992, an increase in car production in 1994–95, and a marked upturn in the chemical sector in 1997. In recent years the textile industry has been badly affected by competition from China and other Asian manufacturers, and the sector has become dependent on government subsidies for survival. Since the opening in 2007 of the UPM paper mill, cellulose and other timber products have become an important part of the country's industrial base. It was expected that construction of a second cellulose plant would start in 2011, with possibly a third plant to follow in the second half of the decade.

Manufacturing GDP increased at an average annual rate of 2.0% between 1998 and 2008, according to the World Bank. In 2009 the sector was badly affected by the world-wide recession, declining by 3.7% year on year, but it recovered in the first quarter of 2010, in which it grew by 3% in seasonally adjusted terms. Industrial activity is concentrated in Montevideo. The most important branches of manufacturing are food products (mainly processed meat for export and dairy products), beverages and tobacco, cellulose and timber products, chemicals, metal products, machinery and equipment, textiles, clothing, and leather products. By 2000 the number of people working in industry was only one-half the level of 1988, reflecting both greater productivity (with a consequent loss of jobs) and a major expansion of the service sector, which by 2007 accounted for 58.1% of GDP. Employment in the textile sector in 2000 was one-third of the 1988 level.

ENERGY

The absence of any commercially viable deposits of petroleum, natural gas or coal made Uruguay heavily dependent on the import of crude petroleum, which accounted for some two-thirds of its energy requirements. Prospecting for petroleum began in the 1940s and resumed in the 1970s in the wake of the oil crisis, when attention was focused on offshore possibilities, but these were judged to be economically unviable. In 1999, however, after a further round of oil-price increases, an initiative was announced within Mercosur to investigate the deposits. In 2008 annual consumption was estimated at 1.4m. metric tons of oil equivalent. Refining capacity was 50,000 barrels per day. In 2009 imports of petroleum and petroleum products were valued at US $1,354.0m., accounting for 19.6% of the value of total imports. In August 2005 Venezuelan President Hugo Chávez Frías agreed to supply Uruguay with petroleum on preferential terms for the next 25 years. Controversial legislation enacted in 2001 to allow private sector involvement in the state oil concern, Administración Nacional de Combustibles, Alcohol y Portland (ANCAP), was repealed following the law's rejection in a referendum in December 2003 (see below).

Uruguay consumed an estimated 102.8m. cu m of natural gas in 2007, all imported. A second natural gas pipeline between Uruguay and Argentina, the Gasoducto Cruz del Sur (GCDS), with a transportation capacity of 180m. cu ft per day, was completed in 2002 as part of a greater scheme to link the gas network of the Mercosur countries. The project held a concession for a possible extension of the GCDS to Porto Alegre, Brazil. However, Argentina's declining gas production severely limited exports to Uruguay and hence the utilization of the pipeline. In June 2005 the Presidents of the four Mercosur member countries signed an agreement creating an 'energy ring' (*anillo energético*), which would facilitate the supply and storage of natural gas from the Camisea field in Peru. The project, however, was fraught with political, financial and environmental difficulties, and little progress had been made by mid-2010. Similar initiatives to import gas from Venezuela and Bolivia were also in the preliminary stages.

In 2008 Uruguay's electric power consumption amounted to 7,762.7 GWh, while the country had an installed capacity for producing energy of 2,047.0 MW. In an attempt to reduce the dependence on imported petroleum, successive governments promoted the use of hydroelectricity, which accounted for 87.0% of total electricity production in 2005. Exploitation of hydroelectric resources began in the 1930s, but there was substantial development in the 1970s, as a result of major investments in the 1,800-MW Salto Grande project with Argentina, and the 300-MW Palmar installation with Brazil. The output from these two plants and two others on the Río Negro (Rincón del Bonete and Baygorria), which runs through the middle of the country, made Uruguay a net exporter of electric energy by the 1980s, and hydroelectric power became an important factor in the country's balance of payments from 1992. However, the danger of over-dependency on hydroelectric power became apparent in 2008, when a prolonged drought drastically reduced output from the hydroelectric plants and forced the state energy-generating company, Administración Nacional de Usinas y Transmisiones Eléctricas (UTE), to utilize its expensive oil-fuelled plants. In mid-2010 it was thought that growing demand would increase the likelihood of power shortages in the medium term unless there was significant investment in energy generation. Among the alternatives being considered were nuclear power, increasing energy imports from Brazil and Bolivia, and greater use of renewable energy, particularly wind power and biofuels.

TRANSPORT, INFRASTRUCTURE AND COMMUNICATIONS

Montevideo is the focal point of all Uruguay's transport systems, and the city's port is the principal gateway for foreign trade, but during the 1980s the transport systems suffered from neglect. Major improvements began in the 1990s, stimulated by the growth of tourism and investment in non-traditional exports; by the end of the decade there was a rolling programme of road, rail and port extension. The sector was a growth area even though the country's freight shipment costs were the highest in Mercosur.

The railway system was relatively extensive, with 1,641 km of standard gauge track radiating from Montevideo, and links to the Argentine and Brazilian networks. Most of the track and rolling stock, however, was in need of replacement. After a decade of decline, passenger services ceased completely in 1988. Apart from livestock, principal freight items are stone, cement, rice and fuel. In 1996 a project was launched for a freight railway scheme to connect the forestry industry in the north-east of the country with the coast, but little progress had been made due to a lack of resources. Like the railways, Uruguay's roads linked interior cities with the capital, rather than with each other. However, the 77,432 km of roads were virtually all paved in 2006. The transport, storage and communications sector contributed 9.1% of GDP in 2007, and during the 1990s recorded an average annual growth rate of 8%, owing chiefly to the telecommunications sector. By 2007 Uruguay had around 3.0m. mobile phone owners and some 968,000 internet users. An ambitious project to provide every schoolchild with a laptop computer was launched in 2007 and largely completed by 2009. The communications sector was in the vanguard of government free market reforms. Although opposition to privatization halted the proposed sale of the state telecommunications concern, Administración Nacional de Telecomunicaciones (ANTEL, see below), cellular-telephone services, road maintenance, and port and airport administration were opened to private sector participation in the mid-1990s.

PRIVATIZATION

The process of privatization in Uruguay was much slower than in other South American countries, in part because the state sector had been more efficient than its counterparts and also because of more effective political opposition to the policy. Government attempts to introduce a major privatization programme in the early 1990s met with resistance from the Frente Amplio (FA) and the trade unions, which initially were successful in reversing plans by demanding a referendum on each individual sale. Consequently, many initiatives were presented on more than one occasion. In 1992 the Government was forced to suspend the sale of shares in ANTEL, and to adopt a more gradual approach to privatization, encouraging competition and the use of private capital in state concerns.

The state monopolies on insurance and the financing and construction of new homes were ended in 1993 and 1996, respectively, and the national airline, Primeras Líneas Uruguayas de Navegación Aérea (PLUNA), was privatized in 1995.

The restructuring of the social-security system undertaken by the Government of Julio María Sanguinetti (1995–2000) proved less controversial. President Sanguinetti had made four previous attempts at such a reform, and his arguments were reinforced by the pressing need to alleviate the fiscal pressure exerted by pensions. In 1995 only 65% of the social-security budget was raised by contributions from those currently employed, while the number of people of pensionable age was over one-half of the economically active population. The new legislation, approved in August 1996, increased the period of contribution, raised the retirement age, and established a mixed capitalization and distribution system. The reforms aimed to eliminate the system's structural deficit within 10 years. The first pension-fund administration company (fondo de ahorro previsional—Afap) was inaugurated in April 1996, and by 2000 some 85% of the work-force had joined a new private pension scheme. Private savings accrued in Afaps accounted for more than 10% of GDP by late 2004. In 1996 ANCAP lost its monopoly over the manufacture of alcohol and cement, and in 1997 the Government ended the state monopoly on the generation of electricity and introduced legislation allowing the use of private capital in electricity distribution.

When President Jorge Batlle Ibáñez came to office in March 2000 he continued a cautious liberalization policy, opting for the introduction of competition rather than the dismantling of state concerns, although this strategy was still opposed by the FA and the trade unions. Further efforts were made to deregulate the telecommunications sector, and the Government enabled ANCAP to use private sector partners to develop its refining capacity. The privatization programme gained impetus in 2002 when the Government sought IMF assistance to counter the effects of the Argentine default. Under the agreement reached in March, the Government undertook to end the remaining state monopolies in the energy and telecommunications sectors, eliminate the pension-fund deficit, and allow private companies into the administration of roads and airports. In December 2003, however, the legislation to allow private sector involvement in ANCAP was rejected in a referendum. The FA Government of President Tabaré Ramón Vázquez Rosas (2005–10) renationalized two water companies in the department of Maldonado, but otherwise did not reverse the privatizations carried out by previous administrations. The new FA Government of José Alberto Mujica Cordano, which succeeded Vázquez's administration in March 2010, was committed to increasing the use of public-private partnerships in order to attract much-needed private investment to the public sector.

INVESTMENT AND FINANCE

In the 1970s Uruguay experienced a high level of public sector investment, largely in hydroelectricity and bridge-construction programmes, but during the 1980s and 1990s an increasing amount of investment came from the private sector. A law adopted in 1987 allowed for the establishment of free trade zones, both publicly and privately owned, for various manufacturing and service industries. In the mid-1990s the opening up of the public sector to private capitalization and joint-venture schemes encouraged significant levels of foreign direct investment for the first time. A new investment law, approved in 1998, promised further opportunities for private finance, with incentives including tax and tariff exemptions and a reduction of employers' social-security contributions. Its main consequence was to boost foreign investment, although indications were that investment funds were growing in response to the decline in interest rates and inflation and the 'pegging' of the exchange rate. Like internal investment, domestic savings and stock-exchange trading were relatively low for the region.

In conformity with the terms of agreements reached with the IMF in 1985, 1990, 1992 and 1996, successive governments reduced the fiscal deficit, to 1.4% of GDP in 1998. Notably, the number of public sector employees was reduced from 240,000 in 1990 to 150,000 in 1997, the social-security system was reformed in 1996 and taxes were increased. Further fiscal measures were attached to IMF stand-by credits approved in January 1999 and May 2000, but with the economy in decline the fiscal deficit increased rapidly to 4.3% of GDP in 2001. In 2004 the fiscal deficit stood at 2.9% of GDP, following the impressive economic growth recorded in the previous year. The Vázquez administration expressed its commitment to fiscal prudence and macroeconomic equilibriums. As part of an agreement with the IMF for a stand-by loan worth some US $1,110m., formally approved in July 2005, a primary fiscal surplus equivalent to 3.5% of GDP was set as a target for 2005. The IMF agreed additional disbursements in September 2005 ($44.4m.) and in January and March 2006 ($44.3m. and $123.6m., respectively). Between 2005 and 2009 the fiscal deficit remained below 2% of GDP, with a balanced budget in 2007 and a maximum deficit of 1.9% of GDP in 2009.

During the 1990s successive governments made considerable efforts to counter inflation, which had risen as high as 112.5% in 1990. The rate was brought down to 44.7% in 1994, mainly through the use of exchange controls and public sector wage restraints. In 1993 the peso uruguayo replaced the peso nuevo at the rate of one to 1,000. The currency entered a floating exchange-rate system, supervised by the Government at a monthly devaluation rate of approximately 1%. The inflation rate continued to decline, to 4.4% in 2001, assisted by the recession in Brazil and Argentina. In the wake of the financial crisis, consumer prices rose rapidly, averaging 13.9% in 2002 and 19.4% in 2003. However, they increased at a more moderate 9.2% in 2004 and 4.9% in 2005. Inflation rose again to 6.4% in 2006, 8.5% in 2007 and 9.2% in 2008 before decreasing back to 5.9% in 2009.

The Uruguayan economy experienced serious difficulties following the Argentine default of January 2002. Argentine citizens had long sought to insure against the chronic financial instability of their own country by holding substantial assets in Uruguayan banks. In May the Argentine Government drastically restricted monthly withdrawals from Argentine banks, precipitating a run on Uruguay's banking sector. On 19 July the Uruguayan Government floated the peso, increasing pressure on the banks, and 10 days later closed all banks for four days and suspended four of them (including the two already under its administration); national reserves had declined to US $655m., from $3,000m. in January. During the bank closure legislation was approved to prevent customers from accessing long-term foreign-exchange deposits at the two state banks for periods ranging from one to three years. The banks reopened with the assistance of an emergency loan of $1,500m. from the US Administration, which also facilitated the disbursement of IMF and other international funds. By the end of 2005 total international reserves were estimated at $3,078m., compared with $772m. at the end of 2002. Reserves continued to grow, as economic expansion attracted high levels of foreign investment. In December 2009 foreign reserves reached a record $8,000m.

The effective devaluation of the peso in 2002 dramatically affected the Government's economic targets, particularly on the national debt, and for several months it was anticipated that the country might be obliged to default. Before the flotation the exchange rate had been 17 pesos to the US dollar, and the rate decreased to 35 pesos before stabilizing at around 28 pesos. In December 2002 Uruguay failed to meet IMF requirements; the Fund expressed particular concern at the continuing uncertainty regarding the four suspended banks. The two sides held further discussions to allow for the release of US $3,000m. in IMF funding. The IMF agreed a plan in February 2003, which included a commitment from the Government to implement banking reforms and restructure at least part of the debt. In March, in compliance with IMF demands, a new state-owned bank (Nuevo Banco Comercial—NBC) was created from the merger of three of the suspended banks. (The NBC was privatized in mid-2006.) In many respects, the economy began to recover faster than anticipated, prompting the IMF to revise its forecasts favourably following a team visit in June 2003. The improvement in Uruguay's economic and financial situation was demonstrated by the Government's announcement in November 2006 of early repayment of all outstanding obligations with the IMF, as well as the cancellation of the stand-by arrangement, which extended until 2008. In January 2007 Uruguay was upgraded by credit rating agency Moody's from B3 to B1 on the basis of improvements in its fiscal status and the reduction in its debt ratio; in May another credit rating agency, Standard & Poor's, confirmed that it considered Uruguay's long-term B+ rating to be 'positive' rather than 'stable'. At mid-July 2010 one US dollar was equivalent to 21.3 Uruguayan pesos.

In March 2009 Uruguay was included in the Organisation for Economic Co-operation and Development (OECD) blacklist of tax havens that had not agreed to respect international standards, alongside Costa Rica, Malaysia and the Philippines. The Government promptly endorsed OECD's standards and in April was moved to the so-called 'grey list' of territories that had committed to but not yet fully implemented the agreed standards of transparency measures.

DEBT

Uruguay's total foreign debt rose from US $2,156m. in 1981 to $4,279m. by the end of 1987; nearly 90% of it was publicly held. A series of agreements with creditors reduced interest payments, and by 1990 the total debt had been reduced to $3,707m. By 1997 the country's debt profile had improved sufficiently for it to be accorded an investment-grade rating. The picture changed drastically in 2002. The investment-grade rating was forfeited in February, and the flotation of the peso increased the debt from $8,500m. in July to $10,000m. in August. In 2004 the total reached $12,376m. ($7,251m. of which was long-term public debt), and debt payments made during that year amounted to some $1,543m. In relation to GDP, the debt rose from the equivalent of 38% in 1998 to some 90% in 2002 and 2003. In May 2003 the Government reached a debt-exchange agreement on about one-half of the current debt, with a grace period of up to five years. Although the external debt increased in nominal terms in 2005, in relation to GDP it declined to the equivalent of 78.8%, primarily as a result of strong economic growth and exchange-rate appreciation. In 2006–07 all IMF indebtedness was replaced by longer-tenured capital market debt and additional debt swaps made to take advantage of market conditions. As a result, the debt/GDP ratio of the non-financial public sector declined to 63%, although it rose again slightly, to 67%, in 2007. According to preliminary figures, the external debt stood at $13,435m. at the end of December 2009, up from $12,393m. in 2008.

FOREIGN TRADE AND THE BALANCE OF PAYMENTS

Exports of goods (free on board) in 2009 amounted to US $5,385,509m. The principal exports were food and live animals, and basic manufactures. The main export partners in that year were Brazil (20.4%), Argentina (6.4%), China (4.3%) Venezuela (3.5%) and the USA (3.3%). Imports of goods were worth $6,529,291m. The principal goods imported were machinery and transport equipment, mineral fuels, and chemicals and related products. The main import partners were Brazil (23.2%), Argentina (22.1%), Venezuela (11.4%), China (9.7%), the USA (7.4%) and Russia (3.5%).

Uruguay's traditional exports were meat, wool and other unprocessed animal products, which, until the mid-1970s, provided about 80% of the country's total export earnings. By the 1990s that proportion had contracted to 20%–25%, although these primary commodities were still crucial to overall export performance. Non-traditional exports include dairy products, textiles, leather goods, fish, wheat, soya beans and rice, and by the 1990s tourism had also become a major contributor. Despite this growth, the trade balance, which had recorded surpluses in 1990 and 1991, registered a deficit in the rest of the 1990s, chiefly because of rising imports of capital goods. In 1999 the imbalance increased to US $897m., largely as a result of the Brazilian devaluation; lower demand in Brazil helped to reduce exports by 24%, while imports declined by only 14%. In 2000 the trade deficit reached $927m., but there was a major change with the recession of 2002: a sharp reduction in imports resulted in a visible trade surplus of $48.3m. Exports of goods and services increased by an average of just over 8% and imports by 8.7% between 2005 and 2009. The higher growth of imports was a result of the demand for capital goods, strong domestic consumption and rising oil prices. The balance of trade was in deficit between 2006 and 2009 but was offset by surpluses in the services balance. After declining by 9.4% year on year in 2009 because of the international recession, merchandise exports rose by almost 25% in the first four months of 2010.

In the 1990s over 44% of Uruguay's exports were purchased by the countries of Mercosur, mainly Argentina and Brazil. Following the currency devaluation of 2002, Uruguay started to diversify its exports, and by 2005 the USA had become the second largest market for Uruguayan goods after Brazil. In the following years the USA declined in significance as a destination for Uruguayan exports, while China, Russia and Venezuela emerged as important markets. In 2009 Uruguay exported 28.4% of its goods to the countries of Mercosur, 15.1% to the EU, 7.5% to the countries of the North American Free Trade Agreement (NAFTA—comprising Canada, Mexico and the USA) and 8.5% to Asian markets. However, the countries of Mercosur were still the main source of imports, with Argentina and Brazil accounting for 25.2% and 21.5% of imports, respectively.

From 1992 the current account of the balance of payments stayed in deficit as a result of the deteriorating trade balance, rising to US $566.2m. in 2000, before declining to $487.7m. in 2001. The balance regained a surplus (of $322.2m.) in 2002, equivalent to 2.1% of GDP. This surplus was reduced to $3.1m. in 2004 and rose slightly, to $24.3m., in 2005. However, owing to the sharp deterioration in the trade balance, a current account deficit of $369.2m. was recorded in 2006; in the following year the deficit decreased to $220m., but it rose again to a record $1,510m. in 2008. In 2009 the steep decline in imports resulted in the first balance of payments surplus, of $253m., in four years. Current account deficits were offset by surpluses in the capital account.

MERCOSUR

Argentina, Brazil, Paraguay and Uruguay signed the Treaty of Asunción in March 1991, forming a regional common market, Mercosur, with its headquarters in Montevideo, which came into effect on 1 January 1995. (Venezuela joined in mid-2006, although ratification of that country's membership had not been completed by mid-2010.) In preparation for the implementation of Mercosur, Uruguay continued to liberalize its trade, reducing its three-tier tariffs in March 1992 and again in January 1993. The country generally recorded a trade deficit within Mercosur, and closer ties increased Uruguay's vulnerability to economic events in the other member countries, notably the Argentine economic crises in 1995 and 2001, austerity measures in Brazil in 1996, and the Brazilian devaluation in January 1999. However, membership of the common market did bring economic advantages through the presence of the Mercosur secretariat in Uruguay, reduced tariffs and interest in investment from a number of multinational companies. By the end of the 1990s most duties between the member countries had been eliminated and a common external tariff had been established for trade outside Mercosur. However, by the time of the Mercosur Heads of State Summit in December 2000 there were evident strains within the organization, which were not addressed effectively. In June 2005 the Uruguayan Minister of Economy and Finance, Danilo Astori, expressed grave concerns that progress in free trade and customs union within Mercosur was being reversed and that macroeconomic co-ordination had been extremely poor.

At a meeting of the Uruguay-US Joint Commission of Trade and Investment in October 2006 the two countries agreed to start negotiations towards a bilateral agreement to strengthen their trading relations. In January 2007 a Trade and Investment Framework Agreement (TIFA) was signed in Montevideo, which established a Uruguay-US Council on Trade and Investment and detailed a work programme. In October 2008 two bilateral TIFA protocols were signed to further trade facilitation.

TOURISM

Tourism and financial services had become the major contributors to the country's balance of payments by the mid-1990s, with tourism revenues outstripping receipts from exports of wool and meat. Uruguay's principal attractions for tourists are the fashionable resort of Punta del Este and the chain of beaches between it and Montevideo. The sector expanded considerably in the 1980s, with the number of summer-season visitors rising from just over 316,000 in 1980/81, to nearly 690,000 in 1990/91. Although the 1990s saw an increase in visitors from other neighbouring countries, and also the USA and Europe, in 2003 visitors from Argentina still accounted for 57% of total arrivals. The recession in Argentina and Brazil severely affected tourism receipts from 1999; in January 2002 the number of Argentine tourists in Punta del Este was estimated at only 10% of its usual level, and this downward trend continued. The total number of visitors declined steadily, from 2.3m. in 1998 to 1.4m. in 2002. Thereafter, however, a recovery in tourist numbers was experienced, with 1.9m. visitors in 2004. Receipts from tourism also began to increase, from US $409m. in 2002 to $494m. in 2004.

It was estimated that in the 2005/06 summer season there was a 12% decline in the number of visitors from Argentina, primarily as a result of the bridge blockades by Argentines protesting against the construction of the new pulp mills (see above). However, arrivals from Brazil rose considerably between 2003 and 2006 owing to the strength of the real, and in 2006 receipts from tourism were valued at US $597m. The Government announced a Social Tourism Plan in 2006, with the aim of encouraging domestic tourism; agreements were also signed with Argentina and Brazil to promote tourism within the region. Also in 2006 Uruguay was granted Approved Destination Status by China. In 2008 Uruguay received 2,242,278 tourists, a 15% year-on-year increase. Argentine tourists represented 52.4% of total arrivals, compared with 65% in 1998, while Brazilian visitors comprised 14.9%. There was also a significant increase in the number of tourists from the USA and Europe. Receipts from tourism rose steadily, exceeding $1,000m. in 2008.

THE ENVIRONMENT

By the mid-1990s certain recreational areas in Montevideo were severely damaged by industrial pollution from meat-processing and tannery plants in the Miguelete river. There was also concern over the possible consequences of a proposed five-nation (the Mercosur countries and Bolivia) scheme to dredge a waterway to allow large shipping up the River Plate Estuary into the interior as far as the Bolivian border. In December 2000 a Brazilian judge suspended licences for dredging and construction projects along the waterway out of concern for wildlife in the Pantanal, a 140,000 sq km area in western Brazil. A petroleum spill, which occurred 20 km off the coast of the resort of Punta del Este in February 1998, polluted not only the beach, but also affected local seal and sea-lion colonies. The oil leak halted the harvesting of mussels, which accounted for a major part of the country's shellfish catch. Like other Latin American countries, Uruguay suffered from abnormal weather conditions caused by El Niño in 1997–98, with severe flooding in the west of the country, and considerable damage to the rice crop. In mid-2003 Uruguay, Brazil, Argentina and Paraguay began work on an agreement covering the future usage and protection of the Guaraní aquifer. Fear that effluent from the proposed pulp mills on the Uruguay river would pollute both the river and the River Plate estuary was a major factor in Argentine hostility to the proposed development, although subsequent studies indicated that no significant damage had been caused.

In early 2007 the Government announced the creation of seven 'protected areas' (with additional areas to follow) under the Sistema Nacional de Areas Protegidas (National System of Protected Areas) to safeguard biological diversity and natural resources in the country. These would include the sparsely populated Cabo Polonio in Rocha, well known for its sand dunes and sea-lion colonies.

Like other smaller agricultural countries, Uruguay is vulnerable to abnormal weather conditions. In August 2005 an unpredicted wind and rain storm struck the southern and eastern parts of the country, where 70% of the population lives, destroying infrastructure in the capital, Montevideo, and in the departments of Canelones, San José, Colonia and Maldonado. Hurricane force winds reached 175 km per hour, and, according to the UN Office for the Co-ordination of Humanitarian Affairs (OCHA), eight people were killed, thousands of homes lost their roofs, nearly 1,000 families had no access to drinking water, and approximately 20,000 households had no electricity and telephone services.

In early May 2007, in the worst flooding for half a century, some 12,000 people in and around Durazno and Mercedes in central Uruguay were driven from their homes for several days by heavy rains and overflowing rivers. According to OCHA, most schools in seven of the 19 departments were closed, electricity and phone lines were disrupted temporarily, and some 30,000 people were left without access to clean drinking water. In 2008–09 a prolonged drought led to severe losses in the agricultural sector, and the decline in water volumes in the Uruguay and Rio Negro rivers resulted in decreased output from the hydroelectric plants that provided most of the country's power. In June 2008 the collision of two ships near Montevideo harbour created a 21-km oil spill that threatened Uruguay's coastline and beaches.

CONCLUSION

The economy remains vulnerable to the fluctuations in the price of crude petroleum on the world market and also to the misfortunes of neighbouring countries, as exemplified by the ramifications for Uruguay of the economic crises in Brazil and Argentina, notably in 2002. Indeed, the recovery of the economy since mid-2003 has been fuelled by an increase in trade with Brazil and Argentina, and by higher international prices for beef and dairy products, aided also by a boom in agricultural production. In recent years the Government has promoted the diversification of the country's exports, and also sought to attract alternative trading partners in order to reduce dependence on Argentina and Brazil.

Although in March 2005 international financial markets reacted with caution to the inauguration of the new left-wing Encuentro Progresista—Frente Amplio—Nueva Mayoría Government, headed by Tabaré Vázquez, the appointment of orthodox economist Danilo Astori as Minister of Economy and Finance, and commitments to structural reform, low inflation and fiscal prudence, proved reassuring. In July the IMF formally agreed a three-year stand-by arrangement worth US $1,110m., contingent on the successful continuation of reforms, including the rationalization of the public sector and of government spending, liberalization of the banking sector, continuation of the privatization programme, and the reduction of the national debt (to less than an equivalent of 60% of GDP) by 2009. Certain reforms, including those regarding fiscal prudence and privatization, met with resistance from within the ruling coalition. The Plan de Atención Nacional de Emergencia Social, an ambitious programme of social spending with the aim of reducing poverty in the country, was launched in March 2005; it was financed partly through funds derived from sustained economic growth, and also through greater foreign investment and a radical reform of the taxation system. Between 2004 and 2008 indigence halved, while the level of poverty decreased from 31.9% to 21.7%. Meanwhile, a programme to give each schoolchild between the ages of six and 12 a laptop computer was launched in late 2007. By June 2009 the XO laptops (at a cost of just $100 each) were in use in more than 1,000 schools; it was hoped that a total of 300,000 such laptops would be in use by the end of that year. New tax legislation entered into force on 1 July 2007; among other measures, it introduced a personal income tax, reduced the rate of corporation tax to 25%, and lowered both the minimum and maximum general rates of value-added tax (VAT). Other provisions were specifically aimed at encouraging inward foreign investment.

Strong rates of economic growth were recorded in 2005–08 (6.6%, 4.6%, 7.6% and 8.9%, respectively). Foreign investment rose by 25% in 2008, with foreign reserves totalling $6,200m., double their pre-crisis level. Tourism receipts rose significantly, as did exports, not least because of operations commencing at the Botnia paper mill. However, inflation also increased, from less than 4% in 2005 to 9.2% in 2008 (and remained high, at 5.9%, in 2009), in part the result of high commodity prices. Record low rainfall in 2007 and 2008 necessitated the use of fossil fuel power generation in order to supplement hydroelectric energy and also had a negative impact on agricultural production. GDP growth slowed considerably in 2009, to 2.9%, primarily as a result of the international financial crisis; merchandise exports decreased by 9.4% and imports by 24.1%. However, after a contraction in the first quarter of 2009, GDP growth resumed in the second quarter and accelerated in the second half of the year. All economic sectors, with the exception of manufacturing, registered positive growth, with transport and communications and water production and energy generation demonstrating rapid expansion (the latter largely due to the growth in hydroelectric generation as a result of the end of the drought). Public sector demand was the main source of growth, with a rise in public spending of 9.5% over the year. In contrast, private consumption grew by just 1.5% and gross fixed capital formation by the private sector decreased by over 10%. Sustained by the growth in public spending, the investment rate declined by just 1%, to 19.1%, compared with 2008. The economic recovery continued in the first quarter of 2010, with an 8.9% year-on-year increase in GDP prompted by domestic demand, which grew by 11% in seasonally adjusted terms. Economic growth was expected to reach between 5.5% and 6% in 2010.

The new FA Government of President Mujica, which took office in March 2010, largely continued the orthodox economic policies of the previous administration. Mujica identified a technologically advanced agricultural sector, tourism and regional logistics as the country's strategic development sectors, with infrastructure, particularly railways, ports and telecommunications, energy and social housing as the main investment priorities. In the short term, the Government's attention was focused on restraining the growth in salaries and public spending to avoid overheating the economy and increasing the budgetary primary surplus to reduce the public debt, which, after declining in the first four years of the Vázquez administration, had risen again in 2009.

Statistical Survey

Sources (unless otherwise stated): Instituto Nacional de Estadística, Río Negro 1520, 11100 Montevideo; tel. (2) 9027303; internet www.ine.gub.uy; Banco Central del Uruguay, Avda Juan P. Fabini, esq. Florida 777, Casilla 1467, 11100 Montevideo; tel. (2) 9085629; fax (2) 9021634; e-mail info@bcu.gub.uy; internet www.bcu.gub.uy; Cámara Nacional de Comercio y Servicios del Uruguay, Edif. Bolsa de Comercio, Rincón 454, 2°, Casilla 1000, 11000 Montevideo; tel. (2) 9161277; fax (2) 9161243; e-mail info@cncs.com.uy; internet www.cncs.com.uy.

Area and Population

AREA, POPULATION AND DENSITY

Area (sq km)	
Land area	175,016
Inland water	1,199
Total	176,215*
Population (census results)†	
22 May 1996	3,163,763
May–July 2004	
Males	1,565,533
Females	1,675,470
Total	3,241,003
Population (official estimates at mid-year)	
2008	3,334,052
2009	3,344,938
2010	3,356,584
Density (per sq km) at mid-2010	19.2

* 68,037 sq miles.

† Excluding adjustment for underenumeration.

POPULATION BY AGE AND SEX

(official estimates at mid-2010)

	Males	Females	Total
0–14	386,912	370,067	756,979
15–64	1,054,499	1,088,602	2,143,101
65 and over	180,117	276,387	456,504
Total	1,621,528	1,735,056	3,356,584

DEPARTMENTS

(population estimates at mid-2010)

	Area (sq km)	Population	Density (per sq km)	Capital
Artigas	11,928	79,270	6.6	Artigas
Canelones	4,536	525,980	116.0	Canelones
Cerro Largo	13,648	90,883	6.7	Melo
Colonia	6,106	120,894	19.8	Colonia del Sacramento
Durazno	11,643	62,155	5.3	Durazno
Flores	5,144	25,726	5.0	Trinidad
Florida	10,417	70,811	6.8	Florida
Lavalleja	10,016	61,994	6.2	Minas
Maldonado	4,793	152,523	31.8	Maldonado
Montevideo	530	1,336,878	2,522.4	Montevideo
Paysandú	13,922	116,387	8.4	Paysandú
Río Negro	9,282	56,513	6.1	Fray Bentos
Rivera	9,370	112,084	12.0	Rivera
Rocha	10,551	70,374	6.7	Rocha
Salto	14,163	128,669	9.1	Salto
San José	4,992	110,714	22.2	San José de Mayo
Soriano	9,008	88,449	9.8	Mercedes
Tacuarembó	15,438	96,783	6.3	Tacuarembó
Treinta y Tres	9,529	49,497	5.2	Treinta y Tres
Total	175,016*	3,356,584	19.2	

* Land area only.

PRINCIPAL TOWNS

(population at 22 May 1996 census)

Montevideo (capital)	1,378,707	Mercedes	50,800
Salto	93,420	Maldonado	50,420
Paysandú	84,160	Melo	47,160
Las Piedras	66,100	Tacuarembó	42,580
Rivera	63,370		

Mid-2010 ('000, incl. suburbs, UN estimate): Montevideo 1,635 (Source: UN, *World Urbanization Prospects: The 2009 Revision*).

BIRTHS, MARRIAGES AND DEATHS*

	Registered live births		Registered marriages		Registered deaths	
	Number	Rate (per 1,000)	Number	Rate (per 1,000)	Number	Rate (per 1,000)
2001	51,959	15.7	13,988	4.2	31,228	9.4
2002	51,953	15.7	14,073	4.3	31,628	9.6
2003	50,631	15.3	14,147	4.3	32,587	9.9
2004	50,052	15.2	13,123	4.0	32,222	9.8
2005	46,944†	14.2†	13,075	4.0	32,319†	9.8†
2006	47,410†	14.2†	12,415	3.7	31,056†	9.4†
2007	47,373	14.3	12,771	3.8	33,706†	10.3†
2008	47,484	14.2	12,180	3.7	31,363†	9.4†

* Data are tabulated by year of registration rather than by year of occurrence and have not been adjusted to take account of the most recent census.
† Preliminary.

Life expectancy (years at birth, WHO estimates): 75 (males 72; females 79) in 2008 (Source: WHO, *World Health Statistics*).

ECONOMICALLY ACTIVE POPULATION
(ISIC major divisions, '000 persons aged 14 years and over, urban areas)

	2001	2002	2003
Agriculture, hunting, forestry and fishing	45.4	43.7	46.9
Mining and quarrying	1.3	1.2	1.2
Manufacturing (incl. electricity, gas and water)	167.1	154.2	151.1
Construction	87.9	77.4	69.6
Trade, restaurants, hotels and repair of vehicles and household goods	240.8	228.9	225.4
Transport, storage and communications	66.8	62.4	61.1
Financing, insurance, real estate and business services	97.4	96.5	91.0
Public administration and defence, compulsory social security	85.1	86.9	91.2
Education	57.2	62.2	61.6
Health and social work	72.5	76.7	76.7
Community, social and personal services	56.2	52.2	54.8
Private households with employed persons	98.5	96.0	100.9
Sub-total	—	—	1,031.7
Activities not adequately defined	—	—	0.3
Total employed	1,076.2	1,038.3	1,032.0
Males	617.7	597.9	589.7
Females	458.5	440.4	442.3
Unemployed	193.2	211.3	208.5
Total labour force	1,269.4	1,250.1	1,240.5

Source: ILO.

2007 ('000 persons aged 14 years and over, estimates): Total employed 1,482; Unemployed 149; Total labour force 1,631 (males 913, females 718).

Mid-2010 ('000, estimates): Agriculture, etc. 186; Total labour force 1,654 (Source: FAO).

Health and Welfare

KEY INDICATORS

Total fertility rate (children per woman, 2008)	2.1
Under-5 mortality rate (per 1,000 live births, 2008)	16
HIV/AIDS (% of persons aged 15–49, 2007)	0.6
Physicians (per 1,000 head, 2002)	3.7
Hospital beds (per 1,000 head, 2006)	2.9
Health expenditure (2007): US $ per head (PPP)	916
Health expenditure (2007): % of GDP	8.0
Health expenditure (2007): public (% of total)	74.0
Total carbon dioxide emissions ('000 metric tons, 2006)	6,859.0
Carbon dioxide emissions per head (metric tons, 2006)	2.1
Human Development Index (2007): ranking	50
Human Development Index (2007): value	0.865

For sources and definitions, see explanatory note on p. vi.

Agriculture

PRINCIPAL CROPS
('000 metric tons)

	2006	2007	2008
Wheat	611.2	697.1	1,288.0
Rice, paddy	1,292.4	1,145.7	1,330.0
Barley	432.1	310.2	405.5
Maize	205.0	337.8	334.7
Oats	42.9	21.1	19.0
Sorghum	61.3	162.8	151.2
Potatoes	148.0	118.4	106.6
Sweet potatoes	68.0*	70.0*	22.0
Sugar cane	144.5	293.2	334.1
Sunflower seed	80.6	43.1	54.2
Tomatoes	46.1	41.5	39.8
Onions, dry	27.8	40.0	19.6
Carrots and turnips	27.2	23.9	24.9
Oranges	138.3	186.3	128.9
Tangerines, mandarins, clementines and satsumas	88.2	117.7	88.5
Lemons and limes	42.9	37.7	40.0
Apples	61.3	66.9	51.3
Pears	17.7	18.7	15.8
Peaches and nectarines	17.3	17.6	18.6
Grapes	130.2	133.0	112.9

* FAO estimate.

Aggregate production ('000 metric tons, may include official, semi-official or estimated data): Total cereals 2,647.7 in 2006, 2,677.5 in 2007, 3,531.4 in 2008; Total fruits (excl. melons) 517.5 in 2006, 595.3 in 2007, 467.9 in 2008; Total vegetables (incl. melons) 188.1 in 2006, 179.7 in 2007, 162.2 in 2008.

Source: FAO.

LIVESTOCK
('000 head, year ending September)

	2006	2007	2008*
Cattle	12,437	12,368	12,368
Sheep	11,087	10,323	10,323
Pigs	240	245	243
Horses	525	427	427
Chickens*	14,000	14,000	16,000

* FAO estimates.

Source: FAO.

LIVESTOCK PRODUCTS
('000 metric tons)

	2006	2007	2008
Cattle meat*	600.0	560.0	588.0
Sheep meat†	31.0	27.0	27.0
Pig meat	18.5	21.1	20.9
Chicken meat†	60.3	50.1	75.3
Cows' milk	1,620.0	1,576.0	1,576.0†
Hen eggs*	42.3	43.6	53.5
Wool, greasy	46.7	45.6	45.0†

* Unofficial figures.
† FAO estimate(s).

Source: FAO.

Forestry

ROUNDWOOD REMOVALS
('000 cubic metres, excl. bark)

	2006	2007	2008
Sawlogs and veneer logs	734	1,168	1,150
Pulpwood	3,497	3,929	6,080
Other industrial wood	23	14	14
Fuel wood	2,111	2,062	2,210
Total	6,365	7,173	9,454

Source: FAO.

SAWNWOOD PRODUCTION
('000 cubic metres, incl. railway sleepers)

	2006	2007	2008
Coniferous (softwood)	104	109	105
Broadleaved (hardwood)	189	199	179
Total	293	308	284

Source: FAO.

Fishing

('000 metric tons, live weight)

	2006	2007	2008
Capture	134.0	108.7	110.7
Argentine hake	31.2	30.6	34.1
Striped weakfish	10.0	8.9	11.2
Whitemouth croaker	28.9	27.7	28.1
Argentine anchovy	12.9	n.a.	n.a.
Castaneta	3.9	1.0	4.4
Rays, stingrays and mantas	2.8	3.6	1.9
Argentine shortfin squid	16.3	15.9	10.9
Aquaculture	0.0	0.0	0.0
Total catch	134.0	108.8	110.7

Note: Figures exclude aquatic mammals, recorded by number rather than by weight. The number of South American fur seals and sea lions caught was: 35 in 2006; 88 in 2007; 63 in 2008.

Source: FAO.

Mining

('000 metric tons, unless otherwise indicated)

	2006	2007	2008
Gold (kg)	3,000	2,820	2,182
Gypsum*	1,150	1,150	1,150
Feldspar (metric tons)	2,470	2,500	2,500

* Estimates.

Source: US Geological Survey.

Industry

SELECTED PRODUCTS
('000 metric tons unless otherwise indicated)

	2005	2006	2007
Raw sugar*	6	6	6
Wine	89.2	95.9	94.0
Motor spirit (petrol) ('000 barrels)†	1,830	1,850	1,850
Kerosene ('000 barrels)†	67	100	100
Distillate fuel oils ('000 barrels)†	8,476	8,500	8,500
Residual fuel oils ('000 barrels)†	3,650	3,650	3,650
Cement (hydraulic)†	620	620	620
Electric energy (million kWh)	7,683	5,618	9,424

* Unofficial figures.
† US Geological Survey estimate(s).

Sources: FAO; US Geological Survey; UN Industrial Commodity Statistics Database.

2008 ('000 barrels unless otherwise indicated): Motor spirit (petrol) 1,850; Kerosene 100; Distillate fuel oil 8,500; Residual fuel oils 3,650; Cement (hydraulic) 620,000 metric tons (Source: US Geological Survey).

Finance

CURRENCY AND EXCHANGE RATES

Monetary Units
100 centésimos = 1 peso uruguayo.

Sterling, Dollar and Euro Equivalents (30 April 2010)
£1 sterling = 29.430 pesos;
US $1 = 19.200 pesos;
€1 = 25.565 pesos;
1,000 pesos uruguayos = £33.98 = $52.08 = €39.12.

Average Exchange Rate (pesos per US $)
2007 23.471
2008 20.949
2009 22.568

Note: On 1 March 1993 a new currency, the peso uruguayo (equivalent to 1,000 former new pesos), was introduced.

CENTRAL GOVERNMENT BUDGET*
(million pesos uruguayos)

Revenue	2006	2007	2008
Tax revenue	100,293	113,947	132,986
Taxes on income, profits, etc.	20,448	22,724	33,499
Individual taxes	6,235	9,638	15,780
Corporate taxes	13,694	11,952	5,867
Taxes on property	7,951	8,276	8,941
Domestic taxes on goods and services	65,804	75,868	82,010
General sales, take-over or value-added tax	51,749	61,119	69,578
Taxes on international trade and transactions	2,524	3,275	4,182
Taxes on leisure activities	50	52	59
Other taxes and rates	3,516	3,752	4,295
Non-tax revenue	7,462	8,347	7,240
Transfers	3,318	3,700	4,368
Other income	248	938	1,891
Total	111,321	126,932	146,485

Expenditure	2004	2005	2006
General public services	23,204	25,519	28,230
Government administration	13,444	15,058	16,290
Defence	4,376	4,660	5,187
Public order and safety	5,385	5,801	6,753
Special and community services	37,148	38,747	58,271
Education	11,873	12,573	14,392
Health	6,521	7,135	8,654
Social security and welfare	16,817	17,109	32,375
Housing and community amenities	1,259	1,371	2,029
Recreational, cultural and religious affairs	679	559	821
Economic affairs and services	3,353	5,931	6,435
Fuel and energy	186	179	194
Agriculture, fishing, forestry and hunting	1,421	2,033	1,584
Mining and mineral resources	253	273	275
Transport and communications	2,530	2,728	3,725
Other economic services	964	718	657
Debt-servicing and governmental transfers	22,805	20,322	24,289
Total	88,510	90,519	117,225

* Figures represent the consolidated accounts of the central Government, which include social security revenue and expenditure.

2007: Total expenditure 133,728.

2008: Total expenditure 155,686.

General government finances (consolidated accounts of general government, million pesos uruguayos, preliminary figures): *Revenue:* Total 173,315 (taxes 157,913) in 2006; total 201,035 (taxes 184,322) in 2007; total 225,173 in 2008. *Expenditure:* Total 180,122 (social security 54,720) in 2006; total 206,193 (social security 59,897) in 2007; total 231,646 in 2008.

INTERNATIONAL RESERVES
(US $ million at 31 December)

	2007	2008	2009
Gold	7	7	9
IMF special drawing rights	—	4	385
Foreign exchange	4,114	6,349	7,644
Total	4,121	6,360	8,038

Source: IMF, *International Financial Statistics*.

MONEY SUPPLY
(million pesos uruguayos at 31 December)

	2007	2008	2009
Currency outside depository corporations	18,892.5	21,406.7	24,306.0
Transferable deposits	71,624.0	98,811.7	97,072.6
Other deposits	125,875.9	163,607.5	155,599.1
Securities other than shares	6,661.0	2,943.3	2,193.1
Broad money	223,053.4	286,769.3	279,170.8

Source: IMF, *International Financial Statistics*.

COST OF LIVING
(Consumer Price Index for Montevideo; base: March 1997 = 100)

	2007	2008	2009
Food and beverages	256.9	292.0	310.0
Housing	251.2	279.2	309.0
Clothing and footwear	161.5	166.3	174.2
Transport and communications	252.4	255.6	260.7
All items (incl. others)	238.5	257.3	275.4

NATIONAL ACCOUNTS
(million pesos uruguayos at current prices, preliminary figures)

Expenditure on the Gross Domestic Product

	2007	2008	2009
Government final consumption expenditure	63,709.7	76,956.7	91,582.8
Private final consumption expenditure	395,765.2	456,349.1	485,285.8
Increase in stocks	4,553.8	16,191.0	−8,349.5
Gross fixed capital formation	104,315.0	132,140.2	135,858.3
Total domestic expenditure	568,343.7	681,637.0	704,377.4
Exports of goods and services	159,784.8	190,486.2	188,353.9
Less Imports of goods and services	165,952.0	218,972.2	181,593.9
GDP in market prices	562,176.5	653,151.0	711,137.4
GDP at constant 2005 prices	476,489.3	517,158.9	531,937.9

Gross Domestic Product by Economic Activity

	2007	2008	2009
Agriculture, hunting and forestry	48,088.3	60,142.4	57,921.6
Fishing and mining	2,780.2	3,275.7	3,187.8
Manufacturing	79,991.1	102,110.7	98,790.7
Electricity, gas and water	18,379.3	3,954.7	10,739.1
Construction	33,970.4	42,248.8	51,850.0
Trade, restaurants and hotels	76,721.5	98,107.1	103,068.6
Transport, storage and communications	44,512.8	51,848.2	53,649.4
Finance and insurance	26,175.1	27,129.1	31,296.6
Real estate and business services	77,507.7	88,581.0	101,735.1
General government services	28,049.9	31,893.5	37,922.1
Other community, social and personal services	65,550.1	78,523.1	91,398.5
Sub-total	501,726.3	587,814.3	641,559.4
Less Financial intermediation services indirectly measured	15,777.2	15,577.6	17,233.0
Gross value added in basic prices	485,949.1	572,236.7	624,326.4
Taxes, less subsidies, on products	76,227.4	80,914.3	86,811.1
GDP in market prices	562,176.5	653,151.0	711,137.4

BALANCE OF PAYMENTS
(US $ million)

	2007	2008	2009
Exports of goods f.o.b.	5,099.9	7,112.3	6,388.9
Imports of goods f.o.b.	–5,647.6	–8,666.6	–6,663.7
Trade balance	–547.7	–1,554.3	–274.7
Exports of services	1,836.6	2,221.5	2,162.3
Imports of services	–1,122.9	–1,416.0	–1,091.3
Balance on goods and services	166.0	–748.8	796.2
Other income received	885.0	753.9	519.2
Other income paid	–1,400.9	–1,380.6	–1,198.5
Balance on goods, services and income	–349.9	–1,375.4	117.0
Current transfers received	164.6	187.7	177.6
Current transfers paid	–27.1	–37.3	–35.8
Current balance	–212.4	–1,225.0	258.8
Capital account (net)	3.7	0.2	—
Direct investment abroad	–89.4	–0.7	–13.0
Direct investment from abroad	1,320.8	2,205.1	1,138.8
Portfolio investment assets	195.2	–52.3	–707.4
Portfolio investment liabilities	995.3	–519.0	–30.5
Other investment assets	–2,027.5	179.9	–832.4
Other investment liabilities	1,143.1	1,470.5	2,353.3
Net errors and omissions	–283.5	173.5	–580.7
Overall balance	1,005.4	2,232.3	1,586.9

Source: IMF, *International Financial Statistics*.

External Trade

PRINCIPAL COMMODITIES
(US $ million)

Imports c.i.f.	2006	2007	2008*
Food industry products; beverages, tobacco, alcohol and vinegars	223.6	257.0	373.2
Mineral products	1,366.9	1,303.5	2,820.2
Mineral fuels, petroleum and petroleum products	1,344.2	1,274.5	2,769.0
Chemicals and related products	606.5	841.0	1,171.7
Fertilizers	98.4	215.9	304.8
Plastics and plastic products; rubber and manufactures thereof	379.0	458.6	575.7
Plastics and plastic products	284.3	349.2	424.3
Textiles and textile manufactures	200.3	235.9	312.5
Base metals and metal manufactures	250.1	281.4	409.5
Machinery and appliances, electrical materials, audio-visual recording and reproducing apparatus	763.5	967.2	1,457.6
Nuclear reactors, boilers, etc. machinery and apparatus	388.6	535.7	867.3
Transport equipment	354.6	457.9	882.9
Automobiles, tractors, cycles, parts and accessories	347.3	453.4	711.0
Total (incl. others)	4,806.1	5,627.7	9,069.4

Exports f.o.b.	2006	2007*	2008*
Live animals and animal products	1,511.0	1,492.2	2,110.6
Chilled beef products	257.5	229.1	319.0
Frozen beef products	678.1	566.8	877.4
Fish, crustaceans, molluscs and preparations thereof	153.6	171.2	192.2
Dairy products and birds' eggs	273.2	353.1	455.4
Crops and vegetable products	548.4	747.0	1,229.5
Rice	218.0	279.8	444.3
Food industry products; beverages, tobacco, alcohol and vinegars	140.1	154.6	143.7
Mineral products	153.3	208.2	210.1
Chemicals and related products	181.8	236.4	320.3
Plastics and plastic products; rubber and manufactures thereof	203.5	246.7	301.7
Pelts, skins, hides and products thereof	342.1	339.9	289.1
Hides and leathers	305.5	305.0	258.4
Wood, charcoal, cork, etc. and products thereof	190.1	247.4	421.6
Textiles and textile manufactures	272.8	306.8	289.6
Total (incl. others)	3,989.3	4,514.4	5,948.9

* Preliminary.

PRINCIPAL TRADING PARTNERS
(US $ million)

Imports c.i.f.	2006	2007	2008
Argentina	1,103.3	1,254.8	1,431.2
Brazil	1,084.3	1,314.3	1,584.2
Canada	18.3	19.3	222.9
Chile	71.2	77.3	101.9
China, People's Republic	350.9	540.2	908.3
France (incl. Monaco)	82.2	83.7	102.4
Germany	99.3	112.0	141.6
India	34.9	49.4	74.5
Iran	130.2	1.1	1.3
Italy	81.9	94.0	117.3
Japan	50.4	60.9	88.7
Korea, Republic	55.8	59.8	94.9
Mexico	60.6	83.8	119.5
Nigeria	0.0	0.0	120.0
Russia	43.5	195.6	283.9
Spain	56.0	71.5	94.0
United Kingdom	45.7	42.9	56.0
USA	326.2	413.2	596.7
Venezuela	599.5	637.6	163.0
Total (incl. others)	4,806.1	5,627.7	7,088.6

Exports f.o.b.	2006	2007	2008
Argentina	301.9	441.2	507.0
Brazil	582.5	728.4	986.6
Canada	45.1	72.3	33.0
Chile	165.3	108.0	133.9
China, People's Republic	164.3	161.5	171.5
France (incl. Monaco)	33.2	35.5	34.1
Germany	165.2	205.6	212.5
Iran	51.0	29.6	102.1
Israel	56.6	44.9	83.2
Italy	112.8	101.1	143.8
Japan	43.3	32.5	44.0
Mexico	136.4	207.3	177.5
Netherlands	68.1	94.1	162.7
Paraguay	58.4	76.9	106.9
Russia	224.8	113.3	332.0
Spain	121.0	147.4	240.5
United Kingdom	96.0	120.4	172.4
USA	523.1	493.1	214.2
Venezuela	78.4	98.6	237.2
Total (incl. others)	3,986.0	4,496.0	5,948.9

Transport

RAILWAYS
(traffic)

	2002	2003	2004
Passenger-km (million)	8	11	11
Net ton-km (million)	178	188	297

Source: UN, *Statistical Yearbook*.

ROAD TRAFFIC
(motor vehicles in use at 31 December)

	1995	1996	1997
Passenger cars	464,547	485,109	516,889
Buses and coaches	4,409	4,752	4,984
Lorries and vans	41,417	43,656	45,280
Road tractors	12,511	14,628	15,514
Motorcycles and mopeds	300,850	328,406	359,824

Source: International Road Federation, *World Road Statistics*.

2005: Passenger cars and vans 523,866; Coaches and minibuses 6,990; Lorries and road tractors 77,364; Motorcycles and mopeds 473,967.

2006: Passenger cars and vans 553,204; Coaches and minibuses 7,049; Lorries and road tractors 83,958; Motorcycles and mopeds 536,220.

SHIPPING

Merchant Fleet
(registered at 31 December)

	2006	2007	2008
Number of vessels	123	127	130
Total displacement ('000 grt)	97.4	111.5	108.8

Source: Lloyd's Register-Fairplay, *World Fleet Statistics*.

CIVIL AVIATION
(traffic on scheduled services)

	2004	2005	2006
Kilometres flown (million)	9.3	7.7	7.6
Passenger-km (million)	1,075.9	979.6	940.4
Total ton-km (million)	4.5	4.3	4.2

Source: UN Economic Commission for Latin America and the Caribbean, *Statistical Yearbook*.

Tourism

ARRIVALS BY NATIONALITY*

	2005	2006	2007
Argentina	1,107,514	975,027	908,116
Brazil	197,672	228,353	286,319
Chile	42,154	43,800	43,219
Germany	14,187	14,421	14,923
Italy	15,335	15,334	16,642
Mexico	17,008	16,261	16,747
Paraguay	20,155	21,670	23,888
Peru	12,609	10,975	13,637
Spain	30,214	31,332	33,075
United Kingdom	12,623	15,684	13,310
United States	62,287	62,834	64,933
Total (incl. others)	1,917,049	1,824,340	1,815,281

* Figures refer to arrivals at frontiers of visitors from abroad, including Uruguayan nationals permanently resident elsewhere.

Tourism receipts (US $ million, excl. passenger transport): 598 in 2006; 809 in 2007; 1,042 in 2008 (provisional).

Source: World Tourism Organization.

Communications Media

	2007	2008	2009
Telephones ('000 main lines in use)	965.2	959.3	953.4
Mobile cellular telephones ('000 subscribers)	3,004.3	3,507.8	3,802.0
Internet users ('000)	968	1,340	1,855
Broadband subscribers ('000)	243.5	244.5	n.a.

Personal computers: 450,000 (136.1 per 1,000 persons) in 2005.

Television receivers (2000): 1,770,000 in use.

Radio receivers (1997): 1,970,000 in use.

Book production (1996): 934 titles.

Daily newspapers (1996): 36 (estimated average circulation 950,000).

Sources: UNESCO, *Statistical Yearbook*; UN, *Statistical Yearbook*; International Telecommunication Union.

Education

(2007, unless otherwise indicated)

	Institutions	Teachers	Students
Pre-primary	1,405	3,984	106,878
Primary	2,395	18,884	348,579
Secondary: general	436	25,168*†	213,550
Secondary: vocational	131	n.a.	70,184
University and equivalent institutions*‡	6	7,723	72,100

* Public education only.
† 2003.
‡ 2005.

Students (2008): Pre-primary 109,654; primary 342,498; secondary: vocational 70,110.

Pupil-teacher ratio (primary education, UNESCO estimate): 15.5 in 2006/07 (Source: UNESCO Institute for Statistics).

Adult literacy rate (UNESCO estimates): 98.2% (males 97.8%; females 98.5%) in 2008 (Source: UNESCO Institute for Statistics).

Directory

The Constitution

The Constitution of Uruguay was ratified by plebiscite, on 27 November 1966, when the country voted to return to the presidential form of government after 15 years of 'collegiate' government. The main points of the Constitution, as amended in January 1997, are as follows:

GENERAL PROVISIONS

Uruguay shall have a democratic republican form of government, sovereignty being exercised directly by the Electoral Body in cases of election, by initiative or by referendum, and indirectly by representative powers established by the Constitution, according to the rules set out therein.

There shall be freedom of religion; there is no state religion; property shall be inviolable; there shall be freedom of thought. Anyone may enter Uruguay. There are two forms of citizenship: natural, being persons born in Uruguay or of Uruguayan parents, and legal, being people established in Uruguay with at least three years' residence in the case of those with family, and five years' for those without family. Every citizen has the right and obligation to vote.

LEGISLATURE

Legislative power is vested in the Congreso (Congress or General Assembly), comprising two houses, which may act separately or together according to the dispositions of the Constitution. It elects in joint session the members of the Supreme Court of Justice, of the Electoral Court, Tribunals, Administrative Litigation and the Accounts Tribunal.

Elections for both houses, the President and the Vice-President shall take place every five years on the last Sunday in October; sessions of the Assembly begin on 1 March each year and last until 15 December (15 September in election years, in which case the new Congress takes office on 15 February). Extraordinary sessions can be convened only in case of extreme urgency.

CHAMBER OF REPRESENTATIVES

The Chamber of Representatives has 99 members elected by direct suffrage according to the system of proportional representation, with at least two representatives for each Department. The number of representatives can be altered by law by a two-thirds' majority in both houses. Their term of office is five years and they must be over 25 years of age and be natural citizens or legal citizens with five years' exercise of their citizenship. Representatives have the right to bring accusations against any member of the Government or judiciary for violation of the Constitution or any other serious offence.

SENATE

The Senate comprises 31 members, including the Vice-President, who sits as President of the Senate, and 30 members elected directly by proportional representation on the same lists as the representatives, for a term of five years. They must be natural citizens or legal citizens with seven years' exercise of their rights, and be over 30 years of age. The Senate is responsible for hearing cases brought by the representatives and can deprive a guilty person of a post by a two-thirds' majority.

THE EXECUTIVE

Executive power is exercised by the President and the Council of Ministers. There is a Vice-President, who is also President of the Congress and of the Senate. The President and Vice-President are directly elected by absolute majority, and remain in office for five years. They must be over 35 years of age and be natural citizens.

The Council of Ministers comprises the office holders in the ministries or their deputies, and is responsible for all acts of government and administration. It is presided over by the President of the Republic, who has a vote.

THE JUDICIARY

Judicial power is exercised by the five-member Supreme Court of Justice and by Tribunals and local courts; members of the Supreme Court must be over 40 years of age and be natural citizens, or legal citizens with 10 years' exercise and 25 years' residence, and must be lawyers of 10 years' standing, eight of them in public or fiscal ministry or judicature. Members serve for 10 years and can be re-elected after a break of five years. The Court nominates all other judges and judicial officials.

The Government

HEAD OF STATE

President: José Alberto Mujica Cordano (took office on 1 March 2010).

Vice-President: Danilo Astori (AU).

COUNCIL OF MINISTERS

(July 2010)

A coalition of the Movimiento de Participación Popular (MPP), the Asamblea Uruguay (AU), the Partido Comunista de Uruguay (PCU), the Partido Socialista del Uruguay (PS), the Vertiente Artiguista (VA) and one Independent.

Minister of the Interior: Eduardo Bonomi (MPP).

Minister of Foreign Affairs: Luis Leonardo Almagro Lemes (MPP).

Minister of National Defence: Luís Rosadilla (MPP).

Minister of Social Development: Ana María Vignoli (PCU).

Minister of Economy and Finance: Fernando Lorenzo (AU).

Minister of Industry, Energy and Mining: Roberto Kreimerman (PS).

Minister of Livestock, Agriculture and Fishing: Tabaré Aguerre (Ind.).

Minister of Tourism and Sport: Dr Héctor Lescano (AP).

Minister of Transport and Public Works: Enrique Pintado (AU).

Minister of Labour and Social Security: Eduardo Brenta (VA).

Minister of Education and Culture: Ricardo Ehrlich (MPP).

Minister of Public Health: Daniel Olesker (PS).

Minister of Housing, Territorial Regulation and the Environment: Graciela Muslera (MPP).

Director of the Planning and Budget Office: Gabriel Frugoni (MPP).

Secretary to the Presidency: Alberto Raúl Breccia Guzzo.

Pro-Secretary to the Presidency: Daniel Cánepa.

MINISTRIES

Office of the President: Casa de Gobierno, Plaza Independencia 710, Torre Ejecutiva, 1° y 2°, 11000 Montevideo; tel. (2) 1502647; fax (2) 9171121; e-mail sci@presidencia.gub.uy; internet www.presidencia.gub.uy.

Ministry of Economy and Finance: Colonia 1089, 3°, 11100 Montevideo; tel. (2) 7122910; fax (2) 7122919; e-mail seprimef@mef.gub.uy; internet www.mef.gub.uy.

Ministry of Education and Culture: Reconquista 535, 9°, 11000 Montevideo; tel. (2) 9161174; fax (2) 9161048; e-mail centrodeinformacion@mec.gub.uy; internet www.mec.gub.uy.

Ministry of Foreign Affairs: Palacio Santos, Avda 18 de Julio 1205, 11100 Montevideo; tel. (2) 9021010; fax (2) 9021349; e-mail webmaster@mrree.gub.uy; internet www.mrree.gub.uy.

Ministry of Housing, Territorial Regulation and the Environment: Zabala 1432, esq. 25 de Mayo, 11000 Montevideo; tel. (2) 9170710; fax (2) 9163914; e-mail ministro@mvotma.gub.uy; internet www.mvotma.gub.uy.

Ministry of Industry, Energy and Mining: Paysandú s/n, esq. Avda Libertador Brig. Gral Lavalleja, 4º, Montevideo; tel. (2) 9002600; fax (2) 9021245; e-mail ministro@miem.gub.uy; internet www.miem.gub.uy.

Ministry of the Interior: Mercedes 993, 11100 Montevideo; tel. (2) 9089024; fax (2) 9023142; e-mail secmin@minterior.gub.uy; internet www.minterior.gub.uy.

Ministry of Labour and Social Security: Juncal 1511, 4°, Planta Baja, 11000 Montevideo; tel. (2) 9162681; fax (2) 9162708; e-mail consultas@mtss.gub.uy; internet www.mtss.gub.uy.

Ministry of Livestock, Agriculture and Fishing: Avda Constituyente 1476, 1°, 11200 Montevideo; tel. (2) 4126326; fax (2) 4184051; e-mail ministro@mgap.gub.uy; internet www.mgap.gub.uy.

Ministry of National Defence: Edif. General Artigas, Avda 8 de Octubre 2628, Montevideo; tel. (2) 4872828; fax (2) 4814833; e-mail rrpp.secretaria@mdn.gub.uy; internet www.mdn.gub.uy.

Ministry of Public Health: Avda 18 de Julio 1892, 11100 Montevideo; tel. (2) 4000101; fax (2) 4085360; e-mail comunicaciones@msp.gub.uy; internet www.msp.gub.uy.

Ministry of Social Development: Avda 18 de Julio 1453, esq. Dr Javier Barrios Amorín, 2°, 11200 Montevideo; tel. and fax (2)

4000302; e-mail ministra@mides.gub.uy; internet www.mides.gub.uy.

Ministry of Tourism and Sport: Rambla 25 de Agosto 1825, esq. Yacaré s/n, Montevideo; tel. (2) 1885100; fax (2) 9162487; e-mail webmaster@mintur.gub.uy; internet www.mintur.gub.uy.

Ministry of Transport and Public Works: Rincón 561, 11000 Montevideo; tel. (2) 9160509; fax (2) 9162883; e-mail difusion@mtop.gub.uy; internet www.mtop.gub.uy.

Planning and Budget Office: Plaza Independencia 710, Torre Ejecutivo, 11000 Montevideo; tel. (2) 1503581; fax (2) 2099730; e-mail direccion@opp.gub.uy; internet www.opp.gub.uy.

President and Legislature

PRESIDENT

Election, 25 October and 29 November 2009

Candidate	First round % of vote	Second round % of vote
José Alberto Mujica Cordano (Frente Amplio)	47.96	52.39
Luis Alberto Lacalle de Herrera (Partido Nacional)	29.07	43.51
Pedro Bordaberry Herrán (Partido Colorado)	17.02	—
Pablo Mieres Gómez (Partido Independiente)	2.49	—
Raúl Rodríguez da Silva (Asamblea Popular)	0.67	—
Invalid votes	2.79	4.10
Total	100.00	100.00

CONGRESO

Cámara de Senadores
(Senate)

President: Vice-Pres. DANILO ASTORI.

Election, 25 October 2009

Party	Seats
Frente Amplio	16
Partido Nacional	9
Partido Colorado	5
Total*	30

* An additional seat is reserved for the Vice-President, who sits as President of the Senate.

Cámara de Representantes
(Chamber of Representatives)

President: IVONNE PASSADA.

Election, 25 October 2009

Party	Seats
Frente Amplio	50
Partido Nacional	30
Partido Colorado	17
Partido Independiente	2
Total	99

Election Commission

Corte Electoral: Ituzaingó 1467, Montevideo; tel. (2) 9158950; fax (2) 9165088; e-mail corelect@adinet.com.uy; internet www.corteelectoral.gub.uy; f. 1967; Pres. Dr RONALD HERBERT.

Political Organizations

Alianza Libertadora Nacionalista: Montevideo; extreme right-wing; Leader OSVALDO MARTÍNEZ JAUME.

Asamblea Popular Izquierda Unida: Avda Daniel Fernández Crespo 1910 bis, esq. La Paz, Montevideo; tel. (2) 9290861; internet www.asambleapopular.webcindario.com; f. 2008; extreme left-wing; mems include:

Movimiento de Defensa de los Jubilados: Leader HÉCTOR MORALES.

Movimiento 26 de Marzo: Durazno 1118, 11200 Montevideo; tel. (2) 9023903; e-mail paginaweb@26demarzo.org.uy; internet www.26demarzo.org.uy; f. 1971; socialist; Pres. EDUARDO RUBIO; Sec.-Gen. FERNANDO VÁZQUEZ.

Partido Comunista Revolucionario: e-mail pcruruguay@yahoo.com; internet www.pcr.org.uy; Sec.-Gen. RICARDO COHEN.

Partido Humanista: Avda 18 de Julio 907, local 3 de Galería Caubarrere, Montevideo; tel. 098001969 (mobile); e-mail partidohumanistauy@gmail.com; internet partidohumanistauy.jimdo.com; Leader DANIEL ROCCA.

Frente Amplio (FA): Colonia 1367, 2°, 11100 Montevideo; tel. (2) 9026666; e-mail comunicacion@frenteamplio.org.uy; internet www.frenteamplio.org.uy; f. 1971; left-wing grouping; Pres. JORGE BROVETTO; mems include:

Alianza Progresista 738 (AP): Colonia 1831, Montevideo; tel. and fax (2) 4016365; e-mail a738@adinet.com.uy; internet alianza738.com.uy; f. 1998; left-wing; Leader RODOLFO NIN NOVOA.

Asamblea Uruguay (AU): Carlos Quijano 1273, Montevideo; tel. (2) 9032121; fax (2) 9241147; e-mail info@2121.org.uy; internet www.2121.org.uy; f. 1994; centre-left; Leader DANILO ASTORI.

Frente Izquierda de Liberación (FIDEL): Mercedes 1244, Montevideo; tel. (2) 9087530; e-mail contacto@fidel.com.uy; internet www.fidel.com.uy; f. 1962; socialist; Sec.-Gen. DOREEN IBARRA.

Movimiento de Participación Popular (MPP): Mercedes 1368, 11200 Montevideo; tel. (2) 9088900; fax (2) 9032248; e-mail info@mppuruguay.org.uy; internet www.mpp.org.uy; f. 1989; grouping of left-wing parties incl. MLN—Tupamaros (see below); Leader LUCÍA TOPOLANSKY.

Movimiento de Liberación Nacional (MLN)—Tupamaros: Tristán Narvaja 1578, 11200 Montevideo; tel. (2) 4092298; fax (2) 4099957; e-mail mln@chasque.apc.org; internet www.chasque.net/mlnweb; f. 1962; radical socialist; during 1962–73 the MLN, operating under its popular name of the Tupamaros, conducted a campaign of urban guerrilla warfare until it was defeated by the Armed Forces in late 1973; following the return to civilian rule, in 1985, the MLN announced its decision to abandon its armed struggle; legally recognized in May 1989; Sec.-Gen. JOSÉ ALBERTO MUJICA CORDANO.

Nuevo Espacio: Eduardo Acevedo 1615, 11200 Montevideo; tel. (2) 4026990; fax (2) 4026989; e-mail internacionales@nuevoespacio.org.uy; internet www.nuevoespacio.org.uy; f. 1994; social-democratic; allied to the FA since Dec. 2002; moderate left-wing; Leader RAFAEL MICHELINI; Sec. EDGARDO CARVALHO.

Partido Comunista de Uruguay (PCU): Río Negro 1525, 11100 Montevideo; tel. (2) 9017171; fax (2) 9011050; e-mail comitecentral@webpcu.org; f. 1920; Sec.-Gen. EDUARDO LORIER; c. 42,000 mems.

Partido Socialista del Uruguay (PS): Casa del Pueblo, Soriano 1218, 11100 Montevideo; tel. (2) 9013344; fax (2) 9082548; e-mail info@ps.org.uy; internet www.ps.org.uy; f. 1910; Pres. REINALDO GARGANO; Sec.-Gen. EDUARDO (LALO) FERNÁNDEZ.

Partido por la Victoria del Pueblo (PVP): Mercedes 1469, esq. Tacuarembó, Montevideo; tel. (2) 4020370; e-mail info@pvp.org.uy; internet www.pvp.org.uy; f. 1975 in Buenos Aires, Argentina; left-wing; Sec.-Gen. (vacant); Spokesman ANGEL VERA.

Vertiente Artiguista (VA): San José 1191, 11200 Montevideo; tel. (2) 9000177; e-mail vertient@vertiente.org.uy; internet portal.vertiente.org.uy; f. 1989; left-wing; Leader EDUARDO BRENTA.

Partido Azul Demócrata (PA): Paul Harris 1722, Montevideo; tel. and fax (2) 6016327; e-mail hablacon@partidoazul.s5.com; internet www.partidoazul.s5.com; liberal; f. 1993; Leader Dr ROBERTO CANESSA; Gen. Sec. Ing. ARMANDO VAL.

Partido Colorado: Andrés Martínez Trueba 1271, 11100 Montevideo; tel. (2) 4090180; e-mail info@partidocolorado.com.uy; internet www.partidocolorado.com.uy; f. 1836; Sec.-Gen. PEDRO BORDABERRY; factions include:

Foro Batllista: Col. 1243, 11100 Montevideo; tel. (2) 9030154; e-mail info@forobatllista.com; internet www.forobatllista.com; Leader Dr JULIO MARÍA SANGUINETTI CAIROLO.

Lista 15: Leader JORGE LUIS BATLLE IBÁÑEZ.

Vanguardia Batllista: Casa de Vanguardia, Paysandú 1333, entre Ejido y Curiales, Montevideo; tel. (2) 9027779; e-mail albertoscavarelli@yahoo.com; internet www.scavarelli.com; f. 1999; Leader Dr ALBERTO SCAVARELLI.

Partido Demócrata Cristiano (PDC): Aquiles Lanza 1318 bis, 11100 Montevideo; tel. and fax (2) 9030704; e-mail pdc@chasque.apc

.org; internet www.chasque.apc.org/pdc; f. 1962; fmrly Unión Cívica del Uruguay; allied to the Alianza Progresista since 1999; Pres. Dr Héctor Lescano; Sec.-Gen. Juan A. Roballo.

Partido Independiente: Avda 18 de Julio 2015, Montevideo; tel. (2) 4020120; e-mail info@partidoindependiente.org; internet www.partidoindependiente.org.uy; Leader Pablo Mieres.

Partido Nacional (Blanco): Juan Carlos Gómez 1384, Montevideo; tel. (2) 9163831; fax (2) 9163758; e-mail partidonacional@partidonacional.com.uy; internet www.partidonacional.com.uy; f. 1836; Exec. Pres. Luis Alberto Lacalle de Herrera; Sec.-Gen. Alberto Zumarán; tendencies within the party include:

Alianza Nacional: Avda 18 de Julio 2060, Montevideo; tel. (2) 4022020; e-mail info@alianzanacional.com.uy; internet alianzanacional.com.uy; Leader Jorge Larrañaga.

Concordia Nacional 747: Avda 18 de Julio 2139, esq. Juan Paullier, Montevideo; tel. (2) 4014320; internet www.concordianacional.com.uy.

Consejo Nacional Herrerista: Leader Luis Alberto Lacalle.

Desafío Nacional: Leader Juan Andrés Ramírez.

Línea Nacional de Florida: Leader Arturo Heber.

Partido del Sol: Peatonal Yi 1385, 11000 Montevideo; tel. (2) 9001616; fax (2) 9006739; e-mail partidodelsol@adinet.com.uy; internet www.partidodelsoluruguay.org; ecologist, federal, pacifist; Leader Homero Mieres.

Unión Cívica: Montevideo; tel. (2) 9005535; e-mail info@unioncivica.org; internet www.dreamsmaker.com.uy/trabajos/union-civica; f. 1912; recognized Christian Democrat faction, split from the Partido Demócrata Cristiano in 1980; Leader W. Gerardo Azambuya.

Diplomatic Representation

EMBASSIES IN URUGUAY

Argentina: Cuareim 1470, 11800 Montevideo; tel. (2) 9028166; fax (2) 9028172; e-mail emargrou@adinet.com.uy; internet emb-uruguay.mrecic.gov.ar; Ambassador Miguel Dante Dovena.

Bolivia: Dr Prudencio de Peña 2469, entre Campbell y Ponce, Casilla 11600, 11300 Montevideo; tel. (2) 7083573; fax (2) 7080066; e-mail embouy@adinet.com.uy; Ambassador Salvador Ric Riera.

Brazil: Blvd Artigas 1328, 11300 Montevideo; tel. (2) 7072119; fax (2) 7072086; e-mail montevideu@brasemb.org.uy; internet www.brasil.org.uy; Ambassador José Eduardo Felicio.

Canada: Plaza Independencia 749, Of. 102, 11100 Montevideo; tel. (2) 9022030; fax (2) 9022029; e-mail mvdeo@international.gc.ca; internet www.canadainternational.gc.ca/uruguay; Ambassador Alain Latulippe.

Chile: 25 de Mayo 575, Montevideo; tel. (2) 9164090; fax (2) 9164083; e-mail echileuy@netgate.com.uy; Ambassador Andrés Rebolledo.

China, People's Republic: Miraflores 1508, esq. Pedro Blanes Viale, Carrasco, Casilla 18966, Montevideo; tel. (2) 6016126; fax (2) 6018508; e-mail embchina@adinet.com.uy; internet uy.china-embassy.org; Ambassador Li Zhongliang.

Colombia: Edif. Tupí, Juncal 1305, 18°, esq Buenos Aires, 11000 Montevideo; tel. (2) 9161592; fax (2) 9161594; e-mail embajada@colombia.com.uy; internet www.colombia.com.uy; Ambassador Claudia Turbay Quintero.

Costa Rica: Roque Graseras 740, entre Solano Antuña y Juan María Pérez, Casilla 12242, Montevideo; tel. (2) 7116408; fax (2) 7120872; e-mail embarica@adinet.com.uy; Ambassador Marco Vinicio Vargas Pereira.

Cuba: Cristóbal Echevarriarza 3471, Montevideo; tel. (2) 6232803; fax (2) 6232805; e-mail emcuburu@adinet.com.uy; internet embacu.cubaminrex.cu/uruguay; Ambassador Carmen Zilia Pérez Mazón.

Dominican Republic: Tomás de Tezanos 1186, entre Arturo Prat y Miguel Grau, 11300 Montevideo; tel. (2) 6287766; fax (2) 6289655; e-mail embajadomuruguay@adinet.com.uy; Ambassador Daniel Guerrero Taveras.

Ecuador: Juan María Pérez 2810, Montevideo; tel. (2) 7110448; fax (2) 7102492; e-mail embajadaecuador@netgate.com.uy; Chargé d'affaires a.i. René Fernández.

Egypt: Avda Brasil 2663, 11300 Montevideo; tel. (2) 7096412; fax (2) 7080977; e-mail embassy.montevideo@mfa.gov.eg; Ambassador Mohamed Abou Eldahab.

El Salvador: Arq. Raúl Lerena Acevedo 1453, Punta Gorda, 11300 Montevideo; tel. (2) 6134143; fax (2) 6199473; e-mail embasauy@dedicado.net.uy; Ambassador Vladimiro P Villalta.

France: Avda Uruguay 853, Casilla 290, 11100 Montevideo; tel. (2) 7050000; fax (2) 7050110; e-mail ambafranceuruguay@gmail.com; internet www.ambafranceuruguay.org; Ambassador Jean-Christophe Potton.

Germany: La Cumparsita 1435, Plaza Alemania, Casilla 20014, 11200 Montevideo; tel. (2) 9025222; fax (2) 9023422; e-mail info@montevideo.diplo.de; internet www.montevideo.diplo.de; Ambassador Karl-Otto König.

Greece: Blvr José G. Artigas 1231, 11600 Montevideo; tel. (2) 4089224; fax (2) 4020360; e-mail gremb.mvd@mfa.gr; internet www.mfa.gr/montevideo; Ambassador Nicolaos Dictakis.

Guatemala: Costa Rica 1538, Carrasco, Montevideo; tel. and fax (2) 6012225; fax (2) 6014057; e-mail embaguate-uruguay@minex.gob.gt; Ambassador Juan José Barrios Taracena.

Holy See: Blvd Artigas 1270, Casilla 1503, 11300 Montevideo (Apostolic Nunciature); tel. (2) 7072016; fax (2) 7072209; e-mail nuntius@adinet.com.uy; Apostolic Nuncio Most Rev. Anselmo Guido Pecorari (Titular Archbishop of Populonia).

Iran: Blvr Artigas 531, Montevideo; tel. (2) 7116657; fax (2) 7116659; e-mail embajada.iran@adinet.com.uy; Ambassador Morteza Tafrishi.

Israel: Blvr Artigas 1585, 11200 Montevideo; tel. (2) 4004164; fax (2) 4095821; e-mail info@montevideo.mfa.gov.il; internet montevideo.mfa.gov.il; Ambassador Dori Goren.

Italy: José Benito Lamas 2857, Casilla 268, 11300 Montevideo; tel. (2) 7084916; fax (2) 7084148; e-mail ambasciata.montevideo@esteri.it; internet www.ambmontevideo.esteri.it; Ambassador Guido Scalici.

Japan: Blvr Artigas 953, 11300 Montevideo; tel. (2) 4187645; fax (2) 4187980; e-mail embjapon@adinet.com.uy; internet www.uy.emb-japan.go.jp; Ambassador Kenichi Sakuma.

Korea, Republic: Edif. World Trade Center, Avda Luis Alberto de Herrera 1248, Torre 2, 10°, Montevideo; tel. (2) 6289374; fax (2) 6289376; e-mail koemur@gmail.com; internet ury.mofat.go.kr; Ambassador Kie-Cheon Lee.

Lebanon: Avda General Rivera 2278, Montevideo; tel. (2) 4086640; fax (2) 4086365; e-mail embliban@adinet.com.uy; Chargé d'affaires a.i. Nmeir Noureddine.

Mexico: 25 de Mayo 512/514 esq. Treinta y Tres, 11100 Montevideo; tel. (2) 9166034; fax (2) 9166098; e-mail embajada-mexico@embamex.com.uy; internet www.sre.gob.mx/uruguay; Ambassador Cassio Manuel Luiselli Fernández.

Netherlands: Leyenda Patria 2880, Of. 202, 2°, Casilla 1519, 11300 Montevideo; tel. (2) 7112956; fax (2) 7113301; e-mail mtv@minbuza.nl; internet www.holanda.org.uy; Ambassador H. E. C. M. (Rasha) ter Braack.

Panama: Juan Benito Blanco 3388, Montevideo; tel. (2) 6230301; fax (2) 6230300; e-mail empanuru@netgate.com.uy; Ambassador Digna M. Donado F.

Paraguay: Blvr Artigas 1256, Montevideo; tel. (2) 7072138; fax (2) 7083682; e-mail embapur@netgate.com.uy; Chargé d'affaires a.i. Carlos Scavone Godoy.

Peru: Obligado 1384, 11300 Montevideo; tel. (2) 7076862; fax (2) 7077793; e-mail emba8@embaperu.org.uy; internet www.angelfire.com/country/embaperu; Ambassador William Beleván McBride.

Portugal: Avda Dr Francisco Soca 1128, Apto 701, 11300 Montevideo; tel. (2) 7084061; fax (2) 7096456; e-mail embport@montevideu.dgaccp.pt; Ambassador Luisa Bastos de Almeida.

Romania: Echevarriarza 3452, Casilla 12040, 11000 Montevideo; tel. (2) 6220135; fax (2) 6220685; e-mail ambromvd@adinet.com.uy; Ambassador Gheorghe Petre.

Russia: Blvr España 2741, 11300 Montevideo; tel. (2) 7081884; fax (2) 7086597; e-mail embaru@montevideo.com.uy; internet www.uruguay.mid.ru; Ambassador Serguey N. Koshkin.

South Africa: Dr Gabriel Otero 6337, Carrasco, 11300 Montevideo; tel. (2) 6017591; fax (2) 6003165; e-mail montevideo.general@foreign.gov.za; Ambassador Anthony Leon (resident in Argentina).

Spain: Avda Libertad 2738, 11300 Montevideo; tel. (2) 7086010; fax (2) 7083291; e-mail emb.montevideo@mae.es; internet www.maec.es/embajadas/montevideo; Ambassador Aurora Díaz-Rato Revuelta.

Switzerland: Ing. Federico Abadie 2936/40, 11°, Casilla 12261, 11300 Montevideo; tel. (2) 7115545; fax (2) 7115031; e-mail vertretung@mtv.rep.admin.ch; internet www.eda.admin.ch/montevideo; Ambassador Hans-Ruedi Bortis.

United Kingdom: Marco Bruto 1073, Casilla 16024, 11300 Montevideo; tel. (2) 6223630; fax (2) 6223650; e-mail ukinuruguay@gmail.com; internet ukinuruguay.fco.gov.uk; Ambassador Patrick Mullee.

USA: Lauro Muller 1776, 11200 Montevideo; tel. (2) 4187777; fax (2) 4188611; e-mail webmastermvd@state.gov; internet uruguay.usembassy.gov; Ambassador David Daniel Nelson.

Venezuela: Iturriaga 3589, esq. Tomás de Tezanos, Puerto Buceo, Montevideo; tel. (2) 6221262; fax (2) 6282530; e-mail despacho@embvenezuelauy.org; internet www.embvenezuelauy.org; Ambassador FRANKLIN RAMÓN GONZÁLEZ.

Judicial System

The Supreme Court of Justice comprises five members appointed at the suggestion of the executive, for a period of five years. It has original jurisdiction in constitutional, international and admiralty cases, and hears appeals from the appellate courts, of which there are seven, each with three judges.

Cases involving the functioning of the state administration are heard in the ordinary Administrative Courts and in the Supreme Administrative Court, which consists of five members appointed in the same way as members of the Supreme Court of Justice.

In Montevideo there are 19 civil courts, 10 criminal and correctional courts, 19 courts presided over by justices of the peace, three juvenile courts, three labour courts and courts for government and other cases. Each departmental capital, and some other cities, have a departmental court; each of the 224 judicial divisions has a justice of the peace.

The administration of justice became free of charge in 1980, with the placing of attorneys-at-law in all courts to assist those unable to pay for the services of a lawyer.

Supreme Court of Justice

H. Gutiérrez Ruiz 1310, Montevideo; tel. (2) 9001041; fax (2) 902350; e-mail secparga@poderjudicial.gub.uy; internet www.poderjudicial.gub.uy.

President of the Supreme Court of Justice: Dr DANIEL GUTIÉRREZ.

Supreme Administrative Court: Mercedes 961, 11100 Montevideo; tel. (2) 9013090; fax (2) 9080539; e-mail sgianarelli.@tca.gub.uy; internet www.tca.gub.uy.

Religion

Under the Constitution, the Church and the State are declared separate and toleration for all forms of worship was proclaimed. Roman Catholicism predominates.

CHRISTIANITY

Federación de Iglesias Evangélicas del Uruguay: Avda 8 de Octubre 3324, 11600 Montevideo; tel. and fax (2) 4875907; e-mail fieu@dcd.com.uy; internet www.chasque.net/obra/skontakt.htm; f. 1956; eight mem. churches; Pres. OSCAR BOLIOLI; Sec. OBED BODYAJIAN.

The Roman Catholic Church

Uruguay comprises one archdiocese and nine dioceses. Some 71% of the population are Roman Catholics.

Bishops' Conference

Conferencia Episcopal Uruguaya, Avda Uruguay 1319, 11100 Montevideo; tel. (2) 9002642; fax (2) 9011802; e-mail ceusecre@adinet.com.uy; internet www.iglesiauruguaya.com.

f. 1972; Pres. Rt Rev CARLOS MARÍA COLLAZZI IRAZÁBAL (Bishop of Mercedes).

Archbishop of Montevideo: Most Rev. NICOLÁS COTUGNO FANIZZI, Arzobispado, Treinta y Tres 1368, Casilla 356, 11000 Montevideo; tel. (2) 9158127; fax (2) 9158926; e-mail info@arquidiocesis.net; internet www.arquidiocesis.net.

The Anglican Communion

Uruguay constitutes a diocese in the Province of the Southern Cone of America. The presiding Bishop of the Iglesia Anglicana del Cono Sur de América is the Bishop of Northern Argentina.

Bishop of Uruguay: Rt Rev. MIGUEL TAMAYO ZALDÍVAR, Centro Diocesano, Reconquista 522, Casilla 6108, 11000 Montevideo; tel. (2) 9159627; fax (2) 9162519; e-mail mtamayo@netgate.com.uy; internet www.uruguay.anglican.org.

Other Churches

Baptist Evangelical Convention of Uruguay: Mercedes 1487, 11100 Montevideo; tel. and fax (2) 2167012; e-mail suspasos@adinet.com.uy; f. 1948; 4,500 mems; Pres. Dr JUAN CARLOS OTORMÍN.

Iglesia Adventista (Adventist Church): Castro 167, Montevideo; f. 1901; 4,000 mems; Principal Officers Dr GUILLERMO DURÁN, Dr ALEXIS PIRO.

Iglesia Evangélica Metodista en el Uruguay (Evangelical Methodist Church in Uruguay): San José 1457, 11200 Montevideo; tel. (2) 4136552; fax (2) 4136554; e-mail iemu@adinet.com.uy; internet www.gbgm-umc.org/iemu; f. 1878; 1,193 mems (1997); Pres. Rev. OSCAR BOLIOLI.

Iglesia Evangélica Valdense (Waldensian Evangelical Church): Avda 8 de Octubre 3039, 11600 Montevideo; tel. and fax (2) 4879406; e-mail ievm@internet.com.uy; f. 1952; 15,000 mems; Pastor ALVARO MICHELIN SALOMÓN.

Iglesia Pentecostal Unida Internacional en Uruguay (United Pentecostal Church International in Uruguay): Helvecia 4032, Piedras Blancas, 12200 Montevideo; tel. (2) 5133618; e-mail lrodrigu@montevideo.com.uy; internet members.tripod.com/~lrodrigu; Pastor LUIS RODRÍGUEZ.

Primera Iglesia Bautista (First Baptist Church): Avda Daniel Fernández Crespo 1741, Casilla 5051, 11200 Montevideo; tel. (2) 4098744; fax (2) 4094356; e-mail piebu@adinet.com.uy; f. 1911; 314 mems; Pastor LEMUEL J. LARROSA.

Other denominations active in Uruguay include the Iglesia Evangélica del Río de la Plata and the Iglesia Evangélica Menonita (Evangelical Mennonite Church).

BAHÁ'Í FAITH

National Spiritual Assembly of the Bahá'ís: Blvr Artigas 2440, 11600 Montevideo; tel. (2) 4875890; fax (2) 4802165; e-mail bahai@multi.com.uy; f. 1938; mems resident in 140 localities.

The Press

DAILIES

Montevideo

El Diario Español: Cerrito 551–555, Casilla 899, 11000 Montevideo; tel. (2) 9159481; fax (2) 9157389; e-mail marcelo.reinante@eldiarioespanol.com.uy; f. 1905; morning (except Monday); newspaper of the Spanish community; Editor MARCELO REINANTE; circ. 20,000.

Diario Oficial: Avda 18 de Julio 1373, Montevideo; tel. (2) 9085042; fax (2) 9023098; e-mail impo@impo.com.uy; internet www.impo.com.uy; f. 1905; biweekly; publishes laws, official decrees, parliamentary debates, judicial decisions and legal transactions; Dir Gen. GONZALO REBOLEDO.

El Observador: Cuareim 2052, 11800 Montevideo; tel. (2) 9247000; fax (2) 9248698; e-mail elobservador@observador.com.uy; internet www.observa.com.uy; f. 1991; morning; Chief Editor GABRIEL PREYRA; circ. 26,000.

El País: Zelmar Michelini 1287, 4°, 11100 Montevideo; tel. (2) 9020115; fax (2) 9020464; e-mail cartas@elpais.com.uy; internet www.elpais.com.uy; f. 1918; morning; supports the Partido Nacional; Editor MARTÍN AGUIRRE REGULES; circ. 106,000.

La República: Avda Gral Garibaldi 2579, 11600 Montevideo; tel. (2) 4873565; fax (2) 4873824; e-mail ffasano@chasque.net; internet www.larepublica.com.uy; f. 1988; morning; Editor FEDERICO FASANO MERTENS; Gen. Man. PABLO FASANO MÁRQUEZ; circ. 25,000.

Ultimas Noticias: Paysandú 1179, 11100 Montevideo; tel. (2) 9020452; fax (2) 9024669; e-mail contacto@ultimasnoticias.com.uy; internet www.ultimasnoticias.com.uy; f. 1981; evening (except Saturday); owned by Impresora Polo; Publr Dr ALPHONSE EMANUILOFF-MAX; circ. 25,000.

Florida

El Heraldo: Independencia 824, 94000 Florida; tel. (35) 22229; fax (35) 24546; e-mail elheraldo@elheraldo.com.uy; internet www.diarioelheraldo.com.uy; f. 1919; morning; independent; Dir ALVARO RIVA REY; circ. 20,000.

Maldonado

Correo de Punta del Este: Zelmar Michelini 815 bis, 20000 Maldonado; tel. and fax (42) 35633; e-mail gallardo@adinet.com.uy; internet www.diariocorreo.com; f. 1993; morning; Editor MARCELO GALLARDO; circ. 2,500.

Paysandú

El Telégrafo: Avda 18 de Julio 1027, 60000 Paysandú; tel. (722) 3141; fax (722) 7999; e-mail correo@eltelegrafo.com; internet www.eltelegrafo.com; f. 1910; morning; independent; Dir FERNANDO A. BACCARO; circ. 8,500.

Salto

El Pueblo: Avda 18 de Julio 151, entre Artigas y Rivera, Salto; tel. (733) 4133; e-mail dipueblo@adinet.com.uy; internet www.diarioelpueblo.com.uy; f. 1959; morning; Dir Adriana Martínez.

PERIODICALS

Montevideo

Brecha: Avda Uruguay 844, 11100 Montevideo; tel. (2) 9025042; fax (2) 9020388; e-mail brecha@brecha.com.uy; internet www.brecha.com.uy; f. 1985; weekly; politics, current affairs; Dir Gabriel Papa; Editor-in-Chief Roberto López Belloso; circ. 8,500.

Búsqueda: Avda Uruguay 1146, 11100 Montevideo; tel. (2) 9021300; fax (2) 9022036; e-mail info@busqueda.com.uy; internet www.busqueda.com.uy; f. 1972; weekly (Thurs.); independent; politics and economics; Dir Claudio Paolillo; circ. 25,000.

Charoná: Gutiérrez Ruiz 1276, Of. 201, Montevideo; tel. (2) 9086665; e-mail administracion@charona.com; internet www.charona.com; f. 1968; fortnightly; children's; Dir Sergio Boffano; circ. 25,000.

Crónicas Económicas: Avda Libertador Brig.-Gen. Lavalleja 1532, Montevideo; tel. (2) 9004790; fax (2) 9020759; e-mail cronicas@netgate.com.uy; internet www.cronicas.com.uy; f. 1981; weekly; independent; business and economics; Dirs Julio Ariel Franco, Walter Hugo Pagés, Jorge Estellano.

El Derecho Digital: Montevideo; tel. (2) 4099643; e-mail ddu@elderechodigital.com.uy; internet www.elderechodigital.com.uy; legal; Dir Luis Fernando Iglesias; Editor Fernando Vargas.

El Diario Medico: Avda 18 de Julio 1485, 2°, Montevideo; tel. and fax (2) 4083797; e-mail eldiariomedico@eldiariomedico.com.uy; internet www.eldiariomedico.com.uy; f. 1997; health; Dir Elbio D. Alvarez.

Guambia: Rimac 1576, 11400 Montevideo; tel. and fax (2) 6132703; e-mail info@guambia.com.uy; internet www.guambia.com.uy; f. 1983; monthly; satirical; Dir and Editor Antonio Dabezies.

La Justicia Uruguaya: Avda 25 de Mayo 555, Apto 404, 11000 Montevideo; tel. (2) 9157587; fax (2) 9159721; e-mail lajusticiauruguaya@lju.com.uy; internet www.lajusticiauruguaya.com.uy; f. 1940; bimonthly; jurisprudence; Dirs Eduardo Albanell Martino, Adolfo Albanell Martino (Editor); circ. 3,000.

Marketing Directo: Guaná 2237 bis, 11200 Montevideo; tel. (2) 650602; fax (2) 4087221; e-mail consumo@adinet.com.uy; internet www.ciecc.org; f. 1988; monthly; Dir Edgardo Martínez Zimarioff; circ. 9,500.

Opinar: Río Negro 1192/60, Montevideo; tel. 099686125 (mobile); e-mail cgarcia@opinar.com; internet www.opinar.com.uy; communist; Dir Tabaré Viera Duarte; Editor César García Acosta.

Patria: Montevideo; e-mail semanariopatria@gmail.com; internet www.patria.com.uy; weekly; organ of the Partido Nacional; right-wing; Dir Luis A. Heber; Editor Dr José Luis Bellani.

Propiedades: Bvar. España 2586, Montevideo; tel. (2) 7118384; fax (2) 7121674; e-mail redaccion@revistapropiedades.com.uy; internet www.revistapropiedades.com.uy; f. 1987; construction and real estate; Dir Julio C. Villamide.

Uruguay Natural: Ibiray 2293, 11300 Montevideo; tel. (2) 7114900; fax (2) 712 3421; e-mail info@uruguaynatural.com.uy; internet www.uruguaynatural.com.uy; tourism; Pres. Javier Santomé Sosa Dias; Dir Fernando Rojo Santana.

Voces: Chaná 2389, Montevideo; tel. (2) 4018298; e-mail vocesfa@montevideo.com.uy; internet www.vocesfa.com.uy; political; Editor Alfredo García.

PRESS ASSOCIATIONS

Asociación de Diarios del Uruguay: Río Negro 1308, 6°, 11100 Montevideo; f. 1922; Pres. Guillermo Scheck.

Asociación de la Prensa Uruguaya: San José 1330, Montevideo; tel. and fax (2) 9013695; e-mail apu@adinet.com.uy; internet www.apu.org.uy; f. 1944; Pres. Daniel Lema; Sec.-Gen. Rúben Hernández.

Publishers

Autores Uruguayos: Paysandú 1561, 11200 Montevideo; e-mail mensajes@autoresuruguayos.com.uy; internet www.autoresuruguayos.com; publishes works by Uruguayan authors; Man. Adriana Dos Santos.

Editorial Arca: Ana Monterroso 2231, Montevideo; tel. (2) 4099796; fax (2) 4099788; f. 1963; general literature, social science and history; Man. Dir Enrique Piqué.

Ediciones de la Banda Oriental: Gaboto 1582, 11200 Montevideo; tel. (2) 4083206; fax (2) 4098138; e-mail ebo@chasque.net; general literature; Man. Dir Heber Raviolo.

CENCI—Uruguay (Centro de Estadísticas Nacionales y Comercio Internacional): Juncal 1327D, Of. 1603, Casilla 1510, 11000 Montevideo; tel. (2) 9152930; fax (2) 9154578; e-mail cenci@cenci.com.uy; internet www.cenci.com.uy; f. 1956; economics, statistics; Dir Kenneth Brunner.

Editorial y Librería Jurídica Amalio M. Fernández SRL: 25 de Mayo 589, 11000 Montevideo; tel. and fax (2) 9151782; e-mail amflibrosjurid@movinet.com.uy; f. 1951; law and sociology; Man. Dir Carlos W. Deamestoy.

Editorial La Flor del Itapebí: Luis Piera 1917/401, Montevideo; tel. and fax (2) 7109267; internet www.itapebi.com.uy; f. 1991; cultural, technical, educational.

Fundación de Cultura Universitaria: 25 de Mayo 568, Casilla 1155, 11000 Montevideo; tel. (2) 9152532; fax (2) 9152549; e-mail ventas@fcu.com.uy; internet www.fcu.com.uy; f. 1968; law and social sciences; Pres. Dr Pablo Donnángelo.

Hemisferio Sur: Buenos Aires 335, Casilla 1755, 11000 Montevideo; tel. (2) 9164515; fax (2) 9164520; e-mail editorial@hemisferiosur.com; internet www.hemisferiosur.com; f. 1951; agronomy and veterinary science.

Editorial Idea: Misiones 1424, 5°, 11000 Montevideo; tel. (2) 9165456; fax (2) 9150868; e-mail vescovi@fastlink.com.uy; law; Dir Dr Guillermo Vescovi.

Librería Linardi y Risso: Juan C. Gómez 1435, 11000 Montevideo; tel. (2) 9157129; fax (2) 9157431; e-mail lyrbooks@linardiyrisso.com.uy; internet www.linardiyrisso.com.uy; f. 1944; general; Man. Dirs Alvaro Risso, Andrés Linardi.

Editorial Medina SRL: Gaboto 1521, Montevideo; tel. (2) 4085800; f. 1933; general; Pres. Marcos Medina Vidal.

A. Monteverde & Cía, SA: Treinta y Tres 1475, Casilla 371, 11000 Montevideo; tel. (2) 9152939; fax (2) 9152012; f. 1879; educational; Man. Dir Liliana Mussini.

Mosca Hermanos SA: Avda 18 de Julio 1578, 11300 Montevideo; tel. (2) 4093141; fax (2) 4088059; e-mail mosca@attmail.com.uy; f. 1888; general; Pres. Lic. Zsolt Agardy.

Librería Selecta Editorial: Guayabo 1865, 11200 Montevideo; tel. (2) 4086989; fax (2) 4086831; f. 1950; academic books; Dir Fernando Masa.

Ediciones Trilce: Durazno 1888, 11200 Montevideo; tel. (2) 4127662; fax (2) 4127722; e-mail trilce@trilce.com.uy; internet www.trilce.com.uy; f. 1985; science, politics, history.

Vintén Editor: Hocquart 1771, 11804 Montevideo; tel. (2) 2090223; internet vinten-uy.com; poetry, theatre, history, art, literature.

PUBLISHERS' ASSOCIATION

Cámara Uruguaya del Libro: Juan D. Jackson 1118, 11200 Montevideo; tel. (2) 4015732; fax (2) 4011860; e-mail camurlib@adinet.com.uy; f. 1944; Pres. Ernesto Sanjinés; Man. Ana Cristina Rodríguez.

Broadcasting and Communications

TELECOMMUNICATIONS

Regulatory Authority

Unidad Reguladora de Servicios de Comunicaciones (URSEC): Uruguay 988, Casilla 11100, Montevideo; tel. (2) 9028082; fax (2) 9005708; e-mail webmaster@ursec.gub.uy; internet www.ursec.gub.uy; regulates telecommunications and postal sectors; Pres. Jaime Igorra.

Service Providers

Administración Nacional de Telecomunicaciones (ANTEL): Complejo Torre de las Telecomunicaciones, Guatemala 1075, Montevideo; e-mail antel@antel.com.uy; internet www.antel.com.uy; f. 1974; state-owned; Pres. Edgardo Carvalho; Gen. Man. José Luis Saldías.

ANCEL: Pablo Galarza 3537, Montevideo; internet www.ancel.com.uy; f. 1974; state-owned mobile telephone co.

CTI Móvil: Montevideo; internet www.cti.com.uy; owned by América Móvil, SA de CV (Mexico); mobile cellular telephone services; launched wireless services in Dec. 2004.

Movistar Uruguay: Avda Constituyente, Edif. Torre el Gaucho, 1467 Montevideo; tel. (2) 4087502; internet www.movistar.com.uy; owned by Telefónica Móviles, SA (Spain); mobile telephone services.

BROADCASTING

Regulatory Authority

Asociación Nacional de Broadcasters Uruguayos (ANDEBU): Carlos Quijano 1264, 11100 Montevideo; tel. (2) 9021525; fax (2) 9021540; e-mail andebu@internet.com.uy; internet www.andebu.com.uy; f. 1933; 101 mems; Pres. CARLOS FALCO; Vice-Pres. Dr WALTER C. ROMAY.

Radio

El Espectador: Río Branco 1481, 11100 Montevideo; tel. (2) 9023531; fax (2) 9083192; e-mail ventas@espectador.com.uy; internet www.espectador.com; f. 1923; commercial; Gen. Man. ESTELA BARTOLIC.

Radio Carve: Mercedes 973, 11100 Montevideo; tel. (2) 9026162; fax (2) 9020126; e-mail carve@sadrep.com.uy; internet www.carve850.com.uy; f. 1928; commercial; Dir HÉCTOR CARLOS VERA.

Radio Montecarlo: Avda 18 de Julio 1224, 1°, 11100 Montevideo; tel. (2) 9030703; fax (2) 9017762; f. 1928; commercial; Dir DANIEL ROMAY.

Radio Sarandí: Enriqueta Compte y Riqué 1250, 11800 Montevideo; tel. (2) 2082612; fax (2) 2036906; e-mail direccion@sarandi690.com.uy; internet www.radiosarandi.com.uy; f. 1931; commercial; Pres. RAMIRO RODRÍGUEZ VALLAMIL RIVIERE.

Radio del Sol: tel. (2) 6283314; e-mail comoestamos@fmdelsol.com; internet www.comoestamos.com.uy.

Radio Universal: Avda 18 de Julio 1220, 3°, 11100 Montevideo; tel. (2) 9026022; fax (2) 9026050; e-mail info@22universal.com; internet www.22universal.com; f. 1929; commercial; Pres. OSCAR IMPERIO.

Radiodifusión Nacional SODRE: Sarandí 430, 11000 Montevideo; tel. (2) 957865; fax (2) 9161933; f. 1929; state-owned; Pres. JULIO CÉSAR OCAMPOS.

In 2002 there were some 16 AM and six FM radio stations in the Montevideo area. In addition, there were approximately 41 AM and 56 FM radio stations outside the capital.

Television

The Uruguayan Government holds a 10% stake in the regional television channel Telesur (q.v.), which began operations in May 2005 and is based in Caracas, Venezuela.

Canal 4 Monte Carlo: Paraguay 2253, 11800 Montevideo; tel. (2) 9244444; fax (2) 9247929; e-mail secretarias@montecarlotv.com.uy; internet www.canal4.com.uy; f. 1961; Dir HUGO ROMAY SALVO.

SAETA TV—Canal 10: Dr Lorenzo Carnelli 1234, 11200 Montevideo; tel. (2) 4102120; fax (2) 4009771; internet www.canal10.com.uy; f. 1956; Pres. JORGE DE FEO.

SODRE (Servicio Oficial de Difusión Radiotelevisión y Espectáculos): Blvr Artigas 2552, 11600 Montevideo; tel. (2) 4806448; fax (2) 4808515; e-mail direccion@tveo.com.uy; internet www.sodre.gub.uy; f. 1963; Pres. NELLY GOITIÑO.

Teledoce Televisora Color—Canal 12: Enriqueta Compte y Riqué 1276, 11800 Montevideo; tel. (2) 2083555; fax (2) 2037623; e-mail latele@teledoce.com; internet www.teledoce.com; f. 1962; Gen. Man. HORACIO SCHECK.

Tevé Ciudad: Javier Barrios Amorín 1460, Montevideo; tel. (2) 4001908; fax (2) 4029369; e-mail griselda.diaz@imm.gub.uy; internet www.teveciudad.com; f. 1996; state-owned; Gen. Dir GRISELDA DÍAZ LARREA.

Finance

BANKING

(cap. = capital; res = reserves; dep. = deposits; m. = million; brs = branches; amounts in pesos uruguayos unless otherwise indicated)

State Banks

Banco Central del Uruguay: Avda Juan P. Fabini 777, Casilla 1467, 11100 Montevideo; tel. (2) 9085629; fax (2) 9021634; e-mail info@bcu.gub.uy; internet www.bcu.gub.uy; f. 1967; note-issuing bank, also controls private banking; cap. 1,547.7m., res –13,844.4m., dep. 103,138.6m. (Dec. 2005); Pres. MARIO BERGARA DUQUE; Dir JORGE LUIS GAMARRA SEBASTIÁN.

Banco Hipotecario del Uruguay (BHU): Avda Daniel Fernández Crespo 1508, Montevideo; tel. (2) 4090000; fax (2) 4090782; e-mail info@bhu.net; internet www.bhu.net; f. 1892; state mortgage bank; in 1977 assumed responsibility for housing projects in Uruguay; Pres. JORGE POLGAR.

Banco de la República Oriental del Uruguay (BROU): Cerrito y Zabala 351, 11000 Montevideo; tel. (2) 9150157; fax (2) 9162064; e-mail broupte@adinet.com.uy; internet www.brounet.com.uy; f. 1896; cap. 12,517.6m., res 2,825.1m., dep. 124,856.8m. (Dec. 2006); Pres. FERNANDO CALLOIA RAFFO; Gen. Man. FERNANDO JORAJURÍA; 117 brs.

Principal Commercial Banks

ABN AMRO Bank Uruguay NV: Julio Herrera y Obes 1365, Casilla 888, 11100 Montevideo; tel. (2) 9031073; fax (2) 9025011; internet www.abnamro.com.uy; f. 1952; owned by ABN AMRO Bank NV (Netherlands); Country Rep. FRANCISCO DI ROBERTO, Jr; 24 brs.

Banco Bilbao Vizcaya Argentaria Uruguay SA (BBVA): 25 de Mayo 401, esq. Zabala, 11000 Montevideo; tel. (2) 9161444; fax (2) 9162821; internet www.bbvabanco.com.uy; f. 1968; fmrly Unión de Bancos del Uruguay, and later Banesto Banco Uruguay, SA and Banco Francés Uruguay, SA; adopted current name in 2000 following merger with Banco Exterior de América, SA; cap. 883.0m., res 674.1m., dep. 10,336.3m. (Dec. 2004); Pres. TOMÁS DEANE; Vice-Pres. and Gen. Man. ANGEL SORIA; 14 brs.

Banco Galicia Uruguay, SA: Edif. World Trade Center, Luis A. Herrera 1248, 22°, Montevideo; tel. 6281230; e-mail contactenos@bancogalicia.com.uy; internet www.bancogalicia.com.uy; f. 1999.

Banco Surinvest SA: Rincón 530, 11000 Montevideo; tel. (2) 9160177; fax (2) 9160241; e-mail bancosurinvest@surinvest.com.uy; internet www.surinvest.com.uy; f. 1981 as Surinvest Casa Bancaria; name changed as above 1991; cap. 249.3m., res 71.4m., dep. 2,351.2m. (Dec. 2004); Gen. Man. ALBERTO A. MELLO.

Crédit Uruguay Banco SA: Rincón 500, 11000 Montevideo; tel. (2) 9150095; fax (2) 9164282; internet www.credituruguay.com.uy; f. 1998 as Banco Acac SA; adopted current name 2004; owned by Crédit Agricole (France); cap. 413.4m., res 18.4m., dep. 11,616.1m. (Dec. 2005); Pres. GERMÁN VILLAR; Gen. Man. MARCELO OTEN.

Discount Bank (Latin America), SA: Rincón 390, 11000 Montevideo; tel. (2) 9164848; fax (2) 9160890; e-mail mensajes@discbank.com.uy; internet www.discbank.com.uy; f. 1978; owned by Israel Discount Bank of New York (USA); cap. US $12.8m., res $0.62m., dep. $179.3m. (Dec. 2002); Pres. and Chair. REUVEN SPIEGEL; Dir and Gen. Man. VALENTIN D. MALACHOWSKI; 4 brs.

HSBC Bank (Uruguay), SA: Ituzaingó 1389, 11000 Montevideo; tel. (2) 9153395; fax (2) 9160125; f. 1995; owned by HSBC Bank PLC (United Kingdom); CEO ALAN WILKINSON.

Nuevo Banco Comercial, SA (NBC): Misiones 1399, CP 11000 Montevideo; tel. (2) 1401300; fax (2) 1401185; e-mail servicioalcliente@nbc.com.uy; internet www.nbc.com.uy; f. 2003 by merger of Banco Comercial, Banco La Caja Obrera and Banco de Montevideo; fmrly state-owned, privatized in June 2006; dep. US $923m., total assets $1,153m. (July 2006); Pres. ERNEST BACHRACH; Gen. Man. JOSÉ FUENTES; 46 brs.

Credit Co-operative

There are several credit co-operatives, which permit members to secure small business loans at preferential rates.

Federación Uruguaya de Cooperativas de Ahorro y Crédito (FUCAC): Blvr Artigas 1472, Montevideo; tel. and fax (2) 7088888; e-mail info@fucac.com.uy; internet www.fucac.com.uy; f. 1972; Pres. CARLOS ALBERTO ICASURIAGA SAMANO; Gen. Man. JAVIER HUMBERTO PI LEÓN.

Development Bank

Banco Bandes Uruguay: Sarandí 402, CP 111000, Montevideo; tel. (2) 9160100; internet www.cofac.com.uy; owned by the Banco de Desarrollo Económico y Social (BANDES) of Venezuela.

Bankers' Association

Asociación de Bancarios del Uruguay (Bankers' Association of Uruguay—AEBU): Camacuá 575, Montevideo; tel. (2) 9161060; e-mail secprensa@aebu.org.uy; internet www.aebu.org.uy; f. 1945; 7 mem. banks; Dir OSCAR JORGE VISSANI.

STOCK EXCHANGE

Bolsa de Valores de Montevideo: Edif. Bolsa de Comercio, Misiones 1400, 11000 Montevideo; tel. (2) 9165051; fax (2) 9161900; e-mail info@bolsademontevideo.com.uy; internet www.bolsademontevideo.com.uy; f. 1867; 75 mems; Pres. IGNACIO ROSPIDE.

INSURANCE

From mid-1994, following the introduction of legislation ending the state monopoly of most types of insurance, the Banco de Seguros del Estado lost its monopoly on all insurance except life, sea transport and fire risks, which have been traditionally open to private underwriters.

AIG Uruguay Compañía de Seguros, SA (USA): Colonia 993, 1°, Montevideo; tel. (2) 9000330; fax (2) 9084552; e-mail aig.uruguay@

aig.com; internet www.aig.com; f. 1996; all classes; Gen. Man. JORGE FERRANTE.

Alico Compañía de Seguros de Vida, SA (USA): 18 de Julio 1738, Montevideo; tel. (2) 4033939; fax (2) 4033938; e-mail alico@alico.com.uy; internet www.alico.com; f. 1996; life; Gen. Man. JUAN ETCHEVERRY.

Banco de Seguros del Estado: Avda Libertador 1465, Montevideo; tel. (2) 9089303; fax (2) 9017030; e-mail directorio@bse.com.uy; internet www.bse.com.uy; f. 1912; state insurance org.; all risks; Pres. ENRIQUE ROIG CURBELO; Gen. Man. CARLOS VALDÉS.

Compañía de Seguros Aliança da Bahia Uruguay, SA (Brazil): Río Negro 1394, 7°, Montevideo; tel. (2) 9021086; fax (2) 9021087; e-mail avivo@netgate.com.uy; f. 1995; transport; Gen. Man. BERNARDO VIVO.

Mapfre Compañía de Seguros, SA (Spain): Blvr Artigas 459, Montevideo; tel. and fax (2) 7116595; e-mail info@mapfre.com.uy; internet www.mapfre.com.uy; f. 1994; general; Gen. Man. DIEGO SOBRINI.

Porto Seguro, Seguros del Uruguay SA (Brazil): Blvr Artigas 2025, Montevideo; tel. (2) 4028000; fax (2) 4030097; e-mail admin@portoseguro.com.uy; internet www.portoseguro.com.uy; f. 1995; property; Pres. LEANDRO SUÁREZ.

Real Uruguaya de Seguros SA (Netherlands): Avda 18 de Julio 988, Montevideo; tel. (2) 9025858; fax (2) 9024515; e-mail realseguros@abnamro.com; internet www.realseguros.com.uy; f. 1900; life and property; part of the ABN AMRO Group; Gen. Man. JOSÉ LUIZ TOMAZINI.

Royal & SunAlliance Seguros, SA (United Kingdom): Peatonal Sarandí 620, Montevideo; tel. (2) 9170505; fax (2) 9170490; internet www.royalsunalliance.com.uy; f. 1997; life and property; Dir Dr JUAN QUARTINO.

Surco, Compañía Cooperativa de Seguros: Blvr Artigas 1320, Montevideo; tel. (2) 7090089; fax (2) 7077313; e-mail surco@surco.com.uy; internet www.surco.com.uy; f. 1995; insurance co-operative; all classes; Gen. Man. ANDRÉS ELOLA.

L'UNION de Paris Compañía Uruguaya de Seguros, SA (France): Misiones 1549, Montevideo; tel. (2) 9160850; fax (2) 9160847; e-mail gabriel.penna@axa-seguros.com.uy; internet www.axa-seguros.com.uy; f. 1897 as L'Union IARD; present name adopted 2004; general; Gen. Man. GABRIEL PENNA.

INSURANCE ASSOCIATION

Asociación Uruguaya de Empresas Aseguradoras (AUDEA): Juncal 1305, Of. 1901, 11000 Montevideo; tel. (2) 9161465; fax (2) 9165991; e-mail audea@adinet.com.uy; Pres. MANUEL RODRÍGUEZ; Gen. Man. MAURICIO CASTELLANOS.

Trade and Industry

GOVERNMENT AGENCIES

Administración Nacional de Combustibles, Alcohol y Portland (ANCAP): Payasandú y Avda del Libertador Brig.-Gen. Lavalleja, 11100 Montevideo; tel. (2) 9020608; fax (2) 9021136; e-mail webmaster@ancap.com.uy; internet www.ancap.com.uy; f. 1931; deals with transport, refining and sale of petroleum products, and the manufacture of alcohol, spirits and cement; tanker services, also river transport; Pres. RAÚL SENDIC; Sec.-Gen. MIGUEL A. TATO.

Oficina de Planeamiento y Presupuesto de la Presidencia de la República: Plaza Independencia 710, 11000 Montevideo; tel. (2) 4872110; fax (2) 2099730; e-mail direccion@opp.gub.uy; internet www.opp.gub.uy; f. 1976; responsible for the implementation of devt plans; co-ordinates the policies of the various ministries; advises on the preparation of the budget of public enterprises; Dir GABRIEL FRUGONI; Sub-Dir Dr CONRADO RAMOS.

Uruguay XXI (Instituto de Promoción de Inversiones y Exportaciones de Bienes y Servicios): Rincón 518/528, 11100 Montevideo; tel. (2) 9153838; fax (2) 9163059; e-mail info@uruguayxxi.gub.uy; internet www.uruguayxxi.gub.uy; f. 1996; govt agency to promote economic investment and export; Exec. Dir ROBERTO VILLAMIL; Gen. Man. ROBERTO BENNETT.

DEVELOPMENT ORGANIZATIONS

Corporación Nacional para el Desarrollo (CND): Rincón 528, 7°, Casilla 977, 11000 Montevideo; tel. (2) 9162800; fax (2) 9159662; e-mail cnd@cnd.org.uy; internet www.cnd.org.uy; f. 1985; national devt corpn; mixed-capital org.; obtains 60% of funding from state; Pres. LUIS PORTO; Gen. Man. PABLO GUTIÉRREZ.

Asociación Nacional de Micro y Pequeños Empresarios (ANMYPE): Miguelete 1584, Montevideo; tel. (2) 9241010; e-mail info@anmype.org.uy; internet www.anmype.org.uy; promotes small businesses; f. 1988; Pres. ALEXIS VERA; Sec. SUSANA CRESPO.

Asociación Nacional de Organizaciones No Gubernamentales Orientadas al Desarrollo: Avda del Libertador 1985 esq. 202, Montevideo; tel. and fax (2) 9240812; e-mail anong@anong.com.uy; internet www.anong.org.uy; f. 1992; umbrella grouping of devt NGOs; Pres. ANA LAURA SCARENZIO; Sec. MARCELO VENTOS.

Centro Interdisciplinario de Estudios sobre el Desarrollo, Uruguay (CIEDUR): 18 de Julio 1645-7, 11200 Montevideo; tel. and fax (2) 4084520; e-mail ciedur@ciedur.org.uy; internet www.ciedur.org.uy; f. 1977; devt studies and training; Pres. ALMA ESPINO; Exec. Sec. ALFREDO BLUM.

Fundación Uruguaya de Cooperación y Desarrollo Solidario (FUNDASOL) (Uruguayan Foundation for Supportive Co-operation and Development): Blvr Artigas 1165, esq. Maldonado, 11200 Montevideo; tel. (2) 4002020; fax (2) 4081485; e-mail consultas@fundasol.org.uy; internet www.fundasol.org.uy; f. 1979; Pres. EDUARDO PIETRA; Gen. Man. JORGE NAYA.

CHAMBERS OF COMMERCE

Cámara de Industrias del Uruguay (Chamber of Industries): Avda Italia 6101, 11500 Montevideo; tel. (2) 6040464; fax (2) 6040501; e-mail ciu@ciu.com.uy; internet www.ciu.com.uy; f. 1898; Pres. DIEGO BALESTRA; Gen. Man. MIGUEL VILARIÑO.

Cámara Nacional de Comercio y Servicios del Uruguay (National Chamber of Commerce): Edif. Bolsa de Comercio, Rincón 454, 2°, Casilla 1000, 11000 Montevideo; tel. (2) 9161277; fax (2) 9161243; e-mail info@cncs.com.uy; internet www.cncs.com.uy; f. 1867; 1,500 mems; Pres. ALFONSO VARELA; Man. Dr CLAUDIO PIACENZA.

Cámara Mercantil de Productos del País (Chamber of Commerce for Local Products): Avda General Rondeau 1908, 1°, 11800 Montevideo; tel. (2) 9240644; fax (2) 9244701; e-mail info@camaramercantil.com.uy; internet www.camaramercantil.com.uy; f. 1891; 180 mems; Pres. CHRISTIAN BOLZ; Gen. Man. GONZALO GONZÁLEZ PIEDRAS.

EMPLOYERS' ORGANIZATIONS

Asociación de Importadores y Mayoristas de Almacén (Importers' and Wholesalers' Asscn): Edif. Bolsa de Comercio, Of. 317/319, Rincón 454, 11000 Montevideo; tel. (2) 9156103; fax (2) 9160796; e-mail fmelissari@nidera.com.uy; f. 1926; 52 mems; Pres. FERNANDO MELISSARI.

Asociación Rural del Uruguay (ARU): Avda Uruguay 864, 11100 Montevideo; tel. (2) 9020484; fax (2) 9020489; e-mail aru@netgate.com.uy; internet www.aru.com.uy; f. 1871; 1,800 mems; Pres. MANUEL LUSSICH TORRENDEL; Gen. Man. Dr GONZALO ARROYO FACELLO.

Federación Rural: Avda 18 de Julio 965, 1°, 11100 Montevideo; tel. (2) 9005583; fax (2) 9004791; e-mail fedrural@gmail.com; internet www.federacionrural.org; f. 1915; 2,000 mems; Pres. MIGUEL BIDEGAIN.

Unión de Exportadores del Uruguay (Uruguayan Exporters' Asscn): Avda Uruguay 917, 1°, esq. Convención, 11100 Montevideo; tel. (2) 9170105; fax (2) 9165967; e-mail info@uruguayexporta.com; internet www.uruguayexporta.com; Pres. ALEJANDRO BZUROVSKI; Exec. Sec. TERESA AISHEMBERG.

MAJOR COMPANIES

Acindar Uruguay: Edif. World Trade Center, Avda Luis A. de Herrera 1248, Of. 321, 11300 Montevideo; tel. and fax (2) 6286655; e-mail acindar@multi.com.uy; internet www.acindar.com.ar; part of Grupo ArcelorMittal; production of iron and steel; Gen. Man. JUAN OSCAR AVILA; Controller JORGE SCIANDRO.

Azucarera del Litoral, SA (AZUCARLITO): Meriggi y Libertad, 60000 Paysandú; tel. (2) 9160868; fax (2) 9161192; e-mail azupay@azucarlito.com; f. 1943; processors of raw cane sugar; Gen. Man. RAÚL CONCELO; 495 employees.

Chery Automobile: Montevideo; f. 2007; jtly owned by Chery Automobile (People's Republic of China, 51%) and Socma (Argentina, 49%); car assembly plant.

Compañía Industrial de Tabacos Monte Paz, SA: San Ramón 716, Montevideo; tel. (2) 2008821; fax (2) 2037890; e-mail info@montepaz.com.uy; internet www.montepaz.com.uy; f. 1930; tobacco and cigarette manufacturers; Pres. JORGE LUIS MAILHOS; 425 employees.

Compañía Sudamericana de Empresas Eléctricas, Mecánicas y Obras Públicas (SACEEM): Treinta y Tres 1468, 11800 Montevideo; tel. (2) 9160208; fax (2) 9163939; e-mail saceem@saceem.com.uy; internet www.saceem.com.uy; f. 1951; construction of industrial buildings and warehouses; Chair. MARTÍN CARRIQUIRY; 800 employees.

Compañía Uruguaya de Transportes Colectivos, SA (CUTCSA): Sarandí 528, 11000 Montevideo; tel. (2) 915933; fax (2) 2032037; e-mail cac@cutcsa.com.uy; internet www.cutcsa.com .uy; f. 1937; passenger transport services; Pres. JUAN ANTONIO SALGADO VILA; Gen. Man. FERNANDO BARCIA; 5,250 employees.

COOPDY: Thompson 3077, 11600 Montevideo; tel. (2) 4870812; fax (2) 4872786; f. 1962 as Dymac, SA; clothing manufacturers; workers' co-operative; Gen. Man. ALICIA PAIVA; 520 employees.

Cooperativa Nacional de Productores de Leche, SA (CONAPROLE): Magallanes 1871, 11200 Montevideo; tel. (2) 9247171; fax (2) 9246672; e-mail jfernandez@conaprole.com.uy; internet www .conaprole.com.uy; f. 1936; manufacturers and wholesalers of milk and dairy products; Pres. JORGE PANIZZA TORRENS; CEO RUBÉN NÚÑEZ HERNÁNDEZ; 2,200 employees.

Fábrica Nacional de Papel, SA (FANAPEL): Rincón 477, 6°, 11000 Montevideo; tel. (2) 9150917; fax (2) 9163096; e-mail secretaria .comercial@fanapel.com.uy; internet www.fanapel.com.uy; f. 1898; pulp and paper mill; Pres. RICARDO ZERBINO CAVAJANI; Gen. Man. LIBERATO TURINELLI DUCASSOU; 1,065 employees.

Fábrica Uruguaya de Neumáticos, SA (FUNSA): Corrales 3076, Casilla 15175, Montevideo; tel. (2) 5083141; fax (2) 5070611; e-mail funsa@ciu.com.uy; internet www.funsa.com.uy; f. 1935; manufacturers of rubber tyres, gloves, shoes and insulated electrical cables; workers' co-operative since 2004; Pres. ENRIQUE ROMERO; 210 employees (2007).

FNC, SA (Fábricas Nacionales de Cerveza): Entre Ríos 1060, Montevideo; tel. (2) 2001683; fax (2) 2034525; e-mail fnc@multi .com.uy; f. 1932; bought by Anheuser-Busch InBev (Belgium) in 2007; brewery; Pres. (South America Zone) BERNANDO PINTO PAIVA; Country Man. GABRIEL TOBARÍAS; 500 employees.

FRIPUR, SA: Avda General Rondeau 2260, Montevideo; tel. (2) 9245821; fax (2) 9243149; e-mail informes@fripur.com.uy; internet www.fripur.com.uy; f. 1976; foodstuffs and fish processing; Pres. ALBERTO FERNÁNDEZ; 1,185 employees.

Industrias Philips del Uruguay, SA: Rambla ÓHiggins 5303, 11400 Montevideo; tel. (2) 6196666; fax (2) 6197777; internet customerphilips@philips.com.ar; internet www.philips.com.uy; f. 1957; subsidiary of NV Philips (Netherlands); manufacturers of lighting and other electrical goods; Gen. Man. LUIS PENNA; Contact MARTÍN RICARDO SPINELLI; 300 employees.

Montevideo Refrescos, SA: Camino Carrasco 6173, 12100 Montevideo; tel. (2) 6008401; fax (2) 6042541; f. 1946; owned by Coca-Cola Corpn of the USA; producers of carbonated beverages; Pres. GREGORIO AZNARES; 560 employees.

Motociclo, SA: Avda Uruguay 1171, 11100 Montevideo; tel. (2) 9020070; fax (2) 9021702; e-mail ventas@motociclo.com.uy; internet www.motociclo.com.uy; f. 1931; bicycle and motorcycle manufacturers; annual capacity of 370,000 units; Pres. LEONARDO ROZENBLUM; 450 employees.

Paysandú Industrias del Cuero, SA (PAYCUEROS): Cerrito 572, 2°, 11100 Montevideo; tel. (2) 9155255; fax (2) 9152305; e-mail omar.tkacz@sadesa.com; internet www.sadesa.com; f. 1946; tannery, manufacturing handbags and other leather products; owned by SADESA (Argentina); Contact OMAR TKACZ; 700 employees.

Sociedad Anónima Arroceros Nacionales (SAMAN): Rambla Baltasar Brum 2772, Montevideo; tel. (2) 2081421; fax (2) 2037007; e-mail info@saman.com.uy; internet www.saman.com.uy; f. 1942; rice mills; Pres. RICARDO FERRÉS BLANCO; Gen. Man. LEOMAR GOLDONI; 538 employees.

Supermercados Disco del Uruguay: Jaime Zudáñez 2627, Montevideo; tel. (2) 7107421; fax (2) 7117903; internet www.disco.com.uy; f. 1960; Uruguayan subsidiary of Disco, SA, Argentina; Gen. Man. LUIS EDUARDO CORDUZO.

UPM Fray Bentos: Ruta Puente Puerto, Km 307, 65000 Fray Bentos; tel. (5) 625740; fax (5) 626971; internet www.upmuruguay .com.uy; f. 2005; operates pulp mill in Fray Bentos; bought 91% of mill from Botnia in 2010; also operates Forestal Oriental forestry co; Pres. TAPIO KORPEINEN.

UTILITIES

Electricity

Administración Nacional de Usinas y Transmisiones Eléctricas (UTE): Palacio de la Luz, Paraguay 2431, 10°, 11100 Montevideo; tel. (2) 2003424; fax (2) 2037082; e-mail ute@ute.com.uy; internet www.ute.com.uy; f. 1912; autonomous state body; sole purveyor of electricity until 1997; Pres. GONZALO CASARAVILLA; Gen. Man. ALEJANDRO PERRONI.

Gas

Conecta: Avda Giannattasio, Km 20, 800 Ciudad de la Costa, Canelones, Montevideo; tel. (2) 6826817; fax (2) 6006732; internet www.conecta.com.uy; gas distribution; Dir FRANCISCO LLANO.

MontevideoGas: Plaza Independencia 831, 10°, 11000 Montevideo; tel. (2) 9017454; e-mail mlcoitino@montevideogas.com.uy; internet www.montevideogas.com.uy; gas producers and service providers; Pres. CLOVIS CORREA; Gen. Man. PEDRO BORGES.

Water

Aguas de la Costa: Calle 1 y 20, La Barra, Maldonado; tel. (42) 771930; fax (42) 771932; e-mail adlcosta@adinet.com.uy; internet www.aguasdelacosta.com.uy; subsidiary of Aguas de Barcelona (Spain); operating in Uruguay since 1994, contract due to expire in 2019; management of water supply in Maldonado Dept.

Obras Sanitarias del Estado (OSE): Carlos Roxlo 1275, 11200 Montevideo; tel. (2) 4001151; fax (2) 4088069; e-mail info@ose.com .uy; internet www.ose.com.uy; f. 1962; processing and distribution of drinking water, sinking wells, supplying industrial zones of the country; Pres. JORGE CARLOS COLACCE MOLINARI.

TRADE UNION

Plenario Intersindical de Trabajadores—Convención Nacional de Trabajadores (PIT—CNT): Jackson 1283, 11200 Montevideo; tel. (2) 4096680; fax (2) 4004160; e-mail pitcnt@adinet.com.uy; internet www.pitcnt.org.uy; f. 1966; org. comprising 83 trade unions, 17 labour federations; 320,000 mems; Pres. JORGE CASTRO; Exec. Sec. JUAN CASTILLO.

Transport

Dirección Nacional de Transporte: Rincón 575, 5°, 11000 Montevideo; tel. (2) 9163122; fax (2) 9163122; e-mail pitcnt@adinet.com .uy; internet www.dnt.gub.uy; co-ordinates national and international transport services.

RAILWAYS

Administración de los Ferrocarriles del Estado (AFE): Avda del Libertador 1672, Montevideo; tel. (2) 9033030; e-mail rrpp-afe@ adinet.com.uy; internet www.afe.com.uy; f. 1952; state org.; 3,002 km of track connecting all parts of the country; there are connections with the Argentine and Brazilian networks; passenger services ceased in 1988; passenger services linking Montevideo with Florida and Canelones were resumed in mid-1993; Pres. ANTONIO GALLICCHIO QUEIROLO.

ROADS

In 2008 Uruguay had an estimated 8,696 km of motorways (forming the densest motorway network in South America), connecting Montevideo with the main towns of the interior and the Argentine and Brazilian frontiers. There was also a network of approximately 40,000 km of paved roads under departmental control.

Corporación Vial del Uruguay, SA: Rincón 528, 5°, 11000 Montevideo; tel. (2) 9261680; fax (2) 9170114; e-mail cvu@cnd.org .uy; internet www.cvu.com.uy; road construction agency; 100% owned by the Corporación Nacional para el Desarrollo; Pres. ALVARO GARCÍA; Gen. Man. ANDRÉS PEREYRA.

INLAND WATERWAYS

There are about 1,250 km of navigable waterways, which provide an important means of transport.

Nobleza Naviera, SA: Avda General Rondeau 2257, Montevideo; tel. (2) 9243222; fax (2) 9243218; e-mail nobleza@netgate.com.uy; operates cargo services on the River Plate, and the Uruguay and Paraná rivers; Chair. AMÉRICO DEAMBROSI; Man. Dir DORIS FERRARI.

SHIPPING

Administración Nacional de Puertos (ANP): Rambla 25 de Agosto de 1825 160, Montevideo; tel. (2) 9151441; fax (2) 9161704; e-mail presidencia@anp.com.uy; internet www.anp.com.uy; f. 1916; national ports admin; Pres. FERNANDO PUNTIGLIANO; Gen. Man. ALBERTO DÍAZ.

Prefectura Nacional Naval: Edif. Comando General de la Armada, 4°, Rambla 25 de Agosto de 1825 s/n, esq. Maciel, Montevideo; tel. (2) 9155500; fax (2) 9156786; internet www.armada.gub .uy/Prena; f. 1829; maritime supervisory body, responsible for rescue services, protection of sea against pollution, etc.; Prefect Rear-Adm. OSCAR DEBALI DE PALLEJA.

Navegación Atlántida, SA: Río Branco 1373, 11100 Montevideo; tel. (2) 9084449; f. 1967; ferry services for passengers and vehicles between Argentina and Uruguay; Pres. H. C. PIETRANERA.

Transportadora Marítima de Combustibles, SA (TRAMACO, SA): Rincón 540, Puerta Baja, 11000 Montevideo; tel. (2) 9165754; fax (2) 9165755; e-mail tramaco@tramaco.com.uy; owned by the Christopherson Group; Pres. JORGE FERNÁNDEZ BAUBETA.

CIVIL AVIATION

Civil aviation is controlled by the Dirección General de Aviación Civil and the Dirección General de Infraestructura Aeronáutica. The main airport is at Carrasco, 21 km from Montevideo, and there are also airports at Paysandú, Rivera, Salto, Melo, Artigas, Punta del Este and Durazno.

Primeras Líneas Uruguayas de Navegación Aérea (PLUNA): Colonia 1013, 9°, 11000 Montevideo; tel. (2) 9013559; fax (2) 9020231; e-mail presidenciapluna@adinet.com.uy; internet www.flypluna.com; f. 1936; nationalized 1951; partially privatized in 1994; 75% stake acquired by Leadgate Investment Corpn in 2007; operates international services to Argentina, Brazil, Chile, El Salvador, Paraguay, Spain and the USA; Pres. CARLOS BOUZAS.

Aeromás, SA: Avda de las Americas 5120, Montevideo; tel. (2) 6046359; e-mail aeromas@aeromas.com; internet www.aeromas.com; private hire, cargo, and air ambulance flights; internal mass transit services to Salto, Paysandú, Rivera, Tacuarembó and Artigas; f. 1983; Dir DANIEL DALMÁS.

Tourism

The sandy beaches and woodlands on the coast and the grasslands of the interior, with their variety of fauna and flora, provide the main tourist attractions. About 52% of tourists came from Argentina and 15% from Brazil in 2008. Uruguay received an estimated 2.0m. visitors in that year, while tourism revenues totalled a provisional US $1,042m.

Asociación Uruguaya de Agencias de Viajes (AUDAVI): Río Branco 1407, Of. 205, 11100 Montevideo; tel. (2) 9012326; fax (2) 9021972; e-mail audavi@netgate.com.uy; internet www.audavi.com.uy; f. 1951; 100 mems; Pres. GIORGIO VALENTI; Man. LEDO SILVA.

Cámara Uruguaya de Turismo: San José 942, 2°, Of. 4, 11200 Montevideo; tel. and fax (2) 9000453; internet camtur.com.uy; Pres. LUIS BORSARI.

Uruguay Natural: Rambla 25 de Agosto de 1825, esq. Yacaré, Montevideo; tel. (2) 1885100; e-mail webmaster@mintur.gub.uy; internet www.uruguaynatural.com; f. 2003; state-run tourism promotion agency; Dir-Gen. Dr ANTONIO CARÁMBULA.

Defence

As assessed at November 2009, Uruguay's Armed Forces consisted of 24,621 volunteers between the ages of 18 and 45 who contract for one or two years of service. There was an army of 16,234, a navy of 5,403 and an air force of 2,984. There were also paramilitary forces numbering 920.

Defence Budget: an estimated 7,730m. pesos uruguayos in 2009.

Commander-in-Chief of the Army: Lt-Gen. JORGE WASHINGTON ROSALES SOSA.

Commander-in-Chief of the Navy: (vacant).

Commander-in-Chief of the Air Force: Brig.-Gen. JOSÉ R. BONILLA.

Education

All education, including university tuition, is provided free of charge. Education is officially compulsory for six years between six and 14 years of age. Primary education begins at the age of six and lasts for six years. Secondary education, beginning at 12 years of age, lasts for a further six years, comprising two cycles of three years each. In 2007 primary enrolment included 98% of children in the relevant age-group (males 97%; females 98%), while the equivalent ratio for secondary enrolment was 68% (males 64%; females 71%). The programmes of instruction are the same in both public and private schools and private schools are subject to certain state controls. There are six universities in Uruguay, including the state Universidad de la República. Central government expenditure on education in 2006 was 14,392m. pesos uruguayos (12.3% of central government spending).

Bibliography

For works on South America generally, see Select Bibliography (Books)

Alexander, R. J. *A History of Organized Labor in Uruguay and Paraguay*. Westport, CT, Praeger Publrs, 2005.

Barahona de Brito, A. *Human Rights and Democratization in Latin America: Uruguay and Chile*. Oxford, Oxford University Press, 1997.

Gillespie, C. G. 'Negotiating Democracy: Politicians and Generals in Uruguay', in *Cambridge Latin American Studies*, No. 72. Cambridge, Cambridge University Press, 1992 and 2006.

Gregory, S. *Intellectuals and Left Politics in Uruguay, 1958-2006*. Eastbourne, Sussex Academic Press, 2008.

Heinz, W., and Fruhling, H. *Determinants of Gross Human Rights Violations by State and State-sponsored Actors in Brazil, Uruguay, Chile and Argentina*. Zoetermeer, Martinus Nijhoff Publrs, 1999.

Lavin, A. *Women, Feminism and Social Change in Argentina, Chile and Uruguay, 1840–1940*. Lincoln, NE, University of Nebraska, 1998.

Markarian, V. *Left in Transformation: Uruguayan Exiles and the Latin American Human Rights Network, 1967–1984*. Abingdon, Routledge, 2005.

Nuñéz, R. C. *The Politics of Social Policy Change in Chile and Uruguay: Retrenchment versus Maintenance, 1973–1998*. London, Routledge, 2005.

Palermo, V., and Reboratti, C. *Del otro lado del río. Ambientalismo y política entre uruguayos y argentinos*. Buenos Aires, Edhasa, 2007.

Roniger, L., and Sznajder, M. *The Legacy of Human-Rights Violations in the Southern Cone: Argentina, Chile and Uruguay*. Oxford, Oxford University Press, 1999.

Vanger, M. I. *Uruguay's José Batlle y Ordoñez: The Determined Visionary, 1915–1917*. Boulder, CO, Lynne Rienner Publrs, 2009.

Weschler, L. *A Miracle, a Universe: Settling Accounts with Torturers*. Chicago, IL, University of Chicago Press, 1998.

VENEZUELA

Geography

PHYSICAL FEATURES

The Bolivarian Republic of Venezuela is on the northern coast of South America. Colombia lies to the west of the country, pushing into it in the south-west. This border (2,050 km or 1,73 miles) is only a little shorter than that with Brazil (2,200 km), which lies to the south. To the east is Guyana—beyond a 743-km frontier, which Venezuela claims should be further east still, along the Essequibo river. There is also a dispute over maritime boundaries in the Gulf of Venezuela with Colombia, and several Caribbean nations object to Venezuelan possession of the isolated Isla de Aves (Island of Birds), 565 km north of the mainland, on a similar latitude to northern Dominica (over 200 km to the east). There are islands that are not Venezuelan territory much closer to the mainland: northern Trinidad (Trinidad and Tobago) is 11 km off shore, to the east of the Paria peninsula and dropping south above the Orinoco delta; at the other end of the country, in the west, the Dutch island of Aruba is 25 km north of the Paraguaná peninsula (at the mouth of the Gulf of Venezuela); while a little further east is Curaçao (55 km off shore), and then Bonaire (80 km), both part of the Netherlands Antilles, although Bonaire is further from the mainland than it is from the Venezuelan dependencies in the Lesser Antilles (specifically, the Islas Las Aves—not to be confused with the single, northerly Aves island mentioned above). Aves is the most northerly of the 72 Caribbean islands, islets or cays included within the territory of Venezuela, which totals 916,445 sq km (353,841 sq miles).

Venezuela stretches along a mainly north-facing coast, the west penetrating less deeply inland than the east, but with a southern extension in the centre of the country thrusting towards the Amazon basin to include the headwaters of the Orinoco. More than 2,700 km of coast is mainly along the Caribbean; it is narrow, steep and deeply indented, owing to the mountains coming so close to the sea. Only in the far east is it low and marshy, around the delta through which the Orinoco debouches into the Atlantic. Just north of this delta is the Gulf of Paria, between Venezuela and the island of Trinidad, and most of the shore runs west from here to the Gulf of Venezuela, near the Colombian border. Parallel to this coast are most of Venezuela's Caribbean islands, the largest being Isla de Margarita. The Gulf of Venezuela is between two peninsulas, that of Paraguaná and that of Guajira, the latter on the west, its head being Colombian territory. Leading south from the Gulf is a channel of 8 km–15 km in width (dredged to a depth of 11 m—36 ft—in 1956, to make it navigable for larger vessels) into Lake Maracaibo, the largest lake in South America (210 km by 120 km). In all, Venezuela has about 30,000 sq km of inland waters. The country can be divided into four topographical regions: the Maracaibo lowlands; the Andean highlands of the north-west and the Caribbean coast; the vast plains (Llanos) of the centre-north; and the Guianan highlands, which dominate the east and south.

The lowlands around Lake Maracaibo, surrounded by heights and giving on to coastal lowlands along the Gulf of Venezuela, constitute the smallest natural region of the country (about 15% of its territory). The fairly brackish lake is in the far north-west, and the original stilt-supported villages of the local Amerindians along its shores inspired the Spanish name for the country ('little Venice'). Maracaibo is famous for its petroleum wealth, although it also has a diverse natural environment—semi-arid brush cloaks the dry north, with wooded savannah intervening before the tropical forest and swampy lagoons of the south. Forests continue up the flanks of the mountains, as Maracaibo is cupped between two Andean ranges. The Andes of Colombia's Cordillera Oriental split just before they enter western Venezuela, the crest of the more westerly Sierra de Perijá heading northwards to form much of the border between the two countries. Some of the Perijá peaks reach over 3,400 m, but the higher range, the Cordillera de Mérida, runs in a north-easterly direction, towards the Caribbean. Here is the highest point in Venezuela, the Pico Bolívar, or La Columna, at 5,007 m (16,433 ft). Before hitting the Caribbean coast, the general alignment of the heavily forested mountains turns east, and the main range runs between the sea and the Orinoco plains, to peter out and then briefly rear up again before descending into the flat, marshy Orinoco delta. The south-eastern half of western Venezuela is occupied by the uplands of the broad Llanos, tropical grasslands that lap the foothills of the Cordillera de Mérida and the coastal range. The Llanos, which covers about one-third of the country, seldom itself exceeds 215 m above sea level and slopes steadily towards the Orinoco delta. All this area, indeed four-fifths of the country, is drained by the Orinoco, which forms some of the western border of Venezuela's southern extension, before heading east and a little north, between the coastal and Guianan highlands, towards the sea. The plains stretch a considerable distance to the north and west of the main river, and vast tracts are flood prone in May–November, yet are parched in summer. The lower reaches remain wetter and there are permanent wetlands and mangroves in the delta. A further one-third of the country comprises the Guianan highlands of the south-east. The centre of the country is dominated by the rugged, hilly plateau that marks the start of the highlands that stretch eastwards to divide the Guiana coast from the Amazon basin. In Venezuela the central heights push south to cup the westward-opening basin of the Orinoco headwaters, and east to fall steeply into the Orinoco valley to the north. The landscape alternates between open grasslands and dense forests. Some of the mountains exceed 2,700 m, and the precipitous terrain allows for some dramatic scenery, such as the Angel Falls, the highest waterfall in the world. Deforestation and irresponsible mining threaten this environment, with industrial pollution more of an issue in the west, but over one-half of the country is still wooded, and one-fifth is classed as pastureland. The type of vegetation is determined more by elevation than latitude, with plants common to a temperate zone established above 900 m, tropical forests in the lower country, mangroves in the Orinoco delta and long prairie grass on the Llanos.

CLIMATE

The country lies entirely in the Tropic of Cancer, and its climate is tropical on the Llanos and on the coast, but temperate in the mountains. Altitude is very important, with hot, temperate and cold climates distinguished locally. There is a wet season in May–November, with more rain falling on the southern slopes than the northern, annual averages ranging from about 1,400 mm (55 ins) in the Andes to 280 mm on the coast. Caracas, the national capital in the mountains immediately above the Caribbean coast, has an average daily temperature range of 59°F–78°F (15°C–26°C) in January and 63°F–80°F (17°C–26°C) in July. Lowland Maracaibo has ranges of 73°F–90°F (23°C–32°C) and 76°F–94°F (24°C–34°C), respectively.

POPULATION

The population is predominantly Mestizo (67%), with 21% as largely unmixed European (predominantly of Spanish descent, but also Italian, Portuguese and German, for instance). Most of the rest of the population are black or mulatto, although there are small communities from other ethnic groups, including Arabs, and 2% are Amerindian. There are at least 40 Amerindian groups, mainly in the Amazon basin, the more isolated ones retaining principal use of their native languages, rather than the more widely used official language, Spanish. The country is overwhelmingly Roman Catholic (some 88%), with about 2% Protestants, and some Jews and adherents of other faiths (including native, animist faiths). The cultural dominance of the Roman Catholic, Spanish-speaking majority is not much disturbed by the presence of a large expatriate community, as it is mainly constituted of Colombians.

The total population was estimated at 28.8m. in mid-2010. Most people live in the coastal highlands, and 87% are urbanized. Society is also divided between extremes of rich and poor. Caracas, the federal capital (with a population of almost 3.1m. at mid-2010), is in the central coastal highlands, its port being La Guaira. The second city of the country is Maracaibo (2.2m.), in the west, on the north-western shore of the lake that shares its name. Another important city is the manufacturing centre of Valencia (1.8m.), mid-way between Caracas and Barquisimeto (1.2m.), a transport hub situated at the northern end of the main Cordillera de Mérida and the western end of the coastal range. The country is a federal republic constituted of 23 states, a Capital District (Caracas) and 11 federally controlled Caribbean island groups (totalling 72 islands) described as federal dependencies.

History

Dr JULIA BUXTON

Revised for this edition by PABLO NAVARRETE

Europeans first discovered Venezuela in 1498, during the navigator Christopher Columbus's third Spanish expedition to the New World. Following the re-establishment of Nueva Granada as a Viceroyalty in 1739, the Spanish administered Venezuela from Lima, in modern-day Peru. In 1777 Venezuela became a Spanish Captaincy-General, with an enhanced degree of administrative autonomy from Bogotá, the capital of Nueva Granada.

INDEPENDENCE

In 1724 a company of Basque merchants, the Caracas Company, obtained a monopoly of foreign trade out of Venezuelan territory and developed new markets in Europe and the Caribbean for local produce, including cocoa and coffee. The export market fostered a small élite of native European planters, the so-called *Marqueses de Chocolate*, and it was a member of this class, Simón Bolívar, who led the successful campaign for independence of the Andean region from the Spanish. Venezuela gained independence in 1819 and joined Colombia, Ecuador and Panama to form the 'Gran Colombia' federation. Bolívar viewed regional integration as a defensive counter to the emerging power of the USA, but this was undermined by infighting between Venezuelan and Colombian élites. In 1830 the federation was dissolved and Venezuela became a separate republic. For the following 80 years, military oligarchs (caudillos) fought each other for control of the country. It was only after one of these caudillos, Juan Vicente Gómez, seized power that centralization of the national territory progressed and a semblance of stability emerged. The repressive Gómez dictatorship (1908–35) coincided with the discovery and exploitation of petroleum reserves, which fuelled rapid economic growth. This in turn catalysed rapid social change and pressure for democratic reform. A fledgling opposition student movement emerged in the 1930s. This was led by Rómulo Betancourt and Dr Rafael Caldera Rodríguez, who went on to form Venezuela's first mass parties, the social democratic Acción Democrática (AD—Democratic Action) and the Christian democratic Comité de Organización Política Electoral Independiente (COPEI—Committee of Independent Electoral Political Organization). State repression failed to stem pressure for political change, and after the death of Gómez his military successors, Eleízar López Contreras (who ruled during 1935–41) and Isaías Medina Angarita (1941–45), were forced to concede political space to the AD and COPEI.

Collaboration between AD and progressive elements of the military led to a coup in 1945 that brought democratic elections and propelled AD to power for three years. However, the radically reformist AD Government was weakened by partisan conflict and unrest in the military, which led to a military coup in 1948 and the seizure of power by Gen. Marcos Pérez Jiménez. Pérez Jiménez occupied the presidency for 10 years. His regime was notable for its nation-building projects but also corruption, economic mismanagement and political oppression. A military rebellion and general strike forced the dictator to flee to Spain in January 1958. Prior to the launch of the co-ordinated uprising against Pérez Jiménez, AD, COPEI, and representatives from the private sector, the union movement and the Roman Catholic Church had signed the Pact of Punto Fijo in 1957. This established a political alliance and centrist policy consensus between the two parties, the so-called *coincidencia*. This institutional engineering aimed to ensure political stability and avoid further military intrusions into national politics. The Pact committed AD and COPEI to share appointments to the state administration (including the election administration and senior positions in the military and judiciary) and to balance the interests of business and labour. Petroleum export revenues facilitated the consolidation of the new democratic system that was established following elections in 1959, which brought Betancourt to the presidency. The distribution of petroleum revenues through the network of clientelist interests affiliated to AD and COPEI and to potentially destabilizing actors, such as the military and the Roman Catholic Church, created strong support for the Punto Fijo system and the two parties that had created it. The revenues ensured that the demands of the majority of organized and sectoral interests could be met, enabling Venezuela largely to avoid class-based conflicts.

THE DEVELOPMENT OF PETROLEUM RESOURCES

Venezuela was the world's third largest producer of coffee in the 19th century, after Brazil and Java (the latter now part of Indonesia). Following the discovery of petroleum resources at the end of that century, oil overtook coffee as the country's primary export commodity. Venezuela's importance as a petroleum exporter was enhanced by the nationalization of Mexico's oil industry in 1938 and the outbreak of the Second World War in Europe in 1939. As Venezuelan dependence on petroleum increased, and the country's role in global supply became more important, Venezuelan oil policy became increasingly nationalistic. In 1943 reforms to national oil legislation revised earlier profit-sharing agreements between the private sector and the Governments of Gómez and López Contreras, ensuring that the Venezuelan state received a 50% share of oil production and export profits. This 'oil nationalism' also led Venezuela to defend oil producer interests through co-operation efforts with other producer countries in the Middle East from 1949 onwards. This culminated in the formation of the Organization of the Petroleum Exporting Countries (OPEC) in Iraq in September 1960.

Venezuela's petroleum industry was nationalized in 1976 following the expiry of private sector concessions. In the early 1990s the Governments of President Carlos Andrés Pérez and Rafael Caldera pursued an *apertura* or opening of the national oil sector to private investors through joint venture agreements with the state petroleum company Petróleos de Venezuela, SA (PDVSA). This prompted a powerful nationalist backlash from emerging political organizations such as La Causa Radical (La Causa R—Radical Cause), which argued that the contracts violated the national oil law, that they had not been subject to congressional scrutiny and that they went against the national economic interest. Under the agreements the Venezuelan state, through PDVSA, paid a fixed amount for the petroleum extracted by private sector partners. This meant that when the price of oil declined towards the end of the 1990s, PDVSA was producing oil at a loss. La Causa R's oil specialist, Alí Rodríguez Araque, who subsequently assumed various high-level posts under Hugo Rafael Chávez Frías' presidency including President of PDVSA, argued that PDVSA was operating as a 'state within a state' outside the jurisdiction of the energy ministry. The Chávez Government, which took office in 1999, reversed the opening and reasserted oil 'sovereignty' through the 1999 Constitution and the hydrocarbons law in 2001, which required PDVSA to have a stake greater than 50% in new production and exploration activities. PDVSA's strategy of 'internationalizing' operations was reversed and the 32 operating service agreements negotiated with foreign private oil companies in 1996 were revised, increasing the taxes and royalties paid to the Venezuelan state. As with AD administrations of the 1960s and 1970s, the Chávez Government pursued a strongly nationalistic oil policy, assuming an uncompromising position in OPEC and using domestic oil revenues as a motor for economic development in the country. In 2006 PDVSA allocated over US $13,700m. in profits to social development, a figure that rose to over $14,100m. in 2007, and to more than $14,733m. in 2008. This figure decreased dramatically to $2,369m. in 2009 as oil-export earnings declined from $91,500m. in 2008 to $54,201m. in 2009. Under the Chávez Government, Venezuela's oil wealth was also used as a tool for promoting regional integration and energy sovereignty through Venezuelan initiatives such as Petrocaribe, which supplied oil at discounted cost to 18 oil-importing Central American and Caribbean countries. In 2007 heavy shale sand reserves in the Orinoco Belt, which had been opened to private sector exploration and drilling, were classified as conventional reserves, rendering Venezuela the country with the world's largest oil reserves. In June 2007 Rafael Ramírez Carreño, the Minister of Energy and Petroleum (and PDVSA President), renegotiated the original exploration contracts, thereby providing PDVSA with a majority stake in the Orinoco projects. The capacity of PDVSA to maintain both its social expenditure commitments, in addition to much needed investment in exploration, production and technology, was subject to increasing scrutiny amid a sharp decline in oil prices between the fourth quarter of 2008 and the first quarter of 2009, and concerns of under-investment in drilling, production and refining.

THE ADMINISTRATION OF CARLOS PÉREZ RODRÍGUEZ

Following the overthrow of the Pérez Jiménez dictatorship in 1958 Venezuela's democracy was seen to be rapidly consolidated. In the 1960s and 1970s major social progress was made as successive AD and COPEI Governments channelled petroleum export earnings into state subsidies and social investment. A comprehensive welfare-state system was established and a programme of land distribution implemented. After the national elections of 1973, which brought the AD candidate, Carlos Andrés Pérez Rodríguez, to power, Venezuela experienced a dramatic change in economic fortunes as the Middle East oil embargo led to a sharp rise in international petroleum prices. This coincided with the nationalization of the Venezuelan petroleum industry, leading to a 10-fold increase in central government revenues. However, the oil 'boom' laid the foundations of a subsequent economic crisis that ultimately delegitimized the Punto Fijo model. The extraordinary levels of revenue accruing to the state exacerbated corruption, and led the national administration to become excessively bureaucratic and inefficient. The Government borrowed from international creditors in order to sustain state investment projects when the price of petroleum began to decline towards the end of Pérez's term in office. Despite the steady deterioration in the oil price and increasingly negative international borrowing conditions, successive COPEI and AD Governments were reluctant to reduce fiscal spending, owing to concerns that economic adjustment would undermine support for the parties. During the administration of Luis Herrera Campins (1979–84) the Government used the investment fund of PDVSA, in an attempt to stabilize the economy after a devaluation of the currency in 1983. The move was unsuccessfully resisted by PDVSA managers, who subsequently began to protect PDVSA's revenues from what they considered to be an increasingly incompetent state. This led to a policy of 'internationalization', which resulted in PDVSA investing outside of Venezuela; for example, it bought refineries in Europe and the USA. PDVSA also used 'transfer pricing' to transfer its profits abroad.

In the 1980s there was mounting popular disaffection with AD and COPEI as the economy went into recession and the network of welfare coverage and oil revenue distribution began to shrink. Despite the increasingly negative evaluation of their performance, AD and COPEI remained the dominant political forces as a result of their institutionalized control of the state and election administration and their ability to privilege a progressively narrowing, but powerful, circle of élite interests.

In 1988 Pérez was re-elected to the presidency amid critical economic conditions and popular expectations of a return to the 'boom years' of his first term in office. Expectations of a renewed era of prosperity were immediately frustrated, as an orthodox programme of liberal economic policies was introduced within a month of Pérez taking office. The strict austerity measures, in particular increased fuel and transport prices, provoked serious civil disturbances in February 1989, which were suppressed by security services when the Government requested that they quell riots in the capital. This resulted in the death of 276 people, according to official figures, although other sources reported as many as 2,000–3,000. This event became known as the 'Caracazo' and it proved pivotal in that it exacerbated alienation from the Punto Fijo system among junior ranks of the armed forces and significant sectors of the population.

President Pérez rapidly lost the support of his own party, AD, and the pro-AD Confederación de Trabajadores de Venezuela (CTV—Venezuelan Workers' Confederation), which organized the first general strike since democratization in 1958. In an attempt to enhance the legitimacy of the political system, the Pérez Government introduced a series of reforms in 1989, including administrative and political decentralization and changes to the electoral system. This enabled minor parties of the centre-left, such as La Causa R and the Movimiento al Socialismo (MAS—Movement to Socialism), to win control of a number of state and municipal governments. It also enabled independent figures running on anti-party platforms to win elective office and gain national prominence, such as Irene Sáez, the mayor of Chacao municipality in Caracas, and Henrique Salas Römer, who was twice elected Governor of Carabobo state. However, the reforms failed to relegitimize the Punto Fijo system, and the opening proved to be a double-edged sword for new parties and independent politicians, as it led them to be associated with Punto Fijo institutions and the existing party political system.

FAILED MILITARY COUP

The depth of the political crisis in Venezuela was revealed by an attempted *coup d'état* in February 1992. The rebels belonged to a nationalist faction of junior officers known as the Movimiento Bolivariano Revolucionario-200 (MBR-200—Bolivarian Revolutionary Movement 200), formed by Lt-Col Chávez Frías and three colleagues 10 years earlier. MBR-200 proposed a 'Bolivarian' alternative to the Punto Fijo model that addressed the needs of the poor and marginalized and aimed to realize the ambitions of the Liberator, Simón Bolívar. Although the coup failed, it transformed Chávez into a popular hero, despite his subsequent imprisonment.

The coup attempt, and a second one organized by forces indirectly linked to MBR-200 in November 1992, seriously weakened President Pérez, who came under pressure to resign. He was suspended from office by the AD-controlled Congreso Nacional (National Congress) in May 1993 following allegations of misappropriation of public funds. In May 1996 he was found guilty and sentenced to two years and four months under house arrest.

THE ADMINISTRATION OF RAFAEL CALDERA RODRÍGUEZ

Following the suspension of Pérez, in June 1993 the Congreso elected Ramón José Velásquez, an independent senator, as interim President until fresh elections were held in December. Rafael Caldera Rodríguez, who contested the election as an independent candidate following his expulsion from COPEI in June, won the presidency on an anti-party and anti-economic-liberalization platform. He was supported by a 17-party electoral alliance, Convergencia Nacional (CN—National Convergence), that included representatives of the traditional left. The election, which was marred by allegations of electoral fraud against La Causa R candidate Andrés Velásquez, was also significant in that it was the first time since 1958 that neither AD nor COPEI controlled the executive. However, they remained the dominant force in the bicameral legislature. On taking office, Caldera released the coup plotters of 1992, including Chávez, who was pardoned for his role in the coup and discharged from the army. Chávez subsequently formed the Movimiento Quinta República (MVR—Fifth Republic Movement), which appealed for abstention in the regional elections of 1995 as a means of delegitimizing the Punto Fijo model.

Although Caldera promised to overhaul the 1961 Constitution and address rising poverty, little was achieved, deepening popular frustration and the search for political alternatives to the country's discredited political élite. The Caldera administration was politically and economically weakened by the collapse of the banking sector that occurred within months of him taking office. The Government intervened to support the sector at the cost of precipitating a major economic crisis that forced the administration to renege on electoral promises and sign a US $1,400m. stand-by agreement with the IMF in July 1996. The series of economic and structural reforms, the so-called *Agenda Venezuela*, exacerbated popular discontent and deepened social inequalities. Caldera became increasingly reliant on the AD and COPEI parties in the Congreso in order to adopt austerity legislation as his Convergencia coalition fragmented. Caldera also looked to the AD-affiliated CTV to support a modification of labour legislation that led to the termination of the system of retroactive severance payments, a crucial form of welfare provision. CTV's participation in these negotiations drastically undermined worker support for the confederation, which, like the parties, was seen as corrupt and out of touch with the interests of its members.

A rise in the oil price afforded the Government fiscal leeway in 1997, and structural adjustment measures were postponed. However, in 1998, the year of national elections, the price of petroleum decreased, forcing the Government to reduce spending by US $6,000m. Underscoring the profound popular hostility to the established political parties, all the leading presidential candidates contested the election as independents. The two front-running candidates, Henrique Salas Römer and Irene Sáez, both ran on neo-liberal platforms, but saw their support levels collapse after they accepted the endorsement of AD and COPEI and as popular sentiment turned against orthodox liberal economic proposals. This benefited Chávez, a little-noticed candidate until the closing stages of the election campaign, who was supported by a multiparty alliance, the Polo Patriótico (PP—Patriotic Pole). This comprised Chávez's MVR party, a dissident faction of La Causa R, Patria Para Todos (PPT—Homeland For All), the MAS and the Partido Comunista de Venezuela (PCV—Venezuelan Communist Party). The Chávez manifesto promised a complete break from the Punto Fijo model and a 'Bolivarian revolution' that would rewrite the Constitution, restructure state institutions and terminate the internationalization strategy of PDVSA. Chávez's platform was relatively moderate, emphasizing a 'third way' model of capitalism in which the state only intervened when the market failed. He enjoyed enormous popular support, owing to his nationalist rhetoric and identification with politically and economically marginalized groups, particularly the indigenous and black communities. Being of mixed race and having no historic ties to AD or COPEI further enhanced his credentials.

Despite attempts by COPEI and AD to prevent a victory by Chávez by revising the electoral schedule, Chávez won the presidency with a majority of votes (56%) in the December 1998 contest. AD secured the most congressional seats (55 of the 189 seats in the Cámara de Diputados and 19 of the 48 seats in the Senado) in elections held in November. The PP also performed well, winning 18 upper-house seats and 70 seats in the Cámara de Diputados.

THE ADMINISTRATION OF HUGO CHÁVEZ FRÍAS

President Chávez used his inauguration in February 1999 to launch his Bolivarian revolution. He decreed a national referendum on the convening of a constituent assembly to draft a new constitution. In the plebiscite, held in April, 88% of voters endorsed Chávez's proposals. AD, COPEI and interests affiliated to those parties (such as the CTV and leading business groups) adopted a strategy of withdrawing from the formal political process in protest against the referendum and in order to delegitimize the new Government.

In the election to the 131-member Constituent Assembly, held in July 1999, supporters of Chávez won 125 of the seats. The Constituent Assembly was convened in August and completed its work in November. The new Constitution was approved by 71% of voters in a second popular referendum held in December. The Bolivarian Constitution introduced radical changes to the institutional framework of the Venezuelan state in order to terminate the control historically exercised by AD and COPEI. The changes included: the introduction of a renewable six-year term for the President (replacing the traditional non-renewable five-year term); the replacement of the bicameral legislative arrangements with a 165-seat unicameral chamber (the Asamblea Nacional, or National Assembly); and the abolition of the Supreme Court, which was to be superseded by the Tribunal Suprema de Justicia (TSJ—Supreme Court of Justice). Two new state powers were created: the Consejo Moral Republicano (Moral Republican Council), the principal duty of which was to uphold the Constitution, and the Consejo Nacional Electoral (CNE—National Electoral Council). The post of Vice-President was created, and serving military officers were given the right to vote, with military promotions removed from the hands of the legislature and given to the President. The army, navy and air force were merged into a single unified command. The Constitution changed the official name of the country to the

Bolivarian Republic of Venezuela, and there was a strong emphasis throughout the document on state provision of welfare and citizen participation through a variety of mechanisms that included recall referendums and participation by civil society groups in state appointments.

Following the promulgation of the new Constitution, the Constituent Assembly appointed an unelected 21-person *congresillo* (mini-congress), pending fresh national elections scheduled for May 2000. In a move that fuelled opposition claims of authoritarianism, the *congresillo* began filling the new posts created by the Constitution with individuals closely identified with the PP, on the grounds that the country was in a 'transitional phase', until a new National Assembly could ratify or reverse the appointments. Opposition criticism regarding the democratic credentials of Chávez increased following the appointment of a number of military officers to senior cabinet and administrative positions. Chávez viewed the military as an integral player in his project for national reconstruction, and this was reflected in the Government's first social policy initiative, the Social Emergency and Internal Defence and Development Plan, known as the 'Plan Bolívar 2000', which was launched in February 1999. The Plan was intended to rehabilitate public property and land, and led to the deployment of the armed forces in local communities to build schools and hospitals. Viewed as a means of by-passing the ineffective state administration, the Plan was, nevertheless, repudiated by influential senior and retired military officers, who began linking up with the party political opposition to Chávez.

Throughout 1999 opposition to President Chávez was fierce among the former beneficiaries of the Punto Fijo model in the business, union and media sectors. However, it was uncoordinated, inchoate and lacking in leadership owing to the weakness of the AD and COPEI parties. In February 2000, on the eighth anniversary of the 1992 military coup attempt, Francisco Arias Cárdenas, a former colleague of Chávez, and five other prominent figures within MBR-200 issued the Declaration of Maracay. This argued that Chávez had betrayed the democratic ideals of MBR-200. Arias subsequently announced his intention to contest the presidency.

The 2000 Elections

The elections scheduled for May 2000 were popularly known as the 'mega-elections', since they were intended to 're-legitimize' all publicly elected officials including the President. These elections were the largest and most complex in the country's history, with more than 6,000 posts to be decided. Arias was the only significant challenger to Chávez for the presidency, following the decision by AD and COPEI not to present presidential candidates. Three days before the elections were due to be held, the TSJ ruled in favour of an injunction introduced by civil society organizations against the elections, on the grounds that the CNE was not technically competent to administer the process. Following the postponement, the CNE executive was replaced by new authorities, which separated the election of the president, legislative assembly, state governors and mayors from those for regional and municipal legislatures.

The elections were eventually held in July 2000 and Chávez received 60% of the votes, compared with 38% secured by Arias. In elections to the new 165-seat Asamblea Nacional the MVR-led PP alliance won 104 seats, more than the three-fifths' majority required to make appointments to the positions of Fiscal- and Comptroller-General and to the judiciary. AD opted to contest the Assembly elections and emerged as the largest opposition party, winning 32 seats, while COPEI was eliminated as a significant political force, securing just five assembly seats. In early August the Asamblea Nacional convened for the first time. The primary task of the legislature was to modify existing legislation in accordance with the new Constitution. In November the Asamblea Nacional granted 'enabling powers' to the executive for one year, allowing President Chávez to legislate by decree in a range of areas.

There was a marked increase in political polarization following the 'mega-elections', as the Chávez administration pressed ahead with its project of reform and moved to decree legislation in line with its Bolivarian revolutionary objectives. In October 2000 Chávez decreed a referendum to approve measures to reform the trade union movement through the introduction of direct internal elections. The CTV leadership viewed this as an attack on its monopoly of labour representation and an attempt by the Government to replace the CTV with a new pro-Government trade union movement called the Frente Bolivariana de Trabajadores (FBT—Bolivarian Workers Front). Opposition to the referendum became a platform for mobilization against the Government and the CTV convoked a series of stoppages by affiliated trade unions. This included a costly four-day strike by oil-industry workers in October in protest against management changes introduced by the Government in line with its strategy of reducing PDVSA autonomy. The referendum on trade union reform went ahead in December, and the proposals were supported by 63% of voters. However, with an abstention rate of 78%, the legitimacy of the Government's reforms was questioned. Elections to a unified confederation proceeded in October 2001, and the presidency was won by the opposition CTV candidate, Carlos Ortega, amid claims of violence and intimidation by conflicting union organizations. The Government refused to recognize Ortega's election, leading to a legal stand-off between the union and the Government.

In 2001 the CTV continued to convoke anti-Government demonstrations, which were supported by different groups whose interests were also affected by government policy. These included the Roman Catholic Church, which opposed changes to education funding, the Federación Venezolana de Cámaras y Asociaciones de Comercio y Producción (Fedecámaras—the leading private sector lobby group), landowners and the senior management within PDVSA. Opposition to the Government became more unified following the introduction of 49 new pieces of legislation decreed by President Chávez under enabling powers in November. The legislation formed the legal and programmatic basis of the Bolivarian revolution and covered a range of areas, including tourism, fishing and banking. Particularly contentious were the Hydrocarbons and Agricultural Development Land Reform Laws. The Hydrocarbons Law and gas laws reserved resource ownership to the state, reversing the opening to private sector interests that had been introduced by President Caldera in the mid-1990s. The Land Reform Law allowed for the expropriation of privately held land deemed 'idle' in the national interest. Lobby groups and sectoral interests, some of which received financial support from US quasi-governmental organizations such as the National Endowment for Democracy, substituted the weak and disorganized opposition political parties that were incapable of mounting a viable challenge to the Government. This added to political instability as anti-Government protests were taken outside formal institutional structures and onto the streets. The economic élite used its control of the private sector media to criticize the Government and mobilize support for the union-led demonstrations. There was a second general strike in January 2002, along with appeals by Government opponents for the military to intervene and remove Chávez from power.

President Chávez rejected appeals for negotiations over the contents of the November 2001 legislation, and this led to divisions in the ruling coalition between moderate factions and more radical sections of the alliance grouped in the MVR and PCV. A section of the MAS defected to the opposition in the legislative assembly, reducing the Government's majority to single figures, and the leader of the MVR, Chávez's ideological mentor, Luis Miquilena, left the Government and created his own party, Solidaridad (Solidarity). Inflammatory verbal attacks between Chávez and his opponents increased political instability during this period, and there was a marked rise in pro- and anti-Government street demonstrations.

The April 2002 Coup

Bolstered by significant popular support and positive signals from the US authorities, at the beginning of 2002 the opposition pressed for President Chávez to resign. On 9 April the CTV and Fedecámaras held a third strike in support of striking workers at PDVSA's headquarters in Caracas.

In a highly disputed series of events, at least 19 people were killed and more than 60 people were wounded on 11 April 2002 as pro- and anti-Government demonstrators clashed near the presidential palace. Amid claims in the private media that the President had ordered his supporters to fire on opposition demonstrators, senior military officers, including the Commander-in-Chief of the Armed Forces, Gen. Lucas Rincón Romero, announced that Chávez had resigned and been placed under arrest. Chávez was subsequently transferred to a military base on a nearby Caribbean island. Senior cabinet figures were arrested and an interim junta was installed, headed by the President of Fedecámaras, Pedro Carmona. The break with the constitutional order in Venezuela was condemned by regional organizations, such as the Organization of American States (OAS), but not by the US, British or Spanish Governments. The military and trade unions withdrew their support from the junta, and the USA revised its position when Carmona appointed a cabinet composed of right-wing economists, dissolved the democratically elected legislature and regional assemblies and suspended the Constitution. The junta collapsed on 13 April, following the intervention of senior pro-Government members of the army and mass popular demonstrations demanding the reinstatement of Chávez, who was returned to office the following day.

The 2004 Recall Referendum

In the immediate aftermath of the coup, the Government convened a series of committees to promote national dialogue with the opposition, which created the Coordinadora Democrática (CD—Democratic Co-ordinator) as an umbrella organization for anti-Chávez groups. However, polarization and political tension persisted, and pro- and anti-Government mobilization continued.

As a result of the continuing conflict, a 'tripartite group' comprising the US-based Carter Center, the OAS and the UN Development Programme was invited to Venezuela to mediate. This failed to achieve common ground between representatives of the Government and the opposition, with dialogue undermined by debilitating divisions between moderate and hard-line factions in both groups.

In December 2002 the opposition initiated an indefinite general strike concentrated in strategic sectors of the economy, most significantly the oil industry, to demand that President Chávez stand down. This was a political victory for radical elements of the opposition, which denied the legitimacy of the Government and sought to accelerate its removal. They prevailed over more moderate sections, represented by Primero Justicia (PJ—Justice First) and some civil society organizations that sought to remove the Government through constitutional electoral methods.

The strike was organized by the CTV and Fedecámaras and was observed by managers and technicians at PDVSA. The stoppage lasted until February 2003 and came at a grave fiscal cost to Venezuela. Petroleum production decreased from an average of 2.9m. barrels per day (b/d) to fewer than 25,000 b/d. The Government was deprived of US $17,000m. in petroleum export revenue, technical installations were sabotaged and PDVSA was forced to import petroleum at a loss and declare *force majeure* on existing contracts. Owing to the repercussions of the strike, which heightened unemployment and shortages over the Christmas period, support for the opposition was eroded.

In January 2003 foreign Governments again intervened to mediate the political crisis through a six-country 'Friends of Venezuela' delegation, comprising officials from the USA, Brazil, Mexico, Chile, Spain and Portugal. As the strike fragmented, the Friends and the tripartite group increased pressure for an accord between the Government and the opposition, which was signed in May. The moderate opposition hailed the agreement as a major breakthrough, as it committed all parties to a constitutional resolution to the crisis. The opposition strategy subsequently shifted from stoppages and protests to electoral methods of replacing President Chávez. This was possible through a recall referendum, a mechanism introduced by the 1999 Constitution.

The failure of the opposition coup and PDVSA strike strengthened the Government's hand. The administration dismissed the senior military command and 18,000 of the 33,000 full-time workers at PDVSA for participating in the strike. PDVSA re-staffing followed a pattern of appointment based on political support for the Bolivarian revolution that was seen in other 'disloyal' institutions such as the diplomatic service and the judiciary, after the opposition-dominated senior judges dismissed charges of military rebellion against the coup leaders. The President of Fedecámaras was later arrested and charged with crimes including treason, although he eventually fled to Colombia, while the CTV President, Carlos Ortega, unsuccessfully sought political asylum in Costa Rica and was arrested in 2006.

In order for a recall referendum on the executive to be convened, 20% of the electorate (more than 2.4m. voters) were constitutionally required to sign a petition. A civil society group, Súmate (Join Up), took a lead role in distributing information to voters ahead of the referendum and preparing databases of the electorate. However, as Súmate was financed by the National Endowment for Democracy, this deepened government and *Chavista* suspicions of the opposition and the continued influence of the USA on Venezuelan politics. After a controversial process, in June 2004 the CNE ruled that the opposition had succeeded in gathering the requisite number of signatures after a petition in April and a 'repair' of signatures that had technical irregularities at the end of May. The recall referendum was scheduled for 15 August, and, in the event that a greater proportion of the electorate voted against Chávez than had supported him in the 2000 elections (59.7% of voters), fresh elections were to be convened within 30 days of the recall result being issued. The opposition went into the recall campaign divided, with party factions vying for the CD candidacy in the event of a fresh presidential election. They also lacked a clear proposal for government. By contrast, the *Chavistas* approached the referendum with a solid organizational base, comprising grassroots organizations grouped in new community-based organizations and electoral units, such as the Círculos Bolivarianos (Bolivarian Circles) and the Comando Ayacucho. Higher than expected oil prices in 2004 further strengthened the position of the Government, which used the petroleum revenue to fund a number of social programmes in areas such as health, education and work training, called *misiones*.

Chávez retained executive control, with 59% voting in favour of his presidency and 41% against. Participation in the referendum was high, at 70%. Súmate challenged the results, even though international observers including the Carter Center deemed the referendum to be clean and fair. Among a number of irregularities reported by Súmate was the 'Tascón list', a list of all those who had signed the petition demanding the referendum, which was posted on the website of MVR Asamblea Nacional member Luis Tascón Gutiérrez. It was claimed that this list was used to vet employment in the public sector and was cited by Súmate as evidence of the lack of democracy and secrecy of the vote in Venezuela. This argument was in turn used to justify contentious increases in US 'democracy assistance' to opposition groups in Venezuela that included Súmate.

In the aftermath of his referendum victory Chávez announced a deepening of the Bolivarian revolution. Land distribution programmes were accelerated and the petroleum revenue-financed *misiones* were extended into new areas of welfare provision. Major progress was made in expanding education, health, welfare and credit provision, with over 8,500 clinics (staffed by some 20,000 Cuban doctors) and 2,500 schools built in areas previously lacking access to welfare. As a result of persistent lockouts and strikes led by the opposition, the Government created new subsidized food-distribution schemes, such as the 6,000 Mercal supermarkets, which were maintained in the aftermath of opposition protests. Financial support was also provided by the Government to workers who took over industries shut down by private sector owners, an opposition strategy that had the unintended consequence of facilitating state intervention in the economy. Social production companies based on co-operative practices, and which received financial support from the Government, expanded across the country, and their position in the national economy was enhanced through the introduction of the Social Production Companies Register, upon which public and private sector contractors were required to draw when outsourcing activities. These windfall petroleum-financed measures consolidated support for the Government among poorer sectors. The administration emerged strengthened and more committed to its revolutionary goals following four years of political turmoil. In the aftermath of the recall referendum, President Chávez announced that Venezuela was striving to achieve a model of '21st Century Socialism'. This evolution in Chávez's ideological thinking, away from his endorsement in 1999 of the 'third way' model associated with British Prime Minister Tony Blair, was made possible by the surge in oil prices and accelerated by antagonism between the Government and the USA and the domestic opposition.

The CD went into the regional elections of October 2004 fragmented and demoralized. Pro-Chávez candidates won control of 21 of the country's 23 state governments. The capacity of the CD alliance to convoke anti-Government mobilizations was further restricted in December, when the Government introduced a 'media responsibility law' and other revisions to the Penal Code that made defamation of a public official, incitement to violence and the distribution of inaccurate reports offences punishable by imprisonment. The introduction of the legislation followed the assassination of public prosecutor Danilo Anderson in November. Anderson had been investigating the events surrounding the coup attempt of April 2002. In what Government opponents interpreted as a further curtailment of their activities, in July 2005 the TSJ announced its intention to prosecute the executive of Súmate for violating domestic laws relating to foreign financing of political activity. In May the President of Súmate, María Corina Machado, had been received by President George W. Bush in Washington, DC, USA, in a high-profile press conference at the White House.

A Third Term for Chávez

The political ascendancy of the *Chavista* alliance was further demonstrated in the elections to the Asamblea Nacional in December 2005, which were boycotted by the opposition on the grounds that a fair and free election and secrecy of the vote could not be guaranteed, despite reassurance from the OAS and international election observer groups. By opting not to participate, the opposition effectively handed control of the legislature to the Government, the political victory of which was accompanied by opposition claims that authoritarianism in the country was deepening.

The opposition was also divided going into the presidential election contest of December 2006, with the nomination contested by Julio Borges of the PJ, Teodoro Petkoff, a former minister and editor of the newspaper *Tal Cual*, and Manuel Rosales, Governor of Zulia state. In August Borges and Petkoff deferred their candidacies in favour of Rosales, thereby avoiding a damaging internal debate. The Rosales campaign lost its initial traction owing to a lack of clarity over policy and the future composition of a Rosales government. Rosales was defeated by Chávez, who obtained 7.3m. votes, representing a share of 63% against 37% for Rosales.

The third Chávez term was launched with a flurry of activity as the re-elected President announced plans to accelerate the creation of 21st Century Socialism. In January 2007 Chávez petitioned the Asamblea Nacional for enabling powers. These were granted, allowing the executive the right to decree policy in an extensive range of areas for an 18-month period. Enabling powers formed one of the 'five motors' of the revolution that were intended to reshape Venezuelan politics and institutions in line with the 21st Century Socialism model. The other four included an expansion of communal power, a new geometry of power, constitutional reform, and the promotion of moral and educational values. Taken together, these changes prefigured a redesign of institutions to reflect a redistribution of power down to grass-roots community councils (of which there were some 20,000 in 2009), which the Government aimed to increase through financial disbursements. During the first few months of the new Chávez presidency moves were also made to expand the role of the state in the economy and reclaim national sovereignty in strategic areas such as telecommunications, electricity and hydrocarbons, all of which came under majority state control after the negotiation of compensation packages with private sector owners. Plans to create a single unified socialist party out of the multi-party pro-Government alliance gained momentum, with national discussion meetings on the structure and orientation of the new party convened across the country. However, these plans proved controversial and caused divisions within the government alliance. Nevertheless, in 2008 the Partido Socialista Unido de Venezuela (PSUV—United Socialist Party of Venezuela) was launched, and the party performed well in the November 2008 regional elections, although it lost the crucial mayorship of Greater Caracas. There was particular controversy over plans to revise the Constitution. The proposed reforms, presented by President Chávez in August 2007, included such measures as unlimited presidential terms, executive control over international reserves and a six-hour working day. In a referendum on the reforms held on 2 December, the Government experienced its first, albeit narrow, electoral defeat, amid a high rate of abstention by traditionally loyal Government supporters. The referendum set-back focused the Government's attention on the need to improve policy and welfare delivery and to address key voter concerns such as corruption, food shortages and, in particular, crime. Although the measures were rejected, Chávez proceeded to introduce some of his planned changes on a case-by-case basis through the use of enabling powers. Ahead of the expiry of enabling authority at the beginning of August 2008, a package of 23 measures was introduced. These included laws against financial speculation and hoarding, which became punishable by imprisonment, and the creation of a civil militia that was intended to improve security in communities. In February 2009 the Government convened a referendum on whether term limits for all publicly elected officials should be abolished. Some 55% of voters approved the constitutional amendment, allowing Chávez to run for re-election indefinitely.

Throughout 2009 and 2010 economic issues such as high inflation, shortages of certain goods and a nation-wide power shortage that led to electricity-rationing in late 2009 compromised the Government's popularity. However, the anti-Chávez movement failed to capitalize on the resulting discontent. In 2008 opposition-aligned students led a series of protests against the administration. This injected some vigour into the opposition campaign, which quickly dissipated owing to the continued lack of opposition leadership and its failure to draw support away from the Government. During 2009 and 2010 a number of high-level opposition figures were charged with corruption. This was interpreted by large sectors of the opposition as 'political persecution' by the Chávez Government and renewed the climate of political polarization in the country. Elections to the Asamblea Nacional were scheduled for September 2010, and the opposition was expected to make important gains.

Nevertheless, 11 years into his tenure, President Chávez remained personally popular, although the opposition appeared increasingly emboldened. Discernable weaknesses that needed to be addressed included crime, corruption, and contradictions in development and economic policy, which had the potential to undermine government strategy and erode support for Chávez over the course of his third term. Divisions within the ruling PSUV and disaffection with the performance of individual PSUV officials in national and regional politics pointed to increased reliance on the unifying figure of Chávez, especially following the victory in the February 2009 referendum that abolished presidential term limits.

INTERNATIONAL RELATIONS

President Chávez instituted a dramatic change in Venezuela's international relations. Three central concepts under the rubric of the Government's 'Bolivarian' approach guided foreign affairs: multipolarism; state sovereignty; and the need for close ties with other oil-producing nations. When the Government first assumed power, its capacity to promote these ideas was limited. However, the strong rise in the international oil price, the spread of left-of-centre Governments across Latin America, rising sentiment against US foreign policy, resource nationalism in countries such as Russia and the emergence of the People's Republic of China as an important trading partner provided an opportunity for Chávez to advance his vision of an alternative global order that would dilute Venezuela's historically close ties with the USA, along with that country's power in world politics and global institutions. This, along with the US Government's increased hostility to those critical of its 'war on terror', contributed significantly to a chronic deterioration in relations between Venezuela and the USA.

Bolivarianism is named after South America's 19th-century independence leader, Simón Bolívar. Drawing on Bolívar's vision of an integrated Latin America as a counter to the emerging USA, Chávez pursued regional integration based on principles of social justice. An outspoken opponent of the planned Free Trade Area of the Americas (FTAA) promoted by the USA, Chávez posited a Bolivarian Alternative for the Americas (Alternativa Bolivariana para las Américas—ALBA—renamed the Bolivarian Alliance for the Peoples of our America or Alianza Bolivariana para los Pueblos de Nuestra América, in June 2009) as a counter model that excluded the USA. Launched by Venezuela and Cuba in 2004, by mid-2010 the organization counted eight members, including Bolivia, Nicaragua and Ecuador, with Paraguay considering future membership. (Honduras withdrew from ALBA in January 2010, following the overthrow of President José Manuel Zelaya Rosales in June 2009.) However, this did not enable Venezuela to supplant the FTAA with ALBA, as some South American states, such as Peru, went on to negotiate bilateral trade agreements with the USA. The Venezuelan Government forged strong links with the Governments of Brazil, Argentina and Uruguay, and a number of economic and cultural integration projects based on ALBA principles of social justice and exploitation of comparative advantages were launched, including the broadcasting initiative Telesur, and the Banco del Sur—intended as a regional alternative to the World Bank. Regional energy integration strategies in the gas, electricity and petroleum sectors were also vigorously pursued by the Venezuelan Government, as exemplified by projects such as the planned Gasoducto del Sur gas pipeline from Venezuela and Bolivia to Argentina, and the regional petroleum company PetroSur.

At the beginning of 2006 Venezuela withdrew from the Comunidad Andina de Naciones (CAN—Andean Community of Nations, comprising Bolivia, Colombia, Ecuador and Peru) on the grounds that CAN membership and bilateral trade deals between the USA and individual CAN members were incompatible. This followed the signing of bilateral accords between Colombia, Peru and the USA. Venezuela was admitted to full membership of the Southern Common Market (Mercado Común del Sur—Mercosur) in July 2006 after nearly a decade of negotiating entry, although its membership was subject to ratification by all the group's existing members, a process that had not been completed by mid-2010; moreover, by 2007 it was evident that Venezuela was despondent as to Mercosur's potential as a mechanism for wider regional integration. Venezuela participated in the founding conference of the Union of South American Nations (Unión de Naciones Suramericanas—UNASUR), which was formed by 12 South American countries in May 2008. In September UNASUR achieved its first diplomatic achievement when it played a key role in defusing a serious political crisis in Bolivia between the Government of Juan Evo Morales Aima and the domestic opposition. UNASUR advanced its agenda of creating closer ties between its member states and created the South American Defense Council (SADC), which held its first meeting in March 2009; it also adopted a position of staunch opposition to the June 2009 coup in Honduras, refusing, for instance, to recognize the elections held under the de facto Government.

Relations between Venezuela and Cuba strengthened significantly after President Chávez assumed office. More than 875 reciprocal agreements in areas such as investment, trade, social provision and energy were signed by Chávez and Cuban Presidents Dr Fidel Castro Ruz and Raúl Castro Ruz. In 2008 trade between the two countries amounted to approximately US $11,000m. per year, up from $388m. in 1998, the year that Chávez was first elected. The reinforcement of bilateral ties aggravated US–Venezuelan hostilities. Venezuela remained opposed to the US embargo on Cuba and defended Venezuela's right to trade with the country on the grounds that this was a 'sovereign' right and that the embargo was against international law.

As part of his anti-imperialist Bolivarian vision, President Chávez sought to reduce Venezuela's trade dependence on the USA and to loosen the close economic and political relationship that had existed between the two countries throughout the 20th century. The Chávez Government was critical of the USA's global 'war on terror', and condemned the US-led invasions of Afghanistan and Iraq in 2001 and 2003, respectively. Relations between the two countries were further strained amid allegations by Chávez that the Bush Administration was working with the CD opposition alliance to destabilize his Government and remove him from power. The USA channelled extensive financial resources to the anti-Government movement, through the National Endowment for Democracy, and sought to isolate Venezuela at the regional level. Senior figures in the US Government accused Chávez of 'destabilizing' the Latin American region, as well as being authoritarian in approach and damaging to the security interests of the USA. Senior figures in the Venezuelan Government in turn accused Bush of heading a 'terrorist' Government. In 2005 the USA imposed an arms export embargo on Venezuela, and in 2006 Venezuela was 'decertified' for non-compliance in the USA's counter-narcotics policy, despite an increase in interdiction and enforcement activities and good co-operative relations between Venezuela and other countries on anti-drugs issues. The USA listed Venezuela as a major drugs transit or illicit drugs-producing country for the financial year 2007, and continued to criticize the Chávez administration's record in relation to counter-narcotics policy, human rights and border security. Continued efforts by the USA to isolate Chávez at the regional and international level, and to undermine his influence through small-scale anti-poverty initiatives, served only to increase sympathy for Venezuela and regional opposition to US interference in South America's domestic politics. Bilateral relations deteriorated further as a result of the failure of US authorities to extradite a self-acknowledged terrorist and former employee of its Central Intelligence Agency, Luis Posada Carriles, to Venezuela to face charges relating to the bombing of a Cuban aeroplane in 1976 in which 73 people died. In May 2007 illegal immigration charges against Posada Carriles, a Venezuelan national, were dismissed by a US district judge and he was released from custody. Relations between Venezuela and the USA reached an all-time low in September 2008 when Venezuela expelled its US ambassador in 'solidarity' with the Morales Government in Bolivia, which had expelled the US ambassador for allegedly 'subverting' Bolivia's democracy by colluding with Bolivian opposition groups. The USA responded by expelling Venezuela's ambassador. Hopes were raised of an improvement in US-Venezuelan relations in January 2009 following Barack Obama's assumption of the US presidency; at the Fifth Summit of the Americas in April, a highly publicized encounter between Chávez and Obama was interpreted as increasing the prospects for improved relations. However, this was short-lived as US support for the regime that removed President Zelaya from office in Honduras in June, along with a controversial agreement signed in October that allowed the USA to use Colombian military bases, was interpreted as hostile towards Venezuela by the Chávez Government.

Antagonism between the USA and Venezuela was particularly pronounced in relation to petroleum. The Chávez Government pursued close relations with other oil-producing nations, including Iraq, Libya, Iran and Russia. In August 2000 President Chávez undertook a controversial tour of the Middle East, during which he visited Iraq and Libya and became the first elected head of state to meet the Iraqi leader Saddam Hussain since sanctions were imposed on that country after the war in the region of the Persian (Arabian) Gulf in 1991. The USA condemned the meeting and was also critical of the Caracas Energy Accord of 2000, which extended to Cuba the preferential terms for oil offered by Venezuela and Mexico to other countries in the region. In 2005 Chávez publicly stated his commitment to co-operating with the Iranian Government in the peaceful use of nuclear energy, and bilateral agreements between the two countries were signed in areas including agricultural, manufacturing, cultural and economic development. In improving the traditionally poor relations between Venezuela and other OPEC member countries and seeking close co-operation within the cartel to achieve high and stable oil prices, Venezuela also went against the energy security interests of the USA. These were seen to be most conspicuously threatened by the forging of amicable links with China, underscored by the signing of extensive technical co-operation, oil supply and trade agreements, despite the Venezuelan Government's stated commitment to remaining a reliable supplier of crude petroleum to the US market. Notwithstanding the antagonistic rhetoric of the two countries' Governments, the volume of trade between Venezuela and the USA increased and the two countries maintained vibrant commercial ties. Venezuela remained one of the top four suppliers of oil to the USA, and one of the largest Latin American investors in the USA, while the USA was Venezuela's most important trading partner, representing approximately 60% of Venezuela's export revenues and 25% of its import revenues.

Relations between Venezuela and Colombia swung between strained and amicable during President Chávez's terms in office. The Venezuelan President supported a peaceful resolution of Colombia's civil conflict and sought to facilitate dialogue between the Colombian Government of President Andrés Pastrana Arango (1998–2002) and the left-wing guerrilla group Fuerzas Armadas Revolucionarias de Colombia—Ejército del Pueblo (FARC). Colombian President Alvaro Uribe Vélez, who was first elected in May 2002, adopted a military solution to Colombia's conflict, which was supported by the USA and thereafter conceived as a 'war on terror'. This definition was rejected by the Venezuelan Government, which accused right-wing Colombian paramilitary 'terrorists' of colluding with the Venezuelan opposition. Relations between the two countries deteriorated in December 2004 when a senior figure in the FARC, Rodrigo Granda Escobar, was abducted in Venezuela by Venezuelan security officials paid by Colombian authorities. After initially denying any wrongdoing in the affair, the Colombian Government subsequently expressed its regret, and relations between the two countries were normalized in February 2005 at a meeting between the two countries' Presidents in Caracas. Despite Venezuela's subsequent withdrawal from the CAN and frequent strains in the political relations between Colombia and Venezuela, economic ties remained strong and the two countries deepened co-operation on energy-related issues in early 2006, including on the construction of a major gas pipeline from Ballenas in Colombia to the energy-starved industrial west of Venezuela. Work began on the pipeline in late 2006, and it was expected that the energy flow would be reversed by 2012, when Venezuela's gas production strategy came on line. In mid-2007 Chávez was invited by his Colombian counterpart to facilitate a release of hostages held by the FARC. However, bilateral ties came under severe strain from November after Chávez was dismissed from that role by Uribe, who accused him of violating the terms of the mediation by contacting the head of the Colombian armed forces. In March 2008 Venezuela mobilized troops to its border with Colombia after an incursion into Ecuadorean territory by Colombian troops led to the death of the FARC's second-in-command, Raúl Reyes. The Colombian and US Governments alleged that Venezuela was providing financial support to the FARC, citing evidence supposedly found on two portable computers belonging to Reyes that were seized during the raid. The claims were denied by the Venezuelan Government, and no direct evidence to substantiate the allegations was presented by Colombian authorities. In July 2008 Chávez and Uribe held reconciliation talks in Venezuela, which were seen to ameliorate diplomatic tensions between the two Governments. The restoration of amicable relations between President Chávez and his Colombian counterpart, despite their profoundly different ideological outlooks, highlighted the perennial capacity for pragmatism on the part of Chávez and his preoccupation with advancing regional integration. However, hostilities resumed in July 2009 following accusations by Colombia that Venezuela was supplying weapons to the FARC. In response to this and an expansion of US military activity in Colombia, Chávez ordered the withdrawal of the Venezuelan ambassador and diplomatic staff from Colombia. These hostilities culminated in the exchange of verbal insults between Chávez and Uribe at the Rio Group summit in Mexico in February 2010. Newly elected Uruguayan President José Alberto Mujica Cordano offered to mediate between the two countries in the following month, as the relationship remained tense.

Venezuela's frequently strained relations with neighbouring Guyana, due to territorial and border disputes, improved over the course of the Chávez presidency. Venezuela had historical claims to all territory west of the gas-rich Essequibo river area in Guyana, and in November 1989 a UN mediator was appointed to resolve this territorial dispute. Limited progress was made. Relations deteriorated in July 2000 when Venezuela strongly protested against the decision by the Government of Guyana to lease land to a US company in the disputed Essequibo delta for the purpose of developing a satellite launch facility. In March 2004 President Chávez met his Guyanese counterpart, Bharrat Jagdeo, and the Venezuelan Government changed its position with regard to the area under dispute, no longer opposing Guyana's initiative to grant mineral exploration concessions in the Essequibo region. In mid-2005 Guyana signed the Petrocaribe energy accord with Venezuela, granting Guyana preferential terms for purchasing Venezuelan petroleum. In July 2008 Venezuela, Guyana and Suriname began negotiations to construct a US $1,100m. natural gas pipeline to facilitate regional energy integration within the framework of UNASUR. Opposition parties in Guyana demanded that Venezuela renounce its claim to the Essequibo region as a condition of the project's approval.

Economy

Dr JULIA BUXTON

Revised for this edition by PABLO NAVARRETE

Venezuela's petroleum reserves are among the world's largest, and oil has been the mainstay of the economy since the discovery of deposits at the end of the 19th century. For over a century successive governments relied on oil as the driving force of the economy. This reliance on petroleum export revenues rendered the country vulnerable to variations in the international oil price, with the performance of the domestic economy characterized by 'boom and bust' cycles. High petroleum prices led to expansionary spending policies, which, in turn, led to severe fiscal problems when the petroleum price decreased. The strong rise in the international oil price in 2003–09 boosted economic performance, allowing the Government to increase public sector spending and investment. Venezuela experienced consecutive years of economic growth between 2004 and 2008. The Government's expansionary fiscal policy and low interest rates were important contributors to growth over this period, with the non-oil sector and private economic activity showing strong improvement. However, the economy contracted by 3.3% in 2009 owing to declining oil prices resulting from a global economic downturn and a sharp reduction in public sector investment.

There have been a number of attempts to diversify the economic base away from petroleum. These included a programme of state-led industrialization focusing on heavy industrial development in the mid-1970s, policies to encourage non-oil export growth, led by the private sector in the early 1990s, and the promotion of small and medium-sized industries and diversification into 'downstream' and agricultural activities by the Government of Lt-Col (retd) Hugo Chávez Frías from 1999. All of these programmes were implemented ineffectively, and they failed to break the country's dependence on oil export revenue. In 2009 petroleum accounted for approximately one-half of the Government's annual budget and more than 94% of export revenue.

Venezuela has remained trapped in a development dilemma common to many oil-producing countries and which the Government of President Chávez had difficulty overcoming. Strong petroleum prices have traditionally inflated the value of the domestic currency, the bolívar, making non-oil imports cheap and Venezuelan exports uncompetitive. Declines in the petroleum price, combined with the devaluation of the currency, have prompted attempts to stimulate non-oil sectors over the short term, but this diversification strategy has been repeatedly abandoned when the oil price resumed an upward trend. The Chávez Government has sought fully to exploit the benefits of high international petroleum prices, with the oil sector serving as the economic motor of the Bolivarian revolution. This has reinforced dependency on petroleum export revenues and led to contradictions in the Government's development policy, which aimed to foster what it termed 'endogenous development'.

The 10-fold increase in world petroleum prices in the early 1970s, which coincided with the nationalization of the Venezuelan oil industry, created an illusion of abundance; this led to heavy external borrowing premised on future oil receipts. A decline in petroleum prices combined with rising interest payments generated a severe economic recession in the 1980s; however, successive governments were unwilling to pay the political price of reducing public spending. As a result, austerity policies were deferred and foreign debt accumulated.

Owing to a severe fiscal crisis, the Government adopted an IMF austerity programme in 1989. This initially contributed to a 7.8% contraction in real gross domestic product (GDP), but growth resumed in 1990 and 1993, following an increase in world petroleum prices (after the Iraqi invasion of Kuwait in August 1990), coupled with a strong performance by the non-oil sector. The adoption of a one-year stand-by agreement with the IMF in 1996 corresponded to a slight contraction in GDP in that year. Nevertheless, the liberalization of the petroleum sector aided recovery in 1997. Following the decline of world petroleum prices and a weak performance by the non-petroleum sector, the economy contracted in the remainder of the decade. This negative performance was reversed in 2000 and 2001, but protracted strike activity and attempts by opponents of the Government to oust Chávez from office had a catastrophic effect on the economy in 2002 and 2003. However, the economy rebounded strongly after 2004, recording five consecutive years of growth led by the non-oil sector, which expanded by 16.1% in 2004, 12.2% in 2005, 11.7% in 2006, 9.5% in 2007, and 5.1% in 2008. By contrast, oil sector growth weakened. After growth of 13.7% in 2004, contractions of 1.5%, 2%, 4.2% were recorded in 2005, 2006 and 2007, respectively. Following a slight recovery in the oil sector in 2008, with growth of 2.5%, preliminary figures from the Banco Central de Venezuela for 2009 showed a further contraction of 6.1%. There was also a decline of 1.9% in the non-oil sector, with the largest decreases in mining (10.2%), transport and storage (8.5%), and trade and repair services (8.2%).

As a result of a high birth rate, a comparatively low death rate and significant immigration, the Venezuelan population increased five-fold between 1958 and 2007, reaching an estimated 28.6m. in mid-2010. According to the 2001 census, one-third of the total population of almost 23.1m. was under the age of 15. The population was expected to reach around 28.8m. in 2011. In 2009 the labour force totalled an estimated 12.7m., of whom 45% were believed to have been employed in the informal sector. Employment creation and underemployment have been historically problematic, owing to the traditional dominance of capital-intensive sectors such as petroleum. Government job creation schemes, a freeze on the dismissal of employees and strong economic growth in the non-oil sector led to a decline in unemployment, from a peak of 18.0% in 2003 to just under 7.9% at the end of 2009. Between 1998 and 2009 2.4m. jobs were created in the private sector and 962,000 in the public sector.

The structure of employment and the distribution of the population in the late 2000s were markedly different from the 1960s, when agriculture generated one-third of total employment. By 2009 agriculture accounted for less than 9% of employment, despite government efforts to repopulate rural areas through the distribution of 4m. ha of land and infrastructure investment. Service sector employment accounted for an estimated 68% of the labour force, with the remaining 23% engaged in industry. The public sector continued to be an important and growing source of employment, occupying 19.7% of the total work-force in 2009. Petroleum production and processing employed only around 28,000 workers in 2007, representing less than 1% of the working population.

Poverty in Venezuela has historically been one of the highest in the region. When President Chávez took office in 1999, 43.9% of households lived below the poverty line. Poverty levels decreased slightly during the first few years of the administration but reached 55.1% in the second half of 2003, a result of the highly unstable political conditions in the country. Strong economic growth and sustained increases in social expenditure led to a reduction in the rate of poverty thereafter, which, according to official figures, decreased to 24.2% of the population at the close of 2009, with extreme poverty declining to 6%. There was also progress in reducing inequality, according to the Gini index (a measure of income inequality), with a decrease from 0.4865 in 1998 to 0.4068 in 2009. Although the Government's social welfare programmes, or *misiones*, proved to be an important mechanism for poverty reduction and contributed to improvements in the human development index, which rose from 0.79 in 2003 to 0.83 in 2008, there were concerns with regard to their sustainability and level of institutionalization.

Tripartite committees representing the Government, business (through Fedecámaras) and labour represented by the Confederación de Trabajadores de Venezuela (CTV) were traditionally responsible for setting minimum and public wage levels, which did not cover workers in the informal sector. The Chávez Government disbanded the tripartite committees and imposed minimum wage rates; in April 2008 the minimum wage rose by 30% to US $371.6 per month, the highest minimum wage in Latin America. In April 2009 the minimum wage was increased by 10%; however, as a result of the global economic downturn, the Government implemented austerity measures to reduce costs including executive pay and bonuses in government institutions. In February 2010 it was announced that from September the minimum wage would rise by 25%.

AGRICULTURE

The agriculture sector went into steep decline following the exploitation of petroleum from the beginning of the 20th century. A land redistribution programme in the 1960s failed to reverse a trend of concentration of land ownership. State protection of major agricultural producers reduced competition and dynamism in the sector, and Venezuela failed to achieve self-sufficiency in agricultural production. In 2001 the Chávez Government introduced the Agricultural Development and Land Reform Law, commonly known as the Land Law. This was intended to address food import dependency, rural underdevelopment and inequalities in land holdings. The law transferred, under certain conditions, idle public and privately held land to peasants, with technical, credit and marketing support provided by the Government through the Instituto Nacional de Tierras (INTI—National Land Institute). The legislation was vigorously resisted by those landowners who were unable to demonstrate legal ownership as required under the new law, and peasants added to rural tensions by occupying privately held land. More than 300 peasant leaders and activists were reported to have been assassinated by powerful landholding interests. More than 11m. ha of state-held land controlled by the Instituto Agrario Nacional (IAN—National Agricultural Institute) were distributed to peasant families organized in co-operatives between 2001 and 2007, and five areas—fishing, forestry, maize, palm oil and sugar—received special funding. The 1999 Constitution mandated protectionist tariffs on imports of these products, which led to protests from the World Trade Organization and the Comunidad Andina de Naciones (CAN—Andean Community of Nations). The Government additionally developed a Programme for Food Security and Rural Development in collaboration with FAO under its

Special Programme for Food Security and invested heavily in silo facilities. An acceleration of the land distribution programme from 2004 meant that by the end of 2005 3m. ha of state-owned land had been distributed to over 200,000 families. Nevertheless, this failed to generate a substantial rise in agricultural output, leading to shortages and increased reliance on imports in 2006 and 2007. Food shortages, which continued in 2008 and fuelled inflation, were driven by political and economic components, namely: price controls that disincentivized private sector food production; hoarding by private producers opposed to the Government; and significant increases in food consumption, especially among poorer sectors. In 2009 the Government announced that almost 1m. ha of redistributed land was now producing food for domestic consumption, an amount that accounted for nearly 90% of the total land expropriated for redistribution. In 2010, in order to guarantee access to essential foods amid price inflation and supply shortages of some items, the Government nationalized a major flour producer, granted low-interest credits to small and medium-sized producers, opened new subsidized food markets, sanctioned price speculators and hoarders, and announced reforms of the Land Law. Since the law was approved in 2001, 2.5m. ha of idle privately owned land have been confiscated and either turned over to small farmers or used for state farms and research laboratories.

Aside from the acute political confrontation in the country, a number of factors accounted for the set-back to government plans for the agricultural sector, which generated approximately 4% of GDP in 2009. These included the Government's decision to import agricultural produce in order to overcome problems in the domestic supply chain. The introduction of fixed prices was a further deterrent to productivity in the sector, as was the introduction of a fixed exchange rate in 2003. This encouraged imports of cheaper products from the USA, Brazil and Colombia. In 2008 government intervention in the agricultural sector was increased through a presidential decree that allowed the Government to 'restrict or prohibit the import, export, distribution, exchange or sale' of certain foods or agricultural products and 'take over distribution activities when considered necessary'. In line with the trend of growing state intervention in agriculture, state-controlled dairy and milk production facilities were introduced in 2007 and 2008 to improve supply. By mid-2010 the Government had expanded state-owned agricultural production, processing and distribution.

MINING AND POWER

Metallic Minerals

Venezuela possesses vast metallic mineral wealth, the majority of which is controlled by the state-owned Corporación Venezolana de Guayana (CVG), which employs around 80,000 workers. Recent governments have sought to exploit the country's minerals in order to reduce dependence on petroleum. Under President Chávez, the sector became an integral element of plans for industrial development directed by the Ministry of Basic Industry and Mining.

In 2005 estimated reserves of iron ore and bauxite totalled 18.2m. metric tons and 5.2m. tons, respectively, and there were deposits of zinc, copper, lead, phosphorus, nickel, diamond, silver, uranium and gold reserves estimated at 10,000 tons. In 2000 reform of the sector enhanced legal security and streamlined the concession-granting process. However, this did not lead to a significant expansion of the sector. In accordance with its programme of increasing state control in strategic sectors of the economy, the Government announced a review of mining legislation in 2006, and in 2007 it outlined plans to integrate heavy industry into its socialist model of endogenous development. The Government pursued a number of public-private partnerships with foreign-owned state and private companies, including enterprises from Russia and the People's Republic of China, in order to increase annual aluminium and iron-ore production, which remained broadly stable at 600,000 tons and 21.3m. tons, respectively. In February 2009 the Government announced that iron ore production was expected to rise to 25m. tons per year by 2013, with an investment of US $8,000m. In May 2009 the Government announced the nationalization of a number of iron briquette and steel companies, and Chávez spoke of the need for 'workers' control' in these companies and in the industrial sector in general.

Venezuela possesses substantial gold reserves. However, exploitation of the sector has suffered from prohibitive mining legislation, delays in conducting environmental impact disputes, institutional divisions between the ministries responsible for environment and for mining, and the activities of illegal miners. The sector was identified by the Government as a 'strategic sector' that fell within its plan for endogenous national development. In 2000–05 Venezuelan gold production almost quadrupled, and stood at 10,092 kg metal content in 2007.

Coal

Venezuela is the third largest coal producer in Latin America after Colombia and Brazil, with estimated reserves of 10,200m. metric tons. Poor transport links in the east of the country, where 80% of reserves are located, and low investment ratios, limited the development of the sector. Until 2004 Petróleos de Venezuela (PDVSA) produced and marketed coal through its subsidiary Carbozulia, which was a minority partner in mixed companies that included majority stakes by private companies. Following a reorganization of PDVSA, the company's shareholding in Carbozulia was transferred to the development agency of Zulia state, Corpozulia, enabling PDVSA to concentrate on oil and gas operations. Carbozulia has outsourced mining activities to German and South African commercial partners in an effort to increase coal production. The largest purchasers are the USA and Canada, which account for around 50% of sales, and Western Europe, which accounts for around 40%. In 2008 President Chávez reversed the trend of privatization in the coal sector and announced plans for Corpozulia to acquire 51% of all coal-mining projects in the Zulia region within two years, and to create state-managed 'socialist' enterprises, in line with trends in heavy industry. Coal production in 2007 was estimated to total 9.3m. tons, as investor uncertainty and a lack of infrastructure development continued to impede the expansion of the sector.

Electricity

Electricity consumption in Venezuela is among the highest in Latin America (more than 90% of households have electricity, of which an estimated one-quarter is obtained through illegal connections), a trend that has been encouraged by state subsidization of energy prices. Supply has traditionally not kept pace with demand, growing at an average annual rate of just 3.3% since the mid-1990s. Declining government revenues and a reluctance to increase electricity tariffs made it difficult to maintain investment in the sector. There were major problems within the transmission and distribution infrastructure; shortages and power cuts were relatively frequent in some areas. An estimated 70% of electricity generation comes from hydropower supplied from the Raúl Leoni hydroelectric complex (also known as the Guri dam) on the Caroní river. The remainder is thermally generated using diesel fuel. Around two-thirds of electricity is generated by the state-run Electrificación del Caroní, CA (Edelca). An expansion of electricity coverage and output, financed by 'windfall' petroleum revenues and facilitated by an increase in gas production, was central to the Government's national development strategy. Work began in 2002 on two new hydroelectric facilities, the Yacambu-Quibor project in the west of Venezuela and a US $2,000m. dam next to the Guri site.

In 2007 the Government nationalized the private sector generator Electricidad de Caracas (EDC), paying compensation of US $739m. to the US owner AES Corporation. In 2008 the Government announced plans to expand electricity generation capacity by 38%, adding 8,635 MW to the existing installed capacity of 22,540 MW, to be financed by state investment of $10,300m. in 42 projects across the country. For the period 2008–14 the Government stated that it hoped to have sustainable growth in line with an increase in demand of 5.7%.

However, in 2009 Venezuela experienced nation-wide power shortages that led to electricity-rationing by the end of the year. In December the Government created the Ministry of Electric Energy to increase power production and promote energy conservation amid a national shortage of an estimated 1,600 MW, which was attributed to a 40% increase in demand over the past decade, low seasonal water levels in hydroelectric facilities and poor management in the nationalized electricity sector.

Petroleum and Natural Gas

In 2007 heavy shale sand reserves in the Orinoco Belt, which had been opened to private sector exploration and drilling, were classified as conventional reserves, rendering Venezuela the country with the world's largest petroleum reserves. According to the Government, in June 2010 Venezuela had 212,000m. barrels of petroleum in certified reserves. The petroleum industry is the mainstay of the economy, usually providing some 50% of government revenue and 90% of export revenues. The oil industry was nationalized in 1975, when PDVSA and its subsidiaries became exclusively responsible for extracting and refining Venezuelan petroleum. The Government extracted revenues from PDVSA through taxes, royalties and special dividend payments. Successive governments and management teams of PDVSA have differed over the question of how the country should best exploit and manage its oil wealth. In the 1990s a strategy was pursued of maximizing output, breaking production quotas set by the Organization of the Petroleum Exporting Countries (OPEC) and incorporating the private sector into production, exploration and refining projects. At the same time, PDVSA executives pursued a strategy of internationalizing the assets of PDVSA in order to prevent the Government from drawing on the company's profits to fund fiscal spending and debt payments, as it had done in the first half of the 1980s. The Government of President Chávez reversed this approach, which led to conflict between PDVSA and the Government, and the near-paralysis of production followed a general strike in the industry in December 2002. The defeat of the strike enabled the Government to drive forward the changes to PDVSA and oil policy in accordance with the provisions of the 2001 Hydrocarbons Law. Operations within PDVSA were restructured into regional divisions, with control transferred to the Ministry of Energy and Petroleum. The Government acted decisively against opponents within PDVSA after the disintegration of the strike in 2003, dismissing some 18,000 workers who had participated in the protest actions.

Production of crude petroleum, which derived mostly from the Maracaibo, Apure-Barinas and eastern Venezuela basins, declined from a peak annual average of 3.7m. barrels per day (b/d) in 1970 to 1.6m. b/d in 1985. Venezuela's OPEC quota increased to just below 2m. b/d in 1990 following the Iraqi invasion of Kuwait, which resulted in a suspension of supplies from those two countries. Under President Rafael Caldera Rodríguez (1994–99), a strategy of maximizing output beyond OPEC quotas was pursued. The steep decline in petroleum prices in 1998 forced Venezuela to embrace OPEC-negotiated production decreases in an attempt to stabilize prices. Under President Chávez the Government pursued high and stable prices through the reduction of production levels and co-operation with OPEC and non-OPEC countries. In 2000 Venezuelan petroleum production averaged 3.1m. b/d. OPEC production reductions in 2001 lowered Venezuelan output to 2.7m. b/d. The country exceeded its OPEC quota of 2.5m. b/d during 2002 in order to improve the Government's disastrous fiscal position, although production collapsed during the PDVSA strike, which began in December. Output temporarily declined, leading to oil export revenue losses of about US $14,700m. Venezuela was forced to import oil to cover its domestic needs, and PDVSA declared *force majeure*. PDVSA claimed to have restored production to pre-strike levels within five weeks of the strike ending. Subsequently, there was a lack of clarity in relation to production, following the decision by Venezuela not to submit PDVSA accountancy figures to the US Securities and Exchange Commission after PDVSA renegotiated and restructured its debts with private investors. In 2006 PDVSA reported production levels of 3.1m. b/d; however, this PDVSA figure was contradicted by the US International Energy Agency, which estimated output at 2.5m. b/d. PDVSA's 2008 report stated oil exports to be 2.9m. b/d, a figure the Center for Economic and Policy Research concurred with.

Venezuela used its oil reserves as a tool of regional diplomacy. Exports to the Caribbean and Central America, which were already significant owing to the San José Agreement, under which Venezuela and Mexico sell 160,000 b/d on preferential financial terms to 11 Caribbean and Central American nations, were increased by the 2000 Caracas Energy Accord and the Caribbean regional oil initiative, Petrocaribe. Launched by Venezuela in 2005, Petrocaribe offered discounted oil to 18 oil-importing countries in Central America and the Caribbean. Energy agreements with China, Brazil, Russia and Argentina were also signed in 2005, as the Government expanded its network of partners in domestic and overseas energy ventures. China was posited as an important future market, and in 2006 investments in infrastructure, transport and refining facilities were outlined to make diversification of supply possible. In 2007 and 2008 Russia, Ecuador, Belarus and China signed energy investment and technical co-operation accords with Venezuela. While a series of new state oil company players, such as Ecuador's Petroecuador and Vietnam's PetroVietnam, were encouraged to participate in the development of heavy oil, Venezuela seemed to be focusing on Russia and China as the main source of investment in future heavy oil developments.

An increase in Venezuela's production output, together with rising petroleum prices, generated a substantial increase in petroleum export revenue in the 1990s. Consensus on production reductions between OPEC and non-OPEC countries increased the price of Venezuelan crude petroleum to an average of US $16.10 per barrel in 1999, resulting in export earnings of $16,343m. for the year. Compliance with production quotas and higher global petroleum demand led to a steep increase in the price of Venezuelan petroleum in 2000, to $25.91 per barrel, raising export earnings to $26,643m. This favourable situation was reversed when a decline in the price of Venezuelan petroleum, combined with decreases in production and acute political instability, including a short-lived coup against the Chávez Government, reduced oil export earnings to $20,831m. by 2003. In 2004 the average export price of Venezuelan petroleum increased by 29%, to $33.22 per barrel, and this, rather than production increases, led to a 48% increase in oil export revenue. In 2005 the average price of the Venezuelan basket of crudes rose to $46.03 per barrel, increasing to $56.43 per barrel in 2006 and generating export earnings of $58,400m. In 2007 oil-export earnings increased to $62,500m. despite production declines, as the price per barrel increased to an annual average of $65.2. In 2008 oil-export earnings surged to $91,500m., as the price per barrel increased to an annual average of $86.5. In 2009 the price per barrel decreased to an annual average of $57.02, with oil-export earnings also declining to $54,201m. At the beginning of April 2010 the price per barrel averaged $70.76.

PDVSA contributed some US $3,700m. to government finances in 2004, of which $2,000m. was channelled through the Fondo para el Desarrollo Económico y Social del País (Fondespa—Economic and Social Development Fund) for infrastructural development. A further $600m. was assigned to the social welfare *misiones*, as part of the Government's plans to create a national oil industry at the service of national development. In 2008 PDVSA's spending on social programmes rose to over $14,700m. This figure decreased dramatically to $2,369m. in 2009 as oil-export earnings declined; PDVSA's profits totalled $4,600m. in the same year. PDVSA also became an important channel for public sector borrowing, opening a credit line of $1,000m. with the French bank BNP Paribas and a $3,500m. loan with two Japanese enterprises, Marubeni Corporation and Mitsui, in 2006. According to the Government, PDVSA's assets had risen from $4,900m. to $149,000m. since Chávez had taken office in 1999, and the company employed 91,000 workers.

The Chávez Government reversed the policy of opening (*apertura*) in the petroleum sector, and the 1999 Constitution enshrined state ownership of PDVSA, ending hopes among supporters of the *apertura* that the company would be privatized. In 2001 the new Hydrocarbons Law was introduced, requiring PDVSA to have a stake greater than 50% in new production and exploration agreements. The legislation also increased royalty rates on oil production from 16.6% to 30%, but reduced the level of income tax from 68% to 34%. In 2005 the Ministry of Energy and Petroleum undertook a review of the entire framework of contracts between PDVSA and the private sector in order to bring these into line with the 2001 legislation, enhancing Venezuela's share of 'windfall' oil revenues and reasserting 'national sovereignty' in the petroleum sector. The 32 operating service agreements signed with foreign companies were redrafted as joint ventures. PDVSA's share in these new joint ventures was increased to 70%, and the income tax rate was adjusted upwards, from 34% to 50%. The legislative and contractual changes were extended to strategic associations in the Orinoco Belt in 2007, with royalty payments increased from 1.0% (reflecting high start-up costs) to 16.7% and a requirement that the state have at least a 60% stake in all oil projects. PDVSA acquired the shares of two private companies, Exxon Mobil Corpn and ConocoPhillips, which rejected the new contract terms. This led to a protracted legal dispute with Exxon Mobil, which unsuccessfully pursued court orders to freeze PDVSA assets. (In June 2010 the International Centre for Settlement of Investment Disputes ruled in favour of Venezuela.) In 2008 there was a significant change in the Government's position towards the private sector, with emphasis placed on attracting more private sector partners into PDVSA-led projects. Bidding was opened for exploration around the Carabobo I block in the Orinoco heavy crude belt, the first major bidding process since the initial *apertura* of the 1990s.

As the Government consolidated its control over PDVSA, concerns were expressed that the company had become too politicized and that little progress was being made in training new staff, a pressing concern in view of the impending retirement of over one-half of senior managers by the end of 2010. The transfer of PDVSA profits to the Government also raised concerns that the company would not have sufficient resources for investment and upgrades, specifically given that PDVSA wells required investment of at least US $2,000m. annually in order to offset a natural rate of decline in the region of 25% per year. Capital expenditure figures for 2006 were opaque, although estimated to be in the region of $6,000m., in line with the $5,600m. projected in PDVSA's 10-year business plan. The Chávez Government came to office committed to implementing a series of policies intended to reduce Venezuelan dependence on petroleum revenue through diversification into petrochemicals and the production of coal and gas. However, limited progress was made in raising petrochemical production. In a redevelopment drive, in 2005 Pequiven, PDVSA's petrochemical subsidiary, was renamed Corporación Petroquímica de Venezuela (CPV) and was to operate independently from PDVSA. In its strategic plan for 2005–12, CPV looked to increase investment in petrochemicals by $10,000m., with the aim of raising production to 25m. tons and annual sales to $12,000m. The plan included the modernization of the El Tablazo and Morón plants, the construction of a new site in Guiria, and a new $700m. fertilizer plant near the Morón site. New legislation intended to expand the domestic petrochemicals sector was being drafted by the Asamblea Nacional (National Assembly). This followed Chávez's criticism of the high domestic costs of petrochemical products manufactured in joint ventures with foreign companies.

The exploitation of the country's massive natural gas reserves was a central element of the Government's diversification programme. With an estimated 176,000,000m. cu ft (4,983,765m. cu m) of proven gas reserves in 2010 and with potential reserves of 196,000,000m. cu ft (50% off shore), Venezuela had the second largest proven gas reserves in the western hemisphere, behind the USA. However, these resources were underdeveloped, and in 2008 Venezuela produced an estimated 848,000m. cu ft (24,012m. cu m) of natural gas, of which some 70% was consumed by the petroleum industry.

The exploitation and production of natural gas was undertaken by PDV Servicios, a subsidiary of PDVSA. The price of natural gas was fixed at artificially low levels, making it an attractive energy source. The petroleum industry remained the largest consumer, absorbing some 70% of domestically produced gas for reinjection into oilfields for flaring. PDVSA introduced a series of investment and production plans in the 1990s to increase capacity. A US $3,000m. public-private initiative, the Cristóbal Colón project, was also inaugurated to develop gas reserves in the Gulf of Paria. The project was relaunched in early 2002 as the Mariscal Sucre project, and concessions were awarded to a consortium of Shell, of the United Kingdom and the Netherlands, and Mitsubishi, of Japan. In 2006 Shell and Mitsubishi were removed from the project and replaced by the Brazilian national oil company, Petrobras. Other concessions in the Deltana Platform offshore gasfield near the maritime border with Trinidad and Tobago were awarded to ChevronTexaco of the USA and Statoil of Norway in 2003. Legislation introduced in 1999 restructured PDVSA Gas, introduced a new regulatory agency, ENAGAS, and permitted foreign investment in exploration and production, distribution, transmission and gasification. The law also imposed price controls and denied the right of international arbitration to foreign investors, creating uncertainty in the sector as to profit margins, contract security and volumes available for export.

Ambitious plans for the development of the gas sector were part of the 2000–09 PDVSA business strategy, which proposed to raise production from 6,300m. cu ft per day to 11,500m. cu ft per day by 2010. Development of the sector gained a new sense of urgency in 2007 after PDVSA acquired a majority stake in the Orinoco Belt oil projects, which required gas injections for pumping, and as the Chávez Government advanced plans for regional energy integration through the US $25,000m. Gasoducto del Sur project to develop a major export pipeline to Brazil and Argentina. The Gasoducto del Sur would extend for 7,000 km and take an estimated eight years to build. Work on Phase 1, connecting the gas fields of Mariscal Sucre to Porto de Sauipe near Recife in Brazil, began in 2007. In 2004 the Governments of Venezuela and Colombia agreed to the construction of a 225-km natural gas pipeline supplying 150m. cu ft of natural gas per day from the Ballenas oilfield in Colombia to western Venezuela. The project, which commenced in 2006, was intended as part of a wider Andean gas distribution network. Underscoring Venezuela's commitment to become a leading international gas producer, President Chávez launched the Organización de Países Productores y Exportadores de Gas de América del Sur (Opegasur), an OPEC-style organization for South American gas producers, in early 2007. In 2008 PDVSA announced a co-operation agreement with the Bolivian government-owned operation Yacimientos Petrolíferos Fiscales Bolivianos (YPFB) to explore for additional gas reserves in the eastern lowlands region of Bolivia. In November Chávez announced that the Caribbean Gas Belt along Venezuela's coastline contained 200,000,000m. cu ft of natural gas reserves. PDVSA and Russian gas company Gazprom began drilling for these reserves that same month. In 2009 Venezuela increased its co-operation with Argentina in gas production and PDVSA and Argentina's gas company Galileo initiated a feasibility study on the creation of a binational company to produce natural gas compressors, transport natural gas, and construct gas stations for natural gas-powered vehicles. As of mid-2010 there was limited private participation in the gas sector, with Repsol-YPF the largest private natural gas producer in the country.

FINANCE

A banking crisis in 1994 forced the Government to intervene in one-third of the country's financial institutions, which were typically family-owned. After the introduction of legislation in 1996 to improve supervision of the sector and create universal banks, many of the largest banks were privatized. This increased the foreign presence in the sector and led to a series of mergers and acquisitions that resulted in an estimated 40,000 job losses. By 2007 the sector had consolidated around 48 private banks, four of which were foreign owned, and 10 public banks, which included four special public banks created by the Chávez Government: the Banco de Desarrollo Económico y Social de Venezuela (BANDES), the Banco del Pueblo Soberano, the Fondo de Desarrollo Microfinanciero and the Banco de Desarrollo de la Mujer (BANMUJER). There were 22 universal banks, 14 commercial banks, five investment banks, two mortgage banks, three savings and loan associations, six development banks, two money-market funds and one public financial leasing company. The trend of financial sector liberalization went into reverse in July 2008, when the Government announced plans to nationalize with compensation the country's third largest privately held bank, Banco de Venezuela, a subsidiary of the Spanish bank Santander with assets of US $11,000m. In May 2009 the Government announced the purchase of Banco de Venezuela from Santander Group for $1,050m., payable in three instalments ending in December 2009. In further interventions in the banking sector, at the end of 2009 the Government opened national investigations into eight private banks, one state-owned bank and several stock brokerage firms for alleged fraud. Two of the banks were liquidated, two were rehabilitated, and four were merged into a new state-owned bank, Bicentenario Banco Universal. Reforms to the General Law on Banks and Other Financial Institutions were also approved, which increased the bank deposit guarantee from 10,000 bolívars ($4,650) to 30,000 bolívars ($13,950) per depositor, increased banks' mandatory contributions to the public deposit insurance fund, and granted the Government more power to enforce this, and placed prohibitions on long-term credits in some sectors of the economy. With the reforms and the recent bank interventions, which increased the state's share to nearly one-quarter of the national banking sector, the Government argued that it sought gradually to change Venezuela's capitalist economy into one that reflected the values of '21st Century Socialism'. A long-term blueprint for this transition was detailed in a seven-year development plan after Chávez was re-elected in 2006, while a series of laws approved in 2008 outlined new types of social and communal property that could co-exist with private property.

The Chávez Government sought to expand credit facilities to those sectors of the population traditionally excluded from formal lending. The special banks played an important role in developing the 'social economy' by lending to targeted sectors that included small and medium-sized industries, indigenous groups, and women. Pressure on the privately owned banks to increase access to credit caused tensions between the financial sector and the Chávez administration. A new banking law in 2001 reduced the operating autonomy of the central bank, and required banks to increase agricultural loans from 8% to 15% of loan portfolios and from 1% to 3% in the case of small businesses. It also increased minimum capital requirements by US $8m. and empowered the President to decree a financial emergency. Follow-up legislation in 2005 increased mandatory allocations to 45% of total lending, with banks required to grant 21% of their loans to agriculture, 10% to housing, 3% to micro credit and 2.5% to tourism. The sector was adversely affected by political instability in 2001 and 2002, which led to an increase in deposit withdrawals and a reduction in savings accounts. After the imposition of exchange controls in 2003, deposits grew strongly, while credit demand remained low. As a result, the banking system increased its purchase of government securities, such as the central bank's *certificados de depósito*. After decreasing to 22.5% in 2001, the lending rate rose to 36.6% in 2002, amid escalating capital flight and mounting perceptions of political and economic risk. The deposit rate increased to 29% (from 15.5% in 2001). In April 2003 the central bank, the Government and representatives of the banking system signed an accord that partially regulated interest rates. In 2003 both the average lending rates and deposit rates declined, to 26.2% and 16.7%, respectively. The trend of state intervention continued into 2005 when the central bank established a maximum lending rate and minimum deposit rates. As a result, the maximum that could be charged for loans was 16.1%, while savings accounts and time deposits had to pay a minimum of 8.0% and 11.0%, respectively. Interest rate increases became an important element of the Government's efforts to counter rising inflation. In April 2008 the central bank increased the interest rates on credit cards, to 33% from 32%, and on savings deposits, which were raised by 2% to 15%, in order to encourage saving and reduce consumption. Timed deposit rates increased to 17% from 14%. Commercial, consumer and mortgage lending all rose sharply in 2007 as a result of negative real interest rates and strong private consumption. After a 400% increase in the portfolio of loans between mid-2003 and mid-2008, Venezuelan banks confronted significant operating challenges as the economy slowed in 2008–10, as interest rates remained below the rate of inflation and as the risk surrounding consumer lending increased.

Foreign participation in the insurance sector increased following the introduction of the Insurance and Reinsurance Company Law of 1994, which removed restrictions on foreign shareholdings. As with the banking system, this resulted in an increase in mergers and acquisitions by foreign companies, leading to a high level of consolidation, with the market dominated by Seguros de Caracas. A revised Insurance and Reinsurance Law was introduced in 2001, which extended the regulatory authority of the Superintendency of Insurance, and raised reserves and minimum capital requirements. Take-up of private life and other insurance remained low, owing to high inflation and a lack of public trust in private provision. Take-up was highest in the non-life sector, which represented nearly three-quarters of premiums, specifically car and hospital insurance.

Two of the country's three stock markets closed in 2000, rendering the Bolsa de Valores de Caracas the only forum to trade equities and fixed-income instruments. Venezuela was removed by the International Finance Corporation from its Latin America Investable Index in 2001 for failing to meet minimum liquidity requirements. However, interest in the stock exchange grew rapidly from 2003, when investors realized that equities could be exchanged for US currency, circumventing the Government's exchange-rate restrictions. In 2006 improvements in perceptions of the country's credit-worthiness—buoyed by enhanced oil revenues—led to a surge in emerging-market assets and a small private bank, Banco Nacional de Crédito, launched the first public offering in more than 10 years. In 2007 the Government's nationalization strategy, commencing with the nationalization of the telecommunications firm Compañía Anónima Nacional Teléfonos de Venezuela (CANTV) and the electricity firm EDC, had a depreciating effect on the stock market, with the index contracting by 20%. There were 60 listed companies in April 2007, with less than one-half being traded regularly.

TELECOMMUNICATIONS

Following the introduction of what was recognized as a model telecommunications law in 2000, the sector has been one of the most dynamic areas of the economy. Dissatisfaction with the fixed-line services monopolized by the state-owned telecommunications company, CANTV, which was privatized in 1991, led to a surge in mobile cellular telephone use. As a result, Venezuela had one of the highest mobile phone penetration rates in South America, at 68.8 per 100 population in 2006. Two service providers—Movistar of Spain and CANTV's subsidiary, Movilnet—dominated the cellular market with 40% of market share, while Digitel was a minor but growing presence in the market. The mobile penetration rate was 71.3% in 2007 and was projected to rise to 95% by 2011. In 2000 legislation was introduced that ended CANTV's monopoly on basic telephone services in accord with the 1991 privatization legislation. Movistar acquired a 15% share of the fixed line market, which remained underdeveloped with a penetration rate of just 16 per 100 population in 2007. In May 2009 the Government launched a mobile phone made by state-owned telecommunications company Vetelca at a price approximately 25% cheaper than the next cheapest mobile phone then available. The Government stated that it aimed to produce 250,000 phones in 2009 for sale in Venezuela and Latin America. Internet access experienced strong growth in the late 1990s and early 2000s, increasing from 4.1% of the population in 2000 to 22.5% (5.9m. people) in 2008. This followed the launch by the Government of a project, supported by the UN Development Programme, to provide Wi-Fi wireless local area networking technology to expand internet access nation-wide. However, levels of computer ownership were low, at 111 personal computers per 1,000.

Growth of cable subscription television was also pronounced, with an estimated 600,000 of the 4.5m. televisions in Venezuela connected to a cable network in 2005. In that year the Government launched Televisora del Sur (Telesur—Television of the South), a media venture in partnership with the Governments of Cuba, Argentina and Uruguay. The Venezuelan Government held a 51% stake in Telesur. The initiative was intended to promote regional integration and a news agenda ready to contest US foreign policy in the region and economic policies of the so-called 'Washington Consensus'. In July the US Congress approved an amendment allowing the USA to commence broadcasts to the region, intended to act as a check on the influence of Telesur. This followed the decision by the Venezuelan Government not to renew the public broadcasting licence of the privately owned television channel Radio Caracas Televisión (RCTV). The move brought strong international condemnation and led to domestic protests against perceived limitations on media freedom. The Government accused RCTV of orchestrating the April 2002 coup attempt and repeatedly violating broadcasting regulations. RCTV's broadcast spectrum, one of the few to be national in coverage, was awarded to a new public sector broadcast channel, while RCTV continued to broadcast on cable. Private media groups continued to dominate broadcast and print media output, despite the increase in public broadcasts and government financial support for community-based media initiatives.

MANUFACTURING

The manufacturing sector in Venezuela historically has been weak and heavily protected, with growth correlating with government spending levels and the international oil price. Small and medium-sized industries in the private sector concentrated on the production of consumer goods for the domestic market, while the major capital-intensive industries were state-owned and located in the Ciudad Guayana development region, in the east of the country. Structural reform in 1989 and free trade agreements within the CAN generated strong manufacturing growth at the beginning of the 1990s. This was not consolidated, owing to the volatility of the exchange rate and economic recession. Political uncertainty and instability in 2002 and 2003 had a deleterious effect on manufacturing, and the main groups representing private sector manufacturers supported and participated in industrial action and anti-Government protests launched by the opposition. Government support for idle factories taken over by workers exacerbated perceptions of insecurity among private sector manufacturing groups, while the promotion of state-financed *empresas de producción social* (social production companies) further undermined the private sector's market share. The strong improvement recorded in manufacturing in 2004 and 2005, with growth of 21.4% and 11.1%, respectively, was based on economic growth, expansionist economic policies and a strong rise in consumer demand. This continued into 2006 and 2007, with manufacturing activity rising by 7.2% in both years. However, growth in manufacturing declined sharply in 2008 to just 1.3%, and the manufacturing sector shrank by 1.1% in the first quarter of 2009, with GDP contracting by 0.3%. In the first quarter of 2010 the manufacturing sector shrank by a further 9.9%, with a 5.8% decrease in the country's GDP. The most severely affected manufacturing sectors were furniture (contracting by 46.8%), metals (39.7%), tires and plastics (25.9%), and vehicles (19.2%).

CONSTRUCTION

Growth in Venezuela's construction industry has followed trends in the petroleum economy. Periods of high oil prices have led to increased levels of public spending and growth of the sector, with decreases in the petroleum price leading to pronounced contractions. In 2007 construction activity grew by 13.3%, although the sector struggled to meet the demand for new housing and infrastructure. In order to fulfil an ambitious target of constructing 85,000–95,000 residential units during 2007, the Government nationalized a number of cement plants and redirected cement exports to national construction projects. In 2008, in line with an overall slowing of the economy, construction sector growth declined to 4.5%. Despite a contraction in GDP in the first quarter of 2010, according to government figures public housing construction increased by 67.7%.

TRANSPORT

Historically high levels of public investment in the transport infrastructure allowed for the development of an extensive highway network that totalled 96,200 km in 2006, of which 32,300 km were paved. A decline in public spending led to a deterioration of the road network, which was the principal means of transport for freight and people. Schemes to boost revenue, such as road tolls, lacked popular support, and attempts to increase private sector participation were constrained by the weak regulatory environment and political uncertainty. The Government committed a significant level of public spending to infrastructure repair and upgrading. The Government allocated US $5,000m. to road and highway construction programmes that were scheduled for completion in 2009 and that formed part of its strategy for national integration. Plans to construct a strategic highway corridor connecting Venezuela to Guyana, Suriname and Brazil were approved by the Venezuelan Government as part of the South American Regional Infrastructure Integration strategy.

The railway network was underdeveloped and small, at 584 km, one-half of which was privately owned. A railway project linking industrial towns in the east to the northern Caribbean coast was announced as part of the 2001–07 National Development Plan. In 2002 construction of a 9.5-km railway between Caracas and the commuter belt area of Los Teques began, at a cost of US $384m. Agreements signed with the Government of China led to an increase in Chinese investment in railway construction in the west of the country. Work on extensions to the Caracas underground system began in 2002, with a fourth line completed in 2006 at a cost of $800m. In 2008 the Government announced a series of regional rail network projects, which included a connection to Colombia and a trilateral regional airline and train network with Argentina and Brazil. The country has 280 registered airstrips, of which 122 have paved runways and 30 receive scheduled air services. There are 11 international airports, with 90% of international flights handled by Maiquetía in Caracas, which underwent a major upgrade in 2005. A national state airline, Consorcio Venezolano de Industrias Aeronáutica y Servicios Aéreos (CONVIASA), was launched by the Chávez Government in 2005 with an investment of $16m. A further $95m. investment was planned in order to extend the fleet from two to 12 aeroplanes for use on international routes. The country has 13 major ports and harbours. La Guaira, Puerto Cabello and Maracaibo handle 80% of bulk trade. The Orinoco river was navigable for about 1,120 km, and in 2000 a $10m. study began to investigate suitable areas for development in order to increase barge transport along the Orinoco and Apure rivers.

TOURISM

Despite a vast array of potential tourist attractions, including the world's highest waterfall (Angel Falls, with an overall drop of 979 m), a 2,718-km Caribbean coastline and an Andean mountain range extending from the south-west to the north-east of the country, the Venezuelan tourism industry remained underdeveloped, with the exception of Margarita Island, which was visited by 90% of tourists to Venezuela. Political instability, a lack of facilities and problems of personal security impeded growth in the sector. After an upturn in hotel development in the mid-1990s, particularly in the provision of five-star facilities by foreign operators, investment decreased and there was no subsequent expansion of hotel capacity. Nevertheless, the Ministry of Tourism's vigorous promotion of the sector, under the National Tourism Development Plan (2007–12), contributed to growth. Foreign tourist arrivals increased to 770,567 in 2007, compared with 747,930 in the previous year. Tourism receipts increased from US $843m. in 2006 to $894m. in 2007. The Americas and Europe accounted for the majority of tourist visitors to Venezuela.

PUBLIC FINANCE

The adoption of an IMF-sponsored austerity programme in 1989 reduced, and then eliminated, the fiscal deficit by 1990. An increase in public spending and a decline in petroleum prices heralded a return to deficit in the rest of the decade. In 2000 a dramatic recovery in the petroleum price led to a 106.5% increase in oil revenue. However, the fiscal accounts registered a deficit of 1.7% of GDP, owing to a 46% increase in public spending as the Government attempted to accelerate economic recovery. High public spending led to further increases in the deficit in the early 2000s. At the end of 2003 the fiscal deficit had widened to an estimated 4.4% of GDP. In 2004, despite a substantial increase in the international oil price, financial transfers from the Government and PDVSA, and also a strong improvement in non-oil taxation collection, an estimated deficit of 1.9% of GDP was recorded as the Government accelerated its public spending plans. The Government achieved a fiscal surplus of 1.6% in 2005. The 2006 budget provided for a further 30% increase in expenditure, and central government spending rose by an estimated 48% in 2006, ahead of the presidential election that was held at the end of the year. A 90% increase in non-oil taxes and a 36% increase in oil income taxes did offset this rise in expenditure, leading to fiscal parity. In 2007, driven by record oil revenues, the Government recorded a fiscal surplus of 3% of GDP. However, in 2009, partly as a result of the global economic downturn and its effects on the price of oil, a fiscal deficit of around 6% was registered. In January 2010 Chávez announced a devaluation of the official exchange rate of the bolívar from US $1 = 2.15 bolívares to $1 = 2.6 bolívares, and the creation of a second rate for non-essential imports, the 'oil bolívar', set at $1 = 4.3 bolívares. It was expected that this two-tier exchange rate would contribute to the fiscal deficit reaching around 3% of GDP in 2010. Corruption, tax evasion and high levels of informal sector employment rendered the non-petroleum tax base in Venezuela a source of fiscal weakness. Following the introduction of more stringent tax collection measures by the Government, in 2004 non-oil taxation revenues increased by 85%.

COST OF LIVING

Inflation in Venezuela was historically low. The strategy adopted in the 1980s of devaluing the currency in order to boost the bolívar equivalent of dollar oil revenue generated inflationary cycles, which subsequent administrations sought to contain through the periodic imposition of price controls. This, in turn, exacerbated inflation, which remained in double figures and at one of the highest rates on the continent. The adjustment programme and liberalization of the exchange rate in 1989 led to a surge in inflation, which reached 84% at the end of the year. Devaluation of the bolívar in 1994, coupled with wage rises, contributed to inflation increasing to 60.8%. In 1995 annual average inflation decreased slightly, to 59.9%, but in the following year it reached a record 103.2%, as a result of two further devaluations and the liberalization of the exchange rate under the Agenda Venezuela adjustment programme.

In 1996 the central bank adopted a new anti-inflationary strategy. A 'crawling peg' banded exchange rate was introduced. This succeeded in reducing the rate of inflation, but at the cost of an increasingly overvalued domestic currency. Depressed domestic demand after 1999 allowed for a progressive decline in the inflation rate to an annual average of 12.3% in 2001. In February 2002 the crawling peg was abandoned, with the devaluation of the currency leading to an acceleration of price increases, and annual inflation rose to 31.2%. A new exchange-rate regime in February 2003 fixed the rate at 1,600 bolívares to US $1. The measures were successful in containing escalating prices and allaying fears of a hyperinflationary cycle, although they created a 'black' market for currency where US $1 was valued at around 3,000 bolívares. The exchange rate was readjusted to 2,150 bolívares to US $1 in 2007, but this was still an estimated 48% overvaluation relative to the dollar. The two-tier exchange rate devaluation announced in January 2010 was seen as positive for diversifying the economy away from oil; however, there were concerns that this could cause further increases in the inflation rate.

In 2006 the Government sought to contain mounting inflationary pressures, which had been generated by expansionary economic policies, negative real interest rates and the oil-induced consumer boom. Certain basic food items and food transport costs were exempt from value-added tax (VAT); this resulted in central government revenue losses of about US $1,700m. Another element of the heterodox anti-inflationary strategy was the introduction in January 2008 of the bolívar fuerte (strong bolívar) whereby three zeros were removed from the domestic currency. In July the Government announced a strategy of expanding production in order to counter rising price pressures. The annual inflation rate reached 30.9% in 2008; in 2009 it contracted to 25.1%, thus bringing consumer price inflation under the Chávez Government for the period 1999–2009 to 21.2%, compared with an average of 52.5% in the decade prior to Chávez taking office.

In 2004 the central bank came under intense pressure from the Government to transfer its profits from 'windfall' oil revenues and the foreign-exchange regime in order to fund social projects and development programmes through the newly created development fund, FONDEN. Following intense political dispute, the central bank transferred US $1,700m. to the Government in February 2005. An estimated $25,000m. in reserves have been transferred from the central bank to FONDEN since its creation in 2005, with the level of optimal reserves ahead of fund transfer calculated at the discretion of the executive. Opposition groups were critical of the creation of FONDEN, which, they argued, reduced transparency in government accounts. By the end of 2008 FONDEN was estimated to have funds of around $40,000m. In January 2010 international reserves, excluding gold, totalled $31,300m., according to government figures. This figure did not include the funds held in FONDEN and in joint development schemes with Russia and China.

FOREIGN DEBT

Declining petroleum revenues, an overvalued bolívar and the accumulation of debt maturities made it increasingly difficult for Venezuela to service its debt during the 1980s, 85% of which was owed to foreign creditors. Between 1986 and 1990 the debt was restructured under a relief programme, and the debt service was lightened. As a result of the crisis in the financial sector in 1994, Venezuela fell behind on repayment of its obligations to the 'Paris Club' of Western creditor nations. A structural adjustment programme was introduced in 1996, which secured a US $1,400m. stand-by agreement from the IMF, and a strong rise in petroleum export revenues enabled the Government to repay the bulk of the debt that had been acquired during the previous three years. Heightened perceptions of risk surrounding the country restricted access to foreign borrowing, and the stock of external debt remained broadly stable at $32,000m.–$36,000m. in 2002. Sentiment towards Venezuela changed after 2003 as international reserves rose and the international oil price increased. This allowed for a series of highly successful debt issues. The Chávez Government pledged to reschedule the debt burden with the aim of progressively reducing the public external debt service ratio from 36.5% of GDP in 2004 to 9.8% by 2008. The Government relied increasingly on domestic debt for deficit financing, and this led to a strong increase in levels of domestic internal public debt, from 8.5% of GDP in 2000 to 14.2% by 2004. In the period 2002–03 the total stock of public debt (external and domestic) peaked at 47.7% of GDP, but this was reduced to 13.8% in 2008. In 2009, as the economy contracted, public debt increased to 19.9% of GDP (26% including PDVSA). In May 2007 Venezuela announced its intention to withdraw from the IMF and the World Bank and to launch a South American development bank, Banco del Sur. Brazil, Argentina, Paraguay, Uruguay, Ecuador, Colombia and Bolivia also participated in the new bank, which was formally established in December. Gross foreign direct investment (FDI) contracted sharply in 2006, turning negative for the first time, by an estimated $600m., amid investor concerns of contractual stability. The total stock of FDI stood at $46,000m., equivalent to 25% of GDP. Gross FDI grew in 2007 and amounted to an estimated $600m.

BALANCE OF PAYMENTS AND TRADE

Venezuela's external trade is dominated by petroleum. The performance of the non-oil sector was weak, owing to the small and uncompetitive profile of the private sector and the overvaluation of the bolívar. This increased reliance on petroleum revenues, which remained volatile and generated a high level of import dependence. In 1994 exchange controls were introduced to stem foreign reserve losses after the collapse of the banking sector. This generated a surplus on the trade and current accounts as imports decreased. In 1995–98 imports grew strongly as the exchange controls were abolished and the currency became increasingly overvalued. In 1999 an increase in the oil price, in conjunction with a deep recession, moved the current account back into a surplus. Non-traditional exports registered strong performance in 2000 following a recovery in demand in the Andean market. Imports grew by 22% as a result of improved domestic demand. This was offset by a 72% increase in petroleum export revenues as oil prices rose sharply and export volumes increased, and surpluses on the trade and current accounts were recorded. These surpluses declined in 2001 as international petroleum prices decreased, but in 2002 economic recession led to a reduction in exports and an increase in surpluses. In 2003 the imposition of exchange controls led to a decline in imports, while export earnings rose slightly, to US $27,170m., generating an improvement on the current account, which was $11,428m. in surplus (14.2% of GDP). The current account surplus reached $15,519m. in 2004 (13.8% of GDP), rising sharply in 2005, to $25,534m. (17.7% of GDP), reflecting strong growth in exports owing primarily to high oil prices. In 2006 a new record on the current account was posted, with a surplus of $27,167m. (14.7% of GDP). This resulted from a 22% increase in petroleum export revenues, to $58,000m., from $48,235m. in 2005. Non-oil exports decreased by 9%, to $7,320m. Amid surging domestic demand, imports continued to rise strongly, increasing by 36%, to $32,498m. In 2007 strong growth in imports, which totalled $44,463m., and a modest improvement in exports, which totalled $69,534m., led to a narrowing of the current account surplus to $21,779m. (8.8% of GDP). In 2008 the Government posted a current account surplus that represented 14.5% of GDP. A $7,200m. current account surplus was recorded in the first quarter of 2010, compared with a deficit of $3,700m. in the same period in 2009.

The USA remained Venezuela's main trading partner, despite efforts by the Government to diversify trading partners. In 2008 the USA accounted for approximately 60% of Venezuela's export revenues and 22% of its import costs, compared with 46.4% of its export revenues and 30.6% of import costs in 2006. However, Venezuela exported an estimated US $28,100m. in oil and other goods to the USA in 2009, a 45% decline from the previous year, as crude petroleum prices decreased and oil output contracted. The country imported $9,300m. in goods from the USA in 2009, a 26% reduction compared with 2008.

Bilateral accords with Russia, China, Iran and Cuba led to significant inward investment to Venezuela, but these agreements did not immediately translate into a diversification of bilateral trading relations. However, by 2008 Venezuela had become China's fourth largest oil supplier and fifth most significant trading partner in Latin America, with bilateral trade reaching a record US $9,850m., a year-on-year increase of 68.2%. A new bilateral trade and energy integration agreement signed by Venezuela and Colombia in 2006 was expected to raise trade volumes. However, the antagonism that characterized relations between the Chávez Government and the Government of Colombian President Alvaro Uribe Vélez during 2007–10 created high levels of uncertainty regarding expected increases in trade volumes between the two countries.

Venezuela was a member of the CAN and, with Mexico and Colombia, a member of the 'Group of Three' that implemented a free trade agreement in 1994. However, in 2006 the Chávez Government announced the withdrawal of Venezuelan membership from both organizations in protest against the desire of other member states to negotiate bilateral trade agreements with the USA. Venezuela participated in the Latin American Economic System, which promoted intra-regional economic and social co-operation. In December 2005 Venezuela received the rights of full membership of the Southern Common Market (Mercado Común del Sur—Mercosur), prior to its formal integration. However, Venezuela's membership was subject to ratification by all the group's existing members, a process that had not been completed by mid-2010. Despite an initially positive assessment of Mercosur membership, Venezuelan sentiment towards the body began to shift in 2007, as Mercosur was progressively weakened by internal discord and as Venezuela looked to expand the Alternativa Bolivariana para las Américas (ALBA—Bolivarian Alternative for the Americas), launched by Venezuela and Cuba in 2004, as a socially orientated regional integration mechanism. (In January 2010 Honduras withdrew from ALBA following the overthrow of President José Manuel Zelaya Rosales in June 2009.) By mid-2010 ALBA counted eight members, including Bolivia, Nicaragua and Ecuador, with Paraguay considering future membership. Venezuela was also a member of UNASUR (Union of South American Nations), which was formally established in May 2008 as an intergovernmental union between Mercosur and the CAN.

CONCLUSION

In 1999 the new Government of Hugo Chávez inherited a dire economic legacy. Growing poverty, informality and unemployment were the main trends after two decades of political and economic turmoil. The objectives of regaining state sovereignty in strategic sectors of the economy, improving distribution to the most deprived sectors of society and promoting regional integration shaped government economic policy. Strategies to overcome the profound inequalities that characterized Venezuelan society, including land reform and improved taxation collection, were negatively received by the wealthiest sectors, which protested against the changes. The opposition movement's failure to dislodge the Government through constitutional and unconstitutional means, combined with a strong rise in the international oil price, strengthened the Government's position, both domestically and internationally, and allowed Chávez to advance his programme of revolutionary change and regional integration. Despite making considerable progress in identifying and addressing the needs of the poor and the excluded, by 2008 the Government had deepened the country's dependence on petroleum export revenue, thereby casting into doubt the sustainability of the Government's long-term development strategy of diversifying the economy away from oil. Moreover, the Government encountered severe difficulties in devising effective economic management methods that would enable it to implement its model of endogenous socialist development at the height of an economic oil boom. The political confrontation between the Venezuelan and US Governments and the promotion of a more active role for the state in the economy weakened investor sentiment in Venezuela and heightened perceptions of political and economic risk. As the price of oil declined dramatically during 2008 and early 2009, as a result of the global financial crisis, and the macroeconomic environment became more difficult, there were mounting concerns that the Government would not have the capacity to make the necessary adjustments to fiscal spending.

The persistence of structural rigidities, production constraints and an overvalued exchange rate (despite a devaluation) were serious economic challenges by 2010. Nevertheless, Venezuela's comparatively low debt levels, access to international credit lines, significant international reserves, and control over its foreign exchange, monetary, and fiscal policies gave it significant leverage to manage its economic challenges.

Statistical Survey

Sources (unless otherwise stated): Instituto Nacional de Estadística (formerly Oficina Central de Estadística e Informática), Edif. Fundación La Salle, Avda Boyacá, Caracas 1050; tel. (212) 782-1133; fax (212) 782-2243; e-mail ocei@platino.gov.ve; internet www.ine.gov.ve; Banco Central de Venezuela, Avda Urdaneta, esq. de las Carmelitas, Caracas 1010; tel. (212) 801-5111; fax (212) 861-0048; e-mail mbatista@bcv.org.ve; internet www.bcv.org.ve.

Area and Population

AREA, POPULATION AND DENSITY

Area (sq km)	916,445*
Population (census results)	
20 October 1990†	18,105,265
30 October 2001‡	
Males	11,402,869
Females	11,651,341
Total	23,054,210
Population (official postcensal estimates at mid-year)§	
2008	27,934,783
2009	28,384,132
2010	28,833,845
Density (per sq km) at mid-2010	31.5

* 353,841 sq miles.

† Excluding Indian jungle population and adjustment for underenumeration, estimated at 6.7%.

‡ Excluding Indian jungle population, enumerated at 183,143 in a separate census of indigenous communities in 2001. Also excluding adjustment for underenumeration, estimated at 6.7%.

§ Based on results of 2001 census, including Indian jungle population and adjustment for underenumeration.

POPULATION BY AGE AND SEX

(postcensal estimates at mid-2010)

	Males	Females	Total
0–14	4,329,000	4,143,332	8,472,332
15–64	9,370,120	9,355,106	18,725,226
65 and over	757,167	879,120	1,636,287
Total	14,456,287	14,377,558	28,833,845

ADMINISTRATIVE DIVISIONS

(official postcensal estimates at mid-2010)

	Area (sq km)	Population	Density (per sq km)	Capital
Capital District	433	2,103,404	4,857.7	Caracas
Amazonas	177,617	153,580	0.9	Puerto Ayacucho
Anzoátegui	43,300	1,550,581	35.8	Barcelona
Apure	76,500	508,783	6.7	San Fernando
Aragua	7,014	1,735,981	247.5	Maracay
Barinas	35,200	805,308	22.9	Barinas
Bolívar	240,528	1,620,359	6.7	Ciudad Bolívar
Carabobo	4,650	2,331,564	501.4	Valencia
Cojedes	14,800	318,277	21.5	San Carlos
Delta Amacuro	40,200	163,360	4.1	Tucupita
Falcón	24,800	950,057	38.3	Coro
Guárico	64,986	788,264	12.1	San Juan de los Morros
Lara	19,800	1,881,595	95.0	Barquisimeto
Mérida	11,300	892,031	78.9	Mérida
Miranda	7,950	2,987,968	375.8	Los Teques
Monagas	28,900	908,626	31.4	Maturín
Nueva Esparta	1,150	456,454	396.9	La Asunción
Portuguesa	15,200	925,144	60.9	Guanare
Sucre	11,800	960,610	81.4	Cumaná
Táchira	11,100	1,242,153	111.9	San Cristóbal
Trujillo	7,400	752,163	101.6	Trujillo
Vargas	1,497	340,337	227.3	La Guaira
Yaracuy	7,100	634,337	89.3	San Felipe
Zulia	63,100	3,821,068	60.6	Maracaibo
Federal Dependencies	120	1,841	15.3	—
Total	916,445	28,833,845	31.5	—

PRINCIPAL TOWNS

(city proper, estimated population at 1 July 2000)

Caracas (capital)	1,975,787	Mérida	230,101
Maracaibo	1,764,038	Barinas	228,598
Valencia	1,338,833	Turmero	226,084
Barquisimeto	875,790	Cabimas	214,000
Ciudad Guayana	704,168	Baruta	213,373
Petare	520,982	Puerto la Cruz	205,635
Maracay	459,007	Los Teques	183,142
Ciudad Bolívar	312,691	Guarenas	170,204
Barcelona	311,475	Puerto Cabello	169,959
San Cristóbal	307,184	Acarigua	166,720
Maturín	283,318	Coro	158,763
Cumaná	269,428		

Mid-2010 ('000, incl. suburbs, UN estimates): Caracas 3,090; Maracaibo 2,192; Valencia 1,770; Barquisimeto 1,180; Maracay 1,057 (Source: UN, *World Urbanization Prospects: The 2009 Revision*).

BIRTHS, MARRIAGES AND DEATHS*

	Registered live births		Registered marriages		Registered deaths	
	Number	Rate (per 1,000)	Number	Rate (per 1,000)	Number	Rate (per 1,000)
2001	529,552	23.2	81,516	3.3	107,867	5.0
2002	492,678	22.9	73,163	2.9	105,388	5.0
2003	555,614	22.6	74,562	2.9	118,562	5.0
2004	637,799	22.3	74,103	2.8	110,946	5.0
2005	665,997	22.0	86,093	3.2	110,301	5.0
2006	646,225	21.8	89,772	3.2	115,348	5.1
2007	615,371	21.5	93,003	3.4	118,594	5.1
2008	581,480	20.8	93,741	3.4	124,062	4.4

* Figures for numbers of births and deaths exclude adjustment for underenumeration. Rates are calculated using adjusted data.

Life expectancy (years at birth, WHO estimates): 75 (males 71; females 78) in 2008 (Source: WHO, *World Health Statistics*).

ECONOMICALLY ACTIVE POPULATION

(labour force survey, '000 persons aged 15 years and over, 2008)*

	Males	Females	Total
Agriculture, hunting, forestry and fishing	920.1	85.8	1,005.9
Mining and quarrying	91.2	15.6	106.8
Manufacturing	985.4	431.0	1,416.4
Electricity, gas and water	42.8	11.9	54.7
Construction	1,099.9	53.9	1,153.7
Wholesale and retail trade, restaurants and hotels	1,340.2	1,468.8	2,808.9
Transport, storage and communications	943.1	99.4	1,042.5
Financing, insurance, real estate business services	386.2	227.8	614.0
Community, social and personal services	1,440.1	2,193.7	3,633.8
Sub-total	7,248.9	4,587.9	11,836.8
Activities not adequately defined	15.5	10.7	26.3
Total employed	7,264.4	4,598.6	11,863.1
Unemployed	506.3	366.6	872.9
Total labour force	7,770.7	4,965.2	12,736.0

* Figures exclude members of the armed forces.

Source: ILO.

Health and Welfare

KEY INDICATORS

Total fertility rate (children per woman, 2008)	2.5
Under-5 mortality rate (per 1,000 live births, 2008)	18
HIV/AIDS (% of persons aged 15–49, 2005)	0.7
Physicians (per 1,000 head, 2001)	1.94
Hospital beds (per 1,000 head, 2003)	0.9
Health expenditure (2007): US $ per head (PPP)	697
Health expenditure (2007): % of GDP	5.8
Health expenditure (2007): public (% of total)	46.5
Access to water (% of persons, 2004)	83
Access to sanitation (% of persons, 2004)	68
Total carbon dioxide emissions ('000 metric tons, 2006)	171,467.9
Carbon dioxide emissions per head (metric tons, 2006)	6.3
Human Development Index (2007): ranking	58
Human Development Index (2007): value	0.844

For sources and definitions, see explanatory note on p. vi.

Agriculture

PRINCIPAL CROPS

('000 metric tons)

	2005	2006	2007
Rice, paddy	1,004.5	1,122.9	1,054.9
Maize	2,193.5	2,336.8	2,570.9
Sorghum	385.4	584.4	382.1
Potatoes	443.1	454.1	456.7
Cassava (Manioc)	531.3	489.0	416.9
Yautia (Cocoyam)	59.2	86.0	79.7
Yams	76.9	87.2	88.6
Sugar cane	9,654.4	9,322.9	9,690.8
Coconuts	146.9	173.4	190.7
Oil palm fruit	304.5	307.4	327.8
Cabbages and other brassicas	92.6	101.4	100.3
Tomatoes	211.7	195.9	209.4
Chillies and peppers, green	94.1	101.1	124.1
Onions, dry	265.4	255.0	256.2
Carrots and turnips	185.0	211.6	221.0
Watermelons	285.7	150.7	206.0
Cantaloupes and other melons	293.6	131.6	207.5
Bananas	529.7	509.0	512.2
Plantains	492.0	335.3	390.3
Oranges	374.4	377.9	389.8
Tangerines, mandarins, etc.	95.7	93.0	67.2
Lemons and limes	65.5	49.6	57.8
Guavas, mangoes and mangosteens	74.9	74.4	67.8
Avocados	63.1	58.7	83.3
Pineapples	349.2	356.9	363.1
Papayas	118.1	151.4	132.0
Coffee, green	64.5	74.3	70.3

Aggregate production ('000 metric tons, may include official, semi-official or estimated data): Total cereals 3,584 in 2005, 4,044 in 2006, 4,008 in 2007; Total roots and tubers 1,159 in 2005, 1,175 in 2006, 1,097 in 2007; Total vegetables (incl. melons) 1,676 in 2005, 1,390 in 2006, 1,578 in 2007; Total fruits (excl. melons) 2,370 in 2005, 2,217 in 2006, 2,289 in 2007.

2008: Figures assumed to be unchanged from 2007 (FAO estimates).

Source: FAO.

LIVESTOCK

('000 head, year ending September)

	2006	2007	2008*
Horses	500*	510*	510
Asses	440*	440*	440
Mules	72*	72*	72
Cattle	16,739	16,778	16,900
Pigs	3,303	2,971	3,000
Sheep	538	564	570
Goats	1,362	1,426	1,450
Chickens	110,000*	120,000*	120,000

* FAO estimate(s).

Source: FAO.

LIVESTOCK PRODUCTS

('000 metric tons)

	2005	2006	2007
Cattle meat	424.7	489.9	493.9
Pig meat	126.2	137.5	152.6
Chicken meat	739.4	707.2	776.8
Cows' milk	1,347.7	1,431.2	1,703.5
Hen eggs*	173.6	160.5	149.6

* FAO estimates.

2008: Figures assumed to be unchanged from 2007 (FAO estimates).

Source: FAO.

Forestry

ROUNDWOOD REMOVALS

('000 cubic metres, excl. bark)

	2006	2007	2008*
Sawlogs, veneer logs and logs for sleepers	1,051	1,289	1,428
Pulpwood	622	847	920
Fuel wood*	3,884	3,925	3,968
Total	5,557	6,061	6,316

* FAO estimates.

Source: FAO.

SAWNWOOD PRODUCTION

('000 cubic metres, incl. railway sleepers)

	2006	2007	2008
Coniferous (softwood)	538	598	670
Broadleaved (hardwood)	300	250	280
Total	838	848	950

Source: FAO.

Fishing

('000 metric tons, live weight)

	2006	2007	2008
Capture*	315.3	256.4	295.4
Freshwater fishes*	41.8	33.3	24.8
Sea catfishes*	7.8	5.6	10.8
Round sardinella	80.0	60.0	36.2*
Skipjack tuna	26.6	20.4	28.4
Yellowfin tuna	24.9	29.2	25.6
Marine crabs*	8.3	5.9	11.5
Ark clams*	52.0	49.0	64.5
Aquaculture*	23.4	20.0	18.6
Whiteleg shrimp	21.2	17.7	16.0
Total catch*	338.7	276.3	314.0

* FAO estimates.

Note: Figures exclude crocodiles, recorded by number rather than by weight. The number of spectacled caimans caught was: 60,864 in 2006; 23,201 in 2007; 15,489 in 2008.

Source: FAO.

Mining

('000 metric tons, unless otherwise indicated)

	2006	2007	2008
Hard coal	7,459	7,457	7,457*
Crude petroleum ('000 barrels)	916,515	920,000*	920,000*
Natural gas (million cu metres)*†	56,000	56,000	56,000
Iron ore: gross weight*	23,000	23,000	23,000
Iron ore: metal content*	15,200	15,200	15,200
Nickel ore (metric tons)*‡	20,000	20,000	20,000
Bauxite	5,928	5,500	5,500*
Gold (kilograms)‡	11,600	10,092	10,100
Phosphate rock*	400	400	400
Salt (evaporated)*	350	350	350
Diamonds (carats): Gem*	45,000	45,000	45,000
Diamonds (carats): Industrial*	70,000	70,000	70,000

* Estimated production.

† Figures refer to the gross volume of output: estimated marketed production (in million cu metres) was: 28,500 in 2006–08.

‡ Figures refer to the metal content of ores and concentrates.

Source: US Geological Survey.

Crude petroleum ('000 metric tons): 144,223 in 2006; 133,861 in 2007; 131,512 in 2008; 124,777 in 2009 (Source: BP, *Statistical Review of World Energy*).

Natural gas (million cu metres, excl. flared or recycled): 31,483 in 2006; 32,052 in 2007; 29,182 in 2008; 27,923 in 2009 (Source: BP, *Statistical Review of World Energy*).

Industry

PETROLEUM PRODUCTS

('000 barrels)

	2004	2005*	2006*
Motor spirit (petrol)	131,929	75,000	85,000
Kerosene	179	120	120
Jet fuel	29,412	32,000	32,000
Distillate fuel oils	109,555	109,000	109,000
Residual fuel oils	101,481	90,000	90,000

* Estimated production.

2007–08: Figures assumed to be unchanged from 2006 (estimates).

Source: US Geological Survey.

SELECTED OTHER PRODUCTS

('000 metric tons, unless otherwise indicated)

	2005	2006	2007
Raw sugar*	690	700	700
Cement†‡	10,000	11,000	11,000
Crude steel†	4,907	4,900‡	5,000
Aluminium†	615	610‡	610‡
Electric energy (million kWh)*	105,990	112,266	114,852

* UN Industrial Commodity Statistics Database.

† Data from US Geological Survey.

‡ Estimate(s).

Finance

CURRENCY AND EXCHANGE RATES

Monetary Units

100 céntimos = 1 bolívar fuerte.

Sterling, Dollar and Euro Equivalents (30 April 2010)

£1 sterling = 3.975 bolívares fuertes;
US $1 = 2.594 bolívares fuertes;
€1 = 3.453 bolívares fuertes;
10 bolívares fuertes = £2.52 = $3.86 = €2.90.

Average Exchange Rate From 1 March 2005 to 8 January 2010 the national currency was pegged to the US dollar at a fixed rate of US $1 = 2.147 bolívares fuertes. From 8 January 2010, when the currency was devalued, a dual fixed rate of US $1 = 2.6 bolívares fuertes for some essential goods (including foods and medicines), and US $1 = 4.3 bolívares fuertes for others, was established.

Note: Venezuela adopted a new currency, the bolívar fuerte, equivalent to 1,000 of the former currency, on 1 January 2008; this became the sole legal tender from the end of June of the same year. Most of the relevant historical data in this survey continue to be presented in terms of Venezuelan bolívares.

BUDGET

('000 million bolívares, preliminary figures)

Revenue	2005	2006	2007
Current revenue	114,385.3	147,865.9	161,881.8
Tax revenue	36,756.2	49,056.5	62,670.2
Taxes on income	7,086.1	12,155.5	17,208.8
Social security contributions	1,889.9	2,743.4	4,217.6
Other	27,780.2	34,157.5	41,243.8
Non-tax revenue	77,599.7	98,801.6	99,211.6
State petroleum company surplus	53,181.0	64,725.6	74,902.5
Transfers	29.3	7.8	—
Capital revenue	27.5	0.5	—
Total revenue	114,412.8	147,866.5	161,881.8

Expenditure*	2005	2006	2007
Current expenditure	64,842.6	94,617.7	109,721.8
Operating expenditure	16,779.6	27,759.0	31,000.2
Wages and salaries	11,594.3	16,270.5	20,852.9
Interest and commission on public debt	9,046.1	8,223.0	8,036.7
Transfers	38,463.3	57,420.5	69,852.0
Other current expenditure	553.7	1,215.2	832.9
Capital expenditure	34,867.9	55,935.9	63,153.9
Acquisition of fixed capital	11,967.9	17,666.9	24,550.9
Capital transfers	22,900.0	38,269.0	38,603.0
Extrabudgetary expenditure	1,415.7	1,894.4	518.6
Total expenditure	101,126.1	152,448.0	173,394.4

* Excluding net lending (preliminary figures): 835.0 in 2005; 1,275.6 in 2006; 1,455.0 in 2007.

CENTRAL BANK RESERVES

(US $ million at 31 December)

	2007	2008	2009
Gold (national valuation)	9,281	9,201	13,297
IMF special drawing rights	1	21	3,511
Reserve position in IMF	509	496	505
Foreign exchange	23,686	32,581	17,687
Total	33,477	42,299	35,000

Source: IMF, *International Financial Statistics*.

MONEY SUPPLY

(million bolívares fuertes at 31 December)

	2006	2007	2008
Currency outside banks	13	17	22
Demand deposits at commercial banks	93,437	115,961	147,572
Total (incl. others)	107,746	135,827	171,799

Source: IMF, *International Financial Statistics*.

COST OF LIVING
(Consumer Price Index for Caracas; Base: 2000 = 100)

	2006	2007	2008
Food	399.3	506.3	738.0
Clothing and footwear	203.3	232.5	232.5
Rent	192.5	205.1	214.0
All items (incl. others)	289.8	343.9	452.1

2009: Food 958.3; All items (incl. others) 581.4.
Source: ILO.

NATIONAL ACCOUNTS
('000 million bolívares at constant 1997 prices, preliminary)

Expenditure on the Gross Domestic Product

	2007	2008	2009
Final consumption expenditure	47,680.8	51,028.1	49,895.8
Households Non-profit institutions serving households	39,089.9	41,862.8	40,521.6
General government	8,590.9	9,165.3	9,374.2
Gross capital formation	23,376.1	23,950.2	19,157.1
Gross fixed capital formation Acquisitions, less disposals, of valuables	19,198.0	18,568.3	17,054.9
Changes in inventories*	4,178.1	5,381.9	2,102.2
Total domestic expenditure	71,056.9	74,978.3	69,052.9
Exports of goods and services	10,569.6	10,280.7	8,956.4
Less Imports of goods and services	26,343.0	27,332.0	21,986.6
GDP in market prices	55,283.5	57,927.0	56,022.7

* Including statistical discrepancy.

Gross Domestic Product by Economic Activity

	2007	2008	2009
Petroleum-related activities	6,807.8	6,974.8	6,471.4
Non-petroleum activities	45,134.4	47,046.9	46,123.8
Mining and quarrying	361.3	346.1	307.4
Manufacturing	9,091.0	9,221.1	8,633.9
Electricity and water	1,173.5	1,240.2	1,292.9
Construction	3,745.1	3,884.3	3,890.8
Wholesale and retail trade; repair of motor vehicles, motorcycles and personal and household goods	5,929.4	6,204.3	5,687.7
Transport and storage	2,116.0	2,196.4	2,009.3
Communications	2,375.9	2,807.6	3,083.2
Financial intermediation and insurance	2,685.8	2,561.4	2,500.8
Real estate, renting and business activities	5,346.3	5,488.2	5,376.5
Community, social and personal services	2,916.7	3,193.9	3,292.8
Government services	6,127.7	6,455.1	6,610.7
Others*	3,265.7	3,448.3	3,437.8
Sub-total	51,942.2	54,021.7	52,595.2
Less Financial intermediation services indirectly measured	2,955.0	2,705.1	2,688.6
Gross value added in basic prices	48,987.2	51,316.6	49,906.6
Taxes on products *Less* Subsidies on products	6,296.4	6,610.3	6,116.0
GDP in market prices	55,283.5	57,927.0	56,022.7

* Including agriculture and hotels and restaurants.

BALANCE OF PAYMENTS
(US $ million)

	2007	2008	2009
Exports of goods f.o.b.	69,010	95,138	57,595
Imports of goods f.o.b.	−46,031	−49,482	−38,442
Trade balance	22,979	45,656	19,153
Exports of services	1,767	2,162	2,005
Imports of services	−8,719	−10,516	−9,622
Balance on goods and services	16,027	37,302	11,536
Other income received	10,194	8,063	2,313
Other income paid	−7,727	−7,365	−4,965
Balance on goods, services and income	18,494	38,000	8,884
Current transfers received	346	345	357
Current transfers paid	−777	−953	−680
Current balance	18,063	37,392	8,561
Direct investment abroad	−30	−1,273	−1,834
Direct investment from abroad	1,008	350	−3,105
Portfolio investment assets	−1,559	2,747	3,928
Portfolio investment liabilities	4,127	299	5,003
Financial derivatives (net)	−5	—	—
Other investment assets	−29,440	−29,363	−24,484
Other investment liabilities	4,225	2,602	5,909
Net errors and omissions	−1,746	−3,302	−4,785
Overall balance	−5,357	9,452	−10,807

Source: IMF, *International Financial Statistics*.

External Trade

PRINCIPAL COMMODITIES
(US $ million)

Imports f.o.b.	2006	2007	2008
Food and live animals	1,813.1	2,441.8	6,480.8
Cereals and cereal preparations	467.8	590.5	1,437.1
Chemicals and related products	3,348.4	3,572.6	6,248.3
Medicinal and pharmaceutical products	931.8	1,184.2	1,764.8
Medicaments (incl. veterinary)	730.6	890.0	1,368.5
Basic manufactures	3,164.5	3,972.8	6,855.0
Textile yarn, fabrics, etc.	521.7	744.5	1,427.5
Machinery and transport equipment	12,668.2	16,206.8	17,483.1
Machinery specialized for particular industries	1,089.3	1,437.0	2,476.0
General industrial machinery equipment and parts	1,681.8	2,108.2	3,395.1
Office machines and automatic data processing machines	988.2	1,228.6	1,365.5
Telecommunications and sound recording and reproducing equipment	2,399.4	2,999.6	3,070.3
Telecommunications equipment parts and accessories	1,761.1	1,850.1	2,485.1
Transmission apparatus for radio-telephony, radio-telegraphy, etc.	1,307.7	1,273.0	1,858.3
Transmission apparatus incorporating reception apparatus	1,299.6	1,267.1	1,845.1
Other electrical machinery, apparatus, etc.	1,261.0	1,608.4	2,638.1
Road vehicles	3,696.1	5,258.6	2,898.7
Passenger motor vehicles (except buses)	1,976.0	2,874.7	1,070.1
Miscellaneous manufactured articles	2,379.9	3,542.8	5,615.6
Articles of apparel and clothing accessories	517.3	797.4	1,593.5
Total (incl. others)	30,559.0	41,911.0	45,128.2

Exports f.o.b.	2005	2006	2008*
Mineral fuels, lubricants and related materials	47,763.5	56,818.4	78,152.4
Petroleum, petroleum products and related materials	47,410.5	56,617.7	77,879.0
Crude petroleum	47,094.8	56,228.5	77,862.0
Basic manufactures	3,908.0	2,983.6	2,760.3
Iron and steel	2,339.9	1,691.7	1,618.7
Total (incl. others)	54,510.1	61,385.2	83,288.2

* Data for 2007 exports were not available.

Source: UN, *International Trade Statistics Yearbook*.

PRINCIPAL TRADING PARTNERS
(US $ million)

Imports f.o.b.	2006	2007	2008
Argentina	505.1	966.7	1,083.7
Brazil	2,456.6	3,003.4	4,072.2
Canada	430.1	373.2	752.2
Chile	405.3	619.8	1,154.4
China, People's Republic	1,652.4	2,076.3	4,221.2
Colombia	2,420.7	3,729.5	6,764.7
France (incl. Monaco)	360.0	376.3	466.2
Germany	702.2	701.2	1,359.5
Italy	587.3	707.5	1,113.6
Japan	843.9	874.6	717.5
Korea, Republic	512.3	608.5	521.3
Mexico	1,638.3	1,569.7	2,096.9
Panama	548.0	1,617.9	979.5
Spain	465.8	686.1	894.5
USA	7,393.3	8,462.2	11,896.5
Total (incl. others)	30,559.0	41,911.0	45,128.2

Exports f.o.b.	2005	2006	2008*
Brazil	1,044.5	1,410.5	2,252.6
Canada	834.0	631.9	158.1
Chile	694.8	887.3	1,476.9
Colombia	1,030.2	585.6	926.0
Netherlands	613.7	1,211.9	1,401.6
Netherlands Antilles	2,765.1	3,516.8	16,810.9
Spain	491.4	1,914.2	1,987.3
United Kingdom	791.8	776.7	1,489.5
USA	28,463.7	31,268.7	33,659.1
Total (incl. others)	54,510.1	61,385.2	83,288.2

* Data for 2007 exports were not available.

Source: UN, *International Trade Statistics Yearbook*.

Transport

RAILWAYS
(traffic)

	1994	1995	1996
Passenger-kilometres (million)	31.4	12.5	0.1
Net ton-kilometres (million)	46.8	53.3	45.5

Net ton-kilometres (million): 54 in 1997; 79 in 1998; 54 in 1999; 59 in 2000; 81 in 2001; 32 in 2002; 12 in 2003; 22 in 2004.

Source: UN, *Statistical Yearbook*.

ROAD TRAFFIC
('000 motor vehicles in use)

	2002	2003	2004
Passenger cars	2,092	2,173	2,466
Commercial vehicles	615	630	677

Source: UN, *Statistical Yearbook*.

2007 ('000 motor vehicles in use): Passenger cars 2,952,129; Buses and coaches 40,440; Lorries and vans 1,051,443 (Source: IRF, *World Road Statistics*).

SHIPPING

Merchant Fleet
(registered at 31 December)

	2006	2007	2008
Number of vessels	321	327	333
Total displacement ('000 grt)	1,034.0	1,068.8	1,016.4

Source: Lloyd's Register-Fairplay, *World Fleet Statistics*.

CIVIL AVIATION
(traffic on scheduled services)

	2004	2005	2006
Kilometres flown (million)	57.4	59.4	61.2
Passenger-km (million)	2,468.9	2,578.7	2,635.0
Freight ton-km (million)	0.6	2.1	2.1

Source: UN Economic Commission for Latin America and the Caribbean.

Tourism

ARRIVALS BY NATIONALITY

	2005	2006	2007
Argentina	26,596	26,287	29,221
Belgium	3,171	3,594	3,181
Brazil	18,574	45,438	51,876
Canada	25,527	28,014	24,643
Chile	15,872	15,020	14,199
Colombia	74,497	84,293	91,958
France	25,464	23,487	21,915
Germany	38,797	37,089	35,915
Italy	56,521	53,177	48,977
Mexico	16,514	18,011	21,414
Netherlands	16,892	18,129	18,786
Peru	28,202	27,671	30,890
Portugal	19,351	19,561	17,719
Spain	66,181	65,894	67,188
Trinidad and Tobago	15,534	18,682	15,696
United Kingdom	25,990	24,057	24,256
USA	89,701	88,825	92,870
Total (incl. others)	706,103	747,930	770,567

2008: Total arrivals 745,000.

Tourism receipts (US $ million, excl. passenger transport): 768 in 2006; 817 in 2007; 895 in 2008 (provisional).

Source: World Tourism Organization.

Communications Media

	2007	2008	2009
Telephones ('000 main lines in use)	5,195.1	6,417.8	6,866.6*
Mobile cellular telephones ('000 subscribers)	23,820.1	27,414.4	28,123.6*
Internet users ('000)	5,719.7	7,221.9*	8,846.5
Broadband subscribers ('000)	857.8	1,330.3*	1,860.7*

* Preliminary.

Personal computers ('000 in use, 2005): 2,475,000 (93.1 per 1,000 persons) in 2005.

Radio receivers ('000 in use, 1997, estimate): 10,750.

Television receivers ('000 in use, 2001): 10,750.

Book production (titles, 1997): 3,851*.

Daily newspapers (2004): 92 (estimated average circulation 2,450,000).

* First editions only.

Sources: UNESCO Institute for Statistics; UN, *Statistical Yearbook*; International Telecommunication Union.

Education

(2003/04)

	Institutions	Teachers	Students*
Pre-school	14,857†	59,178	984,224
Basic education:			
grades 1–6	17,521†	172,322	3,449,579
grades 7–9	4,667†	109,437	1,383,891
Further education:			
general	3,362†	56,458	501,243
professional		8,844	68,372
Adult education	2,402	43,660	506,301
Special needs	1,999	8,723	317,687
Universities	48	51,459	626,837
Other higher	120‡	30,664	447,513‡

* Excluding students in out-of-school education: 720,726 in 2003/04.

† Data may be duplicated for institutions where education is offered at more than one level. The total number of pre-school, basic and further educational establishments in 2003/04 was 24,634.

‡ Estimate.

Sources: Ministry of Education, Caracas; National Council of Universities, Caracas.

2007/08 (UNESCO estimates): *Teachers:* Pre-primary 79,019; Primary 212,425; Secondary 217,516; Tertiary 122,525. *Pupils:* Pre-primary 1,183,816; Primary 3,439,199; Secondary 2,224,214; Tertiary 2,109,331 (Source: UNESCO Institute for Statistics).

Pupil-teacher ratio (primary education, UNESCO estimate): 18.7 in 2004/05 (Source: UNESCO Institute for Statistics).

Adult literacy rate (UNESCO estimates): 93.0% (males 93.3%; females 92.7%) in 2001 (Source: UNESCO Institute for Statistics).

Directory

The Constitution

The Bolivarian Constitution of Venezuela was promulgated on 30 December 1999.

The Bolivarian Republic of Venezuela is divided into States, a Capital District and Federal Dependencies. The States are autonomous but must comply with the laws and Constitution of the Republic.

LEGISLATURE

Legislative power is exercised by the unicameral National Assembly (Asamblea Nacional). This replaced the bicameral Congreso Nacional (National Congress) following the introduction of the 1999 Constitution.

Deputies are elected by direct universal and secret suffrage, the number representing each State being determined by population size on a proportional basis. A deputy must be of Venezuelan nationality and be over 21 years of age. Indigenous minorities have the right to select three representatives. Ordinary sessions of the Asamblea Nacional begin on the fifth day of January of each year and continue until the fifteenth day of the following August; thereafter, sessions are renewed from the fifteenth day of September to the fifteenth day of December, both dates inclusive. The Asamblea is empowered to initiate legislation. The Asamblea also elects a Comptroller-General to preside over the Audit Office (Contraloría General de la República), which investigates Treasury income and expenditure, and the finances of the autonomous institutes.

GOVERNMENT

Executive power is vested in a President of the Republic, elected by universal suffrage for a term of six years. (In February 2009 a constitutional amendment removed any limit on the number of terms a President may serve.) The President is empowered to discharge the Constitution and the laws, to nominate or remove Ministers, to take supreme command of the Armed Forces, to direct foreign relations of the State, to declare a state of emergency and withdraw the civil guarantees laid down in the Constitution, to convene extraordinary sessions of the Asamblea Nacional and to administer national finance.

JUDICIARY

Judicial power is exercised by the Supreme Tribunal of Justice (Tribunal Supremo de Justicia) and by the other tribunals. The Supreme Tribunal forms the highest court of the Republic and the Magistrates of the Supreme Tribunal are appointed by the Asamblea Nacional following recommendations from the Committee for Judicial Postulations, which consults with civil society groups. Magistrates serve a maximum of 12 years.

The 1999 Constitution created two new elements of power. The Moral Republican Council (Consejo Moral Republicano) is comprised of the Comptroller-General, the Attorney-General and the Peoples' Defender (or ombudsman). Its principal duty is to uphold the Constitution. The National Electoral Council (Consejo Nacional Electoral) administers and supervises elections.

The Government

HEAD OF STATE

President of the Republic: Lt-Col (retd) Hugo Rafael Chávez Frías (took office 2 February 1999; re-elected 30 July 2000 and 3 December 2006).

COUNCIL OF MINISTERS

(July 2010)

The Government is formed by the Partido Socialista Unido de Venezuela.

Executive Vice-President: Elías José Jaua Milano.

Minister of the Interior and Justice: Tarek El Aissami.

Minister of Agriculture and Lands: Juan Carlos Loyo Hernández.

Minister of Health: Eugenia Sader Castellanos.

Minister of Planning and Finance: Jorge A. Giordani.

Minister of Science, Technology and Intermediate Industries: Ricardo Menéndez Prieto.

Minister of Energy and Petroleum: Rafael Darío Ramírez Carreño.

Minister of Foreign Affairs: Nicolás Maduro Moros.

Minister of Electric Energy: ALÍ RODRÍGUEZ ARAQUE.

Minister of Basic Industry and Mining: JOSÉ SALAMAT KHAN FERNÁNDEZ.

Minister of Defence: Gen. CARLOS MATA FIGUERO.

Minister of Trade: RICHARD SAMUEL CANÁN.

Minister of Labour and Social Security: MARÍA CRISTINA IGLESIAS.

Minister of Food: CARLOS OSORIO ZAMBRANO.

Minister of Education: JENNIFER GIL LAYA.

Minister of Tourism: ALEJANDRO FLEMING CABRERA.

Minister of University Education: EDGARDO RAMÍREZ.

Minister of Housing and Habitat: RICARDO MOLINA PEÑALOZA.

Minister of the Environment: ALEJANDRO HITCHER MARVALDI.

Minister of Communes and Social Protection: ISIS OCHOA CAÑIZALES.

Minister of Communication and Information: MAURICIO EDUARDO RODRÍGUEZ GELFENSTEIN.

Minister of Sport: HÉCTOR RODRÍGUEZ CASTRO.

Minister of Culture: FRANCISCO (FARRUCO) SESTO NOVAS.

Minister of Indigenous Peoples: NICIA MARINA MALDONADO.

Minister of Women's Affairs and Gender Equality: NANCY PÉREZ SIERRA.

Minister of Transport and Communications: FRANCISCO JOSÉ GARCÉS DA SILVA.

Minister of State for Public Banking: HUMBERTO RAFAEL ORTEGA DÍAZ.

Minister of the Office of the Presidency: MARÍA ISABELLA GODOY PEÑA.

Permanent Secretary: CARLOS GRANADILLO.

MINISTRIES

Ministry of Agriculture and Lands: Avda Urdaneta, entre esq. Platanal a Candilito, a media cuadra de la Plaza la Candelaria, Parroquia la Candelaria, Caracas; tel. (212) 509-0347; e-mail pda2007@mat.gob.ve; internet www.mat.gob.ve.

Ministry of Basic Industry and Mining: Torre Las Mercedes, 9°, Avda La Estancia, Urb. Chuao, Caracas; tel. (212) 950-0311; fax (212) 950-0286; e-mail webmaster@mibam.gob.ve; internet www.mibam.gob.ve.

Ministry of Communes and Social Protection: Edif. INCE, Avda Nueva Granada, Apdo 10340, Caracas 1040; tel. (212) 603-2396; internet www.mpcomunas.gob.ve.

Ministry of Communication and Information: Torre Ministerial, 9° y 10°, Avda Universidad, esq. el Chorro, Caracas 1010; tel. (212) 505-3322; e-mail contactenos@mci.gob.ve; internet www.mci.gob.ve.

Ministry of Culture: Edif. Archivo General de la Nación, Avda Panteón, Foro Libertador, Caracas; tel. (212) 509-5600; e-mail mppc@ministeriodelacultura.gob.ve; internet www.ministeriodelacultura.gob.ve.

Ministry of Defence: Edif. 17 de Diciembre, planta baja, Base Aérea Francisco de Miranda, La Carlota, Caracas; tel. (212) 908-1264; fax (212) 237-4974; e-mail prensamd@mindefensa.gov.ve; internet www.mindefensa.gob.ve.

Ministry of Education: Edif. Sede del MPPE, Mezzanina, esq. de Salas a Caja de Agua, Parroquia Altagracia, Caracas 1010; tel. (212) 569-4111; e-mail atencionsocial@me.gob.ve; internet www.me.gob.ve.

Ministry of Electric Energy: Caracas.

Ministry of Energy and Petroleum: Edif. Petróleos de Venezuela, Torre Oeste, Avda Libertador con Avda Empalme, La Campiña, Porroquia El Recreo, Caracas; tel. (212) 708-7581; fax (212) 708-7598; e-mail atencionalpublico@menpet.gob.ve; internet www.menpet.gob.ve.

Ministry of the Environment: Torre Sur Plaza, 25°, Centro Simón Bolívar, Caracas 1010; tel. (212) 408-1111; internet www.minamb.gob.ve.

Ministry of Food: Edif. Las Fundaciones, Avda Andrés Bello, Caracas; tel. (212) 395-7474; e-mail oirp@minal.gob.ve; internet www.minal.gob.ve.

Ministry of Foreign Affairs: Torre MRE, al lado del Correo de Carmelitas, Avda Urdaneta, Caracas 1010; tel. (212) 806-4400; fax (212) 861-2505; e-mail web.master@mre.gov.ve; internet www.mre.gov.ve.

Ministry of Health: Edif. Sur, 8°, Avda Baralt, Centro Simón Bolívar, El Silencio, Caracas 1010; tel. (212) 408-0033; fax 483-2560; e-mail mpps@mpps.gob.ve; internet www.msds.gov.ve.

Ministry of Housing and Habitat: Torre Este, 50°, Parque Central, Caracas 1010; tel. (212) 201-5551; internet www.mvh.gob.ve.

Ministry of Indigenous Peoples: Antiguo Edif. Sudeban, Avda Universidad, esq. Traposos, 8°, Caracas 1010; tel. (212) 543-1599; fax (212) 543-3100; e-mail atencionlindigena@minpi.gob.ve; internet www.minpi.gob.ve.

Ministry of the Interior and Justice: Edif. Ministerio del Interior y Justicia, esq. de Platanal, Avda Urdaneta, Caracas 1010; tel. (212) 506-1101; fax (212) 506-1559; e-mail webmaster@mij.gov.ve; internet www.mij.gov.ve.

Ministry of Labour and Social Security: Torre Sur, 5°, Centro Simón Bolívar, Caracas 1010; tel. (212) 481-1368; fax (212) 483-8914; internet www.mintra.gov.ve.

Ministry of Planning and Finance: Edif. Ministerio de Finanzas, esq. Carmelitas, Avda Urdaneta, Caracas 1010; tel. (212) 802-1000; e-mail webmaster@mpd.gob.ve; internet www.mpd.gob.ve.

Ministry of the Presidency: Palacio de Miraflores, final Avda Urdaneta, esq. de Bolero, Caracas; tel. (212) 806-3111; fax (212) 806-3229; e-mail dggcomunicacional@presidencia.gob.ve; internet www.presidencia.gob.ve.

Ministry of Science, Technology and Intermediate Industries: Torre MCT, Avda Universidad, esq. El Chorro, Caracas; tel. (212) 555-7410; fax (212) 555-7504; e-mail mcti@mcti.gob.ve; internet www.mct.gob.ve.

Ministry of Sport: Sede Principal, Avda Intercomunal Montalban, Urb. Montalbán, La Vega, Caracas 1020; tel. (212) 443-2682; fax (212) 443-3224; internet www.mindeporte.gob.ve.

Ministry of Tourism: Edif. Mintur, Avda Francisco de Miranda con Avda Principal de la Floresta, Municipio Chacao, Caracas; tel. (212) 208-4651; e-mail auditoria@mintur.gob.ve; internet www.mintur.gob.ve.

Ministry of Trade: Torre Oeste de Parque Central, entrada por el Nivel Lecuna, Avda Lecuna, Caracas 1010; tel. (212) 509-6861; fax (212) 574-2432; e-mail ministro@milco.gob.ve; internet www.milco.gob.ve.

Ministry of Transport and Communications: Caracas; internet www.mtc.gob.ve.

Ministry of University Education: Torre Ministerial, 1°–7°, Avda Universidad, esq. el Chorro, Caracas 1010; tel. (212) 596-5270; fax (212) 569-5261; e-mail webmaster@mppeu.gob.ve; internet www.mppeu.gob.ve.

Ministry of Women's Affairs and Gender Equality: Caracas.

State Agencies

Consejo de Defensa de la Nación (Codena): Edif. 2, 2°, Fuerte Tiuna, Caracas; tel. (212) 690-3222; e-mail secodena@codena.gob.ve; internet www.codena.gob.ve; national defence council; Sec.-Gen. Gen. VIVIAM ANTONIO DURÁN GARCÍA.

Contraloría General de la República (CGR): Edif. Contraloría, Avda Andrés Bello, Guaicaipuro, Caracas 1050; tel. (212) 508-3111; e-mail atencionciudadano@cgr.gov.ve; internet www.cgr.gob.ve; national audit office for Treasury income and expenditure, and for the finances of the autonomous institutes; Comptroller-Gen. CLODOSBALDO RUSSIÁN UZCÁTEGUI.

Defensoría del Pueblo: Edif. Defensoría del Pueblo, 8°, Avda México, Plaza Morelos, Los Caobos, Caracas; tel. (212) 575-4703; fax (212) 575-4467; e-mail prensadefensoria@hotmail.com; internet www.defensoria.gob.ve; acts as an ombudsman and investigates complaints between citizens and the authorities; Ombudsman GABRIELA DEL MAR RAMÍREZ.

Procuraduría General de la República: Paseo Los Ilustres con Avda Lazo Martí, Santa Mónica, Caracas; tel. (212) 597-3300; e-mail webmaster@pgr.gov.ve; internet www.pgr.gob.ve; Procurator-Gen. GLADYS MARÍA GUTIÉRREZ ALVARADO.

President

Election, 3 December 2006

Candidates	Votes	% of total
Lt-Col (retd) Hugo Rafael Chávez Frías (Movimiento V República*)	7,309,080	62.84
Manuel Antonio Rosales Guerrero (Un Nuevo Tiempo)	4,292,466	36.91
Others	28,606	0.25
Total†	11,630,152	100.00

* Dissolved in December 2006 and replaced by the Partido Socialista Unido de Venezuela (PSUV).

† In addition, there were 160,245 blank or spoiled ballots.

Legislature

ASAMBLEA NACIONAL
(National Assembly)

President: CILIA A. FLORES.

First Vice-President: DARIO VIVAS VELASCO.

Second Vice-President: JOSÉ ALBORNOZ.

General Election, 4 December 2005*

Party	Seats
Movimiento V República (MVR)†	114
Por la Democracia Social (PODEMOS)	15
Patria para Todos (PPT)	11
Movimiento Electoral del Pueblo (MEP)‡	11
Partido Comunista de Venezuela (PCV)	8
Unidad Popular Venezolana (UPV)‡	8
Total	167

* The election was boycotted by opposition parties.
† Dissolved in December 2006 and replaced by the Partido Socialista Unido de Venezuela (PSUV).
‡ Merged into the PSUV in 2007–08.

Election Commission

Consejo Nacional Electoral (CNE): Edif. Poder Electoral, antigua torre Teleport, 3°, Plaza Venezuela, Paseo Colón, Caracas; tel. (212) 576-2399; fax (212) 576-5603; internet www.cne.gov.ve; f. 2002; Pres. TIBISAY LUCENA RAMÍREZ.

Political Organizations

Acción Democrática (AD): Casa Nacional Acción Democrática, Calle Los Cedros, La Florida, Caracas 1050; internet www.acciondemocratica.org.ve; f. 1936 as Partido Democrático Nacional; adopted present name and obtained legal recognition in 1941; social democratic; Pres. ISABEL CARMONA DE SERRA; Sec.-Gen. HENRY RAMOS ALLUP.

Alianza Bravo Pueblo: Caracas; e-mail alianzabravopueblo@gmail.com; oppositionist; merged with Visión Emergente in 2010; Pres. ANTONIO LEDEZMA; Co-ordinator CIPRIANO HEREDIA.

La Causa Radical (La Causa R): Santa Teresa a Cipreses, Residencias Santa Teresa, 2°, Ofs 21 y 22, Caracas; tel. (212) 545-7002; f. 1971; radical democratic; Leader ANDRÉS VELÁSQUEZ.

Convergencia Nacional (CN): Edif. Tajamar, 2°, Of. 215, Parque Central, Avda Lecuna, El Conde, Caracas 1010; tel. (212) 578-1177; fax (212) 578-0363; e-mail jjcaldera@convergencia.org.ve; internet www.convergencia.org.ve; f. 1993; Leader Dr RAFAEL CALDERA RODRÍGUEZ; Gen. Co-ordinator JUAN JOSÉ CALDERA.

Movimiento Demócrata Liberal: Quinta El Encuentro, 1º, Avda de Santa Eduvigis, entre 5a y 6a transversal, Caracas; tel. (212) 442-3956; fax (212) 471-3856; e-mail info@democrataliberales.org; internet www.democrataliberales.org; liberal opposition party; Political Dir MARCO POLESEL.

Movimiento Republicano (MR): Reynaldo Hahn 1606, Urb. Santa Mónica, Caracas; tel. (212) 693-2937; e-mail elrepublicano.ve@gmail.com; internet movimientorepublicano.blogspot.com; f. 1997; Pres. CARLOS PADILLA; Sec.-Gen. MANUAL RIVAS.

Movimiento al Socialismo (MAS): Quinta Alemar, Avda Valencia, Las Palmas, Caracas 1050; tel. (212) 793-7800; fax (212) 761-9297; e-mail asamblea07@cantv.net; f. 1971 by PCV dissidents; opposition democratic-socialist party; split in 1997 over issue of support for presidential campaign of Hugo Chávez; Pres. FELIPE MUJICA; Sec.-Gen. LEOPOLDO PUCHI.

Partido Comunista de Venezuela (PCV): Edif. Cantaclaro, Calle Jesús Faría, esq. de San Pedro a San Francisquito, Parroquia San Juan, Caracas; tel. (212) 484-0061; fax (212) 481-9737; internet www.pcv-venezuela.org; f. 1931; Pres. JERÓNIMO CARRERA; Sec. OSCAR FIGUERA.

Partido Social-Cristiano (Comité de Organización Política Electoral Independiente) (COPEI): El Bosque, Avda Principal El Bosque, cruce con Avda Gloria Quinta Cujicito, Chacao, Caracas; tel. (212) 731-4746; fax (212) 731-4953; internet www.partidocopei.org.ve; f. 1946; Christian democratic; Pres. LUIS IGNACIO PLANAS; Sec.-Gen. LUIS CARLOS SOLÓRZANO.

Partido Socialista Unido de Venezuela (PSUV): Calle Lima, cruce con Avda Libertador, Los Caobos, Caracas; tel. (212) 782-3808; fax (212) 782-9720; e-mail contacto@psuv.org.ve; internet www.psuv.org.ve; f. 2007; successor party to the Movimiento V República (dissolved Dec. 2006); promotes Bolivarian revolution; Pres. Lt-Col (retd) HUGO RAFAEL CHÁVEZ FRÍAS.

Patria Para Todos (PPT): Calle Montevideo, Quinta Plaza, Calle Maripérez, Plaza Venezuela, Caracas; tel. (212) 578-3098; fax (212) 577-4545; e-mail partidoppt@gmail.com; internet www.ppt.org.ve; f. 1997; breakaway faction of La Causa Radical; revolutionary humanist party; Nat. Sec.-Gen. JOSÉ ALBORNOZ.

Por la Democracia Social (PODEMOS): Caracas; f. 2001 by dissident mems of MAS (q.v.); abandoned support for the Govt in 2007; Leader ISMAEL GARCÍA.

Primero Justicia: Centro Comercial Chacaíto, Of. 26A, Urb. San Soucy, Caracas; tel. (212) 952-9733; e-mail pjelhaltillo@cantv.net; internet www.primerojusticia.org.ve; f. 2000; opposition party; Nat. Co-ordinator JULIO ANDRÉS BORGES; Nat. Sec. CARLOS GUILLERMO AROCHA.

Proyecto Venezuela (PRVZL): e-mail administrador@vpvonline.com; f. 1998; humanist party; Leader HENRIQUE SALAS RÖMER; Sec.-Gen. CARLOS BERRIZBEITIA.

Un Nuevo Tiempo (UNT): Edif. Montral, Avda Principal de Las Palmas, Municipio Libertador, Caracas; tel. (212) 425-1239; e-mail prensa@partidounnuevotiempo.org; internet www.partidounnuevotiempo.org; f. 2005; opposes Pres. Chávez; Exec. Pres. OMAR BARBOZA; Exec. Sec. ENRIQUE OCHOA ANTICH.

OTHER ORGANIZATIONS

Asociación Civil Queremos Elegir: Edif. Industrial, 4°, Avda Sucre, Los Dos Caminos, Municipio Sucre, Caracas; tel. (212) 286-9785; e-mail info@queremoselegir.org; internet www.queremoselegir.org; f. 1991; opposition grouping promoting citizens' rights; mem. of Alianza Cívica de la Sociedad Venezolana; Principal Co-ordinator ELÍAS SANTANA.

Comité de Familiares Víctimas de los Sucesos de Febrero y Marzo de 1989 (COFAVIC): Edif. El Candil, 1°, Of. 1-A, Avda Urdaneta, esq. El Candilito, Apdo 16150, La Candelaria, Caracas 1011-A; tel. (212) 572-9631; fax (212) 572-9908; e-mail cofavic@cofavic.org.ve; internet www.cofavic.org.ve; f. 1989 as an asscn of relatives of those who had died in demonstrations of Feb.–March; promotes human rights; Exec. Dir LILIANA ORTEGA.

Súmate: Torre A, 5°, Avda Francisco de Miranda, Centro Plaza, Caracas; tel. (212) 285-4562; e-mail info@sumate.org; internet www.sumate.org; f. 2002; opposition grouping promoting citizens' rights; Dir MARÍA CORINA MACHADO.

Diplomatic Representation

EMBASSIES IN VENEZUELA

Algeria: 8a Transversal con 3a Avda, Quinta Azahar, Urb. Altamira, Caracas 1062; tel. (212) 263-2092; fax (212) 261-4254; e-mail ambalgcar@cantv.net; Ambassador RACHID BLADEHANE.

Argentina: Edif. Fedecámaras, 3°, Avda El Empalme, El Bosque, Apdo 569, Caracas; tel. (212) 731-3311; fax (212) 731-2659; e-mail evene@cancilleria.gov.ar; internet www.venezuela.embajada-argentina.gov.ar; Ambassador ALICIA AMALIA CASTRO.

Austria: Edif. Torre D&D, Piso PT, Of. PTN, Avda Orinoco, entre Mucuchíes y Perijá, Urb. Las Mercedes, Apdo 61381, Caracas 1060-A; tel. (212) 999-1211; fax (212) 993-2753; e-mail caracas-ob@bmeia.gv.at; internet www.aussenministerium.at/caracas; Ambassador THOMAS SCHULLER-GÖTZBURG.

Barbados: Edif. Los Frailes, 5°, Of. 501, Avda Principal de Chuao, Chuao, Apdo 68829, Caracas 1060; tel. (212) 992-0545; fax (212) 991-0333; e-mail caracas@foreign.gov.bb; Ambassador (vacant).

Belarus: Quinta Campanera, 3a Transversal (Calle Aveledo) con Avda 7, Urb. Los Chorros, Municipio Sucre, Caracas 1071; tel. (212) 239-2760; fax (212) 239-0419; e-mail venezuela@belembassy.org; internet www.venezuela.belembassy.org; Ambassador GURINOVICH VALENTIN ARKADJEVICH.

Belgium: 10a Transversal con 9a Transversal, Apdo del Este 61550, Altamira, Caracas 1060; tel. (212) 263-3334; fax (212) 261-1333; e-mail caracas@diplobel.fed.be; internet www.diplomatie.be/caracas; Ambassador LÉOPOLD CARREWYN.

Bolivia: Edif. Los Llanos, 1°, Avda Francisco Zolano, esq. San Gerónimo, Zabana Grande, Caracas; tel. (212) 263-3015; fax (212) 261-3386; e-mail embaboliviaven@hotmail.com; internet www.embajada-boliviana-venezuela.com; Chargé d'affaires a.i. JORGE ALVARADO RIVAS.

Brazil: Avda Mohedano con Calle Los Chaguaramos, Centro Gerencial Mohedano, 6°, La Castellana, Caracas 1060; tel. (212) 918-6000; fax (212) 261-9601; e-mail brasembcaracas@embajadabrasil

.org.ve; internet www.brasil.org.ve; Ambassador José Antonio Marcondes de Carvalho.

Bulgaria: Quinta Sofía, Calle Las Lomas, Urb. Las Mercedes, Apdo 68389, Caracas; tel. (212) 993-2714; fax (212) 993-4839; e-mail embulven@cantv.net; internet www.mfa.bg/caracas; Ambassador Kiril Georgiev Kotsaliev.

Canada: Edif. Embajada de Canadá, Avda Francisco de Miranda con Avda Sur, Altamira, Apdo 62302, Caracas 1060-A; tel. (212) 600-3101; fax (212) 261-8741; e-mail crcas@international.gc.ca; internet www.canadainternational.gc.ca/venezuela; Ambassador Perry Calderwood.

Chile: Edif. Torre La Noria, 10°, Of. 10A, Paseo Enrique Eraso, Urb. Las Mercedes, Caracas; tel. (212) 992-3378; fax (212) 992-0614; e-mail echileve@cantv.net; internet www.embachileve.org; Ambassador Claudio Herrera Alamos.

China, People's Republic: Avda El Paseo, Quinta El Oriente, Prados del Este, Caracas; tel. (212) 977-4949; fax (212) 978-0876; e-mail embcnven@cantv.net; internet ve.chineseembassy.org; Ambassador Zhao Rongxian.

Colombia: Torre Credival, 11°, 2A Calle de Campo Alegre con Avda Francisco de Miranda, Apdo 60887, Caracas; tel. (212) 216-9596; fax (212) 261-1358; e-mail ecaracas@minrelext.gov.co; Ambassador José Fernando Bautista (designate).

Costa Rica: Edif. For You, 11°, Avda San Juan Bosco, entre 1a y 2a Transversal, Urb. Altamira, Chacao, Apdo 62239, Caracas; tel. (212) 267-1104; fax (212) 265-4660; e-mail embaricavene@yahoo.com.mx; Ambassador Manuel Vladimir de la Cruz de Lemos.

Cuba: Calle Roraima, entre Río de Janeiro y Choroní, Chuao, Caracas 1060; tel. (212) 991-6661; fax (212) 993-5695; e-mail embajadorcubavzl@cantv.net; internet embacu.cubaminrex.cu/venezuela; Ambassador Rogelio Polanco Fuentes.

Czech Republic: Calle Los Cedros, Quinta Isabel, Urb. Country Club, Altamira, Caracas 1060; tel. (212) 261-8528; fax (212) 266-3987; e-mail caracas@embassy.mzv.cz; internet www.mfa.cz/caracas; Ambassador Stanislav Slavický.

Dominica: Caracas; Ambassador Dr Philbert Aaron.

Dominican Republic: Edif. Argentum, Ofs 1 y 2, 2a Transversal, entre 1a Avda y Avda Andrés Bello, Los Palos Grandes, Caracas 1060; tel. (212) 283-3709; fax (212) 283-3965; e-mail embajadominicana@cantv.net; Ambassador Jaime Durán Hernández.

Ecuador: Centro Andrés Bello, Torre Oeste, 13°, Avda Andrés Bello, Maripérez, Apdo 62124, Caracas 1060; tel. (212) 265-0801; fax (212) 264-6917; e-mail embajadaecuador@cantv.net; Ambassador Gen. (retd) René Vargas Pazos.

Egypt: Calle Caucagua con Calle Guaicaipuro, Quinta Maribel, Urb. San Román, Municipio Baruta, Apdo 49007, Caracas 1042-A; tel. (212) 992-6259; fax (212) 993-1555; e-mail embassy.caracas@mfa.gov.eg; internet www.mfa.gov.eg/Missions/venezuela/caracas/embassy/ar-eg; Ambassador Ali Saleh Murad.

El Salvador: Avda Nicólas Copérnico, Quinta Cuscatlán, Urb. Valle Arriba, Sector Los Naranjos, Municipio Baruta, Miranda, Caracas; tel. (212) 991-4472; fax (212) 959-3920; e-mail embasalve@cantv.net; Ambassador Romnán Antonio Moyorga Quiroz.

Finland: Edif. Atrium, 1°, Calle Sorocaima, El Rosal, Caracas; tel. (212) 952-4111; fax (212) 952-7536; e-mail sanomat.car@formin.fi; internet www.finland.org.ve; Ambassador Mikko Pyhälä.

France: Calle Madrid con Avda Trinidad, Las Mercedes, Apdo 60385, Caracas 1060; tel. (212) 909-6500; fax (212) 909-6630; e-mail infos@francia.org.ve; Ambassador Jean-Marc Laforet.

The Gambia: 4a Avda con 8a Transversal, Quinta La Paz, Urb. Los Palos Grandes, Chacao, Caracas; tel. (212) 285-2554; fax (212) 285-6250; Ambassador Bala Garba Jahumpa.

Germany: Torre La Castellana, 10°, Avda Eugenio Mendoza, cruce con Avda José Angel Lamas, La Castellana, Apdo 2078, Caracas 1010-A; tel. (212) 219-2500; fax (212) 261-0641; e-mail info@caracas.diplo.de; internet www.caracas.diplo.de; Ambassador Georg-Clemens Dick.

Greece: Quinta Maryland, Avda Principal del Avila, Alta Florida, Caracas 1050; tel. (212) 730-3833; fax (212) 731-0429; e-mail gremb.car@mfa.gr; Ambassador Efstathios Daras.

Grenada: Avda Norte 2, Quinta 330, Los Navajos del Cafetal, Caracas; tel. (212) 985-5461; fax (212) 985-6391; e-mail egrenada@cantv.net; internet www.grenadaembassycaracas.org; Ambassador George MacLeish.

Guatemala: Avda de Francisco de Miranda, Torre Dozsa, 1°, Urb. El Rosal, Caracas; tel. (212) 952-5247; fax (212) 954-0051; e-mail embaguat@cantv.net; Ambassador Erick Molina.

Guyana: Quinta 'Roraima', Avda El Paseo, Prados del Este, Apdo 51054, Caracas 1050; tel. (212) 977-1158; fax (212) 976-3765; e-mail embaguy@cantv.net; Ambassador Odeen Ishmael.

Haiti: Quinta Flor 59, Avda Las Rosas, La Florida, Caracas; tel. (212) 730-7220; fax (212) 730-4605; Chargé d'affaires a.i. Christian Toussaint.

Holy See: Avda La Salle, Los Caobos, Apdo 29, Caracas 1010-A (Apostolic Nunciature); tel. (212) 781-8939; fax (212) 793-2403; e-mail nunapos@cantv.net; Apostolic Nuncio Most Rev. Pietro Parolin (Titular Archbishop of Acquapendente).

Honduras: Edif. Banco de Lara, 8°, Of. B2, Avda Principal de la Castellana con 1a Transversal de Altamira, La Castellana, Apdo 68259, Caracas; tel. (212) 264-0606; fax (212) 263-4379; e-mail honduven@cantv.net; Chargé d'affaires a.i. Fernando Suárez Lovo.

India: Quinta Tagore, No. 12, Avda San Carlos, La Floresta, Apdo 61585, Caracas; tel. (212) 285-7887; fax (212) 286-5131; e-mail info@embindia.org; internet www.embindia.org; Ambassador Lal Dingliana.

Indonesia: Quinta 'Indonesia', Avda El Paseo, con Calle Maracaibo, Prados del Este, Apdo 80807, Caracas 1080; tel. (212) 976-2725; fax (212) 976-0550; e-mail kbricaracas1@yahoo1.com; internet www.caracas.deplu.go.id; Ambassador Alfred T. Palembangan.

Iran: Quinta Ommat, Calle Kemal Atatürk, Urb. Valle Arriba, Apdo 68460, Caracas; tel. (212) 992-3575; fax (212) 992-9989; e-mail embairanve@cantv.net; Ambassador Abdul Reza Mesri.

Iraq: Quinta Babilonia, Avda Nicolás Copérnico con Calle Los Malabares, Urb. Valle Arriba, Caracas; tel. (212) 993-3446; fax (212) 993-0819; e-mail crcemb@iraqmfamail.com; Chargé d'affaires a.i. Hisham A. Muhammad.

Italy: Edif. Atrium PH, Calle Sorocaima, entre Avdas Tamanaco y Venezuela, El Rosal, Apdo 3995, Caracas 1060; tel. (212) 952-7311; fax (212) 952-4960; e-mail ambcaracas@esteri.it; internet www.ambcaracas.esteri.it; Ambassador Luigi Maccotta.

Jamaica: Edif. Los Frailes, 5°, Calle La Guairita, Urb. Chuao, Caracas 1062; tel. (212) 916-9055; fax (212) 991-5708; e-mail embjaven@cantv.net; Ambassador Delrose Montague.

Japan: Edif. Bancaracas, 10°, Avda San Felipe con 2a Transversal, La Castellana, Caracas; tel. (212) 261-8333; fax (212) 261-6780; e-mail ajapon@genesisbci.net; internet www.ve.emb-japan.go.jp; Ambassador Shuji Shimokoji.

Korea, Republic: Avda Francisco de Miranda, Centro Lido, Torre B, 9°, Ofs 91-B y 92-B, El Rosal, Caracas; tel. (212) 954-1270; fax (212) 954-0619; e-mail venezuela@mofat.go.kr; internet ven.mofat.go.kr; Ambassador Choi Won Sun.

Kuwait: Quinta El-Kuwait, Avda Las Magnolias con Calle Los Olivos, Los Chorros, Caracas; tel. (212) 235-3864; fax (212) 238-1752; e-mail caracas@mofa.gov.kw; Ambassador Yousef Hussain al-Gabandi.

Lebanon: Edif. Embajada del Líbano, Prolongación Avda Parima, Colinas de Bello Monte, Calle Motatán, Caracas 1041; tel. (212) 751-5943; fax (212) 753-0726; e-mail emblibano@cantv.net; Ambassador Charbel Wehbe.

Malaysia: Centro Profesional Eurobuilding, 6°, Ofs 6D–G, Calle La Guairita, Apdo 65107, Chuao, Caracas 1060; tel. (212) 992-1011; fax (212) 992-1277; e-mail malcaracas@kln.gov.my; internet www.embajadamalasia.com; Ambassador Ramlan Kimin.

Mexico: Edif. Forum, Calle Guaicaipuro con Principal de las Mercedes, 5°, El Rosal, Chacao, Apdo 61371, Caracas; tel. (212) 952-5777; fax (212) 952-3003; e-mail mexico@embamex.com.ve; internet www.embamex.com.ve; Ambassador Jesús Mario Chacón Carrillo.

Netherlands: Edif. San Juan, 9°, Avda San Juan Bosco con 2a Transversal de Altamira, Caracas; tel. (212) 276-9300; fax (212) 276-9311; e-mail car@minbuza.nl; internet www.mfa.nl/car; Ambassador Johannes Gerardus Van Vloten Dissevetl.

Nicaragua: Avda El Paseo, Quinta Doña Dilia, Prados del Este, Caracas; tel. (212) 977-3289; fax (212) 977-3973; e-mail spoveda@cancilleria.gob.ni; Ambassador Ramón Enrique Leets Castillo.

Nigeria: Calle Chivacoa cruce con Calle Taría, Quinta Leticia, Urb. San Román, Apdo 62062, Chacao, Caracas 1060-A; tel. (212) 993-1520; fax (212) 993-7648; e-mail embnig@cantv.net; Ambassador Felix Oboro.

Norway: Centro Lido, Torre A-92A, Avda Francisco de Miranda, El Rosal, Apdo 60532, Chacao, Caracas 1060-A; tel. (212) 953-0269; fax (212) 953-6877; e-mail emb.caracas@mfa.no; internet www.noruega.org.ve; Ambassador Ingunn Klepsvik.

Panama: Edif. Los Frailes, 6°, Calle La Guairita, Chuao, Apdo 1989, Caracas; tel. (212) 992-9093; fax (212) 992-8107; e-mail empanve@cantv.net; Ambassador Pedro Pereira.

Paraguay: Quinta Helechales, 4a Avda, entre 7a y 8a Transversal, Urb. Altamira, Municipio Chacao, Caracas; tel. and fax (212) 267-5543; e-mail embaparven@cantv.net; Chargé d'affaires a.i. Miguel Angel Romero Alvaréz.

Peru: Edif. San Juan, 5°, Avda San Juan Bosco con 2a Transversal, Altamira, Caracas; tel. (212) 264-1483; fax (212) 265-7592; e-mail leprucaracas@cantv.net; Ambassador José Romero Cevallos.

Philippines: 5a Transversal de Altamira, Quinta Filipinas, Altamira, Municipio Chacao, Caracas 1060; tel. (212) 266-4725; fax (212) 266-6443; e-mail caracas@embassyph.com; Ambassador Jocelyn Batoon-García.

Poland: Quinta Ambar, Calle Nicolás Copérnico, Sector Los Naranjos, Valle Arriba, Apdo 62293, Chacao, Caracas; tel. (212) 991-1461; fax (212) 992-2164; e-mail ambcarac@cantv.net; internet www.caracas.polemb.net; Ambassador Krzysztof Jacek Hinz (also serves Guyana).

Portugal: Torre La Castellana, 3°, Avda Eugénio Mendoza, cruce con Calle José Angel Lamas, Urb. La Castellana, Caracas 1062; tel. (212) 263-2529; fax (212) 267-9766; e-mail embajadaportugal@cantv.net; Ambassador João José Gomes Caetano da Silva.

Qatar: Avda Principal Lomas El Mirador, Quinta Alto Claro, Municipio Baruta, Caracas; tel. (212) 993-7925; fax (212) 993-2917; e-mail qatarven@cantv.net; Ambassador Rashid Mubarak al-Kuwari.

Romania: 4a Avda de Altamira, entre 8a y 9a Transversales, Quinta Guardatinajas 49-19, Chacao, Caracas; tel. (212) 261-9480; fax (212) 263-5697; e-mail ambasadaccs@cantv.net; Chargé d'affaires a.i. Elena Lincan.

Russia: Quinta Soyuz, Calle Las Lomas, Las Mercedes, Apdo 60313, Caracas; tel. (212) 993-4395; fax (212) 993-6526; e-mail rusemb@cantv.net; internet www.venezuela.mid.ru; Ambassador Vladimir F. Zaemsky.

Saudi Arabia: Calle Andrés Pietri, Quinta Makkah, Los Chorros, Caracas 1071; tel. (212) 239-0290; fax (212) 239-6494; e-mail saudiembassycaracas@cantv.net; Ambassador Judiya al-Hathal.

South Africa: Edif. Atrium PH-1A, Sorocaima con Avda Venezuela, Urb. El Rosal, Chacao, Apdo 2613, Caracas 1064; tel. (212) 952-0026; fax (212) 952-0277; e-mail embajador.caracas@foreign.gov.za; Ambassador Bheki Wisdom Gila.

Spain: Avda Mohedano entre 1a y 2a Transversal, La Castellana, Apdo 62297, Caracas; tel. (212) 263-2855; fax (212) 261-0892; e-mail emb.caracas@mae.es; internet www.maec.es/embajadas/caracas; Ambassador Dámaso de Lario Ramírez.

Sudan: Caracas; Ambassador Abdurrahman Ahmed Klalid Sharfi.

Suriname: 4a Avda entre 7a y 8a Transversal, Quinta 41, Altamira, Caracas; Apdo 61140, Chacao, Caracas; tel. (212) 261-2724; fax (212) 263-9006; e-mail emsurl@cantv.net; Ambassador Samuel Pawironadi.

Switzerland: Centro Letonia, Torre Ing-Bank, 15°, Avda Eugenio Mendoza y San Felipe, La Castellana, Apdo 62555, Chacao, Caracas 1060-A; tel. (212) 267-9585; fax (212) 267-7745; e-mail car.vertretung@eda.admin.ch; internet www.eda.admin.ch/caracas; Ambassador Armin Ritz.

Syria: Avda Casiquiare, Quinta Damasco, Colinas de Bello Monte, Caracas; tel. (212) 753-5375; fax (212) 751-6146; Ambassador Ghassan Suleiman Abbas.

Trinidad and Tobago: Quinta Poshika, 3a Avda entre 7 y 8 Transversales, Altamira, Municipio Chacao, Caracas; tel. (212) 261-5796; fax (212) 261-9801; e-mail embassytt@cantv.net; Ambassador Razia Ali.

Turkey: Calle Kemal Atatürk, Quinta Turquesa 6, Valle Arriba, Apdo 62078, Caracas 1060-A; tel. (212) 991-0075; fax (212) 992-0442; e-mail turkishemb@cantv.net; internet karakas.be.mfa.gov.tr; Ambassador Nihat Akyol.

United Kingdom: Torre La Castellana, 11°, Avda Principal La Castellana, Caracas 1061; tel. (212) 263-8411; fax (212) 267-1275; e-mail britishembassy@internet.ve; internet ukinvenezuela.fco.gov.uk; Ambassador Catherine Elizabeth Nettleton.

USA: Calle Suapure con Calle F, Urb. Colinas de Valle Arriba, Caracas 1080; tel. (212) 975-6411; fax (212) 975-6710; e-mail embajada@state.gov; internet caracas.usembassy.gov; Chargé d'affaires a.i. John Caulfield.

Uruguay: Torre Seguros Altamira, 4°, Of. D y E, 4a Avda de los Palos Grandes, Apdo 60366, Caracas 1060-A; tel. (212) 285-3549; fax (212) 286-6777; e-mail uruvene@cantv.net; Ambassador Jorge Ernesto Mazzarovich Severi.

Viet Nam: 9a Transversal, entre 6a y 7a Avdas, Quinta Las Mercedes, Urb. Altamira, Chacao 1060-025, Caracas; tel. (212) 635-7402; fax (212) 264-7324; e-mail embavive@yahoo.com.vn; internet www.vietnamembassy-venezuela.org; Ambassador Tran Thanh Huan.

Judicial System

The judicature is headed by the Supreme Tribunal of Justice, which replaced the Supreme Court of Justice after the promulgation of the December 1999 Constitution. The judges are divided into penal and civil and mercantile judges; there are military, juvenile, labour, administrative litigation, finance and agrarian tribunals. In each state there is a superior court and several secondary courts which act on civil and criminal cases. A number of reforms to the judicial system were introduced under the Organic Criminal Trial Code of March 1998. The Code replaced the inquisitorial system, based on the Napoleonic code, with an adversarial system in July 1999. In addition, citizen participation as lay judges and trial by jury was introduced, with training financed by the World Bank.

SUPREME TRIBUNAL OF JUSTICE

The Supreme Tribunal comprises 32 judges appointed by the Asamblea Nacional for 12 years. It is divided into six courts, each with three judges: political-administrative, civil, constitutional, electoral, social and criminal. When these act together the court is in full session. It has the power to abrogate any laws, regulations or other acts of the executive or legislative branches conflicting with the Constitution. It hears accusations against members of the Government and high public officials, cases involving diplomatic representatives and certain civil actions arising between the State and individuals.

Tribunal Supremo de Justicia

Final Avda Baralt, esq. Dos Pilitas, Foro Libertador, Caracas 1010; tel. (212) 801-9178; fax (212) 564-8596; e-mail cperez@tsj.gov.ve; internet www.tsj.gov.ve.

President: Luisa Estella Morales Lamuño.

President of the Constitutional Court: Luisa Estella Morales Lamuño.

President of the Political-Administrative Court: Evelyn Margarita Marrero Ortíz.

President of the Court of Civil Cassation: Yris Armenia Peña Espinoza.

President of the Court of Penal Cassation: Eladio Ramón Aponte Aponte.

President of the Court of Social Cassation: Omar Alfredo Mora Díaz.

President of the Electoral Court: Luis Alfredo Sucre Cuba.

Attorney-General: Luisa Ortega Díaz.

Religion

Roman Catholicism is the religion of the majority of the population, but there is complete freedom of worship.

CHRISTIANITY

The Roman Catholic Church

For ecclesiastical purposes, Venezuela comprises nine archdioceses, 23 dioceses and four Apostolic Vicariates. There are also apostolic exarchates for the Melkite and Syrian Rites. Some 88% of the population are Roman Catholics.

Latin Rite

Bishops' Conference

Conferencia Episcopal de Venezuela, Prolongación Avda Páez, Montalbán, Apdo 4897, Caracas 1010; tel. (212) 471-6284; fax (212) 472-7029; e-mail prensa@cev.org.ve; internet www.cev.org.ve.

f. 1985; statutes approved in 2000; Pres. Most Rev. Ubaldo Ramón Santana Sequera (Archbishop of Maracaibo).

Archbishop of Barquisimeto: Most Rev. Antonio José López Castillo, Arzobispado, Venezuela con Calle 29 y 30 Santa Iglesia Catedral, Nivel Sótano, Barquisimeto 3001; tel. (251) 231-3446; fax (251) 231-3724; e-mail arquidiocesisdebarquisimeto@hotmail.com.

Archbishop of Calabozo: Manuel Felipe Díaz Sánchez, Arzobispado, Calle 4, No 11–82, Apdo 954, Calabozo 2312; tel. (246) 871-0483; fax (246) 871-2097; e-mail el.real@telcel.net.ve.

Archbishop of Caracas (Santiago de Venezuela): Cardinal Jorge Liberato Urosa Savino, Arzobispado, Plaza Bolívar, Apdo 954, Caracas 1010-A; tel. (212) 542-1611; fax (212) 542-0297; e-mail arzobispado@cantv.net.

Archbishop of Ciudad Bolívar: Most Rev. Medardo Luis Luzardo Romero, Arzobispado, Avda Andrés Eloy Blanco con Calle Naiguatá, Apdo 43, Ciudad Bolívar 8001; tel. (285) 654-4960; fax (285) 654-0821; e-mail arzcb@cantv.net.ve.

Archbishop of Coro: Most Rev. Roberto Lückert León, Arzobispado, Calle Federación esq. Palmasola, Apdo 7342, Coro; tel. (268) 251-7024; fax (268) 251-1636; e-mail dioceco@reaccium.ve.

Archbishop of Cumaná: Most Rev. Diego Rafael Padrón Sánchez, Arzobispado, Calle Bolívar 34 con Catedral, Apdo 134, Cumaná 6101-A; tel. (293) 431-4131; fax (293) 433-3413; e-mail dipa@cantv.net.

Archbishop of Maracaibo: Most Rev. Ubaldo Ramón Santana Sequera, Arzobispado, Calle 95, entre Avdas 2 y 3, Apdo 439, Maracaibo; tel. (261) 722-5351; fax (261) 721-0805; e-mail ubrasan@hotmail.com.

Archbishop of Mérida: Most Rev. Baltazar Enrique Porras Cardozo, Arzobispado, Avda 4, Plaza Bolívar, Apdo 26, Mérida 5101-A; tel. (274) 252-5786; fax (274) 252-1238; e-mail arquimer@latinmail.com.

Archbishop of Valencia: Most Rev. Reinaldo del Prette Lissot, Arzobispado, Avda Urdaneta 100-54, Apdo 32, Valencia 2001-A; tel. (241) 858-5865; fax (241) 857-8061; e-mail arqui_valencia@cantv.net.

Melkite Rite

Apostolic Exarch: Rt Rev. Georges Kahhalé Zouhaïraty, Iglesia San Jorge, Final 3a Urb. Montalbán II, Apdo 20120, Caracas; tel. (212) 472-5367; fax (212) 443-0131; e-mail georgeskhhale@cantv.net.

Syrian Rite

Apostolic Exarch: Iwannis Louis Awad, Parroquia Nuestra Señora de la Asunción, 1a Calle San Jacinto, Apdo 11, Maracay; tel. (243) 235-0821; fax (243) 235-7213.

The Anglican Communion

Anglicans in Venezuela are adherents of the Episcopal Church in the USA, in which the country forms a single, extra-provincial diocese attached to Province IX.

Bishop of Venezuela: Rt Rev. Orlando de Jesús Guerrero, Avda Caroní 100, Apdo 49-143, Colinas de Bello Monte, Caracas 1042-A; tel. (212) 753-0723; fax (212) 751-3180; e-mail iglanglicanavzla@cantv.net.

Protestant Churches

Convención Nacional Bautista de Venezuela: Avda Santiago de Chile 12–14, Urb. Los Caobos, Caracas 1050; Apdo 61152, Chacao, Caracas 1060-A; tel. (212) 782-2308; fax (212) 781-9043; e-mail cnbv@telcel.net.ve; internet www.cnbv.org.ve; f. 1951; Pres. Rev. Iván Martínez; Dir-Gen. Rev. Alexander Montero.

Iglesia Evangélica Luterana en Venezuela: Apdo 68738, Caracas 1062-A; tel. and fax (212) 264-1868; e-mail iglesia_ielv@cantv.net; internet ielv.tripod.com; Pres. Akos V. Puky; 4,000 mems.

JUDAISM

Confederación de Asociaciones Israelitas de Venezuela: Avda Washington, al lado del Hotel Avila, San Bernardino, Caracas; tel. (212) 551-0368; fax (212) 551-0377; internet www.caiv.org; f. 1966; federation of five Jewish orgs; Pres. Abraham Levy Benshimol.

ISLAM

Mezquita Sheikh Ibrahim bin-Abdulaziz bin-Ibrahim: Calle Real de Quebrada Honda, Los Caobos, Caracas; tel. (212) 577-7382; f. 1994; Leader Omar Kadwa.

BAHÁ'Í FAITH

National Spiritual Assembly of the Bahá'ís: Colinas de Bello Monte, Apdo 49133, Caracas; tel. and fax (212) 751-7669; e-mail aenbaven@telcel.net.ve; internet www.bci.org/venezuela; f. 1961; mems resident in 954 localities.

The Press

PRINCIPAL DAILIES

Caracas

The Daily Journal: Avda Principal de Boleíta Norte, Apdo 76478, Caracas 1070-A; tel. (212) 237-9644; fax (212) 232-6831; e-mail redaccion@dj.com.ve; internet www.dj.com.ve; f. 1945; morning; English; Chief Editor Russell M. Dallen, Jr.

Diario 2001: Edif. Bloque DeArmas, 2°, final Avda San Martín cruce con Avda La Paz, Caracas; tel. (212) 406-4111; fax (212)443-4961; e-mail contacto@dearmas.com; internet www.2001.com.ve; f. 1973; Pres. Martín de Armas S.; Dir Israel Márquez.

El Diario de Caracas: Calle Los Laboratorios, Torre B, 1°, Of. 101, Los Ruices, Caracas 1070; tel. (212) 238-0386; e-mail editor@eldiariodecaracas.net; internet www.eldiariodecaracas.net; f. 2003; distributed free of charge; Editor Julio Augusto López.

Meridiano: Edif. Bloque DeArmas, final Avda San Martín cruce con Avda La Paz, Caracas 1010; tel. (212) 406-4040; fax (212) 442-5836; e-mail meridian@dearmas.com; internet www.meridiano.com.ve; f. 1969; morning; sport; Pres. Martín de Armas S.; Dir Víctor José López.

El Mundo: Torre de la Prensa, 4°, Plaza del Panteón, Apdo 1192, Caracas; tel. (212) 596-1911; fax (212) 596-1478; e-mail olugo@cadena-capriles.com; internet www.elmundo.com.ve; f. 1958; morning; independent; economics and business; Pres. Miguel Angel Capriles López; Dir Omar Lugo.

El Nacional: Avda Principal de Los Cortijos de Lourdes con 3a Transversal, Caracas 1071-A; tel. (212) 203-3243; fax (212) 203-3158; e-mail contactenos@el-nacional.com; internet www.el-nacional.com; f. 1943; morning; right-wing; independent; Pres. and Editor Miguel Henrique Otero.

El Nuevo País: Pinto a Santa Rosalía 44, Caracas; tel. (212) 541-5211; fax (212) 545-9675; e-mail enpais1@telcel.net.ve; f. 1988; Dir and Editor Rafael Polea.

Reporte (Diario de la Economía): Edif. Jimmy, 1°, Of. 6, California con Mucuchíes, Urb. Las Mercedes, Caracas 1060; tel. (212) 993-3505; e-mail diarioreporte@yahoo.com; internet www.diarioreportedelaeconomia.com; f. 1988; Pres. Tannous Gerges.

TalCual: Edif. Menegrande, 5°, Of. 51, Avda Francisco de Miranda, Caracas; tel. (212) 286-7446; fax (212) 232-7446; e-mail tpetkoff@talcualdigital.com; internet www.talcualdigital.com; f. 2000; evening; right-wing; Pres. Teodoro Petkoff; Editor-in-Chief Maye Primera.

Ultimas Noticias: Torre de la Prensa, 3°, Plaza del Panteón, Apdo 1192, Caracas; tel. (212) 596-1911; fax (212) 596-1433; e-mail edrangel@cadena-capriles.com; internet www.ultimasnoticias.com.ve; f. 1941; morning; independent; Pres. Miguel Angel Capriles López; Dir Eleazar Díaz Rangel.

El Universal: Edif. El Universal, Avda Urdaneta, esq. de Animas, Apdo 1909, Caracas; tel. (212) 505-2314; fax (212) 505-3710; e-mail consejoeditorial@eluniversal.com; internet www.eluniversal.com; f. 1909; morning; Dir Andrés Mata Osorio; Chief Editor Elides Rojas.

Vea: Edif. San Martín, Sótano Uno, Parque Central, Caracas 1010; tel. (212) 516-1004; fax (212) 578-3031; e-mail webmaster@diariovea.com.ve; internet www.diariovea.com.ve; f. 2003; morning; left-wing; Dir Guillermo García Ponce; Editor-in-Chief Mercedes Orduño.

Barcelona

El Norte: Avda Intercomunal Jorge Rodríguez, Sector Las Garzas, Grupo UP, Entre el Banco Exterior y el BOD, Barcelona; tel. (281) 286-2484; e-mail fmartinez@elnorte.com.ve; internet www.elnorte.com.ve; f. 1989; morning; Dir Albertina Petricca; Exec. Dir Fernando Martínez.

Barquisimeto

El Impulso: Avda Los Comuneros, entre Avda República y Calle 1a, Urb. El Parque, Apdo 602, Barquisimeto; tel. (251) 250-2222; fax (251) 250-2129; e-mail reaccion@elimpulso.com; internet www.elimpulso.com; f. 1904; morning; independent; Dir and Editor Carlos Carmona.

El Informador: Edif. El Informador, Carrera 21, esq. Calle 23, Barquisimeto; tel. (251) 231-1811; fax (251) 231-0624; e-mail mauriciogomez@elinformador.com.ve; internet www.elinformador.com.ve; f. 1968; morning; Dir-Gen. Mauricio Gómez Sigala.

Ciudad Bolívar

El Bolivarense: Calle Igualdad 26, Apdo 91, Ciudad Bolívar; tel. (414) 893-4443; fax (285) 632-5667; e-mail publicidad@elbolivarense.com; f. 1957; morning; independent; Dir Alvaro Natera.

El Expreso: Paseo Gáspari con Calle Democracia, Ciudad Bolívar; tel. and fax (285) 632-0334; e-mail webmaster@diarioelexpreso.com.ve; internet www.diarioelexpreso.com.ve; f. 1969; morning; independent; Dir Luis Alberto Guzmán.

Maracaibo

Panorama: Avda 15, No 95–60, Apdo 425, Maracaibo; tel. (261) 725-6888; fax (261) 725-6911; e-mail editor@panodi.com; internet www.panodi.com; f. 1914; morning; independent; Pres. Esteban Pineda Belloso; Editorial Dir María Inés Delgado; circ. 16,000.

Maracay

El Aragüeño: Calle 3a Oeste con Avda 1 Oeste, Urb. Ind. San Jacinto, Maracay; tel. (243) 235-9018; fax (243) 235-7866; e-mail el-aragueno@cantv.net; internet www.el-aragueno.com.ve; f. 1972; morning; Editors ROSELYS PEÑA, PEDRO ELÍAS HERNÁNDEZ.

El Periodiquito: Calle Páez Este 178, Maracay; tel. (243) 322-1422; fax (243) 233-6987; e-mail redaccion@elperiodiquito.com; internet www.elperiodiquito.com; f. 1986; Pres. RAFAEL RODRÍGUEZ R.; Editor-in-Chief YHOSSELINE LUNA GALLARDO.

El Siglo: Edif. 'El Siglo', Avda Bolívar Oeste 244, La Romana, Maracay; tel. (243) 554-9521; fax (243) 554-5154; e-mail direccion@elsiglo.com.ve; internet www.elsiglo.com.ve; f. 1973; morning; independent; Editor TULIO CAPRILES.

Puerto la Cruz

El Tiempo: Edif. Diario El Tiempo, Avda Municipal 153, Puerto La Cruz; tel. (281) 260-0600; fax (281) 260-0660; e-mail buzon@eltiempo.com.ve; internet www.eltiempo.com.ve; f. 1958; independent; Dir and Editor GIOCONDA DE MÁRQUEZ.

San Cristóbal

Diario Católico: Carrera 4a, No 3–41, San Cristóbal; tel. (276) 343-2819; fax (276) 343-4683; e-mail catolico@truevision.net; internet www.diariocatolico.com.ve; f. 1924; morning; Catholic; Man. Dir Mgr JOSÉ LAUREANO BALLESTEROS BLANCO.

Diario La Nación: Edif. La Nación, Calle 4 con Carrera 6 bis, La Concordia, Apdo 651, San Cristóbal; tel. (276) 346-4263; fax (276) 346-5051; e-mail lanacion@lanacion.com.ve; internet www.lanacion.com.ve; f. 1968; morning; independent; Editor JOSÉ RAFAEL CORTEZ.

El Tigre

Antorcha: Edif. Antorcha, Avda Francisco de Miranda, El Tigre; tel. (283) 235-2383; fax (283) 235-3923; e-mail yurbina@diarioantorcha.com; internet www.diarioantorcha.com; f. 1954; morning; independent; Pres. and Editor ANTONIO BRICEÑO AMPARÁN.

Valencia

El Carabobeño: Edif. El Carabobeño, Avda Universidad, Urb. La Granja, Naguanagua, Valencia; tel. (241) 867-2918; fax (241) 867-3450; e-mail website@el-carabobeno.com; internet www.el-carabobeno.com; f. 1933; morning; Dir EDUARDO ALEMÁN PÉREZ.

Notitarde: Edif. Carabobo, Avda Boyacá, entre Navas Spínola y Flores, Valencia; tel. (241) 850-1666; fax (241) 850-1534; e-mail lauodr@notitarde.com; internet www.notitarde.com; evening; Dir LAURENTZI ODRIOZOLA ECHEGARAY.

SELECTED PERIODICALS

Artesanía y Folklore de Venezuela: C. C. Vista Mar, Local 20, Urbaneja, Lecherías, Estado Anzoátegui; tel. and fax (212) 286-2857; e-mail ismandacorrea@cantv.net; handicrafts and folklore; Dir ISMANDA CORREA.

Automóvil de Venezuela: Avda Caurimare, Quinta Expo, Colinas de Bello Monte, Caracas 1041; tel. (212) 751-1355; fax (212) 751-1122; e-mail ortizauto@cantv.net; internet www.automovildevenezuela.com; f. 1961; monthly; automotive trade; circ. 6,000; Editor MARÍA A. ORTIZ.

Barriles: Centro Parque Carabobo, Torre B, 20°, Of. 2003, Avda Universidad, La Candelaria, Caracas; e-mail informaciones@camarapetrolera.org; publ. of the Cámara Petrolera de Venezuela; Editor HAYDÉE REYES.

Business Venezuela: Torre Credival, Avda de Campo Alegre, Apdo 5181, Caracas 1010-A; tel. (212) 263-0833; fax (212) 263-2060; e-mail yrojas@venamcham.org; internet www.bvonline.com.ve; every two months; business and economics journal in English; published by the Venezuelan-American Chamber of Commerce and Industry; Editor-in-Chief CARLOS TEJERA.

ComputerWorld Venezuela: Edif. Marystella, Avda Carabobo, El Rosal, Caracas; tel. (212) 952-7427; fax (212) 953-3950; e-mail cernic@cwv.com.ve; internet www.cwv.com.ve; Editor CLELIA SANTAMBROGIO.

Dinero: Torre Sur, 1°, Centro Comercial El Recreo, Avda Venezuela, Caracas 1050; tel. (212) 750-5011; fax (212) 750-5005; e-mail mcastillo@gep.com.ve; internet www.dinero.com.ve; monthly; business and finance; Dir SALVATORE LOMONACO.

Exceso: Edif. Karam, Avda Urdaneta, 5°, Caracas; tel. (212) 564-1702; fax (212) 564-6760; e-mail baf-exceso@cantv.net; lifestyle; Dir BEN AMÍ FIHMAN; Editor ARMANDO COLL.

Gerente Venezuela: Avda Orinoco 3819, entre Muchuchies y Monterrey, Las Mercedes, Caracas 1060; tel. (212) 267-3733; fax (212) 267-6583; business and management; Editor LUIS RODÁN; circ. 15,000.

Nueva Sociedad: Edif. IASA, 6°, Of. 606, Plaza La Castellana, Apdo 61712, Caracas; tel. (212) 265-9975; fax (212) 267-3397; e-mail nuso@nuso.org; internet www.nuso.org; f. 1972; Latin American affairs; Dir JOACHIM KNOOP.

Producto: Torre Sur, 1°, Centro Comercial El Recreo, Avda Venezuela, Caracas 1050; tel. (212) 750-5011; fax (212) 750-5005; e-mail mcastillo@producto.com.ve; internet www.producto.com.ve; f. 1983; monthly; business; Editor ERNESTO LOTITTO.

Quinto Día: Avda Principal de Los Ruices con Avda Rómulo Gallegos, Residencia Los Almendros, nivel mezzanina, Of. 5, Los Ruices, Caracas; tel. (212) 237-9809; fax (212) 239-2955; e-mail acarrera@quintodia.com; internet www.quintodia.com; weekly; current affairs; Dir CARLOS CROES.

La Razón: Edif. Valores, Sótano 'A', Avda Urdaneta, esq. de Urapal, Apdo 16362, La Candelaria, Caracas; tel. (212) 578-3143; fax (212) 578-2397; e-mail larazon@internet.ve; internet www.larazon.net; weekly, on Sun.; independent; Dir PABLO LÓPEZ ULACIO.

La Red: Urb. Vista Alegre, Calle 7, Quinta Luisa Amelia, Caracas; tel. (212) 472-0703; fax (212) 471-7749; e-mail vdiaz@lared.com.ve; internet www.lared.com.ve; f. 1996; information technology; Editor LUIS MANUEL DÁVILA.

Ronda: Edif. Bloque DeArmas, final Avda San Martín cruce con Avda La Paz, Caracas 1020; tel. (212) 406-4018; fax (212) 406-4018; e-mail martinjr@dearmas.com; fortnightly; celebrities and entertainment; Dir JENNIFER MIRANDA.

Sic: Edif. Centro de Valores, esq. de Luneta, Centro Gumilla, Caracas; tel. (212) 564-9803; fax (212) 564-7557; e-mail sic@gumilla.org; internet www.gumilla.org; f. 1938; Compañía de Jesús; monthly; liberal Jesuit publ; Dir ARTURO PERAZA.

Tendencia: Torre Tendencia, 5°, Avda El Milagro, Sector Gonzaga, Maracaibo; tel. (261) 743-7674; fax (261) 742-0960; e-mail kmanrique@tendencia.com; internet www.tendencia.com; every two months; lifestyle; Dir E. PATRICIO PARDO.

Variedades: Edif. Bloque DeArmas, 6°, final Avda San Martín cruce con Avda La Paz, Caracas 1020; tel. (212) 406-4390; fax (212) 451-0762; e-mail jfeijoo@dearmas.com; f. 1963; monthly; women's interest; Dir MARÍA JESÚS RODRÍGUEZ.

VenEconomía: Edif. Gran Sabana, 1°, Avda Abraham Lincoln 174, Blvr de Sabana Grande, Caracas 1050; tel. (212) 761-8121; fax (212) 762-8160; e-mail editor@veneconomia.com; internet www.veneconomia.com; f. 1982; weekly and monthly edns; Spanish and English; business, economic and political issues; Editor ROBERT BOTTOME.

Zeta: Pinto a Santa Rosalía 44, Apdo 14067, Santa Rosalía, Caracas; tel. (212) 541-5211; fax (212) 545-9675; e-mail enpaiscolumna@hotmail.com; f. 1974; weekly; politics and current affairs; Dir JURATE ROSALES; Editor RAFAEL POLEO.

PRESS ASSOCIATIONS

Asociación de Prensa Extranjera en Venezuela (APEX): Hotel Caracas Hilton, Torre Sur, 3°, Of. 301, Avda México, Caracas; tel. (212) 503-5301; fax (212) 576-9284; e-mail caracashilton@hotmail.com; Pres. PHILIP GUNSON.

Bloque de Prensa Venezolano (BEV): Edif. El Universal, 5°, Of. C, Avda Urdaneta, Caracas; tel. (212) 561-7704; fax (212) 561-9409; e-mail contacto@bloquedeprensavenezolano.com; internet www.bloquedeprensavenezolano.com; asscn of newspaper owners; Pres. Dr DAVID NATERA FEBRES.

Colegio Nacional de Periodistas (CNP): Casa Nacional del Periodista, 2°, Avda Andrés Bello, Caracas; tel. and fax (212) 781-7601; e-mail colegiodeperiodistasjdn@yahoo.com; internet www.cnp.org.ve; journalists' asscn; Pres. WILLIAM ECHEVERRÍA; Sec.-Gen. SILVIA ALEGRETT.

STATE PRESS AGENCY

Agencia Bolivariana de Noticias: Avda Bolívar, Torre Oeste, 16°, Parque Central, Caracas; tel. (212) 572-6543; fax (212) 571-0563; internet www.abn.info.ve; fmrly Venpress; Pres. FREDDY FERNÁNDEZ TORRES.

Publishers

Alfadil Ediciones: Calle Las Flores con Calle Paraíso, Sábana Grande, Apdo 50304, Caracas 1020-A; tel. (212) 762-3036; fax (212) 762-0210; f. 1980; general; Pres. LEONARDO MILLA A.

Armitano Editores, CA: Centro Industrial Boleita Sur, 4a Transversal de Boleita, Apdo 50853, Caracas 1070; tel. (212) 234-2565; fax (212) 234-1647; e-mail armiedit@telcel.net.ve; internet www.alfagrupo.com; art, architecture, ecology, botany, anthropology, history, geography; Pres. ERNESTO ARMITANO.

Ediciones La Casa Bello: Mercedes a Luneta, Apdo 134, Caracas 1010; tel. (212) 562-7100; f. 1973; literature, history; Pres. OSCAR SAMBRANO URDANETA.

Editorial El Ateneo, CA: Complejo Cultural, Plaza Morelos, Los Caobos, Apdo 662, Caracas; tel. (212) 573-4622; f. 1931; school-books and reference; Pres. MARÍA TERESA CASTILLO; Dir ANTONIO POLO.

Editorial Cincel Kapelusz Venezolana, SA: Avda Cajigal, Quinta K No 29, entre Avdas Panteón y Roraima, San Bernardino, Apdo 14234, Caracas 1011-A; f. 1963; school-books; Pres. DANTE TONI; Man. MAYELA MORGADO.

Colegial Bolivariana, CA: Edif. COBO, 1°, Avda Diego Cisneros (Principal), Los Ruices, Apdo 70324, Caracas 1071-A; tel. (212) 239-1433; internet www.co-bo.com; f. 1961; Dir ANTONIO JUZGADO ARIAS.

Ediciones Ekaré: Edif. Banco del Libro, Avda Luis Roche, Altamira Sur, Caracas 1062; tel. (212) 264-7615; fax (212) 263-3291; e-mail editorial@ekare.com.ve; internet www.ekare.com; f. 1978; children's literature; Pres. CARMEN DIANA DEARDEN; Exec. Dir MARÍA FRANCISCA MAYOBRE.

Editora Ferga, CA: Torre Bazar Bolívar, 5°, Of. 501, Avda Francisco de Miranda, El Marqués, Apdo 16044, Caracas 1011-A; tel. (212) 239-1564; fax (212) 234-1008; e-mail ddex1@ibm.net; internet www.ddex.com; f. 1971; Venezuelan Exporters' Directory; Dir NELSON SÁNCHEZ MARTÍNEZ.

Fundación Biblioteca Ayacucho: Centro Financiero Latino, 12°, Ofs 1, 2 y 3, Avda Urdaneta, Animas a Plaza España, Apdo 14413, Caracas 1010; tel. (212) 561-6691; fax (212) 564-5643; e-mail biblioayacucho@cantv.net; internet www.bibliotecayacucho.gob.ve/fba; f. 1974; literature; Pres. STEFANIA MOSCA.

Fundación Bigott: Casa 10-11, Calle El Vigia, Plaza Sucre, Centro Histórico de Petare, Caracas 1010-A; tel. (212) 272-2020; fax (212) 272-5942; e-mail contacto@fundacionbigott.com; internet www.fundacionbigott.com; f. 1936; Venezuelan traditions, environment, agriculture; Admin. Co-ordinator NELSON REYES.

Fundación Editorial Salesiana: Paradero a Salesianos 6, Apdo 369, Caracas; tel. (212) 571-6109; fax (212) 574-9451; e-mail administracion@salesiana.com.ve; internet www.salesiana.com.ve; f. 1960; education; Gen. Man. JAIME GARCÍA.

Fundarte: Edif. Tajamar P. H., Avda Lecuna, Parque Central, Apdo 17559, Caracas 1015-A; tel. (212) 573-1719; fax (212) 574-2794; internet www.fundarte.gob.ve; f. 1975; literature, history; Pres. ALFREDO GOSEN; Dir ROBERTO LOVERA DE SOLA.

Editorial González Porto: Sociedad a Traposos 8, Avda Universidad, Caracas; Pres. Dr PABLO PERALES.

Ediciones IESA: Edif. IESA, 3°, Final Avda IESA, San Bernardino, Apdo 1640, Caracas 1010-A; tel. (212) 555-4298; e-mail ediesa@iesa.edu.ve; internet www.iesa.edu.ve/publicaciones/ediciones; f. 1984; economics, business; Pres. RAMÓN PIÑANGO.

Ediciones María Di Mase: Caracas; f. 1979; children's books; Pres. MARÍA DI MASE; Gen. Man. ANA RODRÍGUEZ.

Monte Avila Editores Latinoamericana, CA: Avda Principal La Castellana, Quinta Cristina, Apdo 70712, Caracas 1070; tel. (212) 265-6020; fax (212) 263-8783; e-mail maelca@telcel.net.ve; internet www.monteavila.gob.ve; f. 1968; general; Pres. MARIELA SÁNCHEZ URDANETA.

Nueva Sociedad: Edif. IASA, 6°, Of. 606, Plaza La Castellana, Apdo 61712, Chacao, Caracas 1060-A; tel. (212) 265-0593; fax (212) 267-3397; e-mail nuso@nuevasoc.org.ve; internet www.nuevasoc.org.ve; f. 1972; social sciences; Dir DIETMAR DIRMOSER.

Ediciones Panamericanas EP, SRL: Edif. Freites, 2°, Avda Libertador cruce con Santiago de Chile, Apdo 14054, Caracas; tel. (212) 782-9891; Man. JAIME SALGADO PALACIO.

Oscar Todtmann Editores: Avda Libertador, Centro Comercial El Bosque, Local 4, Caracas 1050; tel. (212) 763-0881; fax (212) 762-5244; science, literature, photography; Dir CARSTEN TODTMANN.

Vadell Hermanos Editores, CA: Edif. Golden, Avda Sur 15, esq. Peligro a Pele el Ojo, Caracas; tel. (212) 572-3108; fax (212) 572-5243; e-mail edvadell1@cantv.net.ve; internet www.vadellhermanos.com; f. 1973; science, social science; Gen. Man. MANUEL VADELL GRATEROL.

Ediciones Vega, SRL: Edif. Odeon, Plaza Las Tres Gracias, Los Chaguaramos, Caracas 1050-A; tel. (212) 662-2092; fax (212) 662-1397; f. 1965; educational; Man. Dir FERNANDO VEGA ALONSO.

PUBLISHERS' ASSOCIATION

Cámara Venezolana del Libro: Centro Andrés Bello, Torre Oeste, 11°, Of. 112-0, Avda Andrés Bello, Caracas 1050-A; tel. (212) 793-1347; fax (212) 793-1368; f. 1969; Pres. HANS SCHNELL; Sec. ISIDORO DUARTE.

Broadcasting and Communications

TELECOMMUNICATIONS

Regulatory Authority

Comisión Nacional de Telecomunicaciones (CONATEL): Avda Veracruz con Cali, Edif. Conatel, 6°, Las Mercedes, Municipio Baruta, Caracas; tel. (212) 909-0510; fax (212) 993-6122; e-mail conatel@conatel.gov.ve; internet www.conatel.gov.ve; regulatory body for telecommunications; Dir-Gen. ELDA RODRÍGUEZ FERNÁNDEZ.

Major Service Providers

AT&T Venezuela: Edif. Centro Banaven, Avda La Estancia A, Chuao, Caracas 1060; internet www.att.com.

Compañía Anónima Nacional Teléfonos de Venezuela (CANTV): Edif. NEA, 20, Avda Libertador, Caracas 1010-A; tel. (212) 500-3016; fax (212) 500-3512; e-mail amora@cantv.com.ve; internet www.cantv.net; privatized in 1991; renationalized in 2007; Pres. SOCORRO HERNÁNDEZ.

Movilnet: Edif. NEA, 20, Avda Libertador, Caracas 1010-A; tel. (202) 705-7901; e-mail info@movilnet.com.ve; internet www.movilnet.com.ve; f. 1992; mobile cellular telephone operator; owned by CANTV; 6.3m. subscribers (June 2006); Pres. JACQUELINE FARÍA.

Digicel, CA: Caracas; internet www.digicel.com.ve; owned by Banco Santander Central Hispano of Spain; fixed-line telecommunications; 110,200 subscribers (June 2006).

Digitel TIM: Caracas; e-mail 0412empres@digitel.com.ve; internet www.digitel.com.ve; f. 2000; mobile cellular telephone operator; owned by Telecom Italia, Italy; 2.4m. subscribers (June 2006).

Intercable: Avda La Pedregosa Sur, cruce con Avda Los Próceres, Tapias; e-mail jguerrero@multimedios.net; internet www.intercable.net/default.asp; cable, internet and telecommunications services; Dir JUAN GERARDO GUERRERO.

Movistar: Edif. Parque Cristal, Torre Oeste, Avda Francisco Miranda, 14°, Los Palos Grandes, Caracas 1062; tel. (582) 201-8200; internet www.movistar.com.ve; f. 2005; subsidiary of Telefónica Móviles (Spain); 6.5m. subscribers (June 2006); Pres. LUIS MALVIDO.

NetUno: Edif. Insenica II, planta baja, Calle 7, La Urbina, Caracas; tel. (212) 710-0404; e-mail atccaracas@netuno.net; internet www.netuno.net; f. 1995; voice, data and video transmission services; Pres. GILBERT MINIONIS.

Telecom Venezuela: Puerto Ordaz; tel. (212) 393-1912; e-mail eauverana@cvgtelecom.com.ve; internet www.cvgtelecom.com.ve; f. 2004 as CVG Telecomunicaciones, CA; present name adopted Aug. 2007; state-owned telecommunications co; Pres. CARMEN LEONOR MÁRQUEZ; Man. EVELYN AUVERANA.

Telecomunicaciones Gran Caribe: Caracas; f. 2007; owned by Telecom Venezuela (60%) and Transbit of Cuba (40%); construction and operation of 1,550 km fibre-optic cable connecting La Guaira (Venezuela) and Siboney (Cuba).

BROADCASTING

Regulatory Authorities

Cámara Venezolana de la Industria de Radiodifusión: Avda Antonio José Istúriz entre Mohedano y Country Club, La Castellana, Caracas; tel. (212) 263-2228; fax (212) 261-4783; e-mail camradio@camradio.org.ve; internet www.camradio.org; Pres. CIRO GARCÍA.

Cámara Venezolana de Televisión por Suscripción: Edif. Venevisión, 4°, Colinas de Los Caobos, Caracas; tel. (212) 708-9223; fax (212) 708-9146; e-mail cavetesu@cavetesu.org.ve; internet www.cavetesu.org.ve; regulatory body for private stations; Man. EVELYN GONZÁLEZ.

Radio

Radio Nacional de Venezuela (RNV): Final Calle Las Marías, entre Chapellín y Country Club, La Florida, Caracas 1050; tel. (212) 730-6022; fax (212) 731-1457; e-mail rnv@rnv.gov.ve; internet www.rnv.gov.ve; f. 1936; state broadcasting org.; 15 stations; Gen. Man. HELENA SALCEDO.

There are also 20 cultural and some 500 commercial stations.

Television

Government Stations

Telesur (Televisora del Sur): Edif. Anexo VTV, 4°, Avda Principal Los Ruices, Caracas; tel. (212) 237-6365; e-mail contactenos@telesurtv.net; internet www.telesurtv.net; f. 2005; jtly owned by Govts of Venezuela (51%), Argentina (20%), Cuba (19%) and Uruguay (10%); regional current affairs and general interest; Pres. Lt (retd) ANDRÉS IZARRA; Vice-Pres. ARAM AHARONIAN.

Televisora Venezolana Social—Canal 2 (TVes): Quinta Thaizza, Avda Principal Augusto César Sandino con 10a Transversal, Maripérez, Municipio Libertador, Caracas; tel. (212) 781-8069; e-mail info@tves.com.ve; internet tves.org.ve; f. May 2007 to replace private channel RCTV (q.v.); govt-owned; Pres. LIL RODRÍGUEZ.

Venezolana de Televisión (VTV)—Canal 8: Edif. VTV, Avda Principal Los Ruices, Caracas; tel. (212) 239-4870; fax (212) 239-8102; internet www.vtv.gob.ve; f. 1964; 26 relay stations; Pres. JESÚS ROMERO ANSELMI.

ViVe TV (Visión Venezuela): Edif. Biblioteca Nacional, AP-4, Final Avda Panteón, Foro Libertador, Altagracia, Caracas; tel. (212) 505-1611; e-mail dmercadeo@vive.gov.ve; internet www.vive.gob.ve; f. 2003; govt-run cultural channel; Pres. BLANCA EEKHOUT.

Private Stations

Corporación Venezolana de Televisión (Venevisión)—Canal 4: Edif. Venevisión, final Avda La Salle, Colinas de los Caobos, Apdo 6674, Caracas; tel. (212) 708-9224; fax (212) 708-9535; e-mail mponce@venevision.com.ve; internet www.venevision.net; f. 1961; privately owned; Pres. GUSTAVO CISNEROS.

Globovisión—Canal 33: Quinta Globovisión, Avda Los Pinos, Urb. Alta Florida, Caracas; tel. (212) 730-2290; fax (212) 731-4380; e-mail info@globovision.com; internet www.globovision.com; f. 1994; 24-hour news and current affairs channel; Pres. GUILLERMO ZULOAGA; Dir-Gen. (vacant).

Meridiano Televisión: Caracas; e-mail opina@dearmas.com; f. 1982; sports programming; Pres. MARTÍN DE ARMAS; Dir-Gen. JUAN ANDRÉS DAZA.

Radio Caracas Televisión (RCTV): Edif. RCTV, Dolores a Puente Soublette, Quinta Crespo, Caracas; tel. (212) 401-2222; fax (212) 401-2647; e-mail marriaga@rctv.net; internet www.rctv.net; f. 1953; fmrly broadcast on terrestrial channel as Radio Caracas Televisión—Canal 2; ceased broadcasting in May 2007; subsidiary RCTV International (based in Miami, FL, USA) recommenced broadcasting in Venezuela via cable in July 2007; broadcasting licence of RCTV Internacional temporarily suspended in Jan. 2010; Pres. MARCEL GRANIER.

Televén—Canal 10 (Televisión de Venezuela): Edif. Televén, 4a Transversal con Avda Rómulo Gallegos, Urb. Horizonte, Apdo 1070, Caracas; tel. (212) 280-0011; fax (212) 280-0204; e-mail aferro@televen.com; internet www.televen.com; f. 1988; privately owned; Pres. OMAR CAMERO ZAMORA.

Televisora Andina de Mérida (TAM)—Canal 6: Edif. Imperador, Entrada Independiente, Avda 6 y 7, Calle 23, Mérida 5101; tel. and fax (274) 251-0660; f. 1982; regional channel; Pres. Most Rev. BALTAZAR ENRIQUE PORRAS CARDOZO.

VALE TV (Valores Educativos Televisión)—Canal 5: Quinta VALE TV, final Avda La Salle, Colinas de los Caobos, Caracas 1050; tel. (212) 793-9215; fax (212) 708-9743; e-mail webmaster@valetv.com; internet www.valetv.com; f. 1998; Pres. JORGE CARDENAL L. UROSA SAVINO; Man. MARÍA ISABEL ROJAS.

Zuliana de Televisión—Canal 30: Edif. 95.5 América, Avda 11 (Veritas), Maracaibo; tel. (265) 641-0355; fax (265) 641-0565; e-mail elregionalredac@iamnet.com; Pres. GILBERTO URDANETA FIDOL.

Zuvisión: Maracaibo; f. 2007; regional channel for the state of Zulia; Pres. RAFAEL URDANETA.

Finance

(cap. = capital; res = reserves; dep. = deposits; m. = million; brs = branches; amounts in bolívares unless otherwise indicated)

BANKING

Regulatory Authorities

Corporación de la Banca Pública (CBP): Caracas; f. 2009 to oversee all state-owned financial institutions; Supt EDGAR HERNÁNDEZ BEHRENS.

Superintendencia de Bancos (SUDEBAN): Edif. Centro Empresarial Parque del Este, Avda Francisco de Miranda, Urb. La Carlota, Municipio Sucre del Estado Miranda, Apdo 6761, Caracas; tel. (212) 280-6933; fax (212) 238-2516; e-mail sudeban@sudeban.gob.ve; internet www.sudeban.gob.ve; regulates banking sector; Supt EDGAR HERNÁNDEZ BEHRENS.

Central Bank

Banco Central de Venezuela: Avda Urdaneta, esq. de Carmelitas, Caracas 1010; tel. (212) 801-5111; fax (212) 861-0048; e-mail info@bcv.org.ve; internet www.bcv.org.ve; f. 1940; bank of issue and clearing house for commercial banks; granted autonomy 1992; controls international reserves, interest rates and exchange rates; cap. 10m., res 131,188,625m., dep. 73,298,601m. (Dec. 2007); Pres. and Chair. NELSON JOSÉ MERENTES DÍAZ; 2 brs.

Commercial Banks

Banco del Caribe, CA: Edif. Banco del Caribe, 1°, Dr Paúl a esq. Salvador de León, Apdo 6704, Carmelitas, Caracas 1010; tel. (212) 505-5103; fax (212) 562-0460; e-mail producto@bancaribe.com.ve; internet www.bancaribe.com.ve; f. 1954; cap. 201,000m., res 469,639m., dep. 6,701,991m. (Dec. 2008); Founding Pres. JUAN CARLOS DAO; Pres. MIGUEL IGNACIO PURROY; 70 brs and agencies.

Banco Caroní: Edif. Multicentro Banco Caroní, Vía Venezuela, Puerto Ordaz, Estado Bolívar; tel. (286) 950-5200; fax (286) 920-0995; e-mail contactenos.caroni@bancocaroni.com.ve; internet www.bancocaroni.com.ve; Pres. ARÍSTIDES MAZA TIRADO.

Banco de Comercio Exterior (Bancoex): Central Gerencial Mohedano, 1°, Calle Los Chaguaramos, La Castellana, Caracas 1060; tel. (212) 265-1433; fax (212) 265-6722; e-mail exports@bancoex.com; internet www.bancoex.com; f. 1997 principally to promote non-traditional exports; state-owned; cap. US $200m.; Pres. VÍCTOR ALVAREZ.

Banco Exterior, CA—Banco Universal: Edif. Banco Exterior, 1°, Avda Urdaneta, esq. Urapal a Río, Candelaria, Apdo 14278, Caracas 1011-A; tel. (212) 501-0211; fax (212) 501-0745; e-mail lperez@bancoexterior.com; internet www.bancoexterior.com; f. 1958; cap. 85,050m., res 84,518m., dep. 7,550670m. (Dec. 2008); Chair. JOSÉ LORETO ARISMENDI; Pres. RAÚL BALTAR ESTÉVEZ; 70 brs.

Banco Federal, CA: Torre Federal, Avda Venezuela, Urb. El Rosal, Caracas; tel. (268) 51-4011; e-mail masterbf@bancofederal.com; internet www.bancofederal.com; f. 1982; operations suspended June 2010; Pres. NELSON MEZERHANE; Exec. Pres. ROGELIO TRUJILLO.

Banco de Fomento Regional Coro, CA: Avda Manaure, entre Calles Falcón y Zamora, Coro, Falcón; tel. (268) 51-4421; f. 1950; transferred to private ownership in 1994; Pres. ABRAHAM NAÍN SENIOR URBINA.

Banco Guayana, CA: Edif. Los Bancos, Avda Guayana con Calle Caura, Puerto Ordaz, Bolívar; e-mail atencion.cliente@bancoguayana.net; internet www.bancoguayana.net; f. 1955; state-owned; Pres. OSCAR EUSEBIO JIMÉNEZ AYESA; Exec. Pres. BERNARDO KABCHE.

Banco Industrial de Venezuela, CA: Torre Financiera BIV, Avda Las Delicias de Sabana Grande, cruce con Avda Francisco Solano López, Caracas 1010; tel. (212) 952-4051; fax (212) 952-6282; e-mail webmaster@biv.com.ve; internet www.biv.com.ve; f. 1937; 98% state-owned; cap. 9,840m., res 278,645m., dep. 8,600,674m. (Dec. 2006); Pres. LUIS QUIARO; 60 brs.

Banco Occidental de Descuento Banco Universal, CA: Calle 77, esq. Avda 17, Maracaibo 4001, Apdo 695, Zulia; tel. (261) 759-3011; fax (261) 594-9811; e-mail atclient@bodinternet.com; internet www.bodinternet.com; f. 1957; transferred to private ownership in 1991; cap. 169,674m., res 970,738m., dep. 13,824,285m. (Dec. 2008); Pres. VÍCTOR J. VARGAS IRAUSQUIN; Exec. Pres. TOMÁS NIEMBRO CONCHA; 17 brs.

Banco Standard Chartered: Edif. Banaven, Torre D, 5°, Of. D52, Avda la Estancia, Chuao, Caracas 1060A; tel. (212) 993-0522; fax (212) 993-3130; internet www.standardchartered.com/ve; f. 1980 as Banco Exterior de los Andes y de España; current name adopted in 1998 following acquisition by Standard Chartered Bank (United Kingdom); representative office only; CEO JOHN LETO; 3 brs.

Banco de Venezuela, SA: Torre Banco de Venezuela, 16°, Avda Universidad, esq. Sociedad a Traposos, Apdo 6268, Caracas 1010-A; tel. (212) 501-3333; fax (212) 501-2570; e-mail bancodevenezuela@banvenez.com; internet www.bancodevenezuela.com; f. 1890; nationalized in July 2009; cap. 40,524m., res 496,464m., dep. 16,837,805m. (Dec. 2006); Pres. HUMBERTO RAFAEL ORTEGA DÍAZ; 242 brs.

Banesco Banco Universal, CA: Edif. Banesco, 12°, Avda Guaicaipura con Avda Principal de Las Mercedes, Caracas; tel. (212) 952-4972; fax (212) 952-7124; e-mail atclient@banesco.com; internet www.banesco.com; cap. 1,050,000.0m., res 465,000.0m., dep. 32,749,000.0m. (Dec. 2008); Chair. JUAN CARLOS ESCOTET RODRÍGUEZ; Exec. Pres. LUIS XAVIER LUJÁN PUIGBÓ.

BBVA Banco Provincial, SA: Centro Financiero Provincial, 27°, Avda Vollmer con Avda Este O, San Bernadino, Apdo 1269, Caracas 1011; tel. (212) 504-5098; fax (212) 574-9408; e-mail calidad@provincial.com; internet www.provincial.com; f. 1952; 55.14% owned by Banco Bilbao Vizcaya Argentaria, 26.27% owned by Grupo Polar; cap. 1,078,274.7m., res 1,091,213.4m., dep. 17,131,652.6m. (Dec. 2007); Pres. HERNÁN ANZOLA GIMÉNEZ; Exec. Pres. JOSÉ CARLOS PLA ROYO.

Bicentenario Banco Universal: Caracas; internet www.banfoandes.com.ve; f. 2009 by merger of Banco Bolívar, Banco Confederado, Banfoandes and Banco Central; BaNorte incorporated in Jan. 2010; state-owned; Pres. KIMLEN CHANG DE NEGRÓN.

Corp Banca, CA Banco Universal: Torre Corp Banca, Plaza la Castellana, Chacao, Caracas 1060; tel. (212) 206-3333; fax (212) 206-4950; e-mail calidad@corpbanca.com.ve; internet www.corpbanca.com.ve; f. 1969; fmrly Banco Consolidado, current name adopted in 1997; cap. 40,000m., res 47,740m., dep. 2,754,500m. (Dec. 2006); Chair. JORGE SELUME ZAROR; CEO MARIO CHAMORRO; 116 brs.

Mercantil CA Banco Universal: Edif. Mercantil, 35°, Avda Andrés Bello 1, San Bernardino, Apdo 789, Caracas 1010-A; tel. (212) 503-1111; fax (212) 503-1075; e-mail mercan24@bancomercantil.com; internet www.bancomercantil.com; f. 1925; cap. 268,060m., res 208,730m., dep. 28,807,177m. (Dec. 2008); Chair. and CEO Dr GUSTAVO A. MARTURET; 309 brs.

Unibanca Banco Universal, CA: Torre Grupo Unión, Avda Universidad, esq. El Chorro, Apdo 2044, Caracas; tel. (212) 501-7031; fax (212) 563-0986; internet www.unibanca.com.ve; f. 2001 by merger of Banco Unión (f. 1943) and Caja Familia; Pres. Dr IGNACIO SALVATIERRA; Vice-Pres. JOSÉ Q. SALVATIERRA; 174 brs.

Venezolano de Crédito, SA—Banco Universal: Edif. Banco Venezolano de Crédito, Avda Alameda, San Bernadino, Caracas 1011; tel. (212) 806-6111; fax (212) 541-2757; e-mail info@venezolano.com; internet www.venezolano.com; f. 1925 as Banco Venezolano de Crédito, SACA; name changed as above in 2001; cap. 69,888m., res 118,846m., dep. 3,811,053m. (Dec. 2008); Pres. Dr OSCAR GARCÍA MENDOZA; 95 brs in Venezuela and abroad.

Development Banks

Banco de Desarrollo Económico y Social de Venezuela (BANDES): Torre Bandes, Avda Universidad, Traposos a Colón, Caracas 1010; tel. (212) 505-8010; fax (212) 505-8030; e-mail apublicos@bandes.gov.ve; internet www.bandes.gov.ve; state-owned; Pres. EDMÉE BETANCOURT DE GARCÍA.

Banco de Desarrollo de la Mujer (BANMUJER): Edif. Sudameris, planta baja, Avda Urdaneta, entre Plaza España y esq. de Animas, Caracas 1010; tel. (212) 564-3015; fax (212) 564-4087; e-mail banmujer@cantv.net; internet www.banmujer.gob.ve; f. 2001; state-owned bank offering loans to women; Pres. NORA CASTAÑEDA.

Banco del Pueblo Soberano, CA: Edif. El Gallo de Oro, Gradillas a San Jacinto Parroquia Catedral, Caracas; tel. (212) 505-2800; fax (212) 505-2995; e-mail abarrera@bancodelpueblo.gob.ve; internet www.bancodelpueblo.gob.ve; f. 1999; microfinance; Pres. DARÍO ENRIQUE BAUTE DELGADO.

Banco del Sur: Caracas; e-mail atencionalcliente@@delsur.com.ve; internet www.delsur.com.ve; f. 2007 by Govts of Argentina, Bolivia, Brazil, Ecuador, Paraguay, Uruguay and Venezuela; regional devt bank; brs in Buenos Aires (Argentina) and La Paz (Bolivia); Pres. CÉSAR NAVARRETE.

Fondo de Desarrollo Microfinanciero (FONDEMI): Edif. Sudameris, 2°, Avda Urdaneta con Fuerzas Armadas, esq. Plaza España, Caracas 1030; tel. (212) 287-7611; fax (212) 287-7658; e-mail fondemi@fondemi.gob.ve; internet www.fondemi.gob.ve; f. 2001; microfinancing devt fund; Pres. ISA MERCEDES SIERRA FLORES.

Banking Association

Asociación Bancaria de Venezuela: Torre Asociación Bancaria de Venezuela, 1°, Avda Venezuela, El Rosal, Caracas; tel. (212) 951-4711; fax (212) 951-3696; e-mail abvinfo@asobanca.com.ve; internet www.asobanca.com.ve; f. 1959; 49 mems; Pres. JUAN CARLOS ESCOTET; Exec. Dir LARRY M. DE CRACCO.

STOCK EXCHANGE

Bolsa de Valores de Caracas, CA: Edif. Atrium, Nivel C-1, Calle Sorocaima entre Avdas Tamanaco y Venezuela, Urb. El Rosal, Apdo 62724-A, Caracas 1060-A; tel. (212) 905-5511; fax (212) 952-2640; e-mail bvc@bolsadecaracas.com; internet www.bolsadecaracas.com; f. 1947; 65 mems; Pres. NELSON ORTIZ CUSNIER.

INSURANCE

Supervisory Board

Superintendencia de Seguros: Edif. Torre del Desarollo, PH, Avda Venezuela, El Rosal, Chacao, Caracas 1060; tel. (212) 905-1611; fax (212) 953-8615; e-mail sudeseg@sudeseg.gob.ve; internet www.sudeseg.gob.ve; Supt JOSÉ LUÍS PÉREZ.

Principal Insurance Companies

Adriática, CA de Seguros: Edif. Adriática de Seguros, Avda Andrés Bello, esq. de Salesianos, Caracas; tel. (212) 571-5702; fax (212) 571-0812; e-mail adriatica@adriatica.com.ve; internet www.adriatica.com.ve; f. 1952; Pres. FRANÇOIS THOMAZEAU; Exec. Vice-Pres. GHISLAIN FABRE.

Avila, CA de Seguros: Edif. Torre Británica de Seguros, PH, Avda José Felix Sosa, Urb. El Dorado, Altamira, Chacao, Caracas; tel. (212) 238-2470; fax (212) 239-9743; f. 1936; Pres. RAMÓN RODRÍGUEZ; Vice-Pres. JUAN LUIS CASAÑAS.

Bolivariana de Seguros: Caracas; f. 2010; state-owned; Pres. JESÚS TOVAR JIMÉNEZ.

Carabobo, CA de Seguros: Edif. Mene Grande, 7°, Avda Francisco de Miranda, Urb. Los Palos Grandes, Caracas; tel. (212) 620-7193; fax (212) 620-7320; e-mail aehernandez@seguroscarabobo.com; internet www.seguroscarabobo.com; f. 1955; Pres. PAUL FRAYND; Gen. Man. ANDRÉS HERNÁNDEZ.

Mapfre La Seguridad, CA de Seguros: Calle 3A, Frente a La Torre Express, La Urbina Sur, Apdo 473, Caracas 1010; tel. (212) 213-8000; fax (212) 204-8751; e-mail endirecto@mapfre.com.ve; internet www.mapfre.com.ve; f. 1943; owned by Seguros Mapfre (Spain); Pres. ARISTÓBULO BAUSELA.

La Occidental, CA de Seguros: Edif. Seguros Occidental, Avda 4 (Bella Vista) esq. con Calle 71, No 10126, Maracaibo, Zulia; tel. (261) 796-2226; fax (261) 796-2293; e-mail clientes@laoccidental.com; internet www.laoccidental.com; f. 1956; Pres. TOBÍAS CARRERO NÁCAR; Dir CARLOS MONÍZ ROCHA.

La Oriental, CA de Seguros: Torre Oriental de Seguros, Avda Venezuela, entre Calle Sojo y Avda Sorocaima, Urb. El Rosal, Chacao, Caracas 1060; tel. (212) 905-9999; fax (212) 905-9652; internet www.laoriental.com; f. 1975; Pres. GONZALO LAURÍA ALCALÁ.

Seguros Los Andes, CA: Edif. Central, 5°, Avda San Felipe, entre 1a y 2a Transversal, La Castellana, Caracas; tel. (276) 266-5020; fax (276) 340-2596; internet www.seguroslosandes.com; Pres. RAMÓN RODRÍGUEZ.

Seguros Caracas de Liberty Mutual, CAV: Torre Seguros Caracas C-4, Centro Comercial El Parque, Avda Francisco de Miranda, Los Palos Grandes, Caracas; tel. (212) 209-9111; fax (212) 209-9556; e-mail informatica@seguroscaracas.com; internet www.seguroscaracas.com; f. 1943; Pres. ROBERTO SALAS; Regional Man. ANDRÉS VERROCCHI.

Seguros Catatumbo, CA: Edif. Seguros Catatumbo, Avda 4 (Bella Vista), No 77–55, Apdo 1083, Maracaibo; tel. (261) 700-5555; fax (261) 216-0037; e-mail mercado@seguroscatatumbo.com; internet www.seguroscatatumbo.com; f. 1957; cap. 9,300m. (2003); Pres. ERNESTO PINEDA HERNÁNDEZ; Dir-Gen. RAFAEL ARRAGA HUERTA.

Seguros Mercantil, CA: Edif. Seguros Mercantil, Avda Libertador con calle Andrés Galarraga, Chacao, Caracas; tel. (212) 276-2000; fax (212) 276-2596; e-mail cat@segurosmercantil.com; internet www.segurosmercantil.com; f. 1988; acquired Seguros Orinoco in 2002; Pres. ALBERTO BENSHIMOL; Gen. Man. MARÍA SILVIA RODRÍGUEZ FEO.

Seguros Nuevo Mundo, SA: Torre Nuevo Mundo, Avda Luis Roche con 3a Transversal, Urb. Altamira, Apdo 2062, Caracas; tel. (212) 201-1111; fax (212) 201-1428; e-mail luis.sanelli@nuevomundo.com.ve; internet www.nuevomundo.com.ve; f. 1856; cap. 100m. (2003); Pres. RAFAEL PEÑA ALVAREZ; Sec. JUAN CARLOS TRIVELLA.

Seguros La Previsora, CNA: Torre La Previsora, Avda Abraham Lincoln, Sábana Grande, Caracas; tel. (212) 709-1555; fax (212) 709-1976; internet www.previsora.com; f. 1914; nationalized in Dec. 2009; Pres. ALBERTO QUINTANA; Exec. Vice-Pres. JUAN CARLOS MALDONADO.

Seguros Venezuela, CA: Edif. Seguros Venezuela, 8° y 9°, Avda Francisco de Miranda, Urb. Campo Alegre, Caracas; tel. (212) 901-7111; fax (212) 901-7218; e-mail carmen.guillen@segurosvenezuela.com; internet www.segurosvenezuela.com; f. 1948; part of American International group; Exec. Pres. ENRIQUE BANCHIERI ORTIZ.

Universitas de Seguros, CA: Edif. Impres Médico, 2°, Avda Tamanaco, El Rosal, Caracas; tel. (212) 951-6711; fax (212) 901-7506; e-mail tbarrera@universitasdeseguros.com; internet www.universitasdeseguros.com; cap. 6,500m; Pres. ANA TERESA FERRINI.

Insurance Association

Cámara de Aseguradores de Venezuela: Torre Taeca, 2°, Avda Guaicaipuro, Urb. El Rosal, Apdo 3460, Caracas 1010-A; tel. (212) 952-4411; fax (212) 951-3268; e-mail rrpp@camaraseg.org; internet www.camaraseg.org; f. 1951; 42 mems; Pres. GONZALO LAURIA ALCALA; Exec. Pres. ALESIA RODRIGUÉZ PARDO.

Trade and Industry

GOVERNMENT AGENCIES

Comisión de Administración de Divisas (CADIVI): Antiguo Edif. PDVSA Servicios, 6°, Avda Leonardo Da Vinci, Los Chaguaramos, Caracas; tel. (212) 606-3904; fax (212) 606-3026; e-mail info@cadivi.gov.ve; internet www.cadivi.gob.ve; f. 2003; regulates access to foreign currency; Pres. WILLIAM CONTRERAS.

Corporación Venezolana de Guayana (CVG): Edif. General, 2°, Avda La Estancia, Apdo 7000, Chuao, Caracas; tel. (212) 992-1813;

fax (212) 993-4306; e-mail presidenciaccs@cvg.com; internet www.cvg.com; f. 1960 to organize devt of Guayana area, particularly its metal ore and hydroelectric resources; Pres. José Salamat Khan Fernández (Minister of Basic Industry and Mining); 15 subsidiaries; 18,000 employees.

Instituto Nacional de Tierras (INTI): Quinta La Barranca, Calle San Carlos, Urb. Vista Alegre, Caracas; tel. (212) 574-8554; fax (212) 576-2201; internet www.inti.gob.ve; f. 1945 as Instituto Agrario Nacional (IAN); present name adopted in 2001; established under Agrarian Law to assure ownership of the land to those who worked on it; now authorized to expropriate and redistribute idle or unproductive lands; Pres. Juan Carlos Loyo.

Instituto Nacional de la Vivienda: Torre Inavi, Avda Francisco de Miranda, Chacao, Caracas; tel. (212) 206-9279; e-mail comunica@inavi.gov.ve; internet www.inavi.gob.ve; f. 1975; administers govt housing projects; Pres. Pablo José Peña Chaparro; Gen. Man. Aldo Reyes Chacón.

Mercal, CA: Edif. Torres Seguros Orinoco, Avda Fuerzas Armadas, esq. Socarras, Caracas; tel. (212) 564-3856; e-mail fosorio@correo.mercal.gob.ve; internet www.mercal.gob.ve; responsible for marketing agricultural products; fmrly Corporación de Mercadeo Agrícola; Pres. Lt-Col Félix Osorio Guzmán.

Ministry of Energy and Petroleum: see The Government—Ministries.

Superintendencia de Inversiones Extranjeras (SIEX): Edif. La Perla, esq. La Bolsa a Mercaderes, 3° y 5°, Capitolio, Caracas 1010; tel. (212) 483-6666; fax (212) 484-4368; e-mail siexdespacho@cantv.net; internet www.siex.gob.ve; f. 1974; supervises foreign investment in Venezuela; Supt Manuel Figueroa.

DEVELOPMENT ORGANIZATIONS

Fondo para el Desarrollo Agrario Socialista (FONDAS): Edif. FONDAFA, esq. Salvador de León a Socarras, La Hoyada, Caracas; tel. (212) 542-3570; fax (212) 542-5887; internet www.fondas.gob.ve; f. 1974; devt of agriculture, fishing and forestry; Pres. Ricardo Javier Sánchez.

Fondo de Desarrollo Microfinanciero (FONDEMI): see Finance—Development Banks.

Instituto de Desarrollo de la Pequeña y Mediana Industria (INAPYMI): Torre Británica, 14°, 15°, 16° y planta baja, Avda José Felix Sosa, Altamira Sur, Caracas; tel. (212) 276-9511; e-mail zcarrillo@inapymi.gob.ve; internet www.inapymi.gob.ve; f. 2001; govt agency; promotes the devt of small and medium-sized industries; Pres. Patricia Febles Montes; Exec. Dir Zaida María Carrillo.

CHAMBERS OF COMMERCE AND INDUSTRY

Federación Venezolana de Cámaras y Asociaciones de Comercio y Producción (Fedecámaras): Edif. Fedecámaras, Avda El Empalme, Urb. El Bosque, Apdo 2568, Caracas; tel. (212) 731-1711; fax (212) 730-2097; e-mail presidencia@fedecamaras.org.ve; internet www.fedecamaras.org.ve; f. 1944; 307 mems; Pres. Noel Alvarez C.; Gen. Man. Gilberto Delgado G.

Cámara de Comercio, Industria y Servicios de Caracas: Edif. Cámara de Comercio de Caracas, 8°, Avda Andrés Eloy Blanco 215, Los Caobos, Caracas; tel. (212) 571-3222; fax (212) 571-0050; e-mail administración@lacamaradecaracas.org.ve; internet www.lacamaradecaracas.org.ve; f. 1893; 650 mems; Pres. Dr Diana Mayoral; Exec. Dir Víctor Maldonado.

Cámara Venezolano-Americana de Industria y Comercio (Venamcham): Torre Credival, 10°, Of. A, 2a Avda Campo Alegre, Apdo 5181, Caracas 1010-A; tel. (212) 263-0833; fax (212) 263-2060; e-mail venam@venamcham.org; internet www.venamcham.org; f. 1950; Pres. Carlos Henrique Blohm; Gen. Man. Carlos Tejera.

There are chambers of commerce and industry in all major provincial centres.

EMPLOYERS' ORGANIZATIONS

Caracas

Asociación Nacional de Industriales Metalúrgicos y de Minería de Venezuela (AIMM): Centro Empresarial Senderos, 3°, Ofs 302 y 303A, Avda Principal Los Cortijos de Lourdes, 2a Transversal, Sucre, Caracas 1071; tel. and fax (212) 237-5169; e-mail aimmv@cantv.net; internet www.aimm-ven.org; metallurgy and mining; Pres. Eduardo Garmendia; Exec. Dir María Graciela Ferreira.

Asociación Textil Venezolana: Edif. Textilera Gran Colombia, Calle el Club 8, Los Cortijos de Lourdes, Caracas; tel. (212) 238-1744; fax (212) 239-4089; f. 1957; textiles; Pres. David Fihman; 68 mems.

Asociación Venezolana de Exportadores (AVEX): Centro Comercial Concresa, Of. 435, 2°, Prados del Este, Avda Río Caura, Baruta, Caracas; tel. (212) 979-5042; fax (212) 979-4542; e-mail asistentedepresidencia@avex.com.ve; internet www.avex.com.ve; Pres. Alba Guevara; Gen. Man. María Isabel Sáez.

Cámara Petrolera: Torre Domus, 3°, Of. 3-A, Avda Abraham Lincoln con Calle Olimpo, Sábana Grande, Caracas; tel. (212) 794-1222; fax (212) 793-8529; e-mail informacion@camarapetrolera.org; internet www.camarapetrolera.org; f. 1978; assn of petroleum-sector cos; Pres. Mauricio Canard Mendoza; Exec. Dir Ronald Rivas.

Confederación Nacional de Asociaciones de Productores Agropecuarios (FEDEAGRO): Edif. Casa de Italia, planta baja, Avda La Industria, San Bernardino, Caracas 1010; tel. (212) 571-4035; fax (212) 573-4423; e-mail fedeagro@fedeagro.org; internet www.fedeagro.org; f. 1960; agricultural producers; 133 affiliated assns; Pres. Pedro Rivas Ismayel.

Confederación Venezolana de Industriales (CONINDUSTRIA): Edif. CIEMI, Avda Principal de Chuao, Caracas 1061; tel. (212) 991-2116; fax (212) 991-7737; e-mail conindustria@conindustria.org; internet www.conindustria.org; assn of industrialists; Pres. Carlos Larrazabal; Exec. Pres. Ismael Pérez Vigil.

Federación Nacional de Ganaderos de Venezuela (FEDENAGA): Avda Urdaneta, Centro Financiero Latino, 18°, Ofs 18-2 y 18-4, La Candelaria, Caracas; tel. (212) 563-2153; fax (212) 564-7273; e-mail fedenagat@cantv.net; internet www.fedenaga.org; f. 1962; cattle owners; Pres. Manuel Cipriano Heredia C.

Unión Patronal Venezolana del Comercio: Edif. General Urdaneta, 2°, Marrón a Pelota, Apdo 6578, Caracas; tel. (582) 561-7025; fax (582) 561-4321; trade; Sec. H. Espinoza Banders.

Other Towns

Asociación de Comerciantes e Industriales del Zulia (ACIZ): Edif. Los Cerros, 9°, Calle 77 con Avda 3C, Apdo 91, Maracaibo, Zulia; tel. (261) 91-7064; fax (261) 92-0907; e-mail info@aciz.org; f. 1941; traders and industrialists; Pres. Daniel Hómez.

Asociación Nacional de Cultivadores de Algodón (ANCA) (National Cotton Growers' Association): Edif. Portuguesa, Avda Los Pioneros, Sector Aspiga-Acarigua; tel. (255) 621-5111; fax (255) 621-4368; e-mail anca@asoanca.com; Pres. Concepción Quijada G.

Asociación Nacional de Empresarios y Trabajadores de la Pesca: Cumaná; fishermen's org.

Unión Nacional de Cultivadores de Tabaco: Urb. Industrial La Hamaca, Avda Hustaf Dalen, Maracay; tobacco growers.

STATE HYDROCARBONS COMPANIES

PDVSA Petróleo SA: Edif. Petróleos de Venezuela, Torre Este, Avda Libertador, La Campiña, Apdo 169, Caracas 1010-A; tel. (212) 708-4743; fax (212) 708-4661; e-mail saladeprensa@pdvsa.com; internet www.pdvsa.com; f. 1975; responsible for petrochemical sector since 1978 and for devt of coal resources in western Venezuela since 1985; in 1997 the three operating branches (Lagoven SA, Maraven SA and Corpoven SA) were reintegrated to form PDVSA Petróleo y Gas; in 2001 gas related activity passed to PDVSA Gas; state-owned, under control of the Ministry of Energy and Petroleum; Pres. Rafael Darío Ramírez Carreño (Minister of Energy and Petroleum); Vice-Pres. of Exploration and Production Eulogio del Pino; Vice-Pres. of Refining Asdrúbal Chávez; the following are subsidiaries of PDVSA:

Bariven, SA: Edif. PDVSA Los Chaguaramos, 6°, Avda Leonardo Da Vinci, Urb. Los Chaguaramos, Apdo 1889, Caracas 1010-A; tel. (212) 606-4060; fax (212) 606-2741; handles the petroleum, petrochemical and hydrocarbons industries' overseas purchases of equipment and materials.

Corporación Venezolana del Petróleo (CVP): Edif. Pawa, Calle Cali con Avda Veracruz, Las Mercedes, Caracas; f. 1960, reformed 2003; responsible for PDVSA's negotiations with other petroleum cos.

Deltaven, SA: Edif. PDVSA Deltaven, Avda Principal de La Floresta, La Floresta, Caracas 1060; tel. (212) 208-1111; f. 1997; markets PDVSA products and services within Venezuela.

Intevep, SA: Centro de Investigación y Apoyo Tecnológico, Edif. Sede Central, Urb. Santa Rosa, Sector El Tambor, Los Teques, Apdo 76343, Caracas 1070-A; tel. (212) 330-6011; fax (212) 330-6448; f. 1973 as Fundación para la Investigación de Hidrocarburos y Petroquímica; present name adopted in 1979; research and devt br. of PDVSA.

Palmaven: Avda Principal de la Urbina, Torre Olimpia, 7°, Caracas; tel. (212) 204-4511; sustainable devt agency of PDVSA; Man. Dir Eddie Ramírez.

PDV Marina: Edif. Petróleos de Venezuela Refinación, Suminstro y Comercio, Torre Oeste, 9°, Avda Libertador, La Campiña, Apdo 2103, Caracas 1010-A; tel. (212) 708-1111; fax (212) 708-2200;

f. 1990; responsible for the distribution, by ship, of PDVSA products.

PDVSA Gas: Edif. Sucre, Avda Francisco de Miranda, La Floresta, Caracas; tel. (212) 208-6212; fax (212) 208-6288; e-mail messina@pdvsa.com; f. 1998; gas exploration and extraction; Pres. WUILMAN PAREIRA.

Pequiven (Petroquímica de Venezuela, SA): Zona Industrial Municipal Sur, Avda 73, con Calle 79B, Valencia, Carabobo; tel. (241) 839-4665; e-mail deinterespequiven@pequiven.com; internet www.pequiven.com; f. 1956 as Instituto Venezolano de Petroquímica; became Pequiven in 1977; involved in many joint ventures with foreign and private Venezuelan interests for expanding petrochemical industry; active in regional economic integration; an affiliate of PDVSA from 1978 until 2005; thereafter state-owned, under Ministry of Energy and Petroleum; Pres. CLARK INCIARTE.

MAJOR COMPANIES

The following is a selection of major industrial and commercial enterprises, in terms of sales and employment, operating in Venezuela:

Metals and Mining

CVG Aluminio del Caroní, SA (ALCASA): Avda Fuerzas Armadas, Zona Industrial Matanzas, Apdo 115, Ciudad Guayana, Bolívar; tel. (286) 980-1567; fax (286) 980-1891; internet www.alcasa.com.ve; f. 1976; state-owned manufacturer of aluminium products; Pres. CÉSAR AGUILAR; 1,700 employees.

CVG Bauxilum, CA (Industria Integrado de Aluminio): Edif. Administrativo-CVG Bauxilum, Avda Fuerzas Armadas, Zona Industrial Matanzas, Ciudad Guayana, Bolívar; tel. (286) 950-6271; fax (286) 950-6270; e-mail asuntos.publicos@bauxilum.com.ve; internet www.bauxilum.com; f. 1994; state-owned manufacturer of aluminium products; Pres. JESÚS CALDO.

CVG Ferrominera Orinoco, CA: Edif. Administrativo I, Puerto Ordaz, Apdo 399, Vía Caracas, Bolívar 8015; tel. (286) 930-3267; fax (286) 930-3050; e-mail contacto@ferrominera.com; internet www.ferrominera.com; f. 1976; subsidiary of the state-owned Corporación Venezolana de Guayana (see section on Government Agencies); iron ore mining; Pres. RADWAN SABBAGH; 4,100 employees.

Siderúrgica del Orinoco, CA (SIDOR): Edif. General de Seguros, 7°, Avda La Estancia, Chuao, Caracas; tel. (212) 600-7696; fax (212) 993-2930; e-mail ncolon@sidor.com; internet www.sidor.com; f. 1964; fmrly state-owned, privatized in 1997; renationalized in 2008; Ternium (Argentina) retains 10% stake; steel-processing; Pres. CARLOS D'OLIVEIRA; 13,000 employees.

Siderúrgica del Turbio, SA (SIDETUR): Avda Intercomunal de Antímano, Zona Industrial La Yaguara, Caracas 1060; tel. (212) 407-0300; fax (212) 407-0350; internet www.sidetur.com.ve; f. 1972; manufacturers of steel products including galvanized wire and steel rods; owned by SIVENSA (see below); Gen. Man. NICOLÁS IZQUIERDO; 600 employees.

Siderúrgica Venezolana, SACA (SIVENSA): Edif. Torre América, 12°, Avda Venezuela, Urb. Bello Monte, Caracas 1060; tel. (212) 707-6280; fax (212) 707-6352; e-mail antonio.osorio@sivensa.com; internet www.sivensa.com.ve; f. 1948; manufacturers of briquetted iron, steel products, wire and wire products; Pres. OSCAR AUGUSTO MACHADO KOENEKE; 2,906 employees.

UNICON: Avda Beethoven, Torre Financiera, 9°, Collinas de Bello Monte, Caracas 1050; tel. (212) 753-4111; fax (212) 751-1542; e-mail reclamos@unicon.com.ve; internet www.unicon.com.ve; f. 1959 as Conduven; manufacturers of welded pipe for use in petroleum industry, fluid conduction, electrical installations; Pres. ELIYAU WEISZ.

Unión Industrial Venezolana, SA (UNIVENSA): Carrera 3, No 30–30 Zona Industrial Comdibar 1, Barquisimeto, Lara; tel. (251) 237-0133; fax (251) 237-3845; e-mail jorge.baduell@grupounivensa.com; f. 1965; manufacturers of stainless steel tubing; Pres. MIGUEL GONZÁLEZ; 400 employees.

Rubber and Tobacco

Bridgestone Firestone Venezolana, CA: Carrera Nacional Valencia-Los Guayos, cruce con San Diego, Zona Industrial, Valencia, Apdo 194, Carabobo; tel. (241) 874-7758; fax (241) 832-8254; internet www.bfvz.com; f. 1954; subsidiary of Bridgestone Corpn (USA); rubber tyre producers; Pres. ALFREDO ORÁN; 1,111 employees.

Cigarrera Bigott Sucs, SA: Edif. Cigarrera Bigott, Avda Francisco de Miranda, Los Ruices, Caracas 1071; tel. (212) 203-7524; fax (212) 237-9320; e-mail cigarrera_bigott@bat.com; internet www.bigott.com.ve; f. 1921; tobacco products; part of British American Tobacco; Pres. BENJAMIN J. KEMBALL; Gen. Man. CARLOS WAGNER; 609 employees.

Tabacalera Nacional, CA: Torre KPMG, 6°, Avda Francisco de Miranda, Campo Alegre, Chacao, Caracas 1060; tel. (212) 276-3572; fax (212) 901-7766; internet www.philipmorrisinternational.com; f. 1953; subsidiary of Philip Morris Int. (USA); cigarette manufacturers; Pres. JOSÉ ANTONIO CORDIBO-FREYTÉS; 340 employees.

Food and Drink

CA Cervecería Regional: Avda 17 (Los Haticos) 112-13, Apdo 255, Maracaibo; tel. (261) 65-1411; fax (261) 65-1477; internet www.cerveceriaregional.com; brewing co; Pres. JOSÉ R. ODÓN; 135 employees.

Empresas Polar: Edif. Centro Empresarial Polar, 2da Avda de Los Cortijos de Lourdes, Caracas 1010; internet www.empresas-polar.com; f. 1941 as Cervecería Polar; food and drink manufacturers; brands include Cervecería Polar, CA, Alimentos Polar, and Pepsi-Cola Venezuela; Pres. LORENZO MENDOZA.

Mavesa, SA: Edif. Mavesa, Avda Principal, Urb. Industrial Los Cortijos de Lourdes, Caracas 1071; tel. (212) 238-1633; fax (212) 239-2506; f. 1949; acquired by Empresas Polar in 2001; manufacturers and distributors of consumer processed food and cleaning products; Chair. JONATHAN COLES; 2,827 employees.

Parmalat Venezuela (INDULAC): Edif. Parmalat, entre Avda San Francisco y Palmarito, Apdo 1546, Urb. Colinas de la California, Caracas 1010-A; tel. (212) 257-1422; fax (212) 257-7195; internet jperezor@parmalat.com.ve; internet www.parmalat.com.ve; f. 1966; manufacturers and distributors of dairy products; owned by Parmalat of Italy; 2,198 employees.

Chemicals

Clariant (Venezuela), SA: Edif. Clariant, Zona Industrial San Vicente I, Avda Anton Philips, Apdo 34, Maracay 2101; tel. (435) 503-3131; fax (435) 503-3134; internet www.clariant.com.ve; f. 1952; subsidiary of Clariant Int. of Switzerland; manufacturers and distributors of chemicals, textiles, leather, paper, paint, adhesives, plastics; Gen. Man. DARIO GAETA; 207 employees.

Corimón, CA: Edif. Corimón, Urb. Los Cortijos de Lourdes, Calle Hans Neumann, Caracas; tel. (212) 400-5530; e-mail info@corimon.com; internet www.corimon.com; f. 1949; holding co. for subsidiaries producing paint, packaging and processed food; Pres. CARLOS GILL RAMÍREZ; Dir-Gen. ESTEBAN SZEKELY; 2,655 employees.

DuPont Venezuela, CA: Edif. Los Frailes, 1°, Calle La Guairita, Urb. Chuao, Caracas 1060A; tel. (212) 992-6022; fax (212) 991-5683; e-mail vanessa.carrasquel@ven.dupont.com; internet www2.dupont.com/Venezuela_Country_Site/es_VE; f. 1956; manufacturers of industrial chemicals, plastics, pesticides, resins and films; Chair. and CEO ELLEN J. KULLMAN; Pres. for Latin America EDUARDO W. WANICK; Gen. Man. SERGIO RODRÍGUEZ; 260 employees.

Pfizer, SA: Edif. Pfizer, Avda Diego Cisneros, entre 2da y 3ra, Transversal, Caracas 1071; tel. (212) 630-2990; e-mail soporte.ventas.ve@pfizer.com; internet www.pfizer.com.ve; f. 1953; subsidiary of Pfizer Inc (USA); manufacturers of pharmaceutical products; Pres. JOSÉ CLAVIER; 250 employees.

Plastiflex, CA: Torre Phelps, 4°, Avda La Salle, Plaza Venezuela, Caracas 1050; tel. (212) 793-3133; fax (212) 793-3636; f. 1957; manufacturers of plastic sheeting and film; Man. JONA MISHAAN; 415 employees.

Procter and Gamble de Venezuela, SA: Edif. P&G, Sorokaima, Trinidad, Apdo 66349, Caracas 1080; tel. (212) 903-7408; fax (212) 206-6364; e-mail robles.c@pg.com; internet www.sra-robles.com; subsidiary of Procter and Gamble Co (USA); manufacturers of soaps, detergents and pharmaceuticals; Pres. ALBERTO DUEÑAS; 380 employees.

Electrical Equipment

Asea Brown Boveri, SA: Edif. ABB, Avda Diego Cisneros, Los Ruices, Caracas 1070; tel. (212) 203-1740; fax (212) 203-1910; internet www.abb.com; f. 1957; subsidiary of The ABB Group (Switzerland); manufacturers of power transmission machinery and equipment; Regional Man. (South America) SERGIO GOMES; 300 employees.

General Electric de Venezuela, SA: Edif. Centro Banaven, Torre A, 6°, Avda La Estancia, Caracas; tel. (212) 902-5122; fax (212) 902-5300; e-mail corpcommunicationsvenezuela@ge.com; internet www.ge.com/ve; f. 1927; subsidiary of General Electric Corpn (USA); manufacturers of television sets, radio receivers and household electrical appliances; Pres. (Venezuela, Suriname & Guyana) FABIOLA SOJET; 2,600 employees.

Miscellaneous

Cerámica Carabobo, SA: Avda Lisandro Alvarado, Calle de Servicio, Sector C-04, Valencia, Carabobo; tel. (241) 813-4299; fax (241) 813-4194; e-mail infocc@ceramica-carabobo.com; internet www.ceramica-carabobo.com; f. 1956; manufacturers of ceramic floor and wall tiles; also owns Cerámica Industrial del Caribe and Pan-American Ceramics; Gen. Man. JULIO SEVILLA; 3,000 employees.

Constructora Camsa, CA: Edif. CAMSA, Avda 28, No 12A–95, Sector El Manzanillo, Antigua Carretera San Francisco, Apdo 637-4001A, Maracaibo, Zulia; tel. (261) 763-0000; fax (261) 762-5690; e-mail edward.mendez@camsa.com.ve; internet www.camsa.com.ve; f. 1948 as Constructora Heerema; civil engineering and construction, including services to petroleum and gas sectors; Gen. Man. EDWARD MÉNDEZ; 390 employees.

Ford Motors de Venezuela, SA: Avda Henry Ford, Zona Industrial Sur, Valencia, Carabobo 1041; tel. (241) 406-111; fax (241) 406-483; internet www.ford.com.ve; f. 1962; subsidiary of Ford Motor Co (USA); assembly and production of motor vehicles, trucks and farm machinery; Pres. GABRIEL LÓPEZ; 1,500 employees.

Nardi de Venezuela, CA: Zona Industrial Comdivar, Avda 3 con Calle 30, Barquisimeto, Lara; tel. (251) 237-2244; fax (251) 237-3884; internet www.ivemasa.com; f. 1971; manufacturers of agricultural sub-soilers, skimmer scoops and trench diggers; part of Nardi SPA (Italy); Man. GIANCARLO VITALI; 40 employees.

Promociones Ferroca, SA (CVG FERROCASA): Calle Caicara con Carretera El Miamo, Centro Empresarial Ferrocasa, Torre A, Puerto Ordaz, Bolivar; tel. (286) 9230319; e-mail fierro@cantv.net; internet www.cvgferrocasa.com; f. 1987; state-owned construction co involved in devt of Guayana region; Pres. JUAN VINCENTE CABEZA.

UTILITIES

Electricity

Corporación Eléctrica Nacional (Corpoelec): Edif. Centro Eléctrico Nacional, Avda Sanz, Urb. El Marqués, Sucre, Caracas; tel. (212) 280-8111; internet www.corpoelec.gob.ve; f. 2007; generation, transmission, distribution and marketing of electric power and energy; incorporated Edelca, La Nueva Electricidad de Caracas, ENELVEN, ENELCO, ENELBAR, CADAFE, GENEVAPCA, ELEBOL, ELEVAL, Seneca, ENAGAS, TURBOVEN into one corpn in 2010; state-owned; Chair. HIPÓLITO IZQUIERDO GARCÍA; Dir (Generation) JESÚS RANGEL; Dir (Distribution) KHALED ORTÍZ VILLEGAS; Dir (Commercial) JAVIER ALVARADO OCHOA.

CADAFE (Compañía de Administración y Fomento Eléctrico): Edif. Centro Eléctrico Nacional, 14°, Avda Sanz, Urb. El Marqués, Sucre, Caracas; tel. (212) 280-8583; fax (212) 280-8667; e-mail dirgestion@cadafe.com.ve; internet www.cadafe.com.ve; f. 1958; electricity transmission.

La Electricidad de Caracas (EDC): Edif. La Electricidad de Caracas, Avda Vollmer, Urb. San Bernadino, Apdo 2299, Caracas 1010-A; tel. (212) 502-2111; e-mail info@edc-ven.com; internet www.laedc.com.ve; supplies electricity to Caracas.

Electrificación del Caroní, CA (Edelca): Edif. General, planta baja, Avda La Estancia, Chuao, Caracas; tel. (212) 950-2111; fax (212) 950-2808; e-mail asuntos-publicos@edelca.com.ve; internet www.edelca.com.ve; supplies some 70% of the country's electricity.

Enelbar (Energía Eléctrica de Barquisimeto): Edif. Sede, Avda Francisco de Miranda, Carora, Barquisimento; tel. (251) 239-4050; internet www.enelbar.com.ve.

Enelco (Energía Eléctrica de la Costa Oriental): Edif. Sumnistro, Calle Rosario 32, Urb. La Rosa, Cabimas, Miranda; tel. (264) 370-5555; e-mail atencionalcliente@enelco.com.ve; internet www.enelco.com.ve; electricity services to the eastern coast of the Lago de Maracaibo region.

Enelven (Energía Eléctrica de Venezuela): Calle 77, entre Avda 10 y 11, Maracaibo; tel. (261) 790-3800; e-mail asuntospublicos@enelven.com.ve; internet www.enelven.gob.ve.

Gas

ENAGAS (Ente Nacional del Gas): Calle Panamá con Avda Libertador, 8°, Urb. Los Caobos, Caracas; tel. (212) 706-6654; fax (212) 706-6471; e-mail presidencia@enagas.gov.ve; internet www.enagas.gob.ve; f. 1999; subsidiary of Corpoelec; Pres. JORGE LUIS SÁNCHEZ.

Water

Hidroven: Edif. Hidroven, Avda Augusto César Sandino con 9a Transversal, Maripérez, Caracas; tel. (212) 781-4778; fax (212) 781-6424; e-mail ngamboa@cantv.net; internet www.hidroven.gov.ve; national water co; owns Hidroandes, Hidrocapital, Hidrocaribe, Hidrofalcon, Hidrolago, Hidrollanos, Hidropaez, Hidrosuroeste, Aguas de Monagas, Aguas de Ejido, Hidrolara, Aguas de Anaco, Aguas de Cojedes, Aguas de Mérida, Aguas de Apure, Aguas de Yaracuy, Aguas de Portuguesa; Pres. CRISTÓBAL FRANCISCO ORTIZ; Vice-Pres. FRANCISCO DURÁN.

Compañía Anónima Hidrológica de la Región Capital (Hidrocapital): Edif. Hidrocapital, Avda Augusto César Sandino con 9a Transversal, Maripérez, Caracas; tel. (212) 793-1638; fax (212) 793-6794; internet www.hidrocapital.com.ve; f. 1992; operates water supply in Federal District and states of Miranda and Vargas; Pres. ALEJANDRO HITCHER.

TRADE UNIONS

About one-quarter of the labour force in Venezuela belongs to a trade union. Most unions in Venezuela are legally recognized. The country's union movement is strongest in the public sector.

Confederación de Trabajadores de Venezuela (CTV) (Confederation of Venezuelan Workers): Edif. José Vargas, 17°, Avda Este 2, Los Caobos, Caracas; tel. (212) 574-1049; e-mail ctv@ctv.org.ve; internet www.ctv.org.ve; f. 1936; largest trade union confederation; principally active in public sector; Chávez Govt disputes legitimacy of election of CTV leadership; Pres. CARLOS ALFONSO ORTEGA CARVAJAL; Sec.-Gen. MANUEL JOSÉ COVA FERMÍN; 26 regional and 57 industrial feds.

Fedepetrol: union of petroleum workers; Pres. RAFAEL ROSALES.

Federación Campesina (FC): peasant union; CTV affiliate; Leader RUBÉN LANZ.

Fetrametal: union of metal workers; Leader JOSÉ MOLLEGAS.

Fuerza Bolivariana de Trabajadores (FBT): f. 2000; pro-Govt union.

Unión Nacional de Trabajadores (UNT): f. 2003; pro-Govt federation; Nat. Co-ordinators STALIN PÉREZ BORGES, ORLANDO CHIRINO.

Other trade union federations include the Alianza Sindical Independiente (ASI), the Central Unitaria de Trabajadores de Venezuela (CUTV), the Confederación de Sindicatos Autónomos de Venezuela (CODESA) and the Confederación General de Trabajadores de Venezuela (CGT).

Transport

RAILWAYS

The 1999 Constitution included provision for renovation of the national rail network. In 2010 several rail modernization projects were still at the planning stage. A line linking Puerto Cabello and La Encrucijada in central Venezuela was scheduled for completion in 2011, while a line connecting Anaco and Tinaco was expected to be completed in 2013. In October 2006 a 70-km railway line from Caracas to Cúa was opened. Services on the Caracas underground system began in 1983.

CVG Ferrominera Orinoco, CA: Vía Caracas, Puerto Ordaz, Apdo 399, Bolívar; tel. (286) 930-3775; fax (286) 930-3783; e-mail contacto@ferrominera.com; internet www.ferrominera.com; f. 1976; part of state-owned Corporación Venezolana de Guayana (see Trade and Industry—Government Agencies); operates two lines, San Isidro mine–Puerto Ordaz (316 km) and El Pao–Palua (55 km), for transporting iron ore; Pres. RADWAN SABBAGH (acting).

Ferrocarril de CVG Bauxilum—Operadora de Bauxita: Avda Fuerzas Armadas, Zona Industrial Matanzas, Ciudad Guayana, Bolívar; tel. (286) 950-6271; fax (286) 950-6270; internet www.bauxilum.com; f. 1989; state-owned; operates line linking Los Pijiguaos with river Orinoco port of Gumilla (52 km) for transporting bauxite; Pres. JESÚS CALDO.

Instituto Autónomo de Ferrocarriles del Estado (IAFE): Edif. Torre Británica de Seguros, 7° y 8°, Avda José Félix Sosa, Urb. Altamira, Chacao, Caracas 1062-A; tel. (212) 201-8736; fax (212) 201-6902; e-mail info@iafe.gov.ve; state co; operates 336 km of track; Pres. ANGEL GARCÍA ONTIVEROS.

CA Metro de Caracas: Multicentro Empresarial del Este, Edif. Miranda, Torre B, 7°, Avda Francisco de Miranda, Apdo 61036, Caracas; tel. (212) 206-7111; fax (212) 266-3346; internet www.metrodecaracas.com.ve; f. 1976 to supervise the construction and use of the underground railway system; state-owned; Pres. CLAUDIO ROMÁN FARÍAS ARIAS.

ROADS

In 2004 there were an estimated 96,200 km of roads, of which 32,300 km were paved. Responsibility for road maintenance generally lies with state governments; however, legislation adopted in 2009 allowed the central Government to take control of motorways and major roads, as well as ports and airports.

INLAND WATERWAYS

Instituto Nacional de Canalizaciones: Edif. INC, Calle Caracas, al lado de la Torre Diamen, Chuao, Caracas; tel. (212) 908-5106; fax (212) 959-6906; e-mail rrpp@incanal.gov.ve; internet www.incanal.gov.ve; f. 1952; semi-autonomous institution; Pres. JUAN CARLOS FERRER SÁNCHEZ; Vice-Pres. SEGUNDO RAMÓN JUSTO PINTO.

SHIPPING

There are 13 major ports, 34 petroleum and mineral ports and five fishing ports. The main ports for imports are La Guaira, the port for Caracas, and Puerto Cabello, which handles raw materials for the industrial region around Valencia. Maracaibo is the chief port for the petroleum industry. Puerto Ordaz, on the Orinoco River, was also developed to deal with the shipments of iron from Cerro Bolívar.

Consolidada de Ferrys, CA (CONFERRY): Torre Banhorient, 3°, Avda Las Acacias y Avda Casanova, Apdo 87, Sabana Grande, Caracas 1010-A; tel. (212) 781-9711; fax (212) 781-8739; internet www.conferry.com; f. 1970; ferry services to Margarita island; Pres. RODOLFO JOSÉ TOVAR MATA.

Consorcio Naviero Venezolano (Conavén): Torre Uno, 4°, Avda Orinoco, Las Mercedes, Caracas; tel. (212) 993-2922; fax (212) 993-1636; e-mail conavent@conaven.com.

Corpoven, SA: Edif. Petróleos de Venezuela, Avda Libertador, La Campiña, Apdo 61373, Caracas 1060-A; tel. (212) 708-1111; fax (212) 708-1833; Pres. Dr ROBERTO MANDINI; Vice-Pres. JUAN CARLOS GÓMEZ; 2 oil tankers.

Lagoven, SA: Edif. Lagovén, Avda Leonardo da Vinci, Los Chaguaramos, Apdo 889, Caracas; tel. (212) 606-3311; fax (212) 606-3637; f. 1978 as a result of the nationalization of the petroleum industry; fmrly Creole Petroleum Group; transports crude petroleum and by-products between Maracaibo, Aniba and other ports in the area; Pres. B. R. NATERA; Marine Man. P. D. CAREZIS; 10 tankers.

Tacarigua Marina, CA: Torre Lincoln 7A-B, Avda Lincoln, Apdo 51107, Sábana Grande, Caracas 1050-A; tel. (212) 781-1315; Pres. R. BELLIZZI.

Transpapel, CA: Edif. Centro, 11°, Of. 111, Centro Parque Boyaca, Avda Sucre, Los Dos Caminos, Apdo 61316, Caracas 1071; tel. (212) 283-8366; fax (212) 285-7749; e-mail nmaldonado@cantv.net; f. 1985; Chair. GUILLERMO ESPINOSA F.; Man. Dir Capt. NELSON MALDONADO.

Transporte Industrial, SA: Edif. Anzoátegui, Planta Vencemos, Pertigalete, Carretera Guanta, Km 5, Apdo 4356, Puerto la Cruz; tel. (281) 68-5607; fax (281) 68-5683; f. 1955; bulk handling and cement bulk carrier; Chair. VÍCTOR ROMO; Man. Dir RAFAEL ANEE.

CIVIL AVIATION

There are two adjacent airports 13 km from Caracas: Maiquetía for domestic and Simón Bolívar for international services. There are 11 international airports.

Regulatory Authority

Instituto Nacional de Aeronáutica Civil: Torre Británica, Urb. Altamira Sur, Avda José Félix Sosa, Chacao, Caracas 1060; tel. (212) 277-4411; e-mail contacto@inac.gov.ve; internet www.inac.gov.ve; f. 2005; Pres. JOSÉ LUIS MARTÍNEZ BRAVO.

National Airlines

Aeropostal (Alas de Venezuela): Torre Polar Oeste, 22°, Plaza Venezuela, Los Caobos, Caracas 1051; tel. (212) 708-6211; fax (212) 782-6323; internet www.aeropostal.com; f. 1933; transferred to private ownership in Sept. 1996, acquired by Venezuelan/US consortium Corporación Alas de Venezuela; domestic services and flights to destinations in the Caribbean, South America and the USA; Pres. and CEO NELSON RAMIZ.

Aerovías Venezolanas, SA (AVENSA): Torre Humboldt, 1°, Avda Rio Caura, Prados del Este, Caracas; tel. (212) 976-5240; fax (212) 563-0225; e-mail info@avensa.com.ve; internet www.avensa.com.ve; f. 1943; provides domestic services from Caracas and services to Europe and the USA; govt-owned; Pres. WILMAR CASTRO SOTELDO.

Aserca Airlines: Torre Exterior, 8°, Avda Bolívar Norte, Valencia, Carabobo 2002; tel. (241) 237-111; fax (241) 220-210; e-mail rsv@asercaairlines.com; internet www.asercaairlines.com; f. 1968; domestic services and flights to Caribbean destinations; Pres. SIMEÓN GARCÍA.

Consorcio Venezolano de Industrias Aeronáutica y Servicios Aéreos, SA (CONVIASA): Avda Lecuna, Parque Central, Torre Oeste, 49°, Caracas; e-mail mercadeo@conviasa.aero; internet www.conviasa.aero; f. 2004; state-owned; Pres. FRANKLIN FERNÁNDEZ MARTÍNEZ.

LASER (Línea Aérea de Servicio Ejecutivo Regional): Torre Bazar Bolívar, 8°, Avda Francisco de Miranda, El Marqués, Caracas; tel. (212) 202-0100; fax (212) 235-8359; internet www.laser.com.ve; f. 1994; scheduled and charter passenger and cargo services to domestic and international destinations; Pres. INOCENCIO ALVAREZ; Gen. Man. JORGE ANDRADE HIDALGO.

Línea Turística Aereotuy, CA: Edif. Gran Sábana, 5°, Blvd de Sábana Grande, Apdo 2923, Carmelitas, Caracas 1050; tel. (212) 761-6231; fax (212) 762-5254; e-mail tuysales@etheron.net; internet www.tuy.com; f. 1982; operates on domestic and international routes; Pres. PETER BOTTOME; Gen. Man. JUAN C. MÁRQUEZ.

Santa Barbara Airlines: Avda 3H, No 78-51, Res. República, Local 01, Maracaibo; tel. (261) 922-090; fax (261) 927-977; internet www.sbairlines.com; f. 1996; domestic and international services; Pres. FRANCISCO GONZÁLEZ YANES.

Tourism

In 2008 Venezuela received an estimated 745,000 tourists. Receipts from tourism in that year amounted to a provisional US $895m. An estimated 90% of tourists visit the island of Margarita, while only 20% of tourists visit the mainland.

Asociación Venezolana de Agencias de Viajes y Turismo (AVAVIT): Caracas; e-mail turvspecialtours@cantv.net; internet www.avavit.com; Pres. ELIAS M. RAJBE S.

Instituto Nacional de Turismo (INATUR): Hotel Caracas Hilton, Torre Sur, 4°, Of. 424, Caracas; tel. (212) 576-4193; fax (212) 576-5138; e-mail inatur@inatur.gob.ve; internet www.inatur.gob.ve; f. 2001; govt tourism devt agency; Pres. YEAN LUIS DURÁN; Exec. Dir ANTONIO SALVUCHI.

Venezolana de Turismo, SA (VENETUR): Edif. Mintur, Avda Francisco de Miranda con Avda Principal de La Floresta, Torre Norte, 3°, Municipio Chacao, Caracas; tel. (212) 208-4812; fax (212) 208-8160; e-mail informacion@venetur.gob.ve; internet www.venetur.gob.ve; govt tourism promotion agency; Dir JORGE GONZÁLEZ VÁSQUEZ.

Defence

As assessed at November 2009, the armed forces numbered 115,000 men: an army of 63,000, a navy of 17,500 (including an estimated 7,000 marines), an air force of 11,500 and a National Guard of 23,000. In October 2009 legal status was accorded to a fifth unit of the armed forces, the Bolivarian National Militia, and in February 2010 the creation was announced within the National Militia of a peasant force. There was also an army reserve numbering 8,000. Military service is selective and the length of service varies by region for all services. The President is Commander-in-Chief of the Armed Forces.

Defence Budget: 8,970m. bolívares in 2009.

Inspector-General of the National Armed Forces: Vice-Adm. MANUEL ALFREDO YÁNEZ VILLEGAS.

Chief of Staff: Gen. JULIO RAMÓN FERNÁNDEZ.

Commander-General of the Navy: Adm. CARLOS MÁXIMO ANIASI TURCHIO.

Commander of the Army: Maj.-Gen. EUCLIDES AMADOR CAMPOS APONTE.

Commander-General of the Air Force: Maj.-Gen. JORGE AREVALO OROPEZA PERNALETE.

Commander-General of the Army Reserves: Gen. GUSTAVO ENRIQUE GONZÁLEZ LÓPEZ.

Education

Primary education in Venezuela is free and compulsory between the ages of six and 15 years. Secondary education begins at the age of 15 years and lasts for a further two years. In 2008 enrolment at primary schools included 90% of children in the relevant age-group, while the equivalent ratio for secondary enrolment was 69% (males 66%; females 74%). In 2003/04 there were 48 universities. In 2003 the Government, with assistance from Cuba, initiated Misión Robinson, a project intended to eradicate illiteracy and innumeracy in Venezuela. Expenditure by the central Government on education and sport was an estimated 29,601.6m. bolívares in 2004.

Bibliography

For works on the region generally, see Select Bibliography (Books)

Baena, C. E. *The Policy Process in a Petro-State: An Analysis of PDVSA's (Petróleos de Venezuela, SA's) Internationalisation Strategy*. Aldershot, Ashgate Publishing Ltd, 1999.

Buxton, J. 'Venezuela', in Buxton, J., and Phillips, N. *Case Studies in Latin American Political Economy*. Manchester, Manchester University Press, 1999.

The Failure of Political Reform in Venezuela. Aldershot, Ashgate Publishing Ltd, 2001.

Canache, D. *Venezuela: Public Opinion and Protest in a Fragile Democracy*. Boulder, CO, Lynne Rienner Publrs, 2001.

Cannon, B. *Hugo Chávez and the Bolivarian Revolution*. Manchester, Manchester University Press, 2009.

Castro, F., Deutschmann, D. (Ed.), and Salado, J. (Ed.) *Venezuela y Chávez*. Havana, Ocean Press, 2007.

Chávez, H., Deutschmann, D., and Salado, J. *Chávez: Venezuela and the New Latin America*. New York, Consortium, 2004.

Corrales, J. *Presidents Without Parties: The Politics of Economic Reform in Argentina and Venezuela in the 1990s*. Pennsylvania, PA, Penn State University Press, 2002.

Crisp, B. F. *Democratic Institutional Design: The Powers and Incentives of Venezuelan Politicians and Interest Groups*. Stanford, CA, Stanford University Press, 2000.

Ellner, S. *Rethinking Venezuelan Politics: Class, Conflict, and the Chávez Phenomenon*. Boulder, CO, Lynne Rienner Publrs, 2008.

Ellner, S., and Hellinger, D. (Eds). *Venezuelan Politics in the Chávez Era*. Boulder, CO, Lynne Rienner Publrs, 2003.

Ellner, S., and Tinker Salas, M. (Eds). *Venezuela: Hugo Chávez and the Decline of an Exceptional Democracy*. Lanham, MD, Rowman and Littlefield Publrs, 2007.

Friedman, E. J. *Unfinished Transitions: Women and the Gendered Development of Democracy in Venezuela, 1936–1996*. University Park, PA, Penn State University Press, 2000.

Gates, L. C. *Electing Chávez: The Business of Anti-Neoliberal Politics in Venezuela*. Pittsburgh, PA, University of Pittsburgh Press, 2010.

Gott, R. *In the Shadow of the Liberator: The Impact of Hugo Chávez on Venezuela and Latin America*. London and New York, Verso, 2000.

Hugo Chávez and the Bolivarian Revolution. London and New York, Verso, 2005.

Guevara, A. *Chávez: Venezuela and the New Latin America—Hugo Chávez Interviewed by Aleida Guevara*. New York, Ocean Press, 2005.

Harnecker, M. *Understanding the Venezuelan Revolution: Hugo Chávez Talks to Marta Harnecker*. New York, Fordham University Press, 2005.

Hawkins, K. A. *Venezuela's Chavismo and Populism in Comparative Perspective*. Cambridge, Cambridge University Press, 2010.

Jones, B. *Hugo!: The Hugo Chavez Story from Mud Hut to Perpetual Revolution*. Hanover, NH, Steerforth Press, 2007.

Kelly, J., and Romero, C. A. *United States and Venezuela: Rethinking a Relationship*. London, Routledge, 2001.

United States and Venezuela: Relations Between Friends. London, Routledge, 2002.

Kozloff, N. *Hugo Chávez: Oil, Politics, and the Challenge to the U.S.* Basingstoke, Palgrave Macmillan, 2006.

Landau, S. *The Chávez Code: Cracking US Intervention in Venezuela*. Redford, MI, Olive Branch Press, 2006.

Levin, J. *Hugo Chávez*. New York, Chelsea House Publrs, 2007.

McBeth, B. S. *Juan Vicente Gómez and the Oil Companies in Venezuela, 1908–1935*. Cambridge, Cambridge University Press, 2002.

McCaughan, M. *The Battle of Venezuela*. London, Latin America Bureau, 2004.

McCoy, J., and Myers, D. J. (Eds). *The Unraveling of Representative Democracy in Venezuela*. Baltimore, MD, Johns Hopkins University Press, 2005.

Nelson, B. A. *The Silence and the Scorpion: The Coup Against Chávez and the Making of Modern Venezuela*. New York, NY, Nation Books, 2009.

Sullivan, M., and Olhero, N. *Venezuela: Political Conditions and U.S. Policy*. Hauppuage, NY, Nova Science Publishers, 2008.

Tarver, H. M. *The Rise And Fall Of Venezuelan President Carlos Andrés Pérez: The Early Years, 1936–1973*. Lewiston, NY, Edwin Mellen Press, 2001.

Wilbert, G. *Changing Venezuela by Taking Power: The History and Policies of the Chávez Government*. London and New York, Verso, 2006.

PART THREE
Regional Information

REGIONAL ORGANIZATIONS

THE UNITED NATIONS

Address: United Nations, New York, NY 10017, USA.

Telephone: (212) 963-1234; **fax:** (212) 963-4879; **internet:** www.un.org.

The United Nations (UN) was founded on 24 October 1945. The organization, which has 192 member states, aims to maintain international peace and security and to develop international co-operation in addressing economic, social, cultural and humanitarian problems. The principal organs of the UN are the General Assembly, the Security Council, the Economic and Social Council, the International Court of Justice and the Secretariat. The General Assembly, which meets for three months each year, comprises representatives of all UN member states. The Security Council investigates disputes between member countries, and may recommend ways and means of peaceful settlement: it comprises five permanent members (the People's Republic of China, France, Russia, the United Kingdom and the USA) and 10 other members elected by the General Assembly for a two-year period. The Economic and Social Council comprises representatives of 54 member states, elected by the General Assembly for a three-year period: it promotes co-operation on economic, social, cultural and humanitarian matters, acting as a central policy-making body and co-ordinating the activities of the UN's specialized agencies. The International Court of Justice comprises 15 judges of different nationalities, elected for nine-year terms by the General Assembly and the Security Council: it adjudicates in legal disputes between UN member states.

Secretary-General: BAN KI-MOON (Republic of Korea) (2007–11).

MEMBER STATES IN SOUTH AMERICA, CENTRAL AMERICA AND THE CARIBBEAN

(with assessments for percentage contributions to UN budget for 2010–12, and year of admission)

Antigua and Barbuda	0.002	1981
Argentina	0.287	1945
Bahamas	0.018	1973
Barbados	0.008	1966
Belize	0.001	1981
Bolivia	0.007	1945
Brazil	1.611	1945
Chile	0.236	1945
Colombia	0.144	1945
Costa Rica	0.034	1945
Cuba	0.071	1945
Dominica	0.001	1978
Dominican Republic	0.042	1945
Ecuador	0.040	1945
El Salvador	0.019	1945
Grenada	0.001	1974
Guatemala	0.028	1945
Guyana	0.001	1966
Haiti	0.003	1945
Honduras	0.008	1945
Jamaica	0.014	1962
Mexico	2.356	1945
Nicaragua	0.003	1945
Panama	0.022	1945
Paraguay	0.007	1945
Peru	0.090	1945
Saint Christopher and Nevis	0.001	1983
Saint Lucia	0.001	1979
Saint Vincent and the Grenadines	0.001	1980
Suriname	0.003	1975
Trinidad and Tobago	0.044	1962
Uruguay	0.027	1945
Venezuela	0.314	1945

Diplomatic Representation

PERMANENT MISSIONS TO THE UNITED NATIONS

(August 2010)

Antigua and Barbuda: 305 East 47th St, 6th Floor, New York, NY 10017; tel. (212) 541-4117; fax (212) 757-1607; e-mail unmission@abgov.org; internet www.abgov.org; Permanent Representative JOHN W. ASHE.

Argentina: One United Nations Plaza, 25th Floor, New York, NY 10017; tel. (212) 688-6300; fax (212) 980-8395; e-mail argentina@un.int; internet www.un.int/argentina; Permanent Representative JORGE ARGÜELLO.

Bahamas: 231 East 46th St, New York, NY 10017; tel. (212) 421-6925; fax (212) 759-2135; e-mail mission@bahamasny.com; Permanent Representative PAULETTE A. BETHEL.

Barbados: 820 Second Ave, 9th Floor, New York, NY 10017; tel. (212) 551-4300; fax (212) 986-1030; e-mail prun@foreign.gov.bb; Permanent Representative CHRISTOPHER F. HACKETT.

Belize: 675 Third Ave, Suite 1911, New York, NY 10017; tel. (212) 986-1240; fax (212) 593-0932; e-mail blzun@aol.com; internet www.belizemission.com; Permanent Representative (vacant).

Bolivia: 211 East 43rd St, 8th Floor, Rm 802, New York, NY 10017; tel. (212) 682-8132; fax (212) 682-8133; e-mail bolivia@un.int; internet www.bolivia-un.org; Permanent Representative PABLO SOLÓN.

Brazil: 747 Third Ave, 9th Floor, New York, NY 10017; tel. (212) 372-2600; fax (212) 371-5716; e-mail delbrasonu@delbrasonu.org; internet www.un.int/brazil; Permanent Representative MARIA LUIZA RIBEIRO VIOTTI.

Chile: One Dag Hammarskjöld Plaza, 885 Second Ave, 40th Floor, New York, NY 10017; tel. (917) 322-6800; fax (917) 322-6890; e-mail chile@un.int; internet www.un.int/chile; Permanent Representative OCTAVIO ERRÁZURIZ GUILISASTI.

Colombia: 140 East 57th St, 5th Floor, New York, NY 10022; tel. (212) 355-7776; fax (212) 371-2813; e-mail colombia@colombiaun.org; internet www.colombiaun.org; Permanent Representative CLAUDIA BLUM.

Costa Rica: 211 East 43rd St, Rm 903, New York, NY 10017; tel. (212) 986-6373; fax (212) 986-6842; e-mail missioncostaricaun@yahoo.com; internet www.un.int/costarica; Permanent Representative EDUARDO ULIBARRI-BILBAO.

Cuba: 315 Lexington Ave and 38th St, New York, NY 10016; tel. (212) 689-7215; fax (212) 779-1697; e-mail cuba@un.int; internet www.un.int/cuba; Permanent Representative PEDRO NÚNEZ MOSQUERA.

Dominica: 800 Second Ave, Suite 400H, New York, NY 10017; tel. (212) 949-0853; fax (212) 808-4975; e-mail domun@onecommonwealth.org; Permanent Representative VINCE HENDERSON.

Dominican Republic: 144 East 44th St, 4th Floor, New York, NY 10017; tel. (212) 867-0833; fax (212) 297-2509; e-mail drun@un.int; internet www.un.int/dr; Permanent Representative FEDERICO ALBERTO CUELLO CAMILO.

Ecuador: 866 United Nations Plaza, Rm 516, New York, NY 10017; tel. (212) 935-1680; fax (212) 935-1835; e-mail missionecuador@nyct.net; internet www.ecuadoronu.com; Permanent Representative MARIA FERNANDA ESPINOSA GARCES.

El Salvador: 46 Park Ave, New York, NY 10016; tel. (212) 679-1616; fax (212) 725-7831; e-mail elsalvador@un.int; Permanent Representative CARMEN MARÍA GALLARDO HERNÁNDEZ.

Grenada: 800 Second Ave, Suite 400K, New York, NY 10017; tel. (212) 599-0301; fax (212) 599-1540; e-mail grenada@un.int; Permanent Representative DESSIMA M. WILLIAMS.

Guatemala: 57 Park Ave, New York, NY 10016; tel. (212) 679-4760; fax (212) 685-8741; e-mail guatemala@un.int; internet www.un.int/guatemala; Permanent Representative GERT ROSENTHAL.

Guyana: 801 Second Ave, 5th Floor, New York, NY 10017; tel. (212) 573-5828; fax (212) 573-6225; e-mail guyana@un.int; Permanent Representative (vacant).

Haiti: 801 Second Ave, Rm 600, New York, NY 10017; tel. (212) 370-4840; fax (212) 661-8698; e-mail haiti@un.int; Permanent Representative LÉO MÉRORÈS.

Honduras: 866 United Nations Plaza, Suite 417, New York, NY 10017; tel. (212) 752-3370; fax (212) 223-0498; e-mail honduras_un@hotmail.com; internet www.un.int/honduras; Permanent Representative MARY ELIZABETH FLORES FLAKE.

Jamaica: 767 Third Ave, 9th Floor, New York, NY 10017; tel. (212) 935-7509; fax (212) 935-7607; e-mail jamaica@un.int; internet www

.un.int/jamaica; Permanent Representative RAYMOND OSBOURNE WOLFE.

Mexico: Two United Nations Plaza, 28th Floor, New York, NY 10017; tel. (212) 752-0220; fax (212) 688-8862; e-mail mexico@un.int; internet www.sre.gob.mx/onu; Permanent Representative CLAUDE HELLER.

Nicaragua: 820 Second Ave, 8th Floor, New York, NY 10017; tel. (212) 490-7997; fax (212) 286-0815; e-mail nicaragua@un.int; internet www.un.int/nicaragua; Permanent Representative MARIA RUBIALES DE CHAMORRO.

Panama: 866 United Nations Plaza, Suite 4030, New York, NY 10017; tel. (212) 421-5420; fax (212) 421-2694; e-mail emb@panama-un.org; Permanent Representative PABLO ANTONIO THALASSINÓS.

Paraguay: 211 East 43rd St, Suite 400, New York, NY 10017; tel. (212) 687-3490; fax (212) 818-1282; e-mail paraguay@un.int; Permanent Representative JOSÉ ANTONIO DOS SANTOS.

Peru: 820 Second Ave, Suite 1600, New York, NY 10017; tel. (212) 687-3336; fax (212) 972-6975; e-mail onuper@aol.com; internet www.un.int/peru; Permanent Representative GONZALO GUTIÉRREZ.

Saint Christopher and Nevis: 414 East 75th St, 5th Floor, New York, NY 10021; tel. (212) 535-1234; fax (212) 535-6854; e-mail sknmission@aol.com; internet www.stkittsnevis.org; Permanent Representative DELANO FRANK BART.

Saint Lucia: 800 Second Ave, 9th Floor, New York, NY 10017; tel. (212) 697-9360; fax (212) 697-4993; e-mail slumission@aol.com; internet www.un.int/stlucia; Permanent Representative DONATUS ST. AIMEE.

Saint Vincent and the Grenadines: 800 Second Ave, Suite 400G, New York, NY 10017; tel. (212) 599-0950; fax (212) 599-1020; e-mail svgun@aol.com; Permanent Representative CAMILLO M. GONSALVES.

Suriname: 866 United Nations Plaza, Suite 320, New York, NY 10017; tel. (212) 826-0660; fax (212) 980-7029; e-mail suriname@un.int; internet www.un.int/suriname; Permanent Representative HENRY LEONARD MACDONALD.

Trinidad and Tobago: 122 East 42nd St, 39th Floor, New York, NY 10017; tel. (212) 697-7620; fax (212) 682-3580; e-mail tto@un.int; internet www.un.int/trinidadandtobago; Permanent Representative MARINA ANNETTE VALERE.

Uruguay: 866 United Nations Plaza, Suite 322, New York, NY 10017; tel. (212) 752-8240; fax (212) 593-0935; e-mail uruguay@un.int; internet www.un.int/uruguay; Permanent Representative JOSÉ LUIS CANCELA GÓMEZ.

Venezuela: 335 East 46th St, New York, NY 10017; tel. (212) 557-2055; fax (212) 557-3528; e-mail venezuela@un.int; internet www.un.int/venezuela; Permanent Representative JORGE VALERO BRICEÑO.

OBSERVERS

Inter-governmental organizations, etc., active in the region that participate in the sessions and the work of the UN General Assembly as Observers, maintaining permanent offices at the UN.

Caribbean Community (CARICOM): 88 Burnett Ave, Maplewood, NJ 07040; tel. (973) 378-9333; fax (973) 327-2671; e-mail caripoun@gmail.com; Permanent Observer NOEL SINCLAIR.

Central American Integration System: 211 East 43rd St, Suite 701, New York, NY 10017; tel. (212) 682-1550; fax (212) 682-2155; e-mail ccampos@sgsica-ny.org; Permanent Observer CARLOS CAMPOS.

Commonwealth Secretariat: 800 Second Ave, 4th Floor, New York, NY 10017; tel. (212) 599-6190; fax (212) 808-4975; e-mail comsec@thecommonwealth.org.

International Development Law Organization: 336 East 45th St, New York, NY 10017; tel. (212) 867-9707; fax (212) 867-9717; e-mail pcivili@idlo.int; Permanent Observer PATRIZIO M. CIVILI.

International Institute for Democracy and Electoral Assistance: 336 East 45th St, 14th Floor, New York, NY 10017; tel. (212) 286-1084; fax (212) 286-0260; e-mail unobserver@idea.int; Permanent Observer MASSIMO TOMMASOLI.

International Trade Union Confederation: 211 East 43rd St, Suite 710, New York, NY 10017, USA; tel. (212) 370-0180; fax (212) 370-0188; e-mail unoffice@ituc-csi.org; Perm. Rep. GEMMA ADABA.

Inter-Parliamentary Union: 220 East 42nd St, Suite 3002, New York, NY 10017; tel. (212) 557-5880; fax (212) 557-3954; e-mail ny-office@mail.ipu.org; Permanent Observer ANDA FILIP.

IUCN (International Union for Conservation of Nature): 801 Second Ave, 13th Floor, New York, NY 10017; tel. (212) 286-1076; fax (212) 286-1079; e-mail iucn@un.int; Permanent Observer NARINDER KAKAR (India).

Partners in Population and Development: 336 East 45th St, 14th Floor, New York, NY 10017; tel. (212) 286-1082; fax (212) 286-0260; e-mail jsingh@ppdsec.org; Permanent Observer SETHURAMIAH L.N. RAO.

University for Peace: 801 Second Ave, 13th Floor, New York, NY 10017; tel. (212) 286-1076; fax (212) 286-1079; e-mail nyinfo@upeace.org; Permanent Observer NARINDER KAKAR (India).

The African, Caribbean and Pacific Group of States, Agency for the Prohibition of Nuclear Weapons in Latin America and the Caribbean, Andean Community, Central American Integration System, Inter-American Development Bank, Latin American Economic System, Latin American Integration Association, Latin American Parliament, the Organisation of Eastern Caribbean States and the Organization of American States are among a number of intergovernmental organizations that have a standing invitation to participate as Observers, but do not maintain permanent offices at the United Nations.

United Nations Information Centres/Services

Argentina: Junín 1940, 1°, 1113 Buenos Aires; tel. (11) 4803-7671; fax (11) 4804-7545; e-mail unic.buenosaires@unic.org; internet www.unic.org.ar; also covers Uruguay.

Bolivia: Calle 14 esq. Sánchez Bustamante, Ed. Metrobol II, Calacoto, La Paz; tel. (2) 2624512; fax (2) 2795820; e-mail unic.lapaz@unic.org; internet www.nu.org.bo.

Brazil: Palacio Itamaraty, Avda Marechal Floriano 196, 20080-002 Rio de Janeiro; tel. (21) 2253-2211; fax (21) 2233-5753; e-mail unic.brazil@unic.org; internet rio.unic.org.

Chile: Edif. Naciones Unidas, Avda Dag Hammarskjöld, Casilla 179-D, Santiago; tel. (2) 210-2000; fax (2) 228-1947; e-mail dpisantiago@eclac.cl.

Colombia: Calle 100, No. 8A-55, 10°, Edificio World Trade Center, Torre C, Bogotá 2; tel. (1) 257-6044; fax (1) 257-7936; e-mail unic.bogota@unic.org; internet www.nacionesunidas.org.co; also covers Ecuador and Venezuela.

Mexico: Presidente Masaryk 29, 2°, Col. Chapultepec Morales, México 11 570, DF; tel. (55) 5263-9725; fax (55) 5203-8638; e-mail unicmex@un.org.mx; internet www.cinu.org.mx; also covers Cuba and the Dominican Republic.

Panama: UN House Bldg 128, Ciudad del Saber, Clayton, Panama City; tel. (7) 301-0035; fax (7) 301-0037; e-mail unic.panama@unic.org; internet www.cinup.org.

Paraguay: Casilla de Correo 1107; Edif. Naciones Unidas, Avda Mariscal López, Asunción; tel. (21) 614443; fax (21) 611988; e-mail unic.py@undp.org; internet asuncion.unic.org.

Peru: POB 14-0199, Lord Cochrane 130, San Isidro, Lima 27; tel. (1) 441-8745; fax (1) 441-8735; e-mail unic.lima@unic.org; internet www.uniclima.org.pe.

Trinidad and Tobago: 2nd Floor, Bretton Hall, 16 Victoria Ave, Port of Spain; tel. 623-4813; fax 623-4332; e-mail unic.portofspain@unic.org; internet www.unicpos.org.tt; also covers Antigua and Barbuda, Aruba, the Bahamas, Barbados, Belize, Dominica, Grenada, Guyana, Jamaica, the Netherlands Antilles, Saint Christopher and Nevis, Saint Lucia, Saint Vincent and the Grenadines, and Suriname.

Economic Commission for Latin America and the Caribbean—ECLAC

Address: Edif. Naciones Unidas, Avda Dag Hammarskjöld 3477, Vitacura, Casilla 179-D, Santiago, Chile.

Telephone: (2) 2102000; **fax:** (2) 2080252; **e-mail:** secepal@eclac.cl; **internet:** www.eclac.org.

The UN Economic Commission for Latin America was founded by the UN Economic and Social Council (ECOSOC) in 1948 to co-ordinate policies for the promotion of economic development in the Latin American region. The current name of the Commission was adopted in 1984.

MEMBERS

Antigua and Barbuda	El Salvador	Paraguay
Argentina	France	Peru
Bahamas	Germany	Portugal
Barbados	Grenada	Saint Christopher and Nevis
Belize	Guatemala	Saint Lucia
Bolivia	Guyana	Saint Vincent and the Grenadines
Brazil	Haiti	Spain
Canada	Honduras	Suriname
Chile	Italy	Trinidad and Tobago
Colombia	Jamaica	United Kingdom
Costa Rica	Japan	USA
Cuba	Korea, Republic	Uruguay
Dominica	Mexico	Venezuela
Dominican Republic	Netherlands	
Ecuador	Nicaragua	
	Panama	

ASSOCIATE MEMBERS

Anguilla	Cayman Islands	Puerto Rico
Aruba	Montserrat	Turks and Caicos
British Virgin Islands	Netherlands Antilles	United States Virgin Islands

Organization

(August 2010)

COMMISSION

The Commission, comprising representatives of every member state, normally meets every two years at ministerial level. It considers matters relating to the economic and social development of the region, reviews activities of the organization, and adopts programmes of work. The 33rd session was held in Brasília, Brazil, in May–June 2010; the 34th session was scheduled to be convened in El Salvador, in 2012. Member states may meet between Commission meetings in an ad hoc Committee of the Whole. The Commission has established the following ad hoc and permanent bodies:

Caribbean Development and Co-operation Committee;

Committee of High-level Government Experts;

Committee on Central American Economic Co-operation;

Committee on South-South Co-operation;

Regional Conference on Women;

Regional Council for Planning of ILPES;

Statistical Conference of the Americas.

SECRETARIAT

The Secretariat employs more than 500 staff and is headed by the Offices of the Executive Secretary and of the Secretary of the Commission. ECLAC's work programme is carried out by the following divisions: Economic Development (including a Development Studies Unit); Economic and Social Planning (ILPES, see below); International Trade and Integration; Natural Resources and Infrastructure (including a Transport Unit); Population (CELADE, see below); Production, Productivity and Management (including an Agricultural Development Unit, a joint ECLAC/UNIDO Industrial and Technological Development Unit and a Unit on Investment and Corporate Strategies); Social Development; Statistics and Economic Projections; Sustainable Development and Human Settlements; and Women and Development. There are also units for information and conference services, and special studies, an electronic information section, and support divisions of administration, of documents and publications, and of programme planning and management.

Executive Secretary: ALICIA BÁRCENA IBARRA (Mexico).

SUB-REGIONAL OFFICES

Caribbean: 1 Chancery Lane, POB 1113, Port of Spain, Trinidad and Tobago; tel. 623-5595; fax 623-8485; e-mail registry@eclacpos.org; internet www.eclacpos.org; f. 1956; covers non-Spanish-speaking Caribbean countries; functions as the secretariat for the Caribbean Development and Co-operation Committee; Dir NEIL PIERRE.

Central America and Spanish-speaking Caribbean: Avda Presidente Masaryk 29, Apdo Postal 6-718, 11570 México, DF; tel. (55) 5263-9600; fax (55) 5531-1151; e-mail cepal@un.org.mx; internet www.cepal.org.mx; f. 1951; covers Central America and Spanish-speaking Caribbean countries; Dir HUGO E. BETETA.

There are also national offices, in Buenos Aires, Argentina; Brasília, Brazil; Bogotá, Colombia; and Montevideo, Uruguay; and a liaison office in Washington, DC, USA.

Activities

ECLAC collaborates with regional governments in the investigation and analysis of regional and national economic problems, and provides guidance in the formulation of development plans. The activities of its different divisions include research, monitoring of trends and policies, and comparative studies; analysis; publication of information; provision of technical assistance; organizing and participating in workshops, seminars and conferences; training courses; and co-operation with national, regional and international organizations, including non-governmental organizations and the private sector.

In April 1996 the Commission, meeting in San José, Costa Rica, considered means of strengthening the economic and social development of the region, within the framework of a document prepared by ECLAC's Secretariat, and adopted a resolution which defined ECLAC as a centre of excellence, charged with undertaking an analysis of specific aspects of the development process, in collaboration with member governments. The 27th session of the Commission, held in Oranjestad, Aruba, in May 1998, approved the ongoing reform programme, and in particular efforts to enhance the effectiveness and transparency of ECLAC's activities. ECLAC's 28th session, convened in Mexico City in April 2000, debated a document which proposed that the pursuit of social equity, sustainable development and 'active citizenship' (with emphasis on the roles of education and employment) should form the basis of future policy-making in the region.

ECLAC's 29th session, held in Brasília, Brazil, in May 2002, adopted the Brasília Resolution, which outlined a strategic agenda to meet the challenges of globalization. Proposed action included the consolidation of democracy, strengthening social protection, the formulation of policies to reduce macroeconomic and financial vulnerability, and the development of sustainable and systemic competitiveness, in order to build, gradually, an international social agenda based on rights. The 30th session, held in June–July 2004, in San Juan, Puerto Rico, discussed proposals in a new ECLAC study entitled 'Productive Development in Open Economies', and activities to be undertaken, with UNESCO, to promote education in the region. The Commission's 31st session, convened in March 2006, in Montevideo, Uruguay, approved the proposals outlined in a document entitled 'Shaping the Future of Social Protection', which addressed social conditions in member countries. A work programme for ECLAC, covering the period 2008–09, was adopted by the 31st session, which also adopted a resolution supporting the UN Stabilization Mission in Haiti and recognizing efforts undertaken by the Commission on behalf of the operation. The 32nd session of the Commission was convened in June 2008 in Santo Domingo, Dominican Republic. It considered a report, prepared by the Secretariat, entitled 'Structural Change and Productivity Growth—20 years later. Old problems, new opportunities'. The meeting endorsed its conclusions and voted to pursue further study of productive development and innovation policies and best practices. The Commission also requested that the Secretariat research challenges facing the region caused by escalating fuel and food costs at that time. The meeting approved a new programme of work for the period 2010–11, which aimed to promote policies to reduce vulnerability, to foster long-term production development strategies, to improve sustainable development policies, to improve the management of global issues at a regional level, and to strengthen social cohesion, reduce social risks and reinforce gender mainstreaming. In June 2009 ECLAC hosted a meeting of experts and officials from the region's ministries of finance to pursue discussions on structural reform and other measures to counter the impact of the global financial and economic crisis.

The 33rd session of the Commission, held in Brasilía, Brazil, in May–June 2010, adopted a new work programme for the two year period 2012–13. The programme's main areas of activity aimed: to strengthen the region's access to financing for development; to contribute to improving the global, regional and national financial architecture; to heighten the productive potential of the region and reduce productivity gaps, with special emphasis on innovation and new technologies; to improve the region's position in the global economy through trade, co-operation and regional integration; to promote a social covenant through greater social equality, lower social risks and further inclusion of a gender perspective in public policies; to improve policies for sustainable development and energy efficiency and address the effects of climate change; and to improve the development of institutions that deal with the management of global and cross-border issues and the provision of public goods at a regional level. The focus of the Commission meeting was a report entitled 'Time for Equality: Closing gaps, opening trails', which identified economic, social and structural disparities throughout the region. Representatives of member states determined to pursue development efforts with a stronger equality agenda.

ECLAC works closely with other agencies within the UN system and with other regional and multinational organizations. In January 2010 ECLAC offered its total co-operation in the immediate humanitarian tasks resulting from the earthquake that caused extensive damage and loss of life in Haiti and in any future reconstruction process. In March, following a massive earthquake in Chile, ECLAC established a joint working group, with UNDP, OCHA and the Chilean authorities, to define priority areas for emergency funding.

ECLAC supports member countries in negotiations of bilateral or sub-regional free trade agreements, in particular with the USA. In January 2002 ECLAC hosted an Interregional Conference on Financing for Development, held in Mexico City, which it had organized as part of the negotiating process prior to the World Summit on Financing for Development, held in March. In June senior representatives of ECLAC, UNDP, the World Bank and the Inter-American Development Bank agreed to co-ordinate activities in pursuit of the development goals proclaimed by the Millennium Summit meeting of the UN General Assembly in September 2000. ECLAC was to adapt the objectives of the so-called Millennium Development Goals (MDGs) to the reality of countries in the region. In July 2004 the 30th session of the Commission approved the establishment of an intergovernmental forum to monitor the implementation of decisions emerging from the World Summit on Sustainable Development, held in Johannesburg, South Africa, in September 2002. In January 2006 ECLAC organized the first Regional Implementation Forum on Sustainable Development, as mandated by the UN Commission on Sustainable Development. In January 2003 a regional conference was convened, in the Dominican Republic, in preparation for the World Summit on the Information Society (WSIS), the first phase of which was held in December, in Geneva, Switzerland. In July 2004 delegates to the 30th session of the Commission requested that ECLAC co-ordinate a regional preparatory meeting to define objectives and proposals for the second phase of the Summit in 2005. The regional ministerial meeting was convened in Rio de Janeiro, Brazil, in June 2005, and a Regional Action Plan, eLAC 2007, was approved to support national and regional projects that incorporate information and communications technology for use in economic and social development in the region. A second plan, eLAC2010, was adopted by ministers in February 2008, to assist countries to attain the global targets identified by the WSIS. The first Follow-up Meeting of eLAC2010 was convened in April 2009.

In November 2003 a Regional Intergovernmental Conference on Ageing was convened, in Santiago, Chile, to further the objectives of a World Assembly on Ageing that had been held in Madrid, Spain, in April 2002. A second Regional Intergovernmental Conference on Ageing was held in Brasília, Brazil, in December 2007. In November 2003 ECLAC launched REDESA, a web-based network of institutions and experts in social and environmental statistics. The first phase of a Macroeconomic Dialogue Network (REDIMA I) was established in 2003, to assist communication on macroeconomic issues between economists from the region's central banks and ministries of finance: a second phase, REDIMA II, was initiated in 2005. In July 2007 ECLAC organized the fourth Statistical Conference of the Americas (SCA), which is convened every two years to promote the development and improvement of national statistics (in particular their comparability), and to encourage co-operation between national statistical offices and regional and international organizations. The fifth SCA was held in Bogotá, Colombia, in August 2009. ECLAC organizes an annual competition to encourage small-scale innovative social projects in local communities. In June 2008 ECLAC launched an internet website (ideea.cepal.org/ideea/ideea.htm) aimed at publicizing and sharing knowledge about activities being implemented by member states towards attaining the MDGs. Also in that month ECLAC signed an agreement with the UN's International Research and Training Institute for the Advancement of Women (INSTRAW) to establish an observatory on gender equality in Latin America and the Caribbean. In July 2009 ECLAC signed a further agreement with the UN World Tourism Organization to strengthen co-operation in measuring and analysing tourism statistics and indicators. In January 2010 ECLAC initiated a joint project with the Inter-American Development Bank to conduct an economic analysis of the impact of climate change on the region.

In July 2006 Japan became the first Asian nation to be granted full membership of ECLAC. The membership of the Republic of Korea was formally approved in July 2007.

Latin American and Caribbean Institute for Economic and Social Planning (Instituto Latinoamericano y del Caribe de Planificacion Economica y Social—ILPES): Edif. Naciones Unidas, Avda Dag Hammarskjöld 3477, Vitacura, Casilla 179-D, Santiago, Chile; tel. (2) 2102000; fax (2) 2060252; e-mail secretaria.se@cepal.org; internet www.eclac.org/ilpes/; f. 1962; supports regional governments through the provision of training, advisory services and research in the field of public planning policy and co-ordination; Dir JORGE MATTAR-MÁRQUEZ (Mexico).

Latin American Demographic Centre (Centro Latinoamericano y Caribeno de Demografia—CELADE): Edif. Naciones Unidas, Avda Dag Hammarskjöld 3477, Casilla 179-D, Santiago, Chile; tel. (2) 2102000; fax (2) 2080252; e-mail celade@eclac.cl; internet www.eclac.org/celade; f. 1957, became an autonomous entity within ECLAC in 1971 and was fully incorporated into ECLAC as its Population Division in 1997; provides technical assistance to governments, universities and research centres in demographic analysis, population policies, integration of population factors in development planning, and data processing; conducts courses on demographic analysis for development and various national and regional seminars; provides demographic estimates and projections, documentation, data processing, computer packages and training; Dir DIRK JASPERS-FAIJER.

Finance

For the two-year period 2010–11 ECLAC's proposed regular budget, an appropriation from the UN, amounted to US $111.7m. In addition, extra-budgetary activities are financed by governments, other organizations, and UN agencies, including UNDP, UNFPA and UNICEF.

Publications

(in English and Spanish)

CEPAL Review (3 a year).

Challenges / Desafíos (2–3 a year, with UNICEF).

Demographic Observatory (2 a year).

ECLAC Notes (quarterly).

Economic Survey of Latin America and the Caribbean (annually).

FAL Bulletin (Trade Facilitation and Transport in Latin America) (monthly).

Foreign Investment in Latin America and the Caribbean (annually).

Latin America and the Caribbean in the World Economy (annually).

Notas de Población (2 a year).

Preliminary Overview of the Economies of Latin America and the Caribbean (annually).

Social Panorama of Latin America (annually).

Statistical Yearbook for Latin America and the Caribbean.

Water Resources Newsletter (2 a year).

Studies, reports, bibliographical bulletins.

United Nations Development Programme—UNDP

Address: One United Nations Plaza, New York, NY 10017, USA.

Telephone: (212) 906-5300; **fax:** (212) 906-5364; **e-mail:** hq@undp.org; **internet:** www.undp.org.

The Programme was established in 1965 by the UN General Assembly. Its central mission is to help countries to eradicate poverty and achieve a sustainable level of human development, an approach to economic growth that encompasses individual well-being and choice, equitable distribution of the benefits of development, and conservation of the environment. UNDP advocates for a more inclusive global economy. UNDP co-ordinates global and national efforts to achieve the UN Millennium Development Goals.

Organization

(August 2010)

UNDP is responsible to the UN General Assembly, to which it reports through ECOSOC.

EXECUTIVE BOARD

The Executive Board is responsible for providing intergovernmental support to, and supervision of, the activities of UNDP and the UN Population Fund (UNFPA). It comprises 36 members: eight from Africa, seven from Asia and the Pacific, four from eastern Europe, five from Latin America and the Caribbean and 12 from western Europe and other countries. Members serve a three-year term.

SECRETARIAT

Offices and divisions at the Secretariat include: an Operations Support Group; Offices of the United Nations Development Group, the Human Development Report, Development Studies, Audit and Performance Review, Evaluation, and Communications; and Bureaux for Crisis Prevention and Recovery, Resources and Strategic Partnerships, Development Policy, and Management. Five regional bureaux, all headed by an assistant administrator, cover: Africa; Asia and the Pacific; the Arab states; Latin America and the Caribbean; and Europe and the Commonwealth of Independent States. UNDP's Administrator (the third most senior UN official, after the Secretary-General and the Deputy Secretary-General) is in charge of strategic policy and overall co-ordination of UN development activities (including the chairing of the UN Development Group), while the Associate Administrator supervises the operations and management of UNDP programmes.

Administrator: Helen Clark (New Zealand).

Associate Administrator: Rebeca Grynspan (Costa Rica).

Assistant Administrator and Director, Regional Bureau for Latin America and the Caribbean: (vacant).

COUNTRY OFFICES

In almost every country receiving UNDP assistance there is an office, headed by the UNDP Resident Representative, who usually also serves as the UN Resident Co-ordinator, responsible for the co-ordination of all UN technical assistance and development activities in that country, so as to ensure the most effective use of UN and international aid resources.

OFFICES OF UN RESIDENT CO-ORDINATORS IN SOUTH AMERICA, CENTRAL AMERICA AND THE CARIBBEAN

Argentina: Esmeralda 130, Piso 13, CPA C1035ABD, Buenos Aires; tel. (1) 4320-8700; fax (1) 4320-8754; e-mail registry.ar@undp.org; internet www.undp.org.ar; Resident Co-ordinator Martín Santiago.

Barbados: Marine Gardens, Hastings, Christ Church; tel. 467-6000; fax 429-2448; e-mail communications.bb@undp.org; internet www.bb.undp.org; also covers Anguilla, Antigua and Barbuda, British Virgin Islands, Dominca, Grenada, Montserrat, Saint Christopher and Nevis, Saint Lucia, Saint Vincent and the Grenadines; Resident Co-ordinator Michelle Gyles-McDonnough.

Bolivia: Calle 14 Eq. Avda Sánchez Bustamante, Edif. Metrobol II, Calacoto, Casilla 9072, La Paz, Bolivia; tel. (2) 279-5544; fax (2) 279-5820; e-mail registry.bo@undp.org; internet www.pnud.bo; Resident Co-ordinator Yoriko Yasukawa.

Brazil: CP 0285, 70359 Brasília, DF; tel. (61) 3329-2000; fax (61) 3329-0099; e-mail fo.bra@undp.org; internet www.br.undp.org; Resident Co-ordinator Jorge Chediek.

Chile: Avda Dag Hammarskjöld, 3241 Vitacura, 7630412 Santiago; tel. (2) 654-1000; fax (2) 654-1099; e-mail fo.chi@undp.org; internet www.pnud.cl; Resident Co-ordinator Enrique Ganuza.

Colombia: Avda 82, 10-62, Piso 3, Bogotá; tel. (1) 488-9000; fax (1) 214-0110; e-mail fo.col@pnud.org; internet www.pnud.org.co; Resident Co-ordinator Bruno Moro.

Costa Rica: Apdo Postal 4540-1000, San José; tel. 22961544; fax 22961545; e-mail registry.cr@undp.org; internet www.nu.or.cr/pnud; Resident Co-ordinator Luiza Carvalho.

Cuba: Calle 18 No. 110 (entre 1ra y 3ra), Miramar, Playa, Havana; tel. (7) 204-1512; fax (7) 204-1516; e-mail registry.cu@undp.org; internet www.undp.org.cu; Resident Co-ordinator Barbara Pesce-Monteiro.

Dominican Republic: Casa de las Naciones Unidas, Av. Anacaona 9, Mirador Sur. Apdo 1424, Santo Domingo; tel. 537-0909; fax 537-3507; e-mail registry.do@undp.org; internet www.pnud.org.do; Resident Co-ordinator Valerie Julliand (acting).

Ecuador: Avda Amazonas 2889 y la Granja, Quito; tel. (2) 2460-330; fax (2) 2461-960; e-mail registry.ec@undp.org; internet www.pnud.org.ec; Resident Co-ordinator José Manuel Hermida.

El Salvador: POB 1114, San Salvador; tel. 22630066; fax 22093588; e-mail fo.slv@undp.org; internet www.pnud.org.sv; Resident Co-ordinator Jessica Faieta; also covers Belize.

Guatemala: 5a Av. 5-55, Zona 14, Edificio Europlaza, Torre IV, Nivel 10, 01014 Guatemala City; tel. (2) 3843100; fax (2) 3843200; e-mail webpnud@undp.org.gt; internet www.undp.org.gt; Resident Co-ordinator René Mauricio Valdés.

Guyana: 42 Brickdam and Boyle Place, POB 10960, Georgetown, Guyana; tel. (2) 64040; fax (2) 62942; e-mail registry.gy@undp.org; internet www.undp.org.gy; Resident Co-ordinator M. Kiari Liman-Tinguiri.

Haiti: 387 Av. John Brown, BP 557, Port-au-Prince; tel. 2244-9350; fax 2244-9366; e-mail registry.ht@undp.org; internet www.ht.undp.org; Resident Co-ordinator Nigel Fisher.

Honduras: Colonia Palmira, Apdo Postal 976, Tegucigalpa DC; tel. 220-1100; fax 239-8010; e-mail webmaster.hn@undp.org; internet www.undp.un.hn; Resident Co-ordinator Sergio Guimaraes.

Jamaica: 1-3 Lady Musgrave Rd, POB 280, Kingston; tel. 978-2390; fax 946-2163; e-mail registry.jm@undp.org; internet www.jm.undp.org; Resident Co-ordinator Minh Pham; also covers Bahamas, Cayman Islands, Turks and Caicos Islands.

Mexico: Presidente Masaryk 29, 8°, Col. Polanco 11570, México, DF; tel. (55) 5263-9600; fax (55) 5255-0095; e-mail fo.mex@undp.org; internet www.undp.org.mx; Resident Co-ordinator Magdy Martínez-Solimán.

Nicaragua: Apdo Postal 3260, Managua; tel. 266-1701; fax 266-6909; e-mail registry.ni@undp.org; internet www.undp.org.ni; Resident Co-ordinator Pablo Mandeville.

Panama: Apdo 0816-1914, Casa de las Naciones Unidas, Ciudad del Saber, Edificio 129, Panamá; tel. 302-4545; fax 302-4546; e-mail info@undp.org.pa; internet www.undp.org.pa; Resident Co-ordinator Kim Bolduc.

Paraguay: Avda Mcal. López esq. Saraví, Edificio Naciones Unidas, Asunción; tel. (21) 611980; fax (21) 611981; e-mail registry.py@undp.org; internet www.undp.org.py; Resident Co-ordinator Lorenzo Jimenez de Luis.

Peru: Calle Los Cedros 269, San Isidro; tel. (1) 2156969; fax (1) 4212304; e-mail foper@pnud.org; internet www.pnud.org.pe; Resident Co-ordinator Rebeca Arias.

Trinidad and Tobago: POB 1113, Port of Spain; tel. 623-7056; fax 623-1658; e-mail registry@undp.org.tt; internet www.undp.org.tt; Deputy Resident Co-ordinator Dr Marcia de Castro; also covers Aruba, Netherlands Antilles and Suriname.

Uruguay: J. Barrias Amorín 870, 3°, Montevideo; tel. (2) 4123356; fax (2) 4123360; e-mail fouru@undp.org.uy; internet www.undp.org.uy; Resident Co-ordinator Susan McDade.

Venezuela: Avda Francisco de Miranda, Torre Hewlett-Packard, 6°, oficina 6a, Urb. Los Palos Grandes, Caracas; tel. (212) 208-4444; fax (212) 263-8179; e-mail recepcion.ven@undp.org; internet www.pnud.org.ve; Resident Co-ordinator Alfredo Missair.

Activities

UNDP describes itself as the UN's global development network, advocating for change and connecting countries to knowledge, experience and resources to help people build a better life. In 2010 UNDP was active in 166 countries. It provides advisory and support services to governments and UN teams with the aim of advancing sustainable human development and building national development capabilities. Assistance is mostly non-monetary, comprising the provision of experts' services, consultancies, equipment and training for local workers. Developing countries themselves contribute significantly to the total project costs in terms of personnel, facilities, equipment and supplies. UNDP also supports programme countries in attracting aid and utilizing it efficiently.

From the mid-1990s UNDP assumed a more active co-ordinating role within the UN system. In 1997 the UNDP Administrator was appointed to chair the UN Development Group (UNDG), which was established as part of a series of structural reform measures initiated by the UN Secretary-General, with the aim of preventing duplication and strengthening collaboration between all UN agencies, programmes and funds concerned with development. The UNDG promotes coherent policy at country level through the system of UN Resident Co-ordinators (see above), the Common Country Assessment mechanism (CCA, a process for evaluating national development needs), and the UN Development Assistance Framework (UNDAF, for planning and co-ordination development operations at country level, based on the CCA).

During the late 1990s UNDP undertook an extensive internal process of reform, which placed increased emphasis on its activities in the field and on performance and accountability. In 2001 UNDP established a series of Thematic Trust Funds to enable increased support of priority programme activities. In accordance with the more results-oriented approach developed under the reform process UNDP introduced a new Multi-Year Funding Framework (MYFF), which outlined the country-driven goals around which funding was to be mobilized, integrating programme objectives, resources, budget and outcomes. The MYFF was to provide the basis for the Administrator's Business Plans for the same duration and enables policy coherence in the implementation of programmes at country, regional and global levels. A Results-Oriented Annual Report (ROAR) was produced for the first time in 2000 from data compiled by country offices and regional programmes. New measures were introduced in 2006 to improve UNDP's management accountability, internal auditing, evaluation and procurement procedures.

In accordance with the third phase of the MYFF, covering 2008–11, UNDP adopted a Strategic Plan that focused on the following five areas: democratic governance; poverty reduction; energy and the environment; crisis prevention and recovery; and combating HIV/AIDS. Other important 'cross-cutting' themes, to be incorporated throughout the programme areas, included gender equality and the empowerment of women, information and communication technologies, and human rights. The 2008–11 Strategic Plan emphasized UNDP's 'overarching' contribution to achieving sustainable human development through capacity development strategies, to be integrated into all areas of activity. (The UNDP Capacity Development Group, established in 2002 within the Bureau for Development Policy, organizes UNDP capacity development support at local and national level.) Other objectives identified by the 2008–11 Plan included strengthening national ownership of development projects and promoting and facilitating South-South co-operation.

MILLENNIUM DEVELOPMENT GOALS

UNDP, through its leadership of the UNDG and management of the Resident Co-ordinator system, has a co-ordinating function as the focus of UN system-wide efforts to achieve the so-called Millennium Development Goals (MDGs), pledged by UN member governments attending a summit meeting of the UN General Assembly in September 2000. The objectives were to establish a defined agenda to reduce poverty and improve the quality of lives of millions of people and to serve as a framework for measuring development. There are eight MDGs, as follows, for which one or more specific targets have been identified:

i) to eradicate extreme poverty and hunger, with the aim of reducing by 50% (compared with the 1990 figure) the number of people with an income of less than US $1 a day and those suffering from hunger by 2015, and to achieve full and productive employment and decent work for all, including women and young people;

ii) to achieve universal primary education by 2015;

iii) to promote gender equality and empower women, in particular to eliminate gender disparities in primary and secondary education by 2005 and at all levels by 2015;

iv) to reduce child mortality, with a target reduction of two-thirds in the mortality rate among children under five by 2015 (compared with the 1990 level);

v) to improve maternal health, specifically to reduce by 75% the numbers of women dying in childbirth and to achieve universal access to reproductive health by 2015 (compared with the 1990 level);

vi) to combat HIV/AIDS, malaria and other diseases, with targets to have halted and begun to reverse the incidence of HIV/AIDS, malaria and other major diseases by 2015 and to achieve universal access to treatment for HIV/AIDS for all those who need it by 2010;

vii) to ensure environmental sustainability, including targets to integrate the principles of sustainable development into country policies and programmes, to reduce by 50% (compared with the 1990 level) the number of people without access to safe drinking water by 2015, and to achieve significant improvement in the lives of at least 100m. slum dwellers by 2020;

viii) to develop a global partnership for development, including an open, rule-based, non-discriminatory trading and financial system, and efforts to deal with international debt, to address the needs of least developed countries and landlocked and small island developing states, to provide access to affordable, essential drugs in developing countries, and to make available the benefits of new technologies.

UNDP plays a leading role in efforts to integrate the MDGs into all aspects of UN activities at country level and to ensure that the MDGs are incorporated into national development strategies. The Programme supports efforts by countries, as well as regions and subregions, to report on progress towards achievement of the goals, and on specific social, economic and environmental indicators, through the formulation of MDG reports. These form the basis of a global report, issued annually by the UN Secretary-General since mid-2002. UNDP also works to raise awareness of the MDGs and to support advocacy efforts at all levels, for example through regional publicity campaigns, target-specific publications and the Millennium Campaign to generate support for the goals in developing and developed countries. UNDP provides administrative and technical support to the Millennium Project, an independent advisory body established by the UN Secretary-General in 2002 to develop a practical action plan to achieve the MDGs. Financial support of the Project is channelled through a Millennium Trust Fund, administered by UNDP. In January 2005 the Millennium Project presented its report, based on extensive research conducted by teams of experts, which included recommendations for the international system to support country level development efforts and identified a series of 'Quick Wins' to bring conclusive benefit to millions of people in the short-term. International commitment to achieve the MDGs by 2015 was reiterated at a World Summit, convened in September 2005. In December 2006 UNDP and the Spanish Government concluded an agreement on the establishment of the MDG Achievement Fund (MDG-F), which aims to support the acceleration of progress towards the achievement of the MDGs and to enhance co-operation at country level between UN development partners. UNDP and the UN Department of Economic and Social Affairs are lead agencies in co-ordinating the work of the Millennium Development Goals Gap Task Force, which was established by the UN Secretary-General in May 2007 to track, systematically and at both international and country level, existing international commitments in the areas of official development assistance, market access, debt relief, access to essential medicines and technology. In November the UN, in partnership with two major US companies, launched an online MDG Monitor (www.mdgmonitor.org) to track progress and to support organizations working to achieve the goals.

DEMOCRATIC GOVERNANCE

UNDP supports national efforts to ensure efficient and accountable governance, to improve the quality of democratic processes, and to build effective relations between the state, the private sector and civil society, which are essential to achieving sustainable development. As in other practice areas, UNDP assistance includes policy advice and technical support, capacity-building of institutions and individuals, advocacy and public information and communication, the promotion and brokering of dialogue, and knowledge networking and sharing of good practices.

UNDP works to strengthen parliaments and other legislative bodies as institutions of democratic participation. It assists with constitutional reviews and reform, training of parliamentary staff, and capacity-building of political parties and civil organizations as part of this objective. UNDP undertakes missions to help prepare for and ensure the conduct of free and fair elections. It helps to build the long-term capacity of electoral institutions and practices within a country, for example by assisting with voter registration, the establishment of electoral commissions, providing observers to verify that elections are free and fair, projects to educate voters, and training journalists to provide impartial election coverage.

Within its justice sector programme UNDP undertakes a variety of projects to improve access to justice, in particular for the poor and disadvantaged, and to promote judicial independence, legal reform and understanding of the legal system. UNDP also works to promote access to information, the integration of human rights issues into activities concerned with sustainable human development, and support for the international human rights system.

Since 1997 UNDP has been mandated to assist developing countries to fight corruption and improve accountability, transparency and integrity (ATI). It has worked to establish national and international partnerships in support of its anti-corruption efforts and used its role as a broker of knowledge and experience to uphold ATI principles at all levels of public financial management and governance. UNDP publishes case studies of its anti-corruption efforts and assists governments to conduct self-assessments of their public financial management systems.

In March 2002 a UNDP Governance Centre was inaugurated in Oslo, Norway, to enhance the role of UNDP in support of democratic governance and to assist countries to implement democratic reforms in order to achieve the MDGs. The mandate for the work of the Centre during the period 2005–09 incorporated activities in the following areas: governance and poverty eradication; governance and conflict prevention; civil society, empowerment and governance; and learning and capacity development. The Democratic Governance Network (DGP-Net) allows discussion and the sharing of information. In 2007 UNDP also helped to establish the iKnow Politics Network, which aims to help women become involved in politics.

In February 2004 a UNDP-sponsored report entitled *Democracy in Latin America: Towards a Citizens' Democracy* was published, with the aim of promoting regional debate on means of strengthening democratic institutions. In April 2007 UNDP convened a conference in Mexico City, Mexico, on ways to prevent the manipulation for political gain of social programmes intended to help poor families in Latin America.

Within the democratic governance practice area UNDP supports more than 300 projects at international, country and city levels designed to improve conditions for the urban poor, in particular through improvement in urban governance. The Local Initiative Facility for Urban Environment (LIFE) undertakes small-scale projects in low-income communities, in collaboration with local authorities, the private sector and community-based groups, and promotes a participatory approach to local governance. UNDP also works closely with the UN Capital Development Fund to implement projects in support of decentralized governance, which it has recognized as a key element to achieving sustainable development goals.

UNDP aims to ensure that, rather than creating an ever-widening 'digital divide', ongoing rapid advancements in information and communications technology (ICT) are harnessed by poorer countries to accelerate progress in achieving sustainable human development. UNDP advises governments on ICT policy, promotes digital entrepreneurship in programme countries and works with private sector partners to provide reliable and affordable communications networks. The Bureau for Development Policy operates the Information and Communication Technologies for Development Programme, which aims to establish technology access centres in developing countries. A Sustainable Development Networking Programme focuses on expanding internet connectivity in poorer countries through building national capacities and supporting local internet sites. UNDP has used mobile internet units to train people even in isolated rural areas. In 1999 UNDP, in collaboration with an international communications company, Cisco Systems, and other partners, launched NetAid, an internet-based forum (accessible at www.netaid.org) for mobilizing and co-ordinating fundraising and other activities aimed at alleviating poverty and promoting sustainable human development in the developing world. With Cisco Systems and other partners, UNDP has worked to establish academies of information technology to support training and capacity-building in developing countries. UNDP and the World Bank jointly host the secretariat of the Digital Opportunity Task Force, a partnership between industrialized and developing countries, business and non-governmental organizations (NGOs) that was established in 2000. UNDP is a partner in the Global Digital Technology Initiative, launched in 2002 to strengthen the role of ICT in achieving the development goals of developing countries. In January 2004 UNDP and Microsoft Corporation announced an agreement to develop jointly ICT projects aimed at assisting developing countries to achieve the MDGs.

POVERTY REDUCTION

UNDP's activities to facilitate poverty eradication include support for capacity-building programmes and initiatives to generate sustainable livelihoods, for example by improving access to credit, land and technologies, and the promotion of strategies to improve education and health provision for the poorest elements of populations (especially women and girls). UNDP aims to help governments to reassess their development priorities and to design initiatives for sustainable human development. In 1996, following the World Summit for Social Development, which was held in Copenhagen, Denmark, in March 1995, UNDP launched the Poverty Strategies Initiative (PSI) to strengthen national capacities to assess and monitor the extent of poverty and to combat the problem. All PSI projects were to involve representatives of governments, the private sector, social organizations and research institutions in policy debate and formulation. Following the introduction, in 1999, by the World Bank and IMF of Poverty Reduction Strategy Papers (PRSPs), UNDP has helped governments to draft these documents, and, since 2001, has linked the papers to efforts to achieve and monitor progress towards the MDGs. In early 2004 UNDP inaugurated the International Poverty Centre, in Brasília, Brazil, which fosters the capacity of countries to formulate and implement poverty reduction strategies and encourages South-South co-operation in all relevant areas of research and decision-making. In particular, the Centre aims to assist countries to meet MDGs through research into and implementation of pro-poor policies that encourage social protection and human development, and through the monitoring of poverty and inequality. UNDP's Secretariat hosts the Special Unit for South-South Co-operation (SU/SSC), which was established by the United Nations General Assembly in 1978.

UNDP country offices support the formulation of national human development reports (NHDRs), which aim to facilitate activities such as policy-making, the allocation of resources, and monitoring progress towards poverty eradication and sustainable development. In addition, the preparation of Advisory Notes and Country Co-operation Frameworks by UNDP officials helps to highlight country-specific aspects of poverty eradication and national strategic priorities. In January 1998 the Executive Board adopted eight guiding principles relating to sustainable human development that were to be implemented by all country offices, in order to ensure a focus to UNDP activities. Since 1990 UNDP has published an annual *Human Development Report*, incorporating a Human Development Index, which ranks countries in terms of human development, using three key indicators: life expectancy, adult literacy and basic income required for a decent standard of living. In 1997 a Human Poverty Index and a Gender-related Development Index, which assesses gender equality on the basis of life expectancy, education and income, were introduced into the Report for the first time. Jointly with the International Labour Organization (ILO) UNDP operates a Programme on Employment for Poverty Reduction, which undertakes analysis and studies, and supports countries in improving their employment strategies. Microstart, a UNDP scheme to support private sector and community-based initiatives in generating employment opportunities, has been in operation since 1997.

UNDP is committed to ensuring that the process of economic and financial globalization, including national and global trade, debt and capital flow policies, incorporates human development concerns. It aimed to ensure that the Doha Development Round of World Trade Organization (WTO) negotiations (suspended in 2006) should achieve an expansion of trade opportunities and economic growth to less developed countries. With the UN Conference on Trade and Development (UNCTAD), UNDP manages a Global Programme on Globalization, Liberalization and Sustainable Human Development, which aims to support greater integration of developing countries into the global economy. UNDP manages a Trust Fund for the Integrated Framework for Trade-related Technical Assistance to Least-Developed Countries, which was inaugurated in 1997 by UNDP, the IMF, the International Trade Centre, UNCTAD, the World Bank and the WTO.

In 1996 UNDP initiated a process of collaboration between city authorities world-wide to promote implementation of the commitments made at the 1995 Copenhagen summit for social development and to help to combat aspects of poverty and other urban problems, such as poor housing, transport, the management of waste disposal, water supply and sanitation. The World Alliance of Cities Against Poverty was formally launched in October 1997, in the context of the International Decade for the Eradication of Poverty. The sixth global Forum of the Alliance (convened every two years) took place in March 2008.

UNDP sponsors the International Day for the Eradication of Poverty, held annually on 17 October.

ENVIRONMENT AND ENERGY

UNDP plays a role in developing the agenda for international co-operation on environmental and energy issues, focusing on the relationship between energy policies, environmental protection, poverty and development. UNDP promotes development practices that are environmentally sustainable, for example through the formulation and implementation of Poverty Reduction Strategies and National Strategies for Sustainable Development. Together with the UN Environment Programme (UNEP) and the World Bank, UNDP is an implementing agency of the Global Environment Facility (GEF), which was established in 1991 to finance international co-operation in projects to benefit the environment.

UNDP recognizes that desertification and land degradation are major causes of rural poverty and promotes sustainable land management, drought preparedness and reform of land tenure as means of addressing the problem. It also aims to reduce poverty caused by land degradation through implementation of environmental conventions at a national and international level. In 2002 UNDP inaugurated an Integrated Drylands Development Programme which aimed to ensure that the needs of people living in arid regions are met and considered at a local and national level. The Drylands Development Centre implements the programme in 19 African, Arab and West Asian countries. UNDP is also concerned with sustainable management of forestries, fisheries and agriculture. Its Biodiversity Global Programme assists developing countries and communities to integrate issues relating to sustainable practices and biodiversity into national and global practices. Since 1992 UNDP has administered a Small Grants Programme, funded by the GEF, to support community-based initiatives concerned with biodiversity conservation, prevention of land degradation and the elimination of persistent organic pollutants. The Equator Initiative was inaugurated in 2002 as a partnership between UNDP, representatives of governments, civil society and businesses, with the aim of reducing poverty in communities along the equatorial belt by fostering local partnerships, harnessing local knowledge and promoting conservation and sustainable practices.

UNDP's 2007/08 *Human Development Report* concentrated on climate change and the urgent need to prevent an irreversible ecological catastrophe as a result of global warming caused by gas emissions. UNDP promotes clean energy technologies (through the Clean Development Mechanism) and aims to extend access to sustainable energy services, including the introduction of renewable alternatives to conventional fuels, as well as access to investment financing for sustainable energy. In December 2005 UNDP (in collaboration with Fortis, a private sector provider of financial services) launched the MDG Carbon Facility, whereby developing countries that undertake projects to reduce emissions of carbon dioxide, methane and other gases responsible for global warming may sell their 'carbon credits' to finance further MDG projects. The first projects under the MDG Carbon Facility were inaugurated in February 2008, in Uzbekistan, the former Yugoslav republic of Macedonia, Yemen and Rwanda.

UNDP supports efforts to promote international co-operation in the management of chemicals. It was actively involved in the development of a Strategic Approach to International Chemicals Management which was adopted by representatives of 100 governments at an international conference convened in Dubai, UAE, in February 2006.

UNDP works to ensure the effective governance of freshwater and aquatic resources, and promotes co-operation in transboundary water management. It works closely with other agencies to promote safe sanitation, ocean and coastal management, and community water supplies. In 1996 UNDP, with the World Bank and the Swedish International Development Agency, established a Global Water Partnership to promote and implement water resources management. UNDP, with the GEF, supports an extensive range of projects which incorporate development and ecological requirements in the sustainable management of international waters. These include the Global Mercury Project, a project for improved municipal waste-water management in coastal cities of the African, Caribbean and Pacific states, a Global Ballast Water Management Programme and an International Waters Learning Exchange and Resources Network.

UNDP projects concerned with protecting international waters in South America and the Caribbean include the conservation of biodiversity in the Lake Titicaca Basin, protection of the Rio de la Plata, and management of coastal areas and watersheds in small Caribbean island states.

CRISIS PREVENTION AND RECOVERY

UNDP is not primarily a relief organization, but collaborates with other UN agencies in countries in crisis and with special circumstances to promote relief and development efforts, in order to secure the foundations for sustainable human development and thereby increase national capabilities to prevent or mitigate future crises. In particular, UNDP is concerned to achieve reconciliation, reintegration and reconstruction in affected countries, as well as to support emergency interventions and management and delivery of programme aid. It aims to facilitate the transition from relief to longer-term recovery and rehabilitation. Special development initiatives in post-conflict countries include the demobilization of former combatants and destruction of illicit small armaments, rehabilitation of communities for the sustainable reintegration of returning populations and the restoration and strengthening of democratic institutions. UNDP is seeking to incorporate conflict prevention into its development strategies. It has established a mine action unit within its Bureau for Crisis Prevention and Recovery in order to strengthen national and local de-mining capabilities including surveying, mapping and clearance of anti-personnel landmines. It also works to increase awareness of the harm done to civilians by cluster munitions, and participated in the negotiations that culminated in May 2008 with the adoption of an international Convention on Cluster Munitions, which in February 2010 received its 30th ratification, enabling its entry into force on 1 August. UNDP also works closely with UNICEF to raise awareness and implement risk reduction education programmes, and manages global partnership projects concerned with training, legislation and the socio-economic impact of anti-personnel devices. In late 2006 UNDP began to administer a new UN fund, the Peacebuilding Fund, the purpose of which is to strengthen essential services to maintain peace in countries that have undergone conflict. During 2008 UNDP developed a new global programme aimed at strengthening the rule of law in conflict and post-conflict countries; the programme placed particular focus on women's access to justice, institution-building and transitional justice.

In 2006 UNDP launched an Immediate Crisis Response programme (known as 'SURGE') aimed at strengthening its capacity to respond quickly and effectively in the recovery phase following a conflict or natural disaster. Under the programme Immediate Crisis Response Advisors—UNDP staff with special expertise in at least one of 12 identified areas, including early recovery, operational support and resource mobilization—are swiftly deployed, in a 'SURGETeam', to UNDP country offices dealing with crises. In 2008 Immediate Crisis Response Advisors were deployed to northern Cameroon (in February) in response to a sudden influx of Chadian refugees; to Chad (also in February) to review the destruction of the local UNDP office in a period of violent unrest; to Myanmar (May) to assess the aftermath of Cyclone Nargis; and to Haiti (September) following a series of hurricanes there. In January 2009 a SURGETeam was deployed to assess the situation in Gaza, in view of the onset in December 2008 of an intense period of conflict. Following the earthquake that devastated Haiti in January 2010 a SURGETeam, comprising four experts on operations, recovery and security, was deployed immediately to assess the operational requirements of UNDP's office there; subsequently 24 SURGE advisers developed a SURGE work plan for the country.

UNDP is the focal point within the UN system for strengthening national capacities for natural disaster reduction (prevention, preparedness and mitigation relating to natural, environmental and technological hazards). UNDP's Bureau of Crisis Prevention and Recovery, in conjunction with the Office for the Co-ordination of Humanitarian Affairs and the secretariat of the International Strategy for Disaster Reduction, oversees the system-wide Capacity for Disaster Reduction Initiative (CADRI), which was inaugurated in 2007, superseding the former United Nations Disaster Management Training Programme. In February 2004 UNDP introduced a Disaster Risk Index that enabled vulnerability and risk to be measured and compared between countries and demonstrated the correspondence between human development and death rates following natural disasters. UNDP was actively involved in preparations for the second World Conference on Disaster Reduction, which was held in Kobe, Japan, in January 2005. Following the Kobe Conference UNDP initiated a new Global Risk Identification Programme. During 2005 the Inter-Agency Standing Committee, concerned with co-ordinating the international response to humanitarian disasters, developed a concept of providing assistance through a 'cluster' approach, comprising core areas of activity (see OCHA). UNDP was designated the lead agency for the Early Recovery cluster, linking the immediate needs following a disaster with medium- and long-term recovery efforts.

UNDP co-operates with the Co-ordination Centre for the Prevention of Natural Disasters in Central America (CEPREDENAC) and with the Caribbean Disaster Emergency Response Agency (CDERA). In 2010 UNDP was working to support the long-term recovery under way in Haiti following the severe earthquake that struck that country in January. Projects being undertaken by UNDP in Haiti in mid-2010 included cash-for-work initiatives that aimed to inject cash into the fragile local economy, support the local population in providing shelter, food and education for their families; and provide labour for rehabilitation work. During the period January–August 2010 cash-for-work projects employed more than 120,000 Haitians. A UNDP project aimed at managing debris in six earthquake-affected neighbourhoods of Port-au-Prince was to be initiated in the second half of 2010.

HIV/AIDS

UNDP regards the HIV/AIDS pandemic as a major challenge to development, and advocates making HIV/AIDS a focus of national planning and national poverty reduction strategies; supports decentralized action against HIV/AIDS at community level; helps to strengthen national capacities at all levels to combat the disease; and aims to link support for prevention activities, education and treatment with broader development planning and responses. UNDP places a particular focus on combating the spread of HIV/AIDS through the promotion of women's rights. UNDP is a co-sponsor, jointly with the World Health Organization (WHO) and other UN bodies, of the Joint UN Programme on HIV/AIDS (UNAIDS), which became operational on 1 January 1996. UNAIDS co-ordinates UNDP's HIV and Development Programme. Since 2003 UNDP has worked in partnership with the Global Fund to Fight HIV/AIDS, Tuberculosis and Malaria, in particular to support the local principal recipient of grant financing and to help to manage fund projects.

UNDP administers a global programme concerned with intellectual property and access to HIV/AIDS drugs, to promote wider and cheaper access to antiretroviral drugs, in accordance with the agreement on Trade-Related Aspects of Intellectual Property Rights (TRIPS), amended by the WTO in 2005 to allow countries without a pharmaceutical manufacturing capability to import generic copies of patented medicines.

Finance

UNDP and its various funds and programmes are financed by the voluntary contributions of members of the UN and the Programme's participating agencies, cost-sharing by recipient governments and third-party donors. In 2008 UNDP's gross regular (core) income was US $1,100m., and total non-core contributions amounted to $3,700m. Of total provisional programme expenditure of $4,096m. in 2008, some 34.9% was allocated to fostering democratic governance; 30.6% to achieving the MDGs and reducing human poverty; 16.0% to supporting crisis prevention and recovery; and 9.9% to managing energy and the environment for sustainable development. Some 28% of provisional total programme expenditure was allocated to Latin America and the Caribbean; 22% to Asia and the Pacific; 21% to Africa; 12% to the Arab states; and 8% to Europe and the CIS. For the period 2008–11 total voluntary contributions were projected at $20,600m., of which $5,300m. constituted regular (core) resources, $5,000m. bilateral donor contributions, $5,500m. contributions from multilateral partners, and $4,800m. cost-sharing by recipient governments.

Publications

Annual Report of the Administrator.

Choices (quarterly).

Human Development Report (annually).

Poverty Report (annually).

Results-Oriented Annual Report.

Associated Funds and Programmes

UNDP is the central funding, planning and co-ordinating body for technical co-operation within the UN system. A number of associated funds and programmes, financed separately by means of voluntary contributions, provide specific services through the UNDP network. UNDP manages a trust fund to promote economic and technical co-operation among developing countries.

GLOBAL ENVIRONMENT FACILITY (GEF)

The GEF, which is managed jointly by UNDP, the World Bank (which hosts its secretariat) and UNEP, began operations in 1991 and was restructured in 1994. Its aim is to support projects in the six thematic areas of: climate change, the conservation of biological diversity, the protection of international waters, reducing the depletion of the ozone layer in the atmosphere, arresting land degradation and addressing the issue of persistent organic pollutants. Capacity-building to allow countries to meet their obligations under international environmental agreements, and adaptation to climate change, are priority cross-cutting components of these projects. The GEF acts as the financial mechanism for the Convention on Biological Diversity and the UN Framework Convention on Climate Change. UNDP is responsible for capacity-building, targeted research, pre-investment activities and technical assistance. UNDP also administers the Small Grants Programme of the GEF, which supports community-based activities by local NGOs, and the Country Dialogue Workshop Programme, which promotes dialogue on national priorities with regard to the GEF. In August 2006 some 32 donor countries pledged US $3,130m. for the fourth periodic replenishment of GEF funds (GEF-4), covering the period 2007–10. At February 2009 UNDP GEF-funded projects amounted to $8,740m. for 570 full and medium-size initiatives and more than 370 enabling activities. An additional $738.7m. had been committed under the Small Grants Programme.

Chair. and CEO: MONIQUE BARBUT (France).

Executive Co-ordinator of UNDP-GEF Unit: YANNICK GLEMAREC; 304 East 45th St, 9th Floor, New York, NY 10017, USA; fax (212) 906-6998; e-mail gefinfo@undp.org; internet www.undp.org/gef/05/.

MDG ACHIEVEMENT FUND (MDG-F)

The Fund, established in accordance with an agreement concluded in December 2006 between UNDP and the Spanish Government, and with funding from the Spanish Government of nearly €528m. to cover the period 2007–10, aims to support the acceleration of progress towards the achievement of the MDGs and to advance country-level co-operation between UN development partners. The Fund operates through the UN development system and focuses mainly on financing collaborative UN activities addressing multi-dimensional development challenges. By 2010 some 128 programmes were under way in 50 countries, in the thematic areas of children and nutrition; climate change; conflict prevention; culture and development; economic governance; gender equality and women's empowerment; and youth employment.

Director of MDG-F Secretariat: SOPHIE DE CAEN (Canada); MDG-F Secretariat, c/o UNDP, One United Nations Plaza, New York, NY 10017, USA; tel. (212) 906-6180; fax (212) 906-5364; e-mail pb.mdgf.secretariat@undp.org; internet www.mdgfund.org.

MONTREAL PROTOCOL

Through its Montreal Protocol/Chemicals Unit UNDP collaborates with public and private partners in developing countries to assist them in eliminating the use of ozone-depleting substances (ODS), in accordance with the Montreal Protocol to the Vienna Convention for the Protection of the Ozone Layer, through the design, monitoring and evaluation of ODS phase-out projects and programmes. In particular, UNDP provides technical assistance and training, national capacity-building and demonstration projects and technology transfer investment projects. By December 2007 the Executive Committee of the Montreal Protocol had approved grants for projects and activities that had resulted in the elimination of an estimated 175,864 metric tons of ODS production.

SPECIAL UNIT FOR SOUTH-SOUTH CO-OPERATION (SU/SSC)

The SU/SSC, established in 1978 by the UN General Assembly and hosted by UNDP, aims to co-ordinate and support South-South co-operation in the political, economic, social, environmental and technical areas, and to support 'triangular' collaboration on a UN system-wide and global basis. The Special Unit organizes the annual UN Day for South-South Co-operation (December 19), and manages the UN Trust Fund for South-South Co-operation (UNFSC) and the Perez-Guerrero Trust Fund for Economic and Technical Co-operation among Developing Countries (PGTF), as well as undertaking programmes financed by UNDP.

Director: YIPING ZHOU; 304 East 45th St, 12th Floor, New York, NY 11017, USA; tel. (212) 906-6944; fax (212) 906-6352; e-mail ssc.info@undp.org; internet ssc.undp.org.

UNDP DRYLANDS DEVELOPMENT CENTRE (DDC)

The Centre, based in Nairobi, Kenya, was established in February 2002, superseding the former UN Office to Combat Desertification and Drought (UNSO). (UNSO had been established following the conclusion, in October 1994, of the UN Convention to Combat Desertification in Those Countries Experiencing Serious Drought and/or Desertification, Particularly in Africa; in turn, UNSO had replaced the former UN Sudano-Sahelian Office.) The DDC was to focus on the following areas: ensuring that national development planning takes account of the needs of dryland communities, particularly in poverty reduction strategies; helping countries to cope with the effects of climate variability, especially drought, and to prepare for future climate change; and addressing local issues affecting the utilization of resources.

Director: PHILIP DOBIE (United Kingdom); UN Gigiri Compound, United Nations Ave, POB 30552, 00100 Nairobi, Kenya; tel. (20) 7624640; fax (20) 7624648; e-mail ddc@undp.org; internet www.undp.org/drylands.

UNDP-UNEP POVERTY-ENVIRONMENT INITIATIVE (UNPEI)

UNPEI, inaugurated in February 2007, supports countries in developing their capacity to launch and maintain programmes that mainstream poverty-environment linkages into national development planning processes, such as MDG achievement strategies and PRSPs.

Director: PHILIP DOBIE (United Kingdom); UN Gigiri Compound, United Nations Avenue, POB 30552, 00100, Nairobi, Kenya; e-mail facility.unpei@unpei.org; internet www.unpei.org.

UNITED NATIONS CAPITAL DEVELOPMENT FUND (UNCDF)

The Fund was established in 1966 and became fully operational in 1974. It invests in poor communities in least-developed countries

(LDCs) through local governance projects and microfinance operations, with the aim of increasing such communities' access to essential local infrastructure and services and thereby improving their productive capacities and self-reliance. UNCDF encourages participation by local people and local governments in the planning, implementation and monitoring of projects. The Fund aims to promote the interests of women in community projects and to enhance their earning capacities. A Special Unit for Microfinance (SUM), established in 1997 as a joint UNDP/UNCDF operation, was fully integrated into UNCDF in 1999. UNCDF/SUM helps to develop financial services for poor communities and supports UNDP's MicroStart initiative. UNCDF hosts the UN high-level Advisors Group on Inclusive Financial Sectors, established in respect of recommendations made during the 2005 International Year of Microcredit. In November 2008 UNCDF launched MicroLead, a US $26m. fund that was to provide loans to leading microfinance institutions and other financial service providers (MFIs/FSPs) in developing countries; MicroLead was also to focus on the provision of early support to countries in post-conflict situations. In 2009 UNCDF had a programme portfolio with a value of around $125m., in support of initiatives ongoing in 28 LDCs.

Executive Secretary: DAVID MORRISON (United Kingdom); Two United Nations Plaza, 26th Floor, New York, NY 10017, USA; fax (212) 906-6479; e-mail info@uncdf.org; internet www.uncdf.org.

UNITED NATIONS DEVELOPMENT FUND FOR WOMEN (UNIFEM)

UNIFEM is the UN's lead agency in addressing the issues relating to women in development and promoting the rights of women worldwide. The Fund provides direct financial and technical support to enable low-income women in developing countries to increase earnings, gain access to labour-saving technologies and otherwise improve the quality of their lives. It also funds activities that include women in decision-making related to mainstream development projects. UNIFEM has supported the preparation of national reports in 30 countries and used the priorities identified in these reports and in other regional initiatives to formulate a Women's Development Agenda for the 21st century. Through these efforts, UNIFEM played an active role in the preparation for the UN Fourth World Conference on Women, which was held in Beijing, People's Republic of China, in September 1995. UNIFEM participated at a special session of the General Assembly convened in June 2000 to review the conference, entitled Women 2000: Gender Equality, Development and Peace for the 21st Century (Beijing + 5). In March 2001 UNIFEM, in collaboration with International Alert, launched a Millennium Peace Prize for Women. UNIFEM maintains that the empowerment of women is a key to combating the HIV/AIDS pandemic, in view of the fact that women and adolescent girls are often culturally, biologically and economically more vulnerable to infection and more likely to bear responsibility for caring for the sick. UNIFEM was a co-founder of WomenWatch (accessible online at www.un.org/womenwatch), a UN system-wide resource for the advancement of gender equality. UNIFEM manages the UN's Trust Fund in Support of Actions to Eliminate Violence Against Women (established in 1996), which in 2008 awarded US $22m. in support of 28 initiatives in 38 countries and territories. During November 2007–November 2008 UNIFEM undertook a campaign entitled 'Say NO to Violence against Women', to raise awareness of the issue and generate world-wide support for efforts to address it. UNIFEM programme expenditure in 2008 totalled $118.2m.

In July 2010 the UN General Assembly approved the establishment of a new UN Entity for Gender Equality and the Empowerment of Women (UN Women), which was to incorporate UNIFEM, as well as the functions of other gender specific UN bodies. UN Women was scheduled to become operational in January 2011.

Director: INÉS ALBERDI (Spain); 304 East 45th St, 15th Floor, New York, NY 10017, USA; tel. (212) 906-6400; fax (212) 906-6705; e-mail unifem@undp.org; internet www.unifem.org.

UNITED NATIONS VOLUNTEERS (UNV)

The United Nations Volunteers is an important source of middle-level skills for the UN development system supplied at modest cost, particularly in the least-developed countries (LDCs). Volunteers expand the scope of UNDP project activities by supplementing the work of international and host-country experts and by extending the influence of projects to local community levels. UNV also supports technical co-operation within and among the developing countries by encouraging volunteers from the countries themselves and by forming regional exchange teams comprising such volunteers. UNV is involved in areas such as peace-building, elections, human rights, humanitarian relief and community-based environmental programmes, in addition to development activities.

The UN International Short-term Advisory Resources (UNISTAR) Programme, which is the private sector development arm of UNV, has increasingly focused its attention on countries in the process of economic transition. Since 1994 UNV has administered UNDP's Transfer of Knowledge Through Expatriate Nationals (TOKTEN) programme, which was initiated in 1977 to enable specialists and professionals from developing countries to contribute to development efforts in their countries of origin through short-term technical assignments. In March 2000 UNV established an Online Volunteering Service to connect development organizations and volunteers using the internet; in 2008 3,742 online volunteers made their skills available through the Online Volunteering Service.

By 2010 the total number of people who had served as UNVs amounted to around 40,000, deployed to more than 140 countries. During 2008–09 some 7,600 national and international UNVs were deployed in 136 countries.

Executive Co-ordinator: FLAVIA PANSIERI (Italy); POB 260111, 53153 Bonn, Germany; tel. (228) 8152000; fax (228) 8152001; e-mail information@unvolunteers.org; internet www.unv.org.

United Nations Environment Programme—UNEP

Address: POB 30552, Nairobi 00100, Kenya.

Telephone: (20) 621234; **fax:** (20) 623927; **e-mail:** unepinfo@unep.org; **internet:** www.unep.org.

The United Nations Environment Programme was established in 1972 by the UN General Assembly, following recommendations of the 1972 UN Conference on the Human Environment, in Stockholm, Sweden, to encourage international co-operation in matters relating to the human environment.

Organization

(August 2010)

GOVERNING COUNCIL

The main functions of the Governing Council (which meets every two years in ordinary sessions, with special sessions taking place in the alternate years) are to promote international co-operation in the field of the environment and to provide general policy guidance for the direction and co-ordination of environmental programmes within the UN system. It comprises representatives of 58 states, elected by the UN General Assembly, for four-year terms, on a regional basis. The Global Ministerial Environment Forum (first convened in 2000) meets annually as part of the Governing Council's regular and special sessions. The Governing Council is assisted in its work by a Committee of Permanent Representatives.

SECRETARIAT

Offices and divisions at UNEP headquarters include the Offices of the Executive Director and Deputy Executive Director; the Secretariat for Governing Bodies; Offices for Evaluation and Oversight, Programme Co-ordination and Management, and Resource Mobilization; and divisions of communications and public information, early warning and assessment, environmental policy implementation, technology, industry and economics, regional co-operation and representation, environmental law and conventions, and Global Environment Facility co-ordination.

Executive Director: ACHIM STEINER (Germany).

Deputy Executive Director: ANGELA CROPPER (Trinidad and Tobago).

REGIONAL OFFICES

UNEP maintains six regional offices. These work to initiate and promote UNEP objectives and to ensure that all programme formulation and delivery meets the specific needs of countries and regions. They also provide a focal point for building national, sub-regional and regional partnership and enhancing local participation in UNEP initiatives. A co-ordination office has been established at headquarters to promote regional policy integration, to co-ordinate programme planning, and to provide necessary services to the regional offices.

Latin America and the Caribbean: Ciudad del Saber, Edif. 103, Avda Morse, Corregimiento de Ancón, Ciudad de Panamá, Panama;

tel. 305-3100; fax 305-3105; e-mail enlace@pnuma.org; internet www.pnuma.org.

UNEP Brasília Office: EQSW 103/104 Lote 1, Bloco C, CEP 70670-350, Setor Sudoeste, Brasília, Brazil; tel. (61) 3038-9233; fax (61) 3038-9239; e-mail pnuma.brasil@unep.org; internet www.pnuma.org/brasil/.

OTHER OFFICES

Convention on International Trade in Endangered Species of Wild Fauna and Flora (CITES): 15 chemin des Anémones, 1219 Châtelaine, Geneva, Switzerland; tel. 229178139; fax 227973417; e-mail info@cites.org; internet www.cites.org; Sec.-Gen. JOHN SCANLON (Australia).

Global Programme of Action for the Protection of the Marine Environment from Land-based Activities: POB 16227, 2500 BE The Hague, Netherlands; tel. (70) 3114460; fax (70) 3456648; e-mail gpa@unep.nl; internet www.gpa.unep.org; Sec.-Gen. DAVID OSBORN (Australia).

Regional Co-ordinating Unit for the Caribbean Environment Programme: 14–20 Port Royal St, Kingston, Jamaica; tel. 922-9267; fax 922-9292; e-mail rcu@cep.unep.org; internet www.cep.unep.org; Co-ordinator NELSON ANDRADE COLMENARES.

Secretariat of the Basel Convention: CP 356, 13–15 chemin des Anémones, 1219 Châtelaine, Geneva, Switzerland; tel. 229178218; fax 227973454; e-mail sbc@unep.ch; internet www.basel.int; Exec. Sec. KATHERINA KUMMER PEIRY.

Secretariat of the Multilateral Fund for the Implementation of the Montreal Protocol: 1800 McGill College Ave, 27th Floor, Montréal, QC, Canada H3A 3J6; tel. (514) 282-1122; fax (514) 282-0068; e-mail secretariat@unmfs.org; internet www.multilateralfund.org; Chief Officer MARIA NOLAN.

UNEP/CMS (Convention on the Conservation of Migratory Species of Wild Animals) Secretariat: Hermann-Ehlers-Str. 10, 53113 Bonn, Germany; tel. (228) 8152402; fax (228) 8152449; e-mail secretariat@cms.int; internet www.cms.int; Exec. Sec. ELIZABETH MARUMA MREMA.

UNEP Chemicals: International Environment House, 11–13 chemin des Anémones, 1219 Châtelaine, Geneva, Switzerland; tel. 229178192; fax 227973460; e-mail chemicals@unep.ch; internet www.chem.unep.ch; Head PER MENZONY BAKKEN (Norway).

UNEP Division of Technology, Industry and Economics: 15 rue de Milan, 75441 Paris, Cedex 09 France; tel. 1-44-37-14-50; fax 1-44-37-14-74; e-mail unep.tie@unep.fr; internet www.unep.fr; Dir SILVIE LEMMET (France).

UNEP International Environmental Technology Centre (IETC): 2–110 Ryokuchi koen, Tsurumi-ku, Osaka 538-0036, Japan; tel. (6) 6915-4581; fax (6) 6915-0304; e-mail ietc@unep.or.jp; internet www.unep.or.jp; Exec. Dir TAKEHIRO NAKAMURA.

UNEP Ozone Secretariat: POB 30552, Nairobi, Kenya; tel. (20) 762-3851; fax (20) 762-4691; e-mail ozoneinfo@unep.org; internet ozone.unep.org; Exec. Sec. MARCO GONZÁLEZ (Costa Rica).

UNEP-SCBD (Convention on Biological Diversity—Secretariat): 413 St Jacques St, Suite 800, Montréal, QC, Canada H2Y 1N9; tel. (514) 288-2220; fax (514) 288-6588; e-mail secretariat@cbd.int; internet www.cbd.int; Exec. Sec. AHMED DJOGHLAF (Algeria).

UNEP Secretariat for the UN Scientific Committee on the Effects of Atomic Radiation: Vienna International Centre, Wagramerstrasse 5, POB 500, 1400 Vienna, Austria; tel. (1) 26060-4330; fax (1) 26060-5902; e-mail malcolm.crick@unscear.org; internet www.unscear.org; Sec. Dr MALCOLM CRICK.

Activities

UNEP represents a voice for the environment within the UN system. It is an advocate, educator, catalyst and facilitator, promoting the wise use of the planet's natural assets for sustainable development. It aims to maintain a constant watch on the changing state of the environment; to analyse the trends; to assess the problems using a wide range of data and techniques; and to undertake or support projects leading to environmentally sound development. It plays a catalytic and co-ordinating role within and beyond the UN system. Many UNEP projects are implemented in co-operation with other UN agencies, particularly UNDP, the World Bank group, FAO, UNESCO and WHO. About 45 intergovernmental organizations outside the UN system and 60 international non-governmental organizations (NGOs) have official observer status on UNEP's Governing Council, and, through the Environment Liaison Centre in Nairobi, UNEP is linked to more than 6,000 non-governmental bodies concerned with the environment. UNEP also sponsors international conferences, programmes, plans and agreements regarding all aspects of the environment.

In February 1997 the Governing Council, at its 19th session, adopted a ministerial declaration (the Nairobi Declaration) on UNEP's future role and mandate, which recognized the organization as the principal UN body working in the field of the environment and as the leading global environmental authority, setting and overseeing the international environmental agenda. In June a special session of the UN General Assembly, referred to as 'Rio + 5', was convened to review the state of the environment and progress achieved in implementing the objectives of the UN Conference on Environment and Development (UNCED—known as the Earth Summit), that had been held in Rio de Janeiro, Brazil, in June 1992. UNCED had adopted Agenda 21 (a programme of activities to promote sustainable development in the 21st century) and the 'Rio + 5' meeting adopted a Programme for Further Implementation of Agenda 21 in order to intensify efforts in areas such as energy, freshwater resources and technology transfer. The meeting confirmed UNEP's essential role in advancing the Programme and as a global authority promoting a coherent legal and political approach to the environmental challenges of sustainable development. An extensive process of restructuring and realignment of functions was subsequently initiated by UNEP, and a new organizational structure reflecting the decisions of the Nairobi Declaration was implemented during 1999. UNEP played a leading role in preparing for the World Summit on Sustainable Development (WSSD), held in August–September 2002 in Johannesburg, South Africa, to assess strategies for strengthening the implementation of Agenda 21. Governments participating in the conference adopted the Johannesburg Declaration and WSSD Plan of Implementation, in which they strongly reaffirmed commitment to the principles underlying Agenda 21 and also pledged support to all internationally agreed development goals, including the UN Millennium Development Goals adopted by governments attending a summit meeting of the UN General Assembly in September 2000. Participating governments made concrete commitments to attaining several specific objectives in the areas of water, energy, health, agriculture and fisheries, and biodiversity. These included a reduction by one-half in the proportion of people world-wide lacking access to clean water or good sanitation by 2015, the restocking of depleted fisheries by 2015, a reduction in the ongoing loss in biodiversity by 2010, and the production and utilization of chemicals without causing harm to human beings and the environment by 2020. Participants determined to increase usage of renewable energy sources and to develop integrated water resources management and water efficiency plans. A large number of partnerships between governments, private sector interests and civil society groups were announced at the conference.

In May 2000 UNEP's first annual Global Ministerial Environment Forum (GMEF), was held in Malmö, Sweden, attended by environment ministers and other government delegates from more than 130 countries. Participants reviewed policy issues in the field of the environment and addressed issues such as the impact on the environment of population growth, the depletion of earth's natural resources, climate change and the need for fresh water supplies. The Forum issued the Malmö Declaration, which identified the effective implementation of international agreements on environmental matters at national level as the most pressing challenge for policy-makers. The Declaration emphasized the importance of mobilizing domestic and international resources and urged increased co-operation from civil society and the private sector in achieving sustainable development. The GMEF was subsequently convened annually.

EARLY WARNING AND ASSESSMENT

The Nairobi Declaration resolved that the strengthening of UNEP's information, monitoring and assessment capabilities was a crucial element of the organization's restructuring, in order to help establish priorities for international, national and regional action, and to ensure the efficient and accurate dissemination of information on emerging environmental trends and emergencies.

UNEP's Division of Early Warning and Assessment analyses the world environment, provides early warning information and assesses global and regional trends. It provides governments with data and helps them to use environmental information for decision-making and planning.

UNEP's Global Environment Outlook (GEO) process of environmental analysis and assessment, launched in 1995, is supported by an extensive network of collaborating centres. The fourth 'umbrella' report on the GEO process (*GEO-4*) was issued in October 2007, identifying climate change, land degradation and loss of biodiversity as the world's greatest environmental challenges. In recent years regional and national GEO reports have been issued focusing on Africa, the Andean region, the Atlantic and Indian oceans, Brazil, the Caucasus, Latin America and the Caribbean, North America, and the Pacific; and the following thematic GEO reports have been produced: *The Global Deserts Outlook* (2006) and *The Global Outlook for Ice and Snow* (2007). Various GEO technical reports have also been published.

In 1998 UNEP and the World Meteorological Organization (WMO) established the Intergovernmental Panel on Climate Change (IPCC, see below), as an objective source of scientific information about the warming of the earth's atmosphere. UNEP's Global International Waters Assessment (GIWA) considers all aspects of the world's water-related issues, in particular problems of shared transboundary waters, and of future sustainable management of water resources. UNEP is also a sponsoring agency of the Joint Group of Experts on the Scientific Aspects of Marine Environmental Pollution and contributes to the preparation of reports on the state of the marine environment and on the impact of land-based activities on that environment. In November 1995 UNEP published a Global Biodiversity Assessment, which was the first comprehensive study of biological resources throughout the world. The UNEP-World Conservation Monitoring Centre (UNEP-WCMC), established in June 2000 in Cambridge, United Kingdom, manages and interprets data concerning biodiversity and ecosystems, and makes the results available to governments and businesses. In October 2008 UNEP-WCMC, in partnership with the IUCN, launched a new online database of the world's national parks and protected areas; detailed images of more than 100,000 sites could be viewed on the site. In 2007 the Centre undertook the 2010 Biodiversity Indicators Programme, with the aim of supporting decision-making by governments so as to reduce the threat of extinction facing vulnerable species. UNEP is a partner in the International Coral Reef Action Network—ICRAN, which was established in 2000 to monitor, manage and protect coral reefs world-wide. In June 2001 UNEP launched the Millennium Ecosystem Assessment, which was completed in March 2005. Other major assessments undertaken include the International Assessment of Agricultural Science and Technology for Development; the Solar and Wind Energy Resource Assessment; the Regionally Based Assessment of Persistent Toxic Substances; the Land Degradation Assessment in Drylands; and the Global Methodology for Mapping Human Impacts on the Biosphere (GLOBIO) project.

In June 2010 delegates from 85 countries, meeting in Busan, Republic of Korea, at the third conference addressing the creation of a new Intergovernmental Science-Policy Platform on Biodiversity and Ecosystem Services (IPBES), adopted the Busan Outcome Document finalizing details of the establishment of the IPBES. The Platform, to be inaugurated pending approval of the Outcome Document by the UN General Assembly later in 2010, was to undertake, periodically, assessments, based on current scientific literature, of biodiversity and ecosystem outputs beneficial to humans, including timber, fresh water, fish and climatic stability.

UNEP's environmental information network includes the UNEP-INFOTERRA programme, which facilitates the exchange of environmental information through an extensive network of national 'focal points' (national environmental information centres, usually located in the relevant government ministry or agency). By August 2010 177 countries were participating in the network, whereby UNEP promotes public access to environmental information, as well as participation in environmental concerns. UNEP's information, monitoring and assessment structures also serve to enhance early-warning capabilities and to provide accurate information during an environmental emergency.

In September 2008 the UN Reduced Emissions from Deforestation and Forest Degradation (UN-REDD) Programme, a collaboration between UNEP, UNDP and FAO, was launched. Through a trust fund, established in July 2008, UN-REDD aimed to enable donors to pool resources to promote a transformation of forest resource use patterns.

ENVIRONMENTAL LAW AND CONVENTIONS

UNEP promotes international environmental legislation and the development of policy tools and guidelines in order to achieve the sustainable management of the world environment. It helps governments to implement multilateral environmental agreements, and to report on their results. At a national level it assists governments to develop and implement appropriate environmental instruments and aims to co-ordinate policy initiatives. Training in various aspects of environmental law and its applications is provided. The eighth Global Training Programme on Environmental Law and Policy was conducted by UNEP in November 2007, with participants from 62 countries; regional training programmes are also offered. UNEP supports the development of new legal, economic and other policy instruments to improve the effectiveness of existing environmental agreements. It updates a register of international environmental treaties, and publishes handbooks on negotiating and enforcing environmental law. It acts as the secretariat for a number of regional and global environmental conventions (see list above).

UNEP worked in collaboration with WMO to formulate the 1992 UN Framework Convention on Climate Change (UNFCCC), with the aim of reducing the emission of gases that have a warming effect on the atmosphere (known as greenhouse gases). (See Secretariat of the UN Framework Convention on Climate Change, below.)

In late June 2009 the first meeting was convened, in Belgrade, Serbia, of a new Consultative Group of Ministers and High-level Representatives on International Environment Governance; the meeting reviewed UNEP's role and stressed the linkages between sustainable environmental policies and development. From end-June–early July five successive UNEP Executive Directors and other prominent environmentalists met, in Glion, Switzerland, to discuss means of bringing about change in the functioning of the world economy to prioritize a sustainable approach to using and preserving the environment for the benefit of long-term human welfare.

UNEP was instrumental in the drafting of a Convention on Biological Diversity (CBD) to preserve the immense variety of plant and animal species, in particular those threatened with extinction. The Convention entered into force at the end of 1993; by August 2010 192 states and the European Union (EU) were parties to the CBD. The CBD's Cartagena Protocol on Biosafety (so called as it had been addressed at an extraordinary session of parties to the CBD convened in Cartagena, Colombia, in February 1999) was adopted at a meeting of parties to the CBD in January 2000, and entered into force in September 2003; by August 2010 the Protocol had been ratified by 159 states parties and the EU. The Protocol regulates the transboundary movement and use of living modified organisms resulting from biotechnology, in order to reduce any potential adverse effects on biodiversity and human health. It establishes an Advanced Informed Agreement procedure to govern the import of such organisms. In January 2002 UNEP launched a major project aimed at supporting developing countries with assessing the potential health and environmental risks and benefits of genetically modified (GM) crops, in preparation for the Protocol's entry into force. In February the parties to the CBD and other partners convened a conference on ways in which the traditional knowledge and practices of local communities could be preserved and used to conserve highly threatened species and ecosystems. The sixth conference of parties to the CBD, held in April 2002, adopted detailed voluntary guidelines concerning access to genetic resources and sharing the benefits attained from such resources with the countries and local communities where they originate; a global work programme on forests; and a set of guiding principles for combating alien invasive species. UNEP supports co-operation for biodiversity assessment and management in selected developing regions and for the development of strategies for the conservation and sustainable exploitation of individual threatened species (e.g. the Global Tiger Action Plan). It also provides assistance for the preparation of individual country studies and strategies to strengthen national biodiversity management and research. UNEP administers the Convention on International Trade in Endangered Species of Wild Flora and Fauna (CITES), which entered into force in 1975 and comprised 175 states parties at August 2010. CITES has special programmes on the protection of elephants, falcons, great apes, hawksbill turtles, sturgeons, tropical timber (jointly with the International Tropical Timber Organization), and bigleaf mahogany.

The Convention on the Conservation of Migratory Species of Wild Animals (CMS, also referred to as the Bonn Convention), concluded under UNEP auspices in 1979, aims to conserve migratory avian, marine and terrestrial species throughout the range of their migration. The secretariat of the CMS is hosted by UNEP. At August 2010 there were 114 states parties to the Convention. A number of agreements and memoranda of understanding (MOUs) have been concluded under the CMS.

An Agreement on the Conservation of Albatrosses and Petrels (ACAP) was concluded, under CMS auspices, in 2001 and entered into force in 2004. It is envisaged that the scope of ACAP, currently covering only the Southern Hemisphere, will be extended to include species from the Northern Hemisphere.

MoU have been concluded under the CMS relating to: the Ruddy-headed Goose (of Argentina and Chile), Grassland Birds of Southern South America, and High Andean Flamingoes and their Habitats.

UNEP is the principal UN agency for promoting environmentally sustainable water management. It regards the unsustainable use of water as one of the most urgent environmental issues, and estimates that two-thirds of the world's population will suffer chronic water shortages by 2025, owing to rising demand for drinking water as a result of growing populations, decreasing quality of water because of pollution, and increasing requirements of industries and agriculture. In 2000 UNEP adopted a new water policy and strategy, comprising assessment, management and co-ordination components. The Global International Waters Assessment (see above) is the primary framework for the assessment component. The management component includes the Global Programme of Action (GPA) for the Protection of the Marine Environment from Land-based Activities (adopted in November 1995), which focuses on the effects of pollution on freshwater resources, marine biodiversity and the coastal ecosystems of small island developing states. UNEP promotes international co-operation in the management of river basins and coastal areas and for the development of tools and guidelines to achieve the sustainable management of freshwater and coastal resources. In 2007 UNEP initiated a South-South Co-operation programme on technology and capacity-building for the management of water resources. UNEP provides scientific, technical and administrative support to facilitate the implementation and co-ordination of 14 regional seas conventions and 13 regional plans of action. UNEP's Regional Seas Programme aims to protect marine and coastal ecosystems, particularly by helping governments to put relevant legislation into practice.

UNEP administers the Basel Convention on the Control of Transboundary Movements of Hazardous Wastes and their Disposal, which entered into force in 1992 with the aim of preventing the uncontrolled movement and disposal of toxic and other hazardous wastes, particularly the illegal dumping of waste in developing countries by companies from industrialized countries. At August 2010 173 countries and the EU were parties to the Convention.

In 1996 UNEP, in collaboration with FAO, began to work towards promoting and formulating a legally binding international convention on prior informed consent (PIC) for hazardous chemicals and pesticides in international trade, extending a voluntary PIC procedure of information exchange undertaken by more than 100 governments since 1991. The Convention was adopted at a conference held in Rotterdam, Netherlands, in September 1998, and entered into force in February 2004. It aims to reduce risks to human health and the environment by restricting the production, export and use of hazardous substances and enhancing information exchange procedures. UNEP played a leading role in formulating a multilateral agreement to reduce and ultimately eliminate the manufacture and use of Persistent Organic Pollutants (POPs), which are considered to be a major global environmental hazard. The Stockholm Convention on POPs, targeting 12 particularly hazardous pollutants, was adopted by 127 countries in May 2001 and entered into force in May 2004. In May 2009 the fourth conference of parties to the Stockholm Convention agreed on a list of nine further POPs which were to be incorporated into the Convention in an amendment that was to enter into force in late August 2010.

In February 2009 140 governments agreed, under the auspices of UNEP, to launch negotiations on the development of an international treaty to combat toxic mercury emissions world-wide; pending the adoption of the planned treaty, it was agreed that a voluntary Global Mercury Partnership would be formed to address mercury pollution.

UNEP was the principal agency in formulating the 1987 Montreal Protocol to the Vienna Convention for the Protection of the Ozone Layer (1985), which provided for a 50% reduction in the production of chlorofluorocarbons (CFCs) by 2000. An amendment to the Protocol was adopted in 1990, which required complete cessation of the production of CFCs by 2000 in industrialized countries and by 2010 in developing countries. The Copenhagen Amendment, adopted in 1992, stipulated the phasing out of production of hydrochlorofluorocarbons (HCFCs) by 2030 in developed countries and by 2040 in developing nations. Subsequent amendments aimed to introduce a licensing system for all controlled substances, and imposed stricter controls on the import and export of HCFCs, and on the production and consumption of bromochloromethane (Halon-1011, an industrial solvent and fire extinguisher). In September 2007 the states parties to the Vienna Convention agreed to advance the deadline for the elimination of HCFCs: production and consumption were to be frozen by 2013, and were to be phased out in developed countries by 2020 and in developing countries by 2030. A Multilateral Fund for the Implementation of the Montreal Protocol was established in June 1990 to promote the use of suitable technologies and the transfer of technologies to developing countries. UNEP, UNDP, the World Bank and UNIDO are the sponsors of the Fund, which by 2009 had approved financing for more than 6,000 projects and activities in 148 developing countries at a cost of more than US $2,300m. The Fund's total budget for 2009–11 was $490m. In September 2009, following ratification by Timor-Leste, the Montreal Protocol, with 196 states parties, became the first agreement on the global environment to attain universal ratification.

GLOBAL ENVIRONMENT FACILITY

UNEP, together with UNDP and the World Bank, is an implementing agency of the Global Environment Facility (GEF), established in 1991 to help developing countries, and those undergoing economic transition, to meet the costs of projects that benefit the environment in six specific areas: biological diversity, climate change, international waters, depletion of the ozone layer, land degradation and persistent organic pollutants. Important cross-cutting components of these projects include capacity-building to allow countries to meet their obligations under international environmental agreements (described above), and adaptation to climate change. During 1991–2008 some 433 projects were approved by the GEF to be implemented by UNEP, with a total value amounting to US $708m. UNEP services the Scientific and Technical Advisory Panel, which provides expert advice on GEF programmes and operational strategies.

TECHNOLOGY, INDUSTRY AND ECONOMICS

UNEP's Division of Technology, Industry and Economics encourages governments and the private sector to develop and adopt policies and practices that are cleaner and safer, make efficient use of natural resources, incorporate environmental costs, ensure the environmentally sound management of chemicals, and reduce pollution and risks to human health and the environment. In collaboration with other organizations UNEP works to formulate international guidelines and agreements to address these issues. UNEP also promotes the transfer of appropriate technologies and organizes conferences and training workshops to provide sustainable production practices. Relevant information is disseminated through the International Cleaner Production Information Clearing House. UNEP, together with UNIDO, has established 34 National Cleaner Production Centres to promote a preventive approach to industrial pollution control. In October 1998 UNEP adopted an International Declaration on Cleaner Production, with a commitment to implement cleaner and more sustainable production methods and to monitor results. In 1997 UNEP and the Coalition for Environmentally Responsible Economies initiated the Global Reporting Initiative, which, with participation by corporations, business associations and other organizations, develops guidelines for voluntary reporting by companies on their economic, environmental and social performance. In April 2002 UNEP launched the 'Life Cycle Initiative', which evaluates the impact of products over their entire life cycle (from manufacture to disposal) and aims to assist governments, businesses and other consumers with adopting environmentally sound policies and practice, in view of the upward trend in global consumption patterns. UNEP Finance Initiatives (FI) is a programme encouraging banks, insurance companies and other financial institutions to invest in an environmentally responsible way: an annual FI Global Roundtable meeting is held, together with regional meetings. In April 2007 UNEP hosted the first Business for Environment meeting, on corporate environmental responsibility, in Singapore, and in October UNEP's 24th annual consultative meeting with representatives of business and industry took place in Sao Paulo, Brazil. During 2007 UNEP's Programme on Sustainable Consumption and Production established an International Panel for Sustainable Resource Management (comprising experts whose initial subjects of study were to be the environmental risks of biofuels and of metal recycling), and initiated forums for businesses and NGOs in this field.

In October 2008, in response to the global economic, fuel and food crises that escalated during that year, UNEP launched the *Green Economy Initiative (GEI)*, also known as the 'Global Green New Deal', which aimed to mobilize and refocus the global economy towards investments in clean technologies and the natural infrastructure (for example the infrastructures of forests and soils), with a view to, simultaneously, combating climate change and promoting employment. The UNEP Executive Director stated that the global crises were in part related to a broad market failure that promoted speculation while precipitating escalating losses of natural capital and nature-based assets, compounded by an over-reliance on finite, often subsidized fossil fuels. The GEI, which was initially to be operational for a two-year period, was to have three key dimensions: the compilation of the *Green Economy* report, to provide an analysis of how public policy might support markets in accelerating the transition towards a low-carbon green economy; the Green Jobs Initiative, a partnership launched by UNEP, the ILO and the International Trade Union Confederation in 2007 (and joined in 2008 by the International Organisation of Employers); and the Economics of Ecosystems and Biodiversity (TEEB) partnership project, focusing on valuation issues. In February 2009 UNEP issued a report, entitled *The environmental food crisis: environment's role in averting future food crises*, that urged a transformation in the way that food is produced, handled and disposed of, in order to feed the world's growing population and protect the environment; at that time the UNEP Executive Director emphasized the need for a 'Green revolution in a Green Economy'.

In 2009 UNEP was organizing the fifth regional meeting on sustainable consumption and production in Latin America and the Caribbean, to be held in Cartagena, Colombia, in September.

In 1994 UNEP inaugurated the International Environmental Technology Centre (IETC), based in Osaka, Japan. The Centre promotes and implements environmentally sound technologies for disaster prevention and post-disaster reconstruction; sustainable production and consumption; and water and sanitation (in particular waste-water management and more efficient use of rain-water).

The Division's Chemicals branch was established to promote the sound management of hazardous substances, central to which has been the International Register of Potentially Toxic Chemicals (IRPTC). UNEP aims to facilitate access to data on chemicals and hazardous wastes, in order to assess and control health and environmental risks, by using the IRPTC as a clearing house facility of relevant information and by publishing information and technical reports on the impact of the use of chemicals. UNEP provides technical support for implementing the Convention on Persistent Organic Pollutants (see above), encouraging the use of alternative pesticides, and monitoring the emission of pollutants through the burning of waste. UNEP administers the Strategic Approach to International Chemicals Management, adopted by the International Conference on Chemicals in 2006. With UNDP, UNEP helps governments to integrate sound management of chemicals into their development planning.

A Pollutant Release and Transfer Register (PRTR), for collecting and disseminating data on toxic emissions, is in effect in Mexico; the so-called *Registro de Emisiones y Transferencia de Contaminantes* was made mandatory in 2004.

The Division's OzonAction branch promotes information exchange, training and technological awareness, helping governments and industry in developing countries to undertake measures towards the cost-effective phasing-out of ozone-depleting substances (see under Environmental Law and Conventions, above).

UNEP also encourages the development of alternative and renewable sources of energy, as part of its efforts to mitigate climate change. To achieve this, UNEP has created the Global Network on Energy for Sustainable Development, linking 20 centres of excellence in industrialized and developing countries to conduct research and exchange information on environmentally sound energy technology resources. UNEP's Rural Energy Enterprise Development (REED) initiative helps the private sector to develop affordable 'clean' energy technologies, such as solar crop-drying and water-heating, wind-powered water pumps and efficient cooking stoves. UNEP is a member of the Global Bioenergy Partnership initiated by the G8 group of industrialized countries to support the sustainable use of biofuels. Through its Sustainable Transport Programme UNEP promotes the use of renewable fuels and the integration of environmental factors into transport planning, while the Sustainable Buildings and Construction Initiative promotes energy efficiency in the construction industry. In conjunction with UN-Habitat, UNDP, the World Bank and other organizations and institutions, UNEP promotes environmental concerns in urban planning and management through the Sustainable Cities Programme, and projects concerned with waste management, urban pollution and the impact of transportation systems.

During 2007 UNEP (with WMO and WTO) convened a second International Conference on Climate Change and Tourism, together with two meetings on sustainable tourism development and a conference on global eco-tourism.

In June 2009 UNEP and WTO jointly issued a report entitled *Trade and Climate Change*, reviewing the intersections between trade and climate change from the perspectives of: the science of climate change; economics; multilateral efforts to combat climate change; and the effects on trade of national climate change policies. During that month UNEP welcomed the OECD's 'Green Growth' declaration, which urged the adoption of targeted policy instruments to promote green investment, and emphasized commitment to the realization of an ambitious and comprehensive post-2012 global climate agreement.

REGIONAL CO-OPERATION AND REPRESENTATION

UNEP maintains six regional offices. These work to initiate and promote UNEP objectives and to ensure that all programme formulation and delivery meets the specific needs of countries and regions. They also provide a focal point for building national, sub-regional and regional partnerships and enhancing local participation in UNEP initiatives. UNEP's Division of Regional Co-operation promotes regional policy integration, co-ordinates programme planning, and provides necessary services to the regional offices. UNEP provides administrative support to several regional conventions, and organizes regional conferences and training programmes.

COMMUNICATIONS AND PUBLIC INFORMATION

UNEP's public education campaigns and outreach programmes promote community involvement in environmental issues. Further communication of environmental concerns is undertaken through coverage in the press, broadcasting and electronic media, publications (see below), an information centre service and special promotional events, including World Environment Day (whose slogan in 2010 was 'Many Species, One Planet, One Future'), the Focus on your World photography competition, and the awarding of the annual Sasakawa Prize (to recognize distinguished service to the environment by individuals and groups) and of the Champions of the Earth awards (for outstanding environmental leaders from each of UNEP's six regions). An annual Global Civil Society Forum (preceded by regional consultative meetings) is held in association with UNEP's Governing Council meetings. In April 2007 UNEP began a two-year programme on strengthening trade unions' participation in environmental processes. UNEP's Tunza programme for children and young people includes conferences, online discussions and publications. UNEP co-operates with the International Olympic Committee, the Commonwealth Games organizing body and international federations for football, athletics and other sports to encourage 'carbon neutral' sporting events and to use sport as a means of outreach. UNEP's Billion Tree Campaign, initiated in February 2007, encouraged governments, community organizations and individuals to plant 1,000m. trees before the end of the year, and exceeded that target; by August 2010 some 11,832m. trees had been planted under the continuing campaign.

Finance

The projected budget approved by the Governing Council for UNEP's activities during 2010–11 totalled US $493.9m. UNEP is allocated a contribution from the regular budget of the United Nations, and derives most of its finances from voluntary contributions to the Environment Fund and to trust funds.

Publications

Annual Report.

CBTF (Capacity Building Task Force on Trade, Environment and Development) Newsletter.

DEWA / GRID Europe Quarterly Bulletin. E+ (Energy, Climate and Sustainable Development).

The Environment and Poverty Times.

Global 500.

Great Apes Survival Project Newsletter.

IETC (International Environmental Technology Centre) Insight.

Life Cycle Initiatives Newsletter.

Our Planet (quarterly).

Planet in Peril: Atlas of Current Threats to People and the Environment.

ROA (Regional Office for Africa) News (2 a year).

Tourism Focus (2 a year).

RRC.AP (Regional Resource Centre for Asia and the Pacific) Newsletter.

Sustainable Consumption Newsletter.

Tunza (quarterly magazine for children and young people).

UNEP Chemicals Newsletter.

UNEP Year Book.

World Atlas of Biodiversity.

World Atlas of Coral Reefs.

World Atlas of Desertification.

Studies, reports (including the *Global Environment Outlook* series), legal texts, technical guidelines, etc.

Associated Bodies

Intergovernmental Panel on Climate Change (IPCC): established in 1988 by WMO and UNEP; comprises some 3,000 scientists as well as other experts and representatives of all UN member governments. Approximately every five years the IPCC assesses all available scientific, technical and socio-economic information on anthropogenic climate change. The IPCC provides, on request, scientific, technical and socio-economic advice to the Conference of the Parties to the UN Framework Convention on Climate Change (UNFCCC) and to its subsidiary bodies, and compiles reports on specialized topics, such as *Aviation and the Global Atmosphere* and *Regional Impacts of Climate Change.* The IPCC informs and guides, but does not prescribe, policy. In December 1995 the IPCC presented evidence to 120 governments, demonstrating 'a discernible human influence on global climate'. In 2001 the Panel issued its *Third Assessment Report,* in which it confirmed this finding and presented new and strengthened evidence attributing most global climate warming over the past 50 years to human activities. The IPCC's *Fourth Assessment Report*, the final instalment of which was issued in November 2007, concluded that increases in global average air and ocean temperatures, widespread melting of snow and ice, and the rising global average sea level, demonstrate that the warming of the climate system is unequivocal; that observational evidence from all continents and most oceans indicates that many natural systems are being affected by regional climate changes; that a global assessment of data since 1970 has shown that it is likely that anthropogenic warming has had a discernable influence on many physical and biological systems; and that other effects of regional climate changes are emerging. The *Fourth Assessment Report* was awarded a share of the Nobel Peace Prize for 2007. In January 2010 the IPCC accepted criticism that an assertion in the 2007 *Report*, concerning the rate at which Himalayan glaciers were melting, was exaggerated, and in February 2010 the Panel agreed that the *Report* had overstated the proportion of the Netherlands below sea level. In late February it was announced that an independent board of scientists would be appointed to review the work of the IPCC. The *Fifth Assessment Report* of the IPCC was to be published in 2014.

Chair.: RAJENDRA K. PACHAURI (India).

Secretariat of the UN Framework Convention on Climate Change: Haus Carstanjen, Martin-Luther-King-Strasse 8, 53175 Bonn, Germany; tel. (228) 815-1000; fax (228) 815-1999; e-mail secretariat@unfccc.int; internet unfccc.int; WMO and UNEP worked together to formulate the Convention, in response to the first report of the IPCC, issued in August 1990, which predicted an increase in the concentration of 'greenhouse' gases (i.e. carbon dioxide and other gases that have a warming effect on the atmosphere) owing to human activity. The UNFCCC was signed in May 1992 and formally adopted at the UN Conference on Environment and Development, held in June. It entered into force in March 1994. It committed countries to submitting reports on measures being taken to reduce the emission of greenhouse gases and recommended stabilizing these emissions at 1990 levels by 2000; however, this was not legally binding. In July 1996, at the second session of the Conference of the Parties (COP) of the Convention, representatives of developed countries declared their willingness to commit to legally binding objectives for emission limitations in a specified timetable. Multilateral negotiations ensued to formulate a mandatory treaty on greenhouse gas emissions. At the third COP, held in Kyoto, Japan, in December 1997, 38 industrial nations endorsed mandatory reductions of combined emissions of the six major gases by an average of 5.2% during the five-year period 2008–12, to pre-1990 levels. The so-called Kyoto Protocol was to enter into force on being ratified by at least 55 countries party to the UNFCCC, including industrialized countries with combined emissions of carbon dioxide in 1990 accounting for at least 55% of the total global greenhouse gas emissions by developed nations. Many of the Protocol's operational details, however, remained to be determined. The fourth COP, convened in Buenos Aires, Argentina, in November 1998, adopted a plan of action to promote implementation of the UNFCCC and to finalize the operational details of the Kyoto Protocol. These included the Clean Development Mechanism, by which industrialized countries may obtain credits towards achieving their reduction targets by assisting developing countries to implement emission-reducing measures, and a system of trading emission quotas. The fifth COP, held in Bonn, Germany, in October–November 1999, and the first session of the sixth COP, convened in The Hague, Netherlands, in November 2000, failed to reach agreement on the implementation of the Buenos Aires plan of action, owing to a lack of consensus on several technical matters, including the formulation of an effective mechanism for ascertaining compliance under the Kyoto Protocol, and adequately defining a provision of the Protocol under which industrialized countries may obtain credits towards achieving their reduction targets in respect of the absorption of emissions resulting from activities in the so-called land-use, land-use change and forestry (LULUCF) sector. Further, informal, talks were held in Ottawa, Canada, in early December. Agreement on implementing the Buenos Aires action plan was finally achieved at the second session of the sixth COP, held in Bonn in July 2001. The seventh COP, convened in Marrakech, Morocco, in October–November, formally adopted the decisions reached in July, and elected 15 members to the Executive Board of the Clean Development Mechanism. The eighth COP, convened in New Delhi, India, in October–November 2002, issued the Delhi Declaration, urging states parties that had not done so already to ratify the Kyoto Protocol, and urging the integration of climate change objectives in key areas into national sustainable development strategies. In March the USA (the most prolific national producer of harmful gas emissions) announced that it would not ratify the Kyoto Protocol. A major advance achieved at the ninth COP was agreement on the modalities and scope for carbon-absorbing forest management projects in the Clean Development Mechanism. The Kyoto Protocol eventually entered into force on 16 February 2005, 90 days after its ratification by Russia. By December 2009 the Protocol had received ratifications from 189 states and the European Community, including ratifications by industrialized nations with combined responsibility for 63.7% of greenhouse gas emissions by developed nations in 1990 (although excluding participation by the USA). Negotiations commenced in May 2007 on establishing an international agreement to succeed the Kyoto Protocol after its expiry in 2012. Participants in COP 13, convened in Bali, Indonesia, in December 2007, adopted the Bali Roadmap, detailing a two-year process leading to the planned conclusion of the schedule of negotiations in December 2009. Further rounds of talks were held during 2008 in Bangkok, Thailand (March–April); Bonn (June); and in Accra, Ghana (August). The UN Climate Change Conference (COP 14), convened in Poznań, Poland, in December 2008, finalized the Kyoto Protocol's Adaptation Fund, which was to finance projects and programmes in developing signatory states that were particularly vulnerable to the adverse effects of climate change. Addressing the Conference, the UN Secretary-General urged the advancement of a 'Green New Deal', to address simultaneously the ongoing global climate and economic crises. COP 15 was held, concurrently with the fifth meeting of parties to the Kyoto Protocol, in Copenhagen, Denmark, in December 2009. Heads of state and government and other delegates attending the Conference approved the Copenhagen Accord, which determined that international co-operative action should be taken, in the context of sustainable development, to reduce global greenhouse gas emissions so as to hold the ongoing increase in global temperature below 2°C. It was agreed that enhanced efforts should be undertaken to reduce vulnerability to climate change in developing countries, with special reference to least developed countries, small island states and Africa. Developed countries agreed to pursue the achievement by 2020 of strengthened carbon emissions targets, while developing nations were to implement actions to slow down growth in emissions. The need to reduce deforestation and forest degradation, and thereby enhance removals of greenhouse gas emissions, was emphasized by the Accord. A new Copenhagen Green Climate Fund was inaugurated to support climate change mitigation actions in developing countries, and a Technology Mechanism was also established, with the aim of accelerating technology development and transfer in support of climate change adaptation and mitigation activities.

Executive Secretary: CHRISTIANA FIGUERES (Costa Rica).

United Nations High Commissioner for Refugees—UNHCR

Address: CP 2500, 1211 Geneva 2 dépôt, Switzerland.

Telephone: 227398111; **fax:** 227397312; **e-mail:** unhcr@unhcr.org; **internet:** www.unhcr.org.

The Office of the High Commissioner was established in 1951 to provide international protection for refugees and to seek durable solutions to their problems. In 1981 UNHCR was awarded the Nobel Peace Prize.

Organization

(August 2010)

HIGH COMMISSIONER

The High Commissioner is elected by the United Nations General Assembly on the nomination of the Secretary-General, and is responsible to the General Assembly and to the UN Economic and Social Council (ECOSOC).

High Commissioner: ANTÓNIO MANUEL DE OLIVEIRA GUTERRES (Portugal).

Deputy High Commissioner: L. CRAIG JOHNSTONE (USA).

EXECUTIVE COMMITTEE

The Executive Committee of the High Commissioner's Programme (ExCom), established by ECOSOC, gives the High Commissioner policy directives in respect of material assistance programmes and advice in the field of international protection. In addition, it oversees UNHCR's general policies and use of funds. ExCom, which comprises representatives of 66 states, both members and non-members of the UN, meets once a year.

ADMINISTRATION

Headquarters, based in Geneva, Switzerland, include the Executive Office, comprising the offices of the High Commissioner, the Deputy High Commissioner and the two Assistant High Commissioners (for Operations and Protection). The Inspector General, the Director of the UNHCR liaison office in New York, and the Director of the Ethics Office (established in 2008) report directly to the High Commissioner. The principal administrative Divisions cover: International Protection; Programme and Support Management; Emergency Security and Supply; Financial and Administrative Management; Human Resources Management; External Relations; and Information Systems and Telecommunications. A UNHCR Global Service Centre, based in Budapest, Hungary, was inaugurated in 2008 to provide administrative support to the Headquarters. There are five regional bureaux covering Africa, Asia and the Pacific, Europe, the Americas, and North Africa and the Middle East. In 2009 UNHCR employed around 6,600 regular staff, of whom more than 5,800 were working in the field. At that time there were 260 UNHCR offices in 118 countries.

All UNHCR personnel are required to sign, and all interns, contracted staff and staff from partner organizations are required to acknowledge, a Code of Conduct, to which is appended the UN Secretary-General's bulletin on special measures for protection from sexual exploitation and sexual abuse. The post of Senior Adviser to the High Commissioner on Gender Issues, within the Executive Office, was established in 2004.

OFFICES IN SOUTH AND CENTRAL AMERICA AND THE CARIBBEAN

Regional Office for the USA and the Caribbean: 1775 K St, NW, Suite 300, Washington, DC 20006, USA; e-mail usawa@unhcr.ch.

Regional Office for Northern South America: Apdo 69045, Caracas 1062-A, Venezuela; e-mail venca@unhcr.ch.

Regional Office for Southern South America: Cerrito 836, 10°, Buenos Aires 1010, Argentina; e-mail argbu@unhcr.ch.

Activities

The competence of the High Commissioner extends to any person who, owing to well-founded fear of being persecuted for reasons of race, religion, nationality or political opinion, is outside the country of his or her nationality and is unable or, owing to such fear or for reasons other than personal convenience, remains unwilling to accept the protection of that country; or who, not having a nationality and being outside the country of his or her former habitual residence, is unable or, owing to such fear or for reasons other than personal convenience, is unwilling to return to it. This competence may be extended, by resolutions of the UN General Assembly and decisions of ExCom, to cover certain other 'persons of concern', in addition to refugees meeting these criteria. Refugees who are assisted by other UN agencies, or who have the same rights or obligations as nationals of their country of residence, are outside the mandate of UNHCR.

In recent years there has been a significant shift in UNHCR's focus of activities. Increasingly UNHCR has been called upon to support people who have been displaced within their own country (i.e. with similar needs to those of refugees but who have not crossed an international border) or those threatened with displacement as a result of armed conflict. In addition, greater support has been given to refugees who have returned to their country of origin, to assist their reintegration, and UNHCR is working to enable local communities to support the returnees, frequently through the implementation of Quick Impact Projects (QIPs). In 2004 UNHCR led the formulation of a UN system-wide Strategic Plan for internally displaced persons (IDPs). During 2005 the UN's Inter-Agency Standing Committee (IASC), concerned with co-ordinating the international response to humanitarian disasters, developed a concept of organizing agency assistance to IDPs through the institutionalization of a 'Cluster Approach', currently comprising 11 core areas of activity (see OCHA). UNHCR is the lead agency for the clusters on Camp Co-ordination and Management (in conflict situations; the International Organization for Migration leads that cluster in natural disaster situations), Emergency Shelter, and (jointly with OHCHR and UNICEF) Protection.

In the mid-2000s UNHCR widened its scope from its (mandate to protect and assist people fleeing persecution and violence) in response to the enormous impact of two devastating natural disasters. Following the series of tidal waves (tsunamis), emanating from an earthquake in the Indian Ocean, that devastated coastal regions in 14 countries in South and South-East Asia and East Africa in December 2004, UNHCR requested emergency funding totalling US $77m. in support of a 12-month relief operation to provide shelter, non-food relief supplies and logistical support for survivors in Aceh, Indonesia (close to the epicentre of the earthquake), Sri Lanka and Somalia. This was part of a pan-UN inter-agency appeal for $1,100m. In October 2005 UNHCR provided an immediate response to support survivors of the South Asian earthquake that struck northern Pakistan and bordering areas of India and Afghanistan. In May 2008 UNHCR donated tents to provide shelter for some 55,000 people following a devastating earthquake in Sichuan province, People's Republic of China.

UNHCR has been increasingly concerned with the problem of statelessness, where people have no legal nationality, and promotes new accessions to the 1954 Convention Relating to the Status of Stateless Persons and the 1964 Convention on the Reduction of Statelessness. UNHCR maintains that a significant proportion of the global stateless population has not hitherto been systematically identified. In October 2006 ExCom urged member states to share with UNHCR data on stateless persons and on persons with undetermined nationality.

In July 2006 UNHCR issued a '10 Point Plan of Action on Refugee Protection and Mixed Migration' (*10 Point Plan*), a framework document detailing 10 principal areas in which UNHCR might make an impact in supporting member states with the development of comprehensive migration strategies. The 10 areas covered by the Plan were as follows: co-operation among key players; data collection and analysis; protection-sensitive entry systems; reception arrangements; mechanisms for profiling and referral; differentiated processes and procedures; solutions for refugees; addressing secondary movements; return of non-refugees and alternative migration options; and information strategy. A revised version of the *10 Point Plan* was published in January 2007. Addressing the annual meeting of ExCom in October 2007 the High Commissioner, while emphasizing that UNHCR was not mandated to manage migration, urged a concerted international effort to raise awareness and comprehension of the broad patterns (including the scale, complexity, and causes—such as poverty and the pursuit of improved living standards) of global displacement and migration. In order to fulfil UNHCR's mandate to support refugees and others in need of protection within ongoing mass movements of people, he urged better recognition of the mixed nature of many 21st century population flows, often comprising both economic migrants and refugees, asylum-seekers and victims of trafficking who required detection and support. It was also acknowledged that conflict and persecution—the traditional reasons for flight—were being increasingly compounded by factors such as environmental degradation and the detrimental effects of climate change. A Dialogue on Protection Challenges, convened by the High Commissioner in December 2007, agreed that the *10 Point Plan* should be elaborated further. Regional activities based on the Plan have been focused on Central America, Western Africa, Eastern Africa and Southern Asia; and on countries along the Eastern and South-Eastern borders of European Union member states.

In 2009 UNHCR launched the first annual Global Needs Assessment (GNA), with the aim of mapping comprehensively the situation and needs of populations of concern falling under the mandate of the Office. The GNA was to represent a blueprint for planning and decision-making for UNHCR, populations of concern, governments and other partners. In 2008 a pilot GNA, undertaken in eight countries, revealed significant unmet protection needs including in education, food security and nutrition, distribution of non-food items, health, access to clean water and sanitation, shelter, and prevention of sexual violence.

At December 2008 the total global population of concern to UNHCR, based on provisional figures, amounted to 34.4m. At that time the refugee population world-wide totalled 10.5m. UNHCR was also concerned with some 603,943 recently returned refugees, 14.4m. IDPs, 1.4m. returned IDPs, 6.6m. stateless persons, 827,323 asylum-seekers, and 166,857 others. UNHCR maintains an online statistical population database, accessible at www.unhcr.org/statistics/populationdatabase.

World Refugee Day, sponsored by UNHCR, is held annually on 20 June.

INTERNATIONAL PROTECTION

As laid down in the Statute of the Office, UNHCR's primary function is to extend international protection to refugees and its second function is to seek durable solutions to their problems. In the exercise of its mandate UNHCR seeks to ensure that refugees and asylum-seekers are protected against *refoulement* (forcible return), that they receive asylum, and that they are treated according to internationally recognized standards. UNHCR pursues these objectives by a variety of means that include promoting the conclusion and ratification by states of international conventions for the protection of refugees. UNHCR promotes the adoption of liberal practices of asylum by states, so that refugees and asylum-seekers are granted admission, at least on a temporary basis.

The most comprehensive instrument concerning refugees that has been elaborated at the international level is the 1951 United Nations Convention relating to the Status of Refugees. This Convention, the scope of which was extended by a Protocol adopted in 1967, defines the rights and duties of refugees and contains provisions dealing with a variety of matters which affect the day-to-day lives of refugees. The application of the Convention and its Protocol is supervised by UNHCR. Important provisions for the treatment of refugees are also contained in a number of instruments adopted at the regional level. These include the 1969 Convention Governing the Specific Aspects of Refugee Problems adopted by the Organization of African Unity (now the African Union—AU) member states in 1969, the European Agreement on the Abolition of Visas for Refugees, and the 1969 American Convention on Human Rights. In October 2009 AU member states adopted the AU Convention for the Protection and Assistance of IDPs in Africa, the first legally binding international treaty providing legal protection and support to internally displaced populations.

UNHCR has actively encouraged states to accede to the 1951 United Nations Refugee Convention and the 1967 Protocol: 147 states had acceded to either or both of these basic refugee instruments by January 2010. An increasing number of states have also adopted domestic legislation and/or administrative measures to implement the international instruments, particularly in the field of procedures for the determination of refugee status. UNHCR has sought to address the specific needs of refugee women and children, and has also attempted to deal with the problem of military attacks on refugee camps, by adopting and encouraging the acceptance of a set of principles to ensure the safety of refugees. In recent years it has formulated a strategy designed to address the fundamental causes of refugee flows. In 2001, in response to widespread concern about perceived high numbers of asylum-seekers and large-scale international economic migration and human trafficking, UNHCR initiated a series of Global Consultations on International Protection with the signatories to the 1951 Convention and 1967 Protocol, and other interested parties, with a view to strengthening both the application and scope of international refugee legislation. A consultation of 156 Governments, convened in Geneva, in December 2001, reaffirmed commitment to the central role played by the Convention and Protocol. The final consultation, held in May 2002, focused on durable solutions and the protection of refugee women and children. Subsequently, based on the findings of the Global Consultations process, UNHCR developed an Agenda on Protection with six main objectives: strengthening the implementation of the 1951 Convention and 1967 Protocol; the protection of refugees within broader migration movements; more equitable sharing of burdens and responsibilities and building of capacities to receive and protect refugees; addressing more effectively security-related concerns; increasing efforts to find durable solutions; and meeting the protection needs of refugee women and children. The Agenda was endorsed by ExCom in October 2002. In September of that year the High Commissioner for Refugees launched the *Convention Plus* initiative, which aimed to address contemporary global asylum issues by developing, on the basis of the Agenda on Protection, international agreements and measures to supplement the 1951 Convention and 1967 Protocol.

UNHCR is one of the 10 co-sponsors of UNAIDS.

ASSISTANCE ACTIVITIES

The first phase of an assistance operation uses UNHCR's capacity of emergency response. This enables UNHCR to address the immediate needs of refugees at short notice, for example, by employing specially trained emergency teams and maintaining stockpiles of basic equipment, medical aid and materials. A significant proportion of UNHCR expenditure is allocated to the next phase of an operation, providing 'care and maintenance' in stable refugee circumstances. This assistance can take various forms, including the provision of food, shelter, medical care and essential supplies. Also covered in many instances are basic services, including education and counselling.

As far as possible, assistance is geared towards the identification and implementation of durable solutions to refugee problems—this being the second statutory responsibility of UNHCR. Such solutions generally take one of three forms: voluntary repatriation, local integration or resettlement in another country. Where voluntary repatriation, increasingly the preferred solution, is feasible, the Office assists refugees to overcome obstacles preventing their return to their country of origin. This may be done through negotiations with governments involved, or by providing funds either for the physical movement of refugees or for the rehabilitation of returnees once back in their own country. UNHCR supports the implementation of the Guidance Note on Durable Solutions for Displaced Persons, adopted in 2004 by the UN Development Group.

When voluntary repatriation is not an option, efforts are made to assist refugees to integrate locally and to become self-supporting in their countries of asylum. This may be done either by granting loans to refugees, or by assisting them, through vocational training or in other ways, to learn a skill and to establish themselves in gainful occupations. One major form of assistance to help refugees re-establish themselves outside camps is the provision of housing. In cases where resettlement through emigration is the only viable solution to a refugee problem, UNHCR negotiates with governments in an endeavour to obtain suitable resettlement opportunities, to encourage liberalization of admission criteria and to draw up special immigration schemes. During 2008 an estimated 67,000 refugees were resettled under UNHCR auspices.

In the 1990s UNHCR consolidated efforts to integrate certain priorities into its programme planning and implementation, as a standard discipline in all phases of assistance. The considerations include awareness of specific problems confronting refugee women, the needs of refugee children, the environmental impact of refugee programmes and long-term development objectives. In an effort to improve the effectiveness of its programmes, UNHCR has initiated a process of delegating authority, as well as responsibility for operational budgets, to its regional and field representatives, increasing flexibility and accountability. A Policy Development and Evaluation Service reviews systematically UNHCR's operational effectiveness.

THE AMERICAS AND THE CARIBBEAN

In December 1994 a meeting was held, in San José, Costa Rica, to commemorate the 10th anniversary of the November 1984 Cartagena Declaration, which had provided a comprehensive framework for refugee protection in the region. The meeting adopted the San José Declaration on Refugees and Displaced Persons, which aimed to harmonize legal criteria and procedures to consolidate actions for durable solutions of voluntary repatriation and local integration in the region. UNHCR's efforts in the region subsequently emphasized legal issues and refugee protection, while assisting governments to formulate national legislation on asylum and refugees. UNHCR's activities in Central and South America are currently guided by the Mexico Plan of Action (MPA), adopted in November 2004 by regional leaders convened in Mexico City to commemorate the 20th anniversary of the Cartagena Declaration. The MPA aims to address ongoing population displacement problems in Latin America, with a particular focus on the humanitarian crisis in Colombia and the border areas of its neighbouring countries (see below), and the increasing numbers of refugees concentrated in urban centres in the region. The Cities of Solidarity pillar of the MPA assists UNHCR with facilitating the local integration and self-sufficiency of people in urban areas who require international protection; the Borders of Solidarity pillar addresses protection at international borders; and the Resettlement in Solidarity pillar promotes co-operation in resettling refugees. A Regional Conference on Refugee Protection and International Migration in the Americas was held in San José, Costa Rica, in November 2009.

In May 1989, when an International Conference on Central American Refugees (CIREFCA) was held in Guatemala, there were some 146,400 refugees receiving UNHCR assistance (both for emergency relief and for longer-term self-sufficiency programmes) in the region, as well as an estimated 1.8m. other refugees and displaced persons. UNHCR and UNDP were designated as the principal UN organizations to implement the CIREFCA plan of action for the repatriation or resettlement of refugees, alongside national co-ordinating committees. UNHCR QIPs were implemented in the transport, health, agricultural production and other sectors to support returnee reintegration (of both refugees and IDPs) into local communities, and to promote the self-sufficiency of the returning populations. Implementation of UNHCR's programme for the repatriation of some 45,000 Guatemalan refugees in Mexico began in January 1993. UNHCR initiated projects to support the reintegration of Guatemalan returnees, and in 1994–95 undertook a campaign to clear undetonated explosives in forest areas where they had resettled. The CIREFCA process was formally concluded in June 1994, by which time some 118,000 refugees had voluntarily returned to their countries of origin under the auspices of the programme, while thousands of others had integrated into their host countries. From 1996 several thousand Guatemalan refugees have received Mexican citizenship under a fast-track naturalization scheme; the programme to naturalize long-standing Guatemalan refugees was terminated in 2005. At December 2008 1,073 refugees remained in Mexico.

In 1999 the Colombian Government approved an operational plan proposed by UNHCR to address a massive population displacement that had arisen in that country in recent years (escalating from 1997), as a consequence of ongoing internal conflict and alleged human rights abuses committed by armed groups. Significant cross-border movements of Colombian refugees into neighbouring countries prompted UNHCR to intensify its border-monitoring activities during the early 2000s to enhance its capacity to forecast and react to new population movements. UNHCR has assisted with the implementation of an IDP registration plan, provided training in emergency response to displacements, and supported ongoing changes in Colombia's legislative framework for IDPs. UNHCR has also co-operated with UNICEF to improve the provision of education to displaced children. UNHCR works to provide legal and humanitarian support to more than 400,000 IDPs within Colombia and to provide legal protection and educational and medical support to around 500,000 Colombians who have fled to but not sought asylum in neighbouring countries. The Office's strategy for supporting countries receiving displaced Colombians (of whom the majority were not registered as refugees) have included border-monitoring activities, entailing the early warning of potential refugee movements, and provision of detailed country-of-origin data. Within Colombia UNHCR's protection activities have included ensuring an adequate, functioning legal framework for the protection of IDPs and enabling domestic institutions to supervise compliance with national legislation regarding the rights of IDPs; strengthening representation for IDPs and other vulnerable people; and developing local protection networks. UNHCR also aimed to advise on public policy formulation in the areas of emergency response, IDP registration, health, education, housing, income-generation and protection of policy rights; and to promote durable solutions for IDPs, in particular local integration. Conditions in most areas are regarded as unsafe for voluntary returns. The Office has built up stockpiles of relief items in neighbouring countries and has developed contingency plans with other partners to enable the rapid deployment of personnel to border areas should the exodus of refugees from Colombia intensify further. At the end of 2008 around 3m. IDPs within Colombia remained of concern to UNHCR. By that time an estimated 100,637 Colombians (18,337 UNHCR-assisted) were living as refugees in Ecuador, while 201,094 (20,776 UNHCR-assisted) Colombians were sheltering in Venezuela; the majority of these (in both countries) had not sought official protection but were living in 'refugee-like' situations.

Following the devastating earthquake that struck Haiti in January 2010, UNHCR provided assistance to the international humanitarian response operation in the areas of camp registration and profiling matters; shelter co-ordination; and supporting OHCHR in its efforts to assist the displaced population outside Port-au-Prince and earthquake survivors living outside registered camps. UNHCR also implemented a number of Quick Impact Projects, and provided material support to Haitian evacuees in the neighbouring Dominican Republic.

In 2008 Ecuador participated in a pilot project for UNHCR's Global Needs Assessment (formally inaugurated in 2009, see above). Consequently, in July 2008, UNHCR and the Ecuadorian authorities determined to formulate a comprehensive plan of action to assist the population of concern in Ecuador over a two-year period.

CO-OPERATION WITH OTHER ORGANIZATIONS

UNHCR works closely with other UN agencies, intergovernmental organizations and non-governmental organizations (NGOs) to increase the scope and effectiveness of its operations. Within the UN system UNHCR co-operates, principally, with the WFP in the distribution of food aid, UNICEF and WHO in the provision of family welfare and child immunization programmes, OCHA in the delivery of emergency humanitarian relief, UNDP in development-related activities and the preparation of guidelines for the continuum of emergency assistance to development programmes, and the Office of the UN High Commissioner for Human Rights. UNHCR also has close working relationships with the International Committee of the Red Cross and the International Organization for Migration. In 2009 UNHCR was working with 640 NGOs as 'implementing partners', enabling UNHCR to broaden the use of its resources while maintaining a co-ordinating role in the provision of assistance.

TRAINING

UNHCR organizes training programmes and workshops to enhance the capabilities of field workers and non-UNHCR staff, in the following areas: the identification and registration of refugees; people-orientated planning; resettlement procedures and policies; emergency response and management; security awareness; stress management; and the dissemination of information through the electronic media.

Finance

The United Nations' regular budget finances a proportion of UNHCR's administrative expenditure. The majority of UNHCR's programme expenditure (about 98%) is funded by voluntary contributions, mainly from governments. The Private Sector and Public Affairs Service aims to increase funding from non-governmental donor sources, for example by developing partnerships with foundations and corporations. Following approval of the Unified Annual Programme Budget any subsequently identified requirements are managed in the form of Supplementary Programmes, financed by separate appeals. The total Unified Annual Programme Budget for 2009 was projected at US $1,275.5m.

Publications

Global Trends (annually).

Refugees (quarterly, in English, French, German, Italian, Japanese and Spanish).

Refugee Resettlement: An International Handbook to Guide Reception and Integration.

Refugee Survey Quarterly.

Refworld (annually).

Sexual and Gender-based Violence Against Refugees, Returnees and Displaced Persons: Guidelines for Prevention and Response.

The State of the World's Refugees (every 2 years).

Statistical Yearbook (annually).

UNHCR Handbook for Emergencies.

Press releases, reports.

Statistics

PERSONS OF CONCERN TO UNHCR IN LATIN AMERICA AND THE CARIBBEAN
(at 31 December 2008, provisional figures*)

Host Country	Refugees†	Asylum-seekers	Returnees	Others
Argentina	2,845	730	1	—
Brazil	3,852	517	—	—
Chile	1,613	890	—	—
Colombia	170	82	31	3,000,011‡
Costa Rica	18,136	463	105	—
Ecuador	101,398	33,919	—	—
Mexico	1,055	18	—	—
Panama	16,913	601,587	—	1
Peru	1,075	587	1	—
Venezuela	201,161	11,936	—	—

* Countries with fewer than 1,000 persons of concern to UNHCR are not listed.
† Includes persons in refugee-like situations.
‡ Mainly internally displaced persons.

United Nations Peace-keeping

Address: Department of Peace-keeping Operations, Room S-3727-B, United Nations, New York, NY 10017, USA.

Telephone: (212) 963-8077; **fax:** (212) 963-9222; **internet:** www.un.org/Depts/dpko/.

United Nations peace-keeping operations have been conceived as instruments of conflict control. The UN has used these operations in various conflicts, with the consent of the parties involved, to maintain international peace and security, without prejudice to the positions or claims of parties, in order to facilitate the search for political settlements through peaceful means such as mediation and the good offices of the UN Secretary-General. Each operation is established with a specific mandate, which requires periodic review by the UN Security Council. In 1988 the United Nations Peace-keeping Forces were awarded the Nobel Peace Prize.

United Nations peace-keeping operations fall into two categories: peace-keeping forces and observer missions. Peace-keeping forces are composed of contingents of military and civilian personnel, made available by member states. These forces assist in preventing the recurrence of fighting, restoring and maintaining peace, and promoting a return to normal conditions. To this end, peace-keeping forces are authorized as necessary to undertake negotiations, persuasion, observation and fact-finding. They conduct patrols and interpose physically between the opposing parties. Peace-keeping forces are permitted to use their weapons only in self-defence.

Military observer missions are composed of officers (usually unarmed), who are made available, on the Secretary-General's request, by member states. A mission's function is to observe and report to the Secretary-General (who, in turn, informs the Security Council) on the maintenance of a cease-fire, to investigate violations and to do what it can to improve the situation. Peace-keeping forces and observer missions must at all times maintain complete impartiality and avoid any action that might affect the claims or positions of the parties.

The UN's peace-keeping forces and observer missions are financed in most cases by assessed contributions from member states of the organization. In recent years a significant expansion in the UN's peace-keeping activities has been accompanied by a perpetual financial crisis within the organization, as a result of the increased financial burden and some member states' delaying payment. At 30 April 2010 outstanding assessed contributions to the peace-keeping budget amounted to some US $1,240m.

By July 2010 the UN had deployed a total of 64 peace-keeping operations, of which 13 were authorized in the period 1948–88 and 51 since 1988. At 31 May 2010 115 countries were contributing some 101,536 uniformed personnel to the ongoing operations, of whom 85,902 were peace-keeping troops, 13,407 police and 2,227 military observers.

United Nations Stabilization Mission in Haiti—MINUSTAH

Address: Port-au-Prince, Haiti.

Special Representative of the UN Secretary-General: EDMOND MULET (Guatemala).

Force Commander: Maj.-Gen. LUIZ GUILHERME PAUL CRUZ (Brazil).

Police Commissioner: GERALDO CHAUMONT (Argentina).

Establishment and Mandate: In early 2004 political tensions within Haiti escalated as opposition groups demanded political reforms and the resignation of President Jean-Bertrand Aristide. Increasingly violent public demonstrations took place throughout the country, in spite of diplomatic efforts by regional organizations to resolve the crisis, and in February armed opposition forces seized control of several northern cities. At the end of that month, with opposition troops poised to march on the capital and growing pressure from the international community, President Aristide tendered his resignation and fled the country. On that same day the UN Security Council, acting upon a request by the interim President, authorized the establishment of a Multinational Interim Force (MIF) to help to secure law and order in Haiti. The Council also declared its readiness to establish a follow-on UN mission. In April the Security Council agreed to establish MINUSTAH, which was to assume authority from the MIF with effect from 1 June. MINUSTAH was mandated to create a stable and secure environment, to support the transitional government in institutional development and organizing and monitoring elections, and to monitor the human rights situation. Among its declared objectives was the improvement of living conditions of the population through security measures, humanitarian actions and economic development.

Activities, 2004–09: In September 2004 MINUSTAH worked closely with other UN agencies and non-governmental organizations to distribute food and other essential services to thousands of people affected by a tropical storm. By the end of 2004 MINUSTAH's priority continued to be the security situation in the country. By that time the following civil units had become fully operational: electoral assistance; child protection; gender; civil affairs; human rights; and HIV/AIDS. In January 2005 MINUSTAH, with the UN Development Programme, the Haitian Government and the Provisional Electoral Council, signed an agreement on the organization of local, parliamentary and presidential elections, to be held later in that year. In May the UN Secretary-General expressed concern at the security environment with respect to achieving political transition. In the following month the Security Council approved a temporary reinforcement of MINUSTAH to provide increased security in advance of the elections. The military component was to comprise up to 7,500 troops (an additional strength of 750 troops) and the civilian police force up to 1,897 officers. From mid-2005 MINUSTAH forces worked to improve security in the country, in particular to reduce the criminal activities of armed groups in poorer urban areas. In November MINUSTAH deployed experts to train electoral agents and supervisors; however, the electoral timetable was delayed. Presidential and legislative elections were conducted in early February 2006. MINUSTAH officers provided security during the voting and maintained order as the results were being clarified. The mission subsequently pledged to support a post-election process of national dialogue and reconciliation and measures to strengthen the country's police force in order to re-establish law and order in areas of the capital, Port-au-Prince. A second round of voting in the legislative election was conducted in April. In August the UN Security Council determined that the mission should strengthen its role in preventing crime and reducing community violence, in particular kidnappings and other activities by local armed groups. In February 2007 MINUSTAH launched a large-scale operation in the Cité Soleil quarter of Port-au-Prince in order to extend its security presence in the most vulnerable locations and to counter the activities of criminal gangs. At the same time UN personnel helped to rehabilitate education, youth and medical facilities in those areas. In April MINUSTAH provided security and logistical support during the conduct of local municipal and mayoral elections. By November an estimated 9,000 local police officers had graduated from MINUSTAH training institutes. Efforts to control gang violence and uphold security in the poorest urban areas were ongoing in 2007–09. In February 2008 MINUSTAH announced that it was to fund six local infrastructure improvement projects to generate temporary employment for 7,000 people in the Cité Soleil and Martissant districts of Port-au-Prince. In April there were violent local demonstrations concerning the rising cost of living, during which several MINUSTAH personnel were attacked and property was damaged. A contingent of the mission subsequently distributed food aid to some 3,000 families in the poorest quarters of the capital. In August–September MINUSTAH personnel undertook emergency relief and rehabilitation activities, including evacuation of local residents and the distribution of humanitarian aid, to assist some of the 800,000 people affected by tropical storms which struck the country consecutively during a period of three weeks. From mid-2008 MINUSTAH strengthened its presence along the country's border with the Dominican Republic to counter illegal drugs-trafficking and improve security in the region. In December the mission undertook its first joint operation with the local police authorities to seize illegal drugs. Later in that month it was announced that the first and second rounds of planned partial senatorial elections would be held, respectively, in April and June 2009; during December 2008–February 2009 MINUSTAH and the police authorities jointly conducted a security assessment of new voting centres. Also during December 2008 MINUSTAH, international donors and representatives of the Haitian Government participated in a workshop that resulted in the adoption of a legislative agenda for 2009. During 2009 MINUSTAH, as well as implementing projects aimed at reducing violence in the community, was providing technical security capacity-building support to the national police.

2010: The MINUSTAH headquarters in Port-au-Prince was destroyed by a major earthquake that struck Haiti in January 2010. Subsequently it was confirmed that more than 60 mission staff had been killed, among them Hédi Annabi, the then Special Representative of the Secretary-General, his deputy, and the acting police commissioner for the mission; almost 180 further UN personnel were unaccounted for. In January, following the natural disaster, the UN Security Council adopted a resolution increasing the strength of the mission, to enable it to support the immediate recovery, reconstruction and stability efforts in Haiti. The temporary deployment of an additional 680 police officers was authorized by the Security Council in June, in order to strengthen the capacity of the Haitian national police force.

Operational Strength: At 30 June 2010 MINUSTAH comprised 8,609 troops and 2,969 civilian police; there is a support team of 473 international civilian staff, 1,235 local civilian staff (as at 31 May), and 208 UN Volunteers.

Finance: The mission is financed by assessments in respect of a Special Account. The budget for the period 1 July 2010–31 December 2010 amounted to US $380.0m.

World Food Programme—WFP

Address: Via Cesare Giulio Viola 68, Parco dei Medici, 00148 Rome, Italy.

Telephone: (06) 65131; **fax:** (06) 6513-2840; **e-mail:** wfpinfo@wfp.org; **internet:** www.wfp.org.

WFP, the principal food assistance organization of the United Nations, became operational in 1963. It aims to alleviate acute hunger by providing emergency relief following natural or man-made humanitarian disasters, and supplies food assistance to people in developing countries to eradicate chronic undernourishment, to support social development and to promote self-reliant communities.

Organization

(August 2010)

EXECUTIVE BOARD

The governing body of WFP is the Executive Board, comprising 36 members, 18 of whom are elected by the UN Economic and Social Council (ECOSOC) and 18 by the Council of the Food and Agriculture Organization (FAO). The Board meets four times each year at WFP headquarters.

SECRETARIAT

WFP's Executive Director is appointed jointly by the UN Secretary-General and the Director-General of FAO and is responsible for the management and administration of the Programme. In 2008 there were 10,200 staff members, of whom 91% were working in the field. WFP administers some 87 country offices, in order to provide operational, financial and management support at a more local level, and maintains six regional bureaux, located in Bangkok, Thailand (for Asia), Cairo, Egypt (for the Middle East, Central Asia and Eastern Europe), Panama City, Panama (for Latin America and the Caribbean), Johannesburg, South Africa (for Southern Africa), Kampala, Uganda (for Central and Eastern Africa), and Dakar, Senegal (for West Africa).

Executive Director: JOSETTE SHEERAN (USA).

Activities

WFP is the only multilateral organization with a mandate to use food assistance as a resource. It is the second largest source of assistance in the UN, after the World Bank group, in terms of actual transfers of resources, and the largest source of grant aid in the UN system. WFP handles more than one-third of the world's food assistance. WFP is also the largest contributor to South–South trade within the UN system, through the purchase of food and services from developing countries (at least three-quarters of the food purchased by the Programme originates in developing countries). WFP's mission is to provide food assistance to save lives in refugee and other emergency situations, to improve the nutrition and quality of life of vulnerable groups and to help to develop assets and promote the self-reliance of poor families and communities. WFP aims to focus its efforts on the world's poorest countries and to provide at least 90% of its total assistance to those designated as 'low-income food-deficit'. At the World Food Summit, held in November 1996, WFP endorsed the commitment to reduce by 50% the number of undernourished people, no later than 2015. During 2009 WFP food assistance, distributed through development projects, emergency operations (EMOPs) and protracted relief and recovery operations (PRROs), benefited some 101.8m. people, including 84.1m. women and children, in 73 countries. Total food deliveries in 2009 amounted to 4.6m. metric tons, compared with 3.9m. metric tons in 2008.

WFP rations comprise basic food items (staple foods such as wheat flour or rice; pulses such as lentils and chickpeas; vegetable oil fortified with vitamins A and D; sugar; and iodized salt). Where possible basic rations are complemented with special products designed to improve the nutritional intake of beneficiaries. These include fortified blended foods, principally 'Corn Soya Blend', containing important micronutrients; ready-to-use foods, principally peanut-based pastes enriched with vitamins and minerals trademarked as 'Plumpy Doz' and 'Supplementary Plumpy', which are better suited to meeting the nutritional needs of young and moderately malnourished children; high energy biscuits, distributed in the first phases of emergencies when cooking facilities may be scarce; micronutrient powder ('sprinkles'), which can be used to fortify home cooking; and compressed food bars, given out during disaster relief operations when the distribution and preparation of local food is not possible. The Programme's food donations must meet internationally agreed standards applicable to trade in food products. In May 2003 WFP's Executive Board approved a policy on donations of genetically modified (GM) foods and other foods derived from biotechnology, determining that the Programme would continue to accept donations of GM/biotech food and that, when distributing it, relevant national standards would be respected. It is WFP policy to buy food as near to where it is needed as possible, with a view to saving on transport costs and helping to sustain local economies. From 2009 targeted cash and voucher schemes started to be implemented, as a possible alternative to food rations (see below).

WFP aims to address the causes of chronic malnourishment, which it identifies as poverty and lack of opportunity. It emphasizes the role played by women (who are most likely to sow, reap, harvest and cook household food) in combating hunger, and endeavours to address the specific nutritional needs of women, to increase their access to food and development resources, and to promote girls' education. WFP estimates that females represent four-fifths of people engaged in farming in Africa and three-fifths of people engaged in farming in Asia, and that globally women are the sole breadwinners in one-third of households. Increasingly WFP distributes food assistance through women, believing that vulnerable children are more likely to be reached in this way. The Programme also focuses resources on supporting the nutrition and food security of households and communities affected by HIV/AIDS, and on promoting food security as a means of mitigating extreme poverty and vulnerability and thereby combating the spread and impact of HIV/AIDS. In February 2003 WFP and the Joint UN Programme on HIV/AIDS (UNAIDS) concluded an agreement to address jointly the relationship between HIV/AIDS, regional food shortages and chronic hunger, with a particular focus on Africa, South-east Asia and the Caribbean. In October of that year WFP became a co-sponsor of UNAIDS. WFP also urges the development of new food assistance strategies as a means of redressing global inequalities and thereby combating the threat of conflict and international terrorism.

WFP is a participant in the High Level Task Force (HLTF) on the Global Food Security Crisis, which was established by the UN Secretary-General in April 2008, with the aim of addressing the global impact of soaring levels of food and commodity prices, and of formulating a comprehensive framework for action. WFP participated in the High-Level Conference on World Food Security and the Challenges of Climate Change and Bioenergy that was convened by FAO in June. At that time WFP determined to allocate some US $1,200m. in extra-budgetary funds to alleviate hunger in the worst-affected countries. In January 2009 the HLTF participated in a follow-up high level meeting convened in Madrid, Spain, and attended also by 62 government ministers and representatives from 126 countries. The meeting agreed to initiate a consultation process with regard to the establishment of a Global Partnership for Agriculture, Food Security and Nutrition. WFP participated in a World Summit on Food Security, organized by FAO, in Rome, in November 2009, with the aim of securing greater coherence in the global governance of food security and setting a 'new world food order'. In March 2008 WFP launched an Emergency Market Mitigation Account, appealing for US $755m. to cover additional costs, generated by the higher commodity and fuel price levels, that needed to be met in that year; by end-2008 more than $5,000m. had been donated to the Account. In September 2009 the WFP Executive Director appealed to the international donor community for a further $3,000m. to fund the Programme's commitments until end-2009.

In mid-June 2008 WFP's Executive Board approved a four-year strategic plan, covering the period 2008–11, that shifted the focus of WFP's activities from the supply of food aid to the supply of food assistance, and aimed to provide a new institutional framework to support vulnerable populations affected by the ongoing global food crisis and by possible future effects of global climate change. The five principal objectives of the 2008–11 plan were: saving lives and protecting livelihoods in emergencies; preparing for emergencies; restoring and rebuilding lives after emergencies; reducing chronic hunger and undernutrition everywhere; and strengthening the capacity of countries to reduce hunger. The plan emphasized prevention of hunger through early warning systems and analysis; local purchase of food; the maintenance of efficient and effective emergency response systems; and the use of focused cash and voucher programmes to ensure the accessibility to vulnerable people in urban environments of food that was locally available but, owing to the high level of market prices and increasing unemployment, beyond their financial means. It was envisaged that the cash and voucher approach would reduce the cost to WFP of transporting and storing food supplies, and would also benefit local economies (both being long-term WFP policy objectives).

WFP has developed a range of mechanisms to enhance its preparedness for emergency situations (such as conflict, drought and other natural disasters) and to improve its capacity for responding effectively to crises as they arise. Through its Vulnerability Analysis and Mapping (VAM) project, WFP aims to identify potentially vulnerable groups by providing information on food security and the capacity of different groups for coping with shortages, and to enhance emergency contingency-planning and long-term assistance objectives. VAM produces food security analysis reports, guidelines, reference documents and maps. In 2009 VAM field units were operational in 43 countries world-wide. The key elements of WFP's emergency response capacity are its strategic stores of food and logistics equipment (drawn from 'stocks afloat': ships loaded with WFP food supplies that can be rerouted to assist in crisis situations; development project stocks redesignated as emergency project contingency reserves; and in-country borrowing from national food reserves enabled by bilateral agreements); stand-by arrangements to enable the rapid deployment of personnel, communications and other essential equipment; and the Augmented Logistics Intervention Team for Emergencies (ALITE), which undertakes capacity assessments and contingency-planning. When engaging in a crisis WFP dispatches an emergency preparedness team to quantify the amount and type of food assistance required, and to identify the beneficiaries of and the timescale and logistics (e.g. means of transportation; location of humanitarian corridors, if necessary; and designated food distribution sites, such as refugee camps, other emergency shelters and therapeutic feeding centres) underpinning the ensuing EMOP. Once the EMOP has been drafted, WFP launches an appeal to the international donor community for funds and assistance to enable its implementation. WFP special operations are short-term logistics and infrastructure projects that are undertaken to facilitate the movement of food aid, regardless of whether the food is provided by the Agency itself. Special operations typically complement EMOPs or longer rehabilitation projects.

During 2000 WFP led efforts, undertaken with other UN humanitarian agencies, for the design and application of local UN Joint Logistics Centre facilities, which aimed to co-ordinate resources in an emergency situation. In 2001 a UN Humanitarian Response Depot was opened in Brindisi, Italy, under the direction of WFP experts, for the storage of essential rapid response equipment. In that year the Programme published a set of guidelines on contingency planning. Since 2003 WFP has been mandated to provide aviation transport services to the wider humanitarian community. During 2005 the UN's Inter-Agency Standing Committee (IASC), concerned with co-ordinating the international response to humanitarian disasters, developed a concept of organizing agency assistance to IDPs through the institutionalization of a 'Cluster Approach', currently comprising 11 core areas of activity. WFP was designated the lead agency for the clusters on Emergency Telecommunications (jointly with OCHA and UNICEF) and Logistics. During January 2008–June 2009 WFP implemented a Special operation to improve country-specific communications services in order to enhance country-level cluster capacities.

WFP aims to link its relief and development activities to provide a continuum between short-term relief and longer-term rehabilitation and development. In order to achieve this objective, WFP aims to promote capacity-building elements within relief operations, e.g. training, income-generating activities and environmental protection measures; and to integrate elements that strengthen disaster mitigation into development projects, including soil conservation, reafforestation, irrigation infrastructure, and transport construction and rehabilitation. In all its projects WFP aims to assist the most vulnerable groups (such as nursing mothers and children) and to ensure that beneficiaries have an adequate and balanced diet. Through its development activities, WFP aims to alleviate poverty in developing countries by promoting self-reliant families and communities. No individual country is permitted to receive more than 10% of the Programme's available development resources. WFP's Food-for-Assets development operations pay workers living in poverty with food in return for participation in self-help schemes and labour-intensive projects, with the aim of enabling vulnerable households and communities to focus time and resources on investing in lasting assets with which to raise themselves out of poverty (rather than on day-to-day survival). Food-for-Assets projects provide training in new techniques for achieving improved food security (such as training in new agricultural skills or in the establishment of home gardening businesses); and include, for example, building new irrigation or terracing infrastructures; soil and water conservation activities; and allocating food rations to villagers to enable them to devote time to building schools and clinics. In areas undermined by conflict WFP offers food assistance as an incentive for former combatants to put down their weapons and learn new skills. WFP's School feeding activities aim to expand educational opportunities for poor children (given that it is difficult for children to concentrate on studies without adequate food and nutrition, and that food-insecure households frequently have to choose between educating their children or making them work to help the family to survive), and to improve the quality of the teaching environment. During 2009 school feeding projects benefited 20.7m. children. As an incentive to promote the education of vulnerable children, including orphans and children with HIV/AIDS, and to encourage families to send their daughters to school, WFP also implements 'take-home ration' projects, under which it provides basic food items to certain households, usually including sacks of rice and cans of cooking oil. WFP's Purchase for Progress (P4P) programme, launched in September 2008, expands the Programme's long-term 'local procurement' policy, enabling smallholder and low-income farmers in developing countries to supply food to WFP's global assistance operations. Under P4P farmers are taught techniques and provided with tools to enable them to compete competitively in the market-place. P4P also aims to identify and test specific successful local practices that could be replicated to benefit small-scale farmers on a wider scale. During 2008–13 P4P initiatives were being piloted in 21 countries, in Africa, Latin America and Asia.

In 1999 WFP began implementing PRROs, where the emphasis is on fostering stability, rehabilitation and long-term development for victims of natural disasters, displaced persons and refugees. PRROs are introduced no later than 18 months after the initial EMOP and last no more than three years. When undertaken in collaboration with UNHCR and other international agencies, WFP has responsibility for mobilizing basic food commodities and for related transport, handling and storage costs. Some 15 new PRROs were approved in 2008.

In 2009 WFP operational expenditure in Latin America and the Caribbean amounted to US $243.0m. Of the total regional expenditure in 2009, $113.9m. was for emergency relief operations, $22.4m. for agricultural, rural and human resource development projects, and $4.2m. for special operations. In April 2008 WFP launched a $93m. PRRO for Colombia, covering the period 2008–11, that was aimed at supporting annually 530,000 IDPs and individuals in food-insecure communities affected by violent unrest. A country programme being undertaken in Nicaragua over the period 2008–12, at a cost of $18.6m. and with 225,000 planned beneficiaries, was to focus on improving mother-and-child health, and on the implementation of food for education and food for training projects. Over the period June 2009–May 2011 a PRRO (costing $12.3m. and aimed at 200,000 beneficiaries) was being implemented in Bolivia to enable food-insecure households to recover from the effects of consecutive natural disasters (including floods, mudslides, landslides and droughts). A country programme (costing $10m. and aimed at 125,000 beneficiaries) was being undertaken in that country during 2008–12, with a focus on providing food-based interventions for children aged from two–five years; giving food assistance to primary schoolchildren and street children; and offering technical assistance in emergency preparedness and response to government institutions. WFP was implementing a $7.5m. PRRO in Ecuador during December 2007–November 2010, targeting food assistance at Colombian refugees. During 2008–13 WFP's new P4P programme (see above) was being piloted in El Salvador, Honduras, Guatemala and Nicaragua.

WFP estimated in 2008 that around one-half of Haiti's population was malnourished, and it has supported vulnerable people in that country who have been affected by the political and civil unrest, and natural disasters, through education, nutrition and health, and disaster mitigation activities. During 2008–09 WFP implemented a US $124m. PRRO aimed at assisting Haitians in vulnerable groups (including female-headed households in crisis areas, school children, and people infected with HIV); the scope of the PRRO was expanded in June 2008 from 1.4m. to 2.3m. beneficiaries. In 2008 WFP provided emergency food aid, at a cost of $31m., to more than 800,000 people affected by three hurricanes and a tropical storm that struck Haiti during late August and early September. In that year WFP extended school feeding projects over the school summer holidays to assist up to 200,000 Haitian children, and provided take-home rations to the families of 1.1m. children in that country. In January 2010 WFP appealed for $475.3m. to fund a complex emergency humanitarian operation in response to the earthquake that caused devastation in Haiti in that month. WFP's relief activities aimed to target food assistance towards the most vulnerable survivors of the disaster, and were focused on the provision of school meals (aiming initially to reach 72,000 children in 148 schools in the Port-au-Prince area); a scheme to distribute nutritious food products (such as Supplementary Plumpy) to 53,000 children aged under five years, and to 16,000 pregnant and breast-feeding mothers; and the carefully targeted distribution to around 300,000 vulnerable families (comprising an estimated 1.5m. beneficiaries) of full food baskets including rice, beans, corn soya blend, oil and salt. In February WFP hosted a high-level meeting in Rome to launch a global partnership aimed at developing a future food security plan for Haiti.

Finance

The Programme is funded by voluntary contributions from donor countries, intergovernmental bodies such as the European Commission, and the private sector. Contributions are made in the form of commodities, finance and services (particularly shipping). Commitments to the International Emergency Food Reserve (IEFR), from which WFP provides the majority of its food supplies, and to the Immediate Response Account of the IEFR (IRA), are also made on a voluntary basis by donors. WFP's operational expenditures in 2009 amounted to some US $3,986m. Contributions by donors in that year totalled $4,022m.

Publications

Annual Report.
Food and Nutrition Handbook.
School Feeding Handbook.
World Hunger Series.

Food and Agriculture Organization of the United Nations—FAO

Address: Viale delle Terme di Caracalla, 00100 Rome, Italy.

Telephone: (06) 5705-1; **fax:** (06) 5705-3152; **e-mail:** fao-hq@fao.org; **internet:** www.fao.org.

FAO, the first specialized agency of the UN to be founded after the Second World War, aims to alleviate malnutrition and hunger, and serves as a co-ordinating agency for development programmes in the whole range of food and agriculture, including forestry and fisheries. It helps developing countries to promote educational and training facilities and to create appropriate institutions.

Organization

(August 2010)

CONFERENCE

The governing body is the FAO Conference of member nations. It meets every two years, formulates policy, determines the organization's programme and budget on a biennial basis, and elects new members. It also elects the Director-General of the Secretariat and the Independent Chairman of the Council. Regional conferences are also held each year.

COUNCIL

The FAO Council is composed of representatives of 49 member nations, elected by the Conference for rotating three-year terms. It is the interim governing body of FAO between sessions of the Conference. There are eight main Governing Committees of the Council: the Finance and Programme Committees, and the Committees on Commodity Problems, Fisheries, Agriculture, Forestry, World Food Security, and Constitutional and Legal Matters.

SECRETARIAT

There are some 3,600 FAO staff, of whom about one-half are based at headquarters. FAO maintains five regional offices (see below), nine sub-regional offices, five liaison offices (in Yokohama, Japan; Washington, DC, USA, liaison with North America; Geneva, Switzerland and New York, USA, with the UN; and Brussels, Belgium, with the European Union), and some 74 country offices. Work is undertaken by the following departments: Agriculture and Consumer Protection; Economic and Social Development; Fisheries and Aquaculture; Forestry; Human, Financial and Physical Resources; Knowledge and Communication; Natural Resource Management and Environment; and Technical Co-operation.

Director-General: JACQUES DIOUF (Senegal).

REGIONAL OFFICES

Latin America and the Caribbean: Avda Dag Hammarskjöld 3241, Casilla 10095, Vitacura, Santiago, Chile; tel. (2) 923-2100; fax (2) 923-2101; e-mail fao-rlc@field.fao.org; internet www.rlc.fao.org; Regional Rep. JOSÉ GRAZIANO DA SILVA.

Sub-regional Office for the Caribbean: POB 631-C, Bridgetown, Barbados; tel. 426-7110; fax 427-6075; e-mail fao-slac@fao.org; Sub-regional Rep. L. BARBARA GRAHAM.

Activities

FAO aims to raise levels of nutrition and standards of living by improving the production and distribution of food and other commodities derived from farms, fisheries and forests. FAO's ultimate objective is the achievement of world food security, 'Food for All'. The organization provides technical information, advice and assistance by disseminating information; acting as a neutral forum for discussion of food and agricultural issues; advising governments on policy and planning; and developing capacity directly in the field.

In November 1996 FAO hosted the World Food Summit, which was held in Rome and was attended by heads of state and senior government representatives of 186 countries. Participants approved the Rome Declaration on World Food Security and the World Food Summit Plan of Action, with the aim of halving the number of people afflicted by undernutrition, then estimated to total 828m. worldwide, by no later than 2015. A review conference to assess progress in achieving the goals of the summit, entitled World Food Summit: Five Years Later, held in June 2002, reaffirmed commitment to this objective, which is also incorporated into the UN Millennium Development Goals (MDGs). During that month FAO announced the formulation of a global 'Anti-Hunger Programme', which aimed to promote investment in the agricultural sector and rural development, with a particular focus on small-scale farmers, and to enhance food access for those most in need, for example through the provision of school meals, schemes to feed pregnant and nursing mothers and food-for-work programmes. FAO hosts the UN System Network on Rural Development and Food Security, comprising some 20 UN bodies, which was established in 1997 as an inter-agency mechanism to follow-up the World Food Summits.

In November 1999 the FAO Conference approved a long-term Strategic Framework for the period 2000–15, which emphasized national and international co-operation in pursuing the goals of the 1996 World Food Summit. The Framework promoted interdisciplinarity and partnership, and defined three main global objectives: constant access by all people to sufficient, nutritionally adequate and safe food to ensure that levels of undernourishment were reduced by 50% by 2015 (see above); the continued contribution of sustainable agriculture and rural development to economic and social progress and well-being; and the conservation, improvement and sustainable use of natural resources. It identified five corporate strategies (each supported by several strategic objectives), covering the following areas: reducing food insecurity and rural poverty; ensuring enabling policy and regulatory frameworks for food, agriculture, fisheries and forestry; creating sustainable increases in the supply and availability of agricultural, fisheries and forestry products; conserving and enhancing sustainable use of the natural resource base; and generating knowledge. In October 2007 the report of an Independent External Evaluation (IEE) into the role and functions of FAO recommended that the organization elaborate a plan for reform to ensure its continued efficiency and effectiveness. In November 2008 a Special Conference of member countries approved a three-year Immediate Plan of Action to reform the governance and management of the organization based on the recommendations of the IEE.

During 2006–08 international prices for many basic food commodities increased by around 60%, and the international price of grain doubled. In December 2007 FAO inaugurated an Initiative on Soaring Food Prices to help to boost food production in low-income developing countries and improve access to food and agricultural supplies in the short term, with a view to countering the escalating commodity prices. In April 2008 the UN Secretary-General appointed FAO's Director-General as Vice-Chairman of a High Level Task Force (HLTF) on the Global Food Security Crisis, which aimed to address the impact of soaring levels of food and fuel prices and formulate a comprehensive framework for action. In June FAO hosted a High Level Conference on World Food Security and the Challenges of Climate Change and Bioenergy. The meeting adopted a Declaration on Food Security, urging the international donor community to increase its support to developing countries and countries with economies in transition. The Declaration also noted an urgent need to develop the agricultural sectors and expand food production in such countries and for increased investment in rural development, agriculture and agribusiness. In January 2009 a follow-up high level meeting was convened in Madrid, Spain, and attended by 62 government ministers and representatives from 126 countries. The meeting agreed to initiate a consultation process with regard to the establishment of a Global Partnership for Agriculture, Food Security and Nutrition to strengthen international co-ordination and governance for food security. FAO's long-standing Committee on World Food Security (CFS) underwent reform in 2009; henceforth the Committee was to be a central component of the new Global Partnership, and was to influence hunger elimination programmes at global, regional and national level, taking into account that food security relates not just to agriculture but also to economic access to food, adequate nutrition, social safety nets and human rights.

In May 2009 the European Union donated €106m. to FAO, to support farmers and improve food security in 10 developing countries in Africa, Asia and the Caribbean that were particularly badly affected by the 2007–08 global food crisis. Addressing the World Grain Forum, convened in St Petersburg, Russia, in June 2009, the FAO Director-General demanded a more effective and coherent global governance system to ensure future world food security, and urged that a larger proportion of development aid should be allocated to agriculture, to enable developing countries to invest in rural infrastructures. During June it was estimated that, in 2009, the number of people world-wide suffering chronic, daily hunger had risen to an unprecedented 1,020m., of whom an estimated 642m. were in Asia and the Pacific; 265m. in sub-Saharan Africa; 53m. in Latin America and the Caribbean; and 42m. in the Middle East and North Africa. Around 15m. people resident in developed countries were estimated at that time to be afflicted by chronic hunger. The *OECD-FAO Agricultural Outlook 2009–18*, issued in June 2009, found the global agriculture sector to be showing more resilience to the ongoing world-wide economic crisis than other sectors, owing to the status of food as a basic human necessity. However, the report warned that the state of the agriculture sector could become more fragile if the ongoing global downturn were to worsen. In July the FAO Director-General welcomed the L'Aquila Joint Statement on Global Food Security (promoting sustainable agricultural development), and the Food Security Initiative with commitments of US $20,000m., that were approved in that month by G8 leaders.

In mid-October 2009 a high-level forum of experts was convened by FAO to discuss policy on the theme 'How to Feed the World in 2050'. In November 2009 FAO organized a World Summit on Food Security, in Rome, with the aim of achieving greater coherence in the global governance of food security and setting a 'new world food order'. Leaders attending the Summit issued a declaration in which they adopted a number of strategic objectives, including: ensuring urgent action towards achieving World Food Summit objectives/the UN MDG relating to reducing undernutrition; promoting the new Global Partnership for Agriculture, Food Security and Nutrition and fully committing to reform of the CFS; reversing the decline in national and international funding for agriculture, food security and rural development in developing countries, and encouraging new investment to increase sustainable agricultural production; reducing poverty and working towards achieving food security and access to 'Food for All'; and confronting proactively the challenges posed by climate change to food security. The Summit determined to base its pursuit of these strategic objectives on the following *Five Rome Principles for Sustainable Global Food Security*: (i) investment in country-owned plans aimed at channelling resources to efficient results-based programmes and partnerships; (ii) fostering strategic co-ordination at national, regional and global level to improve governance, promote better allocation of resources, avoid duplication of efforts and identify response gaps; (iii) striving for a comprehensive twin-track approach to food security comprising direct action to combat hunger in the most vulnerable, and also medium- and long-term sustainable agricultural, food security, nutrition and rural development programmes to eliminate the root causes of hunger and poverty, including through the progressive realization of the right to adequate food; (iv) ensuring a strong role for the multilateral system by sustained improvements in efficiency, responsiveness, co-ordination and effectiveness of multilateral institutions; and (v) ensuring sustained and substantial commitment by all partners to investment in agriculture and food security and nutrition, with provision of necessary resources in a timely and reliable fashion, aimed at multi-year plans and programmes.

With other UN agencies, FAO attended the Summit of the World's Regions on Food Insecurity, held in Dakar, Senegal, in January 2010. The summit urged that global governance of food security should integrate players on every level, and expressed support for the developing Global Partnership for Agriculture, Food Security and Nutrition.

World Food Day, commemorating the foundation of FAO, is held annually on 16 October. In May 2010 FAO launched an on-line petition entitled the *1billionhungry project*, with the aim of raising awareness of the plight of people world-wide suffering from chronic hunger.

AGRICULTURE AND CONSUMER PROTECTION

FAO's overall objective is to lead international efforts to counter hunger and to improve levels of nutrition. Within this context FAO is concerned to improve crop and grassland productivity and to develop sustainable agricultural systems to provide for enhanced food security and economic development. It provides member countries with technical advice for plant improvement, the application of plant biotechnology, the development of integrated production systems and rational grassland management. There are groups concerned with the main field cereal crops, i.e. rice, maize and wheat, which *inter alia* identify means of enhancing production, collect and analyse relevant data and promote collaboration between research institutions, government bodies and other farm management organizations. In 1985 and 1990 FAO's International Rice Commission endorsed the use of hybrid rice, which had been developed in the People's Republic of China, as a means of meeting growing demand for the crop, in particular in the Far East, and has subsequently assisted member countries to acquire the necessary technology and training to develop hybrid rice production. In Africa FAO has collaborated with the West African Rice Development Association to promote and facilitate the use of new rice varieties and crop management practices. FAO was the lead agency for the International Year of the Potato (2008), which aimed to highlight the importance of the potato in combating world hunger. FAO actively promotes the concept of Conservation Agriculture, which aims to minimize the need for mechanical soil tillage or additional farming resources and to reduce soil degradation and erosion.

FAO is also concerned with the development and diversification of horticultural and industrial crops, for example oil seeds, fibres and medicinal plants. FAO collects and disseminates data regarding crop trials and new technologies. It has developed an information processing site, Ecocrop, to help farmers identify appropriate crops and environmental requirements. FAO works to protect and support the sustainable development of grasslands and pasture, which contribute to the livelihoods of an estimated 800m. people world-wide.

FAO's plant protection service incorporates a range of programmes concerned with the control of pests and the use of pesticides. In February 2001 FAO warned that some 30% of pesticides sold in developing countries did not meet internationally accepted quality standards. In November 2002 FAO adopted a revised International Code of Conduct on the Distribution and Use of Pesticides (first adopted in 1985) to reduce the inappropriate distribution and use of pesticides and other toxic compounds, particularly in developing countries. In September 1998 a new legally binding treaty on trade in hazardous chemicals and pesticides was adopted at an international conference held in Rotterdam, Netherlands. The so-called Rotterdam Convention required that hazardous chemicals and pesticides banned or severely restricted in at least two countries should not be exported unless explicitly agreed by the importing country. It also identified certain pesticide formulations as too dangerous to be used by farmers in developing countries, and incorporated an obligation that countries halt national production of those hazardous compounds. The treaty entered into force in February 2004. FAO was co-operating with UNEP to provide an interim secretariat for the Convention. FAO has promoted the use of Integrated Pest Management (IPM) initiatives to encourage the use, at local level, of safer and more effective methods of pest control, such as biological control methods and natural predators.

FAO hosts the secretariat of the International Plant Protection Convention (first adopted in 1951, revised in 1997) which aims to prevent the spread of plant pests and to promote effective control measures. The secretariat helps to define phytosanitary standards, promote the exchange of information and extend technical assistance to contracting parties (173 at August 2010).

FAO is concerned with the conservation and sustainable use of plant and animal genetic resources. It works with regional and international associations to develop seed networks, to encourage the use of improved seed production systems, to elaborate quality control and certification mechanisms and to co-ordinate seed security activities, in particular in areas prone to natural or man-made disasters. FAO has developed a World Information and Early Warning System (WIEWS) to gather and disseminate information concerning plant genetic resources for food and agriculture and to undertake periodic assessments of the state of those resources. FAO is also developing, as part of the WIEWS, a Seed Information Service to extend information to member states on seeds, planting and new technologies. In June 1996 representatives of more than 150 governments convened in Leipzig, Germany, at an International Technical Conference organized by FAO to consider the use and conservation of plant genetic resources as an essential means of enhancing food security. The meeting adopted a Global Plan of Action, which included measures to strengthen the development of plant varieties and to promote the use and availability of local varieties and locally adapted crops to farmers, in particular following a natural disaster, war or civil conflict. In November 2001 the FAO Conference adopted the International Treaty on Plant Genetic Resources for Food and Agriculture (also referred to as the Seed Treaty), which was to provide a framework to ensure access to plant genetic resources and to related knowledge, technologies and funding. The Treaty entered into force in June 2004, having received the required number of ratifications, and the first meeting of the Treaty's Governing Body was convened in June 2006. At August 2010 125 states were parties to the Treaty.

FAO's Animal Production and Health Division is concerned with the control and management of major animal diseases, and, in recent years, with safeguarding humans from livestock diseases. Other programmes are concerned with the contribution of livestock to poverty alleviation, the efficient use of natural resources in livestock production, the management of animal genetic resources, promoting the exchange of information and mapping the distribution of livestock around the world. In 2001 FAO established a Pro-Poor Livestock Policy Initiative to support the formulation and implementation of livestock-related policies to improve the livelihood and nutrition of the world's rural poor, with an initial focus on the Andean region, the Horn of Africa, West Africa, South Asia and the Mekong.

The Emergency Prevention System for Transboundary Animal and Plant Pests and Diseases (EMPRES) was established in 1994 to strengthen FAO's activities in the prevention, early warning, control and, where possible, eradication of pests and highly contagious livestock diseases (which the system categorizes as epidemic diseases of strategic importance, such as rinderpest or foot-and-mouth; diseases requiring tactical attention at international or regional level, e.g. Rift Valley fever; and emerging diseases, e.g. bovine spongiform encephalopathy—BSE). EMPRES has a desert locust component, and has published guidelines on all aspects of desert locust monitoring. FAO has assumed responsibility for technical leadership and co-ordination of the Global Rinderpest Eradication Programme (GREP), which has the objective of eliminating the disease by 2011. In November 1997 FAO initiated a Programme Against African Trypanosomiasis, which aimed to counter the disease affecting cattle in almost one-third of Africa. In November 2004 FAO established a specialized Emergency Centre for Transboundary Animal Disease Operations (ECTAD) to enhance FAO's role in assisting member states to combat animal disease outbreaks and in co-ordinating international efforts to research, monitor and control transboundary disease crises. In May 2004 FAO and the World Organisation for Animal Health (OIE) signed an agreement to clarify their respective areas of competence and improve co-operation, in response to an increase in contagious transboundary animal diseases (such as foot-and-mouth disease and avian influenza, see below). The two bodies agreed to establish a global framework on the control of transboundary animal diseases, entailing improved international collaboration and circulation of information. In early 2006 FAO, OIE and the World Health Organization (WHO) agreed on the establishment of a Global Early Warning and Response System for Major Animal Diseases, including Zoonoses (GLEWS), in order to strengthen their joint capacity to detect, monitor and respond to animal disease threats. In October 2006 FAO inaugurated a new Crisis Management Centre (CMC) to co-ordinate (in close co-operation with OIE) the organization's response to outbreaks of H5N1 and other major emergencies related to animal or food health.

In September 2004 FAO and WHO declared an ongoing epidemic in certain east Asian countries of the H5N1 strain of highly pathogenic avian influenza (HPAI) to be a 'crisis of global importance': the disease was spreading rapidly through bird populations and was also transmitting to human populations through contact with diseased birds (mainly poultry). In that month FAO published *Recommendations for the Prevention, Control and Eradication of Highly Pathogenic Avian Influenza in Asia*. In April 2005 FAO and OIE established an international network of laboratories and scientists (OFFLU) to exchange data and provide expert technical advice on avian influenza. In the following month FAO, with WHO and OIE, launched a global strategy for the progressive control of the disease. In November a conference on Avian Influenza and Human Pandemic Influenza, jointly organized by FAO, WHO and OIE and the World Bank, issued a plan of action identifying a number of responses, including: supporting the development of integrated national plans for H5N1 containment and human pandemic influenza preparedness and response; assisting countries with the aggressive control of H5N1 and with establishing a more detailed understanding of the role of wild birds in virus transmission; nominating rapid response teams of experts to support epidemiological field investigations; expanding national and regional capacity in surveillance, diagnosis, and alert and response systems; expanding the network of influenza laboratories; establishing multi-country networks for the control or prevention of animal transboundary diseases; expanding the global antiviral stockpile; strengthening veterinary infrastructures; and mapping a global strategy and work plan for co-ordinating antiviral and influenza vaccine research and development. In June 2006 FAO and OIE convened a scientific conference on the spread of H5N1 that advocated as a basis for H5N1 management early detection of the disease in wild birds, improved biosecurity and hygiene in the poultry trade, rapid response to disease outbreaks, and the establishment of a global tracking and monitoring facility involving participation by all relevant organizations, as well as by scientific centres, farmers' groupings, bird-watchers and hunters, and wildlife and wild bird habitat conservation bodies. The conference also urged investment in telemetry/satellite technology to improve tracking capabilities. International conference and pledging meetings on the disease were convened in Washington, DC, USA, in October 2005, Beijing, People's Republic of China (PRC), in January 2006, Bamako, Mali, in December and in New Delhi, India, in December 2007. In August 2008 a new strain of HPAI not previously recorded in sub-Saharan Africa was detected in Nigeria. In October the sixth international ministerial conference on avian influenza was convened in Sharm esh-Sheikh, Egypt. FAO, with WHO, UNICEF, OIE, the World Bank and the UN System Influenza Co-ordinator, presented a new strategic framework, within the concept of 'One World, One Health', to improve understanding and co-operation with respect to emerging infectious diseases, to strengthen animal and public health surveillance and to enhance response mechanisms. During 2003–end-June 2010 outbreaks of H5N1 were recorded in 63 countries and territories, with 17 countries affected in 2009. In early 2010 Cambodia, Hong Kong, Israel, Myanmar, Nepal and Viet Nam reported cases of H5N1 in domestic poultry and wildlife.

In April 2009, in response to a major outbreak in humans of the swine influenza variant pandemic (H1N1) 2009, the FAO Crisis Management Centre mobilized a team of experts to increase animal disease surveillance and maintain response readiness to protect the global pig sector from infection with the emerging virus. In early May FAO, OIE, WHO and WTO together issued a statement stressing that pork products handled in accordance with hygienic practices could not be deemed a source of infection

In December 1992 FAO, with WHO, organized an International Conference on Nutrition, which approved a World Declaration on Nutrition and a Plan of Action, aimed at promoting efforts to combat malnutrition as a development priority. Since the conference, more than 100 countries have formulated national plans of action for nutrition, many of which were based on existing development plans such as comprehensive food security initiatives, national poverty alleviation programmes and action plans to attain the targets set by the World Summit for Children in September 1990. FAO promotes other efforts, at household and community level, to improve nutrition and food security, for example a programme to support home gardens. It aims to assist the identification of food-insecure and vulnerable populations, both through its *State of Food Insecurity in the World* reports and taking a lead role in the development of Food Insecurity and Vulnerability Information and Mapping Systems (FIVIMS), a recommendation of the World Food Summit. In 1999 FAO signed a memorandum of understanding with UNAIDS on strengthening co-operation to combat the threat posed by the HIV/AIDS epidemic to food security, nutrition and rural livelihoods. FAO is committed to incorporating HIV/AIDS into food security and livelihood projects, to strengthening community care and to highlighting the importance of nutrition in the care of those living with HIV/AIDS.

FAO is committed to promoting food quality and safety in all different stages of food production and processing. It supports the development of integrated food control systems by member states, which incorporate aspects of food control management, inspection, risk analysis and quality assurance. The joint FAO/WHO Codex Alimentarius Commission, established in 1962, aims to protect the health of consumers, ensure fair trade practices and promote the co-ordination of food standards activities at an international level. In January 2001 a joint team of FAO and WHO experts issued a report concerning the allergenicity of foods derived from biotechnology (i.e. genetically modified—GM—foods). In July the Codex Alimentarius Commission agreed the first global principles for assessing the safety of GM foods, and approved a series of maximum levels of environmental contaminants in food. In June 2004 FAO published guidelines for assessing possible risks posed to plants by living modified organisms (LMOs). In July 2001 the Codex Alimentarius Commission adopted guidelines on organic livestock production, covering organic breeding methods, the elimination of growth hormones and certain chemicals in veterinary medicines, and the use of good quality organic feed with no meat or bone meal content. In January 2003 FAO organized a technical consultation on biological risk management in food and agriculture which recognized the need for a more integrated approach to so-called biosecurity, i.e. the prevention, control and management of risks to animal, human and plant life and health. FAO has subsequently developed a *Toolkit*, which was published in 2007, to help countries to develop and implement national biosecurity systems and to enhance biosecurity capacity.

FAO aims to assist member states to enhance the efficiency, competitiveness and profitability of their agricultural and food enterprises. FAO extends assistance in training, capacity-building and the formulation of agribusiness development strategies. It promotes the development of effective 'value chains' connecting primary producers with consumers and supports other linkages within the agribusiness industry. Similarly, FAO aims to strengthen marketing systems, links between producers and retailers and training in agricultural marketing, and works to improve the regulatory framework for agricultural marketing. FAO promotes the use of new machinery and technologies to increase agricultural production and extends a range of services to support mechanization, including training, maintenance, testing and the promotion of labour saving technologies. Other programmes are focused on farm management, post-harvest management, food and non-food processing, rural finance, and rural infrastructure. FAO helps reduce immediate post-harvest losses, with the introduction of improved processing methods and storage systems. FAO participates in PhAction, a forum of 12 agencies that was established in 1999 to promote post-harvest research and the development of effective post-harvest services and infrastructure.

FAO's Joint Division with the International Atomic Energy Agency (IAEA) is concerned with the use of nuclear techniques in food and agriculture. It co-ordinates research projects, provides scientific and technical support to technical co-operation projects and administers training courses. A joint laboratory in Seibersdorf, Austria, is concerned with testing biotechnologies and in developing non-toxic fertilizers (especially those that are locally available) and improved strains of food crops (especially from indigenous varieties). In the area of animal production and health, the Joint Division has developed progesterone-measuring and disease diagnostic kits. Other sub-programmes of the Joint Division are concerned with soil and water, plant breeding and nutrition, insect pest control and food and environmental protection.

NATURAL RESOURCES MANAGEMENT AND ENVIRONMENT

FAO is committed to promoting the responsible and sustainable management of natural resources and other activities to protect the environment. FAO assists member states to mitigate the impact of climate change on agriculture, to adapt and enhance the resilience of agricultural systems to climate change, and to promote practices to reduce the emission of greenhouse gases from the agricultural sector. In recent years FAO has strengthened its work in the area of using natural biomass resources as fuel, both at grassroots level and industrial processing of cash crops. In 2006 FAO established the International Bioenergy Platform to serve as a focal point for research, data collection, capacity-building and strategy formulation by local, regional and international bodies concerned with bioenergy. FAO also serves as the secretariat for the Global Bioenergy Partnership, which was inaugurated in May 2006 to facilitate the collaboration between governments, international agencies and representatives of the private sector and civil society in the sustainable development of bioenergy.

FAO aims to enhance the sustainability of land and water systems, and as a result to secure agricultural productivity, through the improved tenure, management, development and conservation of those natural resources. The organization promotes equitable access to land and water resources and supports integrated land and water management, including river basin management and improved irrigation systems. FAO has developed AQUASTAT as a global information system concerned with water and agricultural issues, comprising databases, country and regional profiles, surveys and maps. AquaCrop, CropWat and ClimWat are further productivity models and databases which have been developed to help to assess crop requirements and potential yields. Since 2003 FAO has participated in UN Water, an inter-agency initiative to co-ordinate existing approaches to water-related issues. In December 2008 FAO organized a Ministerial Conference on Water for Agriculture and Energy in Africa: 'the Challenges of Climate Change', in Sirte, Libya, which was attended by representatives of 48 African member countries and other representatives of international, regional and civil organizations.

Within the FAO's Natural Resources Management and Environment Department is a Research and Extension Division, which provides advisory and technical services to support national capacity-building, research, communication and education activities. It maintains several databases which support and facilitate the dissemination of information, for example relating to proven transferable technologies and biotechnologies in use in developing countries. The Division advises countries on communication strategies to strengthen agricultural and rural development, and has actively supported the use of rural radio. FAO is the UN lead agency of an initiative, 'Education for Rural People', which aims to improve the quality of and access to basic education for people living in rural areas and to raise awareness of the issue as an essential element of achieving the MDGs. The Research and Extension Division hosts the secretariat of the Global Forum on Agricultural Research, which was established in October 1996 as a collaboration of research centres, non-governmental and private sector organizations and development agencies. The Forum aims to strengthen research and promote knowledge partnerships concerned with the alleviation of poverty, the increase in food security and the sustainable use of natural resources. The Division also hosts the secretariat of the Science Council of the Consultative Group on International Agricultural Research (CGIAR), which, specifically, aims to enhance and promote the quality, relevance and impact of science within the network of CGIAR research centres and to mobilize global scientific expertise.

In September 2009 FAO published, jointly with the Centre for Indigenous People's Nutrition and Environment (CINE—based in McGill University, Montreal, Canada) a report entitled *Indigenous People's Food Systems: The Many Dimensions of Culture, Diversity and Environment for Nutrition and Health*, which aimed to demonstrate the wealth of knowledge on nutrition retained within indigenous communities world-wide.

FISHERIES AND AQUACULTURE

FAO aims to facilitate and secure the long-term sustainable development of fisheries and aquaculture, in both inland and marine waters, and to promote its contribution to world food security. In March 1995 a ministerial meeting of fisheries adopted the Rome Consensus on World Fisheries, which identified a need for immediate action to eliminate overfishing and to rebuild and enhance depleting fish stocks. In November the FAO Conference adopted a Code of Conduct for Responsible Fishing, which incorporated many global fisheries and aquaculture issues (including fisheries resource conservation and development, fish catches, seafood and fish processing, commercialization, trade and research) to promote the sustainable development of the sector. In February 1999 the FAO Committee on Fisheries adopted new international measures, within the framework of the Code of Conduct, in order to reduce over-exploitation of the world's fish resources, as well as plans of action for the conservation and management of sharks and the reduction in the incidental catch of seabirds in longline fisheries. The voluntary measures were endorsed at a ministerial meeting, held in March and attended by representatives of some 126 countries, which issued a declaration to promote the implementation of the Code of Conduct and to achieve sustainable management of fisheries and aquaculture. In March 2001 FAO adopted an international plan of action to address the continuing problem of so-called illegal, unreported and unregulated fishing (IUU). In that year FAO estimated that about one-half of major marine fish stocks were fully exploited, one-quarter under-exploited, at least 15% over-exploited, and 10% depleted or recovering from depletion. IUU was estimated to account for up to 30% of total catches in certain fisheries. In October FAO and the Icelandic Government jointly organized the Reykjavík Conference on Responsible Fisheries in the Marine Ecosystem, which adopted a declaration on pursuing responsible and sustainable fishing activities in the context of ecosystem-based fisheries management (EBFM). EBFM involves determining the boundaries of individual marine ecosystems, and maintaining or rebuilding the habitats and biodiversity of each of these so that all species will be supported at levels of maximum production. In March 2005 FAO's Committee of Fisheries adopted voluntary guidelines for the so-called eco-labelling and certification of fish and fish products, i.e. based on information regarding capture management and the sustainable use of resources. In March 2007 the Committee agreed to initiate a process of negotiating an internationally-binding agreement to deny port access to fishing vessels involved in IUU activities. Substantive agreement was reached by representatives of 60 countries, meeting in Rome, Italy, in January–February 2008, and the final text of the proposed 'Agreement on Port State Measures to Prevent, Deter and Eliminate Illegal, Unreported and Unregulated Fishing' was agreed in September 2009.

FAO undertakes extensive monitoring, publishing every two years *The State of World Fisheries and Aquaculture*, and collates and maintains relevant databases. It formulates country and regional profiles and has developed a specific information network for the fisheries sector, GLOBEFISH, which gathers and disseminates information regarding market trends, tariffs and other industry issues. FAO aims to extend technical support to member states with regard to the management and conservation of aquatic resources, and other measures to improve the utilization and trade of products, including the reduction of post-harvest losses, preservation marketing and quality assurance. FAO promotes aquaculture (which contributes almost one-third of annual global fish landings) as a valuable source of animal protein and income-generating activity for rural communities. It has undertaken to develop an ecosystem approach to aquaculture (EAA) and works to integrate aquaculture with agricultural and irrigation systems. In February 2000 FAO and the Network of Aquaculture Centres in Asia and the Pacific (NACA) jointly convened a Conference on Aquaculture in the Third Millennium, which was held in Bangkok, Thailand, and attended by participants representing more than 200 governmental and non-governmental organizations. The Conference debated global trends in aquaculture and future policy measures to ensure the sustainable development of the sector. It adopted the Bangkok Declaration and Strategy for Aquaculture Beyond 2000.

FORESTRY

FAO is committed to the sustainable management of trees, forests and forestry resources. It aims to address the critical balance of ensuring the conservation of forests and forestry resources while maximising their potential to contribute to food security and social and economic development. In March 2009 the Committee on Forestry approved a new 10-year FAO Strategic Plan for Forestry, replacing a previous strategic plan initiated in 1999. The new plan, which was 'dynamic' and was to be updated regularly, covered the social, economic and environmental aspects of forestry. The first World Forest Week was held in March 2009, on the themes of sustainable forest management and climate change, and institutional change in a dynamic world.

FAO assists member countries to formulate, implement and monitor national forestry programmes, and encourages the participation of all stakeholders in developing plans for the sustainable management of tree and forest resources. FAO also helps to implement national assessments of those programmes and of other forestry activities. At a global level FAO undertakes surveillance of the state of the world's forests and publishes a report every two years. A separate Forest Resources Assessment is published every five years, the latest (for 2010) was initiated in March 2008. FAO is committed to collecting and disseminating accurate information and data on forests. It maintains the Forestry Information System (FORIS) to make relevant information and forest-related databases widely accessible.

FAO is a member of the Collaborative Partnership on Forests, which was established in April 2004 on the recommendation of the UN's Economic and Social Council. FAO organizes a World Forestry Congress, generally held every six years; the 13th Congress was convened in Buenos Aires, Argentina, in October 2009.

ECONOMIC AND SOCIAL DEVELOPMENT

FAO provides a focal point for economic research and policy analysis relating to food security and sustainable development. It produces studies and reports on agricultural development, the impact of development programmes and projects, and the world food situation, as well as on commodity prices, trade and medium-term projections. It supports the development of methodologies and guidelines to improve research into food and agriculture and the integration of wider concepts, such as social welfare, environmental factors and nutrition, into research projects. In November 2004 the FAO Council adopted a set of voluntary Right to Food Guidelines, and established a dedicated administrative unit, that aimed to 'support the progressive realization of the right to adequate food in the context of national food security' by providing practical guidance to countries in support of their efforts to achieve the 1996 World Food Summit commitment and UN MDG relating to hunger reduction. FAO's Statistical Division assembles, analyses and disseminates statistical data on world food and agriculture and aims to ensure the consistency, broad coverage and quality of available data. The Division advises member countries on enhancing their statistical capabilities. It maintains FAOSTAT as a core database of statistical information relating to nutrition, fisheries, forestry, food production, land use, population etc. In 2004 FAO developed a new statistical framework to provide for the organization and integration of statistical data and metadata from sources within a particular country. CountrySTAT was piloted in Kenya, Kyrgyzstan and Ghana in 2005 and in 15 more developing countries in 2006/07. FAO's internet-based interactive World Agricultural Information Centre (WAICENT) offers access to agricultural publications, technical documentation, codes of conduct, data, statistics and multimedia resources. FAO compiles and co-ordinates an extensive range of international databases on agriculture, fisheries, forestry, food and statistics, the most important of these being AGRIS (the International Information System for the Agricultural Sciences and Technology) and CARIS (the Current Agricultural Research Information System). In June 2000 FAO organized a high-level Consultation on Agricultural Information Management (COAIM), which aimed to increase access to and use of agricultural information by policy-makers and others. The second COAIM was held in September 2002 and the third meeting was convened in June 2007.

FAO's Global Information and Early Warning System (GIEWS), which become operational in 1975, maintains a database on and monitors the crop and food outlook at global, regional, national and sub-national levels in order to detect emerging food supply difficulties and disasters and to ensure rapid intervention in countries experiencing food supply shortages. It publishes regular reports on the weather conditions and crop prospects in sub-Saharan Africa and in the Sahel region, issues special alerts which describe the situation in countries or sub-regions experiencing food difficulties, and recommends an appropriate international response. FAO has also supported the development and implementation of Food Insecurity and Vulnerability Information and Mapping Systems (FIVIMS) and hosts the secretariat of the inter-agency working group on development of the FIVIMS. In October 2007 FAO inaugurated an online Global Forum on Food Security and Nutrition, to contribute to the compilation and dissemination of information relating to food security and nutrition throughout the world. In December 2008 a regular report issued by GIEWS identified 33 countries as being in crisis and requiring external assistance, of which 20 were in Africa, 10 in Asia and the Near East and three in Latin America and the Caribbean. All countries were identified as lacking the resources to deal with critical problems of food insecurity, including many severely affected by the high cost of food and fuel. The publication *Crop Prospects and Food Situation* reviews the global situation, and provides regional updates and a special focus on countries experiencing food crises and requiring external assistance, on a quarterly basis. *Food Outlook*, issued in June and November, analyses developments in global food and animal feed markets.

In May 2008 GIEWS published a special report on the situation in Bolivia, based on an FAO/WFP Crop and Food Supply Evaluation Mission, conducted in April, to evaluate the affect on crop and cereal production of adverse climate-related conditions.

TECHNICAL CO-OPERATION

The Technical Co-operation Department has responsibility for FAO's operational activities, including policy development assistance to member countries; the mobilization of resources; investment support; field operations; emergency operations and rehabilitation; and the Technical Co-operation Programme.

FAO provides policy advice to support the formulation, implementation and evaluation of agriculture, rural development and food security strategies in member countries. It administers a project to assist developing countries to strengthen their technical negotiating skills, in respect to agricultural trade issues. FAO also aims to co-ordinate and facilitate the mobilization of extrabudgetary funds from donors and governments for particular projects. It administers a range of trust funds, including a Trust Fund for Food Security and Food Safety, established in 2002 to generate resources for projects to combat hunger, and the Government Co-operative Programme. FAO's Investment Centre, established in 1964, aims to promote greater external investment in agriculture and rural development by assisting member countries to formulate effective and sustainable projects and programmes. The Centre collaborates with international financing institutions and bilateral donors in the preparation of projects, and administers cost-sharing arrangements, with, typically, FAO funding 40% of a project. The Centre is a co-chair (with the German Government) of the Global Donor Platform for Rural Development, which was established in 2004, comprising multilateral, donor and international agencies, development banks and research institutions, to improve the co-ordination and effectiveness of rural development assistance.

FAO's Technical Co-operation Programme, which was inaugurated in 1976, provides technical expertise and funding for small-scale projects to address specific issues within a country's agriculture, fisheries or forestry sectors. An Associate Professional Officers programme co-ordinates the sponsorship and placement of young professionals to gain experience working in an aspect of rural or agricultural development.

FAO's Special Programme for Food Security (SPFS), initiated in 1994, assists low-income countries with a food deficit to increase food production and productivity as rapidly as possible, primarily through the widespread adoption by farmers of improved production technologies, with emphasis on areas of high potential. Within the SPFS framework are national and regional food security initiatives, all of which aim towards the MDG objective of reducing the incidence of hunger by 50% by 2015. The SPFS is operational in more than 100 countries. The Programme promotes South-South co-operation to improve food security and the exchange of knowledge and experience. Some 39 bilateral co-operation agreements are in force, for example, between Gabon and the People's Republic of China, Egypt and Cameroon, and Viet Nam and Benin. In 2010 some 77 countries were categorized formally as 'low-income food-deficit'.

FAO organizes an annual series of fund-raising events, 'TeleFood', some of which are broadcast on television and the internet, in order to raise public awareness of the problems of hunger and malnutrition. Since its inception in 1997 public donations to TeleFood have exceeded some US $28m. (2010), financing more than 2,700 'grass-roots' projects in 130 countries. The projects have provided tools, seeds and other essential supplies directly to small-scale farmers, and have been especially aimed at helping women.

The Technical Co-operation Division co-ordinates FAO's emergency operations, concerned with all aspects of disaster and risk prevention, mitigation, reduction and emergency relief and rehabilitation, with a particular emphasis on food security and rural populations. FAO works with governments to develop and implement disaster prevention policies and practices. It aims to strengthen the capacity of local institutions to manage and mitigate risk and provides technical assistance to improve access to land for displaced populations in countries following conflict or a natural disaster. Other disaster prevention and reduction efforts include dissemination of information from the various early-warning systems and support for adaptation to climate variability and change, for example by the use of drought-resistant crops or the adoption of conservation agriculture techniques. Following an emergency FAO works with governments and other development and humanitarian partners to assess the immediate and longer-term agriculture and food security needs of the affected population. It has developed an Integrated Food Security and Humanitarian Phase Classification Scheme to determine the appropriate response to a disaster situation. Emergency co-ordination units may be established to manage the local response to an emergency and to facilitate and co-ordinate the delivery of inter-agency assistance. In order to rehabilitate agricultural production following a natural or man-made disaster FAO provides emergency seed, tools, other materials and technical and training assistance. During 2005 the UN's Inter-Agency Standing Committee, concerned with co-ordinating the international response to humanitarian disasters, developed a concept of providing assistance through a 'cluster' approach, comprising core areas of activity. FAO was designated the lead agency for the Agriculture cluster. FAO also contributes the agricultural relief and rehabilitation component of the UN's Consolidated Appeals Process, which aims to co-ordinate and enhance the effectiveness of the international community's response to an emergency. In April 2004 FAO established a Special Fund for Emergency and Rehabilitation Activities to enable it to respond promptly to a humanitarian crisis before making an emergency appeal for additional resources.

During 2008 emergency projects were undertaken in some 95 countries under the framework of the Initiative on Soaring Food Prices (see above), many of which were funded in the form of Technical Co-operation Programme projects, providing fertilizers, seeds and other support necessary to ensure the success of that year's harvest, at a cost of US $36m.

Following the severe earthquake that caused devastation in Haiti in January 2010, FAO and the Haitian authorities distributed agricultural inputs to some 72,000 farming households with a view to facilitating the production and consumption of locally produced food; it was envisaged that through the sale of surplus produce local people would also be enabled to meet health and education expenses. Fostering urban agriculture, reforestation and disaster risk reduction activities were a further focus of FAO's reconstruction efforts in Haiti.

FAO Statutory Bodies

(based at the Rome headquarters, unless otherwise indicated)

Caribbean Plant Protection Commission: c/o FAO Sub-Regional Office for the Caribbean, POB 631-C, Bridgetown, Barbados; tel. 426-7110; fax 427-6075; e-mail fao-slac@fao.org; internet www.fao.org/world/subregional/slac; f. 1967 to preserve the existing plant resources of the area; 13 member states.

Codex Alimentarius Commission (Joint FAO/WHO Food Standards Programme): e-mail codex@fao.org; internet www.codexalimentarius.net; f. 1962 to make proposals for the co-ordination of all international food standards work and to publish a code of international food standards; Trust Fund to support participation by least-developed countries was inaugurated in 2003; there are numerous specialized Codex committees, e.g. for food labelling, hygiene, additives and contaminants, pesticide and veterinary residues, milk and milk products, and processed fruits and vegetables; and an intergovernmental task force on antimicrobial resistance; 181 member states and the European Union.

Commission for Inland Fisheries of Latin America: Avda Dag Hammarskjöld 3241, Casilla 10095, Vitacura, Santiago, Chile; f. 1976 to promote, co-ordinate and assist national and regional fishery and limnological surveys and programmes of research and development leading to the rational utilization of inland fishery resources; 21 member states.

Commission on Livestock Development for Latin America and the Caribbean: Avda Dag Hammarskjöld 3241, Casilla 10095, Vitacura, Santiago, Chile; f. 1986; 24 member states.

Latin American and Caribbean Forestry Commission: 1948 to advise on formulation of forest policy and review and co-ordinate its implementation throughout the region; to exchange information and advise on technical problems; meets every two years; 31 member states.

Finance

FAO's Regular Programme, which is financed by contributions from member governments, covers the cost of FAO's Secretariat, its Technical Co-operation Programme (TCP) and part of the cost of several special action programmes. The budget for the two-year period 2008–09 totalled US $929.8m. Much of FAO's technical assistance programme is funded from extra-budgetary sources, predominantly by trust funds that come mainly from donor countries and international financing institutions.

Publications

Commodity Review and Outlook (annually).

Crop Prospects and Food Situation (5/6 a year).

Ethical Issues in Food and Agriculture.

FAO Statistical Yearbook (annually).

FAOSTAT Statistical Database (online).

Food Outlook (2 a year).

Food Safety and Quality Update (monthly; electronic bulletin).

Forest Resources Assessment.

The State of Agricultural Commodity Markets (every 2 years).

The State of Food and Agriculture (annually).

The State of Food Insecurity in the World (annually).

The State of World Fisheries and Aquaculture (every 2 years).

The State of the World's Forests (every 2 years).

Unasylva (quarterly).

Yearbook of Fishery Statistics.

Yearbook of Forest Products.

Commodity reviews; studies, manuals. A complete catalogue of publications is available at www.fao.org/icatalog/inter-e.htm.

International Bank for Reconstruction and Development—IBRD (World Bank)

Address: 1818 H St, NW, Washington, DC 20433, USA.

Telephone: (202) 473-1000; **fax:** (202) 477-6391; **e-mail:** pic@worldbank.org; **internet:** www.worldbank.org.

The IBRD was established in December 1945. Initially it was concerned with post-war reconstruction in Europe; since then its aim has been to assist the economic development of member nations by making loans where private capital is not available on reasonable terms to finance productive investments. Loans are made either directly to governments, or to private enterprises with the guarantee of their governments. The World Bank, as it is commonly known, comprises the IBRD and the International Development Association (IDA). The affiliated group of institutions, comprising the IBRD, IDA, the International Finance Corporation (IFC), the Multilateral Investment Guarantee Agency (MIGA) and the International Centre for Settlement of Investment Disputes (ICSID, see below), is referred to as the World Bank Group.

Organization

(August 2010)

Officers and staff of the IBRD serve concurrently as officers and staff in IDA. The World Bank has offices in New York, Brussels, Paris (for Europe), Frankfurt, London, Geneva and Tokyo, as well as in more than 100 countries of operation. Country Directors are located in some 30 country offices.

BOARD OF GOVERNORS

The Board of Governors consists of one Governor appointed by each member nation. Typically, a Governor is the country's finance minister, central bank governor, or a minister or an official of comparable rank. The Board normally meets once a year.

EXECUTIVE DIRECTORS

The general operations of the Bank are conducted by a Board of 24 Executive Directors. Five Directors are appointed by the five members having the largest number of shares of capital stock, and the rest are elected by the Governors representing the other members. The President of the Bank is Chairman of the Board.

PRINCIPAL OFFICERS

The principal officers of the Bank are the President of the Bank, three Managing Directors, two Senior Vice-Presidents and 25 Vice-Presidents.

President and Chairman of Executive Directors: ROBERT B. ZOELLICK (USA).

Vice-President, Latin America and the Caribbean: PAMELA COX (USA).

Activities

The World Bank's primary objectives are the achievement of sustainable economic growth and the reduction of poverty in developing countries. In the context of stimulating economic growth the Bank promotes both private sector development and human resource development and has attempted to respond to the growing demands by developing countries for assistance in these areas. In March 1997 the Board of Executive Directors endorsed a 'Strategic Compact' to increase the effectiveness of the Bank in achieving its central objective of poverty reduction. The reforms included greater decentralization of decision-making, and investment in front-line operations, enhancing the administration of loans, and improving access to information and co-ordination of Bank activities through a knowledge management system comprising four thematic networks: Human Development; Environmentally and Socially Sustainable Development; Finance, Private Sector and Infrastructure Development; and Poverty Reduction and Economic Management. In 2000/01 the Bank adopted a new Strategic Framework which emphasized two essential approaches for Bank support: strengthening the investment climate and prospects for sustainable development in a country, and supporting investment in the poor. In September 2001 the Bank announced that it was to become a full partner in implementing the UN Millennium Development Goals (MDGs), and was to make them central to its development agenda. The objectives, which were approved by governments attending a special session of the UN General Assembly in September 2000, represented a new international consensus to achieve determined poverty reduction targets. The Bank was closely involved in preparations for the International Conference on Financing for Development, which was held in Monterrey, Mexico, in March 2002. The meeting adopted the Monterrey Consensus, which outlined measures to support national development efforts and to achieve the MDGs. During 2002/03 the Bank, with the IMF, undertook to develop a monitoring framework to review progress in the MDG agenda. The first *Global Monitoring Report* was issued by the Bank and the IMF in April 2004.

In October 2007 the Bank's President defined the following six strategic themes as priorities for Bank development activities: the poorest countries; fragile and post-conflict states; middle-income countries; global public goods; the Arab world; and knowledge and learning. In May 2008 the Bank established a Global Food Crisis Response Programme (GFRP, see below) to assist developing countries affected by the escalating cost of food production. In December the Bank resolved to establish a new facility to accelerate the provision of funds, through IDA, for developing countries affected by the global decline in economic and financial market conditions. The Bank participated in the meeting of heads of state and government of the Group of 20 (G20) leading economies, that was held in Washington, DC, USA, in November 2008 to address the global economic situation, and pursued close collaboration with other multinational organizations, in particular the IMF and OECD, to analyse the impact of the ongoing economic instability. In January 2009 the Bank's President proposed the establishment of a Vulnerability Fund to support essential investment projects in developing countries, to be financed by developed economies appropriating 0.7% of their economic stimulus measures to the Fund. During early 2009 the Bank elaborated its operational response to the global economic crisis. Three operational platforms were devised to address the areas identified as priority themes, i.e. protecting the most vulnerable against the effects of the crisis; maintaining long-term infrastructure investment programmes; and sustaining the potential for private sector-led economic growth and employment creation. Consequently, a new Vulnerability Financing Facility was established, incorporating the GFRP and a new Rapid Social Response Programme, to extend immediate assistance to the poorest groups in affected low- and middle-income countries. Infrastructure investment was to be supported through a new Infrastructure Recovery and Assets Platform, which was mandated to release funds to secure existing infrastructure projects and to finance new initiatives in support of longer-term economic development. Private sector support for infrastructure projects, bank recapitalization, microfinance, and trade financing was to be led by IFC.

The Bank's efforts to reduce poverty include the compilation of country-specific assessments and the formulation of country assistance strategies (CASs) to review and guide the Bank's country programmes. In 1998/99 the Bank's Executive Directors endorsed a Comprehensive Development Framework (CDF) to effect a new approach to development assistance based on partnerships and country responsibility, with an emphasis on the interdependence of the social, structural, human, governmental, economic and environmental elements of development. The CDF, which aimed to enhance the overall effectiveness of development assistance, was formulated after a series of consultative meetings organized by the Bank and attended by representatives of governments, donor agencies, financial institutions, non-governmental organizations, the private sector and academics. In December 1999 the Bank introduced a new approach to implement the principles of the CDF, as part of its strategy to enhance the debt relief scheme for heavily indebted poor countries (HIPCs, see below). Applicant countries were requested to formulate, in consultation with external partners and other stakeholders, a results-oriented national strategy to reduce poverty, to be presented in the form of a Poverty Reduction Strategy Paper (PRSP). In cases where there might be some delay in issuing a full PRSP, it was permissible for a country to submit a less detailed 'interim' PRSP (I-PRSP) in order to secure the preliminary qualification for debt relief. The approach also requires the publication of annual progress reports. In 2001 the Bank introduced a new Poverty Reduction Support Credit to help low-income countries to implement the policy and institutional reforms outlined in their PRSP. Increasingly, PRSPs have been considered by the international community to be the appropriate country-level framework to assess progress towards achieving the MDGs.

FINANCIAL OPERATIONS

IBRD capital is derived from members' subscriptions to capital shares, the calculation of which is based on their quotas in the IMF. At 30 June 2009 the total subscribed capital of the IBRD was US $189,918m., of which the paid-in portion was $11,491m. (6.1%); the remainder is subject to call if required. Most of the IBRD's lendable funds come from its borrowing, on commercial terms, in world capital markets, and also from its retained earnings and the flow of repayments on its loans. IBRD loans carry a variable interest rate, rather than a rate fixed at the time of borrowing.

IBRD loans usually have a 'grace period' of five years and are repayable over 15 years or fewer. Loans are made to governments, or must be guaranteed by the government concerned, and are normally made for projects likely to offer a commercially viable rate of return. In 1980 the World Bank introduced structural adjustment lending, which (instead of financing specific projects) supports programmes and changes necessary to modify the structure of an economy so that it can restore or maintain its growth and viability in its balance of payments over the medium-term.

The IBRD and IDA together made 302 new lending and investment commitments totalling US $46,906.0m. during the year ending 30 June 2009. During 2008/09 the IBRD alone approved commitments totalling $32,910.8m. (compared with $13,467.6m. in the previous year), of which the largest share, $13,828.5m. (42%), was allocated to projects in Latin America and the Caribbean. Total disbursements by the IBRD in the year ending 30 June 2009 amounted to $18,564m.

In September 1996 the World Bank/IMF Development Committee endorsed a joint initiative to assist heavily indebted poor countries (HIPCs) to reduce their debt burden to a sustainable level, in order to make more resources available for poverty reduction and economic growth. A new Trust Fund was established by the World Bank in November to finance the initiative. The Fund, consisting of an initial allocation of US $500m. from the IBRD surplus and other contributions from multilateral creditors, was to be administered by IDA. Of the 41 HIPCs identified by the Bank, 33 were in sub-Saharan Africa. In early 1999 the World Bank and IMF initiated a comprehensive review of the HIPC initiative. By April meetings of the Group of Seven industrialized nations (G7) and of the governing bodies of the Bank and IMF indicated a consensus that the scheme needed to be amended and strengthened, in order to allow more countries to benefit from the initiative, to accelerate the process by which a country may qualify for assistance, and to enhance the effectiveness of debt relief. In June the G7 and Russia (the G8), meeting in Cologne,

Germany, agreed to increase contributions to the HIPC Trust Fund and to cancel substantial amounts of outstanding debt, and proposed more flexible terms for eligibility. In September the Bank and IMF reached an agreement on an enhanced HIPC scheme, with further revenue to be generated through the revaluation of a percentage of IMF gold reserves. Under the enhanced initiative it was agreed that, during the initial phase of the process to ensure suitability for debt relief, each applicant country should formulate a PRSP, and should demonstrate prudent financial management in the implementation of the strategy for at least one year, with support from IDA and IMF. At the pivotal 'decision point' of the process, having thus developed and successfully applied the poverty reduction strategy, applicant countries still deemed to have an unsustainable level of debt were to qualify for interim debt relief from the IMF and IDA, as well as relief on highly concessional terms from other official bilateral creditors and multilateral institutions. During the ensuing 'interim period' countries were required successfully to implement further economic and social development reforms, as a final demonstration of suitability for securing full debt relief at the 'completion point' of the scheme. Data produced at the decision point was to form the base for calculating the final debt relief (in contrast to the original initiative, which based its calculations on projections of a country's debt stock at the completion point). In the majority of cases a sustainable level of debt was targeted at 150% of the net present value (NPV) of the debt in relation to total annual exports (compared with 200%–250% under the original initiative). Other countries with a lower debt-to-export ratio were to be eligible for assistance under the scheme, providing that their export earnings were at least 30% of GDP (lowered from 40% under the original initiative) and government revenue at least 15% of GDP (reduced from 20%). In June 2005 finance ministers of the G8 proposed providing additional resources to achieve the full cancellation of debts owed by eligible HIPCs, in order to assist those countries to meet their MDG targets. Countries that had reached their completion point were to qualify for immediate assistance. In July the heads of state and government of G8 countries requested that the Bank ensure the effective delivery of the additional funds and provide a framework for performance measurement. In September the Bank's Development Committee and the International Monetary and Financial Committee of the IMF endorsed the proposal, subsequently referred to as the Multilateral Debt Relief Initiative (MDRI). By July 2010 30 countries had reached completion point under the enhanced HIPC initiative, including Bolivia ($1,302m. in NPV terms approved in June 2001), Guyana ($1,553m. in April 2003), Nicaragua ($3,308m. in January 2004), Honduras ($556m. in April 2005) and Haiti ($140m. in June 2009). A further six countries had reached their decision point at that time. At March 2010 assistance committed under the HIPC initiative amounted to an estimated $75,600m. (in 2009 NPV terms), of which the World Bank Group had committed $15,000m. An additional $31,000m. had been pledged under the MDRI, of which $20,000m. was by the Bank.

During 2000/01 the World Bank strengthened its efforts to counter the problem of HIV and AIDS in developing countries. In November 2001 the Bank appointed its first Global HIV/AIDS Adviser. In 2001 a Multi-Country HIV/AIDS Prevention and Control Programme for the Caribbean was launched, with an allocated budget of US $155m. Under this initiative loans and grants have been made available to Barbados, Dominican Republic, Jamaica, Grenada, Guyana, Saint Christopher and Nevis, Trinidad and Tobago and a Pan-Caribbean Partnership against HIV/AIDS. In addition, the Bank has extended some $425m. to an AIDS/sexually transmitted disease control project in Brazil. In July 2009 the Bank published a report, with UNAIDS, concerned with the impact of the global economic crisis on HIV prevention and treatment programmes.

In March 2007 the Board of Executive Directors approved an action plan to develop further its Clean Energy for Development Investment Framework, which had been formulated in response to a request by the G8 heads of state, meeting in Gleneagles, United Kingdom, in July 2005. The action plan focused on efforts to improve access to clean energy, in particular in sub-Saharan Africa; to accelerate the transition to low carbon-emission development; and to support adaptation to climate change. In October 2008 the Bank Group endorsed a new Strategic Framework on Development and Climate Change, which aimed to guide the Bank in supporting the efforts of developing countries to achieving growth and reducing poverty, while recognizing the operational challenges of climate change. In June 2010 the Bank appointed a Special Envoy to lead the Bank's representation in international discussions on climate change.

TECHNICAL ASSISTANCE AND ADVISORY SERVICES

In addition to providing financial services, the Bank also undertakes analytical and advisory services, and supports learning and capacity-building, in particular through the World Bank Institute (see below), the Staff Exchange Programme and knowledge-sharing initiatives. The Bank has supported efforts, such as the Global Development Gateway, to disseminate information on development issues and programmes, and, since 1988, has organized the Annual Bank Conference on Development Economics (ABCDE) to provide a forum for the exchange and discussion of development-related ideas and research. In September 1995 the Bank initiated the Information for Development Programme (InfoDev) with the aim of fostering partnerships between governments, multilateral institutions and private-sector experts in order to promote reform and investment in developing countries through improved access to information technology.

The provision of technical assistance to member countries has become a major component of World Bank activities. The economic and sector work (ESW) undertaken by the Bank is the vehicle for considerable technical assistance and often forms the basis of CASs and other strategic or advisory reports. In addition, project loans and credits may include funds earmarked specifically for feasibility studies, resource surveys, management or planning advice, and training. The World Bank Institute has become one of the most important of the Bank's activities in technical assistance. It provides training in national economic management and project analysis for government officials at the middle and upper levels of responsibility. It also runs overseas courses aiming to build up local training capability, and administers a graduate scholarship programme.

Technical assistance (usually reimbursable) is also extended to countries that do not need Bank financial support, e.g. for training and transfer of technology. The Bank encourages the use of local consultants to assist with projects and stimulate institutional capability.

The Project Preparation Facility (PPF) was established in 1975 to provide cash advances to prepare projects that may be financed by the Bank. In 1992 the Bank established an Institutional Development Fund (IDF), which became operational on 1 July; the purpose of the Fund was to provide rapid, small-scale financial assistance, to a maximum value of US $500,000, for capacity-building proposals. In 2002 the IDF was reoriented to focus on good governance, in particular financial accountability and system reforms.

ECONOMIC RESEARCH AND STUDIES

In the 1990s the World Bank's research, conducted by its own research staff, was increasingly concerned with providing information to reinforce the Bank's expanding advisory role to developing countries and to improve policy in the Bank's borrowing countries. The principal areas of current research focus on issues such as maintaining sustainable growth while protecting the environment and the poorest sectors of society, encouraging the development of the private sector, and reducing and decentralizing government activities.

The Bank chairs the Consultative Group on International Agricultural Research (CGIAR), which was founded in 1971 to raise financial support for international agricultural research work for improving crops and animal production in developing countries; it supports 15 research centres.

CO-OPERATION WITH OTHER ORGANIZATIONS

The World Bank co-operates with other international partners with the aim of improving the impact of development efforts. It collaborates with the IMF in implementing the HIPC scheme and the two agencies work closely to achieve a common approach to development initiatives. The Bank has established strong working relationships with many other UN bodies, in particular through a mutual commitment to poverty reduction objectives. In May 2000 the Bank signed a joint statement of co-operation with OECD. The Bank holds regular consultations with other multilateral development banks and with the European Union with respect to development issues. The Bank-NGO Committee provides an annual forum for discussion with non-governmental organizations (NGOs). Strengthening co-operation with external partners was a fundamental element of the Comprehensive Development Framework, which was adopted in 1998/99 (see above). In 2001/02 a Partnership Approval and Tracking System was implemented to provide information on the Bank's regional and global partnerships. In June 2007 the World Bank and the UN Office on Drugs and Crime launched a joint Stolen Asset Recovery (StAR) initiative, as part of the Bank's new Governance and Anti-Corruption (GAC) strategy. In April 2009 the G20 recommended that StAR review and propose mechanisms to strengthen international co-operation relating to asset recovery.

In 1997 the Bank, in partnership with the IMF, UNCTAD, UNDP, the World Trade Organization (WTO) and the International Trade Commission, established an Integrated Framework for Trade-related Assistance to Least Developed Countries, at the request of the WTO, to assist those countries to integrate into the global trading system and improve basic trading capabilities. Also in 1997 a Partnerships Group was established to strengthen the Bank's work with development institutions, representatives of civil society and the private sector. The Group established a new Development Grant Facility, which became operational in October, to support partnership initiatives and to co-ordinate all of the Bank's grant-making activities. The Bank establishes trust funds, open to contributions from member countries and multilateral organizations, NGOs, and private sector institutions, in order to support development partnerships. By 30 June 2009 the Bank had a portfolio of 1,046 active trust funds.

In June 1995 the World Bank joined other international donors (including regional development banks, other UN bodies, Canada, France, the Netherlands and the USA) in establishing a Consultative Group to Assist the Poorest (CGAP), which was to channel funds to the most needy through grass-roots agencies. An initial credit of approximately US $200m. was committed by the donors. The Bank manages the CGAP Secretariat, which is responsible for the administration of external funding and for the evaluation and approval of project financing. The CGAP provides technical assistance, training and strategic advice to microfinance institutions and other relevant bodies. As an implementing agency of the Global Environment Facility (GEF) the Bank assists countries to prepare and supervise GEF projects relating to biological diversity, climate change and other environmental protection measures. It is an example of a partnership in action which addresses a global agenda, complementing Bank country assistance activities. Other funds administered by the Bank include the Global Program to Eradicate Poliomyelitis, launched during the financial year 2002/03, the Least Developed Countries Fund for Climate Change, established in September 2002, an Education for All Fast-Track Initiative Catalytic Trust Fund, established in 2003/04, a Carbon Finance Assistance Trust Fund, established in 2004/05, and a Trust Fund for Anti-Money Laundering and Combating Financing of Terrorism for Asia-Pacific and for Central America and the Caribbean, established in 2005/06. In 2006/07 the Bank established a Global Facility for Disaster Reduction and Recovery. In September 2007 the Bank's Executive Directors approved a Carbon Partnership Facility and a Forest Carbon Partnership Facility to support its climate change activities. In May 2008 the Bank inaugurated the Global Food Crisis Response Programme (GFRP) to provide financial support, with resources of some $1,200m., to help meet the immediate needs of countries affected by the escalating cost of food production and by food shortages. Grants and loans were to be allocated on the basis of rapid needs assessments, conducted by the Bank with the FAO, the WFP and IFAD. As part of the facility a Multi-Donor Trust Fund was established to facilitate co-ordination among donors and to leverage financial support for the rapid delivery of seeds and fertilizer to small-scale farmers. In April 2009 the Bank increased the resources available under the GFRP to $2,000m. By April 2010 $1,170m. had been approved under the GFRP for initiatives in 35 countries, of which $884m. had been disbursed.

The Bank is a lead organization in providing reconstruction assistance following natural disasters or conflicts, usually in collaboration with other UN agencies or international organizations, and through special trust funds. In May–June 2004 the Bank, jointly with the Inter-American Development Bank, the European Commission and the UN, assisted the Haitian Government to prepare an Interim Co-operation Framework (ICF) as an assessment of the country's technical and financial needs in the next two years. In July the ICF was presented to an International Donor Conference on Haiti, held in Washington, DC. Participants to the conference, which was hosted by the four lead institutions, pledged some US $1,085m. to support Haiti's economic, social and political recovery. In February 2007 the World Bank hosted a donor conference to raise funds for the establishment of a Caribbean Catastrophe Risk Insurance Facility. In June the Bank hosted a Conference on the Caribbean, organized jointly with the Inter-American Development Bank and the Organization of American States, at which some 15 heads of state or government met with policy makers and representatives of the private, academic and social sectors to discuss the growth and development of the Caribbean region and strengthening relations with the USA. In January 2010 the Bank issued $100m. in immediate emergency funding to support recovery efforts in Haiti following an earthquake which caused extensive damage and loss of life. By June the Bank had extended some $479m. in grants to support Haiti reconstruction and rehabilitation; at the end of May it cancelled the remaining $36m. outstanding debt owed by Haiti. The Bank acts as trustee of a multi-donor Haiti Reconstruction Fund, which was established in March at an international donors' conference.

The Bank has worked with FAO, WHO and the World Organisation of Animal Health (OIE) to develop strategies to monitor, contain and eradicate the spread of highly pathogenic avian influenza. In September 2005 the Bank organized a meeting of leading experts on the issue and in November it co-sponsored, with FAO, WHO and OIE, an international partners' conference, focusing on control of the disease and preparedness planning for any future related influenza pandemic in humans. In January 2006 the Bank's Board of Directors approved the establishment of a funding programme (the Global Program for Avian Influenza Control and Human Pandemic Preparedness and Response—GPAI), with resources of up to US $500m., to assist countries to combat the disease. Later in that month the Bank co-sponsored, with the European Commission and the People's Republic of China, an International Ministerial Pledging Conference on Avian and Human Pandemic Influenza (AHI), convened in Beijing. Participants pledged some $1,900m. to fund disease control and pandemic preparedness activities at global, regional and country levels. Commitments to the AHI facility amounted to $126m. at January 2009. In June the Bank approved an additional $500m. to expand the GPAI in order to fund emergency operations required to prevent and control outbreaks of the new swine influenza variant pandemic (H1N1).

The Bank conducts co-financing and aid co-ordination projects with official aid agencies, export credit institutions, and commercial banks to leverage additional concessional funds for recipient countries. During the year ending 30 June 2009 65 Bank projects leveraged US $5,500m. in co-financing.

EVALUATION

The Independent Evaluation Group is an independent unit within the World Bank. It conducts Country Assistance Evaluations to assess the development effectiveness of a Bank country programme, and studies and publishes the results of projects after a loan has been fully disbursed, so as to identify problems and possible improvements in future activities. In addition, the department reviews the Bank's global programmes and produces the *Annual Review of Development Effectiveness*. In 1996 a Quality Assurance Group was established to monitor the effectiveness of the Bank's operations and performance. In March 2009 the Bank published an Action Plan on Aid Effectiveness, based on the Accra Agenda for Action that had been adopted in September 2008 during the Third High Level Forum on Aid Effectiveness, held in Ghana.

In September 1993 the Bank established an independent Inspection Panel, consistent with the Bank's objective of improving project implementation and accountability. The Panel, which became operational in September 1994, was to conduct independent investigations and report on complaints from local people concerning the design, appraisal and implementation of development projects supported by the Bank. By mid-2009 the Panel had received 58 formal requests for inspection.

IBRD INSTITUTIONS

World Bank Institute (WBI): founded in March 1999 by merger of the Bank's Learning and Leadership Centre, previously responsible for internal staff training, and the Economic Development Institute (EDI), which had been established in 1955 to train government officials concerned with development programmes and policies. The new Institute aimed to emphasize the Bank's priority areas through the provision of training courses and seminars relating to poverty, crisis response, good governance and anti-corruption strategies. The Institute supports a Global Knowledge Partnership, which was established in 1997 to promote alliances between governments, companies, other agencies and organizations committed to applying information and communication technologies for development purposes. Under the EDI a World Links for Development programme was also initiated to connect schools in developing countries with partner establishments in industrialized nations via the internet. In 1999 the WBI expanded its programmes through distance learning, a Global Development Network, and use of new technologies. A new initiative, Global Development Learning Network (GDLN), aimed to expand access to information and learning opportunities through the internet, video conferences and organized exchanges. By early 2010 the GDLN comprised more than 120 recognized global institutions, or Affiliates, in some 80 countries. At that time the WBI had also established 60 formal partnership arrangements with learning centres and public, private and non-governmental organizations to support joint capacity building programmes; many other informal partnerships were also in place. During 2009/10 new South-South Learning Middle-income country (MIC)–OECD Knowledge Exchange facilities were to be established. In July 2009 the Institute began implementing a renewal strategy to refocus its work on the following key development areas: fragile and conflict-affected states; the global economic crisis; governance; climate change; health systems; public-private partnerships in infrastructure; and sustainable urban development; Vice-Pres. SANJAY PRADHAN (India); publs *Annual Report*, *Development Outreach* (quarterly), other books, working papers, case studies.

International Centre for Settlement of Investment Disputes (ICSID): founded in 1966 under the Convention of the Settlement of Investment Disputes between States and Nationals of Other States. The Convention was designed to encourage the growth of private foreign investment for economic development, by creating the possibility, always subject to the consent of both parties, for a Contracting State and a foreign investor who is a national of another Contracting State to settle any legal dispute that might arise out of such an investment by conciliation and/or arbitration before an impartial, international forum. The governing body of the Centre is its Administrative Council, composed of one representative of each Contracting State, all of whom have equal voting power. The President of the World Bank is (*ex officio*) the non-voting Chairman of the Administrative Council. At early 2010 310 cases had been registered with the Centre, of which 183 had been concluded and 127 were pending consideration. At that time 144 countries had signed and ratified the Convention to become ICSID Contracting States; Sec.-Gen. MEG KINNEAR (Canada).

Publications

Abstracts of Current Studies: The World Bank Research Program (annually).
African Development Indicators (annually).
Annual Report on Operations Evaluation.
Annual Report on Portfolio Performance.
Annual Review of Development Effectiveness.
Doing Business (annually).
Global Commodity Markets (quarterly).
Global Development Finance (annually).
Global Economic Prospects (annually).
ICSID Annual Report.
ICSID Review—Foreign Investment Law Journal (2 a year).
Joint BIS-IMF-OECD-World Bank Statistics on External Debt (quarterly).
News from ICSID (2 a year).
Poverty Reduction and the World Bank (annually).
Poverty Reduction Strategies Newsletter (quarterly).
Research News (quarterly).
Staff Working Papers.
World Bank Annual Report.
World Bank Atlas (annually).
World Bank Economic Review (3 a year).
The World Bank and the Environment (annually).
World Bank Research Observer.
World Development Indicators (annually).
World Development Report (annually).

Statistics

IBRD OPERATIONS APPROVED IN LATIN AMERICA AND THE CARIBBEAN, 1 JULY 2008–30 JUNE 2009
(US $ million)

Country	Purpose	Amount
Argentina	Social and fiscal national identification system	20.0
	Mining environmental restoration	30.0
	Second provincial agricultural development specific investment loan	300.0
	Unleashing productive innovation	150.0
	Renewable Energy in the Rural Market Project (PERMER) (additional financing)	50.0
	Basic social protection	450.0
	Matanza-Riachuelo Basin sustainable development	840.0
Barbados	Second HIV/AIDS specific investment loan	35.0
Brazil	Second provincial agricultural development specific investment loan	35.6
	Uruguaiana, Rio Grande do Sul (RS), integrated municipal development	6.8
	Bagé, RS, integrated municipal development	6.6
	Rio Grande do Sul fiscal sustainability for growth	1,100.0
	Sergipe State integrated project: rural poverty	20.8
	Ceará inclusive growth (SWAP II) program loan	240.0
	Paraiba second rural poverty reduction specific investment loan	20.9
	Acre social and economic inclusion and sustainable development (PROACRE)	120.0
	Ceará integrated water resource management (additional financing)	103.0
	Santa Maria, RS, integrated municipal development	14.0
	Brazil health formation and quality improvement	235.0
	Brazil Espirito Santo water and coastal pollution management (additional financing)	71.5
	Ceará regional economic development	46.0
	Brazil sustainable environmental management	1,300.0
	Federal District multisector public management loan	130.0
	Pernambuco education results and accountability	154.0
Chile	Promoting innovation and competitiveness	30.0
Colombia	Bogotá urban services	30.0
	Strengthening public information, monitoring, evaluation for results management	8.5
	Third sustainable development policy loan	450.0
	Disaster risk management with catastrophe deferred draw down option	150.0
	Second social safety net specific investment loan	636.5
Costa Rica	Costa Rica catastrophe deferred draw down option	65.0
	Public finance, education and competitiveness enhancing development loan	500.0
Dominican Republic	Water and sanitation in tourist areas	27.5
El Salvador	El Salvador public finance and social sector development	450.0
Guatemala	Fiscal and institutional development	200.0
	Disaster risk management with a catastrophe deferred draw down option	85.0
Jamaica	Jamaica fiscal and debt sustainability	100.0
Mexico	Mexico information technology development	80.0
	Savings and rural finance (second phase)	50.0
	Mexico environmental sustainability	300.8
	Private housing finance markets strengthening	1,010.0
	Results-based management and budgeting technical assistance loan	17.2

Country—*continued*	Purpose	Amount
	Mexico environmental sustainability (supplemental financing)	401.0
	Mexico sustainable rural development	50.0
	Support to Oportunidades project	1,503.8
	Customs institutional strengthening	10.0
Panama	Health quality and performance improvement	40.0
	Basic education quality improvement	35.0
	Protecting the poor under global uncertainty policy loan	80.0
	Second competitiveness and public financial management development policy loan	100.0
Paraguay	Water and sanitation sector modernization	64.0
	First public sector reform development policy loan	100.0
Peru	Second programmatic fiscal management and competitiveness development policy loan	370.0
	Second programmatic fiscal management and competitiveness development policy loan (supplemental financing)	330.0
	Second health reform adaptable program loan	15.0
	Environmental development	330.0
	Second results and accountability development policy loan	330.0
Uruguay	Second programmatic reform implementation development policy loan	400.0

Source: World Bank, *Annual Report 2009*.

International Development Association—IDA

Address: 1818 H Street, NW, Washington, DC 20433, USA.

Telephone: (202) 473-1000; **fax:** (202) 477-6391; **internet:** www.worldbank.org/ida.

The International Development Association began operations in November 1960. Affiliated to the IBRD, IDA advances capital to the poorer developing member countries on more flexible terms than those offered by the IBRD.

Organization

(August 2010)

Officers and staff of the IBRD serve concurrently as officers and staff of IDA.

President and Chairman of Executive Directors: Robert B. Zoellick (USA).

Activities

IDA assistance is aimed at the poorer developing countries (i.e. those with an annual GNP per capita of less than US $1,135 were to qualify for assistance in 2009/10) in order to support their poverty reduction strategies. Under IDA lending conditions, credits can be extended to countries whose balance of payments could not sustain the burden of repayment required for IBRD loans. Terms are more favourable than those provided by the IBRD; credits are for a period of 35 or 40 years, with a 'grace period' of 10 years, and carry no interest charges. At mid-2010 79 countries were eligible for IDA assistance, including several small-island economies with a GNP per head greater than $1,135, but which would otherwise have little or no access to Bank funds, and 14 so-called 'blend borrowers' which are entitled to borrow from both IDA and the IBRD.

IDA's total development resources, consisting of members' subscriptions and supplementary resources (additional subscriptions and contributions), are replenished periodically by contributions from the more affluent member countries. Negotiations on the 15th replenishment of IDA funds (IDA15) commenced in March 2007, in Paris, France. Participants selected the following 'special themes' for further discussion: the role of IDA in global aid architecture; the effectiveness of IDA assistance at country level; and IDA's role in fragile states. In December an agreement was concluded to replenish IDA resources by some US $41,600m., for the period 1 July 2008–30 June 2011, of which $25,100m. was pledged by 45 donor countries.

During the year ending 30 June 2009 IDA commitments amounted to US $14,041m. for 176 projects, compared with $11,235m. for 199 projects in the previous year. More than one-third of lending was for infrastructure projects (including energy and mining, transportation, water sanitation and flood protection, and information and communications and technologies sectors).

In December 2008 the Bank's Board of Executive Directors approved a new IDA facility, the Financial Crisis Response Fast Track Facility, to accelerate the provision of up to US $2,000m. of IDA15 resources to help the poorest countries to counter the impact of the global economic and financial crisis. The first operations approved under the Facility, in February 2009, were for Armenia (amounting to $35m.) and the Democratic Republic of Congo ($100m.) in support of employment creation and infrastructure development initiatives and meeting the costs of essential services. In December the Board of Executive Directors approved a Crisis Response Window to deploy an additional $1,300m. of IDA funds to support the poorest countries affected by the economic crisis until the end of the IDA15 period (June 2011). The new facility was proposed during a mid-term review of IDA15, held in November, with the aim of assisting those countries to maintain spending on sectors critical to achieving the Millennium Development Goals.

IDA administers a Trust Fund, which was established in November 1996 as part of a World Bank/IMF initiative to assist heavily indebted poor countries (HIPCs). In September 2005 the World Bank's Development Committee and the International Monetary and Financial Committee of the IMF endorsed a proposal of the Group of Eight (G8) industrialized countries to cancel the remaining multilateral debt owed by HIPCs that had reached their completion point under the scheme (see IBRD). In December IDA convened a meeting of donor countries to discuss funding to uphold its financial capability upon its contribution to the so-called Multilateral Debt Relief Initiative (MDRI). The scheme was approved by the Board of Executive Directors in March 2006 and entered into effect on 1 July. By July 2010 30 countries had reached completion point, including Bolivia, Guyana, Haiti, Honduras and Nicaragua.

Publication

Annual Report.

Statistics

IDA CREDITS APPROVED IN SOUTH AMERICA AND THE CARIBBEAN, 1 JULY 2008–30 JUNE 2009
(US $ million)

Country/Region	Purpose	Amount
Bolivia	Rural alliances project (additional financing)	30.0
Grenada	OECS education development (additional financing)	1.9
	OECS skills for inclusive growth credit	3.0
Haiti	Avian influenza control and human influenza emergency preparedness and control	1.6
	Emergency bridge reconstruction and vulnerability reduction	20.0
	Community-driven development (additional financing)	8.0
	Haiti emergency school reconstruction	5.0
	Strengthening the management of agricultural public services	5.0
Honduras	Food prices crisis (supplemental financing to the first programmatic financial sector development policy credit)	10.0
	Honduras power sector efficiency enhancement	30.0
	Second road reconstruction and improvement specific investment credit	25.0
Nicaragua	Development policy credit	20.0
	Greater Managua water and sanitation specific investment credit/grant	20.0/20.0
Saint Lucia	Disaster management II specific investment credit	3.0

Source: World Bank, *Annual Report 2009*.

International Finance Corporation—IFC

Address: 2121 Pennsylvania Ave, NW, Washington, DC 20433, USA.

Telephone: (202) 473-3800; **fax:** (202) 974-4384; **e-mail:** information@ifc.org; **internet:** www.ifc.org.

IFC was founded in 1956 as a member of the World Bank Group to stimulate economic growth in developing countries by financing private-sector investments, mobilizing capital in international financial markets, and providing technical assistance and advice to governments and businesses.

Organization

(August 2010)

IFC is a separate legal entity in the World Bank Group. Executive Directors of the World Bank also serve as Directors of IFC. The President of the World Bank is *ex officio* Chairman of the IFC Board of Directors, which has appointed him President of IFC. Subject to his overall supervision, the day-to-day operations of IFC are conducted by its staff under the direction of the Executive Vice-President. The senior management team includes 10 Vice-Presidents responsible for regional and thematic groupings. At the end of June 2009 IFC had 3,402 staff members, of whom 54% were based in field offices in 86 countries.

PRINCIPAL OFFICERS

President: ROBERT B. ZOELLICK (USA).

Executive Vice-President: LARS THUNELL (Sweden).

Vice-President, Europe, Central Asia, and Latin America and the Caribbean (and Global Financial Markets): JYRKI KOSKELO (Finland).

Director, Latin America and the Caribbean Department: ATUL MEHTA.

MISSIONS AND OFFICES IN SOUTH AMERICA, CENTRAL AMERICA AND THE CARIBBEAN

IFC Advisory Services in Latin America and the Caribbean: Avda Alvarez Calderón 185, 2°, San Isidro, Lima; tel. (11) 6112501; fax (11) 6112525; Gen. Man. LUKE HAGGARTY.

Argentina: Bouchard Plaza, Bouchard 557, 11°, 1106 Buenos Aires; tel. (11) 4114-7200; fax (11) 4312-7184; 'hub' for Chile, Paraguay and Uruguay; Country Man. SALEM ROHANA.

Bolivia: Edif. Victor, 8°, Calle Fernando Guachalla 342, La Paz; tel. (2) 211-5400; fax (2) 244-5499; Country Man. ENRIQUE CAÑAS.

Brazil (Rio de Janeiro): Rua Redentor 14, Ipanema, 22421-030, Rio de Janeiro; tel. (21) 2525-5850; fax (21) 2525-5879; Country Man. ANDREW GUNTHER.

Brazil (São Paulo): Edif. Torre Sul, Rua James Jouse 65, Ciudade Monções, São Paulo; tel. (11) 5185-6888; fax (11) 5185-6890.

Colombia: Carrera 7, 71-21, Torre A, 14°, Edif. Fiduagraria, Bogotá, DC; tel. (1) 319-2330; fax (1) 319-2359; 'hub' for Bolivia, Ecuador, Peru and Venezuela; Country Man. ENRIQUE CAÑAS.

Dominican Republic: Calle Virgilio Diaz Ordoñez 36, esq. Gustavo Mejía Ricart, Edif. Mezzo Tempo, Suite 401, Santo Domingo; tel. 566-6815; fax 566-7746; Country Man. JUN ZHANG.

El Salvador: Blvd Orden de Malta Sur, Edif. Naciones Unidas, Urb. Santa Elena, Antigua Cuscatlan, La Libertad, San Salvador; tel. 2263-4877; fax 2526-5936; Operations Officer ERNESTO MARTÍN-MONTERO.

Guatemala: 13 calle 3-40, Zona 10, Edif. Atlantis Nivel 14, Of. 1402, Guatemala City; tel. 2329-8047; fax 2329-8099; Senior Investment Officer BERNARDO RICO.

Haiti: 7 rue Oge, Petion-Ville; tel. 2256-4260; fax 2256-0848; Investment Officer JENNIFER FIEVRE.

Honduras: Centro Financiero Citi, 4°, blvd San Juan Bosco, Col. Payaqui, Tegucigalpa; tel. 239-4551; fax 239-4555; Senior Investment Officer EDGAR RESTREPO.

Jamaica: Island Life Center, 6 St Lucia Ave, Suite 8 South, Kingston 5; tel. 960-0459; fax 960-0463; also serves Guyana; Resident Rep. KALIM SHAH.

Mexico: Montes Urales, Of. 503, Col. Lomas de Chapultepec, 11000 México, DF; tel. (55) 3098-0130; fax (55) 3098-0146; 'hub' for Costa Rica, El Salvador, Guatemala, Honduras, Nicaragua and Panama; Senior Man. ROBERTO ALBISETTI.

Nicaragua: Plaza Santo Domingo, Km 6 1/2 Carretera a Masaya, Edif. Cobirsa 2, Managua; tel. 270-0000; fax 270-0077; Investment Officer JUAN CARLOS PEREIRA.

Peru: Calle Miguel Dasso 104, 5°, San Isidro, Lima; tel. (11) 6112500; fax (11) 6112525; Country Man. ENRIQUE CAÑAS.

Trinidad and Tobago: SW Penthouse, SAGICOR Bldg, 3rd Floor, 16 Queen's Park West, POB 751, Port of Spain; tel. 628-5074; fax 622-1003; regional 'hub' for Belize, Dominican Republic, Guyana, Haiti, Jamaica and OECS countries; Country Man. JUN ZHANG.

Activities

IFC aims to promote economic development in developing member countries by assisting the growth of private enterprise and effective capital markets. It finances private sector projects, through loans, the purchase of equity, quasi-equity products, and risk management services, and assists governments to create conditions that stimulate the flow of domestic and foreign private savings and investment. IFC may provide finance for a project that is partly state-owned, provided that there is participation by the private sector and that the project is operated on a commercial basis. IFC also mobilizes additional resources from other financial institutions, in particular through syndicated loans, thus providing access to international capital markets. IFC provides a range of advisory services to help to improve the investment climate in developing countries and offers technical assistance to private enterprises and governments. In 2008 IFC formulated a policy document to help to increase its impact in the three-year period 2009–11. The IFC Road Map identified five strategic 'pillars' as priority areas of activity: strengthening the focus on frontier markets (i.e. the lowest-income countries or regions of middle-income countries, those affected by conflict, or underdeveloped industrial sectors); building long-term partnerships with emerging 'players' in developing countries; addressing climate change and securing environmental and social sustainability; promoting private sector growth in infrastructure, health and education; and developing local financial markets. From late 2008 IFC's overriding concern was to respond effectively to the difficulties facing member countries affected by the global economic and financial crisis and to maintain a sustainable level of development. In particular it aimed to preserve and create employment opportunities, to support supply chains for local businesses, and to provide credit.

To be eligible for financing projects must be profitable for investors, as well as financially and economically viable; must benefit the economy of the country concerned; and must comply with IFC's environmental and social guidelines. IFC aims to promote best corporate governance and management methods and sustainable business practices, and encourages partnerships between governments, non-governmental organizations and community groups. In 2001/02 IFC developed a Sustainability Framework to help to assess the longer-term economic, environmental and social impact of projects. The first Sustainability Review was published in mid-2002. In 2002/03 IFC assisted 10 international banks to draft a voluntary set of guidelines (the Equator Principles), based on IFC's environmental, social and safeguard monitoring policies, to be applied to their global project finance activities. A revised set of Equator Principles was released in July 2006. In September 2009 IFC initiated a Performance Standards Review Process to define new standards to be applied within the Equator Principles framework. At June 2010 68 financial institutions had signed up to the Equator Principles.

In November 2004 IFC announced the establishment of a Global Trade Finance Programme (GTFP), with initial funding of some US $500m., which aimed to support small-scale importers and exporters in emerging markets, and to facilitate South–South trade in goods and services, by providing guarantees for trade transactions, as well as extending technical assistance and training to local financial institutions. Additional funding of $500m. was approved in January 2007, and in October 2008, by which time there were 147 confirming banks from 70 countries participating in the initiative and 126 issuing banks in 66 countries. In December, as part of a set of measures to support the global economy, the Board of Directors approved an expansion of the GTFP, doubling its funding to $3,000m. Other initiatives included the establishment of an Infrastructure Crisis Facility to provide investment for existing projects affected by a lack of private funding, and a new Bank Capitalization Fund (to be financed, up to $3,000m., with the Japan Bank for International Co-operation) to provide investment and advisory services to banks in emerging markets. In May 2009 IFC established an Asset Management Company, as a wholly owned subsidiary, to administer the Capitalization Fund. IFC committed $1,000m. in funds to a new Global Trade Liquidity Program, which was inaugurated by the World Bank Group in April, with the aim of mobilizing support of up to $50,000m. in trade transactions through financing extended by governments, other development banks and the private sector.

IFC's authorized capital is US $2,450m. At 30 June 2009 paid-in capital was $2,369m. The World Bank was originally the principal source of borrowed funds, but IFC also borrows from private capital markets. IFC's net income amounted to –$151m. in 2008/09 (after a $450m. transfer to IDA), compared with $1,547m. in the previous year. In December 2008 the Board of Directors approved a Sovereign Funds Initiative to enable IFC to raise and manage commercial capital from sovereign funds.

In the year ending 30 June 2009 project financing approved by IFC amounted to US $12,405m. for 447 projects in 103 countries (compared with $14,649m. for 372 projects in the previous year). Of the total approved in 2008/09, $10,547m. was for IFC's own account, while $1,858m. was in the form of loan syndications and underwriting of securities issues and investment funds by more than 100 participating banks and institutional investors. Generally, IFC limits its financing to less than 25% of the total cost of a project, but may take up to a 35% stake in a venture (although never as a majority shareholder). Disbursements for IFC's account amounted to $5,640m. in 2008/09 (compared with $7,539m. in the previous year).

IFC has identified the following as priority strategic areas for future activity in Latin America and the Caribbean: to improve the environment to promote and support businesses; to broaden and facilitate access to finance; to increase private sector participation in infrastructure and advise on reforms of the regulatory framework; and to promote sustainability through higher standards for corporate governance and environmental and social performance. In 2008/09 IFC committed some US $2,721m. in financing for 124 projects in 21 countries in the region. An additional $670m. was mobilized in the form of loan participation, parallel loans and structured finance. During that year IFC participated, with other International Financial Institutions, in establishing a Latin American and Caribbean (LAC) Multilateral Crisis Initiative, committing some $7,900m. of the total $90,000m. over a two-year period. IFC pledged $150m. in support of an $850m. Caribbean Joint Action Plan which was signed in May 2010.

IFC's Advisory Services are a major part of the organization's involvement with member countries to support the development of private enterprises and efforts to generate funding, as well as to enhance private sector participation in developing infrastructure. Advisory services cover the following five main areas of expertise: the business enabling environment (i.e improving the investment climate in a country); access to financing (including developing financing institutions, improving financial infrastructure and strengthening regulatory frameworks); infrastructure (mainly encouraging private sector participation); environment and social sustainability; and corporate advice (in particular in support of small and medium-sized enterprises—SMEs). In December 2008 the Board of Directors determined to provide additional funding to IFC advisory services in order to strengthen the capacity of financial institutions and governments to respond to the crisis in the global financial markets. IFC manages, jointly financed with the World Bank and MIGA, the Foreign Investment Advisory Service (FIAS), which provides technical assistance and advice on promoting foreign investment and strengthening the country's investment framework at the request of governments. Under the Technical Assistance Trust Funds Program (TATF), established in 1988, IFC manages resources contributed by various governments and agencies to provide finance for feasibility studies, project identification studies and other types of technical assistance relating to project preparation. In 2004 a Grassroots Business Initiative was established, with external donor funding, to support businesses that provide economic opportunities for disadvantaged communities in Africa, Latin America, and South and Southeast Asia. Since 2002 IFC has administered an online SME Toolkit to enhance the accessibility of business training and advice. By 2009 the service was available in 16 languages.

Since 2004 IFC has presented an annual Client Leadership Award to a chosen corporate client who more represents IFC values in innovation, operational excellence and corporate governance.

Publications

Annual Report.

Doing Business (annually).

Emerging Stock Markets Factbook (annually).

Lessons of Experience (series).

Outcomes (quarterly).

Results on the Ground (series).

Review of Small Businesses (annually).

Sustainability Report (annually).

Other handbooks, discussion papers, technical documents, policy toolkits, public policy journals.

Multilateral Investment Guarantee Agency—MIGA

Address: 1818 H Street, NW, Washington, DC 20433, USA.

Telephone: (202) 473-6163; **fax:** (202) 522-2630; **internet:** www.miga.org.

MIGA was founded in 1988 as an affiliate of the World Bank. Its mandate is to encourage the flow of foreign direct investment to, and among, developing member countries, through the provision of political risk insurance and investment marketing services to foreign investors and host governments, respectively.

Organization

(August 2010)

MIGA is legally and financially separate from the World Bank. It is supervised by a Council of Governors (comprising one Governor and one Alternate of each member country) and an elected Board of Directors (of no less than 12 members).

President: ROBERT B. ZOELLICK (USA).

Executive Vice-President: IZUMI KOBAYASHI (Japan).

Activities

The convention establishing MIGA took effect in April 1988. Authorized capital was US $1,082m. In April 1998 the Board of Directors approved an increase in MIGA's capital base. A grant of $150m. was transferred from the IBRD as part of the package, while the capital increase (totalling $700m. callable capital and $150m. paid-in capital) was approved by MIGA's Council of Governors in April 1999. A three-year subscription period then commenced, covering the period April 1999–March 2002 (later extended to March 2003). At 30 June 2009 110 countries had subscribed $749.9m. of the new capital increase. At that time total subscriptions to the capital stock amounted to $1,899.9m., of which $362.4m. was paid-in.

MIGA guarantees eligible investments against losses resulting from non-commercial risks, under four main categories:

(i) transfer risk resulting from host government restrictions on currency conversion and transfer;

(ii) risk of loss resulting from legislative or administrative actions of the host government;

(iii) repudiation by the host government of contracts with investors in cases in which the investor has no access to a competent forum;

(iv) the risk of armed conflict and civil unrest.

Before guaranteeing any investment, MIGA must ensure that it is commercially viable, contributes to the development process and is not harmful to the environment. During the fiscal year 1998/99 MIGA and IFC appointed the first Compliance Advisor and Ombudsman to consider the concerns of local communities directly affected by MIGA- or IFC-sponsored projects. In February 1999 the Board of Directors approved an increase in the amount of political risk insurance available for each project, from US $75m. to $200m. In April 2009 the Board of Directors approved modifications to MIGA's policies and operational regulations in order to enhance operational flexibility and efficiency, in particular in the poorest countries and those affected by conflict.

During the year ending 30 June 2009 MIGA issued 30 investment insurance contracts for 26 projects with a value of US $1,400m. (compared with 38 contracts amounting to $2,100m. in the previous year). Since 1988 the total investment guarantees issued amounted to some $20,900m., through 952 contracts in support of 600 projects.

MIGA works with local insurers, export credit agencies, development finance institutions and other organizations to promote insurance in a country, to ensure a level of consistency among insurers and to support capacity-building within the insurance industry. MIGA also offers investment marketing services to help to promote foreign investment in developing countries and in transitional economies, and to disseminate information on investment opportunities. In early 2007 MIGA's technical assistance services were amalgamated into the Foreign Advisory Investment Service (FIAS, see IFC), of which MIGA became a lead partner, along with IFC and the World Bank.

In October 1995 MIGA established a new network on investment opportunities, which connected investment promotion agencies (IPAs) throughout the world on an electronic information network. The so-called IPA*net* aimed to encourage further investments among developing countries, to provide access to comprehensive information on investment laws and conditions and to strengthen links between governmental, business and financial associations and investors. A new version of IPA*net* was launched in 1997 (and can be accessed at www.ipanet.net). In June 1998 MIGA initiated a new internet-based facility, 'PrivatizationLink', to provide information on investment opportunities resulting from the privatization of industries in developing economies. In October 2000 a specialized facility within the service was established to facilitate investment in Russia (russia.privatizationlink.com). During 2000/01 an office was established in Paris, France, to promote and co-ordinate European investment in developing countries, in particular in Africa and Eastern Europe. In March 2002 MIGA opened a regional office, based in Johannesburg, South Africa. In September a new regional office was inaugurated in Singapore, in order to facilitate foreign investment in Asia.

In April 2002 MIGA launched a new service, 'FDIXchange', to provide potential investors, advisors and financial institutions with up-to-date market analysis and information on foreign direct investment opportunities in emerging economies (accessible at www.fdixchange.com). An FDIXchange Investor Information Development Programme was launched in January 2003. In January 2004 a new FDI Promotion Centre became available on the internet (www.fdipromotion.com) to facilitate information exchange and knowledge-sharing among investment promotion professionals, in particular in developing countries. (A Serbian language version was launched in June 2005.) During 2003/04 MIGA established a new fund, the Invest-in-Development Facility, to enhance the role of foreign investment in attaining the Millennium Development Goals. In 2005/06 MIGA supported for the first time a project aimed at selling carbon credits gained by reducing greenhouse gas emissions; it provided US $2m. in guarantee coverage to the El Salvador-based initiative. A new internet service, relating to political risk management and insurance, was launched during 2006/07 (www.pri-center.com).

Publications

Annual Report.

MIGA News (online newsletter; every 2 months).

Other guides, brochures and regional briefs.

International Fund for Agricultural Development—IFAD

Address: Via Paolo di Dono 44, 00142 Rome, Italy.

Telephone: (06) 54591; **fax:** (06) 5043463; **e-mail:** ifad@ifad.org; **internet:** www.ifad.org.

IFAD was established in 1977, following a decision by the 1974 UN World Food Conference, with a mandate to combat hunger and eradicate poverty on a sustainable basis in the low-income, food-deficit regions of the world. Funding operations began in January 1978.

Organization

(August 2010)

GOVERNING COUNCIL

Each member state is represented in the Governing Council (the Fund's highest authority) by a Governor and an Alternate. Sessions are held annually with special sessions as required. The Governing Council elects the President of the Fund (who also chairs the

Executive Board) by a two-thirds majority for a four-year term. The President is eligible for re-election.

EXECUTIVE BOARD

Consists of 18 members and 18 alternates, elected by the Governing Council, who serve for three years. The Executive Board is responsible for the conduct and general operation of IFAD and approves loans and grants for projects; it holds three regular sessions each year. An independent Office of Evaluation reports directly to the Board.

The governance structure of the Fund is based on the classification of members. Membership of the Executive Board is distributed as follows: eight List A countries (i.e. industrialized donor countries), four List B (petroleum-exporting developing donor countries), and six List C (recipient developing countries), divided equally among the three Sub-List C categories (i.e. for Africa, Europe, Asia and the Pacific, and Latin America and the Caribbean).

President and Chairman of Executive Board: KANAYO F. NWANZE (Nigeria).

Vice-President: YUKIKO OMURA (Japan).

Activities

IFAD provides financing primarily for projects designed to improve food production systems in developing member states and to strengthen related policies, services and institutions. In allocating resources IFAD is guided by: the need to increase food production in the poorest food-deficit countries; the potential for increasing food production in other developing countries; and the importance of improving the nutrition, health and education of the poorest people in developing countries, i.e. small-scale farmers, artisanal fishermen, nomadic pastoralists, indigenous populations, rural women, and the rural landless. All projects emphasize the participation of beneficiaries in development initiatives, both at the local and national level. Issues relating to gender and household food security are incorporated into all aspects of its activities. IFAD is committed to achieving the Millennium Development Goals (MDGs), pledged by governments attending a special session of the UN General Assembly in September 2000, and, in particular, the objective to reduce by 50% the proportion of people living in extreme poverty by 2015. In 2001 the Fund introduced new measures to improve monitoring and impact evaluation, in particular to assess its contribution to achieving the MDGs.

In December 2006 the Executive Board adopted IFAD's Strategic Framework for 2007–10, in which it reiterated its commitment to enabling the rural poor to achieve household food security and to overcome their poverty. Accordingly, the Fund's efforts were to focus on ensuring that poor rural populations have improved and sustainable access to, and sufficiently developed skills to take advantage of: natural resources; better agricultural technologies and production services; a broad range of financial services; transparent competitive agricultural input and produce markets; opportunities for rural off-farm employment and enterprise development; and local and national policy and programming processes. Within this Framework the Fund has also formulated regional strategies for rural poverty reduction, based on a series of regional poverty assessments. In 2003 a new Policy Division was established under the External Affairs Department to co-ordinate policy work at the corporate level. A Policy Forum was launched in 2004, comprising IFAD senior management and staff. During 2007–09 IFAD implemented a performance-enhancing action plan for improving its development effectiveness.

IFAD is a participant in the High Level Task Force (HLTF) on the Global Food Security Crisis, which was established by the UN Secretary-General in April 2008 and aims to address the impact of soaring global levels of food and fuel prices and to formulate a comprehensive framework for action. In June IFAD participated in the High-Level Conference on World Food Security and the Challenges of Climate Change and Bioenergy, convened by FAO in Rome, Italy. The meeting adopted a Declaration on Food Security, which noted an urgent need to develop the agricultural sectors and expand food production in developing countries and countries with economies in transition, and for increased investment in rural development, agriculture and agribusiness. In January 2009 the HLTF participated in a follow-up high level meeting convened in Madrid, Spain, and attended also by 62 government ministers and representatives from 126 countries. The meeting agreed to initiate a consultation process with regard to the establishment of a Global Partnership for Agriculture, Food Security and Nutrition.

IFAD is a leading repository of knowledge, resources and expertise in the field of rural hunger and poverty alleviation. In 2001 it renewed its commitment to becoming a global knowledge institution for rural poverty-related issues. Through its technical assistance grants, IFAD aims to promote research and capacity-building in the agricultural sector, as well as the development of technologies to increase production and alleviate rural poverty. In recent years IFAD has been increasingly involved in promoting the use of communication technology to facilitate the exchange of information and experience among rural communities, specialized institutions and organizations, and IFAD-sponsored projects. Within the strategic context of knowledge management, IFAD has supported initiatives to establish regional electronic networks, such as Electronic Networking for Rural Asia/Pacific (ENRAP, currently in its third phase), and FIDAMERICA in Latin America and the Caribbean (established in 1995 and currently in its fourth phase), as well as to develop other lines of communication between organizations, local agents and the rural poor.

IFAD is empowered to make both loans and grants. Loans are available on highly concessionary, intermediate and ordinary terms. Highly concessionary loans carry no interest but have an annual service charge of 0.75% and a repayment period of 40 years, including a 10-year grace period. New Debt Sustainability Framework (DSF) grant financing was introduced in 2007 in place of highly concessional loans for heavily indebted poor countries (HIPCs). Intermediate term loans are subject to a variable interest charge, equivalent to 50% of the interest rate charged on World Bank loans, and are repaid over 20 years. Ordinary loans carry a variable interest charge equal to that levied by the World Bank, and are repaid over 15–18 years. In 2009 highly concessionary loans represented some 41.9% of total lending in that year, DSF grants 28.9%, intermediate loans 13.1%, and ordinary loans 16.1%. Research and technical assistance grants are awarded to projects focusing on research and training, and for project preparation and development. In order to increase the impact of its lending resources on food production, the Fund seeks as much as possible to attract other external donors and beneficiary governments as cofinanciers of its projects. Some 15 of the 26 projects approved in 2009 that were designed and initiated by IFAD were to receive external cofinancing, accounting for some 23.8% of their total cost; meanwhile, domestic contributions, i.e. from recipient governments and other local sources, accounted for 20.5%.

In October 2007 the HIPC Trust Fund, administered by the World Bank, transferred US $104.1m. to IFAD, representing the first instalment of about $282m. which was to offset the impact of IFAD's debt relief commitments to post-decision point HIPC countries (see under IBRD) on the Fund's available resources for the disbursement of loans and grants. At 31 December 2009 IFAD had fulfilled its debt relief requirements to all of the 34 HIPCs that had met their decision points at that time.

IFAD's development projects usually include a number of components, such as infrastructure (e.g. improvement of water supplies, small-scale irrigation and road construction); input supply (e.g. improved seeds, fertilizers and pesticides); institutional support (e.g. research, training and extension services); and producer incentives (e.g. pricing and marketing improvements). IFAD also attempts to enable the landless to acquire income-generating assets: by increasing the provision of credit for the rural poor, it seeks to free them from dependence on the capital market and to generate productive activities.

In addition to its regular efforts to identify projects and programmes, IFAD organizes special programming missions to certain selected countries to undertake a comprehensive review of the constraints affecting the rural poor, and to help countries to design strategies for the removal of these constraints. In general, projects based on the recommendations of these missions tend to focus on institutional improvements at the national and local level to direct inputs and services to small farmers and the landless rural poor. Monitoring and evaluation missions are also sent to check the progress of projects and to assess the impact of poverty reduction efforts.

The Fund supports projects that are concerned with environmental conservation, in an effort to alleviate poverty that results from the deterioration of natural resources. In addition, it extends environmental assessment grants to review the environmental consequences of projects under preparation. In October 1997 IFAD was appointed to administer the Global Mechanism of the Convention to Combat Desertification in those Countries Experiencing Drought and Desertification, particularly in Africa, which entered into force in December 1996. The Mechanism was envisaged as a means of mobilizing and channelling resources for implementation of the Convention. A series of collaborative institutional arrangements were to be concluded between IFAD, UNDP and the World Bank in order to facilitate the effective functioning of the Mechanism. IFAD is an executing agency of the Global Environmental Facility, specializing in the area of combating rural poverty and environmental degradation.

In Latin America and the Caribbean IFAD has aimed to formulate and implement projects that integrate the rural poor into the mainstream economy as well as local and centralized decision-making processes, enhance the productivity and market competitiveness of small-scale farmers, promote sustainable production and utilization of natural resources in environmentally fragile areas, and encourage the participation of women in rural development programmes. During 2009 IFAD approved six loans for projects in the Latin America and Caribbean region, amounting to US $102m. (or 15.1% of total IFAD lending in that year). At end-2009 31 programmes and projects were ongoing in the region.

During 1998 the Executive Board endorsed a policy framework for the Fund's provision of assistance in post-conflict situations, with the aim of achieving a continuum from emergency relief to a secure basis from which to pursue sustainable development. In July 2001 IFAD and UNAIDS signed a memorandum of understanding on developing a co-operation agreement. A meeting of technical experts from IFAD, FAO, WFP and UNAIDS, held in December, addressed means of mitigating the impact of HIV/AIDS on food security and rural livelihoods in affected regions.

During the late 1990s IFAD established several partnerships within the agribusiness sector, with a view to improving performance at project level, broadening access to capital markets, and encouraging the advancement of new technologies. Since 1996 it has chaired the Support Group of the Global Forum on Agricultural Research (GFAR), which facilitates dialogue between research centres and institutions, farmers' organizations, non-governmental bodies, the private sector and donors. In October 2001 IFAD became a co-sponsor of the Consultative Group on International Agricultural Research (CGIAR). In 2006 IFAD reviewed the work of the International Alliance against Hunger, which was established in 2004 to enhance co-ordination among international agencies and non-governmental organizations concerned with agriculture and rural development, and national alliances against hunger. In November 2009 IFAD and the Islamic Development Bank concluded a US $1,500m. framework cofinancing agreement for jointly financing priority projects during 2010–12 in many of the 52 countries that had membership of both organizations.

In February 2010 the Governing Council decided that the Executive Board should submit a revised set of Lending Policies and Criteria for approval by the 34th session of the Governing Council, scheduled to be held in 2011.

Finance

In accordance with the Articles of Agreement establishing IFAD, the Governing Council periodically undertakes a review of the adequacy of resources available to the Fund and may request members to make additional contributions. A target of US $1,200m. was set for the eighth replenishment of IFAD funds, covering the period 2010–12. The provisional budget for administrative expenses for 2010 amounted to $132.0m., while some $6.2m. was budgeted in that year to the Fund's Office of Evaluation and some $3.5m. to its capital budget.

Publications

Annual Report.

IFAD Update (2 a year).

Rural Poverty Report.

Staff Working Papers (series).

Statistics

PROJECTS IN LATIN AMERICA AND THE CARIBBEAN APPROVED IN 2009

Country	Purpose	Loan amount (SDRm.*)
Bolivia	Plan to eradicate extreme poverty, phase I	5.1
Brazil	Semi-arid sustainable development project in Piauí	12.8
	Carirí and Seridó sustainable development project	15.6
Dominican Rep.	Development project for rural poor economic organizations in the border region	9.5
Ecuador	Ibarra-San Lorenzo development project	8.2
Mexico	Community-based forestry development project in southern states (Campeche, Chiapas and Oaxaca)	3.2

* The average value of the SDR—Special Drawing Right—in 2009 was US $1.56769.

International Monetary Fund—IMF

Address: 700 19th St, NW, Washington, DC 20431, USA.

Telephone: (202) 623-7000; **fax:** (202) 623-4661; **e-mail:** publicaffairs@imf.org; **internet:** www.imf.org.

The IMF was established at the same time as the World Bank in December 1945, to promote international monetary co-operation, to facilitate the expansion and balanced growth of international trade and to promote stability in foreign exchange.

Organization

(August 2010)

Managing Director: DOMINIQUE STRAUSS-KAHN (France).

First Deputy Managing Director: JOHN LIPSKY (USA).

Deputy Managing Directors: MURILO PORTUGAL (Brazil), NAOYUKI SHINOHARA (Japan).

Director, Western Hemisphere Department: NICOLÁS EYZAGUIRRE (Chile).

BOARD OF GOVERNORS

The highest authority of the Fund is exercised by the Board of Governors, on which each member country is represented by a Governor and an Alternate Governor. The Board normally meets annually. The voting power of each country is related to its quota in the Fund. An International Monetary and Financial Committee (IMFC, formerly the Interim Committee) advises and reports to the Board on matters relating to the management and adaptation of the international monetary and financial system, sudden disturbances that might threaten the system and proposals to amend the Articles of Agreement.

BOARD OF EXECUTIVE DIRECTORS

The 24-member Board of Executive Directors is responsible for the day-to-day operations of the Fund. The USA, United Kingdom, Germany, France and Japan each appoint one Executive Director. There is also one Executive Director from the People's Republic of China, Russia and Saudi Arabia, while the remainder are elected by groups of the remaining countries.

REGIONAL REPRESENTATION

There is a network of regional offices and Resident Representatives in more than 90 member countries. In addition, special information and liaison offices are located in Tokyo, Japan (for Asia and the Pacific), in New York, USA (for the United Nations), and in Europe (Paris, France; Geneva, Switzerland; Belgium, Brussels; and Warsaw, Poland, for Central Europe and the Baltic states).

Activities

The purposes of the IMF, as defined in the Articles of Agreement, are:

(i) To promote international monetary co-operation through a permanent institution which provides the machinery for consultation and collaboration on monetary problems;

(ii) To facilitate the expansion and balanced growth of international trade, and to contribute thereby to the promotion and maintenance of high levels of employment and real income and to the development of members' productive resources;

(iii) To promote exchange stability, to maintain orderly exchange arrangements among members, and to avoid competitive exchange depreciation;

(iv) To assist in the establishment of a multilateral system of payments in respect of current transactions between members and in the elimination of foreign exchange restrictions which hamper the growth of trade;

(v) To give confidence to members by making the general resources of the Fund temporarily available to them, under adequate safeguards, thus providing them with the opportunity to correct maladjustments in their balance of payments, without resorting to measures destructive of national or international prosperity;

(vi) In accordance with the above, to shorten the duration of and lessen the degree of disequilibrium in the international balances of payments of members.

In joining the Fund, each country agrees to co-operate with the above objectives. In accordance with its objective of facilitating the expansion of international trade, the IMF encourages its members to accept the obligations of Article VIII, Sections two, three and four, of the Articles of Agreement. Members that accept Article VIII undertake to refrain from imposing restrictions on the making of payments and transfers for current international transactions and from engaging in discriminatory currency arrangements or multiple currency practices without IMF approval. At the end of 2009 some 90% of members had accepted Article VIII status.

In 2000/01 the Fund established an International Capital Markets Department to improve its understanding of financial markets and a separate Consultative Group on capital markets to serve as a forum for regular dialogue between the Fund and representatives of the private sector. In mid-2006 the International Capital Markets Department was merged with the Monetary and Financial Systems Department to create the Monetary and Capital Markets Department, with the intention of strengthening surveillance of global financial transactions and monetary arrangements. In June 2008 the Managing Director presented a new Work Programme, comprising the following four immediate priorities for the Fund: to enable member countries to deal with the current crises of reduced economic growth and escalating food and fuel prices, including efforts by the Fund to strengthen surveillance activities; to review the Fund's lending instruments; to implement new organizational tools and working practices; and to advance further the Fund's governance agenda.

The deceleration of economic growth in the world's major economies in 2007 and 2008 and the sharp decline in global financial market conditions, in particular in the second half of 2008, focused international attention on the adequacy of the governance of the international financial system and of regulatory and supervisory frameworks. The IMF aimed to provide appropriate and rapid financial and technical assistance to low-income and emerging economies most affected by the crisis and to support a co-ordinated, multinational recovery effort. The Fund worked closely with the Group of 20 (G20) leading economies to produce an Action Plan, in November 2008, concerned with strengthening regulation, transparency and integrity in financial markets and reform of the international financial system. In March 2009 the IMF released a study on the 'Impact of the Financial Crisis on Low-income Countries', and in that month convened, with the Government of Tanzania, a high-level conference, held in Dar es Salaam, to consider the effects of the global financial situation on African countries, as well as areas for future partnership and growth. Later in that month the Executive Board approved a series of reforms to enhance the effectiveness of the Fund's lending framework, including new conditionality criteria, a new flexible credit facility and increased access limits (see below).

In April 2009 a meeting of G20 heads of state and government, convened in London, United Kingdom, determined to make available substantial additional resources through the IMF and other multinational development institutions in order to strengthen global financial liquidity and support economic recovery. There was a commitment to extend US $250,000m. to the IMF in immediate bilateral financial contributions (which would be incorporated into an expanded New Arrangements to Borrow facility) and to support a general allocation of special drawing rights (SDRs), amounting to a further $250,000m. It was agreed that additional resources from sales of IMF gold were to be used to provide $6,000m. in concessional financing for the poorest countries over the next two to three years. The G20 meeting also resolved to implement several major reforms to strengthen the regulation and supervision of the international financial system, which envisaged the IMF collaborating closely with a new Financial Stability Board. In September G20 heads of state and government endorsed a mutual assessment programme, which aimed to achieve sustainable and balanced growth, with the IMF providing analysis and technical assistance. In 2010 the IMF was undertaking a review of its mandate and role in the 'post-crisis' global economy. Short-term priorities included advising countries on moving beyond the policies they implemented during the crisis; reviewing the Fund's mandate in surveillance and lending, and investigating ways of improving the stability of the international monetary system; strengthening macro-financial and cross-country analyses, including early warning exercises; and studying ways to make policy frameworks more resilient to crises.

In August 2009 the Fund's Board of Governors approved the new general allocation of SDRs, amounting to SDR 161,200m., which became available to all members, in proportion to their existing quotas, from 28 August. A further SDR 21,400m, (equivalent to US $33,000m.) became available on 9 September under a special allocation provided for by the Fourth Amendment to the Articles of Agreement, which entered into force in the previous month having been ratified by members holding 85% of the total voting power.

In February 2002 a newly-appointed Director for Special Operations immediately assumed leadership of the staff team working with the authorities in Argentina to help that country to overcome its extreme economic and social difficulties. Detailed consideration ensued of means of orderly resolution of financial crises.

QUOTAS

IMF MEMBERSHIP AND QUOTAS IN LATIN AMERICA AND THE CARIBBEAN
(million SDR*)

Country	August 2010
Antigua and Barbuda	13.5
Argentina	2,117.1
The Bahamas	130.3
Barbados	67.5
Belize	18.8
Bolivia	171.5
Brazil	3,036.1
Chile	856.1
Colombia	774.0
Costa Rica	164.1
Dominica	8.2
Dominican Republic	218.9
Ecuador	302.3
El Salvador	171.3
Grenada	11.7
Guatemala	210.2
Guyana	90.9
Haiti	81.9
Honduras	129.5
Jamaica	273.5
Mexico	3,152.8
Nicaragua	130.0
Panama	206.6
Paraguay	99.9
Peru	638.4
Saint Christopher and Nevis	8.9
Saint Lucia	15.3
Saint Vincent and the Grenadines	8.3
Suriname	92.1
Trinidad and Tobago	335.6
Uruguay	306.5
Venezuela	2,659.1

* The Special Drawing Right (SDR) was introduced in 1970 as a substitute for gold in international payments, and was intended eventually to become the principal reserve asset in the international monetary system. Its value (which was US $1.52754 at 10 August 2010 and averaged $1.54205 in 2009) is based on a basket of international currencies comprising the US dollar, Japanese yen, euro and pound sterling. Each member is assigned a quota related to its national income, monetary reserves, trade balance and other economic indicators; the quota approximately determines a member's voting power and the amount of foreign exchange it may purchase from the Fund. A member's subscription is equal to its quota. Quotas are reviewed at intervals of not more than five years, to take into account the state of the world economy and members' different rates of development. In January 1998 the Board of Governors approved an increase of some 45% of total IMF resources, bringing the total value of quotas to approximately SDR 212,000m. By January 1999 member states having at least 85% of total quotas (as at December 1997) had consented to the new subscriptions enabling the increase to enter into effect. The Twelfth General Review was concluded in January 2003 without an increase in quotas. In September 2006 the Board of Governors adopted a resolution on Quota and Voice Reform in the IMF, representing a two-year reform package aimed at improving the alignment of the quota shares of member states to represent more accurately their relative positions in the global economy and also to enhance the participation and influence of emerging market and low-income countries. An immediate ad hoc quota increase was approved for the People's Republic of China, the Republic of Korea, Mexico and Turkey. A Thirteenth General Review was concluded,

without an increase in quotas, in January 2008. At August 2010 total quotas in the Fund amounted to SDR 217,433.5m.

RESOURCES

Members' subscriptions form the basic resource of the IMF. They are supplemented by borrowing. Under the General Arrangements to Borrow (GAB), established in 1962, the Group of Ten industrialized nations (G10—Belgium, Canada, France, Germany, Italy, Japan, the Netherlands, Sweden, the United Kingdom and the USA) and Switzerland (which became a member of the IMF in May 1992 but which had been a full participant in the GAB from April 1984) undertake to lend the Fund as much as SDR 17,000m. in their own currencies to assist in fulfilling the balance of payments requirements of any member of the group, or in response to requests to the Fund from countries with balance of payments problems that could threaten the stability of the international monetary system. In 1983 the Fund entered into an agreement with Saudi Arabia, in association with the GAB, making available SDR 1,500m., and other borrowing arrangements were completed in 1984 with the Bank for International Settlements, the Saudi Arabian Monetary Agency, Belgium and Japan, making available a further SDR 6,000m. In 1986 another borrowing arrangement with Japan made available SDR 3,000m. In May 1996 GAB participants concluded an agreement in principle to expand the resources available for borrowing to SDR 34,000m., by securing the support of 25 countries with the financial capacity to support the international monetary system. The so-called New Arrangements to Borrow (NAB) was approved by the Executive Board in January 1997. It was to enter into force, for an initial five-year period, as soon as the five largest potential creditors participating in NAB had approved the initiative and the total credit arrangement of participants endorsing the scheme had reached at least SDR 28,900m. While the GAB credit arrangement was to remain in effect, the NAB was expected to be the first facility to be activated in the event of the Fund's requiring supplementary resources. In July 1998 the GAB was activated for the first time in more than 20 years in order to provide funds of up to US $6,300m. in support of an IMF emergency assistance package for Russia (the first time the GAB had been used for a non-participant). The NAB became effective in November, and was used for the first time as part of an extensive programme of support for Brazil, which was adopted by the IMF in early December. (In March 1999, however, the activation was cancelled.) In November 2002 NAB participants approved Chile's Central Bank as the 26th participant. In November 2008 the Executive Board initiated an assessment of IMF resource requirements and options for supplementing resources in view of an exceptional increase in demand for IMF assistance. In February 2009 the Board approved the terms of a borrowing agreement with the Government of Japan to extend some SDR 67,000m. (some $100,000m.) in supplemental funding, for an initial one-year period. In April G20 heads of state and government resolved to expand the NAB facility, to incorporate all G20 economies, in order to increase its resources by up to $500,000m. The G20 summit meeting held in September confirmed that it had contributed the additional resources to the NAB.

FINANCIAL ASSISTANCE

The Fund makes resources available to eligible members on an essentially short-term and revolving basis to provide members with temporary assistance to contribute to the solution of their payments problems. Before making a purchase, a member must show that its balance of payments or reserve position makes the purchase necessary. Apart from this requirement, reserve tranche purchases (i.e. purchases that do not bring the Fund's holdings of the member's currency to a level above its quota) are permitted unconditionally. Exchange transactions within the Fund take the form of members' purchases (i.e. drawings) from the Fund of the currencies of other members for the equivalent amounts of their own currencies.

With further purchases, however, the Fund's policy of conditionality means that a recipient country must agree to adjust its economic policies, as stipulated by the IMF. All requests other than for use of the reserve tranche are examined by the Executive Board to determine whether the proposed use would be consistent with the Fund's policies, and a member must discuss its proposed adjustment programme (including fiscal, monetary, exchange and trade policies) with IMF staff. New guidelines on conditionality, which, *inter alia*, aimed to promote national ownership of policy reforms and to introduce specific criteria for the implementation of conditions given different states' circumstances, were approved by the Executive Board in September 2002. In March 2009 the Executive Board approved reforms to modernize the Fund's conditionality policy, including greater use of pre-set qualification criteria and monitoring structural policy implementation by programme review (rather than by structural performance criteria).

Purchases outside the reserve tranche are made in four credit tranches, each equivalent to 25% of the member's quota; a member must reverse the transaction by repurchasing its own currency (with SDRs or currencies specified by the Fund) within a specified time. A credit tranche purchase is usually made under a 'Stand-by Arrangement' with the Fund, or under the Extended Fund Facility. A Stand-by Arrangement is normally of one or two years' duration, and the amount is made available in instalments, subject to the member's observance of 'performance criteria'; repurchases must be made within three-and-a-quarter to five years. An Extended Arrangement is normally of three years' duration, and the member must submit detailed economic programmes and progress reports for each year; repurchases must be made within four-and-a-half to 10 years. In October 1994 the Executive Board approved an increase in members' access to IMF resources, on the basis of a recommendation by the then Interim Committee. The annual access limit under IMF regular tranche drawings, Stand-by Arrangements and Extended Fund Facility credits was increased from 68% to 100% of a member's quota, with the cumulative access limit set at 300%. In March 2009 the Executive Board agreed to double access limits for non-concessional loans to 200% and 600% of a member's quota for annual and cumulative access respectively. In 2008/09 regular funding arrangements approved (and augmented) amounted to SDR 66,736m., compared with SDR 1,333m. in the previous financial year.

In addition, special-purpose arrangements have been introduced, all of which are subject to the member's co-operation with the Fund to find an appropriate solution to its difficulties. In December 1997 the Executive Board established a new Supplemental Reserve Facility (SRF) to provide short-term assistance to members experiencing exceptional balance of payments difficulties resulting from a sudden loss of market confidence. In December 1998 some SDR 9,100m. was extended to Brazil under the SRF as part of a new Stand-by Arrangement. In January 2001 some SDR 2,100m. in SRF resources were approved for Argentina as part of an SDR 5,187m. Stand-by Arrangement augmentation. The SDR 22,821m. Stand-by credit approved for Brazil in September 2002 included some SDR 7,600m. committed under the SRF. In March 2009 the Executive Board decided to terminate the SRF.

In October 1995 the Interim Committee of the Board of Governors endorsed recent decisions of the Executive Board to strengthen IMF financial support to members requiring exceptional assistance. An Emergency Financing Mechanism was established to enable the IMF to respond swiftly to potential or actual financial crises, while additional funds were made available for short-term currency stabilization. The Mechanism was activated for the first time in July 1997, in response to a request by the Philippines Government to reinforce the country's international reserves, and was subsequently used during that year to assist Thailand, Indonesia and the Republic of Korea. It was used in 2001 to accelerate lending to Turkey. In September 2008 the Mechanism was activated to facilitate approval of a Stand-by Arrangement amounting to SDR 477.1m. for Georgia, which urgently needed to contain its fiscal deficit and undertake rehabilitation measures following a conflict with Russia in the previous month. In November the Board approved a Stand-by Arrangement of SDR 5,169m., under the Emergency Financing Mechanism procedures, to support an economic stabilization programme in Pakistan, one for Ukraine, amounting to SDR 11,000m., and another of SDR 10,538m. for Hungary, which constituted 1,015% of its quota, to counter exceptional pressures on that country's banking sector and the Government's economic programme. An arrangement for Latvia, amounting to SDR 1,522m., was approved in the following month. In May 2010 the Board endorsed a Stand-by Arrangement for Greece amounting to SDR 26,400m., 3,200% of that country's quota. The Arrangement was approved under the Emergency Financing Mechanism, as part of a joint IMF-European Union financial assistance package to alleviate Greece's sovereign debt crisis and to support an economic recovery and reform programme. In October 2008 the Executive Board approved a new Short-Term Liquidity Facility (SLF) to extend exceptional funds (up to 500% of quotas) to emerging economies affected by the turmoil in international financial markets and economic deceleration in advanced economies. Eligibility for lending under the new Facility was to be based on a country's record of strong macroeconomic policies and having a sustainable level of debt. In March 2009 the Executive Board decided to replace the SLF with a Flexible Credit Line (FCL) facility, which, similarly, was to provide credit to countries with strong economic foundations, but was also to be primarily considered as precautionary. In addition, it was to have a longer repayment period (of up to five years) and have no access 'cap'. The first arrangement under the FCL was approved in April for Mexico, making available funds of up to SDR 31,528m. for a one-year period. Other arrangements were approved in May for Poland (SDR 13.7m.) and Colombia (SDR 7.0m.)

In January 2006 a new Exogenous Shocks Facility (ESF) was established to provide concessional assistance to economies adversely affected by events deemed to be beyond government control, for example commodity price changes, natural disasters, or conflicts in neighbouring countries that disrupt trade. Loans under the ESF were to be offered on the same terms as those of the Poverty Reduction and Growth Facility (PRGF) for low-income countries without a PRGF in place. In September 2008 modifications to the ESF were approved, including a new rapid-access component (to provide up to 25% of a country's quota) and a high-access component (to provide up to 75% of quota). These came into effect in late November. Commitments under the ESF were approved for Saint Vincent and the Grenadines (SDR 3.7m.) in May 2009 and for Dominica (SDR 3,3m.) and Saint Lucia (SDR 6.9m.) in July.

In January 2010 the Fund introduced new concessional facilities for low-income countries as part of broader reforms to enhance flexibility of lending and to focus support closer to specific national requirements. The three new facilities aimed to support country-owned programmes to achieve macroeconomic positions consistent with sustainable poverty reduction and economic growth. They carried zero interest rate, although this was to be reviewed every two years. An Extended Credit Facility (ECF) succeeded the existing PRGF to provide medium-term balance of payments assistance to low-income members. ECF loans were to be repayable over 10 years, with a five-and-a-half-year grace period. A Standby Credit Facility (SCF) replaced the high-access component of the Exogenous Shocks Facility (see above) in order to provide short-term balance of payments financial assistance, including on a precautionary basis. SCF loans were to be repayable over eight years, with a grace period of four years. A new Rapid Credit Facility was to provide rapid financial assistance to members requiring urgent balance of payments assistance, under a range of circumstances. Loans were repayable over 10 years, with a five-and-a-half-year grace period.

In May 2001 the Executive Board decided to provide a subsidized loan rate for emergency post-conflict assistance for PRGF-eligible countries, in order to facilitate the rehabilitation of their economies and to improve their eligibility for further IMF concessionary arrangements. In January 2005 the Executive Board decided to extend the subsidized rate for natural disasters. During 2008/09 the Fund approved assistance for Lebanon (of SDR 25.4m.), Comoros (SDR 1.1m.) and Guinea-Bissau (SDR 1.8m.) under the emergency post-conflict assistance facility and for Belize (SDR 4.7m.) and Saint Christopher and Nevis (SDR 2.2m.) under the emergency natural disaster component.

During 2008/09 the IMF approved 11 new Stand-by Arrangements amounting to SDR 34,249.3m., (compared with three Arrangements totalling some SDR 556m. in the previous year). In 2008/09 10 new PRGF arrangements, amounting to SDR 631.4m., were approved, in addition to the augmentation of 13 existing arrangements (totalling SDR 160.6m.). During 2008/09 members' purchases from the general resources account amounted to SDR 16,363m., compared with SDR 1,468m. in the previous year. Outstanding IMF credit at 30 April 2009 totalled SDR 24,625m., compared with SDR 9,844m. in the previous year.

The arrangement approved in September 2002, in support of the Brazilian Government's efforts to secure economic and financial stability, was the largest ever Stand-by credit agreed by the Fund at that time, amounting to SDR 22,821m. In April 2009 the Fund approved a 12-month flexible credit arrangement for Mexico amounting to SDR 31,528.0m. During the financial year 2008/09 new Stand-by Arrangements in the Latin American and Caribbean region were agreed for Costa Rica (amounting to SDR 492.3m.), El Salvador (SDR 513.9m.) and Guatemala (SDR 630.6m.). Increases in existing PRGF arrangements were approved for Grenada (SDR 1.5m.), Haiti (SDR 41.0m.) and Nicaragua (SDR 6.5m.).

IMF participates in an initiative to provide exceptional assistance to heavily indebted poor countries (HIPCs), in order to help them to achieve a sustainable level of debt management. The initiative was formally approved at the September 1996 meeting of the Interim Committee, having received the support of the 'Paris Club' of official creditors, which agreed to increase the relief on official debt from 67% to 80%. In all 41 HIPCs were identified, of which 33 were in sub-Saharan Africa. Resources for the HIPC initiative were channelled through the PRGF Trust. In early 1999 the IMF and the World Bank initiated a comprehensive review of the HIPC scheme, in order to consider modifications of the initiative and to strengthen the link between debt relief and poverty reduction. A consensus emerged among the financial institutions and leading industrialized nations to enhance the scheme, in order to make it available to more countries, and to accelerate the process of providing debt relief. In September the IMF Board of Governors expressed its commitment to undertaking an off-market transaction of a percentage of the Fund's gold reserves (i.e. a sale, at market prices, to central banks of member countries with repayment obligations to the Fund, which were then to be made in gold), as part of the funding arrangements of the enhanced HIPC scheme; this was undertaken during the period December 1999–April 2000. Under the enhanced initiative it was agreed that countries seeking debt relief should first formulate, and successfully implement for at least one year, a national poverty reduction strategy (see above). In May 2000 Uganda became the first country to qualify for full debt relief under the enhanced scheme. In September 2005 the IMF and the World Bank endorsed a proposal of the Group of Eight (G8) nations to achieve the cancellation by the IMF, IDA and the African Development Bank of 100% of debt claims on countries that had reached completion point under the HIPC initiative, in order to help them to achieve their Millennium Development Goals. The debt cancellation was to be undertaken within the framework of a Multilateral Debt Relief Initiative (MDRI). The IMF's Executive Board determined, additionally, to extend MDRI debt relief to all countries with an annual per caput GDP of US $380, to be financed by IMF's own resources. Other financing was to be made from existing bilateral contributions to the PRGF Trust Subsidy Account. In December the Executive Board gave final approval to the first group of countries assessed as eligible for 100% debt relief under the MDRI, including 17 countries that had reached completion point at that time, as well as Cambodia and Tajikistan. The initiative became effective in January 2006 once the final consent of the 43 contributors to the PRGF Trust Subsidy Account had been received. By July 2010 a further 13 countries had qualified for MDRI relief. At March 2010 the IMF had committed some $6,500m. in debt relief under the HIPC initiative, of a total of $75,600m. pledged for the initiative (in 2009 net present value terms).

SURVEILLANCE

Under its Articles of Agreement, the Fund is mandated to oversee the effective functioning of the international monetary system. Accordingly, the Fund aims to exercise firm surveillance over the exchange rate policies of member states and to assess whether a country's economic situation and policies are consistent with the objectives of sustainable development and domestic and external stability. The Fund's main tools of surveillance are regular, bilateral consultations with member countries conducted in accordance with Article IV of the Articles of Agreement, which cover fiscal and monetary policies, balance of payments and external debt developments, as well as policies that affect the economic performance of a country, such as the labour market, social and environmental issues and good governance, and aspects of the country's capital accounts, and finance and banking sectors. In April 1997 the Executive Board agreed to the voluntary issue of Press Information Notices (PINs) following each member's Article IV consultation, to those member countries wishing to make public the Fund's views. Other background papers providing information on and analysis of economic developments in individual countries continued to be made available. The Executive Board monitors global economic developments and discusses policy implications from a multilateral perspective, based partly on World Economic Outlook reports and Global Financial Stability Reports. In addition, the IMF studies the regional implications of global developments and policies pursued under regional fiscal arrangements. The Fund's medium-term strategy, initiated in 2006, determined to strengthen its surveillance policies to reflect new challenges of globalization for international financial and macroeconomic stability. In June 2007 the Executive Board approved a Decision on Bilateral Surveillance to update and clarify principles for a member's exchange rate policies and to define best practice for the Fund's bilateral surveillance activities. In October 2008 the Board adopted a Statement of Surveillance Priorities, based on a series of economic and operational policy objectives, for the period 2008–11. The need to enhance surveillance and economic transparency was a priority throughout 2009 as the Fund assessed the global economic and financial crisis and its own role in future crisis prevention.

In April 1996 the IMF established the Special Data Dissemination Standard (SDDS), which was intended to improve access to reliable economic statistical information for member countries that have, or are seeking, access to international capital markets. In March 1999 the IMF undertook to strengthen the Standard by the introduction of a new reserves data template. By September 2009 64 countries had subscribed to the Standard. The financial crisis in Asia, which became apparent in mid-1997, focused attention on the importance of IMF surveillance of the economies and financial policies of member states and prompted the Fund further to enhance the effectiveness of its surveillance through the development of international standards in order to maintain fiscal transparency. In December 1997 the Executive Board approved a new General Data Dissemination System (GDDS), to encourage all member countries to improve the production and dissemination of core economic data. The operational phase of the GDDS commenced in May 2000. By June 2009 96 countries were participating in the GDDS. The Fund maintains a Dissemination Standards Bulletin Board (accessible at dsbb.imf.org), which aims to ensure that information on SDDS subscribing countries is widely available.

In April 1998 the then Interim Committee adopted a voluntary Code of Good Practices on Fiscal Transparency: Declaration of Principles, which aimed to increase the quality and promptness of official reports on economic indicators, and in September 1999 it adopted a Code of Good Practices on Transparency in Monetary and Financial Policies: Declaration of Principles. The IMF and World Bank jointly established a Financial Sector Assessment Programme (FSAP) in May 1999, initially as a pilot project, which aimed to promote greater global financial security through the preparation of confidential detailed evaluations of the financial sectors of individual countries. As at the end of June 2009 125 FSAP assessments had been completed (including three regional assessments), as well as 48 updated assessments. In September the IMF and World Bank determined to enhance the FSAP's surveillance effectiveness with new features, for example introducing a risk assessment matrix, targeting it more closely to country needs, and improving its cross-country analysis and perspective. As part of the FSAP Fund staff may conclude a Financial System Stability Assessment (FSSA), addressing issues relating to macroeconomic stability and the strength of a country's financial system. A separate component of the FSAP are Reports on the Observance of Standards and Codes (ROSCs), which are compiled after an assessment of a country's implementation and observance of internationally recognized financial standards.

In April 2001 the Executive Board agreed on measures to enhance international efforts to counter money-laundering, in particular through the Fund's ongoing financial supervision activities and its programme of assessment of offshore financial centres (OFCs). In November the IMFC, in response to the terrorist attacks against targets in the USA, which had occurred in September, resolved, *inter alia*, to strengthen the Fund's focus on surveillance, and, in particular, to extend measures to counter money-laundering to include the funds of terrorist organizations. It determined to accelerate efforts to assess offshore centres and to provide technical support to enable poorer countries to meet international financial standards. In March 2004 the Board of Directors resolved that an anti-money laundering and countering the financing of terrorism (AML/CFT) component be introduced into regular OFC and FSAP assessments conducted by the Fund and the World Bank, following a pilot programme undertaken from November 2002 with the World Bank, the Financial Action Task Force and other regional supervisory bodies. The first phase of the OFC assessment programme was concluded in February 2005, at which time 41 of 44 contacted jurisdictions had been assessed and the reports published. In May 2008 the IMF's Executive Board agreed to integrate the OFC programme into the FSAP.

TECHNICAL ASSISTANCE

Technical assistance is provided by special missions or resident representatives who advise members on every aspect of economic management, while more specialized assistance is provided by the IMF's various departments. In 2000/01 the IMFC determined that technical assistance should be central to the IMF's work in crisis prevention and management, in capacity-building for low-income countries, and in restoring macroeconomic stability in countries following a financial crisis. Technical assistance activities subsequently underwent a process of review and reorganization to align them more closely with IMF policy priorities and other initiatives.

Since 1993 the IMF has delivered some technical assistance, aimed at strengthening local capacity in economic and financial management, through regional centres. The first, established in that year, was a Pacific Financial Technical Assistance Center, located in Fiji. A Caribbean Regional Technical Assistance Centre (CARTAC), located in Barbados, began operations in November 2001. In October 2002 an East African Regional Technical Assistance Centre (East AFRITAC), based in Dar es Salaam, Tanzania, was inaugurated and a second AFRITAC was opened in Bamako, Mali, in May 2003, to cover the West African region. In October 2004 a new technical assistance centre for the Middle East (METAC) was inaugurated, based in Beirut, Lebanon. A regional technical assistance centre for Central Africa, located in Libreville, Gabon, was inaugurated in 2006/07. A Regional Technical Assistance Centre for Central America, Panama and the Dominican Republic (CAPTAC-DR), was inaugurated in June 2009, in Guatemala City, Guatemala. In September 2002 the IMF signed a memorandum of understanding with the African Capacity Building Foundation to strengthen collaboration, in particular within the context of a new IMF Africa Capacity-Building Initiative.

The IMF Institute, which was established in 1964, trains officials from member countries in macroeconomic management, financial analysis and policy, balance of payments methodology and public finance. The IMF Institute also co-operates with other established regional training centres and institutes in order to refine its delivery of technical assistance and training services. The IMF is a co-sponsor, with UNDP and the Japan administered account, of the Joint Vienna Institute, which was opened in the Austrian capital in October 1992 and which trains officials from former centrally-planned economies in various aspects of economic management and public administration. In May 1998 an IMF-Singapore Regional Training Institute (an affiliate of the IMF Institute) was inaugurated, in collaboration with the Singaporean Government, in order to provide training for officials from the Asia-Pacific region. In January 1999 the IMF, in co-operation with the African Development Bank and the World Bank, announced the establishment of a Joint Africa Institute, in Abidjan, Côte d'Ivoire, which was to offer training to officials from African countries. (It relocated to Tunis, Tunisia, in 2003.) Also in 1999 a Joint Regional Training Programme, administered with the Arab Monetary Fund, was established in the United Arab Emirates. During 2000/01 the Institute established a new joint training programme for government officials of the People's Republic of China, based in Dalian, Liaoning Province. A Joint Regional Training Centre for Latin America became operational in Brasília, Brazil, in 2001. In July 2006 a Joint India-IMF Training Programme was inaugurated in Pune, India.

Publications

Annual Report.
Balance of Payments Statistics Yearbook.
Civil Society Newsletter (quarterly).
Direction of Trade Statistics (quarterly and annually).
Emerging Markets Financing (quarterly).
F & D—Finance and Development (quarterly).
Financial Statements of the IMF (quarterly).
Global Financial Stability Report (2 a year).
Global Monitoring Report (annually, with the World Bank).
Government Finance Statistics Yearbook.
Handbook on Securities Statistics (published jointly by IMF, BIS and the European Central Bank).
IMF Commodity Prices (monthly).
IMF Financial Activities (weekly, online).
IMF in Focus (annually).
IMF Research Bulletin (quarterly).
IMF Survey (monthly, and online).
International Financial Statistics (monthly and annually).
Joint BIS-IMF-OECD-World Bank Statistics on External Debt (quarterly).
Quarterly Report on the Assessments of Standards and Codes.
Staff Papers (quarterly).
World Economic Outlook (2 a year).
Other country reports, regional outlooks, economic and financial surveys, occasional papers, pamphlets, books.

United Nations Educational, Scientific and Cultural Organization—UNESCO

Address: 7 place de Fontenoy, 75352 Paris 07 SP, France.

Telephone: 1-45-68-10-00; **fax:** 1-45-67-16-90; **e-mail:** bpi@unesco.org; **internet:** www.unesco.org.

UNESCO was established in 1946 'for the purpose of advancing, through the educational, scientific and cultural relations of the peoples of the world, the objectives of international peace and the common welfare of mankind'.

Organization

(August 2010)

GENERAL CONFERENCE

The supreme governing body of the Organization, the Conference meets in ordinary session once in two years and is composed of representatives of the member states. It determines policies, approves work programmes and budgets and elects members of the Executive Board.

EXECUTIVE BOARD

The Board, comprising 58 members, prepares the programme to be submitted to the Conference and supervises its execution; it meets twice a year.

SECRETARIAT

The organization is headed by a Director-General, appointed for a four-year term. There are Assistant Directors-General for the main thematic sectors, i.e education, natural sciences, social and human sciences, culture, and communication and information, as well as for the support sectors of external relations and co-operation and of administration.

Director-General: IRINA BOKOVA (Bulgaria).

CO-OPERATING BODIES

In accordance with UNESCO's constitution, national Commissions have been set up in most member states. These help to integrate work within the member states and the work of UNESCO. Most member states also have their own permanent delegations to UNESCO. UNESCO aims to develop partnerships with cities and local authorities.

FIELD CO-ORDINATION

UNESCO maintains a network of offices to support a more decentralized approach to its activities and enhance their implementation at field level. Cluster offices provide the main structure of the field co-ordination network. These cover a group of countries and help to co-ordinate between member states and with other UN and partner agencies operating in the area. In 2010 there were 27 cluster offices covering 148 states. In addition 21 national offices serve a single country, including those in post-conflict situations or economic transition and the nine most highly-populated countries. The regional bureaux (see below) provide specialized support at a national level.

UNESCO Caribbean Office: The Towers, 3rd Floor, 25 Dominica Drive, Kingston 5, Jamaica; tel. 929-7087; fax 929-8468; e-mail kingston@unesco.org; Dir KWAME BOAFO.

REGIONAL BUREAUX

Regional Bureau for Culture in Latin America and the Caribbean (ORCALC): Calzada 551, esq. D, Vedado, Havana 4, Cuba; tel. (7) 833-3438; fax (7) 833-3144; e-mail habana@unesco.org.cu; internet www.unesco.org.cu; f. 1950; activities include research and programmes of cultural development and cultural tourism; maintains a documentation centre and a library of 14,500 vols; Dir HERMAN VAN HOOFF; publs *Oralidad* (annually), *Boletín Electrónico* (quarterly).

Regional Bureau for Education in Latin America and the Caribbean: Calle Enrique Delpiano 2058, Providencia, Santiago, Chile; Casilla 127, Correo 29, Providencia, Santiago, Chile; tel. (2) 472-4600; fax (2) 655-1046; e-mail santiago@unesco.org; internet www.unesco.cl; Dir ROSA BLANCO GUIJARRO.

Regional Bureau for Science for Latin America and the Caribbean: Calle Dr Luis Piera 1992, 2°, Casilla 859, 11000 Montevideo, Uruguay; tel. (2) 413-2075; fax (2) 413-2094; e-mail orcyt@unesco.org.uy; internet www.unesco.org.uy; also cluster office for Argentina, Brazil, Chile, Paraguay, Uruguay; Dir JORGE GRANDI.

Activities

In the implementation of all its activities UNESCO aims to contribute to achieving the UN Millennium Development Goal (MDG) of halving levels of extreme poverty by 2015, as well as other MDGs concerned with education and sustainable development. UNESCO was the lead agency for the International Decade for a Culture of Peace and Non-violence for the Children of the World (2001–10). In November 2007 the General Conference approved a medium-term strategy to guide UNESCO during the period 2008–13. UNESCO's central mission as defined under the strategy was to contribute to building peace, the alleviation of poverty, sustainable development and intercultural dialogue through its core programme sectors (Education; Natural Sciences; Social and Human Sciences; Culture; and Communication and Information). The strategy identified five 'overarching objectives' for UNESCO in 2008–13, within this programme framework: Attaining quality education for all; Mobilizing scientific knowledge and science policy for sustainable development; Addressing emerging ethical challenges; Promoting cultural diversity and intercultural dialogue; and Building inclusive knowledge societies through information and communication.

EDUCATION

UNESCO recognizes education as an essential human right, and an overarching objective for 2008–13 was to attain quality education for all. Through its work programme UNESCO is committed to achieving the MDGs of eliminating gender disparity at all levels of education and attaining universal primary education in all countries by 2015. The focus of many of UNESCO's education initiatives are the nine most highly-populated developing countries (Bangladesh, Brazil, the People's Republic of China (PRC), Egypt, India, Indonesia, Mexico, Nigeria and Pakistan), known collectively as the E-9 ('Education-9') countries.

UNESCO leads and co-ordinates global efforts in support of 'Education for All' (EFA), which was adopted as a guiding principle of UNESCO's contribution to development following a world conference, convened in March 1990. In April 2000 several UN agencies, including UNESCO and UNICEF, and other partners sponsored the World Education Forum, held in Dakar, Senegal, to assess international progress in achieving the goal of Education for All and to adopt a strategy for further action (the 'Dakar Framework'), with the aim of ensuring universal basic education by 2015. The Dakar Framework, incorporating six specific goals, emphasized the role of improved access to education in the reduction of poverty and in diminishing inequalities within and between societies. UNESCO was appointed as the lead agency in the implementation of the Framework, focusing on co-ordination, advocacy, mobilization of resources, and information-sharing at international, regional and national levels. It was to oversee national policy reforms, with a particular focus on the integration of EFA objectives into national education plans. An EFA Global Action Plan was formulated in 2006 to reinvigorate efforts to achieve EFA objectives and, in particular, to provide a framework for international co-operation and better definition of the roles of international partners and of UNESCO in leading the initiative. UNESCO's medium-term strategy for 2008–13 committed the organization to strengthening its role in co-ordinating EFA efforts at global and national levels, promoting monitoring and capacity-building activities to support implementation of EFA objectives, and facilitating mobilization of increased resources for EFA programmes and strategies (for example through the EFA-Fast Track Initiative, launched in 2002 to accelerate technical and financial support to low-income countries).

UNESCO advocates 'Literacy for All' as a key component of Education for All, regarding literacy as essential to basic education and to social and human development. UNESCO is the lead agency of the UN Literacy Decade (2003–12), which aims to formulate an international plan of action to raise literacy standards throughout the world and to assist policy-makers to integrate literacy standards and goals into national education programmes. The Literacy Initiative for Empowerment (LIFE) was developed as an element of the Literacy Decade to accelerate efforts in some 35 countries where illiteracy is a critical challenge to development. UNESCO is also the co-ordinating agency for the UN Decade of Education for Sustainable Development (2005–14), through which it aims to establish a global framework for action and strengthen the capacity of education systems to incorporate the concepts of sustainable development into education programmes. The April 2000 World Education Forum recognized the global HIV/AIDS pandemic to be a significant challenge to the attainment of Education for All. UNESCO, as a co-sponsor of UNAIDS, takes an active role in promoting formal and non-formal preventive health education. Through a Global Initiative on HIV/AIDS and Education (EDUCAIDS) UNESCO aims to develop comprehensive responses to HIV/AIDS rooted in the education sector, with a particular focus on vulnerable children and young people. An initiative covering the 10-year period 2006–15, the Teacher Training Initiative in sub-Saharan Africa, aims to address the shortage of teachers in that region (owing to HIV/AIDS, armed conflict and other causes) and to improve the quality of teaching.

A key priority area of UNESCO's education programme is to foster quality education for all, through formal and non-formal educational opportunities. It assists members to improve the quality of education provision through curricula content, school management and teacher training. UNESCO aims to expand access to education at all levels and to work to achieve gender equality. In particular, UNESCO aims to strengthen capacity-building and education in natural, social and human sciences and promote the use of new technologies in teaching and learning processes.

The Associated Schools Project (ASPnet—comprising more than 8,500 institutions in 180 countries in 2010) has, since 1953, promoted the principles of peace, human rights, democracy and international co-operation through education. It provides a forum for dialogue and for promoting best practices. At tertiary level UNESCO chairs a University Twinning and Networking (UNITWIN) initiative, which was established in 1992 to establish links between higher education institutions and to foster research, training and programme development. A complementary initiative, Academics Across Borders, was inaugurated in November 2005 to strengthen communication and the sharing of knowledge and expertise among higher education professionals. In October 2002 UNESCO organized the first Global Forum on International Quality Assurance, Accreditation and the Recognition of Qualifications to establish international standards and promote capacity-building for the sustainable development of higher education systems.

Within the UN system UNESCO is responsible for providing technical assistance and educational services in the context of emergency situations. This includes establishing temporary schools, providing education to refugees and displaced persons, as well as assistance for the rehabilitation of national education systems. In Palestine, UNESCO collaborates with UNRWA to assist with the training of teachers, educational planning and rehabilitation of schools. In February 2010 UNESCO agreed to form an International Co-ordination Committee in support of Haitian culture, in view of the devastation caused by an earthquake that had struck that country in January, causing 230,000 fatalities and the destruction of local infrastructure and architecture.

In February 2010 a high-level meeting on Education for All, comprising ministers of education and international co-operation, and representatives from international and regional organizations, civil society and the private sector, was held to assess the impact on education of the ongoing global economic crisis, and to consider related challenges connected to social marginalization.

NATURAL SCIENCES

The World Summit on Sustainable Development, held in August–September 2002, recognised the essential role of science (including mathematics, engineering and technology) as a foundation for achieving the MDGs of eradicating extreme poverty and ensuring environmental sustainability. UNESCO aims to promote this function within the UN system and to assist member states to utilise and foster the benefits of scientific and technical knowledge. A key objective for the medium-term strategy (2008–13) was to mobilize science knowledge and policy for sustainable development. Throughout the natural science programme priority was to be placed on Africa, least developed countries and small island developing states. The Local and Indigenous Knowledge System (LINKS) initiative aims to strengthen dialogue among traditional knowledge holders, natural and social scientists and decision-makers to enhance the conservation of biodiversity, in all disciplines, and to secure an active and equitable role for local communities in the governance of resources.

In November 1999 the General Conference endorsed a Declaration on Science and the Use of Scientific Knowledge and an agenda for action, which had been adopted at the World Conference on Science, held in June–July 1999, in Budapest, Hungary. By leveraging scientific knowledge, and global, regional and country level science networks, UNESCO aims to support sustainable development and the sound management of natural resources. It also advises governments on approaches to natural resource management, in particular the collection of scientific data, documenting and disseminating good practices and integrating social and cultural aspects into management structures and policies. UNESCO's Man and the Biosphere Programme supports a world-wide network of biosphere reserves (comprising 564 biosphere reserves in 109 countries in 2010), which aim to promote environmental conservation and research, education and training in biodiversity and problems of land use (including the fertility of tropical soils and the cultivation of sacred sites). The third World Congress of Biosphere Reserves, held in Madrid, Spain, in February 2008, adopted the Madrid Action Plan, which aimed to promote biosphere reserves as the main internationally-designated areas dedicated to sustainable development. UNESCO also supports a Global Network of National Geoparks (66 in 20 countries at August 2010) which was inaugurated in 2004 to promote collaboration among managed areas of geological significance to exchange knowledge and expertise and raise awareness of the benefits of protecting those environments. In June 2008 UNESCO organized the third International Geoparks Conference.

UNESCO promotes and supports international scientific partnerships to monitor, assess and report on the state of Earth systems. With the World Meteorological Organization and the International Council of Science, UNESCO sponsors the World Climate Research Programme, which was established in 1980 to determine the predictability of climate and the effect of human activity on climate. UNESCO hosts the secretariat of the World Water Assessment Programme (WWAP), which prepares the periodic *World Water Development Report*. UNESCO is actively involved in the 10-year project, agreed by more than 60 governments in February 2005, to develop a Global Earth Observation System of Systems (GEOSS). The project aims to link existing and planned observation systems in order to provide for greater understanding of the earth's processes and dissemination of detailed data, for example predicting health epidemics or weather phenomena or concerning the management of ecosystems and natural resources. UNESCO's Intergovernmental Oceanographic Commission serves as the Secretariat of the Global Ocean Observing System. The International Geoscience Programme, undertaken jointly with the International Union of Geological Sciences (IUGS), facilitates the exchange of knowledge and methodology among scientists concerned with geological processes and aims to raise awareness of the links between geoscience and sustainable socio-economic development. The IUGS and UNESCO jointly initiated the International Year of Planet Earth (2008).

UNESCO is committed to contributing to international efforts to enhance disaster preparedness and mitigation. Through education UNESCO aims to reduce the vulnerability of poorer communities to disasters and improve disaster management at local and national levels. It also co-ordinates efforts at an international level to establish monitoring networks and early-warning systems to mitigate natural disasters, in particular in developing tsunami early-warning systems in Africa, the Caribbean, the South Pacific, the Mediterranean Sea and the North East Atlantic similar to those already established for the Indian and Pacific oceans. Other regional partnerships and knowledge networks were to be developed to strengthen capacity-building and the dissemination of information and good practices relating to risk awareness and mitigation and disaster management. Disaster education and awareness were to be incorporated as key elements in the UN Decade of Education for Sustainable Development (see above). UNESCO is also the lead agency for the International Flood Initiative, which was inaugurated in January 2005 at the World Conference on Disaster Reduction, held in Kobe, Japan. The Initiative aimed to promote an integrated approach to flood management in order to minimize the damage and loss of life caused by floods, mainly with a focus on research, training, promoting good governance and providing technical assistance.

A priority of the natural science programme for 2008–09 was to promote policies and strengthen human and institutional capacities in science, technology and innovation. At all levels of education UNESCO aimed to enhance teaching quality and content in areas of science and technology and, at regional and sub-regional level, to strengthen co-operation mechanisms and policy networks in training and research. With the International Council of Scientific Unions and the Third World Academy of Sciences, UNESCO operates a short-term fellowship programme in the basic sciences and an exchange programme of visiting lecturers.

UNESCO is the lead agency of the New Partnership for Africa's Development (NEPAD) Science and Technology Cluster and the NEPAD Action Plan for the Environment.

SOCIAL AND HUMAN SCIENCES

UNESCO is mandated to contribute to the world-wide development of the social and human sciences and philosophy, which it regards as of great importance in policy-making and maintaining ethical vigilance. The structure of UNESCO's Social and Human Sciences programme takes into account both an ethical and standard-setting dimension, and research, policy-making, action in the field and future-oriented activities. One of UNESCO's so-called overarching objectives in the period 2008–13 was to address emerging ethical challenges.

A priority area of UNESCO's work programme on Social and Human Sciences for 2008–09 was to promote principles, practices and ethical norms relevant for scientific and technological development. It fosters international co-operation and dialogue on emerging issues, as well as raising awareness and promoting the sharing of knowledge at regional and national levels. UNESCO supports the activities of the International Bioethics Committee (IBC—a group of 36 specialists who meet under UNESCO auspices) and the Intergovernmental Bioethics Committee, and hosts the secretariat of the 18-member World Commission on the Ethics of Scientific Knowledge and Technology (COMEST), established in 1999, which aims to serve as a forum for the exchange of information and ideas and to promote dialogue between scientific communities, decision-makers and the public.

The priority Ethics of science and technology element aims to promote intergovernmental discussion and co-operation; to conduct explorative studies on possible UNESCO action on environmental ethics and developing a code of conduct for scientists; to enhance public awareness; to make available teaching expertise and create regional networks of experts; to promote the development of international and national databases on ethical issues; to identify ethical issues related to emerging technologies; to follow up relevant declarations, including the Universal Declaration on the Human Genome and Human Rights (see below); and to support the Global Ethics Observatory, an online world-wide database of information on applied bioethics and other applied science- and technology-related areas (including environmental ethics) that was launched in December 2005 by the IBC.

UNESCO itself provides an interdisciplinary, multicultural and pluralistic forum for reflection on issues relating to the ethical dimension of scientific advances, and promotes the application of international guidelines. In May 1997 the IBC approved a draft version of a Universal Declaration on the Human Genome and Human Rights, in an attempt to provide ethical guidelines for developments in human genetics. The Declaration, which identified some 100,000 hereditary genes as 'common heritage', was adopted by the UNESCO General Conference in November and committed states to promoting the dissemination of relevant scientific knowledge and co-operating in genome research. In October 2003 the General Conference adopted an International Declaration on Human Genetic Data, establishing standards for scientists working in that field, and in October 2005 the General Conference adopted the Universal Declaration on Bioethics and Human Rights. At all levels UNESCO aims to raise awareness and foster debate about the ethical implications of scientific and technological developments and promote exchange of experiences and knowledge between governments and research bodies.

UNESCO recognizes that globalization has a broad and significant impact on societies. It is committed to countering negative trends of social transformation by strengthening the links between research and policy formulation by national and local authorities, in particular concerning poverty eradication. In that respect, UNESCO promotes the concept that freedom from poverty is a fundamental human right. In 1994 UNESCO initiated an international social science research programme, the Management of Social Transformations (MOST), to promote capacity-building in social planning at all levels of decision-making. In 2003 the Executive Board approved a continuation of the programme but with a revised strategic objective of strengthening links between research, policy and practice. In 2008–13 UNESCO aimed to promote new collaborative social science research programmes and to support capacity-building in developing countries.

UNESCO aims to monitor emerging social or ethical issues and, through its associated offices and institutes, formulate preventative action to ensure they have minimal impact on the attainment of UNESCO's objectives. As a specific challenge UNESCO is committed to promoting the International Convention against Doping in Sport, which entered into force in 2007. UNESCO also focuses on the educational and cultural dimensions of physical education and sport and their capacity to preserve and improve health.

Fundamental to UNESCO's mission is the rejection of all forms of discrimination. It disseminates information aimed at combating racial prejudice, works to improve the status of women and their access to education, promotes equality between men and women, and raises awareness of discrimination against people affected by HIV/AIDS, in particular among young people. In 2004 UNESCO inaugurated an initiative to enable city authorities to share experiences and collaborate in efforts to counter racism, discrimination, xenophobia and exclusion. As well as the International Coalition of Cities against Racism, regional coalitions were to be formed with more defined programmes of action. A Latin American and Caribbean coalition was inaugurated in October 2006 and its first General Conference was convened, in Montevideo, Uruguay, in September 2007. An International Youth Clearing House and Information Service (Infoyouth) aims to increase and consolidate the information available on the situation of young people in society, and to heighten awareness of their needs, aspirations and potential among public and private decision-makers. Supporting efforts to facilitate dialogue among different cultures and societies and promoting opportunities for reflection and consideration of philosophy and human rights, for example the celebration of World Philosophy Day, are also among UNESCO's fundamental aims.

CULTURE

In undertaking efforts to preserve the world's cultural and natural heritage UNESCO has attempted to emphasize the link between culture and development. In December 1992 UNESCO established the World Commission on Culture and Development, to strengthen links between culture and development and to prepare a report on the issue. The first World Conference on Culture and Development was held in June 1999, in Havana, Cuba. In November 2001 the General Conference adopted the UNESCO Universal Declaration on Cultural Diversity, which affirmed the importance of intercultural dialogue in establishing a climate of peace. UNESCO's medium-term strategy for 2008–13 recognized the need for a more integrated approach to cultural heritage as an area requiring conservation and development and one offering prospects for dialogue, social cohesion and shared knowledge.

A priority element of UNESCO's draft work programme on Culture for 2008–09 was promoting cultural diversity through the safeguarding of heritage and enhancement of cultural expressions. In January 2002 UNESCO inaugurated the Global Alliance on Cultural Diversity, to promote partnerships between governments, non-governmental bodies and the private sector with a view to supporting cultural diversity through the strengthening of cultural industries and the prevention of cultural piracy. In October 2005 the General Conference approved an International Convention on the Protection of the Diversity of Cultural Expressions. It entered into force in March 2007 and the first session of the intergovernmental committee servicing the Convention was convened in Ottawa, Canada, in December.

UNESCO's World Heritage Programme, inaugurated in 1978, aims to protect historic sites and natural landmarks of outstanding universal significance, in accordance with the 1972 UNESCO Convention Concerning the Protection of the World Cultural and Natural Heritage, by providing financial aid for restoration, technical assistance, training and management planning. The medium-term strategy for 2008–13 acknowledged that new global threats may affect natural and cultural heritage. It also reinforced the concept that conservation of sites contributes to social cohesion. During mid-2010–mid-2011 the 'World Heritage List' comprised 911 sites globally, of which 704 had cultural significance, 180 were natural landmarks, and 27 were of 'mixed' importance. Examples include the city of Potosí (Bolivia), the Galápagos Islands (Ecuador), the Inca city of Machu Picchu in Peru, the Pitons Management Area in Saint Lucia, and numerous other historic sites and nature reserves in the region. UNESCO also maintains a list of World Heritage in Danger; during mid-2010–mid-2011 this numbered 34 sites, including the Belize Barrier Reef Reserve System (inscribed in 2009), the Humberstone and Santa Laura saltpeter works in Chile, Los Katíos National Park in Colombia (inscribed in 2009), the Chan Chan Archaeological Zone in Peru, and the colonial port town of Coro in Venezuela.

UNESCO supports the safeguarding of humanity's non-material 'intangible' heritage, including oral traditions, music, dance and medicine. An Endangered Languages Programme was initiated in 1993. By 2010 the Programme estimated that, of some 6,700 languages spoken world-wide, about one-half were endangered. It works to raise awareness of the issue, for example through publication of the *Atlas of the World's Languages in Danger of Disappearing*, to strengthen local and national capacities to safeguard and document languages, and administers a Register of Good Practices in Language Preservation. In October 2003 the UNESCO General Conference adopted a Convention for the Safeguarding of Intangible Cultural Heritage, which provided for the establishment of an intergovernmental committee and for participating states to formulate national inventories of intangible heritage. The Convention entered into force in April 2006 and the intergovernmental committee convened its inaugural session in November. The second session was held in Tokyo, Japan, in September 2007. A List of Intangible Cultural Heritage in Need of Urgent Safeguarding was inaugurated in November 2008; in September 2009 76 new elements were inscribed on the List, including several dances, such as the tango, which originated in Argentina and Uruguay; the dances of the Ainu in Japan; of the Ashiqs in Azerbaijan; and of Korean and Tibetan ethnic groups in the PRC; as well as dances from India, the Republic of Korea, Mexico, and from Réunion. In May 2001, November 2003 and November 2005 (i.e. before the Convention entered into effect) UNESCO awarded the title of 'Masterpieces of the Oral and Intangible Heritage of Humanity' to a total of 90 examples of intangible heritage deemed to be of outstanding value. UNESCO's culture programme also aims to safeguard movable cultural heritage and to support and develop museums as a means of preserving heritage and making it accessible to society as a whole.

In November 2001 the General Conference authorized the formulation of a Declaration against the Intentional Destruction of Cultural Heritage. In addition, the Conference adopted the Convention on the Protection of the Underwater Cultural Heritage, covering the protection from commercial exploitation of shipwrecks, submerged historical sites, etc., situated in the territorial waters of signatory states. UNESCO also administers the 1954 Hague Convention on the Protection of Cultural Property in the Event of Armed Conflict and the 1970 Convention on the Means of Prohibiting and Preventing the Illicit Import, Export and Transfer of Ownership of Cultural Property. In 1992 a World Heritage Centre was established to enable rapid mobilization of international technical assistance for the preservation of cultural sites. Through the World Heritage Information Network (WHIN), a world-wide network of more than 800 information providers, UNESCO promotes global awareness and information exchange.

UNESCO aims to support the development of creative industries and or creative expression. Through a variety of projects UNESCO promotes art education, supports the rights of artists, and encourages crafts, design, digital art and performance arts. In October 2004 UNESCO launched a Creative Cities Network to facilitate public and private sector partnerships, international links, and recognition of a city's unique expertise. At August 2010 21 cities were participating in the Network, including Buenos Aires, Argentina (City of Design) and Popayan, Colombia (City of Gastronomy). UNESCO is active in preparing and encouraging the enforcement of international legislation on copyright, raising awareness on the need for copyright protection to uphold cultural diversity, and is contributing to the international debate on digital copyright issues and piracy.

Within its ambition of ensuring cultural diversity, UNESCO recognizes the role of culture as a means of promoting peace and dialogue. Several projects have been formulated within a broader concept of Roads of Dialogue. In Central Asia a project on intercultural dialogue follows on from an earlier multi-disciplinary study of the ancient Silk Roads trading routes linking Asia and Europe, which illustrated many examples of common heritage. Other projects include a study of the movement of peoples and cultures during the slave trade, a Mediterranean Programme, the Caucasus Project and the Arabia Plan, which aims to promote world-wide knowledge and understanding of Arab culture. UNESCO has overseen an extensive programme of work to formulate histories of humanity and regions, focused on ideas, civilizations and the evolution of societies and cultures. These have included the *General History of Africa*, *History of Civilizations of Central Asia*, and *History of Humanity*. In 2008–09 UNESCO endeavoured to consider and implement the findings of the Alliance of Civilizations, a high-level group convened by the UN Secretary-General that published a report in November 2006.

UNESCO was designated as the lead UN agency for organizing the International Year for the Rapprochement of Cultures (2010). In February 2010, at the time of the launch of the International Year, the UNESCO Director-General established a High Panel on Peace and Dialogue among Cultures, which was to provide guidance on means of advancing tolerance, reconciliation and balance within societies world-wide.

COMMUNICATION AND INFORMATION

UNESCO regards information, communication and knowledge as being at the core of human progress and well-being. The Organization advocates the concept of knowledge societies, based on the principles of freedom of expression, universal access to information and knowledge, promotion of cultural diversity, and equal access to quality education. In 2008–13 it determined to consolidate and implement this concept, in accordance with the Declaration of Principles and Plan of Action adopted by the World Summit on the Information Society (WSIS) in November 2005.

A key strategic objective of building inclusive knowledge societies was to be through enhancing universal access to communication and information. At national and global levels UNESCO promotes the rights of freedom of expression and of access to information. It promotes the free flow and broad diffusion of information, knowledge, data and best practices, through the development of communications infrastructures, the elimination of impediments to freedom of expression, and the development of independent and pluralistic media, including through the provision of advisory services on media legislation, particularly in post-conflict countries and in countries in transition. UNESCO recognizes that the so-called global 'digital divide', in addition to other developmental differences between countries, generates exclusion and marginalization, and that increased participation in the democratic process can be attained through strengthening national communication and information capacities. UNESCO promotes policies and mechanisms that enhance provision for marginalized and disadvantaged groups to benefit from information and community opportunities. Activities at local and national level include developing effective 'infostructures', such as libraries and archives and strengthening low-cost community media and information access points, for example through the establishment of Community Multimedia Centres (CMCs). Many of UNESCO's principles and objectives in this area are pursued through the Information for All Programme, which entered into force in 2001. It is administered by an intergovernmental council, the secretariat of which is provided by UNESCO. UNESCO also established, in 1982, the International Programme for the Development of Communication (IPDC), which aims to promote and develop independent and pluralistic media in developing countries, for example by the establishment or modernization of news agencies and newspapers and training media professionals, the promotion of the right to information, and through efforts to harness informatics for development purposes and strengthen member states' capacities in this field. In February 2010 IPDC allocated more than US $2.1m. towards 84 proposed media development projects in 61 developing and emerging countries.

UNESCO supports cultural and linguistic diversity in information sources to reinforce the principle of universal access. It aims to raise awareness of the issue of equitable access and diversity, encourage good practices and develop policies to strengthen cultural diversity in all media. In 2002 UNESCO established Initiative B@bel as a multidisciplinary programme to promote linguistic diversity, with the aim of enhancing access of under-represented groups to information sources as well as protecting under-used minority languages. In December 2009 UNESCO and the Internet Corporation for Assigned Names and Numbers (ICANN) signed a joint agreement which aimed to promote the use of multilingual domain names using non-Latin script, with a view to promoting linguistic diversity. UNESCO's Programme for Creative Content supports the development of and access to diverse content in both the electronic and audio-visual media. The Memory of the World project, established in 1992, aims to preserve in digital form, and thereby to promote wide access to, the world's documentary heritage. By end-2009 193 inscriptions had been included on the project's register; three inscriptions originated from international organizations: the Archives of the ICRC's former International Prisoners of War Agency, 1914–23, submitted by the ICRC, and inscribed in 2007; the League of Nations Archives, 1919–46, submitted by the UN Geneva Office, and inscribed in 2009; and the UNRWA Photo and Film Archives of Palestinian Refugees' Documentary Heritage, submitted by UNRWA, and also inscribed in 2009. UNESCO also supports other efforts to preserve and disseminate digital archives and, in 2003, adopted a Charter for the Preservation of Digital Heritage. In April 2009 UNESCO launched the internet based World Digital Library, accessible at www.wdl.org, which aims to display primary documents (including texts, charts and illustrations), and authoritative explanations, relating to the accumulated knowledge of a broad spectrum of human cultures.

UNESCO promotes freedom of expression, of the press and independence of the media as fundamental human rights and the basis of democracy. It aims to assist member states to formulate policies and legal frameworks to uphold independent and pluralistic media and infostructures and to enhance the capacities of public service broadcasting institutions. In regions affected by conflict UNESCO supports efforts to establish and maintain an independent media service and to use it as a means of consolidating peace. UNESCO also aims to develop media and information systems to respond to and mitigate the impact of disaster situations, and to integrate these objectives into wider UN peace-building or reconstruction initiatives. UNESCO is the co-ordinating agency for 'World Press Freedom Day', which is held annually on 3 May. The theme for 2010 was 'Freedom of Information: The Right to Know'. It also awards an annual World Press Freedom Prize. UNESCO maintains an Observatory on the Information Society, which provides up-to-date information on the development of new ICTs, analyses major trends, and aims to raise awareness of related ethical, legal and societal issues. UNESCO promotes the upholding of human rights in the use of cyberspace. In 1997 it organized the first International Congress on Ethical, Legal and Societal Aspects of Digital Information ('INFOethics').

UNESCO promotes the application of information and communication technology for sustainable development. In particular it supports efforts to improve teaching and learning processes through electronic media and to develop innovative literacy and education initiatives, such as the ICT-Enhanced Learning (ICTEL) project. UNESCO also aims to enhance understanding and use of new technologies and support training and ongoing learning opportunities for librarians, archivists and other information providers.

Finance

UNESCO's activities are funded through a regular budget provided by contributions from member states and extrabudgetary funds from other sources, particularly UNDP, the World Bank, regional banks and other bilateral Funds-in-Trust arrangements. UNESCO co-operates with many other UN agencies and international non-governmental organizations.

UNESCO's proposed Regular Programme budget for the two years 2008–09 was US $631m.

Publications

(mostly in English, French and Spanish editions; Arabic, Chinese and Russian versions are also available in many cases)

Atlas of the World's Languages in Danger of Disappearing (online).
Copyright Bulletin (quarterly).
Encyclopedia of Life Support Systems (online).
Education for All Global Monitoring Report.
International Review of Education (quarterly).
International Social Science Journal (quarterly).
Museum International (quarterly).
Nature and Resources (quarterly).
The New Courier (quarterly).
Prospects (quarterly review on education).
UNESCO Sources (monthly).
UNESCO Statistical Yearbook.
World Communication Report.
World Educational Report (every 2 years).
World Heritage Review (quarterly).
World Information Report.
World Science Report (every 2 years).
Books, databases, video and radio documentaries, statistics, scientific maps and atlases.

Specialized Institutes and Centres

Abdus Salam International Centre for Theoretical Physics: Strada Costiera 11, 34151 Trieste, Italy; tel. (040) 2240111; fax (040) 224163; e-mail sci_info@ictp.it; internet www.ictp.it; f. 1964; promotes and enables advanced study and research in physics and mathematical sciences; organizes and sponsors training opportunities, in particular for scientists from developing countries; aims to provide an international forum for the exchange of information and ideas; operates under a tripartite agreement between UNESCO, IAEA and the Italian Government; Dir FERNANDO QUEVEDO (Guatemala).

International Bureau of Education (IBE): POB 199, 1211 Geneva 20, Switzerland; tel. 229177800; fax 229177801; e-mail doc .centre@ibe.unesco.org; internet www.ibe.unesco.org; f. 1925, became an intergovernmental organization in 1929 and was incorporated into UNESCO in 1969; the Council of the IBE is composed of representatives of 28 member states of UNESCO, designated by the General Conference; the Bureau's fundamental mission is to deal with matters concerning educational content, methods, and teaching/learning strategies; an International Conference on Education is held periodically; Dir CLEMENTINA ACEDO (Venezuela); publs *Prospects* (quarterly review), *Educational Innovation* (newsletter), educational practices series, monographs, other reference works.

UNESCO Institute for Information Technologies in Education: 117292 Moscow, ul. Kedrova 8, Russia; tel. (495) 129-29-90; fax (495) 129-12-25; e-mail info@iite.ru; internet www.iite.ru; the Institute aims to formulate policies regarding the development of, and to support and monitor the use of, information and communication technologies in education; it conducts research and organizes training programmes; Chair Prof. BERNARD CORNU.

UNESCO Institute for Life-long Learning: Feldbrunnenstr. 58, 20148 Hamburg, Germany; tel. (40) 448-0410; fax (40) 410-7723; e-mail uil@unesco.org; internet www.unesco.org/uil/index.htm; f. 1951, as the Institute for Education; a research, training, information, documentation and publishing centre, with a particular focus on adult basic and further education and adult literacy; Dir ADAMA OUANE (Mali).

UNESCO Institute for Statistics: CP 6128, Succursale Centre-Ville, Montréal, QC, H3C 3J7, Canada; tel. (514) 343-6880; fax (514) 343-6882; e-mail uis@unesco.org; internet www.uis.unesco.org; f. 2001; collects and analyses national statistics on education, science, technology, culture and communications; Dir HENDRIK VAN DER POL (Netherlands).

UNESCO Institute for Water Education: Westvest 7, 2611 AX Delft, Netherlands; tel. (15) 2151-715; fax (15) 2122-921; e-mail info@unesco-ihe.org; internet www.unesco-ihe.org; f. 2003; activities include education, training and research; and co-ordination of a global network of water sector organizations; advisory and policy-making functions; setting international standards for postgraduate education programmes; and professional training in the water sector; Rector ANDRÁS SZÖLLÖSI-NAGY.

UNESCO International Centre for Technical and Vocational Education and Training: UN Campus, Hermann-Ehlers-Str. 10, 53113 Bonn, Germany; tel. (228) 8150-100; fax (228) 8150-199; e-mail info@unevoc.unesco.org; internet www.unevoc.unesco.org; f. 2002; promotes high-quality lifelong technical and vocational education in UNESCO's member states, with a particular focus on young people, girls and women, and the disadvantaged; Officer-in-Charge L. EFISON MUNJANGANJA (Zimbabwe).

UNESCO International Institute for Educational Planning (IIEP): 7–9 rue Eugène Delacroix, 75116 Paris, France; tel. 1-45-03-77-00; fax 1-40-72-83-66; e-mail info@iiep.unesco.org; internet www .unesco.org/iiep; f. 1963; serves as a world centre for advanced training and research in educational planning; aims to help all member states of UNESCO in their social and economic development efforts, by enlarging the fund of knowledge about educational planning and the supply of competent experts in this field; legally and administratively a part of UNESCO, the Institute is autonomous, and its policies and programme are controlled by its own Governing Board, under special statutes voted by the General Conference of UNESCO; a satellite office of the IIEP is based in Buenos Aires, Argentina; Dir MARK BRAY (United Kingdom).

UNESCO International Institute for Higher Education in Latin America and the Caribbean: Avda Los Chorros con Calle Acueducto, Edif. Asovincar, Altos de Sebucán, Apdo 68394, Caracas 1062-A, Venezuela; tel. (212) 286-0555; fax (212) 286-0527; e-mail prensa@unesco.org.ve; internet www.iesalc.unesco.org.ve; Dir JOSÉ RENATO CARVALHO.

World Health Organization—WHO

Address: Ave Appia 20, 1211 Geneva 27, Switzerland.

Telephone: 227912111; **fax:** 227913111; **e-mail:** info@who.int; **internet:** www.who.int.

WHO, established in 1948, is the lead agency within the UN system concerned with the protection and improvement of public health.

Organization

(August 2010)

WORLD HEALTH ASSEMBLY

The Assembly meets in Geneva, once a year. It is responsible for policy making and the biennial programme and budget; appoints the Director-General; admits new members; and reviews budget contributions.

EXECUTIVE BOARD

The Board is composed of 34 health experts designated by a member state that has been elected by the World Health Assembly to serve on the Board; each expert serves for three years. The Board meets at least twice a year to review the Director-General's programme, which it forwards to the Assembly with any recommendations that seem necessary. It advises on questions referred to it by the Assembly and is responsible for putting into effect the decisions and policies of the Assembly. It is also empowered to take emergency measures in case of epidemics or disasters.

Chairman: Dr MIHALY KÖKÉNY (Hungary).

SECRETARIAT

Director-General: Dr MARGARET CHAN (People's Republic of China).

Deputy Director-General: Dr ANARFI ASAMOA-BAAH (Ghana).

Assistant Directors-General: ALA ALWAN (Iraq) (Non-communicable Diseases and Mental Health), Dr CARISSA F. ETIENNE (Dominica) (Health Systems and Services), MOHAMED ABDI JAMA (Somalia) (General Management), Dr ERIC LAROCHE (France) (Health Action in Crises), HIROKI NAKATANI (Japan) (HIV/AIDS, TB, Malaria and Neglected Tropical Diseases), ANDREY V. PIROGOV (Russia) (Executive Director of the WHO Office at the UN), NAMITA PRADHAM (India) (Partnerships and UN Reform), SUZANNE WEBER-MOSDORF (Germany) (Executive Director of the WHO Office at the EU).

PRINCIPAL OFFICES

Each of WHO's six geographical regions has its own organization, consisting of a regional committee representing relevant member states and associate members, and a regional office staffed by experts in various fields of health.

WHO Centre for Health Development: I. H. D. Centre Bldg, 9th Floor, 5–1, 1-chome, Wakinohama-Kaigandori, Chuo-ku, Kobe, Japan; tel. (78) 230-3100; fax (78) 230-3178; e-mail wkc@wkc.who.int; internet www.who.or.jp; f. 1995 to address health development issues; Dir Dr JACOB KUMARESAN (India).

WHO Lyon Office for National Epidemic Preparedness and Response: 58 ave Debourg, 69007 Lyon, France; tel. 4-72-71-64-70; fax 4-72-71-64-71; e-mail oms@lyon.who.int; internet www.who.int/ihr/lyon/en/index.html; supports global capacity-building for detection of and response to epidemics of infectious diseases; provides bridging role between WHO headquarters, the regional offices and ongoing activities in the field; Dir Dr GUÉNAËL RODIER.

Activities

WHO's objective is stated in its constitution as 'the attainment by all peoples of the highest possible level of health'. 'Health' is defined as 'a state of complete physical, mental and social well-being and not merely the absence of disease and infirmity'.

WHO has developed a series of international classifications, including the *International Statistical Classification of Disease and Related Health Problems (ICD)*, providing an etiological framework of health conditions, and currently in its 10th edition; and the complementary *International Classification of Functioning, Disability and Health (ICF)*, which describes how people live with their conditions.

WHO acts as the central authority directing international health work, and establishes relations with professional groups and government health authorities on that basis.

It provides, on request from member states, technical and policy assistance in support of programmes to promote health, prevent and control health problems, control or eradicate disease, train health workers best suited to local needs and strengthen national health systems. Aid is provided in emergencies and natural disasters.

A global programme of collaborative research and exchange of scientific information is carried out in co-operation with about 1,200 national institutions. Particular stress is laid on the widespread communicable diseases of the tropics, and the countries directly concerned are assisted in developing their research capabilities.

It keeps diseases and other health problems under constant surveillance, promotes the exchange of prompt and accurate information and of notification of outbreaks of diseases, and administers the International Health Regulations (the most recently revised version of which entered into force in June 2007). It sets standards for the quality control of drugs, vaccines and other substances affecting health. It formulates health regulations for international travel.

It collects and disseminates health data and carries out statistical analyses and comparative studies in such diseases as cancer, heart disease and mental illness.

It receives reports on drugs observed to have shown adverse reactions in any country, and transmits the information to other member states.

It promotes improved environmental conditions, including housing, sanitation and working conditions. All available information on effects on human health of the pollutants in the environment is critically reviewed and published.

Co-operation among scientists and professional groups is encouraged. The organization negotiates and sustains national and global partnerships. It may propose international conventions and agreements, and develops and promotes international norms and standards. The organization promotes the development and testing of new technologies, tools and guidelines. It assists in developing an informed public opinion on matters of health.

WHO's first global strategy for pursuing 'Health for all' was adopted in May 1981 by the 34th World Health Assembly. The objective of 'Health for all' was identified as the attainment by all citizens of the world of a level of health that would permit them to lead a socially and economically productive life, requiring fair distribution of available resources, universal access to essential health care, and the promotion of preventive health care. In May 1998 the 51st World Health Assembly renewed the initiative, adopting a global strategy in support of 'Health for all in the 21st century', to be effected through regional and national health policies. The new framework was to build on the primary health care approach of the initial strategy, but aimed to strengthen the emphasis on quality of life, equity in health and access to health services. The following have been identified as minimum requirements of 'Health for all':

Safe water in the home or within 15 minutes' walking distance, and adequate sanitary facilities in the home or immediate vicinity;

Immunization against diphtheria, pertussis (whooping cough), tetanus, poliomyelitis, measles and tuberculosis;

Local health care, including availability of essential drugs, within one hour's travel;

Trained personnel to attend childbirth, and to care for pregnant mothers and children up to at least one year old.

In the implementation of all its activities WHO aims to contribute to achieving by 2015 the UN Millennium Development Goals (MDGs) that were agreed by the September 2000 UN Millennium Summit. WHO has particular responsibility for the MDGs of: reducing child mortality, with a target reduction of two-thirds in the mortality rate among children under five; improving maternal health, with a specific goal of reducing by 75% the numbers of women dying in childbirth; and combating HIV/AIDS, malaria and other diseases. In addition, it directly supports the following Millennium 'targets': halving the proportion of people suffering from malnutrition; halving the proportion of people without sustainable access to safe drinking water and basic sanitation; and providing access, in co-operation with pharmaceutical companies, to affordable, essential drugs in developing countries. Furthermore, WHO reports on 17 health-related MDG indicators; co-ordinates, jointly with the World Bank, the High-Level Forum on the Health MDGs, comprising government ministers, senior officials from developing countries, and representatives of bilateral and multilateral agencies, foundations, regional organizations and global partnerships; and undertakes technical and normative work in support of national and regional efforts to reach the MDGs.

The Eleventh General Programme of Work, for the period 2006–15, defined a policy framework for pursuing the principal objectives of building healthy populations and combating ill health. The Programme took into account: increasing understanding of the social, economic, political and cultural factors involved in achieving better health and the role played by better health in poverty reduction; the increasing complexity of health systems; the importance of safeguarding health as a component of humanitarian action; and the need for greater co-ordination among development organizations. It incorporated four interrelated strategic directions: lessening excess mortality, morbidity and disability, especially in poor and marginalized populations; promoting healthy lifestyles and reducing risk factors to human health arising from environmental, economic, social and behavioural causes; developing equitable and financially fair health systems; and establishing an enabling policy and an institutional environment for the health sector and promoting an effective health dimension to social, economic, environmental and development policy. WHO is the sponsoring agency for the Health Workforce Decade (2006–15).

In its work WHO adheres to a six-point agenda covering: promoting development; fostering health security; strengthening health systems; harnessing research, information and evidence; enhancing partnerships; and improving performance.

During 2005 the UN's Inter-Agency Standing Committee (IASC), concerned with co-ordinating the international response to humanitarian disasters, developed a concept of organizing agency assistance to IDPs through the institutionalization of a 'Cluster Approach', comprising 11 core areas of activity. WHO was designated the lead agency for the clusters on Health.

COMMUNICABLE DISEASES

WHO identifies infectious and parasitic communicable diseases as a major obstacle to social and economic progress, particularly in developing countries, where, in addition to disabilities and loss of productivity and household earnings, they cause nearly one-half of all deaths. Emerging and re-emerging diseases, those likely to cause epidemics, increasing incidence of zoonoses (diseases or infections passed from vertebrate animals to humans by means of parasites, viruses, bacteria or unconventional agents), attributable to factors such as environmental changes and changes in farming practices, outbreaks of unknown etiology, and the undermining of some drug therapies by the spread of antimicrobial resistance, are main areas of concern. In recent years WHO has noted the global spread of communicable diseases through international travel, voluntary human migration and involuntary population displacement.

WHO's Communicable Diseases group works to reduce the impact of infectious diseases world-wide through surveillance and response; prevention, control and eradication strategies; and research and product development. The group seeks to identify new technologies and tools, and to foster national development through strengthening health services and the better use of existing tools. It aims to strengthen global monitoring of important communicable disease problems. The group advocates a functional approach to disease control. It aims to create consensus and consolidate partnerships around targeted diseases and collaborates with other groups at all stages to provide an integrated response. In 2000 WHO and several partner institutions in epidemic surveillance established the Global Outbreak Alert and Response Network (GOARN). Through the Network WHO aims to maintain constant vigilance regarding outbreaks of disease and to link world-wide expertise to provide an immediate response capability. From March 2003 WHO, through the Network, was co-ordinating the international investigation into the global spread of Severe Acute Respiratory Syndrome (SARS), a previously unknown atypical pneumonia. From the end of that year WHO was monitoring the spread through several Asian countries of the virus H5N1 (a rapidly mutating strain of zoonotic highly pathogenic avian influenza—HPAI) that was transmitting to human populations through contact with diseased birds, mainly poultry. It was feared that H5N1 would mutate into a form transmissable from human to human. In March 2005 WHO issued a *Global Influenza Preparedness Plan*, and urged all countries to develop national influenza pandemic preparedness plans and to stockpile antiviral drugs. In May, in co-operation with the UN Food and Agriculture Organization (FAO) and the World Organisation for Animal Health (OIE), WHO launched a Global Strategy for the Progressive Control of Highly Pathogenic Avian Influenza. A conference on Avian Influenza and Human Pandemic Influenza that was jointly organized by WHO, FAO, OIE and the World Bank in November 2005 issued a plan of action identifying a number of responses, including: supporting the development of integrated national plans for H5N1 containment and human pandemic influenza preparedness and response; assisting countries with the aggressive control of H5N1 and with establishing a more detailed understanding of the role of wild birds in virus transmission; nominating rapid response teams of experts to support epidemiological field investigations; expanding national and regional capacity in surveillance, diagnosis, and alert and response systems; expanding the network of influenza laboratories; establishing multi-country networks for the control or prevention of animal trans-boundary diseases; expanding the global antiviral stockpile; strengthening veterinary infrastructures; and mapping a global strategy and work plan for co-ordinating antiviral and influenza vaccine research and development. An International Pledging Conference on Avian and Human Influenza, convened in January 2006 in Beijing, People's Republic of China (PRC), and co-sponsored by the World Bank, European Commission and PRC Government, in co-operation with WHO, FAO and OIE, requested a minimum of US $1,200m. in funding towards combating the spread of the virus. By 12 August 2010 a total of 504 human cases of H5N1 had been laboratory confirmed, in Azerbaijan, Bangladesh, Cambodia, PRC, Djibouti, Egypt, Indonesia, Iraq, Laos, Myanmar, Nigeria, Pakistan, Thailand, Turkey and Viet Nam, resulting in 299 deaths. Cases in poultry had become endemic in parts of Asia and Africa, and outbreaks in poultry had also occurred in some European and Middle Eastern countries.

In April 2009 GOARN sent experts to Mexico to work with health authorities there in response to an outbreak of confirmed human cases of a new variant of swine influenza A(H1N1) that had not previously been detected in animals or humans. In late April, by which time cases of the virus had been reported in the USA and Canada, the Director-General of WHO declared a 'public health emergency of international concern'. All countries were instructed to activate their national influenza pandemic preparedness plans (see above). At the end of April the level of pandemic alert was declared to be at phase five of a six-phase (phase six being the most severe) warning system that had been newly revised earlier in the year. Phase five is characterized by human-to-human transmission of a new virus into at least two countries in one WHO region. On 11 June WHO declared a global pandemic (phase six on the warning scale, characterized by human-to-human transmission in two or more WHO regions). The status and development of pandemic influenza vaccines was the focus of an advisory meeting of immunization experts held at the WHO headquarters in late October. In June 2010 the WHO Director-General refuted allegations, levelled by a British medical journal and by the Parliamentary Assembly of the Council of Europe, regarding the severity of pandemic (H1N1) 2009 and the possibility that the Organization had, in declaring the pandemic, used advisers with a vested commercial interest in promoting pharmaceutical industry profitability. In August 2010 the WHO Director-General declared that transmission of the new H1N1 virus had entered a post-pandemic phase.

One of WHO's major achievements was the eradication of smallpox. Following a massive international campaign of vaccination and surveillance (begun in 1958 and intensified in 1967), the last case was detected in 1977 and the eradication of the disease was declared in 1980. In May 1996 the World Health Assembly resolved that, pending a final endorsement, all remaining stocks of the smallpox virus were to be destroyed on 30 June 1999, although 500,000 doses of smallpox vaccine were to remain, along with a supply of the smallpox vaccine seed virus, in order to ensure that a further supply of the vaccine could be made available if required. In May 1999, however, the Assembly authorized a temporary retention of stocks of the virus until 2002. In late 2001, in response to fears that illegally-held virus stocks could be used in acts of biological terrorism (see below), WHO reassembled a team of technical experts on smallpox. In January 2002 the Executive Board determined that stocks of the virus should continue to be retained, to enable research into more effective treatments and vaccines.

In 1988 the World Health Assembly launched the Global Polio Eradication Initiative (GPEI), which aimed, initially, to eradicate poliomyelitis by the end of 2000; this target was subsequently extended to 2013 (see below). Co-ordinated periods of Supplementary Immunization Activity (SIA, facilitated in conflict zones by the negotiation of so-called 'days of tranquillity'), including National Immunization Days (NIDs), Sub-National Immunization Days (SNIDs), mop-up campaigns, VitA campaigns (Vitamin A is administered in order to reduce nutritional deficiencies in children and thereby boost their immunity), and Follow up/Catch up campaigns, have been employed in combating the disease, alongside the strengthening of routine immunization services. Since the inauguration of the GPEI WHO has declared the following regions 'polio-free': the Americas (1994); Western Pacific (2000); and Europe (2002). Furthermore, type 2 wild poliovirus has been eradicated globally (since 1999), although a type 2 circulating vaccine-derived poliovirus (cVDPV) was reported to be active in northern Nigeria during 2006–early 2010. In January 2004 ministers of health of affected countries, and global partners, meeting under the auspices of WHO and UNICEF, adopted the Geneva Declaration on the Eradication of Poliomyelitis, in which they made a commitment to accelerate the drive towards eradication of the disease, by improving the scope of vaccination programmes. Significant progress in eradication of the virus was reported in Asia during that year. In sub-Saharan Africa, however, an outbreak originating in northern Nigeria in mid-2003—caused by a temporary cessation of vaccination activities in response to local opposition to the vaccination programme—had spread, by mid-2004, to 10 previously polio-free countries. These included Côte d'Ivoire and Sudan, where ongoing civil unrest and population displacements impeded control efforts. During 2004–05 some 23 African governments, including those of the affected West and Central African countries, organized, with support from the African Union, a number of co-ordinated mass vaccination drives, which resulted in the vaccination of about 100m. children. By mid-2005 the sub-regional epidemic was declared over; it was estimated that since mid-2003 it had resulted in the paralysis of nearly 200 children. In Nigeria itself, however, the number of confirmed wild poliovirus cases had by 2006 escalated to 1,122 from 202 in 2002. In February 2007 the GPEI launched an intensified eradication effort aimed at identifying and addressing the outstanding operational, technical and financial barriers to eradication. The May 2008 World Health Assembly adopted a resolution urging all remaining polio-affected member states to ensure the vaccination of every child during each SIA. By the end of 2008, having received independent advice that the intensified eradication effort initiated in 2007 had demonstrated that the remaining challenges to eradication were surmountable, the GPEI endorsed a strategic plan covering the period 2009–13 (replacing a previous plan for 2004–08). The new strategic plan aimed to achieve the interruption of type 1 wild poliovirus transmission in India, and the cessation of all prolonged outbreaks in Africa by the end of 2009; the interruption of all poliovirus transmission in Afghanistan, India and Pakistan, of type 1 wild poliovirus transmission in Nigeria, and of all wild poliovirus transmission elsewhere in Africa, by end-2010; the interruption of type 3 wild poliovirus transmission in Nigeria by end-2011; and the eradication of new cVDPVs within six months of detection by end-2013. During February–March 2009 WHO and UNICEF co-ordinated a synchronized cross-border polio vaccination initiative, implemented in two simultaneous rounds, throughout the following eight West African countries: Benin, Burkina Faso, Côte d'Ivoire, Ghana, Mali, Niger, Togo, and Nigeria, with the aim of reaching a critical mass of immunization coverage. Some 1,606 polio cases were confirmed world-wide in 2009, of which 1,256 were in the countries designated at that time as polio-endemic (Nigeria, 388 cases; India, 741 cases; Pakistan, 89 cases; and Afghanistan, 38 cases). (In 1988 35,000 cases had been confirmed in 125 countries, with the actual number of cases estimated at around 350,000.)

The Onchocerciasis Elimination Programme in the Americas (OEPA), launched in 1992, co-ordinates work to control the disease in six Latin American countries where it is endemic. In January 1998 a new 20-year programme to eliminate lymphatic filariasis was initiated, with substantial funding and support from two major pharmaceutical companies, and in collaboration with the World Bank, the Arab Fund for Economic and Social Development and the governments of Japan, the United Kingdom and the USA. South American trypanosomiasis ('Chagas disease') is endemic in Central and South America, causing the deaths of some 45,000 people each year and infecting a further 16m.–18m. A regional intergovernmental commission is implementing a programme to eliminate Chagas from the Southern Cone region of Latin America. The countries of the Andean region of Latin America initiated a plan for the elimination of transmission of Chagas disease in February 1997, and a similar plan was launched by Central American governments in October. In July 2007, to combat the expansion of Chagas disease into some European countries, the Western Pacific, and the USA, as well as the re-emergence of the disease in areas such as the Chaco, in Argentina and Bolivia, where it was thought to have been eradicated, WHO established a Global Network for Chagas Disease Elimination.

WHO is committed to the elimination of leprosy (the reduction of the prevalence of leprosy to less than one case per 10,000 population). The use of a highly effective combination of three drugs (known as multi-drug therapy—MDT) resulted in a reduction in the number of leprosy cases world-wide from 10m.–12m. in 1988 to 213,036 registered cases in January 2010. In 2008 some 249,007 cases were detected in 121 countries. The number of countries having more than one case of leprosy per 10,000 had declined to four by January 2007 (Brazil, Democratic Republic of the Congo, Mozambique and Nepal), compared with 122 in 1985. The country with the highest prevalence of leprosy cases in 2007 was Brazil (3.21 per 10,000 population) and the country with the highest number of cases was India (139,252). The Global Alliance for the Elimination of Leprosy, launched in November 1999 by WHO, in collaboration with governments of affected countries and several private partners, including a major pharmaceutical company, aims to support the eradication of the disease through the provision until end-2010 of free MDT treatment. In June 2005 WHO adopted a Strategic Plan for Further Reducing the Leprosy Burden and Sustaining Leprosy Control Activities, covering the period 2006–10 and following on from a previous strategic plan for 2000–05. In 1998 WHO launched the Global Buruli Ulcer Initiative, which aimed to co-ordinate control of and research into Buruli ulcer, another mycobacterial disease. In July of that year the Director-General of WHO and representatives of more than 20 countries, meeting in Yamoussoukro, Côte d'Ivoire, signed a declaration on the control of Buruli ulcer. In May 2004 the World Health Assembly adopted a resolution urging improved research into, and detection and treatment of, Buruli ulcer.

The Special Programme for Research and Training in Tropical Diseases, established in 1975 and sponsored jointly by WHO, UNDP and the World Bank, as well as by contributions from donor countries, involves a world-wide network of some 5,000 scientists working on the development and application of vaccines, new drugs, diagnostic kits and preventive measures, and applied field research on practical community issues affecting the target diseases.

The objective of providing immunization for all children by 1990 was adopted by the World Health Assembly in 1977. Six diseases (measles, whooping cough, tetanus, poliomyelitis, tuberculosis and diphtheria) became the target of the Expanded Programme on Immunization (EPI), in which WHO, UNICEF and many other organizations collaborated. As a result of massive international and national efforts, the global immunization coverage increased from 20% in the early 1980s to the targeted rate of 80% by the end of 1990. In 2006 WHO, UNICEF and other partners launched the Global Immunization Vision and Strategy (GIVS), a global 10-year framework, covering 2006–15, aimed at reducing deaths due to vaccine-preventable diseases by at least two-thirds compared to 2000 levels, by 2015; and increasing national vaccination coverage levels to at least 90%. In 2009 the global child vaccination coverage rate was estimated at 82%.

In June 2000 WHO released a report entitled 'Overcoming Antimicrobial Resistance', in which it warned that the misuse of antibiotics could render some common infectious illnesses unresponsive to treatment. At that time WHO issued guidelines which aimed to mitigate the risks associated with the use of antimicrobials in livestock reared for human consumption.

HIV/AIDS, TB, MALARIA AND NEGLECTED DISEASES

Combating the human immunodeficiency virus/acquired immunodeficiency syndrome (HIV/AIDS), tuberculosis (TB) and malaria are organization-wide priorities and, as such, are supported not only by their own areas of work but also by activities undertaken in other areas. TB is the principal cause of death for people infected with the HIV virus and an estimated one-third of people living with HIV/AIDS globally are co-infected with TB. In July 2000 a meeting of the Group of Seven industrialized nations and Russia, convened in Genoa, Italy, announced the formation of a new Global Fund to Fight AIDS, TB and Malaria (as previously proposed by the UN Secretary-General and recommended by the World Health Assembly).

The HIV/AIDS epidemic represents a major threat to human well-being and socio-economic progress. Some 95% of those known to be infected with HIV/AIDS live in developing countries, and AIDS-related illnesses are the leading cause of death in sub-Saharan Africa. It is estimated that more than 25m. people world-wide died of AIDS during 1981–2008. WHO supports governments in developing effective health-sector responses to the HIV/AIDS epidemic through enhancing their planning and managerial capabilities, implementation capacity, and health systems resources. The Joint UN Programme on HIV/AIDS (UNAIDS) became operational on 1 January 1996, sponsored by WHO and other UN agencies; the UNAIDS secretariat is based at WHO headquarters. Sufferers of HIV/AIDS in developing countries have often failed to receive advanced antiretroviral (ARV) treatments that are widely available in industrialized countries, owing to their high cost. (It was estimated in 2005 that only 15% of HIV/AIDS patients were receiving the optimum treatment.) In May 2000 the World Health Assembly adopted a resolution urging WHO member states to improve access to the prevention and treatment of HIV-related illnesses and to increase the availability and affordability of drugs. A WHO-UNAIDS HIV Vaccine Initiative was launched in that year. In June 2001 governments participating in a special session of the UN General Assembly on HIV/AIDS adopted a Declaration of Commitment on HIV/AIDS. WHO, with UNAIDS, UNICEF, UNFPA, the World Bank, and major pharmaceutical companies, participates in the 'Accelerating Access' initiative, which aims to expand access to care, support and ARVs for people with HIV/AIDS. In March 2002, under its 'Access to Quality HIV/AIDS Drugs and Diagnostics' programme, WHO published a comprehensive list of HIV-related medicines deemed to meet standards recommended by the Organization. In April WHO issued the first treatment guidelines for HIV/AIDS cases in poor communities, and endorsed the inclusion of HIV/AIDS drugs in its *Model List of Essential Medicines* (see below) in order to encourage their wider availability. The secretariat of the International HIV Treatment Access Coalition, founded in December of that year by governments, non-governmental organizations, donors and others to facilitate access to ARVs for people in low- and middle-income countries, is based at WHO headquarters. In 2006 WHO, UNAIDS and partner organizations negotiated a framework approach, covering 2007–10, aimed at accelerating universal access to HIV/AIDS prevention, treatment, care and support. WHO supports the following *Three Ones* principles, endorsed in April 2004 by a high-level meeting organized by UNAIDS, the United Kingdom and the USA, with the aim of strengthening national responses to the HIV/AIDS pandemic: for every country there should be one agreed national HIV/AIDS action framework; one national AIDS co-ordinating authority; and one agreed monitoring and evaluation system.

At December 2007 some 230,000 people in the Caribbean region and 1.6m. in Latin America were reported to have HIV/AIDS. The Caribbean has the second highest rate of HIV prevalence in the world, after sub-Saharan Africa. National adult prevalence rates are estimated to exceed 1% in Barbados, Dominican Republic, Jamaica and Suriname, 2% in the Bahamas, Guyana and Trinidad and Tobago, and to stand at 3.6% in Haiti (reduced from more than 6% in the early 1990s).

In 1995 WHO established a Global Tuberculosis Programme to address the challenges of the TB epidemic, which had been declared a global emergency by the Organization in 1993. According to WHO estimates, one-third of the world's population carries the TB bacillus. In 2007 this generated 9.3m. new active cases (1.4m. in people co-infected with HIV), and killed 1.8m. people (0.5m. of whom were also HIV-positive). Some 22 high-burden countries account for four-fifths of global TB cases. The largest concentration of TB cases is in South-East Asia. WHO provides technical support to all member countries, with special attention given to those with high TB prevalence, to establish effective national tuberculosis control programmes. WHO's strategy for TB control includes the use of the expanded DOTS (direct observation treatment, short-course) regime, involving the following five tenets: sustained political commitment to increase human and financial resources and to make TB control in endemic countries a nation-wide activity and an integral part of the national health system; access to quality-assured TB sputum microscopy; standardized short-course chemotherapy for all cases of TB under proper case-management conditions; uninterrupted supply of quality-assured drugs; and maintaining a recording and reporting system to enable outcome assessment. Simultaneously, WHO is encouraging research with the aim of further advancing DOTS, developing new tools for prevention, diagnosis and treatment, and containing new threats (such as the HIV/TB co-epidemic). Inadequate control of DOTS in some areas, leading to partial and inconsistent treatments, has resulted in the development of drug-resistant and, often, incurable strains of TB. The incidence of so-called Multidrug Resistant TB (MDR-TB) strains, that are unresponsive to at least two of the four most commonly used anti-TB drugs, has risen in recent years, and WHO estimates that about four-fifths are 'super strains', resistant to at least three of the main anti-TB drugs; some 0.5m. cases of TB in 2007 were reported to be MDR. WHO has developed DOTS-Plus, a specialized strategy for controlling the spread of MDR-TB in areas of high prevalence.

The 'Stop TB' partnership, launched by WHO in 1999, in partnership with the World Bank, the US Government and a coalition of non-governmental organizations, co-ordinates the Global Plan to Stop TB, which represents a 'roadmap' for TB control. The current phase of the plan, covering the period 2006–15, aims to facilitate the achievement of the MDG of halting and beginning to reverse by 2015 the incidence of TB by means of access to quality diagnosis and treatment for all; to supply ARVs to 3m. TB patients co-infected with HIV; to treat nearly 1m. people for MDR-TB; to develop a new anti-TB drug by 2010 and a new vaccine by 2015; and to develop rapid and inexpensive diagnostic tests at the point of care. The Global TB Drug Facility, launched by 'Stop TB' in 2001, aims to increase access to high-quality anti-TB drugs for sufferers in developing countries.

In September 2006 WHO expressed strong concern at the emergence of strains of Extensive Drug Resistant TB (XDR-TB) that are virtually untreatable with most existing anti-TB drugs. XDR-TB is believed to be most prevalent in Eastern Europe and Asia.

In October 1998 WHO, jointly with UNICEF, the World Bank and UNDP, formally launched the Roll Back Malaria (RBM) programme. The disease acutely affects at least 350m.–500m. people, and kills an estimated 1m. people, every year. Some 90% of all malaria cases occur in sub-Saharan Africa. It is estimated that the disease directly causes 18% of all child deaths in that region. The global RBM Partnership, linking governments, development agencies, and other parties, aims to mobilize resources and support for controlling malaria. The RBM Partnership Global Strategic Plan for the period 2005–15, adopted in November 2005, lists steps required to intensify malaria control interventions with a view to attaining targets set by the Partnership for 2010 and 2015 (the former targets include: ensuring the protection of 80% of people at risk from malaria and the diagnosis and treatment within one day of 80% of malaria patients, and reducing the global malaria burden by one-half compared with 2000 levels; and the latter: achieving a 75% reduction in malaria morbidity and mortality over levels at 2005). WHO recommends a number of guidelines for malaria control, focusing on the need for prompt, effective antimalarial treatment, and the issue of drug resistance; vector control, including the use of insecticide-treated bednets; malaria in pregnancy; malaria epidemics; and monitoring and evaluation activities. WHO, with several private- and public-sector partners, supports the development of more effective anti-malaria drugs and vaccines through the 'Medicines for Malaria' venture.

Joint UN Programme on HIV/AIDS (UNAIDS): 20 ave Appia, 1211 Geneva 27, Switzerland; tel. 227913666; fax 227914187; e-mail communications@unaids.org; internet www.unaids.org; established in 1996 to lead, strengthen and support an expanded response to the global HIV/AIDS pandemic; activities focus on prevention, care and support, reducing vulnerability to infection, and alleviating the socioeconomic and human effects of HIV/AIDS; launched the Global Coalition on Women and AIDS in Feb. 2004; guided by UN Security Council Resolution 1308, focusing on the possible impact of AIDS on social instability and emergency situations, and the potential impact of HIV on the health of international peace-keeping personnel; by the UN Millennium Development Goals adopted in Sept. 2000; by the Declaration of Commitment on HIV/AIDS agreed in June 2001 by the first-ever Special Session of the UN General Assembly on HIV/AIDS, which acknowledged the AIDS epidemic as a 'global emergency'; and the Political Declaration on HIV/AIDS, adopted by the June 2006 UN General Assembly High Level Meeting on AIDS; launched the Global Coalition on Women and AIDS in Feb. 2004; co-sponsors: WHO, UNICEF, UNDP, UNFPA, UNODC, the ILO, UNESCO, the World Bank, WFP, UNHCR; Exec. Dir MICHEL SIDIBÉ (Mali).

NON-COMMUNICABLE DISEASES AND MENTAL HEALTH

The Non-communicable Diseases (NCDs) and Mental Health group comprises departments for the surveillance, prevention and management of uninfectious diseases, and departments for health promotion, disability, injury prevention and rehabilitation, substance abuse and mental health. Surveillance, prevention and management of NCDs, tobacco, and mental health are organization-wide priorities.

Addressing the social and environmental determinants of health is a main priority of WHO. Tobacco use, unhealthy diet and physical inactivity are regarded as common, preventable risk factors for the four most prominent NCDs: cardiovascular diseases, cancer, chronic respiratory disease and diabetes. It is estimated that the four main NCDs are collectively responsible for an estimated 35m. deaths—60% of all deaths—globally each year, and that up to 80% of cases of heart disease, stroke and type 2 diabetes, and more than one-third of cancers, could be prevented by eliminating shared risk factors, the main ones being: tobacco use, unhealthy diet, physical inactivity and harmful use of alcohol. WHO envisages that the disease burden and mortality from these diseases will continue to increase, most rapidly in Africa and the Eastern Mediterranean, and that the highest number of deaths will occur in the Western Pacific region and in South-East Asia. WHO aims to monitor the global epidemiological situation of NCDs, to co-ordinate multinational research activities concerned with prevention and care, and to analyse determining factors such as gender and poverty. The 53rd World Health Assembly, convened in May 2000, endorsed a Global Strategy for the Prevention and Control of NCDs. In May 2008 the 61st World Health Assembly endorsed a new Action Plan for 2008–13 for the Global Strategy for the Prevention and Control of NCDs, based on the vision of the 2000 Global Strategy. The Action Plan aimed to provide a roadmap establishing and strengthening initiatives on the surveillance, prevention and management of NCDs, and emphasized the need to invest in NCD prevention as part of sustainable socio-economic development planning.

The sixth Global Conference on Health Promotion, convened jointly by WHO and the Thai Government, in Bangkok, Thailand, in August 2005, adopted the Bangkok Charter for Health Promotion in a Globalized World, which identified ongoing key challenges, actions and commitments.

In May 2004 the World Health Assembly endorsed a Global Strategy on Diet, Physical Activity and Health; it is estimated that more than 1,000m. adults world-wide are overweight, and that, of these, some 300m. are clinically obese. WHO has studied obesity-related issues in co-operation with the International Association for the Study of Obesity (IASO). The International Task Force on Obesity, affiliated to the IASO, aims to encourage the development of new policies for managing obesity. WHO and FAO jointly commissioned an expert report on the relationship of diet, nutrition and physical activity to chronic diseases, which was published in March 2003.

WHO's programmes for diabetes mellitus, chronic rheumatic diseases and asthma assist with the development of national initiatives, based upon goals and targets for the improvement of early detection, care and reduction of long-term complications. WHO's cardiovascular diseases programme aims to prevent and control the major cardiovascular diseases, which are responsible for more than 14m. deaths each year. It is estimated that one-third of these deaths could have been prevented with existing scientific knowledge. The programme on cancer control is concerned with the prevention of cancer, improving its detection and cure, and ensuring care of all cancer patients in need. In May 2004 the World Health Assembly adopted a resolution on cancer prevention and control, recognizing an increase in global cancer cases, particularly in developing countries, and stressing that many cases and related deaths could be prevented. The resolution included a number of recommendations for the improvement of national cancer control programmes. In May 2009 WHO and the IAEA launched a Joint Programme on Cancer Control, aimed at enhancing efforts to fight cancer in the developing world. WHO is a co-sponsor of the Global Day Against Pain, which is held annually on 11 October. The Global Day highlights the need for improved pain management and palliative care for sufferers of diseases such as cancer and AIDS, with a particular focus on patients living in low-income countries with minimal access to opioid analgesics, and urges recognition of access to pain relief as a basic human right.

The WHO Human Genetics Programme manages genetic approaches for the prevention and control of common hereditary diseases and of those with a genetic predisposition representing a major health factor. The Programme also concentrates on the further development of genetic approaches suitable for incorporation into health care systems, as well as developing a network of international collaborating programmes.

WHO works to assess the impact of injuries, violence and sensory impairments on health, and formulates guidelines and protocols for the prevention and management of mental problems. The health promotion division promotes decentralized and community-based health programmes and is concerned with developing new approaches to population ageing and encouraging healthy life-styles and self-care. It also seeks to relieve the negative impact of social changes such as urbanization, migration and changes in family structure upon health. WHO advocates a multi-sectoral approach—involving public health, legal and educational systems—to the prevention of injuries, which represent 16% of the global burden of disease. It aims to support governments in developing suitable strategies to prevent and mitigate the consequences of violence, unintentional injury and disability. Several health promotion projects have been undertaken, in collaboration between WHO regional and country offices and other relevant organizations, including: the Global School Health Initiative, to bridge the sectors of health and education and to promote the health of school-age children; the Global Strategy for Occupational Health, to promote the health of the working population and the control of occupational health risks; Community-based Rehabilitation, aimed at providing a more enabling environment for people with disabilities; and a communication strategy to provide training and support for health communications personnel and initiatives. In 2000 WHO, UNESCO, the World Bank and UNICEF adopted the joint Focusing Resources for Effective School Health (FRESH Start) approach to promoting life skills among adolescents.

WHO supports the UN Convention, and its Optional Protocol, on the Rights of Persons with Disabilities, which came into force in May 2008, and seeks to address challenges that prevent the full participation of people with disabilities in the social, economic and cultural lives of their communities and societies; at that time the WHO Director-General appointed a Taskforce on Disability to ensure that WHO was reflecting the provisions of the Convention overall as an organization and in its programme of work.

In February 1999 WHO initiated a new programme, 'Vision 2020: the Right to Sight', which aimed to eliminate avoidable blindness (estimated to be as much as 80% of all cases) by 2020. Blindness was otherwise predicted to increase by as much as twofold, owing to the increased longevity of the global population.

The Tobacco or Health Programme aims to reduce the use of tobacco, by educating tobacco-users and preventing young people from adopting the habit. In 1996 WHO published its first report on the tobacco situation world-wide. According to WHO, about one-third of the world's population aged over 15 years smoke tobacco, which causes approximately 3.5m. deaths each year (through lung cancer, heart disease, chronic bronchitis and other effects). In 1998 the 'Tobacco Free Initiative', a major global anti-smoking campaign, was established. In May 1999 the World Health Assembly endorsed the formulation of a Framework Convention on Tobacco Control (FCTC) to help to combat the increase in tobacco use (although a number of tobacco growers expressed concerns about the effect of the convention on their livelihoods). The FCTC entered into force in February 2005. The greatest increase in tobacco use is forecast to occur in developing countries. In 2008 WHO published a comprehensive analysis of global tobacco use and control, the *WHO Report on the Global Tobacco Epidemic*, which designated abuse of tobacco as one of the principal global threats to health, and predicted that during the latter part of the 21st century the vast majority of tobacco-related deaths would occur in developing countries. The Report identified and condemned a global tobacco industry strategy to target young people and adults in the developing world, and it detailed six key proven strategies, collectively known as the 'MPOWER package', that were aimed at combating global tobacco use: monitoring tobacco use and implementing prevention policies; protecting people from tobacco smoke; offering support to people to enable them to give up tobacco use; warning about the dangers of tobacco; enforcing bans on tobacco advertising, promotion and sponsorship; and raising taxes on tobacco. The MPOWER package provided a roadmap to support countries in building on their obligations under the FCTC. The FCTC obligates its states parties to require 'health warnings describing the harmful effects of tobacco use' to appear on packs of tobacco and their outside packaging, and recommends the use of warnings that contain pictures. WHO provides technical and other assistance to countries to support them in meeting this obligation through the Tobacco Free Initiative. During 2009 WHO planned to encourage governments to adopt tobacco health warnings meeting the agreed criteria for maximum effectiveness in convincing consumers not to smoke: these were to appear on both the front and back of a cigarette pack, to cover more than half of the pack, and to contain pictures.

WHO's Mental Health and Substance Abuse department was established in 2000 from the merger of formerly separate departments to reflect the many common approaches in managing mental health and substance use disorders.

WHO defines mental health as a 'state of well-being in which every individual realizes his or her own potential, can cope with the normal stresses of life, can work productively and fruitfully, and is able to make a contribution to her or his community'. WHO's Mental Health programme is concerned with mental health problems that include unipolar and bipolar affective disorders, psychosis, epilepsy, dementia, Parkinson's disease, multiple sclerosis, drug and alcohol dependency, and neuropsychiatric disorders such as post-traumatic stress disorder, obsessive compulsive disorder and panic disorder. Although, overall, physical health has improved, mental, behavioural and social health problems are increasing, owing to extended life expectancy and improved child mortality rates, and factors such as war and poverty. WHO aims to address mental problems by increasing awareness of mental health issues and promoting improved mental health services and primary care. In October 2008 WHO launched the so-called mental health Gap Action Programme (mhGAP), which aimed to improve services addressing mental, neurological and substance use disorders, with a special focus on low and middle income countries. It was envisaged that, with proper care, psychosocial assistance and medication, many millions of patients in developing countries could be treated for depression, schizophrenia, and epilepsy; prevented from attempting suicide; and encouraged to begin to lead normal lives. A main focus of mhGAP concerns forging strategic partnerships to enhance countries' capacity to combat stigma commonly associated with mental illness, reduce the burden of mental disorders, and promote mental health. WHO is a joint partner in the Global Campaign against Epilepsy: Out of the Shadows, which aims to advance understanding, treatment, services and prevention of epilepsy world-wide.

The Substance Abuse programme addresses the misuse of all psychoactive substances, irrespective of legal status and including alcohol. WHO provides technical support to assist countries in formulating policies with regard to the prevention and reduction of the health and social effects of psychoactive substance abuse, and undertakes epidemiological surveillance and risk assessment, advocacy and the dissemination of information, strengthening national and regional prevention and health promotion techniques and strategies, the development of cost-effective treatment and rehabilitation approaches, and also encompasses regulatory activities as required under the international drugs-control treaties in force.

FAMILY AND COMMUNITY HEALTH

WHO's Family and Community Health group addresses the following areas of work: child and adolescent health, research and programme development in reproductive health, making pregnancy safer and men's and women's health. Making pregnancy safer is an organization-wide priority. The group's aim is to improve access to sustainable health care for all by strengthening health systems and fostering individual, family and community development. Activities include newborn care; child health, including promoting and protecting the health and development of the child through such approaches as promotion of breast-feeding and use of the mother-baby package, as well as care of the sick child, including diarrhoeal and acute respiratory disease control, and support to women and children in difficult circumstances; the promotion of safe motherhood and maternal health; adolescent health, including the promotion and development of young people and the prevention of specific health problems; women, health and development, including addressing issues of gender, sexual violence, and harmful traditional practices; and human reproduction, including research related to contraceptive technologies and effective methods. In addition, WHO aims to provide technical leadership and co-ordination on reproductive health and to support countries in their efforts to ensure that people: experience healthy sexual development and maturation; have the capacity for healthy, equitable and responsible relationships; can achieve their reproductive intentions safely and healthily; avoid illnesses, diseases and injury related to sexuality and reproduction; and receive appropriate counselling, care and rehabilitation for diseases and conditions related to sexuality and reproduction.

In September 1997 WHO, in collaboration with UNICEF, formally launched a programme advocating the Integrated Management of Childhood Illness (IMCI). IMCI recognizes that pneumonia, diarrhoea, measles, malaria and malnutrition cause some 70% of the approximately 11m. childhood deaths each year, and recommends screening sick children for all five conditions, to obtain a more accurate diagnosis than may be achieved from the results of a single assessment. WHO's Division of Diarrhoeal and Acute Respiratory Disease Control encourages national programmes aimed at reducing childhood deaths as a result of diarrhoea, particularly through the use of oral rehydration therapy and preventive measures. The Division is also seeking to reduce deaths from pneumonia in infants through the use of a simple case-management strategy involving the recognition of danger signs and treatment with an appropriate antibiotic.

SUSTAINABLE DEVELOPMENT AND HEALTHY ENVIRONMENTS

The Sustainable Development and Healthy Environments group focuses on the following areas of work: health in sustainable development; nutrition; health and environment; food safety; and emergency preparedness and response. Food safety is an organization-wide priority.

WHO promotes recognition of good health status as one of the most important assets of the poor. The Sustainable Development and Healthy Environment group seeks to monitor the advantages and disadvantages for health, nutrition, environment and development arising from the process of globalization (i.e. increased global flows of capital, goods and services, people, and knowledge); to integrate the issue of health into poverty reduction programmes; and to promote human rights and equality. Adequate and safe food and nutrition is a priority programme area. WHO collaborates with FAO, the World Food Programme, UNICEF and other UN agencies in pursuing its objectives relating to nutrition and food safety. It has been estimated that 780m. people world-wide cannot meet basic needs for energy and protein, more than 2,000m. people lack essential vitamins and minerals, and that 170m. children are malnourished. In December 1992 WHO and FAO hosted an international conference on nutrition, at which a World Declaration and Plan of Action on Nutrition was adopted to make the fight against malnutrition a development priority. Following the conference, WHO promoted the elaboration and implementation of national plans of action on nutrition. WHO aims to support the enhancement of member states' capabilities in dealing with their nutrition situations, and addressing scientific issues related to preventing, managing and monitoring protein-energy malnutrition; micronutrient malnutrition, including iodine deficiency disorders, vitamin A deficiency, and nutritional anaemia; and diet-related conditions and NCDs such as obesity (increasingly affecting children, adolescents and adults, mainly in industrialized countries), cancer and heart disease. In 1990 the World Health Assembly resolved to eliminate iodine deficiency (believed to cause mental retardation); a strategy of universal salt iodization was launched in 1993. In collaboration with other international agencies, WHO is implementing a comprehensive strategy for promoting appropriate infant, young child and maternal nutrition, and for dealing effectively with nutritional emergencies in large populations. Areas of emphasis include promoting healthcare practices that enhance successful breast-feeding; appropriate complementary feeding; refining the use and interpretation of body measurements for assessing nutritional status; relevant information, education and training; and action to give effect to the International Code of Marketing of Breast-milk Substitutes. The food safety programme aims to protect human health against risks associated with biological and chemical contaminants and additives in food. With FAO, WHO establishes food standards (through the work of the Codex Alimentarius Commission and its subsidiary committees) and evaluates food additives, pesticide residues and other contaminants and their implications for health. The programme provides expert advice on such issues as food-borne pathogens (e.g. listeria), production methods (e.g. aquaculture) and food biotechnology (e.g. genetic modification). In July 2001 the Codex Alimentarius Commission adopted the first global principles for assessing the safety of genetically modified (GM) foods. In March 2002 an intergovernmental task force established by the Commission finalized 'principles for the risk analysis of foods derived from biotechnology', which were to provide a framework for assessing the safety of GM foods and plants. In the following month WHO and FAO announced a joint review of their food standards operations. In February 2003 the FAO/WHO Project and Fund for Enhanced Participation in Codex was launched to support the participation of poorer countries in the Commission's activities.

WHO's programme area on environmental health undertakes a wide range of initiatives to tackle the increasing threats to health and well-being from a changing environment, especially in relation to air pollution, water quality, sanitation, protection against radiation, management of hazardous waste, chemical safety and housing hygiene. In 2008 it was estimated that some 1,200m. people worldwide had no access to clean drinking water, while a further 2,600m. people are denied suitable sanitation systems. WHO helped launch the Water Supply and Sanitation Council in 1990 and regularly updates its *Guidelines for Drinking Water Quality*. In rural areas the emphasis continues to be on the provision and maintenance of safe and sufficient water supplies and adequate sanitation, the health aspects of rural housing, vector control in water resource management, and the safe use of agrochemicals. In urban areas assistance is provided to identify local environmental health priorities and to improve municipal governments' ability to deal with environmental conditions and health problems in an integrated manner; promotion of the 'Healthy City' approach is a major component of the programme. Other programme activities include environmental health information development and management, human resources development, environmental health planning methods, research and work on problems relating to global environment change, such as UV-radiation. The WHO Global Strategy for Health and Environment, developed in response to the WHO Commission on Health and Environment which reported to the UN Conference on Environment and Development in June 1992, provides the framework for programme activities. In May 2008 the 61st World Health Assembly adopted a resolution urging member states to take action to address the impact of climate change on human health.

Through its International EMF Project WHO is compiling a comprehensive assessment of the potential adverse effects on human health deriving from exposure to electromagnetic fields (EMF). In June 2004 WHO organized a workshop on childhood sensitivity to EMF.

WHO's work in the promotion of chemical safety is undertaken in collaboration with the ILO and UNEP through the International Programme on Chemical Safety (IPCS), the Central Unit for which is located in WHO. The Programme provides internationally evaluated scientific information on chemicals, promotes the use of such information in national programmes, assists member states in establishment of their own chemical safety measures and programmes, and helps them strengthen their capabilities in chemical emergency preparedness and response and in chemical risk reduction. In 1995 an Inter-organization Programme for the Social Management of Chemicals was established by UNEP, the ILO, FAO, WHO, UNIDO and OECD, in order to strengthen international co-operation in the field of chemical safety. In 1998 WHO led an international assessment of the health risk from bendocine disruptors (chemicals which disrupt hormonal activities).

Since the major terrorist attacks perpetrated against targets in the USA in September 2001, WHO has focused renewed attention on the potential malevolent use of bacteria (such as bacillus anthracis, which causes anthrax), viruses (for example, the variola virus, causing smallpox) or toxins, or of chemical agents, in acts of biological or chemical terrorism. In September 2001 WHO issued draft guidelines entitled 'Health Aspects of Biological and Chemical Weapons'.

Within the UN system, WHO's Department of Emergency and Humanitarian Action co-ordinates the international response to emergencies and natural disasters in the health field, in close co-operation with other agencies and within the framework set out by the UN's Office for the Co-ordination of Humanitarian Affairs. In this context, WHO provides expert advice on epidemiological surveillance, control of communicable diseases, public health information and health emergency training. Its emergency preparedness activities include co-ordination, policy-making and planning, awareness-building, technical advice, training, publication of standards and guidelines, and research. Its emergency relief activities include organizational support, the provision of emergency drugs and supplies and conducting technical emergency assessment missions. The Division's objective is to strengthen the national capacity of member states to reduce the adverse health consequences of disasters. In responding to emergency situations, WHO always tries to develop projects and activities that will assist the national authorities concerned in rebuilding or strengthening their own capacity to handle the impact of such situations. Under the UN's inter-agency Consolidated Appeals Process (CAP) for 2010, launched in November 2009, WHO appealed for US $114.9m. to fund its emergency humanitarian operations.

HEALTH TECHNOLOGY AND PHARMACEUTICALS

WHO's Health Technology and Pharmaceuticals group, made up of the departments of essential drugs and other medicines, vaccines and other biologicals, and blood safety and clinical technology, covers the following areas of work: essential medicines—access, quality and rational use; immunization and vaccine development; and worldwide co-operation on blood safety and clinical technology. Blood safety and clinical technology are an organization-wide priority.

In January 1999 the Executive Board adopted a resolution on WHO's Revised Drug Strategy which placed emphasis on the inequalities of access to pharmaceuticals, and also covered specific aspects of drugs policy, quality assurance, drug promotion, drug donation, independent drug information and rational drug use. Plans of action involving co-operation with member states and other international organizations were to be developed to monitor and analyse the pharmaceutical and public health implications of international agreements, including trade agreements. In April 2001 experts from WHO and the World Trade Organization participated in a workshop to address ways of lowering the cost of medicines in less developed countries. In the following month the World Health Assembly adopted a resolution urging member states to promote equitable access to essential drugs, noting that this was denied to about one-third of the world's population. WHO participates with other partners in the 'Accelerating Access' initiative, which aims to expand access to antiretroviral drugs for people with HIV/AIDS (see above).

WHO reports that 2m. children die each year of diseases for which common vaccines exist. In September 1991 the Children's Vaccine Initiative (CVI) was launched, jointly sponsored by the Rockefeller Foundation, UNDP, UNICEF, the World Bank and WHO, to facilitate the development and provision of children's vaccines. The CVI has as its ultimate goal the development of a single oral immunization shortly after birth that will protect against all major childhood diseases. An International Vaccine Institute was established in Seoul, Republic of Korea, as part of the CVI, to provide scientific and technical services for the production of vaccines for developing countries. The first edition of a comprehensive survey, entitled *State of the World's Vaccines and Immunization*, was published by WHO, jointly with UNICEF, in 1996; a revised edition of the survey was issued in 2003. In 1999 WHO, UNICEF, the World Bank and a number of public and private sector partners formed the Global Alliance for Vaccines and Immunization (GAVI), which aimed to expand the provision of existing vaccines and to accelerate the development and introduction of new vaccines and technologies, with the ultimate goal of protecting children of all nations and from all socio-economic backgrounds against vaccine-preventable diseases.

WHO supports states in ensuring access to safe blood, blood products, transfusions, injections, and healthcare technologies.

INFORMATION, EVIDENCE AND RESEARCH

The Information, Evidence and Research group addresses the following areas of work: evidence for health policy; health information management and dissemination; and research policy and promotion and organization of health systems. Through the generation and dissemination of evidence the Information, Evidence and Research group aims to assist policy-makers assess health needs, choose intervention strategies, design policy and monitor performance, and thereby improve the performance of national health systems. The group also supports international and national dialogue on health policy.

WHO co-ordinates the Health InterNetwork Access to Research Initiative (HINARI), which was launched in July 2001 to enable relevant authorities in developing countries to access biomedical journals through the internet at no or greatly reduced cost, in order to improve the world-wide circulation of scientific information; by July 2008 more than 3,750 publications were being made available to health institutions in 113 countries.

Finance

WHO's regular budget is provided by assessment of member states and associate members. An additional fund for specific projects is provided by voluntary contributions from members and other sources, including UNDP and UNFPA.

A regular budget of US $5,382.7m. was proposed for the two years 2010–11, of which some 5.3%, or $286.0m., was provisionally allocated to the Americas.

Publications

Bulletin of WHO (monthly).

Eastern Mediterranean Health Journal (annually).

International Classification of Functioning, Disability and Health—ICF.

International Pharmacopoeia.

International Statistical Classification of Disease and Related Health Problems.

International Travel and Health.

Model List of Essential Medicines (every two years).

Pan-American Journal of Public Health (annually).

3 By 5 Progress Report.

Toxicological Evaluation of Certain Veterinary Drug Residues in Food (annually).

Weekly Epidemiological Record (in English and French, paper and electronic versions available).

WHO Drug Information (quarterly).

WHO Global Atlas of Traditional, Complementary and Alternative Medicine.

WHO Model Formulary.

WHO Report on the Global Tobacco Epidemic.

World Health Report (annually, in English, French and Spanish).

World Cancer Report.

World Malaria Report (with UNICEF).

Zoonoses and Communicable Diseases Common to Man and Animals.

Technical report series; catalogues of specific scientific, technical and medical fields available.

Other UN Organizations Active in the Region

OFFICE FOR THE CO-ORDINATION OF HUMANITARIAN AFFAIRS—OCHA

Address: United Nations Plaza, New York, NY 10017, USA.

Telephone: (212) 963-1234; **fax:** (212) 963-1312; **e-mail:** ochany@un.org; **internet:** ochaonline.un.org.

The Office was established in January 1998 as part of the UN Secretariat, with a mandate to co-ordinate international humanitarian assistance and to provide policy and other advice on humanitarian issues. It administers the Humanitarian Early Warning System, as well as Integrated Regional Information Networks (IRIN), to monitor the situation in different countries, and a Disaster Response System. A complementary service, Reliefweb, which was launched in 1996, monitors crises and publishes information on the internet.

Under-Secretary-General for Humanitarian Affairs and Emergency Relief Co-ordinator: VALERIE AMOS (United Kingdom) (from 1 September 2010).

UNITED NATIONS OFFICE ON DRUGS AND CRIME—UNODC

Address: Vienna International Centre, POB 500, 1400 Vienna, Austria.

Telephone: (1) 26060-0; **fax:** (1) 26060-5866; **e-mail:** unodc@unodc.org; **internet:** www.unodc.org.

The Office was established in November 1997 (as the UN Office of Drug Control and Crime Prevention) to strengthen the UN's integrated approach to issues relating to drug control, crime prevention and international terrorism. It comprises two principal components: the United Nations Drug Programme and the Crime Programme.

Executive Director: ANTONIO MARIA COSTA (Italy).

OFFICE OF THE UNITED NATIONS HIGH COMMISSIONER FOR HUMAN RIGHTS—OHCHR

Address: Palais Wilson, 52 rue de Paquis, 1201 Geneva, Switzerland.

Telephone: 229179290; **fax:** 229179022; **e-mail:** infodesk@ohchr.org; **internet:** www.ohchr.org.

The Office is a body of the UN Secretariat and is the focal point for UN human-rights activities. Since September 1997 it has incorporated the Centre for Human Rights. The High Commissioner is the UN official with principal responsibility for UN human rights activities.

High Commissioner: NAVANETHEM PILLAY (South Africa).

UNITED NATIONS HUMAN SETTLEMENTS PROGRAMME—UN-HABITAT

Address: POB 30030, Nairobi, Kenya.

Telephone: (20) 621234; **fax:** (20) 624266; **e-mail:** infohabitat@unhabitat.org; **internet:** www.unhabitat.org.

UN-Habitat was established, as the United Nations Centre for Human Settlements, in October 1978 to service the intergovernmental Commission on Human Settlements. It became a full UN programme on 1 January 2002, serving as the focus for human settlements activities in the UN system.

Executive Director: ANNA KAJUMULO TIBAIJUKA (Tanzania).

UNITED NATIONS CHILDREN'S FUND—UNICEF

Address: 3 United Nations Plaza, New York, NY 10017, USA.

Telephone: (212) 326-7000; **fax:** (212) 888-7465; **e-mail:** info@unicef.org; **internet:** www.unicef.org.

UNICEF was established in 1946 by the UN General Assembly as the UN International Children's Emergency Fund, to meet the emergency needs of children in post-war Europe and China. In 1950 its mandate was changed to emphasize programmes giving long-term benefits to children everywhere, particularly those in developing countries who are in the greatest need.

Executive Director: ANTHONY LAKE (USA).

UNITED NATIONS CONFERENCE ON TRADE AND DEVELOPMENT—UNCTAD

Address: Palais des Nations, 1211 Geneva 10, Switzerland.

Telephone: 229171234; **fax:** 229070043; **e-mail:** info@unctad.org; **internet:** www.unctad.org.

UNCTAD was established in 1964. It is the principal organ of the UN General Assembly concerned with trade and development, and is the focal point within the UN system for integrated activities relating to trade, finance, technology, investment and sustainable development. It aims to maximize the trade and development opportunities of developing countries, in particular least-developed countries, and to assist them to adapt to the increasing globalization and liberalization of the world economy. UNCTAD undertakes consensus-building activities, research and policy analysis and technical co-operation.

Secretary-General: DR SUPACHAI PANITCHPAKDI (Thailand).

UNITED NATIONS POPULATION FUND—UNFPA

Address: 220 East 42nd St, New York, NY 10017, USA.

Telephone: (212) 297-5020; **fax:** (212) 297-4911; **internet:** www.unfpa.org.

Created in 1967 as the Trust Fund for Population Activities, the UN Fund for Population Activities (UNFPA) was established as a Fund of the UN General Assembly in 1972 and was made a subsidiary organ of the UN General Assembly in 1979, with the UNDP Governing Council (now the Executive Board) designated as its governing body. In 1987 UNFPA's name was changed to the United Nations Population Fund (retaining the same acronym).

Executive Director: THORAYA A. OBAID (Saudi Arabia).

UN Specialized Agencies

INTERNATIONAL CIVIL AVIATION ORGANIZATION—ICAO

Address: 999 University St, Montréal, QC H3C 5H7, Canada.

Telephone: (514) 954-8219; **fax:** (514) 954-6077; **e-mail:** icaohq@icao.org; **internet:** www.icao.int.

ICAO was founded in 1947, on the basis of the Convention on International Civil Aviation, signed in Chicago, in 1944, to develop the techniques of international air navigation and to help in the planning and improvement of international air transport.

Secretary-General: RAYMOND BENJAMIN (France).7

INTERNATIONAL LABOUR ORGANIZATION—ILO

Address: 4 route des Morillons, 1211 Geneva 22, Switzerland.

Telephone: 227996111; **fax:** 227988685; **e-mail:** ilo@ilo.org; **internet:** www.ilo.org.

ILO was founded in 1919 to work for social justice as a basis for lasting peace. It carries out this mandate by promoting decent living standards, satisfactory conditions of work and pay and adequate employment opportunities. Methods of action include the creation of international labour standards; the provision of technical co-operation services; and training, education, research and publishing activities to advance ILO objectives.

Director-General: JUAN O. SOMAVÍA (Chile).

Regional Office for Latin America and the Caribbean: Las Flores 275 San Isidro, Apdo 14-124 Lima, Peru; tel. (1) 6150300; fax (1) 6150400; e-mail oit@oit.org.pe; internet www.oit.org.pe/portal/index.php; Regional Dir JEAN MANINAT (Venezuela).

INTERNATIONAL MARITIME ORGANIZATION—IMO

Address: 4 Albert Embankment, London, SE1 7SR, United Kingdom.

Telephone: (20) 7735-7611; **fax:** (20) 7587-3210; **e-mail:** info@imo.org; **internet:** www.imo.org.

The Inter-Governmental Maritime Consultative Organization (IMCO) began operations in 1959, as a specialized agency of the UN to facilitate co-operation among governments on technical matters affecting international shipping. Its main aims are to improve the safety of international shipping, and to prevent pollution caused by ships. IMCO became IMO in 1982.

Secretary-General: EFTHIMIOS MITROPOULOS (Greece).

INTERNATIONAL TELECOMMUNICATION UNION—ITU

Address: Place des Nations, 1211 Geneva 20, Switzerland.

Telephone: 227305111; **fax:** 227337256; **e-mail:** itumail@itu.int; **internet:** www.itu.int.

Founded in 1865, ITU became a specialized agency of the UN in 1947. It acts to encourage world co-operation for the improvement and use of telecommunications, to promote technical development, to harmonize national policies in the field, and to promote the extension of telecommunications throughout the world.

Secretary-General: HAMADOUN TOURÉ (Mali).

UNITED NATIONS INDUSTRIAL DEVELOPMENT ORGANIZATION—UNIDO

Address: Vienna International Centre, POB 300, 1400 Vienna, Austria.

Telephone: (1) 260260; **fax:** (1) 2692669; **e-mail:** unido@unido.org; **internet:** www.unido.org.

UNIDO began operations in 1967 and became a specialized agency in 1985. Its objectives are to promote sustainable and socially equitable industrial development in developing countries and in countries with economies in transition. It aims to assist such countries to integrate fully into global economic system by mobilizing knowledge, skills, information and technology to promote productive employment, competitive economies and sound environment.

Director-General: KANDEH YUMKELLA (Sierra Leone).

UNIVERSAL POSTAL UNION—UPU

Address: Weltpoststr., 3000 Bern 15, Switzerland.

Telephone: 313503111; **fax:** 313503110; **e-mail:** info@upu.int; **internet:** www.upu.int.

The General Postal Union was founded by the Treaty of Berne (1874), beginning operations in July 1875. Three years later its name was changed to the Universal Postal Union. In 1948 UPU became a specialized agency of the UN. It aims to develop and unify the international postal service, to study problems and to provide training.

Director-General: EDOUARD DAYAN (France).

WORLD INTELLECTUAL PROPERTY ORGANIZATION—WIPO

Address: 34 chemin des Colombettes, 1211 Geneva 20, Switzerland.

Telephone: 223389111; **fax:** 227335428; **e-mail:** wipo.mail@wipo.int; **internet:** www.wipo.int.

WIPO was established in 1970. It became a specialized agency of the UN in 1974 concerned with the protection of intellectual property (e.g. industrial and technical patents and literary copyrights) throughout the world. WIPO formulates and administers treaties embodying international norms and standards of intellectual property, establishes model laws, and facilitates applications for the protection of inventions, trademarks etc. WIPO provides legal and technical assistance to developing countries and countries with economies in transition and advises countries on obligations under the World Trade Organization's agreement on Trade-Related Aspects of Intellectual Property Rights (TRIPS).

Director-General: FRANCIS GURRY (Australia).

WORLD METEOROLOGICAL ORGANIZATION—WMO

Address: 7 bis, ave de la Paix, 1211 Geneva 2, Switzerland.

Telephone: 227308111; **fax:** 227308181; **e-mail:** wmo@wmo.int; **internet:** www.wmo.int.

WMO was established in 1950 and was recognized as a Specialized Agency of the UN in 1951, aiming to improve the exchange of information in the fields of meteorology, climatology, operational hydrology and related fields, as well as their applications. WMO jointly implements, with UNEP, the UN Framework Convention on Climate Change.

Secretary-General: MICHEL JARRAUD (France).

WORLD TOURISM ORGANIZATION—UNWTO

Address: Capitán Haya 42, 28020 Madrid, Spain.

Telephone: (91) 5678100; **fax:** (91) 5713733; **e-mail:** omt@world-tourism.org; **internet:** www.world-tourism.org.

The World Tourism Organization was established in 1975 and was recognized as a Specialized Agency of the UN in December 2003. It works to promote and develop sustainable tourism, in particular in support of socio-economic growth in developing countries.

Secretary-General: TALEB RIFAI (Jordan).

ANDEAN COMMUNITY OF NATIONS

(COMUNIDAD ANDINA DE NACIONES—CAN)

Address: Paseo de la República 3895, San Isidro, Lima 27; Apdo 18-1177, Lima 18, Peru.

Telephone: (1) 4111400; **fax:** (1) 2213329; **e-mail:** contacto@comunidadandina.org; **internet:** www.comunidadandina.org.

The organization was established in 1969 as the Acuerdo de Cartagena (the Cartagena Agreement), also referred to as the Grupo Andino (Andean Group) or the Pacto Andino (Andean Pact). In March 1996 member countries signed a Reform Protocol of the Cartagena Agreement, in accordance with which the Andean Group was superseded in August 1997 by the Andean Community of Nations (CAN). The Andean Community was to promote greater economic, commercial and political integration within a new Andean Integration System (Sistema Andino de Integración), comprising the organization's bodies and institutions.

MEMBERS

Bolivia   Colombia   Ecuador   Peru

Note: Argentina, Brazil, Chile, Paraguay and Uruguay are associate members of the Community. Mexico and Panama have observer status. Venezuela withdrew from the Community in April 2006.

Organization

(August 2010)

ANDEAN PRESIDENTIAL COUNCIL

The presidential summits, which had been held annually since 1989, were formalized under the 1996 Reform Protocol of the Cartagena Agreement as the Andean Presidential Council. The Council is the highest-level body of the Andean Integration System, and provides the political leadership of the Community.

COMMISSION

The Commission consists of a plenipotentiary representative from each member country, with each country holding the presidency in turn. The Commission is the main policy-making organ of the Andean Community, and is responsible for co-ordinating Andean trade policy.

COUNCIL OF FOREIGN MINISTERS

The Council of Foreign Ministers meets annually or whenever it is considered necessary, to formulate common external policy and to co-ordinate the process of integration.

GENERAL SECRETARIAT

In August 1997 the General Secretariat assumed the functions of the Board of the Cartagena Agreement. The General Secretariat is the body charged with implementation of all guidelines and decisions issued by the bodies listed above. It submits proposals to the Commission for facilitating the fulfilment of the Community's objectives. Members are appointed for a three-year term. Under the reforms agreed in March 1996 the Secretary-General is elected by the Council of Foreign Ministers for a five-year term, and has enhanced powers to adjudicate in disputes arising between member states, as well as to manage the sub-regional integration process. There are three Directors-General.

Secretary-General: Dr Adalid Contreras Baspineiro (Bolivia) (acting).

PARLIAMENT

Parlamento Andino: Avda 13, No. 70-61, Bogotá, Colombia; tel. (1) 217-3357; fax (1) 348-2805; e-mail correo@parlamentoandino.org; internet www.parlamentoandino.org; f. 1979; comprises five members from each country, and meets in each capital city in turn; makes recommendations on regional policy; in April 1997 a new protocol was adopted that provided for the election of members by direct and universal voting; Pres. Wilbert Bendezu Carpio (Peru).

COURT OF JUSTICE

Tribunal de Justicia de la Comunidad Andina: 33-65, Calle Augusto Egas y Bosmediano, Sector Bella-Vista, Quito, Ecuador; tel. (22) 446448; fax (22) 2922462; e-mail tjca@tribunalandino.org.ec; internet www.tribunalandino.org.ec; f. 1979, began operating in 1984; a protocol approved in May 1996 (which came into force in August 1999) modified the Court's functions; its main responsibilities are to resolve disputes among member countries and interpret community legislation; comprises one judge from each member country, appointed for a renewable period of six years; the Presidency is assumed annually by each judge in turn; Pres. (2010) Leonor Perdomo Perdomo (Colombia).

Activities

In May 1979, at Cartagena, Colombia, the Presidents of the then five member countries signed the 'Mandate of Cartagena', which envisaged greater economic and political co-operation, including the establishment of more sub-regional development programmes (especially in industry). In May 1989 the Group undertook to revitalize the process of Andean integration, by withdrawing measures that obstructed the programme of trade liberalization, and by complying with tariff reductions that had already been agreed upon. In May 1991, in Caracas, Venezuela, a summit meeting of the Andean Group agreed the framework for the establishment of a free trade area on 1 January 1992 (achieved in February 1993) and for an eventual Andean common market.

In March 1996 heads of state, meeting in Trujillo, Peru, agreed to a substantial restructuring of the Andean Group. The heads of state signed the Reform Protocol of the Cartagena Agreement, providing for the establishment of the Andean Community of Nations, which was to have greater ambitious economic and political objectives. Consequently, in August 1997 the Andean Community was inaugurated, and the Group's Junta was replaced by a new General Secretariat, headed by a Secretary-General with enhanced executive and decision-making powers. The initiation of these reforms was designed to accelerate harmonization in economic matters. In April 1997 the Peruvian Government announced its intention to withdraw from the Cartagena Agreement, owing to disagreements about the terms of Peru's full integration into the Community's trading system. Later in that month the heads of state of the four other members attended a summit meeting, in Sucre, Bolivia, and reiterated their commitment to strengthening regional integration. A high-level group of representatives was established to pursue negotiations with Peru regarding its future relationship with the Community (agreement was reached in June—see below). In January 2002 a special Andean presidential summit, held in Santa Cruz, Bolivia, reiterated the objective of creating a common market and renewing efforts to strengthen sub-regional integration, including the adoption of a common agricultural policy and the standardization of macroeconomic policies.

In April 2006 the President of Venezuela announced his intention to withdraw that country from the Andean Community, with immediate effect, expressing opposition to the bilateral free trade agreements signed by Colombia and Peru with the USA on the grounds that they would undermine efforts to achieve regional economic integration. The Community countered that Venezuela's commitment to Andean integration had been placed in doubt by its declared allegiance to other regional groupings, in particular Mercosur.

POLITICAL CO-OPERATION

In June 2002 ministers of defence and of foreign affairs of the Andean Community approved an Andean Charter for Peace and Security, establishing principles and commitments for the formulation of a policy on sub-regional security, the establishment of a zone of peace, joint action in efforts to counter terrorism, and the limitation of external defence spending. Other provisions of the Charter included commitments to eradicate illegal trafficking in firearms, ammunition and explosives, to expand and reinforce confidence-building measures, and to establish verification mechanisms to strengthen dialogue and efforts in those areas. In January 2003 the Community concluded a co-operation agreement with Interpol providing for collaboration in combating national and transnational crime, and in June the presidential summit adopted an Andean Plan for the Prevention, Combating and Eradication of Small, Light Weapons. The heads of state, convened in Quirama, Colombia, also endorsed a new strategic direction for the Andean integration process based on the following core themes: developing the Andean common market; common foreign policy and social agenda; the physical integration of South America; and sustainable development. In July 2004 the 15th presidential summit, held in Quito, Ecuador, formulated priority objectives for a New Strategic Scheme. A sub-regional workshop to formulate an Andean Plan to Fight Corruption was held in April 2005, organized by the General Secretariat and the European Commission. In June 2007 heads of state expressed their commitment to the Plan. In September 2008 Offices of the Controller General and other supervisory bodies in Andean countries agreed to implement the Plan. In November a meeting was convened, at the request of heads of state, of a Community Council of treasury or finance ministers, heads of central banks and ministers responsible for economic planning, in order to analyse the effects on the region of the severe global economic and financial downturn. The Council met again in February 2009 to consider various technical studies that had been undertaken.

At the 13th presidential summit, held in Valencia, Venezuela, in June 2001, heads of state adopted an Andean Co-operation Plan for the Control of Illegal Drugs and Related Offences, which was to promote a united approach to combating these problems. An executive committee was to be established under the accord to oversee implementation of an action plan. In July 2005 the Council of Foreign Ministers approved an Andean Alternative Development Strategy, which aimed to support sustainable local development initiatives, including alternatives to the production of illegal drug crops. In August 2009 the Council approved a financing agreement with the EU to implement an Anti-Illegal Drug Program in the Andean Community.

In June 2003 ministers of foreign affairs and foreign trade adopted 16 legal provisions aimed at giving maximum priority to the social dimension of integration within the Community, including a measure providing for mobility of workers between member countries. A new Andean passport system, which had been approved in 2001, entered into effect in December 2005.

TRADE

A council for customs affairs met for the first time in January 1982, aiming to harmonize national legislation within the group. In December 1984 the member states launched a common currency, the Andean peso, aiming to reduce dependence on the US dollar and to increase regional trade. The new currency was to be supported by special contributions to the Fondo Andino de Reservas (now the Fondo Latinoamericano de Reservas) amounting to US $80m., and was to be 'pegged' to the US dollar, taking the form of financial drafts rather than notes and coins.

The 'Caracas Declaration' of May 1991 provided for the establishment of an Andean free trade area (AFTA), which entered into effect (excluding Peru—see below) in February 1993. Heads of state also agreed in May 1991 to create a common external tariff (CET), to standardize member countries' trade barriers in their dealings with the rest of the world, and envisaged the eventual creation of an Andean common market. In December heads of state defined four main levels of external tariffs (between 5% and 20%). In August 1992 the Group approved a request by Peru for the suspension of its rights and obligations under the Pact, thereby enabling the other members to proceed with hitherto stalled negotiations on the CET. Peru was readmitted as a full member of the Group in 1994, but participated only as an observer in the ongoing negotiations.

In November 1994 ministers of trade and integration, meeting in Quito, Ecuador, concluded a final agreement on a four-tier structure of external tariffs (although Bolivia was to retain a two-level system). The CET agreement came into effect on 1 February 1995. The agreement covered 90% of the region's imports which were to be subject to the following tariff bands: 5% for raw materials; 10%–15% for semi-manufactured goods; and 20% for finished products. In order to reach an agreement, special treatment and exemptions were granted, while Peru, initially, was to remain a 'non-active' member of the accord. In June 1997 an agreement was concluded to ensure Peru's continued membership of the Community, which provided for that country's integration into AFTA. The Peruvian Government determined to eliminate customs duties on some 2,500 products with immediate effect. The process of incorporating Peru into AFTA was completed by January 2006.

In May 1999 the 11th presidential summit agreed to establish the Andean Common Market by 2005; the Community adopted a policy on border integration and development to prepare the border regions of member countries for the envisaged free circulation of people, goods, capital and services, while consolidating sub-regional security. In June 2001 the Community agreed to recognize national identification documents issued by member states as sufficient for tourist travel in the sub-region. Community heads of state, meeting in January 2002 at a special Andean presidential summit, agreed to consolidate and improve the free trade zone by mid-2002 and apply a new CET (with four levels, i.e. 0%, 5%, 10% and 20%). To facilitate this process a common agricultural policy was to be adopted and macro-economic policies were to be harmonized. In June 2002 ministers of foreign affairs approved a schedule of activities relating to the new CET. In October member governments determined the new tariff levels applicable to 62% of products and agreed the criteria for negotiating levels for the remaining 38%. The new CET was to become effective on 1 January 2004. This date was subsequently postponed. In January 2006 ministers of trade approved a working programme to define the Community's common tariff policy, which was to incorporate a flexible CET. The value of intra-Community trade totalled some US $5,774m. in 2009.

EXTERNAL RELATIONS

In September 1995 heads of state of member countries identified the formulation of common positions on foreign relations as an important part of the process of relaunching the integration initiative. A Protocol Amending the Cartagena Agreement was signed in June 1997 to confirm the formulation of a common foreign policy. During 1998 the General Secretariat held consultations with government experts, academics, representatives of the private sector and other interested parties to help formulate a document on guidelines for a common foreign policy. The guidelines, establishing the principles, objectives and mechanisms of a common foreign policy, were approved by the Council of Foreign Ministers in 1999. In July 2004 Andean ministers of foreign affairs approved new guidelines for an Andean common policy on external security, which aimed to prevent and counter new security threats more effectively. The ministers, meeting in Quito, Ecuador, also adopted a Declaration on the Establishment of an Andean Peace Zone, free from nuclear, chemical or biological weapons. In April 2005 the Community Secretariat signed a memorandum of understanding with the Organization for the Prohibition of Chemical Weapons, which aimed to consolidate the Andean Peace Zone, assist countries to implement the Chemical Arms Convention and promote further collaboration between the two groupings.

The Community has sought to strengthen relations with the EU, and a co-operation agreement was signed between the two blocs in April 1993, establishing a Mixed Commission to further deliberation and co-operation between the two organizations. A Euro-Andean Forum is held periodically to promote mutual co-operation, trade and investment. In February 1998 the Community signed a co-operation and technical assistance agreement with the EU in order to combat drugs trafficking. At the first summit meeting of Latin American and Caribbean (LAC) and EU leaders held in Rio de Janeiro, Brazil, in June 1999, Community-EU discussions were held on strengthening economic, trade and political co-operation and on the possibility of concluding an Association Agreement. In May 2002 the EU adopted a Regional Strategy for the Andean Community covering the period 2002–06. The second LAC and EU summit meeting, held in May 2002 in Madrid, Spain, welcomed a new initiative to negotiate an accord on political dialogue and co-operation, envisaging that this would strengthen the basis for subsequent bilateral negotiations. Consequently, the Political Dialogue and Co-operation Agreement was negotiated during May–October 2003, and signed in December. In May 2004 a meeting of the two sides held during the third LAC-EU summit, in Guadalajara, Mexico, confirmed that an EU-CAN Association Agreement was a common strategic objective. In January 2005 an ad hoc working group was established in order to undertake a joint appraisal exercise on regional economic integration. The fourth LAC and EU summit meeting, held in Vienna, Austria, in May 2006, approved the establishment of an EU-LAC Parliamentary Assembly; this was inaugurated in November. The meeting also welcomed the proposed EU-CAN Association Agreement. Negotiations on an agreement were formally inaugurated at the meeting of Andean heads of state held in Tarifa, Bolivia, in June 2007, and the first round of negotiations was held in September. A second round was held in Brussels, Belgium, in December and a third round in Quito, Ecuador, in April 2008. In May heads of state of the Andean Community confirmed that they would continue to negotiate the agreement as a single group. In December, however, the EU announced that it was to commence negotiations for separate free trade agreements with Colombia and Peru. Bolivia criticized the decision as undermining the Andean integration process. In March 2010 the EU-CAN Mixed Commission agreed on a programme of co-operation in 2011–13, with funding commitments of €17.5m. for projects concerned with economic integration, countering illicit drugs production and trafficking, and environmental protection. An EU-CAN summit meeting was held in Madrid, Spain, in May 2010.

Since December 1991 exports from Andean Community countries have benefited from preferential access to US markets under the Andean Trade Preference Act. In August 2002 the legislation was renewed and amended under a new Andean Trade Preference and Drug Eradication Act, which provided duty free access for more than 6,000 products with the objective of supporting legal trade transactions in order to help to counter the production and trafficking of illegal narcotic drugs. The Act was initially scheduled to expire in December 2006, but has been periodically extended by the US Congress. In December 2008 the US President suspended Bolivia's eligibility under the Act owing to its failure to meet its counter-narcotics requirements.

In March 2000 the Andean Community concluded an agreement to establish a political consultation and co-operation mechanism with the People's Republic of China. At the first ministerial meeting within this framework, which took place in October 2002, it was agreed that consultations would be held thereafter on a biennial basis. The first meeting of the Council of Foreign Ministers with the Chinese Vice-President took place in January 2005. A high-level meeting between senior officials from Community member states and Japan was organized in December 2002; further consultations were to be convened, aimed at cultivating closer relations.

In April 1998, at the 10th Andean presidential summit, an agreement was signed with Panama establishing a framework for negotiations providing for the conclusion of a free trade accord by the end of 1998 and for Panama's eventual associate membership of the Community. A political dialogue and co-operation agreement, a requirement for Panama's associate membership status, was signed by the two sides in September 2007. Mexico was invited to assume observer status in September 2004. In November 2006 Mexico and the Andean Community signed an agreement to establish a mechanism for political dialogue and co-operation in areas of mutual interest. The first meeting of the mechanism was held in New York, USA, in September 2007.

Also in April 1998 the Community signed a framework agreement with the Mercado Común del Sur (Mercosur) on the establishment of a free trade accord. Although negotiations between the Community and Mercosur were subsequently delayed, bilateral agreements between the countries of the two groupings were extended. A preferential tariff agreement was concluded between Brazil and the Community in July 1999; the accord entered into effect, for a period of two years, in August. In August 2000 a preferential tariff agreement concluded with Argentina entered into force. The Community commenced negotiations on drafting a preferential tariff agreement with (jointly) El Salvador, Guatemala and Honduras in March of that year. In September leaders of the Community and Mercosur, meeting at a summit of Latin American heads of state, determined to relaunch negotiations, with a view to establishing a free trade area. In July 2001 ministers of foreign affairs of the two groupings approved the establishment of a formal mechanism for political dialogue and co-ordination in order to facilitate negotiations and to enhance economic and social integration. In December 2003 Mercosur and the Andean Community signed an Economic Complementary Agreement providing for free trade provisions, according to which tariffs on 80% of trade between the two groupings were to be phased out by 2014 and tariffs to be removed from the remaining 20% of, initially protected, products by 2019. The entry into force of the accord, scheduled for 1 July 2004, was postponed owing to delays in drafting the tariff reduction schedule. Members of the Latin American Integration Association (Aladi) remaining outside Mercosur and the Andean Community—Cuba, Chile and Mexico—were to be permitted to apply to join the envisaged larger free trade zone. In July 2005 the Community granted Argentina, Brazil, Paraguay and Uruguay associate membership of the grouping, as part of efforts to achieve a reciprocal association agreement. In December 2004 the Andean Community agreed to grant observer status to Chile, and in September 2006 Chile was formally invited to join the organization as an associate member. In December the first meeting of the CAN-Chile Joint Commission was convened in Cochabamba, Bolivia. An agreement on Chile's full participation in all Community bodies and mechanisms was approved in July 2007. In February 2010 foreign ministers of the Community and Mercosur agreed to establish a CAN–Mercosur Mixed Commission to facilitate enhanced co-operation between the countries of the two organizations.

In March 1998 ministers of trade from 34 countries, meeting in San José, Costa Rica, concluded an agreement on the structure of negotiations for the establishment of a Free Trade Area of the Americas (FTAA). The process was formally initiated by heads of state, meeting in Santiago, Chile, in the following month. The Community negotiated as a bloc to obtain chairmanship of three of the nine negotiating groups: on market access (Colombia), on competition policy (Peru), and on intellectual property (Venezuela). In April 2001, convened in Québec, Canada, leaders of the participating countries determined to conclude negotiations on the FTAA by January 2005. At a special summit of the Americas, held in January 2004 in Monterrey, Mexico, the leaders adopted a declaration committing themselves to its eventual establishment although failed to specify a completion date for the process. Negotiations remained stalled in 2010.

In December 2004 leaders from 12 Latin American countries attending a pan-South American summit, convened in Cusco, Peru, approved in principle the creation of a new South American Community of Nations (SACN). It was envisaged that negotiations on the formation of the new Community, which was to entail the merger of the Andean Community, Mercosur and Aladi (with the participation of Chile, Guyana and Suriname), would be completed within 15 years. In April 2005 a region-wide meeting of ministers of foreign affairs was convened, within the framework of establishing the SACN. The first South American Community meeting of heads of state was held in September, in Brasília, Brazil. The meeting issued mandates to the heads of sub-regional organizations to consider integration processes, the convergence of economic agreements and common plans of action. In April 2007, at the first South American Energy Summit, convened in Margarita Island, Venezuela, heads of state endorsed the establishment of a Union of South American Nations (UNASUR), to replace the SACN as the lead organization for regional integration. It was envisaged that UNASUR would have political decision-making functions, supported by a small permanent secretariat, to be located in Quito, Ecuador, and would co-ordinate on economic and trade matters with the Andean Community, Mercosur and Aladi. A summit meeting formally to inaugurate UNASUR, scheduled to be convened in December, was postponed. A rescheduled meeting, to be held in March 2008, was also postponed, owing to the diplomatic dispute between Ecuador and Colombia. It was later convened in May, in Brasília, Brazil, at which a constitutional document formally establishing UNASUR was signed. In December Brazil hosted a Latin American and Caribbean Summit on Integration and Development, which aimed to strengthen the commitment by all countries in the region to work together in support of sustainable development. The meeting issued the Salvador Declaration, which pledged support to strengthen co-operation among the regional and sub-regional groupings, to pursue further consultation and joint efforts to counter the effects of the global financial crisis on the region, and to promote closer collaboration on a range of issues including energy, food security, social development, physical infrastructure and natural disaster management. The first informal meeting of the General Secretariat of the Andean Community and UNASUR was held in January 2010, in Lima, Peru.

In August 1999 the Secretary-General of the Community visited Guyana in order to promote bilateral trading opportunities and to strengthen relations with the Caribbean Community. The Community held a meeting on trade relations with the Caribbean Community during 2000.

INDUSTRY AND ENERGY

In May 1987 member countries signed the Quito Protocol, modifying the Cartagena Agreement, to amend the strict rules that had formerly been imposed on foreign investors in the region. In March 1991 the Protocol was amended, with the aim of further liberalizing foreign investment and stimulating an inflow of foreign capital and technology. External and regional investors were to be permitted to repatriate their profits (in accordance with the laws of the country concerned) and there was no stipulation that a majority shareholding must eventually be transferred to local investors. A further directive, adopted in March, covered the formation of multinational enterprises in order to ensure that at least two member countries have a shareholding of 15% or more of the capital, including the country where the enterprise was to be based. These enterprises were entitled to participate in sectors otherwise reserved for national enterprises, subject to the same conditions as national enterprises in terms of taxation and export regulations, and to gain access to the markets of all member countries. In September 1999 Colombia, Ecuador and Venezuela signed an accord to facilitate the production and sale of vehicles within the region. The agreement became effective in January 2000, with a duration of 10 years.

In November 1988 member states established a bank, the Banco Intermunicipal Andino, which was to finance public works. In October 2004 a sub-regional committee on small and medium-sized enterprises (SMEs) endorsed efforts by the Community Secretariat to establish an Andean System of SME Guarantees to facilitate their access to credit.

In May 1995 the Group initiated a programme to promote the use of cheap and efficient energy sources and greater co-operation in the energy sector. The programme planned to develop a regional electricity grid. During 2003 efforts were undertaken to establish an Andean Energy Alliance, with the aim of fostering the development of integrated electricity and gas markets, as well as other objectives of developing renewable energy sources, promoting 'energy clusters' and ensuring regional energy security. The first meeting of ministers of energy, electricity, hydrocarbons and mines, convened in Quito, Ecuador, in January 2004, endorsed the Alliance.

TRANSPORT AND COMMUNICATIONS

The Andean Community has pursued efforts to improve infrastructure throughout the region. In 1983 the Commission formulated a plan to assist land-locked Bolivia, particularly through improving roads connecting it with neighbouring countries and the Pacific Ocean. An 'open skies' agreement, giving airlines of member states equal rights to airspace and airport facilities within the grouping, was signed in May 1991. In June 1998 the Commission approved the establishment of an Andean Commission of Land Transportation Authorities, which was to oversee the operation and development of land transportation services. Similarly, an Andean Committee of Water Transportation Authorities has been established to ensure compliance with Community regulations regarding ocean transportation activities. The Community aims to facilitate the movement of goods throughout the region by the use of different modes of transport ('multimodal transport') and to guarantee operational standards. It also intends to harmonize Community transport regulations and standards with those of Mercosur countries. In September 2005 the first summit meeting of the proposed SACN issued a declaration to support and accelerate infrastructure, transport and communications integration throughout the region.

In August 1996 a regulatory framework was approved for the development of a commercial Andean satellite system. In December 1997 the General Secretariat approved regulations for granting authorization for the use of the system; the Commission subsequently granted the first Community authorization to an Andean multinational enterprise (Andesat), comprising 48 companies from all five member states. In 1994 the Community initiated efforts to establish digital technology infrastructure throughout the Community: the resulting Andean Digital Corridor comprises ground, underwater and satellite routes providing a series of cross-border interconnections between the member countries. The Andean Internet System, which aims to provide internet protocol-based services throughout the Community, was operational in Colombia, Ecuador and Venezuela in 2000, and was due to be extended to all five member countries. In May 1999 the Andean Committee of Telecommunications Authorities agreed to remove all restrictions to free trade in telecommunications services (excluding sound broadcasting and television) by 1 January 2002. The Committee also determined to formulate provisions on interconnection and the safeguarding of free competition and principles of transparency within the sector. In November 2006 the Andean Community approved a new regulatory framework for the commercial exploitation of the Andean satellite system belonging to member states.

Asociación de Empresas de Telecomunicaciones de la Comunidad Andina (ASETA): Calle La Pradera 510 y San Salvador, Casilla 17-1106042, Quito, Ecuador; tel. (2) 256-3812; fax (2) 256-2499; e-mail info@aseta.org; internet www.aseta.org; f. 1974; coordinates improvements in national telecommunications services, in order to contribute to the further integration of the countries of the Andean Community; Sec.-Gen. MARCELO LÓPEZ ARJONA.

RURAL DEVELOPMENT AND FOOD SECURITY

An Andean Agricultural Development Programme was formulated in 1976 within which 22 resolutions aimed at integrating the Andean agricultural sector were approved. In 1984 the Andean Food Security System was created to develop the agrarian sector, replace imports progressively with local produce, and improve rural living conditions. In April 1998 the Presidential Council instructed the Commission, together with ministers of agriculture, to formulate an Andean Common Agricultural Policy, including measures to harmonize trade policy instruments and legislation on animal and plant health. The 12th Andean presidential summit, held in June 2000, authorized the adoption of the concluded Policy and the enforcement of a plan of action for its implementation. In January 2002, at the special Andean presidential summit, it was agreed that all countries in the bloc would adopt price stabilization mechanisms for agricultural products.

In July 2004 Andean ministers of agriculture approved a series of objectives and priority actions to form the framework of a Regional Food Security Policy, as requested by heads of state in the previous year. Also in July 2004 Andean heads of state endorsed the Andean Rural Development and Agricultural Competitiveness Programme to promote sub-regional efforts in areas such as rural development, food security, production competitiveness, animal health and technological innovation. In October 2005 ministers of trade and of agriculture approved the establishment of a special fund to finance the programme. Regulations formally to inaugurate the fund, to be called the Fund for Rural Development and Agricultural Productivity, were approved by ministers meeting in December 2008.

ENVIRONMENT

In March–April 2005 the first meeting of an Andean Community Council of Ministers of the Environment and Sustainable Development was convened, in Paracas, Peru. An Andean Environmental Agenda, covering the period 2006–10, aims to strengthen the capacities of member countries with regard to environmental and sustainable development issues, in particular biodiversity, climate change and water resources. In accordance with the Agenda the Community was working to establish an Andean Institute for Biodiversity, and to establish and implement regional strategies on integrated water resource management and on climate change. In June 2007 the Secretariat signed an agreement with Finland to develop a regional biodiversity programme in the Amazon region of Andean member countries (BioCAN). The Council of Foreign Ministers, meeting in February 2010, approved implementation of BioCAN. In October 2007 the Secretariat organized Clima Latino, hosted by two city authorities in Ecuador, comprising conferences, workshops and cultural events at which climate change was addressed. The Community represented member countries at the conference of parties to the UN Framework Convention on Climate Change, held in Bali, Indonesia, in December, and demanded greater international political commitment and funding to combat the effects of climate change, in particular to monitor and protect the Amazon rainforest.

In July 2002 an Andean Committee for Disaster Prevention and Relief (CAPRADE) was established to help to mitigate the risk and impact of natural disasters in the sub-region. The Committee was to be responsible for implementing the Andean Strategy for Disaster Prevention and Relief, which was approved by the Council of Foreign Ministers in July 2004. A new Strategy for Natural Disaster Prevention and Relief was approved in August 2009, which aimed to link activities for disaster prevention and relief to those related to the environmental agenda, climate change and integrated water management. An Andean University Network in Risk Management and Climate Change promotes information exchange between some 32 institutions.

SOCIAL INTEGRATION

Several formal agreements and institutions have been established within the framework of the Andean Integration System to enhance social development and welfare. In May 1999 the 11th Andean presidential summit adopted a 'multidimensional social agenda' focusing on job creation and on improvements in the fields of education, health and housing throughout the Community. In June 2000 the 12th presidential summit instructed the Andean institutions to prepare individual programmes aimed at consolidating implementation of the Community's integration programme and advancing the development of the social agenda, in order to promote greater involvement of representatives of civil society. In July 2004 Community heads of state declared support for a new Andean Council of Social Development Ministers. Other bodies established in 2003/04 included Councils of Ministers of Education and of Ministers responsible for Cultural Policies, and a Consultative Council of Municipal Authorities. During 2009 work was ongoing to develop and implement an Integral Plan for Social Development, first approved by the Council of Foreign Ministers in Sept. 2004. In August 2009 the Council of Foreign Ministers endorsed the establishment of an Andean Council of Authorities of Women's Affairs as a forum for regional consideration of equal opportunities and gender issues. In March 2010 representatives of Andean cultural authorities determined to initiate an Andean Development Plan for Cultural Industries. In the previous month a Permanent Working Network on Andean Cinema was established.

In June 2007 Community heads of state approved the establishment of a Working Committee on Indigenous People's Rights. In the following month the Community convened the first forum of intellectuals and researchers to strengthen the debate on indigenous issues and their incorporation into the integration process. A resolution to establish a Consultative Council enabling the participation of representatives of indigenous communities in the Andean integration process was approved in September.

INSTITUTIONS

Consejo Consultivo de Pueblos Indígenos de la Comunidad Andina (Consultative Council of Indigenous Peoples of the Andean Community): Paseo de la República 3895, Lima, Peru; tel. (1) 4111400; fax (1) 2213329; f. 2007; first meeting held in September 2008; aims to strengthen the participation of indigenous peoples in the sub-regional integration process.

Consejo Consultivo Empresarial Andino (Andean Business Advisory Council): Paseo de la República 3895, Lima, Peru; tel. (1) 4111400; fax (1) 2213329; e-mail rsuarez@comunidadandina.org; first meeting held in Nov. 1998; an advisory institution within the framework of the Sistema Andino de Integración; comprises elected representatives of business organizations; advises Community ministers and officials on integration activities affecting the business sector; Chair. EDUARDO FARAH (Peru).

Consejo Consultivo Laboral Andino (Andean Labour Advisory Council): Paseo de la República 3832, Of. 502, San Isidro, Lima 27, Peru; tel. (1) 4217334; fax (1) 2226124; e-mail cutperujcb@gmail.com; internet www.ccla.org.pe; f. 1998; an advisory institution within the framework of the Sistema Andino de Integración; comprises elected representatives of labour organizations; advises Community ministers and officers on related labour issues; Chair. JULIO CÉSAR BAZÁN (Peru).

Convenio Andrés Bello (Andrés Bello Agreement): Avda 13 85-60, Bogotá, Colombia; tel. (1) 644-9292; fax (1) 610-0139; e-mail ecobello@col1.telecom.com.co; internet www.cab.int.co; f. 1970, modified in 1990; aims to promote integration in the educational, technical and cultural sectors; a new Interinstitutional Co-operation Agreement was signed with the Secretariat of the CAN in Aug. 2003; mems: Bolivia, Chile, Colombia, Cuba, Ecuador, Panama, Paraguay, Peru, Spain, Venezuela; Exec. Sec. Dr FRANCISCO HUERTA MONTALVO (Ecuador).

Convenio Hipólito Unanue (Hipólito Unanue Agreement): Edif. Cartagena, Paseo de la República 3832, 3°, San Isidro, Lima, Peru; tel. (1) 2210074; fax (1) 2222663; e-mail postmaster@conhu.org.pe; internet www.orasconhu.org; f. 1971 on the occasion of the first meeting of Andean ministers of health; became part of the institutional structure of the Community in 1998; aims to enhance the development of health services, and to promote regional co-ordination in areas such as environmental health, disaster preparedness and the prevention and control of drug abuse; Exec. Sec. Dr OSCAR FEO ISTÚRIZ (Venezuela).

Convenio Simón Rodríguez (Simón Rodríguez Agreement): Paseo de la República 3895, esq. Aramburú, San Isidro, Lima 27, Peru; tel. (1) 4111400; fax (1) 2213329; promotes a convergence of social and labour conditions throughout the Community, for example, working hours and conditions, employment and social security policies, and to promote the participation of workers and employers in the sub-regional integration process; Protocol of Modification signed in June 2001; ratification process ongoing.

Corporación Andina de Fomento (CAF) (Andean Development Corporation): Torre CAF, Avda Luis Roche, Altamira, Apdo 5086, Caracas, Venezuela; tel. (212) 2092111; fax (212) 2092444; e-mail infocaf@caf.com; internet www.caf.com; f. 1968, began operations in 1970; aims to encourage the integration of the Andean countries by specialization and an equitable distribution of investments; conducts research to identify investment opportunities, and prepares the resulting investment projects; gives technical and financial assistance; and attracts internal and external credit; auth. cap. US $5,000m.; subscribed or underwritten by the governments of member countries, or by public, semi-public and private sector institutions authorized by those governments; the Board of Directors comprises representatives of each country at ministerial level; mems: the Andean Community, Argentina, Brazil, Chile, Costa Rica, Jamaica, Mexico, Panama, Paraguay, Spain, Trinidad and Tobago, Uruguay, Venezuela, and 15 private banks in the Andean region; Exec. Pres. ENRIQUE GARCÍA RODRÍGUEZ (Bolivia).

Fondo Latinoamericano de Reservas (FLAR) (Latin American Reserve Fund): Avda 82 12–18, 7°, POB 241523, Bogotá, Colombia; tel. (1) 634-4360; fax (1) 634-4384; e-mail flar@flar.net; internet www.flar.net; f. 1978 as the Fondo Andino de Reservas to support the balance of payments of member countries, provide credit, guarantee loans, and contribute to the harmonization of monetary and financial policies; adopted present name in 1991, in order to allow the admission of other Latin American countries; in 1992 the Fund began extending credit lines to commercial cos for export financing; it is administered by an Assembly of the ministers of finance and economy of the member countries, and a Board of Directors comprising the Presidents of the central banks of the member states; mems: Bolivia, Colombia, Costa Rica, Ecuador, Peru, Uruguay, Venezuela; subscribed cap. US $2,343.8m. cap. p.u. $1,774.6m. (July 2009); Exec. Pres. RODRIGO BOLAÑOS ZAMORA; Sec.-Gen. ANA MARÍA CARRASQUILLA.

Universidad Andina Simón Bolívar (Simón Bolívar Andean University): Calle Real Audiencia 73, Casilla 545, Sucre, Bolivia; tel. (64) 60265; fax (64) 60833; e-mail uasb@uasb.edu.bo; internet www.uasb.edu.bo; f. 1985; institution for postgraduate study and research; promotes co-operation between other universities in the Andean region; branches in Quito (Ecuador), La Paz (Bolivia), Caracas (Venezuela) and Cali (Colombia); Pres. Dr JULIO GARRETT AILLÓN.

Publications

Reports, working papers, sector documents, council proceedings.

CARIBBEAN COMMUNITY AND COMMON MARKET—CARICOM

Address: POB 10827, Georgetown, Guyana.

Telephone: (2) 222-0001; **fax:** (2) 222-0171; **e-mail:** info@caricom.org; **internet:** www.caricom.org.

CARICOM was formed in 1973 by the Treaty of Chaguaramas, signed in Trinidad, as a movement towards unity in the Caribbean; it replaced the Caribbean Free Trade Association (CARIFTA), founded in 1965. A revision of the Treaty of Chaguaramas (by means of nine separate Protocols), in order to institute greater regional integration and to establish a CARICOM Single Market and Economy (CSME), was instigated in the 1990s and completed in July 2001. The single market component of the CSME was formally inaugurated on 1 January 2006.

MEMBERS

Antigua and Barbuda	Jamaica
Bahamas*	Montserrat
Barbados	Saint Christopher and Nevis
Belize	Saint Lucia
Dominica	Saint Vincent and the Grenadines
Grenada	Suriname
Guyana	Trinidad and Tobago
Haiti	

* The Bahamas is a member of the Community but not the Common Market.

ASSOCIATE MEMBERS

Anguilla	Cayman Islands
Bermuda	Turks and Caicos Islands
British Virgin Islands	

Note: Aruba, Colombia, Dominican Republic, Mexico, the Netherlands Antilles, Puerto Rico and Venezuela have observer status with the Community.

Organization

(August 2010)

HEADS OF GOVERNMENT CONFERENCE AND BUREAU

The Conference is the final authority of the Community and determines policy. It is responsible for the conclusion of treaties on behalf of the Community and for entering into relationships between the Community and international organizations and states. Decisions of the Conference are generally taken unanimously. Heads of government meet annually, although inter-sessional meetings may be convened.

At a special meeting of the Conference, held in Trinidad and Tobago in October 1992, participants decided to establish a Heads of Government Bureau, with the capacity to initiate proposals, to update consensus and to secure the implementation of CARICOM decisions. The Bureau became operational in December, comprising the Chairman of the Conference, as Chairman, as well as the incoming and outgoing Chairmen of the Conference, and the Secretary-General of the Conference, in the capacity of Chief Executive Officer.

COMMUNITY COUNCIL OF MINISTERS

In October 1992 CARICOM heads of government agreed that a Caribbean Community Council of Ministers should be established to replace the existing Common Market Council of Ministers as the second highest organ of the Community. Protocol I amending the Treaty of Chaguaramas, to restructure the organs and institutions of the Community, was formally adopted at a meeting of CARICOM heads of government in February 1997 and was signed by all member states in July. The inaugural meeting of the Community Council of Ministers was held in Nassau, Bahamas, in February 1998. The Council consists of ministers responsible for community affairs, as well as other government ministers designated by member states, and is responsible for the development of the Community's strategic planning and co-ordination in the areas of economic integration, functional co-operation and external relations.

COURT OF JUSTICE

Caribbean Court of Justice (CCJ): 134 Henry St, POB 1768, Port of Spain, Trinidad and Tobago; tel. 623-2225; e-mail info@caribbeancourtofjustice.org; internet www.caribbeancourtofjustice.org; inaugurated in April 2005; an agreement establishing the Court was formally signed by 10 member countries in February 2001; in January 2004 a revised agreement on the establishment of the CCJ, which incorporated provision for a Trust Fund, entered into force; serves as a tribunal to enforce rights and to consider disputes relating to the CARICOM Single Market and Economy; intended to replace the Judicial Committee of the Privy Council as the Court of Final Appeal (effective for Barbados, Belize and Guyana as at August 2010); Pres. MICHAEL DE LA BASTIDE.

MINISTERIAL COUNCILS

The principal organs of the Community are assisted in their functions by the following bodies, established under Protocol I amending the Treaty of Chaguaramas: the Council for Trade and Economic Development (COTED); the Council for Foreign and Community Relations (COFCOR); the Council for Human and Social Development (COHSOD); and the Council for Finance and Planning (COFAP). The Councils are responsible for formulating policies, promoting their implementation and supervising co-operation in the relevant areas.

SECRETARIAT

The Secretariat is the main administrative body of the Caribbean Community. The functions of the Secretariat are to service meetings of the Community and of its Committees; to take appropriate follow-up action on decisions made at such meetings; to carry out studies on questions of economic and functional co-operation relating to the region as a whole; to provide services to member states at their request in respect of matters relating to the achievement of the objectives of the Community. The Secretariat incorporates Directorates, each headed by an Assistant Secretary-General, for Trade and Economic Integration; Foreign and Community Relations; Human and Social Development; and CARIFORUM.

Secretary-General: EDWIN W. CARRINGTON (Trinidad and Tobago).

Deputy Secretary-General: LOLITA APPLEWHAITE (Barbados).

Activities

In January 2010 CARICOM provided immediate assistance to Haiti, which had suffered extensive damage and loss of life as a result of a massive earthquake. A Tactical Mission was rapidly deployed to assess relief requirements and logistics, in particular in providing health services. A Special Co-ordinator, to be based in Haiti, was appointed to ensure the effectiveness of the Community's assistance, working closely with the Caribbean Disaster Emergency Management Agency and other international relief efforts. CARICOM was a member of a co-ordination committee to organize an international conference on Haiti. At the International Donors' Conference Towards a New Future for Haiti, held in New York, USA, in March, UN member countries and other international partners pledged US $5,300m. in support of an Action Plan for the National Recovery and Development of the country. CARICOM pledged to support the Haitian Government in working with the international community and to provide all necessary institutional and technical assistance during the rehabilitation process. CARICOM was represented on the Board of the Interim Commission for the Reconstruction of Haiti, which was inaugurated in June following a World Summit on the Future of Haiti, held to discuss the effective implementation of the Action Plan. In July 2010 CARICOM heads of government expressed serious concern at the slow disbursement of international pledges towards the reconstruction effort.

The Heads of Government meeting, convened in Montego Bay, Jamaica, in July 2010, agreed to establish a seven-member high level committee to draft proposals on a new governance structure for CARICOM, in order to address concerns regarding the implementation of community decisions.

ECONOMIC CO-OPERATION

The Caribbean Community's main field of activity is economic integration, by means of a Caribbean Common Market. The Secretariat and the Caribbean Development Bank undertake research on the best means of facing economic difficulties, and meetings of the Chief Executives of commercial banks and of central bank officials are also held with the aim of strengthening regional co-operation. In March 2009 Heads of Government, meeting in Belize City, Belize, resolved to pursue a regional strategy to counter the effects on the region of the severe global economic and financial downturn. A new Heads of Government Task Force on the Regional Financial and Economic Crisis held its inaugural meeting in August, in Jamaica.

In July 1984 heads of government agreed to establish a common external tariff (CET) on certain products, in order to protect domestic industries. They also urged the necessity of structural adjustment in the economies of the region, including measures to expand production and reduce imports. In 1989 the Conference of Heads of Government agreed to implement, by July 1993, a series of measures to encourage the creation of a single Caribbean market. These included the establishment of a CARICOM Industrial Programming Scheme; the inauguration of the CARICOM Enterprise Regime; facilitation of travel for CARICOM nationals within the region; full implementation of the rules of origin and the revised scheme for the harmonization of fiscal incentives; free movement of skilled workers; removal of all remaining regional barriers to trade; establishment of a regional system of air and sea transport; and the introduction of a scheme for regional capital movement. A CARICOM Export Development Council, established in November 1989, undertook a three year export development project to stimulate trade within CARICOM and to promote exports outside the region.

In August 1990 CARICOM heads of government mandated the governors of CARICOM members' central banks to begin a study of the means to achieve a monetary union within CARICOM; they also institutionalized meetings of CARICOM ministers of finance and senior finance officials, to take place twice a year.

The initial deadline of 1991 for the establishment of a CET was not achieved. At a special meeting, held in October 1992, CARICOM heads of government agreed to reduce the maximum level of tariffs from 45% to between 30% and 35%, to be in effect by 30 June 1993 (the level was to be further lowered, to 25%–30% by 1995). The Bahamas, however, was not party to these trading arrangements (since it is a member of the Community but not of the Common Market), and Belize was granted an extension for the implementation of the new tariff levels. At the Heads of Government Conference, held in July 1995 in Guyana, Suriname was admitted as a full member of CARICOM and acceded to the treaty establishing the Common Market. It was granted until 1 January 1996 for implementation of the tariff reductions.

The 1995 Heads of Government Conference approved additional measures to promote the single market. The free movement of skilled workers (mainly graduates from recognized regional institutions) was to be permitted from 1 January 1996. At the same time an agreement on the mutual protection and provision of social security benefits was to enter into force. In July 1996 the heads of government decided that CARICOM ministers of finance, central bank governors and planning agencies should meet more frequently to address single market issues and agreed to extend the provisions of free movement to sports men and women, musicians and others working in the arts and media.

In July 1997 the Conference, meeting in Montego Bay, Jamaica, agreed to accelerate economic integration, with the aim of completing a single market by 1999. At the meeting 11 member states signed Protocol II amending the Treaty of Chaguaramas, which constituted a central element of a CARICOM Single Market and Economy (CSME), providing for the right to establish enterprises, the provision of services and the free movement of capital and labour throughout participating countries. A regional collaborative network was established to promote the CSME. In July 1998, at the meeting of heads of government, held in Saint Lucia, an agreement was signed with the Insurance Company of the West Indies to accelerate the establishment of a Caribbean Investment Fund, which was to mobilize foreign currency from extra-regional capital markets for investment in new or existing enterprises in the region. Some 60% of all funds generated were to be used by CARICOM countries and the remainder by non-CARICOM members of the Association of Caribbean States.

In November 2000 a special consultation on the single market and economy was held in Barbados, involving CARICOM and government officials, academics, and representatives of the private sector, labour organizations, the media, and other regional groupings. In February 2001 heads of government agreed to establish a new high-level sub-committee to accelerate the establishment of the CSME and to promote its objectives. The sub-committee was to be supported by a Technical Advisory Council, comprising representatives of the public and private sectors. By June all member states had signed and declared the provisional application of Protocol II. By May 2007 12 countries had completed the fourth phase of the CET.

In October 2001 CARICOM heads of government, meeting in a special emergency meeting, considered the impact on the region's economy of the terrorist attacks perpetrated against targets in the USA in the previous month. The meeting resolved to enhance aviation security, to implement promotion and marketing campaigns in support of the tourist industry, and to approach international institutions to assist with emergency financing. The economic situation, which had been further adversely affected by the reduced access to the EU banana market, the economic downturn in the USA, and the effects on the investment climate of the OECD Harmful Taxation Initiative, was considered at the Heads of Government Conference, held in Guyana, in July 2002. Heads of government agreed to meet in August in special session to elaborate a programme to revive the economy, on the basis of the work of a newly appointed technical team. A technical committee was also established in July to develop proposals for a regional stabilization programme.

On 1 January 2006 the single market component of the CSME was formally inaugurated, with Barbados, Belize, Guyana, Jamaica, Suriname and Trinidad and Tobago as active participants. Six more countries (Antigua and Barbuda, Dominica, Grenada, Saint Christopher and Nevis, Saint Lucia, Saint Vincent and the Grenadines) formally joined the single market in July. At the same time CARICOM heads of government approved a contribution formula allowing for the establishment of a regional Development Fund. In February 2007 an inter-sessional meeting of the Conference of Heads of Government, held in Saint Vincent and the Grenadines, approved a timetable for the full implementation of the CSME: phase I (mid-2005–08) for the consolidation of the single market and the initiation of a single economy; phase II (2009–15) for the consolidation and completion of the single economy process, including the harmonization and co-ordination of economic policies in the region and the establishment of new institutions to implement those policies. In July 2007 CARICOM heads of government endorsed the report, *Towards a Single Development Vision and the Role of the Single Economy*, on which the elaboration of the CSME was based. In January 2008 a Caribbean Competition Commission was inaugurated, in Paramaribo, Suriname, to enforce the rules of competition within the CSME. In February Haiti signed the revised Treaty of Chaguaramas. The Caribbean Development Fund was launched in mid-2008, with initial finances of US $60m. It commenced full operations in late August 2009. A Convocation on the CSME was convened in Bridgetown, Barbados, in October, as part of a wider appraisal of the CSME.

In December 2007 a special meeting of the Conference of Heads of Government, convened in Georgetown, Guyana, considered issues relating to regional poverty and the rising cost of living in member states. The meeting resolved to establish a technical team to review the CET on essential commodities to determine whether it should be removed or reduced to deter inflationary pressures. The meeting also agreed to review the supply and distribution of food throughout the region, including transportation issues affecting the price of goods and services, and determined to expand agricultural production and agro-processing. Efforts to harness renewable energy sources were to be strengthened to counter rising fuel prices.

REGIONAL INTEGRATION

In 1989 CARICOM heads of government established the 15-member West Indian Commission to study regional political and economic integration. The Commission's final report, submitted in July 1992, recommended that CARICOM should remain a community of sovereign states (rather than a federation), but should strengthen the integration process and expand to include the wider Caribbean region. It recommended the formation of an Association of Caribbean States (ACS), to include all the countries within and surrounding the Caribbean Basin. In November 1997 the Secretaries-General of CARICOM and the ACS signed a Co-operation Agreement to formalize the reciprocal procedures through which the organizations work to enhance and facilitate regional integration. Suriname was admitted to CARICOM in July 1995. In July 1997 the Heads of Government Conference agreed to admit Haiti as a member, although the terms and conditions of its accession to the organization were not finalized until July 1999. In July 2001 the CARICOM Secretary-General formally inaugurated a CARICOM Office in Haiti, which aimed to provide technical assistance in preparation of Haiti's accession to the Community. In January 2002 a CARICOM special mission visited Haiti, following an escalation of the political violence that had started in the previous month. Ministers of foreign affairs emphasized the need for international aid for Haiti when they met their US counterpart in February. Haiti was admitted as the 15th member of CARICOM at the Heads of Government Conference, held in July.

During 1998 CARICOM was concerned by the movement within Nevis to secede from its federation with Saint Christopher. In July heads of government agreed to dispatch a mediation team to the country (postponed until September). The Heads of Government Conference held in March 1999 welcomed the establishment of a Constitutional Task Force by the local authorities to prepare a draft constitution, on the basis of recommendations of a previous constitutional commission and the outcome of a series of public meetings. In July 1998 heads of government expressed concern at the hostility between the Government and opposition groupings in Guyana. The two sides signed an agreement, under CARICOM auspices, and in September a CARICOM mediation mission visited Guyana to promote further dialogue. CARICOM has declared its support for Guyana in its territorial disputes with Venezuela and Suriname. In July 2008 CARICOM observers monitored the general election that was held in Guyana.

In February 1997 Community heads of government signed a new Charter of Civil Society for the Community, which set out principles in the areas of democracy, government, parliament, freedom of the press and human rights. In July 2002 a conference was held, in Liliendaal, Guyana, attended by representatives of civil society and the CARICOM heads of government. The meeting issued a statement of principles on 'Forward Together', recognizing the role of civil society in meeting the challenges to the region. It was agreed to hold regular meetings and to establish a task force to develop a regional strategic framework for pursuing the main recommendations of the conference. In February 2007 an inter-sessional meeting of CARICOM heads of government determined to add security (including crime) as a fourth pillar of regional integration, in addition to those identified: economic integration; co-ordination of foreign policy; and functional co-operation.

CO-ORDINATION OF FOREIGN POLICY

The co-ordination of foreign policies of member states is listed as one of the main objectives of the Community in its founding treaty. Activities include: strengthening of member states' position in international organizations; joint diplomatic action on issues of particular interest to the Caribbean; joint co-operation arrangements with third countries and organizations; and the negotiation of free trade agreements with third countries and other regional groupings. In April 1997 CARICOM inaugurated a Caribbean Regional Negotiating Machinery (CRNM) body, based in Kingston, Jamaica, to co-ordinate and strengthen the region's presence at external economic negotiations. The main areas of activity were negotiations to establish a Free Trade Area of the Americas (FTAA—now stalled), ACP relations with the European Union (EU), and multilateral trade negotiations under the World Trade Organization (WTO). In July 2009 the CRNM was renamed the Office of Trade Negotiations, reporting directly to the Council for Trade and Economic Development. The mandate of the new Office was expanded to include responsibility for all external trade negotiations on behalf of the Community, with immediate priority to be placed on negotiations with Canada.

In July 1991 Venezuela applied for membership of CARICOM, and offered a non-reciprocal free trade agreement for CARICOM exports to Venezuela, over an initial five-year period. In October 1993 the newly established Group of Three (Colombia, Mexico and Venezuela) signed joint agreements with CARICOM and Suriname on combating drugs-trafficking and environmental protection. In June 1994 CARICOM and Colombia concluded an agreement on trade, economic and technical co-operation, which, *inter alia*, gives special treatment to the least-developed CARICOM countries. CARICOM has observer status in the Latin American Rio Group.

In 1992 Cuba applied for observer status within CARICOM, and in July 1993 a joint commission was inaugurated to establish closer ties between CARICOM and Cuba and to provide a mechanism for regular dialogue. In July 1997 the heads of government agreed to pursue consideration of a free trade accord between the Community and Cuba. A Trade and Economic Agreement was signed by the two sides in July 2000, and a CARICOM office was established in Cuba, in February 2001. The first meeting of heads of state and government was convened in Havana, Cuba, in December 2002, at which it was agreed to commemorate the start of diplomatic relations between the two sides, some 30 years previously, on 8 December each year as Cuba/CARICOM Day. The second summit meeting, held in December 2005 in Bridgetown, Barbados, agreed to strengthen co-operation in education, cultural and the environment, access to health care and efforts to counter international terrorism. A second meeting of CARICOM-Cuba ministers of foreign affairs was convened in May 2007 (the first having taken place in July 2004). The third meeting at the level of heads of state and government was held in December 2008 in Santiago de Cuba, Cuba. CARICOM leaders urged the new US administration to reconsider its restrictions on trade with Cuba.

In February 1992 ministers of foreign affairs from CARICOM and Central American states met to discuss future co-operation, in view of the imminent conclusion of the North American Free Trade Agreement (NAFTA) between the USA, Canada and Mexico. It was agreed that a consultative forum would be established to discuss the possible formation of a Caribbean and Central American free trade zone. In October 1993 CARICOM declared its support for NAFTA, but requested a 'grace period', during which the region's exports would have parity with Mexican products, and in March 1994 requested that it should be considered for early entry into NAFTA.

In May 1997 a meeting of CARICOM heads of government and the US President established a partnership for prosperity and security, and arrangements were instituted for annual consultations between the ministers of foreign affairs of CARICOM countries and the US Secretary of State. However, the Community failed to secure a commitment by the USA to grant the region's exports 'NAFTA-parity' status, or to guarantee concessions to the region's banana industry. The USA's opposition to a new EU banana policy (which was to terminate the import licensing system, extending import quotas to 'dollar' producers, while maintaining a limited duty-free quota for Caribbean producers) was strongly criticized by CARICOM leaders, meeting in July 1998. In March 1999 the Inter-Sessional meeting of the Conference of Heads of Government issued a statement condemning the imposition by the USA of sanctions against a number of EU imports, in protest at the revised EU banana regime, and the consequences of this action on Caribbean economies, and agreed to review its co-operation with the USA under the partnership for prosperity and security.

In August 1998 CARICOM and the Dominican Republic signed a free trade accord, covering trade in goods and services, technical barriers to trade, government procurement, and sanitary and phytosanitary measures and standards. A protocol to the agreement was signed in April 2000, following the resolution of differences concerning exempted items. The accord was ratified by the Dominican Republic in February 2001 and entered partially into force on 1 December. A Task Force to strengthen relations between the two sides was established in 2007 and held its first meeting in November 2008. In November 2001 the CARICOM Secretary-General formally inaugurated a Caribbean Regional Technical Assistance Centre (CARTAC), in Barbados, to provide technical advice and training to officials from member countries and the Dominican Republic in support of the region's development, with particular focus on fiscal management, financial sector supervision and regulation, and the compilation of statistics. The IMF was to manage the Centre's operations, while UNDP was to provide administrative and logistical support.

In March 2000 heads of government issued a statement supporting the territorial integrity and security of Belize in that country's ongoing border dispute with Guatemala. CARICOM subsequently urged both countries to implement the provisions of an agreement signed in November and has continued regularly to monitor the situation.

In July 2000 the Heads of Government meeting issued a statement strongly opposing the OECD Harmful Tax Initiative, under which punitive measures had been threatened against 35 countries, including CARICOM member states, if they failed to tighten taxation legislation. The meeting also condemned a separate list, issued by the OECD's Financial Action Task Force on Money Laundering (FATF), which identified 15 countries, including five Caribbean states, of failing to counter effectively international money-laundering. The statement reaffirmed CARICOM's commitment to fighting financial crimes and support for any necessary reform of supervisory practices or legislation, but insisted that national taxation jurisdictions, and specifically competitive regimes designed to attract offshore business, was not a matter for OECD concern. CARICOM remained actively involved in efforts to counter the scheme, and in April 2001 presented its case to the US President. In September the FATF issued a revised list of 19 'un-co-operative jurisdictions', including Dominica, Grenada, Saint Christopher and Nevis and Saint Vincent and the Grenadines. In early 2002 most Caribbean states concluded a provisional agreement with the OECD to work to improve the transparency and supervision of offshore sectors.

In February 2002 the first meeting of heads of state and of government of CARICOM and the Central American Integration System (SICA) was convened in Belize City, Belize. The meeting aimed to strengthen co-operation between the groupings, in particular in international negotiations, efforts to counter transnational organized crime, and support for the regions' economies. In late 2002 a joint CARICOM-Spain commission was inaugurated to foster greater co-operation between the two parties. In March 2004 CARICOM signed a free trade agreement with Costa Rica.

In January 2004 CARICOM heads of government resolved to address the escalating political crisis in Haiti. Following a visit by a high-level delegation to that country early in the month discussions were held with representatives of opposition political parties and civil society groups. At the end of January several CARICOM leaders met with Haiti's President Aristide and members of his Government and announced a Prior Action Plan, incorporating opposition demands for political reform. The Plan, however, was rejected by opposition parties since it permitted Aristide to complete his term-in-office. CARICOM, together with the OAS, continued to pursue diplomatic efforts to secure a peaceful solution to the crisis. On 29 February Aristide resigned and left the country and a provisional president was appointed. In March CARICOM heads of government determined not to allow representatives of the new interim administration to participate in the councils of the Community until constitutional rule had been reinstated. In July heads of government resolved to send a five-member ministerial team to Haiti to discuss developments in that country with the interim authorities. In July 2005 CARICOM heads of government expressed concern at the deterioration of the situation in Haiti, but reiterated their readiness to provide technical assistance for the electoral process, under the auspices of the UN mission. In March 2006 the CARICOM Chairman endorsed the results of the presidential election, which had been conducted in the previous month, and pledged fully to support Haiti's return to democratic rule. In July 2010 CARICOM agreed to send a joint election observation mission, with representatives of the OAS, to monitor preparations for presidential and legislative elections in Haiti, scheduled to be conducted in November.

In July 2005 CARICOM heads of government issued a statement protesting against proposals by the European Commission, issued in the previous month, to reform the EU sugar regime. Particular concern was expressed at a proposed price reduction in the cost of refined sugar of 39% over a four-year period. The heads of government insisted that, in accordance with the ACP-EU Cotonou Agreement, any review of the Sugar Protocol was required to be undertaken with the agreement of both parties and with regard to safeguarding benefits. In December CARICOM heads of government held a special meeting to discuss the EU sugar and banana regimes, in advance of a ministerial meeting of the WTO, held in Hong Kong later in that month. The Conference reiterated the potentially devastating effects on regional economies of the sugar price reduction and proposed new banana tariffs, and expressed the need for greater compensation and for the WTO multilateral negotiations to address fairly issues of preferential access. Negotiations between the ACP Caribbean signatory countries (the so-called CARIFORUM) and the EU on an Economic Partnership Agreement to succeed the Cotonou Agreement, which had commenced in April 2004, were concluded in December 2007. In January 2008 CARICOM's Council for Trade and Economic Development resolved to conduct an independent review of the new agreement. The EPA was signed (initially, with the exception of Guyana and Haiti) in October.

In March 2006 a CARICOM-Mexico Joint Commission signed an agreement to promote future co-operation, in particular in seven priority areas including: disaster management, energy conservation and regional statistics. The first summit level meeting between heads of state and government of Mexico and CARICOM was held in February 2010, in Riviera Maya, Mexico. In February 2007 the Secretaries-General of CARICOM and SICA signed a plan of action on future co-operation between the two groupings. A second CARICOM-SICA meeting of heads of state and of government was convened in May, in Belize. The meeting endorsed the plan of action and, in addition, instructed their ministers of foreign affairs and of trade to pursue efforts to negotiate a free trade agreement, to be based on that signed by CARICOM with Costa Rica (see above). Trade negotiations were formally inaugurated in August.

In March 2006 CARICOM ministers of foreign affairs met with the US Secretary of State and agreed to strengthen co-operation and enhance bilateral relations. In June 2007 a major meeting, the 'Conference on the Caribbean: a 20/20 Vision', was held in Washington, DC, USA. A series of meetings was held to consider issues and challenges relating to CARICOM's development and integration efforts and to the strengthening of relations with other countries in the region and with the USA. An Experts' Forum was hosted by the World Bank, a Private Sector Dialogue was held at the headquarters of the Inter-American Development Bank, and a Diaspora Forum was convened at the OAS. A summit meeting of CARICOM heads of government and the US President, George W. Bush, was held in the context of the Conference, at which issues concerning trade, economic growth and development, security and social investment were discussed. A second Conference on the Caribbean was held in New York, USA, in June 2008. In April 2010 the new US President, Barack Obama, announced a Caribbean Basin Security Initiative (CBSI), which was to structure its regional security policy around a bilateral partnership with CARICOM, in particular to advance public safety and security, to reduce substantially trafficking of illicit substances and to promote social justice. In May 2010 an inaugural Caribbean–US Security Co-operation Dialogue was held, in Washington, DC, to pursue discussion of the CBSI. A meeting of CARICOM foreign ministers with the US Secretary of State was held in the following month, in Barbados, at which a series of commitments was concluded to enhance co-operation on a range of issues including energy security, climate change, health and trade relations.

In April 2009 Trinidad and Tobago hosted, in Port of Spain, the fifth Summit of the Americas.

CRIME AND SECURITY

In December 1996 CARICOM heads of government determined to strengthen comprehensive co-operation and technical assistance to combat illegal drugs-trafficking. The Conference decided to establish a Caribbean Security Task Force to help formulate a single regional agreement on maritime interdiction, incorporating agreements already concluded by individual members. A Regional Drugs Control Programme at the CARICOM Secretariat aims to co-ordinate regional initiatives with the overall objective of reducing the demand and supply of illegal substances. In July 2001 heads of government resolved to establish a task force to be responsible for producing recommendations for a forthcoming meeting of national security advisers. In October heads of government convened an emergency meeting in Nassau, the Bahamas, to consider the impact of the terrorist attacks against the USA that had occurred in September. The meeting determined to convene immediately the so-called Task Force on Crime and Security in order to implement new policy directives. It was agreed to enhance co-ordination and collaboration of security services throughout the region, in particular in intelligence gathering, analysis and sharing in relation to crime, illicit drugs and terrorism, and to strengthen security at airports, seaports and borders. In July 2002 heads of government agreed on a series of initiatives recommended by the Task Force to counter the escalation in crime and violence. These included strengthening border controls, preparing national anti-crime master plans, establishing broad-based National Commissions on law and order and strengthening the exchange of information and intelligence. In July 2005 CARICOM heads of government endorsed a new Management Framework for Crime and Security, which provided for regular meetings of a Council of Ministers responsible for national security and law enforcement, a Security Policy Advisory Committee, and the establishment of an Implementation Agency for Crime and Security. Several co-ordinated security measures were implemented during the cricket world cup, which was held across the region in early 2007. In July CARICOM heads of government agreed in principle to extend these security efforts, including the introduction of a voluntary CARICOM Travel Card, CARIPASS, to facilitate the establishment of a single domestic space. An agreement to implement CARIPASS, was signed by heads of state and government meeting in Dominica, in March 2010; it was expected to be introduced for use later in that year.

INDUSTRY, ENERGY AND THE ENVIRONMENT

A protocol relating to the CARICOM Industrial Programming Scheme (CIPS), approved in 1988, is the Community's instrument for promoting the co-operative development of industry in the region. Protocol III amending the Treaty of Chaguaramas, with respect to industrial policy, was opened for signature in July 1998. The Secretariat has established a national standards bureau in each member country to harmonize technical standards. In 1999 members agreed to establish a new CARICOM Regional Organisation for Standards and Quality (CROSQ), as a successor to the Caribbean Common Market Standards Council. The agreement to establish CROSQ, to be located in Barbados, was signed in February 2002.

The CARICOM Alternative Energy Systems Project provides training, assesses energy needs and conducts energy audits. Efforts in regional energy development are directed at the collection and analysis of data for national energy policy documents. Implementation of a Caribbean Renewable Energy Development Programme, a project initiated in 1998, commenced in 2004. The Programme aimed to remove barriers to renewable energy development, establish a foundation for a sustainable renewable energy industry, and to create a framework for co-operation among regional and national renewable energy projects. A Caribbean Renewable Energy Fund was to be established to provide equity and development financing for renewable energy projects.

In January 2001 the Council for Trade and Economic Development approved the development of a specialized CARICOM agency to co-ordinate the gathering of information and other activities relating to climate change. The Caribbean Community Climate Change Centre became operational in early 2004 and was formally inaugurated, in Belmopan, Belize, in August 2005. It serves as an official clearing house and repository of data relating to climate change in the Caribbean region, provides advice to governments and other expertise for the development of projects to manage and adapt to climate change, and undertakes training. The results of the Centre's Mainstreaming Adaptation to Climate Change (MACC) Project were presented to governments at a Caribbean Climate Change Conference, held in Saint Lucia, in March 2009. In July 2008 CARICOM heads of government established a Task Force on Climate Change and Development to consider future action in relation to developments in energy and climate change, and in particular food insecurity caused by global rising food and fuel prices. The inaugural meeting of the Task Force was held in November, in Saint Lucia.

TRANSPORT, COMMUNICATIONS AND TOURISM

A Summit of Heads of Government on Tourism, Trade and Transportation was held in Trinidad and Tobago, in August 1995, to which all members of the ACS and regional tourism organizations were invited. In 1997 CARICOM heads of government considered a number of proposals relating to air transportation, tourism, human resource development and capital investment, which had been identified by Community ministers of tourism as critical issues in the sustainable development of the tourist industry. The heads of government requested ministers to meet regularly to develop tourism policies, and in particular to undertake an in-depth study of human resource development issues in early 1998. A regional summit on tourism, in recognition of the importance of the industry to the economic development of the region, was held in the Bahamas, in December 2001. A new Caribbean passport was introduced in January 2005; all 12 member countries participating in the CSME were issuing the document by 2009.

A Caribbean Confederation of Shippers' Councils represents the interests of regional exporters and importers. A Multilateral Agreement Concerning the Operations of Air Services within the Caribbean Community entered into force in November 1998, providing a formal framework for the regulation of the air transport industry and enabling CARICOM-owned and -controlled airlines to operate freely within the region. In July 1999 heads of government signed Protocol VI amending the Treaty of Chaguaramas providing for a common transportation policy, with harmonized standards and practices, which was to be an integral component of the development of a single market and economy. In November 2001 representatives of national civil aviation authorities signed a memorandum of understanding, providing for the establishment of a regional body, the Regional Aviation Safety Oversight System. This was succeeded, in July 2008, by a Caribbean Aviation Safety and Security Oversight System upon the signing of an agreement by Barbados, Guyana, Saint Lucia and Trinidad and Tobago.

In 1989 the Caribbean Telecommunications Union was established to oversee developments in regional telecommunications. In July 2006 the Conference of heads of government, convened in Saint Christopher and Nevis, mandated the development of C@ribNET, a project to extend the availability of high speed internet access throughout the region. In May 2007 the inaugural meeting of a Regional Information Communications and Technology Steering Committee was held, in Georgetown, Guyana, to determine areas of activity for future co-operation in support of the establishment of a Caribbean Information Society.

AGRICULTURE AND FISHERIES

In July 1996 the CARICOM summit meeting agreed to undertake wide-ranging measures in order to modernize the agricultural sector and to increase the international competitiveness of Caribbean agricultural produce. The CARICOM Secretariat was to support national programmes with assistance in policy formulation, human resource development and the promotion of research and technology development in the areas of productivity, marketing, agri-business and water resources management. Protocol V amending the Treaty of Chaguaramas, which was concerned with agricultural policy, was opened for signature by heads of government in July 1998. In July 2002 heads of government approved an initiative to develop a CARIFORUM Special Programme for Food Security. CARICOM Governments have continually aimed to generate awareness of the economic and social importance of the banana industry to the region, in particular within the framework of the WTO multilateral trade negotiations.

A Caribbean Regional Fisheries Mechanism was established in 2002 to promote the sustainable use of fisheries and aquaculture resources in the region. It incorporates a Caribbean Fisheries Forum, which serves as the main technical and scientific decision-making body of the Mechanism. In March 2010 a Caribbean Agricultural Health and Food Safety Agency (CAHFSA) was inaugurated in Paramaribo, Suriname.

HEALTH AND EDUCATION

In 1986 CARICOM and the Pan-American Health Organization launched 'Caribbean Co-operation in Health' with projects to be undertaken in six main areas: environmental protection, including the control of disease-bearing pests; development of human resources; chronic non-communicable diseases and accidents; strengthening health systems; food and nutrition; maternal and child health care; and population activities. In 2001 CARICOM established the Pan-Caribbean Partnership against HIV/AIDS (PANCAP), with the aim of reducing the spread and impact of HIV and AIDS in member countries. In February 2002 PANCAP initiated regional negotiations with pharmaceutical companies to secure reductions in the cost of anti-retroviral drugs. A Caribbean Environmental Health Institute (see below) aims to promote collaboration among member states in all areas of environmental management and human health. In July 2001 heads of government, meeting in the Bahamas, issued the Nassau Declaration on Health, advocating greater regional strategic co-ordination and planning in the health sector and institutional reform, as well as increased resources. In February 2006 PANCAP and UNAIDS organized a regional consultation on the outcomes of country-based assessments of the HIV/AIDS crisis that had been undertaken in the region, and formulated a Regional Roadmap for Universal Access to HIV and AIDS Prevention, Care, Treatment and Support over the period 2006–10. A special meeting of COHSOD, convened in June 2006, in Trinidad and Tobago, issued the Port of Spain Declaration on the Education Sector Response to HIV and AIDS, which committed member states to supporting the Roadmap through education policy. In September 2007 a special regional summit meeting on chronic non-communicable diseases was held in Port of Spain, Trinidad and Tobago. In July 2008 CARICOM heads of government endorsed a new Caribbean Regional Strategy Framework on HIV and AIDS for the period 2008–12. In March 2010 Caribbean heads of government approved the establishment of a Caribbean Public Health Agency (CARPHA), which was intended to promote a co-ordinated approach to public health issues, in accordance with the Nassau Declaration.

CARICOM education programmes have included the improvement of reading in schools through assistance for teacher-training and ensuring the availability of low-cost educational material throughout the region. In July 1997 CARICOM heads of government adopted the recommendations of a ministerial committee, which identified priority measures for implementation in the education sector. These included the objective of achieving universal, quality secondary education and the enrolment of 15% of post-secondary students in tertiary education by 2005, as well as improved training in foreign languages and science and technology. In March 2004 CARICOM ministers of education endorsed the establishment of a Caribbean Knowledge and Learning Network to strengthen tertiary education institutions throughout the region and to enhance knowledge sharing. The Network was formally inaugurated in July, in co-operation with the OECS, in Grenada. A Caribbean Vocational Qualification was introduced in 2007.

From the late 1990s youth activities have been increasingly emphasized by the Community. These have included new programmes for disadvantaged youths, a mechanism for youth exchange and the convening of a Caribbean Youth Parliament. CARICOM organizes a biennial Caribbean Festival of Arts (CARIFESTA). CARIFESTA X was staged in Georgetown, Guyana, in August 2008.

EMERGENCY ASSISTANCE

A Caribbean Disaster Emergency Response Agency (CDERA) was established in 1991 to co-ordinate immediate disaster relief, primarily in the event of hurricanes. In January 2005, meeting on the sidelines of the fifth Summit of the Alliance of Small Island States, in Port Louis, Mauritius, the Secretaries-General of CARICOM, the Commonwealth, the Pacific Islands Forum and the Indian Ocean Commission determined to take collective action to strengthen the disaster preparedness and response capabilities of their member countries in the Caribbean, Pacific and Indian Ocean areas. In September 2006 CARICOM, the European Union and the Caribbean ACP states signed a Financing Agreement for Institutional Support and Capacity-Building for Disaster Management in the Caribbean, which aimed to support CDERA by providing €3.4m. to facilitate the implementation of revised legislation, improved co-ordination between countries in the region and the increased use of information and communications technology in emergency planning. A new Caribbean Catastrophe Risk Insurance Facility (CCRIF), a multi-country initiative enabling participating states to draw funds for responding immediately to adverse natural events, such as earthquakes and hurricanes, became operational in June 2007, with support from international donors, including the Caribbean Development Bank and the World Bank. In July 2009 an agreement to establish a new Caribbean Disaster Emergency Management Agency (CDEMA) was opened for signature. It was inaugurated in September 2009, formally replacing the CDERA, at which time it had 18 participating states. CDEMA co-ordinated the immediate regional response to the devastating earthquake that struck Haiti in January 2010. It identified priority areas for emergency assistance and collated donations and other offers of support, in close collaboration with other regional organizations.

INSTITUTIONS

The following are among the institutions formally established within the framework of CARICOM:

Assembly of Caribbean Community Parliamentarians: c/o CARICOM Secretariat; an intergovernmental agreement on the establishment of a regional parliament entered into force in August 1994; inaugural meeting held in Barbados, in May 1996. Comprises up to four representatives of the parliaments of each member country, and up to two of each associate member. It aims to provide a forum for wider community involvement in the process of integration and for enhanced deliberation on CARICOM affairs; authorized to issue recommendations for the Conference of Heads of Government and to adopt resolutions on any matter arising under the Treaty of Chaguaramas.

Caribbean Agricultural Research and Development Institute (CARDI): UWI Campus, St Augustine, Trinidad and Tobago; tel. 645-1205; fax 645-1208; e-mail sking@cardi.org; internet www.cardi.org; f. 1975; aims to contribute to the competitiveness and sustainability of Caribbean agriculture by generating and transferring new and appropriate technologies and by developing effective partnerships with regional and international entities; Exec. Dir Dr Arlington Chesney; publs *CARDI Weekly*, *CARDI Review*, technical bulletin series.

Caribbean Centre for Development Administration (CARICAD): Weymouth Corporate Centre, 1st Floor, Roebuck St, St Michael, Barbados; tel. 427-8535; fax 436-1709; e-mail caricad@caricad.net; internet www.caricad.net; f. 1980; aims to assist governments in the reform of the public sector and to strengthen their managerial capacities for public administration; promotes the involvement of the private sector, non-governmental organizations and other bodies in all decision-making processes; Exec. Dir Jennifer Astaphan.

Caribbean Community Climate Change Centre: Lawrence Nicholas Bldg, 2nd Floor, Ring Rd, POB 563, Belmopan, Belize; tel. 822-1094; fax 822-1365; e-mail kleslie1@caribbeanclimate.bz; internet www.caribbeanclimate.bz; f. 2005 to co-ordinate the region's response to climate change; Exec. Dir Dr Kenrick Leslie.

Caribbean Competition Commission: Paramaribo, Suriname; f. 2008; to enforce the rules of competition of the CARICOM Single Market and Economy; Chair. Kusha Haraksingh (Trinidad and Tobago); Exec. Dir Barbara Lee (Jamaica).

Caribbean Disaster Emergency Management Agency (CDEMA): Bldg 1, Manor Lodge, Lodge Hill, St Michael, Barbados; tel. 425-0386; fax 425-8854; e-mail cdera@caribsurf.com; internet www.cdera.org; f. 1991; aims to respond with immediate assistance following a request by a participating state in the event of a natural or man-made disaster; co-ordinates other relief efforts; assists states to establish disaster preparedness and response capabilities; incorporates national disaster organizations, headed by a co-ordinator, in each participating state; Exec. Dir Jeremy Collymore.

Caribbean Environmental Health Institute (CEHI): POB 1111, The Morne, Castries, St Lucia; tel. 4522501; fax 4532721; e-mail cehi@candw.lc; internet www.cehi.org.lc; f. 1980 (began operations in 1982); provides technical and advisory services to member states in formulating environmental health policy legislation and in all areas of environmental management (for example, solid waste management, water supplies, beach and air pollution, and pesticides control); promotes, collates and disseminates relevant research; conducts courses, seminars and workshops throughout the region; Exec. Dir Patricia Aquing (Trinidad and Tobago).

Caribbean Examinations Council: The Garrison, St Michael 20, Barbados; tel. 436-6261; fax 429-5421; e-mail cxcezo@cxc.org; internet www.cxc.org; f. 1972; develops syllabuses and conducts examinations for the Caribbean Advanced Proficiency Examination (CAPE), the Caribbean Secondary Education Certificate (CSEC) and the Caribbean Certificate of Secondary Level Competence (CCSLC); mems: govts of 16 English-speaking countries and territories; Registrar and CEO Dr Didicus Jules.

Caribbean Food and Nutrition Institute (CFNI): UWI Campus, POB 140, St Augustine, Trinidad and Tobago; tel. 645-2917; fax 663-1544; e-mail cfni@cablenett.net; internet www.cfni.paho.org; f. 1967 to serve the governments and people of the region and to act as a catalyst among persons and organizations concerned with food and nutrition through research and field investigations, training in nutrition, dissemination of information, advisory services and production of educational material; a specialized centre of the Pan American Health Organization; mems: all English-speaking Caribbean territories, including the mainland countries of Belize and Guyana; Dir Dr Fitzroy Henry; publs *CAJANUS* (quarterly), *Nyam News* (monthly), *Nutrient-Cost Tables* (quarterly), educational material.

Caribbean Meteorological Organization (CMO): POB 461, Port of Spain, Trinidad and Tobago; tel. 622-4711; fax 622-0277; e-mail cmohq@cmo.org.tt; internet www.cmo.org.tt; f. 1951 to co-ordinate regional activities in meteorology, operational hydrology and allied sciences; became a specialized institution of CARICOM in 1973; comprises a Council of Government Ministers, a Headquarters Unit, the Caribbean Meteorological Foundation and the Caribbean Institute for Meteorology and Hydrology, located in Barbados; mems: govts of 16 countries and territories represented by the National Meteorological and Hydro-meteorological Services; Co-ordinating Dir Tyrone W. Sutherland.

Caribbean Telecommunications Union (CTU): Victoria Park Suites, 3rd Floor, 14–17 Victoria Sq., Port of Spain, Trinidad and Tobago; tel. 627-0281; fax 623-1523; internet www.ctu.int/ctu; f. 1989; aims to co-ordinate the planning and development of telecommunications in the region; encourages the development of regional telecommunications standards, the transfer of technology and the exchange of information among national telecommunications administrations; membership includes mems of CARICOM and other countries in the region, private sector orgs and non-governmental orgs; Pres. Clive Mullings (Jamaica); Sec.-Gen. Bernadette Lewis (Trinidad and Tobago).

CARICOM Implementation Agency for Crime and Security (IMPACS): Sagicor Bldg, Ground Floor, 16 Queen's Park West, Port of Spain, Trinidad and Tobago; tel. 622-0245; fax 628-9795; e-mail enquiries@caricomimpacs.org; internet www.caricomimpacs.org; f. 2006 as a permanent institution to co-ordinate activities in the region relating to crime and security; incorporates two sub-agencies: a Joint Regional Communications Centre and a Regional Intelligence Fusion Centre; Exec. Sec. Lynne Anne Williams (Trinidad and Tobago).

CARICOM Regional Organisation for Standards and Quality: 'The Heritage', 35 Pine Rd Belleville, St Michael, Barbados; tel. 437-8146; fax 437-4569; e-mail crosq.caricom@crosq.org; internet www.crosq.org; f. 2002; aims to enhance and promote the implementation of standards and quality verification throughout the region and liaise with international standards orgs; CEO Vyjayanthi Lopez.

Council of Legal Education: c/o Gordon St, St Augustine, Trinidad and Tobago; tel. 662-5860; fax 662-0927; internet www.clecaribbean.com; f. 1971; responsible for the training of members of the legal profession; administers law schools in Jamaica, Trinidad and Tobago, and the Bahamas; mems: govts of 12 countries and territories; Chair. E. ANN HENRY (Antigua and Barbuda).

ASSOCIATE INSTITUTIONS

Caribbean Development Bank: POB 408, Wildey, St Michael, Barbados; tel. 431-1600; fax 426-7269; e-mail info@caribank.org; internet www.caribank.org; f. 1969 to stimulate regional economic growth through support for agriculture, industry, transport and other infrastructure, tourism, housing and education; in 2008 new loans, grants and equity investments approved totalled US $348.2m., bringing the cumulative total to $3,305.7m.; in May 2010 the Board of Governors approved an ordinary capital increase of some $1,000m., including a paid-up component of $216m.; mems: CARICOM states, and Canada, the People's Republic of China, Colombia, Germany, Italy, Mexico, United Kingdom, Venezuela; Pres. Dr. COMPTON BOURNE.

Caribbean Law Institute: University of the West Indies, Cave Hill Campus, POB 64, Bridgetown, Barbados; tel. 417-4560; fax 417-4138; internet www.law.fsu.edu/centers/cli/index.html; f. 1988 to harmonize and modernize commercial laws in the region; Exec. Dir Dr WINSTON C. ANDERSON.

Other Associate Institutions of CARICOM, in accordance with its constitution, are the University of Guyana, the University of the West Indies and the Secretariat of the Organisation of Eastern Caribbean States.

Publications

CARICOM Perspective (annually).

CARICOM View (6 a year).

CENTRAL AMERICAN INTEGRATION SYSTEM

(SISTEMA DE LA INTEGRACIÓN CENTROAMERICANA—SICA)

Address: Blv. Orden de Malta 470, Santa Elena, Antiguo Cuscatlán, San Salvador, El Salvador.

Telephone: 2248-8800; **fax:** 2248-8899; **e-mail:** info.sgsica@sica.int; **internet:** www.sica.int.

Founded in December 1991, when the heads of state of six Central American countries signed the Protocol of Tegucigalpa to the agreement establishing the Organization of Central American States (f. 1951), creating a new framework for regional integration. A General Secretariat of the Sistema de la Integración Centroamericana (SICA) was inaugurated in February 1993 to co-ordinate the process of political, economic, social cultural and environmental integration and to promote democracy and respect for human rights throughout the region.

In September 1997 Central American Common Market (CACM) heads of state, meeting in the Nicaraguan capital, signed the Managua Declaration in support of further regional integration and the establishment of a political union. A commission was to be established to consider all aspects of the policy and to formulate a timetable for the integration process. In February 1998 heads of state resolved to establish a Unified General Secretariat to integrate the institutional aspects of the grouping in a single office, to be located in San Salvador. The process was ongoing in 2010.

Secretary-General: JUAN DANIEL ALEMÁN GURDIÁN.

MEMBERS

Belize	Guatemala	Nicaragua
Costa Rica	Honduras	Panama
El Salvador		

ASSOCIATE MEMBER

Dominican Republic

Note: Argentina, Brazil, Chile, Germany, Italy, Japan, Mexico, Spain and Taiwan have observer status with SICA.

Organization

(August 2010)

SUMMIT MEETINGS

The meetings of heads of state of member countries serve as the supreme decision-making organ of SICA.

COUNCIL OF MINISTERS

Ministers for foreign affairs of member states meet regularly to provide policy direction for the process of integration.

CONSULTATIVE COMMITTEE

The Committee comprises representatives of business organizations, trade unions, academic institutions and other federations concerned with the process of integration in the region. It is an integral element of the integration system and assists the Secretary-General in determining the policies of the organization.

President: CARLOS MOLINA.

GENERAL SECRETARIAT

The General Secretariat of SICA was established in February 1993 to co-ordinate the process of enhanced regional integration. It comprises the following divisions: inter-institutional relations; research and co-operation; legal and political affairs; economic affairs; and communications and information.

SPECIALIZED TECHNICAL SECRETARIATS

Secretaría Ejecutiva de la Comisión Centroamericana de Ambiente y Desarrollo (SE-CCAD): Blv. Orden de Malta 470, Santa Elena, Antiguo Cuscatlán, San Salvador, El Salvador; tel. 2248-8800; fax 2248-8894; e-mail info.ccad@sica.int; internet www.ccad.ws; f. 1989 to enhance collaboration in the promotion of sustainable development and environmental protection; Exec. Sec. Dr MARCO ANTONIO GONZÁLEZ PASTORA.

Secretaría General de la Coordinación Educativa y Cultural Centroamericana (SG-CECC): 100m norte de la Nunciatura, Casa 8815, Rohrmoser, San José, Costa Rica; tel. and fax 2232-2891; e-mail sgcecc@racsa.co.cr; internet www.cecc.mep.go.cr; f. 1982; promotes development of regional programmes in the fields of education and culture; Sec.-Gen. MARVIN HERRERA ARAYA.

Secretaría de Integración Económica Centroamericana (SIECA): 4 A Avda 10–25, Zona 14, Apdo 1237, 01901 Guatemala City, Guatemala; tel. 2368-2151; fax 2368-1071; e-mail info@sieca.int; internet www.sieca.int; f. 1960 to assist the process of economic integration and the creation of a Central American Common Market (CACM—established by the organization of Central American States under the General Treaty of Central American Economic Integration, signed in December 1960 and ratified by Costa Rica, Guatemala, El Salvador, Honduras and Nicaragua in September 1963); supervises the correct implementation of the legal instruments of economic integration, carries out relevant studies at the request of the CACM, and arranges meetings; comprises departments covering the working of the CACM: negotiations and external trade policy; external co-operation; systems and statistics; finance and administration; also includes a unit for co-operation with the private sector and finance institutions, and a legal consultative committee; Sec.-Gen. YOLANDA MAYORA DE GAVIDIA; publs *Anuario Estadístico Centroamericano de Comercio Exterior*, *Carta Informativa* (monthly), *Cuadernos de la SIECA* (2 a year), *Estadísticas Macroeconómicas de Centroamérica* (annually), *Series Estadísticas Seleccionadas de Centroamérica* (annually), *Boletín Informativo* (fortnightly).

Secretaría de la Integración Social Centroamericana (SISCA): Blv. Orden de Malta 470, Santa Elena, Antiguo Cuscatlán, San Salvador, El Salvador; tel. 2248-8857; fax 2248-8896; e-mail info.sisca@sica.int; internet www.sica.int/sisca; f. 1995; Sec. ANA HAZEL ESCRICH.

OTHER SPECIALIZED SECRETARIATS

Secretaría Técnica del Consejo Centroamericano de Turismo: Blv. Orden de Malta 470, Santa Elena, Antiguo Cuscatlán,

San Salvador, El Salvador; tel. 2248-8837; fax 2248-8897; e-mail info .stcct@sica.int; internet www.sica.int/cct; f. 1965 to develop regional tourism activities; Dir MERCEDES MELÉNDEZ DE MENA.

Secretaría del Consejo Agropecuario Centroamericano (SCAC): 600 m noreste del Cruce de Ipis-Coronado, San Isidro de Coronado, Apdo Postal 55-2200, San José, Costa Rica; tel. 2216-0303; fax 2216-0285; e-mail coreca@iica.ac.cr; internet www.coreca.org; f. 1991 to determine and co-ordinate regional policies and programmes relating to agriculture and agroindustry; Exec. Sec. RÓGER GUILLÉN BUSTOS.

Secretaría Ejecutiva del Consejo Monetario Centroamericano (SECMCA) (Central American Monetary Council): 400 m suroeste de la Rotonda La Bandera, Barrio Dent, Contiguo al BANHVI, San José, Costa Rica; tel. 2280-9522; fax 2524-1062; e-mail secma@secmca.org; internet www.secmca.org; f. 1964 by the presidents of Central American central banks, to co-ordinate monetary policies; Exec. Sec. WILLIAM CALVO VILLEGAS; publs *Boletín Estadístico* (annually), *Informe Económico* (annually).

Comisión Centroamericana de Transporte Marítimo (COCATRAM): Frente al Costado Oeste del Hotel Mansión Teodolinda, Barrio Bolonia, Apdo Postal 2423, Managua, Nicaragua; tel. 222-2754; fax 222-2759; e-mail drojas@cocatram.org.ni; internet www .cocatram.org.ni; f. 1981; Exec. Dir OTTO NOACK SIERRA; publ. *Boletín Informativo*.

AD HOC INTERGOVERNMENTAL SECRETARIATS

Consejo Centroamericano de Instituciones de Seguridad Social (COCISS) (Central American Council of Social Security Institutions): Barrio Abajo 555, 10°, Tegucigalpa, Honduras; tel. 222-8412; fax 222-8414; e-mail cociss@ccss.sa.cr; internet www.ccss .sa.cr/cociss/idcociss.htm; f. 1992; Sec. RICHARD ZABLAH.

Comisión para el Desarrollo Científico y Tecnológico de Centroamérica y Panamá (CTCAP) (Committee for the Scientific and Technological Development of Central America and Panama): Antigua base de Clayton, Edif. 213, Panama; tel. 317-0014; fax 317-0026; e-mail espinoza@ns.hondunet.net; f. 1976; Pres. ROSA MARIA AMAYA DE LÓPEZ.

Consejo del Istmo Centroamericano de Deportes y Recreación (CODICADER) (Committee of the Central American Isthmus for Sport and Recreation): Ministerio de Cultura, Artes y Deportes, Contiguo a Migración, Tegucigalpa, Honduras; tel. 221-3877; fax 236-9532; f. 1992; Sec.-Gen. JORGE MEJÍA.

Unidad Técnica del Consejo Centroamericano de Vivienda y Asentamientos Humanos (CCVAH) (Central American Council on Housing and Human Settlements): Blv. Orden de Malta 470, Santa Elena, Antiguo Cuscatlán, San Salvador, El Salvador; tel. and fax 2248-8856; f. 1992.

Secretaría Ejecutiva del Consejo de Electrificación de América Central (CEAC) (Central American Electrification Council): 9A Calle Pte 950, Edif. CEL, Centro de Gobierno, San Salvador, El Salvador; tel. 2211-6175; fax 2211-6239; e-mail jmontesi@cel.gob.sv; f. 1985; Exec. Sec. JULIO ROBERTO ALVAREZ.

Organización Centroamericana y del Caribe de Entidades Fiscalizadores Superiores (OCCEFS): Tribunal Superior de Cuentas de la República de Honduras Centro Cívico Gubernamental, Col. Las Brisas Comayagüela, Honduras; tel. 234-5210; fax 234-5210; internet www.occefs.org; f. 1995 as the Organización Centroamericana de Entidades Fiscalizadores Superiores, within the framework of the Organización Latinoamericana y del Caribe de Entidades Fiscalizadoras Superiores; assumed present name in 1998; Exec. Sec. RENÁN SAGASTUME FERNÁNDEZ.

CORE INSTITUTIONS

Central American Parliament (PARLACEN)

12 Avda 33-04, Zona 5, 01005 Guatemala City, Guatemala; tel. 2424-4600; fax 2424-4610; e-mail guatemala@parlacen.org.gt; internet www.parlacen.org.gt.; officially inaugurated in 1991; comprises elected representatives of El Salvador, Guatemala, Honduras, Nicaragua and Panama; Pres. JACINTO SUÁREZ (Nicaragua); Sec.-Gen. WERNER VARGAS.

Central American Court of Justice

Apdo Postal 907, Managua, Nicaragua; tel. 266-6273; fax 266-4604; e-mail cortecen@ccj.org.ni; internet www.ccj.org.ni.; officially inaugurated in 1994; tribunal authorized to consider disputes relating to treaties agreed within the regional integration system; in February 1998 Central American heads of state agreed to limit the number of magistrates in the Court to one per country; Pres. SILVIA ISABEL ROSALES BOLAÑOS (Nicaragua); Sec.-Gen. Dr ORLANDO GUERRERO MAYORGA.

OTHER REGIONAL INSTITUTIONS

Finance

Banco Centroamericano de Integración Económica (BCIE) (Central American Bank for Economic Integration): Blv. Suyapa, Contigua a Banco de Honduras, Apdo 772, Tegucigalpa, Honduras; tel. 240-2243; fax 240-2185; e-mail MNunez@bcie.org; internet www .bcie.org; f. 1961 to promote the economic integration and balanced economic development of member countries; finances public and private development projects, particularly those related to industrialization and infrastructure; auth. cap. US $2,000m; regional mems: Costa Rica, El Salvador, Guatemala, Honduras, Nicaragua; non-regional mems: Argentina, the People's Republic of China, Colombia, Mexico, Spain; Exec. Pres. NICK RISCHBIETH; publs *Annual Report*, *Revista de la Integración y el Desarrollo de Centroamérica*.

Public Administration

Centro de Coordinación para la Prevención de Desastres Naturales en América Central (CEPREDENAC): Avda Hincapié 21-72, Zona 13 Guatemala City, Guatemala; tel. 2362-1980; e-mail info.cepredenac@sica.int; internet www.sica.int/cepredenac; f. 1988, integrated into SICA in 1995; aims to strengthen the capacity of the region to reduce its vulnerability to natural disasters; Exec. Sec. IVAN MORALES.

Instituto Centroamericano de Administración Pública (ICAP) (Central American Institute of Public Administration): Apdo Postal 10025-1000, San José, Costa Rica; tel. 2234-1011; fax 2225-2049; e-mail info@icap.ac.cr; internet www.icap.ac.cr; f. 1954 by the five Central American Republics and the UN, with later participation by Panama; the Institute aims to train the region's public servants, provide technical assistance and carry out research leading to reforms in public administration; Dir Dr HUGO ZELAYA CÁLIX.

Secretaría Ejecutiva de la Comisión Regional de Recursos Hidráulicos (SE-CRRH): Apdo Postal 21–2300, Curridabat, San José, Costa Rica; tel. 2231-5791; fax 2296-0047; e-mail crrhcr@sol .racsa.co.cr; internet aguayclima.com; f. 1966; mems: Belize, Costa Rica, El Salvador, Guatemala, Honduras, Nicaragua, Panama; Exec. Sec. MAX CAMPOS ORTIZ.

Agriculture and Fisheries

Organismo Internacional Regional de Sanidad Agropecuaria (OIRSA) (International Regional Organization of Plant Protection and Animal Health): Calle Ramón Belloso, Final Pasaje Isolde, Colonia Escalón, Apdo (01) 61, San Salvador, El Salvador; tel. 2263-1123; fax 2263-1128; e-mail oirsa@oirsa.org; internet www .oirsa.org; f. 1953 for the prevention of the introduction of animal and plant pests and diseases unknown in the region; research, control and eradication programmes of the principal pests present in agriculture; technical assistance and advice to the ministries of agriculture and livestock of member countries; education and qualification of personnel; mems: Belize, Costa Rica, Dominican Republic, El Salvador, Guatemala, Honduras, Mexico, Nicaragua, Panama; Exec. Dir GUILLERMO ENRIQUE ALVARADO DOWNING.

Unidad Coordinadora de la Organización del Sector Pesquero y Acuícola del Istmo Centroamericano (OSPESCA): Blv. Orden de Malta 470, Santa Elena, Antiguo Cuscatlán, San Salvador, El Salvador; tel. 2248-8841; fax 2248-8899; e-mail info .ospesca@sica.int; internet www.sica.int/ospesca; f. 1995, incorporated into SICA in 1999; Regional Co-ordinator MARIO GONZÁLEZ RECINOS.

Education and Health

Comité Coordinador Regional de Instituciones de Agua Potable y Saneamiento de Centroamérica, Panamá y República Dominicana (CAPRE): Avda Bo. 1A, El Obelisco Comayagüela, Tegucigalpa, Honduras; tel. 237-8552; fax 237-2575; e-mail capregtz@sol.racsa.co.cr; f. 1979; Dir LILIANA ARCE UMAÑA.

Consejo Superior Universitario Centroamericano (CSUCA) (Central American University Council): Avda Las Américas 1–03, Zona 14, International Club Los Arcos, 01014 Guatemala City, Guatemala; tel. 2367-1833; fax 2367-4517; e-mail sg@listas.csuca .org; internet www.csuca.org; f. 1948 to guarantee academic, administrative and economic autonomy for universities and to encourage regional integration of higher education; maintains libraries and documentation centres; Council of 32 mems; mems: 18 universities, in Belize, Costa Rica (four), Dominican Republic, El Salvador, Guatemala, Honduras (two), Nicaragua (four) and Panama (four); Sec.-Gen. EFRAÍN MEDINA GUERRA; publs *Estudios Sociales Centroamericanos* (quarterly), *Cuadernos de Investigación* (monthly), *Carta Informativa de la Secretaría General* (monthly).

Instituto de Nutrición de Centroamérica y Panamá (INCAP) (Institute of Nutrition of Central America and Panama): Calzada

Roosevelt 6–25, Zona 11, Apdo Postal 1188-01901, Guatemala City, Guatemala; tel. 2472-3762; fax 2473-6529; e-mail email@incap.int; internet www.new.paho.org/incap; f. 1949 to promote the development of nutritional sciences and their application and to strengthen the technical capacity of member countries to reach food and nutrition security; provides training and technical assistance for nutrition education and planning; conducts applied research; disseminates information; maintains library (including about 600 periodicals); administered by the Pan American Health Organization and the World Health Organization; mems: CACM mems, Belize and Panama; Dir Dr JOSÉ ADÁN MONTES FIGUEROA (a.i.); publ. *Annual Report*.

Transport and Communications

Comisión de Telecomunicaciones de Centroamérica (COMTELCA) (Commission for Telecommunications in Central America): Col. Palmira, Edif. Alpha 608, Avda Brasil, Apdo 1793, Tegucigalpa, Honduras; tel. 220-6666; fax 220-1197; e-mail sec@comtelca.org; internet www.comtelca.org; f. 1966 to co-ordinate and improve the regional telecommunications network; Dir-Gen. RAFAEL A. MARADIAGA.

Corporación Centroamericana de Servicios de Navegación Aérea (COCESNA) (Central American Air Navigation Services Corporation): Apdo 660, Aeropuerto de Toncontín, Tegucigalpa, Honduras; tel. 234-3360; fax 234-2550; e-mail sec-interna@cocesna.org; internet www.cocesna.org; f. 1960; offers radar air traffic control services, aeronautical telecommunications services, flight inspections and radio assistance services for air navigation; provides support in the areas of safety, aeronautical training and aeronautical software; Exec. Pres. EDUARDO MARÍN J.

Activities

In June 1990 the presidents of the CACM countries (Costa Rica, El Salvador, Guatemala, Honduras and Nicaragua) signed a declaration welcoming peace initiatives in El Salvador, Guatemala and Nicaragua, and appealing for a revitalization of CACM, as a means of promoting lasting peace in the region. In December the presidents committed themselves to the creation of an effective common market, proposing the opening of negotiations on a comprehensive regional customs and tariffs policy by March 1991, and the introduction of a regional 'anti-dumping' code by December 1991. They requested the support of multilateral lending institutions through investment in regional development, and the cancellation or rescheduling of member countries' debts. In December 1991 the heads of state of the five CACM countries and Panama signed the Protocol of Tegucigalpa, and in February 1993 the General Secretariat of SICA was inaugurated to co-ordinate the integration process in the region.

In October 1993 the presidents of the CACM countries and Panama signed a protocol to the 1960 General Treaty, committing themselves to full economic integration in the region (with a common external tariff of 20% for finished products and 5% for raw materials and capital goods) and creating conditions for increased free trade. The countries agreed to accelerate the removal of internal non-tariff barriers, but no deadline was set. Full implementation of the protocol was to be 'voluntary and gradual', owing to objections on the part of Costa Rica and Panama. In May 1994, however, Costa Rica committed itself to full participation in the protocol. In March 1995 a meeting of the Central American Monetary Council discussed and endorsed a reduction in the tariff levels from 20% to 15% and from 5% to 1%. However, efforts to adopt this as a common policy were hindered by the implementation of these tariff levels by El Salvador on a unilateral basis, from 1 April, and the subsequent modifications by Guatemala and Costa Rica of their external tariffs. In March 2002 Central American leaders adopted the San Salvador Plan of Action for Central American Economic Integration, establishing several objectives as the basis for the future creation of a regional customs union, with a single tariff.

In October 1999 the heads of state adopted a strategic framework for the period 2000–04 to strengthen the capacity for the physical, social, economic and environmental infrastructure of Central American countries to withstand the impact of natural disasters. In particular, programmes for the integrated management and conservation of water resources, and for the prevention of forest fires were to be implemented.

In June 2001 the heads of state and representatives of Belize, Costa, Rica, El Salvador, Guatemala, Honduras, Mexico, Nicaragua and Panama agreed to activate a Puebla-Panamá Plan (PPP) to promote sustainable social and economic development in the region and to reinforce integration efforts among Central America and the southern states of Mexico (referred to as Mesoamerica). The heads of state identified the principal areas for PPP initiatives, including tourism, road integration, telecommunications, energy interconnection, and the prevention and mitigation of disasters. In June 2002 the heads of state of seven countries, and the Vice-President of Panama, convened in Mérida, Mexico, during an investment fair to promote the Plan and reiterated their support for the regional initiatives. The meeting was also held within the framework of the Tuxtla dialogue mechanism, so-called after an agreement signed in 1991 between Mexico and Central American countries, to discuss co-ordination between the parties, in particular in social matters, health, education and the environment. Regular 'Tuxtla' summit meetings have subsequently been convened. A Centre for the Promotion of Small and Medium-sized Enterprises was established in June 2001. In June 2006 representatives of SICA and of Colombia, the Dominican Republic and Mexico adopted the Declaration of Romana, wherein they agreed to implement the Mesoamerican Energy Integration Program, aimed at developing regional oil, electricity and natural gas markets, promoting the use of renewable energy, and increasing electricity generation and interconnection capacity across the region. In the following month, at the 8th Tuxtla summit, convened in Panama, SICA member states approved the legal framework for the Central American Electrical Connection System (known as SIEPAC), which was to be co-funded by the Central American Bank for Economic Integration and the Inter-American Development Bank. In June 2008 the 10th Tuxtla summit meeting, convened in Villahermosa, Mexico, agreed to establish the Mesoamerican Integration and Development Project to supersede the PPP. The new Project was to incorporate ongoing initiatives on highways and infrastructure and implement energy, electricity and information networks.

In January 2007 the Treaty on Payment Systems and the Liquidation of Assets in Central America and the Dominican Republic was presented to the Secretary-General of SICA. The treaty aimed to increase greater financial co-operation and further to develop the financial markets in the region.

A meeting of Central American heads of state, held in December 2004, was concerned with economic and regional security issues. In March 2005 SICA ministers responsible for security, defence and the interior resolved to establish a special regional force to combat crime, drugs and arms trafficking and terrorism. In June 2008 SICA heads of state and government, convened in San Salvador, El Salvador, agreed to establish a peace-keeping operations unit within the secretariat in order to co-ordinate participation in international peace-keeping missions.

In November 2007 SICA heads of state endorsed a Sustainable Energy Strategy for Central America 2020. Its main areas of concern were: access to energy by the least advantaged populations; the rational and efficient use of energy; renewable sources of energy; biofuels for the transport sector; and climate change. A joint summit on the environment and climate change in Central America and the Caribbean was held with representatives of Caribbean Community and Common Market (CARICOM) in San Pedro Sula, Honduras, in May 2008. In June the SICA summit meeting, convened in San Salvador, El Salvador, reiterated concerns regarding escalating petroleum and food prices, and welcomed several initiatives concerned with strengthening the region's food security (see above). In July 2010 heads of state ratified an agreement to accelerate efforts to reduce the region's vulnerability to natural disasters and the effects of climate change. They determined to establish a special regional fund to finance the initiative.

In December 2008 a summit meeting, convened in San Pedro Sula, Honduras, adopted a plan of urgent measures to address the effects of the global economic and financial downturn, including a commitment of greater investment in infrastructure projects and the establishment of a common credit fund. Heads of state also ratified an agreement to establish a Central American Statistical Commission (Centroestad), which aimed to development a regional statistics service, to provide technical statistical assistance to member countries and to harmonize national and regional statistics.

In late June 2009 SICA ministers for foreign affairs, convened in Managua, Nicaragua, issued a special declaration condemning the removal, by military force, of the Honduran President Manuel Zelaya and the illegal detention of members of his Government. SICA heads of state subsequently met in an extraordinary session and agreed a series of immediate measures, including the suspension of all meetings with the new Honduran authorities, the suspension—through the Central American Bank for Economic Integration—of all loans and disbursements to Honduras, and support for an OAS resolution demanding a reinstatement of the democratically-elected government. Costa Rica and Panama recognised the results of a general election, held in November. In July 2010 SICA heads of state (excluding the Nicaraguan President) signed a Special Declaration on Honduras, permitting that country's full participation in the grouping and supporting its readmission into the OAS.

EXTERNAL RELATIONS

In February 1993 the European Community (now European Union—EU) signed a new framework co-operation agreement with the CACM member states extending the programme of economic assistance and political dialogue initiated in 1984; a further co-operation agreement with the EU was signed in early 1996. In May 2002 ministers of foreign affairs of Central America and the EU agreed upon a new agenda for a formalized dialogue and on priority areas of action, including environmental protection, democracy and governance, and poverty reduction. The meeting determined to work towards the eventual conclusion of an Association Agreement, including an agreement on free trade, although the latter was to be conditional upon the completion of the Doha Round of multilateral negotiations on trade liberalization and upon the attainment of a sufficient level of economic integration in Central America. It was agreed that meetings between the two sides, at ministerial level, were to be held each year. In December 2003 a new EU-Central America Political Dialogue and Co-operation Agreement was signed to replace an existing (1993) framework accord. A new Regional Strategy, for 2007–13, was concluded in March 2007, with an allocation of €75.0m. In May 2006 a meeting of EU and Central American heads of state resolved to initiate negotiations to conclude an Association Agreement. The first round of negotiations was concluded in San José, Costa Rica, in October 2007; subsequent rounds were held in Brussels, Belgium, in February 2008, in El Salvador, San Salvador, in April, in Brussels in July, in Guatemala City, Guatemala, in October, and in Brussels, in January 2009. In April the seventh round of negotiations, being held in Tegucigalpa, Honduras, was suspended when the delegation from Nicaragua withdrew from the talks. The process was suspended in July owing to the political crisis in Honduras. Negotiations to conclude the accord were resumed in February 2010;Panama participated in the negotiations as a full member for the first time in March. The Association Agreement was formally signed by both sides in May. It provided for immediate duty-free access into the EU for some 92% of Central American products into the EU (48% for EU goods entering Central America), with the remainder of tariffs (on all but 4% of products) being phased out over a 15-year period. The accord also incorporated new import quotas for meat, dairy products and rice, and market access agreements for car manufacturers and the service industry.

In December 1994 member states and the USA signed a joint declaration (CONCAUSA), covering co-operation in the following areas: conservation of biodiversity, sound management of energy, environmental legislation, and sustainable economic development. In June 2001 both sides signed a renewed and expanded CONCAUSA, now also covering co-operation in addressing climate change, and in disaster preparedness. In May 1997 the heads of state of CACM member countries, together with the Prime Minister of Belize, conferred with the then US President, Bill Clinton, in San José, Costa Rica. The leaders resolved to establish a Trade and Investment Council to promote trade relations; however, Clinton failed to endorse a request from CACM members that their products receive preferential access to US markets, on similar terms to those from Mexico agreed under the NAFTA accord. During the 1990s the Central American Governments pursued negotiations to conclude free trade agreements with Mexico, Panama and the members of the CARICOM. Nicaragua signed a bilateral accord with Mexico in December (Costa Rica already having done so in 1994). El Salvador, Guatemala and Honduras jointly concluded a free trade arrangement with Mexico in May 2000. In November 1997, at a special summit meeting of CACM heads of state, an agreement was reached with the President of the Dominican Republic to initiate a gradual process of incorporating that country into the process of Central American integration, with the aim of promoting sustainable development throughout the region. The first sectors for increased co-operation between the two sides were to be tourism, health, investment promotion and air transport. A free trade accord with the Dominican Republic was concluded in April 1998, and formally signed in November.

In April 2001 Costa Rica concluded a free trade accord with Canada; the other four CACM countries commenced negotiations with Canada in November with the aim of reaching a similar agreement. In February 2002 Central American heads of state convened an extraordinary summit meeting in Managua, Nicaragua, at which they resolved to implement measures to further the political and economic integration of the region. The leaders determined to pursue initial proposals for a free trade accord with the USA during the visit to the region of the then US President George W. Bush in the following month, and, more generally, to strengthen trading relations with the EU. They also pledged to resolve all regional conflicts by peaceful means. Earlier in February the first meeting of heads of state or government of Central American and CARICOM countries took place in Belize, with the aim of strengthening political and economic relations between the two groupings. The meeting agreed to work towards concluding common negotiating positions, for example in respect of the World Trade Organization. The summit meeting of CACM heads of state, convened in December 2002, in Costa Rica, adopted the 'Declaration of San José', supporting the planned establishment of the Central American customs union (see above), and endorsing the initiation of negotiations with the USA on the creation of a new Central American Free Trade Area (CAFTA). The establishment of a new Central American Tourism Agency was also announced at the meeting.

Negotiations on CAFTA between the CACM countries and the USA were initiated in January 2003. An agreement was concluded between the USA and El Salvador, Guatemala, Honduras and Nicaragua in December, and with Costa Rica in January 2004. Under the resulting US-Central America Free Trade Agreement some 80% of US exports of consumer and industrial goods and more than 50% of US agricultural exports to CAFTA countries were to become duty-free immediately upon its entry into force, with remaining tariffs to be eliminated over a 10-year period for consumer and industrial goods and over a 15-year period for agricultural exports. Almost all CAFTA exports of consumer and industrial products to the USA were to be duty-free on the Agreement's entry into force. The Agreement was signed by the US Trade Representative and CACM ministers of trade and economy, convened in Washington, DC, in May 2004. It required ratification by all national legislatures before entering into effect. Negotiations on a US-Dominican Republic free trade agreement, to integrate the Dominican Republic into CAFTA, were concluded in March and the agreement was signed in August. The so-called DR-CAFTA accord was formally ratified by the USA in August 2005. Subsequently the agreement has entered into force with El Salvador on 1 March 2006, Honduras and Nicaragua on 1 April, Guatemala on 1 July, and the Dominican Republic on 1 March 2007. It was endorsed by a popular referendum held in Costa Rica, in October, and ratified by the country's legislative assembly, after lengthy negotiations, in November 2008. It entered into effect on 1 January 2009.

In February 2007 the Secretaries-General of SICA and CARICOM signed a plan of action to foster greater co-operation in areas including foreign policy, international trade relations, security and combating crime, and the environment. Meetings of ministers of foreign affairs and of the economy and foreign trade were convened in the same month at which preparations were initiated for trade negotiations between the two groupings. In May the second Central American-CARICOM summit meeting was convened, in Belize City, Belize. Heads of state and of government endorsed the efforts to enhance co-operation between the organizations and approved the elaboration of a free trade agreement, based on the existing bilateral accord signed between CARICOM and Costa Rica. Formal negotiations were inaugurated at a meeting of ministers of trade in August. Proposals to convene a third SICA-CARICOM summit meeting, in Nicaragua, were under consideration in 2009.

In May 2008 SICA heads of state and government met their Brazilian counterparts in San Salvador, El Salvador. The summit meeting reaffirmed the willingness of both sides to enhance political and economic co-operation with the grouping of Southern Common Market (Mercosur) countries and determined to establish mechanisms, in particular, to promote trade and political dialogue. Brazil was invited to become an observer of SICA.

In June 2009 the Council of Ministers agreed to admit Japan as an extra-regional observer of the grouping. The agreement was formalized with the Japanese Government in January 2010.

THE COMMONWEALTH

Address: Commonwealth Secretariat, Marlborough House, Pall Mall, London, SW1Y 5HX, United Kingdom.

Telephone: (20) 7747-6500; **fax:** (20) 7930-0827; **e-mail:** info@commonwealth.int; **internet:** www.thecommonwealth.org.

The Commonwealth is a voluntary association of 53 independent states (at August 2010), comprising about one-quarter of the world's population. It includes the United Kingdom and most of its former dependencies, and former dependencies of Australia and New Zealand (themselves Commonwealth countries). All Commonwealth countries accept Queen Elizabeth II as the symbol of the free association of the independent member nations and as such the Head of the Commonwealth.

MEMBERS IN SOUTH AMERICA AND THE CARIBBEAN

Antigua and Barbuda
Bahamas
Barbados
Belize
Dominica
Grenada
Guyana
Jamaica
Saint Christopher and Nevis
Saint Lucia
Saint Vincent and the Grenadines
Trinidad and Tobago
UK Overseas Territories:
Anguilla
Bermuda
British Virgin Islands
Cayman Islands
Falkland Islands
Montserrat
Turks and Caicos Islands

Organization

(August 2010)

The Commonwealth is not a federation: there is no central government nor are there any rigid contractual obligations such as bind members of the United Nations.

The Commonwealth has no written constitution but its members subscribe to the ideals of the Declaration of Commonwealth Principles unanimously approved by a meeting of heads of government in Singapore in 1971. Members also approved the Gleneagles Agreement concerning apartheid in sport (1977); the Lusaka Declaration on Racism and Racial Prejudice (1979); the Melbourne Declaration on relations between developed and developing countries (1981); the New Delhi Statement on Economic Action (1983); the Goa Declaration on International Security (1983); the Nassau Declaration on World Order (1985); the Commonwealth Accord on Southern Africa (1985); the Vancouver Declaration on World Trade (1987); the Okanagan Statement and Programme of Action on Southern Africa (1987); the Langkawi Declaration on the Environment (1989); the Kuala Lumpur Statement on Southern Africa (1989); the Harare Commonwealth Declaration (1991); the Ottawa Declaration on Women and Structural Adjustment (1991); the Limassol Statement on the Uruguay Round of multilateral trade negotiations (1993); the Millbrook Commonwealth Action Programme on the Harare Declaration (1995); the Edinburgh Commonwealth Economic Declaration (1997); the Fancourt Commonwealth Declaration on Globalization and People-centred Development (1999); the Coolum Declaration on the Commonwealth in the 21st Century: Continuity and Renewal (2002); the Aso Rock Commonwealth Declaration and Statement on Multilateral Trade (2003); the Malta Commonwealth Declaration on Networking for Development (2005); the Munyonyo Statement on Respect and Understanding (2007); the Marlborough House Statement on Reform of International Institutions (2008); and the Commonwealth Climate Change Declaration (2009).

MEETINGS OF HEADS OF GOVERNMENT

Commonwealth Heads of Government Meetings (CHOGMs) are private and informal and operate not by voting but by consensus. The emphasis is on consultation and exchange of views for co-operation. A communiqué is issued at the end of every meeting. Meetings are normally held every two years in different capitals in the Commonwealth. The 2009 meeting was held in Trinidad and Tobago, in November. The 2011 meeting was to be held in Perth, Australia, in October.

OTHER CONSULTATIONS

The Commonwealth Ministerial Action Group on the Harare Declaration (CMAG) was formed in 1995 to support democracy in member countries (see Activities, below). It comprises a group of nine ministers of foreign affairs, with rotating membership. In November 2009 the membership of CMAG was reconstituted for the ensuing two-year period, to comprise the ministers responsible for foreign affairs of Australia, Bangladesh, Ghana, Jamaica, Maldives, Namibia, New Zealand, Vanuatu and Trinidad and Tobago.

Since 1959 Commonwealth finance ministers have met in the week prior to the annual meetings of the IMF and the World Bank. Ministers responsible for civil society, education, the environment, foreign affairs, gender issues, health, law, tourism and youth also hold regular meetings.

Senior officials—cabinet secretaries, permanent secretaries to heads of government and others—meet regularly in the year between meetings of heads of government to provide continuity and to exchange views on various developments.

COMMONWEALTH SECRETARIAT

The Secretariat, established by Commonwealth heads of government in 1965, operates as an intergovernmental organization at the service of all Commonwealth countries. It organizes consultations between governments and runs programmes of co-operation. Meetings of heads of government, ministers and senior officials decide these programmes and provide overall direction. A Board of Governors, on which all eligible member governments are represented, meets annually to review the Secretariat's work and approve its budget. The Board is supported by an Executive Committee which convenes four times a year to monitor implementation of the Secretariat's work programme. The Secretariat is headed by a secretary-general, elected by heads of government.

In 2002 the Secretariat was restructured, with a view to strengthening the effectiveness of the organization to meet the priorities determined by the meeting of heads of government held in Coolum, Australia, in March 2002. Under the reorganization the number of deputy secretaries-general was reduced from three to two. Certain work divisions were amalgamated, while new units or sections, concerned with youth affairs, human rights and good offices, were created to strengthen further activities in those fields. Accordingly, the Secretariat's divisional structure is as follows: Legal and constitutional affairs; Political affairs; Corporate services; Communications and public affairs; Strategic planning and evaluation; Economic affairs; Governance and institutional development; Social transformation programmes; Youth affairs (from 2004); and Special advisory services. (Details of some of the divisions are given under Activities, below.) In addition there are units responsible for human rights and project management and referrals, and an Office of the Secretary-General.

The Secretariat's strategic plan for 2008/09–2011/12, approved by the Board of Governors in May 2008, set out two main, long-term objectives for the Commonwealth. The first, 'Peace and Democracy', was to support member countries in preventing or resolving conflicts, to strengthen democracy and the rule of law, and to achieve greater respect for human rights. The second, 'Pro-Poor Growth and Sustainable Development', was to support policies for economic growth and sustainable development, particularly for the benefit of the poorest people, in member countries. Four programmes were to facilitate the pursuit of the first objective: Good Offices for Peace; Democracy and Consensus Building; Rule of Law; and Human Rights. The second objective was to be pursued through the following four programmes: Public Sector Development; Economic Development; Environmentally Sustainable Development; and Human Development.

Secretary-General: Kamalesh Sharma (India).

Deputy Secretaries-General: Mmasekgoa Masire-Mwamba (Botswana), Ransford Smith (Jamaica).

Assistant Secretary-General for Corporate Affairs: Stephen Cutts (United Kingdom).

Activities

PROMOTING DEMOCRACY, HUMAN RIGHTS AND DEVELOPMENT

In October 1991 heads of government, meeting in Harare, Zimbabwe, issued the Harare Commonwealth Declaration, in which they reaffirmed their commitment to the Commonwealth Principles declared in 1971, and stressed the need to promote sustainable development and the alleviation of poverty. The Declaration placed emphasis on the promotion of democracy and respect for human rights and resolved to strengthen the Commonwealth's capacity to assist countries in entrenching democratic practices. In November 1995 Commonwealth heads of government, convened in New Zealand, formulated and adopted the Millbrook Commonwealth Action Programme on the Harare Declaration, to promote adherence by member countries to the fundamental principles of democracy and human rights (as proclaimed in the 1991 Declaration). The Programme incorporated a framework of measures to be pursued in support of democratic processes and institutions, and actions to be taken in response to violations of the Harare Declaration principles, in particular the unlawful removal of a democratically-elected government. A Commonwealth Ministerial Action Group on the Harare Declaration (CMAG) was to be established to implement this process and to assist the member country involved to comply with the Harare principles. On the basis of this Programme, the leaders suspended Nigeria from the Commonwealth with immediate effect, following the execution by that country's military Government of nine environmental and human rights protesters and a series of other violations of human rights. The meeting determined to expel Nigeria from the Commonwealth if no 'demonstrable progress' had been made towards the establishment of a democratic authority by the time of the next summit meeting. In addition, the Programme formulated measures to promote sustainable development in member countries, which was considered to be an important element in sustaining democracy, and to facilitate consensus-building within the international community.

In December 1995 CMAG convened for its inaugural meeting in London, United Kingdom, and considered efforts to restore democratic government in the three Commonwealth countries then under military regimes, i.e. The Gambia, Nigeria and Sierra Leone. At the second meeting of the Group, in April 1996, ministers commended the conduct of presidential and parliamentary elections in Sierra Leone and the announcement by The Gambia's military leaders that there would be a transition to civilian rule. In June a three-member CMAG delegation visited The Gambia to reaffirm Commonwealth support of the transition process in that country and to identify possible areas of further Commonwealth assistance. In August the Gambian authorities issued a decree removing the ban on political activities and parties, although shortly afterwards they prohibited certain parties and candidates involved in political life prior to the military take-over from contesting the elections. CMAG recommended that in such circumstances no Commonwealth observers should be sent to either the presidential or parliamentary elections, which were held in September 1996 and January 1997 respectively. Following the restoration of a civilian Government in early 1997, CMAG requested the Commonwealth Secretary-General to extend technical assistance to The Gambia in order to consolidate the democratic transition process. In April 1996 it was noted that the human rights situation in Nigeria had continued to deteriorate. CMAG, having pursued unsuccessful efforts to initiate dialogue with the Nigerian authorities, outlined a series of punitive and restrictive measures (including visa restrictions on members of the administration, a cessation of sporting contacts and an embargo on the export of armaments) that it would recommend for collective Commonwealth action in order to exert further pressure for reform in Nigeria. Following a meeting of a senior delegation of the Nigerian Government and CMAG in June, the Group agreed to postpone the implementation of the sanctions, pending progress on the dialogue. (Canada, however, determined, unilaterally, to impose the measures with immediate effect; the United Kingdom did so in accordance with a decision of the European Union to implement limited sanctions against Nigeria.) A proposed CMAG mission to Nigeria was postponed from August until November, owing to restrictions imposed by the military authorities on access to political detainees and other civilian activists in that country. In October 1997 Commonwealth heads of government endorsed CMAG's recommendation that the imposition of sanctions against Nigeria be held in abeyance, pending the scheduled completion of a transition programme towards democracy by October 1998. In October 1998 CMAG, convened for its 10th formal meeting, acknowledged Gen. Abdulsalam Abubakar's efforts towards restoring a democratic government and recommended that member states begin to remove sanctions against Nigeria and that it resume participation in certain Commonwealth activities. The Commonwealth Secretary-General subsequently announced a programme of technical assistance to support Nigeria in the planning and conduct of democratic elections. Staff teams from the Commonwealth Secretariat observed local government, and state and governorship elections, held in December and in January 1999, respectively. A Commonwealth Observer Group was also dispatched to Nigeria to monitor preparations and conduct of legislative and presidential elections, held in February. While the Group reported several irregularities in the conduct of the polling, it confirmed that, in general, the conditions had existed for free and fair elections and that the elections were a legitimate basis for the transition of power to a democratic, civilian government. In April CMAG voted to readmit Nigeria to full membership on 29 May, upon the installation of the new civilian administration.

In July 1997 the Group CMAG reiterated the Commonwealth Secretary-General's condemnation of a military coup in Sierra Leone in May, and decided that the country's participation in meetings of the Commonwealth should be suspended pending the restoration of a democratic government. In March 1998 CMAG commended the efforts of the Economic Community of West African States (ECOWAS) in restoring the democratically-elected Government of President Ahmed Tejan Kabbah in Sierra Leone, and agreed to remove all restrictions on Sierra Leone's participation in Commonwealth activities. Later in that month, a representative mission of CMAG visited Sierra Leone to express its support for Kabbah's administration and to consider the country's needs in its process of reconstruction. At the CMAG meeting held in October members agreed that Sierra Leone should no longer be considered under the Group's mandate; however, they urged the Secretary-General to continue to assist that country in the process of national reconciliation and to facilitate negotiations with opposition forces to ensure a lasting cease-fire. A Special Envoy of the Secretary-General was appointed to co-operate with the UN, ECOWAS and the Organization of African Union (OAU, now African Union—AU) in monitoring the implementation of the Sierra Leone peace process, and the Commonwealth supported the rebuilding of the Sierra Leone police force. In September 2001 CMAG recommended that Sierra Leone be removed from its remit, but that the Secretary-General should continue to monitor developments there.

In 1999 the Commonwealth Secretary-General appointed a Special Envoy to broker an agreement in order to end a civil dispute in Honiara, Solomon Islands. An accord was signed in June, and it was envisaged that the Commonwealth would monitor its implementation. In October a Commonwealth Multinational Police Peace Monitoring Group was stationed in Solomon Islands; this was renamed the Commonwealth Multinational Police Assistance Group in February 2000. Following further internal unrest, however, the Group was disbanded. In June CMAG determined to send a new mission to Solomon Islands in order to facilitate negotiations between the opposing parties, to convey the Commonwealth's concern and to offer assistance. The Commonwealth welcomed the peace accord concluded in Solomon Islands in October, and extended its support to the International Peace Monitoring Team that was established to oversee implementation of the peace accords. CMAG welcomed the conduct of parliamentary elections held in Solomon Islands in December 2001. CMAG removed Solomon Islands from its agenda in December 2003 but was to continue to receive reports from the Secretary-General on future developments.

In mid-October 1999 a special meeting of CMAG was convened to consider the overthrow of the democratically-elected Government of Pakistan in a military coup. The meeting condemned the action as a violation of Commonwealth principles and urged the new authorities to declare a timetable for the return to democratic rule. CMAG also resolved to send a four-member delegation to discuss this future course of action with the military regime. Pakistan was suspended from participation in meetings of the Commonwealth with immediate effect. The suspension, pending the restoration of a democratic government, was endorsed by heads of government, meeting in November, who requested that CMAG keep the situation in Pakistan under review.

In November 1999 heads of government also agreed to establish a new ministerial group on Guyana and to reconvene a ministerial committee on Belize, in order to facilitate dialogue in ongoing territorial disputes with neighbouring countries.

In June 2000, following the overthrow in May of the Fijian Government by a group of armed civilians, and the subsequent illegal detention of members of the elected administration, CMAG suspended Fiji's participation in meetings of the Commonwealth pending the restoration of democratic rule. In September, upon the request of CMAG, the Secretary-General appointed a Special Envoy to support efforts towards political dialogue and a return to democratic rule in Fiji. The Special Envoy undertook his first visit in December. In December 2001, following the staging of democratic legislative elections in August–September, Fiji was readmitted to Commonwealth meetings on the recommendation of CMAG. Fiji was removed from CMAG's agenda in May 2004, although the Group determined to continue to note developments there, as judgments were still pending in the Fiji Supreme Court on unresolved matters concerning the democratic process. In December 2006, following the overthrow of the Fijian Government by the military, an extraordinary meeting of CMAG determined that Fiji should once again be suspended from meetings of the Commonwealth, pending the reinstatement of democratic governance. In September 2007 the Group urged the Fijian authorities to hold a democratic general election by March 2009 and determined to keep the situation in that country under review; the March 2009 election deadline was not, however, met by the Fijian authorities. CMAG expressed support at the March meeting for ongoing political dialogue in Fiji, jointly mediated by the Commonwealth and the UN. In April the Commonwealth Secretary-General condemned the unconstitutional conduct of the Fijian authorities in abrogating the Constitution, dismissing the judiciary and announcing that democratic elections were to be postponed to 2014, following a judgment by Fiji's Court of Appeal declaring the appointment of the current interim government to be unlawful and urging the prompt restoration of democracy. Meeting at the end of July, CMAG demanded that the Fijian regime reactivate by 1 September 2009 the Commonwealth- and UN-mediated political dialogue process, leading to the staging of elections no later than October 2010. At the beginning of September 2009 the Commonwealth Secretary-General announced that the Fijian regime had not acted to meet CMAG's demands and that Fiji's Commonwealth membership was consequently fully suspended with immediate effect.

In March 2001 CMAG resolved to send a ministerial mission to Zimbabwe, in order to relay to the government the Commonwealth's concerns at the ongoing violence and abuses of human rights in that country, as well as to discuss the conduct of parliamentary elections and extend technical assistance. The mission was rejected by the Zimbabwe Government, which queried the basis for CMAG's intervention in the affairs of an elected administration. In September, under the auspices of a group of Commonwealth foreign ministers partly derived from CMAG, the Zimbabwe Government signed the Abuja Agreement, which provided for the cessation of illegal occupations of white-owned farms and the resumption of the rule of law, in return for financial assistance to support the ongoing process of land reform in that country. In January 2002 CMAG expressed strong concern at the continuing violence and political intimidation in Zimbabwe. The summit of Commonwealth heads of government convened in early March (see below) also expressed concern at the situation in Zimbabwe, and, having decided on the principle that CMAG should be permitted to engage with any member Government deemed to be in breach of the organization's core values, mandated a Commonwealth Chairperson's Committee on Zimbabwe to determine appropriate action should an impending presidential election (scheduled to be held during that month) be found not to have been conducted freely and fairly. Following the publication by a Commonwealth observer team of an unfavourable report on the conduct of the election, the Committee decided to suspend Zimbabwe from meetings of the Commonwealth for one year. In March 2003 the Committee concluded that the suspension should remain in force pending consideration by the next summit of heads of government.

In March 2002, meeting in Coolum, near Brisbane, Australia, Commonwealth heads of government adopted the Coolum Declaration on the Commonwealth in the 21st Century: Continuity and Renewal, which reiterated commitment to the organization's principles and values. Leaders at the meeting condemned all forms of terrorism and endorsed a Plan of Action for combating international terrorism, establishing a Commonwealth Committee on Terrorism, convened at ministerial level, to oversee the implementation of the Plan. The leaders welcomed the Millennium Development Goals (MDGs) adopted by the UN General Assembly; requested the Secretary-General to constitute an expert group on implementing the objectives of the Fancourt Commonwealth Declaration on Globalization and People-Centred Development (see Economic Co-operation, below); pledged continued support for small states; and urged renewed efforts to combat the spread of HIV/AIDS. They also endorsed a Commonwealth Local Government Good Practice Scheme, to be managed by the Commonwealth Local Government Forum (established in 1995). The heads of government adopted a report on the future of the Commonwealth drafted by the High Level Review Group. The document recommended strengthening the Commonwealth's role in conflict prevention and resolution and support of democratic practices; enhancing the 'good offices' role of the Secretary-General; better promoting member states' economic and development needs; strengthening the organization's role in facilitating member states' access to international assistance; and promoting increased access to modern information and communications technologies. The meeting expanded CMAG's mandate to enable the Group to consider action against serious violations of the Commonwealth's core values perpetrated by elected administrations (such as that in Zimbabwe, see above) as well as by military regimes.

A Commonwealth team of observers dispatched to monitor legislative and provincial elections that were held in Pakistan, in October 2002, found them to have been well-organized and conducted in a largely transparent manner. The team made several recommendations on institutional and procedural issues. CMAG subsequently expressed concern over the promulgation of new legislation in Pakistan following the imposition earlier in the year of a number of extra-constitutional measures. CMAG determined that Pakistan should continue to be suspended from meetings of the Commonwealth, pending a review of the role and functioning of its democratic institutions. Pakistan's progress in establishing democratic institutions was welcomed by a meeting of CMAG in May 2003.

In November 2002 a Commonwealth Expert Group on Papua New Guinea, established in the previous month to review the electoral process in that country (in view of unsatisfactory legislative elections that were conducted there in July), made several recommendations aimed at enhancing the future management of the electoral process.

In December 2003 the meeting of heads of government, held in Abuja, Nigeria, resolved to maintain the suspension of Pakistan and Zimbabwe from participation in Commonwealth meetings. President Mugabe of Zimbabwe responded by announcing his country's immediate withdrawal from the Commonwealth and alleging a pro-Western bias within the grouping. Support for Zimbabwe's position was declared by a number of members, including South Africa, Mozambique, Namibia and Zambia. A Commonwealth committee, consisting of six heads of government, was established to monitor the situation in Zimbabwe.

In concluding the 2003 meeting heads of government issued the Aso Rock Commonwealth Declaration, which emphasized their commitment to strengthening development and democracy, and incorporated clear objectives in support of these goals. Priority areas identified included efforts to eradicate poverty and attain the MDGs, to strengthen democratic institutions, empower women, promote the involvement of civil society, combat corruption and recover assets (for which a working group was to be established), facilitate finance for development, address the spread of HIV/AIDS and other diseases, combat illicit trafficking in human beings, and promote education. The leaders also adopted a separate statement on multilateral trade, in particular in support of the stalled Doha Round of World Trade Organization negotiations.

In response to the earthquake and tsunami that devastated coastal areas of several Indian Ocean countries in late December 2004, the Commonwealth Secretary-General appealed for assistance from Commonwealth Governments for the mobilization of emergency humanitarian relief. In early January 2005 the Secretariat dispatched a Disaster Relief Co-ordinator to the Maldives to assess the needs of that country and to co-ordinate ongoing relief and rehabilitation activities, and later in that month the Secretariat sent emergency medical doctors from other member states to the Maldives. In mid-January, meeting during the fifth Summit of the Alliance of Small Island States, in Port Louis, Mauritius, the Secretaries-General of the Commonwealth, the Caribbean Community and Common Market (CARICOM), the Pacific Islands Forum and the Indian Ocean Commission determined to take collective action to strengthen the disaster-preparedness and response capacities of their member countries in the Caribbean, Pacific and Indian Ocean areas.

In May 2004 Pakistan was readmitted to the Commonwealth. However, CMAG urged the prompt separation of the military and civilian offices held by the President Musharraf, deeming this arrangement to be undemocratic. In February 2005 CMAG expressed serious concern that Musharraf had failed to relinquish the role of chief of army staff. Noting President Musharraf's own undertaking not to continue as chief of army staff beyond 2007, the Group stated its view that the two offices should not be combined in one person beyond the end (in that year) of the current presidential term. In November 2005, following Musharraf's re-election as President of Pakistan in early October, CMAG condemned the recent abrogation of Pakistan's Constitution and the institution there of a non-constitutional state of emergency; expressed grave concern at the recent dismissal of the Chief Justice and several other members of the judiciary and their placement under house arrest, and at other actions taken against lawyers, opposition politicians and civil society leaders, and at the suspension of all private media broadcasts and restrictions on the press; and noted with alarm a recent legislation that retrospectively gave military courts the right to try civilians on charges of 'anti-national activities'. While welcoming an announcement by President Musharraf that parliamentary elections would be staged in early 2008, CMAG maintained that such elections would only be credible if the state of emergency were revoked and constitutional rights restored. CMAG also noted with concern that Musharraf continued to retain the role of chief of army staff. The Group urged the Government of Pakistan to fulfil its obligations in accordance with Commonwealth principles through the implementation of the following measures: immediate repeal of the state of emergency, immediate release of political party leaders, lawyers, journalists and other activists detained under the state of emergency, and full restoration of the Constitution and of the independence of the judiciary; and for President Musharraf to relinquish his role as chief of army staff. Meeting on 22 November CMAG noted that these measures had not been implemented, as a consequence of which Pakistan was once again suspended from the Councils of the Commonwealth 'pending restoration of democracy and rule of law in the country'. President Musharraf relinquished his command of the Pakistan military at the end of November and the state of emergency was lifted in the following month. Meeting in May 2008 CMAG commended the transition to a democratically-elected government in Pakistan, though it urged reform of the electoral system, and welcomed recent positive actions made by the Pakistan regime, including the relaxation of restrictions on the media and the release of political detainees. CMAG concluded that Pakistan should be readmitted to meetings of the Councils of the Commonwealth, and requested the Secretary-General to continue to provide technical assistance to the Pakistan Government towards strengthening the country's democratic institutions and processes.

The 2007 meeting of Commonwealth heads of government, convened in Kampala, Uganda, in November, issued the Munyonyo Statement on Respect and Understanding, which commended the work of the Commonwealth Commission on Respect and Understanding (established in 2005) and endorsed its recently published report entitled *Civil Paths to Peace* aimed at building tolerance and understanding of diversity.

In November 2009 Commonwealth heads of government, meeting in Trinidad and Tobago, welcomed recent progress in the discussion of border disputes between Belize and Guatemala, and between Guyana and Venezuela. They expressed support for negotiations on the reunification of Cyprus, initiated in 2008, and welcomed the recent agreement on power-sharing in Zimbabwe. They urged the renewal of commitment to the non-proliferation of nuclear weapons at the next Non-Proliferation Treaty review conference (convened in May 2010), and the negotiation of a comprehensive Arms Trade Treaty (on conventional weapons) at a conference to be held in 2012. Heads of government also urged the conclusion of a UN treaty on international terrorism and discussed combating piracy and human trafficking. In July 2010, in view of a decision of the 2009 heads of government meeting, a new Commonwealth Eminent Persons Group (EPG) was inaugurated; the EPG was to make recommendations on means of strengthening the organization. During July 2010 the Commonwealth Secretariat hosted the first Small States Biennial Conference, comprising representatives of small states from the Africa, Asia-Pacific and Caribbean regions.

Political Affairs Division: assists consultation among member governments on international and Commonwealth matters of common interest. In association with host governments, it organizes the meetings of heads of government and senior officials. The Division services committees and special groups set up by heads of government dealing with political matters. The Secretariat has observer status at the United Nations, and the Division manages a joint office in New York to enable small states, which would otherwise be unable to afford facilities there, to maintain a presence at the United Nations. The Division monitors political developments in the Commonwealth and international progress in such matters as disarmament and the Law of the Sea. It also undertakes research on matters of common interest to member governments, and reports back to them. The Division is involved in diplomatic training and consular co-operation.

In 1990 Commonwealth heads of government mandated the Division to support the promotion of democracy by monitoring the preparations for and conduct of parliamentary, presidential or other elections in member countries at the request of national governments. Commonwealth observer groups were dispatched to observe legislative elections in Sri Lanka and Saint Christopher and Nevis in January 2010, in the Solomon Islands in July, and in Rwanda in August.

Under the reorganization of the Secretariat in 2002 a Good Offices Section was established within the Division to strengthen and support the activities of the Secretary-General in addressing political conflict in member states and in assisting countries to adhere to the principles of the Harare Declaration. The Secretary-General's good offices may involve discreet 'behind the scenes' diplomacy to prevent or resolve conflict and assist other international efforts to promote political stability. In 2010 Special Envoys of the Secretary-General were active in Guyana, Fiji and Tonga.

Human Rights Unit: undertakes activities in support of the Commonwealth's commitment to the promotion and protection of fundamental human rights. It develops programmes, publishes human rights materials, co-operates with other organizations working in the field of human rights, in particular within the UN system, advises the Secretary-General, and organizes seminars and meetings of experts; it provides training for police forces, magistrates and government officials in awareness of human rights. The Unit aims to integrate human rights standards within all divisions of the Secretariat.

Legal and Constitutional Affairs Division: promotes and facilitates co-operation and the exchange of information among member governments on legal matters and assists in combating financial and organized crime, in particular transborder criminal activities. It administers, jointly with the Commonwealth of Learning (see below), a distance training programme for legislative draftsmen and assists governments to reform national laws to meet the obligations of international conventions. The Division organizes the triennial meeting of ministers, Attorneys General and senior ministry officials concerned with the legal systems in Commonwealth countries. It has also initiated four Commonwealth schemes for co-operation on extradition, the protection of material cultural heritage, mutual assistance in criminal matters and the transfer of convicted offenders within the Commonwealth. It liaises with the Commonwealth Magistrates' and Judges' Association, the Commonwealth Legal Education Association, the Commonwealth Lawyers' Association (with which it helps to prepare the triennial Commonwealth Law Conference for the practising profession), the Commonwealth Association of Legislative Counsel, and with other international non-governmental organizations. The Division provides in-house legal advice for the Secretariat. The Commonwealth Law Bulletin, published four times a year, reports on legal developments in and beyond the Commonwealth. The Commonwealth Human Rights Law Digest (three a year) contains details of decisions relating to human rights cases from across the Commonwealth.

ECONOMIC AND ENVIRONMENTAL CO-OPERATION

In May 1998 the Commonwealth Secretary-General appealed to the Group of Eight industrialized nations (G8) to accelerate and expand the initiative to ease the debt burden of the most heavily indebted poor countries (HIPCs—see World Bank and IMF). In October Commonwealth finance ministers reiterated their appeal to international financial institutions to accelerate the HIPC initiative. The meeting also issued a Commonwealth Statement on the global economic crisis and endorsed proposals to help to counter the difficulties experienced by several countries. These measures included a mechanism to enable countries to suspend payments on all short-term financial obligations at a time of emergency without defaulting, assistance to governments to attract private capital and to manage capital market volatility, and the development of international codes of conduct regarding financial and monetary policies and corporate governance. In March 1999 the Commonwealth Secretariat hosted a joint IMF-World Bank conference to review the HIPC scheme and initiate a process of reform. In November Commonwealth heads of government, meeting in South Africa, declared their support for measures undertaken by the World Bank and IMF to enhance the HIPC initiative. At the end of an informal retreat the leaders adopted the Fancourt Commonwealth Declaration on Globalization and People-Centred Development, which emphasized the need for a more equitable spread of wealth generated by the process of globalization, and expressed a renewed commitment to the elimination of all forms of discrimination, the promotion of people-centred development and capacity-building, and efforts to ensure that developing countries benefit from future multilateral trade liberalization measures. In June 2002 the Commonwealth Secretary-General urged more generous funding of the HIPC initiative. Meetings of ministers of finance from Commonwealth member countries participating in the HIPC initiative are convened twice a year, as the Commonwealth Ministerial Debt Sustainability Forum. The Secretariat aims to assist HIPCs and other small economies through its Debt Recording and Management System (DRMS), which was first used in 1985 and updated in 2002; in July 2010 Liberia became the 60th country to join the System. In July 2005 the Commonwealth Secretary-General welcomed an initiative of the G8 to eliminate the debt of those HIPCs that had reached their completion point in the process, in addition to a commitment substantially to increase aid to Africa.

In February 1998 the Commonwealth Secretariat hosted a meeting of intergovernmental organizations to promote co-operation between small island states and the formulation of a unified policy approach to international fora. A second meeting was convened in March 2001, where discussions focused on the forthcoming WTO ministerial meeting and OECD's Harmful Tax Competition Initiative. In September 2000 Commonwealth finance ministers, meeting in Malta, reviewed the OECD initiative and agreed that the measures, affecting many member countries with offshore financial centres, should not be imposed on governments. The ministers mandated the involvement of the Commonwealth Secretariat in efforts to resolve the dispute; a joint working group was subsequently established by the Secretariat with the OECD. In April 2002 a meeting on international co-operation in the financial services sector, attended by representatives of international and regional organizations, donors and senior officials from Commonwealth countries, was held under Commonwealth auspices in Saint Lucia. In September 2005 Commonwealth finance ministers, meeting in Barbados, considered new guidelines for Public Financial Management Reform.

In November 2005 Commonwealth heads of government issued the Malta Declaration on Networking the Commonwealth for Development, expressing their commitment to making available to all the benefits of new technologies and to using information technology networks to enhance the effectiveness of the Commonwealth in supporting development. The meeting endorsed a new Commonwealth Action Programme for the Digital Divide and approved the establishment of a special fund to enable implementation of the programme's objectives. Accordingly a Commonwealth Connects programme was established in August 2006 to develop partnerships and help to strengthen the use of and access to information technology in all Commonwealth countries. The 2005 Heads of Government Meeting also issued the Valletta Statement on Multilateral Trade, emphasizing their concerns that the Doha Round of WTO negotiations proceed steadily, on a development-oriented agenda, to a successful conclusion and reiterating their objectives of achieving a rules-based and equitable international trading system. A separate statement drew attention to the specific needs and challenges of small states and urged continued financial and technical support, in particular for those affected by natural disasters.

The Commonwealth Climate Change Action Plan, adopted by heads of government in November 2007, acknowledged that climate change posed a serious threat to the very existence of some small island states within the Commonwealth, and to the low-lying coastal areas of others. It offered unqualified support for the UN Framework Convention on Climate Change, and recognized the need to overcome technical, economic and policy-making barriers to reducing carbon emissions, to using renewable energy, and to increasing energy efficiency. The Plan undertook to assist developing member states in international negotiations on climate change; to support improved land use management, including the use of forest resources; to investigate the 'carbon footprint' of agricultural exports from member countries; to increase support for management of natural disasters in member countries; and to provide technical assistance to help least-developed members and small states to assess the implications of climate change and adapt accordingly.

In June 2008 the Commonwealth issued the Marlborough House Statement on Reform of International Institutions, declaring that ongoing global financial turbulence and soaring food and fuel prices highlighted the poor responsiveness of some international organizations mandated to promote economic stability, and determining to identify underlying principles and actions required to reform the international system. In November 2009 heads of government reiterated the need for reform in the UN system, demanding greater representation for developing countries in international economic decision-making, with particular reference to the IMF and the World

Bank. They expressed concern that many Commonwealth countries were falling behind the MDG targets, and resolved to strengthen existing networks of co-operation: in particular, they undertook to take measures to improve the quality of data used in policy-making, and to strengthen the links between research and policy-making. A new Commonwealth Partnership Platform Portal was to provide practical support for sharing ideas and best practices. Heads of government also undertook to promote investment in science, technology and innovation.

Economic Affairs Division: organizes and services the annual meetings of Commonwealth ministers of finance and the ministerial group on small states and assists in servicing the biennial meetings of heads of government and periodic meetings of environment ministers. It engages in research and analysis on economic issues of interest to member governments and organizes seminars and conferences of government officials and experts. The Division actively supports developing Commonwealth countries to participate in the Doha Round of multilateral trade negotiations and is assisting the ACP group of countries to negotiate economic partnership agreements with the European Union. It continues to help developing countries to strengthen their links with international capital markets and foreign investors. The Division also services groups of experts on economic affairs that have been commissioned by governments to report on, among other things, protectionism; obstacles to the North-South negotiating process; reform of the international financial and trading system; the debt crisis; management of technological change; the impact of change on the development process; environmental issues; women and structural adjustment; and youth unemployment. A separate section within the Division addresses the specific needs of small states and provides technical assistance. The work of the section covers a range of issues including trade, vulnerability, environment, politics and economics. A Secretariat Task Force services a Commonwealth Ministerial Group of Small States which was established in 1993 to provide strategic direction in addressing the concerns of small states and to mobilize support for action and assistance within the international community. The Economic Affairs Division also co-ordinates the Secretariat's environmental work and manages the Iwokrama International Centre for Rainforest Conservation and Development.

The Division supported the establishment of a Commonwealth Private Investment Initiative (CPII) to mobilize capital, on a regional basis, for investment in newly-privatized companies and in small and medium-sized businesses in the private sector. The first regional fund under the CPII, the Commonwealth Africa Investment Fund (Comafin), was operational during the period July 1996–end-December 2006, and made 19 investments (of which three were subsequently written off) to assist businesses across nine sectors in seven countries in sub-Saharan Africa. A Pan-Commonwealth Africa Partners Fund was launched in 2002, which aimed to help existing businesses expand to become regional or pan-African in scope. In August 1997 an investment fund for the Pacific Islands (known as the Kula Fund) was launched, with an initial capital of $15.0m.; a successor fund (Kula Fund II), with financing of some $20m., was launched in October 2005, with the aim of injecting capital into the smaller Pacific Island countries. A $200m. South Asia Regional Fund (SARF) was established at the heads of government meeting in October 1997. In October 1998 the Tiona Fund for the Commonwealth Caribbean was inaugurated, at a meeting of Commonwealth finance ministers; this was subsequently absorbed into the Caribbean Investment Fund (established in 1993 by member states of CARICOM).

SOCIAL WELFARE

Social Transformation Programmes Division: consists of three sections concerned with education, gender and health.

The **Education Section** arranges specialist seminars, workshops and co-operative projects, and commissions studies in areas identified by ministers of education, whose meetings it also services. Its areas of work include improving the quality of and access to basic education; strengthening science, technology and mathematics education in formal and non-formal areas of education; improving the quality of management in institutions of higher learning and basic education; improving the performance of teachers; strengthening examination assessment systems; and promoting the movement of students between Commonwealth countries. The Section also promotes the elimination of gender disparities in education, support for education in difficult circumstances, such as areas affected by conflict or natural disasters, and mitigating the impact of HIV and AIDS on education.It attempts to address the problems of scale particular to smaller member countries, and encourages collaboration between governments, the private sector and other non-governmental organizations.

The **Gender Affairs Section** is responsible for the implementation of the Commonwealth Plan of Action for Gender Equality, covering the period 2005–15, which succeeded the Commonwealth Plan of Action on Gender and Development (adopted in 1995 and updated in 2000). The Plan of Action supports efforts towards achieving the MDGs, and the objectives of gender equality adopted by the 1995 Beijing Declaration and Platform for Action and the follow-up Beijing + 5 review conference, held in 2000, and Beijing + 10 in 2005. Gender equality, poverty eradication, promotion of human rights, and strengthening democracy are recognized as intrinsically inter-related, and the Plan has a particular focus on the advancement of gender mainstreaming in the following areas: democracy, peace and conflict; human rights and law; poverty eradication and economic empowerment; and HIV/AIDS.

The **Health Section** organizes ministerial, technical and expert group meetings and workshops, to promote co-operation on health matters, and the exchange of health information and expertise. The Section commissions relevant studies and provides professional and technical advice to member countries and to the Secretariat. It also supports the work of regional health organizations and promotes health for all people in Commonwealth countries.

The **Youth Affairs Division**, reporting directly to a Deputy Secretary-General, was established within the Secretariat in 2002. The unit acquired divisional status in 2004.

The Division administers the Commonwealth Youth Programme (CYP), which was initiated in 1973 to promote the involvement of young people in the economic and social development of their countries. The CYP, funded through separate voluntary contributions from governments, was awarded a budget of £2.8m. for 2009/10. The Programme's activities are in three areas: Youth Enterprise and Sustainable Livelihoods; Governance, Development and Youth Networks; and Youth Work Education and Training. Regional centres are located in Zambia (for Africa), India (for Asia), Guyana (for the Caribbean), and Solomon Islands (for the Pacific). The Programme administers a Youth Study Fellowship scheme, a Youth Project Fund, a Youth Exchange Programme (in the Caribbean), and a Youth Development Awards Scheme. It also holds conferences and seminars, carries out research and disseminates information. The CYP Diploma in Youth Development Work is offered by partner institutions in 45 countries, primarily through distance education. The Commonwealth Youth Credit Initiative, initiated in 1995, provides funds and advice for young entrepreneurs setting up small businesses. A Plan of Action for Youth Empowerment, covering the period 2007–15, was approved by the sixth meeting of Commonwealth ministers responsible for youth affairs, held in Nassau, Bahamas, in May 2006. The first Commonwealth Youth Games was held in Edinburgh, United Kingdom in 2000, and has been convened every four years since. The seventh Commonwealth Youth Forum was convened in Trinidad and Tobago, in November 2009.

TECHNICAL ASSISTANCE

Commonwealth Fund for Technical Co-operation (CFTC): f. 1971 to facilitate the exchange of skills between member countries and to promote economic and social development; it is administered by the Commonwealth Secretariat and financed by voluntary subscriptions from member governments. The CFTC responds to requests from member governments for technical assistance, such as the provision of experts for short- or medium-term projects, advice on economic or legal matters, and training programmes. Public-sector development, allowing member states to build on their capacities, is the principal element in CFTC activities. This includes assistance for improvement of supervision and combating corruption; improving economic management, for example by advising on exports and investment promotion; strengthening democratic institutions, such as electoral commissions; and improvement of education and health policies. The CFTC also administers the Langkawi awards for the study of environmental issues, which is funded by the Canadian Government; the CFTC budget for 2009/10 amounted to £29.2m, supplemented by external resources through partnerships.

CFTC activities are mainly implemented by the following divisions:

Governance and Institutional Development Division: strengthens good governance in member countries, through advice, training and other expertise in order to build capacity in national public institutions. The Division administers the Commonwealth Service Abroad Programme (CSAP), which is funded by the CFTC. The Programme extends short-term technical assistance through highly qualified volunteers. The main objectives of the scheme are to provide expertise, training and exposure to new technologies and practices, to promote technology transfers and sharing of experiences and knowledge, and to support community workshops and other local activities.

Special Advisory Services Division: provides advice and technical assistance in four principal areas: debt management; economic and legal services; enterprise and agriculture; and trade.

Finance

The Secretariat's budget for 2009/10 amounted to £15.0m. Member governments meet the cost of the Secretariat through subscriptions on a scale related to income and population.

Publications

Advisory (annual newsletter of the Special Advisory Services Division).

Global (electronic magazine).

Commonwealth News (weekly e-mail newsletter).

Report of the Commonwealth Secretary-General (every 2 years).

Numerous reports, studies and papers (catalogue available).

Commonwealth Organizations

(in the United Kingdom, unless otherwise stated)

The two principal intergovernmental organizations established by Commonwealth member states, apart from the Commonwealth Secretariat itself, are the Commonwealth Foundation and the Commonwealth of Learning. In 2010 there were nearly 90 other professional or advocacy organizations bearing the Commonwealth's name and associated with or accredited to the Commonwealth, a selection of which are listed below.

PRINCIPAL INTERGOVERNMENTAL ORGANIZATIONS

Commonwealth Foundation: Marlborough House, Pall Mall, London, SW1Y 5HY; tel. (20) 7930-3783; fax (20) 7839-8157; e-mail geninfo@commonwealth.int; internet www.commonwealthfoundation.com; f. 1966; intergovernmental body promoting people-to-people interaction, and collaboration within the non-governmental sector of the Commonwealth; supports non-governmental organizations, professional associations and Commonwealth arts and culture; awards an annual Commonwealth Writers' Prize; funds are provided by Commonwealth govts; Chair. SIMONE DE COMARMOND (Seychelles); Dir Dr MARK COLLINS (United Kingdom); publ. *Commonwealth People* (quarterly).

Commonwealth of Learning (COL): 1055 West Hastings St, Suite 1200, Vancouver, BC V6E 2E9, Canada; tel. (604) 775-8200; fax (604) 775-8210; e-mail info@col.org; internet www.col.org; f. 1987 by Commonwealth Heads of Government to promote the devt and sharing of distance education and open learning resources, including materials, expertise and technologies, throughout the Commonwealth and in other countries; implements and assists with national and regional educational programmes; acts as consultant to international agencies and national governments; conducts seminars and studies on specific educational needs; core financing for COL is provided by Commonwealth governments on a voluntary basis; COL had a budget of C $11.2m. for the two-year period 2009–10; Pres. and CEO Sir JOHN DANIEL (Canada/UK); publs *Connections, EdTech News*.

The following represents a selection of other Commonwealth organizations:

ADMINISTRATION AND PLANNING

Commonwealth Association for Public Administration and Management (CAPAM): 1075 Bay St, Suite 402, Toronto, ON M5S 2B1, Canada; tel. (416) 920-3337; fax (416) 920-6574; e-mail capam@capam.org; internet www.capam.org; f. 1994; aims to promote sound management of the public sector in Commonwealth countries and to assist those countries undergoing political or financial reforms; an international awards programme to reward innovation within the public sector was introduced in 1997, and is awarded every 2 years; more than 1,200 individual mems and 80 institutional memberships in some 80 countries; Pres. GERALDINE FRASER-MOLEKETI (South Africa); Exec. Dir and CEO DAVID WAUNG.

Commonwealth Association of Planners: c/o Royal Town Planning Institute in Scotland, 57 Melville St, Edinburgh, EH3 7HL; tel. (131) 226-1959; fax (131) 226-1909; e-mail annette.odonnell@rtpi.org.uk; internet www.commonwealth-planners.org; aims to develop urban and regional planning in Commonwealth countries, to meet the challenges of urbanization and the sustainable development of human settlements.

Commonwealth Local Government Forum: 16A Northumberland Ave, London, WC2N 5AP; tel. (20) 7389-1490; fax (20) 7389-1499; e-mail info@clgf.org.uk; works to promote democratic local government in Commonwealth countries, and to encourage good practice through conferences, programmes, research and the provision of information; regional offices in Fiji, India and South Africa.

AGRICULTURE AND FORESTRY

Commonwealth Forestry Association: Crib, Dinchope, Craven Arms, Shropshire, SY7 9JJ; tel. (1588) 672868; fax (870) 0116645; e-mail cfa@cfa-international.org; internet www.cfa-international.org; f. 1921; produces, collects and circulates information relating to world forestry and promotes good management, use and conservation of forests and forest lands throughout the world; mems: 1,200; Pres. DAVID BILLS (Australia/UK); publs *International Forestry Review* (quarterly), *Commonwealth Forestry News* (quarterly), *Commonwealth Forestry Handbook* (irregular).

Royal Agricultural Society of the Commonwealth: Ingliston House, Royal Highland Centre, Edinburgh, EH28 8NB; tel. (131) 335-6200; fax (131) 335 6229; e-mail rasc@commagshow.org; internet www.commagshow.org; f. 1957 to promote development of agricultural shows and good farming practice, in order to improve incomes and food production in Commonwealth countries.

Standing Committee on Commonwealth Forestry: Forestry Commission, 231 Corstorphine Rd, Edinburgh, EH12 7AT; tel. (131) 314-6137; fax (131) 316-4344; e-mail libby.jones@forestry.gsi.gov.uk; internet www.cfc2010.org; f. 1923 to provide continuity between Confs, and to provide a forum for discussion on any forestry matters of common interest to mem. govts which may be brought to the Cttee's notice by any mem. country or organization; 54 mems; June 2010 Conference: Edinburgh, United Kingdom; Sec. LIBBY JONES; publ. *Newsletter* (quarterly).

BUSINESS

Commonwealth Business Council: 18 Pall Mall, London, SW1Y 5LU; tel. (20) 7024-8200; fax (20) 7024-8201; e-mail info@cbcglobal.org; internet www.cbcglobal.org; f. 1997 by the Commonwealth Heads of Government Meeting to promote co-operation between governments and the private sector in support of trade, investment and development; the Council aims to identify and promote investment opportunities, in particular in Commonwealth developing countries, to support countries and local businesses to work within the context of globalization, to promote capacity-building and the exchange of skills and knowledge (in particular through its Information Communication Technologies for Development programme), and to encourage co-operation among Commonwealth members; promotes good governance; supports the process of multilateral trade negotiations and other liberalization of trade and services; represents the private sector at government level; Dir-Gen. and CEO Dr MOHAN KAUL.

COMMONWEALTH STUDIES

Institute of Commonwealth Studies: South Block, 2nd Floor, Senate House, Malet Street, London, WC1E 7HU; tel. (20) 7862-8844; fax (20) 7862-8813; e-mail ics@sas.ac.uk; internet commonwealth.sas.ac.uk/; f. 1949 to promote advanced study of the Commonwealth; provides a library and meeting place for postgraduate students and academic staff engaged in research in this field; offers postgraduate teaching; Dir Prof. PHILIP MURPHY; publs *Annual Report*, *Collected Seminar Papers*, *Newsletter*, *Theses in Progress in Commonwealth Studies*.

EDUCATION AND CULTURE

Association of Commonwealth Universities (ACU): Woburn House, 20-24 Tavistock Sq., London, WC1H 9HF; tel. (20) 7380-6700; fax (20) 7387-2655; e-mail info@acu.ac.uk; internet www.acu.ac.uk; f. 1913; promotes international co-operation and understanding; provides assistance with staff and student mobility and development programmes; researches and disseminates information about universities and relevant policy issues; organizes major meetings of Commonwealth universities and their representatives; acts as a liaison office and information centre; administers scholarship and fellowship schemes; operates a policy research unit; mems: c. 500 universities in 36 Commonwealth countries or regions; Sec.-Gen. Prof. JOHN TARRANT; publs include *Yearly Review*, *Commonwealth Universities Yearbook*, *ACU Bulletin* (quarterly), *Who's Who of Executive Heads: Vice-Chancellors, Presidents, Principals and Rectors*, *International Awards*, student information papers (study abroad series).

Commonwealth Association of Museums: R.R.1, De Winton, Alberta, T0L 0X0, Canada; tel. and fax (403) 938-3190; e-mail rvinel@fclc.com; internet www.maltwood.uvic.ca/cam; f. 1985; professional asscn working for the improvement of museums throughout the Commonwealth; encourages links between museums and assists professional development and training through distance learning, workshops and seminars; general assembly held every three or four years; c. 700 mems in 32 Commonwealth countries; Pres. Prof. LOIS IRVINE.

Commonwealth Association of Science, Technology and Mathematics Educators (CASTME): c/o Dr Egan, Faculty of Education, University of Winchester, SO22 4NR; e-mail Bridget.Egan@winchester.ac.uk; internet www.castme.org; f. 1974; special emphasis is given to the social significance of education in these subjects; organizes an Awards Scheme to promote effective teaching and learning in these subjects, and biennial regional seminars; Chair. BRIDGET EGAN; publ. *CASTME Journal* (3 a year).

Commonwealth Council for Educational Administration and Management: Suite 161, Private Bag X9, Melville 2109, Johannesburg, South Africa; tel. (18) 302200; fax (866) 312639; e-mail zandileK@mgsl.co.za; internet www.cceam.org; f. 1970; aims to foster quality in professional development and links among educational administrators; holds nat. and regional confs, as well as visits and seminars; mems: 24 affiliated groups representing 3,000 persons; Pres. ZANDILE KUNENE; publ. *International Studies in Educational Administration* (2 a year).

Commonwealth Education Trust: New Zealand House, 80 Haymarket, London, SW1Y 4TQ; tel. (20) 7024-9822; fax (20) 7024-9833; e-mail information@commonwealth-institute.org; internet www.commonwealth-institute.org; f. 2007 as the successor trust to the Commonwealth Institute; funds the Centre of Commonwealth Education, established in 2004 as part of Cambridge University; supports the Lifestyle of Our Kids (LOOK) project initiated in 2005 by the Commonwealth Institute (Australia).

League for the Exchange of Commonwealth Teachers: 7 Lion Yard, Tremadoc Rd, London, SW4 7NQ; tel. (870) 7702636; fax (870) 7702637; e-mail info@lect.org.uk; internet www.lect.org.uk; f. 1901; promotes educational exchanges between teachers throughout the Commonwealth; Dir ANNA TOMLINSON; publ. *Annual Review*.

HEALTH AND WELFARE

Commonwealth Medical Trust (COMMAT): BMA House, Tavistock Sq., London, WC1H 9JP; tel. (20) 7272-8492; fax (1689) 890609; e-mail office@commat.org; internet www.commat.org; f. 1962 (as the Commonwealth Medical Association) for the exchange of information; provision of tech. co-operation and advice; formulation and maintenance of a code of ethics; promotes the Right to Health; liaison with WHO and other UN agencies on health issues; meetings of its Council are held every three years; mems: medical asscns in Commonwealth countries; Dir MARIANNE HASLEGRAVE.

Commonwealth Nurses' Federation: c/o Royal College of Nursing, 20 Cavendish Sq., London, W1G 0RN; tel. (20) 7647-3593; fax (20) 7647-3413; e-mail jill@commonwealthnurses.org; internet www.commonwealthnurses.org; f. f. 1973 to link national nursing and midwifery asscns in Commonwealth countries; aims to influence health policy, develop nursing networks, improve nursing education and standards, and strengthen leadership; Exec. Sec. JILL ILIFFE.

Commonwealth Organization for Social Work: Melbourne, Australia; tel. (3) 9489-3774; e-mail cosw@aasw.asn.au; internet www.sasw.org.sg/cosw; promotes communication and collaboration between social workers in Commonwealth countries; provides network for information and sharing of expertise.

Commonwealth Pharmacists Association: 1 Lambeth High St, London, SE1 7JN; tel. (20) 7572-2364; fax (20) 7572-2508; e-mail admin@commonwealthpharmacy.org; internet www.commonwealthpharmacy.org; f. 1970 (as the Commonwealth Pharmaceutical Association) to promote the interests of pharmaceutical sciences and the profession of pharmacy in the Commonwealth; to maintain high professional standards, encourage links between members and the creation of nat. asscns; and to facilitate the dissemination of information; holds confs (every four years) and regional meetings; mems: pharmaceutical asscns from over 40 Commonwealth countries; Pres. IVAN KOTZÉ; publ. *Quarterly Newsletter*.

Commonwealth Society for the Deaf (Sound Seekers): 34 Buckingham Palace Rd, London, SW1W 0RE; tel. (20) 7233-5700; fax (20) 7233-5800; e-mail sound.seekers@btinternet.com; internet www.sound-seekers.org.uk; f. 1959; undertakes initiatives to establish audiology services in developing Commonwealth countries, including mobile clinics to provide outreach services; aims to educate local communities in aural hygiene and the prevention of ear infection and deafness; provides audiological equipment and organizes the training of audiological maintenance technicians; conducts research into the causes and prevention of deafness; Chief Exec. GARY WILLIAMS; publ. *Annual Report*.

Royal Commonwealth Ex-Services League: Haig House, 199 Borough High St, London, SE1 1AA; tel. (20) 3207-2413; fax (20) 3207-2115; e-mail mgordon-roe@commonwealthveterans.org.uk; internet www.commonwealthveterans.org.uk; links the ex-service orgs in the Commonwealth, assists ex-servicemen of the Crown who are resident abroad; holds conferences every 4 years; 56 mem. orgs in 48 countries; Grand Pres. HRH The Duke of EDINBURGH; publ. *Annual Report*.

Sightsavers (Royal Commonwealth Society for the Blind): Grosvenor Hall, Bolnore Rd, Haywards Heath, West Sussex, RH16 4BX; tel. (1444) 446600; fax (1444) 446688; e-mail info@sightsavers.org; internet www.sightsavers.org; f. 1950 to prevent blindness and restore sight in developing countries, and to provide education and community-based training for incurably blind people; operates in collaboration with local partners in some 30 developing countries, with high priority given to training local staff; Chair. Lord NIGEL CRISP; Chief Exec. Dr CAROLINE HARPER; publ. *Sight Savers News*.

INFORMATION AND THE MEDIA

Commonwealth Broadcasting Association: 17 Fleet St, London, EC4Y 1AA; tel. (20) 7583-5550; fax (20) 7583-5549; e-mail cba@cba.org.uk; internet www.cba.org.uk; f. 1945; gen. confs are held every two years (2010: Johannesburg, South Africa); mems: c. 100 in more than 50 countries; Pres. ABUBAKAR JIJIWA; Sec.-Gen. ELIZABETH SMITH; publs *Commonwealth Broadcaster* (quarterly), *Commonwealth Broadcaster Directory* (annually).

Commonwealth Journalists Association: c/o Canadian Newspaper Association, 890 Yonge St, Suite 200, Toronto, ON M4W 3P4, Canada; tel. (416) 575-5377; fax (416) 923-7206; e-mail cantleyb@commonwealthjournalists.com; internet www.commonwealthjournalists.com; f. 1978 to promote co-operation between journalists in Commonwealth countries, organize training facilities and confs, and foster understanding among Commonwealth peoples; Exec. Dir BRYAN CANTLEY; publ. *Newsletter* (3 a year).

CPU Media Trust (Association of Commonwealth Newspapers, News Agencies and Periodicals): ; e-mail webform@cpu.org.uk; internet www.cpu.org.uk; f. 2008 as a 'virtual' organization charged with carrying on the aims of the Commonwealth the Commonwealth Press Union (CPU, f. 1950, terminated 2008); promotes the welfare of the Commonwealth press; Chair. GUY BLACK.

LAW

Commonwealth Lawyers' Association: c/o Institute of Advanced Legal Studies, 17 Russell Sq., London, WC1B 5DR; tel. (20) 7862-8824; fax (20) 7862-8816; e-mail cla@sas.ac.uk; internet www.commonwealthlawyers.com; f. 1983 (fmrly the Commonwealth Legal Bureau); seeks to maintain and promote the rule of law throughout the Commonwealth, by ensuring that the people of the Commonwealth are served by an independent and efficient legal profession; upholds professional standards and promotes the availability of legal services; organizes the biannual Commonwealth Law Conference; Sec.-Gen. CLAIRE MARTIN; publs *The Commonwealth Lawyer*, *Clarion*.

Commonwealth Legal Advisory Service: c/o British Institute of International and Comparative Law, Charles Clore House, 17 Russell Sq., London, WC1B 5DR; tel. (20) 7862-5151; fax (20) 7862-5152; e-mail info@biicl.org; internet www.biicl.org; f. 1962; financed by the British Institute and by contributions from Commonwealth govts; provides research facilities for Commonwealth govts and law reform commissions; Chair. Rt Hon. Lord BROWNE-WILKINSON; publ. *New Memoranda* series.

Commonwealth Legal Education Association: c/o Legal and Constitutional Affairs Division, Commonwealth Secretariat, Marlborough House, Pall Mall, London, SW1Y 5HX; tel. (20) 7747-6415; fax (20) 7004-3649; e-mail clea@commonwealth.int; internet www.clea-web.com; f. 1971 to promote contacts and exchanges and to provide information regarding legal education; Gen. Sec. SELINA GOULBOURNE; publ. *Commonwealth Legal Education Association Newsletter* (3 a year).

Commonwealth Magistrates' and Judges' Association: Uganda House, 58–59 Trafalgar Sq., London, WC2N 5DX; tel. (20) 7976-1007; fax (20) 7976-2394; e-mail info@cmja.org; internet www.cmja.org; f. 1970 to advance the administration of the law by promoting the independence of the judiciary, to further education in law and crime prevention and to disseminate information; confs and study tours; corporate membership for asscns of the judiciary or courts of limited jurisdiction; assoc. membership for individuals; Pres. Hon. Mrs Justice NORMA WADE-MILLER; Exec. Vice-Pres. Sir PHILIP BAILHACHE; publs *Commonwealth Judicial Journal* (2 a year), *CMJA News*.

PARLIAMENTARY AFFAIRS

Commonwealth Parliamentary Association: Westminster House, Suite 700, 7 Millbank, London, SW1P 3JA; tel. (20) 7799-1460; fax (20) 7222-6073; e-mail hq.sec@cpahq.org; internet www.cpahq.org; f. 1911 to promote understanding and co-operation between Commonwealth parliamentarians; organization: Exec. Cttee of 35 MPs responsible to annual Gen. Assembly; 175 brs in national, state, provincial and territorial parliaments and legislatures throughout the Commonwealth; holds annual Commonwealth Parliamentary Confs and seminars; also regional confs and seminars; Sec.-Gen. Dr WILLIAM F. SHIJA; publ. *The Parliamentarian* (quarterly).

SCIENCE AND TECHNOLOGY

Commonwealth Association of Architects: POB 508, Edgware, Middx, HA8 9XZ; tel. and fax (20) 8951-0550; e-mail info@comarchitect.org; internet comarchitect.org; f. 1964; an asscn of 38 socs of architects in various Commonwealth countries; objectives: to facilitate the reciprocal recognition of professional qualifications; to provide a clearing house for information on architectural practice; and to encourage collaboration. Plenary confs every three years; regional confs are also held; Exec. Dir TONY GODWIN; publs *Handbook, Objectives and Procedures: CAA Schools Visiting Boards, Architectural Education in the Commonwealth* (annotated bibliography of research), *CAA Newsnet* (2 a year), a survey and list of schools of architecture.

Commonwealth Engineers' Council: c/o Institution of Civil Engineers, 1 Great George St, London, SW1P 3AA; tel. (20) 7665-2005; fax (20) 7223-1806; e-mail neil.bailey@ice.org.uk; internet www.ice.org.uk/cec; f. 1946; links and represents engineering institutions across the Commonwealth, providing them with an opportunity to exchange views on collaboration and mutual support; holds international and regional conferences and workshops; mems: 45 institutions in 44 countries; Pres. TOM FOULKES; Sec.-Gen. NEIL BAILEY.

Commonwealth Telecommunications Organization: 26–28 Hammersmith Grove, London, W6 7BA; tel. (870) 7777697; fax (870) 0345626; e-mail info@cto.int; internet www.cto.int; f. 1967 as an international development partnership between Commonwealth and non-Commonwealth governments, business and civil society organizations; aims to help to bridge the digital divide and to achieve social and economic development by delivering to developing countries knowledge-sharing programmes in the use of information and communication technologies in the specific areas of telecommunications, IT, broadcasting and the internet; CEO Dr EKWOW SPIO-GARBRAH; publs *CTO Update* (quarterly), *Annual Report*, *Research Reports*.

Conference of Commonwealth Meteorologists: c/o International Branch, Meteorological Office, FitzRoy Rd, Exeter, EX1 3PB; tel. (1392) 886435; fax (1392) 885681; e-mail commonwealth@metoffice.gov.uk; internet internet www.commonwealthmet.org; links national meteorological and hydrological services in Commonwealth countries; conferences held every four years.

SPORT AND YOUTH

Commonwealth Games Federation: 2nd Floor, 138 Piccadilly, London, W1J 7NR; tel. (20) 7491-8801; fax (20) 7409-7803; e-mail info@thecgf.com; internet www.thecgf.com; the Games were first held in 1930 and are now held every four years; participation is limited to competitors representing the mem. countries of the Commonwealth; 2010 games: New Delhi, India, in October; mems: 72 affiliated bodies; Pres. MICHAEL FENNELL; CEO MICHAEL HOOPER.

Commonwealth Youth Exchange Council: 7 Lion Yard, Tremadoc Rd, London, SW4 7NQ; tel. (20) 7498-6151; fax (20) 7622-4365; e-mail mail@cyec.org.uk; internet www.cyec.org.uk; f. 1970; promotes contact between groups of young people of the United Kingdom and other Commonwealth countries by means of educational exchange visits, provides information for organizers and allocates grants; provides host governments with technical assistance for delivery of the Commonwealth Youth Forum, held every two years (2009: Trinidad and Tobago); mems: 222 orgs; Chief Exec. V. S. G. CRAGGS; publs *Contact* (handbook), *Exchange* (newsletter), *Final Communiqués* (of the Commonwealth Youth Forums), *Safety and Welfare* (guidelines for Commonwealth Youth Exchange groups).

RELATIONS WITHIN THE COMMONWEALTH

Commonwealth Countries League: 37 Priory Ave, Sudbury, Middx, HA0 2SB; tel. (20) 8248- 3275; e-mail rennie158@btinternet.com; internet www.ccl-int.org; f. 1925; aims to secure equality of liberties, status and opportunities between women and men and to promote friendship and mutual understanding throughout the Commonwealth; promotes women's political and social education and links together women's organizations in most countries of the Commonwealth; an education sponsorship scheme was established in 1967 to finance the secondary education of bright but needy girls in their own Commonwealth countries; the CCL Education Fund was sponsoring more than 243 girls throughout the Commonwealth (2010); Exec. Chair. MARJORIE RENNIE; publs *News Update* (3 a year), *Annual Report*.

Commonwealth War Graves Commission: 2 Marlow Rd, Maidenhead, Berks, SL6 7DX; tel. (1628) 634221; fax (1628) 771208; internet www.cwgc.org; casualty and cemetery enquiries; e-mail casualty.enq@cwgc.org; f. 1917 (as Imperial War Graves Commission); responsible for the commemoration in perpetuity of the 1.7m. members of the Commonwealth Forces who died during the wars of 1914–18 and 1939–45; provides for the marking and maintenance of war graves and memorials at some 23,000 locations in 150 countries; mems: Australia, Canada, India, New Zealand, South Africa, United Kingdom; Pres. HRH The Duke of KENT; Dir-Gen. RICHARD KELLAWAY.

Council of Commonwealth Societies: c/o Royal Commonwealth Society, 25 Northumberland Ave, London, WC2N 5AP; tel. (20) 7766-9200; fax (20) 7930-9705; e-mail ccs@rcsint.org; internet www.rcsint.org/day; f. 1947; provides a forum for the exchange of information regarding activities of mem. orgs which promote understanding among countries of the Commonwealth; co-ordinates the distribution of the Commonwealth Day message by Queen Elizabeth, organizes the observance of and promotes Commonwealth Day, and produces educational materials relating to the occasion; seeks to raise the profile of the Commonwealth; mems: 30 official and unofficial Commonwealth orgs; Chair. Lord ALAN WATSON; Sec. ALICE KAWOWA.

Royal Commonwealth Society: 25 Northumberland Ave, London, WC2N 5AP; tel. (20) 7766-9200; fax (20) 7930-9705; e-mail info@thercs.org; internet www.thercs.org; f. 1868; to promote international understanding of the Commonwealth and its people; organizes meetings and seminars on topical issues, projects for young people, a youth leadership programme, and cultural and social events; Chair. Baroness PRASHAR; Dir Dr DANNY SRISKANDARAJAH; publs *RCS Exchange* (3 a year), conference reports.

Royal Over-Seas League: Over-Seas House, Park Place, St James's St, London, SW1A 1LR; tel. (20) 7408-0214; fax (20) 7499-6738; e-mail info@rosl.org.uk; internet www.rosl.org.uk; f. 1910 to promote friendship and understanding in the Commonwealth; clubhouses in London and Edinburgh; membership is open to all British subjects and Commonwealth citizens; Dir-Gen. ROBERT F. NEWELL; publ. *Overseas* (quarterly).

Victoria League for Commonwealth Friendship: 55 Leinster Sq., London, W2 4PW; tel. (20) 7243-2633; fax (20) 7229-2994; e-mail victorialeaguehq@btconnect.com; internet www.victorialeague.co.uk; f. 1901; aims to further personal friendship among Commonwealth peoples and to provide hospitality for visitors; maintains Student House, providing accommodation for students from Commonwealth countries; has brs elsewhere in the UK and abroad; Chair. LYN D. HOPKINS; Gen. Sec. JOHN M. W. ALLAN; publ. *Annual Report*.

EUROPEAN UNION—EU

Presidency of the Council of the European Union: Belgium (July–December 2010); Hungary (January–June 2011).

President of the European Council: HERMAN VAN ROMPUY (Belgium).

High Representative of the Union for Foreign Affairs and Security Policy: CATHERINE ASHTON (United Kingdom).

Latin America

A non-preferential trade agreement was signed with Uruguay in 1974, and economic and commercial co-operation agreements with Mexico in 1975 and with Brazil in 1980. A five-year co-operation agreement with the members of the Central American Common Market and with Panama entered into force in 1987, as did a similar agreement with the member countries (see below) of the Andean Group (now the Andean Community). Co-operation agreements were signed with Argentina and Chile in 1990, and in that year tariff preferences were approved for Bolivia, Colombia, Ecuador and Peru, in support of those countries' efforts to combat drugs trafficking. In May 1992 an inter-institutional co-operation agreement was signed with the Southern Common Market (Mercosur); in the following month the European Community (EC) and the member states of the Andean Group (Bolivia, Colombia, Ecuador, Peru and Venezuela) initialled a new co-operation agreement, which was to broaden the scope of economic and development co-operation and enhance trade relations, and a new co-operation agreement was signed with Brazil. In July 1993 the EC introduced a tariff regime to limit the import of bananas from Latin America, in order to protect the banana-producing countries of the African, Caribbean and Pacific (ACP) group, then linked to the EC by the Lomé Convention. (In December 2009, in resolution to a long dispute over the tariff regime, the EU and Latin American states initialled the EU-Latin America Bananas Agreement, which provided for a gradual reduction in the tariff rate.)

From 1996 the European Union (EU, as the EC became in 1993) forged closer links with Latin America, by means of strengthened political ties, an increase in economic integration and free trade, and co-operation in other areas. In April 1997 the EU extended further trade benefits to the countries of the Andean Community. In July the EU and Mexico concluded an Economic Partnership, Political Co-ordination and Co-operation Agreement (the 'Global Agreement') and an interim agreement on trade. The accords were signed in December, and entered into effect in 2000. In November 1999 the EU and Mexico concluded a free trade agreement, which provided for the removal of all tariffs on bilateral trade in industrial products by 2007. The first meeting of the Joint Council established by the Economic Partnership, Political Co-ordination and Co-operation Agreement between the EU and Mexico was held in February 2001; further meetings have since been held on a regular basis. In July 2008, in acknowledgement of the gradual strengthening of EU-Mexico relations, the European Commission proposed the establishment of a Strategic Partnership with Mexico. An EU-Mexico summit meeting was held in Comillas, Spain, in May 2010.

In June 1996 the EU and Chile signed a framework agreement on political and economic co-operation, which provided for a process of bilateral trade liberalization, as well as co-operation in other industrial and financial areas. An EU-Chile Joint Council was established. In November 1999 the EU and Chile commenced practical negotiations on developing closer political and economic co-operation, within the framework of a proposed Association Agreement. In November 2002 the EU and Chile signed an association and free trade agreement, which entered into force in March 2005; it provided for the liberalization of trade within seven years for industrial products and 10 years for agricultural products. The first meeting of the Association Council set up by the agreement took place in Athens, Greece, in March 2003, and the second was held in Luxembourg in May 2005. Representatives of civil society met within the framework of the Association Agreement for the first time in late 2006. In May 2008 the EU and Chile determined to establish a joint Association for Development and Innovation. The first EU-Chile dialogue on human rights was convened in Santiago, Chile, in April 2009. The fourth EU-Chile summit meeting was held in Madrid, Spain, in May 2010.

In May 2007 the European Commission proposed launching a Strategic Partnership with Brazil, in recognition of its increasing international prominence and strong bilateral ties with Europe. The first EU-Brazil summit was duly held in Lisbon, Portugal, in July. The inaugural EU-Brazil Macroeconomic and Financial Dialogue was convened in Brasilia, Brazil, in July 2009. The fourth EU-Brazil summit took place in Brasília, Brazil, in July 2010.

In late December 1994 the EU and Mercosur signed a joint declaration that aimed to promote trade liberalization and greater political co-operation. In September 1995, at a meeting in Montevideo, Uruguay, a framework agreement on the establishment of a free trade regime between the two organizations was initialled. The agreement was formally signed in December. In July 1998 the European Commission voted to commence negotiations towards an interregional Association Agreement with Mercosur, which would strengthen existing co-operation agreements. Negotiations were initiated in April 2000 (focusing on the three pillars of political dialogue, co-operation, and establishing a free trade area), and were extended in May 2008 to cover the additional pillars of science and technology, infrastructure, and renewable energy.

The first ministerial conference between the EC and the Rio Group of Latin American and Caribbean states took place in April 1991; since then high-level joint ministerial meetings have been held every two years. The 14th ministerial conference between the EU and the 19 Rio Group states took place in Prague, the Czech Republic, in May 2009, and discussed maintaining a sustainable approach to energy security and climate change, as well as recovering financial security and global economic growth. The conference also adopted a declaration of solidarity and support with the countries in the region most affected by the swine influenza variant pandemic (H1N1) in 2009, with particular reference to Mexico. The next meeting is due to take place in Chile, in 2011. The first summit meeting of all EU and Latin American and Caribbean heads of state or government was held in Rio de Janeiro, Brazil, in June 1999, when a strategic partnership was launched. A second EU-Latin America/Caribbean (EU-LAC) summit took place in Madrid, Spain, in May 2002, and covered co-operation in political, economic, social and cultural fields. A political dialogue and co-operation agreement with the Andean Community and its member states was signed in December 2003. At the third EU-LAC summit meeting, held in Guadalajara, Mexico, in May 2004 it was agreed by the two parties that an Association Agreement, including a free trade area, was a common objective. In December 2005 the European Commission proposed a renewed strategy for strengthening the strategic partnership with Latin America, ahead of the fourth EU-LAC summit, held in Vienna, Austria, in May 2006. Its proposals included increasing political dialogue between the two regions, stimulating economic and commercial exchanges, encouraging regional integration, addressing inequality and adapting the EU's development and aid policy to correspond more closely to conditions in Latin America. At the fourth EU-LAC summit it was decided that negotiations for Association Agreements with Central America and with the Andean Community should be initiated. The summit also endorsed a proposal to establish an EU-Latin America parliamentary assembly. The assembly met for the first time in November 2006. The fifth EU-LAC summit was held in Lima, Peru, in May 2008, and concentrated on the themes of poverty, inequality and inclusion, and sustainable development (climate change, the environment and energy). An EU-LAC Forum on Corporate Social Responsibility was held in October 2009, in Buenos Aires, Argentina, and, in May 2010, the sixth EU-LAC summit was convened, in Madrid, Spain, on the theme 'Innovation and technology for sustainable development and social inclusion'. In June 2007 the EU and the Andean Community initiated negotiations on the planned Association Agreement in Tarija, Bolivia. However, negotiations were suspended in June 2008, reportedly owing to divergent views of the aims and scope of the trade provisions. In January 2009 negotiations recommenced between three of the Andean Community countries, Colombia, Ecuador and Peru, with the goal of concluding a multi-party trade agreement; Ecuador provisionally suspended its participation in the negotiations in July. Negotiations were concluded on 1 March 2010, with an agreement on trade between the EU and Colombia and Peru, providing for the liberalization of trade in 65% of industrial products with Colombia, and 80% with Peru. Talks on an Association Agreement between the EU and the countries of Central America (Costa Rica, El Salvador, Guatemala, Honduras, Nicaragua and Panama) commenced in Costa Rica in October 2007, but negotiations were suspended temporarily during 2009 owing to the unstable political situation in Honduras. In May 2010 the EU concluded negotiations on an Association Agreement with Central America, covering three areas: trade, political dialogue and co-operation. In July 2008 the European Commission allocated some €10m. in support of Andean Community projects focusing on regional economic integration and combating the trade in illegal drugs. The European Commission was expected to provide total funding of some €50m. for the period 2007–13. In 2007 the EU also concluded negotiations for an Economic Partnership Agreement with the Caribbean Forum (CARIFORUM) grouping of 16 Caribbean states.

Cuba remained the only Latin American country that did not have a formal economic co-operation agreement with the EU. In June 1995 a Commission communication advocated greater economic co-operation with Cuba. This policy was strongly supported by a resolution of the European Parliament in January 1996, but was criticized by the US Government, which continued to maintain an economic embargo against Cuba. Later that year the EU agreed to make the extent of economic co-operation with Cuba (a one-party state) contingent on progress towards democracy. In 2000 Cuba withdrew its application to join the successor to the Lomé Convention, the Cotonou Agreement, following criticism by some European governments of its human rights record. Improvements in bilateral relations between Cuba and the EU led to the opening of an EU legation office in the Cuban capital, Havana, in March 2003 and support for Cuba's renewed application to join the Cotonou Agreement. However, human rights abuses perpetrated by the Cuban regime in April (the imprisonment of a large number of dissidents) led to the downgrading of diplomatic relations with Cuba by the EU, the instigation of an EU policy of inviting dissidents to embassy receptions in Havana (the so-called cocktail wars) and the indefinite postponement of Cuba's application to join the Cotonou Agreement. In May Cuba withdrew its application for membership, and in July the Cuban President, Fidel Castro, announced that the Government would not accept aid from the EU and would terminate all political contact with the organization. In December 2004 the EU proposed a compromise—namely not to invite any Cubans, whether government ministers or dissidents, to future embassy receptions—but reiterated its demand that Cuba unconditionally release all political prisoners who remained in detention (several dissidents had already been released). In response to this improvement in relations, Cuba announced in January 2005 that it was restoring diplomatic ties with all EU states. At the end of that month the EU temporarily suspended the diplomatic sanctions imposed on Cuba in mid-2003 and announced its intention to resume a 'constructive dialogue' with the Cuban authorities. In March 2005 the European Commissioner responsible for Development and Humanitarian Aid visited Cuba, where he held meetings with the Cuban President, as well as several dissidents. The EU extended the temporary suspension of diplomatic sanctions against Cuba for one year in June, and again in mid-2006 and mid-2007, in the hope that constructive dialogue would bring about reform in the areas of human rights and democratization and the release of further political prisoners. Sanctions were lifted in June 2008, although the decision was to be subject to an annual review.

The EU's natural disaster prevention and preparedness programme (Dipecho) has targeted earthquake, flood, hurricane, and volcanic eruption preparedness throughout Latin America and the Caribbean. In December 2008 some €10m. was allocated to Latin America for 2009, and in May and August 2009, respectively, €5m. and €2m. were allocated to the Caribbean region, under Dipecho. Humanitarian aid granted to countries in the region in 2009 included €12m. to assist displaced persons and survivors of natural disasters in Colombia; €7m. in support of people affected by multiple challenges, including food insecurity and natural disasters, in Haiti; and €2m. to assist people affected by hurricanes Gustav, Ike and Paloma in Cuba. The EU has adopted the following decentralized programmes to provide economic assistance to Latin America: AL-INVEST (supporting European investment in Latin America-based small and medium-sized enterprises that seek to operate internationally); ALFA (promoting bilateral co-operation in higher education); URB-AL (promoting links between European and Latin American cities); ALBAN (promoting higher education through the provision of scholarships); @LIS (supporting the use of information technologies); OBREAL (aimed at establishing a network of non-profit-making institutions from both regions); and EUROSociAL (inaugurated in May 2004 to assist Latin American countries with developing and implementing social policies aimed at strengthening social cohesion). The budget for the EU's Regional Indicative Programme for Latin America was €556m. for the period 2007–13.

It was announced in late January 2010 that at least 300 EU military police would be deployed to Haiti to support law and order in the aftermath of the earthquake that devastated the country's infrastructure earlier in that month. The EU was also to send engineers and equipment to help rehabilitate damaged roads. By March 2010 EU humanitarian assistance for Haiti, including planned pledges, totalled more than €320m. (from member states and the European Commission). Emergency relief from the European Commission was worth over €120m., including €3m. in emergency funding allocated within 24 hours of the earthquake taking place.

African, Caribbean and Pacific (ACP) Countries

In June 2000, meeting in Cotonou, Benin, heads of state and of government of the EU and African, Caribbean and Pacific (ACP) countries concluded a new 20-year partnership accord between the EU and ACP states. The EU-ACP Partnership Agreement, known as the Cotonou Agreement, entered into force on 1 April 2003 (although many of its provisions had been applicable for a transitional period since August 2000), following ratification by the then 15 EU member states and more than the requisite two-thirds of the ACP countries. Previously, the principal means of co-operation between the Community and developing countries were the Lomé Conventions. The First Lomé Convention (Lomé I), which was concluded at Lomé, Togo, in February 1975 and came into force on 1 April 1976, replaced the Yaoundé Conventions and the Arusha Agreement. Lomé I was designed to provide a new framework of co-operation, taking into account the varying needs of developing ACP countries. The Second Lomé Convention entered into force on 1 January 1981 and the Third Lomé Convention on 1 March 1985 (trade provisions) and 1 May 1986 (aid). The Fourth Lomé Convention, which had a 10-year commitment period, was signed in December 1989: its trade provisions entered into force on 1 March 1990, and the remainder entered into force in September 1991.

The Cotonou Agreement was to cover a 20-year period from 2000 and was subject to revision every five years. A financial protocol was attached to the Agreement, which indicated the funds available to the ACP through the European Development Fund (EDF), the main instrument for Community aid for development co-operation in ACP countries. The ninth EDF, covering the initial five-year period from March 2000, provided a total budget of €13,500m., of which €1,300m. was allocated to regional co-operation and €2,200m. was for the new investment facility for the development of the private sector. In addition, uncommitted balances from previous EDFs amounted to a further €2,500m. The new Agreement envisaged a more participatory approach with more effective political co-operation to encourage good governance and democracy, increased flexibility in the provision of aid to reward performance, and a new framework for economic and trade co-operation. Its objectives were to alleviate poverty, contribute to sustainable development and integrate the ACP economies into the global economy. Negotiations to revise the Cotonou Agreement were initiated in May 2004 and concluded in February 2005. The political dimension of the Agreement was broadly strengthened and a reference to co-operation in counter-terrorism and the prevention of the proliferation of weapons of mass destruction was included. The revised Cotonou Agreement was signed on 24 June 2005.

Under the provisions of the new accord, the EU was to finalize free trade arrangements (replacing the previous non-reciprocal trade preferences) with the most developed ACP countries during 2000–08; these would be structured around a system of six regional free trade zones, and would be designed to ensure full compatibility with World Trade Organization (WTO) provisions. Once in force, the agreements would be subject to revision every five years. The first general stage of negotiations for the Economic Partnership Agreements (EPA), involving discussions with all ACP countries regarding common procedures, began in September 2002. The regional phase of EPA negotiations to establish a new framework for trade and investment commenced in October 2003. Negotiations had been scheduled for completion in mid-2007 to allow for ratification by 2008, when the WTO exception for existing arrangements expired. However, the negotiation period was subsequently extended. By June 2009 36 ACP states had signed full or interim EPAs, covering the liberalization of goods and agricultural products. The EPAs attracted some criticism for their focus on trade liberalization and their perceived failure to recognize the widespread poverty of ACP countries. Meanwhile, the EU had launched an initiative to allow free access to the products of the least-developed ACP nations by 2005. Stabex and Sysmin, instruments under the Lomé Conventions designed to stabilize export prices for agricultural and mining commodities, respectively, were replaced by a system called FLEX, introduced in 2000, to compensate ACP countries for short-term fluctuations in export earnings. In February 2001 the EU agreed to phase out trade barriers on imports of everything but military weapons from the world's 48 least-developed countries, 39 of which were in the ACP group. Duties on sugar, rice, bananas and some other products were to remain until 2009 (these were withdrawn from October of that year). In May 2001 the EU announced that it would cancel all outstanding debts arising from its trade accords with former colonies of member states.

One major new programme set up on behalf of the ACP countries and financed by the EDF was Pro€Invest, which was launched in 2002, with funding of €110m. over a seven-year period. In October 2003 the Commission proposed to incorporate the EDF into the EU budget (it had previously been a fund outside the EU budget, to which the EU member states made direct voluntary contributions). The cost-sharing formula for the 25 member states would automatically apply, obviating the need for negotiations about contributions for the 10th EDF. The Commission proposal was endorsed by the European Parliament in April 2004. Despite the fears of ACP countries that the enlargement of the EU could jeopardize funding, the 10th EDF was agreed in December 2005 by the European Council and provided funds of €22,682m. for the period 2008–13.

On 1 July 1993 the EC introduced a regime to allow the preferential import into the Community of bananas from former French and British colonies in the Caribbean. This was designed to protect the banana industries of ACP countries from the availability of cheaper bananas, produced by countries in Latin America. Latin American and later US producers brought a series of complaints before the WTO, claiming that the EU banana import regime was in contravention of free trade principles. The WTO upheld their complaints on each occasion leading to adjustments of the complex quota and tariffs systems in place. Following the WTO authorization of punitive US trade sanctions, in April 2001 the EU reached agreement with the USA and Ecuador on a new banana regime. Under the new accord, the EU was granted the so-called Cotonou waiver, which allowed it to maintain preferential access for ACP banana exports, in return for the adoption of a new tariff-only system for bananas from Latin American countries from 1 January 2006. The Latin American producers were guaranteed total market access under the agreement and were permitted to seek arbitration if dissatisfied with the EU's proposed tariff levels. Following the WTO rejection of EU proposals for tariff levels of €230 and €187 per metric ton (in comparison with existing rates of €75 for a quota of 2.2m. tons and €680 thereafter), in November 2005 the EU announced that a tariff of €176, with a duty-free quota of 775,000 metric tons for ACP producers, would be implemented on 1 January 2006. In late 2006 Ecuador initiated a challenge to the EU's proposals at the WTO. Twelve other countries subsequently initiated third-party challenges to the proposals at the WTO, in support of the challenge by Ecuador. In April 2008 the WTO upheld the challenge initiated by Ecuador, and ordered the EU to bring its tariffs into conformity with WTO regulations. In December 2009 representatives from the EU and Latin American countries initialled the EU-Latin America Bananas Agreement, which aimed to end the dispute. Under the Agreement, which made no provision for import quotas, the EU was gradually to reduce its import tariff on bananas from Latin American countries, to €114 per metric ton from €176, by 2017. The EU also pledged to mobilize up to €200m. to support the main ACP banana-exporting countries with adjusting to the envisaged increased market competition from Latin America. (ACP countries would continue to enjoy duty- and quota-free access to EU markets.) On their side, Latin American banana-producing countries undertook not to demand further tariff reductions; and to withdraw several related cases against the EU pending at the WTO. In response to the Agreement, the US authorities determined to settle ongoing parallel complaints lodged with the WTO against the EU relating to bananas.

Following a WTO ruling at the request of Brazil, Australia and Thailand in 2005 that the EU's subsidized exports of sugar breached legal limits, reform of the EU's sugar regime was required by May 2006. Previously, the EU purchased fixed quotas of sugar from ACP producers at two or three times the world price, the same price that it paid to sugar growers in the EU. In November 2005 the EU agreed to reform the sugar industry through a phased reduction of its prices for white sugar of 36% by 2009 (which was still double the market price in 2005). Compensation to EU producers was generous, amounting to €6,300m. over the four years beginning in January 2006, but compensation to ACP producers was worth just €40m. in 2006. Development campaigners and impoverished ACP countries, notably Jamaica and Guyana, condemned the plans.

In May 2003 Timor-Leste joined the ACP and the ACP-EC Council of Ministers approved its accession to the ACP-EC Partnership Agreement. Cuba, which had been admitted to the ACP in December 2000, was granted observer status. Cuba withdrew its application to join the Cotonou Agreement in July 2003.

Article 96 of the Cotonou Agreement, which provides for suspension of the Agreement in specific countries in the event of violation of one of its essential elements (respect for human rights, democratic principles and the rule of law), was invoked against Haiti in 2001, and this was extended annually to December 2004. However, relations with Haiti were in the process of normalization from September of that year.

INTER-AMERICAN DEVELOPMENT BANK—IDB

Address: 1300 New York Ave, NW, Washington, DC 20577, USA.
Telephone: (202) 623-1000; **fax:** (202) 623-3096; **e-mail:** pic@iadb.org; **internet:** www.iadb.org.

The Bank was founded in 1959 to promote the individual and collective development of Latin American and Caribbean countries through the financing of economic and social development projects and the provision of technical assistance. From 1976 membership was extended to include countries outside the region.

MEMBERS

Argentina	Ecuador	Nicaragua
Austria	El Salvador	Norway
Bahamas	Finland	Panama
Barbados	France	Paraguay
Belgium	Germany	Peru
Belize	Guatemala	Portugal
Bolivia	Guyana	Slovenia
Brazil	Haiti	Spain
Canada	Honduras	Suriname
Chile	Israel	Sweden
China, People's Rep.	Italy	Switzerland
Colombia	Jamaica	Trinidad and Tobago
Costa Rica	Japan	United Kingdom
Croatia	Republic of Korea	USA
Denmark	Mexico	Uruguay
Dominican Republic	Netherlands	Venezuela

Organization

(August 2010)

BOARD OF GOVERNORS

All the powers of the Bank are vested in a Board of Governors, consisting of one Governor and one alternate appointed by each member country (usually ministers of finance or presidents of central banks). The Board meets annually, with special meetings when necessary. The 51st annual meeting was held in Cancún, Mexico, in March 2010. The meeting in 2011 was to be convened in Calgary, Canada.

BOARD OF EXECUTIVE DIRECTORS

The Board of Executive Directors is responsible for the operations of the Bank. It establishes the Bank's policies, approves loan and technical co-operation proposals that are submitted by the President of the Bank, and authorizes the Bank's borrowings on capital markets.

There are 14 executive directors and 14 alternates. Each Director is elected by a group of two or more countries, except the Directors representing Canada and the USA. The USA holds 30% of votes on the Board, in respect of its contribution to the Bank's capital. The Board has five permanent committees, relating to: Policy and evaluation; Organization, human resources and board matters; Budget, financial policies and audit; Programming; and a Steering Committee.

ADMINISTRATION

In December 2006 the Board of Executive Directors approved a new structure which aimed to strengthen the Bank's country focus and improve its operational efficiency. Three new positions of Vice-Presidents were created. Accordingly the executive structure comprised the President, Executive Vice-President and Vice-Presidents for Countries (with responsibility for four regional departments); Sectors and Knowledge; Private Sector and Non-sovereign Guaranteed Operations; and Finance and Administration. The principal Offices were of the Auditor-General, Outreach and Partnerships, External Relations, Risk Management, and Strategic Planning and Development Effectiveness. The Bank has country offices in each of its borrowing member states, and special offices in Paris, France and in Tokyo, Japan. There are some 1,800 Bank staff (excluding the Board of Executive Directors and the Evaluation Office), of whom almost 30% are based in country offices. The total Bank group administrative expenses for 2009 amounted to US $542m.

President: Luis Alberto Moreno (Colombia).

Executive Vice-President: Daniel M. Zelikow (USA).

Activities

Loans are made to governments and to public and private entities for specific economic and social development projects and for sectoral reforms. These loans are repayable in the currencies lent and their terms range from 12 to 40 years. Total lending authorized by the Bank amounted to US $183,171.5m. by the end of 2009. During 2009 the Bank approved loans and guarantees amounting to $15,507m., of which Ordinary Capital loans totalled $15,278m. (compared with $11,085m. in 2008). Disbursements on Ordinary Capital loans amounted to $11,424m. in 2009, compared with $7,149m. in the previous year. In October 2008 the Bank announced measures to help to counter the effects on the region of the downturn in the world's major economies and the restrictions on the availability of credit. It resolved to accelerate lending and establish an emergency liquidity facility, with funds of up to $6,000m., in order to sustain regional economic growth and to support social welfare programmes.

The subscribed Ordinary Capital stock, including inter-regional capital, which was merged into it in 1987, totalled US $104,980m. at the end of 2009, of which $4,339m. was paid-in and $100,641m. was callable. The callable capital constitutes, in effect, a guarantee of the securities that the Bank issues in the capital markets in order to increase its resources available for lending. In March 2009 the Board of Governors agreed to initiate a capital review, in recognition of unprecedented demand for Bank resources owing to the sharp contraction of international capital markets. An agreement to increase the Bank's authorized capital by $70,000m. was concluded in March 2010 and endorsed by the Board of Governors in July. Of the total increase, $1,700m. was expected to be paid in by member countries over a five-year period, commencing 2011.

In 2009 the Bank borrowed the equivalent of US $17,886m. on the international capital markets, bringing total borrowings outstanding to $57,641m. at the end of the year. In 2009 operating income amounted to $1,294m., compared with –$972m. in 2008.

The Fund for Special Operations (FSO) enables the Bank to make concessional loans for economic and social projects where circumstances call for special treatment, such as lower interest rates and longer repayment terms than those applied to loans from the ordinary resources. Assistance may be provided to countries adversely affected by economic crises or natural disasters through an Emergency Lending Program. In March 2007 the Board of Governors approved a reform of the Bank's concessional lending (at the same time as endorsing arrangements for participation in the Multilateral Debt Relief Initiative, see below), and resolved that FSO lending may be 'blended' with Ordinary Capital loans by means of a parallel lending mechanism. In June a new grant facility was established, funded by transfers from the FSO, to make available resources for specific projects or countries in specific circumstances. During 2009 the FSO approved 24 parallel loans amounting to $716m. (of which $228m. was from FSO resources and $488m. from Ordinary Capital funds). At 31 December 2009 cumulative FSO lending amounted to $18,870.5m. In March 2010 the Board of Governors agreed to guarantee a full replenishment of FSO resources.

In 1998 the Bank agreed to participate in an initiative of the IMF and the World Bank to assist heavily indebted poor countries (HIPCs) to maintain a sustainable level of debt. Also in 1998, following projections of reduced resources for the Fund for Special Operations, borrowing member countries agreed to convert about US $2,400m. in local currencies held by the Bank, in order to maintain a convertible concessional Fund for poorer countries, and to help to reduce the debt-servicing payments under the HIPC initiative. In mid-2000 a committee of the Board of Governors endorsed a financial framework for the Bank's participation in an enhanced HIPC initiative, which aimed to broaden the eligibility criteria and accelerate the process of debt reduction. The Bank was to provide $896m. (in net present value), in addition to $204m. committed under the original scheme, of which $307m. was for Bolivia, $65m. for Guyana, $391m. for Nicaragua and $133m. for Honduras. The Bank assisted the preparation of national Poverty Reduction Strategy Papers, a condition of reaching the 'completion point' of the process. In January 2007 the Bank concluded an agreement to participate in the Multilateral Debt Relief Initiative (MDRI), which had been approved by the World Bank and IMF in 2005 as a means of achieving 100% cancellation of debts for eligible HIPCs. The agreement to support the MDRI was endorsed by the Bank's Board of Governors in March 2007. Under the initiative the eligible completion point countries, along with Haiti (which had reached 'decision point' in November 2006) were to receive additional debt relief amounting to some $3,370m. in principal payments and $1,000m. in future interest payments, cancelling loan balances with the FSO (outstanding as of 31 December 2004). Haiti reached 'completion point' under the HIPC initiative in June 2009. Accordingly FSO delivered debt relief under the enhanced HIPC initiative and the MDRI amounting to some $419m. The capital increase, approved in 2010, intended to provide for cancellation of all Haiti's outstanding debts to the Bank.

In June 2006 the Bank inaugurated a new initiative, Opportunities for the Majority, to improve conditions for low-income communities throughout the region. Under the scheme the Bank was to support the development of partnerships between communities, private sector bodies and non-governmental organizations to generate employment, deliver services and integrate poorer members of society into the productive economy. At the end of 2009 the initiative was supporting 13 projects in low-income communities, of which nine were approved during that year.

In March 2007 the Bank's Board of Governors endorsed the Sustainable Energy and Climate Change Initiative (SECCI), which aimed to expand the development and use of biofuels and other sources of renewable energy, to enhance energy efficiency and to facilitate adaptation to climate change. A Bank fund, with an initial US $20m. in resources, was established to finance feasibility studies and technical co-operation projects. By the end of 2009 SECCI had approved more than 60 technical co-operation projects amounting to $34.7m. and three investment grants totalling $2.25m. In November 2009 the Bank signed a memorandum of understanding with the Asian Development Bank to support projects and programmes that promote sustainable, low-carbon transport in both regions. In accordance with the priorities of the lending agreement approved along with the capital increase in July 2010, support for climate change adaptation initiatives and other projects concerned with renewable energy and environmental sustainability was expected to reach 25% of total lending by the end of 2015.

The Bank supports a range of consultative groups in order to strengthen donor co-operation with countries in the Latin America and Caribbean region, in particular to co-ordinate emergency relief and reconstruction following a natural disaster or to support peace efforts within a country. In November 2001 the Bank hosted the first meeting of a Network for the Prevention and Mitigation of Natural Disasters in Latin America and the Caribbean, which was part of a regional policy dialogue, sponsored by the Bank to promote broad debate on strategic issues. In April 2006 the Bank established the Disaster Prevention Fund, financed through Ordinary Capital funds, to help countries to improve their disaster preparedness and reduce their vulnerability to natural hazards. A separate Multi-donor Disaster Prevention Trust Fund was established at the end of 2006 to finance technical assistance and investment in preparedness projects.

In July 2004 the Bank co-hosted an international donor conference, together with the World Bank, the EU and the UN, to consider the immediate and medium-term needs for Haiti following a period of political unrest. Some US $1,080m. was pledged at the conference, of which the Bank's contribution was $260m. In April 2009 international donors, meeting under the Bank's auspices, pledged further contributions of $324m. to Haiti's economic and social development. In January 2010 the Bank determined to redirect undisbursed funds of up to $90m. to finance priority emergency assistance and reconstruction efforts in Haiti following a devastating earthquake. In March the Board of Governors agreed to cancel Haiti's outstanding debt, requiring contributions by member countries of $479m., and to convert undisbursed loans in order to provide grant assistance amounting to $2,000m. over the coming 10 years. In mid-March the Bank organized a conference of representatives of the private sector in Haiti, in preparation for the International Donors' Conference, which was then held at the end of that month in New York, USA. The Bank also supported the Haitian Government in preparing, jointly with the UN, World Bank and European Commission, a Preliminary Damage and Needs Assessment report for presentation at the Conference.

An increasing number of donor countries have placed funds under the Bank's administration for assistance to Latin America, outside the framework of the Ordinary Resources and the Bank's Special Operations. These include the Social Progress Trust Fund (set up by the USA in 1961); the Venezuelan Trust Fund (set up in 1975); the Japan Special Fund (1988); and other funds administered on behalf of Austria, Belgium, Canada, Chile, Denmark, Finland, France, Israel, Italy, Japan, the Netherlands, Norway, Portugal, Spain, Sweden, Switzerland, the United Kingdom and the EU. A Program for the Development of Technical Co-operation was established in 1991, which is financed by European countries and the EU. During 2009 co-financing by bilateral and multilateral sources, mainly the World Bank and the Central American Bank for Economic Integration, amounted to some US $3,391.8m.

The Bank provides technical co-operation to help member countries to identify and prepare new projects, to improve loan execution, to strengthen the institutional capacity of public and private agencies, to address extreme conditions of poverty and to promote small- and micro-enterprise development. The Bank has established a special co-operation programme to facilitate the transfer of experience and technology among regional programmes. Technical co-operation operations are mainly financed by income from the FSO and donor trust funds. The Bank supports the efforts of the countries of the region to achieve economic integration and has provided extensive technical support for the formulation of integration strategies in the Andean, Central American and Southern Cone regions. In 2001 the Bank took a lead role in a Central American regional initiative, the Puebla-Panamá Plan, which aimed to consolidate integration and support for social and economic development. In June 2010 the Bank agreed to collaborate with the Spanish Government, the Bill and Melinda Gates Foundation and the Carlos Slim Health Institute in administering a new 'Salud Mesoamérica 2015' initiative, which aimed to support efforts to achieve the millennium development health objectives in the region over a five-year period. The Bank is a member of the technical co-ordinating committee of the Integration of Regional Infrastructure in South America initiative, which aimed to promote multinational development projects, capacity-building and integration in that region. In September 2006 the Bank established a new fund to support the preparation of infrastructure projects, InfraFund, with an initial US $20m. in resources. In 2005 the Bank inaugurated a Trade Finance Facilitation Program (TFFP) to support economic growth in the region by expanding the financing available for international trade activities. The programme was given permanent status in November 2006. In May 2008 the Bank launched a training initiative within the framework of the TFFP. In January 2009 the Bank determined to expand the TFFP to include loans, as well as guarantees, and to increase the programme limit from $400m. to $1,000m. By March 2010 there were 62 issuing banks from 18 Latin American and Caribbean countries participating in the programme, and 227 confirming banks from 87 international banking groups. At that time the programme had issued guarantees in support of international trade transactions totalling $865m. In September 2009 the Bank supported the establishment, jointly with the MIF, IIC, Andean Development Corporation, the US private investment corporation and a Swiss investment management company, of a Microenterprise Growth Facility (MIGROF), which aimed to provide up to $250m. to microfinance institutions in Latin America and the Caribbean.

AFFILIATES

Inter-American Investment Corporation (IIC): 1350 New York Ave, NW, Washington, DC 20577, USA; tel. (202) 623-3900; fax (202) 623-2360; e-mail iicmail@iadb.org; internet www.iic.int; f. 1986 as a legally autonomous affiliate of the Inter-American Development Bank, to promote the economic development of the region; commenced operations in 1989; initial capital stock was US $200m., of which 55% was contributed by developing member nations, 25.3% by the USA, and the remainder by non-regional members; in 2001 the Board of Governors of the Bank agreed to increase the IIC's capital to $500m; places emphasis on investment in small and medium-sized enterprises without access to other suitable sources of equity or long-term loans; in 2009 the IIC approved 40 operations amounting to $294m., bringing the cumulative total since 1989 to some $3,660m. for more than 600 projects; mems: 44 countries as shareholders; Gen. Man. JACQUES ROGOZINSKI; publ. *Annual Report* (in English, French, Portuguese and Spanish).

Multilateral Investment Fund (MIF) (Fondo Multilateral de Inversiones (FOMIN): 1300 New York Ave, NW, Washington, DC 20577, USA; tel. (202) 942-8211; fax (202) 942-8100; e-mail mifcontact@iadb.org; internet www.iadb.org/mif; f. 1993 as an autonomous fund administered by the Bank, to promote private sector development in the region; the 21 Bank members who signed the initial draft agreement in 1992 to establish the Fund pledged to contribute US $1,200m.; the Fund's activities are undertaken through three separate facilities concerned with technical co-operation, human resources development and small enterprise development; in 2000 a specialist working group, established to consider MIF operations, recommended that it target its resources on the following core areas of activity: small business development; market functioning; and financial and capital markets; the Bank's Social Entrepreneurship Program makes available credit to individuals or groups without access to commercial or development loans; some $10m. is awarded under the programme to fund projects in 26 countries; a Microenterprise Forum, 'Foromic', is held annually (Oct. 2010: Montevideo, Uruguay); in April 2005 38 donor countries agreed to establish MIF II, and replenish the Fund's resources with commitments totalling $502m.; MIF II came into effect in March 2007; in 2009 MIF approved $115.7m. for 134 operations; in mid-2010 MIF supported the establishment of an Emergency Liquidity Program for Haiti; Gen. Man. JULIE T. KATZMAN.

INSTITUTIONS

Instituto para la Integración de América Latina y el Caribe (INTAL) (Institute for the Integration of Latin America and the Caribbean): Esmeralda 130, 17°, 1035 Buenos Aires, Argentina; tel. (11) 4320-1850; fax (11) 4320-1865; e-mail int/inl@iadb.org; internet www.iadb.org/intal; f. 1965 under the auspices of the Inter-American Development Bank; forms part of the Bank's Integration and Regional Programmes Department; undertakes research on all aspects of regional integration and co-operation and issues related to international trade, hemispheric integration and relations with other regions and countries of the world; activities come under four main headings: regional and national technical co-operation projects on integration; policy fora; integration fora; and journals and information; hosts the secretariat of the Integration of Regional Infrastructure in South America (IIRSA) initiative; maintains an extensive Documentation Center and various statistical databases; Dir RICARDO CARCIOFI; publs *Integración y Comercio / Integration and Trade* (2 a year), *INTAL Monthly Newsletter, Informe Andino / Andean Report, CARICOM Report, Informe Centroamericano / Central American Report, Informe Mercosur / Mercosur Report* (2 a year).

Inter-American Institute for Social Development (INDES): 1350 New York Ave, NW, Washington, DC 20057, USA; fax (202) 623-2008; e-mail indes@iadb.org; internet indes.iadb.org; commenced operations in 1995; aims to support the training of senior officials from public sector institutions and organizations involved with social policies and social services; organizes specialized sub-regional courses and seminars and national training programmes; produces teaching materials and also serves as a forum for the exchange of ideas on social reform.

Publications

Annual Report (in English, French, Portuguese and Spanish).

Development Effectiveness Overview.

IDB Edu (quarterly).

Puentes (periodic civil society newsletter).

Revelation of Expectations in Latin America (periodic analysis of market expectations of inflation and growth).

Brochure series, occasional papers, working papers, reports.

Statistics

Distribution of loans and guarantees by sector
(US $ million)

Sector	2009	%	1961–2009	%
Competitiveness				
Energy	2,096.4	13.5	25,243.6	13.8
Transportation and communication	1,450.3	9.4	21,195.9	11.6
Agriculture and fisheries	838.6	5.4	15,885.9	8.7
Industry, mining and tourism	25.0	0.2	13,580.3	7.4
Multisector credit and preinvestment	1,055.0	6.8	5,972.1	3.3
Capital markets	2,351.5	15.2	3,912.8	2.1
Productive infrastructure	32.0	0.2	2,771.4	1.5
Science and technology	100.0	0.6	3,247.6	1.8
Trade financing	46.0	0.3	2,019.4	1.1
Social Development				
Social investment	2,594.1	16.7	23,573.0	12.9
Water and sanitation	1,808.8	11.7	12,950.2	7.1
Urban development	389.1	2.5	9,408.3	5.1
Education	154.8	1.0	6,939.6	3.8
Environment	741.0	4.8	4,567.6	2.5
Health	94.0	0.6	3,488.8	1.9
Microenterprise	10.8	0.1	520.2	0.3
Reform and Modernization of the State				
Reform and public sector support	201.1	1.3	12,338.6	6.7
Financial sector reform	400.0	2.6	8,360.3	4.6
Fiscal reform	1,096.7	7.1	5,609.8	3.1
Decentralization policies	—	0.0	1,131.8	0.6
Modernization and administration of justice	21.4	0.1	454.3	0.2
Total	15,506.5	100.0	183,171.5	100.0

Yearly and cumulative loans and guarantees, 1961–2009
(US $ million; after cancellations and exchange adjustments)

Country	Total Amount* 2009†	Total Amount* 1961–2009	Ordinary Capital 1961–2009	Fund for Special Operations 1961–2009	Funds in Administration 1961–2009
Argentina	1,601.0	28,594.3	27,900.2	644.9	49.2
Bahamas	—	486.6	484.6	—	2.0
Barbados	80.0	532.3	471.8	41.5	19.0
Belize	27.5	164.2	164.2	—	—
Bolivia	191.1	4,136.6	1,566.9	2,497.4	72.3
Brazil	2,958.8	37,318.2	35,628.3	1,555.9	134.0
Chile	66.5	6,401.2	6,151.1	205.5	44.6
Colombia	1,347.2	16,468.3	15,632.9	769.4	66.0
Costa Rica	45.0	3,429.5	2,924.5	367.0	138.0
Dominican Republic	992.3	3,844.8	2,999.9	756.2	88.7
Ecuador	515.0	5,662.2	4,569.5	997.4	95.3
El Salvador	327.0	3,829.6	2,876.6	805.2	147.8
Guatemala	672.0	4,139.2	3,357.9	711.2	70.1
Guyana	34.8	1,177.7	177.2	993.6	6.9
Haiti	—	1,304.9	—	1,298.6	6.3
Honduras	71.0	3,170.1	793.3	2,308.9	67.9
Jamaica	401.0	2,464.5	2,091.8	173.8	198.9
Mexico	3,126.9	25,407.9	24,786.1	559.0	62.8
Nicaragua	173.4	2,849.3	470.9	2,310.6	67.8
Panama	705.0	3,461.9	3,122.9	296.4	42.6
Paraguay	239.8	2,648.6	1,974.3	661.9	12.4
Peru	447.0	9,528.0	8,868.4	438.5	221.1
Suriname	15.0	203.8	197.4	6.4	—
Trinidad and Tobago	48.8	1,199.6	1,143.8	30.6	25.2
Uruguay	325.5	5,112.4	4,966.1	104.5	41.8
Venezuela	1,000.0	6,118.9	5,944.6	101.4	72.9
Regional	95.0	3,516.9	3,268.1	234.7	14.1
Total	15,506.5	183,171.5	162,533.3	18,870.5	1,767.7

* Includes non-sovereign guaranteed loans, net of participations, and guarantees, as applicable. Excludes lines of credit approved and guarantees issued under the Trade Finance Facilitation Program.
† Includes US $800m. of loan approvals cancelled during that year.
Source: IADB, *Annual Report 2009*.

LATIN AMERICAN INTEGRATION ASSOCIATION—LAIA

(ASOCIACIÓN LATINOAMERICANA DE INTEGRACIÓN—ALADI)

Address: Cebollatí 1461, Casilla 20.005, 11200 Montevideo, Uruguay.

Telephone: (2) 410-1121; **fax:** (2) 419-0649; **e-mail:** sgaladi@aladi.org; **internet:** www.aladi.org.

The Latin American Integration Association was established in August 1980 to replace the Latin American Free Trade Association, founded in February 1960.

MEMBERS

Argentina	Colombia	Paraguay
Bolivia	Cuba	Peru
Brazil	Ecuador	Uruguay
Chile	Mexico	Venezuela

Observers: People's Republic of China, Costa Rica, Dominican Republic, El Salvador, Guatemala, Honduras, Italy, Japan, Republic of Korea, Nicaragua, Panama, Portugal, Romania, Russia, Spain, Switzerland and Ukraine; also the UN Economic Commission for Latin America and the Caribbean (ECLAC), the UN Development Programme (UNDP), the Andean Development Corporation, the European Union, the Ibero-American General Secretariat (SEGIB), the Inter-American Development Bank, the Inter-American Institute for Co-operation on Agriculture, the Latin American Economic System, the Organization of American States, and the Pan American Health Organization/World Health Organization.

Organization

(August 2010)

COUNCIL OF MINISTERS

The Council of Ministers of Foreign Affairs is responsible for the adoption of the Association's policies. It meets when convened by the Committee of Representatives.

CONFERENCE OF EVALUATION AND CONVERGENCE

The Conference, comprising plenipotentiaries of the member governments, assesses the integration process and encourages negotiations between members. It also promotes the convergence of agreements and other actions on economic integration. The Conference meets when convened by the Committee of Representatives.

COMMITTEE OF REPRESENTATIVES

The Committee, the permanent political body of the Association, comprises a permanent and a deputy representative from each member country. The Committee is the main forum for the negotiation of ALADI's initiatives and is responsible for the correct implementation of the Treaty and its supplementary regulations. There are the following auxiliary bodies:

Advisory Commission for Financial and Monetary Affairs.

Advisory Commission on Customs Valuation.

Advisory Council for Enterprises.

Advisory Council for Export Financing.

Advisory Council for Customs Matters.

Budget Commission.

Commission for Technical Support and Co-operation.

Council for Financial and Monetary Affairs: comprises the Presidents of member states' central banks, who examine all aspects of financial, monetary and exchange co-operation.

Council of National Customs Directors.

Council on Transport for Trade Facilitation.

Labour Advisory Council.

Nomenclature Advisory Commission.

Sectoral Councils.

Tourism Council.

GENERAL SECRETARIAT

The General Secretariat is the technical body of the Association; it submits proposals for action, carries out research and evaluates activities. The Secretary-General is elected for a three-year term, which is renewable. There are two Assistant Secretaries-General.

Secretary-General: José Félix Fernández Estigarribia (Paraguay).

Activities

The Latin American Free Trade Association (LAFTA) was an intergovernmental organization, created by the Treaty of Montevideo in February 1960 with the object of increasing trade between the Contracting Parties and of promoting regional integration, thus contributing to the economic and social development of the member countries. The Treaty provided for the gradual establishment of a free trade area, which would form the basis for a Latin American Common Market. Reduction of tariff and other trade barriers was to be carried out gradually until 1980.

By 1980, however, only 14% of annual trade among members could be attributed to LAFTA agreements. In June it was decided that LAFTA should be replaced by a less ambitious and more flexible organization, the Latin American Integration Association (Asociación Latinoamericana de Integración—ALADI), established by the 1980 Montevideo Treaty, which came into force in March 1981, and was fully ratified in March 1982. The Treaty envisaged an area of economic preferences, comprising a regional tariff preference for goods originating in member states (in effect from 1 July 1984) and regional and partial scope agreements (on economic complementation, trade promotion, trade in agricultural goods, scientific and technical co-operation, the environment, tourism, and other matters), taking into account the different stages of development of the members, and with no definite timetable for the establishment of a full common market.

The members of ALADI are divided into three categories: most developed (Argentina, Brazil and Mexico); intermediate (Chile, Colombia, Peru, Uruguay and Venezuela); and least developed (Bolivia, Cuba—which joined the Association in August 1999, Ecuador and Paraguay), enjoying a special preferential system. By 2007 intra-ALADI exports were estimated to total US $94,410m., an increase of almost 20% compared with the previous year.

Certain LAFTA institutions were retained and adapted by ALADI, e.g. the Reciprocal Payments and Credits Agreement (1965, modified in 1982) and the Multilateral Credit Agreement to Alleviate Temporary Shortages of Liquidity, known as the Santo Domingo Agreement (1969, extended in 1981 to include mechanisms for counteracting global balance of payments difficulties and for assisting in times of natural disaster).

Agreements concluded under ALADI auspices include a regional tariff preference agreement, whereby members allow imports from other member states to enter with tariffs 20% lower than those imposed on imports from other countries, and a Market Opening Lists agreement in favour of the three least developed member states, which provides for the total elimination of duties and other restrictions on imports of certain products. Other 'partial scope agreements' (in which two or more member states participate), include: renegotiation agreements (pertaining to tariff cuts under LAFTA); trade agreements covering particular industrial sectors; the agreements establishing the Southern Common Market (Mercosur) and the Group of Three (G-3); and agreements covering agriculture, gas supply, tourism, environmental protection, books, transport, sanitation and trade facilitation. A new system of tariff nomenclature, based on the 'harmonized system', was adopted from 1 January 1990 as a basis for common trade negotiations and statistics. General regimes on safeguards and rules of origin entered into force in 1987.

The Secretariat convenes meetings of entrepreneurs in various private industrial sectors, to encourage regional trade and co-operation. In 2001 ALADI conducted a survey on small and medium-sized enterprises in order to advise the Secretary-General in formulating a programme to assist those businesses and enhance their competitiveness.

ALADI has worked to establish multilateral links or agreements with Latin American non-member countries or integration organizations, and with other developing countries or economic groups outside the continent. In February 1994 the Council of Ministers of Foreign Affairs urged that ALADI should become the co-ordinating body for the various bilateral, multilateral and regional accords (with the Andean Community, Mercosur and G-3, etc.), with the aim of eventually forming a region-wide common market. The General Secretariat initiated studies in preparation for a programme to undertake this co-ordinating work. At the same meeting in February there was a serious disagreement regarding the proposed adoption of a protocol to the Montevideo Treaty to enable Mexico to participate in the North American Free Trade Agreement (NAFTA), while remaining a member of ALADI. Brazil, in particular, opposed such a solution. However, in June the first Interpretative Protocol to the Montevideo Treaty was signed by the Ministers of Foreign Affairs: the Protocol allows member states to establish preferential trade agreements with developed nations, with a temporary waiver of the most-favoured nation clause, subject to the negotiation of unilateral compensation.

Mercosur (comprising Argentina, Brazil, Paraguay and Uruguay) aims to conclude free trade agreements with the other members of ALADI. In March 2001 ALADI signed a co-operation agreement with the Andean Community to facilitate the exchange of information and consolidate regional and subregional integration. In December 2003 Mercosur and the Andean Community signed an Economic Complementary Agreement, and in April 2004 they concluded a free trade agreement, to come into effect on 1 July 2004 (although later postponed). Those ALADI member states remaining outside Mercosur and the Andean Community—Cuba, Chile and Mexico—would be permitted to apply to join the envisaged larger free trade zone.

Publications

Empresarios en la Integración (monthly, in Spanish).

Noticias ALADI (monthly, in Spanish).

Estadísticas y Comercio (quarterly, in Spanish).

Reports, studies, brochures, texts of agreements.

NORTH AMERICAN FREE TRADE AGREEMENT—NAFTA

Address: *(Canadian section)* Royal Bank Centre, 90 Sparks St, Suite 705, Ottawa, ON K1P 5B4.

Telephone: (613) 992-9388; **fax:** (613) 992-9392; **e-mail:** canada@nafta-sec-alena.org; **internet:** www.nafta-sec-alena.org/canada.

Address: *(Mexican section)* Blvd Adolfo López Mateos 3025, 2°, Col Héroes de Padierna, 10700 México, DF.

Telephone: (55) 5629-9630; **fax:** (55) 5629-9637; **e-mail:** mexico@nafta-sec-alena.org.

Address: *(US section)* 14th St and Constitution Ave, NW, Room 2061, Washington, DC 20230.

Telephone: (202) 482-5438; **fax:** (202) 482-0148; **e-mail:** usa@nafta-sec-alena.org; **internet:** www.nafta-sec-alena.org.

The North American Free Trade Agreement (NAFTA) grew out of the free trade agreement between the USA and Canada that was signed in January 1988 and came into effect on 1 January 1989. Negotiations on the terms of NAFTA, which includes Mexico in the free trade area, were concluded in October 1992 and the Agreement was signed in December. The accord was ratified in November 1993 and entered into force on 1 January 1994; the full implementation of the provisions of the accord was achieved in January 2008. The NAFTA Secretariat is composed of national sections in each member country.

MEMBERS

Canada Mexico USA

MAIN PROVISIONS OF THE AGREEMENT

Under NAFTA almost all restrictions on trade and investment between Canada, Mexico and the USA were removed over the period 1 January 1994–1 January 2008. Tariffs on trade between the USA and Mexico in 94% of agricultural products were eliminated immediately, with trade restrictions on further agricultural products initially protected by tariff-rate quotas (TRQs) and eliminated more gradually; tariffs on the most import-sensitive staple agricultural commodities, including Mexican exports to the USA of sugar and selected horticultural products and US exports to Mexico of corn, high fructose corn syrup, dry edible beans and non-fat dry milk, were abolished on 1 January 2008.

NAFTA also provided for the phasing out by 2004 of tariffs on automobiles and textiles between all three countries; and for Mexico to open its financial sector to US and Canadian investment, with all restrictions to be removed by 2008. Mexico was to liberalize government procurement, removing preferential treatment for domestic companies over a 10-year period. Barriers to investment were removed in most sectors, with exemptions for petroleum in Mexico, culture in Canada and airlines and radio communications in the USA. In April 1998 the fifth meeting of the three-member ministerial Free Trade Commission (see below), held in Paris, France, agreed to remove tariffs on some 600 goods, including certain chemicals, pharmaceuticals, steel and wire products, textiles, toys, and watches, from 1 August. As a result of that agreement, a number of tariffs were eliminated as much as 10 years earlier than had been originally planned.

In transport, it was initially planned that heavy goods vehicles would have complete freedom of movement between the three countries by 2000. However, owing to concerns on the part of the US Government relating to the implementation of adequate safety standards by Mexican truck-drivers, the 2000 deadline for the free circulation of heavy goods vehicles was not met. In February 2001 a five-member NAFTA panel of experts appointed to adjudicate on the dispute ruled that the USA was violating the Agreement. In December the US Senate approved legislation entitling Mexican long-haul trucks to operate anywhere in the USA following compliance with rigorous safety checks to be enforced by US inspectors.

In the case of a sudden influx of goods from one country to another that adversely affects a domestic industry, the Agreement makes provision for the imposition of short-term 'snap-back' tariffs.

Disputes are to be settled in the first instance by intergovernmental consultation. If a dispute is not resolved within 30 to 40 days, a government may call a meeting of the Free Trade Commission. The Commission's Advisory Committee on Private Commercial Disputes and its Advisory Committee on Private Commercial Disputes Regarding Agricultural Goods recommend procedures for the resolution of such complex disputes. If the Commission is unable to settle an issue a panel of experts in the relevant field is appointed to adjudicate. In June 1996 Canada and Mexico announced their decision to refer the newly enacted US 'Helms-Burton' legislation on trade with Cuba to the Commission. They claimed that the legislation, which provides for punitive measures against foreign companies that engage in trade with Cuba, imposed undue restrictions on Canadian and Mexican companies and was, therefore, in contravention of NAFTA. However, at the beginning of 1997 certain controversial provisions of the Helms-Burton legislation were suspended for a period of six months by the US administration. The relevant provisions continued to be suspended at six-monthly intervals, most recently in July 2010.

In December 1994 NAFTA members issued a formal invitation to Chile to seek membership of the Agreement. Formal discussions on Chile's entry began in June 1995, but were stalled in December when the US Congress failed to approve 'fast-track' negotiating authority for the US Government, which was to have allowed the latter to negotiate a trade agreement with Chile, without risk of incurring a line-by-line veto from the US Congress. In February 1996 Chile began high-level negotiations with Canada on a wide-ranging bilateral free trade agreement. Chile, which already had extensive bilateral trade agreements with Mexico, was regarded as advancing its position with regard to NAFTA membership by means of the proposed accord with Canada. The bilateral agreement, which provided for the extensive elimination of customs duties by 2002, was signed in November 1996 and ratified by Chile in July 1997. However, in November 1997 the US Government was obliged to request the removal of the 'fast-track' proposal from the legislative agenda, owing to insufficient support within Congress.

In April 1998 heads of state of 34 countries, meeting in Santiago, Chile, agreed formally to initiate the negotiating process to establish a Free Trade Area of the Americas (FTAA). The US Government had originally proposed creating the FTAA through the gradual extension of NAFTA trading privileges on a bilateral basis. However, the framework agreed upon by ministers of trade of the 34 countries, meeting in March, provided for countries to negotiate and accept FTAA provisions on an individual basis and as part of a sub-regional economic bloc. It was envisaged that the FTAA would exist alongside the sub-regional associations, including NAFTA. At a special summit of the Americas, held in January 2004 in Monterrey, Mexico, the leaders adopted a declaration committing themselves to the eventual establishment of the FTAA; however, they did not specify a completion date for the negotiations. In March the negotiations were suspended, and at 2010 it appeared likely that they would remain stalled.

ADDITIONAL AGREEMENTS

During 1993, as a result of domestic pressure, the new US Government negotiated two 'side agreements' with its NAFTA partners, which were to provide safeguards for workers' rights and the environment. A Commission for Labour Co-operation was established under the North American Agreement on Labour Co-operation (NAALC) to monitor implementation of labour accords and to foster co-operation in that area. Panels of experts, with representatives from each country, were established to adjudicate in cases of alleged infringement of workers' rights or environmental damage. The panels were given the power to impose fines and trade sanctions, but only with regard to the USA and Mexico; Canada, which was opposed to such measures, was to enforce compliance with NAFTA by means of its own legal system. The Commission for Environmental Co-operation (CEC), initiated in 1994 under the provisions of the 1993 North American Agreement on Environmental Co-operation (which complements the relevant environmental provisions of NAFTA), addresses regional environmental concerns, assists in the prevention of potential trade and environmental conflicts, advises on the environmental impact of trade issues, encourages private-sector investment in environmental trade issues, and promotes the effective enforcement of environmental law. In co-operation with mapping agency partners CEC produces the *North American Environmental Atlas*. During 1994–2009 the CEC adopted numerous resolutions, including on the sound management of chemicals, the environmentally sound management and tracking of hazardous wastes and hazardous recyclable materials, the conservation of butterflies and birds, the availability of pollutant release and transfer data, and on co-operation in the conservation of biodiversity. The CEC-financed North American Fund for Environmental Co-operation (NAFEC), established in 1995, supports community environmental projects.

With regard to the NAALC, National Administration Offices have been established in each of the three NAFTA countries in order to monitor labour issues and to address complaints about non-compliance with domestic labour legislation. However, punitive measures in the form of trade sanctions or fines (up to US $20m.) may only be imposed in the specific instances of contravention of national legislation regarding child labour, a minimum wage or health and safety standards. A Commission for Labour Co-operation has been established (see below) and incorporates a council of ministers of labour of the three countries.

In August 1993 the USA and Mexico agreed to establish a Border Environmental Co-operation Commission (BECC) to assist with the co-ordination of projects for the improvement of infrastructure and to monitor the environmental impact of the Agreement on the US–Mexican border area, where industrial activity was expected to intensify. The Commission is located in Ciudad Juárez, Mexico. By August 2010 the BECC had certified 173 projects, at a cost of US $3,864.4m. The North American Development Bank (NADB or NADBank), established by an agreement concluded between the USA and Mexico in October 1993, is mandated to finance environmental and infrastructure projects along the US–Mexican border.

Commission for Environmental Co-operation (CEC): 393 rue St Jacques Ouest, Bureau 200, Montréal, QC H2Y IN9, Canada; tel. (514) 350-4300; fax (514) 350-4314; e-mail info@cec.org; internet www.cec.org; f. 1994; Exec. Dir EVAN LLOYD; publs *Annual Report*, *Taking Stock* (annually), industry reports, policy studies.

Commission for Labour Co-operation: 1211 Connecticut Ave, NW Suite 400, Washington, DC 20036, USA; tel. (202) 464-1100; fax (202) 464-9490; e-mail info@naalc.org; internet www.naalc.org; f. 1994; Exec. Dir (vacant); publ. *Annual Report*.

North American Development Bank (NADB/NADBank): 203 South St Mary's, Suite 300, San Antonio, TX 78205, USA; tel. (210) 231-8000; fax (210) 231-6232; internet www.nadbank.org; at August 2010 the NADB had authorized capital of US $3,000m., subscribed equally by Mexico and the USA, of which $450m. was paid-up; Man. Dir JORGE C. GARCÉS (USA); publs *Annual Report*, *NADBank News*.

ORGANIZATION OF AMERICAN STATES—OAS

(ORGANIZACIÓN DE LOS ESTADOS AMERICANOS—OEA)

Address: 17th St and Constitution Ave, NW, Washington, DC 20006, USA.

Telephone: (202) 458-3000; **fax:** (202) 458-6319; **e-mail:** pi@oas .org; **internet:** www.oas.org.

The ninth International Conference of American States (held in Bogotá, Colombia, in 1948) OAS by adopting the Charter of the Organization of American States; the OAS succeeded the Commercial Bureau of American Republics, founded in 1890, and the Pan-American Union. The Charter was subsequently amended by the Protocol of Buenos Aires (creating the annual General Assembly), signed in 1967 and enacted in 1970; by the Protocol of Cartagena de Indias, which was signed in 1985 and enacted in 1988; and by the Protocol of Washington, signed in 1992 and enacted in 1997. The purpose of the OAS is to strengthen the peace and security of the continent; to promote human rights and to promote and consolidate representative democracy, with due respect for the principle of non-intervention; to prevent possible causes of difficulties and to ensure the peaceful settlement of disputes that may arise among the member states; to provide for common action in the event of aggression; to seek the solution of political, juridical and economic problems that may arise among the member states; to promote, by co-operative action, their economic, social and cultural development; to achieve an effective limitation of conventional weapons; to devote the largest amount of resources to the economic and social development of the member states; and to confront shared problems such as poverty, terrorism, the trade in illegal drugs, and corruption. The OAS is the principal regional multilateral forum. It plays a leading role in implementing mandates established by the hemisphere's leaders through the Summits of the Americas.

MEMBERS

Antigua and Barbuda	Guyana
Argentina	Haiti
Bahamas	Honduras†
Barbados	Jamaica
Belize	Mexico
Bolivia	Nicaragua
Brazil	Panama
Canada	Paraguay
Chile	Peru
Colombia	Saint Christopher and Nevis
Costa Rica	Saint Lucia
Cuba*	Saint Vincent and the Grenadines
Dominica	
Dominican Republic	Suriname
Ecuador	Trinidad and Tobago
El Salvador	USA
Grenada	Uruguay
Guatemala	Venezuela

* The Cuban Government was suspended from OAS activities in 1962; the suspension was revoked by the OAS General Assembly in June 2009, although Cuba's participation in the organization was to be subject to further review.

† Membership suspended in July 2009.

Permanent Observers: Algeria, Angola, Armenia, Austria, Azerbaijan, Belgium, Benin, Bosnia and Herzegovina, Bulgaria, People's Republic of China, Croatia, Cyprus, Czech Republic, Denmark, Egypt, Equatorial Guinea, Estonia, Finland, France, Georgia, Germany, Ghana, Greece, Holy See, Hungary, Iceland, India, Ireland, Israel, Italy, Japan, Kazakhstan, Republic of Korea, Latvia, Lebanon, Lithuania, Luxembourg, Morocco, Netherlands, Nigeria, Norway, Pakistan, Philippines, Poland, Portugal, Qatar, Romania, Russia, Saudi Arabia, Serbia, Slovakia, Slovenia, Spain, Sri Lanka, Sweden, Switzerland, Thailand, Tunisia, Turkey, Ukraine, United Kingdom, Yemen and the European Union.

Organization

(August 2010)

GENERAL ASSEMBLY

The Assembly meets annually and may also hold special sessions when convoked by the Permanent Council. As the highest decision-making body of the OAS, it decides general action and policy. The 40th General Assembly was convened in Lima, Peru, in June 2010; the 41st General Assembly was scheduled to be convened in San Salvador, El Salvador, in June 2011.

MEETINGS OF CONSULTATION OF MINISTERS OF FOREIGN AFFAIRS

Meetings are convened, at the request of any member state, to consider problems of an urgent nature and of common interest to member states, or to serve as an organ of consultation in cases of armed attack or other threats to international peace and security. The Permanent Council determines whether a meeting should be convened and acts as a provisional organ of consultation until ministers are able to assemble.

PERMANENT COUNCIL

The Council meets regularly throughout the year at OAS headquarters. It is composed of one representative of each member state with the rank of ambassador; each government may accredit alternate representatives and advisers and when necessary appoint an interim representative. The office of Chairman is held in turn by each of the representatives, following alphabetical order according to the names of the countries in Spanish. The Vice-Chairman is determined in the same way, following reverse alphabetical order. Their terms of office are three months.

The Council guides ongoing policies and actions and oversees the maintenance of friendly relations between members. It supervises the work of the OAS and promotes co-operation with a variety of other international bodies including the United Nations. It comprises a General Committee and Committees on Juridical and Political Affairs, Hemispheric Security, Inter-American Summits Management and Civil Society Participation in OAS Activities, and Administrative and Budgetary Affairs. There are also ad hoc working groups. The official languages are English, French, Portuguese and Spanish.

INTER-AMERICAN COUNCIL FOR INTEGRAL DEVELOPMENT (CIDI)

The Council was established in 1996, replacing the Inter-American Economic and Social Council and the Inter-American Council for Education, Science and Culture. Its aim is to promote co-operation among the countries of the region, in order to accelerate economic and social development. An Executive Secretariat for Integral Development provides CIDI with technical and secretarial services and co-ordinates a Special Multilateral Fund of CICI (FEMCIDI), the New Programming Approaches programme, a Hemispheric Integral Development Program, a Universal Civil Identity Program in the Americas, and Migration and Development Innovative Programs. Technical co-operation and training programmes are managed by a subsidiary body of the Council, the Inter-American Agency for Co-operation and Development, which was established in 1999.

Executive Secretary: ALFONSO QUIÑÓNEZ.

INTER-AMERICAN JURIDICAL COMMITTEE (IAJC)

The Committee's purposes are: to serve as an advisory body to the OAS on juridical matters; to promote the progressive development and codification of international law; and to study juridical problems relating to the integration of the developing countries in the hemisphere, and, in so far as may appear desirable, the possibility of attaining uniformity in legislation. It comprises 11 jurists, nationals of different member states, elected for a period of four years, with the possibility of re-election.

Chairman: GUILLERMO FERNÁNDEZ DE SOTO (Colombia); Av. Marechal Floriano 196, 3° andar, Palácio Itamaraty, Centro, 20080-002, Rio de Janeiro, Brazil; tel. (21) 2206-9903; fax (21) 2203-2090; e-mail cjioea.trp@terra.com.br.

INTER-AMERICAN COMMISSION ON HUMAN RIGHTS

The Commission was established in 1960 to promote the observance and protection of human rights in the member states of the OAS. It examines and reports on the human rights situation in member countries and considers individual petitions relating to alleged human rights violations by member states. A Special Rapporteurship on the Rights of People of Afro-Descendants, and against Racial Discrimination was established in 2005. Other rapporteurs analyse and report on the rights of children, women, indigenous peoples, migrant workers, prisoners and displaced persons, and on freedom of expression.

Executive Secretary: SANTIAGO A. CANTON; 1889F St, NW, Washington, DC 20006, USA; tel. (202) 458-6002; fax (202) 458-3992; e-mail cidhoea@oas.org; internet www.cidh.oas.org.

GENERAL SECRETARIAT

The Secretariat, the central and permanent organ of the Organization, performs the duties entrusted to it by the General Assembly, Meetings of Consultation of Ministers of Foreign Affairs and the Councils. There is an Administrative Tribunal, comprising six elected members, to settle staffing disputes.

Secretary-General: JOSÉ MIGUEL INSULZA (Chile).

Assistant Secretary-General: ALBERT R. RAMDIN (Suriname).

INTER-AMERICAN COMMITTEES AND COMMISSIONS

Inter-American Committee Against Terrorism (Comité Interamericano Contra el Terrorismo—CICTE): 1889 F St, NW, Washington, DC 20006, USA; tel. (202) 458-6960; fax (202) 458-3857; e-mail cicte@oas.org; internet www.cicte.oas.org; f. 1999 to enhance the exchange of information via national authorities, formulate proposals to assist member states in drafting counter-terrorism legislation in all states, compile bilateral, sub-regional, regional and multilateral treaties and agreements signed by member states and promote universal adherence to international counter-terrorism conventions, strengthen border co-operation and travel documentation security measures, and develop activities for training and crisis management; Exec. Sec. GONZALO GALLEGOS (USA).

Inter-American Committee on Ports (Comisión Interamericana de Puertos—CIP): 1889 F St, NW, Washington, DC 20006, USA; tel. (202) 458-3871; fax (202) 458-3517; e-mail cip@oas.org; internet www.oas.org/cip; f. 1998; serves as the permanent inter-American forum to strengthen co-operation on port-related issues among the member states, with the active participation of the private sector; the Committee, comprising 34 mem. states, meets every two years; its Executive Board, which executes policy decisions, meets annually; four technical advisory groups have been established to advise on logistics and competition (formerly port operations), port security, navigation control, and environmental protection; Sec. CARLOS M. GALLEGOS.

Inter-American Court of Human Rights (IACHR) (Corte Interamericana de Derechos Humanos): Apdo Postal 6906-1000, San José, Costa Rica; tel. (506) 2234-0581; fax (506) 2234-0584; e-mail corteidh@corteidh.or.cr; internet www.corteidh.or.cr; f. 1979 as an autonomous judicial institution whose purpose is to apply and interpret the American Convention on Human Rights (which entered into force in 1978); comprises seven jurists from OAS member states; Pres. DIEGO GARCÍA-SAYÁN (Peru); Exec. Sec. PABLO SAAVEDRA ALESSANDRI (Chile); publ. *Annual Report*.

Inter-American Defense Board (Junta Interamericana de Defensa—JID): 2600 16th St, NW, Washington, DC 20441, USA; tel. (202) 939-6041; fax (202) 387-2880; e-mail iadc-registrar@jid.org; internet www.jid.org; promotes co-operative security interests in the Western Hemisphere; new statutes adopted in 2006 formally designated the Board as an OAS agency; works on issues such as disaster assistance and confidence-building measures directly suporting the hemispheric security goals of the OAS and of regional ministers of defence; also provides a senior-level academic programme in security studies for military, national police and civilian leaders at the Inter-American Defense College; Dir-Gen. Brig. ANCIL W. ANTOINE (Trinidad and Tobago).

Inter-American Drug Abuse Control Commission (Comisión Interamericana para el Control del Abuso de Drogas—CICAD): 1889 F St, NW, Washington, DC 20006, USA; tel. (202) 458-3178; fax (202) 458-3658; e-mail oidcicad@oas.org; internet www.cicad.oas.org; f. 1986 by the OAS to promote and facilitate multilateral co-operation in the control and prevention of the trafficking, production and use of illegal drugs, and related crimes; reports regularly, through the Multilateral Evaluation Mechanism, on progress against illegal drugs in each member state and region-wide; mems: 34 countries; Exec. Sec. JAMES F. MACK; publs *Statistical Survey* (annually), *Directory of Governmental Institutions Charged with the Fight Against the Illicit Production, Trafficking, Use and Abuse of Narcotic Drugs and Psychotropic Substances*, *Evaluation of Progress in Drug Control*, *Progress Report on Drug Control—Implementation and Recommendations* (2 a year).

Inter-American Telecommunication Commission (Comisión Interamericana de Telecomunicaciones—CITEL): 1889 F St, NW, Washington, DC 20006, USA; tel. (202) 458-3004; fax (202) 458-6854; e-mail citel@oas.org; internet www.citel.oas.org; f. 1993 to promote the development and harmonization of telecommunications in the region, in co-operation with governments and the private sector; CITEL has more than 200 associate members representing private associations or companies, permanent observers, and international organizations; under its Permanent Executive Committee specialized consultative committees focus on telecommunication standardization and radiocommunication, including broadcasting; mems: 35 countries; Exec. Sec. CLOVIS JOSÉ BAPTISTA NETO.

Activities

STRENGTHENING DEMOCRACY

The OAS promotes and supports good governance in its member states through various activities, including electoral observations, crisis-prevention missions, and programmes to strengthen government institutions and to support a regional culture of democracy. In September 2001 the member states adopted the Inter-American Democratic Charter, which details the essential elements of representative democracy, including free and fair elections; respect for human rights and fundamental freedoms; the exercise of power in accordance with the rule of law; a pluralistic political party system; and the separation and independence of the branches of government. Transparency and responsible administration by governments, respect for social rights, freedom of expression and citizen participation are among other elements deemed by the Charter to define democracy.

The observation of elections is one of the most important tasks of the OAS. Depending on the specific situation and the particular needs of each country, missions vary from a few technical experts sent for a limited time to a large country-wide team of monitors dispatched to observe the full electoral process for an extended period commencing with the political parties' campaigns. The missions present their observations to the OAS Permanent Council, along with recommendations for how each country's electoral process might be strengthened. Twelve electoral observer missions were conducted in 2009; in early 2010 missions were dispatched to federal elections in Saint Christopher and Nevis (in January), a general election conducted in Costa Rica (February), and legislative elections in Colombia (March). In August a joint electoral observation mission, with representatives from CARICOM, was deployed to oversee the presidential and legislative electoral processes in Haiti, where polling was scheduled to take place in November.

The OAS has responded to numerous political crises in the region. In some cases, at the request of member states, it has sent special missions to provide critical support to the democratic process. During 2005–06 the OAS was particularly active in Nicaragua. In June 2005, responding to issues raised by the Government of President Enrique Bolaños, the OAS General Assembly expressed concern about developments that posed a threat to the separation and independence of branches of government. Citing the Inter-American Democratic Charter and the OAS Charter, the General Assembly authorized an OAS mission to help establish a broad national dialogue in that country; accordingly, the OAS Secretary-General led a high-level mission to Nicaragua to support efforts to find democratic solutions to the situation, and also appointed a special envoy to facilitate dialogue there. In 2006 the OAS Special Mission to Accompany the Democratic and Electoral Process in Nicaragua monitored regional elections, conducted in March, and a general election in November. In a subsequent report to the OAS Permanent Council, the Chief-of-Mission noted that Nicaragua had made significant steps forward in its democratic development and that its elections were 'increasingly clean and competitive'.

In 2005, following an institutional crisis in Ecuador, the OAS offered support for the establishment of an impartial, independent Supreme Court of Justice. The OAS Secretary-General appointed two distinguished jurists as his special representatives to observe the selection process; members of Ecuador's new Supreme Court were sworn in during November. The OAS also played a role in Bolivia in 2005, following the resignation in June of President Carlos Mesa. The OAS Secretary-General appointed a special representative to facilitate political dialogue and to head the OAS observation mission on the electoral process that resulted in Evo Morales winning the presidency.

In August 2000 the OAS Secretary-General undertook the first of several high-level missions to negotiate with the authorities in Haiti in order to resolve the political crisis resulting from a disputed general election in May. In January 2001, following a meeting with the Haitian Prime Minister, the Assistant Secretary-General recommended that the OAS renew its efforts to establish a dialogue between the Government, opposition parties and representatives of civil society in that country. In May and June the OAS and the Caribbean Community and Common Market (CARICOM) undertook joint missions to Haiti in order to assess and promote prospects for a democratic resolution to the political uncertainties. Following political and social unrest in Haiti in December, the OAS and CARICOM pledged to conduct an independent investigation into the violence, and in March 2002 an agreement to establish a Special OAS Mission for Strengthening Democracy in Haiti was signed in the capital, Port-au-Prince. The independent commission of inquiry reported to the OAS at the beginning of July, and listed a set of recommendations relating to law reform, security and other confidence-building measures to help to secure democracy in Haiti. In January 2004 the OAS Special Mission condemned the escalation of political violence in Haiti and in February took a lead in drafting a plan of action to implement a CARICOM-brokered action plan to resolve the crisis. In late February the Permanent Council met in special session, and urged the UN to take necessary and appropriate action to address the deteriorating situation in Haiti. On 29 February President Jean-Bertrand Aristide resigned and left the country; amid ongoing civil unrest, a provisional leader was sworn in. The OAS Mission continued to attempt to maintain law and order, in co-operation with a UN-authorized Multinational Interim Force, and facilitated political discussions on the establishment of a transitional government. From March the Special Mission participated in the process to develop an Interim Co-operation Framework, identifying the urgent and medium-term needs of Haiti, which was presented to a meeting of international donors held in July. In June the OAS General Assembly adopted a resolution instructing the Permanent Council to undertake all necessary diplomatic initiatives to foster the restoration of democracy in Haiti, and called upon the Special Mission to work with the new UN Stabilization Mission in Haiti in preparing, organizing and monitoring future elections. During 2005 OAS technical experts, together with UN counterparts, assisted Haiti's Provisional Electoral Council (PEC) with the process of voter registration for legislative and presidential elections, initially scheduled for later in that year, as well as to formulate an electronic vote tabulation system, which was to serve as the basis for a permanent civil registry. In January 2006 the OAS Permanent Council declared its grave concern at a further postponement of the elections. In the following month, however, the Council expressed its satisfaction that polling had taken place in a free and fair manner. The Secretary-General visited Haiti to meet with officials and offer his support for the declared President-elect, René Préval. The OAS has continued to extend support to the country and to co-ordinate international assistance, mainly through its Haiti Task Force, chaired by the Assistant Secretary-General. In February 2008 a special mission of the Permanent Council visited Haiti to assess priorities for future support. In July the Assistant Secretary-General announced the establishment of an OAS Haiti Fund to support the organization's mandate and priorities in that country. In September the Assistant Secretary-General, visiting Haiti after it had been struck by a series of tropical cyclones, reiterated OAS commitment to Haiti's socio-economic development and stability. In early 2009 the OAS pledged to support the electoral process in Haiti, and to monitor forthcoming senate elections.

In April 2002 a special session of the General Assembly was convened to discuss the ongoing political instability in Venezuela. The Assembly applied its authority granted under the Inter-American Democratic Charter to condemn the alteration of the constitutional order in Venezuela which forced the temporary eviction of President Hugo Chávez from office. In January 2003 the OAS announced the establishment of a Group of Friends, composed of representatives from Brazil, Chile, Mexico, Spain, Portugal and the USA, to support its efforts to resolve the ongoing crisis in Venezuela. In March the OAS Secretary-General was invited by Venezuelan opposition groupings to mediate negotiations with the Government. The talks culminated in May with the signing of an OAS-brokered agreement which, it was hoped, would lead to mid-term referendums on elected officials, including the presidency. The OAS, with the Carter Center, subsequently oversaw and verified the collection of signatures to determine whether referendums should be held. Following the staging of a recall referendum on the Venezuelan presidency in August 2004, OAS member states urged that there should be a process of reconciliation in that country.

In June 2009 the OAS Secretary-General and Permanent Council condemned the forced expulsion from power of President José Manuel Zelaya of Honduras by members of that country's armed forces. A special session of the General Assembly was convened, which urged the Secretary-General to pursue diplomatic efforts to restore constitutional order and the rule of law. When this was not achieved within the required 72 hour period, the Assembly, on 4 July, resolved to suspend the membership rights of Honduras to participate in the organization. President Óscar Arias of Costa Rica agreed to lead efforts on behalf of the OAS to mediate with the new authorities in Honduras in order to resolve the crisis. In August the OAS organized a delegation of foreign ministers to visit Honduras and promote a settlement based on the San José Accord formulated by President Arias, which envisaged Zelaya returning to the country as head of a government of national unity, and the holding of a general election a month earlier than scheduled, in late October. Political amnesty was to be offered to all sides under the proposed agreement. The interim authorities permitted the delegation's visit conditional on the OAS Secretary-General participating only as an observer. The opposing leaders signed an accord in October, although it was soon rejected by Zelaya after he was excluded from an interim national unity government. A special session of the Permanent Council was convened in December to consider the political situation in Honduras following a general election conducted in late November. The Council urged the newly elected leader, Porfirio Lobo, fully to re-establish respect for human rights, to end 'persecution' of Zelaya, and to establish a national unity government to serve until the original presidential term ended in January 2010. In June the OAS General Assembly determined to establish a high level commission to assess the political and human rights situation in Honduras. The commission's report, issued in late July, included the following recommendations: the termination of legal proceedings initiated against former President Zelaya; support for Zelaya's application to membership of the Central American Parliament with the status of a former constitutional president; continued investigation into alleged human rights violations; and implementation, by the new government, of further measures to protect activists, journalists, judges and others who had opposed the coup d'etat.

In special situations, when both or all member states involved in a dispute ask for its assistance, the OAS plays a longer-term role in supporting countries to resolve bilateral or multilateral issues. In September 2005 Belize and Guatemala signed an agreement at the OAS establishing a framework for negotiations and confidence-building measures to help maintain good bilateral relations while they sought a permanent solution to a long-standing territorial dispute. Following a series of negotiations under OAS auspices, both sides signed a Special Agreement to resolve the dispute in December 2008. In April 2006 another OAS-supported effort was concluded successfully when El Salvador and Honduras signed an accord settling differences over the demarcation of their common border. In March 2008 a Meeting of Consultation of OAS ministers of foreign affairs was convened following an escalation of diplomatic tension between Colombia and Ecuador resulting from a violation of Ecuador's borders by Colombian soldiers in pursuit of opposition insurgents. The meeting approved a resolution to establish a Good Offices Mission to restore confidence between the two countries and to negotiate an appropriate settlement to the dispute. A Verification Commission of the Good Offices Mission presented a report in July 2009, which included proposals to strengthen bilateral relations.

The OAS places a high priority on combating corruption in recognition of the undermining effect this has on democratic institutions. In 1996 the OAS member states adopted the Inter-American Convention against Corruption, which by mid-2009 had been ratified or acceded to by 33 member states. In 2002 the treaty's signatory states initiated a peer review process to examine their compliance with the treaty's key provisions. The Follow-Up Mechanism for the Implementation of the Inter-American Convention against Corruption assesses progress and recommends concrete measures that the states parties can implement to improve compliance. Representatives of civil society organizations are also given the opportunity to meet with experts and present information for their consideration. A second round of the review process commenced in 2006 and was concluded in December 2008, at which time 28 country reports had been adopted. All participating countries have been assessed at least once and the completed progress reports are available to the public. The OAS has also held seminars and training sessions in the region on such matters as improving transparency in government and drafting model anti-corruption legislation.

In recent years, the OAS has expanded its outreach to civil society. More than 200 non-governmental organizations (NGOs) are registered to take part in OAS activities. Civil society groups are encouraged to participate in workshops and round-tables in advance of the OAS General Assembly to prepare proposals and recommendations to present to the member states. This is also the case with Summits of the Americas and the periodic ministerial meetings, such as those on education, labour, culture, and science and technology. NGOs contributed ideas to the development of the Inter-American Democratic Charter and have participated in follow-up work on hemispheric treaties against corruption and terrorism.

The OAS has also focused on strengthening ties with the private sector. In 2006 it concluded a co-operation agreement with the business forum Private Sector of the Americas which aimed to promote dialogue and to support public–private alliances with a view to creating jobs, combating poverty and strengthening development. Business leaders from the region develop proposals and recommendations to present to the OAS General Assembly and to the Summits of the Americas.

Under the Democratic Charter a 'respect for human rights and fundamental freedoms' is deemed to be an essential element of a democracy. The Inter-American Commission on Human Rights and the Inter-American Court of Human Rights are the pillars of a system designed to protect individuals in the Americas who have suffered violations of their rights. A key function of the Commission is to consider petitions from individuals who claim that a state has violated a protected right and that they have been unable to find justice. The Commission brings together the petitioner and the state to explore a 'friendly settlement'. If such an outcome is not possible, the Commission may recommend specific measures to be carried out by the state to remedy the violation. If a state does not follow the recommendations the Commission has the option to publish its report or take the case to the Inter-American Court of Human Rights, as long as the state involved has accepted the Court's compulsory jurisdiction. The Commission convenes for six weeks each year.

In addition to hearing cases the Court may exercise its advisory jurisdiction to interpret the human rights treaties in effect in the region. The Commission, for its part, may conduct an on-site visit to a country, at the invitation of its Government, to analyse and report on the human rights situation. The Commission has also created rapporteurships focusing on particular human rights issues. In 2005 it created a rapporteurship on the rights of persons of African descent and against racial discrimination. Other rapporteurs analyse and report on the rights of children, women, indigenous peoples migrant workers, prisoners and displaced persons, and on freedom of expression. The Commission also has a special unit on human rights defenders. The OAS also works beyond the inter-American human rights system to promote the rights of vulnerable groups. The member states are in the process of negotiating the draft American Declaration on the Rights of Indigenous Peoples, which is intended to promote and protect a range of rights covering such areas as family, spirituality, work, culture, health, the environment, and systems of knowledge, language and communication. A special fund was established for voluntary contributions by member states and permanent observers in order to help cover the costs involved in broadening indigenous participation. The OAS also works to promote and protect women's rights. The Inter-American Commission of Women (CIM), established in 1928, has had an impact on shaping laws and policies in many countries. One of its key initiatives led to the adoption of the Inter-American Convention on the Prevention, Punishment and Eradication of Violence against Women, also known as the Convention of Belém do Pará, which was adopted in 1994 by the OAS General Assembly and, by 2010, had been ratified by 32 OAS member states. Since 2005 parties to the Belém do Pará Convention have been participating in a follow-up mechanism designed to determine how the countries are complying with the treaty and progress achieved in preventing and punishing violence against women. In 2006 the CIM also initiated an examination of strategies for reversing the spread of HIV/AIDS among women in the region. The Commission has urged greater efforts to integrate a gender perspective into every aspect of the OAS agenda. An Inter-American Year of Women was inaugurated in February 2010.

SOCIAL AND ECONOMIC DEVELOPMENT

Combating poverty and promoting social equity and economic development are priority concerns of the OAS. In 2007 the member states were negotiating the text of a new Social Charter of the Americas. The OAS works on a number of fronts to combat poverty and promote development, in partnership with regional and global agencies, the private sector and the international community. In 2006 the OAS General Assembly approved a new Strategic Plan for Partnership for Integral Development 2006–09, which was to guide OAS actions in this area. (In June 2009 the General Assembly resolved to extend the Strategic Plan by one year, until 31 December 2010.) OAS development policies and priorities are determined by the organization's political bodies, including the General Assembly, the Permanent Council and the Inter-American Council for Integral Development (CIDI), with direction from the Summits of the Americas. The OAS Executive Secretariat for Integral Development (SEDI) implements the policies through projects and programmes. Specialized departments within SEDI focus on education, culture, science and technology; sustainable development; trade, tourism and competitiveness; and social development and employment. SEDI also supports the regional ministerial meetings on topics such as culture, education, labour and sustainable development that are held periodically as part of the Summit of the Americas process. These regional meetings foster dialogue and strengthen co-operation in specific sectors and ensure that Summit policies are implemented at the national level. The OAS convenes the ministerial meetings, prepares documents for discussion and tracks the implementation of Summit mandates. In June 2009 the General Assembly adopted a resolution committing members to strengthening co-operation to control the spread of communicable diseases, in particular the outbreak of the swine influenza variant pandemic (H1N1), through greater surveillance and other disease control methods.

In June 2008 a technical secretariat was established in Panama City, Panama, to co-ordinate the implementation of an action plan in support of the Decade of the Americas for the Rights and Dignity of Persons with Disabilities (2006–2016). The theme of the Decade, which had been inaugurated in Santo Domingo, Dominican Republic, was 'Equality, Dignity, and Participation'. In July 2008 the first Meeting of Ministers and High Authorities of Social Development, within the framework of CIDI, was convened in Valparaiso, Chile.

The OAS Department of Sustainable Development assists member states with formulating policies and executing projects that are aimed at integrating environmental protection with rural development and poverty alleviation, and that ensure high levels of transparency, public participation and gender equity. Its projects, which receive substantial external funding, focus on several key areas. In December 2006 regional ministers of the environment met in Santa Cruz de la Sierra, Bolivia, to define strategies and goals related to sustainable development, environmental protection, the management of resources and the mitigation of natural disasters. Water resource management projects include initiatives that support member states in managing transboundary water resources in the major river basins of South and Central America, in partnership with UNEP, the World Bank and the Global Environment Facility (GEF). The OAS is also active in various international fora that address water-related issues.

Projects focusing on natural disasters and climate adaptation include a new programme, launched in April 2006, which is aimed at assisting member countries to reduce the risk of natural disasters, particularly those related to climatic variations that have been linked to rises in sea levels. The OAS also works with CARICOM on the Main-streaming Adaptation to Climate Change project. Activities include incorporating risk reduction into development and economic planning; supporting good governance in such areas as the use of appropriate building codes and standards for public and residential buildings; supporting innovative financial instruments related to risk transfer; and supporting regional collaboration with different agencies and organizations.

The OAS serves as the technical secretariat for the Renewable Energy in the Americas initiative, which offers governments access to information on renewable energy and energy-efficient technologies, and facilitates contacts between the private sector and state energy entities in the Americas. The OAS also provides technical assistance for developing renewable energy projects and facilitating their funding.

Various OAS-supported activities help member countries to improve the management of biological diversity. The Inter-American Biodiversity Information Network (IABIN), which has been supported since 2004 by the GEF, World Bank and other sources, is a principal focus of OAS biodiversity efforts. The Department of Sustainable Development also supports the work of national conservation authorities in areas such as migratory species and biodiversity corridors. It co-operates with the private sector to support innovative financing through payment for ecological services, and maintains a unique online portal regarding land tenure and land title, which is used throughout the Americas.

In the areas of environmental law, policy and economics the OAS conducts environmental and sustainability assessments to help member states to identify key environmental issues that impact trade. Efforts include working with countries to develop priorities for capacity-building in such areas as domestic laws, regulations and standards affecting market access of goods and services. Other initiatives include supporting countries in water and renewable energy legislation; supporting efforts towards the more effective enforcement of domestic laws; and facilitating natural disaster risk reduction and relief.

In mid-2006 the OAS launched a programme aimed at supporting countries with managing pesticides and industrial chemicals. The programme was to co-ordinate its work closely with UNEP Chemicals, the UN Stockholm Convention and other entities.

The OAS supports member states at national, bilateral and multilateral level to cope with trade expansion and economic integration. Through its Department of Trade, Tourism and Competitiveness the OAS General Secretariat provides support in strengthening human and institutional capacities; and in enhancing trade opportunities and competitiveness, particularly for micro, small and medium-sized enterprises. One of the Department's key responsibilities is to help member states (especially smaller economies) to develop the capacity they need to negotiate, implement and administer trade agreements and to take advantage of the benefits offered by free trade and expanded markets. Many member states seek assistance from the OAS to meet successfully the challenges posed by increasing globalization and the need to pursue multiple trade agendas. The OAS also administers an Inter-American Foreign Trade Information System (SICE), which acts as a repository for information about trade and trade-related issues in the region, including the texts of trade agreements, information on trade disciplines, data, and national legislation. In October 2008 a meeting of Ministers and High Authorities on Science and Technology, convened in Mexico City, Mexico, declared their commitment to co-ordinate activities to promote and enhance policies relating to science, technology, engineering and innovation as tools of development, increasing productivity, and sustainable natural resource management.

The OAS provided support to the Free Trade Area of the Americas (FTAA) process, endorsed by the First Summit of the Americas, held in December 1994 (see below), as well as supporting sub-regional and bilateral trade agreements. A trade unit was established in 1995 in order to strengthen the organization's involvement in trade issues and the process of economic integration, which became a priority area following the First Summit of the Americas. The trade unit provided technical assistance in support of the establishment of the FTAA and co-ordinated activities between regional and sub-regional integration organizations. At the Special Summit of the Americas, held in January 2004 in Monterrey, Mexico, the leaders failed to specify a completion date for the negotiations, although they adopted a declaration committing themselves to its eventual establishment. Negotiations on the FTAA subsequently stalled. The unit also supports a Hemispheric Co-operation Programme, which was established by ministers of trade of the Americas, meeting in November 2002, to assist smaller economies to gain greater access to resources and technical assistance.

MULTIDIMENSIONAL SECURITY

The promotion of hemispheric security is a fundamental purpose of the OAS. In October 2003, at a Special Conference on Security convened in Mexico City, the member states established a 'multidimensional' approach that recognized both traditional security concerns and newer threats such as international terrorism, drugs-trafficking, money-laundering, illegal arms dealing, trafficking in persons, institutional corruption and organized crime. In some countries problems such as poverty, disease, environmental degradation and natural disasters increase vulnerability and undermine human security. In March 2006, during a special session of the OAS General Assembly, the member states determined to enhance co-operation on defence issues by formally designating the Inter-American Defense Board (IADB) as an OAS agency. Under its new mandate the operations and structure of the IADB were to be in keeping with the OAS Charter and the Inter-American Democratic Charter, including 'the principles of civilian oversight and the subordination of military institutions to civilian authority'. The IADB provides technical and educational advice and consultancy services to the OAS and its member states on military and defence matters. The OAS Secretary-General chairs the Inter-American Committee on Natural Disaster Reduction, which was established in 1999 comprising the principal officers of regional and international organizations concerned with the prevention and mitigation of natural disasters. In January 2010 the OAS established an emergency committee to help to co-ordinate relief efforts for Haiti, which had suffered extensive damage and loss of life as a result of a massive earthquake. A joint mission of the OAS and representatives of four inter-American institutions visited Haiti at the end of that month to assess its immediate relief and reconstruction needs. In March the OAS hosted a Haiti Diaspora Meeting, with the collaboration of the Haitian Government, which made recommendations, in particular concerning nation-building, recovery and development, for the forthcoming International Donors' Conference, held in New York, USA, at the end of that month.

Following the 11 September 2001 terrorist attacks perpetrated against targets in the USA, the OAS member states strengthened their co-operation against the threat of terrorism. The Inter-American Convention against Terrorism, which seeks to prevent the financing of terrorist activities, strengthen border controls and increase co-operation among law enforcement authorities in different countries, was opened for signature in June 2002 and entered into force in July 2003. At mid-2009 it had been signed by all 34 active member states and ratified or acceded to by 24. The Inter-American Committee against Terrorism (CICTE) offers technical assistance and specialized training in key counter-terrorism areas including port security, airport security, customs and border security, and legislation and legal assistance. In 2006 CICTE provided training to security officials in the Caribbean countries that were preparing to host the 2007 Cricket World Cup. Through CICTE member countries have also improved co-operation in improving the quality of identification and travel documents, strengthening cyber-security and adopting financial controls to prevent money-laundering and the funding of terrorist activities. In October 2008 the first meeting of ministers responsible for public security in the Americas was convened, in Mexico City, Mexico. In June 2009 the General Assembly, meeting in Honduras, adopted the Declaration of San Pedro Sula, promoting the theme 'Towards a Culture of Non-violence'.

The Inter-American Drug Abuse Control Commission (CICAD) seeks to reduce the supply of and demand for illegal drugs, building on the 1996 Anti-Drug Strategy in the Hemisphere. The CICAD Executive Secretariat implements programmes aimed at preventing and treating substance abuse; reducing the supply and availability of illicit drugs; strengthening national drug-control institutions; improving practices to control firearms and money laundering; developing alternate sources of income for growers of coca, poppy and marijuana; and helping member governments to improve the gathering and analysis of data. The Multilateral Evaluation Mechanism (MEM) measures drug-control progress in the member states and the hemisphere as a whole, based on a series of objective indicators. The national reports on the third evaluation round, completed in 2006, included 506 specific recommendations designed to help countries strengthen their policies to combat drugs-related activities, and to increase multilateral co-operation. Following each evaluation round the MEM process examines how countries are carrying out the recommendations. In June 2009 the OAS General Assembly agreed to initiate a review of the organization's anti-drug strategy and its instruments to counter drugs-trafficking and abuse.

In 1997 the member states adopted the Inter-American Convention against the Illicit Manufacturing of and Trafficking in Firearms, Ammunition, Explosives, and other Related Materials (known as CIFTA), which, by early 2009, had been ratified by 29 member states. These countries have strengthened co-operation and information-sharing on CIFTA-related issues. In 2005 the OAS convened the first meeting of national authorities that make operational decisions on granting export, import and transit licenses for firearms, with a view to creating an information-exchange network to prevent illegal manufacturing and trafficking.

Since the 1990s the OAS has co-ordinated a comprehensive international programme to remove many thousands of antipersonnel landmines posing a threat to civilians in countries that have been affected by conflict. The OAS co-ordinates activities, identifying, obtaining and delivering the necessary resources, including funds, equipment and personnel; the IADB oversees technical demining operations, working with field supervisors from various countries; and the actual demining is executed by teams of trained soldiers, security forces or other personnel from the affected country. In addition to supporting landmine clearance the OAS Program for Comprehensive Action against Anti-personnel Mines helps with mine risk education; victim assistance and the socio-economic reintegration of formerly mined zones; the establishment of a mine action database; and support for a ban on the production, use, sale, transfer and stockpiling of antipersonnel landmines. It has also helped to destroy more than 1m. stockpiled mines in Argentina, Colombia, Chile, Ecuador, Honduras, Nicaragua and Peru. By mid-2009 Costa Rica, El Salvador, Guatemala, Honduras and Suriname had declared their territory to be clear of anti-personnel landmines. Nicaragua was officially declared to be free of landmines in June 2010.

The OAS Trafficking in Persons Section organizes seminars and training workshops for law-enforcement officials and others to raise awareness on human trafficking, which includes human exploitation, smuggling and other human rights violations. In March 2006 the Venezuelan Government hosted the first Meeting of National Authorities on Trafficking in Persons in order to study ways to strengthen co-operation and to develop regional policies and strategies to prevent human trafficking. Gang violence is another growing public security concern in the region. A second Meeting was convened in Buenos Aires, Argentina, in March 2009.

In June 2010 the 40th meeting of the OAS General Assembly, meeting in Lima, Peru, adopted the Declaration of Lima, aimed at strengthening collective commitment to peace, security and co-operation, as the principal means of confronting threats to the region.

SUMMITS OF THE AMERICAS

Since December 1994, when the First Summit of the Americas was convened in Miami, USA (see below), the leaders of the region's 34 democracies have met periodically to examine political, economic and social development priorities and to determine common goals and forge a common agenda. This process has increasingly shaped OAS policies and priorities and many OAS achievements, for example the adoption of the Inter-American Democratic Charter and the creation of mechanisms to measure progress against illicit drugs and corruption, have been attained as a result of Summit mandates. The Summits of the Americas have provided direction for the OAS in the areas of human rights, hemispheric security, trade, poverty reduction, gender equity and greater civil society participation. The OAS serves as the institutional memory and technical secretariat to the Summit process. It supports the countries in follow-up and planning, and provides technical, logistical and administrative support. The OAS Summits Secretariat co-ordinates the implementation of mandates assigned to the OAS and chairs the Joint Summit Working Group, which includes the institutions of the inter-American system. The OAS also has responsibility for strengthening outreach to civil society to ensure that nongovernmental organizations, academic institutions, the private sector and other interests can contribute ideas and help to monitor and implement Summit initiatives.

In December 1994 the First Summit of the Americas was convened in Miami, USA. The meeting endorsed the concept of a Free Trade Area of the Americas, and also approved a Plan of Action to strengthen democracy, eradicate poverty and promote sustainable development throughout the region. The OAS subsequently embarked on an extensive process of reform and modernization to strengthen its capacity to undertake a lead role in implementing the Plan. The organization realigned its priorities in order to respond to the mandates emerging from the Summit and developed a new institutional framework for technical assistance and co-operation, although many activities continued to be undertaken by the specialized or associated organizations of the OAS (see below). In 1996 the OAS member states participated in the interim Summit of the Americas on Sustainable Development, convened in Santa Cruz de la Sierra, Bolivia, which established sustainable development goals that incorporated economic, social and environmental concerns. The Second Summit of the Americas, which took place in 1998 in Santiago, Chile, focused on education, as well as such issues as strengthening democracy, justice and human rights; promoting integration and free trade; and eradicating poverty and discrimination. In 1998, following the Second Summit, the OAS established an Office of Summit Follow-Up, in order to strengthen its servicing of the meetings, and to co-ordinate tasks assigned to it. The Third Summit, convened in Québec, Canada, in April 2001, reaffirmed the central role of the OAS in implementing decisions of the summit meetings and instructed the organization to pursue the process of reform in order to enhance its operational capabilities, in particular in the areas of human rights, combating trade in illegal drugs, and enforcement of democratic values. The Summit declaration stated that commitment to democracy was a requirement for a country's participation in the summit process. The Third Summit urged the development of an Inter-American Democratic Charter to reinforce OAS instruments for defending and promoting democracy; the Democratic Charter was adopted in September of that year. The Third Summit also determined that the OAS was to be the technical secretariat for the summit process, assuming many of the responsibilities previously incumbent on the host country. Further to its mandate, the OAS established a Summits of the Americas Secretariat, which assists countries in planning and follow-up and provides technical, logistical and administrative support for the Summit Implementation Review Group and the summit process. An interim Special Summit of the Americas was held in January 2004, in Monterrey, Mexico, to reaffirm commitment to the process; the Special Summit established a range of concrete goals on three main issues: achieving economic growth to reduce poverty; promoting social development; and strengthening democratic governance. The Fourth Summit of the Americas was convened in Mar del Plata, Argentina, in November 2005, on the theme 'creating jobs to fight poverty and strengthen democracy'. The meeting approved a plan of action, incorporating both hemispheric co-operation and national commitments, to achieve employment growth and security. The Fifth Summit was held in Port of Spain, Trinidad and Tobago, in April 2009, focusing on the theme: 'Securing our citizens' future by promoting human prosperity, energy security and environmental sustainability'. The meeting adopted a Declaration of Commitment of the Port of Spain. All governments determined to enhance co-operation to restore global economic growth and to reduce social inequalities. The meeting mandated the OAS to pursue various objectives, including the establishment of an Inter-American Social Protection Network, to facilitate the exchange of information with regard to policies, programmes and best practices; the convening of a Conference on Development; organizing regional consultations on climate change; and strengthening the leadership of the Joint Summit Working Group. The Sixth Summit was to be hosted by Colombia, in 2012. A Summits of the Americas follow-up and implementation system was inaugurated in January 2010.

TOURISM AND CULTURE

A specialized unit for tourism was established in 1996 in order to strengthen and co-ordinate activities for the sustainable development of the tourism industry in the Americas. The unit supports regional and sub-regional conferences and workshops, as well as the Inter-American Travel Congress, which was convened for the first time in 1993 to serve as a forum to formulate region-wide tourism policies. The unit also undertakes research and analysis of the industry. In April 2006 the OAS, the Caribbean Tourism Organization and the Caribbean Hotel Association signed an agreement on the provision of training and assistance aimed at improving the capacity of the Caribbean tourism industry.

In 1998 the OAS approved an Inter-American Programme of Culture to support efforts being undertaken by member states and to promote co-operation in areas such as cultural diversity; protection of cultural heritage; training and dissemination of information; and the promotion of cultural tourism. The OAS also assists with the preparation of national and multilateral cultural projects, and co-operates with the private sector to protect and promote cultural assets and events in the region. In July 2002 the first Inter-American meeting of ministers of culture approved the establishment of an Inter-American Committee on Culture, within the framework of CIDI, to co-ordinate high-level dialogue and co-operation on cultural issues. In November 2006 regional ministers of culture met in Montréal, Canada, to address the contribution of the cultural sector towards promoting development and combating poverty. In 2009 the General Assembly declared 2011 as the Inter-American Year of Culture.

Finance

The OAS programme budget for 2010, approved by the General Assembly in September 2009, amounted to US $178m., of which $90.1m. was from the regular fund, and $88m. from voluntary funds and contributions to specific projects.

Publications

(in English and Spanish)

Américas (6 a year).

Annual Report.

Numerous cultural, legal and scientific reports and studies.

Specialized Organizations and Associated Agencies

Inter-American Children's Institute (Instituto Americano del Niño, la Niña y Adolescentes—IIN): Avda 8 de Octubre 2904, POB 16212, Montevideo 11600, Uruguay; tel. (2) 487-2150; fax (2) 487-3242; e-mail iin@oas.org; internet www.iin.oea.org; f. 1927; promotes the regional implementation of the Convention on the Rights of the Child, assists in the development of child-oriented public policies; promotes co-operation between states; and aims to develop awareness of problems affecting children and young people in the region. The Institute organizes workshops, seminars, courses, training programmes and conferences on issues relating to children, including, for example, the rights of children, children with disabilities, and the child welfare system. It also provides advisory services, statistical data and other relevant information to authorities and experts throughout the region. A Pan-American Child Congress was scheduled to be convened in Lima, Peru, in September 2009; Dir-Gen. María de los Dolores Aguilar Marmolejo; publ. *iinfancia* (annually).

Inter-American Commission of Women (Comisión Interamericana de Mujeres—CIM): 1889 F St, NW, Suite 350 Washington, DC 20006, USA; tel. (202) 458-6084; fax (202) 458-6094; e-mail spcim@oas.org; internet www.oas.org/cim; f. 1928 as the first ever official intergovernmental agency created expressly to ensure recognition of the civil and political rights of women; the CIM is the principal forum for generating hemispheric policy to advance women's rights and gender equality; comprises 34 principal delegates; the Assembly of Delegates, convened every two years, is the highest authority of the Commission, establishing policies and a plan of action for each biennium and electing the seven-member Executive Committee; Pres. Wanda K. Jones (USA); Exec. Sec. Carmen Lomellin (USA).

Inter-American Indigenous Institute (Instituto Indigenista Interamericano—III): Avda de las Fuentes 106, Col. Jardines del Pedregal, Delegación Álvaro Obregón, 01900 México, DF, Mexico; tel. (55) 5595-8410; fax (55) 5595-4324; e-mail ininin@data.net.mx; internet www.indigenista.org; f. 1940; conducts research on the situation of the indigenous peoples of America; assists the exchange of information; promotes indigenous policies in member states aimed at the elimination of poverty and development within Indian communities, and to secure their position as ethnic groups within a democratic society; Hon. Dir Dr Guillermo Espinosa Velasco (Mexico); publs *América Indígena* (quarterly), *Anuario Indigenista*.

Inter-American Institute for Co-operation on Agriculture (IICA) (Instituto Interamericano de Cooperación para la Agricultura): Apdo Postal 55–2200 San Isidro de Coronado, San José, Costa Rica; tel. (506) 216-0222; fax (506) 216-0233; e-mail iicahq@iica.ac.cr; internet www.iica.int; f. 1942 (as the Inter-American Institute of Agricultural Sciences, present name adopted 1980); supports the efforts of member states to improve agricultural development and rural well-being; encourages co-operation between regional organizations, and provides a forum for the exchange of experience; Dir-Gen. Víctor M. Villalobos (Mexico).

Justice Studies Center of the Americas (Centro de Estudios de Justicia de las Américas): Rodó 1950, Providencia, Santiago, Chile; tel. (2) 2742933; fax (2) 3415769; e-mail info@cejamericas.org; internet www.cejamericas.org; f. 1999; aims to support the modernization of justice systems in the region; Exec. Dir Cristián Riego Ramírez (Chile).

Pan American Development Foundation (PADF) (Fundación Panamericana para el Desarrollo): 1889 F St, NW, Washington, DC 20006, USA; tel. (202) 458-3969; fax (202) 458-6316; e-mail padf-dc@padf.org; internet www.padf.org; f. 1962 to promote and facilitate economic and social development in Latin America and the Caribbean by means of innovative partnerships and integrated involvement of the public and private sectors; provides low-interest credit for small-scale entrepreneurs, vocational training, improved health care, agricultural development and reafforestation, and strengthening local non-governmental organizations; provides emergency disaster relief and reconstruction assistance; Exec. Dir JOHN SANBRAILO.

Pan American Health Organization (PAHO) (Organización Panamericana de la Salud): 525 23rd St, NW, Washington, DC 20037, USA; tel. (202) 974-3000; fax (202) 974-3663; e-mail webmaster@paho.org; internet www.paho.org; f. 1902; co-ordinates regional efforts to improve health; maintains close relations with national health organizations and serves as the Regional Office for the Americas of the World Health Organization; Dir Dr MIRTA ROSES PERIAGO (Argentina).

Pan-American Institute of Geography and History (PAIGH) (Instituto Panamericano de Geografía e Historia–IPGH): Ex-Arzobispado 29, 11860 México, DF, Mexico; tel. (55) 5277-5888; fax (55) 5271-6172; e-mail secretariageneral@ipgh.org; internet www.ipgh.org.mx; f. 1928; co-ordinates and promotes the study of cartography, geophysics, geography and history; provides technical assistance, conducts training at research centres, distributes publications, and organizes technical meetings; Sec.-Gen. SANTIAGO BORRERO MUTIS (Colombia); Publs *Revista Cartográfica* (2 a year), *Revista Geográfica* (2 a year), *Revista de Historia de América* (2 a year), *Revista Geofísica* (2 a year), *Revista de Arqueología Americana* (annually), *Folklore Americano* (annually), *Boletín de Antropología Americana* (annually).

SOUTHERN COMMON MARKET—MERCOSUR/ MERCOSUL

(MERCADO COMÚN DEL SUR/MERCADO COMUM DO SUL)

Address: Edif. Mercosur, Luis Piera 1992, 1°, 11200 Montevideo, Uruguay.

Telephone: (2) 412-9024; **fax:** (2) 418-0557; **e-mail:** secretaria@mercosur.org.uy; **internet:** www.mercosur.int/msweb.

Mercosur (known as Mercosul in Portuguese) was established in March 1991 by the heads of state of Argentina, Brazil, Paraguay and Uruguay with the signature of the Treaty of Asunción. The primary objective of the Treaty is to achieve the economic integration of member states by means of a free flow of goods and services between member states, the establishment of a common external tariff, the adoption of common commercial policy, and the co-ordination of macroeconomic and sectoral policies. The Ouro Preto Protocol, which was signed in December 1994, conferred on Mercosur the status of an international legal entity with the authority to sign agreements with third countries, groups of countries and international organizations.

MEMBERS

Argentina	Brazil	Paraguay	Uruguay

Note: Venezuela was admitted as a full member of Mercosur in July 2006, pending ratification by each country's legislature. By August 2010 that had still not been achieved. Bolivia, Chile, Colombia, Ecuador and Peru are associate members.

Organization

(August 2010)

COMMON MARKET COUNCIL

The Common Market Council (Consejo del Mercado Común) is the highest organ of Mercosur and is responsible for leading the integration process and for taking decisions in order to achieve the objectives of the Asunción Treaty.

COMMON MARKET GROUP

The Common Market Group (Grupo Mercado Común) is the executive body of Mercosur and is responsible for implementing concrete measures to further the integration process.

TRADE COMMISSION

The Trade Commission (Comisión de Comercio del Mercosur) has competence for the area of joint commercial policy and, in particular, is responsible for monitoring the operation of the common external tariff (see below). The Brasília Protocol may be referred to for the resolution of trade disputes between member states.

CONSULTATIVE ECONOMIC AND SOCIAL FORUM

The Consultative Economic and Social Forum (Foro Consultivo Económico-Social) comprises representatives from the business community and trade unions in the member countries and has a consultative role in relation to Mercosur.

PARLIAMENT

Parlamento del Mercosur: Edif. Mercosur, Luis Piera 1992, 1°, 11200 Montevideo, Uruguay; tel. (2) 410-2298; e-mail secadministrativa@parlamentodelmercosur.org; internet www.parlamentodelmercosur.org; f. 2005, as successor to the Joint Parliamentary Commission (Comisión Parlamentaria Conjunta); aims to facilitate implementation of Mercosur decisions and regional co-operation.

ADMINISTRATIVE SECRETARIAT

Director: Dr AGUSTÍN COLOMBO SIERRA (Argentina).

Activities

Mercosur's free trade zone entered into effect on 1 January 1995, with tariffs removed from 85% of intra-regional trade. A regime of gradual removal of duties on a list of special products was agreed, with Argentina and Brazil given four years to complete this process while Paraguay and Uruguay were allowed five years. Regimes governing intra-zonal trade in the automobile and sugar sectors remained to be negotiated. Mercosur's customs union also came into force at the start of 1995, comprising a common external tariff (CET) of 0%–20%. A list of exceptions from the CET was also agreed; these products were to lose their special status and were to be subject to the general tariff system concerning foreign goods by 2006.

In December 1995 Mercosur presidents affirmed the consolidation of free trade as Mercosur's 'permanent and most urgent goal'. To this end they agreed to prepare norms of application for Mercosur's customs code, accelerate paper procedures and increase the connections between national computerized systems. It was also agreed to increase co-operation in the areas of agriculture, industry, mining, energy, communications, transport and tourism, and finance. At this meeting Argentina and Brazil reached an accord aimed at overcoming their dispute regarding the trade in automobiles between the two countries. They agreed that cars should have a minimum of 60% domestic components and that Argentina should be allowed to complete its balance of exports of cars to Brazil, which had earlier imposed a unilateral quota on the import of Argentine cars. In June 1995 Mercosur ministers responsible for the environment agreed to harmonize environmental legislation and to form a permanent sub-group of Mercosur.

In May 1996 Mercosur parliamentarians met with the aim of harmonizing legislation on patents in member countries. In December Mercosur heads of state, meeting in Fortaleza, Brazil, approved agreements on harmonizing competition practices (by 2001), integrating educational opportunities for post-graduates and human resources training, standardizing trading safeguards applied against third-country products (by 2001) and providing for intra-regional cultural exchanges. An Accord on Sub-regional Air Services was signed at the meeting (including by the heads of state of Bolivia and Chile) to liberalize civil transport throughout the region. In addition, the heads of state endorsed texts on consumer rights that were to be incorporated into a Mercosur Consumers' Defence Code.

In June 1996 Mercosur heads of state, meeting in San Luis de Mendoza, Argentina, endorsed a 'Democratic Guarantee Clause', whereby a country would be prevented from participation in Mercosur unless democratic, accountable institutions were in place. At the summit meeting, the presidents approved the entry into Mercosur of Bolivia and Chile as associate members. An Economic Complementation Accord with Bolivia, which includes Bolivia in Mercosur's free trade zone, but not in the customs union, was signed in December

1995 and was to come into force on 1 January 1997. later extended until 30 April 1997. Measures of the free trade agreement, which was signed in October 1996, were to be implemented over a transitional period commencing on 28 February 1997 (revised from 1 January). Chile's Economic Complementation Accord with Mercosur entered into effect on 1 October 1996, with duties on most products to be removed over a 10-year period (Chile's most sensitive products were given 18 years for complete tariff elimination). Chile was also to remain outside the customs union, but was to be involved in other integration projects, in particular infrastructure projects designed to give Mercosur countries access to both the Atlantic and Pacific Oceans (Chile's Pacific coast was regarded as Mercosur's potential link to the economies of the Far East).

In June 1997 the first meeting of tax administrators and customs officials of Mercosur member countries was held, with the aim of enhancing information exchange and promoting joint customs inspections. During 1997 Mercosur's efforts towards regional economic integration were threatened by Brazil's adverse external trade balance and its Government's measures to counter the deficit, which included the imposition of import duties on certain products. In November the Brazilian Government announced that it was to increase its import tariff by 3%, in a further effort to improve its external balance. The measure was endorsed by Argentina as a means of maintaining regional fiscal stability. The new external tariff, which was to remain in effect until 31 December 2000, was formally adopted by Mercosur heads of state at a meeting held in Montevideo, Uruguay, in December 1997. At the summit meeting a separate Protocol was signed providing for the liberalization of trade in services and government purchases over a 10-year period. In order to strengthen economic integration throughout the region, Mercosur leaders agreed that Chile, while still not a full member of the organization, should be integrated into the Mercosur political structure, with equal voting rights. In December 1998 Mercosur heads of state agreed on the establishment of an arbitration mechanism for disputes between members, and on measures to standardize human, animal and plant health and safety regulations throughout the grouping. In March 1998 the ministers of the interior of Mercosur countries, together with representatives of the Governments of Chile and Bolivia, agreed to implement a joint security arrangement for the border region linking Argentina, Paraguay and Brazil. In particular, the initiative aimed to counter drugs-trafficking, money-laundering and other illegal activities in the area.

Tensions within Mercosur were compounded in January 1999 owing to economic instability in Brazil and its Government's decision effectively to devalue the national currency, the real. In March the grouping's efforts at integration were further undermined by political instability in Paraguay. Argentina imposed tariffs on imports of Brazilian steel and demanded some form of temporary safeguards on certain products as compensation for their perceived loss of competitiveness resulting from the devalued real. An extraordinary meeting of the Common Market Council was convened, at Brazil's request, in August, in order to discuss the dispute, as well as measures to mitigate the effects of economic recession throughout the sub-region. However, little progress was made and the bilateral trade dispute continued to undermine Mercosur's integration objectives. Argentina imposed new restrictions on textiles and footwear, while, in September, Brazil withdrew all automatic import licences for Argentine products, which were consequently to be subject to the same quality control, sanitary measures and accounting checks applied to imports from non-Mercosur countries. In January 2000, however, the Argentine and Brazilian Governments agreed to refrain from adopting potentially divisive unilateral measures and resolved to accelerate negotiations on the resolution of ongoing differences. In March Mercosur determined to promote and monitor private accords to cover the various areas of contention, and also established a timetable for executing a convergence of regional macroeconomic policies. In June Argentina and Brazil signed a bilateral automobile agreement. The motor vehicle agreement, incorporating new tariffs and a nationalization index, was endorsed by all Mercosur leaders at a meeting convened in Florianopolis, Brazil, in December. (In July 2002 the summit meeting, convened in Buenos Aires, Argentina, adopted an agreement providing for reduced tariffs and increased quotas in the grouping's automotive sector, with a view to establishing a fully liberalized automotive market by 2006.) The summit meeting held in December 2000 approved criteria, formulated by Mercosur finance ministers and central bank governors, determining monetary and fiscal targets which aimed to achieve economic convergence, to promote economic stability throughout the region, and to reduce competitive disparities affecting the unity of the grouping. The Florianopolis summit meeting also recommended the formulation of social indicators to facilitate achieving targets in the reduction of poverty and the elimination of child labour. However, political debate surrounding the meeting was dominated by the Chilean Government's announcement that it had initiated bilateral free trade discussions with the USA, which was considered, in particular by the Brazilian authorities, to undermine Mercosur's unified position at multilateral free trade negotiations. Procedures to incorporate Chile as a full member of Mercosur were suspended. (Chile and the USA concluded negotiations on a bilateral free trade agreement in December 2002.) In July 2008 Mercosur and Chile concluded a protocol on trade in services.

In early 2001 Argentina imposed several emergency measures to strengthen its domestic economy, in contradiction of Mercosur's external tariffs. In March Brazil was reported to have accepted the measures, which included an elimination of tariffs on capital goods and an increase in import duties on consumer goods, as an exceptional temporary trade regime; this position was reversed by mid-2001 following Argentina's decision to exempt certain countries from import tariffs. In February 2002, at a third extraordinary meeting of the Common Market Council, held in Buenos Aires, Argentina, Mercosur heads of state expressed their support for Argentina's application to receive international financial assistance, in the wake of that country's economic crisis. Although there were fears that the crisis might curb trade and stall economic growth across the region, Argentina's adoption of a floating currency made the prospect of currency harmonization between Mercosur member countries appear more viable. In December 2002 Mercosur ministers of justice signed an agreement permitting citizens of Mercosur member and associate member states to reside in any other Mercosur state, initially for a two-year period. At a summit convened in June 2003, in Asunción, Paraguay, heads of state of the four member countries agreed to strengthen integration of the bloc and to harmonize all import tariffs by 2006, thus creating the basis for a single market. They also agreed to establish a directly elected Mercosur legislature, as a successor to the Joint Parliamentary Commission. The July 2004 summit of Mercosur heads of state announced that an Asunción-based five-member tribunal (comprising one legal representative from each of Mercosur's four member countries, plus one 'consensus' member) responsible for ruling on appeals in cases of disputes between member countries was to become operational in the following month. In September 2006 the tribunal criticized the Argentine Government for allowing blockades of international bridges across the River Uruguay by protesters opposing the construction of two pulp mills on the Uruguayan side of the river. (In April 2010 the International Court of Justice delivered a judgment supporting the ongoing operations of the mills; both sides subsequently agreed to co-operate in the implementation of environmental protection measures to limit pollution of the River Uruguay.)

In June 2005 Mercosur heads of state announced a US $100m. structural convergence fund to support education, job creation and infrastructure projects in the poorest regions, in particular in Paraguay and Uruguay, in order to remove some economic disparities within the grouping. The meeting also endorsed a multilateral energy project to link gasfields in Camisea, Peru, to existing supply pipelines in Argentina, Brazil and Uruguay, via Tocopilla, Chile. In July 2008 Mercosur heads of state considered the impact of escalating food costs and the production of biofuels. In December a summit meeting, convened in Bahía, Brazil, agreed to establish a $100m. guarantee fund to facilitate access to credit for small and medium-sized businesses operating in the common market in order to alleviate the impact of the global financial crisis. In August 2010 Mercosur heads of state, meeting in San Juan, Argentina, endorsed a new common customs code, incorporating agreements on the redistribution of external customs revenue and elimination of the double taxation on goods imported from outside the group.

In May 2007 the Mercosur parliament, the so-called Parlasur, which initially was to serve as an advisory committee, held its inaugural session in Montevideo, Uruguay. In April 2009 a new agreement was concluded providing for representation in the parliament to be proportionally allocated based on each country's population and introduced in two stages, in 2010 and in 2014. Thus the distribution of seats was envisaged as 36 (75 in 2014) for Brazil, 26 (43) for Argentina and 18 each for Paraguay and Uruguay. The accord required ratification by the Common Market Council. In July final consideration of the proposal was postponed owing to a demand by the Paraguayan authorities that it should be conditional on a parallel approval to establish a supranational justice tribunal to adjudicate on trade disputes.

EXTERNAL RELATIONS

During 1997 negotiations to establish a free trade accord with the Andean Community were hindered by differences regarding schedules for tariff elimination and Mercosur's insistence on a local content of 60% to qualify for rules of origin preferences. However, in April 1998 the two groupings signed an accord that committed them to the establishment of a free trade area by January 2000. Negotiations in early 1999 failed to conclude an agreement on preferential tariffs between the two blocs, and the existing arrangements were extended on a bilateral basis. In March the Andean Community agreed to initiate free trade negotiations with Brazil; a preferential tariff agreement was concluded in July. In August 2000 a similar agreement between the Community and Argentina entered into force. In September leaders of Mercosur and the Andean Community, meeting at a summit of Latin American heads of state, determined to relaunch negotiations. The establishment of a mechanism to support political dialogue and co-ordination between the two groupings, which aimed to enhance the integration process, was approved at the first joint meeting of ministers of foreign affairs in July 2001. In April 2004 Mercosur and the Andean Community signed a free trade accord, providing for tariffs on 80% of trade between the two groupings to be phased out by 2014 and for tariffs to be removed from the remaining 20% of, initially protected, products by 2019. The entry into force of the accord, scheduled for 1 July 2004, was postponed owing to delays in drafting the tariff reduction schedule. Peru became an associate member of Mercosur in December 2003, and Colombia and Ecuador were granted associate membership in December 2004. In July 2004 Mexico was invited to attend all meetings of the organization with a view to future accession to associate membership. Bilateral negotiations on a free trade agreement between Mexico and Mercosur were initiated in 2001. In 2005 Mercosur and the Andean Community formulated a reciprocal association agreement, to extend associate membership to all member states of both groupings. In February 2010 foreign ministers agreed to establish an Andean Community-Mercosur Mixed Commission to facilitate and strengthen co-operation between member countries of both organizations. In December 2005 Bolivia was invited to join as a full member. At the summit meeting of heads of state held in January 2007 in Rio de Janeiro, Brazil, Bolivia stated two conditions on which its membership would be dependent: continued membership of the Andean Community and exemption from Mercosur's CET. Also in December 2005 Mercosur heads of state agreed to a request by Venezuela (which had been granted associate membership in December 2004) to become a member with full voting rights. The leaders signed a protocol, in July 2006, formally to admit Venezuela to the group. The accord, however, required ratification by each country's legislature. In August 2010, at which time the Paraguayan parliament had yet to endorse the protocol, Mercosur heads of state urged a quick conclusion to Venezuela's incorporation into the organization in order to enhance regional integration.

In December 1995 Mercosur and the European Union (EU) signed a framework agreement for commercial and economic co-operation, which provided for co-operation in the economic, trade, industrial, scientific, institutional and cultural fields and the promotion of wider political dialogue on issues of mutual interest. In June 1997 Mercosur heads of state, convened in Asunción, reaffirmed the group's intention to pursue trade negotiations with the EU, Mexico and the Andean Community, as well as to negotiate as a single economic bloc in discussions with regard to the establishment of a Free Trade Area of the Americas (FTAA). Chile and Bolivia were to be incorporated into these negotiations. Negotiations between Mercosur and the EU on the conclusion of an Interregional Association Agreement commenced in 1999. Specific discussion of tariff reductions and market access commenced at the fifth round of negotiations, held in July 2001, at which the EU proposed a gradual elimination of tariffs on industrial imports over a 10-year period and an extension of access quotas for agricultural products; however, negotiations stalled in 2005 owing to differences regarding farm subsidies. In July 2008 Mercosur heads of state condemned a new EU immigration policy that would permit the detention and forcible return of illegal immigrants. Leaders attending a Mercosur-EU summit meeting, convened in Madrid, Spain, in May 2010, determined to restart promptly the Association Agreement negotiations. The first discussions subsequently took place in Buenos Aires, Argentina, in July.

In March 2003 Argentina and Brazil, with the support of other Mercosur member states, formed the Southern Agricultural Council (CAS), which was to represent the interests of the grouping as a whole in negotiations with third countries. In December 2004 leaders from 12 Latin American countries (excluding Argentina, Ecuador, Paraguay and Uruguay) attending a pan-South American summit, convened in Cusco, Peru, approved in principle the creation of a new South American Community of Nations (SACN). It was envisaged that negotiations on the formation of the new Community, which was to entail the merger of Mercosur, the Andean Community and the Latin American Integration Association (ALADI), would be completed within 15 years. In April 2005 a region-wide meeting of ministers of foreign affairs was convened within the framework of establishing the SACN. A joint SACN communiqué was released, expressing concern at the deterioration of constitutional rule and democratic institutions in Ecuador and announcing its intention to send a ministerial mission to that country. The first SACN summit meeting was convened in September, in Brasília, Brazil. In April 2007, at the first South American Energy Summit, convened in Margarita Island, Venezuela, heads of state endorsed the establishment of a Union of South American Nations (UNASUR), to replace SACN as the lead organization for regional integration. UNASUR was to have political decision-making functions, supported by a small permanent secretariat, to be located in Quito, Ecuador, and was to co-ordinate on economic and trade matters with Mercosur, the Andean Community and ALADI. A summit meeting formally to inaugurate UNASUR, scheduled to be convened in December, was postponed. A rescheduled meeting, to be convened in March 2008, was also postponed, owing to a diplomatic dispute between Ecuador and Colombia. It was later convened in May, in Brasília, Brazil, when the constitutional document formally establishing UNASUR was signed. In December Brazil hosted a Latin American and Caribbean Summit on Integration and Development, which aimed to strengthen the commitment by all countries in the region to work together in support of sustainable development. It issued the Salvador Declaration, which pledged support to strengthen co-operation among the regional and sub-regional groupings, to pursue further consultation and joint efforts to counter the effects of the global financial crisis on the region, and to promote closer collaboration on a range of issues including energy, food security, social development, physical infrastructure and natural disaster management. In February 2010 a summit meeting of the Rio Group, convened in Cancún, Mexico, approved in principle the establishment of a new Community of Latin American and Caribbean States, to strengthen regional co-operation.

In March 1998 ministers of trade of 34 countries agreed a detailed framework for negotiations on the establishment of the FTAA. Mercosur secured support for its request that a separate negotiating group be established to consider issues relating to agriculture, as one of nine key sectors to be discussed. The FTAA negotiating process was formally initiated by heads of state of the 34 countries meeting in Santiago, Chile, in April 1998. In June Mercosur and Canada signed a Trade and Investment Co-operation Arrangement, which aimed to remove obstacles to trade and to increase economic co-operation between the two signatories. The summit meeting held in December 2000 was attended by the President of South Africa, and it was agreed that Mercosur would initiate free trade negotiations with that country. (These commenced in October 2001.) In June 2001 Mercosur leaders agreed to pursue efforts to conclude a bilateral trade agreement with the USA, an objective previously opposed by the Brazilian authorities, while reaffirming their commitment to the FTAA process. Leaders attending a special summit of the Americas, convened in January 2004 in Monterrey, Mexico, failed to specify a completion date for the FTAA process, although they adopted a declaration committing themselves to its eventual establishment. However, negotiations were suspended in March, and remained stalled in 2010.

In December 2007 Mercosur signed a free trade accord with Israel. The agreement entered into effect in December 2009. At the meeting of heads of state, held in San Miguel de Tucumán, Argentina, in July 2008 a preferential trade agreement was signed with the Southern African Customs Union. Framework agreements on the preparation of free trade accords were also signed with Turkey and Jordan. In June 2009 a preferential trade agreement with India, which had been signed in 2004, entered into force. A framework agreement on trade with Morocco, also signed in 2004, entered into effect in April 2010. In August Mercosur signed a free trade agreement with Egypt.

In July 2009 Mercosur heads of state, meeting in Asunción, Paraguay, issued a joint statement, which condemned the removal by military force of President Manuel Zelaya of Honduras, demanded the immediate restoration of democratic and constitutional order, and refused to recognize the legitimacy of the interim authorities in that country.

Finance

The annual budget for the secretariat is contributed by the four full member states.

Publication

Boletín Oficial del Mercosur (quarterly).

OTHER REGIONAL ORGANIZATIONS

Agriculture, Food, Forestry and Fisheries

(for organizations concerned with agricultural commodities, see Commodities)

CAB International (CABI): Nosworthy Way, Wallingford, Oxon, OX10 8DE, United Kingdom; tel. (1491) 832111; fax (1491) 833508; e-mail corporate@cabi.org; internet www.cabi.org; f. 1929 as the Imperial Agricultural Bureaux (later Commonwealth Agricultural Bureaux), current name adopted in 1985; aims to improve human welfare world-wide through the generation, dissemination and application of scientific knowledge in support of sustainable development; places particular emphasis on sustainable agriculture, forestry, human health and the management of natural resources, with priority given to the needs of developing countries; a separate microbiology centre, in Egham, Surrey (UK), undertakes research, consultancy, training, capacity-building and institutional development measures in sustainable pest management, biosystematics and molecular biology, ecological applications and environmental and industrial microbiology; compiles and publishes extensive information (in a variety of print and electronic forms) on aspects of agriculture, forestry, veterinary medicine, the environment and natural resources, and Third World rural development; maintains regional centres in the People's Republic of China, India, Kenya, Malaysia, Pakistan, Switzerland, Trinidad and Tobago, and the USA; mems: 45 countries and territories; Chair. Dr JOHN REGAZZI (USA); CEO Dr TREVOR NICHOLLS (United Kingdom).

Indian Ocean Tuna Commission (IOTC): POB 1011, Victoria, Mahé, Seychelles; tel. 225494; fax 224364; e-mail iotc.secretary@iotc.org; internet www.iotc.org; f. 1996 as a regional fisheries organization with a mandate for the conservation and management of tuna and tuna-like species in the Indian Ocean; mems: Australia, Belize, People's Republic of China, the Comoros, European Union, Eritrea, France, Guinea, India, Indonesia, Iran, Japan, Kenya, Republic of Korea, Madagascar, Malaysia, Mauritius, Oman, Pakistan, Philippines, Seychelles, Sudan, Sri Lanka, Tanzania, Thailand, United Kingdom, Vanuatu; co-operating non-contracting parties: Indonesia, Senegal, South Africa; Exec. Sec. ALEJANDRO ANGANUZZI (Argentina).

Inter-American Association of Agricultural Librarians, Documentalists and Information Specialists (Asociación Interamericana de Bibliotecarios, Documentalistas y Especialistas en Información Agrícolas—AIBDA): c/o IICA-CIDIA, Apdo 55-2200 Coronado, Costa Rica; tel. 2216-0222; fax 2216-0291; e-mail info@aibda.com; internet www.aibda.com; f. 1953 to promote professional improvement through technical publications and meetings, and to promote improvement of library services in agricultural sciences; mems: 653 in 31 countries and territories; Pres. RUBÉN URBIZAGÁSTEGUI (Peru); publ. *Revista AIBDA* (2 a year).

Inter-American Tropical Tuna Commission (IATTC): 8604 La Jolla Shores Drive, La Jolla, CA 92037-1508, USA; tel. (858) 546-7100; fax (858) 546-7133; e-mail info@iattc.org; internet www.iattc.org; f. 1950; administers two programmes, the Tuna-Billfish Programme and the Tuna-Dolphin Programme. The principal responsibilities of the Tuna-Billfish Programme are: to study the biology of the tunas and related species of the eastern Pacific Ocean to estimate the effects of fishing and natural factors on their abundance; to recommend appropriate conservation measures in order to maintain stocks at levels which will afford maximum sustainable catches; and to collect information on compliance with Commission resolutions. The principal functions of the Tuna-Dolphin Programme are: to monitor the abundance of dolphins and their mortality incidental to purse-seine fishing in the eastern Pacific Ocean; to study the causes of mortality of dolphins during fishing operations and promote the use of fishing techniques and equipment that minimize these mortalities; to study the effects of different fishing methods on the various fish and other animals of the pelagic ecosystem; and to provide a secretariat for the International Dolphin Conservation Programme; mems: Colombia, Costa Rica, Ecuador, El Salvador, France, Guatemala, Japan, Mexico, Nicaragua, Panama, Peru, Republic of Korea, Spain, USA, Vanuatu, Venezuela; co-operating non-contracting parties: Belize, Canada, China, Cook Islands, European Union and Chinese Taipei (Taiwan); Dir GUILLERMO A. COMPEÁN; publs *Bulletin* (irregular), *Annual Report*, *Fishery Status Report*, *Stock Assessment Report* (annually), *Special Report* (irregular).

International Centre for Tropical Agriculture (Centro Internacional de Agricultura Tropical—CIAT): Apdo Aéreo 6713, Cali, Colombia; tel. (2) 445-0000; fax (2) 445-0073; e-mail ciat@cgiar.org; internet www.ciat.cgiar.org; f. 1967 to contribute to the alleviation of hunger and poverty in tropical developing countries by using new techniques in agriculture research and training; focuses on production problems in field beans, cassava, rice and tropical pastures in the tropics; Dir-Gen. RUBEN G. ECHEVERRÍA; publs *Annual Report*, *Growing Affinities* (2 a year), *Pasturas Tropicales* (3 a year), catalogue of publications.

International Food Policy Research Institute (IFPRI): 2033 K St, NW, Washington, DC 20006, USA; tel. (202) 862-5600; fax (202) 467-4439; e-mail ifpri@cgiar.org; internet www.ifpri.org; f. 1975; co-operates with academic and other institutions in further research; develops policies for cutting hunger and malnutrition; committed to increasing public awareness of food policies; Dir Gen. SHENGGEN FAN (People's Republic of China).

International Service for National Agricultural Research (ISNAR): IFPRI, ISNAR Division, ILRI, POB 5689, Addis Ababa, Ethiopia; tel. (11) 646-3215; fax (11) 646-2927; e-mail ifpri-addisababa@cgiar.org; fmrly based in The Hague, Netherlands, the ISNAR Program relocated to Addis Ababa in 2004, under the governance of IFPRI; Dir Dr WILBERFORCE KISAMBA-MUGERWA.

South Pacific Regional Fisheries Management Organization: Interim Secretariat, L4, ASB Bank House, POB 3797, Wellington 6140, New Zealand; tel. (4) 499-9889; fax (4) 473-9579; e-mail interim.secretariat@southpacificrfmo.org; internet www.southpacificrfmo.org; international negotiations on the establishment of a South Pacific regional fisheries management body commenced in 2005, led by New Zealand, Australia and Chile; the negotiations were concluded at the 8th international meeting on the establishment of the org., held in Auckland, New Zealand, in Nov. 2009 and the Convention was adopted unanimously; Chair. BILL MANSFIELD; Exec. Sec. Dr ROBIN ALLEN.

World Organisation of Animal Health: 12 rue de Prony, 75017 Paris, France; tel. 1-44-15-18-88; fax 1-42-67-09-87; e-mail oie@oie.int; internet www.oie.int; f. 1924 as Office International des Epizooties (OIE); objectives include promoting international transparency of animal diseases; collecting, analysing and disseminating scientific veterinary information; providing expertise and promoting international co-operation in the control of animal diseases; promoting veterinary services; providing new scientific guidelines on animal production, food safety and animal welfare; launched in May 2005, jointly with FAO and WHO, a Global Strategy for the Progressive Control of Highly Pathogenic Avian Influenza (H5N1), and, in partnership with other organizations, has convened conferences on avian influenza; experts in a network of 156 collaborating centres and reference laboratories; 172 mems; Dir-Gen. BERNARD VALLAT; publs *Disease Information* (weekly), *World Animal Health* (annually), *Scientific and Technical Review* (3 a year), other manuals, codes, etc.

Arts and Culture

Inter-American Music Council (Consejo Interamericano de Música—CIDEM): 2511 P St NW, Washington, DC 20007, USA; f. 1956 to promote the exchange of works, performances and information in all fields of music, to study problems relative to music education, to encourage activity in the field of musicology, to promote folklore research and music creation, and to establish distribution centres for music material of the composers of the Americas; mems: national music societies of 33 American countries.

Organization of World Heritage Cities: 15 rue Saint-Nicolas, Québec, QC G1K 1M8, Canada; tel. (418) 692-0000; fax (418) 692-5558; e-mail secretariat@ovpm.org; internet www.ovpm.org; f. 1993 to assist cities inscribed on the UNESCO World Heritage List to implement the Convention concerning the Protection of the World Cultural and Natural Heritage (1972); promotes co-operation between city authorities, in particular in the management and sustainable development of historic sites; holds an annual General Assembly, comprising the mayors of member cities; mems: 226 cities world-wide; Sec.-Gen. DENIS RICARD; publ. *OWHC Newsletter* (2 a year, in English, French and Spanish).

Commodities

Cocoa Producers' Alliance (CPA): National Assembly Complex, Tafawa Balewa Sq., POB 1718, Lagos, Nigeria; tel. (1) 2635574; fax (1) 2635684; e-mail info@copal-cpa.org; internet www.copal-cpa.org; f. 1962 to exchange technical and scientific information, to discuss problems of mutual concern to producers, to ensure adequate supplies at remunerative prices and to promote consumption; mems: Brazil, Cameroon, Côte d'Ivoire, Dominican Republic, Gabon, Ghana, Malaysia, Nigeria, São Tomé and Príncipe, Togo; Sec.-Gen. HOPE SONA EBAI.

Gas Exporting Countries Forum: Al Dana Tower, 12th floor, POB 3212, Doha, Qatar; tel. 494-6655; fax 494-6433; e-mail GECForum@qp.com.qa; internet www.gecforum.org; f. 2001 to represent and promote the mutual interests of gas exporting countries; aims to increase the level of co-ordination among member countries and to promote dialogue between gas producers and consumers; a ministerial meeting is convened annually; the 7th ministerial meeting, convened in Moscow, Russia, in Dec. 2008, agreed on a charter and a permanent structure for the grouping; mems: Algeria, Bolivia, Egypt, Equatorial Guinea, Iran, Libya, Nigeria, Qatar, Russia, Trinidad and Tobago, Venezuela; observers: Kazakhstan, Netherlands, Norway.

International Cocoa Organization (ICCO): Commonwealth House, 1–19 New Oxford St, London, WC1A 1NU, United Kingdom; tel. (20) 7400-5050; fax (20) 7421-5500; e-mail info@icco.org; internet www.icco.org; f. 1973 under the first International Cocoa Agreement, 1972; the ICCO supervises the implementation of the agreements, and provides member governments with up-to-date information on the world cocoa economy; the sixth International Cocoa Agreement (2001) entered into force in October 2003; mems: 13 exporting countries and 28 importing countries; and the EU; Exec. Dir Dr JAN VINGERHOETS (Netherlands); publs *Quarterly Bulletin of Cocoa Statistics*, *Annual Report*, *World Cocoa Directory*, *Cocoa Newsletter*, studies on the world cocoa economy.

International Coffee Organization (ICO): 22 Berners St, London, W1T 3DD, United Kingdom; tel. (20) 7612-0600; fax (20) 7612-0630; e-mail info@ico.org; internet www.ico.org; f. 1963 under the International Coffee Agreement, 1962, which was renegotiated in 1968, 1976, 1983, 1994 (extended in 1999), 2001 and 2007; aims to improve international co-operation and provide a forum for inter-governmental consultations on coffee matters; to facilitate international trade in coffee by the collection, analysis and dissemination of statistics; to act as a centre for the collection, exchange and publication of coffee information; to promote studies in the field of coffee; and to encourage an increase in coffee consumption; mems: 45 exporting and 32 importing countries; Chair. of Council DAVID BROOKS (USA); Exec. Dir NÉSTOR OSORIO (Colombia).

International Sugar Organization: 1 Canada Sq., Canary Wharf, London, E14 5AA, United Kingdom; tel. (20) 7513-1144; fax (20) 7513-1146; e-mail exdir@isosugar.org; internet www.isosugar.org; administers the International Sugar Agreement (1992), with the objectives of stimulating co-operation, facilitating trade and encouraging demand; aims to improve conditions in the sugar market through debate, analysis and studies; serves as a forum for discussion; holds annual seminars and workshops; sponsors projects from developing countries; mems: 84 countries producing some 83% of total world sugar; Exec. Dir Dr PETER BARON; publs *Sugar Year Book*, *Monthly Statistical Bulletin*, *Market Report and Press Summary*, *Quarterly Market Outlook*, seminar proceedings.

International Tropical Timber Organization (ITTO): International Organizations Center, 5th Floor, Pacifico-Yokohama, 1-1-1, Minato-Mirai, Nishi-ku, Yokohama 220-0012, Japan; tel. (45) 223-1110; fax (45) 223-1111; e-mail itto@itto.or.jp; internet www.itto.int; f. 1985 under the International Tropical Timber Agreement (1983); a new treaty, ITTA 1994, came into force in 1997; provides a forum for consultation and co-operation between countries that produce and consume tropical timber, and is dedicated to the sustainable development and conservation of tropical forests; facilitates progress towards 'Objective 2000', which aims to move as rapidly as possible towards achieving exports of tropical timber and timber products from sustainably managed resources; encourages, through policy and project work, forest management, conservation and restoration, the further processing of tropical timber in producing countries, and the gathering and analysis of market intelligence and economic information; mems: 33 producing and 26 consuming countries and the EU; Exec. Dir EMMANUEL ZE MEKA (Cameroon); publs *Annual Review and Assessment of the World Timber Situation*, *Tropical Timber Market Information Service* (every 2 weeks), *Tropical Forest Update* (quarterly).

Organization of the Petroleum Exporting Countries (OPEC): 1010 Vienna, Helferstorferstrasse 17; tel. (1) 211-12-279; fax (1) 214-98-27; e-mail prid@opec.org; internet www.opec.org; f. 1960 to unify and co-ordinate members' petroleum policies and to safeguard their interests generally; holds regular conferences of member countries to set reference prices and production levels; conducts research in energy studies, economics and finance; provides data services and news services covering petroleum and energy issues; mems: Algeria, Angola, Iran, Iraq, Kuwait, Libya, Nigeria, Qatar, Saudi Arabia, United Arab Emirates, Venezuela; Sec.-Gen. ABDULLA SALEM EL-BADRI (Libya); publs *Annual Report*, *Annual Statistical Bulletin*, *OPEC Bulletin* (10 year), *OPEC Review* (quarterly), *Monthly Oil Market Report*, *World Oil Outlook* (annually).

Petrocaribe: internet www.petrocaribe.org; f. June 2005; an initiative of the Venezuelan Government to enhance the access of countries in the Caribbean region to petroleum on preferential payment terms; aims to co-ordinate the development of energy policies and plans regarding natural resources among signatory countries; 6th summit held in Saint Christopher and Nevis in June 2009; mems: Antigua and Barbuda, Bahamas, Belize, Cuba, Dominica, Dominican Republic, Grenada, Guatemala, Guyana, Haiti, Honduras, Jamaica, Nicaragua, Saint Christopher and Nevis, Saint Lucia, Saint Vincent and the Grenadines, Suriname, Venezuela.

Regional Association of Oil and Natural Gas Companies in Latin America and the Caribbean (Asociación Regional de Empresas de Petróleo y Gas Natural en Latinoamérica y el Caribe—ARPEL): Javier de Viana 2345, Casilla de correo 1006, 11200 Montevideo, Uruguay; tel. (2) 4106993; fax (2) 4109207; e-mail arpel@arpel.org.uy; internet www.arpel.org; f. 1965 as the Mutual Assistance of the Latin American Oil Companies; aims to initiate and implement activities for the development of the oil and natural gas industry in Latin America and the Caribbean; promotes the expansion of business opportunities and the improvement of the competitive advantages of its members; promotes guidelines in support of competition in the sector; and supports the efficient and sustainable exploitation of hydrocarbon resources and the supply of products and services. Works in co-operation with international organizations, governments, regulatory agencies, technical institutions, universities and non-governmental organizations; mems: 28 state-owned enterprises, representing more than 90% of regional operations, in Argentina, Bolivia, Brazil, Canada, Chile, Colombia, Costa Rica, Cuba, Ecuador, Jamaica, Mexico, Nicaragua, Paraguay, Peru, Suriname, Trinidad and Tobago, Uruguay, Venezuela; Exec. Sec. JOSÉ FÉLIX GARCÍA GARCÍA; publ. *Boletín Técnico*.

Sugar Association of the Caribbean (Inc.): 80 Abercromby St, Port of Spain,, Trinidad and Tobago; f. 1942; administers the West Indies Central Sugar Cane Breeding Station (in Barbados) and the West Indies Sugarcane Breeding and Evaluation Network; mems: national sugar cos of Barbados, Belize, Guyana, Jamaica and Trinidad and Tobago, and Sugar Asscn of St Kitts–Nevis–Anguilla; publs *SAC Handbook*, *SAC Annual Report*, *Proceedings of Meetings of WI Sugar Technologists*.

Union of Banana-Exporting Countries (Unión de Paises Exportadores de Banano—UPEB): Apdo 4273, Bank of America, 7°, Panamá 5, Panama; tel. 263-6266; fax 264-8355; e-mail iicapan@pan.gbm.net; f. 1974 as an intergovernmental agency to assist in the cultivation and marketing of bananas and to secure prices; collects statistics; mems: Colombia, Costa Rica, Guatemala, Honduras, Nicaragua, Panama, Venezuela; publs *Informe UPEB*, *Fax UPEB*, *Anuario de Estadísticas*, bibliographies.

West Indian Sea Island Cotton Association (Inc.): c/o Barbados Agricultural Development Corporation, Fairy Valley, Christ Church, Barbados; mems: organizations in Antigua and Barbuda, Barbados, Jamaica, Montserrat and Saint Christopher and Nevis; Pres. LEROY ROACH; Sec. MICHAEL I. EDGHILL.

Development and Economic Co-operation

Amazon Co-operation Treaty Organization: SHIS-QI 05, Conjunto 16, casa 21, Lago Sul, Brasília, DF 71615-160, Brazil; tel. (61) 3248-4119; fax (61) 3248-4238; internet www.otca.org.br; f. 1978, permanent secretariat established 1995; aims to promote the co-ordinated and sustainable development of the Amazonian territories; there are regular meetings of ministers of foreign affairs; there are specialized co-ordinators of environment, health, science technology and education, infrastructure, tourism, transport and communications, and of indigenous affairs; mems: Bolivia, Brazil, Colombia, Ecuador, Guyana, Peru, Suriname, Venezuela; Sec.-Gen. MANUEL ERNESTO PICASSO BOTTO (Peru).

Association of Caribbean States (ACS): 5–7 Sweet Briar Rd, St Clair, POB 660, Port of Spain, Trinidad and Tobago; tel. 622-9575; fax 622-1653; e-mail communications@acs-aec.org; internet www.acs-aec.org; f. 1994 by the Governments of the 13 CARICOM countries and Colombia, Costa Rica, Cuba, Dominican Republic, El Salvador, Guatemala, Haiti, Honduras, Mexico, Nicaragua, Suriname and Venezuela; aims to promote economic integration, sustainable development and co-operation in the region; to preserve the environmental integrity of the Caribbean Sea which is regarded as the common patrimony of the peoples of the region; to undertake concerted action to protect the environment, particularly the Caribbean Sea; and to co-operate in the areas of trade, transport, sustainable tourism, and natural disasters. Policy is determined by a Ministerial Council and implemented by a Secretariat based in Port of Spain. In December 2001 a third Summit of Heads of State and Government was convened in Venezuela, where a Plan of Action focusing on issues of sustainable tourism, trade, transport and natural disasters was agreed. The fourth ACS Summit was held in Panama, in July 2005. A final Declaration included resolutions to strengthen co-operation mechanisms with the EU and to promote a strategy for the Caribbean Sea Zone to be recognized as a special area for the purposes of sustainable development programmes, support for a strengthened social agenda and efforts to achieve the Millennium Development Goals, and calls for member states to sign or ratify the following accords: an ACS Agreement for Regional Co-operation in the area of Natural Disasters; a Convention Establishing the Sustainable Tourism Zone of the Caribbean; and an ACS Air Transport Agreement; mems: 25 signatory states, 4 associate mems, 19 observers, 6 founding observer countries; Sec.-Gen. LUIS FERNANDO ANDRADE FALLA.

Caribbean-Britain Business Council: 2 Belgrave Sq., London, SW1X 8PJ, United Kingdom; tel. (20) 7235-9484; fax (20) 7823-1370; e-mail admin@caribbean-council.org; internet www.caribbean-council.org; f. 2001; promotes trade and investment development between the United Kingdom, the Caribbean and the European Union; Chair. BARRY HUMPHREYS; Exec. Dir DAVID JESSOP; publs *Caribbean Insight* (weekly), *Cuba Briefing* (weekly).

Council of American Development Foundations (Consejo de Fundaciones Americanas de Desarrollo—SOLIDARIOS): Calle 6 No. 10 Paraíso, Apdo Postal 620, Santo Domingo, Dominican Republic; tel. 549-5111; fax 544-0550; e-mail solidarios@codetel.net.do; f. 1972; exchanges information and experience, arranges technical assistance, raises funds to organize training programmes and scholarships; administers development fund to finance programmes carried out by members through a loan guarantee programme; provides consultancy services. Mem. foundations provide technical and financial assistance to low-income groups for rural, housing and microenterprise development projects; mems: 18 institutional mems in 14 Latin American and Caribbean countries; Pres. MERCEDES P. DE CANALDA; Sec.-Gen. ISABEL C. ARANGO; publs *Solidarios* (quarterly), *Annual Report*.

G-20 (Doha Round negotiating group): e-mail g-20@mre.gov.br; internet www.g-20.mre.gov.br/index.asp; f. 2003 with the aim of defending the interests of developing countries in the negotiations on agriculture under the WTO's Doha Development Round and meets regularly to address WTO-related agricultural trade issues; now comprises 23 developing countries; mems: Argentina, Bolivia, Brazil, Chile, People's Republic of China, Cuba, Ecuador, Egypt, Guatemala, India, Indonesia, Mexico, Nigeria, Pakistan, Paraguay, Peru, Philippines, South Africa, Tanzania, Thailand, Uruguay, Venezuela, Zimbabwe.

Group of Three (G-3): c/o Secretaría de Relaciones Exteriores, 1 Tlatelolco, Del. Cuauhtémoc, 06995 México, DF, Mexico; e-mail gtres@sre.gob.mx; f. 1990 by Colombia, Mexico and Venezuela to remove restrictions on trade between the three countries; in November 2004 Panama joined the Group, which briefly became the Group of Four until Venezuela's withdrawal in November 2006; the trade agreement covers market access, rules of origin, intellectual property, trade in services, and government purchases, and entered into force in early 1994. Tariffs on trade between member states were to be removed on a phased basis. Co-operation was also envisaged in employment creation, the energy sector and the fight against cholera. The secretariat function rotates between the member countries on a two-yearly basis; mems: Colombia, Mexico and Panama.

Group of 15 (G15): G15 Technical Support Facility, 1 route des Morillons, CP 2100, 1218 Grand Saconnex, Geneva, Switzerland; tel. 227916701; fax 227916169; e-mail tsf@g15.org; internet www.g15.org; f. 1989 by 15 developing nations during the 9th summit of the Non-Aligned Movement; retains its original name although current membership totals 17; convenes biennial summits to address the global economic and political situation and to promote economic development through South-South co-operation and North-South dialogue; mems: Algeria, Argentina, Brazil, Chile, Egypt, India, Indonesia, Iran, Jamaica, Kenya, Malaysia, Mexico, Nigeria, Senegal, Sri Lanka, Venezuela, Zimbabwe; Head of Office AUDU A. KADIRI.

Group of 77 (G77): c/o UN Headquarters, Rm S-3953, New York, NY 10017, USA; tel. (212) 963-3515; fax (212) 963-1753; e-mail g77off@undp.org; internet www.g77.org/; f. 1964 by the 77 signatory states of the 'Joint Declaration of the Seventy-Seven Countries' (the G77 retains its original name, owing to its historic significance, although its membership has expanded since inception); first ministerial meeting, held in Algiers, Algeria, in Oct. 1967, adopted the Charter of Algiers as a basis for G77 co-operation; subsequently G77 Chapters were established with liaison offices in Geneva (UNCTAD), Nairobi (UNEP), Paris (UNESCO), Rome (FAO/IFAD), Vienna (UNIDO), and the Group of 24 (G24) in Washington, DC (IMF and World Bank); as the largest intergovernmental organization of developing states in the United Nations the G77 aims to enable developing nations to articulate and promote their collective economic interests and to improve their negotiating capacity with regard to global economic issues within the United Nations system; in Sept. 2006 G77 ministers of foreign affairs, and the People's Republic of China, endorsed the establishment of a new Consortium on Science, Technology and Innovation for the South (COSTIS); a chairperson, who also acts as spokesperson, co-ordinates the G77's activities in each Chapter; the chairmanship rotates on a regional basis between Africa, Asia, and Latin America and the Caribbean; the supreme decision-making body of the G77 is the South Summit, convened at five-yearly intervals (2005: Doha, Qatar; the third Summit was scheduled to be convened in Africa, in 2010); the annual meeting of G77 ministers of foreign affairs is convened at the start (in September) of the regular session of the UN General Assembly; periodic sectoral ministerial meetings are organized in preparation for UNCTAD sessions and prior to the UNIDO and UNESCO General Conferences, and with the aim of promoting South-South co-operation; other special ministerial meetings are also convened from time to time; the first G77 Ministerial Forum on Water Resources was convened in February 2009, in Muscat, Oman; mems: 131 developing countries.

Inter-American Planning Society (Sociedad Interamericana de Planificación—SIAP): c/o Revista Interamericana de Planificación, Casilla 01-05-1978, Cuenca, Ecuador; tel. (7) 823860; fax (7) 823949; e-mail siap1@siap.org.ec; f. 1956 to promote development of comprehensive planning; mems: institutions and individuals in 46 countries; Exec. Sec. LUIS E. CAMACHO (Colombia); publs *Correo Informativo* (quarterly), *Inter-American Journal of Planning* (quarterly).

Latin American Association of Development Financing Institutions (Asociación Latinoamericana de Instituciones Financieras para el Desarrollo—ALIDE): Apdo Postal 3988, Paseo de la República 3211, Lima 100, Peru; tel. (1) 4422400; fax (1) 4428105; e-mail sg@alide.org.pe; internet www.alide.org.pe; f. 1968 to promote co-operation among regional development financing bodies; programmes: technical assistance; training; studies and research; technical meetings; information; projects and investment promotion; mems: 67 active, 3 assoc. and 5 collaborating (banks and financing institutions and development organizations in 22 Latin American countries, Slovenia and Spain); Sec.-Gen. ROMMEL ACEVEDO; publs *ALIDE Bulletin* (6 a year), *ALIDENOTICIAS Newsletter* (monthly), *Annual Report*, *Latin American Directory of Development Financing Institutions*.

Latin American Economic System (Sistema Económico Latinoamericano—SELA): Torre Europa, 4°, Urb. Campo Alegre, Avda Francisco de Miranda, Caracas 1060, Venezuela; Apdo 17035, Caracas 1010-A, Venezuela; tel. (212) 955-7111; fax (212) 951-5292; e-mail difusion@sela.org; internet www.sela.org; f. 1975 in accordance with the Panama Convention; aims to foster co-operation and integration among the countries of Latin America and the Caribbean, and to provide a permanent system of consultation and co-ordination in economic and social matters; conducts studies and other analysis and research; extends technical assistance to sub-regional and regional co-ordination bodies; provides library, information service and databases on regional co-operation. The Latin American Council, the principal decision-making body of the System, meets annually at ministerial level and high-level regional consultation and co-ordination meetings are held; there is also a Permanent Secretariat; mems: 28 countries; Perm. Sec. ROBERTO GUARNIERI (Venezuela); publs *Capítulos del SELA* (3 a year), *Bulletin on Latin America and Caribbean Integration* (monthly), *SELA Antenna in the United States* (quarterly).

Mesoamerican Integration and Development Project (Proyecto de Integración y Desarrollo de Mesoamérica): Torre Roble, 8°, San Salvador, El Salvador; tel. 2261-5444; fax 2260-9175; e-mail c.trinidad@proyectomesoamerica.org; internet www.proyectomesoamerica.org; f. 2001 as the Puebla-Panamá Plan (PPP); relaunched with formal institutionalized structure in 2004; current name and mandate approved in June 2008 by the Tuxtla summit meeting; aims to promote economic development and reduce poverty in member countries; eight key areas of activity: energy, transport, telecommunications, tourism, trade environment and competitiveness, human development, sustainable development, prevention and mitigation of natural disasters; administers the Mesoamerica Biological Corridor initiative to enhance the management of the region's biodiversity; mems: Belize, Colombia, Costa

Rica, El Salvador, Guatemala, Honduras, Mexico, Nicaragua, Panama; Exec. Dir MARÍA TERESA ORELLANA DE RENDÓN.

Organization of the Co-operatives of America (Organización de las Cooperativas de América): Apdo Postal 241263, Carrera 11, No 86-32, Of. 101, Bogotá, Colombia; tel. (1) 6103296; fax (1) 6101912; f. 1963 for improving socio-economic, cultural and moral conditions through the use of the co-operatives system; works in every country of the continent; regional offices sponsor plans and activities based on the most pressing needs and special conditions of individual countries; mems: national or local orgs in 23 countries and territories; Exec. Sec. Dr CARLOS JULIO PINEDA SUÁREZ; publs *América Cooperativa* (monthly), *OCA News* (monthly).

Pacific Basin Economic Council (PBEC): Suite 1304, Wing On Centre, 111 Connaught Road Central, Hong Kong, SAR; tel. 2815-6550; fax 2545-0499; e-mail info@pbec.org; internet www.pbec.org; f. 1967; an asscn of business representatives aiming to promote business opportunities in the region, in order to enhance overall economic development; advises governments and serves as a liaison between business leaders and government officials; encourages business relationships and co-operation among members; holds business symposia; mems: 20 economies (Australia, Canada, Chile, People's Republic of China, Colombia, Ecuador, Hong Kong, Indonesia, Japan, Republic of Korea, Malaysia, Mexico, New Zealand, Peru, Philippines, Russia, Singapore, Taiwan, Thailand, USA); Pres. MARTIN CRAIGS; publs *PBEC Update* (quarterly), *Executive Summary* (annual conference report).

Partners in Population and Development (PPD): IPH Bldg, 2nd Floor, Mohakhali, Dhaka 1212, Bangladesh; tel. (2) 988-1882; fax (2) 882-9387; e-mail partners@ppdsec.org; internet www.partners-popdev.org; f. 1994; aims to implement the decisions of the International Conference on Population and Development, held in Cairo, Egypt in 1994, in order to expand and improve South-South collaboration in the fields of family planning and reproductive health; administers a Visionary Leadership Programme, a Global Leadership Programme, and other training and technical advisory services; mems: 24 developing countries; Exec. Dir SANGEET HARRY JOOSEERY.

Trans-Pacific Strategic Economic Partnership Agreement (P4): c/o Ministry of Foreign Affairs and Trade, Private Bag 1890, Wellington, New Zealand; tel. (4) 439-8446; f. 2006 upon entry into force of agreement signed by the four founding mems; eliminated some 90% of tariffs on trade between mems; negotiations on financial services and investment commenced in March 2008; mems: Brunei, Chile, New Zealand, Singapore.

World Economic Forum: 91–93 route de la Capite, 1223 Cologny/Geneva, Switzerland; tel. 228691212; fax 227862744; e-mail contact@weforum.org; internet www.weforum.org; f. 1971; the Forum comprises commercial interests gathered on a non-partisan basis, under the stewardship of the Swiss Government, with the aim of improving society through economic development; convenes an annual meeting in Davos, Switzerland; organizes the following programmes: Technology Pioneers; Women Leaders; and Young Global Leaders; and aims to mobilize the resources of the global business community in the implementation of the following initiatives: the Global Health Initiative; the Disaster Relief Network; the West-Islamic World Dialogue; and the G20/International Monetary Reform Project; the Forum is governed by a guiding Foundation Board; an advisory International Business Council; and an administrative Managing Board; regular mems: representatives of 1,000 leading commercial companies world-wide; selected mem. companies taking a leading role in the movement's activities are known as 'partners'.

Economics and Finance

Banco del Sur (South American Bank): Caracas, Venezuela; f. Dec. 2007; formal agreement establishing the bank signed in Sept. 2009; aims to provide financing for social and investment projects in South America; auth. cap. US $20,000m.; mems: Argentina, Brazil, Bolivia, Ecuador, Paraguay, Uruguay, Venezuela.

Bank for International Settlements (BIS): Centralbahnplatz 2, 4002 Basel, Switzerland; tel. 612808080; fax 612809100; e-mail email@bis.org; internet www.bis.org; f. pursuant to the Hague Agreements of 1930 to promote co-operation among national central banks and to provide additional facilities for international financial operations; provides the secretariat for the Basel Committee on Banking Supervision and the Financial Stability Board; representative offices in Hong Kong SAR, and Mexico; mems: central banks in 55 countries; Chair. CHRISTIAN NOYER (France); Gen. Man. JAIME CARUANA (Spain); publs *Annual Report*, *Quarterly Review: International Banking and Financial Market Developments*, *The BIS Consolidated International Banking Statistics* (every 6 months), *Joint BIS-IMF-OECD-World Bank Statistics on External Debt* (quarterly), *Regular OTC Derivatives Market Statistics* (every 6 months), *Central Bank Survey of Foreign Exchange and Derivatives Market Activity* (every 3 years).

Centre for Latin American Monetary Studies (Centro de Estudios Monetarios Latinoamericanos—CEMLA): Durango 54, Col. Roma, Del. Cuauhtémoc, 06700 México, DF, Mexico; tel. (55) 5533-0300; fax (55) 5525-4432; e-mail estudios@cemla.org; internet www.cemla.org; f. 1952; organizes technical training programmes on monetary policy, development finance, etc; runs applied research programmes on monetary and central banking policies and procedures; holds regional meetings of banking officials; mems: 30 associated members (Central Banks of Latin America and the Caribbean), 20 co-operating members (supervisory institutions of the region and non-Latin American Central Banks); Dir-Gen. KENNETH GILMORE COATES SPRY; publs *Bulletin* (every 2 months), *Monetaria* (quarterly), *Money Affairs* (2 a year).

Eastern Caribbean Central Bank (ECCB): POB 89, Basseterre, St Christopher and Nevis; tel. 465-2537; fax 465-9562; e-mail info@eccb-centralbank.org; internet www.eccb-centralbank.org; f. 1983 by OECS governments; maintains regional currency (Eastern Caribbean dollar) and advises on the economic development of member states; mems: Anguilla, Antigua and Barbuda, Dominica, Grenada, Montserrat, Saint Christopher and Nevis, Saint Lucia, Saint Vincent and the Grenadines; Gov. Sir K. DWIGHT VENNER.

Financial Action Task Force (FATF) (Groupe d'action financière—GAFI): 2 rue André-Pascal, 75775 Paris Cédex 16, France; tel. 1-45-24-79-45; fax 1-44-30-61-37; e-mail contact@fatf-gafi.org; internet www.fatf-gafi.org; f. 1989, on the recommendation of the Group of Seven industrialized nations (G7), to develop and promote policies to combat money laundering and the financing of terrorism; formulated a set of recommendations (40+9) for countries world-wide to implement; established partnerships with regional task forces in the Caribbean, Asia-Pacific, Central Asia, Europe, East and South Africa, the Middle East and North Africa and South America; mems: 35 state jurisdictions, the European Commission, and the Co-operation Council for the Arab States of the Gulf; observers: India, Basel Committee on Banking Supervision, Eurasian Group (EAG) on combating money laundering and financing of terrorism; Pres. LUIS URRUTIA CORRAL (Mexico); Exec. Sec. RICK MCDONELL; publs *Annual Report*, *e-Bulletin*.

Financial Stability Board: c/o BIS, Centralbahnplatz 2, 4002 Basel, Switzerland; tel. 612808298; fax 612809100; e-mail fsb@bis.org; internet www.financialstabilityboard.org; f. 1999 as the Financial Stability Forum, name changed in April 2009; brings together senior representatives of national financial authorities, international financial institutions, international regulatory and supervisory groupings and committees of central bank experts and the European Central Bank; aims to promote international financial stability and strengthen the functioning of the financial markets; in March 2009 agreed to expand its membership to include all Group of 20 (G20) economies, as well as Spain and the European Commission; in April 2009 the meeting of G20 heads of state and government determined to re-establish the then Forum as the Financial Stability Board, strengthen its institutional structure (to include a plenary body, a steering committee and three standing committees concerned with Vulnerabilities Assessment; Supervisory and Regulatory Co-operation; and Standards Implementation) and expand its mandate to enhance its effectiveness as an international mechanism to promote financial stability; the Board was to strengthen its collaboration with the International Monetary Fund, and conduct joint 'early warning exercises'; in December 2009 the Board initiated a peer review of implementation of the Principles and Standards for Sound Compensation Practices; Chair. MARIO DRAGHI.

Group of 20 (G20): internet www.g20.org; f. Sept. 1999 as an informal deliberative forum of finance ministers and central bank governors representing both industrialized and 'systemically important' emerging market nations; aims to strengthen the international financial architecture and to foster sustainable economic growth and development; in 2004 participating countries adopted the G20 Accord for Sustained Growth and stated a commitment to high standards of transparency and fiscal governance; the IMF Managing Director and IBRD President participate in G20 annual meetings (Nov. 2008: São Paulo, Brazil); an extraordinary Summit on Financial Markets and the World Economy was convened in Washington, DC, USA, in November 2008, attended by heads of state or government of G20 member economies; a second summit meeting, held in London, United Kingdom, in April 2009, issued as its final communiqué a *Global plan for recovery and reform* outlining commitments to restore economic confidence, growth and jobs, to strengthen financial supervision and regulation, to reform and strengthen global financial institutions, to promote global trade and investment and to ensure a fair and sustainable economic recovery; detailed declarations were also issued on measures agreed to deliver substantial resources (of some US $850,000m.) through international financial institutions and on reforms to be implemented in order to strengthen the financial system; as a follow-up to the London summit, G20 heads of state met in Pittsburgh, USA, in September 2009; the meeting adopted a *Framework for Strong, Sustainable, and Balanced Growth* and resolved to expand the role of the G20 to be at the centre of future international economic policymaking; summit meetings in 2010 were scheduled to be convened in Canada, in June (at the G8 summit), and Republic of Korea, in November; mems: Argentina, Australia, Brazil, Canada, People's Republic of China, France, Germany, India, Indonesia, Italy, Japan, Republic of Korea, Mexico, Russia, Saudi Arabia, South Africa, Turkey, United Kingdom, USA and the European Union; observers: the Netherlands, Spain.

Intergovernmental Group of 24 (G24) on International Monetary Affairs and Development: 700 19th St, NW, Rm 3-600 Washington, DC 20431, USA; tel. (202) 623-6101; fax (202) 623-6000; e-mail G24@G24.org; internet www.g24.org/; f. 1971; aims to co-ordinate the position of developing countries on monetary and development finance issues; operates at the political level of ministers of finance and governors of central banks, and also at the level of government officials; mems (Africa): Algeria, Côte d'Ivoire, DRC, Egypt, Ethiopia, Gabon, Ghana, Nigeria, South Africa; (Latin America and the Caribbean): Argentina, Brazil, Colombia, Guatemala, Mexico, Peru, Trinidad and Tobago and Venezuela; (Asia and the Middle East): India, Iran, Lebanon, Pakistan, Philippines, Sri Lanka and Syrian Arab Republic; the People's Republic of China has the status of special invitee at G24 meetings; G77 participant states may attend G24 meetings as observers.

Latin American Banking Federation (Federación Latinoamericana de Bancos—FELABAN): Cra 11A No. 93-67 Of. 202 A.A 091959, Bogotá, Colombia; tel. (1) 6218617; fax (1) 6217659; internet www.latinbanking.com; f. 1965 to co-ordinate efforts towards wide and accelerated economic development in Latin American countries; mems: 19 Latin American national banking asscns, representing more than 500 banks and financial institutions; Pres. RICARDO MARINO (Brazil); Sec.-Gen. MARICIELO GLEN DE TOBÓN (Colombia).

Education

Association of Caribbean University and Research Institutional Libraries (ACURIL): Apdo postal 23317, San Juan 00931-3317, Puerto Rico; tel. 790-8054; fax 764-2311; e-mail acurilsec@yahoo.com; internet acuril.uprrp.edu; f. 1968 to foster contact and collaboration between mem. universities and institutes; holds conferences, meetings and seminars; circulates information through newsletters and bulletins; facilitates co-operation and the pooling of resources in research; encourages exchange of staff and students; mems: 250; Pres. BÉA BAZILE (Guadeloupe); Exec.-Sec. ONEIDA R. ORTIZ (Puerto Rico); publ. *Cybernotes*.

Inter-American Centre for Research and Documentation on Vocational Training (Centro Interamericano de Investigación y Documentación sobre Formación Profesional—CINTERFOR): Avda Uruguay 1238, Casilla de correo 1761, Montevideo, Uruguay; tel. (2) 9020557; fax (2) 9021305; e-mail dirmvd@cinterfor.org.uy; internet www.ilo.org/public/english/region/ampro/cinterfor; f. 1964 by the International Labour Organization for mutual help among the Latin American and Caribbean countries in planning vocational training; services are provided in documentation, research, exchange of experience; holds seminars and courses; Dir PEDRO DANIEL WEINBERG; publs *Bulletin CINTERFOR/OIT Heramientas para la transformación*, *Trazos de la formación*, studies, monographs and technical papers.

Inter-American Confederation for Catholic Education (Confederación Interamericana de Educación Católica—CIEC): Calle 78 No 12–16 (of. 101), Apdo Aéreo 90036, Bogotá 8 DE, Colombia; tel. (1) 2553676; fax (1) 2550513; e-mail secretariageneral@ciec.edu.co; internet www.ciec.edu.co; f. 1945 to defend and extend the principles and rules of Catholic education, freedom of education, and human rights; organizes congress every three years (2010: Santo Domingo, Dominican Republic); Pres. JOSÉ MANUEL VELASCO (Mexico); Sec.-Gen. RAMÓN EMILIO RIVAS TORRES; publ. *Educación Hoy*.

Inter-American Organization for Higher Education (IOHE): 333 Grande Allée Est, bureau 230, Québec, QC G1R 2H8, Canada; tel. (418) 650-1515; fax (418) 650-1519; e-mail secretariat@oui-iohe.qc.ca; internet www.oui-iohe.org; f. 1980 to promote co-operation among universities of the Americas and the development of higher education; mems: some 265 institutions and 34 national and regional higher education asscns; Exec. Dir PATRICIA GUDIÑO.

International Council for Adult Education (ICAE): Ave. 18 de Julio 2095/301, CP 11200, Montevideo, Uruguay; tel. and fax (2) 4097982; e-mail secretariat@icae.org.uy; internet www.icae2.org; f. 1973 as a partnership of adult learners, teachers and organizations; General Assembly meets every four years; mems: 7 regional orgs and over 700 literacy, adult and lifelong learning asscns in more than 50 countries; Pres. PAUL BÉLANGER; Sec.-Gen. CELITA ECHER; publs *Convergence*, *ICAE News*.

International Institute of Iberoamerican Literature (Instituto Internacional de Literatura Iberoamericana): 1312 CL, University of Pittsburgh, PA 15260, USA; tel. (412) 624-3359; fax (412) 624-0829; e-mail iili@pitt.edu; internet www.pitt.edu/~hispan/iili; f. 1938 to advance the study of Iberoamerican literature, and intensify cultural relations among the peoples of the Americas; mems: scholars and artists in 37 countries; publs *Revista Iberoamericana*, *Memorias*.

Italian-Latin American Institute: Piazza Benedetto Cairoli 3, 00186 Rome, Italy; tel. (06) 684921; fax (06) 6872834; e-mail info@iila.org; internet www.iila.org/IILA/; f. 1966; aims to promote Italian culture in Latin America; awarded observer status at the UN General Assembly in 2007; Sec.-Gen. PAOLO BRUNI.

Organization of Ibero-American States for Education, Science and Culture (Organización de Estados Iberoamericanos para la Educación, la Ciencia y la Cultura—OEI): Centro de Recursos Documentales e Informáticos, Calle Bravo Murillo 38, 28015 Madrid, Spain; tel. (91) 5944382; fax (91) 5943286; internet www.oei.es; f. 1949 (as the Ibero-American Bureau of Education); promotes peace and solidarity between member countries, through education, science, technology and culture; provides information, encourages exchanges and organizes training courses; the General Assembly (at ministerial level) meets every four years; mems: govts of 20 countries; Sec.-Gen. ÁLVARO MARCHESI ULLASTRES; publ. *Revista Iberoamericana de Educación* (quarterly).

Organization of the Catholic Universities of Latin America (Organización de Universidades Católicas de América Latina—ODUCAL): c/o Dr J. A. Tobías, Universidad del Salvador, Viamonte 1856, CP 1056, Buenos Aires, Argentina; tel. (11) 4813-1408; fax (11) 4812-4625; e-mail udes-rect@salvador.edu.ar; f. 1953 to assist the social, economic and cultural development of Latin America through the promotion of Catholic higher education in the continent; mems: 43 Catholic universities in 15 Latin American countries; Sec.-Gen. Dr JOAQUÍN R. LEDESMA; publs *Anuario*, *Sapientia*, *Universitas*.

Union of Universities of Latin America and the Caribbean (Unión de Universidades de América Latina y el Caribe—UDUAL): Edificio UDUAL, Apdo postal 70-232, Ciudad Universitaria, Del. Coyoacán, 04510 México, DF, Mexico; tel. (55) 5622-0091; fax (55) 5622-0092; e-mail contacto@udual.org; internet www.udual.org; f. 1949 to organize exchanges between professors, students, research fellows and graduates and generally encourage good relations between the Latin American universities; arranges conferences; conducts statistical research; maintains centre for university documentation; mems: 180 universities and 8 university networks; Pres. Dr GUSTAVO GARCÍA DE PAREDES (Panama); Sec.-Gen. Dr RAFAEL CORDERA CAMPOS (Mexico); publs *Universidades* (2 a year), *Gaceta UDUAL* (quarterly), *Censo* (every 2 years).

Environmental Conservation

Caribbean Conservation Association: Savannah Lodge, The Garrison, St Michael, Barbados; tel. 426-5373; fax 429-8483; e-mail cca@caribsurf.com; f. 1967; aims to conserve the environment and cultural heritage of the region through education, legislation, and management of museums and sites; mems: 17 govts, 60 NGOs and 130 associates; Pres. ATHERTON MARTIN (Dominica); Exec. Dir LESLIE JOHN WALLING; publ. *Caribbean Conservation News* (quarterly).

Consortium for Oceanographic Research and Education (CORE): 1201 New York Ave, NW, Suite 420, Washington, DC 20005, USA; tel. (202) 332-0063; fax (202) 332-9751; e-mail coml@coreocean.org; internet www.comlsecretariat.org; f. 1999 to launch and host the International Steering Committee and Secretariat for the Census of Marine Life, a 10-year initiative to assess the diversity, distribution and abundance of marine life being implemented by a network of researchers from more than 70 countries; aims to promote, support and advance the science of oceanography; Pres. RICHARD WEST.

Global Coral Reef Monitoring Network: POB 772, Townsville MC 4810, Australia; tel. (7) 4721-2699; fax (7) 4772-2808; e-mail clive.wilkinson@rrrc.org.au; internet www.gcrmn.org; f. 1994, as an operating unit of the International Coral Reef Initiative; active in more than 80 countries; aims include improving the management and sustainable conservation of coral reefs, strengthening links between regional organizations and ecological and socioeconomic monitoring networks, and disseminating information to assist the formulation of conservation plans; Global Co-ordinator Dr CLIVE WILKINSON (Australia); publ. *Status of Coral Reefs of the World*.

Global Wind Energy Council: Renewable Energy House, rue d'Arlon 63-65, 1040 Brussels, Belgium; tel. (2) 400-10-29; fax (2)

546-19-44; e-mail info@gwec.net; internet www.gwec.net; represents the main national, regional and international institutions, companies and asscns related to wind power; aims to promote the development and growth of wind as a major source of energy; organizes a Global WindPower Conference every two years (2010: India); Sec.-Gen. STEVE SAWYER; publs *Global Wind Energy Outlook*, *Wind Force 12*, other reports, surveys.

International Coral Reef Initiative: internet www.icriforum.org; f. 1994 at the first Conference of the Parties of the Convention on Biological Diversity; a partnership of governments, non-governmental organizations, scientific bodies and the private sector; aims to highlight the degradation of coral reefs and provide a focus for action to ensure the sustainable management and conservation of these and related marine ecosystems; in 1995 issued a Call to Action and a Framework for Action; the Secretariat rotates among members (2009–11, France).

International Renewable Energy Agency: internet www.irena.org; f. 2009 at a conference held in Bonn, Germany; aims to promote the development and application of renewable sources of energy; to act as a forum for the exchange of information and technology transfer; and to organize training seminars and other educational activities; mems: 81 countries.

International Seabed Authority: 14–20 Port Royal St, Kingston, Jamaica; tel. 922-9105; fax 922-0195; e-mail postmaster@isa.org.jm; internet www.isa.org.jm; f. Nov. 1994 upon the entry into force of the 1982 United Nations Convention on the Law of the Sea; the Authority is the institute through which states parties to the Convention organize and control activities in the international seabed area beyond the limits of national jurisdiction, particularly with a view to administering the resources of that area; Sec.-Gen. NII ALLOTEY ODUNTON (Ghana).

IUCN—International Union for Conservation of Nature: 28 rue Mauverney, 1196 Gland, Switzerland; tel. 229990000; fax 229990002; e-mail webmaster@iucn.org; internet www.iucn.org; f. 1948, as the International Union for Conservation of Nature and Natural Resources; supports partnerships and practical field activities to promote the conservation of natural resources, to secure the conservation of biological diversity as an essential foundation for the future; to ensure wise use of the earth's natural resources in an equitable and sustainable way; and to guide the development of human communities towards ways of life in enduring harmony with other components of the biosphere, developing programmes to protect and sustain the most important and threatened species and eco-systems and assisting governments to devise and carry out national conservation strategies; incorporates the Species Survival Commission (SSC), a science-based network of volunteer experts aiming to ensure conservation of present levels of biodiversity; compiles annually updated Red List of Threatened Species, comprising in 2009 some 47,677 species, of which 17,291 were threatened with extinction; maintains a conservation library and documentation centre and units for monitoring traffic in wildlife; mems: more than 1,000 states, government agencies, non-governmental organizations and affiliates in some 140 countries; Pres. ASHOK KHOSLA (India); Dir-Gen. JULIA MARTON-LEFÈVRE (USA); publs *World Conservation Strategy*, *Caring for the Earth*, *Red List of Threatened Plants*, *Red List of Threatened Species*, *United Nations List of National Parks and Protected Areas*, *World Conservation* (quarterly), *IUCN Today*.

Permanent Commission of the South Pacific (Comisión Permanente del Pacífico Sur): Av. Carlos Julio Arosemena, Km 3 Edificio Inmaral, Guayaquil, Ecuador; e-mail cpps_pse@cpps-int.org; internet www.cpps-int.org; f. 1952 to consolidate the presence of the zonal coastal states; Sec.-Gen. Dr GONZALO PEREIRA.

Secretariat of the Antarctic Treaty: Av. Leandro Alem 884, piso 4, C1001AAQ Buenos Aires, Argentina; tel. (11) 5169-1500; fax (11) 5169-1513; e-mail secret@ats.aq; internet www.ats.aq; f. 2004 to administer the Antarctic Treaty (signed in 1959); has developed an Electronic Information Exchange System; organizes annual Consultative Meeting (2010: Punta del Este, Uruguay); mems: 49 states party to the Treaty; Exec. Sec. MANFRED REINKE.

World Association of Zoos and Aquariums (WAZA): Lindenrain 3, 3012 Bern, Switzerland; e-mail secretariat@waza.org; internet www.waza.org; f. 1946, current name adopted 2000; aims to provide leadership and support for zoos and aquariums and to promote biodiversity, environmental education, and global sustainability; adopted WAZA Code of Ethics and Animal Welfare, and a Consensus Document on Responsible Reproductive Management, in 2003; in 2005 WAZA launched a World Zoo and Aquarium Conservation Strategy, adopted Research Guidelines, and participated for the first time in Conferences of the Parties to the Ramsar Convention and the Convention of Migratory Species; mems: leading zoos and aquariums and related regional and national asscn; affiliate conservation orgs; Exec. Dir GERALD DICK.

World Rainforest Movement (WRM): Maldonado 1858, Montevideo 11200, Uruguay; tel. (2) 4132989; fax (2) 4100985; e-mail wrm@wrm.org.uy; internet www.wrm.org.uy; f. 1986; aims to secure the lands and livelihoods of rainforest peoples and supports their efforts to defend rainforests from activities including commercial logging, mining, the construction of dams, the development of plantations, and shrimp farming; issued the Penang Declaration in 1989 setting out the shared vision of an alternative model of rainforest development based on securing the lands and livelihoods of forest inhabitants; released in 1998 the Montevideo Declaration, campaigning against large-scale monocrop plantations, for example of pulpwood, oil palm and rubber; and issued the Mount Tamalpais Declaration in 2000, urging governments not to include tree plantations as carbon sinks in international action against climate change; publ. *WRM Bulletin* (monthly).

WWF International: 27 ave du Mont-Blanc, 1196 Gland, Switzerland; tel. 223649111; fax 223648836; e-mail info@wwfint.org; internet www.panda.org; f. 1961 (as World Wildlife Fund), name changed to World Wide Fund for Nature in 1986, current nomenclature adopted 2001; aims to stop the degradation of natural environments, conserve bio-diversity, ensure the sustainable use of renewable resources, and promote the reduction of both pollution and wasteful consumption; addresses six priority issues: forests, freshwater, marine, species, climate change, and toxics; has identified, and focuses its activities in, 200 'ecoregions' (the 'Global 200'), believed to contain the best part of the world's remaining biological diversity; actively supports and operates conservation programmes in more than 90 countries; mems: 54 offices, 5 associate orgs, c. 5m. individual mems world-wide; Pres. YOLANDA KAKABADSE (Ecuador); Dir-Gen. JAMES P. LEAPE; publs *Annual Report*, *Living Planet Report*.

Government and Politics

Agency for the Prohibition of Nuclear Weapons in Latin America and the Caribbean (Organismo para la Proscripción de las Armas Nucleares en la América Latina y el Caribe—OPANAL): Schiller 326, 5°, Col. Chapultepec Morales, 11570 México, DF, Mexico; tel. (55) 5255-2914; fax (55) 5255-3748; e-mail info@opanal.org; internet www.opanal.org; f. 1969 to ensure compliance with the Treaty for the Prohibition of Nuclear Weapons in Latin America (Treaty of Tlatelolco), 1967; to ensure the absence of all nuclear weapons in the application zone of the Treaty; to contribute to the movement against proliferation of nuclear weapons; to promote general and complete disarmament; to prohibit all testing, use, manufacture, acquisition, storage, installation and any form of possession, by any means, of nuclear weapons; the organs of the Agency comprise the General Conference, meeting every two years, the Council, meeting every two months, and the secretariat; a General Conference is held every two years; mems: 33 states that have fully ratified the Treaty; the Treaty has two additional Protocols: the first signed and ratified by France, the Netherlands, the United Kingdom and the USA, the second signed and ratified by China, the USA, France, the United Kingdom and Russia; Sec.-Gen. GIOCONDA UBEDA RIVERA.

Alliance of Small Island States (AOSIS): c/o 800 Second Ave, Suite 400K, New York, NY 10017, USA; tel. (212) 599-0301; fax (212) 599-1540; e-mail slumission@aol.com; internet www.sidsnet.org/aosis; f. 1990 as an ad hoc intergovernmental grouping to focus on the special problems of small islands and low-lying coastal developing states; mems: 43 island nations; Chair. Dr ANGUS FRIDAY (Grenada); publ. *Small Islands, Big Issues*.

Bolivarian Alliance for the Americas (Alianza Bolivariana para las Américas—ALBA): internet www.alianzabolivariana.org; f. 2002 (as the Bolivarian Alternative for the Americas) by the President of Venezuela, Hugo Chávez, to promote an alternative model of political, economic and social co-operation and integration between Caribbean and Latin American countries sharing geographic, historical and cultural bonds; aims to reduce disparities in development between countries in the region and to combat poverty and social exclusion; in June 2007 ministers of foreign affairs convened for the inaugural meeting of ALBA's Council of Ministers agreed to the establishment of joint enterprises, as an alternative to transnational corporations, a joint bank to finance projects supported by the grouping and to develop bilateral agreements; the establishment of a Bank of ALBA was endorsed at the 6th summit meeting of heads of state, convened in January 2008; an emergency summit meeting was convened in April to consider the global food crisis; mems: Antigua and Barbuda, Bolivia, Cuba, Dominica, Ecuador, Nicaragua, Saint Vincent and the Grenadines, Venezuela.

Club of Madrid: Calle Goya 5-7, Pasaje 2A, 28001 Madrid, Spain; tel. (91) 1548230; fax (91) 1548240; e-mail clubmadrid@clubmadrid.org; internet www.clubmadrid.org; f. 2001, following Conference on Democratic Transition and Consolidation; forum of former Presidents and Prime Ministers; aims to strengthen democratic values and leadership; maintains office in Brussels, Belgium; Sec.-Gen. FERNANDO PERPIÑÁ (Spain).

Comunidade dos Países de Língua Portuguesa (CPLP) (Community of Portuguese-Speaking Countries): rua S. Caetano 32, 1200-829 Lisbon, Portugal; tel. (21) 392-8560; fax (21) 392-8588; e-mail comunicacao@cplp.org; internet www.cplp.org; f. 1996; aims to produce close political, economic, diplomatic and cultural links between Portuguese-speaking countries and to strengthen the influence of the Lusophone commonwealth within the international community; dispatched an observer mission to oversee presidential elections held in Timor-Leste in May 2007; mems: Angola, Brazil, Cape Verde, Guinea-Bissau, Mozambique, Portugal, São Tomé and Príncipe, Timor-Leste; associate observers: Equatorial Guinea, Mauritius, Senegal; Exec. Sec. DOMINGOS SIMÕES PEREIRA (Guinea-Bissau).

Group of Eight (G8): an informal meeting of developed nations, originally comprising France, Germany, Italy, Japan, United Kingdom and the USA, first convened in Nov. 1975, at Rambouillet, France, at the level of heads of state and government; Canada became a permanent participant in 1976, forming the Group of Seven major industrialized countries—G7; from 1991 Russia was invited to participate in the then G7 summit outside the formal framework of co-operation; from 1994 Russia contributed more fully to the G7 political dialogue and from 1997 Russia became a participant in nearly all of the summit process scheduled meetings, excepting those related to finance and the global economy; from 1998 the name of the co-operation framework was changed to Group of Eight—G8, and since 2003 Russia has participated fully in all scheduled summit meetings, including those on the global economy; the European Union is also represented at G8 meetings, although it may not chair fora; G8 heads of government and the President of the European Commission and President of the European Council convene an annual summit meeting, the chairmanship and venue of which are rotated in the following order: France, USA, United Kingdom, Russia, Germany, Japan, Italy, Canada (July 2009: L'Aquila, Italy; June 2010: Huntsville, Ontario, Canada); G8 summit meetings address and seek consensus, published in a final declaration, on social and economic issues confronting the international community; the following ('+8') nations: Australia, Brazil, People's Republic of China, India, Indonesia, Mexico, Republic of Korea and South Africa were guest participants at the June 2008 G8 summit; G8 sectoral ministerial meetings (covering areas such as energy, environment, finance and foreign affairs) are held on the fringes of the annual summit, and further G8 sectoral ministerial meetings are convened through the year; mems: Canada, France, Germany, Italy, Japan, Russia, United Kingdom and the USA; European Union representation.

Ibero-American General Secretariat (Secretaría General Iberoamericana—SEGIB): Calle Serrano 187, 28002 Madrid, Spain; tel. (91) 5901980; e-mail info@segib.org; internet www.segib.org; f. 2003; aims to provide institutional and technical support to the annual Iberoamerican summit meetings, to monitor programmes agreed at the meetings and to strengthen the Ibero-American community; meetings of Ibero-American heads of state and government (the first of which was convened in Guadalajara, Mexico in 1991) aim to promote political, economic and cultural co-operation among the 19 Spanish- and Portuguese-speaking Latin American countries and three European countries; Sec.-Gen. ENRIQUE IGLESIAS (Uruguay).

International Institute for Democracy and Electoral Assistance (IDEA): Strömsborg, 103 34 Stockholm, Sweden; tel. (8) 698-3700; fax (8) 20-2422; e-mail info@idea.int; internet www.idea.int; f. 1995; aims to promote sustainable democracy in new and established democracies; works with practitioners and institutions promoting democracy in Africa, Asia, Arab states and Latin America; 25 mem. states; Sec.-Gen. VIDAR HELGESEN (Norway).

Inter-Parliamentary Union (IPU): 5 chemin du Pommier, CP 330, 1218 Le Grand-Saconnex/Geneva, Switzerland; tel. 229194150; fax 229194160; e-mail postbox@mail.ipu.org; internet www.ipu.org; f. 1889 to promote peace, co-operation and representative democracy by providing a forum for multilateral political debate between representatives of national parliaments; mems: national parliaments of 155 sovereign states; 9 assoc. mems; Sec.-Gen. ANDERS B. JOHNSSON (Sweden); publs *Chronicle of Parliamentary Elections* (annually), *The World of Parliaments* (quarterly), *World Directory of Parliaments* (annually).

Latin American Parliament (Parlamento Latinoamericano): Avda Auro Soares de Moura Andrade 564, São Paulo, Brazil; tel. (11) 3824-6325; fax (11) 3824-0621; e-mail secgeneral@parlatino.org; internet www.parlatino.org; f. 1965; permanent democratic institution, representative of all existing political trends within the national legislative bodies of Latin America; aims to promote the movement towards economic, political and cultural integration of the Latin American republics, and to uphold human rights, peace and security; Sec.-Gen. SONIA ESCUDERO; publs *Acuerdos, Resoluciones de las Asambleas Ordinarias* (annually), *Parlamento Latinoamericano–Actividades de los Órganos*, *Revista Patria Grande* (annually), statements and agreements.

Non-aligned Movement (NAM): c/o Permanent Representative of Cuba to the UN, 315 Lexington Ave, New York, NY 10016; tel. (212) 689-7215; fax (212) 779-1697; e-mail cuba@un.int; internet www.canada.cubanoal.cu; f. 1961 by a meeting of 25 Heads of State, with the aim of linking countries that had refused to adhere to the main East/West military and political blocs; co-ordination bureau established in 1973; works for the establishment of a new international economic order, and especially for better terms for countries producing raw materials; maintains special funds for agricultural development, improvement of food production and the financing of buffer stocks; South Commission promotes co-operation between developing countries; seeks changes in the United Nations to give developing countries greater decision-making power; holds summit conference every three years; 15th conference (July 2008): Tehran, Iran; mems: 118 countries.

Organisation of Eastern Caribbean States (OECS): Morne Fortune, POB 179, Castries, Saint Lucia; tel. 452-2537; fax 453-1628; e-mail oesec@oecs.org; internet www.oecs.org; f. 1981 by the seven states which formerly belonged to the West Indies Associated States (f. 1966); aims to promote the harmonized development of trade and industry in member states; single market created on 1 January 1988; principal institutions are: the Authority of Heads of Government (the supreme policy-making body), the Foreign Affairs Committee, the Defence and Security Committee, and the Economic Affairs Committee; other functional divisions include an Export Development and Agricultural Diversification Unit (EDADU, based in Dominica), a Pharmaceutical Procurement Service (PPS), a Regional Integration Unit, a Regional E-Government Unit and an HIV/AIDS Project Unit; an OECS Technical Mission to the World Trade Organization in Geneva, Switzerland, was inaugurated in June 2005; in Aug. 2008 heads of government determined to achieve economic union by 2011 and political union by 2013; an agreement to establish an economic union was signed in December 2009, and, accordingly, a Revised Treaty of Basseterre Establishing the OECS Economic Union was signed by heads of government in June 2010; a new governance structure, in which an OECS Commission was to be established as a supranational executive institution, was scheduled to be operational by Jan. 2011; mems: Antigua and Barbuda, Dominica, Grenada, Montserrat, Saint Christopher and Nevis, Saint Lucia, Saint Vincent and the Grenadines; assoc. mems: Anguilla, British Virgin Islands; Dir-Gen. Dr LEN ISHMAEL.

Organization of Solidarity of the Peoples of Africa, Asia and Latin America (OSPAAAL) (Organización de Solidaridad de los Pueblos de Africa, Asia y América Latina): Apdo 4224, Calle C No 670 esq. 29, Vedado, Havana 10400, Cuba; tel. (7) 830-5136; fax (7) 833-3985; e-mail ospaaal1966@enet.cu; internet www.tricontinental.cubaweb.cu; f. 1966 at the first Conference of Solidarity of the Peoples of Africa, Asia and Latin America, to unite, co-ordinate and encourage national liberation movements in the three continents, to oppose foreign intervention in the affairs of sovereign states, colonial and neo-colonial practices, and to fight against racialism and all forms of racial discrimination; favours the establishment of a new international economic order; mems: 56 orgs in 46 countries; publ. *Tricontinental* (quarterly).

Rio Group: f. 1987 at a meeting in Acapulco, Mexico, of eight Latin American government leaders, who agreed to establish a 'permanent mechanism for joint political action'; additional countries subsequently joined the Group (see below); holds annual summit meetings at presidential level. At the ninth presidential summit (Quito, Ecuador, September 1995) a 'Declaration of Quito' was adopted, which set out joint political objectives, including the strengthening of democracy; combating corruption, drugs-production and -trafficking and money-laundering; and the creation of a Latin American and Caribbean free trade area (supporting the efforts of the various regional groupings). Opposes US legislation (the 'Helms-Burton' Act), which provides for sanctions against foreign companies that trade with Cuba; admitted Cuba as a member in November 2008; also concerned with promoting sustainable development in the region, the elimination of poverty, and economic and financial stability. The Rio Group holds regular ministerial conferences with the European Union; summit meeting in Cancún, Mexico, in February 2010, determined to establish a new regional grouping of Latin American and Caribbean states; mems: Argentina, Belize, Bolivia, Brazil, Chile, Colombia, Costa Rica, Cuba, Dominican Republic, Ecuador, El Salvador, Guatemala, Guyana, Haiti, Honduras, Jamaica, Mexico, Nicaragua, Panama, Paraguay, Peru, Suriname, Uruguay, Venezuela.

Union of South American Nations (UNASUR): Secretaria General de la UNASUR, Quito, Ecuador; tel. (2) 2502770; e-mail unasur@mmrree.gov.ec; internet www.unasur.org; in Dec. 2004 leaders from 12 Latin American countries attending a pan-South American summit, convened in Cusco, Peru, approved in principle the creation of a new South American Community of Nations (SACN), to entail the merger of the Andean Community, Mercosur and Aladi (with the participation of Chile, Guyana and Suriname); the first South American Community meeting of heads of state was held in September, in Brasília, Brazil; in April 2007, at the first South American Energy Summit, convened in Margarita Island, Venezuela, heads of state endorsed the establishment of a Union of South American Nations (UNASUR), to replace SACN as the lead organization for regional integration; it was envisaged that UNASUR would have political decision-making functions, supported by a small permanent secretariat, to be located in Quito, Ecuador, and would co-ordinate on economic and trade matters with the Andean Community, Mercosur and Aladi; a regional parliament was to be established in Cochabamba, Bolivia; summit meetings formally to inaugurate UNASUR were scheduled to be held in December 2007, then March 2008; both were postponed; the constituent treaty to establish UNASUR was signed by heads of state meeting in Brasília, Brazil, in May; a South American Defence Council (Consejo de Defensa Suramericano—CDS) was inaugurated in Santiago, Chile, in March 2009; in April 2009 UNASUR ministers of health approved the establishment of a South American Council on Health; the third ordinary summit meeting of heads of state was held in Quito, Ecuador, in August, followed by an extraordinary summit at the end of that month, in Bariloche, Argentina, to consider a military agreement between Colombia and the USA; a summit meeting in May 2010 elected the organization's first Secretary-General; as at July 2010 the constituent treaty had been ratified by Argentina, Bolivia, Ecuador, Guyana, Peru and Venezuela; Sec.-Gen. NÉSTOR KIRCHNER (Argentina); Pres. pro-tempore RAFAEL CORREA (Ecuador).

Industrial and Professional Relations

Caribbean Congress of Labour: NUPW Bldg, Dalkeith Rd, POB 90 B, St Michael, Barbados; tel. 427-5067; fax 427-2496; e-mail cclres@caribsurf.com; f. 1960; fights for the recognition of trade union organizations; to build and strengthen the ties between the free trade unions of the Caribbean and the rest of the world; supports the work of the International Trade Union Confederation; encourages the formation of national groupings and centres; mems: 30 unions in 17 countries; Pres. JACQUELINE JACK (Trinidad and Tobago); Gen.-Sec. LINCOLN LEWIS (Guyana).

Central American Confederation of Workers (Confederación Centroamericana de Trabajadores): Apdo 226, 2200 Coronado, San José, Costa Rica; tel. 229-0152; fax 229-3893; e-mail icaesca@sol.racsa.co.cr; f. 1963; mems: national confederations in 7 countries; Sec.-Gen. ALSIMIRO HERRERA TORRES.

Inter-American Regional Organization of Workers (ORIT) (Organización Regional Interamericana de Trabajadores): Edif. José Vargas, Avda Andrés Eloy Blanco No 2, 15°, Los Caobos, Caracas, Venezuela; tel. (212) 578-3538; fax (212) 578-1702; e-mail sedeorit@cioslorit; internet www.cioslorit.org/; f. 1951 by the International Confederation of Free Trade Unions (now International Trade Union Confederation), to link and represent democratic labour organizations in the region; sponsors training; mems: trade unions in 29 countries (including Canada and the USA) with over 45m. individuals; Gen. Sec. VICTOR BÁEZ MOSQUEIRA.

International Confederation of Energy Regulators: e-mail office@icer-regulators.net; internet www.iern.net; f. 2009; mems: 11 regional energy regulatory asscns, representing more than 200 regulatory authorities world-wide.

International Trade Union Confederation (ITUC): 5 blvd Roi Albert II, 1210 Brussels, Belgium; tel. (2) 224-02-10; fax (2) 201-58-15; e-mail info@ituc-csi.org; internet www.ituc-csi.org; f. 2006 by the merger of the International Confederation of Free Trade Unions, the World Confederation of Labour and eight national trade union organizations; aims to promote the interests of working people and to secure recognition of workers' orgs as free bargaining agents; mems: 312 organizations in 157 countries (March 2009); Gen. Sec. GUY RYDER (United Kingdom).

Latin American Confederation of Trade Unions (Central Latinoamericano de Trabajadores—CLAT): Apdo 6681, Caracas 1010A, Venezuela; tel. (212) 372-1549; fax (212) 372-0463; e-mail clat@telcel.net.ve; internet www.clat.org; f. 1954; affiliated to the World Confederation of Labour; mems: over 50 national and regional orgs in Latin America and the Caribbean; Sec.-Gen. EDUARDO GARCÍA MOURE.

Latin American Federation of Agricultural Workers (Federación Latinoamericana de Trabajadores Agrícolas, Pecuarios y Afines—FELTRA): Antiguo Local Conadi, B° La Granja, Comayaguela, Tegucigalpa, Honduras; tel. 2252526; fax 2252525; e-mail feltra@123.hn; internet www.acmoti.org; f. 1999 by reorganization of FELTACA (f. 1961) to represent the interests of workers in agricultural and related industries in Latin America; mems: national unions in 28 countries and territories; Sec.-Gen. MARCIAL REYES CABALLERO; publ. *Boletín Luchemos* (quarterly).

Law

Inter-American Bar Association (IABA): 1211 Connecticut Ave, NW, Suite 202, Washington, DC 20036, USA; tel. (202) 466-5944; fax (202) 466-5946; e-mail iaba@iaba.org; internet www.iaba.org; f. 1940 to promote the rule of law and to establish and maintain relations between asscns and organizations of lawyers in the Americas; mems: 90 asscns and 3,500 individuals in 27 countries; Sec.-Gen. HARRY A. INMAN (USA); publs *Newsletter* (quarterly), *Conference Proceedings*.

International Criminal Police Organization (INTERPOL): 200 quai Charles de Gaulle, 69006 Lyon, France; tel. 4-72-44-70-00; fax 4-72-44-71-63; e-mail info@interpol.int; internet www.interpol.int; f. 1923, reconstituted 1946; aims to promote and ensure mutual assistance between police forces in different countries; co-ordinates activities of police authorities of member states in international affairs; works to establish and develop institutions with the aim of preventing transnational crimes; centralizes records and information on international criminals; operates a global police communications network linking all member countries; holds General Assembly annually; mems: 188 countries; Sec.-Gen. RONALD K. NOBLE (USA); publ. *Annual Report*.

International Development Law Organization (IDLO): Viale Vaticano, 106 00165 Rome, Italy; tel. (06) 40403200; fax (06) 404032327; e-mail idlo@idlo.int; internet www.idlo.int; f. 1983; aims to promote the rule of law and good governance in developing countries, transition economies and nations emerging from conflict and to assist countries to establish effective infrastructure to achieve sustainable economic growth, security and access to justice; activities include Policy Dialogues, Technical Assistance, Global Network of Alumni and Partners, Training Programs, Research and Publications; maintains Regional Offices in Cairo, Egypt, covering Arabic-speaking countries and in Sydney, Australia, covering the Asia Pacific area; also operates Project Offices in Afghanistan, Indonesia, Sudan and Kyrgyzstan; mems: 22 mems (21 states and OPEC Fund for International Development); Dir-Gen. ANTONIO BADINI (Italy).

International Union of Latin Notaries (Union Internationale du Notariat Latin—UINL): Alsina 2280, 2°, 1090 Buenos Aires, Argentina; tel. (11) 4952-8848; fax (11) 4952-7094; e-mail onpiuinl@onpi.org.ar; internet www.uinl.org; f. 1948 to study and standardize notarial legislation and promote the progress, stability and advancement of the Latin notarial system; mems: organizations and individuals in 76 countries; Pres. Dr EDUARDO GALLINO; publs *Revista Internacional del Notariado* (quarterly), *Notarius International*.

Medicine and Health

Council for International Organizations of Medical Sciences (CIOMS): c/o WHO, ave Appia, 1211 Geneva 27, Switzerland; tel. 227913467; fax 227914286; e-mail cioms@who.int; internet www.cioms.ch; f. 1949 to serve the scientific interests of the international biomedical community; aims to facilitate and promote activities in biomedical sciences; runs long-term programmes on bioethics, health policy, ethics and values, drug development and use, and the international nomenclature of diseases; maintains collaborative relations with the UN; holds a general assembly every three years; mems: 66 orgs; Pres. Prof. MICHEL B. VALLOTTON; Sec.-Gen. Dr GOTTFRIED KREUTZ; publs *Reports on Drug Development and Use*, *Proceedings of CIOMS Conferences*, *International Nomenclature of Diseases*, *International Ethical Guidelines for Biomedical Research Involving Human Subjects*.

Global Fund to Fight AIDS, TB and Malaria: 6–8 chemin Blandonnet, 1214 Vernier-Geneva, Switzerland; tel. 587911700; fax 587911701; e-mail info@theglobalfund.org; internet www.theglobalfund.org; f. 2000 as a partnership between governments, civil society, private sector interests, UN bodies (including WHO, UNAIDS, the IBRD and UNDP), and other agencies to raise resources for combating AIDS, TB and malaria; the Fund supports but does not implement assistance programmes; US $9,700m. was pledged by international donors at a conference convened in Sept. 2007 to replenish the Fund during 2008–10; by 30 June 2009 the Fund had approved $15,907m. (of which $7,974m. had been disbursed) in respect of more than 572 programmes supporting prevention and treatment programmes in 140 countries; by that time the cumulative allocation of grant funding by region was as follows: Africa (57%), the Middle East and North Africa and South Asia (14%),

East Asia and the Pacific (14%), Eastern Europe and Central Asia (8%), and Latin America and the Caribbean (8%); while the approximate distribution by health sector was: HIV/AIDS (61%), malaria (25%), and TB (14%); Exec. Dir Dr MICHEL KAZATCHKINE (France).

Inter-American Association of Sanitary and Environmental Engineering (Asociación Interamericana de Ingeniería Sanitaria y Ambiental—AIDIS): Rua Nicolau Gagliardi 354, 05429-010 São Paulo, SP, Brazil; tel. (11) 3812-4080; fax (11) 3814-2441; e-mail aidis@aidis.org.br; internet www.aidis.org.br; f. 1948 to assist in the development of water supply and sanitation; aims to generate awareness on environmental, health and sanitary problems and assist in finding solutions; mems: 32 countries; Pres. ADALBERTO NOYOLA (Mexico); Exec. Dir LUIZ AUGUSTO DE LIMA PONTES (Brazil); publs *Revista Ingeniería Sanitaria* (quarterly), *Desafío* (quarterly).

International Association of Hydatidology: Florida 460, 3°, 1005 Buenos Aires, Argentina; tel. (11) 4322-2030; fax (11) 4325-8231; f. 1941; mems: 1,200 in 41 countries; publs *Archivos Internacionales de la Hidatidosis* (every 2 years), *Boletín de Hidatidosis* (quarterly).

Latin American Federation of Societies for Ultrasound in Medicine and Biology: Obst/Gyn, Roman Diaz 205, Of. 205, Santiago, Chile; tel. and fax (2) 235-0133; fax (2) 235-1294; e-mail obgynuch@ctcinternet.cl; f. 1983; mems: some 6,000 mems in 13 countries; Pres. Dr HERNAN MUNOZ SALAZAR (Chile).

Latin American Odontological Federation (Federación Odontológica Latinoamericana): c/o Federación Odontológica Colombiana, Calle 71 No 11-10, Of. 1101, Apdo Aéreo 52925, Bogotá, Colombia; e-mail arn@codetel.net.do; internet www.folaoral.com; f. 1917; linked to FDI World Dental Federation; mems: national orgs in 12 countries; Sec. Dr MARCOS ALVALLERO.

Pan-American Association of Ophthalmology (PAAO): 1301 South Bowen Rd, Suite 365, Arlington, TX 76013, USA; tel. (817) 275-7553; fax (817) 275-3961; e-mail info@paao.org; internet www.paao.org; f. 1939 to promote friendship within the profession and the dissemination of scientific information; holds biennial Congress (2011: Buenos Aires, Argentina); mems: national ophthalmological societies and other bodies in 39 countries; Pres. Dr CRISTIAN LUCO; Exec. Dir TERESA BRADSHAW; publ. *Vision Panamerica* (quarterly).

Pan-American Medical Association (Asociación Médica Panamericana): 745 Fifth Ave, New York, NY 10151, USA; tel. (212) 753-6033; f. 1925; holds inter-American congresses, conducts seminars and grants post graduate scholarships to Latin American physicians; mems: 6,000 in 30 countries.

World Medical Association (WMA): 13 chemin du Levant, CIB-Bâtiment A, 01210 Ferney-Voltaire, France; tel. 4-50-40-75-75; fax 4-50-40-59-37; e-mail wma@wma.net; internet www.wma.net; f. 1947 to achieve the highest international standards in all aspects of medical education and practice, to promote closer ties among doctors and national medical asscns by personal contact and all other means, to study problems confronting the medical profession, and to present its views to appropriate bodies; holds an annual General Assembly; mems: 83 national medical asscns; Pres. Dr YORAM BLACHER (Israel); Sec.-Gen. Dr OTMAR KLOIBER (Germany); publ. *The World Medical Journal* (quarterly).

Posts and Telecommunications

International Telecommunications Satellite Organization (INTELSAT): 3400 International Drive, NW, Washington, DC 20008-3098, USA; tel. (202) 944-6800; fax (202) 944-8125; internet www.intelsat.com; f. 1964 to establish a global commercial satellite communications system; Assembly of Parties attended by representatives of member governments, meets every two years to consider policy and long-term aims and matters of interest to members as sovereign states; meeting of Signatories to the Operating Agreement held annually; 24 INTELSAT satellites in geosynchronous orbit provide a global communications service; provides most of the world's overseas traffic; in 1998 INTELSAT agreed to establish a private enterprise, incorporated in the Netherlands, to administer six satellite services; mems: 143 governments; CEO DAVID MCGLADE (USA).

Internet Corporation for Assigned Names and Numbers (ICANN): 4676 Admiralty Way, Suite 330, Marina del Rey, CA 90292-6601, USA; tel. (310) 823-9358; fax (310) 823-8649; e-mail icann@icann.org; internet www.icann.org; f. 1998; non-profit, private sector body; aims to co-ordinate the technical management and policy development of the internet; comprises three Supporting Organizations to assist, review and develop recommendations on internet policy and structure relating to addresses, domain names, and protocol; Pres. and CEO ROD BECKSTROM (USA).

Postal Union of the Americas, Spain and Portugal (Unión Postal de las Américas, España y Portugal): Cebollatí 1468/70, 1°, Casilla de Correos 20.042, Montevideo, Uruguay; tel. (2) 4100070; fax (2) 4105046; e-mail secretaría@upaep.com.uy; internet www.upaep.com.uy; f. 1911 to extend, facilitate and study the postal relationships of member countries; mems: 27 countries; Sec.-Gen. SERRANA BASSINI CASCO.

Press, Radio and Television

Inter-American Press Association (IAPA) (Sociedad Interamericana de Prensa): Jules Dubois Bldg, 1801 SW 3rd Ave, Miami, FL 33129, USA; tel. (305) 634-2465; fax (305) 635-2272; e-mail info@sipiapa.org; internet www.sipiapa.org; f. 1942 to guard the freedom of the press in the Americas; to promote and maintain the dignity, rights and responsibilities of the profession of journalism; to foster a wider knowledge and greater interchange among the peoples of the Americas; mems: 1,400; Exec. Dir JULIO E. MUÑOZ; publ. *IAPA News* (monthly).

International Association of Broadcasting (Asociación Internacional de Radiodifusión—AIR): Carlos Quijano 1264, 1110 Montevideo, Uruguay; tel. (2) 9011319; fax (2) 9080458; e-mail mail@airiab.com; internet www.airiab.com; f. 1946 (as the Interamerican Association of Broadcasting) to preserve free and private broadcasting; to promote co-operation between the corporations and public authorities; to defend freedom of expression; mems: national asscns of broadcasters; Pres. LUIS PARDO SAINZ (Chile); Dir-Gen. Dr HÉCTOR OSCAR AMENGUAL; publ. *La Gaceta de AIR* (every 2 months).

World Catholic Association for Communication (SIGNIS): 310 rue Royale, 1210 Brussels, Belgium; tel. (2) 734-97-08; fax (2) 734-70-18; e-mail sg@signis.net; internet www.signis.net; f. 2001; brings together professionals working in radio, television, cinema, video, media education, internet, and new technology; Sec.-Gen. ALVITO DE SOUZA.

Religion

Bahá'í International Community: Bahá'í World Centre, POB 155, 31001 Haifa, Israel; tel. (4) 8358394; fax (4) 8313312; e-mail opi@bwc.org; internet www.bahai.org; f. 1844; the aim of the Bahá'í International Community is to promote the unity of mankind and world peace through the teachings of the Bahá'í religion, including the equality of men and women and the elimination of all forms of prejudice; maintains schools for children and adults world-wide, operates educational and cultural radio stations in the USA, Asia and Latin America; and works to promote health education in many countries around the world; has 33 publishing trusts throughout the world, which have translated literature into 802 languages; governing body: Universal House of Justice (nine mems elected by 183 National Spiritual Assemblies); mems: in 101,969 local communities, 2,112 different indigenous tribes, races and ethnic groups (in 191 countries and 47 dependent territories or overseas departments); Sec.-Gen. ALBERT LINCOLN (USA); publs *Bahá'í World* (annually), *One Country* (quarterly, in 6 languages).

Caribbean Conference of Churches: POB 876, Port of Spain, Trinidad and Tobago; tel. 662-3064; fax 662-1303; e-mail trinidad-headoffice@ccc-caribe.org; internet www.ccc-caribe.org; f. 1973; governed by a General Assembly which meets every five years (June 2005: Panama City, Panama) and appoints a 15-member Continuation Committee (board of management) to establish policies and direct the work of the organization between Assemblies; maintains three sub-regional offices in Antigua, Jamaica and Trinidad with responsibility for programme implementation in various territories; mems: 33 member churches in 34 territories in the Dutch-, English-, French-, and Spanish-speaking territories of the region; Gen. Sec. GERARD GRANADO; publ. *Ecuscope Caribbean*.

Latin American Council of Churches (Consejo Latinoamericano de Iglesias—CLAI): Casilla 17-08-8522, Calle Inglaterra N.32–113 y Mariana de Jesús, Quito, Ecuador; tel. (2) 255-9933; fax (2) 256-8373; e-mail nilton@claiweb.org; internet www.claiweb.org; f. 1982; mems: some 150 churches in 21 countries; Pres. Rev. JULIO MURRAY (Panama); Gen. Sec. Rev. NILTON GUISE (Brazil); publs *Nuevo Siglo* (monthly, in Spanish), *Latin American Ecumenical News* (quarterly), *Signos de Vida* (quarterly), other newsletters.

Latin American Episcopal Council (Consejo Episcopal Latinoamericano—CELAM): Carrera 5A 118–31, Apartado Aéreo 51086, Bogotá, Colombia; tel. (1) 5879710; fax (1) 5879117; e-mail celam@celam.org; internet www.celam.org; f. 1955 to co-ordinate Church activities in and with the Latin American and the Caribbean Catholic Bishops' Conferences; mems: 22 Episcopal Conferences of Central and South America and the Caribbean; Pres. Archbishop RAYMUNDO DAMASCENO ASSIS (Brazil); publ. *Boletín* (6 a year).

World Council of Churches (WCC): 150 route de Ferney, Postfach 2100, 1211 Geneva 2, Switzerland; tel. 227916111; fax 227910361; e-mail info@wcc-coe.org; internet www.wcc-coe.org; f. 1948 to promote co-operation between Christian Churches and to prepare for a clearer manifestation of the unity of the Church; activities are grouped under the following programmes: The WCC and the ecumenical movement in the 21st century; Unity, mission, evangelism and spirituality; Public witness: addressing power, affirming peace; Justice, *diakonia* and responsibility for creation; Education and ecumenical formation; and Inter-religious dialogue and co-operation; mems: 349 Churches in more than 110 countries; Gen. Sec. Dr OLAV FYKSE TVEIT (Norway); publs *Current Dialogue* (2 a year), *Ecumenical News International* (weekly), *Ecumenical Review* (quarterly), *International Review of Mission* (quarterly), *WCC News* (quarterly), *WCC Yearbook*.

World Union of Catholic Women's Organisations: 37 rue Notre-Dame-des-Champs, 75006 Paris, France; tel. 1-45-44-27-65; fax 1-42-84-04-80; e-mail wucwosecgen@gmail.com; internet www.wucwo.org; f. 1910 to promote and co-ordinate the contribution of Catholic women in international life, in social, civic, cultural and religious matters; General Assembly held every four or five years (2010: Jerusalem, Israel, in Oct.); mems: some 100 orgs representing 5m. women; Pres. KAREN M. HURLEY (USA); Sec.-Gen. LILIANE STEVENSON; publ. *Women's Voice* (quarterly, in 4 languages).

Science

International Council for Science (ICSU): 5 rue Auguste Vacquerie 75116 Paris, France; tel. 1-45-25-03-29; fax 1-42-88-94-31; e-mail secretariat@icsu.org; internet www.icsu.org; f. 1919 as International Research Council; present name adopted 1931; new statutes adopted 1996; incorporates national scientific bodies and International Scientific Unions, as well as more than 20 Interdisciplinary Bodies (international scientific networks established to address specific areas of investigation); through its global network co-ordinates interdisciplinary research to address major issues of relevance to both science and society; advocates for freedom in the conduct of science, promotes equitable access to scientific data and information, and facilitates science education and capacity-building; General Assembly of representatives of national and scientific members meets every three years to formulate policy. Interdisciplinary Bodies and Joint Initiatives: Scientific Committee on Problems of the Environment (SCOPE); Committee on Space Research (COSPAR); International Polar Year (IPY); Scientific Committee on Antarctic Research (SCAR); Scientific Committee on Oceanic Research (SCOR); Scientific Committee on Solar-Terrestrial Physics (SCOSTEP); Integrated Research on Disaster Risk (IRDR); Programme on Ecosystem Change and Society (PECS); DIVERSITAS; International Geosphere-Biosphere Programme (IGBP); International Human Dimensions Programme on Global Environmental Change (IHDP); World Climate Research Programme (WCRP); Global Climate Observing System (GCOS); Global Ocean Observing System (GOOS); Global Terrestrial Observing System (GTOS); Committee on Data for Science and Technology (CODATA); International Network for the Availability of Scientific Publications (INASP); Scientific Committee on Frequency Allocations for Radio Astronomy and Space Science (IUCAF); World Data System (WDS); mems: 119 national mems from 139 countries, 30 International Scientific Unions; Pres. CATHERINE BRÉCHIGNAC (France); Exec. Dir DELIANG CHEN (Sweden); publs *Insight* (quarterly), *Annual Report*.

Social Sciences

International Peace Institute: 777 United Nations Plaza, New York, NY 10017-3521, USA; tel. (212) 687-4300; fax (212) 983-8246; e-mail ipi@ipinst.org; internet www.ipacademy.org; f. 1970 (as the International Peace Academy) to promote the prevention and settlement of armed conflicts between and within states through policy research and development; educates government officials in the procedures needed for conflict resolution, peace-keeping, mediation and negotiation, through international training seminars and publications; off-the-record meetings are also conducted to gain complete understanding of a specific conflict; Chair. RITA E. HAUSER; Pres. TERJE ROD-LARSEN.

Social Welfare and Human Rights

Co-ordinator of the Indigenous Organizations of the Amazon Basin (COICA): Calle Sevilla 24–358 y Guipuzcoa, La Floresta, Quito, Ecuador; e-mail com@coica.org; internet www.coica.org; f. 1984; aims to co-ordinate the activities of national organizations concerned with the indigenous people and environment of the Amazon basin, and promotes respect for human rights and the self-determination of the indigenous populations; 9 member orgs; Co-ordinator-Gen. JOCELYN ROGER THERESE; publ. *Nuestra Amazonia* (quarterly, in English, Spanish, French and Portuguese).

Global Humanitarian Forum: 9 ave de la Paix, 1202 Geneva, Switzerland; tel. 229197500; fax 229197519; e-mail ghf-geneva@ghf-geneva.org; internet www.ghf-geneva.org; f. 2007 to support dialogue and encourage partnerships to focus international attention on and generate increased investment towards addressing key humanitarian concerns; also seeks to place international migration issues on the global agenda; CEO WALTER FUST (Switzerland).

Global Migration Group: f. 2003, as the Geneva Migration Group; renamed as above in 2006; mems: ILO, IOM, UNCTAD, UNDP, United Nations Department of Economic and Social Affairs (UNDESA), UNFPA, OHCHR, UNHCR, UNODC, and the World Bank; holds regular meetings to discuss issues relating to int. migration, chaired by mem. orgs on a six-month rotational basis.

Inter-American Conference on Social Security (Conferencia Interamericano de Seguridad Social—CISS): c/o F. Flores, Instituto Mexicano del Seguro Social, Paseo de la Reforma 476, 1°, Col. Juarez, Del. Cuauhtemoc, CP 06600, México, DF, Mexico; tel. (55) 5211-4853; fax (55) 5211-2623; e-mail ciss@ciss.org.mx; internet www.ciss.org.mx; f. 1942 to contribute to the development of social security in the countries of the Americas and to co-operate with social security institutions; CISS bodies are: the General Assembly, the Permanent Inter-American Committee on Social Security, the Secretariat General, six American Commissions of Social Security and the Inter-American Center for Social Security Studies; mems: 66 social security institutions in 36 countries; Pres. FERNANDO FLORES (Mexico); Sec.-Gen. Dr GABRIEL MARTÍNEZ GONZÁLEZ (Mexico); publs *Social Security Journal / Seguridad Social* (every 2 months), *The Americas Social Security Report* (annually), *Social Security Bulleting* (monthly, online), monographs, study series.

World Social Forum (WSF): Support Office: Rua General Jardim 660, 7th Floor, São Paulo, Brazil 01223-010; e-mail forumsocialmundial.org.br; internet www.forumsocialmundial.org; f. 2001 as an annual global meeting of civil society bodies; a Charter of Principles was adopted in June 2002; the WSF is a permanent global process which aims to pursue alternatives to neo-liberal policies and commercial globalization; its objectives include the development and promotion of democratic international systems and institutions serving social justice, equality and the sovereignty of peoples, based on respect for the universal human rights of citizens of all nations and for the environment; the 9th (2009) WSF was held in Belém do Pará, Brazil, in January; an International Council, comprising 129 civil society organizations and commissions, guides the Forum and considers general political questions and methodology; the Support Office in São Paulo, Brazil, provides administrative assistance to the Forum process, to the International Council and to the specific organizing committees for each annual event; mems: civil society orgs and movements world-wide.

Sport and Recreations

International Federation of Association Football (Fédération internationale de football association—FIFA): FIFA-Str. 20, POB 8044, Zürich, Switzerland; tel. 432227777; fax 432227878; e-mail media@fifa.org; internet www.fifa.com; f. 1904 to promote the game of association football and foster friendly relations among players and national asscns; to control football and uphold the laws of the game as laid down by the International Football Association Board; to prevent discrimination of any kind between players; and to provide arbitration in disputes between national asscns; organizes World Cup competition every four years (2010: South Africa); mems: 208 national asscns, 6 continental confederations; Pres. JOSEPH S. BLATTER (Switzerland); Gen. Sec. JÉRÔME VALCKE (France); publs *FIFA News* (monthly), *FIFA Magazine* (every 2 months) (both in English, French, German and Spanish), *FIFA Directory* (annually), *Laws of the Game* (annually), *Competitions' Regulations* and *Technical Reports* (before and after FIFA competitions).

Technology

Latin American Association of Pharmaceutical Industries (Asociación Latinoamericana de Industrias Farmaceuticas—ALIFAR): Av. Libertador 602, 6°, 1001 ABT Buenos Aires, Argentina; tel. and fax (11) 4812-4532; e-mail mlevis@cilfa.org.ar; f. 1980; mems: about 400 enterprises in 15 countries; Sec.-Gen. RUBÉN ABETE; Exec. Sec. MIRTA LEVIS.

Latin-American Energy Organization (Organización Latinoamericana de Energía—OLADE): Avda Mariscal Antonio José de Sucre, No N58–63 y Fernándes Salvador, Edif. OLADE, Sector San Carlos, POB 17-11-6413 CCI, Quito, Ecuador; tel. (2) 2598-122; fax (2) 2531-691; e-mail oladel@olade.org.ec; internet www.olade.org.ec; f. 1973 to act as an instrument of co-operation in using and conserving the energy resources of the region; mems: 26 Latin-American and Caribbean countries; Exec. Sec. ÁLVARO RÍOS ROCA; publ. *Energy Magazine*.

Latin American Iron and Steel Institute: Benjamín 2944, 5° piso, Las Condes, Santiago, Chile; tel. (2) 233-0545; fax (2) 233-0768; e-mail ilafa@ilafa.org; internet www.ilafa.org; f. 1959 to help achieve the harmonious development of iron and steel production, manufacture and marketing in Latin America; conducts economic surveys on the steel sector; organizes technical conventions and meetings; disseminates industrial processes suited to regional conditions; prepares and maintains statistics on production, end uses, etc., of raw materials and steel products within this area; mems: 18 hon. mems; 49 active mems; 36 assoc. mems; Chair. ANDRÉ BIER GERDAU JOHANNPETER; Sec.-Gen. GUILLERMO MORENO; publs *Acero Latinoamericano* (every 2 months), *Statistical Year Book*, *Directory of Latin American Iron and Steel Companies* (every 2 years).

Tourism

Caribbean Hotel and Tourism Association: 2655 Le Jeune Road, Suite 910 Coral Gables, FL 33134, USA; tel. (305) 443-3040; fax (305) 443-3005; internet www.caribbeanhotelassociation.com; f. 1962 (as the Caribbean Hotel Assn; name changed July 2008); represents and promotes the hotel and tourism industry in the Caribbean region; jointly owns and operates, with the Caribbean Tourism Organization, the Caribbean Tourism Development Co; mems: 849 hotels in 36 national hotel asscns; Pres. ENRIQUE DE MARCHENA KALUCHE; CEO and Dir-Gen. ALEC SANGUINETTI; publ. *CHA Weekly News*.

Caribbean Tourism Organization: One Financial Pl., Collymore Rock, St Michael, Barbados; tel. 427-5242; fax 429-3065; e-mail ctobar@caribsurf.com; internet www.onecaribbean.org; f. 1989, by merger of the Caribbean Tourism Association (f. 1951) and the Caribbean Tourism Research and Development Centre (f. 1974); aims to encourage tourism in the Caribbean region; organizes annual Caribbean Tourism Conference, Sustainable Tourism Development Conference and Tourism Investment Conference; conducts training and other workshops on request; maintains offices in New York, Canada and London; mems: 34 Caribbean govts, 400 allied mems; Sec.-Gen. HUGH RILEY; publs *Caribbean Tourism Statistical News* (quarterly), *Caribbean Tourism Statistical Report* (annually).

Latin-American Confederation of Tourist Organizations (Confederación de Organizaciones Turísticas de la América Latino—COTAL): Viamonte 640, 8°, 1053 Buenos Aires, Argentina; tel. (11) 4322-4003; fax (11) 4393-5696; e-mail cotal@cotal.org.ar; internet www.cotal.org.ar; f. 1957 to link Latin American national asscns of travel agents and their members with other tourist bodies around the world; mems: in 21 countries; Pres. LUIS FELIPE AQUINO; publ. *Revista COTAL* (every 2 months).

Trade and Industry

Cairns Group: (no permanent secretariat); e-mail agriculture.negotiations@dfat.gov.au; internet www.cairnsgroup.org; f. 1986 by major agricultural exporting countries; aims to bring about reforms in international agricultural trade, including reductions in export subsidies, in barriers to access and in internal support measures; represents members' interests in WTO negotiations; mems: Argentina, Australia, Bolivia, Brazil, Canada, Chile, Colombia, Costa Rica, Guatemala, Indonesia, Malaysia, New Zealand, Pakistan, Paraguay, Peru, Philippines, South Africa, Thailand, Uruguay; Chair. STEPHEN SMITH (Australia).

Caribbean Association of Industry and Commerce (CAIC): Ground Floor, 27A Saddle Rd, Maraval, Trinidad and Tobago; tel. 628-9859; fax 622-7810; e-mail info@caic.org.tt; internet www.caic.org.tt; f. 1955; aims to encourage economic development through the private sector; undertakes research and training and gives assistance to small enterprises; encourages export promotion; mems: chambers of commerce and enterprises in 20 countries and territories; Pres. CAROL EVELYN (Saint Christopher and Nevis); publ. *Caribbean Investor* (quarterly).

CropLife International: 326 ave Louise, POB 35, 1050 Brussels, Belgium; tel. (2) 542-04-10; fax (2) 542-04-19; e-mail croplife@croplife.org; internet www.croplife.org; f. 1960 as European Group of National Asscns of Pesticide Manufacturers, international body since 1967, present name adopted in 2001, evolving from Global Crop Protection Federation; represents the plant science industry, with the aim of promoting sustainable agricultural methods; aims to harmonize national and international regulations concerning crop protection products and agricultural biotechnology; promotes observation of the FAO Code of Conduct on the Distribution and Use of Pesticides; holds an annual General Assembly; mems: 6 regional bodies and national asscns in 85 countries; Dir-Gen. CHRISTIAN VERSCHUEREN.

Federación de Cámaras de Comercio del Istmo Centroamericano (Federation of Central American Chambers of Commerce): 10A Calle 3-80, Zona 1, 01001 Guatemala City, Guatemala; tel. 2326-8840; fax 2220-9393; e-mail aechevarria@fecamco.com; internet www.fecamco.com; f. 1961; plans and co-ordinates industrial and commercial exchanges and exhibitions; Exec. Dir ALEJANDRA ECHEVARRIA VALENZUELA.

Instituto Centroamericano de Administración de Empresas (INCAE) (Central American Institute for Business Administration): Apdo 960, 4050 Alajuela, Costa Rica; tel. 2443-9908; fax 2433-9983; e-mail costarica@incae.edu; internet www.incae.edu; f. 1964; provides a postgraduate programme in business administration; runs executive training programmes; carries out management research and consulting; maintains a second campus in Nicaragua; libraries of 85,000 vols; Rector ARTURO CONDO; publs *Alumni Journal* (in Spanish), *Bulletin* (quarterly), books and case studies.

Inter-American Commercial Arbitration Commission: OAS Administration Bldg, Rm 211, 19th and Constitution Ave, NW, Washington, DC 20006, USA; tel. (202) 458-3249; fax (202) 458-3293; f. 1934 to establish an inter-American system of arbitration for the settlement of commercial disputes by means of tribunals; mems: national committees, commercial firms and individuals in 22 countries; Dir-Gen. Dr ADRIANA POLANIA.

Transport

Pan American Railway Congress Association (Asociación del Congreso Panamericano de Ferrocarriles): Av. Dr. José María Ramos Mejía 1302, Planta Baja, 1104 Buenos Aires, Argentina; tel. (11) 4315-3445; fax (11) 4312-3834; e-mail acpf@acpf.com.ar; internet www.acpf.com.ar; f. 1907, present title adopted 1941; aims to promote the development and progress of railways in the American continent; holds Congresses every three years; mems: government representatives, railway enterprises and individuals in 21 countries; Pres. LORENZO PEPE; Gen. Sec. JULIO SOSA; publ. *Boletín ACPF* (5 a year).

Youth and Students

Latin American and Caribbean Confederation of Young Men's Christian Associations (Confederación Latinoamericana y del Caribe de Asociaciones Cristianas de Jóvenes): Culpina 272, 1406 Buenos Aires, Argentina; tel. (11) 4373-4156; fax (11) 4374-4408; e-mail clacj@wamani.apc.org; f. 1914; aims to encourage the moral, spiritual, intellectual, social and physical development of young men; to strengthen the work of national Asscns and to sponsor the establishment of new Asscns; mems: affiliated YMCAs in 25 countries (comprising 350,000 individuals); Pres. GERARDO VITUREIRA (Uruguay); Gen. Sec. MARCO ANTONIO HOCHSCHEIT (Brazil); publs *Diecisiete/21* (bulletin), *Carta Abierta*, *Brief*, technical articles and other studies.

WFUNA Youth: c/o WFUNA, 1 United Nations Plaza, Room DC1-1177, New York, NY 10017, USA; tel. (212) 963-5610; fax (212) 963-0447; e-mail coordinating.committee@qmail.com; internet www.wfuna-youth.org; f. 1948 by the World Federation of United Nations Associations (WFUNA) as the International Youth and Student Movement for the United Nations (ISMUN), independent since 1949; an international non-governmental organization of students and young people dedicated especially to supporting the principles embodied in the United Nations Charter and Universal Declaration of Human Rights; encourages constructive action in building economic, social and cultural equality and in working for national independence, social justice and human rights on a world-wide scale; maintains regional offices in Austria, France, Ghana, Panama and the USA; mems: asscns in over 100 mem. states of the UN.

World Alliance of Young Men's Christian Associations: 12 Clos. Belmont, 1208 Geneva, Switzerland; tel. 228495100; fax 228495110; e-mail office@ymca.int; internet www.ymca.int; f. 1855; organizes World Council every four years (2010: Hong Kong, SAR); mems: federation of YMCAs in 124 countries with a membership of over 45m.; Pres. KEN COLLOTON (USA); Sec.-Gen. Rev. JOHAN VILHELM ELTRIK (from 1 Jan. 2011); publ. *YMCA World* (quarterly).

MAJOR COMMODITIES OF LATIN AMERICA

Note: For each of the commodities in this section, there is a statistical table relating to recent levels of production. Each production table shows estimates of output for the world and for Latin America. In addition, the table lists the main Latin American producing countries and, for comparison, the leading producers from outside the region.

ALUMINIUM AND BAUXITE

Aluminium (known as aluminum in the USA and, generally, Canada) is the second most abundant metallic element in the earth's crust after silicon, comprising about 8% of the total. However, it is much less widely used than steel, despite having about the same strength and only half the weight. Aluminium has important applications as a metal because of its lightness, ease of fabrication and other desirable properties. Other products of alumina (aluminium oxide trihydrate, into which bauxite, the commonest aluminium ore, is refined) are materials in refractories, abrasives, glass manufacture, other ceramic products, catalysts and absorbers. Alumina hydrates are used for the production of aluminium chemicals, fire retardant in carpet-backing, and industrial fillers in plastics and related products.

The major markets for aluminium are in transportation, packaging, building and construction, electrical and other machinery and equipment, and consumer durables. Transportation was estimated to have accounted for about one-third, and containers and packaging for about 26%, of all US aluminium end-use in 2009, for example. Although the production of aluminium is energy-intensive, its light weight results in a net saving, particularly in the transportation industry, where the use of the metal as a substitute for steel, in particular in the manufacture of road motor vehicles and components, is well established. Aluminium is valued by the aerospace industry for its weight-saving characteristics and for its low cost relative to alternative materials. Aluminium-lithium alloys command considerable potential for use in this sector, although the traditional dominance of aluminium in the aerospace industry has been challenged since the 1990s by 'composites' such as carbonepoxy, a fusion of carbon fibres and hardened resins, the lightness and durability of which can exceed that of many aluminium alloys.

Bauxite is the principal aluminium ore. Nepheline syenite, kaolin, shale, anorthosite and alunite are all potential alternative sources of alumina, but these are not currently economic to process. Of all bauxite mined, approximately 85% is converted to alumina (Al_2O_3) for the production of aluminium metal. The developing countries, in which at least 70% of known bauxite reserves are located, supply some 60% of the ore required. According to the US Geological Survey (USGS), 32% of potential world bauxite resources lie in Africa, 23% in Oceania, 21% in Latin America and the Caribbean, and 18% in Asia. Total world bauxite production in 2009 was estimated at 201,000 metric tons by the USGS, compared with 205,000 tons in 2008. Australia was by far the largest producer, providing 63,000 tons, or 31%, of the 2009 total, followed by the People's Republic of China (18%), Brazil (14%), India (11%), Guinea (8%) and Jamaica (4%).

The industry is structured in three stages: bauxite mining, alumina refining, and smelting. While the high degree of 'vertical integration' (i.e. the control of successive stages of production) in the industry means that a significant proportion of trade in bauxite and alumina is in the form of intra-company transfers, and the increasing tendency to site alumina refineries near to bauxite deposits has resulted in a shrinking bauxite trade, there is a growing free market in alumina, serving the needs of the increasing number of independent (i.e. non-integrated) smelters.

The alumina is separated from the ore by the Bayer process. After mining, bauxite is fed direct to process if mine-run material is adequate (as in Jamaica), or else it is crushed and beneficiated. Where the ore 'as mined' presents handling problems, or weight reduction is desirable, it may be dried prior to shipment.

At the alumina plant the ore is slurried with spent-liquor direct, if the soft Caribbean type is used, or, in the case of other types, it is ball-milled to reduce it to a size that will facilitate the extraction of the alumina. The bauxite slurry is then digested with caustic soda to extract the alumina from the ore while leaving the impurities as an insoluble residue. The digest conditions depend on the aluminium minerals in the ore and the impurities. The liquor, with the dissolved alumina, is then separated from the insoluble impurities by combinations of sedimentation, decantation and filtration, and the residue washed to minimize the soda losses. The clarified liquor is concentrated and the alumina precipitated by seeding with hydrate. The precipitated alumina is then filtered, washed and calcined to produce alumina. The ratio of bauxite to alumina is approximately 1.95:1.

Production of Bauxite
(crude ore, '000 metric tons)

	2008	2009*
World total (excl. USA)	205,000	201,000
Latin America and Caribbean	48,800	46,000
Latin American and Caribbean producers		
Brazil	28,000	22,000
Guyana	2,100	1,200
Jamaica	14,000	8,000
Suriname	5,200	4,000
Venezuela	5,500	4,800
Other leading producers		
Australia	61,400	63,000
China, People's Repub.	35,000	37,000
Guinea	18,500	16,800
India	21,200	22,300
Kazakhstan	4,900	4,900
Russia	6,300	3,300

* Estimated production.

Source: US Geological Survey.

The smelting of the aluminium is generally by electrolysis in molten cryolite. Owing to the high consumption of electricity by the smelting process, alumina is usually smelted in areas where low-cost electricity is available. However, most of the electricity now used in primary smelting in the Western world is generated by hydro-electricity—a renewable energy source.

The recycling of aluminium is economically, as well as environmentally, desirable, as the process uses only 5% of the electricity required to produce a similar quantity of primary aluminium. Aluminium recycled from scrap accounted for approximately one-third of the total annual world output of primary aluminium in 2008, according to the International Aluminium Institute (IAI). With the added impetus of environmental concerns, considerable growth occurred world-wide in the recycling of used beverage cans (UBC) during the 1990s and 2000s. From the mid-1990s, according to aluminium industry estimates, the recycling rate of UBC rose from some 55% to approximately 69% world-wide in 2007. The IAI reckoned that in 2007 some 69% of UBC globally were being collected for recycling, making this the world's most recycled container (the industry was aiming for a recycling rate of 75% by 2015).

Brazil was the world leader in aluminium can recycling in each year in 2001–07. In 2007, according to the Associação Brasileira do Aluminío and the Associação Brasileira dos Fabricantes de Latas de Alta Reciclabilidade, 96.5% of all aluminium cans sold in Brazil were recycled—a rate equivalent to 160,600 tons of aluminium can scrap. Recycling aluminium cans in Brazil is of major commercial significance. Those individuals, known as catadores, whose livelihood is based on the collection of UBC (and other discarded waste) from the streets in urban areas, themselves generate revenues totalling hundreds of millions of reais by selling what they find to recycling centres. Brazilian organizations like the Corporation Commitment for Recycling have encouraged recycling and sought to organize catadores in order to maximize UBC collection. In 2006 more than 160,000 Brazilians were reported to depend on collecting aluminium cans for their livelihood, selling UBC at more than 6,000 deposit points country-wide.

At the end of the 20th century world markets for finished and semi-finished aluminium products were dominated by six Western producers—Alcan (Canada), Alcoa, Reynolds, Kaiser (all USA), Pechiney (France) and algroup (formerly Alusuisse, of Switzerland). From 2000 the picture began to change dramatically, through mergers and the emergence of new international players from Russia and the People's Republic of China. In mid-2000 Alcoa merged with Reynolds.

In October Alcan took over algroup; a tripartite merger proposal from the previous year, which had also included Pechiney, was effectively achieved in 2003. Concerns regarding the safeguarding of competition were met by divestment of some of the new group's rolled aluminium assets into a new group, Novelis, in 2005; two years later Novelis was bought by India's Hindalco, which thus became the world's largest aluminium rolling company and one of Asia's biggest producers of primary aluminium. Meanwhile, in 2002, after the purchase of Germany's VAW, Norway's Norsk Hydro became the world's third largest integrated aluminium concern. (Hydro separated out its fertilizer business in 2005 and its petroleum and gas concerns, through a merger with Norway's Statoil, in 2007.) The level of dominance of the six major Western producers was already being challenged by a significant geographical shift in the location of alumina and aluminium production to countries where cheap power is available, such as Australia, Brazil, Norway, Canada and Venezuela. In the Persian (Arabian) Gulf, Bahrain and Dubai (United Arab Emirates), with the advantage of low energy costs, also produce primary aluminium. From the mid-1990s Russia emerged as a significant force in the world aluminium market, and in 2000 the country's principal producers, together with a number of plants located in other former Soviet states, joined together to form the Russian Aluminium Co (RUSAL). In March 2007 United Company RUSAL was formed by RUSAL's merger with Russia's second largest aluminium producer, Siberian-Urals Aluminium Company (SUAL), and the alumina assets of Switzerland's Glencore International AG. At mid-2009 United Company RUSAL claimed to be the world's largest aluminium company, accounting for almost 12% of world output of primary aluminium and 15% of global alumina production. In late 2007 the multinational mining concern Rio Tinto purchased Canada's Alcan Inc.—like United Company RUSAL, Rio Tinto Alcan, as the Rio Tinto division formed by the purchase was named (administratively, still based in Canada, although the aluminium and bauxite subdivision is based in Australia), also claims to be the world's biggest aluminium company. In February 2008 China's principal aluminium producer, Aluminium Corpn of China (Chinalco), and the USA's Alcoa jointly purchased a 12% stake in Rio Tinto in a move that was perceived as intended to obstruct an attempt by the Anglo-Australian company BHP Billiton, the world's largest mining company (and the sixth largest primary aluminium producer), to take over Rio Tinto. In June 2009 Rio Tinto ended moves towards greater integration with Chinalco (or, more specifically, its listed subsidiary, Chalco) amid some recriminations.

In 2009, according to USGS estimates, world output of primary aluminium totalled 36.9m. metric tons–compared with some 39,000 tons in 2008, when eastern Asia accounted for 34.5% of the global total (overwhelmingly because of China, but with some production in Indonesia and a little in Japan), with an additional 5.9% in Oceania (mainly Australia, but also New Zealand). North America provided 14.8% of world production in that year, Europe 13.8%, Russia and the other Soviet successor states 11.3%, Latin America (mainly Brazil, but also Venezuela and some in Argentina) 6.7%, the Middle East and North Africa 6.0%, sub-Saharan Africa (South Africa, Mozambique, Cameroon and some in Nigeria) 3.7% and South Asia (India) 3.4%. In 2009 China alone provided 35.2% of estimated world primary aluminium production, followed by Russia (8.9%), Canada (8.1%) and Australia (5.3%).

China displaced the USA as the most significant country for the international aluminium industry in the 2000s, accounting for about one-third of both consumption and production globally by 2009. The USA was for many years the world's principal producing country, but in 2001 US output of primary aluminium was surpassed by that of Russia and China. From 2002 Canadian production also exceeded that of the USA. In 2009 production of primary aluminium by China was estimated to have been almost eight times that by the USA.

Brazil possesses extensive bauxite reserves in Minas Gerais state and in the Amazon region. Until 2005 the country rivalled China for the position of second largest producer of the ore in the world. From that year, however, according to the USGS, Brazil's ore production remained fluctuating just above 22m. metric tons annually, while Chinese bauxite output increased steadily—even a 27% increase in Brazilian production in 2009, to an estimated 28m. tons (13.9% of the world total), left the country in third place after Australia and China. A joint venture, Mineração Rio do Norte SA, accounted for almost 73% of bauxite output in 2007 and was the world's third largest bauxite producer and exporter. Brazilian exports of bauxite totalled 5.8m. tons in 2007, generating revenues of US $240m. According to the USGS, Brazil's output of alumina increased slowly from 2005, reaching some 7m. tons by 2008; in the previous year alumina exports had amounted to 3.8m. tons, earning $1,300m. The country's principal alumina producer was Alumínio do Norte do Brasil (Alunorte), which accounted for one-half of output in 2006. Primary aluminium production in 2007 increased by 6.3%, to 1.7m. tons, helping supply exports of 1.1m. tons (worth $2,900m.); 27.7% of output was produced by Alumínio Brasileiro SA (Albras), 27.2% by Companhia Brasileira de Alumínio (CBA), 22.1% by Alcoa, 10.8% by BHP Billiton and 5.7% by Vale do Sul Alumínio SA (Aluvale). Primary aluminium production in Brazil remained steady in 2008, at almost 1.7m. tons, but declined to an estimated 1.6m. tons in 2009, according to the USGS, in which year Brazil slipped behind India in the world production rankings to seventh place.

Venezuela's aluminium industry achieved rapid growth in the 1980s, as a result of the availability of raw materials and cheap hydroelectric power. Aluminium production, based on imported alumina, subsequently overtook iron ore to become Venezuela's main export industry after petroleum. The country also has native bauxite resources, based on reserves of 320m. metric tons (as of 2008). Mining expanded rapidly after 1992, when output exceeded 1m. tons. In 1997 and 1998, and from 2002, more than 5m. tons of bauxite were mined annually. Output peaked at some 5.9m. tons annually in 2005–07, before falling back to 5.5m. tons in 2008 and to an estimated 4.8m. tons in 2009, according to the USGS. The country is the third bauxite producer in Latin America and the Caribbean, after Brazil and Jamaica. Venezuela's alumina production, levels of which are more often matched or exceeded by other producer countries in the region, continued at around 1.9m. tons per year from the mid-2000s. Primary aluminium is produced at two smelters, in both of which state-controlled Corporación Venezolana de Guayana has a majority share. According to the USGS, Venezuela's production of primary aluminium reached a record 634,000 tons in 1997, thereafter falling back to about 570,000 tons annually, before rising significantly, to 605,000 tons, in 2002. Aluminium production reached 624,000 tons in 2004, but declined to an estimated 610,000 tons per year in 2006–08 and 550,000 tons in 2009. Aluminium sold abroad earned the country US $1,057m. in 2006, or 1.7% of total export revenue (compared with 2.4% in 2004).

The only other regional player in the aluminium industry is Argentina, which has a smelter that produces almost 0.3m. metric tons of primary aluminium annually (an estimated 343,000 tons in 2008, according to the USGS). An expansion in capacity was planned. There have also been intermittent plans for a smelter in Trinidad and Tobago, which is strategically placed on the shipping lanes from the bauxite-rich South American Guiana coast. In 2004, the Government and Alcoa signed a memorandum of understanding that envisaged the construction of a primary aluminium smelter at La Brea, in the south-west of Trinidad island, but a judicial challenge in 2009 to the integrity of the environmental impact process left the project awaiting a final Court of Appeal decision in the first half of 2010.

Suriname and Guyana, as well as Venezuela, have bauxite reserves. The economy of Suriname relies heavily on the mining and export of bauxite. In 1993 bauxite, alumina and aluminium accounted for 91.5% of Suriname's annual export earnings, whereas in 1978 the corresponding proportion had been 83.8%. In early 2005 the expansion of the alumina refinery operated by Suriname Aluminium Co, LLC (Suralco)—owned by Alcoa World Alumina and Chemicals—at Paranam was completed, raising the facility's annual capacity to some 2.2m. metric tons. In 2005 exports of alumina contributed about 48% of total export revenue. The other main producer in Suriname is BHP Billiton. Bauxite production rose steadily, from 4.1m. tons in 2004 to an estimated 5.2m. tons in 2008. However, preliminary USGS estimates for 2009 recorded a dramatic decline in bauxite production, to some 4.0m. tons, a level not seen since 2002. After the early 2000s alumina production fluctuated around 2.0m. tons per year (the figure for 2008), ranging between 1.9m. tons in 2005 and 2.3m. tons in 2007. In line with bauxite production, and in response to economic recession in the country's main North American and European markets, alumina production in 2009 registered a significant decline. (Suralco alone reduced alumina production by about one-third.) Provisional figures from the Bank of Jamaica put exports of alumina and raw bauxite (the latter worth only 9% of alumina exports) up slightly in value in 2008; together, these accounted for 52.9% of general merchandise exports.

Guyana's bauxite production industry is a major source of the country's export revenue (excluding revenue from re-exports), of which bauxite provided almost 17% in 2008. Bauxite production in Guyana declined on average in the first half of the 2000s, but increased in 2005 to 1.7m. metric tons. Production dipped to 1.5m. tons in the 2006, but reached 2.2m. tons in 2007 and 2.1m. tons in 2008, reflecting the impact of foreign investment in the previously nationalized industry. However, in January 2010 the USGS put Guyanan bauxite production at only 1.2m. tons in 2009, owing to the impact of global recession and falling demand. Most of the country's production is by the Aroaima Bauxite Co, in which Russia's United Company RUSAL holds a 90% stake (bought from the Government, which retains the other 10%, in 2006—Aroaima was previously a Reynolds concern). Rising production costs forced the temporary closure of Omai Bauxite Mines Incorporated (OBMI) in mid-2006, after escalating fuel costs had reduced the profit margin on production. Bosai Minerals of China then acquired a 70% stake in OBMI from the Canadian-based IAMGOLD Corpn; the Government of

Guyana held the residual 30% share. Production was expected to shift towards lower grade bauxite, which was considerably cheaper to refine, and that trend could already be seen from late 2006, when the plant reopened—output of high-grade bauxite declined to an estimated 15,000 tons per month, compared with average monthly production of 30,000 tons before the closure. In 2007 Bosai Minerals announced plans for a new refinery, smelter and hydroelectric facility, while continuing to raise capacity at the Omai mine. Any expansion was likely to be delayed in the global economic conditions prevalent from 2009.

A production levy on the Jamaican bauxite industry, which has operated since 1974, provides an important source of government revenue. Production capacity was increased in the second half of the 1980s in order to supply the strategic mineral stockpiles of both the USA and the USSR (sales of aluminium ores and concentrates, including alumina, accounted for 63% of total export earnings in 1990), but, post-Cold War, depressed conditions in the international market affected Jamaican income adversely in the 1990s. Measures to revitalize Jamaica's bauxite and alumina industry were announced in July 1998 (in which year output of bauxite was 12.6m. metric tons, its highest level for 25 years), but production declined by 7.1% in 1999, owing to the closure of a US refinery that used Jamaican ore. Since 2002, however, output of both bauxite and alumina has, generally, risen. On the basis of figures published by the USGS in January 2010, Jamaica remained the world's sixth largest producer of bauxite in 2009; however, its share of global production fell from 6.8% in 2008 to 4.0% in 2009, as output declined by more than two-fifths to an estimated 8.0m. tons. Production had been more than 14.0m. tons annually since the mid-2000s, while alumina production had been around the 4.0m. tons recorded for 2008. The impact of the global recession, as well as oversupply problems in the parent company, meant that the two United Company RUSAL alumina refineries in Jamaica (Alumina Partners of Jamaica—Alpart and the West Indies Alumina Co—Windalco, both majority-owned by RUSAL since 2007) suspended operations in 2009, and a halving of Windalco bauxite production was announced. Continuing uncertainty in the world market was reflected in United Company RUSAL's announcement of the final closure of its Jamaican operations at the end of March 2010, followed by its raising some weeks later of the possibility of a partial reactivation of production later in the year. Alcoa's Jamaica Aluminium Co (Jamalco), which had recently expanded refinery capacity at its plant near Clarendon, maintained its alumina production levels in 2009. Noranda Aluminum, also of the USA, reduced bauxite production at the St Ann mine by about 30% in 2009, but overall bauxite output in Jamaica was down 67% in the first three quarters of 2009. The Jamaican Government put the earnings of the bauxite industry at J $5,000m. in 2007/08, $4,400m. still in 2008/09, but only a projected $139m. in 2009/10.

The Dominican Republic, which revived exploitation of its bauxite reserves in the 2000s, reached production of some 0.5m. metric tons each year in 2005–07, but fell back to 0.4m. tons in 2008. By 2009 it was clear that any consolidation of production levels, given the global economic situation, was unlikely.

In 2005 the average settlement price for aluminium (unalloyed primary ingots, high grade—minimum 99.7% purity) traded on the London Metal Exchange (LME) was, at US $1,898 per metric ton, 10.6% higher than in 2004 (cash price). During the year aluminium traded within a range of $1,675–$2,289 per ton. Stocks of metal held by the Exchange declined steadily during the first half of 2005, from 654,025 tons at the end of January to 535,525 tons at 30 June. By December 2005, however, inventories had recovered to 643,700 tons.

At US $2,567 per metric ton, the average price of aluminium traded on the LME in 2006 was 35.2% higher than that recorded in 2005. During the year the metal traded within a range of $2,267–$3,275 per ton. Generally, stocks of aluminium held by the LME rose in the first half of 2006, reaching 710,075 tons at the end of January and 779,100 tons at the end of March. At the end of June inventories totalled 760,900 tons. In the second half of the year, however, stocks declined steadily in September–November, before rising in December to total 698,425 tons. Key market influences in 2006 were increased Chinese consumption and the renewed interest of investment funds in aluminium, in combination with restructuring in European and US aluminium.

In 2007 the average price of aluminium traded on the LME increased by 2.8%, compared with the previous year, to US $2,639 per metric ton. During 2007 aluminium traded within a range of $2,317–$2,953 per ton. Prices fluctuated throughout the year, but, generally, were lower in the second half of the year than in the first. Chinese consumption remained a key market influence in 2007. In January–May, according to analysts, Chinese utilization rose by 47%, while consumption world-wide in the same period grew at a substantially lower rate of 10.5%. LME inventories of aluminium rose steadily in January–May, totalling 833,525 tons at the end of that period. In June, however, they declined to 823,625 tons. By the end of September stocks had risen to 937,400 tons, but they fell in October, to 918,250 at the end of that month. At the end of 2007 LME stocks of aluminium totalled 929,450 tons.

In 2008 the average LME price for aluminium per metric ton was US $2,573, part of a dramatic escalation in commodity prices until the onset of global economic anxieties in the second half of the year. By July 2008 the monthly average price of aluminium traded on the LME had soared to a record $3,380 per ton. Stocks of the metal held by the LME, meanwhile, had risen to more than 1.1m. tons by the end of May, compared with 956,475 tons at the end of January. The general trend in the prices of base metals was downward, but aluminium prices were supported by a continued decline in the value of the US dollar and by concern about possible shortages. However, weak demand in the West and the generally weak economic context world-wide caused the average monthly aluminium price to collapse, falling below $1,800 per ton by February 2009.

During 2009 the average LME aluminium price was US $1,665 per metric ton. In the first quarter an average price of only $1,360 per ton was recorded, but there was some recovery thereafter. Although demand in the USA, Japan and Europe remained weak, and stocks continued to increase, aluminium prices rose later in 2009 because there were expectations of recovering demand, as well as a resurgence in Chinese growth. There was a realization that many of the stocks were committed, aluminium production had lessened, and car-makers had returned to the market. In July prices exceeded $1,800 per ton for the first time since the previous November, and they then spiked beyond $2,000 per ton: the average quarterly price for October–December was $2,003 per ton. LME stocks were put at 4.6m. tons in July 2009, having doubled since the end of 2008.

In the first seven months of 2010 the average price for aluminium on the LME was US $2,110 per metric ton. After early rises at the beginning of the year, the average price fell back into February before beginning to recover in the latter part of that month. Prices peaked in April, with a monthly average of $2,317 per ton, but then fell back to just above $1,800 per ton in June, before regaining some ground. The average monthly price in July was $1,988 per ton. LME stocks were put at just above 4.4m. tons in mid-August.

The IAI, based in London, United Kingdom, is a global forum of producers of aluminium dedicated to the development and wider use of the metal. In 2010 the IAI had 27 member companies, representing every part of the world, including Russia and China, and responsible for more than 80% of global primary aluminium production and a significant proportion of the world's secondary output.

BANANA (*Musa sapientum*)

Although it is often erroneously termed a 'tree', the banana plant is, in fact, a giant herb. It grows to a height of 3–9 m (10–30 ft) and bears leaves which are very long and broad. The stem of the plant is formed by the overlapping bases of the leaves above. Bananas belong to the genus *Musa*, but the cultivated varieties are barren hybrid forms which cannot therefore be assigned specific botanical names. These banana hybrids, producing edible seedless fruits, are now grown throughout the tropics, but originally diversified naturally or were developed by humans in prehistoric times from wild bananas which grow in parts of South-East Asia. The plantain hybrid has grown in Central Africa for thousands of years, and traders and explorers gradually spread this and other varieties to Asia Minor and East Africa. The Spanish and Portuguese introduced them to West Africa and took them across the Atlantic to the Caribbean islands and the American continent. However, the varieties which are now most commonly traded internationally were not introduced to the New World until the 19th century.

The banana is propagated by the planting of suckers or shoots growing from the rhizome, which is left in the ground after the flowering stem, having produced its fruit, has died and been cut down. Less than one year after planting, a flowering stem begins to emerge from the tip of the plant. As it grows, the stem bends and hangs downwards. The barren male flowers which grow at the end of the stem eventually wither and fall off. The seedless banana fruits develop, without fertilization, from the clusters of female flowers further up the stem. Each stem usually bears between nine and 12 'hands' of fruit, each hand comprising 12–16 fruits. Before it is ripe, the skin of the banana fruit is green, turning yellow as it ripens. When ripe, the fruit is most commonly eaten raw, owing to its high sugar content (17%–19%). To obtain edible white flesh, the skin is peeled back. The process of fruiting and propagation can repeat itself indefinitely. In commercial cultivation the productive life of a banana field is usually limited to between five and 20 years before it is replanted, although small producers frequently allow their plants to continue fruiting for up to 60 years. Banana plantations are vulnerable to disease and to severe weather (particularly tropical storms), but the banana plant is fast-growing, and a replanted field can be ready to produce again within a year, albeit at a high cost.

Production of Bananas
('000 metric tons, excluding plantains)

	2007	2008
World total	89,100	90,706
Latin America and the Caribbean	25,279	25,390
Leading Latin American and Caribbean producers		
Brazil	7,098	7,117
Colombia	1,820	1,820*
Costa Rica	2,350*	1,882
Cuba	386	281
Dominican Republic	496	440
Ecuador	6,002	6,701
Guatemala	1,569	1,569*
Honduras*	910	910
Mexico	1,965	2,159
Panama	545	358
Venezuela	512	512*
Other leading producers		
Burundi*	1,850	1,850
China, People's Repub.	8,038	8,043
Egypt	945	1,062
India	23,205	23,205*
Indonesia	5,454	5,741
Philippines	7,484	8,688
Tanzania*	3,500	3,500
Thailand*	2,000	2,000
Viet Nam*	1,355	1,355

* FAO estimates.

Dessert bananas are the leading exported fresh fruit in terms of volume, while their exports rank second in terms of value, after those of citrus fruits. Only about one-fifth of banana production is traded internationally. Since the 1950s international trade has been almost exclusively based on the Cavendish variety, which gained predominance after the formerly mass-produced Gros Michel variety became virtually extinct as a result of Panama disease—caused by a fungus that attacks the roots of the banana plant. Apart from the trade in fresh, sweet bananas, the fruit has few commercial uses, although there is a small industry in dried bananas and banana flour as well as in fibre production. Although international trade is principally in the sweet dessert fruit, this type comprises less than one-fifth of total annual world banana production. On the basis of gross value of production, bananas are the world's fourth most important food crop, after rice, wheat and maize. In 2007 they were cultivated in around 130 countries. Many types of sweet banana, unsuitable for export, are consumed locally. Indeed, most types of bananas and the vast majority of bananas grown in the tropics are produced by small-scale farmers either for home consumption or for local markets. The numerous high-starch varieties with a lower sugar content, which are not eaten in their raw state, are used in cooking, mostly in the producing areas. Such varieties are picked when their flesh is unripe and more readily resistant to damage during transport, although they are occasionally of a type that would become sweet if left to ripen. Cooking bananas, sometimes called 'plantains' (though this term is also applied to types of dessert banana in some countries), form the staple diet of millions of inhabitants of the tropics, in particular in Eastern and Central Africa. Since they produce fruits all year round, bananas, like plantains, are of vital importance to food security in these countries. Bananas can also be used for making beer, and in East Africa special varieties are cultivated for that purpose. Advances in production methods, packaging, storage and transport (containerization) have made bananas available world-wide.

The banana was introduced into Latin America and the Caribbean by the Spanish and the Portuguese during the 16th century. The expansion of the banana industry in the small Latin American (so-called 'green' or 'banana') republics between 1880 and 1910 had a decisive effect in establishing this region as the centre of the world banana trade. Favourable soil and climatic conditions, combined with the ease of access around the Caribbean and to a major market in the USA, were important factors in the initial commercial success of the Latin American banana industry. Although advances in storage and transportation made the US market more accessible to producers in other areas, they also made available an equally important market in Europe (see below). Owing to considerably lower production costs than in other producing areas, bananas from South and Central America and the Caribbean command the major portion of the world export market (69% in 2007, according to FAO). Ecuador, Costa Rica, Colombia and Guatemala were among the five leading banana exporters in 2007, with Ecuador alone providing 29% of global banana exports in that year. It is there that the large multinational companies (notably Chiquita Brands International, Del Monte Foods and Dole Food Co) that dominate the world banana market are established. According to FAO, in 2007 Ecuador was followed by Costa Rica, which sold 13% of world banana exports, Colombia 9% and Guatemala 8% (the main non-regional rival was the Philippines, at 10%). Compared to an 80% contribution to the world banana export market in the 1970s, Latin America and the Caribbean still accounted for over 70% for most of the 2000s, but South America had displaced Central America as the principal supplier; Central America's share of world exports declining from 42% in the 1970s to 27% in 2007, and the Caribbean's from 8% to less than 2%, while South America's share rose from 28% to 40% over the same period.

Bananas are grown in most Latin American countries. The Americas accounted for one-half of world banana production in the 1970s and Asia little more than one-third, but by 2007 the respective shares were 28% and 57%, although Latin America remains dominant in the export market. India alone grows between one-fifth and one-quarter of world production (23.2m. metric tons, or 26%, in 2008), but little for export, followed by the Philippines (8.7m. tons) and the People's Republic of China (8.0m. tons). Brazil has traditionally been the region's leading producer (7.1m. tons in 2008), but again the crop is mainly for local consumption and bananas contribute only a small proportion of the country's total export earnings. In Ecuador, however, where production in 1996–2000 surpassed that of Brazil (6.7m. tons in 2008), bananas are the leading cash crop. Ecuador is the world's leading exporter of bananas, with shipments valued at an estimated US $1,282.0m. in 2007, or 18% of the total worth of world exports (FAO figures). In the same year banana exports accounted for 9.1% of the country's total export earnings (the relative contribution of banana sales to Ecuador's total export revenues had declined from 13.4% in 2004, mainly because increases in the price of petroleum inflated its contribution to receipts from foreign sales). One in seven of the population is reportedly dependent on the banana trade in Ecuador. Banana shipments also make a marked contribution to the export receipts of Honduras (providing 14.6% of the total in 2009), Belize (13.3% in 2009), Panama (8.6% in 2008) and Costa Rica (7.7% in 2006), and are a useful source of foreign exchange in the Dominican Republic (6.8% in 2006—less since then), Guatemala (5.7% in 2009), Colombia (where they provided 3.7% of total export earnings in 2000 and where they are the second most important agricultural export in terms of value after coffee) and Nicaragua (3.6% in 2006, but only 0.8% in 2009). The territories most dependent on bananas for export revenue tend to be the smaller producers, including Dominica (where bananas represented 20.0% of total exports, by value, in 2008), Saint Lucia (13.3%—down from 19.7% in 2006) and Saint Vincent and the Grenadines (22.3% in 2006—down from 38% of total exports, including re-exports, in 2004). The French overseas departments of Guadeloupe (22% in 1997) and Martinique (40% in 2003) also remained highly dependent on banana exports. Banana exports from the region are frequently adversely affected by tropical storms and hurricanes, which can have a devastating effect on banana harvests.

There is no international agreement governing trade in bananas, but there are various associations—such as the Union of Banana-Exporting Countries (UPEB), comprising Colombia, Costa Rica, Ecuador, Guatemala, Honduras, Nicaragua and Panama; the Caribbean Banana Exporters' Association, comprising Jamaica, Belize, the Windward Islands and Suriname; and WIBDECO, the Windward Islands Banana Development Co—which have been formed by producer countries to protect their commercial interests. Prices have varied greatly, depending on relative wages and yields in the producing countries, freight charges, and various trade agreements negotiated under the Lomé Conventions or the later Cotonou Agreement between the European Community (EC, now the European Union—EU) and 71 African, Caribbean and Pacific (ACP) countries. The Lomé arrangements included a banana protocol, which ensured producers an export market, a fixed quota and certain customs duty concessions. The importance of these arrangements come from the fact that the major producers are not ACP countries, while the EU market is the most valuable in the world—the EU and the USA are the world's largest markets for bananas. According to FAO, in 2007 the EU took 42% of world banana imports (by weight) and the USA 25%; the EU purchased 60% of the total value of world banana imports in that year. There was, therefore, a lot at stake in the negotiations and disputes that evolved into the so-called 'banana wars'.

Given the importance of the European market, the prospect of a withdrawal of internal barriers to intra-EC trade, as a result of the completion of a single market with effect from January 1993, was the cause of considerable anxiety to most major banana exporters (see below). Under the market arrangements prior to the end of 1992, just over one-half of banana imports were subject to quota controls under the Lomé Convention. Approximately 20% of market supplies were imported, duty-free, from former British, French and Italian colonies. The Windward Islands of Saint Lucia, Dominica and Grenada together accounted for some 90% of banana exports to the EC under the Lomé Convention's banana protocol, Jamaica and Belize also being parties to the Convention. About 70% of bananas from the Windward Islands were exported to the United Kingdom. France maintained similar arrangements with its traditional suppliers (overseas territories such as Guadeloupe and Martinique), as did Italy (Somalia). Another 25% of EC demand was satisfied internally, mainly from Spain (the Canary Islands), with smaller quantities from Portugal (Madeira and the Azores) and Greece (Crete). The remainder of quota imports (representing 10% of overall market demand) were imported, duty-free, into Germany, mainly from Latin and Central American countries. Banana imports into the residual free market originated mainly from the same countries, but attracted a 20% import tariff.

This complex market structure, which strongly favoured the Caribbean islands, was maintained by barriers to internal trade. These prevented the re-export of imports into Germany from, for instance, Honduras or Ecuador to the United Kingdom and France. Without these restrictions, Central and Latin American exporters, enjoying the cost advantages of modern technology and large-scale production, and subject to a 20% import tariff on their EC exports, would have substantially expanded their market share, and possibly displaced Caribbean producers altogether in the longer term.

The intention of the EC Commission that the tariff-free quota system would cease after 1992 held serious implications for Caribbean producers, who, with the ACP secretariat, sought to persuade the EC to devise a new preference system to protect their existing market shares, possibly taking the form of quota allocations, which would accord with the obligations of the EC countries in relation to trade with the ACP under the terms of the Lomé Convention. These guarantee that 'no ACP state shall be placed, as regards access to its traditional markets ... in a less favourable position than in the past or present'.

In December 1992 it was announced by the EC Commission that ACP banana producers were to retain their preferential status under the EC's single-market arrangements that were to enter into force in July 1993. These would guarantee 30% of the European banana market to ACP producers, by way of an annual duty-free quota of approximately 750,000 metric tons. Imports of Latin American bananas were to be limited to 2m. tons per year at a tariff of 20%, with any additional shipments to be subject to a tariff rate of 170%, equivalent to 850 European Currency Units (ECU) per ton. It was asserted that, as the proposals linked tariffs with quotas, the EC was not in contravention of the General Agreement on Tariffs and Trade (GATT) regulations on the restriction of market access.

These arrangements were opposed by Germany, Denmark, Belgium and Luxembourg, as well as by the Latin American banana producers, who forecast that their shipments to the EC, totalling approximately 2.6m. metric tons annually, could decline by as much as 20%. In early 1993 the German Government unsuccessfully sought a declaration from the Court of Justice of the European Communities that the EC Commission was in violation of GATT free trade regulations. In June Ecuador, Guatemala, Honduras, Mexico and Panama obtained agreement by GATT to examine the validity of the EC proposals. In the mean time, the new arrangements covering EC banana imports duly took effect on 1 July.

In February 1994 a GATT panel ruled in favour of the five Latin American producers, declaring that the policy on bananas unfairly favoured the ACP banana exporters and was in contravention of free trade principles. The Latin American producers accordingly demanded that the EU (as the EC was now known) increase its annual quota to 3.2m. metric tons and reduce the tariff level on excess shipments. The EU responded to the ruling by offering to increase the Latin American banana quota to 2.1m. tons in 1994 (with effect from 1 October) and to 2.2m. tons in 1995, and to reduce the tariff rate by one-quarter. This compromise was accepted by Colombia, Costa Rica, Nicaragua and Venezuela, but rejected by Ecuador and the other Latin American producers. The Latin American exporters assenting to the plan were each to receive specific quotas, based on their past share of the market, within the overall 2.1m.-ton quota. In October 1994 the Court of Justice of the European Communities rejected a petition by Germany seeking a quota of 2.5m. tons in that year, with subsequent annual increases of 5%.

With the accession to the EU in January 1995 of Austria, Finland and Sweden, it was anticipated that the quota for duty-free bananas would be increased by up to 350,000 metric tons annually to accommodate the community's enlarged membership (a proposal viewed as inadequate by Germany). In February 1995 the EU came under further pressure from a number of African banana-producing countries seeking further improvements in their access to EU markets under ACP arrangements. The dispute to which the new arrangements covering European banana imports had given rise was further complicated, from early 1995, by the involvement of the US Government—although the USA is only a marginal producer of bananas, US business interests hold substantial investments in the multinational companies operating in Central and South America. In September the USA formally instituted a complaint against the EU with the World Trade Organization (WTO), the successor organization to GATT. Further representations to the WTO by the US Government, supported by the Ecuador, Guatemala, Honduras and Mexico, followed in February 1996. This dispute remained, essentially, unresolved when the European Commission proposed in mid-2000 the possible introduction of a banana import regime based on a tariff quota system that would involve the distribution of licences on a 'first come, first served' basis. However, the European Commission also suggested that, if a consensus was not reached, a tariff-only solution, whereby no restrictions would be imposed on quantities but which would give ACP countries preferable rates, would be the only viable solution; the latter option was rejected by a number of EU governments as potentially damaging to EU banana-growers. Moreover, the granting of licences on a 'first come, first served' basis was subsequently rejected by representatives of Latin American banana-producing states, while the USA stated that the proposed regime did not adequately address its concerns.

In October 2000 the European Commission formally approved the introduction of a tariff quota system for bananas on a 'first come, first served' basis. Such a system would retain the use of three quotas until 2006, the Commission favouring the introduction of a tariff-only regime thereafter. The third quota would permit annual imports of 850,000 metric tons and would be available to all exporters. However, ACP exporters would be granted a tariff preference of US $264 per ton, rather than $275 per ton as had previously been proposed. The proposed new tariff quota system was immediately rejected by Colombia, Costa Rica, Guatemala, Honduras, Nicaragua and Panama, which threatened renewed action with the WTO. The USA also questioned whether the new regime was 'WTO-compatible'. Shortly after the announcement of the details of the proposed new regime EU governments declared that it provided 'a basis for settling the banana dispute'.

In March 2001 the EU announced that it would delay the introduction of the new tariff quota system for bananas in order to consider an alternative proposal, by the US company Chiquita Brands International, which would effectively grant quotas based on historical market share. In April the dispute over bananas appeared finally to have been resolved after the EU agreed temporarily to reallocate to Chiquita a larger share of the European banana market from 1 July 2001, the date set as a target for the introduction of the new tariff quota system. Under the settlement negotiated, the EU agreed to transfer 100,000 metric tons of bananas from the quota reserved mainly for ACP producers to that set for Latin American producers. From 1 July most import licences to the EU would be allocated on the basis of traditional shipment levels. Some 17% of licences would be reserved for new exporters or for companies that had significantly increased their imports since a 1994–96 reference period. The arrangements detailed above were supplemented in 2004 by what was termed an 'additional quantity' quota in order to allow imports of bananas into the 10 new member states of the enlarged EU.

In November 2004 negotiations between the EU and Latin American banana-exporting countries commenced in respect of the transfer to a tariff-only EU banana import regime from 1 January 2006, the European Commission stating that it would continue to seek some protection for domestic and ACP producers. In January 2005 Colombia, Costa Rica, Ecuador, Guatemala, Honduras, Nicaragua and Panama rejected the tariff—€230 per metric ton, on a most favoured nation (MFN) basis—proposed by the EU for the new banana import regime, arguing that it was not consistent with the obligations that the EU had assumed at a ministerial meeting of the WTO held in Doha, Qatar, in 2001. (At the Doha meeting the EU obtained a waiver from the WTO that allows it to grant ACP countries a quota for duty-free exports of bananas to its market.) According to the European Commission, the tariff had been set by computing the gap between internal and external EU prices. Many Latin American banana-exporting countries had reportedly urged that the tariff be set no higher than €75 per ton, while ACP banana-exporting countries were reported to favour a new single tariff of €275 per ton.

In January 2006 the EU abandoned its tariff quota banana import regime in favour of a tariff-only system of €176 per metric ton for MFN suppliers. The new regime included a duty-free quota of 775,000 tons for ACP suppliers, which was mostly to be allocated on a 'first come, first served' basis. Provisional figures issued by the EU showed that import volumes and domestic banana prices remained unchanged under the new regime in the first quarter of 2006 compared with the corresponding period of 2005. However, interested parties reportedly continued to question the suitability of the selected tariff, with some stating their intention to challenge it once again at the WTO on the grounds that it was too high. In November 2006 Ecuador was the first to resume the long-standing dispute at the WTO, on the grounds that its banana exports were still unfairly discriminated against. The other main banana producers followed suit in March 2007, and the USA lodged a separate complaint in July. The complainants requested that the WTO review the conformity of the EU's import regime with the WTO's former recommendations and rulings. In February 2008 a WTO panel ruled that the EU's banana import regime, the tariff in particular, violated international trade rules and requested that the EU bring its regime into conformity with its obligations under GATT. In May the EU considered appealing against the ruling on the grounds that the USA was not an interested party and should not have been allowed to intervene (an EU appeal was rejected in November). In June, however, the WTO agreed to extend the compliance deadline until the end of August to allow ongoing negotiations to continue. In July indications by the European Commission that it would accept a compromise solution proposed by the Director-General of the WTO whereby the tariff applied to non-ACP bananas would be reduced and there would be a so-called 'peace clause' devised to end ongoing WTO banana-dispute procedures. The ACP banana-producing countries favoured a longer period for the introduction of the new regime, by 2020 instead of 2015, as well as more compensatory support for their growers, while the Latin American producers urged that the new tariff be lowered still further. Generally, efforts to resolve the banana dispute over the year from mid-2008 became mired in the complex negotiations around the stalled WTO Doha Round of negotiations on world trade liberalization. In July 2009 Ecuador, backed by Colombia and Peru, broke off further negotiations with the EU about bananas. However, in December the 'banana wars' seemed to be over, when the EU agreed to reduce the import tariffs for Latin American bananas from €176 per ton to €114 per ton over a transition period of eight years. The cases before the WTO were suspended, pending European compliance with the agreement concluded with the banana producers and the USA. The European Commission adopted the relevant proposals on 17 January 2010 (as well as proposing the Bananas Accompanying Measures, to assist the disadvantaged ACP suppliers, which were not party to the agreement, with €190m. in 2011–13).

Meanwhile, under the terms of the Cotonou Agreement, the successor convention to the fourth Lomé Convention which covers the period 2000–20, the system of trade preferences hitherto pertaining for the ACP countries was to be gradually replaced by new economic partnerships based on the progressive and reciprocal removal of trade barriers. In a protocol to the Cotonou Agreement (the Second Banana Protocol), the 'overwhelming importance to the ACP banana suppliers of their exports to the Community (EU) market' was acknowledged, and the EU agreed to seek to ensure the continued viability of their banana export industries, and the continued access of their bananas to the EU market. (Given such provision, the ACP countries complained that they were not involved in the December 2009 agreement with the Latin American banana producers.) In a parallel move, in May 2010, at the EU-Latin American summit in Spain, the EU signed free trade agreements with a number of Central American countries and, separately, with Colombia and Peru, which promised a further reduction in tariffs, from €114 per metric ton to €75 per ton by 2020. Ecuador, however, rejected such an arrangement, arguing that its small economy had little chance against the weight of the European economy if openness was reciprocal. Instead, the country sought an 'accord for development', leaving the country a measure of protection, before tariff reductions for its regional competitors began to take effect.

Bananas were included by the UN Conference on Trade and Development (UNCTAD) on a list of 18 commodities in its proposed integrated programme for the regulation of international trade in primary products, based on commodity agreements backed by a common fund for financial support. The UN's Food and Agriculture Organization (FAO) and UNCTAD are seeking, through an intergovernmental group, to formulate such an international agreement on bananas, involving producers and consumers, which would ensure a proper balance of supply and demand, regulating trade in order to provide regular supplies for consumers at a price remunerative to producers. The main impediments to a trade pact are disagreements on the means by which the market would be stabilized, in particular on the definition and use of export quotas, which producers consider to be restrictive, and on the lowering of trade barriers to allow reciprocal trade, which is opposed by countries with high production costs.

In 2005, according to data compiled by the World Bank, average US import prices for main-brand bananas from Central and South America (c.o.t., US Gulf ports) increased by 15%, to US $603 per metric ton. The stronger prices recorded were attributed to a shortage of Latin American and African supplies, as the consequence of an exceptionally intense Atlantic hurricane season. Import prices were further boosted by higher shipping rates. Average EU import prices for main-brand bananas from Central and South America (c.i.f., Hamburg) increased to an even greater extent, by 30%, to $1,176 per ton—a situation that was attributed by some observers to a shortage of import licences, in addition to higher shipping rates and tight supplies. In 2006 US import prices rose by a further 13%, to $677 per ton, while EU import prices fell by 24%, to $897 per ton. As a possible explanation, it was noted that some exporters had transferred sales from the USA to European destinations. However, it was stated to be difficult to gauge the effect of the EU's new banana import regime (see above), among the range of other factors that had possibly been responsible for the decline in European import prices. In 2007 there was a significant recovery, of 16%, to $1,037 per ton, in EU import prices, while US import prices fell marginally, to $676 per ton. In 2008 banana import prices in the EU increased by 15%, to $1,188 per ton, while in the USA they rose substantially, by 25%, to $844 per ton, continuing the rise over 2009, to give an annual average US price of $847 per ton. The US market remained essentially stable into 2010, recording an average price of $845 per ton in January–July. The EU price, however, fell slightly to $1,145 per ton in 2009 and $1,013 per ton in January–July 2010, the market weakening upon the conclusion of the 'banana wars' in favour of the Latin American producers. Given that within the EU retail prices have remained comparatively high—the EU banana market is one of the world's most profitable—owing to the former operation of a tariff quota import regime, it is no surprise that the average EU price in 2009 was 20% higher than the US price (55% higher, on average, in 2004–07), but in July 2010 the US price of an average $985 per ton actually exceeded the EU price of $959 per ton for the first time.

COCOA (*Theobroma cacao*)

This tree, up to 14 m (46 ft) tall, originated in the tropical forests of Central and South America. The first known cocoa plantations were in southern Mexico around AD 600, although the crop may have been cultivated for some centuries earlier. Cocoa first came to Europe in the 16th century, when Spanish explorers found the beans being used in Mexico as a form of primitive currency as well as the basis of a beverage. The Spanish and Portuguese introduced cocoa into West Africa at the beginning of the 19th century.

Cocoa is now widely grown in the tropics, usually at altitudes less than 300 m above sea-level, where it needs a fairly high rainfall and good soil. Cocoa trees can take up to four years from planting before producing enough fruit to merit harvesting. They may live for 80 years or more, although the fully productive period is usually about 20 years. The tree is very vulnerable to pests and diseases, and it is highly sensitive to climatic changes. Its fruit is a large pod, about 15–25 cm (6–10 in) long, which at maturity is yellow in some varieties and red in others. The ripe pods are cut from the tree, on which they grow directly out of the trunk and branches. When opened, cocoa pods disclose a mass of seeds (beans) surrounded by white mucilage. After harvesting, the beans and mucilage are scooped out and fermented. Fermentation lasts several days, allowing the flavour to develop. The mature fermented beans, dull red in colour, are then dried, ready to be bagged as raw cocoa which may be further processed or exported.

Cultivated cocoa trees may be broadly divided into three groups. Most cocoas belong to the Amazonian Forastero group, which now accounts for more than 80% of world cocoa production. It includes Amelonado varieties, suitable for chocolate-manufacturing, and widely cultivated in Brazil and in West Africa. Criollo cocoa is rarely grown and is used only for luxury confectionery. The third group is Trinitario—descending from a cross between the Criollo and Forastero varieties—which comprises about 15% of world output and is cultivated mainly in Central America and the northern regions of South America.

The cocoa production chain is extremely labour-intensive: the International Cocoa Organization (ICCO) estimated that in the 2000s some 3m. smallholders accounted for 90% of global cocoa output. Large-scale plantations are found only in Brazil and Indonesia. The cocoa-processing industry, meanwhile, is highly concentrated. In the 2003/04 cocoa year three major companies (Archer Daniel Midland, Barry Callebaut and Cargill) processed about 42% of global cocoa production. Most cocoa-processing takes place in importing countries, mainly in the USA and the Netherlands. The processes include shelling, roasting and grinding the beans. The primary product of grinding is chocolate liquor, a part of which is sold directly to chocolate-manufacturers; the remainder is then processed further, in order to extract a fat—cocoa butter—and chocolate powder. Almost half of each bean after shelling consists of cocoa butter. Cocoa powder for use as a beverage is largely fat-free. Cocoa is a mildly stimulating drink, because of its caffeine content, and, unlike coffee and tea, is highly nutritious.

The most important use of cocoa liquor is in the manufacture of chocolate, of which it is the main ingredient. About 90% of all cocoa liquor produced is used in chocolate-making, for which extra cocoa butter is added, as well as other substances, such as sugar and, in the case of milk chocolate, milk. Cocoa butter is also used in cosmetic products, while the by-products of cocoa beans—the husks and shells—are used to make fertilizers and animal feed. Proposals initially announced in 1993 (and subsequently amended in 1997) by the consumer countries of the European Union (EU), permitting chocolate-manufacturers in member states to add as much as 5% vegetable fats to cocoa solids and cocoa fats in the manufacture of chocolate products, were perceived by producers as potentially damaging to the world cocoa trade. In 1998 it was estimated that the implementation of this plan could reduce world demand for cocoa beans by 130,000–200,000 metric tons annually. In July 1999, despite protests from Belgium, which, with France, Germany, Greece, Italy, Luxembourg, the Netherlands and Spain, prohibits the manufacture or import of chocolate containing non-cocoa-butter vegetable fats, the European Commission cleared the way to the abolition of this restriction throughout the EU countries, which took effect in June 2000. The implementation of the new regulations by all member states ensued in 2003. Producers identified another, potentially more damaging threat, when, in March 2007, the US Chocolate Manufacturers Association, following a similar request at the end of 2006 from the Grocery Manufacturers of America, began to lobby the US Food and Drug Administration (FDA) to change the legal definition of chocolate, in order to allow them to substitute at will vegetable fats and oils for cocoa butter in products labelled as chocolate. In response, the FDA initiated a public consultation period. In order to allay consumers' concerns, in June 2007 the FDA provisionally assured that 'cacao fat, as one of the signature characteristics of the product, will remain a principal component of standardized chocolate'. Meanwhile, an EU study on the evaluation of the new regulations, published in June 2006, found that the rate of growth of net cocoa imports had increased to 3.5% by 2005, despite a saturated market for chocolate products. The study attributed this growth mainly to an increase in consumer demand for products with a high cocoa content. According to an ICCO report published in June 2008, changes in consumption behaviour had had a significant impact on demand for cocoa beans in terms of both quality and quantity. Between 2001/02 and 2006/07 world cocoa consumption expanded at an average annual rate of 3.8%. In 2006/07 consumption increased by 2.5% from the previous season. A significant part of the increase resulted from higher consumption in Europe (where it rose by 6%), where consumers were increasingly inclined to purchase organic, fine-flavour and high-cocoa-content products. In particular, the growing demand for products with a high cocoa content was influenced by research findings on the beneficial health properties of cocoa, and led in turn to increased demand for cocoa beans of higher quality—which command higher prices. In the same year, global consumption of dark chocolate was estimated to constitute 5%–10% of the total consumption of chocolate bars, with the highest share (20%) in continental Europe, particularly in the Netherlands, France, Belgium and Switzerland. Consumption of dark chocolate in the USA increased at an average annual rate of 9% between 2001 and 2005. In addition, concerns about food safety and environmental issues led to increased demand for organic chocolate, the share of which in global production was, however, still estimated at less than 0.5% in 2005. According to the ICCO, such changes in consumption have mainly benefited the economies of those countries recognized by the International Cocoa Council (ICC) as exporters of premium cocoa (Colombia, Costa Rica, Dominica, Ecuador, Grenada, Indonesia, Jamaica, Madagascar, Papua New Guinea, Peru, Saint Lucia, São Tomé and Príncipe, Trinidad and Tobago, and Venezuela). At the same time as this qualitative shift in consumption, which has expanded existing, saturated markets, increased consumption in emerging and newly industrialized countries, in particular in Russia and in Asia, has sustained demand for bulk cocoa.

A combination of growing consumer concerns about poverty in less developed countries and a more organized fair-trade movement has established steady growth in sales of fair-trade products since the early 1990s. Sales of cocoa labelled 'fair-trade' increased from 700 metric tons in 1996 to 5,657 tons in 2005, equivalent to annual growth averaging 23%, although at the end of that period the share of fair-trade cocoa was still estimated to represent less than 0.2% of global production. In 2005 83% of sales of fair-trade cocoa world-wide were distributed among only six countries: the United Kingdom (40%), Germany and France (13% each), Austria, Italy and Switzerland (6% each).

Production of Cocoa Beans
('000 metric tons)

	2007	2008
World total	4,150	4,300
Latin America and the Caribbean	484	501
Leading Latin American and Caribbean producers		
Brazil	202	208
Colombia	40	45
Dominican Republic	42	42*
Ecuador	86	94
Mexico	30	28
Peru	31	31*
Other leading producers		
Cameroon†	179	188
Côte d'Ivoire	1,384	1,370†
Ghana†	615	700
Indonesia	740	793
Malaysia	35	30
Nigeria	500†	500*
Papua New Guinea†	47	49
Togo†	78	80

* FAO estimate.
† Unofficial figure(s).

In 2008, according to FAO, the most important producing area in the world was Africa, which accounted for 67% of total output, followed by eastern Asia and Oceania, at 21%, and Latin America and the Caribbean, at 12%. In 2007 Africa accounted for 65% of foreign sales of cocoa beans world-wide, by volume, eastern Asia and Oceania 16% and Latin America and the Caribbean 5% (the balance includes re-exports). According to ICCO figures, the largest single producer of cocoa beans in 2009/10, despite falling output, remained Côte d'Ivoire, with a forecast 1.19m. metric tons (down from 1.22m. tons in 2008/09), followed by Ghana with 645,000 tons (down from 662,000 tons), Indonesia with 525,000 tons (up from 490,000 tons), Nigeria with 260,000 tons (250,000 tons), Cameroon with 205,000 tons (227,000 tons), Brazil with 158,000 tons (157,000 tons) and Ecuador with 140,000 tons (130,000 tons). World output of cocoa beans, according to FAO, was 4.15m. tons in 2007 and 4.30m. in 2008. ICCO figures for production tend to be lower: world production was put at 3.73m. tons of cocoa beans in 2007/08, 3.59m. tons in 2008/09 and a projected 3.60m. tons in 2009/10. Since two-fifths of the processing (grinding) of cocoa beans does not take place in the country of origin, the Netherlands is the world leader, accounting for 12.6% of the world total of 3.49m. tons in 2008/09, followed by Côte d'Ivoire (12.0%), the USA (10.3%), Germany (9.8%), Malaysia (8.0%) and Brazil (6.2%). Overall, Europe accounted for 41% of grindings, the Americas 22%, Asia and Oceania 19% and Africa 18%. Global consumption of chocolate products is dominated by the European Union (53%); and by Northern America (26%).

In 2008 FAO figures put Brazil as the world's fifth largest producer of cocoa beans, after Côte d'Ivoire, Indonesia, Ghana and Nigeria. Output of cocoa beans in 2006, affected by weather conditions related to El Niño (an aberrant current which periodically causes the warming of the Pacific coast of South America, disrupting usual weather patterns), fell by 15%, compared with 2005, and by a further 5% in 2007, before increasing by 3.3% in 2008. Brazil's exports of cocoa beans, however, were far exceeded regionally by those of Ecuador and the Dominican Republic, and comfortably by Haiti, Mexico and Colombia—in 2007 they totalled 718 metric tons. This indicated the greater degree of processing that took place in the country: regionally, Brazil was the leading exporter of cocoa butter (32,744 tons in 2007) and cocoa paste (12,258 tons). In 2007 exports of cocoa beans from Ecuador amounted to 80,093 tons, representing 2.9% of global exports, and earning US $190.4m. Following devastation caused to the cocoa crop as a result of El Niño in 1997–98, and fluctuating fortunes thereafter, in 2001–05 Ecuador's exports of cocoa beans increased by 41%, from 55,420 tons to 78,348 tons, while earnings from the sale of cocoa beans rose by 107% during the same period, when the country began to benefit both from its efforts to focus increasingly on the production of high-quality chocolate, and from rising world prices for cocoa beans. At the same time, the share of earnings from the sale of cocoa in Ecuador's total export revenue declined from 2.3% in 1999 to 1.2% in 2006. In 2005 the Dominican Republic derived about 3% of its export earnings from cocoa and cocoa products (excluding exports from free trade zones), compared with 4.5% in 2003. The country's cocoa crop was severely damaged by Hurricane Georges in September 1998. The Dominican Republic's production of cocoa beans—42,154 tons in 2007 and estimated at a similar level in 2008—has never fully recovered, and is barely three-fifths the volume achieved in 1996 (67,196 tons). However, the Dominican Republic's export earnings from the sale of cocoa and cocoa products began to recover in 2002, when they increased by 58%, compared with 2001. In 2002–05 the country's revenues from foreign sales of cocoa beans continued to rise, by an average annual rate of 20.6%. Exports of 39,512 tons of cocoa beans in 2007 earned $81.0m.

World prices for cocoa are highly sensitive to changes in supply and demand, making its market position volatile. Negotiations to secure international agreement on stabilizing the cocoa industry began in 1956. Full-scale cocoa conferences, under UN auspices, were held in 1963, 1966 and 1967, but all proved abortive. A major difficulty was the failure to agree on a fixed minimum price. In 1972 the fourth UN Cocoa Conference took place in Geneva, Switzerland, and resulted in the first International Cocoa Agreement (ICCA), adopted by 52 countries, although the USA, the world's principal cocoa importer at that time, did not sign. The ICCA took formal effect in October 1973. It operated for three quota years and provided for an export quota system for producing countries, a fixed price range for cocoa beans and a buffer stock to support the agreed prices. In accordance with the ICCA, the ICCO, based in London, United Kingdom, was established in 1973. By January 2010 the membership of the 2001 ICCA (see below) comprised 43 countries (14 exporting members, 29 importing members), representing about 85% of world cocoa production and some 60% of world cocoa consumption. The European Union (EU) is also an inter-governmental party to the 2001 Agreement. However, the USA, a leading importer of cocoa, is not a member. Nor is Indonesia, which is now the third largest producer in the world. The governing body of the ICCO is the ICC, established to supervise implementation of the ICCA. The ICC is also based in London.

A second ICCA operated during 1979–81. This was followed by an extended agreement, which was in force in 1981–87. A fourth ICCA took effect in 1987. During the period of these ICCAs the effective operation of cocoa price stabilization mechanisms was frequently impeded by a number of factors, principally by crop and stock surpluses, which continued to overshadow the cocoa market in the early 1990s. In addition, the achievement of ICCA objectives was affected by the divergent views of producers, led by Côte d'Ivoire, and consumers, led by the USA, as to appropriate minimum price levels. Disagreements also developed over the allocation of members' export quotas and the conduct of price support measures by means of the buffer stock (which ceased to operate during 1983–88), and subsequently over the disposal of unspent buffer stock funds. The effectiveness of financial operations under the fourth ICCA was severely limited by the accumulation of arrears of individual members' levy payments, notably by Côte d'Ivoire and Brazil. The fourth ICCA was extended for a two-year period from October 1990, although the suspension of the economic clauses relating to cocoa price support operations rendered the agreement ineffective in terms of exerting any influence over cocoa market prices.

Preliminary discussions on a fifth ICCA, again held under UN auspices, ended without agreement in May 1992, when consumer members, while agreeing to extend the fourth ICCA for a further year (until October 1993), refused to accept producers' proposals for the creation of an export quota system as a means of stabilizing prices, on the grounds that such arrangements would not impose sufficient limits on total production to restore equilibrium between demand and supply. Additionally, no agreement was reached on the disposition of cocoa buffer stocks, then totalling 240,000 metric tons. In March 1993 ICCO delegates abandoned efforts to formulate arrangements whereby prices would be stabilized by means of a stock-withholding scheme. At a further negotiating conference in July, however, terms were finally agreed for a new ICCA, to take effect from October, subject to its ratification by at least five exporting countries (accounting for at least 80% of total world exports) and by importing countries (representing at least 60% of total imports). Unlike previous commodity agreements sponsored by the UN, the fifth ICCA aimed to achieve stable prices by regulating supplies and promoting consumption, rather than through the operation of buffer stocks and export quotas.

The fifth ICCA, operating until September 1998, entered into effect in February 1994. Under the new agreement, buffer stocks totalling 233,000 metric tons that had accrued from the previous ICCA were to be released on the market at the rate of 51,000 tons annually over a maximum period of four-and-a-half years, beginning in the 1993/94 crop season. At a meeting of the ICCO held in October 1994, it was agreed that, following the completion of the stocks reduction programme, the extent of stocks held should be limited to the equivalent of three months' consumption. ICCO members also assented to a voluntary reduction in output of 75,000 tons annually, beginning in 1993/94 and terminating in 1998/99. Further measures to achieve a closer balance of production and consumption, under which the levels of cocoa stocks would be maintained at 34% of world grindings during the 1996/97 crop year, were introduced by the ICCO in September 1996. The ICCA was subsequently extended until September 2001. In April 2000 the ICCO agreed to implement measures to remedy low levels of world prices (see below), which were to centre on the elimination of sub-grade cocoa in world trade: these cocoas were viewed by the ICCO as partly responsible for the downward trend in prices. In mid-July Côte d'Ivoire, Ghana, Nigeria and Cameroon disclosed that they had agreed to destroy a minimum of 250,000 tons of cocoa at the beginning of the 2000/01 crop season, with a view to assisting prices to recover and to 'improving the quality of cocoa' entering world markets.

A sixth ICCA was negotiated, under the auspices of the UN, in February 2001. Like its predecessor, the sixth ICCA aimed to achieve stable prices through the regulation of supplies and the promotion of consumption, but it also incorporated into its objectives the development of a sustainable cocoa economy. The Agreement took provisional effect on 1 October 2003. In December, in accordance with its terms, the ICC established a Consultative Board on the World Cocoa Economy, a private sector board comprising seven exporting and seven importing members, with a mandate to 'contribute to the development of a sustainable cocoa economy; identify threats to supply and demand and propose actions to meet the challenges; facilitate the exchange of information of production, consumption and stocks; and advise on other cocoa-related matters within the scope of the Agreement'. In November 2005, on its ratification by the Dominican Republic, the sixth ICCA entered definitively into force. (This was the first time that an ICCA had ever entered definitively into force.) The Agreement was to remain open to new signatories until 2010.

International prices for cocoa were generally very low until the early 2000s. In 1998 the average of the ICCO's daily prices (based on selected quotations from the London and New York markets) was US $1,676 per metric ton (49.9 US cents per lb), its highest level since 1982, but in 1999 it slumped to $1,140 (a fall of 32.0%). In 2000 the average of the ICCO's daily prices again declined steeply, falling well below that recorded in 1992—$1,099.5 per ton—to only $888 per ton, a reduction of some 22%. (The average ICCO quotation ranged between $942 per ton in June 2000 and $801 per ton in November, the lowest monthly average since March 1973.) Prices recovered somewhat in 2001, but, even so, the ICCO's daily quotation averaged only $1,089 per ton in that year, the second lowest average price recorded since 1972. In 2002, however, the average price rebounded by almost 63%, compared with the previous year, to reach $1,778 per ton. In 2003 the ICCO's average daily price fell slightly, by 1.3%, to $1,755 per ton. A more substantial decline, of 11.8%, was recorded in 2004, when the ICCO's daily quotation averaged $1,548 per ton. In 2005 the average quotation fell marginally, by 0.6%, to $1,538 per ton. The ICCO's average daily price recovered by 3.5% in 2006, to $1,592 per ton. The average daily price increased substantially, by 22.6%, to $1,952 per ton in 2007, and again, by 32.0%, to $2,577 per ton in 2008. Global economic concerns, which had depressed cocoa quotations in the second half of 2008 and had affected all commodity prices, were pronounced into the first half of 2009, despite continued expectation of a production deficit. Nevertheless, the average price for 2009 was $2,889 per ton, the price having risen considerably later in the year (the final quarter average was $3,418 per ton). Prices fell back somewhat from late-2009 heights during the first seven months of 2010, but still recorded an average of $3,249 per ton over January–July. The monthly average of the ICCO daily price in July was $3,222 per ton. In that month some controversy hit the London market. A cocoa futures contract saw the largest delivery of cocoa in 14 years, leaving the bulk of the available graded stock in the hands of one firm, sparking fears of supply being tight in September, as well as allegations of excessive speculation in London. Prices seemed more likely to be maintained by declining output in Côte d'Ivoire, the leading producer, and the continued threat of a cocoa deficit.

The Cocoa Producers' Alliance (COPAL), with headquarters in Lagos, Nigeria, had 10 members as of 2010: Brazil, Cameroon, Côte d'Ivoire, the Dominican Republic, Gabon, Ghana, Malaysia, Nigeria, São Tomé and Príncipe, and Togo. The alliance was formed in 1962 with the aim of preventing excessive price fluctuations by regulating the supply of cocoa. Members of COPAL currently account for about three-quarters of world cocoa production. COPAL has acted in concert with successive ICCAs.

The principal centres for cocoa-trading in the industrialized countries are the London Cocoa Terminal Market, in the United Kingdom, and the New York Coffee, Sugar and Cocoa Exchange, in the USA.

COFFEE (*Coffea*)

The coffee plant is an evergreen shrub or small tree, generally 5–10 m tall, indigenous to Asia and tropical Africa. Wild trees grow to 10 m, but cultivated shrubs are usually pruned to a maximum of 3 m. The dried seeds (beans) are roasted, ground and brewed in hot water to provide one of the most popular of the world's non-alcoholic beverages. Coffee is drunk in every country in the world, and its consumers comprise an estimated one-third of the world's adult population. Although it has little nutrient value, coffee acts as a mild stimulant, owing to the presence of caffeine, an alkaloid also present in tea and cocoa.

There are about 40 species of *Coffea*, most of which grow wild in the eastern hemisphere. The two species of chief economic importance are *C. arabica* (native to Ethiopia), which in the mid-2000s accounted for about 60%–65% of world production, and *C. canephora* (the source of Robusta coffee), which accounted for almost all of the remainder. Arabica coffee is more aromatic, but Robusta, as the name implies, is a stronger plant. Coffee grows in the tropical belt, between 20°N and 20°S, and from sea-level to as high as 2,000 m above. The optimum growing conditions are found at 1,250–1,500 m above sea-level, with an average temperature of around 17°C and an average annual rainfall of 1,000–1,750 mm. Trees begin bearing fruit three to five years after planting, depending upon the variety, and give their maximum yield (up to 5 kg of fruit per year) from the sixth to the 15th year. Few shrubs remain profitable beyond 30 years.

Arabica coffee trees are grown mostly in the American tropics and supply the largest quantity and the best quality of coffee beans. The yield of Arabica trees has a propensity to follow a biennial cycle, whereby a heavy crop alternates with a light crop. In Africa and Asia Arabica coffee is vulnerable in lowland areas to a serious leaf disease, and consequently cultivation has been concentrated in highland areas. Some highland Arabicas, such as those grown in Kenya, are renowned for their high quality.

The Robusta coffee tree, grown mainly in East and West Africa, and in the Far East, has larger leaves than Arabica, but the beans are generally smaller and of lower quality and, consequently, fetch a lower price. However, Robusta coffee has a higher yield than Arabica, as the trees are more resistant to disease. It can also be grown at lower elevations than Arabica, from 500 m to 1,500 m above sea level. About 60% of African coffee belongs to the Robusta variety. It is more suitable for the production of soluble ('instant') coffee, and is favoured by multinational roasters and instant coffee producers because of its lower cost. Soluble coffee accounts for more than one-fifth of world coffee consumption. In the mid-2000s four main roaster companies

(Kraft Foods, Nestlé, Procter & Gamble and Sarah Lee) purchased more than 50% of global Robusta coffee production.

Each coffee berry, green at first but red when ripe, usually contains two beans (white in Arabica, light brown in Robusta) which are the commercial product of the plant. To produce the best quality Arabica beans—known in the trade as 'mild' coffee—the berries are opened by a pulping machine and the beans fermented briefly in water before being dried and hulled into green coffee. Much of the crop is exported in green form. Robusta beans are generally prepared by dry-hulling. Roasting and grinding are usually undertaken in the importing countries, for economic reasons, and because roasted beans rapidly lose their freshness when exposed to air.

Apart from beans, coffee produces a few minor by-products. When the coffee beans have been removed from the fruit, what remains is a wet mass of pulp and, at a later stage, the dry material of the 'hull' or fibrous sleeve that protects the beans. Coffee pulp is used as cattle feed; the fermented pulp makes a good fertilizer; and coffee bean oil is an ingredient in soaps, paints and polishes.

More than one-half of the world's coffee is produced on smallholdings of less than 5 ha in area. In most producing countries coffee is almost entirely an export crop, for which (with the exception of Brazil, after the USA the world's second largest coffee consumer) there is little domestic demand. Green coffee accounts for some 96% of all the coffee that is exported, with soluble and roasted coffee comprising the balance. Tariffs on green/raw coffee are usually low or non-existent, but those applied to soluble coffee may be as high as 30%. The USA is the largest single importer, although its volume of coffee purchases was overtaken in 1975 by the combined imports of the (then) nine countries of the European Community (EC, now the European Union—EU).

After petroleum, coffee is the major raw material of world trade, and it is the single most valuable agricultural export of the tropics. In the 2000s about 25m. small producers world-wide depended on coffee. Coffee is the most important cash crop of Latin America, with a number of countries heavily dependent on it as a source of foreign exchange. Of the estimated total world crop of coffee beans in 2009/10, Latin American and Caribbean countries accounted for 58.2% (Brazil alone contributed 32.7% of the world total). Africa, which formerly ranked second, was overtaken in 1992/93 by Asian producers. In 2009/10 African producers accounted for 11.2% of the estimated world coffee crop, compared with 25.9% for countries in eastern Asia and Oceania. South Asia—India and Sri Lanka—harvested a further 4.0% of the world coffee crop in the same year. (The above shares have been calculated on the basis of data released by the International Coffee Organization—ICO. Non-members of the ICO accounted for 0.6% of the world coffee crop in 2009/10.) The largest single producer after Brazil is Viet Nam (14.9% of world production), followed by Indonesia (8.8%) and Colombia (7.5%). Forecasts for 2010/11 reckoned on record Brazilian and world coffee harvests.

Brazil and Colombia together consistently accounted for more than 32% of world trade in green (unroasted) coffee during the 1990s. In 1999 their share of the world coffee trade rose to 39%, reflecting the bumper crop from Brazil, and in 2002 more than 43% of all coffee traded world-wide emanated from Brazil and Colombia. In the ICO year to June 2010 exports by Brazil and Colombia represented about 40% of all coffee exported world-wide. Coffee's traditional status as Brazil's most important agricultural export has been gradually eroded; by 1990 earnings from soybeans were more than double those from coffee. Unroasted coffee provided 2.1% of Brazil's total exports in 2008. In terms of volume, Brazilian coffee exports reached a record level of 31.4m. bags (each of 60 kg) in 2008/09, compared with 27.4m. bags in 2007/08, but fell back to 29.7m. bags in 2009/10. The state of Minas Gerais—which grows mainly Arabica trees—accounted for an average 48% of total Brazilian coffee production and 63.4% of Brazil's Arabica output in 2001/02–2006/07, according to data compiled by the US Department of Agriculture (USDA). About three-quarters of Brazil's harvest (73.7% in 2009/10) comes from Arabica trees, and the country's coffee output (and all the more so that of Minas Gerais) is largely determined by the tree's biennial cycle.

Coffee remains the leading legal cash export crop in Colombia, although its relative importance in the country's economy declined in the 1990s, when it was overtaken by petroleum and its derivatives as the main source of export earnings. Colombia produces only Arabica varieties of coffee. 'Colombian Mild' Arabica coffee beans, to which the country has given its name, are regarded as being of a superior quality to other coffee types and are grown primarily in Colombia, Kenya and Tanzania. (Colombian Milds are one of four internationally designated coffee groups, the others being Other Milds, which are produced primarily in Central America; Brazilian Natural Arabicas, which are produced primarily in Brazil and Ethiopia; and Robustas, of which the main producers are Viet Nam, Indonesia and Brazil.) According to the ICO, Colombian coffee output in 2002/03–2007/08 averaged 12.1m. bags. Production ranged from 11.2 bags in 2003/04 to 12.5m. bags in 2007/08; however, it only reached 8.7m. bags in 2008/09 and rather less in 2009/10. Shipments of coffee from Colombia accounted for 6.9% of the country's total export earnings in 2005, 6.0% in 2006, 5.7% in 2007, 5.0% in 2008 and 4.7% in 2009, reflecting the decline in coffee production. Coffee consumption in Colombia (around 2 kg per caput per year) is far below the consumption levels of neighbouring countries, and Colombia exports 90% of its production. Colombian exports of coffee totalled 12.2m. bags in 2006/07 and 11.9m. bags in 2007/08, but fell to 9.6m. bags in 2008/09 and 7.0m. bags in 2009/10. A modest recovery was forecast for the following crop year, although problems persisted. In response to the mounting competition from Brazilian or Vietnamese producers—who benefit from extremely low labour costs—from the 1990s onward, the Colombian coffee sector has focused increasingly on 'gourmet' coffee, which commands a higher profit margin. In 2002 the coffee sector launched a series of high-quality specialist brands under the 'Café de Colombia' name. By 2008, according to USDA, high-quality 'specialty' coffee exports had quadrupled since 2002. The USA is consistently the most important single market for Colombian coffee, accounting for 35% of total shipments in 2007. Overall, however, the EU is the most important market for Colombian coffee. In 2007 Colombian coffee exports to the EU represented 38% of total shipments. Germany was the most important European destination for shipments, accounting for an estimated 12.7% of Colombia's total exports of coffee.

Traditionally, Arabica coffee was the principal export crop in El Salvador, Guatemala, Haiti, Mexico, Nicaragua and Peru, and the second most important crop in Costa Rica, the Dominican Republic, Ecuador, Honduras and Puerto Rico. Sales of coffee contributed 33.2% of El Salvador's total export earnings in 1996, and 38.2% in 1997. Unfavourable weather, disease (rust), civil war and falling coffee prices reduced production thereafter, and from 2001 the contribution of coffee to the country's export revenue was less than 10%. In 2008 exports of coffee (excluding the *maquila* zones), bolstered by high international prices, represented 12.7% of total export earnings, compared with 8.6% in 2007 and 9.8% in 2006. In 2009 coffee exports constituted 10.0% of the total. Coffee provided 8.4% of Guatemala's export earnings in 2007, 8.4% in 2008 and 8.1% in 2009. Sales of Nicaraguan coffee, which also exhibit signs of the biennial fluctuation of the Arabica crop, accounted for 15.4% of the country's export revenue in 2007, 18.7% in 2008 and 17.0% in 2009.

In Costa Rica coffee ranks second to bananas as the principal export commodity. The country grows only Arabica highland coffee, which commands a premium on the world market, and achieves some of the highest yields in the world. None the less, coffee contributes a diminishing share of the country's export revenue on account of Costa Rica's successful economic diversification away from cash crops since the 1960s. In 2007 coffee accounted for 2.6% of Costa Rica's total export earnings, compared with 10.8% in 1997. A continued decline in export volumes was forecast for 2010/11. In Honduras coffee has displaced bananas as the country's principal agricultural export commodity, contributing 20.3% of export revenue (excluding the *maquila* zones) in 2006, 21.1% in 2007, a record 21.9% in 2008 and another record of 23.7% in 2009. In 2008/09 Honduras surpassed Guatemala as Central America's largest producer, although the latter's export volumes remained greater. Mexico, which produces more coffee than any of the Central American countries (regionally, only exceeded by Brazil and Colombia), has a large domestic market and is not as important an exporter as Guatemala or Honduras. Moreover, its varied economy means that it is not dependent on coffee exports in any way. Panama produces a small amount of coffee for local consumption.

Coffee provided 23.1% of Haiti's export earnings in 1989/90, but its contribution has declined sharply since then, amounting to 0.8% in 2007/08 and 0.5% in 2008/09. The neighbouring Dominican Republic earned 7.3% of its total export revenue from coffee (including exports from free trade zones) in 1998, but by 2005 exports of green coffee beans contributed only 1.1% of the country's total export earnings. Cocoa, sugar and tobacco were more important exports. Elsewhere in the Caribbean, Cuba also produces a small amount of coffee, though not for export, and Jamaica grows even less, although its noted, speciality Blue Mountain coffee is much sought after, particularly in Japan. Trinidad and Tobago exports most of its minimal production.

Coffee's share in Ecuador's export revenue, which was 10.8% in 1994, declined sharply in the second half of the 1990s and by 2005 sales of coffee contributed less than 1% of Ecuador's export revenue. Coffee accounted for 2.3% of Peru's total export earnings in 2004, 1.8% in 2005, only 0.6% in 2006, but 1.5% in 2007. Nevertheless, Peru's exports exceeded those of any Central American country or Mexico. Venezuela produces a fairly significant amount of coffee, some for export, while Paraguay produces a small amount. Bolivia produces some coffee for local consumption. Guyana, which is not a member of the ICO, grows some coffee as well.

Since the last decades of the 20th century Latin American Arabica production has been inhibited by the coffee berry borer beetle, which has been described as the most damaging pest to coffee world-wide. Endemic to Central Africa, the beetle was first detected in Brazil in 1926. Guatemala and Mexico were affected in the 1970s, followed by Colombia in the late 1980s and the Dominican Republic in the 1990s. It was identified in Puerto Rico in August 2007. The beetle has been estimated to cost Latin American producers US $500m. annually in lost production. Infestation has been particularly acute in Colombia, where, at one time, the beetle, which cannot be effectively eliminated by pesticides, depredated two-thirds of the total area under coffee. From the late 1990s experimental research aimed at eliminating the beetle through biotechnological methods was proceeding in Ecuador, Guatemala, Honduras, Jamaica, Mexico and India.

Effective international attempts to stabilize coffee prices began in 1954, when a number of producing countries made a short-term agreement to fix export quotas. After three such agreements, a five-year International Coffee Agreement (ICA), covering both producers and consumers and introducing a quota system, was signed in 1962. This led to the establishment in 1963 of the ICO, with its headquarters in London, United Kingdom. In October 2009 the International Coffee Council, the highest authority of the ICO, comprised 77 members (45 exporting countries and 32 importing countries). Successive ICAs took effect in 1968, 1976, and 1983. The system of export quotas to stabilize prices was eventually abandoned in July 1989. In October 1993 the USA withdrew from the ICO (it did not rejoin it until 2005), which was increasingly perceived at that time to have been eclipsed by the Association of Coffee Producing Countries (ACPC—see below). In 1994 the ICO agreed provisions for a new ICA, again with primarily consultative and administrative functions, to operate for a five-year period, until September 1999. In November of that year it was agreed to extend this limited ICA until September 2001. A successor ICA took effect provisionally in October 2001, and definitively in May 2005. By May 2007 the new ICA had been endorsed by 74 of the International Coffee Council's 77 members. Among the principal objectives of the 2001 ICA were the promotion of international co-operation with regard to coffee, and the provision of a forum for consultations, both intergovernmental and with the private sector, with the aim of achieving a reasonable balance between world supply and demand in order to guarantee adequate supplies of coffee at fair prices for consumers, and markets for coffee at remunerative prices for producers. A seventh ICA, agreed between the 77 members of the ICC, was formally adopted in September 2007. The new agreement reiterated the objectives contained in the sixth ICA, emphasizing the need to support the advancement of a sustainable coffee economy to benefit small-scale farmers. It established in particular a Consultative Forum of Coffee Sector Finance that was to facilitate access to financial and market information in the coffee sector, and a Promotion and Market Development Committee that was to co-ordinate information campaigns, research and studies.

Production of Green Coffee Beans
('000 bags, each of 60 kg, coffee years)

	2008/09	2009/10
World total*	128,086	120,613
Latin America and the Caribbean*	77,992	70,231
Leading Latin American and Caribbean producers		
Brazil	45,992	39,470
Colombia	8,664	9,000*
Costa Rica	1,320	1,462
Ecuador	691	813
El Salvador	1,547	1,065
Guatemala	3,785	3,500*
Honduras	3,450	3,527*
Mexico	4,651	4,200*
Nicaragua	1,615	1,686*
Peru	3,872	3,315
Other leading producers		
Cameroon	750	690*
Côte d'Ivoire	2,353	1,850*
Ethiopia	4,350	4,500*
India	4,371	4,827
Indonesia	9,350	10,632
Kenya	572	750*
Papua New Guinea	1,028	1,003
Tanzania	1,186	667*
Thailand	675	930*
Uganda	3,200	3,200*
Viet Nam	18,500	18,000*

* Estimated figure(s).

Source: International Coffee Organization.

During each ICA up to and including the one implemented in 1994, contention arose over the allocation of members' export quotas, the operation of price support mechanisms, and, most importantly, illicit sales by some members of surplus stocks to non-members of the ICO (notably to the USSR and to countries in Eastern Europe and the Middle East). These 'leaks' of low-price coffee, often at less than one-half of the official ICA rate, also found their way to consumer members of the ICO through free ports, depressing the general market price and making it more difficult for exporters to fulfil their quotas. The issue of coffee export quotas had become further complicated in the 1980s, as consumers in the main importing market, the USA, and, to a lesser extent, in the EC came to prefer the milder Arabica coffees grown in Central America at the expense of the Robustas exported by Brazil and the main African producers. Disagreements over a new system of quota allocations, taking account of coffee by variety, had the effect of undermining efforts in 1989 to preserve the economic provisions of the ICA, pending the negotiation of a new agreement. The ensuing deadlock between consumers and producers, as well as among the producers themselves, led in July to the collapse of the quota system and the suspension of the economic provisions of the ICA. The administrative clauses of the agreement, however, continued to operate and were subsequently extended until October 1993, pending an eventual settlement of the quota issue and the entry into force of a successor ICA.

With the abandonment of the ICA quotas, coffee prices fell sharply in world markets, and were further depressed by a substantial accumulation of coffee stocks held by consumers. The response by some Latin American producers was to seek to revive prices by imposing temporary suspensions of exports; this strategy, however, merely increased losses of coffee revenue. By early 1992 there had been general agreement among the ICO exporting members that the export quota mechanism should be revived. However, disagreements persisted over the allocation of quotas, and in April 1993 it was announced that efforts to achieve a new ICA with economic provisions had collapsed. In the following month Brazil and Colombia, the two largest coffee producers at that time, were joined by some Central American producers in a scheme to limit their annual coffee production and exports in the 1993/94 coffee year. Although world consumption of coffee exceeded the level of shipments, prices were severely depressed by surpluses of coffee stocks totalling 62m. bags, with an additional 21m. bags held in reserve by consumer countries. Prices, in real terms, stood at historic 'lows'.

In September 1993 the Latin American producers announced the formation of an Association of Coffee Producing Countries (ACPC) to implement an export-withholding, or coffee-retention, plan. In the following month the 25-member Inter-African Coffee Organization (IACO) agreed to join the Latin American producers in a new plan to withhold 20% of output whenever market prices fell below an agreed level. With the participation of Asian producers, a 28-member ACPC, with headquarters in London, was formally established in August. Its signatory member countries numbered 28 in 2001, 14 of which were ratified. Production by the 14 ratified members in 1999/2000 accounted for 61.4% of coffee output world-wide.

The ACPC coffee-retention plan came into operation in October 1993 and gradually generated improved prices; by April 1994 market quotations for all grades and origins of coffee had achieved their highest levels since 1989. Ultimately, however, in spite of this initial success, the ACPC was unable—even with the support of non-members—to bring about lasting price stability by pursuing coffee/export-retention strategy. In September 2001 the ICO daily composite indicator price reached a low point, unseen for decades, averaging 41.17 US cents per lb—the average for the whole year was 45.59 cents per lb, compared with an average of 64.24 cents per lb for the whole of 2000, itself the lowest annual average since 1973. In October 2001 the ACPC announced that it would dissolve itself in January 2002. The Association's relevance had been increasingly compromised by the failure of some of its members to comply with the retention plan in operation at that time, and by some members' inability to pay operating contributions to the group owing to the depressed state of the world market for coffee. Meanwhile, in May 2001 the collapse in the price of coffee had been described as the most serious crisis in a global commodity market since the 1930s, with prices at their lowest level ever in real terms. The collapse of the market was regarded, fundamentally, as the result of an ongoing increase in world production at twice the rate of growth in consumption, this over-supply having led to an overwhelming accumulation of stocks. In this connection, some observers highlighted the role of Viet Nam, which had substantially increased its production and exports of coffee in recent years: by mid-2000 Viet Nam had overtaken Indonesia to become the world's leading supplier of Robusta coffee and was rivalling Colombia as the second largest coffee-producing country overall.

In early July 2001 the price of the Robusta coffee contract for September delivery fell below US $540 per metric ton, marking a record 30-year 'low'. At about the same time the ICO recorded its lowest composite price ever. Despite a recovery beginning in October, the average composite price recorded by the ICO for 2001 was 29% lower than the average composite price recorded in 2000. In 2001 coffee prices were at their lowest level since 1973 in nominal terms, and at a record low level in real terms. Although prices began to recover slowly, the low returns for producers in the early 2000s created what was sometimes called the 'coffee crisis'. In 2005 the average composite price recorded by the ICO, at 89.36 US cents per lb, was 43.8% higher than in 2004, with the price of Robustas recovering strongly. In its review of the 2004/05 crop year the ICO noted that the crisis in the coffee economy of exporting countries had abated somewhat. The ICO composite indicator price continued its steady recovery through the mid-2000s, regaining the levels of the mid-1990s by 2008: 95.75 cents per lb in 2006, 107.68 cents in 2007 and 124.25 cents in 2008.

In common with other commodities, coffee prices were stronger in the first half of 2008, before economic uncertainties set in, although the ICO also attributed the upward trend in its composite average price to a 4% reduction in coffee supply in the second half of 2007, when exports from both Kenya—which consist exclusively of Arabicas—and Uganda were affected by social and political unrest in Kenya. The shortage in supply was exacerbated by producers slowing down exports to take advantage of anticipated sharper increases and by the concomitant intensification of speculative activity on the future market from investment funds. According to the ICO, the composite average price for February 2008, at 138.82 US cents per lb, was the highest since June 1997, but the year ended with an average price of only 103.07 cents per lb in December. The annual average ICO composite price for 2009 was 115.67 cents per lb, indicating a gradual if erratic recovery of prices through the year, after the lows of late 2008. That the 2009 average price had not fallen by more than 6.9% on the previous year's price was largely a result of the strength of the Arabica price—the annual average price for Colombian Mild Arabicas increased by 24.0% and Other Mild Arabicas by 2.9% (the 2009 average price for Robustas fell by a massive 29.2%, and the price for Brazilian Natural Arabicas by 8.9%, on 2008). The Colombian Mild price remained particularly strong into 2010, and the Robusta price stabilized, so that the monthly averages for the ICO composite price, from December 2009, consistently remained above the levels seen since October 2008. Prices surged up in July 2010, for all the four main coffee groups, driven by tight supplies and the efforts of major producers to replenish stocks and, although a record harvest was forecast for the 2010/11 crop year, prices were expected to remain strong at least until the end of 2010. The average July price (daily weighted average) for Colombian Milds was 235.52 cents per lb (up 32.7% on the 2009 average), for Other Milds 203.21 cents per lb (41.3%), Brazilian Naturals 156.87 cents per lb (36.0%) and Robustas 85.27 cents per lb (14.3%), giving an ICO composite price of 153.41 cents per lb (32.6% higher than the average for 2009).

COPPER

The ores containing copper are mainly copper sulphide or copper oxide. They are mined both underground and by open-cast or surface mining. After break-up of the ore body by explosives, the lumps of ore are crushed, ground and mixed with reagents and water, in the case of sulphide ores, and then subjected to a flotation process by which copper-rich minerals are extracted. The resulting concentrate, which contains about 30% copper, is then dried, smelted and cast into anode copper, which is further refined to about 99.98% purity by electrolysis (chemical decomposition by electrical action). The cathodes are then cast into convenient shapes for working or are sold as such. Oxide ores, less important than sulphides, are treated in ways rather similar to the solvent extraction process described below.

Two alternative copper extraction processes have been developed in recent years. The first of these techniques, and as yet of minor importance in the industry, is known as 'Torco' (treatment of refractory copper ores) and is used for extracting copper from silicate ores that were previously not treatable.

The second, and relatively low-cost, technique is the solvent extraction process. This is suited to the treatment of very low-grade oxidized ores and is currently being used on both new ores and waste dumps that have accumulated over previous years from conventional copper working. The copper in the ore or waste material is dissolved in acid, and the copper-bearing leach solution is then mixed with a special organic-containing chemical reagent which selectively extracts the copper. After allowing the two layers to separate, the layer containing the copper is separated from the acid leach solution. The copper is extracted from the concentrated leach solution by means of electrolysis to produce refined cathodes.

Copper is ductile, resists corrosion, and is an excellent conductor of heat and electricity. Its industrial uses are mainly in the electrical industry (about 60% of copper is made into wire for use in power cables, telecommunications, domestic and industrial wiring) and the building, engineering and chemical industries. Bronzes and brasses are typical copper alloys used for both industrial and decorative purposes. There are, however, substitutes for copper in almost all of its industrial uses, and in recent years aluminium has presented a challenge in the electrical and transport industries.

According to the International Copper Study Group (ICSG), mined production of copper world-wide increased steadily in the second half of the 2000s, reaching 15.5m. metric tons in 2008 and a provisional 15.8m. tons in 2009. Using ICSG figures, the US Geological Survey (USGS), the largest single producer in 2009 was Chile, which alone accounted for 34% of global output, followed by Peru (8.0%) and the USA (7.5%). The People's Republic of China (6.1%), Indonesia (6.0%), Australia (5.7%), Russia (4.7%), Zambia (4.1%) and Canada (3.3%) were also important producers. Regionally, Latin America and the Caribbean mined the bulk of world copper (46.8% in 2008), followed by eastern Asia and Oceania (19.6%). Africa provided only 6.1% of world mine output of copper in 2008, but almost three-fifths of its total was from one country, Zambia.

The major copper-importing countries are China, the member states of the European Union (EU), Japan and the USA. According to provisional figures from the ICSG, world-wide usage of refined copper peaked in 2007 at 18.2m. metric tons, decreasing by 1.0% in 2008, to a provisional 18.0m. tons. Production, including secondary output (recovery from scrap), continued to increase in 2008 (by 1.7% compared with 2007), to 18.3m. tons. Consequently, in 2008 the ICSG reckoned that a copper surplus of 238,000 tons was achieved, compared with a deficit of 231,000 tons in 2007. Identified stocks of refined copper throughout the world fell by 104,000 tons during 2007, but increased by 137,000 tons over 2008, to total 1.0m. tons at the end of the year. Provisional data from the ICSG indicated that world-wide usage of refined copper during January–April 2009 reached 5.9m. tons, a decrease of about 2.9% compared with the corresponding period of 2008. Over the same 2009 period total production (primary and secondary) was 5.9m. tons: 1.1% lower than in January–April 2008. As a result, there was a deficit of 37,000 tons in world copper supplies for the first four months of 2009, which was less than in the same period one year earlier, given that fears of global recession had contracted demand faster than it had production. Identified stocks of refined copper at the end of April stood at 1.3m. tons.

Since 1982, when it overtook the USA, Chile—where, according to the USGS, about 30% of world copper reserves are located—has been the world's leading producer of copper. It is also the biggest exporter. The world's three largest copper mines (Chuquicamata, El Teniente and La Escondida) are located within the country. In 1996 La Escondida overtook Chuquicamata as the world's largest copper mine. Production at the Escondida Norte open pit copper mine, which is adjacent to the original Escondida open pit mine, began in 2005. Annual production capacity at the two Escondida facilities rose to 1.25m. metric tons on the completion of Escondida Norte's development—according to the mine operator, output in 2006 was, at a record 1.26m. tons, rising to 1.48m. tons in 2007, representing about 10% of world and some 28% of Chilean production, although it fell back to 1.24m. tons in 2008. According to the USGS, Chile's output of copper rose above 5.0m. tons in 2004, but declined slightly in 2005, to 5.3m. tons. Output in 2006 was put at 5.4m. tons, 5.6m. tons in 2007, 5.3m. tons in 2008 and an estimated 5.3m. tons in 2009 (34% of world production). The Chilean economy relies heavily on the copper industry, and in 2008 copper mine production was estimated to contribute 15.5% of gross domestic product. Total copper exports of 5.4m. tons in that year accounted for about 85% of the total value of all mining exports and 52% of all Chilean exports. Chile's copper industry benefited from the 2004 conclusion of a free trade agreement with the USA and high international prices in the latter years of the decade. Although the industry has been vulnerable to labour unrest and to geographical and climatic adversities, foreign investment in Chilean mining development has risen. The state-owned copper corporation CODELCO is the world's leading copper mining company. Chile also has significant refinery.

Production of Copper Ore
(copper content, '000 metric tons)

	2008	2009*
World total	15,400	15,800
Latin America†	6,847	6,830
Leading Latin American producers		
Chile	5,330	5,320
Mexico	247	250
Peru	1,270	1,260
Other leading producers		
Australia	886	900
Canada	607	520
China, People's Repub.	950	960
Indonesia	651	950
Kazakhstan	420	410
Poland	430	440
Russia	750	750
USA	1,310	1,190
Zambia	546	655

* Estimated production.

† Figures represent the sum of output in listed countries. Smaller quantities of copper-bearing ores are also produced in Argentina, Bolivia, Brazil, Colombia, Cuba, Ecuador and Honduras.

Source: US Geological Survey.

After Chile, the Latin American country to which the copper industry is most important is Peru. Over a decade until the mid-

1990s, however, the industry was adversely affected by the country's economic instability and by guerrilla attacks on the mines. The restoration of relative internal stability, together with the phased privatization of the state-owned mining corporation, Centromín, stimulated foreign investment in mining exploration ventures. In June 1999 it was announced that financing had been secured for the proposed development of the Antamina copper-zinc mine, which began operations in late 2001, and by April 2002 was already the most productive in Peru. In 2005, Antamina's proven and probable ore reserves were assessed at 559m. metric tons. In 2008, according to the Ministry of Energy and Mines, investment by mining companies in Peruvian copper was expected to exceed US $24,700m. Chinese investment had become increasingly evident in the 2000s. Earnings from foreign sales of copper (including copper and copper alloys and copper ores and concentrates), valued at $7,700m., accounted for one-quarter of Peru's total export revenues in 2008. Peru displaced the USA as the world's second largest copper producer in 2007 and (according to provisional estimates) in 2009. The USA, China, Canada and Japan are the major markets for Peru's exports of copper and other metals and minerals.

The development of deposits of copper in Argentina, estimated to total 700m. metric tons, commenced in 1997. In 2008 mined copper output—almost all of it from Minera Alumbrera's Bajo de la Alumbrera facility—totalled a reported 156,900 tons, compared with about 180,200 tons in 2007. In 2007 Brazil's production of copper concentrate totalled 205,728 tons, an increase of 39% compared with the previous year, and in 2008 was estimated to be at similar levels. The leading producers in 2008 were Companhia Vale do Rio Doce (CVRD, now generally known as Vale)—57% of the total, from the Sossego mine in Carajás, Pará—and Mineração Caraíba SA (10%), which exploited deposits located in Bahia. Caraíba Metais was the only producer of electrolytic copper in Brazil in 2008 (almost 220,000 tons, a little up on 2007); the company planned to be producing up to a further 500,000 tons at another plant by 2010. The ongoing feasibility study by CVRD subsidiary Salobo Metais on the Salobo copper project, located at the site of the country's largest copper deposit at Marabá, Pará, was due to be completed in 2011. Salobo was the country's largest copper field, containing estimated ore resources of 928.5m. metric tons, as well as gold deposits. The project's development was soon expected to produce 127,000 tons of copper concentrate per year, from investment of US $1,200m., and 254,000 tons per year upon further investment of $855m. Thus, with other projects, Brazil hoped to achieve self-sufficiency in copper supplies before 2015. In Panama, as of 2009, two of the world's largest copper deposits, one in Cerro Colorado district, Chiriqui province, the other in Cerro Petaquilla district, province of Colon, remained undeveloped. In 2009 Mexico's output of copper recovered slightly, to an estimated 250,000 tons, having fallen to 246,593 tons in 2008 (compared with 429,051 tons as recently as 2005), mainly as a consequence of disputes and industrial action at the country's two leading mines—the Cananea mine in the state of Sonara, operated by Mexicana de Cananea, and Mexicana de Cobre's La Caridad mine. In 2008 copper still accounted for the largest share of the value of Mexican mineral production (21%).

There is no international agreement between producers and consumers governing the stabilization of supplies and prices. Although most of the world's supply of primary and secondary copper is traded direct between producers and consumers, prices quoted on the London Metal Exchange (LME) and the New York Commodity Exchange (COMEX) provide the principal price-setting mechanism for world copper trading.

In 2005 the average settlement price of Grade 'A' copper (minimum purity 99.9935%) traded on the LME was US $3,684 per metric ton, an increase of 28.5% compared with 2004. In the final quarter of 2005 the average price of copper was $4,297 per ton. During the year copper traded within a range of $3,072–$4,650 per ton. Refined stocks of the metal world-wide fell 6.1% on the previous year to some 867,000 tons (on top of a 48% fall the year before), according to the ICSG, with the LME recording its lowest level of stocks for more than 30 years in June. During the second half of 2005, however, stocks recovered steadily. Analysts noted that, unusually, the sustained growth in the price of copper in 2005 had not been accompanied by correspondingly strong growth in global demand, despite the continued rise in Chinese consumption.

The average price of copper traded on the LME rose consistently in each of the first five months of 2006, reaching US $8,045 per metric ton in May. In June, the average price fell, to $7,198 per ton. During the first half of 2006 copper traded within a price range of $4,537–$8,788 per ton. Stagnating production and escalating demand placed upward pressure on international prices. The average price of copper traded on the LME increased by 82.6%, to $6,727 per ton over 2006. International stocks, meanwhile, began to recover, rising to 1.13m. tons.

In 2007 the year's average price of copper traded on the LME reached the height of US $7,126 per metric ton. During the year prices ranged between $5,226 and $8,301 per ton. World stocks of refined copper fell back over the year, ending at 1.03m. tons, although this level was a recovery from earlier in the year.

The average LME copper price for 2008 was US $6,952 per metric ton, owing to the collapse in commodity prices in the last months of the year. During the first four months of 2008 the price of copper traded on the LME rose steadily, from an average of $7,601 per ton in January to an average of $8,685 per ton in April. In May, however, the average price of copper declined to $8,397 per ton. The average price of copper recorded in the first quarter of 2008, at $7,763 per ton, was 7.2% higher than that recorded in the final quarter of 2007 and more than 30% higher than that recorded in the corresponding period of 2007. Daily prices ranged from $6,666 to $8,885 per ton in January–May 2008. According to analysts, key market influences in mid-2008 were, rightly, concern about the prospects of the US economy and static demand from China. Although not as high in real terms as in 1974, the international price of copper remained expensive until September 2008. In April 2008 copper prices had peaked, with a record high of $8,985 per ton, but fears of a global recession gained ground thereafter, particularly from October, when prices plummeted. In November prices were their lowest in three years. At the end of the year, international stocks had increased somewhat, to 1.16m. tons.

In 2009 the average settlement price of copper on the LME was down to US $5,164 per metric ton, because of continuing low prices at the beginning of the year, which offset the later recovery. In fact, the average price over the first four months of 2009 was only $3,673 per ton, compared with $7,361 per ton in the corresponding period in 2010. Generally, prices recovered, strengthened and remained generally high into the first quarter of 2010, although they fell back somewhat from May. According to World Bank figures for the LME average copper price, it was $7,074 per ton in January–July, although the July price was $6,735 per ton. World stocks of refined copper ended 2009 23% up on one year before, at 1.43m. tons, and at the end of April 2010 were 1.51m. tons (31% up on one year previously). Although recovering production in 2010 and 2011 is expected to help satisfy increasing copper usage world-wide, the continuing repercussions of the global recession and the uncertainties of the economic recovery in many of the major markets seemed likely to help maintain copper prices into 2011.

The ICSG, initially comprising 18 producing and importing countries, was formed in 1992 to compile and publish statistical information and to provide an intergovernmental forum on copper. In 2010 ICSG members and observers totalled 21 countries, plus the EU, accounting for more than 80% of world trade in copper. The ICSG, which is based in Lisbon, Portugal, does not participate in trade or exercise any form of intervention in the market.

IRON ORE

The main economic iron-ore minerals are magnetite and haematite, which are used almost exclusively to produce pig-iron and direct-reduced iron (DRI). These comprise the principal raw materials for the production of crude steel. Most iron ore is processed after mining to improve its chemical and physical characteristics, and is often agglomerated by pelletizing or sintering. The transformation of the ore into pig-iron is achieved through reduction by coke in blast furnaces; the proportion of ore to pig-iron yielded is usually about 1.5:1 or 1.6:1. Pig-iron is used to make cast iron and wrought iron products, but most of it is converted into steel by removing most of the carbon content. Particular grades of steel (e.g. stainless) are made by the addition of ferro-alloys such as chromium, nickel and manganese. From the 1990s processing technology was being developed in the use of high-grade ore to produce DRI, which, unlike the iron used for traditional blast furnace operations, requires no melting or refining. The DRI process, which is based on the use of natural gas, has expanded rapidly in Venezuela, but, owing to technological limitations, is not expected within the foreseeable future to replace more than a small proportion of the world's traditional blast-furnace output. In 1998 Mexico overtook Venezuela as the leading producer of DRI.

Iron is, after aluminium, the second most abundant metallic element in the earth's crust, and its ore volume production is far greater than that of any other metal. Some ores contain 70% iron, while a grade of only 25% is commercially exploitable in certain areas. As the basic feedstock for the production of steel, iron ore is a major raw material in the world economy and in international trade. Mining the ore usually involves substantial long-term investment, so about 60% of trade is conducted under long-term contracts, and the mine investments are financed with some participation from consumers.

Iron ore is widely distributed throughout Latin America. Brazil is by far the dominant producer in the region, and its ore is of a high quality (68% iron). In terms of iron content, Brazil was the largest producer in the world, accounting for some 22% of estimated global output in 2007, although by that year the People's Republic of China produced only a little less, exceeding it in 2008 and 2009 (China an estimated 39% of global output by the latter year, Brazil 17%, only a little ahead of Australia). Brazil's vast open-cast mine in the Serra do Carajás began production in 1986. The project was developed by the

Companhia Vale do Rio Doce (CVRD—now known as Vale), which also operates several other mines in the state of Minas Gerais. The Carajás deposit has been stated to contain 18,000m. metric tons of high-grade reserves (66% iron). Improved rail links have facilitated the transportation of iron ore for export from Carajás, in the country's interior. Following the construction of the Igarapava dam, in north-east Minas Gerais, the Carajás complex was expected to become partially self-sufficient in energy. Annual production capacity at Carajás was expanded to 85m. tons in 2006 and to a planned 130 tons from 2010. In all, Vale planned to invest US $18,000m. in the Brazilian mining sector in 2009–13, in order to protect its leading global position in the iron ore industry. In 2008 Vale produced 221.8m. tons of beneficiated iron ore, of a Brazilian total of 351.7m. tons (less than 1% down on the previous year); the next most important companies were Minerações Brasileiras Reunidas—MBR (61.7m. tons), SAMARCO Mineração (16.2m. tons) and Companhia Siderúrgica Nacional—CSN (14.9m. tons). In 2007 MMX Mineração e Metalicos SA had been engaged in the development of a project, together with associated transport infrastructure, to exploit iron ore deposits in the state of Amapá. The company reportedly planned to invest more than $3,500m. in iron ore projects, with the aim of raising total annual output from mines in Amapá, Mato Grosso do Sul and Minas Gerais to some 37m. tons by 2011. Potential development in the future could raise capacity by a further 30m. tons annually. Iron ore is the main mineral export commodity in Brazil, which is the major supplier to the world market after Australia (Brazilian exports briefly exceeded Australia's in the mid-2000s). Sales of iron ore and concentrates provided 8.4% of Brazil's total export earnings in 2008. Brazil also has a major iron and steel industry, primary forms accounting for a further 2.0% of export revenue in 2008.

Production of Iron Ore
(iron content, '000 metric tons)

	2006	2007*
World total	950,000	1,050,000
Latin America	239,769	266,906
Leading Latin American producers		
Brazil	207,524	233,700
Chile	5,235	5,350
Mexico	6,590	7,323
Peru	4,861	5,185
Venezuela	15,200*	15,000
Other leading producers		
Australia	170,934	186,000
Canada†	21,341	20,751
China, People's Repub.*	198,000	233,000
India	102,000*	115,000
Russia	59,100*	60,800
South Africa	26,100*	26,600
Ukraine	40,700*	42,800
USA	33,300	33,100

* Estimated production.

† Including the metal content of by-product ore.

Source: US Geological Survey.

Venezuela has proven reserves of more than 4,000m. metric tons of crude ore. About one-half of total proven reserves is classified as high-grade ore. Iron ore vies with aluminium to be the second most important export industry (after petroleum). In the early 1990s there was installed capacity for the production of as much as 20m. tons annually, but, generally, output declined after 1997. In 2003, however, production of iron ore by Ferrominera Orinoco (FO), the country's sole producer, reached its highest level since 1997. Venezuelan production increased steadily from 2003, when the gross weight of ore shipped amounted to 18.0m. metric tons, to reach an estimated 23.0m. tons by 2006. In May 2007 Orinoco was operating at 70% of capacity, with a monthly output of some 149,249 tons, owing to a shortage of pellets, which helped restrain production in 2007 to the same level as in 2006. In 2008, at some 21m. tons, iron ore output levels were maintained, but in 2009 only an estimated 16m. tons were produced. Sales of iron ore and concentrates provided only 0.3% of Venezuela's total export earnings in 2000. Sales of iron and steel, however, provided 2.7% of total export revenue in that year, and 3.1% in 2001. The contribution of foreign sales of iron and steel to total export revenue rose to 4.1% in 2002, 4.2% in 2003 and 5.1% in 2004, but fell to 4.3% in 2005, 2.8% in 2006, owing to lower commodity prices, and 1.9% in 2007.

In 2005 Mexico's output of iron totalled some 7.0m. metric tons. The largest mine in operation that year was Peña Colorado, in the state of Colima, with an annual capacity of 3.5m. tons. Production was estimated to have declined slightly, to about 6.6m. tons, in 2006, with a reported recovery in 2007 to 7.3m. tons, although later figures put the actual figure for 2007 slightly lower than in the previous year, at a little less than 6.6m. tons, postponing the recovery until 2007, when mine output (metal content) was 7.0m. tons.

In 2009, on the basis of data compiled by the UN Conference on Trade and Development (UNCTAD) Trust Fund on Iron Ore, world exports of iron ore decreased, after seven successive years of increase, by 6.2%, to some 1,600m. metric tons (crude ore). Based on converted iron ore content, the largest producer in 2009 was Australia (394m. tons), followed by Brazil (300m. tons) and India (257m. tons), while China had fallen right back into fourth place, with 234m. tons. Iron ore exports continued to expand in 2009, however, world exports reaching 955m. tons, 7.4% up on 2008. The Americas accounted for 40% of total world exports of iron ore in 2006, followed by Oceania, with 33%. In regional terms, Africa was the least significant exporter, contributing only 5% of total world exports. Iron ore exports globally doubled between 1999 and 2008, mainly owing to increased demand from China, which was the leading importer of iron ore. In 2008 China received 49% of total world imports—or 444m. tons, an increase of 16% compared with 2007. Japan (the second largest importer) was the destination for 140m. tons, an increase of 1.1% compared with 2007. The largest iron ore companies in the world are Vale, Rio Tinto and BHP Billiton, which accounted for 35.4% of global iron ore production in 2009, up slightly on the year before. The three companies are even more significant in export markets, controlling 61% of the world seaborne trade of iron ore.

Until 2010 world reference prices for iron ore were decided annually at a series of meetings between producers and purchasers (the steel industry accounts for about 95% of all iron ore consumption), but when China failed to agree prices with major producers in 2009, and with 'spot' prices for iron ore soaring in the latter half of the year when miners were still selling at prices agreed in March, the system effectively collapsed. The USA and the republics of the former USSR, although major steel producers, rely on domestic ore production and had taken little part in the price negotiations. It was generally accepted that, because of its diversity in form and quality, iron ore was ill-suited to price stabilization through an international buffer stock arrangement. Given the complexity of the old pricing system, a general trend can be indicated from the prices cited by the World Bank. The average contract price to Europe for Brazilian iron ore (f.o.b., Ponta da Madeira) in 2008 was 140.6 US cents per dry metric ton unit, or US $94.91 per dry metric ton (multiplying by the percentage of metal content, which is 67.50% in 2005 to 2010—i.e. by 0.675—converts the price in cents per dry metric ton unit to a price in dollars per dry metric ton). The average price in 2008 was $67.18 per ton in 2009 and $93.62 per ton in January–July 2010. The average quarterly prices changed from $67.18 per ton throughout 2009 and into 2010 until the second quarter of the latter year, when the average price changed to $112.73 per ton (which still pertained in July). Falling Chinese production had not abated the country's expanding need for iron, which helped maintain iron ore prices. Although new production capacity was being added steadily around the world (75m. tons in 2009), supply remained tight and, while prices were likely to relax into 2011, they were still strong in the first half of 2010 and unlikely to lapse beyond 2008 levels thereafter. The 40-year-old annual series of bench mark negotiations to determine iron ore prices finally ended in early 2010. Even the commercially dominant Chinese steel companies, as well as the Japanese and European steel industry organizations, could not resurrect the process, which was replaced by a general model of quarterly semi-negotiated prices. Criticism of the new system in the iron ore market concerns the inherent uncertainties and the lack of transparency, according to UNCTAD Trust Fund on Iron Ore: price settlements were no longer announced and the published 'spot' prices are still not fully reliable.

The Association of Iron Ore Exporting Countries (Association des Pays Exportateurs de Minerai de Fer—APEF) was established in 1975 to promote close co-operation among members, to safeguard their interests as iron ore exporters, to ensure the orderly growth of international trade in iron ore and to secure 'fair and remunerative' returns from its exploitation, processing and marketing. Since 1975 APEF, which also collects and disseminates information on iron ore from its secretariat in Geneva, Switzerland, has had nine members: Algeria, Australia, Chile, India, Mauritania, Peru, Sierra Leone, Tunisia and Venezuela. UNCTAD compiles statistics on iron ore production and trade, and in recent years has sought to establish a permanent international forum for discussion of issues affecting the industry.

MAIZE (Indian Corn, Mealies) (*Zea mays*)

Maize is one of the world's three principal cereal crops, with wheat and rice. The main varieties are dent maize (which has large, soft, flat grains) and flint maize (which has round, hard grains). Dent maize is the predominant type world-wide, but flint maize is widely grown in southern Africa and parts of South America. Maize may be white or yellow (there is little nutritional difference) but the former is preferred for human consumption. Native to the Americas, maize was brought to Europe by Christopher Columbus and has since been dispersed to many parts of the world. It is an annual crop, planted from seed, and matures within three to five months. It requires a warm climate and ample water supplies during the growing season. Genetically modified varieties of maize, with improved resistance to pests, are now being cultivated, particularly in the USA and also in Argentina and the People's Republic of China. However, further development of genetically modified maize may be slowed by consumer resistance in importing countries and doubts about its possible environmental impact.

Maize is an important food source in regions such as sub-Saharan Africa and the tropical zones of Latin America, where the climate precludes the extensive cultivation of other cereals. It is, however, inferior in nutritive value to wheat, being especially deficient in lysine, and tends to be replaced by wheat in diets when the opportunity arises. As food for human consumption, the grain is ground into meal, or it can be made into (unleavened) corn bread and breakfast cereals. In Latin America maize meal is made into cakes, called tortillas. Maize is also the source of an oil used in cooking.

The high starch content of maize makes it highly suitable as a compound feed ingredient, especially for pigs and poultry. Animal feeding is the main use of maize in the USA, Europe and Japan, and large amounts are also used for feed in developing countries in the Far East Asia, Latin America and, to some extent, in North Africa. Maize has a large variety of industrial uses, including the preparation of ethyl alcohol (ethanol), which may be added to petrol to produce a blended motor fuel. Maize is also a source of dextrose and fructose, which can be used as artificial sweeteners, many times sweeter than sugar. The amounts of maize used for these purposes depend, critically, on its price to the users relative to those of petroleum, sugar and other potential raw materials. Maize cobs, previously regarded as a waste product, may be used as feedstock to produce various chemicals (e.g. acetic acid and formic acid).

Since 2000 global production has averaged about 670m. metric tons annually. From 2006 the world maize crop grew steadily, to reach a record 823m. tons in 2008 (FAO figure). The USA is by far the largest producer, with annual harvests of, on average, about 270m. tons in 2000–07; the 2006 harvest of 270m. tons increasing to 331m. tons in 2007, before contracting to 307m. tons in 2008. (In years of drought or excessive heat, however, US output can fall significantly: in 1995, for example, the maize crop totalled only 188m. tons.) In the crop year 2009/10 US output accounted for 41% of global maize production, according to the US Department of Agriculture (USDA). China, whose maize output has been expanding rapidly, is the second largest producer—its harvest averaged about 133m. tons annually in 2000–08, reaching a height of 166m. tons in the final year of that series. China's production, however, is mainly destined for the domestic market, whereas US output makes the country the world's largest exporter by far (a low 57% of global exports in 2009/10). Argentina (16% in 2009/10) and Brazil (9%) follow, with Ukraine emerging in a clear fourth place in 2008/09 (6% in 2009/10) and forecast to maintain the position into 2010/11 at least.

Maize production in Latin America and the Caribbean increased rapidly from the early 1990s, stabilized in the second half of that decade and began to rise again in the early 2000s. In 2008 production was estimated to have totalled some 120m. metric tons, compared with 109m. metric tons in 2007. In most years, three countries—Argentina, Brazil and Mexico—between them account for a clear majority of the region's annual maize crop (about 88% in 2008). Brazil is the largest producer, with output totalling an estimated 59.0m. tons in 2008. In the north and north-east of the country, which account for about 10% of Brazil's production, maize is an important food for human consumption, and is largely grown by subsistence farmers. The droughts to which these regions are prone can occasion considerable hardship. Most of Brazil's maize is grown commercially for use as animal feed in the centre and south of the country. Production there varies according to the amount of government support (mostly in the form of subsidized credit) and the prices of alternative crops, especially oilseeds. Although Brazil's animal feed requirements are growing rapidly, many of the feed mills are located in the far south of the country, where maize supplies may be obtained more cheaply from Argentina than from domestic sources. Brazil's maize imports increased in the second half of the 2000s, totalling 1.1m. tons in 2008/09 and 0.7m. tons in 2009/10 (compared with exports of 7.2m. tons and 7.5m. tons, respectively), according to USDA.

Mexico is usually Latin America's second largest maize producer, with harvests averaging about 21m. metric tons annually in 2000–08. Much of the Mexican crop consists of white corn rather than the yellow variety. The establishment of CIMMYT (Centro Internacional del Mejoramiento de Maíz y Trigo—the International Wheat and Maize Improvement Centre) at Sonora, in northern Mexico, has made the country the testing-ground for many of the technical advances in the development of different maize varieties since the 1960s. Local production, however, has been hampered by the small size of most agricultural holdings, competition for irrigated land from other crops, and the inability of small producers to afford enough fertilizers. Shortages of irrigation water commonly result in poor crops. Maize in Mexico is mainly used for human consumption, particularly in the form of tortillas. Domestic maize is mostly reserved for this purpose, with animal feed manufacturers traditionally preferring to use sorghum and, increasingly, yellow corn imported from the USA.

Policy changes implemented since the 1980s, with the aim of completely liberalizing the agricultural sector by 2008, have affected maize production and consumption trends in Mexico. The Compañía Nacional de Subsistencias Populares (CONASUPO), the parastatal food distribution company that traditionally supported the maize market by purchasing 20% of the annual crop at subsidized prices, was dismantled, while controls on the prices of tortillas—a staple food in Mexico—were removed. Annual imports of cheaper, US-produced white maize have increased since the inception of the North American Free Trade Agreement (NAFTA) in 1994, and have made a further contribution towards discouraging local farmers from maize production. While the volume of Mexican maize production remained stable in 1994–2006, imports of maize more than doubled during the same period. According to USDA, in the 2005/06 crop year Mexico's imports of maize totalled about 6.8m. metric tons. As part of the Government's response to the so-called 'tortilla crisis' in early 2007 (when a shortage of maize in the country and a concomitant sharp increase in the price of tortillas provoked mass protests), imports rose by 32%, to 8.9m. tons in 2006/07. In 2007/08 imports increased by a further 8%, to an estimated 9.7m. tons, but fell back to 8.0m. tons in 2009/10.

Argentina is Latin America's most substantial maize-exporting country, and, in world terms, ranks second only to the USA in amounts sold—Brazil is third in the world, and Paraguay too conducts a healthy export trade. Market liberalization in the early 1990s, particularly the abolition of export taxes, encouraged maize production in Argentina. Farmers were able to plan their activities more rationally, and to make longer-term investments in land improvement and up-to-date equipment. At the same time, privatization and decontrol of the ports and transport systems resulted in much greater efficiency in grain movement. However, farmers are no longer shielded from international price trends, and the low prices of the late 1990s caused many to switch from maize to oilseeds or other more profitable crops. Argentina's maize production was 21.8m. metric tons in 2007, compared with only 14.4m. tons in 2006, and 22.0m. tons in 2008. Commercial plantings of genetically modified maize started in 1999. In 2007/08 Argentina exported 15.7m. tons of maize, but only 8.5m. tons in the following year (compared with Brazil's 7.2m. tons—Brazil's much larger production is largely for domestic consumption, but exports expanded after 2006). Exports recovered to 14.0m. tons in 2009/10.

Maize is grown widely as a subsistence crop in Central America. It is one of the most important foods in El Salvador and Guatemala, where consumption per head is around 100 kg per year. In South America food use is generally declining, although it remains important in some countries, notably Bolivia, Colombia, Paraguay and Venezuela, in each of which consumption averages 40–50 kg per year.

Production of Maize
('000 metric tons)

	2007	2008
World total*	788,112	822,713
Latin America and the Caribbean*	112,180	120,232
Leading Latin American producers		
Argentina	21,755	22,017
Bolivia	770	770*
Brazil	52,112	59,018
Chile	1,123	1,365
Colombia	1,733	1,727
Ecuador	945	805
El Salvador	837	1,000
Guatemala	1,294	1,294*
Mexico	23,513	24,320
Paraguay	1,900	1,900
Peru	1,362	1,362*
Venezuela	2,571	2,571*
Other leading producers		
Canada	11,649	10,592
China, People's Repub.	152,419	166,035
Egypt	6,243	6,544
France	14,357	15,819
Hungary	4,027	8,963
India	18,955	19,290
Indonesia	13,288	16,324

—continued	2007	2008
Italy	9,809	9,491
Nigeria	6,724	7,525
Philippines	6,737	6,928
Romania	3,854	7,849
South Africa	7,125	11,597
Ukraine	7,421	11,447
USA	331,175	307,384

* FAO estimate(s).

The world's principal maize importer is Japan. However, the volume of Japanese imports remained stable through the 2000s, as the domestic livestock industry was rationalized to compete with imported meat. Japanese imports of maize totalled about 16.3m. metric tons in 2009/10. Rapidly growing livestock industries elsewhere in eastern Asia made the region the major world market for maize, although in terms of individual countries Mexico sometimes challenges the Republic of Korea (South Korea) for the title of second largest importer: 8.0m. tons and 8.2m. tons, respectively, in 2009/10). Feed users in South Korea are willing to substitute other grains for maize, particularly feed wheat, when prices are attractive, so that maize imports are variable. Taiwan regularly imported about 5.0m. tons of maize annually in the first half of the 2000s, but more like 4.5m. tons on average in the second half of the decade, so Egypt overtook it, importing 5.0m. tons in 2009/10.

Export prices of maize are mainly influenced by the level of supplies and demand in the USA, and the intensity of competition between the exporting countries. Record quotations were achieved in April 1996, when the price of US No. 2 Yellow Corn (f.o.b. Gulf ports) reached US $210 per metric ton. The quotation subsequently declined, however. In each of the five years in 2000–04 an increase in the quotation was recorded, the average price reaching $111.7 in 2004. In 2005 the average export price declined to $98.5 per ton. However, the price began to rise again in 2006, averaging $122.1 per ton over the year. This was attributed to, largely, the increased use of maize for the production of ethanol in the USA and Europe. Prices continued to increase in 2007, to $162.65 per metric ton, rising to $223.13 in 2008, as global stocks fell to a 24-year low at the end of the 2007/08 crop year, despite a 9.5% increase in global production and a 24% increase in US output. The global recession that had gained momentum by the end of 2008 restrained prices in 2009, so that the average US No. 2 Yellow Corn price for the year fell to $165.64. The average for the first seven months of 2010 was $160.70, although expectations were for prices to be maintained. Maize and grain prices were generally projected to increase in line with the expanding market for ethanol, which is closely linked to the price of petroleum. New energy legislation in 2007, in both the European Union and the USA, stipulated the greater use of biofuels for motor vehicles. According to the World Bank, the share of global maize production used for ethanol increased from 2.5% in 2000 to 11.0% in 2007, and the trend remained evident thereafter. However, maize-based ethanol production remained a heavily subsidized industry in the USA, and it remained a costly and relatively inefficient substitute for its sugar-based equivalent (see below). Critics remained sceptical regarding the long-term prospects for the industry, especially as sugar-based ethanol was already being produced more cheaply in Latin America.

PETROLEUM

Crude oils, from which petroleum is derived, consist essentially of a wide range of hydrocarbon molecules which are separated by distillation in the refining process. Refined oil is treated in different ways to make the different varieties of fuel. More than four-fifths of total world oil supplies are used as fuel for the production of energy in the form of power or heating.

Petroleum, together with its associated mineral fuel, natural gas, is extracted both from onshore and offshore wells in many areas of the world. It is the leading raw material in international trade. Worldwide, demand for this commodity totalled an estimated 84.1m. barrels per day (b/d) in 2009, a decline—only the second recorded since 1993—of 1.4% compared with the previous year. The world's 'published proven' reserves of petroleum and natural gas liquids at 31 December 2009 were estimated to total 181,700m. metric tons, equivalent to about 1,333,000m. barrels (1 metric ton is equivalent to approximately 7.3 barrels, each of 42 US gallons or 34.97 imperial gallons, i.e. 159 litres). The dominant producing region is the Middle East, whose proven reserves in December 2009 accounted for 56.1% of known world deposits of crude petroleum, gas condensate and natural gas liquids. The Middle East accounted for 30.5% of world output in 2009. Latin America (including Mexico) contained 30,100m. tons of proven reserves (16.6% of the world total) at the end of 2009, and accounted for 12.7% of world production in that year.

From storage tanks at the oilfield wellhead, crude petroleum is conveyed, frequently by pumping for long distances through large pipelines, to coastal depots where it is either treated in a refinery or delivered into bulk storage tanks for subsequent shipment for refining overseas. In addition to pipeline transportation of crude petroleum and refined products, natural (petroleum) gas is, in some areas, also transported through networks of pipelines. The properties of different crude petroleums (e.g. colour, viscosity, etc.) vary considerably, and these variations are a determinant both of price and of end-use after refining.

In the refining process, crude petroleum is heated until vaporized. The vapours are then separately condensed, according to their molecular properties, passed through airless steel tubes and pumped into the lower section of a high, cylindrical tower, as a hot mixture of vapours and liquid. The heavy unvaporized liquid flows out at the base of the tower as a 'residue' from which is obtained heavy fuel and bitumen. The vapours passing upwards then undergo a series of condensation processes that produce 'distillates', which form the basis of the various petroleum products.

The most important of these products is fuel oil, composed of heavy distillates and residues, which is used to produce heating and power for industrial purposes. Products in the kerosene group have a wide number of applications, ranging from heating fuels to the powering of aviation gas turbine engines. Gasoline (petrol) products fuel internal combustion engines (principally in road motor vehicles), and naphtha, a gasoline distillate, is a commercial solvent that can also be processed as a feedstock. Propane and butane, the main liquefied petroleum gases, have a wide range of industrial applications and are also used for domestic heating and cooking.

Mexico's oil industry was nationalized in 1938 and it remains in the control of a government agency, Petróleos Mexicanos—PEMEX—which is divided into four subsidiaries, with responsibility, respectively, for exploration and production, natural gas and basic petrochemicals, petrochemicals, and refining. In 2008, with the aim of arresting an ongoing decline in national oil production (see below), the Government enacted a number of reforms, including the extension of seats on PEMEX's administrative board to external oil industry specialists, the establishment of an advisory board with long-term strategic functions, and the creation of a regulatory authority for the sector. Other measures granted PEMEX a greater degree of flexibility *vis-à-vis* procurement and investment. Mexico was the world's leading petroleum producer in 1921, but by 1938 output had fallen dramatically.The discovery of extensive deposits of petroleum in the states of Tabasco and Chiapas, and off shore in the Bay of Campeche, enabled output to increase significantly in the 1970s. However, the country's reserves of petroleum and other hydrocarbons are now in decline. In 2004, in terms of oil equivalence, according to the US Geological Survey (USGS), reserves had fallen by 17% compared with 1999. Mexico's proven reserves of petroleum stood at 1,600m. metric tons at the end of 2009. In 2009 about 80% of Mexico's crude oil was sourced off shore, in the Gulf of Campeche. The country's largest oilfield, and one of the largest in the world, is the Cantarell field, but production there is now in steep decline. In 2004, according to the Energy Information Administration (EIA) of the US Department of Energy, Cantarell contributed about 62% of Mexico's total output of crude oil. In 2008 Cantarell was the source of only 24% of total production. Output from the Cantarell field in 2009 was 38% lower than in 2008, according to the EIA, and 70% lower than at its peak, in 2004. Thanks to a nitrogen re-injection programme, output from the Ku-Maloob-Zaap (KMZ) production centre—also located in the Gulf of Campeche—has compensated to some extent for that lost from Cantarell. KMZ's output reportedly doubled in 2006–09—but production there, too, is forecast to peak in the near future. Output from onshore fields contributes only about one-fifth of Mexico's total production of crude petroleum, but it is hoped that this may be boosted by the development of the Chicontepec project, which comprises 29 oilfields located north-east of Mexico City. In 2009 output from Chicontepec reportedly amounted to some 30,000 b/d, and PEMEX aims to increase this to 700,000 b/d by 2017. In 2008 tenders were invited to drill 1,000 wells at Chicontepec; this was followed, in 2009, by an invitation for bids to drill more than 150 development wells there. The heavy crude Maya generally accounts for about 60% of total Mexican production, with the remainder comprising the lighter crudes Isthmus and Olmeca. Mexico was the world's seventh largest producer of petroleum in 2009, with estimated output of 147.5m. tons, a decline of 6.5% compared with 2008. Mexico's foreign sales of petroleum largely comprise heavy crude, with the country retaining the lighter grades produced for domestic consumption. In 2007 exports totalled some 653m. barrels, of which the USA was the destination for about 95%. In 2008, according to the EIA, exports of petroleum totalled some 511m. barrels, of which about 86% was destined for the USA. Foreign sales reportedly fell to some 450m. barrels in 2009, the USA receiving about 89% of the total. Mexico is usually one of the USA's three leading suppliers of crude petroleum—the others are Canada and Saudi Arabia. In 2009 Mexico ranked second, after Canada. The largest of Mexico's six oil refineries is the Salina Cruz complex, which has a capacity of 330,000 b/d. In 2009 PEMEX announced plans to construct, at a cost of some $10,000m., a seventh refinery at Tula, in the state of Hidalgo. Work on the new facility is scheduled to commence in 2011. The Tula plant is to be specially adapted to refine Mexico's heavy crudes, with the aim of reducing the country's continued reliance—despite its high ranking in world terms as a producer of crude oil—on imports of refined petroleum products, of which it remains a net purchaser. Imports totalled about 190m. barrels in 2009, while exports amounted to some 90m. barrels. Gasoline accounted for about 60% of Mexico's total refined imports in 2009.

With 1,800m. metric tons at the end of 2009, Brazil had the second largest national petroleum resource in the region, after that of Venezuela. It is anticipated that Brazilian reserves will continue to rise as Petróleo Brasileiro (Petrobras), the state-owned petroleum company, will make substantial investments in exploration—for both petroleum and natural gas—up to 2012. The offshore (Santos Basin) Tupi oilfield, the discovery of which was announced in 2006, has been described by Petrobras as comparable with the most important fields already in production world-wide, constituting a recoverable resource of 5,000m.–8,000m. barrels. The Tupi field—and others like it that were discovered subsequently—has further significance for exploration in that, unlike Brazil's older oilfields, it is located in a geological formation referred to as the sub-salt layer and comprises lighter, sweeter crude than has hitherto, for the most part, been located in the country. While they have not accepted Petrobras' assessment of these sub-salt layer resources without reservation, analysts have acknowledged the potential of the Tupi and similar fields to wreak a huge impact on world markets for oil. In 2009 Petrobras commenced an extended test at the Tupi field, with the aim of achieving initial annual output of about 5m. barrels as well as elaborating production methods suitable for pre-salt resources. The extended well test represents the first of three phases into which the development of pre-salt resources—both at Tupi and elsewhere—has been divided in a strategic plan published by Petrobras in 2009. In that year details of how the Government proposed to regulate the country's pre-salt reserves were also announced. These include new production-sharing agreements (PSAs) rather than the concessions that have been employed for existing resources. The creation of a new agency—Petrosal—is also envisaged to manage a Petrobras stake of at least 30% in each PSA. Revenues accruing to the Government from the development of the pre-salt reserves are to be channelled into a development fund. Finally, a new law will permit the Government to capitalize Petrobras by allocating it pre-salt reserves that are unlicensed at present. Brazil's current production is already overwhelmingly focused on deep-water reserves off shore in the state of Rio de Janeiro. Potential output has been boosted considerably by the completion of production/expansion projects undertaken by Petrobras at, in 2006, the Albacore Leste, Golfinho and Jubarte fields, and, in 2007, at the Piranema and Espadarte fields. In 2009 Brazil's production of crude petroleum amounted to an estimated 100.4m. metric tons, an increase of about 7% compared with 2008. Annual output rose consistently in 1999–2009 (with the exception of 2004, when a small decline was recorded), and the EIA forecast in September 2009 that the Brazilian Government would achieve its aim of transforming the country into a net exporter of petroleum in that year. Petrobras operates 11 of the country's 13 petroleum refineries. National refining capacity at September 2009 was, at some 1.9m. b/d, by far the largest in the region. The largest refinery is the Paulínia facility, operated by Petrobras in São Paulo, which has a daily capacity of 360,000 barrels. In 2007 Petrobras began preparatory work for the construction of a new, 230,000 b/d refinery ('Abreu e Lima') in the north-eastern state of Pernambuco. The project, whose cost has been estimated at US $12,000m., was initially intended to be undertaken as a joint venture with Petróleos de Venezuela SA (PDVSA), with each partner providing one-half of the refinery's new feedstock. However, as of September 2009 the terms of the joint venture had still not been finalized. Overall, Brazil aims to raise national refining capacity to 3m. b/d by 2020. Brazil has aimed to increase its capacity for refining the predominantly heavy crudes that it produces. Although the country's production of these crudes has risen steadily in recent years, it remains insufficient to meet domestic demand and has to be supplemented by imports of lighter crudes. Brazil is also an exporter of heavy crudes to, for example, the People's Republic of China. Petrobras's monopoly of the Brazilian petroleum sector was ended in 1997 by the adoption of legislation allowing private sector investment in all parts of the industry. At the same time, a National Petroleum Agency (Agência National do Petróleo) was established. These and other reforms of the sector were undertaken as part of Brazil's pursuit of self-sufficiency in petroleum supply. Foreign participation has proceeded slowly, however, and Petrobras remains by far the country's dominant producer. The Bijupira-Salema oilfield, in the Campos Basin, where Royal Dutch Shell commenced production in 2003, was the first Brazilian oilfield to be operated independently of Petrobras, while Devon Energy's Polvo field, where output began in 2007, was the first Brazilian upstream project in which Petrobras had no participation. In 2009 other foreign oil companies that were actively engaged on projects in Brazil included Chevron and StatoilHydro. Private competition is not, however, confined to foreign oil companies. In 2008 a Brazilian firm, OGX, was reported to have bid successfully for concessions in the country's ninth round of licensing.

The production of petroleum is the dominant economic activity in Venezuela. In 2008, according to the USGS, the value of the country's petroleum exports amounted to US $62,500m., representing about 90% of the total value of the country's export earnings, and petroleum revenues contributed about 30% of gross domestic product (GDP) and some 50% of federal budget revenues. The country is consistently one of the four leading suppliers of petroleum to the USA. In 2009 Venezuela ranked as the USA's third largest supplier, shipping 1.1m. b/d of crude petroleum. Exports of crude petroleum and petroleum products amounted to 1.19m. b/d in 2008, with petroleum products accounting for 149,000 b/d of the total. Venezuela supplied about 9% of the USA's total petroleum imports (including derivatives) in 2008. According to the Energy Information Administration (EIA) of the US Department of Energy, the country ranked eighth among the world's leading net exporters of petroleum in 2008. In both 2007 and 2008 Venezuela's petroleum exports (net) averaged about 1.9m. b/d. In addition to the USA, Venezuela finds markets for its oil elsewhere in South America, in Europe and in the Caribbean. China has gained rapidly in significance as an outlet for Venezuelan crude in recent years: in 2008, according to the EIA, China's imports totalled some 44m. barrels, compared with about 14m. barrels in 2005. Venezuela also supplies crude petroleum and derivatives on favourable terms (including discounted prices) to a number of neighbouring, Caribbean and Central American countries. Under another agreement, Venezuela supplies Cuba with some 30m. barrels of crude petroleum and petroleum products annually. In 2009, when Venezuela accounted for 25.7% of Latin American production, it ranked as the world's eighth largest producer. The country's proven reserves were estimated at 24,800m. metric tons at the end of 2009. In 1992, for the first time since the nationalization of PDVSA in 1976, exploration and production were opened up to foreign participation, via PDVSA subsidiary Corporación Venezolana de Petróleo (CVP). Since 1998, however, the Government of President Hugo Chávez Frías has significantly modified policy in respect of foreign companies' involvement in the country's petroleum sector. New hydrocarbons legislation adopted in 2001 stipulated, among other provisions, that PDVSA must take a 51% share in all new production and exploration projects; and that in future joint ventures would supersede existing operating service agreements, risk/profit-sharing agreements and strategic associations as the only permitted vehicles for foreign participation. According to the EIA, the conversion of all joint ventures, risk/profit-sharing agreements and strategic associations—which had been transferred from PDVSA to CVP in 2003—had been completed by the end of 2007. Investment in the oil sector has subsequently been sought from foreign national oil companies, including those of China and Russia. In 2004 PDVSA announced plans to invest $26,000m. in oil (and natural gas) exploration and production activities in 2004–09. Petroleum resources that have been estimated to amount to as much as 270,000m. barrels in Venezuela's Orinoco Belt are currently the focus of much development effort, via the so-called 'Magna Reserva' programme, for which PDVSA's partners include the national oil companies of Brazil, Iran, China and India—respectively, Petrobras, Petropars (a wholly owned subsidiary of the National Iranian Oil Co), China National Petroleum Corpn (CNPC) and Oil and Natural Gas Corpn Ltd. In late 2008 Venezuela invited bids for the development of extra-heavy oil resources at three projects extending over seven blocks in the Carabobo area. In early 2010 it was announced that Repsol YPF of Spain had tendered successfully for Carabobo 1, while a Chevron-led consortium was awarded Carabobo 3. Carabobo 2 remained allocated. Industry sources assessed Venezuela's domestic petroleum-refining capacity in 2010 at some 1.3m. b/d. This was supplemented by additional capacity overseas, including in the USA and Europe. PDVSA is reportedly collaborating in a joint venture with Petrobras of Brazil to construct a new refinery in the north-eastern (Brazilian) state of Pernambuco (see above). As of September 2009, however, the terms of the joint venture had still to be finalized.

Production of Crude Petroleum

('000 metric tons, including natural gas liquids)

	2008	2009
World total	3,934,700	3,820,500
Latin America and the Caribbean	493,200	486,000
Leading Latin American and Caribbean producers		
Argentina	34,100	33,800
Brazil	93,900	100,400
Colombia	30,500	34,100
Ecuador	26,200	25,200
Mexico	157,700	147,500
Peru	5,300	6,400
Trinidad and Tobago	6,900	6,800
Venezuela	131,500	124,800

—continued	2008	2009
Other leading producers		
Algeria	85,600	77,600
Angola	92,200	87,400
Canada	157,700	155,700
China, People's Repub.	195,100	189,000
Iran	209,900	202,400
Iraq	119,300	121,800
Kuwait	137,200	121,300
Libya	85,300	77,100
Nigeria	103,100	99,100
Norway	114,100	108,300
Russia	488,500	494,200
Saudi Arabia	515,300	459,500
United Arab Emirates	137,300	120,600
United Kingdom	71,700	68,000
USA	304,900	325,300

Source: BP, *Statistical Review of World Energy 2010*.

Ecuador's petroleum industry has been a significant contributor to the economy since 1972, when petroleum was exported for the first time, after the completion of the 480-km (300-mile) trans-Andean pipeline, linking the oilfields of Oriente Province with the tanker-loading port of Esmeraldas. The country's most important oilfields lie in the north east of the country, and, of these, Shushufindi, operated by state-owned Petroecuador, is the largest, providing about 9% of total output. Petroecuador is the country's most important producer of crude, accounting for 51% of total output in 2007. However, private producers have begun to play a greater part in the sector, and Petroecuador's production has declined in recent years. The most significant private producers are foreign-owned. Spain's Repsol YPF is the largest private foreign oil company active in Ecuador, accounting, as of early 2009, according to the EIA, for about 13% of the country's total output of crude. CNPC is also active in Ecuador, leading a consortium (Andes Petroleum) that purchased production and pipeline assets in 2005. In the first half of 2007 Andes Petroleum accounted for 12% of total crude production. Perenco and Italy's Agip have also entered the sector, although Perenco's contracts were cancelled in 2010 after the Government claimed the company had failed to fulfil the terms they contained. Having declined significantly in 2001–05, Petroecuador's share of national production was boosted in 2006 as a result of the company's takeover of the production assets of Occidental Petroleum. The Government had alleged, prior to the takeover, that Occidental had failed to meet contractual obligations by transferring assets to another oil company. A legal claim by Occidental for compensation totalling US $3,200m. in respect of the takeover remained unresolved as of mid-2010. Ecuador's output of crude comprises two varieties: Oriente, a medium-heavy, medium-sour grade; and Napo, a heavy, sour crude. As of early 2009 Ecuador's three refineries had a total capacity of some 176,000 b/d. In 2008, as part of its effort to reduce the country's dependence on foreign supplies of refined petroleum products, of which it is a net importer, the Government concluded an agreement with Venezuela and established a joint venture for the construction of a new refinery in Manabi province, with daily capacity of 300,000 barrels. Operations at the new refinery, the cost of which has been estimated at $7,000m., are expected to begin in 2013. The upgrading of Ecuador's three existing refineries is also pending, most notably that of the largest, the 100,000 b/d facility at Esmeraldas, which South Korea's SK Engineering is contracted to undertake at an estimated cost of $200m. In September 2003 the entry into operation of the Oleoducto de Crudos Pesados (OCP), the country's second pipeline, raised Ecuador's potential oil transportation capacity to 850,000 b/d. OCP links oilfields in the Amazon region with port facilities on the Pacific Ocean and has a maximum capacity of 450,000 b/d. More than 50% of Ecuador's exports of petroleum and petroleum derivatives are destined for the USA, of which it was the third largest Latin American supplier after Mexico and Venezuela in 2009. In that year, according to the EIA, Ecuador exported, on average, about 221,000 b/d of crude oil and refined products to the USA, thus supplying about 2% of all US oil imports in that year. Ecuador's proven published reserves of petroleum at the end of 2009 amounted to 900m. metric tons. Petroleum and petroleum products accounted for 36.3% of export revenue in 1996, but by 1998 the proportion had declined to 23.6%, reflecting lower prices. Their contribution has subsequently risen steadily, to total about 64% in 2008. The oil industry generally accounts for about one-third of all tax revenue accruing to the Government. The future growth of Ecuador's oil sector will probably depend on the development of the Ishpingo-Tapococha-Tiputini (ITT) block, which is located in the Amazon region. The Government reportedly intends to offer foreign operators licences to operate in the block, where proven reserves have been assessed at 900m. barrels. It has been estimated that the ITT block may supply at least 190,000 b/d of crude when fully developed. However, according to the EIA, the block's reserves mainly consist of a very heavy variety of crude which would require blending before distribution. The development of Amazonian reserves has been impeded in the past by opposition from indigenous groups and environmentalist groups, and it is thought that the ITT block's development would provoke particularly strong resistance. In 2007 Ecuador's President, Rafael Correa, proposed a measure to protect the environment involving the payment to Ecuador by developed countries of at least one-half of the estimated total revenues that exploitation of some 850m. barrels of heavy crude oil in the Yasuní National Park, located in the Amazon region, would generate. A fund was reportedly being established in late 2009 to help implement the project, although no firm financial commitment had been made by potential contributor countries at that time.

The economy of Trinidad and Tobago has relied heavily on the petroleum industry since the 1940s. The industry received a fillip from the discovery of offshore fields in 1955, and by the 1970s petroleum accounted for about 50% of the country's gross domestic product and about 90% of its export income. Until 1998 no significant onshore discoveries had been made since the early 1970s, although there are substantial reserves of natural gas. A series of offshore discoveries in 1998–2000 was reported to constitute the largest discovery of gas and petroleum in the history of the nation, equivalent to 630m. barrels. At 1 January 2010 Trinidad and Tobago's proven reserves of petroleum amounted to 100m. metric tons. Generally, the country's output has increased since 2000. In 2007, however, it declined sharply, by 13.3%, to 7.2m. tons, compared with 8.3m. tons in both 2006 and 2005. A further decline in production, to 6.9m. tons, was registered in 2008. In 2009 output fell again, albeit marginally, to 6.8m. tons. The challenge for the oil sector in Trinidad and Tobago is to discover new reserves, as it is feared that those currently exploited may be fully depleted by around 2015. Exports of crude petroleum and refined petroleum products accounted for 49.1% of the country's export revenue (excluding re-exports) in 2002, 46.9% in 2003, and 26.3% in 2004. In 2007, according to the USGS, energy sector exploration and output contributed about one-quarter of Trinidad and Tobago's real GDP, while refining operations (including liquefied natural gas) contributed a further 6%. Trinidad and Tobago's principal producers of crude petroleum are the state-owned operator, Petrotrin, and the Anglo-Australian BHP Billiton.

In December 2009 Colombia's proven reserves of petroleum were estimated at 200m. metric tons. The country's importance as a producer of petroleum increased dramatically in 1984, when vast oil reserves were discovered at Caño-Limón, near the Venezuelan border. This deposit, the largest petroleum discovery ever made in Colombia (with initial proven reserves of 192m. tons, of which 80m.–140m. tons were assessed as recoverable), doubled the country's recoverable petroleum reserves and transformed its prospects as a producer. The Caño-Limón discovery was followed in 1991 by the discovery of the Cusiana field, in the Andes foothills, with reserves estimated at 178m. tons. A further discovery, north of Cusiana at Cupiagua, with reserves estimated at 70m. tons, followed in 1992. Large areas of Colombia remain unexplored for petroleum. The most recent exploration licensing round, in September 2008, awarded permits to prospect in the Llanos Basin, close to the border with Venezuela, where there is believed to be potential for the discovery of heavy crudes. Although the reserves at Cusiana and Cupiagua maintained Colombia's production and export capacity until the end of the 1990s, production declined from its highest ever recorded level of 41.6m. tons in 1999 to 35.3m. tons in 2000, and to 31.0m. tons in 2001. Output subsequently continued either to fall or to stagnate, totalling 29.7m. tons in 2002, 27.9m. tons in 2003 and 27.3m. tons in each of 2004 and 2005. In 2006, however, production rose to 27.5m. tons, and a further small increase, to 27.6m. tons, was recorded in 2007. In 2008 output rose by 10.5%, to 30.5m. tons. Another increase, of almost 12%, to an estimated 34.1m. tons, was registered in 2009. In that year Colombia ranked as the fourth largest producer of crude petroleum in Latin America and the Caribbean, contributing 7% of the region's output. According to the EIA, the increases in production recorded in 2006–09 were the result of regulatory changes and greater security, which have encouraged investment in the oil sector. From the late 1990s, in response to fears that without new discoveries, for which there was substantial potential, naturally declining production levels, technical difficulties and political instability would soon transform Colombia into a net importer of petroleum, the Government sought—successfully—to revive the interest of foreign companies in exploration investment by, for example, permitting 100% participation in upstream projects, and compelling state-owned Empresa Colombiana de Petróleos (Ecopetrol) to compete with private enterprises. Foreign direct investment (FDI) in the country's oil industry totalled $2,950m. in 2009 and was expected to rise to $3,500m. in 2010, according to government sources. Although Colombia is a net exporter of petroleum, the country is obliged to import petroleum products as domestic refining capacity is insufficient to meet local demand. The country's refining capacity was assessed by industry sources at about 285,850 b/d in 2009, all of it controlled by Ecopetrol. The refinery at Barrancabermeja-Santander is Colombia's largest. In 2009 Ecopetrol approved plans to expand capacity at the Cartagena facility from 75,000 b/d to 165,000 b/d, at a cost of $3,800m. The company took complete control of the plant in 2009 by purchasing a stake held by Glencore International AG of Switzerland. Ecopetrol also reportedly plans to raise capacity at Barrancabermeja-Santander to 300,000 b/d and to enable it to refine more heavy crude. Expenditure on imports of petroleum products amounted to $262m. in 2004. Colombia currently exports about 50% of all of the petroleum it produces, mainly to the USA, which received shipments averaging 278,000 b/d in 2009. Export earnings from petroleum and its derivatives accounted for 25.9% of total foreign revenue in 2006, 24.4% in 2007 and 32.5% in 2008. The value of Colombia's exports of petroleum and its derivatives totalled $12,213m. in 2008.

Argentina had estimated proven reserves of crude petroleum totalling 300m. metric tons in December 2009. In 1993 the Government relinquished its monopoly in the petroleum sector and transferred the state corporation, Yacimientos Petrolíferos Fiscales (YPF), to private ownership. Production increased substantially during the 1990s, allowing the country, the fourth largest consumer of petroleum in Latin America (after Mexico, Brazil and Venezuela), to become a significant regional exporter, shipping mainly to Brazil and Chile. Failure to compensate for declining output at mature fields, however, has led to a steady decline in overall production since 2002. Output amounted to an estimated 33.8m. tons in 2009, compared with 41.5m. tons in 2001. In 2007, according to the USGS, the value of Argentina's exports of crude petroleum amounted to US $1,300m., compared with $2,400m. in 2006. US imports of Argentinian crude were reported to have totalled 22m. barrels in 2007, worth $708m. A further 11m. barrels were exported to other destinations for a total of $588m. The value of Argentina's exports of gasoline (excluding aviation fuel) in 2007 totalled $1,037m. Gasoline exports to the USA in that year were reported to have totalled 4m. barrels, generating revenue of $310m., while Mexico was the destination for exports totalling 2m. barrels, worth $188m. Sales of gasoline to Nigeria also amounted to 2m. barrels, worth $172m. A further 5m. barrels of gasoline were exported to various other destinations, for $367m. Repsol of Spain merged with YPF in 1999, and Repsol YPF became the principal producer, explorer and refiner in Argentina's petroleum sector. In 2007, according to the USGS, a total of 48 companies were involved in national petroleum production, with Repsol YPF retaining the rank of leading producer, accounting for 38% of output. Pan American Energy LLC Sucursal Argentina contributed an additional 16% to the total, and Chevron Argentina SRL 8%. According to the USGS, 28% of total FDI in Argentina in 2007 targeted the petroleum sector. Of total FDI in this branch, Spain accounted for 51%, the USA 16%, the Netherlands 7%, and Canada and France 4% each. In 2000 Chile imported more than 90% of its petroleum requirements. The national oil company, ENAP, was reported in 1999 to have begun to search for partners in proposed joint ventures, with the objective of increasing domestic production. Deposits in the Strait of Magellan constitute Chile's richest reserves, but access to new technology is required in order to maximize their and other fields' potential. In 2008 proven reserves amounted to 150m. barrels, according to *Oil and Gas Journal*. In that year, according to the USGS, the value of imports of petroleum and petroleum refinery products amounted to some $14,000m. Angola was the leading supplier of crude petroleum to Chile in 2006, with sales totalling $1,320m. in value, while the USA was the principal supplier of petroleum products, making shipments with a total value of $1,160m. Domestic output of crude petroleum and concentrates was reported to have amounted to 966,000 barrels in 2008, compared with 931,000 barrels in 2007 and 1.1m. barrels in 2006. Production of refinery products totalled 82.6m. barrels in 2008, compared with 82.2m. barrels in 2007 and 88.1m. barrels in 2006. Peru had proven petroleum reserves of 200m. tons in December 2009. Having generally declined since the mid-1990s, output subsequently rose fairly steadily, from 4.4m. tons in 2004 to an estimated 6.4m. tons in 2009. Formerly an exporter of petroleum that was surplus to domestic demand, Peru has become a net importer, purchasing mainly from South American suppliers. According to the USGS, the value of Peru's exports of crude petroleum and petroleum derivatives amounted to $2,200m. in 2007, compared with $1,800m. in 2006. None the less, the country recorded a negative trade balance in crude oil totalling $1,242m. in 2007 as imports of crude and demand for derivatives rose. Daily imports of crude petroleum and derivatives reportedly averaged 136,800 barrels, while daily domestic consumption averaged 170,000 barrels. In 2008 imports of crude petroleum and petroleum products were reported to have fallen to an average of 52,000 b/d, while average daily consumption remained approximately constant, at 172,000 barrels. Foreign participation in the development of new deposits had, by 2002, failed to check Peru's increasing reliance on imported petroleum, prompting the Government to introduce new legislation with the aim of encouraging exploration by improving the terms for investment. Exploration has since burgeoned, and in 2004 Occidental announced a substantial discovery in the Amazon Basin. In 2006 Barrett Resources announced that it would spend $1,000m. to develop, from 2010, resources located likewise in Peru's Amazon region. In 2005 Petro-Tech announced the discovery of Peru's first offshore resource. The company made another major offshore discovery in 2008, estimating that production there could begin as early as 2010. In 2007 Perúpetro, a state agency which promotes investments in the Peruvian hydrocarbons sector, reportedly secured foreign investment totalling more than $1,100m. In total, 25 new oil exploration and production contracts were signed in 2007. Pluspetrol SA was responsible for 56.7% of total national output of crude petroleum in 2007, while Petrobrás accounted for 17.3% and Petrotech for 15.4%. Some 60% of national output was reportedly sourced from oilfields located in the jungle zones of the Loreto and Ucayali regions. In 2008 a total of six oil refineries were in operation in Peru, of which the two largest, La Pampilla and Talara, belonged to Perúpetro. Guatemala, the only country in Central America that produces petroleum on a commercial scale, commenced petroleum exports in 1980. According to *Oil and Gas Journal*, Guatemala's proven reserves amounted to 83m. barrels in 2007. Production has hitherto derived mainly from the Mexican border region, but the Government reportedly planned to award licences for offshore resources in 2007–08. Domestic consumption exceeds both domestic production and refining capacity, and Guatemala is, accordingly, a net importer of petroleum. Most domestic crude is exported to the USA. Petroleum accounted for 3.9% of Guatemala's export earnings in 2006, 3.6% in 2007 and 4.8% in 2008. In 2008 production of crude petroleum totalled an estimated 4.5m. barrels, compared with 4.6m. barrels in 2007 and 5.9m. barrels in 2006.

Discoveries of oil in Cuba have hitherto been mainly of low-gravity, highly sulphurated crudes, according to the USGS. However, there is believed to be more promising potential for discoveries off shore in deep waters in the Gulf of Mexico. Domestic output of petroleum and natural gas generates about 90% of the country's electricity. In 2004 Spain's Repsol YPF was awarded exploration rights in five offshore blocks, and the Government reportedly invited Petrobras of Brazil to explore off shore in the Gulf of Mexico. Cuba and Venezuela were also reported to have discussed the development of Cuba as a distribution centre for Venezuelan crude. In late 2004 Cuba and Venezuela concluded the Bolivarian Alternative for the Americas Agreement (ALBA), under the terms of which Venezuela was to supply Cuba with as much as 90,000 b/d of petroleum in 2005, at a price of not less than US $27 per barrel. In 2004, according to the USGS, Venezuela supplied Cuba with 78,000 b/d of petroleum, some of which Cuba subsequently resold (via negotiations with PDVSA) to Guatemala, Honduras, El Salvador, Nicaragua and Panama. Venezuela was to supply Cuba with enough petroleum to meet all of its needs above domestic production in 2005. In that year, according to the USGS, petroleum was produced in Cuba by Sheritt International Corporation (SIC), mainly from the country's Canasi, Puerto Escondido, Seboruco, Varadero West and Yumuri oilfields. Most of SIC's output was sold to the Cuban Government for consumption in state-owned power plants. SIC reportedly planned to continue an exploration and development programme in 2006, and to invest some $40m. in maintaining existing production. In late 2004 an estimated 100m.-barrel reserve was discovered by SIC at Cuba's Santa Cruz field, off shore of Havana. The petroleum discovered was reportedly of better quality than that previously discovered in Cuba. The company reportedly planned to drill two appraisal wells in 2009. In early 2005 PDVSA opened an agency in Havana in order to participate in petroleum exploration and production, and in refining activities with Cubapetróleo. Pebercan Inc. of Canada had an interest in five Cuban blocks in 2005. In that year the company drilled more than 10 wells, at a cost of some $60m. Cuba operates four refineries in total, with combined capacity of 300,000 b/d. However, two are reported to be technologically outdated and environmentally harmful. Having been closed in the mid-1990s, a Soviet-designed facility at Cienfuegos resumed operations in late 2007 as a joint venture between Cuba Petróleo (CUPET) and PDVSA. In 2008 it was reported that the two partners planned to raise processing capacity at Cienfuegos from 65,000 b/d to 150,000 b/d. Plans also exist to renovate a 189-km pipeline that runs between Cuba's northern and southern coasts, in order to distribute refined products from Cienfuegos; to boost capacity at the outdated Hermanos Diaz refinery from 22,000 b/d to 65,000 b/d; and to construct a new refinery—to be operated, again, as a CUPET/PDVSA joint venture—at the port of Matanzas, at an estimated cost of $4,300m. In 2008, according to the USGS, Cuban production of crude petroleum totalled 19.3m. barrels, while that of refinery products amounted to 10.1m. barrels.

International petroleum prices are strongly influenced by the Organization of the Petroleum Exporting Countries (OPEC), founded in 1960 to co-ordinate the production and marketing policies of those countries whose main source of export earnings is petroleum. In 2010 OPEC had 12 members. Venezuela and Ecuador are the only Latin American participants. Ecuador, which had withdrawn from OPEC in 1992 owing to disagreements regarding its membership fee and production quota, rejoined the organization in 2007. It was anticipated that the country would align itself with those members, including Venezuela and Iran, seeking to ensure that a greater proportion of oil revenues accrued to national authorities at the expense of that appropriated by international oil companies involved in production activities. Elsewhere in Latin America, Mexico, like some other non-members, has collaborated closely with OPEC in recent years.

In each year in 2000–03 the average price of the OPEC reference 'basket' of crude oils fell within a range of US $22–$28 per barrel—the acknowledged 'preferred trading range' that the market management strategy pursued by the Organization during that period was designed to sustain. The average price of the 'basket' recorded in 2004, however, at $36.05 per barrel, rose significantly above the upper limit of the range, reflecting, perhaps, OPEC's assessment, in July 2004, that apparently 'the market has entered a new reality, one where tightness in upstream spare capacity due to lack of capacity expansion and surprisingly robust oil demand growth promises to set the scene for a new market dynamic'.

In January 2005 the average price of the OPEC reference 'basket' of crude oils, at US $40.24 per barrel, was 12.7% higher than in December 2004. At the same time, the average 'spot' quotation of Brent increased by 11.6%, to $44.01 per barrel, and that of West Texas Intermediate (WTI) by 8.2%, to $44.39 per barrel. The average price of the OPEC reference 'basket' in January 2005 was 33% higher than in the corresponding month of 2004. Among the factors that were cited as having contributed to the increase in prices at the beginning of 2005 were instability in Iraq, anticipated of industrial action in Venezuela and declines in US stocks of crude. At an extraordinary meeting of the OPEC conference held on 30 January, OPEC noted that supplies of oil world-wide exceeded demand, and that commercial stocks had risen to above five-year average levels. The market remained volatile, however, due to concerns over interruption of supply and predicted continued strong demand. In view of forecasts indicating that markets would remain balanced in the first quarter of 2005, OPEC agreed to maintain crude output at its prevailing level. The conference noted, moreover, that prices had remained outside of the Organization's preferred $22–$28-per barrel trading range for more than one year and that the range was now 'unrealistic'. The decision was taken therefore to suspend the price range 'pending completion of further studies on the subject'.

In February 2005 the average price of the OPEC reference 'basket', at US $41.68 per barrel, was 3.6% higher than in January. The average 'spot' quotation of Brent increased by almost 2% in February, to $44.87 per barrel, while that of WTI rose by 2.3%, to $47.69 per barrel. During the first two weeks of February prices generally declined in response to factors such as the predicted warmer weather conditions. Gains occurred in the latter part of the month, in response to a decline in the value of the US dollar, among other factors.

At US $49.07 per barrel, 17.7% higher than in February 2005, the average price of the OPEC reference 'basket' in March was the highest ever recorded. During March the average 'spot' quotations of Brent and WTI rose, respectively, by 17.2%, to $52.60 per barrel, and by 13.4%, to $54.09 per barrel. Projected high demand was a key determinant of market movements in the early part of March. Fears that demand would exceed supply propelled prices to close to $50 per barrel in the second week of March. In the second half of the month prices rose above $50 per barrel in response, among other things, to declines in US stocks of gasoline, distillates and heating oil. Towards the end of March the price of the OPEC 'basket' of crudes rose to a record high level of $50.72 per barrel after an accident occurred at a US refinery. The price declined in the final days of the month, however. On 16 March, meeting in Esfahan, Iran, the OPEC conference agreed to raise the Organization's production 'ceiling' to 27.5m. b/d, with immediate effect, and authorized OPEC's President to announce a further increase of 500,000 b/d in the 'ceiling' before the next meeting of the conference, should 'oil prices remain at current levels or continue to rise further'. OPEC noted that world crude oil prices had begun to rise again even though all indicators pointed to a market that was fundamentally well supplied. In explanation, OPEC's concluding statement referred to late cold weather conditions in the northern hemisphere, the anticipated continued strength of demand, speculative activity in oil futures markets, geopolitical tensions and downstream bottlenecks.

In April 2005 the average price of the OPEC reference 'basket' increased by 1.1%, to US $49.63 per barrel. The average 'spot' quotation of both Brent and WTI also declined in April, by 1.4%, to $51.87 per barrel, and by 1.8%, to $53.09 per barrel, respectively. Early in the month prices rose in response to a report by the investment bank Goldman Sachs in which the possibility that oil prices might double from their current levels was discussed. Indeed, in the first week of April the average price of OPEC 'basket' crudes, at $52.07 per barrel, was the highest ever recorded. In the second week of April, however, continued increases in US stocks of crude, high OPEC output and a revised, lower forecast of world demand for oil in 2005 by the International Energy Agency (IEA) combined to bring down prices.

In May 2005 the average price of the OPEC reference 'basket' fell by more than 5%, to US $46.96 per barrel. At the same time, the average 'spot' quotation of Brent declined by 5.7%, compared with the previous month, to $48.90 per barrel, while that of WTI declined by 5.3%, to $50.25 per barrel. During the first three weeks of May OPEC's reference price fell steadily in response to such factors as the ready availability of OPEC crudes and, in particular, the high level of US crude inventories. In the final week of the month, however, prices were supported by fears that supplies of refined products would be disrupted in advance of the US driving season.

At an extraordinary meeting of the OPEC conference on 15 June 2005, the Organization decided to raise its production 'ceiling' by 500,000 b/d, with effect from 1 July. OPEC noted that although markets were well supplied, world crude prices had remained high and volatile owing to concerns over a lack of effective global oil refining capacity. Refiners' difficulties, moreover, were being exacerbated by geopolitical developments and speculative investment activity on futures markets. OPEC's decision also took into account anticipated continued strong growth in demand for crude oil in 2005 and renewed price increases. The conference also authorized its President to announce an additional increase of 500,000 b/d in the production 'ceiling' if crude prices remained at their current levels or continued to rise. Separately, the conference announced its decision to change the composition of the OPEC reference 'basket' from 16 June 2005. The new 'basket' would comprise the main export crudes (Saharan Blend—Algeria; Minas—Indonesia; Iran Heavy—Iran; Basra Light—Iraq; Kuwait Export—Kuwait; Es Sider—Libya; Bonny Light—Nigeria; Qatar Marine—Qatar; Arabian Light—Saudi Arabia; Murban—UAE; BCF 17—Venezuela) of all OPEC member states and would be weighted according to production and exports to the principal markets. The new 'basket' would also better reflect the average quality of member countries' crudes.

In June 2005 the average price of the OPEC reference 'basket' (calculated on the basis of both the old and the new components of the 'basket'—see above) rose by 11%, to US $52.04 per barrel. The average price of the 'basket' as composed until 16 June increased by 12%, to $52.72 per barrel, while that of its newly defined counterpart rose by 13%, to $52.92 per barrel. In June the average 'spot' quotation of Brent increased by 11.9%, to $54.73 per barrel, while that of WTI rose by 12.6%, to $56.60 per barrel. Concern over possible shortages of refined products was identified as the key determinant of price movements in June.

In July 2005 the average price of the OPEC reference 'basket' increased by 2%, to US $53.13 per barrel. At the same time, the average quotation of Brent for immediate delivery rose by 5%, to $54.47 per barrel, while that of WTI strengthened by 3.6%, to $58.66 per barrel. Oil prices were reported to have been boosted in the early part of the month by stormy weather conditions in the Gulf of Mexico that had revived fears of possible shortages of crude and petroleum products. Having eased somewhat, oil prices were subsequently driven upwards again by a recurrence of adverse weather in the Gulf of Mexico, although they were checked on this occasion by reported accumulations of stocks of distillate fuels. In the third week of July the average price of the OPEC reference 'basket' declined in response to lower Chinese consumption of oil, and to forecasts of slower growth in demand for oil. In the final week of the month prices were supported by concern that supplies would be disrupted by adverse weather conditions and by problems at US refineries.

In August 2005 the average price of the OPEC reference 'basket' rose by US $4.69, equivalent to almost 9%, to $57.82 per barrel. The average 'spot' quotation of Brent blend increased by $6.59 in August, to $64.06 per barrel, while that of WTI rose by $6.3, to $64.96 per barrel. During the course of the month prices were propelled to record levels owing to concern that 'refinery outages' would be aggravated by hurricane weather conditions. In its review of the markets for oil in July, OPEC had identified 'refinery outages' as a key factor behind the recent price volatility of oil and urged 'rapid and sizeable investment in the refining sector, particularly in conversion capacity, which has persistently lagged market requirements . . .'. Strike action in Ecuador was another factor behind the volatile market conditions in August. In late August the price of US light crude rose to more than $70 per barrel in response to damage to US production and refining facilities caused by hurricane weather conditions in the Gulf of Mexico. Upward pressure on prices was subsequently checked by the decision of the US Administration to release stocks from the US strategic petroleum reserve (SPR); and by the announcement by the IEA on 2 September that its signatory countries would begin to release a total of 60m. barrels from American, Asian and European strategic stocks.

In September 2005 the average price of the OPEC reference 'basket' increased marginally, by US $0.06 per barrel, to $57.88 per barrel. The average 'spot' quotation of Brent declined by $1.31, to $62.75 per barrel, while that of WTI rose slightly, by $0.32, to $65.28 per barrel. In the first week of the month upward movement was checked by the release of US and IEA strategic stocks. In the second week of September downward pressure was reinforced by the IEA's prediction that global demand for oil in 2005 would be lower than previously forecast and by speculative sales on futures markets. Prices subsequently strengthened in response to fears of damage to oil production and refining facilities in the Gulf of Mexico by Hurricane Rita, but eased again towards the end of the month as, among other factors, speculators took profits on futures markets. At the OPEC ministerial conference held on 19–20 September, in response to the continued rise in crude prices, the Organization undertook, if necessary, to make available to the market spare capacity of some 2m. b/d for a period of three months from 1 October 2005. At the same time, the Organization emphasized that 'the continuing shortage of appropriate refining capacity remains one of the main reasons behind recent oil price increases and price volatility'.

In October 2005 the average price of the OPEC reference 'basket' fell by US $3.25, equivalent to 5.6%, to $54.63 per barrel. The average 'spot' quotation of Brent declined by $4, to $58.75 per barrel, while that of WTI fell by $2.61, to $62.67 per barrel. In the first week of the month prices of OPEC crudes were reportedly depressed by a wider divergence in the price of sweet/sour grades and by the US Administration's stated intention to resort to the SPR for supplies of crude and heating oil, should this be required. In the second week prices strengthened initially, in response, among other things, to growing Asian demand for winter fuels and to a lower assessment by the IEA of OPEC supply in 2005, while growth in demand world-wide was expected to continue well into 2006; but were subsequently depressed by such factors as ample supply of OPEC crudes and weaker US demand for gasoline. In mid-October prices strengthened in response to fears that US production and refining facilities in the Gulf of Mexico would suffer further damage from an imminent hurricane, but began to weaken once it appeared that Hurricane Wilma would strike the US coast elsewhere. The downward trend persisted throughout the remainder of the month, reinforced, *inter alia*, by reportedly substantial growth in US crude inventories. The price of the OPEC reference 'basket' remained under pressure from abundant supplies in the final week of October.

Further declines in the price of the OPEC reference 'basket' occurred in November 2005, the price of its components averaging US $51.29 per barrel, a decline of $3.34, equivalent to more than 6%, compared with the previous month. At the same time the average 'spot' price of Brent declined by $3.34, to $55.41 per barrel, while that of WTI fell by $4.25, to $58.42 per barrel. Growth in crude oil inventories was among the factors that caused prices to ease marginally in the first two weeks of the month. Prices also came under pressure from a lower estimate of global demand for oil by the IEA, in combination with ongoing and projected increases in OPEC's production capacity. In the third week of the month profit-taking on futures markets added further downward pressure to prices, but declines were checked by a fall in US crude inventories and forecasts of colder weather conditions in the northern hemisphere. In the final week of November, for the first time in nine weeks, prices strengthened overall as concerns over colder weather conditions intensified. In the final days of the month, however, the prices of some crudes declined sharply in response to unusually warm winter weather conditions in some northern areas of the USA.At an extraordinary meeting of the OPEC ministerial conference on 12 December 2005, OPEC assessed the ceiling of 28m. b/d adopted in June as adequate to maintain market equilibrium in the first quarter of 2006, but determined to hold a further extraordinary meeting at the end of January 2006 in order to decide upon the appropriate level of production for the second and third quarters of the year. The conference urged consumers and industry to take action to reduce 'refinery bottlenecks', which it described as the main determinant of price in the prevailing market conditions of abundant supply.

In December 2005 the average price of the OPEC reference 'basket' increased by US $1.36, equivalent to 2.6%, to $52.65 per barrel. The average 'spot' quotation of Brent, meanwhile, rose by $1.61, to $57.02 per barrel and that of WTI by $0.94, to $59.36 per barrel. During the whole of 2005 the price of the OPEC 'basket' averaged $50.46 per barrel, an increase of 40% compared with 2004. In early December 2005 forecasts of warmer weather in the northern hemisphere were among the factors that caused the composite price to decline marginally, but during the second week of the month the price rose by more than 5%, partly in response to concerns over the adequacy of supplies of heating fuels. The price of OPEC crudes rose further in the third week of the month as cold weather persisted and the IEA revised upwards its forecast of demand for oil world-wide in 2006, but upward pressure was relieved by profit-taking on futures markets. In the final week of December 2005 the price of the OPEC reference 'basket' declined by more than 4% in response, according to OPEC, to the publication of 'bearish data' in the USA and forecasts of warmer weather. Prices had begun to rise again before the end of the year, however, as Nigerian supplies were disrupted and Japanese demand for sweet crudes increased after heavy snowfalls caused the closure of some of the country's nuclear facilities.

The price of the OPEC reference 'basket' rose substantially in January 2006, to US $58.47 per barrel. Substantial increases also occurred in the average 'spot' quotations of both Brent, which rose to $63.05 per barrel, and WTI, which rose to $65.39 per barrel. During the first week of January the price of the OPEC reference 'basket' rose by more than 7% in response to disruption of the supply of Russian natural gas to European markets. Tension in the Middle East—in particular concerns over the health of the Israeli Prime Minister, ongoing instability in Iraq and, most seriously, an escalating international dispute concerning Iran's nuclear programme, and its possible consequences in view of Iran's position as the world's fourth largest exporter of crude petroleum—in combination with disruption to Nigerian supplies reportedly kept prices firm in the second week of the month. Concerns over tension in the Middle East remained a key concern in the third week of January, although prices were checked at the same time by, among other things, forecasts of warmer weather in the northern hemisphere. Geopolitical issues, combined in the final week of the month with a reduction in Russian supplies as a consequence of cold weather conditions and continued disruption of supplies from Nigeria, maintained the upward pressure on prices, although increases were restrained by OPEC members' assurances that production would be maintained at an adequate level and by low seasonal demand from US refineries. At an extraordinary meeting of the OPEC conference on 31 January it was decided to maintain OPEC's output at 28m. b/d, as part of the effort to restrain prices.

The average price of the OPEC reference 'basket' in February 2006, at US $56.62 per barrel, declined by 3%, or $1.85. Declines were also registered in the average 'spot' quotation of Brent, which fell by $2.93, to $60.12 per barrel, and in that of WTI, which fell by $3.9, to $61.49 per barrel. In the first week of February OPEC's recent decision to maintain its output unchanged caused prices generally to ease, although Iran's announcement that it would no longer allow unscheduled inspections of its nuclear facilities caused prices to rise sharply on 6 February. Other factors that contributed to a further, more substantial decline in the price of the OPEC reference 'basket' in the second week of February were reportedly abundant Middle Eastern supplies and a substantial increase in US stocks of gasoline. The downward trend was reinforced in the third week of the month by, among other things, an IEA report that indicated that growth in supplies world-wide was increasing at a faster rate than incremental demand in 2006. The price of the reference 'basket' subsequently recovered somewhat, in response, partly, to the disruption of supplies from Nigeria. Other factors responsible for the recovery in prices in late February were ongoing tension in the Middle East, growing demand for light, sweet crudes and an attempt by militants to disrupt activity at Saudi Arabia's Abqaiq oil-processing facility.

In March 2006 the average price of the OPEC reference 'basket' rose by US $1.24—more than 2%—to $57.86 per barrel. At the same time the price of Brent increased by $1.96, to $62.08 per barrel, and that of WTI by $1.33, to $62.82 per barrel. Prices strengthened in the first week of the month in response to fears of disruption to some Middle Eastern and West African supplies. OPEC's decision, taken at the ministerial conference held on 8 March, to maintain output at 28m. b/d, in combination with an increase in US inventories of crude, subsequently checked upward movement, but prices quickly began to rise again under the influence of concerns over the adequacy of US gasoline supplies. OPEC's decision not to reduce production was taken explicitly in the light of geopolitical threats to supplies—threats that were underlined on 20 March when militants were reported to have carried out an attack on a pipeline in Nigeria, further boosting prices. In the fourth week of the month prices weakened in response to the perceived abundance of crude supplies world-wide and anticipated lower growth in world demand for oil. Prices rose substantially in the final week of the month in response to conflict in southern Iraq and to a heavy fall in US gasoline inventories.

At the ministerial conference held in Vienna, Austria, on 8 March 2006 (at which it was decided to maintain the Organization's output unchanged at 28m. b/d), OPEC noted that, despite indications that markets were well supplied and the high level of inventories in countries of the Organisation for Economic Co-operation and Development (OECD), prices remained volatile as a result of geopolitical tensions and 'downstream bottlenecks'.

At US $64.44 per barrel, $6.57 or 11.35% higher than in March, the average price of the OPEC reference 'basket' in April 2006 was the highest ever recorded. At the same time the average 'spot' quotation of Brent increased by $8.27, to $70.35 per barrel, and that of WTI by $6.64, to $69.46 per barrel. The price of both Brent and US light, sweet crudes rose to record levels in April. Geopolitical issues, in particular an escalation of the international dispute over Iran's nuclear programme, continued to exert the strongest influence on markets for OPEC crudes. Other inflationary influences were the publication, on 19 April, of data that indicated a greater-than-expected decline in US inventories of gasoline. Prices moved upwards consistently during the first three weeks of the month, but stabilized during the final week in response to the interplay of profit-taking on futures markets and strong Chinese demand for crude. Another factor that exerted a calming influence on the market in late April was a speech (on 25 April) by US President Bush in which he undertook, among other things, to boost supplies to US markets at the expense of increasing the US SPR.

In May 2006, as in April, the average price of the OPEC reference 'basket' was the highest ever recorded, rising to US $65.11, an increase of more than 1%. The average price of Brent, meanwhile, declined fractionally, to $69.83 per barrel, while that of WTI increased by some 2%, to $70.89 per barrel. The key determinants of price movements during the early part of May were, on the one hand, continued geopolitical tension and conditions—especially in the USA—of abundant supply. During the first three weeks of the month, markets remained volatile, but prices generally moved downwards, in response, notably, to fears that the level to which they had risen had begun to cause demand to weaken. In the third week of May, the average price of the OPEC crudes was, at $63.72 per barrel, the lowest for six weeks. In the final week of May, however, geopolitical tensions came to the fore once again, reinforced, according to OPEC, by concern over the approaching hurricane season in the Gulf of Mexico. Strong US demand was an additional factor that supported prices in the final week of the month.

At an extraordinary ministerial conference held in Caracas, Venezuela, on 1 June 2006, OPEC decided to maintain output of crude by its members at the prevailing level. The decision proceeded from the Organization's assessment of markets for oil as 'over-supplied' and its identification as the key influence on markets characterized by high prices and volatility of 'the lack of effective global oil refining capacity, in the short and medium term, coupled with anxiety about the ability of oil producers to meet anticipated future oil demand'.

In June 2006 the average price of the OPEC 'basket', at US $64.69 per barrel, was fractionally lower than in May. Geopolitical tensions having eased somewhat in the first week of the month, in the second week the average price declined by almost 3% in response to data indicating that OPEC stocks of crude were the highest for 20 years, and to fears that demand was under threat from higher interest rates and inflation. In the final week of the month prices strengthened in response to renewed fears regarding the adequacy of gasoline supplies in the summer months, forecast strong Chinese demand and disruption to US refining operations.

The average price of OPEC 'basket' crudes rose substantially, by more than 6%, to US $68.92 per barrel in July 2006. At the same time the average price of North Sea Brent crude increased by more than 7%, to $73.66 per barrel, while that of WTI rose by nearly 5%, to $74.33. Among the key influences on petroleum prices in July were increased seasonal demand and, especially, conflict in the Middle East—both between the Israeli armed forces and Palestinian fighters in the Gaza Strip and the West Bank, and between Israeli forces and the militant Shi'a organization Hezbollah in Lebanon. On 14 July the average price of OPEC crudes rose to $71.71 per barrel, a record high, prompting the Organization to reaffirm its commitment to market stability and to emphasize, again, that markets for oil continued, fundamentally, to be characterized by excess of supply.

The closure of a pipeline (operated by BP) at Prudhoe Bay, Alaska, USA, led OPEC on 10 August 2006 to issue another statement in which it sought to calm the volatility of oil markets by re-emphasizing the adequacy of crude supplies *vis-à-vis* demand. Already, during the first week of August, the average price of OPEC reference crudes had risen to more than US $70 per barrel, in response to the continued effects of conflict in the Middle East and damage to Russia's Druzhba pipeine. Further inflationary pressure, in the form of adverse weather conditions in the Gulf of Mexico and anxiety, in the light of newly released data, about the adequacy of US crude inventories, propelled the average price of the OPEC reference 'basket' to a new record level of $72.67 per barrel. In the second half of August, generally, prices eased as political tension in the Middle East subsided somewhat and a perception of the adequacy of crude supplies overrode previous concerns. For the whole of August an average price of $68.81 per barrel was recorded for OPEC crudes, representing a slight decline, of only about 0.1%, compared with the previous month. During August the average price of Brent fell (by less than 1%) to $73.11 per barrel, while that of WTI declined by $1.32 per barrel, or 1.8%, to $73.01.

During the first week of September 2006 the average price of OPEC reference crudes eased further, to US $63.14 per barrel, as political tension in the Middle East continued to subside and the availability of supplies from both the Gulf of Mexico and Nigeria improved. This downward trend became more pronounced in the second week of the month, in response to, among other factors, OPEC's decision, taken at a ministerial conference on 11 September, to leave its production 'ceiling' unchanged. In the third week of August the average price of OPEC reference crudes declined further, by some 4%, to $57.16 per barrel, as markets remained confident of the adequacy of OPEC supplies and Asian refiners' demand for oil was reduced. An average price of $56.35 per barrel was recorded for OPEC crudes in the final week of September. Overall, the average price of the OPEC reference 'basket' fell substantially in September, by more than $10 per barrel, equivalent to 14%. At the same time the average price of Brent registered a decline of more than $11 per barrel, to $61.71, while that of WTI fell by more than 12%, to $64 per barrel.

During October 2006 the average price of the OPEC reference 'basket' declined by a further 7.4% (US $4.37), to $54.97 per barrel—its lowest level of the year to date. At the same time the average price of Brent crude declined by 6.3%, to $57.80 per barrel, while that of WTI fell by more than 8%, to $58.82 per barrel. The ready availability of crude oil was the key influence on markets throughout the month. At a consultative meeting of the OPEC conferenceon 19–20 October, delegates observed with concern that markets were characterized by excess of supply and had been destabilized as a consequence. The consultative meeting decided to address this by reducing OPEC output by some 1.2m. b/d, to 26.3m. b/d, from 1 November. The reduction was to be reviewed at an extraordinary meeting of the OPEC conference scheduled for mid-December.

At the extraordinary meeting of the OPEC conference that was duly convened in mid-December 2006, it was observed 'with satisfaction' that the decision to reduce member states' output from 1 November had achieved a better balance between supply and demand, although an element of volatility remained. In November the average price of the OPEC reference 'basket' rose slightly, by less than US $0.5, to $55.42 per barrel. During November an increase of $1.12, to $58.92 per barrel, was registered in the average price of Brent, while the average price of WTI rose marginally, by $0.12, to $58.94 per barrel. In spite of the reduction in OPEC output from 1 November, it was not until the final week of the month that there was decisive upward movement in prices, markets having been influenced by such depressive factors as, in particular, ample OECD crude inventories, during the first three weeks of the month. Having noted at the extraordinary meeting held in December that markets continued to be characterized by residual volatility, it was agreed that an additional reduction in OPEC members' output, of 500,000 b/d, should be implemented from 1 February 2007 in order to maintain market equilibrium.

During the first week of December 2006 the average price of the OPEC reference 'basket' continued to strengthen, in response to anticipated normal winter demand and to the perceived likelihood of an additional reduction in OPEC output. At US $59.06 per barrel, the average price of OPEC reference crudes recorded in the the first week of the month was the highest since mid-September. However, the average price retreated in the second week of the month, owing to the effect on demand of forecasts of warmer winter weather in the northern hemisphere. A lack of clear direction in the third week of December was succeeded by a decline in the average price of more than 2.5%, to $56.50 per barrel, in response to mild weather in the western hemisphere and the perceived adequacy of supplies. For the whole of December, none the less, the average price of the OPEC reference 'basket' increased by $2.53, equivalent to 4.6%, to $57.95 per barrel. The average price of Brent, meanwhile, rose by some 5.8%, to $62.33 per barrel, in December, while that of WTI increased by about 5.1%, to $61.96 per barrel.

During the first week of 2007 the average price of OPEC reference crudes declined by more than 5%, to US $53.99 per barrel, as a consequence of warm winter weather. Unseasonably high temperatures, especially in the USA, exerted further downward pressure on markets for crude in the second week of January, the average price of the OPEC reference 'basket' falling by more than 8%, to $50.27 per barrel. This pressure was checked somewhat in the third week of the month as colder weather returned, but, even so, the average weekly price, at $48.45 per barrel, was the lowest recorded since May 2005. In the final week of January cold weather combined with the US Administration's decision to replenish the SPR with some 100,000 b/d of crude caused the average price of OPEC reference crudes to strengthen to $50.42 per barrel. For the whole of January 2007 the average price of the OPEC reference 'basket' fell by more than 12%, to $50.73 per barrel, the lowest monthly average since May 2005. The average price of North Sea Brent, meanwhile, declined by almost 14%, to $53.68 per barrel, while that of WTI fell by more than 12%, to $54.40 per barrel. At the extraordinary meeting of the OPEC conference held in mid-December 2006 it was decided to admit Angola as the Organization's 12th member, with effect from 1 January 2007, from which time, accordingly, Angola's Cabinda crude was to be included in calculations of OPEC production, although it was not immediately to be included as a constituent of the OPEC reference 'basket'.

In February 2007 the supplementary reduction (from 1 February) in OPEC output agreed upon in December 2006, continued cold weather in the USA, an increase in political tension in the Middle East and an upward adjustment to forecast world demand for oil were the predominant influences on markets for crude petroleum, overriding OPEC member states' assurances of steady supply, lower demand for winter fuels as mild weather returned and an abrupt reversal in Chinese equity values to raise the average price of the OPEC reference 'basket' by more than 7%, to US $54.45 per barrel. During February the average price of Brent rose by almost 7%, to $57.43 per barrel, while that of WTI increased by 8.8%, to $59.21 per barrel.

During the first week of March 2007 a marginal increase, of 0.6%, to US $57.85 per barrel, was recorded in the average price of the

OPEC reference 'basket'. A possible increase in demand for crude, owing to the recent lower prices, was among the factors to which stronger prices were attributed at the beginning of March. As the month progressed, factors such as improved weather conditions and concern about the prospects for economic growth world-wide came to the fore, causing the average price of OPEC reference crudes to decline by more than 1%, to $57.12 per barrel. Having risen marginally in the third week, in the final week of March the average price of OPEC reference crudes increased by 7.5%, to $61.58 per barrel, influenced in particular by political tension in the Middle East and by lower US inventories of summer fuels. For the whole of March, at $58.47 per barrel, an increase of 7.4% compared with February, the average price recorded for the OPEC reference 'basket' was the highest for six months. During March the average price of Brent rose by some $4.7, to $62.15 per barrel, while that of WTI increased by about $1.4, to $60.63 per barrel. At a meeting of the OPEC conference on 15 March, ministers decided to leave the Organization's output unchanged, noting that markets remained well supplied and that commercial inventories of crude oil in OECD countries were 'healthy'.

Concern about the adequacy of summer fuel supplies was the dominant market influence in the first week of April 2007, causing the average price of the OPEC reference 'basket' to rise by 3.4%, to US $63.73 per barrel, the highest weekly average since August 2006. A decline of 1.7% in the average price in the third week of April was cancelled in the final week of the month, when the average price of OPEC reference crudes increased by 1.7% in response to concern about possible shortages of some West African crudes and falls in US gasoline inventories. For the whole of April the average price of the OPEC reference 'basket' increased by 8.4%, to $63.39 per barrel, the third consecutive monthly increase, which raised the 'basket' price by one-quarter compared with that recorded in January. During April an average price of $67.51 per barrel was recorded for North Sea Brent, while the average price of WTI rose by some $3.2, to $63.85 per barrel.

During May 2007 the upward trend in the price of OPEC crudes continued: an average price of US $64.36 per barrel was recorded, an increase of $0.97, or 1.5%, compared with the previous month. Increases in US inventories of crude exerted a depressive influence on prices during the first half of May, although declines were checked by concern regarding disruption to West African supplies and the adequacy of summer fuel supplies. In the third week of May the average price of the OPEC reference 'basket' rose by 3.7%, to $64.55 per barrel, as concern about disruption to supplies from Nigeria was reinforced by technical problems at some US refineries. In the final week of the month the average price of the reference 'basket' increased by a further 3%, in response to industrial action planned in Nigeria and a rise in political tension in the Middle East. During May the average price of Brent, meanwhile, declined slightly, compared with the previous month, to $67.38 per barrel, while that of WTI fell by 0.6%, to $63.46 per barrel.

A further increase, of 2.41%, to US $66.77 per barrel, was recorded in the average price of OPEC crudes in June 2007. Concern as to whether US gasoline supplies would be sufficient to meet demand during the driving season exerted a key influence on markets for crude in the first week of the month, as did concern about the possible effect of Cyclone Gonu on production in Oman and on transportation of oil from Middle Eastern locations. In the second week of the month, despite continued concern about US gasoline supplies, the average price of the OPEC reference 'basket' eased marginally, but it was driven upward again in the third week of June, to $67.74 per barrel, the highest weekly average of the year to date, by enduring concern about US gasoline supplies, among other factors. In the final week of the month the average price of the reference 'basket' eased somewhat, to $67.49 per barrel. The average price of Brent rose by more than 6% in June, compared with the previous month, to $71.55 per barrel, while that of WTI likewise rose by more than 6%, to $67.44 per barrel.

In July 2007 the average price of the OPEC reference 'basket' increased by almost US $5 per barrel, to reach a record high of $71.75 per barrel. The price of North Sea Brent, meanwhile, rose by $5.46, to $77.01 per barrel, while a gain of more than $6.50, to $73.98 per barrel, was registered in the price of WTI. Previously existing concerns about the adequacy of gasoline supplies to meet US demand were reportedly exacerbated in early July by restricted Nigerian output of gasoline-rich crude, and these exerted a key influence on markets throughout the month.

Official price data published by OPEC in August 2007 reflected for the first time the inclusion of Angola's Girassol crude in the reference 'basket'. On the basis of this revision, the average price of the reference 'basket' declined by US $3.18 per barrel, equivalent to 4.4%, in August. The average price of Brent, meanwhile, fell by $6.27 per barrel, or 8.1%, to $70.74. A smaller decline, of $1.61 per barrel, or 2.2%, to $72.37, was recorded in the average price of WTI. Declines in the prices of OPEC crudes were most marked in the first half of the month, in response to growing concern regarding the consequences for the US economy of the 'sub-prime' crisis (stemming from low-income borrowers' inability to meet repayment obligations on lending). This concern was alleviated by such factors as, in the third week, fears that supplies of Mexican crude would be disrupted by Hurricane Dean and falls in US inventories of crude oil and gasoline.

At the meeting of the OPEC conference that was convened on 11 September 2007, OPEC announced its decision to increase overall output by its members (excluding Angola and Iraq) by 500,000 b/d, from 1 November. This decision proceeded from an analysis of current market conditions that emphasized the priority of maintaining supplies in the winter season, in the context of 'ongoing tightness' in the US market for petroleum products, and the consequences for inventory levels of a recent shift into 'backwardation' of petroleum futures markets.

In September 2007, despite the decision of the OPEC conference to increase supplies from 1 November, the average price of the OPEC reference 'basket' rose by almost 8%, compared with the previous month, or US $5.47, to a new record high of $74.18 per barrel. An increase of $6.13, or 8.7%, to $76.87, was recorded in the average price per barrel of Brent blend, while the average price of WTI, at $79.69, was $7.32 per barrel, or 10.1%, higher than that recorded in August. In the first week of the month concern that supplies would be disrupted by stormy weather conditions in the Caribbean Sea was one factor that lent strength to prices. In the second week the influence of OPEC's decision to increase member states' output by 500,000 b/d was overridden by attacks on oil and gas pipelines in Mexico, even though it quickly became apparent that the effect of these on Mexican crude exports would be minimal. Prices received a further boost in the days following OPEC's announcement from data indicating that US inventories of crude oil had fallen to their lowest level for eight months. However, price increases were reportedly checked in the second half of September by continued concern about the prospects of the US economy, and by speculators' profit-taking.

In October 2007 the average price of the OPEC reference 'basket' rose by US $5.18, or almost 7%, to a new record level of $79.36 per barrel. Increases of $5.63 (7.3%), to $82.50 per barrel, and of $6.18 (7.8%), to $85.87 per barrel, were recorded, respectively, in the average prices of Brent and WTI. In the second week of October the price of light crude traded in New York and of London Brent rose in response to, among other factors, a report released by the IEA which concluded that stocks of crude oil held by major industrialized countries had declined below five-year average levels. In a press statement issued in mid-October, however, OPEC Secretary-General Abdallah Salem el-Badri attributed the high price of oil at this time to, above all, speculative activity. In the third week of October prices were propelled upward by an escalation in a conflict between Turkish and Kurdish armed forces in northern Iraq. Towards the end of the month the decision by state-owned Mexican producer PEMEX to cut output by 600,000 b/d, owing to bad weather in the Gulf of Mexico, lent strength to world prices.

Upward momentum in the price of oil was maintained in November 2007, when the average price of the OPEC reference 'basket' reached US $88.99 per barrel—an increase of $9.63, equivalent to more than 12%. An increase of $10.12, or 12.3%, was recorded in the average price of Brent, while the corresponding price of WTI rose by $9, or 10.5%. Prices rose strongly on the first day of November, in response to a sharp decline in US inventories of crude. Other factors that influenced the price of oil during the first week of November were fears that political turmoil in Pakistan could lead to a disruption of supplies, and the continued weakness of the US dollar: in response, the price of the OPEC reference 'basket' rose to a new record high of $90.71 per barrel, before declining to an average price of $87.35 per barrel in the second week of the month. At a press conference held in Riyadh, Saudi Arabia, OPEC's Secretary-General denied that OPEC was responsible for recent rises in the price of oil, identifying, rather, weakness of the US dollar and a lack of investment in refining capacity as among the principal factors. In the third week of November, none the less, in response to strong winter demand for petroleum, the average price of the OPEC 'basket' increased by 4%, to a record weekly high of $90.71 per barrel. This strength was initially maintained in the final week of the month, when a new daily record high, of $91.91 per barrel, was recorded. Overall, however, the average price of the 'basket' declined by more than 2% in the final week of November, to $88.78 per barrel.

In early December 2007 expectations that OPEC would raise production combined with forecasts of lower demand for oil and reduced tension in the Middle East to exert downward pressure on the price of oil. In the first week of the month the average price of the OPEC reference 'basket' declined by more than 4%, to US $84.97 per barrel. In the second week—after OPEC had decided to make no change to its output, but to conduct a further review of markets at the end of January 2008—the average price of the OPEC reference price recovered some of the lost ground, rising to $86.43 per barrel in response to expectations that growth in demand for oil would be fuelled by a cut in interest rates by the US Federal Reserve and measures taken by other leading central banks to support financial markets. In the third week of December, when key influences on markets for oil included a strengthening of the US dollar against other major currencies and declining US inventories of petroleum products, the average price of the OPEC reference 'basket' rose by a further 1.2%, to $87.45 per barrel. In the final week of 2007 a further influx of speculative funds into markets for oil propelled the average price of the OPEC reference 'basket' to $89.70, an increase of 2.6% compared with the previous week. On a monthly basis, the price of the OPEC reference 'basket' declined by $1.80, or 2%, to $87.19 per barrel in December. The average price of Brent, meanwhile, fell by $1.37, or 1.5%, to $91.25 per barrel, while that of WTI, at $91.69 per barrel, was $3.22, or 3.4% lower.

In a statement issued on 5 December 2007, at the conclusion of an extraordinary meeting of the OPEC conference, the Organization noted that abundance of supplies remained the key fundamental factor affecting markets for oil. The statement reiterated the concern expressed by OPEC in October that price volatility was being exacerbated by speculation. In view of this assessment, the conference resolved to maintain members' output at the prevailing level. It was also announced that Angola and Ecuador (Ecuador had rejoined OPEC in November, having withdrawn from the Organization in 1992) had been allocated production quotas of 1.9m. b/d and 520,000 b/d, respectively.

In the first week of January 2008—when the price of light crude oil traded in New York rose above US $100 per barrel—the average price of the OPEC reference 'basket' reached a new record daily high of $93.78 per barrel, rising in response to a combination of strong demand for winter fuels, speculative purchasing activity on oil futures markets, concerns arising from the ongoing dispute between Western powers—principally the USA—and Iran over its civil nuclear programme and reports of unrest in Port Harcourt, the centre of Nigeria's oil industry. The average price of the 'basket' in the first week of the year, at $92.68, was more than 3% higher than in the previous week. Upward movement was reportedly checked, however, by fears of economic recession in the USA and declines in share prices on world markets. The average price of the OPEC reference 'basket' declined by $1.67, or 1.8%, to $90.81 per barrel in the second week of January. There was a more marked decline in the third week of the month, when concern about possible economic recession and weaker demand for oil exerted the strongest influences on markets: the average price of the reference 'basket' fell by more than 4%, to $87.18 per barrel. A further decline, of 2.4%, to $85.07 per barrel—the lowest average price recorded for eight weeks—was registered in the fourth week of January. In monthly terms, the average price of the OPEC reference 'basket' rose by $1.31, or 1.5%, to $88.50 per barrel in January. The average price of Brent increased by less than $1, to $92 per barrel, relative to December 2007, while a slightly higher increase, of $1.18, to $92.87 per barrel, was recorded in the average price of WTI.

In February 2008 the average price of the OPEC reference 'basket', in which Ecuador's Oriente crude was now included, rose by US $2.29, or 2.59%, compared with the previous month, to a new record monthly high of $90.64 per barrel. The average price of Brent, meanwhile, increased by $2.98, or 3.2%, to $94.98 per barrel—the price of Brent rose above $100 per barrel for the first time in February—and an increase, of $2.45 (or 2.6%), to $95.32, was recorded in the average price of WTI. Increases in the prices of crude oil were especially marked from late in the second week of the month, influenced by such factors as the escalation of an ongoing dispute between the Government of Venezuela and the multinational oil company ExxonMobil, strong winter demand for petroleum, and concern that OPEC would respond to data indicating that the global economy was likely to slow later in 2008—thus reducing demand for oil—by formally cutting output at its forthcoming conference in March. An explosion at the Big Spring oil refinery in Texas, USA, in mid-February was an additional factor lending strength to oil prices in that month. Inflows of speculative funds into commodities in general and oil in particular, at the expense of shares and currencies, reportedly continued on a large scale in February.

Speculative investment interest in commodity markets, in particular those for petroleum, remained strong in March 2008, spurred by the continued weakness of the US dollar. The average price of the OPEC reference 'basket' rose by US $8.39, or more than 9%, compared with the previous month, to $99.03 per barrel, while the average price of Brent, at $103.58, was $8.6, or 9.1%, higher. At $105.41 per barrel, the average price of WTI was $10.1, or 10.6%, higher, relative to February. Gains in the price of oil were especially marked in the second week of March, when the average price of the OPEC 'basket' rose to a new record of $101.34 per barrel; an all-time daily high, of $102.88 per barrel, was also recorded in that week. In a statement issued on 5 March, at the conclusion of its 148th conference, OPEC reiterated the view that it had frequently expressed in the recent past: that the fundamental characteristics of oil markets did not justify the record highs to which the price of oil had risen. On the contrary, the deceleration of economic growth in the USA, together with a worsening crisis in financial markets world-wide, pointed to the likelihood that demand for oil would decline in coming months. At the time of the statement, the Organization noted that markets remained well supplied and that commercial inventories of oil were above five-year average levels.

At a new record level of US $105.20 per barrel, the average price of the OPEC reference 'basket' was more than 6%, or $6.13, higher in April 2008, compared with the previous month. The average price of Brent, meanwhile, increased by $5.39, or 5.2%, to $108.97 per barrel, while that of WTI rose by $7.23, or 6.9%, relative to March, to $112.64 per barrel. On 17 April, despite indications that the US economy was likely to move into recession and that economic growth would slow in other major economies, the price of light crude traded in New York rose above $115 per barrel after the announcement of unexpected declines in US inventories of crude oil and gasoline prompted concern about the adequacy of stocks *vis-à-vis* demand during the forthcoming summer driving season. At the same time, the price of Brent crude in London rose to $113.29 per barrel. Oil was thus trading at its highest level ever, in real terms. As in other recent months, the weakness of the US dollar was again identified as a key factor behind the continued, unprecedented strength of oil markets, in combination, in the third week of April, with strong Chinese demand for crude.

In May 2008 a further substantial increase, of US $14.23, or 13.5%, was recorded in the average price of the OPEC reference 'basket', which reached a new record level of $119.39 per barrel. The average price of North Sea Brent, meanwhile, rose by $14.08, or 12.9%, compared with the previous month, to $123.05 per barrel, while that of WTI increased by $13.02, or 11.6%, to $125.66 per barrel. In the first half of the month the price of both light crude traded in New York and of London Brent rose above $125 per barrel, in response to, among other factors: forecasts by some observers that the price of crude oil could rise as high as $150–$200 per barrel in the second half of 2008; concern that attacks on oil wells and pipelines by forces opposed to the Government in Nigeria would endanger supplies from that country; renewed cross-border conflict between Turkish government forces and Kurdish insurgents in northern Iraq; and violent unrest in Lebanon involving Hezbollah and other factions there. Already, in the third week of May, when the price of oil on some markets rose to $135 per barrel, the prospect that it would increase to $150 per barrel had begun to appear entirely realistic, prompting some analysts to reflect on the likely economic repercussions if it were to remain at such a high level for an extended period of time. In a press statement issued on 8 May, the Secretary-General of OPEC, Abdallah Salem el-Badri, had again identified speculative purchases of oil futures contracts, fuelled by the continued weakness of the US dollar, as the key factor responsible for the high price of oil, dismissing the argument that the higher price of oil was a consequence of a shortage of supplies with reference to the high level of commercial inventories of crude oil in OECD countries and high output by OPEC member states. A number of commentators expressed support for this view, arguing that, since the key factors frequently cited as being responsible for the increases in the price of oil since the start of 2008—the so-called 'peak oil' phenomenon and the beginning of a transition to a post-oil era; strong demand from emerging economies, in particular China and India; and supplementary capacity among major producers that was no greater than 3% of total production—had long been familiar, they should, assuming rational market conditions, already be fully reflected in prices, leaving speculation as the most plausible explanation for the increases recorded in May.

During June 2008 the price of oil on world markets was subject to unprecedented volatility. On 5 June, in response to a warning by an Israeli government minister that an attack by Israel on Iranian nuclear facilities appeared to be 'inevitable', and to a heavy fall in the value of the US dollar against a 'basket' of other currencies, the price of US light crude traded in New York rose by US $10.75 per barrel—the highest 'spike' ever—to $136.79 per barrel. On 9 June, in an attempt to calm the markets, Saudi Arabia announced that it would convene an extraordinary conference to discuss ways of tackling the high price of oil, which it again referred to as 'unjustified'. Almost immediately after the announcement had been made, however, Nigeria's Minister of State for Energy in charge of Petroleum, Odein Ajumogobia, dismissed the need for such a conference, claiming that there was nothing that OPEC could do to reduce the price of oil. Saudi Arabia's efforts to calm the markets were perceived as having been further undermined the following day, when the Chairman of Russia's state-owned oil and gas producer, Gazprom, insisted that strong demand was responsible for the high price of oil and claimed that the price might rise as high as $250 per barrel within 18 months. On 16 June, after talks had been held between the UN Secretary-General, Ban Ki-Moon, King Abdullah of Saudi Arabia and the Saudi Arabian Minister of Petroleum and Mineral Resources, Ali ibn Ibrahim al-Nuami, Saudi Arabia indicated that it was willing to increase output from 9.45m. b/d to 9.7m. b/d. Immediately prior to the extraordinary conference, the President of OPEC, Chakib Khelil, dismissed as 'irrational and illogical' an appeal to the Organization by the British Prime Minister, Gordon Brown, to increase its production of oil; Khelil insisted that the high price of oil was due to geopolitical tensions, speculation and shortage of refining capacity, rather than a lack of supplies. The conference was widely perceived as having failed to achieve any progress towards calming markets for oil. Indeed, on the day after it was held the price of light crude traded in New York rose in response to a warning by the Iranian Minister of Defence and Armed Forces Logistics that Iran's response to any attack against it would be 'devastating'. Fears were expressed at the same time that attacks on Nigerian oil infrastructure by forces opposed to the Nigerian Government in the previous week would reduce Nigeria's output to such an extent that the announced increase in Saudi Arabian output would be immediately cancelled out. On the final day of the month, two days after Iran had threatened to impose controls on shipping in the Gulf, the price of light crude traded in New York rose to $143.67 per barrel.

At the end of the first week of July 2008 the leaders of the Group of Eight (G8) industrial nations announced the formation of a new World Energy Forum in a further international attempt to address economic issues arising from the 100% increase in the price of oil that had occurred over the previous 12 months, indicating that one of the aims of the new forum would be to seek to persuade oil-producing countries to make 'stable investment to meet rising global demand'. On 11 July the price of Brent traded in London increased to a new record of US $147.02 per barrel, and that of US light crude to $146.90 per barrel. This followed tests by Iran of missiles that were capable of striking Israel, prompting a pledge to defend Israel by the USA; and a threat by the Movement for the Emancipation of the Niger Delta to resume attacks on Nigeria's oil infrastructure. In July the average price of the OPEC reference 'basket' increased by $2.89, equivalent to 2%, compared with the previous month, to $131.22 per barrel. The average price of London-traded Brent crude, meanwhile, rose by $0.75 per barrel—less than 1%—to $133.19 per barrel, while that of WTI fell slightly, by $0.11, to $133.82 per barrel. Sharp increases in the price of the OPEC reference 'basket' in the first half of July were attributed to the continued geopolitical tension in the Middle East noted above, and to the continued weakness of the US dollar. As the month progressed, however, concerns over future growth in demand for oil, in combination with a stronger dollar and a high level of exports by OPEC member states, dominated market sentiment, exerting downward pressure to the extent that by late July the price of the OPEC 'basket' had fallen to its lowest level for some two months.

At US $112.41 per barrel, the average price of the OPEC reference 'basket' recorded in August 2008 was $18.81—more than 14%—lower than that registered in the previous month. Brent blend, meanwhile, traded on average at $20.16, roughly 15%, lower, at $113.03 per barrel, while the average price of WTI, at $116.58 per barrel, was $17.24, or some 13%, lower than in July. As in late July, the prices of the crudes comprising the 'basket' were weak in the opening week of August, with demand reportedly subdued in response to data indicating slow economic growth in key world economies, in particular that of the USA. US demand for crude oil was reported by OPEC to have declined by some 900,000 b/d in January–August 2008, with consumption in June having fallen to its lowest level since 1998. Other factors that tended to depress the prices of 'basket' crudes in the first week of August included profit-taking by investment funds and fears that supplies from the Gulf of Mexico would be disrupted by a gathering tropical storm. Overall, the average price of the reference 'basket' declined by 5% in the first week of August. A further decline, of 5.3%, to $109.73 per barrel, ensued in the second week, when markets were defined by a stronger US dollar and growth in output of petroleum from the North Sea. On 13 August prices were boosted by US government data indicating an unexpected fall in US inventories of oil and gasoline, and in the third week of the month, for the first time in seven weeks, according to OPEC, a higher weekly average price—$111.08 per barrel—was recorded for the reference 'basket'. A key factor at this time was the conflict in the Caucasus involving Russia, South Ossetia, Abkhazia and Georgia. A further, marginal increase in the average OPEC reference price, to $111.20 per barrel, was recorded in the final week of August.

In September 2008 the average price of the OPEC reference 'basket' declined by US $15.56—a drop of almost 14% compared with the previous month—to $96.85 per barrel, its lowest level for eight months. The average price of WTI, meanwhile, fell by $12.43, or about 10.7%, to $116.58 per barrel, while that of Brent blend declined by $14.90, some 13.2%, to $113.03 per barrel. Declining prices were reported to reflect deteriorating conditions on world financial markets and their tangible economic impact, in particular in the USA where there was increasing evidence of recession. During the first week of September a combination of factors, including unfavourable US economic data and slowing demand for oil from China, caused the price of the OPEC reference 'basket' to decline, on average, by more than 6% ($6.81), to $104.39 per barrel. In the following week factors including the continued appreciation of the US dollar and low demand for crude oil from US refineries exerted further pressure, with the average price of the OPEC reference 'basket' falling by a further $7.02, or 6.7%, to $97.37 per barrel. In the third week of September the bankruptcy—the largest in US corporate history at that time—of the US-based global financial services company Lehman Brothers exerted decisive downward pressure on markets for oil, with the withdrawal of investment funds from dollar-denominated commodities causing a sharp fall in the value of the US dollar, although this factor was mitigated to some extent by fundamental factors, such as declining US inventories of crude oil, that tended to strengthen prices: the average price of the OPEC reference 'basket' declined by $8.17, or 8.4%, to $89.20 per barrel. In the final week of the month markets for crude oil were supported, notably, by a limited return of speculative funds, with the average price of the OPEC reference 'basket' rising by $9.0, or 10.2%, to $98.2 per barrel. On 9–10 September the 149th meeting of the OPEC conference took place in Vienna. With regard to market developments, the conference observed that action taken by OPEC member states had ensured that the market for oil was well supplied and inventories at a satisfactory level. In view of recent declines in the price of crude oil in response to lower growth in demand for oil, the conference agreed that production allocations (adjusted to include Angola and Ecuador and excluding Indonesia and Iraq) fixed in September 2007 to total 28.8m. b/d should remain in force, as markets were now oversupplied.

In October 2008 the average price of the OPEC reference 'basket' plunged by $27.69—almost 29%, the highest month-on-month decline ever—compared with the previous month, to $69.16 per barrel, the lowest average monthly OPEC price registered since March 2007. WTI, meanwhile, declined by $27.53, or 26.4%, to an average price of $76.62 per barrel, while the average price of Brent fell by $26.26, or 26.8%, to $71.87 per barrel. Continued disarray on world financial markets together with abundant supplies of crude oil were key influences on markets for oil in the first week of October, when the price of the OPEC reference 'basket' declined by $8.27, equivalent to 8.4%, to average $90.01 per barrel. The withdrawal of institutional investments from US dollar-denominated commodities exerted further pressure on crude oil prices in the second week of October, the average price of the OPEC reference 'basket' falling by a further $12.03, more than 13%, to $77.98 per barrel. This trend was maintained in the following week, when the average OPEC reference price slipped further, by $10.10—almost 13%—to $67.88 per barrel. On 24 October the 150th (extraordinary) meeting of the OPEC conference was held in Vienna. The meeting, which had been brought forward from November, was convened so that OPEC members could address the ongoing world financial crisis and its impact on markets for oil. The conference observed at the outset that the financial crisis had already weakened demand for oil—and for energy generally—thereby aggravating a situation of prolonged over-supply. The conference observed, too, that there had been a collapse in oil prices that was unprecedented in terms of both its speed and depth. In view of these factors, the decision was taken to reduce output by member states (excluding Iraq) by 1.5m. b/d from 28.8m. b/d with effect from 1 November. The reductions to be implemented by member states were as follows: Algeria, 71,000; Angola, 99,000; Ecuador, 27,000; Iran, 199,000; Kuwait, 132,000; Libya, 89,000; Nigeria, 113,000; Qatar, 43,000; Saudi Arabia, 466,000; UAE, 134,000; Venezuela, 129,000. The decision to reduce supplies was to be reviewed at a further extraordinary meeting scheduled to take place in Algeria on 17 December. Prior to the October OPEC conference, some traders were reported to have indicated that a cut of at least 3m. b/d in OPEC members' output would be needed effectively to support prices. Declines in the price of US crudes and a 6.5% drop in the price of Brent in the aftermath of OPEC's announcement of a 1.5m. b/d were reported to reflect disappointment and the perception that more had needed to be done. Markets for oil remained under pressure in the fourth week of October, sinking in response to, notably, declines in the share values of major oil compaines. The OPEC reference price fell by $6.35, or 9.4%, to $61.35 per barrel. In the final week of October the average price of the OPEC reference 'basket' declined by $3.89, or 6.3%, to $57.64 per barrel, its lowest level since March 2007.

Markets for crude oil were reportedly volatile in early November 2008, pulled in a positive direction by a weaker US dollar, some upward movement on global equity markets and rumours that Saudi Arabia had already reduced its output of crude. Also in early November the IEA forecast in its latest World Energy Outlook report that the price of oil would return above US $100 per barrel once normal economic conditions had been restored and that it would exceed $200 per barrel by 2030. Claiming that the era of cheap oil had ended, the IEA warned that the prevailing low price of oil was a temporary phenomenon and predicted an average price for crude oil of more than $100 per barrel in the period to 2015 as deficit of supply became the norm. The IEA estimated that production from oilfields world-wide was declining at an annual rate of 9% and claimed that prevailing patterns of energy supply and consumption were unsustainable. In the first week of November, none the less, fears of global economic recession set the tone for trading on oil markets, with the average price of the OPEC reference 'basket' declining to $56.83 per barrel. In the second week of the month lower forecasts of growth in demand for crude oil by the IEA and the EIA were judged partially responsible for a fall of $6.08, almost 11%, in the OPEC reference price, to $50.75 per barrel. In the third week of the month an escalation of the global financial crisis in combination with signs of recession in some countries caused the average price of the reference basket to decline again, by $6.41, or 10.5%, to $45.40 per barrel. Figures released by the EIA on 19 November showed US inventories of crude oil had increased by 1.6m. barrels in the previous week, twice as much as expected. In the final week of the month, however, the pressure on markets for crude was reportedly checked by the European stimulus plan put forward by the European Commission to tackle the global economic crisis and speculation that OPEC was about to implement further cuts in members' output. The average price of the OPEC reference 'basket' increased by $0.63, or 1.4%, to $46.03 in the fourth week of November. In November the OPEC reference price fell below $50 per barrel for the first time since 2005, averaging $49.76 per barrel, $19.40—28%—lower than in October. At the same time, the average price of WTI fell by $19.50, or 25.4%, to $57.12 per barrel, while that of Brent declined by $19.36, or almost 27%, to $52.51 per barrel.

In early December 2008 markets for crude oil remained under the negative influence of the official declaration of recession in the US economy by the US National Bureau of Economic Research that had prompted selling pressure across commodity markets generally; and of OPEC's decision at its November conference to leave its output unchanged. On 5 December the price of crude oil traded in New York sank below US $42 per barrel, almost its lowest level for four years, while the retail price of gasoline in the USA was reported to have declined to less than $1 per gallon. Also in early December, the price of London-traded Brent crude oil for January delivery declined to $46.02, its lowest level since February 2005. The US investment bank Merrill Lynch cautioned that oil prices might fall—albeit temporarily—to as low as $25 per barrel in 2009 if economic recession and declining demand for oil were to extend to China. This warning coincided with the announcement by the IEA that it was reducing its forecast for growth in demand for crude oil in 2009 to 220,000 b/d, compared with a previous forecast of 350,000 b/d. On 12 December it was announced that investment bank Goldman Sachs had lowered its forecast for the average of crude oil in 2009 to only $45 per barrel in 2009—earlier in 2008 the bank had suggested that the price of crude oil might 'spike' as high as $200 per barrel. However, bank analysts also forecast that prices would reach their nadir in early 2009 and that so-called 'demand destruction' would thereafter give way to 'supply destruction', rekindling the rally in the price of crude oil.

In the opening week of December 2008, in response to the factors outlined above, a decline of $5.26, or 11.4%, was registered in the price of OPEC crudes, which averaged $40.77 per barrel. The downward trend was limited to some extent in the second week of the month by the strengthening of the US dollar, which boosted investment in oil futures. The average price of the OPEC reference 'basket' declined by a further $1.71, or 4.2%, to $39.06 per barrel. Broadly, when the OPEC conference convened in Oran, Algeria, on 17 December for its 151st (extraordinary) meeting, the global financial crisis had begun to extend to the 'real' economy in the form of recession in all of the principal OECD regions and was spreading to developing countries, notably in Asia. The economic downturn had begun to sharply reduce demand for oil in the OECD countries; and there had been contraseasonal build-ups in commercial crude oil inventories, resulting in over-supply. In view of the prevailing supply/demand equation, oil inventories were expected to increase further still, to the top of the five-year range. The conference observed that there had been 'unprecedented down pressure ... on prices, which have fallen by more than US $90 per barrel since early July 2008. The organization's response to a situation which, if unaddressed, could lead to the fall of prices 'to levels which would place at jeopardy the investments required to guarantee adequate energy supplies in the medium-to-long term' was to reduce member states' output by 4.2m. b/d from the actual level of production by OPEC-11 in September 2008—29.045m b/d—from 1 January 2009. Greater than observers had anticipated, OPEC's reduction was reported to have lent considerable support to markets for crude in the third week of December, when the average price of the OPEC reference 'basket' increased by $1.22, equivalent to 3%, to $40.28 per barrel. On 19 December, at the initiative of the British Prime Minister, Gordon Brown, the London Energy Meeting was held in an attempt to address the issue of volatility in crude oil prices, which Brown, in his opening address to the meeting, described as 'the most pressing challenge' that faced the international community. Emphasizing the cost of wide variations in the price of oil to the international community, Brown urged transparency in prices, a new partnership between oil producers and consumers and the extension of the 'visionary internationalism' with which the global financial crisis had been tackled to energy challenges. However, subsequently, in a radio inteview, OPEC's secretary-general, Abdallah Salem el-Badri, claimed Brown was 'confused' regarding oil prices and suggested he should reduce the duty levied on oil if he was worried about prices. In the fourth week of December concerns about demand for crude oil, in combination with weak US new homes sales data, a heavy fall in the price of shares traded on Wall Street and data indicating a decline in Japanese exports, returned to dominate markets, the average price of the OPEC reference 'basket' falling by $5.36—13.3%—to $34.92 per barrel, the lowest monthly average price recorded since December 2004. In the final week of the year conflict between Israeli and Palestinian forces in Gaza, together with China's announcement that it was to accelerate the replenishment of its SPR, lent support to markets for oil. The average price of the OPEC reference 'basket' rose by $0.15, to $35.07 per barrel, in the final week of December. In December 2008 the average OPEC reference price thus declined by $11.16—equivalent to 22.4%—to $38.60 per barrel. At the same time, the average price of WTI fell by $15.67, or 27.4%, to $41.45 per barrel, while that of Brent declined by $12.16, or 23.2%, to $40.35 per barrel. For the whole of 2008 the average price of the OPEC reference 'basket' was $94.45 per barrel, having peaked at $131.22 in July.

In January 2009 the average price of the OPEC reference 'basket' (in which Indonesia's Minas crude blend was no longer included) rose by US $2.92, or 7.6%, to $41.52 per barrel. At the same time the average price of WTI increased by $0.05 per barrel, to $41.50 per barrel, while that of Brent rose by $3.24 (8%), to $43.59 per barrel. In the first week of January markets for crude were supported by continued conflict in Gaza and by an escalating dispute between Russia and Ukraine over Ukraine's failure to pay for natural gas supplied by Russia. The average price of the OPEC reference 'basket' leapt by 21% in the first week of 2009, to $43.98 per barrel. In the second week of the month markets were influenced by the interplay of such factors as the resolution of the dispute between Russia and Ukraine and the implementation of supply cuts by OPEC member states, with the average OPEC reference price declining by $3.07, or 7%, to $40.91 per barrel. Markets remained in a downward trend in the third week of January, although losses were limited by cold weather in the northern hemisphere. The average price of the OPEC reference 'basket' declined by $0.83, or 2%, to $40.08 per barrel in the third week of the month. In the final week of January the reduction in supplies from OPEC member states, cold weather conditions in North America and a decline in the value of the US dollar outweighed continued concern about the prospects of the world economy and demand for crude oil—on 22 January official US figures showed there had been an unexpected rise in US oil and gasoline stocks, causing some crudes to shed as much as $2 per barrel. The average OPEC reference price increased by $1.35, or 3.4%, to $41.43 per barrel in the final week of January.

In February 2009 there was little change in the price of the OPEC reference 'basket', which averaged US $41.35 per barrel, an increase of $0.17 or 0.4%. The average price of WTI, meanwhile, declined by $2.42 (5.8%), to $39.08 per barrel, while that of Brent rose by $0.52—1.2%—to $43.07 per barrel. During the first week of the month the average OPEC reference price increased by $0.97, or 2.2%, to $42.23 per barrel, in response to the announcement in more detail by the US Administration of measures to tackle the financial crisis, together with the continued effect of supply reductions by OPEC members. Markets were reinforced in the second week of February, too, by, among other factors, limited availability of crude on European markets. However, the gloomy prospects for the world economy—including further downward revisions of forecasted growth in demand for oil—continued to weigh heavily on markets, offsetting positive factors. The average price of the OPEC reference 'basket' increased by $0.48, or 1%, to $42.71 per barrel in the second week of February. Markets were dominated by pessimistic sentiment in the third week of the month, when the OPEC reference price declined by $3.26, or 7%, to an average of $29.45 per barrel. There was limited upward movement in the final week of the month, in response, notably, to strong demand for gasoline in the US and a lower-than-expected increase in inventories of crude. The price of the OPEC reference 'basket' increased by $1.56, or 3.9%, to an average of $41.01 per barrel in the final week of February.

In March 2009 the average price of the OPEC reference 'basket' increased by US $4.37, or 10.5%, to $45.78 per barrel. At the same time the average price of WTI rose by $8.92 (22.8%), to $48 per barrel, while that of Brent gained $3.48—8.1%—to reach $46.55 per barrel. In the first week of the month infrastructural problems affecting supplies from West Africa and the Russian port of Novorossiysk were reported to have outweighed declines registered in Wall Street trading, while markets for crude oil mustered additional support from an apparent increase in demand for gasoline. The OPEC reference price increased by $1.87, or 4.5%, to $43 per barrel in the first week of March. Positive factors dominated once again in the second week of the month, when the average price of the reference 'basket' rose by $0.26, equivalent to 0.6%, to $43.26 per barrel. On 16 March the price of some crudes declined by almost 5% as traders reacted to OPEC's decision, taken at its 152nd conference on the previous day, not to cut its output further. According to some observers, OPEC's decision proceeded in part from its eagerness not to risk antagonizing the USA by precipitating a harmful crude oil price 'spike'. In the third week of the month markets for crude oil were reported to have been dominated less ambiguously than in the two preceding weeks by positive factors, including continued observance by OPEC member states of measures adopted to curb supplies, the weakness of the US dollar and the publication of more details of measures the US Federal Reserve planned to take to counter the problems of the US banking sector. The price of the OPEC reference 'basket' increased by $2.65 (6.3%), to an average of $45.91 per barrel, in the third week of March. The continued weakness of the US dollar and renewed investment by funds in energy markets—prompted by rises in the value of shares traded on Wall Street—contributed to an increase of $4.48, or almost 10%, in the average OPEC reference price in the fourth week of March. At $50.39 per barrel, the weekly average price was the highest recorded since November 2008.

The average OPEC reference price recorded in April 2009—US $50.20 per barrel, $4.42, almost 10%, higher than in March—was the highest recorded since October 2008. The average price of WTI, meanwhile, increased by $1.82, or 3.8%, to $49.82 per barrel, while that of Brent rose by $3.89 (8.4%), to $50.44 per barrel. OPEC reported that markets for crude oil were weak in the early part of April, but were reinforced to some extent by decisions taken at the Group of Twenty (G20) finance minister and central bank governors summit meeting in London at the beginning of the month. The average price of the OPEC reference 'basket' declined by 3.7%—$1.84—to $48.55 per barrel in the first week of April. In the following week prices were reported to have been supported by continued adjustments to supplies by OPEC member states, among other factors, the average OPEC reference price rising by $2.79, equivalent to almost 6%, to $51.34 per barrel. The high level of US crude inventories, in combination with generally weak economic data, put markets for crude oil under pressure in the third week of April, although the average price of the OPEC reference 'basket' did, none the less, increase marginally, by $0.09 (less than 0.2%), to $51.43 per barrel. In the fourth week of the month the withdrawal of large-scale investments from energy markets in favour of media perceived to be more secure maintained downward pressure on crude oil prices, with the average OPEC reference price falling by $2.40, or 4.7%, to $49.03 per barrel. In the final week of the month markets were generally without direction. The price of the OPEC reference 'basket' stood at $49.73 per barrel at the end of April.

In May 2009 the average price of the OPEC reference 'basket' increased by US $6.78, nearly 14%, to $56.98 per barrel, the highest monthly average price recorded for seven months. At the same time the average price of WTI increased by $9.39, or nearly 19%, to $59.21 per barrel, while that of Brent rose by $6.83 (13.5%), to $57.27 per barrel. During the first week of the month positive US economic data prevailed over concerns about the likelihood of a global epidemic of swine flu to exercise, overall, a positive influence on markets, with the price of the OPEC reference basket increasing by $4.53, or more than 10%, to $56.35 per barrel. In the following week data that appeared to support hopes for a recovery in demand for crude vied with profit-taking by investment funds to exert the key influence, with a decline in the value of the US dollar—which prompted investment in energy products and other dollar-denominated commodities—tipping the balance in favour of the former. The price of the OPEC reference basket increased by $2.22, or 4%, to average $56.37 per barrel. Markets lacked direction in the third week of May, with the continued weakness of the US dollar remaining a key factor. The average price of the OPEC reference 'basket' rose by $1.30, or 2.3%, to $57.78 per barrel. In the the final week of the month markets for crude moved upwards again as hopes for global economic recovery, the perceived likelihood of strong US demand for gasoline during the driving season and the continued weakness of the US dollar dominated sentiment. The average OPEC reference price increased by $2.92, equivalent to almost 5%, to $60.70 per barrel in the final week of May, its highest level for seven months. On 28 May the 153rd (extraordinary) meeting of the OPEC conference took place in Vienna. In its review of markets for oil, the conference observed that 'the severe and broad impact of the ongoing global economic downturn, precipitated by the financial crisis, has led to a weakness in global oil demand, which is likely to remain for some time. Indeed, since the second half of 2008, world oil demand growth has witnessed its first decline since the early 1980s.' The conference noted, further, that while measures implemented by OPEC with the aim of correcting this imbalance had stabilized oil prices to some extent, supplies of oil world-wide remained in excess of demand and global inventories were still high, close, in fact, to the record level registered in early 1998). Citing the need to safeguard producers' ability to maintain the investments needed to guarantee adequate energy supplies in the medium-to-long term, OPEC voted to maintain output at its current level and to review this decision at its next ordinary meeting in September.

In June 2009 the average price of the OPEC reference 'basket' soared by US $11.38—almost 20%—to $68.36 per barrel. At the same time the average price of WTI rose by $10.47 (17.7%), to $69.68 per barrel, while that of London-traded Brent gained $11.28, equivalent to 19.7%, reaching $68.55 per barrel. In the first week of June the average OPEC reference price increased by $6 (almost 10%), to $66.67 per barrel. On 2 June oil prices rose to their highest levels since the beginning of 2009, with US light crude reported to have traded at more than $68 per barrel, and Brent blend registering a daily gain of $1.77 to reach $67.46. Crude oil was thus trading at almost twice the level of $35—the lowest to date in 2009—to which it had fallen in February. According to some analysts, the increases recorded in early June were due to (generally) improved factory output world-wide, booming trade in stocks and shares and the weakness of the US dollar. Others cautioned, however, that markets were disregarding more negative fundamental factors, such as continued weak demand and very high US inventories by focusing on disconnected examples of good news. Prices remained in an upward trend in the second week of June, when the average price of the OPEC reference 'basket' increased by $2.50—equivalent to 3.8%—to $69.17 per barrel. On 11 June the price of crude traded on the New York Mercantile Exchange (NYMEX) rose above $71 per barrel in response to industry data which showed that proven reserves had fallen for the first time in 10 years and a prediction—by Alexei Miller, Chairman of the Russian energy organization Gazprom—that the price of crude oil might eventually rise as high as $250 per barrel. Markets were more subdued in the third week of June as the US dollar strengthened. A marginal increase, of $0.33, to $69.50 per barrel, was recorded in the average OPEC reference price. Fears for the prospects of the global economy and a continued rise in the value of the US dollar dominated in the final week of the month, with the average price of the OPEC reference 'basket' falling by $1.80 (2.6%), to $67.70 per barrel.

The average price of the OPEC reference 'basket' declined by US $3.77 (6%) in July 2009, to $64.59 per barrel. The average price of London-traded Brent blend, meanwhile, fell by $3.94 (5.7%), to $64.61, while a fall of $5.45 (7.8%) was registered in the average price of WTI. Markets for oil were subject to conflicting influences throughout the month. In early July concerns about global economic prospects, in particular those of the USA, were prevalent, and by 13 July the average OPEC reference price had fallen to $59.66 per barrel. Markets subsequently responded positively to demand assessments published earlier in the month, however, including forecasts by analysts at US investment bank Merrill Lynch that the price of (US) crude oil in 2009 and 2010 would average, respectively, $58.50 per barrel and $75 per barrel. On 10 July the IEA forecast that world demand for crude oil would increase by 1.4m. b/d, or 1.7%, to 85.2m. b/d in 2010, driven mainly by demand from China and India. The July forecast was the first issued by the IEA in 2009 that predicted an increase in demand in 2010. In the final week of the month the average price of the OPEC 'basket' recovered to $67.66 per barrel. Overall, however, analysts noted that markets for oil in July had continued to be characterized by underlying weakness of demand, citing a decline in the utilization of US inventories as one example of this. Leading oil industry executives, including the chief executive of Royal Dutch Shell and the chairman and chief executive of Exxon Mobil, concurred in this assessment of demand in statements that accompanied the announcement of their companies' most recent quarterly results towards the end of the month. On 30 July, after the price of US light crude had risen to $67.01 per barrel and that of Brent blend to $70.21 per barrel, some commentators expressed concern at the continued volatility of oil markets, observing that the day's increases had been triggered by higher share prices in the USA, Japan and Europe rather than any significant change in fundamental market conditions. Financial regulators in the USA were reported to have initiated an inquiry in late July into the role played by speculation in oil-price volatility throughout 2008 and in June 2009.

In August 2009 the average price of the OPEC reference 'basket' recovered by some 10.5% (US $6.76), to $71.35 per barrel. At the same time an increase of $8.23 (13%) in the average price of Brent, to $72.84 per barrel, was recorded, while the average price of WTI rose by 10.6% ($6.82), to $71.05 per barrel. Markets for oil were supported in the early part of August by data that indicated good prospects for the US manufacturing and European banking sectors, as well as strong economic data from China. As the middle of the month approached, the price of some OPEC 'basket' components had risen above $72 per barrel, having fallen as low as $66.42 late in July. These positive factors subsequently gave way, in the second half of the month, to currency and technical factors, including, profit-taking, with the average price of the OPEC 'basket' declining to $68.04 by 17 August. Before the end of the month, the average price had risen above $70 per barrel again, however, in response to positive US and European economic data, including increased utilization of US inventories of crude oil. On 25 August the prices of US light crude and London-traded Brent rose to $75 per barrel—their highest level to date in 2009—in response to data indicating improved US consumer confidence. Markets for these crudes closed lower, however, owing to profit-taking by institutional investors. Analysts noted that, fundamentally, markets for crude remained weak, and forecast continued price volatility in the near term.

The average price of the OPEC reference 'basket' declined by 5.9% (US $4.18), in September 2009, to $67.17 per barrel. The average price of Brent fell by $5.45 per barrel (7.5%), to $67.39 per barrel, while that of WTI eased by 2.4% ($1.71), to $69.34 per barrel. Markets for crude petroleum were reported to have weakened at the beginning of September in response to increased supplies of the commodity, in combination with 'technical' sales triggered by lower share prices in China. A rise in the value of the US dollar was another factor that exerted pressure on prices at this time. Immediately prior to a meeting of the OPEC conference on 9 September, however, the price of US light crude rose by $0.59, to $71.69 per barrel, while that of London-traded Brent rose by $0.67, to $70.09 per barrel. At the conclusion of its September meeting OPEC noted that in spite of some signs of economic recovery world-wide, concerns remained regarding the extent and tempo of the upturn, especially in the OECD countries. Although there had been some decline in excessive stocks of oil, market fundamentals remained weak, refinery utilization rates were low, and large refined-product inventories had accumulated. In view of a continued excess of supply, the conference agreed to retain current production levels until its 155th (extraordinary) meeting, scheduled for December. Subsequently, in September, markets for oil were supported by forecasts—notably one by the IEA—of stronger demand for crude oil and a greater-than-expected decline in US inventories of crude, among other influences. On 16 September, in response to lower stocks data, the price of NYMEX-traded crude rose by $1.58, to $72.51 per barrel, while that of London-traded Brent increased by $1.81, to $71.67 per barrel. On 17 September the price of the OPEC reference 'basket' had risen above $70 per barrel again. On 24 September, however, the price of US light crude fell by more than $3, to $65.89 per barrel, while a decline of $3.17, to $64.82 per barrel, was recorded in the price of Brent. On 28 September the price of the OPEC reference 'basket' declined to $64 per barrel.

In October 2009 the average price of the OPEC reference 'basket' increased by US $5.50, equivalent to 8.2%, to $72.67 per barrel. At the same time the average price of WTI rose by $6.39, or 9.2%, to $75.73 per barrel, while that of Brent increased by some 8%, or $5.37, to $72.76 per barrel. Markets were influenced in the first two full weeks of October by sanguine assessments of economic prospects world-wide, in combination with a decline in the value of the US dollar, in particular relative to the euro. Early in the month the IMF forecast global economic growth of 3.1% in 2010, compared with a prediction of 2.5% published in July. Also, both the IEA and OPEC raised their projections for world oil consumption in 2010. Markets were subsequently reported to have remained under the influence of these—and other—positive factors, including, according to industry sources, unexpectedly high demand for crude from US gasoline inventories and the presence in the market of so-called 'technical' buyers. The price of the OPEC 'basket' averaged $76.64 per barrel in the week ending 23 October, compared with $72.21 in the previous week. On 29 October the price of US light crude rose sharply, by 3.4%, to $80.08 per barrel, after the publication of data that showed that the US economy had returned to growth for the first time in more than a year in July–September. At the same time the price of Brent increased to $78.24 per barrel. Analysts noted, however, that markets continued to be driven by sentiment that left out of account weak fundamental factors, such as unused oil-industry capacity and stagnant demand. In late October the President of OPEC, José Botelho de Vasconcelos, indicated that any increase in the price of oil beyond the $80-per-barrel level might prompt OPEC member states to increase supplies in the interest of global economic recovery. Data published in late October indicated that Chinese demand for oil in September had grown at its fastest rate for more than three years, by 12.5%, to 8.17m. b/d.

The average price of the OPEC reference 'basket' increased by US $3.62, equivalent to some 5%, in November 2009, to $76.29 per barrel. At the same time the average price of Brent blend rose by $3.90 (5.4%), to $76.66 per barrel, while an increase of $2.11 (2.8%), to $77.84 per barrel, was recorded in the average price of WTI. On 3 November the price of both US light crude and Brent rose by more than $1 per barrel, in response to strong manufacturing data in the USA. In the week to 6 November, likewise under the influence of positive assessments of economic prospects, and of the continued weakness of the US dollar, the average price of the OPEC reference 'basket' rose to $76.36 per barrel. In the following week, however, in response to a rise in the value of the dollar, together with profit-taking, the average price of the reference 'basket' eased somewhat, to $76.25 per barrel. In mid-November, in a monthly report which noted that the price of oil had risen by more than 70% since the beginning of 2009, the IEA warned that recent rises in the price of oil could jeopardize economic recovery world-wide and retard growth in demand for oil. The agency observed that demand for oil at this time was being driven principally by Chinese consumption, and revised upwards its global demand forecast for 2010, to 86.2m. b/d. The price of the reference 'basket'—and the prices of US light crude and London-traded Brent—subsequently rose as the dollar depreciated again and US Gulf Coast production was disrupted by Hurricane Ida, averaging $76.77 per barrel in the week to 20 November. In the last full week of the month, 'technical' selling, together with increased US inventories of crude, among other factors, caused the average price of the reference 'basket' to fall to $75.79 per barrel.

In December 2009 the average price of the OPEC reference 'basket' declined by US $2.28 (3%), to $74.01 per barrel. At the same time, the average price of WTI fell by $3.43 (4.4%), to $74.41 per barrel, while that of Brent eased by $2.38 (3.1%), to $74.28 per barrel. In the early part of the month prices were exposed to strong negative influences, in particular high US inventories of crude, doubts about the strength of global economic prospects and, consequently, the likely future strength of demand for petroleum. Early in the month the price of Brent crude (for January 2010 delivery) declined to its lowest level for three-and-a-half years, in response to data that indicated that the number of jobs lost in November in the USA had been the highest in 34 years. On 14 December the average price of the OPEC reference 'basket', at $70.64 per barrel, was the lowest recorded for two months. On 22 December the 155th (extraordinary) meeting of the OPEC conference was convened in Luanda, Angola. At its conclusion OPEC observed, 'with great concern', that the global economy remained confronted by the deepest and most widespread contraction since the 1940s, including declining industrial output, weak private consumption and high unemployment. In 2009, for the first time since the 1980s, demand for oil world-wide had contracted for a second, successive year. In the absence of any firm indications of how strong or durable economic recovery might be, OPEC decided to maintain existing production levels unchanged. In the second half of December, none the less, the average OPEC price rose from the 14 December 'low' to close at $77.16 per barrel on 31 December. The recovery was reported to have been spurred by higher futures prices, due, in turn, to cold weather in the northern hemisphere. Despite the overall decline registered, the average price of the OPEC reference 'basket' in December was the second highest in 2009, after that of November. For the whole of 2009 the OPEC reference price averaged $61.06 per barrel, 35% lower than that—$94.45 per barrel—recorded in 2008.

The average price of the OPEC reference 'basket' increased by US $2 (2.7%) in January 2010, to $76.01 per barrel. At the same time, the average price of Brent rose by $1.91 (2.6%), to $78.30 per barrel, while that of WTI increased by 5.2%, or $3.89, to $78.30 per barrel. Prices were reported to have been propelled upwards in the early part of January by cold weather in the northern hemisphere and by renewed investment interest. In the second week of January the price of US crude oil for February delivery rose to $83.95 per barrel—the highest price recorded since October 2008. This and other gains were reported to have been fuelled by the publication of Chinese economic data showing that demand for oil in China had soared by 25% in December 2009. Continued cold weather in the USA and Europe was another factor that supported oil prices at this time, together with depreciation in the value of the US dollar. On 11 January the price of the reference 'basket' rose to its highest level since October 2008, $80.29 per barrel. Throughout the remainder of the month, however, warmer northern-hemisphere temperatures, a stronger US dollar and lower share prices combined to push prices lower.

Markets for oil remained subject to negative influences in February 2010. In the first week of the month the price of the OPEC reference 'basket' of crudes fell below US $69 per barrel, in response to pessimistic assessments of the prospects for economic recovery world-wide and, in particular, an appreciation in the value of the US dollar relative to the euro, the European currency having fallen as a result of the sovereign debt crisis in Greece. On 5 February a decline of $3 per barrel was registered in the price of the OPEC reference 'basket', the biggest decline in one day for some six months. Prices subsequently recovered somewhat, in response, notably, to higher global share prices. Overall, for the whole of February, the average price of the OPEC reference 'basket' declined by $3.02 (about 4%), to $72.99 per barrel. The average price of WTI, meanwhile, fell by $1.96 (2.5%), to $76.34 per barrel. At $73.64 per barrel, the average price of London-traded Brent was 3.3%, or $2.55, lower than that recorded in January.

In March 2010, at US $77.21—$4.22 per barrel, or 5.8%, higher than in February—the average price of the OPEC reference 'basket' was the highest recorded since September 2008. Gains were also registered in the average price of Brent, which rose by $5.26 (7.1%), to $78.90 per barrel, and that of WTI, which increased by $4.91 (6.4%), to $81.25 per barrel. Analysts noted that, at this level, the price of the OPEC reference 'basket' was some 70% higher than one year previously. The gains registered in March were attributed to renewed forecasts of higher economic growth world-wide, together with a decline in the value of the US dollar relative, in particular, to the euro, which had risen as it appeared increasingly likely that the debt crisis in Greece would be resolved satisfactorily. Prior to a meeting of the OPEC conference the IEA forecast that demand for oil in 2010 would be driven by rising demand from emerging countries, with half of all growth coming from Asia, in particular China, where an 'astonishing' increase in demand of 28% had been recorded in January compared with January 2009. At the same time, however, the IEA forecasted a decline of 0.3% in demand for oil from developed countries in 2010. The agency increased its forecast for global demand for oil in 2010 by 1.8%, to 86.6m. b/d. At the conclusion of the 156th OPEC conference, which convened in Vienna on 17 March, OPEC observed that the global economy was clearly recovering from the recession of 2008 and early 2009, but that serious threats to that recovery remained, including high public debt in the most advanced economies, high unemployment, weak demand and increased protectionism. OPEC expressed concern, too, that while world oil demand was forecast to rise marginally in 2010, the rise was expected to be more than offset by increased non-OPEC supply. Demand for OPEC oil was thus likely to decline for a third successive year. Persistently high OECD stock levels indicated that there had been a contraseasonal accumulation in January–March, and excessive forward-cover was judged likely to persist for the remainder of the year. In the light of this analysis, OPEC decided, once again, to maintain output unchanged, at 24.84m. b/d. In the immediate aftermath of OPEC's decision the price of the United Kingdom's benchmark Brent crude rose by $0.72, to $81.25 per barrel. The price of US light, sweet crude likewise rose, by $0.77, to $82.47 per barrel.

The average price of the OPEC reference 'basket' increased by 6.6% (US $5.12) in April 2010, to $82.33 per barrel. At the same time the average price of Brent rose by 7.5% ($5.89), to $84.79 per barrel, while that of WTI gained 3.9% ($3.19), reaching $84.44 per barrel. At the beginning of April oil prices rose to their highest level for 17 months, propelled upwards by better-than-expected manufacturing data in China and the euro zone. The price of US light, sweet crude (for delivery in May) increased by $0.70, to $84.46 per barrel, while the price of Brent gained $0.74 to reach to $83.44 per barrel. The rise of the price of some crudes to as high as $87 per barrel in early April prompted the IEA to warn that the price of oil was 'overheated'. Another factor driving early-April price increases was news of a rise in the number of new jobs created in the USA in March to its highest level since March 2007. Concerns were expressed at this time that the effect on the price of oil of 'benign' economic data from the USA was being compounded, in the absence of supply/demand data that would support price increases, by speculation. Early in the month the price of the OPEC reference 'basket' rose above $80 per barrel for the first time since January, and by the end of the month it had reached $84.13 per barrel, the highest price recorded since October 2008.

Markets for oil were characterized by renewed volatility in May 2010, the price of the OPEC reference 'basket' averaging US $74.48 per barrel—$7.85, or 9.5%, lower than in April. The average price of Brent blend, meanwhile, declined by 10.9%, or $9.22, to $75.57 per barrel, while that of WTI fell by $10.79 (12.8%), to $73.65 per barrel. In monthly terms, the decline in the price of the reference 'basket' recorded in May was the greatest since December 2008. Analysts attributed the fall to renewed pessimism about global economic prospects, in particular concerns that the Greek debt crisis could extend to other countries in the eurozone. By late May the price of the reference 'basket' had descended to an eight-month 'low' of less than $67 per barrel, compared with more than $84 per barrel at the beginning of May. In late May a rise in the value of the US dollar relative to the euro caused the price of New York-traded WTI to fall below $68 per barrel, its lowest level for five months. The price of Brent crude (for July delivery), meanwhile, fell by 2.2%, to $69.55 per barrel.

The price of the OPEC reference 'basket' continued to decline in June 2010, averaging US $72.95 per barrel, $1.53 (2.1%) lower than the average price recorded in May. The average price of Brent also fell in June, by $0.72 (less than 1%), to $74.85 per barrel. However, an increase of $1.64 (2.2%), to $75.29, was recorded in the average price of WTI. In the second week of June the price of some crudes rose by as much as 4% in response to renewed optimism about global economic growth, a greater-than-expected decline in US inventories of crude and stronger demand for refined petroleum products at the beginning of the US driving season. Analysts noted that while the average price recorded for the reference 'basket' in June was the lowest since October 2009, prices had been considerably less volatile than in May. The continued weakness of markets for oil was attributed to abundant supplies of crude and to high global inventories. In late June the price of oil traded in New York rose to $79.38, its highest level for seven weeks, in response to fears of hurricane weather conditions in the Gulf of Mexico. In the first week of July the price of the OPEC reference 'basket' fell below $70 per barrel, in response, according to industry sources, to unfavourable macroeconomic data. By 8 July, however, the average OPEC price had recovered to $71.86 per barrel after the IMF revised upwards its global economic growth projection for 2010.

In July 2010, at US $72.51 per barrel, the average price of the OPEC reference 'basket' was $0.44—less than 1%—lower than that recorded in June. The average price of Brent, meanwhile, rose by $0.79, equivalent to about 1%, to $75.64 per barrel. A slight increase, of $0.82, or 1.1%, to $76.11 per barrel, was likewise recorded in the average price of WTI. The decline in OPEC's reference price in July was reported to have been determined mainly by the ready availability of Middle Eastern crudes, which faced strong competition from Russian ESPO (Eastern Siberia–Pacific Ocean) crude amid weak demand overall. Early in August the price of the reference 'basket' increased to $78.28 per barrel, its highest level for three months, in response to the strength of share markets world-wide, the weakness of the US dollar and positive economic data from the USA. By 17 August, however, the price had declined to $73.25 per barrel. On 21 August US petroleum inventories were reported to have risen to their highest level for 20 years—in fact their highest level since the US Department of Energy had begun to collect combined weekly data—prompting speculation that the price of oil would soon decline below $70 per barrel and that OPEC, in response, would initiate action to enforce observance of existing quotas and further restrict production.

The Regional Association of Oil and Natural Gas Companies in Latin America and the Caribbean (Asociación Regional de Empresas de Petróleo y Gas Natural en Latinoamérica y el Caribe—ARPEL) exists to promote co-operation in matters of technical and economic development. ARPEL, with headquarters in Montevideo, Uruguay, has 28 members, including companies based outside the region.

SILVER

Known since prehistoric times, silver is a white metal which is extremely malleable and ductile. It is one of the best metallic conductors of heat and electricity, hence its use in electrical contacts and in electroplating. Silver's most important compounds are the chloride and bromide, which darken on exposure to light and form the basis of photographic emulsions.

World-wide, almost 70% of silver production in 2009 was generated as a by-product, or co-product, of gold, copper, lead, zinc and other mining operations. Methods of recovery depend upon the composition of the silver-bearing ore. The exploitation of primary sources of silver ore accounted for 30% of silver output in 2009.

In 2009 the world-wide use of silver in fabricated products totalled 729.8m. troy ounces (a decrease of almost 12% compared with the 2008 level). The figure was the lowest seen since the early 1990s, mainly because of reduced usage in industry and photography, reflecting lower volumes of world trade in time of recession. Industrial purposes (including the manufacture of electronic equipment and batteries in the major industrialized countries) consumed the majority, 48% or 352.2m. oz (compared with 443.4m. oz in 2008). Jewellery and silverware absorbed 216.1m. oz (30%), the small fall in jewellery demand, which took it an 11-year low, more than compensated for by silverware reversing its generally declining trend over the decade with a 5% rise to 59.5m. oz. The use of silver in the production of photographic material (including X-ray film)—increasingly affected by the uptake of digital products in consumer markets—fell by a further 21%, to 82.9m. oz (compared with 218.3m. oz at the beginning of the decade, in 2000), to represent 11% of global demand for fabrication in 2009 (24% in 2000). The remainder, 78.7m. oz of silver (representing 7% of total fabrication demand), was consumed in the manufacture of coins and medals; that 2009 figure represented a further, atypical, substantial increase on the previous year, of 21%, following the 64% of 2008 on 2007. Coins and medals used a usual amount of about 40m. oz in the mid-2000s and some 30m. oz at the turn of the century. Other industrial uses for silver include the production of brazing alloys, mirrors and catalysts. New areas of growth for the use of silver in recent years are reported to be in the fields of electronics (plasma screens), health (antibacterial dressings) and renewable energy (photovoltaic cells). In 2009 the principal user of silver in fabricated products (including the use of scrap) remained the USA, which consumed 164.4m. oz (23% of the world total). India, the only major market to record an increase in industrial demand, surged into second place, with 104.3m. oz (14%), while Japan's 39% fall in demand saw it slip into fourth place, with 66.6m. oz (9%), while the People's Republic of China, with 70.7m. oz (10%) took third place. Europe accounted for usage of 149.0m. oz (20%—the main countries being Italy, with 33.6m. oz, and Germany, with 32.8m.oz). Thailand was the world's seventh heaviest user of silver for fabrication (third in eastern Asia), followed by Belgium, the United Kingdom and Ireland, the Republic of Korea (South Korea), Mexico, Taiwan, France and Austria. Other regions of the world were less significant, demand in Africa being negligible (1.7m. oz in total—2009 figures) and the only significant user in Latin America apart from Mexico (16.4m. oz) being Brazil (6.6m. oz).

World mine production of silver was estimated to have increased by 25% during the period 1979–85, as a result of generally higher (although widely fluctuating) prices. However, while output advanced, consumption declined, resulting in a world surplus of silver in each year during 1980–89. In 1990 this trend was reversed, and, according to the Silver Institute (an international association of miners, refiners, fabricators and manufacturers, with its headquarters in Washington, DC, USA), world demand exceeded mine and secondary (recycled and scrap silver) production, creating the first silver market supply deficit since 1978. In each of the years 1991–97 world consumption of silver outpaced mine production, which declined by 13.8% over 1990–94. Output began a steady recovery in 1995, increasing by around 36% between then and 2002. In 2002 world output of mined silver rose by 2.6% to a new record level (for the fifth consecutive year) of 606.2m. oz. In 2002, however, world mined production fell by 2.1%, to 593.9m. oz. Sharp falls in the mined output of the USA and Chile were among the factors contributing to the world-wide decline. In 2003 world mined production recovered slightly, to 596.6m. oz, and a little more strongly in 2004, to a new record level of 613.0m. oz. Increased output by the world's four major producers—Mexico, Peru, Australia and China—was reported to have accounted for most of the increase in that year. In 2005 global mined production of silver increased by 3.9%, to 636.8m. oz. Record output at the world's two largest primary silver mines—Mexico's Proaño mine and BHP Billiton's Cannington mine in Australia—was among the factors that boosted world production of silver in 2005. World mined production of silver increased only fractionally in 2006, to 640.9m. oz, when continued growth in output in Peru, Mexico and China was counterbalanced by a sharp decline in mine production in Australia, where the two largest mines—including the Cannington mine—had to undergo rehabilitation owing to structural and metallurgical problems. In 2007 world mine output of silver increased by 3.7%, to 664.4m. oz, partly as a result of new developments in Mexico and Bolivia. The recovery of output at the Cannington mine in Australia and continued steady growth in overall Chinese output also contributed to the global increase in 2007. A 3.1% increase in 2008 took world-wide mine production of silver to 684.7m. oz, following significant increases in Latin American production, despite a contraction in Chilean output. The pattern was repeated in 2009, although China and Turkey also recorded increases in production, while Australia's contraction in ongoing operations exceeded the decline in Chile. A 3.6% rise in global mine production took primary silver output to 709.6m. oz (22,072 metric tons) in 2009. In that year Latin America and the Caribbean, including Mexico, accounted for 48% of mined silver production (Peru alone 17.5%, Mexico 15%), while eastern Asia and Oceania accounted for 22% (China 13%, Australia 7%).

In 2002 Peru overtook Mexico as the world's leading producer of silver, retaining the top rank in each year in 2003–09. Peruvian mined output of silver, which rose steadily throughout the 2000s, reached production of 102.6m. oz in 2005, 111.1m. oz in 2006, 112.6m. oz in 2007, 118.3m. oz in 2008 and 123.9m. oz in 2009. Peru possessed an estimated 15% of total reserves of silver worldwide in 2009, according to the US Geological Survey (USGS). Mexican output has fluctuated somewhat in the 2000s, but remained above 80.0m. oz from 2000, rising substantially in 2005, by 12.7%, to 93.1m. oz, and continuing to increase each year thereafter: to 95.5m. oz in 2006, 100.8m. oz in 2007, 104.2m. oz in 2008 and 104.7m. oz in 2009. The country's Proaño mine, operated by Industria Peñoles near Fresnillo (in the state of Zacatecas), was the largest primary silver mine in the world (in terms of production) in 2009—again surpassing the declining production of Australia's Cannington mine, having first done so in 2006. Mexico's reserves of silver ore in 2009 were estimated by the USGS to represent 9% of total reserves world-wide. Chile, despite its continuing problems in the silver sector, is reckoned to have the world's largest reserves (18% of total in 2009), but the country was displaced by Bolivia as the region's third largest producer in 2009. In that year Chile, now the fourth most important regional producer and seventh in the world (having also slipped behind Russia), accounted for 5.9% of estimated world production, down from 9.1% in 2007, following a 33% decline in output over the two years, to 41.8m. oz, which was below the 2003 level. This was mainly attributable to developments in the primary silver-mining sector, with La Coipa mine returning to primary gold operations in 2008 and another mine suspending operations at the end of that year. Bolivian production, however, increased by 19% in 2009, to 42.6m. oz (6.0% of world output—the fifth largest mine production). This followed a doubling in the previous year, from 16.9m. oz in 2007, to 35.8m. oz, mainly as a result of mining beginning in earnest at San Cristóbal, in the silver-zinc-lead deposits of Potosí department in southern Bolivia. San Cristóbal has proven and probable silver reserves that total 251m. metric tons of ore, containing 1.8 oz of silver per ton, and it is one of the world's largest open-pit silver projects. San Cristóbal alone provides about three-quarters of Bolivian mined silver production. Although a relatively minor producer, Argentina almost quadrupled its silver output between 1998 and 2007, as the result of the entry into production of two new mines in the earlier year. In 2007 output amounted to 7.8m. oz, compared with 6.2m. oz in 2006, an increase of 26%; a further 32% increase in production took output to 10.3m. oz in 2008, while a 66% increase in 2009 reached 17.1m. oz (10th in the world). The dramatic rise was mainly the result of two new projects coming on line during 2009, at the Manantial Espejo and Pirquitas mines. Honduras produced a little over 1.6m. oz annually in the early 2000s, but this rose in the second half of the decade, to some 1.9m. oz in 2008 and 2009. Meanwhile, Guatemala, which only began production in 2005, exceeded Honduras in 2007 and reached some 4.2m. oz in 2009. In the latter year the Dominican Republic became the region's eighth largest producer of mined silver, with 0.6m. oz, when output began at its Cerro de Maimón site.

As an investment metal (an estimated 80% of the world's silver bullion stocks are speculative holdings), silver is highly sensitive to factors other than the comparative levels of supply and demand. Silver, like gold and platinum, is customarily measured in troy weight. The now otherwise obsolete troy pound contains 12 ounces (oz), each of 480 grains. One troy ounce is equal to 31.1 grams (1 kg = 32.15 troy oz), compared with the avoirdupois ounce of 28.3 grams.

Fluctuations in the price of silver bullion traditionally tended to follow trends in prices for gold and other precious metals. However, silver has come to be viewed increasingly as an industrial raw material and hence likely to decrease in price in times of economic recession. Two of the main centres for trading in silver are the London Bullion Market (LBM) and the New York Commodity Exchange (COMEX). Dealings in silver on the LBM are only on the basis of 'spot' contracts (for prompt delivery), while COMEX contracts are also for silver 'futures' (options to take delivery at specified future dates).

Silver Prices on the New York Commodity Exchange
(average 'spot' quotations, US $ per troy ounce)

	Average	Highest month(s)	Lowest month(s)
2000	4.965	—	—
2007	13.378	15.449 (Nov.)	12.130 (Jan.)
2008	14.960	15.499 (March)	8.790 (Oct.)
2009	14.693	17.858 (Nov.)	11.386 (Jan.)

Sources: The Silver Institute; Gold Fields Mineral Services Ltd.

From a peak in 1998, the annual average London price of silver declined steadily until 2001. A rise of 5.2% in the annual average in 2002 took the London price to US $4.60 per troy oz, and the rise continued, through $11.55 per oz in 2006 (its highest nominal level for 26 years—a 58% rise on the previous year), to $13.38 per oz in 2007 (the highest real level in 23 years) and $14.99 per oz in 2008. Analysts attributed the increase recorded in 2007 to, above all, investment demand for silver, especially in October–December. Strong demand for silver for fabrication purposes was an additional factor that buoyed the price of the metal, and this continued into the first months of 2008. The average annual price of silver in 2008, however, concealed volatile price fluctuations as the world entered recession in the last months of the year. In March the daily price reached $20.92, the highest figure since 1980 (when there was a record $49.45 per oz price), while in late October the nadir was a price of $8.88. The silver price recovered steadily through 2009 (increasing by 53%), but at $14.67 for the year was still down on the 2008 annual average. The 2009 silver price rally, although fluctuating over the year, was driven by investment, industrial demand and the gold price rise—illustrating silver's dual nature as both a precious metal ('safe haven') and an industrial commodity. After falling in January 2010, prices began to recover in the first half of the year, and the average price for January–July was $17.69 per oz.

Production of Silver Ore
(provisional figures, silver content, metric tons)

	2008	2009
World total	21,297	22,072
Latin America	9,943	10,551
Leading Latin American producers		
Argentina	321	533
Bolivia	1,114	1,326
Chile	1,396	1,301
Guatemala	100	129
Mexico	3,241	3,256
Peru	3,681	3,854
Other leading producers		
Australia	1,926	1,635
Canada	670	609
China, People's Repub.	2,578	2,771
Kazakhstan	629	674
Poland	1,209	1,220
Russia	1,232	1,312
USA	1,120	1,239

Sources: The Silver Institute; Gold Fields Mineral Services Ltd.

SOYBEANS

The soybean plant (*Glycine max* or *G. soya*) is a legume, a member of the pea family (*fabaceae*). Like other legumes it is able to collect its own nitrogen from the air and release it into the soil. The soybean has accordingly played an important role in the maintenance of soil fertility under traditional crop rotation regimes. Owing to the plant's sensitivity to light, it has been possible to optimize cultivation through the selection of varieties adapted, according to the length of their crop durations, to geographical differences in daylight hours. It is the breeding of such varieties that has allowed successful cultivation to extend from northern, temperate zones, where the soybean originated, to, for example, subtropical and tropical regions of the USA and South America. In North America, the main area of cultivation, soybeans are generally planted in the late spring. The plant flowers in the summer, producing 60–80 pods from which two to four pea-sized beans are harvested in the autumn.

Cultivation of the soybean plant is thought to have originated more than 5,000 years ago in northern China, and to have spread southwards from there to Korea, Japan and throughout South-East Asia. In the regions of its origin and early dissemination the soybean has for centuries been a primary source of protein for human consumption. However, it was not until the mid-20th century that soybeans began to be traded internationally to a significant degree.

During the Second World War, and into the 1950s and 1960s, US soybean production was greatly expanded, with the aim of substituting domestically produced soybean oil for imported oils and fats. Thereafter, the protein-rich meal, which is a by-product of crushing for oil, was used to boost livestock production in the USA. Until recently the soybean had for long been the most important source of vegetable oil world-wide. Today, however, the oil palm surpasses it as the most important source, production of palm oil superseding soybean oil definitively in 2004 (FAO figures). Soybean meal, meanwhile, accounts for about 70% of the world's supply of protein-rich animal feedstuffs. The meal (also known as cake), almost all of which is used for livestock feed, is the most valuable product obtained from processing, generally accounting for 50%–75% of total value, depending on the difference in the prices of meal and oil. Furthermore, in addition to the traditional foods derived from soy for human consumption, the plant's derivatives are widely employed in processed foods marketed in Europe and North America. Among many industrial applications, the soybean also provides a raw material for the manufacture of ink, soap, paint, polymers and a fuel for diesel engines. It remains uncertain, however, the extent to which demand will increase for soybeans as a biofuel feedstock, since, under production and trading regimes as of the beginning of 2010, especially in the European Union (EU), the economic viability of many other crop-derived feedstocks was superior to that of soybeans.

The USA has dominated world production of soybeans since the 1950s, when its output overtook that of the People's Republic of China. In 2009/10, according to the US Department of Agriculture (USDA), US production amounted to some 91.4m. metric tons, equivalent to 35.2% of total world output of some 259.9m. tons. Earlier in the decade, US output in 2005/06 was about 84m. tons (38% of the global total of 221m. tons), in 2006/07 87m. tons, out of world-wide production of 237m. tons (37%), and in 2007/08 only 73m. tons, out of 221m. tons (33%), but in 2008/09 81m. tons out of 211m. tons (38%). Thus, despite consistently improving harvests (except in 2007/08), the USA's share of world production has been in decline since the 1970s, when the country was regularly the source of more than two-thirds of global output. Soybeans are also grown in Canada—in 2009/10, with output totalling about 3.5m. tons, Canada ranked as the world's seventh largest producer.

Production of Soybeans
('000 metric tons)

	2008/09	2009/10
World total	211,964	259,896
Latin America*	93,800	130,700
Major Latin American producers		
Argentina	32,000	54,500
Brazil	57,800	69,000
Paraguay	4,000	7,200
Other major producers		
Canada	3,336	3,500
China, People's Rep.	15,540	14,700
India	9,100	8,750
USA	80,749	91,417

* Figures represent the sum of output in listed countries only.

Source: US Department of Agriculture, *Oilseeds: World Markets and Trade* (July 2010).

One of the reasons for the decline in the USA's share of world production has been the very substantial increases in the output of Latin America and the Caribbean, which since 2002 (with the exception of 2004, when North America—the USA and Canada—regained primacy) has ranked as the world's largest producer region, even in 2008/09, when most countries in the region experienced a dip in harvest levels. In 2009/10 the three main producers of Latin America accounted for one-half (50.3%) of the world total. Brazil is the largest producer in the region, and the second largest world-wide, with strongly recovering output of 69.0m. metric tons in 2009/10 (USDA). Production by Argentina, the world's third largest grower, amounted to about 54.5m. tons in 2009/10, while Paraguay, with output of about 7.2m. tons, is the other major producer among Latin American and Caribbean countries. According to FAO, the next largest producer is Bolivia, with estimated output of soybeans amounting to some 1.6m. tons in 2008 (compared with some 60m. tons in Brazil).

China and India complement the list of major world producers, with estimated output, respectively, of about 14.7m. metric tons and some 8.8m. metric tons in 2009/10, according to USDA. Both harvests were down on the previous year.

The pattern of production of soybean meal is similar to that of unprocessed soybeans, except that the USA, hitherto the dominant world producer, was edged out of the leading position in 2009/10 by China, the output of which USDA put at 38.4m. metric tons, or 23% of total world production of 163.5m. tons. The USA produced output of 37.7m. tons (23% of world production) in that year. On a regional basis, however, world output is dominated by Latin America—Argentina, Brazil and, to a lesser extent, Mexico—where aggregated production totalled about 53m. tons in 2009/10 (Argentina 26.2m. tons, Brazil 25.8m. tons and Mexico 2.8m. tons—33% of world production); in 2008/09 Brazil replaced Argentina as the main regional producer, only for the previous position to be restored the next year. With output of about 9.8m. tons, the 27 member states of the EU ranked as the world's fifth largest producer of soybean meal in 2009/10. India was the remaining major producer in that crop year, with production of some 5.3m. tons.

Production of Soybean Meal
('000 metric tons)

	2008/09	2009/10
World total	151,433	163,552
Latin America*	51,790	54,700
Major Latin American producers		
Argentina	24,363	26,150
Brazil	24,700	25,790
Mexico	2,727	2,760
Other major producers		
China, People's Rep.	32,475	38,367
European Union	10,131	9,848
India	5,746	5,310
USA	35,473	37,671

* Figures represent the sum of output in listed countries only.

Source: US Department of Agriculture, *Oilseeds: World Markets and Trade* (July 2010).

As with soybean meal, as a producer of soybean oil China was expected to displace the USA as the world leader, but not until 2010/11, according to USDA estimates. In 2009/10 the USA remained the world's leading individual producer of soybean oil, with output totalling some 8.9m. metric tons, or 23% of world production amounting to about 38.4m. tons in that crop year. On a regional basis, Latin America—again, Argentina, Brazil and Mexico—dominates world output, the region's aggregated production totalling about 13.4m. tons in 2009/10 (Argentina 6.4m. tons, Brazil 6.4m. tons, Mexico 0.6m. tons), equivalent to some 35% of output world-wide in that year. In 2009/10 China still ranked as the world's second largest producer of soybean oil, just behind the USA with production totalling 8.6m. tons. The members states of the EU occupied fifth position, with output amounting to some 2.3m. tons. India complemented the list of major producers of soybean oil in 2009/10, with production totalling about 1.2m. tons.

Production of Soybean Oil
('000 metric tons)

	2008/09	2009/10
World total	35,695	38,402
Latin America*	12,643	13,396
Major Latin American producers		
Argentina	5,914	6,390
Brazil	6,120	6,390
Mexico	609	616
Other major producers		
China, People's Rep.	7,314	8,641
European Union	2,314	2,250
India	1,287	1,190
USA	8,503	8,870

* Figures represent the sum of output in listed countries only.

Source: US Department of Agriculture, *Oilseeds: World Markets and Trade*.

Soybeans are by far the most important oilseed in international trade. In 2009/10, according to USDA, soybean imports, totalling about 87m. metric tons, accounted for some 86% of all world oilseed imports (including, additionally, those of copra, cottonseed, palm kernels, groundnuts, rapeseed and sunflowerseed), totalling about 101m. tons, while exports of soybeans, at some 90m. tons, were equivalent to about 85% of world exports of oilseeds amounting to 105m. tons. Rapeseed, which ranks as the second largest oilseed in international trade (and of increasing significance in the second half of the 2000s, until a significant decline in 2009/10), accounted for about 10% of all oilseeds imported and exported (down from 13% the year before). China was the principal importer of soybeans in 2009/10, receiving shipments totalling almost 50m. tons, or about 57% of total world imports, followed by the member states of the EU (15%), Japan (4%) and Mexico (4%). Taiwan, Thailand, Egypt, Indonesia, Turkey and the Republic of Korea (South Korea) are other leading importers. The USA is the leading exporter of soybeans, with foreign sales totalling some 40m. tons in 2009/10—equivalent to about 45% of world exports. On a regional basis, Latin America ranks as the leading world exporter of soybeans, with the aggregated exports of Brazil, Argentina and Paraguay still accounting for 50% of global exports in 2009/10, recovering strongly from a collapse in Argentina and Paraguay's production in the previous year. Brazil ranked as the world's second largest exporter country in 2009/10, with foreign sales totalling some 28m. tons, followed by Argentina (11m. tons), Paraguay (5m. tons) and Canada (2m. tons).

Soybean meal is the leading protein meal in international trade, accounting for 77% of all world exports of protein meal in 2009/10, according to USDA. In comparison, exports of palm kernel meal—the second most widely traded protein meal—accounted for almost 7% of total world exports of protein meal in that year. International trade in soybean meal has increased steadily since the 1970s. Latin America is the leading exporting region, Argentina and Brazil between them accounting for about 68% of world exports totalling 56m. metric tons in 2009/10, according to USDA. Within the region, Argentina overtook Brazil as the leading exporter in the late 1990s. In 2009/10 Argentina exported 25m. tons and Brazil almost 13m. tons. The USA ranked as the world's third largest exporter of soybean meal in 2009/10, with foreign sales totalling about 10m. tons—some 19% of total world exports—followed by India (5%) and China (3%). In 2009/10 the member states of the EU accounted for by far the largest share—41%—of world imports of soybean meal totalling about 56m. tons. Most other significant importers of soybean meal—Viet Nam, Indonesia, Thailand, Japan, South Korea and the Philippines—were located in South-East and East Asia, with their aggregated imports accounting for some 24% of the world total. Mexico (at 3% of world imports in 2009/10, a little more than the Philippines) and Canada and Iran (each on 2%) are also significant importers of soybean meal.

While soybeans dominate international trade in unprocessed oilseeds, and soybean meal dominates world trade in protein meals, trade in vegetable oils is now increasingly dominated by palm oil. In 2009/10, according to USDA, palm oil accounted for about 33% of vegetable oil production (soybean oil 28%); palm oil contributed 62% of world exports of vegetable oils (including, additionally, coconut, cottonseed, olive, palm, palm kernel, groundnut, rapeseed—canola, soybean and sunflowerseed oils) totalling about 58m. metric tons, and for some 63% of vegetable oil imports—amounting to about 55m. tons—world-wide. Soybean oil, which costs about one-fifth more than palm oil to produce, ranks second, accounting for 15% of world vegetable oil exports and about 16% of world vegetable oil imports in 2009/10. In that year Argentina ranked as the world's leading exporter of soybean oil, its foreign sales, at about 4m. tons (down from almost 6m. tons since 2006/07), accounting for about 49% of world exports totalling some 9m. tons. The combined exports of Argentina, Brazil, Paraguay and Bolivia represented about 70% of world exports of soybean oil in 2009/10, far greater than those of any other region or trading bloc; the USA was the third largest exporter, supplying more than 1m. tons. China was the world's leading importer of soybean oil in 2009/10, accounting for 19% of world imports totalling some 9m. tons, but this was considerably down on the 28% of the previous year. China was more closely followed by India in 2009/10 (17%), then by the member states of the EU (5%). Bangladesh imported almost 5% of the world total, followed by Morocco 4% and Algeria (each on a little over 4%). Among the next four top importing countries were two Latin American countries, Venezuela and Peru, with Iran and South Korea between. According to some forecasts, it is anticipated that demand, supply and trade in vegetable oil might increase substantially. Owing to the complexity of the calculations involved, increasing demand for biofuels has not always been factored into medium-term predictions. Soybean oil has hitherto accounted for only a small proportion—relative to, above all, rapeseed oil and sunflowerseed oil—of biodiesel derived from vegetable oil, and, under current production and trading conditions, in terms of economic viability trails palm oil and rapeseed oil, as well as other crops (e.g. sugar and cassava) that can be used as biodiesel feedstocks.

As there are relatively few major producers of soybeans world-wide, and as soybeans are the most important oilseed in world trade, US policy has influenced not only the world market for soybeans, but also the markets for the seven major competing oilseeds—rapeseed, sunflowerseed, cottonseed, groundnuts, flaxseed, copra and palm kernels. Moreover, with regard to unprocessed soybeans, US influence has been reinforced by the fact that international trade has historically been comparatively free of tariffs and other restrictions on imports. (Tariffs applied to protect the oilseed-processing industries of importing countries, however, have typically been fixed at about twice the rate applied to the unprocessed commodity.) Since the mid-1970s, however, the USA's dominance of the international soybean market has steadily declined, in spite of growth in both production and export volume. Above all, this has been due to the rapid expansion in production and exports by Argentina and Brazil, whose individual exports of soybean meal and soybean oil have both overtaken those of the USA. Lower-cost production of soybeans in Argentina and Brazil has given those countries a considerable competitive advantage in international markets.

The leading role of the USA in the production and export of soybeans means that US prices are the most accurate and readily available guide to the international market. According to USDA, the US farm price for soybeans averaged US $205 per metric ton in 2005/06 (October–September), rising to $254 per ton in 2006/07. (A decade earlier, in 1996/97, the US farm price averaged $274 per ton.) In the 2007/08 crop year the average price rose steeply, to $414 per ton for the whole year, but ranging between $307 per ton in October, at the beginning of the year, and a peak of $489 per ton in July. The average price in 2008/09 was only $368 per ton, falling to a monthly low of £330 per ton three months into the year (December 2008), and maintaining the best prices in May–August 2009 (including a June high point of $419 per ton). A dip in prices meant that the monthly average for October, the first month of the 2009/10 crop year, was $347 per ton. However, the monthly fluctuations in soybean oilseed prices proved to be much flatter during the year—or at least its first 10 months—ranging only between $345 per ton (March) and $360 per ton (December, January and, according to preliminary figures, July), to give an average US farm price for the first 10 months of the 2009/10 year (October–July) of $351.

Fluctuations in prices for soybean products tend to follow variations in the price of unprocessed beans, with an additional vulnerability to market conditions for alternatives, especially in the case of soybean oil. In 2005/06 (October–September) the average US wholesale price for soybean meal (48% protein) was US $192 per metric ton, rising to $226 per ton in 2006/07 and $370 in 2007/08. The price did not fall back as much in 2008/09 as it did for unprocessed soybeans, averaging $365 per ton, but this concealed monthly fluctuations between $287 per ton in October and $461 per ton in June. In October 2009–July 2010 the average US wholesale price fell to $340 per ton, ranging between $306 per ton in March and $368 per ton in December; the preliminary July figure had risen to $359 per ton. In 2005/06 the quotation (f.o.b.) for Brazilian soybean meal (45%–46%) protein at Rio Grande was $176 per ton. The representative Brazilian quotation rose to $199 per ton in 2006/07 and $337 in 2007/08, before falling back to $333 per ton in 2008/09. In October 2009–July 2010 an average price of $321 per ton was recorded at Rio Grande, the quotation ranging between $268 per ton (March) and $354 per ton (October and November). The price of Argentinian soybean meal pellets (f.o.b.) at Buenos Aires averaged $158 per ton in 2005/06, rising to $181 per ton in 2006/07 and $299 in 2007/08, before falling back to $290 per ton in 2008/09. In October 2009–July 2010 the average representative Argentinian quotation was $301 per ton (the only one of the four major price quotations to record a rise on the previous year), soybean meal having traded within a range of $239–$333 per ton in that period. In 2005/06 the average import price (f.o.b., ex-mill) of soybean meal recorded at Hamburg, Germany, was $215 per ton. In 2006/07 the average import price recorded at Hamburg rose to $276 per ton, and it increased further in 2007/08, to $469 per ton, but fell back to $401 per ton in 2008/09. In October 2009–July 2010 the average import price recorded at Hamburg fell to $390 per ton, having traded between $342 per ton (June) and $430 per ton (October—at the beginning of the year) in that period.

According to USDA, the average US price of soybean oil (wholesale tank, crude) was US $516 per metric ton in 2005/06 (October–September). In 2006/07 the average US price increased to $684 per ton, and in 2007/08 it increased dramatically to $1,147 per ton, before falling back to $709 per ton in 2008/09. In October 2009–July 2010 a recovery in the US price for soybean oil saw it average $782 per ton over the 10 months, ranging between $731 per ton in October and $818 per ton in April. Similar annual fluctuations were observed in the other main price quotations. The representative Brazilian quotation (f.o.b. bulk rate) for soybean oil averaged $474 per ton in 2005/06, $673 per ton in 2006/07, $1,190 per ton in 2007/08 and $740 per ton in 2008/09. In the first 10 months of 2009/10 the average Brazilian quotation increased further to $832 per ton, having traded between $802 per ton (October) and $857 per ton (December) in that period. In 2005/06 the representative quotation (f.o.b.) for soybean oil of Argentine origin averaged $467 per ton, rising to $667 per ton in 2006/07 and $1,191 in 2007/08, before falling back to $741 per ton in

2008/09. In October 2009–July 2010 the average Argentine quotation recovered to $811 per ton, having ranged between $773 per ton (June) and $852 per ton (January). At Rotterdam, Netherlands, an average import price (Dutch f.o.b., ex-mill) of $573 per ton was registered for soybean oil in 2005/06. In 2006/07 the average Rotterdam quotation increased to $771 per ton, and in 2007/08 it rose substantially, to $1,327, before falling back to $826 per ton in 2008/09. In October 2009–July 2010 the average import price at Rotterdam ranged between $859 per ton (June) and $935 per ton (December), averaging $905 per ton for the 10 months.

At mid-2010 USDA reported that Chinese imports were continuing to keep prices high. The process of replenishing stocks by the leading exporters had contributed to maintaining rising price levels into 2010.

SUGAR

Sugar is a sweet crystalline substance which may be derived from the juices of various plants. Chemically, the basis of sugar is sucrose, one of a group of soluble carbohydrates which are important sources of energy in the human diet. It can be obtained from trees, including the maple and certain palms, but virtually all manufactured sugar is derived from two plants, sugar beet (*Beta vulgaris*) and sugar cane, a giant perennial grass of the genus *Saccharum*.

Sugar cane, found in tropical areas, grows to a height of up to 5 m (16 ft). The plant is native to Polynesia, but its distribution is now widespread. It is not necessary to plant cane every season as, if the root of the plant is left in the ground, it will grow again in the following year. This practice, known as 'ratooning', may be continued for as long as three years, when yields begin to decline. Cane is ready for cutting 12–24 months after planting, depending on local conditions. More than one-half of the world's sugar cane is still cut by hand, but rising costs are hastening the change to mechanical harvesting. The cane is cut as close as possible to the ground, and the top leaves, which may be used as cattle fodder, are removed.

After cutting, the cane is loaded by hand or by machine into trucks or trailers and transported directly to a factory for processing. Sugar cane rapidly deteriorates after it has been cut and should be processed as soon as possible. At the factory the cane passes first through shredding knives or crushing rollers, which break up the hard rind and expose the inner fibre, and then to squeezing rollers, where the crushed cane is subjected to high pressure and sprayed with water. The resulting juice is heated, and lime is added for clarification and the removal of impurities. The clean juice is then concentrated in evaporators. This thickened juice is next boiled in steam-heated vacuum pans until a mixture or 'massecuite' of sugar crystals and 'mother syrup' is produced. The massecuite is then spun in centrifugal machines to separate the sugar crystals (raw cane sugar) from the residual syrup (cane molasses).

After the milling of sugar, the cane has dry fibrous remnants known as bagasse, which is usually burned as fuel in sugar mills. Bagasse can also be pulped and used for making fibreboard, particle board and most grades of paper. As the costs of imported wood pulp have risen, cane-growing regions have turned increasingly to the manufacture of paper from bagasse. In view of rising energy costs, some countries (such as Cuba) have encouraged the use of bagasse as fuel for electricity production in order to conserve foreign exchange expended on imports of petroleum. Another by-product, cachaza, has been utilized as an animal feed.

The production of beet sugar follows the same process as sugar from sugar cane, except that the juice is extracted by osmotic diffusion. Its manufacture produces white sugar crystals that do not require further refining. In most producing countries, it is consumed domestically, and a fall in the production of beet sugar by the European Union (EU), which only accounted for about one-20th of total world sugar output in 2008, has meant that it has become a net importer of white refined sugar. Beet sugar accounted for only 11.5% of estimated world production in 2008, according to FAO. The production data in the first table, therefore, is for sugar cane, covering all crops harvested, except crops grown explicitly for feed. The second table covers the production of raw sugar by the centrifugal process. While global output of non-centrifugal sugar (i.e. produced from sugar cane which has not undergone centrifugation) is not insignificant, it tends to be destined for domestic consumption. The main producer of non-centrifugal sugar is India, but countries such as Brazil and Colombia are also significant producers.

Most of the raw cane sugar produced in the world is sent to refineries outside the country of origin, unless the sugar is for local consumption. Cuba, Thailand, Brazil and India are among the few cane-producers that export part of their output as refined sugar. The refining process further purifies the sugar crystals and eventually results in finished products of various grades, such as granulated, icing or castor sugar. The ratio of refined to raw sugar is usually about 0.9:1.

As well as providing sugar, quantities of cane are grown in some countries for seed, feed, fresh consumption, the manufacture of alcohol and other uses. Molasses may be used as cattle feed or fermented to produce alcoholic beverages for human consumption, such as rum, a distilled spirit manufactured in Caribbean countries. Sugar cane juice may be used to produce ethyl alcohol (ethanol). This chemical can be utilized, either exclusively or mixed with petroleum derivatives, as a fuel for motor vehicles. The steep rise in the price of petroleum after 1973 made the large-scale conversion of sugar cane into ethanol economically attractive (particularly to developing countries), especially as sugar, unlike petroleum, is a renewable source of energy. Several countries developed ethanol production by this means in order to reduce petroleum imports and to support cane growers. Ethanol-based fuel, a type of biofuel that generates fewer harmful exhaust hydrocarbons than petroleum-based fuel, may be known as 'gasohol', 'alcogas', 'green petrol' or, as in Brazil, simply as alcohol. Brazil was the pioneer in this field, establishing in 1975, in the wake of the first global oil crisis, the largest ethanol-based fuel production programme—PROALCOOL—in the world. Public subsidies and tax concessions encouraged farmers to plant more sugar cane, investors to construct more distilleries, and designers to blueprint cars fuelled exclusively by ethanol. By the early 1980s almost every new car sold in Brazil was fuelled exclusively by ethanol. In the 1990s, however, a shortage of ethanol, in conjunction with lower world petroleum prices and the Government's withdrawal of ethanol subsidies, resulted in a sharp fall in Brazil's output of such vehicles. Research to improve efficiency in ethanol production continued none the less, so that by the time petroleum prices reached new heights, in the mid-2000s, the production cost of ethanol had been reduced by two-thirds. Most Brazilian filling stations now offer as vehicle fuels, in addition to gasoline (petrol), a choice of pure ethanol or a blend of gasoline and 20% ethanol. By 2010 more than 90% of new cars sold in the country were so-called 'flex-fuel' models (first introduced in 2003), and by 2011 flex-fuel vehicles were expected to account for almost 50% of the light vehicles fleet. Moreover, Brazil was becoming a significant exporter of ethanol, as interest in biofuel increased world—in 2007 Brazil exported 20% of its production, accounting for almost one-half of world exports. Although Asian attempts to establish 'gasohol' production were less successful (e.g. in the Philippines and Papua New Guinea), other Latin American countries were encouraged by free trade agreements with the USA, where the Energy Independence and Security Act of 2007 requires the greater use of biofuel. The EU also adopted similar legislation in 2007. Global output of ethanol (including ethanol derived from crops other than sugar, such as maize) had already increased by 70% in 2000–06, from 30,000m. litres to 51,000m. litres, while production in 2010 was expected to reach some 103,000m. litres—equivalent to 2% of world petroleum consumption. Sugar cane cultivation is projected to expand in line with ethanol production, as it is the most cost-effective feedstock for biofuel production, and as demand is expected to increase by 80% between 2010 and 2015.

By the mid-2000s, however, the promotion of biofuels was also becoming increasingly controversial. In April 2008 a report compiled by the World Bank argued that the drive for biofuels by US and European governments had been the most important factor responsible for the rapid increase in the prices of internationally traded food commodities since 2002. In the same month a UN report warned that unchecked expansion of the production of biofuel jeopardized food security in developing countries, not only by raising food prices, but also by making 'substantial demands on the world's land and water resources at a time when demand for both food and forest products is also rising rapidly'. The UN urged governments to put in place regulations to manage the growth of the biofuel industry.

Production of Sugar Cane
('000 metric tons)

	2007	2008
World total	1,627,451	1,743,093
Latin America and the Caribbean	780,110	882,695
Leading Latin American and Caribbean producers		
Argentina*	29,950	29,950
Bolivia	6,419	6,419
Brazil	549,707	648,921
Colombia*	38,500	38,500
Cuba	11,900	15,700
Ecuador	8,360	9,341
El Salvador	4,956	5,250
Guatemala	25,437	25,437
Honduras	5,958	5,958
Mexico	52,089	51,107
Peru	8,229	8,229
Venezuela	9,691	9,691
Other leading producers		
Australia	36,397	33,973
China, People's Repub.	113,732	124,918

—continued	2007	2008
India	355,520	348,178
Indonesia†	25,300	26,000
Pakistan	54,742	63,920
Philippines	32,500†	26,601
South Africa*	20,300	20,500
Thailand	64,365	73,502
USA	27,751	27,603
Viet Nam	17,397	16,128

* FAO estimates.
† Unofficial estimate(s).

Production of Centrifugal Sugar
(raw value, '000 metric tons, Oct.–Sept. marketing year)

	2008/09	2009/10*
World total	143,540	163,836
Latin America and the Caribbean	51,603	55,499
Leading Latin American and Caribbean producers		
Argentina	2,420	2,230
Brazil	31,850	36,400
Colombia	2,277	2,200
Cuba	1,250	1,000
Guatemala	2,381	2,415
Mexico	5,260	4,900
Other leading producers		
Australia	4,814	4,700
China	13,317	11,566
India	15,960	19,460
Pakistan	3,512	3,420
Thailand	7,200	6,940
USA	6,833	7,118

* Advance estimates.

Source: US Department of Agriculture (USDA), Foreign Agricultural Service.

From the last part of the 20th century sugar encountered increased competition from other sweeteners, including maize-based products, such as isoglucose (a form of high-fructose corn syrup, or HFCS), and chemical additives, such as saccharine, aspartame and xylitol. Aspartame (APM) was the most widely used high-intensity artificial sweetener in the early 1990s, its market dominance then came under challenge from sucralose, which is about 600 times as sweet as sugar (compared with 200–300 times for other intense sweeteners) and is more resistant to chemical deterioration than APM. In 1998 the US Government approved the domestic marketing of sucralose, the only artificial sweetener made from sugar. Sucralose was stated to avoid many of the taste problems associated with other artificial sweeteners. From the late 1980s research was conducted in the USA to formulate means of synthesizing thaumatin, a substance derived from the fruit of the West African katemfe plant, *Thaumatococcus daniellii*, which is about 2,500 times as sweet as sugar. As of 2005, the use of thaumatin had been approved in the EU, Israel and Japan, while in the USA its use as a flavouring agent had been endorsed.

Production of sugar cane is dominated by Latin America and the Caribbean, which grow about one-half of the world total: 51% in 2008, according to FAO (South America 43%, Central America 6% and Caribbean 1%). South Asia grew 24%, eastern Asia and Oceania 16%, and Africa 5%. The area under sugar cane cultivation in the whole of Latin America and the Caribbean more than doubled in 40 years. The area from which sugar cane was harvested went from 4.6m. ha in 1968 to 11.3m. ha in 2008 (FAO), as part of an attempt to satisfy greater domestic consumption and to diversify from predominant industries (such as coffee and cocoa), but this figure conceals important sub-regional variations. In Central America the area harvested increased by 81% between 1968 and 2008, to 1.3m. ha, meaning that in importance to sugar production it displaced the Caribbean, where the area harvested fell by 37% over the same period. In South America, however, the area harvested for sugar cane increased almost fourfold between 1968 and 2008, from 2.4m. ha to 9.4m. ha. Moreover, South America enjoyed productive yields, whereas the Caribbean yield was the lowest in the world. In 2008 Oceania, closely followed by South America, had the highest average yields. Egypt and Peru had the highest yields, followed by Senegal, Malawi, Ethiopia, Zambia, Tanzania and Colombia—thus, despite strong individual industries, Africa as a whole had poor productivity in sugar cane. Latin America and the Caribbean also dominate world trade in sugar. According to the US Department of Agriculture (USDA), exports of (centrifugal) sugar from Latin American and Caribbean countries contributed 58% of total world sales abroad in 2008/09, compared with 21% from (eastern and southern) Asia and Oceania, notably Thailand and Australia (major producers such as India and China being net importers). The main importing region was also Asia and Oceania (34% in 2008/09, mainly India and Indonesia), followed by the Middle East (20%), Africa (excluding Egypt—16%), Europe (Eastern Europe—mainly Russia—9%; and Western Europe—mainly the EU—7%) and the USA and Canada (9%).

Brazil is firmly established as the world's largest producer of sugar cane and sugar, and as a leading producer of ethanol (see above). According to FAO, output of sugar cane has more than doubled during the 2000s, from 328m. metric tons in 2000 (26% of the world total) to 649m. tons in 2008 (37%). Brazil's output of centrifugal sugar in 2008/09 was 31.9m. tons, according to USDA, and in 2009/10 it was an estimated 36.4m. tons. In 2010/11 production was expected to reach 40.7m. tons. Increases through the 2000s correspond in part to the continued expansion of the area under sugar cane in the central-southern region, which is the most important producing area (in 2009/10 it accounted for about 90% of national output, while the remaining 10% was produced in the north-east, in particular the states of Pernambuco and Alagoas). The central-southern region also produced 86% of the country's centrifugal sugar. Owing to the relatively greater economic significance of sugar production to the north-eastern region, the Government has tended to grant it the entire annual US sugar import quota allocation, for which premium prices are obtained. Brazil is one of the world's most efficient sugar producers, and, because it possesses the infrastructure to process cane into either sugar or ethanol, the country is able to respond swiftly to market conditions. As the world's largest producer of sugar cane, Brazil exerts considerable influence on the world market price of sugar, of which the balance in the country between ethanol and raw sugar production is a major determinant. The ratio of ethanol to raw sugar as products of the sugar crop increased in ethanol's favour during the 2000s as a consequence of rising national consumption of ethanol. In 2008/09 the share of ethanol production increased to 56.5% but in 2009/10 it was forecast at 55.4%, as the temptation of high international sugar prices diverted manufacturers from the policy maintaining domestic supplies of ethanol. Domestic demand for ethanol and for sugar itself determine export availability, since Brazil is a leading consumer as well as exporter of each. Exports of sugar continued to rise, from 21.6m. tons in 2008/09 to an estimated 24.m. tons in 2009/10, and a projected rise to 28.4m. tons in 2010/11 (78% raw sugar, the rest refined). However, exports of ethanol were predicted to fall to 2,500m. litres, from 3,100m. litres in 2009/10, owing to reduced direct exports to the USA and India (US regulations and import quotas meant that a significant amount of Brazilian ethanol went as re-exports through countries of the Caribbean Basin Initiative). In 2005 exports of sugar generated US $2,382m., equivalent to 2.0% of Brazil's total export revenues. Income from exports fluctuated in line with commodity prices, currency values and the amount of sugar cane processed for ethanol, so raw sugar exports earned less in 2006 and 2007 ($3,936m. and $3,130m., respectively), but increased in 2008, to $3,650m. (1.8% of total exports).

Of Brazil's neighbours to the south and west, Argentina is a major producer of sugar, while Peru is the second largest ethanol producer of the region. According to USDA, Argentina produced 2.4m. metric tons of centrifugal sugar in 2008/09 and an estimated 2.2m. tons in 2009/10; output of 2.3m. tons was projected for 2010/11. Argentina vies with Colombia to hold second place to Brazil in South America, but they are far behind Mexico, while Guatemalan sugar output now exceeds both Argentina and Colombia. In terms of the volume of sugar cane production, in 2008 Mexico was followed by Colombia, Argentina, Guatemala, Cuba, Ecuador and Peru. Peru's output of sugar cane was about 8.2m. tons in each of 2007 and 2008. The country boasts the highest sugar cane yields in the region (and among the highest in the world), with the intensive use of fertilizers and irrigation compensating for the natural disadvantages of light soil and aridity. In 2007 Peru was the second largest producer of sugar cane ethanol in the region, although the quantity that it produced in that year—29m. litres—was equivalent to only a fraction of Brazil's output. In response to expanding ethanol demand, the US, Texas-based company Maple purchased 10,684 ha of land in north-western Peru in January 2007. Maple used the land to develop a vertically integrated ethanol production project, including the cultivation of sugar cane and the building of a new ethanol processing facility. The scheme was scheduled to begin production in 2011, with anticipated initial capacity of about 160m. litres per year.

The sugar sector in Colombia has undergone a major expansion since the 1960s, in an attempt to diversify the economy away from coffee. The area planted to sugar cane increased by 45% between 1961 and 2006, stayed much the same in 2007, but contracted by almost 7% in 2008. Production of sugar cane was estimated by FAO to average about 38.8m. metric tons annually in 2005–08. According to USDA, Colombia produced 2.3m. tons of centrifugal sugar in 2008/09 and an estimated 2.2m. tons in 2009/10 (2.2m. tons was projected for 2010/11). In 2009/10 Colombia was the region's fourth largest exporter of sugar, after Brazil, Guatemala and, for the first time, Argentina, although it was expected to regain third place in 2010/11. In the main production zone, the Cauca river valley in south-western Colombia, climatic conditions permit the cultivation of sugar uninterrupted throughout the year, resulting in exceptionally low fixed investment costs per ton of sugar produced. Colombia has also developed considerable capacity in the production of ethanol since it commenced output in 2005. In 2007 there were five refineries operating in the country's sugar-producing Cauca valley, with combined annual production of some 1.2m. litres. This output, however, met only 70% of the country's requirement—the achievement of a target, contained in a government decree issued in 2001, that all gasoline sold in cities of more than 500,000 inhabitants should comprise 10% ethanol by 2005 was deferred. In 2009 and 2010 new projects to meet the shortfall were to use cassava as a feedstock instead of sugar cane.

Venezuela, by contrast, has a much smaller sugar industry. It has become a substantial importer of sugar (about 40% of its requirements were imported in 1997), owing partly to the demands of its petroleum industry, which have reduced the availability of labour to other industries, necessitated the introduction of costly mechanized techniques, and also obviated the need for ethanol use.

The sugar industry in Guatemala has been expanded rapidly, and annual production of sugar cane increased from 2.5m. metric tons in 1966 to an estimated 25.4m. tons in 2008. Output averaged about 18.2m. tons annually in 2000–08. USDA put centrifugal sugar production in the country at 2.4m. tons in both 2008/09 and 2009/10, and projected output of 2.5m. tons for 2010/11. Guatemala is now the second largest regional exporter of raw centrifugal sugar, after Brazil, having overtaken Cuba in 2006. In 2009 sugar exports earned the country US $507.7m., or 7.0% of total exports. According to preliminary figures, in 2009/10 the equivalent of about 68% of Guatemala's total sugar output was expected to be exported. Guatemala has also supplied a higher percentage than any other country of 'above quota' sugar to the USA, under that country's re-export programme. International labour organizations have criticized some aspects of working conditions in the Guatemalan sugar industry. Guatemala is a party to the Dominican Republic-Central American Free Trade Agreement (DR-CAFTA, see below) and one of the principal objections of opponents of that Agreement, both in Guatemala and the USA, has been its scant provision for safeguarding and enforcing national labour legal rights.

Mexico was a sugar exporter until 1979, but has been only intermittently since then (such as in 2008/09). The low domestic price of sugar, which the Government traditionally set below the cost of production, discouraged the purchase of modern equipment and the renovation of sugar plants. The result was stagnation in sugar production, a steady rise in domestic sugar consumption to a level among the highest in the world (45 kg per head per year), and the need to import sugar. Since 1980, as part of a plan to increase production, to slow the rate of increase in demand and to allow the Government to reduce the subsidy on sugar, domestic sugar prices have been set above the level of production costs. During 1980–85 as much as an additional 170,000 ha were planted to sugar cane. Under the North American Free Trade Agreement (NAFTA), which entered into operation in January 1994, Mexico was permitted to increase substantially its sugar exports to the USA and Canada after NAFTA arrangements for the duty-free access of Mexican sugar to the US market took effect in 2001. However, the USA's interpretation of the sugar-related provisions of NAFTA prevented Mexico from obtaining a significant sugar quota for the US market, which was believed to have been a factor motivating a 2002 Mexican tax on sweeteners in soft drinks—the dispute was settled in the USA's favour in 2006 by a ruling of the World Trade Organization (WTO). Mexico reportedly planned to raise its output of bioethanol as part of its efforts to improve the competitiveness of its sugar sector prior to market liberalization under NAFTA in 2008. Mexican output of sugar cane remained above 50m. metric tons per year in 2005–08. According to USDA, output of centrifugal sugar recovered to 5.9m. tons in 2007/08, after hurricane damage and drought. However, production was only 5.3m. tons in 2008/09 and 4.9m. tons in 2009/10, although a recovery to 5.5m. tons was projected for 2010/11.

The Cuban economy has traditionally relied heavily on sales of sugar and sugar products. The share of these exports in Cuba's total earnings from trade has been as high as 90%, but low world prices in the 1980s, occasionally not even covering producers' costs, affected all sugar exporters. Sugar and sugar products accounted for 73.2% of export revenue in 1989, compared with about 43% in the late 1990s. In 2000 exports of raw sugar accounted for 26.7% of Cuba's export revenue. Prior to the revolution of 1959–60, Cuba exported more than 50% of its sugar to the USA. Following the trade embargo imposed by the USA, approximately 60% of annual exports were taken by the USSR and other Eastern bloc countries, mostly under long-term trade and barter agreements at preferential prices. (In 1990 the USSR supplied Cuba with 95% of its total petroleum requirements.) After 1991, however, these arrangements ceased, and the Cuban sugar trade with the successor republics of the USSR, as well as with Eastern European countries and China, is now conducted on the basis of full market prices. Cuba has sought new markets in Canada, North Africa, the Middle East and the Far East. However, Cuban sugar production has declined sharply since the early 1990s, owing both to adverse weather conditions, especially drought, and to disruptions in the procurement of fuel, fertilizers, mill equipment and other essential production inputs, as a result of the US embargoes. These factors (which resulted in the 1994/95 harvest declining to the lowest level in 50 years) necessitated over-extended harvests and the use of reserves of cane intended for future crops, so in 1993 sugar exports were temporarily suspended. Difficulties arose in meeting subsequent export commitments, such as to Russia and China, but some investment in the mid-1990s failed to improve the situation significantly. In 2002 a restructuring programme was initiated that involved the closure of 71 of Cuba's 156 sugar mills and, reportedly, the reassignment of as much as 60% of sugar plantation land to pasture. In 2005, however, the failure of the programme to revitalize the sector was apparent, and the closure of more mills was forecast. Output of centrifugal sugar in 2006/07, at 1.1m. metric tons, was at its lowest level since 1908, necessitating imports in order to satisfy contractual obligations and domestic consumption. In 2007 the Government reversed its programme to downsize the industry further, in view of higher world prices and increased global demand for ethanol. Several mills reopened at the end of 2007, and there were plans to modernize and expand the country's ethanol production facilities: in contrast to Brazilian refineries, Cuban sugar refineries only produce sugar cane alcohol for human consumption, after the removal of nutrients, which restricts the industrial flexibility of use required for global competitiveness. According to USDA, a large amount of investment would be needed to convert the Cuban sugar industry. There is also, reportedly, high-level political resistance in Cuba to the diversion of much of the country's land resources into large-scale production of ethanol, and Cuba's current access to low-cost petroleum imports from Venezuela may act as a further disincentive. USDA assessed that Cuba produced about 1.4m. tons of centrifugal sugar in 2007/08, falling to 1.3m. tons in 2008/09 and an anticipated 1.0m. tons in 2009/10, as a consequence of poor infrastructure and low productivity (a recovery to 1.1m. tons was expected for 2010/11). Cane production, meanwhile, reached a low point of 11.1m. tons in 2006, but recovered to 15.7m. tons by 2008. In 2008 exports of sugar, sugar preparations and honey increased in value by 16% on the previous year, generating 233.4m. pesos in export revenue, equivalent to 6.3% of total exports; the 225.0m. pesos earned in 2009 were equivalent to 7.8% of total exports.

The next largest Caribbean sugar producer is the Dominican Republic. Sugar cane is the principal commercial crop in the country, but inefficient production techniques, lack of investment and falling international sugar prices depressed the industry throughout the 1980s, although it achieved production levels of some 0.8m. metric tons again in the 1990s. By the second half of the 2000s, however, a more typical level was the 0.5m. tons of sugar produced annually each year from 2007/08 to 2009/10. After two years of modest rises, production was expected to fall back slightly in 2010/11, while still remaining about 0.5m. tons. Exports of sugar and sugar cane derivatives, worth US $119.6m. (raw sugar $91.7m.), accounted for an estimated 7.1% of the Dominican Republic's total export revenue (excluding exports from free trade zones) in 2009.

In some of the smaller American countries and the Caribbean islands, sugar cultivation is the main bulwark of the economy. Sugar is the most important agricultural product of the Caribbean Community and Common Market (CARICOM) economic and political grouping, for instance. In Belize sugar cane plantations occupy about 50% of the total cultivated area, while the sugar industry employs about one-quarter of the labour force. In 2009 sales of sugar contributed 17.8% of total export revenue. In Guyana sugar contributed 15.6% of total export revenue (excluding re-exports) in 2009. In other countries, the tradition of sugar exporting has been all but abandoned: in 2005 it was reported that Barbadian production had declined to the point that the island was unable to meet its EU export quota (in 2003 sugar and molasses had contributed an estimated 9.2% of total export revenue, including re-exports), although domestic consumption and the local rum industry remained important; and in Saint Christopher and Nevis, where 21% of total export revenue was derived from sales of raw sugar in 2001, the Government announced in 2005 that that year's sugar harvest would be the country's last, as rising production costs and a fall in revenues had left the state-owned sugar company heavily in debt. Rising sugar prices in the second half of the decade helped the industry, but it remained in decline in the Caribbean generally.

Representatives of US sugar cane and sugar beet producers have strongly opposed the free trade agreement concluded (as CAFTA) between the USA and Costa Rica, El Salvador, Guatemala, Honduras, Nicaragua and the Dominican Republic in 2004 (the agreement first came into force in El Salvador in March 2006; Costa Rica was the last among the Latin American countries to implement it, at the end of 2007, after a referendum had been held). Under the terms of what is now DR-CAFTA, which was approved by the US Congress in July 2005, most tariffs on goods traded between the USA and the

Central American and Caribbean participants would be eliminated. The US Administration of George W. Bush undertook to maintain a 'ceiling' on sugar imports from its DR-CAFTA partners. Quotas were to be gradually increased over a period of 16 years.

The first International Sugar Agreement (ISA) was negotiated in 1958, and its economic provisions operated until 1961. A second ISA did not come into operation until 1969. It included quota arrangements and associated provisions for regulating the price of sugar traded on the open market, and established the International Sugar Organization (ISO) to administer the agreement. However, the USA and the six original members of the European Community (EC, now the EU) did not participate in the ISA and, following its expiry in 1974, it was replaced by a purely administrative interim agreement; this remained operational until the finalization of a third ISA, which took effect in 1978. The new agreement's implementation was supervised by an International Sugar Council (ISC), which was empowered to establish price ranges for sugar-trading and to operate a system of quotas and special sugar stocks. Owing to the reluctance of the USA and of EC countries (which were not party to the agreement) to accept export controls, the ISO ultimately lost most of its power to regulate the market, and since 1984 the activities of the organization have been restricted to recording statistics and providing a forum for discussion between producers and consumers. Subsequent ISAs, without effective regulatory powers, have been in operation since 1985. At the end of 1992 the USA withdrew from the ISO, following a disagreement over the formulation of members' financial contributions. The Group of Latin American and Caribbean Sugar Exporting Countries (GEPLACEA), founded in 1975, which represents 23 Latin American and Caribbean countries and the Philippines, complements the activities of the ISO as a forum for co-operation and research.

Special arrangements for the sugar trade were incorporated into the successive Lomé Conventions that were in operation from 1975 between the EU and a group of African, Caribbean and Pacific (ACP) countries. A special protocol on sugar, forming part of each Convention, required the EU to import specified quantities of raw sugar annually from ACP countries. In June 1998, however, the EU indicated its intention to phase out preferential sugar prices paid to ACP countries within three years. Under the terms of the Cotonou Agreement, a successor to the fourth Lomé Convention covering the period 2000–2020, the protocol on sugar was to be maintained initially, but would become subject to review within the framework of negotiations for new trading arrangements (negotiations for more WTO-compatible Economic Partnership Agreements—EPAs began in 2002). In 2001 the EU Council adopted the EBA (Everything but Arms) regulation, whereby the least developed countries were granted unlimited duty-free access to the EU for all goods except arms and ammunition. EBA was to apply to sugar from October 2009. Meanwhile, in September 2007 the EU Council of Ministers criticized the protocol on sugar on the grounds that it was not compatible with EU sugar reforms (themselves undertaken in response to upheld complaints before the WTO by Australia, Brazil and Thailand about export subsidies for the ACP countries) and did not take into account the specific needs of different ACP regions. The EU offered duty- and quota-free access to the ACP countries after 2015, in compensation for the loss of subsidies and quotas. A transitional period from October 2009 until September 2015 was to effect the progressive removal of reciprocal trade barriers. However, there was concern that the benefits that ACP countries were intended to derive from unlimited access to the EU market would be undermined by falling sugar prices. It was also uncertain whether some countries that had refused to embrace the EPA arrangements, such as Malawi, would be allowed to continue trading under EBA in order to take advantage of unrestricted access to the EU market sooner (i.e. from 2009 instead of 2015), while sugar prices were still guaranteed to be maintained at a relatively high level.

In tandem with world output of cane and beet sugars, stock levels (of centrifugal sugar) are an important factor in determining the prices at which sugar is traded internationally. These stocks, which were at relatively low levels in the late 1980s, increased significantly in the 1990s, although not, according to USDA data, in each successive trading year (September–August). In 2005/06, when world production of sugar amounted to about 145m. metric tons and world consumption to some 144m. tons, world sugar stocks fell for a third consecutive year, to about 31m. tons. In 2006/07, when world production of sugar totalled 164m. tons and world consumption 151m. tons, world sugar stocks increased to some 40m. tons. World stocks of sugar increased to 41m. tons in 2007/08, in which year world production amounted to 166m. tons and consumption to 155m. tons. In 2008/09, on the basis of the decline in world production to 144m. tons and reasonably steady consumption at 154m. tons, USDA assessed that stocks fell sharply, to 28m. tons. In 2009/10, estimating an increase in world production to 152m. tons and continuing steady consumption of 154m. tons, USDA had stocks slipping back to less than 27m. tons, and for 2010/11 the forecast was for stocks to rise only just above 27m. tons (on production of 164m. tons and consumption of 158m. tons).

After reasonably steady sugar prices during 2005 (the average ISA daily price for the year was 9.90 US cents per lb), in 2006 they displayed a high level of volatility. Overall, the average ISA daily price rose by 49%, to 14.75 cents per lb, in 2006. The highest average monthly price was 18.05 cents per lb in February; the lowest—11.65 cents per lb—was recorded in December. In 2007 prices declined by 32%, compared with 2006, to 10.07 cents per lb. The lowest average monthly price, 9.38 cents per lb, was recorded in June, and the highest, 11.01 cents per lb, in January. This decline in prices was largely attributed to continued substantial excess of supply, and was exacerbated by the weakness of the US dollar. According to the ISO, prices in real terms were too low to cover production costs. However, the relative weakness of sugar prices, compared with those of other agricultural commodities, subsequently spurred speculative investment, and sugar prices recovered in 2008 to peak at 14.51 cents per lb in August. The average ISA daily price was 12.79 cents per lb for that year, rising to 18.00 cents per lb in 2009, because of the basic underlying deficit in the world sugar market and because of the impact of high petroleum prices on demand for ethanol. Average monthly prices in 2009 recorded a steady increase from the beginning of the year, rising from 12.49 cents per lb in January to 22.93 cents per lb in September. The price fell slightly thereafter, although remaining above 22.00 cents per lb, but there was a jump back up in December, to 23.23 cents per lb. This marked the start of a speculative rise in the price in the course of January 2010, with an average of 26.46 cents per lb over the month, a 30-year high. After a small decline in February prices fell considerably, recording a 43% decline by May, as the markets adjusted to better-than-expected production in India and Brazil. Prices rose slightly in June, with their general level being sustained by the production shortfall, which was expected to be eliminated in 2010/11 to produce the first production surplus in three years.

The World Bank records three sugar prices, to reflect the major markets. The world price that it quotes is the ISA daily price for raw sugar (f.o.b., stowed at greater Caribbean ports), but using different measurements to the prices cited above: the average price for 2008 was 28.21 US cents per kg, for 2009 it was 40.00 cents per kg, and for the first seven months of 2010 the average was 42.68 cents per kg. The average ISA daily price for both the last quarter of 2009 and the first quarter of 2010 was above 50.00 cents per kg, but for the second quarter of 2010 it was only 34.93 cents per kg; the average price was 33.51 cents per kg in May, recovering to 38.49 cents per kg by July. The US price, under nearby futures contract (c.i.f.), recorded similar but more pronounced fluctuations: 46.86 cents per kg in 2008, 54.88 cents per kg in 2009 and 76.44 cents per kg in January–July 2010. An average US price of 84.31 cents per kg in the first quarter of 2010 fell to 69.62 cents per kg in the second quarter; the low May price of 68.11 cents per kg recovered to 73.28 cents per kg by July. The increasingly anachronistic EU negotiated import price for raw, unpackaged sugar from ACP countries under the Lomé Conventions (c.i.f., European ports) recorded a decline from an annual average of 69.69 cents per kg in 2008 to 52.44 cents per kg in 2009, and to 44.27 in January–July 2010; such averages mask some fluctuation in price, such as the arrest of the falling price since early 2010 in June at 40.91 cents per kg, and the subsequent rise to 42.77 cents per kg for July.

The 84 members of the ISO together account for (on the basis of data for 2007) 82% of world sugar production, 66% of world sugar consumption, 93% of world sugar exports and 38% of world sugar imports. The ISO is based in London, United Kingdom.

TIN

The world's known tin reserves, estimated by the US Geological Survey (USGS) to total 5.6m. metric tons in 2009, are located mainly in the equatorial zones of Asia and Africa, in central South America and in Australia. Cassiterite is the only economically important tin-bearing mineral, and it is generally associated with tungsten, silver and tantalum minerals. There is a clear association of cassiterite with igneous rocks of granitic composition, and 'primary' cassiterite deposits occur as disseminations, or in veins and fissures in or around granites. If the primary deposits are eroded, as by rivers, cassiterite may be concentrated and deposited in 'secondary', sedimentary deposits. These secondary deposits form the bulk of the world's tin reserves. The ore is treated, generally by gravity method or flotation, to produce concentrates prior to smelting.

Tin owes its special place in industry to its unique combination of properties: low melting point, the ability to form alloys with most other metals, resistance to corrosion, non-toxicity and good appearance. Its main uses are in tinplate (about 40% of world tin consumption), in alloys (tin-lead solder, bronze, brass, pewter, bearing and type metal), and in chemical compounds (in paints, plastics, medicines, coatings and as fungicides and insecticides). Since the late 1990s a number of possible new applications for tin have been under study, including its use in fire-retardant chemicals and as an environmentally preferable substitute for cadmium in zinc alloy anti-corrosion coatings on steel. The possible development of a lead-free tin solder has also receiving consideration.

According to the USGS, the People's Republic of China (37% of estimated global production in 2009) and Indonesia (33%) each produce more tin than Latin America (21%), even though the region includes the world's next two largest producers and its sixth largest. In 2002 Bolivian production of tin surpassed that of Brazil, making it the region's second largest producer (after Peru). Bolivia's largest tin mine is located south-east of La Paz, at Huanuni, where, in 2000, most of the Posokoni tin deposit that it works was sold to United Kingdom-based Allied Deals. The mine was subsequently operated as a joint venture between Allied Deals and Bolivia's state-owned mining company, Corporación Minera de Bolivia (COMIBOL). In 2002, after Allied Deals (known at that time as RGB Resources) had been declared bankrupt, COMIBOL successfully pursued legal action for the right to administer mining activities at Huanuni. This right derived from newly drafted legislation. However, as a consequence of the failure to enact the new law, the Huanuni mine continued to be operated as a joint venture between COMIBOL, which employed a salaried mining work-force, and independent miners organized co-operatively. In 2006, following violent unrest at Huanuni, 4,000 independent miners formally became COMIBOL employees and the Government took control of the Huanuni mine in October. It was planned subsequently to expand capacity at the mine and at its associated Santa Elená concentrator, and to construct a new concentrator. In February 2007 the Government seized control of Bolivia's principal tin smelter, the Vinto smelter, which had been sold to Glencore International AG of Switzerland in 2005. At the time of the seizure, owing to the very high price of tin on international markets, the smelter was a highly profitable venture, control over which the Government sought as an outlet for tin produced at the Huanuni mine. (There was speculation, in late 2007, that the Government would seek control of all tin production in Bolivia, including other mining operations undertaken by Glencore.) Glencore subsequently demanded compensation. The Government's denial of any liability to pay this resulted in a legal dispute that remained ongoing—in May 2020 compounded by nationalization of a Glencore subsidiary's antimony smelter. in 2008. In 2009 Bolivia was the world's fourth largest mine producer of tin (after China, Indonesia and Peru). In the same year it was the seventh largest producer of refined tin—an additional blast furnace at the Vinto smelter was planned for 2011, as part of the Government's plan to reactivate processing of minerals in the country. In 2001 foreign sales of primary tin accounted for 3.8% of the country's export revenue, compared with almost 60% in 1978. From the 1970s Bolivian output of tin had declined as a result of internal economic conditions and the low world price of tin. Burgeoning foreign demand (particularly from China) caused tin prices to soar during 2005–06, increasing Bolivian export revenues to US $27.9m. in the latter year. However, zinc remained Bolivia's most lucrative mineral commodity, and tin—contributing less than 1% of export revenues in both 2005 and 2006—remained a marginal sector in comparison.

Brazil possesses the world's largest tin mine, located at Pitinga, in Amazonas state, with identified reserves of 420,000 metric tons, although it was suggested in the late 1990s that the mine's total reserves could exceed 800,000 tons. In late 2008 the mine was purchased by Peruvian tin-mining interests. Following a period of decline in output, from the early 1990s, as a result of adverse market conditions, Brazil's annual production of tin, from the early 2000s, stabilized at about 11,000–12,000 tons. In 2006 the country's leading tin-mining company, Grupo Paranapanema, estimated, on the basis of expansion work under way, that national output could rise as high as 20,000 tons per year in the short-to-medium term. In 2006, however, mine production of refined tin fell to its lowest level—less than 9,000 tons—since 1982. Figures for 2007 indicated a recovery to more than 12,000 tons in 2007, falling back in the following year, but maintaining a similar level that year and in 2009. From 2008 Brazil was displaced by the Democratic Republic of the Congo as the world's fifth largest tin producer. In 2008, according to the International Trade Centre, Brazil's revenue from exports of tin (mainly semi-manufactured, non-alloyed metal) was reported to have increased by 35% on the year before, which itself was about double the value of exports in the previous two years.

In 1994 Peru emerged as the region's leading producer of tin and the world's third largest source, a position it has maintained. Until the 1990s almost all of Peru's tin exports were in the form of ores and concentrates, which provided 1.5% of the country's total export earnings in 1996. However, Peru's first tin smelter, at Pisco, began operating in 1997, with an initial production capacity of 15,000 metric tons of metal per year. In 2007 Peru was the third largest producer of primary tin in the world, with reported output of 39,019 tons—little more than 1% higher than in 2006 and still down on production levels earlier in the decade (particularly the 2004 peak of 67,675 tons). Production in 2008 was estimated to be slightly down on 2007, but still equivalent to about 11% of total world production. Minsur, Peru's only fully integrated supplier of tin, exported 38,100 tons of the metal, worth US $332.1m., in 2006. Elsewhere in Latin America, Canada's Silver Standard Resources Inc. estimated in 2006 that some 25% of future revenues from its Pirquitas silver project in Argentina could derive from tin resources located there, while Mexico produced about 25 tons annually in 2006 and 2007.

During the period 1956–85 much of the world's tin production and trade was covered by successive international agreements, administered by the International Tin Council (ITC), based in London, United Kingdom. The aim of each successive International Tin Agreement (ITA), of which there were six, was to stabilize prices within an agreed range by using a buffer stock to regulate the supply of tin. The buffer stock was financed by producing countries, with voluntary contributions by some consuming countries. 'Floor' and 'ceiling' prices were fixed, and market operations conducted by a buffer stock manager who intervened, as necessary, to maintain prices within these agreed limits. For added protection, the ITA provided for the imposition of export controls if the 'floor' price was being threatened. The ITA was effectively terminated in October 1985, when the ITC's buffer stock manager informed the London Metal Exchange (LME) that he no longer had the funds with which to support the tin market. The factors underlying the collapse of the ITA included its limited membership (Bolivia and the USA, leading producing and consuming countries, were not signatories) and the accumulation of tin stocks which resulted from the widespread circumvention of producers' quota limits. The LME responded by suspending trading in tin, leaving the ITC owing more than £500m. to some 36 banks, tin smelters and metals traders. The crisis was eventually resolved in March 1990, when a financial settlement of £182.5m. was agreed between the ITC and its creditors. The ITC was itself dissolved in July of that year. Transactions in tin contracts were resumed on the LME in 1989.

These events lent new significance to the activities of the Association of Tin Producing Countries (ATPC), founded in 1983 by Malaysia, Indonesia and Thailand and later joined by Bolivia, Nigeria, Australia and Zaire (now the Democratic Republic of the Congo—DRC). Prior to the withdrawal of Australia and Thailand in 1996 (see below), members of the ATPC accounted for almost two-thirds of world production. The ATPC, which was intended to operate as a complement to the ITC and not in competition with it, introduced export quotas for tin for the year from 1 March 1987. Brazil and China agreed to co-operate with the ATPC in implementing these supply restrictions, which, until their suspension in 1996 (see below), were renegotiated to cover succeeding years, with the aim of raising prices and reducing the level of surplus stocks. The ATPC membership also took stringent measures to control smuggling. Brazil and China (jointly accounting for more than one-third of world tin production) both initially held observer status at the ATPC. China became a full member in 1994, but Brazil remained as an observer, together with Peru and Viet Nam. China and Brazil agreed to participate in the export quota arrangements, for which the ATPC had no power of enforcement.

The ATPC members' combined export quota was fixed at 95,849 metric tons for 1991, and was reduced to 87,091 tons for 1992. However, the substantial level of world tin stocks, combined with depressed demand, led to mine closures and reductions in output, with the result that members' exports in 1991 were below quota entitlements. The progressive depletion of stock levels prompted a forecast by the ATPC, in May 1992, that export quotas would be removed in 1994 if these disposals continued at their current rate. The ATPC had previously set a target level for stocks of 20,000 tons, representing five weeks of world tin consumption. Projections that world demand for tin would remain at about 160,000 tons annually, together with continued optimism about the rate of stock disposals, led the ATPC to increase its members' 1993 export quota to 89,700 tons. The persistence, however, of high levels of annual tin exports by China (estimated to have exceeded 30,000 tons in 1993 and 1994, compared with its ATPC quota of 20,000 tons), together with sales of surplus defence stocks of tin by the US Government, necessitated a reduction of the quota to 78,000 tons for 1994. In late 1993 prices had fallen to a 20-year 'low', and world tin stocks were estimated at 38,000–40,000 tons, owing partly to the non-observance of quota limits by Brazil and China, as well as to increased production by non-ATPC members. World tin stocks resumed their rise in early 1994, reaching 48,000 tons in June. However, the effects of reduced output, from both ATPC and non-ATPC producing countries, helped to reduce stock levels to 41,000 tons at the end of December. In 1995 exports by ATPC members exceeded the agreed voluntary quotas by 10%, and in May 1996, when world tin stocks were estimated to have been reduced to 31,000 tons, the ATPC suspended its quota arrangements. Shortly before the annual meeting of the ATPC was convened in September, Australia and Thailand announced their withdrawal from the organization. Although China and Indonesia indicated that they would continue to support the ATPC, together with Bolivia, Malaysia and Nigeria (Zaire had ceased to be an active producer of tin), the termination of its quota arrangements in 1996, together with the continuing recovery of the tin market, indicated that its future role would be that of a forum for tin-producers and consumers. Malaysia, Australia and Indonesia left the ATPC in 1997, and Brazil became a full member in 1998. In June 1999, when the organization's headquarters were moved from Kuala Lumpur, Malaysia, to Rio de

Janeiro, Brazil, the membership comprised Brazil, Bolivia, China, the DRC and Nigeria.

Production of Tin Concentrates
(tin content, metric tons)

	2007	2008
World total (excl. USA)*	303,000	299,000
Latin America†	67,612	67,971*
Leading Latin American producers		
Bolivia	15,972	17,319
Brazil*	12,596	11,600
Peru	39,019	39,037*
Other leading producers		
Australia	2,071	1,783
China, People's Repub.*	146,000	110,000
Congo, Democratic Repub.*	8,900	11,800
Indonesia	66,137	96,000*
Malaysia	2,263	2,200*
Russia*	2,500	1,500
Viet Nam*	3,500	3,500

* Estimated production.

† Figures represent the sum of output in listed countries and Mexico, which is a minor producer of tin-bearing ores and concentrates.

Source: US Geological Survey.

After consumption, and prices, of tin suffered something of a decline in the early 2000s, demand for tin world-wide was estimated to have increased by about 7% in 2003, and provisional figures indicated a similar level of growth in 2004, when output surged in response to the growth that had occurred in the previous year. The price of tin in London (i.e. the average quotation for tin for immediate delivery traded on the LME) increased by almost 75% in 2004—a larger increase than that recorded for any other metal traded on the LME—to an average of US $8,513 per metric ton. Stocks of tin held by the Exchange declined precipitously in 2004, totalling 8,160 tons at the end of the year. In 2005 the average price of tin traded on the LME declined by 13.4%, relative to the previous year, to $7,370 per ton. In mid-2005 the market for tin was characterized by uncommonly low stocks—LME inventories totalled only 3,855 tons at the end of June. By the end of the year, however, LME stocks had recovered to 16,725 tons. This recovery reflected the return of tin markets to surplus, a consequence of a surge in Indonesian production, among other factors. The average price of tin traded on the LME increased by 18.9% in 2006, to $8,763 per ton. During 2006 the price of tin traded in London ranged between $6,595 and $11,900 per ton. At the end of the year LME stocks of tin totalled 12,970 tons. The average price of tin traded on the LME rose in each month in January–May 2007. In May an average price of $14,148 per ton was recorded, but in June the average price fell to $14,107 per ton. The average price rose, by 4.5%, to $14,747 per ton in July, when speculative funds were reported to have exerted a strong influence on the tin market. On the final day of July the 'spot' or cash price for tin in London rose to a record 'high' of $16,480 per ton. Concern about the level of future supplies from Bolivia, China and Indonesia were cited by analysts as the key drivers of the rise in the price of tin and, with rising demand in China and Europe, far outweighed data indicating weak demand for tin in the USA and Japan. The price of tin traded on the LME continued to rise in the second half of 2007, peaking at an average price of $16,692 per ton in November. For the whole of 2007 an average price of tin traded on the LME of $14,536 per ton was recorded, an increase (in nominal terms) of 65.9%. Stocks of tin held by the LME declined fairly substantially in January–April 2007, but by the end of July they had recovered to 13,680 tons. The LME's inventories of tin at the end of July totalled 12,150 tons. In January–May 2008 the price of tin traded in London rose steeply, from an average of $16,337 per ton in January to $24,214 per ton in May. The average price recorded in May represented an all-time 'high', and, on a daily basis, the 'spot' price of $25,000 per ton recorded on 15 May was also a record. According to analysts, a key factor behind the rise in the price of tin in early 2008 were data confirming China's evolution from a tin exporter to a net importer of the metal, including tin concentrates. Stocks of tin held by the LME declined from 11,590 tons at the end of January to 7,435 tons at the end of May. Prices declined dramatically in the final quarter of 2008, owing to the onset of global recession, but average prices for the year remained higher than in 2007. According to the World Bank (based on LME figures), the average price of tin in the final quarter of 2008 was $13,100 per ton, restraining the average price for the whole of 2008 to $18,510 per ton. In the first quarter of 2009 the price fell further, to an average of $11,030 per ton, but by the second quarter prices were recovering, following strong demand in China and supply problems in Indonesia. Prices rose fairly steadily thereafter into mid-2010, as global economic recovery, notably in China, set in, averaging $13,570 per ton for 2009 as a whole. The final quarter of 2009 had an average price of $15,170 per ton. By the second quarter of 2010 the average London price for tin was $17,860 per ton, although that figure masked a dip in the price over June. However, the average monthly price for July had risen again, reaching $18,440 per ton, while daily prices were pushing past $20,000 per ton again by early August, given the restraint on production by the rains in Indonesia, as well as rebounding demand in Europe.

The success, after 1985, of the ATPC in restoring orderly conditions in tin trading (partly by the voluntary quotas and partly by working towards the reduction of tin stockpiles) unofficially established it as the effective successor to the ITC as the international co-ordinating body for tin interests. The International Tin Study Group (ITSG), comprising 36 producing and consuming countries, was established by the ATPC in 1989 to assume the informational functions of the ITC. In 1991 the secretariat of the United Nations Conference on Trade and Development (UNCTAD) assumed responsibility for the publication of statistical information on the international tin market. The International Tin Research Institute (ITRI), founded in 1932 and based in London, United Kingdom, promotes scientific research and technical development in the production and use of tin.

ACKNOWLEDGEMENTS

We gratefully acknowledge the assistance of the following organizations in the preparation of this section: the Food and Agriculture Organization of the United Nations (FAO); the International Aluminium Institute; the International Cocoa Organization; the International Coffee Organization; the International Copper Study Group; the International Iron and Steel Institute; the International Monetary Fund; the International Sugar Organization; The Silver Institute; the US Department of Agriculture; the US Department of Energy; and the US Geological Survey, US Department of the Interior. Unless otherwise indicated, FAO is the source for all agricultural production tables.

RESEARCH INSTITUTES

ASSOCIATIONS AND INSTITUTIONS STUDYING LATIN AMERICA AND THE CARIBBEAN

ARGENTINA

Centro Argentino de Datos Oceanográficos (CEADO) (Argentine Centre of Oceanographic Data): Avda Montes de Oca 2124, C1270ABV Buenos Aires; tel. and fax (11) 4303-2240; e-mail ceado@hidro.gov.ar; internet www.hidro.gov.ar/ceado/ceado.asp; f. 1974; stores oceanographic data of national area, provides information to the scientific community, private and public enterprises and other marine users; Dir ARIEL HERNÁN TROISI.

Centro Argentino de Información Científica y Tecnológica (CAICYT) (Argentine Centre for Scientific and Technological Information): Saavedra 15, 1°, C1083ACA Buenos Aires; tel. (11) 4951-6975; fax (11) 4951-7310; e-mail caicyt@caicyt.gov.ar; internet www.caicyt-conicet.gov.ar; f. 1958; attached to Consejo Nacional de Investigaciones y Técnicas; Dir MARIO ALBORNOZ.

Centro de Investigaciones Económicas (CIE) (Economic Research Centre): Instituto Torcuato de Tella, Miñones 2177, 1428 Buenos Aires; tel. (11) 4783-8680; fax (11) 4783-3061; e-mail postmaster@itdtar.edu.ar; internet www.itdt.edu; library of 60,000 vols and 1,400 domestic and foreign periodicals; publ. *Documentos de Trabajo*.

Consejo Argentino para las Relaciones Internacionales (CARI) (Argentine Council for International Relations): Uruguay 1037, 1°, 1016 Buenos Aires; tel. (11) 4811-0071; fax (11) 4815-4742; e-mail cari@cari.org.ar; internet www.cari.org.ar; f. 1978; Pres. Dr ADALBERTO RODRÍGUEZ GIAVARINI.

Instituto para la Integración de América Latina y el Caribe (Institute for the Integration of Latin America and the Caribbean): Esmeralda 130, 16°, 1035 Buenos Aires; tel. (11) 4223-2350; fax (11) 4323-2365; e-mail intal@iadb.org; internet www.iadb.org/intal; f. 1965 under auspices of Inter-American Devt Bank's Integration and Regional Program Dept; research on all aspects of regional integration and co-operation; activities are channelled through four lines of action: regional and national technical projects on integration; policy forums; integration forums; journals and information; documentation centre includes 100,000 documents, 12,000 books, 400 periodicals; Dir RICARDO CARCIOFI; publs *Integración y Comercio* (2 a year), *INTAL Carta Mensual* (monthly newsletter), *Serie Informes Subregionales de Integración*.

AUSTRALIA

Australian Institute of International Affairs: 32 Thesiger Court, Deakin, ACT 2600; tel. (2) 6282-2133; fax (2) 6285-2334; e-mail ceo@aiia.asn.au; internet www.aiia.asn.au; f. 1933; 1,800 mems; brs in all states; Pres. CLIVE HILDEBRAND; Exec. Dir MELISSA H. CONLEY TYLER; publ. *The Australian Journal of International Affairs* (4 a year).

AUSTRIA

Österreichische Forschungsstiftung für Entwicklungshilfe (Austrian Foundation for Development Research): 1090 Vienna, Berggasse 7; tel. (1) 317-40-10; fax (1) 317-40-15; e-mail office@oefse.at; internet www.oefse.at; f. 1967; documentation and information on development aid, developing countries and international development, particularly relating to Austria; library of 40,000 vols, 250 periodicals; Pres. GERHARD BITTNER; publs *Österreichische Entwicklungspolitik* (annually), Läander-profile.

Österreichische Gesellschaft für Aussenpolitik und Internationale Beziehungen (Austrian Association for Foreign Policy and International Relations): 1010 Vienna, Hofburg/Schweizerhof/Brunnenstiege; tel. (1) 535-46-27; e-mail una.austria@afa.at; internet afa.at; f. 1958; lectures, discussions; approx. 400 mems; Pres. MICHAEL F PFEIFER; publ. *Österreichisches Jahrbuch für Internationale Politik*.

Österreichisches Lateinamerika Institut (Austrian Latin American Institute): 1090 Vienna, Schlickgasse 1; tel. and fax (1) 310-74-65; e-mail office@lai.at; internet www.lai.at; f. 1965; Dir STEFANIE REINBERG; publs *Atención: Jahrbuch des Österreichischen Lateinamerika Instituts* (annually), *Diálogo Austria-América Latina* (annually).

BARBADOS

Sir Arthur Lewis Institute of Social and Economic Studies: University of the West Indies, Cave Hill Campus, POB 64, Bridgetown; tel. 417-4478; fax 424-7291; e-mail salises@cavehill.uwi.edu; internet www.cavehill.uwi.edu/salises; f. 1948; applied research and graduate teaching programme relating to the Caribbean; Dir Prof. ANDREW DOWNES; publ. *Journal of Eastern Caribbean Studies* (quarterly).

BELGIUM

Académie Royale des Sciences d'Outre-Mer/Koninklijke Academie voor Overzeese Wetenschappen (Royal Academy for Overseas Sciences): rue Defacqz 1/3, 1000 Brussels; tel. (2) 538-02-11; fax (2) 539-23-53; e-mail kaowarsom@skynet.be; internet www.kaowarsom.be; f. 1928; the promotion of scientific knowledge of overseas areas, especially those with particular development problems; 128 mems, 67 assoc. mems, 100 correspondent mems; Perm. Sec. Prof. DANIELLE SWINNE; publs *Bulletin des Séances / Mededelingen der Zittingen*, *Mémoires / Verhandelingen*, *Recueils d'Etudes Historiques / Historische bijdragen*, *Biographie belge d'Outre-Mer / Belgische Overzeese Biographie*, *Actes Symposiums / Acta Symposia*.

EGMONT—The Royal Institute for International Relations: 69 rue de Namur, 1000 Brussels; tel. (2) 223-41-14; fax (2) 223-41-16; e-mail info@egmontinstitute.be; internet www.egmontinstitute.be; f. 1947 as Institut Royal des Relations Internationales—Koninklijk Instituut Voor Internationale Betrekkingen; adopted current name in 2007; research in foreign policy, international relations, law, economics, European issues, environment and defence; specialist library of 700 vols and 1,200 periodicals; archives; organizes lectures and conferences; Pres. ÉTIENNE DAVIGNON; Dir-Gen. R. VAN HELLEMONT; publs *Studia Diplomatica* (4 a year).

Institut d'Etudes du Développement (Institute for Development Studies): Université Catholique de Louvain, 1 pl. des Doyens, 1348 Louvain-La-Neuve; tel. (10) 47-39-35; fax (10) 47-28-05; e-mail vandenbossche@dvlp.ucl.ac.be; internet www.uclouvain.be/dvlp; f. 1961; incorporates the Groupe de Recherches Interdisciplinaires sur l'Amerique Latine (Interdisciplinary Latin America Research Group); Pres. JEAN-MARIE WAUTELET.

Institute of Development Policy and Management: Prinsstraat 13, 2000 Antwerp; tel. (3) 265-57-70; fax (3) 265-57-71; e-mail dev@ua.ac.be; internet www.ua.ac.be/dev; f. 1965; autonomous institution of the University of Antwerp; courses in development studies; library of 50,000 vols; Dir ROBRECHT RENARD.

BRAZIL

Instituto Brasileiro de Economia (Brazilian Institute of Economics): Getúlio Vargas Foundation, Praia de Botafogo 190, Botafogo, 22253-900 Rio de Janeiro, RJ; tel. (21) 2559-6087; fax (21) 2553-6372; e-mail conjunturaeconomica@fgv.br; internet www.fgv.br/ibre; f. 1951; Dir A. SALAZAR BRANDÃO; publs *National Accounts* (annually), *Conjuntura Econômica* (monthly), *Agroanalysis* (monthly).

Instituto Brasileiro de Relações Internacionais (Brazilian Institute of International Relations): Avda R. Marquês de São Vicente 225, Casa 20, Gávea 22453-900, Rio de Janeiro, RJ; tel. and fax (21) 3527-1557; e-mail iripuc@puc-rio.br; internet www.puc-rio.br/iri; f. 1954; 4,100 vols; Dir Prof. MÔNICA HERZ; publ. *Revista Brasileira de Política Internacional* (quarterly).

Instituto Nacional de Pesquisas Da Amazônia (INPA) (National Institute for Amazonian Research): Avda André Araújo 2936, Aleixo, CEP 69060-001, Manaus, AM; tel. (92) 3643-3377; e-mail ascom@inpa.gov.br; internet www.inpa.gov.br; f. 1952; basic and applied research on Amazonian biodiversity, including botany, entomology, aquatic biology, ecology, earth sciences, human health, agriculture, aquaculture, forestry, forest products, natural products and food technology; postgraduate programme in tropical biology and natural resources; Dir ADALBERTO LUIS VAL.

Instituto de Pesquisa Econômica Aplicada (Institute of Applied Economic Research): Avda Presidente Antônio Carlos 51, 13° andar, CP 2672, 20020-010 Rio de Janeiro, RJ, Brazil; tel. (21) 3315-5185; e-mail faleconosco@ipea.gov.br; internet www.ipea.gov.br; library of 60,000 vols; Pres. MARCIO POCHMANN; publs *Jornal* (monthly).

Superintendência de Estudos Econômicos e Sociais da Bahia (SEI) (Bahia Economic and Social Studies Superintendency): Centro Administrativo da Bahia, 4a Avda 435, 41745 002 Salvador, BA; tel. (71) 3115-4704; fax (71) 3116-1781; e-mail diger@sei.ba.gov.br; internet www.sei.ba.gov.br; f. 1995; statistics, natural resources, economic indicators; library of 25,000 vols; Dir JOSÉ GERALDO DOS REIS SANTOS; publ. *Bahia Análise e Dados* (every 4 months).

CANADA

Canadian Association for Latin American and Caribbean Studies/Association Canadienne des Etudes Latino-Américaines et des Caraïbes (CALACS/ACELAC): c/o Dept of History, University of Windsor, 401 Sunset Ave, Windsor, ON N9B 3P4; tel. (519) 253-3000; fax (519) 971-3610; e-mail calacs_acelac@bellnet.ca; internet www.can-latam.org; f. 1969; Pres. STUART MCCOOK; publ. *Canadian Journal of Latin American and Caribbean Studies* (2 a year), *Newsletter* (2 a year).

Canadian Council for International Co-operation/Conseil canadien pour la coopération internationale: 450 Rideau St, Suite 200, Ottawa, ON K1N 5Z4; tel. (613) 241-7007; fax (613) 241-5302; e-mail info@ccic.ca; internet www.ccic.ca; f. 1968 (formerly Overseas Institute of Canada, f. 1961); co-ordination centre for voluntary agencies working in international development; 100 mems; Chair. KAREN TAKACS; publs *Newsletter* (2 a year), *Directory of Canadian NGOs*.

Canadian International Council: 45 Willcocks St, Rm 210, Toronto, ON M5C 1C7; tel. (416) 946-7209; fax (416) 946-7319; e-mail mailbox@canadianinternationalcouncil.org; internet www.canadianinternationalcouncil.org; f. 2007; Chair. and CEO JIM BALSILLIE; publs *International Journal* (quarterly), Annual Report.

Centre for Research on Latin America and the Caribbean (CERLAC): York University, 240 York Lanes, 4700 Keele St, North York, ON M3J 1P3; tel. (416) 736-5237; fax (416) 736-5737; e-mail cerlac@yorku.ca; internet www.yorku.ca/cerlac; f. 1978; interdisciplinary research organization; seeks to build academic and cultural links with the region; research findings made available through publs, lectures, seminars, etc.; Dir EDUARDO CANEL.

Institute of Island Studies: University of Prince Edward Island, 550 University Ave, Charlottetown, PE C1A 4P3; tel. (902) 566-0386; fax (902) 566-0756; e-mail iis@upei.ca; internet www.upei.ca/iis; f. 1985; public policy research and facilitation of public debate; comparative island studies; Chair. IRENE NOVACZEK.

International Development Research Centre: POB 8500, Ottawa, ON K1G 3H9; tel. (613) 236-6163; fax (613) 563-2476; e-mail info@idrc.ca; internet www.idrc.ca; f. 1970 by the Government of Canada; est. to support research in developing countries to promote growth and devt; has regional offices incl. Montevideo; Pres. DAVID M. MALONE; publs include *IDRC Bulletin* (monthly), online e-books, and the IDRC in_focus collection.

CHILE

Centro de Estudios Públicos: Monseñor Sótero Sanz 162, Santiago, Chile; tel. (2) 3282441; fax (2) 2335253; e-mail biblioteca@cepchile.cl; internet www.cepchile.cl; f. 1980; Dir ARTURO FONTAINE TALAVERA; publ. *Estudios Públicos* (quarterly).

Centro Latinoamericano y Caribeño de Demografía (CELADE): Avda Dag Hammarskjöld 3477, Casilla 179-D, Santiago; tel. (2) 2102021; fax (2) 2080196; e-mail celade@eclac.cl; internet www.eclac.cl/celade; f. 1957; Population Division of the UN Economic Commission for Latin American and the Caribbean (ECLAC); analysis of demographic trends, population and development research, teaching and training, and diverse information on population; Dir DIRK JASPARS-FAIJER.

Centro Latinoamericano de Desarrollo Sustentable (CLADES) (Latin American Centre for Sustainable Development): Casilla 97, Correo 9, Santiago; tel. (2) 2341141; fax (2) 2338918; e-mail adm@clades.mic.cl; internet www.clades.cl; f. 1989; aims to prevent the collapse of rural agriculture by the adoption of efficient and sustainable practices; undertakes research, oversees training programmes and facilitates information exchange; Pres. ANDRÉS YURJEVIC.

Corporación de Investigaciones Económicas para Latinoamérica (CIEPLAN): Avda Dag Hammarskjöld 3269, 3°, Vitacura, Santiago; tel. (2) 3781250; fax (2) 4269989; e-mail cieplan@cieplan.cl; internet www.cieplan.cl; f. 1976; economic research; Dir JOAQUIN VIAL.

Facultad Latinoamericana de Ciencias Sociales (FLACSO): Avda Dag Hammarskjöld 3269, Vitacura, Santiago; tel. (2) 2900200; fax (2) 2900263; e-mail flacso@flacso.cl; internet www.flacso.cl; f. 1957; research in sociology, education, political science, international affairs; library of 18,000 vols, 592 periodicals; Dir JOSÉ JARA; publs *Nueva Serie*, *Serie Libros FLACSO*, *Fuerzas Armadas y Sociedad* (quarterly).

Instituto Antártico Chileno (INACH): Plaza Muñoz Gamero 1055, Punta Arenas; tel. (61) 298100; e-mail inach@inach.cl; internet www.inach.cl; f. 1964; a centre for technological and scientific development on matters relating to the Antarctic; 43 mems; library of 2,550 vols and 400 periodicals; Dir JOSÉ RETAMALES ESPINOZA; publs *Serie Científica* (annually), *Boletín Antártico Chileno* (2 a year).

Instituto de Estudios Internacionales: Universidad de Chile, Avda Condell 249, Suc. 21, Providencia, Casilla 14187, Santiago; tel. (2) 4961200; fax (2) 2740155; e-mail inesint@uchile.cl; internet www.iei.uchile.cl; f. 1966; research and teaching institute for international relations, political science, international law, economics and studies on Pacific Basin; Dir Prof. JOSÉ MORANDÉ LEVIN; publ. *Revista de Estudios Internacionales* (quarterly).

Instituto Latinoamericano y del Caribe de Planificación Económica y Social (ILPES) (Latin American and Caribbean Institute for Economic and Social Planning): Edif. Naciones Unidas, Avda Dag Hammarskjöld 3477, Vitacura, Casilla 179-D, Santiago; tel. (2) 2102507; fax (2) 2066104; e-mail alejandra.naser@cepal.org; internet www.ilpes.cl; f. 1962 by UN Economic Commission for Latin America; provides technical assistance, training for govt officials and research on planning techniques; Dir JORGE MATTAR; publs *Cuadernos del ILPES*, *Boletín* (2 a year).

PEOPLE'S REPUBLIC OF CHINA

Institute of Latin American Studies, Chinese Academy of Social Sciences: 3 Zhang Zi Zeng Rd, Dong Cheng District, POB 1113, Beijing; tel. (10) 64014011; e-mail latinlat@public.bta.net.cn; internet www.cass.net.cn; f. 1961; 60 mems; library of 40,000 vols; Dir LI MINGDE; publ. *Latin-American Studies*.

Institute of World Economics and Politics, Chinese Academy of Social Sciences: 5 Jianguomen Nei Da Jie, Beijing 100732; tel. (10)85196063; fax (10) 65126180; e-mail cassrose9@gmail.com; internet en.iwep.org.cn; f. 1980; advises the Govt on economic reform through its 8 areas of research; conducts academic exchanges with foreign institutions; Dir YU YONGDING; publ. *The Yellow Book of International EconomyThe Yellow Book of International Politics*.

COLOMBIA

Centro de Estudios sobre Desarrollo Económico (CEDE) (Centre for Economic Development Studies): Carrera 1E, No 18A-10, Apdo Aéro 4976, Bogotá, DC; tel. (1) 339-4949; fax (1) 332-4492; e-mail infcede@uniandes.edu.co; internet economia.uniandes.edu.co; f. 1958; research in all aspects of economic development; 40 research staff; library of 40,000 vols; Dir FABIO JOSÉ SÁNCHEZ TORRES; publs *Desarrollo y Sociedad* (quarterly), *Cuadernos CEDE*, documents series.

Centro de Información y Documentación Biblioteca José Fernández de Madrid: Universidad de Cartagena, Centro Carrera 6, No 36-100, Cartagena; tel. and fax (95) 660-0682; e-mail biblioteca@unicartagena.edu.co; internet www.unicartagena.edu.co; f. 1827; Rector GERMÁN ARTURO SIERRA ANAYA; publs *Revista Unicarta*, *Revista Palobra (Palabra que Obra)*.

Centro Latinoamericano (CLAM) (Latin American Centre): Pontifíca Universidad Javeriana, Edif. José Rafael Arboleda, S.J., 4°, Transv. 4, No-42–00, Bogotá, DC; tel. and fax (1) 320-8320; e-mail dl-clam@javeriana.edu.co; internet www.javeriana.edu.co/Facultades/comunicacion_lenguaje/centro_lat; academic unit within the university's School of Communication and Language; concerned with teaching Spanish as a foreign language and increasing knowledge of Latin American and Colombian culture; Dir E. CRISTINA MONTAÑA.

Centro Regional para el Fomento del Libro en América Latina y el Caribe (CERLALC) (Regional Centre for the Promotion of Books in Latin America and the Caribbean): Calle 70, No 9-52, Apdo Aereo 57348, Bogotá, DC; tel. (1) 540-2071; fax (1) 541-6398; e-mail libro@cerlalc.org; internet www.cerlalc.org; f. 1972 by UNESCO and Colombian Govt; promotes production and circulation of books and development of libraries; provides training; promotes protection of copyright; 21 mem. countries; Dir ISADORA DE NORDEN; publs *El Libro en América Latina y el Caribe* (quarterly), *Boletín Informativo* CERLALC (quarterly).

Instituto de Estudios Políticos y Relaciones Internacionales: Universidad Nacional de Colombia, Edif. Manuel Ancizar, 3°, Of. 3026, Ciudad Universitaria, Bogotá, DC; tel. and fax (1) 316-5217; e-mail maeep.bog@unal.edu.co; internet www.unal.edu.co/institutos/iepri; international relations; Dir Dr GABRIEL MISAS.

COSTA RICA

Centro Agronómico Tropical de Investigación y Enseñanza (CATIE) (Tropical Agricultural Research and Higher Education Center): Apdo 65, 7170 Cartago, Turrialba 30501; tel. 2558-2000; fax 2558-2060; e-mail comunicacion@catie.ac.cr; internet www.catie.ac.cr; f. 1973; applied research, graduate and short-term training; mems: Inter-American Institute for Co-operation on Agriculture—IICA, Belize, Brazil, Colombia, Costa Rica, Dominican Republic, Ecuador, El Salvador, Guatemala, Honduras, Mexico, Nicaragua, Panama, Venezuela; library of 80,000 vols; Dir-Gen. Dr JOSÉ JOAQUÍN

Campos; publs *Boletín de Semillas Forestales*, *Revista MIP*, *Revista Forestal Centroamericana*, *Revista Agroforestería—las Américas*, *Noticias de Turrialba* (quarterly), *Informe Anual*.

Instituto Centroamericano de Administración Pública (ICAP) (Central American Institute of Public Administration): Apdo 10025-1000, San José; tel. 2234-1011; fax 2225-2049; e-mail info@icap.ac.cr; internet www.icap.ac.cr; f. 1954; technical assistance from UNDP; public administration, economic development and integration; library of 30,800 vols; Dir Dr Hugo Zelaya Calix; publ. *Revista* (2 a year).

Instituto de Estudios Centroamericanos (Institute of Central American Studies): Apdo 1524, 2050 San Pedro; tel. 2253-3195; fax 2234-7682; e-mail mesoamerica@ice.co.cr; internet www.mesoamericaonline.net; f. 1981; Exec. Dir Linda J. Holland.

Instituto de Estudios de Desarrollo Centroamericanos (Institute for Central American Development Studies—ICADS): Apdo 300-2050, San Pedro de Montes de Oca; tel. 2225-0508; fax 2234-1337; e-mail info@icads.org; internet www.icads.org; Dir Dr Sandra Neil Kinghorn.

Inter-American Institute for Co-operation on Agriculture: Apdo 55, 2200 San Isidro de Coronado, San José; tel. 2216-0222; fax 2216-0233; e-mail iicahq@iica.ac.cr; internet www.iica.int; f. 1942; agricultural development and rural well-being; mems: 32 countries of the Americas and Caribbean; library of 75,000 vols; Dir-Gen. Dr Chelston W. D. Brathwaite; publ. *Turrialba* (quarterly).

CUBA

Centro de Información Bancaria y Económica, Banco Central de Cuba (CIBE) (Banking and Economic Information Centre, Central Bank of Cuba): Cuba 410, Havana 10100; tel. (7) 60-4811; fax (7) 66-6601; e-mail chely@bc.gov.cu; internet www.bc.gov.cu; f. 1950; library of 32,000 vols; Pres. Ernesto Medina Villaveirán; Librarian Aracelis Cejas Rodríguez; publs *Cuba: Half Yearly Economic Report* (annually), *Journal of the Central Bank of Cuba*.

Instituto de Política Internacional (Institute of International Politics): Ministerio de Relaciones Exteriores, Calzada 360, Vedado, Havana; tel. (7) 32-3279; f. 1962; 11 mems; Dir René Alvárez Ríos.

CZECH REPUBLIC

Ústav mezinárodních vztahů (Institute of International Relations): 118 50 Prague 1, Nerudova 3; tel. 251108111; fax 251108222; e-mail umv@iir.cz; internet www.iir.cz; f. 1957; research on international relations and foreign and security policy of the Czech Republic, publishing, training, education; Dir Petr Drulák; Deputy Dir Ing. Mgr Petr Kratochvíl; publs include *International Relations* (quarterly) in Czech, *International Politics* (monthly) in Czech, and *Perspectives* (2 a year) in English.

DENMARK

Institute for International Studies (IIS): Strandgade 56, 1401 Copenhagen V; tel. 32-69-87-87; fax 32-69-87-00; e-mail diis@diis.dk; internet www.diis.dk; f. 2002 following merger of Centre for Development Research, Danish Institute of International Affairs, Copenhagen Peace Research Institute and Danish Centre for Holocaust and Genocide Studies; forms part of Danish Centre for International Studies and Human Rights; Chair. Georg Sørensen; publs *Den Ny Verden* (quarterly).

Udenrigspolitiske Selskab (Danish Foreign Policy Society): Amaliegade 40A, 1256 Copenhagen K; tel. 33-14-88-86; fax 33-14-85-20; e-mail udenrigs@udenrigs.dk; internet www.udenrigs.dk; f. 1946; studies, debates, courses and conferences on international affairs; library of 150 periodicals and publs from UN, OECD, WTO, EU; Dir Klaus Carsten Pedersen; publs *Udenrigs*, *Udenrigspolitiske SkrifterLandeLommofermal*.

DOMINICAN REPUBLIC

Centro de Investigación Económica para el Caribe (CIECA) (Economic Research Centre for the Caribbean): Calle Juan Parada Bonilla 8A, Plaza Winnie, La Arboleda Ans. Naco, Apdo 3117, Santo Domingo, DN; tel. 563-9838; fax 227-2533; e-mail ciecard@verizon.net.do; f. 1987; Pres. Pável Isa Contreras.

ECUADOR

Centro Internacional de Estudios Superiores de Comunicación para América Latina (CIESPAL): Diego de Almagro 2155 y Andrade Marín, Apdo 484, Quito; tel. (2) 2254-8011; fax (2) 2502-487; e-mail info@ciespal.net; internet www.ciespal.net; f. 1959; research in communications and training of communicators; library of 16,500 documents, 2,000 vols; Dir Dr Fernando Checa Montúfar; publ. *Revista Chasqui* (quarterly).

Instituto Latinoamericano de Investigaciones Sociales (ILDIS) (Latin American Social Sciences Research Institute): Avdo República 500 y Diego de Almagro, Edif. Pucará, 4°, Casilla 17 03 367, Quito; tel. (2) 2562-103; fax (2) 2504-337; e-mail ildis1@fes.ec; internet www.ildis.org.ec; f. 1974; research in economics, sociology, political science and education; library of 15,000 vols; Dir Hans-Ulrich Bünger.

FRANCE

Académie du Monde Latin: 217 blvd Saint-Germain, 75007 Paris; aims to encourage contact between leading personalities of countries whose language, culture and civilization are of Latin origin; 100 co-opted mems; Pres. Paulo de Berredo Carneiro (Brazil).

Association d'Etudes et d'Informations Politiques Internationales: 86 blvd Haussmann, 75008 Paris; f. 1949; Dir G. Albertini; publs *Est & Ouest* (Paris, 2 a month), *Documenti sul Comunismo* (Rome), *Este y Oeste* (Caracas).

Centre de Coopération Internationale en Recherche Agronomique pour le Développement (CIRAD): 42 rue Scheffer, 75116 Paris; tel. 1-53-70-20-00; fax 1-47-55-15-30; e-mail patrick.herbin@cirad.fr; internet www.cirad.fr; f. 1992; scientific and technical research; experimental stations, industrial plantations; researchers based in over 50 countries; Dir-Gen. Gérard Matheron; publ. *Plantations Recherche Développement* (every 2 months).

Centre d'Etudes Prospectives et d'Informations Internationales (CEPII): 9 rue Georges Pitard, 75740 Paris Cédex 15; tel. 1-53-68-55-00; fax 1-53-68-55-01; e-mail cepiiweb@cepii.fr; internet www.cepii.fr; f. 1978; study of international economics; affiliated with the Centre d'analyse stratégique; 50 mems; library of 20,000 vols, 400 periodicals; Dir Agnès Bénassy-Quéré; Sec.-Gen. Frédérique Abiven; publs *L'economie mondiale* (annual), *Economie Internationale* (quarterly), *La Lettre du CEPII* (monthly), *CEPII News-letter* (quarterly), books, working papers.

Ecole des Hautes Etudes Internationales et L'Ecole des Hautes Etudes Politiques (HEI-HEP): 54 ave Marceau, 75008 Paris; tel. 1-47-20-57-47; fax 1-47-20-57-30; e-mail contact@hei-hep.com; internet www.hei-hep.com; f. 1889; Pres. Odile Launay.

Ibero-American Centre for Study and Research: Institut Catholique de Paris, 21 rue d'Assas, Paris Cédex 06; tel. 1-44-39-52-00; Dirs J. Descola, J. Pingle.

Institut d'Etudes Ibéroaméricaines: Université de Bordeaux III, Domaine Universitaire, 33607 Pessac Cédex; tel. 5-57-12-44-04; fax 5-57-12-47-57; e-mail nadinely@club-internet.fr; f. 1943; teaching and research; 30 staff; library of 51,000 vols; Dir Nadine Ly.

Institut des Hautes Etudes de l'Amérique Latine: 28 rue Saint-Guillaume, 75007 Paris; tel. 1-44-39-86-00; fax 1-45-48-79-58; teaching and research unit of Université de Paris III Sorbonne Nouvelle; shares its library, publications service and website with Centre de recherche et de documentation sur l'Amerique latine—CREDAL; Dir Jean-Michel Blanquer; publs *Cahiers des Amériques latines* (3 a year), *Travaux et Mémoires*.

Institut Européen des Hautes Etudes Internationales (IEHEI): 10 ave des Fleurs, 06000 Nice; tel. 4-93-97-93-70; fax 4-93-97-93-71; e-mail iehei@wanadoo.fr; internet www.iehei.org; f. 1964; library of 4,000 vols; Dir Matthias Waechter.

Institut Français des Relations Internationales (IFRI): 27 rue de la Procession, 75740 Paris Cédex 15; tel. 1-40-61-60-00; fax 1-40-61-60-60; e-mail campagne@ifri.org; internet www.ifri.org; f. 1979; international politics and economy, security issues and regional studies; library of 30,000 vols and 200 periodicals; Pres. Thierry de Montbrial; publs *Politique Etrangère* (quarterly), *Notes*, *Travaux et recherches*, *Cahiers et Conférences*, *Rapport Annuel sur le Système Economique et les Stratégies—RAMSES* (annually).

Institut Pluridisciplinaire d'Etudes sur l'Amérique Latine de Toulouse (IPEALT): Maison de la Recherche, Université de Toulouse Le Mirail, 5 allée Antonio Machado, 31058 Toulouse Cédex; tel. 5-61-50-43-93; fax 5-61-50-36-25; e-mail ipealt@univ-tlse2.fr; internet w3.ipealt.univ-tlse2.fr; f. 1985; specialized research; economic documentation centre; 31 staff; Dir Modesta Suárez; publs *Caravelle*, *L'Ordinaire latino américain*, *Les Ateliers de Caravelle*.

Institut de Recherche pour le Développement (IRD): 44 blvd de Dunkerque, 13002 Marseille; tel. 4-91-99-92-00; fax 4-91-99-92-22; e-mail webmaster@ird.fr; internet www.ird.fr; f. 1944; a public corporation mandated to aid developing countries through research, with special application to human environment problems, tropical climate and diseases, water resources, biodiversity and food production; library and documentation centre; Pres. Jean-François Girard; Dir-Gen. Michel Laurent; *Sciences au Sud* (5 a year).

Institut de Recherches Agronomiques Tropicales et des Cultures Vivrières (IRAT): 110 rue de l'Université, 75340 Paris Cédex; tel. 1-45-50-32-10; fax 1-93-37-79-39; f. 1960; works in numerous stations in Africa, the Antilles, French Guiana, Brazil; research into general agronomy, the cultivation of food crops, sugar cane, forages, spices, etc; 220 research workers and technicians; library of 28,000 vols; Dir F. Bour; publ. *L'Agronomie Tropicale* (quarterly).

Laboratoire Interdisciplinaire de Recherche sur Les Amériques (LIRA): Université de Rennes II, Place du Recteur Henri Le Moal, Rennes Cedex; tel. 2-99-14-17-53; e-mail jean-pierre.sanchez@uhb.fr; f. 1966; general and musical studies on region; Dir Jean-Pierre Sánchez.

Musée de l'Homme: Palais de Chaillot, place du Trocadéro, 75116 Paris; tel. 1-44-05-72-06; fax 1-44-05-72-91; e-mail bmhweb@mnhn.fr; internet mussi.mnhn.fr; f. 1878; library of 250,000 vols, 5,000 periodicals; ethnography, anthropology, pre-history; attached to the Muséum National d'Histoire Naturelle; also a research and education centre; Dir André Langaney; publ. *Objets et mondes* (quarterly).

Société des Américanistes: Maison René Ginouvès, 21 allée de l'Université, 92023 Nanterre; tel. 1-46-69-26-34; fax 1-46-69-25-08; e-mail jsa@mae.u-paris10.fr; f. 1896; 500 mems; Pres. Philippe Descola; Gen. Sec. Dominique Michelet; publ. *Journal*.

GERMANY

Deutsche Gesellschaft für Auswärtige Politik eV (DGAP) (German Council on Foreign Relations): 10787 Berlin, Rauchstr. 17–18; tel. and fax (30) 2542310; fax (30) 25423116; e-mail info@dgap.org; internet www.dgap.org; f. 1955; 1,600 mems; discusses and promotes research on problems of international politics; research library of 78,000 vols; Pres. Dr Arend Oetker; Exec. Vice-Pres. Fritjof von Nordenskjöld; Dir, Research Institute Prof. Dr Eberhard Sandschneider; publs *Die Internationale Politik* (annually), *Internationale Politik: Transatlantic Edition* (quarterly), *Internationale Politik* (6 a year).

Ibero-Amerikanisches Institut Preussischer Kulturbesitz (IAI): 10785 Berlin, Potsdamer Str. 37, Postfach 1247; tel. (30) 266451500; fax (30) 266351550; e-mail iai@iai.spk-berlin.de; internet www.iai.spk-berlin.de; f. 1930; library and research institute; 1.2m. vols (830,000 monographs); Dir Dr Barbara Göbel; publs *Revista Internacional de Lingüística Iberoamericana*, *Indiana*, *Iberoamericana*, *Bibliotheca Ibero-Americana*, *Biblioteca Luso-BrasileiraRevista Internacional de Lingüística Iberoamericana*,*Estudios Indiana*,*Ibero-Online*,*Ibero-Bibliographien*.

Institut für Lateinamerika-Studien (ILAS) (Institute for Latin American Studies): 20354 Hamburg 36, Neuer Jungfernstieg 21; tel. (40) 42825561; fax (40) 42825562; e-mail ilas@giga-hamburg.de; internet www.giga-hamburg.de/ilas; f. 1962; part of the German Institute of Global and Area Studies (GIGA); Dir Dr Detlef Nolte.

Stiftung Wissenschaft und Politik (SWP): Deutsches Institut für Internationale Politik und Sicherheit (German Institute for International and Security Affairs), 10719 Berlin, Ludwigkirchpl. 3–4; tel. (30) 880070; fax (30) 88007100; e-mail swp@swp-berlin.org; internet www.swp-berlin.org; f. 1962; Dir Prof. Dr Volker Perthes.

ZI Lateinamerika-Institut der Freien Universität Berlin (Institute for Latin American Studies): 14197 Berlin, Rüdesheimer Str. 54–56; tel. (30) 83853072; fax (30) 83855464; e-mail lai@zedat.fu-berlin.de; internet www.lai.fu-berlin.de; f. 1970; teaching and research; part of the Freie Universität Berlin; Chair. Prof. Dr Stefan Rinke.

GUATEMALA

Instituto Centroamericano de Investigación y Tecnología Industrial (ICAITI) (Central American Research Institute for Industry): Guatemala City; tel. 2331-0631; fax 2331-7470; e-mail general@icaiti.org.gt; f. 1956; research on marketing, development of new industries and manufacturing techniques, microbiology, geology and energy research projects, establishment of Central American standards, information services to industry, and professional advice; library of 36,000 vols; Dir Ing. Luis Fidel Cifuentes E. (acting).

Instituto de Nutrición de Centroamérica y Panamá (INCAP) (Institute of Nutrition of Central America and Panama): Calzada Roosevelt, Zona 11, Apdo 1188, 01001 Guatemala City; tel. 2472-3762; fax 2473-6529; e-mail info.incap@sica.int; internet www.sica.int/incap; f. 1949; represents the following countries: Belize, Costa Rica, El Salvador, Guatemala, Honduras, Nicaragua, Panama; administered by Pan American Health Organization (PAHO)/World Health Organization (WHO); programmes to promote food and nutrition security among Central American countries through: technical co-operation; human resources; development research; dissemination of information and resources mobilization; main areas of interest are: Food Protection; Nutritionally Improved Foods; Food Nutrition and Security in Disaster Areas; Health and Nutrition of Vulnerable Groups; library of 70,500 vols; Dir José Adán Montes; publs various documents.

Instituto de Relaciones Internacionales y de Investigaciones para la Paz (IRIPAZ) (International Relations and Peace Research Institute): 1a Calle 9-52, Zona 1, 01001 Guatemala City; tel. 2232-8260; fax 2253-1532; e-mail iripaz@iripaz.org; internet www.iripaz.org; f. 1989; research, training and lobbying in international relations and peace studies; Dir Luis Andrés Padilla Vassaux.

GUYANA

Guyana Institute of International Affairs: POB 101176, Georgetown; tel. 227-7768; fax 222-9542; f. 1965; 175 mems; library of 5,000 vols; Pres. Donald A. B. Trotman; publs *Annual Journal of International Affairs*, occasional papers.

INDIA

Indian Council of World Affairs: Sapru House, Barakhamba Rd, New Delhi 110 001; tel. (11) 23317246; fax (11) 23310638; e-mail dg@icwa.in; internet www.icwa.in; f. 1943; non-governmental institution for the study of Indian and international questions; 2,625 mems; library of more than 125,000 vols; Pres. M. Hamid Ansari; publs *India Quarterly*, *Foreign Affairs Reports* (monthly).

ISRAEL

International Institute for Development, Labour and Co-operative Studies (Afro-Asian Institute of the Histradut): 7 Nehardea St, POB 16201, Tel-Aviv 64235; tel. and fax 3-5229195; f. 1958; seminars and courses for leadership of trade unions, co-operative and development institutions, community organizations, women's and youth groups, etc., in African, Asian, Caribbean and Pacific regions; library of 15,000 vols; Dir and Principal Dr Y. Paz.

ITALY

Istituto Affari Internazionali (IAI): Palazzo Rondinini, Via Angelo Brunetti 9, 00186 Roma; tel. (06) 3224360; fax (06) 3224363; e-mail iai@iai.it; internet www.iai.it; f. 1965; research on European integration, the international political economy, the Mediterranean and the Middle East; defence and security; transatlantic relations; library of 24,000 vols and 280 periodicals; Pres. Stefano Silvestri; Dir Ettore Greco; publs *The International Spectator* (quarterly, in English), *L'Italia e la politica internazionale* (annually, in Italian), *IAI Quaderni* (monograph series, in Italian and English), *Documenti IAI* (working papers, in Italian and English), *Affarinternazionali* (online, in Italian).

Istituto Italo-Latino Americano: Palazzo Santacroce, Pasolini Piazza Benedetto Cairoli 3, 00186 Roma; tel. (06) 684921; fax (06) 6872834; e-mail info@iila.org; internet www.iila.org; f. 1966 by 20 Latin American states and Italy; cultural activities, commercial exchanges, economic and sociological, scientific and technical research, etc; awards student grants; library of 90,000 vols; Sec.-Gen. Paolo Bruni.

Istituto per le relazioni tra l'Italia e i paesi dell'Africa, America Latina e Medio Oriente (IPALMO) (Institute for Relations between Italy and the Countries of Africa, Latin America and the Middle East): Via degli Scipioni 147, 00192 Roma; tel. (06) 32699701; fax (06) 32699750; e-mail ipalmo@ipalmo.com; internet www.ipalmo.com; f. 1971; library and archive of over 20,000 vols; Pres. Gianni De Michelis; Sec.-Gen. Antonio Loche; publ. *Politica Internazionale* (every 2 months).

Istituto per gli Studi di Politica Internazionale (ISPI): Palazzo Clerici, Via Clerici 5, 20121 Milano; tel. (02) 8633131; fax (02) 8692055; e-mail ispi.eventi@ispionline.it; internet www.ispionline.it; f. 1933 for the promotion of the study and knowledge of all problems concerning international relations; operates under supervision of foreign affairs ministry; seminars at postgraduate level; library of 100,000 vols; Dir Paolo Magri; publs *Relazioni Internazionali* (quarterly), *Working Papers*, *Policy Brief*.

JAMAICA

Asociación de Universidades e Institutos de Investigación del Caribe (UNICA) (Association of Caribbean Universities and Research Institutes): c/o Office of Administration and Special Initiatives, University of the West Indies, Kingston 7; tel. 977-6065; fax 977-7525; e-mail unica@uwimona.edu.jm; internet oficinacentral.inter.edu/vaaps/unica; f. 1968 to foster contact and collaboration between member universities and institutes; conferences, meetings, seminars, etc; circulation of information; facilitates co-operation and the pooling of resources in research; encourages exchanges of staff and students; mems: 50 institutions; Pres. Dr Orville Kean; Sec.-Gen. Mervyn Alleyne; publ. *Caribbean Educational Bulletin* (quarterly).

Caribbean Food and Nutrition Institute: University of the West Indies, POB 140, Mona, Kingston 7; tel. 927-1540; fax 927-2657; e-mail e-mail@cfni.paho.org; internet www.cfni.paho.org; f. 1967; specialized centre of the Pan American Health Organization (PAHO); research and field investigations, training in nutrition, dissemination of information, advisory services, production of educational material; mems: all English-speaking Caribbean territories, Belize, Guyana and Suriname; library of 4,500 vols; Dir Dr FITZROY HENRY; publs *Cajanus* (quarterly), *Nyam News Nutrient-Cost Tables* (quarterly).

JAPAN

Ajia Keizai Kenkyusho (IDE-JETRO) (Institute of Developing Economies): Wakaba 3-2-2, Mihamaku, Chiba 261-8545; tel. (4) 3299-9500; fax (4) 3299-9724; e-mail info@ide.go.jp; internet www.ide.go.jp; f. 1960; merged with Japan External Trade Organization in 1998; researches industrial devt and political change in Latin America; library of 545,000 vols; Pres. TAKASHI SHIRAISHI; publ. *Developing Economies* (quarterly), *Latin America Report* (2 a year).

Centre for Latin American Studies: Nanzan University, 18 Yamazato-cho, Showa-ku, Nagoya 466; tel. (52) 832-3111; fax (52) 832-6825; e-mail centro-latino@ic.nanzan-u.ac.jp; internet www.nanzan-u.ac.jp/LATIN; f. 1983; an institute specializing in the study of contemporary Latin America (social sciences); Dir TAKAHIRO KATO.

Institute of Developing Economies—Japan External Trade Organization (JETRO): 3-2-2 Wakaba, Mihama-ku, China-shi, Chiba 261-8545, Japan; tel. (43) 299-9500; fax (43) 299-9726; internet www.ide.go.jp; Pres. TAKASHI SHIRAISHI.

Tokyo University of Foreign Studies: 3-11-1, Asahi-cho, Fuchu-shi, Tokyo 183; tel. (42) 330-5126; fax (42) 330-5599; e-mail ml-zenhp@tufs.ac.jp; internet www.tufs.ac.jp; f. 1899; programmes of study into world languages, cultures and international relations; Pres. IKUO KAMEYAMA.

REPUBLIC OF KOREA

Institute of Brazilian Studies: Kyung Hee University, 1 Hoiki Dong, Dongdaemun-ku, Seoul 131; tel. (2) 965-8000; f. 1978.

MEXICO

Centro de Cooperación Regional para la Educación de Adultos en América Latina y el Caribe (CREFAL) (Regional Co-operation Centre for Adult Education in Latin America and the Caribbean): Avda Lázaro Cardenas 525, Col. Revolución, 61609 Pátzcuaro, Mich.; tel. (434) 342-8200; fax (434) 342-8151; e-mail crefal@crefal.edu.mx; internet www.crefal.edu.mx; f. 1951 by UNESCO and OAS; admin. by Board of Directors from mem. countries; regional technical assistance, specialist training in literary and adult education, research; library of 42,799 vols; Dir MERCEDES CALDERÓN GARCÍA; publs *Revista Interamericana de Educación de Adultos* (quarterly).

Centro de Estudios Educativos, AC (Education Studies Centre): Avda Revolución 1291, Col. Tlacopoa, San Angel, 01040 México, DF; tel. (55) 5593-5719; fax (55) 5651-6374; e-mail ceemexico@cee.edu.mx; internet www.cee.edu.mx; f. 1963; scientific research into the problems of education in Mexico and Latin America; 20 researchers; library of 35,000 vols and 600 periodicals; Dir-Gen. LUIS MORFÍN LÓPEZ; publ. *Revista Latinoamericana de Estudios Educativos* (quarterly).

Centro de Estudios Históricos (Historical Studies Centre): Colegio de México, AC, Camino al Ajusco 20, Col. Pedregal de Santa Teresa, 10740 México, DF; tel. (55) 5449-3000; fax (55) 5645-0464; e-mail webmaster@colmex.mx; internet www.colmex.mx; Pres. Dr JAVIER GARCIADIEGO DANTÁN.

Centro de Estudios Internacionales (Centre for International Studies): Colegio de México, Camino al Ajusco 20, Col. Pedregal de Santa Teresa, 10740 México, DF; tel. (55) 5449-3000; fax (55) 5645-0464; e-mail posto@colmex.mx; internet www.colmex.mx/centros/cei/org.htm; f. 1960; research and teaching in international relations and public administration; Dir GUSTAVO VEGA CANOVAS.

Centro de Estudios Monetarios Latinoamericanos (Centre for Latin American Monetary Studies): Durango 54, Col. Roma, Del. Cuauhtémoc, 06700 México, DF; tel. (55) 5061-6640; fax (55) 5525-4432; e-mail informacion@cemla.org; internet www.cemla.org; f. 1952; organizes technical training programmes on monetary policy, development finance, etc; applied research programmes, regional meetings of banking officials; 50 mems; Dir-Gen. Dr KENNETH GILMORE COATES SPRY; Deputy Dir LUÍZ BARBOSA; publs *Boletín* (every 2 months), *Monetaria* (quarterly), *Money Affairs* (2 a year).

Centro de Investigaciones sobre América Latina y el Caribe (CIALC): Torre II de Humanidades 8°, Ciudad Universitaria, 04510 México, DF; tel. (55) 5623-0211; fax (55) 5623-0219; e-mail camposg@servidor.unam.mx; internet www.ccydel.unam.mx; f. 1978; fmrly Centro Coordinador y Difusor Estudios Latinoamericanos; attached to Universidad Nacional de México; study of Latin America and the Caribbean in all disciplines (history, literature, philosophy, etc.); library of over 22,000 vols; Dir Dr ADALBERTO SANTANA HERNÁNDEZ; publs *Latinoamérica: Revista de estudios latinoamericanos* (3 a year).

Centro de Relaciones Internacionales (CRI) (Centre for International Relations): Ciudad Universitaria, FCPM, 04510 México, DF; tel. (55) 5622-9412; internet www.politicas.unam.mx/carreras/ri/index.htm; f. 1970; attached to the Faculty of Political and Social Sciences of the Universidad Nacional Autónoma de México; co-ordinates and promotes research in all aspects of international relations and Mexico's foreign policy, as well as the training of researchers in different fields: disciplinary construction problems, co-operation and international law, developing nations, current problems in world society, Africa, Asia, peace research; 30 full mems; library of 16,000 vols; Dir CONSUELO DÁVILA PÉREZ; publs *Relaciones Internacionales* (quarterly), *Cuadernos*, *Boletín Informativo del CRI*.

Consejo Latinoamericano de Investigación para la Paz (CLAIP) (Latin American Peace Research Council): Calle Magnolia 39, Col. San Jeronimo Lidice, 10200 México, DF; e-mail sarahorowitz@respuestaparalapaz.org.ar; f. 1978; holds conferences; Sec.-Gen. (vacant); publ. *Boletín Informativo CLAIP*.

Pan American Institute of Geography and History: Ex-Arzobispado 29, Col. Observatorio, 11860 México, DF; tel. (55) 5277-5888; fax (55) 5271-6172; e-mail secretariageneral@ipgh.org; internet www.ipgh.org; f. 1928; promotes, co-ordinates, and publicizes studies in cartography, geography, geophysics, history, anthropology and archaeology in the Americas; mems: nations of the Organization of American States; library of 228,285 vols; Sec.-Gen. SANTIAGO BORRERO; publs *Revista Cartográfica*, *Revista Geográfica*, *Revista de Historia de América*, *Revista Geofísica*, *Boletín de Antropología Americana*, *Revista de Arqueología Americana*, more than 500 books and monographs.

THE NETHERLANDS

Institute of Social Studies: POB 29776, 2502 LT The Hague; tel. (70) 4260460; fax (70) 4260799; e-mail information@iss.nl; internet www.iss.nl; f. 1952; university institute of Erasmus University Rotterdam from 1 July 2009; postgraduate courses, research and consultancy in development studies; Rector Prof. LOUK DE LA RIVE BOX; publs *Development and Change* (5 a year), *Development Issues* (3 a year), *Working Papers*.

NICARAGUA

Coordinadora Regional de Investigaciones Económicas y Sociales (CRIES) (Regional Co-ordinating Committee of Economic and Social Research): De Iglesia El Carmen 1c. al Largo, Apdo 3516, Managua; tel. 22-5137; fax 22-6180; e-mail aserbin@cries.org; internet www.cries.org; research into economic development and other socio-economic and socio-political issues in Central America and the Caribbean; Pres. Dr ANDRÉS SERBÍN; publs *Cuadernos de Pensamiento Propio*, *Revista Pensamiento Propio* (monthly), *Servicios Especiales* (2 a month).

Instituto Histórico Centroamericano (IHCA) (Central American Historical Institute): Universidad Centroamericana, Apdo A-194, Managua; tel. (2) 278-2557; fax (2) 278-1402; e-mail envio@ns.uca.edu.ni; internet www.envio.org.ni; f. 1981; Dir P. ANDREU OLIVA; publ. *Envío* (monthly).

PAKISTAN

Area Study Centre for Africa, North and South America: Quaidi-i-Azam University, Islamabad; tel. (51) 2896006; fax (51) 2896007; f. 1978; teaching and research; library of 11,915 vols, microfilm/microfiche collection; Dir Dr RUKHSANA QAMBER; publ. *Pakistan Journal of American Studies* (2 a year).

PANAMA

Centro de Estudios Latinoamericanos 'Justo Arosemena' (CELA) (Justo Arosemena Centre for Latin American Studies): Apdo 63093, El Dorado, Panamá; tel. 223-0028; fax 269-2032; e-mail cela@cableonda.net; internet bibliotecavirtual.clacso.org.ar/ar/cela.html; f. 1977 for the analysis and dissemination of international agreements and intervention and other foreign affairs issues; Exec. Sec. MARCO A. GANDÁSEGUI.

Instituto Interamericano de Estadística (Inter-American Statistical Institute—IASI): INEC, POB 0816-01521, Panamá; tel. 510-4890; fax 223-6535; e-mail fabpan@cwpanama.net; internet www.indec.gov.ar/iasi; f. 1940; research, seminars, technical meetings; co-ordination and co-operation with the Organization of American States; consultative status with the UN Economic and Social Council; affiliated to the International Statistical Institute; Tech. Sec. EVELIO O. FABBRONI; publs *Estadística* (2 a year), *Newsletter* (4 a year); br. in Buenos Aires, Argentina.

PARAGUAY

Servicio Técnico Interamericano de Cooperación Agrícola (Inter-American Technical Service for Agricultural Co-operation):

Casilla de Correo 819, Asunción; f. 1943; 10,000 vols; Librarian LUCILA M. I. CARDUS.

PERU

Centro Peruano de Estudios Internacionales (CEPEI) (Peruvian Centre for International Studies): San Ignacio de Loyola 554, Miraflores 8, Lima 18; tel. (1) 4457225; fax (1) 4451094; f. 1983; external relations, incl. Peru's border relations; Exec. Pres. Dr EDUARDO FERRERO COSTA; publ. *Cronología de Las Relaciones Internacionales del Peru* (quarterly).

Instituto de Economía de Libre Mercado (IELM) (Institute of Free Market Economics): Avda Santa Cruz 398, San Isidro, Lima 27; fax (1) 4216242; f. 1993; studies economic, political and social history of the area; Exec. Pres. CARLOS BOLOÑA BEHR.

POLAND

Centre for Latin American Studies (CESLA): University of Warsaw, ul. Smyczkowa 14, 02-678 Warsaw; tel. (22) 5534209; fax (22) 5534210; e-mail cesla@uw.edu.pl; internet www.cesla.uw.edu.pl; f. 1988; documentation, publications and library service; Dir Prof. Dr ANDRZEJ DEMBICZ; publs *CESLA 'Estudios y Memorias' Series*, *Documentos de Trabajo*, *Revista de CESLA*.

Polski Instytut Spraw Międzynarodowych (Polish Institute for International Affairs): 00-950 Warsaw, Warecka 1A; tel. (22) 5568000; fax (22) 5568099; e-mail pism@pism.pl; internet www.pism.pl; f. 1999; international relations; library of 155,000 vols; Dir Dr SŁAWOMIR DĘBSKI; publs *Polski Przeglad Dyplomatyczny* (6 a year), *Polish Foreign Affairs Digest* (quarterly, in English), *Europa* (quarterly, in Russian).

PUERTO RICO

Institute of Caribbean Studies: POB 23361, University Station, Río Piedras, PR 00931; tel. (787) 764-0000; fax (787) 764-3099; e-mail iec@uprrp.edu; internet graduados.uprrp.edu/icaribe; f. 1959; research and publishing; 10 mems; library of 150 vols; Dir Dr HUMBERTO GARCÍA-MUNIZ; publ. *Caribbean Studies*.

RUSSIA

Institute of Latin America of the Russian Academy of Sciences: 113035 Moscow, B. Ordynka 21; tel. (495) 951-53-23; fax (495) 953-40-70; e-mail ilac-ran@mtu-ntt.ru; internet www.ilaran.ru; f. 1961; concerned with the economic, social, political and cultural development of Latin American countries; Dir Dr VLADIMIR M. DAVYDOV; publ. *Latinskaya Amerika* (monthly).

Institute of World Economics and International Relations: 117859 Moscow, Profsoyuznaya 23; tel. (495) 120-43-32; fax (495) 310-70-27; e-mail imemoran@glasnet.ru; f. 1956; Dir V. A. MARTYNOV (acting).

SENEGAL

Centre des Hautes Etudes Afro-Ibéro-Américaines: Université Cheikh Anta Diop de Dakar, Dakar-Fann, Dakar; tel. 22-05-30; concerned with all matters relating to Africa and Latin America in the fields of law, science and the arts.

SERBIA

Institute of International Politics and Economics: 11000 Belgrade, POB 750, Makedonska 25; tel. (11) 3373633; fax (11) 3373835; e-mail iipe@diplomacy.bg.ac.yu; internet www.diplomacy.bg.ac.yu; f. 1947; international relations, world economy, international law, social, economic and political development in all countries; library of more than 150,000 vols; Dir Dr DUŠKO DIMITRIJEVIČ (acting); publs *International Problems* (annually), *Review of International Affairs* (quarterly).

SPAIN

Agencia Española de Cooperación Internacional (AECID) (Spanish Agency for International Co-operation): Avda de los Reyes Católicos 4, Ciudad Universitaria, 28040 Madrid; tel. (91) 5838100; fax (91) 5838310; e-mail centro.informacion@aecid.es; internet www.aecid.es; f. 1988; promotes cultural understanding and promotes international co-operation by organizing conferences, exhibitions and exchanges, scholarships; finances programmes of cultural, scientific, economic and technical co-operation; information department; library of more than 600,000 vols; Pres. SORRAYA RODRÍGUEZ RAMOS; Sec.-Gen. JUAN PABLO DE LAIGLESIA Y GONZÁLEZ DE PEREDO; Dir-Gen. for Co-operation with Latin America AURORA DÍAZ-RATO REVUELTA; numerous publs on international development and co-operation.

Escuela de Estudios Hispanoamericanos: Alfonso XII 16, 41002 Seville; tel. (95) 4500972; fax (95) 4224331; e-mail bibescu@cica.es; f. 1943; studies history of the Americas; Library Dir ISABEL REAL DÍAZ.

Instituto de Cuestiones Internacionales y Política Exterior (INCIPE) (Institute of International Affairs and Foreign Policy): Alberto Aguilera 7, 6°, 28015 Madrid; tel. (91) 4455847; fax (91) 4457489; e-mail info@incipe.org; internet www.incipe.org; f. 1988; Pres. JOSÉ LLADÓ FERNÁNDEZ-URRUTÍA; Dir VICENTE GARRIDO REBOLLEDO; publ. *Ensayos*, *Informes*.

Instituto de Relaciones Europeo-Latinoamericanas (IRELA) (Institute for European-Latin American Relations): Calle Pedro de Valdivia 10, Apdo 2600, 28002 Madrid; tel. (91) 5617200; fax (91) 5626499; e-mail info@ivcla.org; f. 1984; research, conferences, etc.; Pres. ROLF LINKOHR; Dir WOLF GRABENDORFF; publs *Dossiers* (8 a year), *Working Papers* (6 a year).

Real Academia Hispano-Americana (Royal Spanish-American Academy): Plaza Fragela s/n, 4°, 11003 Cádiz; tel. (956) 221680; fax (956) 222124; e-mail raha@raha.es; internet www.insacan.org/rahcla/rahcla.html; f. 1910; 29 mems; Dir RAFAEL CABRERA AFONSO; publs *Anuario*, *Boletín*.

Real Instituto Elcano: Príncipe de Vergara 51, 28006 Madrid; tel. (91) 7816770; fax (91) 4262157; e-mail info@rielcano.org; internet www.realinstitutoelcano.org; f. 2001; independent body for the study of international affairs; Pres. GUSTAVO SUÁREZ PERTIERRA; Dir GIL CARLOS RODRÍGUEZ IGLESIAS; publs *Analysis of the Real Instituto Elcano (ARI)*, *Barometer of the Real Instituto Elcano* (3 a year), *ARI Magazine* (monthly).

SWEDEN

Latinamerika-Institutet i Stockholm (Institute of Latin American Studies, Stockholm University): Universitetsvägen 10B, 106 91 Stockholm; tel. (8) 16-34-36; fax (8) 15-85-78; e-mail lai@lai.su.se; internet www.lai.su.se; f. 1951; research on economic, political and social development in the region; library of 50,000 vols; Dir MONA ROSENDAHL; publ. *Iberoamericana: Nordic Journal of Latin American and Caribbean Studies* (2 a year).

SWITZERLAND

Institut de Hauts Etudes Internationales et du Développement (Graduate Institute of International and Development Studies): 132 rue de Lausanne, CP 136, 1211 Geneva 21; tel. 229085700; fax 229085710; e-mail info@graduateinstitute.ch; internet graduateinstitute.ch; f. 2008 by merger of Institut Universitaire de Hautes Etudes Internationales (f. 1927) and Institut Universitaire d'Etudes du Développement (f. 1961); African history, Middle Eastern and Latin American studies, international relations, Switzerland–Developing World economic relations; Dir PHILIPPE BURRIN.

Schweizerisches Institut für Auslandforschung (Swiss Institute of International Studies): Augustinerhof 1, 8001 Zürich; tel. 2121313; fax 2127854; e-mail info@siaf.ch; internet www.siaf.ch; f. 1943; Man. Dir Dr MARTIN MEYER.

Zentrum für Vergleichende und Internationale Studien (Centre for Comparative and International Studies): Seilergraben 45–53, 8001 Zürich; tel. 6327968; fax 6321942; e-mail cispostmaster@sipo.gess.ethz.ch; internet www.cis.ethz.ch; f. 1997; international relations, comparative politics, security studies and conflict research; Dir Prof. KATHARINA MICHAELOWA.

TRINIDAD AND TOBAGO

Caribbean Agricultural Research and Development Institute (CARDI): University of the West Indies, St Augustine Campus, St Augustine; tel. 645-1205; fax 645-1208; e-mail infocentre@cardi.org; internet www.cardi.org; f. 1975; mems: CARICOM countries (see Regional Organizations); provides technical assistance, technology devt and transfer in agriculture and animal sciences; library of 3,000 vols; Exec. Dir Dr ARLINGTON CHESNEY; publs *CARDI Weekly*, *CARDI Review*, *technical bulletins and papers*.

Caribbean Association of Industry and Commerce (CAIC): 27a Saddle Road, Ground Floor, Maraval; tel. 628-9859; fax 622-7810; e-mail caic.admin@gmail.com; internet www.caic.org.tt; policy advocacy to improve trading conditions for regional private sector; CEO CAROL AYOUNG; publ. *CAIC Newsletter* (monthly).

Institute of International Relations: University of the West Indies, St Augustine Campus, St Augustine; tel. 662-2002; fax 663-9685; e-mail iirt@sta.uwi.edu; internet sta.uwi.edu/iir; f. 1966; diplomatic training and postgraduate teaching and research; library of some 20,000 vols; Dir Prof. TIMOTHY SHAW.

UNITED KINGDOM

Centre of Latin American Studies: 17 Mill Lane, Cambridge, CB2 1RX; tel. (1223) 335390; fax (1223) 335397; e-mail general@latin-american.cam.ac.uk; internet www.latin-american.cam.ac.uk; f. 1969; research and graduate teaching, mainly in comparative history and anthropology, and in Latin American culture, sociology, politics and economics; Dir Dr GEOFFREY KANTARIS; publs *Cambridge Latin American Miniatures*, *Working Paper Series*.

Hispanic and Luso-Brazilian Council: Canning House, 2 Belgrave Sq., London, SW1X 8PJ; tel. (20) 7235-2303; fax (20) 7838-9258; e-mail enquiries@canninghouse.com; internet www.canninghouse.com; f. 1943; cultural, educational, corporate and economic links with Latin America, Spain and Portugal; 130 corporate mems; library of 60,000 vols; Dir-Gen. NIGEL MCCOLLUM; publ. *British Bulletin of Publications on Latin America, the Caribbean, Portugal and Spain* (2 a year).

Institute of Commonwealth Studies: 28 Russell Sq., London, WC1B 5DS; tel. (20) 7862-8844; fax (20) 7862-8820; e-mail ics@sas.ac.uk; internet www.sas.ac.uk/commonwealthstudies; f. 1949; attached to University of London; for postgraduate research in social sciences and recent history relating to the Commonwealth; lead institution of CASBAH project (Caribbean Studies Black and Asian History); library of 190,000 vols, includes library of West India Committee; Dir Prof. WARWICK GOULD (acting).

Institute of Development Studies: University of Sussex, Falmer, Brighton, BN1 9RE; tel. (1273) 606261; fax (1273) 621202; e-mail ids@ids.ac.uk; internet www.ids.ac.uk; f. 1966; research, training, post-graduate teaching, advisory work, information services; Dir Prof. LAWRENCE HADDAD; publs *IDS Bulletin* (quarterly), research reports, working papers development bibliographies, discussion papers, policy briefings, annual report, publications catalogue.

Institute of Latin American Studies: University of Liverpool, 86 Bedford St South, Liverpool, L69 7WW; tel. (1517) 94-3079; fax (1517) 94-3080; e-mail smurph@liverpool.ac.uk; internet www.liv.ac.uk/ILAS; f. 1966; university centre for the development of teaching and research on Latin America; library of 50,000 vols; Dir Dr STEVEN RUBENSTEIN; publs monographs, research papers.

Institute for the Study of the Americas: Senate House, Malet Street, London, WC1E 7HU; tel. (20) 7862-8870; fax (20) 7862-8886; e-mail americas@sas.ac.uk; internet americas.sas.ac.uk; f. 2004; graduate study centre within the School of Advanced Study of the University of London; co-ordinates national information on the Americas in the United Kingdom; post-graduate courses on politics, economics, history, sociology, globalization and development of Latin America and the Caribbean; library of bibliographies, guides and research aids; wide range of seminars, workshops and conferences on Latin America and the Caribbean; Dir Prof. MAXINE MOLYNEUX; publs monographs, research papers and miscellaneous documents.

Latin American Centre: St Antony's College, Oxford, OX2 6JF; tel. (1865) 274486; fax (1865) 274489; e-mail enquiries@lac.ox.ac.uk; internet www.lac.ox.ac.uk; f. 1964; promotes research on Latin America, particularly with regard to the post-Independence period and in the fields of history, the social sciences, literature and geography; organizes seminars; library of 12,000 vols; Dir TIMOTHY POWER.

Overseas Development Institute: Overseas Development Institute, 111 Westminster Bridge Rd, London, SE1 7JD; tel. (20) 7922-0300; fax (20) 7922-0399; e-mail odi@odi.org.uk; internet www.odi.org.uk; f. 1960 to act as a research and information centre on overseas development issues and problems; library of 16,000 vols; Dir ALISON EVANS; publs *Development Policy Review* (quarterly), *Disasters: the Journal of Disaster Studies, Policy and Management* (quarterly), books, pamphlets, briefing papers.

Progressio: Unit 3, Canonbury Yard, 190a New North Rd, London, N1 7BJ; tel. (20) 7354-0883; fax (20) 7359-0017; e-mail enquiries@progressio.org.uk; internet www.progressio.org.uk; f. 1940, known as the Catholic Institute for International Relations (CIIR) until 2006; information and analysis of socio-economic, political, church and human rights issues in the developing countries, incl. the Dominican Repub., Ecuador, El Salvador, Haiti, Honduras, Nicaragua and Peru; Exec. Dir CHRISTINE ALLEN; publs include specialized studies on EU development policy.

Royal Commonwealth Society: 25 Northumberland Ave, London, WC2N 5AP; tel. (20) 7766-9200; fax (20) 7766 9222; e-mail info@thercs.org; internet www.thercs.org; f. 1868; int. educational charity; Chair. Sir MICHAEL MCWILLIAM; Dir DANNY SRISKANDARAJAH; publs *Annual Review*, *The View* (e-newsletter, monthly), *RCS Exchange* (3 a year).

Royal Institute of International Affairs (Chatham House): 10 St James's Sq., London, SW1Y 4LE; tel. (20) 7957-5700; fax (20) 7957-5710; e-mail contact@chathamhouse.org.uk; internet www.chathamhouse.org.uk; f. 1920; an independent body that aims to promote the study and understanding of international affairs; over 300 corporate mems and many individual mems; library of 160,000 vols, 650 periodicals; Chair. Dr DEANNE JULIUS; Dir Dr ROBIN NIBLETT; publs *The World Today* (monthly), *International Affairs* (6 a year).

Yesu Persaud Centre for Caribbean Studies: University of Warwick, Coventry, CV4 7AL; tel. (24) 7652-3443; fax (24) 7652-3473; e-mail caribbeanstudies@warwick.ac.uk; internet www.warwick.ac.uk/fac/arts/ccs; f. 1984 as the Centre for Caribbean Studies; renamed 2010; MA and PhD programme, conferences and symposia, lectures, publishing; Dir Dr CECILY JONES; publs *Warwick/Macmillan Caribbean Series*.

USA

Brookings Institution: 1775 Massachusetts Ave, NW, Washington, DC 20036; tel. (202) 797-6000; fax (202) 797-6004; e-mail brookinfo@brookings.edu; internet www.brookings.edu; f. 1916; research, education and publishing in the fields of economics, government and foreign policy; library of 80,000 vols; Pres. STROBE TALBOTT.

Center for International Policy (CIP): 1717 Massachusetts Ave NW, Suite 801, Washington, DC 20036; tel. (202) 232-3317; fax (202) 232-3440; e-mail cip@ciponline.org; internet www.ciponline.org; f. 1975; promotes international co-operation and demilitarization; Pres. ROBERT E. WHITE; Exec. Dir WILLIAM GOODFELLOW; publ. *International Policy Reports*.

Center for International Studies: Massachusetts Institute of Technology, Bldg E40, 1 Amherst St, Cambridge, MA 02139; tel. (617) 253-8093; internet web.mit.edu/cis; f. 1952; development, migration, defence and arms control studies, environment, trade, political economy; Dir RICHARD SAMUELS.

Center for Latin American Studies: University of Florida, 319 Grinter Hall, POB 115530, Gainesville, FL 32611-5530; tel. (352) 392-0375; fax (352) 392-7682; e-mail info@latam.ufl.edu; internet www.latam.ufl.edu; f. 1931; graduate teaching and research; tropical conservation and development, business, crime, Haitian Creole and Portuguese language programmes; extensive Latin American collection in library; Dir PHILIP J. WILLIAMS; publ. *The Latinamericanist* (2 a year).

Council on Foreign Relations, Inc: The Harold Pratt House, 58 East 68th St, New York, NY 10065; tel. (212) 434-9400; fax (212) 434-9800; e-mail communications@cfr.org; internet www.cfr.org; f. 1921; 4,000 mems; Foreign Relations Library of 5,000 vols, 300 periodicals; Pres. RICHARD N. HAASS; Co-Chair. CARLA A. HILLS, RICHARD E. SALOMON; publs *Foreign Affairs* (6 a year) and books on major issues of US foreign policy.

Council on Hemispheric Affairs: 1250 Connecticut Ave, NW, Suite 1C, Washington, DC 20036; tel. (202) 223-4975; fax (202) 223-4979; e-mail coha@coha.org; internet www.coha.org; f. 1975; conducts research into relations between North and South America; Dir LARRY BIRNS; publ. *News and Analysis* (2 a week).

Hispanic Society of America: 613 West 155th St, New York, NY 10032; tel. (212) 926-2234; fax (212) 690-0743; e-mail info@hispanicsociety.org; internet www.hispanicsociety.org; f. 1904; maintains a public museum, rare book room, research staff, publishing section; 400 hon. mems; library of 250,000 vols and 15,000 rare books; Dir MITCHELL A. CODDING.

Institute of Latin American and Iberian Studies: Rm 830, 420 West 118th St, Columbia University, New York, NY 10027; tel. (212) 854-4643; fax (212) 854-4607; internet www.columbia.edu/cu/ilas; f. 1961; co-ordinates events, lectures and seminars on subjects relating to Latin America and Spain; Dir PABLO PICCATO; publs *Newsletter* (3 a year), working paper series.

Inter-American Dialogue: 1211 Connecticut Ave, Suite 510, Washington, DC 20036; tel. (202) 822-9002; fax (202) 822-9553; e-mail iad@thedialogue.org; internet www.thedialogue.org; f. 1982; centre for policy analysis, communication and exchange on Western affairs; 100 mems; Co-Chair. CARLA A. HILLS, RICARDO LAGOS; Pres. PETER HAKIM; publ. *Dialogue* (2 a year), *Latin America Advisor* (newsletter).

Kellogg Institute for International Studies: University of Notre Dame, 130 Hesburgh Center for International Studies, Notre Dame, IN 46556-5677; tel. (574) 631-6580; fax (574) 631-6717; e-mail kellogg@nd.edu; internet kellogg.nd.edu; f. 1982; international research, particularly focused upon Latin America; Dir EDWARD BEATTY (acting); publs *Working Papers*, *Newsletter* (2 a year), monograph series.

Latin American and Caribbean Center: Florida International University, University Park, Miami, FL 33199; tel. (305) 348-2894; fax (305) 348-3593; e-mail lacc@fiu.edu; internet lacc.fiu.edu; f. 1979; university research institute; Dir CRISTINA EGUIZÁBAL; publ. *Hemisphere* (2 a year), *Journal of Latin American Anthropology*.

Latin American and Iberian Institute: University of New Mexico, 801 Yale NE, MSC02 1690, Albuquerque, NM 87131-0001; tel. (505) 277-2961; fax (505) 277-5989; e-mail info@laii.unm.edu;

internet www.laii.unm.edu; Dir Dr SUSAN TIANO; publ. research papers.

Latin American Institute: University of California, Los Angeles (UCLA), 10343 Bunche Hall, Hilgard Ave, POB 951447, Los Angeles, CA 90095-1447; tel. (310) 825-4571; e-mail latinamctr@international.ucla.edu; internet www.international.ucla.edu/lac; Dir RANDAL JOHNSON.

Latin American Studies Association: 416 Bellefield Hall, University of Pittsburgh Pittsburgh, PA 15260; tel. (412) 648-7929; fax (412) 624-7145; e-mail lasa@pitt.edu; internet lasa.international.pitt.edu; Exec. Dir MILAGROS PEREYRA; publs Latin American Research Review (3 a year), LASA Forum (4 a year).

Library of International Relations: 565 West Adams, Chicago, IL 60661; tel. (312) 906-5600; fax (312) 906-5685; f. 1932; aims to stimulate interest and research in international problems; conducts seminars, etc; library of over 200,000 books, documents and periodicals; Pres. HOKEN SEKI.

Middle American Research Institute: Tulane University, New Orleans, LA 70118; tel. (504) 865-5110; fax (504) 862-8778; e-mail mari@tulane.edu; internet www.tulane.edu/~mari; f. 1924; publs on archaeology in Mesoamerica and related subjects; Dir MARCELLO A. CANUTO; publs books, miscellaneous papers.

Paul H. Nitze School of Advanced International Studies (SAIS): Johns Hopkins University, 1740 Massachusetts Ave, NW, Washington, DC 20036; tel. (202) 663-5734; fax (202) 663-5737; e-mail sais-westernhemisphere@jhu.edu; internet www.sais-jhu.edu/latinamerica; Dean RIORDAN ROETT.

Pre-Columbian Studies, Dumbarton Oaks: 1703 32nd St, NW, Washington, DC 20007; tel. (202) 339-6440; fax (202) 625-0284; e-mail pre-Columbian@doaks.org; internet www.doaks.org/research/pre_columbian; f. 1962; residential fellowships, annual symposia, seminars, etc; Pre-Columbian art collection; library of 26,000 vols on Pre-Columbian history; Dir of Studies JOANNE PILLSBURY; publs annual symposia vols and occasional monographs.

Princeton Institute for International and Regional Studies (PIIRS): Aaron Burr Hall, Princeton University, Princeton, NJ 08544; tel. (609) 258-4851; fax (609) 258-3988; e-mail piirs@princeton.edu; internet www.princeton.edu/~piirs/index.html; f. 2003; an academic institute of Princeton University; international relations; 65 faculty associates; Dir KATHERINE S. NEWMAN; publs *World Politics* (quarterly), monographs, occasional papers.

School of International and Public Affairs (SIPA): Columbia University, 420 West 118th St, Rm 1414, New York, NY 10027; tel. (212) 854-3239; fax (212) 864-5765; internet www.sipa.columbia.edu; Dean JOHN H. COATSWORTH; publ. *Journal of International Affairs* (2 a year).

Teresa Lozano Long Institute of Latin American Studies (LLILAS): Sid Richardson Hall 1.310, University of Texas, Austin, TX 78712; tel. (512) 471-5551; fax (512) 471-3090; e-mail ilas@uts.cc.utexas.edu; internet www.utexas.edu/cola/insts/llilas; f. 1940; Dir CHARLES R. HALE.

Washington Office on Latin America (WOLA): Suite 400, 1666 Connecticut Ave, NW, Washington, DC, USA; tel. (202) 797-2171; fax (202) 797-2172; e-mail wola@wola.org; internet www.wola.org; f. 1974; resource and interlocutor for Latin American non-governmental organizations working for human rights and social justice; Exec. Dir JOY OLSON.

Woodrow Wilson Center—Latin American Program: 1 Woodrow Wilson Plaza, 1300 Pennsylvania Ave, NW, Washington, DC 20004; tel. (202) 691-4170; fax (202) 691-4001; e-mail sharon.mccarter@wilsoncenter.org; internet www.wilsoncenter.org; f. 1977; residential fellowship programme: inter-American dialogue, inter-American economic issues, conferences, history and culture of Latin America, administration of social policy and governance, resolution of civil conflict; Dir LEE H. HAMILTON; publ. *Centerpoint* (monthly newsletter), *The Wilson Quarterly*, *Working Paper Series*.

URUGUAY

Asociación Sudamericana de Estudios Geopolíticos e Internacionales (South American Association of Geopolitical and International Studies): Quiebrayugos 4814, Casilla Correo 18.112, 11400 Montevideo; tel. (2) 6192953; fax (2) 9161923; f. 1979; research into inter-American issues, including that of economic integration in the Southern Cone; Sec.-Gen. Prof. BERNARDO QUAGLIOTTI DE BELLIS; publ. *Geosur* (6 a year).

Centro de Estadísticas Nacionales y Comercio Internacional del Uruguay (CENCI Uruguay) (Centre for National Statistics and International Trade): Juncal 1327 D, 16°, Of. 1603, Montevideo; tel. (2) 9152930; fax (2) 9154578; e-mail cenci@cenci.com.uy; internet www.cenci.com.uy; f. 1956; economic and statistical information on all Latin American countries, import tariffs on commodities; mem. of ALADI and CEPAL; library of 900 vols; Dir KENNETH BRUNNER; publs *Anuario Estadístico sobre el intercambio comercial* (annually), *Boletines: Noticias Latinoamericanas, Dictámenes de Clasificacíon Arancelaria—MERCOSUR, Estudios del Mercado, Industrias por sectores de actividad, Manual Práctico del Importador* (monthly), *Manual Práctico del Exportador* (monthly), *Manual Práctico Aduanero* (monthly), *Manual Práctico del Contribuyente* (monthly), *Régimen de Origen—ALADI y MERCOSUR*.

Centro Latinoamericano de Economía Humana (CLAEH) (Latin American Centre for Human Economy): Zelmar Michelini 1220, POB 5021, 11100 Montevideo; tel. (2) 9007194; e-mail info@claeh.org.uy; internet www.claeh.org.uy; f. 1958 to conduct research into economics and other social sciences; Dir JAVIER MIRANDA; publ. *Cuadernos del CLAEH* (3 a year).

VENEZUELA

Centro de Estudios del Desarrollo (CENDES) (Centre for Development Studies): Universidad Central de Venezuela, Edif. FUNDAVAC, Avda Neverí, Colinas de Bello Monte, Apdo 47604, Caracas 1041-A; tel. (212) 753-3475; fax (212) 751-2691; e-mail contacto@cendes-ucv.edu.ve; internet www.cendes-ucv.edu.ve; f. 1961; centre for research and graduate studies on all aspects of development in Venezuela and Latin America; library of 30,000 vols; Dir CARLOS WALTER; publs *Anuario de Estudios del Desarrollo*, *CENDES Newsletter* (3 a year), *Cuadernos del CENDES* (3 a year).

Centro Experimental de Estudios Latinoamericanos (CEELA) (Experimental Centre for Latin American Studies): Universidad del Zulia, Apdo de Correos 526, Maracaibo 4011, Zulia; tel. (261) 596703; internet www.viceacademico.luz.edu.ve/VACLUZ/dependencias_ceela.php; research in socio-economic development, especially the Andean Pact model, inflation and crises in Latin America; conferences and seminars; Dir Dr GASTON PARRA LUZARDO; publ. *Cuadernos Latinoamericanos*.

Instituto de Altos Estudios de América Latina (IAEAL) (Institute for Advanced Latin American Studies): Apdo 17271, El Conde, Caracas 1010; tel. (212) 573-8824; e-mail iaeal@usb.ve; internet www.iaeal.usb.ve; f. 1975; research, seminars, publs on Latin America; attached to the Universidad Simón Bolívar; library of 3,000 vols; Dir Prof. MAKRAM HALUANI; publs *Mundo Nuevo: Revista de Estudios Latinoamericanos* (quarterly), working papers, books.

Instituto de Investigaciones Económicas y Sociales (IIES) (Institute of Economic and Social Research): Universidad Católica Andrés Bello, Urb. Montalbán, La Vega, Caracas 1020; tel. (212) 407-4496; fax (212) 407-4349; e-mail iies@ucab.edu.ve; internet www.ucab.edu.veiies.html; studies labour and demographic economics; Dir LUIS PEDRO ESPAÑA.

SELECT BIBLIOGRAPHY (BOOKS)

South America

Adams, F. *The United Nations in Latin America: Aiding Development*. Abingdon, Routledge, 2009.

Alcántara Sáez, M. (Ed.). *Politicians and Politics in Latin America*. Boulder, CO, Lynne Rienner Publrs, 2007.

Albert, B. *South America and the First World War*. Cambridge, Cambridge University Press, 2002.

Allison, G. T. *Essence of Decision: Explaining the Cuban Missile Crisis*. Boston, MA, Little Brown, 1971.

Almond, G. A., and Verba, S. *The Civic Culture: Political Attitudes and Democracy in Five Nations*, 2nd edn. Newbury Park, CA, Sage Publications, 1989.

Andolina, R., Laurie, N., and Radcliffe, S. A. *Indigenous Development in the Andes: Culture, Power and Transnationalism*. Durham, NC, Duke University Press, 2010.

Angell, A. *et al. Decentralizing Development: The Political Economy of Institutional Change in Colombia and Chile*. Oxford, Oxford University Press, 2001.

Democracy after Pinochet: Politics, Parties and Elections in Chile. London, Institute for the Study of the Americas, 2007.

Anglade, C., and Fortín, C. *The State and Capital Accumulation in Latin America*. London, Macmillan, 1985.

Arceneaux, C. L. *Bounded Missions: Military Regimes and Democratization in the Southern Cone and Brazil*. Pennsylvania, PA, Penn State University Press, 2001.

Archetti, E. P., Cammack, P., and Roberts, B. (Eds). *Sociology of 'Developing Societies': Latin America*. Basingstoke, Macmillan, 1987.

Arias, E. D., Goldstein, D. (Eds). *Violent Democracies in Latin America: The Cultures and Practice of Violence*. Durham, NC, Duke University Press, 2010.

Aviel, J. F. 'Political Participation of Women in Latin America', in *Western Political Quarterly*, Vol. 34. 1981.

Baloyra, E. A. (Ed.). *Comparing New Democracies: Transition and Consolidation in Mediterranean Europe and the Southern Cone*. Boulder, CO, Westview Press, 1987.

Bethell, L., and Roxborough, I. (Eds). *Latin America between the Second World War and the Cold War, 1944–1948*. Cambridge, Cambridge University Press, 1993.

Black, J. K. 'Elections and Other Trivial Pursuits: Latin America and the New World Order', in *Third World Quarterly*, Vol. 14, No. 3. 1993.

Latin America: Its Problems and Its Promise, 3rd edn. Boulder, CO, Westview Press, 1998.

Bouvier, V. *Alliance or Compliance, Implications of the Chilean Experience for the Catholic Church in Latin America*. Syracuse, NY, Syracuse University Press, 1983.

Boville, B. *The Cocaine War: Drugs, Politics, and the Environment*. New York, NY, Algora Publishing, 2004.

Bowman, K. S. *Militarization, Democracy and Development: The Perils of Praetorianism in Latin America*. Pennsylvania, PA, Penn State University Press, 2004.

Brands, H. *Latin America's Cold War*. Cambridge, MA, Harvard University Press, 2010.

Brannstrom, C. (Ed.). *Territories, Commodities and Knowledges: Latin American Environmental Histories in the Nineteenth and Twentieth Centuries*. London, Institute for the Study of the Americas, 2005.

Brass, T. *Latin American Peasants*. London, Frank Cass, 2003.

Bruneau, T. C. *The Political Transformation of the Brazilian Catholic Church*. Cambridge, Cambridge University Press, 1974.

Bulmer-Thomas, V. *The Economic History of Latin America Since Independence*. Cambridge, Cambridge University Press, 1994.

The New Economic Model in Latin America and its Impact on Income Distribution and Poverty. Basingstoke, Macmillan, 1996.

Britain and Latin America: A Changing Relationship. Cambridge, Cambridge University Press, 2008.

Calleros-Alarcón, J. C. *The Unfinished Transition to Democracy in Latin America*. Abingdon, Routledge, 2008.

Calvert, P. *A Study of Revolution*. Oxford, Clarendon Press, 1970.

'Latin America: Laboratory of Revolution', in O'Sullivan, N. (Ed.), *Revolutionary Theory and Political Reality*. Brighton, Harvester Press, 1983.

'Demilitarisation in Latin America', in *Third World Quarterly*, Vol. 7. 1985.

(Ed.). *Political and Economic Encyclopedia of South America and the Caribbean*. Harlow, Essex, Longman, 1991.

The International Politics of Latin America. Manchester, Manchester University Press, 1994.

A Political and Economic Dictionary of Latin America. London, Europa Publications, 2004.

Calvert, P., and Calvert, S. *Latin America in the Twentieth Century*, 2nd edn. Basingstoke, Macmillan, 1993.

Calvert, P., and Milbank, S. *The Ebb and Flow of Military Government in South America*, (Conflict Studies No. 198). London, Institute for the Study of Conflict, 1987.

Cameron, M. A., and Hershberg, E. (Eds). *Latin America's Left Turns: Politics, Policies, and Trajectories of Change*. Boulder, CO, Lynne Rienner Publishers, 2010.

Camp, R. A. *Democracy in Latin America: Patterns and Cycles*. Wilmington, DE, SR Books, 1996.

Carruthers, D. V. (Ed.). *Environmental Justice in Latin America: Problems, Promise, and Practice*. Cambridge, MA, MIT Press, 2008.

Cason, Jeffrey, W. *The Political Economy of Integration: The Experience of Mercosur*. Abingdon, Routledge, 2010.

Castañeda, J. G. *Utopia Unarmed: The Latin American Left after the Cold War*. New York, NY, Vintage Books, 1994.

Castro, D. (Ed.). *Revolution and Revolutionaries, Guerrilla Movements in Latin America*. Scholarly Review Books, 1999.

Chávez, D., and Goldfrank, B. (Eds). *The Left in the City: Participatory Local Governments in Latin America*. London, Latin America Bureau, 2004.

Clawson, P., and Lee, R. *The Andean Cocaine Industry*. Basingstoke, Palgrave Macmillan, 1999.

Clissold, S. *Soviet Relations with Latin America, 1918–1968: A Documentary Survey*. London, Oxford University Press for Royal Institute of International Affairs, 1969.

Collinson, H. (Ed.). *Green Guerrillas: Environmental Conflicts and Initiatives in Latin America*. London, Latin America Bureau, 1996.

Cooper, A. F., and Heine, J. (Eds). *Which Way Latin America?: Hemispheric Politics Meets Globalization*. Tokyo, United Nations University, 2009.

Couso, J., Huneeus, A., Sieder, R. (Eds). *Cultures of Legality: Judicialization and Political Activism in Latin America*. Cambridge, Cambridge University Press, 2010.

Cubitt, T. *Latin American Society*, 2nd edn. Harlow, Longman, 1995.

Dabène, O. *The Politics of Regional Integration in Latin America*. Basingstoke, Palgrave Macmillan, 2009.

De Janvry, A. *The Agrarian Question and Reformism in Latin America*. Baltimore, MD, Johns Hopkins University Press, 1981.

DeHart, M. C. *Ethnic Entrepreneurs: Identity and Development Politics in Latin America*. Palo Alto, CA, Stanford University Press, 2010.

Desch, M. C. *When the Third World Matters: Latin America and United States Grand Strategy*. Baltimore, MD, Johns Hopkins University Press, 1993.

De Soto, H. *The Other Path: The Invisible Revolution in the Third World*. New York, NY, Harper Row, 1989.

Deutsch, S. M. *Las Derechas: The Extreme Right in Argentina, Brazil and Chile, 1890–1939*. Stanford, CA, Stanford University Press, 1999.

Devereux, S., and Justino, P., (Eds). *Overcoming Inequality in Latin America: Issues and Challenges for the 21st Century*. Abingdon, Routledge, 2005.

Di Tella, T. S. *Latin American Politics: A Theoretical Framework*. Austin, TX, University of Texas Press, 1990.

Dix, R. H. 'The Breakdown of Authoritarian Regimes', in *Western Political Quarterly*, Vol. 35. 1982.

'Populism: Authoritarian and Democratic', in *Latin American Research Review*, Vol. 20. 1985.

Domínguez, F. (Ed.). *Identity and Discursive Practices: Spain and Latin America*. Bern, Peter Lang AG, 2000.

Domínguez, F., and Guedes de Oliveira, M. (Eds). *Mercosur: Between Integration and Democracy*. New York, NY, Peter Lang Publrs, Inc, 2004.

Domínguez, J. I., and Fernández de Castro, R. (Eds). *Contemporary US–Latin American Relations: Cooperation or Conflict in the 21st Century?* Abingdon, Routledge, 2010.

Domínguez, J., and Shifter, M. (Eds). *Constructing Democratic Governance in Latin America*. Baltimore, MD, Johns Hopkins University Press, 2003.

Dunkerley, J. *Bolivia: Revolution and the Power of History in the Present*. London, Institute for the Study of the Americas, 2007.

Duran, E. (Ed.). *Power and Popular Protest: Latin American Social Movements*. Berkeley, CA, University of California Press, 1989.

Edwards, S. *Left Behind: Latin America and the False Promise of Populism*. Chicago, IL, Chicago University Press, 2010.

Farcau, B. W. *The Ten Cents War: Chile, Peru, and Bolivia in the War of the Pacific, 1879–1884*. Westport, CT, Praeger Publrs, 2000.

Ferrell, R. H. *Latin American Diplomacy: The Twentieth Century*. New York, NY, W. W. Norton, 1988.

Fisher, J. *Out of the Shadows: Women, Resistance and Politics in South America*. London, Latin America Bureau, 1993.

Foders, F., and Feldsieper, M. *The Transformation of Latin America: Economic Development in the Early 1990s*. Northampton, MA, Edward Elgar Publishing, 2000.

Foweraker, J. *Theorizing Social Movements*. London, Pluto Press, 1995.

Fowler, W. *Ideologues and Ideologies in Latin America*. Westport, CT, Greenwood Press, 1997.

Frieden, J. A. *Debt, Development and Democracy: Modern Political Economy and Latin America, 1965–1985*. Princeton, NJ, Princeton University Press, 1992.

Frieden, J. A., Pastor, M., and Tomz, M. *Modern Political Economy and Latin America: Theory and Policy*. Boulder, CO, Westview Press, 2000.

Gardini, G. L. *The Origins of Mercosur: Democracy and Regionalization in South America*. Basingstoke, Palgrave Macmillan, 2010.

Gilbert, A. *Latin America*. London, Routledge, 1990.

Gill, L. *School of the Americas: Military Training and Political Violence in the Americas (American Encounters/Global Interactions)*. Durham, NC, Duke University Press, 2004.

The Latin American City, revised edn. London, Latin America Bureau, 1998.

Grandin, G., and Joseph, G. M. (Eds). *A Century of Revolution: Insurgent and Counterinsurgent Violence during Latin America's Long Cold War*. Durham, NC, Duke University Press, 2010.

Green, D. *Faces of Latin America*. London, Latin America Bureau, 1997.

Silent Revolution: The Rise of Market Economics in Latin America. 2nd edn, London, Cassell/Latin America Bureau, 2003.

Grosse, R. *Government Responses to the Latin American Debt Problem*. Boulder, CO, Lynne Rienner Publrs, 1996.

Grugel, J., and Riggirozzi, P. (Eds). *Governance after Neoliberalism in Latin America*. Basingstoke, Palgrave Macmillan, 2009.

Guillermoprieto, A. *Looking for History: Dispatches from Latin America*. New York, NY, Pantheon Books, 2001.

Gwynne, R. N., and Kay, C. (Eds). *Latin America Transformed: Globalization and Modernity*. London, Arnold, 1999.

Hall, A. (Ed.). *Global Impact, Local Action: New Environmental Policy in Latin America*. London, Institute for the Study of the Americas, 2005.

Hall, A., and Patrinos, H. A. (Eds). *Indigenous Peoples, Poverty and Human Development in Latin America: 1994–2004*. Basingstoke, Palgrave Macmillan, 2005.

Hammergren, L. A. *Envisioning Reform: Improving Judicial Performance in Latin America*. University Park, PA, Penn State University Press, 2007.

Harrison, L. E. *Underdevelopment is a State of Mind: The Latin American Case*. Lanham, MD, University Press of America, 1985.

Heinz, W. S., and Fruhling, H. *Determinants of Gross Human Rights Violations by State and State-sponsored Actors in Brazil, Uruguay, Chile and Argentina*. Leiden, Martinus Nijhoff Publrs, 1999.

Hellin, J., and Higman, S. *Feeding the Market: South American Farmers, Trade and Globalization*. ITDG Publrs, Colchester, 2003.

Hinds, H. E., Jr, and Tatum, C. M. (Eds). *Handbook of Latin American Popular Culture*. Westport, CT, Greenwood Press, 1985.

Jones, G. A., and Varley, A. 'The Contest for the City Centre: Street Traders versus Buildings', in *Bulletin of Latin American Research*, Vol. 13, No. 1 (Jan.). 1994.

Keegan, J. (Ed.). *World Armies*. London, Macmillan, 1983.

Kennedy, J. J. *Catholicism, Nationalism and Democracy in Argentina*. South Bend, IN, University of Notre Dame Press, 1958.

Kilty, K. M., and Segal, E. (Eds). *Poverty and Inequality in the Latin American-U.S. Borderlands: Implications of U.S. Interventions*. Binghamton, NY, Haworth Press, Inc, 2005.

Kingstone, P. *The Political Economy of Latin America: Reflections on Neoliberalism and Development*. Abingdon, Routledge, 2010.

Kirk, J. 'John Paul II and the Exorcism of Liberation Theology...', in *Bulletin of Latin American Research*, Vol. 4, No. 1. 1985.

Koonings, K., and Kruijt, D. *Fractured Cities: Social Exclusion, Urban Violence and Contested Spaces in Latin America*. London, Zed Books, 2007.

Kozloff, N. *Revolution!: South America and the Rise of the New Left*. Basingstoke, Palgrave Macmillan, 2008.

Larson, B. *Trials of Nation Making: Liberalism, Race and Ethnicity in the Andes, 1810–1910*. Cambridge, Cambridge University Press, 2004.

Lehmann, D. *Democracy and Development in Latin America*. Cambridge, Polity Press, 1990.

LeoGrande, W. 'Enemies Evermore: US Policy Towards Cuba After Helms-Burton', in *Journal of Latin American Studies*, Vol. 29, 1997.

Levine, D. H. (Ed.). *Churches and Politics in Latin America*. Beverley Hills, CA, Sage Publications, 1979.

Lockhart, J., and Schwartz, S. B. *Early Latin America: A History of Colonial Spanish America and Brazil*. New York, NY, Cambridge University Press, 1983.

Lopez-Calva, L. F., and Lustig, N. C. (Eds). *Declining Inequality in Latin America: A Decade of Progress?* Washington, DC, Brookings Institution, 2010.

Lora E. (Ed.) *The State of State Reforms in Latin America*. Washington, DC, World Bank Publications, 2006.

Loveman, B., and Davies, T. M. (Eds). *The Politics of Antipolitics: The Military in Latin America*. Lincoln, NE, University of Nebraska Press, 1978.

Loveman, B. *The Constitution of Tyranny: Regimes of Exception in Latin America*. Pittsburgh, PA, University of Pittsburgh Press, 1994.

Lowenthal, A. F. (Ed.). *Armies and Politics in Latin America*. New York, NY, Holmes and Meier, 1976.

MacDonald, S. B., and Fauriol, G. A. *Fast Forward: Latin America on the Edge of the 21st Century*. Piscataway, NJ, and London, Transaction Publrs, 1997.

Mace, G., Cooper, A. F., and Shaw, T. M. (Eds). *Inter-American Cooperation at a Crossroads*. Basingstoke, Palgrave Macmillan, 2010.

Mahoney, J. *Colonialism and Postcolonial Development: Spanish America in Comparative Perspective*. Cambridge, Cambridge University Press, 2010.

Mainwaring, S., O'Donnell, G., and Valenzuela, J. S. (Eds). *Issues in Democratic Consolidation: The New South American Democracies in Comparative Perspective*. South Bend, IN, University of Notre Dame Press, 1992.

Mainwaring, S., Scully, T. R. (Eds). *Democratic Governance in Latin America*. Palo Alto, CA, Stanford University Press, 2009.

Malloy, J. M., and Seligson, M. A. (Eds). *Authoritarians and Democrats: Regime Transition in Latin America*. Pittsburgh, PA, University of Pittsburgh Press, 1987.

Martz, J. D. (Ed.). *United States Policy in Latin America: A Quarter Century of Crisis and Challenge, 1961–1986*. Lincoln, NE, University of Nebraska Press, 1988.

Martz, J. D., and Schoultz, L. (Eds). *Latin America, the United States and the Inter-American System*. Boulder, CO, Westview Press, 1980.

McKinney, J. A., and Gardner, H. S. (Eds). *Economic Integration in the Americas*. Abingdon, Routledge, 2009.

Meade, T. A. *A History of Modern Latin America: 1800 to the Present*. Hobeken, NJ, Wiley-Blackwell, 2009.

Meso-Lago, C. *Market, Socialist, and Mixed Economies: Comparative Policy and Performance in Chile, Cuba, and Costa Rica*. Baltimore, MD, Johns Hopkins University Press, 2000.

Middlebrook, K. J. *Conservative Parties, the Right and Democracy in Latin America*. Baltimore, MD, Johns Hopkins University Press, 2000.

Millett, R. L., Holmes J. S., and Pérez, O. J. *Latin American Democracy: Emerging Reality or Endangered Species?* Abingdon, Routledge, 2008.

Morgenstern, S., and Nacif, B. *Legislative Politics in Latin America*. Cambridge, Cambridge University Press, 2002.

Munck, R. *Politics and Dependency in the Third World: The Case of Latin America*. London, Zed Books, 1984.

Contemporary Latin America. Basingstoke, Palgrave Macmillan, 2007.

Muñoz, H., and Tulchin, J. S. (Eds). *Latin American Nations in World Politics*. Boulder, CO, Westview Press, 1984.

Murillo, M. V. *Labour Unions, Partisan Coalitions and Market Reforms in Latin America*. Cambridge, Cambridge University Press, 2001.

Nunn, F. M. *The Time of the Generals: Latin American Professional Militarism in World Perspective*. Lincoln, NE, University of Nebraska Press, 1992.

Yesterday's Soldiers: European Military Professionalism in South America, 1890–1940. Lincoln, NE, University of Nebraska Press, 1983.

O'Donnell, G. *Delegative Democracy*. South Bend, IN, University of Notre Dame Press, 1992.

Counterpoints: Selected Essays on Authoritarianism and Democratization. Notre Dame, IN, University of Notre Dame, 2000.

Organisation for Economic Co-operation and Development (OECD). *Challenges to Fiscal Adjustment in Latin America: The Cases of Argentina, Brazil, Chile and Mexico*. Paris, OECD Publishing, 2007.

Oxhorn, P., and Starr, P. *Markets and Democracy in Latin America: Conflict or Convergence?* Boulder, CO, Lynne Rienner Publrs, 1998.

Painter, M., and Durham, W. H. *The Social Causes of Environmental Destruction in Latin America*. Ann Arbor, MI, University of Michigan Press, 1995.

Pang, E. *The International Political Economy of Transformation in Argentina, Brazil and Chile since 1960*. Basingstoke, Palgrave Macmillan, 2002.

Parkinson, F. *Latin America, the Cold War and the World Powers, 1945–1973*. Beverley Hills, CA, Sage Publications, 1974.

Pastor, R. A. *Condemned to Repetition: The United States and Nicaragua*. Princeton, NJ, Princeton University Press, 1987.

Pearce, J. (Ed.). *The European Challenge: Europe's New Role in Latin America*. London, Latin America Bureau, 1982.

Petras, J., and Morley, M. *Latin America in the Time of Cholera: Electoral Politics, Market Economy, and Permanent Crisis*. New York, NY, Routledge, 1992.

Philip, G. *Oil and Politics in Latin America: Nationalist Movements and State Companies*. Cambridge, Cambridge University Press, 1982.

The Military and South American Politics. London, Croom Helm, 1985.

'The New Economic Liberalism in Latin America: Friends or Enemies?', in *Third World Quarterly*, Vol. 14, No. 3. 1993.

Phillips, N. *The Southern Cone Model: The Political Economy of Regional Capitalist Development in Latin America*. London, Routledge, 2004.

The United States and Latin America: Myths and Stereotypes of Civilization and Nature. Austin, TX, University of Texas Press, 1992.

Portes, A. 'Latin American Urbanization During the Years of the Crisis', in *Latin American Research Review*, Vol. 24, No. 3. 1989.

Posada-Carbó, E., and Malamud, C. (Eds). *The Financing of Politics: Latin American and European Perspectives*. London, Institute for the Study of the Americas, 2005.

Rakowski, C. A. (Ed.). *Contrapunto: The Informal Sector Debate in Latin America*. Albany, NY, State University of New York Press, 1994.

Randall, L. 'Lies, Damn Lies and Argentine GDP', in *Latin American Research Review*, Vol. 11. 1974.

Reid, M. *Forgotten Continent: The Battle for Latin America's Soul*. New Haven, CT, Yale University Press, 2007.

Roberts, B. R. *The Making of Citizens: Cities of Peasants Revisited*. London, Arnold, 1995.

Roberts, K. M. *Deepening Democracy? The Modern Left and Social Movements in Chile and Peru*. Stanford, CA, Stanford University Press, 2000.

Santiso, J. *Latin America's Political Economy of the Possible: Beyond Good Revolutionaries and Free Marketeers*. Cambridge, MA, MIT Press, 2006.

Schwindt-Bayer, L. A. *Political Power and Women's Representation in Latin America*. New York, NY, Oxford University Press USA, 2010.

Seckinger, R. 'The Central American Militaries: A Survey of the Literature', in *Latin American Research Review*, Vol. 16. 1981.

Segura-Ubierga, A. *The Political Economy of the Welfare State in Latin America: Globalization, Democracy, and Development*, Cambridge, Cambridge University Press, 2007.

Shafer, D. M. *Deadly Paradigms: The Failure of US Counterinsurgency Policy*. Princeton, NJ, Princeton University Press, 1988.

Sherman, J. W. *Latin America in Crisis*. Boulder, CO, Westview Press, 2000.

Sieder, R., Schjolden, L., and Angell, A. (Eds). *The Judicialization of Politics in Latin America*. London, Institute for the Study of the Americas, 2005.

Silva, E. *Challenging Neoliberalism in Latin America*. Cambridge, Cambridge University Press, 2009.

Silvert, K. H. *The Conflict Society: Reaction and Revolution in Latin America*. New York, NY, American Universities Field Staff Inc, 1966.

Skidmore, T. E., and Smith, P. H. *Modern Latin America*. Oxford, Oxford University Press, 2000.

Smith, B. *The Church and Politics in Chile: Challenges to Modern Catholicism*. Princeton, NJ, Princeton University Press, 1982.

Spalding, H. A. *Organised Labor in Latin America: Historical Case Studies of Urban Workers in Dependent Societies*. New York, NY, Harper and Row, 1977.

Stein, E., and Tommasi, M. (Eds). *Policymaking in Latin America: How Politics Shapes Policies*. Cambridge, MA, Harvard University Press, 2008.

Tamarin, D. *The Argentine Labor Movement, 1930–1945: A Study in the Origins of Peronism*. Albuquerque, NM, University of New Mexico Press, 1985.

Teichman, J. A. *The Politics of Freeing Markets in Latin America: Chile, Argentina and Mexico*. Chapel Hill, NC, University of North Carolina Press, 2001.

Thomas, J. R. *Bibliographical Dictionary of Latin American Historians and Historiography*. Westport, CT, Greenwood Press, 1984.

Thorp, R. (Ed.). *Latin America in the 1930s: The Role of the Periphery in World Crisis*. Basingstoke, Macmillan, 1984.

Thorp, R., and Whitehead, L. (Eds). *Latin American Debt and the Adjustment Crisis*. Basingstoke, Macmillan, 1987.

Tiano, S. 'Authoritarianism and Political Culture in Argentina and Chile in the Mid 1960s', in *Latin American Research Review*, Vol. 31. 1986.

Timerman, J. *Prisoner without a Name, Cell without a Number*. Harmondsworth, Penguin, 1982.

Tokman, V. E., and Klein, E. *Regulation and the Informal Economy: Microenterprises in Chile, Ecuador and Jamaica*. Boulder, CO, Lynne Rienner Publrs, 1995.

Trubowitz, P. *Defining the National Interest: Conflict and Change in American Foreign Policy*. Chicago, IL, University of Chicago Press, 1998.

Tulchin, J. S., and Garland, A. M. (Eds). *Social Development in Latin America*. Boulder, CO, Lynne Rienner Publrs, 2000.

Tulchin, J. S., and Espach, R. H. *Latin America in the New International System*. Boulder, CO, Lynne Rienner Publrs, 2000.

Turner, B. (Ed.). *Latin America Profiled: Essential Facts on Society, Business and Politics in Latin America* (Syb Factbook). New York, NY, St Martin's Press, 2000.

Ungar, M. *Policing Democracy: Overcoming Obstacles to Citizen Security in Latin America*. Baltimore, MD, John Hopkins University Press, 2010.

Van Cott, D. L. *The Friendly Liquidation of the Past: The Politics of Diversity in Latin America* (Pitt Latin American Series). Pittsburgh, PA, University of Pittsburgh Press, 2000.

Weyland, K. G. *The Politics of Market Reform in Fragile Democracies: Argentina, Brazil, Peru and Venezuela*. Princeton, NJ, Princeton University Press, 2002.

Wilgus, A. C. (Ed.). *South American Dictators During the First Century of Independence*. New York, NY, Russell and Russell, 1963.

Wilkie, J. W., and Perkal, A. (Eds). *Statistical Abstract of Latin America*. Los Angeles, CA, University of California (Los Angeles) Latin American Center, annual.

Youngers, C., and Rosin, E. *Drugs and Democracy in Latin America: The Impact of US Policy*. London, Lynne Rienner Publrs, 2004.

Central America

Aguilera, G. *El fusil y el olivo: la cuestión militar en Centroamérica*. USA, FLACSO/DEI, 1988.

Anderson, T. P. *Politics in Central America: Guatemala, El Salvador, Honduras and Nicaragua*. New York, NY, Praeger Publrs, 1988.

Barry, T. *Roots of Rebellion: Land and Hunger in Central America*. Cambridge, MA, South End Press, 1987.

Bendaña, A. *Demobilization and Reintegration in Central America: Peace Building Challenges and Responses*. Managua, Centro de Estudios Internacionales, 1999.

Binational Study: The State of Migration Flows Between Costa Rica and Nicaragua—An Analysis of Economic and Social Implications for Both Countries. Geneva, Intergovernmental Committee for Migration, 2003.

Blachman, M., et al. *Confronting Revolution: Security through Diplomacy in Central America*. New York, NY, Pantheon, 1986.

Booth, J. A. *Understanding Central America: Global Forces, Development and Change*, 5th edn. Boulder, CO, Westview Press, 2010.

Booth, J., and Seligson, M. *Elections and Democracy in Central America*. Chapel Hill, NC, University of North Carolina Press, 1989.

Booth, J. A., and Walker, T. W. *Understanding Central America*, 3rd edn. Boulder, CO, Westview Press, 1999.

Brockett, C. D., et al. (Eds). *Political Movements and Violence in Central America*. Cambridge, Cambridge University Press, 2005.

Bulmer-Thomas, V. *Studies in the Economics of Central America*. London, Macmillan, 1989.

Calvert, P. (ed.). *The Central American Security System: North-South or East-West?* Cambridge, Cambridge University Press, 2008.

Chomsky, A., and Lauria-Santiago, A. (Eds). *Identity and Struggle at the Margins of the Nation-State: The Laboring Peoples of Central America and the Hispanic Caribbean*. Durham, NC, Duke University Press, 1998.

Colburn, F. D., and Cruz S., A. J. *Varieties of Liberalism in Central America: Nation-States as Works in Progress*. Austin, TX, University of Texas, 2007.

Domínguez, J., and Fernández de Castro, R. *United States and Mexico*. Abingdon, Routledge, 2009.

Dunkerley, J. *Power in the Isthmus: A Political History of Modern Central America*. London, Verso, 1988.

The Pacification of Central America. London and New York, NY, Verso, 1994.

Flora, J., and Torres-Rivas, E. (Eds). *Central America*. Austin, TX, Central America Resource Center, 1989.

Goodman, L. W., Leogrande, W. M., and Mendelson Forman, J. (Eds). *Political Parties and Democracy in Central America*. Boulder, CO, Westview Press, 1992.

Greentree, T. R. *Crossroads of Intervention: Insurgency and Counterinsurgency Lessons from Central America*. Santa Barbara, CA, Praeger Security International, 2008.

Holden, R. H. *Armies Without Nations: Public Violence and State Formation in Central America, 1821–1960*. Oxford, Oxford University Press, 2004.

Horton, L. R. *Grassroots Struggles for Sustainability in Central America*. Boulder, CO, University Press of Colorado, 2007.

Karnes, T. L. *The Failure of Union in Central America, 1824–1960*. Chapel Hill, NC, University of North Carolina Press.

Keeley, J. *Containing the Communists: America's Foreign Policy Entanglements*. San Diego, CA, Lucent Books, 2003.

Kirk, J. M., and Schuyler, G. V. (Eds). *Central America: Democracy, Development and Change*. New York, NY, Praeger Publrs, 1989.

Krenn, M. L. *The Chains of Interdependence: US Policy toward Central America, 1945–1954*. Armonk, NY, M. E. Sharpe, 1996.

Krujit, D. *Guerrillas: War and Peace in Central America*. London, Zed Books, 2008.

Landau, S. *The Guerrilla Wars of Central America*. London, Weidenfeld & Nicolson, 1993.

Mahoney, J. *The Legacies of Liberalism: Path Dependence and Political Regimes in Central America*. Baltimore, MD, Johns Hopkins University Press, 2002.

Meara, W. R. *Contra Cross: Insurgency and Tyranny in Central America, 1979-1989*. Annapolis, MD, Naval Institute Press, 2006.

Paige, J. M. *Coffee and Power: Revolution and the Rise of Democracy in Central America*. Cambridge, MA, Harvard University Press, 1998.

Pearce, J. *The Report of the President's National Bipartisan Commission on Central America*. London, Collier Macmillan, 1984.

Pérez-Brignoli, H. *A Brief History of Central America*. Berkeley, CA, University of California Press, 1989.

Putnam, L. *The Company They Kept: Migrants and the Politics of Gender in Caribbean Costa Rica, 1870–1960*. Chapel Hill, NC, University of North Carolina Press, 2002.

Rockwell, R. J., and Janus, N. *Media Power in Central America*. Champaign, IL, University of Illinois Press, 2003

Rosenberg, M. B., and Solís-Rivera, L. G. *United States and Central America: Geopolitical Realities and Regional Fragility, Vol. 4*. Abingdon, Routledge, 2007.

Saint-Germain, M. A., and Chávez Metoyer, C. *Women Legislators in Central America: Politics, Democracy, and Policy*. Austin, TX, University of Texas Press, 2008.

Sánchez Sánchez, R. *The Politics of Central American Integration*. Abingdon, Routledge, 2008.

Sandoval-García, C. *Threatening Others: Nicaraguans and the Formation of National Identities in Costa Rica*. Columbus, OH, Ohio University Press, 2004.

Schooley, H. *Conflict in Central America*. Harlow, Keesing's International—Longman, 1987.

Scranton, M. E. *The Noriega Years: US-Panamanian Relations, 1981–1990*. Boulder, CO, Lynne Rienner Publrs, 1991.

Sieder, R. (Ed.). *Central America: Fragile Transition*. London and Basingstoke, Macmillan with Institute of Latin American Studies Series, 1996.

Torres-Rivas, E. *Repression and Resistance: The Struggle for Democracy in Central America*. Boulder, CO, Westview Press, 1989.

Vilas, C. *Between Earthquakes and Volcanoes, Market, State, and the Revolutions in Central America*. New York, NY, Monthly Review Press, 1995.

Wearne, P., and Menchu, R. *Return of the Indian: Conquest and Revival in the Americas*. Philadelphia, PA, Temple University Press, 1996.

Wiarda, H. J. (Ed.). *US Policy in Central America: Consultant Papers for the Kissinger Commission*. Washington, DC, American Enterprise Institute for Public Policy Research, 1984.

Woodward, R. L. *Central America: Historical Perspectives on the Contemporary Crises*. London, Greenwood, 1988.

The Caribbean

Ahmed, B., and Afroz, S. *The Political Economy of Food and Agriculture in the Caribbean*. Kingston, Ian Randle Publrs, 1996.

Anderson, T. D. *Geopolitics of the Caribbean: Ministates in a Wider World*. New York, NY, Praeger Publrs, 1985.

Ayala, C. J. *American Sugar Kingdom: The Plantation Economy of the Spanish Caribbean 1898–1934*. Chapel Hill, NC, University of North Carolina Press, 1999.

Baker, G. (Ed.). *No Island is an Island: The Impact of Globalization on the Commonwealth Caribbean*. London, Chatham House, 2007.

Barnes, N. *Cultural Conundrums: Gender, Race, Nation, and the Making of Caribbean Cultural Politics*. Ann Arbor, MI, University of Michigan Press, 2006.

Besson, J., and Momsen, J. (Eds). *Caribbean Land and Development Revisited*. Basingstoke, Palgrave Macmillan, 2007.

Birbalsingh, F. (Ed.). *Indo-Caribbean Resistance*. Toronto, TSAR, 1993.

Braveboy-Wagner, J. A. *Small States in Global Affairs: The Foreign Policies of the Caribbean Community (CARICOM)*. Basingstoke, Palgrave Macmillan, 2008.

Burton, R. D. E., and Reno, F. (Eds). *French and West Indian: Martinique, Guadeloupe, and French Guiana Today*. Charlottesville, VA, University of Virginia Press, 2006.

Buxton, J., and Phillips, N. *Case Studies in Latin American Political Economy*. Manchester, Manchester University Press, 1999.

Chamberlain, M. (Ed.). *Caribbean Migration: Globalised Identities*. London, Routledge, 1998.

Clegg, P. (Ed.). *Governance in the Non-independent Caribbean: Challenges and Opportunities in the Twenty-first Century*. Kingston, Ian Randle Publrs, 2009.

Craton, M. and the Cayman Islands New History Committee. *A History of the Cayman Islands and Their Peoples*. Kingston, Ian Randle Publrs, 2004.

Desch, M. C., Domínguez, J. I., Serbin, A. (Eds). *From Pirates to Druglords, the Post-Cold War Caribbean Security Environment*. Oxford, Heinemann, 1998.

Domínguez, J. I. *Democratic Politics in Latin America and the Caribbean*. Baltimore, MD, Johns Hopkins University Press, 1998.

Dubois, L. *A Colony of Citizens: Revolution and Slave Emancipation in the French Caribbean, 1787–1804*. Chapel Hill, NC, University of North Carolina Press, 2004.

Dunn, H. S. (Ed.). *Globalization, Communications and Caribbean Identity*. Kingston, Ian Randle Publrs, 1995.

Flint, A. *Trade, Poverty and The Environment: The EU, Cotonou and the African-Caribbean-Pacific Bloc*. Basingstoke, Palgrave Macmillan, 2008.

Forte, M. C. *Indigenous Resurgence in the Contemporary Caribbean: Amerindian Survival and Revival*. New York, NY, Peter Lang Publishing, 2006.

Frazier, E. F., and Williams, E. *The Economic Future of the Caribbean*. Dover, MA, Majority Press, 2004.

Gaspar, D. B., and Geggus, D. P. (Eds). *A Turbulent Time: The French Revolution and the Greater Caribbean*. Bloomington, IN, Indiana University Press, 1997.

Gleijeses, P. *The Dominican Crisis: The 1965 Constitutional Revolt and American Intervention*. Baltimore, MD, Johns Hopkins University Press, 1979.

Griffith, I. L., and Sedoc-Dahlberg, B. N. (Eds). *Democracy and Human Rights in the Caribbean*. Boulder, CO, Westview Press, 1997.

Grossman, L. S. *The Political Ecology of Bananas, Contract Farming, Peasants and Agrarian Change in the Eastern Caribbean*. Chapel Hill, NC, University of North Carolina Press, 1998.

Hall, K., and Benn, D. (Eds.). *Contending with Destiny: The Caribbean in the 21st Century*. Kingston, Ian Randle Publrs, 2000.

Hallward, P. *Damming the Flood: Haiti, Aristide, and the Politics of Containment*. London, Verso, 2008.

Harrison, M. *King Sugar: Jamaica, the Caribbean and the World Sugar Industry*. New York, NY, New York University Press, 2001.

Hennessy, A. (Ed.). *Intellectuals in the Twentieth Century Caribbean—Unity in Variety*, Vol. II: *The Hispanic and Francophone Caribbean*. Basingstoke, Macmillan, 1992.

Heron, T. *The New Political Economy of United States-Caribbean Relations: The Apparel Industry and the Politics of Nafta Parity*. Aldershot, Ashgate Publishing, 2004.

Hodge, A. *The Caribbean*. Hove, East Sussex, Macdonald Young, 1998.

Holme, P. *Colonial Encounters: Europe and the Native Caribbean 1492–1797*. London, Methuen, 1986.

Hope, K. *Urbanization in the Commonwealth Caribbean*. Boulder, CO, Westview Press, 1986.

Hope, K. R. *Economic Development in the Caribbean*. New York, NY, Praeger Publrs, 1986.

Development Finance and the Development Process: A Case Study of Selected Caribbean Countries. London, Greenwood, 1987.

Jayawardena, C. (Ed.). *Caribbean Tourism: More Than Sun, Sand and Sea*. Kingston, Ian Randle Publrs, 2006.

Klak, T. *Globalization and Neoliberalism: The Caribbean Context*. Lanham, MD, Rowman & Littlefield Publrs, 1998.

Klein, A., Harriott, A., and Day, M. (Eds). *Caribbean Drugs: From Criminalization to Harm Reduction*. London, Zed Books, 2004.

Klein, H. S. *African Slavery in Latin America and the Caribbean*. New York, NY, Oxford University Press, 1986.

Lewis, G. K., and Maingot, A. P. *Main Currents in Caribbean Thought: The Historical Evolution of Caribbean Society in its Ideological Aspects, 1492–1900*. Lincoln, NE, University of Nebraska Press, 2004.

Maingot, A. P. *US Power and Caribbean Security: Geopolitics in a Sphere of Influence*. London, Lynne Rienner Publrs, 1989.

Mandle, J. R. *Persistent Underdevelopment: Change and Economic Modernization in the West Indies*. Newark, NJ, Gordon & Breach, 1996.

Mars, P., and Young, A. H. *Caribbean Labor and Politics: Legacies of Cheddi Jagan and Michael Manley*. Detroit, MI, Wayne State University Press, 2004.

Marshall, D. D. *Caribbean Political Economy at the Crossroads: NAFTA and Regional Developmentalism*. Basingstoke, Macmillan, 1998.

Martínez-Fernández, L. *Protestantism and Political Conflict in the Nineteenth-Century Hispanic Caribbean*. Piscataway, NJ, Rutgers University Press, 2002.

Moberg, M. *Slipping Away: Banana Politics and Fair Trade in the Eastern Caribbean*. Oxford, Berghahn Books, 2010.

Mora, F. O., and Hey, J. A. K. (Eds). *Latin America and Caribbean Foreign Policy*. Lanham, MD, Rowman and Littlefield Publrs, 2003.

Olwig, K. F. (Ed.). *Small Islands, Large Questions: Society, Culture and Resistance in the Post-Emancipation Caribbean*. London, Frank Cass, 1995.

Palmer, C. A. *Eric Williams and the Making of the Modern Caribbean*. Chapel Hill, NC, University of North Carolina Press, 2006.

Palmer, R. W. (Ed.). *US-Caribbean Relations, Their Impact on Peoples and Culture*. Westport, CT, Greenwood Press, 1998.

Pattullo, P. *Last Resorts*. London, Cassell, 1996.

Fire from the Mountain: The Story of the Montserrat Volcano. London, Constable and Co Ltd, 2000.

Payne, A., and Sutton, P. (Eds). *Modern Caribbean Politics*. Baltimore, MD, Johns Hopkins University Press, 1993.

Potter, R. B. *The Contemporary Caribbean*. Harlow, Prentice Hall, 2004.

Puri, S. (Ed.). *The Legacies of Caribbean Radical Politics*. Abingdon, Routledge, 2010.

Randall, S. J., and Mount, G. S. *The Caribbean Basin: An International History*. London, Routledge, 1998.

Reinhart, C. *Claims to Memory: Beyond Slavery and Emancipation in the French Caribbean*. Oxford, Berghahn, 2008.

Richardson, B. C. *The Caribbean in the Wider World, 1492–1992: A Regional Geography*. Cambridge, Cambridge University Press, 1992.

Economy and Environment in the Caribbean. Jamaica, University of the West Indies Press, 1997.

Ritter, A. R. M., and Kirk, J. M. *Cuba in the International System: Normalization and Integration*. London, Macmillan, 1995.

Sanders, R. *Crumbled Small: The Commonwealth Caribbean in World Politics*. London, Hansib Publishing (Caribbean) Ltd, 2005.

Sutton, P. *Dual Legacies in the Contemporary Caribbean: Continuing Aspects of British and French Domination*. London, Frank Cass, 1986.

Thomas, C. Y. *The Poor and the Powerless: Economic Policy and Change in the Caribbean*. New York, NY, Monthly Review Press, 1989.

Thomas-Hope, E. M. (Ed.). *Explanation in Caribbean Migration, Perception and the Image: Jamaica, Barbados, Saint Vincent*. London, Macmillan, 1992.

Thompson, A. O. *The Haunting Past: Politics, Economics and Race in Caribbean Life*. Oxford, James Curry Publrs, 1997.

Williams, E. E. *From Columbus to Castro: The History of the Caribbean 1492-1969*. London, André Deutsch, 1970.

Wright, T. C. *Latin America in the Era of the Cuban Revolution*. New York, NY, Praeger Publrs, 2000.

Wucker, M. *Why the Cocks Fight: Dominicans, Haitians, and the Struggle for Hispaniola*. New York, NY, Hill & Wang Publishing, 2000.

Young, A. H., and Phillips, D. E. *Militarization in the Non-Hispanic Caribbean*. London, Lynne Rienner Publrs, 1986.

SELECT BIBLIOGRAPHY (PERIODICALS)

Amazonía Peruana: Gonzales Prada 626, Magdalena, Apdo 14-0166, Lima 14, Peru; tel. (1) 4615223; f. 1976; Amazon anthropology, ethnology and linguistics, community development, bilingual education; Spanish, but with abstracts in English, French and German; Dir Pierre Guérig; 2 a year.

AméricaEconomía: Santiago, Chile; tel. (2) 290-9442; internet www.americaeconomia.com; f. 1986; Latin American business, economics and finance; Spanish; monthly; Editorial Dir Felipe Aldunate.

América Indígena: Nubes 232, Col. Pedregal de San Angel, México, DF, Mexico; tel. (55) 5568-0819; fax (55) 5652-1274; f. 1940; anthropology, rural development, Indians of the Americas, ethnology; Spanish and Portuguese, with abstracts in English; Editorial Dir Dr José Matos Mar (Instituto Indigenista Interamericano); quarterly.

Américas Magazine: Organization of American States, Suite 300, 19th and Constitution Ave, NW, Washington, DC 20006, USA; tel. (202) 458-6218; fax (202) 458-6217; f. 1949; culture, history, literature, travel, art, music, book reviews, Inter-American System; English and Spanish edns; Editor James Patrick Kiernan; 6 a year.

Americas Review: CEB Ltd, 2 Market St, Saffron Walden, CB10 1HZ, United Kingdom; tel. (1799) 521150; e-mail woi-subs@btconnect.com; internet www.worldinformation.com; f. 1979; business, economic and political issues concerning North, South and Central America and the Caribbean; English; Editor Tony Axon; annual.

Andean Report: Pasaje Los Pinos 156, Of. B6, Casilla 531, Miraflores, Lima 100, Peru; tel. (1) 4472552; fax (1) 4467888; f. 1975; commerce, development, economics and politics of Peru, including mining and petroleum; English; Editor Nicholas Asheshov; monthly.

Anuario de Estudios Americanos: Escuela de Estudios Hispano-Americanos, Alfonso XII, 16, 41002 Seville, Spain; tel. (95) 4501120; fax (95) 4224331; e-mail anuario@eehaa.csic.es; internet www.estudiosamericanos.revistas.csic.es/index.php/estudiosamericanos; f. 1944; humanities and social sciences of the Americas; Spanish, Portuguese, English and French; Editor-in-Chief Consuela Varela; 2 a year.

Anuario de Estudios Centroamericanos: Editorial de la Universidad de Costa Rica, Apdo 75, 2060 Ciudad Unversitaria Rodrigo Facio, San José, Costa Rica; tel. 2207-3505; e-mail oscarf@cariari.ucr.ac.cr; internet cariari.ucr.ac.cr/~anuario/index.html; f. 1974; published by the Social Sciences Research Institute of the University of Costa Rica; history, society, politics and economics relating to Central America; Spanish; Dir Eugenia Ibarra; Editor Ronald Solano; 2 a year.

Anuario Indigenista: Nubes 232, Col. Pedregal de San Angel, México, DF, Mexico; tel. (55) 5568-0819; fax (55) 5652-1274; f. 1962; Indians of the Americas, policies, anthropology, government, minorities; Spanish, Portuguese; Dir José Matos Mar (Instituto Indigenista Interamericano); annual.

Apuntes del CENES: Centro de Estudios Económicos—CENES, Universidad Pedagógica y Tecnológica de Colombia, Apdo Aéreo 1234, Carretera Central del Norte, Tunja, Boyacá, Colombia; tel. and fax (87) 42-5237; f. 1983; national economic and development studies, politics and culture; Spanish; Editor Luis E. Vallejo Zamudio; 2 a year.

Archivo Ibero Americano: Joaquín Costa 36, 28002 Madrid, Spain; tel. (91) 5619900; f. 1914; history of Spain and Hispanic America, mainly relating to the Franciscan Order; quarterly.

¡Basta!: Chicago Religious Task Force on Central America, Suite 1400, 59 East Van Buren, Chicago, IL 60605, USA; tel. (312) 663-4398; fax (312) 427-4171; f. 1984; analysis of social and political events in Central America: theological debate, news and information; English; 3 a year.

Boletín de la Academia Nacional de la Historia: Balcarce 139, 1064 Buenos Aires, Argentina; tel. (11) 4343-4416; fax (11) 4331-4633; e-mail admite@an-historia.org.ar; f. 1924; history of Argentina and the Americas, principally as review of activities of the Academia Nacional de la Historia; Spanish; annual.

Boletín Americanista: Universitat de Barcelona, Facultat de Geografia i Història, Departament d'Anthropologia Social i d'Historia d'Amèrica i d'Africa, Montagegre 6, 08001 Barcelona, Spain; tel. (93) 4037767; fax (93) 4037774; e-mail pgarciajordan@ub.edu; internet www.raco.cat/index.php/BoletinAmericanista; f. 1959; anthropology, economics, geography, history of America; Spanish, English and French; Editor Pilar García Jordán; annual.

Brazil: Brasília, DF, Brazil; tel. (61) 223-5180; deals with trade and industry of Brazil and is published by Fundação Visconde de Cabo Frio under the auspices of the Trade Promotion Department of the Ministry of Foreign Affairs and of the Vice-Presidency of Resources and Operations of the Banco do Brasil; Editor Fernando Luz; Portuguese, German and French edns (quarterly), English and Spanish edns (monthly).

Bulletin of Hispanic Studies: University of Liverpool, 18 Oxford St, Liverpool, L69 7ZN, United Kingdom; tel. and fax (151) 794-2773; fax (151) 794-1459; e-mail bhs@liv.ac.uk; internet www.bulletinofhispanicstudies.org; f. 1923; language, literature and civilization of Spain, Portugal and Latin America; mainly English and Spanish, occasionally Portuguese, Catalan and French; Gen. Editor Dr Claire Taylor; quarterly.

Bulletin de l'Institut Français d'Etudes Andines: IFEA, Ave Arequipa 4500, Lima 18, Peru; tel. (1) 4476070; fax (1) 4457650; e-mail postmaster@ifea.org.pe; internet www.ifeanet.org; f. 1972; geology and human and social sciences in the Andes; French, Spanish and English; Editor Anne-Marie Brougère; 3 a year.

Bulletin of Latin American Research: Wiley-Blackwell Publishing, 9600 Garsington Rd, Oxford, OX4 2DQ, United Kingdom; tel. (1865) 776868; fax (1865) 714591; internet www.blackwellpublishing.com/blar; on behalf of The Society for Latin American Studies; current interest research in social sciences and humanities; English; Editors David Howard, Geoffrey Kantaris, Tony Kapcia, Jasmine Gideon, Lucy Taylor; quarterly.

Bulletin of Spanish Studies: Hispanic Studies and Researches on Spain, Portugal and Latin America: Routledge, Taylor & Francis, 4 Park Sq., Milton Park, Abingdon, Oxon, OX14 4RN, United Kingdom; tel. (20) 7017-6000; fax (20) 7017-6336; e-mail authorqueries@tandf.co.uk; internet www.tandf.co.uk/journals/cbhs; f. 1923; fmrly Bulletin of Hispanic Studies; publ. by University of Glasgow; language, literature, history and civilization of Spain, Portugal and Latin America; mainly English and Spanish, occasionally Portuguese, Catalan and French; Gen. Editors Prof. Ann L. Mackenzie, James Whiston, Jeremy Robbins; 8 a year.

Cahiers des Amériques Latines: Institut des Hautes Etudes de l'Amérique Latine, 28 rue Saint-Guillaume, 75007 Paris, France; tel. 1-44-39-86-00; fax 1-45-48-79-58; e-mail iheal.edition@univ-paris3.fr; f. 1968; political science, economy, urbanism, geography, history, sociology, ethnology, etc; mainly French, but also Spanish and English; 3 a year.

Canadian Journal of Latin American and Caribbean Studies (CJLACS): University of Guelph, College of Arts, MacKinnon, 279 Ontario, N1G 2W1, Canada; tel. (514) 343-6569; fax (514) 343-7716; e-mail rogomez@uoguelph.ca; internet www.can-latam.org; f. 1976; political, economic, cultural, etc; English, French, Portuguese and Spanish; Editor Victor Armony; 2 a year.

Caribbean Affairs: 93 Frederick St, Port of Spain, Trinidad and Tobago; tel. 624-2477; fax 627-3013; f. 1988; business, political and social affairs of the Caribbean; English; Editor Owen Baptiste; quarterly.

Caribbean Business: Casiano Communications, 1700 Fernández Juncos Ave, San Juan, PR 00909, Puerto Rico; tel. 728-3000; fax 268-1001; internet www.casiano.com/html/cb.html; f. 1975; business and finance; English; Man. Editor Manuel A. Casiano, Jr; weekly.

Caribbean Handbook: FT Caribbean (BVI) Ltd, 19 Mercers Rd, London, N19 4PH, United Kingdom; tel. (20) 7281-5746; fax (20) 7281-7157; e-mail ftcaribbean@btinternet.com; internet www.candoo.com/ftcarribean/; f. 1983; business, economic and political information on the Caribbean region, including country profiles; English; Editor Lindsay Maxwell; annual.

Caribbean Insight: c/o Caribbean Council, 2 Belgrave Sq., London, SW1X 8PJ, United Kingdom; tel. (20) 7235-9484; fax (20) 7823-1370; e-mail insight@caribbean-council.org; internet www.caribbean-council.org; f. 1978; business, political and social; English; Publr David Jessop; Editor Dr Chris Brogan; weekly.

Caribbean Investor and the CAIC Times: Caribbean Asscn of Industry and Commerce, 27A Saddle Rd, Maraval, Trinidad & Tobago; tel. 628-9859; fax 622-7810; e-mail caic.admin@gmail.com; internet www.caic.org.tt; finance and trading; CEO Carol Ayoung; quarterly.

Caribbean Quarterly: POB 130, Kingston 7, Jamaica; tel. 977-1689; fax 970-3261; e-mail cq@uwimena.edu.jm; f. 1949; general; English; Editor Rex Nettleford; quarterly.

Caribbean Review: 9700 SW 67th Ave, Miami, FL 33156-3272, USA; tel. (305) 284-8466; fax (305) 284-1019; f. 1969; all subjects relating to the Caribbean, Latin America and their emigrant groups; quarterly.

Caribbean Studies: Institute of Caribbean Studies, POB 23361, University Station, Río Piedras, PR 00931, Puerto Rico; tel. (787) 764-0000; fax (787) 764-3099; e-mail iec@rrpac.upr.clu.edu; Caribbean affairs; English; Editor OSCAR MENDOZA; 2 a year.

Caribbean Update: 116 Myrtle Ave, Millburn, NJ 07041, USA; tel. (973) 885-6897; e-mail kalwagenheim@cs.com; internet www.caribbeanupdate.org; f. 1985; business and economic news and opportunities in the Caribbean and Central America; English; Editor and Publr KAL WAGENHEIM; monthly.

El Caribe Contemporáneo: Centro de Estudios Latinoamericanos, Facultad de Ciencias Políticas y Sociales, Universidad Nacional Autónoma de México, 04510 México, DF, Mexico; tel. (55) 5655-1344; f. 1980; political organization and government; Spanish; Dir Dr PABLO A. MARÍÑEZ A.; 2 a year.

Carta Internacional: Programa de Pesquisa de Relações Internacionais, Universidade de São Paulo, Rua do Anfiteatro 181, Colméia, Cidade Universitária, 05508-900 São Paulo, SP, Brazil; tel. (11) 3091-3061; fax (11) 3091-3044; e-mail nupri@edu.usp.br; internet www.usp.br/cartainternacional; Brazilian foreign and economic policy, regional integration, NAFTA and Mercosur; English, Portuguese and Spanish; Dir Prof. Dr JOSÉ AUGUSTO GUILHON ALBUQUERQUE; monthly.

Central America Report: Inforpress Centroamericana, Calle Mariscal o Diagonal 21 6-58 Zona 11, Guatemala City, Guatemala; tel. 2473-7001; fax 2473-2231; e-mail inforpre@inforpressca.com; internet www.inforpressca.com/CAR; f. 1972; review of economics and politics of Central America; English; Dir MATTHEW CREELMAN; weekly.

Centroamerica Internacional: Latin American Faculty of Social Sciences, Costa Rica—FLACSO, General Secretariat, Apdo 5429, 1000 San José, Costa Rica; tel. 2257-0533; fax 2221-5671; f. 1989; Central American, South American and Caribbean international relations, regional integration; Spanish; 2 a month.

CEPAL Review/Revista de la CEPAL: Casilla 179-D, Santiago, Chile; tel. (2) 2102000; fax (2) 2080252; f. 1976; a publication of the UN Economic Commission for Latin America and the Caribbean dealing with socio-economic topics; English and Spanish; Dir ANDRÉ HOFMAN; 3 a year.

Chile Ahora: Ministry of Foreign Affairs, Palacio de la Moneda, Santiago, Chile; all aspects of life in Chile; Spanish; Editor M. ANGELICA HUIDOBRO G. H.; monthly.

Colombia Internacional: Centro de Estudios Internacionales, Universidad de los Andes, Calle 19, No 1–46, Apdo 4976, Bogotá, Colombia; tel. (1) 286-7504; fax (1) 284-1890; f. 1988; international co-operation, Latin American integration, drugs-trafficking controls; Spanish; quarterly.

Colonial Latin American Review: Routledge, Taylor & Francis, 4 Park Sq., Milton Park, Abingdon, Oxon, OX14 4RN, United Kingdom; tel. (20) 7017-6000; fax (20) 7017-6336; e-mail authorqueries@tandf.co.uk; internet www.tandf.co.uk/journals/ccla; f. 1992; colonial period in Latin America; English, with articles in Portuguese and Spanish; Gen. Editor KRIS LANE; 3 a year.

Comercio Exterior: Banco Nacional de Comercio Exterior, SNC, Camino a Santa Teresa 1679, Col. Jardines del Pedregal, 01900 México, DF, Mexico; tel. (55) 5481-6220; e-mail revcomer@bancomext.gob.mx; internet www.bancomext.com; f. 1951; international trade, analysis of Latin America's economics, general economics; Spanish with English abstracts; monthly.

Contexto Internacional: Instituto de Relações Internacionais, Pontifíca Universidade Católica de Rio de Janeiro, Rua Marquês de São Vicente 225, Gávea, 22453-900 Rio de Janeiro, RJ, Brazil; tel. and fax (21) 3527-1557; e-mail iripuc@rdc.puc-rio.br; internet www.puc-rio.br/iri; international relations, Brazilian foreign policy, Latin American and European integration, US-Latin American relations; Portuguese; Editor SONIA DE CAMARGO; 3 a year.

The Courier ACP-European Union: European Commission, 200 rue de la Loi, 1049 Brussels, Belgium; tel. (2) 299-11-11; fax (2) 299-30-02; internet www.europa.eu.int/comm/development/body/publications_courier_en.htm; affairs of the African, Caribbean and Pacific countries and the European Union; English and French edns; Editor SIMON HORNER; 6 a year.

Cronología de las Relaciones Internacionales del Peru: Peruvian Centre for International Studies, San Ignacio de Loyola 554, Miraflores 8, Lima 18, Peru; tel. (1) 4457225; fax (1) 4451094; economic and political international relations of Peru; Spanish; quarterly.

Cuadernos de Economía (Latin American Journal of Economics): Instituto de Economía, Pontificia Universidad Católica de Chile, Casilla 76, Correo 17, Santiago, Chile; tel. (2) 3544303; fax (2) 5532377; e-mail cuadecon@faceapuc.cl; internet www.cuadernosdeeconomia.cl; f. 1963; applied economies as contribution to economic policy, with special emphasis in Latin America; Spanish, with English abstracts; Editors JOSÉ MIGUEL SÁNCHEZ, JUAN PABLO MONTERO, RAIMUNDO SOTO; 2 a year.

Cuadernos Hispanoamericanos: Avda de los Reyes Católicos 4, 28040 Madrid, Spain; tel. (91) 5838399; e-mail cuadernos@hispanoamericanosaeci.es; f. 1948; humanities, particularly relating to Hispanic America; Spanish; Editor BLAS MATAMORO; monthly.

Cuba Internacional: Calle 21, No 406, Vedado, Havana 4; Apdo B603, Havana 3, Cuba; tel. (7) 329-3531; f. 1959; politics and foreign affairs; Spanish and Russian; monthly.

Cuba Update: Center for Cuban Studies, 124 West 23rd St, New York, NY 10011, USA; tel. (212) 242-0559; fax (212) 242-1937; e-mail cubanctr@igc.org; internet www.cubaupdate.org; f. 1977; Cuban foreign affairs, culture and development; English; Editor SANDRA LEVINSON; quarterly.

The Developing Economies: Nihon Boeki Shinkokiko Ajia Keizai Kenkyusho (Institute of Developing Economies, Japan External Trade Organization—JETRO), 3-2-2 Wakaba, Mihama-ku, Chinashi, Chiba 261-8545, Japan; tel. (43) 299-9500; fax (43) 299-9726; internet www.ide.go.jp; f. 1962; quarterly; Pres. TAKASHI SHIRAISHI.

Development Policy Review: Overseas Development Institute, 111 Westminster Bridge Rd, London, SE1 7JD, United Kingdom; tel. (20) 7922-0399; fax (20) 7922-0399; internet www.odi.org.uk; f. 1982; Editor DAVID BOOTH; 6 a year.

Economia Brasileira e Suas Perspectivas: Associação Promotora de Estudos de Economia, Rua Sorocaya 295, Botafogo, Rio de Janeiro, RJ, Brazil; fax (21) 266-3597; f. 1962; Brazilian economic issues, published by the Asscn for the Promotion of Economic Studies; Portuguese and English; Editor BASÍLIO MARTINS; annual.

Economía Mexicana Nueva Época: Centro de Investigación y Docencia Económicas—CIDE, Carretera México-Toluca 3655 (km 16.5), Col. Lomas de Santa Fe, Del. Alvaro Obregón, 01210 México, DF, Mexico; tel. (55) 5727-9800; fax (55) 5727-9878; e-mail ecomex@cide.edu; internet www.economiamexicana.cide.edu; f. 1992; economic problems in Mexico and Latin America; Spanish and English; Editor DAVID MAYER FOULKES; 2 a year.

Economic Development and Cultural Change: University of Chicago Press, 1427 East 60th St, Chicago, IL 60637, USA; tel. (213) 702-8116; fax (213) 753-0811; e-mail edcc@press.uchicago.edu; internet www.journals.uchicago.edu/EDCC; f. 1952; multidisciplinary journal of development economics; English; Editor CHARLOTTE ROBINSON; quarterly.

Economic and Social Progress in Latin America: Inter-American Development Bank, 1300 New York Ave, NW, Washington, DC 20577, USA; tel. (202) 623-1403; internet www.iadb.org; f. 1961; socio-economic conditions and development; topical reports; English and Spanish; annual.

Estudios de Coyuntura: Universidad del Zulia, Facultad de Ciencias Ecónomicas y Sociales, Apdo 526, Maracaibo 4011, Estado Zulia, Venezuela; tel. (261) 51-7697; fax (261) 51-2525; f. 1989; business and economics; Editor HERNAN PARDO; Spanish; 2 a year.

Estudios de Cultura Maya: Centro de Estudios Mayas, Instituto de Investigaciones Filológicas, Circuito Mario de la Cueva, Ciudad Universitaria, 04510 México, DF, Mexico; tel. and fax (55) 5622-7490; e-mail cem@servidor.uma.mx; internet filologicas.unam.mx/indices/estculmay_col.htm; f. 1961; anthropology, archaeology, history, epigraphy and linguistics of the Mayan groups; Spanish, English and French; Editor MARICELA AYALA; 2 a year.

Estudios Económicos: Universidad Nacional del Sur, Departamento de Economía, 12 de Octubre y San Juan, 8000 Bahía Blanca, Argentina; tel. and fax (91) 25432; f. 1962; Spanish; Editor RICARDO BARA; annual.

Estudios de Historia Moderna y Contemporánea de México: Instituto de Investigaciones Históricas, Circuito Metropolitano Mario de la Cueva, Del. Coyoacán, Ciudad Universitaria, 04510 México, DF, Mexico; tel. (55) 5622-7520; internet www.iih.unam.mx/moderna/index.html; f. 1967; history of Mexico from independence war (1810) to present; Spanish; Editor MARCELA TERRAZAS Y BASANTE; 2 a year.

Estudios Internacionales: International Relations and Peace Research Institute, 1a Calle 9-52, Zona 1, 01001 Guatemala City, Guatemala; international relations; Spanish; 2 a year.

Estudios Internacionales: Institute of International Studies, University of Chile, Avda Condell 249, Casilla 14187, Santiago 9, Chile; tel. (2) 4961200; fax (2) 2740155; e-mail inesint@uchile.cl; internet www.iei.uchile.cl; f. 1966; contemporary international relations, particularly concerning Latin America; Spanish; Editor ROSE CAVE S.; quarterly.

Estudios Paraguayos: Universidad Católica, Casilla 1718, Asunción, Paraguay; tel. (21) 446251; fax (21) 445245; f. 1973; philosophy, politics, law, history, linguistics, economics, literature; Spanish; 2 a year.

Estudios Políticos: Facultad de Ciencias Políticas y Sociales, Universidad Nacional Autónoma de México, Ciudad Universitaria, Apdo 70-266, 04510 México, DF, Mexico; tel. (55) 5665-1233; fax (55) 5666-8334; e-mail igarza@sociolan.politicas.unam.mx; f. 1975; politics of government, political science; Spanish; quarterly.

Estudios Públicos: Centro de Estudios Públicos, Monseñor Sótero Sanz 162, Santiago, Chile; tel. (2) 3282441; fax (2) 2335253; e-mail biblioteca@cepchile.cl; internet www.cepchile.cl; f. 1980; forum of ideas and commentary on diverse issues in Latin America, incl. philosophy and literature, economics, politics and sociology; English, Spanish; quarterly.

Estudios Sociales: Miguel Claro 1460, Santiago, Chile; tel. (2) 2043418; fax (2) 2741828; e-mail cpu@cpu.cl; internet www.cpu.cl; f. 1973; sociology, history, anthropology, economics, political science, education, philosophy, social psychology, law; Spanish; Editor RAÚL ATRIA; 2 a year.

EURE Revista Latinoamericana de Estudios Urbanos y Regionales: Instituto de Estudios Urbanos, Universidad Católica de Chile, Casilla 16002, Correo 9, Santiago, Chile; tel. (2) 36865511; fax (2) 2328805; e-mail eure@puc.cl; internet www.scielo.cl/eure.htm; f. 1970; urban and regional development in Latin America; Spanish, with English abstracts; Dir CARLOS DE MATTOS; quarterly.

European Review of Latin American and Caribbean Studies / Revista Europea de Estudios Latinoamericanos y del Caribe: Centre for Latin American Research and Documentation (CEDLA), Keizersgracht 395-397, 1016 EK Amsterdam, Netherlands; tel. (20) 525-34-98; fax (20) 625-51-27; e-mail secretariat@cedla.uva.nl; internet www.cedla.uva.nl; f. 1989; social scientific and historical research on Latin America and the Caribbean (anthropology, economics, geography, history, politics, sociology, etc.); English and Spanish; Man. Editor Prof. Dr MICHIEL BAUD; 2 a year.

FIDE, Coyuntura y Desarrollo: Development Research Foundation—FIDE, 1241 Buenos Aires, Argentina; tel. and fax (11) 4964-3331; e-mail info@fide.com.ar; internet www.fide.com.ar; national and international socio-economic analysis and economic theory; Spanish; Dir MERCEDES MARCÓ DEL PONT; monthly.

Foro Internacional: Colegio de México, Camino al Ajusco 20, Col. Pedregal de Santa Teresa, 10740 México, DF, Mexico; tel. (5) 5449-3013; fax (5) 5645-0464; e-mail revfi@colmex.mx; internet revistas.colmex.mx; f. 1960; international relations, Latin American politics, comparative politics; Mexican politics, public administration and public policy; Spanish, with English abstracts; Editor REYNALDO YUNUEN ORTEGA ORTIZ; quarterly.

Fuerzas Armadas y Sociedad: Latin American Faculty of Social Sciences—FLACSO Chile, Avda Dag Hammarskjöld 3269, Vitacura, Santiago; tel. 2900200; fax 2900270; e-mail flacso@flacso.cl; internet www.flacso.cl; military affairs and international relations; Spanish; quarterly.

GIGA Focus Lateinamerika: 21 Neuer Jungfernstieg, 20354 Hamburg, Alsterglacis 8, Germany; tel. (40) 42825561; fax (40) 42825562; e-mail ilas@giga-hamburg.de; internet www.giga-hamburg.de/ilas; f. 1962; political, economic and social development; German; monthly.

Global Studies: Latin America: McGraw Hill Higher Education, 2460 Kerper Blvd, Dubuque, IA 52001, USA; tel. (203) 453-4351; fax (203) 453-6000; e-mail nichole_altman@mcgraw-hill.com; internet www.dushkin.com; f. 1991; articles on Mexico, Central America, South America and the Caribbean; English; Editor PAUL GOODWIN; every 2 years.

Handbook of Latin American Studies: University of Texas Press, POB 7819, Austin, TX 78713-7819; tel. (512) 471-7233; fax (512) 232-7178; e-mail utpress@uts.cc.utexas.edu; internet www.utexas.edu/utpress; f. 1936; edited by the Hispanic Division of the US Library of Congress; bibliography of Latin American articles and publications; annual, alternating between humanities and social science topics, online edn published weekly.

Hemisphere: Latin American and Caribbean Center, Florida International University, University Park, Miami, FL 33199, USA; tel. (305) 348-2894; fax (305) 348-3593; e-mail lacc@fiu.edu; internet lacc.fiu.edu; f. 1988; Latin American and Caribbean Affairs; English; Editor EDUARDO A. GAMARRA; 2 a year.

Hispanic American Historical Review (HAHR): Duke University Press, 905 W Main St, Suite 18B, Durham, NC 27701, USA; tel. (919) 687-3600; fax (919) 688-4574; e-mail subscriptions@dukeupress.edu; internet www.dukeupress.edu; f. 1918; published in co-operation with the American Historial Asscn; Man. Editor SARA LICKEY; quarterly.

Historia: Casilla 6277, Santiago 22, Chile; tel. (2) 3547831; e-mail revhist@puc.cl; internet www.hist.puc.cl; f. 1961; history of Chile and related subjects; mainly Spanish; Editor NICOLÁS CRUZ; 2 a year.

Historia Mexicana: Colegio de México, Camino al Ajusco 20, Pedregal de Santa Teresa, 01000 México, DF, Mexico; tel. (55) 5449-3000; fax (55) 5645-0464; internet historiamexicana.colmex.mx; f. 1951; history of Mexico; Spanish; Editor OSCAR MAZIN; quarterly.

Iberoamericana: 60594 Frankfurt am Main, Elisabethenstr. 3–9, Verlag Klaus Dieter Vervuert, Germany; tel. (69) 5974617; fax (69) 5978743; e-mail info@iberoamericanalibros.com; internet www.ibero-americana.net; f. 2001; comprises fmrly separate journals *Iberoamericana*, *Ibero-Amerikanisches Archiv* and *Notas*; Latin American literature, history and social sciences; Spanish, Portuguese, English and German; quarterly.

Iberoamericana: Nordic Journal of Latin American and Caribbean Studies: Institute of Latin American Studies, Stockholm University, Universitetsvägen 10B, 106 91 Stockholm, Sweden; tel. (8) 16-28-86; fax (8) 15-65-82; e-mail lai@lai.su.se; internet www.lai.su.se; f. 1960; articles on economic, political and local developments in Latin America and the Caribbean; English, Portuguese, Spanish; Chief Editor Prof. JAIME BEHAR; 2 a year.

Indicadores Económicos: Contraloría-General de la República, Avda Balboa y Federico Boyd, Apdo 0816-01521, Panamá, Panama; tel. 510-4777; fax 510-4355; e-mail comsocial@cwpanama.net; internet www.contraloria.gob.pa; f. 1996; economic indicators for Panama; Spanish; annual.

Industri-Noticias: Publi-News Latinoamericano, SACV, Colina 436, México, DF, Mexico; f. 1966; business, economics and industry; Spanish; Editor ROBERTO J. MÁRQUEZ; monthly.

Industria: Sindicato de Industriales de Panamá, Apdo 6-4798, El Dorado, Panamá, Panama; tel. 230-0169; fax 230-0805; e-mail sip@cableonda.net; internet www.industriales.org; f. 1953; economics and industry in Panama; Spanish; Editor FLOR ORTEGA; quarterly.

Industria Venezolana: Editorial Guía Industrial, Apdo 60772, Chacao, Caracas 101, Venezuela; f. 1971; economics and industry in Venezuela; Spanish; Editor JOSÉ PRECEDO; 6 a year.

Información Sistemática: Valencia 84, Insurgentes Mixcoac, Del. Benito Juárez, 03920 México, DF, Mexico; tel. (55) 5598-6043; e-mail bac@infosis21.com.mx; f. 1976; clippings archive since 1976; electronic database since 1988; research on media impact on public opinion and the correlation between media statistics and public opinion polls; daily summary of 11 newspapers; Spanish; Dirs BERNARDO AVALOS, LUPITA FLORES; customized frequency.

Information Services Latin America: POB 6103, Albany, CA 94706, USA; tel. (510) 996-23181; e-mail isla@lmi.net; internet isla.lmi.net; f. 1970; selected articles from major daily news sources in the USA and the United Kingdom; English; online edn; Dir KAREN CRUMP; monthly.

Integración y Comercio: Institute for the Integration of Latin America and the Caribbean, Esmeralda 130, 16°, CADB1035 Buenos Aires, Argentina; tel. (11) 4320-1850; fax (11) 4320-1865; e-mail int/inl@iadb.org; internet www.iabd.org/intal; f. 1965; Latin American integration; Spanish and English; Dir RICARDO CARCIOFI; 2 a year.

Integración Financiera—pasado, presente y futuro de las finanzas en Colombia y el mundo: Medios and Medios Publicidad Cía Ltda, No 11–45, Of. 802, Calle 63, Apdo 036943, Bogotá, DC, Colombia; tel. (1) 255-0992; fax (1) 249-4696; f. 1984; financial sector development in Colombia and the rest of Latin America; Spanish; Editor RAÚL RODRÍGUEZ PUERTO; 6 a year.

Investigaciones y Ensayos: Balcarce 139, 1064 Buenos Aires, Argentina; tel. (11) 4343-4416; e-mail adminte@an-historia.org.ar; internet www.an-historia.org.ar; f. 1966; history of Argentina and the Americas; Spanish; published by the Academia Nacional de la Historia; 2 a year.

Jahrbuch für Geschichte Lateinamerikas: 20146 Hamburg, Von-Melle-Park 6, Universität Hamburg Historisches Seminar, Germany; e-mail horst.pietschmann@uni-hamburg.de; internet www-gewi.uni-graz.at/jbla; published by Böhlau-Verlag, Cologne and Vienna; f. 1964; political, economic, social and cultural history of Latin America from colonial period to present; articles in Spanish, English, French, German and Portuguese; Dir Prof. Dr HORST PIETSCHMANN; annual.

Journal of Development Studies: Routledge, Taylor & Francis, 4 Park Sq., Milton Park, Abingdon, Oxon, OX14 4RN, United Kingdom; tel. (20) 7017-6000; fax (20) 7017-6336; internet www.tandf.co.uk/journals; f. 1964; Editors STUART CORBRIDGE, OLIVER MORRISSEY, Dr RICHARD PALMER-JONES, HOWARD WHITE; 10 a year.

Journal of Iberian and Latin American Research: Routledge, Taylor & Francis, 4 Park Sq., Milton Park, Abingdon, Oxon, OX14 4RN, United Kingdom; tel. (20) 7017-6000; fax (20) 7017-6336; e-mail tf.enquiries@tandf.co.uk; internet www.tandf.co.uk/journals; f. 2010; research on the histories, political economies, sociologies, literatures, and cultures of Latin America and the Iberian peninsula; Man. Editors JEFF BROWITT, BLANCA TOVÍAS; 2 a year.

Journal of Iberian and Latin American Studies: Routledge, Taylor & Francis, 4 Park Sq., Milton Park, Abingdon, Oxon, OX14 4RN, United Kingdom; tel. (20) 7017-6000; fax (20) 7017-6336; e-mail tf.enquiries@tandf.co.uk; internet www.tandf.co.uk/journals; fmrly *Tesserae*; language, literature, history and culture of Latin America and Iberian peninsula; English, with articles in Catalan and Spanish; Editors JORDI LARIOS, MONTSERRAT LUNATI; 3 a year.

Journal of Latin American Cultural Studies: Routledge, Taylor & Francis, 4 Park Sq., Milton Park, Abingdon, Oxon, OX14 4RN,

United Kingdom; tel. (20) 7017-6000; fax (20) 7017-6336; e-mail authorqueries@tandf.co.uk; internet www.tandf.co.uk/journals/cjla; f. 1992; history and analysis of Latin American culture; English; Editors JENS ANDERMANN, BEN BOLLIG, PHILLIP DERBYSHIRE, JOHN KRANIAUSKAS, LORRAINE LEU, DAVID WOOD; 3 a year.

Journal of Latin American Studies: Institute for the Study of the Americas, University of London, Senate House, Malet St, London, WC1E 7HU, United Kingdom; tel. (20) 7862-8877; fax (20) 7862-8886; e-mail journals@cambridge.org; internet www.journals.cambridge.org/jid_LAS; Editors Dr GARETH JONES, Dr RORY MILLER, FIONA MACAULAY; 4 a year.

Journal de la Société des Américanistes: Musée de l'Homme, 17 place du Trocadéro, 75116 Paris, France; tel. 1-46-69-26-34; fax 1-46-69-25-08; e-mail jsa@mae.u-paris10.fr; f. 1896; archaeology, ethnology, ethnohistory and linguistics of the American continent; French, Spanish, English and Portuguese; Editor DOMINIQUE MICHELET; annual.

Kañina: Revista de Artes y Letras: Facultad de Letras, Ciudad Universitaria Rodrigo Facio, Universidad de Costa Rica, San Pedro, San José, Costa Rica; tel. 2207-5107; fax 2207-5089; e-mail kanina@cariari.ucr.ac.cr; f. 1976; arts and literature; mainly Spanish, but also French, English and Italian; Editor VICTOR SÁNCHEZ CORRALES; 2 a year.

LARF Report: Latin America Reserve Fund—LARF, Bogotá, DC, Colombia; tel. (1) 285-8511; fax (1) 288-1117; f. 1979; economic summary of Bolivia, Colombia, Ecuador, Peru and Venezuela; Spanish and English; annual.

Lateinamerika Analysen: GIGA German Institute of Global and Area Studies, 20354 Hamburg, Neuer Jungfernstieg 21, Germany; tel. (40) 42825593; fax (40) 42825547; e-mail info@giga-hamburg.de; internet www.giga-hamburg.de; f. 2002; fmrly *Lateinamerika: Analysen-Daten-Dokumentation*; political, economic and social development, regional integration and international relations of Latin America; German, Spanish and Portuguese; Editor WOLFGANG HEIN; 3 a year.

Lateinamerika Anders Panorama: Informationsgruppe Lateinamerika, Postfach 123, 1061 Vienna, Austria; e-mail igla@aon.at; internet www.lateinamerika-anders.org; f. 1976; news and analysis of Latin American affairs; German; Editors WERNER HÖRTNER, HERMANN KLOSIUS; 5 a year.

Latin American Business Review: Routledge, Taylor & Francis, 4 Park Sq., Milton Park, Abingdon, Oxon, OX14 4RN, United Kingdom; tel. (20) 7017-6000; fax (20) 7017-6336; e-mail tf.enquiries@tandf.co.uk; internet www.tandf.co.uk/journals; f. 2008; Editor CESAR GONÇALVES NETO.

Latin America and Caribbean Contemporary Record: Holmes and Meier Publishers Inc, 160 Broadway East Wing, New York, NY 10038, USA; tel. (212) 374-0100; fax (212) 374-1313; e-mail info@holmesandmeier.com; internet www.holmesandmeier.com; f. 1981; analysis of events and trends in Latin America and the Caribbean; English; Editors JAMES MALLOY, EDUARDO GAMARRA; annual.

Latin American and Caribbean Ethnic Studies: Routledge, Taylor & Francis, 4 Park Sq., Milton Park, Abingdon, Oxon, OX14 4RN, United Kingdom; tel. (20) 7017-6000; fax (20) 7017-6336; e-mail authorqueries@tandf.co.uk; internet www.tandf.co.uk/journals/rlac; f. 2006; ethnicity, race relations and indigenous peoples in Latin America and the Caribbean; Editor-in-Chief LEON ZAMOSC; 3 a year.

Latin American Economy and Business: Latin American Newsletters, 61 Old St, London, EC1V 9HW, United Kingdom; tel. (20) 7251-0012; fax (20) 7253-8193; e-mail subs@latinnews.com; internet www.latinnews.com; economic data and indicators; English; Editor WILL OLLARD; monthly.

Latin American Index: Welt Publishing LLC, Washington, DC, USA; tel. (202) 371-0555; fax (202) 408-9369; political, economic and social affairs of Latin America, and US-Latin American relations; English; Editor WILLIAM KNEPPER; 23 a year.

Latin American Monitor: Business Monitor International, Mermaid House, 2 Puddle Dock, Blackfriars, London, EC4V 3DS, United Kingdom; tel. (20) 7248-0468; fax (20) 7248-0467; e-mail subs@businessmonitor.com; internet www.businessmonitor.com; publishes 6 regional reports covering Mexico, Brazil, Central America, Andean Group, Southern Cone and Caribbean; English; monthly.

Latin American Perspectives: University of California, POB 5703, Riverside, CA 92517-5703, USA; tel. (951) 827-1571; fax (951) 827-5685; e-mail laps@ucr.edu; internet www.latinamericanperspectives.com; economics, political science, international relations, philosophy, history, sociology, geography, anthropology and literature; English; Man. Editor RONALD H. CHILCOTE; 6 a year.

Latin American Politics and Society: Center for Latin American Studies, University of Miami, POB 248123, Coral Gables, FL 33124C, USA; tel. (1305) 284-5554; fax (305) 284-4406; e-mail laps.sis@miami.edu; internet www.wiley.com/bw/journal.asp?ref=1531-426X; f. 1959; fmrly Journal of Interamerican Studies and World Affairs; Latin American comparative politics, democratization, Latin American-US relations; English; Editor WILLIAM C. SMITH; quarterly.

Latin American Regional Reports: Latin American Newsletters, 61 Old St, London, EC1V 9HW, United Kingdom; tel. (20) 7251-0012; fax (20) 7253-8193; e-mail subs@latinnews.com; internet www.latinnews.com; 4 regional reports covering Andean Group, Mexico and Nafta, Brazil and Southern Cone, and Caribbean and Central America; English; Editors EILEEN GAVIN, KATHERINE CALDER, SARAH SHELDON, WILL OLLARD; monthly.

Latin American Research Review (LARR): McGill University, Peterson Hall Room 238, 3460 McTavish St, Montreal, QC H3A 1X9, Canada; tel. (514) 398-3507; fax (514) 398-8432; e-mail larr.editorial@mcgill.ca; internet lasa.international.pitt.edu/eng/larr/index.asp; f. 1965; articles, research notes and essays dealing with contemporary issues; English, Spanish and Portuguese; Editor-in-Chief Dr PHILIP OXHORN; 3 a year.

Latin American Special Reports: Latin American Newsletters, 61 Old St, London, EC1V 9HW, United Kingdom; tel. (20) 7251-0012; fax (20) 7253-8193; e-mail subs@latinnews.com; internet www.latinnews.com; each edn provides detailed information on and analysis of one specific subject; English and Spanish; Editor EDUARDO CRAWLEY; 6 a year.

Latin American Studies in Asia: K. K. Roy (Pvt) Ltd, 55 Gariahat Rd, POB 10210, Kolkata 700 019, India; tel. (33) 4754872; f. 1991; Latin American and Caribbean affairs; English; Editor Dr K. K. ROY; quarterly.

Latin American Weekly Report/Informe Latinoamericano: Latin American Newsletters, 61 Old St, London, EC1V 9HW, United Kingdom; tel. (20) 7251-0012; fax (20) 7253-8193; e-mail subs@latinnews.com; internet www.latinnews.com; political, economic and general news; English and Spanish edns; Editor JON FARMER; weekly.

Latinskaya Amerika: Institute of Latin American Studies, Russian Academy of Sciences, 119034 Moscow, per. Kropotkinskii 24, Russia; tel. (095) 201-56-64; fax (095) 200-42-14; e-mail revistala@mtu-net.ru; f. 1969; politics, economic development, history and culture of Latin American countries; Russian; Editor VLADIMIR E. TRAVKIN; monthly.

Latin Studies Journal: Center for Latino Research, North-Eastern University, Dept of Sociology and Anthropology, 521 Holmes Hall, Boston, MA 02115, USA; tel. (617) 373-2000; f. 1990; Latin American affairs; Latin American-North American relations; Editor FELIX PADILLA; 3 a year.

Lecturas de Economía: Centro de Investigaciones y Consultorías, Universidad de Antioquia, Calle 67, No 53–108, Bloque 13, Of. 121, Ciudad Universitaria, Medellín, Antioquia, Colombia; tel. (4) 219-5840; fax (4) 233-1249; e-mail lecturas@economicas.udea.edu.co; internet http://economicas.udea.edu.co/lecturas/rev_lectecono/rev_lectecono.html; f. 1980; economic issues; Spanish; Editor ALEXANDER TOBÓN ARIAS; 2 a year.

Luso-Brazilian Review: University of Wisconsin Press, Journals Division, 1930 Monroe St, Madison, WI 53711, USA; tel. (608) 263-0668; fax (608) 263-1173; e-mail journals@uwpress.wisc.edu; internet www.wisc.edu/wisconsinpress/journals/Luso-Brazilian_Review.html; f. 1964; history, social sciences and literature; English and Portuguese; Editors PETER M. BEATTIE, ELLEN W. SAPEGA, SEVERINO J. ALBUQUERQUE; 2 a year.

Mesoamérica: Skidmore College, 815 North Broadway, Saratoga Springs, NY 12866, USA; tel. (518) 580-5272; fax (518) 580-5258; e-mail editores@mesoamericarevista.org; internet www.mesoamericarevista.org; f. 1980; Plumsock Mesoamerican Studies; anthropology, history, linguistics and social sciences of southern Mexico and Central America; Spanish; Editors JORDANA DYM, CHRISTOPHE BELAUBRE; annual.

Mexico Watch: Orbis Publications Ltd, 1924 47th St, NW, Washington, DC 20007, USA; tel. (202) 298-7936; fax (202) 298-7938; e-mail orbis@orbispub.com; politics, economics and business of Mexico; English; Publr STEPHEN M. FOSTER; monthly.

Mundo Nuevo. Revista de Estudios Latínoamericanos: Apdo 17271, Caracas 1015-A, Venezuela; tel. (212) 573-8824; internet www.iaeal.usb.ve; f. 1975; international relations, politics, economy of Latin America; Spanish, but some articles are published in their original languages, English, French and Portuguese; published by the Instituto de Altos Estudios de América Latina, Universidad Simón Bolívar; quarterly.

Mundus: Wissenschaftliche Verlagsgesellschaft GmbH, Birkenwaldstr. 44, 70191 Stuttgart, Germany; tel. (711) 25820; fax (711) 2582290; f. 1965; review of German research on Latin America, Asia and Africa; English; Editor JÜRGEN HOHNHOLZ (Institute for Scientific Co-operation); quarterly.

NACLA Report on the Americas: North American Congress on Latin America, 38 Greene St, 4th Floor, New York, NY 10013, USA; tel.

(646) 613-1440; fax (646) 613-1443; e-mail nacla@igv.apc.org; internet www.nacla.org; f. 1966; publication of North American Congress on Latin America covering US foreign policy towards Latin America and the Caribbean, and domestic developments in the region; English; Editor PABLO MORALES; 6 a year.

Negobancos—Negocios y Bancos: Bolívar 8-103, Apdo 1907, 06000 México, DF, Mexico; tel. (55) 5510-1884; fax (55) 5512-9411; f. 1951; business and economics; Spanish; Dir ALFREDO FARRUGIA REED; fortnightly.

Nordeste: Análise Conjuntural: Banco do Nordeste do Brasil, Escritório Técnico de Estudos Econômicos do Nordeste, Praça Murilo Borges, No 1, CP 628, Fortaleza, CE, Brazil; e-mail nego_bancos@mexico.com; f. 1972 as Análise Conjuntural de Economia Nordestina; adopted current name in 1974; Brazilian economy, including statistics; Portuguese; Editor JOÃO DE AQUINO LIMAVERDE.

NotiCen: University of New Mexico, Latin American and Iberian Institute, Latin American Data Base, 801 Yale NE, Albuquerque, NM 87131, USA; tel. (505) 277-6839; fax (505) 277-5989; e-mail info@ladb.unm.edu; internet ladb.unm.edu/noticen; online news digest; sustainable development, economic and political affairs in Central America and the Caribbean; Editor MICHAEL LEFFERT; weekly.

Noticias Indigenistas de América/Indian News of the Americas: Instituto Indigenista Interamericano, Avda Insurgentes Sur 1690, Col. Florida, 01030 México, DF, Mexico; tel. (55) 5660-0007; fax (55) 5534-8090; internet www.ini.gob.mx/iii/noticiasindi.html; f. 1978; news of the Indians of the Americas, government policies, anthropology; Spanish and English edns; Editor Dr JOSÉ MATOS MAR; 3 a year.

Noticias de Latino América Documentos: 41 rue de Suède, 1060 Brussels, Belgium; tel. (2) 538-78-81; extracts from Latin American press; Spanish; Editor KRISTIN MINNE; every two months.

NotiSur: University of New Mexico, Latin American and Iberian Institute, Latin America Data Base, 801 Yale, NE, Albuquerque, NM 87131, USA; tel. (505) 277-6389; fax (505) 277-5989; e-mail info@ladb.unm.edu; internet ladb.unm.edu/notisur; online news digest; provides alternative viewpoints on political and economic affairs in South America, particularly on human rights and peace issues and sustainable development; English; Editor JOE GARDNER WESSELY; weekly.

Opciones: Territorial, esq. Gen Suárez, Plaza de la Revolución, Havana, Cuba; tel. (7) 881-8934; fax (7) 881-8621; e-mail opciones@jrebelde.cip.cu; internet www.opciones.cu; f. 1994; economics and politics; Spanish; weekly; Editor HERIBERTO ROSABAL ESPINOSA.

Panorama Económico: Bancomer, SA, Grupo Investigaciones Económicas, Centro Bancomer, Avda Universidad 1200, 03339 México, DF, Mexico; tel. (55) 5534-0034; fax (55) 5621-3230; f. 1966; Mexican economy, in particular the automobile and textiles industries; Spanish and English; Editor EDUARDO MILLAN LOZANO; 6 a year.

Panorama Económico Latinoamericano (PEL): Ediciones Cubanas, Obispo 527, Apdo 605, Havana, Cuba; tel. (7) 63-1981; fax (7) 33-8943; f. 1960; book reviews and statistics; available on micro-film; Spanish; Editor JOSÉ BODES GÓMEZ; 2 a month.

Panorama Latinoamericano: Moscow, Zubovskii bul. 4, Russia; tel. (095) 201-55-79; review of economic, political, cultural, and social life of Latin America drawn from Russian Press and published by RIA—Novosti (Russian Information Agency—News); Spanish; fortnightly.

Paz: South American Commission for Peace, Regional Security and Democracy, Santiago, Chile; tel. (2) 232-8329; fax (2) 233-3502; Spanish; 2 a year.

Pesquisa e Planejamento Econômico: Institute of Applied Economic Research, Avda Antônio Carlos 51, 16° andar, CP 2672, 20.020-010 Rio de Janeiro, RJ, Brazil; tel. (21) 3804-8118; fax (21) 2220-5533; e-mail editrj@ipea.gov.br; internet ppe.ipea.gov.br; f. 1970; economics and planning; Portuguese and English; Editor MARCO ANTONIO CAVALCANTI; quarterly.

Política Externa: Programa de Pesquisa de Relações Internacionais, Universidade de São Paulo, Rua do Anfiteatro 181, Colméia, favo 14, Cidade Universitária, 05508-900 São Paulo, SP, Brazil; tel. (11) 3091-3061; fax (11) 3032-4154; e-mail guilhon@usp.br; internet www.usp.br/relint; f. 1990; Brazilian foreign and economic policy, regional integration, NAFTA and Mercosur; Portuguese; Dir RAFAEL VILLA; quarterly.

Problemas del Desarrollo—revista latinoamericana de economía: Instituto de Investigaciones Económicas de la Universidad Nacional Autónoma de México, Ciudad Universitaria, Del. Coyoacán, 04510, México, DF, Mexico; tel. (55) 5623-0105; fax (55) 5623-0097; e-mail revprode@servidor.unam.mx; f. 1969; economic, political and social affairs of Mexico, Latin America and the developing world; Spanish, with English and French abstracts; quarterly.

Puerto Rico Business Review/Puerto Rico Economic Indicators: Government Development Bank for Puerto Rico, POB 42001, San Juan, PR 00940-2001, Puerto Rico; tel. 722-2525; fax 268-5496; e-mail bgf.gobierno.pr; internet www.gdb-pur.com/economy/latest-information-monthly-indicators_pub.htm; f. 1976; English; Editor ANABEL HERNÁNDEZ; quarterly.

Quarterly Economic Review: Central Bank of the Bahamas, Research Dept, Frederick St, POB N-4868, Nassau, Bahamas; tel. 322-2193; fax 356-4321; e-mail cbob@centralbankbahamas.com; internet www.bahamascentralbank.com; review of Bahamian economy; English; quarterly.

Quehacer: Centro de Estudios y Promoción del Desarrollo—DESCO, León de la Fuente 110, Magdalena del Mar, Lima 17, Peru; tel. (1) 6138300; fax (1) 6138308; e-mail postmaster@desco.org.pe; internet www.desco.org.pe; f. 1979; business development and research; Spanish; Dir ABELARDO SÁNCHEZ-LEÓN; quarterly.

Relaciones Internacionales: Facultad de Ciencias Políticas y Sociales, Universidad Nacional Autónoma de México, México, DF, Mexico; tel. (55) 5622-9412; f. 1973; international relations; Spanish; Editor ROBERTO DOMÍNGUEZ; Dir CONSUELO DÁVILA; 3 a year.

Review: Literature and Arts of the Americas: Routledge, Taylor & Francis, 4 Park Sq., Milton Park, Abingdon, Oxon, OX14 4RN, United Kingdom; tel. (20) 7017-6000; fax (20) 7017-6336; e-mail authorqueries@tandf.co.uk; internet www.tandf.co.uk/journals/rrev; f. 1967; Latin American literature in translation, articles on visual arts, theatre, music, cinema, book reviews; English, but poetry is, in addition, published in the vernacular; Man. Editor DANIEL SHAPIRO; 2 a year.

Revista Análisis: Revistas Interamericanos SA, Apdo 8038, Panama 7, Panama; tel. 26-0073; fax 26-3758; f. 1979; economic and political analysis; academic; Spanish; Editor MARIO A. ROGNONI; monthly.

Revista Argentina de Estudios Estratégicos: Argentine Centre of Strategic Studies, Viamonte 494, 3°, Of. 11, 1053 Buenos Aires, Argentina; tel. (11) 4312-1605; fax (11) 4312-5802; the armed forces; Spanish; quarterly.

Revista de Biología Tropical: Universidad de Costa Rica, Ciudad Universitaria Rodrigo Facio, San José, Costa Rica; tel. and fax 2207-5550; e-mail rbt@cariari.ucr.ac.cr; f. 1953; biology, ecology, taxonomy, etc., of Neotropics and African tropics; Spanish and English; Dir J. MONGE-NAJERA; quarterly, with supplements, and online edn.

Revista Brasileira de Economia: Escola de Pós-Graduaçao em Economia, Praia de Botafogo 190, Of. 1100, 22.253-900 Rio de Janeiro, RJ, Brazil; tel. (21) 2559-5860; fax (21) 2552-4898; e-mail rbe@fgv.br; internet www.fgv.br/epge/home/publi/RBE; f. 1947; economic theory, economic policy and econometrics; Portuguese and English; Editor RICARDO CAVALCANTI; quarterly.

Revista Brasileira de Estatística: Fundação Instituto Brasileiro de Geografia e Estatística, Avda Chile 500, 10° andar, 20.031-170 Rio de Janeiro, RJ, Brazil; tel. (21) 2142-4551; fax (21) 2142-4548; e-mail salbieri@ibge.gov.br; f. 1940; statistical subjects by means of articles, analysis, etc; Portuguese; Editor FRANCISCO LOUZADA NETO; 2 a year.

Revista Brasileira de Estudos Políticos: Av. Alvares Cabral 211, salá 1206, CP 1301, 30170-000 Belo Horizonte, MG, Brazil; tel. (31)3224-5856; e-mail rbep@direito.ufmg.br; f. 1956; public law, political science, economics, history; Portuguese; published by Universidade Federal de Minas Gerais; Dir ALOÍSIO GONZAGA ARAÚJO; 2 a year.

Revista Brasileira de Geografia: Fundação Instituto Brasileiro de Geografia e Estatistica, Directoria de Geociências, Av. Brasil 15.671, Parada de Lucas, 21.241-051 Rio de Janeiro, RJ, Brazil; tel. (21) 2142-4990; fax (21) 2142-4910; internet www.ibge.gov.br; f. 1936; advanced geographic, socio-economic and scientific articles, also news and translations; Portuguese, with English summaries; Dir of Geosciences LUIZ PAULO S. FORTES; 2 a year.

Revista Chilena de Historia y Geografía: Sociedad Chilena de Historia y Geografía, Londres 65, Casilla 1386, Santiago, Chile; tel. (2) 6382489; f. 1911; history, geography, anthropology, archaeology, genealogy, numismatics; Spanish; Dir YSIDORO VÁSQUEZ DE AMIÑA; annual.

Revista de Ciencias Sociales de la Universidad de Costa Rica: Vicerectoría de Investigación, Apdo 49-2060, Montes de Oca 2050, Costa Rica; tel. 2511-3450; e-mail revista.cs@ucr.ac.cr; internet revistacienciassociales.ucr.ac.cr; f. 1956; sociology, anthropology, geography, history, etc., with special reference to Costa Rica and Central America; Spanish; Editor CECILIA ARGUEDAS; Dir DANIEL CAMACHO; quarterly.

Revista Ecuador Debate: Centro Andino de Acción Popular—CAAP, Utreras 733 y Selva Alegre, Quito, Ecuador; tel. (2) 252-2763; fax (2) 256-8452; e-mail caap1@caap.org.ec; internet www.dlh.lahora.com.ec; f. 1983; economic conditions and agriculture; Spanish; Editor FREDDY RIVERA VÉLEZ; 3 a year.

Revista Educación: Facultad de Educación, Universidad de Costa Rica, 2060 San Pedro, Montes de Oca, San José, Costa Rica; tel. 2511-5387; fax 2511-4244; e-mail revedu@gmail.com; f. 1977; education; Spanish; Dir FLORA EUGENIA SALAS MADRIZ; Editor CARMEN GRACE SALAZAR SALAS; 2 a year.

Revista Estudios Sociales Centroamericanos: CSUCA, Apdo 37 Ciudad Universitaria Rodrigo Facio, San José, Costa Rica; f. 1972; socio-economic and political aspects of Central America; Spanish; Editor MARIO LUNGO UCLÉS; 3 a year.

Revista Geológica de América Central: Escuela Centroamericana de Geología, Apdo 214-2060 Universidad de Costa Rica, San José, Costa Rica; tel. 2207-4042; fax 2207-5311; e-mail pdenyer@geologia.ucr.ac.cr; internet www.geologia.ucr.ac.cr; f. 1983; geology and geophysics of Central America; Spanish, with abstracts in English, and English, with abstracts in Spanish; Editor SIEGFRIED KUSSMAUL; 2 a year.

Revista Homines: Dept of Social Sciences, Universidad Interamericana de Puerto Rico, Apdo 191293, Hato Rey, PR 00919, Puerto Rico; internet coqui/metro.inter.edu/homines/homines.htm; f. 1957; sociology, anthropology, history, economics, geography, political sciences, psychology; Spanish; Editorial Dir ALINE FRAMBES BUXEDA DE ALZÉRRECA; 2 a year.

Revista do Instituto Histórico e Geográfico Brasileiro: Av. Augusto Severo 8, 10° andar, 20.021-040 Rio de Janeiro, RJ, Brazil; tel. (21) 232-1312; fax (21) 252-4430; f. 1838; history and geography; Portuguese; quarterly.

Revista do Mercado Comum do Sul—Mercosul / Revista del Mercado Común del Sur—Mercosur: Rua Teófilo Ontoni 123, 3° andar, 20090-3001 Rio de Janeiro, Brazil; tel. (21) 2223-1180; fax (21) 2223-3001; e-mail revistadomercosul@etm.com.br; internet www.uol.com.br/revistadomercosul; f. 1992; Latin American integration; Portuguese and Spanish; Editor ANTÔNIO CARLOS DA CUNHA; monthly.

Revista Mexicana de Ciencias Políticas y Sociales: Facultad de Ciencias Políticas y Sociales, Universidad Autónoma de México, 04510 México, DF, Mexico; tel. (55) 5622-9433; fax (55) 5665-1786; e-mail bokser@mail.politicas.unam.mx; f. 1955; political and social sciences; Spanish; Dir JUDIT BOKSER MISSES; quarterly.

Revista Mexicana de Política Exterior: Matias Romero Institute for Diplomatic Studies, Ricardo Flores Magón No 2, Col. Guerrero, 06200 México, DF, Mexico; tel. (55) 3686-5100; fax (55) 3686-5041; e-mail imrinfo@sre.gob.mx; internet www.sre.gob.mx/imr; Spanish; quarterly.

Revista Repertorio Americano: Instituto de Estudios Latinoamericanos, Universidad Nacional, Apdo 86-3000, Heredia, Costa Rica; tel. and fax 2562-4240; e-mail idela@una.ac.cr; internet www.una.ac.cr; f. 1919; Latin American and Spanish culture; Spanish; Dir JULIÁN GONZÁLEZ ZÚÑIGA; 2 a year.

Revista Venezolana de Análisis de Coyuntura: Research Institute of the Faculty of Economic and Social Sciences, Universidad Central de Venezuela, Of. de Publicaciones, Apdo 54057, Caracas 1051-A, Venezuela; tel. and fax (212) 605-2523; e-mail coyuntura@cantv.net; f. 1980 as Boletín de Indicadores Socio-económicos; adopted existing name in 1995; socio-economic issues; Spanish; 2 a year.

Revista Venezolana de Economía y Ciencias Sociales: Research Institute of the Faculty of Economic and Social Sciences, Universidad Central de Venezuela, Of. de Publicaciones, Apdo 54057, Caracas 1051-A, Venezuela; tel. and fax (212) 605-2523; f. 1958 as Economía y Ciencias Sociales; changed name as above in 1995; Spanish; Editor LUIS E. LANDER; 3 a year.

Semana Económica: Apoyo Publicaciones, Calle Juan de la Fuente 625, San Antonio, Lima 18, Peru; tel. (1) 2130600; fax (1) 4445240; e-mail redaccion@semanaeconomica.com; internet www.semanaeconomica.com; f. 1985; economic affairs; Spanish; Editor-in-Chief AUGUSTO TOWNSEND K.; weekly.

Síntesis Económica: Bogotá, DC, Colombia; tel. (1) 212-5121; fax (1) 212-8365; f. 1975; Spanish; Dir FÉLIX LAFAURIE RIVERA; weekly.

Sourcemex: University of New Mexico, Latin American and Iberian Institute, Latin America Data Base, 801 Yale, NE, Albuquerque, NM 87131, USA; tel. (505) 277-6839; fax (505) 277-5989; e-mail info@ladb.unm.net; internet ladb.unm.edu/sourcemex; online news digest; political and economic news and analysis in Mexico; weekly.

Suplemento Antropológico: Centro de Estudios Antropológicos de la Universidad Católica, Casilla 1718, Asunción, Paraguay; tel. (21) 446251; fax (21) 445245; f. 1965; practical and theoretical problems of the indigenous peoples of the River Plate basin (Bolivia, Brazil, Uruguay, Argentina and Paraguay); Spanish; 2 a year.

Third World Quarterly: Dept of Geography, Royal Holloway, University of London, Egham, Surrey, TW20 0EX, United Kingdom; fax (20) 8947-1243; e-mail editor@thirdworldquarterly.com; internet www.tandf.co.uk/journals; f. 1979; Editor SHAHID QADIR; 8 a year.

Tricontinental: Organization of Solidarity of the Peoples of Asia, Africa and Latin America, Calle C, No 668, esq. 29, Vedado, Apdo 4224, Havana, Cuba; tel. (7) 30-4941; fax (7) 33-3985; f. 1967; analysis of cultural, political and social developments in Cuba and other developing countries; Spanish, French and English; Editor ANA MARÍA PELLÓN SÁEZ; quarterly.

El Trimestre Económico: Fondo de Cultura Económica, Carretera Picacho Ajusco 227, Col. Bosques del Pedregal, Del. Tlaplan, 14200 México, DF, Mexico; tel. (55) 5227-4671; fax (55) 5227-4640; e-mail trimestre@fondodeculturaeconomica.com; internet www.fondodeculturaeconomica.com/trimestre.asp; f. 1934; theoretical or empirical investigation with special interest in economies of Latin America and Spain; economic development and economic theory, employment and investment policy; Spanish; Editor FAUSTO HERNÁNDEZ TRILLO; quarterly.

Uruguay Económico: Ministerio de Economía y Finanzas, Asesoría Economico-Financiera, Col. 1013, 8°, Montevideo, Uruguay; f. 1978; economy of Uruguay; published by the Economic and Financial Advisory Office of the Uruguayan Ministry of Economy and Finance; Spanish; 2 a year.

Uruguay Síntesis Económico: Banco Central del Uruguay, Departamento de Estadísticas Económicas, Paysando y Florida, Casilla 1467, Montevideo, Uruguay; tel. (2) 917117; fax (2) 921634; economic conditions in Uruguay; publication of the Economic Statistics Department of the Central Bank of Uruguay; Spanish; 2 a year.

Visión (La Revista Latinoamericana Visión): Arguímedes 199, 6° y 7°, Col. Polanco, 11570 México, DF, Mexico; tel. (5) 203-6091; f. 1950; news and analysis of Latin America; Spanish Gen. Man. ROBERTO BELLO; 2 a month.

INDEX OF REGIONAL ORGANIZATIONS

(Main reference only)

A

B

C

D

E

F

G

H

I

J

L

M

N

O

P